Sourcebook of ZIP Code Demographics

23rd Edition

2009

The source of business information in the 23rd Edition of the *Sourcebook of ZIP Code Demographics* is *info*USA Inc., Omaha, NE.

The source for ZIP Code boundaries is Tele Atlas, Lebanon, NH.

NOTICE: The data contained in this book have been prepared using generally accepted statistical techniques. ESRI cannot and does not guarantee that the data collected in this book are completely error-free.

ISBN Number: 978-1-58948-225-8

TABLE OF CONTENTS

Appendixes

ZIP Code Maps

Introduction

ESRI provides customer and market intelligence solutions to help businesses, government agencies, and nonprofit organizations with

- Customer profiling and segmentation analysis
- Site evaluation and selection
- Market evaluation and selection
- Custom target analysis
- Direct mail campaign implementation
- Media planning
- Merchandise mix analysis
- Target marketing
- Sales forecasting

By combining demographics, consumer spending data, and lifestyle segmentation with innovative technology, ESRI empowers you to make better business decisions.

Since 1969, ESRI® has been giving customers around the world the power to think and plan geographically. The market leader in GIS, ESRI software is used in more than 300,000 organizations worldwide including each of the 200 largest cities in the United States, most national governments, more than two-thirds of Fortune 500 companies, and more than 7,000 colleges and universities. ESRI applications, running on more than one million desktops and thousands of Web and enterprise servers, provide the backbone for the world's mapping and spatial analysis. ESRI is the only vendor that provides complete technical solutions for desktop, mobile, server, and Internet platforms.

For more information about
ESRI's products, services, and solutions, visit www.esri.com.

ESRI
380 New York Street
Redlands, California 92373

Features of the 23rd Edition

This edition of the *Sourcebook of ZIP Code Demographics* contains the most accurate demographic information based on ESRI's release of the 2009 updates and 2014 forecasts of key population and income data. Updated variables for population, households, families, income, race, age, and spending potential for a wide variety of products and services are included in this reference tool. The *Sourcebook of ZIP Code Demographics* contains:

Residential and Non-Residential ZIP Codes – residential ZIP Codes are profiled using more than 70 demographic variables. An appendix references the non-residential ZIP Codes with their enclosing residential ZIP Codes.

Profile Sections - demographic variables are grouped by section into profiles for Population Change, Population Composition, Income and Spending Potential. Updated demographics include population, age, race, Hispanic origin, household type and household income.

Summaries - the state and local data summaries provide a quick comparison of a ZIP Code to state and national information.

Explanation of Variables - definitions of the demographic variables and key terms used in the Sourcebook are included.

Business Data - the predominant industry by ZIP Code is listed in the Business Data section. Information about the total number of businesses and the total employment in each ZIP Code is also included.

ESRI's segmentation system, Tapestry™ Segmentation - includes information about the dominant Tapestry Segmentation summary group in each ZIP Code and the proportion of households represented by the group.

Demographic and ZIP Code Update Methodologies - current data methodology statements explain how the population and income data are forecast from the Census 2000 base as well as how ZIP Code data is estimated.

ZIP Code Ranges - to find specific ZIP Codes, refer to the ZIP Code ranges listed on each page.

ZIP Code Maps – individual state maps delineating three-digit ZIP Code boundaries are included as reference.

Complementary sourcebook products include the 21st edition of the *Sourcebook of County Demographics* and the Sourcebook • America with ArcReader™ CD. Bound in a handsome soft cover, the county sourcebook includes more than 80 demographic, consumer spending, and business variables for all 3,141 U.S. counties, along with important reference materials and state maps. Sourcebook • America with ArcReader contains all of the data from the ZIP Code and county sourcebooks with our proprietary query, sort, and report software and the ArcReader map display software.

For more information about the sourcebook products, please visit www.esri.com/sourcebooks. If you would like to speak with an account representative, please call 800-292-2224.

ZIP Code to State Cross-Reference

01000-02799 Massachusetts

02800-02999 Rhode Island

03000-03899 New Hampshire

03900-04999 Maine

05000-05999 Vermont

06000-06999 Connecticut

07000-08999 New Jersey

09000-14999 New York

15000-19699 Pennsylvania

19700-19999 Delaware

20000-20599 District of Columbia

20600-21999 Maryland

22000-24699 Virginia

24700-26899 West Virginia

27000-28999 North Carolina

29000-29999 South Carolina

30000-31999 Georgia

32000-34999 Florida

35000-36999 Alabama

37000-38599 Tennessee

38600-39799 Mississippi

40000-42799 Kentucky

43000-45899 Ohio

46000-47999 Indiana

48000-49999 Michigan

50000-52899 Iowa

53000-54999 Wisconsin

55000-56799 Minnesota

57000-57799 South Dakota

58000-58899 North Dakota

59000-59999 Montana

60000-62999 Illinois

63000-65899 Missouri

66000-67999 Kansas

68000-69399 Nebraska

70000-71499 Louisiana

71600-72999 Arkansas

73000-74999 Oklahoma

75000-79999 Texas

80000-81699 Colorado

82000-83199 Wyoming

83200-83899 Idaho

84000-84799 Utah

85000-86599 Arizona

87000-88499 New Mexico

89000-89899 Nevada

90000-96699 California

96700-96899 Hawaii

97000-97999 Oregon

98000-99499 Washington

99500-99999 Alaska

There are 81 exceptions to these ranges in 6 states: Georgia (39813-39897), Kentucky (45275), New York (06390), Tennessee (42223), Virginia (20041 and 20105-20198), and Wyoming (83414).

There are six residential ZIP Codes that physically exist in two states. The state that contains the largest portion of the ZIP Code is listed.

ZIP CODE	LISTED IN THIS STATE	NOT LISTED IN THIS STATE
42223	Tennessee	Kentucky
57724	South Dakota	Montana
63673	Missouri	Illinois
71749	Arkansas	Louisiana
72395	Arkansas	Tennessee
73949	Oklahoma	Texas

ESRI

Update Methodology: 2009/2014

2009 DEMOGRAPHIC UPDATE METHODOLOGY

Forecasts are prepared initially for counties and block groups (BGs). From the county database, forecasts are aggregated to CBSAs, states, or higher levels. From the block group database, forecasts can be retrieved for census tracts; places; county subdivisions; ZIP Codes; congressional districts for the 111th Congress; DMAs; or any user-defined site, circle, or polygon.

County Totals

The change in total population is a function of changes in household population and the population in group quarters, which are subject to different trends. The addition of a prison, for example, produces a sudden increase in the group quarters' population that is unlikely to yield an attendant change in the household population or the projected population growth of a county. A military base closing effects an immediate decrease in the household population with the reduction of not only military personnel but also their families and civilian personnel; however, this drop is unlikely to continue. To address local changes specifically in the military, ESRI has analyzed the 2005 Defense Base Realignment and Closure (BRAC) plan. The Department of Defense (DoD) has undergone four BRAC rounds since 1988 and is currently implementing its fifth round—the 2005 round. The recommendations became effective on November 9, 2005, and DoD has until September 15, 2011, to complete the implementation of all BRAC recommendations. To summarize, the plans include more than 800 closures or realignments, with the relocation of approximately 123,000 personnel.[1] The disparity of trends in household versus group quarters' population is best accommodated by separate projections. The group quarters' population is the Census 2000 count of group quarters, with CQR revisions and updates culled from a variety of federal, state, and local sources.

Forecasting change in the size and distribution of the household population begins at the county level with several sources of data. ESRI begins with a time series from the U.S. Census Bureau that includes county estimates through 2007.[2] Because testing has revealed improvement in accuracy by using a variety of different sources to track county population trends, ESRI also employs a time series of county-to-county migration data from the Internal Revenue Service, building permits and housing starts, and residential postal delivery counts. Finally, local data sources that tested well against Census 2000 are reviewed.

Block Group Totals

Measuring the change in population or households at the county level is facilitated by the array of data reported for counties. Unfortunately, there is no current data reported specifically for block groups. Past trends can be calculated from previous census counts, but nothing is current. To measure current population change by block group, ESRI models the change in households from three primary sources: the InfoBase-X™ database from Acxiom Corporation, residential delivery statistics from the U.S. Postal Service, and residential construction data from Hanley Wood Market Intelligence, in addition to several ancillary sources.

The USPS publishes monthly counts of residential deliveries for every U.S. postal carrier route. This represents the most comprehensive and current information available for small, subcounty geographic areas. The USPS establishes carrier routes to enable efficient mail delivery. Carrier routes are a fluid geographic construct and are redefined continually to incorporate real changes in the housing inventory and occupancy along with administrative changes in staffing and budgets of local post offices. These frequent changes in the carrier routes are not the only difficulty.

Converting delivery statistics from postal carrier routes to census block groups is a complex challenge. Carrier routes are defined to deliver the mail, while block groups are constructed to collect and report census data. Comparing two different areas that are defined for wholly different purposes provides one significant conversion issue. Carrier routes also commonly overlap multiple block groups. In many cases, a carrier route encompasses disjointed areas that can be distant from each other, but block groups are rarely divided into multiple polygons. These overlaps require an effective method of allocating the postal delivery counts across multiple block groups.

One way to distribute delivery statistics among component block groups is to create a correspondence using boundary files. Changes in postal carrier routes can be tracked through quarterly updates of carrier route boundaries, and delivery statistics can be assigned to block groups with Census 2000 block data. There is another way that also employs boundary files but assumes a uniform distribution of households within the area. Using standard geodemographic tools, it is possible to estimate the change in households from carrier route delivery statistics and apply that change to any block group(s) in the area. However, the estimated change is simply being redistributed from one summary area to another.

ESRI has developed another way to link a carrier route to the correct block group(s)—using the actual locations of mail deliveries. Its proprietary Address-Based Allocation (ABA) solves the complex challenge of converting delivery counts from carrier routes to block groups.[3] This allocation method uses the addresses from Acxiom's InfoBase-X household database. Addresses in the database are geocoded with carrier route and block group codes, using an enhanced geocoding technique and locator database, and serve as the foundation for the conversion. This approach is unbounded by geographic borders or arbitrary assumptions about the distribution of households or postal deliveries.

ABA results have been tested extensively. The tests include benchmarking against the 2000 Census. Manual reviews confirm the capability of the method to identify areas with high growth. The ABA allocation method reveals sprawls and new developments across the country since Census 2000.

---

[1] United States Government Accountability Office, "Military Base Realignments and Closures: DoD Faces Challenges in Implementing Recommendations on Time and Is Not Consistently Updating Savings Estimates," http://www.gao.gov/new.items/d09217.pdf.

[2] U.S. Bureau of the Census, Population Division, Table CO-EST2007-ALLDATA.

[3] Patent pending.

Assessments based on other data sources verify the efficacy and precision of ABA. For the small portion of block groups where addresses are not available from the InfoBase-X database, delivery statistics are allocated from a correspondence file. The correspondence between census block groups and postal carrier routes is developed using quarterly updated data from Tele Atlas®.

The effectiveness of ABA relies on the precision of block group assignment to InfoBase-X addresses. ESRI improved the geocoding accuracy of the InfoBase-X file by applying ArcGIS® 9.3 with the Dynamap®/Address Points database from Tele Atlas, which provides coordinates that are accurate *to the building*. It offers a new development in large-scale geographic databases, where addresses are represented as points rather than approximations estimated from address ranges or street segments. The database currently covers the most densely populated areas in the United States, with continually increasing geographic coverage. Addresses that fall outside the coverage were geocoded with the conventional approach, based on address ranges.

Post office delivery counts or address counts provide less coverage in rural areas. Sparsely populated areas tend to have post office box ZIP Codes because there are few rural addressing systems and little comparability to urban street delivery. The same problems characterize rural addresses in the InfoBase-X database. To track new housing developments—especially in previously unpopulated areas—in 2006, ESRI licensed a new data source from Hanley Wood Market Intelligence: new and planned residential construction in the top 75 U.S. housing markets, including new markets added through 2008.

The residential construction database from Hanley Wood Market Intelligence adds a unique component to ESRI's strategy for producing accurate demographic forecasts. This database identifies individual construction projects—for instance, a complex of single-family homes or townhomes or a condominium building with their exact location by latitude and longitude. It also pinpoints conversions of apartments into condominiums. The construction information includes

- Total number of units planned
- Inventory of units under construction, sold and/or closed
- Type of housing—detached homes, townhomes, condominiums, etc.
- Target markets—families, seniors, empty nesters, etc.

The use of this type of information in demographic forecasts has traditionally been confined to small-scale implementation, such as producing forecasts for a specific county. ESRI partners with Hanley Wood Market Intelligence to introduce this information in a large-scale forecasting effort. The construction database complements and corroborates the postal delivery statistics. More importantly, it tabulates planned construction to be completed in upcoming years. This information is incorporated in ESRI's five-year forecasts. Tracking residential development since 2000 with enhanced demographic and spatial analysis tools provides better information for the five-year forecasts than past trends.

A revised housing unit methodology applies the change in households estimated from address counts, delivery counts, and new housing construction to update household population by block group. The best techniques are derived from a combination of models and data sources. Discrepant trends are checked extensively against independent sources. Finally, totals for block groups are controlled by the county totals. Despite the appeal of microforecasting, there is simply more information available to track population change by county than by household. Ignoring the advantage of county-level data is throwing away information.

Population and Household Characteristics

ESRI's population and household characteristics include population by sex and age, race and Hispanic origin, sex by age by race and Hispanic origin, marital status, educational attainment, and household type. Population by sex and age includes estimates by five-year age groups and by single years from less than 1 year to 84 years.

The population by age and sex is projected via a cohort survival model that calculates the components of population change separately, by age and sex. Applying survival rates specific to the cohort carries the 2000 population forward. Changes in the population by age and sex diverge at the household level. For example, an area that is losing population can age more rapidly with the loss of population in prime migrant ages—20–34 years—unless there is a college nearby. An influx of college students can offset the loss of youthful outmigrants.

To capture these variations, ESRI's model first separates the group quarters' population from the household population then keys the calculations to the size and characteristics of the population. This stratification identifies several different patterns of change by age and sex that are applied in the cohort survival model. Births are projected from area-specific, child-woman ratios. Migration is computed as a residual, the difference between the survived household population and independent projections of the total household population.

The changing profile of the U.S. population would be incomplete without measuring the growth of population by race and Hispanic origin. Immigration to the United States has diversified the U.S. population. ESRI's database includes a Diversity Index to summarize racial and ethnic diversity. This measure shows the likelihood that two persons, chosen at random from the same area, belong to different races or ethnic groups. The index ranges from 0 (no diversity) to 100 (complete diversity).

The U.S. Diversity Index currently stands at 60.5, an increase of 1.1 percent annually since 2000. Led primarily by the growth of the Hispanic population, California, New Mexico, and Texas are the most diverse mainland states, with 2009 diversity indexes higher than 74. The process of diversification in these states is advanced; therefore, these areas are among the states with slow rates of change in diversification. Although immigration is still rising in these states, it has a smaller impact on the diversity level. Traditionally nondiverse states, such as Maine, Vermont, and Connecticut, are experiencing some of the highest rates of diversification. Pockets of diversity are evident in less diverse states. For example, the Liberal, Garden City, and Dodge City micropolitan statistical areas in Kansas have diversity indexes of 82, 80, and 76, respectively, although the state's index is 41.6.

The Hispanic population now stands at 48.7 million, or 15.7 percent of the total U.S. population. The influence of this ethnic group on American culture is on the rise due to growth rates of 3.5 percent per year since 2000 and a projected total of 56.8 million by 2014 (17.5 percent of the U.S. population).

Asian and non-Hispanic multiracial populations are following Hispanic trends closely with growth rates of 3.4 percent and 3 percent, respectively, from 2000 to 2009, although they are smaller population groups. The proportion of the non-Hispanic white population in the country has declined from 69 percent in 2000 to 64.5 percent in 2009. By 2014, the ratio is forecast to drop to 61.9 percent. At this rate of decline, the proportion of non-Hispanic whites will be less than 50 percent by 2040.

Historical trends in race and Hispanic origin play an important role in the analysis and forecasting process. Tracking intercensal population change by race was encumbered by the new reporting method in Census 2000. Race was reported as a multiple-choice item—not "one person–one race," as reported in past censuses or estimates. The Census 2000 data is not directly comparable to 1990 Census data or to any earlier estimates or projections.

Comparisons made between single-race reporters in 2000 and 1990 underestimate the change by race. Excluding the rapid growth of the multiracial population minimizes the change by race from 1990 to 2000. Alternatively, combining single-race reporters with races reported in any combination can cut down the 63 racial groups reported in Census 2000. For example, a person who reports "White and Asian" is counted as both "White" and "Asian." This combination of single-race and multiracial reporters overcounts multiracial reporters and overestimates the change by race from 1990 to 2000. To achieve a true picture of population change by race, it is important to account for the change in multiracial reporting.

ESRI takes an innovative approach in analyzing this data to make effective use of the additional information from Census 2000.[4] The Census Bureau released most race-related data for six single-race groups and one multiple-race group. ESRI's data preserves this format and enables a comparison of 1990 and 2000 data for six single races and one multiracial group. Assuming that the probability of reporting more than one race varies by race group and geographic area as shown in Census 2000, ESRI estimates the number of likely multiple race reporters from 1990 Census data. The same approach is adopted for the population of Hispanic origin by race.

The most current data sources by race and Hispanic origin are 2007 data available by county and state from the Census Bureau's estimates. Survey data is analyzed in conjunction with ESRI's estimate of change from 1990 to 2000 by race and Hispanic origin to establish county population by race and Hispanic origin. Forecasts by block group combine local changes in the distributions by race and projected change for counties. The last step controls block group distributions to county projections.

The composition of the American household continues the slow change from married-couple families to nontraditional families and single-person households. Between 1990 and 2000, the dominant share of households remained married-couple families in most states but decreased from 55 percent of all households to 52 percent in 2000. Increased shares of single-parent and single-person units comprise the difference. The attendant change in average household size is the decline from 2.63 in 1990 to 2.59 in 2000. Through 2009, these changes continue but even more gradually than in the 1990s.

The gradual change in household size makes it uniquely suitable to forecasting the change in households from the change in household population. Average household size is one of the most stable and predictable components of the forecasts. Household forecasts are predicated upon local patterns of change, which are controlled by the more constant trends for states and counties. Nationally, household change stabilized in the 1990s and remains at 2.59 in 2009.

Local change, however, is affected more by the singular composition of the population, and trends often vary from the national norm. Nationally, average household size decreased by less than 0.4 percent annually from 1990 to 2000. By county, the change varied from a low of -2.1 percent to a high of 1.3 percent. An increase in household size can result from higher rates of fertility locally or from an increase in multigenerational households. Census 2000 has documented the increase in multigenerational households in areas where there is high immigration or areas with housing shortages and higher costs. From 2000 through 2009, the annual change in household size by county ranges from -1.1 to a high of 0.6 percent.

Few block groups represent a cross-section of U.S. households. In areas that gained population from immigration in the 1990s, the trend in average household size actually reversed and increased. To distinguish local variation, ESRI's model is keyed to the characteristics of households at the block group level. This stratification identifies several different patterns of change by household type that are applied to forecast trends in the characteristics of households—both family composition and tenure. Local change is emphasized in the 2009/2014 forecasts of households and families for counties and block groups. National and state trends are monitored with sources such as the Current Population Survey (CPS) and the American Community Survey (ACS) from the Census Bureau, then applied as controls.

In 2008, ESRI added two new characteristics—marital status and educational attainment. Four marital status categories are updated for the population 15 years and older: never married, married (includes the separated population), divorced, and widowed. Seven categories of educational attainment are reported for the population 25 years and older. Educational attainment levels are categorized as less than a ninth-grade level of education, some high school, high school graduate (including GED equivalent), some college, associate degree, bachelor degree, and graduate degree.

Data from the 2000–2007 American Community Surveys is evaluated against long-term trends in census data. Intercensal trends identify the progress of important social factors such as the labor force participation among women, later age at first marriage, and delayed childbearing. Generational changes in the U.S. population from the baby boomers to their children, Generation Y, are key factors in ESRI's analysis of change in marital status and educational attainment. Once regional profiles for marital status and education are established, local area estimates link expected regional change to local changes in the distributions.

Housing

ESRI's housing updates include total housing units, occupancy, tenure, and home value. With the mortgage crisis extending beyond the subprime market and credit tightening, the housing market represents a major concern for not only homeowners and Wall Street but also all levels of government. Many local governments have stepped up their efforts to deal with the rising incidences of foreclosures.

Home prices have dropped from a historical high in recent years, with a median of $162,000 for the United States in 2009 compared with $183,000 in 2008. The last time the United States faced a widespread decline in home prices occurred in the early 1990s. That recovery started around the mid-1990s, with homeownership surging at the same time.

[4] A more detailed discussion of ESRI's 1990–2000 race analysis is available from Sangita Vashi's paper, *Trends in the U.S. Multiracial Population 1990–2000*, presented at the 2001 Southern Demographic Association's annual meeting.

In 2009, the U.S. homeownership rate fell to 66.2 percent. The rate hovered around 64 percent throughout the first half of the 1990s. From the mid-1990s, the rate climbed rapidly until 2004, then leveled off for the next few years before declining. Although the housing market crisis contributes to the recent decline in the homeownership rate, demographics play a key role. Due to the changing composition of the age cohorts in the United States, the homeownership rate is unlikely to climb back up to its historic high over the next few years. The echo boomers, or Generation Y, represent a sizable share of the population that is more likely to rent than own as they begin to form households. In contrast, the baby boomers are primarily homeowners because of their financial position, desire to own a home, or both.

Current data on change in the housing inventory encumbers the application of past trends. From 1990 to 2000, the housing stock increased by less than 1.4 million annually. From 2000 to 2008, the annual increment was more than 1.7 million units; however, the collapse of the housing market has slowed construction significantly in the past year. Total housing units are updated from the Census 2000 base by recorded changes in the housing inventory and estimated changes in occupancy rates since April 2000. Recorded change in the housing inventory is culled from several data sources, including construction data from Hanley Wood Market Intelligence, building permits for permit-issuing places and counties, and data for new manufactured homes placed by state from the Census Bureau. Dozens of independent sources were consulted to retrieve detailed information on housing development data where no building permits existed. Fewer than half the counties have complete coverage with building permits. Independent estimates of change in occupancy were calculated from U.S. Postal Service residential lists, vacancy durations from the Department of Housing and Urban Development, and data from the Current Population Survey and the Housing Vacancy Survey from the Census Bureau.

The data for tenure represents owner- and renter-occupied housing units. Together, the two components add up to total households, or total occupied housing units. A time series model based on data from the Housing Vacancy Survey, combined with changes in the Current Population Survey and the latest census data, guide tenure forecasts. With a blend of top-down and bottom-up techniques, the forecasts take advantage of the latest information from survey data at higher levels of geography while employing local characteristics at the lower levels. The data from the lower levels of geography are controlled to the higher levels to produce the tenure updates. Changes in owner-versus-renter occupancy are forecast independently and controlled to the total households.

ESRI tracks the change in home value using the HPI from the OFHEO. The HPI is designed to monitor changes in average home prices based on repeat sales or refinancing of the same properties. The index is derived from mortgage loans purchased or secured by Fannie Mae or Freddie Mac. The OFHEO affirms the significant advantages of the HPI over Commerce Department surveys or other data collections based on snapshots of sales figures. Employing the repeat-sales methodology renders the index less susceptible to compositional effects, especially with data for smaller geographic areas. If a higher proportion of lower-end homes are sold in the current period than in an earlier period, the survey data will give the misleading impression over time that home prices have fallen.

The OFHEO index series is released quarterly for states, metropolitan areas, and nonmetropolitan areas within states and with county or county group data for larger metropolitan areas. In 2008, ESRI began to incorporate trends in the purchase-only House Price Index series for states and the United States from the OFHEO. Traditionally, the OFHEO has combined loan data from purchases and refinancing to compute the index. For refinanced loans, the appraised value of a home is used in lieu of the sales value to estimate the change in home prices. ESRI has applied time series' analysis to extrapolate both short-term (2009) and long-range (2014) trends in home value from states and metropolitan areas to block groups. The 2008 update introduced sophisticated new techniques to capture the local relationship between the House Price Index and home value of all owner-occupied units. Local estimates of home value incorporate supply-demand characteristics, the socioeconomic traits of householders in the area, and HPI trends assessed for larger markets.

ESRI's 2009 estimates incorporate a new series from the OFHEO. Since Census 2000, ESRI has employed its State and Metropolitan Area series as a primary data source. The OFHEO has provided the Rural HPI series that tracks change in home prices for all nonmetropolitan counties in a state (including micropolitan counties). ESRI's 2009 estimates target growth or decline in home value to counties and smaller areas more accurately.

This has resulted in a realignment of growth between metropolitan and rural counties. Because ESRI's 2008 estimates did not benefit from information on rural trends, the 2008–2009 change in median home value is emphasized in some areas. States with the largest difference between the rural HPI trend line and the state HPI trend line will show this. Long-term trends between 2000 and 2009 are more reliable than short-term trends in these states.

Based on the OFHEO data, the majority of states show higher growth in rural counties compared to the parent state. In other words, metropolitan areas are experiencing the brunt of the downturn. Major metropolitan areas that have seen new homeownership increase rapidly since 2000 are the very areas that are now the heart of the housing crisis.

The 2009 update employs sophisticated new techniques to capture the local relationship between the House Price Index and home value. Local estimates of home value incorporate supply-demand characteristics, the socioeconomic traits of householders in the area, and HPI trends assessed for larger markets. Given the rise in unemployment and loss of income and the resetting of adjustable rate mortgages in the near future, it is clear that foreclosures have not yet hit their peak. According to Mark Zandi of Economy.com, foreclosures will peak around the fourth quarter of 2009, and growth in housing prices will only resume in the second half of 2010. ESRI's five-year recovery estimate is predicated on both short- and long-term trends in the OFHEO's House Price Index. ESRI estimates that home prices will grow at a rate of 2.7 percent per year between 2009 and 2014.

INCOME UPDATE METHODOLOGY

The recent slowdown in economic activity did not affect the job market until early 2008. This year, the labor force surplus is expected to cause downward pressure on wages and salaries. With the country now more than 16 months into a recession, the impact of this downturn is taking a toll on the earnings of every U.S. worker. ESRI's 2009 income estimates capture the 2008 calendar year income, the first year after the start of the current recession. Income declines during a recession for a number of reasons. Job cuts, reduced overtime hours, minimal wage growth, and even pay cuts are implemented as businesses try to cut costs.

Data Sources

ESRI's projection base is the income reported in Census 2000. Technically, 2000 income data represents income from 1999, because the Census Bureau tabulated income in the last year before the decennial census. Similarly, ESRI's 2009 income updates represent income received in 2008, expressed in 2008 dollars. Projections for 2014 are shown in 2013 dollars, assuming a continuation of the current rate of inflation, 2.9 percent.

ESRI uses the definition of money income used by the Census Bureau, which enables the direct comparison of income updates and decennial census data. For each person 15 years of age or older, money income received in the preceding calendar year is tallied from each of the following sources: earnings, unemployment compensation, Social Security, Supplemental Security Income, public assistance, veterans' payments, survivor benefits, disability benefits, pension or retirement income, interest, dividends, rent, royalties, estates and trusts, educational assistance, alimony, child support, financial assistance from outside the household, and other income.

Data for consumer income collected by the Census Bureau covers money income received (exclusive of certain money receipts such as capital gains) before payments for personal income taxes, Social Security, union dues, Medicare deductions, and so forth. Therefore, money income does not reflect the fact that some families receive part of their income in the form of noncash benefits, such as food stamps, health benefits, rent-free housing, or goods produced and consumed on a farm. In addition, money income does not include noncash benefits, such as the use of business transportation and facilities; full or partial payments by business for retirement, medical, and educational expenses; and so forth.

Income Methods

To estimate income for all households including family households, ESRI evaluated several federal data sources, including the CPS and ACS, and the personal and per capita income data and the Census of Employment and Wages from the Bureau of Labor Statistics.

After Census 2000, ESRI conducted a detailed evaluation of data sources employed in past income forecasts and an analysis of more recent data from the Supplementary and American Community Surveys. Data for 2000 from each source varied from the income that was reported in Census 2000. It was concluded that one point in time is not a good measure of a data series. For any given year, any estimate of income is likely to vary from the true population value. However, the sources that ESRI employed throughout the 1990s proved to be effective measures of change in income. Testing revealed the power of time series' data in tracking income. ESRI's postcensal updates emphasize the use of time series' data from household surveys to establish a base trend line. Annual updates evaluate current trends in wage inflation and other economic shocks that impact income growth. For the 2009 and 2014 forecasts, an evaluation of recessionary income trends that focused on dates, duration, and recovery periods was necessary.

After forecasting state income distributions, household income is estimated for counties, then block groups. ESRI's income forecasts are uniquely designed to distinguish local variation, changes in income inequality, and urbanicity as differentiators of income growth. The model correlates the characteristics of households at the block group geography level with changes in income. This stratification identifies several different patterns of change by household type that are applied to forecast trends in income. The annual change in income is derived from national surveys. Modeling links the current income change to all households with similar socioeconomic characteristics. Separate forecasts of the change in income by strata are aggregated to compose the income distributions.

Once the base 2000 income tabulations are updated, the distributions are extended to provide additional data for the wealthiest households. The Pareto function is employed to extend the upper interval of the income distributions from $200,000 or more to include the intervals $200,000–$249,999, $250,000–$499,999, and $500,000 or more. Finally, the models are calibrated to distinguish the change in average household income, for example, from the change in median income.

Average and median income for 2009 and 2014 are calculated in the same way that the Census 2000 average and median income were computed. Medians are calculated from the distributions using linear or Pareto interpolation, and averages are from aggregate household income.[5] Differences arise from the distributions. The 2000 income base from the Census Bureau is different from the income tables that are reported to the public. ESRI's 2009/2014 income base is also different from the Census 2000 reported tables. Medians and averages for 2009/2014 represent the extended income distributions to $500,000 or more. It is the extended income distributions that provide the base for updating aggregate income. Using the midpoints of income intervals in the extended distribution, aggregate household income is calculated to be consistent with the distribution of household income and the aggregate incomes that are estimated for the extended distributions of income by age of householder.

Household income reported by age of householder is updated to be consistent with the 2009/2014 distributions of household income and age of householder. To update the age distribution of householders, the ratio of householders by age to population by age in 2000 is extrapolated to 2009/2014 and applied to the current age distributions. After the targets are set, the 2000 distributions of household income by age of householder by block group are fitted to current distributions of households by income and by age of householder.

Use of Projections

Projections are necessarily derived from current events and past trends. The past and the present are known; the future must be extrapolated from this knowledge base. Even though projections represent the unknown, they are not uninformed. Guidelines for the development of projections also inform the use of those projections:

- The recent past provides a reasonable clue as to the course of future events, especially if that information is tempered with a historical perspective.
- A stable rate of growth is easier to anticipate than rapid growth or decline.
- The risk inherent in projections is inversely related to the size of an area: the smaller the area, the greater the risk.
- The risk increases with the length of the projection interval. Any deviation of the projected trends from actual events is amplified over time.

ESRI revises its projections annually to draw on the most recent estimates and projections of local trends. However, this data can be complemented with personal knowledge of an area to provide the qualitative, anecdotal detail that is not captured in a national database. It is incumbent upon the data user and the producers to incorporate as much information as

[5] For more information on calculations used with Census 2000 data, see *Census 2000 Summary File 3 Technical Documentation* prepared by the U.S. Bureau of the Census, 2002.

possible when assessing local trends, especially for areas that are subject to boom-bust cycles.

Changes in Geography

Change is inevitable with any geographic area—political or statistical. Identifying changes in the areas for which data is tabulated and reported is critical to the analysis of trends. In the past year, there have been minor changes to metropolitan areas by the Office of Management and Budget, boundary revisions for designated market areas (DMAs) by Nielsen Media Research, and the usual adjustment of ZIP Codes by the U.S. Postal Service (USPS).

Metropolitan changes include the latest revisions to core-based statistical areas (CBSAs), released in November 2008. Changes include three micropolitan areas that have been redefined as metropolitan areas: Cape Girardeau-Jackson, Missouri-Illinois (CBSA Code 16020); Manhattan, Kansas (CBSA Code 31740); and Mankato-North Mankato, Minnesota (CBSA Code 31860). There is also one name change that includes a code revision, The Dalles, Oregon, micropolitan statistical area (CBSA Code 45520, formerly 17180), as well as five other name changes. There are still 940 CBSAs, 366 metropolitan areas, and 574 micropolitan areas.

DMAs represent the 2008–2009 markets as defined by Nielsen Media Research. Most DMAs correspond to whole counties, but there are a few exceptions where counties are split into different DMAs. Finally, ZIP Codes, which are defined solely to expedite mail delivery, are updated to reflect the November 2008 inventory from the U.S. Postal Service.

ZIP CODE UPDATE METHODOLOGY

Data for residential ZIP Codes is estimated by ESRI. Census 2000 geographic areas are the building blocks for ESRI's ZIP Codes. Because ZIP Code boundaries change frequently, census geography provides a comparatively stable base for the development of ZIP Code data. ZIP Code data has been estimated from block groups. Block groups are assigned to residential ZIP Codes by overlaying the centroids of component blocks onto ZIP Code boundaries. Expressed as latitude/longitude coordinates, centroids approximate the geographic centers of blocks. If the centroid of a block falls within a ZIP Code, it is included in the residential inventory; otherwise, it is classified as nonresidential. Block data is then aggregated, and the ratio of block totals to block group data is used to apportion demographic characteristics to a ZIP Code.

The 2009/2014 updates include data for 30,094 residential ZIP Codes. This geodemographic method does not provide data for ZIP Codes with no assigned boundary. If a polygon is not defined for a ZIP Code, or no blocks are assigned to a ZIP Code polygon, data cannot be retrieved. In most cases, information about post office box ZIP Codes or single address ZIP Codes is incorporated with the data for the enclosing residential ZIP Code.

Data Source for Boundaries

Tele Atlas creates boundary files for ZIP Codes. The complete ZIP Code inventory includes both point and boundary ZIP Codes. ZIP Code boundaries are current as of November 2008.

Comparisons over Time

ZIP Codes are not amenable to time series' analysis, a fact which prevents a direct comparison with ZIP Codes from earlier updates. Changes typically include new residential ZIP Codes (40), dropped ZIP Codes (13), and boundary revisions. The 2009 inventory of residential ZIP Codes includes 5,315 ZIP Codes that have the same geocode as the 2008 inventory but a different population base as a result of boundary changes or slightly different block allocations. These changes reflect revisions of ZIP Codes by the U.S. Postal Service in addition to any changes in the techniques used by Tele Atlas to define ZIP Code boundaries.

ESRI'S DATA DEVELOPMENT TEAM

Led by chief demographer Lynn Wombold, ESRI's data development team has a 30-year history of excellence in market intelligence. The combined expertise of the team's economists, statisticians, demographers, geographers, and analysts totals nearly a century of data and segmentation development experience. The team has crafted data methodologies, such as the demographic update, segmentation, the Diversity Index, and the Retail MarketPlace database, that are now industry benchmarks.

Spending Potential Indices
Methodology Statement

Spending potential data measure the likely expenditure for a product or service in a county, ZIP Code, or other trade area. The ESRI database includes the average expenditure per household, total expenditures and a Spending Potential Index (SPI) for over 700 products and services. The Sourcebook contains the SPIs for 20 key products or services. The SPI compares the average local expenditure for a product to the average amount spent nationally. An index of 100 is average. An SPI of 120 shows that the average spent by local consumers is 20 percent above the national average. An SPI of 85 shows that the average spent is 15 percent below the national average.

Methodology
ESRI has combined the latest Consumer Expenditure Surveys (CEX), 2005 and 2006, from the Bureau of Labor Statistics (BLS) to estimate current spending patterns. The continuing surveys include a Diary Survey for daily purchases and an Interview Survey for general purchases. The Diary Survey represents record keeping by consumer units (CU) for two consecutive weeklong periods. This component of the CEX collects data on small, daily purchases that could be overlooked by the quarterly Interview Survey. The Interview Survey collects expenditure data from consumers in five interviews conducted every three months. ESRI integrates data from both surveys to provide a comprehensive database on all consumer expenditures. To compensate for the relatively small CEX survey bases and the variability of single-year data, expenditures are combined from the 2005 and 2006 surveys.

Over the years, both the BLS and ESRI have updated their methods of collecting and estimating the consumer spending data. In 2004, the BLS introduced multiple imputations of income data to estimate data for missing records and in 2001, the BLS revised the Interview Survey to collect income by using ranges in addition to discrete totals. The goal is to improve the accuracy of income reporting, but the changes also affects expenditures derived directly from income data, such as Social Security deductions. Additionally, the values reported in the surveys vary for select data items due to coding and definition changes.

For example, items like investments are commonly topcoded to a select upper limit. Topcoding replaces data when the value of the reported item exceeds prescribed critical values. The critical values for each topcoded variable are estimated in accordance with Census Disclosure Review Board guidelines. The topcoded value represents the mean of the subset of all outlying observations and, therefore, is subject to large changes from year to year. Any average, including average expenditures, can be influenced by the presence of extreme values. Therefore, when the topcode is changed, the average also changes. BLS may include other coding changes.

ESRI has updated the models used to estimate consumer spending with its segmentation system, Tapestry™ Segmentation. The model that links the spending of consumer units in CEX surveys to all households with similar socioeconomic characteristics is a conditional probability model that integrates consumer spending with Tapestry Segmentation, ESRI's market segmentation system. Tapestry truly differentiates consumer spending by market—especially among the smallest U.S. market areas, where distinctions can be difficult to measure, and for the largest ticket items, where consumer preferences are more pronounced. However, changes in the method of estimating consumer spending, like changes in the methods of data collection, preclude direct comparison with previous CEX databases.

Spending patterns are developed by Tapestry markets and updated to 2009 by adjusting to current levels of income. Expenditures represent 2009 annual averages and totals.

Computation of a Spending Potential Index
For any trade area, the expenditure per household for a particular product or service can be computed by linking the expenditure data to the demographic characteristics of the population. The SPI is defined as the ratio of the local average to the U.S. average expenditure. This equation shows how the index is derived:

$$SPI = \left[\frac{\text{Local Average Expenditure}}{\text{U.S. Average Expenditure}}\right] \times 100$$

How High is High?
The Spending Potential Index exhibits different value ranges for different products or services. In general, products pertaining to specific lifestyles or income levels will show a wider range of SPI values than the products or services purchased by everybody.

The SPI has an average value of 100, but the distribution of SPIs among ZIP Codes varies by product. The table on the next page shows the upper range of values for select SPIs by ZIP Code. This is a rough guide for determining "how high is high":

Medians and Percentiles of Spending Potential Indices: All U.S. ZIP Codes

		Somewhat High	Very High	Extremely High
		Percentiles		
	Median	***75th***	***90th***	***95th***
Financial Services:				
Auto Loan	86	99	125	150
Home Loan	72	97	141	177
Investments	84	103	142	181
Retirement Plans	71	98	141	179
The Home:				
Home Improvements				
Home Repair	73	97	142	181
Lawn & Garden	88	103	132	162
Furnishings	74	95	131	160
Computers and Hardware-Personal	83	99	131	161
Major Appliances	78	95	126	152
TV, Radio, Sound Equipment	70	94	135	168
Furniture	73	97	142	181
Entertainment:				
Dine Out/Carry Out	77	95	128	154
Sports Equipment	64	77	101	124
Fees & Tickets	66	95	140	177
Toys & Games	78	96	128	154
Travel	73	96	137	172
Cable TV	82	97	124	148
Personal:				
Apparel & Services	52	66	91	112
Auto Repairs	80	97	129	156
Health Insurance	87	101	126	151
Pets & Supplies	99	117	151	183

Variable Definitions

Here are definitions of the 2009 Sourcebook Spending Potential Indices:

Financial Services

Auto Loan
Reduction of principal vehicle loan, automobile finance charges, truck finance charges, motorcycle finance charges, and other vehicle finance charges. Other vehicles include motorized campers, trailer-type campers, other attachable type campers, scooters, mopeds, and boats.

Home Loan
Payments of mortgage interest and principal, property taxes, homeowners insurance, and ground rent.

Investments
Purchase price of stocks, bonds, or mutual funds.

Retirement Plans
Amount of private pension funds deducted from last pay, annualized for all consumer unit members.

The Home

Home Improvements

Home Repair
Maintenance and repair services associated with painting or papering, plumbing or water heating installation or repair, heating, air conditioning or electrical work, roofing and gutters, and other repair and maintenance work (including repair and replacement of hard surface flooring, and repair of built-in appliances such as dishwashers, garbage disposals, or range hoods). Maintenance and repair products associated with paints, wallpaper and supplies; painting and wallpapering tools and equipment; plumbing supplies and equipment; electrical supplies; heating and air conditioning; materials for hard surface flooring, roofing, gutters, downspouts, materials for plaster, panel, and siding, materials for patios, walks, fences, brick or stucco work; landscaping maintenance materials, insulation materials, materials for additions, finishing attics, remodeling rooms, construction materials for jobs not started, hard surface flooring material, material for landscape maintenance.

Lawn & Garden
Gardening and lawn care services, supplies, and equipment. Expenditures for indoor plants and fresh flowers, repairs/rentals of lawn and garden equipment.

Furnishings

Computers and Hardware - Personal
Computers, computer systems, and related hardware for non-business use.

Major Appliances
Purchase of dishwashers, garbage disposals, refrigerators, freezers, washing and drying machines, cooking ovens and stoves, microwave ovens, window air conditioning units, electric floor cleaning equipment, and miscellaneous household appliances such as sewing machines, etc.

TV, Radio, Sound Equipment
Community antenna or cable TV; portion of management fees for utilities in condos or co-ops. TV and video expenditures that include purchase of TVs , VCRs, video cameras/camcorders, disc players, video cassettes, tapes, and discs, video game hardware and software, satellite dishes and rental of videos (tapes, films, and discs). Expenditures for sound equipment include sound components and component systems, CD, tape, record and video mail order clubs, records, CDs, tapes, needles, tape recorders, radios, miscellaneous equipment/accessories, musical instruments and accessories, repair and rental of musical instruments, rental and repair of TV, VCR, radio and sound equipment.

Furniture
Mattresses and box springs, other bedroom furniture, sofas, living room chairs and tables, kitchen and dining room furniture infant furniture, outdoor furniture, wall units, cabinets and other furniture.

Entertainment

Dine Out/Carry-Out
Breakfast, lunch, dinner, or snacks at fast food or full service establishments, place of employment, or vending machines.

Sports Equipment
Equipment and gear for exercise, camping, hunting, fishing and sports (water, winter, etc.), game tables, and bicycles. Also, rental or repair of miscellaneous sports equipment.

Fees and Tickets
Fees and admissions for social, recreation, or civic club memberships, dating services, sports participation, movie, theater, opera, ballet, sporting events, or recreational lessons.

Toys & Games
Toys, games, hobbies, tricycles, playground equipment, play on arcade pinball/video games, and other entertainment and games.

Travel
Transportation expenditures for airline fares, intercity trains, ships, and intercity buses. Also includes trip expenditures such as local transport, taxis and limousines, auto and truck rentals, gasoline, motor oil, parking fees, tolls, and lodging; Expenditures on food and drink on trips (alcoholic beverages and food); Entertainment-related expenses on trips for recreation, participant sports, admission to movies, sporting events, etc.

Cable TV
Community antenna service, cable, or satellite.

Personal

Apparel and Services
Men's suits, sport coats, coats and jackets, underwear, socks, nightwear, uniforms, costumes, sweaters and vests, active sportswear, shirts, pants, shorts, and accessories. Women's coats and jackets, dresses, sport coats and tailored jackets, sweaters and vests, shirts, tops, and blouses, skirts, pants, shorts, active sportswear, sleepwear, uniforms, costumes, suits, undergarments, hosiery, and accessories. Boys' and girls' coats and jackets, sweaters, shirts, underwear, sleepwear, socks and hosiery, suits, dresses and skirts, shirts and blouses, sport coats, vests, pants, shorts, active sportswear, uniforms, costumes, and accessories. Footwear, jewelry, and watches. Apparel products and services, such as material for making clothes, sewing patterns and notions, shoe repair and other shoe services, laundry and dry cleaning, alteration, repair and tailoring of apparel, clothing rental and storage, and watch and jewelry repair.

Auto Repairs
Expenditures for vehicle maintenance and repairs such as coolant, additives, brake and transmission fluid, tires (purchased, replaced, installed), parts, equipment, and accessories, vehicle products, audio/video equipment, GPS services, miscellaneous auto repair and servicing, body work and painting, clutch, transmission, rear-end, and drive shaft repairs, brake work, steering, front end, and engine cooling system repair, motor tune up, lube, oil change, oil filters, front end alignment, wheel balance and rotation, shock absorber replacement, tire repair, air conditioning, exhaust and electrical system repair, motor repair and replacement, and auto repair service policies.

Health Insurance
Commercial health insurance coverage from traditional service health plans and preferred provider plans, health maintenance organizations, and Medicare payments. Coverage from Blue Cross/Blue Shield, which includes traditional service health plans, preferred provider plans, health maintenance organizations, commercial Medicare supplements, long-term care insurance plans, and other health insurance.

Pets & Supplies
Pets, pet food, pet supplies, pet services, medicine for pets, and veterinary services.

Tapestry™ Segmentation Methodology Statement

Based on the foundation of proven segmentation methodology introduced more than 30 years ago, the Tapestry™ Segmentation system classifies U.S. neighborhoods into 65 market segments. Neighborhoods with the most similar characteristics are grouped together, while neighborhoods showing divergent characteristics are separated.

Attributes Used to Build Tapestry Segmentation

Each U.S. neighborhood is analyzed and sorted by more than 60 attributes including income, employment, home value, housing type, education, household composition, age, and other key determinants of consumer behavior. U.S. consumer markets are multidimensional and diverse. Using a large array of attributes captures this diversity with the most powerful data available. Data sources include Census 2000 data, ESRI's proprietary demographic updates, the InfoBase® consumer database from Acxiom Corporation, and other sources to capture the subtlety and vibrancy of the U.S. marketplace.

Optimal Number of Segments

A frequently asked question about geodemographic segmentation is: Why does Tapestry Segmentation have 65 segments? Why not 60 or some other number? Tapestry Segmentation's 65 segments serve to effectively describe the U.S. markets. ESRI employed several statistical methods to ensure the optimal number of segments. The most intuitive measure among the batch of statistics used is the concept of stability. By examining how many neighborhoods would change their assignment, we could assess the stability of a solution. From an analysis of multiple solutions with different numbers of segments, the solution with 65 segments proved to be the most stable.

Statistical Methods

Tapestry Segmentation combines the traditional statistical methodology of cluster analysis with the latest data-mining techniques to provide a robust and compelling segmentation of U.S. neighborhoods. ESRI incorporated and developed these data-mining techniques to complement and strengthen traditional methods to work with a large geodemographic database.

Many neighborhoods contain large or small values in their geodemographic attributes. Robust methods are less susceptible to extreme values and, therefore, crucial to dealing with neighborhood data. The traditional methodology of cluster analysis has a long track record in developing segmentation systems. Complementary use of data-mining techniques and implementation of robust methods enhance the effectiveness of traditional statistical methodology in developing Tapestry Segmentation.

For a broader view of the consumer markets, cluster analysis was also used to develop Tapestry Segmentation's summary groups. The 65 segments are combined into 12 LifeMode groups based on lifestyle and lifestage. The 11 Urbanization groups present an alternative way of combining the 65 segments based on the segments' geographic and physical features and income. The summary groups are ideal when users want to work with fewer than all 65 segments.

Verification Procedures

Verification procedures follow the creation of the segments to ensure their stability and validity. Replicating the segments with independent samples checks stability. Validity is checked through the use of characteristics that are not used to generate the segments. Linking the Tapestry Segmentation system to the latest consumer survey data is the critical test. A market segmentation system must be able to distinguish consumer behavior—spending patterns and lifestyle choices—as expected. The validity check provides the answer to the most important question: Does it work?

Tapestry™ Segmentation Summary Descriptions

1. Top Rung

Top Rung is the wealthiest consumer market, representing less than one percent of all U.S. households. The median household income of $200,449 is more than three and one-half times that of the national median, and the median net worth of more than a million dollars is nearly ten times that of the national level. The median home value is $1,042,864. These educated residents are in their peak earning years, 45–64, in married-couple households, with or without children. The median age is 42.4 years. With the purchasing power to indulge any choice, Top Rung residents travel in style, both domestically and overseas. This is the top market for owning or leasing a luxury car; residents favor new imported vehicles, especially convertibles. Avid readers, these residents find time to read two or more daily newspapers and countless books.

2. Suburban Splendor

These successful suburbanites are the epitome of upward mobility, just a couple of rungs below the top, situated in growing neighborhoods of affluent homes with a median value of $442,916. Most households are composed of two-income, married-couple families with or without children. The population is well educated and well employed, with a median age of 41.5 years. Home improvement and remodeling are a main focus of Suburban Splendor residents. Their homes feature the latest amenities and reflect the latest in home design. Residents travel extensively in the United States and overseas for business and pleasure. Leisure activities include physical fitness, reading, visiting museums, or attending the theater. This market is proactive in tracking investments, financial planning, and holding life insurance policies.

3. Connoisseurs

Second in wealth to Top Rung but first for conspicuous consumption, Connoisseurs residents are well educated and somewhat older, with a median age of 47.3 years. Although residents appear closer to retirement than child rearing age, many of these married couples have children who still live at home. Their neighborhoods tend to be older bastions of affluence where the median home value is $706,720. Growth in these neighborhoods is slow. Residents spend money for nice homes, cars, clothes, and vacations. Exercise is a priority; they work out weekly at a club or other facility, ski, play golf, snorkel, play tennis, practice yoga, and jog. Active in the community, they work for political candidates or parties, write or visit elected officials, and participate in local civic issues.

4. Boomburbs

The newest additions to the suburbs, Boomburbs communities are home to younger families who live a busy, upscale lifestyle. The median age is 33.7 years. This market has the highest population growth at 5.3 percent annually—more than four and one-half times the national figure. The median home value is $334,829, and most households have two earners and two vehicles. This is the top market for households to own projection TVs, MP3 players, scanners, and laser printers as well as owning or leasing full-sized SUVs. It is the second-ranked market for owning flat-screen or plasma TVs, video game systems, and digital camcorders as well as owning or leasing minivans. Family vacations are a top priority. Popular vacation destinations are Disney World and Universal Studios, Florida. For exercise, residents play tennis and golf, ski, and jog.

5. Wealthy Seaboard Suburbs

Wealthy Seaboard Suburbs neighborhoods are established quarters of affluence located in coastal metropolitan areas, primarily along the California, New York, New Jersey, and New England coasts. Neighborhoods are older and slow to change, with a median home value that exceeds $471,252. Households consist of married-couple families. Over half of employed persons are in management and professional occupations. The median age is 42.3 years. Residents enjoy traveling and shopping. They prefer to shop at Macy's, and Nordstrom as well as BJ's Wholesale Club and Costco. They also purchase many items online or by phone. Residents take nice vacations, traveling in the United States and abroad. Europe; Hawaii; Atlantic City, New Jersey; Las Vegas, Nevada; and Disneyland are popular destinations. Leisure activities include going to the beach, skiing, ice skating, and attending theater performances.

6. Sophisticated Squires

Sophisticated Squires residents enjoy cultured country living in newer home developments with low density and a median home value of $268,921. These urban escapees are primarily married-couple families, educated, and well employed. They prefer to commute to maintain their semi-rural lifestyle. The median age is 38.3 years. They do their own lawn and landscaping work as well as home improvement and remodeling projects such as installing carpet or hardwood floors and interior painting. They like to barbeque on their gas grills and make bread with their bread-making machines. This is the top market for owning three or more vehicles. Vehicles of choice are minivans and full-sized SUVs. Family activities include playing volleyball, bicycling, playing board games and cards, going to the zoo, and attending soccer and baseball games.

7. Exurbanites
Open areas with affluence define these neighborhoods. Empty nesters comprise 40 percent of these households; married couples with children occupy 32 percent. Over half of the householders are between the ages of 45 and 64 years. The median age is 44.8 years. Approximately half of those who work hold professional or managerial positions. The median home value is $288,301; the median household income is $88,531. Financial health is a priority for the Exurbanites market; they consult with financial planners and track their investments online. They own a diverse investment portfolio and hold long-term care and substantial life insurance policies. Residents work on their homes, lawns, and gardens. Leisure activities include boating, hiking, kayaking, playing Frisbee, photography, and bird-watching. Many are members of fraternal orders and participate in civic activities.

8. Laptops and Lattes
Tapestry Segmentation's most eligible and unencumbered market, Laptops and Lattes residents are affluent, single, and still renting. They are highly educated, professional, and partial to city life, preferring major metropolitan areas such as New York, Los Angeles, San Francisco, Boston, and Chicago. The median household income is $101,325; the median age is 38.5 years. Technologically savvy, this is the top market for owning a laptop or notebook PC; they use the Internet on a daily basis, especially to shop. Their favorite department store, by far, is Banana Republic. Leisure activities include going to the movies, rock concerts, shows, museums, and nightclubs. These residents exercise regularly and take vitamins. They enjoy yoga, jogging, skiing, reading, watching foreign films on DVD, dining out, and traveling abroad. They embrace liberal philosophies and work for environmental causes.

9. Urban Chic
Urban Chic residents are well-educated professionals living an urban, exclusive lifestyle. Most own expensive single-family homes with a median value of $659,997. Married-couple families and singles comprise most of these households. The median age is 42 years. Urban Chic residents travel extensively, visit museums, attend dance performances, play golf, and go hiking. They use the Internet frequently to trade or track investments or to shop, buying concert and sports tickets, clothes, flowers, and books. They appreciate a good cup of coffee while reading a book or newspaper and prefer to listen to classical music, all-talk, or public radio programs. Civic minded, residents are likely to volunteer in their communities.

10. Pleasant-Ville
Prosperous domesticity distinguishes the settled homes of Pleasant-Ville neighborhoods. Most residents live in single-family homes with a median value of $339,930; approximately half were built in the 1950s and 1960s. Located primarily in the Northeast and California, these households are headed by middle-aged residents, some nearing early retirement. The median age is 39.8 years. Approximately 40 percent of households include children. Home remodeling is a priority for residents who live in older homes. Shopping choices are eclectic, ranging from upscale department stores to warehouse or club stores. Sports fanatics, they attend ball games, listen to sports programs and games on the radio, and watch a variety of sports on TV.

11. Pacific Heights
Pacific Heights neighborhoods are found in the high-rent districts of California and Hawaii. The median home value is $604,866; residents prefer single-family homes or townhomes. This market is small but affluent; one in two households earns $81,128 annually. The median age is 39.1 years. Distance does not deter Pacific Heights residents from keeping in touch with family living overseas, as they make frequent phone calls and travel overseas to visit. Many households own three or more cell phones. Residents generally visit Disneyland or Las Vegas, Nevada, during the year and enjoy playing chess, reading history books, and renting classic movies on DVD to watch on their giant screen or projection TVs. This is one the top markets for owning an Apple brand PC.

12. Up and Coming Families
Up and Coming Families represents the second highest household growth market and, with a median age of 31.9 years, is the youngest of Tapestry Segmentation's affluent family markets. The profile for these neighborhoods is young, affluent families with young children. Approximately half of the households are concentrated in the South, with another half in the West and Midwest. Neighborhoods are located in suburban outskirts of midsized metropolitan areas. The homes are newer, with a median value of $213,306. Because family and home priorities dictate their consumer purchases, they frequently shop for baby and children's

products and household furniture. Leisure activities include playing softball, going to the zoo, and visiting theme parks (generally SeaWorld or Disney World). Residents enjoy watching science fiction, comedy, and family-type movies on DVD.

13. In Style
In Style residents live in affluent neighborhoods of metropolitan areas. More suburban than urban, they nevertheless embrace an urban lifestyle. Townhome ownership is more than double that of the national level; however, more than half of the households are traditional single-family homes. Labor force participation is high, and professional couples predominate. The median household income is $72,326. Nearly one-third of these households include children. The median age is 40.3 years. In Style residents are computer savvy; they use the Internet daily to research information, track investments, or shop. They own a diverse investment portfolio, contribute to retirement savings plans, and hold long-term care and life insurance policies. They enjoy going to the beach, snorkeling, playing golf, casino gambling, and domestic travel.

14. Prosperous Empty Nesters
Prosperous Empty Nesters neighborhoods are well established, located throughout the United States; approximately one-third are on the eastern seaboard. The median age is 48.7 years. More than half of the householders are aged 55 or older. Forty percent of household types are married couples with no children living at home. Educated and experienced, residents are enjoying the life stage transition from child rearing to retirement. The median household income is $70,623. Residents place a high value on their physical and financial well-being and take an active interest in their homes and communities. They travel extensively, both at home and abroad. Leisure activities include refinishing furniture, playing golf, attending sports events, and reading mysteries. Civic participation includes joining civic clubs, engaging in fund-raising, and working as volunteers.

15. Silver and Gold
Silver and Gold residents are the second oldest of the Tapestry segments and the wealthiest seniors, with a median age of 59.7 years; most are retired from professional occupations. Their affluence has allowed them to move to sunnier climates. More than 60 percent of the households are in the South (mainly in Florida); 25 percent reside in the West, primarily in California and Arizona. Neighborhoods are exclusive, with a median home value of $369,808 and a high proportion of seasonal housing. Residents enjoy traveling, woodworking, playing cards, bird-watching, target shooting, saltwater fishing, and power boating. Golf is more a way of life than a mere leisure pursuit; they play golf, attend tournaments, watch golf on TV, and listen to golf programs on the radio. They are avid readers but also find the time to watch their favorite TV shows and a multitude of news programs.

16. Enterprising Professionals
This fast-growing market is home to young, educated, working professionals, with a median age of 32.4 years. Single or married, they prefer newer neighborhoods with townhomes or apartments. The median household income is $71,018. This segment is ranked second of all the Tapestry Segmentation markets for labor force participation, at 75 percent. Their lifestyle reflects their youth, mobility, and growing consumer clout. Residents rely on cell phones and PCs to stay in touch. They use the Internet to find their next job or home, track their investments, and shop. They own the latest electronic gadgets. Leisure activities include yoga, playing Frisbee and football, jogging, going to the movies, and attending horse races and basketball games. These residents also travel frequently, both domestically and overseas.

17. Green Acres
A "little bit country", Green Acres residents live in pastoral settings of developing suburban fringe areas, mainly in the Midwest and South. The median age is 40.7 years. Married couples with and without children comprise most of the households, which are primarily in single-family dwellings. This upscale market has a median household income of $65,074 and a median home value of $197,519. These do-it-yourselfers maintain and remodel their homes, painting, installing carpet, or adding a deck, and own all the necessary tools to accomplish these tasks. They also take care of their lawn and gardens, again, with the right tools. Vehicles of choice are motorcycles and full-sized pickup trucks. For exercise, residents ride their bikes and go water skiing, canoeing, and kayaking. Other activities include bird-watching, power boating, target shooting, hunting, and attending auto races.

18. Cozy and Comfortable
Cozy and Comfortable residents are settled, married, and still working. Many couples are still living in the pre-1970s, single-family homes in which they raised their children. Households are located primarily in suburban areas of the Midwest, Northeast, and South. The median age is 42.1 years, and the median home value is $174,687. Home improvement and remodeling are important to Cozy and Comfortable residents. Although some work is contracted, homeowners take an active part in many projects, especially painting and lawn care. They play softball and

golf, attend ice hockey games, watch science fiction films on DVD, and gamble at casinos. Television is significant; many households have four or more sets. Preferred cable stations include QVC, Home & Garden Television, and The History Channel.

19. Milk and Cookies
Milk and Cookies households are composed mainly of young, affluent married-couple families. Approximately half of the households include children. The median age for this market is 34 years. Residents prefer single-family homes in suburban areas, chiefly in the South, particularly in Texas. Smaller concentrations of households are located in the West and Midwest. The median home value is $148,781. Families with two or more workers, more than one child, and two or more vehicles is the norm for this market. Residents are well insured for the future. The presence of children drives their large purchases of baby and children's products and timesavers such as fast food. For fun, residents play video games, chess, backgammon, basketball and football, or fly kites. Favorite cable channels include Toon Disney, The Discovery Health Channel, ESPNews, and Lifetime Movie Network.

20. City Lights
City Lights neighborhoods are diverse, situated primarily in the Northeast. This dense, urban market is a mixture of housing, household types, and cultures, sharing the same city sidewalks. Housing types include single-family homes, townhomes, and apartments. Thirty-five percent of households are apartments in buildings with two to four units, almost four times the national level. Approximately two-thirds of the housing units were built before 1960. Households include both families and singles. The median age of 37.8 years is slightly older than the U.S. median. City Lights residents are more likely to spend for household furnishings than home maintenance. They shop at a variety of stores, especially Macy's, Disney Store, Gap, and BJ's Wholesale Club. They favor overseas travel. Being conservative investors, they own U.S. savings bonds.

21. Urban Villages
Urban Villages neighborhoods are multicultural enclaves of young families, unique to U.S. gateway cities located primarily in California. The median age is 30.5 years. All family types dominate this market. The average family size of 4.18 is the second highest of all the Tapestry segments. Many households have two wage earners, chiefly employed in the manufacturing, health care, retail trade, construction, and educational services industries. The median household income is $63,363. Most residents own older, single-family homes with a median value of $346,721, and multiple vehicles. Family and home dictate purchases. To maintain their older homes, time and money are spent on home remodeling and repairs. Leisure activities include playing soccer and tennis, renting foreign films, listening to Hispanic and variety radio, and visiting Disneyland, SeaWorld, or Six Flags theme parks.

22. Metropolitans
Metropolitans residents favor city living in older neighborhoods. Approximately half of the households are composed of singles who live alone or with others. However, married-couple families comprise 40 percent of the households. The median age is 37.7 years. Over half of employed persons hold professional or management positions. These neighborhoods are an eclectic mix of single-family homes and multiunit structures, with a median home value of $215,587. The median household income is $62,812. Residents lead busy, active lifestyles. They travel frequently and participate in numerous civic activities. They enjoy going to museums and zoos and listening to classical music and jazz on the radio. Refinishing furniture and playing a musical instrument are favorite hobbies. Exercise includes yoga, using Rollerblades, and hiking/backpacking.

23. Trendsetters
These neighborhoods are located primarily on the West Coast. On the cutting edge of urban style, Trendsetters residents are young, diverse, mobile, educated professionals with substantive jobs. The median age is 35.5 years. More than half of the households are single-person or shared. Most still rent, preferring upscale, multiunit dwellings in older city districts. The median household income is $64,002. Residents are spenders; they shop in stores, online, and via the phone. They own the latest laptop computers, cell phones, and MP3 players, and use the Internet daily. Exercise includes playing tennis, volleyball, baseball, and golf as well as ice skating, snorkeling, and yoga. Leisure activities include traveling, attending rock concerts, and reading biographies. Residents also enjoy syndicated TV shows such as Access Hollywood and Seinfeld.

24. Main Street, USA
Main Street, USA neighborhoods are a mix of single-family homes and multiunit dwellings found in the suburbs of smaller metropolitan cities, mainly in the Northeast, West, and Midwest. This market is similar to the United States when comparing household type, age, educational attainment, housing type, occupation, industry, and household income type distributions. The median age of 36.8 years matches that of the U.S. median. The median household income is a

comfortable $56,882. Homeownership is at 65 percent, and the median home value is $205,391. Active members of the community, residents participate in local civic issues and work as volunteers. They take care of their lawns and gardens, and work on small home projects. They enjoy going to the beach and visiting theme parks as well as playing chess, going bowling or ice skating, and participating in aerobic exercise.

25. Salt of the Earth
A rural or small-town lifestyle best describes the Salt of the Earth market. The median age is 41.4 years. Labor force participation is higher than the U.S. level, and unemployment is lower. Above-average numbers of employed residents work in the manufacturing, construction, mining, and agricultural industries. The median household income is $50,913. Households are dominated by married-couple families who live in single-family dwellings, with homeownership at 85 percent. Twenty-eight percent of the households own three or more vehicles. Most homes own a truck; many own a motorcycle. Residents are settled, hardworking, and self-reliant, taking on small home projects as well as vehicle maintenance. Families often own two or more pets, usually dogs or cats. Residents enjoy fishing, hunting, target shooting, attending country music concerts and auto races, and flying kites.

26. Midland Crowd
Approximately 11.9 million people represent Midland Crowd, Tapestry Segmentation's largest market. The median age of 37 is similar to the US Median. Most households are composed of married-couple families, half with children and half without. The median household income is $50,462. Housing developments are generally in rural areas throughout the United States (more village or town than farm), mainly in the South. Home ownership is at 83 percent. Two-thirds of households are single-family structures; 28 percent are mobile homes. This is a somewhat conservative market politically. These do-it-yourselfers take pride in their homes, lawns, and vehicles. Hunting, fishing, and woodworking are favorite pursuits. Pet ownership, especially birds or dogs, is common. Many households have a satellite dish, and TV viewing includes various news programs as well as shows on CMT and Outdoor Life Network.

27. Metro Renters
Metro Renters residents are young (approximately 30 percent are in their 20s), well-educated singles beginning their professional careers in some of the largest U.S. cities such as New York City, Chicago, and Los Angeles. The median age is 33.8 years; the median household income is $59,730. As the name Metro Renters implies, most residents are renting apartments in high-rise buildings, living alone or with a roommate. Their interests include traveling, reading two or more daily newspapers, listening to classical music and public radio programs, and surfing the Internet. For exercise, they work out regularly at clubs, play tennis and volleyball, practice yoga, ski, and jog. They enjoy dancing, attending rock concerts, going to museums or the movies, and throwing a Frisbee. Painting and drawing are favorite hobbies. Politically, this market is liberal.

28. Aspiring Young Families
Aspiring Young Families neighborhoods are located in large, growing metropolitan areas in the South and West, with the highest concentrations in California, Florida, and Texas. Mainly composed of young, married-couple families or single parents with children, the median age for this segment is 30.6 years. Nearly half of the households are owner-occupied, single-family dwellings or townhomes, and over half are occupied by renters, many living in newer, multiunit buildings. Residents spend much of their discretionary income on baby and children's products and toys as well as home furnishings. Recent electronic purchases include cameras and video game systems. Leisure activities include dining out, dancing, going to the movies, attending professional football games, fishing, weight lifting, and playing basketball. Typically, vacations would include visits to theme parks. Internet usage mainly involves chat room visits.

29. Rustbelt Retirees
Most Rustbelt Retirees neighborhoods can be found in older, industrial cities in the Northeast and Midwest, especially in Pennsylvania and other states surrounding the Great Lakes. Households are mainly occupied by married couples with no children and singles who live alone. The median age is 45 years. Although many residents are still working, labor force participation is below average. More than 40 percent of the households receive Social Security benefits. Most residents live in owned, single-family homes, with a median value of $129,157. Unlike many retirees, these residents are not inclined to move. They are proud of their homes and gardens and participate in community activities. Some are members of veterans' clubs. Leisure activities include playing bingo, gambling in Atlantic City, going to the horse races, working crossword puzzles, and playing golf.

30. Retirement Communities
Retirement Communities neighborhoods are found mostly in cities scattered across the United States. The majority of households are multiunit dwellings. Congregate housing, which commonly

includes meals and other services in the rent, is a trait of this segment dominated by singles who live alone. This educated, older market has a median age of 51.9 years. One-third of residents are aged 65 years or older. Although the median household income is a modest $48,889, the median net worth is $119,873. Good health is a priority; residents visit their doctors regularly, diet and exercise, purchase low-sodium food, and take vitamins. They spend their leisure time working crossword puzzles, playing bingo, gardening indoors, canoeing, gambling, and traveling overseas. They like to spend time with their grandchildren and spoil them with toys. Home remodeling projects are usually in the works.

31. Rural Resort Dwellers

Favoring milder climates and pastoral settings, Rural Resort Dwellers residents live in rural, nonfarm areas. These small, growing communities mainly consist of single-family and mobile homes, with a significant inventory of seasonal housing. This somewhat older market has a median age of 47.1 years. Most households consist of married couples with no children living at home or singles who live alone. A higher-than-average proportion of residents are self employed and work from home. The median household income is $47,908. Modest living and simple consumer tastes describe this market. The rural setting calls for more riding lawn mowers and satellite dishes. Lawn maintenance and gardening is a priority, and households own a plethora of tools and equipment. Many households own or lease a truck. Residents enjoy boating, hunting, fishing, snorkeling, canoeing, and listening to country music.

32. Rustbelt Traditions

Rustbelt Traditions neighborhoods are the backbone of older, industrial cities in states bordering the Great Lakes. Most employed residents work in the service, manufacturing, and retail trade industries. Most residents own and live in modest single-family homes that have a median value of $102,391. Households are primarily a mix of married-couple families, single-parent families, and singles who live alone. The median age is 36.1 years; the median household income is $51,436. Residents prefer to use a credit union and invest in certificates of deposit. They use coupons regularly, especially at Sam's Club, work on home remodeling or improvement projects, and buy domestic vehicles. Favorite leisure activities include hunting, bowling, fishing, and attending auto races, country music shows, and ice hockey games (in addition to listening to games on the radio).

33. Midlife Junction

Midlife Junction communities are found in suburbs across the country. Residents are phasing out of their child-rearing years. Approximately half of the households are composed of married-couple families; 31 percent are singles who live alone. The median age is 41.2 years; the median household income is $49,031. One-third of the households receive Social Security benefits. Nearly two-thirds of the households are single-family structures; most of the remaining dwellings are apartments in multiunit buildings. These residents live quiet, settled lives. They spend their money prudently and do not succumb to fads. They prefer to shop by mail or phone from catalogs such as J.C. Penney, L.L. Bean, and Lands' End. They enjoy yoga, attending country music concerts and auto races, refinishing furniture, and reading romance novels.

34. Family Foundations

Family is the cornerstone of life in Family Foundations communities. A family mix of married couples, single parents, grandparents, and young and adult children populate these small, urban neighborhoods located in large metropolitan areas, primarily in the South and Midwest. This market represents stability. Hardly any household growth has occurred since 2000; these neighborhoods experience little turnover. The median age is 39.0 years; the median household income is $46,308. Most households are single-family structures built before 1970, occupied by owners. Many residents are members of church boards or religious clubs and participate in fund-raising. Basketball is a favorite sport; residents play it, attend professional games, watch games on TV and listen to games on the radio. They watch courtroom TV shows, sports, and news programs on TV and listen to gospel, urban, and jazz radio formats.

35. International Marketplace

Located primarily in cities in coastal gateway states, International Marketplace neighborhoods are developing, urban markets with a rich blend of cultures and household types. Approximately 70 percent of households are occupied by families. Married couples with children and single parents with children represent 44 percent of households. A typical family rents an apartment in an older, multiunit structure. Most of the households are located in California and northeastern states. The median age is 30.3 years, and the median household income is $47,207. Top purchases include groceries and children's clothing. Residents shop at stores such as Marshalls and Costco, but for convenience, they stop at 7-Eleven or other similar convenience stores. They are loyal listeners of Hispanic radio programs and prefer to watch movies and sports on TV.

36. Old and Newcomers
Old and Newcomers neighborhoods are in transition, populated by those who are starting their careers or retiring. The proportion of householders in their 20s or aged 75 years or older is higher than the national level. The median age is 37.1 years. Spread throughout metropolitan areas of the United States, these neighborhoods have more single-person and shared households than families. Many residents have moved in the last five years. Over sixty percent of households are occupied by renters; approximately half live in mid-rise or high-rise buildings. Residents have substantial life insurance policies and investments in certificates of deposit, bonds, and annuities. Leisure activities include roller skating, using Rollerblades, playing golf, gambling at casinos, playing bingo, and attending college ball games. They listen to classic hits on the radio. Many residents are members of fraternal orders or school boards.

37. Prairie Living
Agriculture plays an important part of the Prairie Living economy; small, family-owned farms dominate this stable market located mainly in the Midwest. Two-thirds of the households are married-couple families; the median age is 41.3 years. Homeownership is at 80 percent; the median home value is $106,220. Although single-family dwellings are characteristic of these communities, 11 percent of the households live in mobile homes. More than a third of the housing units were built before 1940. These residents are big country music fans and enjoy hunting, fishing, target shooting, and horseback riding. They work on their vegetable gardens, vehicles, and home projects. Many are members of church boards or civic clubs and get involved in civic issues. Because cable TV can be unavailable in these rural areas, many households have a satellite dish. Families with pet cats or dogs are common.

38. Industrious Urban Fringe
Industrious Urban Fringe neighborhoods are found on the fringe of metropolitan cities. Approximately half of these households are located in the West; 40 percent are in the South. Most employed residents work in the manufacturing, construction, retail trade, and service industries. Family is central, and children are present in more than half of the households. Many live in multigenerational households. The median age is 28.6 years; the median household income is $43,007. Two-thirds of the households own their single-family dwellings, with a median value of $146,678. Necessities for babies and children are among their primary purchases along with toys and video games. Big movie fans, residents visit the cinema several times a month and watch movies at home frequently. They prefer to watch syndicated TV and listen to Hispanic radio.

39. Young and Restless
Change is the constant in this diverse market. With a median age of 28.7 years, the population is young and on the go. About 85 percent of householders moved in the last five years. Young and Restless householders are primarily renters, living in apartments in multiunit buildings. Almost 60 percent are single-person or shared households. This educated market has the highest labor force participation among all the Tapestry segments, at 76 percent, and the highest female labor force participation, at 73 percent. The median household income is $45,236. Residents use the Internet daily to visit chat rooms, play games, obtain the latest news, and search for employment. They read computer and music magazines and listen to public radio. They watch movies in the theater and on DVD, attend rock concerts, play pool, go dancing, and exercise weekly at a gym.

40. Military Proximity
Military Proximity communities depend upon the military for their livelihood. More than 75 percent of the labor force is in the armed forces, and others work in civilian jobs on military bases. The median household income is $45,232, and the median age is 22.5 years. Two-thirds of the households are composed of married couples with children. Housing types are mainly townhomes and apartments in small, multiunit buildings; 93 percent are occupied by renters. Residents participate in civic activities and are members of business clubs. Many homes have a pet, most likely a dog. Residents use the Internet to trade stocks and make purchases. For exercise, they snorkel, play tennis, practice yoga, and jog. Families visit theme parks and the zoo, throw Frisbees, and go bowling. Recent purchases include MP3 players, digital cameras, video game systems, cell phones, apparel, and jewelry.

41. Crossroads
Young families living in mobile homes typify Crossroads neighborhoods, found in small towns throughout the South, Midwest, and West. These growing communities are home to married-couple and single-parent families. The median age is 32.1 years. Homeownership is at 75 percent, and the median home value is $73,224. More than half of the householders live in mobile homes; 36 percent live in single-family dwellings. Employment is chiefly in the manufacturing, construction, retail trade, and service industries. Many homes have dogs. Residents generally

shop at discount stores but also frequent convenience stores. They prefer domestic cars and trucks, often buying and servicing used vehicles. Residents go fishing, attend auto races, participate in auto racing, and play the lottery. An annual family outing to SeaWorld is common.

42. Southern Satellites

Southern Satellites neighborhoods are rural settlements found primarily in the South, with employment chiefly in the manufacturing and service industries. Married-couple families dominate this market. The median age is 37.7 years, and the median household income is $39,758. Most housing is newer, single-family dwellings or mobile homes with a median value of $90,801, occupied by owners. Residents enjoy country living. They listen to gospel and country music on the radio and attend country music concerts. They participate in fishing, hunting, and auto racing. Favorite TV stations are CMT and Outdoor Life Network. Satellite dishes are popular in these rural locations. Households own older, domestic vehicles, particularly trucks and two-door sedans. Residents invest time in vegetable gardening, and households are likely to own riding mowers, garden tractors, and tillers.

43. The Elders

The Elders residents' median age of 73.5 years represents Tapestry Segmentation's oldest market. The highest concentration of retiree residents prefer communities designed for senior living, primarily in warm climates. Half of these households are located in Florida, and 30 percent are situated in Arizona or California. Approximately 80 percent of households collect Social Security benefits; 48 percent receive retirement income. These residents are members of veterans' clubs and fraternal orders. Health conscious, they take vitamins, visit doctors regularly, and watch their diets. Leisure activities include traveling, working crossword puzzles, fishing, attending horse races, gambling at casinos, going to the theater, and dining out. They play golf, listen to golf on the radio, and watch tournaments on The Golf Channel. Their daily routine includes watching TV and reading newspapers.

44. Urban Melting Pot

The ethnically rich Urban Melting Pot neighborhoods are made up of recently settled immigrants; more than half of whom were born abroad. Half of the foreign-born residents immigrated to the United States in the last 10 years. Most rent apartments in high-density, urban canyons of large cities, primarily in New York and California. Approximately half of the housing units were built before 1950. The median age is 36.4 years, and the median household income is $42,129. These fashion- and cost-conscious residents love to shop, from upscale retailers to warehouse/club stores. Leisure activities include going to the beach, visiting theme parks and museums, playing football, ice skating, and using Rollerblades. Distance does not deter these residents from contacting family living outside the United States. They keep in touch with phone calls and overseas travel.

45. City Strivers

City Strivers members are urban denizens of densely settled neighborhoods in major metropolitan areas such as New York City and Chicago, Illinois. Most households are composed of a mix of family types. The median age is 32.3 years, and the median household income is $41,376. Employment is concentrated in the city, with over half of employed residents working in the service industry, particularly in health care. Twenty-two percent are government workers. Unemployment is more than twice that of the U.S. level. Housing is mostly older, rented apartments in smaller, multiunit buildings. Primary spending is for groceries, baby products, and children's essentials. Residents enjoy going to dance performances, football and basketball games, and Six Flags theme parks. They listen to urban, all-news, and jazz radio formats and watch TV, especially movies, sitcoms, news programs, courtroom TV and talk shows, tennis, and wrestling.

46. Rooted Rural

Rooted Rural neighborhoods are located in rural areas throughout the country; however, more than three-fifths of the households are located in the South. Households are dominated by married-couple families. One-third of the households receive Social Security benefits. The median age is 42.2 years. Housing is predominantly single-family dwellings, with a strong presence of mobile homes and some seasonal housing. The median home value is $101,198. Stable and settled, residents tend to move infrequently. They are do-it-yourselfers, constantly working on their homes, gardens, and vehicles. Many families have pets. Residents enjoy hunting, fishing, target shooting, boating, attending country music concerts, and listening to country music on the radio. Many households have a satellite dish; favorite stations include Outdoor Life Network and CMT.

47. Las Casas

Las Casas residents are the latest wave of western pioneers. Settled primarily in California, approximately half were born outside the United States. Young, Hispanic families dominate these households; 63 percent include children. This market has the highest average household size

(4.28) among all the Tapestry segments. The median age is 25.7 years, and the median household income is $38,689. Most households are occupied by renters, although homeownership is at 41 percent. The median home value is $280,115. Housing is a mix of older apartment buildings, single-family homes, and townhomes. This is a strong market for the purchase of baby and children's products. Residents enjoy listening to Hispanic radio, reading adventure stories, and playing soccer. Many treat their children to a family outing at a theme park, especially Disneyland. When taking a trip, Mexico is a popular destination.

48. Great Expectations
Great Expectations neighborhoods are located throughout the country, with higher proportions found in the Midwest and South. Young singles and married-couple families dominate. The median age is 33.2 years. Labor force participation is high. Manufacturing, retail, and service industries are the primary employers. Approximately half of the households are owners living in single-family dwellings with a median value of $110,922; the other half are renters, mainly living in apartments in low-rise or mid-rise buildings. Most of the housing units in these older, suburban neighborhoods were built before 1960. Residents enjoy a young and active lifestyle. They go out to dinner, to the movies, to bars, and to nightclubs. They enjoy roller skating; using Rollerblades; playing Frisbee, chess, and pool; and attending auto races. They read music magazines and listen to rock music on the radio.

49. Senior Sun Seekers
The Senior Sun Seekers market is one of the faster growing markets, located mainly in the South and West, especially in Florida. Escaping from cold winter climates, many residents have permanently relocated to warmer areas; others are "snowbirds" who move south for the winter. Most residents are retired or are anticipating retirement. The median age is 52.5 years; 63 percent of the householders are aged 55 years or older. Most households are single-family dwellings or mobile homes with a median value of $129,580. There is a high proportion of seasonal housing. Many residents are members of veterans' clubs or fraternal orders. They own high-paying insurance policies and consult with financial advisors. Leisure activities include dining out, reading (especially boating magazines), watching TV, fishing, playing backgammon and bingo, working crossword puzzles, and gambling at casinos.

50. Heartland Communities
Heartland Communities neighborhoods are preferred by approximately six million people. These neighborhoods can be found primarily in small towns in the Midwest and South. More than 75 percent of the households are single-family dwellings with a median home value of $82,080. Most homes are older, built before 1960. The median age is 42.0 years; nearly one-third of the householders are aged 65 years or older. The distinctly country lifestyle of these residents is reflected in their interest in hunting, fishing, woodworking, playing bingo, and listening to country music. In addition to working on home improvement projects, they are avid gardeners and read gardening magazines. They participate in civic activities and take an interest in local politics. Residents order items from catalogs, QVC, and Avon sales representatives.

51. Metro City Edge
Metro City Edge residents live in older, suburban neighborhoods of large, metropolitan cities, primarily in the Midwest and South. This market is home to married-couple, single-parent, and multigenerational families. The median age is 29.4 years, and the median household income is $32,291. Nearly half of employed residents work in the service industry. Most households live in single-family dwellings; 14 percent live in buildings with two to four units, many of them duplexes. Homeownership is at 54 percent, and the median home value is $78,213. Prudent shoppers, residents buy household and children's items at superstores and wholesalers. They enjoy watching TV (especially sitcoms and courtroom TV shows), going to the movies, visiting theme parks, roller skating, and playing basketball. They read music, gardening, and baby magazines and listen to urban and gospel radio.

52. Inner City Tenants
Inner City Tenants neighborhoods are a microcosm of urban diversity, located primarily in the South and West. This multicultural market is young, with a median age of 27.9 years. Households are a mix of singles and families. Most residents rent economical apartments in mid- or high-rise buildings. Recent household purchases by this market include video game systems, baby food, baby products, and furniture. Internet access at home is not typical; those who have no access at home surf the Internet at school or at the library. Playing games and visiting chat rooms are typical online activities. Residents frequently eat at fast-food restaurants. They enjoy going to the movies; attending football and basketball games; water skiing; and playing football, basketball, and soccer. Some enjoy the nightlife, visiting bars and nightclubs to go dancing.

53. Home Town
These low-density, settled neighborhoods, located chiefly in the Midwest and South, rarely

change. Home Town residents stay close to their home base. Although they may move from one house to another, they rarely cross the county line. Household types are a mix of singles and families. The median age is 34.0 years. Single-family homes predominate in this market. Homeownership is at 59 percent, and the median home value is $66,885. The manufacturing, retail trade, and service industries are the primary sources of employment. Residents enjoy fishing and playing baseball, bingo, backgammon, and video games. Favorite cable TV stations include CMT, Nick-at-Nite, Game Show Network, and TV Land. Belk and Wal-Mart are favorite shopping destinations stops; residents also purchase items from Avon sales representatives.

54. Urban Rows
With 1.1 million people, Urban Rows is the smallest Tapestry segment. Row houses are characteristic of these neighborhoods found primarily in large, northeastern cities, with much smaller concentrations in the South. Two-thirds of the households are in Pennsylvania; one-fifth are in Maryland. Homeownership is at 61 percent, and the median home value is $92,746. Most housing was built before 1950. Households are a mix of family types. Nearly half of the households do not own a vehicle. The median age is 33.3 years. These residents rarely eat out. They prefer BJ's Wholesale Club for general shopping; preferred grocery stores are Acme, Pathmark, and Giant. Residents enjoy roller skating; playing baseball; attending basketball games; listening to urban, variety, and jazz radio programs; and watching sitcoms and sports on TV. Many households do not subscribe to cable TV.

55. College Towns
Education is the key focus for College Towns residents. College and graduate school enrollment is 41 percent. The median age for this market is 24.4 years, with a high concentration of 18–24-year-olds. One out of eight residents lives in a dorm on campus. Students in off-campus housing rent low-income apartments. Twenty-nine percent of the households are occupied by owners, who are typically town residents living in single-family dwellings. The median home value is $148,030. Convenience is the primary consideration for food purchases; residents frequently eat out, order in, or eat easy-to-prepare food. Many own a laptop computer. In their leisure time, they jog, go horseback riding, practice yoga, play tennis, rent videos, play chess or pool, attend concerts, attend college football or basketball games, and go to bars. They listen to classical music and public radio programs.

56. Rural Bypasses
Open space, undeveloped land, and farmland are found in Rural Bypasses neighborhoods located almost entirely in the South. This market is home to families who live in small towns along country back roads. The median age is 38.0 years. Higher-than-average proportions of employed residents work in the agricultural, mining, manufacturing, and construction industries. Labor force participation is low, and unemployment is high. Although most households are single-family dwellings, 32 percent are mobile homes. Homeownership is at 77 percent, and the median home value is $66,625. Residents save money by maintaining their homes, gardens, and vehicles themselves. They enjoy hunting, reading fishing and hunting magazines, and listening to gospel radio. They prefer to watch courtroom TV and talk shows as well as cartoons. Recent purchases include baby products, clothes, and toys.

57. Simple Living
Simple Living neighborhoods are found in urban outskirts or suburban areas throughout the United States. Half of the households are singles who live alone or share housing, and 32 percent consist of married-couple families. The median age is 40.7 years. Approximately one-third of householders are aged 65 years or older; 19 percent are aged 75 years or older. Housing is a mix of single-family dwellings and multiunit buildings of varying stories. Some seniors live in congregate housing (assisted living). Fifty-six percent of households are occupied by renters. Forty percent of households receive Social Security benefits. Younger residents enjoy going out dancing, whereas seniors prefer going to bingo night. To stay fit, residents play softball and volleyball. Many households do not own a computer, cell phone, or DVD player. Residents watch hours of TV a day, especially sitcoms and science fiction shows.

58. NeWest Residents
Most NeWest Residents members rent apartments in mid- or high-rise buildings, primarily in major cities in the West and South. California has the largest concentration of these households, followed by Texas. Families dominate this market. Children reside in 54 percent of the households, either in married-couple or single-parent families. Approximately half of the population is foreign-born. This young market has a median age of 25.4 years. Most of the employed residents work in service and skilled labor occupations. These residents lead a strongly family-oriented lifestyle. Budget constraints restrict their purchases to essentials such as baby food, equipment, and products as well as children's clothing. For fun, families go to the movies, visit theme parks, and play soccer.

They like to watch sports on TV, especially wrestling and soccer, and listen to Hispanic radio.

59. Southwestern Families
These families are the bedrock of the Hispanic culture in the Southwest, more with children than without. Two-thirds of the households live in owner-occupied, single-family dwellings with a median home value of $60,100. Most employed residents work in blue collar or service occupations. Southwestern Families is an ethnically diverse market, with a median age of 28.6 years and a median household income of $27,863. Recent purchases include baby and children's products. Households generally own or lease a two-door sedan. The grocery store of choice is H.E. Butt. When eating fast food, Whataburger is a favorite stop. Residents enjoy fishing, water skiing, playing soccer, and going to the movies. They read gardening and parenthood magazines and listen to Hispanic and urban radio formats. Typical TV viewing includes comedies as well as wrestling and boxing.

60. City Dimensions
Diversity in household type and ethnicity characterize City Dimensions neighborhoods that are located in large, urban cities. Population density remains high, with approximately 2,900 people per square mile. This market is young, with a median age of 29.2 years. Sixty-five percent of the households rent. More than half are apartments in multiunit structures. Most of the real estate is older. Approximately 70 percent of the housing units were built before 1960, 42 percent of which were built before 1940. Many households lease their vehicles, preferring Mercury or Ford models. Residents shop at BJ's Wholesale Club, Kmart, Marshalls, and T.J. Maxx. They enjoy roller skating, playing soccer and chess, attending auto races and shows, going to the movies, and renting movies on DVD (especially classics, horror, and science fiction). Video game systems are also popular.

61. High Rise Renters
This segment has the highest percentage of renters among all the Tapestry segments; more than nine in ten households are renters in these densely populated neighborhoods. Over 40 percent of the households are in buildings with 50 or more units. High Rise Renters communities are located almost entirely in the Northeast; 86 percent of the households are in New York. Residents represent a diverse mix of cultures; many speak a language other than English. The median age is 30.1 years. Household types are mainly single parent and single person. Part-time work is just as common as full time. Residents do aerobics and play soccer. They enjoy dancing; attending basketball and football games; watching movies on DVD; and listening to all-news, urban, and Hispanic radio. They watch a variety of news programs and are avid viewers of daytime TV.

62. Modest Income Homes
Modest Income Homes neighborhoods are found primarily in the older suburbs of metropolitan areas. Single-family dwellings represent more than two-thirds of the housing; 15 percent are duplexes. The median home value is $57,381. Household types are mainly single person and single parent. However, 64 percent of households are family types. The median age is 35.7 years. Slightly more employed residents work part time than full time, mainly in service and blue collar occupations. At 20 percent, unemployment is high. These frugal residents shop at discount stores, do not pay for Internet access, and rarely eat out. They are content to wait for movies to be shown on TV instead of going to the theater. They watch daytime and primetime TV, especially courtroom TV shows and sitcoms, and listen to urban and gospel radio. A favorite cable channel is BET.

63. Dorms to Diplomas
Dorms to Diplomas is Tapestry Segmentation's youngest market, with a median age of 21.7 years. College and graduate school enrollment is 81 percent. Nearly three-fourths of employed residents work part time in low-paying service industry jobs. Forty-three percent of residents live in on-campus dormitories; the remainder rent apartments in off-campus, multiunit buildings. Ninety percent of households are renters. Computers are a necessity, and the Internet is easily accessible to research assignments, search for jobs, obtain the latest news, and keep in touch with family. For exercise, residents participate in a variety of sports. They enjoy going to college football and basketball games, rock concerts, movies, and bars as well as dancing, playing pool, and renting movies on DVD. They listen to classic hits, public, and rock radio programs.

64. City Commons
City Commons neighborhoods are found in cities of large metropolitan areas, mainly in the South and Midwest. This younger market has a median age of 24.6 years. Single- parent families and singles dominate these households, and children abound. Almost 80 percent of the households are renters; 63 percent of the rentals are apartments in multiunit buildings, primarily with fewer than 20 units. More residents work part time instead of full time. This market has the highest unemployment rate among all the Tapestry segments. Baby and children's products are the major purchases. Residents enjoy playing basketball, softball, and backgammon. A yearly family outing to a theme

park is common. They prefer to watch courtroom TV shows; listen to gospel, urban, and jazz programs on the radio; and read music, baby, parenthood, and fashion magazines.

65. Social Security Set
Four in ten householders in the Social Security Set segment are aged 65 years or older; the median age is 45.8 years. Most of these residents live alone. Located in large cities scattered across the United States, these communities are dispersed among business districts and around city parks. The service industry provides more than half of the jobs held by residents who work. Households subsist on very low, fixed incomes. Most residents rent apartments in low-rent, high-rise buildings. Many rely on public transportation, because more than half of these households do not own a vehicle. Limited resources somewhat restrict the purchases and activities of these residents, although many have invested their savings in stock. They enjoy going to movies and soccer games and reading science fiction. Many households subscribe to cable TV; residents particularly enjoy watching game shows, sports, and entertainment news shows.

66. Unclassified
Unclassified neighborhoods include unpopulated areas such as parks, golf courses, open spaces, or other types of undeveloped land. Institutional group quarters, such as prisons, juvenile detention homes, mental hospitals, or any area with insufficient data for classification, are also included in this category.

Business Data Note

ESRI business data are extracted from a comprehensive list of businesses licensed from *info*USA. The *info*USA business list contains data for over twelve million U.S. businesses including the business name, location, franchise code, North American Industry Classification System (NAICS) code, number of employees and sales volume. These statistics are current as of January 2009.

Data Sources

*info*USA collects and maintains its business database by referencing several sources, including directory listings (yellow pages and business white pages), annual reports, 10K's and SEC information, federal, state, and municipal government data, business magazines, newsletters and newspapers, and U.S. Postal Service information. *info*USA conducts annual telephone verifications with each business to ensure accurate and complete information.

ESRI provides reports and file extracts from the *info*USA database that include the number of businesses by NAICS code and employment size or sales volume, total employment, and total sales, where available. Industry classifications include the standard NAICS code hierarchy, plus *info*USA's proprietary industry code which expands upon the NAICS code hierarchy. Also, a special industry code for select industries is available that provides more detailed information, such as the number of rooms in hotels/motels or the number of beds in hospitals and nursing homes. Sales data are reported for business locations.

In the January 2009 database, *info*USA supplied ESRI with an improved, more comprehensive business record extract. In the past, affiliated businesses that shared a common address and at least one other element (e.g., phone number, business name, contact name, linkage to the same parent company) were removed to represent a single business per location. Now, all of these businesses will be included. This change will increase the total number of records in the database by approximately five percent.

The Business Data section shows the total number of companies and employees by ZIP Code for all industries. Also shown is the top industry as determined by total employment for each ZIP Code. Industries are represented by three-digit NAICS industry. A complete list of NAICS definitions is included in Appendix II.

Business Locations

*info*USA compiles an address list of businesses from its sources and telephone verification. The addresses are geocoded to assign latitude and longitude coordinates to the business site and to append a census geographic code. Most businesses are coded at the address level and assigned to a census block group. Of course, the quality of the local address system varies: address matching is better in an urban area with street-level address systems than in rural areas. Overall, 88 percent of the businesses are coded at the address level; 99.7 percent are assigned to a census block group. Businesses that cannot be assigned to a block group are assigned to a census tract or county.

ESRI uses the geographic codes to report business data for summary areas--states, counties, census tracts and block groups. Aggregations by ZIP Codes are created from the business database. *info*USA's ZIP Codes may differ from the residential ZIP Codes in ESRI's demographic databases due to the inclusion of business-only ZIP Codes, which are unique to a particular establishment and include no residential area.

Explanation of Variables*

Tapestry Segmentation Type
Tapestry Segmentation is ESRI's market segmentation system. There are 65 distinct residential Tapestry segments and one unclassified segment.

Top Tapestry Segmentation Type
The top Tapestry Segmentation type is determined by the household distribution of the ZIP Code among the 66 Tapestry segments. The top Tapestry Segmentation type has the largest share of households in a ZIP Code, usually the majority of households. However, in a large diverse ZIP Code, the top Tapestry Segmentation type may not represent most of the households, but a smaller share.

Age
Age is reported for five-year age groups and select summary groups such as 18 years and over. These data are ESRI's 2009 projections.

Median Age
Median age is calculated from the distribution of age by five-year groups. ESRI's 2009 projections. See Median.

Average Household Size
See Household.

Census Tract
Tracts are small statistical subdivisions of a county. The boundaries are delineated by local committees to represent relatively homogeneous neighborhoods and to maintain stable boundaries. Census tracts generally have 1,500 to 8,000 residents.

Centile
Same as Percentile.

County
Counties are the primary legal subdivisions of a state and are identified by a two-digit state FIPS code and a three-digit county FIPS code. Because ZIP Code boundaries do not follow county lines, the dominant county reported for each ZIP Code represents the county with the largest proportion of land area in a ZIP Code. See FIPS Code.

Families
Households in which one or more persons in the household are related to the householder (formerly, the head of the household) by birth, marriage or adoption. The Census tabulates only one family per household. These data are Census 2000 and ESRI 2009 projections.

FIPS Code
Federal Information Processing Standards for numeric codes used to identify states and counties.

Hispanic Origin
Defined by self-identification, Hispanic origin refers to ethnicity, not race. Persons of Hispanic origin may be of any race. These data are Census 2000 and ESRI's 2009 projections.

Home Value
The estimate of value is presented for total owner-occupied units. For a discussion of home value projections, see the Update Methodology. These data are ESRI's 2009 projections.

Median Home Value
This estimate divides the distribution of home value into two equal parts. Linear interpolation is used if the median home value falls below $1,000,000. If the median falls in the upper home value interval of $1,000,000+, it is represented by $1,000,001.

Home Value Base
This is the sum of the home value distribution.

Household
A household is an occupied housing unit. Household type is identified by the presence of relatives and the number of persons living in the household. Family households, with or without children, include married couples and other families--a male or female householder with no spouse present. Non-family households may be a group of unrelated persons or a single person living alone. These data are Census 2000 and ESRI's 2009 and 2014 projections.

Average Household Size
The average size is calculated by dividing the number of persons in households by the number of households.

Household Income
See Income.

Household Income Base
The sum of the household income distribution.

Income
2009 Income is a forecast of Income for the calendar year 2008. Income amounts are expressed in current dollars, including an adjustment for inflation or cost-of-living increases. For a discussion of income projections, see the Update Methodology. These data are ESRI's 2009 and 2014 projections.

Median
Median is a value that divides a distribution into two equal parts. A median is a positional measure that is unaffected by extremely high or low values in a distribution that can affect an average.

---

* Note: For more information about Census 2000 data, please see the 2000 Census of Population and Housing, Summary Files 1 and 3 Technical Documentation prepared by the U.S. Bureau of the Census.

Median Household Income
This is the value that divides the distribution of household income into two equal parts. Pareto interpolation is used if the median falls in an income interval other than the first or last. For the lowest interval, <$10,000, linear interpolation is used. If the median falls in the upper income interval of $500,000+, it is represented by the value of $500,001.

Per Capita Income
This is the average income for all persons calculated from the aggregate income of persons 15 years and older.

Percentile
This is another measure that can be used to locate the position of a value for a select area relative to that value for other areas. Percentiles show the proportion of areas that have a lower value. For example, ZIP Codes are ranked on 2009 median household income by percentile, 0 to 100, in each state and nationwide. A ZIP Code with a rank of 95 on median household income has a higher median value than 95 percent of the ZIP Codes in a state or the U.S.

Population
This is the total number of residents in an area. Residence refers to the "usual place" where a person lives, not necessarily the legal residence. For example, college students are counted where they attend school. These data are Census 2000 and ESRI's 2009 and 2014 projections.

Post Office Name
Typically, the post office name is the name that appears on the city/state address line. If multiple post office names are assigned to a ZIP Code, the city name is used.

Race
Defined by self-identification, race detail from Census 2000 was expanded to include a multiracial component. For the first time, each individual could report up to six race categories, resulting in 63 possible race combinations. The six basic race categories are White, Black or African American, American Indian or Alaskan Native, Asian, Native Hawaiian or Other Pacific Islander, and "some other" race for persons who do not identify with one of the specified groups. ESRI forecasts race for all single and multiracial populations that are consistent with 2000 Census tabulations. Data are Census 2000 and ESRI's 2009 projections of White, Black, and Asian/Pacific Islander populations.

Rate, Annual Percent
Calculated as an annual compound rate of change from 2000 to 2009 for population, households, and families. For example:

$$Rate = \left[\left(\frac{P_{09}}{P_{00}} \right)^{1/9.25} - 1 \right] \times 100$$

The rate of population change is ranked by percentile within each state. See Percentile.

Spending Potential Index
See the Spending Potential Indices Methodology.

State
States are identified by a two-digit FIPS code. The District of Columbia is included as a state-equivalent area in the ESRI database. See FIPS Code.

ZIP Code
Created by the U.S. Postal Service to deliver the mail, ZIP Codes do not represent standard census geographic areas for data reporting. Because the ZIP Code boundaries are not contiguous with census geographic areas or stable over time, data estimated for ZIP Codes are also subject to change. The ZIP Codes in this Sourcebook are current as of November 2008. See the ZIP Code Update Methodology for a description of data estimation for ZIP Codes.

Residential ZIP Code Data by State

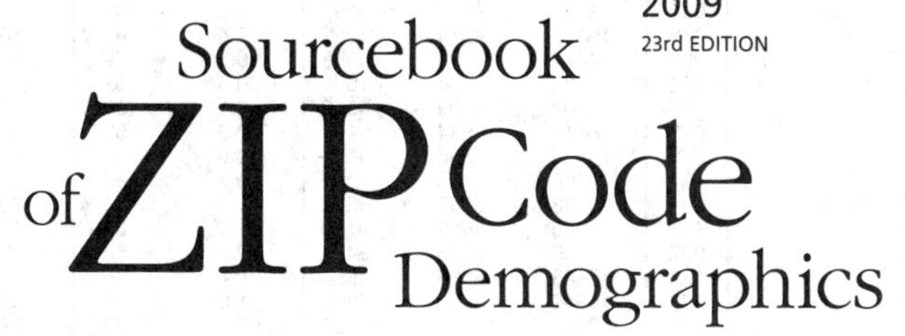

ZIP CODE #	POST OFFICE NAME	COUNTY FIPS CODE	POPULATION 2000	POPULATION 2009	POPULATION 2014	2000-2009 ANNUAL RATE % Rate	2000-2009 ANNUAL RATE State Centile	HOUSEHOLDS 2000	HOUSEHOLDS 2009	HOUSEHOLDS 2014	HOUSEHOLDS % Annual Rate 2000-2009	HOUSEHOLDS 2009 Average HH Size	FAMILIES 2000	FAMILIES 2009	FAMILIES % Annual Rate 2000-2009
35004	MOODY	115	6779	8641	9739	2.7	94	2632	3400	3847	2.8	2.53	1970	2487	2.6
35005	ADAMSVILLE	073	9139	8681	8499	-0.6	16	3530	3473	3431	-0.2	2.49	2670	2561	-0.4
35006	ADGER	073	3170	3283	3317	0.4	62	1211	1302	1328	0.8	2.52	926	970	0.5
35007	ALABASTER	117	22452	27044	30919	2.0	90	8121	10091	11661	2.4	2.64	6504	7949	2.2
35010	ALEXANDER CITY	123	20602	19877	19350	-0.4	25	8167	8110	7963	-0.1	2.35	5672	5510	-0.3
35014	ALPINE	121	4190	4297	4325	0.3	58	1571	1644	1668	0.5	2.38	1177	1207	0.3
35016	ARAB	095	15679	16665	17278	0.7	70	6361	6780	7041	0.7	2.44	4611	4816	0.5
35019	BAILEYTON	043	2211	2322	2378	0.5	64	863	930	960	0.8	2.50	643	678	0.6
35020	BESSEMER	073	31407	29194	28402	-0.8	9	12111	11534	11294	-0.5	2.49	8144	7507	-0.9
35022	BESSEMER	073	14657	18520	19980	2.6	93	5720	7472	8136	2.9	2.45	4409	5653	2.7
35023	BESSEMER	073	25246	25009	24842	-0.1	39	9397	9632	9647	0.3	2.42	7076	7088	0.0
35031	BLOUNTSVILLE	009	7849	8787	9212	1.2	80	3073	3503	3689	1.4	2.51	2312	2588	1.2
35033	BREMEN	043	3571	4044	4238	1.4	84	1355	1571	1658	1.6	2.57	1079	1232	1.4
35034	BRENT	007	5257	5133	5242	-0.3	29	1505	1683	1747	1.2	2.66	1095	1200	1.0
35035	BRIERFIELD	007	1491	1531	1553	0.3	58	545	584	600	0.7	2.62	437	462	0.6
35036	BROOKSIDE	073	142	138	147	-0.3	29	61	61	65	0.0	2.21	46	45	-0.2
35040	CALERA	117	7126	12796	15214	6.5	99	2691	5022	6024	7.0	2.54	2048	3768	6.8
35041	CARDIFF	073	8	15	16	7.0	100	3	6	6	7.8	2.50	2	4	7.8
35042	CENTREVILLE	007	5259	5749	5767	1.0	77	2099	2206	2241	0.5	2.35	1515	1559	0.3
35043	CHELSEA	117	4394	7814	9446	6.4	99	1564	2894	3527	6.9	2.69	1275	2309	6.6
35044	CHILDERSBURG	121	7820	8029	8067	0.3	58	2930	3046	3082	0.4	2.60	2118	2155	0.2
35045	CLANTON	021	12989	13680	13965	0.6	67	5109	5499	5649	0.8	2.43	3624	3819	0.6
35046	CLANTON	021	4699	5049	5191	0.8	74	1925	2124	2201	1.1	2.38	1443	1561	0.9
35049	CLEVELAND	009	3654	4047	4212	1.1	79	1351	1522	1591	1.3	2.65	1047	1160	1.1
35051	COLUMBIANA	117	7281	8804	9953	2.1	90	2734	3397	3879	2.4	2.55	2038	2464	2.1
35053	CRANE HILL	043	2450	2852	3006	1.7	88	1002	1198	1272	2.0	2.38	783	919	1.7
35054	CROPWELL	115	3356	4073	4535	2.1	90	1351	1643	1836	2.1	2.48	1005	1199	1.9
35055	CULLMAN	043	18511	18659	18757	0.1	49	7844	8030	8114	0.3	2.25	5108	5101	0.0
35057	CULLMAN	043	11809	12287	12554	0.4	62	4551	4858	5008	0.7	2.53	3550	3722	0.5
35058	CULLMAN	043	9822	10212	10419	0.4	62	3765	3999	4108	0.7	2.54	2920	3044	0.5
35061	DOLOMITE	073	1642	1576	1548	-0.4	25	576	573	568	-0.1	2.68	437	423	-0.4
35062	DORA	073	8372	8642	8647	0.3	58	3212	3398	3427	0.6	2.54	2512	2606	0.4
35063	EMPIRE	127	4833	4911	4871	0.2	52	1827	1889	1885	0.4	2.60	1381	1401	0.2
35064	FAIRFIELD	073	12490	11789	11496	-0.6	16	4645	4461	4376	-0.4	2.50	3176	2955	-0.8
35068	FULTONDALE	073	5819	6454	6658	1.1	79	2399	2754	2867	1.5	2.34	1691	1891	1.2
35071	GARDENDALE	073	13419	15210	15635	1.4	84	5409	6337	6571	1.7	2.37	4031	4605	1.4
35072	GOODWATER	027	4725	4638	4549	-0.2	34	1793	1836	1823	0.3	2.50	1321	1328	0.1
35073	GRAYSVILLE	073	2922	3005	3036	0.3	58	1161	1232	1253	0.6	2.42	854	882	0.3
35077	HANCEVILLE	043	12982	13772	14164	0.6	67	5071	5547	5760	1.0	2.42	3666	3915	0.7
35078	HARPERSVILLE	117	2650	2922	3133	1.1	79	1005	1143	1236	1.4	2.53	757	839	1.1
35079	HAYDEN	009	7061	7598	7829	0.8	74	2618	2879	2980	1.0	2.61	2061	2230	0.9
35080	HELENA	117	11591	15866	18221	3.5	97	4319	6005	6928	3.6	2.64	3417	4681	3.5
35083	HOLLY POND	043	2950	3092	3156	0.5	64	1132	1218	1254	0.8	2.54	857	903	0.6
35085	JEMISON	021	8066	8793	9111	0.9	76	3013	3372	3517	1.2	2.60	2292	2520	1.0
35087	JOPPA	103	1909	2067	2142	0.9	76	753	833	870	1.1	2.48	564	611	0.9
35089	KELLYTON	037	2915	2906	2862	0.0	45	1126	1166	1161	0.4	2.48	832	845	0.2
35091	KIMBERLY	073	1707	1881	1936	1.1	79	618	699	725	1.3	2.69	482	532	1.1
35094	LEEDS	073	11985	12327	12787	0.3	58	4927	5214	5439	0.6	2.36	3457	3572	0.4
35096	LINCOLN	121	6641	7165	7362	0.8	74	2588	2870	2974	1.1	2.49	1902	2064	0.9
35097	LOCUST FORK	009	1264	1438	1516	1.4	84	462	539	573	1.7	2.67	372	428	1.5
35098	LOGAN	043	1200	1253	1281	0.5	64	465	499	514	0.8	2.51	362	381	0.6
35111	MC CALLA	073	10762	14610	15946	3.4	97	3803	5395	5963	3.9	2.66	3172	4404	3.6
35114	MAYLENE	117	4066	6611	7704	5.4	99	1464	2435	2862	5.7	2.71	1153	1873	5.4
35115	MONTEVALLO	117	12018	13652	14990	1.4	84	4445	5273	5872	1.9	2.42	3013	3449	1.5
35116	MORRIS	073	3977	4121	4142	0.4	62	1483	1572	1590	0.6	2.62	1168	1213	0.4
35117	MOUNT OLIVE	073	4870	5546	5916	1.4	84	1863	2186	2353	1.7	2.51	1459	1664	1.4
35118	MULGA	073	3624	3639	3624	0.0	45	1400	1458	1467	0.4	2.50	1066	1083	0.2
35120	ODENVILLE	115	8743	12281	13900	3.7	97	3204	4534	5180	3.8	2.57	2568	3578	3.7
35121	ONEONTA	009	14176	15234	15656	0.8	74	5368	5848	6028	0.9	2.53	3912	4178	0.7
35124	PELHAM	117	17410	23484	26554	3.3	96	6705	9104	10350	3.4	2.58	4932	6555	3.1
35125	PELL CITY	115	9397	10694	11605	1.4	84	3562	4084	4461	1.5	2.56	2615	2933	1.2
35126	PINSON	073	20292	22032	22597	0.9	76	7078	7926	8191	1.2	2.77	5844	6442	1.1
35127	PLEASANT GROVE	073	9969	10284	10319	0.3	58	3566	3792	3839	0.7	2.66	2885	3009	0.5
35128	PELL CITY	115	9006	11037	12186	2.2	91	3408	4222	4686	2.3	2.59	2596	3157	2.1
35130	QUINTON	127	3772	3753	3688	-0.1	39	1520	1545	1531	0.2	2.43	1140	1134	-0.1
35131	RAGLAND	115	3853	4497	4952	1.7	88	1467	1719	1902	1.7	2.59	1138	1310	1.5
35133	REMLAP	009	3201	3604	3790	1.3	82	1197	1379	1460	1.5	2.61	958	1087	1.4
35135	RIVERSIDE	115	1499	1728	1880	1.5	86	644	744	814	1.6	2.32	459	522	1.4
35136	ROCKFORD	037	1876	1936	1924	0.3	58	784	843	849	0.8	2.26	548	577	0.6
35143	SHELBY	117	3357	3973	4366	1.8	89	1364	1662	1842	2.2	2.39	1002	1187	1.8
35146	SPRINGVILLE	115	8593	10101	11037	1.8	89	2763	3297	3629	1.9	2.82	2182	2562	1.8
35147	STERRETT	117	2698	5924	7390	8.9	100	1023	2301	2897	9.2	2.57	795	1754	8.9
35148	SUMITON	127	2829	2791	2738	-0.1	39	1162	1166	1153	0.0	2.36	831	817	-0.2
35150	SYLACAUGA	121	19087	18845	18682	-0.1	39	7765	7745	7723	0.0	2.40	5255	5123	-0.3
35151	SYLACAUGA	037	8508	8306	8188	-0.3	29	3319	3308	3289	0.0	2.50	2506	2450	-0.2
35160	TALLADEGA	121	28199	27071	26737	-0.4	25	10361	10198	10134	-0.2	2.41	7255	6969	-0.4
35171	THORSBY	021	3295	3743	3921	1.4	84	1261	1458	1537	1.6	2.55	980	1115	1.4
35172	TRAFFORD	009	2730	3055	3192	1.2	80	1095	1259	1325	1.5	2.43	860	971	1.3
35173	TRUSSVILLE	073	19487	24254	26052	2.4	92	6893	8799	9514	2.7	2.73	5549	6979	2.5
35175	UNION GROVE	095	4477	4791	4988	0.7	70	1764	1897	1980	0.8	2.53	1350	1425	0.6
35176	VANDIVER	117	809	838	1009	0.4	62	310	332	403	0.7	2.52	247	260	0.6
35178	VINCENT	117	3403	4109	4552	2.1	90	1357	1676	1871	2.3	2.45	1015	1224	2.0
35179	VINEMONT	043	8717	8934	9104	0.3	58	3347	3529	3626	0.6	2.53	2558	2644	0.4
35180	WARRIOR	073	12235	12896	13151	0.6	67	4584	4941	5067	0.8	2.61	3608	3817	0.6
35183	WEOGUFKA	037	116	113	111	-0.3	29	52	53	52	0.2	2.11	39	39	0.0
35184	WEST BLOCTON	007	5583	6045	6201	0.9	76	2091	2337	2428	1.2	2.56	1613	1773	1.0
35186	WILSONVILLE	117	4060	4689	5159	1.6	87	1569	1844	2046	1.8	2.52	1231	1417	1.5
35188	WOODSTOCK	007	2359	2398	2434	0.2	52	837	882	906	0.6	2.70	651	676	0.4
35203	BIRMINGHAM	073	3693	3559	3554	-0.4	25	1199	1203	1229	0.0	1.68	443	417	-0.7
35204	BIRMINGHAM	073	14942	13002	12389	-1.5	1	5934	5238	5001	-1.3	2.22	3419	2896	-1.8
35205	BIRMINGHAM	073	20669	20092	19722	-0.3	29	10904	10819	10680	-0.1	1.65	3389	3115	-0.9
35206	BIRMINGHAM	073	21706	20872	20393	-0.4	25	8247	7854	7676	-0.5	2.57	5500	5055	-0.9
35207	BIRMINGHAM	073	11173	9595	9098	-1.6	0	4266	3811	3650	-1.2	2.51	2870	2476	-1.6
35208	BIRMINGHAM	073	17875	16577	16034	-0.8	9	6681	6234	6051	-0.7	2.61	4731	4292	-1.0
35209	BIRMINGHAM	073	26939	26645	26336	-0.1	39	13102	13021	12903	-0.1	2.00	6463	6101	-0.6
	ALABAMA					0.6					0.9	2.44			0.6
	UNITED STATES					1.0					1.1	2.59			0.9

#	POST OFFICE NAME	RACE (%) White 2000	White 2009	Black 2000	Black 2009	Asian/Pacific 2000	Asian/Pacific 2009	% Hispanic Origin 2000	% Hispanic Origin 2009	2009 AGE DISTRIBUTION (%) 0-4	5-9	10-14	15-19	20-24	25-44	45-64	65-84	85+	18+	MEDIAN AGE 2009	% 2009 Males	% 2009 Females
35004	MOODY	94.4	93.3	3.4	3.7	0.3	0.4	1.2	2.1	6.9	6.9	6.9	6.4	5.8	28.3	27.4	10.1	1.2	75.4	37.9	49.3	50.7
35005	ADAMSVILLE	77.9	69.7	20.6	28.3	0.2	0.3	0.5	1.0	5.5	5.8	6.2	6.4	4.8	26.1	28.6	14.6	1.9	78.6	41.7	48.1	51.9
35006	ADGER	92.5	88.8	6.3	9.5	0.1	0.1	0.4	0.8	5.2	5.5	6.5	6.9	5.5	26.3	31.6	11.4	1.1	78.6	41.5	50.8	49.2
35007	ALABASTER	87.8	85.1	9.5	10.8	0.6	0.8	2.1	3.8	8.9	8.3	7.8	6.0	4.3	32.4	24.4	6.8	1.1	71.2	34.9	48.6	51.4
35010	ALEXANDER CITY	71.9	69.6	26.9	28.8	0.2	0.4	0.6	0.9	6.4	6.4	6.5	6.2	5.5	24.7	26.6	14.7	3.0	76.9	40.7	47.5	52.5
35014	ALPINE	44.0	42.0	54.8	56.9	0.2	0.2	0.7	0.7	6.5	6.8	6.7	7.1	6.8	28.3	25.8	10.9	1.1	76.1	36.9	53.0	47.0
35016	ARAB	98.2	97.5	0.1	0.1	0.3	0.4	0.9	1.7	6.2	6.3	6.5	6.5	5.2	25.7	28.1	13.6	1.9	76.9	40.7	49.0	51.0
35019	BAILEYTON	97.2	95.8	0.0	0.0	0.1	0.2	2.3	4.2	7.3	7.3	7.4	6.5	5.5	27.3	25.8	11.3	1.5	74.0	37.5	50.2	49.8
35020	BESSEMER	24.5	18.8	73.9	79.2	0.2	0.2	1.3	1.8	7.4	7.4	7.0	7.0	6.7	24.3	25.3	12.4	2.5	74.0	36.9	46.3	53.7
35022	BESSEMER	68.0	64.9	30.4	32.9	0.3	0.5	0.8	1.4	7.6	7.0	6.7	6.2	5.3	24.9	27.7	12.6	1.9	74.9	39.4	47.4	52.6
35023	BESSEMER	82.8	78.1	16.2	20.5	0.1	0.2	0.5	0.9	5.2	5.4	5.8	5.7	5.4	28.6	28.4	13.2	2.3	80.1	40.9	51.4	48.6
35031	BLOUNTSVILLE	95.5	93.0	0.1	0.1	0.2	0.3	6.7	11.6	6.6	6.6	6.8	6.3	5.1	27.8	26.8	12.5	1.5	76.2	38.8	50.7	49.3
35033	BREMEN	98.4	98.0	0.5	0.5	0.1	0.2	0.6	1.1	6.4	6.6	6.7	6.1	5.2	26.0	29.2	12.7	1.3	76.7	40.0	49.6	50.4
35034	BRENT	53.2	50.2	45.5	47.3	0.2	0.6	1.1	2.1	5.6	6.0	6.2	6.1	9.3	34.6	22.4	8.6	1.2	79.3	34.3	60.1	39.9
35035	BRIERFIELD	85.2	84.2	13.5	14.0	0.1	0.2	0.9	1.6	6.1	6.2	6.6	6.5	4.6	26.9	28.9	12.9	1.3	77.1	40.6	49.1	50.9
35036	BROOKSIDE	95.0	91.3	3.5	6.5	0.0	0.0	0.7	0.7	5.8	6.5	6.5	5.8	4.3	26.1	30.4	12.3	2.2	77.5	41.8	50.0	50.0
35040	CALERA	84.4	83.5	12.7	12.6	0.3	0.4	2.5	4.2	7.2	7.3	7.4	6.5	5.1	28.3	27.5	9.6	1.1	74.0	37.3	49.9	50.1
35041	CARDIFF	100.0	93.3	0.0	6.7	0.0	0.0	0.0	0.0	0.0	6.7	6.7	0.0	0.0	33.3	53.3	0.0	0.0	86.7	46.3	46.7	53.3
35042	CENTREVILLE	73.9	71.5	25.2	27.1	0.1	0.2	1.2	2.0	5.7	5.5	5.7	6.1	7.0	29.5	26.1	11.9	2.4	79.8	38.5	53.6	46.4
35043	CHELSEA	96.3	95.1	1.4	1.9	0.3	0.4	1.2	2.3	7.5	7.3	7.3	6.8	5.5	29.6	27.1	8.1	0.8	73.4	35.4	49.2	50.8
35044	CHILDERSBURG	70.8	69.6	27.9	29.2	0.2	0.2	0.6	0.6	7.3	7.1	7.0	6.6	6.1	25.8	25.9	12.7	1.5	74.7	37.5	47.6	52.4
35045	CLANTON	82.1	79.8	14.9	15.6	0.3	0.4	3.1	5.1	6.8	6.8	6.7	6.3	5.3	26.3	25.9	13.6	2.3	75.8	39.0	49.1	50.9
35046	CLANTON	97.2	96.3	1.1	1.2	0.2	0.3	2.1	3.6	6.2	6.4	6.6	6.1	4.6	27.3	28.6	13.0	1.2	77.0	40.0	50.5	49.5
35049	CLEVELAND	94.5	91.9	0.8	0.8	0.1	0.2	7.8	13.4	7.2	7.0	7.0	6.4	5.7	26.7	26.9	11.8	1.3	74.8	38.0	51.3	48.7
35051	COLUMBIANA	88.3	85.5	9.6	11.6	0.2	0.2	1.7	2.9	6.6	7.0	7.0	6.5	5.7	29.1	27.1	9.8	1.2	75.6	36.8	50.6	49.4
35053	CRANE HILL	98.7	98.4	0.0	0.0	0.2	0.3	0.5	0.9	5.4	5.3	6.3	5.4	4.2	22.9	33.9	14.7	1.8	79.7	45.2	50.7	49.3
35054	CROPWELL	86.3	84.7	12.4	13.5	0.2	0.3	0.7	1.2	5.1	5.4	5.8	5.4	4.0	21.9	33.6	17.2	1.5	80.3	46.4	49.5	50.5
35055	CULLMAN	96.9	95.7	0.3	0.3	0.4	0.5	4.1	6.8	6.3	6.1	6.1	5.8	5.3	25.6	25.6	15.7	3.6	78.0	41.0	48.1	51.9
35057	CULLMAN	97.9	97.2	0.3	0.4	0.1	0.2	1.3	2.4	6.7	6.7	6.9	6.5	5.3	27.3	27.6	11.7	1.2	75.6	38.6	50.2	49.8
35058	CULLMAN	97.1	95.8	0.1	0.1	0.3	0.4	2.7	4.7	6.8	6.9	7.1	6.5	5.0	26.9	27.1	12.3	1.5	75.2	38.7	50.1	49.9
35061	DOLOMITE	33.8	24.9	65.9	74.7	0.1	0.1	0.5	0.6	5.1	5.7	6.2	6.2	5.3	24.8	29.7	14.0	3.0	79.2	42.4	46.2	53.8
35062	DORA	93.5	92.0	4.3	5.0	0.1	0.2	0.3	0.6	6.5	6.7	6.9	6.3	4.8	26.7	28.4	12.3	1.4	76.0	39.6	49.7	50.3
35063	EMPIRE	91.8	90.6	6.8	7.3	0.1	0.1	0.8	1.3	7.1	7.2	7.2	6.8	5.6	26.3	27.7	11.0	1.2	74.5	37.7	49.8	50.2
35064	FAIRFIELD	10.6	6.9	88.5	92.1	0.2	0.2	0.6	0.6	5.7	6.0	6.7	9.2	8.6	23.1	27.5	10.6	2.7	76.6	36.7	44.7	55.3
35068	FULTONDALE	92.8	89.6	4.6	6.5	0.6	0.9	1.1	2.0	6.0	5.9	5.9	5.5	5.3	27.1	27.4	14.8	2.0	78.8	40.6	47.4	52.6
35071	GARDENDALE	96.4	94.6	2.0	2.9	0.4	0.6	0.8	1.6	5.3	5.7	6.0	5.8	4.5	24.2	29.6	16.2	2.6	79.3	43.8	47.5	52.5
35072	GOODWATER	60.7	59.7	38.0	38.9	0.0	0.1	0.4	0.5	6.5	6.7	6.7	6.2	5.6	25.8	28.7	12.0	2.0	76.5	39.6	50.0	50.0
35073	GRAYSVILLE	79.0	72.1	19.1	25.3	0.3	0.4	0.8	1.4	5.6	5.8	6.0	6.0	4.9	24.7	28.8	15.7	2.6	78.8	42.9	47.2	52.8
35077	HANCEVILLE	93.3	92.2	4.7	5.0	0.2	0.2	1.6	2.8	6.2	6.1	6.1	6.0	5.4	27.5	26.6	13.7	2.3	78.1	39.5	49.7	50.3
35078	HARPERSVILLE	73.6	70.2	24.4	27.1	0.4	0.6	0.6	1.1	6.3	6.5	7.1	7.2	5.4	25.9	28.2	11.9	1.4	75.5	39.1	49.3	50.7
35079	HAYDEN	96.2	94.8	1.0	1.2	0.2	0.3	1.9	3.4	7.1	7.3	7.2	6.5	5.0	27.5	26.8	11.3	1.3	74.3	37.9	50.9	49.1
35080	HELENA	93.4	91.8	3.9	4.3	0.8	1.3	1.8	3.0	9.3	8.8	8.1	5.9	4.3	35.4	22.4	5.2	0.6	70.1	34.3	48.3	51.7
35083	HOLLY POND	98.2	97.4	0.0	0.0	0.1	0.1	1.4	2.7	7.1	7.1	7.1	6.2	4.8	27.2	26.6	12.5	1.4	74.9	38.4	50.0	50.0
35085	JEMISON	88.7	85.9	8.0	8.9	0.1	0.2	3.9	6.5	7.0	7.1	7.3	6.4	5.4	28.5	26.5	10.6	1.2	74.6	37.1	50.3	49.7
35087	JOPPA	98.1	97.3	0.1	0.0	0.1	0.1	2.4	4.6	6.9	7.0	7.1	6.2	5.5	27.2	28.1	10.8	1.3	75.3	38.7	50.8	49.2
35089	KELLYTON	50.4	45.3	47.9	51.7	0.0	0.6	1.9	3.1	5.6	5.8	7.1	6.3	5.6	29.5	27.2	11.5	1.5	78.4	38.6	52.5	47.5
35091	KIMBERLY	97.2	95.5	1.2	2.0	0.2	0.4	0.6	1.3	6.6	6.8	7.0	7.2	4.9	27.0	27.9	11.4	1.2	75.2	38.6	49.8	50.2
35094	LEEDS	83.6	79.2	14.4	17.9	0.6	0.8	1.3	2.3	6.4	6.4	6.6	6.4	5.4	25.7	28.4	13.1	1.5	76.6	40.4	48.3	51.7
35096	LINCOLN	74.8	73.7	23.9	24.9	0.1	0.1	0.8	0.8	5.9	6.1	6.4	6.2	4.7	25.8	31.2	12.4	1.2	78.1	41.2	50.0	50.0
35097	LOCUST FORK	98.6	98.2	0.1	0.1	0.1	0.1	0.5	0.7	6.5	6.7	7.0	7.0	5.2	27.5	27.4	11.6	1.0	75.5	38.9	50.3	49.7
35098	LOGAN	98.2	97.5	0.0	0.0	0.1	0.2	1.4	2.7	6.5	6.5	6.9	6.9	5.6	27.3	27.7	11.3	1.4	75.9	38.6	49.7	50.3
35111	MC CALLA	92.7	89.5	5.7	8.2	0.1	0.2	0.9	1.7	6.5	6.9	7.1	6.2	4.5	26.2	29.3	11.4	1.9	75.6	39.9	49.0	51.0
35114	MAYLENE	92.5	90.0	5.3	6.7	0.7	1.1	1.6	3.0	9.3	8.6	7.8	5.8	4.7	35.6	22.6	5.2	0.5	70.7	33.4	49.4	50.6
35115	MONTEVALLO	80.9	78.7	17.0	18.4	0.2	0.3	2.4	4.2	6.0	5.9	6.0	9.4	12.7	26.1	23.1	9.4	1.3	78.1	32.2	48.1	51.9
35116	MORRIS	96.6	94.8	1.9	3.1	0.2	0.2	0.8	1.6	6.8	6.8	7.1	7.4	5.2	27.5	27.8	10.4	1.1	74.8	38.0	49.6	50.4
35117	MOUNT OLIVE	95.8	93.4	2.5	4.1	0.1	0.2	0.8	1.4	6.0	6.4	6.7	6.1	4.4	25.8	30.7	12.4	1.6	77.1	41.6	49.2	50.8
35118	MULGA	81.6	75.4	17.2	23.1	0.1	0.1	0.5	0.8	5.4	5.7	5.9	5.7	5.0	25.8	29.0	15.5	2.1	79.6	42.6	48.6	51.4
35120	ODENVILLE	88.7	87.9	9.6	9.8	0.2	0.2	0.9	1.6	6.6	6.6	6.8	6.7	6.0	28.5	27.5	10.0	1.3	75.8	37.9	52.1	47.9
35121	ONEONTA	91.9	89.1	2.9	3.0	0.1	0.2	9.4	15.8	6.8	6.8	6.8	6.2	5.4	26.1	26.1	13.4	2.4	75.8	39.1	49.7	50.3
35124	PELHAM	91.5	88.7	4.2	5.0	1.6	2.3	4.3	6.9	7.5	7.7	7.7	6.2	4.3	29.7	27.9	8.1	0.9	73.0	37.3	49.1	50.9
35125	PELL CITY	91.7	90.3	6.2	6.9	0.2	0.2	1.2	2.2	7.1	6.8	6.8	6.8	6.5	27.6	25.5	10.9	2.0	75.0	37.1	49.1	50.9
35126	PINSON	94.3	91.5	4.3	6.3	0.4	0.7	0.7	1.3	6.4	6.7	7.1	7.2	5.5	26.9	29.8	9.5	1.0	75.2	38.6	49.1	50.9
35127	PLEASANT GROVE	82.2	75.2	16.8	23.5	0.2	0.3	0.3	0.5	5.3	5.8	6.3	6.4	4.7	23.8	30.8	14.4	2.5	78.6	43.3	47.4	52.6
35128	PELL CITY	89.2	87.6	9.6	10.7	0.2	0.3	0.8	1.5	6.2	6.5	6.9	6.5	4.9	25.2	29.1	13.2	1.7	76.4	40.9	49.4	50.6
35130	QUINTON	90.4	88.5	6.9	7.9	0.1	0.2	0.4	0.8	5.4	5.5	5.9	6.4	4.7	25.9	30.2	14.2	1.7	79.1	42.6	49.7	50.3
35131	RAGLAND	91.2	90.1	8.0	8.8	0.1	0.1	0.5	0.8	7.2	7.2	7.2	6.6	5.4	27.2	26.6	11.5	1.2	74.4	37.9	49.9	50.1
35133	REMLAP	98.1	97.5	0.2	0.2	0.1	0.2	1.2	2.0	7.1	7.3	7.5	6.8	4.5	26.7	27.4	11.8	1.0	73.9	38.7	50.5	49.5
35135	RIVERSIDE	84.4	82.4	13.3	14.5	0.1	0.1	1.0	1.8	5.9	6.0	6.5	6.8	4.7	27.3	29.0	12.7	1.0	77.2	40.4	49.1	50.9
35136	ROCKFORD	71.4	68.2	25.8	28.0	0.1	0.2	1.8	2.7	5.8	6.1	6.0	6.5	4.8	23.6	30.4	14.5	2.3	77.7	42.9	51.4	48.6
35143	SHELBY	92.8	90.5	5.7	7.4	0.1	0.2	1.8	3.3	5.6	6.2	6.4	5.6	4.5	25.5	31.7	13.4	1.1	78.3	42.1	50.9	49.1
35146	SPRINGVILLE	88.4	86.7	9.7	10.8	0.2	0.3	1.6	2.5	6.4	6.7	6.9	6.2	5.4	29.7	28.1	9.7	0.9	76.2	38.1	54.4	45.6
35147	STERRETT	93.5	94.1	4.2	2.9	0.3	0.4	1.1	2.3	6.6	6.7	7.1	6.8	5.5	25.7	29.3	11.1	1.3	75.5	39.1	49.8	50.2
35148	SUMITON	94.2	92.7	3.0	3.5	0.1	0.2	0.7	1.3	6.1	6.6	6.3	7.2	5.7	24.1	29.6	12.9	1.5	77.3	40.1	48.0	52.0
35150	SYLACAUGA	69.7	68.4	28.7	30.0	0.3	0.3	0.9	0.9	6.7	6.6	6.4	6.4	6.0	24.6	26.8	14.0	2.5	77.2	39.7	46.2	53.8
35151	SYLACAUGA	86.5	85.3	12.3	13.3	0.0	0.0	0.7	0.9	6.7	6.7	6.7	6.3	5.2	25.7	28.6	12.7	1.4	76.1	40.2	50.0	50.0
35160	TALLADEGA	59.1	58.3	39.5	40.1	0.2	0.3	1.5	1.5	5.5	5.9	6.2	6.9	6.6	27.0	27.3	12.6	2.0	79.0	38.8	50.9	49.1
35171	THORSBY	89.9	87.0	5.9	6.4	0.2	0.3	4.9	8.1	6.9	7.0	7.0	6.4	5.4	27.9	26.9	11.0	1.5	75.3	37.9	51.0	49.0
35172	TRAFFORD	98.1	97.3	0.3	0.5	0.1	0.1	0.5	0.9	6.8	6.9	7.1	6.7	5.1	28.1	27.3	10.9	1.0	75.0	37.9	50.3	49.7
35173	TRUSSVILLE	96.0	93.7	2.4	3.8	0.4	0.6	0.8	1.5	6.1	6.7	7.4	7.2	4.7	25.4	30.7	10.3	1.6	75.1	40.4	49.1	50.9
35175	UNION GROVE	97.2	96.1	0.2	0.3	0.2	0.4	1.0	2.0	6.1	6.4	6.6	6.1	4.8	26.7	30.2	11.9	1.1	77.1	40.5	49.3	50.7
35176	VANDIVER	95.4	94.2	2.2	2.6	0.6	1.0	0.9	1.6	6.8	7.3	7.8	6.3	4.1	26.3	30.0	10.6	1.0	74.2	39.8	50.4	49.6
35178	VINCENT	81.4	78.7	17.0	19.4	0.2	0.2	0.8	1.4	5.9	6.2	6.4	5.9	4.8	24.5	30.6	14.3	1.5	77.9	42.6	48.8	51.2
35179	VINEMONT	97.6	96.9	0.1	0.1	0.2	0.3	1.0	1.9	6.2	6.3	6.6	6.6	5.4	27.0	28.9	11.7	1.4	77.0	39.5	50.3	49.7
35180	WARRIOR	93.6	91.4	4.7	6.4	0.2	0.2	0.4	0.8	6.6	6.8	6.8	6.2	5.1	27.5	27.7	12.0	1.3	75.9	39.0	49.7	50.3
35183	WEOGUFKA	94.0	93.8	2.6	2.7	0.0	0.0	0.9	1.8	5.3	5.3	5.3	6.2	4.4	23.9	31.0	16.8	1.8	80.5	44.7	49.6	50.4
35184	WEST BLOCTON	90.6	90.1	8.5	8.8	0.0	0.0	0.8	1.3	7.9	7.7	7.9	7.2	5.5	27.7	25.0	10.0	1.1	72.0	35.7	50.8	49.2
35186	WILSONVILLE	93.4	91.9	5.1	6.0	0.4	0.7	0.5	0.9	6.4	6.7	7.0	6.3	5.1	24.9	29.3	12.8	1.3	76.2	40.3	49.4	50.6
35188	WOODSTOCK	92.1	91.0	6.3	6.9	0.0	0.0	0.8	1.4	8.0	8.0	7.9	6.7	4.8	30.2	24.3	9.3	0.9	72.0	35.6	50.5	49.5
35203	BIRMINGHAM	19.5	15.3	79.0	82.7	0.4	0.6	0.8	1.1	6.4	4.3	2.3	4.2	11.2	37.9	23.7	7.9	2.2	85.3	36.7	60.4	39.6
35204	BIRMINGHAM	8.2	6.5	90.1	91.4	0.2	0.3	1.7	2.1	5.7	6.0	6.0	9.2	9.3	20.9	26.0	13.6	3.4	78.0	38.7	45.7	54.3
35205	BIRMINGHAM	51.9	44.3	40.0	45.4	4.8	6.0	2.5	4.1	4.4	3.6	3.1	6.3	11.7	40.1	20.3	8.1	2.4	87.2	33.2	49.8	50.2
35206	BIRMINGHAM	29.5	21.8	68.6	75.8	0.4	0.5	1.1	1.5	6.7	7.2	7.6	8.3	6.7	24.9	25.8	10.3	2.6	73.6	36.3	46.3	53.7
35207	BIRMINGHAM	5.7	3.6	93.5	95.5	0.0	0.1	0.7	0.8	6.9	7.2	6.9	7.5	6.4	22.3	27.4	13.4	2.0	74.4	38.2	46.4	53.6
35208	BIRMINGHAM	8.9	5.9	89.8	92.7	0.2	0.2	0.9	1.1	6.5	7.3	7.6	8.9	7.5	24.7	28.0	8.1	1.4	73.3	35.0	45.3	54.7
35209	BIRMINGHAM	68.0	60.4	26.0	31.7	2.9	3.7	4.1	6.4	7.0	5.5	4.8	5.8	12.1	37.3	19.7	6.3	1.4	80.1	31.0	48.6	51.4
	ALABAMA	71.1	69.3	26.0	26.7	0.7	1.0	1.7	2.8	6.6	6.6	6.6	6.9	6.6	26.4	26.7	11.7	1.8	76.1	37.8	48.6	51.4
	UNITED STATES	75.1	72.0	12.3	12.7	3.8	4.6	12.5	15.7	6.8	6.7	6.6	7.1	6.9	27.0	26.0	10.9	1.9	75.7	36.9	49.2	50.8

#	POST OFFICE NAME	2009 Per Capita Income	2009 HH Income Base	2009 HOUSEHOLD INCOME DISTRIBUTION (%) Less than $25,000	$25,000 to $49,999	$50,000 to $99,999	$100,000 to $149,999	$150,000 or More	MEDIAN HOUSEHOLD INCOME 2009	2014	2009 National Centile	2009 State Centile	2009 Home Value Base	2009 HOME VALUE DISTRIBUTION (%) Less than $50,000	$50,000 to $89,999	$90,000 to $174,999	$175,000 to $399,999	$400,000 or More	2009 Median Home Value
35004	MOODY	21244	3400	21.6	30.8	38.4	7.3	1.8	48039	49904	57	87	2617	19.1	12.1	45.0	21.1	2.7	130147
35005	ADAMSVILLE	21870	3473	21.6	30.0	39.0	7.8	1.6	48555	50022	58	88	3004	17.0	30.4	47.5	4.9	0.3	93074
35006	ADGER	19113	1302	28.0	33.1	33.9	3.8	1.2	41771	43584	39	71	1109	28.3	36.2	28.7	5.4	1.4	75054
35007	ALABASTER	32026	10091	10.8	15.7	41.7	24.4	7.4	74631	77787	89	99	8673	8.3	4.8	37.1	46.1	3.8	174839
35010	ALEXANDER CITY	20035	8110	35.0	28.9	27.9	5.6	2.6	35805	36325	20	48	5606	18.6	31.6	35.2	10.8	3.9	89840
35014	ALPINE	16667	1644	36.1	31.4	27.3	4.9	0.3	35548	36371	19	47	1448	34.1	24.7	22.9	16.1	2.2	74576
35016	ARAB	20841	6780	27.5	31.7	31.6	6.8	2.3	42135	42642	40	73	5192	12.2	21.5	43.6	20.2	2.5	115765
35019	BAILEYTON	17437	930	31.0	37.1	27.3	3.5	1.1	36998	38539	24	54	776	23.6	25.4	36.5	11.7	2.8	92353
35020	BESSEMER	13190	11534	50.3	28.1	18.6	2.3	0.6	24774	26220	3	11	6927	31.3	47.7	18.8	2.2	0.1	63049
35022	BESSEMER	23990	7472	24.5	27.0	34.5	10.1	4.0	48377	50561	57	87	5782	9.0	20.6	41.4	27.5	1.5	123978
35023	BESSEMER	22815	9632	20.5	29.6	39.9	7.8	2.1	49802	50841	61	89	8043	8.0	31.0	50.3	10.1	0.5	102455
35031	BLOUNTSVILLE	17286	3503	34.3	30.3	29.9	4.6	1.0	36817	39673	23	53	2726	22.2	22.0	37.2	16.0	2.6	97512
35033	BREMEN	18416	1571	27.6	37.2	29.1	4.0	2.2	37870	38895	26	58	1381	26.8	26.4	26.9	15.9	4.0	84765
35034	BRENT	14104	1683	44.5	24.4	25.9	4.3	1.0	28570	30531	6	18	1286	32.3	25.0	27.8	13.5	1.4	73500
35035	BRIERFIELD	20138	584	22.4	25.5	44.2	7.0	0.9	51101	51276	64	90	506	26.5	24.1	21.9	25.9	1.6	88235
35036	BROOKSIDE	20858	61	32.8	31.1	31.1	3.3	1.6	36721	38599	23	52	50	24.0	22.0	38.0	16.0	0.0	94000
35040	CALERA	23991	5022	21.6	25.7	38.3	11.2	3.2	53666	54579	69	93	4213	14.8	16.0	32.8	28.9	7.5	138496
35041	CARDIFF	18675	6	33.3	0.0	66.7	0.0	0.0	65822	45000	84	97	5	0.0	0.0	100.0	0.0	0.0	120833
35042	CENTREVILLE	17003	2206	38.3	26.7	29.5	5.0	0.5	34578	37035	17	42	1659	26.2	23.4	34.1	15.6	0.8	90722
35043	CHELSEA	29112	2894	14.4	19.7	37.6	22.3	5.9	67442	70578	85	97	2534	14.5	9.1	18.4	47.3	10.8	210945
35044	CHILDERSBURG	16279	3046	41.3	26.4	26.6	4.6	1.1	31489	33009	11	26	2338	24.6	32.2	32.3	9.5	1.4	80914
35045	CLANTON	18073	5499	34.2	30.1	29.4	5.2	1.1	37000	39104	24	54	4120	18.5	21.9	40.6	17.0	2.0	106039
35046	CLANTON	19889	2124	30.3	28.6	34.9	5.0	1.2	42946	44143	42	76	1825	23.1	22.6	30.8	21.9	1.6	98722
35049	CLEVELAND	18563	1522	25.8	30.2	36.9	5.8	1.2	44949	46449	48	82	1270	22.4	18.4	38.2	17.1	3.9	105189
35051	COLUMBIANA	21783	3397	27.1	25.1	36.7	8.2	2.9	47346	47393	55	86	2617	20.4	17.7	30.7	26.1	5.1	117879
35053	CRANE HILL	22122	1198	27.1	29.9	32.8	6.3	3.8	43727	45055	45	78	1078	17.6	12.2	30.3	35.2	4.6	140870
35054	CROPWELL	25473	1643	23.3	29.4	33.4	8.2	5.8	46712	49215	53	85	1443	18.8	11.4	26.0	29.9	13.8	157989
35055	CULLMAN	20498	8030	34.0	30.3	28.4	5.2	2.0	36653	38299	23	52	5101	8.6	18.5	48.8	21.1	3.1	124544
35057	CULLMAN	18608	4858	31.3	34.3	28.1	4.2	2.1	38317	39297	28	60	4011	21.5	19.4	37.1	17.7	4.3	106864
35058	CULLMAN	20253	3999	25.4	32.0	35.1	5.6	2.0	42643	43789	41	75	3261	15.7	20.6	41.3	18.4	3.9	115848
35061	DOLOMITE	17778	573	29.8	32.8	33.2	3.7	0.5	41099	42764	36	70	463	12.7	50.3	33.9	3.0	0.0	78176
35062	DORA	19140	3398	32.5	28.9	32.0	5.2	1.4	37777	38756	26	57	2847	22.3	25.5	40.5	11.6	0.1	93378
35063	EMPIRE	14793	1889	40.5	30.8	24.7	3.5	0.5	31045	32763	10	24	1565	37.3	30.9	24.7	6.8	0.3	63384
35064	FAIRFIELD	16712	4461	40.1	26.2	27.1	5.8	0.7	32464	34901	12	31	2757	13.1	40.6	41.1	5.2	0.0	86339
35068	FULTONDALE	21783	2754	24.9	32.2	35.5	6.1	1.3	43784	45749	45	78	2029	4.1	29.7	58.9	6.9	0.4	105984
35071	GARDENDALE	25445	6337	19.3	28.4	41.0	7.7	3.5	52153	52876	66	91	5288	8.5	15.7	52.4	22.0	1.3	124815
35072	GOODWATER	15984	1836	39.7	31.3	25.3	2.7	1.0	32238	33783	12	30	1561	34.3	27.8	29.5	7.5	0.9	68008
35073	GRAYSVILLE	18999	1232	33.5	28.0	33.0	4.1	1.4	39246	40458	30	64	1023	19.2	40.4	33.4	6.9	0.1	83229
35077	HANCEVILLE	17898	5547	32.1	34.0	28.5	4.0	1.4	37506	38695	25	56	4324	22.7	25.3	37.2	13.0	1.9	93973
35078	HARPERSVILLE	19284	1143	34.7	26.9	29.5	7.0	1.9	37514	38258	25	57	915	36.3	25.7	19.7	11.1	7.2	65448
35079	HAYDEN	18946	2879	26.8	30.8	35.2	5.8	1.5	42375	44472	41	74	2540	21.7	18.1	38.1	20.4	1.8	106891
35080	HELENA	37626	6005	6.8	12.8	42.2	27.9	10.4	81994	85110	93	100	5496	9.3	4.6	29.6	50.4	6.1	185834
35083	HOLLY POND	19072	1218	29.8	31.5	31.9	4.8	1.9	41262	42321	37	71	994	18.1	22.2	39.4	15.3	4.9	109150
35085	JEMISON	18151	3372	27.6	33.8	32.1	5.3	1.2	39766	42248	32	65	2847	22.9	23.7	33.4	17.5	2.4	96349
35087	JOPPA	20216	833	33.7	31.0	28.3	4.2	2.8	38751	40095	29	62	694	22.8	29.0	32.6	13.4	2.3	86842
35089	KELLYTON	17111	1166	35.6	36.5	22.9	2.8	2.1	34234	35586	16	40	950	37.6	28.7	28.3	4.9	0.4	67692
35091	KIMBERLY	19153	699	26.3	28.0	38.6	5.3	1.7	45586	47608	50	82	598	18.4	24.6	38.6	16.6	1.8	103667
35094	LEEDS	25975	5214	27.0	26.9	32.5	8.9	4.7	45965	48379	51	83	3687	13.4	24.1	35.1	20.9	6.6	114572
35096	LINCOLN	19346	2870	31.1	29.8	31.3	6.2	1.5	38151	38462	27	59	2424	28.8	24.3	25.5	15.6	5.8	84565
35097	LOCUST FORK	18148	539	26.7	29.7	37.5	5.2	0.9	43895	46241	45	79	469	20.5	22.0	34.8	20.7	2.1	104167
35098	LOGAN	16576	499	36.5	32.5	25.7	4.0	1.4	35076	36846	18	44	421	22.8	22.8	37.1	13.8	3.6	99250
35111	MC CALLA	21628	5395	17.1	29.5	43.4	8.6	1.4	52301	52186	66	92	4783	12.4	15.0	39.0	30.8	2.7	138367
35114	MAYLENE	31356	2435	10.4	15.9	42.7	23.7	7.3	73703	77510	89	99	2085	11.2	5.3	35.0	46.0	2.4	172794
35115	MONTEVALLO	21241	5273	32.1	28.0	28.3	8.6	3.0	39880	41351	32	65	3666	21.6	21.8	34.6	18.5	3.5	100000
35116	MORRIS	20075	1572	21.9	31.5	39.9	5.4	1.3	47153	48457	54	86	1329	21.7	17.9	40.7	17.5	2.2	108198
35117	MOUNT OLIVE	21834	2186	25.3	26.1	39.2	7.1	2.3	48328	49884	57	87	1872	12.1	17.7	47.2	22.6	0.4	117927
35118	MULGA	20292	1458	26.0	30.4	37.5	4.8	1.3	44145	46038	46	80	1227	21.0	31.5	38.6	7.9	1.0	86648
35120	ODENVILLE	19809	4534	25.2	31.8	34.6	6.3	2.2	44658	46492	47	81	3911	22.3	21.5	27.5	24.4	4.3	104817
35121	ONEONTA	18287	5848	33.4	29.8	28.6	6.2	2.0	37603	39523	26	57	4518	22.9	20.4	35.3	16.7	4.8	100870
35124	PELHAM	33926	9104	10.0	18.1	41.7	21.6	8.6	71874	75840	88	99	7888	12.9	3.1	27.9	46.7	9.5	187348
35125	PELL CITY	18848	4084	29.6	33.4	29.9	5.0	2.1	37444	38745	25	56	3062	20.6	20.1	38.5	17.6	3.2	105214
35126	PINSON	23987	7926	14.5	25.6	46.3	9.9	3.6	60650	59831	78	95	7076	9.3	12.2	51.7	25.1	1.8	125890
35127	PLEASANT GROVE	24577	3792	16.1	22.8	47.1	11.4	2.6	61525	61003	79	96	3367	1.8	13.8	61.3	22.7	0.4	133161
35128	PELL CITY	22025	4222	23.2	30.4	32.9	9.7	3.8	46427	48739	53	84	3654	12.3	17.0	30.5	33.2	7.1	144766
35130	QUINTON	17482	1545	33.3	32.1	31.3	2.7	0.7	35298	36646	19	46	1293	30.3	36.0	26.1	6.7	0.8	72863
35131	RAGLAND	16776	1719	30.2	32.8	33.0	3.1	0.9	39076	40370	30	63	1464	24.9	22.8	33.3	15.1	3.8	97500
35133	REMLAP	21376	1379	18.8	32.4	40.5	6.7	1.6	48863	48721	59	88	1224	15.5	21.3	36.9	24.2	2.0	115512
35135	RIVERSIDE	21369	744	28.1	33.2	30.4	5.6	2.7	38455	39358	28	61	519	22.0	15.2	27.9	29.3	5.6	121991
35136	ROCKFORD	18812	843	32.7	30.5	33.1	3.4	0.2	37819	38758	26	58	679	33.0	25.3	30.0	11.3	0.3	79912
35143	SHELBY	22951	1662	24.7	27.6	37.7	7.6	2.4	45480	45429	50	82	1396	35.2	15.5	21.4	25.3	2.5	87609
35146	SPRINGVILLE	19370	3297	22.5	27.7	39.7	7.4	2.6	49780	51029	61	89	2857	18.8	15.4	29.4	29.8	6.7	131033
35147	STERRETT	25592	2301	24.1	25.0	35.6	10.2	5.0	51017	51764	64	90	2088	12.3	14.4	22.6	37.0	13.8	179620
35148	SUMITON	17622	1166	39.0	28.1	26.6	5.3	0.9	32785	34807	13	33	885	30.5	25.0	32.0	11.4	1.1	82652
35150	SYLACAUGA	17695	7745	39.5	27.3	26.7	4.9	1.6	33437	35317	14	36	5255	27.3	26.5	32.7	12.3	1.3	83536
35151	SYLACAUGA	18429	3308	31.5	31.8	30.0	5.2	1.5	37720	38371	26	57	2857	28.5	21.0	34.7	13.3	2.6	91076
35160	TALLADEGA	17246	10198	38.5	29.0	26.1	4.9	1.5	34807	36115	17	43	7356	26.1	27.8	32.0	12.6	1.5	84034
35171	THORSBY	18736	1458	27.0	34.0	32.4	5.3	1.2	41946	43387	39	72	1234	20.2	24.4	36.5	16.1	2.8	99306
35172	TRAFFORD	19265	1259	29.3	28.2	37.3	4.2	1.0	43067	45544	43	76	1069	27.8	23.2	31.7	15.4	1.9	88521
35173	TRUSSVILLE	26873	8799	14.4	21.8	43.9	13.7	6.2	64414	63843	83	97	7768	10.1	9.1	36.4	40.3	4.1	158046
35175	UNION GROVE	20408	1897	27.9	28.8	34.7	5.9	2.6	42427	43573	41	74	1629	20.3	17.1	39.0	16.8	6.9	113127
35176	VANDIVER	43714	332	21.1	14.8	30.7	16.6	16.9	68549	75753	86	98	289	15.9	19.0	11.4	27.0	26.6	235417
35178	VINCENT	22078	1676	30.2	26.8	33.2	6.4	3.4	41191	41526	37	71	1409	27.5	24.8	25.7	15.7	6.3	85290
35179	VINEMONT	18836	3529	31.9	31.2	29.5	5.4	1.9	38411	39439	28	61	2930	25.8	19.5	32.3	18.5	3.9	102975
35180	WARRIOR	19618	4941	24.9	30.4	37.3	6.4	1.0	44168	46341	46	80	4133	14.2	19.5	44.1	20.9	1.4	116465
35183	WEOGUFKA	22389	53	30.2	30.2	34.0	5.7	0.0	42356	40000	40	73	47	14.9	34.0	36.2	12.8	2.1	91250
35184	WEST BLOCTON	17625	2337	32.3	34.1	26.4	6.2	1.0	38294	39876	28	60	1929	29.0	33.8	27.3	8.0	2.0	73305
35186	WILSONVILLE	25262	1844	22.3	26.7	37.6	9.1	4.3	51319	51955	64	91	1596	19.0	16.0	27.0	29.6	8.3	129895
35188	WOODSTOCK	17978	882	27.0	29.4	37.8	4.9	1.0	43717	44896	44	78	713	19.8	28.1	31.4	18.2	2.5	95000
35203	BIRMINGHAM	13775	1203	70.8	10.7	15.7	1.7	1.0	11956	13209	1	0	147	7.5	2.7	81.0	8.8	0.0	135192
35204	BIRMINGHAM	13436	5238	57.4	26.0	13.8	1.9	0.9	19929	20763	1	3	2258	28.3	50.9	19.6	0.9	0.3	66715
35205	BIRMINGHAM	24312	10819	42.4	31.2	20.1	3.6	2.7	30176	31351	8	22	2704	12.6	22.9	36.6	19.4	8.4	111772
35206	BIRMINGHAM	15103	7854	40.4	33.2	22.7	2.3	1.4	31162	32466	10	25	5202	14.3	57.1	24.8	3.7	0.2	73811
35207	BIRMINGHAM	12752	3811	59.0	24.2	13.8	1.5	1.5	18998	19535	1	3	2185	39.9	43.7	15.7	0.5	0.2	57500
35208	BIRMINGHAM	16448	6234	35.7	32.5	27.5	2.8	1.6	34886	36496	17	43	4049	19.4	61.4	18.3	0.9	0.0	70930
35209	BIRMINGHAM	29247	13021	24.4	31.3	31.0	8.3	5.0	43991	45810	45	79	5435	1.9	5.8	33.3	53.0	6.0	193655
	ALABAMA	21187		31.4	27.9	30.6	6.9	3.2	40822	42202				18.1	22.4	35.8	19.6	4.0	107730
	UNITED STATES	27277		20.9	24.4	35.3	11.7	7.6	54719	56938				9.3	13.1	31.6	32.6	13.5	162279

ZIP CODE		FINANCIAL SERVICES				THE HOME						ENTERTAINMENT						PERSONAL			
						Home Improvements		Furnishings													
#	POST OFFICE NAME	Auto Loan	Home Loan	Invest-ments	Retire-ment Plans	Home Repair	Lawn & Garden	Comput-ers & Hard-ware-Personal	Major Appli-ances	TV, Radio, Sound Equip-ment	Furni-ture	Dine out/ Carry out	Sports Equip-ment	Fees & Tickets	Toys & Games	Travel	Cable TV	Apparel & Services	Auto Repairs	Health Insur-ance	Pets & Supplies
35004	MOODY	87	78	71	75	76	81	75	79	78	78	78	59	70	81	71	80	53	77	80	95
35005	ADAMSVILLE	78	80	80	79	79	89	73	81	77	72	77	60	75	78	77	82	53	78	87	95
35006	ADGER	87	62	79	60	63	85	64	78	71	61	70	59	51	73	61	78	47	73	81	94
35007	ALABASTER	131	139	118	133	130	120	123	125	118	132	120	99	124	126	122	113	84	119	111	144
35010	ALEXANDER CITY	80	60	71	60	61	79	65	74	71	61	69	56	55	72	61	77	47	71	80	89
35014	ALPINE	75	51	69	48	50	73	54	66	61	51	60	51	41	63	50	68	40	62	70	81
35016	ARAB	83	69	74	69	69	84	69	78	75	67	74	59	62	76	67	80	50	75	83	93
35019	BAILEYTON	79	56	65	55	56	75	59	68	65	57	64	52	47	68	53	71	43	65	72	83
35020	BESSEMER	48	40	38	41	39	47	45	44	50	45	49	33	42	49	41	53	33	47	52	55
35022	BESSEMER	85	86	79	87	84	89	83	85	84	82	84	66	83	85	83	85	58	83	88	100
35023	BESSEMER	83	82	80	82	80	90	78	84	82	76	81	63	78	82	79	86	56	82	90	99
35031	BLOUNTSVILLE	77	57	65	56	57	74	59	68	64	56	63	52	48	67	54	70	42	64	72	82
35033	BREMEN	86	61	75	59	61	83	63	76	71	61	69	58	50	73	59	77	46	71	80	92
35034	BRENT	67	48	58	47	47	64	51	59	58	50	56	46	42	59	47	63	38	57	63	73
35035	BRIERFIELD	85	73	75	75	74	88	73	83	76	67	75	63	65	78	71	81	51	77	86	97
35036	BROOKSIDE	83	60	86	58	62	85	61	78	68	57	67	59	49	68	61	75	44	72	81	93
35040	CALERA	99	88	83	86	86	95	85	91	88	87	88	68	79	92	81	92	60	88	92	109
35041	CARDIFF	83	60	86	58	62	85	61	78	68	57	67	59	49	68	61	75	44	72	81	93
35042	CENTREVILLE	70	52	63	51	52	69	56	64	61	53	60	49	47	62	52	67	41	61	68	77
35043	CHELSEA	123	122	105	118	116	113	112	115	111	118	112	88	109	117	108	110	77	110	108	134
35044	CHILDERSBURG	69	56	58	55	54	68	58	63	63	56	62	48	52	64	54	68	42	62	68	76
35045	CLANTON	71	58	62	58	58	71	61	67	66	57	64	51	54	66	58	70	44	65	72	80
35046	CLANTON	85	61	76	59	62	83	63	76	70	60	69	58	51	72	59	77	46	71	80	92
35049	CLEVELAND	87	65	72	63	64	83	67	76	73	66	72	58	55	76	61	79	48	73	80	93
35051	COLUMBIANA	93	79	80	76	78	88	77	85	81	78	81	63	69	84	73	85	55	81	86	101
35053	CRANE HILL	89	70	108	69	76	92	70	88	75	67	74	65	60	72	74	80	49	82	88	103
35054	CROPWELL	104	85	124	83	91	110	84	104	89	81	88	76	75	87	89	95	59	97	105	121
35055	CULLMAN	69	62	63	62	62	71	65	69	69	62	67	51	61	68	63	72	46	68	75	81
35057	CULLMAN	81	64	69	62	64	78	64	73	69	64	68	55	55	72	60	74	46	69	75	87
35058	CULLMAN	86	70	75	70	70	85	71	80	75	68	74	61	62	78	67	80	50	76	83	95
35061	DOLOMITE	77	62	77	61	63	82	64	76	70	59	69	56	56	69	63	77	46	72	83	89
35062	DORA	83	66	75	64	66	82	66	76	71	64	70	58	57	73	63	76	47	72	79	91
35063	EMPIRE	71	48	66	45	47	69	50	62	57	48	56	48	39	59	47	64	37	58	65	76
35064	FAIRFIELD	61	56	50	57	53	61	58	57	63	59	62	42	57	62	55	65	43	60	65	71
35068	FULTONDALE	70	72	67	72	71	77	71	72	73	68	73	53	73	73	72	77	51	72	80	85
35071	GARDENDALE	83	90	85	90	89	96	83	89	86	82	85	65	87	85	87	89	59	86	96	103
35072	GOODWATER	73	51	65	48	50	71	53	64	60	51	59	50	41	62	49	66	39	61	68	78
35073	GRAYSVILLE	77	59	78	57	61	81	61	75	68	56	66	55	52	67	61	74	44	70	81	88
35077	HANCEVILLE	74	56	64	55	56	72	59	67	65	57	64	51	50	66	55	70	43	65	72	81
35078	HARPERSVILLE	88	63	73	62	63	84	66	77	73	64	72	59	53	76	60	80	48	73	81	93
35079	HAYDEN	85	69	70	67	68	80	68	76	73	68	72	57	59	76	63	77	49	72	78	91
35080	HELENA	150	166	135	160	155	135	145	144	136	158	139	115	150	147	144	127	98	136	124	164
35083	HOLLY POND	83	65	71	65	65	82	66	76	71	63	70	58	56	74	62	77	47	71	80	91
35085	JEMISON	85	61	70	59	61	81	64	74	71	62	69	57	51	74	58	77	47	70	78	90
35087	JOPPA	91	65	75	63	65	86	68	79	75	66	73	61	54	78	62	82	49	75	83	96
35089	KELLYTON	78	53	72	50	53	76	56	68	64	54	62	53	43	65	52	70	41	65	72	84
35091	KIMBERLY	87	72	71	70	71	82	71	78	75	72	75	58	63	79	66	79	51	75	80	93
35094	LEEDS	96	84	90	84	84	97	85	93	89	83	88	70	78	90	83	93	60	90	96	110
35096	LINCOLN	82	65	82	64	67	82	65	77	70	63	69	57	56	70	65	74	46	72	79	91
35097	LOCUST FORK	84	66	69	64	65	79	66	74	71	66	71	56	57	74	61	76	48	71	77	90
35098	LOGAN	73	55	63	54	55	70	56	65	62	55	61	49	47	64	52	66	41	62	68	79
35111	MC CALLA	90	85	78	85	84	90	81	87	83	80	83	65	78	86	80	86	57	83	88	102
35114	MAYLENE	131	140	114	134	130	116	124	124	117	134	120	99	125	127	121	111	84	117	109	141
35115	MONTEVALLO	85	70	71	69	69	79	76	78	78	73	78	60	67	80	70	81	53	78	81	93
35116	MORRIS	84	78	69	75	76	79	73	78	76	76	76	56	69	79	70	78	52	75	78	92
35117	MOUNT OLIVE	86	79	88	78	78	93	74	85	78	72	78	64	71	79	77	83	53	80	88	101
35118	MULGA	75	72	75	70	71	84	67	76	73	66	72	55	67	73	69	78	49	73	84	89
35120	ODENVILLE	88	72	72	70	71	83	71	79	76	72	76	59	63	79	67	81	51	76	81	95
35121	ONEONTA	82	60	70	59	60	79	63	73	70	61	68	55	52	71	58	76	46	69	77	88
35124	PELHAM	130	137	120	135	132	124	125	126	122	132	123	97	127	127	125	119	86	122	118	147
35125	PELL CITY	82	63	68	62	62	78	67	73	73	64	71	57	57	75	61	78	48	72	78	89
35126	PINSON	97	103	89	103	99	99	94	96	93	96	94	74	96	96	95	93	65	93	95	113
35127	PLEASANT GROVE	88	103	93	103	100	104	90	95	92	90	92	71	99	92	97	94	64	92	101	111
35128	PELL CITY	93	80	85	79	80	95	78	87	83	78	82	66	71	85	76	88	56	83	91	105
35130	QUINTON	76	54	72	53	55	75	56	69	63	53	61	52	45	64	54	69	41	64	72	83
35131	RAGLAND	77	58	66	56	57	73	59	68	65	58	64	52	49	67	55	70	43	65	71	82
35133	REMLAP	95	77	78	75	76	90	76	85	82	77	81	64	67	85	71	87	55	81	88	102
35135	RIVERSIDE	82	71	67	69	70	77	68	74	72	70	72	55	62	75	65	75	49	72	76	89
35136	ROCKFORD	74	55	75	52	57	76	56	69	63	56	61	51	47	62	55	69	41	65	74	83
35143	SHELBY	92	75	93	73	77	91	74	87	79	73	78	64	65	79	74	84	53	82	88	103
35146	SPRINGVILLE	90	82	78	81	80	89	78	85	81	79	81	64	74	84	76	84	55	81	86	101
35147	STERRETT	115	89	95	86	88	109	90	101	97	89	96	77	76	101	83	104	65	97	105	123
35148	SUMITON	76	52	73	50	53	75	55	68	62	52	61	52	43	63	52	69	40	64	72	83
35150	SYLACAUGA	67	55	58	54	55	68	59	63	64	56	62	47	52	64	55	68	42	63	70	76
35151	SYLACAUGA	80	61	71	59	61	78	62	72	68	61	67	55	52	70	59	73	45	69	76	87
35160	TALLADEGA	70	55	63	54	55	70	58	65	64	56	62	48	50	64	55	69	42	63	71	78
35171	THORSBY	86	62	71	61	62	82	65	75	72	63	70	58	52	75	59	78	47	71	79	91
35172	TRAFFORD	80	64	66	62	63	76	64	71	69	64	68	54	55	72	59	73	46	68	74	86
35173	TRUSSVILLE	105	115	107	116	113	112	103	108	102	106	102	83	109	104	108	102	72	104	105	126
35175	UNION GROVE	88	71	73	69	70	83	71	79	76	71	75	59	62	79	66	80	51	75	81	95
35176	VANDIVER	170	167	153	164	165	166	153	162	156	161	156	120	152	162	151	158	108	156	158	191
35178	VINCENT	97	69	93	67	71	95	72	87	80	69	78	67	58	81	69	87	52	82	91	106
35179	VINEMONT	83	64	69	62	63	79	65	74	70	64	69	56	54	73	60	76	47	70	77	89
35180	WARRIOR	85	71	74	69	70	82	70	78	75	70	74	58	62	77	66	79	50	75	80	93
35183	WEOGUFKA	85	61	87	59	63	86	62	80	69	58	68	60	50	69	62	76	45	73	83	94
35184	WEST BLOCTON	79	60	67	58	59	75	62	70	67	61	66	54	51	70	57	72	45	67	72	85
35186	WILSONVILLE	103	94	84	91	92	96	89	94	92	93	92	69	84	96	85	95	63	91	95	112
35188	WOODSTOCK	83	68	69	65	67	78	67	74	71	67	71	55	58	74	62	76	48	71	76	89
35203	BIRMINGHAM	36	24	24	28	23	27	37	29	40	35	40	24	32	39	31	42	28	36	35	39
35204	BIRMINGHAM	44	35	33	36	34	42	41	40	46	41	45	29	38	44	37	50	31	43	48	50
35205	BIRMINGHAM	63	44	43	49	41	45	67	50	65	61	67	45	56	66	54	64	47	61	54	65
35206	BIRMINGHAM	56	51	44	52	48	55	54	52	58	53	58	39	53	58	51	61	40	55	59	64
35207	BIRMINGHAM	47	38	36	39	36	45	43	42	49	44	48	30	40	47	39	52	33	45	51	53
35208	BIRMINGHAM	62	58	51	59	54	63	58	58	64	60	63	42	59	63	56	67	43	61	66	72
35209	BIRMINGHAM	89	70	66	75	67	68	89	75	88	87	89	63	80	89	78	86	62	85	76	92
	ALABAMA	83	70	73	70	69	80	73	77	76	71	76	59	66	77	69	80	52	76	80	92
	UNITED STATES	100	100	100	100	100	100	100	100	100	100	100	100	100	100	100	100	100	100	100	100

ZIP CODE #	POST OFFICE NAME	COUNTY FIPS CODE	POPULATION 2000	POPULATION 2009	POPULATION 2014	2000-2009 ANNUAL RATE % Rate	2000-2009 ANNUAL RATE State Centile	HOUSEHOLDS 2000	HOUSEHOLDS 2009	HOUSEHOLDS 2014	HOUSEHOLDS % Annual Rate 2000-2009	HOUSEHOLDS 2009 Average HH Size	FAMILIES 2000	FAMILIES 2009	FAMILIES % Annual Rate 2000-2009
35210	BIRMINGHAM	073	14113	13972	13864	-0.1	39	5643	5749	5747	0.2	2.31	3715	3675	-0.1
35211	BIRMINGHAM	073	31283	28851	28000	-0.9	6	12212	11656	11409	-0.5	2.45	8214	7586	-0.9
35212	BIRMINGHAM	073	15451	13760	13222	-1.2	2	5862	5364	5197	-1.0	2.53	3741	3287	-1.4
35213	BIRMINGHAM	073	14231	13834	13599	-0.3	29	6302	6262	6196	-0.1	2.19	3854	3688	-0.5
35214	BIRMINGHAM	073	21515	20296	19834	-0.6	16	8436	8213	8098	-0.3	2.45	6094	5774	-0.6
35215	BIRMINGHAM	073	46221	46563	46367	0.1	49	17982	18471	18506	0.3	2.51	12928	12936	0.0
35216	BIRMINGHAM	073	31796	31679	31324	0.0	45	14453	14721	14662	0.2	2.13	8272	8089	-0.2
35217	BIRMINGHAM	073	15764	14328	13784	-1.0	4	6126	5701	5526	-0.8	2.49	4162	3745	-1.1
35218	BIRMINGHAM	073	9773	8480	8081	-1.5	1	3726	3292	3157	-1.3	2.54	2475	2121	-1.7
35221	BIRMINGHAM	073	6302	5767	5583	-1.0	4	2387	2265	2212	-0.6	2.51	1709	1576	-0.9
35222	BIRMINGHAM	073	8376	8344	8298	0.0	45	3911	4003	4010	0.3	2.06	1952	1899	-0.3
35223	BIRMINGHAM	073	11561	11222	11020	-0.3	29	4630	4608	4563	-0.1	2.43	3378	3282	-0.3
35224	BIRMINGHAM	073	7434	7073	6913	-0.5	19	2818	2734	2689	-0.3	2.59	1998	1881	-0.7
35226	BIRMINGHAM	073	26935	27402	27503	0.2	52	10408	11002	11137	0.6	2.46	7424	7648	0.3
35228	BIRMINGHAM	073	11543	10923	10662	-0.6	16	4346	4196	4122	-0.4	2.56	3051	2851	-0.7
35229	BIRMINGHAM	073	2013	2011	1997	0.0	45	95	93	91	-0.2	2.55	39	35	-1.2
35233	BIRMINGHAM	073	259	271	271	0.5	64	101	116	120	1.5	1.43	20	21	0.5
35234	BIRMINGHAM	073	8051	7149	6861	-1.3	2	2782	2523	2431	-1.1	2.52	1826	1601	-1.4
35235	BIRMINGHAM	073	18449	19199	19362	0.4	62	7612	8160	8290	0.8	2.35	5538	5783	0.5
35242	BIRMINGHAM	117	32454	45113	51340	3.6	97	12941	18184	20810	3.7	2.48	8964	12378	3.6
35243	BIRMINGHAM	073	17219	18548	19027	0.8	74	7283	8173	8467	1.3	2.27	4616	5020	0.9
35244	BIRMINGHAM	117	26501	31584	34111	1.9	89	10466	12602	13652	2.0	2.50	7464	8855	1.9
35401	TUSCALOOSA	125	37766	35354	34970	-0.7	13	14255	14072	14067	-0.1	2.02	6310	5817	-0.9
35404	TUSCALOOSA	125	19137	20687	20968	0.8	74	7851	8318	8521	0.6	2.37	4836	4828	0.0
35405	TUSCALOOSA	125	30001	33318	34842	1.1	79	12079	13917	14731	1.5	2.38	8315	9221	1.1
35406	TUSCALOOSA	125	10833	12653	13447	1.7	88	4554	5369	5720	1.8	2.35	3073	3578	1.7
35441	AKRON	065	1432	1439	1426	0.1	49	589	615	618	0.5	2.34	409	418	0.2
35442	ALICEVILLE	107	5912	5641	5517	-0.5	19	2148	2104	2075	-0.2	2.62	1508	1446	-0.5
35443	BOLIGEE	063	1091	1039	997	-0.5	19	406	401	391	-0.1	2.59	276	266	-0.4
35444	BROOKWOOD	125	3108	3538	3753	1.4	84	1149	1369	1470	1.9	2.56	893	1031	1.6
35446	BUHL	125	1581	1626	1647	0.3	58	598	644	660	0.8	2.51	469	490	0.5
35447	CARROLLTON	107	4251	4160	4105	-0.2	34	1599	1609	1601	0.1	2.58	1150	1134	-0.2
35452	COKER	125	3553	3590	3711	0.1	49	1323	1393	1460	0.6	2.53	1034	1056	0.2
35453	COTTONDALE	125	9015	9428	9676	0.5	64	3473	3801	3954	1.0	2.48	2627	2774	0.6
35456	DUNCANVILLE	125	4012	4059	4087	0.1	49	1436	1514	1545	0.6	2.68	1126	1150	0.2
35457	ECHOLA	125	155	155	155	0.0	45	62	64	65	0.3	2.42	48	49	0.2
35458	ELROD	125	510	526	529	0.3	58	194	205	209	0.6	2.57	146	149	0.2
35459	EMELLE	119	807	781	761	-0.4	25	315	319	315	0.1	2.45	221	219	-0.1
35460	EPES	119	962	942	922	-0.2	34	362	369	365	0.2	2.51	236	235	0.0
35461	ETHELSVILLE	107	1837	1674	1620	-1.0	4	764	720	704	-0.6	2.33	540	499	-0.9
35462	EUTAW	063	6306	6211	6068	-0.2	34	2519	2625	2603	0.4	2.34	1699	1730	0.2
35463	FOSTERS	125	1471	1646	1735	1.2	80	560	657	702	1.7	2.51	438	498	1.4
35464	GAINESVILLE	119	263	264	262	0.0	45	101	106	106	0.5	2.49	70	72	0.3
35466	GORDO	107	5433	5333	5276	-0.2	34	2162	2185	2181	0.1	2.44	1579	1563	-0.1
35469	KNOXVILLE	063	533	515	505	-0.4	25	213	217	216	0.2	2.37	138	138	0.0
35470	LIVINGSTON	119	5432	4991	4762	-0.9	6	2202	2099	2026	-0.5	2.31	1312	1215	-0.8
35473	NORTHPORT	125	13268	14454	15019	0.9	76	5358	6050	6354	1.3	2.39	3843	4223	1.0
35474	MOUNDVILLE	065	5361	5451	5461	0.2	52	2015	2123	2154	0.6	2.53	1500	1548	0.3
35475	NORTHPORT	125	10395	12914	13904	2.4	92	3802	4878	5312	2.7	2.65	3076	3824	2.4
35476	NORTHPORT	125	7070	7138	7100	0.1	49	2905	2938	2952	0.1	2.19	1703	1626	-0.5
35480	RALPH	125	917	1020	1072	1.2	80	340	397	423	1.7	2.57	265	300	1.4
35481	REFORM	107	4170	3914	3813	-0.7	13	1646	1588	1561	-0.4	2.42	1170	1106	-0.6
35487	TUSCALOOSA	125	609	1263	1263	8.2	100	391	415	415	0.6	1.18	82	76	-0.8
35490	VANCE	125	2780	3314	3550	1.9	89	1010	1246	1351	2.3	2.66	815	978	2.0
35501	JASPER	127	10715	9962	9601	-0.8	9	4435	4175	4041	-0.7	2.28	2936	2693	-0.9
35503	JASPER	127	9254	9098	8910	-0.2	34	3644	3645	3596	0.0	2.46	2701	2648	-0.2
35504	JASPER	127	12901	12786	12572	-0.1	39	5104	5142	5086	0.1	2.44	3752	3704	-0.1
35540	ADDISON	133	2593	2565	2526	-0.1	39	1056	1075	1069	0.2	2.39	774	770	-0.1
35541	ARLEY	133	3198	3630	3702	1.4	84	1282	1507	1550	1.8	2.40	974	1123	1.6
35542	BANKSTON	057	1200	1172	1141	-0.3	29	453	461	456	0.2	2.54	348	347	0.0
35543	BEAR CREEK	093	1130	1083	1050	-0.5	19	459	452	442	-0.2	2.40	347	336	-0.3
35544	BEAVERTON	075	893	858	834	-0.4	25	365	364	357	0.0	2.36	261	254	-0.3
35546	BERRY	057	3938	4241	4292	0.8	74	1553	1726	1768	1.1	2.46	1155	1252	0.9
35548	BRILLIANT	093	1796	1681	1616	-0.7	13	737	711	690	-0.4	2.32	523	494	-0.6
35549	CARBON HILL	127	4469	4294	4174	-0.4	25	1887	1846	1807	-0.2	2.29	1322	1263	-0.5
35550	CORDOVA	127	6441	6150	5975	-0.5	19	2612	2529	2471	-0.3	2.39	1825	1728	-0.6
35552	DETROIT	093	1069	1054	1034	-0.2	34	446	456	452	0.2	2.31	333	334	0.0
35553	DOUBLE SPRINGS	133	4712	4726	4680	0.0	45	1872	1941	1940	0.4	2.33	1347	1366	0.2
35554	ELDRIDGE	057	1235	1191	1159	-0.4	25	486	483	474	-0.1	2.45	375	366	-0.3
35555	FAYETTE	057	10996	10147	9746	-0.9	6	4554	4355	4225	-0.5	2.25	3141	2936	-0.7
35563	GUIN	093	4274	4095	3977	-0.5	19	1808	1789	1753	-0.1	2.24	1237	1198	-0.3
35564	HACKLEBURG	093	2542	2442	2372	-0.4	25	1075	1070	1049	-0.1	2.28	743	724	-0.3
35565	HALEYVILLE	133	14128	13227	12766	-0.7	13	5742	5490	5338	-0.5	2.39	4081	3818	-0.7
35570	HAMILTON	093	11117	10895	10679	-0.2	34	4451	4504	4452	0.1	2.27	3135	3105	-0.1
35571	HODGES	059	1068	999	964	-0.7	13	437	419	407	-0.5	2.38	329	310	-0.6
35572	HOUSTON	133	1327	1281	1252	-0.4	25	548	547	540	0.0	2.34	405	396	-0.2
35574	KENNEDY	075	1434	1353	1294	-0.6	16	589	575	556	-0.3	2.35	437	419	-0.5
35575	LYNN	133	1344	1292	1264	-0.4	25	553	548	541	-0.1	2.36	416	404	-0.3
35576	MILLPORT	075	3566	3399	3277	-0.5	19	1442	1425	1389	-0.1	2.38	1054	1022	-0.3
35578	NAUVOO	127	5755	5698	5598	-0.1	39	2296	2318	2296	0.1	2.45	1727	1710	-0.1
35579	OAKMAN	127	3273	3283	3248	0.0	45	1285	1311	1304	0.2	2.50	956	955	0.0
35580	PARRISH	127	4590	4623	4560	0.1	49	1833	1873	1858	0.2	2.47	1380	1384	0.0
35581	PHIL CAMPBELL	059	5631	5708	5646	0.1	49	2220	2298	2285	0.4	2.48	1670	1697	0.2
35582	RED BAY	059	4595	4568	4501	-0.1	39	1905	1931	1908	0.1	2.32	1357	1348	-0.1
35585	SPRUCE PINE	059	1468	1429	1398	-0.3	29	590	586	575	-0.1	2.44	442	430	-0.3
35586	SULLIGENT	075	4966	4702	4518	-0.6	16	2023	1974	1915	-0.3	2.34	1474	1410	-0.5
35587	TOWNLEY	127	1191	1134	1099	-0.5	19	478	463	452	-0.3	2.44	359	341	-0.6
35592	VERNON	075	5040	4683	4452	-0.8	9	2032	1957	1880	-0.4	2.33	1472	1390	-0.6
35593	VINA	059	1874	1842	1809	-0.2	34	752	758	748	0.1	2.42	580	575	-0.1
35594	WINFIELD	093	7779	7735	7603	-0.1	39	3128	3206	3182	0.3	2.37	2270	2281	0.1
35601	DECATUR	103	34844	33800	33501	-0.3	29	14017	13759	13694	-0.2	2.38	9145	8712	-0.5
35603	DECATUR	103	25464	28355	29738	1.2	80	10111	11573	12234	1.5	2.43	7382	8279	1.2
35610	ANDERSON	077	2027	2176	2244	0.8	74	830	907	941	1.0	2.40	636	680	0.7
35611	ATHENS	083	22828	24323	25449	0.7	70	9286	10024	10533	0.8	2.37	6289	6628	0.6
35613	ATHENS	083	12653	15856	17446	2.5	92	4678	5885	6514	2.5	2.66	3692	4568	2.3
	ALABAMA					0.6					0.9	2.44			0.6
	UNITED STATES					1.0					1.1	2.59			0.9

#	POST OFFICE NAME	RACE (%) White 2000	White 2009	Black 2000	Black 2009	Asian/Pacific 2000	Asian/Pacific 2009	% Hispanic Origin 2000	% Hispanic Origin 2009	2009 AGE DISTRIBUTION (%) 0-4	5-9	10-14	15-19	20-24	25-44	45-64	65-84	85+	18+	MEDIAN AGE 2009	% 2009 Males	% 2009 Females
35210	BIRMINGHAM	76.1	69.6	21.0	26.3	1.0	1.4	2.0	3.7	5.6	5.7	6.0	5.6	5.0	25.1	28.4	13.7	4.9	79.1	42.9	46.3	53.7
35211	BIRMINGHAM	4.3	4.3	94.6	94.4	0.2	0.2	0.8	0.9	7.4	7.6	7.4	7.6	6.9	23.4	25.4	12.2	2.0	73.1	36.0	44.0	56.0
35212	BIRMINGHAM	17.9	14.2	78.0	80.5	0.2	0.3	4.6	6.1	8.6	8.6	7.6	7.4	6.9	26.7	24.4	8.3	1.5	70.7	32.7	46.8	53.2
35213	BIRMINGHAM	90.5	86.1	7.5	11.0	1.1	1.7	0.9	1.7	7.1	6.2	6.2	4.9	5.7	26.6	25.9	14.2	3.2	77.1	40.2	46.1	53.9
35214	BIRMINGHAM	33.8	28.6	65.0	69.9	0.2	0.2	0.7	0.9	6.0	6.5	6.7	6.6	5.5	24.6	28.5	13.2	2.4	76.8	40.1	45.9	54.1
35215	BIRMINGHAM	57.6	47.5	40.0	49.3	0.5	0.6	1.8	3.0	8.1	7.5	7.0	6.8	6.6	28.6	23.7	10.1	1.6	73.2	34.5	47.0	53.0
35216	BIRMINGHAM	86.0	79.8	7.0	9.9	3.3	4.7	5.5	9.4	5.8	5.0	4.9	5.6	9.3	30.2	24.4	11.5	3.3	81.1	36.6	48.1	51.9
35217	BIRMINGHAM	52.0	45.6	46.0	51.5	0.1	0.2	1.8	3.1	6.4	6.6	6.5	7.2	6.8	24.3	27.1	12.6	2.5	76.1	38.8	46.4	53.6
35218	BIRMINGHAM	5.8	3.9	93.2	95.0	0.1	0.1	1.0	1.1	7.4	7.8	7.8	8.5	7.7	25.4	25.7	8.0	1.7	71.8	33.1	45.2	54.8
35221	BIRMINGHAM	2.6	1.7	96.7	97.6	0.0	0.1	0.2	0.2	6.6	7.4	7.6	7.6	5.7	22.3	26.7	13.3	2.7	73.6	38.0	43.8	56.2
35222	BIRMINGHAM	54.6	47.3	42.2	48.4	1.2	1.5	2.7	4.0	6.3	6.4	6.0	5.3	7.1	29.3	25.6	11.6	2.5	78.1	38.0	47.5	52.5
35223	BIRMINGHAM	97.3	95.8	1.3	2.1	0.8	1.3	0.6	1.1	5.8	6.7	8.4	7.2	4.2	20.0	32.4	12.9	2.5	74.3	43.5	48.5	51.5
35224	BIRMINGHAM	41.7	33.3	56.5	64.7	0.4	0.5	0.5	0.6	6.5	7.1	7.8	7.5	5.8	24.3	25.7	12.9	2.4	73.9	37.6	46.3	53.7
35226	BIRMINGHAM	89.6	84.2	5.6	8.5	3.1	4.7	1.8	3.4	6.0	5.8	5.9	5.6	5.9	28.7	27.8	12.0	2.4	79.0	39.1	48.0	52.0
35228	BIRMINGHAM	20.2	14.1	78.8	84.9	0.2	0.2	0.3	0.4	6.5	7.0	7.5	7.9	6.7	24.5	27.0	10.6	2.3	74.2	37.3	45.2	54.8
35229	BIRMINGHAM	92.7	88.4	4.4	7.0	1.9	3.0	0.7	1.5	1.6	1.7	1.2	28.3	39.2	10.5	8.3	7.4	1.8	94.7	22.2	39.0	61.0
35233	BIRMINGHAM	37.5	31.7	49.0	53.9	10.8	11.4	1.9	2.6	3.3	2.2	1.8	12.9	17.7	32.1	17.0	10.3	2.6	90.8	31.0	50.2	49.8
35234	BIRMINGHAM	4.7	3.1	94.7	96.3	0.1	0.1	0.4	0.4	6.0	6.6	6.2	6.4	6.3	25.9	27.2	12.7	2.7	77.3	39.4	46.0	54.0
35235	BIRMINGHAM	78.9	71.2	18.7	25.4	0.8	1.2	1.3	2.2	6.2	6.3	6.4	6.0	4.9	27.4	28.0	12.8	2.0	77.3	40.1	47.6	52.4
35242	BIRMINGHAM	92.8	90.8	4.0	4.6	2.1	3.0	1.7	2.8	6.8	7.0	7.5	6.6	4.7	30.5	28.8	7.6	0.6	74.5	37.3	49.3	50.7
35243	BIRMINGHAM	96.3	93.9	1.5	2.4	1.3	2.1	0.9	1.9	5.2	5.1	5.7	6.1	7.3	30.5	28.5	10.2	1.5	80.4	37.8	49.3	50.7
35244	BIRMINGHAM	90.2	86.3	5.8	7.9	2.3	3.4	2.2	3.7	6.8	7.0	7.5	6.6	5.4	29.7	28.4	7.7	1.0	74.6	36.9	49.4	50.6
35401	TUSCALOOSA	40.7	36.9	56.0	58.6	1.8	2.6	1.1	1.8	5.0	4.6	4.5	13.8	22.0	21.2	17.5	9.2	2.1	82.0	25.0	46.3	53.7
35404	TUSCALOOSA	61.7	55.2	35.8	41.4	0.6	0.8	1.7	2.9	6.3	6.3	6.2	7.2	9.6	26.8	23.4	11.8	2.2	77.8	35.1	48.8	51.2
35405	TUSCALOOSA	61.0	55.4	36.4	41.0	1.0	1.4	1.5	2.3	7.3	6.9	6.7	7.0	7.3	30.6	24.4	8.7	1.1	74.8	33.9	48.3	51.7
35406	TUSCALOOSA	89.3	87.0	7.6	8.3	2.1	3.3	0.7	1.1	5.9	6.4	7.0	6.8	7.7	22.0	30.3	11.9	1.9	76.6	40.7	48.4	51.6
35441	AKRON	47.1	44.1	52.4	55.0	0.0	0.0	0.7	1.1	7.8	8.2	7.9	6.3	5.2	23.7	27.0	12.2	1.8	72.2	37.9	47.6	52.4
35442	ALICEVILLE	29.2	27.2	69.7	71.4	0.1	0.2	0.8	1.0	7.4	7.3	7.3	7.7	6.4	23.0	25.5	12.8	2.6	73.0	37.3	46.5	53.5
35443	BOLIGEE	11.5	10.8	87.9	88.5	0.0	0.0	1.2	1.3	9.2	10.1	9.2	7.7	6.2	21.2	25.3	9.1	1.9	66.6	30.7	44.4	55.6
35444	BROOKWOOD	97.0	95.9	1.3	1.8	0.1	0.1	0.5	0.9	7.0	6.9	7.1	7.2	5.7	27.9	27.6	9.5	1.1	74.5	37.3	49.5	50.5
35446	BUHL	91.1	88.3	7.0	8.9	0.1	0.1	2.0	3.5	5.9	6.3	6.6	6.5	5.5	25.0	30.2	12.6	1.4	77.2	40.7	49.1	50.9
35447	CARROLLTON	44.5	41.3	54.3	57.0	0.1	0.1	0.8	1.1	7.9	7.4	7.3	7.1	5.6	24.3	26.6	11.5	2.3	72.9	36.9	47.1	52.9
35452	COKER	92.4	90.1	5.2	6.3	0.2	0.3	1.7	3.0	7.2	7.2	7.1	6.2	5.5	27.1	26.5	11.9	1.3	74.5	37.8	50.0	50.0
35453	COTTONDALE	89.9	86.9	8.2	10.5	0.3	0.4	0.9	1.5	6.6	6.7	6.8	6.2	5.0	28.9	28.2	10.4	1.1	76.1	38.0	49.6	50.4
35456	DUNCANVILLE	84.3	80.4	13.6	16.9	0.5	0.7	0.7	1.2	6.9	6.7	6.8	7.4	7.4	28.0	27.5	8.4	0.8	75.0	35.6	49.4	50.6
35457	ECHOLA	94.9	93.5	2.6	3.2	0.0	0.0	1.9	3.2	6.5	6.5	6.5	6.5	5.2	25.2	29.0	13.5	1.3	76.8	40.7	49.7	50.3
35458	ELROD	95.1	93.2	2.7	3.4	0.0	0.2	1.4	2.5	5.9	6.3	6.7	6.1	4.0	25.3	31.0	13.5	1.3	77.4	42.3	49.2	50.8
35459	EMELLE	25.9	23.8	73.6	75.5	0.0	0.0	0.9	1.2	6.7	6.7	6.9	8.5	6.7	23.9	26.6	11.9	2.2	74.6	37.4	47.6	52.4
35460	EPES	21.9	20.1	77.3	78.7	0.1	0.2	1.2	1.6	7.6	7.7	7.9	8.1	9.0	23.6	23.6	10.4	2.1	72.3	32.3	46.9	53.1
35461	ETHELSVILLE	62.1	58.7	36.9	40.0	0.1	0.1	0.4	0.6	6.1	6.3	6.6	6.2	5.3	25.9	27.8	14.3	1.6	77.4	40.4	48.9	51.1
35462	EUTAW	19.6	17.8	79.7	81.4	0.1	0.2	0.5	0.5	7.1	7.4	7.2	7.6	6.1	22.3	26.8	12.5	2.9	73.6	38.0	46.9	53.1
35463	FOSTERS	65.9	59.1	33.4	40.1	0.0	0.0	0.5	0.9	6.1	6.6	6.7	5.8	4.7	25.5	30.1	12.8	1.6	76.9	41.1	49.3	50.7
35464	GAINESVILLE	17.1	15.9	81.7	82.2	0.0	0.0	1.5	1.9	8.3	8.7	8.3	8.0	6.4	23.5	24.6	10.2	1.9	69.7	33.0	47.0	53.0
35466	GORDO	81.9	79.7	17.1	18.8	0.2	0.2	0.8	1.3	6.2	6.3	6.5	6.2	4.8	25.1	28.8	14.4	1.7	77.2	41.5	49.5	50.5
35469	KNOXVILLE	26.8	25.4	72.8	74.2	0.0	0.0	1.5	1.6	5.2	5.8	5.8	6.2	5.0	24.7	30.1	15.1	1.9	79.4	42.9	51.3	48.7
35470	LIVINGSTON	31.9	29.5	67.0	69.1	0.2	0.3	1.0	1.2	7.0	6.8	6.6	7.9	14.4	22.4	22.8	9.6	2.5	75.9	30.3	46.8	53.2
35473	NORTHPORT	83.3	78.9	13.4	16.5	1.3	1.7	1.9	3.2	6.5	6.4	6.6	6.7	7.2	28.1	26.6	10.7	1.3	76.5	36.6	49.1	50.9
35474	MOUNDVILLE	64.4	60.8	33.4	36.4	0.5	0.5	1.2	1.8	7.2	7.1	7.0	6.7	6.1	26.7	26.9	10.4	1.8	74.4	37.3	48.2	51.8
35475	NORTHPORT	93.8	91.8	4.9	6.3	0.1	0.2	0.9	1.6	6.4	6.8	7.0	6.4	4.8	27.6	30.1	10.1	0.9	75.8	39.4	50.6	49.4
35476	NORTHPORT	57.0	51.6	41.2	45.9	0.4	0.6	1.4	2.1	7.0	6.5	6.1	5.9	8.1	25.9	20.9	14.8	4.7	77.5	37.0	43.2	56.8
35480	RALPH	65.8	59.4	33.6	39.8	0.0	0.0	0.5	0.9	6.2	6.6	6.8	5.9	4.7	25.4	30.0	12.9	1.6	77.0	41.1	49.3	50.7
35481	REFORM	65.1	62.7	33.6	35.7	0.1	0.2	0.6	0.8	6.8	7.0	6.9	6.6	5.1	23.4	27.1	14.3	2.7	75.1	40.6	46.8	53.2
35487	TUSCALOOSA	59.5	56.2	38.7	40.5	0.7	1.4	1.0	2.5	3.7	3.6	3.3	10.7	24.1	23.3	16.9	11.1	3.3	86.0	28.3	50.0	50.0
35490	VANCE	93.8	91.4	3.7	4.6	0.1	0.1	1.9	3.5	8.1	8.4	8.0	6.4	5.2	29.2	25.4	8.4	0.9	71.5	35.0	50.1	49.9
35501	JASPER	80.3	78.4	17.4	18.2	0.3	0.5	1.7	2.9	6.1	6.0	6.0	5.8	5.7	25.5	27.0	14.9	2.9	78.4	40.7	48.0	52.0
35503	JASPER	97.7	97.0	0.6	0.7	0.4	0.5	1.0	1.7	6.3	6.5	6.7	6.1	4.7	25.5	29.0	13.3	1.9	76.9	40.7	49.7	50.3
35504	JASPER	97.5	96.8	1.2	1.4	0.4	0.6	0.9	1.5	6.2	6.3	6.4	5.7	4.9	25.4	28.5	14.5	2.1	77.7	41.6	48.4	51.6
35540	ADDISON	98.2	97.7	0.2	0.3	0.1	0.1	0.4	0.7	6.1	6.2	6.4	6.7	5.4	26.7	28.2	12.8	1.4	77.2	40.0	50.1	49.9
35541	ARLEY	99.1	98.8	0.0	0.0	0.0	0.0	0.8	1.4	6.6	6.8	6.8	5.6	5.1	25.5	28.7	13.4	1.5	76.3	40.6	49.0	51.0
35542	BANKSTON	97.4	96.8	1.8	2.1	0.0	0.0	0.5	0.9	6.1	6.2	6.6	6.2	5.3	26.8	27.5	13.9	1.4	77.2	39.7	50.0	50.0
35543	BEAR CREEK	98.3	97.7	0.1	0.1	0.2	0.3	0.9	1.6	6.6	6.6	6.7	6.6	5.6	28.0	28.5	10.3	0.9	75.8	38.2	52.0	48.0
35544	BEAVERTON	93.4	92.8	5.5	5.8	0.2	0.3	0.3	0.3	5.4	5.7	5.7	6.1	5.0	27.7	27.2	15.5	1.7	79.4	40.9	49.3	50.7
35546	BERRY	95.4	94.0	3.1	3.7	0.1	0.1	1.0	1.7	6.9	6.9	7.0	6.6	5.1	26.5	27.2	12.4	1.4	75.1	38.6	49.7	50.3
35548	BRILLIANT	98.5	98.2	0.7	0.8	0.1	0.1	1.0	1.7	6.1	6.4	6.5	5.7	5.1	25.5	28.3	14.6	1.8	77.6	40.9	50.6	49.4
35549	CARBON HILL	94.7	93.8	4.2	4.8	0.0	0.0	0.7	1.2	6.0	6.5	6.6	5.7	4.4	24.4	29.2	14.8	2.5	77.6	42.3	47.3	52.7
35550	CORDOVA	91.6	90.0	7.3	8.4	0.0	0.0	0.7	1.2	6.2	6.6	6.7	6.1	5.4	24.9	27.8	13.5	2.8	76.7	40.3	47.1	52.9
35552	DETROIT	92.4	91.2	5.7	6.3	0.2	0.2	0.8	1.6	6.3	6.2	6.7	6.3	4.9	27.7	26.7	13.5	1.8	76.9	39.9	49.8	50.2
35553	DOUBLE SPRINGS	98.4	97.9	0.1	0.2	0.1	0.1	0.8	1.3	5.8	5.6	5.9	6.1	5.0	26.8	28.3	13.9	2.6	79.1	41.3	49.1	50.9
35554	ELDRIDGE	96.4	95.3	2.8	3.4	0.0	0.1	1.1	1.8	6.0	6.3	6.5	6.0	5.0	26.8	28.1	13.4	2.0	77.6	40.2	48.9	51.1
35555	FAYETTE	81.7	79.5	17.2	19.0	0.2	0.3	0.9	1.5	5.6	5.7	5.9	6.6	5.6	24.2	28.2	15.0	3.2	79.0	42.2	48.2	51.8
35563	GUIN	91.0	89.9	7.4	8.0	0.1	0.1	0.9	1.6	6.3	6.3	6.3	5.4	5.1	25.3	26.2	16.0	3.0	77.6	41.5	49.3	50.7
35564	HACKLEBURG	98.9	98.6	0.1	0.1	0.0	0.0	0.4	0.9	5.9	5.9	6.1	6.6	5.1	25.6	27.0	15.9	2.0	78.1	41.3	48.5	51.5
35565	HALEYVILLE	96.3	94.5	0.6	0.6	0.2	0.3	2.4	4.4	6.4	6.4	6.4	6.2	5.3	26.3	28.0	13.3	1.7	77.0	40.1	49.4	50.6
35570	HAMILTON	92.5	91.2	5.6	6.1	0.4	0.6	1.3	2.2	5.9	5.8	6.1	5.7	5.1	27.1	27.7	14.3	2.3	78.8	41.1	51.5	48.5
35571	HODGES	98.5	97.9	0.1	0.1	0.1	0.1	0.2	0.4	6.9	6.8	6.7	5.8	4.7	27.2	26.0	14.1	1.7	75.9	39.3	50.3	49.7
35572	HOUSTON	96.5	95.3	0.1	0.2	0.2	0.2	1.1	1.8	5.6	5.9	6.0	5.7	4.7	25.4	29.4	15.8	1.6	79.1	42.8	50.4	49.6
35574	KENNEDY	85.1	83.4	14.1	15.4	0.0	0.1	0.7	1.2	6.4	6.5	6.6	5.9	5.0	26.2	27.4	14.3	1.6	76.9	40.6	48.4	51.6
35575	LYNN	98.7	98.4	0.1	0.1	0.1	0.2	0.4	0.7	6.1	6.3	6.5	6.4	5.3	26.3	28.3	13.5	1.3	77.2	40.5	47.9	52.1
35576	MILLPORT	84.6	82.8	14.6	16.2	0.1	0.1	0.9	1.6	6.1	6.1	6.3	6.1	4.9	25.3	28.9	14.2	2.0	77.8	41.4	49.9	50.1
35578	NAUVOO	98.9	98.6	0.1	0.2	0.1	0.1	0.6	1.0	6.5	6.7	6.8	5.9	4.7	27.0	28.8	12.2	1.4	76.4	39.9	49.7	50.3
35579	OAKMAN	92.7	91.3	6.3	7.5	0.1	0.1	0.5	0.8	6.4	6.5	6.6	6.2	5.2	25.2	29.2	13.2	1.6	76.7	40.7	50.3	49.7
35580	PARRISH	90.2	88.1	8.4	9.9	0.1	0.2	0.5	0.8	6.1	6.4	6.7	6.3	5.0	25.2	29.2	13.4	1.7	77.0	41.0	49.4	50.6
35581	PHIL CAMPBELL	96.2	94.0	0.4	0.4	0.1	0.2	3.4	6.1	6.1	6.1	6.3	6.3	5.9	26.9	27.2	13.6	1.6	77.7	39.6	50.2	49.8
35582	RED BAY	97.1	95.9	1.4	1.7	0.0	0.1	0.8	1.6	5.8	5.8	6.0	6.0	5.5	26.0	27.4	14.8	2.9	78.9	41.4	47.1	52.9
35585	SPRUCE PINE	96.3	94.2	1.0	1.3	0.1	0.1	2.2	4.5	6.0	6.2	6.6	6.5	5.3	27.3	28.1	12.4	1.6	77.2	39.4	49.3	50.7
35586	SULLIGENT	82.8	81.0	15.8	16.9	0.0	0.1	1.7	2.9	6.1	6.1	6.2	6.1	5.3	26.7	27.5	13.5	2.6	78.0	40.4	48.1	51.9
35587	TOWNLEY	98.8	98.6	0.4	0.4	0.3	0.4	0.4	0.8	6.3	7.0	7.0	6.1	4.9	25.5	28.5	12.8	2.0	76.0	40.1	50.5	49.5
35592	VERNON	89.4	88.0	9.3	10.0	0.1	0.1	1.5	2.6	5.9	6.1	6.2	6.1	5.3	25.9	28.1	13.8	2.6	78.2	41.0	47.9	52.1
35593	VINA	98.6	97.7	0.3	0.3	0.0	0.0	1.0	1.8	6.4	6.4	6.5	6.4	5.4	27.1	27.1	12.9	1.7	76.5	39.2	49.7	50.3
35594	WINFIELD	94.9	93.9	3.8	4.3	0.2	0.3	1.0	1.7	6.1	6.2	6.2	5.9	5.1	25.1	27.8	14.8	2.9	77.9	41.8	49.0	51.0
35601	DECATUR	69.4	65.5	24.9	26.1	0.6	0.8	7.8	13.2	6.6	6.5	6.3	6.6	6.3	26.5	25.5	13.3	2.4	76.7	38.4	49.0	51.0
35603	DECATUR	87.4	84.1	9.2	11.1	1.0	1.4	1.6	3.2	6.7	6.5	6.4	6.6	6.5	27.1	28.8	10.2	1.1	76.3	37.9	48.1	51.9
35610	ANDERSON	98.2	97.7	0.6	0.8	0.1	0.2	0.3	0.6	6.6	6.7	6.8	6.2	5.4	26.7	28.3	11.9	1.5	76.1	39.6	50.1	49.9
35611	ATHENS	78.8	75.7	17.5	18.9	0.5	0.6	4.2	7.1	6.6	6.6	6.5	6.3	5.5	26.9	26.5	12.7	2.4	76.5	39.0	48.0	52.0
35613	ATHENS	88.0	86.7	9.5	9.8	0.4	0.5	1.8	3.0	6.5	6.9	7.3	6.8	4.8	27.4	29.2	10.2	1.0	75.1	38.9	50.3	49.7
	ALABAMA	71.1	69.3	26.0	26.7	0.7	1.0	1.7	2.8	6.6	6.6	6.6	6.9	6.6	26.4	26.7	11.7	1.8	76.1	37.8	48.6	51.4
	UNITED STATES	75.1	72.0	12.3	12.7	3.8	4.6	12.5	15.7	6.8	6.7	6.6	7.1	6.9	27.0	26.0	10.9	1.9	75.7	36.9	49.2	50.8

INCOME

ZIP CODE #	POST OFFICE NAME	2009 Per Capita Income	2009 HH Income Base	2009 Household Income Distribution (%): Less than $25,000	$25,000 to $49,999	$50,000 to $99,999	$100,000 to $149,999	$150,000 or More	Median Household Income: 2009	2014	2009 National Centile	2009 State Centile	2009 Home Value Base	2009 Home Value Distribution (%): Less than $50,000	$50,000 to $89,999	$90,000 to $174,999	$175,000 to $399,999	$400,000 or More	2009 Median Home Value
35210	BIRMINGHAM	27425	5749	21.6	26.5	37.0	10.3	4.6	51450	52337	65	91	4307	9.3	14.8	50.1	19.8	6.0	121786
35211	BIRMINGHAM	14098	11656	47.8	28.6	20.1	2.5	1.0	26479	28083	4	14	6170	23.4	54.5	19.2	2.6	0.3	68148
35212	BIRMINGHAM	13749	5364	50.9	26.8	17.4	3.5	1.3	24111	25752	3	10	2438	24.7	40.4	29.3	5.4	0.2	72735
35213	BIRMINGHAM	46507	6262	12.0	25.3	32.7	11.1	18.9	64727	64817	83	97	4606	0.7	1.9	28.8	35.3	33.3	259717
35214	BIRMINGHAM	20260	8213	30.5	30.1	30.1	7.3	2.0	40197	40819	33	66	6111	14.0	30.5	46.0	9.2	0.3	97172
35215	BIRMINGHAM	20690	18471	23.2	30.8	38.9	5.7	1.3	46042	47818	51	84	12321	3.3	29.1	60.2	7.3	0.1	104333
35216	BIRMINGHAM	33007	14721	18.3	29.2	34.3	10.9	7.3	52415	53261	67	92	7826	0.6	7.7	28.3	54.6	8.8	201780
35217	BIRMINGHAM	16087	5701	40.3	31.4	23.7	3.4	1.2	31786	33880	11	28	3758	21.5	51.4	23.3	3.4	0.5	70743
35218	BIRMINGHAM	12113	3292	53.6	30.6	13.3	1.9	0.5	22494	23572	2	7	1634	28.0	61.9	9.5	0.4	0.2	60786
35221	BIRMINGHAM	14346	2265	44.9	31.4	20.0	3.4	0.3	29440	30601	7	21	1547	25.3	56.6	17.6	0.1	0.4	68286
35222	BIRMINGHAM	27535	4003	34.0	28.6	25.5	6.7	5.1	39824	39557	32	65	2010	7.9	7.7	51.5	22.6	10.3	143284
35223	BIRMINGHAM	56423	4608	8.9	16.2	28.9	16.4	29.5	90722	92516	95	100	3900	1.2	1.0	10.2	43.9	43.7	368421
35224	BIRMINGHAM	15139	2734	42.3	29.8	24.4	2.2	1.4	30070	31525	8	22	2014	34.3	47.3	16.8	1.6	0.0	60961
35226	BIRMINGHAM	35836	11002	10.5	21.2	38.6	16.9	12.9	70298	70310	87	98	7847	0.5	2.1	27.6	62.4	7.4	205519
35228	BIRMINGHAM	16362	4196	35.2	33.3	26.8	3.7	0.9	34286	36167	16	41	3090	16.7	62.0	19.9	1.3	0.0	72480
35229	BIRMINGHAM	10584	93	21.5	40.9	24.7	7.5	5.4	36400	37727	22	51	31	0.0	12.9	29.0	51.6	6.5	203571
35233	BIRMINGHAM	18708	116	45.7	31.9	19.8	2.6	0.0	28414	28416	6	18	14	14.3	7.1	64.3	14.3	0.0	130000
35234	BIRMINGHAM	12218	2523	54.3	30.0	13.6	1.3	0.8	22053	23511	2	6	1135	34.5	51.5	13.7	0.3	0.0	58603
35235	BIRMINGHAM	27392	8160	14.4	27.0	45.7	9.4	3.6	56821	56178	74	94	6652	2.3	13.5	67.0	16.0	1.2	122406
35242	BIRMINGHAM	49303	18184	8.8	17.7	29.8	22.5	21.2	86430	89431	94	100	12399	3.9	2.7	5.5	53.5	34.4	316006
35243	BIRMINGHAM	46810	8173	12.8	20.2	35.0	15.4	16.6	69845	69907	87	98	5135	1.0	2.3	21.7	48.3	26.8	248838
35244	BIRMINGHAM	42445	12602	8.2	18.3	35.7	19.3	18.5	78625	81160	91	100	8967	2.3	2.3	12.0	66.9	16.6	255024
35401	TUSCALOOSA	14988	14072	57.6	25.1	14.1	1.8	1.5	19946	20432	1	4	4792	15.4	30.4	41.9	11.0	1.4	95259
35404	TUSCALOOSA	18617	8318	36.9	27.9	29.2	4.5	1.6	34370	36238	16	41	4587	12.0	24.1	44.6	17.4	1.9	111030
35405	TUSCALOOSA	23532	13917	26.1	27.1	34.7	8.7	3.3	46602	47871	53	84	8279	9.9	7.7	43.3	36.3	2.8	153067
35406	TUSCALOOSA	37141	5369	19.9	22.3	28.5	14.3	15.0	60193	61926	78	95	4281	7.6	5.3	18.6	44.1	24.4	232874
35441	AKRON	15325	615	44.1	30.7	21.6	2.9	0.7	30048	31236	8	22	503	38.0	26.4	17.9	16.7	1.0	56954
35442	ALICEVILLE	14278	2104	47.5	26.0	22.7	2.5	1.3	26445	27471	4	14	1604	37.8	25.9	25.0	9.9	1.3	69082
35443	BOLIGEE	11263	401	54.6	30.4	13.7	1.2	0.0	22424	22934	2	7	284	36.6	34.2	21.5	7.7	0.0	58261
35444	BROOKWOOD	18520	1369	29.5	29.1	36.2	4.5	0.7	44079	45740	46	80	1148	31.4	22.7	30.2	15.4	0.2	82836
35446	BUHL	18336	644	35.4	22.2	36.3	4.7	1.4	42018	45000	39	73	563	25.2	23.3	33.7	13.0	4.8	93269
35447	CARROLLTON	14877	1609	45.9	26.5	23.6	2.8	1.2	27590	28650	5	17	1295	36.3	25.2	29.1	8.6	0.8	72765
35452	COKER	20312	1393	27.1	25.8	39.5	5.5	2.1	46230	47670	52	84	1140	20.4	15.7	37.5	23.9	2.5	119483
35453	COTTONDALE	20867	3801	23.8	29.2	40.5	4.9	1.5	46765	47809	53	85	3147	25.9	15.1	35.7	22.4	1.0	111213
35456	DUNCANVILLE	18278	1514	26.7	28.4	38.8	5.6	0.5	44828	46715	48	81	1307	32.4	16.4	26.9	22.0	2.4	93370
35457	ECHOLA	19391	64	26.6	35.9	31.3	6.3	0.0	40000	40561	33	66	55	14.5	34.5	40.0	10.9	0.0	91667
35458	ELROD	21027	205	24.4	41.5	25.4	6.8	2.0	38410	40386	28	61	175	19.4	30.3	31.4	17.1	1.7	90833
35459	EMELLE	14125	319	48.6	28.5	21.6	0.6	0.6	26051	28221	4	14	255	47.8	23.1	17.6	10.6	0.8	52895
35460	EPES	12397	369	54.2	26.3	17.6	1.4	0.5	21692	22500	2	6	266	46.6	21.8	22.9	7.1	1.5	54286
35461	ETHELSVILLE	17370	720	35.1	32.2	28.6	3.5	0.6	32259	33097	12	30	656	34.9	28.2	31.4	5.5	0.0	72182
35462	EUTAW	14961	2625	55.0	23.5	17.3	2.8	1.4	21182	22133	2	5	1874	35.9	25.3	28.9	8.4	1.4	73364
35463	FOSTERS	18397	657	32.1	30.3	32.3	3.8	1.5	36763	38403	23	53	580	27.4	26.0	29.0	14.3	3.3	85556
35464	GAINESVILLE	12093	106	50.9	27.4	20.8	0.9	0.0	24046	25000	3	10	79	49.4	16.5	24.1	8.9	1.3	51000
35466	GORDO	18512	2185	36.6	26.3	31.4	4.0	1.7	37076	38828	24	55	1702	20.4	26.2	39.5	13.0	0.9	95179
35469	KNOXVILLE	15460	217	42.9	29.0	22.1	4.1	1.8	28941	30200	7	20	191	49.2	24.1	23.0	3.7	0.0	50750
35470	LIVINGSTON	13274	2099	56.7	22.5	18.2	1.8	0.7	19396	19740	1	3	1322	41.5	22.7	26.0	8.2	1.7	62551
35473	NORTHPORT	25059	6050	22.8	24.6	39.1	11.0	2.6	52353	52249	67	92	4209	7.5	5.3	45.6	40.4	1.2	162268
35474	MOUNDVILLE	17893	2123	32.6	25.4	37.1	4.4	0.4	43053	44424	43	76	1722	26.1	20.6	34.4	17.4	1.6	95743
35475	NORTHPORT	23886	4878	17.6	25.0	44.3	10.0	3.1	56443	55649	73	94	4207	15.3	11.7	30.2	39.6	3.2	154861
35476	NORTHPORT	17300	2938	42.9	28.2	25.4	2.5	1.1	29335	30459	7	20	1480	16.2	16.1	61.4	5.5	0.9	112749
35480	RALPH	17896	397	32.5	30.0	32.2	3.8	1.5	36817	38341	23	53	350	28.0	25.7	29.1	14.3	2.9	85185
35481	REFORM	15547	1588	44.3	27.1	23.1	4.5	0.9	28056	28904	6	18	1240	32.3	28.6	30.2	7.9	1.0	75375
35487	TUSCALOOSA	17594	415	73.7	10.8	8.9	3.4	3.1	14641	14416	1	1	48	4.2	4.2	37.5	50.0	4.2	180556
35490	VANCE	19036	1246	22.8	31.1	39.6	5.9	0.5	46023	47033	51	83	1052	26.8	16.9	36.8	18.6	0.9	103000
35501	JASPER	19359	4175	38.7	28.6	24.8	5.4	2.4	32214	34321	12	30	2877	25.3	32.6	29.9	10.9	1.3	80602
35503	JASPER	18957	3645	30.8	33.6	29.5	3.9	2.2	38905	39533	29	63	3043	21.2	26.7	38.6	12.1	1.4	93750
35504	JASPER	21176	5142	27.1	31.5	32.4	6.2	2.9	42700	42967	41	75	4128	23.2	20.0	35.6	19.1	2.1	101842
35540	ADDISON	16853	1075	37.3	30.5	28.3	3.2	0.7	32706	34058	13	33	903	33.8	18.4	30.1	12.0	5.8	86905
35541	ARLEY	17941	1507	32.8	36.6	24.0	4.2	2.3	35128	35929	18	45	1279	32.1	20.3	27.7	13.4	6.6	86067
35542	BANKSTON	15699	461	33.6	34.3	29.1	2.6	0.4	35089	36326	18	45	398	38.2	24.9	31.4	5.0	0.5	72857
35543	BEAR CREEK	16680	452	36.3	32.1	28.8	2.2	0.7	33811	35293	15	39	389	35.2	30.6	27.0	6.9	0.3	69423
35544	BEAVERTON	15710	364	40.9	33.8	22.0	2.2	1.1	30970	32216	10	23	297	34.7	45.5	13.1	6.7	0.0	67500
35546	BERRY	15743	1726	39.9	32.1	24.3	3.1	0.6	32570	34886	13	32	1382	36.8	23.9	26.9	11.1	1.2	70484
35548	BRILLIANT	16483	711	41.5	27.6	27.8	2.3	0.8	31529	32912	11	26	576	44.4	23.8	22.0	6.9	2.8	58421
35549	CARBON HILL	15857	1846	43.0	32.3	21.2	2.9	0.7	29005	30192	7	20	1472	33.8	35.9	24.3	5.8	0.2	66535
35550	CORDOVA	15134	2529	45.4	29.9	20.4	3.6	0.7	27610	29046	5	17	1889	41.5	32.3	21.3	4.9	0.1	58545
35552	DETROIT	16347	456	36.8	35.5	24.1	3.1	0.4	33916	35370	15	39	368	35.6	29.3	23.9	10.3	0.8	67500
35553	DOUBLE SPRINGS	17100	1941	36.1	39.7	19.2	3.5	1.6	32506	33608	12	32	1563	37.7	23.5	25.3	12.3	1.3	70309
35554	ELDRIDGE	17995	483	30.8	32.5	31.5	4.6	0.6	38095	38958	27	59	417	32.9	28.8	30.9	6.7	0.7	69125
35555	FAYETTE	18376	4355	36.6	31.6	26.8	3.9	1.1	33984	35685	15	40	3193	24.4	30.1	34.3	10.7	0.6	85000
35563	GUIN	19250	1789	39.9	27.8	25.3	5.2	1.8	33347	35067	14	36	1243	32.1	24.9	32.4	9.6	1.0	79675
35564	HACKLEBURG	17610	1070	38.3	35.9	22.2	2.2	1.3	31105	32180	10	25	865	37.6	28.6	26.4	6.7	0.8	65635
35565	HALEYVILLE	17596	5490	40.3	32.3	22.5	2.9	1.9	31630	32853	11	27	4197	30.3	34.1	26.4	7.2	2.0	73747
35570	HAMILTON	18342	4504	38.1	33.9	22.9	3.1	2.0	33310	35094	14	35	3411	26.9	27.6	33.6	11.0	1.0	82827
35571	HODGES	18971	419	37.5	32.5	24.3	2.6	3.1	32001	33313	11	29	353	36.5	28.0	28.0	7.4	0.0	66731
35572	HOUSTON	14501	547	45.3	32.4	20.1	1.6	0.5	27172	28466	5	16	468	47.6	13.5	25.0	12.2	1.7	56111
35574	KENNEDY	16365	575	35.5	36.5	25.7	2.1	0.2	34241	35329	16	40	466	34.1	35.2	25.1	5.4	0.2	67805
35575	LYNN	17865	548	35.0	35.6	24.3	4.2	0.9	34832	35575	17	43	449	47.0	20.5	27.6	4.5	0.4	54500
35576	MILLPORT	17314	1425	37.1	30.2	28.2	3.8	0.7	35114	35877	18	45	1142	31.0	30.1	28.8	9.5	0.6	74536
35578	NAUVOO	16441	2318	39.4	30.0	25.9	3.8	0.8	31826	33650	11	28	2007	31.9	32.9	28.8	6.2	0.2	72232
35579	OAKMAN	16203	1311	37.5	32.3	25.1	3.5	1.5	31912	33700	11	29	1048	37.6	28.3	29.2	3.4	1.4	71286
35580	PARRISH	16518	1873	37.6	31.8	25.0	5.0	0.6	33546	35714	14	37	1621	37.3	34.7	23.8	3.6	0.6	64280
35581	PHIL CAMPBELL	16194	2298	39.9	31.9	23.7	3.3	1.3	32286	33806	12	30	1813	27.6	30.4	32.3	8.9	0.7	76837
35582	RED BAY	17144	1931	39.0	32.7	23.1	4.1	1.0	31318	32087	10	26	1389	24.4	35.6	31.4	8.5	0.1	77713
35585	SPRUCE PINE	16663	586	40.6	28.0	27.1	3.4	0.9	31754	32864	11	28	469	27.1	24.7	40.1	7.7	0.4	87500
35586	SULLIGENT	16599	1974	39.0	33.0	23.8	3.1	1.0	31562	32820	11	26	1493	33.8	33.3	25.3	6.4	1.3	68259
35587	TOWNLEY	15274	463	39.3	35.6	21.8	2.2	1.1	31977	33647	11	29	392	34.9	23.2	31.6	7.9	2.3	79500
35592	VERNON	17652	1957	39.3	27.6	28.9	2.8	1.4	32973	34514	13	34	1444	27.2	30.3	30.7	10.4	1.3	78305
35593	VINA	16097	758	40.5	30.2	25.6	2.4	1.3	31232	32453	10	25	648	35.8	30.9	22.7	10.3	0.3	69778
35594	WINFIELD	18645	3206	34.2	31.7	27.8	5.0	1.3	36993	37614	24	54	2528	26.4	27.1	33.9	11.8	0.8	85742
35601	DECATUR	19825	13759	34.2	29.7	27.8	5.9	2.4	37018	38008	24	54	8422	8.2	30.1	47.6	12.2	1.9	102784
35603	DECATUR	25701	11573	21.2	25.5	38.5	10.4	4.3	53546	53931	69	92	8146	7.9	10.9	45.0	33.0	3.3	143884
35610	ANDERSON	19282	907	29.5	33.5	30.1	5.2	1.7	37969	39782	27	59	770	23.1	22.3	45.6	8.3	0.6	98537
35611	ATHENS	20048	10024	35.8	27.1	28.8	5.9	2.5	36295	38047	21	50	6686	11.6	21.8	44.6	19.4	2.6	113168
35613	ATHENS	22566	5885	20.5	28.3	37.4	10.4	3.4	51083	51633	64	90	4894	10.4	13.4	39.1	32.0	5.0	145080
	ALABAMA	21187		31.4	27.9	30.6	6.9	3.2	40822	42202				18.1	22.4	35.8	19.6	4.0	107730
	UNITED STATES	27277		20.9	24.4	35.3	11.7	7.6	54719	56938				9.3	13.1	31.6	32.6	13.5	162279

ZIP CODE		FINANCIAL SERVICES				THE HOME						ENTERTAINMENT						PERSONAL			
						Home Improvements		Furnishings													
#	POST OFFICE NAME	Auto Loan	Home Loan	Invest-ments	Retire-ment Plans	Home Repair	Lawn & Garden	Comput-ers & Hard-ware-Personal	Major Appli-ances	TV, Radio, Sound Equip-ment	Furni-ture	Dine out/ Carry out	Sports Equip-ment	Fees & Tickets	Toys & Games	Travel	Cable TV	Apparel & Services	Auto Repairs	Health Insur-ance	Pets & Supplies
35210	BIRMINGHAM	93	95	93	95	94	95	92	93	92	93	92	71	93	92	93	92	64	93	94	109
35211	BIRMINGHAM	49	43	39	45	41	48	47	45	52	48	51	33	46	50	44	54	35	49	53	57
35212	BIRMINGHAM	50	40	36	42	38	44	49	44	53	48	53	34	45	53	43	56	37	49	51	56
35213	BIRMINGHAM	132	154	170	159	162	143	147	144	139	154	140	113	162	137	158	134	102	143	135	165
35214	BIRMINGHAM	71	70	65	70	67	76	67	70	72	68	72	52	69	72	68	76	49	70	77	84
35215	BIRMINGHAM	76	74	63	74	70	72	75	72	75	75	75	56	73	77	72	75	52	73	74	86
35216	BIRMINGHAM	99	94	92	98	93	90	103	94	101	103	102	75	102	102	99	100	72	100	95	113
35217	BIRMINGHAM	59	53	49	53	51	59	56	56	59	55	59	42	53	59	53	62	40	57	62	68
35218	BIRMINGHAM	45	37	33	38	34	42	42	40	47	42	46	30	40	46	38	50	32	43	47	51
35221	BIRMINGHAM	51	49	45	49	47	54	48	49	53	50	53	35	49	51	47	56	36	51	57	61
35222	BIRMINGHAM	78	71	71	75	71	72	82	75	83	81	83	59	80	81	78	84	59	81	80	91
35223	BIRMINGHAM	168	217	254	228	236	203	193	196	180	206	181	151	228	178	219	174	136	187	178	220
35224	BIRMINGHAM	62	48	54	48	47	62	52	57	59	51	57	42	46	58	49	64	39	57	65	70
35226	BIRMINGHAM	122	135	131	139	134	126	126	125	122	132	124	97	135	124	131	120	88	124	120	146
35228	BIRMINGHAM	61	56	52	57	54	62	57	58	62	58	61	43	56	61	55	65	42	60	65	71
35229	BIRMINGHAM	83	72	71	76	70	72	90	77	89	86	90	63	84	87	83	89	63	87	84	95
35233	BIRMINGHAM	47	28	30	33	27	31	58	37	53	47	54	35	43	51	41	51	38	48	41	49
35234	BIRMINGHAM	45	37	34	38	35	43	41	41	47	42	46	29	39	45	38	51	32	44	49	51
35235	BIRMINGHAM	93	97	86	96	94	95	91	93	91	92	91	70	92	93	91	91	63	91	93	109
35242	BIRMINGHAM	169	195	184	202	194	173	174	172	165	186	167	139	192	172	183	157	122	166	154	198
35243	BIRMINGHAM	145	154	152	161	153	143	153	144	148	157	150	116	161	149	155	143	108	147	139	171
35244	BIRMINGHAM	151	165	152	172	162	145	153	148	145	164	148	121	164	152	156	137	107	145	132	171
35401	TUSCALOOSA	48	33	32	35	31	37	52	40	50	44	50	33	41	49	39	50	35	46	44	51
35404	TUSCALOOSA	66	58	56	59	56	64	65	62	66	62	66	48	60	66	60	68	45	65	68	76
35405	TUSCALOOSA	82	76	68	78	73	74	81	76	81	82	82	60	79	83	77	80	57	80	77	91
35406	TUSCALOOSA	121	131	138	134	135	131	124	127	121	128	121	97	131	120	129	120	86	123	123	146
35441	AKRON	66	44	62	42	44	64	47	58	54	45	52	45	36	55	44	60	35	55	61	71
35442	ALICEVILLE	69	46	68	44	47	68	49	62	56	46	55	48	37	56	46	62	36	58	65	75
35443	BOLIGEE	44	34	33	34	33	42	38	39	45	40	43	27	36	43	35	49	30	42	48	49
35444	BROOKWOOD	85	62	71	60	62	81	64	75	71	63	70	57	52	74	59	77	47	71	78	91
35446	BUHL	82	60	77	58	61	80	62	74	68	59	67	56	50	69	59	74	44	69	77	89
35447	CARROLLTON	71	47	69	45	48	70	50	63	57	47	56	49	38	58	47	63	37	59	66	77
35452	COKER	84	75	68	72	73	78	72	76	75	74	75	57	67	78	68	77	51	74	77	91
35453	COTTONDALE	84	72	71	71	71	81	71	77	75	71	75	58	65	78	68	79	51	75	80	93
35456	DUNCANVILLE	80	69	65	67	67	74	69	72	71	70	71	55	62	74	64	74	49	71	73	87
35457	ECHOLA	84	61	77	59	61	82	63	76	69	60	68	58	50	71	59	76	45	71	79	91
35458	ELROD	96	69	99	67	72	98	71	90	79	66	77	68	57	78	70	86	51	83	94	107
35459	EMELLE	64	42	62	39	42	63	45	56	52	43	51	44	34	53	42	58	33	53	60	70
35460	EPES	58	38	56	36	38	57	40	51	47	38	46	40	30	47	38	52	30	48	54	63
35461	ETHELSVILLE	73	52	61	51	52	69	54	63	60	53	59	49	43	63	49	66	40	60	67	77
35462	EUTAW	58	40	50	40	40	55	47	51	53	45	52	39	39	53	42	58	35	52	57	63
35463	FOSTERS	82	59	85	57	61	84	60	77	67	56	66	58	48	67	60	74	44	71	80	92
35464	GAINESVILLE	56	37	54	34	36	55	39	49	45	37	44	38	29	46	36	50	29	46	52	61
35466	GORDO	81	58	80	56	60	81	60	75	66	56	65	56	48	66	58	73	43	69	78	89
35469	KNOXVILLE	67	44	64	42	44	66	48	59	55	46	54	46	36	56	44	61	36	56	63	73
35470	LIVINGSTON	54	35	48	34	35	49	44	47	47	39	46	38	33	47	37	50	31	47	49	58
35473	NORTHPORT	89	84	76	85	82	84	85	83	86	86	87	64	84	88	82	87	60	85	85	99
35474	MOUNDVILLE	79	61	71	58	59	75	61	71	67	61	66	54	52	69	58	72	45	68	73	86
35475	NORTHPORT	97	95	88	95	93	98	88	94	89	90	90	71	87	92	88	91	62	90	93	111
35476	NORTHPORT	56	50	49	51	50	56	55	54	58	53	57	40	52	57	52	61	39	56	61	65
35480	RALPH	82	59	84	57	61	83	60	77	67	56	66	58	48	67	60	74	43	70	80	91
35481	REFORM	70	47	68	44	47	69	49	62	56	47	55	48	38	57	47	62	36	58	65	76
35487	TUSCALOOSA	38	26	30	30	27	31	45	34	46	39	46	28	37	42	37	47	32	42	44	44
35490	VANCE	84	72	70	70	71	80	70	76	74	71	73	56	63	77	66	77	50	73	78	91
35501	JASPER	74	57	67	56	57	73	61	69	67	58	65	52	52	67	58	72	44	67	74	82
35503	JASPER	84	60	77	58	61	82	63	76	69	59	68	57	50	71	59	76	45	71	80	91
35504	JASPER	89	68	81	67	69	88	71	82	77	67	75	62	59	78	67	83	51	78	87	98
35540	ADDISON	73	52	60	51	52	69	54	63	60	53	59	48	43	63	49	66	40	60	67	77
35541	ARLEY	78	56	64	54	56	74	58	68	65	57	63	52	47	67	53	70	43	64	71	82
35542	BANKSTON	72	52	59	50	51	68	54	63	60	52	58	48	43	62	49	65	39	59	66	76
35543	BEAR CREEK	72	52	60	50	51	69	54	63	60	52	59	48	43	62	49	65	39	59	66	76
35544	BEAVERTON	67	48	55	47	48	63	50	58	55	49	54	45	40	58	45	60	36	55	61	71
35546	BERRY	69	50	60	48	50	66	52	61	58	51	57	47	42	60	48	63	38	58	64	74
35548	BRILLIANT	70	49	61	47	49	67	51	61	58	49	56	47	40	60	47	63	38	58	65	75
35549	CARBON HILL	67	45	64	42	45	66	48	59	54	45	53	46	36	56	44	61	35	56	63	73
35550	CORDOVA	62	46	58	44	45	61	48	57	54	47	53	43	40	54	46	59	35	55	61	69
35552	DETROIT	68	49	56	48	49	65	51	59	56	50	55	46	41	59	46	62	37	56	63	72
35553	DOUBLE SPRINGS	73	52	63	51	52	70	54	64	60	52	59	49	43	62	50	66	40	60	67	78
35554	ELDRIDGE	80	57	68	55	57	76	59	70	66	57	65	54	47	68	54	72	43	66	73	85
35555	FAYETTE	71	54	64	53	54	70	56	65	62	54	61	49	48	63	53	68	41	62	70	78
35563	GUIN	77	55	68	54	56	75	58	69	65	55	63	53	47	66	54	71	42	65	74	83
35564	HACKLEBURG	71	51	63	49	51	70	54	64	60	51	58	49	43	61	50	66	39	60	69	77
35565	HALEYVILLE	74	54	63	53	54	72	57	66	63	55	62	50	47	65	53	68	41	63	70	80
35570	HAMILTON	75	54	62	53	54	71	58	66	64	56	63	50	47	66	53	69	42	63	70	80
35571	HODGES	82	59	67	57	58	77	61	71	68	59	66	54	49	70	55	74	45	67	75	86
35572	HOUSTON	62	43	55	41	43	60	45	54	51	43	50	42	35	52	41	56	33	51	57	66
35574	KENNEDY	69	50	58	48	50	66	52	61	58	50	56	46	42	60	47	63	38	57	64	74
35575	LYNN	76	55	63	53	54	72	57	66	63	55	62	51	46	66	52	69	41	63	70	80
35576	MILLPORT	75	52	71	50	52	74	54	67	61	52	60	52	42	62	51	68	40	63	71	82
35578	NAUVOO	74	51	66	49	51	71	53	65	60	51	59	50	42	62	49	66	39	61	68	79
35579	OAKMAN	74	51	67	49	52	72	54	65	60	52	59	50	42	62	50	66	39	61	69	79
35580	PARRISH	75	51	70	48	51	73	53	66	61	51	59	51	41	62	50	67	40	62	70	81
35581	PHIL CAMPBELL	72	51	62	50	52	70	54	64	60	51	59	49	43	62	50	66	39	60	68	77
35582	RED BAY	70	51	56	50	51	66	55	61	60	53	59	47	45	62	49	65	40	59	65	75
35585	SPRUCE PINE	73	53	63	51	53	70	54	64	60	53	59	49	44	62	50	66	40	61	68	78
35586	SULLIGENT	71	50	62	48	49	68	52	62	58	50	57	48	41	60	48	64	38	59	66	76
35587	TOWNLEY	69	46	67	44	46	68	49	61	55	46	54	47	37	56	46	62	36	57	65	75
35592	VERNON	75	52	69	50	53	73	55	67	62	52	60	51	43	63	52	68	40	63	71	81
35593	VINA	70	51	58	49	50	67	53	61	58	51	57	47	42	61	48	64	38	58	65	75
35594	WINFIELD	78	57	72	55	58	78	60	72	66	56	64	54	48	67	56	72	43	67	76	86
35601	DECATUR	68	63	60	64	62	70	67	67	70	64	69	50	64	70	64	74	48	68	75	80
35603	DECATUR	92	91	85	92	89	89	90	89	89	91	89	69	89	91	89	88	62	89	87	105
35610	ANDERSON	83	60	69	58	60	79	62	73	69	61	68	56	50	72	57	75	46	69	77	88
35611	ATHENS	76	63	67	62	62	75	66	72	71	63	69	54	59	71	63	75	47	70	77	85
35613	ATHENS	93	89	84	89	88	95	83	90	86	84	86	68	82	88	84	89	59	86	92	107
	ALABAMA	83	70	73	70	69	80	73	77	76	71	76	59	66	77	69	80	52	76	80	92
	UNITED STATES	100	100	100	100	100	100	100	100	100	100	100	100	100	100	100	100	100	100	100	100

ZIP CODE #	POST OFFICE NAME	COUNTY FIPS CODE	POPULATION 2000	POPULATION 2009	POPULATION 2014	2000-2009 ANNUAL RATE % Rate	2000-2009 ANNUAL RATE State Centile	HOUSEHOLDS 2000	HOUSEHOLDS 2009	HOUSEHOLDS 2014	HOUSEHOLDS % Annual Rate 2000-2009	HOUSEHOLDS 2009 Average HH Size	FAMILIES 2000	FAMILIES 2009	FAMILIES % Annual Rate 2000-2009
35614	ATHENS	083	6602	7037	7440	0.7	70	2557	2772	2947	0.9	2.54	1933	2046	0.6
35616	CHEROKEE	033	4817	4669	4589	-0.3	29	1959	1965	1952	0.0	2.38	1466	1443	-0.2
35618	COURTLAND	079	2260	2145	2092	-0.6	16	929	924	913	-0.1	2.32	633	615	-0.3
35619	DANVILLE	079	5419	5402	5415	0.0	45	2041	2091	2112	0.3	2.58	1586	1595	0.1
35620	ELKMONT	083	7876	8697	9300	1.1	79	2904	3260	3506	1.3	2.67	2308	2533	1.0
35621	EVA	103	2970	3193	3294	0.8	74	1133	1249	1297	1.1	2.56	887	959	0.8
35622	FALKVILLE	103	7019	7551	7829	0.8	74	2527	2790	2916	1.1	2.60	1947	2105	0.8
35630	FLORENCE	077	30862	30612	30390	-0.1	39	13798	13803	13805	0.0	2.07	7842	7577	-0.4
35633	FLORENCE	077	19552	19955	20133	0.2	52	7616	8001	8151	0.5	2.49	5925	6083	0.3
35634	FLORENCE	077	10991	10913	10885	-0.1	39	4193	4265	4295	0.2	2.54	3376	3378	0.0
35640	HARTSELLE	103	21355	23271	24244	0.9	76	8384	9364	9826	1.2	2.48	6367	6957	1.0
35643	HILLSBORO	079	3285	3233	3185	-0.2	34	1255	1296	1293	0.3	2.49	942	955	0.1
35645	KILLEN	077	11341	11755	11922	0.4	62	4306	4584	4694	0.7	2.55	3417	3570	0.5
35646	LEIGHTON	033	5512	5287	5180	-0.4	25	2162	2158	2137	0.0	2.45	1624	1592	-0.2
35647	LESTER	083	1063	1118	1177	0.5	64	405	434	460	0.8	2.58	322	337	0.5
35648	LEXINGTON	077	3905	3932	3941	0.1	49	1548	1597	1614	0.3	2.46	1145	1154	0.1
35650	MOULTON	079	13810	13700	13490	-0.1	39	5400	5553	5534	0.3	2.43	4018	4058	0.1
35651	MOUNT HOPE	079	1302	1317	1303	0.1	49	500	522	522	0.5	2.52	397	407	0.3
35652	ROGERSVILLE	077	7913	8382	8560	0.6	67	3233	3487	3587	0.8	2.40	2396	2525	0.6
35653	RUSSELLVILLE	059	10708	10347	10098	-0.4	25	4130	4014	3920	-0.3	2.50	2924	2783	-0.5
35654	RUSSELLVILLE	059	8354	8383	8276	0.0	45	3188	3231	3197	0.1	2.59	2385	2372	-0.1
35660	SHEFFIELD	033	9662	9266	9085	-0.5	19	4249	4204	4160	-0.1	2.20	2720	2620	-0.4
35661	MUSCLE SHOALS	033	15687	16119	16202	0.3	58	6227	6596	6695	0.6	2.41	4657	4836	0.4
35670	SOMERVILLE	103	7683	8126	8366	0.6	67	2933	3177	3295	0.9	2.56	2283	2423	0.6
35671	TANNER	083	2158	2512	2726	1.7	88	842	1004	1097	1.9	2.47	625	725	1.6
35672	TOWN CREEK	079	6715	6500	6376	-0.4	25	2661	2688	2666	0.1	2.42	2006	1989	-0.1
35673	TRINITY	079	7373	7633	7723	0.4	62	2773	2974	3045	0.8	2.56	2224	2348	0.6
35674	TUSCUMBIA	033	17534	17776	17757	0.1	49	7187	7514	7577	0.5	2.32	5046	5162	0.2
35677	WATERLOO	077	1839	1879	1900	0.2	52	744	784	801	0.6	2.40	571	589	0.3
35739	ARDMORE	083	3839	4645	5009	2.1	90	1520	1861	2020	2.2	2.50	1112	1330	2.0
35740	BRIDGEPORT	071	3851	3838	3790	0.0	45	1602	1667	1666	0.4	2.30	1115	1132	0.2
35741	BROWNSBORO	089	2794	3173	3570	1.4	84	1042	1208	1372	1.6	2.62	856	974	1.4
35744	DUTTON	071	2663	2743	2725	0.3	58	1030	1094	1099	0.7	2.50	781	813	0.4
35745	ESTILLFORK	071	314	307	301	-0.2	34	131	133	132	0.2	2.31	100	99	-0.1
35746	FACKLER	071	591	589	581	0.0	45	223	232	231	0.4	2.54	170	173	0.2
35747	GRANT	095	4799	5394	5699	1.3	82	1951	2191	2320	1.3	2.45	1448	1596	1.1
35748	GURLEY	089	5249	5641	5952	0.8	74	1975	2200	2347	1.2	2.56	1514	1638	0.9
35749	HARVEST	089	14700	20739	23526	3.8	98	4310	6594	7665	4.7	2.82	3524	5276	4.5
35750	HAZEL GREEN	089	11921	13540	14577	1.4	84	4267	4993	5433	1.7	2.70	3437	3919	1.4
35751	HOLLYTREE	071	394	371	360	-0.6	16	108	104	102	-0.4	3.33	80	75	-0.7
35752	HOLLYWOOD	071	2334	2304	2265	-0.1	39	928	955	951	0.3	2.41	694	699	0.1
35754	LACEYS SPRING	103	5058	5259	5369	0.4	62	1992	2126	2192	0.7	2.47	1476	1536	0.4
35755	LANGSTON	095	492	507	511	0.3	58	231	241	245	0.5	2.10	169	174	0.3
35756	MADISON	083	4095	6757	7933	5.6	99	1564	2640	3118	5.8	2.56	1158	1909	5.6
35757	MADISON	089	7831	11724	13393	4.5	98	2769	4242	4916	4.7	2.67	2245	3366	4.5
35758	MADISON	089	30425	39610	44026	2.9	95	11636	15277	17062	3.0	2.58	8340	10682	2.7
35759	MERIDIANVILLE	089	4235	5256	5784	2.4	92	1546	1990	2214	2.8	2.64	1282	1616	2.5
35760	NEW HOPE	089	5124	5595	5934	1.0	77	2056	2319	2486	1.3	2.41	1517	1656	1.0
35761	NEW MARKET	089	7569	10003	11204	3.1	95	2828	3860	4370	3.4	2.58	2188	2899	3.1
35763	OWENS CROSS ROADS	089	7036	11304	13144	5.3	99	2463	3970	4631	5.3	2.83	2043	3267	5.2
35764	PAINT ROCK	071	449	476	476	0.6	67	183	200	203	1.0	2.38	141	151	0.7
35765	PISGAH	071	4033	4173	4151	0.4	62	1609	1724	1735	0.7	2.42	1227	1290	0.5
35766	PRINCETON	071	244	229	222	-0.7	13	95	91	89	-0.5	2.42	70	66	-0.6
35768	SCOTTSBORO	071	11630	11215	10952	-0.4	25	4746	4719	4653	-0.1	2.29	3246	3158	-0.3
35769	SCOTTSBORO	071	9723	9737	9730	0.0	45	4080	4208	4236	0.3	2.31	2960	2997	0.1
35771	SECTION	071	3631	3858	3869	0.7	70	1422	1554	1574	1.0	2.47	1081	1158	0.7
35772	STEVENSON	071	5260	5234	5169	-0.1	39	2103	2182	2180	0.4	2.36	1520	1541	0.1
35773	TONEY	089	9737	12241	13548	2.5	92	3544	4579	5116	2.8	2.66	2784	3494	2.5
35774	TRENTON	071	266	250	243	-0.7	13	108	104	102	-0.4	2.28	80	76	-0.6
35775	VALHERMOSO SPRINGS	103	588	600	609	0.2	52	230	241	247	0.5	2.49	165	169	0.3
35776	WOODVILLE	071	3675	3783	3791	0.3	58	1426	1513	1531	0.6	2.49	1124	1172	0.5
35801	HUNTSVILLE	089	23000	23001	23573	0.0	45	10556	10931	11344	0.4	2.00	6075	5982	-0.2
35802	HUNTSVILLE	089	19429	20567	21508	0.6	67	8875	9771	10338	1.0	2.09	5657	5947	0.5
35803	HUNTSVILLE	089	25288	26536	27800	0.5	64	9741	10611	11250	0.9	2.50	7440	7852	0.6
35805	HUNTSVILLE	089	22086	22295	22848	0.1	49	10029	10424	10806	0.4	2.05	5223	5153	-0.1
35806	HUNTSVILLE	089	13470	17492	19729	2.9	95	6092	7979	9036	3.0	2.11	3627	4658	2.7
35808	HUNTSVILLE	089	2365	2172	2101	-0.9	6	487	435	418	-1.2	3.40	444	393	-1.3
35810	HUNTSVILLE	089	28674	29245	30266	0.2	52	10854	11516	12061	0.6	2.53	7888	8039	0.2
35811	HUNTSVILLE	089	23875	27904	30130	1.7	88	8735	10596	11588	2.1	2.47	6469	7664	1.8
35816	HUNTSVILLE	089	13431	14128	14724	0.5	64	5629	6135	6486	0.9	2.13	2793	2846	0.2
35824	HUNTSVILLE	089	2996	4194	4748	3.7	97	1453	2101	2409	4.1	2.00	778	1094	3.8
35898	HUNTSVILLE	089	4	4	4	0.0	45	3	3	3	0.0	1.33	3	0	-100.0
35901	GADSDEN	055	20757	20314	20133	-0.2	34	8400	8447	8435	0.1	2.28	5455	5354	-0.2
35903	GADSDEN	055	18467	18225	18118	-0.1	39	7667	7766	7780	0.1	2.33	5088	5033	-0.1
35904	GADSDEN	055	15204	14221	13861	-0.7	13	6260	6029	5926	-0.4	2.31	4364	4096	-0.7
35905	GADSDEN	055	6314	6391	6424	0.1	49	2420	2545	2584	0.5	2.42	1859	1912	0.3
35906	GADSDEN	055	8811	9183	9320	0.4	62	3721	4030	4134	0.9	2.26	2627	2763	0.5
35907	GADSDEN	055	6958	7996	8388	1.5	86	2646	3177	3364	2.0	2.51	2172	2563	1.8
35950	ALBERTVILLE	095	17319	19106	20046	1.1	79	6667	7247	7601	0.9	2.62	4754	5064	0.7
35951	ALBERTVILLE	095	11165	12201	12748	1.0	77	4028	4364	4563	0.9	2.76	3034	3220	0.6
35952	ALTOONA	055	7538	8061	8244	0.7	70	2898	3179	3276	1.0	2.52	2221	2386	0.8
35953	ASHVILLE	115	6700	8246	9142	2.3	91	2473	3064	3420	2.3	2.63	1895	2309	2.2
35954	ATTALLA	055	13092	12880	12780	-0.2	34	5138	5224	5232	0.2	2.43	3726	3694	-0.1
35956	BOAZ	055	8206	8396	8455	0.2	52	3186	3364	3419	0.6	2.49	2490	2575	0.4
35957	BOAZ	095	13338	14085	14548	0.6	67	5408	5691	5889	0.6	2.45	3820	3934	0.3
35958	BRYANT	071	3513	3572	3545	0.2	52	1336	1413	1417	0.6	2.53	1052	1093	0.4
35959	CEDAR BLUFF	019	4383	4576	4617	0.5	64	1848	2010	2051	0.9	2.26	1371	1464	0.7
35960	CENTRE	019	9460	9567	9485	0.1	49	3884	4086	4098	0.5	2.28	2816	2903	0.3
35961	COLLINSVILLE	049	5527	5798	5948	0.5	64	2031	2130	2192	0.5	2.64	1453	1491	0.3
35962	CROSSVILLE	049	6931	7529	7815	0.9	76	2585	2789	2898	0.8	2.66	1964	2081	0.6
35963	DAWSON	049	1478	1548	1581	0.5	64	573	597	612	0.4	2.59	435	445	0.2
35966	FLAT ROCK	071	3832	3928	3961	0.3	58	1469	1540	1564	0.5	2.55	1138	1173	0.3
35967	FORT PAYNE	049	16240	16647	16844	0.3	58	6351	6423	6504	0.1	2.54	4479	4436	-0.1
35968	FORT PAYNE	049	3803	4085	4228	0.8	74	1483	1582	1638	0.7	2.57	1129	1180	0.5
35971	FYFFE	049	4597	4929	5098	0.8	74	1783	1904	1975	0.7	2.53	1326	1389	0.5
	ALABAMA					0.6					0.9	2.44			0.6
	UNITED STATES					1.0					1.1	2.59			0.9

ZIP CODE #	POST OFFICE NAME	RACE (%) White 2000	White 2009	Black 2000	Black 2009	Asian/Pacific 2000	Asian/Pacific 2009	% Hispanic Origin 2000	% Hispanic Origin 2009	2009 AGE DISTRIBUTION (%) 0-4	5-9	10-14	15-19	20-24	25-44	45-64	65-84	85+	18+	MEDIAN AGE 2009	% 2009 Males	% 2009 Females
35614	ATHENS	92.2	90.6	5.0	5.5	0.3	0.4	2.8	4.9	7.0	7.0	7.2	6.3	5.0	27.6	28.2	10.8	0.9	74.8	38.5	50.9	49.1
35616	CHEROKEE	86.8	84.6	11.5	13.1	0.0	0.0	1.0	1.8	5.9	6.2	6.4	5.8	4.5	23.8	29.2	16.3	1.8	77.9	42.9	50.2	49.8
35618	COURTLAND	47.9	44.8	48.5	51.0	0.1	0.1	1.0	1.3	6.7	6.5	6.9	7.5	6.6	24.3	26.9	12.4	2.1	75.2	38.9	46.5	53.5
35619	DANVILLE	88.9	87.1	4.8	5.5	0.0	0.1	0.8	1.5	7.0	7.0	7.1	6.7	5.8	28.2	27.2	10.0	1.0	74.8	37.5	51.1	48.9
35620	ELKMONT	94.3	93.2	4.1	4.6	0.1	0.1	1.0	1.7	6.5	6.6	7.0	7.1	5.6	28.0	28.5	9.9	0.9	75.6	38.4	51.0	49.0
35621	EVA	97.6	96.6	0.3	0.4	0.1	0.1	1.2	2.4	6.7	6.8	7.0	6.5	5.2	28.0	27.9	10.7	1.2	75.4	38.5	51.8	48.2
35622	FALKVILLE	96.5	95.3	1.4	1.8	0.2	0.3	1.0	1.9	6.5	6.5	6.7	6.3	5.5	25.7	27.5	12.9	2.5	76.6	40.2	49.1	50.9
35630	FLORENCE	75.8	73.1	21.6	23.3	0.6	0.9	1.5	2.4	5.8	5.2	5.1	7.1	9.3	25.6	22.9	15.0	4.1	80.7	37.7	45.7	54.3
35633	FLORENCE	92.7	91.1	5.9	7.0	0.3	0.4	0.9	1.7	5.6	6.0	6.4	6.3	4.8	26.8	29.9	12.6	1.4	78.0	41.0	48.8	51.2
35634	FLORENCE	97.1	96.3	1.5	1.8	0.3	0.4	0.8	1.5	5.5	5.9	6.6	6.5	4.7	25.2	31.7	12.5	1.5	77.9	42.2	49.7	50.3
35640	HARTSELLE	94.0	91.9	3.5	4.6	0.3	0.4	1.1	2.3	6.1	6.3	6.6	6.5	5.0	26.4	29.4	12.4	1.5	77.0	40.5	49.5	50.5
35643	HILLSBORO	61.0	57.4	32.3	34.6	0.1	0.2	1.2	2.0	6.1	6.3	6.6	6.9	5.4	26.5	29.6	11.4	1.2	76.6	39.9	48.9	51.1
35645	KILLEN	96.2	95.1	2.3	2.7	0.3	0.4	0.9	1.7	6.5	6.9	7.1	6.4	4.6	26.4	28.9	11.8	1.4	75.5	40.0	49.4	50.6
35646	LEIGHTON	74.7	71.8	23.1	25.4	0.3	0.4	1.1	1.8	6.1	6.3	6.5	6.5	5.0	24.5	29.5	13.8	1.7	76.9	41.5	48.9	51.1
35647	LESTER	97.0	96.4	1.9	2.1	0.1	0.1	0.8	1.5	7.1	7.2	7.2	7.0	6.0	26.7	27.5	10.5	1.1	74.2	38.0	50.8	49.2
35648	LEXINGTON	98.8	98.5	0.2	0.2	0.1	0.1	0.5	1.0	6.5	6.7	6.8	5.8	4.5	25.8	28.7	13.4	1.8	76.2	41.0	49.4	50.6
35650	MOULTON	85.1	82.5	5.3	6.0	0.2	0.2	0.9	1.5	6.3	6.3	6.5	6.5	5.3	27.3	27.3	12.7	1.9	77.1	39.9	49.1	50.9
35651	MOUNT HOPE	86.6	84.3	4.5	5.3	0.0	0.0	0.5	0.8	7.3	7.1	7.1	6.5	5.8	27.2	25.7	12.0	1.4	74.6	38.0	49.2	50.8
35652	ROGERSVILLE	94.0	92.8	4.8	5.7	0.2	0.2	0.4	0.6	5.9	6.0	6.3	6.0	4.6	24.9	29.1	15.5	1.7	78.0	42.4	49.4	50.6
35653	RUSSELLVILLE	82.2	77.0	9.4	9.7	0.3	0.4	11.0	18.2	6.4	6.3	6.4	6.6	5.6	26.0	26.1	13.8	2.8	76.9	39.3	48.4	51.6
35654	RUSSELLVILLE	88.7	83.7	2.9	3.4	0.2	0.3	10.2	16.9	6.9	6.7	6.8	7.1	5.9	27.5	26.4	11.6	1.1	75.3	37.0	51.3	48.7
35660	SHEFFIELD	71.2	69.1	26.2	27.4	0.3	0.5	1.5	2.4	6.4	6.4	6.2	6.2	5.3	24.3	26.9	15.1	3.1	77.1	41.1	46.4	53.6
35661	MUSCLE SHOALS	83.2	81.1	15.0	16.5	0.4	0.6	1.1	1.8	5.8	6.2	6.6	6.5	5.1	25.5	29.2	13.4	1.7	77.6	40.9	47.7	52.3
35670	SOMERVILLE	94.8	93.3	2.6	3.4	0.2	0.4	0.6	1.2	6.4	6.6	7.0	6.6	5.6	26.8	30.0	10.3	0.9	76.1	38.9	50.7	49.3
35671	TANNER	67.2	63.0	27.6	29.1	0.3	0.4	4.6	8.0	6.4	6.7	6.8	7.6	6.2	26.7	28.7	9.8	1.0	75.6	37.4	50.8	49.2
35672	TOWN CREEK	68.5	65.0	22.0	23.7	0.1	0.1	1.5	2.4	6.3	6.8	7.1	6.9	5.8	26.3	28.2	11.0	1.6	75.5	38.5	50.0	50.0
35673	TRINITY	89.2	86.9	4.3	5.3	0.2	0.3	0.9	1.7	6.4	6.7	6.9	6.7	5.2	27.5	29.0	10.5	1.0	75.8	39.3	49.5	50.5
35674	TUSCUMBIA	85.4	83.6	13.1	14.4	0.2	0.3	1.0	1.7	6.0	6.1	6.2	6.0	5.3	25.2	28.0	14.5	2.6	77.9	41.4	48.4	51.6
35677	WATERLOO	98.1	97.4	0.9	1.1	0.0	0.0	0.7	1.3	4.7	5.4	6.2	6.9	5.2	27.0	30.2	12.7	1.6	79.5	41.4	50.7	49.3
35739	ARDMORE	92.9	89.1	4.3	6.7	0.4	0.6	1.4	2.6	6.8	6.8	6.9	6.6	5.5	27.6	27.3	11.2	1.1	75.4	38.4	48.9	51.1
35740	BRIDGEPORT	88.5	86.6	6.6	7.4	0.2	0.4	1.0	1.7	6.5	6.5	6.6	6.0	5.2	26.4	27.8	13.1	1.7	76.6	39.6	48.9	51.1
35741	BROWNSBORO	90.5	88.2	6.7	8.2	0.5	0.9	1.0	1.8	8.0	8.6	8.4	7.0	3.7	24.6	29.8	9.2	0.8	70.9	38.5	49.5	50.5
35744	DUTTON	94.1	92.7	0.1	0.1	0.1	0.1	1.3	2.2	6.8	6.9	7.1	6.0	4.9	27.6	27.1	12.2	1.3	75.8	38.7	49.3	50.7
35745	ESTILLFORK	97.5	96.7	0.0	0.0	0.0	0.0	0.6	1.0	5.5	5.9	5.9	6.5	6.5	28.3	27.4	12.7	1.3	78.8	40.1	49.5	50.5
35746	FACKLER	87.0	84.6	7.6	8.8	0.5	0.5	0.8	1.4	5.6	5.8	6.1	6.5	5.1	29.0	28.5	12.4	1.0	78.9	39.5	52.3	47.7
35747	GRANT	97.8	97.1	0.3	0.3	0.3	0.4	0.6	1.1	5.8	6.0	6.3	6.3	4.8	25.2	30.3	13.8	1.4	77.9	41.9	49.9	50.1
35748	GURLEY	87.1	84.1	9.7	11.8	0.2	0.3	1.2	2.1	6.5	6.7	7.1	6.9	5.1	25.4	29.8	11.1	1.4	75.3	40.1	50.3	49.7
35749	HARVEST	71.7	67.6	24.6	27.4	0.9	1.4	1.4	2.4	7.5	7.6	7.5	7.2	6.2	31.4	26.1	6.0	0.5	73.6	35.5	53.2	46.8
35750	HAZEL GREEN	93.3	91.5	3.0	3.7	0.5	0.7	1.1	2.0	7.4	7.4	7.4	7.1	6.0	28.1	27.2	8.4	0.8	73.3	36.4	49.6	50.4
35751	HOLLYTREE	95.7	94.1	0.3	0.3	0.3	0.3	1.5	2.7	5.1	5.4	6.7	11.1	5.4	25.6	26.7	12.4	1.6	74.1	38.4	50.1	49.9
35752	HOLLYWOOD	86.4	84.0	8.8	10.0	0.2	0.3	1.4	2.3	6.2	6.4	6.7	6.6	5.2	27.6	28.6	11.6	1.0	76.6	38.8	50.0	50.0
35754	LACEYS SPRING	95.3	93.4	1.1	1.4	0.3	0.4	1.2	2.6	6.7	6.8	6.8	6.5	5.4	26.1	29.4	11.4	0.8	75.7	39.2	50.7	49.3
35755	LANGSTON	95.7	94.5	0.6	0.6	0.2	0.2	1.0	2.0	4.7	5.1	5.5	5.3	3.9	21.9	33.1	18.7	1.6	81.3	47.5	51.3	48.7
35756	MADISON	58.7	61.8	38.0	33.0	0.8	1.2	2.3	4.4	8.0	7.6	7.2	6.4	5.4	31.6	25.3	7.4	1.0	73.1	34.9	49.8	50.2
35757	MADISON	76.4	72.1	19.5	22.5	1.1	1.6	1.6	2.7	8.4	8.2	8.0	7.7	5.0	29.7	25.6	6.8	0.6	71.0	35.1	48.6	51.4
35758	MADISON	79.6	74.3	13.4	16.0	3.6	5.3	2.4	4.1	7.7	7.5	7.7	7.3	5.9	29.4	27.6	6.3	0.6	72.4	34.4	48.8	51.2
35759	MERIDIANVILLE	82.7	78.8	13.6	16.3	0.7	1.0	0.9	1.6	6.4	7.0	7.4	6.9	4.7	24.8	31.4	10.5	0.9	74.8	40.5	49.2	50.8
35760	NEW HOPE	95.6	94.3	0.6	0.7	0.2	0.3	0.8	1.5	6.3	6.5	6.7	6.3	5.0	27.0	29.1	11.7	1.4	76.7	39.8	48.7	51.3
35761	NEW MARKET	86.8	83.3	7.7	9.6	0.3	0.4	1.8	3.1	6.9	6.9	7.1	6.9	5.6	27.4	28.5	9.6	1.1	74.5	37.8	50.2	49.8
35763	OWENS CROSS ROADS	94.4	92.3	2.3	3.5	0.8	1.4	0.9	1.7	8.3	8.7	7.6	6.3	3.1	25.9	30.2	8.9	0.9	72.3	39.1	49.6	50.4
35764	PAINT ROCK	93.8	92.4	0.7	0.8	0.2	0.2	0.7	1.3	7.1	7.4	7.4	5.7	4.8	26.9	27.5	11.6	1.7	74.4	38.6	51.1	48.9
35765	PISGAH	95.2	94.2	0.0	0.0	0.1	0.1	0.9	1.5	6.7	6.9	7.0	6.1	4.8	27.7	26.7	12.5	1.5	75.6	38.5	50.9	49.1
35766	PRINCETON	95.9	95.2	0.0	0.0	0.0	0.0	0.8	1.7	4.8	5.2	6.1	8.7	5.2	26.6	28.4	12.7	2.2	77.7	40.4	50.7	49.3
35768	SCOTTSBORO	89.4	87.8	6.6	7.0	0.5	0.7	1.4	2.4	5.6	5.6	6.0	6.7	5.5	25.6	27.5	14.9	2.6	78.5	41.4	47.9	52.1
35769	SCOTTSBORO	95.2	94.1	1.8	2.0	0.4	0.6	1.2	2.0	5.7	6.1	6.3	6.3	4.7	24.7	30.7	14.1	1.4	78.2	42.3	48.8	51.2
35771	SECTION	94.7	93.5	0.6	0.7	0.1	0.1	1.0	1.8	6.1	6.1	6.5	6.4	5.2	27.8	28.3	12.4	1.2	77.6	39.3	49.7	50.3
35772	STEVENSON	85.8	83.5	9.9	11.0	0.2	0.2	1.1	1.8	6.3	6.5	6.6	5.9	5.0	26.7	28.3	12.6	2.2	76.7	40.2	48.9	51.1
35773	TONEY	84.9	81.3	11.4	13.9	0.3	0.5	1.2	2.1	7.6	7.7	7.7	6.8	5.4	27.5	27.7	9.0	0.7	72.8	36.9	49.8	50.2
35774	TRENTON	96.2	94.4	0.0	0.0	0.0	0.0	1.1	2.4	4.8	5.2	6.4	8.0	5.6	26.4	28.0	13.6	2.0	78.0	40.8	50.4	49.6
35775	VALHERMOSO SPRINGS	89.5	86.3	8.5	10.8	0.2	0.3	0.5	0.8	5.3	6.0	6.5	6.0	5.7	26.2	31.0	12.3	1.0	78.7	41.1	51.5	48.5
35776	WOODVILLE	95.1	94.1	0.5	0.6	0.1	0.1	0.8	1.5	6.4	6.5	6.8	6.6	4.8	27.1	28.2	12.3	1.2	76.1	39.5	49.4	50.6
35801	HUNTSVILLE	87.1	84.4	9.5	10.8	1.2	1.8	1.3	2.3	5.4	5.1	5.2	5.4	5.7	24.1	27.8	17.7	3.5	81.0	44.3	48.1	51.9
35802	HUNTSVILLE	89.1	85.8	5.4	6.6	3.3	4.8	1.5	2.5	4.3	4.4	5.0	5.6	5.0	21.8	29.7	21.4	2.9	83.0	47.6	47.4	52.6
35803	HUNTSVILLE	90.4	86.7	2.4	2.9	4.2	6.3	2.1	3.8	5.4	6.2	7.2	7.5	5.1	23.2	32.9	11.6	0.9	76.3	41.9	49.3	50.7
35805	HUNTSVILLE	57.8	52.3	34.7	37.7	2.6	3.6	4.0	6.3	8.1	6.9	5.8	6.0	9.4	29.9	22.5	9.7	1.6	76.1	33.2	49.0	51.0
35806	HUNTSVILLE	64.8	61.6	29.1	30.6	2.6	3.5	1.7	2.7	7.0	6.8	6.6	7.5	7.8	30.4	25.0	8.2	0.7	76.0	34.0	49.2	50.8
35808	HUNTSVILLE	56.9	50.6	31.7	34.2	2.8	3.6	9.3	14.3	8.4	10.8	8.9	13.4	11.7	41.2	5.3	0.1	0.1	68.1	23.6	61.0	39.0
35810	HUNTSVILLE	27.2	23.5	69.2	72.2	0.7	0.9	1.4	1.9	6.2	6.5	6.7	7.3	6.2	24.7	28.1	12.7	1.7	76.2	39.2	46.5	53.5
35811	HUNTSVILLE	71.7	69.1	25.2	26.8	0.5	0.8	1.0	1.8	6.3	6.6	6.7	9.3	6.9	24.7	27.2	11.1	1.2	76.5	37.6	49.8	50.2
35816	HUNTSVILLE	33.5	29.0	60.5	63.3	2.3	3.0	3.4	4.9	7.1	5.9	5.1	9.2	12.6	29.6	18.8	9.9	1.7	78.6	29.9	47.1	52.9
35824	HUNTSVILLE	67.8	61.2	23.0	26.3	5.3	7.5	2.5	4.0	7.7	6.1	5.6	5.7	9.1	36.7	22.5	6.3	0.4	77.5	32.9	49.1	50.9
35898	HUNTSVILLE	66.7	75.0	33.3	25.0	0.0	0.0	0.0	0.0	0.0	0.0	0.0	0.0	50.0	50.0	0.0	0.0	0.0	100.0	27.5	50.0	50.0
35901	GADSDEN	63.6	60.6	33.5	35.4	0.7	1.0	2.2	3.5	6.2	6.0	5.8	6.9	6.1	23.7	26.6	15.6	3.2	77.9	41.2	47.2	52.8
35903	GADSDEN	67.2	63.7	29.6	32.1	0.6	0.7	2.4	3.7	6.5	6.4	6.4	6.4	5.8	26.3	26.6	13.2	2.4	76.9	39.2	47.9	52.1
35904	GADSDEN	90.2	87.8	7.8	9.4	0.2	0.3	1.3	2.2	6.5	6.5	6.6	6.3	4.8	24.2	26.0	16.2	2.9	76.5	41.0	47.6	52.4
35905	GADSDEN	97.0	95.8	1.6	2.3	0.2	0.3	0.3	0.7	5.1	5.3	5.7	6.1	4.7	24.8	30.8	14.8	2.6	80.1	43.6	48.7	51.3
35906	GADSDEN	93.3	90.4	3.5	4.6	1.4	2.1	1.4	2.6	6.1	6.5	6.5	5.8	4.9	26.2	28.6	13.5	1.9	77.4	40.7	47.7	52.3
35907	GADSDEN	98.1	97.2	0.6	0.8	0.2	0.4	0.7	1.3	6.0	6.3	6.7	5.9	4.3	27.0	30.3	12.3	1.3	77.4	41.4	49.3	50.7
35950	ALBERTVILLE	88.5	83.3	1.8	1.8	0.2	0.3	13.3	21.4	7.8	7.6	7.1	6.7	5.7	28.2	24.0	11.2	1.6	73.4	35.8	48.9	51.1
35951	ALBERTVILLE	91.5	86.8	0.9	1.0	0.3	0.5	9.5	16.1	7.5	7.5	7.5	6.7	5.1	28.3	25.0	10.6	1.7	73.4	36.3	50.2	49.8
35952	ALTOONA	96.1	93.9	0.6	0.8	0.1	0.2	3.1	5.6	6.9	7.0	7.1	6.3	5.2	27.0	27.0	11.9	1.6	75.0	38.4	49.1	50.9
35953	ASHVILLE	85.6	83.1	11.9	13.4	0.2	0.2	1.5	2.6	6.6	6.6	6.8	6.7	5.9	27.3	27.3	11.6	1.2	76.0	38.3	51.2	48.8
35954	ATTALLA	89.2	86.2	8.4	10.1	0.1	0.2	2.2	4.0	6.4	6.6	6.6	6.1	5.1	26.4	27.3	13.3	2.2	76.6	39.8	49.0	51.0
35956	BOAZ	98.1	97.0	0.2	0.3	0.2	0.3	1.5	3.0	6.5	6.7	7.0	6.3	4.6	26.6	28.6	12.3	1.4	75.8	39.5	50.5	49.5
35957	BOAZ	93.9	90.3	0.9	1.0	0.3	0.4	6.1	10.8	6.8	6.6	6.4	6.6	5.3	26.1	25.9	14.0	2.3	76.1	39.1	48.2	51.8
35958	BRYANT	95.7	94.6	0.0	0.0	0.1	0.2	0.9	1.4	7.0	6.9	7.0	6.2	5.1	27.2	27.9	11.8	1.0	75.3	38.8	49.4	50.6
35959	CEDAR BLUFF	92.4	91.4	6.0	6.6	0.1	0.2	0.7	1.3	5.9	6.1	6.4	6.3	4.6	25.2	27.9	15.8	1.7	77.6	41.5	49.2	50.8
35960	CENTRE	91.2	89.9	7.3	8.1	0.2	0.3	0.6	1.1	5.4	5.7	5.8	5.4	4.2	24.1	29.6	17.3	2.5	79.7	44.5	49.1	50.9
35961	COLLINSVILLE	83.2	76.7	6.0	6.5	0.3	0.4	14.1	23.2	6.9	6.8	7.0	6.9	5.9	26.8	24.6	12.3	2.7	74.8	37.2	49.6	50.4
35962	CROSSVILLE	97.0	95.2	0.1	0.1	0.1	0.2	3.8	6.9	7.1	7.0	7.1	6.7	5.4	27.1	26.6	10.9	2.1	74.7	37.6	49.5	50.5
35963	DAWSON	96.4	94.3	0.0	0.0	0.1	0.3	3.2	6.3	6.2	6.3	6.7	6.5	5.0	26.5	28.2	12.7	1.9	76.9	39.9	50.1	49.9
35966	FLAT ROCK	95.5	94.5	0.1	0.1	0.1	0.1	0.7	1.2	7.1	7.1	7.2	6.7	4.9	27.7	26.0	12.0	1.2	74.4	38.0	49.9	50.1
35967	FORT PAYNE	85.4	79.6	4.0	4.2	0.6	0.8	10.3	16.8	6.6	6.4	6.5	6.3	5.9	27.8	26.0	12.3	2.2	76.8	38.3	49.0	51.0
35968	FORT PAYNE	95.6	93.1	0.6	0.7	0.2	0.3	2.7	5.2	6.3	6.4	6.6	6.5	5.2	27.5	28.5	11.8	1.4	77.0	39.2	50.8	49.2
35971	FYFFE	96.6	95.2	0.7	0.9	0.1	0.1	1.3	2.6	6.7	6.8	6.8	6.1	4.6	27.8	27.0	12.7	1.5	76.1	39.1	48.8	51.2
	ALABAMA	71.1	69.3	26.0	26.7	0.7	1.0	1.7	2.8	6.6	6.6	6.6	6.9	6.6	26.4	26.7	11.7	1.8	76.1	37.8	48.6	51.4
	UNITED STATES	75.1	72.0	12.3	12.7	3.8	4.6	12.5	15.7	6.8	6.7	6.6	7.1	6.9	27.0	26.0	10.9	1.9	75.7	36.9	49.2	50.8

C 35614-35971

#	POST OFFICE NAME	2009 Per Capita Income	2009 HH Income Base	2009 Household Income Distribution (%): Less than $25,000	$25,000 to $49,999	$50,000 to $99,999	$100,000 to $149,999	$150,000 or More	Median Household Income: 2009	2014	2009 National Centile	2009 State Centile	2009 Home Value Base	2009 Home Value Distribution (%): Less than $50,000	$50,000 to $89,999	$90,000 to $174,999	$175,000 to $399,999	$400,000 or More	2009 Median Home Value
35614	ATHENS	18675	2772	29.0	32.2	31.5	6.0	1.4	40872	41870	36	70	2196	21.1	22.5	40.1	15.1	1.1	97609
35616	CHEROKEE	19280	1965	34.6	33.3	25.3	4.0	2.8	33492	36023	14	37	1639	24.2	38.7	29.3	7.2	0.6	79485
35618	COURTLAND	16569	924	45.7	27.8	21.4	3.1	1.9	27835	29696	5	18	700	31.7	35.9	24.1	7.4	0.9	69184
35619	DANVILLE	18150	2091	32.7	28.0	32.2	5.5	1.5	40529	42498	34	68	1758	24.6	23.5	33.8	16.6	1.5	93367
35620	ELKMONT	18408	3260	27.6	29.9	34.8	6.2	1.4	42357	43422	40	73	2780	18.6	18.1	42.9	19.1	1.3	108394
35621	EVA	18812	1249	27.4	32.3	33.7	4.8	1.8	41250	42459	37	71	1061	24.9	27.0	34.3	11.7	2.1	86894
35622	FALKVILLE	17271	2790	33.3	32.1	27.4	5.7	1.5	36426	38152	22	51	2297	26.9	27.2	32.3	10.8	2.7	83438
35630	FLORENCE	19484	13803	44.8	26.3	22.2	4.3	2.3	28643	30601	6	19	7416	13.3	30.9	40.8	13.8	1.2	97105
35633	FLORENCE	21636	8001	26.7	27.8	35.7	7.1	2.7	45895	47089	51	83	6589	12.9	23.6	43.7	18.0	1.8	110592
35634	FLORENCE	23971	4265	18.9	32.0	36.9	8.1	4.1	49023	49396	59	88	3716	11.4	18.2	39.5	25.1	5.9	123045
35640	HARTSELLE	22849	9364	23.9	27.9	37.3	7.6	3.2	47875	49867	56	87	7283	11.2	22.3	42.1	22.2	2.3	115702
35643	HILLSBORO	19611	1296	31.3	29.0	33.3	4.8	1.6	40494	41178	34	68	1082	28.6	32.4	28.7	9.7	0.6	78696
35645	KILLEN	23815	4584	20.4	27.9	39.2	8.5	3.9	51178	51524	64	90	3896	10.7	22.0	38.6	23.8	4.9	119891
35646	LEIGHTON	16093	2158	37.1	31.9	26.7	3.5	0.8	32398	35092	12	31	1812	26.0	33.7	29.8	8.7	1.8	81767
35647	LESTER	19037	434	28.3	28.6	35.3	6.0	1.8	42469	43391	41	74	360	20.3	18.6	45.8	15.0	0.3	104365
35648	LEXINGTON	17897	1597	32.1	34.6	27.6	4.8	0.9	35432	37915	19	46	1329	19.9	27.8	40.8	10.3	1.2	93144
35650	MOULTON	19030	5553	32.3	30.6	29.5	5.7	1.9	37947	39356	27	59	4467	21.5	28.9	30.4	18.0	1.2	89488
35651	MOUNT HOPE	18669	522	33.3	29.9	28.9	5.6	2.3	40584	41478	35	69	446	26.2	21.7	39.0	10.5	2.5	93214
35652	ROGERSVILLE	19939	3487	29.2	32.3	31.3	5.8	1.4	40732	42159	35	69	2845	18.0	20.9	41.5	18.0	1.6	108648
35653	RUSSELLVILLE	16467	4014	39.6	27.4	27.3	4.6	1.1	31177	31836	10	25	2790	21.2	30.3	34.9	12.9	0.7	87657
35654	RUSSELLVILLE	16616	3231	37.4	29.1	27.5	4.7	1.3	33110	34640	13	35	2453	23.6	25.5	39.1	10.5	1.3	91178
35660	SHEFFIELD	18491	4204	38.9	31.2	24.6	4.4	1.0	31854	34419	11	28	2660	12.8	44.5	32.4	9.2	1.1	85138
35661	MUSCLE SHOALS	22469	6596	24.5	30.7	35.2	7.7	2.0	46310	46875	52	84	5119	10.9	22.3	41.0	21.2	4.6	115324
35670	SOMERVILLE	19339	3177	25.3	32.5	34.5	6.3	1.4	43532	45517	44	77	2690	22.1	24.4	35.8	15.5	2.2	95689
35671	TANNER	23036	1004	31.9	25.8	28.9	8.4	5.1	42232	43051	40	73	781	23.6	14.2	22.4	31.5	8.3	128009
35672	TOWN CREEK	18217	2688	33.9	30.5	29.4	5.0	1.3	36641	38218	22	52	2234	30.4	24.9	33.8	10.0	0.9	80407
35673	TRINITY	21354	2974	26.3	28.0	35.8	7.4	2.5	45922	47334	51	83	2599	19.5	20.3	40.8	18.7	0.7	108062
35674	TUSCUMBIA	19993	7514	34.4	29.5	28.1	5.8	2.2	35297	37802	19	46	5592	17.3	32.7	36.1	12.5	1.4	90000
35677	WATERLOO	16779	784	38.1	39.5	18.1	2.9	1.3	31830	34838	11	28	663	29.3	33.2	31.4	5.1	1.1	78141
35739	ARDMORE	19636	1861	29.6	28.1	35.5	5.7	1.1	42733	43859	42	75	1453	14.9	20.1	45.2	18.7	1.1	111716
35740	BRIDGEPORT	19118	1667	31.9	37.0	25.6	4.1	1.4	33723	35648	15	38	1222	32.0	23.6	31.1	12.3	1.0	80548
35741	BROWNSBORO	34273	1208	10.3	19.3	43.2	15.3	11.9	69094	69987	86	98	1090	5.8	10.6	29.2	38.6	15.8	197642
35744	DUTTON	17713	1094	33.4	31.8	28.8	5.0	1.0	36605	37892	22	52	868	25.7	28.0	32.7	12.2	1.4	85676
35745	ESTILLFORK	18211	133	30.8	35.3	30.8	3.0	0.0	36760	37227	23	53	115	35.7	27.0	27.8	8.7	0.9	69545
35746	FACKLER	19049	232	27.2	40.1	28.0	3.0	1.7	40372	40487	34	67	192	28.6	35.4	18.8	15.6	1.6	70000
35747	GRANT	20078	2191	29.9	31.6	30.0	6.3	2.1	41062	41446	36	70	1832	23.9	18.9	36.0	17.6	3.7	104251
35748	GURLEY	19505	2200	29.1	27.4	35.2	6.9	1.5	41816	42300	39	72	1793	17.5	20.2	38.4	21.1	2.8	116278
35749	HARVEST	24762	6594	12.1	20.3	45.1	18.0	4.5	65134	66748	83	97	5954	6.2	8.4	47.2	35.2	2.9	155045
35750	HAZEL GREEN	18915	4993	22.9	30.7	40.1	5.1	1.2	45013	46369	48	82	4207	13.6	20.4	49.6	15.1	1.3	113980
35751	HOLLYTREE	13208	104	29.8	37.5	27.9	2.9	1.9	38867	39545	29	62	89	33.7	32.6	24.7	6.7	2.2	72500
35752	HOLLYWOOD	18939	955	30.6	34.6	28.9	4.6	1.4	37764	38719	26	57	777	28.8	32.4	26.6	10.7	1.4	74245
35754	LACEYS SPRING	19763	2126	30.0	30.6	31.5	4.6	3.3	39908	40941	32	66	1753	33.1	21.3	25.7	16.1	3.7	79375
35755	LANGSTON	22678	241	27.4	32.0	34.4	5.0	1.2	44327	45098	46	80	209	21.1	23.9	29.7	20.6	4.8	103500
35756	MADISON	23867	2640	23.9	21.4	40.3	10.3	4.0	53609	55385	69	93	2143	10.2	12.4	60.8	13.8	2.8	120318
35757	MADISON	30785	4242	9.7	19.6	41.8	19.5	9.5	70372	72303	87	98	3785	7.0	5.5	42.9	39.4	5.3	162406
35758	MADISON	32764	15277	13.0	17.9	39.9	18.8	10.4	71654	72100	88	99	10465	2.6	4.7	36.0	48.6	8.1	193777
35759	MERIDIANVILLE	27890	1990	11.1	22.5	48.6	13.0	4.9	61660	63305	80	96	1757	7.5	3.1	55.3	31.5	2.7	143488
35760	NEW HOPE	19588	2319	30.6	28.8	35.3	4.5	0.8	39326	39947	31	64	1834	20.0	24.3	42.1	12.3	1.3	99907
35761	NEW MARKET	19422	3860	27.8	28.3	35.9	6.7	1.3	42531	43215	41	74	3288	16.8	21.7	41.9	17.0	2.6	108591
35763	OWENS CROSS ROADS	35930	3970	13.1	15.2	36.9	16.5	18.4	74378	75069	89	99	3540	6.6	6.2	23.4	38.8	25.1	246649
35764	PAINT ROCK	17878	200	27.5	43.0	26.5	2.0	1.0	38452	38919	28	61	165	20.0	29.1	33.3	17.0	0.6	91154
35765	PISGAH	17468	1724	34.4	30.7	31.1	2.8	1.0	34573	36690	17	42	1395	33.9	25.7	31.4	8.5	0.5	74931
35766	PRINCETON	18176	91	28.6	37.4	28.6	3.3	2.2	39049	39751	30	63	78	33.3	32.1	25.6	6.4	2.6	73333
35768	SCOTTSBORO	19489	4719	33.4	31.7	28.6	4.9	1.4	36326	37546	22	51	3388	22.0	29.9	36.2	10.2	1.7	87684
35769	SCOTTSBORO	22786	4208	30.8	26.8	31.1	8.4	2.9	42723	44129	42	75	3149	18.3	16.1	38.1	22.3	5.1	121602
35771	SECTION	18424	1554	34.0	28.2	31.6	4.9	1.3	38366	39363	28	60	1252	26.5	32.0	27.2	12.5	1.8	80000
35772	STEVENSON	18523	2182	31.9	32.6	30.2	4.2	1.1	36590	37617	22	51	1689	34.0	29.5	27.6	6.9	2.0	74076
35773	TONEY	20045	4579	20.0	31.1	41.2	6.3	1.4	48534	50140	58	88	3963	14.3	18.8	46.8	18.7	1.4	116045
35774	TRENTON	18860	104	28.8	37.5	28.8	2.9	1.9	39367	39511	31	64	89	32.6	31.5	27.0	6.7	2.2	72778
35775	VALHERMOSO SPRINGS	18651	241	19.5	45.2	30.7	3.3	1.2	43801	45303	45	79	206	19.9	35.4	32.5	10.2	1.9	84211
35776	WOODVILLE	18537	1513	27.0	36.6	31.7	3.9	0.9	40751	41259	35	69	1275	20.1	25.9	41.3	12.1	0.6	96280
35801	HUNTSVILLE	33519	10931	26.5	21.6	33.3	10.9	7.7	51506	53075	65	91	7196	1.9	7.5	36.8	39.5	14.2	186565
35802	HUNTSVILLE	37131	9771	14.5	21.4	41.9	14.9	7.4	61649	63443	80	96	6268	0.3	4.4	32.2	54.7	8.3	200884
35803	HUNTSVILLE	32272	10611	10.3	17.6	45.5	19.7	6.9	70659	71933	87	98	8774	3.8	4.4	49.9	39.3	2.6	162203
35805	HUNTSVILLE	15729	10424	50.2	28.4	19.2	1.9	0.4	24904	26027	3	12	3581	11.4	47.3	39.3	2.0	0.0	85330
35806	HUNTSVILLE	32952	7979	19.6	22.6	36.4	13.5	7.8	58060	61467	75	94	4504	4.2	9.4	35.9	44.9	5.6	176509
35808	HUNTSVILLE	14313	435	12.9	42.5	38.2	6.2	0.2	43391	43298	44	77	10	0.0	0.0	80.0	20.0	0.0	164286
35810	HUNTSVILLE	20621	11516	26.8	26.1	39.3	5.5	2.3	44946	46967	48	82	8543	3.9	32.2	56.5	7.0	0.4	101055
35811	HUNTSVILLE	23900	10596	18.5	24.9	44.8	8.9	2.9	54022	55970	70	93	8683	6.1	14.2	51.8	25.5	2.3	135019
35816	HUNTSVILLE	16204	6135	49.7	24.9	21.2	3.3	0.9	25208	26728	3	13	1882	7.3	31.9	54.5	6.0	0.3	105376
35824	HUNTSVILLE	32572	2101	17.2	23.5	44.5	10.6	4.2	56337	58678	73	94	652	9.2	3.8	39.3	40.8	6.9	170130
35898	HUNTSVILLE	0	0	0.0	0.0	0.0	0.0	0.0	0	0	0	0	0	0.0	0.0	0.0	0.0	0.0	0
35901	GADSDEN	20269	8447	39.2	25.8	26.9	5.2	2.8	34866	37181	17	43	5543	23.5	24.6	29.7	18.5	3.8	95495
35903	GADSDEN	17820	7766	37.5	30.2	27.3	3.7	1.2	33904	36405	15	39	5296	23.6	35.1	33.7	6.8	0.8	77921
35904	GADSDEN	17888	6029	38.3	33.1	23.9	3.1	1.6	32667	35600	13	32	4587	36.5	29.3	27.0	6.0	1.2	63590
35905	GADSDEN	21169	2545	23.6	30.2	39.4	5.6	1.3	46748	46895	53	85	2099	19.4	22.2	40.4	17.5	0.4	104153
35906	GADSDEN	24857	4030	22.0	31.0	36.4	7.1	3.4	47143	47147	54	85	2778	11.1	13.4	44.7	29.0	1.8	138210
35907	GADSDEN	27446	3177	14.8	22.9	43.9	14.0	4.4	61916	61344	80	96	2889	6.6	10.2	54.0	27.1	2.0	134507
35950	ALBERTVILLE	17254	7247	34.4	30.0	29.2	4.9	1.6	37361	38779	25	56	4983	13.3	30.7	38.7	15.7	1.7	97835
35951	ALBERTVILLE	17227	4364	32.6	34.2	25.3	5.2	2.8	35420	36948	19	46	3249	20.9	28.0	33.5	14.8	2.7	91530
35952	ALTOONA	15919	3179	37.9	30.9	26.8	3.5	0.9	32910	35534	13	34	2500	31.5	28.4	29.0	9.0	2.2	74172
35953	ASHVILLE	17474	3064	28.6	33.5	32.4	4.1	1.4	39582	41023	31	64	2607	22.8	26.9	32.7	13.5	4.2	90683
35954	ATTALLA	17753	5224	37.4	29.3	27.8	4.1	1.5	34425	36738	16	42	3858	27.0	36.0	28.4	7.1	1.5	73659
35956	BOAZ	17186	3364	33.5	33.0	28.7	3.9	0.8	35850	37801	20	49	2823	21.3	32.0	31.3	14.0	1.5	85933
35957	BOAZ	17239	5691	37.3	30.6	26.7	3.9	1.5	33473	35235	14	36	4036	16.3	30.3	39.5	11.6	2.2	95290
35958	BRYANT	17076	1413	31.1	31.7	33.3	3.5	0.4	39883	40726	32	66	1194	21.9	30.2	37.7	9.5	0.8	87475
35959	CEDAR BLUFF	19422	2010	33.2	30.0	31.7	4.0	1.0	37939	38565	26	58	1592	29.5	18.3	35.0	15.0	2.2	94487
35960	CENTRE	19036	4086	34.7	31.3	27.7	5.0	1.3	35109	36370	18	45	3185	21.9	22.9	34.5	16.7	4.0	98092
35961	COLLINSVILLE	15062	2130	40.3	32.1	23.1	3.7	0.9	31452	32778	10	26	1604	30.4	32.4	24.4	10.2	2.6	72353
35962	CROSSVILLE	16197	2789	35.0	31.3	28.9	3.4	1.4	34313	35413	16	41	2211	21.9	26.2	35.6	13.4	2.8	92455
35963	DAWSON	14927	597	36.0	35.0	26.3	2.0	0.7	33684	34085	15	38	493	18.7	31.8	34.3	8.9	6.3	89390
35966	FLAT ROCK	16209	1540	32.5	34.5	28.9	3.7	0.4	33961	35388	15	40	1293	32.6	28.7	30.0	8.0	0.8	77061
35967	FORT PAYNE	19595	6423	32.0	30.0	30.0	5.3	2.7	38266	38622	27	60	4609	18.8	27.1	37.2	14.5	2.4	96649
35968	FORT PAYNE	17723	1582	32.6	33.9	28.2	3.3	2.1	37039	37185	24	55	1315	20.7	28.8	36.8	11.1	2.6	90985
35971	FYFFE	17004	1904	35.0	34.0	25.4	4.3	1.3	34888	35595	17	44	1571	26.7	26.4	32.0	12.1	2.9	85855
	ALABAMA	21187		31.4	27.9	30.6	6.9	3.2	40822	42202				18.1	22.4	35.8	19.6	4.0	107730
	UNITED STATES	27277		20.9	24.4	35.3	11.7	7.6	54719	56938				9.3	13.1	31.6	32.6	13.5	162279

ZIP CODE #	POST OFFICE NAME	FINANCIAL SERVICES: Auto Loan	FINANCIAL SERVICES: Home Loan	FINANCIAL SERVICES: Investments	FINANCIAL SERVICES: Retirement Plans	THE HOME: Home Improvements: Home Repair	THE HOME: Home Improvements: Lawn & Garden	THE HOME: Furnishings: Computers & Hardware-Personal	THE HOME: Furnishings: Major Appliances	THE HOME: Furnishings: TV, Radio, Sound Equipment	THE HOME: Furnishings: Furniture	ENTERTAINMENT: Dine out/ Carry out	ENTERTAINMENT: Sports Equipment	ENTERTAINMENT: Fees & Tickets	ENTERTAINMENT: Toys & Games	ENTERTAINMENT: Travel	ENTERTAINMENT: Cable TV	PERSONAL: Apparel & Services	PERSONAL: Auto Repairs	PERSONAL: Health Insurance	PERSONAL: Pets & Supplies
35614	ATHENS	82	63	68	62	62	79	65	73	70	62	69	56	54	73	60	76	47	70	77	88
35616	CHEROKEE	82	58	80	56	60	82	60	75	67	57	66	57	48	68	58	74	44	70	79	90
35618	COURTLAND	71	47	67	45	47	69	50	62	58	48	56	48	38	59	47	64	37	59	66	76
35619	DANVILLE	85	61	70	59	60	80	63	73	70	61	69	56	51	73	57	76	46	70	78	89
35620	ELKMONT	86	66	71	64	65	82	67	76	73	66	72	58	56	76	61	78	48	72	79	92
35621	EVA	87	62	72	61	62	82	65	75	72	63	70	58	52	75	59	78	47	71	80	92
35622	FALKVILLE	81	59	68	57	59	78	61	71	68	59	66	55	49	70	56	74	45	68	75	87
35630	FLORENCE	60	50	50	52	50	57	60	57	62	56	61	43	54	61	54	65	42	60	64	68
35633	FLORENCE	84	78	77	78	77	87	74	81	77	73	77	61	71	79	74	81	52	78	84	96
35634	FLORENCE	96	88	89	88	88	98	84	92	87	84	87	69	80	89	83	92	60	88	95	109
35640	HARTSELLE	90	80	80	80	80	92	78	87	82	75	81	66	72	84	77	86	55	82	90	103
35643	HILLSBORO	89	62	77	60	62	85	65	77	73	63	72	60	52	76	60	80	48	73	82	95
35645	KILLEN	94	88	84	90	88	98	84	92	87	82	86	71	81	89	84	90	59	87	94	109
35646	LEIGHTON	72	50	69	48	50	71	52	64	58	49	57	49	41	59	49	64	38	60	68	78
35647	LESTER	89	64	73	62	63	84	66	77	73	64	72	59	53	76	60	80	48	73	81	94
35648	LEXINGTON	78	57	73	56	58	78	59	71	65	55	64	54	48	66	56	71	42	66	75	85
35650	MOULTON	80	60	70	59	60	78	63	73	69	60	68	55	52	71	59	75	46	69	77	87
35651	MOUNT HOPE	85	61	70	59	61	81	63	74	70	62	69	57	51	73	58	77	46	70	78	90
35652	ROGERSVILLE	83	62	80	61	64	83	64	77	70	61	69	58	53	71	62	76	46	72	81	92
35653	RUSSELLVILLE	69	53	62	53	53	68	57	64	62	53	60	49	48	62	53	66	41	62	68	77
35654	RUSSELLVILLE	77	56	66	55	56	74	58	68	64	56	63	52	47	66	54	70	42	64	72	83
35660	SHEFFIELD	59	52	54	52	52	62	55	59	60	53	59	43	52	59	54	64	40	59	66	70
35661	MUSCLE SHOALS	86	76	79	75	76	88	75	83	79	73	78	61	69	80	73	83	53	79	87	98
35670	SOMERVILLE	89	64	74	63	64	85	67	78	74	65	72	60	54	77	61	80	49	73	82	94
35671	TANNER	96	81	83	78	80	92	78	88	83	79	83	65	70	86	75	88	56	84	89	105
35672	TOWN CREEK	80	56	70	54	56	77	59	70	66	57	64	54	46	68	54	72	43	66	74	86
35673	TRINITY	92	75	78	74	75	90	75	84	80	73	79	64	65	83	71	85	54	80	87	101
35674	TUSCUMBIA	76	61	68	60	61	76	64	72	69	61	68	53	56	70	61	74	46	69	77	85
35677	WATERLOO	72	52	68	50	53	71	53	65	59	51	58	50	43	60	51	65	39	61	68	78
35739	ARDMORE	83	66	72	64	65	81	67	76	72	65	71	57	57	74	63	77	48	72	80	91
35740	BRIDGEPORT	80	56	69	54	56	77	59	70	66	57	64	54	46	68	54	72	43	66	74	85
35741	BROWNSBORO	128	144	123	147	139	134	127	131	123	132	125	103	136	129	132	121	88	124	123	152
35744	DUTTON	80	57	66	56	57	76	60	70	66	58	65	53	48	69	54	72	44	66	73	85
35745	ESTILLFORK	76	54	63	53	54	72	57	66	63	55	62	51	45	66	51	69	41	62	70	80
35746	FACKLER	87	63	72	61	62	83	65	76	72	63	71	58	52	75	59	79	48	72	80	92
35747	GRANT	85	65	77	65	66	85	67	79	72	63	71	60	56	74	64	78	48	73	82	94
35748	GURLEY	78	73	66	72	71	76	70	73	72	70	72	55	67	74	67	74	49	72	75	87
35749	HARVEST	110	118	101	116	113	107	105	108	102	111	104	83	108	108	106	101	72	103	100	125
35750	HAZEL GREEN	86	72	71	70	70	81	71	77	75	72	74	58	63	78	66	78	50	74	79	93
35751	HOLLYTREE	80	57	66	56	57	76	60	69	66	58	65	53	48	69	54	72	44	66	73	84
35752	HOLLYWOOD	81	60	67	59	60	78	62	72	68	60	67	55	51	71	57	74	45	68	75	87
35754	LACEYS SPRING	82	68	67	66	67	77	68	73	72	69	71	55	60	75	63	75	48	71	75	88
35755	LANGSTON	83	63	87	61	66	83	64	78	69	61	68	58	53	69	64	74	45	73	79	92
35756	MADISON	97	93	87	89	88	91	86	91	86	90	87	71	83	91	83	87	60	87	86	106
35757	MADISON	122	141	118	139	134	117	121	122	113	132	116	98	130	122	124	107	82	114	105	138
35758	MADISON	124	130	113	132	124	112	124	117	117	130	120	96	127	124	122	112	85	117	106	137
35759	MERIDIANVILLE	102	115	101	117	112	114	102	106	102	103	103	81	110	104	108	103	72	103	108	125
35760	NEW HOPE	85	61	74	59	61	82	63	75	70	61	69	57	51	72	59	77	46	71	79	91
35761	NEW MARKET	86	70	70	67	69	81	69	76	74	69	73	57	60	77	64	78	49	73	79	92
35763	OWENS CROSS ROADS	152	161	152	164	158	156	143	152	140	149	141	121	149	147	148	138	100	142	141	176
35764	PAINT ROCK	77	55	63	54	55	73	57	67	64	56	62	51	46	66	52	69	42	63	70	81
35765	PISGAH	76	55	63	53	54	72	57	66	63	55	62	51	46	66	52	69	42	63	70	81
35766	PRINCETON	80	58	66	56	57	76	60	70	67	58	65	54	48	69	55	73	44	66	74	85
35768	SCOTTSBORO	74	58	64	57	58	73	62	69	67	59	66	52	53	68	58	73	45	67	75	82
35769	SCOTTSBORO	82	71	80	71	73	86	72	80	77	69	75	60	66	76	71	82	51	77	86	95
35771	SECTION	82	59	68	57	59	78	61	71	68	60	67	55	49	71	56	74	45	68	75	87
35772	STEVENSON	80	56	68	54	56	76	59	69	66	57	64	54	47	68	54	72	43	66	73	85
35773	TONEY	86	78	72	76	76	82	74	79	77	76	77	59	69	80	71	80	52	77	80	95
35774	TRENTON	79	57	65	55	56	75	59	69	66	58	64	53	47	68	54	71	43	65	73	84
35775	VALHERMOSO SPRINGS	84	60	69	58	60	80	63	73	69	61	68	56	50	72	57	76	46	69	77	89
35776	WOODVILLE	83	60	70	58	60	79	62	73	69	60	68	56	50	72	57	75	45	69	76	88
35801	HUNTSVILLE	93	95	99	97	97	101	97	97	99	96	98	72	99	96	99	101	69	98	105	114
35802	HUNTSVILLE	105	111	114	113	114	115	108	110	109	111	110	80	115	107	114	111	77	110	118	127
35803	HUNTSVILLE	112	128	121	129	126	118	114	116	110	120	111	88	123	112	120	108	79	112	110	134
35805	HUNTSVILLE	48	37	33	39	35	39	48	41	49	46	49	34	43	50	41	50	34	47	45	52
35806	HUNTSVILLE	105	98	90	103	95	92	107	96	102	107	103	80	103	106	99	99	73	100	92	114
35808	HUNTSVILLE	92	48	36	56	43	41	87	60	82	81	86	60	66	98	63	75	60	77	54	73
35810	HUNTSVILLE	73	73	67	73	70	79	71	73	76	71	75	54	73	75	71	79	52	74	81	88
35811	HUNTSVILLE	88	91	82	91	89	91	85	88	86	87	86	65	87	88	86	88	60	86	90	103
35816	HUNTSVILLE	51	37	36	40	36	39	53	43	54	50	54	36	46	53	45	54	38	51	48	55
35824	HUNTSVILLE	98	86	76	91	81	77	97	84	94	98	96	72	92	99	88	90	68	91	80	102
35898	HUNTSVILLE	0	0	0	0	0	0	0	0	0	0	0	0	0	0	0	0	0	0	0	0
35901	GADSDEN	69	61	62	63	61	69	66	67	69	64	68	49	62	68	63	73	47	68	74	80
35903	GADSDEN	64	54	55	54	53	65	58	61	62	54	60	46	52	62	54	66	41	61	67	73
35904	GADSDEN	67	53	61	52	53	68	56	63	62	53	60	47	49	61	54	67	41	61	70	75
35905	GADSDEN	85	70	79	70	71	89	71	83	76	65	74	63	62	77	69	82	50	77	87	98
35906	GADSDEN	80	83	73	85	81	84	80	81	80	79	80	62	81	81	80	81	56	80	83	95
35907	GADSDEN	92	109	96	110	105	107	95	99	95	96	96	76	105	97	103	96	67	96	102	116
35950	ALBERTVILLE	75	60	62	59	60	72	63	69	67	61	66	52	55	69	59	71	45	67	72	82
35951	ALBERTVILLE	83	63	71	61	63	79	65	74	71	64	69	57	54	73	60	76	47	71	77	89
35952	ALTOONA	73	52	62	50	52	70	54	64	60	52	59	49	43	62	49	65	39	60	67	77
35953	ASHVILLE	82	61	68	59	61	78	63	72	69	62	68	55	52	72	57	74	46	68	75	87
35954	ATTALLA	75	55	66	54	55	74	58	68	65	55	63	52	48	66	54	70	42	65	73	82
35956	BOAZ	75	56	67	55	57	74	58	68	63	55	62	52	47	65	54	69	42	64	72	82
35957	BOAZ	69	54	60	54	55	68	58	65	63	55	61	49	50	64	54	68	42	62	69	77
35958	BRYANT	78	56	64	54	56	74	58	68	65	57	63	52	47	67	53	70	43	64	71	82
35959	CEDAR BLUFF	79	57	65	55	57	75	59	69	66	58	64	53	48	69	54	72	43	65	73	84
35960	CENTRE	75	57	76	55	60	76	58	71	64	57	63	52	49	63	58	69	42	66	75	84
35961	COLLINSVILLE	71	53	59	51	52	67	54	62	59	54	58	48	45	62	50	64	39	59	65	75
35962	CROSSVILLE	77	57	63	55	56	73	59	67	64	57	63	52	48	67	53	70	43	64	71	82
35963	DAWSON	70	50	58	49	50	66	52	61	58	51	57	47	42	60	47	63	38	57	64	74
35966	FLAT ROCK	75	54	62	52	53	71	56	65	62	54	61	50	45	64	51	67	41	61	68	79
35967	FORT PAYNE	83	66	72	65	65	81	69	76	74	67	73	58	59	76	64	79	49	74	80	92
35968	FORT PAYNE	81	59	68	58	59	78	62	72	68	60	67	55	50	71	57	74	45	68	75	87
35971	FYFFE	77	56	67	55	56	75	58	69	64	56	63	53	47	66	54	70	42	65	72	83
	ALABAMA	83	70	73	70	69	80	73	77	76	71	76	59	66	77	69	80	52	76	80	92
	UNITED STATES	100	100	100	100	100	100	100	100	100	100	100	100	100	100	100	100	100	100	100	100

35972-36262

# POST OFFICE NAME	COUNTY FIPS CODE	POPULATION 2000	POPULATION 2009	POPULATION 2014	2000-2009 ANNUAL RATE % Rate	2000-2009 ANNUAL RATE State Centile	HOUSEHOLDS 2000	HOUSEHOLDS 2009	HOUSEHOLDS 2014	HOUSEHOLDS % Annual Rate 2000-2009	HOUSEHOLDS 2009 Average HH Size	FAMILIES 2000	FAMILIES 2009	FAMILIES % Annual Rate 2000-2009
35972 GALLANT	055	795	877	911	1.1	79	306	346	362	1.3	2.53	244	270	1.1
35973 GAYLESVILLE	019	3077	3231	3267	0.5	64	1177	1282	1312	0.9	2.48	882	943	0.7
35974 GERALDINE	049	1377	1427	1449	0.4	62	585	603	615	0.3	2.36	416	420	0.1
35975 GROVEOAK	049	1145	1179	1199	0.3	58	458	469	478	0.3	2.51	343	345	0.1
35976 GUNTERSVILLE	095	15700	17243	18090	1.0	77	6417	7074	7447	1.1	2.38	4481	4839	0.8
35978 HENAGAR	049	5035	5299	5419	0.6	67	1956	2062	2117	0.6	2.57	1485	1536	0.4
35979 HIGDON	049	1151	1244	1294	0.8	74	438	476	496	0.9	2.61	342	365	0.7
35980 HORTON	095	4293	4601	4776	0.8	74	1589	1713	1783	0.8	2.69	1255	1331	0.6
35981 IDER	049	2426	2639	2755	0.9	76	977	1057	1104	0.9	2.50	734	780	0.7
35983 LEESBURG	019	3161	3290	3282	0.4	62	1295	1400	1414	0.8	2.34	975	1036	0.7
35984 MENTONE	049	1783	2042	2162	1.5	86	753	860	914	1.4	2.37	528	590	1.2
35986 RAINSVILLE	049	6748	7548	7929	1.2	80	2771	3084	3247	1.2	2.43	2021	2207	1.0
35987 STEELE	115	2645	2972	3217	1.3	82	1020	1153	1252	1.3	2.55	787	875	1.2
35988 SYLVANIA	049	1683	1826	1896	0.9	76	669	722	751	0.8	2.53	517	549	0.7
35989 VALLEY HEAD	049	2918	3357	3562	1.5	86	1126	1288	1369	1.5	2.61	839	939	1.2
36003 AUTAUGAVILLE	001	1859	2112	2291	1.4	84	695	820	899	1.8	2.57	491	565	1.5
36005 BANKS	109	1353	1299	1273	-0.4	25	535	519	510	-0.3	2.50	395	378	-0.5
36006 BILLINGSLEY	001	1357	1560	1685	1.5	86	516	608	663	1.8	2.56	393	454	1.6
36009 BRANTLEY	041	2798	2780	2792	-0.1	39	1182	1217	1235	0.3	2.28	821	828	0.1
36010 BRUNDIDGE	109	4582	4860	4936	0.6	67	1955	2130	2179	0.9	2.28	1303	1399	0.8
36013 CECIL	101	537	547	552	0.2	52	199	208	212	0.5	2.63	150	152	0.1
36016 CLAYTON	005	5416	5609	5564	0.4	62	1582	1651	1653	0.5	2.58	1111	1133	0.2
36017 CLIO	005	2951	2982	2928	0.1	49	727	710	698	-0.3	2.62	507	485	-0.5
36020 COOSADA	051	1228	1413	1539	1.5	86	429	500	548	1.7	2.83	343	393	1.5
36022 DEATSVILLE	051	9515	12239	13560	2.8	94	3338	4373	4878	3.0	2.71	2673	3447	2.8
36024 ECLECTIC	051	5288	6050	6517	1.5	86	2040	2367	2565	1.6	2.56	1563	1776	1.4
36025 ELMORE	051	4714	5839	6318	2.3	91	876	1160	1314	3.1	3.43	722	944	2.9
36026 EQUALITY	037	1161	1195	1213	0.3	58	477	505	516	0.6	2.37	360	378	0.5
36027 EUFAULA	005	17285	16598	16225	-0.4	25	6769	6692	6609	-0.1	2.44	4820	4671	-0.3
36028 DOZIER	041	839	833	832	-0.1	39	360	366	369	0.2	2.28	243	242	0.0
36029 FITZPATRICK	011	1043	949	899	-1.0	4	409	388	373	-0.6	2.45	297	276	-0.8
36030 FOREST HOME	013	1008	1048	1032	0.4	62	355	380	380	0.7	2.76	269	282	0.5
36031 FORT DAVIS	011	106	98	94	-0.8	9	41	40	39	-0.3	2.45	26	24	-0.9
36032 FORT DEPOSIT	085	2859	2821	2742	-0.1	39	1038	1074	1059	0.4	2.61	740	750	0.1
36033 GEORGIANA	013	4394	4068	3887	-0.8	9	1804	1753	1698	-0.3	2.27	1239	1177	-0.6
36034 GLENWOOD	109	622	610	636	-0.2	34	263	270	286	0.3	2.26	193	195	0.1
36035 GOSHEN	109	1748	2178	2293	2.4	92	734	940	999	2.7	2.32	500	627	2.5
36036 GRADY	101	2104	2188	2223	0.4	62	846	917	943	0.9	2.39	616	651	0.6
36037 GREENVILLE	013	14245	13438	12914	-0.6	16	5540	5442	5296	-0.2	2.44	3884	3734	-0.4
36038 GANTT	039	3564	3532	3500	-0.1	39	1461	1482	1482	0.2	2.38	1032	1025	-0.1
36039 HARDAWAY	087	394	393	385	0.0	45	146	152	151	0.4	2.58	98	99	0.1
36040 HAYNEVILLE	085	4719	4407	4231	-0.7	13	1637	1615	1574	-0.1	2.71	1219	1181	-0.3
36041 HIGHLAND HOME	041	1135	1126	1120	-0.1	39	438	446	447	0.2	2.52	319	319	0.0
36042 HONORAVILLE	041	1126	1110	1098	-0.2	34	438	444	443	0.1	2.50	326	325	0.0
36043 HOPE HULL	085	3434	3434	3410	0.0	45	1296	1353	1363	0.5	2.52	951	968	0.2
36046 LAPINE	041	1715	1722	1726	0.0	45	667	688	695	0.3	2.50	500	505	0.1
36047 LETOHATCHEE	085	2020	1988	1952	-0.2	34	744	771	768	0.4	2.57	538	544	0.1
36048 LOUISVILLE	005	1872	1745	1693	-0.8	9	707	688	675	-0.3	2.54	520	496	-0.5
36049 LUVERNE	041	5252	5034	4939	-0.5	19	2159	2137	2115	-0.1	2.28	1473	1425	-0.4
36051 MARBURY	001	2062	2372	2551	1.5	86	714	842	913	1.8	2.76	547	632	1.6
36052 MATHEWS	101	682	767	799	1.3	82	266	311	328	1.7	2.47	189	216	1.5
36053 MIDWAY	011	2416	2347	2297	-0.3	29	954	954	943	0.0	2.25	651	637	-0.2
36054 MILLBROOK	051	10872	13800	15548	2.6	93	3814	4899	5551	2.7	2.82	3029	3821	2.5
36061 PEROTE	011	251	216	200	-1.6	0	107	96	90	-1.2	2.25	74	65	-1.4
36064 PIKE ROAD	101	4038	5152	5647	2.7	94	1438	1900	2107	3.1	2.71	1169	1510	2.8
36066 PRATTVILLE	001	13180	17559	19827	3.1	95	4884	6706	7642	3.5	2.62	3876	5229	3.3
36067 PRATTVILLE	001	22923	25202	26694	1.0	77	8347	9426	10074	1.3	2.65	6369	7066	1.1
36069 RAMER	101	2221	2384	2448	0.8	74	896	1004	1044	1.2	2.37	618	670	0.9
36071 RUTLEDGE	041	865	838	826	-0.3	29	343	346	344	0.1	2.42	241	238	-0.1
36075 SHORTER	087	2119	2264	2263	0.7	70	775	861	873	1.1	2.63	554	600	0.9
36078 TALLASSEE	051	12475	13148	13584	0.6	67	4919	5263	5469	0.7	2.47	3521	3680	0.5
36079 TROY	109	9199	9816	9945	0.7	70	3747	4122	4216	1.0	2.38	2478	2651	0.7
36080 TITUS	051	2154	2437	2600	1.3	82	912	1049	1128	1.5	2.32	656	737	1.3
36081 TROY	109	13337	13344	13279	0.0	45	5337	5498	5515	0.3	2.27	3243	3255	0.0
36082 TROY	109	325	312	311	-0.4	25	0	0	0	0.0	0.00	0	0	0.0
36083 TUSKEGEE	087	11575	10543	10049	-1.0	4	4575	4339	4187	-0.6	2.28	2773	2541	-0.9
36088 TUSKEGEE INSTITUTE	087	5251	4820	4630	-0.9	6	1540	1360	1288	-1.3	2.29	841	717	-1.7
36089 UNION SPRINGS	011	9651	9139	8823	-0.6	16	3154	3066	2973	-0.3	2.49	2141	2033	-0.6
36091 VERBENA	021	2987	3421	3592	1.5	86	1169	1378	1460	1.8	2.48	870	1006	1.6
36092 WETUMPKA	051	18584	21556	23067	1.6	87	6130	7228	7871	1.8	2.48	4549	5239	1.5
36093 WETUMPKA	051	6607	9060	10397	3.5	97	2437	3387	3906	3.6	2.67	2055	2804	3.4
36104 MONTGOMERY	101	12681	10587	10028	-1.9	0	4991	4237	4025	-1.8	2.17	2672	2155	-2.3
36105 MONTGOMERY	101	14973	13742	13354	-0.9	6	5486	5220	5131	-0.5	2.63	3930	3636	-0.8
36106 MONTGOMERY	101	15370	15344	15362	0.0	45	5853	6053	6122	0.4	2.18	3500	3501	0.0
36107 MONTGOMERY	101	9880	9338	9129	-0.6	16	4313	4174	4115	-0.4	2.18	2351	2169	-0.9
36108 MONTGOMERY	101	25377	23268	22668	-0.9	6	9333	8888	8751	-0.5	2.58	6453	5976	-0.8
36109 MONTGOMERY	101	24713	24787	24888	0.0	45	10405	10822	10985	0.4	2.24	7100	7153	0.1
36110 MONTGOMERY	101	13170	12918	12842	-0.2	34	4907	4981	5005	0.2	2.51	3435	3377	-0.2
36111 MONTGOMERY	101	12296	12173	12084	-0.1	39	5340	5325	5315	0.0	2.27	3310	3176	-0.4
36112 MONTGOMERY	101	5786	5492	5398	-0.6	16	542	448	421	-2.0	2.91	461	375	-2.2
36115 MONTGOMERY	101	845	829	828	-0.2	34	193	197	199	0.2	3.28	187	190	0.2
36116 MONTGOMERY	101	38778	39597	39852	0.2	52	14880	15529	15773	0.5	2.52	10130	10214	0.1
36117 MONTGOMERY	101	37601	45713	48733	2.1	90	15230	19102	20558	2.5	2.28	9835	12341	2.5
36201 ANNISTON	015	21517	19843	19256	-0.9	6	8697	8281	8123	-0.5	2.33	5750	5347	-0.8
36203 OXFORD	015	17170	17494	17590	0.2	52	6745	7056	7159	0.5	2.46	4948	5073	0.3
36205 ANNISTON	015	19	503	507	42.5	100	9	217	218	41.1	2.31	3	143	51.9
36206 ANNISTON	015	11970	11267	10995	-0.7	13	4873	4750	4690	-0.3	2.36	3449	3292	-0.5
36207 ANNISTON	015	18084	18621	18780	0.3	58	7802	8169	8290	0.5	2.24	5135	5301	0.3
36250 ALEXANDRIA	015	3939	4116	4185	0.5	64	1476	1608	1657	0.9	2.56	1151	1232	0.7
36251 ASHLAND	027	5495	5338	5221	-0.3	29	2202	2219	2197	0.1	2.31	1552	1529	-0.2
36255 CRAGFORD	027	1146	1116	1087	-0.3	29	442	442	436	0.0	2.52	332	326	-0.2
36256 DAVISTON	123	1586	1534	1488	-0.4	25	625	621	609	-0.1	2.47	457	445	-0.3
36258 DELTA	027	1776	1773	1782	0.0	45	714	741	752	0.4	2.39	532	542	0.2
36260 EASTABOGA	121	4073	4185	4234	0.3	58	1614	1719	1756	0.7	2.43	1212	1265	0.5
36262 FRUITHURST	029	1255	1393	1453	1.1	79	488	560	591	1.5	2.48	364	411	1.3
ALABAMA					0.6					0.9	2.44			0.6
UNITED STATES					1.0					1.1	2.59			0.9

ZIP CODE #	POST OFFICE NAME	RACE (%) White 2000	White 2009	Black 2000	Black 2009	Asian/Pacific 2000	Asian/Pacific 2009	% Hispanic Origin 2000	% Hispanic Origin 2009	2009 AGE DISTRIBUTION (%) 0-4	5-9	10-14	15-19	20-24	25-44	45-64	65-84	85+	18+	MEDIAN AGE 2009	% 2009 Males	% 2009 Females
35972	GALLANT	97.5	96.4	0.6	0.9	0.1	0.1	1.4	2.7	5.9	5.9	6.4	6.4	5.1	26.7	28.3	13.8	1.5	77.8	40.8	49.9	50.1
35973	GAYLESVILLE	96.3	95.6	2.1	2.3	0.1	0.2	0.3	0.5	6.1	6.3	6.4	6.3	5.2	26.0	27.5	14.4	1.9	77.4	40.6	49.0	51.0
35974	GERALDINE	98.3	97.8	0.0	0.0	0.1	0.1	0.8	1.5	6.9	7.0	7.2	6.6	5.1	24.9	26.3	13.5	2.3	75.0	39.1	48.8	51.2
35975	GROVEOAK	97.6	96.6	0.0	0.0	0.0	0.0	0.7	1.4	6.5	6.7	6.8	6.0	4.7	25.4	28.6	13.7	1.5	76.2	40.2	49.9	50.1
35976	GUNTERSVILLE	93.1	91.7	4.1	4.3	0.3	0.4	2.3	4.2	5.5	5.7	6.0	6.1	5.2	24.1	29.7	15.5	2.2	79.0	43.0	49.0	51.0
35978	HENAGAR	96.7	95.8	0.1	0.1	0.1	0.1	0.8	1.6	7.1	7.3	7.3	6.0	4.8	26.9	26.4	12.7	1.4	74.6	38.2	49.2	50.8
35979	HIGDON	97.9	97.5	0.1	0.1	0.1	0.1	0.6	1.2	6.7	6.4	6.8	6.9	5.2	28.1	26.1	12.5	1.3	75.9	38.9	49.8	50.2
35980	HORTON	94.2	90.2	0.1	0.1	0.1	0.2	5.7	10.4	7.4	7.4	7.5	6.6	5.2	28.5	26.0	10.2	1.1	73.5	36.5	50.6	49.4
35981	IDER	97.5	96.8	0.0	0.0	0.0	0.1	0.5	0.9	6.6	6.7	6.9	6.7	5.2	26.4	26.7	13.5	1.4	75.6	39.4	48.7	51.3
35983	LEESBURG	94.5	93.0	3.1	3.3	0.2	0.2	2.0	3.3	6.0	6.2	6.5	5.8	4.8	25.6	29.1	14.2	1.6	77.5	41.2	50.2	49.8
35984	MENTONE	94.7	92.6	1.1	1.4	0.1	0.2	1.1	2.4	5.4	5.7	6.1	6.0	5.0	24.6	31.4	13.9	1.8	78.9	42.6	49.7	50.3
35986	RAINSVILLE	96.7	94.9	0.2	0.2	0.2	0.3	2.2	4.4	6.4	6.6	6.8	6.5	4.6	26.8	28.0	12.7	1.6	76.2	39.8	48.9	51.1
35987	STEELE	95.1	93.1	1.7	1.9	0.1	0.1	3.3	5.7	6.2	6.3	6.4	6.1	4.9	26.8	28.2	13.5	1.6	77.1	40.3	49.5	50.5
35988	SYLVANIA	96.3	94.6	0.1	0.2	0.2	0.3	1.6	3.3	7.2	7.2	7.1	5.8	5.0	27.5	27.0	11.8	1.3	74.9	38.1	49.3	50.7
35989	VALLEY HEAD	93.9	90.4	0.8	1.0	0.1	0.2	4.2	8.5	6.8	6.9	7.1	6.5	4.8	26.8	27.9	11.8	1.4	75.1	38.5	49.3	50.7
36003	AUTAUGAVILLE	41.7	38.5	57.2	60.3	0.1	0.0	0.6	0.8	7.3	7.2	7.3	6.9	5.8	25.0	27.1	11.7	1.5	73.8	37.5	48.6	51.4
36005	BANKS	77.5	74.4	19.4	21.5	0.0	0.0	0.7	1.2	5.5	5.6	6.5	7.5	5.0	24.8	30.1	13.0	2.0	77.8	41.5	48.6	51.4
36006	BILLINGSLEY	75.2	72.4	22.8	24.9	0.1	0.3	1.2	1.9	7.6	7.6	7.4	7.1	5.7	26.5	26.0	10.7	1.3	73.1	36.2	49.5	50.5
36009	BRANTLEY	75.3	72.8	23.5	25.7	0.0	0.1	0.4	0.7	5.7	5.9	6.2	6.6	5.3	23.4	29.9	14.5	2.4	78.1	42.6	47.1	52.9
36010	BRUNDIDGE	55.5	55.5	42.0	41.5	0.2	0.2	0.9	1.3	5.7	6.0	6.2	6.5	5.6	23.1	28.9	15.5	2.3	78.1	42.5	46.8	53.2
36013	CECIL	58.7	50.5	40.0	47.5	0.0	0.0	1.1	2.0	6.0	6.2	6.8	6.4	5.5	22.5	34.4	10.4	1.8	77.3	42.3	48.3	51.7
36016	CLAYTON	41.2	37.6	56.8	59.7	0.1	0.1	1.6	2.3	5.7	5.7	5.8	6.3	8.8	34.7	22.9	8.6	1.5	79.1	34.7	60.8	39.2
36017	CLIO	48.8	44.9	46.8	49.0	0.3	0.4	3.3	5.0	3.6	3.6	3.9	5.0	9.5	39.5	24.0	9.3	1.6	86.2	37.0	68.2	31.8
36020	COOSADA	50.8	46.8	47.4	51.0	0.2	0.4	0.7	0.9	8.1	7.9	7.9	8.1	5.9	26.0	24.3	10.8	1.1	71.3	35.1	49.3	50.7
36022	DEATSVILLE	90.0	87.5	7.8	9.4	0.3	0.4	1.3	2.2	7.5	7.2	7.1	6.9	6.5	29.7	25.8	8.4	0.9	74.0	35.4	50.8	49.2
36024	ECLECTIC	85.6	83.9	12.8	14.0	0.1	0.1	1.1	1.7	6.3	6.2	6.5	6.4	5.4	24.2	30.1	13.3	1.6	77.1	41.4	49.3	50.7
36025	ELMORE	64.7	62.8	32.8	34.1	0.3	0.4	1.5	2.3	5.7	5.7	5.6	7.2	11.3	35.5	21.1	6.7	1.2	79.4	32.6	64.1	35.9
36026	EQUALITY	82.9	81.9	15.5	16.2	0.0	0.1	0.6	0.8	5.5	5.6	5.8	4.9	2.6	21.2	34.6	18.2	1.7	79.7	47.9	50.1	49.9
36027	EUFAULA	56.3	54.1	41.5	42.9	0.4	0.6	1.3	2.1	7.0	7.0	7.1	7.3	6.2	24.6	26.7	12.0	2.1	74.3	37.9	47.6	52.4
36028	DOZIER	76.9	74.3	21.9	24.0	0.0	0.1	0.4	0.6	5.8	6.0	6.2	7.1	5.5	23.3	29.9	13.7	2.5	77.7	42.0	46.7	53.3
36029	FITZPATRICK	37.7	34.5	61.4	64.4	0.2	0.3	1.5	2.1	6.2	6.4	6.8	6.3	4.8	24.3	29.4	13.9	1.7	76.4	40.7	48.8	51.2
36030	FOREST HOME	51.3	47.3	48.3	52.3	0.0	0.0	0.4	0.6	7.0	7.2	7.1	6.9	5.7	24.3	28.5	11.3	2.1	74.8	38.2	50.3	49.7
36031	FORT DAVIS	12.3	10.2	86.8	88.8	0.0	0.0	0.9	1.0	8.2	8.2	7.1	7.1	7.1	20.4	26.5	12.2	3.1	72.4	37.0	43.9	56.1
36032	FORT DEPOSIT	34.7	32.9	64.8	66.4	0.2	0.3	0.6	0.8	7.9	7.9	7.7	7.5	6.1	23.1	26.2	11.6	2.1	71.9	36.9	46.1	53.9
36033	GEORGIANA	57.9	55.7	41.5	43.6	0.0	0.0	0.6	0.8	6.2	6.3	6.4	6.2	5.3	22.4	28.3	15.7	3.2	77.1	42.5	47.0	53.0
36034	GLENWOOD	84.6	83.1	12.5	13.3	0.0	0.0	1.0	1.5	5.2	5.9	7.0	7.5	4.9	24.8	29.7	13.0	2.0	77.0	40.9	49.5	50.5
36035	GOSHEN	75.7	74.9	22.6	23.2	0.0	0.0	1.4	1.7	5.9	6.2	6.4	6.2	4.5	23.4	30.8	14.4	2.3	77.7	43.0	49.8	50.2
36036	GRADY	63.6	58.0	35.4	40.7	0.0	0.0	0.8	1.1	5.9	6.3	6.4	6.4	4.8	24.2	30.9	13.3	2.0	77.5	41.9	49.5	50.5
36037	GREENVILLE	56.9	54.3	42.2	44.6	0.2	0.3	0.7	1.0	6.7	6.5	6.7	7.2	6.1	23.9	27.6	12.7	2.6	75.7	39.3	47.2	52.8
36038	GANTT	95.1	94.5	3.6	3.8	0.1	0.1	0.3	0.5	5.6	5.8	6.1	6.0	5.5	24.1	29.8	15.0	2.1	78.9	42.7	50.6	49.4
36039	HARDAWAY	10.4	8.9	88.8	90.3	0.0	0.0	0.5	0.5	7.1	7.6	9.2	8.1	6.1	23.4	25.2	10.7	2.5	70.7	35.7	44.3	55.7
36040	HAYNEVILLE	10.1	8.7	89.3	90.6	0.1	0.1	0.5	0.6	7.6	7.6	9.2	9.1	7.6	24.2	23.4	9.5	1.7	70.0	32.2	46.5	53.5
36041	HIGHLAND HOME	74.5	72.4	24.1	26.0	0.1	0.1	0.9	1.4	6.6	6.6	6.8	6.9	5.3	26.0	27.9	12.3	1.6	75.8	38.6	50.0	50.0
36042	HONORAVILLE	77.6	75.2	21.0	22.8	0.2	0.3	0.9	1.4	6.4	6.4	6.7	6.8	5.4	26.1	28.3	12.3	1.5	76.3	39.1	49.6	50.4
36043	HOPE HULL	57.4	51.2	41.4	47.3	0.1	0.1	0.8	1.2	6.0	6.3	6.7	6.3	4.8	24.0	30.9	13.6	1.4	77.1	42.0	48.4	51.6
36046	LAPINE	74.8	70.3	23.8	27.8	0.1	0.1	0.9	1.5	6.3	6.2	6.6	6.6	5.0	25.7	29.2	13.0	1.5	76.8	40.1	49.9	50.1
36047	LETOHATCHEE	38.5	35.1	60.7	63.9	0.1	0.2	0.6	1.0	7.6	7.8	7.7	7.5	5.8	23.1	28.0	10.8	1.6	72.2	37.4	47.6	52.4
36048	LOUISVILLE	41.3	38.5	56.7	58.5	0.0	0.0	2.2	3.6	6.1	6.0	6.1	7.0	6.1	25.2	28.1	13.2	2.1	77.4	39.2	45.8	54.2
36049	LUVERNE	72.3	69.5	26.4	28.9	0.1	0.2	0.5	0.8	5.8	5.9	6.3	6.5	5.5	23.3	27.5	15.6	3.7	78.0	42.1	47.0	53.0
36051	MARBURY	82.6	80.6	14.9	16.5	0.3	0.4	1.9	3.2	6.6	6.6	6.9	7.1	5.9	26.9	27.3	11.0	1.6	75.3	37.9	49.9	50.1
36052	MATHEWS	59.6	54.0	39.4	44.7	0.3	0.4	0.9	1.4	5.6	6.3	6.6	7.3	4.8	24.1	32.7	11.2	1.3	76.7	41.4	50.7	49.3
36053	MIDWAY	19.4	17.9	79.6	80.9	0.1	0.1	0.6	0.9	5.7	5.7	6.0	7.4	7.2	26.8	27.1	11.4	2.8	78.3	38.4	50.7	49.3
36054	MILLBROOK	78.4	76.1	19.1	20.5	0.5	0.7	1.3	2.1	8.4	8.0	7.8	7.5	6.5	30.3	23.9	7.0	0.7	71.2	32.9	47.9	52.1
36061	PEROTE	37.5	35.2	61.4	63.4	0.0	0.0	1.2	1.9	6.9	6.9	7.4	6.9	5.1	22.2	27.8	13.9	2.8	73.1	40.4	47.2	52.8
36064	PIKE ROAD	57.2	54.0	41.3	43.9	0.7	1.2	0.5	0.9	7.2	7.6	7.6	7.4	5.3	25.3	29.8	9.0	0.8	72.8	37.7	48.7	51.3
36066	PRATTVILLE	89.6	87.1	7.7	9.1	0.9	1.2	1.9	3.2	7.4	7.2	7.2	7.3	5.9	28.0	26.3	9.7	0.9	73.7	35.7	47.9	52.1
36067	PRATTVILLE	77.7	74.7	20.1	22.5	0.4	0.5	1.2	2.0	7.0	7.0	7.0	7.4	6.2	27.3	26.7	10.2	1.2	74.5	36.4	48.2	51.8
36069	RAMER	57.7	49.0	41.5	50.0	0.1	0.1	0.5	0.6	5.3	5.6	5.8	5.9	5.3	23.9	31.2	15.3	1.7	79.7	43.5	49.4	50.6
36071	RUTLEDGE	73.1	70.0	25.1	27.3	0.5	0.7	0.9	1.3	6.0	6.2	6.3	6.3	4.9	26.1	28.3	13.8	2.0	77.3	40.5	48.0	52.0
36075	SHORTER	19.0	16.1	80.1	82.8	0.0	0.1	0.2	0.4	6.8	6.9	8.1	8.2	5.6	24.1	27.6	10.5	2.2	72.8	37.3	46.0	54.0
36078	TALLASSEE	77.7	75.5	20.8	22.6	0.2	0.3	1.0	1.6	7.0	6.8	6.9	6.9	5.7	25.2	26.5	12.7	2.4	75.1	38.7	48.4	51.6
36079	TROY	71.6	68.5	25.5	27.9	0.2	0.3	1.4	2.2	7.3	6.8	6.3	6.1	7.5	31.7	23.4	9.6	1.2	76.0	33.2	49.1	50.9
36080	TITUS	88.1	86.3	10.5	12.0	0.1	0.2	0.7	1.1	4.9	5.3	5.7	5.9	3.4	21.6	34.7	16.7	1.8	80.4	46.9	51.1	48.9
36081	TROY	53.3	50.8	44.0	45.9	0.6	0.9	1.1	1.8	6.7	6.5	6.4	9.4	12.6	24.1	22.0	10.2	2.1	76.6	31.1	46.5	53.5
36082	TROY	67.3	63.5	29.6	31.7	1.2	1.9	1.5	2.9	0.3	0.3	0.0	39.1	52.2	3.5	0.3	1.6	2.6	99.4	21.0	44.2	55.8
36083	TUSKEGEE	7.5	6.9	91.4	91.7	0.2	0.2	0.8	0.9	6.8	7.2	7.3	9.0	8.1	21.1	25.2	12.7	2.6	74.0	35.9	45.7	54.3
36088	TUSKEGEE INSTITUTE	2.5	2.2	94.9	94.5	1.3	1.8	0.6	0.6	4.8	4.7	4.3	19.2	22.3	18.8	14.5	9.4	2.0	83.6	23.8	46.3	53.7
36089	UNION SPRINGS	25.5	24.8	72.7	72.9	0.2	0.3	3.1	4.9	6.5	6.6	6.5	7.3	7.9	28.9	24.3	9.7	2.3	75.8	35.2	54.8	45.2
36091	VERBENA	84.0	81.8	14.3	15.9	0.2	0.3	1.2	1.9	7.0	7.1	7.3	7.0	5.5	25.4	27.8	11.5	1.3	74.2	37.6	51.0	49.0
36092	WETUMPKA	68.7	65.0	28.5	31.2	0.5	0.7	1.4	2.2	6.1	6.0	6.0	6.3	7.4	32.2	24.9	9.4	1.8	78.2	36.3	50.5	49.5
36093	WETUMPKA	90.2	88.4	7.7	8.8	0.7	1.0	1.0	1.6	5.9	6.6	7.3	6.6	4.0	23.4	33.2	11.9	1.1	76.0	42.5	49.3	50.7
36104	MONTGOMERY	14.0	11.6	85.0	87.2	0.2	0.2	0.7	0.8	8.3	7.5	6.4	9.7	9.0	25.8	20.8	10.0	2.5	73.2	31.5	48.2	51.8
36105	MONTGOMERY	11.6	10.1	87.3	88.6	0.2	0.2	0.7	0.8	6.8	7.2	7.5	8.1	6.9	24.5	26.1	11.3	1.6	73.6	36.0	45.7	54.3
36106	MONTGOMERY	67.3	63.0	30.7	34.2	0.8	1.1	1.0	1.6	5.0	5.1	5.4	11.3	11.1	22.6	25.1	11.8	2.6	81.4	36.3	46.5	53.5
36107	MONTGOMERY	65.5	58.9	31.8	37.5	0.8	1.1	1.1	1.8	7.0	6.5	6.3	6.8	7.3	29.2	24.1	9.7	3.0	76.2	35.9	46.7	53.3
36108	MONTGOMERY	15.7	13.7	82.8	84.6	0.3	0.3	0.9	1.1	7.8	8.1	7.9	8.9	6.8	22.7	24.9	11.2	1.6	70.8	33.8	45.4	54.6
36109	MONTGOMERY	89.9	86.4	7.7	10.1	1.1	1.6	1.0	1.8	5.3	5.3	5.6	6.3	6.0	23.0	28.9	16.6	3.1	80.2	43.8	46.6	53.4
36110	MONTGOMERY	45.1	38.8	51.9	57.3	1.4	1.8	0.9	1.4	6.9	7.2	7.1	7.5	6.8	27.1	24.8	11.1	1.4	74.3	36.0	47.7	52.3
36111	MONTGOMERY	62.6	56.7	35.3	40.5	0.7	1.0	1.4	2.1	5.9	6.1	6.4	6.3	6.9	22.6	26.0	15.7	4.1	77.8	41.5	45.2	54.8
36112	MONTGOMERY	62.7	55.1	31.2	37.3	1.3	1.8	3.4	5.4	3.6	3.4	1.9	9.9	37.3	37.1	6.7	0.2	0.1	90.4	24.2	74.8	25.2
36115	MONTGOMERY	63.6	55.2	29.1	35.0	3.9	5.1	3.3	5.2	10.5	10.1	9.0	8.9	14.8	42.6	3.7	0.2	0.0	65.9	23.8	53.9	46.1
36116	MONTGOMERY	29.5	25.6	67.8	71.2	1.0	1.3	1.3	1.8	8.2	7.9	7.6	7.7	7.9	29.8	23.0	6.5	1.4	71.6	31.7	45.8	54.2
36117	MONTGOMERY	69.2	64.3	26.4	30.0	2.4	3.1	1.7	2.7	6.7	6.5	6.4	6.5	7.0	30.6	26.3	8.8	1.1	76.5	36.4	49.8	50.2
36201	ANNISTON	53.0	50.7	45.1	46.9	0.2	0.3	1.2	1.9	6.6	6.8	6.7	7.1	5.9	24.6	26.8	13.3	2.2	75.6	39.3	47.3	52.7
36203	OXFORD	82.7	79.5	14.2	16.3	0.6	0.7	2.8	4.4	6.1	6.2	6.4	6.5	5.4	27.1	28.8	11.6	1.8	77.3	39.8	48.0	52.0
36205	ANNISTON	84.2	79.7	0.0	0.0	15.8	20.3	0.0	0.0	6.2	5.8	6.2	6.4	5.2	22.7	27.6	16.9	3.2	78.7	43.2	48.7	51.3
36206	ANNISTON	79.8	75.8	16.9	19.9	1.0	1.3	1.9	3.1	6.4	6.1	6.1	6.4	5.8	26.8	27.2	13.8	1.4	77.5	39.0	47.6	52.4
36207	ANNISTON	79.9	77.8	17.8	19.2	0.9	1.1	1.5	2.6	5.4	5.6	6.0	5.8	4.6	23.7	29.7	15.8	3.4	79.4	44.2	47.7	52.3
36250	ALEXANDRIA	91.2	89.0	7.0	8.6	0.5	0.7	0.6	1.0	6.5	6.7	6.9	6.5	5.2	28.9	28.9	9.6	0.8	75.9	37.7	48.5	51.5
36251	ASHLAND	85.6	84.9	13.0	13.6	0.1	0.1	2.1	2.2	6.2	5.9	6.5	6.6	5.3	24.9	26.8	14.5	3.4	77.5	41.2	48.6	51.4
36255	CRAGFORD	96.7	96.7	1.5	1.5	0.2	0.2	1.0	1.0	6.8	6.6	7.0	6.4	5.4	27.3	26.4	12.4	1.7	75.6	38.2	51.5	48.5
36256	DAVISTON	83.2	80.1	15.8	18.6	0.1	0.1	0.8	1.1	6.0	5.9	6.3	6.6	5.7	26.7	28.0	13.0	1.8	77.8	40.6	48.1	51.9
36258	DELTA	93.2	92.3	4.3	4.6	0.1	0.1	2.1	3.3	5.5	5.8	6.0	6.1	5.2	26.9	29.0	13.7	1.6	78.7	41.4	49.7	50.3
36260	EASTABOGA	85.2	82.6	12.6	14.6	0.1	0.1	0.9	1.5	5.9	6.2	6.7	6.3	5.1	27.5	30.2	10.9	1.2	77.3	39.7	49.6	50.4
36262	FRUITHURST	97.4	96.9	1.2	1.3	0.1	0.1	0.3	0.5	6.5	6.5	6.8	6.6	5.2	26.6	29.4	11.3	1.1	76.3	39.3	50.1	49.9
	ALABAMA	71.1	69.3	26.0	26.7	0.7	1.0	1.7	2.8	6.6	6.6	6.6	6.9	6.6	26.4	26.7	11.7	1.8	76.1	37.8	48.6	51.4
	UNITED STATES	75.1	72.0	12.3	12.7	3.8	4.6	12.5	15.7	6.8	6.7	6.6	7.1	6.9	27.0	26.0	10.9	1.9	75.7	36.9	49.2	50.8

ZIP CODE #	POST OFFICE NAME	2009 Per Capita Income	2009 HH Income Base	2009 HOUSEHOLD INCOME DISTRIBUTION (%) Less than $25,000	$25,000 to $49,999	$50,000 to $99,999	$100,000 to $149,999	$150,000 or More	MEDIAN HOUSEHOLD INCOME 2009	2014	2009 National Centile	2009 State Centile	2009 Home Value Base	2009 HOME VALUE DISTRIBUTION (%) Less than $50,000	$50,000 to $89,999	$90,000 to $174,999	$175,000 to $399,999	$400,000 or More	2009 Median Home Value
35972	GALLANT	18480	346	30.6	30.3	33.8	3.8	1.4	38266	39814	27	60	294	26.5	22.1	40.5	8.8	2.0	92667
35973	GAYLESVILLE	14853	1282	40.1	35.0	23.0	1.4	0.5	32112	33757	12	29	1108	28.2	28.1	34.7	8.0	0.9	81667
35974	GERALDINE	16984	603	39.6	34.5	21.2	3.8	0.8	31964	32678	11	29	480	21.9	21.5	42.1	12.3	2.3	97619
35975	GROVEOAK	18174	469	29.0	32.4	33.9	3.2	1.5	40214	39873	33	67	406	26.8	11.6	42.1	16.3	3.2	110674
35976	GUNTERSVILLE	21013	7074	31.0	30.9	29.2	5.8	3.1	37843	38858	26	58	5324	15.8	17.5	38.3	19.9	8.5	122546
35978	HENAGAR	16723	2062	32.9	33.0	29.5	3.6	0.9	35791	36592	20	48	1709	24.9	26.3	38.5	10.1	0.2	88304
35979	HIGDON	17383	476	33.8	29.6	32.1	2.9	1.5	36286	37254	21	50	401	33.9	30.7	26.7	8.7	0.0	71250
35980	HORTON	15332	1713	35.3	33.5	26.8	3.3	1.1	33795	35842	15	38	1354	29.5	22.2	34.0	11.8	2.4	86806
35981	IDER	16876	1057	35.0	30.7	30.4	2.7	1.2	34177	35134	16	40	859	30.2	27.5	33.4	8.4	0.6	80076
35983	LEESBURG	18840	1400	31.5	35.4	27.9	3.3	1.9	37921	38485	26	58	1198	27.6	24.9	32.3	13.0	2.2	86429
35984	MENTONE	17215	860	36.4	32.4	26.0	4.8	0.3	33763	34930	15	38	712	26.4	25.6	33.4	10.7	3.9	86818
35986	RAINSVILLE	17682	3084	35.7	28.5	30.4	4.2	1.2	35815	36602	20	49	2429	20.9	23.3	40.2	12.9	2.7	97818
35987	STEELE	18658	1153	28.6	34.6	30.4	4.2	2.1	39527	39493	31	64	955	24.2	25.8	36.5	10.8	2.7	90094
35988	SYLVANIA	16387	722	34.5	32.5	29.5	2.2	1.2	35711	36366	20	48	588	24.8	27.9	35.9	10.2	1.2	86000
35989	VALLEY HEAD	17392	1288	33.1	34.1	27.3	3.7	1.9	35129	35830	18	45	1047	26.6	26.6	31.6	12.3	2.9	84924
36003	AUTAUGAVILLE	15006	820	43.5	29.8	24.4	1.1	1.2	30073	31670	8	22	689	40.3	29.8	19.3	8.0	2.6	59925
36005	BANKS	16371	519	41.2	37.2	19.7	1.0	1.0	33051	35406	13	34	427	29.0	36.1	20.6	13.3	0.9	70104
36006	BILLINGSLEY	16894	608	35.5	28.6	32.1	2.6	1.2	35761	37524	20	48	527	34.5	23.0	28.7	11.6	2.3	74423
36009	BRANTLEY	16609	1217	45.9	32.7	17.0	2.1	2.3	27283	27997	5	16	945	35.8	29.3	24.0	9.7	1.2	67986
36010	BRUNDIDGE	14355	2130	52.3	28.4	16.1	2.5	0.8	23638	25265	3	9	1592	31.4	39.7	21.6	5.8	1.4	65275
36013	CECIL	23316	208	33.7	13.0	26.0	24.5	2.9	52624	52623	67	92	175	24.0	15.4	14.9	36.0	9.7	119318
36016	CLAYTON	13259	1651	50.2	26.2	20.2	2.1	1.3	24848	26332	3	12	1280	36.9	34.4	23.0	4.9	0.8	63981
36017	CLIO	12514	710	58.2	21.3	16.8	2.1	1.7	20663	21452	2	4	570	49.1	25.4	18.9	4.6	1.9	50980
36020	COOSADA	16671	500	32.2	30.2	32.2	3.2	2.2	40492	41599	34	68	411	32.4	17.8	36.5	11.9	1.5	89821
36022	DEATSVILLE	22469	4373	15.8	27.4	45.1	9.1	2.6	55370	56675	72	93	3716	16.3	13.2	42.1	26.2	2.1	129106
36024	ECLECTIC	20489	2367	26.1	31.1	34.6	5.7	2.5	42835	44457	42	75	1984	15.0	21.2	34.4	20.1	9.3	115335
36025	ELMORE	17126	1160	13.6	26.9	43.1	12.2	4.1	58343	59526	76	94	1020	12.2	13.4	47.8	26.0	0.6	130508
36026	EQUALITY	29531	505	24.8	24.2	34.3	8.7	8.1	51506	52319	65	91	445	9.2	16.0	26.5	32.1	16.2	167788
[illegible]27	EUFAULA	17578	6692	42.6	24.6	25.8	4.8	2.2	32172	33402	12	30	4622	20.9	28.6	32.5	15.5	2.5	90878
[illegible]28	DOZIER	15179	366	49.5	30.6	16.4	1.9	1.6	25316	26119	3	13	270	35.2	30.0	28.9	5.6	0.4	68095
[illegible]29	FITZPATRICK	16407	388	37.9	29.6	29.4	1.8	1.3	36208	37239	21	50	337	32.3	22.3	30.3	12.5	2.7	80882
[illegible]030	FOREST HOME	13451	380	46.8	26.8	21.8	3.4	1.1	26672	26646	4	15	321	35.8	28.0	20.6	14.6	0.9	71667
[illegible]031	FORT DAVIS	14694	40	47.5	25.0	22.5	5.0	0.0	30000	32372	8	21	32	37.5	25.0	31.3	6.3	0.0	60000
[illegible]6032	FORT DEPOSIT	14752	1074	48.8	22.5	23.3	3.3	2.1	25789	27061	4	13	856	39.5	26.5	25.7	6.2	2.1	63725
[illegible]6033	GEORGIANA	16390	1753	47.5	28.6	20.0	2.4	1.5	26936	27745	5	16	1384	45.5	28.8	16.8	7.9	0.9	55082
36034	GLENWOOD	19545	270	36.7	28.1	31.1	2.6	1.5	37058	38292	24	55	230	37.0	27.0	21.3	10.9	3.9	65500
36035	GOSHEN	18555	940	34.6	29.7	30.6	4.3	0.9	37019	38791	24	54	794	30.4	31.1	26.6	10.1	1.9	75636
36036	GRADY	17681	917	41.4	24.2	30.9	1.5	2.0	33351	35363	14	36	772	29.0	27.1	32.6	9.6	1.7	82295
36037	GREENVILLE	17168	5442	45.5	27.8	20.9	3.6	2.1	28836	29314	6	19	4013	30.1	28.9	29.8	10.0	1.2	75204
36038	GANTT	18301	1482	37.2	27.7	30.0	3.2	1.9	32456	33644	12	31	1231	25.7	28.6	29.9	13.2	2.6	79741
36039	HARDAWAY	12231	152	57.9	23.7	15.8	2.6	0.0	20838	21284	2	4	116	37.1	22.4	30.2	9.5	0.9	66250
36040	HAYNEVILLE	11502	1615	54.9	26.0	16.8	1.7	0.6	21407	22502	2	6	1277	41.3	30.7	20.0	5.9	2.2	58139
36041	HIGHLAND HOME	16151	446	38.3	33.2	24.0	2.9	1.6	33105	34567	13	35	384	33.6	33.3	26.3	6.0	0.8	71333
36042	HONORAVILLE	15847	444	36.0	33.8	26.6	3.4	0.2	35163	35875	18	46	369	32.2	29.3	29.8	7.0	1.6	74259
36043	HOPE HULL	20793	1353	30.2	30.7	31.3	4.9	3.0	40689	41635	35	69	1134	32.4	20.4	27.9	18.1	1.3	83542
36046	LAPINE	16955	688	34.3	30.7	31.5	2.3	1.2	37441	38433	25	56	581	29.9	28.2	31.3	8.4	2.1	79205
36047	LETOHATCHEE	15167	771	44.1	29.1	22.6	3.0	1.3	29192	31025	7	20	624	36.7	27.1	23.4	10.7	2.1	65116
36048	LOUISVILLE	13079	688	55.1	23.7	17.0	2.8	1.5	22785	23761	2	8	582	41.8	28.5	22.3	5.3	2.1	61463
36049	LUVERNE	17289	2137	43.1	27.0	24.7	4.2	1.1	30084	30903	8	22	1470	24.7	33.8	28.8	11.0	1.7	82188
36051	MARBURY	17034	842	29.5	28.7	37.6	2.6	1.5	40869	42760	36	70	738	31.4	22.6	30.2	12.7	3.0	80909
36052	MATHEWS	24808	311	27.3	24.4	29.9	12.5	5.8	46848	49104	54	85	250	26.4	22.0	13.6	20.8	17.2	95714
36053	MIDWAY	14661	954	55.9	24.3	14.5	3.8	1.6	21300	22224	2	5	755	43.6	26.2	20.1	6.5	3.6	56929
36054	MILLBROOK	19752	4899	18.5	31.9	41.1	6.8	1.7	49621	50859	60	88	3800	11.0	15.2	52.5	20.1	1.2	123336
36061	PEROTE	12311	96	55.2	30.2	12.5	2.1	0.0	22231	22437	2	7	75	33.3	10.7	44.0	10.7	1.3	102604
36064	PIKE ROAD	29696	1900	17.6	22.3	31.7	17.9	10.5	61211	61748	79	95	1705	13.0	19.5	23.4	27.0	17.1	152567
36066	PRATTVILLE	27690	6706	13.2	21.2	44.5	16.2	4.9	63753	66463	82	96	5036	3.4	8.6	50.3	35.2	2.4	151997
36067	PRATTVILLE	20287	9426	26.5	26.7	38.5	5.9	2.4	46659	48195	53	85	7592	24.1	21.1	33.1	19.2	2.5	99840
36069	RAMER	18809	1004	36.1	26.3	31.1	3.9	2.7	35084	36541	18	44	819	26.9	33.0	23.6	12.6	4.0	76250
36071	RUTLEDGE	16309	346	42.2	28.6	24.0	4.9	0.3	33188	35143	14	35	276	29.3	34.1	22.1	12.3	2.2	74063
36075	SHORTER	12875	861	52.3	23.2	22.0	2.2	0.3	23587	24428	3	9	709	29.6	24.7	33.3	10.9	1.6	83646
36078	TALLASSEE	18182	5263	37.0	28.3	28.4	4.1	2.1	35290	36962	19	46	3879	24.7	25.2	34.6	13.6	1.8	90177
36079	TROY	17957	4122	40.0	28.7	26.2	3.1	2.0	32804	35179	13	33	2976	32.3	21.4	29.1	14.9	2.4	81406
36080	TITUS	22861	1049	20.6	29.3	45.1	3.4	1.6	50083	51419	61	89	913	7.7	18.5	33.0	33.1	7.8	151806
36081	TROY	16633	5498	48.2	24.4	21.2	4.5	1.7	26835	29292	5	15	3159	25.6	25.0	31.8	14.4	3.1	89049
36082	TROY	10888	0	0.0	0.0	0.0	0.0	0.0	0	0	0	0	0	0.0	0.0	0.0	0.0	0.0	0
36083	TUSKEGEE	15280	4339	51.6	25.7	18.2	3.5	1.0	23686	25244	3	9	2647	19.0	33.5	39.9	7.1	0.5	87031
36088	TUSKEGEE INSTITUTE	15061	1360	51.5	22.9	19.8	3.9	2.0	23718	25820	3	9	709	16.2	34.7	41.9	7.2	0.0	88860
36089	UNION SPRINGS	12646	3066	52.5	28.2	16.1	2.7	0.6	22989	23664	2	8	2201	33.3	28.1	29.1	6.7	2.8	74185
36091	VERBENA	16491	1378	33.7	36.3	25.8	3.3	0.9	35521	37490	19	47	1142	29.2	20.0	27.7	18.3	4.9	91961
36092	WETUMPKA	18502	7228	26.3	34.4	32.2	5.2	1.9	41838	42761	39	72	5749	20.1	21.9	37.0	18.7	2.3	106512
36093	WETUMPKA	31393	3387	10.2	19.8	43.5	17.5	9.0	70946	71058	87	99	3062	6.1	6.7	29.8	49.4	8.0	190833
36104	MONTGOMERY	11807	4237	65.9	21.8	10.1	1.3	0.9	15775	15575	1	2	1172	35.7	25.3	28.0	9.0	2.1	65714
36105	MONTGOMERY	13999	5220	44.9	30.4	20.3	3.6	0.8	29373	30767	7	20	3244	23.0	45.3	23.2	7.6	0.9	70590
36106	MONTGOMERY	29781	6053	17.1	29.0	35.3	11.6	7.1	55209	54311	72	93	4031	2.6	8.8	48.5	33.1	7.1	154571
36107	MONTGOMERY	17328	4174	38.3	35.9	22.8	2.2	0.7	33124	35123	14	35	2068	7.7	66.0	24.9	1.0	0.4	76476
36108	MONTGOMERY	12750	8888	50.9	27.7	18.3	2.4	0.7	24272	25582	3	11	5193	30.5	46.8	20.9	1.6	0.3	68876
36109	MONTGOMERY	24939	10822	20.2	29.9	39.4	8.8	1.6	49859	50137	61	89	8508	4.2	16.5	65.3	13.1	0.8	120399
36110	MONTGOMERY	14352	4981	38.9	37.0	21.9	1.8	0.4	31053	32072	10	24	3436	22.1	55.7	21.3	0.6	0.3	67258
36111	MONTGOMERY	29267	5325	23.6	26.6	33.2	10.4	6.2	49764	50288	60	88	3461	0.6	17.8	48.6	25.1	7.8	140269
36112	MONTGOMERY	12840	448	27.2	36.8	29.9	5.4	0.7	41209	42049	37	71	2	0.0	100.0	0.0	0.0	0.0	85000
36115	MONTGOMERY	17016	197	4.1	23.9	70.1	2.0	0.0	62186	61763	80	96	0	0.0	0.0	0.0	0.0	0.0	0
36116	MONTGOMERY	20167	15529	28.6	31.9	29.8	7.4	2.3	41980	43080	39	72	8950	10.8	27.0	49.0	11.9	1.3	104488
36117	MONTGOMERY	33566	19102	14.1	24.0	38.1	14.5	9.4	61263	61036	79	95	12920	2.0	6.4	45.3	36.7	9.5	164471
36201	ANNISTON	14533	8281	50.7	28.2	17.6	2.5	1.0	24470	26032	3	11	5366	38.2	39.0	19.5	2.8	0.4	60468
36203	OXFORD	20729	7056	26.9	28.7	36.7	6.0	1.8	44485	45518	47	81	5210	13.0	24.1	46.3	14.8	1.8	106805
36205	ANNISTON	17974	217	0.0	100.0	0.0	0.0	0.0	40921	40355	36	70	76	0.0	28.9	50.0	18.4	2.6	113462
36206	ANNISTON	22181	4750	24.5	33.1	34.4	5.8	2.3	44121	45359	46	80	3473	18.3	30.7	40.5	9.7	0.8	91172
36207	ANNISTON	25568	8169	27.1	29.3	31.8	7.4	4.3	42999	44306	42	76	5864	13.5	19.5	40.3	21.7	5.0	123922
36250	ALEXANDRIA	20565	1608	21.4	33.6	37.1	5.7	2.2	47201	47540	55	86	1367	14.4	19.1	51.5	14.1	0.9	110410
36251	ASHLAND	16326	2219	37.1	34.9	24.5	3.1	0.4	31746	33094	11	27	1634	29.3	27.2	33.0	9.8	0.7	78374
36255	CRAGFORD	15779	442	34.2	37.6	25.3	2.3	0.7	33566	35282	15	37	376	22.6	37.2	31.6	8.2	0.3	76286
36256	DAVISTON	16568	621	30.9	38.6	26.7	3.1	0.6	35789	35738	20	48	501	27.7	37.9	28.7	5.2	0.4	72556
36258	DELTA	18235	741	27.1	39.0	30.0	3.2	0.7	37331	37377	25	56	642	28.3	23.7	36.9	8.7	2.3	87045
36260	EASTABOGA	19954	1719	28.2	32.2	33.4	4.7	1.6	40120	41006	33	66	1449	30.0	28.2	36.6	4.7	0.6	82922
36262	FRUITHURST	17707	560	30.7	36.1	29.6	2.7	0.9	38692	38902	29	62	456	33.1	26.3	24.8	14.5	1.3	76154
	ALABAMA	21187		31.4	27.9	30.6	6.9	3.2	40822	42202				18.1	22.4	35.8	19.6	4.0	107730
	UNITED STATES	27277		20.9	24.4	35.3	11.7	7.6	54719	56938				9.3	13.1	31.6	32.6	13.5	162279

ZIP CODE #	POST OFFICE NAME	FINANCIAL SERVICES: Auto Loan	Home Loan	Invest-ments	Retire-ment Plans	THE HOME: Home Improvements: Home Repair	Lawn & Garden	Furnishings: Comput-ers & Hard-ware-Personal	Major Appli-ances	TV, Radio, Sound Equip-ment	Furni-ture	ENTERTAINMENT: Dine out/ Carry out	Sports Equip-ment	Fees & Tickets	Toys & Games	Travel	Cable TV	PERSONAL: Apparel & Services	Auto Repairs	Health Insur-ance	Pets & Supplies
35972	GALLANT	84	61	72	59	61	81	63	74	70	61	68	57	50	72	58	76	46	70	78	90
35973	GAYLESVILLE	67	48	55	47	48	63	50	58	55	49	54	45	40	58	45	60	36	55	61	71
35974	GERALDINE	72	52	60	50	52	69	54	63	60	53	59	48	43	62	49	65	39	60	66	76
35975	GROVEOAK	82	59	71	58	60	79	62	72	68	60	67	55	50	70	57	74	45	68	76	87
35976	GUNTERSVILLE	83	66	79	66	68	83	69	79	74	66	73	58	60	74	67	79	49	75	83	93
35978	HENAGAR	78	56	64	54	55	74	58	67	64	56	63	52	46	67	53	70	42	64	71	82
35979	HIGDON	82	59	68	57	59	78	61	71	68	60	67	55	49	71	56	74	45	67	75	87
35980	HORTON	74	53	61	52	53	71	56	65	62	54	60	50	45	64	50	67	41	61	68	79
35981	IDER	76	55	63	53	54	72	57	66	63	55	62	51	46	66	52	69	42	63	70	80
35983	LEESBURG	80	57	66	56	57	76	59	69	66	58	65	53	48	69	54	72	43	66	73	84
35984	MENTONE	73	53	68	51	53	72	54	66	60	52	59	50	44	61	52	66	39	62	69	80
35986	RAINSVILLE	76	56	68	55	57	75	58	69	64	55	62	53	47	65	55	69	42	64	72	83
35987	STEELE	86	61	81	60	63	85	63	78	70	60	69	59	51	71	61	77	46	72	81	93
35988	SYLVANIA	75	54	62	52	53	71	56	65	62	54	61	50	45	65	51	68	41	62	69	79
35989	VALLEY HEAD	82	59	67	57	59	78	61	71	68	59	66	55	49	71	56	74	45	67	75	86
36003	AUTAUGAVILLE	71	48	65	46	48	69	51	62	58	49	56	48	39	59	47	64	38	59	66	76
36005	BANKS	73	52	73	51	54	74	54	68	60	51	59	51	43	60	53	66	39	63	71	81
36006	BILLINGSLEY	79	55	67	54	55	75	58	68	65	56	63	53	46	67	53	71	43	65	72	84
36009	BRANTLEY	70	47	66	45	47	68	50	62	57	47	55	48	38	58	46	63	37	58	65	75
36010	BRUNDIDGE	58	40	52	38	39	56	43	51	49	42	48	39	34	50	40	54	32	49	55	63
36013	CECIL	89	94	86	96	91	96	85	91	85	85	86	71	88	87	89	87	59	87	90	107
36016	CLAYTON	65	44	61	41	43	63	46	57	53	45	52	44	36	54	43	58	34	54	60	70
36017	CLIO	63	41	61	39	41	62	44	55	51	42	49	43	33	51	41	57	33	52	58	68
36020	COOSADA	85	60	74	58	60	82	63	74	70	61	69	57	50	73	58	77	46	71	78	91
36022	DEATSVILLE	100	91	84	89	88	93	87	92	89	89	89	71	81	93	83	90	61	88	90	109
36024	ECLECTIC	90	71	84	69	72	87	71	82	76	70	75	61	61	78	69	81	51	78	84	98
36025	ELMORE	108	102	94	98	98	100	95	100	95	99	96	77	90	100	92	96	66	96	95	117
36026	EQUALITY	111	95	138	93	105	121	93	114	98	93	97	80	86	93	100	105	65	106	118	132
36027	EUFAULA	73	56	62	55	55	70	58	65	64	58	63	49	50	66	54	69	43	64	70	79
36028	DOZIER	64	42	61	40	42	63	45	56	52	43	50	44	34	53	42	58	33	53	60	69
36029	FITZPATRICK	72	51	73	49	53	73	53	67	59	49	58	50	42	58	52	65	38	62	70	80
36030	FOREST HOME	68	46	63	44	46	66	49	60	55	47	54	46	37	57	45	61	36	56	63	73
36031	FORT DAVIS	67	44	65	41	43	66	47	59	54	44	53	46	35	55	44	60	35	55	62	72
36032	FORT DEPOSIT	66	47	61	46	47	65	51	60	58	49	56	44	42	57	48	64	38	58	66	73
36033	GEORGIANA	68	46	67	44	47	68	49	62	56	46	54	47	37	56	46	62	36	58	65	75
36034	GLENWOOD	81	55	76	53	56	79	58	72	66	55	64	55	45	67	55	73	43	67	76	87
36035	GOSHEN	77	54	78	52	56	78	56	71	63	53	62	54	44	63	55	70	41	66	75	86
36036	GRADY	76	53	77	51	54	77	55	70	62	52	61	53	43	62	54	69	40	65	73	84
36037	GREENVILLE	71	53	65	51	52	71	55	64	63	54	61	48	47	63	52	69	41	63	70	78
36038	GANTT	77	56	74	55	57	77	58	71	64	54	63	54	47	65	56	70	42	66	74	85
36039	HARDAWAY	56	39	52	37	38	55	41	49	47	40	46	39	33	48	38	52	31	48	53	61
36040	HAYNEVILLE	58	38	56	36	38	57	40	51	47	38	46	40	30	47	38	52	30	48	54	63
36041	HIGHLAND HOME	75	51	67	49	51	72	54	65	61	52	60	51	42	63	50	67	40	62	69	80
36042	HONORAVILLE	72	50	66	48	50	70	52	64	59	50	58	49	41	60	49	65	38	60	67	78
36043	HOPE HULL	90	70	86	68	70	89	70	83	77	68	76	62	60	78	68	83	51	78	86	100
36046	LAPINE	76	54	70	53	55	75	56	68	63	54	62	52	45	64	53	69	41	64	72	83
36047	LETOHATCHEE	67	48	62	46	48	66	51	60	58	50	57	45	42	58	48	64	38	59	66	74
36048	LOUISVILLE	62	40	60	38	40	61	43	54	50	41	48	42	32	50	40	55	32	51	57	67
36049	LUVERNE	69	49	69	47	50	71	53	65	59	48	57	49	41	59	51	65	38	61	71	78
36051	MARBURY	81	65	69	63	64	77	64	72	69	65	69	54	56	72	60	74	46	69	74	87
36052	MATHEWS	100	85	105	84	86	104	82	96	87	81	86	73	75	88	83	93	59	90	97	115
36053	MIDWAY	62	41	60	38	41	61	44	55	50	41	49	43	33	51	41	56	32	52	58	67
36054	MILLBROOK	88	82	72	80	79	79	79	80	80	83	80	61	75	84	75	80	55	79	78	95
36061	PEROTE	52	34	50	32	34	51	36	45	41	34	40	35	27	42	34	46	27	43	48	56
36064	PIKE ROAD	114	127	115	127	124	118	113	116	111	120	112	88	121	113	117	109	79	112	112	135
36066	PRATTVILLE	109	115	98	112	109	104	103	106	101	109	102	82	105	106	103	99	71	101	99	122
36067	PRATTVILLE	85	78	72	76	76	81	75	79	78	77	78	60	72	80	73	80	53	77	80	94
36069	RAMER	80	57	80	54	57	80	58	73	66	56	64	56	47	66	57	72	43	68	76	88
36071	RUTLEDGE	71	48	73	47	50	72	53	66	58	46	56	52	40	57	51	64	37	61	70	80
36075	SHORTER	63	41	61	39	41	62	44	55	50	42	49	43	33	51	41	56	33	52	59	68
36078	TALLASSEE	77	58	67	57	58	75	61	70	67	59	66	53	52	68	57	72	44	67	74	84
36079	TROY	71	55	60	54	53	63	60	63	63	60	63	50	52	65	55	65	43	63	63	76
36080	TITUS	91	70	106	68	75	95	71	89	76	66	75	66	59	74	73	82	49	82	90	105
36081	TROY	58	48	46	48	47	53	56	53	58	53	57	41	50	58	49	60	40	56	57	64
36082	TROY	0	0	0	0	0	0	0	0	0	0	0	0	0	0	0	0	0	0	0	0
36083	TUSKEGEE	54	43	43	44	41	52	48	49	53	48	53	37	44	53	44	57	36	51	55	61
36088	TUSKEGEE INSTITUTE	56	45	44	47	44	52	55	52	59	52	57	39	49	58	49	61	40	56	59	63
36089	UNION SPRINGS	56	38	51	37	38	55	42	50	48	41	47	38	33	48	39	53	31	48	54	61
36091	VERBENA	74	53	65	51	53	71	55	65	61	53	60	50	44	62	51	66	40	61	69	79
36092	WETUMPKA	82	66	71	65	66	80	68	75	72	66	71	57	59	74	64	77	48	72	79	90
36093	WETUMPKA	116	132	119	136	130	129	117	123	115	119	116	95	127	117	125	115	81	118	121	143
36104	MONTGOMERY	37	27	26	29	26	31	36	32	40	35	39	24	32	38	31	42	27	36	38	40
36105	MONTGOMERY	54	47	45	47	45	54	49	50	55	50	54	36	48	54	47	59	37	52	58	62
36106	MONTGOMERY	95	105	104	107	105	103	101	100	99	103	100	76	107	99	105	99	71	100	101	117
36107	MONTGOMERY	55	48	44	49	46	53	55	52	57	51	56	41	51	57	50	59	39	55	57	63
36108	MONTGOMERY	50	41	41	42	40	48	45	45	49	45	49	33	42	48	42	52	33	47	51	56
36109	MONTGOMERY	76	82	78	82	82	86	78	80	80	78	80	59	82	79	81	83	55	80	88	94
36110	MONTGOMERY	55	47	45	47	45	54	50	51	54	49	53	38	46	54	46	57	36	52	57	62
36111	MONTGOMERY	91	93	94	95	94	97	93	93	95	94	95	69	96	93	95	97	66	95	100	110
36112	MONTGOMERY	82	43	32	49	38	36	77	53	73	72	76	53	59	87	56	67	54	68	48	65
36115	MONTGOMERY	107	55	41	64	49	47	100	69	94	93	99	69	76	113	72	87	70	88	63	84
36116	MONTGOMERY	76	68	60	69	64	67	73	68	74	74	75	54	70	76	68	74	52	72	70	83
36117	MONTGOMERY	113	114	106	118	112	105	114	108	111	118	112	86	116	114	112	108	80	110	104	127
36201	ANNISTON	56	41	48	41	41	54	45	50	51	45	50	37	39	51	42	56	34	50	56	61
36203	OXFORD	80	71	71	70	70	79	71	76	74	70	74	57	66	75	68	78	50	74	79	90
36205	ANNISTON	70	51	71	49	53	73	55	68	62	49	59	51	44	61	53	68	40	64	74	80
36206	ANNISTON	79	71	72	71	69	81	73	77	76	69	75	59	68	77	71	79	52	76	82	92
36207	ANNISTON	86	80	86	80	81	91	79	86	83	79	82	63	77	82	80	87	56	84	91	101
36250	ALEXANDRIA	84	78	69	75	76	79	73	78	76	76	76	56	69	79	70	78	52	75	78	92
36251	ASHLAND	67	49	62	47	49	67	50	60	57	49	55	46	41	58	47	62	37	57	64	73
36255	CRAGFORD	72	52	59	50	51	68	54	62	60	52	58	48	43	62	49	65	39	59	66	76
36256	DAVISTON	74	53	61	52	53	70	55	64	61	54	60	49	44	64	50	67	40	61	68	78
36258	DELTA	79	57	65	55	56	75	59	68	65	57	64	53	47	68	53	71	43	65	72	83
36260	EASTABOGA	87	63	74	61	63	84	65	76	72	63	71	59	52	75	60	79	48	72	81	93
36262	FRUITHURST	79	57	65	55	57	75	59	69	66	58	64	53	47	68	54	72	43	65	73	84
	ALABAMA	83	70	73	70	69	80	73	77	76	71	76	59	66	77	69	80	52	76	80	92
	UNITED STATES	100	100	100	100	100	100	100	100	100	100	100	100	100	100	100	100	100	100	100	100

POPULATION CHANGE

ZIP CODE #	POST OFFICE NAME	COUNTY FIPS CODE	POPULATION 2000	POPULATION 2009	POPULATION 2014	2000-2009 ANNUAL RATE % Rate	2000-2009 ANNUAL RATE State Centile	HOUSEHOLDS 2000	HOUSEHOLDS 2009	HOUSEHOLDS 2014	HOUSEHOLDS % Annual Rate 2000-2009	HOUSEHOLDS 2009 Average HH Size	FAMILIES 2000	FAMILIES 2009	FAMILIES % Annual Rate 2000-2009
36263	GRAHAM	111	733	755	750	0.3	58	263	275	274	0.5	2.75	197	202	0.3
36264	HEFLIN	029	8828	8980	9112	0.2	52	3475	3651	3741	0.5	2.43	2538	2613	0.3
36265	JACKSONVILLE	015	16543	17608	17922	0.7	70	6446	7089	7318	1.0	2.27	4091	4343	0.6
36266	LINEVILLE	027	5028	5253	5249	0.5	64	2093	2279	2303	0.9	2.28	1445	1540	0.7
36267	MILLERVILLE	027	56	57	57	0.2	52	25	27	27	0.8	2.11	19	20	0.6
36268	MUNFORD	121	5186	5366	5422	0.4	62	1971	2065	2100	0.5	2.60	1506	1549	0.3
36269	MUSCADINE	029	1217	1352	1411	1.1	79	477	547	576	1.5	2.46	354	398	1.3
36271	OHATCHEE	015	5492	5770	5876	0.5	64	2137	2333	2406	1.0	2.46	1608	1721	0.7
36272	PIEDMONT	019	13560	13590	13543	0.0	45	5484	5669	5708	0.4	2.40	3995	4045	0.1
36273	RANBURNE	029	2692	2875	2958	0.7	70	1073	1180	1226	1.0	2.44	815	880	0.8
36274	ROANOKE	111	11484	11073	10790	-0.4	25	4380	4302	4212	-0.2	2.48	3068	2944	-0.4
36276	WADLEY	111	2382	2319	2275	-0.3	29	913	913	901	0.0	2.41	651	637	-0.2
36277	WEAVER	015	5157	5287	5336	0.3	58	2018	2151	2198	0.7	2.46	1536	1603	0.5
36278	WEDOWEE	111	3690	4300	4359	1.7	88	1474	1765	1804	2.0	2.40	1077	1269	1.8
36279	WELLINGTON	015	2433	2453	2465	0.1	49	966	1013	1030	0.5	2.41	719	740	0.3
36280	WOODLAND	111	3642	3714	3680	0.2	52	1450	1503	1497	0.4	2.47	1093	1110	0.2
36301	DOTHAN	069	32384	34781	36280	0.8	74	13426	14542	15244	0.9	2.37	9171	9721	0.6
36303	DOTHAN	069	28506	30187	31418	0.6	67	11405	12186	12753	0.7	2.43	7822	8185	0.5
36305	DOTHAN	069	9629	12954	14490	3.3	96	3875	5310	5979	3.5	2.39	2783	3719	3.2
36310	ABBEVILLE	067	7171	7145	7131	0.0	45	2860	2952	2978	0.3	2.36	2047	2070	0.1
36311	ARITON	045	2828	2852	2842	0.1	49	1161	1200	1209	0.4	2.18	841	852	0.1
36312	ASHFORD	069	5390	6080	6478	1.3	82	2142	2439	2613	1.4	2.49	1558	1732	1.2
36314	BLACK	061	503	492	487	-0.2	34	199	199	198	0.0	2.46	146	143	-0.2
36316	CHANCELLOR	061	2019	2060	2106	0.2	52	824	867	897	0.6	2.38	601	618	0.3
36317	CLOPTON	067	625	579	563	-0.8	9	247	239	234	-0.4	2.42	186	176	-0.6
36318	COFFEE SPRINGS	061	1248	1220	1217	-0.2	34	504	509	512	0.1	2.40	371	367	-0.1
36319	COLUMBIA	067	2495	2820	2991	1.3	82	1026	1188	1269	1.6	2.37	725	820	1.3
36320	COTTONWOOD	069	3656	4124	4394	1.3	82	1440	1641	1759	1.4	2.51	1083	1208	1.2
36321	COWARTS	069	1384	1512	1591	1.0	77	545	603	639	1.1	2.51	423	461	0.9
36322	DALEVILLE	045	7515	7255	7112	-0.4	25	3143	3144	3117	0.0	2.31	2087	2041	-0.2
36323	ELBA	031	8155	8188	8281	0.0	45	3147	3271	3345	0.4	2.40	2285	2322	0.2
36330	ENTERPRISE	031	28876	31525	32997	1.0	77	11595	13114	13870	1.3	2.38	8170	9056	1.1
36340	GENEVA	061	5678	5565	5523	-0.2	34	2349	2370	2372	0.1	2.28	1598	1573	-0.2
36343	GORDON	069	1372	1680	1826	2.2	91	525	651	711	2.4	2.58	393	477	2.1
36344	HARTFORD	061	5471	5469	5455	0.0	45	2183	2233	2247	0.2	2.40	1566	1570	0.0
36345	HEADLAND	067	5583	6357	6654	1.4	84	2206	2600	2755	1.8	2.44	1628	1880	1.6
36346	JACK	031	1497	1656	1768	1.1	79	608	695	750	1.5	2.38	460	516	1.2
36349	MALVERN	061	193	217	226	1.3	82	78	91	96	1.7	2.38	59	68	1.5
36350	MIDLAND CITY	045	6989	7273	7243	0.4	62	2839	3052	3072	0.8	2.37	2036	2125	0.5
36351	NEW BROCKTON	031	3251	3458	3585	0.7	70	1270	1402	1472	1.1	2.40	956	1034	0.9
36352	NEWTON	069	4597	4935	5118	0.8	74	1801	1977	2065	1.0	2.49	1364	1465	0.8
36353	NEWVILLE	067	1994	1809	1745	-1.0	4	799	753	734	-0.6	2.40	591	547	-0.8
36360	OZARK	045	19371	18850	18524	-0.3	29	7855	7939	7888	0.1	2.32	5488	5418	-0.1
36362	FORT RUCKER	045	6091	6087	6044	0.0	45	1412	1468	1473	0.4	3.33	1358	1402	0.3
36370	PANSEY	069	867	961	1030	1.1	79	336	377	406	1.3	2.55	251	276	1.0
36373	SHORTERVILLE	067	996	1026	1039	0.3	58	404	434	446	0.8	2.36	286	301	0.6
36374	SKIPPERVILLE	045	1092	1178	1185	0.8	74	414	460	468	1.1	2.56	320	350	1.0
36375	SLOCOMB	061	6497	6984	7195	0.8	74	2578	2838	2945	1.0	2.46	1904	2055	0.8
36376	WEBB	069	2201	2190	2212	-0.1	39	854	859	872	0.1	2.54	641	631	-0.2
36401	BURNT CORN	035	8118	7896	7663	-0.3	29	3338	3387	3334	0.2	2.31	2242	2219	-0.1
36420	ANDALUSIA	039	12710	12386	12221	-0.3	29	5315	5330	5307	0.0	2.28	3628	3563	-0.2
36421	ANDALUSIA	039	4555	4879	4974	0.7	70	1819	2028	2092	1.2	2.37	1259	1366	0.9
36425	BEATRICE	099	1399	1368	1347	-0.2	34	550	563	561	0.3	2.43	367	367	0.0
36426	BREWTON	053	15847	15296	14938	-0.4	25	6404	6382	6297	0.0	2.34	4466	4352	-0.3
36432	CASTLEBERRY	035	3491	3272	3148	-0.7	13	1419	1381	1343	-0.3	2.37	993	948	-0.5
36435	COY	131	876	832	816	-0.6	16	328	330	327	0.1	2.52	213	209	-0.2
36436	DICKINSON	025	751	668	632	-1.3	2	260	242	232	-0.8	2.76	190	173	-1.0
36441	FLOMATON	053	3718	3795	3762	0.2	52	1475	1560	1564	0.6	2.43	1087	1128	0.4
36442	FLORALA	039	3541	3434	3387	-0.3	29	1565	1563	1555	0.0	2.20	991	964	-0.3
36444	FRANKLIN	099	924	884	867	-0.5	19	366	369	366	0.1	2.40	269	265	-0.2
36445	FRISCO CITY	099	5628	5548	5454	-0.2	34	2206	2252	2243	0.2	2.45	1625	1628	0.0
36446	FULTON	025	269	251	241	-0.7	13	99	97	94	-0.2	2.59	74	71	-0.4
36451	GROVE HILL	025	5303	5071	4905	-0.5	19	2064	2050	2008	-0.1	2.44	1483	1442	-0.3
36453	KINSTON	031	2182	2261	2312	0.4	62	907	971	1003	0.7	2.33	660	692	0.5
36454	LENOX	035	548	511	489	-0.8	9	235	227	220	-0.4	2.25	170	162	-0.5
36456	MC KENZIE	013	1286	1189	1134	-0.8	9	545	532	515	-0.3	2.23	366	348	-0.5
36460	MONROEVILLE	099	12149	11902	11694	-0.2	34	4651	4760	4739	0.3	2.46	3350	3359	0.0
36467	OPP	039	10054	9735	9615	-0.3	29	4189	4190	4174	0.0	2.28	2947	2887	-0.2
36471	PETERMAN	099	1347	1390	1387	0.3	58	540	586	592	0.9	2.37	351	371	0.6
36473	RANGE	035	313	292	279	-0.7	13	119	115	111	-0.4	2.54	86	82	-0.5
36474	RED LEVEL	039	2099	2033	2002	-0.3	29	855	854	851	0.0	2.37	613	600	-0.2
36475	REPTON	035	1762	1623	1552	-0.9	6	706	677	655	-0.5	2.40	485	456	-0.7
36477	SAMSON	061	4578	4868	4983	0.7	70	1912	2098	2165	1.0	2.32	1340	1443	0.8
36480	URIAH	099	1564	1727	1751	1.1	79	611	708	729	1.6	2.44	459	523	1.4
36481	VREDENBURGH	099	963	933	915	-0.3	29	322	328	326	0.2	2.84	246	246	0.0
36482	WHATLEY	025	866	771	730	-1.2	2	329	304	292	-0.9	2.53	235	213	-1.1
36483	WING	039	1629	1439	1377	-1.3	2	654	599	579	-0.9	2.40	479	431	-1.1
36502	ATMORE	053	18494	18146	17801	-0.2	34	6283	6301	6231	0.0	2.43	4429	4350	-0.2
36505	AXIS	097	1710	1749	1773	0.2	52	598	616	627	0.3	2.84	504	510	0.1
36507	BAY MINETTE	003	18838	22034	24219	1.7	88	6802	8323	9271	2.2	2.55	5114	6141	2.0
36509	BAYOU LA BATRE	097	2602	2407	2344	-0.8	9	860	801	785	-0.8	3.00	682	621	-1.0
36511	BON SECOUR	003	482	698	871	4.1	98	187	276	348	4.3	2.53	140	201	4.0
36515	CARLTON	025	29	27	26	-0.8	9	11	11	10	0.0	2.45	9	8	-1.3
36518	CHATOM	129	3290	3255	3226	-0.1	39	1245	1283	1287	0.3	2.47	925	936	0.1
36521	CHUNCHULA	097	5130	5587	5776	0.9	76	1789	1960	2036	1.0	2.84	1457	1565	0.8
36522	CITRONELLE	097	6145	6374	6465	0.4	62	2167	2265	2308	0.5	2.75	1698	1735	0.2
36523	CODEN	097	3198	3193	3213	0.0	45	1178	1188	1201	0.1	2.69	889	870	-0.2
36524	COFFEEVILLE	025	1367	1358	1324	-0.1	39	592	612	605	0.4	2.22	380	384	0.1
36525	CREOLA	097	1561	1536	1534	-0.2	34	558	552	554	-0.1	2.78	428	416	-0.3
36526	DAPHNE	003	20153	27246	31303	3.3	96	7805	10714	12369	3.5	2.52	5670	7722	3.4
36527	SPANISH FORT	003	7405	10609	12466	4.0	98	2769	4010	4742	4.1	2.62	2122	3024	3.9
36528	DAUPHIN ISLAND	097	1369	1415	1441	0.4	62	600	624	638	0.4	2.27	433	436	0.1
36529	DEER PARK	129	997	961	945	-0.4	25	338	335	332	-0.1	2.87	262	255	-0.3
36530	ELBERTA	003	6289	8412	9744	3.2	96	2514	3468	4050	3.5	2.42	1833	2468	3.3
36532	FAIRHOPE	003	22069	28372	32310	2.8	94	9081	12019	13793	3.1	2.34	6379	8330	2.9
	ALABAMA					0.6					0.9	2.44			0.6
	UNITED STATES					1.0					1.1	2.59			0.9

ZIP CODE #	POST OFFICE NAME	RACE (%) White 2000	White 2009	Black 2000	Black 2009	Asian/Pacific 2000	Asian/Pacific 2009	% Hispanic Origin 2000	% Hispanic Origin 2009	2009 AGE DISTRIBUTION (%) 0-4	5-9	10-14	15-19	20-24	25-44	45-64	65-84	85+	18+	MEDIAN AGE 2009	% 2009 Males	% 2009 Females
36263	GRAHAM	86.8	84.1	11.2	13.0	0.3	0.4	2.0	3.2	6.0	6.2	6.5	7.2	5.8	25.3	29.9	11.9	1.2	76.8	40.5	48.1	51.9
36264	HEFLIN	92.2	90.7	6.1	6.8	0.2	0.2	1.9	3.3	6.2	6.3	6.5	6.4	5.2	26.1	27.8	13.6	1.8	77.0	40.5	50.6	49.4
36265	JACKSONVILLE	84.2	80.6	12.6	15.1	1.0	1.2	1.5	2.6	5.4	5.2	5.2	9.4	13.7	24.3	24.4	10.7	1.7	81.2	33.3	48.3	51.7
36266	LINEVILLE	74.7	74.2	23.4	23.9	0.2	0.2	2.1	2.2	6.2	6.2	6.4	6.3	5.2	24.8	27.3	15.2	2.4	77.4	41.0	49.0	51.0
36267	MILLERVILLE	62.5	61.4	35.7	36.8	0.0	0.0	0.0	0.0	5.3	7.0	7.0	5.3	7.0	26.3	31.6	10.5	0.0	77.2	39.4	50.9	49.1
36268	MUNFORD	79.4	78.1	19.3	20.5	0.2	0.2	0.6	0.6	6.3	6.4	6.8	7.1	5.5	27.7	27.7	11.4	1.1	76.2	38.4	48.8	51.2
36269	MUSCADINE	98.8	98.4	0.1	0.1	0.2	0.3	0.2	0.4	7.2	7.3	7.3	6.4	5.1	27.1	27.7	10.8	1.0	74.3	37.5	50.8	49.2
36271	OHATCHEE	93.4	91.7	4.8	5.9	0.2	0.2	0.6	1.1	6.3	6.5	6.6	5.9	5.4	26.8	30.3	11.2	1.0	77.0	39.6	50.3	49.7
36272	PIEDMONT	92.4	90.8	6.2	7.3	0.1	0.1	0.9	1.6	6.4	6.4	6.5	6.2	5.1	26.3	28.2	13.3	1.6	76.8	40.4	49.8	50.2
36273	RANBURNE	99.1	98.9	0.0	0.0	0.1	0.2	0.8	1.4	6.1	6.3	6.5	6.5	5.0	26.9	27.9	13.1	1.6	77.1	39.9	51.0	49.0
36274	ROANOKE	69.5	66.6	29.3	31.6	0.3	0.4	1.0	1.6	7.1	7.2	7.2	6.6	5.1	25.1	25.6	13.0	3.0	74.5	38.5	48.0	52.0
36276	WADLEY	76.0	72.4	22.3	25.4	0.1	0.1	1.4	2.2	6.2	6.3	6.7	10.0	6.9	23.2	25.9	12.9	1.9	76.7	37.2	48.2	51.8
36277	WEAVER	87.7	84.7	8.0	9.8	1.7	2.0	1.6	2.7	6.1	6.1	6.6	6.4	5.9	25.6	29.2	12.8	1.2	77.1	40.1	48.1	51.9
36278	WEDOWEE	78.6	77.7	20.1	20.5	0.2	0.3	1.1	2.0	6.0	6.0	6.3	6.3	5.3	24.7	28.6	14.9	1.9	77.9	41.5	50.2	49.8
36279	WELLINGTON	95.6	94.2	2.5	3.1	0.3	0.4	0.8	1.5	5.7	5.9	6.4	6.4	5.3	27.6	30.4	11.1	1.2	78.2	40.0	49.5	50.5
36280	WOODLAND	88.1	85.9	10.5	12.2	0.1	0.2	1.3	2.3	6.2	6.3	6.6	6.9	5.5	25.3	28.5	13.1	1.6	76.6	40.3	49.0	51.0
36301	DOTHAN	75.7	72.7	21.6	23.8	0.7	0.9	1.4	2.2	6.8	6.6	6.5	6.3	6.1	26.6	26.6	12.5	1.9	76.1	38.5	47.5	52.5
36303	DOTHAN	57.8	54.5	40.0	42.6	0.7	1.0	1.2	1.8	6.7	6.9	7.1	7.2	6.1	24.6	27.6	11.7	2.2	74.8	38.1	47.5	52.5
36305	DOTHAN	90.3	87.5	6.5	7.9	1.3	2.0	1.8	3.0	7.2	7.1	6.9	6.0	4.9	29.1	26.5	10.0	2.3	75.1	37.7	47.9	52.1
36310	ABBEVILLE	60.0	55.9	37.4	39.8	0.1	0.1	2.5	4.4	6.1	6.1	6.5	6.3	5.2	23.2	28.6	15.2	3.0	77.5	42.3	48.2	51.8
36311	ARITON	74.2	71.8	23.2	24.7	0.2	0.4	1.4	2.2	5.7	6.1	6.2	5.9	5.5	27.2	27.9	13.4	2.1	78.4	40.4	54.1	45.9
36312	ASHFORD	83.9	80.6	14.9	17.7	0.0	0.1	0.9	1.3	6.3	6.4	6.7	6.5	5.3	25.3	28.7	12.8	1.9	76.5	40.6	48.8	51.2
36314	BLACK	94.8	94.1	3.8	4.3	0.2	0.2	0.4	0.6	5.5	5.5	5.7	6.1	6.3	25.8	31.3	12.0	1.8	79.7	41.8	49.8	50.2
36316	CHANCELLOR	84.9	82.7	13.3	14.8	0.7	1.1	0.8	1.4	5.4	6.2	7.3	6.1	5.1	24.1	29.5	14.2	2.1	77.4	41.7	48.8	51.2
36317	CLOPTON	58.1	54.1	41.1	45.1	0.0	0.0	0.3	0.5	5.5	5.7	6.2	6.7	5.2	25.2	28.7	15.0	1.7	78.6	41.8	49.7	50.3
36318	COFFEE SPRINGS	94.2	93.1	4.0	4.6	0.2	0.3	0.5	0.7	5.5	5.7	5.9	5.5	4.3	24.3	31.1	15.9	1.9	79.3	44.2	48.4	51.6
36319	COLUMBIA	80.7	77.0	17.6	21.0	0.0	0.1	0.8	1.4	5.9	6.2	6.2	5.7	4.8	22.8	31.0	15.1	2.2	78.2	43.6	48.5	51.5
36320	COTTONWOOD	85.9	83.1	12.1	14.4	0.2	0.3	1.3	2.0	6.8	6.7	7.0	6.4	5.4	26.5	27.3	12.5	1.5	75.5	39.3	49.1	50.9
36321	COWARTS	86.9	83.8	11.0	13.4	0.0	0.1	0.9	1.5	6.2	6.2	6.5	6.5	5.4	26.5	28.7	12.7	1.3	77.1	39.8	48.5	51.5
36322	DALEVILLE	70.8	66.5	21.1	22.3	2.8	4.0	3.2	5.3	6.6	6.7	6.3	6.1	6.3	27.6	27.8	11.7	0.9	76.7	37.6	49.4	50.6
36323	ELBA	73.5	71.4	24.1	25.5	0.1	0.1	1.0	1.5	6.1	6.0	6.1	6.6	5.7	25.4	27.4	14.0	2.7	77.8	40.7	50.1	49.9
36330	ENTERPRISE	73.9	70.7	20.4	21.5	1.7	2.3	4.2	6.7	6.5	6.3	6.3	6.5	6.6	27.1	26.6	12.3	1.9	77.0	37.8	48.8	51.2
36340	GENEVA	85.9	83.8	12.6	14.1	0.1	0.2	1.0	1.7	5.6	5.8	6.1	6.3	5.7	23.6	28.2	15.6	3.1	78.5	42.7	48.2	51.8
36343	GORDON	64.8	59.6	33.7	38.6	0.0	0.1	1.0	1.4	6.3	6.3	6.5	6.9	6.2	24.5	28.7	13.2	1.4	76.6	40.4	50.0	50.0
36344	HARTFORD	88.2	86.8	10.2	11.0	0.1	0.2	1.5	2.7	5.5	5.6	6.0	6.5	5.2	23.5	28.3	16.4	2.9	78.9	43.2	48.7	51.3
36345	HEADLAND	73.5	71.7	25.1	26.6	0.1	0.1	0.5	0.6	6.2	6.8	7.1	7.1	4.9	25.3	28.9	11.6	2.2	75.4	39.6	48.2	51.8
36346	JACK	91.4	89.5	4.4	5.5	0.0	0.1	1.0	1.6	5.7	5.9	6.3	7.0	5.3	24.9	29.2	13.8	1.9	77.7	41.4	48.9	51.1
36349	MALVERN	95.3	93.5	2.6	2.8	0.0	0.0	2.1	3.7	6.5	6.5	6.5	6.0	5.5	29.0	28.1	10.6	1.4	76.5	39.0	49.3	50.7
36350	MIDLAND CITY	82.9	81.2	14.2	15.1	0.3	0.6	1.1	1.8	6.5	6.6	6.6	6.6	5.7	25.8	28.2	12.4	1.6	76.3	39.1	48.8	51.2
36351	NEW BROCKTON	84.3	82.0	10.9	12.1	0.3	0.5	1.4	2.3	5.3	5.6	6.3	6.6	5.1	23.5	31.1	15.0	1.7	78.7	43.3	50.2	49.8
36352	NEWTON	89.8	88.7	8.0	8.3	0.2	0.3	1.4	2.4	6.4	6.4	6.6	6.4	5.6	25.4	29.2	12.4	1.6	76.4	39.8	50.5	49.5
36353	NEWVILLE	67.4	63.4	30.9	34.3	0.1	0.1	1.1	1.8	6.4	6.4	7.1	6.6	4.7	24.8	28.5	13.7	1.9	76.0	41.1	49.5	50.5
36360	OZARK	71.4	69.2	25.6	26.7	0.7	1.0	1.9	3.2	6.4	6.1	5.9	6.4	5.9	24.7	27.8	14.2	2.6	77.7	40.7	47.5	52.5
36362	FORT RUCKER	68.6	63.5	18.1	18.4	2.8	3.5	11.6	18.1	15.6	11.2	6.2	6.2	13.0	44.7	2.9	0.2	0.0	64.7	24.2	56.7	43.3
36370	PANSEY	66.8	61.9	31.1	35.7	0.1	0.1	0.7	1.0	6.0	6.0	6.3	7.6	6.3	23.5	29.7	13.0	1.5	77.1	40.7	49.7	50.3
36373	SHORTERVILLE	67.9	63.2	29.7	33.3	0.3	0.5	1.5	2.5	5.8	6.0	6.1	6.1	5.2	25.1	30.4	13.4	1.8	78.2	41.7	47.8	52.2
36374	SKIPPERVILLE	84.0	81.6	14.2	15.9	0.1	0.2	0.7	1.4	4.9	6.7	7.7	8.1	3.5	24.7	30.5	12.6	1.4	75.4	40.7	50.8	49.2
36375	SLOCOMB	87.3	85.5	9.9	10.7	0.1	0.2	3.0	4.9	6.0	6.2	6.5	6.8	5.5	25.5	28.7	12.9	1.9	77.2	40.4	49.8	50.2
36376	WEBB	82.5	79.1	16.1	19.1	0.0	0.1	0.7	1.1	7.0	7.1	7.1	6.5	5.5	26.3	28.0	11.2	1.3	74.5	38.3	48.4	51.6
36401	BURNT CORN	51.5	49.0	47.6	49.9	0.2	0.2	0.7	1.0	6.2	6.7	6.9	7.2	5.6	22.7	27.3	14.3	3.0	75.6	40.5	46.4	53.6
36420	ANDALUSIA	81.6	80.6	16.9	17.5	0.2	0.3	0.8	1.3	6.2	6.3	6.1	6.3	5.4	24.0	27.6	15.0	3.1	77.6	41.6	47.9	52.1
36421	ANDALUSIA	84.6	79.8	13.9	18.3	0.2	0.3	0.7	1.1	5.7	5.7	6.0	6.8	6.0	24.4	27.9	15.0	2.6	78.5	41.7	48.9	51.1
36425	BEATRICE	21.8	19.3	77.2	79.5	0.4	0.4	0.6	0.7	5.0	5.5	6.1	8.3	6.5	23.5	29.2	13.2	2.7	78.4	40.5	48.6	51.4
36426	BREWTON	71.9	69.3	25.6	27.3	0.3	0.5	1.1	1.9	5.9	5.8	6.1	6.9	5.7	24.2	28.5	14.4	2.5	78.1	41.4	47.8	52.2
36432	CASTLEBERRY	63.2	61.2	35.5	37.0	0.2	0.3	0.6	0.9	5.9	6.1	6.4	6.8	5.2	24.8	29.2	13.9	1.8	77.4	41.2	48.4	51.6
36435	COY	18.7	17.2	81.2	82.7	0.0	0.0	0.3	0.2	7.2	7.2	7.0	7.1	5.4	25.6	26.1	12.4	2.0	74.4	37.1	45.6	54.4
36436	DICKINSON	42.2	40.0	57.0	59.0	0.0	0.0	0.9	1.0	7.8	7.8	7.8	7.8	5.7	25.0	26.0	10.6	1.5	72.0	36.2	48.2	51.8
36441	FLOMATON	87.8	85.3	8.9	10.7	0.0	0.0	1.2	1.9	6.2	6.2	6.5	6.8	5.6	26.5	27.9	12.8	1.6	77.0	39.2	49.1	50.9
36442	FLORALA	83.5	82.1	13.8	14.2	0.4	0.6	2.1	3.4	5.4	5.7	5.7	5.8	4.7	22.8	29.6	17.5	2.6	79.5	44.8	48.9	51.1
36444	FRANKLIN	42.8	39.1	56.4	60.0	0.0	0.0	0.5	0.7	7.1	7.4	7.4	6.6	5.3	24.5	26.5	13.5	1.8	74.1	38.3	49.9	50.1
36445	FRISCO CITY	68.4	65.2	28.9	31.5	0.3	0.4	0.8	1.2	7.6	7.7	7.8	6.9	5.5	25.5	26.6	10.8	1.7	72.6	37.1	49.0	51.0
36446	FULTON	51.5	47.8	47.8	51.0	0.0	0.0	0.7	0.8	8.0	8.0	7.6	7.6	6.4	24.7	27.5	9.2	1.2	71.7	35.5	48.2	51.8
36451	GROVE HILL	60.8	57.7	38.4	41.3	0.0	0.0	0.6	0.9	6.8	7.0	7.1	7.1	5.8	24.8	27.1	12.6	1.8	74.9	38.4	48.0	52.0
36453	KINSTON	94.1	92.9	1.7	2.1	0.1	0.1	0.5	1.0	5.8	6.1	6.4	5.4	4.6	24.9	30.2	14.8	1.8	78.3	42.6	50.6	49.4
36454	LENOX	86.8	84.9	10.4	11.5	0.0	0.0	1.3	2.2	6.5	6.8	7.0	6.1	4.5	26.4	28.2	13.1	1.4	76.1	39.4	51.5	48.5
36456	MC KENZIE	75.9	73.8	23.1	25.0	0.1	0.1	0.7	0.9	5.3	5.6	5.4	5.8	5.9	22.5	31.3	15.5	2.9	80.4	44.7	47.3	52.7
36460	MONROEVILLE	60.1	57.5	38.1	40.2	0.4	0.5	0.8	1.2	7.9	7.4	7.4	7.0	5.7	24.3	26.1	12.0	2.3	73.0	37.4	47.0	53.0
36467	OPP	87.6	86.5	11.2	11.9	0.2	0.2	0.6	1.0	6.1	6.1	6.2	6.2	5.0	23.8	28.1	15.4	3.2	77.8	42.4	46.9	53.1
36471	PETERMAN	30.0	26.9	69.6	72.6	0.1	0.1	0.7	0.7	6.0	6.2	6.6	8.2	5.9	24.2	28.6	12.1	2.2	76.2	39.6	47.3	52.7
36473	RANGE	86.6	84.9	10.5	11.3	0.0	0.0	1.3	2.4	6.2	6.8	7.2	6.2	4.5	25.7	28.8	13.4	1.4	76.0	39.8	51.0	49.0
36474	RED LEVEL	93.0	92.5	5.9	6.3	0.0	0.0	0.3	0.6	5.8	5.7	5.9	5.7	6.0	25.5	29.1	14.4	2.1	79.1	41.6	51.3	48.7
36475	REPTON	56.0	53.5	42.8	45.1	0.0	0.0	0.6	0.9	6.3	6.4	6.6	6.3	5.5	25.9	28.5	12.8	1.7	76.8	40.1	49.6	50.4
36477	SAMSON	85.8	84.8	11.0	11.2	0.1	0.2	1.9	3.0	5.8	6.0	6.4	6.4	4.8	24.6	28.8	15.2	2.0	77.9	42.1	49.8	50.2
36480	URIAH	76.9	73.5	16.7	19.1	0.3	0.3	1.1	1.7	6.6	6.8	7.3	7.1	4.8	25.6	27.6	12.9	1.3	74.9	39.2	48.8	51.2
36481	VREDENBURGH	28.0	25.3	71.0	73.6	0.0	0.0	0.4	0.6	7.3	8.7	8.4	7.5	5.3	24.4	23.9	12.9	1.7	70.6	35.7	47.8	52.2
36482	WHATLEY	41.2	39.3	58.3	60.2	0.0	0.0	0.8	1.0	6.9	7.1	7.3	8.0	5.6	24.6	26.1	12.3	2.1	73.9	37.9	47.7	52.3
36483	WING	96.4	95.9	2.6	2.8	0.1	0.1	0.8	1.5	5.5	5.7	5.8	5.8	5.1	24.7	30.6	14.9	1.9	79.4	42.9	50.5	49.5
36502	ATMORE	52.3	49.2	40.5	42.6	0.3	0.4	0.8	1.3	6.3	6.4	6.1	6.5	7.5	29.9	24.8	10.5	1.8	77.5	36.5	54.6	45.4
36505	AXIS	88.1	82.7	9.4	14.5	0.2	0.3	0.6	0.9	7.3	7.3	7.4	7.0	5.7	27.6	28.0	9.0	0.7	73.6	36.5	49.2	50.8
36507	BAY MINETTE	76.3	74.5	21.6	23.1	0.3	0.3	1.1	1.4	7.3	7.1	7.0	7.3	6.4	26.5	25.3	11.5	1.5	74.6	36.3	49.7	50.3
36509	BAYOU LA BATRE	62.7	53.7	10.3	13.3	24.1	29.7	1.3	1.7	7.0	7.4	7.4	8.4	6.6	25.7	26.1	10.3	1.0	73.2	35.3	50.8	49.2
36511	BON SECOUR	96.1	95.4	0.6	0.7	0.4	0.4	3.5	4.6	6.3	6.4	6.6	6.3	4.7	24.5	29.8	13.8	1.6	76.8	41.5	48.6	51.4
36515	CARLTON	32.1	29.6	67.9	70.4	0.0	0.0	0.0	0.0	7.4	7.4	7.4	7.4	7.4	29.6	29.6	3.7	0.0	70.4	33.8	48.1	51.9
36518	CHATOM	78.1	75.2	21.3	24.0	0.1	0.1	0.7	1.1	7.2	7.0	7.0	6.9	6.3	24.4	25.6	13.1	2.7	74.6	38.0	49.0	51.0
36521	CHUNCHULA	84.0	78.1	12.2	17.4	0.1	0.1	0.6	0.8	7.4	7.3	7.6	7.7	6.0	27.5	26.7	9.1	0.8	73.0	35.5	50.0	50.0
36522	CITRONELLE	78.7	72.4	15.5	21.1	0.1	0.2	0.7	1.0	7.7	7.6	7.5	6.9	5.9	26.5	25.7	10.8	1.5	73.1	35.9	48.4	51.6
36523	CODEN	83.8	80.4	3.5	4.6	9.7	11.4	1.2	1.6	5.9	6.0	6.3	6.8	5.1	24.1	31.9	13.0	1.1	77.5	42.3	52.0	48.0
36524	COFFEEVILLE	57.8	54.2	41.4	44.8	0.3	0.4	1.0	1.0	7.8	8.0	7.7	5.7	4.9	22.5	24.8	16.1	2.6	72.9	39.7	47.5	52.5
36525	CREOLA	70.7	63.0	26.9	34.5	0.1	0.2	0.9	1.0	7.1	7.2	7.2	6.8	5.2	25.5	28.5	11.1	1.4	74.3	38.6	49.0	51.0
36526	DAPHNE	84.4	82.1	13.3	15.2	0.6	0.7	1.6	2.2	6.4	6.5	6.9	6.9	5.9	25.8	29.7	10.6	1.3	75.8	39.4	48.6	51.4
36527	SPANISH FORT	92.0	89.9	6.1	7.8	0.7	0.8	0.9	1.3	5.7	6.6	7.6	7.3	4.1	21.3	32.9	11.9	2.6	75.0	43.3	48.8	51.2
36528	DAUPHIN ISLAND	95.2	93.2	1.2	2.0	0.6	0.8	1.0	1.6	4.8	4.8	5.3	6.1	4.7	22.8	36.1	14.3	1.0	81.0	45.7	52.7	47.3
36529	DEER PARK	76.1	73.3	21.4	23.4	0.1	0.1	0.5	0.9	7.5	7.3	7.5	7.1	5.5	25.2	26.8	11.8	1.4	73.3	37.7	49.0	51.0
36530	ELBERTA	96.1	95.2	0.9	1.1	0.3	0.4	1.9	2.6	6.4	6.6	6.8	6.4	4.5	24.9	28.5	14.4	1.5	76.2	41.0	50.1	49.9
36532	FAIRHOPE	88.7	86.9	9.3	10.7	0.5	0.6	1.2	1.7	5.7	5.9	6.4	6.4	4.6	23.3	30.2	14.6	2.9	77.8	43.3	47.7	52.3
	ALABAMA	71.1	69.3	26.0	26.7	0.7	1.0	1.7	2.8	6.6	6.6	6.6	6.9	6.6	26.4	26.7	11.7	1.8	76.1	37.8	48.6	51.4
	UNITED STATES	75.1	72.0	12.3	12.7	3.8	4.6	12.5	15.7	6.8	6.7	6.6	7.1	6.9	27.0	26.0	10.9	1.9	75.7	36.9	49.2	50.8

ALABAMA

INCOME

36263-36532

ZIP CODE #	POST OFFICE NAME	2009 Per Capita Income	2009 HH Income Base	2009 HOUSEHOLD INCOME DISTRIBUTION (%) Less than $25,000	$25,000 to $49,999	$50,000 to $99,999	$100,000 to $149,999	$150,000 or More	MEDIAN HOUSEHOLD INCOME 2009	2014	2009 National Centile	2009 State Centile	2009 Home Value Base	2009 HOME VALUE DISTRIBUTION (%) Less than $50,000	$50,000 to $89,999	$90,000 to $174,999	$175,000 to $399,999	$400,000 or More	2009 Median Home Value
36263	GRAHAM	14447	275	37.1	32.7	25.8	3.3	1.1	33421	34775	14	36	231	30.3	26.8	31.6	8.2	3.0	80294
36264	HEFLIN	17299	3651	35.0	32.9	27.1	3.9	1.2	34901	36135	17	44	2875	29.8	21.1	33.3	13.7	2.1	88268
36265	JACKSONVILLE	19161	7089	38.6	25.8	28.1	5.2	2.3	33787	36030	15	38	4571	19.6	21.7	39.8	17.9	1.1	105294
36266	LINEVILLE	17355	2279	38.6	32.0	25.1	3.1	1.3	31633	33010	11	27	1672	25.6	25.9	35.7	10.5	2.3	87863
36267	MILLERVILLE	17018	27	44.4	22.2	33.3	0.0	0.0	32357	18539	12	31	23	17.4	34.8	39.1	8.7	0.0	85000
36268	MUNFORD	18182	2065	28.9	32.2	33.9	3.3	1.6	40345	40270	34	67	1713	29.9	29.9	30.1	8.5	1.6	74675
36269	MUSCADINE	17792	547	33.6	37.1	24.9	2.7	1.6	36284	37255	21	50	445	29.2	29.9	26.3	11.7	2.9	76875
36271	OHATCHEE	19484	2333	30.1	30.6	33.6	3.6	2.1	40267	41293	34	67	2004	21.9	27.6	34.6	12.6	3.3	90687
36272	PIEDMONT	17347	5669	35.8	32.9	26.2	3.9	1.2	33939	36028	15	39	4492	29.7	28.6	32.1	8.2	1.4	80362
36273	RANBURNE	16814	1180	37.1	31.4	27.2	3.5	0.8	35583	36601	19	47	975	28.6	18.8	34.9	13.4	4.3	95543
36274	ROANOKE	16653	4302	35.4	33.8	26.8	2.6	1.5	34241	35358	16	40	3252	27.7	28.0	33.3	10.1	1.0	82009
36276	WADLEY	16774	913	36.1	37.6	21.0	3.8	1.4	31398	32169	10	26	706	26.2	27.8	38.8	7.1	0.1	83000
36277	WEAVER	20787	2151	26.5	32.6	33.6	5.0	2.3	42659	43356	41	75	1711	21.9	26.8	41.8	9.2	0.3	91490
36278	WEDOWEE	16814	1765	41.2	28.0	26.5	3.2	1.1	30760	32535	9	23	1431	27.0	21.9	33.1	14.5	3.5	91686
36279	WELLINGTON	18380	1013	28.3	37.5	28.9	4.2	1.0	37103	38063	24	55	843	24.3	24.3	38.1	12.5	0.8	92300
36280	WOODLAND	17224	1503	33.4	33.5	28.7	3.7	0.7	36060	36542	21	49	1275	28.9	22.4	32.3	14.6	1.8	87500
36301	DOTHAN	19532	14542	32.5	30.4	31.0	4.4	1.7	38657	40555	29	62	9574	15.1	29.7	42.5	11.7	1.0	96318
36303	DOTHAN	21077	12186	35.5	26.1	27.2	7.3	3.8	38622	40516	29	62	7884	12.4	21.4	38.2	24.8	3.3	120863
36305	DOTHAN	30957	5310	17.6	24.2	37.6	13.9	6.7	57591	56771	75	94	3731	4.6	12.0	45.8	29.5	8.1	149552
36310	ABBEVILLE	17117	2952	43.8	26.5	24.4	3.6	1.6	29906	31790	8	21	2357	27.2	33.7	27.3	10.6	1.2	77038
36311	ARITON	16819	1200	44.5	25.8	26.8	1.9	1.1	29383	31231	7	20	962	35.3	26.7	26.2	9.7	2.1	71972
36312	ASHFORD	17676	2439	33.1	32.3	29.5	3.6	1.4	38301	40075	28	60	1930	23.3	30.9	33.1	11.7	1.0	85773
36314	BLACK	17918	199	27.1	38.2	30.2	4.5	0.0	38979	40000	30	63	167	28.1	32.3	29.3	10.2	0.0	76538
36316	CHANCELLOR	18251	867	38.9	28.3	27.9	3.2	1.7	32552	34176	12	32	744	31.9	20.6	30.1	12.9	4.6	85135
36317	CLOPTON	15382	239	43.1	26.8	27.2	2.9	0.0	30156	31768	8	22	203	38.9	35.0	21.7	3.4	1.0	58333
36318	COFFEE SPRINGS	17771	509	34.8	36.0	25.0	2.6	1.8	33958	35313	15	39	445	25.4	26.3	33.9	12.8	1.6	86875
36319	COLUMBIA	17377	1188	38.5	33.9	21.6	3.5	2.5	31712	33431	11	27	968	31.7	30.1	31.9	5.1	1.2	74107
36320	COTTONWOOD	16229	1641	36.4	29.5	30.6	3.2	0.4	35757	37532	20	48	1336	23.9	31.1	32.6	11.9	0.5	83832
36321	COWARTS	18322	603	29.7	31.2	34.7	2.8	1.7	40329	41913	34	67	511	23.7	34.1	33.5	7.6	1.2	83730
36322	DALEVILLE	19360	3144	31.4	29.2	34.3	4.6	0.5	40272	41168	34	67	2009	25.4	26.7	39.1	8.0	0.7	86805
36323	ELBA	17279	3271	38.9	34.6	21.1	3.1	2.3	32515	35313	12	32	2446	28.2	27.5	29.3	13.2	1.8	79733
36330	ENTERPRISE	22529	13114	27.7	29.7	32.1	7.8	2.8	43680	44791	44	78	8549	11.6	21.5	47.2	17.8	1.9	115662
36340	GENEVA	17029	2370	46.5	24.3	24.9	3.0	1.4	27447	28604	5	17	1809	24.2	39.4	26.0	8.8	1.7	73417
36343	GORDON	15726	651	38.9	30.0	28.0	2.5	0.8	36497	38359	22	51	545	35.2	22.0	33.4	8.3	1.1	80125
36344	HARTFORD	16890	2233	37.9	30.5	27.2	3.7	0.6	33024	34544	13	34	1805	25.8	32.1	31.4	9.4	1.3	77344
36345	HEADLAND	20628	2600	29.0	27.5	34.8	6.7	2.0	43605	44118	44	78	2033	11.2	23.8	39.2	23.5	2.5	114486
36346	JACK	16618	695	34.4	36.3	25.9	2.2	1.3	34559	36201	17	42	602	29.7	31.9	29.9	7.0	1.5	68028
36349	MALVERN	18911	91	31.9	31.9	30.8	4.4	1.1	39594	40000	31	65	78	20.5	28.2	42.3	7.7	1.3	91111
36350	MIDLAND CITY	19093	3052	34.3	29.5	29.5	5.3	1.4	36906	38713	23	53	2182	23.6	30.7	30.7	10.8	4.2	82879
36351	NEW BROCKTON	19074	1402	33.0	32.8	28.0	3.9	2.4	36314	37639	21	50	1173	22.1	31.1	27.3	17.1	2.5	85968
36352	NEWTON	18824	1977	28.0	32.5	33.8	4.7	1.0	41795	43096	39	71	1613	22.9	23.8	36.9	15.2	1.2	94612
36353	NEWVILLE	16349	753	39.3	28.0	29.3	3.1	0.3	32640	34308	13	32	636	30.2	35.2	30.8	3.1	0.6	68769
36360	OZARK	18638	7939	36.9	28.5	29.4	3.9	1.3	35482	37140	19	47	5379	17.5	29.0	42.4	10.0	1.2	94715
36362	FORT RUCKER	14046	1468	15.7	44.2	35.4	4.1	0.5	43126	43594	43	77	65	36.9	35.4	27.7	0.0	0.0	55313
36370	PANSEY	15768	377	38.2	36.9	20.4	2.4	2.1	34290	36451	16	41	312	36.2	29.8	28.2	5.1	0.6	70000
36373	SHORTERVILLE	16294	434	40.8	30.4	26.0	1.6	1.2	33568	36017	15	37	366	39.6	30.1	24.0	5.7	0.5	61667
36374	SKIPPERVILLE	16236	460	35.7	32.4	27.6	3.0	1.3	35931	37038	20	49	395	29.9	23.3	37.0	8.4	1.5	83750
36375	SLOCOMB	17348	2838	39.0	26.6	28.6	4.1	1.8	32814	34720	13	33	2322	22.4	31.6	35.9	9.0	1.1	84598
36376	WEBB	17433	859	30.5	33.6	31.9	2.6	1.4	37832	39822	26	58	726	26.3	35.8	25.3	11.2	1.4	77222
36401	BURNT CORN	16053	3387	46.6	27.9	20.7	3.0	1.7	27004	27878	5	16	2538	35.8	26.4	30.7	6.3	0.8	69195
36420	ANDALUSIA	19235	5330	39.5	29.5	24.9	3.9	2.2	32465	33845	12	31	4064	27.2	29.3	31.5	9.7	2.3	79520
36421	ANDALUSIA	18952	2028	37.2	27.6	28.6	4.4	2.1	34910	36120	17	44	1518	23.7	26.9	33.1	12.8	3.4	89048
36425	BEATRICE	12121	563	51.5	31.1	15.5	1.8	0.2	23881	25964	3	10	450	56.2	22.0	14.7	2.9	4.2	43488
36426	BREWTON	19452	6382	37.5	26.1	29.1	4.8	2.5	35130	36578	18	45	4916	27.8	27.5	33.1	10.0	1.6	80582
36432	CASTLEBERRY	14717	1381	50.3	26.4	19.8	2.3	1.1	24712	26173	3	11	1218	35.7	28.8	27.3	7.6	0.7	68280
36435	COY	10476	330	57.0	24.8	18.2	0.0	0.0	18593	19634	1	3	291	50.5	21.3	22.7	3.8	1.7	39250
36436	DICKINSON	12774	242	51.7	21.9	21.1	5.4	0.0	23784	25540	3	9	214	44.4	26.2	28.5	0.5	0.5	59231
36441	FLOMATON	18131	1560	36.5	27.2	32.1	2.9	1.3	37290	38066	24	55	1263	32.1	30.9	28.8	7.9	0.2	71869
36442	FLORALA	14486	1563	55.2	28.3	13.6	1.8	1.1	22110	23409	2	7	1157	40.3	30.7	20.7	7.0	1.4	60722
36444	FRANKLIN	14250	369	42.8	30.9	25.5	0.8	0.0	31272	32143	10	25	328	39.0	28.4	31.4	0.6	0.6	66154
36445	FRISCO CITY	16114	2252	38.1	30.8	27.5	2.5	1.1	33627	34281	15	37	1826	36.5	28.1	28.2	7.1	0.1	63776
36446	FULTON	14873	97	45.4	20.6	29.9	4.1	0.0	30444	33636	9	23	86	41.9	26.7	30.2	1.2	0.0	70000
36451	GROVE HILL	16414	2050	43.6	25.1	24.9	5.9	0.5	30000	31726	8	21	1693	28.8	33.3	25.8	11.4	0.7	68404
36453	KINSTON	18324	971	33.9	37.5	23.5	2.8	2.4	35684	36578	20	47	790	27.2	31.6	31.9	8.6	0.6	77656
36454	LENOX	18084	227	38.8	29.5	27.3	4.4	0.0	32869	34491	13	33	206	38.3	18.0	30.1	11.7	1.9	74615
36456	MC KENZIE	16133	532	47.9	28.0	20.7	2.4	0.9	26727	27387	4	15	411	45.7	30.2	13.9	10.2	0.0	53302
36460	MONROEVILLE	19240	4760	36.1	28.2	27.6	5.8	2.3	36290	36499	21	50	3597	24.1	23.2	37.1	14.8	0.8	95107
36467	OPP	18105	4190	37.7	33.2	24.1	3.4	1.6	32120	33033	12	30	3157	26.7	35.6	28.1	7.6	1.9	74911
36471	PETERMAN	14260	586	48.8	29.0	19.6	2.0	0.5	25883	27306	4	14	503	47.9	22.9	24.1	3.2	2.0	52838
36473	RANGE	16026	115	38.3	29.6	27.0	5.2	0.0	33054	35372	13	34	104	38.5	18.3	28.8	12.5	1.9	74286
36474	RED LEVEL	16257	854	37.8	34.4	24.9	1.9	0.9	31001	31734	10	24	749	43.3	27.4	22.7	6.0	0.7	56733
36475	REPTON	14504	677	46.7	28.2	22.2	2.5	0.4	27702	29160	5	17	609	33.2	26.6	29.4	10.5	0.3	70185
36477	SAMSON	16368	2098	44.1	33.9	18.2	2.2	1.6	28773	30020	6	19	1614	26.3	35.3	28.9	7.1	2.4	74453
36480	URIAH	17556	708	35.3	30.8	28.8	4.4	0.7	36073	36257	21	49	635	34.6	35.9	19.8	9.6	0.0	62925
36481	VREDENBURGH	11094	328	44.5	37.5	17.1	0.6	0.3	30000	30639	8	21	277	53.4	22.4	22.7	0.4	1.1	45870
36482	WHATLEY	13706	304	53.9	24.3	14.8	6.6	0.3	22745	24095	2	8	260	39.2	28.1	26.2	6.2	0.4	61667
36483	WING	15918	599	39.7	34.9	20.7	4.3	0.3	30888	31673	10	23	514	27.6	30.4	29.6	11.9	0.6	79149
36502	ATMORE	15747	6301	41.5	29.6	24.1	3.6	1.1	31077	32528	10	24	4696	32.0	25.1	32.7	9.3	0.8	76426
36505	AXIS	19234	616	23.7	24.5	43.8	6.7	1.3	51308	51159	64	90	538	13.6	13.2	45.5	24.5	3.2	126220
36507	BAY MINETTE	18545	8323	30.8	31.0	31.6	4.9	1.7	40419	41100	34	68	6436	22.0	23.3	34.4	18.2	2.1	96779
36509	BAYOU LA BATRE	12845	801	44.6	28.1	24.2	2.1	1.0	28523	30262	6	18	582	44.8	24.9	21.3	7.4	1.5	57143
36511	BON SECOUR	19666	276	25.7	33.7	34.8	4.7	1.1	43986	45281	45	79	229	18.8	17.9	29.7	33.6	0.0	124479
36515	CARLTON	14259	11	45.5	27.3	27.3	0.0	0.0	27273	32500	5	16	10	30.0	40.0	20.0	10.0	0.0	70000
36518	CHATOM	19189	1283	35.0	24.9	33.1	5.1	1.9	39289	39822	31	64	1054	30.1	24.8	37.0	7.4	0.8	81207
36521	CHUNCHULA	15134	1960	30.5	31.8	33.2	4.2	0.3	40519	42197	34	68	1718	29.5	23.9	33.1	11.9	1.6	84727
36522	CITRONELLE	15685	2265	36.0	29.1	30.4	3.5	1.0	36674	39224	23	52	1763	25.6	30.2	34.8	8.7	0.7	81542
36523	CODEN	17030	1188	33.8	31.0	29.7	3.8	1.8	38109	40773	27	59	933	27.7	17.7	30.3	17.5	6.9	99886
36524	COFFEEVILLE	15065	612	46.1	34.3	16.7	2.8	0.2	26648	27624	4	15	524	41.6	25.4	24.8	7.6	0.6	65625
36525	CREOLA	15509	552	40.9	23.2	29.3	5.4	1.1	33857	36311	15	39	417	24.0	19.9	38.1	15.6	2.4	102579
36526	DAPHNE	28872	10714	15.9	20.8	43.6	13.0	6.6	61453	60948	79	95	8262	3.1	5.0	35.1	43.2	13.6	191588
36527	SPANISH FORT	31933	4010	12.5	20.9	38.8	16.9	10.9	65438	65126	84	97	3374	6.6	7.4	22.9	51.0	12.0	223278
36528	DAUPHIN ISLAND	22285	624	27.9	30.8	34.6	4.8	1.9	43073	44678	43	76	508	19.1	13.2	28.7	27.4	11.6	136000
36529	DEER PARK	13649	335	43.9	21.8	30.4	2.4	1.5	29862	30500	8	21	304	31.6	23.7	33.9	5.9	4.9	79286
36530	ELBERTA	20151	3468	28.8	35.2	29.1	5.0	1.9	39238	39712	30	63	2803	16.5	13.9	26.7	30.4	12.4	149720
36532	FAIRHOPE	26328	12019	22.1	27.5	36.9	9.1	4.4	50333	50651	62	90	9467	9.3	6.7	24.3	42.7	17.0	207928
	ALABAMA	21187		31.4	27.9	30.6	6.9	3.2	40822	42202				18.1	22.4	35.8	19.6	4.0	107730
	UNITED STATES	27277		20.9	24.4	35.3	11.7	7.6	54719	56938				9.3	13.1	31.6	32.6	13.5	162279

ZIP CODE #	POST OFFICE NAME	FINANCIAL SERVICES: Auto Loan	Home Loan	Invest-ments	Retire-ment Plans	THE HOME: Home Improvements: Home Repair	Lawn & Garden	Furnishings: Comput-ers & Hard-ware-Personal	Major Appli-ances	TV, Radio, Sound Equip-ment	Furni-ture	ENTERTAINMENT: Dine out/ Carry out	Sports Equip-ment	Fees & Tickets	Toys & Games	Travel	Cable TV	PERSONAL: Apparel & Services	Auto Repairs	Health Insur-ance	Pets & Supplies
36263	GRAHAM	72	51	59	50	51	68	53	62	59	52	58	48	43	62	49	65	39	59	66	76
36264	HEFLIN	76	54	67	52	54	74	56	67	63	54	62	52	45	65	52	69	41	63	71	82
36265	JACKSONVILLE	69	57	59	57	57	65	66	64	67	61	66	50	58	67	59	69	46	66	68	77
36266	LINEVILLE	72	50	66	48	50	70	53	64	59	50	58	49	41	60	49	65	39	60	68	78
36267	MILLERVILLE	65	47	54	45	46	62	48	56	54	47	53	43	39	56	44	59	35	53	59	69
36268	MUNFORD	84	62	70	61	62	80	64	74	70	63	69	56	53	73	59	76	46	70	77	89
36269	MUSCADINE	79	57	65	55	56	75	59	69	66	58	64	53	47	68	54	71	43	65	73	84
36271	OHATCHEE	84	65	70	63	64	80	65	74	71	65	70	56	55	74	61	76	47	71	77	90
36272	PIEDMONT	73	53	64	52	53	71	56	66	62	53	60	50	45	63	52	68	41	62	70	79
36273	RANBURNE	74	53	61	52	53	70	55	64	61	54	60	49	44	64	50	67	40	61	68	78
36274	ROANOKE	75	53	63	52	53	71	56	65	63	54	61	50	45	65	51	68	41	62	69	80
36276	WADLEY	75	52	66	50	52	72	54	65	61	53	60	51	43	63	50	68	40	62	69	80
36277	WEAVER	82	71	75	70	70	83	70	78	74	68	73	59	64	75	68	78	50	75	81	93
36278	WEDOWEE	73	51	68	50	52	72	54	66	60	51	59	50	42	61	51	66	39	61	69	79
36279	WELLINGTON	77	60	67	58	60	74	60	69	65	59	64	52	51	67	57	70	43	65	72	83
36280	WOODLAND	77	55	67	53	55	74	57	68	63	55	62	52	46	65	53	69	42	64	71	82
36301	DOTHAN	72	62	61	62	61	70	65	68	68	64	67	51	59	69	61	71	46	67	72	81
36303	DOTHAN	74	72	68	73	71	75	72	72	74	74	74	54	72	74	71	76	51	73	77	86
36305	DOTHAN	112	116	103	113	112	107	107	108	105	112	106	83	108	110	106	103	74	105	102	126
36310	ABBEVILLE	73	51	70	49	52	72	54	66	60	52	59	50	43	61	51	67	39	62	70	80
36311	ARITON	69	47	68	44	47	68	49	62	56	46	54	48	38	56	47	62	36	58	65	75
36312	ASHFORD	80	56	71	54	56	77	59	71	66	56	64	54	46	67	55	72	43	66	74	86
36314	BLACK	80	57	66	56	57	76	59	69	66	58	65	53	48	69	54	72	43	65	73	84
36316	CHANCELLOR	78	54	77	52	55	78	57	71	64	53	63	55	45	65	55	71	42	66	75	86
36317	CLOPTON	69	46	67	43	46	68	48	61	56	46	54	47	37	56	46	62	36	57	64	75
36318	COFFEE SPRINGS	76	55	76	53	56	77	56	71	62	53	61	53	45	62	55	68	40	65	74	84
36319	COLUMBIA	73	52	73	50	53	74	54	68	61	50	59	51	43	60	53	67	39	63	72	81
36320	COTTONWOOD	72	54	62	52	54	69	55	64	60	54	59	49	45	62	51	65	40	61	67	77
36321	COWARTS	83	60	68	58	59	78	62	72	69	61	67	55	50	72	56	75	45	68	76	87
36322	DALEVILLE	70	61	59	60	60	67	63	65	65	62	65	49	58	67	59	68	44	65	68	78
36323	ELBA	74	53	67	52	54	73	56	67	62	53	61	51	45	63	53	68	41	63	71	81
36330	ENTERPRISE	81	73	71	74	72	78	77	77	78	75	78	60	72	79	73	80	54	78	80	92
36340	GENEVA	70	49	67	47	50	70	52	64	58	48	57	49	41	59	49	64	38	60	68	77
36343	GORDON	74	51	65	49	51	71	54	65	61	52	59	50	42	63	49	67	40	61	68	79
36344	HARTFORD	70	53	68	51	54	72	54	65	60	51	59	49	45	60	52	66	39	61	69	78
36345	HEADLAND	82	68	79	67	68	84	68	79	73	65	72	60	61	74	67	78	49	75	82	94
36346	JACK	72	50	67	48	51	71	52	64	59	50	57	49	41	60	50	64	38	60	68	78
36349	MALVERN	78	62	64	60	61	74	62	69	67	62	66	52	53	69	57	71	44	66	71	83
36350	MIDLAND CITY	73	62	65	61	61	72	63	69	66	61	65	52	56	67	60	70	44	67	71	82
36351	NEW BROCKTON	83	59	83	57	61	83	61	77	68	57	66	58	49	68	60	74	44	71	80	91
36352	NEWTON	76	66	66	64	66	75	64	71	68	64	68	53	59	70	62	72	46	68	74	84
36353	NEWVILLE	71	50	72	48	51	71	51	65	58	48	56	49	41	58	50	64	37	60	68	78
36360	OZARK	67	58	59	58	57	67	61	64	64	58	63	48	56	64	58	67	43	63	69	76
36362	FORT RUCKER	85	44	33	51	40	38	80	56	75	75	79	55	61	91	58	69	56	71	50	68
36370	PANSEY	74	50	69	47	50	72	53	65	60	50	59	50	40	62	49	67	39	61	69	80
36373	SHORTERVILLE	71	47	68	45	47	70	50	63	57	48	56	49	38	58	47	64	37	59	66	77
36374	SKIPPERVILLE	75	53	76	51	55	75	54	69	61	51	60	52	43	61	54	67	39	64	72	83
36375	SLOCOMB	75	55	71	53	56	74	57	69	63	54	62	52	46	64	54	69	41	64	72	82
36376	WEBB	79	58	66	56	58	76	60	69	66	58	65	53	48	69	55	72	44	66	73	84
36401	BURNT CORN	62	45	56	44	45	61	50	56	56	47	54	43	41	56	46	61	37	55	62	69
36420	ANDALUSIA	74	56	70	55	57	75	60	70	65	56	64	52	50	65	57	71	43	66	75	83
36421	ANDALUSIA	76	57	69	56	58	76	61	71	67	58	65	53	51	67	58	73	44	68	76	84
36425	BEATRICE	55	36	53	34	36	54	38	48	44	36	43	38	29	45	36	49	28	45	51	59
36426	BREWTON	77	59	71	58	59	77	62	72	68	59	66	54	52	68	59	74	45	69	77	86
36432	CASTLEBERRY	64	43	62	40	43	63	45	57	52	43	51	44	34	53	43	58	34	53	60	70
36435	COY	49	32	47	30	32	48	34	43	40	33	39	34	26	40	32	44	26	41	46	53
36436	DICKINSON	66	43	63	40	43	64	46	58	53	43	52	45	34	54	43	59	34	54	61	71
36441	FLOMATON	79	57	67	55	57	76	59	70	66	57	64	53	48	68	54	72	43	66	74	84
36442	FLORALA	56	39	56	37	40	57	42	52	47	38	46	40	33	47	40	52	30	49	56	62
36444	FRANKLIN	64	41	61	39	41	62	44	56	51	42	50	44	33	52	41	57	33	53	59	69
36445	FRISCO CITY	73	49	66	47	49	70	52	64	59	50	58	49	40	61	48	65	38	60	67	78
36446	FULTON	72	47	69	44	47	70	50	63	58	47	56	49	37	59	47	64	37	59	66	77
36451	GROVE HILL	74	50	67	48	50	71	53	64	60	51	59	50	41	62	49	67	39	61	68	79
36453	KINSTON	77	55	71	53	56	75	57	69	63	54	62	53	45	64	54	69	41	64	72	83
36454	LENOX	73	53	61	51	52	70	55	64	61	53	60	49	44	63	50	66	40	60	67	78
36456	MC KENZIE	67	44	65	41	44	66	47	59	54	44	53	46	35	55	44	60	35	55	62	72
36460	MONROEVILLE	80	61	72	60	60	79	64	74	71	61	69	56	54	72	60	76	47	71	79	89
36467	OPP	72	52	66	50	52	71	56	66	62	52	60	50	45	62	52	68	40	63	71	79
36471	PETERMAN	63	41	60	39	41	61	44	55	51	42	49	43	33	52	41	56	33	52	58	68
36473	RANGE	73	53	61	51	52	70	55	64	61	53	60	49	44	63	50	66	40	60	67	78
36474	RED LEVEL	70	50	58	48	49	66	52	61	58	50	56	47	41	60	47	63	38	57	64	74
36475	REPTON	63	44	56	42	44	61	46	55	52	45	51	43	36	54	42	57	34	52	58	68
36477	SAMSON	68	47	68	46	49	69	50	63	56	46	55	48	39	56	48	62	36	58	66	75
36480	URIAH	77	55	64	54	55	73	58	67	64	56	63	52	46	67	52	70	42	64	71	82
36481	VREDENBURGH	59	38	57	36	38	58	41	52	47	39	46	40	31	48	38	53	31	49	55	63
36482	WHATLEY	63	42	59	40	42	62	45	56	52	44	51	43	35	53	42	58	34	53	59	68
36483	WING	68	49	69	47	51	69	50	63	56	47	55	48	40	56	49	61	36	58	66	76
36502	ATMORE	69	50	62	49	50	68	53	62	60	51	58	47	44	60	50	65	39	60	67	76
36505	AXIS	88	81	71	78	79	82	76	80	79	79	79	59	72	82	72	81	54	78	81	96
36507	BAY MINETTE	80	64	67	63	63	77	66	72	71	65	70	55	58	73	61	75	47	70	76	87
36509	BAYOU LA BATRE	71	48	67	46	48	69	51	63	58	48	56	48	39	59	47	64	37	59	66	77
36511	BON SECOUR	89	64	91	62	66	90	65	83	72	61	71	62	52	72	65	80	47	76	86	99
36515	CARLTON	63	45	52	44	45	60	47	55	52	46	51	42	38	55	43	57	34	52	58	67
36518	CHATOM	85	61	75	59	61	83	64	76	71	61	70	58	51	73	59	78	47	72	81	92
36521	CHUNCHULA	76	58	62	56	57	72	59	67	64	58	63	51	49	67	54	69	42	63	69	81
36522	CITRONELLE	78	55	68	53	55	76	58	69	65	56	63	53	46	67	53	71	43	65	73	84
36523	CODEN	80	59	91	58	63	82	60	77	66	57	65	57	50	64	62	71	43	71	78	91
36524	COFFEEVILLE	62	41	60	38	40	61	43	55	50	41	49	43	33	51	40	56	32	51	58	67
36525	CREOLA	75	58	67	55	57	72	58	67	63	58	63	51	49	65	55	68	42	64	69	81
36526	DAPHNE	104	110	101	112	108	104	105	104	102	107	103	81	108	104	106	100	72	103	101	122
36527	SPANISH FORT	114	136	136	139	138	129	117	124	113	124	114	92	130	114	128	112	81	117	117	142
36528	DAUPHIN ISLAND	84	67	109	66	74	89	67	86	71	63	70	63	58	67	73	75	46	79	85	99
36529	DEER PARK	72	49	66	46	48	70	52	63	59	49	57	49	40	60	48	65	38	59	67	77
36530	ELBERTA	81	68	78	66	69	80	66	76	70	66	70	56	60	71	66	74	47	72	77	90
36532	FAIRHOPE	91	92	94	91	93	98	85	92	87	87	87	68	86	87	88	89	60	89	95	108
	ALABAMA	83	70	73	70	69	80	73	77	76	71	76	59	66	77	69	80	52	76	80	92
	UNITED STATES	100	100	100	100	100	100	100	100	100	100	100	100	100	100	100	100	100	100	100	100

36535-36849

ZIP CODE #	POST OFFICE NAME	COUNTY FIPS CODE	POPULATION 2000	POPULATION 2009	POPULATION 2014	2000-2009 ANNUAL RATE % Rate	2000-2009 ANNUAL RATE State Centile	HOUSEHOLDS 2000	HOUSEHOLDS 2009	HOUSEHOLDS 2014	HOUSEHOLDS % Annual Rate 2000-2009	HOUSEHOLDS 2009 Average HH Size	FAMILIES 2000	FAMILIES 2009	FAMILIES % Annual Rate 2000-2009
36535	FOLEY	003	17327	24505	28896	3.8	98	6990	10230	12190	4.2	2.37	4993	7133	3.9
36538	FRANKVILLE	129	499	467	455	-0.7	13	196	191	188	-0.3	2.45	145	139	-0.5
36539	FRUITDALE	129	963	922	902	-0.5	19	352	345	341	-0.2	2.67	273	263	-0.4
36540	GAINESTOWN	025	854	807	780	-0.6	16	277	273	267	-0.2	2.96	211	204	-0.4
36541	GRAND BAY	097	13460	15476	16465	1.5	86	4605	5348	5714	1.6	2.88	3725	4243	1.4
36542	GULF SHORES	003	7576	10297	11804	3.4	97	3537	4955	5739	3.7	2.08	2339	3227	3.5
36544	IRVINGTON	097	10945	12432	13053	1.4	84	3662	4187	4413	1.5	2.96	2973	3327	1.2
36545	JACKSON	025	10424	10151	9876	-0.3	29	3881	3923	3862	0.1	2.56	2914	2891	-0.1
36548	LEROY	129	1023	886	841	-1.5	1	388	349	335	-1.1	2.54	288	256	-1.3
36549	LILLIAN	003	4370	5798	6752	3.1	95	2061	2845	3353	3.5	2.04	1526	2059	3.3
36550	LITTLE RIVER	003	429	496	542	1.6	87	165	199	220	2.0	2.49	116	137	1.8
36551	LOXLEY	003	6040	7893	8957	2.9	95	2044	2811	3245	3.5	2.62	1555	2097	3.3
36553	MC INTOSH	129	4725	4514	4425	-0.5	19	1636	1610	1594	-0.2	2.80	1251	1211	-0.4
36555	MAGNOLIA SPRINGS	003	579	752	870	2.9	95	263	354	415	3.3	2.12	173	224	2.8
36558	MILLRY	129	3244	3498	3552	0.8	74	1284	1442	1482	1.3	2.43	936	1031	1.1
36560	MOUNT VERNON	097	4461	4435	4424	-0.1	39	1442	1441	1441	0.0	2.83	1103	1076	-0.3
36561	ORANGE BEACH	003	4417	6844	8154	4.8	99	2048	3261	3928	5.2	2.10	1299	2008	4.8
36562	PERDIDO	003	1551	1795	1961	1.6	87	569	685	756	2.0	2.62	446	526	1.8
36567	ROBERTSDALE	003	10371	13364	15315	2.8	94	3817	5065	5856	3.1	2.63	2937	3825	2.9
36569	SAINT STEPHENS	129	964	911	888	-0.6	16	341	335	330	-0.2	2.72	260	251	-0.4
36571	SARALAND	097	13665	14016	14185	0.3	58	5285	5453	5535	0.3	2.54	3981	4006	0.1
36572	SATSUMA	097	5785	6265	6467	0.9	76	2047	2232	2314	0.9	2.80	1682	1799	0.7
36574	SEMINOLE	003	1196	1528	1720	2.7	94	459	607	690	3.1	2.52	366	476	2.9
36575	SEMMES	097	14732	15506	15826	0.6	67	5162	5471	5607	0.6	2.83	4226	4396	0.4
36576	SILVERHILL	003	3591	3802	4050	0.6	67	1339	1462	1574	1.0	2.60	1028	1098	0.7
36578	STAPLETON	003	1208	1550	1840	2.7	94	436	575	691	3.0	2.68	355	461	2.9
36579	STOCKTON	003	1871	2044	2180	1.0	77	727	829	895	1.4	2.47	539	600	1.2
36580	SUMMERDALE	003	4568	6092	7036	3.2	96	1685	2292	2666	3.4	2.66	1300	1731	3.1
36582	THEODORE	097	20901	22664	23517	0.9	76	7680	8396	8748	1.0	2.69	5904	6300	0.7
36583	TIBBIE	129	313	301	295	-0.4	25	120	118	117	-0.2	2.55	91	88	-0.4
36584	VINEGAR BEND	129	418	397	389	-0.6	16	168	165	163	-0.2	2.41	132	128	-0.3
36585	WAGARVILLE	129	1674	1541	1491	-0.9	6	642	614	602	-0.5	2.51	483	454	-0.7
36587	WILMER	097	8188	8693	9004	0.6	67	2842	3041	3163	0.7	2.85	2296	2406	0.5
36602	MOBILE	097	922	937	947	0.2	52	552	558	564	0.1	1.38	124	115	-0.8
36603	MOBILE	097	12369	11149	10861	-1.1	3	4143	3710	3614	-1.2	2.77	2628	2273	-1.6
36604	MOBILE	097	11682	11178	11036	-0.5	19	4739	4538	4488	-0.5	2.33	2617	2390	-1.0
36605	MOBILE	097	32617	31383	31009	-0.4	25	12085	11635	11527	-0.4	2.68	8597	8031	-0.7
36606	MOBILE	097	18559	17705	17424	-0.5	19	8034	7643	7534	-0.5	2.31	4767	4348	-1.0
36607	MOBILE	097	8483	8008	7866	-0.6	16	3557	3362	3314	-0.6	2.24	1963	1775	-1.1
36608	MOBILE	097	34950	35084	35403	0.0	45	14062	14141	14287	0.1	2.41	9189	8991	-0.2
36609	MOBILE	097	24535	24488	24416	0.0	45	10737	10704	10703	0.0	2.29	6370	6079	-0.5
36610	MOBILE	097	19235	16897	16320	-1.4	1	6664	5862	5678	-1.4	2.77	4827	4130	-1.7
36611	MOBILE	097	6364	6026	5929	-0.6	16	2747	2618	2584	-0.5	2.30	1766	1621	-0.9
36612	MOBILE	097	5210	4812	4697	-0.9	6	1895	1765	1729	-0.8	2.73	1365	1233	-1.1
36613	EIGHT MILE	097	12547	12994	13232	0.4	62	4344	4527	4626	0.4	2.84	3476	3546	0.2
36615	MOBILE	097	528	482	469	-1.0	4	155	140	137	-1.1	3.26	118	104	-1.4
36617	MOBILE	097	16640	15517	15184	-0.8	9	5974	5593	5488	-0.7	2.69	4332	3935	-1.0
36618	MOBILE	097	15689	15823	15924	0.1	49	5862	5945	6002	0.2	2.65	4468	4427	-0.1
36619	MOBILE	097	14372	14972	15331	0.4	62	5360	5583	5729	0.4	2.67	4172	4264	0.2
36688	MOBILE	097	1555	1556	1556	0.0	45	4	4	4	0.0	2.25	3	3	0.0
36693	MOBILE	097	18520	18525	18577	0.0	45	7383	7415	7455	0.0	2.45	5234	5096	-0.3
36695	MOBILE	097	31201	41164	44568	3.0	95	11402	15005	16287	3.0	2.72	8744	11369	2.9
36701	SELMA	047	24443	22656	21750	-0.8	9	9536	9169	8906	-0.4	2.44	6746	6357	-0.6
36703	SELMA	047	14289	13027	12464	-1.0	4	5347	5062	4898	-0.6	2.52	3708	3436	-0.8
36720	ALBERTA	131	1179	1108	1081	-0.7	13	399	397	393	-0.1	2.79	298	291	-0.3
36722	ARLINGTON	131	648	613	598	-0.6	16	222	220	217	-0.1	2.79	169	164	-0.3
36726	CAMDEN	131	5267	5300	5282	0.1	49	1926	2085	2104	0.9	2.48	1337	1418	0.6
36727	CAMPBELL	025	104	98	94	-0.6	16	39	38	37	-0.3	2.58	27	26	-0.4
36728	CATHERINE	131	662	673	664	0.2	52	221	234	234	0.6	2.88	162	168	0.4
36732	DEMOPOLIS	091	9047	8406	8043	-0.8	9	3586	3468	3364	-0.4	2.40	2500	2366	-0.6
36736	DIXONS MILLS	091	1199	1210	1193	0.1	49	437	464	464	0.7	2.61	327	342	0.5
36738	FAUNSDALE	091	838	786	754	-0.7	13	315	310	302	-0.2	2.54	217	209	-0.4
36740	FORKLAND	063	1994	1864	1789	-0.7	13	773	762	743	-0.2	2.45	525	506	-0.4
36742	GALLION	091	2290	2274	2249	-0.1	39	874	907	909	0.4	2.51	634	643	0.2
36744	GREENSBORO	065	7644	8803	8778	1.5	86	2826	2970	2993	0.5	2.56	2010	2070	0.3
36748	LINDEN	091	4249	3990	3861	-0.7	13	1673	1637	1604	-0.2	2.38	1188	1136	-0.5
36749	JONES	001	1208	1215	1228	0.1	49	452	473	484	0.5	2.57	330	338	0.3
36750	MAPLESVILLE	021	2983	3186	3274	0.7	70	1105	1211	1254	1.0	2.63	845	909	0.8
36751	LOWER PEACH TREE	131	419	398	389	-0.6	16	136	137	136	0.1	2.91	101	99	-0.2
36752	LOWNDESBORO	085	1883	1754	1684	-0.8	9	773	763	746	-0.1	2.30	538	519	-0.4
36754	MAGNOLIA	091	348	328	317	-0.6	16	139	138	135	-0.1	2.38	101	98	-0.3
36756	MARION	105	7713	7147	6853	-0.8	9	2821	2706	2624	-0.4	2.46	1977	1856	-0.7
36758	PLANTERSVILLE	047	1621	1667	1684	0.3	58	615	656	671	0.7	2.54	442	461	0.5
36759	MARION JUNCTION	047	1772	1747	1713	-0.2	34	680	699	695	0.3	2.50	483	485	0.0
36761	MINTER	047	1434	1408	1377	-0.2	34	529	548	545	0.4	2.57	383	387	0.1
36765	NEWBERN	065	1348	1383	1399	0.3	58	482	523	537	0.9	2.46	349	371	0.7
36767	ORRVILLE	047	2230	2040	1951	-1.0	4	832	794	769	-0.5	2.57	572	533	-0.8
36768	PINE APPLE	131	1205	1118	1080	-0.8	9	471	457	448	-0.3	2.44	316	300	-0.6
36769	PINE HILL	131	3304	3118	3043	-0.6	16	1199	1197	1183	0.0	2.60	877	859	-0.2
36773	SAFFORD	047	525	539	536	0.3	58	201	217	219	0.8	2.48	134	140	0.5
36775	SARDIS	047	1052	989	954	-0.7	13	426	422	412	-0.1	2.34	285	276	-0.3
36776	SAWYERVILLE	065	1900	2123	2209	1.2	80	667	778	819	1.7	2.73	485	554	1.4
36782	SWEET WATER	091	2497	2525	2486	0.1	49	948	1003	1002	0.6	2.52	729	757	0.4
36783	THOMASTON	091	1230	1186	1151	-0.4	25	486	487	478	0.0	2.44	350	343	-0.2
36784	THOMASVILLE	025	8950	8545	8260	-0.5	19	3426	3407	3335	-0.1	2.44	2474	2409	-0.3
36785	TYLER	085	1049	950	903	-1.1	3	406	390	376	-0.4	2.44	297	280	-0.6
36786	UNIONTOWN	105	3883	3745	3632	-0.4	25	1404	1412	1387	0.1	2.65	993	977	-0.2
36790	STANTON	021	281	301	309	0.7	70	118	130	135	1.1	2.32	87	94	0.8
36792	RANDOLPH	007	1043	1114	1141	0.7	70	391	432	448	1.1	2.58	301	327	0.9
36793	LAWLEY	007	656	677	684	0.3	58	243	259	265	0.7	2.61	183	192	0.5
36801	OPELIKA	081	20249	20601	21192	0.2	52	8020	8496	8827	0.6	2.35	5354	5474	0.2
36804	OPELIKA	081	14893	16979	18429	1.4	84	5416	6393	7003	1.8	2.65	4234	4880	1.5
36830	AUBURN	081	27490	32221	34840	1.7	88	12242	14636	15890	1.9	2.15	5778	6960	2.0
36832	AUBURN	081	18949	23968	26396	2.6	93	8688	11538	12873	3.1	1.98	2844	3579	2.5
36849	AUBURN UNIVERSITY	081	2189	1984	2028	-1.1	3	0	6	7	0.0	2.50	0	2	0.0
	ALABAMA					0.6					0.9	2.44			0.6
	UNITED STATES					1.0					1.1	2.59			0.9

#	POST OFFICE NAME	RACE (%) White 2000	White 2009	Black 2000	Black 2009	Asian/Pacific 2000	Asian/Pacific 2009	% Hispanic Origin 2000	% Hispanic Origin 2009	2009 AGE DISTRIBUTION (%) 0-4	5-9	10-14	15-19	20-24	25-44	45-64	65-84	85+	18+	MEDIAN AGE 2009	% 2009 Males	% 2009 Females
36535	FOLEY	85.0	81.3	11.9	14.9	0.5	0.6	3.7	4.8	6.3	6.4	6.5	6.1	4.9	25.1	27.4	15.1	2.2	77.1	41.0	48.3	51.7
36538	FRANKVILLE	73.5	70.2	26.1	29.1	0.0	0.0	0.4	0.6	7.3	7.3	7.1	6.6	5.8	25.5	27.8	10.7	1.9	74.1	37.7	50.1	49.9
36539	FRUITDALE	85.7	83.4	12.1	13.6	0.0	0.0	1.1	2.0	8.9	9.0	8.6	7.2	5.5	26.9	23.4	9.2	1.3	69.0	32.8	51.0	49.0
36540	GAINESTOWN	20.4	18.5	78.8	80.7	0.0	0.0	0.8	1.0	8.4	9.2	8.7	9.0	5.9	26.4	22.4	8.3	1.6	68.2	31.6	47.2	52.8
36541	GRAND BAY	86.8	81.4	10.2	14.8	1.2	1.7	1.0	1.4	7.4	7.5	7.7	7.5	6.1	26.8	26.1	9.8	1.0	72.8	35.7	50.0	50.0
36542	GULF SHORES	96.8	96.4	0.3	0.5	0.3	0.4	1.5	2.0	3.6	3.9	4.4	4.8	4.1	21.7	35.3	20.0	2.1	84.8	49.7	49.8	50.2
36544	IRVINGTON	79.9	72.6	12.5	17.7	5.7	7.5	0.9	1.1	8.0	7.9	8.0	8.0	6.7	27.0	25.5	8.3	0.7	71.3	33.1	49.0	51.0
36545	JACKSON	54.8	52.2	44.0	46.3	0.2	0.3	0.5	0.8	7.9	8.1	7.7	6.7	5.1	25.0	25.9	11.7	2.0	72.2	37.1	47.3	52.7
36548	LEROY	63.3	60.0	34.7	37.4	0.1	0.2	0.3	0.6	5.8	6.0	6.8	7.6	6.1	25.6	29.3	11.2	1.7	76.9	38.4	50.5	49.5
36549	LILLIAN	95.1	94.3	2.8	3.3	0.3	0.4	1.0	1.3	2.1	2.2	2.5	2.7	2.0	9.7	30.1	44.8	4.0	91.6	64.5	47.5	52.5
36550	LITTLE RIVER	57.8	54.4	37.5	40.3	0.2	0.2	1.2	1.4	5.8	6.0	6.0	6.3	5.8	23.0	30.2	14.5	2.2	78.4	42.7	50.0	50.0
36551	LOXLEY	79.9	77.5	16.2	17.9	0.2	0.3	2.9	3.6	6.4	6.5	6.7	7.2	6.7	28.1	26.8	10.4	1.1	76.0	37.1	52.4	47.6
36553	MC INTOSH	33.7	29.5	38.8	39.3	0.1	0.2	1.1	1.4	8.4	8.4	8.4	8.0	5.9	26.1	24.9	9.1	0.8	69.8	33.8	49.0	51.0
36555	MAGNOLIA SPRINGS	96.0	95.3	0.5	0.7	1.2	1.5	1.7	2.3	4.3	4.9	5.5	5.5	3.6	21.1	35.6	17.3	2.3	82.2	48.4	49.3	50.7
36558	MILLRY	76.6	74.4	22.6	24.6	0.1	0.1	1.2	1.9	6.3	6.3	6.7	7.3	5.8	25.6	28.2	12.3	1.6	76.2	39.3	49.5	50.5
36560	MOUNT VERNON	36.2	29.4	44.8	50.9	0.2	0.2	0.2	0.3	6.7	6.7	6.9	7.1	5.6	24.9	28.3	12.1	1.6	75.0	38.8	48.4	51.6
36561	ORANGE BEACH	95.9	95.1	0.3	0.3	0.2	0.2	2.0	2.7	3.9	3.6	4.1	4.6	5.2	22.3	37.1	17.8	1.4	85.5	49.0	51.9	48.1
36562	PERDIDO	91.0	89.6	6.6	7.5	0.1	0.2	1.1	1.5	7.4	7.2	7.3	6.5	5.5	27.5	26.6	11.0	0.9	74.0	37.4	49.5	50.5
36567	ROBERTSDALE	94.7	93.6	2.8	3.3	0.2	0.2	1.3	1.9	7.4	7.2	7.1	6.9	6.4	27.0	26.1	10.8	1.1	74.0	36.2	49.2	50.8
36569	SAINT STEPHENS	78.5	75.5	20.6	23.4	0.1	0.2	0.7	1.2	6.6	6.6	6.8	7.0	5.8	26.1	28.6	10.8	1.6	75.5	38.4	51.3	48.7
36571	SARALAND	85.8	79.8	11.6	17.1	0.4	0.6	1.1	1.4	6.4	6.3	6.3	6.5	5.9	27.5	26.6	13.0	1.6	77.3	38.6	48.5	51.5
36572	SATSUMA	90.6	87.5	7.8	10.4	0.2	0.3	0.7	1.0	6.5	6.8	7.1	6.7	4.7	25.7	29.0	12.2	1.4	75.6	39.4	49.4	50.6
36574	SEMINOLE	96.4	95.8	0.4	0.5	0.3	0.3	1.6	2.3	6.7	7.1	6.9	6.2	5.4	25.3	29.6	11.7	1.0	75.6	39.5	51.0	49.0
36575	SEMMES	94.6	92.4	3.4	5.1	0.3	0.4	1.3	1.9	7.5	7.6	7.7	6.9	5.1	28.9	27.0	8.7	0.7	72.8	36.2	49.9	50.1
36576	SILVERHILL	92.4	91.2	4.9	5.4	0.4	0.4	2.0	2.9	7.2	7.2	7.3	6.7	5.5	27.1	26.7	11.1	1.2	73.8	37.5	48.7	51.3
36578	STAPLETON	87.2	85.9	10.9	11.7	0.2	0.2	1.2	1.7	7.0	6.9	7.3	7.5	5.9	26.8	27.3	10.5	1.0	74.1	37.0	51.4	48.6
36579	STOCKTON	63.5	59.4	34.4	38.3	0.1	0.1	1.0	1.1	6.4	6.5	6.8	6.8	5.8	24.6	28.4	13.1	1.8	76.1	40.0	49.2	50.8
36580	SUMMERDALE	87.4	85.9	9.2	10.1	0.3	0.3	2.7	3.7	7.9	7.8	7.8	6.9	5.1	26.8	25.7	11.0	1.0	72.2	36.3	49.5	50.5
36582	THEODORE	84.1	79.2	12.8	16.9	0.9	1.3	1.1	1.5	7.4	7.4	7.4	6.6	5.3	26.7	27.6	10.5	1.0	73.8	37.1	49.5	50.5
36583	TIBBIE	93.9	92.4	3.2	3.7	0.0	0.0	0.6	1.0	8.3	8.0	8.0	6.6	5.3	26.2	24.3	12.0	1.3	71.4	35.6	49.8	50.2
36584	VINEGAR BEND	68.2	64.2	30.1	33.5	0.0	0.0	0.5	1.0	6.8	7.1	7.3	7.6	5.5	24.9	27.5	11.8	1.5	74.3	38.6	48.6	51.4
36585	WAGARVILLE	70.7	67.9	27.1	29.1	0.1	0.2	0.5	1.0	6.8	6.9	6.9	7.3	5.5	24.9	27.1	13.1	1.5	74.8	38.5	48.9	51.1
36587	WILMER	92.4	89.0	5.3	8.2	0.1	0.1	1.2	1.7	8.1	8.0	7.9	7.2	5.7	27.7	26.0	8.7	0.8	71.5	35.2	50.2	49.8
36602	MOBILE	52.0	40.9	44.4	55.1	1.4	1.7	1.4	1.5	2.6	2.3	2.1	3.2	4.9	22.0	30.6	26.4	5.9	91.4	53.9	49.7	50.3
36603	MOBILE	4.6	3.4	94.1	95.4	0.2	0.2	0.8	0.8	10.3	9.1	7.9	7.9	8.8	22.3	20.9	10.2	2.5	68.1	29.6	46.2	53.8
36604	MOBILE	44.3	36.3	53.4	61.2	0.8	1.0	1.1	1.2	7.4	7.0	6.6	8.5	7.6	26.5	25.9	8.5	2.1	73.4	34.8	48.2	51.8
36605	MOBILE	37.4	30.6	60.0	66.6	0.7	0.8	1.3	1.5	8.1	8.3	7.8	8.1	6.6	23.6	25.2	10.6	1.7	70.7	34.3	46.6	53.4
36606	MOBILE	56.3	48.8	40.7	47.8	0.8	1.0	1.7	2.1	7.4	6.9	6.4	6.7	7.2	28.0	24.6	10.7	2.2	75.3	36.3	46.5	53.5
36607	MOBILE	39.1	33.3	59.5	65.1	0.3	0.3	1.0	1.2	6.6	6.5	6.3	6.0	7.1	23.9	24.3	14.4	4.9	77.1	39.5	44.1	55.9
36608	MOBILE	76.8	71.8	19.1	23.2	2.3	2.8	1.5	1.9	6.6	6.5	6.3	7.2	8.0	27.8	23.9	11.4	2.3	76.7	35.3	48.0	52.0
36609	MOBILE	64.0	55.4	29.0	36.3	4.3	5.3	2.2	2.7	8.4	6.8	6.0	6.4	9.5	32.1	20.7	8.8	1.4	75.2	31.7	47.8	52.2
36610	MOBILE	5.4	4.0	93.5	95.1	0.1	0.1	0.7	0.7	8.5	8.6	8.1	9.0	8.0	22.4	23.7	9.7	2.0	69.5	31.3	46.6	53.4
36611	MOBILE	87.5	82.5	9.6	14.0	0.3	0.3	1.1	1.5	7.3	7.2	6.9	6.2	5.6	24.6	24.0	14.8	3.4	74.9	38.6	47.7	52.3
36612	MOBILE	11.2	7.6	87.2	91.0	0.1	0.1	0.5	0.5	6.6	7.9	7.9	8.8	6.4	22.7	26.6	11.6	1.6	72.0	36.1	45.2	54.8
36613	EIGHT MILE	66.7	58.9	31.2	38.9	0.2	0.2	0.6	0.8	6.9	7.2	7.2	7.2	6.3	25.6	28.0	10.5	1.1	74.5	36.7	48.2	51.8
36615	MOBILE	7.2	3.9	90.0	92.9	1.5	1.7	0.6	0.8	8.9	8.9	8.9	11.6	11.0	23.4	21.8	5.0	0.4	67.0	25.4	47.5	52.5
36617	MOBILE	1.3	0.8	98.0	98.6	0.0	0.0	0.6	0.6	7.1	7.2	7.2	8.2	6.4	21.0	24.6	15.6	2.6	73.3	38.4	45.3	54.7
36618	MOBILE	60.5	51.5	37.3	46.0	0.5	0.7	1.0	1.2	6.6	6.9	7.0	6.9	6.3	25.6	27.3	12.0	1.5	75.3	37.7	47.5	52.5
36619	MOBILE	93.9	91.3	3.2	4.9	0.8	1.2	1.1	1.6	6.5	6.7	7.0	6.5	4.7	26.1	29.3	12.0	1.2	75.7	39.6	49.5	50.5
36688	MOBILE	70.6	60.9	22.1	30.1	4.3	5.5	3.0	3.9	0.0	0.0	0.1	37.5	57.7	4.5	0.2	0.0	0.0	99.7	21.1	39.5	60.5
36693	MOBILE	81.7	74.5	15.4	21.9	1.3	1.8	1.4	1.9	5.9	5.9	6.1	6.0	5.1	23.2	27.9	16.3	3.6	78.3	43.2	47.6	52.4
36695	MOBILE	86.5	81.5	9.2	13.2	2.1	2.7	1.9	2.5	7.7	7.4	7.2	6.5	6.3	29.5	27.5	7.1	0.8	73.6	34.9	49.0	51.0
36701	SELMA	43.0	40.7	55.5	57.4	0.6	0.8	0.7	0.9	7.2	7.2	7.0	7.1	6.1	24.1	26.6	12.4	2.2	74.3	37.8	46.1	53.9
36703	SELMA	24.6	22.9	74.5	76.0	0.2	0.2	0.5	0.7	8.4	8.3	8.1	8.4	7.1	23.4	23.9	10.8	1.7	70.6	33.0	44.8	55.2
36720	ALBERTA	3.9	3.7	94.6	94.0	0.0	0.0	1.8	2.8	7.6	7.2	7.8	8.2	7.5	25.6	23.7	10.5	1.9	72.4	33.8	46.2	53.8
36722	ARLINGTON	36.7	34.4	63.1	65.4	0.0	0.0	0.3	0.3	9.6	9.6	8.3	6.4	6.0	23.5	23.8	11.3	1.5	68.5	33.4	48.1	51.9
36726	CAMDEN	34.2	30.0	65.2	69.2	0.3	0.3	0.9	1.1	7.9	8.0	7.8	7.0	6.7	23.4	24.8	11.9	2.4	71.9	35.9	47.0	53.0
36727	CAMPBELL	8.7	7.1	90.4	91.8	0.0	0.0	0.0	0.0	5.1	9.2	7.1	8.2	5.1	28.6	21.4	13.3	2.0	71.4	37.1	48.0	52.0
36728	CATHERINE	22.4	20.4	77.3	79.2	0.0	0.0	0.3	0.4	6.8	8.9	7.7	9.1	5.1	23.0	26.3	10.1	3.0	70.3	35.8	45.9	54.1
36732	DEMOPOLIS	47.1	44.8	51.6	53.4	0.2	0.3	1.0	1.5	7.1	7.5	7.4	7.6	5.9	23.6	26.2	12.3	2.4	73.3	37.6	46.4	53.6
36736	DIXONS MILLS	23.3	20.7	76.3	78.8	0.2	0.2	0.3	0.4	6.4	8.3	7.7	7.2	6.0	22.7	27.6	11.7	2.4	72.7	37.1	48.3	51.7
36738	FAUNSDALE	31.5	29.1	67.5	69.7	0.2	0.3	2.0	2.9	7.4	7.1	7.4	8.8	6.5	23.4	25.7	12.1	1.7	72.9	37.5	48.6	51.4
36740	FORKLAND	19.8	18.7	79.9	81.0	0.0	0.0	0.4	0.5	7.9	8.1	7.9	7.5	5.3	21.7	28.1	11.7	1.7	71.4	38.0	48.6	51.4
36742	GALLION	62.6	59.9	36.5	39.0	0.4	0.5	1.0	1.6	6.7	6.9	7.3	8.4	6.2	23.5	28.7	10.9	1.4	73.7	37.5	49.0	51.0
36744	GREENSBORO	32.6	33.3	66.5	65.2	0.1	0.2	0.9	1.4	7.8	7.6	7.6	8.0	6.9	23.8	24.4	11.2	2.6	72.6	35.3	47.6	52.4
36748	LINDEN	51.9	48.7	47.1	49.9	0.2	0.3	1.0	1.5	6.7	7.2	7.4	7.2	5.3	22.0	26.4	14.6	3.3	74.0	40.2	46.6	53.4
36749	JONES	50.0	45.6	49.1	53.5	0.0	0.0	0.7	0.9	6.6	6.7	6.9	7.5	5.9	23.2	29.3	12.3	1.6	75.4	39.4	48.9	51.1
36750	MAPLESVILLE	76.0	73.6	22.5	24.1	0.1	0.1	1.5	2.5	7.3	7.0	7.3	7.4	6.2	26.4	25.8	11.0	1.5	73.9	36.4	51.4	48.6
36751	LOWER PEACH TREE	6.7	6.0	93.1	93.5	0.0	0.0	0.5	0.5	9.8	10.1	8.3	10.3	7.8	22.6	20.9	9.5	0.8	65.6	28.0	47.2	52.8
36752	LOWNDESBORO	55.3	50.6	42.8	46.7	0.4	0.6	0.7	1.1	5.5	6.1	6.3	6.6	4.8	21.8	31.0	16.2	1.7	78.1	44.2	47.1	52.9
36754	MAGNOLIA	43.8	40.5	55.6	58.8	0.0	0.0	0.6	0.6	7.3	7.3	7.6	7.3	5.5	23.8	25.3	13.7	2.1	72.9	37.9	47.9	52.1
36756	MARION	41.3	38.8	57.7	59.8	0.1	0.1	0.8	1.2	6.6	6.6	6.8	10.5	6.6	21.4	24.8	13.7	3.2	74.8	37.2	46.3	53.7
36758	PLANTERSVILLE	65.2	60.7	33.2	37.1	0.1	0.1	0.6	1.0	7.1	5.8	7.2	8.8	5.7	28.2	26.1	9.4	1.7	74.6	36.5	50.0	50.0
36759	MARION JUNCTION	35.6	31.2	64.0	68.2	0.0	0.0	0.8	1.0	6.2	6.4	6.6	7.1	6.2	23.5	29.5	12.3	2.1	76.4	40.0	47.2	52.8
36761	MINTER	20.7	17.8	79.1	82.0	0.0	0.0	0.3	0.4	6.8	6.5	8.0	8.2	6.0	22.3	24.8	13.8	3.6	73.6	38.1	46.7	53.3
36765	NEWBERN	24.6	25.4	73.9	73.0	0.1	0.2	0.5	0.9	8.1	7.8	7.5	7.5	7.2	24.1	25.3	10.8	1.6	72.2	34.4	49.1	50.9
36767	ORRVILLE	15.5	12.7	83.9	86.5	0.0	0.0	1.0	1.2	6.9	7.0	7.2	7.7	5.7	25.1	26.6	11.7	2.1	74.2	36.9	45.5	54.5
36768	PINE APPLE	24.6	22.8	74.9	76.6	0.2	0.4	0.2	0.4	7.8	7.7	7.2	6.1	5.5	22.8	27.5	12.4	3.0	73.7	38.6	47.5	52.5
36769	PINE HILL	32.1	30.2	67.4	69.2	0.1	0.1	0.5	0.6	8.8	8.5	7.7	8.8	6.3	23.8	23.7	11.2	1.3	69.5	33.3	47.9	52.1
36773	SAFFORD	27.2	23.0	72.6	76.8	0.0	0.0	0.8	0.7	6.5	6.7	6.5	6.5	5.2	22.6	27.5	15.4	3.2	76.1	41.2	47.1	52.9
36775	SARDIS	25.1	21.1	74.0	77.9	0.4	0.5	0.3	0.3	4.4	5.7	7.2	7.2	5.5	22.6	28.1	15.6	3.7	78.0	43.0	46.7	53.3
36776	SAWYERVILLE	15.2	13.8	84.3	85.6	0.0	0.0	0.8	0.8	9.8	8.2	8.9	9.3	5.8	25.5	21.8	9.2	1.5	67.2	30.4	45.8	54.2
36782	SWEET WATER	53.0	50.4	46.5	48.8	0.0	0.0	0.9	1.2	6.8	7.2	7.1	5.9	5.3	23.6	29.0	13.2	1.9	75.3	40.3	49.7	50.3
36783	THOMASTON	32.6	29.8	66.3	68.6	0.2	0.3	1.1	1.6	6.3	6.2	6.4	7.5	6.4	22.9	29.1	12.7	2.4	76.6	40.4	46.9	53.1
36784	THOMASVILLE	59.2	56.4	39.7	42.1	0.2	0.3	0.7	1.1	7.2	7.1	7.1	7.3	6.2	25.0	26.0	12.1	2.1	74.1	37.4	47.6	52.4
36785	TYLER	20.6	18.6	79.2	81.2	0.0	0.0	0.6	0.6	6.8	7.4	8.1	7.4	6.2	23.5	27.5	11.7	1.5	73.3	37.1	45.9	54.1
36786	UNIONTOWN	9.5	8.7	90.1	90.9	0.0	0.0	1.0	1.1	10.1	9.4	8.7	8.5	8.0	22.0	21.6	9.9	1.9	66.5	29.0	43.7	56.3
36790	STANTON	80.1	78.1	18.9	20.9	0.0	0.0	0.7	1.0	7.0	6.6	6.6	7.3	7.0	26.6	26.2	11.3	1.3	75.1	37.1	51.2	48.8
36792	RANDOLPH	88.2	86.7	9.4	9.9	0.1	0.2	2.2	3.5	7.5	7.4	7.5	6.7	5.0	27.2	25.9	11.5	1.3	73.5	37.4	48.3	51.7
36793	LAWLEY	82.9	81.7	15.7	16.5	0.0	0.1	1.4	2.2	6.9	6.9	7.1	6.5	5.2	26.3	27.0	12.4	1.6	75.0	38.8	49.3	50.7
36801	OPELIKA	55.6	53.7	42.4	43.5	0.8	1.3	1.2	1.9	7.2	7.0	6.9	7.2	6.8	26.5	25.2	11.1	2.2	74.7	36.5	46.5	53.5
36804	OPELIKA	71.4	67.5	26.2	29.2	1.3	1.9	0.7	1.2	7.5	7.4	7.4	7.2	6.2	28.2	26.7	8.6	0.8	73.2	35.6	49.5	50.5
36830	AUBURN	77.4	73.2	17.5	19.8	3.2	4.4	1.8	2.8	5.4	5.2	5.2	8.8	21.1	26.2	19.8	7.3	1.2	81.3	27.5	50.0	50.0
36832	AUBURN	70.8	68.4	24.9	25.7	2.8	3.9	1.2	2.0	3.5	3.2	3.3	15.5	41.9	17.9	10.6	3.7	0.5	87.8	22.9	52.8	47.2
36849	AUBURN UNIVERSITY	90.0	87.8	7.6	8.9	0.9	1.5	1.0	1.6	0.7	0.3	0.4	52.9	38.2	5.3	1.7	0.4	0.2	98.4	19.6	28.2	71.8
	ALABAMA	71.1	69.3	26.0	26.7	0.7	1.0	1.7	2.8	6.6	6.6	6.6	6.9	6.6	26.4	26.7	11.7	1.8	76.1	37.8	48.6	51.4
	UNITED STATES	75.1	72.0	12.3	12.7	3.8	4.6	12.5	15.7	6.8	6.7	6.6	7.1	6.9	27.0	26.0	10.9	1.9	75.7	36.9	49.2	50.8

ZIP CODE				2009 HOUSEHOLD INCOME DISTRIBUTION (%)					MEDIAN HOUSEHOLD INCOME					2009 HOME VALUE DISTRIBUTION (%)					
#	POST OFFICE NAME	2009 Per Capita Income	2009 HH Income Base	Less than $25,000	$25,000 to $49,999	$50,000 to $99,999	$100,000 to $149,999	$150,000 or More	2009	2014	2009 National Centile	2009 State Centile	2009 Home Value Base	Less than $50,000	$50,000 to $89,999	$90,000 to $174,999	$175,000 to $399,999	$400,000 or More	2009 Median Home Value
36535	FOLEY	21081	10230	28.4	33.1	30.7	5.4	2.4	40741	41330	35	69	7800	13.1	15.0	34.1	30.7	7.1	144994
36538	FRANKVILLE	17754	191	40.3	22.0	31.4	5.2	1.0	33743	35447	15	38	174	43.1	29.3	25.9	1.7	0.0	56000
36539	FRUITDALE	17014	345	25.8	35.9	33.6	3.5	1.2	41859	41567	39	72	314	37.3	17.8	36.0	6.4	2.5	82381
36540	GAINESTOWN	10988	273	50.5	28.9	18.3	1.5	0.7	24664	25649	3	11	241	41.5	36.1	16.2	5.4	0.8	56212
36541	GRAND BAY	17111	5348	27.2	30.9	36.1	4.2	1.5	43229	45030	43	77	4572	22.6	23.0	40.2	11.1	3.1	96506
36542	GULF SHORES	26354	4955	25.7	30.4	34.9	5.3	3.9	44637	45463	47	81	3647	4.7	4.4	26.3	41.9	22.7	226397
36544	IRVINGTON	15771	4187	31.9	32.2	30.8	3.5	1.7	36838	38633	23	53	3507	27.8	28.2	34.6	8.0	1.5	81586
36545	JACKSON	18549	3923	37.0	25.5	29.2	5.8	2.5	36397	37111	22	51	3167	29.2	28.0	29.7	11.8	1.2	78836
36548	LEROY	19145	349	33.2	18.1	42.1	6.6	0.0	48167	48884	57	87	315	28.9	21.3	36.5	13.0	0.3	89643
36549	LILLIAN	26795	2845	22.0	31.7	39.4	4.6	2.4	47182	47818	55	86	2609	10.8	21.8	30.9	28.7	7.8	129284
36550	LITTLE RIVER	20209	199	42.7	34.2	15.6	3.0	4.5	31981	34197	11	29	178	34.8	19.1	35.4	10.7	0.0	80000
36551	LOXLEY	17894	2811	29.6	29.5	34.8	4.6	1.5	41957	43502	39	72	2280	21.6	18.3	30.5	25.3	4.3	114364
36553	MC INTOSH	13792	1610	36.8	34.8	25.2	2.9	0.3	34266	35518	16	41	1418	41.6	21.0	31.5	4.4	1.4	69565
36555	MAGNOLIA SPRINGS	26917	354	30.2	31.6	28.5	4.5	5.1	43298	44281	43	77	293	5.1	6.5	21.8	43.7	22.9	221354
36558	MILLRY	17784	1442	37.4	28.6	29.3	3.5	1.1	34608	35740	17	43	1282	32.6	28.5	32.0	5.9	1.0	66311
36560	MOUNT VERNON	12591	1441	46.4	28.3	22.0	2.8	0.4	27576	29373	5	17	1212	36.6	33.4	27.1	2.3	0.6	63690
36561	ORANGE BEACH	31715	3261	25.1	28.4	32.0	7.9	6.5	45888	47166	51	83	2390	3.5	2.1	18.3	33.7	42.4	333333
36562	PERDIDO	16200	685	27.3	38.0	32.0	2.8	0.0	37527	38363	25	57	598	32.8	29.8	30.4	6.4	0.7	70000
36567	ROBERTSDALE	19465	5065	27.2	28.3	37.6	4.5	2.4	45795	46521	51	82	4091	14.6	17.9	38.9	23.8	4.9	123496
36569	SAINT STEPHENS	17881	335	30.7	20.6	41.8	6.3	0.6	47648	47679	56	86	305	32.1	29.5	29.5	8.2	0.7	71591
36571	SARALAND	19762	5453	26.4	31.9	35.0	5.0	1.7	43523	45347	44	77	4107	11.8	22.0	53.8	11.2	1.2	108187
36572	SATSUMA	23061	2232	17.6	28.0	40.4	11.3	2.7	54398	53769	70	93	1886	8.1	15.3	50.0	25.2	1.4	128171
36574	SEMINOLE	21489	607	19.4	30.0	44.8	4.0	1.8	50323	50071	62	89	528	16.9	14.2	33.5	28.6	6.8	137791
36575	SEMMES	18261	5471	22.1	30.3	41.6	4.9	1.1	47716	48544	56	86	4696	16.0	20.2	51.0	11.9	0.8	106816
36576	SILVERHILL	20158	1462	22.4	34.7	35.9	5.0	1.9	43947	44635	45	79	1201	15.7	18.9	31.1	29.6	4.7	129258
36578	STAPLETON	18818	575	24.3	31.7	36.9	5.6	1.6	45889	46612	51	83	498	17.7	29.3	25.9	23.1	4.0	96250
36579	STOCKTON	17118	829	37.4	31.7	26.1	4.0	0.8	36689	37885	23	52	730	41.1	22.2	20.8	13.8	2.1	66078
36580	SUMMERDALE	17748	2292	30.7	30.6	31.7	5.8	1.3	40119	40699	33	66	1917	17.4	18.0	38.0	22.2	4.4	118981
36582	THEODORE	17195	8396	31.7	30.6	31.7	4.3	1.7	40535	41985	34	68	6415	18.1	20.9	44.0	13.7	3.3	104021
36583	TIBBIE	18993	118	29.7	23.7	42.4	4.2	0.0	44212	44540	46	80	108	22.2	26.9	36.1	11.1	3.7	91111
36584	VINEGAR BEND	15379	165	46.7	24.2	24.8	1.8	2.4	27562	28604	5	17	148	39.9	21.6	31.8	3.4	3.4	63000
36585	WAGARVILLE	18898	614	33.2	24.8	36.0	4.7	1.3	40705	40598	35	69	546	26.9	33.0	29.9	10.1	0.2	78113
36587	WILMER	16569	3041	30.9	31.1	33.2	3.1	1.7	40786	42418	35	70	2632	26.3	20.1	36.9	14.1	2.7	96906
36602	MOBILE	20673	558	64.5	15.8	14.9	2.7	2.2	15651	15091	1	1	126	4.8	19.0	27.8	43.7	4.8	170833
36603	MOBILE	9278	3710	70.0	15.7	11.9	1.4	0.9	13441	13366	1	1	1207	30.3	33.0	28.3	6.3	2.1	72344
36604	MOBILE	17107	4538	43.7	28.8	20.9	4.5	2.2	28885	29952	7	19	2344	12.7	20.8	39.2	25.3	2.0	117141
36605	MOBILE	13834	11635	45.4	28.1	22.6	2.9	1.1	28730	30340	6	19	7219	17.1	48.2	28.0	3.9	2.9	77277
36606	MOBILE	18815	7643	36.6	32.3	25.3	4.1	1.7	34376	36708	16	41	4464	6.2	36.6	45.9	10.6	0.7	96730
36607	MOBILE	17156	3362	50.2	26.7	16.4	4.1	2.6	24831	25891	3	12	1597	17.6	32.5	31.4	13.8	4.7	89872
36608	MOBILE	25822	14141	27.5	28.1	30.0	7.7	6.7	43795	45898	45	78	8862	5.5	13.0	43.7	27.1	10.7	140181
36609	MOBILE	21162	10704	32.4	28.0	32.4	4.8	2.4	39129	41431	30	63	4873	1.2	17.0	58.4	22.1	1.2	129681
36610	MOBILE	9580	5862	65.6	21.6	10.3	1.7	0.8	16729	16732	1	2	2822	43.7	38.6	16.2	1.4	0.1	54986
36611	MOBILE	16348	2618	40.8	32.9	22.8	3.1	0.4	31635	33609	11	27	1703	10.9	51.7	34.8	2.6	0.0	79111
36612	MOBILE	12238	1765	48.4	30.9	17.7	2.9	0.2	26010	27197	4	14	1019	30.4	42.8	25.8	1.0	0.0	67415
36613	EIGHT MILE	17667	4527	28.4	31.1	32.9	6.1	1.4	42618	44273	41	74	3832	17.6	30.5	43.1	7.9	0.9	92239
36615	MOBILE	8737	140	58.6	26.4	14.3	0.7	0.0	20590	21258	2	4	21	19.0	66.7	14.3	0.0	0.0	63571
36617	MOBILE	12802	5593	52.0	26.0	18.4	2.8	0.8	23529	25023	2	9	3595	21.5	42.2	33.4	2.9	0.0	76434
36618	MOBILE	19836	5945	24.5	30.0	36.8	6.7	2.0	46284	47345	52	84	4806	5.7	33.0	53.5	7.3	0.6	100730
36619	MOBILE	21954	5583	24.5	27.4	35.5	9.7	2.9	48148	49067	57	87	4364	7.9	22.8	47.5	19.4	2.5	114617
36688	MOBILE	11890	4	0.0	100.0	0.0	0.0	0.0	42500	42500	41	74	0	0.0	0.0	0.0	0.0	0.0	0
36693	MOBILE	25404	7415	19.7	27.5	40.1	8.7	4.0	52390	52119	67	92	5459	2.5	7.5	61.1	25.9	2.9	140511
36695	MOBILE	26427	15005	15.3	22.9	41.4	14.8	5.6	61468	61310	79	95	11590	4.8	5.8	47.2	38.5	3.6	156010
36701	SELMA	17353	9169	41.5	26.8	25.2	4.9	1.7	31870	34348	11	28	6177	23.9	29.0	35.9	9.9	1.4	85384
36703	SELMA	13056	5062	54.7	22.3	19.0	3.4	0.6	21173	22419	2	5	2714	40.3	26.5	24.7	8.1	0.4	59034
36720	ALBERTA	7955	397	66.8	21.9	9.3	2.0	0.0	15125	15310	1	1	356	47.5	27.8	11.2	13.5	0.0	53333
36722	ARLINGTON	11321	220	55.0	27.7	14.1	1.8	1.4	21162	22104	2	5	201	51.2	24.4	14.9	5.0	4.5	47222
36726	CAMDEN	13354	2085	53.2	25.2	16.9	3.5	1.1	21574	22252	2	6	1629	35.5	23.6	30.5	8.4	2.0	68820
36727	CAMPBELL	10529	38	47.4	44.7	7.9	0.0	0.0	25549	25839	4	13	34	67.6	32.4	0.0	0.0	0.0	33333
36728	CATHERINE	9806	234	62.0	22.6	13.2	1.3	0.9	19600	19798	1	3	210	44.3	32.4	14.8	4.8	3.8	55455
36732	DEMOPOLIS	18563	3468	44.3	25.0	21.4	6.1	3.1	30990	32812	10	24	2437	23.7	20.8	39.0	15.6	0.9	97472
36736	DIXONS MILLS	11501	464	58.0	20.3	18.5	2.8	0.4	18537	19705	1	3	415	47.7	29.6	17.1	1.0	4.6	52794
36738	FAUNSDALE	11945	310	57.4	23.9	14.8	3.5	0.3	20482	22046	2	4	254	50.8	26.0	11.4	9.8	2.0	49167
36740	FORKLAND	14343	762	51.2	30.6	14.2	2.1	2.0	23882	25224	3	10	668	39.1	28.0	27.7	3.1	2.1	60678
36742	GALLION	17291	907	35.7	27.1	30.9	5.3	1.0	34503	36316	17	42	789	38.4	22.2	22.6	13.4	3.4	77439
36744	GREENSBORO	14062	2970	47.2	27.2	20.5	3.9	1.1	26633	27919	4	15	2207	36.2	23.9	29.2	8.7	2.0	68699
36748	LINDEN	17015	1637	42.8	23.7	28.6	4.2	0.7	30979	32034	10	23	1236	31.3	34.0	28.0	6.3	0.4	72143
36749	JONES	14688	473	47.6	23.7	26.0	1.7	1.1	26950	28284	5	16	397	38.3	16.1	34.8	9.6	1.3	79211
36750	MAPLESVILLE	16667	1211	33.4	29.8	31.6	4.9	0.3	37478	39290	25	56	1031	24.6	23.2	42.7	8.7	0.8	93571
36751	LOWER PEACH TREE	9573	137	65.7	19.0	11.7	2.2	1.5	14132	14673	1	1	111	50.5	20.7	24.3	1.8	2.7	49583
36752	LOWNDESBORO	23681	763	32.4	22.4	35.1	6.8	3.3	43869	44701	45	79	642	29.1	19.3	33.2	16.7	1.7	93333
36754	MAGNOLIA	15304	138	50.0	22.5	22.5	5.1	0.0	25000	26234	3	12	111	42.3	26.1	27.9	3.6	0.0	57727
36756	MARION	14616	2706	46.7	24.9	23.8	3.5	1.0	27839	29684	5	18	2071	37.7	27.6	26.8	6.8	1.1	64020
36758	PLANTERSVILLE	13881	656	50.3	27.0	17.8	4.9	0.0	24778	26228	3	11	552	52.0	15.0	26.3	6.7	0.0	46207
36759	MARION JUNCTION	15344	699	52.2	17.5	26.0	2.6	1.7	23114	24795	2	8	561	42.2	23.5	21.7	7.8	4.6	64464
36761	MINTER	11875	548	55.8	30.8	9.5	2.2	1.6	20857	21620	2	5	445	44.9	17.3	25.8	6.5	5.4	59783
36765	NEWBERN	12165	523	54.7	24.1	19.7	1.5	0.0	21916	23150	2	6	450	35.3	31.8	20.4	12.0	0.4	74510
36767	ORRVILLE	10538	794	60.2	24.7	12.6	2.5	0.0	17701	18827	1	2	603	38.0	30.5	26.4	4.6	0.5	60273
36768	PINE APPLE	12119	457	63.7	17.7	16.0	1.5	1.1	16425	16697	1	2	397	58.7	15.4	17.1	8.8	0.0	34853
36769	PINE HILL	12882	1197	53.5	23.7	19.0	3.0	0.8	21665	23292	2	6	1014	44.3	26.3	21.8	5.4	2.2	59063
36773	SAFFORD	12415	217	61.3	26.3	7.4	2.3	2.8	17790	17684	1	2	171	43.3	20.5	26.3	7.0	2.9	63889
36775	SARDIS	15820	422	50.0	24.2	22.7	1.2	1.9	25000	29495	3	12	335	27.5	21.5	36.1	14.3	0.6	92188
36776	SAWYERVILLE	12036	778	52.1	30.3	14.3	2.1	1.3	23454	24106	2	8	686	53.2	23.3	20.1	3.4	0.0	46857
36782	SWEET WATER	17386	1003	40.3	24.5	28.3	5.2	1.7	33613	35000	15	37	889	45.8	25.9	18.4	6.2	3.7	56148
36783	THOMASTON	15587	487	51.3	20.7	23.2	2.1	2.7	23869	25287	3	10	426	45.3	24.2	24.4	5.4	0.7	55405
36784	THOMASVILLE	16840	3407	38.6	27.8	27.8	4.9	0.9	32397	33524	12	31	2620	32.1	27.8	29.2	8.6	2.2	76583
36785	TYLER	14388	390	49.2	24.4	23.6	1.8	1.0	25628	27072	4	13	327	35.8	29.7	24.5	8.3	1.8	65690
36786	UNIONTOWN	10091	1412	63.2	23.4	11.8	0.8	0.8	17586	17740	1	2	955	49.4	28.8	18.0	2.6	1.2	50663
36790	STANTON	19274	130	33.8	30.0	31.5	4.6	0.0	38599	39791	28	61	109	33.0	26.6	33.9	6.4	0.0	77500
36792	RANDOLPH	17094	432	28.9	35.9	30.3	4.4	0.5	38704	40110	29	62	370	30.8	25.9	23.8	16.8	2.7	79545
36793	LAWLEY	16676	259	29.0	37.5	29.7	3.5	0.4	38384	39553	28	60	220	33.2	24.5	28.2	12.7	1.4	79286
36801	OPELIKA	19439	8496	37.4	25.0	30.3	5.1	2.0	37040	38680	24	55	4959	19.5	14.4	41.8	21.3	3.0	125913
36804	OPELIKA	19377	6393	26.2	29.1	36.8	6.1	1.7	44405	45342	47	81	5279	30.4	19.2	30.5	14.1	5.8	90874
36830	AUBURN	23205	14636	42.3	18.6	27.2	8.2	3.7	34810	37740	17	43	7105	12.9	6.7	29.8	39.5	11.1	177326
36832	AUBURN	13760	11538	66.1	18.9	10.9	2.7	1.3	15055	15092	1	1	4972	50.3	11.0	13.8	20.4	4.4	49317
36849	AUBURN UNIVERSITY	9089	6	0.0	83.3	16.7	0.0	0.0	35000	32225	18	44	1	0.0	0.0	0.0	100.0	0.0	225000
	ALABAMA	21187		31.4	27.9	30.6	6.9	3.2	40822	42202				18.1	22.4	35.8	19.6	4.0	107730
	UNITED STATES	27277		20.9	24.4	35.3	11.7	7.6	54719	56938				9.3	13.1	31.6	32.6	13.5	162279

#	POST OFFICE NAME	FINANCIAL SERVICES: Auto Loan	FINANCIAL SERVICES: Home Loan	FINANCIAL SERVICES: Invest-ments	FINANCIAL SERVICES: Retire-ment Plans	THE HOME: Home Improvements: Home Repair	THE HOME: Home Improvements: Lawn & Garden	THE HOME: Furnishings: Comput-ers & Hard-ware-Personal	THE HOME: Furnishings: Major Appli-ances	THE HOME: Furnishings: TV, Radio, Sound Equip-ment	THE HOME: Furnishings: Furni-ture	ENTERTAINMENT: Dine out/ Carry out	ENTERTAINMENT: Sports Equip-ment	ENTERTAINMENT: Fees & Tickets	ENTERTAINMENT: Toys & Games	ENTERTAINMENT: Travel	ENTERTAINMENT: Cable TV	PERSONAL: Apparel & Services	PERSONAL: Auto Repairs	PERSONAL: Health Insur-ance	PERSONAL: Pets & Supplies
36535	FOLEY	82	68	80	67	70	82	69	79	73	67	72	58	61	73	68	77	48	75	81	93
36538	FRANKVILLE	80	53	76	50	53	78	57	70	65	54	63	55	43	66	53	72	42	66	74	87
36539	FRUITDALE	82	59	69	57	58	78	61	71	68	59	67	55	49	71	56	74	45	68	75	87
36540	GAINESTOWN	55	40	46	39	39	53	43	48	49	43	48	36	36	49	39	54	32	48	54	60
36541	GRAND BAY	86	66	72	64	65	82	67	76	73	66	72	58	56	76	62	78	48	73	79	92
36542	GULF SHORES	88	73	112	73	81	94	74	90	77	71	76	65	67	72	79	81	51	84	91	104
36544	IRVINGTON	81	63	67	61	62	76	64	72	69	64	68	54	55	72	59	73	46	69	74	86
36545	JACKSON	83	62	77	61	62	83	64	76	70	60	69	59	52	72	61	77	46	71	80	92
36548	LEROY	88	63	73	61	62	84	65	76	73	64	71	59	52	76	60	79	48	72	81	93
36549	LILLIAN	72	76	103	68	89	99	69	88	76	77	73	51	76	66	83	83	48	82	109	96
36550	LITTLE RIVER	92	63	84	60	63	89	66	81	75	64	74	63	51	77	61	83	49	76	85	99
36551	LOXLEY	84	64	75	61	63	80	65	75	71	64	70	57	55	73	61	76	47	71	77	91
36553	MC INTOSH	71	49	63	47	48	68	51	62	58	49	57	48	40	60	47	64	38	58	65	76
36555	MAGNOLIA SPRINGS	95	78	114	76	84	98	77	95	80	74	80	69	68	78	82	85	53	88	94	110
36558	MILLRY	78	56	65	54	55	74	58	68	64	56	63	52	46	67	53	70	42	64	71	82
36560	MOUNT VERNON	66	44	63	42	44	64	47	58	53	45	52	45	36	54	44	59	35	55	61	71
36561	ORANGE BEACH	101	89	125	89	97	108	90	103	94	90	93	74	86	88	96	98	63	100	108	121
36562	PERDIDO	76	55	63	54	55	73	57	67	63	56	62	51	46	66	52	69	42	63	70	81
36567	ROBERTSDALE	82	73	68	71	72	78	72	76	75	73	74	56	66	77	68	77	51	74	77	90
36569	SAINT STEPHENS	89	62	77	59	61	85	65	77	73	63	71	60	51	75	59	80	48	73	82	94
36571	SARALAND	73	71	65	71	70	76	70	72	73	69	72	54	69	74	69	76	50	72	78	86
36572	SATSUMA	92	97	83	100	93	100	91	94	91	89	91	73	93	93	93	93	63	91	97	111
36574	SEMINOLE	87	80	71	77	78	81	75	80	78	78	78	58	71	81	72	80	53	77	80	95
36575	SEMMES	79	78	68	77	76	79	72	76	73	74	74	57	72	76	71	75	51	73	76	90
36576	SILVERHILL	84	76	70	74	75	80	73	78	76	75	76	57	68	78	70	78	51	75	78	92
36578	STAPLETON	90	67	74	65	67	85	69	78	75	68	74	60	57	78	63	81	50	75	82	95
36579	STOCKTON	77	54	67	52	53	74	56	67	63	54	62	52	44	65	52	69	41	63	71	82
36580	SUMMERDALE	78	67	70	64	66	76	64	73	68	65	68	53	58	70	62	72	46	69	74	86
36582	THEODORE	78	64	68	62	63	76	63	71	68	62	67	54	56	69	60	72	45	68	74	86
36583	TIBBIE	87	63	72	61	62	83	65	76	72	64	71	58	52	76	59	79	48	72	80	92
36584	VINEGAR BEND	68	45	64	43	45	67	48	60	55	46	54	47	37	57	45	62	36	57	63	74
36585	WAGARVILLE	86	60	75	58	60	83	63	75	71	61	69	58	50	73	58	78	46	71	80	92
36587	WILMER	82	64	67	62	63	78	64	73	70	64	69	55	55	73	60	75	47	69	75	88
36602	MOBILE	39	30	34	34	31	35	45	37	47	41	47	29	41	42	40	49	33	44	48	47
36603	MOBILE	37	28	26	29	26	32	34	32	39	34	38	24	31	38	30	41	26	36	38	40
36604	MOBILE	58	52	47	53	50	55	58	54	60	56	60	42	55	60	53	62	41	58	60	66
36605	MOBILE	57	46	46	47	44	55	51	52	56	49	55	40	46	55	47	59	37	54	59	64
36606	MOBILE	63	56	52	57	54	60	63	59	64	59	64	46	59	64	58	66	44	62	65	72
36607	MOBILE	55	47	46	49	46	52	55	51	59	54	58	39	51	57	50	62	40	56	60	64
36608	MOBILE	89	87	83	88	86	89	90	87	91	89	91	67	89	90	88	92	63	89	93	104
36609	MOBILE	70	59	55	62	57	58	72	62	71	70	72	51	67	72	65	70	50	69	65	77
36610	MOBILE	39	29	28	30	28	36	35	34	41	36	39	25	32	39	31	44	27	37	41	43
36611	MOBILE	59	46	52	46	46	59	52	56	56	48	55	43	45	56	48	60	37	56	62	67
36612	MOBILE	48	43	40	43	41	49	44	45	50	46	49	32	44	48	42	53	33	47	53	56
36613	EIGHT MILE	77	72	67	71	69	78	69	73	73	70	73	54	67	74	67	76	49	72	78	88
36615	MOBILE	42	35	29	37	32	38	39	36	42	39	42	28	37	43	35	44	29	39	41	46
36617	MOBILE	49	44	40	45	42	49	46	46	52	48	51	33	45	50	44	55	35	49	54	57
36618	MOBILE	73	75	63	76	70	79	73	72	76	72	76	55	75	77	72	79	52	74	81	88
36619	MOBILE	87	86	84	86	85	94	81	88	83	80	83	67	80	85	83	86	57	84	91	103
36688	MOBILE	65	28	27	34	25	32	92	45	73	62	74	49	54	71	49	66	52	64	45	61
36693	MOBILE	89	91	91	92	92	94	88	91	89	89	89	67	90	88	90	90	61	90	95	106
36695	MOBILE	109	112	94	110	106	97	105	102	101	111	103	81	105	107	102	97	72	100	93	119
36701	SELMA	64	56	55	56	55	64	58	61	63	57	62	45	55	63	56	66	42	61	67	73
36703	SELMA	53	39	41	39	38	49	44	46	50	44	49	35	39	50	40	54	33	48	52	57
36720	ALBERTA	41	27	40	25	27	40	29	36	33	27	32	28	22	34	27	37	21	34	38	45
36722	ARLINGTON	59	38	57	36	38	58	41	52	47	39	46	40	31	48	38	53	31	49	54	63
36726	CAMDEN	61	41	59	39	41	60	43	54	49	41	48	42	33	50	41	55	32	51	58	66
36727	CAMPBELL	51	33	49	31	33	50	35	44	41	33	40	35	26	41	33	45	26	42	47	55
36728	CATHERINE	52	34	51	32	34	51	37	46	42	35	41	36	27	43	34	47	27	43	49	57
36732	DEMOPOLIS	69	58	60	58	57	69	61	64	66	60	65	48	56	66	58	70	45	65	70	78
36736	DIXONS MILLS	56	36	54	34	36	55	39	49	45	37	44	38	29	46	36	50	29	46	52	60
36738	FAUNSDALE	56	37	54	35	37	55	39	49	45	37	44	39	29	46	37	51	29	47	52	61
36740	FORKLAND	65	43	63	40	42	64	46	57	53	43	51	45	34	53	42	59	34	54	61	71
36742	GALLION	80	54	72	52	54	77	57	70	65	55	63	54	44	67	53	72	42	66	73	85
36744	GREENSBORO	65	44	60	42	44	63	49	58	56	46	54	44	39	56	45	61	36	56	63	71
36748	LINDEN	74	50	73	48	51	74	53	67	61	50	59	51	41	61	50	67	39	63	71	81
36749	JONES	70	46	68	43	46	69	49	62	56	47	55	48	37	57	46	63	37	58	65	76
36750	MAPLESVILLE	79	57	65	55	56	75	59	69	66	58	64	53	47	68	54	71	43	65	73	84
36751	LOWER PEACH TREE	41	32	31	33	31	40	37	37	43	38	41	26	34	41	33	47	28	40	45	46
36752	LOWNDESBORO	98	69	99	66	70	99	71	90	80	67	78	69	56	80	69	88	52	84	94	108
36754	MAGNOLIA	68	44	65	42	44	66	47	59	54	45	53	46	35	55	44	61	35	56	63	73
36756	MARION	64	44	59	42	44	63	48	57	55	46	53	44	38	55	44	61	36	55	62	70
36758	PLANTERSVILLE	65	44	61	41	43	63	46	57	53	44	52	44	35	54	43	59	34	54	60	70
36759	MARION JUNCTION	70	48	65	45	47	68	50	61	57	49	56	48	39	59	47	63	37	58	65	75
36761	MINTER	57	37	55	35	37	56	40	50	46	38	45	39	30	46	37	51	30	47	53	61
36765	NEWBERN	56	36	54	34	36	55	39	49	45	37	44	38	29	46	36	50	29	46	52	60
36767	ORRVILLE	50	33	49	31	33	49	35	44	41	33	40	35	26	41	33	45	26	42	47	54
36768	PINE APPLE	55	36	53	34	36	54	38	48	44	36	43	38	29	45	36	49	29	45	51	59
36769	PINE HILL	59	40	54	39	40	57	44	52	51	43	49	39	35	51	40	56	33	51	57	64
36773	SAFFORD	57	37	55	35	37	56	40	50	46	38	45	39	30	47	37	51	30	47	53	62
36775	SARDIS	69	45	67	43	45	68	48	61	55	46	54	47	36	56	45	62	36	57	64	74
36776	SAWYERVILLE	61	40	59	37	40	60	43	54	49	40	48	42	32	50	40	55	32	51	57	66
36782	SWEET WATER	80	55	78	53	56	79	57	72	65	54	63	55	45	65	55	71	42	67	76	87
36783	THOMASTON	70	46	68	43	46	69	49	62	57	47	55	48	37	58	46	63	37	58	66	76
36784	THOMASVILLE	73	52	63	51	52	70	56	65	62	53	61	50	45	64	51	68	41	62	69	79
36785	TYLER	65	43	63	41	43	64	46	58	52	43	51	44	35	53	43	58	34	54	61	70
36786	UNIONTOWN	40	29	29	30	28	36	36	35	42	36	40	26	32	40	31	45	28	38	42	44
36790	STANTON	81	58	66	56	57	76	60	70	67	59	65	54	48	70	55	73	44	66	74	85
36792	RANDOLPH	80	57	66	56	57	76	59	69	66	58	65	53	48	69	54	72	43	65	73	84
36793	LAWLEY	78	56	69	55	57	76	58	69	65	56	64	53	47	67	54	71	43	65	73	84
36801	OPELIKA	70	59	58	60	58	66	65	64	69	64	68	49	60	69	60	71	47	67	70	78
36804	OPELIKA	82	75	69	72	73	78	72	76	74	74	74	57	67	77	69	76	51	74	76	90
36830	AUBURN	74	58	57	62	57	61	83	65	77	72	77	56	69	77	67	75	54	73	66	80
36832	AUBURN	42	23	22	26	21	25	54	31	45	40	46	31	36	45	33	42	32	41	32	41
36849	AUBURN UNIVERSITY	51	52	50	53	51	50	53	50	53	54	53	40	54	53	53	52	37	52	51	60
	ALABAMA	83	70	73	70	69	80	73	77	76	71	76	59	66	77	69	80	52	76	80	92
	UNITED STATES	100	100	100	100	100	100	100	100	100	100	100	100	100	100	100	100	100	100	100	100

POPULATION CHANGE

#	POST OFFICE NAME	COUNTY FIPS CODE	POPULATION 2000	POPULATION 2009	POPULATION 2014	2000-2009 ANNUAL RATE % Rate	2000-2009 ANNUAL RATE State Centile	HOUSEHOLDS 2000	HOUSEHOLDS 2009	HOUSEHOLDS 2014	HOUSEHOLDS % Annual Rate 2000-2009	HOUSEHOLDS 2009 Average HH Size	FAMILIES 2000	FAMILIES 2009	FAMILIES % Annual Rate 2000-2009
36850	CAMP HILL	123	2822	2718	2648	-0.4	25	1142	1141	1124	0.0	2.37	790	771	-0.3
36852	CUSSETA	017	2043	2427	2564	1.9	89	772	945	1006	2.2	2.57	579	692	1.9
36853	DADEVILLE	123	8165	8432	8352	0.3	58	3271	3508	3512	0.8	2.31	2378	2501	0.5
36854	VALLEY	017	14153	14098	14103	0.0	45	5690	5831	5887	0.3	2.39	4040	4061	0.1
36855	FIVE POINTS	017	1745	1724	1694	-0.1	39	720	744	740	0.4	2.32	512	517	0.1
36856	FORT MITCHELL	113	1577	2342	2590	4.4	98	559	851	949	4.6	2.75	421	628	4.4
36858	HATCHECHUBBEE	113	917	926	932	0.1	49	362	380	386	0.5	2.44	243	248	0.2
36860	HURTSBORO	113	1725	1691	1678	-0.2	34	736	752	755	0.2	2.24	460	455	-0.1
36861	JACKSONS GAP	123	3522	3498	3442	-0.1	39	1420	1458	1448	0.3	2.40	1064	1075	0.1
36862	LAFAYETTE	017	7052	6924	6795	-0.2	34	2646	2711	2691	0.3	2.44	1856	1860	0.0
36863	LANETT	017	13511	12476	11991	-0.9	6	5382	5139	4990	-0.5	2.41	3760	3515	-0.7
36866	NOTASULGA	087	3579	3528	3457	-0.2	34	1459	1503	1490	0.3	2.35	992	989	0.0
36867	PHENIX CITY	113	18497	19951	20652	0.8	74	7790	8639	9019	1.1	2.29	5107	5570	0.9
36869	PHENIX CITY	113	19464	19878	20147	0.2	52	7358	7782	7970	0.6	2.50	5173	5346	0.4
36870	PHENIX CITY	081	12859	15479	16929	2.0	90	4623	5703	6282	2.3	2.71	3625	4403	2.1
36871	PITTSVIEW	113	1720	1795	1838	0.5	64	658	711	737	0.8	2.51	471	498	0.6
36874	SALEM	081	6669	7691	8397	1.6	87	2424	2883	3177	1.9	2.67	1923	2240	1.7
36875	SEALE	113	4691	4951	5146	0.6	67	1732	1881	1976	0.9	2.63	1289	1372	0.7
36877	SMITHS STATION	081	9590	11476	12613	2.0	90	3557	4388	4867	2.3	2.62	2806	3387	2.1
36879	WAVERLY	017	1234	1574	1710	2.7	94	497	656	719	3.0	2.40	340	430	2.6
36904	BUTLER	023	4807	4937	4961	0.3	58	1978	2131	2173	0.8	2.26	1379	1454	0.6
36907	CUBA	119	2016	1811	1703	-1.2	2	770	713	680	-0.8	2.54	534	484	-1.1
36908	GILBERTOWN	023	2363	2274	2226	-0.4	25	964	967	957	0.0	2.35	718	708	-0.2
36910	JACHIN	023	350	433	461	2.3	91	146	190	205	2.9	2.28	100	128	2.7
36912	LISMAN	023	2151	2294	2327	0.7	70	844	946	974	1.2	2.42	582	638	1.0
36915	NEEDHAM	023	770	732	712	-0.5	19	306	305	301	0.0	2.40	232	227	-0.2
36916	PENNINGTON	023	668	648	640	-0.3	29	281	287	287	0.2	2.26	192	192	0.0
36919	SILAS	023	2632	2720	2739	0.4	62	993	1081	1103	0.9	2.52	753	806	0.7
36921	TOXEY	023	1495	1398	1353	-0.7	13	587	574	562	-0.2	2.42	431	414	-0.4
36922	WARD	023	809	791	788	-0.2	34	316	324	327	0.3	2.44	219	221	0.1
36925	YORK	119	4626	4228	3997	-1.0	4	1705	1596	1525	-0.7	2.56	1129	1031	-1.0
	ALABAMA					0.6					0.9	2.44			0.6
	UNITED STATES					1.0					1.1	2.59			0.9

ZIP CODE #	POST OFFICE NAME	RACE (%) White 2000	White 2009	Black 2000	Black 2009	Asian/Pacific 2000	Asian/Pacific 2009	% Hispanic Origin 2000	% Hispanic Origin 2009	2009 AGE DISTRIBUTION (%) 0-4	5-9	10-14	15-19	20-24	25-44	45-64	65-84	85+	18+	MEDIAN AGE 2009	% 2009 Males	% 2009 Females
36850	CAMP HILL	34.6	32.2	64.2	66.3	0.0	0.0	1.0	1.4	6.5	6.8	7.1	7.2	4.8	23.1	30.1	12.5	1.8	74.9	39.9	47.6	52.4
36852	CUSSETA	77.6	76.3	20.7	21.4	0.3	0.4	0.8	1.4	7.6	7.3	7.1	6.9	6.3	29.4	25.8	8.8	0.9	73.9	35.3	49.0	51.0
36853	DADEVILLE	73.6	71.8	24.9	26.3	0.2	0.3	0.7	1.1	5.3	5.5	5.8	5.6	4.4	21.8	31.1	17.9	2.6	79.8	46.1	48.9	51.1
36854	VALLEY	76.9	75.6	21.9	22.8	0.3	0.4	0.9	1.4	6.9	6.8	6.9	6.4	5.4	26.2	26.2	12.8	2.4	75.5	38.8	47.7	52.3
36855	FIVE POINTS	64.2	62.4	35.2	36.8	0.0	0.0	0.4	0.6	6.0	6.3	6.7	6.4	4.6	24.3	29.4	14.4	2.0	77.0	41.9	48.5	51.5
36856	FORT MITCHELL	61.9	57.8	33.2	36.0	1.1	1.1	3.1	5.1	8.5	8.0	7.6	7.5	6.9	27.2	25.0	8.5	0.8	71.3	33.2	49.1	50.9
36858	HATCHECHUBBEE	28.4	24.5	70.7	74.3	0.1	0.1	1.1	1.3	6.4	7.5	7.6	7.1	4.8	21.9	29.5	13.4	1.9	74.2	40.5	49.2	50.8
36860	HURTSBORO	18.0	15.3	81.4	84.1	0.0	0.0	0.5	0.5	6.4	7.6	7.7	6.9	4.8	22.2	28.2	13.7	2.6	74.2	40.5	47.6	52.4
36861	JACKSONS GAP	90.1	88.5	9.0	10.2	0.2	0.3	0.7	1.2	5.0	5.2	5.6	5.3	4.2	22.0	34.7	17.0	1.1	80.9	46.9	51.0	49.0
36862	LAFAYETTE	43.1	39.4	56.0	59.4	0.1	0.2	0.9	1.2	5.7	6.0	6.1	6.4	5.5	25.4	27.9	13.7	3.2	78.3	41.1	48.2	51.8
36863	LANETT	58.4	56.1	40.5	42.4	0.2	0.2	0.7	1.2	7.0	7.0	6.8	6.7	5.7	25.1	26.3	13.1	2.3	75.1	38.7	47.9	52.1
36866	NOTASULGA	59.0	53.8	39.8	44.5	0.1	0.2	0.9	1.4	6.5	6.5	7.0	6.5	5.8	24.4	28.8	12.7	1.7	76.0	39.6	48.5	51.5
36867	PHENIX CITY	70.7	68.5	27.0	28.3	0.6	1.0	1.6	2.6	7.3	6.7	6.4	6.2	7.1	26.9	24.5	12.8	2.0	75.8	36.8	46.6	53.4
36869	PHENIX CITY	46.7	44.8	51.0	52.3	0.3	0.4	1.4	2.0	7.2	7.2	7.0	7.2	6.8	26.9	25.7	10.6	1.5	74.1	35.8	48.3	51.7
36870	PHENIX CITY	83.8	80.5	13.4	15.6	0.5	0.7	2.3	4.0	9.0	8.1	7.6	6.9	5.4	33.9	21.6	6.9	0.6	71.1	32.8	49.2	50.8
36871	PITTSVIEW	54.4	49.1	42.4	46.9	0.2	0.2	1.7	2.6	6.6	6.9	7.0	6.9	5.8	23.7	29.4	12.3	1.4	75.3	39.8	50.4	49.6
36874	SALEM	78.1	74.2	20.1	23.5	0.3	0.4	0.9	1.4	6.6	6.8	6.9	6.7	5.4	26.5	29.3	11.0	0.8	75.7	39.0	49.7	50.3
36875	SEALE	61.0	56.1	35.4	39.2	0.4	0.5	2.2	3.3	6.9	7.0	7.2	7.1	5.9	25.6	28.5	10.7	1.1	74.5	37.8	50.1	49.9
36877	SMITHS STATION	85.1	82.2	12.6	14.7	0.4	0.7	1.6	2.7	7.6	7.4	7.4	7.1	5.3	30.0	26.1	8.5	0.7	73.3	36.0	49.2	50.8
36879	WAVERLY	52.3	51.7	46.6	46.4	0.2	0.6	0.8	1.5	6.3	6.2	6.2	6.4	6.4	27.3	30.6	9.5	1.3	77.4	38.9	48.5	51.5
36904	BUTLER	60.3	58.3	39.0	41.0	0.0	0.1	0.6	0.9	6.3	5.7	5.8	6.5	5.5	22.9	29.5	15.0	2.7	78.0	42.7	46.8	53.2
36907	CUBA	29.9	26.9	69.3	71.8	0.0	0.1	1.7	2.1	7.6	7.8	7.6	7.2	5.7	24.0	26.3	11.9	1.9	72.6	36.8	48.4	51.6
36908	GILBERTOWN	81.2	79.0	18.1	20.1	0.0	0.1	0.9	1.4	7.3	7.5	7.2	5.1	4.5	23.9	28.4	14.1	2.1	74.8	40.5	49.3	50.7
36910	JACHIN	21.4	20.6	77.1	77.8	0.0	0.0	2.0	2.3	6.7	6.9	6.7	6.9	6.0	23.8	28.9	11.5	2.5	75.3	38.7	44.6	55.4
36912	LISMAN	16.2	15.6	82.8	83.3	0.0	0.0	0.7	1.0	6.4	6.4	6.5	6.9	6.4	23.5	29.3	12.9	1.9	76.6	39.8	44.8	55.2
36915	NEEDHAM	79.1	77.6	20.2	21.7	0.1	0.1	0.3	0.4	6.7	6.7	7.0	6.1	4.9	24.5	28.7	14.1	1.4	75.7	40.5	48.9	51.1
36916	PENNINGTON	38.8	36.7	60.9	63.0	0.0	0.0	0.4	0.5	6.6	8.0	9.0	6.2	3.9	25.2	28.7	11.1	1.4	71.9	39.4	49.4	50.6
36919	SILAS	48.6	46.5	50.6	52.5	0.0	0.1	0.6	0.8	7.9	8.0	7.7	6.6	5.0	24.8	26.9	11.7	1.4	72.2	37.4	48.1	51.9
36921	TOXEY	83.8	82.3	15.7	17.0	0.1	0.3	0.3	0.6	7.3	7.2	7.4	6.4	4.7	24.7	27.0	13.7	1.7	74.1	39.5	48.1	51.9
36922	WARD	20.3	18.8	79.2	80.7	0.0	0.0	1.1	1.0	7.0	7.2	9.1	7.5	5.2	23.9	25.9	12.0	2.3	71.4	37.6	45.5	54.5
36925	YORK	20.8	19.5	78.5	79.7	0.1	0.1	1.1	1.1	7.1	7.3	7.5	8.1	6.5	23.1	25.3	11.6	3.4	73.1	36.6	44.9	55.1
	ALABAMA	71.1	69.3	26.0	26.7	0.7	1.0	1.7	2.8	6.6	6.6	6.6	6.9	6.6	26.4	26.7	11.7	1.8	76.1	37.8	48.6	51.4
	UNITED STATES	75.1	72.0	12.3	12.7	3.8	4.6	12.5	15.7	6.8	6.7	6.6	7.1	6.9	27.0	26.0	10.9	1.9	75.7	36.9	49.2	50.8

#	POST OFFICE NAME	2009 Per Capita Income	2009 HH Income Base	2009 Household Income Distribution (%): Less than $25,000	$25,000 to $49,999	$50,000 to $99,999	$100,000 to $149,999	$150,000 or More	Median Household Income: 2009	2014	2009 National Centile	2009 State Centile	2009 Home Value Base	2009 Home Value Distribution (%): Less than $50,000	$50,000 to $89,999	$90,000 to $174,999	$175,000 to $399,999	$400,000 or More	2009 Median Home Value
36850	CAMP HILL	16288	1141	44.3	32.2	19.3	2.9	1.3	28846	30487	6	19	849	36.7	34.9	20.6	6.1	1.6	62635
36852	CUSSETA	18608	945	23.2	38.0	33.7	3.9	1.3	42864	43051	42	76	764	35.7	18.8	28.9	14.3	2.2	80278
36853	DADEVILLE	21054	3508	32.0	29.2	30.4	5.7	2.6	38465	38299	28	61	2973	20.8	25.0	26.0	19.6	8.6	100672
36854	VALLEY	18940	5831	31.6	30.7	32.7	3.9	1.1	39881	40516	32	65	4494	25.7	32.0	29.8	10.6	1.8	78980
36855	FIVE POINTS	17495	744	35.9	31.7	29.0	2.4	0.9	32909	34720	13	34	639	25.2	27.7	33.0	13.0	1.1	85132
36856	FORT MITCHELL	17173	851	25.5	36.2	32.5	5.1	0.7	39831	40597	32	65	588	25.0	18.9	44.9	10.7	0.5	102344
36858	HATCHECHUBBEE	13632	380	48.2	28.4	21.8	1.1	0.5	26302	28440	4	14	312	42.0	26.6	18.9	7.7	4.8	61600
36860	HURTSBORO	13863	752	55.6	24.5	18.0	1.6	0.4	20610	22119	2	4	565	45.5	25.7	20.0	6.2	2.7	54474
36861	JACKSONS GAP	21164	1458	28.4	30.9	32.0	5.8	2.8	42296	41571	40	73	1254	19.9	22.1	23.4	28.1	6.5	109677
36862	LAFAYETTE	15801	2711	42.1	27.7	26.5	2.8	0.8	31583	33659	11	27	2044	24.6	27.9	37.0	8.9	1.6	84900
36863	LANETT	17781	5139	38.3	29.2	27.4	3.6	1.5	34378	36123	16	42	3680	23.4	36.5	29.4	9.2	1.4	77021
36866	NOTASULGA	17087	1503	41.3	31.3	23.0	2.7	1.8	31063	32321	10	24	1194	32.4	29.8	28.1	8.0	1.7	76667
36867	PHENIX CITY	20281	8639	34.2	27.1	31.2	5.8	1.7	36981	38815	24	54	4997	11.3	18.5	44.7	22.8	2.6	125551
36869	PHENIX CITY	14973	7782	41.9	30.0	24.4	3.1	0.6	30835	32631	9	23	4723	20.0	25.0	46.8	7.0	1.1	95573
36870	PHENIX CITY	20803	5703	22.0	25.3	42.0	8.8	1.9	51888	53327	66	91	4283	14.8	15.7	53.8	14.5	1.1	123524
36871	PITTSVIEW	15507	711	39.4	28.1	29.1	3.4	0.0	33185	35616	14	35	576	27.3	27.8	27.8	16.0	1.2	80938
36874	SALEM	18810	2883	27.4	28.8	37.1	5.0	1.6	44354	45177	46	81	2397	18.4	19.9	35.6	22.7	3.3	117281
36875	SEALE	16623	1881	32.6	30.4	32.6	3.9	0.6	35664	37125	20	47	1516	27.4	22.6	33.0	15.8	1.2	89894
36877	SMITHS STATION	21833	4388	21.3	28.5	39.0	8.5	2.7	50170	50084	62	89	3550	18.4	16.2	39.5	20.5	5.4	124138
36879	WAVERLY	17618	656	39.5	25.5	28.8	5.2	1.1	32755	35982	13	33	512	20.3	21.1	33.8	17.4	7.4	109677
36904	BUTLER	19012	2131	41.5	28.8	22.4	5.7	1.5	31165	32546	10	25	1739	27.6	27.8	32.1	9.4	3.2	83074
36907	CUBA	13996	713	47.4	25.0	24.7	2.4	0.6	26594	27957	4	15	608	48.2	19.1	26.0	5.8	1.0	53438
36908	GILBERTOWN	20140	967	39.6	20.3	32.0	6.3	1.9	36121	37980	21	49	852	31.7	17.1	35.8	12.8	2.6	92564
36910	JACHIN	14723	190	58.4	26.3	8.9	3.7	2.6	21144	21544	2	5	164	36.0	30.5	20.1	13.4	0.0	68182
36912	LISMAN	14254	946	54.2	25.3	15.4	3.5	1.6	22285	24068	2	7	826	43.0	27.1	17.7	10.9	1.3	60952
36915	NEEDHAM	16622	305	49.8	24.9	20.7	2.6	2.0	25222	28749	3	13	275	47.6	26.2	21.1	3.6	1.5	51857
36916	PENNINGTON	14574	287	53.7	23.3	18.8	3.8	0.3	22809	24384	2	8	246	46.7	29.3	15.9	8.1	0.0	55000
36919	SILAS	14218	1081	51.6	25.3	19.6	2.6	0.9	24008	25676	3	10	963	44.4	25.5	22.8	5.6	1.6	56605
36921	TOXEY	17569	574	39.5	23.9	31.2	4.5	0.9	33363	35165	14	36	516	37.6	19.4	29.5	10.5	3.1	70526
36922	WARD	13775	324	50.0	29.6	17.0	3.1	0.3	25000	26785	3	12	282	43.3	30.9	21.6	3.9	0.4	55278
36925	YORK	12802	1596	53.7	27.0	15.4	2.7	1.3	22385	22895	2	7	1167	38.8	31.3	26.0	3.3	0.6	63188
	ALABAMA	21187		31.4	27.9	30.6	6.9	3.2	40822	42202				18.1	22.4	35.8	19.6	4.0	107730
	UNITED STATES	27277		20.9	24.4	35.3	11.7	7.6	54719	56938				9.3	13.1	31.6	32.6	13.5	162279

ZIP CODE	FINANCIAL SERVICES				THE HOME						ENTERTAINMENT						PERSONAL			
					Home Improvements		Furnishings													
# POST OFFICE NAME	Auto Loan	Home Loan	Invest-ments	Retire-ment Plans	Home Repair	Lawn & Garden	Comput-ers & Hard-ware-Personal	Major Appli-ances	TV, Radio, Sound Equip-ment	Furni-ture	Dine out/ Carry out	Sports Equip-ment	Fees & Tickets	Toys & Games	Travel	Cable TV	Apparel & Services	Auto Repairs	Health Insur-ance	Pets & Supplies
36850 CAMP HILL	71	48	67	46	48	69	51	62	58	49	56	48	39	59	47	64	37	59	66	76
36852 CUSSETA	78	68	63	65	66	72	67	70	70	69	69	53	61	73	63	72	47	69	71	84
36853 DADEVILLE	86	64	96	62	67	88	66	82	71	62	70	62	54	70	66	77	47	76	84	98
36854 VALLEY	75	59	65	58	59	74	62	70	67	60	66	52	54	69	58	72	45	67	74	83
36855 FIVE POINTS	74	51	64	50	51	71	54	64	61	52	59	50	42	63	49	67	40	61	68	79
36856 FORT MITCHELL	75	68	61	65	65	68	67	68	68	70	68	52	62	71	63	69	47	68	68	82
36858 HATCHECHUBBEE	62	40	60	38	40	61	43	54	50	41	49	42	32	51	40	55	32	51	57	67
36860 HURTSBORO	57	38	55	36	37	56	40	50	47	39	45	39	31	47	38	52	30	48	54	62
36861 JACKSONS GAP	90	66	93	64	68	89	68	83	74	64	73	63	55	74	66	81	48	78	85	99
36862 LAFAYETTE	71	48	65	46	49	69	51	63	58	49	57	49	40	59	48	64	38	59	67	77
36863 LANETT	73	54	61	53	53	70	59	65	65	56	63	50	49	66	53	70	43	64	71	79
36866 NOTASULGA	73	50	68	48	50	71	53	64	60	51	59	50	41	61	49	66	39	61	68	79
36867 PHENIX CITY	70	59	57	60	58	65	66	65	69	64	68	50	61	69	61	72	47	67	70	78
36869 PHENIX CITY	61	47	48	47	45	56	52	53	56	51	56	41	45	57	47	60	38	55	58	66
36870 PHENIX CITY	88	87	77	84	83	80	81	83	80	85	80	65	79	84	78	78	56	79	77	96
36871 PITTSVIEW	72	48	66	46	48	70	51	63	58	49	57	49	39	60	47	65	38	59	66	77
36874 SALEM	82	72	71	70	72	78	69	76	72	71	72	55	64	75	67	75	49	73	76	90
36875 SEALE	77	58	66	56	57	73	59	68	65	58	64	52	49	67	55	70	43	65	71	83
36877 SMITHS STATION	89	87	75	85	84	84	80	84	81	84	82	63	78	85	78	82	56	81	81	99
36879 WAVERLY	68	59	59	58	58	64	59	62	61	60	61	48	54	63	56	63	42	61	63	75
36904 BUTLER	77	53	74	50	53	76	57	69	65	54	63	53	44	65	54	72	42	66	74	85
36907 CUBA	66	43	64	41	43	65	46	58	53	44	52	45	35	54	43	59	34	55	61	71
36908 GILBERTOWN	86	60	83	57	61	85	62	78	70	59	69	59	49	71	60	77	45	72	81	94
36910 JACHIN	62	41	60	38	41	61	44	55	50	41	49	43	33	51	41	56	32	52	58	67
36912 LISMAN	64	42	62	39	42	63	45	56	52	43	51	44	34	53	42	58	33	53	60	69
36915 NEEDHAM	74	48	72	46	48	73	52	65	60	49	58	51	39	61	48	67	39	61	69	80
36916 PENNINGTON	61	40	59	38	40	60	43	54	49	41	48	42	32	50	40	55	32	51	57	66
36919 SILAS	67	43	64	41	43	65	46	58	54	44	52	46	35	54	43	60	35	55	62	72
36921 TOXEY	77	54	69	52	54	75	57	68	63	54	62	52	45	65	53	70	41	64	72	83
36922 WARD	63	41	60	38	41	61	44	55	50	41	49	43	33	51	41	56	33	52	58	68
36925 YORK	57	39	52	38	39	56	43	51	49	41	48	39	35	49	40	55	32	49	56	62
ALABAMA	83	70	73	70	69	80	73	77	76	71	76	59	66	77	69	80	52	76	80	92
UNITED STATES	100	100	100	100	100	100	100	100	100	100	100	100	100	100	100	100	100	100	100	100

99501-99671

#	POST OFFICE NAME	COUNTY FIPS CODE	POPULATION 2000	POPULATION 2009	POPULATION 2014	2000-2009 ANNUAL RATE % Rate	2000-2009 ANNUAL RATE State Centile	HOUSEHOLDS 2000	HOUSEHOLDS 2009	HOUSEHOLDS 2014	HOUSEHOLDS % Annual Rate 2000-2009	HOUSEHOLDS 2009 Average HH Size	FAMILIES 2000	FAMILIES 2009	FAMILIES % Annual Rate 2000-2009
99501	ANCHORAGE	020	16545	17432	17494	0.6	77	7360	7504	7552	0.2	1.97	3097	2970	-0.5
99502	ANCHORAGE	020	21730	23583	24325	0.9	86	7845	8522	8808	0.9	2.75	5673	6003	0.6
99503	ANCHORAGE	020	13847	14369	14507	0.4	70	6067	6263	6331	0.3	2.20	2903	2849	-0.2
99504	ANCHORAGE	020	36961	39529	40328	0.7	79	13370	14361	14675	0.8	2.72	9391	9793	0.5
99505	FORT RICHARDSON	020	5322	5442	5367	0.2	63	1231	1165	1145	-0.6	3.34	1137	1068	-0.7
99506	ELMENDORF AFB	020	6621	7825	8186	1.8	95	1584	1863	1979	1.8	3.60	1559	1831	1.8
99507	ANCHORAGE	020	31546	37010	39380	1.7	94	11513	13612	14528	1.8	2.71	8044	9200	1.5
99508	ANCHORAGE	020	34098	35837	36233	0.5	73	12480	12929	13074	0.4	2.62	7752	7726	0.0
99515	ANCHORAGE	020	18342	22620	24445	2.3	95	6302	7835	8487	2.4	2.88	4845	5869	2.1
99516	ANCHORAGE	020	17313	20189	21392	1.7	94	5730	6768	7204	1.8	2.97	4825	5587	1.6
99517	ANCHORAGE	020	16557	17501	17681	0.6	77	6660	7098	7175	0.7	2.45	4016	4114	0.3
99518	ANCHORAGE	020	9245	9853	10036	0.7	79	3794	4108	4207	0.9	2.39	2306	2387	0.4
99540	INDIAN	020	237	265	275	1.2	90	116	132	137	1.4	2.01	56	61	0.9
99546	ADAK	016	363	279	269	-2.8	4	159	131	128	-2.1	1.98	95	76	-2.4
99547	ATKA	016	96	74	71	-2.8	4	34	28	27	-2.1	2.46	20	16	-2.4
99549	PORT HEIDEN	164	119	99	90	-2.0	8	41	35	31	-1.7	2.83	27	23	-1.7
99551	AKIACHAK	050	585	586	577	0.0	55	133	131	128	-0.2	4.47	113	110	-0.3
99552	AKIAK	050	309	310	305	0.0	55	69	68	66	-0.2	4.56	59	57	-0.4
99553	AKUTAN	013	713	752	744	0.6	77	34	32	31	-0.7	5.16	18	17	-0.6
99554	ALAKANUK	270	1419	1545	1613	0.9	86	328	352	365	0.8	4.39	271	286	0.6
99555	ALEKNAGIK	070	221	214	212	-0.3	45	70	68	68	-0.3	3.15	54	52	-0.4
99556	ANCHOR POINT	122	2412	2587	2706	0.8	83	899	986	1039	1.0	2.62	603	645	0.7
99557	ANIAK	050	435	470	462	0.8	83	137	147	143	0.8	3.20	96	102	0.7
99558	ANVIK	290	173	146	133	-1.8	15	58	49	45	-1.8	2.98	43	36	-1.9
99559	BETHEL	050	8459	9193	9345	0.9	86	2436	2612	2651	0.8	3.41	1732	1822	0.5
99561	CHEFORNAK	050	394	399	395	0.1	59	75	75	74	0.0	5.32	65	64	-0.2
99563	CHEVAK	270	3	3	3	0.0	55	1	1	1	0.0	3.00	1	1	0.0
99564	CHIGNIK	164	79	66	60	-1.9	12	29	24	22	-2.0	2.75	19	16	-1.8
99565	CHIGNIK LAGOON	164	103	86	78	-1.9	12	33	28	25	-1.8	3.07	22	18	-2.1
99567	CHUGIAK	020	7666	8546	8977	1.2	90	2623	2961	3121	1.3	2.86	2070	2289	1.1
99568	CLAM GULCH	122	357	401	419	1.3	91	133	153	161	1.5	2.61	88	98	1.2
99569	CLARKS POINT	070	112	108	107	-0.4	43	31	30	30	-0.4	3.60	24	23	-0.5
99571	COLD BAY	013	175	181	179	0.4	70	70	68	66	-0.3	1.59	43	40	-0.8
99572	COOPER LANDING	122	354	376	394	0.7	79	154	167	177	0.9	2.18	92	97	0.6
99573	COPPER CENTER	261	1785	1716	1668	-0.4	43	691	676	660	-0.2	2.54	443	422	-0.5
99574	CORDOVA	261	2597	2371	2280	-1.0	34	969	911	882	-0.7	2.53	604	552	-1.0
99575	CROOKED CREEK	050	4	4	4	0.0	55	2	2	2	0.0	2.00	1	1	0.0
99576	DILLINGHAM	070	3326	3310	3303	-0.1	49	1105	1106	1106	0.0	2.96	776	760	-0.2
99577	EAGLE RIVER	020	22231	25270	26452	1.4	92	7254	8335	8768	1.5	2.98	6009	6791	1.3
99578	EEK	050	555	549	538	-0.1	49	137	133	130	-0.3	4.13	105	101	-0.4
99579	EGEGIK	164	110	92	83	-1.9	12	41	35	31	-1.7	2.63	27	23	-1.7
99580	EKWOK	070	130	126	125	-0.3	45	42	41	41	-0.3	3.07	33	31	-0.7
99583	FALSE PASS	013	64	67	67	0.5	73	22	21	21	-0.5	2.57	12	11	-0.9
99585	MARSHALL	270	651	724	769	1.2	90	162	178	188	1.0	4.07	136	148	0.9
99586	GAKONA	261	328	310	300	-0.6	40	149	143	139	-0.4	2.17	88	82	-0.8
99587	GIRDWOOD	020	1484	1736	1854	1.7	94	672	795	853	1.8	2.18	312	350	1.3
99588	GLENNALLEN	261	1118	1046	1009	-0.7	38	408	388	377	-0.5	2.66	274	255	-0.8
99589	GOODNEWS BAY	050	230	228	223	-0.1	49	71	69	68	-0.3	3.30	54	52	-0.4
99591	SAINT GEORGE ISLAND	016	152	117	113	-2.8	4	51	42	41	-2.1	2.60	30	24	-2.4
99602	HOLY CROSS	290	227	191	174	-1.8	15	64	54	50	-1.8	3.54	47	40	-1.7
99603	HOMER	122	9220	9361	9520	0.2	63	3587	3713	3799	0.4	2.48	2324	2347	0.1
99604	HOOPER BAY	270	1779	1943	2024	1.0	88	394	422	438	0.7	4.60	322	340	0.6
99606	ILIAMNA	164	392	334	304	-1.7	20	122	105	96	-1.6	3.18	91	77	-1.8
99607	KALSKAG	050	230	228	225	-0.1	49	62	61	60	-0.2	3.74	48	46	-0.5
99610	KASILOF	122	1775	1965	2049	1.1	88	691	782	822	1.3	2.51	471	520	1.1
99611	KENAI	122	14634	15918	16514	0.9	86	5226	5769	6022	1.1	2.69	3742	4043	0.8
99612	KING COVE	013	792	805	792	0.2	63	170	170	168	0.0	2.98	115	112	-0.3
99613	KING SALMON	060	388	312	276	-2.3	5	176	145	129	-2.1	2.15	99	80	-2.3
99614	KIPNUK	050	644	652	645	0.1	59	137	136	135	-0.1	4.79	118	117	-0.1
99615	KODIAK	150	13864	13395	13064	-0.4	43	4408	4275	4157	-0.3	3.10	3245	3086	-0.5
99620	KOTLIK	270	591	644	672	0.9	86	117	125	130	0.7	5.15	97	102	0.5
99621	KWETHLUK	050	713	714	704	0.0	55	153	150	147	-0.2	4.76	130	127	-0.3
99622	KWIGILLINGOK	050	697	705	698	0.1	59	152	151	149	-0.1	4.67	131	130	-0.1
99625	LEVELOCK	164	215	183	166	-1.7	20	66	57	52	-1.6	3.21	49	42	-1.7
99626	LOWER KALSKAG	050	267	265	261	-0.1	49	66	65	63	-0.2	4.08	51	49	-0.4
99627	MC GRATH	290	486	409	374	-1.8	15	176	152	140	-1.6	2.69	113	95	-1.9
99628	MANOKOTAK	070	399	386	383	-0.4	43	93	90	90	-0.4	4.29	72	69	-0.5
99630	MEKORYUK	050	210	212	210	0.1	59	73	72	71	-0.1	2.94	57	56	-0.2
99631	MOOSE PASS	122	502	533	559	0.6	77	219	238	251	0.9	2.17	132	138	0.5
99632	MOUNTAIN VILLAGE	270	928	1003	1046	0.8	83	221	236	245	0.7	4.23	173	182	0.5
99634	NAPAKIAK	050	390	387	382	-0.1	49	82	80	78	-0.3	4.84	65	63	-0.3
99636	NEW STUYAHOK	070	653	635	630	-0.3	45	158	153	153	-0.3	4.15	124	118	-0.5
99638	NIKOLSKI	016	39	30	29	-2.8	4	15	12	12	-2.4	2.33	9	7	-2.7
99639	NINILCHIK	122	1006	1081	1112	0.8	83	411	451	468	1.0	2.40	283	303	0.7
99640	NONDALTON	164	221	188	171	-1.7	20	68	58	53	-1.7	3.24	51	43	-1.8
99645	PALMER	170	18505	25163	29689	3.4	98	6253	8628	10247	3.5	2.86	4713	6410	3.4
99647	PEDRO BAY	164	49	42	38	-1.7	20	16	14	13	-1.4	3.00	12	10	-2.0
99648	PERRYVILLE	164	107	89	81	-2.0	8	33	28	25	-1.8	3.18	22	18	-2.1
99649	PILOT POINT	164	109	91	83	-1.9	12	35	29	27	-2.0	3.14	23	19	-2.0
99650	PILOT STATION	270	466	503	524	0.8	83	94	100	104	0.7	5.00	73	76	0.4
99654	WASILLA	170	34554	52565	63905	4.6	98	11862	18148	22120	4.7	2.89	8821	13257	4.5
99655	QUINHAGAK	050	284	282	278	-0.1	49	78	76	74	-0.3	3.71	62	60	-0.4
99656	RED DEVIL	050	51	50	50	-0.2	45	18	17	17	-0.6	2.94	13	12	-0.9
99658	SAINT MARYS	270	625	674	703	0.8	83	167	178	185	0.7	3.77	129	135	0.5
99659	SAINT MICHAEL	180	369	391	402	0.6	77	91	97	100	0.7	4.03	72	76	0.6
99660	SAINT PAUL ISLAND	016	532	410	395	-2.8	4	177	146	142	-2.1	2.60	106	84	-2.5
99661	SAND POINT	013	953	946	925	-0.1	49	230	220	214	-0.5	2.59	156	145	-0.8
99662	SCAMMON BAY	270	467	510	531	1.0	88	97	104	108	0.8	4.90	79	84	0.7
99664	SEWARD	122	4720	5105	5342	0.9	86	1660	1826	1936	1.0	2.43	1019	1088	0.7
99665	SHAGELUK	290	125	105	96	-1.9	12	32	27	25	-1.8	3.89	24	20	-2.0
99667	SKWENTNA	170	20	31	38	4.9	99	5	8	10	5.2	3.88	3	5	5.7
99668	SLEETMUTE	050	13	13	13	0.0	55	6	6	6	0.0	2.17	4	4	0.0
99669	SOLDOTNA	122	11602	12433	12916	0.8	83	4334	4741	4963	1.0	2.60	3102	3321	0.7
99670	SOUTH NAKNEK	060	870	702	620	-2.3	5	314	260	233	-2.0	2.70	202	162	-2.4
99671	STEBBINS	180	547	580	596	0.6	77	123	131	135	0.7	4.43	98	102	0.4
	ALASKA					1.1					1.1	2.74			0.9
	UNITED STATES					1.0					1.1	2.59			0.9

ZIP CODE #	POST OFFICE NAME	RACE (%) White 2000	White 2009	Black 2000	Black 2009	Asian/Pacific 2000	Asian/Pacific 2009	% Hispanic Origin 2000	% Hispanic Origin 2009	2009 AGE DISTRIBUTION (%) 0-4	5-9	10-14	15-19	20-24	25-44	45-64	65-84	85+	18+	MEDIAN AGE 2009	% 2009 Males	% 2009 Females
99501	ANCHORAGE	60.6	55.3	8.8	7.8	7.6	8.3	8.2	11.2	5.8	5.0	4.4	5.7	8.1	32.1	26.1	10.4	2.4	81.8	38.2	52.7	47.3
99502	ANCHORAGE	75.4	70.4	3.2	2.9	8.6	10.2	4.3	6.2	7.3	7.2	7.2	7.4	6.1	29.9	28.4	6.2	0.4	73.5	35.1	49.2	50.8
99503	ANCHORAGE	59.8	53.9	4.7	4.3	12.3	13.6	9.1	12.3	7.0	6.3	5.7	5.9	8.5	32.1	25.5	8.0	0.9	77.6	34.4	51.7	48.3
99504	ANCHORAGE	67.2	62.2	9.9	9.1	5.2	6.1	5.4	7.6	8.1	7.3	7.1	7.4	7.2	29.7	25.5	7.0	0.8	73.0	33.0	49.0	51.0
99505	FORT RICHARDSON	68.3	65.3	20.2	19.3	2.1	2.5	9.2	13.7	13.9	8.5	5.4	7.7	22.2	37.6	3.8	0.9	0.0	70.4	23.3	60.5	39.5
99506	ELMENDORF AFB	77.2	73.6	12.3	11.7	3.1	4.0	7.2	10.6	15.4	12.1	8.4	6.7	18.5	37.0	1.8	0.1	0.0	61.2	22.0	54.5	45.5
99507	ANCHORAGE	73.3	68.0	5.0	4.7	6.6	7.9	6.1	8.8	8.0	7.4	7.2	7.7	8.6	30.8	25.5	4.5	0.3	72.8	31.4	49.9	50.1
99508	ANCHORAGE	58.5	53.6	9.0	7.9	9.2	10.1	7.5	10.2	8.3	7.3	6.8	8.9	8.9	28.3	23.2	7.4	0.8	72.7	30.9	49.4	50.6
99515	ANCHORAGE	77.5	72.1	2.5	2.4	6.1	7.3	5.6	8.1	7.6	7.7	8.0	7.9	5.8	27.5	28.8	6.3	0.4	71.5	35.4	49.3	50.7
99516	ANCHORAGE	89.7	86.9	1.0	0.9	2.8	3.5	2.3	3.4	5.3	7.1	9.0	8.5	3.8	22.4	37.7	5.8	0.3	72.8	41.4	50.6	49.4
99517	ANCHORAGE	71.5	65.7	3.0	2.7	10.6	12.5	5.0	7.1	6.6	6.5	6.2	6.6	6.8	29.2	29.1	8.2	0.8	76.7	36.8	49.8	50.2
99518	ANCHORAGE	74.1	68.9	5.9	5.6	6.2	7.4	5.6	8.1	7.6	7.2	6.8	6.2	6.7	32.2	25.9	7.0	0.4	74.7	34.3	49.3	50.7
99540	INDIAN	92.4	89.8	0.0	0.0	0.4	0.8	1.7	2.6	4.2	6.4	6.8	5.3	4.5	30.6	35.5	6.8	0.0	80.0	41.3	55.1	44.9
99546	ADAK	25.1	20.1	0.6	0.7	3.6	3.2	1.9	2.2	5.7	5.7	5.7	6.1	7.5	32.6	29.4	6.8	0.4	78.5	36.3	56.3	43.7
99547	ATKA	24.7	20.3	1.0	0.0	4.1	4.1	2.1	1.4	5.4	5.4	5.4	5.4	6.8	33.8	31.1	6.8	0.0	78.4	37.0	58.1	41.9
99549	PORT HEIDEN	14.2	12.1	0.0	0.0	0.8	1.0	1.7	3.0	9.1	8.1	8.1	10.1	7.1	26.3	25.3	6.1	0.0	68.7	29.2	49.5	50.5
99551	AKIACHAK	4.5	4.6	0.0	0.0	0.2	0.2	0.5	0.5	12.6	11.1	9.7	10.8	10.2	25.4	15.4	4.4	0.3	60.4	22.8	54.6	45.4
99552	AKIAK	4.5	4.5	0.0	0.0	0.3	0.3	0.3	0.3	11.9	11.0	9.7	10.6	10.3	25.8	15.5	4.5	0.6	60.6	23.3	53.9	46.1
99553	AKUTAN	28.6	26.9	2.1	2.1	32.7	33.4	17.4	17.0	1.3	1.1	1.2	3.3	9.8	44.9	36.2	1.9	0.3	94.9	40.3	74.6	25.4
99554	ALAKANUK	4.1	4.3	0.1	0.1	0.1	0.1	0.5	0.5	12.6	11.0	9.8	11.5	10.6	25.1	14.2	4.9	0.4	59.7	22.4	53.9	46.1
99555	ALEKNAGIK	9.0	9.3	0.0	0.0	0.0	0.0	0.5	0.0	10.3	8.9	8.4	10.3	13.1	25.7	17.8	5.1	0.5	66.8	24.6	53.7	46.3
99556	ANCHOR POINT	89.7	86.4	0.1	0.1	0.5	0.6	1.5	2.4	6.6	6.8	9.6	8.8	4.5	22.3	34.0	6.8	0.6	71.0	39.8	53.3	46.7
99557	ANIAK	14.9	19.6	0.0	0.4	0.0	0.2	1.6	2.3	7.2	10.2	11.7	8.7	6.2	24.7	23.4	7.4	0.4	68.5	30.7	53.8	46.2
99558	ANVIK	5.8	4.8	0.0	0.0	0.0	0.0	0.6	0.7	8.2	9.6	15.1	10.3	4.8	23.3	20.5	8.2	0.0	60.3	26.7	54.1	45.9
99559	BETHEL	19.3	19.6	0.7	0.6	2.0	2.1	1.2	1.5	10.2	10.1	9.2	9.2	8.0	27.3	20.8	4.7	0.5	64.5	27.3	52.1	47.9
99561	CHEFORNAK	2.0	2.0	0.0	0.0	0.0	0.0	0.5	0.3	11.8	10.5	10.0	11.5	8.8	24.6	17.3	5.0	0.5	60.9	23.5	54.4	45.6
99563	CHEVAK	0.0	0.0	0.0	0.0	0.0	0.0	0.0	0.0	0.0	0.0	0.0	0.0	33.3	66.7	0.0	0.0	0.0	100.0	27.5	66.7	33.3
99564	CHIGNIK	15.4	12.1	0.0	0.0	0.0	0.0	1.3	0.0	7.6	7.6	7.6	9.1	6.1	28.8	28.8	4.5	0.0	72.7	30.0	48.5	51.5
99565	CHIGNIK LAGOON	14.4	11.6	0.0	0.0	1.0	1.2	1.9	3.5	8.1	8.1	8.1	9.3	7.0	26.7	26.7	5.8	0.0	70.9	29.4	51.2	48.8
99567	CHUGIAK	87.2	83.2	1.0	0.9	1.2	1.5	2.9	4.4	5.9	7.2	8.1	7.9	4.8	25.2	34.5	5.8	0.7	73.5	39.4	50.7	49.3
99568	CLAM GULCH	89.7	86.5	0.3	0.2	0.8	1.0	1.4	2.0	5.5	7.5	9.2	8.5	3.0	24.4	32.9	8.5	0.5	71.6	40.9	54.4	45.6
99569	CLARKS POINT	9.0	9.3	0.0	0.0	0.0	0.0	0.0	0.0	10.2	9.3	9.3	10.2	11.1	25.9	18.5	5.6	0.0	65.7	25.0	52.8	47.2
99571	COLD BAY	21.7	20.4	1.7	1.7	29.1	29.3	12.0	11.6	3.3	2.8	2.8	4.4	9.9	42.5	31.5	2.8	0.0	89.0	38.1	67.4	32.6
99572	COOPER LANDING	90.4	87.5	0.6	0.8	1.1	1.3	1.1	1.6	4.5	5.1	6.9	6.6	3.5	23.4	36.4	12.5	1.1	78.7	45.0	54.3	45.7
99573	COPPER CENTER	71.8	66.9	0.2	0.2	0.5	0.6	1.9	2.6	6.4	6.9	9.2	8.0	4.9	21.7	33.0	8.9	1.1	72.8	40.6	53.7	46.3
99574	CORDOVA	70.0	64.1	0.4	0.4	9.6	11.3	2.9	4.0	5.9	7.1	7.4	7.4	6.1	26.3	31.2	7.8	0.9	74.6	39.4	54.0	46.0
99575	CROOKED CREEK	25.0	25.0	0.0	0.0	0.0	0.0	0.0	0.0	0.0	0.0	0.0	0.0	25.0	50.0	25.0	0.0	0.0	100.0	40.0	100.0	0.0
99576	DILLINGHAM	28.2	28.8	0.5	0.5	0.9	0.9	2.9	2.9	9.8	8.9	9.3	7.8	6.6	24.1	25.9	6.9	0.6	66.3	30.9	50.9	49.1
99577	EAGLE RIVER	87.5	84.1	2.0	2.0	2.2	2.6	3.5	5.4	6.6	7.7	8.5	8.1	5.9	28.9	29.6	4.3	0.3	71.8	35.7	50.2	49.8
99578	EEK	4.1	4.2	0.0	0.0	0.0	0.0	0.5	0.5	9.3	8.2	8.0	9.7	9.1	26.0	21.3	7.8	0.5	68.7	29.6	52.5	47.5
99579	EGEGIK	14.5	12.0	0.0	0.0	0.9	1.1	1.8	3.3	7.6	7.6	7.6	8.7	6.5	28.3	28.3	5.4	0.0	72.8	29.6	51.1	48.9
99580	EKWOK	6.2	6.3	0.0	0.0	0.0	0.0	1.5	1.6	11.1	9.5	9.5	10.3	12.7	24.6	18.3	4.0	0.0	64.3	23.8	56.3	43.7
99583	FALSE PASS	28.6	26.9	1.6	1.5	33.3	34.3	17.5	16.4	1.5	1.5	1.5	4.5	10.4	43.3	35.8	1.5	0.0	94.0	39.7	74.6	25.4
99585	MARSHALL	5.5	5.9	0.0	0.0	0.0	0.0	0.2	0.3	10.4	12.4	12.8	11.6	8.1	22.0	17.8	4.7	0.1	55.9	21.7	51.1	48.9
99586	GAKONA	60.6	54.8	0.0	0.0	0.0	0.0	0.9	0.6	5.5	6.8	9.0	5.5	4.2	21.6	36.8	9.0	1.6	77.7	43.5	57.4	42.6
99587	GIRDWOOD	94.8	93.1	0.0	0.0	0.8	1.0	1.8	2.7	5.8	4.8	4.6	4.3	7.0	40.3	28.8	4.2	0.3	82.5	35.6	55.4	44.6
99588	GLENNALLEN	78.2	73.4	0.1	0.1	0.9	1.0	0.6	1.0	7.1	8.1	8.3	9.3	5.6	23.2	31.1	6.5	0.8	70.7	36.7	52.9	47.1
99589	GOODNEWS BAY	3.9	4.4	0.0	0.0	0.0	0.0	0.4	0.4	9.2	8.3	7.9	9.6	8.8	25.9	21.5	7.9	0.9	68.4	30.0	53.1	46.9
99591	SAINT GEORGE ISLAND	25.0	20.5	0.7	0.9	3.3	3.4	2.0	1.7	5.1	5.1	5.1	6.0	6.8	35.0	31.6	5.1	0.0	80.3	36.4	58.1	41.9
99602	HOLY CROSS	5.7	4.7	0.0	0.0	0.0	0.0	0.4	0.5	8.4	9.9	14.1	9.4	4.7	25.1	20.9	7.3	0.0	60.7	27.5	53.4	46.6
99603	HOMER	88.1	85.3	0.2	0.3	0.7	0.9	2.1	3.1	6.9	7.4	7.9	7.6	5.6	22.4	33.1	8.3	0.9	72.9	39.4	50.5	49.5
99604	HOOPER BAY	3.7	3.8	0.1	0.1	0.1	0.1	0.3	0.4	10.7	13.9	15.5	12.0	5.9	22.5	14.4	4.6	0.5	51.3	19.1	50.5	49.5
99606	ILIAMNA	22.2	18.6	0.0	0.0	0.0	0.0	0.8	0.9	9.0	8.1	8.4	9.3	8.4	23.4	25.1	7.8	0.6	68.6	29.3	51.5	48.5
99607	KALSKAG	16.5	16.7	0.4	0.4	0.4	0.4	0.4	0.4	9.6	9.2	8.3	10.5	10.5	24.6	21.9	5.3	0.0	66.2	25.9	50.4	49.6
99610	KASILOF	90.9	87.9	0.3	0.5	0.8	0.9	1.1	1.7	4.6	7.2	9.2	8.4	3.0	24.6	34.2	8.3	0.3	72.3	41.4	53.3	46.7
99611	KENAI	84.2	80.3	0.5	0.7	1.5	1.7	2.8	4.1	7.2	7.6	7.8	7.9	5.9	27.3	28.6	7.1	0.5	72.3	35.7	51.0	49.0
99612	KING COVE	15.1	13.8	1.5	1.5	24.6	24.2	6.7	6.5	5.8	5.1	4.3	5.1	9.4	38.9	26.2	4.8	0.2	81.6	35.7	59.0	41.0
99613	KING SALMON	53.4	48.7	1.0	1.3	0.8	1.0	0.5	0.6	6.1	7.1	7.7	7.4	5.1	24.0	36.5	5.8	0.3	74.4	40.0	54.5	45.5
99614	KIPNUK	2.0	2.0	0.0	0.0	0.0	0.0	0.5	0.3	11.8	10.7	10.1	11.2	8.7	24.2	17.3	5.2	0.6	60.6	23.5	54.4	45.6
99615	KODIAK	59.7	54.0	1.0	0.8	16.9	18.9	6.1	8.3	9.0	8.3	8.0	7.0	7.1	28.5	25.5	6.0	0.5	70.2	32.0	52.1	47.9
99620	KOTLIK	4.1	4.3	0.2	0.2	0.2	0.2	0.5	0.6	12.7	11.0	9.8	11.5	11.0	24.8	14.1	4.7	0.3	59.3	22.3	54.3	45.7
99621	KWETHLUK	4.5	4.6	0.0	0.0	0.3	0.3	0.4	0.4	12.6	11.1	9.7	10.6	10.4	25.4	15.4	4.3	0.6	60.4	22.9	54.6	45.4
99622	KWIGILLINGOK	2.0	2.0	0.0	0.0	0.0	0.0	0.4	0.4	11.5	10.6	10.1	11.3	8.7	24.5	17.6	5.1	0.6	60.9	23.7	54.3	45.7
99625	LEVELOCK	22.0	18.6	0.0	0.0	0.0	0.0	0.5	0.5	8.7	8.2	8.2	9.3	8.7	23.5	26.2	7.1	0.0	68.3	29.5	52.5	47.5
99626	LOWER KALSKAG	16.5	17.0	0.4	0.4	0.4	0.4	0.4	0.4	9.8	9.1	8.3	10.6	12.1	23.8	21.5	4.9	0.0	66.8	25.1	50.6	49.4
99627	MC GRATH	42.3	35.9	0.0	0.0	0.4	0.5	1.0	1.5	6.6	6.1	6.6	9.0	9.0	20.5	30.3	11.0	0.7	75.3	35.9	53.1	46.9
99628	MANOKOTAK	9.0	9.1	0.2	0.3	0.5	0.5	0.5	0.8	10.1	9.1	8.3	10.1	11.4	26.2	18.4	6.0	0.5	67.1	25.5	52.1	47.9
99630	MEKORYUK	3.3	3.3	0.0	0.0	0.0	0.0	0.0	0.0	9.0	11.3	11.3	11.3	7.5	25.5	18.4	5.2	0.5	59.4	24.7	53.8	46.2
99631	MOOSE PASS	90.4	87.2	0.6	0.8	1.2	1.5	1.0	1.7	4.5	5.1	6.8	6.9	3.4	22.9	37.0	12.4	1.1	78.8	45.2	54.4	45.6
99632	MOUNTAIN VILLAGE	6.0	6.3	0.0	0.0	0.2	0.3	0.3	0.3	12.3	10.8	9.5	10.4	10.8	26.4	15.0	4.6	0.4	60.6	23.3	53.7	46.3
99634	NAPAKIAK	1.8	2.1	0.5	0.5	0.0	0.0	0.3	0.3	10.3	9.6	9.6	11.6	8.8	25.1	17.6	6.7	0.8	63.3	25.1	55.6	44.4
99636	NEW STUYAHOK	6.1	6.3	0.0	0.0	0.0	0.0	1.4	1.4	10.6	9.6	9.1	10.7	11.0	24.7	18.9	4.7	0.6	64.6	24.5	55.1	44.9
99638	NIKOLSKI	25.6	20.0	0.0	0.0	2.6	3.3	2.6	0.0	6.7	6.7	6.7	6.7	6.7	33.3	33.3	0.0	0.0	73.3	37.5	50.0	50.0
99639	NINILCHIK	84.6	80.9	0.0	0.0	0.7	0.7	1.5	2.1	4.7	5.5	6.6	7.6	3.9	22.1	35.2	13.0	1.5	78.5	44.8	53.8	46.2
99640	NONDALTON	22.2	18.6	0.0	0.0	0.0	0.0	0.9	0.5	8.5	8.5	8.0	9.6	8.5	23.9	25.5	7.4	0.0	69.7	29.3	51.6	48.4
99645	PALMER	87.9	84.9	0.8	0.7	0.9	1.0	2.2	3.2	6.8	7.3	8.3	8.9	6.0	25.4	29.0	7.5	0.8	71.7	36.0	50.6	49.4
99647	PEDRO BAY	22.4	19.0	0.0	0.0	0.0	0.0	0.0	0.0	9.5	9.5	9.5	9.5	9.5	23.8	21.4	7.1	0.0	61.9	26.3	52.4	47.6
99648	PERRYVILLE	14.8	12.4	0.0	0.0	0.9	1.1	1.9	3.4	7.9	7.9	7.9	9.0	6.7	28.1	27.0	5.6	0.0	71.9	29.3	51.7	48.3
99649	PILOT POINT	14.5	12.1	0.0	0.0	0.9	1.1	1.8	3.3	7.7	7.7	7.7	8.8	6.6	28.6	27.5	5.5	0.0	72.5	29.4	51.6	48.4
99650	PILOT STATION	6.5	6.8	0.0	0.0	0.2	0.2	0.2	0.2	12.3	10.7	9.3	9.9	10.7	26.8	15.1	4.6	0.4	60.8	23.6	53.9	46.1
99654	WASILLA	87.8	84.2	0.6	0.6	0.8	1.0	2.8	4.2	7.4	7.6	8.1	8.1	6.3	27.7	28.1	6.3	0.5	71.6	34.5	51.1	48.9
99655	QUINHAGAK	1.8	2.1	0.7	0.4	0.0	0.0	0.4	0.4	10.3	9.2	9.6	11.3	8.9	25.2	18.1	6.7	0.7	63.8	25.6	55.3	44.7
99656	RED DEVIL	15.4	20.0	0.0	0.0	0.0	0.0	1.9	2.0	6.0	12.0	12.0	10.0	6.0	22.0	28.0	4.0	0.0	70.0	30.0	52.0	48.0
99658	SAINT MARYS	6.4	6.8	0.0	0.0	0.3	0.3	0.3	0.3	12.3	10.5	9.3	10.1	10.8	26.9	15.1	4.6	0.3	60.8	23.6	53.7	46.3
99659	SAINT MICHAEL	5.7	4.9	0.0	0.0	0.0	0.0	0.0	0.0	10.7	13.3	13.6	10.0	9.0	22.5	16.9	3.1	1.0	56.0	21.4	52.7	47.3
99660	SAINT PAUL ISLAND	25.0	20.0	0.8	0.5	3.6	3.4	1.9	2.0	5.9	5.9	5.6	6.3	7.1	33.4	29.0	6.6	0.2	77.8	36.6	56.6	43.4
99661	SAND POINT	27.8	26.2	1.5	1.4	23.5	23.4	13.5	13.4	5.1	4.8	4.4	4.9	8.6	37.8	29.5	4.8	0.2	82.7	37.3	61.8	38.2
99662	SCAMMON BAY	3.6	3.7	0.0	0.0	0.0	0.0	0.2	0.2	10.6	13.9	15.5	12.0	5.9	22.7	14.3	4.5	0.6	51.6	19.2	50.8	49.2
99664	SEWARD	75.7	70.4	1.6	2.0	1.7	2.0	2.2	3.2	5.6	5.1	5.2	6.4	9.0	29.6	31.3	7.2	0.6	79.9	37.3	57.8	42.2
99665	SHAGELUK	5.6	4.8	0.0	0.0	0.0	0.0	0.8	0.0	8.6	9.5	15.2	10.5	4.8	24.8	20.0	6.7	0.0	59.0	26.1	53.3	46.7
99667	SKWENTNA	90.0	90.3	0.0	0.0	0.0	0.0	0.0	0.0	0.0	6.5	6.5	9.7	0.0	25.8	41.9	9.7	0.0	77.4	45.6	54.8	45.2
99668	SLEETMUTE	15.4	23.1	0.0	0.0	0.0	0.0	0.0	0.0	7.7	15.4	15.4	7.7	15.4	23.1	15.4	0.0	0.0	61.5	21.3	61.5	38.5
99669	SOLDOTNA	90.0	87.1	0.3	0.4	1.2	1.4	2.2	3.3	6.3	7.1	8.0	7.8	4.9	25.3	31.5	8.4	0.6	73.3	38.6	50.2	49.8
99670	SOUTH NAKNEK	52.2	47.4	0.3	0.4	0.7	0.9	0.6	0.9	6.6	7.4	8.0	7.8	5.1	23.5	35.0	6.3	0.3	73.1	39.3	53.7	46.3
99671	STEBBINS	5.8	4.7	0.2	0.2	0.0	0.0	0.2	0.2	10.7	13.3	13.6	10.0	8.8	22.9	16.6	3.3	0.9	55.9	21.4	53.6	46.4
	ALASKA	69.3	66.7	3.5	3.2	4.5	5.0	4.1	5.7	7.6	7.3	7.4	7.8	7.4	28.4	26.9	6.5	0.6	72.9	33.6	51.3	48.7
	UNITED STATES	75.1	72.0	12.3	12.7	3.8	4.6	12.5	15.7	6.8	6.7	6.6	7.1	6.9	27.0	26.0	10.9	1.9	75.7	36.9	49.2	50.8

INCOME

99501-99671

#	POST OFFICE NAME	2009 Per Capita Income	2009 HH Income Base	2009 HOUSEHOLD INCOME DISTRIBUTION (%) Less than $25,000	$25,000 to $49,999	$50,000 to $99,999	$100,000 to $149,999	$150,000 or More	MEDIAN HOUSEHOLD INCOME 2009	2014	2009 National Centile	2009 State Centile	2009 Home Value Base	2009 HOME VALUE DISTRIBUTION (%) Less than $50,000	$50,000 to $89,999	$90,000 to $174,999	$175,000 to $399,999	$400,000 or More	2009 Median Home Value
99501	ANCHORAGE	30744	7504	27.0	25.3	29.9	11.0	6.8	46962	48705	54	51	2267	1.5	1.7	25.1	51.8	19.9	243735
99502	ANCHORAGE	35125	8522	6.9	13.5	43.9	23.6	12.1	81273	83627	93	96	5666	0.2	1.3	11.7	71.9	14.9	264320
99503	ANCHORAGE	25415	6263	24.3	30.5	32.2	9.7	3.4	45346	47246	49	47	1884	15.5	3.0	20.0	56.7	4.9	210169
99504	ANCHORAGE	30207	14361	11.4	20.0	42.3	17.9	8.4	69916	73294	87	90	9134	9.3	4.5	13.9	66.9	5.3	236149
99505	FORT RICHARDSON	19189	1165	6.4	39.6	43.4	7.0	3.6	52098	52687	66	61	59	0.0	0.0	47.5	45.8	6.8	204688
99506	ELMENDORF AFB	19267	1863	4.9	38.1	40.5	12.9	3.5	57132	59627	74	72	18	0.0	5.6	66.7	27.8	0.0	143750
99507	ANCHORAGE	33707	13612	10.1	18.9	39.1	19.4	12.5	76997	78837	91	95	8903	6.0	3.9	13.6	61.0	15.6	261328
99508	ANCHORAGE	25695	12929	18.0	26.1	38.1	12.4	5.4	54551	55676	71	65	6185	9.5	4.7	20.4	59.3	6.1	220912
99515	ANCHORAGE	34663	7835	6.8	13.7	42.0	23.3	14.2	84335	86100	94	97	5963	5.0	2.0	14.9	60.6	17.5	276963
99516	ANCHORAGE	46747	6768	4.0	5.9	27.2	29.5	33.4	125473	125346	99	100	5992	0.3	0.5	2.7	52.2	44.3	382779
99517	ANCHORAGE	35452	7098	10.1	23.0	38.2	17.3	11.4	70963	74690	87	91	4074	2.4	1.6	20.0	63.7	12.3	244622
99518	ANCHORAGE	32508	4108	10.2	19.9	44.5	18.8	6.5	65450	67678	84	85	2293	0.5	0.8	22.8	71.8	4.1	225515
99540	INDIAN	36130	132	22.0	18.2	36.4	16.7	6.8	57793	61128	75	73	86	1.2	0.0	33.7	46.5	18.6	236364
99546	ADAK	36121	131	12.2	21.4	42.0	19.8	4.6	64415	64304	83	83	50	6.0	28.0	50.0	16.0	0.0	105000
99547	ATKA	29404	28	10.7	21.4	46.4	17.9	3.6	63927	62826	82	82	11	9.1	36.4	45.5	9.1	0.0	95000
99549	PORT HEIDEN	25201	35	17.1	28.6	31.4	14.3	8.6	52516	53240	67	62	27	7.4	14.8	44.4	29.6	3.7	120313
99551	AKIACHAK	10785	131	29.0	32.1	29.8	6.9	2.3	41192	42094	37	37	104	34.6	21.2	25.0	16.3	2.9	78000
99552	AKIAK	10576	68	27.9	33.8	30.9	5.9	1.5	41265	42313	37	37	54	33.3	24.1	22.2	16.7	3.7	76667
99553	AKUTAN	18197	32	25.0	28.1	40.6	3.1	3.1	45000	44057	48	47	14	14.3	14.3	50.0	7.1	14.3	133333
99554	ALAKANUK	11773	352	25.9	29.3	36.1	8.0	0.9	43844	46156	45	44	266	44.0	12.8	13.2	28.2	1.9	63333
99555	ALEKNAGIK	18502	68	32.4	30.9	20.6	10.3	5.9	36134	41141	21	22	54	16.7	14.8	35.2	33.3	0.0	150000
99556	ANCHOR POINT	20602	986	24.0	28.9	36.6	8.4	2.0	46859	48335	54	50	827	10.3	20.0	35.2	29.6	5.0	133285
99557	ANIAK	9311	147	47.6	38.1	12.2	2.0	0.0	26283	26077	4	6	107	13.1	17.8	36.4	27.1	5.6	140833
99558	ANVIK	12427	49	42.9	32.7	20.4	4.1	0.0	29277	30418	7	10	38	55.3	15.8	13.2	13.2	2.6	46000
99559	BETHEL	21510	2612	18.2	24.4	29.7	19.8	7.9	59533	61777	77	74	1336	17.4	11.5	16.0	45.0	10.0	205705
99561	CHEFORNAK	10822	75	24.0	30.7	29.3	10.7	5.3	44529	46151	47	45	57	33.3	21.1	19.3	12.3	14.0	77500
99563	CHEVAK	0	0	0.0	0.0	0.0	0.0	0.0	0	0	0	0	0	0.0	0.0	0.0	0.0	0.0	0
99564	CHIGNIK	23220	24	16.7	20.8	45.8	12.5	4.2	60000	52835	77	75	18	11.1	16.7	38.9	27.8	5.6	118750
99565	CHIGNIK LAGOON	19797	28	17.9	17.9	50.0	10.7	3.6	55982	58032	73	69	21	9.5	14.3	42.9	28.6	4.8	118750
99567	CHUGIAK	35642	2961	6.4	14.9	34.1	29.4	15.2	90375	93660	95	98	2335	0.6	3.6	10.8	69.9	15.0	278522
99568	CLAM GULCH	21621	153	25.5	28.1	35.9	7.2	3.3	46813	48409	54	50	131	21.4	11.5	30.5	28.2	8.4	141346
99569	CLARKS POINT	16236	30	26.7	33.3	23.3	10.0	6.7	40000	42343	33	31	24	16.7	16.7	33.3	33.3	0.0	150000
99571	COLD BAY	35467	68	22.1	26.5	38.2	7.4	5.9	51198	52463	64	59	36	5.6	11.1	41.7	25.0	16.7	156250
99572	COOPER LANDING	29386	167	20.4	23.4	37.7	13.8	4.8	56613	59608	74	70	122	2.5	1.6	34.4	36.1	25.4	231818
99573	COPPER CENTER	19313	676	32.5	24.7	33.7	7.0	2.1	41904	45328	39	39	515	13.8	14.8	28.0	31.5	12.0	152365
99574	CORDOVA	28221	911	19.3	24.0	34.9	16.6	5.2	57554	58455	75	73	545	18.5	4.6	10.5	52.8	13.6	225459
99575	CROOKED CREEK	0	0	0.0	0.0	0.0	0.0	0.0	0	0	0	0	0	0.0	0.0	0.0	0.0	0.0	0
99576	DILLINGHAM	24994	1106	20.9	19.4	35.4	15.5	8.8	62191	63930	80	78	613	12.2	10.9	30.0	39.0	7.8	167008
99577	EAGLE RIVER	36076	8335	4.5	11.2	36.4	30.4	17.5	96612	98723	96	99	6574	1.2	0.6	4.6	77.4	16.2	289195
99578	EEK	9564	133	39.1	35.3	19.5	5.3	0.8	31903	32073	11	16	87	49.4	25.3	14.9	8.0	2.3	51000
99579	EGEGIK	27119	35	17.1	28.6	31.4	14.3	8.6	52516	53240	67	62	27	7.4	14.8	44.4	29.6	3.7	120313
99580	EKWOK	17636	41	29.3	26.8	29.3	9.8	4.9	41151	46156	37	35	28	21.4	10.7	53.6	14.3	0.0	131250
99583	FALSE PASS	32743	21	23.8	28.6	38.1	4.8	4.8	47375	47375	55	52	9	11.1	22.2	44.4	11.1	11.1	134375
99585	MARSHALL	10925	178	30.3	38.8	25.3	3.9	1.7	36519	38626	22	23	111	31.5	5.4	25.2	27.9	9.9	122321
99586	GAKONA	19406	143	42.7	23.8	25.2	7.7	0.7	30968	30372	10	15	106	17.9	13.2	32.1	18.9	17.9	147500
99587	GIRDWOOD	44210	795	7.8	18.7	40.9	18.0	14.6	72395	76612	88	93	452	0.7	0.4	16.2	60.8	21.9	291279
99588	GLENNALLEN	20463	388	25.0	28.1	35.1	9.8	2.1	47454	48903	55	53	239	11.7	10.9	28.5	37.7	11.3	171875
99589	GOODNEWS BAY	11935	69	37.7	36.2	18.8	5.8	1.4	32277	33148	12	17	45	44.4	24.4	15.6	11.1	4.4	58333
99591	SAINT GEORGE ISLAND	27973	42	11.9	21.4	42.9	19.0	4.8	63927	63185	82	82	16	6.3	25.0	56.3	12.5	0.0	106250
99602	HOLY CROSS	10482	54	46.3	29.6	20.4	3.7	0.0	27294	28586	5	7	42	59.5	14.3	11.9	11.9	2.4	45556
99603	HOMER	25868	3713	21.7	24.5	37.3	11.1	5.4	53672	55212	69	63	2638	7.1	5.9	26.9	46.8	13.3	213098
99604	HOOPER BAY	9558	422	32.0	36.7	23.0	5.7	2.6	32775	33266	13	18	290	50.0	14.1	14.8	15.5	5.5	50000
99606	ILIAMNA	14827	105	39.0	25.7	24.8	10.5	0.0	36136	37857	21	23	64	17.2	14.1	20.3	31.3	17.2	168750
99607	KALSKAG	16058	61	24.6	36.1	23.0	11.5	4.9	43232	45000	43	43	46	2.2	6.5	19.6	63.0	8.7	233333
99610	KASILOF	23686	782	26.0	26.3	34.1	9.1	4.5	47505	49083	55	55	666	17.3	6.3	31.1	33.2	12.2	165190
99611	KENAI	25834	5769	19.4	22.9	35.6	16.2	6.0	60591	62183	78	75	4046	8.0	5.9	33.9	44.8	7.4	181583
99612	KING COVE	22718	170	20.0	24.1	38.8	9.4	7.6	55067	57547	71	67	106	0.0	5.7	47.2	32.1	15.1	170833
99613	KING SALMON	30472	145	12.4	23.4	48.3	13.1	2.8	61389	61564	79	76	66	4.5	9.1	28.8	51.5	6.1	195833
99614	KIPNUK	12097	136	24.3	30.1	30.1	10.3	5.1	44439	45985	47	45	104	31.7	22.1	20.2	12.5	13.5	80000
99615	KODIAK	27474	4275	12.0	20.4	38.0	18.3	11.3	70201	72079	87	90	2321	5.5	4.9	19.8	54.2	15.7	242622
99620	KOTLIK	10075	125	25.6	30.4	36.0	7.2	0.8	42376	45650	41	40	94	43.6	12.8	12.8	28.7	2.1	65000
99621	KWETHLUK	10182	150	29.3	32.0	30.0	6.7	2.0	41180	42316	37	36	119	35.3	21.8	24.4	16.0	2.5	75833
99622	KWIGILLINGOK	12413	151	25.2	30.5	29.8	9.9	4.6	43842	45858	45	43	115	31.3	22.6	20.0	13.0	13.0	78750
99625	LEVELOCK	14640	57	40.4	22.8	26.3	10.5	0.0	35752	38194	20	21	35	14.3	14.3	17.1	34.3	20.0	203571
99626	LOWER KALSKAG	14707	65	24.6	36.9	23.1	10.8	4.6	42820	45361	42	41	49	2.0	8.2	18.4	63.3	8.2	236111
99627	MC GRATH	22834	152	30.3	22.4	28.3	11.2	7.9	45933	46895	51	48	94	18.1	22.3	51.1	6.4	2.1	100000
99628	MANOKOTAK	13628	90	31.1	32.2	20.0	10.0	6.7	36854	40000	23	24	71	15.5	16.9	32.4	35.2	0.0	143750
99630	MEKORYUK	18113	72	26.4	37.5	26.4	6.9	2.8	41463	41910	38	38	48	43.8	8.3	25.0	16.7	6.3	80000
99631	MOOSE PASS	29478	238	20.6	22.7	38.2	13.9	4.6	56901	58620	74	71	174	3.4	1.1	35.1	35.6	24.7	225000
99632	MOUNTAIN VILLAGE	13753	236	23.7	28.4	35.2	9.3	3.4	47381	48436	55	52	131	42.0	14.5	25.2	18.3	0.0	71000
99634	NAPAKIAK	9638	80	33.8	33.8	23.8	6.3	2.5	37668	39065	26	26	64	53.1	17.2	9.4	15.6	4.7	48182
99636	NEW STUYAHOK	13165	153	29.4	28.8	27.5	10.5	3.9	40281	44607	34	32	103	21.4	11.7	46.6	18.4	1.9	129861
99638	NIKOLSKI	28645	12	8.3	25.0	50.0	16.7	0.0	63804	65822	82	81	5	0.0	0.0	100.0	0.0	0.0	98333
99639	NINILCHIK	21497	451	31.5	27.9	29.0	9.3	2.2	40661	43530	35	32	375	11.2	12.5	37.3	33.9	5.1	137202
99640	NONDALTON	14682	58	34.5	27.6	27.6	10.3	0.0	38621	37346	29	29	35	14.3	14.3	17.1	34.3	20.0	204167
99645	PALMER	26506	8628	15.0	20.6	41.8	15.0	7.5	65131	67935	83	84	6714	3.9	4.6	16.7	56.9	17.8	255184
99647	PEDRO BAY	13631	14	35.7	35.7	21.4	7.1	0.0	35000	37321	18	20	9	0.0	0.0	44.4	55.6	0.0	208333
99648	PERRYVILLE	19129	28	17.9	17.9	50.0	10.7	3.6	55982	58032	73	69	21	9.5	14.3	42.9	28.6	4.8	118750
99649	PILOT POINT	23405	29	17.2	27.6	34.5	10.3	10.3	53219	55684	68	62	22	9.1	18.2	40.9	27.3	4.5	120000
99650	PILOT STATION	11942	100	23.0	29.0	34.0	10.0	4.0	47384	47878	55	53	51	37.3	15.7	33.3	13.7	0.0	82500
99654	WASILLA	26372	18148	15.7	19.5	41.3	16.0	7.6	65761	69391	84	86	14078	4.3	4.3	16.2	61.3	13.8	250157
99655	QUINHAGAK	12530	76	32.9	32.9	25.0	6.6	2.6	38170	40622	27	28	61	52.5	18.0	9.8	14.8	4.9	48750
99656	RED DEVIL	10214	17	52.9	29.4	17.6	0.0	0.0	22287	26058	2	5	12	8.3	25.0	33.3	25.0	8.3	150000
99658	SAINT MARYS	15802	178	23.0	28.7	34.3	10.1	3.9	48010	49695	57	56	91	39.6	15.4	31.9	13.2	0.0	76250
99659	SAINT MICHAEL	11939	97	33.0	34.0	21.6	8.2	3.1	34676	35747	17	19	69	31.9	26.1	13.0	29.0	0.0	80833
99660	SAINT PAUL ISLAND	27717	146	11.6	19.9	43.8	19.9	4.8	65115	64450	83	84	56	5.4	26.8	50.0	17.9	0.0	108333
99661	SAND POINT	28596	220	12.7	23.6	33.2	19.1	11.4	65455	64954	84	86	128	11.7	11.7	55.5	21.1	0.0	122727
99662	SCAMMON BAY	8965	104	32.7	37.5	22.1	5.8	1.9	32441	33122	12	18	71	49.3	14.1	15.5	15.5	5.6	51000
99664	SEWARD	26704	1826	18.2	23.3	41.5	12.0	4.9	60824	62026	79	76	1091	8.1	5.7	21.2	52.1	13.0	221509
99665	SHAGELUK	9534	27	44.4	29.6	18.5	7.4	0.0	28592	30699	6	9	21	42.9	19.0	14.3	19.0	4.8	65000
99667	SKWENTNA	10726	8	50.0	12.5	37.5	0.0	0.0	27500	47500	5	9	7	0.0	28.6	14.3	28.6	28.6	225000
99668	SLEETMUTE	9231	6	66.7	33.3	0.0	0.0	0.0	11833	20000	1	2	4	0.0	0.0	100.0	0.0	0.0	150000
99669	SOLDOTNA	27551	4741	16.5	21.5	41.6	13.4	7.0	61654	62796	80	77	3565	6.1	6.8	30.7	46.9	9.5	196108
99670	SOUTH NAKNEK	24961	260	13.8	20.8	48.5	13.8	3.1	62818	65010	81	80	133	6.0	8.3	27.8	52.6	5.3	198864
99671	STEBBINS	10879	131	32.8	33.6	21.4	8.4	3.8	35217	36787	18	20	93	30.1	23.7	15.1	31.2	0.0	85000
	ALASKA	28744		15.0	21.0	38.1	16.8	9.1	65464	68018				7.3	5.5	18.9	55.0	13.4	236447
	UNITED STATES	27277		20.9	24.4	35.3	11.7	7.6	54719	56938				9.3	13.1	31.6	32.6	13.5	162279

#	POST OFFICE NAME	FINANCIAL SERVICES: Auto Loan	FINANCIAL SERVICES: Home Loan	FINANCIAL SERVICES: Invest-ments	FINANCIAL SERVICES: Retire-ment Plans	THE HOME: Home Improvements: Home Repair	THE HOME: Home Improvements: Lawn & Garden	THE HOME: Furnishings: Comput-ers & Hard-ware-Personal	THE HOME: Furnishings: Major Appli-ances	THE HOME: Furnishings: TV, Radio, Sound Equip-ment	THE HOME: Furnishings: Furni-ture	ENTERTAINMENT: Dine out/ Carry out	ENTERTAINMENT: Sports Equip-ment	ENTERTAINMENT: Fees & Tickets	ENTERTAINMENT: Toys & Games	ENTERTAINMENT: Travel	ENTERTAINMENT: Cable TV	PERSONAL: Apparel & Services	PERSONAL: Auto Repairs	PERSONAL: Health Insur-ance	PERSONAL: Pets & Supplies
99501	ANCHORAGE	91	72	72	77	71	72	95	80	95	92	97	66	87	94	85	94	68	92	86	99
99502	ANCHORAGE	138	150	133	151	145	133	140	136	134	146	136	108	146	139	141	129	96	135	126	159
99503	ANCHORAGE	83	67	61	70	63	64	85	71	84	83	85	59	76	85	74	82	59	81	73	88
99504	ANCHORAGE	119	121	108	121	116	110	120	114	116	123	118	90	120	120	117	113	83	116	110	135
99505	FORT RICHARDSON	110	57	43	66	51	49	103	71	97	96	102	71	78	117	74	89	72	91	64	87
99506	ELMENDORF AFB	121	63	47	73	56	53	114	79	107	106	112	78	86	128	82	98	79	100	71	96
99507	ANCHORAGE	136	131	116	133	125	116	135	124	129	140	132	101	133	136	128	124	93	128	115	147
99508	ANCHORAGE	99	88	82	90	85	83	100	90	98	100	100	72	95	101	93	96	70	97	89	108
99515	ANCHORAGE	141	158	141	158	153	140	143	141	137	150	139	111	152	142	147	132	99	138	130	164
99516	ANCHORAGE	181	234	233	242	238	210	194	202	182	208	185	157	228	186	217	175	136	189	179	229
99517	ANCHORAGE	124	124	117	126	122	114	127	119	122	131	124	94	128	125	124	119	88	122	115	141
99518	ANCHORAGE	111	112	99	113	107	100	114	105	110	115	112	86	114	114	110	106	79	109	101	125
99540	INDIAN	99	108	106	111	108	104	103	102	101	106	102	78	109	100	107	99	72	101	100	119
99546	ADAK	113	117	95	112	109	101	106	106	103	113	105	80	106	109	103	100	72	103	98	123
99547	ATKA	113	117	95	112	109	101	106	106	103	114	105	80	106	109	103	100	72	103	98	123
99549	PORT HEIDEN	109	113	92	108	105	98	102	102	100	110	102	77	102	105	99	97	70	99	94	119
99551	AKIACHAK	72	72	62	64	71	59	71	70	67	77	68	52	67	68	69	63	48	70	61	77
99552	AKIAK	72	72	62	64	71	59	71	70	67	77	68	52	67	68	69	63	48	70	61	77
99553	AKUTAN	78	67	57	69	63	69	82	71	82	74	81	58	74	82	71	83	56	78	77	88
99554	ALAKANUK	77	77	66	68	76	63	76	75	71	82	73	56	72	73	74	67	52	75	65	82
99555	ALEKNAGIK	87	87	74	77	85	71	86	85	80	93	83	63	81	83	83	76	58	84	73	93
99556	ANCHOR POINT	92	71	114	70	77	97	73	92	76	66	75	69	61	73	77	81	50	85	92	108
99557	ANIAK	55	36	53	34	36	54	39	49	44	37	43	38	29	45	36	49	29	46	51	60
99558	ANVIK	55	47	38	49	42	50	51	48	56	52	55	38	49	56	46	58	38	52	54	61
99559	BETHEL	109	103	90	100	100	94	106	101	105	109	106	77	102	107	101	103	75	104	98	118
99561	CHEFORNAK	97	78	58	65	74	73	77	83	84	87	85	51	67	85	69	87	59	84	81	91
99563	CHEVAK	0	0	0	0	0	0	0	0	0	0	0	0	0	0	0	0	0	0	0	0
99564	CHIGNIK	97	101	82	97	94	88	92	92	89	98	91	69	91	94	89	87	63	89	84	107
99565	CHIGNIK LAGOON	93	96	78	92	90	84	87	87	85	94	87	66	87	89	85	83	60	85	80	102
99567	CHUGIAK	139	169	148	170	163	152	145	148	138	150	140	117	160	143	155	134	100	141	137	171
99568	CLAM GULCH	94	75	122	74	83	100	76	96	79	71	78	70	65	75	82	84	52	89	95	111
99569	CLARKS POINT	87	87	75	77	85	71	86	85	81	93	83	63	82	83	83	76	59	85	74	93
99571	COLD BAY	85	85	77	86	83	83	92	84	91	87	91	68	91	92	88	92	64	89	88	101
99572	COOPER LANDING	108	86	140	85	95	114	87	110	91	81	89	80	75	86	94	97	59	101	109	127
99573	COPPER CENTER	81	67	94	66	72	83	66	80	69	64	69	59	59	67	69	73	46	75	80	94
99574	CORDOVA	112	99	121	100	101	117	101	110	101	93	101	89	92	100	102	104	69	107	112	133
99575	CROOKED CREEK	0	0	0	0	0	0	0	0	0	0	0	0	0	0	0	0	0	0	0	0
99576	DILLINGHAM	105	108	104	107	108	103	106	105	103	108	104	81	107	104	107	102	74	105	103	122
99577	EAGLE RIVER	151	176	157	179	172	153	155	154	146	165	148	124	170	153	162	139	107	148	137	177
99578	EEK	66	53	40	44	51	50	53	57	58	59	58	35	46	59	48	60	41	58	56	63
99579	EGEGIK	109	113	92	108	105	98	102	102	100	110	102	77	102	105	99	97	70	99	94	119
99580	EKWOK	81	81	69	71	79	66	80	79	75	86	77	59	76	77	77	71	54	79	68	86
99583	FALSE PASS	77	66	56	68	62	68	80	70	80	73	80	57	73	81	70	82	55	77	76	86
99585	MARSHALL	66	56	46	58	50	60	62	57	67	62	66	45	59	68	55	69	45	62	65	73
99586	GAKONA	70	56	91	55	62	74	56	71	59	53	58	52	49	56	61	63	39	66	71	83
99587	GIRDWOOD	137	136	127	140	132	127	140	130	137	142	139	105	141	140	137	134	98	135	128	156
99588	GLENNALLEN	90	75	105	73	80	92	74	89	77	71	76	65	66	75	77	81	51	83	88	104
99589	GOODNEWS BAY	66	53	40	44	51	50	53	57	58	59	58	35	46	58	48	60	41	58	55	63
99591	SAINT GEORGE ISLAND	113	117	95	112	109	101	106	106	103	114	105	80	106	109	103	100	72	103	98	123
99602	HOLY CROSS	55	47	38	49	42	50	51	48	56	52	55	38	49	56	46	58	38	52	54	61
99603	HOMER	96	93	102	94	94	100	90	97	90	89	90	74	88	90	92	92	62	94	97	114
99604	HOOPER BAY	66	56	45	58	50	60	61	57	66	61	66	45	59	67	55	69	45	62	64	73
99606	ILIAMNA	76	70	62	67	68	71	66	70	68	68	68	51	62	71	63	70	46	67	70	83
99607	KALSKAG	89	89	77	79	88	73	89	87	83	96	85	65	84	85	85	78	60	87	76	96
99610	KASILOF	99	79	128	78	87	105	79	101	83	74	82	74	69	79	86	88	54	93	100	117
99611	KENAI	104	104	94	104	101	100	99	101	98	102	99	77	98	101	98	98	69	99	98	119
99612	KING COVE	91	106	100	104	105	98	103	99	100	100	101	78	110	101	107	100	73	101	99	115
99613	KING SALMON	81	92	79	94	89	90	82	85	80	82	81	66	87	83	86	81	57	82	84	100
99614	KIPNUK	98	78	58	65	75	73	78	84	85	87	86	52	68	86	70	88	60	85	82	92
99615	KODIAK	122	121	116	122	119	111	126	118	120	126	122	96	124	124	123	116	86	121	112	139
99620	KOTLIK	77	77	66	68	76	63	77	75	72	83	74	56	72	74	74	68	52	75	65	83
99621	KWETHLUK	72	72	62	64	71	59	72	70	67	77	69	52	68	69	69	63	49	70	61	77
99622	KWIGILLINGOK	98	78	58	65	75	73	78	84	85	87	86	52	68	86	70	88	60	85	81	92
99625	LEVELOCK	75	69	61	67	68	71	65	69	68	68	68	50	62	71	62	70	46	67	69	82
99626	LOWER KALSKAG	89	89	77	79	88	73	88	87	83	96	85	65	84	85	85	78	60	87	76	95
99627	MC GRATH	92	81	84	82	84	93	87	91	90	84	88	67	80	89	84	93	60	90	97	106
99628	MANOKOTAK	87	87	75	77	85	71	86	85	81	93	83	63	82	83	83	76	59	85	74	93
99630	MEKORYUK	90	72	54	60	69	67	72	77	78	80	79	48	63	79	64	81	55	78	75	85
99631	MOOSE PASS	108	86	139	85	95	114	86	110	90	81	89	80	75	86	94	96	59	101	108	127
99632	MOUNTAIN VILLAGE	87	87	74	77	85	71	86	84	80	93	82	63	81	82	83	76	58	84	73	93
99634	NAPAKIAK	78	63	47	53	60	59	63	67	68	70	69	42	55	69	56	70	48	68	66	74
99636	NEW STUYAHOK	81	81	70	72	80	67	81	79	75	87	78	59	76	78	78	71	55	79	69	87
99638	NIKOLSKI	104	107	88	103	100	93	98	98	95	104	97	74	97	100	94	92	67	95	90	114
99639	NINILCHIK	86	69	111	68	76	91	69	88	72	65	71	64	60	68	75	77	47	81	86	101
99640	NONDALTON	76	70	62	68	69	72	66	70	69	69	69	51	63	72	63	71	47	68	70	83
99645	PALMER	111	117	106	117	114	112	108	110	106	111	107	85	111	109	110	105	75	107	107	129
99647	PEDRO BAY	66	60	53	58	59	62	57	60	59	59	59	44	54	61	54	61	40	58	60	72
99648	PERRYVILLE	93	96	78	92	90	84	87	87	85	94	87	66	87	89	85	83	60	85	80	102
99649	PILOT POINT	112	116	95	112	109	101	105	105	103	113	105	79	105	108	102	100	72	102	97	123
99650	PILOT STATION	89	89	76	79	87	73	88	86	82	95	85	64	83	85	85	78	60	86	75	95
99654	WASILLA	114	116	109	115	113	111	108	112	106	111	107	86	108	110	109	105	75	108	106	130
99655	QUINHAGAK	78	63	47	52	60	59	62	67	68	70	69	41	55	69	56	70	48	68	65	74
99656	RED DEVIL	56	36	54	34	36	55	39	49	45	37	44	38	29	46	36	50	29	46	52	60
99658	SAINT MARYS	89	89	76	78	87	72	88	86	82	95	84	64	83	84	85	77	60	86	75	95
99659	SAINT MICHAEL	72	61	49	63	54	65	67	62	72	67	72	49	64	73	60	75	49	68	70	80
99660	SAINT PAUL ISLAND	113	117	95	112	109	101	106	106	103	113	105	80	106	108	102	100	72	103	97	123
99661	SAND POINT	111	131	123	128	129	120	126	121	123	123	124	95	135	123	131	122	89	123	121	141
99662	SCAMMON BAY	66	56	45	58	50	60	61	57	66	61	66	45	59	67	55	69	45	62	64	73
99664	SEWARD	100	97	90	96	94	96	95	95	96	97	97	72	94	98	93	97	67	95	96	113
99665	SHAGELUK	55	47	38	49	42	50	51	48	56	52	55	38	49	56	46	58	38	52	54	61
99667	SKWENTNA	69	55	90	55	61	73	56	71	58	52	57	52	48	55	60	62	38	65	70	82
99668	SLEETMUTE	37	24	36	23	24	36	26	33	30	25	29	25	19	30	24	33	19	31	35	40
99669	SOLDOTNA	107	104	101	105	103	106	102	105	102	102	102	80	100	103	101	102	70	103	104	124
99670	SOUTH NAKNEK	94	106	91	109	103	104	94	98	93	95	93	77	101	95	100	93	65	94	97	116
99671	STEBBINS	72	61	49	63	54	65	67	62	73	67	72	49	64	73	60	75	49	68	70	80
	ALASKA	116	114	108	115	111	108	115	111	112	116	113	88	114	115	112	110	80	112	107	131
	UNITED STATES	100	100	100	100	100	100	100	100	100	100	100	100	100	100	100	100	100	100	100	100

ZIP CODE #	POST OFFICE NAME	COUNTY FIPS CODE	POPULATION 2000	POPULATION 2009	POPULATION 2014	2000-2009 ANNUAL RATE % Rate	2000-2009 ANNUAL RATE State Centile	HOUSEHOLDS 2000	HOUSEHOLDS 2009	HOUSEHOLDS 2014	HOUSEHOLDS % Annual Rate 2000-2009	HOUSEHOLDS 2009 Average HH Size	FAMILIES 2000	FAMILIES 2009	FAMILIES % Annual Rate 2000-2009
99672	STERLING	122	2743	3015	3125	1.0	88	1000	1122	1173	1.3	2.68	779	859	1.1
99674	SUTTON	170	945	1271	1475	3.3	97	221	346	428	5.0	2.53	140	215	4.7
99676	TALKEETNA	170	1729	2835	3524	5.5	100	770	1273	1589	5.6	2.23	433	698	5.3
99679	TULUKSAK	050	428	429	422	0.0	55	86	84	83	-0.3	5.11	73	71	-0.3
99681	TUNUNAK	050	1065	1074	1065	0.1	59	235	233	230	-0.1	4.61	184	180	-0.2
99682	TYONEK	122	173	188	200	0.9	86	61	66	70	0.9	2.85	41	43	0.5
99684	UNALAKLEET	180	749	768	770	0.3	66	225	232	234	0.3	3.31	175	178	0.2
99685	UNALASKA	016	4283	3820	3799	-1.2	31	834	787	789	-0.6	2.41	476	436	-0.9
99686	VALDEZ	261	4493	4200	4066	-0.7	38	1670	1593	1551	-0.5	2.60	1152	1074	-0.8
99688	WILLOW	170	2810	4568	5693	5.4	99	1099	1800	2244	5.5	2.54	729	1169	5.2
99689	YAKUTAT	282	378	311	301	-2.1	6	144	125	122	-1.5	2.18	86	73	-1.8
99691	NIKOLAI	290	100	84	77	-1.9	12	40	35	32	-1.4	2.40	26	21	-2.3
99701	FAIRBANKS	090	17673	19038	19838	0.8	83	7211	7475	7778	0.4	2.44	4120	4189	0.2
99702	EIELSON AFB	090	5400	5122	4983	-0.6	40	1448	1308	1272	-1.1	3.59	1414	1275	-1.1
99703	FORT WAINWRIGHT	090	5815	5947	5879	0.2	63	1437	1340	1318	-0.8	3.46	1371	1274	-0.8
99704	CLEAR	290	484	452	430	-0.7	38	204	193	183	-0.6	2.34	119	109	-0.9
99705	NORTH POLE	090	16368	20642	22751	2.5	96	5627	6928	7639	2.3	2.98	4246	5133	2.1
99709	FAIRBANKS	090	25186	29018	31004	1.5	92	9725	10887	11674	1.2	2.55	6121	6668	0.9
99712	FAIRBANKS	090	11326	12851	13688	1.4	92	3913	4337	4638	1.1	2.88	2939	3181	0.9
99714	SALCHA	090	1072	1363	1509	2.6	97	416	514	569	2.3	2.65	292	352	2.0
99720	ALLAKAKET	290	99	89	83	-1.1	33	42	38	35	-1.1	2.34	27	24	-1.3
99721	ANAKTUVUK PASS	185	282	248	234	-1.4	25	84	75	71	-1.2	3.31	64	57	-1.2
99722	ARCTIC VILLAGE	290	152	131	121	-1.6	20	52	46	42	-1.3	2.85	34	29	-1.7
99723	BARROW	185	662	584	550	-1.3	29	166	149	141	-1.2	3.92	129	114	-1.3
99724	BEAVER	290	84	73	67	-1.5	21	31	27	25	-1.5	2.70	20	17	-1.7
99726	BETTLES FIELD	290	118	101	93	-1.7	20	46	40	37	-1.5	2.53	27	23	-1.7
99727	BUCKLAND	188	406	419	425	0.3	66	84	86	87	0.3	4.87	69	70	0.2
99729	CANTWELL	068	276	267	263	-0.4	43	130	133	132	0.2	2.01	72	71	-0.2
99730	CENTRAL	290	143	126	117	-1.4	25	68	61	57	-1.2	2.05	40	35	-1.4
99733	CIRCLE	290	25	22	20	-1.4	25	11	10	9	-1.0	2.20	6	6	0.0
99734	PRUDHOE BAY	185	5	5	5	0.0	55	1	1	1	0.0	5.00	1	1	0.0
99736	DEERING	188	105	108	110	0.3	66	29	30	30	0.4	3.60	24	24	0.0
99737	DELTA JUNCTION	240	3909	4552	4984	1.7	94	1241	1517	1677	2.2	2.87	924	1109	2.0
99739	ELIM	180	285	295	300	0.4	70	73	76	77	0.4	3.88	54	55	0.2
99740	FORT YUKON	290	610	536	499	-1.4	25	231	208	194	-1.1	2.56	136	118	-1.5
99741	GALENA	290	23	21	19	-1.0	34	9	8	8	-1.3	2.63	6	5	-2.0
99742	GAMBELL	180	649	679	697	0.5	73	159	167	172	0.5	4.07	123	128	0.4
99743	HEALY	068	1571	1455	1428	-0.8	36	673	685	681	0.2	2.12	390	385	-0.1
99744	ANDERSON	068	149	114	113	-2.9	1	20	21	21	0.5	5.33	13	14	0.8
99745	HUGHES	290	61	55	51	-1.1	33	20	18	17	-1.1	3.06	13	11	-1.8
99746	HUSLIA	290	293	262	245	-1.2	31	88	79	74	-1.2	3.32	57	50	-1.4
99747	KAKTOVIK	185	294	259	244	-1.4	25	90	81	76	-1.1	3.20	69	61	-1.3
99748	KALTAG	290	230	197	181	-1.7	20	69	60	56	-1.5	3.28	52	45	-1.6
99749	KIANA	188	524	536	545	0.2	63	135	139	141	0.3	3.86	111	112	0.1
99750	KIVALINA	188	1069	1072	1084	0.0	55	182	188	191	0.4	4.45	156	159	0.2
99751	KOBUK	188	367	373	377	0.2	63	83	85	86	0.3	4.39	71	72	0.2
99752	KOTZEBUE	188	3498	3595	3651	0.3	66	957	988	1006	0.3	3.58	717	727	0.1
99753	KOYUK	180	297	307	313	0.4	70	80	83	85	0.4	3.70	59	60	0.2
99755	DENALI NATIONAL PARK	068	67	62	60	-0.8	36	28	28	27	0.0	2.18	16	16	0.0
99756	MANLEY HOT SPRINGS	290	136	88	84	-4.6	1	60	42	40	-3.8	2.10	35	24	-4.0
99757	LAKE MINCHUMINA	290	23	19	18	-2.0	8	11	9	9	-2.1	2.11	7	6	-1.7
99758	MINTO	290	265	227	209	-1.7	20	77	67	62	-1.5	3.39	45	38	-1.8
99759	POINT LAY	185	247	218	206	-1.3	29	61	55	52	-1.1	3.95	49	43	-1.4
99760	NENANA	290	62	58	55	-0.7	38	22	21	20	-0.5	2.76	13	12	-0.9
99762	NOME	180	3819	3908	3949	0.2	63	1278	1312	1330	0.3	2.81	818	817	0.0
99763	NOORVIK	188	772	801	817	0.4	70	172	179	183	0.4	4.47	147	151	0.3
99765	NULATO	290	792	694	645	-1.4	25	250	222	206	-1.3	2.96	180	157	-1.5
99766	POINT HOPE	185	757	668	630	-1.3	29	186	168	159	-1.1	3.96	149	133	-1.2
99767	RAMPART	290	45	38	35	-1.8	15	20	17	16	-1.7	2.24	12	10	-2.0
99768	RUBY	290	191	171	159	-1.2	31	70	63	59	-1.1	2.71	46	40	-1.5
99769	SAVOONGA	180	294	308	316	0.5	73	62	65	67	0.5	4.74	48	50	0.4
99771	SHAKTOOLIK	180	105	108	108	0.3	66	32	33	33	0.3	3.27	25	25	0.0
99772	SHISHMAREF	180	562	576	582	0.3	66	142	146	148	0.3	3.95	102	103	0.1
99773	SHUNGNAK	188	203	206	208	0.2	63	54	55	56	0.2	3.75	46	47	0.2
99777	TANANA	290	158	135	124	-1.7	20	54	47	43	-1.5	2.87	32	27	-1.8
99778	TELLER	180	75	79	81	0.6	77	21	22	22	0.5	3.45	17	17	0.0
99780	TOK	240	2265	2849	3187	2.5	96	857	1090	1226	2.6	2.61	582	724	2.4
99781	VENETIE	290	90	78	72	-1.5	21	28	25	23	-1.2	3.12	18	15	-2.0
99782	WAINWRIGHT	185	546	483	455	-1.3	29	148	133	126	-1.1	3.63	119	106	-1.2
99783	WALES	180	298	305	308	0.3	66	93	96	97	0.3	3.18	67	67	0.0
99784	WHITE MOUNTAIN	180	269	278	283	0.4	70	89	92	94	0.4	3.02	66	67	0.2
99785	BREVIG MISSION	180	276	290	297	0.5	73	68	71	73	0.5	3.93	54	56	0.4
99786	AMBLER	188	10	10	10	0.0	55	2	2	2	0.0	5.00	2	2	0.0
99788	CHALKYITSIK	290	40	35	32	-1.4	25	19	17	15	-1.2	2.06	12	10	-2.0
99789	NUIQSUT	185	3	3	3	0.0	55	1	1	1	0.0	3.00	1	1	0.0
99801	JUNEAU	110	28506	28475	28028	0.0	55	10574	10590	10432	0.0	2.63	7112	6961	-0.2
99820	ANGOON	232	620	523	482	-1.8	15	203	180	169	-1.3	2.91	144	126	-1.4
99824	DOUGLAS	110	2080	2187	2192	0.5	73	922	973	975	0.6	2.25	499	508	0.2
99825	ELFIN COVE	232	37	34	32	-0.9	35	18	17	16	-0.6	1.94	10	10	0.0
99826	GUSTAVUS	232	429	389	365	-1.1	33	199	190	181	-0.5	2.04	116	108	-0.8
99827	HAINES	100	2531	2430	2406	-0.4	43	1035	1016	1015	-0.2	2.39	686	657	-0.5
99829	HOONAH	232	1299	1147	1072	-1.3	29	487	451	426	-0.8	2.50	338	306	-1.1
99833	PETERSBURG	280	4169	3684	3448	-1.3	29	1585	1429	1346	-1.1	2.55	1084	955	-1.4
99835	SITKA	220	8912	8993	9018	0.1	59	3309	3422	3458	0.4	2.56	2240	2263	0.1
99840	SKAGWAY	232	862	797	754	-0.8	36	401	389	372	-0.3	2.05	215	202	-0.7
99901	KETCHIKAN	130	13953	13156	12723	-0.6	40	5350	5090	4945	-0.5	2.53	3595	3339	-0.8
99903	MEYERS CHUCK	201	21	18	16	-1.7	20	9	8	7	-1.3	2.25	5	4	-2.4
99919	THORNE BAY	201	409	346	321	-1.8	15	153	135	126	-1.3	2.56	109	94	-1.6
99921	CRAIG	201	1767	1573	1474	-1.2	31	647	593	562	-0.9	2.58	435	387	-1.3
99922	HYDABURG	201	69	55	50	-2.4	4	28	23	22	-2.1	2.39	19	15	-2.5
99923	HYDER	201	108	90	84	-2.0	8	54	47	45	-1.5	1.91	29	25	-1.6
99925	KLAWOCK	201	966	853	801	-1.3	29	354	324	308	-1.0	2.63	244	217	-1.3
99926	METLAKATLA	201	1564	1654	1654	0.6	77	540	576	580	0.7	2.87	394	410	0.4
99927	POINT BAKER	201	132	110	102	-2.0	8	56	47	44	-1.9	2.11	34	28	-2.1
99929	WRANGELL	280	2421	2163	2052	-1.2	31	963	877	837	-1.0	2.45	655	582	-1.3
	ALASKA					1.1					1.1	2.74			0.9
	UNITED STATES					1.0					1.1	2.59			0.9

ZIP CODE #	POST OFFICE NAME	RACE (%) White 2000	White 2009	Black 2000	Black 2009	Asian/Pacific 2000	Asian/Pacific 2009	% Hispanic Origin 2000	% Hispanic Origin 2009	2009 AGE DISTRIBUTION (%) 0-4	5-9	10-14	15-19	20-24	25-44	45-64	65-84	85+	18+	MEDIAN AGE 2009	% 2009 Males	% 2009 Females
99672	STERLING	92.5	90.1	0.4	0.5	0.7	0.8	1.3	2.0	6.3	7.8	8.8	8.1	4.0	25.2	31.4	8.1	0.4	71.9	38.3	51.7	48.3
99674	SUTTON	66.0	66.1	5.4	3.9	0.7	0.8	1.6	1.8	3.3	5.2	5.3	6.3	5.8	35.6	32.3	5.8	0.4	82.4	39.9	67.3	32.7
99676	TALKEETNA	87.3	83.3	0.3	0.4	0.4	0.5	1.7	2.5	4.5	5.4	7.2	8.0	2.6	27.4	37.0	7.2	0.7	77.7	42.5	54.0	46.0
99679	TULUKSAK	4.4	4.7	0.0	0.0	0.2	0.2	0.5	0.5	12.6	11.2	9.6	10.7	10.7	25.6	15.2	4.0	0.5	60.4	22.8	55.0	45.0
99681	TUNUNAK	3.2	3.3	0.0	0.0	0.0	0.0	0.2	0.2	10.2	11.3	11.2	11.3	7.4	24.8	18.1	5.1	0.7	59.1	24.1	54.7	45.3
99682	TYONEK	18.5	15.4	0.0	0.0	0.0	0.0	2.3	2.1	7.4	11.2	10.1	6.9	3.7	26.1	27.7	6.4	0.5	66.0	33.9	57.4	42.6
99684	UNALAKLEET	10.7	8.9	0.3	0.3	0.0	0.0	0.3	0.3	9.9	8.9	7.9	8.6	7.7	26.6	22.4	7.3	0.8	68.0	29.0	53.4	46.6
99685	UNALASKA	44.2	38.8	3.7	3.0	31.2	32.5	12.9	16.5	4.5	3.4	3.7	4.8	7.4	45.9	28.5	1.8	0.1	85.7	36.7	65.5	34.5
99686	VALDEZ	80.8	76.6	0.4	0.4	2.7	3.2	3.7	5.3	6.6	7.0	7.5	6.9	6.5	26.0	33.7	5.6	0.4	74.4	37.7	51.3	48.7
99688	WILLOW	89.2	85.9	0.1	0.1	0.5	0.6	1.6	2.4	5.1	6.9	7.7	8.0	4.9	25.0	33.0	9.0	0.4	74.8	40.4	52.6	47.4
99689	YAKUTAT	50.3	44.7	0.0	0.0	2.1	2.6	0.8	0.6	4.8	5.8	6.1	8.7	5.5	26.7	35.7	6.8	0.0	76.8	41.1	57.6	42.4
99691	NIKOLAI	42.9	35.7	0.0	0.0	0.0	0.0	1.0	1.2	7.1	6.0	7.1	9.5	11.9	19.0	28.6	10.7	0.0	75.0	31.3	54.8	45.2
99701	FAIRBANKS	66.9	62.0	7.8	7.4	3.0	3.4	4.4	6.4	7.8	6.6	6.2	7.4	8.7	28.6	24.6	8.8	1.5	74.9	33.3	50.0	50.0
99702	EIELSON AFB	81.7	78.1	9.4	9.4	2.3	2.8	5.8	8.9	15.1	12.5	9.5	5.6	17.0	38.8	1.3	0.2	0.0	59.9	22.2	52.9	47.1
99703	FORT WAINWRIGHT	63.6	59.4	20.8	19.9	2.9	3.1	11.6	16.8	15.7	9.7	5.2	7.4	24.6	35.8	1.5	0.1	0.0	67.3	22.4	58.2	41.8
99704	CLEAR	60.9	54.0	0.4	0.2	1.2	1.3	1.7	2.2	5.3	6.0	9.7	7.1	4.0	21.9	35.6	9.1	1.3	77.4	42.7	55.3	44.7
99705	NORTH POLE	84.4	80.4	2.8	2.9	1.7	2.0	2.9	4.4	7.6	7.3	7.0	7.2	7.4	31.6	26.4	5.3	0.3	73.7	32.4	51.4	48.6
99709	FAIRBANKS	79.7	75.7	3.6	3.4	2.7	3.2	3.2	4.7	6.2	6.2	6.3	8.5	9.7	29.0	27.6	6.0	0.4	76.7	33.1	51.2	48.8
99712	FAIRBANKS	85.3	82.1	3.2	2.9	1.5	1.7	3.3	4.8	7.0	6.9	7.0	7.9	7.7	27.3	30.4	5.4	0.4	74.3	35.0	52.7	47.3
99714	SALCHA	89.3	85.9	1.2	1.3	0.9	1.0	2.2	3.5	5.2	5.9	6.9	7.5	4.6	23.6	35.0	10.3	0.9	77.2	42.3	51.1	48.9
99720	ALLAKAKET	8.1	6.7	0.0	0.0	0.0	0.0	2.0	2.2	9.0	9.0	9.0	9.0	9.0	22.5	23.6	9.0	0.0	68.5	28.2	51.7	48.3
99721	ANAKTUVUK PASS	11.4	10.1	0.4	0.8	0.4	0.4	0.4	0.4	10.5	9.3	8.1	9.3	7.3	28.6	19.8	6.9	0.4	66.1	28.0	55.2	44.8
99722	ARCTIC VILLAGE	5.3	3.8	0.0	0.0	0.0	0.0	0.7	0.8	9.2	9.2	8.4	9.2	8.4	26.7	23.7	4.6	0.8	67.9	28.1	54.2	45.8
99723	BARROW	9.7	8.6	0.3	0.5	0.3	0.3	0.2	0.2	10.6	9.6	8.6	9.1	8.4	27.9	19.0	6.3	0.5	65.6	27.0	55.3	44.7
99724	BEAVER	4.8	4.1	0.0	0.0	0.0	0.0	1.2	0.0	8.2	8.2	8.2	9.6	8.2	24.7	28.8	4.1	0.0	71.2	29.6	53.4	46.6
99726	BETTLES FIELD	21.2	17.8	0.0	0.0	0.0	0.0	0.8	1.0	5.9	7.9	9.9	14.9	5.0	23.8	24.8	5.9	2.0	65.3	32.5	55.4	44.6
99727	BUCKLAND	3.9	4.1	0.0	0.0	0.0	0.0	1.0	1.0	9.3	12.2	15.8	13.4	6.9	23.6	14.1	4.8	0.0	52.7	19.8	53.0	47.0
99729	CANTWELL	86.6	83.1	0.7	0.7	2.2	2.2	1.8	3.0	4.9	4.9	5.2	5.6	6.7	24.0	41.2	7.1	0.4	81.3	44.0	55.4	44.6
99730	CENTRAL	25.4	20.6	0.0	0.0	0.0	0.0	1.4	2.4	7.1	7.1	7.1	8.7	6.3	22.2	29.4	11.1	0.8	73.0	35.8	50.0	50.0
99733	CIRCLE	25.0	22.7	0.0	0.0	0.0	0.0	0.0	0.0	9.1	9.1	9.1	9.1	9.1	36.4	18.2	0.0	0.0	68.2	27.5	50.0	50.0
99734	PRUDHOE BAY	50.0	40.0	0.0	0.0	0.0	0.0	0.0	0.0	0.0	0.0	0.0	20.0	20.0	20.0	40.0	0.0	0.0	100.0	27.5	60.0	40.0
99736	DEERING	3.8	3.7	0.0	0.0	0.0	0.0	1.0	0.9	9.3	12.0	15.7	15.7	6.5	23.1	13.9	3.7	0.0	49.1	19.1	51.9	48.1
99737	DELTA JUNCTION	86.5	83.8	3.1	2.9	1.1	1.3	3.0	4.4	7.4	7.2	8.3	8.8	6.8	24.1	28.2	8.7	0.5	71.5	34.5	51.6	48.4
99739	ELIM	7.7	6.1	0.0	0.0	0.4	0.3	0.4	0.3	9.8	10.2	9.2	10.2	9.2	24.1	21.4	5.4	0.7	64.7	26.0	52.5	47.5
99740	FORT YUKON	24.9	20.5	0.2	0.2	0.2	0.2	1.5	1.7	6.9	6.7	7.1	8.4	6.7	22.0	31.7	9.9	0.6	74.3	37.3	51.9	48.1
99741	GALENA	9.1	4.8	0.0	0.0	0.0	0.0	0.0	0.0	9.5	9.5	9.5	9.5	9.5	33.3	19.0	0.0	0.0	61.9	26.3	52.4	47.6
99742	GAMBELL	4.0	3.4	0.0	0.0	0.3	0.3	0.2	0.3	9.1	8.1	7.8	10.0	8.8	27.8	20.9	6.8	0.6	68.6	28.9	54.2	45.8
99743	HEALY	83.3	79.1	1.2	1.3	1.8	2.2	2.3	3.4	4.9	5.3	6.1	5.9	6.3	24.5	39.8	6.7	0.5	80.4	42.9	55.6	44.4
99744	ANDERSON	83.2	77.2	4.0	5.3	1.3	1.8	4.0	6.1	5.3	6.1	7.0	7.0	4.4	26.3	41.2	2.6	0.0	76.3	41.1	58.8	41.2
99745	HUGHES	8.2	5.5	0.0	0.0	0.0	0.0	1.6	1.8	10.9	10.9	9.1	9.1	10.9	20.0	23.6	5.5	0.0	65.5	24.6	52.7	47.3
99746	HUSLIA	7.9	6.1	0.0	0.0	0.0	0.0	1.7	1.9	9.9	9.9	8.8	9.2	8.4	23.3	22.1	7.6	0.8	65.6	27.5	50.8	49.2
99747	KAKTOVIK	11.6	10.0	0.3	0.8	0.3	0.4	0.3	0.4	10.4	9.3	8.5	8.9	7.7	28.6	19.7	6.6	0.4	66.0	27.7	55.2	44.8
99748	KALTAG	8.3	6.6	0.0	0.0	0.0	0.0	0.4	0.5	8.6	8.6	7.6	10.2	10.2	24.9	22.3	6.6	1.0	69.0	27.8	49.7	50.3
99749	KIANA	7.1	7.3	0.0	0.0	0.2	0.2	0.4	0.4	13.8	11.2	10.4	10.3	9.5	24.3	14.9	5.2	0.4	58.4	22.3	57.1	42.9
99750	KIVALINA	10.0	10.5	0.3	0.3	0.0	0.0	0.7	0.7	9.2	7.6	6.7	8.8	10.5	35.3	17.6	3.8	0.4	70.6	28.1	58.0	42.0
99751	KOBUK	10.1	10.5	0.3	0.3	0.3	0.3	0.8	0.8	13.7	9.9	13.4	9.9	7.5	20.6	18.5	5.6	0.8	56.0	22.1	50.7	49.3
99752	KOTZEBUE	17.3	17.8	0.3	0.3	1.5	1.6	1.0	1.3	11.9	10.1	10.0	9.3	7.6	27.1	19.4	4.3	0.5	62.1	25.7	51.2	48.8
99753	KOYUK	7.4	6.2	0.0	0.0	0.3	0.3	0.7	0.3	10.1	10.1	9.1	9.8	10.4	24.1	20.5	5.2	0.7	64.8	25.3	52.4	47.6
99755	DENALI NATIONAL PARK	79.4	75.8	1.5	1.6	1.5	1.6	1.5	3.2	6.5	4.8	6.5	6.5	6.5	24.2	38.7	6.5	0.0	77.4	41.3	54.8	45.2
99756	MANLEY HOT SPRINGS	60.3	52.3	0.0	0.0	1.5	1.1	1.5	2.3	5.7	6.8	10.2	8.0	4.5	22.7	31.8	8.0	2.3	77.3	40.6	52.3	47.7
99757	LAKE MINCHUMINA	43.5	36.8	0.0	0.0	0.0	0.0	0.0	0.0	10.5	10.5	10.5	10.5	10.5	21.1	26.3	0.0	0.0	63.2	23.8	52.6	47.4
99758	MINTO	22.6	18.5	0.0	0.0	0.0	0.0	1.1	0.9	5.7	7.9	10.1	14.1	4.4	23.3	25.1	7.0	2.2	66.5	33.4	56.4	43.6
99759	POINT LAY	9.3	8.3	0.0	0.0	0.0	0.0	2.0	3.7	9.2	12.4	12.4	12.8	7.3	23.4	17.9	4.6	0.0	57.8	22.2	55.5	44.5
99760	NENANA	61.3	53.4	0.0	0.0	1.6	1.7	1.6	3.4	5.2	6.9	8.6	6.9	3.4	20.7	39.7	8.6	0.0	79.3	44.0	56.9	43.1
99762	NOME	36.6	31.9	0.8	0.8	1.5	1.6	2.0	2.5	7.9	8.0	7.6	9.2	6.5	27.1	26.5	6.2	1.0	70.0	33.3	53.6	46.4
99763	NOORVIK	3.2	3.5	0.1	0.1	0.9	1.0	0.1	0.2	15.7	13.0	9.7	9.4	10.9	24.6	13.4	3.0	0.4	56.1	21.0	49.6	50.4
99765	NULATO	19.5	16.4	0.1	0.1	0.6	0.7	1.1	1.3	8.2	7.8	7.9	10.8	9.1	25.9	23.2	6.6	0.4	68.9	28.8	52.4	47.6
99766	POINT HOPE	9.4	8.4	0.1	0.1	0.3	0.3	1.8	3.6	9.0	11.8	12.6	12.4	7.2	23.7	18.3	4.8	0.3	58.5	22.9	55.2	44.8
99767	RAMPART	21.7	18.4	0.0	0.0	0.0	0.0	0.0	0.0	5.3	7.9	10.5	15.8	2.6	23.7	34.2	0.0	0.0	65.8	32.5	57.9	42.1
99768	RUBY	7.9	6.4	0.0	0.0	0.0	0.0	1.6	1.8	10.5	9.4	8.8	8.8	11.1	23.4	21.6	6.4	0.0	66.7	26.0	49.7	50.3
99769	SAVOONGA	4.1	3.2	0.0	0.0	0.3	0.3	0.0	0.3	9.1	7.8	7.8	10.7	9.1	27.6	20.5	6.8	0.6	68.8	28.5	54.2	45.8
99771	SHAKTOOLIK	10.6	8.3	0.0	0.0	0.0	0.0	0.0	0.0	7.4	8.3	8.3	9.3	7.4	26.9	23.1	9.3	0.0	70.4	30.0	51.9	48.1
99772	SHISHMAREF	6.0	5.0	0.2	0.2	0.0	0.0	0.5	0.5	9.0	8.9	8.5	11.3	9.2	27.6	20.0	5.2	0.3	66.7	26.8	53.5	46.5
99773	SHUNGNAK	10.3	10.7	0.0	0.0	0.0	0.0	0.5	0.5	14.6	9.7	13.6	10.2	7.3	19.4	18.4	5.8	1.0	54.9	21.3	50.5	49.5
99777	TANANA	21.7	17.8	0.0	0.0	0.0	0.0	1.3	0.7	5.9	8.1	9.6	12.6	4.4	24.4	25.2	7.4	2.2	67.4	34.6	56.3	43.7
99778	TELLER	10.7	8.9	0.0	0.0	0.0	0.0	1.3	0.0	10.1	10.1	11.4	10.1	8.9	26.6	16.5	6.3	0.0	63.3	24.6	53.2	46.8
99780	TOK	66.0	61.1	0.1	0.1	0.3	0.4	2.1	3.1	6.7	6.5	7.8	8.4	6.3	23.9	31.8	8.0	0.6	73.7	37.8	51.2	48.8
99781	VENETIE	5.6	3.8	0.0	0.0	0.0	0.0	1.1	0.0	7.7	7.7	7.7	9.0	7.7	25.6	30.8	3.8	0.0	73.1	30.0	52.6	47.4
99782	WAINWRIGHT	6.2	5.6	0.2	0.2	0.2	0.2	0.0	0.0	11.0	10.1	8.9	9.3	9.7	27.5	17.2	5.8	0.4	64.2	25.5	54.9	45.1
99783	WALES	6.1	4.9	0.0	0.0	0.0	0.0	0.3	0.3	9.2	8.9	8.5	11.1	9.5	27.5	20.3	4.6	0.3	66.2	26.6	53.8	46.2
99784	WHITE MOUNTAIN	7.4	6.1	0.0	0.0	0.4	0.4	0.4	0.4	10.1	10.1	9.4	10.1	9.4	24.5	20.5	5.4	0.7	64.0	25.7	51.4	48.6
99785	BREVIG MISSION	10.9	9.0	0.0	0.0	0.0	0.0	0.7	0.7	13.4	10.0	12.1	9.7	7.9	26.9	15.2	4.8	0.0	59.0	23.0	55.9	44.1
99786	AMBLER	10.0	10.0	0.0	0.0	0.0	0.0	0.0	0.0	10.0	10.0	20.0	10.0	20.0	30.0	0.0	0.0	0.0	50.0	20.0	40.0	60.0
99788	CHALKYITSIK	5.0	2.9	0.0	0.0	0.0	0.0	0.0	0.0	11.4	11.4	5.7	8.6	8.6	28.6	25.7	0.0	0.0	65.7	27.5	54.3	45.7
99789	NUIQSUT	66.7	66.7	0.0	0.0	0.0	0.0	0.0	0.0	0.0	0.0	0.0	33.3	66.7	0.0	0.0	0.0	0.0	66.7	21.3	66.7	33.3
99801	JUNEAU	74.5	72.8	0.8	0.8	5.3	5.6	3.4	3.4	6.4	6.3	6.6	7.1	6.5	28.2	30.6	7.4	0.8	76.1	37.5	50.0	50.0
99820	ANGOON	31.5	24.1	0.3	0.4	0.5	0.6	4.7	5.7	6.5	6.3	6.9	8.4	6.3	23.5	31.2	10.1	0.8	75.3	37.0	53.3	46.7
99824	DOUGLAS	78.0	76.1	1.5	1.4	1.6	1.7	3.6	3.7	5.9	5.8	6.0	6.4	5.6	30.0	31.2	8.0	1.1	77.7	38.5	47.0	53.0
99825	ELFIN COVE	86.5	79.4	0.0	0.0	0.0	0.0	0.0	0.0	5.9	5.9	5.9	5.9	0.0	23.5	50.0	2.9	0.0	76.5	46.3	58.8	41.2
99826	GUSTAVUS	85.7	80.2	0.0	0.0	0.7	0.8	1.2	1.8	3.9	6.4	8.2	5.9	1.8	25.2	42.2	5.9	0.5	76.9	44.3	56.8	43.2
99827	HAINES	78.5	77.3	0.1	0.1	0.8	0.8	1.5	1.6	5.4	5.9	7.5	7.3	4.1	24.4	34.8	9.3	1.3	75.6	42.4	50.6	49.4
99829	HOONAH	44.4	36.7	0.2	0.2	0.3	0.3	2.9	3.5	5.8	5.9	6.5	7.0	6.2	27.0	32.0	9.0	0.6	77.2	38.7	54.4	45.6
99833	PETERSBURG	73.1	68.1	0.3	0.3	2.4	2.8	2.5	3.5	6.7	7.0	7.4	7.3	6.0	25.3	31.1	8.0	1.1	73.5	38.5	52.3	47.7
99835	SITKA	68.2	66.1	0.3	0.3	4.1	4.3	3.3	3.3	6.5	6.3	6.0	6.9	7.6	28.0	28.1	9.4	1.1	76.9	36.6	50.8	49.2
99840	SKAGWAY	92.3	88.7	0.0	0.0	0.8	0.9	2.1	3.4	4.5	3.8	4.1	6.1	7.7	28.2	33.9	10.7	1.0	84.1	42.0	51.4	48.6
99901	KETCHIKAN	74.2	69.2	0.5	0.8	4.5	5.2	2.7	3.7	6.9	6.8	6.7	7.2	7.0	26.6	29.2	8.5	1.1	75.8	36.9	50.7	49.3
99903	MEYERS CHUCK	95.2	94.4	0.0	0.0	0.0	0.0	0.0	0.0	0.0	0.0	0.0	5.6	5.6	11.1	77.8	0.0	0.0	94.4	53.3	44.4	55.6
99919	THORNE BAY	89.8	86.7	0.0	0.0	0.2	0.3	1.2	2.3	6.9	7.8	7.5	5.5	5.2	22.3	36.1	8.7	0.0	74.0	39.5	52.6	47.4
99921	CRAIG	68.5	63.8	0.1	0.1	0.5	0.5	2.7	3.4	7.3	6.6	7.1	9.0	8.1	25.9	30.5	5.1	0.3	72.0	34.6	54.9	45.1
99922	HYDABURG	39.1	34.5	0.0	0.0	0.0	0.0	0.0	0.0	5.5	9.1	10.9	9.1	5.5	23.6	29.1	7.3	0.0	67.3	35.6	52.7	47.3
99923	HYDER	95.4	93.3	0.0	0.0	0.0	0.0	0.9	1.1	3.3	3.3	4.4	6.7	5.6	20.0	48.9	7.8	0.0	84.4	47.5	52.2	47.8
99925	KLAWOCK	47.0	42.9	0.0	0.0	0.5	0.6	1.3	1.6	7.3	8.2	7.9	8.0	4.5	27.3	30.9	5.3	0.7	71.4	36.5	55.5	44.5
99926	METLAKATLA	15.7	13.1	0.3	0.2	0.2	0.2	1.7	1.9	8.2	8.5	8.5	8.4	6.7	26.2	25.8	7.1	0.5	69.5	32.0	51.7	48.3
99927	POINT BAKER	88.6	86.4	0.0	0.9	0.8	0.9	1.5	1.8	6.4	3.6	8.2	8.2	3.6	27.3	37.3	5.5	0.0	80.9	41.0	60.9	39.1
99929	WRANGELL	74.1	67.3	0.1	0.1	0.7	0.8	1.0	1.4	6.0	6.7	8.6	7.0	4.0	23.3	32.6	10.2	1.7	73.4	41.8	51.7	48.3
	ALASKA	69.3	66.7	3.5	3.2	4.5	5.0	4.1	5.7	7.6	7.3	7.4	7.8	7.4	28.4	26.9	6.5	0.6	72.9	33.6	51.3	48.7
	UNITED STATES	75.1	72.0	12.3	12.7	3.8	4.6	12.5	15.7	6.8	6.7	6.6	7.1	6.9	27.0	26.0	10.9	1.9	75.7	36.9	49.2	50.8

ZIP CODE #	POST OFFICE NAME	2009 Per Capita Income	2009 HH Income Base	2009 Household Income Distribution (%) Less than $25,000	$25,000 to $49,999	$50,000 to $99,999	$100,000 to $149,999	$150,000 or More	Median Household Income 2009	2014	2009 National Centile	2009 State Centile	2009 Home Value Base	2009 Home Value Distribution (%) Less than $50,000	$50,000 to $89,999	$90,000 to $174,999	$175,000 to $399,999	$400,000 or More	2009 Median Home Value
99672	STERLING	24417	1122	19.0	23.6	40.9	11.4	5.1	56821	58805	74	70	940	6.1	11.8	27.2	44.5	10.4	192424
99674	SUTTON	21941	346	26.9	27.2	35.3	6.9	3.8	46022	48418	51	48	284	7.4	7.4	40.5	36.6	8.1	163971
99676	TALKEETNA	23314	1273	36.5	24.7	29.4	6.7	2.7	40210	42367	33	31	1008	12.8	12.0	31.4	33.4	10.3	165455
99679	TULUKSAK	9526	84	29.8	32.1	28.6	7.1	2.4	41107	43049	36	35	67	37.3	20.9	23.9	14.9	3.0	71667
99681	TUNUNAK	11510	233	26.6	37.8	26.2	6.0	3.4	40963	42296	36	34	154	41.6	8.4	27.3	17.5	5.2	90000
99682	TYONEK	12435	66	42.4	28.8	27.3	1.5	0.0	33875	33878	15	19	50	56.0	24.0	18.0	2.0	0.0	45000
99684	UNALAKLEET	19844	232	19.8	30.6	31.9	11.2	6.5	49651	52789	60	58	137	21.9	14.6	33.6	29.2	0.7	132031
99685	UNALASKA	31688	787	5.5	11.9	34.9	31.1	16.5	95201	96215	96	99	172	8.1	4.1	19.2	51.7	16.9	262121
99686	VALDEZ	32963	1593	12.2	18.3	37.8	19.0	12.6	71978	73340	88	92	1084	21.6	7.0	14.8	48.2	8.4	204167
99688	WILLOW	23703	1800	28.9	22.4	33.8	10.4	4.4	47754	50956	56	55	1505	11.2	7.6	23.1	47.0	11.1	201720
99689	YAKUTAT	28119	125	15.2	29.6	42.4	8.8	4.0	54951	58838	71	66	73	19.2	16.4	39.7	17.8	6.8	123611
99691	NIKOLAI	22381	35	37.1	20.0	25.7	11.4	5.7	37381	50000	25	26	22	18.2	18.2	54.5	4.5	4.5	105000
99701	FAIRBANKS	25272	7475	25.7	25.3	32.8	10.9	5.3	48768	50535	58	57	2944	5.8	6.0	34.7	48.4	5.0	183954
99702	EIELSON AFB	16512	1308	7.1	40.7	45.8	4.1	2.4	51095	51703	64	58	8	0.0	0.0	12.5	50.0	37.5	225000
99703	FORT WAINWRIGHT	17419	1340	7.8	44.1	39.9	6.2	2.0	48233	49625	57	57	17	0.0	0.0	35.3	64.7	0.0	212500
99704	CLEAR	23498	193	31.1	22.8	35.2	7.8	3.1	43031	46980	42	42	127	27.6	22.0	34.6	15.7	0.0	90833
99705	NORTH POLE	27796	6928	10.9	18.0	44.9	17.0	9.1	74260	76233	89	94	4768	5.8	5.8	28.4	57.2	2.8	198058
99709	FAIRBANKS	31442	10887	14.8	19.1	39.1	16.1	10.9	66837	70379	85	87	6235	4.7	7.5	24.5	55.2	8.1	215230
99712	FAIRBANKS	30326	4337	8.3	18.6	41.2	20.9	11.0	76137	78163	90	94	3174	10.1	6.6	22.6	50.0	10.6	220576
99714	SALCHA	25099	514	15.6	19.3	51.8	11.3	2.1	59688	65130	77	74	404	8.4	13.4	39.6	35.9	2.7	146667
99720	ALLAKAKET	17148	38	42.1	31.6	21.1	5.3	0.0	31496	30723	11	16	27	22.2	22.2	29.6	11.1	14.8	97500
99721	ANAKTUVUK PASS	22502	75	9.3	20.0	45.3	21.3	4.0	66433	65817	84	87	45	2.2	17.8	44.4	35.6	0.0	145833
99722	ARCTIC VILLAGE	11385	46	47.8	30.4	17.4	2.2	2.2	26496	26489	4	7	32	34.4	18.8	28.1	15.6	3.1	80000
99723	BARROW	19814	149	13.4	16.8	42.3	22.1	5.4	69743	70644	87	89	92	8.7	17.4	44.6	29.3	0.0	132143
99724	BEAVER	9897	27	55.6	29.6	14.8	0.0	0.0	22222	22211	2	4	19	26.3	21.1	47.4	5.3	0.0	95000
99726	BETTLES FIELD	15787	40	45.0	20.0	30.0	5.0	0.0	30000	28611	8	14	25	40.0	32.0	16.0	8.0	4.0	62500
99727	BUCKLAND	13238	86	9.3	38.4	37.2	9.3	5.8	51501	52717	65	59	41	26.8	24.4	26.8	19.5	2.4	87500
99729	CANTWELL	37547	133	14.3	21.1	39.1	19.5	6.0	67669	67574	85	88	84	8.3	16.7	26.2	34.5	14.3	171875
99730	CENTRAL	25279	61	36.1	21.3	31.1	6.6	4.9	41730	44088	38	39	43	34.9	23.3	27.9	11.6	2.3	77500
99733	CIRCLE	15795	10	50.0	20.0	30.0	0.0	0.0	27500	22222	5	9	7	57.1	0.0	42.9	0.0	0.0	8750
99734	PRUDHOE BAY	9500	1	0.0	100.0	0.0	0.0	0.0	47500	47500	55	54	1	0.0	0.0	100.0	0.0	0.0	162500
99736	DEERING	17731	30	6.7	33.3	50.0	6.7	3.3	57071	52087	74	71	14	21.4	28.6	28.6	21.4	0.0	95000
99737	DELTA JUNCTION	21926	1517	22.4	23.4	38.3	12.2	3.7	55427	55642	72	68	1031	8.6	11.0	33.6	24.7	22.1	167614
99739	ELIM	11616	76	34.2	31.6	26.3	7.9	0.0	37318	38360	25	25	43	20.9	14.0	46.5	18.6	0.0	114063
99740	FORT YUKON	20011	208	35.6	23.1	32.2	4.8	4.3	40967	41868	36	34	146	38.4	22.6	25.3	11.6	2.1	71250
99741	GALENA	10833	8	50.0	37.5	12.5	0.0	0.0	25000	25000	3	6	0	0.0	0.0	0.0	0.0	0.0	0
99742	GAMBELL	12180	167	27.5	30.5	32.9	6.0	3.0	41408	45633	37	38	127	34.6	28.3	18.1	17.3	1.6	70833
99743	HEALY	35099	685	16.2	20.9	38.4	18.5	6.0	65300	66434	84	85	445	13.3	16.9	26.7	32.1	11.0	158056
99744	ANDERSON	14742	21	14.3	14.3	52.4	14.3	4.8	72612	75999	88	93	15	13.3	20.0	33.3	33.3	0.0	154167
99745	HUGHES	13213	18	44.4	27.8	22.2	5.6	0.0	30000	37343	8	14	13	15.4	23.1	30.8	7.7	23.1	112500
99746	HUSLIA	12205	79	44.3	29.1	21.5	5.1	0.0	29428	28870	7	13	56	21.4	19.6	33.9	10.7	14.3	103571
99747	KAKTOVIK	23086	81	11.1	22.2	42.0	21.0	3.7	64284	65875	83	83	49	2.0	16.3	46.9	34.7	0.0	145833
99748	KALTAG	12347	60	36.7	33.3	25.0	5.0	0.0	31234	31619	10	15	34	61.8	8.8	17.6	8.8	2.9	33333
99749	KIANA	18675	139	19.4	19.4	37.4	13.7	10.1	61667	61475	80	77	101	10.9	17.8	38.6	26.7	5.9	129688
99750	KIVALINA	14156	188	27.7	29.8	30.3	8.0	4.3	43196	45477	43	42	140	14.3	22.1	37.9	25.7	0.0	106481
99751	KOBUK	15344	85	21.2	24.7	32.9	12.9	8.2	53426	53964	69	63	56	14.3	5.4	25.0	44.6	10.7	187500
99752	KOTZEBUE	22686	988	14.6	19.1	38.2	18.4	9.7	71083	72995	87	92	471	5.9	12.3	25.7	43.5	12.5	201136
99753	KOYUK	12232	83	34.9	30.1	26.5	8.4	0.0	37311	38619	25	25	47	19.1	12.8	51.1	17.0	0.0	113750
99755	DENALI NATIONAL PARK	33220	28	17.9	17.9	39.3	21.4	3.6	69259	72019	86	88	18	5.6	22.2	38.9	27.8	5.6	125000
99756	MANLEY HOT SPRINGS	26228	42	31.0	21.4	35.7	9.5	2.4	45000	40000	48	47	27	33.3	18.5	33.3	14.8	0.0	87500
99757	LAKE MINCHUMINA	21711	9	44.4	11.1	33.3	11.1	0.0	32265	32265	12	17	5	0.0	40.0	60.0	0.0	0.0	95000
99758	MINTO	11988	67	44.8	22.4	28.4	4.5	0.0	29290	33192	7	12	41	46.3	31.7	12.2	7.3	2.4	55000
99759	POINT LAY	23426	55	16.4	9.1	30.9	29.1	14.5	85811	85646	94	98	34	2.9	5.9	70.6	20.6	0.0	132143
99760	NENANA	19748	21	28.6	19.0	42.9	9.5	0.0	54653	60000	71	66	14	7.1	21.4	42.9	28.6	0.0	116667
99762	NOME	29100	1312	15.3	17.4	37.7	19.4	10.2	71037	72850	87	91	618	9.4	17.0	27.5	40.1	6.0	164474
99763	NOORVIK	11670	179	34.1	28.5	21.8	11.7	3.9	35854	37369	20	21	114	7.9	15.8	28.1	47.4	0.9	167857
99765	NULATO	21494	222	22.5	23.4	34.7	14.9	4.5	54054	55459	70	64	131	39.7	15.3	27.5	14.5	3.1	81875
99766	POINT HOPE	23311	168	16.7	8.9	31.0	29.2	14.3	84641	86182	94	97	104	7.7	12.5	57.7	22.1	0.0	130263
99767	RAMPART	15000	17	47.1	23.5	29.4	0.0	0.0	27313	30000	5	8	10	50.0	40.0	10.0	0.0	0.0	50000
99768	RUBY	14875	63	44.4	30.2	20.6	4.8	0.0	29287	29285	7	11	45	24.4	20.0	28.9	11.1	15.6	103125
99769	SAVOONGA	10470	65	27.7	30.8	33.8	6.2	1.5	41167	45363	37	36	50	36.0	26.0	18.0	18.0	2.0	70000
99771	SHAKTOOLIK	19877	33	21.2	33.3	27.3	12.1	6.1	46145	57209	52	49	19	21.1	10.5	31.6	36.8	0.0	143750
99772	SHISHMAREF	13186	146	33.6	33.6	19.2	8.9	4.8	37837	41535	26	27	98	18.4	10.2	25.5	44.9	1.0	158333
99773	SHUNGNAK	18075	55	21.8	23.6	32.7	14.5	7.3	53684	54505	69	64	36	11.1	2.8	33.3	44.4	8.3	181250
99777	TANANA	13866	47	44.7	23.4	27.7	4.3	0.0	29056	31136	7	10	29	41.4	31.0	13.8	10.3	3.4	61667
99778	TELLER	10564	22	45.5	31.8	22.7	0.0	0.0	30000	25000	8	14	17	35.3	52.9	0.0	11.8	0.0	56250
99780	TOK	19994	1090	35.4	23.2	29.4	8.7	3.3	39530	41728	31	30	753	17.8	15.5	34.3	17.4	15.0	134505
99781	VENETIE	8846	25	56.0	28.0	16.0	0.0	0.0	22211	23559	2	4	18	27.8	22.2	44.4	5.6	0.0	90000
99782	WAINWRIGHT	23382	133	16.5	10.5	42.1	23.3	7.5	79008	79242	92	96	87	14.9	12.6	52.9	19.5	0.0	120833
99783	WALES	16309	96	33.3	33.3	18.8	9.4	5.2	38188	39533	27	28	64	18.8	10.9	28.1	40.6	1.6	146875
99784	WHITE MOUNTAIN	15028	92	32.6	32.6	27.2	7.6	0.0	37944	39197	27	27	52	19.2	11.5	50.0	19.2	0.0	117500
99785	BREVIG MISSION	9409	71	45.1	31.0	22.5	0.0	1.4	29292	31350	7	12	56	35.7	48.2	5.4	10.7	0.0	57273
99786	AMBLER	0	0	0.0	0.0	0.0	0.0	0.0	0	0	0	0	0	0.0	0.0	0.0	0.0	0.0	0
99788	CHALKYITSIK	15570	17	52.9	29.4	17.6	0.0	0.0	23529	23514	2	5	12	25.0	16.7	41.7	16.7	0.0	108333
99789	NUIQSUT	15833	1	0.0	100.0	0.0	0.0	0.0	47500	47500	55	54	1	0.0	0.0	100.0	0.0	0.0	162500
99801	JUNEAU	33418	10590	10.9	17.2	39.0	22.4	10.6	77787	78615	91	95	6881	5.7	4.4	7.1	60.1	22.7	282004
99820	ANGOON	16161	180	32.2	31.1	29.4	5.0	2.2	38676	40988	29	30	97	9.3	15.5	34.0	23.7	17.5	151389
99824	DOUGLAS	33892	973	11.5	24.2	41.1	16.6	6.6	62549	64561	81	79	425	1.9	0.9	19.1	41.9	36.2	307143
99825	ELFIN COVE	28353	17	29.4	35.3	23.5	5.9	5.9	38575	50000	28	29	12	0.0	0.0	25.0	66.7	8.3	233333
99826	GUSTAVUS	27400	190	23.7	30.5	33.7	6.8	5.3	45000	47358	48	47	136	3.7	8.1	27.9	45.6	14.7	211364
99827	HAINES	25915	1016	23.1	29.2	33.8	9.7	4.1	47375	48848	55	52	701	11.7	11.6	24.5	40.9	11.3	187109
99829	HOONAH	22260	451	25.5	27.9	34.8	8.2	3.5	46518	48463	53	49	282	13.1	12.8	34.0	29.8	10.3	150000
99833	PETERSBURG	28447	1429	18.1	24.1	38.6	12.5	6.7	57523	58914	75	72	1025	12.6	4.9	16.6	55.3	10.6	244500
99835	SITKA	30448	3422	14.1	21.3	40.5	15.6	8.5	64215	65758	83	82	1977	9.3	4.2	9.9	48.3	28.2	295700
99840	SKAGWAY	36038	389	11.3	23.1	44.0	16.5	5.1	62692	63865	81	79	234	2.1	5.6	22.2	58.1	12.0	235106
99901	KETCHIKAN	30020	5090	12.8	23.8	39.5	17.7	6.2	63354	64329	82	80	3063	4.4	5.2	16.6	59.1	14.9	250053
99903	MEYERS CHUCK	14306	8	75.0	0.0	25.0	0.0	0.0	15000	15855	1	3	6	0.0	0.0	66.7	0.0	33.3	116667
99919	THORNE BAY	24860	135	17.0	29.6	38.5	8.9	5.9	52087	52820	66	60	86	17.4	11.6	26.7	36.0	8.1	157143
99921	CRAIG	25216	593	16.0	28.2	39.8	11.1	4.9	55718	55388	72	68	417	40.8	4.6	9.8	33.1	11.8	147321
99922	HYDABURG	19368	23	30.4	26.1	39.1	4.3	0.0	42372	50000	41	40	16	6.3	6.3	43.8	37.5	6.3	162500
99923	HYDER	17167	47	63.8	8.5	25.5	2.1	0.0	16353	16785	1	3	34	11.8	5.9	47.1	2.9	32.4	125000
99925	KLAWOCK	18981	324	27.5	29.3	35.2	6.8	1.2	42709	43765	42	41	221	38.0	16.7	18.1	18.6	8.6	73182
99926	METLAKATLA	20875	576	17.4	27.1	42.0	12.0	1.6	54260	54262	70	65	394	15.5	8.6	32.7	39.6	3.6	158125
99927	POINT BAKER	18899	47	31.9	34.0	34.0	0.0	0.0	36699	38182	23	24	38	23.7	13.2	26.3	26.3	10.5	125000
99929	WRANGELL	26364	877	25.8	21.7	35.2	11.9	5.5	52016	53200	66	60	601	15.5	3.0	27.6	44.3	9.7	198500
	ALASKA	28744		15.0	21.0	38.1	16.8	9.1	65464	68018				7.3	5.5	18.9	55.0	13.4	236447
	UNITED STATES	27277		20.9	24.4	35.3	11.7	7.6	54719	56938				9.3	13.1	31.6	32.6	13.5	162279

ZIP CODE #	POST OFFICE NAME	FINANCIAL SERVICES: Auto Loan	Home Loan	Invest-ments	Retire-ment Plans	THE HOME: Home Improvements: Home Repair	Lawn & Garden	Furnishings: Comput-ers & Hard-ware-Personal	Major Appli-ances	TV, Radio, Sound Equip-ment	Furni-ture	ENTERTAINMENT: Dine out/ Carry out	Sports Equip-ment	Fees & Tickets	Toys & Games	Travel	Cable TV	PERSONAL: Apparel & Services	Auto Repairs	Health Insur-ance	Pets & Supplies
99672	STERLING	104	91	127	91	97	111	89	107	91	85	90	79	82	88	95	96	61	100	106	124
99674	SUTTON	96	77	124	75	84	101	77	97	80	72	79	71	66	76	83	86	53	90	96	113
99676	TALKEETNA	87	69	112	68	76	92	69	88	73	65	72	64	60	69	75	77	48	81	87	102
99679	TULUKSAK	72	72	62	64	71	59	72	71	67	78	69	53	68	69	69	63	49	71	61	77
99681	TUNUNAK	89	71	53	60	68	67	71	77	78	80	79	47	62	79	64	80	55	78	75	84
99682	TYONEK	55	43	39	44	42	51	52	49	54	47	52	39	44	55	44	57	36	52	55	60
99684	UNALAKLEET	100	104	85	100	97	90	94	94	92	101	94	71	94	97	91	89	64	91	87	110
99685	UNALASKA	157	137	122	146	129	123	155	135	150	157	154	115	147	158	141	144	108	145	128	164
99686	VALDEZ	123	134	127	133	131	127	122	125	118	124	120	99	127	122	126	117	84	121	118	146
99688	WILLOW	99	84	108	82	88	99	82	96	85	80	85	70	74	84	84	89	57	91	96	113
99689	YAKUTAT	102	94	83	91	92	96	88	94	92	92	92	68	84	96	84	94	62	91	94	111
99691	NIKOLAI	80	71	74	72	73	81	76	79	78	73	77	59	70	78	73	81	53	79	85	93
99701	FAIRBANKS	88	79	75	82	77	76	91	81	90	90	91	65	87	90	85	89	64	88	84	98
99702	EIELSON AFB	102	53	40	62	47	45	96	66	90	89	95	66	73	109	69	83	67	85	60	81
99703	FORT WAINWRIGHT	101	52	39	61	47	45	95	66	89	88	94	65	72	107	68	82	66	84	59	80
99704	CLEAR	92	73	119	72	81	97	74	93	77	69	76	68	64	73	80	82	51	86	92	108
99705	NORTH POLE	124	128	106	125	120	111	120	117	116	127	118	91	120	122	116	112	82	115	108	136
99709	FAIRBANKS	115	117	107	119	113	109	119	111	115	120	117	89	120	117	116	112	82	115	109	132
99712	FAIRBANKS	125	139	121	139	133	122	127	124	121	132	123	99	134	128	129	117	88	122	113	144
99714	SALCHA	96	101	101	103	101	105	92	100	92	92	92	77	95	93	98	93	64	95	99	117
99720	ALLAKAKET	60	51	41	53	45	55	56	52	60	56	60	41	54	61	50	63	41	56	59	66
99721	ANAKTUVUK PASS	114	118	96	113	110	102	107	107	104	114	106	81	107	109	103	101	73	104	98	124
99722	ARCTIC VILLAGE	48	41	33	43	37	44	45	42	49	45	48	33	43	49	40	51	33	46	47	54
99723	BARROW	118	120	100	113	114	103	113	112	108	121	111	84	110	113	109	104	77	110	101	128
99724	BEAVER	40	34	27	35	30	36	37	35	40	37	40	27	36	41	33	42	27	38	39	44
99726	BETTLES FIELD	59	46	45	47	45	57	52	53	61	54	59	37	49	59	48	67	40	57	65	66
99727	BUCKLAND	96	96	82	85	94	79	95	94	89	103	92	70	90	92	92	84	65	94	81	103
99729	CANTWELL	102	114	109	116	113	106	107	105	104	110	105	82	114	105	111	102	75	105	102	123
99730	CENTRAL	88	63	88	61	66	92	69	85	77	62	74	64	55	76	67	85	50	79	93	100
99733	CIRCLE	59	42	59	41	44	61	46	57	52	41	50	43	37	51	45	57	33	53	62	67
99734	PRUDHOE BAY	0	0	0	0	0	0	0	0	0	0	0	0	0	0	0	0	0	0	0	0
99736	DEERING	95	95	82	84	93	78	94	93	88	102	91	69	89	91	91	83	64	93	80	102
99737	DELTA JUNCTION	92	90	84	93	89	93	90	91	89	88	90	71	89	92	90	90	62	90	91	107
99739	ELIM	67	57	46	59	51	61	63	58	68	63	67	46	60	69	56	70	46	63	66	75
99740	FORT YUKON	86	62	86	61	64	90	68	84	76	61	73	62	55	75	66	84	49	78	91	98
99741	GALENA	42	36	29	37	32	39	39	37	43	40	42	29	38	43	35	44	29	40	42	47
99742	GAMBELL	83	67	50	56	64	63	67	72	72	75	73	44	58	73	60	75	51	72	70	79
99743	HEALY	107	109	121	110	111	111	104	109	103	105	104	84	106	103	110	104	73	107	107	128
99744	ANDERSON	127	106	160	105	115	134	105	129	109	100	108	95	94	104	113	115	73	120	127	150
99745	HUGHES	60	51	41	53	46	55	56	52	61	56	60	41	54	61	50	63	41	57	59	67
99746	HUSLIA	60	51	42	53	46	55	56	52	61	56	60	41	54	62	50	63	41	57	59	67
99747	KAKTOVIK	113	117	95	112	109	101	106	106	103	114	105	80	106	109	103	100	72	103	98	123
99748	KALTAG	61	51	42	53	46	55	56	52	61	56	60	41	54	62	51	63	42	57	59	67
99749	KIANA	107	107	92	95	105	88	106	105	99	115	102	78	101	102	102	94	72	104	91	115
99750	KIVALINA	82	82	71	73	81	67	82	80	76	88	78	60	77	78	79	72	55	80	70	88
99751	KOBUK	100	100	86	89	98	82	99	98	93	107	96	73	94	96	96	88	67	98	85	107
99752	KOTZEBUE	114	110	99	109	105	99	118	107	118	117	120	84	115	119	111	117	85	114	106	128
99753	KOYUK	68	57	46	59	51	61	63	58	68	63	67	46	60	69	56	71	46	64	66	75
99755	DENALI NATIONAL PARK	103	108	111	109	108	107	104	106	102	104	103	81	106	102	107	102	72	105	105	124
99756	MANLEY HOT SPRINGS	91	73	116	72	80	96	73	92	77	69	76	67	64	73	79	82	51	86	92	107
99757	LAKE MINCHUMINA	69	60	63	61	62	69	65	68	67	62	66	50	60	66	63	69	45	67	73	79
99758	MINTO	61	47	48	48	46	59	53	55	62	55	60	39	49	60	49	68	41	58	66	68
99759	POINT LAY	138	138	118	122	135	113	137	134	128	148	131	100	129	131	132	121	93	134	117	147
99760	NENANA	91	73	118	72	80	96	73	93	76	68	75	68	63	72	79	81	50	85	91	107
99762	NOME	121	118	105	120	113	108	122	113	118	124	120	91	121	122	117	115	84	117	109	135
99763	NOORVIK	78	78	67	69	76	64	77	76	72	83	74	56	73	74	74	68	52	76	66	83
99765	NULATO	96	92	75	91	84	87	90	87	92	94	93	67	88	95	85	92	64	89	88	106
99766	POINT HOPE	138	138	118	122	135	112	136	134	127	147	131	100	129	131	131	120	93	134	116	147
99767	RAMPART	50	39	38	40	38	48	44	45	52	46	50	31	41	49	40	56	34	48	55	56
99768	RUBY	60	51	41	53	46	55	56	52	61	56	60	41	54	61	50	63	41	57	59	67
99769	SAVOONGA	83	67	50	56	64	63	67	72	73	75	73	44	58	74	60	75	51	73	70	79
99771	SHAKTOOLIK	99	102	83	98	96	89	93	93	91	100	93	70	93	96	90	89	64	91	86	109
99772	SHISHMAREF	78	66	53	68	59	71	72	67	78	72	78	53	69	79	65	81	53	73	76	86
99773	SHUNGNAK	101	101	86	89	99	82	100	98	93	108	96	73	95	96	96	88	68	98	85	108
99777	TANANA	59	46	45	47	45	57	52	53	61	54	59	37	49	59	48	67	40	57	65	66
99778	TELLER	53	45	36	46	40	48	49	45	53	49	53	36	47	54	44	55	36	50	52	58
99780	TOK	85	74	85	72	76	84	72	81	75	72	74	59	66	75	72	78	50	77	81	96
99781	VENETIE	41	35	28	36	31	37	38	36	42	38	41	28	37	42	34	43	28	39	40	46
99782	WAINWRIGHT	126	126	108	112	124	103	125	123	117	135	121	92	119	121	121	111	85	123	107	135
99783	WALES	77	66	53	68	59	70	72	67	78	72	77	53	69	79	65	81	53	73	76	86
99784	WHITE MOUNTAIN	68	57	47	60	51	62	63	59	68	63	68	46	61	69	57	71	46	64	66	75
99785	BREVIG MISSION	53	45	36	46	40	48	49	46	53	49	53	36	47	54	44	55	36	50	52	58
99786	AMBLER	0	0	0	0	0	0	0	0	0	0	0	0	0	0	0	0	0	0	0	0
99788	CHALKYITSIK	48	41	33	42	36	44	44	41	48	45	48	32	43	49	40	50	33	45	47	53
99789	NUIQSUT	0	0	0	0	0	0	0	0	0	0	0	0	0	0	0	0	0	0	0	0
99801	JUNEAU	124	131	122	132	129	121	128	123	124	131	125	96	132	126	128	121	88	124	120	145
99820	ANGOON	75	69	61	67	68	71	65	69	68	68	68	50	62	71	62	70	46	67	69	82
99824	DOUGLAS	103	115	110	117	114	107	109	106	105	111	106	83	115	106	113	103	76	106	103	125
99825	ELFIN COVE	94	76	122	74	83	100	76	96	79	71	78	70	66	75	82	84	52	89	95	111
99826	GUSTAVUS	93	75	121	74	82	99	75	95	78	70	77	69	65	74	81	83	51	88	94	110
99827	HAINES	103	83	131	82	91	108	83	104	87	78	86	76	72	83	89	92	57	97	103	121
99829	HOONAH	90	81	81	78	80	86	77	84	80	79	80	61	72	82	75	83	54	81	84	100
99833	PETERSBURG	111	110	97	109	107	111	102	107	103	104	104	80	101	107	101	105	71	103	107	127
99835	SITKA	108	115	108	116	113	106	114	108	110	114	112	86	117	112	114	108	79	110	106	127
99840	SKAGWAY	102	104	99	106	101	100	107	100	105	107	106	79	108	105	105	104	74	104	102	120
99901	KETCHIKAN	103	113	107	113	111	105	110	106	107	109	108	84	115	108	112	105	77	107	104	125
99903	MEYERS CHUCK	54	43	69	42	47	57	43	55	45	40	44	40	37	43	47	48	30	50	54	63
99919	THORNE BAY	102	94	83	91	92	96	89	94	92	92	92	68	84	96	84	94	63	91	94	112
99921	CRAIG	101	93	79	90	88	88	95	92	95	98	95	71	89	99	88	94	66	94	89	110
99922	HYDABURG	72	65	65	68	67	77	64	73	66	58	65	55	59	68	64	70	45	67	75	85
99923	HYDER	55	44	71	43	48	58	44	56	46	41	45	41	38	44	48	49	30	52	55	65
99925	KLAWOCK	78	73	62	69	69	70	72	71	72	75	72	54	68	75	67	72	50	72	70	85
99926	METLAKATLA	90	89	80	87	87	92	83	88	86	85	86	64	82	88	82	89	59	85	91	103
99927	POINT BAKER	71	49	78	49	51	75	54	67	56	44	56	56	40	55	54	61	36	63	71	83
99929	WRANGELL	105	87	120	86	93	108	88	104	92	84	91	76	79	89	91	97	61	98	105	122
	ALASKA	116	114	108	115	111	108	115	111	112	116	113	88	114	115	112	110	80	112	107	131
	UNITED STATES	100	100	100	100	100	100	100	100	100	100	100	100	100	100	100	100	100	100	100	100

ZIP CODE #	POST OFFICE NAME	COUNTY FIPS CODE	POPULATION 2000	POPULATION 2009	POPULATION 2014	2000-2009 ANNUAL RATE % Rate	2000-2009 ANNUAL RATE State Centile	HOUSEHOLDS 2000	HOUSEHOLDS 2009	HOUSEHOLDS 2014	HOUSEHOLDS % Annual Rate 2000-2009	HOUSEHOLDS 2009 Average HH Size	FAMILIES 2000	FAMILIES 2009	FAMILIES % Annual Rate 2000-2009
99950	KETCHIKAN	201	767	646	597	-1.8	15	307	261	243	-1.7	2.34	200	166	-2.0
	ALASKA					1.1					1.1	2.74			0.9
	UNITED STATES					1.0					1.1	2.59			0.9

ZIP CODE #	POST OFFICE NAME	RACE (%) White 2000	White 2009	Black 2000	Black 2009	Asian/Pacific 2000	Asian/Pacific 2009	% Hispanic Origin 2000	% Hispanic Origin 2009	2009 AGE DISTRIBUTION (%) 0-4	5-9	10-14	15-19	20-24	25-44	45-64	65-84	85+	18+	MEDIAN AGE 2009	% 2009 Males	% 2009 Females
99950	KETCHIKAN	79.8	77.2	0.3	0.5	0.7	0.8	1.3	2.0	6.0	5.7	8.4	7.6	4.3	25.1	35.9	6.5	0.5	76.8	40.4	57.4	42.6
	ALASKA	69.3	66.7	3.5	3.2	4.5	5.0	4.1	5.7	7.6	7.3	7.4	7.8	7.4	28.4	26.9	6.5	0.6	72.9	33.6	51.3	48.7
	UNITED STATES	75.1	72.0	12.3	12.7	3.8	4.6	12.5	15.7	6.8	6.7	6.6	7.1	6.9	27.0	26.0	10.9	1.9	75.7	36.9	49.2	50.8

ZIP CODE #	POST OFFICE NAME	2009 Per Capita Income	2009 HH Income Base	2009 HOUSEHOLD INCOME DISTRIBUTION (%) Less than $25,000	$25,000 to $49,999	$50,000 to $99,999	$100,000 to $149,999	$150,000 or More	MEDIAN HOUSEHOLD INCOME 2009	2014	2009 National Centile	2009 State Centile	2009 Home Value Base	2009 HOME VALUE DISTRIBUTION (%) Less than $50,000	$50,000 to $89,999	$90,000 to $174,999	$175,000 to $399,999	$400,000 or More	2009 Median Home Value
99950	KETCHIKAN	22218	261	28.4	31.4	33.0	3.8	3.4	40668	42449	35	33	191	19.4	12.0	27.2	31.4	9.9	148750
	ALASKA	28744		15.0	21.0	38.1	16.8	9.1	65464	68018				7.3	5.5	18.9	55.0	13.4	236447
	UNITED STATES	27277		20.9	24.4	35.3	11.7	7.6	54719	56938				9.3	13.1	31.6	32.6	13.5	162279

ZIP CODE	FINANCIAL SERVICES				THE HOME						ENTERTAINMENT						PERSONAL			
					Home Improvements		Furnishings													
# POST OFFICE NAME	Auto Loan	Home Loan	Invest-ments	Retire-ment Plans	Home Repair	Lawn & Garden	Comput-ers & Hard-ware-Personal	Major Appli-ances	TV, Radio, Sound Equip-ment	Furni-ture	Dine out/ Carry out	Sports Equip-ment	Fees & Tickets	Toys & Games	Travel	Cable TV	Apparel & Services	Auto Repairs	Health Insur-ance	Pets & Supplies
99950 KETCHIKAN	88	70	87	69	71	91	72	84	75	64	74	66	60	75	71	80	49	79	87	101
ALASKA	116	114	108	115	111	108	115	111	112	116	113	88	114	115	112	110	80	112	107	131
UNITED STATES	100	100	100	100	100	100	100	100	100	100	100	100	100	100	100	100	100	100	100	100

85003-85272

ZIP CODE			POPULATION			2000-2009 ANNUAL RATE		HOUSEHOLDS					FAMILIES		
#	POST OFFICE NAME	COUNTY FIPS CODE	2000	2009	2014	% Rate	State Centile	2000	2009	2014	% Annual Rate 2000-2009	2009 Average HH Size	2000	2009	% Annual Rate 2000-2009
85003	PHOENIX	013	9823	13287	14274	3.3	71	3606	4389	4897	2.1	2.11	1473	1578	0.7
85004	PHOENIX	013	4615	4990	5271	0.8	27	1980	2158	2319	0.9	2.09	791	769	-0.3
85006	PHOENIX	013	33387	35665	37478	0.7	24	9635	9943	10387	0.3	3.50	6415	6288	-0.2
85007	PHOENIX	013	15831	17536	18845	1.1	37	4838	5243	5599	0.9	3.09	2956	3020	0.2
85008	PHOENIX	013	57698	69638	76704	2.1	57	18867	21413	23310	1.4	3.17	11475	12461	0.9
85009	PHOENIX	013	55926	61467	64025	1.0	34	12825	13311	13894	0.4	3.98	9915	9867	-0.1
85012	PHOENIX	013	7079	7255	7535	0.3	11	3237	3329	3463	0.3	2.04	1452	1349	-0.8
85013	PHOENIX	013	21975	23994	25581	1.0	34	10143	11022	11738	0.9	2.16	4777	4724	-0.1
85014	PHOENIX	013	26981	28641	30273	0.6	22	12287	12908	13632	0.5	2.18	5618	5372	-0.5
85015	PHOENIX	013	42736	46868	49648	1.0	34	15538	16275	17119	0.5	2.86	9510	9307	-0.2
85016	PHOENIX	013	35579	39309	42190	1.1	37	16337	17736	18964	0.9	2.20	7887	7840	-0.1
85017	PHOENIX	013	38028	41284	43597	0.9	31	12174	12545	13147	0.3	3.24	8171	7994	-0.2
85018	PHOENIX	013	35161	36096	37580	0.3	11	16034	16424	17082	0.3	2.18	8657	8191	-0.6
85019	PHOENIX	013	28699	30004	31040	0.5	17	8929	8988	9244	0.1	3.33	6464	6196	-0.5
85020	PHOENIX	013	34833	36423	38117	0.5	17	15287	15846	16542	0.4	2.28	8165	7804	-0.5
85021	PHOENIX	013	38580	39845	41507	0.3	11	15460	15724	16348	0.2	2.49	8772	8311	-0.6
85022	PHOENIX	013	46010	51476	55491	1.2	40	19653	21681	23235	1.1	2.37	11993	12469	0.4
85023	PHOENIX	013	33872	35748	37764	0.6	22	13639	14404	15198	0.6	2.48	8557	8411	-0.2
85024	PHOENIX	013	17245	22287	25751	2.8	67	6341	8114	9348	2.7	2.75	4688	5716	2.2
85027	PHOENIX	013	35859	39242	41961	1.0	34	14078	15423	16487	1.0	2.54	9152	9304	0.2
85028	PHOENIX	013	21735	22240	23100	0.2	8	8883	9194	9593	0.4	2.40	6041	5880	-0.3
85029	PHOENIX	013	46078	48465	50611	0.5	17	17515	18197	18917	0.4	2.65	11161	10910	-0.2
85031	PHOENIX	013	27778	30556	32380	1.0	34	7496	7860	8260	0.5	3.89	5861	5937	0.1
85032	PHOENIX	013	66297	70927	74887	0.7	24	24877	26202	27612	0.6	2.67	16038	15929	-0.1
85033	PHOENIX	013	51305	55636	58982	0.9	31	14119	15010	15857	0.7	3.71	11663	11989	0.3
85034	PHOENIX	013	9697	9199	9466	-0.6	1	2844	2820	2960	-0.1	3.12	1846	1669	-1.1
85035	PHOENIX	013	42192	51791	57732	2.2	58	11133	13261	14704	1.9	3.90	8914	10210	1.5
85037	PHOENIX	013	33811	45904	51202	3.4	72	10058	13465	14969	3.2	3.41	8242	10718	2.9
85040	PHOENIX	013	28335	35549	39786	2.5	62	7455	9009	10022	2.1	3.91	5594	6469	1.6
85041	PHOENIX	013	33563	61497	75053	6.8	88	8552	16282	19948	7.2	3.76	7101	12918	6.7
85042	PHOENIX	013	33501	42764	49060	2.7	66	10042	12819	14724	2.7	3.30	7269	8812	2.1
85043	PHOENIX	013	15976	37525	47195	9.7	90	4785	10931	13727	9.3	3.43	3622	7645	8.4
85044	PHOENIX	013	40406	41426	43031	0.3	11	17120	17500	18165	0.2	2.37	10389	9924	-0.5
85045	PHOENIX	013	5860	8435	9999	4.0	79	1950	2801	3318	4.0	3.01	1655	2298	3.6
85048	PHOENIX	013	31384	35025	37568	1.2	40	10898	12115	12967	1.2	2.89	8422	8950	0.7
85050	PHOENIX	013	20920	26839	30432	2.7	66	8147	10392	11758	2.7	2.58	5817	7112	2.2
85051	PHOENIX	013	40637	41488	42978	0.2	8	15155	15410	15928	0.2	2.68	9940	9501	-0.5
85053	PHOENIX	013	28271	30530	32288	0.8	27	10553	11365	12002	0.8	2.68	7317	7447	0.2
85054	PHOENIX	013	2664	7185	9553	11.3	91	1190	3102	4099	10.9	2.32	756	1846	10.1
85083	PHOENIX	013	2193	12442	16516	20.6	97	527	3992	5348	24.5	2.95	436	2991	23.1
85085	PHOENIX	013	849	11987	16426	33.1	99	318	4418	6022	32.9	2.71	253	3122	31.2
85086	PHOENIX	013	8735	37560	50207	17.1	95	2818	13273	17789	18.2	2.78	2196	10171	18.0
85087	NEW RIVER	013	3905	6202	7339	5.1	83	1501	2499	3009	5.7	2.33	1134	1782	5.0
85201	MESA	013	47615	50855	53451	0.7	24	18156	19191	20123	0.6	2.61	10667	10455	-0.2
85202	MESA	013	44067	45830	47827	0.4	14	17953	18504	19236	0.3	2.47	10259	9844	-0.4
85203	MESA	013	36938	38650	40509	0.5	17	12675	13245	13866	0.5	2.90	9000	8913	-0.1
85204	MESA	013	65749	68798	71963	0.5	17	21844	22633	23605	0.4	3.03	15553	15305	-0.2
85205	MESA	013	40127	45674	49718	1.4	44	16307	18659	20371	1.5	2.43	11000	11893	0.8
85206	MESA	013	31207	42644	49566	3.4	72	13211	17241	19744	2.9	2.39	8517	10493	2.3
85207	MESA	013	28499	46957	57424	5.5	85	10121	16696	20421	5.6	2.81	7912	12601	5.2
85208	MESA	013	28907	38899	44742	3.3	71	12236	15705	17789	2.7	2.47	8426	10400	2.3
85209	MESA	013	20700	39650	48153	7.3	89	8211	14969	18074	6.7	2.65	6341	11492	6.6
85210	MESA	013	36505	37197	38335	0.2	8	12941	12978	13317	0.0	2.82	8142	7683	-0.6
85212	MESA	013	7509	20914	27463	11.7	92	2370	6754	8879	12.0	3.09	1904	5396	11.9
85213	MESA	013	30008	33714	36430	1.3	42	10062	11246	12128	1.2	2.98	7770	8424	0.9
85215	MESA	013	15344	16768	18101	1.0	34	6389	6842	7307	0.7	2.44	4724	4898	0.4
85218	APACHE JUNCTION	021	6523	11525	15040	6.3	87	3055	5680	7507	6.9	2.03	2389	4310	6.6
85219	APACHE JUNCTION	021	16094	17906	20600	1.2	40	6810	8134	9438	1.9	2.20	4729	5440	1.5
85220	APACHE JUNCTION	021	28259	30969	34630	1.0	34	12370	14108	15855	1.4	2.18	8170	8825	0.8
85222	CASA GRANDE	021	30633	42896	52578	3.7	75	10855	16514	20615	4.6	2.58	7981	11634	4.2
85224	CHANDLER	013	43417	48246	51588	1.1	37	15648	17359	18535	1.1	2.75	10856	11433	0.6
85225	CHANDLER	013	66369	74696	80934	1.3	42	22139	24983	27107	1.3	2.98	16262	17395	0.7
85226	CHANDLER	013	39242	40866	42725	0.4	14	14357	14826	15453	0.3	2.75	10239	10061	-0.2
85228	COOLIDGE	021	10648	14261	18209	3.2	70	3368	4871	6384	4.1	2.89	2522	3487	3.6
85231	ELOY	021	16761	20143	24824	2.0	55	4851	6742	8552	3.6	2.88	3796	5102	3.2
85232	FLORENCE	021	19885	25534	35809	2.7	66	3263	5674	10414	6.2	2.42	2287	3868	5.8
85233	GILBERT	013	38489	41753	44534	0.9	31	13143	14089	14982	0.8	2.96	10254	10556	0.3
85234	GILBERT	013	42198	53788	60796	2.7	66	13213	16506	18526	2.4	3.26	10927	13452	2.3
85236	HIGLEY	013	18	16	21	-1.3	1	5	6	8	2.0	2.67	4	5	2.4
85237	KEARNY	021	2786	3848	4876	3.6	74	1040	1532	1960	4.3	2.51	768	1091	3.9
85238	MARICOPA	021	1806	33682	48970	37.2	99	520	10370	15251	38.2	3.25	404	7714	37.6
85239	MARICOPA	021	6193	16069	22855	10.9	91	2008	5562	8005	11.6	2.87	1515	3995	11.1
85240	QUEEN CREEK	021	4001	22551	33032	20.6	97	1326	8302	12262	21.9	2.71	1040	6335	21.6
85242	QUEEN CREEK	013	8868	44680	61467	19.1	96	2605	13649	18910	19.6	3.27	2224	11217	19.1
85243	QUEEN CREEK	021	812	32641	47960	49.1	100	278	10618	15738	48.3	3.07	219	8110	47.8
85245	RED ROCK	021	42	52	66	2.3	60	12	17	22	3.8	2.53	9	12	3.2
85247	SACATON	021	8459	10224	12737	2.1	57	2036	2614	3314	2.7	3.74	1690	2113	2.4
85248	CHANDLER	013	22647	31607	37346	3.7	75	10570	14650	17186	3.6	2.16	7923	10483	3.1
85249	CHANDLER	013	5897	42095	56736	23.7	98	2549	12998	17255	19.3	3.24	1833	10117	20.3
85250	SCOTTSDALE	013	16421	16391	16861	0.0	4	8029	7971	8178	-0.1	2.05	4303	3960	-0.9
85251	SCOTTSDALE	013	36074	38993	41676	0.8	27	17961	19540	20925	0.9	1.98	8032	7869	-0.2
85253	PARADISE VALLEY	013	18223	18381	18957	0.1	6	7126	7153	7358	0.0	2.56	5334	5158	-0.4
85254	SCOTTSDALE	013	49649	51639	54065	0.4	14	18440	19236	20159	0.5	2.66	13546	13419	-0.1
85255	SCOTTSDALE	013	27320	39680	47219	4.1	80	10939	15643	18563	3.9	2.54	8517	11642	3.4
85256	SCOTTSDALE	013	4881	5209	5473	0.7	24	1270	1353	1417	0.7	3.82	876	881	0.1
85257	SCOTTSDALE	013	30093	30931	32268	0.3	11	13289	13583	14137	0.2	2.23	7136	6769	-0.6
85258	SCOTTSDALE	013	24803	25085	26431	0.1	6	12044	12197	12865	0.1	2.05	7409	6989	-0.6
85259	SCOTTSDALE	013	19106	23022	25565	2.0	55	7402	8826	9728	1.9	2.61	5180	6010	1.6
85260	SCOTTSDALE	013	35278	37383	39089	0.6	22	14947	15922	16678	0.7	2.31	9630	9728	0.1
85262	SCOTTSDALE	013	5105	9382	11727	6.8	88	2264	4184	5213	6.9	2.24	1816	3260	6.5
85263	RIO VERDE	013	1461	2149	2721	4.3	81	777	1170	1483	4.5	1.84	637	930	4.2
85264	FORT MCDOWELL	013	930	1099	1204	1.8	49	279	333	368	1.9	3.30	223	251	1.3
85266	SCOTTSDALE	013	7113	11282	13419	5.1	83	3051	4785	5656	5.0	2.36	2428	3645	4.5
85268	FOUNTAIN HILLS	013	20235	25409	28763	2.5	62	8653	10834	12227	2.5	2.34	6516	7836	2.0
85272	STANFIELD	021	1149	1446	2115	2.5	62	322	386	570	2.0	3.75	249	286	1.5
	ARIZONA					2.9					2.7	2.69			2.5
	UNITED STATES					1.0					1.1	2.59			0.9

ZIP CODE		RACE (%)						% Hispanic Origin		2009 AGE DISTRIBUTION (%)										MEDIAN AGE		
		White		Black		Asian/Pacific																
#	POST OFFICE NAME	2000	2009	2000	2009	2000	2009	2000	2009	0-4	5-9	10-14	15-19	20-24	25-44	45-64	65-84	85+	18+	2009	% 2009 Males	% 2009 Females
85003	PHOENIX	62.1	56.7	10.9	12.6	1.8	1.7	42.5	44.1	5.1	4.2	3.7	7.8	10.2	37.1	22.0	8.4	1.4	82.3	34.9	65.9	34.1
85004	PHOENIX	65.9	61.5	7.2	8.0	0.9	1.0	46.2	53.6	6.6	5.5	4.7	7.5	9.1	31.9	23.3	9.7	1.8	79.3	34.2	57.1	42.9
85006	PHOENIX	62.7	59.8	4.2	4.0	0.8	0.8	73.1	79.5	11.7	10.2	8.3	8.7	8.8	31.5	15.8	4.3	0.7	64.8	26.2	53.3	46.7
85007	PHOENIX	59.9	57.4	11.2	10.9	0.7	0.7	59.3	66.4	10.4	8.9	7.3	7.7	8.9	29.6	20.2	6.2	0.9	68.9	28.8	53.9	46.1
85008	PHOENIX	58.3	53.7	5.7	5.9	1.4	1.5	57.6	66.1	11.0	9.2	7.5	7.8	10.2	32.6	15.9	4.9	0.8	67.9	27.1	52.4	47.6
85009	PHOENIX	46.7	43.5	4.0	4.0	0.6	0.6	76.4	80.9	10.7	9.1	7.4	9.6	10.4	32.0	15.0	5.1	0.7	67.2	26.4	56.3	43.7
85012	PHOENIX	81.0	75.9	3.8	4.6	1.9	2.4	19.6	26.6	5.2	4.6	4.3	4.6	7.4	30.8	25.1	15.3	2.8	83.6	39.4	54.9	45.1
85013	PHOENIX	76.2	71.4	5.1	5.8	2.1	2.7	24.7	31.9	6.4	5.6	5.2	5.6	7.3	30.3	26.8	10.4	2.5	79.8	38.1	49.9	50.1
85014	PHOENIX	69.5	64.2	4.5	5.0	1.5	1.8	30.3	37.6	7.3	6.2	5.4	6.2	9.2	31.2	24.8	8.3	1.4	77.9	34.2	51.8	48.2
85015	PHOENIX	59.8	54.2	6.7	7.2	3.2	3.6	40.8	49.0	10.2	8.9	7.2	7.3	8.7	31.2	18.6	6.4	1.6	69.5	29.0	50.9	49.1
85016	PHOENIX	73.7	67.8	3.5	3.9	1.9	2.4	27.7	35.6	6.7	5.8	5.3	5.7	7.7	30.7	24.5	11.0	2.6	79.0	36.4	50.1	49.9
85017	PHOENIX	55.7	50.1	5.6	5.6	3.8	4.3	49.1	57.9	10.9	9.4	8.0	8.5	9.5	30.6	16.6	5.7	0.9	67.2	26.9	51.6	48.4
85018	PHOENIX	85.3	81.4	2.4	3.0	1.9	2.5	14.3	19.4	5.8	5.6	5.8	5.7	6.1	26.3	28.4	13.3	3.0	79.4	41.5	49.2	50.8
85019	PHOENIX	57.0	51.7	5.5	5.8	3.6	4.1	51.9	60.0	10.7	9.4	8.0	8.0	8.2	30.9	17.4	6.5	0.8	67.2	28.0	51.9	48.1
85020	PHOENIX	82.7	78.3	2.5	3.0	1.6	2.1	23.1	30.0	6.6	6.0	5.6	5.5	6.4	28.8	26.5	12.0	2.5	78.7	38.6	49.9	50.1
85021	PHOENIX	74.2	69.3	3.7	4.4	3.9	4.6	25.0	30.8	7.7	6.6	5.8	6.8	9.6	29.7	21.6	9.5	2.6	76.4	32.4	51.1	48.9
85022	PHOENIX	87.9	83.8	2.1	2.6	2.8	3.8	11.0	16.0	6.6	6.2	6.1	6.1	6.8	28.7	27.9	10.5	1.3	77.7	37.7	49.2	50.8
85023	PHOENIX	84.5	79.4	2.7	3.3	2.8	3.7	13.5	19.2	8.0	6.8	6.2	6.4	8.5	32.3	23.0	7.9	0.9	75.4	32.2	49.4	50.6
85024	PHOENIX	90.5	87.5	1.8	2.4	2.3	3.3	8.3	11.9	8.0	7.9	7.7	6.5	4.7	32.9	25.1	6.5	0.8	72.4	35.9	49.2	50.8
85027	PHOENIX	88.3	84.4	2.1	2.6	1.5	2.0	10.7	15.5	8.5	7.8	7.0	6.2	7.1	33.6	22.0	7.0	0.9	72.9	32.6	49.7	50.3
85028	PHOENIX	93.2	90.7	1.1	1.5	1.7	2.4	6.2	9.2	4.5	5.1	5.9	6.0	4.6	22.1	34.2	15.1	2.5	80.8	46.0	48.6	51.4
85029	PHOENIX	81.9	76.9	3.2	3.9	2.6	3.4	18.9	25.8	7.7	6.5	6.1	6.8	9.0	30.9	22.2	9.1	1.7	75.9	32.3	50.0	50.0
85031	PHOENIX	56.3	52.1	4.8	4.8	1.4	1.5	62.5	70.9	10.8	9.8	8.8	8.9	8.6	28.5	17.0	6.9	0.8	65.3	26.8	50.4	49.6
85032	PHOENIX	84.3	79.9	1.7	2.0	1.7	2.3	19.1	25.5	7.4	7.0	6.6	6.8	6.9	31.0	24.6	8.2	1.5	74.9	34.5	50.1	49.9
85033	PHOENIX	55.7	50.3	8.1	8.1	1.6	1.7	55.9	65.0	11.5	10.3	9.0	8.7	9.0	29.3	16.7	5.2	0.4	63.9	25.8	50.1	49.9
85034	PHOENIX	46.9	45.5	7.5	7.8	0.7	0.9	76.2	77.8	10.9	9.0	7.6	8.1	10.0	30.7	17.0	5.9	0.9	68.0	27.3	54.0	46.0
85035	PHOENIX	40.6	36.9	7.1	6.9	1.6	1.6	70.8	76.7	11.7	10.4	9.1	9.3	8.8	30.4	15.7	4.2	0.4	63.3	25.4	51.4	48.6
85037	PHOENIX	59.6	50.0	8.2	7.5	2.3	8.4	41.7	47.8	10.7	9.6	8.6	7.6	7.1	33.1	19.0	4.0	0.3	66.4	28.6	49.4	50.6
85040	PHOENIX	38.3	36.7	23.8	22.1	0.7	0.6	65.0	70.6	11.4	10.2	8.8	9.1	8.7	28.9	16.2	6.1	0.8	64.3	26.1	51.6	48.4
85041	PHOENIX	52.2	52.5	9.4	8.1	0.7	0.7	73.7	76.3	9.9	9.5	8.7	8.8	8.1	27.3	19.9	7.1	0.8	66.7	28.2	50.8	49.2
85042	PHOENIX	41.1	37.0	21.4	21.5	1.3	1.3	52.0	58.1	9.6	8.6	7.7	7.9	8.6	30.3	19.9	6.6	0.8	69.4	29.0	49.7	50.3
85043	PHOENIX	51.5	47.2	6.6	4.9	0.9	1.0	66.5	73.2	10.8	9.9	8.6	8.5	8.2	29.7	17.9	5.7	0.6	65.8	27.3	51.0	49.0
85044	PHOENIX	85.8	81.7	3.7	4.5	4.0	5.4	9.5	13.5	6.2	5.9	5.9	5.8	7.2	31.9	26.5	9.3	1.2	78.5	36.5	49.8	50.2
85045	PHOENIX	87.0	83.1	3.5	4.6	5.2	6.9	6.3	9.3	9.4	9.9	9.6	7.1	3.6	31.7	25.7	2.9	0.2	66.4	35.6	50.4	49.6
85048	PHOENIX	86.1	81.3	3.2	4.0	5.3	7.2	8.1	12.1	7.8	8.4	8.4	7.4	5.0	31.8	27.2	3.8	0.2	70.7	34.9	49.7	50.3
85050	PHOENIX	92.0	89.5	1.1	1.3	1.9	2.9	6.9	9.8	8.9	8.7	8.2	5.9	4.1	31.6	23.4	8.1	1.1	70.4	36.2	48.5	51.5
85051	PHOENIX	76.5	70.6	4.7	5.4	3.2	4.1	21.8	29.1	8.1	7.1	6.5	7.2	8.1	28.9	22.8	10.1	1.2	74.2	33.1	50.0	50.0
85053	PHOENIX	86.8	82.8	2.6	3.2	2.2	3.0	12.2	17.2	7.1	6.7	6.5	6.9	7.1	30.2	25.6	8.8	1.0	75.7	34.7	50.1	49.9
85054	PHOENIX	93.1	90.4	1.2	1.5	2.6	3.7	4.0	6.1	6.5	5.3	4.9	4.9	9.3	36.5	25.8	6.3	0.4	80.7	35.0	50.2	49.8
85083	PHOENIX	85.3	85.3	7.1	3.0	2.1	3.7	21.5	14.6	9.7	9.1	8.8	10.2	2.8	35.4	20.2	3.6	0.3	64.4	32.5	51.1	48.9
85085	PHOENIX	96.8	95.8	0.1	0.2	0.5	0.7	4.0	6.1	5.2	6.2	7.2	7.0	3.6	21.8	36.6	11.2	1.2	76.9	44.3	49.2	50.8
85086	PHOENIX	91.8	92.9	3.7	1.5	0.8	1.0	8.4	8.4	6.6	7.4	8.1	7.5	4.3	27.8	30.2	7.5	0.7	73.2	38.5	50.4	49.6
85087	NEW RIVER	95.7	91.9	0.7	2.9	0.5	0.9	4.9	10.0	4.9	5.4	6.2	5.6	4.2	26.7	33.8	12.3	1.0	80.1	43.3	52.7	47.3
85201	MESA	73.1	67.0	3.8	4.3	1.5	1.9	29.5	38.2	9.5	7.9	6.5	6.6	9.6	31.3	18.6	7.9	2.2	72.5	29.8	49.6	50.4
85202	MESA	74.3	68.1	4.5	5.2	3.5	4.5	20.1	27.1	7.8	6.2	5.6	6.6	11.3	34.7	20.8	6.2	0.9	77.0	29.9	50.3	49.7
85203	MESA	83.4	78.7	2.2	2.7	1.3	1.7	18.2	24.6	8.7	8.0	7.6	7.6	8.0	28.8	22.0	8.0	1.4	71.2	30.9	49.9	50.1
85204	MESA	76.0	70.6	2.3	2.7	1.6	1.9	30.3	37.9	9.7	8.5	7.5	7.5	8.7	30.2	18.3	8.2	1.5	69.9	29.1	50.6	49.4
85205	MESA	91.6	88.5	1.5	2.0	1.2	1.7	8.2	12.1	6.1	5.9	5.8	5.8	5.3	20.6	24.1	21.7	4.5	78.5	45.3	46.9	53.1
85206	MESA	92.0	87.9	1.5	2.0	1.2	2.1	8.0	12.7	7.0	6.2	5.6	4.9	4.2	23.8	18.6	22.3	7.4	78.0	43.3	46.8	53.2
85207	MESA	90.7	87.6	1.4	1.9	0.8	1.2	10.8	14.6	8.0	7.7	7.6	6.7	4.9	27.3	25.4	11.3	1.1	72.4	36.6	48.8	51.2
85208	MESA	89.8	85.0	1.3	1.7	0.9	1.4	13.1	20.3	7.5	6.9	6.1	5.1	4.3	24.1	21.1	21.2	3.8	76.3	41.5	48.1	51.9
85209	MESA	89.7	84.9	1.5	2.1	1.4	2.4	11.3	16.3	9.0	8.3	7.2	5.8	4.2	29.7	18.5	15.1	2.2	71.7	35.6	48.6	51.4
85210	MESA	68.1	61.8	3.4	3.8	2.3	2.8	36.5	44.8	9.0	7.7	6.8	7.1	8.8	35.3	19.6	5.2	0.6	72.6	29.9	51.9	48.1
85212	MESA	85.1	81.9	2.4	2.6	1.9	2.8	13.4	17.8	11.5	9.8	8.5	6.5	5.5	35.0	17.1	5.4	0.6	66.2	30.4	49.2	50.8
85213	MESA	89.3	85.2	1.4	1.8	1.7	2.5	10.0	14.4	7.4	7.2	7.2	7.2	6.4	25.7	25.7	11.4	1.8	73.7	35.3	49.2	50.8
85215	MESA	94.5	92.5	1.1	1.4	0.9	1.3	5.5	8.4	5.2	5.6	6.3	5.7	3.6	19.0	27.8	23.2	3.6	79.3	48.1	48.3	51.7
85218	APACHE JUNCTION	95.2	93.7	0.3	0.5	0.8	1.0	5.0	6.6	3.4	3.7	4.1	4.1	3.0	16.0	39.1	24.9	1.7	86.2	54.7	48.3	51.7
85219	APACHE JUNCTION	93.7	91.6	0.6	0.8	0.5	0.9	6.5	8.4	4.2	4.1	4.2	4.2	4.1	16.7	33.0	27.5	2.1	84.9	54.5	48.0	52.0
85220	APACHE JUNCTION	93.0	90.4	0.6	0.9	0.6	0.8	8.7	11.8	6.2	5.8	5.4	4.6	3.8	21.0	25.5	24.3	3.4	79.6	47.9	49.2	50.8
85222	CASA GRANDE	66.5	64.3	3.7	4.5	1.1	1.3	38.4	39.3	8.0	7.5	7.2	7.2	6.5	24.9	24.4	12.6	1.6	72.8	35.5	49.2	50.8
85224	CHANDLER	80.1	74.6	3.5	4.2	4.6	6.1	15.0	20.7	7.5	7.2	6.9	6.7	6.5	33.3	24.5	6.0	1.3	74.2	34.1	49.5	50.5
85225	CHANDLER	69.2	63.8	3.7	4.2	2.8	3.6	34.5	40.9	10.1	9.0	7.9	6.9	7.0	33.8	19.7	5.1	0.6	68.8	30.3	50.2	49.8
85226	CHANDLER	81.3	75.7	3.7	4.5	6.7	9.0	11.6	16.4	8.2	7.8	7.7	7.0	6.5	33.7	24.9	3.8	0.3	71.9	32.8	49.4	50.6
85228	COOLIDGE	57.6	49.3	7.5	10.9	0.7	0.7	36.8	41.9	8.1	7.8	7.7	8.0	6.6	24.0	24.2	11.9	1.6	71.6	34.2	48.8	51.2
85231	ELOY	62.4	62.6	4.0	4.5	1.0	0.8	55.4	54.0	8.5	7.9	7.5	7.7	7.3	25.3	22.1	12.4	1.3	71.5	33.4	51.9	48.1
85232	FLORENCE	59.8	56.2	8.0	8.7	0.7	1.1	34.3	37.5	3.3	3.3	3.4	5.0	9.7	40.5	22.5	11.0	1.3	87.7	37.0	71.8	28.2
85233	GILBERT	82.7	77.3	2.7	3.3	5.4	7.2	13.3	18.6	9.6	9.2	8.5	6.8	5.4	33.7	22.2	4.1	0.3	68.3	31.8	49.6	50.4
85234	GILBERT	88.6	84.9	1.9	2.3	2.3	3.3	10.6	14.7	9.6	9.2	9.0	8.1	5.6	30.8	22.8	4.4	0.4	66.9	30.8	49.2	50.8
85236	HIGLEY	83.3	75.0	0.0	6.3	5.6	6.3	16.7	18.8	12.5	12.5	12.5	0.0	0.0	62.5	0.0	0.0	0.0	62.5	32.5	43.8	56.2
85237	KEARNY	79.5	75.6	0.5	0.6	0.2	0.3	35.5	42.4	7.1	6.4	6.5	6.7	4.7	20.3	29.5	17.0	1.8	75.6	43.4	48.4	51.6
85238	MARICOPA	53.8	46.3	1.8	2.6	0.7	0.9	49.6	63.2	9.8	9.3	8.9	9.2	8.0	24.8	20.4	8.6	1.1	66.4	28.3	49.8	50.2
85239	MARICOPA	61.4	59.8	1.3	1.9	0.3	0.3	36.8	43.3	8.7	7.9	7.3	7.5	8.3	26.7	24.3	8.6	0.8	71.5	31.7	50.6	49.4
85240	QUEEN CREEK	81.6	75.9	0.7	1.0	1.0	0.9	25.5	34.5	7.2	7.2	7.5	7.3	5.5	26.7	27.2	10.4	1.1	73.6	37.1	50.0	50.0
85242	QUEEN CREEK	82.5	78.0	0.5	0.5	0.5	0.6	27.7	34.9	7.9	8.1	8.3	7.7	5.1	28.5	27.0	6.7	0.7	70.8	35.0	50.1	49.9
85243	QUEEN CREEK	79.8	75.5	0.7	1.0	0.6	0.8	28.9	35.3	7.4	7.4	7.6	7.4	5.6	27.3	27.3	9.0	1.0	73.0	36.3	50.1	49.9
85245	RED ROCK	51.2	44.2	4.9	7.7	0.0	0.0	53.7	57.7	5.8	5.8	5.8	7.7	9.6	30.8	23.1	11.5	0.0	76.9	35.8	57.7	42.3
85247	SACATON	4.3	3.0	0.2	0.3	0.0	0.0	8.6	6.8	9.7	10.7	12.0	10.2	7.3	23.5	19.1	6.3	1.2	60.8	25.1	45.8	54.2
85248	CHANDLER	92.0	89.8	1.7	2.3	2.2	3.2	4.3	6.3	4.7	4.7	4.5	3.2	1.5	18.5	23.6	35.2	4.1	84.1	58.0	47.1	52.9
85249	CHANDLER	91.7	81.6	0.7	1.0	0.8	1.5	12.5	31.2	9.3	8.2	7.4	6.2	5.0	32.0	21.4	9.9	0.8	71.2	33.6	49.0	51.0
85250	SCOTTSDALE	95.0	93.3	0.9	1.2	1.2	1.7	5.1	7.8	3.9	3.7	3.8	4.1	4.9	25.2	29.8	21.3	3.3	86.3	48.0	46.9	53.1
85251	SCOTTSDALE	88.9	85.7	1.5	1.9	1.6	2.1	13.7	18.3	4.8	4.3	4.3	4.6	7.6	30.6	24.0	15.8	4.0	84.0	40.2	48.6	51.4
85253	PARADISE VALLEY	94.9	93.1	0.9	1.1	2.3	3.3	3.0	4.6	4.4	5.2	6.9	7.0	4.3	17.6	34.5	17.5	2.5	78.8	47.8	49.4	50.6
85254	SCOTTSDALE	93.6	91.2	1.1	1.4	2.5	3.6	4.3	6.5	5.2	5.9	6.8	7.2	5.7	25.5	32.9	9.5	1.3	77.4	41.0	48.8	51.2
85255	SCOTTSDALE	94.3	92.1	1.2	1.6	2.3	3.3	3.2	4.9	6.3	7.0	7.7	5.8	2.9	22.5	33.0	13.4	1.4	75.0	43.9	49.0	51.0
85256	SCOTTSDALE	20.7	17.2	0.5	0.5	0.2	0.2	16.8	19.8	9.0	9.4	9.1	8.2	7.0	20.8	21.1	12.8	2.5	67.6	31.6	46.4	53.6
85257	SCOTTSDALE	84.5	80.1	1.8	2.2	1.6	2.1	14.1	19.7	5.7	5.3	5.1	5.4	6.0	29.2	24.8	15.1	3.5	80.7	40.5	48.7	51.3
85258	SCOTTSDALE	95.1	93.2	0.7	0.9	2.2	3.2	3.1	4.8	3.4	3.5	3.9	4.4	4.1	20.6	33.9	23.2	3.0	86.6	51.8	46.9	53.1
85259	SCOTTSDALE	93.5	91.3	1.4	1.8	2.4	3.4	3.9	5.6	5.9	6.6	7.5	6.8	4.9	25.4	31.6	10.2	1.0	75.5	40.9	48.7	51.3
85260	SCOTTSDALE	93.9	91.7	1.1	1.4	2.7	3.9	3.8	5.7	5.6	5.9	6.6	6.1	5.0	27.9	29.7	11.2	1.9	77.9	40.6	47.9	52.1
85262	SCOTTSDALE	96.9	95.7	0.6	0.7	0.9	1.3	2.6	4.0	3.0	3.7	4.1	3.6	1.8	13.7	42.7	25.2	2.1	86.8	55.7	49.4	50.6
85263	RIO VERDE	98.2	97.6	0.1	0.0	0.4	0.6	1.6	2.4	2.3	2.4	2.7	2.4	1.6	9.9	30.4	43.6	4.7	91.2	64.2	47.4	52.6
85264	FORT MCDOWELL	13.3	20.2	0.4	0.4	0.1	0.1	10.2	10.6	10.6	9.8	9.4	9.2	8.0	25.4	21.8	5.6	0.3	64.6	26.9	51.0	49.0
85266	SCOTTSDALE	96.2	94.9	0.5	0.6	1.2	1.7	3.1	4.6	4.0	4.8	5.6	5.0	2.6	16.6	38.4	21.0	1.9	82.3	51.3	49.3	50.7
85268	FOUNTAIN HILLS	96.3	94.9	0.6	0.8	0.9	1.4	3.0	4.6	4.3	4.8	5.6	5.1	3.3	19.7	35.9	19.0	2.2	81.9	49.1	48.1	51.9
85272	STANFIELD	52.7	48.4	2.1	2.7	0.9	0.9	61.5	66.3	9.7	9.3	8.8	9.1	8.0	24.8	20.3	8.7	1.2	66.6	28.5	49.9	50.1
	ARIZONA	75.5	72.3	3.1	3.3	1.9	2.4	25.3	30.8	7.6	7.1	6.8	6.9	6.8	26.9	24.0	12.0	1.8	74.5	35.8	49.7	50.3
	UNITED STATES	75.1	72.0	12.3	12.7	3.8	4.6	12.5	15.7	6.8	6.7	6.6	7.1	6.9	27.0	26.0	10.9	1.9	75.7	36.9	49.2	50.8

ZIP CODE #	POST OFFICE NAME	2009 Per Capita Income	2009 HH Income Base	2009 HOUSEHOLD INCOME DISTRIBUTION (%) Less than $25,000	$25,000 to $49,999	$50,000 to $99,999	$100,000 to $149,999	$150,000 or More	MEDIAN HOUSEHOLD INCOME 2009	2014	2009 National Centile	2009 State Centile	2009 Home Value Base	2009 HOME VALUE DISTRIBUTION (%) Less than $50,000	$50,000 to $89,999	$90,000 to $174,999	$175,000 to $399,999	$400,000 or More	2009 Median Home Value
85003	PHOENIX	21346	4389	44.9	23.1	19.1	7.5	5.4	29962	32259	8	12	1434	6.7	7.6	21.8	57.5	6.4	217082
85004	PHOENIX	22130	2158	39.8	20.3	31.3	5.6	3.0	36151	37137	21	24	625	12.2	20.3	45.0	20.6	1.9	117873
85006	PHOENIX	11668	9943	38.9	32.7	22.7	4.4	1.4	31305	32222	10	15	3551	13.5	33.1	46.3	6.8	0.4	93257
85007	PHOENIX	16107	5243	43.4	24.7	19.5	8.7	3.8	30487	30738	9	13	2142	15.0	24.6	24.3	29.8	6.3	123227
85008	PHOENIX	15052	21413	29.6	35.1	27.4	6.0	1.9	38549	40344	28	29	7478	14.3	23.3	52.7	9.0	0.7	100818
85009	PHOENIX	11570	13311	36.9	33.6	24.0	3.9	1.6	33328	35006	14	18	6928	29.7	44.3	24.7	1.1	0.2	69242
85012	PHOENIX	35275	3329	24.4	28.0	26.8	11.0	9.8	47280	51529	55	52	1268	2.8	4.7	20.7	49.1	22.7	267485
85013	PHOENIX	30815	11022	21.7	30.3	31.9	9.5	6.7	47607	52038	56	53	4436	6.7	10.3	50.8	23.2	9.0	142385
85014	PHOENIX	26221	12908	24.0	33.2	29.9	9.2	3.8	43725	47068	45	45	4641	7.1	17.7	47.3	22.7	5.3	126008
85015	PHOENIX	17414	16275	27.5	34.6	29.3	6.4	2.1	39615	42085	32	31	5913	10.1	24.9	58.5	5.9	0.5	103798
85016	PHOENIX	34012	17736	20.6	28.7	31.2	10.0	9.5	50622	53617	63	61	8171	3.9	10.4	43.9	25.6	16.3	151818
85017	PHOENIX	14268	12545	29.9	34.8	29.0	5.0	1.2	38125	40584	27	28	6091	12.3	34.7	51.3	1.4	0.3	91999
85018	PHOENIX	41213	16424	16.6	26.1	31.6	11.2	14.5	57250	60731	74	70	8894	2.0	5.3	29.1	37.5	26.2	227565
85019	PHOENIX	15473	8988	24.3	34.0	32.5	7.6	1.6	43122	46116	43	44	4800	3.5	24.9	69.8	1.3	0.5	103834
85020	PHOENIX	33635	15846	19.6	25.5	32.6	12.6	9.7	54676	57992	71	68	8405	4.1	13.8	40.1	31.4	10.6	146055
85021	PHOENIX	28942	15724	20.0	28.7	32.6	10.4	8.3	51069	54065	64	61	6668	7.6	10.2	42.1	29.2	10.9	145241
85022	PHOENIX	34821	21681	14.2	25.8	35.0	15.3	9.6	59371	62383	77	73	13192	10.8	9.9	35.8	37.7	5.8	159042
85023	PHOENIX	29568	14404	15.9	27.5	36.8	13.4	6.5	56417	59406	73	69	7308	8.6	5.7	52.1	28.5	5.1	145891
85024	PHOENIX	34134	8114	7.3	16.1	40.6	24.4	11.5	79258	82802	92	87	7139	5.2	8.2	39.4	45.8	1.5	170771
85027	PHOENIX	26541	15423	12.4	27.6	43.3	13.3	3.4	58468	61054	76	71	9965	13.1	10.4	66.8	9.4	0.4	120168
85028	PHOENIX	44475	9194	9.0	19.0	33.7	21.7	16.6	79346	82384	92	88	6948	0.6	1.3	30.0	56.1	12.0	210634
85029	PHOENIX	23793	18197	17.5	29.1	37.9	11.8	3.7	52827	55766	68	64	9765	2.3	11.3	76.2	9.3	1.0	122246
85031	PHOENIX	13214	7860	22.0	35.2	34.4	7.3	1.1	44081	47032	46	46	5207	6.3	31.4	61.0	1.3	0.0	95608
85032	PHOENIX	26199	26202	13.8	26.1	41.2	13.8	5.0	58920	61366	76	72	15900	6.7	8.0	54.9	28.8	1.6	142449
85033	PHOENIX	14254	15010	20.0	33.7	37.1	8.1	1.1	46598	50178	53	51	9490	4.8	29.5	63.9	1.6	0.1	98954
85034	PHOENIX	13149	2820	42.3	28.9	22.6	4.9	1.3	30941	33266	10	14	777	34.6	35.3	24.1	6.0	0.0	63819
85035	PHOENIX	12380	13261	26.3	33.4	33.8	5.1	1.4	42428	45392	41	41	7683	5.3	35.8	58.5	0.4	0.1	94129
85037	PHOENIX	21352	13465	8.0	20.2	54.0	14.3	3.5	65611	68604	84	78	10516	2.5	10.4	81.3	5.3	0.5	118989
85040	PHOENIX	10315	9009	38.1	33.8	23.3	3.9	1.0	31671	32962	11	16	4268	17.8	43.3	36.6	1.5	0.8	79742
85041	PHOENIX	13472	16282	27.6	35.0	27.2	8.6	1.6	40769	43118	35	35	11986	13.7	32.0	28.7	22.5	3.1	94301
85042	PHOENIX	18366	12819	20.2	27.6	38.3	10.7	3.2	51888	55083	66	62	8454	11.0	21.9	50.2	14.3	2.5	107303
85043	PHOENIX	14112	10931	22.1	41.2	30.5	4.4	1.7	40483	42865	34	34	6511	11.9	14.1	60.6	11.7	1.7	111758
85044	PHOENIX	41406	17500	7.1	17.0	40.2	22.8	12.9	78377	81118	91	87	10257	1.2	1.1	35.9	52.6	9.3	194236
85045	PHOENIX	58167	2801	1.4	2.5	14.7	31.0	50.4	150433	151876	100	100	2597	0.9	0.2	2.6	69.5	26.8	306589
85048	PHOENIX	46875	12115	3.6	7.5	29.9	28.9	30.0	113183	113749	98	98	9229	0.8	1.0	12.3	67.7	18.2	251563
85050	PHOENIX	38354	10392	8.2	14.7	35.3	27.6	14.1	84490	87351	94	90	8631	15.1	13.6	22.3	45.6	3.4	172576
85051	PHOENIX	21821	15410	19.8	29.8	38.2	9.5	2.7	50322	53222	62	60	8866	3.5	15.7	75.0	5.5	0.3	115691
85053	PHOENIX	25866	11365	11.7	25.8	43.6	15.3	3.6	60927	62643	79	75	7382	0.2	5.0	77.5	16.2	1.1	134150
85054	PHOENIX	53223	3102	5.5	11.9	29.6	28.7	24.4	103489	104372	97	96	1605	0.0	0.0	22.7	55.0	22.4	262500
85083	PHOENIX	35840	3992	7.9	11.6	27.9	36.6	15.9	101909	102505	97	96	3650	1.1	4.2	34.1	54.3	6.3	193186
85085	PHOENIX	28932	4418	12.0	15.8	41.8	25.8	4.5	70973	74469	87	83	3918	0.5	5.1	38.2	50.4	5.8	186398
85086	PHOENIX	34066	13273	7.5	11.7	41.3	29.4	10.1	85344	86540	94	91	12329	1.1	5.3	44.9	39.9	8.8	172189
85087	NEW RIVER	34167	2499	10.7	23.4	36.9	21.7	7.3	67246	71067	85	80	2203	10.1	9.2	23.8	47.8	9.1	192815
85201	MESA	21593	19191	20.7	30.8	37.4	8.5	2.6	48824	51857	58	55	8333	15.2	17.8	56.8	9.4	0.8	109515
85202	MESA	26040	18504	16.7	27.9	38.4	13.2	3.8	54477	57059	70	67	8033	7.5	11.6	55.5	24.3	1.1	136526
85203	MESA	25340	13245	14.9	24.7	37.8	15.7	6.9	60453	63080	78	74	7735	7.8	9.3	50.2	28.7	3.9	146207
85204	MESA	20260	22633	16.6	29.8	40.4	10.3	2.9	52781	55697	68	63	13151	16.6	6.2	66.8	9.2	1.3	120195
85205	MESA	27599	18659	21.0	25.7	34.6	12.6	6.1	53160	55988	68	65	13209	15.8	8.1	52.0	19.8	4.2	127489
85206	MESA	29411	17241	15.0	26.4	37.5	15.6	5.5	58872	63429	76	72	12068	10.5	10.5	52.5	24.6	2.0	143431
85207	MESA	30490	16696	12.9	19.4	37.7	19.4	10.5	68518	73122	86	82	13821	8.1	10.6	41.7	30.1	9.4	149248
85208	MESA	24044	15705	18.8	30.5	36.6	11.4	2.8	50603	54407	63	61	12974	20.2	19.4	43.3	16.6	0.5	106617
85209	MESA	30663	14969	8.9	19.9	41.7	23.7	5.8	70837	75722	87	83	12817	9.2	10.0	38.7	40.0	2.1	161406
85210	MESA	21604	12978	16.9	30.3	37.8	12.2	2.8	52058	54567	66	63	5893	12.4	12.6	55.1	19.5	0.4	125418
85212	MESA	29829	6754	4.9	13.4	43.0	31.7	6.9	83454	85195	93	89	5571	5.6	8.4	41.9	39.5	4.6	164565
85213	MESA	29806	11246	10.9	20.7	37.1	19.9	11.4	69750	73663	87	82	8450	15.2	5.7	30.4	39.1	9.6	172073
85215	MESA	36342	6842	12.4	20.8	37.2	16.7	12.9	67680	71764	85	80	6008	6.0	8.2	35.4	41.8	8.5	175579
85218	APACHE JUNCTION	45164	5680	8.4	18.5	41.5	19.5	12.0	75837	76145	90	85	4940	6.1	4.7	17.0	60.3	12.0	218002
85219	APACHE JUNCTION	27891	8134	19.5	30.5	36.0	9.2	4.7	49956	53057	61	59	6474	22.6	21.0	28.3	23.8	4.3	105457
85220	APACHE JUNCTION	22727	14108	26.0	32.7	34.9	4.6	1.8	43119	46579	43	43	11267	40.1	18.6	33.7	7.2	0.4	65715
85222	CASA GRANDE	21116	16514	25.7	30.4	33.0	7.4	3.5	44660	48745	47	48	10515	20.5	24.7	38.9	15.0	1.0	97785
85224	CHANDLER	30367	17359	9.1	19.1	42.6	20.5	8.7	71548	75757	88	83	11046	0.6	1.2	60.1	34.3	3.7	160595
85225	CHANDLER	25862	24983	11.6	21.6	42.9	18.3	5.7	66293	70009	84	79	16711	9.6	7.2	53.2	29.2	0.8	146181
85226	CHANDLER	37108	14826	5.3	12.7	40.5	27.7	13.8	86455	88270	94	91	10203	1.0	1.4	40.5	52.2	4.9	186806
85228	COOLIDGE	17712	4871	29.9	34.1	26.8	6.2	3.1	38670	41215	29	29	3151	28.2	34.1	32.4	5.1	0.2	74809
85231	ELOY	17540	6742	27.9	31.0	32.0	6.3	2.8	42249	46479	40	39	4530	23.8	36.0	31.3	7.9	0.9	73212
85232	FLORENCE	20601	5674	20.5	29.4	39.4	8.0	2.7	50073	51931	61	60	4252	17.4	28.2	41.0	11.0	2.4	96456
85233	GILBERT	34891	14089	5.9	11.5	36.6	31.7	14.3	92466	94356	95	94	10457	0.6	1.2	31.9	62.7	3.7	199326
85234	GILBERT	32278	16506	4.6	12.2	38.7	32.0	12.5	90783	93300	95	93	13543	1.0	1.7	32.6	57.2	7.6	201821
85236	HIGLEY	43486	6	0.0	0.0	33.3	50.0	16.7	125000	113943	99	98	5	0.0	0.0	40.0	60.0	0.0	187500
85237	KEARNY	21960	1532	23.3	27.7	41.0	6.0	2.0	49133	52007	59	56	1177	32.7	44.8	20.2	1.8	0.5	63018
85238	MARICOPA	14282	10370	31.6	34.6	26.0	5.9	1.9	38163	40461	27	28	7398	4.5	16.3	63.2	13.8	2.2	123900
85239	MARICOPA	20465	5562	19.6	26.6	42.8	8.5	2.5	53167	55299	68	65	4023	12.1	23.9	52.3	10.2	1.5	110816
85240	QUEEN CREEK	22980	8302	15.1	30.7	42.2	9.2	2.8	52933	54897	68	64	7565	3.3	16.3	51.6	24.1	4.6	128641
85242	QUEEN CREEK	25689	13649	13.1	17.9	39.5	19.7	9.8	69836	71654	87	82	12428	3.9	10.0	29.3	48.6	8.2	197659
85243	QUEEN CREEK	20335	10618	15.1	30.6	42.2	9.3	2.8	53007	54946	68	64	9681	2.4	16.4	52.2	24.4	4.6	129250
85245	RED ROCK	18852	17	35.3	23.5	29.4	11.8	0.0	37343	37303	25	26	9	44.4	44.4	11.1	0.0	0.0	55000
85247	SACATON	8904	2614	51.4	30.3	14.7	2.7	1.0	24006	24265	3	6	1548	58.9	30.7	8.4	1.7	0.3	39048
85248	CHANDLER	46875	14650	9.3	18.5	34.2	21.6	16.4	76678	81714	90	86	12473	1.1	2.0	31.8	57.5	7.5	214779
85249	CHANDLER	30852	12998	7.6	11.4	41.6	25.9	13.5	84113	87491	94	89	11379	1.0	3.0	35.7	44.7	15.7	197957
85250	SCOTTSDALE	39949	7971	12.7	22.8	40.1	16.0	8.4	64731	68757	83	77	5685	0.5	2.2	41.7	48.6	7.0	185795
85251	SCOTTSDALE	36728	19540	17.7	28.4	36.2	10.1	7.6	53692	57602	69	66	9533	1.8	6.3	50.1	34.8	7.0	162221
85253	PARADISE VALLEY	78790	7153	5.1	9.5	19.5	14.7	51.2	155374	167141	100	100	5864	0.0	0.4	2.9	12.4	84.4	934923
85254	SCOTTSDALE	43374	19236	5.6	12.1	34.8	27.9	19.6	94514	96259	96	95	13955	1.0	1.0	12.0	69.3	16.8	265396
85255	SCOTTSDALE	68390	15643	5.3	9.7	23.3	19.9	41.8	131729	135640	99	99	12834	0.5	0.1	1.2	37.9	60.3	451922
85256	SCOTTSDALE	11658	1353	36.2	28.7	27.6	6.4	1.1	36032	38364	21	24	1034	60.1	24.0	10.6	4.7	0.6	44348
85257	SCOTTSDALE	28276	13583	20.0	25.2	37.7	13.0	4.1	54300	57722	70	66	8546	12.8	8.9	53.8	24.0	0.6	141518
85258	SCOTTSDALE	59644	12197	8.1	16.7	32.5	19.9	22.8	85703	88730	94	91	8430	0.9	0.2	12.0	56.1	30.7	308493
85259	SCOTTSDALE	54519	8826	8.3	13.3	28.8	18.0	31.6	98893	103716	97	95	6180	0.4	0.3	4.3	41.7	53.3	417826
85260	SCOTTSDALE	50786	15922	8.5	15.2	32.5	21.0	22.8	87089	90615	94	92	10374	0.6	0.1	9.1	59.0	31.2	297527
85262	SCOTTSDALE	84664	4184	7.3	10.0	22.6	16.8	43.2	132418	138781	99	99	3777	0.7	1.7	1.9	24.4	71.3	550393
85263	RIO VERDE	76524	1170	5.5	13.4	28.6	23.5	29.0	103724	106772	97	97	1078	0.0	0.1	5.6	39.9	54.5	423077
85264	FORT MCDOWELL	22393	333	22.5	17.4	40.8	9.3	9.9	57842	59740	75	71	270	24.1	31.5	24.1	13.0	7.4	82857
85266	SCOTTSDALE	66907	4785	4.5	9.0	21.3	27.6	37.5	126413	129177	99	99	4287	0.6	0.7	4.0	34.5	60.1	444246
85268	FOUNTAIN HILLS	42491	10834	7.9	16.6	38.3	22.2	15.0	79301	82562	92	87	8628	0.4	1.6	16.4	56.4	25.3	267619
85272	STANFIELD	12556	386	30.8	35.0	26.4	6.0	1.8	38952	40994	30	30	277	2.2	16.2	65.3	14.1	2.2	125216
	ARIZONA	26377		19.0	25.8	34.8	13.4	7.1	55275	58294				9.3	12.3	42.2	29.4	6.9	143619
	UNITED STATES	27277		20.9	24.4	35.3	11.7	7.6	54719	56938				9.3	13.1	31.6	32.6	13.5	162279

ZIP CODE #	POST OFFICE NAME	FINANCIAL SERVICES: Auto Loan	FINANCIAL SERVICES: Home Loan	FINANCIAL SERVICES: Invest-ments	FINANCIAL SERVICES: Retire-ment Plans	THE HOME: Home Improvements: Home Repair	THE HOME: Home Improvements: Lawn & Garden	THE HOME: Furnishings: Comput-ers & Hard-ware-Personal	THE HOME: Furnishings: Major Appli-ances	THE HOME: Furnishings: TV, Radio, Sound Equip-ment	THE HOME: Furnishings: Furni-ture	ENTERTAINMENT: Dine out/ Carry out	ENTERTAINMENT: Sports Equip-ment	ENTERTAINMENT: Fees & Tickets	ENTERTAINMENT: Toys & Games	ENTERTAINMENT: Travel	ENTERTAINMENT: Cable TV	PERSONAL: Apparel & Services	PERSONAL: Auto Repairs	PERSONAL: Health Insur-ance	PERSONAL: Pets & Supplies
85003	PHOENIX	65	53	55	58	53	55	71	60	73	68	74	49	66	69	65	73	52	69	68	75
85004	PHOENIX	63	53	54	56	53	56	68	60	70	65	71	46	63	67	62	72	50	67	69	73
85006	PHOENIX	59	48	42	47	47	42	60	53	58	61	61	42	54	59	54	55	43	59	48	60
85007	PHOENIX	72	59	54	59	58	55	72	64	72	73	74	50	66	73	65	71	53	71	63	75
85008	PHOENIX	71	55	48	55	52	49	71	60	69	71	72	50	63	71	62	67	51	69	58	71
85009	PHOENIX	65	54	45	48	52	49	60	59	61	64	63	42	54	62	55	60	45	62	55	65
85012	PHOENIX	106	93	98	98	95	91	111	99	108	110	108	80	105	107	104	106	77	107	99	118
85013	PHOENIX	92	85	84	89	84	84	97	88	97	95	98	70	95	95	93	96	69	95	93	106
85014	PHOENIX	82	68	64	71	65	67	86	73	85	83	86	60	79	85	77	84	61	82	76	89
85015	PHOENIX	73	58	52	60	56	56	74	63	73	72	75	52	67	75	66	72	53	72	65	77
85016	PHOENIX	105	94	93	98	93	92	110	97	109	108	110	79	106	109	103	107	78	106	101	118
85017	PHOENIX	68	57	50	56	55	51	69	60	67	69	69	48	62	68	62	64	48	67	58	71
85018	PHOENIX	120	123	128	127	125	120	129	122	127	130	128	95	133	125	131	126	92	127	125	143
85019	PHOENIX	75	67	56	66	63	61	76	68	74	76	76	55	71	76	69	72	54	74	67	80
85020	PHOENIX	106	103	103	105	103	101	111	104	109	112	111	81	111	109	109	108	78	109	106	123
85021	PHOENIX	105	89	85	93	87	86	107	94	106	106	108	76	100	107	98	104	76	104	95	113
85022	PHOENIX	121	116	109	118	113	110	119	113	117	122	119	89	118	120	116	115	83	117	111	134
85023	PHOENIX	109	97	87	100	93	90	108	97	106	110	108	79	103	109	100	103	76	104	94	117
85024	PHOENIX	138	151	128	149	144	129	135	134	129	145	131	105	141	136	135	123	92	129	121	154
85027	PHOENIX	102	98	84	96	92	87	99	93	96	103	98	73	96	100	93	93	68	95	88	110
85028	PHOENIX	139	164	174	167	171	162	148	154	146	156	146	113	166	142	163	146	104	150	156	176
85029	PHOENIX	93	82	73	84	78	78	93	83	92	93	93	67	88	94	85	90	65	90	84	101
85031	PHOENIX	76	72	64	65	71	61	75	73	72	81	74	54	71	73	72	69	52	75	66	81
85032	PHOENIX	104	99	89	99	96	92	102	97	100	105	102	76	99	103	98	98	71	100	94	114
85033	PHOENIX	78	73	63	67	71	61	78	74	74	82	77	56	73	76	73	70	54	77	65	82
85034	PHOENIX	61	43	38	43	41	41	59	51	60	59	62	39	50	60	50	60	44	59	52	60
85035	PHOENIX	72	65	56	60	63	54	72	66	68	76	71	51	66	70	66	64	50	70	59	74
85037	PHOENIX	111	116	94	110	109	96	106	105	101	114	103	82	106	107	103	96	72	101	93	120
85040	PHOENIX	62	50	41	46	48	46	56	54	58	60	60	39	50	59	51	58	42	58	53	61
85041	PHOENIX	80	69	59	63	68	65	71	73	72	76	74	52	65	74	66	72	51	74	69	82
85042	PHOENIX	91	85	73	81	81	75	89	84	86	93	88	65	84	89	83	83	62	87	79	97
85043	PHOENIX	71	67	59	62	67	55	72	68	67	76	70	53	67	69	68	63	49	70	59	75
85044	PHOENIX	140	139	130	144	136	128	142	133	138	147	140	106	144	142	139	134	99	136	129	156
85045	PHOENIX	249	302	260	310	294	247	251	254	231	282	235	211	284	250	264	211	173	231	207	283
85048	PHOENIX	197	222	191	226	213	185	196	193	183	214	187	159	211	197	199	171	135	183	165	219
85050	PHOENIX	147	162	138	160	155	138	143	144	135	155	137	115	150	145	144	128	98	135	126	163
85051	PHOENIX	84	78	68	79	74	75	85	78	85	84	86	62	83	87	80	84	60	83	80	93
85053	PHOENIX	101	99	86	100	94	91	100	94	98	103	100	75	100	102	97	96	70	98	93	112
85054	PHOENIX	187	163	144	173	153	145	184	160	178	187	182	136	174	187	167	171	128	172	152	194
85083	PHOENIX	155	187	162	193	183	154	156	158	143	175	146	131	177	156	164	131	108	144	129	176
85085	PHOENIX	103	128	131	132	131	121	109	115	104	116	106	86	124	104	122	102	76	109	109	132
85086	PHOENIX	129	161	144	160	156	141	135	138	127	142	130	109	152	132	146	123	93	131	125	158
85087	NEW RIVER	113	128	132	129	132	129	113	122	112	119	112	89	123	110	124	112	79	117	122	141
85201	MESA	84	69	62	71	66	66	84	73	83	83	84	60	76	85	75	82	59	81	74	89
85202	MESA	97	81	73	84	77	75	96	83	94	96	96	68	88	97	86	91	67	92	82	101
85203	MESA	105	106	96	106	102	96	107	101	104	109	106	80	107	107	104	101	75	104	97	118
85204	MESA	91	84	76	82	82	78	89	84	88	93	89	65	85	89	84	86	62	88	82	98
85205	MESA	91	98	101	94	102	101	92	98	94	99	93	67	98	90	98	96	64	96	107	111
85206	MESA	96	108	110	100	113	111	97	106	99	107	98	71	107	95	107	100	67	102	117	118
85207	MESA	127	137	124	133	134	123	122	126	118	132	119	96	127	122	124	114	83	120	116	144
85208	MESA	85	89	93	83	92	92	82	89	83	89	82	62	85	81	87	84	56	86	94	101
85209	MESA	117	126	118	119	126	118	115	120	112	125	113	88	119	114	119	110	78	115	118	135
85210	MESA	91	77	68	78	73	69	91	79	89	92	91	65	84	91	82	85	64	88	76	95
85212	MESA	141	149	120	144	139	122	135	132	128	146	130	106	136	138	131	120	91	127	115	151
85213	MESA	121	136	129	136	136	130	125	127	123	131	123	96	135	123	133	121	87	125	127	147
85215	MESA	116	139	145	133	147	142	120	132	121	132	120	90	137	117	136	122	84	126	141	147
85218	APACHE JUNCTION	126	133	167	130	148	151	122	139	126	134	125	91	131	116	137	131	86	134	152	158
85219	APACHE JUNCTION	89	86	103	83	94	100	83	94	87	88	85	63	83	82	88	91	58	91	103	108
85220	APACHE JUNCTION	73	72	81	67	76	80	67	76	70	73	69	51	67	67	71	73	47	73	82	87
85222	CASA GRANDE	85	75	81	73	76	80	77	81	78	78	78	59	71	78	75	80	53	80	81	95
85224	CHANDLER	125	127	108	126	120	110	122	117	117	129	120	93	122	123	118	113	84	116	108	137
85225	CHANDLER	114	113	96	111	108	97	114	107	108	119	111	86	111	114	108	103	78	108	97	123
85226	CHANDLER	151	158	135	160	150	134	150	142	141	159	144	117	153	151	146	134	103	140	126	165
85228	COOLIDGE	84	68	76	65	67	81	70	78	74	70	74	59	61	75	67	78	50	76	80	93
85231	ELOY	80	69	71	64	71	75	69	76	73	73	72	52	63	72	68	76	49	75	79	87
85232	FLORENCE	85	80	88	76	83	88	79	86	82	83	81	60	77	79	81	84	55	85	92	100
85233	GILBERT	151	165	141	165	157	139	150	146	141	162	144	119	157	151	150	133	103	141	128	167
85234	GILBERT	152	173	148	172	166	145	152	151	143	165	145	121	162	152	154	134	104	143	131	172
85236	HIGLEY	165	200	172	206	194	164	166	168	153	186	156	140	188	166	175	140	115	153	137	187
85237	KEARNY	83	78	89	75	80	93	73	85	79	72	78	61	72	77	77	84	53	81	93	99
85238	MARICOPA	78	63	47	52	60	59	62	67	68	70	69	41	54	69	56	70	48	68	65	74
85239	MARICOPA	92	85	72	80	81	82	84	84	85	88	85	63	79	88	79	85	59	85	82	100
85240	QUEEN CREEK	99	92	83	89	90	95	86	92	90	90	90	66	83	93	83	93	61	89	93	109
85242	QUEEN CREEK	123	135	117	133	130	123	119	122	116	126	117	94	125	122	121	114	82	117	113	142
85243	QUEEN CREEK	100	92	82	89	90	94	87	92	90	91	90	67	82	94	83	93	61	89	92	110
85245	RED ROCK	90	59	87	55	59	88	63	79	73	60	71	62	47	74	59	81	47	75	84	98
85247	SACATON	49	39	34	38	37	43	43	43	49	45	48	30	40	48	39	51	33	46	49	52
85248	CHANDLER	133	154	179	149	171	167	134	154	137	153	135	100	154	128	155	140	94	144	169	169
85249	CHANDLER	147	163	141	154	157	141	143	147	137	157	139	111	149	144	146	132	97	139	137	165
85250	SCOTTSDALE	111	120	127	120	124	123	113	117	114	119	114	85	121	111	121	116	80	116	124	136
85251	SCOTTSDALE	100	93	95	97	95	96	105	97	105	105	106	75	104	103	103	106	74	104	105	116
85253	PARADISE VALLEY	244	325	394	339	361	303	283	293	262	308	261	224	343	257	328	249	199	276	260	323
85254	SCOTTSDALE	159	179	176	186	180	163	166	163	158	174	160	129	180	161	174	152	116	160	150	189
85255	SCOTTSDALE	213	286	330	295	312	258	246	256	224	270	223	196	292	219	286	211	167	239	224	283
85256	SCOTTSDALE	69	65	55	61	62	61	64	63	64	67	64	48	60	67	60	63	44	64	62	75
85257	SCOTTSDALE	89	88	85	88	87	89	90	88	91	90	91	67	90	90	90	92	63	91	93	104
85258	SCOTTSDALE	162	182	215	184	198	180	173	179	166	186	166	131	187	159	190	163	118	175	175	203
85259	SCOTTSDALE	189	224	232	234	230	202	202	200	190	215	192	159	228	195	217	182	142	194	179	229
85260	SCOTTSDALE	163	185	181	193	186	165	170	166	160	181	163	134	186	166	177	153	119	162	149	191
85262	SCOTTSDALE	246	294	379	297	333	310	256	289	252	286	249	198	295	235	301	253	178	271	291	322
85263	RIO VERDE	193	203	276	202	234	240	183	216	193	207	189	135	201	174	211	202	130	206	241	244
85264	FORT MCDOWELL	113	107	111	97	108	100	106	112	102	112	104	83	99	103	106	100	73	109	101	125
85266	SCOTTSDALE	194	259	313	264	288	246	219	237	204	245	202	172	263	196	260	197	150	219	218	260
85268	FOUNTAIN HILLS	132	154	172	155	163	157	136	147	135	146	135	104	152	130	152	136	95	141	150	168
85272	STANFIELD	79	63	48	53	61	60	63	68	69	71	70	42	55	70	57	71	48	69	66	75
	ARIZONA	104	101	100	99	102	100	101	102	101	105	102	76	100	101	101	100	71	102	102	118
	UNITED STATES	100	100	100	100	100	100	100	100	100	100	100	100	100	100	100	100	100	100	100	100

ZIP CODE #	POST OFFICE NAME	COUNTY FIPS CODE	POPULATION 2000	POPULATION 2009	POPULATION 2014	2000-2009 ANNUAL RATE % Rate	2000-2009 ANNUAL RATE State Centile	HOUSEHOLDS 2000	HOUSEHOLDS 2009	HOUSEHOLDS 2014	HOUSEHOLDS % Annual Rate 2000-2009	HOUSEHOLDS 2009 Average HH Size	FAMILIES 2000	FAMILIES 2009	FAMILIES % Annual Rate 2000-2009
85273	SUPERIOR	021	3359	3599	4005	0.7	24	1287	1472	1656	1.5	2.44	875	956	1.0
85281	TEMPE	013	54115	66927	74889	2.3	60	21990	27255	30619	2.3	2.30	8388	9300	1.1
85282	TEMPE	013	49683	51722	53976	0.4	14	20685	21458	22322	0.4	2.40	11458	10992	-0.4
85283	TEMPE	013	42078	44646	46945	0.6	22	16128	17107	17992	0.6	2.59	9837	9769	-0.1
85284	TEMPE	013	17514	18448	19389	0.6	22	5945	6254	6559	0.5	2.95	4948	5060	0.2
85286	CHANDLER	013	14885	40750	52372	11.5	91	4961	13543	17364	11.5	3.01	4064	10628	11.0
85287	TEMPE	013	533	538	545	0.1	6	1	1	1	0.0	3.00	0	0	0.0
85292	WINKELMAN	021	2949	3485	4026	1.8	49	1000	1230	1435	2.3	2.83	755	905	2.0
85293	CASA GRANDE	021	3788	4554	5368	2.0	55	1156	1440	1707	2.4	3.15	909	1104	2.1
85294	CASA GRANDE	021	3483	5808	8755	5.7	86	1209	2138	3246	6.4	2.59	950	1599	5.8
85295	GILBERT	013	6564	28803	38736	17.3	95	1986	8612	11607	17.2	3.34	1673	7199	17.1
85296	GILBERT	013	25984	37836	44549	4.1	80	8005	11412	13405	3.9	3.31	6895	9591	3.6
85297	GILBERT	013	1813	23958	32730	32.2	98	526	7275	9921	32.8	3.29	461	6219	32.5
85298	GILBERT	013	1795	23342	31735	32.0	98	540	6851	9296	31.6	3.41	471	5851	31.3
85301	GLENDALE	013	57807	63039	66840	0.9	31	19864	21250	22440	0.7	2.95	13006	13072	0.1
85302	GLENDALE	013	37042	39550	41716	0.7	24	14461	15452	16303	0.7	2.52	9293	9314	0.0
85303	GLENDALE	013	24891	33177	38147	3.2	70	7554	10047	11530	3.1	3.29	5992	7619	2.6
85304	GLENDALE	013	29417	31385	32913	0.7	24	9890	10503	10975	0.7	2.96	7755	7931	0.2
85305	GLENDALE	013	5650	9475	10847	5.7	86	1709	2991	3452	6.2	3.16	1472	2481	5.8
85306	GLENDALE	013	25960	26832	27907	0.4	14	9339	9684	10069	0.4	2.72	6592	6481	-0.2
85307	GLENDALE	013	10447	12098	13860	1.6	46	3355	3786	4369	1.3	3.05	2742	2978	0.9
85308	GLENDALE	013	64461	71773	76772	1.2	40	22559	25059	26759	1.1	2.85	17589	18895	0.8
85309	LUKE AFB	013	682	691	703	0.1	6	0	0	0	0.0	0.00	0	0	0.0
85310	GLENDALE	013	21602	24148	26542	1.2	40	6929	7739	8503	1.2	3.11	5915	6413	0.9
85321	AJO	019	3850	4160	4323	0.8	27	1730	1896	1985	1.0	2.19	1133	1180	0.4
85322	ARLINGTON	013	537	630	693	1.7	47	173	203	223	1.7	3.10	130	139	0.7
85323	AVONDALE	013	17100	38713	48361	9.2	90	4596	10418	12981	9.3	3.70	3599	8064	9.1
85324	BLACK CANYON CITY	025	2751	3666	4373	3.2	70	1265	1681	2013	3.1	2.16	795	1021	2.7
85326	BUCKEYE	013	17058	52222	67771	12.9	92	4787	16245	21258	14.1	3.16	3733	12403	13.9
85328	CIBOLA	012	1363	1409	1424	0.4	14	548	572	582	0.5	2.46	350	358	0.2
85331	CAVE CREEK	013	22851	28992	32689	2.6	64	8910	11251	12682	2.6	2.58	6996	8482	2.1
85332	CONGRESS	025	2134	3121	3761	4.2	81	1004	1460	1757	4.1	2.14	688	973	3.8
85333	DATELAND	027	477	547	625	1.5	45	134	153	178	1.4	3.41	102	113	1.1
85335	EL MIRAGE	013	7640	31475	41967	16.5	94	2127	9048	12050	16.9	3.48	1754	7205	16.5
85337	GILA BEND	013	2365	2626	2785	1.1	37	762	910	996	1.9	1.77	567	640	1.3
85338	GOODYEAR	013	13655	42267	56050	13.0	93	3782	13266	17788	14.5	3.02	3089	10647	14.3
85339	LAVEEN	013	5862	31510	42269	19.9	97	1737	10385	13948	21.3	3.03	1371	7754	20.6
85340	LITCHFIELD PARK	013	7131	22156	28129	13.0	93	2559	8434	10722	13.8	2.62	1992	5959	12.6
85342	MORRISTOWN	013	1046	1213	1735	1.6	46	433	487	703	1.3	2.49	321	336	0.5
85343	PALO VERDE	013	104	122	135	1.7	47	37	43	48	1.6	2.84	28	30	0.7
85344	PARKER	012	15813	16763	17242	0.6	22	6700	7258	7535	0.9	2.27	4527	4813	0.7
85345	PEORIA	013	53654	60071	64562	1.2	40	18929	21017	22537	1.1	2.83	13660	14548	0.7
85347	ROLL	027	1285	1854	2129	4.0	79	386	617	719	5.2	2.93	299	462	4.8
85348	SALOME	012	2367	2660	2798	1.3	42	1049	1202	1273	1.5	2.21	700	787	1.3
85350	SOMERTON	027	27809	39209	45769	3.8	76	6201	9462	11236	4.7	3.91	5725	8669	4.6
85351	SUN CITY	013	29050	29567	30754	0.2	8	17859	18170	18897	0.2	1.60	9330	8739	-0.7
85353	TOLLESON	013	7211	29705	39246	16.5	94	2097	8611	11362	16.5	3.45	1682	6822	16.3
85354	TONOPAH	013	2716	3021	3291	1.2	40	920	1019	1109	1.1	2.96	684	714	0.5
85355	WADDELL	013	2957	5390	6843	6.7	88	886	1633	2069	6.8	3.30	767	1335	6.2
85356	WELLTON	027	5899	7851	9056	3.1	69	2192	3115	3626	3.9	2.51	1703	2351	3.5
85361	WITTMANN	013	3045	4162	5167	3.4	72	1023	1326	1651	2.8	3.14	778	947	2.1
85362	YARNELL	025	766	938	1041	2.2	58	410	498	555	2.1	1.88	250	293	1.7
85363	YOUNGTOWN	013	3013	5308	6555	6.3	87	1643	3062	3806	7.0	1.70	770	1269	5.5
85364	YUMA	027	71754	85284	92640	1.9	52	24042	29451	32219	2.2	2.85	17834	21596	2.1
85365	YUMA	027	36610	48410	54188	3.1	69	13059	18006	20337	3.5	2.59	10046	13494	3.2
85367	YUMA	027	16369	17904	19475	1.0	34	7902	9056	9927	1.5	1.97	5997	6658	1.1
85373	SUN CITY	013	12862	15267	17422	1.9	52	7055	8301	9347	1.8	1.81	4318	4908	1.4
85374	SURPRISE	013	28772	48086	62728	5.7	86	11822	19878	26515	5.8	2.41	9145	14995	5.5
85375	SUN CITY WEST	013	26349	29850	33335	1.4	44	14998	16955	18859	1.3	1.75	10366	11169	0.8
85379	SURPRISE	013	946	35440	48501	48.0	99	343	12003	16392	46.9	2.95	251	8835	47.0
85381	PEORIA	013	22230	25360	27667	1.4	44	7421	8421	9149	1.4	2.97	5872	6412	1.0
85382	PEORIA	013	29363	41867	49195	3.9	78	11811	16373	19079	3.6	2.52	8651	11741	3.4
85383	PEORIA	013	7339	33538	44236	17.9	96	2262	11406	14984	19.1	2.94	1993	9578	18.5
85387	SURPRISE	013	1870	8318	10881	17.5	96	574	3853	5061	22.9	2.16	450	2983	22.7
85388	SURPRISE	013	557	21063	26703	48.1	100	168	6994	8759	49.6	3.01	140	5550	48.9
85390	WICKENBURG	013	9352	11323	14289	2.1	57	4069	4909	6167	2.0	2.30	2656	2991	1.3
85392	AVONDALE	013	18705	37801	47487	7.9	90	6026	12032	15040	7.8	3.14	5109	9613	7.1
85395	GOODYEAR	013	6416	24363	31920	15.5	94	2765	9655	12675	14.5	2.51	2207	7426	14.0
85396	BUCKEYE	013	1705	7529	10227	17.4	95	525	2333	3168	17.5	3.23	444	1865	16.8
85501	GLOBE	007	13446	13923	14208	0.4	14	5116	5306	5421	0.4	2.51	3514	3581	0.2
85530	BYLAS	009	1846	2130	2253	1.6	46	443	516	547	1.7	4.13	366	421	1.5
85533	CLIFTON	011	1186	1179	1217	-0.1	2	428	427	442	0.0	2.71	334	329	-0.2
85534	DUNCAN	011	2988	3004	3095	0.1	6	1138	1148	1187	0.1	2.61	810	804	-0.1
85535	EDEN	009	77	85	89	1.1	37	23	26	27	1.3	3.27	18	20	1.1
85539	MIAMI	007	5973	5892	6025	-0.1	2	2397	2391	2457	0.0	2.46	1628	1591	-0.2
85540	MORENCI	011	4375	4194	4226	-0.5	2	1551	1496	1512	-0.4	2.80	1122	1066	-0.6
85541	PAYSON	007	21168	22902	23730	0.9	31	9140	9848	10215	0.8	2.30	6275	6634	0.6
85542	PERIDOT	007	6344	6835	7134	0.8	27	1585	1701	1777	0.8	3.95	1316	1401	0.7
85543	PIMA	009	3628	4028	4234	1.1	37	1184	1321	1393	1.2	3.05	946	1040	1.0
85544	PINE	007	3142	3495	3657	1.2	40	1454	1619	1696	1.2	2.16	1017	1112	1.0
85545	ROOSEVELT	007	75	81	84	0.8	27	50	54	56	0.8	1.50	29	27	-0.8
85546	SAFFORD	009	18191	18909	19381	0.4	14	5887	6176	6368	0.5	2.70	4257	4387	0.3
85550	SAN CARLOS	009	2574	2893	3027	1.3	42	549	623	655	1.4	4.64	501	565	1.3
85552	THATCHER	009	5909	6371	6627	0.8	27	1856	2027	2120	1.0	3.01	1396	1497	0.8
85601	ARIVACA	019	79	95	105	2.0	55	55	67	75	2.2	1.40	32	27	-1.8
85602	BENSON	003	9064	10745	11728	1.9	52	3822	4588	5028	2.0	2.32	2630	3083	1.7
85603	BISBEE	003	8420	9081	9433	0.8	27	3652	4016	4200	1.0	2.20	2071	2204	0.7
85606	COCHISE	003	1385	1463	1509	0.6	22	627	672	698	0.8	2.18	419	438	0.5
85607	DOUGLAS	003	21238	23090	23914	0.9	31	6083	6717	7004	1.1	3.15	4635	5042	0.9
85610	ELFRIDA	003	1480	1731	1875	1.7	47	532	628	683	1.8	2.71	379	437	1.6
85611	ELGIN	023	622	787	892	2.6	64	257	326	370	2.6	2.41	181	224	2.3
85613	FORT HUACHUCA	003	5107	4280	4118	-1.9	0	868	686	651	-2.5	4.26	824	649	-2.5
85614	GREEN VALLEY	019	14542	22345	27455	4.8	83	8065	11721	14205	4.1	1.89	4992	7161	4.0
85615	HEREFORD	003	6657	8349	9155	2.5	62	2525	3166	3483	2.5	2.63	1897	2337	2.3
85616	HUACHUCA CITY	003	4859	6928	7912	3.9	78	1909	2757	3164	4.1	2.51	1311	1853	3.8
	ARIZONA					2.9					2.7	2.69			2.5
	UNITED STATES					1.0					1.1	2.59			0.9

#	POST OFFICE NAME	RACE (%) White 2000	White 2009	Black 2000	Black 2009	Asian/Pacific 2000	Asian/Pacific 2009	% Hispanic Origin 2000	% Hispanic Origin 2009	2009 AGE DISTRIBUTION (%) 0-4	5-9	10-14	15-19	20-24	25-44	45-64	65-84	85+	18+	MEDIAN AGE 2009	% 2009 Males	% 2009 Females
85273	SUPERIOR	73.2	71.3	0.5	0.8	0.4	0.4	67.8	73.3	6.2	6.0	7.0	7.1	5.4	21.0	26.1	18.8	2.5	76.6	42.3	48.8	51.2
85281	TEMPE	70.8	65.0	3.1	3.4	6.6	8.4	25.1	31.1	5.9	4.5	3.8	11.1	20.6	34.6	13.9	4.7	0.8	83.3	26.4	53.2	46.8
85282	TEMPE	79.2	73.9	4.2	4.9	3.6	4.6	16.7	22.6	6.0	5.1	4.9	5.4	10.5	33.5	21.9	10.5	2.2	81.2	33.8	50.2	49.8
85283	TEMPE	72.2	67.3	4.2	5.2	3.7	4.8	21.8	27.1	6.3	5.8	5.7	6.2	8.4	35.3	23.6	7.7	1.0	78.7	33.3	50.4	49.6
85284	TEMPE	88.2	84.1	1.8	2.3	6.3	8.7	6.9	10.1	5.8	7.2	8.7	7.7	3.9	25.1	34.7	6.2	0.5	73.1	40.4	49.7	50.3
85286	CHANDLER	82.8	78.7	2.6	2.7	5.2	5.3	15.1	26.5	10.9	10.2	9.1	6.2	4.0	35.2	20.1	3.9	0.3	65.7	32.2	49.4	50.6
85287	TEMPE	86.1	81.2	1.3	1.7	3.6	4.8	8.1	11.9	0.9	1.1	0.6	47.6	18.6	20.6	7.8	1.9	0.9	96.8	20.0	53.3	46.7
85292	WINKELMAN	64.1	60.9	0.3	0.3	0.4	0.3	63.3	68.3	7.6	7.5	7.9	7.1	5.7	21.3	29.7	12.2	1.1	72.4	38.3	50.1	49.9
85293	CASA GRANDE	50.3	43.9	1.3	1.7	0.7	0.7	38.7	42.5	8.0	9.0	9.2	8.3	6.1	23.9	24.0	10.5	0.9	68.4	32.8	49.7	50.3
85294	CASA GRANDE	69.8	59.6	5.0	6.2	0.4	0.3	30.1	39.8	6.8	6.7	7.0	8.1	6.2	25.5	27.9	10.8	1.1	75.4	37.4	49.4	50.6
85295	GILBERT	85.1	79.2	2.4	2.7	2.6	2.1	13.4	21.8	10.2	9.8	9.2	7.1	3.9	33.0	22.2	4.3	0.4	66.3	33.0	49.9	50.1
85296	GILBERT	86.6	82.1	2.6	3.2	3.4	4.4	11.2	16.6	11.8	11.0	9.9	6.8	3.6	35.4	18.4	3.0	0.2	62.7	31.1	49.6	50.4
85297	GILBERT	85.0	81.3	1.7	1.6	0.9	1.2	17.3	27.5	10.1	9.2	8.3	6.7	4.8	33.9	21.7	4.8	0.5	68.2	32.0	49.4	50.6
85298	GILBERT	89.1	83.1	0.4	0.4	0.8	1.1	17.0	28.0	10.0	8.9	8.1	6.8	5.4	33.9	21.3	5.1	0.5	68.7	31.4	49.4	50.6
85301	GLENDALE	60.6	54.7	7.0	7.2	1.4	1.9	46.1	53.5	10.4	9.0	7.6	7.6	8.6	29.0	18.3	8.3	1.2	68.7	28.7	50.0	50.0
85302	GLENDALE	80.9	75.5	3.9	4.6	3.1	4.1	17.3	23.8	6.9	6.5	6.3	6.6	7.0	29.3	23.9	11.1	2.4	76.6	34.9	48.8	51.2
85303	GLENDALE	62.8	56.8	7.3	7.8	2.4	2.8	41.8	50.8	10.7	9.3	8.5	8.0	7.8	31.1	19.6	4.6	0.4	66.5	28.2	50.1	49.9
85304	GLENDALE	85.1	80.3	3.1	4.0	3.2	4.3	12.1	17.1	6.3	6.5	6.9	7.6	7.0	27.7	27.9	8.7	1.4	75.7	35.9	49.3	50.7
85305	GLENDALE	75.2	64.0	6.1	5.1	1.8	4.1	26.0	37.7	8.5	8.0	7.7	7.3	6.4	32.6	24.2	4.9	0.4	71.1	31.9	49.5	50.5
85306	GLENDALE	85.9	81.3	2.0	2.5	4.3	5.8	10.9	15.7	6.3	6.5	6.7	7.1	7.2	30.6	25.9	8.1	1.6	76.2	34.7	49.3	50.7
85307	GLENDALE	74.0	67.6	7.6	8.5	2.9	3.7	22.5	31.0	11.9	9.6	7.7	7.2	10.5	34.4	14.6	3.7	0.3	67.1	26.5	51.0	49.0
85308	GLENDALE	89.1	85.4	2.1	2.6	3.4	4.8	8.7	12.4	7.6	7.5	7.4	6.9	5.3	31.1	27.2	6.4	0.6	73.1	35.4	49.6	50.4
85309	LUKE AFB	72.6	66.4	14.2	17.1	3.2	4.1	13.2	18.4	16.1	11.9	7.7	8.4	20.0	34.7	1.2	0.1	0.0	61.9	21.5	55.9	44.1
85310	GLENDALE	91.5	88.5	1.3	1.7	2.0	2.9	7.3	10.8	8.1	8.4	8.6	7.9	4.4	30.1	27.1	4.9	0.4	69.8	35.3	49.5	50.5
85321	AJO	78.5	74.7	0.2	0.3	0.4	0.5	37.1	45.5	5.2	5.3	5.2	5.7	4.7	15.9	26.2	28.4	3.3	80.9	52.6	47.7	52.3
85322	ARLINGTON	77.7	71.3	0.7	0.8	0.2	0.2	33.0	43.7	8.3	7.5	7.3	8.6	8.9	25.2	24.0	9.5	0.8	71.9	31.0	51.9	48.1
85323	AVONDALE	51.2	52.4	3.6	3.9	0.6	0.7	71.7	70.6	9.9	9.2	8.6	8.9	8.3	26.7	20.0	7.4	0.9	66.9	28.3	50.4	49.6
85324	BLACK CANYON CITY	96.1	95.5	0.3	0.4	0.3	0.4	3.7	5.2	3.6	3.8	4.1	5.0	4.0	15.5	36.4	25.1	2.5	84.8	54.1	50.5	49.5
85326	BUCKEYE	72.7	72.4	3.5	2.3	0.4	0.6	34.4	35.8	7.6	7.5	7.7	7.9	6.3	27.1	26.3	8.7	0.9	72.4	35.0	51.1	48.9
85328	CIBOLA	82.8	77.1	1.1	1.2	0.1	0.1	30.0	40.0	6.2	6.6	7.9	7.9	5.6	24.1	28.8	12.3	0.5	74.0	39.1	52.7	47.3
85331	CAVE CREEK	95.3	93.2	0.6	0.9	1.1	1.5	4.9	7.7	6.8	7.3	7.5	5.7	3.2	25.4	31.3	11.9	1.0	74.8	41.7	49.6	50.4
85332	CONGRESS	95.8	94.9	0.2	0.2	0.1	0.1	7.8	10.7	2.7	2.8	3.0	3.7	3.2	11.2	30.9	39.8	2.8	89.3	61.7	49.4	50.6
85333	DATELAND	77.1	75.3	0.4	0.5	0.2	0.2	72.7	79.3	9.9	9.0	8.8	10.4	9.1	23.2	19.4	9.7	0.5	66.2	27.0	55.2	44.8
85335	EL MIRAGE	66.1	69.7	3.4	2.7	0.5	1.1	66.6	57.9	8.7	8.5	8.1	7.5	5.8	25.0	24.6	10.6	1.2	70.2	34.1	50.5	49.5
85337	GILA BEND	48.1	48.1	1.1	4.7	0.3	1.3	44.3	44.9	5.4	5.4	5.4	7.7	10.4	34.8	23.2	6.8	0.7	81.0	33.8	62.6	37.4
85338	GOODYEAR	75.0	75.5	5.5	5.0	1.0	1.6	27.0	29.6	7.8	7.6	7.5	6.8	5.8	31.7	25.0	7.1	0.7	73.0	34.6	50.1	49.9
85339	LAVEEN	51.7	68.9	1.9	3.0	0.6	0.9	25.4	38.7	6.2	6.8	7.5	7.4	4.5	24.0	32.3	10.2	1.1	74.9	40.9	49.5	50.5
85340	LITCHFIELD PARK	86.7	78.7	1.8	2.7	2.6	3.2	14.9	26.3	7.3	7.0	6.7	6.7	6.2	26.5	27.2	11.2	1.2	74.8	37.3	49.7	50.3
85342	MORRISTOWN	85.4	81.1	0.9	1.1	0.3	0.4	20.3	27.0	5.4	5.8	5.9	5.9	4.5	18.1	30.3	21.8	2.3	79.3	48.3	49.7	50.3
85343	PALO VERDE	77.9	70.5	1.0	0.8	0.0	0.0	32.7	44.3	8.2	7.4	7.4	8.2	9.0	25.4	24.6	9.0	0.8	72.1	31.4	50.8	49.2
85344	PARKER	71.1	68.8	0.8	0.9	0.6	0.7	21.7	26.1	4.8	4.6	4.6	4.8	4.9	17.4	27.2	29.0	2.8	83.1	53.4	51.1	48.9
85345	PEORIA	78.4	72.9	3.7	4.2	1.7	2.3	23.5	31.0	8.2	7.7	7.3	7.1	6.5	29.3	22.2	9.8	2.0	72.4	33.6	48.7	51.3
85347	ROLL	74.7	71.3	1.0	1.1	0.2	0.2	58.0	65.7	8.6	8.1	8.0	9.0	7.5	23.5	23.8	10.6	1.0	69.8	32.1	53.7	46.3
85348	SALOME	89.7	86.4	0.2	0.2	0.4	0.5	22.0	30.3	4.0	3.7	3.8	5.4	4.4	14.7	28.1	33.0	2.7	85.2	56.7	50.4	49.6
85350	SOMERTON	53.7	52.8	1.8	1.4	0.3	0.3	87.7	91.4	9.8	9.5	8.9	9.9	9.8	27.6	18.5	5.5	0.5	65.8	26.3	51.7	48.3
85351	SUN CITY	98.3	97.7	0.5	0.7	0.4	0.5	1.1	1.7	0.3	0.2	0.1	0.1	0.2	1.4	13.8	64.7	19.2	99.3	75.5	41.1	58.9
85353	TOLLESON	57.6	58.1	1.2	0.7	0.6	0.4	67.2	56.6	9.3	8.9	8.6	8.6	7.7	26.9	21.3	7.8	1.0	68.0	29.5	50.5	49.5
85354	TONOPAH	76.9	70.3	1.7	1.9	0.1	0.1	30.8	40.6	8.1	8.0	7.7	7.5	6.7	24.2	26.6	10.6	0.5	71.4	35.1	52.2	47.8
85355	WADDELL	86.3	81.5	1.0	1.2	0.7	0.8	19.8	27.8	6.7	7.3	8.0	8.0	4.9	26.1	30.9	7.3	0.7	72.7	37.6	50.4	49.6
85356	WELLTON	73.2	67.5	2.1	2.5	0.5	0.6	32.2	40.4	6.5	6.4	6.1	5.9	5.8	18.8	25.1	23.8	1.6	77.5	45.5	51.3	48.7
85361	WITTMANN	79.5	73.0	1.2	1.7	0.3	0.4	29.3	39.3	7.1	7.5	7.7	7.3	5.0	22.3	28.1	13.5	1.4	73.1	39.3	50.1	49.9
85362	YARNELL	93.5	91.7	0.3	0.3	0.1	0.2	7.5	10.0	2.8	3.2	3.7	4.5	3.5	12.7	35.9	30.7	3.0	87.5	57.8	50.7	49.3
85363	YOUNGTOWN	88.9	86.5	1.4	1.5	0.9	1.1	12.7	16.3	2.4	2.2	2.0	1.7	2.3	9.6	26.5	42.0	11.1	92.3	66.4	41.7	58.3
85364	YUMA	63.5	59.6	2.7	2.9	1.4	1.7	55.0	62.1	9.2	8.5	7.9	7.9	7.5	26.1	21.3	10.0	1.6	69.6	31.0	49.0	51.0
85365	YUMA	77.2	73.1	2.4	2.4	1.2	1.4	33.2	40.7	7.4	6.7	6.5	6.6	7.9	21.4	22.5	18.9	2.2	76.0	39.1	50.7	49.3
85367	YUMA	91.3	89.0	0.4	0.5	0.6	0.8	10.9	14.9	2.6	2.6	2.6	2.5	1.9	9.2	23.3	50.6	4.7	90.6	66.9	48.0	52.0
85373	SUN CITY	96.7	95.3	0.9	1.1	0.5	0.7	3.2	5.0	2.5	2.3	2.1	1.7	1.3	8.3	17.2	50.3	14.4	92.1	70.9	43.8	56.2
85374	SURPRISE	86.8	85.6	2.6	3.0	1.1	1.5	22.4	21.2	6.5	5.9	5.1	3.8	2.9	20.6	18.8	32.8	3.7	80.2	52.3	47.3	52.7
85375	SUN CITY WEST	98.4	97.5	0.5	0.7	0.4	0.6	1.0	1.9	0.3	0.3	0.3	0.3	0.3	1.8	12.5	68.1	16.1	98.9	76.2	42.8	57.2
85379	SURPRISE	82.2	67.8	2.9	3.9	1.8	2.9	18.6	36.3	8.8	8.0	7.4	6.3	5.2	33.0	23.8	6.7	0.8	71.9	33.8	48.9	51.1
85381	PEORIA	88.2	84.4	2.5	3.1	3.2	4.2	10.4	14.9	6.5	7.1	7.5	7.7	5.3	26.3	28.6	7.6	3.5	74.1	37.8	47.9	52.1
85382	PEORIA	91.9	88.6	1.9	2.6	1.7	2.6	7.1	11.0	7.6	7.2	6.5	5.4	3.9	25.2	21.8	18.9	3.6	75.1	40.9	47.4	52.6
85383	PEORIA	93.2	91.4	1.1	1.1	1.3	1.7	7.0	9.7	8.4	8.1	7.6	6.0	3.4	27.7	23.8	13.5	1.6	72.0	38.2	48.8	51.2
85387	SURPRISE	87.5	91.9	1.0	0.8	0.5	0.5	16.7	10.2	1.9	2.0	2.1	2.0	1.5	7.3	21.6	54.5	7.2	92.8	69.1	45.0	55.0
85388	SURPRISE	70.7	71.0	1.3	11.6	0.4	0.4	43.4	27.0	3.5	3.8	4.1	4.1	2.6	15.0	26.5	33.7	6.7	86.0	59.0	46.0	54.0
85390	WICKENBURG	88.5	84.4	0.4	0.5	0.4	0.5	15.8	22.2	4.8	4.7	4.8	5.4	4.9	17.5	30.8	24.0	3.2	82.4	51.3	48.6	51.4
85392	AVONDALE	74.8	69.0	6.7	6.8	3.4	3.8	22.3	33.8	9.8	8.8	8.2	6.9	5.3	34.4	21.9	4.3	0.3	68.8	31.9	49.7	50.3
85395	GOODYEAR	86.2	75.7	3.8	3.6	3.3	2.8	9.8	30.1	5.8	5.7	5.4	5.0	3.9	22.5	28.3	21.7	1.6	79.9	46.3	49.5	50.5
85396	BUCKEYE	84.3	79.1	1.8	2.2	0.8	1.0	17.8	24.8	6.5	7.0	7.8	7.8	4.5	25.5	30.7	9.3	0.9	73.1	39.3	49.8	50.2
85501	GLOBE	81.8	77.5	0.7	0.7	0.8	1.0	28.9	38.6	6.4	6.4	6.6	6.7	5.7	22.9	27.9	15.0	2.5	76.4	41.3	49.7	50.3
85530	BYLAS	1.0	3.5	0.0	0.0	0.1	0.0	2.4	3.2	10.3	12.0	12.3	12.3	7.3	23.6	17.5	4.5	0.4	57.6	22.2	49.5	50.5
85533	CLIFTON	73.8	70.3	0.3	0.3	0.1	0.1	53.8	61.8	7.0	6.8	7.1	7.2	5.2	23.0	27.9	14.3	1.5	74.0	40.0	51.7	48.3
85534	DUNCAN	83.3	79.4	0.2	0.3	0.1	0.1	28.8	36.3	8.2	7.2	7.5	7.8	6.2	22.1	26.7	12.7	1.6	71.6	37.3	51.8	48.2
85535	EDEN	83.1	82.4	0.0	0.0	0.0	0.0	15.6	20.0	9.4	9.4	8.2	5.9	5.9	23.5	22.4	12.9	2.4	67.1	33.8	52.9	47.1
85539	MIAMI	79.6	75.7	0.9	1.0	0.2	0.2	37.6	46.3	6.8	6.5	6.6	6.3	5.1	20.4	28.5	17.6	2.3	76.3	43.6	49.1	50.9
85540	MORENCI	68.0	63.2	0.8	0.9	0.3	0.3	49.9	57.7	8.7	8.6	7.9	8.5	5.9	27.4	25.2	7.0	0.9	69.3	32.5	52.3	47.7
85541	PAYSON	95.1	94.1	0.2	0.2	0.5	0.6	5.1	7.6	4.6	4.7	4.8	5.0	4.2	16.2	32.1	25.0	3.5	82.8	52.7	48.7	51.3
85542	PERIDOT	4.1	4.5	0.1	0.2	0.2	0.3	2.6	3.1	10.2	10.8	10.2	10.7	8.1	24.0	19.4	6.1	0.5	61.9	25.0	49.3	50.7
85543	PIMA	85.4	83.0	0.3	0.4	0.2	0.3	19.3	25.3	10.0	9.7	9.1	7.7	5.7	24.8	21.1	10.6	1.4	66.4	30.9	50.2	49.8
85544	PINE	96.9	96.0	0.1	0.1	0.3	0.4	2.3	3.7	2.7	3.1	3.7	3.9	3.1	10.8	40.3	30.3	2.1	88.1	58.3	50.0	50.0
85545	ROOSEVELT	96.0	96.3	0.0	0.0	0.0	0.0	2.7	3.7	2.5	2.5	2.5	1.2	2.5	12.3	33.3	40.7	2.5	91.4	61.9	51.9	48.1
85546	SAFFORD	75.1	71.8	2.4	2.6	0.8	1.0	36.9	44.8	7.5	6.9	6.5	6.9	7.6	28.6	22.3	11.8	1.9	75.1	34.2	54.9	45.1
85550	SAN CARLOS	1.1	3.4	0.0	0.1	0.0	0.1	3.2	4.6	11.5	12.3	12.9	12.7	7.8	23.0	16.3	3.3	0.3	54.7	20.4	48.9	51.1
85552	THATCHER	84.1	81.0	0.8	0.9	0.6	0.8	20.4	26.6	8.4	7.5	7.4	12.3	10.5	21.4	21.3	9.6	1.7	72.1	27.8	47.1	52.9
85601	ARIVACA	87.3	84.2	0.0	1.1	0.0	0.0	25.3	32.6	4.2	4.2	4.2	6.3	5.3	17.9	37.9	17.9	2.1	82.1	49.7	50.5	49.5
85602	BENSON	90.6	87.6	0.5	0.6	0.5	0.6	15.1	22.0	5.4	5.3	6.0	6.1	4.5	18.3	31.5	20.3	2.6	79.4	48.1	49.8	50.2
85603	BISBEE	79.6	75.0	0.7	0.7	0.5	0.5	39.7	50.8	5.9	5.9	5.8	6.4	5.4	21.8	29.4	16.9	2.6	78.3	44.0	49.0	51.0
85606	COCHISE	91.7	88.2	0.2	0.3	0.8	1.0	12.6	19.0	3.8	3.9	4.4	4.9	4.2	14.3	34.2	26.9	3.5	85.0	55.5	49.1	50.9
85607	DOUGLAS	62.5	59.9	1.4	1.4	0.5	0.5	78.4	84.1	8.7	8.4	8.0	8.7	7.6	26.0	21.2	9.8	1.6	69.8	30.9	51.8	48.2
85610	ELFRIDA	81.6	76.3	0.9	0.9	0.7	0.8	32.5	43.4	5.4	5.3	6.2	8.0	6.1	18.7	29.8	18.7	1.8	77.9	45.2	50.7	49.3
85611	ELGIN	91.2	87.8	0.3	0.3	0.3	0.5	16.2	25.7	3.6	3.9	4.8	3.4	2.8	16.1	44.1	19.2	2.0	85.4	53.8	50.3	49.7
85613	FORT HUACHUCA	61.7	55.1	20.4	22.7	3.2	3.8	14.7	20.9	12.9	8.8	5.4	13.0	24.0	32.9	2.6	0.4	0.0	70.6	22.1	58.8	41.2
85614	GREEN VALLEY	95.8	92.4	0.3	0.4	0.5	0.7	8.2	15.6	2.4	2.5	2.6	2.6	1.9	9.2	21.5	47.4	10.0	90.9	67.9	45.0	55.0
85615	HEREFORD	86.2	82.4	1.4	1.7	1.1	1.4	15.3	22.6	6.0	6.0	6.7	7.1	4.9	21.9	33.3	13.0	1.0	76.3	43.0	49.7	50.3
85616	HUACHUCA CITY	80.7	76.1	4.3	4.7	1.1	1.4	14.7	21.3	5.8	6.3	6.8	7.2	5.7	21.8	30.8	14.2	1.4	76.7	42.3	49.0	51.0
	ARIZONA	75.5	72.3	3.1	3.3	1.9	2.4	25.3	30.8	7.6	7.1	6.8	6.9	6.8	26.9	24.0	12.0	1.8	74.5	35.8	49.7	50.3
	UNITED STATES	75.1	72.0	12.3	12.7	3.8	4.6	12.5	15.7	6.8	6.7	6.6	7.1	6.9	27.0	26.0	10.9	1.9	75.7	36.9	49.2	50.8

ZIP CODE #	POST OFFICE NAME	2009 Per Capita Income	2009 HH Income Base	2009 HOUSEHOLD INCOME DISTRIBUTION (%) Less than $25,000	$25,000 to $49,999	$50,000 to $99,999	$100,000 to $149,999	$150,000 or More	MEDIAN HOUSEHOLD INCOME 2009	2014	2009 National Centile	2009 State Centile	2009 Home Value Base	2009 HOME VALUE DISTRIBUTION (%) Less than $50,000	$50,000 to $89,999	$90,000 to $174,999	$175,000 to $399,999	$400,000 or More	2009 Median Home Value
85273	SUPERIOR	17361	1472	36.8	26.9	32.6	2.2	1.4	34146	37961	16	20	988	39.8	44.3	13.9	1.4	0.6	56392
85281	TEMPE	20843	27255	31.4	31.2	28.4	6.8	2.3	38967	41486	30	30	7335	16.5	13.0	55.9	13.5	1.2	114274
85282	TEMPE	29305	21458	14.7	25.5	39.0	15.6	5.2	59370	62020	77	72	11518	10.1	5.8	56.5	26.9	0.6	142614
85283	TEMPE	31842	17107	12.2	20.4	40.3	18.0	9.1	66533	70284	85	80	9400	3.0	6.6	50.9	37.6	1.9	160417
85284	TEMPE	50012	6254	2.9	8.3	26.2	26.7	35.9	119717	122002	98	98	5692	0.3	0.9	10.4	66.4	22.0	276894
85286	CHANDLER	34702	13543	5.1	11.1	38.9	30.6	14.4	92282	94168	95	94	10768	6.0	1.2	25.6	58.6	8.6	215432
85287	TEMPE	9322	0	0.0	0.0	0.0	0.0	0.0	0	0	0	0	0	0.0	0.0	0.0	0.0	0.0	0
85292	WINKELMAN	18135	1230	28.8	31.0	31.6	5.1	3.5	42907	46400	42	43	992	59.5	23.1	13.2	2.2	2.0	40105
85293	CASA GRANDE	14914	1440	27.2	36.5	29.3	5.3	1.7	40450	42429	34	34	1049	42.4	31.6	19.4	5.9	0.7	56737
85294	CASA GRANDE	22918	2138	13.7	38.4	38.1	6.3	3.5	47435	51515	55	53	1591	12.2	16.5	46.3	23.9	1.1	119259
85295	GILBERT	29947	8612	2.7	15.0	36.3	34.8	11.1	92461	94914	95	94	7529	0.5	0.3	17.3	69.3	12.7	246735
85296	GILBERT	34769	11412	2.4	6.7	33.7	42.6	14.6	107072	108335	98	98	10198	0.7	0.4	27.7	67.2	4.0	203962
85297	GILBERT	31382	7275	6.4	9.2	38.0	32.9	13.6	94207	99504	96	94	6556	0.3	0.0	12.3	68.0	19.5	274774
85298	GILBERT	29709	6851	8.6	10.8	37.0	29.3	14.3	89277	93905	95	93	6183	0.4	2.3	13.0	66.6	17.8	268268
85301	GLENDALE	15643	21250	29.6	33.1	30.8	5.5	1.0	39297	41602	31	31	9631	24.8	26.5	44.2	4.2	0.3	88310
85302	GLENDALE	25396	15452	16.9	26.7	39.3	13.6	3.5	55718	58584	72	69	9358	3.9	12.1	69.5	14.1	0.4	132085
85303	GLENDALE	18881	10047	18.0	27.3	39.9	12.0	2.8	53866	56515	69	66	6168	3.8	11.9	70.8	12.9	0.6	124447
85304	GLENDALE	27500	10503	9.3	21.9	41.0	19.7	8.0	68393	72570	86	81	7515	0.0	2.6	68.5	27.6	1.3	148835
85305	GLENDALE	28431	2991	3.9	11.9	51.7	25.5	7.1	80820	84368	92	88	2404	7.3	2.5	70.5	18.4	1.2	145055
85306	GLENDALE	26744	9684	14.2	21.5	42.3	16.0	5.9	62979	65536	81	76	6058	2.0	7.2	67.0	22.3	1.6	140817
85307	GLENDALE	24184	3786	6.5	26.6	40.1	23.6	3.2	64438	67368	83	77	2447	2.7	6.5	54.2	31.8	4.8	155552
85308	GLENDALE	35849	25059	5.6	13.3	39.7	26.9	14.6	86363	88715	94	91	19709	1.5	2.5	41.1	50.7	4.1	185855
85309	LUKE AFB	2974	0	0.0	0.0	0.0	0.0	0.0	0	0	0	0	0	0.0	0.0	0.0	0.0	0.0	0
85310	GLENDALE	39622	7739	2.4	6.8	33.7	35.9	21.1	107025	107910	98	97	7127	0.9	1.5	31.7	58.6	7.3	203675
85321	AJO	19112	1896	34.9	37.9	21.6	3.3	2.4	32485	33910	12	17	1389	18.9	40.0	34.2	5.5	1.4	78873
85322	ARLINGTON	17184	203	29.6	34.5	26.6	5.4	3.9	34629	37143	17	21	141	31.2	14.2	40.4	11.3	2.8	95417
85323	AVONDALE	14322	10418	25.0	30.4	36.2	7.1	1.2	45448	49680	50	50	6539	15.6	24.8	41.6	16.8	1.1	106542
85324	BLACK CANYON CITY	25476	1681	30.0	28.9	29.8	6.4	5.0	41729	45690	38	38	1369	15.6	28.9	38.8	13.7	3.1	98297
85326	BUCKEYE	19679	16245	20.4	28.0	36.2	12.3	3.1	51335	55007	64	62	13208	7.9	17.3	37.0	34.8	2.9	143265
85328	CIBOLA	21066	572	28.5	24.1	37.1	10.3	0.0	44457	51401	47	47	357	53.8	4.2	35.0	3.6	3.4	45345
85331	CAVE CREEK	48991	11251	5.4	9.7	29.9	30.2	24.8	106321	107194	97	97	9744	2.1	0.6	8.3	60.7	28.3	289957
85332	CONGRESS	24664	1460	29.5	33.1	27.5	6.6	3.4	39820	43182	32	32	1225	13.1	24.4	35.9	16.7	9.8	109541
85333	DATELAND	12160	153	39.2	34.0	19.6	5.2	2.0	30163	31381	8	13	71	64.8	11.3	19.7	4.2	0.0	35500
85335	EL MIRAGE	17245	9048	16.1	34.7	34.9	11.8	2.5	49176	52470	59	56	6734	9.2	20.9	39.4	24.3	6.1	118655
85337	GILA BEND	20731	910	38.0	34.0	23.2	3.4	1.4	33427	35111	14	19	514	56.4	24.3	15.2	2.5	1.6	41316
85338	GOODYEAR	31214	13266	4.7	19.0	41.8	21.6	12.9	76633	79795	90	86	11434	2.6	2.2	59.3	32.1	3.8	154789
85339	LAVEEN	27069	10385	14.2	21.2	35.5	20.6	8.5	65096	68761	83	78	8565	3.2	13.8	25.5	51.4	6.1	196019
85340	LITCHFIELD PARK	32513	8434	10.4	23.0	44.6	14.8	7.2	74936	75949	89	84	6931	3.1	7.4	30.0	49.2	10.3	198966
85342	MORRISTOWN	19828	487	30.6	32.0	27.9	7.0	2.5	39560	42615	31	31	384	25.0	15.9	29.9	25.3	3.9	107353
85343	PALO VERDE	19020	43	30.2	30.2	27.9	7.0	4.7	39070	36525	30	30	30	30.0	13.3	40.0	13.3	3.3	96667
85344	PARKER	19958	7258	34.3	34.3	24.0	4.9	2.5	35049	36562	18	22	5686	30.0	25.9	35.0	7.1	1.9	78462
85345	PEORIA	24409	21017	13.4	24.9	43.7	14.5	3.5	61180	63416	79	75	15814	15.2	12.0	63.3	9.1	0.3	118199
85347	ROLL	15921	617	32.7	34.7	24.5	5.7	2.4	34483	36746	16	20	353	39.1	14.7	36.0	8.5	1.7	78158
85348	SALOME	16923	1202	43.3	35.0	16.6	3.1	2.1	27803	28428	5	10	1000	35.6	28.1	30.6	4.4	1.3	69434
85350	SOMERTON	10265	9462	38.8	36.7	20.1	3.6	0.8	31440	32235	10	16	6720	13.2	27.3	52.2	6.4	0.9	98647
85351	SUN CITY	32592	18170	24.3	36.3	29.8	6.5	3.0	41446	43800	38	37	15412	2.9	21.5	67.1	8.1	0.4	109206
85353	TOLLESON	16404	8611	20.1	30.0	39.1	9.2	1.7	49913	53435	61	59	6177	4.3	33.2	40.9	18.1	3.5	105719
85354	TONOPAH	18028	1019	28.0	32.9	27.6	8.7	2.8	40176	43346	33	33	698	33.2	16.2	37.0	10.5	3.2	90952
85355	WADDELL	27383	1633	8.3	14.5	35.8	34.3	7.2	85034	85808	94	90	1411	6.5	4.0	19.5	60.2	9.7	229011
85356	WELLTON	20178	3115	25.9	34.7	30.6	6.4	2.4	40220	43985	33	33	2261	27.7	19.1	40.7	11.2	1.3	95219
85361	WITTMANN	13395	1326	34.4	34.2	25.6	5.1	0.8	35786	37696	20	24	1027	27.2	26.4	34.8	10.7	1.0	82065
85362	YARNELL	23330	498	37.8	33.7	21.3	5.2	2.0	32244	33808	12	17	403	16.6	22.3	42.4	16.1	2.5	105810
85363	YOUNGTOWN	23812	3062	37.1	36.1	21.7	3.4	1.8	30632	30585	9	13	1769	10.8	47.9	37.6	3.0	0.7	85048
85364	YUMA	19793	29451	27.3	30.0	29.6	9.0	4.0	43398	47697	44	44	18217	15.3	14.9	55.7	12.7	1.5	112974
85365	YUMA	24285	18006	19.7	31.4	34.0	9.9	4.9	48915	52548	59	55	14373	18.7	15.0	40.7	22.3	3.3	121568
85367	YUMA	27501	9056	22.4	34.9	33.8	5.7	3.2	44352	48532	46	46	8115	9.4	21.4	49.5	18.2	1.5	115059
85373	SUN CITY	34672	8301	16.2	29.8	38.7	11.9	3.5	53062	56654	68	65	6956	7.4	8.2	58.5	24.9	0.9	138093
85374	SURPRISE	30060	19878	10.9	23.2	48.1	13.6	4.2	63169	66201	81	77	16870	4.2	7.3	46.8	36.4	5.4	161423
85375	SUN CITY WEST	39990	16955	11.9	30.7	39.7	12.0	5.6	55848	59187	72	69	15341	0.4	2.9	48.0	45.0	3.6	172844
85379	SURPRISE	25215	12003	4.5	10.4	67.4	15.9	1.8	66866	69407	85	80	10137	0.0	0.2	71.2	27.2	1.4	154069
85381	PEORIA	33018	8421	7.3	12.7	37.4	32.2	10.4	86678	88925	94	92	6838	1.0	2.6	42.0	51.1	3.3	181769
85382	PEORIA	34900	16373	8.1	17.2	41.7	24.3	8.7	74345	78409	89	84	13681	1.8	4.2	39.0	53.4	1.7	182308
85383	PEORIA	37486	11406	5.4	12.7	31.6	31.5	18.8	100371	100666	97	96	10422	0.9	1.1	17.9	61.9	18.2	258361
85387	SURPRISE	28374	3853	16.0	32.0	38.9	9.5	3.6	51334	54392	64	62	3428	5.4	13.7	40.1	35.9	5.0	152895
85388	SURPRISE	23790	6994	11.9	31.6	42.3	8.6	5.7	57824	62148	75	71	6006	0.2	0.6	75.7	22.1	1.3	143817
85390	WICKENBURG	22862	4909	30.0	30.0	29.3	7.9	2.8	41173	44765	37	36	3267	26.1	9.0	26.9	31.9	6.1	133121
85392	AVONDALE	31478	12032	3.0	8.9	47.6	29.4	11.1	84328	85634	94	89	10081	3.2	1.1	49.2	46.0	0.5	171090
85395	GOODYEAR	39907	9655	7.0	13.2	40.9	24.3	14.5	75892	79184	90	85	8375	1.5	2.1	20.4	66.0	10.0	230205
85396	BUCKEYE	21407	2333	13.5	26.3	41.1	14.0	5.1	61975	64330	80	75	2079	0.6	9.6	57.1	29.0	3.7	150241
85501	GLOBE	20667	5306	27.6	27.5	35.5	7.3	2.0	44842	47090	48	48	4077	23.9	32.0	35.2	8.0	0.8	80605
85530	BYLAS	6493	516	58.1	28.1	12.6	1.2	0.0	20665	20976	2	4	240	61.3	30.0	8.8	0.0	0.0	37083
85533	CLIFTON	19195	427	18.5	34.9	37.2	8.7	0.7	46725	50901	53	52	332	15.1	26.8	52.4	5.1	0.6	100633
85534	DUNCAN	16365	1148	33.9	32.2	28.7	4.5	0.7	37095	40227	24	26	888	23.6	26.7	44.4	4.7	0.6	89143
85535	EDEN	13299	26	30.8	26.9	38.5	3.8	0.0	40000	42380	33	32	20	5.0	10.0	75.0	10.0	0.0	120833
85539	MIAMI	20160	2391	32.0	30.2	29.0	5.9	2.8	38919	41343	29	29	1833	31.3	32.2	28.6	6.7	1.1	72847
85540	MORENCI	21071	1496	14.8	25.3	50.2	8.1	1.6	54410	55391	70	67	321	22.4	33.3	40.5	3.7	0.0	80263
85541	PAYSON	24075	9848	27.7	30.1	31.2	7.1	3.9	41849	44664	39	39	7766	10.6	12.1	43.6	27.6	6.2	139014
85542	PERIDOT	7472	1701	57.4	24.4	16.7	0.6	0.8	21364	21799	2	4	1221	71.9	21.6	4.8	1.2	0.5	28274
85543	PIMA	14564	1321	32.4	29.4	32.9	4.1	1.2	37821	40938	26	27	1046	15.5	25.1	49.0	9.8	0.6	102340
85544	PINE	30202	1619	21.5	29.1	33.0	10.2	6.2	49302	51160	60	57	1386	4.4	8.4	37.7	43.4	6.1	173849
85545	ROOSEVELT	26959	54	44.4	29.6	22.2	1.9	1.9	28592	32315	6	11	47	25.5	25.5	25.5	17.0	6.4	85000
85546	SAFFORD	17810	6176	31.7	27.5	32.8	6.2	1.8	40932	44473	36	35	4618	17.0	27.6	44.8	9.8	0.7	96640
85550	SAN CARLOS	7298	623	50.2	23.8	23.3	2.2	0.5	24861	26119	3	6	400	51.3	35.8	11.5	0.0	1.5	48718
85552	THATCHER	17640	2027	25.8	32.3	31.9	7.0	3.1	42692	45931	41	42	1494	9.0	23.0	54.4	13.4	0.2	110959
85601	ARIVACA	25521	67	43.3	28.4	26.9	1.5	0.0	27552	31352	5	9	47	25.5	25.5	34.0	10.6	4.3	88333
85602	BENSON	21809	4588	28.7	32.8	29.3	7.0	2.2	40040	42342	33	33	3558	22.4	29.3	35.9	9.3	3.1	86791
85603	BISBEE	20331	4016	33.0	30.9	29.7	5.1	1.4	38091	40976	27	27	2666	12.4	40.5	39.5	6.4	1.2	86652
85606	COCHISE	20858	672	37.9	28.0	25.9	6.8	1.3	34854	36983	17	21	526	17.1	24.0	46.8	9.7	2.5	99592
85607	DOUGLAS	12120	6717	48.1	27.2	20.5	2.8	1.4	26192	26936	4	8	4139	24.7	34.6	36.8	3.7	0.2	77881
85610	ELFRIDA	15077	628	40.1	30.7	24.0	3.8	1.3	30091	31494	8	12	456	27.4	27.0	34.9	7.0	3.7	84118
85611	ELGIN	33505	326	17.2	18.7	37.4	16.3	10.4	64776	65354	83	78	254	3.9	6.3	23.2	44.1	22.4	228205
85613	FORT HUACHUCA	13455	686	12.2	45.9	36.3	4.8	0.7	45000	47933	48	49	22	18.2	27.3	36.4	18.2	0.0	93333
85614	GREEN VALLEY	34450	11721	17.1	30.5	37.1	9.4	5.8	51964	55634	66	63	9829	3.9	11.5	50.2	31.2	3.2	143788
85615	HEREFORD	23180	3166	18.0	26.9	40.0	12.3	2.8	53386	54709	69	65	2642	8.9	16.2	49.8	21.8	3.3	121161
85616	HUACHUCA CITY	18175	2757	30.8	35.7	26.2	6.3	1.1	38507	40722	28	28	2004	15.4	30.0	49.5	4.9	0.1	94292
	ARIZONA	26377		19.0	25.8	34.8	13.4	7.1	55275	58294				9.3	12.3	42.2	29.4	6.9	143619
	UNITED STATES	27277		20.9	24.4	35.3	11.7	7.6	54719	56938				9.3	13.1	31.6	32.6	13.5	162279

ZIP CODE #	POST OFFICE NAME	FINANCIAL SERVICES: Auto Loan	FINANCIAL SERVICES: Home Loan	FINANCIAL SERVICES: Invest-ments	FINANCIAL SERVICES: Retire-ment Plans	THE HOME: Home Improvements: Home Repair	THE HOME: Home Improvements: Lawn & Garden	THE HOME: Furnishings: Comput-ers & Hard-ware-Personal	THE HOME: Furnishings: Major Appli-ances	THE HOME: Furnishings: TV, Radio, Sound Equip-ment	THE HOME: Furnishings: Furni-ture	ENTERTAINMENT: Dine out/ Carry out	ENTERTAINMENT: Sports Equip-ment	ENTERTAINMENT: Fees & Tickets	ENTERTAINMENT: Toys & Games	ENTERTAINMENT: Travel	ENTERTAINMENT: Cable TV	PERSONAL: Apparel & Services	PERSONAL: Auto Repairs	PERSONAL: Health Insur-ance	PERSONAL: Pets & Supplies
85273	SUPERIOR	72	52	72	50	54	75	56	70	63	51	61	52	45	62	55	69	40	65	76	82
85281	TEMPE	73	50	46	54	47	49	81	58	75	71	76	52	64	76	62	72	54	70	59	74
85282	TEMPE	101	94	89	96	92	92	102	95	101	103	102	74	100	102	98	101	71	100	98	113
85283	TEMPE	122	115	102	117	110	104	121	111	118	124	120	89	118	122	114	115	85	116	106	132
85284	TEMPE	195	249	244	259	253	220	206	214	193	225	196	169	242	200	229	183	145	198	186	241
85286	CHANDLER	154	175	146	173	167	144	151	151	141	166	144	123	161	153	153	132	103	141	128	171
85287	TEMPE	0	0	0	0	0	0	0	0	0	0	0	0	0	0	0	0	0	0	0	0
85292	WINKELMAN	84	72	68	66	70	76	71	76	75	74	75	55	64	76	67	77	51	75	77	90
85293	CASA GRANDE	76	66	67	62	65	69	66	70	67	68	68	53	60	69	63	69	46	69	68	83
85294	CASA GRANDE	89	91	80	89	88	90	83	87	85	86	86	64	85	88	84	87	59	85	88	102
85295	GILBERT	142	170	145	169	163	142	144	145	134	156	137	117	158	143	150	126	98	136	124	164
85296	GILBERT	166	197	168	200	190	161	166	167	153	185	156	138	184	166	172	141	114	153	138	187
85297	GILBERT	154	173	142	169	163	141	150	150	140	164	143	121	158	152	151	131	102	141	128	170
85298	GILBERT	154	168	135	161	157	136	148	147	139	161	142	117	151	151	145	131	99	139	127	167
85301	GLENDALE	68	59	52	58	57	55	68	61	67	68	68	48	62	68	62	65	48	66	61	72
85302	GLENDALE	94	87	79	89	84	83	93	87	93	95	94	68	90	94	88	92	65	91	88	103
85303	GLENDALE	94	91	76	87	86	79	91	87	88	96	90	68	87	92	86	85	63	88	80	101
85304	GLENDALE	118	123	107	123	117	110	118	113	114	123	116	89	120	119	116	111	82	114	107	133
85305	GLENDALE	133	146	121	143	137	122	131	129	123	140	126	103	136	132	130	117	89	124	113	147
85306	GLENDALE	108	103	89	104	97	95	106	99	105	109	107	78	104	108	100	103	74	103	97	118
85307	GLENDALE	118	99	85	100	93	86	113	100	108	115	111	84	103	118	100	102	78	106	91	117
85308	GLENDALE	149	164	142	163	157	141	148	146	140	158	143	116	155	148	149	134	101	141	130	168
85309	LUKE AFB	0	0	0	0	0	0	0	0	0	0	0	0	0	0	0	0	0	0	0	0
85310	GLENDALE	175	210	183	212	203	175	177	179	164	195	167	145	197	176	185	153	122	166	151	201
85321	AJO	64	56	74	53	62	71	56	67	60	57	58	45	52	56	59	64	39	63	74	77
85322	ARLINGTON	83	78	66	74	74	74	77	76	77	80	77	58	72	80	72	77	53	77	75	91
85323	AVONDALE	83	72	60	65	70	65	76	75	76	81	78	53	68	78	69	75	54	77	70	85
85324	BLACK CANYON CITY	81	77	99	71	86	92	74	87	78	80	76	57	73	71	80	82	51	83	97	99
85326	BUCKEYE	97	92	84	89	90	93	87	92	89	90	89	69	84	92	85	90	61	89	90	108
85328	CIBOLA	81	76	64	72	72	72	75	74	75	78	75	56	70	78	70	75	52	75	73	88
85331	CAVE CREEK	173	210	205	213	212	186	178	185	168	196	169	143	201	173	194	160	123	172	165	208
85332	CONGRESS	71	74	97	67	86	92	68	83	73	76	71	50	74	65	80	79	47	79	100	92
85333	DATELAND	68	55	41	46	52	51	55	59	59	61	60	36	48	60	49	61	42	59	57	65
85335	EL MIRAGE	97	83	97	76	85	89	82	94	85	85	85	66	74	83	83	87	58	90	90	106
85337	GILA BEND	76	50	73	47	49	74	53	67	61	50	60	52	40	62	49	68	40	63	70	82
85338	GOODYEAR	143	155	141	150	149	139	138	143	132	146	134	111	142	138	141	128	94	135	129	163
85339	LAVEEN	113	128	121	131	128	124	115	120	112	119	113	91	124	113	123	111	80	115	116	139
85340	LITCHFIELD PARK	126	119	128	119	119	121	121	123	120	123	122	94	118	121	121	120	84	124	122	144
85342	MORRISTOWN	78	66	90	62	72	87	65	80	71	66	69	55	60	67	69	76	46	75	88	92
85343	PALO VERDE	84	79	67	75	75	75	78	77	78	81	78	59	73	81	73	78	54	78	75	92
85344	PARKER	63	64	75	58	71	74	60	70	64	67	62	44	63	59	67	67	42	67	80	78
85345	PEORIA	103	105	92	100	102	96	99	100	97	106	98	74	99	100	98	96	68	98	97	114
85347	ROLL	81	61	67	55	60	72	62	73	68	63	68	51	52	69	58	73	46	70	73	84
85348	SALOME	55	52	67	48	58	63	50	59	53	54	51	39	49	48	54	56	35	57	66	67
85350	SOMERTON	62	52	40	44	50	46	54	55	55	59	57	37	48	56	49	55	40	56	51	60
85351	SUN CITY	61	75	98	65	91	96	65	83	72	77	69	43	80	60	84	79	46	78	110	87
85353	TOLLESON	86	83	71	74	81	70	82	82	79	89	81	60	77	81	79	76	57	82	73	91
85354	TONOPAH	83	78	67	74	74	75	76	76	77	79	77	58	72	80	72	77	53	76	75	91
85355	WADDELL	122	153	134	153	147	132	128	130	120	135	123	104	144	125	138	116	88	124	116	149
85356	WELLTON	76	68	86	63	74	82	68	78	72	72	71	53	66	69	72	76	48	76	87	89
85361	WITTMANN	73	54	77	52	57	76	55	70	61	52	60	52	45	60	55	67	40	64	73	83
85362	YARNELL	65	61	79	57	68	74	58	69	62	63	60	45	58	57	64	65	41	66	77	79
85363	YOUNGTOWN	55	51	61	49	56	62	55	60	59	55	58	40	54	55	57	64	39	60	71	68
85364	YUMA	87	78	71	74	76	76	80	81	81	84	82	59	75	82	76	81	57	82	79	93
85365	YUMA	94	90	102	86	95	98	88	96	89	92	89	68	86	87	91	92	61	94	101	110
85367	YUMA	69	77	99	69	90	95	69	85	75	79	73	49	79	65	84	81	49	81	105	93
85373	SUN CITY	77	92	114	81	108	111	80	99	87	94	84	55	95	75	99	93	56	93	124	106
85374	SURPRISE	98	108	119	99	118	117	97	110	100	110	99	70	107	94	109	103	67	105	124	121
85375	SUN CITY WEST	81	100	131	86	122	128	87	111	96	103	92	58	106	80	112	105	61	104	146	117
85379	SURPRISE	110	120	102	117	114	102	108	107	102	116	104	85	112	109	108	98	73	103	96	122
85381	PEORIA	136	161	149	162	160	144	139	143	133	151	135	111	155	137	149	128	96	135	132	162
85382	PEORIA	126	137	134	132	139	132	124	131	122	135	123	95	131	123	130	121	85	125	131	148
85383	PEORIA	151	182	172	180	184	165	154	162	147	173	148	123	174	151	167	141	106	150	152	180
85387	SURPRISE	76	86	114	75	103	112	76	97	85	88	81	54	89	72	95	93	54	91	125	105
85388	SURPRISE	90	107	118	100	118	122	94	109	98	103	96	69	108	90	111	103	65	104	129	121
85390	WICKENBURG	79	72	96	68	79	88	70	83	74	73	73	57	67	69	76	79	49	80	91	96
85392	AVONDALE	149	163	133	157	153	134	144	143	135	156	139	114	148	146	143	128	97	136	124	163
85395	GOODYEAR	143	152	169	149	161	153	138	150	137	153	137	106	147	134	149	136	96	143	149	169
85396	BUCKEYE	96	108	93	112	105	106	97	101	95	97	96	79	103	98	102	95	67	97	100	118
85501	GLOBE	84	69	85	68	72	88	71	82	76	68	74	60	63	75	70	81	50	78	88	97
85530	BYLAS	45	36	27	30	35	34	36	39	39	40	40	24	31	40	32	40	28	39	38	43
85533	CLIFTON	92	67	93	65	69	93	69	86	76	64	75	65	56	76	68	83	49	80	90	102
85534	DUNCAN	74	54	64	54	54	71	58	66	64	55	62	51	48	65	54	69	42	64	71	80
85535	EDEN	78	56	80	54	58	79	57	73	63	53	62	54	46	63	56	70	41	67	76	86
85539	MIAMI	81	66	81	63	68	83	67	78	72	66	71	57	59	71	66	77	47	74	84	92
85540	MORENCI	93	88	82	85	84	87	83	88	84	86	84	66	79	87	81	84	58	84	85	103
85541	PAYSON	83	76	104	74	84	93	74	88	78	77	77	60	72	73	80	83	52	84	94	101
85542	PERIDOT	49	39	31	33	37	38	39	42	42	43	43	27	34	43	35	44	30	42	41	47
85543	PIMA	77	59	74	58	60	76	59	72	65	57	64	53	50	65	58	70	42	67	74	85
85544	PINE	101	90	135	89	101	113	86	106	90	88	89	73	83	84	96	96	60	99	110	122
85545	ROOSEVELT	59	57	72	52	63	68	54	64	57	58	56	42	53	52	59	60	37	61	71	73
85546	SAFFORD	75	68	65	66	67	73	68	71	70	68	69	53	63	72	65	72	48	70	73	84
85550	SAN CARLOS	57	46	34	38	44	43	46	49	50	51	50	30	40	50	41	51	35	50	48	54
85552	THATCHER	80	76	72	75	76	82	73	78	77	74	76	56	72	77	72	79	52	76	82	92
85601	ARIVACA	53	50	64	46	56	60	48	57	51	52	49	37	47	46	52	54	33	54	63	65
85602	BENSON	74	68	85	64	74	81	69	78	73	71	71	53	66	68	72	77	48	76	86	90
85603	BISBEE	73	57	75	56	59	77	60	72	66	55	64	53	51	65	59	72	43	68	78	84
85606	COCHISE	67	64	81	59	71	76	60	71	64	65	62	47	60	58	66	68	42	69	79	82
85607	DOUGLAS	59	52	41	45	50	47	51	53	53	57	54	36	47	54	48	53	37	54	50	59
85610	ELFRIDA	68	54	74	51	57	72	54	67	59	53	58	48	47	57	55	64	38	62	71	78
85611	ELGIN	119	114	164	112	129	140	106	129	112	113	110	86	108	102	120	118	75	121	137	147
85613	FORT HUACHUCA	88	46	34	53	41	39	83	58	78	77	82	57	63	94	60	72	58	73	52	70
85614	GREEN VALLEY	81	94	117	84	110	115	83	102	90	95	87	59	97	78	102	97	58	97	127	111
85615	HEREFORD	98	87	100	85	89	98	84	95	87	84	86	69	78	87	84	90	58	90	94	111
85616	HUACHUCA CITY	78	58	78	57	60	79	61	74	67	57	65	55	51	66	60	72	43	69	78	87
	ARIZONA	104	101	100	99	102	100	101	102	101	105	102	76	100	101	101	100	71	102	102	118
	UNITED STATES	100	100	100	100	100	100	100	100	100	100	100	100	100	100	100	100	100	100	100	100

ZIP CODE #	POST OFFICE NAME	COUNTY FIPS CODE	POPULATION 2000	POPULATION 2009	POPULATION 2014	2000-2009 ANNUAL RATE % Rate	2000-2009 ANNUAL RATE State Centile	HOUSEHOLDS 2000	HOUSEHOLDS 2009	HOUSEHOLDS 2014	HOUSEHOLDS % Annual Rate 2000-2009	HOUSEHOLDS 2009 Average HH Size	FAMILIES 2000	FAMILIES 2009	FAMILIES % Annual Rate 2000-2009
85617	MC NEAL	003	1224	1282	1312	0.5	17	518	558	577	0.8	1.65	346	365	0.6
85618	MAMMOTH	021	1841	2542	3220	3.5	73	592	874	1119	4.3	2.91	464	663	3.9
85619	MOUNT LEMMON	019	132	135	155	0.2	8	58	59	68	0.2	2.25	45	44	-0.2
85621	NOGALES	023	22910	24832	26152	0.9	31	6646	7242	7653	0.9	3.40	5489	5921	0.8
85622	GREEN VALLEY	019	5211	6297	7095	2.1	57	2836	3436	3879	2.1	1.83	2104	2473	1.8
85623	ORACLE	021	4337	6505	8233	4.5	82	1719	2891	3735	5.8	2.22	1290	2101	5.4
85624	PATAGONIA	023	1250	1560	1746	2.4	61	584	735	824	2.5	2.12	352	431	2.2
85625	PEARCE	003	2008	2021	2048	0.1	6	936	959	979	0.3	2.09	621	620	0.0
85629	SAHUARITA	019	6178	21374	28152	14.4	93	2058	6905	9092	14.0	3.08	1585	5254	13.8
85630	SAINT DAVID	003	2716	3250	3537	2.0	55	1050	1274	1395	2.1	2.54	731	867	1.9
85631	SAN MANUEL	021	5441	5768	6517	0.6	22	1835	2101	2407	1.5	2.75	1484	1642	1.1
85632	SAN SIMON	003	1478	1724	1868	1.7	47	624	739	803	1.8	2.31	425	491	1.6
85634	SELLS	019	7483	8610	9204	1.5	45	1993	2318	2492	1.6	3.69	1521	1710	1.3
85635	SIERRA VISTA	003	28920	34268	36567	1.9	52	12085	14396	15401	1.9	2.36	7846	9306	1.9
85637	SONOITA	023	1028	1355	1541	3.0	68	454	603	686	3.1	2.23	333	431	2.8
85638	TOMBSTONE	003	2032	2417	2632	1.9	52	932	1116	1217	2.0	2.16	570	665	1.7
85640	TUMACACORI	023	666	981	1150	4.3	81	311	458	538	4.3	2.14	195	281	4.0
85641	VAIL	019	6540	17223	21770	11.0	91	2437	6148	7787	10.5	2.80	1913	4699	10.2
85643	WILLCOX	009	8987	9763	10180	0.9	31	3034	3346	3512	1.1	2.67	2156	2332	0.9
85645	AMADO	023	2771	3407	4311	2.3	60	1085	1346	1698	2.4	2.52	761	913	2.0
85648	RIO RICO	023	10766	17383	20735	5.3	84	3049	4914	5863	5.3	3.54	2622	4179	5.2
85650	SIERRA VISTA	003	14011	16907	18717	2.1	57	5140	6323	7080	2.3	2.53	4256	5136	2.1
85653	MARANA	019	8978	14177	16657	5.1	83	2944	4781	5672	5.4	2.88	2226	3479	4.9
85658	MARANA	021	2107	8220	10653	15.9	94	867	3408	4430	15.9	2.41	671	2591	15.7
85701	TUCSON	019	4480	4843	5097	0.8	27	2281	2462	2598	0.8	1.87	826	838	0.2
85704	TUCSON	019	30561	33928	35893	1.1	37	13745	15482	16494	1.3	2.14	8182	8708	0.7
85705	TUCSON	019	57084	59393	61129	0.4	14	25122	26144	26984	0.4	2.25	12672	12304	-0.3
85706	TUCSON	019	49132	58983	64007	2.0	55	14890	17632	19147	1.8	3.34	11553	13192	1.4
85707	TUCSON	019	6058	5427	5298	-1.2	1	1452	1294	1265	-1.2	3.65	1395	1239	-1.3
85709	TUCSON	019	31	31	35	0.0	4	14	14	16	0.0	2.21	8	8	0.0
85710	TUCSON	019	53509	56081	57868	0.5	17	24116	25515	26458	0.6	2.19	14065	14115	0.0
85711	TUCSON	019	43437	44830	45920	0.3	11	18136	18850	19402	0.4	2.35	10462	10242	-0.2
85712	TUCSON	019	30654	31989	32972	0.5	17	15022	15836	16409	0.6	1.95	6820	6657	-0.3
85713	TUCSON	019	45189	48873	51137	0.9	31	14908	16180	17014	0.9	2.89	10228	10645	0.4
85714	TUCSON	019	13670	14386	14839	0.6	22	4127	4389	4549	0.7	3.25	3212	3307	0.3
85715	TUCSON	019	19478	21349	22473	1.0	34	8724	9683	10264	1.1	2.19	5402	5663	0.5
85716	TUCSON	019	33834	34175	34737	0.1	6	16728	17012	17366	0.2	2.00	7451	7005	-0.7
85718	TUCSON	019	26550	28810	30306	0.9	31	12174	13456	14292	1.1	2.10	7313	7544	0.3
85719	TUCSON	019	36286	37461	38465	0.3	11	17241	17895	18437	0.4	2.02	6356	6082	-0.5
85721	TUCSON	019	6049	6039	6044	0.0	4	2	2	2	0.0	2.50	0	0	0.0
85730	TUCSON	019	37453	39748	41385	0.6	22	14106	15128	15830	0.8	2.62	10111	10448	0.4
85735	TUCSON	019	8263	10565	11920	2.7	66	2988	3879	4404	2.9	2.72	2229	2793	2.5
85736	TUCSON	019	6195	6702	6999	0.9	31	2184	2379	2504	0.9	2.81	1559	1626	0.5
85737	TUCSON	019	17950	21507	23531	2.0	55	6991	8295	9088	1.9	2.58	5438	6325	1.6
85739	TUCSON	019	11354	16111	19816	3.9	78	4770	7383	9409	4.8	2.15	3722	5497	4.3
85741	TUCSON	019	31125	34264	36121	1.0	34	11537	12860	13653	1.2	2.65	8253	8860	0.8
85742	TUCSON	019	22693	27299	29863	2.0	55	8149	9809	10761	2.0	2.78	6414	7478	1.7
85743	TUCSON	019	18563	30432	36463	5.5	85	6721	11057	13262	5.5	2.75	5244	8474	5.3
85745	TUCSON	019	31071	36385	39309	1.7	47	12038	14350	15640	1.9	2.49	7944	8990	1.3
85746	TUCSON	019	38205	46822	51526	2.2	58	12424	15258	16869	2.2	3.06	9517	11309	1.9
85747	TUCSON	019	13714	27395	33241	7.8	89	4676	9580	11688	8.1	2.86	3927	7764	7.6
85748	TUCSON	019	15434	18653	20485	2.1	57	6019	7316	8068	2.1	2.55	4575	5386	1.8
85749	TUCSON	019	18613	21352	22819	1.5	45	6842	7942	8529	1.6	2.68	5543	6268	1.3
85750	TUCSON	019	24804	26053	26963	0.5	17	10846	11465	11917	0.6	2.26	7251	7341	0.1
85755	TUCSON	019	8917	14540	17342	5.4	84	3966	6458	7728	5.4	2.25	3192	5063	5.1
85756	TUCSON	019	21401	30380	34159	3.9	78	5280	8186	9591	4.9	3.01	4171	6056	4.1
85757	TUCSON	019	8998	17805	21686	7.7	89	2466	5062	6230	8.1	3.52	2081	4111	7.6
85901	SHOW LOW	017	24600	30243	33038	2.3	60	7768	9672	10648	2.4	3.11	6023	7397	2.2
85920	ALPINE	001	267	290	302	0.9	31	136	149	156	1.0	1.95	98	106	0.9
85922	BLUE	011	2	2	2	0.0	4	2	2	2	0.0	1.00	2	0	-100.0
85924	CONCHO	001	2111	2366	2489	1.2	40	862	973	1030	1.3	2.43	606	674	1.2
85925	EAGAR	001	4530	4720	4823	0.4	14	1570	1649	1696	0.5	2.84	1202	1246	0.4
85928	HEBER	017	3683	4788	5400	2.9	68	1568	2065	2347	3.0	2.32	1128	1465	2.9
85929	LAKESIDE	017	7267	8302	8976	1.4	44	2783	3237	3525	1.6	2.55	2060	2349	1.4
85935	PINETOP	017	3470	4937	5700	3.9	78	1424	2056	2389	4.1	2.40	1069	1519	3.9
85936	SAINT JOHNS	001	4090	4193	4266	0.3	11	1155	1193	1221	0.4	3.26	918	938	0.2
85937	SNOWFLAKE	017	9009	11482	12961	2.7	66	2812	3652	4154	2.9	3.13	2223	2849	2.7
85938	SPRINGERVILLE	001	2797	2899	2947	0.4	14	1057	1106	1132	0.5	2.44	775	798	0.3
86001	FLAGSTAFF	005	35894	42153	45185	1.8	49	13551	16283	17639	2.0	2.42	7415	8683	1.7
86004	FLAGSTAFF	005	33883	37258	39202	1.0	34	11936	13290	14062	1.2	2.80	8607	9494	1.1
86021	COLORADO CITY	015	4637	6606	7768	3.9	78	740	1040	1224	3.7	6.35	661	926	3.7
86022	FREDONIA	005	1280	1394	1475	0.9	31	456	506	539	1.1	2.75	343	377	1.0
86025	HOLBROOK	017	5829	5997	6077	0.3	11	1950	2021	2056	0.4	2.88	1425	1454	0.2
86030	HOTEVILLA	017	253	301	319	1.9	52	73	87	93	1.9	3.46	48	56	1.7
86033	KAYENTA	017	8437	10154	11043	2.0	55	2173	2648	2897	2.2	3.83	1767	2128	2.0
86034	KEAMS CANYON	017	3466	4131	4444	1.9	52	952	1149	1243	2.1	3.54	730	869	1.9
86035	LEUPP	005	2738	3056	3267	1.2	40	695	790	851	1.4	3.87	556	626	1.3
86036	MARBLE CANYON	005	594	672	717	1.3	42	287	331	356	1.6	2.03	156	177	1.4
86038	MORMON LAKE	005	97	97	115	0.0	4	46	46	55	0.0	2.11	30	30	0.0
86039	KYKOTSMOVI VILLAGE	017	109	132	146	2.1	57	33	41	45	2.4	3.22	25	30	2.0
86040	PAGE	005	8953	9941	10580	1.1	37	2827	3176	3404	1.3	3.13	2210	2459	1.2
86042	POLACCA	017	1627	1927	2036	1.8	49	418	501	533	2.0	3.85	339	401	1.8
86043	SECOND MESA	017	1587	1878	1985	1.8	49	516	618	657	2.0	3.04	375	442	1.8
86044	TONALEA	005	120	121	124	0.1	6	36	36	37	0.0	3.36	25	24	-0.4
86045	TUBA CITY	005	11715	13022	13860	1.2	40	3001	3383	3624	1.3	3.82	2434	2720	1.2
86046	WILLIAMS	005	8479	10109	10967	1.9	52	3391	4070	4437	2.0	2.47	2229	2631	1.8
86047	WINSLOW	017	19138	21058	22260	1.0	34	5333	5895	6253	1.1	3.28	4078	4463	1.0
86053	KAIBETO	005	7487	8433	9028	1.3	42	1791	2037	2193	1.4	4.12	1472	1662	1.3
86054	SHONTO	017	2033	2402	2542	1.8	49	557	668	711	2.0	3.60	434	513	1.8
86301	PRESCOTT	025	16734	21313	24433	2.6	64	7264	9325	10786	2.7	2.17	4400	5636	2.7
86303	PRESCOTT	025	16398	20723	22881	2.6	64	7777	9464	10429	2.1	2.14	4563	5434	1.9
86305	PRESCOTT	025	14600	18607	20824	2.7	66	6111	7836	8801	2.7	2.27	4079	5113	2.5
86314	PRESCOTT VALLEY	025	25748	34960	40029	3.4	72	9679	13085	14997	3.3	2.66	7108	9406	3.1
86315	PRESCOTT VALLEY	025	1086	7238	9788	22.8	98	410	2644	3581	22.3	2.74	340	2013	21.2
86320	ASH FORK	025	860	1223	1459	3.9	78	305	429	513	3.8	2.85	225	309	3.5
	ARIZONA					2.9					2.7	2.69			2.5
	UNITED STATES					1.0					1.1	2.59			0.9

#	POST OFFICE NAME	RACE (%) White 2000	White 2009	Black 2000	Black 2009	Asian/Pacific 2000	Asian/Pacific 2009	% Hispanic Origin 2000	% Hispanic Origin 2009	2009 AGE DISTRIBUTION (%) 0-4	5-9	10-14	15-19	20-24	25-44	45-64	65-84	85+	18+	MEDIAN AGE 2009	% 2009 Males	% 2009 Females
85617	MC NEAL	70.5	64.4	8.0	8.2	0.2	0.3	25.2	34.6	2.3	2.3	3.4	4.6	9.9	39.5	25.7	11.2	1.1	89.4	38.4	74.2	25.8
85618	MAMMOTH	62.3	60.0	0.1	0.2	0.5	0.6	70.8	76.0	8.4	8.1	7.9	8.3	7.3	24.1	23.8	10.7	1.2	70.5	32.9	50.1	49.9
85619	MOUNT LEMMON	92.4	90.4	0.8	0.7	2.3	3.0	6.9	9.6	3.7	4.4	5.2	6.7	3.7	18.5	37.0	18.5	2.2	82.2	49.8	47.4	52.6
85621	NOGALES	77.5	78.3	0.4	0.4	0.4	0.4	92.5	95.3	9.0	8.8	8.7	9.1	7.4	24.5	22.0	9.1	1.3	67.6	29.9	47.4	52.6
85622	GREEN VALLEY	98.7	98.1	0.1	0.2	0.4	0.5	2.5	4.1	0.7	0.7	0.8	1.0	0.8	3.7	19.9	62.5	10.0	97.2	72.3	45.3	54.7
85623	ORACLE	79.1	77.7	0.2	0.3	0.6	0.7	34.2	36.5	4.9	5.1	5.6	5.7	5.2	18.8	29.7	23.1	1.8	81.0	48.8	48.6	51.4
85624	PATAGONIA	87.7	84.2	0.2	0.3	0.4	0.5	33.8	47.4	4.2	4.6	5.3	4.4	3.7	15.6	38.7	20.8	2.8	82.7	51.3	48.3	51.7
85625	PEARCE	91.0	87.6	0.4	0.5	0.6	0.8	13.0	19.8	3.7	3.8	4.2	4.9	4.5	14.0	35.0	26.8	3.1	85.2	55.7	49.0	51.0
85629	SAHUARITA	86.0	73.3	0.7	0.5	0.6	0.3	25.4	44.7	6.7	6.9	7.3	7.1	5.3	26.2	28.8	10.5	1.2	74.7	38.4	49.9	50.1
85630	SAINT DAVID	92.9	90.3	0.6	0.8	0.5	0.6	9.9	15.1	5.5	6.5	7.6	7.2	3.2	16.3	31.6	19.3	2.7	75.5	47.7	49.9	50.1
85631	SAN MANUEL	68.4	64.0	0.3	0.5	0.4	0.5	48.0	54.9	8.2	8.0	7.5	7.7	6.8	24.7	24.3	11.8	1.0	71.6	33.7	50.5	49.5
85632	SAN SIMON	79.7	73.2	0.2	0.2	0.8	0.8	32.8	44.3	6.6	6.7	7.0	6.0	5.2	19.6	27.2	20.1	1.6	75.8	43.9	52.0	48.0
85634	SELLS	2.2	2.2	0.1	0.1	0.3	0.4	3.1	3.3	10.4	10.4	9.6	9.7	8.4	24.6	19.5	6.8	0.6	63.1	26.1	48.1	51.9
85635	SIERRA VISTA	75.9	72.2	8.1	8.6	4.1	4.8	18.1	24.6	6.4	6.0	5.9	6.2	6.8	24.4	27.0	15.3	2.0	77.8	40.2	47.9	52.1
85637	SONOITA	91.1	87.7	0.5	0.6	0.3	0.4	15.8	24.4	4.0	4.4	5.2	3.5	2.1	17.2	43.2	18.3	2.3	83.8	52.7	49.8	50.2
85638	TOMBSTONE	88.9	85.3	0.5	0.7	0.8	1.0	20.0	29.3	3.8	3.4	6.1	5.9	3.0	17.2	39.1	19.2	2.4	82.7	51.4	49.9	50.1
85640	TUMACACORI	78.0	73.7	0.1	0.1	1.0	1.1	45.7	59.0	5.0	5.4	5.7	5.3	3.9	19.7	32.8	20.0	2.2	80.6	48.8	49.2	50.8
85641	VAIL	88.0	83.2	0.7	0.9	0.6	0.8	17.0	24.9	6.3	6.8	7.3	7.0	4.8	24.5	31.7	10.5	1.0	75.2	40.5	50.0	50.0
85643	WILLCOX	76.6	71.3	1.9	1.9	0.5	0.6	35.1	46.1	6.4	6.4	6.3	6.2	6.6	26.5	26.3	13.3	2.0	76.9	38.0	53.6	46.4
85645	AMADO	84.7	81.0	0.3	0.4	0.5	0.7	34.0	42.7	5.2	5.3	5.6	5.7	4.8	17.6	30.7	21.8	3.3	80.4	49.8	48.1	51.9
85648	RIO RICO	68.0	66.9	0.5	0.5	1.1	1.0	79.1	86.5	9.9	9.6	9.1	9.1	7.7	26.6	21.5	5.9	0.6	65.8	28.1	49.1	50.9
85650	SIERRA VISTA	79.1	76.2	7.5	7.3	3.3	4.2	13.5	19.3	6.2	6.0	6.1	7.3	7.5	21.2	29.4	14.9	1.4	77.8	41.2	50.1	49.9
85653	MARANA	77.9	70.3	2.7	3.4	0.7	1.0	25.1	35.4	6.5	6.5	6.7	7.7	7.0	26.7	27.4	10.5	1.1	75.7	36.9	51.4	48.6
85658	MARANA	92.1	89.5	0.7	1.0	0.6	0.9	11.6	16.8	5.0	5.5	6.0	5.6	3.6	21.9	34.2	16.7	1.5	80.0	46.4	49.8	50.2
85701	TUCSON	68.0	63.8	3.8	3.8	1.6	1.7	48.9	57.5	5.4	4.6	4.5	5.6	9.6	33.2	25.1	10.3	1.9	82.5	36.1	50.3	49.7
85704	TUCSON	90.5	87.5	1.3	1.6	2.2	3.0	11.2	15.8	3.9	3.9	4.3	5.1	5.8	22.3	30.1	19.4	5.4	84.8	48.6	46.4	53.6
85705	TUCSON	70.1	64.3	3.6	3.9	2.8	3.4	32.2	40.5	7.6	6.4	5.6	6.6	10.5	29.7	21.7	10.2	1.8	76.9	32.3	50.3	49.7
85706	TUCSON	51.6	48.1	2.6	2.7	0.8	0.8	77.0	81.9	10.8	9.9	8.6	8.9	8.7	28.5	18.1	5.9	0.6	65.3	26.8	49.8	50.2
85707	TUCSON	67.3	60.7	13.9	15.9	4.2	5.4	15.0	20.3	16.9	11.9	8.1	7.2	16.5	36.5	2.7	0.3	0.0	59.9	21.8	54.2	45.8
85709	TUCSON	71.9	67.7	3.1	3.2	3.1	3.2	43.8	54.8	6.5	6.5	6.5	6.5	6.5	25.8	25.8	16.1	0.0	74.2	38.8	48.4	51.6
85710	TUCSON	84.2	80.0	4.0	4.7	2.2	2.9	15.4	21.2	5.6	5.2	5.3	5.8	6.6	24.5	25.7	17.2	4.0	80.4	42.5	47.0	53.0
85711	TUCSON	72.9	67.5	4.6	5.0	2.8	3.5	29.7	37.5	7.4	6.5	6.0	6.6	8.6	28.4	24.2	10.1	2.3	76.4	34.4	48.7	51.3
85712	TUCSON	81.0	76.1	3.8	4.5	2.8	3.8	18.8	25.1	6.0	5.1	4.7	5.0	7.5	29.4	24.2	13.5	4.6	81.4	38.8	47.7	52.3
85713	TUCSON	51.6	48.4	6.3	6.2	1.0	1.1	62.6	68.2	8.1	7.8	7.4	7.5	6.9	26.2	21.4	12.5	2.0	72.1	33.7	48.4	51.6
85714	TUCSON	43.6	41.5	1.6	1.5	0.5	0.5	86.6	89.8	9.0	8.8	8.3	8.9	7.3	26.9	20.3	9.2	1.3	68.4	30.2	49.2	50.8
85715	TUCSON	87.6	83.9	2.4	2.9	2.7	3.7	12.1	16.8	5.0	5.0	5.5	5.8	5.4	24.2	29.3	16.7	3.0	80.9	44.2	47.7	52.3
85716	TUCSON	79.1	74.0	3.5	4.0	2.9	3.7	21.0	27.6	6.3	5.3	4.8	5.5	10.1	32.7	24.9	8.4	1.9	80.8	34.3	49.5	50.5
85718	TUCSON	91.8	89.1	1.1	1.4	3.1	4.4	7.5	10.8	3.2	3.4	4.1	5.1	6.6	18.5	34.0	20.3	4.8	86.3	51.3	47.4	52.6
85719	TUCSON	77.0	71.6	3.1	3.5	5.3	6.8	20.0	26.3	4.9	4.0	3.4	8.6	21.5	31.1	18.0	6.8	1.7	85.5	28.1	51.2	48.8
85721	TUCSON	81.6	76.1	3.3	4.0	8.1	11.2	10.1	14.2	0.0	0.0	0.0	72.0	26.1	1.3	0.4	0.1	0.0	99.4	18.5	41.6	58.4
85730	TUCSON	76.5	71.3	6.7	7.5	3.3	4.1	20.2	26.7	7.5	7.3	7.0	7.0	6.9	28.1	24.4	10.5	1.3	73.9	34.9	48.6	51.4
85735	TUCSON	77.0	71.1	0.9	1.1	0.3	0.4	33.9	43.9	6.8	6.6	6.6	6.8	5.8	23.5	30.1	12.5	1.2	75.9	40.5	49.5	50.5
85736	TUCSON	73.7	68.1	0.6	0.7	0.5	0.6	36.7	45.8	6.7	6.3	6.5	7.9	8.6	23.9	29.3	9.8	1.0	75.7	36.4	51.2	48.8
85737	TUCSON	92.1	89.4	1.2	1.4	2.3	3.3	8.8	12.7	5.5	6.0	6.8	6.9	4.0	22.4	33.0	14.0	1.3	77.0	43.9	48.5	51.5
85739	TUCSON	90.7	89.5	0.5	0.7	0.6	0.9	14.5	16.2	3.5	3.6	3.9	4.2	3.3	15.6	27.4	35.5	3.0	86.3	58.2	48.2	51.8
85741	TUCSON	85.4	81.1	1.8	2.1	2.3	3.0	19.1	26.0	7.1	6.8	6.9	7.2	7.1	29.8	26.4	7.5	1.2	74.8	34.6	49.1	50.9
85742	TUCSON	89.0	85.6	1.6	2.0	1.8	2.4	13.7	19.3	6.9	7.4	7.5	7.2	4.5	26.9	29.1	9.4	1.2	73.6	38.8	48.5	51.5
85743	TUCSON	87.3	82.4	1.5	2.2	1.8	3.1	15.3	21.9	8.4	7.9	7.8	6.9	5.0	29.0	25.9	8.5	0.6	71.2	35.7	49.4	50.6
85745	TUCSON	66.9	63.8	3.0	3.1	2.0	2.4	47.9	54.1	6.5	6.3	6.2	6.1	6.3	29.2	27.5	10.6	1.4	77.5	37.2	48.1	51.9
85746	TUCSON	56.4	52.0	2.9	2.9	1.0	1.2	59.2	67.4	9.1	8.6	8.0	7.9	7.1	28.0	22.3	7.9	1.0	69.5	30.9	48.8	51.2
85747	TUCSON	81.9	78.3	4.8	4.4	2.4	2.7	16.5	22.1	8.6	8.4	8.2	7.0	5.0	29.6	25.6	7.0	0.6	70.2	35.2	49.7	50.3
85748	TUCSON	88.4	84.5	2.7	3.3	2.9	4.1	10.8	15.6	5.4	6.0	6.6	6.3	4.5	24.1	33.1	12.7	1.4	78.0	43.1	48.7	51.3
85749	TUCSON	93.2	90.8	1.1	1.3	2.0	2.8	7.8	11.1	4.1	5.4	6.9	7.5	4.1	19.4	38.1	13.2	1.2	78.6	46.3	50.0	50.0
85750	TUCSON	90.7	87.6	1.4	1.7	3.8	5.2	7.3	10.5	4.1	4.3	5.0	5.7	5.4	20.4	34.7	18.1	2.2	82.9	48.2	48.1	51.9
85755	TUCSON	95.0	93.2	0.9	1.1	1.6	2.3	4.7	7.0	3.7	3.8	4.0	3.7	2.2	13.0	32.5	33.6	3.5	86.2	58.5	48.0	52.0
85756	TUCSON	59.4	59.2	4.5	4.2	0.5	0.7	58.2	60.4	6.3	6.1	5.8	6.7	8.1	32.4	22.1	11.3	1.2	77.8	34.5	56.1	43.9
85757	TUCSON	39.7	45.5	1.0	1.2	0.3	0.3	47.7	63.5	9.1	8.9	8.7	8.5	7.8	27.4	22.3	6.8	0.6	68.1	29.3	49.1	50.9
85901	SHOW LOW	52.0	51.1	0.3	0.3	0.3	0.5	5.9	8.2	9.0	8.7	8.5	8.8	6.9	23.0	24.1	10.0	0.9	68.0	31.9	48.6	51.4
85920	ALPINE	92.9	91.4	0.4	0.3	0.7	0.7	8.2	10.7	4.1	4.5	5.2	4.8	3.4	16.6	37.2	23.1	1.0	82.8	52.3	50.7	49.3
85922	BLUE	100.0	100.0	0.0	0.0	0.0	0.0	50.0	50.0	0.0	0.0	0.0	0.0	0.0	50.0	50.0	0.0	0.0	100.0	47.5	50.0	50.0
85924	CONCHO	85.5	83.3	1.2	1.3	0.6	0.7	11.5	15.0	5.3	6.3	6.7	6.1	3.1	16.4	39.6	15.5	0.8	77.3	48.1	51.7	48.3
85925	EAGAR	87.0	85.0	0.4	0.4	0.6	0.7	14.2	18.4	7.3	7.2	8.4	8.4	5.8	20.8	28.9	11.8	1.3	71.4	38.5	49.1	50.9
85928	HEBER	95.4	94.0	0.1	0.1	0.2	0.4	5.4	8.1	3.9	4.3	5.0	5.5	3.7	16.2	34.4	25.4	1.7	83.4	52.5	50.6	49.4
85929	LAKESIDE	88.9	85.3	0.7	0.9	0.5	0.6	11.8	17.2	6.2	6.9	7.6	7.2	4.4	21.9	31.5	13.1	1.3	74.5	41.9	50.0	50.0
85935	PINETOP	91.2	89.0	0.9	1.2	0.4	0.6	8.1	11.2	4.7	5.2	6.1	6.5	2.6	17.4	37.6	18.4	1.5	79.8	49.7	49.9	50.1
85936	SAINT JOHNS	79.3	76.5	1.0	1.0	0.4	0.4	23.8	30.0	8.3	7.8	8.3	8.1	7.3	24.4	24.8	9.9	1.2	70.5	32.7	52.0	48.0
85937	SNOWFLAKE	89.1	86.8	0.5	0.7	0.4	0.6	8.0	11.6	9.6	9.4	9.3	8.7	5.4	22.2	25.2	9.2	1.1	66.0	31.4	50.3	49.7
85938	SPRINGERVILLE	83.1	80.6	1.1	1.1	0.4	0.6	18.6	23.6	7.0	7.1	7.4	7.0	6.1	24.0	27.4	12.7	1.3	73.7	38.0	51.9	48.1
86001	FLAGSTAFF	82.7	79.8	1.6	1.8	1.3	1.7	12.0	15.8	6.0	5.0	5.0	8.1	19.0	29.1	21.3	5.8	0.7	80.7	28.4	50.1	49.9
86004	FLAGSTAFF	75.8	73.1	1.3	1.3	1.0	1.2	17.0	21.0	7.7	7.0	7.0	7.2	7.8	29.5	26.5	6.7	0.5	73.9	33.1	49.4	50.6
86021	COLORADO CITY	94.1	93.5	0.1	0.2	0.2	0.3	2.6	3.6	21.1	17.2	13.9	10.1	6.3	22.0	7.8	1.5	0.2	41.3	14.2	50.6	49.4
86022	FREDONIA	86.6	85.2	0.9	1.0	0.2	0.2	1.6	2.2	7.7	7.7	7.7	8.2	6.7	23.7	27.3	10.0	0.9	71.7	35.4	50.6	49.4
86025	HOLBROOK	61.0	57.5	2.2	2.7	1.0	1.3	21.9	28.5	8.6	8.8	8.7	10.2	5.9	23.3	24.3	9.0	1.3	67.1	31.6	47.9	52.1
86030	HOTEVILLA	1.6	1.3	0.0	0.0	0.0	0.0	2.4	2.7	9.3	9.0	9.0	11.3	9.6	21.3	20.9	8.3	1.3	65.8	26.5	48.5	51.5
86033	KAYENTA	4.4	4.0	0.1	0.2	0.1	0.1	0.9	1.1	10.6	10.4	10.6	10.8	8.5	24.3	18.9	5.4	0.5	61.4	24.5	48.5	51.5
86034	KEAMS CANYON	5.7	5.3	0.1	0.1	0.1	0.1	2.5	2.8	10.3	9.2	9.0	10.2	8.4	23.6	21.6	6.9	0.9	65.6	27.1	49.0	51.0
86035	LEUPP	0.8	0.7	0.0	0.0	0.0	0.0	1.4	1.4	8.9	8.4	9.1	10.6	8.7	24.1	20.4	8.8	1.0	67.0	28.2	50.7	49.3
86036	MARBLE CANYON	83.3	81.4	0.3	0.3	0.8	1.2	2.0	2.8	5.4	5.5	6.0	4.5	4.6	23.1	36.2	14.1	0.7	80.5	45.6	53.0	47.0
86038	MORMON LAKE	68.4	67.0	0.0	0.0	1.0	1.0	6.1	7.2	8.2	7.2	8.2	6.2	3.1	27.8	33.0	6.2	0.0	71.1	40.6	49.5	50.5
86039	KYKOTSMOVI VILLAGE	3.7	4.5	1.8	2.3	0.0	0.0	5.5	6.1	9.1	8.3	9.1	9.8	9.8	24.2	21.2	6.8	1.5	65.9	27.8	47.0	53.0
86040	PAGE	51.4	49.4	0.3	0.3	0.7	0.9	3.8	4.9	8.1	8.8	9.7	9.4	6.5	25.5	24.5	6.9	0.7	67.1	30.7	49.5	50.5
86042	POLACCA	1.4	1.2	0.1	0.1	0.1	0.1	0.7	0.8	11.1	10.8	10.1	9.8	8.2	21.8	19.7	7.6	0.9	62.0	25.1	48.5	51.5
86043	SECOND MESA	3.8	3.7	0.5	0.6	0.1	0.2	1.4	1.7	7.1	8.6	8.6	8.2	6.2	22.1	26.9	10.4	1.8	70.9	35.6	48.2	51.8
86044	TONALEA	0.0	0.0	0.0	0.0	0.0	0.0	3.3	3.3	10.7	11.6	7.4	6.6	5.8	24.0	17.4	16.5	0.0	64.5	31.8	54.5	45.5
86045	TUBA CITY	4.2	3.9	0.1	0.1	0.2	0.2	2.4	2.6	10.2	9.5	10.2	11.0	8.6	25.1	19.0	5.5	0.8	63.1	25.3	49.1	50.9
86046	WILLIAMS	80.1	77.5	1.5	1.6	1.0	1.2	19.8	24.3	6.2	6.0	6.8	7.2	5.8	27.0	31.5	8.7	0.8	76.5	39.7	52.0	48.0
86047	WINSLOW	36.0	31.7	2.7	3.0	0.6	0.7	15.7	18.3	9.0	8.8	8.8	9.2	8.6	25.6	20.7	8.0	1.3	67.7	28.6	51.7	48.3
86053	KAIBETO	1.3	1.2	0.1	0.1	0.0	0.0	0.5	0.4	11.1	11.0	11.3	11.1	8.5	23.0	16.4	6.9	0.8	59.6	23.3	49.3	50.7
86054	SHONTO	1.4	1.3	0.0	0.0	0.0	0.0	0.8	0.9	9.7	10.2	11.3	10.7	7.0	22.8	19.8	7.5	1.0	61.7	25.9	50.7	49.3
86301	PRESCOTT	91.2	90.2	0.5	0.6	0.8	1.1	9.4	11.2	3.8	4.0	4.4	5.8	5.8	19.0	29.0	23.5	4.5	84.6	50.4	49.0	51.0
86303	PRESCOTT	94.7	93.9	0.4	0.4	0.6	0.8	6.0	7.7	3.0	3.2	3.5	3.6	3.5	16.5	34.9	28.0	3.8	88.2	56.6	48.3	51.7
86305	PRESCOTT	94.9	93.5	0.4	0.5	0.8	1.2	6.0	8.1	3.7	3.9	4.6	6.5	6.2	15.9	35.9	20.0	3.2	84.9	50.6	50.0	50.0
86314	PRESCOTT VALLEY	90.3	88.3	0.5	0.5	0.6	0.8	12.3	15.8	7.7	7.0	7.0	6.9	6.3	24.6	24.4	13.9	2.2	73.7	37.6	48.9	51.1
86315	PRESCOTT VALLEY	91.4	89.5	0.2	0.2	0.6	0.8	6.7	9.1	4.5	5.1	6.0	6.0	3.7	20.8	35.9	16.3	1.7	80.6	47.3	50.0	50.0
86320	ASH FORK	94.5	94.3	0.9	0.9	0.1	0.1	28.1	35.5	6.1	6.1	6.4	6.2	6.5	24.4	30.3	13.0	1.1	77.7	40.2	54.9	45.1
	ARIZONA	75.5	72.3	3.1	3.3	1.9	2.4	25.3	30.8	7.6	7.1	6.8	6.9	6.8	26.9	24.0	12.0	1.8	74.5	35.8	49.7	50.3
	UNITED STATES	75.1	72.0	12.3	12.7	3.8	4.6	12.5	15.7	6.8	6.7	6.6	7.1	6.9	27.0	26.0	10.9	1.9	75.7	36.9	49.2	50.8

85617-86320

#	POST OFFICE NAME	2009 Per Capita Income	2009 HH Income Base	2009 Household Income Distribution (%): Less than $25,000	$25,000 to $49,999	$50,000 to $99,999	$100,000 to $149,999	$150,000 or More	Median Household Income: 2009	2014	2009 National Centile	2009 State Centile	2009 Home Value Base	2009 Home Value Distribution (%): Less than $50,000	$50,000 to $89,999	$90,000 to $174,999	$175,000 to $399,999	$400,000 or More	2009 Median Home Value
85617	MC NEAL	27411	558	36.2	27.4	28.7	7.0	0.7	34581	36569	17	21	431	15.8	34.8	39.2	8.1	2.1	89306
85618	MAMMOTH	14511	874	33.2	36.3	24.8	5.1	0.6	36709	38325	23	25	635	40.3	41.4	16.1	1.1	1.1	57321
85619	MOUNT LEMMON	54389	59	11.9	13.6	30.5	23.7	20.3	89436	90933	95	93	48	0.0	6.3	8.3	60.4	25.0	275000
85621	NOGALES	12894	7242	43.3	27.5	21.2	5.0	3.1	28840	29562	6	11	4206	19.0	17.0	45.8	14.0	4.2	111236
85622	GREEN VALLEY	49133	3436	10.1	23.1	40.0	13.8	13.0	66129	67163	84	79	3169	0.9	2.8	28.0	58.4	9.9	215731
85623	ORACLE	32245	2891	18.6	25.7	34.0	13.6	8.0	57364	60036	74	70	2254	18.6	13.1	26.3	31.1	10.8	143846
85624	PATAGONIA	22552	735	34.6	28.4	28.4	5.7	2.9	35424	37757	19	22	503	31.4	15.1	24.5	23.9	5.2	105068
85625	PEARCE	21022	959	37.5	30.2	24.3	7.0	0.9	33053	34777	13	18	752	17.8	24.6	45.5	9.4	2.7	98028
85629	SAHUARITA	21712	6905	16.7	26.9	40.6	11.0	4.8	55357	56743	72	68	6164	3.5	7.7	39.1	46.1	3.6	174311
85630	SAINT DAVID	19472	1274	26.4	33.0	32.1	6.6	2.0	41592	44003	38	38	1001	25.5	19.4	41.7	11.1	2.4	99717
85631	SAN MANUEL	21265	2101	20.8	30.9	38.6	6.6	3.1	48645	51494	58	55	1615	30.2	40.5	27.4	1.1	0.7	66020
85632	SAN SIMON	15172	739	46.1	31.7	17.5	4.1	0.7	26875	27765	5	9	552	35.3	36.4	21.9	4.7	1.6	66250
85634	SELLS	8074	2318	54.5	25.5	17.3	2.3	0.3	20758	21324	2	4	1485	57.6	23.6	16.8	1.5	0.5	35054
85635	SIERRA VISTA	25111	14396	20.4	30.0	35.4	10.8	3.4	49599	53109	60	57	8315	6.4	13.7	60.8	18.1	1.1	124012
85637	SONOITA	39153	603	15.8	18.1	35.3	18.2	12.6	68088	68583	86	81	484	2.7	4.1	17.6	50.6	25.0	246154
85638	TOMBSTONE	20608	1116	36.5	27.7	29.7	4.1	2.0	35365	38383	19	22	778	13.6	23.8	53.3	7.5	1.8	103125
85640	TUMACACORI	27911	458	35.2	21.8	21.8	16.4	4.8	41447	45364	38	37	328	20.1	16.2	30.2	23.8	9.8	131061
85641	VAIL	25242	6148	11.8	28.9	41.3	12.3	5.7	60782	61537	79	74	5587	4.4	12.3	51.4	26.8	5.1	143757
85643	WILLCOX	16639	3346	36.0	26.7	29.6	6.3	1.4	38208	41044	27	28	2316	23.3	31.6	38.0	6.3	0.9	80508
85645	AMADO	28994	1346	26.2	24.1	26.7	13.1	9.9	49617	54753	60	58	1065	11.5	14.2	31.5	28.0	14.8	152500
85648	RIO RICO	15937	4914	19.0	35.5	35.5	7.0	3.0	45692	50070	50	50	3855	3.1	8.5	72.8	14.7	0.8	126634
85650	SIERRA VISTA	30128	6323	9.3	23.4	41.0	19.7	6.6	66502	67657	85	79	4825	3.5	10.4	42.3	38.1	5.6	163716
85653	MARANA	17488	4781	26.0	34.0	31.9	5.3	2.9	42355	44926	40	40	3701	14.7	25.5	50.6	7.0	2.3	99181
85658	MARANA	29209	3408	13.8	29.3	41.6	9.5	5.8	56817	58365	74	70	3111	3.6	11.8	46.3	31.4	6.9	152156
85701	TUCSON	18660	2462	48.3	31.0	16.8	2.7	1.3	25913	26547	4	8	642	1.9	13.6	53.3	26.9	4.4	132576
85704	TUCSON	33612	15482	15.2	26.6	37.8	12.9	7.5	59078	59941	76	72	9185	7.8	4.2	31.1	53.3	3.7	189656
85705	TUCSON	17433	26144	40.1	33.2	22.4	3.1	1.2	30924	32057	10	14	11496	42.7	22.4	31.0	3.4	0.5	64516
85706	TUCSON	11949	17632	37.4	34.8	24.0	2.8	1.1	31796	33009	11	17	9650	30.3	31.2	37.4	1.1	0.1	77274
85707	TUCSON	14770	1294	8.3	48.8	39.6	2.6	0.7	46617	49278	53	51	107	68.2	16.8	15.0	0.0	0.0	32500
85709	TUCSON	22903	14	21.4	35.7	35.7	7.1	0.0	45000	50000	48	49	12	0.0	16.7	75.0	8.3	0.0	133333
85710	TUCSON	25352	25515	21.2	33.7	35.9	6.6	2.6	45402	50068	49	50	14441	7.0	7.4	70.9	13.8	1.0	132536
85711	TUCSON	21607	18850	30.0	30.8	30.2	6.4	2.6	40393	42960	34	34	9276	1.1	14.6	66.3	17.1	0.9	120073
85712	TUCSON	24324	15836	30.1	35.0	28.1	4.5	2.3	37361	40387	25	27	6167	8.1	12.8	65.1	11.4	2.6	121777
85713	TUCSON	14890	16180	35.3	34.8	24.4	3.7	1.8	33509	35579	14	19	10163	21.2	41.8	32.6	3.8	0.6	74642
85714	TUCSON	12323	4389	37.6	34.6	24.1	3.0	0.8	33044	34596	13	18	2647	18.4	48.0	32.3	1.3	0.0	77127
85715	TUCSON	34744	9683	13.0	25.5	39.8	13.4	8.4	62473	63233	81	76	6463	3.7	7.4	35.5	48.2	5.1	179831
85716	TUCSON	25240	17012	32.4	32.9	25.2	5.6	3.9	36499	39107	22	24	6580	5.9	9.8	54.0	24.6	5.8	136264
85718	TUCSON	56919	13456	11.8	16.0	31.5	16.9	23.8	82190	83621	93	88	8323	1.2	1.5	8.3	44.9	44.2	368361
85719	TUCSON	21811	17895	40.2	30.0	21.6	5.1	3.1	31024	32476	10	14	5797	9.8	10.2	52.5	24.0	3.5	129950
85721	TUCSON	16734	0	0.0	0.0	0.0	0.0	0.0	0	17500	0	0	0	0.0	0.0	0.0	0.0	0.0	0
85730	TUCSON	22582	15128	15.0	34.4	39.8	7.9	3.0	50471	53140	62	60	10354	7.5	13.2	69.8	8.3	1.2	120899
85735	TUCSON	20177	3879	15.4	37.4	37.5	8.3	1.5	48001	51291	57	53	3256	17.0	22.1	50.6	10.0	0.3	101840
85736	TUCSON	18628	2379	28.8	29.9	31.1	7.1	3.1	40743	44391	35	35	1916	26.0	26.7	38.3	7.8	1.2	84301
85737	TUCSON	41101	8295	6.0	12.5	40.7	23.6	17.1	86511	87941	94	92	6747	1.0	3.3	18.0	66.5	11.2	235934
85739	TUCSON	41259	7383	10.5	21.2	39.6	15.7	13.0	68137	71254	86	81	6370	5.9	6.1	19.8	46.4	21.9	270035
85741	TUCSON	25721	12860	11.7	25.4	46.7	12.3	3.8	59485	60430	77	73	8557	4.3	4.3	73.7	17.4	0.3	141786
85742	TUCSON	32082	9809	6.6	15.4	48.3	20.7	9.0	75998	77330	90	86	8138	2.2	1.4	54.8	38.4	3.1	165949
85743	TUCSON	30844	11057	7.7	18.1	45.2	19.6	9.4	73076	76333	88	84	9364	3.6	10.5	51.1	30.3	4.5	148803
85745	TUCSON	27178	14350	20.1	25.9	35.2	12.5	6.3	54468	56755	70	67	9501	5.6	11.5	41.3	35.8	5.9	158266
85746	TUCSON	18214	15258	20.7	30.9	39.3	6.9	2.2	48265	51855	57	54	10997	16.2	15.4	62.0	6.0	0.4	110717
85747	TUCSON	29093	9580	4.7	19.2	50.9	19.0	6.2	71725	71684	88	83	8681	2.6	6.1	56.2	31.8	3.3	157855
85748	TUCSON	34597	7316	7.3	19.4	44.5	18.8	10.0	75096	75058	89	85	6007	0.1	0.7	46.8	46.0	6.4	178893
85749	TUCSON	45149	7942	7.4	12.0	30.7	27.2	22.7	99771	102115	97	95	6563	0.7	1.3	6.9	59.6	31.5	301580
85750	TUCSON	52198	11465	6.6	16.0	36.5	19.3	21.6	84537	85972	94	90	7606	0.7	0.2	9.7	55.4	34.0	322115
85755	TUCSON	42883	6458	6.0	17.1	42.5	22.2	12.2	79330	79809	92	87	6011	0.0	0.3	17.1	71.8	10.9	232116
85756	TUCSON	16496	8186	25.6	35.9	31.5	5.1	1.9	41350	45066	37	37	6553	17.0	35.5	41.1	5.7	0.7	87441
85757	TUCSON	14396	5062	26.4	30.7	34.6	6.0	2.3	43455	47811	44	45	4029	7.5	23.3	60.8	7.1	1.3	107359
85901	SHOW LOW	14081	9672	34.5	30.3	28.7	5.5	1.0	36854	38093	23	25	7018	22.8	17.8	45.9	11.2	2.3	102728
85920	ALPINE	28182	149	27.5	27.5	32.2	10.1	2.7	45282	50000	49	49	124	4.0	8.1	42.7	35.5	9.7	165625
85922	BLUE	0	0	0.0	0.0	0.0	0.0	0.0	0	0	0	0	0	0.0	0.0	0.0	0.0	0.0	0
85924	CONCHO	16492	973	42.5	26.3	24.0	6.5	0.6	30852	32293	9	13	864	23.4	30.4	37.5	7.2	1.5	85217
85925	EAGAR	18692	1649	25.7	29.5	34.0	9.3	1.6	44454	50283	47	47	1293	7.0	11.1	60.5	19.3	2.1	121324
85928	HEBER	20189	2065	29.8	32.2	31.7	4.4	1.9	41019	43613	36	36	1786	8.4	16.1	46.0	25.7	3.9	125581
85929	LAKESIDE	20292	3237	24.9	31.0	35.4	6.9	1.9	44129	49091	46	46	2450	6.3	15.1	52.9	22.9	2.8	127589
85935	PINETOP	32623	2056	17.0	21.7	35.0	19.0	7.3	62399	63181	80	76	1684	3.3	7.4	33.3	46.6	9.4	196581
85936	SAINT JOHNS	15352	1193	27.9	32.9	28.5	9.5	1.3	41771	45624	39	38	892	14.5	30.0	49.6	5.8	0.1	95698
85937	SNOWFLAKE	15968	3652	25.7	32.7	31.4	8.5	1.6	42634	46143	41	42	3006	11.8	17.8	56.1	11.9	2.5	113064
85938	SPRINGERVILLE	20043	1106	30.3	29.9	30.0	8.4	1.4	41995	45521	39	39	825	9.0	13.7	60.1	14.9	2.3	116585
86001	FLAGSTAFF	24841	16283	23.3	27.3	35.2	9.5	4.7	49390	52685	60	57	8036	9.4	7.7	26.3	44.2	12.3	193015
86004	FLAGSTAFF	27159	13290	14.6	24.0	38.3	15.8	7.3	62293	63206	80	76	8638	9.5	6.7	28.2	48.7	6.9	186941
86021	COLORADO CITY	7482	1040	27.9	41.1	23.7	4.5	2.9	35544	37460	19	23	582	13.6	14.1	41.4	27.8	3.1	138119
86022	FREDONIA	15916	506	27.9	43.3	24.5	3.4	1.0	36895	39628	23	26	388	29.4	38.7	27.3	3.6	1.0	74583
86025	HOLBROOK	17473	2021	31.7	30.6	28.0	7.3	2.4	39974	41009	32	32	1391	24.3	35.6	35.2	4.1	0.8	77903
86030	HOTEVILLA	9833	87	67.8	10.3	10.3	11.5	0.0	16724	16734	1	2	62	30.6	17.7	11.3	19.4	21.0	100000
86033	KAYENTA	11463	2648	42.0	24.9	22.5	9.4	1.3	33697	34978	15	19	1884	59.7	16.6	20.3	1.9	1.6	35915
86034	KEAMS CANYON	10616	1149	48.3	25.2	20.2	5.1	1.1	26470	27367	4	9	795	57.1	15.8	21.9	4.4	0.8	42938
86035	LEUPP	8655	790	49.1	27.7	20.5	2.5	0.1	25550	26255	4	7	617	52.8	22.5	14.9	8.6	1.1	45513
86036	MARBLE CANYON	26668	331	18.7	33.5	39.3	6.9	1.5	48302	51214	57	54	203	39.4	17.2	22.7	15.3	5.4	77813
86038	MORMON LAKE	22335	46	39.1	26.1	28.3	4.3	2.2	31099	34291	10	15	34	26.5	20.6	5.9	32.4	14.7	125000
86039	KYKOTSMOVI VILLAGE	8375	41	51.2	26.8	22.0	0.0	0.0	9762	9783	0	2	36	47.2	36.1	16.7	0.0	0.0	70000
86040	PAGE	22275	3176	19.2	23.1	35.2	16.0	6.4	59670	61174	77	73	2421	28.7	23.0	21.4	25.2	1.7	86327
86042	POLACCA	8404	501	45.5	31.9	19.4	3.0	0.2	26926	28143	5	9	430	57.9	26.7	14.0	1.2	0.2	43929
86043	SECOND MESA	9242	618	54.5	28.0	15.7	1.8	0.0	21610	22426	2	5	482	43.2	28.6	17.2	8.3	2.7	55893
86044	TONALEA	9891	36	11.1	83.3	5.6	0.0	0.0	31738	31885	11	16	33	51.5	9.1	12.1	21.2	6.1	14167
86045	TUBA CITY	13311	3383	31.5	23.9	35.1	7.4	2.1	44516	48728	47	48	2105	62.2	21.6	12.3	3.1	0.8	36985
86046	WILLIAMS	22444	4070	23.1	28.4	38.7	7.1	2.7	48623	52085	58	54	2357	20.7	20.1	31.1	21.4	6.7	109575
86047	WINSLOW	13451	5895	39.9	28.2	22.8	7.7	1.4	32540	33314	12	17	4198	30.7	30.2	31.8	4.2	3.0	75241
86053	KAIBETO	8781	2037	48.6	25.8	20.7	3.4	1.6	25804	26997	4	8	1717	68.0	19.9	9.7	2.0	0.3	28836
86054	SHONTO	10281	668	46.4	29.8	17.2	6.0	0.6	28074	28868	6	10	551	57.9	15.6	22.5	3.1	0.9	37738
86301	PRESCOTT	30096	9325	21.6	29.3	32.7	10.1	6.3	49204	52677	59	57	6355	4.3	9.3	39.5	41.0	5.9	167207
86303	PRESCOTT	30345	9464	21.3	28.9	32.7	11.0	6.2	49844	53231	61	58	6510	5.3	3.3	25.8	48.2	17.4	226538
86305	PRESCOTT	30250	7836	22.4	27.0	31.6	12.3	6.8	50642	54091	63	61	5815	13.7	6.3	16.9	43.2	19.9	231589
86314	PRESCOTT VALLEY	20481	13085	22.7	33.6	34.7	6.4	2.7	45643	49375	50	50	9033	3.5	16.1	62.8	16.9	0.6	125404
86315	PRESCOTT VALLEY	22654	2644	20.2	34.2	31.2	9.5	4.9	46785	50416	53	52	2439	0.2	9.3	43.0	40.1	7.4	170701
86320	ASH FORK	12127	429	43.8	34.0	20.3	1.6	0.2	28747	29618	6	11	334	37.7	29.3	26.0	5.1	1.8	69500
	ARIZONA	26377		19.0	25.8	34.8	13.4	7.1	55275	58294				9.3	12.3	42.2	29.4	6.9	143619
	UNITED STATES	27277		20.9	24.4	35.3	11.7	7.6	54719	56938				9.3	13.1	31.6	32.6	13.5	162279

ZIP CODE #	POST OFFICE NAME	Financial Services: Auto Loan	Financial Services: Home Loan	Financial Services: Investments	Financial Services: Retirement Plans	The Home: Home Improvements: Home Repair	The Home: Home Improvements: Lawn & Garden	The Home: Furnishings: Computers & Hardware-Personal	The Home: Furnishings: Major Appliances	The Home: Furnishings: TV, Radio, Sound Equipment	The Home: Furnishings: Furniture	Entertainment: Dine out/Carry out	Entertainment: Sports Equipment	Entertainment: Fees & Tickets	Entertainment: Toys & Games	Entertainment: Travel	Entertainment: Cable TV	Personal: Apparel & Services	Personal: Auto Repairs	Personal: Health Insurance	Personal: Pets & Supplies
85617	MC NEAL	65	62	79	57	69	74	59	70	62	64	61	46	58	57	64	66	41	67	78	80
85618	MAMMOTH	74	55	57	49	53	64	56	65	62	59	62	45	46	63	51	66	42	63	65	75
85619	MOUNT LEMMON	164	198	199	203	201	187	173	179	166	182	168	135	193	166	190	163	120	172	171	206
85621	NOGALES	70	62	49	54	60	56	61	63	63	67	64	42	55	64	56	63	44	63	60	70
85622	GREEN VALLEY	114	129	173	120	153	159	114	140	123	132	120	80	133	107	140	132	81	133	171	153
85623	ORACLE	120	97	131	94	103	126	95	116	103	94	102	83	85	101	98	111	68	108	123	137
85624	PATAGONIA	71	67	87	62	74	80	64	76	67	68	66	50	62	62	70	71	44	72	83	87
85625	PEARCE	65	62	79	57	69	74	59	69	62	64	61	45	58	57	64	66	41	67	77	79
85629	SAHUARITA	103	100	90	99	98	102	93	99	95	96	95	73	92	98	92	97	65	95	99	117
85630	SAINT DAVID	73	69	88	64	77	83	66	78	70	71	68	51	65	64	72	74	46	75	87	89
85631	SAN MANUEL	86	85	77	80	82	85	82	85	83	83	83	63	80	84	81	84	58	84	87	98
85632	SAN SIMON	60	46	64	44	48	63	46	58	51	44	50	42	39	50	47	55	33	54	61	68
85634	SELLS	46	37	31	36	35	40	40	40	45	42	44	28	37	45	36	47	30	42	44	48
85635	SIERRA VISTA	86	81	79	81	80	84	85	83	86	84	86	63	82	86	82	87	59	85	87	99
85637	SONOITA	123	126	174	125	144	150	114	136	121	127	118	86	123	109	131	126	81	129	150	154
85638	TOMBSTONE	65	62	79	57	69	75	59	70	63	64	61	46	58	58	65	67	41	67	78	80
85640	TUMACACORI	102	79	112	77	84	107	78	98	86	76	84	72	68	84	81	93	56	91	103	116
85641	VAIL	101	111	99	112	108	107	100	104	98	102	98	81	104	100	104	97	68	99	101	121
85643	WILLCOX	76	58	75	55	59	77	59	71	65	57	64	53	49	65	57	71	43	67	75	85
85645	AMADO	110	103	132	98	113	119	98	114	102	105	101	78	96	96	106	106	69	109	120	130
85648	RIO RICO	85	87	73	80	83	73	82	81	78	88	80	61	80	82	79	75	56	80	73	92
85650	SIERRA VISTA	114	113	121	114	118	116	109	114	109	115	110	83	112	110	113	109	76	112	115	131
85653	MARANA	85	70	75	67	69	81	69	78	73	69	73	58	61	75	66	77	49	74	79	93
85658	MARANA	115	95	147	94	104	123	94	118	98	90	97	86	84	94	102	105	65	109	118	137
85701	TUCSON	49	38	37	41	37	39	54	44	53	49	53	36	47	52	46	52	37	51	47	54
85704	TUCSON	96	101	108	102	104	106	101	101	102	103	103	74	106	98	105	105	72	103	111	118
85705	TUCSON	59	46	45	47	45	47	58	52	59	57	59	41	51	59	51	59	41	57	54	63
85706	TUCSON	61	52	44	49	50	46	58	54	57	60	59	41	52	59	53	56	42	58	51	62
85707	TUCSON	93	48	36	56	43	41	87	60	82	81	86	60	66	98	63	75	61	77	54	73
85709	TUCSON	66	76	72	74	76	82	67	74	72	66	71	52	74	70	73	76	49	71	84	84
85710	TUCSON	75	75	75	76	76	80	77	77	80	76	80	57	79	78	78	82	55	79	85	91
85711	TUCSON	73	64	60	67	62	65	74	67	75	72	75	53	70	75	69	75	52	73	71	81
85712	TUCSON	69	56	56	59	56	59	70	62	71	68	71	49	64	70	64	71	50	69	68	76
85713	TUCSON	64	60	55	54	60	59	59	62	61	64	61	42	57	60	58	62	42	62	64	70
85714	TUCSON	63	55	45	49	54	51	56	57	57	60	58	39	51	58	52	58	41	58	55	64
85715	TUCSON	105	109	111	111	110	108	109	107	107	111	108	81	112	106	111	107	76	108	108	125
85716	TUCSON	73	60	57	63	58	59	77	64	75	73	76	54	69	75	68	73	53	73	66	79
85718	TUCSON	159	177	206	184	191	173	172	172	165	183	165	130	187	160	186	161	120	170	166	197
85719	TUCSON	65	46	44	50	44	48	75	54	69	64	70	48	59	69	57	67	49	65	57	69
85721	TUCSON	0	0	0	0	0	0	0	0	0	0	0	0	0	0	0	0	0	0	0	0
85730	TUCSON	87	87	76	86	84	81	85	83	84	89	85	63	85	86	83	82	59	83	81	97
85735	TUCSON	85	79	83	75	82	86	75	83	79	79	78	58	72	78	76	82	53	80	87	97
85736	TUCSON	80	76	72	71	75	76	74	77	75	78	75	56	71	76	72	76	51	76	77	90
85737	TUCSON	146	171	171	174	174	160	148	155	143	162	144	118	165	145	160	139	103	146	147	176
85739	TUCSON	129	130	155	128	141	146	120	135	125	130	124	91	125	119	130	130	85	130	145	156
85741	TUCSON	103	100	85	99	95	89	100	95	97	104	99	74	97	101	94	94	68	96	89	112
85742	TUCSON	125	144	129	143	140	129	126	129	121	134	123	100	136	126	132	118	87	123	121	148
85743	TUCSON	130	136	114	131	129	119	122	124	118	131	120	96	122	126	120	115	83	118	113	143
85745	TUCSON	96	96	90	96	95	93	97	94	96	99	97	72	98	97	96	96	69	96	94	110
85746	TUCSON	84	82	73	78	79	76	80	80	79	84	80	60	77	81	77	77	55	80	76	93
85747	TUCSON	122	134	113	132	128	120	119	121	115	125	116	95	124	120	121	111	81	116	113	140
85748	TUCSON	118	142	132	143	140	132	123	127	119	129	121	96	137	122	133	118	86	122	121	146
85749	TUCSON	159	198	200	204	202	184	169	176	161	180	163	134	194	162	188	157	118	167	163	201
85750	TUCSON	155	175	198	180	186	170	168	169	161	177	162	127	182	156	182	158	116	167	164	194
85755	TUCSON	133	140	190	138	161	165	126	149	133	142	130	93	138	119	145	139	89	142	165	168
85756	TUCSON	75	72	71	66	73	71	69	74	70	74	70	52	67	69	69	70	48	72	73	84
85757	TUCSON	77	74	62	72	70	71	72	71	73	75	73	54	70	76	68	73	50	72	71	85
85901	SHOW LOW	72	59	70	55	61	68	59	68	63	60	62	48	52	62	59	66	42	66	69	78
85920	ALPINE	91	73	118	72	80	97	73	93	77	69	76	68	64	73	79	82	50	86	92	108
85922	BLUE	0	0	0	0	0	0	0	0	0	0	0	0	0	0	0	0	0	0	0	0
85924	CONCHO	61	55	72	51	61	68	53	64	57	56	55	43	51	53	57	61	37	61	70	73
85925	EAGAR	83	79	77	78	78	83	74	80	75	75	75	59	71	77	74	78	52	77	80	94
85928	HEBER	77	63	100	62	69	82	62	79	65	59	65	57	55	62	68	70	43	73	79	91
85929	LAKESIDE	85	72	97	70	75	87	70	84	73	68	73	61	63	72	73	77	49	79	83	98
85935	PINETOP	119	109	161	108	123	136	103	126	108	107	107	86	102	100	116	114	72	119	133	145
85936	SAINT JOHNS	83	69	76	66	68	80	68	77	72	68	71	57	60	73	66	76	48	73	78	91
85937	SNOWFLAKE	82	71	80	69	72	81	68	78	72	68	71	57	62	73	68	75	48	74	78	92
85938	SPRINGERVILLE	81	70	79	68	71	81	68	77	71	67	71	57	61	72	67	75	48	73	78	91
86001	FLAGSTAFF	91	76	74	80	74	76	97	81	91	89	92	68	85	92	83	89	64	88	81	99
86004	FLAGSTAFF	109	111	102	112	108	102	110	105	106	113	108	84	111	110	109	104	76	107	100	124
86021	COLORADO CITY	76	70	62	68	68	71	66	70	69	69	69	51	63	71	63	70	47	68	70	83
86022	FREDONIA	70	63	56	62	62	65	61	64	63	64	64	47	58	66	58	65	43	63	64	76
86025	HOLBROOK	81	66	69	65	65	77	71	74	74	68	73	57	62	76	65	78	50	74	77	89
86030	HOTEVILLA	57	45	35	38	44	43	46	49	50	51	50	30	40	50	41	52	35	50	48	54
86033	KAYENTA	71	62	50	56	59	59	61	63	64	66	64	44	56	66	57	65	44	64	62	73
86034	KEAMS CANYON	61	49	38	43	47	47	51	53	55	55	55	35	45	56	46	56	38	54	53	59
86035	LEUPP	57	44	38	38	43	45	45	49	49	49	49	32	38	50	40	51	34	49	49	55
86036	MARBLE CANYON	85	77	69	75	75	78	76	78	78	78	79	58	72	81	72	80	54	77	79	93
86038	MORMON LAKE	79	63	102	62	69	83	63	80	66	59	65	58	55	63	68	70	43	74	79	93
86039	KYKOTSMOVI VILLAGE	45	36	27	30	35	34	36	39	39	41	40	24	32	40	32	41	28	39	38	43
86040	PAGE	103	107	95	103	104	99	99	101	97	105	98	76	100	100	99	96	69	99	95	117
86042	POLACCA	54	44	33	36	42	41	43	47	47	49	48	29	38	48	39	49	33	47	45	51
86043	SECOND MESA	52	34	49	32	34	50	37	46	42	35	41	35	28	43	34	47	27	43	48	56
86044	TONALEA	55	42	42	40	40	50	46	49	50	45	49	36	38	51	41	53	33	49	52	59
86045	TUBA CITY	80	74	60	68	70	69	71	73	73	76	74	52	68	75	67	73	51	73	71	84
86046	WILLIAMS	89	73	87	73	74	83	78	83	80	76	80	64	70	80	76	82	54	82	83	99
86047	WINSLOW	69	59	49	55	56	60	60	62	63	62	63	44	55	64	55	65	43	62	63	72
86053	KAIBETO	60	49	36	41	46	45	48	52	53	54	53	32	42	53	43	54	37	53	50	57
86054	SHONTO	62	50	37	42	48	47	50	53	54	56	55	33	43	55	45	56	38	54	52	59
86301	PRESCOTT	92	94	107	93	100	104	91	98	94	95	93	67	95	89	97	98	64	97	108	113
86303	PRESCOTT	93	90	118	89	100	106	88	99	92	93	91	67	89	85	95	97	62	97	110	114
86305	PRESCOTT	100	95	122	95	104	110	95	104	99	99	98	72	96	92	102	102	67	103	113	121
86314	PRESCOTT VALLEY	83	76	73	75	75	80	77	79	79	78	78	59	72	80	74	81	54	79	82	93
86315	PRESCOTT VALLEY	103	83	134	82	91	109	83	105	87	78	86	77	72	82	90	92	57	97	104	122
86320	ASH FORK	62	45	52	44	45	59	47	54	52	46	51	41	38	53	43	56	34	51	57	66
	ARIZONA	104	101	100	99	102	100	101	102	101	105	102	76	100	101	101	100	71	102	102	118
	UNITED STATES	100	100	100	100	100	100	100	100	100	100	100	100	100	100	100	100	100	100	100	100

ZIP CODE #	POST OFFICE NAME	COUNTY FIPS CODE	POPULATION 2000	POPULATION 2009	POPULATION 2014	2000-2009 ANNUAL RATE % Rate	2000-2009 ANNUAL RATE State Centile	HOUSEHOLDS 2000	HOUSEHOLDS 2009	HOUSEHOLDS 2014	HOUSEHOLDS % Annual Rate 2000-2009	HOUSEHOLDS 2009 Average HH Size	FAMILIES 2000	FAMILIES 2009	FAMILIES % Annual Rate 2000-2009
86321	BAGDAD	025	1487	1988	2305	3.2	70	540	718	833	3.1	2.77	409	532	2.9
86322	CAMP VERDE	025	9942	14305	16982	4.0	79	3807	5503	6575	4.1	2.53	2648	3730	3.8
86323	CHINO VALLEY	025	12374	17137	20119	3.6	74	4732	6485	7631	3.5	2.64	3557	4781	3.2
86324	CLARKDALE	025	4311	6025	7172	3.7	75	1898	2640	3152	3.6	2.27	1273	1536	2.1
86325	CORNVILLE	025	3950	5982	7100	4.6	82	1571	2398	2857	4.7	2.46	1095	1627	4.4
86326	COTTONWOOD	025	19571	24903	28330	2.6	64	7906	10012	11423	2.6	2.44	5250	6452	2.3
86327	DEWEY	025	6955	10191	12466	4.2	81	3076	4741	5817	4.8	2.15	2234	3372	4.6
86332	KIRKLAND	025	1623	2048	2308	2.5	62	718	901	1018	2.5	2.25	450	548	2.2
86333	MAYER	025	4705	6530	7573	3.6	74	1977	2750	3196	3.6	2.35	1302	1744	3.2
86334	PAULDEN	025	2820	4124	4977	4.2	81	926	1338	1617	4.1	3.08	711	1007	3.8
86335	RIMROCK	025	3362	4850	5802	4.0	79	1477	2119	2544	4.0	2.29	961	1340	3.7
86336	SEDONA	005	12626	15043	16533	1.9	52	6117	7240	7959	1.8	2.07	3582	4120	1.5
86337	SELIGMAN	025	946	1360	1624	4.0	79	435	622	744	3.9	2.19	269	373	3.6
86343	CROWN KING	025	154	215	255	3.7	75	84	117	139	3.6	1.84	47	64	3.4
86351	SEDONA	025	5526	7215	8215	2.9	68	2686	3502	3999	2.9	2.03	1681	2118	2.5
86401	KINGMAN	015	17847	23218	25881	2.9	68	6957	9040	10095	2.9	2.50	4804	6135	2.7
86403	LAKE HAVASU CITY	015	13809	17829	19820	2.8	67	6055	7691	8541	2.6	2.31	3944	4890	2.4
86404	LAKE HAVASU CITY	015	12795	17098	19527	3.2	70	5624	7439	8486	3.1	2.30	4031	5215	2.8
86406	LAKE HAVASU CITY	015	18566	24565	27782	3.1	69	7722	10143	11479	3.0	2.40	5727	7389	2.8
86409	KINGMAN	015	21041	25810	28273	2.2	58	8579	10415	11415	2.1	2.47	5832	6943	1.9
86411	HACKBERRY	015	754	1222	1474	5.4	84	330	537	647	5.4	2.28	233	371	5.2
86413	GOLDEN VALLEY	015	7669	10334	11758	3.3	71	3184	4247	4831	3.2	2.43	2170	2836	2.9
86426	FORT MOHAVE	015	8918	14956	18104	5.7	86	3403	5683	6904	5.7	2.63	2618	4297	5.5
86429	BULLHEAD CITY	015	4605	7997	9813	6.1	87	2041	3507	4308	6.0	2.28	1310	2183	5.7
86432	LITTLEFIELD	015	1584	2725	3344	6.0	87	597	994	1218	5.7	2.74	431	714	5.6
86434	PEACH SPRINGS	005	1325	1879	2207	3.8	76	341	483	569	3.8	3.81	280	392	3.7
86435	SUPAI	005	503	572	613	1.4	44	140	162	175	1.6	3.53	102	115	1.3
86436	TOPOCK	015	2055	3065	3664	4.4	82	1016	1499	1789	4.3	2.04	627	906	4.1
86440	MOHAVE VALLEY	015	6513	8094	8903	2.4	61	2516	3090	3395	2.2	2.60	1792	2169	2.1
86441	DOLAN SPRINGS	015	2006	2383	2809	1.9	52	979	1160	1369	1.9	2.05	580	673	1.6
86442	BULLHEAD CITY	015	29806	36808	40658	2.3	60	12189	14863	16464	2.2	2.47	7959	9488	1.9
86444	MEADVIEW	015	879	975	1096	1.1	37	445	489	549	1.0	1.99	319	344	0.8
86445	WILLOW BEACH	015	220	787	928	14.8	93	89	342	404	15.7	2.30	53	198	15.3
86502	CHAMBERS	001	2266	2619	2774	1.6	46	646	725	766	1.3	3.61	492	546	1.1
86503	CHINLE	001	12475	13128	13495	0.6	22	3322	3520	3644	0.6	3.63	2532	2648	0.5
86505	GANADO	001	24474	25544	26188	0.5	17	6802	7146	7372	0.5	3.53	5227	5419	0.4
86507	LUKACHUKAI	001	1773	1878	1931	0.6	22	486	518	536	0.7	3.63	373	392	0.5
86510	PINON	017	7935	9859	10944	2.4	61	2007	2502	2787	2.4	3.94	1585	1949	2.3
86514	TEEC NOS POS	001	5666	6011	6202	0.6	22	1596	1704	1770	0.7	3.53	1232	1297	0.6
86535	DENNEHOTSO	001	1783	1832	1862	0.3	11	441	456	466	0.4	4.02	347	354	0.2
86538	MANY FARMS	001	4824	5118	5284	0.6	22	1291	1377	1431	0.7	3.71	989	1042	0.6
86556	TSAILE	001	1894	1995	2046	0.6	22	462	490	507	0.6	3.86	363	381	0.5
	ARIZONA					2.9					2.7	2.69			2.5
	UNITED STATES					1.0					1.1	2.59			0.9

ZIP CODE #	POST OFFICE NAME	RACE (%) White 2000	White 2009	Black 2000	Black 2009	Asian/Pacific 2000	Asian/Pacific 2009	% Hispanic Origin 2000	% Hispanic Origin 2009	2009 AGE DISTRIBUTION (%) 0-4	5-9	10-14	15-19	20-24	25-44	45-64	65-84	85+	18+	MEDIAN AGE 2009	% 2009 Males	% 2009 Females
86321	BAGDAD	93.2	91.8	0.9	1.1	0.5	0.6	17.4	22.8	7.7	7.0	6.6	7.7	8.4	26.2	27.5	8.2	0.6	74.1	33.3	50.3	49.7
86322	CAMP VERDE	86.0	83.9	0.4	0.5	0.5	0.7	10.7	14.2	5.9	5.9	6.3	6.6	4.5	20.6	30.4	17.9	2.1	77.8	45.2	50.3	49.7
86323	CHINO VALLEY	93.8	92.5	0.2	0.3	0.3	0.4	9.9	13.6	6.3	6.4	7.0	7.1	5.3	22.4	30.2	14.1	1.3	75.8	41.6	49.6	50.4
86324	CLARKDALE	85.6	83.3	0.4	0.5	0.4	0.5	10.8	14.0	5.1	5.2	5.4	5.3	4.5	18.2	31.9	21.4	3.1	80.7	49.8	48.3	51.7
86325	CORNVILLE	92.6	90.7	0.4	0.4	0.6	0.7	9.2	12.7	4.5	4.9	5.7	6.0	4.1	20.4	37.7	15.2	1.5	81.1	47.6	50.1	49.9
86326	COTTONWOOD	88.4	85.7	0.4	0.4	0.5	0.7	15.6	20.4	6.2	5.8	5.9	6.1	5.6	20.8	28.1	18.1	3.5	78.3	44.7	47.5	52.5
86327	DEWEY	96.1	94.3	0.2	0.2	0.5	0.6	5.2	7.8	3.8	4.4	5.8	5.1	3.3	16.5	34.0	24.2	2.8	82.7	52.5	49.5	50.5
86332	KIRKLAND	93.4	91.7	0.2	0.2	0.2	0.2	8.1	11.1	3.4	3.8	4.2	4.4	3.4	14.2	35.9	28.1	2.6	85.8	56.0	50.2	49.8
86333	MAYER	95.6	94.8	0.2	0.3	0.3	0.4	6.5	8.7	4.4	4.7	5.1	5.3	4.4	17.2	34.5	22.1	2.4	82.1	51.1	50.8	49.2
86334	PAULDEN	93.5	92.2	0.4	0.5	0.4	0.5	11.5	15.4	6.3	6.5	7.0	7.4	5.9	23.6	30.1	12.0	1.2	75.7	39.9	50.6	49.4
86335	RIMROCK	90.8	89.5	0.1	0.1	0.2	0.3	7.5	10.1	5.2	5.5	6.0	5.4	3.2	20.9	34.0	17.6	2.2	79.9	47.5	48.7	51.3
86336	SEDONA	92.6	90.7	0.5	0.5	0.9	1.2	8.5	11.6	2.8	3.0	3.3	3.7	3.0	15.8	40.3	25.1	3.1	88.5	55.6	47.7	52.3
86337	SELIGMAN	85.7	82.9	1.4	1.6	1.2	1.4	14.8	19.1	4.3	4.7	6.0	6.3	3.5	19.7	37.5	17.3	0.7	80.4	48.6	51.6	48.4
86343	CROWN KING	97.4	98.1	0.0	0.0	0.6	0.5	5.2	7.4	1.4	2.8	5.1	3.7	3.7	17.2	52.1	11.6	2.3	88.4	52.6	59.1	40.9
86351	SEDONA	95.2	94.1	0.3	0.4	0.8	1.1	6.7	9.1	2.1	2.3	2.9	3.5	2.1	11.6	38.3	32.3	4.9	90.4	60.2	45.9	54.1
86401	KINGMAN	90.4	88.6	0.5	0.5	1.3	1.6	8.7	11.2	6.0	5.8	5.9	6.2	5.8	21.6	28.8	17.7	2.2	78.4	43.9	49.8	50.2
86403	LAKE HAVASU CITY	92.1	90.0	0.4	0.4	0.7	0.9	10.5	14.3	5.0	5.1	5.2	5.5	4.6	20.1	29.5	21.7	3.2	81.4	48.3	48.8	51.2
86404	LAKE HAVASU CITY	94.6	93.1	0.2	0.3	0.5	0.6	8.0	11.0	4.4	4.4	4.6	4.7	3.9	17.2	31.5	27.0	2.4	83.8	52.8	49.7	50.3
86406	LAKE HAVASU CITY	95.5	94.3	0.3	0.3	0.7	1.0	6.1	8.6	4.3	4.5	4.8	5.2	4.1	17.9	30.9	25.1	3.2	83.1	51.5	48.7	51.3
86409	KINGMAN	91.2	89.3	0.6	0.6	0.9	1.1	8.9	12.0	6.3	6.0	6.0	6.2	5.7	20.8	29.2	17.7	2.2	77.9	44.2	48.7	51.3
86411	HACKBERRY	89.0	86.8	0.5	0.6	0.8	1.1	5.6	7.9	3.2	3.6	4.1	4.4	3.4	17.1	40.9	21.8	1.5	86.3	53.7	52.1	47.9
86413	GOLDEN VALLEY	94.1	92.8	0.5	0.6	0.8	1.0	7.1	9.8	4.3	5.1	5.8	5.3	3.2	18.1	37.8	19.1	1.3	81.1	50.1	51.1	48.9
86426	FORT MOHAVE	90.7	88.6	0.6	0.7	1.2	1.5	11.9	15.6	5.7	5.6	5.7	6.0	4.6	19.6	30.6	20.5	1.6	79.3	46.9	49.6	50.4
86429	BULLHEAD CITY	90.7	88.6	1.1	1.3	1.2	1.6	13.5	17.8	5.2	5.0	5.1	4.9	4.7	22.0	28.9	22.0	2.1	81.6	47.3	49.1	50.9
86432	LITTLEFIELD	83.3	79.0	0.0	0.0	0.5	0.6	23.7	30.7	8.6	7.4	6.1	5.0	6.6	23.0	30.5	12.4	0.6	75.1	38.6	52.6	47.4
86434	PEACH SPRINGS	4.8	4.7	0.1	0.1	0.1	0.1	5.1	5.7	9.8	9.8	9.3	10.8	8.6	25.2	20.5	5.3	0.7	64.1	26.1	47.6	52.4
86435	SUPAI	9.9	9.4	0.0	0.0	0.0	0.0	1.8	1.9	11.0	12.9	11.2	7.7	7.0	25.5	20.6	3.3	0.7	59.4	25.2	48.1	51.9
86436	TOPOCK	95.9	95.0	0.5	0.6	0.5	0.7	5.2	7.2	2.4	2.7	3.0	3.9	3.8	13.0	33.3	34.4	3.5	89.5	59.0	49.8	50.2
86440	MOHAVE VALLEY	85.8	83.7	0.4	0.5	0.8	0.9	13.1	17.2	5.9	6.2	6.3	5.9	4.7	20.4	31.7	17.5	1.5	77.8	45.4	50.5	49.5
86441	DOLAN SPRINGS	93.5	91.9	0.8	1.0	1.3	1.7	6.1	8.4	3.5	3.7	3.9	4.0	3.7	12.3	32.1	33.5	3.2	86.4	58.5	51.3	48.7
86442	BULLHEAD CITY	85.1	82.3	0.9	1.0	1.0	1.4	20.8	25.4	5.9	5.8	5.8	5.7	4.5	20.6	29.4	20.2	2.2	79.1	46.3	49.7	50.3
86444	MEADVIEW	95.0	94.4	0.7	0.8	0.3	0.4	3.2	4.5	3.1	3.3	3.6	3.4	3.2	13.1	32.9	35.3	2.2	87.6	59.2	50.3	49.7
86445	WILLOW BEACH	93.2	91.7	0.9	1.0	1.4	1.8	5.9	8.4	3.4	3.7	3.9	4.1	3.7	12.3	32.3	33.3	3.3	86.4	58.4	51.1	48.9
86502	CHAMBERS	13.0	12.1	0.4	0.4	0.1	0.1	3.6	4.4	11.0	9.9	8.9	10.4	9.9	22.8	19.9	6.5	0.6	63.2	24.9	49.1	50.9
86503	CHINLE	3.2	3.2	0.1	0.1	0.1	0.1	1.4	1.7	10.8	10.6	10.2	11.0	8.6	23.6	18.0	6.3	1.0	61.4	24.3	50.0	50.0
86505	GANADO	3.2	3.2	0.1	0.1	0.1	0.2	1.2	1.4	9.8	9.6	9.3	9.9	8.7	24.2	20.7	7.0	0.8	64.9	26.7	49.0	51.0
86507	LUKACHUKAI	1.2	1.2	0.0	0.0	0.1	0.1	1.0	1.2	9.7	9.6	9.4	11.8	8.8	23.9	18.7	7.2	1.0	64.4	25.5	48.0	52.0
86510	PINON	2.1	1.9	0.0	0.0	0.0	0.0	0.8	0.9	11.8	10.9	10.2	10.2	8.7	23.4	17.5	6.7	0.8	60.9	24.0	49.7	50.3
86514	TEEC NOS POS	1.7	1.6	0.0	0.0	0.1	0.1	0.7	0.7	10.3	9.4	9.1	10.4	9.0	23.5	19.0	8.4	0.9	64.9	26.3	50.1	49.9
86535	DENNEHOTSO	0.8	0.8	0.0	0.0	0.0	0.0	0.8	0.9	10.5	9.3	8.7	11.1	10.9	22.9	17.2	8.4	1.0	64.8	24.7	51.3	48.7
86538	MANY FARMS	3.0	2.9	0.1	0.1	0.1	0.1	0.9	1.0	11.2	11.5	10.4	10.4	8.9	24.0	17.1	6.0	0.6	60.3	23.7	48.6	51.4
86556	TSAILE	2.4	2.3	0.1	0.1	0.1	0.1	0.9	1.0	10.6	10.2	9.3	11.3	10.9	24.5	16.7	5.9	0.7	63.5	24.0	47.8	52.2
	ARIZONA	75.5	72.3	3.1	3.3	1.9	2.4	25.3	30.8	7.6	7.1	6.8	6.9	6.8	26.9	24.0	12.0	1.8	74.5	35.8	49.7	50.3
	UNITED STATES	75.1	72.0	12.3	12.7	3.8	4.6	12.5	15.7	6.8	6.7	6.6	7.1	6.9	27.0	26.0	10.9	1.9	75.7	36.9	49.2	50.8

#	POST OFFICE NAME	2009 Per Capita Income	2009 HH Income Base	2009 Household Income Distribution (%): Less than $25,000	$25,000 to $49,999	$50,000 to $99,999	$100,000 to $149,999	$150,000 or More	Median Household Income: 2009	2014	2009 National Centile	2009 State Centile	2009 Home Value Base	2009 Home Value Distribution (%): Less than $50,000	$50,000 to $89,999	$90,000 to $174,999	$175,000 to $399,999	$400,000 or More	2009 Median Home Value
86321	BAGDAD	22521	718	14.6	22.6	51.5	9.5	1.8	60297	60339	78	74	163	54.0	37.4	6.7	1.8	0.0	45938
86322	CAMP VERDE	20038	5503	24.5	33.4	33.4	7.9	0.8	43302	47143	43	44	4294	16.0	20.9	37.1	22.9	3.1	111889
86323	CHINO VALLEY	22401	6485	22.9	31.6	32.6	8.8	4.1	46194	50136	52	51	5247	8.1	17.0	39.0	28.6	7.4	139396
86324	CLARKDALE	22933	2640	26.9	33.6	29.6	6.9	3.0	40936	44531	36	36	2077	10.9	19.0	40.1	26.3	3.8	124708
86325	CORNVILLE	22920	2398	21.5	30.1	36.5	8.8	3.1	48415	51782	58	54	1831	4.0	13.9	36.9	35.3	9.9	161048
86326	COTTONWOOD	22148	10012	25.6	32.3	32.7	5.9	3.5	43029	47077	42	43	6643	4.2	15.8	49.8	26.0	4.2	140520
86327	DEWEY	30312	4741	18.9	31.3	36.1	8.2	5.6	49827	53031	61	58	3963	6.0	7.5	40.8	38.1	7.7	165147
86332	KIRKLAND	20501	901	36.4	32.2	23.9	5.5	2.0	34048	37370	16	20	719	16.8	20.4	37.8	19.1	5.8	110206
86333	MAYER	21427	2750	32.3	28.1	30.4	5.9	3.2	40820	43416	35	35	2155	18.0	32.3	35.1	12.1	2.5	89589
86334	PAULDEN	18859	1338	22.0	34.7	31.7	7.7	4.0	44273	48183	46	46	1098	4.9	14.8	46.2	29.4	4.7	143056
86335	RIMROCK	20949	2119	27.1	34.5	32.5	4.0	1.9	42710	46027	42	42	1564	5.9	13.1	52.7	23.5	4.7	132143
86336	SEDONA	38473	7240	17.9	26.5	31.3	13.2	11.1	56499	59079	73	69	5297	7.2	3.5	13.3	44.2	31.8	286192
86337	SELIGMAN	17412	622	41.6	31.0	23.0	3.5	0.8	30083	31267	8	12	478	40.6	33.9	23.6	0.6	1.3	57759
86343	CROWN KING	33491	117	24.8	32.5	27.4	5.1	10.3	42309	44742	40	40	83	19.3	14.5	22.9	36.1	7.2	142500
86351	SEDONA	40057	3502	15.7	29.8	30.8	12.1	11.7	55581	58801	72	68	2411	0.0	1.6	11.3	50.5	36.6	326810
86401	KINGMAN	21189	9040	29.2	28.7	31.0	8.7	2.5	42058	46015	39	39	6957	9.8	17.3	49.5	21.6	1.7	119953
86403	LAKE HAVASU CITY	23252	7691	23.9	35.5	29.8	7.6	3.2	42619	46031	41	41	5297	0.6	13.9	61.9	20.8	2.8	127086
86404	LAKE HAVASU CITY	23506	7439	23.3	35.9	29.0	9.5	2.2	42806	46075	42	43	5991	4.5	17.5	50.6	23.1	4.3	134732
86406	LAKE HAVASU CITY	26274	10143	18.1	32.0	35.6	9.8	4.6	49988	52544	61	59	8175	0.9	6.1	60.1	26.0	6.8	148761
86409	KINGMAN	19090	10415	31.5	35.4	25.1	6.1	2.0	36649	38997	23	25	7733	16.2	35.0	39.5	8.5	0.7	88170
86411	HACKBERRY	26092	537	30.2	27.9	28.7	7.8	5.4	42368	46433	41	40	474	10.1	16.2	35.2	30.6	7.8	152459
86413	GOLDEN VALLEY	19300	4247	32.3	35.1	24.9	5.4	2.3	35541	37725	19	23	3562	12.0	37.6	43.6	6.2	0.7	90453
86426	FORT MOHAVE	22725	5683	18.4	32.4	36.0	10.5	2.7	49193	52703	59	56	4498	1.7	17.8	52.2	27.6	0.8	139156
86429	BULLHEAD CITY	23089	3507	23.2	39.0	29.7	5.5	2.7	42484	45783	41	41	1870	10.7	5.7	36.8	42.3	4.5	169843
86432	LITTLEFIELD	19660	994	21.6	35.6	32.7	7.7	2.3	44513	48607	47	47	753	21.0	14.9	47.4	13.1	3.6	117698
86434	PEACH SPRINGS	10271	483	49.3	26.9	18.0	3.3	2.5	25381	25776	3	7	240	27.9	44.2	24.2	3.8	0.0	69259
86435	SUPAI	9781	162	50.0	30.9	12.3	2.5	4.3	25000	26187	3	7	95	69.5	23.2	2.1	5.3	0.0	26500
86436	TOPOCK	21435	1499	32.8	37.1	25.2	3.3	1.7	33729	35665	15	20	1244	14.5	41.1	37.6	6.0	0.7	83636
86440	MOHAVE VALLEY	19367	3090	25.3	32.5	33.9	6.9	1.5	43674	47008	44	45	2343	11.2	25.9	45.7	16.3	1.0	111138
86441	DOLAN SPRINGS	17632	1160	54.1	23.8	15.6	4.9	1.6	22756	23133	2	5	1010	35.1	34.4	26.9	2.7	0.9	66224
86442	BULLHEAD CITY	20039	14863	28.3	36.0	27.6	5.6	2.5	39266	42352	31	31	9359	15.1	29.4	42.8	10.8	1.9	96436
86444	MEADVIEW	23787	489	32.9	35.6	22.7	6.7	2.0	35605	37355	20	23	436	10.3	18.1	58.3	12.2	1.1	117135
86445	WILLOW BEACH	15740	342	54.4	24.0	15.5	4.7	1.5	22651	22838	2	5	298	34.6	34.2	27.9	2.3	1.0	66897
86502	CHAMBERS	10082	725	45.4	27.2	23.6	3.0	0.8	28032	29245	6	10	536	17.7	23.5	50.4	3.5	4.9	100564
86503	CHINLE	9344	3520	50.3	28.1	17.9	2.3	1.4	24585	25565	3	6	2357	59.9	21.1	13.7	2.4	2.8	36725
86505	GANADO	11486	7146	41.8	26.9	24.3	6.0	1.1	31230	32536	10	15	5101	53.7	22.2	18.9	4.0	1.2	44534
86507	LUKACHUKAI	5349	518	73.0	18.9	7.5	0.6	0.0	13010	13277	1	2	413	62.5	9.7	23.2	4.1	0.5	22130
86510	PINON	6650	2502	59.9	24.9	12.9	2.1	0.2	17014	16166	1	2	1809	53.2	19.0	18.1	5.7	3.9	44730
86514	TEEC NOS POS	7750	1704	60.0	20.4	18.1	1.5	0.0	17937	19388	1	3	1404	62.7	20.8	11.3	2.9	2.4	33673
86535	DENNEHOTSO	7145	456	53.1	29.4	14.9	2.6	0.0	19121	19233	1	3	373	51.5	13.7	28.7	4.3	1.9	47609
86538	MANY FARMS	8186	1377	51.9	28.1	17.4	2.3	0.2	23041	23607	2	6	951	51.8	21.7	22.7	2.8	0.9	45270
86556	TSAILE	8162	490	58.6	23.5	13.7	4.1	0.2	19678	20435	1	3	332	57.8	16.9	23.2	1.5	0.6	35000
	ARIZONA	26377		19.0	25.8	34.8	13.4	7.1	55275	58294				9.3	12.3	42.2	29.4	6.9	143619
	UNITED STATES	27277		20.9	24.4	35.3	11.7	7.6	54719	56938				9.3	13.1	31.6	32.6	13.5	162279

ZIP CODE		FINANCIAL SERVICES				THE HOME						ENTERTAINMENT						PERSONAL			
						Home Improvements		Furnishings													
#	POST OFFICE NAME	Auto Loan	Home Loan	Invest-ments	Retire-ment Plans	Home Repair	Lawn & Garden	Comput-ers & Hard-ware-Personal	Major Appli-ances	TV, Radio, Sound Equip-ment	Furni-ture	Dine out/ Carry out	Sports Equip-ment	Fees & Tickets	Toys & Games	Travel	Cable TV	Apparel & Services	Auto Repairs	Health Insur-ance	Pets & Supplies
86321	BAGDAD	97	91	77	86	86	87	90	89	90	93	90	68	85	94	84	90	62	90	87	106
86322	CAMP VERDE	79	70	91	67	76	85	68	81	72	71	71	56	64	68	72	76	48	77	86	93
86323	CHINO VALLEY	95	85	87	82	84	90	82	89	85	84	85	66	77	87	80	87	58	86	88	105
86324	CLARKDALE	79	71	96	69	78	87	70	83	73	71	72	57	67	69	75	78	49	79	88	95
86325	CORNVILLE	94	76	116	75	83	98	76	94	79	72	79	69	67	76	81	84	52	88	93	110
86326	COTTONWOOD	80	73	83	73	76	84	75	81	78	75	77	58	72	76	76	82	53	80	87	94
86327	DEWEY	97	91	127	88	102	111	86	104	91	91	89	69	86	83	96	96	60	98	111	119
86332	KIRKLAND	70	64	87	60	71	78	62	74	65	64	64	50	59	60	67	69	43	71	80	85
86333	MAYER	74	71	90	65	78	84	67	79	71	73	69	52	66	65	73	75	47	76	88	91
86334	PAULDEN	94	84	83	81	84	90	80	88	83	82	83	64	75	86	78	86	56	84	88	104
86335	RIMROCK	80	64	101	63	70	83	64	81	67	61	66	59	56	64	69	71	44	75	80	94
86336	SEDONA	115	113	157	111	129	137	105	125	110	114	108	82	109	101	119	116	74	119	136	143
86337	SELIGMAN	56	53	68	49	59	64	51	60	54	55	52	39	50	49	55	57	35	57	67	68
86343	CROWN KING	101	83	130	81	91	108	82	104	86	78	85	75	72	81	89	92	57	96	104	120
86351	SEDONA	113	119	161	118	137	140	107	126	113	121	111	79	117	101	123	118	76	120	140	143
86401	KINGMAN	78	73	78	73	74	83	74	79	76	72	75	59	71	75	74	80	52	78	85	93
86403	LAKE HAVASU CITY	82	71	92	69	76	87	73	84	77	71	76	60	67	74	75	82	51	81	90	97
86404	LAKE HAVASU CITY	82	74	98	70	82	90	73	86	76	75	75	58	69	71	78	81	50	82	92	98
86406	LAKE HAVASU CITY	92	89	110	86	96	105	85	98	89	87	88	67	84	84	91	94	59	94	106	113
86409	KINGMAN	73	65	74	62	67	73	65	72	68	67	67	52	61	67	65	70	45	70	75	84
86411	HACKBERRY	99	79	128	78	87	105	79	101	83	74	82	74	69	79	86	89	55	93	100	117
86413	GOLDEN VALLEY	69	66	84	61	73	78	63	74	66	68	65	48	62	61	68	70	43	71	82	84
86426	FORT MOHAVE	89	85	101	79	92	98	80	93	85	86	83	62	79	80	86	89	56	89	102	107
86429	BULLHEAD CITY	78	70	78	70	74	82	73	79	76	73	75	57	69	74	73	79	51	78	85	92
86432	LITTLEFIELD	84	79	67	75	75	75	78	77	78	81	78	59	73	81	73	78	54	77	75	92
86434	PEACH SPRINGS	57	49	39	50	43	52	53	50	58	53	57	39	51	58	48	60	39	54	56	64
86435	SUPAI	58	47	35	39	45	44	46	50	51	52	51	31	40	51	42	52	36	50	49	55
86436	TOPOCK	64	61	78	57	68	73	58	69	62	63	60	45	58	56	64	65	40	66	77	79
86440	MOHAVE VALLEY	80	70	90	67	73	82	69	80	71	69	71	58	63	69	71	74	48	76	80	93
86441	DOLAN SPRINGS	53	51	65	47	56	61	48	57	51	52	50	37	48	47	53	54	33	55	63	65
86442	BULLHEAD CITY	74	69	82	64	74	80	67	76	71	71	69	52	65	67	70	74	47	74	83	88
86444	MEADVIEW	69	66	85	61	74	79	63	75	67	68	65	49	62	61	69	71	44	72	83	85
86445	WILLOW BEACH	53	51	65	47	56	61	48	57	51	52	50	37	48	47	53	54	33	55	63	65
86502	CHAMBERS	55	53	46	48	52	47	53	53	51	56	52	39	50	52	50	50	36	53	49	60
86503	CHINLE	55	44	34	39	42	43	45	47	49	49	49	30	40	50	40	51	34	48	47	53
86505	GANADO	65	56	46	51	54	53	56	58	58	61	59	40	51	60	52	59	41	58	56	66
86507	LUKACHUKAI	33	26	20	22	25	25	26	28	28	29	29	17	23	29	23	29	20	28	27	31
86510	PINON	43	35	27	30	33	34	35	38	39	39	39	24	31	39	32	40	27	38	38	42
86514	TEEC NOS POS	46	37	28	31	35	35	37	40	40	41	40	24	32	41	33	41	28	40	38	43
86535	DENNEHOTSO	48	39	29	32	37	36	39	42	42	43	43	26	34	43	35	43	30	42	40	46
86538	MANY FARMS	48	39	31	37	36	40	41	41	45	44	45	29	38	46	37	47	31	44	44	49
86556	TSAILE	50	40	30	33	38	38	40	43	43	45	44	26	35	44	36	45	30	43	42	47
	ARIZONA	104	101	100	99	102	100	101	102	101	105	102	76	100	101	101	100	71	102	102	118
	UNITED STATES	100	100	100	100	100	100	100	100	100	100	100	100	100	100	100	100	100	100	100	100

ZIP CODE #	POST OFFICE NAME	COUNTY FIPS CODE	POPULATION 2000	POPULATION 2009	POPULATION 2014	2000-2009 ANNUAL RATE % Rate	2000-2009 ANNUAL RATE State Centile	HOUSEHOLDS 2000	HOUSEHOLDS 2009	HOUSEHOLDS 2014	HOUSEHOLDS % Annual Rate 2000-2009	HOUSEHOLDS 2009 Average HH Size	FAMILIES 2000	FAMILIES 2009	FAMILIES % Annual Rate 2000-2009
71601	PINE BLUFF	069	20225	18645	17911	-0.9	12	7157	6713	6481	-0.7	2.61	4750	4263	-1.2
71602	WHITE HALL	069	19184	16768	16339	-1.4	3	6736	6747	6638	0.0	2.44	4996	4837	-0.3
71603	PINE BLUFF	069	36151	36166	35170	0.0	40	13889	13701	13418	-0.1	2.46	9773	9275	-0.6
71630	ARKANSAS CITY	041	45	40	37	-1.3	5	13	12	11	-0.9	3.33	9	8	-1.3
71631	BANKS	011	748	748	741	0.0	40	304	312	311	0.3	2.40	201	198	-0.2
71635	CROSSETT	003	13823	13014	12598	-0.6	18	5454	5275	5149	-0.4	2.45	4023	3763	-0.7
71638	DERMOTT	043	4756	4209	3945	-1.3	5	1626	1471	1386	-1.1	2.61	1124	978	-1.5
71639	DUMAS	041	6630	5885	5530	-1.3	5	2473	2274	2160	-0.9	2.57	1768	1570	-1.3
71640	EUDORA	017	4052	3680	3449	-1.0	9	1531	1433	1360	-0.7	2.57	1090	982	-1.1
71642	FOUNTAIN HILL	003	513	526	523	0.3	49	218	229	230	0.5	2.30	163	166	0.2
71643	GOULD	079	2634	3540	3513	3.2	97	657	646	640	-0.2	2.55	464	439	-0.6
71644	GRADY	079	4253	3489	3458	-2.1	0	780	772	766	-0.1	2.76	601	578	-0.4
71646	HAMBURG	003	6907	6655	6483	-0.4	25	2604	2565	2519	-0.2	2.56	1947	1859	-0.5
71647	HERMITAGE	011	2398	2261	2175	-0.6	18	862	811	778	-0.7	2.47	621	564	-1.0
71651	JERSEY	011	400	357	341	-1.2	6	102	91	86	-1.2	2.91	71	60	-1.8
71652	KINGSLAND	025	1083	1120	1117	0.4	54	432	453	454	0.5	2.47	318	322	0.1
71653	LAKE VILLAGE	017	5615	4963	4643	-1.3	5	2183	1995	1881	-1.0	2.30	1526	1346	-1.3
71654	MC GEHEE	041	5491	5076	4846	-0.8	14	2205	2112	2038	-0.5	2.37	1535	1414	-0.9
71655	MONTICELLO	043	15314	15432	15127	0.1	43	6020	6201	6132	0.3	2.38	4140	4104	-0.1
71656	MONTICELLO	043	160	187	188	1.7	89	7	8	8	1.5	2.50	3	3	0.0
71658	MONTROSE	003	997	928	898	-0.8	14	363	347	338	-0.5	2.67	263	243	-0.9
71660	NEW EDINBURG	025	1078	1278	1346	1.9	91	424	509	537	2.0	2.51	317	369	1.7
71661	PARKDALE	003	471	425	405	-1.1	8	183	171	165	-0.7	2.49	136	123	-1.1
71662	PICKENS	041	1037	929	873	-1.2	6	393	365	347	-0.8	2.55	287	257	-1.2
71663	PORTLAND	003	918	818	775	-1.2	6	348	322	308	-0.8	2.54	253	225	-1.3
71665	RISON	025	6140	6203	6185	0.1	43	2322	2391	2398	0.3	2.57	1806	1809	0.0
71666	MC GEHEE	041	639	566	531	-1.3	5	256	231	219	-1.1	2.45	179	156	-1.5
71667	STAR CITY	079	6942	7066	7103	0.2	45	2580	2689	2725	0.4	2.52	1895	1909	0.1
71670	TILLAR	043	1082	1059	1034	-0.2	31	415	422	417	0.2	2.48	298	293	-0.2
71671	WARREN	011	9199	8681	8357	-0.6	18	3620	3472	3356	-0.5	2.38	2535	2342	-0.9
71674	WATSON	041	966	879	828	-1.0	9	382	359	342	-0.7	2.45	277	252	-1.0
71675	WILMAR	043	1862	1871	1838	0.1	43	748	776	770	0.4	2.40	534	535	0.0
71676	WILMOT	003	974	863	822	-1.3	5	370	337	323	-1.0	2.42	242	209	-1.6
71677	WINCHESTER	043	77	76	74	-0.1	35	30	31	30	0.4	2.45	22	22	0.0
71678	YORKTOWN	079	857	834	826	-0.3	27	319	320	319	0.0	2.61	228	220	-0.4
71701	CAMDEN	103	21745	20247	19415	-0.8	14	8796	8370	8079	-0.5	2.37	6075	5563	-0.9
71720	BEARDEN	103	2539	2306	2193	-1.0	9	973	909	871	-0.7	2.52	699	630	-1.1
71722	BLUFF CITY	099	478	543	572	1.4	84	197	230	244	1.7	2.36	144	162	1.3
71725	CARTHAGE	039	1186	1009	939	-1.7	2	473	411	385	-1.5	2.33	303	251	-2.0
71726	CHIDESTER	103	1314	1244	1202	-0.6	18	580	566	553	-0.3	2.19	386	361	-0.7
71730	EL DORADO	139	36074	34441	33386	-0.5	22	14277	13856	13494	-0.3	2.42	9990	9337	-0.7
71740	EMERSON	027	1863	1808	1756	-0.3	27	722	718	703	-0.1	2.51	515	493	-0.5
71742	FORDYCE	039	5887	5435	5202	-0.9	12	2185	2053	1972	-0.7	2.44	1499	1353	-1.1
71743	GURDON	019	4349	4360	4357	0.0	40	1758	1792	1800	0.2	2.43	1237	1214	-0.2
71744	HAMPTON	013	3621	3719	3715	0.3	49	1461	1556	1571	0.7	2.32	1013	1035	0.2
71745	HARRELL	013	821	734	702	-1.2	6	337	312	302	-0.8	2.35	244	219	-1.2
71747	HUTTIG	139	1256	1183	1140	-0.6	18	496	480	467	-0.4	2.46	348	323	-0.8
71748	IVAN	039	318	302	290	-0.6	18	135	132	128	-0.2	2.29	101	95	-0.7
71749	JUNCTION CITY	139	3016	3026	2987	0.0	40	1152	1183	1176	0.3	2.52	861	860	0.0
71751	LOUANN	103	1018	1056	1043	0.4	54	408	438	437	0.8	2.41	307	317	0.3
71752	MC NEIL	027	1265	1195	1152	-0.6	18	483	469	455	-0.3	2.55	340	317	-0.8
71753	MAGNOLIA	027	17505	16835	16304	-0.4	25	6798	6615	6434	-0.3	2.37	4493	4188	-0.8
71758	MOUNT HOLLY	139	552	574	571	0.4	54	222	237	238	0.7	2.42	156	160	0.3
71762	SMACKOVER	139	2752	2656	2583	-0.4	25	1042	1025	1002	-0.2	2.53	743	705	-0.6
71763	SPARKMAN	039	1802	1669	1588	-0.8	14	719	682	655	-0.6	2.45	522	478	-0.9
71764	STEPHENS	103	2358	2119	2008	-1.1	8	928	852	813	-0.9	2.49	654	575	-1.4
71765	STRONG	139	2527	2490	2442	-0.2	31	1015	1025	1014	0.1	2.43	705	686	-0.3
71766	THORNTON	013	1302	1199	1159	-0.9	12	519	493	482	-0.6	2.43	373	343	-0.9
71770	WALDO	027	3316	3129	3019	-0.6	18	1321	1280	1245	-0.3	2.44	917	855	-0.8
71801	HOPE	057	17279	17561	17550	0.2	45	6521	6612	6602	0.1	2.62	4589	4484	-0.2
71822	ASHDOWN	081	9400	9288	9114	-0.1	35	3726	3830	3804	0.3	2.38	2685	2662	-0.1
71825	BLEVINS	057	959	1052	1079	1.0	75	360	398	409	1.1	2.64	272	291	0.7
71826	BRADLEY	073	1869	1723	1648	-0.9	12	762	733	709	-0.4	2.35	520	479	-0.9
71827	BUCKNER	073	1159	1043	989	-1.1	8	436	405	388	-0.8	2.55	318	286	-1.1
71828	CALE	099	329	380	402	1.6	87	117	138	147	1.8	2.75	88	100	1.4
71831	COLUMBUS	057	81	79	78	-0.3	27	29	29	28	0.0	2.72	20	19	-0.6
71832	DE QUEEN	133	9603	10210	10436	0.7	66	3308	3440	3499	0.4	2.92	2450	2467	0.1
71833	DIERKS	061	2473	2481	2454	0.0	40	951	975	969	0.3	2.50	722	717	-0.1
71834	DODDRIDGE	091	1419	1564	1633	1.1	78	603	684	720	1.4	2.29	433	474	1.0
71835	EMMET	099	1577	1761	1840	1.2	80	616	700	735	1.4	2.52	439	479	0.9
71836	FOREMAN	081	2993	2936	2878	-0.2	31	1212	1228	1218	0.1	2.39	853	833	-0.3
71837	FOUKE	091	6366	6773	6951	0.7	66	2283	2491	2578	0.9	2.72	1821	1938	0.7
71838	FULTON	057	1190	1227	1231	0.3	49	444	461	464	0.4	2.66	311	310	0.0
71839	GARLAND CITY	091	546	602	628	1.1	78	210	239	251	1.4	2.49	156	173	1.1
71841	GILLHAM	133	852	909	932	0.7	66	351	374	382	0.7	2.43	265	273	0.3
71842	HORATIO	133	2627	2742	2803	0.5	58	985	1021	1037	0.4	2.69	737	741	0.1
71845	LEWISVILLE	073	2286	2247	2201	-0.2	31	918	931	921	0.2	2.40	641	625	-0.3
71846	LOCKESBURG	133	2748	2854	2908	0.4	54	1095	1137	1153	0.4	2.51	798	800	0.0
71847	MC CASKILL	057	689	749	767	0.9	72	265	290	297	1.0	2.58	206	219	0.7
71851	MINERAL SPRINGS	061	2444	2528	2516	0.4	54	954	1005	1008	0.6	2.52	705	717	0.2
71852	NASHVILLE	061	9613	9571	9454	0.0	40	3645	3689	3660	0.1	2.50	2564	2502	-0.3
71853	OGDEN	081	520	498	483	-0.5	22	220	219	216	0.0	2.27	151	145	-0.4
71854	TEXARKANA	091	32116	34615	35544	0.8	68	12542	13854	14341	1.1	2.42	8671	9205	0.6
71855	OZAN	057	897	913	912	0.2	45	348	358	358	0.3	2.55	247	244	-0.1
71857	PRESCOTT	099	5716	5964	6040	0.5	58	2229	2383	2434	0.7	2.38	1514	1552	0.3
71858	ROSSTON	099	1427	1616	1702	1.4	84	551	643	683	1.7	2.51	406	458	1.3
71859	SARATOGA	061	581	612	614	0.6	62	251	268	271	0.7	2.28	167	171	0.3
71860	STAMPS	073	2856	2609	2487	-1.0	9	1138	1071	1030	-0.7	2.34	769	695	-1.1
71861	TAYLOR	027	1954	1983	1950	0.2	45	802	835	827	0.4	2.33	586	588	0.0
71862	WASHINGTON	057	783	801	803	0.2	45	329	340	341	0.4	2.36	239	238	0.0
71864	WILLISVILLE	099	789	888	935	1.3	82	322	375	398	1.7	2.37	233	261	1.2
71865	WILTON	081	26	25	24	-0.4	25	11	11	11	0.0	2.27	9	8	-1.3
71866	WINTHROP	081	697	674	658	-0.4	25	299	300	297	0.0	2.25	216	210	-0.3
71901	HOT SPRINGS NATIONAL	051	28854	30508	31575	0.6	62	11807	12338	12784	0.5	2.35	7343	7334	0.0
71909	HOT SPRINGS NATIONAL	051	13172	16107	17509	2.2	93	6417	7866	8604	2.2	2.04	4975	5960	2.0
	ARKANSAS					0.9					1.1	2.46			0.7
	UNITED STATES					1.0					1.1	2.59			0.9

ZIP CODE #	POST OFFICE NAME	RACE (%) White 2000	White 2009	Black 2000	Black 2009	Asian/Pacific 2000	Asian/Pacific 2009	% Hispanic Origin 2000	% Hispanic Origin 2009	2009 AGE DISTRIBUTION (%) 0-4	5-9	10-14	15-19	20-24	25-44	45-64	65-84	85+	18+	MEDIAN AGE 2009	% 2009 Males	% 2009 Females
71601	PINE BLUFF	16.1	13.0	82.5	85.6	0.3	0.3	0.9	1.2	7.9	7.8	7.4	10.2	9.9	23.1	21.7	10.1	2.0	72.2	30.4	45.9	54.1
71602	WHITE HALL	74.9	73.9	23.1	23.2	0.6	1.0	1.1	1.7	7.0	6.9	6.8	6.8	6.2	26.9	27.4	10.8	1.2	75.3	37.2	50.2	49.8
71603	PINE BLUFF	50.0	45.4	47.9	52.0	1.0	1.4	0.7	1.0	6.6	6.8	6.7	6.4	6.1	26.0	26.6	12.2	2.6	76.1	38.3	48.7	51.3
71630	ARKANSAS CITY	55.6	50.0	42.2	47.5	0.0	0.0	2.2	2.5	7.5	7.5	7.5	5.0	5.0	20.0	30.0	15.0	2.5	75.0	42.5	47.5	52.5
71631	BANKS	55.7	51.6	41.5	44.5	0.1	0.1	2.4	3.6	5.7	6.0	6.6	7.1	5.7	23.5	26.6	16.0	2.7	77.5	41.6	50.1	49.9
71635	CROSSETT	71.6	68.2	26.4	29.1	0.3	0.4	1.9	2.8	7.2	7.1	7.3	6.9	5.4	25.7	25.9	12.5	2.0	74.1	38.1	48.6	51.4
71638	DERMOTT	38.7	36.5	59.4	60.9	0.3	0.4	1.6	2.3	6.3	6.4	6.6	7.4	6.7	26.7	24.7	12.7	2.6	76.3	37.4	50.6	49.4
71639	DUMAS	40.2	36.8	55.6	57.3	0.4	0.5	4.6	6.7	8.1	8.2	7.8	7.5	6.2	23.6	25.1	11.3	2.1	71.2	35.4	47.2	52.8
71640	EUDORA	29.2	26.3	67.7	69.5	0.1	0.2	3.9	5.4	7.7	7.8	7.4	7.1	6.1	23.7	25.5	13.0	1.7	72.8	36.3	47.3	52.7
71642	FOUNTAIN HILL	79.7	74.3	13.8	16.5	0.0	0.0	5.8	8.7	6.7	6.7	6.5	6.5	5.5	27.2	27.2	12.7	1.1	76.2	38.3	51.0	49.0
71643	GOULD	36.9	37.8	61.2	60.0	0.0	0.1	1.1	1.6	4.2	4.4	4.1	5.2	11.1	42.5	21.5	5.9	1.1	84.5	34.5	71.8	28.2
71644	GRADY	53.5	48.3	43.7	47.5	0.2	0.1	3.0	4.8	4.2	4.2	4.1	5.8	14.2	37.9	21.0	7.6	1.0	84.6	33.5	72.5	27.5
71646	HAMBURG	76.3	71.7	18.3	20.7	0.1	0.2	5.5	8.0	6.7	6.7	6.9	7.0	5.3	26.4	27.2	12.2	1.7	75.3	38.5	49.7	50.3
71647	HERMITAGE	61.7	53.3	17.4	17.2	0.0	0.0	22.3	31.8	6.9	6.8	6.7	6.6	7.3	28.6	24.2	11.5	1.5	75.9	35.7	55.9	44.1
71651	JERSEY	60.3	50.4	15.0	14.8	0.0	0.0	24.2	34.5	3.9	4.2	4.2	5.3	9.2	30.5	26.9	14.0	1.7	84.3	40.4	63.0	37.0
71652	KINGSLAND	78.7	75.9	19.4	21.7	0.2	0.3	1.6	2.3	7.1	6.9	7.2	7.1	5.0	25.4	26.3	13.4	1.7	74.4	38.1	48.3	51.7
71653	LAKE VILLAGE	59.0	54.3	37.8	41.3	0.7	1.0	2.8	4.1	6.6	6.6	6.4	6.5	5.8	24.9	26.2	14.4	2.4	76.3	39.3	49.9	50.1
71654	MC GEHEE	54.2	50.4	43.8	47.1	0.3	0.5	1.5	2.1	7.1	7.2	7.0	6.8	5.9	23.6	26.8	12.9	2.7	74.3	38.6	46.3	53.7
71655	MONTICELLO	71.1	67.7	26.4	29.0	0.5	0.7	1.6	2.4	6.9	6.7	6.8	8.3	7.3	26.8	24.4	10.8	2.0	75.3	34.9	48.5	51.5
71656	MONTICELLO	66.5	62.0	31.7	35.3	0.6	1.1	0.6	1.6	2.7	1.6	0.5	38.0	36.4	9.1	8.0	3.2	0.5	92.5	21.0	54.0	46.0
71658	MONTROSE	54.7	51.0	40.2	41.8	0.0	0.0	6.1	8.7	6.4	6.9	8.7	8.6	5.9	26.0	24.6	10.5	2.5	72.2	34.9	49.1	50.9
71660	NEW EDINBURG	79.5	75.1	18.4	21.9	0.0	0.1	2.1	3.1	5.8	5.9	6.1	6.3	5.9	25.4	29.4	13.8	1.5	78.5	41.0	50.8	49.2
71661	PARKDALE	57.7	52.7	39.5	43.5	0.0	0.0	3.6	5.2	7.3	6.8	7.1	6.8	5.6	25.6	26.8	12.2	1.6	74.6	37.8	48.9	51.1
71662	PICKENS	62.4	57.2	33.7	37.6	0.4	0.4	3.9	5.8	7.3	7.6	7.3	6.6	5.9	24.3	27.6	11.7	1.6	73.6	37.4	48.5	51.5
71663	PORTLAND	52.6	46.8	44.0	48.5	0.0	0.0	5.1	7.1	7.1	7.1	7.0	7.1	5.4	25.1	26.8	12.6	2.0	74.3	38.0	48.9	51.1
71665	RISON	86.3	84.7	11.8	12.8	0.2	0.3	1.5	2.3	6.7	6.8	6.9	6.7	5.3	25.3	27.5	13.0	1.8	75.4	39.7	48.8	51.2
71666	MC GEHEE	56.8	50.5	41.9	47.7	0.0	0.0	2.8	4.1	7.4	7.4	7.2	6.9	5.3	22.8	28.8	12.4	1.8	73.7	40.1	48.4	51.6
71667	STAR CITY	83.6	80.6	14.3	16.9	0.1	0.1	1.5	2.2	6.9	6.9	6.9	7.0	5.5	24.6	25.8	13.4	3.0	75.2	38.8	48.3	51.7
71670	TILLAR	69.7	65.2	27.5	31.4	0.1	0.1	2.1	3.2	6.2	6.2	6.4	6.7	5.7	26.0	28.7	11.7	2.4	76.9	39.3	48.8	51.2
71671	WARREN	65.1	61.1	30.7	32.6	0.1	0.1	4.3	6.7	5.9	5.8	5.9	6.1	5.8	24.6	26.4	16.0	3.5	78.6	41.5	47.3	52.7
71674	WATSON	73.3	67.7	23.1	27.6	0.3	0.3	3.1	4.9	7.1	7.1	6.8	5.3	5.3	22.4	28.4	15.2	2.3	75.9	41.7	49.9	50.1
71675	WILMAR	62.1	58.7	35.5	37.8	0.2	0.3	2.0	2.9	6.3	6.3	6.4	6.1	5.7	26.7	28.8	12.4	1.3	77.1	39.0	50.4	49.6
71676	WILMOT	32.2	28.2	66.7	70.7	0.0	0.0	2.0	2.7	5.3	5.0	5.1	6.6	6.0	23.6	28.0	15.9	4.4	80.4	43.7	44.8	55.2
71677	WINCHESTER	71.8	68.4	24.4	27.6	0.0	0.0	2.6	3.9	6.6	6.6	6.6	7.9	5.3	30.3	26.3	9.2	1.3	75.0	35.0	47.4	52.6
71678	YORKTOWN	49.5	44.6	47.2	51.1	0.0	0.0	2.5	3.7	8.3	8.3	8.0	6.8	5.3	24.0	26.4	11.5	1.4	71.1	36.1	49.9	50.1
71701	CAMDEN	58.8	55.5	39.6	42.5	0.3	0.4	0.7	1.0	6.4	6.4	6.5	6.8	6.1	23.5	27.5	14.0	2.9	76.6	40.5	47.3	52.7
71720	BEARDEN	62.1	56.4	36.0	41.3	0.1	0.1	1.1	1.6	6.5	6.8	7.1	7.0	5.6	24.8	28.5	12.2	1.5	75.2	38.7	50.8	49.2
71722	BLUFF CITY	54.2	49.5	44.8	49.2	0.0	0.2	0.4	0.6	6.4	6.4	6.6	6.1	5.9	23.6	29.8	13.3	1.8	76.6	41.0	51.2	48.8
71725	CARTHAGE	43.0	38.0	54.8	59.3	0.0	0.0	3.2	4.7	5.8	6.1	6.5	6.3	4.7	20.0	30.3	16.9	3.2	77.6	45.3	51.1	48.9
71726	CHIDESTER	64.8	59.2	33.5	38.7	0.4	0.6	0.7	1.0	5.3	5.8	5.4	6.5	4.7	18.7	32.7	17.9	3.0	80.1	47.6	49.8	50.2
71730	EL DORADO	66.0	62.9	32.1	34.7	0.5	0.7	1.1	1.6	6.5	6.4	6.6	6.8	5.6	24.3	27.2	13.5	3.0	76.2	40.1	47.9	52.1
71740	EMERSON	67.5	62.9	31.1	35.5	0.1	0.2	1.1	1.5	5.9	6.0	6.4	7.2	5.5	25.2	29.0	12.6	2.3	77.3	40.6	49.5	50.5
71742	FORDYCE	53.2	49.3	45.1	48.4	0.4	0.5	1.4	2.0	6.2	6.4	7.6	7.5	5.8	23.3	26.7	13.4	3.0	74.9	39.2	47.5	52.5
71743	GURDON	70.7	67.7	25.8	27.3	0.1	0.1	3.3	5.0	7.4	7.2	7.1	6.6	5.6	25.6	26.1	12.5	1.9	74.2	38.0	49.1	50.9
71744	HAMPTON	75.6	73.0	22.2	24.8	0.1	0.1	1.9	1.8	5.2	5.3	5.6	7.0	6.0	23.8	29.6	14.7	2.8	79.6	42.8	48.8	51.2
71745	HARRELL	70.4	68.9	28.1	29.6	0.0	0.0	0.5	0.5	5.7	6.1	6.3	6.3	5.3	25.7	29.6	12.7	2.3	78.1	41.5	48.0	52.0
71747	HUTTIG	54.6	47.7	42.0	48.1	0.1	0.1	2.3	3.5	5.8	6.1	6.5	7.0	5.2	24.4	30.3	13.1	1.6	77.3	41.3	50.0	50.0
71748	IVAN	90.9	88.7	8.5	10.3	0.0	0.0	0.3	0.7	5.0	5.3	5.6	5.0	4.3	20.9	37.7	14.6	1.7	80.5	47.7	52.6	47.4
71749	JUNCTION CITY	71.0	65.9	27.9	32.7	0.0	0.1	0.8	1.2	6.9	6.8	6.9	6.7	5.8	25.4	27.1	12.4	1.9	75.4	38.0	50.6	49.4
71751	LOUANN	80.6	76.4	17.7	21.6	0.3	0.4	0.7	1.0	4.9	6.1	6.7	8.0	4.5	24.5	31.6	11.8	1.8	76.8	42.0	50.2	49.8
71752	MC NEIL	52.6	47.2	45.7	50.9	0.2	0.2	1.0	1.5	7.4	7.4	6.9	7.9	6.2	24.7	25.6	12.4	1.7	73.6	37.0	49.0	51.0
71753	MAGNOLIA	61.9	58.5	36.1	38.8	0.5	0.7	1.1	1.6	6.1	5.9	5.9	8.7	8.3	24.2	24.7	13.4	2.8	78.0	37.2	47.7	52.3
71758	MOUNT HOLLY	73.7	68.1	25.2	30.7	0.0	0.0	1.3	2.1	4.4	6.4	7.1	7.0	5.2	24.2	29.3	13.8	2.6	77.0	42.0	50.5	49.5
71762	SMACKOVER	74.7	70.6	24.3	28.2	0.1	0.1	0.3	0.4	5.8	6.1	5.9	6.4	5.4	23.2	26.7	16.7	3.7	78.4	42.8	48.7	51.3
71763	SPARKMAN	72.1	67.6	24.6	27.7	0.0	0.0	3.2	4.9	6.2	6.3	6.6	6.1	5.5	23.1	30.1	13.9	2.2	77.2	42.0	48.7	51.3
71764	STEPHENS	54.2	49.0	44.7	49.6	0.1	0.2	0.6	0.8	5.3	5.4	6.1	6.9	6.2	24.3	28.7	14.9	2.2	79.0	41.4	47.6	52.4
71765	STRONG	52.7	47.8	44.4	48.4	0.4	0.6	2.7	3.7	6.1	6.2	6.5	6.8	6.1	25.3	28.8	12.1	2.0	77.0	39.9	48.4	51.6
71766	THORNTON	74.1	72.8	23.7	24.9	0.0	0.0	1.2	1.3	6.5	6.8	7.0	6.6	5.1	24.1	29.4	12.9	1.6	75.7	41.0	48.5	51.5
71770	WALDO	55.7	51.2	42.8	46.9	0.1	0.1	1.2	1.7	6.9	6.9	6.8	6.6	5.3	25.6	26.7	13.0	2.1	75.3	38.9	48.4	51.6
71801	HOPE	61.3	57.9	31.7	32.7	0.2	0.3	9.6	13.7	7.7	7.4	7.0	7.0	6.3	25.9	24.4	11.9	2.5	73.6	36.2	48.2	51.8
71822	ASHDOWN	73.3	70.3	23.1	25.4	0.2	0.2	1.4	2.1	6.6	6.7	6.8	6.3	5.3	24.2	28.2	13.4	2.3	76.0	39.9	49.1	50.9
71825	BLEVINS	78.4	72.7	15.8	18.8	0.2	0.3	6.4	10.6	6.4	6.6	6.7	6.6	5.7	25.0	29.7	12.0	1.4	76.3	39.4	50.1	49.9
71826	BRADLEY	67.3	63.4	30.9	34.4	0.7	1.0	1.4	2.1	6.0	6.3	6.3	6.9	6.2	21.1	29.9	15.0	2.3	77.1	42.6	49.0	51.0
71827	BUCKNER	71.7	67.5	26.5	30.5	0.2	0.2	0.4	0.6	6.8	7.2	7.0	7.5	4.5	23.1	29.3	12.5	2.1	74.4	39.7	49.7	50.3
71828	CALE	64.7	60.3	34.3	38.7	0.0	0.0	0.3	0.8	7.1	7.1	6.8	6.8	5.8	26.6	25.5	12.9	1.3	74.5	37.8	50.0	50.0
71831	COLUMBUS	45.7	39.2	53.1	59.5	0.0	0.0	1.2	3.8	6.3	7.6	7.6	7.6	5.1	22.8	27.8	12.7	2.5	75.9	38.1	48.1	51.9
71832	DE QUEEN	75.3	69.0	4.1	3.8	0.2	0.3	27.9	38.3	8.5	8.3	8.1	7.2	5.3	27.9	22.5	10.3	2.0	70.8	34.4	49.7	50.3
71833	DIERKS	95.1	93.5	2.1	2.8	0.1	0.1	2.9	6.2	6.2	6.3	6.5	6.2	5.3	25.9	27.8	12.6	3.1	77.0	40.4	48.6	51.4
71834	DODDRIDGE	85.6	82.2	13.1	16.3	0.2	0.3	0.4	0.6	5.9	6.1	6.2	5.9	4.5	23.9	28.1	16.8	2.6	78.1	43.1	48.2	51.8
71835	EMMET	83.6	80.4	13.4	15.7	0.1	0.2	2.2	3.4	6.2	6.2	6.6	7.1	5.0	27.3	27.2	12.8	1.6	76.7	39.4	49.7	50.3
71836	FOREMAN	77.9	74.6	16.7	19.2	0.2	0.2	2.3	3.5	7.2	7.3	7.4	6.1	5.1	25.1	26.6	13.2	2.0	74.5	38.7	49.2	50.8
71837	FOUKE	95.5	94.2	2.1	2.7	0.1	0.1	1.3	2.1	7.8	7.6	7.2	6.7	6.0	28.3	25.6	9.8	1.0	73.3	35.3	51.4	48.6
71838	FULTON	59.3	52.7	37.4	42.6	0.1	0.2	2.8	4.4	6.8	7.1	7.2	6.4	5.2	23.9	28.4	13.3	1.8	75.0	39.0	49.7	50.3
71839	GARLAND CITY	82.6	78.6	15.2	18.8	0.2	0.3	0.7	1.2	6.6	7.0	7.3	6.5	5.0	25.9	28.9	11.5	1.3	74.8	39.3	51.5	48.5
71841	GILLHAM	89.9	85.0	0.6	0.7	0.1	0.2	10.2	17.2	7.0	7.0	7.2	6.5	5.6	26.8	27.7	11.2	0.9	74.8	37.7	50.9	49.1
71842	HORATIO	87.2	81.8	2.7	3.0	0.1	0.1	10.7	17.5	7.7	7.4	7.5	7.5	5.5	26.8	24.5	11.3	1.7	72.7	36.2	49.2	50.8
71845	LEWISVILLE	57.8	53.2	40.9	45.3	0.0	0.0	1.5	2.2	5.8	5.9	6.1	7.3	5.7	22.3	29.7	14.3	2.8	77.3	42.6	48.1	51.9
71846	LOCKESBURG	84.3	81.0	11.4	13.2	0.1	0.1	2.4	4.3	6.8	6.8	7.0	6.6	5.2	26.1	26.7	13.0	1.8	75.2	38.7	51.0	49.0
71847	MC CASKILL	80.4	75.0	13.9	16.6	0.1	0.1	5.4	9.3	7.2	7.2	7.2	6.7	5.6	25.4	27.2	12.0	1.5	74.4	38.3	49.8	50.2
71851	MINERAL SPRINGS	53.9	48.5	41.3	44.2	0.1	0.1	6.2	10.9	6.8	6.6	7.0	7.7	5.9	26.4	26.5	11.2	1.9	74.9	37.7	49.0	51.0
71852	NASHVILLE	73.5	68.6	21.2	23.1	0.7	0.7	5.3	9.7	7.3	7.1	7.0	6.9	6.2	25.5	25.5	12.0	2.5	74.4	37.4	49.5	50.5
71853	OGDEN	48.6	45.8	43.2	44.0	1.0	1.0	5.8	8.0	6.4	6.4	6.6	7.0	5.0	23.7	29.9	13.1	1.8	76.3	41.6	49.6	50.4
71854	TEXARKANA	69.1	65.7	27.7	30.4	0.5	0.7	1.7	2.6	7.3	7.2	6.9	6.7	6.4	26.5	25.4	11.5	2.2	74.6	36.7	48.8	51.2
71855	OZAN	58.1	51.7	38.3	43.3	0.0	0.0	3.2	5.4	6.7	7.0	7.1	6.7	5.0	23.2	29.7	13.1	1.4	75.0	40.4	49.6	50.4
71857	PRESCOTT	64.3	60.6	33.6	36.4	0.1	0.1	2.0	3.0	6.4	6.4	6.5	6.4	5.3	24.9	27.6	13.3	3.2	76.7	40.4	48.7	51.3
71858	ROSSTON	67.6	63.5	31.0	34.6	0.0	0.1	0.9	1.3	6.6	6.8	6.6	5.9	5.0	24.8	28.0	14.2	2.0	76.3	40.7	48.8	51.2
71859	SARATOGA	53.7	47.2	43.7	49.5	0.2	0.2	1.7	2.8	6.4	6.7	6.9	5.9	4.9	22.9	30.1	14.1	2.3	76.3	41.9	49.8	50.2
71860	STAMPS	54.0	52.1	44.7	46.4	0.1	0.2	0.7	1.0	6.5	6.6	6.6	7.4	5.3	23.4	26.1	14.3	3.9	75.8	40.4	48.1	51.9
71861	TAYLOR	82.4	78.2	16.7	20.7	0.2	0.4	0.4	0.6	5.5	5.8	6.2	5.8	4.6	22.2	30.2	17.0	2.8	78.8	44.9	48.8	51.2
71862	WASHINGTON	54.9	48.6	41.6	46.6	0.0	0.0	3.6	5.7	7.0	7.2	7.4	6.9	5.5	25.0	27.0	12.7	1.4	74.3	37.7	48.8	51.2
71864	WILLISVILLE	66.1	62.2	32.2	35.7	0.0	0.0	1.4	1.7	6.6	7.0	6.5	5.9	4.7	24.2	28.3	14.3	2.5	76.0	41.2	47.0	53.0
71865	WILTON	92.3	88.0	3.8	8.0	0.0	0.0	0.0	0.0	8.0	8.0	8.0	8.0	8.0	32.0	28.0	0.0	0.0	68.0	31.3	48.0	52.0
71866	WINTHROP	94.3	93.5	1.0	1.2	0.0	0.0	1.1	1.8	6.7	6.7	7.0	5.5	4.6	24.2	28.2	15.4	1.8	76.1	41.4	49.9	50.1
71901	HOT SPRINGS NATIONAL	80.7	77.9	15.3	17.0	0.7	1.0	3.3	5.1	6.0	5.7	5.8	6.2	5.9	23.8	28.7	14.7	3.2	78.7	42.4	48.9	51.1
71909	HOT SPRINGS NATIONAL	97.8	97.2	0.7	0.8	0.3	0.5	1.0	1.5	2.0	1.9	2.0	2.1	2.0	8.4	25.4	51.0	4.9	92.6	67.0	47.4	52.6
	ARKANSAS	80.0	78.2	15.7	15.8	0.8	1.2	3.2	5.1	6.8	6.6	6.5	6.9	6.6	26.0	26.1	12.4	2.0	76.1	37.8	49.1	50.9
	UNITED STATES	75.1	72.0	12.3	12.7	3.8	4.6	12.5	15.7	6.8	6.7	6.6	7.1	6.9	27.0	26.0	10.9	1.9	75.7	36.9	49.2	50.8

#	POST OFFICE NAME	2009 Per Capita Income	2009 HH Income Base	2009 HOUSEHOLD INCOME DISTRIBUTION (%) Less than $25,000	$25,000 to $49,999	$50,000 to $99,999	$100,000 to $149,999	$150,000 or More	MEDIAN HOUSEHOLD INCOME 2009	2014	2009 National Centile	2009 State Centile	2009 Home Value Base	2009 HOME VALUE DISTRIBUTION (%) Less than $50,000	$50,000 to $89,999	$90,000 to $174,999	$175,000 to $399,999	$400,000 or More	2009 Median Home Value
71601	PINE BLUFF	14867	6713	43.8	26.8	24.0	4.0	1.4	29804	31599	8	14	3846	41.0	39.2	17.0	2.6	0.3	58032
71602	WHITE HALL	22549	6747	27.8	27.5	33.2	8.1	3.3	44043	45568	46	84	4808	31.2	27.9	31.4	8.9	0.6	78162
71603	PINE BLUFF	22025	13701	28.8	26.4	32.6	8.2	3.9	45270	46763	49	86	9204	22.4	35.5	32.3	8.4	1.4	80644
71630	ARKANSAS CITY	8750	12	50.0	33.3	16.7	0.0	0.0	25000	27273	3	5	9	77.8	11.1	11.1	0.0	0.0	27500
71631	BANKS	11807	312	61.2	26.0	10.6	1.0	1.3	20409	21105	2	1	268	53.0	25.0	18.7	3.4	0.0	46923
71635	CROSSETT	21500	5275	28.5	28.6	33.5	6.4	3.0	43623	43699	44	83	3889	31.3	31.3	27.4	8.7	1.3	72984
71638	DERMOTT	13665	1471	47.8	26.9	21.2	2.7	1.5	26832	28376	5	7	1037	55.3	28.4	12.7	2.3	1.4	45902
71639	DUMAS	16360	2274	41.9	28.5	23.0	4.4	2.2	31757	34285	11	23	1367	42.4	36.4	18.0	3.2	0.1	57518
71640	EUDORA	13681	1433	51.8	25.5	19.2	2.1	1.5	24021	24956	3	3	984	50.6	29.5	12.4	7.4	0.1	49483
71642	FOUNTAIN HILL	19700	229	35.4	33.6	26.6	3.1	1.3	36908	38156	23	57	194	47.9	22.2	22.2	6.2	1.5	52667
71643	GOULD	12403	646	42.4	29.3	23.4	2.5	2.5	30452	31528	9	18	414	59.9	24.6	10.9	4.3	0.2	40889
71644	GRADY	13328	772	34.6	37.6	21.1	3.6	3.1	34297	35258	16	40	574	46.7	28.7	20.0	4.0	0.5	53878
71646	HAMBURG	18645	2565	31.7	31.5	29.8	5.1	1.9	39557	40524	31	72	2054	37.9	24.6	28.9	7.4	1.2	71189
71647	HERMITAGE	17825	811	39.8	28.0	24.5	4.1	3.6	32009	32747	11	24	604	43.5	24.3	25.3	4.8	2.0	60938
71651	JERSEY	13244	91	41.8	29.7	22.0	3.3	3.3	30364	30620	9	18	78	46.2	24.4	21.8	3.8	3.8	56000
71652	KINGSLAND	18270	453	33.8	30.9	30.2	4.2	0.9	38097	40504	27	64	367	57.8	28.6	11.2	2.5	0.0	45169
71653	LAKE VILLAGE	20717	1995	41.6	24.2	25.4	5.1	3.8	35019	38156	18	44	1401	33.5	24.7	19.3	21.1	1.5	76748
71654	MC GEHEE	17755	2112	47.2	25.5	19.6	4.8	2.9	27274	28747	5	8	1362	36.9	33.6	26.1	3.5	0.0	63333
71655	MONTICELLO	21085	6201	34.2	29.1	27.6	5.3	3.8	37159	38130	24	59	4116	32.4	23.8	29.3	13.1	1.5	79889
71656	MONTICELLO	6961	8	50.0	12.5	37.5	0.0	0.0	25000	45000	3	5	3	0.0	66.7	33.3	0.0	0.0	67500
71658	MONTROSE	15888	347	42.7	31.1	20.2	4.6	1.4	31236	33177	10	21	257	52.9	23.3	22.2	1.6	0.0	47727
71660	NEW EDINBURG	17816	509	33.6	35.8	24.0	5.3	1.4	34372	37340	16	40	432	37.0	36.8	21.8	3.5	0.9	65405
71661	PARKDALE	18067	171	37.4	32.7	24.6	4.1	1.2	35182	38396	18	45	140	50.0	24.3	22.1	3.6	0.0	50000
71662	PICKENS	17380	365	42.2	29.6	20.5	4.1	3.6	30260	31314	8	17	229	43.2	35.4	14.8	4.8	1.7	54559
71663	PORTLAND	17146	322	40.1	32.6	21.1	3.7	2.5	32318	35220	12	27	253	56.5	21.3	15.8	5.9	0.4	44310
71665	RISON	19738	2391	29.9	28.4	33.5	5.6	2.5	42117	43981	40	81	1941	33.9	31.2	25.7	7.8	1.4	72659
71666	MC GEHEE	18588	231	45.9	28.6	16.5	5.6	3.5	27983	29459	6	9	179	58.7	21.8	15.6	2.2	1.7	40882
71667	STAR CITY	18834	2689	31.6	29.4	30.5	6.3	2.2	39984	41951	32	74	2105	34.5	33.0	23.6	7.9	1.0	71543
71670	TILLAR	19474	422	35.5	27.3	28.9	4.7	3.6	35000	36006	18	43	324	42.3	28.1	23.5	6.2	0.0	60000
71671	WARREN	18281	3472	41.3	29.5	22.1	3.9	3.3	31984	33252	11	24	2440	35.5	30.7	25.5	7.0	1.4	64024
71674	WATSON	18229	359	44.0	26.5	22.6	3.9	3.1	29625	31856	7	13	263	51.7	25.5	17.9	3.0	1.9	48200
71675	WILMAR	20244	776	39.0	28.7	23.6	5.0	3.6	34010	34504	16	38	627	42.6	23.9	19.1	12.3	2.1	61410
71676	WILMOT	12445	337	60.2	20.5	16.3	1.2	1.8	17837	18280	1	1	244	61.9	26.6	8.2	2.5	0.8	41714
71677	WINCHESTER	16414	31	38.7	25.8	32.3	3.2	0.0	33615	35000	15	36	25	44.0	28.0	20.0	8.0	0.0	57500
71678	YORKTOWN	16334	320	37.2	34.7	22.2	3.4	2.5	33245	34209	14	33	258	51.2	22.5	17.4	8.1	0.8	49231
71701	CAMDEN	19065	8370	36.7	27.6	28.9	4.8	1.9	37094	39398	24	58	5737	34.3	31.5	27.0	6.7	0.5	67360
71720	BEARDEN	16902	909	35.8	34.1	24.2	4.4	1.5	34626	36123	17	41	705	44.5	40.1	14.0	1.3	0.0	55347
71722	BLUFF CITY	18879	230	31.7	36.5	25.2	4.3	2.2	33958	33964	15	37	199	46.2	25.6	23.6	4.0	0.5	55769
71725	CARTHAGE	14897	411	46.7	27.0	23.8	1.7	0.7	26840	28261	5	7	324	59.9	22.8	13.6	2.8	0.9	42381
71726	CHIDESTER	22703	566	35.0	33.7	21.2	6.5	3.5	33968	35693	15	38	446	41.9	25.8	20.9	10.8	0.7	57826
71730	EL DORADO	21079	13856	33.1	28.2	29.0	6.1	3.5	38808	40248	29	68	9741	32.4	27.9	27.6	10.1	2.0	73598
71740	EMERSON	18842	718	33.8	29.5	29.2	5.4	1.9	39491	40850	31	72	579	45.1	24.5	24.4	5.7	0.3	55816
71742	FORDYCE	16823	2053	39.1	33.1	23.7	2.0	2.2	30540	32262	9	18	1426	48.5	27.6	16.1	6.9	0.9	51556
71743	GURDON	18210	1792	33.6	34.9	26.6	3.8	1.1	36155	36947	21	51	1291	42.3	30.0	20.0	5.8	1.9	61862
71744	HAMPTON	19529	1556	36.9	31.9	25.2	3.3	2.7	34893	35904	17	42	1243	45.6	32.8	17.5	3.6	0.5	54698
71745	HARRELL	19602	312	38.8	30.8	21.2	6.1	3.2	31530	33081	11	22	267	47.2	31.5	15.7	4.9	0.7	53409
71747	HUTTIG	16966	480	38.5	30.2	26.5	3.5	1.3	32806	34270	13	30	401	55.6	31.7	11.0	0.7	1.0	45000
71748	IVAN	32886	132	12.1	41.7	28.0	7.6	10.6	47742	47842	56	90	113	28.3	45.1	15.0	11.5	0.0	69375
71749	JUNCTION CITY	18561	1183	35.2	29.3	29.0	4.7	1.7	37063	38718	24	58	997	42.8	26.3	22.4	7.3	1.2	58614
71751	LOUANN	19585	438	26.3	33.6	35.4	4.6	0.2	44104	43885	46	84	374	32.4	28.9	36.9	1.6	0.3	76667
71752	MC NEIL	16422	469	40.7	29.9	23.5	3.6	2.3	31577	32870	11	22	347	45.5	31.1	17.3	5.5	0.6	54189
71753	MAGNOLIA	20581	6615	35.3	27.1	27.7	6.3	3.6	36269	38042	21	52	4515	31.0	25.6	28.9	13.2	1.3	77422
71758	MOUNT HOLLY	18763	237	32.5	36.3	25.7	4.2	1.3	36750	39066	23	56	197	46.7	24.9	18.8	7.1	2.5	54063
71762	SMACKOVER	17309	1025	33.4	34.1	26.4	4.3	1.8	35847	37350	20	49	776	39.0	26.9	25.8	8.1	0.1	67000
71763	SPARKMAN	20101	682	33.4	31.1	28.9	4.5	2.1	37652	38203	26	62	561	50.8	30.1	16.4	2.7	0.0	49100
71764	STEPHENS	16898	852	43.2	27.1	25.0	3.2	1.5	32399	34931	12	28	669	44.1	32.3	19.3	3.4	0.9	57596
71765	STRONG	17190	1025	40.5	30.2	24.6	2.8	1.9	31711	33173	11	23	839	46.8	27.2	22.8	2.3	1.0	52880
71766	THORNTON	20319	493	32.9	35.7	23.5	3.4	4.5	37807	39238	26	63	420	50.5	19.0	21.4	6.0	3.1	49535
71770	WALDO	16769	1280	42.7	26.2	25.2	4.3	1.6	30839	31421	9	20	952	43.2	28.4	22.1	6.0	0.4	56915
71801	HOPE	16978	6612	35.2	30.2	28.4	4.4	1.8	36034	38080	21	50	4322	28.8	34.4	25.8	9.8	1.2	72394
71822	ASHDOWN	20951	3830	32.0	29.3	28.9	7.0	2.7	38108	39879	27	64	2881	31.7	28.0	33.3	6.9	0.1	73803
71825	BLEVINS	18090	398	29.6	32.9	31.4	4.8	1.3	41088	42118	36	78	313	32.6	27.8	28.4	7.0	4.2	71316
71826	BRADLEY	18573	733	46.8	27.3	18.4	3.8	3.7	27421	28569	5	9	540	51.7	22.0	19.4	4.3	2.6	48333
71827	BUCKNER	17721	405	36.5	29.1	27.9	4.4	2.0	33196	34743	14	33	328	48.2	19.5	23.5	7.0	1.8	52069
71828	CALE	16350	138	30.4	36.2	29.0	2.9	1.4	36834	39076	23	56	121	47.1	24.0	20.7	6.6	1.7	53500
71831	COLUMBUS	16209	29	41.4	31.0	17.2	3.4	6.9	31116	32315	10	21	24	45.8	25.0	16.7	12.5	0.0	55000
71832	DE QUEEN	15201	3440	34.4	32.5	26.7	4.8	1.5	36860	37964	23	57	2431	28.3	29.7	32.3	9.0	0.8	76565
71833	DIERKS	18513	975	32.6	32.2	29.0	2.9	3.3	36604	38252	22	54	783	43.9	25.3	20.9	8.0	1.8	57917
71834	DODDRIDGE	19376	684	40.9	27.8	26.0	3.1	2.2	32998	35287	13	31	564	41.7	25.4	23.8	7.4	1.8	60286
71835	EMMET	18618	700	36.3	29.9	27.6	3.4	2.9	36159	37951	21	51	550	38.2	24.9	27.6	7.5	1.8	65556
71836	FOREMAN	18118	1228	34.2	33.5	26.3	4.4	1.6	35162	35962	18	45	960	35.0	27.6	32.1	4.8	0.5	71304
71837	FOUKE	18159	2491	26.9	31.4	33.5	6.6	1.5	43594	45485	44	83	2018	33.0	26.8	30.0	8.8	1.4	75773
71838	FULTON	15996	461	39.7	29.7	24.1	4.3	2.2	32871	34272	13	30	371	40.4	32.1	18.1	8.4	1.1	60676
71839	GARLAND CITY	21862	239	32.2	27.2	26.4	11.7	2.5	42369	45109	41	81	192	31.3	24.0	30.7	13.5	0.5	81667
71841	GILLHAM	20522	374	27.0	36.9	27.8	7.0	1.3	41403	41945	37	79	300	33.7	24.0	32.3	9.0	1.0	69259
71842	HORATIO	17492	1021	29.4	35.3	28.7	4.7	2.0	37705	38341	26	62	797	30.1	31.4	28.4	8.3	1.9	72170
71845	LEWISVILLE	18427	931	39.7	27.2	25.7	5.6	1.8	32145	34273	12	25	758	52.9	20.8	20.2	5.3	0.8	47778
71846	LOCKESBURG	19429	1137	32.2	31.8	27.7	5.6	2.7	37898	38828	26	63	914	32.2	30.5	24.5	9.8	3.0	71017
71847	MC CASKILL	18480	290	30.7	31.4	31.0	5.2	1.7	42048	42992	39	80	230	27.0	27.4	31.7	9.6	4.3	83333
71851	MINERAL SPRINGS	16860	1005	35.0	35.7	23.7	4.0	1.6	35711	36962	20	48	771	38.4	29.2	23.7	7.5	1.2	64100
71852	NASHVILLE	19473	3689	34.6	29.1	29.1	4.0	3.1	36639	38468	22	54	2532	25.0	25.0	33.5	12.8	3.7	90067
71853	OGDEN	19823	219	29.7	42.0	21.9	4.6	1.8	36837	37318	23	57	171	36.8	21.1	34.5	7.6	0.0	74375
71854	TEXARKANA	21451	13854	34.4	25.3	29.8	6.9	3.6	39454	42805	31	71	8908	25.0	31.8	34.0	8.0	1.2	81949
71855	OZAN	17799	358	40.2	29.9	21.2	4.7	3.9	32217	33837	12	26	286	33.9	26.2	25.5	10.5	3.8	71176
71857	PRESCOTT	16819	2383	40.4	27.0	27.1	4.6	0.9	31996	33038	11	24	1614	37.6	27.9	29.6	4.3	0.6	66080
71858	ROSSTON	17707	643	37.6	28.9	27.8	3.3	2.3	32860	33115	13	30	547	42.4	28.5	23.8	4.8	0.5	59881
71859	SARATOGA	17217	268	39.6	34.0	21.3	4.1	1.1	31954	32947	11	24	216	45.4	29.2	17.6	6.5	1.4	56250
71860	STAMPS	17007	1071	40.8	30.7	23.5	3.2	1.8	31755	33601	11	23	818	53.2	25.8	14.9	5.9	0.2	46829
71861	TAYLOR	20711	835	30.7	33.8	28.4	4.1	3.1	37060	38785	24	58	688	43.3	27.2	21.5	7.8	0.1	57667
71862	WASHINGTON	18205	340	40.0	27.9	25.9	3.5	2.6	33016	35110	13	32	276	36.2	28.6	22.5	10.9	1.8	65769
71864	WILLISVILLE	19151	375	41.9	25.6	26.1	2.9	3.5	30832	30578	9	20	316	44.0	29.1	22.5	4.1	0.3	57308
71865	WILTON	19646	11	36.4	27.3	27.3	9.1	0.0	32290	32290	12	26	10	30.0	40.0	30.0	0.0	0.0	70000
71866	WINTHROP	19856	300	35.3	32.7	23.0	6.3	2.7	33546	33970	14	36	255	39.2	23.5	29.4	5.5	2.4	73750
71901	HOT SPRINGS NATIONAL	21406	12338	37.3	27.5	24.6	6.4	4.2	35467	38856	19	47	7581	24.5	22.8	31.6	16.9	4.2	95980
71909	HOT SPRINGS NATIONAL	35317	7866	12.8	25.7	43.2	12.5	5.8	61063	63072	79	98	6893	8.2	8.1	29.1	43.9	10.9	188718
	ARKANSAS	21917		28.7	29.0	32.0	6.7	3.7	42685	44760				21.5	25.6	34.9	15.2	2.9	95077
	UNITED STATES	27277		20.9	24.4	35.3	11.7	7.6	54719	56938				9.3	13.1	31.6	32.6	13.5	162279

ZIP CODE #	POST OFFICE NAME	FINANCIAL SERVICES: Auto Loan	Home Loan	Invest-ments	Retire-ment Plans	THE HOME: Home Improvements: Home Repair	Lawn & Garden	Furnishings: Comput-ers & Hard-ware-Personal	Major Appli-ances	TV, Radio, Sound Equip-ment	Furni-ture	ENTERTAINMENT: Dine out/ Carry out	Sports Equip-ment	Fees & Tickets	Toys & Games	Travel	Cable TV	PERSONAL: Apparel & Services	Auto Repairs	Health Insur-ance	Pets & Supplies
71601	PINE BLUFF	60	49	48	50	47	58	54	54	60	54	59	41	50	59	50	64	40	57	62	68
71602	WHITE HALL	87	77	76	76	75	86	77	82	81	76	80	62	72	83	74	85	55	80	85	98
71603	PINE BLUFF	85	76	76	77	75	87	78	82	83	76	81	62	74	83	75	87	56	81	89	98
71630	ARKANSAS CITY	54	35	52	33	35	53	38	48	44	36	43	37	28	44	35	49	28	45	50	59
71631	BANKS	53	34	51	32	34	52	37	46	42	35	41	36	28	43	34	47	27	44	49	57
71635	CROSSETT	88	70	75	69	69	86	72	80	78	70	77	61	63	80	68	84	52	78	86	97
71638	DERMOTT	61	44	54	43	44	60	48	56	56	47	54	41	41	55	45	61	36	55	62	68
71639	DUMAS	71	51	65	50	51	70	55	65	63	54	62	48	46	62	52	70	41	63	72	79
71640	EUDORA	60	42	55	41	42	59	46	54	53	45	51	40	38	52	43	58	34	53	59	66
71642	FOUNTAIN HILL	82	59	67	57	58	78	61	71	68	59	66	55	49	71	55	74	45	67	75	86
71643	GOULD	68	51	57	50	50	65	55	61	63	56	61	45	48	62	51	68	41	61	68	74
71644	GRADY	80	56	77	54	57	79	58	72	66	56	64	55	46	67	56	72	43	68	76	87
71646	HAMBURG	87	62	76	60	62	84	64	77	72	62	70	59	51	74	59	78	47	72	81	93
71647	HERMITAGE	86	58	85	55	59	85	61	77	69	58	68	59	47	70	58	77	45	72	81	94
71651	JERSEY	77	54	78	53	56	78	56	71	63	52	62	54	45	63	55	69	41	66	74	85
71652	KINGSLAND	81	58	69	57	58	78	61	71	67	59	66	55	49	70	56	74	44	67	75	87
71653	LAKE VILLAGE	85	61	88	59	63	85	67	80	74	62	72	60	54	73	64	80	48	76	84	96
71654	MC GEHEE	71	51	66	51	52	71	57	65	63	53	61	50	47	62	53	69	41	64	72	80
71655	MONTICELLO	85	67	70	66	66	80	72	76	77	70	76	58	62	78	66	81	51	75	81	92
71656	MONTICELLO	55	23	23	29	21	27	77	38	62	52	63	41	46	60	41	56	44	54	38	52
71658	MONTROSE	78	53	72	50	53	76	56	68	64	54	62	53	43	65	52	70	41	65	72	84
71660	NEW EDINBURG	80	58	71	56	58	78	60	72	66	57	65	55	48	68	56	73	44	67	75	86
71661	PARKDALE	82	56	76	53	56	80	59	73	67	56	66	56	46	69	55	74	44	68	77	89
71662	PICKENS	79	55	70	53	54	77	58	69	66	57	65	53	46	68	54	73	43	67	75	85
71663	PORTLAND	80	54	78	51	54	79	57	72	65	54	63	55	43	65	54	72	42	67	75	87
71665	RISON	93	64	86	62	65	91	67	83	76	64	74	63	53	77	63	83	49	77	87	100
71666	MC GEHEE	85	55	82	52	55	83	59	74	68	56	67	58	44	69	55	76	44	70	79	91
71667	STAR CITY	87	61	78	59	61	85	65	78	72	62	71	59	51	74	60	80	47	73	82	94
71670	TILLAR	89	61	82	59	61	87	65	78	72	61	71	61	50	74	60	79	47	74	83	96
71671	WARREN	74	54	71	53	56	75	60	70	67	55	65	52	49	65	57	73	43	67	77	83
71674	WATSON	82	56	75	53	55	79	59	72	67	56	65	56	45	69	54	74	43	68	76	88
71675	WILMAR	87	63	76	61	63	83	65	77	72	64	71	59	53	75	60	79	48	73	80	93
71676	WILMOT	57	37	54	35	37	55	40	50	46	38	45	39	30	47	37	51	30	47	53	61
71677	WINCHESTER	73	52	60	51	52	69	54	63	60	53	59	48	44	63	49	66	40	60	67	77
71678	YORKTOWN	79	52	73	50	52	77	56	69	64	53	62	54	42	65	52	71	41	65	73	85
71701	CAMDEN	74	58	64	58	57	73	63	69	68	59	67	52	54	69	58	73	45	67	75	83
71720	BEARDEN	79	53	73	50	53	77	56	69	64	54	62	54	43	65	52	71	42	65	73	85
71722	BLUFF CITY	82	56	74	53	56	79	59	72	67	57	65	55	46	69	54	74	43	67	76	88
71725	CARTHAGE	66	43	64	41	43	65	46	58	53	44	52	45	34	54	43	59	34	54	61	71
71726	CHIDESTER	79	65	87	62	70	86	66	80	72	66	70	56	59	68	68	78	47	76	88	93
71730	EL DORADO	82	68	73	68	67	82	71	77	76	69	75	58	64	77	67	81	51	76	83	92
71740	EMERSON	87	58	81	56	58	85	62	77	71	59	69	60	47	73	58	79	46	72	81	94
71742	FORDYCE	77	52	76	50	53	77	56	70	63	52	62	54	43	64	53	70	41	65	74	85
71743	GURDON	81	56	74	53	56	79	58	71	66	56	65	55	46	68	54	73	43	67	75	87
71744	HAMPTON	84	58	74	56	58	81	61	73	69	59	67	57	48	71	56	76	45	69	78	90
71745	HARRELL	85	57	77	55	57	82	61	74	69	58	67	58	47	71	56	76	45	70	78	91
71747	HUTTIG	78	51	75	48	51	76	54	68	63	52	61	53	41	64	51	70	40	64	72	84
71748	IVAN	134	96	138	93	100	136	99	126	110	92	108	94	79	109	98	121	71	115	131	149
71749	JUNCTION CITY	86	60	73	58	60	82	63	75	71	61	69	58	50	73	58	77	46	71	79	91
71751	LOUANN	85	61	77	59	62	83	63	76	70	60	68	58	50	71	59	76	46	71	80	92
71752	MC NEIL	76	52	76	50	53	76	55	69	62	51	60	53	42	62	52	68	40	64	72	84
71753	MAGNOLIA	79	65	71	65	65	79	70	75	75	67	74	56	63	75	66	80	50	74	81	90
71758	MOUNT HOLLY	81	58	83	56	60	82	60	76	66	56	65	57	48	66	59	73	43	70	79	90
71762	SMACKOVER	78	54	77	52	55	79	58	72	66	54	64	55	46	66	56	73	42	68	78	87
71763	SPARKMAN	90	62	81	59	61	87	65	79	74	63	72	61	50	76	60	81	48	74	83	96
71764	STEPHENS	75	51	74	49	52	76	55	69	62	51	61	53	43	63	52	69	40	64	74	83
71765	STRONG	77	52	69	50	52	74	55	67	62	53	61	52	43	64	51	69	41	63	71	82
71766	THORNTON	89	64	74	62	64	85	67	77	74	65	72	60	53	77	61	81	49	73	82	94
71770	WALDO	75	51	71	49	51	74	54	67	61	51	60	51	41	62	51	67	40	63	70	81
71801	HOPE	73	56	64	56	56	72	61	68	67	57	65	51	52	67	57	72	44	66	74	82
71822	ASHDOWN	86	65	78	63	66	86	68	79	75	66	73	59	57	75	64	81	49	75	85	95
71825	BLEVINS	86	62	73	60	62	82	64	75	71	62	70	58	51	74	59	78	47	71	79	92
71826	BRADLEY	75	56	78	52	58	77	57	70	64	57	62	52	48	63	57	70	42	67	76	84
71827	BUCKNER	83	56	82	54	57	83	59	75	67	56	66	57	46	68	57	75	44	70	79	91
71828	CALE	81	58	68	57	58	77	61	71	67	59	66	54	49	70	55	73	44	67	75	86
71831	COLUMBUS	82	54	79	50	53	81	57	72	66	54	65	56	43	67	53	74	43	68	76	89
71832	DE QUEEN	79	58	64	55	58	73	60	69	66	60	65	51	49	68	55	71	44	66	72	82
71833	DIERKS	84	60	78	58	61	83	63	76	69	58	68	59	49	70	59	75	45	71	79	92
71834	DODDRIDGE	81	55	80	53	56	81	58	73	66	54	64	56	45	66	55	73	42	68	77	89
71835	EMMET	84	60	82	58	62	84	62	77	69	58	67	58	50	69	60	75	45	71	80	92
71836	FOREMAN	78	56	71	54	57	76	58	70	64	55	63	53	46	65	55	70	42	65	73	84
71837	FOUKE	83	68	70	66	67	79	68	75	72	68	72	57	60	75	64	76	48	72	77	90
71838	FULTON	79	52	73	50	52	77	56	69	64	53	62	54	42	65	52	71	41	65	73	85
71839	GARLAND CITY	98	70	97	68	72	98	72	91	80	68	79	68	58	80	71	88	52	84	94	108
71841	GILLHAM	90	65	75	63	64	86	67	78	74	65	73	60	54	77	61	81	49	74	83	95
71842	HORATIO	85	61	71	59	61	81	63	74	70	61	69	57	51	73	58	76	46	70	78	90
71845	LEWISVILLE	82	54	80	51	54	81	58	73	66	55	65	56	43	67	54	74	43	68	77	89
71846	LOCKESBURG	88	63	80	61	64	86	65	79	72	62	71	60	52	74	61	79	47	73	82	95
71847	MC CASKILL	86	62	77	60	62	84	64	77	71	61	69	58	51	72	60	77	46	72	80	92
71851	MINERAL SPRINGS	77	54	68	51	53	75	56	68	63	54	62	52	44	65	52	70	41	64	71	83
71852	NASHVILLE	85	63	72	62	62	82	67	76	75	65	73	58	56	76	62	81	49	74	83	93
71853	OGDEN	80	57	76	55	57	80	60	73	67	56	65	56	47	68	57	74	44	68	77	88
71854	TEXARKANA	83	68	71	68	67	80	74	77	78	71	77	58	66	78	69	83	53	77	83	92
71855	OZAN	83	57	82	54	58	83	59	75	67	56	66	57	46	67	57	74	43	70	79	91
71857	PRESCOTT	73	51	73	49	52	74	54	68	61	50	59	51	42	60	52	67	39	63	72	81
71858	ROSSTON	81	56	78	54	57	80	59	73	66	55	64	56	46	67	56	73	43	68	76	88
71859	SARATOGA	73	48	71	45	48	72	51	64	59	48	57	50	38	60	48	66	38	60	68	79
71860	STAMPS	73	50	72	47	50	73	53	67	60	49	59	51	41	61	50	67	39	62	71	80
71861	TAYLOR	82	63	87	61	67	86	64	80	71	62	69	58	55	69	65	77	46	74	86	94
71862	WASHINGTON	78	54	71	52	54	76	57	69	64	54	63	53	44	65	53	70	42	65	73	84
71864	WILLISVILLE	83	56	82	54	57	83	59	75	67	56	66	57	46	68	57	74	43	70	79	91
71865	WILTON	81	58	67	56	58	77	60	70	67	59	65	54	48	70	55	73	44	66	74	85
71866	WINTHROP	80	57	82	55	59	81	59	75	65	55	64	56	47	65	58	71	42	68	78	89
71901	HOT SPRINGS NATIONAL	79	67	76	66	68	79	72	76	76	69	75	56	65	74	69	80	51	76	83	91
71909	HOT SPRINGS NATIONAL	90	102	133	90	122	130	91	114	100	105	96	64	105	85	112	109	64	108	145	123
	ARKANSAS	88	73	79	72	73	85	76	82	80	74	79	62	68	81	72	84	54	80	86	98
	UNITED STATES	100	100	100	100	100	100	100	100	100	100	100	100	100	100	100	100	100	100	100	100

#	POST OFFICE NAME	COUNTY FIPS CODE	POPULATION 2000	POPULATION 2009	POPULATION 2014	2000-2009 ANNUAL RATE % Rate	2000-2009 ANNUAL RATE State Centile	HOUSEHOLDS 2000	HOUSEHOLDS 2009	HOUSEHOLDS 2014	HOUSEHOLDS % Annual Rate 2000-2009	HOUSEHOLDS 2009 Average HH Size	FAMILIES 2000	FAMILIES 2009	FAMILIES % Annual Rate 2000-2009
71913	HOT SPRINGS NATIONAL	051	37740	43350	46238	1.5	85	17021	19338	20656	1.4	2.23	11063	12026	0.9
71921	AMITY	019	1847	1988	2030	0.8	68	738	799	819	0.9	2.49	542	566	0.5
71922	ANTOINE	109	93	88	86	-0.6	18	41	40	39	-0.3	2.20	30	28	-0.7
71923	ARKADELPHIA	019	16603	16596	16608	0.0	40	6170	6289	6311	0.2	2.32	3871	3762	-0.3
71929	BISMARCK	059	3846	4481	4702	1.7	89	1495	1730	1821	1.6	2.54	1138	1271	1.2
71933	BONNERDALE	059	1685	1802	1857	0.7	66	650	697	719	0.8	2.59	498	515	0.4
71935	CADDO GAP	097	1300	1356	1364	0.5	58	485	511	515	0.6	2.65	359	366	0.2
71937	COVE	113	2133	2263	2278	0.6	62	817	877	885	0.8	2.58	590	610	0.4
71940	DELIGHT	109	2083	1962	1895	-0.6	18	837	808	787	-0.4	2.43	601	560	-0.8
71941	DONALDSON	059	2186	2292	2326	0.5	58	875	938	958	0.8	2.44	678	703	0.4
71942	FRIENDSHIP	059	144	150	152	0.4	54	58	62	63	0.7	2.42	46	47	0.2
71943	GLENWOOD	109	4814	4980	4938	0.4	54	1830	1918	1910	0.5	2.54	1323	1337	0.1
71944	GRANNIS	113	898	886	872	-0.1	35	329	326	321	-0.1	2.72	253	243	-0.4
71945	HATFIELD	113	1540	1607	1610	0.5	58	588	621	623	0.6	2.59	434	442	0.2
71949	JESSIEVILLE	051	1658	1807	1887	0.9	72	626	678	710	0.9	2.67	482	501	0.4
71950	KIRBY	109	1700	1680	1648	-0.1	35	684	693	685	0.1	2.42	523	516	-0.1
71952	LANGLEY	109	272	260	252	-0.5	22	104	102	100	-0.2	2.55	82	78	-0.5
71953	MENA	113	14403	14349	14187	0.0	40	5873	5896	5842	0.0	2.40	4187	4056	-0.3
71956	MOUNTAIN PINE	051	1782	1866	1923	0.5	58	676	703	725	0.4	2.65	506	504	0.0
71957	MOUNT IDA	097	3050	3220	3257	0.6	62	1330	1430	1455	0.8	2.18	912	944	0.4
71958	MURFREESBORO	109	3007	2866	2781	-0.5	22	1242	1211	1183	-0.3	2.32	891	838	-0.7
71959	NEWHOPE	109	648	672	668	0.4	54	255	271	272	0.7	2.47	193	199	0.3
71960	NORMAN	097	1169	1158	1148	-0.1	35	485	480	475	-0.1	2.41	359	343	-0.5
71961	ODEN	097	933	971	980	0.4	54	377	397	401	0.6	2.45	290	296	0.2
71962	OKOLONA	019	878	900	904	0.3	49	365	377	380	0.4	2.39	269	268	0.0
71964	PEARCY	051	3734	4324	4641	1.6	87	1371	1577	1695	1.5	2.74	1079	1199	1.1
71965	PENCIL BLUFF	097	313	314	312	0.0	40	129	131	130	0.2	2.40	97	95	-0.2
71968	ROYAL	051	3980	4489	4776	1.3	82	1463	1644	1759	1.3	2.61	1140	1237	0.9
71969	SIMS	097	573	568	559	-0.1	35	225	225	223	0.0	2.52	168	162	-0.4
71970	STORY	097	629	604	590	-0.4	25	275	267	262	-0.3	2.26	199	187	-0.7
71971	UMPIRE	061	493	517	517	0.5	58	181	194	196	0.8	2.64	139	145	0.5
71972	VANDERVOORT	113	211	223	223	0.6	62	78	83	84	0.7	2.69	57	58	0.2
71973	WICKES	113	1217	1281	1287	0.6	62	424	451	454	0.7	2.84	325	334	0.3
71998	ARKADELPHIA	019	241	226	225	-0.7	16	15	14	14	-0.7	4.57	7	6	-1.7
72001	ADONA	105	722	776	795	0.8	68	283	309	318	1.0	2.51	214	227	0.6
72002	ALEXANDER	125	10808	13463	14759	2.4	94	4006	5135	5678	2.7	2.59	3106	3869	2.4
72003	ALMYRA	001	803	790	771	-0.2	31	320	324	319	0.1	2.43	237	232	-0.2
72004	ALTHEIMER	069	1589	1426	1369	-1.2	6	558	527	511	-0.6	2.71	393	355	-1.1
72005	AMAGON	067	359	375	372	0.5	58	146	152	152	0.4	2.17	106	106	0.0
72006	AUGUSTA	147	3292	3068	2938	-0.8	14	1336	1280	1236	-0.5	2.37	936	864	-0.9
72007	AUSTIN	085	5150	6694	7712	2.9	96	1863	2595	3019	3.6	2.58	1518	2055	3.3
72010	BALD KNOB	145	6866	7457	7748	0.9	72	2667	2949	3082	1.1	2.52	1952	2081	0.7
72011	BAUXITE	125	3504	4338	4858	2.3	93	1240	1567	1766	2.6	2.77	1003	1235	2.3
72012	BEEBE	145	9032	10820	11640	2.0	91	3433	4162	4493	2.1	2.58	2609	3064	1.8
72013	BEE BRANCH	141	1658	1752	1792	0.6	62	666	718	739	0.8	2.44	502	525	0.5
72014	BEEDEVILLE	067	105	108	107	0.3	49	43	45	45	0.5	2.38	31	32	0.3
72015	BENTON	125	21150	25597	28165	2.1	92	7993	9972	11095	2.4	2.47	5770	6980	2.1
72016	BIGELOW	105	2718	2687	2662	-0.1	35	996	996	990	0.0	2.68	764	742	-0.3
72017	BISCOE	117	1321	1214	1169	-0.9	12	530	503	489	-0.6	2.41	390	359	-0.9
72019	BENTON	125	18171	21136	23014	1.6	87	7001	8423	9264	2.0	2.49	5461	6368	1.7
72020	BRADFORD	067	4322	4497	4537	0.4	54	1699	1808	1840	0.7	2.48	1258	1292	0.3
72021	BRINKLEY	095	5736	5099	4768	-1.3	5	2236	2029	1909	-1.0	2.46	1493	1301	-1.5
72022	BRYANT	125	10074	12568	14054	2.4	94	3718	4813	5455	2.8	2.54	2892	3616	2.4
72023	CABOT	085	25055	33973	38533	3.3	97	8934	12267	14001	3.5	2.75	7228	9648	3.2
72024	CARLISLE	085	3565	4052	4332	1.4	84	1417	1656	1787	1.7	2.37	1000	1113	1.2
72025	CASA	105	818	890	914	0.9	72	322	355	367	1.1	2.51	248	265	0.7
72026	CASSCOE	001	375	361	347	-0.4	25	156	155	150	-0.1	2.33	113	108	-0.5
72027	CENTER RIDGE	029	1350	1444	1484	0.7	66	513	561	581	1.0	2.57	387	409	0.6
72028	CHOCTAW	141	1019	1057	1074	0.4	54	425	450	460	0.6	2.33	299	305	0.2
72029	CLARENDON	095	2908	2671	2539	-0.9	12	1228	1146	1095	-0.7	2.32	821	734	-1.2
72030	CLEVELAND	029	439	551	583	2.5	94	172	223	238	2.8	2.47	129	161	2.4
72031	CLINTON	141	5868	5936	5951	0.1	43	2405	2466	2485	0.3	2.35	1671	1649	-0.1
72032	CONWAY	045	25952	31338	34497	2.1	92	9616	11626	12972	2.1	2.51	6884	8051	1.7
72034	CONWAY	045	31593	42551	48165	3.3	97	12376	16797	19126	3.4	2.46	7920	10347	2.9
72035	CONWAY	045	1864	2826	2826	4.6	99	4	4	4	0.0	1.50	0	0	0.0
72036	COTTON PLANT	147	1503	1313	1235	-1.5	2	627	563	534	-1.2	2.33	417	361	-1.5
72038	CROCKETTS BLUFF	001	42	40	39	-0.5	22	20	20	19	0.0	2.00	14	14	0.0
72039	DAMASCUS	045	825	1111	1270	3.3	97	325	443	509	3.4	2.51	250	331	3.1
72040	DES ARC	117	3511	3339	3245	-0.5	22	1440	1401	1372	-0.3	2.33	1015	950	-0.7
72041	DE VALLS BLUFF	117	1912	1768	1701	-0.8	14	805	771	750	-0.5	2.29	572	528	-0.9
72042	DE WITT	001	5905	5687	5510	-0.4	25	2370	2327	2269	-0.2	2.35	1693	1602	-0.6
72044	EDGEMONT	023	859	1309	1496	4.7	99	387	599	688	4.8	2.19	291	436	4.5
72045	EL PASO	145	1009	1103	1161	1.0	75	388	432	457	1.2	2.53	303	327	0.8
72046	ENGLAND	085	4718	4876	4977	0.4	54	1818	1922	1976	0.6	2.50	1319	1333	0.1
72047	ENOLA	045	723	821	894	1.4	84	265	310	340	1.7	2.65	199	225	1.3
72048	ETHEL	001	77	74	71	-0.4	25	35	34	33	-0.3	2.18	26	25	-0.4
72051	FOX	137	1105	1109	1123	0.0	40	446	459	468	0.3	2.42	331	331	0.0
72052	GARNER	145	76	83	91	1.0	75	27	30	33	1.1	2.77	19	21	1.1
72055	GILLETT	001	977	916	878	-0.7	16	421	407	393	-0.4	2.25	293	272	-0.8
72057	GRAPEVINE	053	1103	1170	1194	0.6	62	402	433	444	0.8	2.70	317	332	0.5
72058	GREENBRIER	045	12276	14284	15654	1.7	89	4458	5273	5816	1.8	2.71	3518	4054	1.5
72060	GRIFFITHVILLE	145	594	601	606	0.1	43	247	255	259	0.3	2.36	173	171	-0.1
72063	HATTIEVILLE	029	1514	1715	1798	1.4	84	590	687	727	1.7	2.50	452	511	1.3
72064	HAZEN	117	1800	1774	1744	-0.2	31	721	735	729	0.2	2.32	514	506	-0.2
72065	HENSLEY	125	4268	4797	5129	1.3	82	1607	1846	1987	1.5	2.42	1260	1411	1.2
72066	HICKORY PLAINS	117	507	476	460	-0.7	16	191	184	179	-0.4	2.59	147	137	-0.8
72067	HIGDEN	023	2529	2680	2719	0.6	62	1099	1184	1208	0.8	2.26	823	856	0.4
72068	HIGGINSON	145	399	440	457	1.1	78	163	182	190	1.2	2.42	123	132	0.8
72069	HOLLY GROVE	095	1224	1019	936	-2.0	1	491	415	384	-1.8	2.46	314	253	-2.3
72070	HOUSTON	105	1203	1217	1218	0.1	43	494	506	509	0.3	2.40	353	349	-0.1
72072	HUMNOKE	085	536	607	644	1.4	84	212	246	263	1.6	2.47	154	171	1.1
72073	HUMPHREY	001	1360	1323	1296	-0.3	27	544	548	541	0.1	2.41	392	382	-0.3
72076	JACKSONVILLE	119	39672	40496	41187	0.2	45	15039	15829	16251	0.6	2.55	11071	11134	0.1
72079	JEFFERSON	069	573	614	618	0.7	66	212	240	244	1.4	2.54	167	182	0.9
72080	JERUSALEM	029	471	581	636	2.3	93	190	242	267	2.6	2.40	141	174	2.3
	ARKANSAS					0.9					1.1	2.46			0.7
	UNITED STATES					1.0					1.1	2.59			0.9

ZIP CODE #	POST OFFICE NAME	RACE (%) White 2000	White 2009	Black 2000	Black 2009	Asian/Pacific 2000	Asian/Pacific 2009	% Hispanic Origin 2000	% Hispanic Origin 2009	2009 AGE DISTRIBUTION (%) 0-4	5-9	10-14	15-19	20-24	25-44	45-64	65-84	85+	18+	MEDIAN AGE 2009	% 2009 Males	% 2009 Females
71913	HOT SPRINGS NATIONAL	91.1	89.0	5.4	6.4	0.5	0.8	2.6	4.1	5.4	5.5	5.6	5.3	4.4	22.9	30.0	18.1	2.9	80.3	45.7	48.2	51.8
71921	AMITY	95.7	94.1	0.5	0.7	0.1	0.1	3.0	4.7	7.1	7.1	7.0	6.1	4.8	26.3	25.5	14.1	2.0	75.0	38.8	51.2	48.8
71922	ANTOINE	75.0	70.5	21.7	25.0	0.0	0.0	1.1	2.3	6.8	6.8	6.8	6.8	6.8	21.6	27.3	14.8	2.3	75.0	40.8	51.1	48.9
71923	ARKADELPHIA	72.8	68.9	23.4	26.1	0.9	1.3	2.2	3.3	5.6	5.1	5.4	10.4	14.0	22.7	22.1	12.4	2.5	80.9	32.9	47.9	52.1
71929	BISMARCK	97.2	96.2	0.4	0.6	0.2	0.3	2.1	3.3	5.8	6.0	6.5	6.6	4.7	24.3	30.6	13.9	1.5	77.5	42.0	50.1	49.9
71933	BONNERDALE	96.4	95.2	0.3	0.4	0.5	0.8	2.0	3.3	6.5	6.6	6.7	6.7	5.2	25.2	29.5	12.3	1.3	76.1	40.1	51.6	48.4
71935	CADDO GAP	93.6	91.0	0.5	0.6	0.2	0.4	5.1	8.0	7.0	7.0	7.2	6.5	5.3	24.0	27.7	13.9	1.5	74.9	40.4	50.8	49.2
71937	COVE	93.4	91.4	0.5	0.5	0.1	0.1	4.1	6.3	7.0	6.8	7.0	7.2	6.0	26.0	26.4	12.2	1.4	74.8	37.7	51.3	48.7
71940	DELIGHT	86.9	84.0	8.5	9.9	0.3	0.5	2.3	3.4	6.5	6.7	6.9	6.3	4.8	23.0	28.5	14.8	2.4	75.8	41.8	51.3	48.7
71941	DONALDSON	97.8	97.1	0.2	0.3	0.1	0.2	1.1	1.7	5.9	6.1	6.4	5.8	5.0	25.9	29.6	13.6	1.7	78.1	40.8	50.8	49.2
71942	FRIENDSHIP	97.2	96.0	0.0	0.0	0.0	0.0	1.4	2.0	6.7	6.7	6.7	6.0	4.7	28.0	26.7	12.7	2.0	76.7	38.8	51.3	48.7
71943	GLENWOOD	92.5	89.1	0.6	0.7	0.2	0.3	7.2	11.0	7.5	6.8	6.8	6.6	5.7	24.2	25.5	14.0	3.1	75.0	39.1	50.1	49.9
71944	GRANNIS	81.2	74.0	0.3	0.3	0.3	0.5	14.9	22.8	7.6	7.3	7.0	6.4	6.4	29.6	23.8	10.8	1.0	74.4	35.2	50.1	49.9
71945	HATFIELD	94.7	93.9	0.1	0.1	0.1	0.1	1.1	1.8	7.5	7.7	7.6	6.2	4.5	23.5	27.9	13.6	1.6	73.3	39.7	48.0	52.0
71949	JESSIEVILLE	98.3	97.7	0.2	0.2	0.3	0.5	0.6	1.0	5.7	5.8	5.7	5.7	4.6	21.5	28.4	20.3	2.3	79.3	45.7	49.1	50.9
71950	KIRBY	97.1	96.1	0.6	0.7	0.1	0.2	1.9	2.8	6.3	6.3	6.6	6.4	5.2	24.5	28.0	15.1	1.7	76.5	41.1	50.7	49.3
71952	LANGLEY	99.3	98.8	0.0	0.0	0.0	0.0	1.1	1.5	6.9	6.9	6.9	5.8	5.4	23.1	27.3	16.2	1.5	75.0	40.7	52.3	47.7
71953	MENA	96.8	96.0	0.1	0.1	0.3	0.5	1.6	2.6	6.4	6.5	6.6	6.1	4.9	22.9	27.0	16.7	2.9	76.7	42.2	49.0	51.0
71956	MOUNTAIN PINE	85.9	81.7	9.9	13.0	0.6	0.9	1.9	3.0	7.2	7.3	7.6	7.0	5.8	26.0	27.2	10.6	1.3	73.6	36.9	50.1	49.9
71957	MOUNT IDA	96.8	96.0	0.2	0.3	0.3	0.5	0.8	1.2	4.5	4.7	4.9	5.3	4.3	19.6	31.0	21.6	4.2	82.5	49.5	47.5	52.5
71958	MURFREESBORO	91.6	89.8	4.9	5.7	0.2	0.3	1.8	2.7	5.6	5.9	6.3	6.1	4.7	24.0	29.8	14.7	2.9	78.0	42.9	49.3	50.7
71959	NEWHOPE	96.9	96.0	0.8	1.0	0.3	0.3	3.4	6.7	5.8	6.1	6.3	6.1	4.3	24.7	29.6	15.5	1.6	78.0	42.7	49.3	50.7
71960	NORMAN	94.8	92.9	0.4	0.5	0.3	0.4	3.2	5.4	6.8	6.8	7.2	6.7	4.9	23.7	27.3	15.0	1.6	75.0	40.6	49.3	50.7
71961	ODEN	95.6	94.5	0.0	0.0	1.0	1.3	0.6	1.0	6.2	6.4	6.7	5.6	4.4	21.8	30.1	17.0	1.9	77.1	44.1	47.9	52.1
71962	OKOLONA	80.1	76.6	17.8	20.9	0.0	0.0	0.8	1.2	6.1	6.2	6.8	5.9	4.4	22.6	30.9	15.4	1.7	77.2	43.5	52.0	48.0
71964	PEARCY	97.3	96.5	0.2	0.3	0.3	0.5	1.7	2.7	6.2	6.4	6.7	6.9	5.6	25.5	30.2	11.4	1.0	76.5	39.6	51.8	48.2
71965	PENCIL BLUFF	96.5	95.9	0.6	0.6	0.3	0.6	0.6	0.6	6.7	7.3	7.3	5.4	3.8	20.1	29.6	17.8	1.9	74.8	44.5	48.7	51.3
71968	ROYAL	93.6	91.6	3.9	5.4	0.1	0.1	1.6	2.7	5.3	5.6	5.9	9.3	6.0	23.0	30.9	12.8	1.1	77.5	40.9	51.5	48.5
71969	SIMS	97.0	96.3	0.7	0.7	0.2	0.4	0.5	0.9	6.5	7.4	7.6	5.5	3.5	19.5	30.1	18.1	1.8	75.0	45.0	48.9	51.1
71970	STORY	96.5	95.9	0.3	0.3	0.2	0.2	0.8	1.3	5.3	6.0	6.3	6.0	3.8	20.2	30.0	20.2	2.3	78.6	46.8	50.3	49.7
71971	UMPIRE	97.0	95.9	1.0	1.4	0.0	0.0	7.9	15.9	6.2	6.6	6.8	5.6	3.5	27.3	28.8	13.5	1.7	77.0	40.6	51.8	48.2
71972	VANDERVOORT	94.3	92.4	0.9	0.9	0.0	0.0	3.8	5.8	6.3	6.3	6.7	7.6	5.8	26.0	26.5	13.5	1.3	75.3	38.7	51.1	48.9
71973	WICKES	83.1	76.8	0.0	0.0	0.2	0.2	17.9	26.6	8.7	8.7	8.3	7.7	5.6	26.2	23.2	10.6	1.1	69.6	34.1	50.5	49.5
71998	ARKADELPHIA	90.8	88.5	5.8	6.6	1.7	2.7	1.3	1.8	1.3	0.9	1.3	30.5	48.7	7.1	6.2	3.5	0.4	94.2	21.6	54.4	45.6
72001	ADONA	97.2	96.8	0.6	0.6	0.1	0.1	1.0	1.3	7.0	6.7	6.7	6.4	5.3	25.6	26.2	14.4	1.7	75.8	39.6	50.6	49.4
72002	ALEXANDER	94.3	92.5	3.0	3.9	0.5	0.8	1.3	2.1	6.5	6.9	7.2	7.0	5.2	28.8	28.5	9.1	0.7	74.8	37.3	50.6	49.4
72003	ALMYRA	91.6	90.0	7.9	9.2	0.0	0.1	0.2	0.4	6.7	7.0	6.7	4.7	4.3	25.9	30.1	12.9	1.6	76.7	41.1	51.9	48.1
72004	ALTHEIMER	38.1	31.7	59.4	65.0	0.5	0.6	2.4	3.3	7.2	7.2	7.1	7.2	6.1	22.6	27.6	13.0	2.0	74.3	38.5	46.2	53.8
72005	AMAGON	89.4	86.7	7.0	8.5	0.3	0.5	2.8	4.3	5.6	5.6	5.6	6.7	9.3	24.5	26.7	13.6	2.4	79.7	40.6	49.9	50.1
72006	AUGUSTA	58.8	54.7	40.1	44.2	0.0	0.0	0.6	0.8	6.6	7.1	6.8	6.8	5.8	23.2	28.4	13.3	2.0	75.4	39.5	49.5	50.5
72007	AUSTIN	97.3	96.4	0.2	0.4	0.3	0.5	1.7	2.8	6.7	6.6	6.8	7.2	6.2	28.2	28.2	9.1	0.9	75.4	37.3	49.8	50.2
72010	BALD KNOB	94.0	92.4	3.0	3.6	0.4	0.6	2.4	3.8	6.8	6.7	7.1	7.0	5.8	26.1	26.8	12.0	1.6	75.1	38.2	49.0	51.0
72011	BAUXITE	97.9	97.5	0.6	0.7	0.2	0.3	1.1	1.7	7.4	7.3	7.1	7.4	6.4	29.6	26.3	7.8	0.7	73.7	35.2	49.0	51.0
72012	BEEBE	93.8	92.6	3.4	3.8	0.5	0.7	1.2	1.9	6.7	6.7	6.8	7.1	6.2	26.5	27.8	10.8	1.5	75.7	37.7	48.7	51.3
72013	BEE BRANCH	97.8	97.2	0.1	0.1	0.3	0.4	1.6	2.3	6.2	6.6	6.8	6.1	4.8	24.7	29.1	14.0	1.8	76.6	41.1	51.0	49.0
72014	BEEDEVILLE	96.1	92.6	1.0	1.9	0.0	0.9	2.9	4.6	6.5	5.6	6.5	5.6	5.6	23.1	29.6	14.8	2.8	77.8	43.3	50.0	50.0
72015	BENTON	92.2	91.3	5.0	5.1	0.4	0.6	2.0	3.0	6.8	6.8	6.7	6.5	5.8	27.8	25.8	11.6	2.2	75.7	37.9	48.7	51.3
72016	BIGELOW	92.7	91.1	4.6	5.6	0.1	0.2	1.0	1.5	6.6	6.7	7.2	7.3	5.7	25.6	29.5	10.2	1.0	74.8	38.6	50.5	49.5
72017	BISCOE	76.2	73.7	22.6	24.6	0.1	0.2	0.8	1.2	5.3	5.4	5.6	6.1	5.5	24.8	31.6	13.6	2.1	80.1	42.9	50.9	49.1
72019	BENTON	97.3	96.5	0.7	0.9	0.5	0.8	1.1	1.7	6.1	6.3	6.7	6.3	5.1	26.2	29.7	12.2	1.3	76.8	40.2	49.7	50.3
72020	BRADFORD	97.8	97.2	0.2	0.3	0.1	0.2	1.3	2.1	6.2	6.2	6.5	6.6	5.4	25.6	27.9	13.9	1.7	77.1	40.3	49.5	50.5
72021	BRINKLEY	57.1	53.0	40.8	44.3	0.2	0.3	1.2	1.8	7.6	7.3	7.6	7.4	5.8	20.5	25.8	14.7	3.2	73.0	39.5	46.2	53.8
72022	BRYANT	95.0	93.2	2.4	3.1	1.0	1.5	1.1	1.8	7.0	6.8	7.0	7.0	5.8	27.6	27.3	9.9	1.7	74.5	37.4	48.3	51.7
72023	CABOT	96.7	95.6	0.4	0.5	0.7	1.0	1.7	2.7	7.5	7.4	7.4	7.2	6.1	29.2	26.0	8.3	0.9	73.1	35.0	49.2	50.8
72024	CARLISLE	87.9	83.5	10.7	14.8	0.3	0.3	0.7	1.1	5.8	6.0	6.4	6.5	4.7	24.3	28.2	14.7	3.4	77.7	42.1	49.2	50.8
72025	CASA	97.4	96.7	0.6	0.8	0.1	0.2	0.5	0.8	7.4	7.2	7.0	6.6	5.4	25.7	25.4	13.7	1.6	74.4	38.7	50.8	49.2
72026	CASSCOE	74.3	69.5	24.3	29.1	0.0	0.0	0.0	0.0	6.4	6.9	6.9	5.0	5.0	23.5	31.3	13.3	1.7	76.5	42.2	51.0	49.0
72027	CENTER RIDGE	91.6	89.7	6.1	7.1	0.2	0.3	1.9	3.0	6.8	6.9	6.9	6.4	4.7	24.5	28.4	13.6	1.7	75.3	40.3	50.6	49.4
72028	CHOCTAW	97.3	96.6	0.1	0.1	0.2	0.3	1.2	1.7	5.5	6.0	6.1	6.0	4.5	21.5	31.1	17.3	2.0	78.3	45.3	50.1	49.9
72029	CLARENDON	69.8	65.5	28.6	32.3	0.1	0.1	1.9	2.7	6.0	6.2	6.6	6.8	5.1	23.6	28.5	14.7	2.5	77.2	41.4	49.6	50.4
72030	CLEVELAND	93.8	91.8	4.6	5.6	0.0	0.0	1.8	2.7	5.8	6.4	6.4	6.5	4.5	24.0	29.4	15.2	1.8	77.3	42.4	50.5	49.5
72031	CLINTON	95.9	94.8	0.5	0.6	0.3	0.5	1.6	2.6	5.5	5.7	5.9	6.3	4.7	22.5	29.0	16.9	3.6	79.0	44.6	49.4	50.6
72032	CONWAY	86.6	84.8	10.4	11.4	0.5	0.8	1.9	2.8	6.9	6.6	6.4	8.3	8.5	29.2	24.5	8.6	1.1	76.3	33.8	49.2	50.8
72034	CONWAY	85.1	83.0	11.0	11.8	1.3	1.8	2.2	3.4	7.7	6.3	5.5	6.6	11.2	33.5	19.8	7.7	1.7	77.1	30.4	48.3	51.7
72035	CONWAY	76.9	73.4	18.5	20.6	2.6	3.7	1.0	1.5	0.0	0.0	0.0	58.8	39.5	1.6	0.0	0.0	0.0	99.8	19.3	38.4	61.6
72036	COTTON PLANT	41.8	38.4	56.6	59.8	0.2	0.3	1.3	1.4	7.9	7.2	7.8	7.6	5.0	19.0	26.2	15.6	3.7	72.1	41.2	44.3	55.7
72038	CROCKETTS BLUFF	75.6	67.5	24.4	30.0	0.0	0.0	0.0	0.0	5.0	5.0	5.0	5.0	5.0	25.0	35.0	15.0	0.0	80.0	45.0	52.5	47.5
72039	DAMASCUS	80.5	77.3	17.5	20.3	0.2	0.4	0.7	0.9	6.8	6.7	6.7	7.0	5.6	25.1	27.9	12.7	1.6	75.7	39.9	50.0	50.0
72040	DES ARC	88.5	86.6	9.7	11.1	0.2	0.4	0.9	1.4	6.0	6.3	6.3	6.1	5.0	23.1	28.5	16.1	2.5	77.5	42.9	49.4	50.6
72041	DE VALLS BLUFF	82.7	80.4	16.5	18.6	0.1	0.1	0.4	0.6	5.7	6.2	6.2	5.8	4.8	23.6	30.7	14.5	2.6	78.4	43.3	48.5	51.5
72042	DE WITT	84.9	82.1	13.9	16.4	0.2	0.2	0.6	1.0	6.3	6.4	6.5	5.9	5.0	24.3	28.2	14.6	2.9	77.1	41.6	48.4	51.6
72044	EDGEMONT	98.3	98.2	0.0	0.0	0.1	0.1	0.2	0.4	3.9	3.9	3.9	4.7	3.8	15.7	29.6	32.0	2.5	85.6	56.9	49.3	50.7
72045	EL PASO	97.1	96.4	0.1	0.1	0.4	0.5	1.4	2.2	6.5	6.5	7.0	6.3	5.5	26.3	28.5	12.1	1.2	76.1	39.2	50.7	49.3
72046	ENGLAND	70.2	62.0	28.3	36.4	0.1	0.1	1.3	1.9	6.8	7.1	7.0	6.6	4.9	24.5	27.9	12.8	2.4	75.1	39.5	47.9	52.1
72047	ENOLA	97.4	96.5	0.0	0.1	0.3	0.2	1.7	2.6	7.6	7.4	7.3	6.8	6.2	26.1	26.3	10.7	1.6	73.4	37.0	51.4	48.6
72048	ETHEL	94.7	93.2	5.3	6.8	0.0	0.0	0.0	1.4	5.4	6.8	6.8	4.1	4.1	24.3	28.4	17.6	2.7	77.0	44.0	48.6	51.4
72051	FOX	97.6	97.1	0.4	0.5	0.1	0.1	1.0	1.4	5.4	5.5	6.0	5.5	4.7	20.1	33.3	17.7	1.9	79.8	46.8	51.3	48.7
72052	GARNER	93.5	91.6	1.3	1.2	0.0	0.0	2.6	4.8	7.2	7.2	7.2	7.2	4.8	26.5	25.3	13.3	1.2	73.5	37.9	50.6	49.4
72055	GILLETT	88.1	85.3	11.1	13.5	0.0	0.0	1.0	1.5	4.4	4.7	5.5	6.8	5.0	23.6	33.7	14.2	2.2	81.2	45.1	48.8	51.2
72057	GRAPEVINE	88.0	86.4	10.1	11.5	0.1	0.1	0.4	0.5	5.8	5.7	6.1	7.0	6.9	25.2	30.3	11.8	1.2	78.4	39.8	51.8	48.2
72058	GREENBRIER	96.3	95.4	1.4	1.6	0.1	0.2	0.9	1.4	7.3	7.2	7.3	7.4	5.7	28.1	26.7	9.3	1.1	73.7	36.4	49.8	50.2
72060	GRIFFITHVILLE	96.1	66.2	1.0	30.8	0.0	0.2	2.4	2.8	7.3	7.5	7.3	6.7	5.0	22.3	27.5	15.0	1.5	73.7	40.5	52.4	47.6
72063	HATTIEVILLE	96.1	94.9	2.0	2.7	0.1	0.2	0.3	0.5	5.8	6.0	6.5	7.0	4.8	23.7	30.0	14.4	1.7	77.3	42.3	48.6	51.4
72064	HAZEN	82.0	79.4	16.9	19.5	0.0	0.0	0.7	1.0	6.0	6.3	6.5	5.8	4.1	22.7	29.3	15.5	3.8	77.2	43.9	49.4	50.6
72065	HENSLEY	85.4	83.7	11.4	11.9	1.0	1.5	0.9	1.3	6.1	6.3	6.5	6.5	5.6	30.7	28.2	9.2	0.8	77.0	38.0	53.2	46.8
72066	HICKORY PLAINS	92.7	91.0	4.1	4.6	1.0	1.5	1.8	2.7	8.4	8.2	8.2	6.1	4.2	25.8	25.8	11.6	1.7	71.4	37.3	51.7	48.3
72067	HIGDEN	97.5	97.2	0.1	0.1	0.2	0.2	1.0	1.5	4.3	4.6	4.8	4.4	4.1	16.0	34.7	24.6	2.4	83.6	52.8	50.7	49.3
72068	HIGGINSON	96.5	95.5	0.0	0.0	0.5	0.7	3.3	5.2	6.6	6.1	6.6	6.8	6.1	28.9	27.5	10.2	1.1	76.6	38.2	51.1	48.9
72069	HOLLY GROVE	38.1	34.1	61.2	65.1	0.1	0.1	0.3	0.4	6.2	6.6	6.5	7.6	5.9	21.7	27.1	15.4	3.1	76.2	41.2	45.0	55.0
72070	HOUSTON	95.1	94.1	2.0	2.4	0.1	0.2	1.2	1.8	6.2	6.4	6.8	6.4	4.7	23.9	28.4	15.5	1.6	76.3	41.7	50.5	49.5
72072	HUMNOKE	69.8	57.7	27.8	39.4	0.2	0.2	1.5	2.1	6.6	6.8	6.6	6.9	5.1	25.7	28.2	12.4	1.8	75.8	39.1	48.8	51.2
72073	HUMPHREY	62.2	57.7	35.5	39.6	0.1	0.2	1.1	1.5	6.1	6.2	6.5	6.8	5.9	24.8	28.9	12.7	2.0	77.1	40.5	48.1	51.9
72076	JACKSONVILLE	74.4	67.8	19.8	24.8	1.7	2.4	3.0	4.6	8.8	7.9	7.1	6.5	7.3	29.5	23.0	9.1	0.8	72.3	32.6	48.9	51.1
72079	JEFFERSON	88.1	83.9	9.6	12.7	0.2	0.3	2.8	4.4	7.3	7.2	6.7	6.4	6.7	28.8	27.7	8.5	0.8	75.2	35.9	51.8	48.2
72080	JERUSALEM	92.2	90.9	6.6	7.7	0.0	0.0	0.4	0.7	4.8	5.3	5.9	6.2	4.5	22.9	32.0	16.7	1.7	80.2	45.2	51.5	48.5
	ARKANSAS	80.0	78.2	15.7	15.8	0.8	1.2	3.2	5.1	6.8	6.6	6.5	6.9	6.6	26.0	26.1	12.4	2.0	76.1	37.8	49.1	50.9
	UNITED STATES	75.1	72.0	12.3	12.7	3.8	4.6	12.5	15.7	6.8	6.7	6.6	7.1	6.9	27.0	26.0	10.9	1.9	75.7	36.9	49.2	50.8

ZIP CODE #	POST OFFICE NAME	2009 Per Capita Income	2009 HH Income Base	2009 HOUSEHOLD INCOME DISTRIBUTION (%) Less than $25,000	$25,000 to $49,999	$50,000 to $99,999	$100,000 to $149,999	$150,000 or More	MEDIAN HOUSEHOLD INCOME 2009	2014	2009 National Centile	2009 State Centile	2009 Home Value Base	2009 HOME VALUE DISTRIBUTION (%) Less than $50,000	$50,000 to $89,999	$90,000 to $174,999	$175,000 to $399,999	$400,000 or More	2009 Median Home Value
71913	HOT SPRINGS NATIONAL	24193	19338	26.8	32.0	30.6	6.8	3.8	42405	44687	41	81	13639	17.5	22.5	35.9	18.6	5.6	106451
71921	AMITY	17307	799	38.3	30.9	25.0	4.0	1.8	33308	34213	14	34	639	40.2	24.3	22.5	10.6	2.3	64500
71922	ANTOINE	18636	40	37.5	37.5	20.0	2.5	2.5	33162	34057	14	32	34	50.0	17.6	26.5	5.9	0.0	50000
71923	ARKADELPHIA	19276	6289	37.8	23.9	29.6	6.0	2.7	37467	39492	25	61	3853	21.7	19.9	40.0	16.1	2.2	102077
71929	BISMARCK	18945	1730	28.1	37.3	26.6	4.9	3.1	38422	40232	28	66	1431	23.7	20.7	38.9	14.0	2.8	97318
71933	BONNERDALE	18521	697	28.8	34.7	29.4	5.0	2.0	38031	40199	27	64	590	26.3	29.5	30.2	12.4	1.7	82609
71935	CADDO GAP	16403	511	32.9	33.1	29.2	3.9	1.0	39193	40163	30	70	422	39.8	19.0	25.6	11.4	4.3	69167
71937	COVE	16530	877	41.3	32.2	20.1	4.7	1.8	29813	30589	8	14	694	41.8	29.0	24.1	4.8	0.4	57403
71940	DELIGHT	18399	808	37.1	34.9	22.5	3.5	2.0	33101	33747	13	32	692	42.9	17.5	27.2	9.8	2.6	62692
71941	DONALDSON	18778	938	26.4	35.8	32.1	5.0	0.6	40142	41302	33	75	799	39.2	24.9	29.9	5.6	0.4	67019
71942	FRIENDSHIP	20924	62	22.6	30.6	40.3	6.5	0.0	45000	44307	48	85	52	36.5	30.8	28.8	3.8	0.0	63333
71943	GLENWOOD	17030	1918	33.8	35.8	24.6	4.6	1.2	35177	35877	18	45	1436	37.8	20.9	27.6	10.7	3.1	75851
71944	GRANNIS	17360	326	31.9	38.0	23.3	4.0	2.8	36199	37851	21	51	243	39.1	24.7	25.5	7.4	3.3	67813
71945	HATFIELD	15581	621	41.9	32.5	20.6	2.7	2.3	29723	30722	8	13	503	29.0	29.4	28.8	9.1	3.6	72045
71949	JESSIEVILLE	21989	678	23.6	31.9	34.1	6.6	3.8	45536	46529	50	86	563	38.4	14.2	31.1	15.8	0.5	85972
71950	KIRBY	19182	693	35.9	32.3	23.2	5.6	2.9	33503	34346	14	35	588	39.1	25.7	21.8	9.5	3.9	64419
71952	LANGLEY	18253	102	35.3	34.3	21.6	4.9	3.9	32498	33949	12	28	84	32.1	32.1	20.2	9.5	6.0	68333
71953	MENA	18081	5896	37.5	33.3	23.8	3.2	2.1	32513	34020	12	28	4606	22.1	29.2	31.5	13.4	3.7	88104
71956	MOUNTAIN PINE	15948	703	33.0	37.4	24.3	4.6	0.7	36273	39826	21	52	553	56.4	20.3	15.4	7.4	0.5	43302
71957	MOUNT IDA	19430	1430	35.6	35.5	22.7	3.6	2.6	33360	33849	14	35	1157	27.6	24.1	31.8	15.2	1.3	87132
71958	MURFREESBORO	19597	1211	34.4	34.7	24.8	4.0	2.1	36367	37017	22	53	924	34.1	33.1	23.8	7.9	1.1	67045
71959	NEWHOPE	19964	271	35.8	28.8	26.2	5.2	4.1	35870	37034	20	49	232	35.8	28.9	25.4	7.3	2.6	66842
71960	NORMAN	16827	480	37.9	31.0	25.8	4.4	0.8	34232	35097	16	39	390	43.1	22.1	23.3	8.5	3.1	59643
71961	ODEN	23488	397	29.7	37.3	22.9	4.3	5.8	38148	39675	27	65	337	26.1	30.9	31.2	9.5	2.4	81897
71962	OKOLONA	18641	377	34.2	30.2	30.8	2.9	1.9	36482	37420	22	53	320	37.2	23.8	26.3	5.3	7.5	77742
71964	PEARCY	19570	1577	25.6	33.7	30.9	6.8	2.9	42847	44846	42	82	1332	24.0	22.0	33.7	16.1	4.1	95464
71965	PENCIL BLUFF	19723	131	34.4	38.2	19.8	3.8	3.8	33719	33588	15	37	113	33.6	25.7	28.3	9.7	2.7	78125
71968	ROYAL	18596	1644	22.9	33.2	38.3	4.6	1.2	46456	46972	53	88	1396	29.3	27.9	24.1	15.6	3.2	81525
71969	SIMS	17367	225	36.4	37.8	19.1	4.0	2.7	32287	32940	12	26	195	35.9	24.1	27.2	9.7	3.1	76538
71970	STORY	17932	267	39.3	31.8	23.2	4.1	1.5	32296	33423	12	27	227	40.1	20.7	27.3	10.1	1.8	73214
71971	UMPIRE	21120	194	32.5	26.8	27.3	7.7	5.7	40000	41869	33	74	162	31.5	27.8	28.4	9.3	3.1	75000
71972	VANDERVOORT	16550	83	36.1	34.9	21.7	6.0	1.2	32298	32315	12	27	68	39.7	30.9	23.5	5.9	0.0	60000
71973	WICKES	14740	451	43.0	32.4	20.0	2.2	2.4	29278	29724	7	12	329	52.0	17.9	24.0	4.6	1.5	47833
71998	ARKADELPHIA	10302	14	21.4	28.6	28.6	14.3	7.1	50000	50000	61	92	7	0.0	0.0	57.1	42.9	0.0	162500
72001	ADONA	19942	309	30.4	33.7	28.2	5.2	2.6	38674	41280	29	67	257	33.9	28.8	26.8	8.2	2.3	74423
72002	ALEXANDER	22408	5135	17.9	29.4	42.2	8.5	2.0	51950	54598	66	94	4316	24.9	22.9	33.0	17.9	1.4	94486
72003	ALMYRA	23926	324	24.1	28.1	39.8	4.6	3.4	48277	47962	57	91	249	36.9	29.7	25.3	6.4	1.6	63214
72004	ALTHEIMER	14644	527	41.9	31.9	21.8	2.5	1.9	30689	32046	9	19	343	57.4	24.8	10.5	7.0	0.3	42917
72005	AMAGON	15524	152	48.0	32.9	17.8	0.7	0.7	26338	27472	4	6	118	59.3	31.4	8.5	0.0	0.8	39286
72006	AUGUSTA	16067	1280	47.3	27.3	20.9	2.9	1.6	27113	28273	5	7	810	51.9	30.0	14.7	3.5	0.0	48571
72007	AUSTIN	22529	2595	16.0	30.9	44.1	6.4	2.5	51922	53898	66	94	2178	20.6	18.8	38.3	19.8	2.6	109772
72010	BALD KNOB	17304	2949	38.0	27.6	28.3	4.6	1.5	35089	36943	18	44	2116	37.1	30.9	25.4	5.9	0.7	62342
72011	BAUXITE	20800	1567	13.7	31.4	48.2	5.2	1.5	53102	55563	68	95	1314	20.4	29.7	39.4	10.3	0.2	89889
72012	BEEBE	21296	4162	24.7	29.3	35.5	7.4	3.1	46823	46802	54	88	3101	15.4	21.0	45.0	15.5	3.2	110505
72013	BEE BRANCH	19860	718	28.8	37.7	26.2	3.5	3.8	36642	37527	22	54	591	28.8	22.5	30.6	13.7	4.4	87917
72014	BEEDEVILLE	14661	45	46.7	35.6	17.8	0.0	0.0	27303	27912	5	8	35	60.0	34.3	5.7	0.0	0.0	36250
72015	BENTON	23598	9972	21.3	27.3	39.2	9.1	3.1	51040	53622	64	93	6956	15.0	30.8	41.2	11.9	1.0	96425
72016	BIGELOW	19990	996	25.8	33.4	31.4	6.2	3.1	39928	41817	32	73	863	25.4	31.4	29.8	11.2	2.2	80714
72017	BISCOE	17570	503	37.4	30.0	27.4	4.0	1.2	33627	34543	15	36	361	47.6	20.5	23.8	6.1	1.9	55313
72019	BENTON	28092	8423	14.1	27.4	41.5	11.4	5.7	57722	60139	75	96	6724	12.0	16.3	45.8	21.8	4.2	121335
72020	BRADFORD	16989	1808	36.7	31.3	28.3	2.9	0.9	35221	37212	18	46	1448	48.6	30.0	16.4	4.4	0.6	51250
72021	BRINKLEY	16264	2029	48.3	26.9	20.4	2.1	2.3	27205	28687	5	8	1275	39.9	34.5	21.3	3.6	0.7	58801
72022	BRYANT	27281	4813	14.6	23.1	43.1	15.1	4.1	62774	64281	81	98	4054	19.0	11.3	42.3	25.2	2.3	126134
72023	CABOT	26261	12267	13.6	21.1	45.3	15.0	5.0	64316	65967	83	99	9555	9.1	16.2	48.7	24.6	1.4	124167
72024	CARLISLE	20712	1656	39.5	21.9	30.7	4.6	3.4	36681	40374	23	55	1146	30.5	35.5	24.0	9.6	0.3	68917
72025	CASA	19115	355	32.7	33.0	26.8	5.4	2.3	37732	40477	26	63	304	36.2	30.9	25.7	4.6	2.6	72059
72026	CASSCOE	23460	155	17.4	29.7	46.5	3.9	2.6	51770	51595	65	94	125	35.2	25.6	27.2	12.0	0.0	72500
72027	CENTER RIDGE	18622	561	35.7	26.0	29.9	5.9	2.5	36181	37209	21	51	486	26.7	29.2	33.7	6.0	4.3	82564
72028	CHOCTAW	20837	450	32.4	36.9	22.9	3.6	4.2	34087	34568	16	39	367	28.1	17.2	31.9	18.5	4.4	101359
72029	CLARENDON	17515	1146	44.4	25.9	25.0	2.8	1.9	30771	31245	9	19	794	52.0	27.8	17.5	2.4	0.3	48384
72030	CLEVELAND	19009	223	37.2	27.4	26.0	6.7	2.7	35978	37183	21	50	193	29.5	27.5	26.9	10.4	5.7	81563
72031	CLINTON	18026	2466	42.3	30.0	22.0	3.2	2.6	30373	31332	9	18	1929	28.7	29.9	28.7	10.6	2.2	79543
72032	CONWAY	23768	11626	20.9	26.5	39.0	9.9	3.6	52498	55692	67	95	8068	12.6	19.3	47.4	18.3	2.5	115291
72034	CONWAY	26688	16797	25.0	23.0	34.3	11.0	6.8	51727	54502	65	94	9783	8.8	11.6	43.3	32.1	4.3	142615
72035	CONWAY	8994	4	75.0	0.0	25.0	0.0	0.0	6667	6667	0	1	0	0.0	0.0	0.0	0.0	0.0	0
72036	COTTON PLANT	12829	563	62.2	22.2	13.9	0.5	1.2	20138	20173	1	1	350	68.6	17.4	10.3	3.4	0.3	32656
72038	CROCKETTS BLUFF	27144	20	15.0	35.0	45.0	5.0	0.0	50000	47368	61	92	16	37.5	25.0	25.0	12.5	0.0	65000
72039	DAMASCUS	19761	443	25.5	32.3	35.4	5.2	1.6	43214	44511	43	83	384	23.7	31.5	32.8	10.7	1.3	83548
72040	DES ARC	19962	1401	35.8	32.1	23.8	5.7	2.6	35076	35566	18	44	1026	37.6	25.4	31.5	4.8	0.7	69091
72041	DE VALLS BLUFF	20057	771	37.6	26.7	31.4	2.6	1.7	36338	37903	22	52	564	40.6	27.1	26.2	5.1	0.9	65135
72042	DE WITT	18118	2327	40.1	27.8	26.6	3.5	2.1	32780	34004	13	29	1591	43.2	27.0	23.6	5.4	0.9	57282
72044	EDGEMONT	21715	599	28.7	33.2	31.7	4.2	2.2	38172	40183	27	65	530	17.9	11.3	37.5	30.2	3.0	140489
72045	EL PASO	22611	432	26.9	28.0	32.6	6.5	6.0	46373	45545	52	88	371	23.2	20.2	36.7	11.1	8.9	104449
72046	ENGLAND	18224	1922	34.8	30.4	28.0	4.9	1.9	36927	39891	23	57	1216	34.5	29.0	25.2	10.2	1.1	66379
72047	ENOLA	17716	310	29.4	35.5	28.4	5.2	1.6	37320	40155	25	60	261	32.2	24.9	27.2	14.2	1.5	80750
72048	ETHEL	20113	34	32.4	35.3	29.4	0.0	2.9	38575	37903	28	67	27	40.7	22.2	29.6	7.4	0.0	65000
72051	FOX	16275	459	40.1	37.9	17.9	1.5	2.6	31630	34329	11	23	395	33.2	29.6	25.3	9.4	2.5	71667
72052	GARNER	13204	30	43.3	30.0	23.3	3.3	0.0	30000	31124	8	16	22	31.8	40.9	27.3	0.0	0.0	65000
72055	GILLETT	22401	407	32.4	33.2	26.3	5.2	2.9	38871	39274	29	68	305	42.0	31.1	23.6	2.6	0.7	61250
72057	GRAPEVINE	18122	433	28.6	31.6	30.5	7.2	2.1	41002	44424	36	78	381	38.8	29.9	21.5	6.0	3.7	71711
72058	GREENBRIER	20977	5273	22.1	27.9	40.8	7.1	2.1	50006	52041	61	92	4215	17.7	23.8	38.2	18.4	1.9	103074
72060	GRIFFITHVILLE	16535	255	36.5	33.3	27.5	2.4	0.4	34004	35813	16	38	199	41.7	23.6	28.1	6.5	0.0	64375
72063	HATTIEVILLE	19571	687	27.9	33.3	30.9	6.1	1.7	40505	40972	34	77	608	23.8	23.5	40.8	9.0	2.8	94571
72064	HAZEN	20152	735	31.0	34.4	27.8	4.2	2.6	37725	38282	26	62	530	29.6	33.8	29.2	7.0	0.4	73585
72065	HENSLEY	24008	1846	19.0	23.3	47.0	9.4	1.4	56565	59517	73	96	1608	23.6	28.0	35.7	11.9	0.8	86905
72066	HICKORY PLAINS	21764	184	31.5	22.3	35.9	4.3	6.0	47640	49308	56	89	152	28.9	22.4	46.7	0.0	2.0	87143
72067	HIGDEN	24339	1184	27.2	30.4	31.7	7.1	3.6	44245	44714	46	84	1024	19.9	19.3	35.4	18.5	6.8	110352
72068	HIGGINSON	17551	182	27.5	39.0	29.1	3.8	0.5	38269	39708	27	65	141	37.6	30.5	24.8	5.7	1.4	67083
72069	HOLLY GROVE	13223	415	55.7	22.9	18.1	2.9	0.5	22003	22772	2	2	271	57.9	26.6	14.0	1.5	0.0	44881
72070	HOUSTON	18462	506	34.8	30.4	28.5	4.0	2.4	35489	37618	19	47	415	27.2	32.3	29.2	8.4	2.9	77821
72072	HUMNOKE	16090	246	44.3	30.1	23.2	0.8	1.6	28316	28877	6	10	181	63.0	29.3	3.9	3.9	0.0	41897
72073	HUMPHREY	17041	548	42.7	25.7	25.4	4.9	1.3	32047	33653	11	25	396	43.9	32.8	19.2	3.8	0.3	57059
72076	JACKSONVILLE	21191	15829	22.3	30.7	39.2	5.9	1.9	47106	49568	54	88	8747	17.1	37.6	36.7	7.7	1.0	85266
72079	JEFFERSON	21120	240	20.0	32.1	39.6	6.7	1.7	47950	49266	56	90	182	39.6	33.0	23.6	3.8	0.0	64167
72080	JERUSALEM	20227	242	35.1	31.0	23.1	8.3	2.5	36976	38034	24	57	211	29.9	24.2	26.5	14.2	5.2	85526
	ARKANSAS	21917		28.7	29.0	32.0	6.7	3.7	42685	44760				21.5	25.6	34.9	15.2	2.9	95077
	UNITED STATES	27277		20.9	24.4	35.3	11.7	7.6	54719	56938				9.3	13.1	31.6	32.6	13.5	162279

#	POST OFFICE NAME	FINANCIAL SERVICES: Auto Loan	FINANCIAL SERVICES: Home Loan	FINANCIAL SERVICES: Invest-ments	FINANCIAL SERVICES: Retire-ment Plans	THE HOME: Home Improvements: Home Repair	THE HOME: Home Improvements: Lawn & Garden	THE HOME: Furnishings: Comput-ers & Hard-ware-Personal	THE HOME: Furnishings: Major Appli-ances	THE HOME: Furnishings: TV, Radio, Sound Equip-ment	THE HOME: Furnishings: Furni-ture	ENTERTAINMENT: Dine out/ Carry out	ENTERTAINMENT: Sports Equip-ment	ENTERTAINMENT: Fees & Tickets	ENTERTAINMENT: Toys & Games	ENTERTAINMENT: Travel	ENTERTAINMENT: Cable TV	PERSONAL: Apparel & Services	PERSONAL: Auto Repairs	PERSONAL: Health Insur-ance	PERSONAL: Pets & Supplies
71913	HOT SPRINGS NATIONAL	84	73	89	71	76	88	74	84	78	72	77	61	68	76	75	83	52	81	89	98
71921	AMITY	77	55	73	54	56	76	57	70	63	54	62	53	46	64	55	70	41	65	73	84
71922	ANTOINE	76	50	74	47	50	75	53	67	61	51	60	52	40	62	50	68	40	63	71	82
71923	ARKADELPHIA	75	59	68	60	60	71	68	70	71	64	70	54	59	71	63	75	48	71	75	84
71929	BISMARCK	87	62	89	60	64	88	64	81	71	59	70	61	51	70	63	78	46	74	84	96
71933	BONNERDALE	81	66	76	64	66	80	65	76	69	64	69	56	56	71	63	74	46	71	77	90
71935	CADDO GAP	78	56	75	54	57	78	58	71	64	54	63	54	46	64	56	70	42	66	75	85
71937	COVE	77	55	65	53	55	74	57	67	64	55	62	52	46	66	52	70	42	64	71	82
71940	DELIGHT	81	56	81	54	57	81	58	74	66	55	64	56	46	66	57	73	43	68	77	89
71941	DONALDSON	83	59	74	57	60	80	61	74	68	59	67	56	49	70	57	74	45	69	77	89
71942	FRIENDSHIP	91	66	75	64	65	87	68	79	76	66	74	61	55	79	62	83	50	75	84	97
71943	GLENWOOD	78	56	72	54	57	77	58	71	65	55	63	53	47	66	55	71	42	66	75	85
71944	GRANNIS	86	60	74	58	60	82	63	75	71	61	69	58	50	73	58	77	46	71	79	91
71945	HATFIELD	72	52	74	50	54	73	53	67	59	49	58	51	42	58	52	65	38	62	70	80
71949	JESSIEVILLE	98	76	108	73	82	106	76	97	84	74	83	69	66	82	79	93	55	89	106	113
71950	KIRBY	83	60	76	58	61	82	62	75	69	59	67	57	50	70	58	75	45	70	79	90
71952	LANGLEY	84	60	69	59	60	80	63	73	70	61	68	56	50	73	57	76	46	69	77	89
71953	MENA	75	54	77	53	56	78	58	72	64	52	62	55	46	63	57	70	41	67	77	86
71956	MOUNTAIN PINE	76	55	63	53	55	73	57	66	63	55	62	51	46	66	52	69	42	63	70	81
71957	MOUNT IDA	74	55	83	54	59	77	57	72	62	53	61	53	47	60	58	67	40	67	74	84
71958	MURFREESBORO	82	59	84	57	61	83	60	77	67	56	66	58	48	67	60	74	43	70	80	91
71959	NEWHOPE	88	62	93	61	65	91	66	83	71	59	70	64	51	71	65	78	46	77	87	100
71960	NORMAN	72	52	74	50	54	74	53	68	59	50	58	51	43	59	53	65	38	62	71	81
71961	ODEN	103	73	105	71	76	104	75	96	84	70	82	72	60	83	75	92	54	88	100	114
71962	OKOLONA	79	57	82	55	59	81	58	74	65	54	64	56	47	64	58	71	42	68	77	88
71964	PEARCY	85	79	72	77	77	82	74	80	77	77	77	59	71	80	72	79	52	77	80	95
71965	PENCIL BLUFF	84	60	87	59	63	86	62	79	69	58	68	59	50	68	61	76	45	72	82	94
71968	ROYAL	84	69	77	66	69	82	67	78	72	67	71	58	59	73	65	76	48	73	80	93
71969	SIMS	78	56	80	54	58	80	58	73	64	54	63	55	46	63	57	70	41	67	76	87
71970	STORY	72	52	74	50	54	74	53	68	59	50	58	51	43	59	53	65	38	62	70	81
71971	UMPIRE	100	69	110	69	72	106	77	95	80	62	79	79	56	78	76	87	51	89	101	117
71972	VANDERVOORT	80	58	66	56	57	76	60	70	66	58	65	54	48	69	54	72	44	66	74	85
71973	WICKES	78	51	75	48	51	76	54	68	63	52	61	53	41	64	51	70	41	64	72	84
71998	ARKADELPHIA	93	60	58	66	58	65	111	76	99	88	99	69	81	100	78	97	70	92	79	96
72001	ADONA	90	65	78	63	65	87	67	79	75	65	73	61	54	77	62	81	49	75	84	96
72002	ALEXANDER	94	86	78	83	84	88	82	86	84	85	84	64	77	88	78	86	57	84	86	102
72003	ALMYRA	104	73	106	72	75	107	79	97	84	68	83	78	60	84	77	92	54	91	102	118
72004	ALTHEIMER	74	48	71	45	48	72	51	65	59	49	58	51	38	60	48	66	38	61	68	80
72005	AMAGON	66	43	64	41	43	65	46	58	53	44	52	45	35	54	43	60	34	55	62	72
72006	AUGUSTA	66	47	59	45	47	65	51	59	58	49	56	44	41	58	47	63	38	57	65	72
72007	AUSTIN	93	85	75	83	83	86	81	85	84	84	84	62	77	87	77	86	57	83	85	101
72010	BALD KNOB	79	55	74	53	55	78	58	71	65	55	63	54	45	66	54	72	42	66	75	86
72011	BAUXITE	92	85	74	82	82	85	81	84	83	84	83	62	76	87	77	85	57	82	84	100
72012	BEEBE	92	76	78	74	75	88	76	84	81	76	80	62	67	83	71	86	54	80	87	100
72013	BEE BRANCH	87	62	85	60	64	87	64	80	71	60	70	60	51	71	62	78	46	74	83	95
72014	BEEDEVILLE	65	42	63	40	42	64	45	57	52	43	51	45	34	53	42	59	34	54	61	70
72015	BENTON	88	85	78	84	82	90	83	86	86	82	86	64	81	87	81	89	59	85	91	102
72016	BIGELOW	94	72	78	70	72	89	73	83	80	73	78	63	62	83	68	85	53	79	86	100
72017	BISCOE	77	53	77	50	54	77	55	70	63	52	61	54	43	63	53	69	41	65	73	85
72019	BENTON	106	104	96	103	103	107	98	103	100	100	100	76	97	102	97	103	69	100	106	122
72020	BRADFORD	77	53	68	51	53	74	56	67	63	54	62	52	44	65	52	69	41	64	71	82
72021	BRINKLEY	67	49	59	49	49	66	55	61	61	51	59	46	46	60	51	66	40	60	68	74
72022	BRYANT	109	105	94	102	102	104	100	103	101	103	101	77	97	104	97	102	69	101	102	121
72023	CABOT	111	112	94	109	107	102	104	105	102	110	103	81	103	108	101	100	72	102	99	122
72024	CARLISLE	89	64	89	61	65	89	66	82	73	62	72	62	53	73	64	80	48	76	86	98
72025	CASA	86	62	73	60	62	83	64	75	72	63	70	58	52	74	59	78	47	71	80	92
72026	CASSCOE	99	71	81	69	70	94	74	86	82	72	80	66	59	85	67	89	54	81	90	104
72027	CENTER RIDGE	86	61	88	59	64	87	63	80	70	59	69	60	50	69	62	77	45	73	83	95
72028	CHOCTAW	87	62	89	60	65	88	64	81	71	60	70	61	51	71	63	78	46	75	85	97
72029	CLARENDON	74	50	74	48	51	74	53	67	60	50	59	51	41	61	51	67	39	62	70	81
72030	CLEVELAND	84	60	86	58	62	85	62	78	68	57	67	59	49	68	61	75	44	72	82	93
72031	CLINTON	76	54	78	53	56	77	56	71	63	52	61	53	45	62	56	69	41	66	75	85
72032	CONWAY	97	87	83	86	85	91	89	90	90	88	90	69	83	93	84	92	62	90	91	108
72034	CONWAY	99	89	79	91	84	84	102	89	98	99	99	74	94	101	91	95	69	95	88	108
72035	CONWAY	32	13	13	16	12	15	44	22	35	30	36	24	26	35	24	32	25	31	22	30
72036	COTTON PLANT	50	36	44	35	36	49	39	45	45	39	44	33	33	44	36	50	29	44	50	55
72038	CROCKETTS BLUFF	98	70	81	68	70	93	73	85	81	71	80	65	59	85	67	89	53	81	90	104
72039	DAMASCUS	86	66	84	64	67	86	66	80	72	64	71	60	56	72	65	78	47	75	83	95
72040	DES ARC	85	59	85	57	61	85	62	78	69	58	68	59	48	70	60	77	45	72	82	94
72041	DE VALLS BLUFF	84	57	85	54	58	85	61	76	68	55	66	60	46	68	58	75	44	71	80	93
72042	DE WITT	75	54	71	54	55	75	59	69	64	54	63	54	47	64	56	70	42	66	74	84
72044	EDGEMONT	70	66	84	61	73	79	63	75	67	68	65	49	62	61	69	71	44	72	83	85
72045	EL PASO	102	76	84	74	75	97	78	90	86	76	84	68	64	89	71	93	57	85	94	109
72046	ENGLAND	80	58	79	57	59	82	61	75	67	55	66	58	49	67	60	74	44	70	79	90
72047	ENOLA	84	61	69	60	61	80	63	73	70	62	69	56	51	73	58	76	46	70	77	89
72048	ETHEL	78	56	80	54	58	79	57	73	64	53	63	55	46	63	57	70	41	67	76	87
72051	FOX	70	50	72	49	52	71	52	66	57	48	56	49	41	57	51	63	37	60	68	78
72052	GARNER	66	47	54	46	47	63	49	57	55	48	54	44	40	57	45	60	36	54	60	70
72055	GILLETT	90	64	93	62	67	92	67	84	73	61	72	64	53	73	66	80	47	78	88	101
72057	GRAPEVINE	88	63	73	62	63	84	66	77	73	64	72	59	53	76	60	80	48	73	81	93
72058	GREENBRIER	92	82	75	80	80	87	79	84	82	81	82	62	74	86	75	85	56	81	85	100
72060	GRIFFITHVILLE	72	48	68	45	48	70	51	63	58	48	57	49	38	60	47	65	38	60	67	78
72063	HATTIEVILLE	87	62	90	61	65	89	64	82	71	60	70	61	51	71	63	78	46	75	85	97
72064	HAZEN	85	60	91	59	63	88	64	80	69	56	68	63	49	68	63	75	44	74	84	97
72065	HENSLEY	103	85	87	82	83	97	83	92	89	84	88	69	74	92	78	94	60	89	94	111
72066	HICKORY PLAINS	102	73	84	71	73	97	76	88	84	74	83	68	61	88	69	92	55	84	93	107
72067	HIGDEN	81	77	98	71	86	92	73	87	78	79	76	57	73	71	80	82	51	83	96	99
72068	HIGGINSON	77	55	63	53	55	73	57	67	63	56	62	51	46	66	52	69	42	63	70	81
72069	HOLLY GROVE	52	38	44	38	37	51	43	47	50	43	48	34	37	48	39	54	32	48	54	58
72070	HOUSTON	80	57	74	55	58	78	59	72	65	56	64	55	47	67	56	72	43	67	75	86
72072	HUMNOKE	74	48	71	45	48	72	52	65	59	49	58	51	39	60	48	66	38	61	69	80
72073	HUMPHREY	75	52	67	50	52	72	55	66	61	53	60	51	43	63	51	67	40	62	69	80
72076	JACKSONVILLE	83	73	63	73	69	73	78	74	79	77	80	59	73	83	72	80	55	77	76	90
72079	JEFFERSON	86	77	67	75	74	76	77	77	78	80	79	58	72	82	72	79	54	77	76	92
72080	JERUSALEM	87	62	89	60	64	88	64	81	71	59	69	61	51	70	63	78	46	74	84	96
	ARKANSAS	88	73	79	72	73	85	76	82	80	74	79	62	68	81	72	84	54	80	86	98
	UNITED STATES	100	100	100	100	100	100	100	100	100	100	100	100	100	100	100	100	100	100	100	100

#	POST OFFICE NAME	COUNTY FIPS CODE	POPULATION 2000	POPULATION 2009	POPULATION 2014	2000-2009 ANNUAL RATE % Rate	2000-2009 ANNUAL RATE State Centile	HOUSEHOLDS 2000	HOUSEHOLDS 2009	HOUSEHOLDS 2014	HOUSEHOLDS % Annual Rate 2000-2009	HOUSEHOLDS 2009 Average HH Size	FAMILIES 2000	FAMILIES 2009	FAMILIES % Annual Rate 2000-2009
72081	JUDSONIA	145	7173	7355	7445	0.3	49	2689	2812	2868	0.5	2.54	2036	2061	0.1
72082	KENSETT	145	1997	2203	2312	1.1	78	784	881	933	1.3	2.37	527	566	0.8
72083	KEO	085	138	155	164	1.3	82	58	67	72	1.6	2.31	44	49	1.2
72084	LEOLA	053	969	1057	1093	0.9	72	364	404	420	1.1	2.62	285	307	0.8
72086	LONOKE	085	9295	10659	11308	1.5	85	3453	4042	4317	1.7	2.57	2564	2902	1.3
72087	LONSDALE	125	1329	1613	1761	2.1	92	510	621	685	2.2	2.59	402	474	1.8
72088	FAIRFIELD BAY	141	2609	3131	3322	2.0	91	1299	1603	1717	2.3	1.89	883	1053	1.9
72099	LITTLE ROCK AIR FORC	119	1291	1360	1387	0.6	62	93	125	138	3.2	2.28	61	82	3.3
72101	MC CRORY	147	4327	4048	3894	-0.7	16	1729	1662	1612	-0.4	2.37	1204	1113	-0.8
72102	MC RAE	145	2362	2979	3281	2.5	94	903	1150	1275	2.6	2.59	686	847	2.3
72103	MABELVALE	125	12078	12633	13158	0.5	58	4545	4913	5165	0.8	2.57	3474	3625	0.5
72104	MALVERN	059	21758	22936	23017	0.6	62	8629	8864	8928	0.3	2.46	6251	6206	-0.1
72105	JONES MILL	059	106	117	122	1.1	78	31	35	36	1.3	3.34	25	27	0.8
72106	MAYFLOWER	045	4183	5253	5865	2.5	94	1710	2186	2449	2.7	2.40	1207	1495	2.3
72110	MORRILTON	029	11405	11398	11460	0.0	40	4509	4591	4641	0.2	2.41	3155	3089	-0.2
72111	MOUNT VERNON	045	1186	1534	1710	2.8	95	461	597	668	2.8	2.57	342	428	2.5
72112	NEWPORT	067	12348	11745	11248	-0.5	22	4483	4180	3998	-0.8	2.34	3030	2711	-1.2
72113	MAUMELLE	119	12272	18226	20614	4.4	98	4788	7246	8249	4.6	2.51	3647	5325	4.2
72114	NORTH LITTLE ROCK	119	14554	13644	13342	-0.7	16	5812	5503	5411	-0.6	2.43	3357	2971	-1.3
72116	NORTH LITTLE ROCK	119	21311	21645	21958	0.2	45	9700	10089	10309	0.4	2.14	6171	6069	-0.2
72117	NORTH LITTLE ROCK	119	12303	12408	12518	0.1	43	4657	4820	4904	0.4	2.57	3272	3237	-0.1
72118	NORTH LITTLE ROCK	119	21998	21505	21628	-0.2	31	9121	9127	9243	0.0	2.32	6030	5747	-0.5
72120	SHERWOOD	119	27007	29832	31215	1.1	78	10801	12319	13015	1.4	2.41	7872	8566	0.9
72121	PANGBURN	145	2378	2574	2662	0.9	72	951	1046	1086	1.0	2.46	725	772	0.7
72122	PARON	125	1032	1152	1266	1.2	80	394	463	516	1.8	2.48	314	358	1.4
72125	PERRY	105	1092	1210	1255	1.1	78	401	455	474	1.4	2.66	298	328	1.0
72126	PERRYVILLE	105	4088	4362	4443	0.7	66	1661	1794	1834	0.8	2.36	1190	1240	0.4
72127	PLUMERVILLE	029	2335	2432	2473	0.4	54	921	985	1011	0.7	2.47	665	683	0.3
72128	POYEN	053	744	793	809	0.7	66	289	312	319	0.8	2.54	224	235	0.5
72129	PRATTSVILLE	053	1325	1458	1518	1.0	75	510	574	601	1.3	2.54	395	433	1.0
72130	PRIM	023	356	397	415	1.2	80	136	155	163	1.4	2.56	106	117	1.1
72131	QUITMAN	023	3671	3858	3971	0.5	58	1537	1639	1694	0.7	2.35	1133	1167	0.3
72132	REDFIELD	069	2531	2583	2570	0.2	45	945	1013	1017	0.8	2.55	730	757	0.4
72133	REYDELL	069	45	45	44	0.0	40	19	20	20	0.6	2.25	14	14	0.0
72134	ROE	095	377	373	368	-0.1	35	146	147	146	0.1	2.50	101	97	-0.4
72135	ROLAND	119	2845	2695	2676	-0.6	18	1090	1070	1073	-0.2	2.52	830	784	-0.6
72136	ROMANCE	145	1500	1744	1871	1.6	87	537	628	675	1.7	2.78	435	496	1.4
72137	ROSE BUD	145	2304	2509	2582	0.9	72	870	960	990	1.1	2.61	665	710	0.7
72140	SAINT CHARLES	001	359	344	332	-0.5	22	154	151	147	-0.2	2.28	115	109	-0.6
72141	SCOTLAND	141	864	910	930	0.6	62	340	363	372	0.7	2.49	236	241	0.2
72142	SCOTT	085	2056	2295	2423	1.2	80	809	928	988	1.5	2.47	613	677	1.1
72143	SEARCY	145	28395	31338	32825	1.1	78	10929	12245	12902	1.2	2.44	7765	8406	0.9
72149	SEARCY	145	1680	1745	1745	0.4	54	1	1	1	0.0	1.00	0	0	0.0
72150	SHERIDAN	053	11616	12311	12556	0.6	62	4386	4743	4869	0.8	2.56	3331	3496	0.5
72152	SHERRILL	069	623	478	447	-2.8	0	249	220	208	-1.3	2.17	161	134	-2.0
72153	SHIRLEY	141	3317	3462	3527	0.5	58	1353	1439	1473	0.7	2.40	976	1002	0.3
72156	SOLGOHACHIA	029	505	527	540	0.5	58	192	205	211	0.7	2.57	149	155	0.4
72157	SPRINGFIELD	029	1441	1485	1505	0.3	49	553	582	595	0.6	2.55	413	421	0.2
72160	STUTTGART	001	11162	10403	9933	-0.8	14	4566	4359	4193	-0.5	2.35	3168	2907	-0.9
72165	THIDA	063	148	151	152	0.2	45	51	53	54	0.4	2.85	38	38	0.0
72166	TICHNOR	001	246	235	225	-0.5	22	105	103	100	-0.2	2.28	81	77	-0.5
72167	TRASKWOOD	125	1610	1793	1938	1.2	80	607	697	760	1.5	2.57	459	508	1.1
72168	TUCKER	069	2221	2113	2073	-0.5	22	326	292	278	-1.2	2.44	215	183	-1.7
72170	ULM	117	356	327	313	-0.9	12	151	143	139	-0.6	2.29	114	105	-0.9
72173	VILONIA	045	6226	7552	8377	2.1	92	2203	2710	3021	2.3	2.77	1798	2166	2.0
72175	WABBASEKA	069	570	524	503	-0.9	12	226	218	211	-0.4	2.40	156	143	-0.9
72176	WARD	085	4650	6843	7851	4.3	98	1634	2452	2833	4.5	2.79	1303	1890	4.1
72179	WILBURN	023	480	474	462	-0.1	35	190	191	188	0.1	2.48	145	141	-0.3
72199	NORTH LITTLE ROCK	119	355	357	360	0.1	43	38	40	41	0.6	2.55	26	26	0.0
72201	LITTLE ROCK	119	498	759	805	4.7	99	191	387	418	7.9	1.59	46	71	4.8
72202	LITTLE ROCK	119	10855	10093	9974	-0.8	14	5298	5133	5164	-0.3	1.86	2264	1973	-1.5
72204	LITTLE ROCK	119	32344	33934	34732	0.5	58	11820	12745	13183	0.8	2.49	7700	7872	0.2
72205	LITTLE ROCK	119	24187	24111	24171	0.0	40	11490	11684	11796	0.2	1.96	5743	5410	-0.6
72206	LITTLE ROCK	119	26833	26311	26374	-0.2	31	10101	10169	10279	0.1	2.48	6810	6551	-0.4
72207	LITTLE ROCK	119	12120	11853	11789	-0.2	31	6081	6061	6071	0.0	1.95	3149	2911	-0.8
72209	LITTLE ROCK	119	32066	31867	31836	-0.1	35	11987	11968	12004	0.0	2.66	8414	8034	-0.5
72210	LITTLE ROCK	119	11101	14837	16499	3.2	97	4649	6418	7203	3.5	2.31	3228	4231	3.0
72211	LITTLE ROCK	119	18034	20426	21252	1.4	84	8549	9687	10119	1.4	2.09	4691	5049	0.8
72212	LITTLE ROCK	119	12568	12819	13299	0.2	45	4951	5179	5421	0.5	2.45	3533	3565	0.1
72223	LITTLE ROCK	119	11287	16610	18803	4.3	98	4438	6320	7104	3.9	2.62	3238	4594	3.9
72227	LITTLE ROCK	119	12111	11776	11680	-0.3	27	5644	5637	5642	0.0	2.07	3365	3158	-0.7
72301	WEST MEMPHIS	035	27440	27795	28004	0.1	43	9960	10351	10519	0.4	2.66	7081	7081	0.0
72310	ARMOREL	093	9	8	8	-1.3	5	3	3	3	0.0	2.67	2	2	0.0
72311	AUBREY	077	47	43	41	-1.0	9	23	22	21	-0.5	1.95	16	15	-0.7
72313	BASSETT	093	48	50	51	0.4	54	15	16	17	0.7	3.13	11	11	0.0
72315	BLYTHEVILLE	093	27255	25095	23953	-0.9	12	10211	9582	9205	-0.7	2.59	7243	6554	-1.1
72320	BRICKEYS	077	1945	1888	1851	-0.3	27	108	101	97	-0.7	2.55	83	76	-0.9
72324	CHERRY VALLEY	037	2170	2226	2226	0.3	49	837	883	893	0.6	2.52	630	643	0.2
72326	COLT	123	2640	2575	2526	-0.3	27	1025	1034	1024	0.1	2.47	767	749	-0.3
72327	CRAWFORDSVILLE	035	1885	1947	1979	0.4	54	702	753	772	0.8	2.58	513	530	0.4
72328	CRUMROD	107	342	287	268	-1.9	1	99	85	80	-1.6	3.38	79	67	-1.8
72329	DRIVER	093	3	3	2	0.0	40	1	1	1	0.0	3.00	1	1	0.0
72330	DYESS	093	919	787	736	-1.7	2	324	284	266	-1.4	2.77	260	222	-1.7
72331	EARLE	035	3929	3727	3666	-0.6	18	1391	1353	1341	-0.3	2.75	965	902	-0.7
72333	ELAINE	107	1373	1200	1131	-1.4	3	508	456	433	-1.2	2.63	355	307	-1.6
72335	FORREST CITY	123	20177	20725	20112	0.3	49	6626	6369	6189	-0.4	2.57	4707	4364	-0.8
72338	FRENCHMANS BAYOU	093	19	19	19	0.0	40	8	8	8	0.0	2.38	6	6	0.0
72339	GILMORE	035	387	402	407	0.4	54	135	145	149	0.8	2.77	106	111	0.5
72340	GOODWIN	123	135	120	114	-1.3	5	40	37	35	-0.8	3.24	30	27	-1.1
72341	HAYNES	077	50	42	39	-1.9	1	22	19	18	-1.6	2.21	17	14	-2.1
72342	HELENA	107	6950	6300	6004	-1.1	8	2548	2338	2236	-0.9	2.59	1723	1518	-1.4
72346	HETH	123	890	795	756	-1.2	6	323	298	286	-0.9	2.67	236	211	-1.2
72347	HICKORY RIDGE	037	939	886	868	-0.6	18	376	369	367	-0.2	2.40	281	268	-0.5
72348	HUGHES	123	3274	3012	2901	-0.9	12	1236	1170	1138	-0.6	2.56	875	796	-1.0
72350	JOINER	093	1453	1244	1167	-1.7	2	538	475	449	-1.3	2.62	380	324	-1.7
	ARKANSAS					0.9					1.1	2.46			0.7
	UNITED STATES					1.0					1.1	2.59			0.9

POPULATION COMPOSITION

#	POST OFFICE NAME	RACE (%) White 2000	White 2009	Black 2000	Black 2009	Asian/Pacific 2000	Asian/Pacific 2009	% Hispanic Origin 2000	% Hispanic Origin 2009	2009 AGE DISTRIBUTION (%) 0-4	5-9	10-14	15-19	20-24	25-44	45-64	65-84	85+	18+	MEDIAN AGE 2009	% 2009 Males	% 2009 Females
72081	JUDSONIA	96.0	94.7	0.9	1.1	0.1	0.2	2.5	4.0	6.8	6.7	6.9	6.5	5.4	26.3	26.7	12.2	2.4	75.5	38.7	49.6	50.4
72082	KENSETT	76.6	71.4	17.3	19.9	0.3	0.3	5.1	7.8	7.5	7.7	7.5	6.5	4.9	23.4	25.1	13.8	3.6	73.7	38.8	46.9	53.1
72083	KEO	84.8	76.8	13.0	20.6	0.0	0.0	2.2	3.2	6.5	6.5	7.7	6.5	3.2	25.8	30.3	11.6	1.9	75.5	41.3	51.0	49.0
72084	LEOLA	89.5	85.1	1.2	1.4	0.3	0.4	8.1	12.6	7.8	7.9	8.0	6.4	5.2	26.4	25.8	11.2	1.3	72.4	36.8	49.5	50.5
72086	LONOKE	84.1	80.3	13.1	16.1	0.3	0.4	2.2	3.3	6.7	6.9	7.0	6.6	5.3	25.2	27.8	12.2	2.2	75.3	39.3	49.3	50.7
72087	LONSDALE	97.1	96.4	0.5	0.7	0.2	0.3	0.9	1.5	6.1	6.0	5.9	5.8	5.3	22.9	27.7	19.1	1.4	78.5	43.5	49.8	50.2
72088	FAIRFIELD BAY	98.1	97.7	0.3	0.4	0.2	0.4	0.7	1.1	2.6	2.5	2.4	2.6	2.3	9.5	25.4	45.0	7.7	90.9	66.0	45.8	54.2
72099	LITTLE ROCK AIR FORC	72.7	65.2	22.4	28.5	1.6	2.3	2.6	4.0	2.4	1.1	1.5	9.3	36.3	43.9	5.1	0.5	0.0	94.8	24.9	80.5	19.5
72101	MC CRORY	86.2	83.3	12.1	14.5	0.3	0.4	0.9	1.3	6.6	6.5	6.5	6.3	5.4	23.0	28.1	14.4	3.2	76.3	41.6	47.2	52.8
72102	MC RAE	96.4	95.3	0.4	0.5	0.0	0.1	1.7	2.7	6.8	6.8	6.9	6.7	5.7	26.8	27.3	11.7	1.3	75.4	38.0	50.5	49.5
72103	MABELVALE	83.1	80.6	13.4	14.8	0.9	1.3	1.7	2.6	7.0	7.1	7.1	7.2	6.0	28.2	27.4	9.3	0.8	74.4	36.8	50.0	50.0
72104	MALVERN	83.4	80.9	14.2	16.2	0.3	0.4	1.1	1.6	6.2	6.0	6.2	6.7	5.8	24.6	27.8	14.0	2.6	77.5	40.7	49.3	50.7
72105	JONES MILL	99.0	98.3	0.0	0.0	0.0	0.9	1.0	0.9	6.8	6.8	6.8	8.5	5.1	25.6	28.2	11.1	0.9	74.4	38.4	49.6	50.4
72106	MAYFLOWER	86.8	83.4	10.7	13.6	0.3	0.4	1.1	1.6	5.6	5.8	6.0	5.8	5.4	25.6	31.5	13.0	1.2	78.7	42.0	49.4	50.6
72110	MORRILTON	83.2	80.5	13.7	15.4	0.3	0.4	2.3	3.5	6.7	6.9	6.9	6.2	5.1	24.6	26.5	14.4	2.6	75.7	39.9	48.7	51.3
72111	MOUNT VERNON	97.1	96.2	0.3	0.3	0.2	0.2	1.5	2.5	7.3	7.3	7.2	6.5	5.7	26.6	26.8	11.0	1.5	74.1	37.5	51.3	48.7
72112	NEWPORT	74.2	71.0	24.0	26.7	0.2	0.3	1.2	1.8	5.3	5.4	5.4	7.5	10.0	24.2	25.3	14.0	2.9	80.4	38.6	47.7	52.3
72113	MAUMELLE	89.1	85.6	8.0	10.4	0.8	1.2	1.8	3.0	7.6	7.6	7.6	6.2	4.8	29.6	28.1	7.6	0.8	73.1	37.0	48.4	51.6
72114	NORTH LITTLE ROCK	24.1	19.6	72.6	76.5	0.4	0.4	2.1	2.9	9.7	9.0	7.6	8.1	7.0	23.8	22.0	10.2	2.7	68.9	31.5	45.3	54.7
72116	NORTH LITTLE ROCK	88.6	84.7	8.5	11.2	1.0	1.4	1.6	2.7	5.0	5.1	5.4	5.1	5.2	25.5	30.0	15.7	3.0	81.4	44.0	47.6	52.4
72117	NORTH LITTLE ROCK	44.2	37.7	52.7	58.8	0.3	0.3	1.4	2.0	6.9	7.0	7.0	7.6	6.7	25.0	26.6	11.6	1.6	74.5	36.7	48.0	52.0
72118	NORTH LITTLE ROCK	74.9	68.5	20.9	25.8	0.5	0.7	3.6	5.5	7.0	6.6	6.3	6.4	6.4	28.3	26.6	10.7	1.8	76.2	37.0	48.8	51.2
72120	SHERWOOD	87.0	81.8	9.4	13.0	0.9	1.4	2.1	3.5	6.7	6.7	6.9	6.4	5.6	28.6	27.2	10.5	1.3	75.7	37.5	48.4	51.6
72121	PANGBURN	98.1	97.4	0.2	0.2	0.0	0.1	1.0	1.7	6.0	6.1	6.5	7.1	5.2	25.7	28.4	13.4	1.6	77.1	40.4	49.3	50.7
72122	PARON	97.3	96.8	0.4	0.4	0.5	0.6	0.7	1.1	3.9	4.1	4.5	4.5	3.2	15.9	28.8	32.9	2.2	84.7	56.3	49.7	50.3
72125	PERRY	97.0	96.3	0.2	0.2	0.2	0.2	1.7	2.4	6.8	6.7	6.8	6.7	6.1	27.6	26.0	12.1	1.2	75.8	37.4	50.7	49.3
72126	PERRYVILLE	97.2	96.5	0.2	0.3	0.2	0.2	1.4	2.1	6.0	6.1	6.2	6.3	5.1	23.3	28.1	15.7	3.2	77.7	42.8	49.2	50.8
72127	PLUMERVILLE	66.1	61.4	31.4	35.5	0.3	0.3	0.9	1.4	6.7	7.0	7.1	6.4	5.3	24.4	29.6	11.8	1.7	75.2	39.6	49.0	51.0
72128	POYEN	97.0	96.2	0.8	0.9	0.0	0.0	1.6	2.5	5.4	5.5	6.1	6.9	5.2	28.4	28.8	12.4	1.4	78.6	40.2	50.9	49.1
72129	PRATTSVILLE	87.0	85.2	11.5	13.0	0.3	0.5	0.5	0.8	6.2	6.3	6.4	6.0	5.5	26.7	28.7	12.5	1.7	77.4	39.7	51.0	49.0
72130	PRIM	99.2	98.5	0.0	0.0	0.0	0.3	0.3	0.3	5.3	5.3	5.8	6.3	4.3	21.2	30.2	19.9	1.8	79.3	46.1	48.9	51.1
72131	QUITMAN	98.2	97.7	0.1	0.1	0.1	0.1	1.6	2.4	6.2	6.4	6.2	5.4	4.8	21.5	29.2	18.2	2.0	77.8	44.5	50.2	49.8
72132	REDFIELD	92.2	88.9	4.5	6.5	0.9	1.2	2.3	3.6	6.2	6.2	6.3	6.7	6.2	28.2	30.5	8.9	0.9	77.3	37.9	49.5	50.5
72133	REYDELL	57.8	48.9	37.8	44.4	0.0	0.0	4.4	4.4	6.7	6.7	6.7	6.7	4.4	22.2	33.3	13.3	0.0	77.8	43.1	44.4	55.6
72134	ROE	83.0	78.8	14.1	17.2	0.3	0.3	1.1	1.6	6.2	6.7	7.2	6.7	4.6	24.9	28.7	12.9	2.1	75.9	40.3	50.9	49.1
72135	ROLAND	91.7	89.1	6.3	8.4	0.1	0.2	0.4	0.6	5.1	5.6	6.4	6.8	5.0	23.5	35.5	11.0	1.3	78.9	43.3	50.3	49.7
72136	ROMANCE	97.5	96.8	0.7	0.8	0.2	0.3	0.9	1.4	7.2	7.2	7.2	6.6	5.6	26.5	27.9	10.8	1.0	74.4	38.0	50.6	49.4
72137	ROSE BUD	97.6	96.9	0.2	0.2	0.2	0.3	1.3	2.0	6.2	6.2	6.5	7.0	5.1	25.1	29.3	13.4	1.4	76.8	40.6	50.7	49.3
72140	SAINT CHARLES	94.4	93.3	5.0	6.1	0.0	0.0	0.3	0.6	6.1	6.7	6.1	3.8	3.8	24.1	30.5	16.9	2.0	78.5	44.6	50.3	49.7
72141	SCOTLAND	96.2	95.1	0.3	0.4	0.8	1.2	1.7	2.6	5.6	6.0	6.2	6.2	4.7	24.0	28.4	16.4	2.6	78.2	42.8	50.3	49.7
72142	SCOTT	75.7	67.7	20.9	27.7	0.1	0.2	3.0	4.3	5.8	5.9	6.1	7.0	4.5	25.2	32.6	11.3	1.6	78.0	42.1	51.5	48.5
72143	SEARCY	92.3	90.3	4.9	6.1	0.4	0.6	1.7	2.6	6.3	6.0	6.0	7.0	8.8	25.7	24.8	12.8	2.6	77.9	37.4	49.2	50.8
72149	SEARCY	92.9	90.5	3.3	4.0	0.8	1.1	3.3	5.3	0.0	0.0	0.0	51.6	47.9	0.5	0.1	0.0	0.0	99.6	19.8	33.1	66.9
72150	SHERIDAN	97.4	96.8	1.0	1.2	0.2	0.3	0.7	1.1	6.5	6.5	6.7	6.5	5.7	26.3	28.4	11.6	1.7	76.2	39.4	49.5	50.5
72152	SHERRILL	49.4	41.0	49.0	56.9	0.2	0.2	1.3	1.7	5.4	5.6	5.9	5.9	6.1	22.0	29.7	16.9	2.5	79.3	44.3	48.1	51.9
72153	SHIRLEY	97.2	96.6	0.3	0.3	0.1	0.2	1.2	1.9	5.7	5.9	5.8	5.4	4.7	21.1	29.8	19.5	2.1	79.2	45.9	49.8	50.2
72156	SOLGOHACHIA	94.5	93.2	3.4	4.0	0.2	0.4	0.8	1.3	5.7	6.8	7.4	6.8	4.7	24.7	28.3	13.7	1.9	75.5	40.6	48.2	51.8
72157	SPRINGFIELD	89.2	87.1	8.7	10.0	0.3	0.4	1.0	1.6	6.6	6.7	6.8	6.5	5.1	25.1	29.0	12.8	1.5	75.8	39.9	51.0	49.0
72160	STUTTGART	66.5	63.1	31.8	34.8	0.6	0.9	0.8	1.2	6.9	6.8	6.8	6.6	5.8	24.0	26.9	13.5	2.7	75.4	39.4	47.2	52.8
72165	THIDA	95.3	94.0	1.4	1.3	0.0	0.0	0.0	0.7	4.6	5.3	6.0	6.6	5.3	26.5	28.5	15.2	2.0	80.1	42.3	49.7	50.3
72166	TICHNOR	94.3	92.8	3.6	4.7	0.0	0.0	2.8	3.8	3.8	4.7	5.1	5.1	4.3	25.5	34.5	15.3	1.7	83.0	46.0	50.6	49.4
72167	TRASKWOOD	97.8	97.2	0.3	0.4	0.1	0.2	0.8	1.2	6.9	6.7	6.9	7.2	6.4	27.6	27.6	10.0	0.9	75.1	36.8	49.0	51.0
72168	TUCKER	51.8	43.0	47.2	55.7	0.1	0.2	0.7	1.0	2.1	2.0	2.0	2.7	11.4	53.6	19.6	5.6	0.8	92.8	35.6	82.1	17.9
72170	ULM	91.6	90.5	7.3	8.3	0.0	0.0	0.6	0.9	5.2	6.4	6.4	4.6	3.7	22.9	33.9	14.7	2.1	78.3	45.5	51.4	48.6
72173	VILONIA	97.5	96.8	0.2	0.2	0.2	0.3	1.4	2.1	7.2	7.2	7.3	7.4	6.1	28.2	27.1	8.4	1.0	73.4	36.2	50.0	50.0
72175	WABBASEKA	29.5	22.9	68.7	75.2	0.0	0.0	1.4	1.9	7.8	7.6	7.6	7.4	5.9	23.1	26.1	11.5	2.9	72.1	36.4	46.2	53.8
72176	WARD	97.6	96.9	0.2	0.3	0.3	0.4	1.6	2.5	8.2	7.8	7.6	7.7	6.4	29.6	23.9	8.0	0.7	71.6	33.9	49.7	50.3
72179	WILBURN	98.5	97.7	0.2	0.2	0.0	0.2	0.4	0.6	5.5	5.9	5.9	5.5	4.4	21.5	31.4	18.4	1.5	79.1	45.7	48.5	51.5
72199	NORTH LITTLE ROCK	94.4	92.2	3.7	5.3	0.0	0.0	1.7	2.5	4.5	4.8	4.8	15.7	6.2	23.0	25.2	11.5	4.5	73.1	38.1	49.0	51.0
72201	LITTLE ROCK	42.1	36.2	54.9	59.7	0.4	0.7	2.0	2.8	2.9	2.6	1.4	2.6	9.0	42.6	27.9	9.5	1.4	91.8	39.3	58.1	41.9
72202	LITTLE ROCK	29.1	26.6	68.3	70.1	0.5	0.8	1.5	2.1	5.7	5.6	5.2	6.8	9.2	27.7	25.6	11.9	2.2	79.8	36.5	48.9	51.1
72204	LITTLE ROCK	28.8	23.8	67.3	71.4	1.1	1.4	3.1	4.3	6.9	7.0	7.0	8.2	8.0	28.2	24.7	8.3	1.8	74.7	33.7	48.0	52.0
72205	LITTLE ROCK	70.8	65.0	25.6	30.1	1.5	2.1	1.8	2.9	5.3	4.6	4.6	5.4	8.0	30.8	25.2	12.0	3.9	82.4	38.8	46.6	53.4
72206	LITTLE ROCK	44.5	42.2	53.1	54.7	0.4	0.6	1.3	1.9	6.4	6.4	6.5	6.8	5.9	25.3	28.3	12.4	2.0	76.6	39.5	49.1	50.9
72207	LITTLE ROCK	90.1	86.7	7.1	9.3	1.3	2.0	1.1	1.8	5.5	5.1	5.0	4.8	6.5	29.1	28.3	12.7	3.0	81.6	40.9	46.1	53.9
72209	LITTLE ROCK	32.3	25.7	61.3	66.3	0.8	0.9	5.7	7.7	9.3	9.4	8.6	8.0	7.1	28.3	21.7	6.7	0.8	67.8	30.0	46.6	53.4
72210	LITTLE ROCK	84.6	78.2	12.4	17.6	0.8	1.2	1.5	2.6	7.0	6.3	5.8	5.7	6.7	28.1	30.3	9.3	0.7	77.3	38.2	48.2	51.8
72211	LITTLE ROCK	79.5	74.1	13.8	17.1	4.0	5.5	2.4	3.5	7.4	6.4	6.0	4.9	7.3	35.2	23.5	7.5	1.8	77.2	34.6	48.0	52.0
72212	LITTLE ROCK	86.4	81.6	8.5	11.3	3.5	5.1	1.2	1.9	5.8	6.2	7.1	6.3	5.2	22.5	32.0	12.6	2.3	77.0	42.7	47.8	52.2
72223	LITTLE ROCK	89.2	85.8	6.2	8.2	2.8	4.0	1.3	2.0	7.5	8.0	8.5	6.9	5.1	26.5	29.3	7.5	0.8	71.4	37.1	50.3	49.7
72227	LITTLE ROCK	81.8	76.2	13.5	17.4	2.3	3.4	2.4	3.8	4.8	4.7	5.0	5.3	6.1	26.1	29.9	15.6	2.6	82.2	43.5	45.9	54.1
72301	WEST MEMPHIS	43.0	40.2	55.1	57.4	0.5	0.8	1.0	1.4	8.6	8.5	7.9	7.8	6.9	25.5	23.1	10.0	1.3	70.1	32.3	46.7	53.3
72310	ARMOREL	88.9	87.5	11.1	12.5	0.0	0.0	0.0	0.0	0.0	0.0	0.0	0.0	0.0	100.0	0.0	0.0	0.0	100.0	31.7	37.5	62.5
72311	AUBREY	47.8	41.9	52.2	58.1	0.0	0.0	2.2	2.3	4.7	7.0	7.0	9.3	4.7	18.6	32.6	14.0	2.3	72.1	43.8	34.9	65.1
72313	BASSETT	64.6	56.0	35.4	42.0	0.0	0.0	2.1	2.0	8.0	8.0	8.0	8.0	6.0	26.0	22.0	12.0	2.0	68.0	33.8	52.0	48.0
72315	BLYTHEVILLE	58.3	54.8	38.5	41.2	0.6	0.9	1.9	2.7	8.6	8.2	7.5	7.2	6.9	26.1	23.0	10.6	1.9	71.3	33.2	47.7	52.3
72320	BRICKEYS	57.2	53.6	41.8	45.2	0.0	0.0	4.9	6.8	2.6	2.6	2.8	3.9	13.8	51.8	16.3	5.7	0.6	90.3	33.0	80.2	19.8
72324	CHERRY VALLEY	91.5	88.5	7.3	10.2	0.1	0.2	0.8	1.3	6.3	6.4	6.8	6.8	5.2	26.1	28.7	12.0	1.7	76.4	39.4	51.3	48.7
72326	COLT	75.4	72.6	23.5	26.2	0.2	0.2	1.2	1.0	7.5	7.7	7.6	7.2	4.9	24.5	27.1	12.2	1.3	72.6	37.3	49.2	50.8
72327	CRAWFORDSVILLE	44.8	36.4	53.4	61.4	0.2	0.2	2.1	2.8	8.0	8.3	8.0	6.9	5.5	23.2	27.5	11.1	1.5	71.2	36.1	49.7	50.3
72328	CRUMROD	36.1	31.7	56.6	58.2	0.3	0.3	10.6	14.6	7.7	11.1	8.7	12.2	7.7	18.8	24.7	8.4	0.7	64.8	27.7	49.8	50.2
72329	DRIVER	100.0	100.0	0.0	0.0	0.0	0.0	0.0	0.0	0.0	0.0	0.0	0.0	0.0	66.7	33.3	0.0	0.0	100.0	38.8	66.7	33.3
72330	DYESS	91.5	87.8	3.1	3.9	0.1	0.1	6.4	10.0	8.4	8.5	8.1	6.6	5.3	27.7	24.3	9.8	0.8	70.9	34.2	48.7	51.3
72331	EARLE	31.6	25.4	66.9	72.9	0.4	0.4	0.9	1.2	9.7	8.8	8.2	9.0	6.3	21.3	22.9	11.5	2.3	67.4	32.8	46.5	53.5
72333	ELAINE	42.7	37.3	53.7	57.7	0.1	0.2	5.9	8.3	8.1	8.3	8.2	8.1	6.4	21.8	25.0	12.0	2.1	70.5	34.3	46.0	54.0
72335	FORREST CITY	44.0	41.8	52.9	54.8	0.6	0.6	6.5	6.5	7.2	6.6	6.1	6.3	7.7	32.6	22.9	9.0	1.7	76.2	34.2	56.8	43.2
72338	FRENCHMANS BAYOU	66.7	57.9	33.3	42.1	0.0	0.0	0.0	0.0	10.5	10.5	10.5	10.5	10.5	36.8	10.5	0.0	0.0	57.9	23.8	47.4	52.6
72339	*GILMORE*	59.0	50.0	37.1	45.8	1.3	1.5	2.3	3.0	7.7	8.0	7.7	6.7	6.0	25.4	26.4	10.7	1.5	72.9	37.4	51.0	49.0
72340	GOODWIN	60.7	58.3	37.8	40.0	0.0	0.0	3.0	2.5	5.8	5.8	6.7	5.8	6.7	25.0	29.2	13.3	1.7	77.5	42.1	46.7	53.3
72341	HAYNES	34.0	31.0	64.0	66.7	0.0	0.0	2.0	2.4	7.1	7.1	7.1	7.1	4.8	19.0	28.6	16.7	2.4	71.4	42.5	45.2	54.8
72342	HELENA	33.9	30.8	64.5	67.1	0.6	0.8	0.9	1.3	8.9	8.0	7.6	8.3	6.9	21.6	22.5	13.4	2.8	70.3	33.9	45.7	54.3
72346	HETH	60.7	57.7	37.1	39.5	0.1	0.1	2.4	2.1	6.5	6.4	6.8	7.7	5.7	26.7	27.3	11.8	1.1	75.8	38.3	50.4	49.6
72347	HICKORY RIDGE	98.3	97.5	0.1	0.2	0.1	0.2	1.6	2.5	6.2	6.5	6.7	6.4	4.3	24.4	29.1	14.6	1.8	76.4	41.5	49.4	50.6
72348	HUGHES	45.8	43.3	51.8	54.0	1.0	1.0	1.5	1.8	7.8	7.7	7.6	7.4	6.2	22.6	26.3	12.7	1.7	72.3	37.2	48.7	51.3
72350	JOINER	65.7	58.4	33.3	40.3	0.0	0.0	0.8	1.1	7.2	7.0	6.8	6.2	6.4	25.4	26.0	12.9	2.0	75.1	38.0	45.4	54.6
	ARKANSAS	80.0	78.2	15.7	15.8	0.8	1.2	3.2	5.1	6.8	6.6	6.5	6.9	6.6	26.0	26.1	12.4	2.0	76.1	37.8	49.1	50.9
	UNITED STATES	75.1	72.0	12.3	12.7	3.8	4.6	12.5	15.7	6.8	6.7	6.6	7.1	6.9	27.0	26.0	10.9	1.9	75.7	36.9	49.2	50.8

ZIP CODE				2009 HOUSEHOLD INCOME DISTRIBUTION (%)					MEDIAN HOUSEHOLD INCOME					2009 HOME VALUE DISTRIBUTION (%)					
#	POST OFFICE NAME	2009 Per Capita Income	2009 HH Income Base	Less than $25,000	$25,000 to $49,999	$50,000 to $99,999	$100,000 to $149,999	$150,000 or More	2009	2014	2009 National Centile	2009 State Centile	2009 Home Value Base	Less than $50,000	$50,000 to $89,999	$90,000 to $174,999	$175,000 to $399,999	$400,000 or More	2009 Median Home Value
72081	JUDSONIA	17177	2812	33.4	31.0	31.4	2.5	1.7	37159	38724	24	59	2208	34.8	31.3	24.3	7.8	1.8	70402
72082	KENSETT	13779	881	46.2	34.5	16.7	1.5	1.1	28676	31419	6	11	552	39.9	41.7	12.9	5.6	0.0	58615
72083	KEO	21543	67	32.8	26.9	32.8	6.0	1.5	39304	40899	31	71	48	27.1	20.8	35.4	14.6	2.1	93333
72084	LEOLA	19345	404	31.9	28.0	30.4	7.4	2.2	39766	43063	32	73	323	51.1	21.7	19.2	4.3	3.7	49205
72086	LONOKE	19856	4042	27.6	28.1	36.6	6.5	1.2	44876	46063	48	85	3015	23.3	29.6	29.4	16.2	1.5	85419
72087	LONSDALE	24168	621	18.7	30.8	37.2	8.2	5.2	50407	51532	62	93	513	24.0	20.7	25.9	22.4	7.0	103827
72088	FAIRFIELD BAY	31268	1603	22.6	31.1	35.9	5.6	4.8	46829	47459	54	88	1335	13.6	26.4	41.2	17.4	1.5	103519
72099	LITTLE ROCK AIR FORC	11236	125	34.4	28.0	32.8	4.8	0.0	41151	41843	37	79	70	80.0	0.0	15.7	0.0	4.3	36579
72101	MC CRORY	17849	1662	41.0	29.9	23.8	3.7	1.6	32769	33925	13	29	1162	49.4	29.1	15.6	4.9	1.0	50654
72102	MC RAE	17992	1150	32.3	32.5	29.3	3.8	2.0	36720	39274	23	55	937	24.3	30.7	30.5	12.3	2.1	82692
72103	MABELVALE	21626	4913	18.1	32.6	40.6	6.8	1.9	49410	51420	60	91	3904	24.3	31.9	37.1	6.6	0.1	82957
72104	MALVERN	18665	8864	30.2	31.8	32.5	4.4	1.2	40121	41769	33	75	6655	24.7	29.8	35.5	9.4	0.5	81466
72105	JONES MILL	14954	35	17.1	37.1	42.9	2.9	0.0	46148	47295	52	87	27	18.5	25.9	40.7	14.8	0.0	97500
72106	MAYFLOWER	21395	2186	23.8	34.4	34.6	5.6	1.6	43049	44608	43	82	1727	24.4	29.0	38.2	7.9	0.6	85909
72110	MORRILTON	20693	4591	32.5	27.4	30.8	6.2	3.0	40036	41313	33	74	3305	20.8	30.9	36.1	10.7	1.5	88011
72111	MOUNT VERNON	18776	597	25.3	39.4	27.6	6.0	1.7	37726	39555	26	63	507	26.2	22.5	31.6	16.8	3.0	91970
72112	NEWPORT	18668	4180	38.7	29.6	23.4	4.3	4.0	32209	33710	12	26	2716	34.6	33.8	23.1	7.3	1.2	64630
72113	MAUMELLE	39086	7246	10.5	15.0	38.9	19.3	16.2	78925	80266	92	100	5762	5.6	6.7	49.5	35.1	3.2	147681
72114	NORTH LITTLE ROCK	13720	5503	51.9	27.7	16.9	2.4	1.1	23563	24599	3	2	1890	43.4	43.2	11.3	2.1	0.0	55081
72116	NORTH LITTLE ROCK	36565	10089	11.7	20.8	46.6	13.1	7.7	65021	66155	83	99	6527	1.9	10.7	58.0	26.6	2.7	135174
72117	NORTH LITTLE ROCK	17154	4820	34.6	32.6	28.7	2.8	1.3	36079	38414	21	51	3160	35.7	47.5	13.6	2.9	0.3	60916
72118	NORTH LITTLE ROCK	24230	9127	22.3	27.9	40.6	6.7	2.5	49796	51763	61	92	5811	13.9	50.1	29.6	6.2	0.2	80018
72120	SHERWOOD	28561	12319	13.1	25.0	45.7	12.1	4.2	60041	61782	77	97	8499	5.3	25.7	53.9	14.4	0.7	110481
72121	PANGBURN	19280	1046	28.5	33.9	31.9	4.4	1.2	40000	41107	33	74	855	24.4	25.6	35.0	13.7	1.3	89898
72122	PARON	31089	463	13.2	22.9	43.2	13.0	7.8	61838	65350	80	98	403	12.9	15.4	24.3	34.0	13.4	164063
72125	PERRY	18396	455	26.8	34.1	32.7	4.4	2.0	39920	42262	32	73	351	33.3	31.3	26.8	6.6	2.0	71806
72126	PERRYVILLE	20787	1794	29.9	30.4	31.0	6.1	2.6	39958	42242	32	73	1417	28.0	32.0	30.1	7.1	2.8	77422
72127	PLUMERVILLE	18507	985	31.4	32.9	30.2	3.8	1.8	38253	38772	27	65	799	31.5	30.9	31.5	5.0	1.0	72636
72128	POYEN	20604	312	23.4	34.0	34.6	5.4	2.6	43787	45682	45	83	254	34.6	24.4	33.1	7.5	0.4	79000
72129	PRATTSVILLE	20754	574	25.1	30.8	32.9	9.2	1.9	45248	47393	49	86	473	30.9	36.4	26.0	5.5	1.3	68659
72130	PRIM	18418	155	29.7	35.5	29.0	2.6	3.2	38391	40133	28	66	134	29.9	14.2	34.3	20.1	1.5	104545
72131	QUITMAN	20306	1639	28.9	35.3	29.7	4.0	2.2	40244	41599	33	75	1344	23.5	22.0	36.8	15.0	2.8	96897
72132	REDFIELD	21457	1013	19.2	30.9	42.8	5.8	1.2	49891	50791	61	92	799	30.8	37.7	27.0	4.5	0.0	72689
72133	REYDELL	18996	20	30.0	40.0	25.0	5.0	0.0	35000	40000	18	43	13	53.8	7.7	15.4	23.1	0.0	45000
72134	ROE	18916	147	35.4	29.9	28.6	4.1	2.0	35245	36548	18	46	98	39.8	39.8	16.3	4.1	0.0	60000
72135	ROLAND	29898	1070	13.4	32.6	32.7	12.1	9.2	53807	56200	69	96	900	17.7	27.0	23.7	22.3	9.3	104567
72136	ROMANCE	22435	628	20.1	31.4	36.8	7.8	4.0	48899	48737	59	91	557	16.3	18.7	37.2	23.0	4.8	115665
72137	ROSE BUD	20227	960	24.3	32.2	37.0	3.8	2.8	44682	45311	47	85	807	23.9	20.1	34.6	19.3	2.1	100825
72140	SAINT CHARLES	19038	151	34.4	33.8	29.8	0.0	2.0	37759	38067	26	63	122	37.7	24.6	31.1	6.6	0.0	71667
72141	SCOTLAND	15476	363	42.4	32.0	21.5	3.3	0.8	30213	31202	8	17	296	30.7	25.7	30.1	10.5	3.0	77222
72142	SCOTT	25701	928	22.2	27.4	40.2	6.7	3.6	50260	51480	62	92	684	21.8	28.9	27.6	17.3	4.4	87727
72143	SEARCY	22258	12245	27.6	28.3	34.3	6.3	3.6	43747	44146	45	83	8362	11.7	18.8	45.5	20.0	4.0	118237
72149	SEARCY	8979	0	0.0	0.0	0.0	0.0	0.0	0	0	0	0	0	0.0	0.0	0.0	0.0	0.0	0
72150	SHERIDAN	22064	4743	23.1	28.8	38.7	6.0	3.4	48124	50396	57	90	3725	24.6	25.7	36.9	11.5	1.3	89504
72152	SHERRILL	17344	220	47.7	26.8	20.0	2.7	2.7	26908	28607	5	7	158	60.8	22.8	15.8	0.6	0.0	42273
72153	SHIRLEY	18647	1439	32.4	37.6	24.4	4.1	1.5	35372	35886	19	46	1196	29.8	24.9	29.8	13.0	2.3	82692
72156	SOLGOHACHIA	18981	205	28.8	27.8	36.6	5.9	1.0	44094	43534	46	84	176	22.7	25.0	41.5	8.0	2.8	94000
72157	SPRINGFIELD	18970	582	31.4	29.4	32.3	5.5	1.4	38038	38552	27	64	507	26.2	30.6	35.9	4.7	2.6	81786
72160	STUTTGART	22146	4359	30.9	29.0	31.1	5.6	3.4	40345	41084	34	76	2843	22.8	34.4	31.5	10.8	0.4	80573
72165	THIDA	15079	53	26.4	39.6	32.1	1.9	0.0	36333	37278	22	52	41	31.7	41.5	24.4	2.4	0.0	67500
72166	TICHNOR	23165	103	29.1	35.9	25.2	7.8	1.9	38281	38751	28	65	75	37.3	28.0	29.3	4.0	1.3	68750
72167	TRASKWOOD	20295	697	23.5	31.4	38.2	5.6	1.3	46542	47820	53	88	572	27.3	32.5	27.8	10.0	2.4	76731
72168	TUCKER	11427	292	46.2	25.7	21.9	3.8	2.4	27703	29396	5	9	210	66.2	18.1	14.8	1.0	0.0	39375
72170	ULM	20724	143	28.7	35.0	32.2	2.8	1.4	40603	41310	35	77	113	27.4	25.7	38.1	8.0	0.9	85625
72173	VILONIA	21194	2710	18.3	30.6	41.4	7.7	1.9	50927	53822	63	93	2232	20.2	19.6	41.9	16.6	1.7	108078
72175	WABBASEKA	14867	218	50.9	24.3	19.7	3.2	1.8	24225	25923	3	3	143	58.7	26.6	11.9	2.1	0.7	43750
72176	WARD	19841	2452	20.5	31.3	38.6	7.0	2.6	48078	50273	57	90	1868	23.2	21.2	39.4	14.5	1.7	99630
72179	WILBURN	20255	191	29.8	30.9	31.9	5.2	2.1	39782	41404	32	73	166	18.1	21.1	35.5	24.1	1.2	109091
72199	NORTH LITTLE ROCK	7624	40	17.5	35.0	42.5	5.0	0.0	45000	47404	48	85	29	24.1	37.9	24.1	13.8	0.0	68333
72201	LITTLE ROCK	20001	387	47.5	34.6	14.5	1.0	2.3	25767	26231	4	5	33	21.2	24.2	36.4	18.2	0.0	101563
72202	LITTLE ROCK	22410	5133	48.4	24.3	21.4	2.9	3.1	25985	26822	4	5	1766	29.5	41.1	17.0	6.9	5.5	71545
72204	LITTLE ROCK	18144	12745	32.0	30.9	31.6	4.0	1.4	38145	40825	27	64	7439	27.2	48.4	23.1	1.1	0.2	70605
72205	LITTLE ROCK	30477	11684	21.9	29.0	36.7	7.4	5.0	49187	51108	59	91	6274	3.2	21.0	55.6	18.5	1.7	116989
72206	LITTLE ROCK	18623	10169	32.0	30.8	30.1	5.1	1.9	38312	41120	28	66	6873	33.0	36.4	24.7	5.8	0.2	69106
72207	LITTLE ROCK	47090	6061	13.2	24.4	38.3	11.8	12.3	63392	64723	82	99	3655	2.1	8.8	41.6	30.6	17.0	167851
72209	LITTLE ROCK	17613	11968	29.2	34.1	31.6	3.5	1.6	38965	41418	30	69	6433	21.2	61.3	17.1	0.4	0.0	68683
72210	LITTLE ROCK	31896	6418	16.8	23.9	38.2	14.4	6.6	60257	61958	78	98	4582	19.1	14.2	43.3	20.0	3.3	122672
72211	LITTLE ROCK	38922	9687	11.3	21.5	43.3	15.0	8.9	67986	69555	86	99	5519	2.5	4.6	56.1	33.7	3.2	150555
72212	LITTLE ROCK	46970	5179	7.1	16.0	35.5	20.9	20.5	86199	86459	94	100	3893	0.8	2.8	29.5	55.7	11.3	224448
72223	LITTLE ROCK	56355	6320	8.1	13.5	25.8	19.1	33.5	105404	108257	97	100	4580	5.1	9.2	15.5	45.8	24.4	253184
72227	LITTLE ROCK	40037	5637	15.9	24.9	35.7	13.1	10.4	59099	61174	76	97	3306	1.5	3.4	53.0	35.1	7.0	164250
72301	WEST MEMPHIS	18504	10351	35.8	26.5	27.8	6.5	3.3	36709	40320	23	55	5864	22.0	41.8	29.1	6.3	0.8	76542
72310	ARMOREL	0	0	0.0	0.0	0.0	0.0	0.0	0	0	0	0	0	0.0	0.0	0.0	0.0	0.0	0
72311	AUBREY	18964	22	50.0	22.7	27.3	0.0	0.0	25000	26079	3	5	17	64.7	29.4	5.9	0.0	0.0	32500
72313	BASSETT	11083	16	43.8	43.8	6.3	6.3	0.0	27230	22287	5	8	11	81.8	0.0	18.2	0.0	0.0	32500
72315	BLYTHEVILLE	19765	9582	33.3	27.1	28.4	8.0	3.2	39086	41363	30	69	5589	24.2	33.1	31.6	10.3	0.9	78821
72320	BRICKEYS	7842	101	35.6	32.7	23.8	5.0	3.0	36235	37760	21	52	70	52.9	34.3	12.9	0.0	0.0	47500
72324	CHERRY VALLEY	19408	883	30.9	38.8	23.8	3.1	3.4	35478	36135	19	47	679	39.5	31.5	23.4	4.9	0.7	63750
72326	COLT	18079	1034	32.2	33.8	28.1	4.3	1.5	37226	40000	24	60	825	37.0	30.7	25.2	5.7	1.5	66181
72327	CRAWFORDSVILLE	15814	753	38.4	33.1	23.0	4.0	1.6	33383	35623	14	35	462	48.1	21.0	25.3	4.8	0.9	56429
72328	CRUMROD	9224	85	54.1	31.8	11.8	2.4	0.0	23709	25000	3	2	34	52.9	20.6	26.5	0.0	0.0	45000
72329	DRIVER	0	0	0.0	0.0	0.0	0.0	0.0	0	0	0	0	0	0.0	0.0	0.0	0.0	0.0	0
72330	DYESS	14581	284	37.7	34.2	23.6	4.2	0.4	32891	34082	13	31	207	67.1	22.7	9.7	0.0	0.5	38375
72331	EARLE	15163	1353	47.2	30.7	16.9	3.2	2.1	26484	27717	4	6	792	63.3	20.1	14.4	1.9	0.4	41322
72333	ELAINE	15605	456	50.2	28.3	15.1	3.1	3.3	24879	27813	3	4	243	55.1	24.7	16.9	3.3	0.0	44318
72335	FORREST CITY	15335	6369	41.1	26.5	26.4	3.6	2.4	33006	35337	13	32	3776	26.8	35.6	27.9	8.7	1.0	76082
72338	FRENCHMANS BAYOU	11316	8	50.0	37.5	12.5	0.0	0.0	22500	22500	2	2	6	66.7	0.0	33.3	0.0	0.0	30000
72339	GILMORE	15503	145	37.9	26.9	29.7	2.8	2.8	35746	38307	20	49	99	55.6	27.3	17.2	0.0	0.0	46765
72340	GOODWIN	9896	37	43.2	35.1	21.6	0.0	0.0	32302	39059	12	27	28	42.9	35.7	17.9	3.6	0.0	54000
72341	HAYNES	16395	19	42.1	36.8	21.1	0.0	0.0	28562	35000	6	11	13	46.2	30.8	23.1	0.0	0.0	55000
72342	HELENA	16374	2338	50.9	23.1	18.4	3.8	3.8	24446	26336	3	4	1164	37.5	26.4	20.4	13.3	2.3	64156
72346	HETH	16093	298	42.6	25.5	24.5	5.0	2.3	30000	33211	8	16	214	52.3	22.9	16.4	8.4	0.0	48148
72347	HICKORY RIDGE	24574	369	34.4	26.0	27.6	4.1	7.9	40755	41946	35	78	265	38.5	34.0	15.8	5.7	6.0	59531
72348	HUGHES	15631	1170	46.2	26.5	21.5	3.9	1.8	29140	31472	7	12	687	41.6	25.6	27.5	4.1	1.2	61889
72350	JOINER	14843	475	41.9	29.5	23.8	4.0	0.8	31106	31885	10	20	337	52.2	23.7	22.6	1.5	0.0	47656
	ARKANSAS	21917		28.7	29.0	32.0	6.7	3.7	42685	44760				21.5	25.6	34.9	15.2	2.9	95077
	UNITED STATES	27277		20.9	24.4	35.3	11.7	7.6	54719	56938				9.3	13.1	31.6	32.6	13.5	162279

ZIP CODE #	POST OFFICE NAME	FINANCIAL SERVICES: Auto Loan	Home Loan	Invest-ments	Retire-ment Plans	THE HOME: Home Improvements: Home Repair	Lawn & Garden	Furnishings: Comput-ers & Hard-ware-Personal	Major Appli-ances	TV, Radio, Sound Equip-ment	Furni-ture	ENTERTAINMENT: Dine out/ Carry out	Sports Equip-ment	Fees & Tickets	Toys & Games	Travel	Cable TV	PERSONAL: Apparel & Services	Auto Repairs	Health Insur-ance	Pets & Supplies
72081	JUDSONIA	79	58	67	56	58	75	60	69	66	58	65	53	49	68	55	71	44	66	73	84
72082	KENSETT	62	40	60	38	40	61	43	54	50	41	49	42	32	51	40	56	32	51	57	67
72083	KEO	89	61	98	61	64	94	68	85	71	55	70	70	50	69	68	77	45	79	89	104
72084	LEOLA	90	67	74	65	66	85	69	79	75	68	74	60	57	78	63	81	50	75	82	95
72086	LONOKE	86	68	78	68	69	86	70	81	76	67	74	61	61	76	68	82	50	77	86	96
72087	LONSDALE	95	91	89	86	93	96	86	93	90	92	89	65	85	90	87	92	60	91	98	108
72088	FAIRFIELD BAY	77	86	111	76	101	107	77	95	84	88	81	54	88	72	94	90	54	90	119	103
72099	LITTLE ROCK AIR FORC	79	41	31	48	37	35	74	51	70	69	74	51	56	84	54	64	52	66	46	63
72101	MC CRORY	74	53	69	52	53	74	58	68	64	53	62	52	46	64	54	70	42	65	73	82
72102	MC RAE	84	60	69	59	60	80	63	73	70	61	68	56	50	73	57	76	46	69	77	89
72103	MABELVALE	90	77	73	75	74	84	77	81	81	78	81	61	71	84	72	84	55	80	84	98
72104	MALVERN	79	62	72	61	62	78	64	73	69	61	68	55	55	70	61	74	46	70	78	87
72105	JONES MILL	80	74	65	71	72	75	70	74	72	72	72	54	66	75	66	74	49	71	74	88
72106	MAYFLOWER	92	66	83	64	67	90	69	82	76	66	75	63	55	78	64	83	50	77	86	99
72110	MORRILTON	87	64	84	63	66	88	68	82	75	63	73	61	56	75	65	81	49	77	87	97
72111	MOUNT VERNON	83	66	68	64	65	78	66	74	71	66	70	55	57	74	61	76	47	70	76	89
72112	NEWPORT	80	60	73	59	60	79	65	74	72	61	70	56	55	72	61	78	48	72	80	89
72113	MAUMELLE	144	158	137	155	151	136	142	141	135	152	137	111	148	142	143	129	97	136	127	162
72114	NORTH LITTLE ROCK	48	37	35	39	35	42	47	43	52	45	51	33	43	50	41	55	35	48	51	54
72116	NORTH LITTLE ROCK	108	111	110	113	112	115	110	111	111	110	111	83	113	110	112	113	77	111	117	130
72117	NORTH LITTLE ROCK	74	55	62	54	53	71	60	66	66	58	65	51	51	67	55	72	44	65	72	81
72118	NORTH LITTLE ROCK	84	78	68	78	74	82	81	80	83	78	82	62	77	85	76	85	57	81	86	96
72120	SHERWOOD	100	102	90	102	98	97	98	97	97	101	99	75	99	100	97	97	69	97	96	114
72121	PANGBURN	86	61	73	60	61	82	64	75	71	62	69	57	51	73	59	77	46	71	79	91
72122	PARON	106	114	121	106	123	128	102	117	108	112	106	75	111	102	114	114	72	112	135	132
72125	PERRY	88	63	73	62	63	84	66	77	73	64	72	59	53	76	60	80	48	73	81	93
72126	PERRYVILLE	87	64	85	62	66	88	66	81	73	62	72	61	54	73	64	80	48	76	85	97
72127	PLUMERVILLE	84	56	79	54	56	82	60	74	68	57	67	58	46	70	56	76	44	70	78	91
72128	POYEN	94	68	78	66	68	90	71	82	78	69	77	63	57	82	64	85	52	78	87	100
72129	PRATTSVILLE	95	68	83	66	68	92	71	84	78	68	77	64	57	81	65	86	51	79	88	102
72130	PRIM	78	63	76	60	66	80	63	74	69	65	67	53	56	68	62	74	45	71	80	88
72131	QUITMAN	80	63	83	60	67	83	63	77	69	63	68	56	55	68	64	75	45	72	82	91
72132	REDFIELD	88	80	72	77	77	82	77	80	79	79	79	60	71	83	72	81	54	79	81	96
72133	REYDELL	80	52	77	49	52	78	55	70	64	53	62	54	41	65	52	71	41	66	74	86
72134	ROE	85	61	87	59	63	86	63	80	69	58	68	60	50	69	62	76	45	73	83	95
72135	ROLAND	120	111	101	108	109	115	104	111	108	108	108	82	100	112	101	111	74	108	112	132
72136	ROMANCE	100	92	81	89	90	94	87	92	90	90	90	67	82	94	83	92	61	89	92	109
72137	ROSE BUD	94	68	88	66	69	93	70	85	78	67	76	65	57	79	67	85	51	80	89	103
72140	SAINT CHARLES	77	55	80	54	58	79	57	72	63	53	62	54	46	63	56	70	41	66	75	86
72141	SCOTLAND	69	49	70	48	51	70	51	64	56	47	55	48	41	56	50	62	37	59	67	77
72142	SCOTT	114	80	120	78	83	117	85	107	92	74	90	84	65	91	84	100	59	99	112	129
72143	SEARCY	86	75	76	75	74	85	79	81	82	76	81	62	72	83	74	85	55	81	87	98
72149	SEARCY	0	0	0	0	0	0	0	0	0	0	0	0	0	0	0	0	0	0	0	0
72150	SHERIDAN	101	75	86	73	75	97	77	89	84	75	83	68	63	87	71	91	56	84	93	108
72152	SHERRILL	70	46	68	43	46	69	49	62	56	46	55	48	37	57	46	63	36	58	65	76
72153	SHIRLEY	75	59	79	56	63	78	59	73	65	59	64	53	51	63	60	70	42	68	77	86
72156	SOLGOHACHIA	87	62	89	60	65	88	64	82	71	60	70	61	51	71	63	78	46	75	85	97
72157	SPRINGFIELD	87	62	84	60	64	86	64	79	71	60	70	60	51	72	62	78	46	74	83	95
72160	STUTTGART	85	67	76	66	67	85	72	80	78	69	76	60	62	78	67	84	52	78	86	95
72165	THIDA	77	55	79	53	57	78	56	72	63	52	61	54	45	62	56	69	41	66	75	85
72166	TICHNOR	95	65	104	65	68	100	72	90	75	58	74	74	53	74	72	82	48	84	95	110
72167	TRASKWOOD	90	71	73	69	70	84	72	79	77	72	76	60	62	80	66	82	52	76	82	96
72168	TUCKER	73	49	69	46	48	71	52	64	59	50	58	50	40	60	48	65	38	61	67	79
72170	ULM	85	59	92	58	61	89	64	80	68	53	67	65	48	66	64	74	43	75	85	98
72173	VILONIA	95	86	78	84	84	89	82	87	85	85	85	64	77	89	78	88	58	84	88	104
72175	WABBASEKA	66	43	64	41	43	65	46	58	53	44	52	46	35	54	43	60	35	55	62	72
72176	WARD	88	81	71	78	79	81	78	81	80	81	80	60	74	83	74	81	55	79	80	96
72179	WILBURN	90	64	92	62	67	91	66	84	73	61	72	63	53	73	65	81	47	77	87	100
72199	NORTH LITTLE ROCK	93	70	76	68	70	88	71	81	78	71	77	62	60	81	66	84	52	78	85	99
72201	LITTLE ROCK	50	32	34	37	31	36	53	41	56	49	56	34	45	52	44	57	39	51	51	53
72202	LITTLE ROCK	60	45	47	49	44	51	61	53	66	59	65	42	55	63	54	68	45	61	63	67
72204	LITTLE ROCK	69	59	51	61	55	64	66	62	70	65	69	48	63	70	60	72	48	66	69	77
72205	LITTLE ROCK	86	80	77	82	79	83	89	83	90	86	90	64	86	89	85	91	63	88	90	100
72206	LITTLE ROCK	75	60	65	59	59	73	64	69	70	63	69	51	57	70	60	75	47	69	76	84
72207	LITTLE ROCK	123	127	129	131	129	127	131	125	130	132	131	96	136	127	133	130	92	130	132	148
72209	LITTLE ROCK	70	61	50	63	55	64	66	62	70	66	69	49	63	71	60	72	48	66	68	77
72210	LITTLE ROCK	110	104	93	105	100	98	107	102	105	109	107	80	104	109	102	104	74	104	100	121
72211	LITTLE ROCK	121	113	100	116	107	102	121	109	117	123	119	89	117	122	113	113	84	115	105	131
72212	LITTLE ROCK	157	174	178	181	178	164	165	162	159	173	160	126	179	160	173	155	115	161	155	188
72223	LITTLE ROCK	212	230	206	240	225	201	214	207	202	229	206	170	227	213	216	191	148	202	184	239
72227	LITTLE ROCK	117	113	120	116	117	120	119	118	119	118	118	89	118	117	119	121	83	120	124	139
72301	WEST MEMPHIS	70	62	55	64	59	67	70	65	74	68	73	50	67	74	64	77	51	70	73	80
72310	ARMOREL	0	0	0	0	0	0	0	0	0	0	0	0	0	0	0	0	0	0	0	0
72311	AUBREY	69	45	66	42	45	68	48	61	55	46	54	47	36	56	45	62	36	57	64	75
72313	BASSETT	64	42	62	40	42	63	45	57	52	43	51	44	34	53	42	58	34	53	60	70
72315	BLYTHEVILLE	78	70	66	69	67	76	72	73	75	72	75	55	68	76	68	78	51	74	78	88
72320	BRICKEYS	83	54	80	51	54	82	58	73	67	55	65	57	43	68	54	75	43	69	77	90
72324	CHERRY VALLEY	88	63	74	61	63	84	66	77	73	64	72	59	53	76	60	80	48	73	81	94
72326	COLT	81	57	70	56	57	78	60	71	67	58	66	55	48	69	55	73	44	67	75	87
72327	CRAWFORDSVILLE	75	50	72	47	50	73	53	66	61	51	60	51	41	62	50	67	40	62	70	81
72328	CRUMROD	58	38	56	36	38	57	40	51	47	38	46	40	30	47	38	52	30	48	54	63
72329	DRIVER	0	0	0	0	0	0	0	0	0	0	0	0	0	0	0	0	0	0	0	0
72330	DYESS	73	52	61	51	52	69	54	63	60	53	59	49	44	63	49	66	40	60	67	77
72331	EARLE	68	50	55	50	49	65	56	60	64	55	62	45	48	63	51	69	42	61	68	74
72333	ELAINE	65	48	53	48	47	63	54	58	63	55	61	42	48	61	49	69	41	60	68	72
72335	FORREST CITY	67	55	53	56	53	63	61	61	66	59	65	47	56	66	56	69	44	63	67	75
72338	FRENCHMANS BAYOU	50	33	48	31	32	49	35	44	40	33	39	34	26	41	33	45	26	41	46	54
72339	GILMORE	80	52	77	49	52	78	56	70	64	53	63	55	42	65	52	72	42	66	74	86
72340	GOODWIN	60	39	58	37	39	59	42	52	48	40	47	41	31	49	39	54	31	49	55	65
72341	HAYNES	67	44	65	41	44	66	47	59	54	45	53	46	35	55	44	61	35	56	63	73
72342	HELENA	66	50	55	51	49	62	58	59	66	57	64	44	52	64	53	70	44	62	68	73
72346	HETH	78	54	69	52	54	75	57	68	64	55	63	53	45	66	52	71	42	65	72	83
72347	HICKORY RIDGE	106	75	108	72	77	107	77	98	86	72	85	74	61	86	76	95	56	91	103	118
72348	HUGHES	69	49	63	48	49	68	53	62	60	51	59	46	43	60	49	66	39	60	68	76
72350	JOINER	72	47	69	45	47	71	51	63	58	48	57	49	38	59	47	65	38	60	67	78
	ARKANSAS	88	73	79	72	73	85	76	82	80	74	79	62	68	81	72	84	54	80	86	98
	UNITED STATES	100	100	100	100	100	100	100	100	100	100	100	100	100	100	100	100	100	100	100	100

ZIP CODE #	POST OFFICE NAME	COUNTY FIPS CODE	POPULATION 2000	POPULATION 2009	POPULATION 2014	2000-2009 ANNUAL RATE % Rate	2000-2009 ANNUAL RATE State Centile	HOUSEHOLDS 2000	HOUSEHOLDS 2009	HOUSEHOLDS 2014	HOUSEHOLDS % Annual Rate 2000-2009	HOUSEHOLDS 2009 Average HH Size	FAMILIES 2000	FAMILIES 2009	FAMILIES % Annual Rate 2000-2009
72351	KEISER	093	963	819	766	-1.7	2	366	323	305	-1.3	2.54	283	242	-1.7
72354	LEPANTO	111	2623	2517	2449	-0.4	25	1019	998	977	-0.2	2.52	735	693	-0.6
72355	LEXA	107	3673	3525	3442	-0.4	25	1325	1298	1274	-0.2	2.65	995	945	-0.6
72358	LUXORA	093	1933	1704	1611	-1.4	3	677	604	572	-1.2	2.52	498	429	-1.6
72360	MARIANNA	077	8770	8076	7721	-0.9	12	3316	3147	3035	-0.6	2.40	2324	2125	-1.0
72364	MARION	035	12574	14697	15615	1.7	89	4573	5517	5924	2.0	2.60	3448	4021	1.7
72365	MARKED TREE	111	3752	3515	3389	-0.7	16	1495	1430	1386	-0.5	2.38	1024	942	-0.9
72366	MARVELL	107	3062	2810	2700	-0.9	12	1188	1111	1074	-0.7	2.49	792	707	-1.2
72367	MELLWOOD	107	84	71	66	-1.8	1	20	17	16	-1.7	4.18	16	13	-2.2
72368	MORO	077	1224	1153	1115	-0.6	18	497	490	481	-0.2	2.35	358	341	-0.5
72369	ONEIDA	107	57	50	48	-1.4	3	19	17	16	-1.2	2.94	14	12	-1.7
72370	OSCEOLA	093	10039	9278	8902	-0.8	14	3559	3366	3247	-0.6	2.66	2600	2376	-1.0
72372	PALESTINE	123	2159	2080	2032	-0.4	25	815	813	802	0.0	2.54	608	587	-0.4
72373	PARKIN	037	1875	1761	1724	-0.7	16	712	694	688	-0.3	2.54	487	455	-0.7
72374	POPLAR GROVE	107	988	915	880	-0.8	14	377	358	347	-0.6	2.55	272	249	-1.0
72376	PROCTOR	035	2199	2219	2236	0.1	43	775	813	829	0.5	2.73	593	602	0.2
72379	SNOW LAKE	041	132	123	116	-0.8	14	53	51	49	-0.4	2.41	37	34	-0.9
72384	TURRELL	035	1413	1466	1494	0.4	54	499	531	545	0.7	2.76	366	374	0.2
72386	TYRONZA	111	2072	2018	1976	-0.3	27	803	805	795	0.0	2.51	596	578	-0.3
72390	WEST HELENA	107	10424	9793	9433	-0.7	16	3829	3667	3553	-0.5	2.67	2673	2461	-0.9
72392	WHEATLEY	123	436	383	361	-1.4	3	176	159	151	-1.1	2.41	132	116	-1.4
72394	WIDENER	123	770	690	657	-1.2	6	277	257	247	-0.8	2.68	197	176	-1.2
72395	WILSON	093	1133	1006	951	-1.3	5	434	398	381	-0.9	2.53	318	282	-1.3
72396	WYNNE	037	14171	13889	13728	-0.2	31	5331	5402	5396	0.1	2.52	3949	3871	-0.2
72401	JONESBORO	031	47457	51353	53645	0.9	72	19046	20529	21496	0.8	2.38	12196	12584	0.3
72404	JONESBORO	031	16516	21797	24431	3.0	96	6217	8306	9359	3.2	2.59	4663	5942	2.7
72410	ALICIA	075	701	687	674	-0.2	31	264	262	258	-0.1	2.62	208	200	-0.4
72411	BAY	031	2337	2588	2752	1.1	78	890	993	1059	1.2	2.60	682	733	0.8
72412	BEECH GROVE	055	494	579	624	1.7	89	196	232	251	1.8	2.50	162	186	1.5
72413	BIGGERS	121	1152	1227	1240	0.7	66	462	500	509	0.9	2.45	340	354	0.4
72414	BLACK OAK	031	790	839	876	0.7	66	305	323	337	0.6	2.59	227	231	0.2
72415	BLACK ROCK	075	1651	1587	1553	-0.4	25	650	631	620	-0.3	2.52	470	439	-0.7
72416	BONO	031	5300	5753	6023	0.9	72	2013	2195	2308	0.9	2.60	1543	1618	0.5
72417	BROOKLAND	031	2643	2845	2980	0.8	68	995	1071	1124	0.8	2.66	775	804	0.4
72419	CARAWAY	031	1635	1731	1798	0.6	62	665	706	734	0.6	2.41	475	480	0.1
72421	CASH	031	779	852	890	1.0	75	326	358	375	1.0	2.38	237	248	0.5
72422	CORNING	021	5637	5195	4967	-0.9	12	2322	2159	2067	-0.8	2.37	1601	1432	-1.2
72424	DATTO	021	63	60	58	-0.5	22	27	26	25	-0.4	2.31	19	17	-1.2
72425	DELAPLAINE	055	498	519	539	0.4	54	192	203	212	0.6	2.56	143	145	0.2
72426	DELL	093	339	310	295	-1.0	9	148	139	133	-0.7	2.23	106	96	-1.1
72428	ETOWAH	093	391	332	310	-1.8	1	151	132	125	-1.4	2.52	117	99	-1.8
72429	FISHER	111	568	531	513	-0.7	16	235	224	217	-0.5	2.37	162	148	-1.0
72430	GREENWAY	021	432	383	361	-1.3	5	194	174	165	-1.2	2.20	136	117	-1.6
72432	HARRISBURG	111	6628	6712	6629	0.1	43	2519	2592	2572	0.3	2.51	1880	1871	-0.1
72433	HOXIE	075	3364	3223	3151	-0.5	22	1325	1291	1268	-0.3	2.48	953	894	-0.7
72434	IMBODEN	121	1794	1861	1876	0.4	54	739	773	781	0.5	2.41	536	543	0.1
72435	KNOBEL	021	563	550	534	-0.3	27	231	227	221	-0.2	2.42	167	158	-0.6
72436	LAFE	055	910	1030	1095	1.3	82	347	400	428	1.5	2.58	272	304	1.2
72437	LAKE CITY	031	3450	3825	4052	1.1	78	1296	1444	1536	1.2	2.59	975	1043	0.7
72438	LEACHVILLE	093	2545	2370	2265	-0.8	14	1000	941	902	-0.7	2.52	718	652	-1.0
72440	LYNN	075	319	321	320	0.1	43	136	139	139	0.2	2.31	103	102	-0.1
72441	MC DOUGAL	021	79	71	67	-1.1	8	34	31	30	-1.0	2.29	25	22	-1.4
72442	MANILA	093	4552	4131	3922	-1.0	9	1771	1627	1552	-0.9	2.50	1264	1121	-1.3
72443	MARMADUKE	055	3117	3350	3508	0.8	68	1229	1340	1411	0.9	2.49	932	983	0.6
72444	MAYNARD	121	1897	1994	2012	0.5	58	783	840	853	0.8	2.37	571	591	0.4
72445	MINTURN	075	19	19	18	0.0	40	6	6	6	0.0	3.17	5	5	0.0
72447	MONETTE	031	1763	1885	1981	0.7	66	743	795	837	0.7	2.29	481	486	0.1
72449	O KEAN	121	208	210	207	0.1	43	89	92	91	0.4	2.28	66	66	0.0
72450	PARAGOULD	055	31770	35233	37157	1.1	78	12576	14138	14976	1.3	2.45	9028	9797	0.9
72453	PEACH ORCHARD	021	319	314	306	-0.2	31	138	137	134	-0.1	2.29	100	95	-0.6
72454	PIGGOTT	021	5738	5555	5402	-0.3	27	2444	2384	2325	-0.3	2.29	1635	1528	-0.7
72455	POCAHONTAS	121	12916	13025	12938	0.1	43	5147	5274	5263	0.3	2.41	3675	3635	-0.1
72456	POLLARD	021	686	668	653	-0.3	27	278	273	269	-0.2	2.45	210	200	-0.5
72457	PORTIA	075	144	140	138	-0.3	27	60	59	59	-0.2	2.34	42	40	-0.5
72458	POWHATAN	075	583	584	580	0.0	40	232	237	236	0.2	2.46	170	167	-0.2
72459	RAVENDEN	075	923	953	954	0.3	49	363	381	383	0.5	2.50	267	270	0.1
72460	RAVENDEN SPRINGS	121	1013	1098	1128	0.9	72	406	447	462	1.0	2.46	300	319	0.7
72461	RECTOR	021	3754	3408	3247	-1.0	9	1615	1484	1418	-0.9	2.30	1088	961	-1.3
72464	SAINT FRANCIS	021	27	27	27	0.0	40	13	13	13	0.0	2.08	9	9	0.0
72465	SEDGWICK	075	23	23	23	0.0	40	8	8	8	0.0	2.88	6	6	0.0
72466	SMITHVILLE	075	888	905	906	0.2	45	353	366	367	0.4	2.47	266	267	0.0
72467	STATE UNIVERSITY	031	28	32	35	1.5	85	11	13	14	1.8	2.46	9	10	1.1
72469	STRAWBERRY	135	1414	1483	1494	0.5	58	555	590	597	0.7	2.51	422	436	0.4
72470	SUCCESS	021	269	256	248	-0.5	22	109	105	101	-0.4	2.44	76	70	-0.9
72471	SWIFTON	067	1239	1133	1076	-1.0	9	485	452	433	-0.8	2.50	356	319	-1.2
72472	TRUMANN	111	9209	9166	9003	-0.1	35	3632	3678	3633	0.1	2.47	2606	2549	-0.2
72473	TUCKERMAN	067	2408	2096	1960	-1.5	2	1022	908	855	-1.3	2.26	711	608	-1.7
72476	WALNUT RIDGE	075	7096	6845	6708	-0.4	25	2844	2756	2708	-0.3	2.28	1898	1764	-0.8
72478	WARM SPRINGS	121	281	275	271	-0.2	31	114	113	112	-0.1	2.33	86	82	-0.5
72479	WEINER	111	1374	1429	1420	0.4	54	550	579	577	0.6	2.47	398	403	0.1
72482	WILLIFORD	135	1288	1448	1527	1.3	82	576	654	692	1.4	2.21	401	439	1.0
72501	BATESVILLE	063	24101	24201	24069	0.0	40	9518	9761	9768	0.3	2.38	6684	6601	-0.1
72512	HORSESHOE BEND	065	3349	3452	3510	0.3	49	1570	1634	1667	0.4	2.07	1045	1042	0.0
72513	ASH FLAT	135	2102	2015	1970	-0.5	22	846	822	809	-0.3	2.36	567	524	-0.8
72515	BEXAR	049	139	127	123	-1.0	9	55	51	50	-0.8	2.49	42	38	-1.1
72517	BROCKWELL	065	730	723	703	-0.1	35	282	284	278	0.1	2.55	212	208	-0.2
72519	CALICO ROCK	005	2830	2938	2990	0.4	54	944	1005	1034	0.7	2.59	656	675	0.3
72520	CAMP	049	470	425	408	-1.1	8	185	170	164	-0.9	2.49	142	127	-1.2
72521	CAVE CITY	135	4262	4534	4635	0.7	66	1640	1776	1824	0.9	2.50	1205	1259	0.5
72522	CHARLOTTE	063	237	276	290	1.7	89	100	120	127	2.0	2.30	78	90	1.6
72523	CONCORD	023	1102	1177	1210	0.7	66	433	472	488	0.9	2.49	322	339	0.6
72524	CORD	063	443	470	479	0.6	62	183	199	204	0.9	2.36	138	145	0.5
72527	DESHA	063	374	393	401	0.5	58	149	161	165	0.8	2.44	112	117	0.5
72528	DOLPH	065	424	419	419	-0.1	35	174	174	174	0.0	1.71	127	123	-0.3
72529	CHEROKEE VILLAGE	049	4837	5261	5428	0.9	72	2264	2479	2564	1.0	2.10	1643	1738	0.6
	ARKANSAS					0.9					1.1	2.46			0.7
	UNITED STATES					1.0					1.1	2.59			0.9

ZIP CODE		RACE (%)						% Hispanic Origin		2009 AGE DISTRIBUTION (%)										MEDIAN AGE		
#	POST OFFICE NAME	White		Black		Asian/Pacific															%	%
		2000	2009	2000	2009	2000	2009	2000	2009	0-4	5-9	10-14	15-19	20-24	25-44	45-64	65-84	85+	18+	2009	2009 Males	2009 Females
72351	KEISER	89.2	86.0	8.1	10.5	0.1	0.1	2.3	3.5	6.2	6.2	6.6	7.0	5.9	25.2	28.7	12.7	1.6	76.6	39.9	50.2	49.8
72354	LEPANTO	84.5	80.6	13.1	16.1	0.0	0.0	2.3	3.6	7.8	7.7	7.5	6.7	5.7	25.2	25.9	11.9	1.5	72.7	36.1	48.6	51.4
72355	LEXA	53.0	49.3	45.1	48.1	0.2	0.4	1.4	2.1	7.0	7.4	7.9	7.9	6.3	23.4	27.3	11.3	1.5	72.8	36.2	47.9	52.1
72358	LUXORA	53.6	48.1	43.5	48.2	0.1	0.1	2.6	3.6	7.4	6.9	6.7	8.2	9.3	26.4	23.8	9.6	1.6	74.5	33.3	53.1	46.9
72360	MARIANNA	34.5	31.1	64.0	67.0	0.4	0.5	1.7	2.3	7.5	7.3	7.0	7.6	7.3	24.1	24.0	12.4	2.8	73.6	35.7	47.7	52.3
72364	MARION	75.0	68.4	22.7	28.4	0.5	0.8	1.9	2.9	7.9	7.7	7.5	7.7	6.5	30.4	24.8	6.7	0.8	72.2	33.7	50.2	49.8
72365	MARKED TREE	72.5	69.0	24.8	27.4	0.2	0.3	2.2	3.2	6.8	6.9	6.9	6.5	5.8	23.2	25.7	15.4	2.9	75.6	39.9	47.9	52.1
72366	MARVELL	40.5	36.7	58.3	61.7	0.0	0.0	0.8	1.2	7.6	7.0	6.9	8.3	6.2	20.1	25.9	15.1	3.0	73.2	39.3	46.4	53.6
72367	MELLWOOD	38.1	33.8	54.8	57.7	0.0	0.0	10.7	14.1	7.0	11.3	8.5	12.7	7.0	21.1	25.4	7.0	0.0	66.2	29.2	47.9	52.1
72368	MORO	62.2	58.2	37.2	40.9	0.2	0.4	1.5	2.2	6.2	7.3	7.3	5.8	4.9	22.7	27.7	15.4	2.8	75.5	41.0	47.7	52.3
72369	ONEIDA	54.4	48.0	40.4	44.0	0.0	0.0	7.0	8.0	8.0	8.0	8.0	8.0	4.0	26.0	26.0	12.0	0.0	74.0	35.0	50.0	50.0
72370	OSCEOLA	52.1	48.3	46.1	49.5	0.2	0.3	1.6	2.3	9.0	8.9	8.1	7.7	7.3	25.6	22.7	9.3	1.5	69.4	31.1	48.6	51.4
72372	PALESTINE	67.0	64.7	32.0	34.1	0.2	0.2	0.1	0.1	6.9	6.9	6.7	7.2	5.4	24.1	28.6	12.5	1.8	74.9	39.0	49.4	50.6
72373	PARKIN	35.1	27.7	63.5	70.8	0.1	0.1	1.0	1.2	6.9	9.1	7.8	8.4	5.7	22.5	24.0	13.6	2.0	70.8	35.4	47.1	52.9
72374	POPLAR GROVE	50.4	46.1	48.5	52.2	0.1	0.1	1.2	1.9	6.0	6.7	7.5	8.5	6.0	21.6	28.9	12.8	2.0	74.3	39.1	48.3	51.7
72376	PROCTOR	48.6	39.8	49.1	57.2	0.2	0.3	1.9	2.6	7.8	7.8	7.7	6.9	5.6	25.4	27.5	10.2	1.2	72.6	36.6	49.9	50.1
72379	SNOW LAKE	65.6	60.2	31.3	36.6	0.0	0.0	3.1	4.1	8.1	8.1	6.5	4.9	4.9	19.5	28.5	17.1	2.4	74.0	43.2	50.4	49.6
72384	TURRELL	36.9	29.5	59.9	66.4	0.2	0.3	3.8	5.2	8.1	8.5	8.4	7.7	5.3	23.3	27.6	9.5	1.7	70.1	35.9	50.3	49.7
72386	TYRONZA	85.8	81.6	12.0	15.4	0.2	0.3	1.2	1.8	7.2	7.2	7.3	6.2	5.4	27.1	26.2	12.0	1.3	74.4	36.9	49.7	50.3
72390	WEST HELENA	36.7	33.3	61.9	64.8	0.3	0.4	1.1	1.6	9.5	9.2	8.4	8.3	6.6	22.5	23.1	10.8	1.6	67.8	31.5	45.9	54.1
72392	WHEATLEY	62.4	60.1	35.8	37.9	0.0	0.0	3.2	2.9	6.5	6.5	6.5	6.3	7.0	24.0	27.2	14.1	1.8	77.0	40.9	48.6	51.4
72394	WIDENER	47.3	44.5	50.8	53.3	0.1	0.1	2.9	2.8	7.8	7.5	7.5	8.4	6.1	24.5	24.6	11.6	1.9	72.0	36.0	50.1	49.9
72395	WILSON	76.2	70.0	21.8	27.1	0.0	0.0	2.7	4.0	6.8	6.5	6.5	6.5	7.2	24.6	30.5	10.1	1.5	76.7	38.7	46.6	53.4
72396	WYNNE	75.8	73.0	22.7	25.0	0.4	0.6	0.9	1.3	7.1	7.1	7.0	6.9	5.7	25.6	26.8	11.9	2.0	74.5	37.8	48.5	51.5
72401	JONESBORO	84.6	82.0	12.0	13.6	0.8	1.1	2.6	3.9	6.8	6.1	5.7	8.1	9.6	27.4	23.3	11.0	2.1	78.0	34.1	48.0	52.0
72404	JONESBORO	93.9	91.6	3.5	4.7	0.7	1.1	1.2	2.1	6.8	6.4	6.4	7.1	9.9	28.8	26.1	7.6	1.0	76.4	33.8	49.7	50.3
72410	ALICIA	99.3	99.3	0.0	0.0	0.0	0.0	0.1	0.3	3.9	8.2	8.3	7.1	4.9	24.5	27.2	14.0	1.9	75.1	40.2	51.4	48.6
72411	BAY	95.9	94.5	2.5	3.2	0.0	0.1	1.5	2.6	7.2	7.2	7.3	6.6	5.9	26.5	26.8	10.9	1.4	74.1	37.2	49.2	50.8
72412	BEECH GROVE	98.0	97.6	0.0	0.0	0.0	0.2	0.4	0.5	6.7	6.9	6.9	5.7	4.8	28.2	27.6	11.7	1.4	75.8	39.6	52.0	48.0
72413	BIGGERS	96.0	95.1	1.6	1.9	0.0	0.1	0.3	0.6	6.8	6.7	6.8	7.1	5.0	23.9	25.9	15.6	2.3	75.5	40.4	48.7	51.3
72414	BLACK OAK	97.2	96.2	0.1	0.1	0.3	0.4	1.3	2.3	5.6	5.7	6.3	5.7	4.8	24.6	31.2	13.9	2.1	78.8	43.3	50.7	49.3
72415	BLACK ROCK	98.5	98.2	0.1	0.1	0.0	0.1	0.5	0.7	5.9	6.2	6.4	6.6	5.5	23.8	29.4	14.1	2.0	77.5	41.5	51.1	48.9
72416	BONO	97.6	96.9	0.6	0.7	0.1	0.2	1.3	2.1	7.5	7.5	7.5	7.0	5.3	28.5	25.6	10.2	0.9	73.1	36.1	49.9	50.1
72417	BROOKLAND	97.4	96.4	0.5	0.7	0.0	0.0	1.2	2.1	8.4	8.1	8.2	7.1	4.9	28.0	24.0	10.1	1.2	70.9	35.7	50.7	49.3
72419	CARAWAY	97.4	95.9	0.0	0.0	0.2	0.2	3.0	5.1	6.6	6.8	7.1	6.5	4.9	24.1	28.2	13.3	2.5	75.8	40.3	48.8	51.2
72421	CASH	98.1	97.4	0.5	0.6	0.4	0.6	1.9	3.2	8.6	7.9	7.9	6.1	3.3	28.1	23.8	12.7	1.8	71.7	37.7	52.2	47.8
72422	CORNING	97.3	96.8	0.2	0.3	0.2	0.3	0.5	0.8	6.4	6.3	6.3	6.6	5.8	25.1	26.0	14.8	2.7	77.1	40.2	49.0	51.0
72424	DATTO	100.0	98.3	0.0	0.0	0.0	0.0	1.6	1.7	6.7	6.7	6.7	6.7	6.7	23.3	26.7	15.0	1.7	73.3	40.0	46.7	53.3
72425	DELAPLAINE	91.6	89.8	0.0	0.0	0.2	0.4	0.8	1.3	5.0	5.0	6.0	7.5	6.0	26.4	28.5	14.1	1.5	79.4	40.8	51.3	48.7
72426	DELL	89.4	85.8	6.5	8.4	0.3	0.3	4.7	7.4	5.8	6.5	6.8	6.8	4.8	22.9	31.3	13.2	1.9	76.8	42.4	50.3	49.7
72428	ETOWAH	93.3	90.1	1.3	1.8	0.0	0.0	6.4	9.6	9.0	8.4	7.8	6.9	5.4	27.4	22.9	11.1	0.9	70.2	34.5	49.7	50.3
72429	FISHER	96.7	95.3	1.1	1.3	0.0	0.0	2.5	4.0	5.3	5.6	6.2	6.8	4.0	23.9	33.7	12.6	1.9	78.7	43.8	51.0	49.0
72430	GREENWAY	99.1	98.7	0.0	0.0	0.0	0.0	0.5	0.8	4.4	4.7	5.5	6.8	4.7	23.8	31.9	16.2	2.1	81.5	45.1	51.7	48.3
72432	HARRISBURG	95.9	94.6	2.3	2.9	0.2	0.3	1.3	2.0	6.3	6.5	6.6	7.1	5.1	26.1	27.2	13.2	1.8	76.0	39.2	50.0	50.0
72433	HOXIE	98.4	98.0	0.4	0.5	0.1	0.1	1.2	1.8	6.8	7.1	7.0	6.7	5.8	26.0	25.6	12.8	2.1	75.0	38.1	48.6	51.4
72434	IMBODEN	97.0	96.2	0.4	0.6	0.0	0.0	0.9	1.5	5.9	6.1	6.6	6.7	4.6	23.4	29.4	15.1	2.1	77.3	42.6	49.9	50.1
72435	KNOBEL	97.7	97.1	0.4	0.4	0.0	0.0	2.0	2.7	6.9	6.9	7.3	6.7	5.5	23.3	26.2	15.5	1.8	74.7	40.6	49.3	50.7
72436	LAFE	94.1	92.8	0.0	0.0	0.0	0.1	1.0	1.5	6.1	6.0	6.1	6.6	6.0	26.1	29.3	12.7	1.0	78.0	40.4	50.3	49.7
72437	LAKE CITY	98.0	97.3	0.1	0.2	0.1	0.1	1.6	2.6	6.3	6.4	6.6	6.9	5.8	26.2	26.6	13.2	2.1	76.7	39.1	49.3	50.7
72438	LEACHVILLE	93.8	91.0	1.3	1.7	0.2	0.3	7.2	11.3	7.0	7.0	7.0	6.6	5.3	25.2	26.8	13.4	1.7	74.9	38.4	50.4	49.6
72440	LYNN	96.9	96.3	0.3	0.3	0.0	0.0	0.6	0.9	6.9	7.5	7.2	5.9	4.0	23.4	29.6	14.0	1.6	74.8	40.7	49.8	50.2
72441	MC DOUGAL	98.7	98.6	0.0	0.0	0.0	0.0	0.0	0.0	7.0	7.0	7.0	5.6	5.6	23.9	26.8	15.5	1.4	73.2	41.3	53.5	46.5
72442	MANILA	97.6	96.6	0.2	0.3	0.0	0.1	2.0	3.1	6.6	6.6	6.8	7.0	5.5	26.9	26.2	12.5	1.9	75.8	38.9	48.1	51.9
72443	MARMADUKE	96.5	95.4	0.0	0.0	0.1	0.1	1.2	1.9	6.6	6.4	6.7	6.7	5.7	26.5	27.1	12.8	1.5	76.2	39.3	49.7	50.3
72444	MAYNARD	97.0	96.3	0.8	1.0	0.1	0.2	0.5	0.7	5.9	5.9	6.4	7.3	5.3	23.6	28.8	15.1	1.7	77.4	41.9	49.8	50.2
72445	MINTURN	100.0	100.0	0.0	0.0	0.0	0.0	0.0	0.0	0.0	5.3	10.5	5.3	0.0	36.8	36.8	5.3	0.0	78.9	41.3	47.4	52.6
72447	MONETTE	96.0	93.6	0.1	0.1	0.0	0.1	3.7	6.4	6.6	6.4	6.3	5.3	4.6	24.1	25.4	17.2	4.1	77.3	42.4	46.6	53.4
72449	O KEAN	98.6	97.1	0.0	0.0	0.0	0.5	0.5	1.0	7.6	7.6	7.1	5.7	5.2	27.1	27.1	11.0	1.4	73.8	37.7	49.5	50.5
72450	PARAGOULD	97.7	97.1	0.2	0.2	0.2	0.3	1.2	1.9	6.8	6.7	6.7	6.5	5.6	27.0	26.1	12.5	2.0	75.7	38.2	49.1	50.9
72453	PEACH ORCHARD	96.9	96.2	0.3	0.3	0.0	0.0	1.9	2.5	6.7	6.7	7.0	7.0	5.4	23.6	26.8	15.0	1.9	75.2	40.7	50.0	50.0
72454	PIGGOTT	98.6	98.2	0.2	0.2	0.0	0.0	0.8	1.3	6.0	6.3	6.3	6.0	4.9	23.3	26.4	17.4	3.4	77.5	42.8	48.6	51.4
72455	POCAHONTAS	97.2	96.6	0.9	1.1	0.1	0.1	0.8	1.3	6.1	6.1	6.2	6.4	5.6	24.4	27.1	15.0	3.0	77.6	41.1	49.0	51.0
72456	POLLARD	99.1	99.0	0.0	0.0	0.0	0.0	0.7	1.0	5.7	5.7	6.1	6.1	5.4	25.4	29.0	14.8	1.6	78.7	41.8	49.9	50.1
72457	PORTIA	98.6	98.6	0.7	0.7	0.0	0.0	0.7	0.7	5.7	5.7	6.4	7.9	5.0	22.1	27.1	17.9	2.1	78.6	43.0	49.3	50.7
72458	POWHATAN	98.3	97.4	0.2	0.3	0.0	0.2	0.7	1.2	5.7	6.0	6.2	6.2	5.0	23.8	30.5	14.9	1.9	78.4	42.8	51.2	48.8
72459	RAVENDEN	96.9	96.1	0.0	0.0	0.0	0.0	0.9	1.5	6.4	6.3	6.5	5.9	6.4	24.2	29.5	13.3	1.5	77.1	40.2	50.2	49.8
72460	RAVENDEN SPRINGS	97.5	97.1	0.3	0.4	0.0	0.0	1.0	1.5	5.8	5.9	6.3	6.1	4.6	24.8	29.9	14.9	1.7	78.1	42.4	50.5	49.5
72461	RECTOR	98.2	97.8	0.2	0.3	0.1	0.1	1.1	1.6	5.9	6.0	6.2	5.8	4.8	23.5	27.4	17.2	3.1	78.2	43.2	48.2	51.8
72464	SAINT FRANCIS	100.0	100.0	0.0	0.0	0.0	0.0	0.0	3.7	7.4	7.4	7.4	7.4	7.4	29.6	29.6	3.7	0.0	70.4	33.8	48.1	51.9
72465	SEDGWICK	100.0	100.0	0.0	0.0	0.0	0.0	0.0	0.0	8.7	8.7	8.7	8.7	4.3	30.4	30.4	0.0	0.0	65.2	32.5	52.2	47.8
72466	SMITHVILLE	97.4	96.8	0.2	0.3	0.1	0.1	0.8	1.1	6.2	6.9	6.6	6.1	4.3	23.1	30.5	14.6	1.8	76.5	42.3	50.5	49.5
72467	STATE UNIVERSITY	100.0	100.0	0.0	0.0	0.0	0.0	0.0	0.0	6.3	6.3	6.3	6.3	6.3	25.0	31.3	12.5	0.0	75.0	40.0	53.1	46.9
72469	STRAWBERRY	98.4	98.1	0.3	0.3	0.1	0.1	0.4	0.6	6.8	7.1	7.4	6.7	4.5	24.0	27.8	14.0	1.6	74.3	39.9	50.8	49.2
72470	SUCCESS	97.8	97.7	0.0	0.0	0.0	0.0	0.7	1.2	6.6	6.6	6.6	6.6	5.5	25.0	25.8	15.6	1.6	75.4	40.0	52.0	48.0
72471	SWIFTON	98.1	97.4	0.4	0.5	0.1	0.1	1.8	2.6	6.2	6.1	6.3	6.8	6.2	25.8	26.7	14.4	1.6	77.4	40.3	47.7	52.3
72472	TRUMANN	94.9	93.5	3.5	4.4	0.2	0.3	1.0	1.6	7.2	7.1	7.0	6.7	6.4	25.6	25.7	12.4	1.9	74.5	37.3	48.8	51.2
72473	TUCKERMAN	88.7	86.6	9.7	11.4	0.0	0.0	0.9	1.3	5.4	5.7	5.7	6.5	6.2	22.9	30.4	14.6	2.5	79.4	43.0	47.7	52.3
72476	WALNUT RIDGE	97.1	96.5	0.8	1.0	0.1	0.2	0.6	1.0	6.5	6.4	5.9	6.7	6.8	23.8	23.9	16.0	4.0	78.0	39.7	47.2	52.8
72478	WARM SPRINGS	93.2	91.6	4.3	5.1	0.0	0.0	1.8	2.9	5.1	5.1	5.8	8.7	5.8	23.3	30.2	14.5	1.5	78.2	41.9	52.4	47.6
72479	WEINER	97.7	96.9	1.0	1.3	0.3	0.5	1.7	2.7	5.4	5.9	6.2	6.5	4.4	25.4	30.6	13.4	2.1	78.4	42.4	50.0	50.0
72482	WILLIFORD	98.3	98.0	0.1	0.1	0.1	0.1	0.8	1.2	4.9	5.1	5.0	5.2	4.1	19.5	30.7	23.3	2.1	81.8	50.0	50.1	49.9
72501	BATESVILLE	94.0	92.4	2.7	3.1	0.9	1.3	1.7	2.7	6.3	6.4	6.5	6.7	6.2	24.7	27.6	13.3	2.4	77.2	39.8	48.6	51.4
72512	HORSESHOE BEND	97.4	97.4	0.2	0.2	0.1	0.1	1.2	1.2	3.5	3.5	3.7	3.4	3.1	13.6	28.3	34.9	5.9	87.1	60.5	48.0	52.0
72513	ASH FLAT	97.4	96.7	0.6	0.7	0.2	0.2	1.1	1.8	5.3	5.2	5.4	6.0	5.4	20.7	28.3	19.8	4.1	80.0	46.5	47.4	52.6
72515	BEXAR	98.6	98.4	0.0	0.0	0.0	0.0	0.7	0.8	4.7	5.5	5.5	6.3	4.7	23.6	31.5	16.5	1.6	81.1	44.7	51.2	48.8
72517	BROCKWELL	97.7	97.6	0.1	0.1	0.0	0.0	1.1	1.0	5.5	6.2	7.2	5.7	4.1	24.3	31.1	14.2	1.5	77.6	42.4	49.0	51.0
72519	CALICO ROCK	94.6	94.1	3.2	3.5	0.2	0.2	1.3	1.3	4.7	4.9	5.3	6.1	6.4	25.9	28.3	16.2	2.4	81.1	42.8	54.4	45.6
72520	CAMP	97.0	96.9	0.0	0.0	0.0	0.0	0.9	0.7	4.7	5.2	5.4	5.2	4.7	20.0	32.5	20.0	2.4	81.2	48.0	50.1	49.9
72521	CAVE CITY	97.1	96.5	1.0	1.1	0.1	0.1	1.1	1.8	7.6	7.4	7.3	6.4	5.3	25.0	25.0	13.3	2.9	73.6	38.5	48.2	51.8
72522	CHARLOTTE	96.2	94.9	0.8	1.1	0.0	0.4	1.7	2.5	6.2	6.2	6.5	5.4	5.4	27.9	30.4	10.9	1.1	77.9	39.3	52.5	47.5
72523	CONCORD	98.1	97.7	0.0	0.0	0.1	0.1	1.0	1.7	5.7	5.6	6.1	7.0	5.9	26.7	26.8	14.5	1.8	78.3	40.6	50.1	49.9
72524	CORD	98.0	97.4	0.5	0.6	0.2	0.2	0.7	1.1	5.7	6.2	6.4	6.0	4.9	24.7	31.5	13.0	1.7	78.1	41.9	52.1	47.9
72527	DESHA	98.1	97.2	0.5	0.5	0.3	0.5	0.8	1.0	5.9	6.4	6.4	5.6	4.8	25.7	30.3	13.5	1.5	77.9	41.7	46.6	53.4
72528	DOLPH	86.6	85.0	11.3	12.9	0.2	0.2	0.5	0.5	3.3	4.1	4.3	4.8	8.6	40.6	25.5	7.6	1.2	85.0	37.3	69.5	30.5
72529	CHEROKEE VILLAGE	96.8	96.2	0.2	0.2	0.3	0.4	0.8	1.3	3.9	3.9	3.9	3.9	3.5	14.2	28.5	33.1	5.1	85.9	58.5	47.5	52.5
	ARKANSAS	80.0	78.2	15.7	15.8	0.8	1.2	3.2	5.1	6.8	6.6	6.5	6.9	6.6	26.0	26.1	12.4	2.0	76.1	37.8	49.1	50.9
	UNITED STATES	75.1	72.0	12.3	12.7	3.8	4.6	12.5	15.7	6.8	6.7	6.6	7.1	6.9	27.0	26.0	10.9	1.9	75.7	36.9	49.2	50.8

ZIP CODE #	POST OFFICE NAME	2009 Per Capita Income	2009 HH Income Base	2009 Household Income Distribution (%) Less than $25,000	$25,000 to $49,999	$50,000 to $99,999	$100,000 to $149,999	$150,000 or More	Median Household Income 2009	2014	2009 National Centile	2009 State Centile	2009 Home Value Base	2009 Home Value Distribution (%) Less than $50,000	$50,000 to $89,999	$90,000 to $174,999	$175,000 to $399,999	$400,000 or More	2009 Median Home Value
72351	KEISER	19247	323	26.0	31.6	35.6	5.9	0.9	44092	44859	46	84	206	34.5	46.6	18.9	0.0	0.0	58000
72354	LEPANTO	16251	998	42.6	28.2	24.5	3.4	1.3	30204	31951	8	16	606	46.2	32.7	18.0	3.0	0.2	54107
72355	LEXA	16481	1298	40.8	29.7	24.2	3.5	1.8	32580	34915	13	28	871	43.4	30.2	20.9	5.4	0.1	57986
72358	LUXORA	14235	604	43.7	29.1	22.4	4.0	0.8	30000	31030	8	16	335	46.0	29.9	19.7	4.5	0.0	55000
72360	MARIANNA	14970	3147	51.5	25.5	18.6	2.5	1.8	24060	24562	3	3	1890	41.8	36.7	20.0	1.5	0.1	56540
72364	MARION	23922	5517	19.2	26.9	37.6	13.2	3.0	53161	53558	68	95	3592	20.0	22.3	40.6	16.3	0.8	101316
72365	MARKED TREE	15918	1430	43.8	29.0	22.7	4.0	0.6	30085	31521	8	16	828	31.4	39.6	23.3	5.1	0.6	69390
72366	MARVELL	16255	1111	48.8	27.7	17.7	3.1	2.7	26333	28234	4	6	730	52.7	32.2	12.2	2.5	0.4	46970
72367	MELLWOOD	6514	17	52.9	35.3	11.8	0.0	0.0	23529	23405	2	2	7	42.9	28.6	28.6	0.0	0.0	55000
72368	MORO	16168	490	48.6	25.3	22.2	2.4	1.4	26260	27140	4	6	386	50.5	29.3	19.7	0.5	0.0	49429
72369	ONEIDA	10950	17	47.1	29.4	23.5	0.0	0.0	27313	30000	5	9	9	66.7	33.3	0.0	0.0	0.0	37500
72370	OSCEOLA	15667	3366	40.5	28.8	25.1	3.3	2.3	32019	33491	11	25	1809	22.1	43.7	26.5	7.1	0.6	72365
72372	PALESTINE	16917	813	37.5	31.9	26.0	3.1	1.6	33733	36228	15	37	626	37.7	31.2	23.6	5.0	2.6	66522
72373	PARKIN	14217	694	51.0	26.7	17.1	3.3	1.9	24400	25308	3	4	435	57.5	27.4	11.3	2.3	1.6	43981
72374	POPLAR GROVE	16217	358	41.6	30.4	22.6	3.6	1.7	33171	35625	14	33	268	43.3	33.2	18.7	4.9	0.0	56923
72376	PROCTOR	17857	813	29.9	35.1	29.2	3.4	2.5	38426	40949	28	66	576	37.7	26.7	28.8	4.5	2.3	71724
72379	SNOW LAKE	16202	51	52.9	23.5	19.6	2.0	2.0	23275	24265	2	2	38	57.9	15.8	23.7	2.6	0.0	42500
72384	TURRELL	15195	531	38.2	31.1	24.7	4.1	1.9	34008	36269	16	38	331	56.8	17.8	19.9	4.5	0.9	46311
72386	TYRONZA	16937	805	35.0	33.4	26.3	4.1	1.1	35040	37633	18	44	534	49.8	29.8	18.4	2.1	0.0	50222
72390	WEST HELENA	14902	3667	46.3	25.6	23.2	3.3	1.5	29742	31468	8	14	1990	35.8	36.4	24.5	3.0	0.3	63831
72392	WHEATLEY	15343	159	37.1	36.5	23.9	2.5	0.0	35399	37309	19	46	118	40.7	38.1	16.1	5.1	0.0	55000
72394	WIDENER	16528	257	47.1	25.3	21.0	4.3	2.3	27154	29113	5	8	175	62.3	26.9	10.9	0.0	0.0	42037
72395	WILSON	21292	398	31.4	27.6	32.7	5.0	3.3	41023	43237	36	78	234	26.9	37.6	31.6	2.1	1.7	73158
72396	WYNNE	19715	5402	33.5	29.1	30.2	4.6	2.6	38437	39823	28	66	3837	26.4	28.6	34.5	9.5	1.1	82801
72401	JONESBORO	20908	20529	31.1	29.1	30.6	6.0	3.1	39162	42147	30	70	12032	16.4	31.2	37.9	12.9	1.6	93212
72404	JONESBORO	28678	8306	17.5	24.1	37.7	12.7	7.9	58571	57037	76	97	5722	10.7	16.0	49.6	19.2	4.4	116792
72410	ALICIA	15403	262	39.3	35.1	19.1	5.0	1.5	31149	31174	10	21	197	62.9	21.3	13.7	2.0	0.0	44900
72411	BAY	18155	993	27.3	35.1	31.8	4.0	1.7	40820	42891	35	78	700	34.4	44.4	16.6	4.4	0.1	59561
72412	BEECH GROVE	21581	232	22.0	32.3	39.7	3.9	2.2	46315	46481	52	87	200	22.0	19.0	35.0	21.5	2.5	108696
72413	BIGGERS	14911	500	41.8	33.8	22.8	1.0	0.6	30420	31165	9	18	392	56.6	31.4	11.0	1.0	0.0	46232
72414	BLACK OAK	17993	323	37.5	28.2	26.9	4.3	3.1	35963	38635	20	49	245	43.3	39.2	11.0	6.5	0.0	54342
72415	BLACK ROCK	16417	631	33.6	38.4	23.6	3.3	1.1	33311	34555	14	34	495	37.6	35.2	21.6	5.7	0.0	63235
72416	BONO	18803	2195	27.5	36.4	29.4	5.0	1.8	38921	41883	30	68	1681	29.0	40.0	23.0	7.0	1.0	70972
72417	BROOKLAND	19375	1071	26.1	33.4	32.5	5.7	2.2	42585	44531	41	81	842	30.0	37.9	27.3	4.0	0.7	73390
72419	CARAWAY	15497	706	42.5	32.4	20.8	3.3	1.0	30306	32416	9	17	498	58.6	32.1	7.4	1.8	0.0	44028
72421	CASH	15457	358	42.5	33.2	19.8	4.5	0.0	29418	31397	7	13	270	44.8	38.5	15.2	1.5	0.0	55000
72422	CORNING	17016	2159	41.2	32.0	22.4	3.1	1.3	30641	31883	9	19	1556	49.3	32.7	16.1	1.7	0.3	50640
72424	DATTO	13250	26	42.3	38.5	19.2	0.0	0.0	30000	36115	8	16	20	65.0	25.0	10.0	0.0	0.0	37500
72425	DELAPLAINE	16438	203	33.5	38.4	22.7	2.0	3.4	36510	38147	22	53	167	47.3	29.9	18.6	4.2	0.0	53750
72426	DELL	21057	139	31.7	27.3	35.3	3.6	2.2	39073	43085	30	69	98	36.7	33.7	18.4	11.2	0.0	61429
72428	ETOWAH	14974	132	38.6	37.9	20.5	1.5	1.5	32059	33228	12	26	89	56.2	21.3	20.2	2.2	0.0	39167
72429	FISHER	16537	224	40.6	31.7	24.6	1.3	1.8	31592	33112	11	22	163	48.5	27.6	17.8	3.7	2.5	51667
72430	GREENWAY	26732	174	31.0	31.6	24.7	6.3	6.3	38181	40675	27	65	139	46.0	29.5	12.9	10.8	0.7	52115
72432	HARRISBURG	16984	2592	40.3	25.5	27.6	5.1	1.5	33793	36845	15	37	1969	44.2	32.4	17.6	5.0	0.8	56341
72433	HOXIE	16790	1291	40.4	30.8	23.4	3.3	2.2	32776	34488	13	29	879	36.6	46.6	13.9	2.8	0.0	60341
72434	IMBODEN	18465	773	36.1	31.8	26.1	3.4	2.6	32718	34310	13	29	611	32.9	33.2	25.4	6.4	2.1	67845
72435	KNOBEL	14337	227	42.7	33.5	22.9	0.9	0.0	31274	34653	10	21	172	66.9	20.3	9.9	1.7	1.2	39615
72436	LAFE	17130	400	30.0	33.5	32.3	2.8	1.5	39672	41741	32	72	348	34.8	34.5	25.6	4.0	1.1	69615
72437	LAKE CITY	17970	1444	28.9	34.9	29.2	5.1	1.9	38955	41177	30	69	1036	40.8	39.6	15.7	3.6	0.3	55864
72438	LEACHVILLE	17646	941	35.6	35.6	23.4	3.1	2.3	34805	36277	17	42	624	50.5	28.0	18.1	3.4	0.0	49639
72440	LYNN	18248	139	36.0	35.3	23.7	4.3	0.7	35197	38477	18	45	114	36.0	33.3	28.9	1.8	0.0	67000
72441	MC DOUGAL	19758	31	35.5	19.4	38.7	6.5	0.0	42386	42343	41	81	26	50.0	30.8	15.4	3.8	0.0	50000
72442	MANILA	16982	1627	38.1	30.8	24.5	5.3	1.2	32782	34051	13	29	1136	42.6	32.7	19.4	5.3	0.0	57304
72443	MARMADUKE	16706	1340	35.9	34.8	24.9	2.5	2.0	34829	37229	17	42	1016	26.1	38.3	28.4	4.7	2.5	74396
72444	MAYNARD	16871	840	41.8	29.0	25.4	2.5	1.3	31454	33198	10	22	658	43.0	29.3	23.6	4.1	0.0	55679
72445	MINTURN	14079	6	0.0	66.7	33.3	0.0	0.0	35000	42500	18	43	4	0.0	50.0	50.0	0.0	0.0	90000
72447	MONETTE	18232	795	36.4	31.2	26.7	4.2	1.6	36078	38843	21	50	543	43.5	38.9	14.5	3.1	0.0	55071
72449	O KEAN	18778	92	35.9	32.6	28.3	1.1	2.2	40000	40959	33	74	68	52.9	35.3	7.4	4.4	0.0	48571
72450	PARAGOULD	20427	14138	30.2	30.3	32.2	4.7	2.6	40051	42473	33	75	9896	13.0	28.9	39.9	16.3	2.0	101910
72453	PEACH ORCHARD	15473	137	41.6	34.3	22.6	0.7	0.7	31938	35000	11	24	105	65.7	21.9	10.5	1.0	1.0	40833
72454	PIGGOTT	18863	2384	36.8	33.5	24.0	2.8	2.9	33299	34833	14	34	1774	31.4	30.5	27.4	9.8	0.9	69756
72455	POCAHONTAS	18913	5274	33.7	32.8	26.4	4.8	2.3	37046	39385	24	58	3785	19.5	34.1	36.0	9.8	0.6	85142
72456	POLLARD	15981	273	36.6	37.0	23.1	2.2	1.1	31611	32921	11	22	227	46.7	26.4	19.4	5.7	1.8	54167
72457	PORTIA	17565	59	42.4	25.4	25.4	5.1	1.7	32340	32340	12	27	44	31.8	52.3	15.9	0.0	0.0	58889
72458	POWHATAN	16139	237	35.9	37.1	22.4	3.4	1.3	33158	34494	14	32	194	36.1	29.4	26.8	7.7	0.0	67647
72459	RAVENDEN	14995	381	45.1	35.4	16.5	1.3	1.6	30525	32415	9	18	299	34.4	46.2	13.0	5.4	1.0	59688
72460	RAVENDEN SPRINGS	17524	447	40.0	29.8	25.3	2.7	2.2	32534	34329	12	28	367	29.2	29.7	22.3	10.1	8.7	74773
72461	RECTOR	18518	1484	41.6	27.7	25.5	3.5	1.6	30716	32260	9	19	1124	47.7	35.1	11.7	5.4	0.2	52063
72464	SAINT FRANCIS	18241	13	30.8	46.2	23.1	0.0	0.0	36045	37321	21	50	11	45.5	36.4	18.2	0.0	0.0	55000
72465	SEDGWICK	9457	8	62.5	12.5	25.0	0.0	0.0	20000	20000	1	1	6	33.3	33.3	33.3	0.0	0.0	70000
72466	SMITHVILLE	16825	366	35.2	35.0	24.9	3.8	1.1	34648	37109	17	41	303	34.7	28.7	28.4	6.9	1.3	70217
72467	STATE UNIVERSITY	16641	13	30.8	38.5	30.8	0.0	0.0	38541	42248	28	67	10	60.0	40.0	0.0	0.0	0.0	40000
72469	STRAWBERRY	18088	590	33.7	28.1	30.8	5.9	1.4	36484	38979	22	53	494	34.4	25.5	27.1	8.1	4.9	68750
72470	SUCCESS	18599	105	37.1	37.1	21.0	0.0	4.8	32038	32619	11	25	79	62.0	24.1	12.7	1.3	0.0	39688
72471	SWIFTON	15182	452	40.7	33.6	21.2	3.8	0.7	30970	32231	10	20	327	46.5	34.3	15.6	3.7	0.0	52396
72472	TRUMANN	16937	3678	37.3	29.9	28.7	2.7	1.4	35220	38140	18	45	2374	33.2	41.0	24.0	1.6	0.2	63616
72473	TUCKERMAN	18561	908	38.2	31.9	25.0	3.9	1.0	34085	36272	16	39	674	40.4	41.2	16.2	1.5	0.7	55909
72476	WALNUT RIDGE	18612	2756	34.5	32.0	28.8	2.2	2.4	36027	38095	21	50	1772	27.9	45.4	22.4	4.3	0.0	68765
72478	WARM SPRINGS	18902	113	36.3	32.7	28.3	1.8	0.9	33592	34423	15	36	88	26.1	39.8	25.0	5.7	3.4	74444
72479	WEINER	21566	579	34.4	26.9	28.5	5.4	4.8	37565	41725	25	61	464	32.5	39.9	22.0	4.7	0.9	71493
72482	WILLIFORD	18501	654	43.4	32.6	18.8	3.1	2.1	28206	28568	6	10	559	30.1	36.9	23.8	8.2	1.1	70738
72501	BATESVILLE	21153	9761	30.8	28.9	32.7	4.6	3.1	40927	42003	36	78	6942	21.3	30.6	32.7	13.4	2.0	87352
72512	HORSESHOE BEND	21391	1634	32.0	35.3	27.8	3.4	1.5	36809	37868	23	56	1373	24.9	30.2	32.5	11.6	0.8	82950
72513	ASH FLAT	16601	822	45.5	29.6	20.1	2.2	2.7	26725	27495	4	7	644	16.6	38.7	30.3	12.4	2.0	83704
72515	BEXAR	16844	51	35.3	37.3	23.5	3.9	0.0	31695	33179	11	23	44	27.3	20.5	29.5	20.5	2.3	100000
72517	BROCKWELL	16201	284	39.8	31.0	22.9	3.9	2.5	33440	35000	14	35	248	31.9	20.6	28.2	15.7	3.6	86000
72519	CALICO ROCK	15632	1005	39.7	32.9	22.0	2.7	2.7	32151	33918	12	25	770	26.2	25.5	33.0	14.8	0.5	87174
72520	CAMP	19675	170	38.8	28.8	24.7	3.5	4.1	33187	36884	14	33	149	17.4	24.8	30.2	26.2	1.3	106250
72521	CAVE CITY	16142	1776	36.0	33.7	26.7	2.9	0.7	33950	35345	15	37	1338	27.4	35.4	26.3	8.4	2.5	74317
72522	CHARLOTTE	21191	120	25.8	31.7	35.8	5.8	0.8	44212	45151	46	84	103	34.0	22.3	31.1	11.7	1.0	77000
72523	CONCORD	18555	472	33.9	32.6	28.6	3.4	1.5	36625	38039	22	54	410	36.8	31.7	22.2	9.3	0.0	64681
72524	CORD	21963	199	28.1	32.2	32.7	4.5	2.5	40682	41842	35	77	168	23.2	28.0	33.3	14.9	0.6	88182
72527	DESHA	21202	161	13.7	41.0	40.4	3.1	1.9	46144	45903	52	87	129	14.7	17.8	56.6	7.0	3.9	110547
72528	DOLPH	19360	174	49.4	22.4	23.0	2.9	2.3	25553	26824	4	5	147	26.5	18.4	32.0	20.4	2.7	100833
72529	CHEROKEE VILLAGE	23052	2479	26.2	44.6	22.1	4.2	2.9	37486	39438	25	61	2023	13.8	40.6	31.8	13.7	0.0	85498
	ARKANSAS	21917		28.7	29.0	32.0	6.7	3.7	42685	44760				21.5	25.6	34.9	15.2	2.9	95077
	UNITED STATES	27277		20.9	24.4	35.3	11.7	7.6	54719	56938				9.3	13.1	31.6	32.6	13.5	162279

ZIP CODE		FINANCIAL SERVICES				THE HOME						ENTERTAINMENT						PERSONAL			
						Home Improvements		Furnishings													
#	POST OFFICE NAME	Auto Loan	Home Loan	Invest-ments	Retire-ment Plans	Home Repair	Lawn & Garden	Comput-ers & Hard-ware-Personal	Major Appli-ances	TV, Radio, Sound Equip-ment	Furni-ture	Dine out/ Carry out	Sports Equip-ment	Fees & Tickets	Toys & Games	Travel	Cable TV	Apparel & Services	Auto Repairs	Health Insur-ance	Pets & Supplies
72351	KEISER	88	63	73	61	63	84	66	76	73	64	72	59	53	76	60	80	48	72	81	93
72354	LEPANTO	75	51	68	49	51	73	54	66	61	52	60	51	42	63	50	68	40	62	69	81
72355	LEXA	77	54	70	52	53	75	58	68	66	56	65	52	47	67	54	73	43	66	74	84
72358	LUXORA	63	46	53	46	46	61	52	57	56	48	55	44	43	57	47	61	37	56	61	69
72360	MARIANNA	61	42	52	42	42	58	49	54	56	48	55	41	41	56	44	62	37	55	61	67
72364	MARION	98	94	81	91	89	89	90	91	90	94	91	70	87	94	86	89	62	90	87	107
72365	MARKED TREE	63	47	56	46	47	63	51	58	58	49	56	43	43	57	48	63	38	57	65	70
72366	MARVELL	70	49	64	47	49	69	53	63	61	51	60	48	43	61	50	68	40	61	70	77
72367	MELLWOOD	51	33	49	31	33	50	35	44	41	34	40	35	26	41	33	45	26	42	47	55
72368	MORO	71	46	68	43	46	69	49	62	57	47	56	48	37	58	46	64	37	59	66	76
72369	ONEIDA	58	39	54	37	38	57	42	51	48	40	47	39	33	49	39	54	31	49	55	63
72370	OSCEOLA	67	53	50	53	50	62	59	59	64	56	63	46	52	65	53	67	43	61	65	73
72372	PALESTINE	79	54	78	51	55	78	56	71	64	53	62	55	44	64	54	71	41	66	75	86
72373	PARKIN	62	43	56	42	43	61	47	55	55	46	53	41	38	54	43	60	36	54	61	68
72374	POPLAR GROVE	75	51	74	49	52	75	54	68	61	51	60	52	42	62	51	68	40	63	72	82
72376	PROCTOR	85	65	77	62	64	82	65	76	72	65	71	58	55	74	61	77	47	73	79	92
72379	SNOW LAKE	73	47	70	45	47	71	51	64	58	48	57	50	38	59	47	65	38	60	67	79
72384	TURRELL	77	52	76	49	53	76	55	69	62	52	61	53	42	63	52	69	40	64	73	84
72386	TYRONZA	77	54	67	52	54	74	57	67	64	55	62	52	45	66	52	70	42	64	71	82
72390	WEST HELENA	61	49	51	50	47	60	53	56	60	53	58	41	49	59	50	64	40	57	64	69
72392	WHEATLEY	69	45	66	42	45	67	48	60	55	46	54	47	36	56	45	62	36	57	64	74
72394	WIDENER	82	54	80	51	54	81	58	73	66	55	65	57	43	67	54	74	43	68	77	89
72395	WILSON	97	70	80	68	69	92	73	84	80	71	79	65	58	84	66	88	53	80	89	103
72396	WYNNE	83	67	73	66	66	82	69	76	74	66	73	58	60	75	65	78	49	74	81	92
72401	JONESBORO	77	68	63	68	66	72	74	72	76	71	75	55	68	76	68	77	52	74	76	86
72404	JONESBORO	113	107	96	109	103	103	108	104	107	110	108	83	105	111	104	105	75	106	101	125
72410	ALICIA	74	50	68	48	50	72	53	65	60	51	59	51	41	62	49	67	39	61	69	80
72411	BAY	85	62	70	60	61	80	64	74	71	62	69	57	52	74	58	77	47	70	78	90
72412	BEECH GROVE	85	75	76	78	76	90	75	85	78	68	76	64	68	80	74	83	52	78	87	99
72413	BIGGERS	65	45	64	43	45	66	48	60	55	44	53	46	37	55	46	60	35	56	64	72
72414	BLACK OAK	84	60	86	58	62	85	61	78	68	57	67	59	49	68	61	75	44	72	81	93
72415	BLACK ROCK	74	53	67	52	54	72	55	66	61	53	60	51	44	62	52	67	40	62	70	80
72416	BONO	87	65	72	63	64	83	67	76	73	66	72	58	55	76	61	79	48	73	80	93
72417	BROOKLAND	93	67	77	65	66	88	69	81	77	68	75	62	56	80	63	84	51	76	85	98
72419	CARAWAY	70	46	68	43	46	68	49	62	56	46	55	48	37	57	46	62	36	58	65	75
72421	CASH	66	46	67	45	47	68	50	61	53	43	52	49	38	53	49	58	34	57	64	75
72422	CORNING	69	51	58	50	50	67	56	62	61	52	59	48	46	62	51	66	40	61	67	75
72424	DATTO	55	40	46	39	39	52	41	48	46	40	45	37	33	48	37	50	30	45	51	58
72425	DELAPLAINE	76	54	63	53	54	72	57	66	63	55	62	51	45	66	51	69	41	62	70	80
72426	DELL	84	60	84	58	62	85	62	78	69	58	67	59	49	69	61	75	45	72	81	93
72428	ETOWAH	68	49	56	47	49	65	51	59	56	49	55	45	41	59	46	61	37	56	62	72
72429	FISHER	70	48	77	48	50	74	54	67	56	43	55	55	39	55	53	61	36	62	70	82
72430	GREENWAY	105	75	106	73	78	106	77	98	86	72	84	74	62	86	76	94	56	90	102	116
72432	HARRISBURG	78	54	72	53	55	76	57	70	64	54	63	53	45	65	54	71	42	66	74	84
72433	HOXIE	73	52	64	50	52	71	56	65	63	53	61	50	45	64	52	68	41	63	70	80
72434	IMBODEN	79	57	81	55	59	81	58	74	65	54	64	56	47	64	58	71	42	68	77	88
72435	KNOBEL	63	45	52	44	45	60	47	54	52	46	51	42	38	54	43	57	34	52	57	66
72436	LAFE	80	57	66	56	57	76	59	69	66	58	65	53	48	69	54	72	43	66	73	84
72437	LAKE CITY	85	61	71	59	61	81	63	74	70	62	69	57	51	73	58	77	46	70	78	90
72438	LEACHVILLE	81	56	76	53	56	80	58	72	66	56	65	56	45	67	55	73	43	68	76	88
72440	LYNN	75	54	77	52	56	76	55	70	61	51	60	53	44	61	55	68	40	65	73	84
72441	MC DOUGAL	82	59	67	57	58	78	61	71	68	59	66	55	49	71	55	74	45	67	75	86
72442	MANILA	77	55	65	54	55	74	58	67	64	56	63	52	46	67	52	70	42	64	71	82
72443	MARMADUKE	75	54	62	52	54	71	56	65	62	55	61	50	45	65	51	68	41	62	69	80
72444	MAYNARD	73	50	73	48	51	73	52	66	59	49	58	51	41	59	51	65	38	61	69	80
72445	MINTURN	80	58	66	56	57	76	60	70	67	59	65	54	48	70	55	73	44	66	74	85
72447	MONETTE	73	53	70	51	54	75	57	69	63	52	61	52	45	63	54	69	41	65	74	82
72449	O KEAN	77	56	64	54	55	73	58	67	64	56	63	52	46	67	53	70	42	64	71	82
72450	PARAGOULD	84	66	72	65	66	82	70	77	75	66	73	59	59	76	65	80	50	75	82	93
72453	PEACH ORCHARD	64	46	53	45	46	61	48	56	53	47	52	43	38	55	43	58	35	53	59	68
72454	PIGGOTT	74	55	70	54	57	76	58	70	64	53	62	53	48	64	56	70	42	66	75	83
72455	POCAHONTAS	76	60	69	59	61	77	63	72	68	59	66	54	54	68	60	73	45	69	77	85
72456	POLLARD	71	51	59	49	50	67	53	61	58	51	57	47	42	61	48	64	38	58	65	75
72457	PORTIA	70	51	70	49	52	73	55	68	61	49	59	51	44	61	53	68	40	63	74	80
72458	POWHATAN	71	51	70	49	52	71	53	65	58	49	57	49	42	59	51	64	38	60	68	78
72459	RAVENDEN	68	49	57	47	48	65	50	59	56	49	55	45	40	58	46	61	37	56	62	72
72460	RAVENDEN SPRINGS	77	55	79	53	57	78	56	72	63	53	62	54	45	62	56	69	41	66	75	85
72461	RECTOR	74	53	69	52	54	74	57	69	63	52	61	52	46	64	54	69	41	64	74	82
72464	SAINT FRANCIS	68	49	56	48	49	65	51	59	57	50	56	46	41	59	46	62	37	56	63	72
72465	SEDGWICK	49	35	50	34	36	49	36	45	40	33	39	34	29	39	35	44	26	42	47	54
72466	SMITHVILLE	74	53	75	52	55	75	55	69	61	51	60	52	44	61	54	67	39	64	72	82
72467	STATE UNIVERSITY	74	53	61	52	53	70	55	64	61	54	60	49	44	64	50	67	40	61	68	78
72469	STRAWBERRY	81	58	78	57	60	81	60	74	67	57	66	56	48	68	58	73	44	69	78	89
72470	SUCCESS	82	59	68	57	58	78	61	71	68	60	66	55	49	71	56	74	45	67	75	87
72471	SWIFTON	70	46	70	44	47	70	50	63	56	46	55	50	37	57	48	62	36	59	66	77
72472	TRUMANN	69	53	54	53	52	66	59	62	63	55	61	48	50	65	53	68	42	62	67	75
72473	TUCKERMAN	75	52	75	50	53	76	56	70	63	51	61	54	43	63	53	70	40	65	75	84
72476	WALNUT RIDGE	74	54	69	54	55	75	60	70	66	54	64	53	49	66	57	72	43	67	77	83
72478	WARM SPRINGS	81	58	67	57	58	77	61	71	67	59	66	54	49	70	55	73	44	67	75	86
72479	WEINER	95	67	100	66	70	98	71	89	77	63	76	70	55	76	70	84	50	83	93	108
72482	WILLIFORD	65	55	74	52	60	71	54	66	59	55	57	46	50	55	57	63	38	62	71	77
72501	BATESVILLE	86	67	76	67	68	85	71	79	75	67	75	60	60	77	66	82	51	76	84	95
72512	HORSESHOE BEND	64	62	82	56	71	79	58	72	63	63	61	45	60	57	66	68	41	68	84	80
72513	ASH FLAT	68	49	69	48	51	71	53	66	59	48	57	49	43	58	51	65	38	61	71	77
72515	BEXAR	75	54	77	52	56	76	55	70	61	51	60	53	44	61	54	67	40	64	73	83
72517	BROCKWELL	74	53	76	51	55	75	54	69	60	50	59	52	43	60	54	66	39	63	72	82
72519	CALICO ROCK	73	54	75	52	56	76	57	70	63	52	61	52	46	61	56	69	41	65	76	83
72520	CAMP	88	63	90	61	65	89	64	82	72	60	70	62	52	71	64	79	46	75	85	97
72521	CAVE CITY	72	52	64	50	52	71	55	65	61	52	59	50	44	62	51	66	40	61	69	78
72522	CHARLOTTE	88	63	73	61	63	84	66	76	73	64	71	59	53	76	60	79	48	72	81	93
72523	CONCORD	83	60	71	58	60	80	62	73	69	60	68	56	50	72	57	75	45	69	77	89
72524	CORD	93	67	88	65	68	92	69	85	76	65	75	64	55	77	66	84	50	79	88	101
72527	DESHA	80	73	72	76	74	86	72	81	74	65	73	62	66	76	72	79	50	75	84	94
72528	DOLPH	69	49	71	48	51	70	50	64	56	47	55	48	40	56	50	62	36	59	67	76
72529	CHEROKEE VILLAGE	69	68	89	63	77	84	64	77	68	70	66	49	66	62	72	73	45	73	88	87
	ARKANSAS	88	73	79	72	73	85	76	82	80	74	79	62	68	81	72	84	54	80	86	98
	UNITED STATES	100	100	100	100	100	100	100	100	100	100	100	100	100	100	100	100	100	100	100	100

ZIP CODE #	POST OFFICE NAME	COUNTY FIPS CODE	POPULATION 2000	POPULATION 2009	POPULATION 2014	2000-2009 ANNUAL RATE % Rate	2000-2009 ANNUAL RATE State Centile	HOUSEHOLDS 2000	HOUSEHOLDS 2009	HOUSEHOLDS 2014	HOUSEHOLDS % Annual Rate 2000-2009	HOUSEHOLDS 2009 Average HH Size	FAMILIES 2000	FAMILIES 2009	FAMILIES % Annual Rate 2000-2009
72530	DRASCO	023	1927	2034	2070	0.6	62	801	866	887	0.8	2.35	606	634	0.5
72531	ELIZABETH	049	742	725	722	-0.3	27	335	337	340	0.1	2.15	238	231	-0.3
72532	EVENING SHADE	135	1494	1621	1678	0.9	72	617	680	707	1.1	2.38	453	482	0.7
72533	FIFTY SIX	137	456	475	487	0.4	54	190	203	210	0.7	2.34	141	146	0.4
72534	FLORAL	063	1267	1296	1286	0.2	45	485	503	502	0.4	2.58	372	374	0.1
72536	FRANKLIN	065	455	453	449	0.0	40	187	189	188	0.1	2.37	140	136	-0.3
72537	GAMALIEL	005	877	989	1051	1.3	82	388	442	471	1.4	2.24	273	298	1.0
72538	GEPP	049	345	386	394	1.2	80	141	160	164	1.4	2.41	104	115	1.1
72539	GLENCOE	049	774	712	688	-0.9	12	303	282	273	-0.8	2.50	236	214	-1.1
72540	GUION	065	267	255	253	-0.5	22	111	108	108	-0.3	2.36	76	71	-0.7
72542	HARDY	135	3254	3506	3614	0.8	68	1370	1490	1538	0.9	2.35	947	990	0.5
72543	HEBER SPRINGS	023	11174	11463	11437	0.3	49	4798	4985	4992	0.4	2.25	3362	3361	0.0
72544	HENDERSON	005	684	754	794	1.1	78	288	322	341	1.2	2.34	202	217	0.8
72546	IDA	023	64	69	71	0.8	68	27	30	31	1.1	2.30	20	22	1.0
72550	LOCUST GROVE	063	842	907	932	0.8	68	337	373	386	1.1	2.43	257	276	0.8
72553	MAGNESS	063	42	42	42	0.0	40	16	16	16	0.0	2.63	11	11	0.0
72554	MAMMOTH SPRING	049	3894	3965	3952	0.2	45	1625	1673	1673	0.3	2.37	1190	1186	0.0
72555	MARCELLA	137	634	612	613	-0.4	25	255	250	251	-0.2	2.45	189	181	-0.5
72556	MELBOURNE	065	2327	2390	2425	0.3	49	1017	1066	1088	0.5	2.17	669	673	0.1
72560	MOUNTAIN VIEW	137	6744	7376	7685	1.0	75	2833	3179	3342	1.3	2.28	2009	2172	0.8
72561	MOUNT PLEASANT	065	1451	1422	1420	-0.2	31	580	580	582	0.0	2.45	429	415	-0.4
72562	NEWARK	063	2160	2382	2453	1.1	78	857	971	1008	1.4	2.45	627	683	0.9
72564	OIL TROUGH	063	510	524	526	0.3	49	223	234	237	0.5	2.24	168	171	0.2
72565	OXFORD	065	891	886	865	-0.1	35	360	365	358	0.1	2.43	264	259	-0.2
72566	PINEVILLE	065	385	379	378	-0.2	31	160	159	160	-0.1	1.70	115	111	-0.4
72567	PLEASANT GROVE	137	858	918	959	0.7	66	343	371	389	0.9	2.47	262	276	0.6
72568	PLEASANT PLAINS	063	1696	1882	1943	1.1	78	652	741	771	1.4	2.54	498	548	1.0
72569	POUGHKEEPSIE	135	621	637	646	0.3	49	244	254	258	0.4	2.51	186	188	0.1
72571	ROSIE	063	495	517	522	0.5	58	177	188	191	0.7	2.75	142	147	0.4
72572	SAFFELL	075	211	226	227	0.7	66	87	94	95	0.8	2.40	64	67	0.5
72573	SAGE	065	248	257	261	0.4	54	102	108	111	0.6	2.31	70	72	0.3
72576	SALEM	049	3252	3273	3248	0.1	43	1354	1395	1393	0.3	2.29	933	921	-0.1
72577	SIDNEY	135	516	597	629	1.6	87	171	202	215	1.8	2.75	132	152	1.5
72578	STURKIE	049	154	159	159	0.3	49	60	63	63	0.5	2.52	45	46	0.2
72579	SULPHUR ROCK	063	1010	1112	1144	1.0	75	387	438	453	1.3	2.54	289	316	1.0
72581	TUMBLING SHOALS	023	943	1113	1179	1.8	90	405	489	521	2.1	2.28	303	353	1.7
72583	VIOLA	049	1188	1191	1180	0.0	40	477	488	486	0.2	2.44	355	353	-0.1
72584	VIOLET HILL	065	311	308	301	-0.1	35	133	134	131	0.1	2.29	100	97	-0.3
72585	WIDEMAN	065	144	143	140	-0.1	35	57	58	57	0.2	2.43	42	41	-0.3
72587	WISEMAN	065	19	19	18	0.0	40	8	8	8	0.0	2.38	6	6	0.0
72601	HARRISON	009	27389	29631	30946	0.9	72	11201	12368	13005	1.1	2.35	7881	8385	0.7
72611	ALPENA	015	1502	1676	1770	1.2	80	581	658	697	1.4	2.55	443	485	1.0
72616	BERRYVILLE	015	9496	10237	10636	0.8	68	3620	3883	4029	0.8	2.61	2579	2663	0.3
72617	BIG FLAT	005	226	274	298	2.1	92	103	128	140	2.4	2.14	75	90	2.0
72619	BULL SHOALS	089	2242	2187	2151	-0.3	27	1118	1107	1095	-0.1	1.97	735	693	-0.6
72623	CLARKRIDGE	005	674	890	970	3.1	96	269	365	402	3.4	2.44	215	283	3.0
72624	COMPTON	101	242	243	239	0.0	40	111	117	117	0.6	2.08	82	83	0.1
72626	COTTER	005	1151	1343	1424	1.7	89	566	678	726	2.0	1.98	357	411	1.5
72628	DEER	101	1436	1394	1361	-0.3	27	590	601	595	0.2	2.32	408	400	-0.2
72629	DENNARD	141	1204	1239	1253	0.3	49	490	516	525	0.6	2.40	353	359	0.2
72631	EUREKA SPRINGS	015	3369	3800	4014	1.3	82	1572	1794	1900	1.4	2.10	1140	1255	1.0
72632	EUREKA SPRINGS	015	4219	4620	4836	1.0	75	1960	2178	2287	1.1	2.08	1139	1196	0.5
72633	EVERTON	009	1252	1365	1432	0.9	72	474	531	561	1.2	2.57	378	411	0.9
72634	FLIPPIN	089	4268	4509	4597	0.6	62	1759	1882	1923	0.7	2.38	1256	1296	0.3
72635	GASSVILLE	005	3058	3479	3705	1.4	84	1210	1412	1517	1.7	2.39	883	991	1.3
72638	GREEN FOREST	015	7095	8157	8673	1.5	85	2579	2954	3139	1.5	2.76	1898	2104	1.1
72639	HARRIET	129	1012	1001	1000	-0.1	35	420	430	434	0.3	2.33	321	320	0.0
72640	HASTY	101	275	283	280	0.3	49	108	116	116	0.8	2.44	82	85	0.4
72641	JASPER	101	1953	1931	1892	-0.1	35	816	841	835	0.3	2.24	532	524	-0.2
72642	LAKEVIEW	005	1902	2079	2184	1.0	75	957	1058	1115	1.1	1.97	664	700	0.6
72644	LEAD HILL	009	2059	2501	2700	2.1	92	871	1076	1169	2.3	2.26	623	742	1.9
72645	LESLIE	129	1853	1954	1994	0.6	62	844	921	950	0.9	2.12	568	595	0.5
72648	MARBLE FALLS	101	892	899	887	0.1	43	350	369	369	0.6	2.43	258	263	0.2
72650	MARSHALL	129	2859	2804	2792	-0.2	31	1225	1239	1246	0.1	2.23	842	819	-0.3
72651	MIDWAY	005	1171	1244	1316	0.7	66	511	552	586	0.8	2.25	364	377	0.4
72653	MOUNTAIN HOME	005	26335	28513	29830	0.9	72	11779	12991	13675	1.1	2.15	8048	8530	0.6
72655	MOUNT JUDEA	101	912	876	855	-0.4	25	375	378	373	0.1	2.30	280	273	-0.3
72658	NORFORK	005	1570	1860	2021	1.8	90	658	804	880	2.2	2.31	483	568	1.8
72660	OAK GROVE	015	548	641	686	1.7	89	207	245	263	1.8	2.62	159	182	1.5
72661	OAKLAND	089	577	651	681	1.3	82	276	317	334	1.5	2.05	209	231	1.1
72662	OMAHA	009	2482	2826	2996	1.4	84	1005	1175	1256	1.7	2.41	749	842	1.3
72663	ONIA	137	477	500	513	0.5	58	196	210	217	0.7	2.38	150	156	0.4
72666	PARTHENON	101	563	554	542	-0.2	31	242	249	247	0.3	2.22	167	165	-0.1
72668	PEEL	089	627	657	656	0.5	58	287	302	303	0.6	2.18	208	210	0.1
72669	PINDALL	129	502	493	489	-0.2	31	194	195	195	0.1	2.53	139	135	-0.3
72670	PONCA	101	288	289	284	0.0	40	114	120	120	0.6	2.41	84	85	0.1
72675	SAINT JOE	129	1591	1933	2019	2.1	92	656	805	844	2.2	2.40	469	561	2.0
72679	TILLY	115	66	72	76	0.9	72	30	34	35	1.4	2.12	23	25	0.9
72680	TIMBO	137	1166	1218	1250	0.5	58	487	519	536	0.7	2.35	367	380	0.4
72682	VALLEY SPRINGS	089	128	228	252	6.4	100	49	87	97	6.4	2.61	37	64	6.1
72683	VENDOR	101	816	784	767	-0.4	25	314	316	313	0.1	2.46	237	232	-0.2
72685	WESTERN GROVE	101	1036	1065	1055	0.3	49	413	441	443	0.7	2.41	315	326	0.4
72686	WITTS SPRINGS	129	671	606	589	-1.1	8	273	255	250	-0.7	2.38	196	176	-1.2
72687	YELLVILLE	089	7899	8322	8472	0.6	62	3116	3328	3400	0.7	2.47	2294	2362	0.3
72701	FAYETTEVILLE	143	33455	40338	44232	2.0	91	12895	15938	17656	2.3	2.23	7006	8343	1.9
72703	FAYETTEVILLE	143	24937	31063	34210	2.4	94	10733	13849	15383	2.8	2.16	5767	6936	2.0
72704	FAYETTEVILLE	143	14572	20596	23762	3.8	98	5824	8347	9665	4.0	2.47	3788	5204	3.5
72712	BENTONVILLE	007	24862	38327	45709	4.8	99	9307	14306	17042	4.8	2.65	6711	9951	4.4
72714	BELLA VISTA	007	6501	10085	12274	4.9	99	2941	4525	5499	4.8	2.22	2238	3340	4.4
72715	BELLA VISTA	007	9500	13178	15518	3.6	98	4680	6441	7570	3.5	2.03	3634	4846	3.2
72717	CANEHILL	143	1086	1254	1341	1.6	87	412	491	529	1.9	2.53	315	359	1.4
72718	CAVE SPRINGS	007	778	1034	1376	3.1	96	297	415	552	3.7	2.49	243	324	3.2
72719	CENTERTON	007	2525	8068	10683	13.4	100	865	2698	3570	13.1	2.99	690	2084	12.7
72721	COMBS	087	669	699	715	0.5	58	256	269	276	0.5	2.60	195	199	0.2
72722	DECATUR	007	2804	3639	4194	2.9	96	994	1283	1476	2.8	2.84	778	976	2.5
	ARKANSAS					0.9					1.1	2.46			0.7
	UNITED STATES					1.0					1.1	2.59			0.9

ZIP CODE #	POST OFFICE NAME	RACE (%) White 2000	White 2009	Black 2000	Black 2009	Asian/Pacific 2000	Asian/Pacific 2009	% Hispanic Origin 2000	% Hispanic Origin 2009	2009 AGE DISTRIBUTION (%) 0-4	5-9	10-14	15-19	20-24	25-44	45-64	65-84	85+	18+	MEDIAN AGE 2009	% 2009 Males	% 2009 Females
72530	DRASCO	98.5	98.3	0.0	0.0	0.1	0.0	0.6	1.0	5.4	5.7	6.1	5.6	3.8	23.1	32.3	16.4	1.8	79.3	45.3	50.0	50.0
72531	ELIZABETH	98.1	97.9	0.1	0.1	0.5	0.7	0.5	0.6	4.3	4.7	5.0	5.0	3.9	20.6	31.4	23.0	2.2	83.2	50.1	51.0	49.0
72532	EVENING SHADE	97.7	97.3	0.5	0.6	0.0	0.0	0.6	0.9	5.1	5.3	5.8	6.5	4.6	23.0	31.7	16.2	1.7	79.8	44.7	48.1	51.9
72533	FIFTY SIX	98.7	98.7	0.0	0.0	0.0	0.0	0.7	0.6	4.8	5.1	5.7	6.1	4.4	20.4	32.4	19.4	1.7	80.8	47.4	48.6	51.4
72534	FLORAL	98.6	98.2	0.1	0.1	0.1	0.2	0.9	1.5	6.1	6.5	6.4	6.1	5.4	24.5	29.9	13.7	1.5	77.2	41.5	49.5	50.5
72536	FRANKLIN	97.6	97.6	0.2	0.2	0.0	0.0	1.1	1.1	5.3	5.7	6.6	6.0	4.2	25.2	29.6	15.5	2.0	78.6	43.0	48.8	51.2
72537	GAMALIEL	98.6	98.4	0.0	0.0	0.1	0.2	0.5	0.6	4.1	4.1	4.3	5.3	3.5	17.2	33.9	26.0	1.5	84.1	53.7	51.3	48.7
72538	GEPP	98.8	99.0	0.0	0.0	0.0	0.0	0.3	0.3	6.2	6.2	6.5	6.0	4.7	24.4	28.5	15.8	1.8	77.2	42.0	47.9	52.1
72539	GLENCOE	97.7	97.6	0.3	0.3	0.1	0.1	0.6	0.6	5.1	5.5	5.9	6.3	4.6	20.9	30.8	18.7	2.2	79.6	46.2	49.7	50.3
72540	GUION	96.6	96.5	1.1	1.2	0.0	0.0	0.7	1.2	5.1	5.1	5.9	5.9	3.9	19.2	30.6	22.4	2.0	80.8	49.8	48.6	51.4
72542	HARDY	96.8	96.2	0.1	0.1	0.3	0.4	1.1	1.7	5.3	5.4	5.6	5.2	4.3	19.8	30.6	21.4	2.4	80.5	48.2	48.6	51.4
72543	HEBER SPRINGS	98.1	97.5	0.2	0.3	0.3	0.4	1.4	2.3	5.1	5.0	5.3	5.8	4.7	20.9	29.2	20.5	3.6	81.0	47.2	47.5	52.5
72544	HENDERSON	98.4	98.0	0.1	0.1	0.3	0.4	0.3	0.5	3.6	3.7	4.0	4.6	3.6	16.0	34.4	28.0	2.1	85.9	55.7	50.9	49.1
72546	IDA	98.4	98.6	0.0	0.0	0.0	0.0	1.6	1.4	5.8	5.8	5.8	5.8	2.9	23.2	33.3	14.5	2.9	76.8	45.4	49.3	50.7
72550	LOCUST GROVE	97.6	96.7	0.2	0.3	0.5	0.9	0.6	1.0	6.0	6.2	6.3	6.0	5.5	26.8	29.7	12.3	1.3	77.8	40.6	49.9	50.1
72553	MAGNESS	97.6	97.6	0.0	0.0	0.0	0.0	2.4	2.4	4.8	4.8	4.8	4.8	4.8	23.8	38.1	11.9	2.4	81.0	46.7	47.6	52.4
72554	MAMMOTH SPRING	96.9	96.8	0.4	0.4	0.1	0.1	0.4	0.5	5.3	5.5	5.8	6.2	4.8	21.0	30.7	18.5	2.2	79.7	46.0	48.7	51.3
72555	MARCELLA	96.8	96.2	0.2	0.2	0.0	0.0	1.1	1.6	5.4	5.7	6.2	6.0	4.7	22.1	29.9	18.1	1.8	78.9	44.9	49.7	50.3
72556	MELBOURNE	97.9	97.9	0.2	0.2	0.1	0.1	0.4	0.5	6.1	6.2	6.4	5.6	4.4	24.0	25.9	18.1	3.3	78.2	42.8	47.7	52.3
72560	MOUNTAIN VIEW	97.0	96.5	0.0	0.0	0.1	0.1	1.1	1.8	5.4	5.5	5.7	5.7	4.9	21.0	30.1	18.7	3.0	79.9	46.3	48.6	51.4
72561	MOUNT PLEASANT	98.5	98.5	0.3	0.3	0.2	0.2	0.9	0.9	6.7	6.8	6.8	5.8	4.8	24.1	28.2	15.4	1.5	76.2	41.4	51.3	48.7
72562	NEWARK	97.1	96.3	0.4	0.5	0.4	0.6	0.8	1.4	7.2	7.1	7.2	6.1	5.4	26.2	28.0	11.0	1.8	74.8	37.9	49.4	50.6
72564	OIL TROUGH	95.9	94.8	1.0	1.1	0.0	0.0	0.4	0.6	5.2	5.7	5.7	6.5	5.5	25.2	30.0	14.7	1.5	79.6	42.4	49.8	50.2
72565	OXFORD	97.1	97.1	0.1	0.1	0.1	0.1	1.0	1.0	5.9	6.3	6.2	5.5	4.7	22.6	31.3	15.6	1.9	78.1	43.8	50.1	49.9
72566	PINEVILLE	89.6	88.4	8.6	9.8	0.0	0.0	0.8	0.8	4.0	4.5	4.5	5.0	7.9	36.4	25.9	10.3	1.6	83.6	38.2	64.4	35.6
72567	PLEASANT GROVE	97.8	97.2	0.1	0.2	0.0	0.0	0.6	1.0	6.1	6.1	6.4	6.4	5.0	21.9	30.0	16.7	1.4	77.3	43.4	50.2	49.8
72568	PLEASANT PLAINS	97.1	95.7	0.1	0.1	0.2	0.3	1.9	3.2	6.3	6.4	6.5	6.8	5.8	25.6	28.2	13.0	1.5	76.8	40.1	51.3	48.7
72569	POUGHKEEPSIE	96.8	95.9	2.1	2.5	0.0	0.0	1.1	1.7	6.1	6.1	6.3	6.1	5.3	24.3	29.0	15.2	1.4	77.6	41.9	50.7	49.3
72571	ROSIE	98.0	97.5	0.2	0.2	0.0	0.0	0.8	1.4	7.7	7.9	7.7	6.2	5.6	23.8	28.6	11.4	1.0	72.7	37.8	51.3	48.7
72572	SAFFELL	99.5	99.6	0.0	0.0	0.0	0.0	0.0	0.4	7.1	7.1	7.5	6.6	4.0	23.5	27.9	14.2	2.2	73.5	40.7	50.9	49.1
72573	SAGE	98.8	98.8	0.0	0.0	0.0	0.0	0.8	0.4	6.2	6.6	6.6	5.8	4.7	24.9	26.1	16.0	3.1	77.4	41.3	49.0	51.0
72576	SALEM	97.8	98.0	0.2	0.2	0.2	0.2	0.6	0.6	6.2	6.3	6.3	5.7	5.0	22.3	27.4	17.2	3.7	77.5	43.5	48.2	51.8
72577	SIDNEY	97.5	97.2	0.2	0.3	0.0	0.0	0.2	0.5	7.0	7.0	7.0	6.2	3.4	25.1	25.3	13.1	5.9	74.9	41.0	48.9	51.1
72578	STURKIE	98.7	98.7	0.0	0.0	0.0	0.0	0.6	0.6	6.3	6.9	6.9	6.3	5.0	24.5	26.4	15.7	1.9	76.1	40.3	50.3	49.7
72579	SULPHUR ROCK	96.7	95.9	0.6	0.8	0.1	0.1	1.6	2.5	6.0	6.1	6.3	5.7	5.7	26.3	30.4	12.0	1.5	78.1	40.1	51.3	48.7
72581	TUMBLING SHOALS	98.8	98.7	0.0	0.0	0.0	0.0	0.4	0.7	4.4	4.7	5.1	4.9	3.2	21.0	34.5	20.4	1.8	82.7	49.1	49.0	51.0
72583	VIOLA	98.7	98.7	0.1	0.1	0.1	0.1	0.7	0.6	6.1	6.4	6.5	6.0	4.8	23.8	29.1	15.5	1.8	77.2	42.3	50.5	49.5
72584	VIOLET HILL	97.7	97.7	0.0	0.0	0.0	0.0	1.0	1.0	5.5	5.8	6.8	5.5	4.5	23.7	31.8	14.6	1.6	78.2	43.4	49.7	50.3
72585	WIDEMAN	97.2	97.2	0.7	0.7	0.0	0.0	0.7	0.7	5.6	5.6	6.3	4.9	4.9	23.1	32.9	14.7	2.1	79.0	44.7	52.4	47.6
72587	WISEMAN	100.0	100.0	0.0	0.0	0.0	0.0	0.0	0.0	10.5	10.5	10.5	5.3	0.0	31.6	31.6	0.0	0.0	63.2	31.3	52.6	47.4
72601	HARRISON	97.6	97.0	0.1	0.1	0.4	0.5	1.1	1.8	6.3	6.0	6.2	6.5	5.8	24.4	27.2	14.8	2.9	77.6	41.0	48.2	51.8
72611	ALPENA	97.6	96.8	0.1	0.1	0.4	0.7	1.4	2.4	6.3	6.4	6.9	6.7	5.4	24.9	29.1	13.1	1.3	76.4	40.6	50.2	49.8
72616	BERRYVILLE	94.0	91.5	0.0	0.0	0.4	0.6	10.5	16.5	7.4	7.3	7.2	6.3	5.5	24.9	26.3	13.0	2.2	74.3	38.3	49.5	50.5
72617	BIG FLAT	97.4	97.1	0.4	0.4	0.4	0.7	0.4	1.1	4.4	4.4	5.1	5.5	3.6	17.9	35.4	20.4	3.3	82.5	50.0	52.2	47.8
72619	BULL SHOALS	98.0	97.6	0.3	0.4	0.4	0.5	0.9	1.4	3.2	3.4	3.5	3.6	2.6	13.6	31.5	33.7	4.8	87.6	60.0	49.2	50.8
72623	CLARKRIDGE	98.2	97.8	0.0	0.0	0.4	0.7	0.9	1.5	3.7	3.9	4.6	6.1	5.1	22.6	35.5	17.0	1.6	84.0	47.3	51.6	48.4
72624	COMPTON	97.9	97.9	0.4	0.4	0.0	0.0	1.2	0.8	5.3	5.8	5.8	5.8	4.5	25.1	32.5	14.0	1.2	79.0	43.0	51.0	49.0
72626	COTTER	97.2	96.6	0.0	0.0	0.2	0.3	1.7	2.6	5.4	5.5	5.5	4.9	4.2	22.3	30.6	19.0	2.5	80.6	46.5	47.7	52.3
72628	DEER	97.1	97.0	0.1	0.1	0.1	0.1	1.0	1.0	4.6	5.2	6.5	6.7	4.2	22.1	34.4	14.3	2.0	79.1	45.4	51.9	48.1
72629	DENNARD	95.4	94.0	0.6	0.6	0.3	0.5	1.2	1.9	5.6	5.8	6.2	6.6	4.5	23.1	30.6	15.8	1.8	78.4	43.5	51.3	48.7
72631	EUREKA SPRINGS	96.7	95.7	0.2	0.2	0.4	0.6	1.7	3.0	2.9	3.3	3.8	4.0	3.5	15.2	38.4	26.3	2.5	87.4	55.6	49.5	50.5
72632	EUREKA SPRINGS	95.3	93.5	0.1	0.1	0.6	0.9	3.3	5.7	3.7	4.0	4.4	3.9	3.8	19.4	37.9	20.0	2.9	85.3	52.1	47.6	52.4
72633	EVERTON	98.5	98.1	0.1	0.1	0.3	0.4	0.7	1.1	5.6	7.3	6.9	7.4	4.7	25.3	30.0	11.3	1.5	75.5	39.4	48.2	51.8
72634	FLIPPIN	96.8	96.1	0.2	0.2	0.3	0.5	0.8	1.2	5.9	6.1	6.2	6.2	5.4	22.1	29.8	15.9	2.4	77.9	43.6	49.0	51.0
72635	GASSVILLE	97.9	97.4	0.1	0.1	0.2	0.3	1.2	1.9	5.9	5.9	6.2	6.9	4.6	23.3	27.6	16.8	2.9	77.5	43.1	47.2	52.8
72638	GREEN FOREST	90.2	87.1	0.2	0.2	0.5	0.6	17.6	24.8	8.1	7.7	7.3	6.8	6.6	27.1	24.6	10.6	1.3	73.0	34.8	50.5	49.5
72639	HARRIET	97.2	97.2	0.1	0.1	0.1	0.1	1.2	1.1	5.2	5.4	5.8	5.3	5.4	22.4	32.2	16.5	1.9	80.5	45.3	51.8	48.2
72640	HASTY	98.2	98.2	0.0	0.0	0.4	0.4	1.1	1.1	6.4	6.4	6.4	6.7	5.3	25.4	29.7	12.7	1.1	77.0	40.4	48.8	51.2
72641	JASPER	96.7	96.7	0.2	0.2	0.2	0.2	1.2	1.2	6.1	6.4	6.4	5.8	4.4	21.9	28.8	17.0	3.2	77.2	44.2	50.0	50.0
72642	LAKEVIEW	98.2	97.7	0.1	0.0	0.5	0.8	1.1	1.7	2.7	3.0	3.0	3.4	3.1	11.8	30.7	37.7	4.5	89.2	60.7	48.3	51.7
72644	LEAD HILL	96.7	96.0	0.0	0.0	0.5	0.8	1.0	1.5	5.1	5.4	5.6	5.7	4.2	20.2	29.8	21.6	2.4	80.2	47.8	50.5	49.5
72645	LESLIE	97.8	98.0	0.0	0.0	0.4	0.4	0.9	0.9	5.7	5.9	6.0	5.6	4.8	22.0	29.3	18.0	2.8	78.9	45.0	48.7	51.3
72648	MARBLE FALLS	97.8	97.8	0.2	0.2	0.2	0.2	1.1	1.1	5.7	6.1	6.1	6.1	4.7	24.9	31.0	13.9	1.4	78.3	42.0	50.2	49.8
72650	MARSHALL	97.8	97.8	0.1	0.1	0.0	0.0	0.8	0.8	5.7	5.6	5.6	5.5	5.3	22.4	28.1	18.2	3.6	79.6	44.9	47.4	52.6
72651	MIDWAY	97.6	97.0	0.0	0.0	0.3	0.3	1.3	1.9	4.2	4.3	4.4	4.4	3.6	16.5	30.7	28.6	3.2	84.3	54.6	49.4	50.6
72653	MOUNTAIN HOME	97.8	97.2	0.1	0.1	0.4	0.6	1.0	1.6	4.4	4.3	4.5	4.8	4.4	18.2	30.3	24.7	4.3	83.8	52.1	47.9	52.1
72655	MOUNT JUDEA	97.6	97.5	0.1	0.1	0.1	0.1	0.9	0.9	6.4	6.4	6.4	5.7	4.9	22.9	29.5	15.9	1.9	76.8	42.7	51.5	48.5
72658	NORFORK	97.5	96.9	0.4	0.5	0.1	0.3	0.6	1.0	4.8	5.1	5.8	6.0	4.5	19.4	33.7	18.7	2.2	80.6	47.9	50.3	49.7
72660	OAK GROVE	96.4	95.2	0.0	0.0	0.4	0.6	1.1	2.0	6.6	6.6	6.9	6.9	5.8	25.1	28.5	12.3	1.4	75.7	38.6	49.9	50.1
72661	OAKLAND	97.9	97.2	0.0	0.0	0.3	0.6	0.2	0.3	2.2	2.5	2.6	3.1	2.8	10.8	34.3	39.6	2.3	90.9	62.3	51.3	48.7
72662	OMAHA	97.1	96.5	0.1	0.1	0.2	0.2	0.8	1.3	6.5	6.8	6.9	5.9	4.5	23.6	29.2	15.3	1.3	76.1	41.9	51.8	48.2
72663	ONIA	97.7	97.0	0.0	0.0	0.0	0.2	1.3	2.2	6.6	6.6	6.6	6.0	4.2	21.2	29.4	17.6	1.8	76.6	44.0	50.6	49.4
72666	PARTHENON	97.0	96.9	0.2	0.2	0.2	0.2	1.2	1.3	4.9	5.4	6.5	6.9	4.3	21.7	33.2	15.3	1.8	78.9	45.2	51.8	48.2
72668	PEEL	97.8	97.4	0.0	0.0	0.0	0.0	0.5	0.8	4.0	3.2	5.2	5.3	3.0	18.4	39.9	19.0	2.0	84.3	51.6	51.9	48.1
72669	PINDALL	97.4	97.4	0.0	0.0	0.2	0.2	1.0	1.0	6.9	6.9	7.1	6.7	6.1	26.2	27.4	11.4	1.4	75.1	38.6	50.5	49.5
72670	PONCA	97.2	97.2	0.3	0.3	0.3	0.3	1.0	1.0	5.2	5.9	6.2	6.2	4.5	24.6	32.5	13.8	1.0	78.5	42.9	51.2	48.8
72675	SAINT JOE	96.0	96.1	0.0	0.0	0.1	0.2	1.3	1.4	6.2	6.4	6.6	6.2	5.1	22.8	30.3	14.6	1.9	77.0	42.5	51.4	48.6
72679	TILLY	98.5	97.2	0.0	0.0	0.0	0.0	1.5	1.4	4.2	8.3	8.3	6.9	4.2	26.4	29.2	11.1	1.4	73.6	40.0	51.4	48.6
72680	TIMBO	97.5	97.1	0.2	0.2	0.2	0.2	1.3	2.1	6.3	6.3	6.6	6.1	4.4	20.9	30.1	17.4	1.9	77.1	44.5	50.7	49.3
72682	VALLEY SPRINGS	98.4	97.4	0.0	0.0	0.0	0.4	0.8	2.2	5.3	6.1	6.1	6.6	5.3	21.1	33.3	14.9	1.3	78.1	44.6	49.1	50.9
72683	VENDOR	97.8	97.7	0.1	0.1	0.1	0.1	1.0	1.0	6.6	6.5	6.6	6.0	5.1	23.0	28.2	16.1	1.9	76.1	41.8	51.8	48.2
72685	WESTERN GROVE	98.1	98.1	0.1	0.1	0.4	0.4	1.2	1.2	6.3	6.3	6.6	6.8	5.4	25.4	29.3	12.9	1.2	76.6	40.3	49.2	50.8
72686	WITTS SPRINGS	96.3	96.4	0.0	0.0	0.3	0.3	2.1	2.0	4.8	5.3	5.6	5.3	4.1	21.5	33.5	17.5	2.5	81.0	47.4	50.0	50.0
72687	YELLVILLE	97.7	97.2	0.1	0.1	0.2	0.3	0.7	1.1	5.4	5.4	5.9	6.3	5.4	21.3	32.0	16.0	2.4	79.3	45.2	49.5	50.5
72701	FAYETTEVILLE	87.5	84.6	4.3	4.6	2.7	3.5	4.3	6.9	5.9	5.1	5.0	11.6	15.0	27.0	21.3	7.7	1.4	81.0	29.2	50.7	49.3
72703	FAYETTEVILLE	89.3	86.4	3.9	4.3	2.2	3.3	4.1	6.3	6.6	5.4	5.0	6.6	15.2	30.5	20.1	8.4	2.2	79.9	30.0	50.3	49.7
72704	FAYETTEVILLE	88.7	86.0	4.2	4.6	1.5	2.3	4.0	6.3	8.0	7.1	6.5	6.6	12.6	31.8	20.6	6.1	0.7	74.9	29.9	50.8	49.2
72712	BENTONVILLE	91.9	88.6	0.8	0.8	2.1	3.0	5.3	9.3	8.3	7.4	7.0	6.9	7.2	29.9	23.0	9.1	1.3	73.2	33.2	48.6	51.4
72714	BELLA VISTA	97.5	96.6	0.1	0.1	0.4	0.6	1.2	2.1	4.7	4.8	4.9	4.6	3.4	17.7	30.2	26.0	3.8	82.7	52.2	48.2	51.8
72715	BELLA VISTA	98.1	97.5	0.2	0.2	0.3	0.4	0.9	1.5	2.8	2.9	3.0	2.7	2.1	11.5	27.7	41.9	5.4	89.6	63.5	47.9	52.1
72717	CANEHILL	92.1	90.4	0.5	0.5	0.1	0.2	2.5	3.9	6.6	7.0	7.1	6.9	4.9	23.8	29.3	13.1	1.3	74.6	40.1	51.6	48.4
72718	CAVE SPRINGS	96.0	95.0	0.5	0.6	0.4	0.7	1.5	2.7	6.7	7.4	7.9	7.2	4.3	25.5	30.6	9.6	1.0	73.5	39.8	49.6	50.4
72719	CENTERTON	95.6	94.5	0.2	0.2	0.2	0.1	3.4	5.4	8.1	8.0	8.1	7.4	5.5	28.1	25.6	8.2	1.0	71.1	35.2	49.3	50.7
72721	COMBS	97.2	96.4	0.0	0.0	0.1	0.1	1.0	1.6	5.9	7.0	7.0	6.9	5.7	24.2	30.2	11.4	1.7	75.3	39.8	48.9	51.1
72722	DECATUR	88.9	84.5	0.0	0.0	0.4	0.6	7.6	13.1	7.9	7.3	7.9	7.3	6.6	26.8	25.6	9.5	1.0	72.4	34.7	52.0	48.0
	ARKANSAS	80.0	78.2	15.7	15.8	0.8	1.2	3.2	5.1	6.8	6.6	6.5	6.9	6.6	26.0	26.1	12.4	2.0	76.1	37.8	49.1	50.9
	UNITED STATES	75.1	72.0	12.3	12.7	3.8	4.6	12.5	15.7	6.8	6.7	6.6	7.1	6.9	27.0	26.0	10.9	1.9	75.7	36.9	49.2	50.8

#	POST OFFICE NAME	2009 Per Capita Income	2009 HH Income Base	2009 Household Income Distribution (%): Less than $25,000	$25,000 to $49,999	$50,000 to $99,999	$100,000 to $149,999	$150,000 or More	Median Household Income: 2009	2014	2009 National Centile	2009 State Centile	2009 Home Value Base	2009 Home Value Distribution (%): Less than $50,000	$50,000 to $89,999	$90,000 to $174,999	$175,000 to $399,999	$400,000 or More	2009 Median Home Value
72530	DRASCO	20118	866	28.9	35.0	29.3	5.1	1.7	40132	41438	33	75	733	24.4	15.1	41.9	16.2	2.3	105603
72531	ELIZABETH	19784	337	36.2	34.4	24.0	4.5	0.9	33905	37365	15	37	290	28.3	20.3	34.5	14.1	2.8	93077
72532	EVENING SHADE	18374	680	35.7	34.4	25.7	2.1	2.1	33187	34729	14	33	581	29.3	31.3	27.4	9.5	2.6	75000
72533	FIFTY SIX	19136	203	39.4	28.6	25.6	4.4	2.0	34298	36934	16	40	172	21.5	26.2	36.0	12.8	3.5	92667
72534	FLORAL	17778	503	31.4	34.4	28.6	4.2	1.4	38137	39670	27	64	429	28.0	34.3	29.4	7.9	0.5	72794
72536	FRANKLIN	17706	189	40.2	30.7	22.2	4.8	2.1	33484	35368	14	35	159	25.8	21.4	32.1	16.4	4.4	93750
72537	GAMALIEL	19608	442	27.8	38.9	29.4	3.8	0.0	36343	37722	22	53	355	16.9	19.7	29.9	32.4	1.1	127232
72538	GEPP	16208	160	34.4	40.6	21.9	1.9	1.3	33162	35401	14	32	129	24.8	32.6	22.5	17.8	2.3	77500
72539	GLENCOE	21978	282	25.9	38.7	28.4	3.5	3.5	38441	41721	28	67	249	19.7	30.9	24.9	17.7	6.8	89063
72540	GUION	16109	108	47.2	27.8	16.7	6.5	1.9	26176	27429	4	6	93	33.3	20.4	28.0	18.3	0.0	84167
72542	HARDY	17411	1490	41.9	32.7	20.7	2.8	1.9	28668	29250	6	11	1174	23.5	32.2	29.2	13.2	1.9	81410
72543	HEBER SPRINGS	23811	4985	30.4	30.3	29.2	5.9	4.2	41307	42501	37	79	3698	9.8	23.1	38.9	22.4	5.7	117188
72544	HENDERSON	19172	322	29.5	37.0	28.6	4.3	0.6	36386	38193	22	53	265	19.2	19.6	30.9	28.3	1.9	115132
72546	IDA	19894	30	33.3	33.3	30.0	3.3	0.0	37333	40727	25	60	25	28.0	16.0	40.0	16.0	0.0	103125
72550	LOCUST GROVE	22225	373	27.3	34.3	30.6	5.4	2.4	39921	40523	32	73	314	28.0	29.6	26.4	13.7	2.2	80769
72553	MAGNESS	16012	16	31.3	37.5	25.0	6.3	0.0	35000	37260	18	43	12	16.7	33.3	33.3	16.7	0.0	95000
72554	MAMMOTH SPRING	17787	1673	40.3	32.5	22.5	2.9	1.8	29945	30982	8	15	1373	31.8	30.7	25.8	10.0	1.7	72429
72555	MARCELLA	14340	250	52.0	28.8	16.4	2.4	0.4	24365	25682	3	3	203	25.6	26.1	32.0	9.9	6.4	84167
72556	MELBOURNE	17197	1066	42.6	30.6	22.3	3.8	0.8	28838	29645	6	12	748	25.0	30.7	29.9	13.2	1.1	80227
72560	MOUNTAIN VIEW	18413	3179	46.1	30.6	17.8	3.3	2.2	27710	29000	5	9	2347	19.0	25.5	38.6	14.5	2.4	96572
72561	MOUNT PLEASANT	16563	580	36.7	34.1	25.0	3.6	0.5	34516	35208	17	40	477	31.0	24.7	26.6	14.0	3.6	77759
72562	NEWARK	18619	971	33.3	31.9	29.2	4.5	1.0	37338	38956	25	60	731	30.5	28.5	28.7	10.9	1.4	75392
72564	OIL TROUGH	20380	234	25.6	37.6	34.2	1.7	0.9	38539	39131	28	67	187	32.6	38.5	24.1	4.8	0.0	67708
72565	OXFORD	15107	365	41.4	36.4	17.8	2.7	1.6	28656	29234	6	11	315	37.5	25.1	29.2	7.9	0.3	71667
72566	PINEVILLE	19033	159	47.2	25.2	22.6	3.1	1.9	27316	27995	5	9	131	26.7	21.4	31.3	18.3	2.3	93125
72567	PLEASANT GROVE	12966	371	53.9	28.3	15.4	2.2	0.3	23867	24333	3	3	316	31.3	23.4	32.0	4.4	8.9	76667
72568	PLEASANT PLAINS	18122	741	31.7	33.3	30.5	2.4	2.0	39258	40647	31	70	644	34.0	28.9	28.6	8.1	0.5	73519
72569	POUGHKEEPSIE	18045	254	29.1	35.8	29.1	4.7	1.2	36782	39153	23	56	220	30.5	25.9	27.7	11.4	4.5	78125
72571	ROSIE	20552	188	25.0	32.4	35.6	2.7	4.3	45551	45385	50	86	163	36.8	30.1	22.1	9.8	1.2	65667
72572	SAFFELL	17960	94	41.5	25.5	24.5	7.4	1.1	30738	32745	9	19	79	36.7	27.8	26.6	6.3	2.5	62500
72573	SAGE	16611	108	37.0	33.3	25.0	3.7	0.9	34072	32756	16	38	75	25.3	29.3	25.3	16.0	4.0	81250
72576	SALEM	18255	1395	42.4	30.3	21.6	3.5	2.2	29022	29854	7	12	1036	21.5	28.8	31.0	14.7	4.1	89538
72577	SIDNEY	14739	202	41.6	26.2	26.2	3.5	2.5	29383	29874	7	13	170	25.9	23.5	30.6	17.1	2.9	90833
72578	STURKIE	14497	63	39.7	38.1	19.0	3.2	0.0	29573	32344	7	13	52	21.2	32.7	25.0	17.3	3.8	83333
72579	SULPHUR ROCK	18799	438	28.5	32.4	32.4	5.5	1.1	40564	42319	35	77	358	30.4	26.3	29.9	12.0	1.4	79167
72581	TUMBLING SHOALS	21385	489	27.8	29.9	32.1	9.6	0.6	43024	43328	42	82	401	14.5	11.2	49.4	22.4	2.5	119243
72583	VIOLA	17600	488	36.1	38.1	20.3	4.1	1.4	32167	33935	12	25	405	21.7	28.9	29.6	16.3	3.5	88750
72584	VIOLET HILL	17609	134	41.0	32.1	21.6	3.7	1.5	31299	32337	10	22	116	31.9	21.6	29.3	13.8	3.4	84286
72585	WIDEMAN	14966	58	39.7	36.2	19.0	3.4	1.7	30000	29569	8	16	50	40.0	22.0	30.0	8.0	0.0	70000
72587	WISEMAN	11579	8	50.0	37.5	12.5	0.0	0.0	25000	25000	3	5	7	42.9	0.0	57.1	0.0	0.0	92500
72601	HARRISON	21274	12368	31.0	32.4	29.0	4.5	3.1	39283	41389	31	71	8795	9.5	23.2	44.3	20.0	3.0	114044
72611	ALPENA	18353	658	33.9	33.9	24.6	5.2	2.4	37273	40154	24	60	530	15.8	29.1	35.7	13.8	5.7	98438
72616	BERRYVILLE	18101	3883	33.3	32.7	27.8	3.8	2.4	35995	37728	21	50	2803	14.3	21.3	40.3	17.6	6.5	112684
72617	BIG FLAT	23331	128	23.4	35.9	34.4	4.7	1.6	41525	42662	38	79	109	16.5	18.3	42.2	21.1	1.8	112500
72619	BULL SHOALS	24140	1107	33.2	34.7	24.2	4.9	3.1	35649	35690	20	48	856	10.3	16.5	51.3	18.8	3.2	117169
72623	CLARKRIDGE	18688	365	28.2	39.7	26.0	4.7	1.4	37669	40000	26	62	325	8.9	19.7	43.7	21.2	6.5	117262
72624	COMPTON	19394	117	33.3	36.8	27.4	1.7	0.9	36775	40243	23	56	92	28.3	27.2	31.5	8.7	4.3	81667
72626	COTTER	21860	678	41.0	28.2	24.5	4.0	2.4	31158	33342	10	21	483	19.0	26.9	35.6	15.1	3.3	96500
72628	DEER	17166	601	43.9	31.6	19.6	3.0	1.8	28320	29116	6	10	516	30.4	24.0	34.1	8.7	2.7	81786
72629	DENNARD	19189	516	39.7	30.6	23.4	3.3	2.9	30915	31975	10	20	426	35.7	31.5	25.8	6.1	0.9	66000
72631	EUREKA SPRINGS	28829	1794	30.7	31.0	26.5	5.9	5.9	38863	41002	29	68	1500	9.1	10.1	34.0	37.5	9.3	165993
72632	EUREKA SPRINGS	23844	2178	37.1	30.4	22.8	5.1	4.5	34662	36131	17	41	1502	6.4	13.8	35.8	34.2	9.8	161111
72633	EVERTON	17867	531	30.1	31.8	31.1	5.1	1.9	39334	41044	31	71	429	17.2	31.2	38.0	12.1	1.4	92241
72634	FLIPPIN	17358	1882	38.4	32.3	25.4	3.2	0.8	32813	33211	13	30	1430	13.8	27.6	37.9	18.0	2.7	102875
72635	GASSVILLE	18572	1412	35.0	31.6	27.8	3.8	1.8	35640	38612	20	48	1091	13.2	31.2	39.0	13.7	3.0	96833
72638	GREEN FOREST	16643	2954	33.6	35.8	24.2	4.1	2.2	35843	37436	20	49	2086	19.7	29.8	33.1	11.3	6.1	90781
72639	HARRIET	14136	430	50.5	31.9	15.1	2.1	0.5	24774	25000	3	4	365	42.7	26.6	24.4	6.0	0.3	58548
72640	HASTY	17711	116	33.6	38.8	22.4	3.4	1.7	35433	35553	19	46	95	24.2	28.4	30.5	15.8	1.1	83750
72641	JASPER	17882	841	44.5	27.9	22.9	2.3	2.4	28592	29272	6	11	622	29.7	25.4	31.4	11.6	1.9	81579
72642	LAKEVIEW	25435	1058	25.3	38.1	28.1	6.6	1.9	40356	42227	34	76	916	9.4	18.8	44.3	25.0	2.5	122667
72644	LEAD HILL	18861	1076	35.1	37.2	21.6	4.2	2.0	34561	36857	17	41	879	19.6	32.1	34.0	12.5	1.8	88210
72645	LESLIE	15449	921	50.8	30.6	15.7	2.0	0.9	24523	24765	3	4	703	32.6	31.2	27.5	7.0	1.8	68534
72648	MARBLE FALLS	16813	369	33.3	37.1	26.6	2.4	0.5	36538	38319	22	54	292	27.7	26.7	31.8	10.3	3.4	82353
72650	MARSHALL	16957	1239	47.5	28.8	19.8	2.7	1.1	27244	27985	5	8	908	32.2	34.1	24.3	7.8	1.5	67849
72651	MIDWAY	22565	552	29.5	38.0	23.7	6.3	2.4	37612	40490	26	62	475	15.2	21.1	38.5	21.3	4.0	114674
72653	MOUNTAIN HOME	23445	12991	28.3	35.0	27.6	6.0	3.2	39222	41527	30	70	10166	10.0	16.7	47.7	22.7	2.8	122631
72655	MOUNT JUDEA	17122	378	41.8	36.8	17.5	2.6	1.3	28812	29052	6	11	326	37.1	24.2	28.2	8.9	1.5	69000
72658	NORFORK	19301	804	31.7	35.4	27.7	2.7	2.4	36694	38499	23	55	685	25.7	17.8	38.4	17.4	0.7	101741
72660	OAK GROVE	17491	245	33.9	36.3	22.0	5.7	2.0	32178	33113	12	26	197	20.8	22.8	32.0	17.3	7.1	106641
72661	OAKLAND	24945	317	35.0	33.1	19.6	8.2	4.1	34173	34095	16	39	284	9.9	29.2	30.6	26.4	3.9	105682
72662	OMAHA	19916	1175	34.7	31.9	26.3	3.1	3.9	35456	38013	19	47	927	20.8	19.4	38.4	16.0	5.4	107585
72663	ONIA	18984	210	40.5	32.9	19.5	4.3	2.9	30000	30509	8	16	178	27.5	30.9	31.5	9.6	0.6	79333
72666	PARTHENON	18521	249	42.6	30.5	21.7	2.8	2.4	28873	29450	7	12	213	26.3	21.6	38.0	12.2	1.9	94091
72668	PEEL	22138	302	36.1	32.1	24.8	4.0	3.0	35000	35248	18	43	271	19.9	18.1	43.9	15.1	3.0	104063
72669	PINDALL	15327	195	42.6	34.9	17.4	3.1	2.1	30221	31658	8	17	159	38.4	28.3	21.4	10.1	1.9	67500
72670	PONCA	16791	120	34.2	35.8	27.5	1.7	0.8	36551	40000	22	54	95	27.4	26.3	33.7	8.4	4.2	84167
72675	SAINT JOE	15139	805	44.0	33.3	20.1	1.5	1.1	29613	30530	7	13	651	25.3	30.6	30.9	10.6	2.6	81444
72679	TILLY	23304	34	32.4	35.3	20.6	5.9	5.9	35000	40735	18	43	28	32.1	35.7	25.0	7.1	0.0	70000
72680	TIMBO	18571	519	40.8	33.9	18.5	3.5	3.3	30055	31124	8	16	440	30.2	31.6	29.3	8.2	0.7	75676
72682	VALLEY SPRINGS	14689	87	36.8	35.6	26.4	0.0	1.1	33254	34046	14	34	73	17.8	30.1	34.2	13.7	4.1	93000
72683	VENDOR	15252	316	41.8	37.3	17.4	2.5	0.9	28402	28592	6	10	271	37.3	22.1	28.8	11.1	0.7	69667
72685	WESTERN GROVE	17945	441	33.8	39.0	22.4	3.2	1.6	35283	36168	19	46	362	25.1	28.5	29.3	15.7	1.4	81333
72686	WITTS SPRINGS	15241	255	47.5	31.4	17.6	2.4	1.2	26527	26650	4	6	210	24.8	35.2	28.6	6.2	5.2	75000
72687	YELLVILLE	16765	3328	36.8	34.6	24.2	2.9	1.5	33382	33651	14	35	2675	19.7	26.8	38.5	12.9	2.2	96097
72701	FAYETTEVILLE	23995	15938	32.2	26.0	27.8	8.3	5.7	41890	45233	39	80	8160	8.4	15.3	38.0	29.8	8.5	138244
72703	FAYETTEVILLE	26397	13849	27.4	29.1	30.4	7.6	5.6	44375	46458	46	85	6141	6.5	9.2	41.9	32.9	9.4	158537
72704	FAYETTEVILLE	23134	8347	22.9	29.8	37.1	6.9	3.3	47871	49988	56	90	5061	12.3	8.5	55.2	19.7	4.2	125328
72712	BENTONVILLE	27645	14306	15.2	27.0	40.8	9.2	7.9	55855	58529	72	96	9469	4.8	11.0	48.4	27.8	8.1	140903
72714	BELLA VISTA	31917	4525	10.3	25.9	48.5	9.1	6.2	58997	61052	76	97	3919	3.8	10.6	48.0	33.7	3.8	151652
72715	BELLA VISTA	36894	6441	10.1	22.2	49.2	11.6	6.9	62609	64177	81	98	5644	2.3	7.0	38.7	44.3	7.7	180009
72717	CANEHILL	18559	491	31.2	34.4	27.5	4.1	2.9	37404	40290	25	61	397	20.2	25.2	34.0	17.4	3.3	99737
72718	CAVE SPRINGS	33359	415	14.9	23.9	37.1	15.2	8.9	65270	66048	84	99	350	2.3	6.0	32.0	41.4	18.3	201754
72719	CENTERTON	19232	2698	19.0	28.9	44.2	5.5	2.4	51327	53609	64	93	2184	4.4	9.4	54.2	23.4	8.6	136340
72721	COMBS	14715	269	35.3	40.1	21.9	2.2	0.4	33250	36217	14	33	229	24.0	32.3	28.8	13.1	1.7	79138
72722	DECATUR	18041	1283	24.2	34.5	32.9	5.5	2.9	42336	43285	40	81	908	21.7	18.9	33.9	19.7	5.7	109655
	ARKANSAS	21917		28.7	29.0	32.0	6.7	3.7	42685	44760				21.5	25.6	34.9	15.2	2.9	95077
	UNITED STATES	27277		20.9	24.4	35.3	11.7	7.6	54719	56938				9.3	13.1	31.6	32.6	13.5	162279

ZIP CODE		FINANCIAL SERVICES				THE HOME						ENTERTAINMENT						PERSONAL			
						Home Improvements		Furnishings													
#	POST OFFICE NAME	Auto Loan	Home Loan	Investments	Retirement Plans	Home Repair	Lawn & Garden	Computers & Hardware Personal	Major Appliances	TV, Radio, Sound Equipment	Furniture	Dine out/ Carry out	Sports Equipment	Fees & Tickets	Toys & Games	Travel	Cable TV	Apparel & Services	Auto Repairs	Health Insurance	Pets & Supplies
72530	DRASCO	82	62	86	60	65	83	63	78	68	60	67	58	52	67	63	74	45	72	81	92
72531	ELIZABETH	70	57	77	54	61	74	56	69	61	56	60	49	50	59	58	66	40	65	74	81
72532	EVENING SHADE	78	56	79	54	58	79	58	73	64	54	63	55	46	64	57	70	41	67	76	87
72533	FIFTY SIX	80	57	82	55	59	81	59	75	65	55	64	56	47	65	58	72	42	69	78	89
72534	FLORAL	82	59	78	57	60	81	61	75	67	58	66	57	49	68	58	74	44	69	78	90
72536	FRANKLIN	75	54	77	52	56	76	55	70	62	51	60	53	44	61	55	68	40	65	73	83
72537	GAMALIEL	64	61	78	57	68	73	58	69	62	63	60	45	58	57	64	65	40	66	77	79
72538	GEPP	69	50	72	49	52	71	51	65	57	48	56	49	42	56	51	62	37	60	68	77
72539	GLENCOE	99	71	101	68	73	100	73	92	81	68	79	69	58	80	72	89	52	85	96	110
72540	GUION	68	49	70	47	50	69	50	64	55	46	54	48	40	55	49	61	36	58	66	75
72542	HARDY	66	54	74	51	59	71	54	66	59	54	57	47	48	56	56	64	38	62	72	77
72543	HEBER SPRINGS	89	71	92	69	74	93	72	86	79	70	77	63	64	77	72	85	52	81	93	101
72544	HENDERSON	66	63	80	58	70	75	60	71	63	65	62	46	59	58	65	67	41	68	79	81
72546	IDA	81	59	87	57	62	83	60	77	66	56	65	57	49	65	61	72	43	70	79	91
72550	LOCUST GROVE	96	70	80	69	70	92	73	85	81	71	79	65	59	84	67	88	53	80	89	103
72553	MAGNESS	76	54	63	53	54	72	57	66	63	55	62	51	45	65	51	69	41	62	70	80
72554	MAMMOTH SPRING	74	54	76	52	56	76	55	70	62	51	60	52	45	61	55	68	40	65	74	83
72555	MARCELLA	64	44	64	42	44	64	46	58	52	43	51	44	35	52	44	57	34	54	61	70
72556	MELBOURNE	65	47	65	45	48	67	50	62	56	45	54	47	40	55	49	62	36	58	67	73
72560	MOUNTAIN VIEW	74	53	76	52	55	76	56	70	62	51	61	53	45	61	55	68	40	65	74	83
72561	MOUNT PLEASANT	72	52	74	50	54	73	53	68	59	49	58	51	43	59	53	65	38	62	71	80
72562	NEWARK	82	59	71	57	59	79	61	73	68	59	67	55	49	70	57	74	45	68	76	88
72564	OIL TROUGH	82	59	80	57	60	82	60	75	67	57	66	57	48	67	59	73	44	69	78	90
72565	OXFORD	65	47	67	45	49	66	48	61	53	45	52	46	39	53	48	59	35	56	64	73
72566	PINEVILLE	69	50	71	48	52	71	51	65	57	48	56	49	41	57	51	63	37	60	68	77
72567	PLEASANT GROVE	60	39	58	37	39	59	42	52	48	40	47	41	31	49	39	54	31	49	55	64
72568	PLEASANT PLAINS	83	60	69	58	59	79	62	72	69	60	67	55	50	72	56	75	45	68	76	88
72569	POUGHKEEPSIE	81	58	71	57	59	79	61	72	67	58	66	55	49	69	56	73	44	68	76	87
72571	ROSIE	102	73	84	71	73	97	76	89	85	74	83	68	61	88	69	92	56	84	94	108
72572	SAFFELL	77	55	79	53	57	78	57	72	63	53	62	54	45	62	56	69	41	66	75	86
72573	SAGE	67	48	68	47	50	69	51	64	57	47	56	48	41	56	50	63	37	59	69	76
72576	SALEM	74	53	75	51	55	76	56	70	62	51	61	52	45	61	55	69	40	65	75	83
72577	SIDNEY	75	51	82	51	54	79	57	71	59	46	59	59	42	58	57	65	38	66	75	87
72578	STURKIE	65	47	67	45	49	66	48	61	53	45	52	46	38	53	48	59	35	56	64	73
72579	SULPHUR ROCK	86	62	71	60	61	82	64	75	71	63	70	57	52	74	58	78	47	71	79	91
72581	TUMBLING SHOALS	82	65	102	63	70	86	65	82	69	61	68	60	55	66	69	73	45	76	82	96
72583	VIOLA	77	55	79	53	57	78	56	72	63	52	61	54	45	62	56	69	41	66	75	85
72584	VIOLET HILL	72	52	74	50	54	73	53	68	59	49	58	51	42	59	53	65	38	62	70	80
72585	WIDEMAN	65	47	67	45	49	66	48	61	53	45	52	46	38	53	48	59	35	56	64	73
72587	WISEMAN	49	35	50	34	37	50	36	46	40	34	39	34	29	40	36	44	26	42	48	55
72601	HARRISON	80	66	74	66	66	80	70	76	74	66	73	58	62	74	67	79	50	75	82	91
72611	ALPENA	84	60	78	58	61	83	62	76	69	59	68	58	50	70	59	76	45	71	79	91
72616	BERRYVILLE	82	61	74	60	62	81	64	75	70	61	69	57	53	71	60	76	46	71	80	90
72617	BIG FLAT	73	70	89	64	78	84	66	79	70	72	69	51	66	64	73	74	46	75	87	90
72619	BULL SHOALS	70	67	85	61	74	80	63	75	67	69	65	49	63	61	69	71	44	72	83	86
72623	CLARKRIDGE	81	58	84	56	60	83	60	76	66	56	65	57	48	66	59	73	43	70	79	90
72624	COMPTON	72	52	74	50	53	73	53	67	59	49	58	50	42	58	52	65	38	62	70	80
72626	COTTER	70	55	74	53	58	75	58	70	63	54	61	51	49	61	58	69	41	66	77	82
72628	DEER	71	51	73	49	53	72	52	67	58	49	57	50	42	58	52	64	38	61	69	79
72629	DENNARD	82	59	84	57	61	83	60	77	67	56	66	58	48	67	60	74	44	71	80	91
72631	EUREKA SPRINGS	95	83	119	79	92	104	81	99	86	82	84	69	76	80	88	91	56	94	105	114
72632	EUREKA SPRINGS	80	67	93	66	72	84	69	81	71	65	70	59	61	69	71	75	47	77	83	94
72633	EVERTON	82	59	84	57	61	83	60	77	67	56	66	58	48	66	60	74	43	70	80	91
72634	FLIPPIN	70	53	67	52	55	72	56	67	61	51	59	50	46	61	54	67	40	62	72	79
72635	GASSVILLE	72	60	73	59	63	77	61	72	65	57	64	53	54	64	61	70	43	68	78	84
72638	GREEN FOREST	83	59	70	58	59	79	62	72	69	60	67	56	50	71	57	75	45	68	76	88
72639	HARRIET	59	42	52	41	43	57	44	52	49	42	48	40	35	50	41	53	32	49	55	63
72640	HASTY	77	55	79	54	57	78	57	72	63	53	62	54	45	63	56	69	41	66	75	86
72641	JASPER	70	51	71	49	52	72	54	67	60	49	58	50	43	59	52	66	38	62	71	79
72642	LAKEVIEW	73	70	89	64	78	84	67	79	70	72	69	51	66	64	73	74	46	75	87	90
72644	LEAD HILL	72	57	78	54	61	76	57	71	62	57	61	51	50	60	58	68	41	66	75	83
72645	LESLIE	57	41	57	40	42	58	43	54	48	39	47	40	35	48	42	53	31	50	58	64
72648	MARBLE FALLS	73	52	75	51	54	74	54	68	60	50	59	51	43	59	53	66	39	63	71	81
72650	MARSHALL	66	47	66	46	49	68	50	63	56	46	54	47	40	56	49	62	36	58	67	74
72651	MIDWAY	78	70	91	65	76	87	67	81	72	71	71	55	64	67	72	77	47	77	89	94
72653	MOUNTAIN HOME	78	68	88	65	74	85	68	80	73	70	71	55	64	69	71	78	48	77	88	93
72655	MOUNT JUDEA	71	51	72	49	52	72	52	66	58	48	57	50	41	57	51	63	37	61	69	78
72658	NORFORK	75	59	81	56	63	79	59	73	64	58	63	52	51	62	61	70	42	68	78	86
72660	OAK GROVE	83	59	68	58	59	78	62	72	68	60	67	55	49	71	56	75	45	68	76	87
72661	OAKLAND	75	72	92	66	80	86	68	81	72	74	70	53	67	66	75	76	47	77	90	92
72662	OMAHA	86	61	88	59	64	87	63	80	70	59	69	60	50	69	62	77	45	73	83	95
72663	ONIA	81	58	83	56	60	82	59	76	66	55	65	57	47	65	59	72	43	69	79	90
72666	PARTHENON	74	53	76	51	55	75	54	69	60	50	59	52	43	60	54	66	39	63	72	82
72668	PEEL	71	67	86	62	75	81	64	76	68	69	66	50	63	62	70	72	44	73	84	87
72669	PINDALL	70	50	58	49	50	67	52	61	58	51	57	47	42	60	48	63	38	58	64	74
72670	PONCA	72	52	74	50	54	73	53	68	59	49	58	51	42	59	53	65	38	62	70	80
72675	SAINT JOE	65	47	64	45	48	65	48	60	53	45	52	45	38	53	47	58	35	55	63	72
72679	TILLY	88	63	90	61	66	89	65	82	72	60	71	62	52	71	64	79	47	76	86	98
72680	TIMBO	78	56	80	54	58	79	57	73	63	53	62	55	46	63	57	70	41	67	76	87
72682	VALLEY SPRINGS	69	49	70	48	51	70	50	64	56	47	55	48	40	56	50	62	36	59	67	76
72683	VENDOR	67	48	69	47	50	68	49	63	55	46	54	47	39	54	49	60	36	58	65	75
72685	WESTERN GROVE	77	55	79	54	58	79	57	72	63	53	62	54	46	63	56	69	41	66	75	86
72686	WITTS SPRINGS	65	46	66	45	48	66	48	61	53	44	52	45	38	52	47	58	34	55	63	72
72687	YELLVILLE	72	54	73	52	56	74	55	68	61	52	59	50	45	60	54	66	39	63	72	81
72701	FAYETTEVILLE	85	71	68	74	70	74	90	77	87	81	87	63	79	87	77	86	61	83	80	94
72703	FAYETTEVILLE	88	68	63	72	65	68	93	75	88	85	89	63	79	90	76	86	62	84	76	92
72704	FAYETTEVILLE	88	75	66	75	72	74	87	78	84	84	85	62	77	87	75	83	59	82	77	94
72712	BENTONVILLE	112	105	94	105	101	100	108	104	106	109	107	82	103	110	101	104	74	105	101	123
72714	BELLA VISTA	109	98	139	92	109	122	94	116	100	97	97	78	90	92	104	106	65	109	124	132
72715	BELLA VISTA	103	108	144	104	125	129	98	117	104	110	102	72	107	93	114	110	69	111	133	131
72717	CANEHILL	84	60	83	59	62	84	62	78	69	59	68	59	50	69	61	76	45	72	81	93
72718	CAVE SPRINGS	116	130	112	134	126	128	116	121	115	117	115	95	124	118	123	115	81	117	120	143
72719	CENTERTON	92	85	75	82	83	87	80	85	83	83	83	62	76	86	76	85	57	82	85	101
72721	COMBS	69	49	65	48	50	68	51	62	56	48	55	47	41	57	49	62	37	58	65	75
72722	DECATUR	91	67	78	65	67	88	69	81	76	66	74	63	56	78	64	82	50	76	85	98
	ARKANSAS	88	73	79	72	73	85	76	82	80	74	79	62	68	81	72	84	54	80	86	98
	UNITED STATES	100	100	100	100	100	100	100	100	100	100	100	100	100	100	100	100	100	100	100	100

72727-72958

ZIP CODE #	POST OFFICE NAME	COUNTY FIPS CODE	POPULATION 2000	POPULATION 2009	POPULATION 2014	2000-2009 ANNUAL RATE % Rate	2000-2009 ANNUAL RATE State Centile	HOUSEHOLDS 2000	HOUSEHOLDS 2009	HOUSEHOLDS 2014	HOUSEHOLDS % Annual Rate 2000-2009	HOUSEHOLDS 2009 Average HH Size	FAMILIES 2000	FAMILIES 2009	FAMILIES % Annual Rate 2000-2009
72727	ELKINS	143	3157	4158	4577	3.0	96	1164	1569	1738	3.3	2.65	904	1174	2.9
72729	EVANSVILLE	143	270	313	335	1.6	87	105	126	136	2.0	2.45	81	93	1.5
72730	FARMINGTON	143	5939	6442	6906	0.9	72	2170	2412	2590	1.1	2.67	1605	1708	0.7
72732	GARFIELD	007	4358	5076	5535	1.7	89	1672	1954	2135	1.7	2.60	1278	1444	1.3
72734	GENTRY	007	6790	8333	9404	2.2	93	2515	3070	3464	2.2	2.71	1924	2271	1.8
72736	GRAVETTE	007	5138	6496	7353	2.6	95	1893	2377	2689	2.5	2.71	1422	1705	2.0
72738	HINDSVILLE	087	1520	1616	1673	0.7	66	572	616	639	0.8	2.62	447	467	0.5
72739	HIWASSE	007	482	529	668	1.0	75	176	197	250	1.2	2.69	142	153	0.8
72740	HUNTSVILLE	087	9184	10351	10911	1.3	82	3500	3988	4219	1.4	2.57	2585	2848	1.1
72742	KINGSTON	087	461	477	486	0.4	54	194	203	207	0.5	2.35	146	149	0.2
72744	LINCOLN	143	4353	5092	5478	1.7	89	1701	2043	2209	2.0	2.49	1255	1441	1.5
72745	LOWELL	007	9240	11780	13886	2.7	95	3462	4345	5097	2.5	2.70	2667	3223	2.1
72747	MAYSVILLE	007	169	202	223	1.9	91	59	70	77	1.9	2.89	46	53	1.5
72749	MORROW	143	33	38	41	1.5	85	7	8	9	1.5	4.75	5	6	2.0
72751	PEA RIDGE	007	3964	5301	6214	3.2	97	1439	1898	2219	3.0	2.79	1147	1471	2.7
72752	PETTIGREW	087	463	474	482	0.3	49	194	201	205	0.4	2.36	132	132	0.0
72753	PRAIRIE GROVE	143	6252	7119	7590	1.4	84	2315	2714	2913	1.7	2.60	1783	2003	1.3
72756	ROGERS	007	35962	42282	46932	1.8	90	13489	15580	17211	1.6	2.69	9810	10902	1.1
72758	ROGERS	007	18578	31282	37804	5.8	100	6696	10950	13165	5.5	2.83	5078	8120	5.2
72760	SAINT PAUL	087	597	614	625	0.3	49	247	257	262	0.4	2.39	173	174	0.1
72761	SILOAM SPRINGS	007	15884	20212	22938	2.6	95	5680	7203	8191	2.6	2.68	4115	5037	2.2
72762	SPRINGDALE	143	26418	33649	37567	2.7	95	9382	12191	13693	2.9	2.73	7134	8897	2.4
72764	SPRINGDALE	143	32200	49005	56941	4.6	99	11464	17267	20022	4.5	2.81	8276	11982	4.1
72768	SULPHUR SPRINGS	007	1519	1770	2004	1.7	89	521	603	683	1.6	2.89	385	431	1.2
72769	SUMMERS	143	915	1057	1126	1.6	87	325	385	413	1.8	2.75	262	301	1.5
72773	WESLEY	087	1662	1751	1796	0.6	62	626	664	683	0.6	2.64	495	513	0.4
72774	WEST FORK	143	5301	5965	6357	1.3	82	1969	2282	2445	1.6	2.61	1540	1718	1.2
72776	WITTER	087	226	234	239	0.4	54	81	85	87	0.5	2.75	59	60	0.2
72801	RUSSELLVILLE	115	16755	18130	18333	0.9	72	6585	6852	6966	0.4	2.28	4122	4061	-0.2
72802	RUSSELLVILLE	115	17669	19980	21018	1.3	82	6553	7527	7968	1.5	2.64	5010	5566	1.1
72820	ALIX	047	91	100	104	1.0	75	36	40	42	1.1	2.50	25	27	0.8
72821	ALTUS	047	1634	1803	1860	1.1	78	645	721	749	1.2	2.50	462	497	0.8
72823	ATKINS	115	6075	6278	6372	0.4	54	2303	2406	2456	0.5	2.55	1748	1768	0.1
72824	BELLEVILLE	149	807	725	698	-1.2	6	315	284	274	-1.1	2.55	243	213	-1.4
72826	BLUE MOUNTAIN	083	59	59	58	0.0	40	21	21	21	0.0	2.81	16	15	-0.7
72827	BLUFFTON	149	163	162	161	-0.1	35	70	70	69	0.0	2.31	52	50	-0.4
72828	BRIGGSVILLE	149	148	147	146	-0.1	35	59	59	58	0.0	2.49	44	42	-0.5
72830	CLARKSVILLE	071	14108	15260	15789	0.9	72	5424	5845	6045	0.8	2.51	3774	3910	0.4
72832	COAL HILL	071	1387	1515	1582	1.0	75	548	594	618	0.9	2.55	395	413	0.5
72833	DANVILLE	149	3974	4016	4005	0.1	43	1313	1292	1281	-0.2	2.94	960	916	-0.5
72834	DARDANELLE	149	10624	11760	12215	1.1	78	4041	4469	4632	1.1	2.60	3004	3204	0.7
72835	DELAWARE	083	832	861	870	0.4	54	341	361	366	0.6	2.38	240	243	0.1
72837	DOVER	115	7265	8132	8547	1.2	80	2730	3111	3288	1.4	2.61	2133	2357	1.1
72838	GRAVELLY	149	166	164	163	-0.1	35	68	67	67	-0.2	2.45	51	49	-0.4
72839	HAGARVILLE	071	396	448	473	1.3	82	159	181	191	1.4	2.48	121	134	1.1
72840	HARTMAN	071	1084	1027	1010	-0.6	18	419	399	392	-0.5	2.57	313	289	-0.9
72841	HARVEY	127	261	250	246	-0.5	22	100	97	96	-0.3	2.58	78	74	-0.6
72842	HAVANA	149	1375	1346	1332	-0.2	31	541	526	521	-0.3	2.51	394	370	-0.7
72843	HECTOR	115	2655	2894	3017	0.9	72	1000	1115	1171	1.2	2.60	777	840	0.8
72845	KNOXVILLE	071	1046	1202	1275	1.5	85	392	449	477	1.5	2.68	307	343	1.2
72846	LAMAR	071	4182	5059	5457	2.1	92	1559	1900	2052	2.2	2.66	1149	1354	1.8
72847	LONDON	115	1807	1954	2033	0.8	68	686	758	794	1.1	2.58	523	559	0.7
72851	NEW BLAINE	083	871	929	946	0.7	66	351	382	390	0.9	2.43	263	275	0.5
72852	OARK	071	247	276	291	1.2	80	103	116	122	1.3	2.38	75	82	1.0
72853	OLA	149	2105	1992	1948	-0.6	18	797	738	717	-0.8	2.62	556	497	-1.2
72854	OZONE	071	351	380	396	0.9	72	136	148	155	0.9	2.57	102	108	0.6
72855	PARIS	083	6888	6807	6736	-0.1	35	2785	2802	2787	0.1	2.36	1912	1849	-0.4
72856	PELSOR	115	63	71	75	1.3	82	26	30	32	1.6	2.37	21	23	1.0
72857	PLAINVIEW	149	1405	1398	1397	-0.1	35	581	578	576	-0.1	2.41	412	396	-0.4
72858	POTTSVILLE	115	2335	2442	2494	0.5	58	880	939	965	0.7	2.60	703	729	0.4
72860	ROVER	149	389	386	384	-0.1	35	144	143	142	-0.1	2.70	107	103	-0.4
72863	SCRANTON	083	1429	1588	1630	1.1	78	539	608	628	1.3	2.61	422	461	1.0
72865	SUBIACO	083	1105	1188	1208	0.8	68	390	428	438	1.0	2.74	303	322	0.7
72901	FORT SMITH	131	22018	22107	22304	0.0	40	9061	9040	9128	0.0	2.34	5153	4826	-0.7
72903	FORT SMITH	131	25124	26462	27286	0.6	62	10584	11139	11497	0.6	2.30	6682	6683	0.0
72904	FORT SMITH	131	19649	20490	21000	0.5	58	7305	7507	7678	0.3	2.71	4931	4828	-0.2
72905	FORT SMITH	131	47	70	76	4.4	98	7	14	15	7.8	4.93	6	10	5.7
72908	FORT SMITH	131	11788	12964	13609	1.0	75	4685	5189	5462	1.1	2.49	3412	3605	0.6
72916	FORT SMITH	131	5307	6579	7101	2.3	93	2138	2653	2873	2.4	2.47	1565	1850	1.8
72921	ALMA	033	11389	13198	14178	1.6	87	4182	4925	5317	1.8	2.68	3294	3770	1.5
72923	BARLING	131	4149	4528	4804	0.9	72	1599	1762	1878	1.1	2.53	1117	1179	0.6
72926	BOLES	127	783	751	739	-0.5	22	317	307	303	-0.3	2.45	252	240	-0.5
72927	BOONEVILLE	083	8456	8472	8453	0.0	40	3172	3215	3218	0.1	2.55	2333	2289	-0.2
72928	BRANCH	047	807	855	869	0.6	62	317	342	349	0.8	2.50	247	260	0.6
72930	CECIL	047	260	254	250	-0.3	27	101	101	100	0.0	2.50	77	75	-0.3
72932	CEDARVILLE	033	1273	1475	1586	1.6	87	450	533	578	1.8	2.77	363	419	1.6
72933	CHARLESTON	047	5073	5317	5401	0.5	58	1971	2106	2148	0.7	2.48	1424	1466	0.3
72934	CHESTER	033	867	926	964	0.7	66	319	348	365	0.9	2.66	243	258	0.6
72936	GREENWOOD	131	12247	14392	15453	1.8	90	4380	5169	5554	1.8	2.75	3533	4046	1.5
72937	HACKETT	131	3410	3947	4222	1.6	87	1319	1532	1639	1.6	2.58	1020	1143	1.2
72938	HARTFORD	131	1407	1535	1610	0.9	72	533	584	613	1.0	2.62	402	424	0.6
72940	HUNTINGTON	131	2699	3031	3224	1.3	82	1015	1145	1219	1.3	2.63	787	856	0.9
72941	LAVACA	131	4634	5077	5325	1.0	75	1721	1890	1988	1.0	2.68	1393	1485	0.7
72943	MAGAZINE	083	2358	2518	2563	0.7	66	894	975	998	0.9	2.58	674	710	0.6
72944	MANSFIELD	127	3131	3383	3515	0.8	68	1185	1290	1343	0.9	2.62	875	915	0.5
72946	MOUNTAINBURG	033	3633	3968	4178	1.0	75	1396	1551	1641	1.1	2.56	1047	1125	0.8
72947	MULBERRY	033	3956	4230	4398	0.7	66	1544	1680	1756	0.9	2.47	1158	1219	0.6
72948	NATURAL DAM	033	503	546	572	0.9	72	188	209	221	1.2	2.61	153	166	0.9
72949	OZARK	047	9833	10088	10102	0.3	49	3761	3912	3933	0.4	2.49	2694	2707	0.1
72950	PARKS	127	460	441	433	-0.5	22	195	189	187	-0.3	2.33	152	144	-0.6
72951	RATCLIFF	083	599	639	649	0.7	66	231	252	258	0.9	2.54	172	181	0.6
72952	RUDY	033	2850	3389	3679	1.9	91	1046	1272	1391	2.1	2.66	845	1002	1.9
72955	UNIONTOWN	033	455	525	565	1.6	87	155	183	198	1.8	2.87	123	141	1.5
72956	VAN BUREN	033	29229	32932	34990	1.3	82	10764	12298	13125	1.5	2.65	8206	9103	1.1
72958	WALDRON	127	7672	8318	8574	0.9	72	3029	3300	3408	0.9	2.48	2124	2228	0.5
	ARKANSAS					0.9					1.1	2.46			0.7
	UNITED STATES					1.0					1.1	2.59			0.9

POPULATION COMPOSITION

ZIP CODE #	POST OFFICE NAME	RACE (%) White 2000	White 2009	Black 2000	Black 2009	Asian/Pacific 2000	Asian/Pacific 2009	% Hispanic Origin 2000	% Hispanic Origin 2009	2009 AGE DISTRIBUTION (%) 0-4	5-9	10-14	15-19	20-24	25-44	45-64	65-84	85+	18+	MEDIAN AGE 2009	% 2009 Males	% 2009 Females
72727	ELKINS	96.2	95.1	0.4	0.5	0.2	0.3	1.7	2.7	7.1	7.3	7.4	6.9	5.5	26.8	28.3	9.7	1.0	73.9	37.2	50.2	49.8
72729	EVANSVILLE	92.6	90.4	0.7	0.6	0.0	0.0	1.9	3.2	6.7	7.0	7.0	7.0	4.8	22.7	30.4	13.1	1.3	74.4	40.7	51.8	48.2
72730	FARMINGTON	93.6	91.8	1.0	1.2	0.5	0.8	3.0	5.0	7.9	7.6	7.4	6.7	7.4	29.9	23.5	8.6	0.9	73.1	33.3	49.8	50.2
72732	GARFIELD	95.6	94.2	0.0	0.0	0.2	0.3	3.2	5.5	5.9	6.1	6.4	6.5	5.2	22.4	32.1	14.3	1.1	77.6	43.2	51.1	48.9
72734	GENTRY	90.5	87.2	0.1	0.1	0.3	0.5	4.8	8.3	7.6	7.5	7.5	7.0	6.1	27.2	26.4	9.6	1.2	73.2	35.8	50.3	49.7
72736	GRAVETTE	92.3	89.8	0.3	0.3	0.3	0.4	3.9	6.9	7.8	7.6	7.5	6.9	6.1	25.5	26.3	10.5	1.7	72.7	36.5	49.0	51.0
72738	HINDSVILLE	96.8	95.9	0.3	0.4	0.1	0.2	2.0	2.9	6.4	6.7	6.8	5.8	4.5	25.6	29.4	13.3	1.5	76.4	41.1	50.9	49.1
72739	HIWASSE	96.7	95.3	0.2	0.2	0.0	0.2	1.9	3.6	6.4	6.4	6.8	6.0	4.5	23.1	26.8	18.1	1.7	76.9	42.6	49.5	50.5
72740	HUNTSVILLE	95.2	93.7	0.1	0.1	0.2	0.2	3.9	6.0	6.7	6.7	6.9	7.0	5.3	24.0	27.8	13.2	2.3	75.3	39.9	49.8	50.2
72742	KINGSTON	96.7	95.8	0.0	0.0	0.0	0.2	0.7	1.0	5.7	6.1	6.5	6.3	4.6	21.2	33.5	14.5	1.7	78.0	44.7	50.5	49.5
72744	LINCOLN	92.8	90.6	0.1	0.1	0.2	0.4	4.0	6.2	7.1	7.2	7.3	6.6	4.9	25.9	27.3	11.8	1.8	74.2	38.5	49.9	50.1
72745	LOWELL	92.1	88.4	0.6	0.6	2.1	3.2	5.6	9.9	9.2	8.6	7.8	5.7	4.4	32.6	22.8	8.1	0.8	71.0	34.4	50.2	49.8
72747	MAYSVILLE	93.5	91.1	0.0	0.0	0.0	0.5	1.2	2.0	8.4	8.9	8.4	6.9	5.0	24.3	27.7	9.4	1.0	69.3	35.7	49.5	50.5
72749	MORROW	93.8	92.1	0.0	0.0	0.0	0.0	3.1	2.6	5.3	7.9	7.9	7.9	5.3	21.1	28.9	15.8	0.0	71.1	40.0	52.6	47.4
72751	PEA RIDGE	96.6	95.2	0.2	0.2	0.4	0.6	2.0	3.4	7.2	7.4	7.4	6.9	5.8	25.1	27.4	11.4	1.4	73.6	37.5	49.9	50.1
72752	PETTIGREW	97.6	97.0	0.0	0.0	0.0	0.0	2.4	3.6	4.2	4.6	4.9	5.5	5.9	20.7	37.8	14.3	2.1	83.1	47.2	52.3	47.7
72753	PRAIRIE GROVE	95.0	93.6	0.3	0.4	0.4	0.5	2.2	3.5	7.1	7.0	6.9	7.0	5.4	25.6	27.3	11.9	1.8	74.5	38.2	48.6	51.4
72756	ROGERS	87.0	82.0	0.4	0.4	1.7	2.4	16.6	24.2	8.1	7.5	7.1	6.7	6.0	27.5	24.2	11.3	1.7	73.2	35.7	49.5	50.5
72758	ROGERS	89.4	85.3	0.5	0.6	1.0	1.3	13.4	19.7	8.4	8.0	7.8	7.0	5.4	28.9	24.0	8.8	1.6	71.4	34.6	49.3	50.7
72760	SAINT PAUL	97.5	97.1	0.0	0.0	0.0	0.0	1.8	2.6	4.6	5.4	5.7	5.7	5.9	21.5	36.0	13.4	2.0	80.8	45.7	51.1	48.9
72761	SILOAM SPRINGS	87.5	82.6	0.3	0.4	0.7	1.0	10.6	17.9	7.6	7.3	7.1	8.1	7.8	27.5	23.3	9.5	1.7	73.8	33.8	49.7	50.3
72762	SPRINGDALE	88.9	85.8	0.5	0.5	2.1	2.9	10.0	13.2	7.6	7.3	7.1	6.8	5.7	28.2	25.7	10.1	1.5	73.9	36.1	48.5	51.5
72764	SPRINGDALE	81.0	75.8	1.0	1.1	3.2	3.9	20.8	28.0	9.5	8.4	7.5	6.6	6.7	31.2	21.1	7.8	1.2	70.7	31.8	50.6	49.4
72768	SULPHUR SPRINGS	91.4	88.6	0.4	0.5	0.3	0.4	5.3	9.1	8.1	7.9	7.8	7.3	6.4	25.1	25.4	10.0	1.9	71.5	35.0	48.8	51.2
72769	SUMMERS	92.0	89.7	0.1	0.1	0.5	0.9	3.6	5.7	7.7	7.6	7.7	6.5	5.2	25.4	27.3	11.5	1.0	73.0	37.3	50.0	50.0
72773	WESLEY	97.1	96.3	0.1	0.1	0.1	0.2	1.5	2.2	6.2	6.8	7.1	6.8	5.9	24.7	30.0	11.1	1.4	75.5	39.5	49.4	50.6
72774	WEST FORK	95.7	94.5	0.4	0.4	0.4	0.6	1.5	2.5	6.7	6.8	7.1	6.9	5.7	26.6	29.3	10.0	1.0	75.2	38.4	50.8	49.2
72776	WITTER	98.2	98.3	0.0	0.0	0.0	0.0	0.9	1.7	4.7	4.7	5.1	6.4	5.1	21.8	34.6	15.8	1.7	82.1	46.2	51.3	48.7
72801	RUSSELLVILLE	88.9	86.3	5.9	6.8	1.0	1.6	3.1	4.8	6.6	5.6	5.2	11.2	11.4	25.7	19.7	11.3	3.4	79.4	31.2	48.8	51.2
72802	RUSSELLVILLE	94.9	93.4	1.8	2.1	0.8	1.2	2.0	3.1	6.8	6.8	6.8	6.8	6.0	27.0	27.8	10.8	1.2	75.6	37.8	49.9	50.1
72820	ALIX	97.8	97.0	0.0	0.0	0.0	1.0	1.1	2.0	7.0	8.0	8.0	6.0	4.0	24.0	27.0	14.0	2.0	73.0	40.0	47.0	53.0
72821	ALTUS	97.2	96.3	0.1	0.2	0.4	0.7	1.7	2.4	7.2	7.5	7.4	6.0	4.4	24.3	28.2	13.4	1.6	74.1	39.9	49.1	50.9
72823	ATKINS	96.0	95.1	1.6	1.8	0.2	0.4	0.9	1.5	6.6	6.6	6.8	6.6	5.4	26.0	27.3	12.4	2.4	76.0	39.4	48.9	51.1
72824	BELLEVILLE	86.1	80.3	2.9	3.3	3.5	5.4	7.3	12.0	5.9	6.2	6.8	6.8	5.7	26.3	27.9	12.7	1.8	77.0	38.7	49.8	50.2
72826	BLUE MOUNTAIN	98.3	98.3	0.0	0.0	0.0	0.0	0.0	0.0	5.1	5.1	6.8	8.5	6.8	23.7	32.2	11.9	0.0	78.0	40.6	45.8	54.2
72827	BLUFFTON	95.1	91.4	0.0	0.0	0.0	0.6	4.3	7.4	5.6	5.6	5.6	7.4	5.6	25.3	28.4	14.8	1.9	78.4	41.4	51.2	48.8
72828	BRIGGSVILLE	94.6	91.2	0.0	0.0	0.0	0.7	4.8	7.5	6.1	6.1	6.1	6.8	5.4	23.1	29.9	14.3	2.0	77.6	41.9	51.7	48.3
72830	CLARKSVILLE	91.9	89.2	2.0	2.3	0.3	0.5	9.3	14.3	6.7	6.6	6.5	6.6	6.4	26.2	25.7	12.7	2.6	76.3	38.1	49.5	50.5
72832	COAL HILL	96.0	94.7	0.1	0.1	0.0	0.0	2.7	4.6	7.7	7.7	7.2	6.5	5.7	27.8	24.0	11.8	1.5	73.4	36.3	48.4	51.6
72833	DANVILLE	78.5	70.4	1.3	1.5	1.0	1.4	25.6	35.8	7.3	6.8	6.2	6.8	6.7	27.4	24.4	11.5	2.9	75.7	36.4	52.0	48.0
72834	DARDANELLE	87.4	83.3	2.1	2.2	0.6	0.8	10.2	15.2	6.2	6.3	6.7	6.8	5.7	26.0	27.4	12.8	2.1	76.7	39.4	49.4	50.6
72835	DELAWARE	98.6	98.3	0.1	0.1	0.1	0.1	1.0	1.6	5.6	5.7	6.0	5.5	4.3	23.2	30.9	17.0	1.9	78.9	44.8	49.4	50.6
72837	DOVER	96.6	95.6	0.2	0.2	0.1	0.2	1.6	2.6	6.5	6.5	6.8	6.8	5.9	26.4	28.5	11.5	1.2	76.0	38.9	49.2	50.8
72838	GRAVELLY	92.8	90.2	0.6	0.6	0.0	0.6	4.8	7.9	4.3	4.9	5.5	6.7	5.5	24.4	31.1	15.9	1.8	81.1	44.1	51.2	48.8
72839	HAGARVILLE	97.0	96.0	0.3	0.2	0.3	0.2	1.5	2.5	5.6	5.8	6.5	6.7	4.5	24.1	30.4	15.0	1.6	78.1	42.7	50.9	49.1
72840	HARTMAN	97.1	96.1	0.4	0.4	0.0	0.1	2.3	3.9	7.8	7.8	7.6	6.4	5.1	26.2	25.2	12.4	1.6	72.8	37.3	49.5	50.5
72841	HARVEY	93.9	92.8	0.8	0.8	1.1	1.6	0.8	1.2	6.4	6.4	7.2	6.8	4.8	23.2	25.6	17.6	2.0	75.2	41.3	50.0	50.0
72842	HAVANA	89.8	84.0	0.1	0.1	1.1	1.8	11.6	18.9	6.4	6.2	6.1	7.1	6.2	25.3	25.6	14.3	2.9	76.9	39.0	49.0	51.0
72843	HECTOR	97.4	96.9	0.2	0.2	0.1	0.1	1.2	1.9	5.6	7.2	8.2	7.1	5.4	25.1	28.2	11.6	1.8	74.5	39.1	51.4	48.6
72845	KNOXVILLE	96.8	95.8	0.1	0.1	0.1	0.2	2.3	3.7	6.4	6.7	7.0	7.6	5.4	26.5	26.6	12.6	1.3	75.4	37.8	52.2	47.8
72846	LAMAR	96.4	95.2	0.5	0.6	0.2	0.3	2.7	4.4	6.4	6.5	7.0	7.1	5.0	25.8	28.5	12.2	1.5	75.8	39.0	51.6	48.4
72847	LONDON	97.3	96.6	0.3	0.3	0.7	1.0	0.8	1.1	5.7	6.0	6.4	6.7	4.8	24.7	30.8	13.6	1.4	77.7	41.9	49.5	50.5
72851	NEW BLAINE	98.2	97.8	0.2	0.2	0.1	0.1	0.9	1.3	6.5	6.5	6.7	6.0	5.0	24.2	28.8	14.6	1.7	76.4	41.5	49.7	50.3
72852	OARK	97.2	96.0	0.0	0.0	0.0	0.0	1.2	1.8	5.1	5.8	6.2	6.5	4.3	21.0	32.2	17.4	1.4	79.3	45.8	51.8	48.2
72853	OLA	88.3	81.4	0.2	0.3	0.3	0.4	11.9	19.9	7.9	7.5	6.8	6.8	5.5	24.7	24.9	13.3	2.5	73.6	37.3	49.6	50.4
72854	OZONE	96.6	95.5	0.3	0.3	0.0	0.0	1.7	2.9	5.5	6.1	6.6	6.6	4.5	23.7	29.7	15.8	1.6	77.4	42.9	49.5	50.5
72855	PARIS	95.2	94.1	2.4	2.8	0.1	0.2	1.6	2.5	6.1	6.1	6.2	6.3	5.3	23.7	27.3	15.7	3.3	77.6	42.2	49.0	51.0
72856	PELSOR	95.2	95.8	0.0	0.0	0.0	0.0	1.6	1.4	5.6	5.6	5.6	7.0	7.0	28.2	29.6	11.3	0.0	80.3	39.5	53.5	46.5
72857	PLAINVIEW	94.0	90.5	0.1	0.1	0.1	0.1	5.8	9.6	6.9	7.2	6.0	6.6	7.0	22.5	24.7	17.0	2.2	76.1	40.1	50.6	49.4
72858	POTTSVILLE	96.2	95.3	1.0	1.2	0.4	0.6	1.2	2.0	6.5	6.5	6.9	7.4	5.8	26.8	29.4	9.7	1.0	75.6	38.7	50.8	49.2
72860	ROVER	94.1	91.2	0.3	0.3	0.3	0.5	4.4	7.8	5.4	5.4	6.0	7.0	5.7	24.1	29.8	14.5	2.1	78.5	42.3	51.8	48.2
72863	SCRANTON	97.8	97.3	0.5	0.6	0.0	0.0	0.7	1.1	6.9	7.0	7.4	6.9	5.6	25.1	27.8	11.8	1.6	74.3	38.4	50.3	49.7
72865	SUBIACO	96.1	95.4	2.0	2.2	0.1	0.3	0.7	1.2	6.4	6.5	6.7	6.5	5.6	24.9	29.1	12.5	1.7	76.3	40.1	51.2	48.8
72901	FORT SMITH	76.5	70.3	8.7	9.6	3.2	4.6	11.1	16.5	7.4	7.0	6.3	6.5	7.3	28.8	24.4	10.4	2.0	75.6	35.2	50.9	49.1
72903	FORT SMITH	86.6	81.7	4.6	5.6	2.4	3.8	5.1	8.2	6.1	5.5	5.5	6.1	6.9	24.5	27.4	14.4	3.6	79.3	41.3	47.0	53.0
72904	FORT SMITH	56.9	47.4	17.7	18.8	10.0	13.2	15.6	22.9	9.1	8.1	7.1	7.0	7.3	26.6	22.5	10.4	1.9	71.5	32.9	48.3	51.7
72905	FORT SMITH	97.8	92.9	0.0	1.4	0.0	1.4	2.2	2.9	5.7	7.1	7.1	7.1	5.7	28.6	30.0	8.6	0.0	75.7	37.9	54.3	45.7
72908	FORT SMITH	90.1	86.3	2.8	3.7	3.0	4.7	1.7	2.9	7.7	7.3	7.2	6.7	5.9	25.6	27.3	11.0	1.4	73.7	37.9	48.0	52.0
72916	FORT SMITH	91.8	88.1	1.2	1.7	2.6	4.4	2.0	3.6	6.6	6.5	6.4	6.0	5.9	29.0	28.1	10.6	1.1	76.9	37.9	50.3	49.7
72921	ALMA	95.3	94.2	0.9	1.0	0.3	0.4	2.2	3.5	7.5	7.4	7.2	6.9	6.1	25.9	27.0	10.8	1.1	73.5	36.5	50.0	50.0
72923	BARLING	86.9	80.9	1.4	1.7	5.5	9.0	3.8	6.5	8.0	7.8	7.4	5.9	5.1	28.9	25.2	9.8	1.9	73.0	35.8	47.4	52.6
72926	BOLES	95.7	94.5	0.1	0.1	0.9	1.3	0.6	0.8	4.8	6.7	7.1	7.3	3.3	22.2	33.8	13.2	1.6	77.1	43.8	51.5	48.5
72927	BOONEVILLE	96.7	95.8	0.3	0.4	0.3	0.4	1.2	1.9	6.8	6.6	6.6	6.7	6.2	24.7	26.8	13.1	2.4	75.6	39.1	49.0	51.0
72928	BRANCH	97.3	96.7	0.1	0.1	0.2	0.4	1.4	2.1	6.0	6.3	6.8	6.7	4.0	25.0	29.5	14.3	1.5	76.6	41.4	52.0	48.0
72930	CECIL	97.3	96.5	0.0	0.0	0.8	0.8	1.5	2.4	5.9	6.3	6.7	6.7	4.3	26.8	29.1	13.0	1.2	77.2	41.3	52.0	48.0
72932	CEDARVILLE	93.7	92.6	0.1	0.1	0.2	0.3	1.3	2.0	6.5	6.6	7.1	7.5	5.8	26.2	28.9	10.2	0.9	75.1	38.2	50.8	49.2
72933	CHARLESTON	95.7	94.4	0.2	0.3	0.4	0.7	1.9	3.1	6.6	6.9	7.0	6.6	4.5	25.1	27.5	13.1	2.8	75.3	40.0	50.3	49.7
72934	CHESTER	94.5	93.4	0.0	0.0	0.2	0.3	1.3	2.1	6.6	6.8	7.2	6.5	4.5	24.2	30.2	12.6	1.3	75.5	40.8	50.0	50.0
72936	GREENWOOD	96.0	94.5	0.3	0.5	0.5	0.8	1.6	2.9	7.6	7.7	7.6	6.8	5.8	28.1	25.1	9.9	1.5	72.8	35.8	49.5	50.5
72937	HACKETT	95.1	93.5	0.3	0.4	0.8	1.4	1.2	2.1	6.1	6.2	6.6	6.6	5.8	25.2	30.3	11.9	1.3	77.1	40.5	50.4	49.6
72938	HARTFORD	95.3	93.4	0.1	0.2	0.6	1.0	1.2	2.3	6.8	6.8	7.1	6.8	5.6	24.3	28.7	12.2	1.6	75.0	39.3	50.7	49.3
72940	HUNTINGTON	95.1	93.3	0.5	0.7	0.7	1.1	1.8	3.3	6.3	6.7	7.1	7.0	5.2	24.6	29.5	12.1	1.6	75.5	40.3	50.7	49.3
72941	LAVACA	95.8	94.1	0.3	0.5	0.1	0.2	1.8	3.3	6.4	6.7	6.9	6.9	4.8	27.9	28.6	10.9	0.9	75.6	39.0	49.6	50.4
72943	MAGAZINE	97.1	96.5	0.1	0.1	0.1	0.1	1.0	1.5	7.2	7.1	7.4	6.9	5.7	24.9	25.9	13.3	1.6	74.0	37.8	52.0	48.0
72944	MANSFIELD	95.2	93.6	0.2	0.3	0.8	1.2	2.0	3.6	7.1	7.4	7.2	6.4	5.4	24.5	28.2	12.1	1.7	74.2	38.7	50.1	49.9
72946	MOUNTAINBURG	96.0	95.2	0.1	0.1	0.2	0.2	1.0	1.6	6.6	6.7	7.1	7.0	5.6	24.7	28.6	12.2	1.3	75.3	39.1	50.0	50.0
72947	MULBERRY	96.0	95.2	0.3	0.3	0.2	0.3	0.8	1.3	5.9	6.1	6.3	6.7	5.3	23.7	29.7	14.6	1.7	77.7	41.9	51.2	48.8
72948	NATURAL DAM	92.4	91.2	0.0	0.0	0.4	0.5	1.2	2.0	7.3	7.1	7.3	6.8	5.1	24.7	29.9	10.6	1.1	73.8	39.3	50.2	49.8
72949	OZARK	96.1	95.1	0.9	1.1	0.2	0.3	1.9	2.9	6.4	6.3	6.5	7.7	5.9	24.6	26.1	13.8	2.7	76.1	39.1	49.2	50.8
72950	PARKS	93.7	92.5	0.9	0.9	1.1	1.6	0.9	1.1	6.8	6.6	7.0	6.6	4.5	22.4	26.5	17.7	1.8	75.5	41.9	51.0	49.0
72951	RATCLIFF	97.5	96.9	0.8	1.1	0.2	0.2	1.2	1.7	5.3	5.5	6.1	7.0	5.3	24.1	31.0	13.9	1.7	78.9	42.6	50.7	49.3
72952	RUDY	94.9	93.8	0.1	0.1	0.5	0.7	1.4	2.2	6.2	6.4	6.9	7.1	5.8	26.5	29.2	10.9	1.0	76.1	39.0	51.6	48.4
72955	UNIONTOWN	92.1	90.9	0.2	0.2	0.2	0.2	1.5	2.3	6.3	6.3	7.0	7.8	5.9	25.3	30.1	10.3	1.0	75.8	38.8	49.1	50.9
72956	VAN BUREN	89.7	86.5	1.2	1.3	2.0	2.9	4.6	7.1	7.9	7.6	7.3	6.9	6.2	27.4	25.3	9.9	1.4	73.0	35.4	49.2	50.8
72958	WALDRON	93.0	90.4	0.2	0.2	0.9	1.3	7.8	11.6	7.7	7.3	7.3	6.6	5.3	24.7	26.0	12.8	2.3	74.0	38.3	50.8	49.2
	ARKANSAS	80.0	78.2	15.7	15.8	0.8	1.2	3.2	5.1	6.8	6.6	6.5	6.9	6.6	26.0	26.1	12.4	2.0	76.1	37.8	49.1	50.9
	UNITED STATES	75.1	72.0	12.3	12.7	3.8	4.6	12.5	15.7	6.8	6.7	6.6	7.1	6.9	27.0	26.0	10.9	1.9	75.7	36.9	49.2	50.8

ZIP CODE #	POST OFFICE NAME	2009 Per Capita Income	2009 HH Income Base	2009 Household Income Distribution (%): Less than $25,000	$25,000 to $49,999	$50,000 to $99,999	$100,000 to $149,999	$150,000 or More	Median Household Income: 2009	2014	2009 National Centile	2009 State Centile	2009 Home Value Base	2009 Home Value Distribution (%): Less than $50,000	$50,000 to $89,999	$90,000 to $174,999	$175,000 to $399,999	$400,000 or More	2009 Median Home Value
72727	ELKINS	20637	1569	20.5	33.1	39.3	5.0	2.1	47610	49064	56	89	1296	15.0	19.1	40.8	20.4	4.6	114213
72729	EVANSVILLE	19239	126	30.2	33.3	30.2	4.0	2.4	38767	41363	29	68	104	19.2	26.0	35.6	17.3	1.9	101786
72730	FARMINGTON	19676	2412	23.9	28.6	39.2	6.8	1.5	47664	49646	56	89	1687	12.7	13.4	48.7	22.5	2.8	123885
72732	GARFIELD	20803	1954	24.0	27.4	41.1	4.6	3.0	48544	50792	58	91	1681	13.2	25.9	29.0	26.9	4.9	114808
72734	GENTRY	19247	3070	24.8	31.5	35.8	5.5	2.4	43184	44438	43	82	2079	19.1	20.0	37.0	18.1	5.8	109375
72736	GRAVETTE	18875	2377	28.6	29.3	33.9	5.1	3.1	41474	43160	38	79	1736	20.9	22.7	33.8	17.3	5.3	103863
72738	HINDSVILLE	19816	616	25.8	33.9	33.8	3.1	3.4	41671	44094	38	80	507	17.9	19.5	35.1	22.3	5.1	107853
72739	HIWASSE	23624	197	17.8	27.4	43.1	7.6	4.1	53142	55614	68	95	164	5.5	8.5	44.5	31.7	9.8	148958
72740	HUNTSVILLE	16985	3988	36.0	33.6	24.2	4.2	2.0	34980	36430	18	42	3049	21.7	25.7	32.3	14.2	6.1	95096
72742	KINGSTON	17487	203	39.4	28.6	27.1	4.9	0.0	32990	34808	13	31	171	20.5	32.2	31.0	11.7	4.7	83571
72744	LINCOLN	18294	2043	32.2	33.3	28.7	4.0	1.8	36945	40678	23	57	1488	17.2	23.5	40.4	13.6	5.3	105039
72745	LOWELL	28372	4345	13.0	17.9	48.4	14.3	6.3	65789	67690	84	99	3371	12.0	6.7	48.3	28.6	4.4	141420
72747	MAYSVILLE	19228	70	20.0	38.6	31.4	7.1	2.9	45622	46925	50	87	55	16.4	18.2	36.4	23.6	5.5	129688
72749	MORROW	6316	8	37.5	50.0	12.5	0.0	0.0	30000	27247	8	16	7	0.0	28.6	71.4	0.0	0.0	131250
72751	PEA RIDGE	20262	1898	18.0	27.5	46.8	5.5	2.1	52506	54422	67	95	1539	6.6	19.4	48.0	20.3	5.7	121467
72752	PETTIGREW	16960	201	43.3	28.9	22.4	3.0	2.5	29793	30789	8	14	168	35.7	27.4	22.6	14.3	0.0	72941
72753	PRAIRIE GROVE	19481	2714	28.7	26.8	37.1	5.4	2.0	45201	47977	49	86	2091	15.7	17.9	45.6	17.6	3.2	115691
72756	ROGERS	23284	15580	21.7	25.5	40.7	6.8	5.2	52087	54383	66	94	10227	8.6	14.6	46.8	25.2	4.8	132325
72758	ROGERS	27913	10950	13.8	22.3	43.5	11.6	8.7	61293	64084	79	98	7962	5.2	8.2	47.6	30.2	8.8	151372
72760	SAINT PAUL	16431	257	42.4	31.1	22.6	2.7	1.2	29853	31888	8	15	217	31.8	30.4	23.5	14.3	0.0	74375
72761	SILOAM SPRINGS	20474	7203	22.4	29.4	40.2	4.7	3.2	47569	50878	56	89	4554	13.0	17.5	44.8	20.7	4.0	118527
72762	SPRINGDALE	24038	12191	16.1	27.6	41.0	11.2	4.1	56072	56860	73	96	8782	5.4	8.5	54.5	26.8	4.8	140071
72764	SPRINGDALE	21043	17267	20.8	32.4	36.2	6.2	4.4	47470	49679	55	89	10095	12.9	16.8	46.7	19.1	4.6	118654
72768	SULPHUR SPRINGS	16395	603	27.7	31.8	35.0	3.5	2.0	42071	43285	39	80	442	22.6	24.7	36.9	12.4	3.4	94615
72769	SUMMERS	17010	385	31.2	32.7	29.9	5.2	1.0	37137	40999	24	59	294	18.4	29.6	22.1	23.1	6.8	94286
72773	WESLEY	16120	664	32.1	41.0	23.0	3.0	0.9	36217	38914	21	51	555	23.6	27.2	34.1	12.8	2.3	88125
72774	WEST FORK	18999	2282	25.8	31.7	36.5	4.6	1.4	44831	46707	48	85	1830	18.5	22.5	37.8	17.6	3.6	105201
72776	WITTER	12498	85	45.9	30.6	21.2	2.4	0.0	28340	30711	6	10	72	16.7	41.7	29.2	12.5	0.0	75556
72801	RUSSELLVILLE	20488	6852	31.2	31.3	28.8	5.7	2.9	38936	41647	30	69	3572	6.0	30.3	48.5	14.1	1.1	103186
72802	RUSSELLVILLE	22370	7527	25.2	26.7	35.7	7.9	4.5	48148	49317	57	91	5834	13.0	21.4	42.6	19.6	3.3	112849
72820	ALIX	16988	40	35.0	35.0	25.0	2.5	2.5	33581	35000	15	36	31	38.7	29.0	25.8	6.5	0.0	67500
72821	ALTUS	17682	721	36.1	32.7	26.4	2.4	2.5	34447	36501	16	40	559	37.0	28.1	27.9	6.3	0.7	72125
72823	ATKINS	18313	2406	33.4	31.1	28.7	4.4	2.3	37109	40407	24	59	1871	23.7	34.9	31.5	8.4	1.5	79868
72824	BELLEVILLE	18868	284	30.3	33.5	30.6	3.2	2.5	37580	38087	25	61	225	32.0	22.2	32.0	10.7	3.1	82692
72826	BLUE MOUNTAIN	11695	21	38.1	42.9	19.0	0.0	0.0	33586	33586	15	36	17	47.1	35.3	11.8	5.9	0.0	52500
72827	BLUFFTON	20453	70	40.0	27.1	27.1	2.9	2.9	32821	35759	13	30	57	40.4	29.8	24.6	3.5	1.8	66250
72828	BRIGGSVILLE	18974	59	39.0	27.1	27.1	3.4	3.4	32954	33866	13	31	48	35.4	33.3	27.1	4.2	0.0	71667
72830	CLARKSVILLE	18088	5845	35.8	31.1	27.3	4.0	1.8	35519	37045	19	47	4080	18.2	32.4	35.7	11.7	2.0	89348
72832	COAL HILL	16054	594	39.9	29.6	25.1	4.0	1.3	30243	31271	8	17	458	33.0	31.0	32.1	3.1	0.9	70333
72833	DANVILLE	15870	1292	34.6	30.1	28.1	4.2	3.0	35060	35579	18	44	888	26.6	34.5	27.4	8.9	2.7	75753
72834	DARDANELLE	18607	4469	30.1	31.5	31.5	5.2	1.7	39658	40674	32	72	3285	17.4	31.6	33.7	15.0	2.3	91071
72835	DELAWARE	18012	361	45.4	23.8	24.1	4.2	2.5	29832	31843	8	14	309	32.4	27.2	28.8	8.1	3.6	79400
72837	DOVER	18083	3111	29.4	31.4	33.3	4.1	1.7	40492	42804	34	76	2549	20.7	30.5	35.7	11.1	2.0	88315
72838	GRAVELLY	19440	67	37.3	29.9	25.4	4.5	3.0	33338	35758	14	34	54	37.0	33.3	25.9	3.7	0.0	62500
72839	HAGARVILLE	18003	181	32.6	34.3	28.2	3.3	1.7	35554	36896	19	47	152	26.3	27.0	26.3	17.1	3.3	84444
72840	HARTMAN	17670	399	38.6	29.6	24.6	3.3	4.0	32360	33477	12	27	315	39.4	30.5	22.9	4.4	2.9	61750
72841	HARVEY	17337	97	32.0	42.3	21.6	2.1	2.1	32747	34067	13	29	84	28.6	26.2	31.0	10.7	3.6	82000
72842	HAVANA	16771	526	38.4	34.6	21.9	3.2	1.9	35093	35052	18	44	395	35.2	32.4	18.0	11.6	2.8	65513
72843	HECTOR	18290	1115	30.9	35.3	25.6	4.9	3.3	37172	40690	24	59	926	31.7	31.4	26.2	8.0	2.6	72000
72845	KNOXVILLE	18280	449	28.5	34.3	29.6	5.3	2.2	40697	42525	35	77	377	19.9	29.7	35.0	12.2	3.2	90625
72846	LAMAR	17026	1900	33.1	35.1	26.1	3.8	2.0	35652	36546	20	48	1452	22.2	32.0	29.6	13.4	2.8	84643
72847	LONDON	21629	758	27.2	31.4	30.7	5.0	5.7	42838	45079	42	82	620	15.0	29.0	36.6	16.8	2.6	97255
72851	NEW BLAINE	19752	382	36.6	29.8	26.7	2.9	3.9	35907	37487	20	49	329	32.5	23.1	30.4	9.4	4.6	81591
72852	OARK	16736	116	44.0	24.1	30.2	0.9	0.9	29284	30000	7	12	99	29.3	29.3	27.3	11.1	3.0	79286
72853	OLA	15257	738	39.3	34.3	20.3	4.5	1.6	30662	31849	9	19	496	37.1	31.5	24.6	5.8	1.0	63333
72854	OZONE	16794	148	35.1	31.1	29.1	4.1	0.7	35000	35749	18	43	126	27.8	24.6	31.0	14.3	2.4	86667
72855	PARIS	18585	2802	36.5	32.4	24.8	3.9	2.3	34768	36350	17	41	2130	24.5	34.7	30.0	9.2	1.6	78283
72856	PELSOR	15623	30	30.0	46.7	23.3	0.0	0.0	35000	35000	18	43	26	34.6	30.8	30.8	3.8	0.0	65000
72857	PLAINVIEW	17052	578	41.3	35.3	18.3	2.4	2.6	30800	31489	9	20	428	43.7	29.2	22.7	3.7	0.7	56429
72858	POTTSVILLE	19760	939	30.0	29.5	30.5	8.1	1.9	40219	42827	33	75	741	21.2	24.4	33.7	19.8	0.8	96132
72860	ROVER	17637	143	37.1	28.7	27.3	2.8	4.2	34225	34520	16	39	115	39.1	30.4	24.3	4.3	1.7	67857
72863	SCRANTON	20264	608	27.3	33.7	33.7	2.0	3.3	40384	41780	34	76	512	24.6	25.0	34.6	10.9	4.9	90488
72865	SUBIACO	17691	428	28.5	34.8	31.5	1.9	3.3	39623	40950	32	72	366	27.0	27.3	31.4	10.4	3.8	82727
72901	FORT SMITH	19630	9040	34.4	32.4	26.4	4.3	2.5	35607	38586	20	48	4415	23.7	42.1	24.8	8.7	0.8	75043
72903	FORT SMITH	31095	11139	20.0	28.3	33.1	10.0	8.5	51774	52915	65	94	6409	4.7	20.1	45.9	24.2	5.1	124011
72904	FORT SMITH	15955	7507	38.8	30.5	25.4	3.3	2.0	32798	35188	13	30	4193	33.2	47.7	16.2	2.2	0.8	61346
72905	FORT SMITH	9155	14	28.6	35.7	28.6	7.1	0.0	40000	42343	33	74	11	0.0	27.3	54.5	18.2	0.0	118750
72908	FORT SMITH	31224	5189	16.3	23.5	38.5	12.8	9.0	59350	57534	77	97	3538	6.7	24.8	46.9	18.7	2.9	111923
72916	FORT SMITH	27108	2653	18.7	27.1	38.8	9.9	5.5	53309	53362	69	96	1850	11.6	19.5	41.2	21.5	6.3	125437
72921	ALMA	19872	4925	27.0	32.0	30.7	6.6	3.7	41879	44541	39	80	3639	18.3	24.2	40.5	15.7	1.2	102466
72923	BARLING	22802	1762	19.6	28.8	41.0	7.7	3.0	50895	51415	63	93	1221	16.7	48.6	31.9	2.0	0.7	78825
72926	BOLES	16537	307	41.0	30.6	26.7	0.3	1.3	34404	35640	16	40	268	36.2	25.0	24.6	11.6	2.6	72667
72927	BOONEVILLE	17306	3215	33.5	34.9	25.7	4.0	1.9	36681	38280	23	55	2321	27.5	31.0	31.7	8.5	1.2	79021
72928	BRANCH	19170	342	33.6	31.6	26.0	6.7	2.0	37096	39871	24	58	289	25.6	22.8	25.3	23.9	2.4	94500
72930	CECIL	19690	101	32.7	28.7	30.7	5.9	2.0	38453	40000	28	67	87	29.9	19.5	40.2	9.2	1.1	90833
72932	CEDARVILLE	16678	533	27.8	37.0	31.1	3.0	1.1	39307	42172	31	71	455	26.6	31.2	27.5	11.9	2.9	78929
72933	CHARLESTON	18877	2106	32.0	28.8	32.9	5.1	1.2	40623	41983	35	77	1638	21.7	34.9	33.0	9.3	1.2	82895
72934	CHESTER	16804	348	35.1	34.8	24.4	3.7	2.0	36980	40418	24	58	294	21.8	30.3	32.0	14.6	1.4	87692
72936	GREENWOOD	20242	5169	18.6	34.7	37.8	7.1	1.9	47563	49302	56	89	4145	11.2	30.6	44.7	12.4	1.1	99351
72937	HACKETT	19851	1532	24.2	32.2	35.8	6.4	1.4	45850	47075	51	87	1290	26.8	32.2	26.6	12.7	1.6	78929
72938	HARTFORD	16956	584	30.3	36.5	27.2	4.8	1.2	37383	40753	25	60	479	41.5	32.8	19.6	4.2	1.9	61912
72940	HUNTINGTON	19420	1145	24.3	34.2	33.9	6.2	1.4	41685	44702	38	80	962	30.0	32.1	26.9	10.4	0.5	75963
72941	LAVACA	22198	1890	18.9	27.7	41.9	8.8	2.6	52489	53183	67	95	1552	17.1	31.7	35.4	14.4	1.4	93396
72943	MAGAZINE	16873	975	35.9	34.4	25.6	2.9	1.2	34296	35616	16	39	773	33.5	32.2	26.0	7.6	0.6	69262
72944	MANSFIELD	18103	1290	31.0	35.3	26.7	5.4	1.6	37939	40732	26	63	1012	32.4	34.0	24.2	8.4	1.0	70680
72946	MOUNTAINBURG	19037	1551	30.6	33.8	29.4	3.9	2.3	39164	42146	30	70	1253	23.5	30.3	31.0	13.6	1.6	85759
72947	MULBERRY	19031	1680	31.0	31.5	30.3	4.8	2.4	39300	42098	31	71	1338	26.9	30.9	30.0	9.5	2.7	81405
72948	NATURAL DAM	17287	209	34.4	30.6	28.2	5.3	1.4	37611	41471	26	61	182	28.0	27.5	34.1	9.9	0.5	81667
72949	OZARK	18073	3912	31.0	33.1	30.5	3.8	1.7	38898	40671	29	68	3013	26.1	32.8	31.5	8.2	1.5	78878
72950	PARKS	19093	189	32.8	42.3	21.2	1.6	2.1	31883	33393	11	23	164	29.9	25.6	30.5	10.4	3.7	80000
72951	RATCLIFF	20522	252	27.8	40.1	25.8	4.0	2.4	36724	38825	23	56	202	20.8	33.7	31.7	11.9	2.0	84706
72952	RUDY	17681	1272	27.0	36.8	30.4	4.5	1.3	40404	42908	34	76	1097	22.5	33.5	27.1	13.6	3.3	80764
72955	UNIONTOWN	17612	183	25.7	33.9	36.1	2.7	1.6	42810	45486	42	82	151	25.8	22.5	36.4	14.6	0.7	92500
72956	VAN BUREN	19619	12298	25.2	31.0	36.0	5.7	2.1	45640	47079	50	87	9067	16.0	32.7	39.5	10.5	1.4	91985
72958	WALDRON	16625	3300	37.2	33.6	24.0	3.8	1.3	32902	35000	13	31	2333	34.6	29.8	23.8	8.8	2.9	68607
	ARKANSAS	21917		28.7	29.0	32.0	6.7	3.7	42685	44760				21.5	25.6	34.9	15.2	2.9	95077
	UNITED STATES	27277		20.9	24.4	35.3	11.7	7.6	54719	56938				9.3	13.1	31.6	32.6	13.5	162279

ZIP CODE #	POST OFFICE NAME	FINANCIAL SERVICES: Auto Loan	FINANCIAL SERVICES: Home Loan	FINANCIAL SERVICES: Investments	FINANCIAL SERVICES: Retirement Plans	THE HOME: Home Improvements: Home Repair	THE HOME: Home Improvements: Lawn & Garden	THE HOME: Furnishings: Computers & Hardware-Personal	THE HOME: Furnishings: Major Appliances	THE HOME: Furnishings: TV, Radio, Sound Equipment	THE HOME: Furnishings: Furniture	ENTERTAINMENT: Dine out/Carry out	ENTERTAINMENT: Sports Equipment	ENTERTAINMENT: Fees & Tickets	ENTERTAINMENT: Toys & Games	ENTERTAINMENT: Travel	ENTERTAINMENT: Cable TV	PERSONAL: Apparel & Services	PERSONAL: Auto Repairs	PERSONAL: Health Insurance	PERSONAL: Pets & Supplies
72727	ELKINS	89	79	73	77	78	85	76	82	79	77	79	60	70	82	72	82	54	79	83	97
72729	EVANSVILLE	85	61	87	59	63	86	62	79	69	58	68	60	50	69	62	76	45	73	83	94
72730	FARMINGTON	83	76	67	74	74	77	74	76	76	76	76	57	70	79	70	77	52	75	76	91
72732	GARFIELD	94	71	96	69	74	94	73	88	79	70	77	66	60	79	71	85	52	82	90	104
72734	GENTRY	92	69	78	67	69	88	71	81	77	69	76	62	59	80	66	83	51	77	85	99
72736	GRAVETTE	87	71	74	69	70	84	70	79	75	69	74	60	61	78	67	80	50	75	82	95
72738	HINDSVILLE	93	66	92	65	68	93	70	85	76	63	74	67	55	76	68	82	49	80	89	104
72739	HIWASSE	98	92	93	91	94	100	87	95	91	90	90	68	85	91	87	94	61	91	98	112
72740	HUNTSVILLE	78	55	75	54	56	78	59	72	64	54	63	55	46	65	56	71	42	67	76	86
72742	KINGSTON	73	51	79	51	54	76	55	69	59	47	58	55	42	58	55	64	38	64	73	84
72744	LINCOLN	80	58	74	57	59	79	61	73	67	57	66	56	49	68	58	73	44	69	77	88
72745	LOWELL	118	120	104	118	115	112	110	115	107	113	108	89	108	114	109	106	75	108	107	132
72747	MAYSVILLE	99	69	104	68	71	103	76	93	80	64	79	76	56	79	74	87	51	87	98	114
72749	MORROW	54	38	55	37	40	54	39	50	44	37	43	38	31	43	39	48	28	46	52	60
72751	PEA RIDGE	84	82	74	83	80	89	79	84	81	76	80	64	77	82	79	84	55	81	88	99
72752	PETTIGREW	71	51	73	50	53	73	52	67	58	49	57	50	42	58	52	64	38	61	69	79
72753	PRAIRIE GROVE	81	71	72	71	70	82	70	77	74	68	73	58	65	75	68	77	49	74	81	92
72756	ROGERS	96	88	88	86	87	92	89	92	90	89	90	70	84	92	87	92	62	91	92	108
72758	ROGERS	119	121	106	118	118	115	113	116	112	117	112	89	113	116	112	111	78	112	112	134
72760	SAINT PAUL	70	50	72	49	52	71	52	65	57	48	56	49	41	57	51	63	37	60	68	78
72761	SILOAM SPRINGS	87	77	73	77	76	85	79	82	82	78	81	61	73	84	75	86	56	81	86	98
72762	SPRINGDALE	97	100	86	99	96	96	94	96	93	95	94	73	94	96	93	93	65	93	94	112
72764	SPRINGDALE	91	82	77	81	79	82	86	85	86	86	86	67	79	88	81	86	60	86	84	100
72768	SULPHUR SPRINGS	85	63	70	61	63	80	65	74	71	64	70	57	53	74	59	77	47	70	78	90
72769	SUMMERS	84	60	71	59	60	80	63	73	70	61	68	57	50	72	58	76	46	70	78	90
72773	WESLEY	77	55	67	53	55	74	57	68	63	55	62	52	46	65	53	69	41	64	71	82
72774	WEST FORK	82	71	69	69	70	78	68	75	72	70	72	55	62	75	65	75	49	72	76	89
72776	WITTER	61	44	63	43	46	62	45	57	50	42	49	43	36	50	45	55	33	53	60	68
72801	RUSSELLVILLE	75	64	61	66	63	70	75	70	76	70	75	55	68	76	68	78	52	74	76	85
72802	RUSSELLVILLE	88	84	80	86	83	88	84	86	84	82	84	67	81	86	83	86	58	85	87	102
72820	ALIX	76	54	78	53	56	77	56	71	62	52	61	53	45	61	55	68	40	65	74	84
72821	ALTUS	77	58	78	57	60	79	59	73	64	54	63	55	48	64	58	70	42	67	76	87
72823	ATKINS	84	61	74	60	62	82	63	75	70	61	69	57	51	72	59	76	46	71	79	91
72824	BELLEVILLE	87	62	75	60	62	83	65	76	72	62	70	58	52	74	60	78	47	72	80	93
72826	BLUE MOUNTAIN	59	43	49	41	42	56	44	52	49	43	48	40	36	51	40	54	32	49	54	63
72827	BLUFFTON	87	59	86	56	59	86	62	78	70	58	69	60	47	71	59	78	45	73	82	95
72828	BRIGGSVILLE	87	59	86	56	59	86	62	78	70	58	68	60	47	71	59	78	45	73	82	95
72830	CLARKSVILLE	80	58	73	57	59	79	62	74	69	58	67	56	51	69	59	75	45	70	79	88
72832	COAL HILL	74	53	61	52	53	70	55	64	61	54	60	49	44	64	50	67	40	61	68	78
72833	DANVILLE	81	60	67	60	60	78	66	73	72	62	70	56	54	73	60	77	47	71	78	88
72834	DARDANELLE	84	61	77	60	62	82	66	77	72	62	71	58	54	73	61	79	48	73	81	92
72835	DELAWARE	77	55	79	53	57	78	56	72	63	52	61	54	45	62	56	69	41	66	75	85
72837	DOVER	80	63	70	62	63	79	64	73	69	62	68	56	55	72	61	75	46	70	77	88
72838	GRAVELLY	86	60	87	58	62	86	62	79	70	58	68	60	49	70	61	77	45	73	83	95
72839	HAGARVILLE	80	57	82	55	59	81	58	74	65	54	64	56	47	64	58	71	42	68	77	88
72840	HARTMAN	82	59	68	57	59	78	61	71	68	60	67	55	49	71	56	74	45	68	75	87
72841	HARVEY	80	57	82	55	59	81	59	75	65	55	64	56	47	65	58	72	42	68	78	89
72842	HAVANA	77	55	63	54	55	73	57	67	64	56	62	51	46	66	52	69	42	63	70	81
72843	HECTOR	85	61	80	59	62	84	63	77	70	60	69	58	51	71	60	77	46	72	81	93
72845	KNOXVILLE	88	63	76	61	63	85	66	78	73	63	71	59	53	75	61	80	48	73	82	94
72846	LAMAR	81	58	74	57	59	80	60	73	67	58	66	56	48	68	57	73	44	68	77	88
72847	LONDON	95	74	94	73	76	98	75	91	81	69	79	69	63	81	74	88	53	84	95	108
72851	NEW BLAINE	86	62	80	60	63	85	64	78	71	61	69	59	51	72	61	78	46	72	82	94
72852	OARK	71	51	73	49	53	72	52	67	58	49	57	50	42	58	52	64	38	61	69	79
72853	OLA	69	51	54	50	50	65	56	61	61	53	59	47	46	63	50	66	40	60	65	74
72854	OZONE	77	55	79	53	57	78	57	72	63	53	62	54	45	62	56	69	41	66	75	86
72855	PARIS	78	55	76	54	57	79	59	73	66	55	64	55	47	66	56	73	43	68	78	87
72856	PELSOR	67	48	55	47	48	63	50	58	55	49	54	45	40	58	45	60	36	55	61	71
72857	PLAINVIEW	76	50	73	47	50	74	54	67	62	51	60	52	40	63	50	69	40	63	71	82
72858	POTTSVILLE	86	71	74	70	70	85	70	79	75	69	74	61	62	78	67	80	50	75	81	95
72860	ROVER	87	59	86	56	60	87	62	78	70	58	69	60	48	71	59	78	46	73	82	95
72863	SCRANTON	95	68	82	66	68	92	71	84	79	69	77	64	57	82	65	86	52	79	88	102
72865	SUBIACO	88	63	77	61	63	85	65	78	72	63	71	59	52	75	61	79	48	73	82	94
72901	FORT SMITH	68	59	55	60	57	65	68	64	71	63	69	50	62	71	61	73	48	68	71	78
72903	FORT SMITH	102	101	97	103	100	103	104	101	105	103	105	78	104	104	103	106	73	104	106	120
72904	FORT SMITH	65	53	50	54	51	61	63	60	66	58	64	46	56	66	55	69	44	63	67	73
72905	FORT SMITH	71	64	59	64	63	67	64	67	65	64	65	50	60	68	61	67	45	65	67	79
72908	FORT SMITH	112	111	99	113	107	111	112	108	112	111	111	85	111	114	109	112	78	110	111	129
72916	FORT SMITH	100	95	85	97	92	94	97	95	96	97	96	75	94	99	94	95	67	95	93	113
72921	ALMA	88	73	74	71	71	86	73	81	78	72	77	61	65	80	69	83	52	78	84	97
72923	BARLING	88	84	70	83	80	85	83	82	84	83	84	63	80	87	79	86	58	83	86	99
72926	BOLES	73	52	63	51	52	70	54	64	60	52	59	49	43	62	50	66	39	61	68	78
72927	BOONEVILLE	77	57	69	55	57	76	61	71	67	57	65	54	50	67	57	73	44	67	76	85
72928	BRANCH	86	61	85	60	63	86	63	79	70	59	69	60	51	70	62	77	46	73	83	95
72930	CECIL	89	62	87	61	64	89	67	81	72	59	71	65	51	72	64	78	47	76	86	99
72932	CEDARVILLE	83	60	71	58	60	80	62	73	69	60	67	56	50	71	57	75	45	69	77	89
72933	CHARLESTON	77	62	75	63	64	82	65	76	69	58	67	58	55	69	64	74	45	71	80	90
72934	CHESTER	80	57	80	56	59	80	59	74	65	55	64	56	47	65	58	72	42	68	77	88
72936	GREENWOOD	89	81	75	80	80	87	78	84	81	78	80	62	73	84	75	84	55	80	85	99
72937	HACKETT	88	68	75	68	68	87	70	80	75	66	74	61	58	78	65	82	50	75	84	96
72938	HARTFORD	80	58	69	56	58	77	60	71	66	58	65	54	48	69	55	72	44	66	74	86
72940	HUNTINGTON	89	68	81	67	69	89	69	82	75	65	74	62	58	77	66	82	50	77	86	98
72941	LAVACA	94	86	81	86	86	95	83	91	86	80	85	68	77	88	81	89	58	86	93	107
72943	MAGAZINE	79	56	66	55	56	75	59	68	65	57	64	53	47	68	54	71	43	65	72	83
72944	MANSFIELD	84	60	79	58	61	84	63	77	70	59	68	59	50	71	60	77	46	72	82	92
72946	MOUNTAINBURG	88	63	77	61	63	85	65	78	72	63	71	59	52	74	61	79	47	73	82	94
72947	MULBERRY	84	60	82	58	62	84	63	78	70	59	68	59	50	70	61	77	45	72	82	93
72948	NATURAL DAM	81	58	79	56	59	81	60	74	66	56	65	56	48	67	58	73	43	69	77	89
72949	OZARK	77	58	68	58	59	76	62	71	68	58	66	54	52	69	58	74	45	68	76	85
72950	PARKS	80	57	81	55	59	81	59	74	65	55	64	56	47	65	58	71	42	68	77	88
72951	RATCLIFF	93	67	95	64	69	94	68	87	76	64	75	65	55	75	68	83	49	80	90	103
72952	RUDY	83	63	70	61	63	79	64	73	70	63	69	55	54	72	59	75	46	70	76	88
72955	UNIONTOWN	91	65	75	64	65	87	68	79	76	66	74	61	55	79	62	82	50	75	84	96
72956	VAN BUREN	83	73	71	71	71	79	73	77	76	73	75	59	67	78	70	78	52	76	79	92
72958	WALDRON	72	52	65	51	53	70	57	65	62	52	60	50	46	62	53	67	41	63	70	79
	ARKANSAS	88	73	79	72	73	85	76	82	80	74	79	62	68	81	72	84	54	80	86	98
	UNITED STATES	100	100	100	100	100	100	100	100	100	100	100	100	100	100	100	100	100	100	100	100

POPULATION CHANGE

ZIP CODE			POPULATION			2000-2009 ANNUAL RATE		HOUSEHOLDS					FAMILIES		
#	POST OFFICE NAME	COUNTY FIPS CODE	2000	2009	2014	% Rate	State Centile	2000	2009	2014	% Annual Rate 2000-2009	2009 Average HH Size	2000	2009	% Annual Rate 2000-2009
72959	WINSLOW	143	2816	3140	3310	1.2	80	1074	1231	1305	1.5	2.55	824	907	1.0
	ARKANSAS					0.9					1.1	2.46			0.7
	UNITED STATES					1.0					1.1	2.59			0.9

ZIP CODE #	POST OFFICE NAME	RACE (%) White 2000	White 2009	Black 2000	Black 2009	Asian/Pacific 2000	Asian/Pacific 2009	% Hispanic Origin 2000	% Hispanic Origin 2009	2009 AGE DISTRIBUTION (%) 0-4	5-9	10-14	15-19	20-24	25-44	45-64	65-84	85+	18+	MEDIAN AGE 2009	% 2009 Males	% 2009 Females
72959	WINSLOW	95.3	94.2	0.4	0.4	0.4	0.5	1.0	1.7	6.1	6.2	7.3	7.1	5.6	23.6	32.2	10.6	1.2	75.8	40.6	50.8	49.2
	ARKANSAS	80.0	78.2	15.7	15.8	0.8	1.2	3.2	5.1	6.8	6.6	6.5	6.9	6.6	26.0	26.1	12.4	2.0	76.1	37.8	49.1	50.9
	UNITED STATES	75.1	72.0	12.3	12.7	3.8	4.6	12.5	15.7	6.8	6.7	6.6	7.1	6.9	27.0	26.0	10.9	1.9	75.7	36.9	49.2	50.8

#	POST OFFICE NAME	2009 Per Capita Income	2009 HH Income Base	2009 HOUSEHOLD INCOME DISTRIBUTION (%) Less than $25,000	$25,000 to $49,999	$50,000 to $99,999	$100,000 to $149,999	$150,000 or More	MEDIAN HOUSEHOLD INCOME 2009	2014	2009 National Centile	2009 State Centile	2009 Home Value Base	2009 HOME VALUE DISTRIBUTION (%) Less than $50,000	$50,000 to $89,999	$90,000 to $174,999	$175,000 to $399,999	$400,000 or More	2009 Median Home Value
72959	WINSLOW	17710	1231	27.6	35.7	32.2	3.7	0.9	39281	42205	31	70	1033	21.8	27.5	30.1	17.3	3.3	91339
	ARKANSAS	21917		28.7	29.0	32.0	6.7	3.7	42685	44760				21.5	25.6	34.9	15.2	2.9	95077
	UNITED STATES	27277		20.9	24.4	35.3	11.7	7.6	54719	56938				9.3	13.1	31.6	32.6	13.5	162279

ZIP CODE	FINANCIAL SERVICES				THE HOME						ENTERTAINMENT						PERSONAL			
					Home Improvements		Furnishings													
# POST OFFICE NAME	Auto Loan	Home Loan	Invest-ments	Retire-ment Plans	Home Repair	Lawn & Garden	Comput-ers & Hard-ware-Personal	Major Appli-ances	TV, Radio, Sound Equip-ment	Furni-ture	Dine out/ Carry out	Sports Equip-ment	Fees & Tickets	Toys & Games	Travel	Cable TV	Apparel & Services	Auto Repairs	Health Insur-ance	Pets & Supplies
72959 WINSLOW	81	58	76	57	59	80	60	73	66	57	65	56	48	67	58	73	43	68	77	88
ARKANSAS	88	73	79	72	73	85	76	82	80	74	79	62	68	81	72	84	54	80	86	98
UNITED STATES	100	100	100	100	100	100	100	100	100	100	100	100	100	100	100	100	100	100	100	100

ZIP CODE		COUNTY FIPS CODE	POPULATION			2000-2009 ANNUAL RATE		HOUSEHOLDS					FAMILIES		
#	POST OFFICE NAME		2000	2009	2014	% Rate	State Centile	2000	2009	2014	% Annual Rate 2000-2009	2009 Average HH Size	2000	2009	% Annual Rate 2000-2009
90001	LOS ANGELES	037	54707	57979	59626	0.6	45	12579	13006	13321	0.4	4.46	10737	11097	0.4
90002	LOS ANGELES	037	44950	50460	52953	1.3	70	10788	11699	12203	0.9	4.30	8835	9600	0.9
90003	LOS ANGELES	037	58069	64840	68215	1.2	68	14450	15752	16479	0.9	4.10	11600	12651	0.9
90004	LOS ANGELES	037	67751	70439	72099	0.4	30	23081	23586	24041	0.2	2.96	15007	15284	0.2
90005	LOS ANGELES	037	40870	44299	46065	0.9	58	14020	14902	15429	0.7	2.96	9109	9681	0.7
90006	LOS ANGELES	037	60562	62794	64173	0.4	30	18079	18352	18643	0.2	3.39	13133	13335	0.2
90007	LOS ANGELES	037	44444	46690	48073	0.5	39	12526	13122	13496	0.5	3.13	7022	7321	0.5
90008	LOS ANGELES	037	30505	31907	32916	0.5	39	13220	13526	13885	0.2	2.35	7432	7597	0.2
90010	LOS ANGELES	037	4015	4344	4530	0.9	58	2225	2354	2441	0.6	1.84	898	948	0.6
90011	LOS ANGELES	037	101637	108560	111674	0.7	50	21785	22616	23196	0.4	4.78	18366	19092	0.4
90012	LOS ANGELES	037	32154	37953	39963	1.8	80	8619	10552	11321	2.2	2.34	4231	5178	2.2
90013	LOS ANGELES	037	8628	9962	10611	1.6	77	3028	3889	4287	2.7	1.52	368	508	3.5
90014	LOS ANGELES	037	3690	4130	4470	1.2	68	2653	2947	3191	1.1	1.16	268	302	1.3
90015	LOS ANGELES	037	17557	21955	23937	2.4	87	5618	7395	8191	3.0	2.87	3392	4164	2.2
90016	LOS ANGELES	037	45512	48625	50251	0.7	50	15946	16633	17095	0.5	2.91	10671	11128	0.5
90017	LOS ANGELES	037	20489	29363	32947	4.0	94	6350	9496	10712	4.4	2.98	4058	5777	3.9
90018	LOS ANGELES	037	50009	52740	54234	0.6	45	16226	16668	17040	0.3	3.11	10844	11144	0.3
90019	LOS ANGELES	037	68613	72911	75326	0.7	50	24173	25180	25879	0.4	2.85	15196	15829	0.4
90020	LOS ANGELES	037	42411	44470	45885	0.5	39	16951	17360	17805	0.3	2.55	9709	9965	0.3
90021	LOS ANGELES	037	3118	3433	3593	1.0	62	1328	1494	1585	1.3	1.73	351	397	1.3
90022	LOS ANGELES	037	67767	70273	71814	0.4	30	16984	17230	17510	0.2	4.07	14127	14337	0.2
90023	LOS ANGELES	037	45397	47165	48178	0.4	30	10302	10480	10663	0.2	4.47	8868	9020	0.2
90024	LOS ANGELES	037	44313	49099	51280	1.1	64	16894	18776	19751	1.1	2.01	5829	6304	0.9
90025	LOS ANGELES	037	40335	42109	43199	0.5	39	20982	21450	21868	0.2	1.94	7688	7888	0.3
90026	LOS ANGELES	037	73282	77057	79175	0.5	39	24484	25160	25682	0.3	3.03	15030	15499	0.3
90027	LOS ANGELES	037	49960	52843	54525	0.6	45	22521	23271	23850	0.4	2.22	10298	10709	0.4
90028	LOS ANGELES	037	29790	32515	33935	1.0	62	14352	15270	15831	0.7	2.08	5085	5513	0.9
90029	LOS ANGELES	037	40546	42560	43751	0.5	39	13239	13622	13930	0.3	3.06	8832	9094	0.3
90031	LOS ANGELES	037	39645	42490	44085	0.8	54	10632	11167	11525	0.5	3.76	8495	8934	0.5
90032	LOS ANGELES	037	46146	48928	50510	0.6	45	12395	12878	13223	0.4	3.76	10072	10471	0.4
90033	LOS ANGELES	037	49047	51922	53401	0.6	45	12300	12808	13135	0.4	3.88	9604	10019	0.5
90034	LOS ANGELES	037	57592	60004	61468	0.4	30	25532	26033	26522	0.2	2.29	12002	12234	0.2
90035	LOS ANGELES	037	28296	29058	29569	0.3	23	13125	13166	13314	0.0	2.16	6331	6358	0.0
90036	LOS ANGELES	037	32520	36624	38553	1.3	70	17104	18687	19540	1.0	1.94	6077	6724	1.1
90037	LOS ANGELES	037	55588	59786	61962	0.8	54	14653	15352	15812	0.5	3.87	11044	11574	0.5
90038	LOS ANGELES	037	32382	34337	35452	0.6	45	12143	12631	12974	0.4	2.70	6569	6842	0.4
90039	LOS ANGELES	037	29401	30472	31146	0.4	30	11428	11592	11780	0.2	2.60	6334	6428	0.2
90040	LOS ANGELES	037	12861	13246	13483	0.3	23	3317	3364	3415	0.2	3.88	2721	2757	0.1
90041	LOS ANGELES	037	28846	30230	31025	0.5	39	9699	9952	10162	0.3	2.87	6574	6755	0.3
90042	LOS ANGELES	037	63487	66595	68425	0.5	39	19173	19743	20202	0.3	3.34	13749	14132	0.3
90043	LOS ANGELES	037	45208	47598	48955	0.6	45	15882	16347	16715	0.3	2.89	10944	11272	0.3
90044	LOS ANGELES	037	88637	94889	98324	0.7	50	24844	25950	26717	0.5	3.64	18939	19799	0.5
90045	LOS ANGELES	037	41052	42511	43679	0.4	30	16475	16833	17263	0.2	2.38	9744	9901	0.2
90046	LOS ANGELES	037	50141	52672	54290	0.5	39	28760	29579	30330	0.3	1.76	8994	9252	0.3
90047	LOS ANGELES	037	47837	50405	51833	0.6	45	15905	16391	16757	0.3	3.07	11566	11925	0.3
90048	LOS ANGELES	037	22111	23490	24249	0.7	50	12252	12798	13167	0.5	1.78	4090	4248	0.4
90049	LOS ANGELES	037	33893	35245	36061	0.4	30	16547	16858	17153	0.2	2.03	7772	7902	0.2
90056	LOS ANGELES	037	8188	8688	8950	0.6	45	3397	3535	3624	0.4	2.46	2322	2415	0.4
90057	LOS ANGELES	037	43460	47468	49478	1.0	62	14579	15557	16147	0.7	2.97	8962	9577	0.7
90058	LOS ANGELES	037	3525	3570	3614	0.1	13	952	949	959	0.0	3.70	748	737	-0.2
90059	LOS ANGELES	037	37565	42135	44282	1.2	68	9237	10030	10468	0.9	4.15	7526	8196	0.9
90061	LOS ANGELES	037	23477	27418	29246	1.7	78	5911	6705	7105	1.4	4.04	4744	5389	1.4
90062	LOS ANGELES	037	28328	29845	30666	0.6	45	8441	8654	8836	0.3	3.41	6018	6170	0.3
90063	LOS ANGELES	037	56328	59063	60581	0.5	39	13220	13565	13855	0.3	4.34	11136	11426	0.3
90064	LOS ANGELES	037	23825	24770	25355	0.4	30	10488	10694	10887	0.2	2.28	5665	5772	0.2
90065	LOS ANGELES	037	47195	48708	49735	0.3	23	14209	14367	14587	0.1	3.37	10362	10479	0.1
90066	LOS ANGELES	037	54762	57559	59115	0.5	39	23250	23991	24494	0.3	2.39	12584	13024	0.4
90067	LOS ANGELES	037	2555	2627	2686	0.3	23	1584	1594	1616	0.1	1.63	642	648	0.1
90068	LOS ANGELES	037	22446	24021	24905	0.7	50	12852	13439	13831	0.5	1.78	3971	4177	0.5
90069	WEST HOLLYWOOD	037	20490	21240	21727	0.4	30	13676	13876	14098	0.2	1.53	2709	2745	0.1
90071	LOS ANGELES	037	7	7	9	0.0	9	1	1	1	0.0	7.00	0	0	0.0
90077	LOS ANGELES	037	9073	9476	9728	0.5	39	3560	3641	3715	0.2	2.56	2470	2527	0.2
90089	LOS ANGELES	037	242	659	660	11.4	99	138	132	131	-0.5	1.79	0	0	0.0
90094	LOS ANGELES	037	0	7088	7392	0.0	9	0	2441	2531	0.0	2.90	0	1409	0.0
90095	LOS ANGELES	037	66	75	79	1.4	72	1	1	1	0.0	3.00	0	0	0.0
90201	BELL	037	104530	109392	111945	0.5	39	23678	24179	24636	0.2	4.49	20825	21271	0.2
90210	BEVERLY HILLS	037	23068	24205	24880	0.5	39	9300	9554	9768	0.3	2.53	6036	6192	0.3
90211	BEVERLY HILLS	037	8082	8464	8693	0.5	39	3634	3717	3792	0.2	2.28	1986	2032	0.2
90212	BEVERLY HILLS	037	11316	11701	11934	0.4	30	5698	5762	5837	0.1	2.03	2658	2691	0.1
90220	COMPTON	037	47167	50834	52974	0.8	54	12237	12856	13305	0.5	3.93	9870	10390	0.6
90221	COMPTON	037	51599	55769	57669	0.8	54	11206	11740	12092	0.5	4.72	9737	10210	0.5
90222	COMPTON	037	29861	32574	33910	0.9	58	7136	7600	7875	0.7	4.27	5886	6270	0.7
90230	CULVER CITY	037	32010	33267	34001	0.4	30	12701	12952	13186	0.2	2.55	7634	7784	0.2
90232	CULVER CITY	037	16736	17468	17909	0.5	39	7144	7296	7438	0.2	2.37	3982	4064	0.2
90240	DOWNEY	037	23157	24524	25127	0.6	45	7355	7482	7604	0.2	3.27	5791	5892	0.2
90241	DOWNEY	037	40446	43098	44196	0.7	50	13736	13985	14236	0.2	3.05	10055	10246	0.2
90242	DOWNEY	037	43612	46061	47038	0.6	45	12874	13010	13201	0.1	3.45	10134	10246	0.1
90245	EL SEGUNDO	037	16033	16599	16947	0.4	30	7060	7150	7256	0.1	2.32	3908	3960	0.1
90247	GARDENA	037	47146	49420	50701	0.5	39	15868	16200	16516	0.2	3.01	10881	11118	0.2
90248	GARDENA	037	9446	10452	10940	1.1	64	3142	3417	3564	0.9	3.06	2351	2546	0.9
90249	GARDENA	037	26216	28581	29797	0.9	58	8825	9376	9704	0.7	3.03	6482	6891	0.7
90250	HAWTHORNE	037	93331	99871	102827	0.7	50	31406	32352	33095	0.3	3.07	22023	22709	0.3
90254	HERMOSA BEACH	037	18689	19693	20234	0.6	45	9538	9836	10045	0.3	1.99	3582	3675	0.3
90255	HUNTINGTON PARK	037	79365	83988	86339	0.6	45	18894	19524	19981	0.4	4.29	16224	16767	0.4
90260	LAWNDALE	037	33641	35559	36515	0.6	45	10174	10375	10575	0.2	3.41	7511	7659	0.2
90262	LYNWOOD	037	68127	72743	74689	0.7	50	14012	14473	14817	0.4	4.87	12598	13013	0.4
90263	MALIBU	037	1525	1595	1625	0.5	39	3	3	3	0.0	2.67	2	2	0.0
90265	MALIBU	037	18015	19838	20740	1.0	62	7246	7809	8131	0.8	2.37	4623	5008	0.9
90266	MANHATTAN BEACH	037	33874	34946	35673	0.3	23	14487	14612	14815	0.1	2.39	8397	8493	0.1
90270	MAYWOOD	037	27725	28396	28824	0.3	23	6406	6423	6490	0.0	4.41	5641	5659	0.0
90272	PACIFIC PALISADES	037	23095	23976	24505	0.4	30	9387	9533	9682	0.2	2.51	6519	6627	0.2
90274	PALOS VERDES PENINSU	037	25027	26234	26973	0.5	39	9297	9545	9751	0.3	2.74	7612	7823	0.3
90275	RANCHO PALOS VERDES	037	41239	42796	43814	0.4	30	15402	15655	15938	0.2	2.70	12254	12459	0.2
90277	REDONDO BEACH	037	33980	35652	36652	0.5	39	16950	17418	17796	0.3	2.04	7908	8139	0.3
90278	REDONDO BEACH	037	37416	39161	40309	0.5	39	15491	15886	16252	0.3	2.46	9431	9681	0.3
	CALIFORNIA					1.2					1.0	2.93			1.1
	UNITED STATES					1.0					1.1	2.59			0.9

ZIP CODE #	POST OFFICE NAME	RACE (%) White 2000	White 2009	Black 2000	Black 2009	Asian/Pacific 2000	Asian/Pacific 2009	% Hispanic Origin 2000	% Hispanic Origin 2009	2009 AGE DISTRIBUTION (%) 0-4	5-9	10-14	15-19	20-24	25-44	45-64	65-84	85+	18+	MEDIAN AGE 2009	% 2009 Males	% 2009 Females
90001	LOS ANGELES	24.6	24.8	14.4	11.5	0.2	0.2	84.5	87.8	11.9	11.0	9.2	9.9	9.4	28.7	14.9	4.3	0.6	61.8	24.2	50.5	49.5
90002	LOS ANGELES	16.7	18.0	35.9	28.8	0.2	0.2	63.1	70.5	11.5	10.9	9.4	10.5	10.2	27.0	15.4	4.5	0.7	61.8	23.8	48.9	51.1
90003	LOS ANGELES	19.5	20.7	31.8	25.5	0.5	0.4	66.7	73.5	11.8	10.9	9.1	9.7	9.8	28.3	15.5	4.3	0.6	62.4	24.3	49.6	50.4
90004	LOS ANGELES	34.1	31.5	3.4	2.9	23.8	23.6	55.6	60.1	8.1	7.4	6.6	7.4	8.6	32.9	21.6	6.5	0.9	73.5	31.7	50.9	49.1
90005	LOS ANGELES	27.8	26.5	4.8	3.9	26.4	25.9	61.1	65.0	8.6	7.9	6.7	7.6	8.3	34.7	19.4	6.0	0.9	72.5	30.9	52.5	47.5
90006	LOS ANGELES	26.6	26.1	4.0	3.1	14.4	13.3	78.0	81.4	9.4	8.5	7.0	8.4	9.5	32.4	18.5	5.7	0.7	70.3	28.8	51.6	48.4
90007	LOS ANGELES	31.6	28.3	13.1	10.5	10.8	12.1	58.2	63.9	7.0	6.4	5.4	12.9	19.6	29.4	14.4	4.3	0.7	77.2	24.7	53.0	47.0
90008	LOS ANGELES	6.9	7.5	78.1	74.0	2.1	2.5	15.7	19.6	7.2	7.2	6.6	6.7	6.4	25.4	25.5	12.6	2.4	74.9	38.0	43.9	56.1
90010	LOS ANGELES	32.5	27.3	8.1	7.3	44.0	47.1	21.8	26.2	5.1	4.5	4.2	4.0	5.5	34.1	24.4	15.8	2.4	84.0	39.9	50.3	49.7
90011	LOS ANGELES	28.0	28.4	13.4	10.3	0.5	0.5	85.3	89.0	12.2	11.2	9.3	9.9	9.3	30.4	14.0	3.4	0.5	61.5	24.0	51.3	48.7
90012	LOS ANGELES	20.4	19.2	16.3	14.0	39.1	36.8	30.1	38.4	4.0	4.0	3.4	5.6	10.0	40.9	19.4	10.6	2.2	86.4	35.3	60.2	39.8
90013	LOS ANGELES	27.0	23.6	37.1	32.1	14.3	18.8	27.3	33.5	2.8	3.0	2.3	2.6	5.1	32.2	33.9	15.5	2.5	90.5	46.0	64.1	35.9
90014	LOS ANGELES	27.2	22.7	33.2	31.0	20.7	22.5	22.9	29.0	2.1	1.9	1.3	1.7	2.8	23.2	38.6	25.2	3.1	93.8	53.0	65.2	34.8
90015	LOS ANGELES	29.9	28.4	4.6	4.2	10.1	13.8	80.3	77.6	8.8	7.4	5.7	8.0	11.4	34.5	16.8	6.5	1.0	73.7	28.5	52.7	47.3
90016	LOS ANGELES	18.1	19.1	47.7	41.8	3.7	4.3	44.1	50.3	8.4	8.0	7.3	8.0	7.9	27.9	22.0	8.9	1.5	71.4	31.8	47.3	52.7
90017	LOS ANGELES	30.2	28.7	4.2	4.7	5.2	6.5	86.2	85.2	10.6	8.9	6.7	7.7	9.9	33.8	15.1	6.2	1.0	69.8	27.7	54.6	45.4
90018	LOS ANGELES	15.9	16.9	44.2	37.5	3.6	3.7	48.2	55.8	8.3	8.3	7.7	8.1	8.1	28.2	20.9	8.4	1.9	70.9	31.2	47.9	52.1
90019	LOS ANGELES	23.5	22.5	31.9	28.1	12.6	13.0	44.1	50.1	7.7	6.9	6.2	7.2	8.9	31.3	22.5	7.9	1.5	75.0	32.5	49.0	51.0
90020	LOS ANGELES	25.8	24.2	7.0	5.8	43.3	43.4	37.7	42.0	7.6	7.1	6.2	6.8	7.4	35.6	22.3	6.3	0.7	75.5	33.8	50.5	49.5
90021	LOS ANGELES	29.9	27.3	25.3	22.6	7.5	7.7	51.1	57.5	4.6	4.2	3.7	4.3	6.5	36.7	32.8	6.9	0.4	85.5	39.6	65.5	34.5
90022	LOS ANGELES	41.4	40.5	0.4	0.4	0.8	0.7	96.3	97.5	10.2	9.8	8.4	9.3	9.0	29.5	16.7	6.2	1.0	66.1	27.0	50.4	49.6
90023	LOS ANGELES	39.3	38.4	0.4	0.4	0.9	0.8	96.9	97.9	10.8	9.9	8.4	9.4	9.4	30.3	15.6	5.3	0.9	65.4	26.2	51.0	49.0
90024	LOS ANGELES	64.6	55.2	2.1	2.2	24.3	30.0	7.3	10.6	2.3	1.8	1.4	14.5	27.6	25.6	15.3	9.0	2.6	93.5	26.2	47.6	52.4
90025	LOS ANGELES	66.2	57.6	2.6	2.7	17.2	21.0	16.2	21.6	3.9	2.9	2.4	2.9	9.6	45.0	21.8	9.3	2.1	89.2	35.0	50.1	49.9
90026	LOS ANGELES	35.9	32.8	2.6	2.2	18.2	17.6	63.8	69.8	8.2	7.1	6.2	7.8	9.3	32.8	20.8	6.8	1.0	74.0	31.1	51.2	48.8
90027	LOS ANGELES	61.8	52.7	3.7	3.7	12.6	15.1	25.1	33.2	4.9	4.5	4.3	5.2	7.6	35.6	25.6	10.4	2.0	83.3	37.7	50.3	49.7
90028	LOS ANGELES	54.9	46.7	7.6	7.1	7.7	8.8	39.4	49.6	5.9	5.0	4.2	6.0	9.9	39.8	20.1	7.9	1.2	81.6	33.0	54.3	45.7
90029	LOS ANGELES	38.2	33.8	2.8	2.3	15.2	15.0	61.0	67.9	8.1	7.3	6.4	7.6	9.3	32.5	20.6	6.9	1.4	73.9	31.0	51.5	48.5
90031	LOS ANGELES	29.4	28.9	1.1	0.9	24.9	23.1	69.1	72.7	9.4	8.8	7.7	8.6	8.5	28.8	19.3	7.5	1.4	69.1	29.1	49.7	50.3
90032	LOS ANGELES	35.7	34.8	2.1	1.7	11.9	11.0	80.6	84.0	9.0	8.6	7.8	8.7	8.6	29.7	19.0	7.6	1.1	69.6	29.4	49.5	50.5
90033	LOS ANGELES	33.6	32.6	1.6	1.3	3.7	3.4	92.2	93.8	10.4	9.8	8.4	9.9	9.1	28.7	16.4	5.8	1.3	65.1	26.3	50.9	49.1
90034	LOS ANGELES	46.4	40.0	15.0	13.6	16.2	18.8	28.8	35.9	6.4	5.1	4.5	5.3	10.6	40.4	20.6	6.0	1.1	81.2	32.2	50.0	50.0
90035	LOS ANGELES	70.9	64.3	12.8	13.0	5.6	7.4	9.4	13.7	5.8	5.0	4.8	4.6	6.0	34.0	25.2	10.9	3.6	81.5	38.6	47.8	52.2
90036	LOS ANGELES	69.4	61.2	7.7	8.0	16.6	21.8	6.7	9.8	4.8	4.0	3.7	3.7	7.4	42.6	21.9	9.1	2.9	85.3	35.4	48.9	51.1
90037	LOS ANGELES	20.8	21.8	30.0	24.1	0.6	0.5	67.7	74.3	11.1	9.9	8.4	9.4	9.9	29.3	16.4	4.9	0.7	65.1	25.7	50.1	49.9
90038	LOS ANGELES	42.4	37.4	4.5	3.8	8.2	8.3	62.1	69.7	7.9	7.1	6.2	7.3	9.4	35.9	19.8	5.6	0.9	74.7	31.1	53.2	46.8
90039	LOS ANGELES	49.6	43.5	2.5	2.4	19.2	20.5	45.0	52.6	6.3	5.8	5.4	6.2	7.3	31.4	26.0	9.8	1.8	78.9	37.4	50.9	49.1
90040	LOS ANGELES	44.3	43.0	1.0	0.9	1.2	1.1	93.5	95.6	9.4	9.0	8.2	9.9	8.4	28.5	18.0	7.5	1.1	67.2	28.1	49.8	50.2
90041	LOS ANGELES	48.3	42.2	2.2	2.0	25.4	27.0	39.3	47.3	6.3	6.1	6.0	8.4	8.4	27.2	25.2	10.4	2.2	77.5	36.0	48.4	51.6
90042	LOS ANGELES	40.8	37.9	3.1	2.6	12.5	12.3	69.9	75.4	9.1	8.3	7.5	8.3	8.7	30.2	20.4	6.6	1.0	70.2	29.6	49.9	50.1
90043	LOS ANGELES	8.4	9.1	72.4	67.4	0.8	0.9	22.6	27.8	7.5	7.5	7.5	8.1	6.9	25.2	24.9	10.8	1.6	72.5	35.3	46.1	53.9
90044	LOS ANGELES	17.1	18.7	45.3	38.1	0.6	0.6	52.6	60.3	11.1	9.8	8.5	9.8	10.2	27.0	17.0	5.8	0.8	64.8	25.4	48.5	51.5
90045	LOS ANGELES	61.5	56.0	16.8	15.7	9.8	12.5	17.1	22.9	5.9	5.8	5.9	8.3	8.2	28.0	26.4	9.4	2.0	79.3	36.9	48.2	51.8
90046	LOS ANGELES	85.5	79.6	3.6	4.2	4.3	6.1	8.1	12.9	2.8	2.4	2.5	2.7	7.0	40.6	26.4	12.6	3.0	90.7	40.3	52.7	47.3
90047	LOS ANGELES	8.5	9.7	73.0	67.8	0.6	0.7	24.3	29.8	7.8	8.2	8.0	8.7	7.2	24.4	23.6	10.8	1.4	70.7	33.5	45.4	54.6
90048	LOS ANGELES	85.8	79.8	2.4	2.8	5.5	7.8	6.1	9.9	3.5	2.6	2.2	2.2	6.3	40.0	24.4	13.0	5.8	90.4	40.6	47.6	52.4
90049	LOS ANGELES	86.9	80.9	1.8	2.2	6.8	9.8	4.7	7.7	4.1	4.1	4.8	4.2	6.2	32.0	27.7	14.1	2.9	84.6	41.2	46.6	53.4
90056	LOS ANGELES	18.8	15.2	71.7	72.5	3.2	3.9	3.9	5.3	5.4	5.7	6.3	5.7	4.0	21.8	31.9	16.4	2.9	79.2	45.7	45.7	54.3
90057	LOS ANGELES	28.7	27.6	5.5	4.4	18.4	17.7	69.5	73.6	9.3	8.5	6.7	7.5	8.9	34.1	17.5	6.3	1.2	71.5	29.5	53.4	46.6
90058	LOS ANGELES	29.2	29.3	12.6	9.7	6.2	5.7	77.7	82.2	10.4	12.3	11.3	10.1	7.1	28.1	16.5	3.6	0.5	59.5	24.1	49.6	50.4
90059	LOS ANGELES	13.5	15.0	45.9	38.5	0.4	0.4	52.3	60.1	11.6	11.0	9.3	10.1	9.8	26.1	16.0	5.2	0.9	62.0	24.1	47.6	52.4
90061	LOS ANGELES	14.1	15.5	45.9	38.5	0.4	0.4	52.6	60.4	10.3	10.0	9.0	9.5	9.2	26.8	17.4	6.9	1.0	64.9	26.2	48.3	51.7
90062	LOS ANGELES	14.4	16.1	51.9	44.3	1.7	1.7	44.1	52.1	8.9	8.8	8.2	8.5	8.0	27.0	21.1	8.0	1.4	68.9	30.2	46.9	53.1
90063	LOS ANGELES	36.7	36.1	0.5	0.4	1.3	1.1	96.8	97.7	10.4	9.8	8.4	9.2	9.0	29.7	16.4	6.2	1.0	65.9	26.8	50.7	49.3
90064	LOS ANGELES	71.9	64.3	2.6	2.6	14.4	18.0	15.7	21.6	5.3	5.1	5.3	4.6	5.1	31.2	27.8	12.1	3.3	81.4	40.8	48.9	51.1
90065	LOS ANGELES	41.5	38.4	2.0	1.7	15.3	15.3	66.3	71.7	8.5	7.8	7.1	8.0	8.1	29.4	21.8	8.2	1.1	71.8	31.8	50.1	49.9
90066	LOS ANGELES	61.4	53.8	4.0	3.8	13.5	16.0	32.1	40.7	6.1	5.3	5.0	5.0	6.4	34.9	25.7	9.7	1.9	80.6	37.3	49.9	50.1
90067	LOS ANGELES	85.6	79.3	2.3	2.7	8.5	12.3	4.0	6.6	2.3	1.5	1.3	1.3	2.4	20.1	31.3	30.7	9.2	94.1	59.4	45.4	54.6
90068	LOS ANGELES	81.4	74.5	4.7	5.3	5.4	7.5	9.2	14.3	3.4	2.7	2.7	2.6	6.4	40.0	30.6	9.9	1.7	89.8	41.0	54.6	45.4
90069	WEST HOLLYWOOD	87.6	82.2	3.0	3.6	3.9	5.5	7.4	12.0	1.8	1.5	1.4	1.2	4.8	44.8	30.2	11.7	2.7	94.7	42.5	58.3	41.7
90071	LOS ANGELES	28.6	28.6	14.3	14.3	57.1	42.9	14.3	28.6	0.0	0.0	0.0	0.0	0.0	100.0	0.0	0.0	0.0	100.0	29.4	57.1	42.9
90077	LOS ANGELES	86.9	80.9	1.7	2.0	6.8	9.9	4.1	6.8	5.1	6.3	7.9	6.0	3.0	20.2	33.1	15.6	2.8	76.9	45.8	48.4	51.6
90089	LOS ANGELES	47.9	39.2	5.0	14.0	28.1	14.7	14.5	37.6	0.9	0.9	0.9	34.3	16.4	34.4	8.8	2.7	0.6	95.4	24.0	67.5	32.5
90094	LOS ANGELES	0.0	50.2	0.0	10.6	0.0	15.8	0.0	35.3	5.7	5.4	5.4	5.2	4.7	27.1	32.3	12.1	2.1	80.4	42.8	48.5	51.5
90095	LOS ANGELES	62.1	52.0	1.5	1.3	21.2	26.7	16.7	24.0	0.0	0.0	2.7	2.7	18.7	30.7	10.7	14.7	20.0	97.3	40.6	40.0	60.0
90201	BELL	47.1	45.7	1.1	1.0	0.9	0.8	92.7	95.2	11.7	10.7	9.0	9.8	9.4	29.9	15.3	3.8	0.5	62.8	24.7	50.6	49.4
90210	BEVERLY HILLS	88.3	82.8	1.4	1.6	5.0	7.2	4.8	8.0	4.7	5.4	6.4	5.6	3.3	21.9	32.0	17.0	3.6	79.7	46.5	47.2	52.8
90211	BEVERLY HILLS	83.2	76.1	1.8	2.1	9.1	12.8	4.3	6.9	3.9	4.6	5.9	6.5	5.4	29.0	29.8	11.7	3.0	81.3	41.4	47.0	53.0
90212	BEVERLY HILLS	84.7	78.1	2.2	2.6	7.7	11.1	4.0	6.5	3.2	4.0	5.4	6.5	4.4	30.2	30.3	12.8	3.2	82.9	42.5	44.5	55.5
90220	COMPTON	15.7	16.6	46.3	39.7	1.9	1.9	47.7	55.1	9.9	9.8	9.1	9.8	8.5	26.2	18.4	7.4	0.8	65.0	26.9	48.5	51.5
90221	COMPTON	20.5	21.5	29.9	24.0	1.1	0.9	67.3	74.0	11.7	10.7	9.1	10.0	9.8	28.0	15.9	4.4	0.4	62.5	24.4	49.9	50.1
90222	COMPTON	18.7	20.0	37.6	31.7	0.4	0.4	61.3	67.5	10.9	10.1	8.9	9.8	9.4	26.6	16.9	6.3	1.1	64.1	25.6	49.5	50.5
90230	CULVER CITY	52.3	46.1	12.9	12.8	12.6	14.7	33.1	39.1	5.8	5.9	6.1	6.4	6.3	28.2	27.8	11.4	2.0	78.2	39.2	48.2	51.8
90232	CULVER CITY	58.5	50.7	7.8	7.6	13.8	16.1	28.3	36.9	5.6	5.2	5.5	5.9	7.6	30.4	28.6	9.3	1.8	80.1	38.2	47.8	52.2
90240	DOWNEY	59.4	53.1	1.8	1.6	10.2	10.7	52.4	63.2	7.1	7.1	7.0	7.5	6.3	27.8	24.3	10.5	2.3	74.1	36.3	48.9	51.1
90241	DOWNEY	55.8	49.7	2.8	2.4	7.2	7.5	57.5	68.0	8.2	7.6	7.1	7.4	7.5	29.7	21.7	8.7	2.1	72.5	32.9	48.0	52.0
90242	DOWNEY	48.2	42.9	5.7	4.8	7.5	7.7	61.0	70.3	8.8	8.3	7.8	9.2	8.2	29.4	20.2	6.9	1.2	69.2	29.7	49.9	50.1
90245	EL SEGUNDO	83.6	76.8	1.2	1.3	6.7	9.2	11.0	17.1	5.8	5.7	5.7	5.6	6.4	31.0	30.1	8.2	1.4	79.3	39.0	49.7	50.3
90247	GARDENA	24.4	22.9	19.2	16.1	27.5	27.9	42.0	48.0	8.2	7.6	7.0	7.6	7.6	29.1	21.8	9.6	1.5	72.7	32.9	49.5	50.5
90248	GARDENA	29.7	26.7	17.8	14.8	31.3	34.1	33.5	38.0	7.0	6.9	6.8	6.6	5.3	26.1	24.3	15.4	1.7	75.5	38.7	49.4	50.6
90249	GARDENA	27.6	24.9	35.1	32.3	16.8	18.4	29.1	34.9	7.7	7.6	7.1	7.7	6.9	27.7	24.4	9.7	1.3	73.0	34.5	49.0	51.0
90250	HAWTHORNE	32.1	30.6	30.1	26.1	8.0	8.3	44.3	52.4	9.7	8.6	7.6	8.3	9.4	30.2	19.7	5.8	0.8	69.2	28.7	48.9	51.1
90254	HERMOSA BEACH	89.5	84.4	0.8	1.0	4.6	6.7	6.8	11.3	4.1	3.0	2.8	2.6	5.6	49.9	24.7	6.2	1.0	88.3	35.0	53.1	46.9
90255	HUNTINGTON PARK	42.2	41.0	0.7	0.6	0.8	0.8	95.6	97.1	10.7	10.0	8.5	9.3	9.2	30.8	16.3	4.7	0.6	65.3	26.3	50.6	49.4
90260	LAWNDALE	43.8	39.1	11.5	9.8	11.5	12.0	50.1	59.1	9.0	8.6	7.9	8.3	7.9	31.0	20.8	5.8	0.7	69.4	30.1	50.6	49.4
90262	LYNWOOD	33.5	33.6	13.7	10.6	1.2	1.0	82.1	86.6	11.0	10.0	8.6	10.1	10.1	29.7	16.0	3.9	0.5	64.5	25.1	51.4	48.6
90263	MALIBU	84.6	78.0	3.4	4.0	5.2	7.5	7.3	11.9	2.7	2.9	2.4	27.0	28.3	13.2	18.9	4.2	0.5	90.7	22.7	44.8	55.2
90265	MALIBU	89.8	84.8	1.6	1.9	3.3	4.8	6.4	10.8	4.4	4.8	5.5	8.4	6.2	22.0	34.3	12.7	1.8	81.0	44.1	49.4	50.6
90266	MANHATTAN BEACH	89.0	83.9	0.6	0.7	6.2	8.9	5.2	8.5	5.9	6.3	7.1	5.6	3.9	29.4	31.0	9.5	1.4	77.0	40.3	50.4	49.6
90270	MAYWOOD	42.9	41.8	0.4	0.3	0.5	0.4	96.3	97.7	11.5	10.9	8.8	9.3	9.0	30.9	15.2	3.9	0.5	63.3	25.3	50.6	49.4
90272	PACIFIC PALISADES	91.3	86.9	0.8	0.9	4.7	7.0	3.6	6.2	5.6	6.8	8.6	6.9	3.0	17.6	34.2	14.6	2.7	74.2	45.8	48.5	51.5
90274	PALOS VERDES PENINSU	76.8	68.0	1.2	1.3	18.1	25.0	3.8	5.9	4.8	5.9	7.5	7.0	3.2	15.9	34.3	18.7	2.9	77.2	48.3	48.3	51.7
90275	RANCHO PALOS VERDES	66.9	57.5	2.3	2.4	25.9	33.2	6.0	8.9	4.8	5.6	6.7	6.5	4.0	18.2	32.8	18.7	2.7	78.6	47.4	48.1	51.9
90277	REDONDO BEACH	83.8	77.2	1.8	2.1	7.7	10.6	9.2	14.4	4.3	4.0	4.3	4.0	4.8	34.7	31.7	10.4	1.8	84.9	41.6	50.2	49.8
90278	REDONDO BEACH	75.1	67.0	2.9	3.1	11.1	14.3	16.0	23.5	6.2	5.5	5.4	5.4	5.9	32.7	29.7	7.9	1.2	79.5	38.8	50.0	50.0
	CALIFORNIA	59.5	54.5	6.7	6.2	11.3	12.5	32.4	38.3	7.5	7.1	6.9	7.5	7.4	28.5	24.2	9.3	1.6	74.1	34.3	49.9	50.1
	UNITED STATES	75.1	72.0	12.3	12.7	3.8	4.6	12.5	15.7	6.8	6.7	6.6	7.1	6.9	27.0	26.0	10.9	1.9	75.7	36.9	49.2	50.8

ZIP CODE #	POST OFFICE NAME	2009 Per Capita Income	2009 HH Income Base	2009 HOUSEHOLD INCOME DISTRIBUTION (%) Less than $25,000	$25,000 to $49,999	$50,000 to $99,999	$100,000 to $149,999	$150,000 or More	MEDIAN HOUSEHOLD INCOME 2009	2014	2009 National Centile	2009 State Centile	2009 Home Value Base	2009 HOME VALUE DISTRIBUTION (%) Less than $50,000	$50,000 to $89,999	$90,000 to $174,999	$175,000 to $399,999	$400,000 or More	2009 Median Home Value
90001	LOS ANGELES	8970	13006	40.9	32.5	22.4	2.9	1.3	30688	32456	9	7	4725	1.2	0.8	9.8	84.8	3.4	244686
90002	LOS ANGELES	9562	11699	43.7	28.8	22.5	3.7	1.3	29296	31255	7	6	4927	1.1	1.0	9.8	85.8	2.4	232097
90003	LOS ANGELES	9277	15752	44.9	30.3	20.4	2.8	1.5	28129	29982	6	5	5556	1.6	0.7	9.2	84.5	3.9	238398
90004	LOS ANGELES	18465	23586	36.2	31.6	21.9	4.6	5.6	34209	36663	16	12	4301	1.2	1.7	1.9	20.6	74.7	644365
90005	LOS ANGELES	13459	14902	45.3	31.9	17.6	2.6	2.5	27323	28494	5	4	1262	2.7	1.8	1.6	26.9	67.0	553697
90006	LOS ANGELES	10599	18352	49.3	31.3	15.4	2.8	1.2	25320	26108	3	3	1636	3.4	1.0	2.7	59.1	33.8	334406
90007	LOS ANGELES	11789	13122	53.4	27.1	15.7	2.6	1.2	21981	23267	2	2	1611	2.0	0.7	4.9	65.5	26.8	312529
90008	LOS ANGELES	23854	13526	35.1	25.5	26.1	7.6	5.7	37535	41068	25	18	4203	0.7	0.2	3.5	38.2	57.5	440269
90010	LOS ANGELES	28606	2354	45.0	26.6	18.3	3.5	6.5	28497	30355	6	5	284	0.4	0.4	14.4	19.4	65.5	769231
90011	LOS ANGELES	8730	22616	41.0	33.6	20.5	3.2	1.7	29971	31505	8	6	6175	1.7	0.8	8.9	79.0	9.6	249408
90012	LOS ANGELES	19535	10552	49.0	23.9	18.3	5.2	3.7	25695	27317	4	3	1304	5.3	0.7	10.5	56.1	27.4	275439
90013	LOS ANGELES	17621	3889	76.8	13.2	6.7	2.1	1.3	10870	11155	0	1	135	6.7	0.0	5.2	70.4	17.8	291129
90014	LOS ANGELES	16820	2947	83.5	10.2	4.8	0.7	0.8	9356	9646	0	1	41	53.7	0.0	4.9	41.5	0.0	38500
90015	LOS ANGELES	14724	7395	52.8	26.3	13.9	3.2	3.8	22472	24223	2	2	818	1.3	0.7	23.6	36.3	38.0	308411
90016	LOS ANGELES	17409	16633	31.7	29.5	29.6	6.1	3.1	39042	42589	30	20	6634	0.4	0.2	7.1	71.6	20.7	280124
90017	LOS ANGELES	9328	9496	63.7	27.1	7.5	0.8	1.0	17390	17791	1	2	268	1.1	0.0	6.7	26.9	65.3	478846
90018	LOS ANGELES	13718	16668	41.3	29.5	23.4	4.1	1.8	31373	33807	10	8	5323	0.4	0.1	3.0	75.0	21.4	292902
90019	LOS ANGELES	19676	25180	31.0	27.8	30.0	6.3	4.8	40535	44350	34	22	6842	0.7	0.5	2.4	30.6	65.8	486067
90020	LOS ANGELES	17562	17360	41.4	32.3	20.3	3.0	2.9	30070	31717	8	6	1467	4.6	2.2	10.2	36.9	46.1	302586
90021	LOS ANGELES	18177	1494	62.7	23.0	9.0	4.4	1.0	16479	16735	1	2	81	0.0	8.6	0.0	24.7	66.7	565972
90022	LOS ANGELES	11218	17230	34.1	32.9	27.4	3.6	1.9	34439	37477	16	13	6262	0.7	0.4	4.9	82.7	11.3	280367
90023	LOS ANGELES	9918	10480	35.5	33.7	25.4	3.5	1.9	33103	35513	13	11	3085	1.0	0.2	6.9	78.3	13.5	274846
90024	LOS ANGELES	46611	18776	28.4	14.9	24.4	12.2	20.1	60666	65547	78	59	6097	0.0	0.1	1.0	13.8	85.1	823805
90025	LOS ANGELES	45345	21450	17.1	20.0	35.8	13.5	13.6	65361	67626	84	66	5024	0.1	0.3	0.4	15.4	83.8	621429
90026	LOS ANGELES	16742	25160	33.2	31.9	25.5	5.9	3.5	35424	38528	19	14	5781	1.2	0.9	3.2	45.4	49.2	396074
90027	LOS ANGELES	29524	23271	29.8	26.8	27.7	8.2	7.5	42758	46281	42	28	4676	0.1	0.4	3.9	20.1	75.3	719119
90028	LOS ANGELES	18634	15270	43.4	30.3	21.6	3.3	1.3	28999	30850	7	5	592	0.7	0.0	8.3	44.6	46.5	376667
90029	LOS ANGELES	12316	13622	43.8	34.4	18.1	2.5	1.2	28155	29695	6	5	1481	2.0	0.4	2.4	38.1	57.1	428630
90031	LOS ANGELES	11820	11167	38.2	32.4	23.3	4.2	1.9	32080	34134	12	9	3424	4.4	0.5	7.1	71.3	16.6	266994
90032	LOS ANGELES	14247	12878	27.8	30.0	32.1	6.9	3.2	42931	46297	42	28	6152	2.3	0.5	6.4	81.1	9.7	263394
90033	LOS ANGELES	9748	12808	45.2	33.3	18.5	1.9	1.2	27501	28728	5	4	2287	0.6	0.2	6.3	77.0	15.9	265550
90034	LOS ANGELES	29131	26033	20.5	29.2	35.5	7.8	7.0	50245	53416	62	43	5051	0.9	0.6	2.6	26.0	69.9	561333
90035	LOS ANGELES	41366	13166	17.7	20.7	33.0	14.5	14.1	65736	68454	84	67	4142	0.0	0.2	0.7	9.1	90.0	763744
90036	LOS ANGELES	45417	18687	16.3	20.5	37.2	12.9	13.1	65805	68139	84	67	3308	0.6	0.2	0.6	5.8	92.7	828503
90037	LOS ANGELES	9313	15352	49.3	29.3	17.4	2.8	1.3	25384	26644	3	3	4147	1.7	1.3	6.7	81.0	9.3	255220
90038	LOS ANGELES	14031	12631	43.7	33.4	18.6	2.5	1.8	28358	29876	6	5	1061	0.2	0.0	2.3	47.9	49.7	398736
90039	LOS ANGELES	29890	11592	17.0	25.0	37.1	11.6	9.4	59587	62200	77	57	5208	0.5	0.1	2.4	39.2	57.8	445506
90040	LOS ANGELES	13561	3364	27.5	29.5	33.8	7.0	2.3	44228	47243	46	31	1585	1.3	0.0	6.9	79.1	12.7	273830
90041	LOS ANGELES	26181	9952	16.6	23.9	36.6	14.2	8.7	61616	64190	80	61	5112	1.5	0.4	2.0	45.9	50.3	401243
90042	LOS ANGELES	17484	19743	25.6	29.1	32.8	8.4	4.1	45924	48561	51	34	8362	1.2	0.4	7.5	74.3	16.6	270415
90043	LOS ANGELES	21536	16347	28.0	27.0	29.3	9.9	5.9	44899	47745	48	32	8541	0.6	0.4	4.0	61.0	34.0	311086
90044	LOS ANGELES	10494	25950	44.4	30.8	20.5	2.9	1.4	28592	30554	6	5	8581	0.8	0.7	9.1	82.5	6.9	248642
90045	LOS ANGELES	39400	16833	12.0	19.5	34.0	17.6	16.9	75770	76601	90	76	8668	0.3	0.6	0.7	10.5	87.9	645741
90046	LOS ANGELES	45579	29579	23.4	24.1	31.9	9.5	11.2	52796	57050	68	47	6607	0.2	0.1	2.9	16.0	80.9	787306
90047	LOS ANGELES	17565	16391	28.8	25.7	36.1	6.7	2.7	44924	48515	48	32	9535	0.4	0.3	3.9	88.4	7.0	270580
90048	LOS ANGELES	50856	12798	16.9	19.5	36.1	13.3	14.2	65326	67435	84	66	3543	0.3	0.1	1.3	8.0	90.3	828135
90049	LOS ANGELES	79371	16858	8.9	10.1	27.7	16.2	37.1	111001	116717	98	94	8596	0.3	0.1	1.3	5.4	92.9	1000001
90056	LOS ANGELES	53134	3535	7.5	12.8	32.2	18.1	29.4	95002	95808	96	89	2438	0.0	0.1	0.0	9.6	90.2	764922
90057	LOS ANGELES	10732	15557	52.4	31.6	13.4	1.9	0.7	23369	24223	2	2	718	6.7	3.1	21.6	54.7	13.9	226163
90058	LOS ANGELES	9528	949	50.7	27.1	17.7	2.7	1.8	24317	24949	3	3	131	0.0	0.0	7.6	77.9	14.5	271875
90059	LOS ANGELES	9713	10030	45.2	27.4	21.6	3.9	1.8	27794	29626	5	4	4312	1.1	0.7	12.9	81.9	3.4	233619
90061	LOS ANGELES	10897	6705	36.8	30.8	26.5	4.0	1.9	33646	36460	15	11	3199	1.2	0.7	7.8	85.7	4.6	242530
90062	LOS ANGELES	14187	8654	36.6	29.5	26.4	4.9	2.6	35308	38964	19	14	3883	1.1	0.9	6.4	85.8	5.8	261628
90063	LOS ANGELES	10971	13565	31.9	32.4	29.3	4.6	1.8	37410	40621	25	17	5195	2.3	0.4	7.3	78.4	11.5	255357
90064	LOS ANGELES	49023	10694	13.3	17.5	32.9	14.0	22.3	76858	78598	90	77	5951	0.4	0.6	0.8	5.9	92.4	796630
90065	LOS ANGELES	18917	14367	22.4	28.6	33.9	9.4	5.8	48888	52197	59	40	7025	0.9	0.7	4.0	58.1	36.2	337216
90066	LOS ANGELES	35530	23991	15.7	24.2	35.7	12.4	12.0	61726	64425	80	61	9403	0.3	0.6	1.2	12.8	85.2	644225
90067	LOS ANGELES	87200	1594	15.4	18.6	19.3	18.8	27.8	91881	98452	95	88	1033	0.0	0.0	0.0	7.0	93.0	857096
90068	LOS ANGELES	65616	13439	15.6	20.0	29.8	12.6	21.9	72150	75325	88	73	5903	0.5	0.1	1.8	11.6	85.9	835695
90069	WEST HOLLYWOOD	69279	13876	15.9	19.3	33.9	12.6	18.3	69085	71344	86	70	5290	0.1	0.0	1.5	28.4	69.9	664021
90071	LOS ANGELES	0	0	0.0	0.0	0.0	0.0	0.0	0	0	0	0	0	0.0	0.0	0.0	0.0	0.0	0
90077	LOS ANGELES	85235	3641	7.1	7.7	18.4	8.7	58.2	199896	203880	100	100	3079	0.2	0.0	0.7	1.1	97.9	1000001
90089	LOS ANGELES	15333	132	93.2	6.8	0.0	0.0	0.0	7952	8086	0	1	0	0.0	0.0	0.0	0.0	0.0	0
90094	LOS ANGELES	153783	2441	0.0	0.0	0.0	0.0	100.0	348129	348520	100	100	1272	0.0	0.0	0.5	35.5	64.1	463028
90095	LOS ANGELES	9578	0	0.0	0.0	0.0	0.0	0.0	0	0	0	0	0	0.0	0.0	0.0	0.0	0.0	0
90201	BELL	10441	24179	29.6	36.1	28.7	3.9	1.6	37338	40420	25	17	6123	9.2	0.9	3.5	63.9	22.5	287001
90210	BEVERLY HILLS	82720	9554	9.1	9.8	21.0	11.2	48.9	145124	157133	100	98	6860	0.1	0.0	0.2	3.5	96.3	1000001
90211	BEVERLY HILLS	51607	3717	13.9	15.7	33.2	14.1	23.1	78942	80689	92	80	1416	0.0	0.3	1.1	2.8	95.8	971393
90212	BEVERLY HILLS	63874	5762	14.1	14.6	28.8	17.1	25.4	84048	87535	94	83	1550	0.0	0.7	1.9	4.5	92.8	1000001
90220	COMPTON	13128	12856	28.9	27.7	35.3	6.2	1.9	43772	46739	45	30	7649	2.3	5.5	11.6	77.7	2.9	232469
90221	COMPTON	10901	11740	29.4	30.0	32.2	5.4	2.9	40648	44405	35	22	6208	1.6	0.3	6.9	89.1	2.1	244442
90222	COMPTON	11854	7600	32.4	30.8	29.0	5.1	2.8	37848	41421	26	18	4039	1.5	0.0	10.0	85.5	3.0	237581
90230	CULVER CITY	32485	12952	15.3	18.6	40.6	14.5	10.9	66009	67966	84	67	7108	0.8	1.1	4.5	34.8	58.9	464585
90232	CULVER CITY	31474	7296	16.1	23.4	41.3	11.3	7.9	60775	63173	78	60	2894	0.0	0.6	1.1	26.8	71.5	548436
90240	DOWNEY	26080	7482	13.3	19.5	41.5	15.8	10.0	70935	72587	87	72	5120	0.6	0.4	0.5	37.0	61.5	442836
90241	DOWNEY	22118	13985	18.7	25.9	38.9	10.3	6.1	54951	58812	71	52	6171	0.7	0.2	2.2	43.3	53.5	413992
90242	DOWNEY	18627	13010	17.9	26.9	40.9	9.8	4.5	54477	58055	70	50	6184	1.6	0.6	2.1	63.7	32.0	345244
90245	EL SEGUNDO	41875	7150	7.0	16.0	41.5	22.8	12.7	78737	79098	91	79	2971	0.0	0.0	1.0	10.8	88.2	677304
90247	GARDENA	17683	16200	26.0	28.7	36.5	6.9	2.0	45093	48481	49	33	6320	7.3	0.8	5.1	65.0	21.8	291967
90248	GARDENA	22505	3417	16.7	27.4	37.9	13.7	4.4	56812	60756	74	54	2364	7.5	2.9	4.5	62.1	23.0	301994
90249	GARDENA	22883	9376	19.3	23.6	38.6	12.8	5.6	59171	62170	76	57	5410	2.2	0.2	2.9	76.5	18.2	324429
90250	HAWTHORNE	17849	32352	25.9	32.3	31.5	6.9	3.4	42988	46181	42	28	9899	0.9	0.1	1.6	64.1	33.3	338737
90254	HERMOSA BEACH	73375	9836	6.4	8.3	30.1	22.6	32.6	110651	113069	98	93	4207	0.5	0.3	0.6	5.4	93.2	871930
90255	HUNTINGTON PARK	11123	19524	29.8	33.9	29.8	4.8	1.7	37685	40624	26	18	6342	0.6	0.3	4.8	79.7	14.6	286390
90260	LAWNDALE	17475	10375	18.7	28.5	41.7	7.8	3.3	52644	56644	67	47	3966	1.0	0.4	4.1	64.6	29.9	325836
90262	LYNWOOD	11134	14473	24.4	32.4	34.9	6.5	1.8	45090	47207	49	33	6833	0.9	0.9	2.7	89.1	6.4	263692
90263	MALIBU	11358	3	0.0	0.0	0.0	0.0	100.0	230236	230236	100	100	2	0.0	0.0	0.0	0.0	100.0	1000000
90265	MALIBU	73006	7809	8.6	9.7	21.5	16.3	43.8	130393	138983	99	97	5661	0.2	0.1	0.9	11.4	87.3	1000001
90266	MANHATTAN BEACH	72712	14612	6.0	7.0	25.7	17.2	44.2	134262	139308	99	97	9281	0.1	0.1	0.6	3.0	96.2	1000001
90270	MAYWOOD	10602	6423	29.7	35.7	29.0	4.2	1.4	37886	40880	26	18	1908	1.2	0.3	0.9	84.7	12.9	277560
90272	PACIFIC PALISADES	80759	9533	5.4	9.0	17.7	17.5	50.4	151577	163873	100	99	7644	0.4	0.4	1.6	5.7	91.8	1000001
90274	PALOS VERDES PENINSU	71438	9545	3.7	8.4	19.3	14.5	54.1	159304	165711	100	99	8256	0.1	0.1	0.9	4.5	94.4	1000001
90275	RANCHO PALOS VERDES	57244	15655	4.8	9.3	29.3	18.4	38.2	119441	124574	98	95	12213	0.2	0.3	1.3	3.6	94.6	925407
90277	REDONDO BEACH	56906	17418	7.7	12.5	37.6	19.0	23.2	87367	88957	94	85	7932	0.3	0.4	1.2	7.9	90.2	779797
90278	REDONDO BEACH	43316	15886	9.3	14.7	34.9	21.7	19.5	85269	85970	94	84	8545	1.8	0.4	0.6	9.4	87.8	608049
	CALIFORNIA	28199		18.5	22.2	33.9	14.0	11.5	61614	64088				3.3	2.6	13.6	41.0	39.5	321752
	UNITED STATES	27277		20.9	24.4	35.3	11.7	7.6	54719	56938				9.3	13.1	31.6	32.6	13.5	162279

ZIP CODE		FINANCIAL SERVICES				THE HOME						ENTERTAINMENT						PERSONAL			
						Home Improvements		Furnishings													
#	POST OFFICE NAME	Auto Loan	Home Loan	Invest-ments	Retire-ment Plans	Home Repair	Lawn & Garden	Comput-ers & Hard-ware-Personal	Major Appli-ances	TV, Radio, Sound Equip-ment	Furni-ture	Dine out/ Carry out	Sports Equip-ment	Fees & Tickets	Toys & Games	Travel	Cable TV	Apparel & Services	Auto Repairs	Health Insur-ance	Pets & Supplies
90001	LOS ANGELES	56	54	44	48	53	39	60	55	53	63	57	45	56	55	58	48	42	59	43	58
90002	LOS ANGELES	57	53	44	48	52	41	61	56	56	63	60	45	57	57	57	52	44	60	46	60
90003	LOS ANGELES	53	50	41	45	49	37	57	52	51	59	55	42	53	52	54	46	40	56	41	54
90004	LOS ANGELES	74	62	61	64	62	54	81	68	78	79	82	56	75	78	74	75	60	78	64	79
90005	LOS ANGELES	55	43	41	44	42	37	59	49	57	58	61	41	53	58	53	54	44	58	45	56
90006	LOS ANGELES	50	38	34	38	37	32	53	44	51	52	55	36	47	52	46	49	40	52	40	50
90007	LOS ANGELES	47	32	29	33	31	28	56	40	50	49	52	35	43	50	42	46	38	48	36	47
90008	LOS ANGELES	65	69	74	72	71	66	80	71	82	73	83	54	81	77	78	85	62	76	75	85
90010	LOS ANGELES	60	56	65	61	59	60	75	64	78	67	79	49	73	71	71	82	57	72	76	78
90011	LOS ANGELES	58	55	45	49	55	41	63	57	56	66	60	47	58	57	60	50	44	61	45	60
90012	LOS ANGELES	55	45	47	48	45	45	64	52	66	59	68	42	59	62	58	67	49	62	59	64
90013	LOS ANGELES	28	21	26	24	22	25	33	27	36	30	35	21	30	31	30	38	25	33	37	35
90014	LOS ANGELES	22	16	20	19	17	20	26	21	28	23	28	16	23	24	23	30	20	26	30	28
90015	LOS ANGELES	60	43	40	45	41	37	63	50	61	61	65	43	54	62	54	58	47	60	47	59
90016	LOS ANGELES	63	66	64	64	66	57	74	67	71	70	74	52	74	70	72	70	55	71	63	75
90017	LOS ANGELES	38	27	24	27	26	23	40	32	38	39	41	27	34	40	34	36	30	39	29	37
90018	LOS ANGELES	52	51	49	51	50	45	62	54	61	58	63	43	60	59	58	61	47	59	53	62
90019	LOS ANGELES	70	68	70	70	69	59	84	71	79	79	83	59	81	78	80	77	61	79	67	83
90020	LOS ANGELES	57	48	47	50	47	44	66	54	66	60	69	43	61	65	59	66	51	62	55	64
90021	LOS ANGELES	37	30	33	33	31	31	43	36	44	40	45	29	40	41	39	45	32	42	42	44
90022	LOS ANGELES	64	61	51	55	61	45	69	63	61	72	66	51	64	63	66	55	48	67	50	66
90023	LOS ANGELES	62	57	47	51	56	42	66	60	59	69	64	49	61	61	63	53	47	65	48	63
90024	LOS ANGELES	147	123	139	138	127	118	183	134	162	160	166	122	160	160	153	153	121	154	128	164
90025	LOS ANGELES	118	105	116	117	106	97	135	109	127	129	131	97	129	127	126	122	95	123	106	134
90026	LOS ANGELES	66	60	60	61	61	51	76	65	71	73	75	55	72	71	72	67	55	72	58	74
90027	LOS ANGELES	84	81	90	87	84	72	100	84	93	95	97	72	97	91	97	89	71	93	79	100
90028	LOS ANGELES	50	40	42	44	40	38	58	46	57	53	59	39	52	55	51	57	43	54	48	56
90029	LOS ANGELES	49	40	39	41	40	35	55	46	54	53	57	38	50	54	50	52	42	53	43	53
90031	LOS ANGELES	62	60	51	54	60	45	66	61	59	69	63	49	62	61	64	53	46	65	49	64
90032	LOS ANGELES	73	77	66	68	77	56	81	76	71	85	75	61	77	72	80	63	55	78	59	80
90033	LOS ANGELES	50	44	37	41	43	34	54	48	50	55	53	39	49	51	50	45	39	53	40	51
90034	LOS ANGELES	92	78	82	85	78	71	103	83	96	99	100	73	95	97	94	91	72	95	80	101
90035	LOS ANGELES	114	120	137	128	126	105	137	119	124	135	128	103	139	122	139	116	94	127	108	140
90036	LOS ANGELES	116	110	123	120	113	99	135	112	125	130	129	99	132	124	130	118	94	124	106	135
90037	LOS ANGELES	51	43	37	40	42	34	54	47	50	55	53	38	49	51	49	46	39	53	40	51
90038	LOS ANGELES	52	40	39	42	39	35	57	46	54	55	58	39	50	55	50	52	42	54	43	54
90039	LOS ANGELES	98	107	114	108	112	90	117	106	106	116	110	87	119	105	119	100	81	111	93	120
90040	LOS ANGELES	72	77	67	68	78	56	80	76	68	85	73	61	77	70	79	61	53	77	58	78
90041	LOS ANGELES	93	113	121	110	119	95	113	107	102	112	105	84	119	101	119	98	78	108	95	118
90042	LOS ANGELES	78	79	74	75	80	63	88	80	79	89	84	65	85	80	86	74	61	84	68	87
90043	LOS ANGELES	76	84	85	84	85	80	87	82	89	83	90	61	92	86	88	92	66	86	85	96
90044	LOS ANGELES	53	47	41	45	46	39	57	50	53	57	56	40	52	54	52	50	41	55	45	56
90045	LOS ANGELES	123	137	156	143	147	123	142	133	131	146	133	107	151	129	150	124	98	136	120	152
90046	LOS ANGELES	106	96	107	107	98	89	123	100	115	117	119	89	118	115	116	110	87	113	97	122
90047	LOS ANGELES	71	74	68	73	72	72	75	72	77	75	78	53	77	75	74	79	55	75	76	86
90048	LOS ANGELES	120	114	130	126	118	105	139	116	130	135	135	102	138	129	135	125	99	127	111	140
90049	LOS ANGELES	203	240	286	258	260	222	237	224	221	245	225	181	268	219	257	212	170	224	204	255
90056	LOS ANGELES	158	208	246	212	230	186	189	192	170	203	170	148	217	164	216	160	127	183	168	212
90057	LOS ANGELES	44	31	28	32	30	27	47	37	45	45	48	31	40	46	40	43	35	45	35	44
90058	LOS ANGELES	49	40	35	39	39	32	52	44	48	52	52	37	46	50	47	44	38	50	38	49
90059	LOS ANGELES	55	51	44	48	50	42	59	53	56	60	58	42	55	56	55	53	42	58	47	59
90061	LOS ANGELES	61	60	51	54	60	48	65	61	59	68	62	48	61	60	63	54	45	64	51	65
90062	LOS ANGELES	60	61	59	61	60	56	69	61	69	64	71	48	69	68	66	71	52	67	63	73
90063	LOS ANGELES	67	64	52	57	64	47	72	66	63	76	68	54	67	65	69	56	50	70	52	69
90064	LOS ANGELES	141	161	187	169	173	142	168	155	151	171	155	129	179	149	178	142	115	158	137	177
90065	LOS ANGELES	84	90	88	85	93	71	96	89	86	99	89	72	95	86	97	78	66	92	74	97
90066	LOS ANGELES	106	115	130	120	121	100	129	114	116	127	120	96	131	113	131	109	88	120	103	132
90067	LOS ANGELES	178	190	224	209	201	174	212	185	198	209	204	158	223	196	217	190	153	194	172	217
90068	LOS ANGELES	151	154	177	168	162	141	175	152	163	173	167	130	179	161	175	155	123	162	142	180
90069	WEST HOLLYWOOD	142	127	141	142	129	120	160	130	152	153	157	115	156	153	150	147	114	146	129	160
90071	LOS ANGELES	0	0	0	0	0	0	0	0	0	0	0	0	0	0	0	0	0	0	0	0
90077	LOS ANGELES	260	372	458	390	417	351	299	323	281	334	279	242	389	280	361	270	218	295	284	351
90089	LOS ANGELES	15	6	6	8	6	7	21	11	17	14	17	11	13	17	11	16	12	15	11	14
90094	LOS ANGELES	557	699	817	712	769	601	665	657	582	713	583	524	728	562	742	533	433	634	551	731
90095	LOS ANGELES	0	0	0	0	0	0	0	0	0	0	0	0	0	0	0	0	0	0	0	0
90201	BELL	65	62	50	55	61	45	70	64	62	73	67	52	65	64	67	56	49	69	50	67
90210	BEVERLY HILLS	251	332	402	349	368	314	290	299	273	314	273	228	354	269	336	264	208	283	273	331
90211	BEVERLY HILLS	145	166	197	179	179	150	173	158	159	175	162	131	187	156	183	151	122	161	143	182
90212	BEVERLY HILLS	162	175	205	190	185	158	193	170	178	191	183	144	203	175	199	170	137	178	156	198
90220	COMPTON	70	75	66	69	74	61	76	73	70	79	73	56	75	70	76	66	52	74	63	79
90221	COMPTON	71	71	59	63	71	52	78	72	68	82	73	58	73	70	75	61	53	75	56	75
90222	COMPTON	70	70	60	65	69	58	74	70	69	78	72	55	72	69	73	64	52	73	62	77
90230	CULVER CITY	105	118	126	120	123	106	122	115	114	122	116	90	127	112	126	111	85	116	107	131
90232	CULVER CITY	96	101	110	104	105	88	113	100	103	112	106	83	113	102	113	98	78	106	91	116
90240	DOWNEY	107	138	144	130	146	114	125	126	111	131	113	96	137	111	138	104	84	121	107	135
90241	DOWNEY	86	96	96	92	98	82	99	93	92	98	95	73	101	92	101	89	70	96	84	103
90242	DOWNEY	86	94	87	86	96	72	97	92	86	101	89	73	95	87	97	79	65	92	74	98
90245	EL SEGUNDO	123	138	158	143	148	118	148	135	130	150	133	114	152	127	155	120	98	138	116	154
90247	GARDENA	68	72	71	69	73	59	80	73	73	79	76	58	78	72	79	69	56	76	63	80
90248	GARDENA	86	107	111	101	112	92	100	99	92	103	93	76	108	90	108	88	68	97	91	109
90249	GARDENA	88	103	103	97	106	85	102	98	94	104	96	76	106	93	106	89	71	99	86	107
90250	HAWTHORNE	75	69	65	68	68	58	83	72	78	81	81	59	78	78	77	74	58	79	66	82
90254	HERMOSA BEACH	183	201	237	218	215	182	217	195	200	218	205	164	231	197	226	190	153	201	177	226
90255	HUNTINGTON PARK	67	62	52	56	62	47	72	65	64	75	69	53	66	66	68	58	50	70	52	69
90260	LAWNDALE	77	83	79	78	84	66	90	82	81	90	85	66	89	81	89	76	63	85	70	90
90262	LYNWOOD	74	72	60	64	71	53	80	74	71	84	76	60	75	72	77	63	55	78	58	77
90263	MALIBU	271	340	398	346	374	292	324	320	283	347	284	255	354	273	361	260	211	308	268	356
90265	MALIBU	222	291	347	300	323	261	263	267	235	285	235	207	304	228	302	220	177	253	231	295
90266	MANHATTAN BEACH	212	267	320	281	293	244	250	246	229	265	231	194	288	224	280	217	174	238	218	275
90270	MAYWOOD	65	63	51	56	62	46	71	65	62	74	67	53	66	64	67	55	49	69	51	67
90272	PACIFIC PALISADES	242	337	409	350	376	312	282	299	260	312	258	225	351	255	335	247	198	276	262	326
90274	PALOS VERDES PENINSU	233	329	401	340	368	307	271	291	250	302	248	216	340	244	326	239	190	267	258	317
90275	RANCHO PALOS VERDES	186	259	308	262	287	235	220	232	200	241	199	174	265	195	260	190	150	216	205	253
90277	REDONDO BEACH	145	167	196	177	180	148	173	160	156	177	159	132	185	153	184	147	119	162	142	183
90278	REDONDO BEACH	134	155	178	160	167	135	160	150	142	164	145	123	168	139	171	132	107	152	132	170
	CALIFORNIA	112	119	122	118	122	107	121	116	114	124	116	92	124	114	124	110	84	118	107	132
	UNITED STATES	100	100	100	100	100	100	100	100	100	100	100	100	100	100	100	100	100	100	100	100

POPULATION CHANGE

ZIP CODE #	POST OFFICE NAME	COUNTY FIPS CODE	POPULATION 2000	POPULATION 2009	POPULATION 2014	2000-2009 ANNUAL RATE % Rate	2000-2009 ANNUAL RATE State Centile	HOUSEHOLDS 2000	HOUSEHOLDS 2009	HOUSEHOLDS 2014	HOUSEHOLDS % Annual Rate 2000-2009	HOUSEHOLDS 2009 Average HH Size	FAMILIES 2000	FAMILIES 2009	FAMILIES % Annual Rate 2000-2009
90280	SOUTH GATE	037	97495	102898	105501	0.6	45	23453	23969	24440	0.2	4.29	20277	20725	0.2
90290	TOPANGA	037	6216	6729	7005	0.9	58	2532	2680	2775	0.6	2.50	1654	1751	0.6
90291	VENICE	037	31446	32106	32705	0.2	18	15752	15798	16017	0.0	2.01	5607	5592	0.0
90292	MARINA DEL REY	037	17482	20789	22216	1.9	81	10584	12234	12990	1.6	1.69	3740	4454	1.9
90293	PLAYA DEL REY	037	9813	10803	11307	1.0	62	5372	5743	5960	0.7	1.87	2142	2310	0.8
90301	INGLEWOOD	037	38157	40302	41479	0.6	45	12179	12576	12880	0.3	3.13	8391	8666	0.3
90302	INGLEWOOD	037	30342	31451	32149	0.4	30	10876	11044	11231	0.2	2.82	7138	7251	0.2
90303	INGLEWOOD	037	26432	27470	28057	0.4	30	7208	7292	7400	0.1	3.76	5854	5927	0.1
90304	INGLEWOOD	037	28990	30506	31346	0.6	45	6560	6739	6888	0.3	4.51	5606	5764	0.3
90305	INGLEWOOD	037	13678	15633	16590	1.5	75	5588	6250	6593	1.2	2.49	3648	4081	1.2
90401	SANTA MONICA	037	5013	6300	6886	2.5	88	3004	3908	4329	2.9	1.43	613	739	2.0
90402	SANTA MONICA	037	12042	12593	12886	0.5	39	5400	5570	5687	0.3	2.26	3129	3216	0.3
90403	SANTA MONICA	037	22544	23451	24033	0.4	30	13279	13543	13808	0.2	1.70	4462	4547	0.2
90404	SANTA MONICA	037	21051	23065	24087	1.0	62	9772	10467	10866	0.7	2.09	3986	4283	0.8
90405	SANTA MONICA	037	25135	26241	26929	0.5	39	13848	14159	14436	0.2	1.84	5068	5183	0.2
90501	TORRANCE	037	40661	43096	44578	0.6	45	13870	14396	14797	0.4	2.98	9715	10073	0.4
90502	TORRANCE	037	17026	17953	18572	0.6	45	5568	5758	5926	0.4	2.98	3933	4072	0.4
90503	TORRANCE	037	42333	45273	46839	0.7	50	16861	17619	18110	0.5	2.53	11090	11667	0.5
90504	TORRANCE	037	31821	33131	33954	0.4	30	11703	11922	12137	0.2	2.77	8373	8540	0.2
90505	TORRANCE	037	35148	36686	37614	0.5	39	14067	14396	14687	0.3	2.52	9538	9762	0.3
90601	WHITTIER	037	31656	32939	33707	0.4	30	10992	11162	11351	0.2	2.92	7978	8106	0.2
90602	WHITTIER	037	25238	26503	27114	0.5	39	7968	8094	8229	0.2	3.18	5566	5663	0.2
90603	WHITTIER	037	18924	19644	20170	0.4	30	6671	6779	6921	0.2	2.86	5125	5212	0.2
90604	WHITTIER	037	38636	40829	42085	0.6	45	11940	12302	12593	0.3	3.31	9468	9763	0.3
90605	WHITTIER	037	38389	40126	40977	0.5	39	10248	10386	10550	0.1	3.84	8535	8654	0.1
90606	WHITTIER	037	32663	34011	34769	0.4	30	8682	8816	8964	0.2	3.74	7090	7203	0.2
90620	BUENA PARK	059	44951	46169	46952	0.3	23	13343	13419	13525	0.1	3.39	10789	10857	0.1
90621	BUENA PARK	059	33360	35547	36369	0.7	50	9960	10259	10395	0.3	3.44	7782	8011	0.3
90623	LA PALMA	059	15478	15894	16112	0.3	23	4988	5058	5088	0.2	3.13	4282	4347	0.2
90630	CYPRESS	059	46850	48378	49161	0.3	23	15894	16206	16348	0.2	2.97	12349	12591	0.2
90631	LA HABRA	059	66806	69126	70301	0.4	30	21520	21719	21909	0.1	3.15	16187	16371	0.1
90638	LA MIRADA	037	45232	47081	48208	0.4	30	14519	14792	15057	0.2	3.14	11514	11734	0.2
90639	LA MIRADA	037	2003	2052	2074	0.3	23	200	201	204	0.1	5.12	113	114	0.1
90640	MONTEBELLO	037	60865	64894	67107	0.7	50	18370	19123	19647	0.4	3.38	14540	15146	0.4
90650	NORWALK	037	103369	109355	111690	0.6	45	26907	27316	27736	0.2	3.91	22542	22891	0.2
90660	PICO RIVERA	037	63417	66604	68450	0.5	39	16464	16888	17260	0.3	3.92	13870	14225	0.3
90670	SANTA FE SPRINGS	037	16167	15896	16333	-0.2	4	4526	4683	4797	0.4	3.35	3511	3629	0.4
90680	STANTON	059	30593	32073	32487	0.5	39	8897	8955	8984	0.1	3.54	6420	6463	0.1
90701	ARTESIA	037	16380	17207	17682	0.5	39	4470	4599	4706	0.3	3.61	3625	3731	0.3
90703	CERRITOS	037	51476	53818	55275	0.5	39	15364	15733	16064	0.3	3.41	13635	13960	0.3
90704	AVALON	037	3696	3951	4077	0.7	50	1281	1325	1362	0.4	2.78	800	828	0.4
90706	BELLFLOWER	037	73333	79294	81809	0.8	54	23478	24209	24786	0.3	3.25	17193	17742	0.3
90710	HARBOR CITY	037	25492	28399	29794	1.2	68	8649	9391	9799	0.9	3.01	6203	6743	0.9
90712	LAKEWOOD	037	31396	33019	33796	0.5	39	11263	11565	11768	0.3	2.85	8271	8490	0.3
90713	LAKEWOOD	037	27381	28155	28690	0.3	23	9562	9616	9740	0.1	2.91	7363	7409	0.1
90715	LAKEWOOD	037	20451	20913	21280	0.2	18	6075	6080	6151	0.0	3.43	4905	4907	0.0
90716	HAWAIIAN GARDENS	037	14898	15562	15901	0.5	39	3489	3541	3599	0.2	4.39	2852	2895	0.2
90717	LOMITA	037	20582	21229	21656	0.3	23	8149	8222	8338	0.1	2.56	5185	5239	0.1
90720	LOS ALAMITOS	059	21745	21819	21913	0.0	9	7927	7858	7835	-0.1	2.72	5986	5936	-0.1
90723	PARAMOUNT	037	54849	58318	59941	0.7	50	13878	14259	14569	0.3	4.07	11270	11594	0.3
90731	SAN PEDRO	037	59989	62537	64237	0.5	39	21880	22295	22844	0.2	2.69	13653	13912	0.2
90732	SAN PEDRO	037	19781	20581	21098	0.4	30	8205	8350	8506	0.2	2.43	5538	5639	0.2
90740	SEAL BEACH	059	23802	24137	24352	0.2	18	12896	12894	12881	0.0	1.85	5866	5895	0.1
90742	SUNSET BEACH	059	836	866	869	0.4	30	449	460	458	0.3	1.88	186	191	0.3
90743	SURFSIDE	059	431	446	449	0.4	30	187	191	190	0.2	2.34	106	108	0.2
90744	WILMINGTON	037	51894	57031	59596	1.0	62	13408	14331	14875	0.7	3.96	11036	11811	0.7
90745	CARSON	037	56068	60357	62640	0.8	54	14881	15686	16202	0.6	3.81	12299	12967	0.6
90746	CARSON	037	25501	27610	28610	0.9	58	7711	8258	8559	0.7	3.27	6264	6640	0.6
90747	CARSON	037	718	723	808	0.1	13	98	98	110	0.0	6.72	65	65	0.0
90755	SIGNAL HILL	037	9441	10675	11314	1.3	70	3662	4127	4375	1.3	2.57	2131	2359	1.1
90802	LONG BEACH	037	39302	44429	46717	1.3	70	18975	21067	22129	1.1	2.06	6941	7557	0.9
90803	LONG BEACH	037	32360	33303	33932	0.3	23	18336	18467	18703	0.1	1.79	7073	7140	0.1
90804	LONG BEACH	037	42440	44979	46066	0.6	45	14883	15270	15581	0.3	2.89	8586	8766	0.2
90805	LONG BEACH	037	90569	96858	99220	0.7	50	25713	25974	26407	0.1	3.69	19791	20011	0.1
90806	LONG BEACH	037	43038	45329	46288	0.6	45	12010	12147	12324	0.1	3.66	8976	9084	0.1
90807	LONG BEACH	037	30427	31696	32350	0.4	30	12177	12322	12502	0.1	2.50	7345	7441	0.1
90808	LONG BEACH	037	37859	39121	39969	0.4	30	14457	14627	14851	0.1	2.66	10354	10481	0.1
90810	LONG BEACH	037	35635	39278	40598	1.1	64	9142	9882	10148	0.8	3.91	7501	8066	0.8
90813	LONG BEACH	037	61667	65604	67643	0.7	50	16093	16818	17295	0.5	3.81	12079	12573	0.4
90814	LONG BEACH	037	18344	19169	19602	0.5	39	8849	8958	9102	0.1	2.10	3633	3679	0.1
90815	LONG BEACH	037	37152	38441	39256	0.4	30	14911	15139	15389	0.2	2.46	9452	9576	0.1
90822	LONG BEACH	037	4	5	5	2.4	87	2	3	3	4.5	1.67	1	2	7.8
90840	LONG BEACH	037	1714	1750	1750	0.2	18	11	12	12	0.9	1.08	0	0	0.0
91001	ALTADENA	037	36183	37405	38197	0.4	30	12388	12543	12740	0.1	2.93	9031	9151	0.1
91006	ARCADIA	037	30382	32190	33174	0.6	45	10550	10900	11164	0.4	2.95	8210	8478	0.3
91007	ARCADIA	037	29582	31194	32062	0.6	45	10815	11112	11351	0.3	2.73	7635	7857	0.3
91008	DUARTE	037	1403	1462	1499	0.4	30	505	517	528	0.3	2.40	308	316	0.3
91010	DUARTE	037	26049	27322	28006	0.5	39	7561	7744	7902	0.3	3.45	5695	5839	0.3
91011	LA CANADA FLINTRIDGE	037	20573	21443	21993	0.4	30	6904	7043	7181	0.2	3.02	5736	5852	0.2
91016	MONROVIA	037	40835	42585	43693	0.5	39	14706	15022	15322	0.2	2.81	10061	10280	0.2
91020	MONTROSE	037	7592	7986	8213	0.5	39	3211	3302	3374	0.3	2.36	1859	1913	0.3
91024	SIERRA MADRE	037	10687	11144	11423	0.5	39	4798	4900	4997	0.2	2.25	2777	2839	0.2
91030	SOUTH PASADENA	037	24295	25592	26348	0.6	45	10477	10804	11059	0.3	2.35	6006	6203	0.3
91040	SUNLAND	037	20624	21722	22385	0.6	45	7675	7916	8109	0.3	2.68	5156	5327	0.4
91042	TUJUNGA	037	26020	27702	28608	0.7	50	9500	9897	10165	0.4	2.76	6376	6643	0.4
91101	PASADENA	037	16486	20199	21911	2.2	85	8603	10473	11348	2.1	1.87	2956	3630	2.2
91103	PASADENA	037	28856	30335	31176	0.5	39	8459	8753	8972	0.4	3.35	6068	6242	0.3
91104	PASADENA	037	37630	38996	39838	0.4	30	12677	12866	13072	0.2	2.98	8714	8855	0.2
91105	PASADENA	037	10850	12065	12671	1.2	68	5018	5479	5729	1.0	2.14	2857	3093	0.9
91106	PASADENA	037	23558	24333	24910	0.4	30	10293	10420	10626	0.1	2.26	5082	5155	0.2
91107	PASADENA	037	31826	33128	33968	0.4	30	12426	12661	12903	0.2	2.59	8107	8275	0.2
91108	SAN MARINO	037	13068	13587	13918	0.4	30	4313	4391	4471	0.2	3.09	3684	3749	0.2
91123	PASADENA	037	32	38	41	1.9	81	7	8	9	1.5	4.63	4	5	2.4
91201	GLENDALE	037	23960	25062	25739	0.5	39	8340	8536	8711	0.3	2.92	6027	6179	0.3
91202	GLENDALE	037	21831	23042	23717	0.6	45	8674	8953	9171	0.3	2.56	5847	6021	0.3
	CALIFORNIA					1.2					1.0	2.93			1.1
	UNITED STATES					1.0					1.1	2.59			0.9

ZIP CODE #	POST OFFICE NAME	RACE (%) White 2000	White 2009	Black 2000	Black 2009	Asian/Pacific 2000	Asian/Pacific 2009	% Hispanic Origin 2000	% Hispanic Origin 2009	2009 AGE DISTRIBUTION (%) 0-4	5-9	10-14	15-19	20-24	25-44	45-64	65-84	85+	18+	MEDIAN AGE 2009	% 2009 Males	% 2009 Females
90280	SOUTH GATE	41.6	39.8	1.0	0.8	1.0	0.9	92.0	94.7	10.3	9.7	8.5	9.5	9.1	30.0	17.5	4.7	0.7	65.8	26.6	50.0	50.0
90290	TOPANGA	90.5	85.6	0.9	1.2	3.6	5.3	5.0	8.5	5.0	5.6	6.9	6.2	4.0	20.2	40.1	11.0	1.0	78.4	45.9	50.3	49.7
90291	VENICE	71.7	65.1	6.7	6.5	3.9	5.0	25.0	33.3	4.7	3.5	3.2	3.5	7.4	44.1	26.2	6.3	1.0	86.6	36.1	52.6	47.4
90292	MARINA DEL REY	82.5	75.2	4.0	4.7	8.1	11.7	6.8	11.4	3.3	2.4	2.3	2.1	4.3	36.9	33.3	13.6	1.8	90.8	44.2	50.8	49.2
90293	PLAYA DEL REY	80.0	73.1	5.2	5.9	7.7	10.4	8.8	13.6	3.8	2.7	2.8	2.7	5.9	37.7	32.6	10.2	1.5	89.1	41.5	49.3	50.7
90301	INGLEWOOD	24.0	24.1	34.8	29.8	2.0	2.0	57.5	64.2	9.4	8.7	7.5	8.4	8.9	29.4	20.6	6.1	1.0	69.3	29.0	48.6	51.4
90302	INGLEWOOD	18.1	18.7	54.5	48.9	1.2	1.3	37.4	44.3	9.3	8.8	7.9	8.0	8.0	30.1	21.6	5.5	0.8	69.2	29.9	46.8	53.2
90303	INGLEWOOD	20.1	20.8	40.2	35.5	1.4	1.2	55.3	60.9	10.1	9.3	8.3	9.7	9.5	27.8	19.0	5.8	0.5	66.6	27.0	49.3	50.7
90304	INGLEWOOD	31.8	30.6	5.5	4.2	2.5	2.1	86.3	90.0	11.0	9.9	8.5	10.3	10.1	29.6	16.5	3.7	0.4	64.5	25.1	51.5	48.5
90305	INGLEWOOD	4.8	4.4	87.7	86.3	0.7	0.7	6.8	8.6	5.8	6.1	6.4	7.1	5.8	23.1	29.1	14.6	2.0	77.2	41.8	44.4	55.6
90401	SANTA MONICA	78.2	71.3	4.3	5.0	6.9	9.1	12.3	17.8	2.8	2.4	2.4	3.0	6.3	38.4	27.5	13.0	4.0	90.5	41.6	51.8	48.2
90402	SANTA MONICA	89.4	84.3	0.6	0.7	6.3	9.3	3.8	6.3	5.0	5.6	6.8	5.6	3.0	22.7	32.9	15.3	3.1	78.9	45.7	48.1	51.9
90403	SANTA MONICA	86.4	80.2	1.4	1.7	6.9	9.9	5.7	9.3	3.4	2.7	3.0	2.7	3.9	38.0	29.1	13.6	3.6	89.2	42.8	46.6	53.4
90404	SANTA MONICA	62.7	54.9	8.4	8.1	8.4	10.2	28.1	37.2	4.5	4.1	3.7	4.9	8.4	36.0	25.6	9.5	3.3	84.8	37.7	48.8	51.2
90405	SANTA MONICA	79.7	72.1	3.2	3.6	7.2	9.7	12.4	18.9	4.2	3.8	4.0	3.4	4.6	36.0	31.4	10.2	2.3	85.9	41.7	49.2	50.8
90501	TORRANCE	48.2	42.0	6.1	5.1	18.8	21.2	39.0	46.2	8.0	7.3	6.6	7.9	8.5	30.1	22.9	7.7	1.1	73.3	32.4	50.6	49.4
90502	TORRANCE	41.2	35.4	7.9	7.0	28.6	30.9	33.0	40.0	6.5	6.5	6.3	6.4	6.1	27.0	26.2	12.7	2.4	76.8	39.0	48.3	51.7
90503	TORRANCE	57.5	48.3	1.8	1.8	33.1	39.8	9.7	13.4	5.6	5.4	5.6	6.1	7.1	26.6	29.2	11.9	2.5	79.6	40.6	48.7	51.3
90504	TORRANCE	46.9	38.6	3.5	3.3	36.1	41.0	17.2	22.4	5.8	5.9	5.8	6.7	6.8	26.8	28.6	11.7	1.8	78.4	39.3	49.2	50.8
90505	TORRANCE	65.9	56.5	1.6	1.7	25.2	31.7	9.1	13.1	5.5	5.7	6.3	6.2	4.9	23.9	31.0	13.7	2.8	78.5	43.4	48.0	52.0
90601	WHITTIER	58.7	53.5	1.3	1.2	6.1	6.3	62.1	71.5	7.7	7.1	6.7	7.5	7.7	28.9	24.0	9.1	1.5	74.4	34.1	48.3	51.7
90602	WHITTIER	52.4	47.3	1.2	1.0	3.2	3.4	68.3	76.9	9.6	8.4	7.4	8.3	8.7	29.6	19.0	7.0	1.9	70.1	29.5	48.6	51.4
90603	WHITTIER	77.8	70.9	0.7	0.7	4.5	5.5	34.8	47.2	6.2	6.3	6.8	7.5	5.5	23.1	28.0	13.5	3.1	76.1	41.1	47.9	52.1
90604	WHITTIER	62.8	56.2	1.6	1.5	3.9	4.2	55.0	66.7	8.1	8.0	7.6	8.3	7.8	28.4	22.4	8.3	1.2	71.2	32.0	49.8	50.2
90605	WHITTIER	52.9	47.6	1.2	1.0	3.1	3.2	68.9	77.5	8.7	8.5	8.1	9.1	8.0	27.8	21.3	7.2	1.2	69.1	30.0	50.0	50.0
90606	WHITTIER	52.9	49.9	1.2	1.0	1.9	1.7	81.7	87.9	8.4	8.1	7.7	10.7	7.8	27.4	20.2	8.2	1.5	69.2	29.9	50.4	49.6
90620	BUENA PARK	57.7	49.7	3.3	3.1	21.5	24.2	27.2	36.1	7.2	7.1	6.9	7.7	6.9	27.8	25.1	9.9	1.4	74.2	35.5	49.2	50.8
90621	BUENA PARK	45.0	39.2	4.7	4.0	21.8	22.7	43.3	51.6	9.4	8.8	7.7	8.0	8.1	30.9	19.6	6.6	0.9	69.3	29.7	50.3	49.7
90623	LA PALMA	43.9	36.5	4.2	4.0	44.2	49.6	11.9	15.9	5.5	5.6	5.8	6.5	6.2	26.1	29.1	13.9	1.2	79.1	40.7	48.7	51.3
90630	CYPRESS	66.2	58.1	2.8	2.8	20.6	24.7	15.6	22.5	6.1	6.3	6.8	7.6	6.2	25.9	28.7	11.2	1.3	76.1	38.9	48.8	51.2
90631	LA HABRA	64.0	56.9	1.5	1.4	7.4	8.5	45.3	55.5	8.2	7.7	7.3	7.6	7.0	27.8	22.9	9.7	1.9	72.2	33.6	49.3	50.7
90638	LA MIRADA	63.7	56.2	1.9	1.8	15.5	18.0	34.1	43.9	6.6	6.6	6.7	7.9	6.8	25.2	26.1	12.1	2.0	75.5	37.9	48.7	51.3
90639	LA MIRADA	77.8	69.8	2.2	2.4	11.0	14.5	15.4	23.1	2.3	2.4	2.2	25.9	30.4	11.2	11.7	8.8	5.1	91.1	22.8	41.3	58.7
90640	MONTEBELLO	47.0	44.6	0.9	0.7	11.3	11.2	75.0	79.7	8.3	8.0	7.1	7.7	7.5	28.8	20.3	10.5	1.8	71.9	32.5	48.3	51.7
90650	NORWALK	44.8	40.8	4.6	4.0	11.9	11.8	62.9	70.5	8.8	8.6	8.1	9.0	8.2	28.3	20.2	7.7	1.2	69.2	29.7	50.0	50.0
90660	PICO RIVERA	49.5	47.5	0.7	0.6	2.8	2.5	88.3	92.1	8.6	8.4	7.9	8.5	7.8	28.0	20.5	9.0	1.3	70.0	30.8	49.2	50.8
90670	SANTA FE SPRINGS	51.5	48.2	4.0	2.2	4.2	4.2	70.0	80.3	7.5	7.4	7.4	8.0	8.0	25.8	22.0	12.2	1.7	73.0	33.7	48.3	51.7
90680	STANTON	49.8	43.0	2.4	2.1	16.7	17.3	46.9	56.1	9.0	8.4	7.6	8.1	7.8	30.0	19.5	7.8	1.8	70.1	30.7	50.6	49.4
90701	ARTESIA	44.2	38.2	3.6	3.2	28.0	30.7	38.3	44.1	7.5	7.3	6.7	7.4	7.5	28.1	23.3	10.2	2.0	74.0	34.0	50.5	49.5
90703	CERRITOS	27.0	21.4	6.7	5.9	58.5	63.1	10.6	13.1	4.9	4.9	5.1	6.7	7.3	25.8	30.4	13.6	1.3	80.8	40.8	48.5	51.5
90704	AVALON	70.8	61.9	0.8	0.9	1.1	1.2	44.3	58.1	7.8	7.9	7.4	7.1	7.9	27.8	25.5	7.3	1.3	72.2	33.8	50.3	49.7
90706	BELLFLOWER	46.0	39.7	13.1	11.7	10.4	11.2	43.3	53.4	9.6	8.9	7.7	8.0	8.1	29.2	20.4	6.8	1.2	69.0	29.5	49.0	51.0
90710	HARBOR CITY	46.5	41.9	14.0	12.9	14.5	15.9	41.8	48.9	8.3	7.6	7.0	7.3	7.1	28.7	22.4	10.1	1.4	72.7	33.5	48.7	51.3
90712	LAKEWOOD	64.8	56.1	8.6	9.0	11.9	14.4	20.7	29.0	6.8	7.0	7.1	7.2	5.9	26.2	27.2	10.3	2.3	74.6	38.2	47.8	52.2
90713	LAKEWOOD	77.6	69.8	3.1	3.3	7.7	10.0	17.3	25.8	6.6	6.9	7.1	7.2	5.8	24.7	29.1	10.4	2.1	74.9	39.5	48.5	51.5
90715	LAKEWOOD	39.9	34.3	11.5	10.3	25.1	27.2	33.4	40.5	8.0	7.5	7.1	8.6	8.5	30.0	22.1	7.5	0.7	72.3	31.0	49.4	50.6
90716	HAWAIIAN GARDENS	38.2	35.6	4.7	3.8	10.2	9.9	72.1	77.8	10.8	9.7	8.3	9.7	10.1	29.8	16.0	4.8	0.7	65.4	25.7	51.3	48.7
90717	LOMITA	66.1	57.6	3.9	3.9	12.3	14.7	26.6	36.2	7.4	6.7	6.6	6.9	6.6	28.0	26.7	9.4	1.7	75.1	36.5	48.4	51.6
90720	LOS ALAMITOS	82.4	76.2	2.0	2.2	8.2	10.7	11.5	17.7	5.0	5.1	6.2	7.7	6.3	22.7	30.1	13.7	3.2	78.9	42.6	47.8	52.2
90723	PARAMOUNT	34.7	33.1	13.5	10.7	4.2	3.9	72.4	79.0	11.1	10.3	8.8	9.6	9.1	29.3	16.6	4.6	0.6	64.1	25.6	49.4	50.6
90731	SAN PEDRO	58.9	53.5	7.6	6.9	4.9	5.4	46.9	56.2	7.9	7.4	6.5	7.2	8.0	30.4	23.1	8.0	1.4	74.1	32.8	50.4	49.6
90732	SAN PEDRO	78.3	72.0	3.4	3.6	6.2	7.8	22.4	31.4	5.5	5.6	6.1	5.9	4.7	24.4	29.4	15.5	3.0	79.4	43.6	47.6	52.4
90740	SEAL BEACH	89.0	84.8	1.4	1.5	5.9	8.0	6.4	10.2	3.2	3.4	3.7	3.7	2.9	18.4	25.0	29.1	10.6	87.5	56.8	44.7	55.3
90742	SUNSET BEACH	88.6	83.4	0.1	0.1	2.4	3.3	5.9	9.9	2.8	3.5	2.2	2.7	6.1	35.9	34.4	10.7	1.7	89.8	42.8	55.2	44.8
90743	SURFSIDE	96.3	94.2	0.0	0.0	1.2	1.6	7.7	12.8	4.9	4.9	5.2	5.6	4.7	27.1	33.6	13.5	0.4	81.6	43.7	52.5	47.5
90744	WILMINGTON	35.8	34.0	3.4	2.6	3.5	3.1	86.0	89.8	10.9	10.1	8.5	9.4	9.0	29.5	16.9	5.1	0.7	64.9	26.2	50.9	49.1
90745	CARSON	29.6	26.9	8.6	7.2	34.9	35.2	40.3	46.0	7.3	7.2	7.0	8.0	7.5	27.8	23.7	10.1	1.4	73.7	33.8	49.1	50.9
90746	CARSON	13.8	13.3	65.5	62.9	7.1	7.5	18.1	21.7	6.4	6.5	6.8	8.5	6.9	24.6	25.8	13.4	1.2	75.6	37.7	47.1	52.9
90747	CARSON	17.7	15.6	67.9	65.8	4.7	5.7	12.0	16.5	4.7	5.3	6.1	11.1	9.1	21.6	26.1	14.5	1.5	80.6	38.0	44.5	55.5
90755	SIGNAL HILL	45.3	39.1	13.1	12.3	18.5	20.2	29.2	36.0	8.0	6.9	6.4	6.4	6.8	30.8	26.3	7.6	0.9	74.9	34.9	49.1	50.9
90802	LONG BEACH	46.5	41.5	17.4	15.5	6.0	6.8	39.7	48.5	7.5	6.0	4.7	5.5	9.8	35.2	22.0	7.4	1.8	78.9	32.9	52.2	47.8
90803	LONG BEACH	85.5	79.5	2.3	2.6	4.8	6.7	10.0	15.9	3.6	3.1	3.1	2.8	5.6	36.5	31.2	12.0	2.3	88.6	42.2	49.2	50.8
90804	LONG BEACH	37.8	33.6	17.0	15.1	15.2	15.8	38.8	46.2	9.6	7.5	6.2	8.4	12.4	34.3	16.7	4.1	1.0	72.1	27.4	49.0	51.0
90805	LONG BEACH	29.5	26.9	23.9	20.6	13.0	13.1	46.0	54.1	10.2	9.5	8.5	9.7	9.3	28.4	18.5	5.1	0.8	65.9	26.6	49.2	50.8
90806	LONG BEACH	25.0	23.2	21.5	18.0	19.8	20.1	45.0	51.6	10.3	9.4	8.2	9.3	9.5	28.4	18.3	5.6	1.1	66.4	26.8	49.5	50.5
90807	LONG BEACH	54.8	47.1	16.2	16.0	14.8	17.7	17.7	24.3	6.2	5.9	6.2	6.4	6.6	26.6	28.2	10.3	3.5	77.8	39.8	47.4	52.6
90808	LONG BEACH	80.6	73.5	2.8	3.1	7.0	9.3	13.8	20.8	6.2	6.5	7.0	6.5	5.0	24.5	30.0	11.7	2.6	76.3	41.5	48.8	51.2
90810	LONG BEACH	23.8	22.2	16.4	13.8	26.2	25.8	45.6	51.8	9.0	8.8	8.2	9.3	8.5	26.8	19.6	8.6	1.4	68.6	29.0	49.2	50.8
90813	LONG BEACH	25.2	24.3	13.5	11.1	16.6	15.9	61.3	66.7	12.6	10.2	7.9	9.8	11.6	29.4	13.8	4.2	0.5	63.6	24.1	51.4	48.6
90814	LONG BEACH	66.8	59.1	9.0	9.1	7.5	9.3	21.1	29.3	5.8	4.9	4.4	4.4	7.8	38.2	25.0	7.7	1.8	82.4	35.8	48.6	51.4
90815	LONG BEACH	76.4	68.5	3.9	4.2	9.5	12.6	12.5	18.8	5.7	5.7	6.1	7.0	7.3	24.9	28.0	12.3	3.0	79.1	40.7	48.1	51.9
90822	LONG BEACH	50.0	60.0	25.0	20.0	0.0	0.0	50.0	40.0	0.0	0.0	0.0	0.0	0.0	100.0	0.0	0.0	0.0	100.0	32.5	100.0	0.0
90840	LONG BEACH	56.2	46.9	11.3	11.6	17.9	21.7	16.5	22.9	0.0	0.0	0.0	67.9	30.9	1.0	0.1	0.0	0.1	99.6	18.7	35.2	64.8
91001	ALTADENA	42.4	38.3	36.5	35.0	3.9	4.8	22.0	28.3	6.6	7.1	7.7	7.4	5.5	23.8	29.1	10.8	2.0	73.7	39.5	48.2	51.8
91006	ARCADIA	48.1	39.3	0.9	0.9	41.9	48.1	13.2	17.5	5.1	5.5	6.2	7.2	5.7	24.2	31.0	12.8	2.2	78.8	42.2	48.0	52.0
91007	ARCADIA	46.5	37.1	1.3	1.3	44.6	51.7	10.4	13.8	4.6	4.7	5.1	6.1	6.0	25.7	29.7	14.3	3.8	81.8	43.4	46.9	53.1
91008	DUARTE	78.3	70.1	1.6	1.8	13.8	18.6	10.5	16.0	3.2	5.3	4.5	3.8	2.9	15.5	23.7	17.9	23.3	84.5	56.8	40.5	59.5
91010	DUARTE	48.4	43.8	10.5	9.1	10.6	12.2	49.0	56.6	7.8	7.5	7.4	7.9	6.9	26.7	23.8	9.9	2.0	72.3	34.3	48.0	52.0
91011	LA CANADA FLINTRIDGE	74.3	65.2	0.8	0.8	20.2	27.2	5.1	7.8	4.9	6.2	8.0	9.0	4.4	16.2	35.4	13.6	2.3	75.1	45.7	48.2	51.8
91016	MONROVIA	63.0	56.9	8.4	7.6	7.1	8.2	35.6	45.4	7.9	7.5	7.2	7.6	7.1	28.2	24.6	8.5	1.6	72.8	34.4	48.6	51.4
91020	MONTROSE	72.1	63.0	0.6	0.7	16.9	21.7	13.0	18.9	5.1	4.9	5.4	6.4	6.9	29.1	28.9	10.6	2.9	80.8	40.0	46.6	53.4
91024	SIERRA MADRE	85.5	79.2	1.2	1.3	6.0	8.3	9.9	15.7	4.8	5.0	5.6	5.1	4.4	23.8	34.9	13.7	2.8	81.3	45.7	47.6	52.4
91030	SOUTH PASADENA	60.3	51.6	3.0	3.0	26.6	32.0	16.1	22.0	4.9	4.6	5.1	6.2	7.3	30.3	29.3	10.4	1.9	81.6	39.6	46.8	53.2
91040	SUNLAND	77.9	70.0	1.6	1.7	6.4	8.2	20.8	30.2	5.9	6.1	6.4	6.8	5.9	24.9	30.5	11.2	2.3	77.4	41.0	49.1	50.9
91042	TUJUNGA	71.8	63.6	2.4	2.4	6.3	7.9	26.6	36.2	7.0	6.8	6.7	7.3	6.7	27.0	28.0	9.1	1.4	75.2	35.9	50.5	49.5
91101	PASADENA	53.9	46.4	11.7	11.0	15.0	19.9	28.8	33.3	5.2	4.1	3.5	4.0	9.8	40.2	20.4	9.4	3.4	85.1	35.3	49.6	50.4
91103	PASADENA	34.5	33.4	27.2	23.1	4.6	5.3	50.8	57.5	8.6	8.2	7.6	8.5	8.6	27.6	21.1	8.2	1.6	70.6	30.4	49.9	50.1
91104	PASADENA	54.4	49.1	14.5	13.0	6.0	7.2	36.4	44.1	7.6	7.1	6.9	7.5	7.3	28.3	25.4	8.3	1.5	73.8	34.8	49.1	50.9
91105	PASADENA	79.5	72.2	4.4	4.9	9.0	11.8	12.3	19.3	4.4	4.9	5.4	4.2	3.5	22.3	32.8	18.3	4.0	82.6	43.1	48.9	51.1
91106	PASADENA	56.8	49.4	9.3	8.6	16.0	19.4	25.8	33.0	6.1	4.8	4.4	5.6	9.2	37.3	22.6	8.4	1.6	82.1	33.9	50.0	50.0
91107	PASADENA	64.0	56.5	5.7	5.7	15.1	18.1	23.6	31.0	6.0	6.0	6.3	5.8	5.3	28.5	27.5	12.0	2.7	78.2	40.2	48.8	51.2
91108	SAN MARINO	48.3	38.3	0.3	0.3	47.9	56.9	4.5	6.1	4.9	5.9	7.5	7.2	4.4	20.4	33.3	14.0	2.5	77.2	44.8	48.4	51.6
91123	PASADENA	84.4	76.3	3.1	2.6	9.4	13.2	6.3	13.2	5.3	2.6	0.0	2.6	2.6	21.1	34.2	26.3	5.3	92.1	55.0	47.4	52.6
91201	GLENDALE	65.6	56.7	1.5	1.4	11.2	13.4	22.1	28.7	6.2	6.1	6.0	6.9	7.7	29.8	25.9	9.7	1.8	77.8	36.7	48.9	51.1
91202	GLENDALE	68.1	58.5	1.1	1.2	18.4	23.2	10.7	15.3	5.0	5.2	5.3	6.0	5.9	28.5	28.5	13.1	2.5	80.8	41.3	47.6	52.4
	CALIFORNIA	59.5	54.5	6.7	6.2	11.3	12.5	32.4	38.3	7.5	7.1	6.9	7.5	7.4	28.5	24.2	9.3	1.6	74.1	34.3	49.9	50.1
	UNITED STATES	75.1	72.0	12.3	12.7	3.8	4.6	12.5	15.7	6.8	6.7	6.6	7.1	6.9	27.0	26.0	10.9	1.9	75.7	36.9	49.2	50.8

INCOME

ZIP CODE				2009 HOUSEHOLD INCOME DISTRIBUTION (%)					MEDIAN HOUSEHOLD INCOME					2009 HOME VALUE DISTRIBUTION (%)					
#	POST OFFICE NAME	2009 Per Capita Income	2009 HH Income Base	Less than $25,000	$25,000 to $49,999	$50,000 to $99,999	$100,000 to $149,999	$150,000 or More	2009	2014	2009 National Centile	2009 State Centile	2009 Home Value Base	Less than $50,000	$50,000 to $89,999	$90,000 to $174,999	$175,000 to $399,999	$400,000 or More	2009 Median Home Value
90280	SOUTH GATE	12541	23969	22.7	32.7	36.4	6.0	2.3	45431	48071	50	34	11116	1.7	0.8	1.6	85.5	10.4	284628
90290	TOPANGA	56811	2680	9.8	12.0	25.3	17.6	35.3	107394	112477	98	93	2048	2.0	0.8	2.2	4.4	90.6	858081
90291	VENICE	44713	15798	15.1	23.1	34.9	13.3	13.6	63533	66370	82	64	4599	0.1	0.3	1.8	7.1	90.7	720792
90292	MARINA DEL REY	77528	12234	11.6	11.2	32.6	17.2	27.4	89908	91997	95	87	3883	0.9	0.7	1.6	7.0	89.8	680271
90293	PLAYA DEL REY	70405	5743	7.5	9.5	35.5	23.2	24.2	94961	96543	96	89	2741	0.2	0.0	0.9	27.1	71.8	703409
90301	INGLEWOOD	15717	12576	31.4	31.4	29.4	6.0	1.7	39791	42540	32	21	3346	0.4	0.2	9.4	75.7	14.3	267177
90302	INGLEWOOD	18042	11044	28.2	32.1	31.9	5.7	2.1	42316	45104	40	26	3108	0.3	0.1	12.6	66.5	20.4	263409
90303	INGLEWOOD	14794	7292	27.4	27.4	35.1	6.9	3.2	45271	48440	49	33	3062	0.5	0.1	1.8	75.7	21.8	316066
90304	INGLEWOOD	10519	6739	32.0	33.4	27.7	4.1	2.8	36796	40176	23	16	2122	0.7	0.3	2.3	78.2	18.5	286556
90305	INGLEWOOD	27640	6250	19.2	22.1	42.2	10.7	5.8	59765	62673	77	58	4097	0.2	0.0	0.2	69.4	30.2	351723
90401	SANTA MONICA	43605	3908	28.4	24.3	30.0	8.9	8.4	47145	48988	54	37	303	0.0	0.0	0.0	6.3	93.7	1000001
90402	SANTA MONICA	86212	5570	8.3	9.0	23.1	12.4	47.3	137269	148632	99	97	3413	0.0	0.0	1.0	3.5	95.4	1000001
90403	SANTA MONICA	62545	13543	14.9	17.3	32.6	15.0	20.2	76469	78085	90	77	3393	0.1	0.2	0.9	7.6	91.2	823891
90404	SANTA MONICA	31883	10467	23.3	24.3	34.4	10.9	7.1	52659	56420	67	47	2288	4.5	0.4	1.4	17.5	76.2	555034
90405	SANTA MONICA	54017	14159	15.3	19.4	33.1	15.0	17.1	70042	72131	87	71	4931	0.4	0.3	1.2	8.1	90.0	845486
90501	TORRANCE	22564	14396	18.6	27.9	36.0	11.1	6.5	53755	57391	69	49	6095	4.0	1.6	2.1	31.9	60.5	465558
90502	TORRANCE	24057	5758	13.2	24.1	43.2	13.9	5.6	62029	63901	80	62	3922	6.4	0.9	9.9	59.6	23.2	302865
90503	TORRANCE	35274	17619	10.9	17.4	41.4	18.5	11.8	74079	75000	89	74	9221	0.8	1.1	1.0	8.7	88.4	623059
90504	TORRANCE	26488	11922	14.8	22.5	41.1	15.3	6.3	62899	64928	81	63	7144	1.8	1.7	0.3	27.5	68.6	453962
90505	TORRANCE	37226	14396	10.7	17.9	39.4	17.6	14.5	74990	76338	89	75	8052	0.7	1.1	2.6	8.5	87.2	716381
90601	WHITTIER	28060	11162	12.7	21.9	40.3	13.8	11.3	66308	68120	84	67	6677	0.4	0.5	2.2	47.8	49.1	396063
90602	WHITTIER	20026	8094	23.7	27.6	33.7	8.7	6.2	48440	51148	58	40	2871	0.3	0.1	1.3	49.7	48.6	393722
90603	WHITTIER	31502	6779	10.6	17.5	41.6	18.3	12.0	74260	75890	89	74	5263	1.3	0.3	0.8	41.6	56.0	419486
90604	WHITTIER	21333	12302	13.8	22.8	44.7	13.7	5.0	63237	65084	81	64	7841	0.9	0.2	1.1	71.6	26.3	342630
90605	WHITTIER	20287	10386	12.2	24.0	43.4	12.8	7.5	63585	65394	82	64	6976	0.8	0.1	2.0	72.3	24.7	324336
90606	WHITTIER	17624	8816	15.5	26.6	43.4	10.3	4.1	57303	60698	74	55	5904	2.2	1.1	2.7	84.7	9.4	294622
90620	BUENA PARK	23702	13419	10.0	20.0	43.1	20.5	6.3	72118	76061	88	73	8591	1.5	1.2	1.4	71.3	24.5	345189
90621	BUENA PARK	20132	10259	16.2	27.0	37.3	13.8	5.7	56040	58092	73	53	4028	0.2	0.3	1.2	65.7	32.6	322602
90623	LA PALMA	33467	5058	6.3	12.4	37.4	26.8	17.0	89316	95056	95	87	3684	0.7	1.0	0.5	20.9	77.0	491774
90630	CYPRESS	32870	16206	8.9	15.6	37.3	24.5	13.6	82094	86350	93	82	10912	1.5	1.0	2.0	40.6	54.8	418688
90631	LA HABRA	27138	21719	13.8	20.8	36.9	18.7	9.8	67919	71714	86	69	13001	2.1	1.8	3.3	50.9	41.9	363144
90638	LA MIRADA	27719	14792	10.0	18.1	42.4	20.0	9.5	76382	77031	90	77	11721	0.6	0.4	3.2	47.8	48.0	393613
90639	LA MIRADA	16680	201	19.9	28.4	37.3	9.0	5.5	53569	61514	69	49	125	0.0	0.0	0.0	31.2	68.8	432192
90640	MONTEBELLO	17840	19123	23.3	28.0	35.5	9.0	4.3	48781	51354	58	40	8906	1.9	0.7	2.9	50.9	43.5	374902
90650	NORWALK	16974	27316	14.3	26.9	44.7	10.2	3.9	59513	61812	77	57	17456	2.2	0.5	3.5	87.2	6.6	281214
90660	PICO RIVERA	15784	16888	20.9	25.2	40.4	9.5	3.9	53959	57823	70	50	11531	1.6	0.7	1.8	82.6	13.3	295856
90670	SANTA FE SPRINGS	19801	4683	17.4	21.8	46.6	9.7	4.5	60121	61914	77	58	2965	5.2	0.3	3.5	84.3	6.7	291969
90680	STANTON	18055	8955	19.9	25.4	40.9	9.8	4.0	54229	56525	70	50	4378	8.8	4.2	5.0	71.5	10.5	256721
90701	ARTESIA	18974	4599	14.3	28.9	41.6	9.9	5.3	57329	60809	74	55	2545	3.6	1.8	4.7	53.2	36.8	339040
90703	CERRITOS	29909	15733	6.4	13.0	41.2	23.3	16.1	84597	86125	94	84	12640	1.7	2.1	1.0	14.2	81.0	543344
90704	AVALON	23617	1325	17.4	32.8	36.5	9.0	4.4	49832	53041	61	42	335	0.9	0.0	1.2	7.5	90.4	722782
90706	BELLFLOWER	18383	24209	20.9	29.3	37.4	8.9	3.4	49736	52321	60	42	9643	9.7	0.9	2.5	64.5	22.5	306250
90710	HARBOR CITY	21879	9391	21.1	25.3	36.2	11.9	5.5	53642	57625	69	49	5053	5.5	5.8	8.9	35.3	44.5	355114
90712	LAKEWOOD	27606	11565	14.4	19.1	40.5	20.1	6.0	70346	72210	87	71	8122	1.5	0.3	0.5	53.6	44.1	383655
90713	LAKEWOOD	29179	9616	8.9	15.6	44.6	24.2	6.7	77988	79278	91	79	7631	0.5	0.1	0.5	47.4	51.5	403534
90715	LAKEWOOD	20563	6080	15.4	22.7	43.2	13.4	5.3	61502	63752	79	61	3191	2.3	0.6	3.6	69.2	24.3	323625
90716	HAWAIIAN GARDENS	11928	3541	25.6	29.0	38.0	5.9	1.5	45200	48794	49	33	1580	10.4	2.1	14.2	68.0	5.3	225953
90717	LOMITA	27427	8222	16.2	25.5	39.7	12.3	6.3	58043	61363	75	56	3878	5.9	1.2	3.1	24.9	64.9	467015
90720	LOS ALAMITOS	40588	7858	7.3	13.4	37.1	20.6	21.5	87940	92349	95	85	5045	0.8	0.8	1.0	16.6	80.9	607048
90723	PARAMOUNT	13490	14259	23.6	30.1	37.8	6.2	2.3	46844	49470	54	36	6124	10.6	3.2	12.7	65.7	7.7	239323
90731	SAN PEDRO	22217	22295	26.8	26.7	32.3	9.2	5.0	46414	48722	53	35	7122	1.3	0.5	2.9	39.3	55.9	429375
90732	SAN PEDRO	38192	8350	11.5	15.9	38.1	20.6	14.0	77865	79058	91	79	6063	0.3	0.2	3.1	24.2	72.3	536973
90740	SEAL BEACH	46622	12894	20.8	23.7	25.1	13.9	16.5	57835	60761	75	56	9657	0.7	8.2	27.4	25.0	38.8	242711
90742	SUNSET BEACH	73815	460	9.1	8.7	32.2	19.8	30.2	100000	107111	97	91	166	0.0	4.8	0.0	6.0	89.2	1000001
90743	SURFSIDE	45706	191	9.4	7.9	38.2	25.1	19.4	90740	98005	95	87	127	0.0	0.0	4.7	0.0	95.3	762500
90744	WILMINGTON	12664	14331	31.0	32.7	28.1	5.2	3.0	37065	40420	24	17	5425	2.7	0.4	6.3	78.7	11.9	278094
90745	CARSON	18790	15686	14.5	22.5	44.4	13.1	5.4	63214	65211	81	63	11187	4.2	2.9	7.4	64.0	21.5	300422
90746	CARSON	24792	8258	11.6	17.9	46.3	16.2	7.9	70630	72302	87	72	7008	2.2	4.4	4.7	53.4	35.4	350267
90747	CARSON	10418	98	22.4	24.5	39.8	9.2	4.1	52602	55560	67	47	83	7.2	10.8	9.6	56.6	15.7	265000
90755	SIGNAL HILL	30387	4127	14.2	20.1	43.9	14.1	7.7	65126	67658	83	66	1988	0.2	1.2	2.3	66.3	30.0	296711
90802	LONG BEACH	22002	21067	37.5	29.7	25.3	4.8	2.7	33141	36062	14	11	4406	2.0	4.4	32.0	38.4	23.2	222907
90803	LONG BEACH	62330	18467	9.4	16.3	37.2	16.9	20.2	79996	80680	92	81	7934	1.2	1.2	3.0	14.5	80.1	699890
90804	LONG BEACH	16982	15270	32.4	29.6	30.4	4.9	2.7	37508	41207	25	18	2954	2.2	0.2	11.8	61.2	24.5	282485
90805	LONG BEACH	13981	25974	28.4	30.9	32.1	6.2	2.3	42030	45238	39	26	11287	6.2	1.3	4.3	83.0	5.2	256114
90806	LONG BEACH	13733	12147	33.8	28.3	28.3	6.9	2.7	36942	40030	23	17	4282	1.1	0.2	4.5	80.2	13.9	295295
90807	LONG BEACH	34787	12322	13.9	22.3	37.6	14.3	12.0	65586	67720	84	66	6756	0.4	0.6	4.6	38.5	55.9	430912
90808	LONG BEACH	34221	14627	10.6	16.4	40.2	21.5	11.2	77426	78469	91	78	11403	0.2	0.1	0.7	29.6	69.5	449521
90810	LONG BEACH	14934	9882	23.8	29.6	35.4	8.0	3.2	47072	49478	54	37	5425	1.1	2.2	4.7	86.5	5.6	258369
90813	LONG BEACH	8810	16818	51.3	31.6	14.3	2.0	0.8	24039	25056	3	3	2135	0.9	1.8	18.5	69.4	9.4	242361
90814	LONG BEACH	34776	8958	17.7	23.6	40.3	10.0	8.4	56812	60118	74	54	2819	0.3	0.1	5.6	31.6	62.4	526724
90815	LONG BEACH	36794	15139	11.2	17.3	40.1	19.1	12.3	74040	75704	89	74	10138	0.4	0.1	1.6	26.9	71.0	462325
90822	LONG BEACH	4500	3	100.0	0.0	0.0	0.0	0.0	7500	7500	0	1	0	0.0	0.0	0.0	0.0	0.0	0
90840	LONG BEACH	20758	12	91.7	8.3	0.0	0.0	0.0	18542	18542	1	2	0	0.0	0.0	0.0	0.0	0.0	0
91001	ALTADENA	35056	12543	11.5	18.2	34.0	18.1	18.3	79079	80262	92	80	9388	0.2	0.1	1.4	34.3	63.9	483323
91006	ARCADIA	32929	10900	10.9	19.5	37.7	16.0	15.9	75018	75785	89	76	7687	3.2	1.8	2.6	18.6	73.8	617589
91007	ARCADIA	32791	11112	14.3	22.6	34.9	15.3	13.0	66253	68906	84	67	6279	1.1	1.7	3.0	18.5	75.8	658765
91008	DUARTE	55424	517	6.4	14.9	29.6	22.2	26.9	98490	101611	96	90	335	0.0	0.0	5.1	6.3	88.7	827899
91010	DUARTE	21379	7744	16.2	21.4	41.4	14.2	6.7	63448	65703	82	64	5383	2.3	0.3	3.3	71.4	22.7	284563
91011	LA CANADA FLINTRIDGE	57911	7043	6.9	8.8	23.4	11.7	49.1	146513	152789	100	98	6030	0.1	0.6	1.9	3.3	94.0	939277
91016	MONROVIA	26049	15022	16.8	25.5	38.1	12.0	7.7	59230	62107	76	57	7514	1.5	0.7	2.4	42.4	53.0	413574
91020	MONTROSE	32084	3302	16.0	23.8	37.7	14.0	8.4	62137	65632	80	62	1282	1.0	1.1	2.0	25.0	70.8	478529
91024	SIERRA MADRE	51169	4900	6.4	15.3	39.7	17.4	21.3	83034	84080	93	82	3012	0.0	0.1	0.4	9.9	89.7	698798
91030	SOUTH PASADENA	41316	10804	12.1	18.0	39.0	13.8	17.0	73702	75095	89	74	4756	0.7	1.2	1.5	15.3	81.2	687548
91040	SUNLAND	30126	7916	14.2	20.3	40.5	15.8	9.2	66494	68609	85	68	5375	2.7	0.5	1.8	50.5	44.4	368971
91042	TUJUNGA	24405	9897	19.1	27.1	37.2	10.9	5.8	53730	56946	69	49	5279	0.8	0.2	5.7	52.3	41.0	350519
91101	PASADENA	34172	10473	26.0	21.5	36.9	9.7	5.9	52056	54522	66	46	1965	1.3	0.0	4.1	71.8	22.8	285631
91103	PASADENA	22004	8753	28.6	25.7	27.5	8.1	10.1	44274	48080	46	31	4054	0.4	0.0	5.4	48.2	46.1	375039
91104	PASADENA	25275	12866	21.6	25.7	29.0	13.5	10.1	53261	57518	68	48	6744	0.6	0.1	1.0	32.1	66.2	476008
91105	PASADENA	68881	5479	11.5	14.0	26.4	15.9	32.1	95481	97225	96	89	3661	0.2	0.1	0.7	7.9	91.2	825718
91106	PASADENA	40327	10420	17.3	22.4	32.9	13.2	14.1	61994	64861	80	61	3827	0.5	0.4	3.4	38.8	56.9	456974
91107	PASADENA	39081	12661	12.4	19.4	35.1	14.5	18.6	73170	74736	88	74	7731	0.3	0.7	1.6	20.0	77.5	593773
91108	SAN MARINO	61766	4391	6.6	7.2	21.4	14.1	50.7	152149	159651	100	99	3829	0.0	1.1	4.6	3.9	90.4	1000001
91123	PASADENA	26374	8	0.0	0.0	75.0	12.5	12.5	85285	95229	94	84	5	0.0	0.0	0.0	0.0	100.0	625000
91201	GLENDALE	22782	8536	23.6	27.0	32.5	9.9	7.0	49307	53113	60	41	2918	1.1	0.6	1.2	23.3	73.7	550545
91202	GLENDALE	32006	8953	17.9	22.0	36.4	12.7	11.0	63026	65258	81	63	4062	0.4	0.4	2.2	24.9	72.1	577231
	CALIFORNIA	28199		18.5	22.2	33.9	14.0	11.5	61614	64088				3.3	2.6	13.6	41.0	39.5	321752
	UNITED STATES	27277		20.9	24.4	35.3	11.7	7.6	54719	56938				9.3	13.1	31.6	32.6	13.5	162279

ZIP CODE #	POST OFFICE NAME	FINANCIAL SERVICES: Auto Loan	Home Loan	Investments	Retirement Plans	THE HOME: Home Improvements: Home Repair	Lawn & Garden	Furnishings: Computers & Hardware-Personal	Major Appliances	TV, Radio, Sound Equipment	Furniture	ENTERTAINMENT: Dine out/Carry out	Sports Equipment	Fees & Tickets	Toys & Games	Travel	Cable TV	PERSONAL: Apparel & Services	Auto Repairs	Health Insurance	Pets & Supplies
90280	SOUTH GATE	75	76	65	67	76	56	81	76	71	86	76	61	77	73	80	64	56	79	60	80
90290	TOPANGA	174	229	273	236	254	204	205	209	184	223	184	163	239	180	235	171	139	198	178	231
90291	VENICE	117	114	128	124	118	102	138	116	127	133	131	101	135	126	134	120	96	127	108	138
90292	MARINA DEL REY	172	170	193	185	177	156	198	170	184	195	189	146	199	183	195	176	138	183	160	203
90293	PLAYA DEL REY	163	181	215	198	193	166	194	174	180	194	186	146	209	178	202	173	139	179	160	202
90301	INGLEWOOD	66	60	56	58	60	50	73	64	69	72	72	52	68	69	68	65	52	71	58	72
90302	INGLEWOOD	68	62	59	62	62	54	76	65	73	73	76	53	71	73	70	71	55	72	62	76
90303	INGLEWOOD	75	77	70	71	77	63	82	76	76	83	80	60	80	77	81	71	58	80	66	83
90304	INGLEWOOD	66	62	53	57	62	47	71	65	64	74	68	53	66	65	68	58	50	70	52	68
90305	INGLEWOOD	86	101	101	99	102	100	94	94	97	92	98	68	103	95	99	101	70	95	102	110
90401	SANTA MONICA	83	76	89	85	79	76	98	82	96	93	98	69	95	91	93	96	71	92	88	100
90402	SANTA MONICA	236	298	360	318	327	277	276	271	257	291	259	215	326	254	309	246	198	263	243	304
90403	SANTA MONICA	134	145	171	159	154	132	159	141	147	158	152	119	168	146	164	141	114	146	129	164
90404	SANTA MONICA	86	83	92	89	86	73	104	87	95	98	100	76	101	94	101	90	73	96	80	103
90405	SANTA MONICA	125	136	159	147	145	122	149	132	136	148	140	112	156	134	154	129	104	138	120	154
90501	TORRANCE	87	91	96	91	95	75	102	92	92	103	95	76	101	91	103	84	70	97	79	103
90502	TORRANCE	90	116	127	111	125	91	111	109	93	118	94	87	117	91	122	83	70	104	86	117
90503	TORRANCE	111	134	151	135	144	115	135	127	119	137	122	104	143	118	145	111	90	128	111	142
90504	TORRANCE	89	112	125	110	122	91	111	107	97	115	98	85	117	93	121	90	73	105	90	118
90505	TORRANCE	115	149	170	148	162	133	136	139	124	145	124	106	153	119	154	118	91	133	126	153
90601	WHITTIER	108	121	122	116	126	99	123	117	110	128	113	93	125	110	127	102	83	118	98	128
90602	WHITTIER	86	83	80	80	84	69	95	86	88	96	92	69	91	88	92	83	67	92	76	95
90603	WHITTIER	107	149	160	142	157	134	126	130	120	126	121	95	148	120	144	121	90	125	124	142
90604	WHITTIER	92	110	105	101	113	88	105	102	94	108	97	79	109	95	109	88	71	101	87	110
90605	WHITTIER	103	124	118	112	129	96	117	116	101	125	105	90	120	102	123	92	77	112	92	122
90606	WHITTIER	88	103	94	91	106	75	100	98	85	107	89	77	100	86	103	76	65	95	75	102
90620	BUENA PARK	100	128	132	120	134	104	119	117	106	122	108	91	128	105	129	100	80	114	100	127
90621	BUENA PARK	92	94	93	92	96	77	104	95	95	106	99	77	102	95	103	89	72	99	82	106
90623	LA PALMA	128	171	192	166	186	142	156	157	135	165	137	122	173	133	176	125	102	150	131	170
90630	CYPRESS	122	155	166	151	163	136	141	141	130	145	132	108	157	130	155	125	97	137	127	156
90631	LA HABRA	110	129	131	123	134	110	125	122	115	128	118	94	133	115	132	110	87	122	109	134
90638	LA MIRADA	107	144	153	135	153	121	127	129	114	131	115	98	142	113	142	109	85	123	113	140
90639	LA MIRADA	78	85	92	85	89	95	86	87	92	86	91	61	93	84	92	98	63	90	109	101
90640	MONTEBELLO	79	86	82	80	88	69	89	85	81	91	85	66	89	81	90	76	62	86	72	91
90650	NORWALK	89	103	95	92	107	76	101	99	86	108	90	77	100	86	104	77	66	96	76	103
90660	PICO RIVERA	84	98	89	86	102	71	95	94	80	103	83	73	94	80	98	70	61	90	70	96
90670	SANTA FE SPRINGS	90	101	97	91	105	81	100	100	89	105	90	76	98	88	102	83	65	96	83	106
90680	STANTON	81	90	86	85	91	75	94	88	87	94	90	69	95	87	95	84	66	91	79	97
90701	ARTESIA	87	103	105	97	109	80	104	100	90	108	93	79	105	88	109	83	69	98	81	107
90703	CERRITOS	128	166	187	161	182	129	158	156	130	171	131	126	167	125	176	114	97	148	120	168
90704	AVALON	82	88	86	85	88	76	97	87	93	92	97	69	97	93	95	92	71	93	83	99
90706	BELLFLOWER	78	82	79	78	83	67	90	82	82	89	85	65	88	82	88	78	62	85	72	91
90710	HARBOR CITY	84	91	92	90	94	79	97	91	90	97	93	72	98	90	99	87	68	94	83	102
90712	LAKEWOOD	99	124	129	118	129	110	112	112	106	113	107	84	124	107	122	105	79	111	105	124
90713	LAKEWOOD	101	142	148	132	147	125	118	122	113	117	114	90	139	114	135	114	85	118	116	134
90715	LAKEWOOD	90	104	102	97	107	83	106	100	95	107	98	79	107	94	108	89	73	101	85	108
90716	HAWAIIAN GARDENS	71	69	59	63	68	53	79	71	71	80	76	58	74	73	75	65	56	76	59	76
90717	LOMITA	87	102	108	101	106	89	103	97	96	101	98	77	109	95	108	94	72	99	90	110
90720	LOS ALAMITOS	140	171	191	172	182	157	160	159	149	165	151	123	178	147	176	144	110	156	148	179
90723	PARAMOUNT	75	75	65	68	75	57	82	76	74	85	79	60	78	75	79	69	58	79	63	81
90731	SAN PEDRO	77	76	77	76	77	66	89	78	84	86	88	64	87	84	86	81	64	85	72	89
90732	SAN PEDRO	117	147	161	147	157	134	134	136	124	140	125	104	149	122	149	120	91	131	125	152
90740	SEAL BEACH	104	128	159	123	147	138	117	130	117	130	115	85	137	106	139	119	81	124	143	141
90742	SUNSET BEACH	173	184	217	203	194	168	206	179	191	202	198	153	216	190	210	184	148	188	166	210
90743	SURFSIDE	133	167	195	170	184	144	159	157	139	170	139	125	174	134	177	127	103	151	132	175
90744	WILMINGTON	70	68	58	61	68	50	76	70	67	79	72	56	71	69	73	61	53	74	55	73
90745	CARSON	96	114	115	104	120	89	109	109	93	115	95	85	110	93	115	85	70	104	86	116
90746	CARSON	103	129	129	123	131	119	113	116	110	116	111	85	126	110	123	111	80	114	114	131
90747	CARSON	87	91	83	92	87	97	84	87	91	88	91	61	90	88	86	95	62	88	100	107
90755	SIGNAL HILL	102	103	104	106	104	91	118	103	109	114	113	87	116	109	115	104	82	111	96	121
90802	LONG BEACH	64	46	46	51	45	45	69	54	68	65	70	46	60	68	59	67	50	65	56	67
90803	LONG BEACH	143	151	175	163	160	137	168	149	154	168	158	126	173	152	171	146	117	156	137	174
90804	LONG BEACH	69	53	52	56	52	47	75	60	71	72	75	52	66	72	66	67	54	71	56	72
90805	LONG BEACH	69	69	63	65	69	55	78	70	71	78	74	57	74	71	75	66	54	74	60	77
90806	LONG BEACH	66	65	60	61	64	53	74	66	69	73	73	53	71	70	71	65	53	72	58	73
90807	LONG BEACH	111	126	138	127	133	113	129	121	120	130	122	96	136	118	135	116	89	124	114	139
90808	LONG BEACH	109	148	161	142	156	133	128	131	121	129	122	98	149	121	146	120	91	127	122	144
90810	LONG BEACH	79	85	77	77	87	65	88	84	77	92	81	66	86	78	88	71	59	84	67	89
90813	LONG BEACH	46	33	30	34	32	28	48	39	47	48	50	33	42	48	42	44	36	47	36	45
90814	LONG BEACH	99	90	98	97	92	80	113	94	104	110	108	82	107	104	107	98	78	105	87	112
90815	LONG BEACH	112	139	153	137	147	130	132	127	125	128	126	97	146	125	141	125	93	128	124	143
90822	LONG BEACH	11	11	10	10	11	9	11	11	10	12	11	8	10	11	11	10	8	11	9	12
90840	LONG BEACH	29	12	12	15	11	14	41	20	33	28	33	22	24	32	22	30	24	29	20	28
91001	ALTADENA	128	168	183	162	181	144	149	152	135	158	136	116	168	133	168	128	101	145	132	165
91006	ARCADIA	119	155	177	154	168	132	143	143	126	152	128	112	160	123	161	118	95	138	122	157
91007	ARCADIA	112	137	157	138	150	113	138	132	119	144	121	107	145	115	150	108	89	130	109	146
91008	DUARTE	183	233	271	236	255	202	218	217	193	232	194	171	242	187	245	179	144	209	185	241
91010	DUARTE	92	115	116	107	120	97	107	106	98	109	101	80	115	98	115	95	74	104	96	115
91011	LA CANADA FLINTRIDGE	209	292	355	303	326	272	244	259	225	270	223	194	304	220	291	214	171	239	229	283
91016	MONROVIA	92	105	107	102	108	88	109	101	100	108	103	80	112	99	112	95	76	104	90	113
91020	MONTROSE	97	104	118	109	110	89	117	104	104	117	107	89	118	102	120	96	78	109	91	120
91024	SIERRA MADRE	143	182	214	186	200	160	170	170	151	182	151	134	190	146	192	140	113	163	146	189
91030	SOUTH PASADENA	123	136	157	143	146	118	148	134	131	150	135	113	152	129	154	121	99	139	117	154
91040	SUNLAND	97	127	135	122	132	114	114	114	110	112	111	85	130	109	126	111	82	112	110	127
91042	TUJUNGA	84	99	102	96	103	86	98	94	91	97	94	73	104	91	103	89	69	95	86	104
91101	PASADENA	89	68	70	76	66	65	98	76	96	92	99	68	88	95	86	93	71	91	80	96
91103	PASADENA	95	97	96	95	99	82	109	98	103	108	107	78	108	102	107	98	79	104	88	110
91104	PASADENA	93	107	115	106	113	93	111	104	103	110	106	81	116	101	115	100	78	106	95	117
91105	PASADENA	182	226	270	237	248	212	215	212	200	227	200	164	245	193	239	193	150	208	197	239
91106	PASADENA	124	113	123	123	116	103	140	117	131	137	136	102	136	131	133	125	99	130	111	141
91107	PASADENA	126	152	172	154	163	132	151	144	135	155	138	116	162	133	163	126	102	143	125	161
91108	SAN MARINO	227	320	389	332	358	295	264	282	243	294	241	212	332	240	315	231	186	259	245	306
91123	PASADENA	152	162	191	179	171	148	181	158	169	178	175	135	191	167	185	162	130	166	147	185
91201	GLENDALE	78	87	92	88	90	78	97	87	94	90	97	68	100	90	97	94	72	92	85	100
91202	GLENDALE	98	111	125	114	118	98	121	110	113	118	116	89	126	109	126	110	86	115	103	126
	CALIFORNIA	112	119	122	118	122	107	121	116	114	124	116	92	124	114	124	110	84	118	107	132
	UNITED STATES	100	100	100	100	100	100	100	100	100	100	100	100	100	100	100	100	100	100	100	100

91203-91763

#	POST OFFICE NAME	COUNTY FIPS CODE	POPULATION 2000	POPULATION 2009	POPULATION 2014	2000-2009 ANNUAL RATE % Rate	2000-2009 ANNUAL RATE State Centile	HOUSEHOLDS 2000	HOUSEHOLDS 2009	HOUSEHOLDS 2014	HOUSEHOLDS % Annual Rate 2000-2009	HOUSEHOLDS 2009 Average HH Size	FAMILIES 2000	FAMILIES 2009	FAMILIES % Annual Rate 2000-2009
91203	GLENDALE	037	14381	15014	15396	0.5	39	5363	5480	5587	0.2	2.71	3555	3633	0.2
91204	GLENDALE	037	17029	17478	17774	0.3	23	5540	5568	5629	0.1	3.05	4009	4031	0.1
91205	GLENDALE	037	41081	42628	43569	0.4	30	13960	14163	14392	0.2	2.95	9719	9865	0.2
91206	GLENDALE	037	32939	34379	35319	0.5	39	13251	13500	13801	0.2	2.51	8678	8847	0.2
91207	GLENDALE	037	10030	10625	10960	0.6	45	4047	4211	4329	0.4	2.52	2749	2857	0.4
91208	GLENDALE	037	15495	16218	16645	0.5	39	6027	6171	6300	0.3	2.59	4144	4244	0.3
91214	LA CRESCENTA	037	29504	30874	31681	0.5	39	10473	10727	10945	0.3	2.86	8108	8305	0.3
91301	AGOURA HILLS	037	25244	27742	28928	1.0	62	8471	9074	9419	0.7	3.05	6750	7204	0.7
91302	CALABASAS	037	24545	27929	29402	1.4	72	8764	9589	10032	1.0	2.90	6753	7391	1.0
91303	CANOGA PARK	037	23799	26251	27698	1.1	64	7622	8024	8422	0.6	3.27	5048	5377	0.7
91304	CANOGA PARK	037	47656	51271	52995	0.8	54	16050	16705	17159	0.4	3.03	11613	12095	0.4
91306	WINNETKA	037	45217	48613	50285	0.8	54	14094	14633	15029	0.4	3.30	10510	10940	0.4
91307	WEST HILLS	111	23608	24573	25180	0.4	30	8072	8245	8400	0.2	2.93	6494	6644	0.2
91311	CHATSWORTH	037	35334	37096	38142	0.5	39	13225	13612	13926	0.3	2.67	9271	9543	0.3
91316	ENCINO	037	25232	27088	28067	0.8	54	11906	12485	12840	0.5	2.17	6537	6878	0.6
91320	NEWBURY PARK	111	36463	42232	44619	1.6	77	12444	14492	15339	1.7	2.89	9705	11305	1.7
91321	NEWHALL	037	31297	35518	37360	1.4	72	10487	11381	11919	0.9	3.05	7148	7796	0.9
91324	NORTHRIDGE	037	24185	25552	26207	0.6	45	8076	8278	8450	0.3	3.06	5652	5801	0.3
91325	NORTHRIDGE	037	30834	32649	33630	0.6	45	11571	11979	12292	0.4	2.59	7387	7649	0.4
91326	PORTER RANCH	037	28080	34803	38033	2.3	86	9729	11669	12628	2.0	2.98	7980	9645	2.1
91330	NORTHRIDGE	037	1963	2086	2145	0.7	50	149	160	166	0.8	2.55	61	66	0.9
91331	PACOIMA	037	97758	104447	107648	0.7	50	21519	22401	23014	0.4	4.64	18580	19340	0.4
91335	RESEDA	037	68567	73985	76578	0.8	54	22071	23039	23691	0.5	3.16	15520	16214	0.5
91340	SAN FERNANDO	037	34941	37565	38854	0.8	54	8246	8619	8871	0.5	4.34	6953	7267	0.5
91342	SYLMAR	037	79709	91509	96902	1.5	75	20797	23307	24617	1.2	3.82	16692	18690	1.2
91343	NORTH HILLS	037	57617	63309	65796	1.0	62	16544	17391	17942	0.5	3.60	13086	13774	0.6
91344	GRANADA HILLS	037	48241	51136	52872	0.6	45	16097	16736	17226	0.4	3.02	12478	12970	0.4
91345	MISSION HILLS	037	17240	18286	18828	0.6	45	5063	5205	5325	0.3	3.44	3889	4004	0.3
91350	SANTA CLARITA	037	25640	31430	34130	2.2	85	7913	9442	10190	1.9	3.31	6802	8132	1.9
91351	CANYON COUNTRY	037	27675	31743	34057	1.5	75	8882	9790	10433	1.1	3.23	6839	7534	1.1
91352	SUN VALLEY	037	45963	49482	51155	0.8	54	11642	12193	12561	0.5	4.03	9501	9959	0.5
91354	VALENCIA	037	18150	31298	34047	6.1	97	6008	10223	11072	5.9	3.06	4846	8045	5.6
91355	VALENCIA	037	27402	42433	46021	4.8	95	10518	15127	16207	4.0	2.77	7209	10677	4.3
91356	TARZANA	037	28882	30661	31692	0.6	45	11527	11950	12263	0.4	2.53	7429	7738	0.4
91360	THOUSAND OAKS	111	42534	43113	43121	0.1	13	14528	14712	14726	0.1	2.82	10766	10867	0.1
91361	WESTLAKE VILLAGE	111	19797	20761	21207	0.5	39	8015	8328	8482	0.4	2.49	5642	5854	0.4
91362	THOUSAND OAKS	111	33954	36866	38103	0.9	58	12491	13501	13923	0.8	2.72	9402	10142	0.8
91364	WOODLAND HILLS	037	23806	24942	25621	0.5	39	9661	9919	10132	0.3	2.46	6497	6670	0.3
91367	WOODLAND HILLS	037	36397	38874	39957	0.7	50	15739	16425	16788	0.5	2.36	9526	9903	0.4
91371	WOODLAND HILLS	037	4	183	204	51.2	100	1	77	85	59.9	2.38	1	38	48.2
91377	OAK PARK	111	14215	14487	14527	0.2	18	5034	5150	5173	0.2	2.81	3851	3927	0.2
91381	STEVENSON RANCH	037	7910	12100	14476	4.7	95	2845	4116	4860	4.1	2.94	2124	3129	4.3
91384	CASTAIC	037	22234	29855	33027	3.2	91	4655	6566	7436	3.8	3.41	3810	5431	3.9
91387	CANYON COUNTRY	037	30797	41559	46116	3.3	92	10525	13448	14708	2.7	3.09	7791	10281	3.0
91390	SANTA CLARITA	037	13665	22691	26275	5.6	96	4453	6954	7945	4.9	3.22	3576	5692	5.2
91401	VAN NUYS	037	41323	43981	45254	0.7	50	14994	15418	15762	0.3	2.84	9655	9929	0.3
91402	PANORAMA CITY	037	66620	73370	75763	1.0	62	17628	18287	18753	0.4	3.99	14077	14612	0.4
91403	SHERMAN OAKS	037	20465	21578	22236	0.6	45	10329	10672	10937	0.4	2.02	4961	5119	0.3
91405	VAN NUYS	037	48410	52423	54118	0.9	58	15374	15879	16274	0.4	3.25	10580	10934	0.4
91406	VAN NUYS	037	53685	57223	59000	0.7	50	18374	18963	19426	0.3	3.00	12372	12776	0.3
91411	VAN NUYS	037	23743	26012	27136	1.0	62	8979	9592	9956	0.7	2.69	5283	5623	0.7
91423	SHERMAN OAKS	037	28040	29229	29984	0.4	30	14144	14437	14724	0.2	2.02	6480	6624	0.2
91436	ENCINO	037	14858	15498	15893	0.5	39	5827	5955	6076	0.2	2.59	4356	4448	0.2
91501	BURBANK	037	19753	21472	22392	0.9	58	8057	8600	8924	0.7	2.49	5033	5358	0.7
91502	BURBANK	037	11466	12423	12925	0.9	58	4741	5068	5262	0.7	2.45	2593	2753	0.6
91504	BURBANK	037	23600	24526	25098	0.4	30	8761	8906	9058	0.2	2.73	6005	6111	0.2
91505	BURBANK	037	29083	30288	31000	0.4	30	13031	13290	13536	0.2	2.26	6811	6942	0.2
91506	BURBANK	037	19201	19874	20290	0.4	30	8024	8138	8268	0.2	2.38	4591	4658	0.2
91522	BURBANK	037	3	3	3	0.0	9	1	1	1	0.0	3.00	0	0	0.0
91601	NORTH HOLLYWOOD	037	38062	41121	42716	0.8	54	15208	16075	16623	0.6	2.53	7754	8175	0.6
91602	NORTH HOLLYWOOD	037	15391	16248	16773	0.6	45	8464	8741	8962	0.3	1.86	3125	3233	0.4
91604	STUDIO CITY	037	24991	26418	27239	0.6	45	13036	13521	13880	0.4	1.92	5539	5721	0.4
91605	NORTH HOLLYWOOD	037	54899	59244	61487	0.8	54	14663	15359	15842	0.5	3.81	11622	12175	0.5
91606	NORTH HOLLYWOOD	037	45128	49643	51775	1.0	62	14544	15493	16047	0.7	3.19	10038	10698	0.7
91607	VALLEY VILLAGE	037	30163	31799	32733	0.6	45	14011	14435	14773	0.3	2.17	6654	6873	0.4
91701	RANCHO CUCAMONGA	071	39329	42560	43757	0.9	58	12829	13431	13694	0.5	3.16	10292	10756	0.5
91702	AZUSA	037	57275	61657	64124	0.8	54	15215	15946	16517	0.5	3.76	11748	12312	0.5
91706	BALDWIN PARK	037	76567	80913	83084	0.6	45	17158	17660	18071	0.3	4.55	15217	15662	0.3
91708	CHINO	071	2700	6436	7850	9.8	98	175	1038	1361	21.2	4.27	149	884	21.2
91709	CHINO HILLS	071	65830	78957	84439	2.0	83	19812	22845	24219	1.6	3.45	16877	19460	1.6
91710	CHINO	071	73237	85030	90145	1.6	77	18998	21597	22851	1.4	3.57	15517	17689	1.4
91711	CLAREMONT	037	34997	37663	38991	0.8	54	11644	12485	12960	0.8	2.57	7971	8547	0.8
91722	COVINA	037	35125	37158	38185	0.6	45	10697	11007	11246	0.3	3.35	8334	8581	0.3
91723	COVINA	037	16063	17507	18225	0.9	58	5755	6086	6293	0.6	2.83	3959	4184	0.6
91724	COVINA	037	25826	27463	28411	0.7	50	8660	8992	9242	0.4	3.02	6663	6924	0.4
91730	RANCHO CUCAMONGA	071	52146	69047	75272	3.1	91	16728	21903	23866	3.0	3.04	12090	15665	2.8
91731	EL MONTE	037	28699	31539	32918	1.0	62	7158	7632	7915	0.7	4.11	5889	6270	0.7
91732	EL MONTE	037	64243	68206	70038	0.6	45	14916	15327	15671	0.3	4.39	12734	13090	0.3
91733	SOUTH EL MONTE	037	45375	47401	48522	0.5	39	9793	9995	10192	0.2	4.72	8713	8899	0.2
91737	RANCHO CUCAMONGA	071	22712	25619	26868	1.3	70	7212	7869	8178	0.9	3.25	5969	6480	0.9
91739	RANCHO CUCAMONGA	071	13742	28241	34367	8.1	97	4172	8222	9915	7.6	3.31	3526	7000	7.7
91740	GLENDORA	037	24620	25633	26223	0.4	30	8099	8273	8425	0.2	3.01	6143	6269	0.2
91741	GLENDORA	037	25771	26997	27877	0.5	39	9050	9285	9546	0.3	2.84	6894	7085	0.3
91744	LA PUENTE	037	84057	88466	90556	0.6	45	18277	18683	19052	0.2	4.73	16178	16544	0.2
91745	HACIENDA HEIGHTS	037	53713	55939	57327	0.4	30	16112	16396	16694	0.2	3.40	13509	13757	0.2
91746	LA PUENTE	037	32295	33885	34698	0.5	39	7142	7327	7481	0.3	4.60	6278	6444	0.3
91748	ROWLAND HEIGHTS	037	46336	48413	49593	0.5	39	13461	13701	13942	0.2	3.53	11421	11633	0.2
91750	LA VERNE	037	33587	34700	35386	0.4	30	11551	11666	11823	0.1	2.90	8653	8749	0.1
91752	MIRA LOMA	065	19186	28946	33573	4.5	95	5843	8434	9680	4.0	3.42	4253	6201	4.2
91754	MONTEREY PARK	037	31896	33543	34517	0.5	39	10784	11104	11361	0.3	3.01	8279	8525	0.3
91755	MONTEREY PARK	037	29061	31388	32617	0.8	54	9139	9655	9972	0.6	3.23	7221	7630	0.6
91759	MT BALDY	071	484	545	604	1.3	70	204	225	251	1.1	2.22	151	166	1.0
91761	ONTARIO	071	56394	60315	62040	0.7	50	14969	15429	15784	0.3	3.89	12563	12872	0.3
91762	ONTARIO	071	54520	59196	60471	0.9	58	15846	16443	16685	0.4	3.57	12290	12707	0.4
91763	MONTCLAIR	071	33938	37444	38938	1.1	64	9066	9655	9988	0.7	3.82	7231	7680	0.7
	CALIFORNIA					1.2					1.0	2.93			1.1
	UNITED STATES					1.0					1.1	2.59			0.9

ZIP CODE #	POST OFFICE NAME	RACE (%) White 2000	White 2009	Black 2000	Black 2009	Asian/Pacific 2000	Asian/Pacific 2009	% Hispanic Origin 2000	% Hispanic Origin 2009	2009 AGE DISTRIBUTION (%) 0-4	5-9	10-14	15-19	20-24	25-44	45-64	65-84	85+	18+	MEDIAN AGE 2009	% 2009 Males	% 2009 Females
91203	GLENDALE	58.2	48.3	1.7	1.7	16.2	18.9	21.1	28.0	5.6	5.3	5.3	6.4	7.9	30.4	26.5	10.7	1.9	80.1	37.6	48.9	51.1
91204	GLENDALE	44.3	37.0	1.5	1.3	19.6	20.8	40.8	48.6	7.2	6.6	6.2	7.4	8.1	31.9	22.5	8.2	1.9	75.8	33.5	49.6	50.4
91205	GLENDALE	57.8	48.6	1.4	1.3	13.5	15.5	28.5	36.7	6.3	5.8	5.8	6.9	8.2	30.3	24.4	10.2	2.1	78.0	35.2	48.3	51.7
91206	GLENDALE	63.6	54.2	1.6	1.6	20.0	24.4	15.1	20.9	5.0	4.9	4.9	5.2	6.4	29.5	28.3	13.3	2.4	82.2	41.2	47.1	52.9
91207	GLENDALE	79.5	71.4	0.7	0.8	10.9	14.7	9.4	14.4	4.9	5.1	5.4	4.6	4.1	26.9	30.9	15.2	2.9	81.6	44.4	47.8	52.2
91208	GLENDALE	75.2	66.6	0.6	0.7	15.0	19.6	9.0	13.4	5.4	5.9	6.5	5.9	4.0	24.0	30.7	14.4	3.2	78.5	44.0	47.4	52.6
91214	LA CRESCENTA	72.6	63.3	0.5	0.6	20.0	26.3	9.1	13.6	5.4	6.0	6.8	7.3	5.9	22.6	32.3	11.7	1.9	77.0	42.2	48.4	51.6
91301	AGOURA HILLS	87.1	81.3	1.3	1.5	6.4	9.1	6.8	11.1	5.8	6.8	8.1	7.8	5.1	23.8	33.6	8.1	0.9	74.1	40.3	49.6	50.4
91302	CALABASAS	87.5	81.6	1.2	1.4	7.2	10.6	4.8	8.1	5.6	6.6	8.1	7.9	5.0	22.0	33.7	10.0	1.1	74.5	41.5	48.8	51.2
91303	CANOGA PARK	50.6	45.4	4.0	3.5	8.9	9.7	59.4	67.2	9.5	8.5	7.2	7.8	9.4	33.1	18.9	4.9	0.6	70.3	28.9	51.7	48.3
91304	CANOGA PARK	61.7	54.3	4.5	4.3	12.3	14.5	32.6	40.6	7.8	7.4	7.1	7.2	6.8	28.4	24.9	8.8	1.6	73.3	35.1	49.7	50.3
91306	WINNETKA	52.4	44.8	4.4	4.0	15.4	16.9	40.4	49.7	7.8	7.5	7.1	7.7	7.1	29.8	23.7	8.0	1.2	72.8	33.6	50.0	50.0
91307	WEST HILLS	79.1	71.5	2.1	2.3	11.5	15.5	10.4	15.7	5.8	6.5	7.3	7.0	4.2	21.8	31.5	13.6	2.2	75.6	43.4	49.1	50.9
91311	CHATSWORTH	73.8	65.9	3.0	3.1	14.2	18.3	13.7	19.8	5.3	5.4	5.8	6.2	5.2	25.0	30.6	14.3	2.2	79.3	43.0	48.3	51.7
91316	ENCINO	82.9	75.5	2.6	3.0	5.1	7.1	10.1	16.0	4.8	4.7	4.9	4.4	4.6	28.6	28.8	15.7	3.7	83.0	43.9	47.1	52.9
91320	NEWBURY PARK	84.5	79.6	1.2	1.3	6.0	8.1	14.2	18.3	7.2	7.6	7.9	6.8	4.4	26.7	28.4	9.5	1.6	73.0	38.7	49.5	50.5
91321	NEWHALL	72.3	66.0	1.9	2.0	4.2	5.4	35.6	44.0	7.9	7.5	7.0	7.5	7.3	29.5	22.7	8.9	1.7	73.4	33.5	50.1	49.9
91324	NORTHRIDGE	59.1	51.6	4.2	4.2	14.8	17.8	31.9	38.7	6.8	6.6	6.4	7.1	7.5	29.5	23.8	10.5	1.7	75.9	34.8	49.5	50.5
91325	NORTHRIDGE	62.9	54.7	6.1	6.0	14.3	17.4	23.1	30.5	5.7	5.4	5.2	8.1	10.1	29.9	23.9	10.0	1.6	80.3	34.1	48.7	51.3
91326	PORTER RANCH	65.5	53.5	2.7	2.7	25.4	35.4	8.8	11.9	5.5	6.3	7.1	6.5	4.2	23.8	32.5	12.6	1.3	76.8	42.8	48.6	51.4
91330	NORTHRIDGE	48.4	40.4	16.6	16.3	19.8	23.5	18.3	24.8	2.6	2.0	1.5	25.6	30.5	24.8	9.8	2.9	0.3	92.6	23.0	45.4	54.6
91331	PACOIMA	36.9	35.2	5.5	4.4	4.7	4.5	81.8	86.1	9.5	9.2	8.3	9.5	8.9	29.9	18.4	5.7	0.7	67.3	27.6	50.6	49.4
91335	RESEDA	57.4	49.9	4.2	3.9	11.3	12.4	41.9	52.0	7.7	7.4	6.9	7.6	7.4	29.7	23.1	8.2	2.1	73.5	33.7	49.2	50.8
91340	SAN FERNANDO	41.2	39.4	2.9	2.2	1.3	1.2	87.8	91.7	10.0	9.4	8.3	8.9	8.9	29.8	18.1	5.6	0.9	66.9	27.5	50.7	49.3
91342	SYLMAR	49.1	45.0	6.6	5.7	3.9	4.0	66.2	74.4	8.6	8.4	8.2	9.4	7.7	28.1	21.2	7.2	1.1	68.8	30.1	50.2	49.8
91343	NORTH HILLS	51.3	46.3	4.9	4.3	12.5	13.6	52.8	60.2	9.5	8.4	7.4	8.6	8.6	28.7	20.4	7.2	1.2	69.5	29.5	50.3	49.7
91344	GRANADA HILLS	65.9	57.1	3.7	3.7	16.4	20.2	20.5	28.2	6.0	6.2	6.7	7.0	5.6	26.2	28.9	11.8	1.8	76.8	40.2	49.2	50.8
91345	MISSION HILLS	52.2	46.6	4.0	3.4	10.7	11.1	54.4	63.7	7.3	7.3	7.2	7.9	6.6	26.4	23.9	10.8	2.5	73.4	35.6	49.1	50.9
91350	SANTA CLARITA	83.2	76.0	1.7	2.0	5.4	7.3	14.9	23.3	7.6	8.0	8.7	8.6	5.0	27.1	28.5	5.8	0.6	70.0	35.2	49.5	50.5
91351	CANYON COUNTRY	74.7	66.5	2.6	2.8	4.9	6.2	26.7	37.3	7.9	7.7	7.6	8.0	6.5	29.0	25.3	7.1	0.8	71.8	33.8	49.4	50.6
91352	SUN VALLEY	49.1	45.3	1.6	1.3	6.5	6.5	70.8	77.0	9.1	8.7	7.9	8.7	8.4	29.2	20.4	6.6	1.0	69.1	29.3	50.9	49.1
91354	VALENCIA	82.7	61.4	1.8	4.8	8.5	15.8	11.3	26.5	10.1	9.5	7.8	6.1	3.6	33.3	23.4	5.4	0.7	68.5	34.7	49.3	50.7
91355	VALENCIA	85.3	67.3	1.5	3.8	6.6	13.2	10.2	21.9	6.9	7.1	7.5	6.9	5.3	26.7	29.2	8.9	1.5	74.1	38.6	49.0	51.0
91356	TARZANA	79.2	72.3	3.7	3.8	5.6	7.4	13.0	18.9	5.7	5.8	6.3	5.9	5.9	26.0	28.7	13.1	2.7	78.4	41.3	48.5	51.5
91360	THOUSAND OAKS	84.5	78.7	0.9	1.1	5.2	6.7	14.9	21.6	6.2	6.5	6.8	7.7	6.4	24.2	27.7	11.7	2.9	76.2	39.7	49.4	50.6
91361	WESTLAKE VILLAGE	90.3	86.0	0.9	1.1	5.1	7.2	5.7	9.3	4.3	4.8	5.9	6.1	4.1	20.9	33.7	17.7	2.6	81.2	47.4	48.7	51.3
91362	THOUSAND OAKS	85.5	80.1	1.1	1.3	6.8	9.2	11.3	16.1	6.6	7.4	8.2	7.2	4.4	23.7	31.4	10.0	1.2	73.3	40.5	48.5	51.5
91364	WOODLAND HILLS	85.0	78.6	2.5	2.9	5.3	7.6	6.9	11.0	5.5	5.8	6.4	5.2	3.7	25.2	32.0	13.4	2.7	78.8	44.0	49.2	50.8
91367	WOODLAND HILLS	82.0	74.4	3.5	4.0	7.5	10.5	7.7	13.0	5.1	5.1	5.4	5.1	5.4	27.9	28.8	14.6	2.6	81.0	42.4	48.8	51.2
91371	WOODLAND HILLS	66.7	46.4	0.0	7.7	0.0	13.1	66.7	51.9	8.2	6.0	4.4	7.1	16.4	39.3	15.3	3.3	0.0	78.1	27.4	53.0	47.0
91377	OAK PARK	88.2	83.5	1.0	1.1	7.2	9.8	4.4	6.8	6.3	7.6	9.1	9.1	4.7	21.7	34.7	6.2	0.6	71.2	40.1	48.4	51.6
91381	STEVENSON RANCH	73.2	64.3	2.7	2.9	14.5	18.9	12.9	18.8	10.0	10.0	9.4	6.4	4.4	32.9	23.2	3.4	0.3	66.3	32.7	50.6	49.4
91384	CASTAIC	68.9	56.3	11.5	8.9	5.3	5.7	32.8	50.5	6.2	6.8	6.0	8.5	11.7	37.8	18.2	3.9	1.0	78.6	31.2	63.6	36.4
91387	CANYON COUNTRY	77.7	70.6	4.1	4.1	5.3	6.9	19.0	28.0	8.2	8.1	8.0	7.9	6.5	29.8	25.4	5.5	0.5	70.8	33.0	49.8	50.2
91390	SANTA CLARITA	85.8	79.0	1.9	2.2	4.5	7.1	12.5	19.0	7.5	8.0	8.7	8.2	4.4	26.3	30.4	5.9	0.6	70.3	36.9	49.3	50.7
91401	VAN NUYS	60.0	53.0	5.0	4.7	4.7	5.4	43.5	53.0	8.1	7.3	6.4	7.1	8.3	31.1	22.7	7.4	1.5	74.0	32.4	50.3	49.7
91402	PANORAMA CITY	35.8	33.0	4.7	3.8	12.4	12.1	69.3	75.1	10.8	9.8	8.3	9.1	9.0	30.2	17.2	4.8	0.8	65.9	26.7	50.6	49.4
91403	SHERMAN OAKS	82.7	75.6	3.5	4.1	5.9	8.3	8.5	13.5	4.9	4.6	4.6	4.0	6.4	34.1	28.0	11.1	2.3	83.5	40.2	48.6	51.4
91405	VAN NUYS	49.2	44.2	6.2	5.3	8.0	8.2	58.0	67.2	9.8	8.8	7.3	7.6	8.6	31.6	18.8	6.1	1.4	69.5	29.3	50.6	49.4
91406	VAN NUYS	54.5	48.4	6.2	5.4	7.0	7.6	51.2	61.0	8.9	8.2	7.4	7.9	7.9	31.3	21.4	6.1	1.0	71.0	31.1	51.0	49.0
91411	VAN NUYS	56.9	51.2	5.1	4.9	5.5	6.3	50.5	58.0	8.0	7.2	6.4	7.0	8.3	34.1	22.2	5.9	1.0	74.5	32.3	51.1	48.9
91423	SHERMAN OAKS	82.5	75.9	4.3	4.9	5.2	7.1	9.8	15.3	5.0	4.6	4.7	4.2	6.7	33.4	28.3	10.6	2.7	83.2	40.1	47.9	52.1
91436	ENCINO	89.0	83.8	1.7	2.0	4.4	6.4	5.0	8.2	5.4	6.2	7.5	5.7	3.1	21.1	31.1	16.7	3.1	77.1	45.5	48.4	51.6
91501	BURBANK	72.2	63.1	1.9	2.0	11.6	14.8	16.0	23.1	5.7	5.4	5.5	5.8	7.3	31.5	27.0	9.9	1.8	80.0	37.7	48.1	51.9
91502	BURBANK	60.4	53.0	2.9	2.7	9.6	11.0	39.5	48.0	6.7	5.9	5.4	7.1	9.2	31.5	21.3	10.7	2.1	77.9	34.7	48.7	51.3
91504	BURBANK	67.8	60.1	2.1	2.0	10.4	12.8	29.0	37.1	6.3	5.9	6.0	7.0	7.3	29.1	25.9	10.5	2.1	77.7	37.4	48.6	51.4
91505	BURBANK	77.6	70.4	2.1	2.3	7.6	9.6	22.3	31.7	5.2	4.9	5.0	5.7	7.5	31.2	28.1	10.0	2.4	81.6	39.4	49.4	50.6
91506	BURBANK	75.6	68.1	1.8	1.8	8.3	10.3	24.9	34.6	5.7	5.5	5.7	5.8	5.9	28.7	28.9	11.0	2.8	79.5	40.7	49.5	50.5
91522	BURBANK	100.0	100.0	0.0	0.0	0.0	0.0	0.0	0.0	0.0	0.0	0.0	0.0	0.0	33.3	66.7	0.0	0.0	100.0	46.3	66.7	33.3
91601	NORTH HOLLYWOOD	52.9	46.7	8.3	7.7	5.2	5.8	49.2	58.3	7.8	6.6	5.6	6.9	10.3	35.2	20.7	5.7	1.0	76.0	31.1	50.7	49.3
91602	NORTH HOLLYWOOD	78.5	71.5	6.1	6.7	6.1	8.1	12.9	19.7	4.2	3.5	3.0	3.1	6.3	41.3	27.6	9.1	1.7	87.4	38.5	49.7	50.3
91604	STUDIO CITY	85.4	79.4	3.5	4.2	5.3	7.6	6.7	10.8	4.4	4.3	4.5	3.6	4.9	33.9	30.3	11.3	2.8	84.6	42.0	49.7	50.3
91605	NORTH HOLLYWOOD	45.2	40.7	3.0	2.5	10.4	10.5	64.1	71.3	9.3	8.9	7.7	8.6	8.9	30.0	19.4	6.2	1.0	69.0	28.9	50.7	49.3
91606	NORTH HOLLYWOOD	52.7	46.5	3.9	3.4	5.1	5.3	57.6	66.8	8.7	8.0	7.3	8.4	8.7	30.6	20.9	6.4	1.0	71.1	30.2	50.7	49.3
91607	VALLEY VILLAGE	73.9	66.2	5.7	6.0	5.3	6.7	19.9	28.7	5.6	4.9	4.6	5.0	7.4	34.3	26.4	9.4	2.4	81.9	37.7	48.6	51.4
91701	RANCHO CUCAMONGA	72.7	65.6	6.0	6.1	6.9	8.6	22.0	30.0	6.6	6.8	7.3	7.7	5.7	28.2	28.7	8.1	1.0	74.5	36.8	48.8	51.2
91702	AZUSA	51.7	47.2	3.4	2.9	6.1	6.3	66.4	74.1	9.4	8.9	8.0	9.5	9.2	29.7	18.5	5.9	0.8	68.5	27.8	49.8	50.2
91706	BALDWIN PARK	40.3	38.7	1.6	1.3	11.7	10.8	78.7	83.0	9.9	9.5	8.5	9.2	8.8	29.2	18.6	5.6	0.7	66.7	27.4	50.1	49.9
91708	CHINO	62.7	60.3	24.4	11.9	0.7	0.8	31.1	50.6	6.5	6.3	5.8	6.2	7.4	42.9	18.9	5.2	0.8	77.7	33.7	35.1	64.9
91709	CHINO HILLS	56.5	50.2	5.6	5.3	22.5	24.4	25.1	33.1	8.7	8.9	8.7	7.7	4.8	31.0	25.0	4.8	0.4	68.7	33.8	49.6	50.4
91710	CHINO	56.4	50.8	7.4	6.6	5.1	5.9	47.3	56.2	7.6	7.4	7.3	8.4	8.6	31.7	22.8	5.4	0.7	72.9	31.5	54.5	45.5
91711	CLAREMONT	73.0	65.4	5.5	5.6	11.2	14.6	16.1	22.9	4.4	4.7	5.3	11.4	11.0	21.4	25.6	13.2	3.0	81.1	37.6	47.4	52.6
91722	COVINA	56.5	50.5	4.9	4.4	9.7	10.3	49.8	60.3	7.7	7.7	7.7	8.6	7.6	28.6	23.0	7.7	1.3	71.7	32.2	48.8	51.2
91723	COVINA	62.7	55.7	4.9	4.3	7.6	8.5	43.0	54.5	8.3	7.6	7.1	7.6	8.0	30.1	22.1	7.7	1.4	72.3	31.9	48.2	51.8
91724	COVINA	66.4	59.1	3.9	3.7	11.4	13.3	33.5	44.3	6.7	6.6	6.9	7.7	6.8	26.3	26.7	10.7	1.7	75.0	36.8	48.3	51.7
91730	RANCHO CUCAMONGA	58.8	52.3	9.6	9.1	5.5	6.7	35.7	43.7	7.8	6.9	6.6	7.4	8.8	34.3	21.9	5.7	0.7	74.5	31.2	50.2	49.8
91731	EL MONTE	38.8	37.4	0.9	0.7	18.0	16.8	72.4	77.1	10.1	9.2	8.1	8.9	8.7	29.3	18.3	6.3	1.0	67.2	27.9	50.6	49.4
91732	EL MONTE	35.2	33.3	0.8	0.7	18.5	17.5	71.7	76.2	10.1	9.6	8.5	9.2	8.6	29.4	18.0	5.7	0.8	66.2	27.3	50.7	49.3
91733	SOUTH EL MONTE	36.5	35.5	0.4	0.3	14.2	13.1	80.3	83.5	10.4	9.8	8.5	9.2	8.6	30.5	16.8	5.5	0.6	65.7	27.0	50.6	49.4
91737	RANCHO CUCAMONGA	72.0	65.5	7.5	7.6	7.7	9.5	19.6	26.7	6.3	6.5	7.2	8.1	5.9	27.5	31.2	6.7	0.7	74.9	36.9	49.4	50.6
91739	RANCHO CUCAMONGA	69.3	62.5	7.2	7.0	4.9	5.0	27.5	38.8	8.0	7.9	7.9	7.9	6.5	30.9	25.7	4.7	0.5	71.5	32.8	50.8	49.2
91740	GLENDORA	74.4	66.6	2.1	2.1	7.5	9.2	28.2	39.2	6.9	7.0	6.9	7.3	6.5	26.7	26.3	10.5	2.0	74.7	37.1	48.6	51.4
91741	GLENDORA	85.8	79.8	0.9	1.1	5.2	7.0	15.5	23.7	5.7	5.9	6.6	8.2	6.7	23.5	29.1	12.3	2.0	76.9	40.4	48.2	51.8
91744	LA PUENTE	40.0	37.9	2.3	1.8	7.9	7.3	80.4	85.0	9.4	9.1	8.3	9.4	8.5	28.9	19.2	6.5	0.7	67.5	28.3	49.8	50.2
91745	HACIENDA HEIGHTS	41.3	36.6	1.6	1.4	35.9	37.5	38.3	44.5	5.9	5.9	6.0	7.3	7.3	26.8	26.8	12.6	1.4	77.9	37.7	48.8	51.2
91746	LA PUENTE	44.3	42.7	2.0	1.6	7.8	7.1	82.2	86.5	9.0	8.6	8.1	8.9	8.2	29.8	19.0	7.6	0.8	69.0	29.3	50.5	49.5
91748	ROWLAND HEIGHTS	28.6	25.1	2.5	2.2	51.2	52.4	28.7	33.1	6.8	6.5	6.4	7.0	6.9	29.7	26.3	9.4	1.1	76.1	35.7	49.4	50.6
91750	LA VERNE	77.2	70.2	3.3	3.4	7.2	9.2	23.0	32.6	5.6	6.0	6.6	7.7	5.9	24.7	29.1	12.2	2.2	77.4	40.2	48.5	51.5
91752	MIRA LOMA	65.4	57.9	2.9	3.1	1.4	1.8	44.5	55.1	8.4	8.0	7.6	8.4	7.7	26.1	23.6	9.0	1.3	70.8	32.1	50.0	50.0
91754	MONTEREY PARK	23.4	22.0	0.4	0.3	58.2	57.7	32.2	35.5	5.6	5.4	5.3	6.3	6.5	27.4	25.8	14.9	2.7	79.9	40.3	48.1	51.9
91755	MONTEREY PARK	19.7	18.3	0.5	0.4	64.9	64.5	26.1	29.0	5.9	5.6	5.4	6.2	7.0	29.3	26.1	12.3	2.3	79.5	38.4	48.6	51.4
91759	MT BALDY	78.8	72.3	3.7	3.7	4.7	6.1	16.5	22.9	4.2	6.1	6.1	7.3	6.1	26.4	33.9	9.2	0.7	79.8	41.5	53.9	46.1
91761	ONTARIO	48.2	43.4	9.1	8.3	5.3	5.8	56.9	64.5	9.6	9.0	8.3	8.7	7.7	30.6	20.9	4.7	0.5	67.9	29.0	50.0	50.0
91762	ONTARIO	49.8	44.4	5.9	5.2	4.0	4.3	59.1	67.5	9.8	9.2	8.0	8.4	7.9	29.4	19.5	6.5	1.1	67.8	28.9	49.5	50.5
91763	MONTCLAIR	44.8	39.8	6.2	5.4	8.2	8.3	60.4	68.3	9.3	8.8	7.7	8.8	8.9	28.6	19.7	7.0	1.2	68.9	28.8	50.1	49.9
	CALIFORNIA	59.5	54.5	6.7	6.2	11.3	12.5	32.4	38.3	7.5	7.1	6.9	7.5	7.4	28.5	24.2	9.3	1.6	74.1	34.3	49.9	50.1
	UNITED STATES	75.1	72.0	12.3	12.7	3.8	4.6	12.5	15.7	6.8	6.7	6.6	7.1	6.9	27.0	26.0	10.9	1.9	75.7	36.9	49.2	50.8

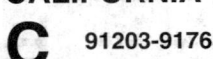

ZIP CODE				2009 HOUSEHOLD INCOME DISTRIBUTION (%)					MEDIAN HOUSEHOLD INCOME					2009 HOME VALUE DISTRIBUTION (%)					
#	POST OFFICE NAME	2009 Per Capita Income	2009 HH Income Base	Less than $25,000	$25,000 to $49,999	$50,000 to $99,999	$100,000 to $149,999	$150,000 or More	2009	2014	2009 National Centile	2009 State Centile	2009 Home Value Base	Less than $50,000	$50,000 to $89,999	$90,000 to $174,999	$175,000 to $399,999	$400,000 or More	2009 Median Home Value
91203	GLENDALE	19160	5480	28.3	30.3	33.0	6.2	2.1	42108	45441	40	26	1268	0.6	0.0	4.1	62.1	33.2	319011
91204	GLENDALE	16406	5568	29.5	27.9	36.0	5.5	1.2	42389	46268	41	27	851	2.2	0.0	1.6	64.2	32.0	292143
91205	GLENDALE	15954	14163	36.1	29.1	27.4	5.0	2.4	35438	39285	19	14	2558	1.8	0.2	7.3	45.0	45.7	373923
91206	GLENDALE	31033	13500	22.4	22.6	34.8	8.3	11.9	55615	60219	72	53	5290	0.3	0.3	4.3	29.3	65.8	570893
91207	GLENDALE	44843	4211	11.9	15.9	30.3	20.5	21.3	82103	82515	93	82	2528	0.2	0.1	2.4	11.4	86.0	745828
91208	GLENDALE	44198	6171	11.2	12.1	33.7	20.5	22.5	84517	84971	94	84	4088	0.5	0.9	0.7	10.7	87.2	721285
91214	LA CRESCENTA	35412	10727	9.2	16.5	37.9	20.1	16.4	80760	81799	92	81	7585	0.6	1.0	1.0	15.4	82.0	568417
91301	AGOURA HILLS	48463	9074	6.3	9.5	29.5	21.3	33.4	111054	113542	98	94	7317	0.3	0.3	1.9	18.6	78.9	676403
91302	CALABASAS	58279	9589	6.4	10.7	27.6	13.3	42.0	122325	128185	99	96	7276	0.5	1.2	1.5	9.3	87.4	901808
91303	CANOGA PARK	17232	8024	21.9	30.5	38.0	6.8	2.8	47763	50510	56	38	2476	0.1	1.1	11.1	67.2	20.5	273909
91304	CANOGA PARK	27303	16705	16.0	22.4	36.5	13.0	12.2	62905	65074	81	63	8768	2.7	3.2	6.0	28.3	59.8	445320
91306	WINNETKA	21376	14633	16.3	25.8	38.4	13.8	5.7	59985	62636	77	58	8083	1.3	0.1	2.7	64.9	31.0	347276
91307	WEST HILLS	39497	8245	6.8	12.4	36.4	21.7	22.6	89988	90629	95	87	6934	0.2	0.0	0.0	21.5	78.3	496836
91311	CHATSWORTH	36288	13612	9.9	15.3	42.3	17.1	15.4	77269	77818	91	78	9106	3.1	2.4	2.3	28.8	63.3	471219
91316	ENCINO	39606	12485	17.4	22.3	37.3	10.7	12.4	61983	64268	80	61	6230	0.2	0.0	7.0	40.5	52.2	415368
91320	NEWBURY PARK	40690	14492	6.3	11.5	30.7	28.9	22.6	102166	105913	97	92	11468	1.5	1.8	3.1	25.7	67.9	483273
91321	NEWHALL	26424	11381	16.8	20.9	36.9	16.2	9.2	62269	66718	83	65	6740	3.9	1.3	7.8	47.3	39.7	318139
91324	NORTHRIDGE	27811	8278	17.3	20.9	34.7	13.7	13.4	65693	67845	84	66	4640	2.6	0.6	0.8	30.0	66.0	482080
91325	NORTHRIDGE	32320	11979	15.4	21.9	37.2	12.3	13.2	63618	65866	82	64	6031	0.3	0.5	1.7	31.0	66.4	503986
91326	PORTER RANCH	46427	11669	6.0	11.1	30.9	18.6	33.5	106680	111684	98	93	9558	0.5	0.6	1.5	15.3	82.1	616471
91330	NORTHRIDGE	12758	160	30.0	23.8	36.3	3.8	6.3	43994	48006	45	31	38	2.6	0.0	0.0	52.6	44.7	377778
91331	PACOIMA	12851	22401	20.7	29.4	37.8	8.6	3.5	49948	52226	61	42	13934	3.1	1.1	7.0	85.7	3.1	255208
91335	RESEDA	19998	23039	19.7	28.2	37.8	9.9	4.4	52263	56520	66	46	11845	0.7	0.4	4.5	74.7	19.7	292515
91340	SAN FERNANDO	13398	8619	20.7	28.3	40.6	8.0	2.3	50823	53652	63	44	4797	1.8	0.6	6.3	86.0	5.3	248363
91342	SYLMAR	19037	23307	14.4	23.2	42.6	12.9	6.9	62547	64338	81	62	16427	2.1	1.5	9.6	66.1	20.7	280428
91343	NORTH HILLS	18176	17391	22.7	25.7	33.5	12.1	6.0	51635	54557	65	45	9107	0.8	0.4	7.4	49.1	42.3	371507
91344	GRANADA HILLS	32600	16736	9.6	17.6	39.1	17.9	15.8	78167	78828	91	79	12147	0.3	0.4	0.8	34.8	63.7	455502
91345	MISSION HILLS	22031	5205	14.0	21.3	43.1	14.7	6.9	66779	68686	85	68	3795	3.2	3.8	5.6	69.5	18.0	308402
91350	SANTA CLARITA	34991	9442	4.3	9.1	39.8	24.4	22.4	95172	95998	96	89	8038	0.4	1.4	3.7	31.7	62.9	441160
91351	CANYON COUNTRY	25774	9790	7.8	19.1	48.3	16.6	8.1	74217	76016	89	74	7311	5.1	4.5	5.8	56.4	28.2	312555
91352	SUN VALLEY	15992	12193	21.5	27.0	36.7	9.2	5.6	51556	55631	65	45	7008	1.8	0.7	5.1	73.6	18.7	278486
91354	VALENCIA	36761	10223	14.8	10.1	28.2	23.3	23.6	94307	96387	96	89	8422	0.1	0.1	1.0	24.0	74.8	501077
91355	VALENCIA	42212	15127	10.5	13.3	30.6	20.3	25.3	90808	94477	95	87	11211	0.1	0.2	1.8	31.5	66.4	485123
91356	TARZANA	44020	11950	15.4	22.2	28.8	10.3	23.2	68170	71070	86	70	6755	0.1	0.1	4.9	20.2	74.6	780237
91360	THOUSAND OAKS	38858	14712	8.3	12.7	32.3	25.8	21.0	93806	99928	96	88	10528	0.3	0.0	1.1	30.6	67.9	479873
91361	WESTLAKE VILLAGE	55444	8328	7.1	12.0	28.1	20.8	31.9	105248	109585	97	92	6072	0.1	0.3	0.7	12.6	86.3	695088
91362	THOUSAND OAKS	52988	13501	8.6	12.8	24.5	20.5	33.7	108999	113278	98	93	10305	0.9	0.5	1.5	20.8	76.2	615097
91364	WOODLAND HILLS	53644	9919	8.2	11.5	32.7	17.8	29.8	95517	97146	96	89	7143	1.2	0.6	0.9	7.8	89.5	691010
91367	WOODLAND HILLS	43643	16425	14.4	16.1	33.2	18.0	18.4	76244	77447	90	77	8988	0.2	0.3	2.3	17.9	79.3	585657
91371	WOODLAND HILLS	20520	77	20.8	39.0	36.4	3.9	0.0	42750	45959	42	28	0	0.0	0.0	0.0	0.0	0.0	0
91377	OAK PARK	51834	5150	6.8	9.6	23.9	26.0	33.7	121357	124523	99	95	3909	0.0	0.2	0.6	21.2	78.1	595105
91381	STEVENSON RANCH	47498	4116	4.2	8.5	32.4	18.2	36.7	113748	119135	98	94	3166	0.0	0.1	2.0	31.2	66.8	523976
91384	CASTAIC	31208	6566	6.5	12.3	33.7	22.9	24.6	95861	96865	96	89	5341	2.0	2.3	2.0	37.4	56.3	421682
91387	CANYON COUNTRY	32279	13448	7.9	15.7	42.3	18.6	15.4	77340	78817	91	78	8399	2.6	1.0	6.0	39.9	50.6	403069
91390	SANTA CLARITA	35519	6954	6.3	9.7	34.8	26.9	22.3	98579	102465	96	90	6013	1.4	1.1	2.7	32.1	62.7	471556
91401	VAN NUYS	22821	15418	23.8	31.7	28.2	9.1	7.2	45406	47861	49	33	5597	0.2	0.3	3.0	32.2	64.3	464378
91402	PANORAMA CITY	12799	18287	26.8	34.7	30.3	6.0	2.2	41301	44284	37	24	6680	0.4	0.5	13.7	78.3	7.1	253842
91403	SHERMAN OAKS	52715	10672	13.6	19.2	33.4	13.3	20.5	72383	74001	88	73	4837	0.1	0.0	0.8	18.2	80.9	758043
91405	VAN NUYS	15143	15879	30.8	32.0	29.0	5.5	2.6	37636	41372	26	18	4529	1.5	0.1	13.0	62.2	23.2	298203
91406	VAN NUYS	19314	18963	23.6	29.9	34.4	8.4	3.8	46567	49522	53	36	7553	2.8	0.3	3.6	68.3	25.0	319208
91411	VAN NUYS	22572	9592	21.5	31.2	34.4	8.0	4.9	47520	49950	55	38	2921	0.3	0.5	5.7	45.9	47.6	387699
91423	SHERMAN OAKS	49406	14437	12.2	19.9	37.0	14.4	16.5	71109	72537	87	72	5960	0.5	0.5	0.5	15.7	82.9	671750
91436	ENCINO	63287	5955	8.5	12.3	21.4	13.4	44.3	127374	135469	99	96	4829	0.0	0.1	0.6	3.8	95.5	937393
91501	BURBANK	31321	8600	17.8	22.4	36.7	13.0	10.0	60470	63189	78	59	3134	0.4	0.5	1.6	23.1	74.3	602336
91502	BURBANK	19855	5068	35.7	26.6	29.5	5.7	2.5	37295	40894	24	17	492	0.2	2.4	2.6	63.0	31.7	329688
91504	BURBANK	30977	8906	14.5	20.7	39.6	13.2	12.1	67865	69700	85	69	4675	0.4	0.0	1.1	29.7	68.8	511945
91505	BURBANK	35278	13290	13.7	21.3	40.2	16.5	8.3	66840	68495	85	69	6503	0.5	0.3	1.7	34.4	63.0	437155
91506	BURBANK	34035	8138	13.4	23.0	38.7	15.6	9.2	64717	66731	83	65	4168	0.7	0.5	0.7	24.9	73.3	478479
91522	BURBANK	0	0	0.0	0.0	0.0	0.0	0.0	0	0	0	0	0	0.0	0.0	0.0	0.0	0.0	0
91601	NORTH HOLLYWOOD	20836	16075	27.2	32.1	32.1	5.6	3.0	42054	45159	39	26	3329	0.0	0.1	2.9	52.5	44.5	369403
91602	NORTH HOLLYWOOD	46900	8741	12.0	23.8	40.2	12.8	11.2	65924	67887	84	67	2840	0.0	0.0	2.7	22.9	74.4	640746
91604	STUDIO CITY	57480	13521	9.8	17.1	37.7	15.0	20.4	78538	79580	91	79	6170	0.0	0.2	0.1	11.8	87.9	777511
91605	NORTH HOLLYWOOD	14031	15359	28.4	30.6	30.0	7.7	3.2	41049	44496	36	24	6461	2.1	0.7	3.2	78.7	15.3	294214
91606	NORTH HOLLYWOOD	16292	15493	28.3	32.2	30.5	6.1	2.9	41031	44333	36	23	5430	0.6	0.1	3.8	75.5	19.8	289969
91607	VALLEY VILLAGE	33124	14435	17.5	27.3	38.4	9.1	7.7	55436	59787	72	52	4516	0.2	0.2	3.4	25.2	71.1	530657
91701	RANCHO CUCAMONGA	31284	13431	9.2	14.6	37.9	22.0	16.2	82534	82807	93	82	10333	4.4	3.0	4.8	70.0	17.7	291189
91702	AZUSA	16964	15946	18.4	26.8	41.5	9.5	3.8	55057	59374	71	52	8966	3.1	1.0	8.0	77.9	9.9	259218
91706	BALDWIN PARK	13691	17660	18.5	27.6	41.5	8.7	3.7	53303	56686	69	48	10676	2.9	0.7	6.3	86.1	3.9	256813
91708	CHINO	19295	1038	16.5	13.5	38.1	24.9	7.1	58287	58489	75	56	794	1.9	0.4	2.0	76.7	19.0	335433
91709	CHINO HILLS	34125	22845	5.6	9.8	35.8	23.7	25.0	97931	99249	96	90	18754	1.8	1.5	5.2	53.6	38.0	357660
91710	CHINO	22264	21597	13.5	18.3	42.5	16.5	9.3	68642	70931	86	70	14758	3.3	1.7	10.9	76.0	8.1	252993
91711	CLAREMONT	37597	12485	13.0	16.0	34.6	17.8	18.6	79473	80405	92	80	8000	1.7	0.6	1.2	31.4	65.1	466667
91722	COVINA	20996	11007	14.6	23.8	44.3	12.4	4.9	62668	64536	81	63	7257	4.1	0.9	2.2	79.6	13.1	293203
91723	COVINA	21763	6086	22.1	25.2	39.4	10.1	3.3	52901	57044	68	47	2423	0.3	0.2	1.2	65.8	32.5	349822
91724	COVINA	28356	8992	11.9	20.4	39.6	17.9	10.3	73061	74879	88	74	6369	4.6	2.3	2.7	48.2	42.2	368949
91730	RANCHO CUCAMONGA	23934	21903	12.6	22.3	43.4	16.7	5.0	63746	65218	82	64	11612	4.7	1.7	17.5	74.0	2.0	211828
91731	EL MONTE	12293	7632	28.0	32.2	31.4	6.1	2.3	39964	43256	32	21	3005	6.9	0.8	3.1	77.3	11.9	276845
91732	EL MONTE	12414	15327	25.9	32.2	32.6	6.3	3.0	42717	45687	42	27	6599	9.7	0.5	3.6	75.1	11.1	261747
91733	SOUTH EL MONTE	11155	9995	25.3	34.7	31.0	6.4	2.6	41716	45023	38	25	4133	9.3	0.6	5.0	75.2	10.0	269619
91737	RANCHO CUCAMONGA	33105	7869	8.7	11.0	42.7	15.7	21.9	83772	84773	93	83	5838	2.1	1.3	2.4	52.5	41.8	360380
91739	RANCHO CUCAMONGA	32499	8222	4.8	9.6	43.0	24.1	18.5	89918	90278	95	87	6412	0.2	0.3	7.9	61.7	29.9	289648
91740	GLENDORA	25456	8273	11.6	20.4	46.5	15.9	5.6	67348	68492	85	69	5715	5.6	1.3	2.9	59.5	30.7	345425
91741	GLENDORA	37116	9285	10.5	16.5	36.6	18.4	18.0	80246	80855	92	81	6717	2.1	1.3	0.7	23.1	72.9	515009
91744	LA PUENTE	14179	18683	14.2	25.3	46.5	10.1	3.9	60761	62685	78	59	13094	3.3	1.3	2.9	89.1	3.4	263615
91745	HACIENDA HEIGHTS	25537	16396	11.5	19.5	40.9	17.5	10.6	71740	73018	88	72	12570	3.1	3.3	1.7	37.0	54.8	425010
91746	LA PUENTE	14354	7327	16.6	26.9	42.8	8.5	5.2	56661	60594	74	54	5014	1.9	0.4	3.3	85.3	9.1	271914
91748	ROWLAND HEIGHTS	23402	13701	15.5	22.1	36.5	14.9	11.0	64946	67177	83	66	8693	4.6	2.7	3.4	39.2	50.0	400322
91750	LA VERNE	32344	11666	12.3	17.8	37.9	17.4	14.6	74482	75350	89	75	8708	5.8	4.8	10.0	25.9	53.6	417003
91752	MIRA LOMA	17061	8434	22.1	32.6	32.5	8.6	4.2	45914	47095	51	34	5217	11.2	7.7	16.8	58.7	5.6	214608
91754	MONTEREY PARK	22173	11104	19.7	28.6	35.0	10.9	5.8	51790	55380	65	45	6360	4.4	1.3	2.5	39.6	52.1	410180
91755	MONTEREY PARK	19679	9655	22.6	25.8	35.4	10.7	5.5	51345	54006	64	44	4715	5.3	1.5	1.8	44.6	46.8	385005
91759	MT BALDY	42746	225	9.3	16.4	44.4	13.8	16.0	75883	77311	90	76	174	9.8	4.0	17.2	31.6	37.4	270000
91761	ONTARIO	17934	15429	13.8	24.5	44.3	12.1	5.3	61293	62550	79	60	9933	7.9	4.6	14.1	70.3	3.1	216449
91762	ONTARIO	16065	16443	22.1	27.7	40.4	7.2	2.7	50229	52440	62	43	8614	2.3	2.2	28.2	64.2	3.2	196019
91763	MONTCLAIR	15316	9655	22.8	27.7	37.8	8.7	2.9	49440	51534	60	41	5539	9.4	1.8	25.3	62.3	1.2	188465
	CALIFORNIA	28199		18.5	22.2	33.9	14.0	11.5	61614	64088				3.3	2.6	13.6	41.0	39.5	321752
	UNITED STATES	27277		20.9	24.4	35.3	11.7	7.6	54719	56938				9.3	13.1	31.6	32.6	13.5	162279

ZIP CODE #	POST OFFICE NAME	FINANCIAL SERVICES: Auto Loan	Home Loan	Investments	Retirement Plans	THE HOME: Home Improvements: Home Repair	Lawn & Garden	Furnishings: Computers & Hardware-Personal	Major Appliances	TV, Radio, Sound Equipment	Furniture	ENTERTAINMENT: Dine out/ Carry out	Sports Equipment	Fees & Tickets	Toys & Games	Travel	Cable TV	PERSONAL: Apparel & Services	Auto Repairs	Health Insurance	Pets & Supplies
91203	GLENDALE	59	60	62	62	60	56	74	63	76	65	79	49	74	72	71	79	58	71	68	76
91204	GLENDALE	58	59	59	60	59	52	73	62	71	65	74	50	71	69	69	72	55	69	62	72
91205	GLENDALE	53	54	57	56	55	51	67	58	68	59	70	45	67	64	64	70	52	64	61	68
91206	GLENDALE	91	102	113	106	107	95	113	102	110	106	113	79	118	105	115	111	84	108	103	119
91207	GLENDALE	139	169	200	176	185	153	166	160	149	174	151	128	184	145	183	140	112	159	143	181
91208	GLENDALE	142	176	207	181	193	160	168	166	152	178	153	130	187	147	188	143	113	162	150	186
91214	LA CRESCENTA	124	164	189	163	179	142	148	150	131	158	132	116	168	128	169	123	98	143	129	164
91301	AGOURA HILLS	192	236	265	244	251	215	211	215	195	226	196	169	240	194	235	185	145	205	189	242
91302	CALABASAS	214	272	310	284	293	250	238	243	223	259	223	188	282	223	268	213	168	231	217	271
91303	CANOGA PARK	77	69	66	69	69	59	85	73	80	84	83	61	79	81	79	75	60	81	66	84
91304	CANOGA PARK	105	118	122	117	122	103	121	114	113	121	116	89	127	113	125	109	86	117	103	127
91306	WINNETKA	89	104	104	99	107	86	104	99	95	105	98	78	108	95	108	91	72	100	87	109
91307	WEST HILLS	138	196	222	192	211	179	162	171	152	169	152	126	196	151	190	149	114	161	157	186
91311	CHATSWORTH	126	151	163	152	159	138	141	140	131	147	132	108	154	130	153	126	96	137	130	158
91316	ENCINO	105	123	138	125	131	117	122	119	117	124	118	92	133	112	132	115	85	121	120	136
91320	NEWBURY PARK	151	192	194	193	197	169	167	169	156	176	159	132	191	159	183	150	117	161	152	189
91321	NEWHALL	104	116	119	114	120	108	115	112	111	118	113	85	122	109	121	109	82	114	110	127
91324	NORTHRIDGE	108	126	135	124	133	107	127	120	114	129	117	97	134	113	134	107	86	121	104	133
91325	NORTHRIDGE	110	114	123	117	118	102	130	114	118	126	121	95	129	118	128	113	89	121	105	132
91326	PORTER RANCH	171	225	252	231	241	204	196	201	180	209	181	155	230	179	224	172	135	190	179	224
91330	NORTHRIDGE	82	53	51	58	51	57	97	66	87	77	87	60	71	88	68	85	62	81	70	85
91331	PACOIMA	82	88	77	78	90	64	91	87	78	97	83	69	87	80	90	69	60	87	67	90
91335	RESEDA	80	91	87	85	93	73	94	88	86	93	89	69	95	86	95	82	66	90	76	96
91340	SAN FERNANDO	81	83	71	74	84	62	88	83	77	93	82	66	83	79	86	69	60	85	65	87
91342	SYLMAR	98	115	107	103	118	89	109	108	95	116	98	83	110	96	113	87	72	105	88	114
91343	NORTH HILLS	86	88	89	86	90	75	96	88	90	96	94	70	96	91	95	86	69	94	79	98
91344	GRANADA HILLS	120	157	171	153	166	139	141	141	131	144	132	108	160	130	157	127	99	138	128	156
91345	MISSION HILLS	100	121	122	110	127	103	110	114	100	115	102	86	116	100	119	96	74	109	99	122
91350	SANTA CLARITA	156	195	181	195	193	169	164	168	154	175	157	132	186	161	177	148	114	158	149	189
91351	CANYON COUNTRY	119	127	114	124	124	111	121	118	115	127	117	93	124	119	122	110	83	117	107	136
91352	SUN VALLEY	86	95	88	86	98	73	96	93	85	101	89	73	96	86	98	77	66	93	75	97
91354	VALENCIA	155	188	172	192	187	158	161	163	149	177	151	133	181	157	172	138	111	152	138	182
91355	VALENCIA	154	186	192	190	192	162	170	167	157	180	159	134	189	159	183	148	117	162	147	189
91356	TARZANA	141	161	182	167	172	147	164	155	152	168	154	124	176	149	173	145	113	157	143	177
91360	THOUSAND OAKS	137	174	193	174	186	156	160	159	148	165	149	123	180	146	178	142	110	156	146	178
91361	WESTLAKE VILLAGE	169	220	263	225	243	204	196	204	180	213	179	153	228	173	226	172	133	193	185	225
91362	THOUSAND OAKS	186	229	242	236	240	204	206	206	191	220	193	162	234	193	226	182	143	198	183	232
91364	WOODLAND HILLS	164	212	251	218	235	188	195	197	174	211	174	154	222	168	222	161	130	188	169	218
91367	WOODLAND HILLS	131	144	163	150	152	131	152	139	141	153	144	114	160	140	158	135	106	145	130	161
91371	WOODLAND HILLS	80	45	39	52	40	44	76	55	76	73	78	50	60	79	58	74	54	71	58	72
91377	OAK PARK	185	242	258	253	255	215	206	211	189	223	191	167	242	190	233	178	143	198	182	238
91381	STEVENSON RANCH	201	227	197	235	219	189	202	197	188	221	192	165	219	203	205	175	140	187	167	224
91384	CASTAIC	167	194	171	195	191	160	172	170	158	187	161	139	186	167	178	146	117	161	143	191
91387	CANYON COUNTRY	143	148	135	151	144	131	145	137	139	151	141	110	149	144	143	133	101	138	126	160
91390	SANTA CLARITA	155	193	181	196	192	168	163	167	152	175	155	133	185	158	177	145	113	156	146	188
91401	VAN NUYS	83	82	85	84	84	70	98	85	90	95	95	72	95	90	95	85	69	93	76	97
91402	PANORAMA CITY	71	64	57	60	63	50	77	68	71	79	75	55	71	72	72	65	55	74	57	74
91403	SHERMAN OAKS	136	139	160	151	147	125	161	139	147	158	152	120	163	146	161	138	112	149	128	164
91405	VAN NUYS	64	58	54	58	57	49	73	62	70	70	73	51	69	70	68	67	54	70	57	71
91406	VAN NUYS	74	78	76	76	78	66	86	77	81	83	84	62	85	81	84	78	62	82	71	87
91411	VAN NUYS	79	74	77	77	75	64	92	78	85	89	90	67	88	85	88	80	65	87	71	91
91423	SHERMAN OAKS	127	134	155	144	142	119	151	133	136	150	141	114	154	135	154	128	104	140	120	155
91436	ENCINO	197	267	323	278	297	246	231	240	212	252	211	183	281	208	270	201	161	225	211	264
91501	BURBANK	98	106	119	110	111	92	118	105	106	116	110	89	120	105	121	100	81	111	94	121
91502	BURBANK	60	55	57	57	55	51	72	60	70	67	72	50	68	67	67	70	52	69	63	72
91504	BURBANK	105	126	136	126	132	111	123	118	114	124	117	93	133	114	131	110	86	118	108	132
91505	BURBANK	100	111	121	113	115	97	119	107	110	116	113	88	123	109	122	106	83	113	99	124
91506	BURBANK	101	121	135	121	129	109	119	115	111	119	112	90	128	109	128	108	83	115	106	129
91522	BURBANK	0	0	0	0	0	0	0	0	0	0	0	0	0	0	0	0	0	0	0	0
91601	NORTH HOLLYWOOD	73	59	59	63	59	53	80	65	76	77	80	56	73	77	72	73	57	76	63	78
91602	NORTH HOLLYWOOD	111	112	128	121	117	97	134	114	120	130	125	100	132	119	133	112	92	123	102	134
91604	STUDIO CITY	142	155	180	166	166	139	167	151	152	169	155	126	175	149	173	143	115	156	136	175
91605	NORTH HOLLYWOOD	73	70	63	65	70	54	80	73	73	83	77	59	75	74	77	66	56	77	60	78
91606	NORTH HOLLYWOOD	68	67	63	64	67	54	78	69	72	76	76	56	75	72	74	68	56	74	61	76
91607	VALLEY VILLAGE	92	94	105	100	98	81	111	95	99	108	103	84	109	98	111	92	75	103	85	112
91701	RANCHO CUCAMONGA	125	161	159	160	163	144	138	140	133	142	135	108	159	135	152	131	99	135	131	158
91702	AZUSA	87	93	84	85	94	72	96	91	85	100	88	72	93	85	96	77	64	92	74	97
91706	BALDWIN PARK	85	93	82	82	95	67	95	91	81	101	86	72	92	82	95	72	63	91	69	94
91708	CHINO	117	117	101	104	115	96	118	114	110	126	113	86	111	113	113	104	80	115	100	126
91709	CHINO HILLS	164	194	177	197	192	164	169	169	157	184	160	137	187	165	178	147	116	160	145	190
91710	CHINO	108	125	116	119	125	104	117	116	107	122	110	91	122	109	121	101	80	112	99	127
91711	CLAREMONT	127	161	179	161	172	148	148	149	139	154	140	113	167	135	165	135	103	145	140	165
91722	COVINA	92	111	105	100	115	85	106	104	92	111	96	81	108	93	111	85	70	101	84	110
91723	COVINA	76	85	84	82	86	72	91	82	85	87	89	66	93	85	91	83	66	87	76	93
91724	COVINA	101	135	143	128	141	120	120	121	115	119	117	90	138	114	134	116	87	119	115	133
91730	RANCHO CUCAMONGA	109	106	91	105	101	92	108	100	103	112	105	81	105	108	102	99	74	103	93	118
91731	EL MONTE	70	68	59	62	69	52	76	70	68	79	72	55	71	69	73	62	53	73	57	74
91732	EL MONTE	75	77	66	68	77	57	82	77	72	86	76	61	77	73	80	65	56	79	61	81
91733	SOUTH EL MONTE	74	74	62	65	74	54	80	74	70	84	75	60	75	72	77	63	55	77	58	77
91737	RANCHO CUCAMONGA	138	176	177	177	180	154	154	155	142	161	144	122	174	144	169	136	106	148	137	175
91739	RANCHO CUCAMONGA	154	179	157	175	175	146	159	158	146	172	149	127	169	154	164	136	108	150	133	176
91740	GLENDORA	96	122	121	114	125	104	111	110	103	111	105	84	121	104	120	100	77	108	99	121
91741	GLENDORA	127	170	190	167	182	154	150	152	141	153	143	115	174	140	170	139	106	148	142	168
91744	LA PUENTE	91	106	95	93	109	76	103	101	86	111	90	79	101	87	106	76	66	98	76	104
91745	HACIENDA HEIGHTS	110	141	149	133	152	109	133	132	112	142	113	104	139	109	145	100	84	125	103	140
91746	LA PUENTE	89	107	98	94	111	77	101	101	85	110	88	78	101	85	105	74	64	96	75	103
91748	ROWLAND HEIGHTS	103	125	133	124	132	102	124	119	109	129	112	96	130	107	132	101	83	117	99	131
91750	LA VERNE	127	147	152	144	152	140	132	138	128	138	129	103	144	128	143	127	92	133	133	156
91752	MIRA LOMA	83	85	78	80	85	76	85	84	81	88	82	64	83	82	84	79	58	84	78	95
91754	MONTEREY PARK	80	99	109	97	107	82	100	96	89	101	91	75	105	86	107	84	68	95	83	105
91755	MONTEREY PARK	75	87	96	87	93	74	95	87	87	92	89	69	97	83	98	84	66	89	79	98
91759	MT BALDY	129	162	167	165	167	153	138	146	132	146	133	108	157	132	155	130	96	138	138	166
91761	ONTARIO	99	108	94	100	107	87	103	102	94	110	97	79	103	97	104	87	69	99	86	111
91762	ONTARIO	78	82	76	76	83	67	85	80	78	87	81	63	84	79	84	74	59	82	70	88
91763	MONTCLAIR	80	84	76	77	85	65	88	83	78	92	82	66	85	80	87	72	59	84	68	89
	CALIFORNIA	112	119	122	118	122	107	121	116	114	124	116	92	124	114	124	110	84	118	107	132
	UNITED STATES	100	100	100	100	100	100	100	100	100	100	100	100	100	100	100	100	100	100	100	100

ZIP CODE			POPULATION			2000-2009 ANNUAL RATE		HOUSEHOLDS					FAMILIES		
#	POST OFFICE NAME	COUNTY FIPS CODE	2000	2009	2014	% Rate	State Centile	2000	2009	2014	% Annual Rate 2000-2009	2009 Average HH Size	2000	2009	% Annual Rate 2000-2009
91764	ONTARIO	071	49567	55005	57472	1.1	64	13388	14232	14736	0.7	3.84	10422	11033	0.6
91765	DIAMOND BAR	037	48340	51851	53737	0.8	54	15179	15875	16334	0.5	3.26	12684	13292	0.5
91766	POMONA	037	70365	77491	80656	1.0	62	17057	18147	18787	0.7	4.24	14277	15193	0.7
91767	POMONA	037	46817	52092	54365	1.2	68	13149	14226	14828	0.9	3.61	9737	10513	0.8
91768	POMONA	037	32821	35662	37012	0.9	58	8100	8550	8832	0.6	3.92	6378	6742	0.6
91770	ROSEMEAD	037	61599	64459	66179	0.5	39	16142	16522	16863	0.3	3.85	13437	13758	0.3
91773	SAN DIMAS	037	34764	36618	37851	0.6	45	12058	12468	12824	0.4	2.84	9030	9353	0.4
91775	SAN GABRIEL	037	24628	26179	26936	0.7	50	8831	9111	9312	0.3	2.85	6418	6621	0.3
91776	SAN GABRIEL	037	37897	39653	40611	0.5	39	11579	11810	12027	0.2	3.31	8826	9015	0.2
91780	TEMPLE CITY	037	33170	34967	36046	0.6	45	11406	11740	12023	0.3	2.95	8644	8904	0.3
91784	UPLAND	071	23236	25991	27068	1.2	68	7950	8717	9039	1.0	2.97	6673	7266	0.9
91786	UPLAND	071	48499	52347	54150	0.8	54	17747	18537	19056	0.5	2.79	12129	12596	0.4
91789	WALNUT	037	45386	47987	49784	0.6	45	12434	12878	13305	0.4	3.58	10973	11362	0.4
91790	WEST COVINA	037	44429	46890	48220	0.6	45	12936	13311	13605	0.3	3.49	10476	10786	0.3
91791	WEST COVINA	037	30608	33959	35589	1.1	64	9778	10641	11104	0.9	3.17	7720	8400	0.9
91792	WEST COVINA	037	31971	35793	37703	1.2	68	9135	9959	10409	0.9	3.59	7571	8251	0.9
91801	ALHAMBRA	037	54933	58002	59769	0.6	45	19602	20292	20799	0.4	2.83	13404	13880	0.4
91803	ALHAMBRA	037	30220	31373	32119	0.4	30	9546	9711	9887	0.2	3.12	7300	7428	0.2
91901	ALPINE	073	16635	17720	18408	0.7	50	5772	6194	6439	0.8	2.76	4408	4717	0.7
91902	BONITA	073	17879	21002	22373	1.8	80	6007	7101	7571	1.8	2.95	4897	5816	1.9
91905	BOULEVARD	073	1448	1638	1741	1.3	70	493	567	607	1.5	2.62	346	396	1.5
91906	CAMPO	073	3049	3684	4009	2.1	84	1024	1260	1378	2.3	2.73	734	896	2.2
91910	CHULA VISTA	073	73537	75173	76306	0.2	18	26445	26715	27034	0.1	2.78	18565	18671	0.1
91911	CHULA VISTA	073	71925	79378	82583	1.1	64	22584	25402	26551	1.3	3.11	17489	19466	1.2
91913	CHULA VISTA	073	13374	46465	56809	14.4	99	4218	13256	16026	13.2	3.51	3539	11443	13.5
91914	CHULA VISTA	073	2321	8769	11189	15.5	99	701	2398	3036	14.2	3.65	632	2116	14.0
91915	CHULA VISTA	073	8337	17390	20741	8.3	98	2443	5395	6443	8.9	3.22	2201	4864	9.0
91916	DESCANSO	073	2250	2380	2484	0.6	45	844	901	943	0.7	2.60	582	615	0.6
91917	DULZURA	073	587	691	744	1.8	80	226	269	290	1.9	2.56	170	201	1.8
91932	IMPERIAL BEACH	073	27001	26800	26957	-0.1	5	9274	9256	9315	0.0	2.82	6453	6399	-0.1
91934	JACUMBA	073	792	858	901	0.9	58	313	338	355	0.8	2.54	195	209	0.8
91935	JAMUL	073	8439	9224	9904	1.0	62	2716	2979	3200	1.0	3.02	2246	2441	0.9
91941	LA MESA	073	43592	43888	44476	0.1	13	18101	18329	18567	0.1	2.36	11237	11313	0.1
91942	LA MESA	073	23990	23831	23958	-0.1	5	10879	10862	10930	0.0	2.13	5769	5708	-0.1
91945	LEMON GROVE	073	24899	24857	25005	0.0	9	8478	8451	8492	0.0	2.88	5998	5954	-0.1
91950	NATIONAL CITY	073	52767	53929	55077	0.2	18	15250	15478	15771	0.2	3.44	12031	12168	0.1
91962	PINE VALLEY	073	2001	2202	2311	1.0	62	766	846	888	1.1	2.51	561	616	1.0
91963	POTRERO	073	1032	1198	1284	1.6	77	341	397	426	1.7	3.00	256	296	1.6
91977	SPRING VALLEY	073	55492	57371	58789	0.4	30	17724	18401	18852	0.4	3.09	13794	14274	0.4
91978	SPRING VALLEY	073	8134	13267	14920	5.4	96	2953	4452	4927	4.5	2.97	2197	3405	4.9
91980	TECATE	073	228	263	281	1.6	77	67	77	82	1.5	3.40	50	58	1.6
92003	BONSALL	073	3753	4159	4398	1.1	64	1386	1551	1641	1.2	2.68	1026	1142	1.2
92004	BORREGO SPRINGS	073	2895	3062	3200	0.6	45	1299	1379	1439	0.6	2.21	826	871	0.6
92007	CARDIFF BY THE SEA	073	11180	11019	11057	-0.2	4	4782	4753	4773	-0.1	2.30	2708	2667	-0.2
92008	CARLSBAD	073	25303	28255	29791	1.2	68	10286	11394	11972	1.1	2.43	6063	6826	1.3
92009	CARLSBAD	073	26220	37303	42216	3.9	93	10169	14084	15818	3.6	2.64	7245	10068	3.6
92010	CARLSBAD	073	10345	15764	17378	4.7	95	4072	5661	6173	3.6	2.76	2877	4060	3.8
92011	CARLSBAD	073	16378	21922	24357	3.2	91	6994	8995	9907	2.8	2.43	4709	6044	2.7
92014	DEL MAR	073	15197	15090	15561	-0.1	5	6526	6636	6842	0.2	2.26	4124	4178	0.1
92019	EL CAJON	073	40619	42632	44054	0.5	39	14271	15012	15491	0.5	2.82	10930	11475	0.5
92020	EL CAJON	073	57393	57743	58327	0.1	13	20709	20784	20968	0.0	2.71	14093	14052	0.0
92021	EL CAJON	073	60714	61743	62833	0.2	18	21809	22239	22632	0.2	2.72	15281	15530	0.2
92024	ENCINITAS	073	46995	50533	53095	0.8	54	18100	19406	20302	0.8	2.58	11635	12419	0.7
92025	ESCONDIDO	073	47476	50027	51479	0.6	45	14480	14956	15353	0.4	3.28	10450	10752	0.3
92026	ESCONDIDO	073	44624	48598	50538	0.9	58	15959	17141	17810	0.8	2.80	11252	12073	0.8
92027	ESCONDIDO	073	47474	51687	53742	0.9	58	15272	16305	16930	0.7	3.14	11277	12052	0.7
92028	FALLBROOK	073	42508	47308	49757	1.2	68	14483	16111	16952	1.2	2.91	11279	12521	1.1
92029	ESCONDIDO	073	18129	19763	20850	0.9	58	6644	7185	7541	0.8	2.74	5005	5395	0.8
92036	JULIAN	073	3504	3771	3946	0.8	54	1450	1571	1646	0.9	2.37	1006	1084	0.8
92037	LA JOLLA	073	42939	43863	44525	0.2	18	17835	18171	18452	0.2	2.07	9531	9662	0.1
92040	LAKESIDE	073	41609	42279	43052	0.2	18	14583	14865	15127	0.2	2.82	10806	10951	0.1
92054	OCEANSIDE	073	40865	42173	42963	0.3	23	14974	15325	15587	0.3	2.73	9083	9243	0.2
92055	CAMP PENDLETON	073	17748	17597	17506	-0.1	5	2340	2235	2211	-0.5	4.17	2276	2172	-0.5
92056	OCEANSIDE	073	51237	52495	53783	0.3	23	18900	19181	19568	0.2	2.72	13416	13576	0.1
92057	OCEANSIDE	073	47158	54087	57229	1.5	75	15706	17757	18751	1.3	3.02	11711	13267	1.4
92058	OCEANSIDE	073	39715	44127	46259	1.1	64	10407	11648	12301	1.2	3.04	8350	9205	1.1
92059	PALA	073	1502	1729	1920	1.5	75	407	462	513	1.4	3.67	319	360	1.3
92061	PAUMA VALLEY	073	2086	2247	2366	0.8	54	668	726	765	0.9	3.09	511	552	0.8
92064	POWAY	073	48155	49282	50324	0.3	23	15509	15921	16248	0.3	3.07	12858	13163	0.3
92065	RAMONA	073	33017	35505	36964	0.8	54	10675	11569	12057	0.9	3.05	8713	9430	0.9
92066	RANCHITA	073	428	445	458	0.4	30	166	174	180	0.5	2.38	111	116	0.5
92067	RANCHO SANTA FE	073	4195	4235	4585	0.1	13	1503	1591	1723	0.6	2.66	1192	1256	0.6
92069	SAN MARCOS	073	38819	47739	52284	2.3	86	11731	14284	15591	2.2	3.33	8970	11013	2.2
92070	SANTA YSABEL	073	1260	1352	1415	0.8	54	519	562	589	0.9	2.38	346	372	0.8
92071	SANTEE	073	53384	54644	55985	0.3	23	18616	19219	19728	0.3	2.78	14098	14474	0.3
92075	SOLANA BEACH	073	12300	12117	12151	-0.2	4	5439	5393	5412	-0.1	2.24	3092	3044	-0.2
92078	SAN MARCOS	073	21261	34231	39539	5.3	96	8969	13944	16025	4.9	2.45	5810	9246	5.2
92081	VISTA	073	25795	27883	29976	0.8	54	9789	10703	11478	1.0	2.50	6739	7345	0.9
92082	VALLEY CENTER	073	16776	18675	19825	1.2	68	5592	6291	6686	1.3	2.95	4458	4991	1.2
92083	VISTA	073	36787	39838	41121	0.9	58	10404	11086	11416	0.7	3.53	7879	8334	0.6
92084	VISTA	073	44402	48548	50424	1.0	62	14092	15140	15724	0.8	3.14	10463	11197	0.7
92086	WARNER SPRINGS	073	1173	1221	1256	0.4	30	466	489	505	0.5	2.33	312	326	0.5
92091	RANCHO SANTA FE	073	2869	2944	3269	0.3	23	1115	1235	1410	1.1	2.38	899	981	0.9
92096	SAN MARCOS	073	91	3311	4154	47.5	100	36	1460	1831	49.2	2.27	22	911	49.6
92101	SAN DIEGO	073	21979	33512	38656	4.7	95	11403	18522	21932	5.4	1.49	2236	3956	6.4
92102	SAN DIEGO	073	46687	46807	47183	0.0	9	14017	13990	14081	0.0	3.29	9335	9271	-0.1
92103	SAN DIEGO	073	29998	29880	30148	0.0	9	17462	17534	17714	0.0	1.66	4954	4897	-0.1
92104	SAN DIEGO	073	48394	49054	49630	0.1	13	21797	21958	22184	0.1	2.22	9508	9461	-0.1
92105	SAN DIEGO	073	72203	74014	74934	0.3	23	20967	20913	21083	0.0	3.53	15660	15536	-0.1
92106	SAN DIEGO	073	18604	21022	21313	1.3	70	7142	8067	8186	1.3	2.34	4233	4805	1.4
92107	SAN DIEGO	073	28198	27944	28063	-0.1	5	14160	14122	14198	0.0	1.92	5912	5839	-0.1
92108	SAN DIEGO	073	12161	16570	18636	3.4	92	7220	9849	11077	3.4	1.67	2112	2915	3.5
92109	SAN DIEGO	073	45711	45200	45428	-0.1	5	23676	23554	23690	-0.1	1.91	7383	7231	-0.2
92110	SAN DIEGO	073	23030	23711	24274	0.3	23	10040	10359	10625	0.3	2.05	4703	4824	0.3
92111	SAN DIEGO	073	46254	46058	46590	0.0	9	16975	16985	17206	0.0	2.69	10809	10728	-0.1
	CALIFORNIA					1.2					1.0	2.93			1.1
	UNITED STATES					1.0					1.1	2.59			0.9

ZIP CODE #	POST OFFICE NAME	RACE (%) White 2000	White 2009	Black 2000	Black 2009	Asian/Pacific 2000	Asian/Pacific 2009	% Hispanic Origin 2000	% Hispanic Origin 2009	2009 AGE DISTRIBUTION (%) 0-4	5-9	10-14	15-19	20-24	25-44	45-64	65-84	85+	18+	MEDIAN AGE 2009	% 2009 Males	% 2009 Females
91764	ONTARIO	45.2	40.4	7.1	6.3	3.4	3.5	64.3	71.8	10.4	9.5	8.3	8.8	8.6	30.3	17.9	5.4	0.9	66.5	27.5	50.8	49.2
91765	DIAMOND BAR	41.2	34.0	4.9	4.4	43.1	48.1	17.5	22.1	5.6	6.0	6.7	7.4	6.1	26.8	31.0	9.5	0.9	77.0	39.2	49.0	51.0
91766	POMONA	39.8	37.0	6.9	5.7	9.2	9.1	69.7	75.8	10.5	9.6	8.7	9.7	9.0	29.1	18.4	4.6	0.5	65.3	26.5	51.1	48.9
91767	POMONA	42.1	38.4	13.7	11.4	5.2	5.3	58.1	66.7	9.4	8.7	7.8	8.8	9.3	28.9	18.8	6.6	1.7	68.8	28.5	49.4	50.6
91768	POMONA	45.6	42.4	8.7	7.2	4.9	4.9	66.7	74.3	10.0	9.2	8.1	9.7	9.6	28.7	18.1	5.6	1.0	67.2	27.1	51.4	48.6
91770	ROSEMEAD	27.2	25.9	0.7	0.6	47.8	46.6	42.2	46.5	7.5	7.6	7.2	7.8	7.3	29.3	22.6	9.1	1.5	72.9	33.4	49.4	50.6
91773	SAN DIMAS	74.6	67.2	3.4	3.4	9.4	11.7	23.7	33.5	5.9	6.1	6.5	7.4	6.3	26.0	28.6	11.2	2.0	76.9	39.0	48.0	52.0
91775	SAN GABRIEL	46.9	39.5	1.4	1.3	39.0	43.6	21.8	27.3	6.3	6.4	6.4	6.3	5.7	26.3	28.1	12.1	2.5	77.0	40.3	48.0	52.0
91776	SAN GABRIEL	28.9	26.5	1.2	1.1	50.5	50.6	34.3	38.8	6.8	6.6	6.2	6.9	7.2	30.5	24.2	9.4	2.1	76.4	35.7	48.7	51.3
91780	TEMPLE CITY	49.3	41.3	1.0	0.9	37.7	42.6	22.0	27.8	5.6	5.6	5.7	6.8	6.7	25.8	28.9	12.2	2.5	79.0	40.3	48.1	51.9
91784	UPLAND	78.9	72.7	3.9	4.2	9.3	11.9	13.3	18.7	4.7	5.4	6.6	6.9	4.3	21.8	34.8	14.1	1.5	78.9	45.2	47.9	52.1
91786	UPLAND	62.7	56.1	8.9	8.5	6.4	7.5	33.4	42.2	8.2	7.4	6.9	7.1	8.4	29.2	22.1	8.9	1.9	73.3	32.3	48.2	51.8
91789	WALNUT	32.5	27.5	4.4	3.9	50.2	53.0	21.3	25.9	5.0	5.3	5.8	8.7	7.9	26.3	30.7	9.3	1.1	79.6	37.6	49.4	50.6
91790	WEST COVINA	47.7	42.8	4.9	4.2	16.5	17.0	53.0	61.6	8.2	8.1	7.7	8.1	7.2	27.4	22.9	9.0	1.4	71.0	32.8	49.0	51.0
91791	WEST COVINA	50.8	44.8	5.4	4.7	20.4	22.1	40.5	49.2	7.0	6.8	6.9	7.7	6.7	27.1	25.5	10.5	1.8	74.7	36.0	48.4	51.6
91792	WEST COVINA	31.8	29.4	8.6	7.1	33.9	34.3	41.7	47.6	7.5	7.3	7.0	7.7	7.8	29.4	24.3	8.2	0.8	73.5	33.3	48.7	51.3
91801	ALHAMBRA	29.0	25.9	1.7	1.4	49.1	49.5	33.1	37.9	6.2	5.9	5.6	6.1	7.2	31.7	24.8	10.0	2.4	78.7	36.8	47.4	52.6
91803	ALHAMBRA	31.4	28.9	1.5	1.3	44.8	44.6	39.5	44.6	6.3	6.0	5.8	7.4	8.3	29.4	23.8	10.2	2.7	77.6	35.8	48.1	51.9
91901	ALPINE	89.2	85.1	1.4	1.6	2.1	2.8	11.0	16.6	5.9	6.3	7.0	7.1	5.6	24.4	31.5	10.9	1.5	76.7	41.0	51.4	48.6
91902	BONITA	69.1	63.2	3.6	3.8	11.6	12.3	31.1	40.6	5.3	5.7	6.4	6.6	5.4	24.8	31.3	12.8	1.7	78.4	42.0	48.4	51.6
91905	BOULEVARD	70.6	65.4	3.5	3.9	0.8	0.9	18.2	26.0	5.7	6.7	6.0	6.5	4.6	27.8	30.2	11.6	1.0	77.3	40.6	56.1	43.9
91906	CAMPO	72.1	64.6	2.4	2.6	1.0	1.1	28.1	38.5	5.7	6.1	6.8	11.1	5.7	21.1	30.4	11.9	1.2	72.5	39.6	53.8	46.2
91910	CHULA VISTA	57.1	51.1	4.5	4.1	11.7	12.4	45.9	55.0	7.8	7.3	6.7	6.8	7.1	29.3	23.0	9.8	2.2	74.1	34.5	48.2	51.8
91911	CHULA VISTA	52.5	47.3	4.7	4.4	7.3	9.1	59.9	65.5	7.9	7.5	7.0	7.8	8.2	28.7	21.8	9.6	1.3	72.9	32.1	48.7	51.3
91913	CHULA VISTA	57.7	43.0	4.6	6.7	18.9	23.3	36.4	45.9	7.9	7.7	7.4	6.7	5.2	30.4	25.7	7.9	1.0	72.8	35.7	49.0	51.0
91914	CHULA VISTA	57.5	52.3	5.8	5.5	19.9	20.7	32.4	39.8	10.5	9.9	9.0	6.6	4.2	34.5	21.0	4.0	0.4	66.4	32.3	49.3	50.7
91915	CHULA VISTA	49.4	42.3	5.5	5.5	29.5	30.5	28.9	40.7	8.6	8.6	8.3	7.1	4.8	30.7	24.5	6.6	0.8	70.0	35.0	49.6	50.4
91916	DESCANSO	87.3	82.7	0.6	0.6	1.2	1.6	9.6	14.8	5.3	5.6	7.3	7.5	4.3	22.1	37.6	9.0	1.3	76.8	43.8	51.7	48.3
91917	DULZURA	90.4	86.4	0.7	0.9	1.0	1.4	22.2	31.8	4.5	6.5	7.2	6.8	3.0	21.9	35.2	13.9	1.0	77.4	45.0	52.4	47.6
91932	IMPERIAL BEACH	62.2	55.6	5.2	5.0	7.2	7.7	40.2	49.7	8.7	7.4	6.7	8.7	11.0	30.4	19.9	6.4	0.9	72.7	28.7	49.9	50.1
91934	JACUMBA	69.7	61.1	4.0	4.4	0.1	0.1	32.3	43.6	6.9	7.1	7.2	6.1	4.4	18.5	33.4	13.9	2.4	75.1	44.8	46.4	53.6
91935	JAMUL	86.3	81.2	1.6	1.8	2.6	3.3	17.0	24.9	5.2	6.8	8.0	8.4	3.7	22.7	34.3	10.0	0.8	74.8	41.9	51.5	48.5
91941	LA MESA	80.2	74.1	5.4	6.0	4.1	5.1	14.1	20.3	6.1	5.8	5.9	5.9	6.5	27.7	27.3	12.1	2.9	78.6	39.6	48.4	51.6
91942	LA MESA	83.3	77.2	3.6	4.1	4.3	5.7	11.1	16.6	5.0	4.6	4.5	5.1	6.7	29.8	25.1	13.6	5.6	83.0	40.8	46.3	53.7
91945	LEMON GROVE	59.7	52.2	12.2	12.1	6.3	7.1	28.8	37.8	6.9	7.1	7.0	7.6	7.6	27.0	25.4	9.3	2.2	74.5	35.2	48.2	51.8
91950	NATIONAL CITY	34.4	31.6	4.6	3.9	19.6	19.1	61.7	66.9	8.8	8.2	7.5	8.6	8.9	27.3	19.6	9.6	1.5	70.4	29.8	49.1	50.9
91962	PINE VALLEY	91.9	87.3	0.7	0.9	0.6	0.9	9.2	15.1	4.4	5.3	6.9	8.7	5.2	17.8	37.3	12.9	1.6	78.2	46.0	51.8	48.2
91963	POTRERO	80.3	73.7	1.3	1.4	0.9	1.1	28.4	39.1	5.5	6.2	6.8	8.1	5.6	21.0	32.8	12.8	1.2	75.3	42.6	51.3	48.7
91977	SPRING VALLEY	57.0	50.3	13.4	13.1	8.7	9.8	28.0	35.8	7.9	7.9	7.5	7.9	7.4	27.8	23.9	8.4	1.4	71.8	32.9	48.8	51.2
91978	SPRING VALLEY	75.1	65.5	6.4	8.0	5.2	8.9	17.3	22.4	6.4	6.7	7.0	6.6	5.0	27.2	29.5	10.1	1.5	75.8	39.1	48.9	51.1
91980	TECATE	78.9	71.9	1.3	1.5	0.9	0.8	29.4	40.3	5.7	6.1	6.5	8.0	6.1	20.9	33.5	12.2	1.1	75.3	42.5	52.1	47.9
92003	BONSALL	85.5	79.5	0.9	1.0	2.5	3.3	18.8	27.5	4.9	5.3	6.2	6.1	3.6	21.4	30.3	18.9	3.3	79.8	46.6	48.6	51.4
92004	BORREGO SPRINGS	82.1	75.5	0.9	0.9	0.4	0.5	31.5	43.3	4.8	5.1	5.3	4.7	3.1	19.6	29.8	24.3	3.4	82.0	50.8	51.4	48.6
92007	CARDIFF BY THE SEA	86.7	81.3	0.8	1.0	2.8	3.7	14.2	20.5	4.7	4.5	4.9	4.8	6.5	33.4	30.7	8.8	1.7	82.8	39.4	50.3	49.7
92008	CARLSBAD	82.3	77.8	0.7	0.8	3.2	4.2	21.7	27.3	5.2	5.0	5.2	5.6	6.1	29.9	28.1	12.2	2.7	81.1	40.1	50.2	49.8
92009	CARLSBAD	89.7	84.7	0.9	1.3	5.0	7.0	6.2	9.9	7.1	7.6	7.8	6.0	3.5	25.8	31.3	9.7	1.3	73.4	40.6	48.4	51.6
92010	CARLSBAD	87.2	80.2	1.5	2.1	4.3	6.9	8.9	14.6	5.8	6.2	6.8	6.7	5.1	23.9	31.0	11.8	2.7	76.9	41.9	48.0	52.0
92011	CARLSBAD	87.4	80.8	1.1	1.5	5.6	7.6	7.3	12.6	6.5	7.1	7.6	5.8	3.3	22.7	31.1	13.5	2.4	75.0	43.3	48.0	52.0
92014	DEL MAR	91.6	87.9	0.6	0.7	4.7	6.6	4.4	6.9	4.1	4.8	5.8	5.3	3.7	22.2	36.4	15.7	2.1	81.8	47.3	50.2	49.8
92019	EL CAJON	83.2	77.6	2.9	3.2	3.4	4.4	13.4	19.2	6.2	6.5	6.9	7.3	6.4	25.7	29.8	10.1	1.2	75.8	38.5	48.9	51.1
92020	EL CAJON	73.4	66.2	5.8	6.0	3.1	3.7	22.4	30.6	8.4	7.3	6.3	6.9	9.2	27.8	21.6	10.2	2.3	73.9	32.3	48.7	51.3
92021	EL CAJON	80.3	74.2	3.6	3.8	2.4	2.9	17.9	25.1	7.5	7.2	6.8	7.0	7.7	27.6	24.7	9.8	1.6	74.2	34.7	49.2	50.8
92024	ENCINITAS	86.6	81.6	0.5	0.6	3.3	4.6	14.9	20.6	5.6	5.8	6.4	6.1	5.6	26.2	32.3	9.6	2.4	78.3	41.1	49.4	50.6
92025	ESCONDIDO	64.0	57.9	2.0	1.9	3.6	4.1	47.2	55.4	9.0	8.3	7.3	8.1	8.2	28.3	20.7	7.9	2.3	70.6	30.7	50.5	49.5
92026	ESCONDIDO	74.7	68.8	2.3	2.3	5.1	6.2	28.3	35.1	7.7	7.1	6.7	7.1	6.8	25.3	24.3	11.9	3.0	74.2	36.6	48.6	51.4
92027	ESCONDIDO	69.8	63.1	2.0	2.0	3.9	4.6	36.0	44.8	8.3	8.0	7.5	7.8	7.1	27.5	23.1	8.9	1.8	71.5	33.0	50.1	49.9
92028	FALLBROOK	76.0	70.2	1.2	1.2	2.1	2.5	30.8	38.9	7.1	6.6	6.6	7.2	6.8	24.2	26.2	13.0	2.3	75.1	37.4	50.5	49.5
92029	ESCONDIDO	82.6	76.7	1.8	2.0	6.0	7.7	14.3	20.3	6.2	6.5	6.9	6.5	5.3	23.1	30.7	12.9	1.9	76.3	41.7	49.2	50.8
92036	JULIAN	89.3	85.5	0.8	1.0	0.4	0.6	8.9	13.7	4.0	5.3	6.7	6.4	3.3	18.0	39.0	15.8	1.5	79.3	48.6	49.1	50.9
92037	LA JOLLA	82.6	77.0	0.8	1.0	11.2	14.4	7.0	10.4	3.6	3.5	3.7	13.7	7.6	24.1	24.8	15.2	3.8	86.9	39.5	47.8	52.2
92040	LAKESIDE	88.2	83.4	1.3	1.5	1.6	2.1	11.6	17.4	7.3	6.8	6.9	6.9	6.6	26.7	27.3	10.2	1.3	74.7	36.9	49.6	50.4
92054	OCEANSIDE	67.0	60.7	4.6	4.5	3.6	4.0	39.7	48.6	8.4	7.3	6.5	7.1	8.3	31.8	21.7	7.6	1.3	73.8	31.8	51.0	49.0
92055	CAMP PENDLETON	63.7	55.1	12.8	13.5	3.9	4.6	22.0	30.5	11.4	5.8	3.4	12.3	42.5	23.5	1.1	0.1	0.0	78.0	22.0	72.0	28.0
92056	OCEANSIDE	73.1	65.9	4.9	5.2	6.7	8.2	20.9	28.1	6.6	6.7	6.5	6.7	6.1	25.6	24.5	14.7	2.5	75.9	38.6	48.5	51.5
92057	OCEANSIDE	63.8	57.8	8.2	8.1	9.2	10.5	27.8	34.9	7.4	7.5	7.4	7.6	6.2	27.0	23.2	11.3	2.3	73.0	35.7	48.8	51.2
92058	OCEANSIDE	58.9	51.3	10.7	10.7	5.9	7.0	31.7	40.2	9.9	7.0	5.6	9.6	22.3	27.4	12.6	4.6	0.9	74.1	24.0	59.1	40.9
92059	PALA	61.5	57.0	1.5	1.5	3.0	3.5	35.0	46.3	8.3	8.4	8.4	9.1	8.0	26.7	23.0	7.3	0.9	68.6	30.5	50.4	49.6
92061	PAUMA VALLEY	44.4	39.7	0.6	0.6	1.2	1.4	41.1	52.3	7.2	8.4	9.7	9.5	6.8	23.5	24.6	9.1	1.2	68.3	33.8	53.0	47.0
92064	POWAY	82.8	76.7	1.7	1.9	7.8	10.1	10.5	15.2	6.0	7.1	8.1	8.1	5.2	24.2	31.3	8.8	1.5	73.6	39.4	49.1	50.9
92065	RAMONA	86.1	81.0	0.7	0.7	1.3	1.7	17.1	24.2	6.9	7.2	7.7	8.1	6.4	23.8	29.7	9.0	1.1	72.9	37.1	50.4	49.6
92066	RANCHITA	83.9	79.8	2.1	2.5	1.6	2.0	12.4	18.7	3.1	3.6	4.3	5.4	4.3	20.7	36.6	19.6	2.5	84.9	50.8	48.3	51.7
92067	RANCHO SANTA FE	93.3	90.1	0.3	0.4	3.2	4.4	4.9	8.0	4.4	5.7	7.9	8.1	3.9	14.1	36.7	15.9	3.2	76.8	48.4	48.6	51.4
92069	SAN MARCOS	64.2	58.2	2.2	2.1	5.1	6.4	41.6	48.1	9.4	8.9	8.0	7.8	6.9	30.7	21.3	6.1	0.9	69.0	30.7	50.4	49.6
92070	SANTA YSABEL	74.2	70.3	1.6	1.8	1.3	1.7	15.3	21.7	4.6	5.2	6.1	6.3	4.2	20.4	35.3	16.2	1.8	80.0	47.5	49.6	50.4
92071	SANTEE	87.0	81.5	1.5	1.7	3.0	3.9	11.2	17.0	6.6	6.6	6.7	7.0	6.2	28.7	28.0	8.9	1.4	75.6	37.1	48.1	51.9
92075	SOLANA BEACH	86.8	82.0	0.5	0.6	3.6	4.8	15.3	20.5	4.7	4.5	4.6	4.8	6.2	27.3	30.0	14.7	3.1	83.2	43.3	49.5	50.5
92078	SAN MARCOS	78.9	75.1	1.3	1.5	4.1	5.7	21.2	24.0	5.8	5.9	6.0	5.5	3.9	20.7	28.1	19.5	4.6	78.6	46.5	47.3	52.7
92081	VISTA	77.8	71.2	4.2	4.5	6.1	7.6	17.1	24.0	6.9	6.3	6.0	6.4	8.1	30.5	24.5	9.5	1.8	77.0	35.1	49.5	50.5
92082	VALLEY CENTER	78.3	72.2	0.6	0.6	1.6	2.0	22.0	31.4	6.0	6.7	7.8	7.6	5.1	22.0	30.8	12.4	1.8	74.6	41.2	50.4	49.6
92083	VISTA	57.2	50.1	4.5	4.3	4.2	4.5	49.0	58.5	9.4	8.6	7.7	8.6	8.9	30.4	19.5	5.7	1.1	69.2	28.8	50.1	49.9
92084	VISTA	67.7	61.6	3.0	2.9	2.9	3.4	38.4	46.4	8.2	7.7	7.4	7.6	6.9	27.1	23.2	9.6	2.3	72.1	33.7	49.7	50.3
92086	WARNER SPRINGS	82.8	78.5	2.0	2.4	1.5	2.0	12.2	18.4	3.3	3.7	4.5	5.5	4.3	20.6	36.4	19.3	2.4	84.4	50.5	48.7	51.3
92091	RANCHO SANTA FE	93.2	90.1	0.2	0.3	3.3	4.6	4.6	7.4	4.7	6.0	7.9	7.9	3.8	15.4	36.4	15.5	2.4	76.0	47.5	49.2	50.8
92096	SAN MARCOS	88.9	83.2	1.1	1.2	2.2	3.0	13.3	19.8	3.8	4.0	4.2	4.2	3.4	17.1	31.2	27.8	4.4	85.5	55.2	48.3	51.7
92101	SAN DIEGO	69.0	62.1	10.2	10.6	5.6	6.8	22.9	31.0	2.9	2.5	2.2	2.9	7.4	39.1	27.2	13.2	2.6	91.3	40.5	59.2	40.8
92102	SAN DIEGO	37.6	35.1	15.0	12.9	6.1	6.0	62.7	69.0	10.1	9.0	7.6	8.7	10.2	31.2	17.1	5.3	0.8	68.2	27.2	50.8	49.2
92103	SAN DIEGO	85.0	79.6	2.6	2.9	3.9	5.0	13.2	19.4	3.0	2.5	2.5	2.8	6.5	37.9	28.5	12.5	3.8	90.3	42.0	51.3	48.7
92104	SAN DIEGO	57.1	50.3	12.1	11.7	5.8	6.4	34.4	43.2	6.9	5.6	5.0	6.1	9.7	35.4	23.5	6.4	1.4	79.0	33.6	51.1	48.9
92105	SAN DIEGO	33.0	30.2	15.3	13.5	17.6	17.5	48.7	54.7	11.3	9.6	7.8	9.3	10.8	29.5	15.9	5.1	0.8	65.8	25.6	50.3	49.7
92106	SAN DIEGO	90.0	84.2	1.6	3.0	2.6	3.8	7.8	12.0	4.3	4.4	4.7	7.2	8.0	26.2	27.8	14.2	3.3	84.3	41.7	51.3	48.7
92107	SAN DIEGO	88.1	83.1	1.6	1.9	2.2	3.0	8.6	13.2	3.9	3.5	3.4	5.2	10.5	38.2	24.9	8.5	1.9	87.1	35.7	51.0	49.0
92108	SAN DIEGO	76.5	69.1	5.3	5.7	8.1	10.5	13.6	19.3	3.5	2.5	1.9	2.6	10.4	46.3	22.1	9.0	1.7	91.1	34.8	50.0	50.0
92109	SAN DIEGO	87.4	82.4	1.4	1.6	3.1	4.2	10.7	15.8	3.5	2.7	2.4	2.8	14.0	45.9	18.7	8.0	1.9	90.0	32.4	53.7	46.3
92110	SAN DIEGO	80.3	73.9	3.9	4.3	5.7	7.2	14.6	21.2	5.2	3.7	3.3	9.0	11.2	31.5	22.2	11.2	2.7	85.6	34.7	50.1	49.9
92111	SAN DIEGO	59.4	53.1	5.5	5.5	19.3	21.5	22.3	28.0	7.0	6.8	6.2	6.3	7.2	30.0	23.8	10.9	1.9	76.2	35.5	49.2	50.8
	CALIFORNIA	59.5	54.5	6.7	6.2	11.3	12.5	32.4	38.3	7.5	7.1	6.9	7.5	7.4	28.5	24.2	9.3	1.6	74.1	34.3	49.9	50.1
	UNITED STATES	75.1	72.0	12.3	12.7	3.8	4.6	12.5	15.7	6.8	6.7	6.6	7.1	6.9	27.0	26.0	10.9	1.9	75.7	36.9	49.2	50.8

#	POST OFFICE NAME	2009 Per Capita Income	2009 HH Income Base	2009 HOUSEHOLD INCOME DISTRIBUTION (%) Less than $25,000	$25,000 to $49,999	$50,000 to $99,999	$100,000 to $149,999	$150,000 or More	MEDIAN HOUSEHOLD INCOME 2009	2014	2009 National Centile	2009 State Centile	2009 Home Value Base	2009 HOME VALUE DISTRIBUTION (%) Less than $50,000	$50,000 to $89,999	$90,000 to $174,999	$175,000 to $399,999	$400,000 or More	2009 Median Home Value
91764	ONTARIO	14621	14232	19.1	33.1	40.0	5.6	2.3	48279	50154	57	39	7207	7.6	1.7	34.2	55.6	0.8	181660
91765	DIAMOND BAR	31612	15875	8.2	12.3	40.2	22.9	16.4	83371	84361	93	83	12560	2.1	1.4	2.5	31.3	62.7	454199
91766	POMONA	15832	18147	22.3	25.8	34.4	11.1	6.4	52045	54878	66	46	10175	3.4	1.2	9.7	66.7	19.0	242671
91767	POMONA	16755	14226	22.8	25.7	39.5	8.0	4.0	51447	54629	65	45	7777	2.4	0.6	7.1	83.8	6.1	242546
91768	POMONA	15395	8550	24.3	29.3	33.9	8.2	4.3	46285	49230	52	35	4872	3.3	1.4	10.9	73.8	10.6	232281
91770	ROSEMEAD	15305	16522	21.8	29.1	37.7	7.8	3.7	49176	51931	59	41	8407	6.2	1.4	2.7	60.5	29.2	318814
91773	SAN DIMAS	34639	12468	8.8	16.5	40.2	19.7	14.8	78175	78705	91	79	8951	3.9	2.0	2.7	36.7	54.8	423021
91775	SAN GABRIEL	29483	9111	13.6	22.1	36.8	16.6	10.9	68828	70678	86	70	5585	2.3	1.9	0.5	19.6	75.7	531752
91776	SAN GABRIEL	17241	11810	20.9	30.6	37.6	8.3	2.5	48437	51518	58	39	4649	5.1	2.1	2.6	47.9	42.4	370664
91780	TEMPLE CITY	24261	11740	13.2	26.3	42.0	13.0	5.5	61500	63729	79	61	7181	4.5	1.9	1.3	31.0	61.2	440510
91784	UPLAND	41375	8717	5.9	8.2	37.3	21.3	27.3	97707	98284	96	90	7490	0.9	0.5	2.7	46.8	49.1	397034
91786	UPLAND	21392	18537	23.9	29.0	34.7	7.6	4.9	47287	49635	55	37	8253	8.0	3.3	16.0	64.1	8.5	233106
91789	WALNUT	30155	12878	8.2	12.6	37.5	21.4	20.4	87669	88836	95	85	10779	3.1	3.8	2.2	19.5	71.5	513688
91790	WEST COVINA	20817	13311	13.1	23.1	44.9	14.0	4.9	63884	65703	82	64	8831	2.0	0.6	1.6	72.8	23.0	335720
91791	WEST COVINA	27376	10641	11.2	21.7	39.1	16.8	11.1	70191	71779	87	71	7298	1.0	0.8	1.5	43.4	53.2	414695
91792	WEST COVINA	21439	9959	9.9	23.3	45.5	15.1	6.2	66179	68605	84	67	6230	3.0	0.8	4.5	63.4	28.3	326929
91801	ALHAMBRA	21102	20292	22.8	28.3	36.2	8.6	4.2	48952	51693	59	40	6896	4.4	1.0	1.5	46.4	46.7	385521
91803	ALHAMBRA	20294	9711	20.7	27.1	37.5	10.4	4.3	52912	58337	68	48	4691	4.2	0.6	1.9	47.5	45.7	383403
91901	ALPINE	34407	6194	12.1	18.6	32.9	23.2	13.2	77390	79961	91	78	4276	5.2	2.1	2.2	25.5	65.0	471064
91902	BONITA	35528	7101	6.9	15.0	38.2	21.9	18.0	84648	86042	94	84	5470	0.0	0.2	3.3	30.9	65.6	475286
91905	BOULEVARD	19161	567	33.2	24.9	33.2	4.9	3.9	42705	45565	42	27	382	6.0	2.1	31.4	49.5	11.0	201299
91906	CAMPO	19701	1260	31.0	25.5	32.3	8.3	2.9	43567	46770	44	30	841	10.3	2.4	14.4	64.0	8.9	224569
91910	CHULA VISTA	24058	26715	19.6	26.1	35.9	12.7	5.6	54292	57630	70	50	12989	6.5	0.7	4.6	62.0	26.2	310876
91911	CHULA VISTA	19862	25402	18.0	29.4	40.5	9.0	3.1	52109	55764	66	46	13781	8.7	2.4	8.2	67.1	13.6	260933
91913	CHULA VISTA	29517	13256	4.2	11.0	43.9	24.2	16.7	87532	89755	94	85	10755	0.7	0.8	3.8	51.5	43.2	376980
91914	CHULA VISTA	29085	2398	3.5	6.5	45.9	31.2	12.8	93214	97592	96	88	2200	0.0	0.0	0.4	61.2	38.3	353442
91915	CHULA VISTA	33767	5395	3.2	8.0	44.2	26.9	17.8	91969	91736	95	88	4681	0.5	0.1	2.9	54.1	42.3	376871
91916	DESCANSO	23430	901	17.9	34.5	35.8	8.8	3.0	48099	49963	57	39	665	11.4	2.9	6.2	58.6	20.9	251263
91917	DULZURA	25099	269	17.8	28.6	35.3	14.9	3.3	52448	54848	67	46	197	9.1	3.6	4.6	41.6	41.1	366346
91932	IMPERIAL BEACH	18803	9256	22.9	33.7	35.4	6.2	1.9	44313	46685	46	31	2678	6.7	2.1	5.5	76.9	8.8	259493
91934	JACUMBA	16172	338	33.4	32.8	27.8	5.9	0.0	37223	39647	24	17	214	9.3	0.0	43.0	34.6	13.1	171324
91935	JAMUL	40671	2979	8.7	11.7	32.5	21.6	25.5	94280	96285	96	89	2465	2.0	1.7	1.5	28.6	66.2	511083
91941	LA MESA	30970	18329	16.7	24.2	38.9	12.3	7.9	59432	62703	77	57	9829	0.9	0.3	4.5	52.4	41.9	361800
91942	LA MESA	28919	10862	17.4	27.7	42.1	9.2	3.6	54254	58058	70	50	4819	1.4	0.4	5.4	79.0	13.9	289327
91945	LEMON GROVE	20603	8451	19.4	28.9	40.8	8.6	2.3	51605	54933	65	45	4616	1.1	0.1	5.2	89.9	3.8	251453
91950	NATIONAL CITY	13555	15478	31.3	32.0	30.4	4.5	1.8	38057	40433	27	18	5331	3.3	1.0	13.8	78.4	3.5	221754
91962	PINE VALLEY	29643	846	12.6	24.5	37.9	18.7	6.3	67156	69853	85	69	643	0.5	0.3	6.1	58.3	34.8	339063
91963	POTRERO	18488	397	29.5	24.9	32.7	9.6	3.3	46096	48318	52	35	278	11.9	2.2	15.5	59.7	10.8	215079
91977	SPRING VALLEY	22047	18401	14.7	26.1	42.8	11.8	4.6	59219	62383	76	57	10995	4.4	1.0	6.2	76.2	12.2	252681
91978	SPRING VALLEY	26583	4452	13.8	22.5	39.8	14.3	9.7	64370	67769	83	65	3308	12.8	2.7	5.4	52.1	26.9	299819
91980	TECATE	15764	77	32.5	24.7	29.9	9.1	3.9	44313	47343	46	31	54	13.0	1.9	18.5	63.0	3.7	200000
92003	BONSALL	34216	1551	10.2	23.5	37.3	16.0	13.0	68618	71766	86	70	1151	0.9	0.0	5.6	39.0	54.6	443388
92004	BORREGO SPRINGS	23791	1379	26.3	32.0	32.1	7.3	2.3	43019	45286	42	29	981	16.0	7.2	20.9	42.6	13.3	190972
92007	CARDIFF BY THE SEA	46391	4753	8.8	14.8	38.2	20.2	18.0	82190	83223	93	82	2602	0.2	0.1	0.5	22.1	77.2	615861
92008	CARLSBAD	36224	11394	14.2	18.9	38.0	16.2	12.7	67783	71457	85	69	5533	0.3	0.6	1.6	30.5	66.9	506589
92009	CARLSBAD	47463	14084	6.0	12.0	32.7	22.7	26.7	98659	101735	96	90	10704	0.0	0.1	0.7	23.6	75.5	583709
92010	CARLSBAD	32746	5661	8.0	17.0	41.3	23.7	10.0	78559	80446	91	79	4182	0.3	0.2	1.3	50.1	48.1	393003
92011	CARLSBAD	49125	8995	10.4	17.8	27.8	17.5	26.5	86443	88083	94	85	6491	0.5	1.1	6.3	17.1	75.1	583052
92014	DEL MAR	73182	6636	7.3	9.4	23.0	20.7	39.6	128103	130654	99	96	4676	0.2	0.1	0.6	8.4	90.8	928404
92019	EL CAJON	31351	15012	12.0	18.9	39.3	18.3	11.5	71185	75052	87	72	10349	4.1	1.0	4.0	44.9	46.1	375675
92020	EL CAJON	21365	20784	24.0	31.1	32.4	8.5	4.0	44874	47222	48	32	7867	4.5	1.5	4.7	50.9	38.4	325936
92021	EL CAJON	21951	22239	20.7	29.1	37.2	9.7	3.3	50187	52993	62	43	11386	15.5	3.7	8.8	50.0	22.0	270101
92024	ENCINITAS	41669	19406	10.5	17.3	33.5	18.4	20.4	79566	81937	92	80	12308	1.6	0.7	2.5	18.7	76.5	583265
92025	ESCONDIDO	20393	14956	21.2	28.7	32.7	10.5	6.9	50123	52789	61	43	6639	2.8	0.2	7.8	48.3	40.9	330437
92026	ESCONDIDO	24518	17141	16.0	25.0	40.4	13.6	5.2	59317	62271	77	57	10069	1.7	0.9	7.3	60.8	29.3	309775
92027	ESCONDIDO	23097	16305	16.0	25.0	38.4	13.9	6.7	59163	62540	76	57	10005	8.4	2.5	6.6	59.7	22.8	271462
92028	FALLBROOK	26698	16111	16.6	23.8	35.7	15.1	8.8	61101	64346	79	60	10661	4.2	0.7	3.9	39.2	52.0	414235
92029	ESCONDIDO	37238	7185	12.3	17.5	34.5	17.4	18.3	77160	78712	91	78	5269	5.0	2.7	8.1	24.7	59.4	490127
92036	JULIAN	26487	1571	19.8	25.3	43.8	7.3	3.9	53685	57055	69	49	1128	4.6	1.2	9.2	48.9	36.1	293960
92037	LA JOLLA	57363	18171	12.5	16.1	28.0	16.6	26.7	85535	87722	94	84	10686	0.1	0.1	1.1	11.9	86.8	890386
92040	LAKESIDE	24131	14865	16.1	24.8	42.0	12.4	4.8	59367	62310	77	57	9449	11.0	5.3	7.1	53.5	23.1	295426
92054	OCEANSIDE	21960	15325	22.9	31.0	32.8	8.9	4.4	46368	48554	52	35	6018	5.0	6.0	5.1	55.0	28.9	297679
92055	CAMP PENDLETON	16299	2235	14.2	44.6	35.3	4.7	1.1	43458	46001	44	29	106	25.5	26.4	19.8	22.6	5.7	85000
92056	OCEANSIDE	27640	19181	12.5	21.5	44.0	15.9	6.1	64774	67240	83	65	13046	2.2	1.2	6.8	59.0	30.8	322906
92057	OCEANSIDE	24662	17757	12.8	23.2	42.1	15.2	6.7	62859	65526	81	63	12568	1.1	1.9	12.6	60.9	23.5	263112
92058	OCEANSIDE	19329	11648	18.4	32.4	39.4	7.0	2.8	49053	52226	59	41	4887	8.6	8.2	11.8	60.7	10.7	229416
92059	PALA	19363	462	18.0	25.3	37.7	13.2	5.8	55726	60085	72	53	318	6.0	2.8	9.4	50.9	30.8	318667
92061	PAUMA VALLEY	19581	726	21.5	32.1	34.7	7.4	4.3	46088	48924	52	35	412	9.5	5.1	13.1	44.9	27.4	280263
92064	POWAY	35941	15921	7.7	14.3	36.6	20.6	20.8	85044	86186	94	84	11836	1.8	1.4	2.1	38.5	56.2	456183
92065	RAMONA	28108	11569	10.8	17.8	42.6	19.3	9.5	72650	76070	88	73	8440	2.1	1.4	2.8	47.9	45.7	384674
92066	RANCHITA	22109	174	27.6	30.5	31.6	8.0	2.3	41153	46024	37	24	128	6.3	4.7	26.6	47.7	14.8	220000
92067	RANCHO SANTA FE	86447	1591	6.8	10.5	13.5	8.2	61.1	208668	212658	100	100	1361	0.0	0.0	0.0	6.1	93.9	1000001
92069	SAN MARCOS	21274	14284	13.4	26.1	39.4	15.9	5.2	60581	64157	78	59	8822	2.6	2.8	9.1	57.9	27.6	305635
92070	SANTA YSABEL	27948	562	28.6	30.4	26.2	7.5	7.3	39395	42101	31	20	381	20.2	2.9	12.9	25.2	38.8	247222
92071	SANTEE	26611	19219	11.3	21.1	45.9	16.9	4.8	66467	68579	85	68	13310	6.8	3.7	10.6	68.1	10.7	266608
92075	SOLANA BEACH	57481	5393	10.2	17.1	28.3	16.3	28.1	88083	89070	95	86	3174	0.3	0.0	0.7	10.5	88.5	711258
92078	SAN MARCOS	33852	13944	13.8	22.9	38.0	16.4	8.9	65253	68979	83	66	10810	3.1	4.8	10.3	40.8	40.9	348451
92081	VISTA	30150	10703	10.5	23.1	45.0	14.6	6.9	62899	65676	81	63	6298	1.9	0.6	3.5	55.3	38.7	363266
92082	VALLEY CENTER	30018	6291	13.2	19.5	37.4	17.5	12.4	71809	74380	88	72	4925	5.2	1.8	6.2	30.1	56.6	438895
92083	VISTA	17490	11086	16.7	30.0	40.4	9.8	3.1	52582	55596	67	47	5579	5.2	1.4	7.6	77.0	8.9	249758
92084	VISTA	22098	15140	16.4	27.5	37.4	12.5	6.2	56263	60585	73	54	8714	5.3	1.7	4.4	51.1	37.5	335537
92086	WARNER SPRINGS	22708	489	27.6	30.9	31.5	7.6	2.5	40857	44655	36	23	358	6.7	4.2	26.0	46.9	16.2	221698
92091	RANCHO SANTA FE	85711	1235	8.9	6.7	20.9	10.8	52.7	169536	184720	100	99	1107	0.0	0.0	0.0	14.5	85.5	1000001
92096	SAN MARCOS	29451	1460	21.1	36.0	24.7	10.6	7.6	42417	45721	41	27	1088	5.4	3.2	29.3	29.2	32.8	198561
92101	SAN DIEGO	31362	18522	43.2	24.5	21.0	6.5	4.8	29770	31923	8	6	4847	1.4	0.0	3.4	39.2	55.9	444145
92102	SAN DIEGO	12922	13990	37.0	33.5	23.8	4.1	1.6	33020	35062	13	10	3937	7.7	1.0	21.8	58.7	10.8	217086
92103	SAN DIEGO	43920	17534	20.1	26.3	34.4	10.4	8.8	53543	57709	69	49	5338	0.5	0.4	4.6	30.5	64.0	529750
92104	SAN DIEGO	22639	21958	28.1	32.8	30.7	6.1	2.4	40545	42814	34	22	5476	0.5	1.4	11.5	63.7	22.9	272864
92105	SAN DIEGO	11680	20913	38.2	33.3	24.0	3.0	1.5	31364	33235	10	8	6266	3.6	2.7	21.1	70.6	2.0	207085
92106	SAN DIEGO	42155	8067	9.4	18.2	29.6	27.5	15.3	84691	87111	94	84	4805	0.8	0.3	1.4	13.9	83.6	663931
92107	SAN DIEGO	37084	14122	15.9	26.9	38.3	12.0	6.9	57022	60901	74	54	5059	0.8	0.7	3.4	27.1	68.0	541713
92108	SAN DIEGO	39530	9849	16.2	25.6	43.0	10.7	4.5	57728	61813	75	55	3750	0.6	0.9	28.2	60.4	9.9	218832
92109	SAN DIEGO	39061	23554	18.0	22.6	38.6	12.5	8.3	60182	63150	78	58	6647	2.1	1.7	4.0	20.6	71.5	576935
92110	SAN DIEGO	31286	10359	20.5	27.5	33.4	12.2	6.5	51975	55260	66	46	4228	1.6	0.2	5.5	38.0	54.7	430685
92111	SAN DIEGO	24038	16985	19.1	25.5	39.6	11.6	4.3	54828	58274	71	51	8512	2.2	1.6	6.5	72.2	17.5	303996
	CALIFORNIA	28199		18.5	22.2	33.9	14.0	11.5	61614	64088				3.3	2.6	13.6	41.0	39.5	321752
	UNITED STATES	27277		20.9	24.4	35.3	11.7	7.6	54719	56938				9.3	13.1	31.6	32.6	13.5	162279

ZIP CODE #	POST OFFICE NAME	FINANCIAL SERVICES: Auto Loan	Home Loan	Invest-ments	Retire-ment Plans	THE HOME: Home Improvements: Home Repair	Lawn & Garden	Furnishings: Comput-ers & Hard-ware-Personal	Major Appli-ances	TV, Radio, Sound Equip-ment	Furni-ture	ENTERTAINMENT: Dine out/ Carry out	Sports Equip-ment	Fees & Tickets	Toys & Games	Travel	Cable TV	PERSONAL: Apparel & Services	Auto Repairs	Health Insur-ance	Pets & Supplies
91764	ONTARIO	79	79	69	73	78	63	84	78	76	87	80	62	80	78	81	71	58	81	66	85
91765	DIAMOND BAR	131	169	182	169	180	140	153	153	133	165	135	122	169	132	170	122	100	145	125	169
91766	POMONA	93	97	85	90	97	76	100	95	90	106	94	76	98	92	99	82	69	97	77	102
91767	POMONA	80	87	82	81	89	69	90	86	81	94	84	67	89	81	91	75	61	87	73	92
91768	POMONA	82	83	73	76	82	65	88	82	80	91	84	65	85	82	86	74	61	86	69	89
91770	ROSEMEAD	79	90	84	81	93	66	90	87	76	96	80	69	88	77	92	68	58	86	67	91
91773	SAN DIMAS	127	159	165	156	165	142	142	142	134	145	135	108	159	136	155	131	99	139	132	160
91775	SAN GABRIEL	103	131	148	130	143	108	127	124	110	132	112	98	136	107	140	102	83	120	104	136
91776	SAN GABRIEL	70	79	81	77	82	64	86	79	77	85	80	63	86	75	87	73	59	81	68	87
91780	TEMPLE CITY	90	116	130	112	127	89	111	109	91	120	92	88	117	88	123	80	68	104	84	118
91784	UPLAND	150	205	233	208	222	186	173	182	159	188	159	137	207	157	202	153	119	170	162	200
91786	UPLAND	81	78	77	79	78	72	88	79	85	86	87	63	86	86	84	83	62	85	77	92
91789	WALNUT	142	180	190	179	191	148	163	164	142	176	143	130	177	141	179	129	105	154	133	180
91790	WEST COVINA	96	117	112	105	122	88	110	109	94	117	97	85	113	94	116	85	71	105	85	114
91791	WEST COVINA	108	140	148	132	148	114	129	128	114	134	116	99	140	112	141	106	86	124	108	138
91792	WEST COVINA	101	122	127	115	131	93	119	116	99	128	101	93	121	98	127	88	74	112	89	124
91801	ALHAMBRA	73	79	82	79	81	67	89	80	83	85	86	64	89	81	89	80	63	84	73	90
91803	ALHAMBRA	79	90	92	87	94	72	96	89	85	96	88	71	96	84	98	80	65	90	75	98
91901	ALPINE	128	150	159	153	155	139	137	139	129	144	130	108	150	129	149	125	94	135	129	159
91902	BONITA	131	171	184	169	180	154	148	152	139	154	140	115	170	138	167	135	102	146	140	170
91905	BOULEVARD	83	66	107	65	73	88	66	85	70	62	69	62	57	66	72	74	46	78	84	98
91906	CAMPO	95	69	99	66	71	97	70	89	78	65	77	67	56	77	70	86	51	82	93	106
91910	CHULA VISTA	90	93	91	93	93	85	97	90	94	96	96	72	99	95	96	92	69	94	87	104
91911	CHULA VISTA	85	89	84	84	90	74	92	87	85	94	87	68	90	86	91	80	63	89	76	96
91913	CHULA VISTA	142	170	165	168	173	141	152	153	137	166	139	122	164	140	162	126	100	144	128	170
91914	CHULA VISTA	157	179	149	176	170	146	154	154	144	169	147	125	164	155	156	134	105	144	131	174
91915	CHULA VISTA	147	183	179	184	188	146	162	162	141	179	143	133	177	146	175	126	105	150	128	178
91916	DESCANSO	102	81	131	80	89	107	81	104	85	76	84	76	71	81	88	91	56	95	102	120
91917	DULZURA	107	86	139	85	94	113	86	109	90	81	89	80	74	85	93	96	59	101	108	127
91932	IMPERIAL BEACH	75	65	61	66	63	59	79	68	77	77	79	56	73	78	72	75	56	76	67	81
91934	JACUMBA	73	53	75	51	55	74	54	69	60	50	59	51	43	59	53	66	39	63	71	82
91935	JAMUL	166	202	223	209	211	194	172	185	164	183	165	141	196	164	194	160	120	173	169	210
91941	LA MESA	95	105	111	106	108	97	107	100	102	107	103	80	112	101	110	99	74	104	97	117
91942	LA MESA	79	82	86	83	84	82	89	82	89	85	89	63	91	86	89	90	64	88	89	97
91945	LEMON GROVE	78	87	83	82	88	74	87	83	81	88	83	65	89	82	89	78	60	84	75	92
91950	NATIONAL CITY	62	61	56	57	61	49	69	63	64	70	67	50	66	64	66	60	49	67	54	69
91962	PINE VALLEY	107	116	134	118	121	121	103	115	102	107	102	85	110	100	114	102	72	108	111	132
91963	POTRERO	98	71	105	69	75	100	73	93	80	68	79	69	59	79	73	88	52	85	96	110
91977	SPRING VALLEY	90	102	98	98	102	87	100	95	93	101	96	75	104	94	102	90	69	96	87	107
91978	SPRING VALLEY	109	122	130	121	124	120	110	116	108	111	109	89	118	109	118	108	78	111	111	133
91980	TECATE	96	69	98	67	71	97	70	90	78	66	77	67	56	78	70	86	51	82	93	107
92003	BONSALL	116	145	157	146	154	146	124	136	123	133	123	96	144	119	143	124	88	128	139	152
92004	BORREGO SPRINGS	84	71	110	69	79	93	70	88	74	68	72	62	64	69	77	79	48	82	91	101
92007	CARDIFF BY THE SEA	133	155	182	163	168	137	159	148	143	164	146	122	171	140	171	135	109	149	131	169
92008	CARLSBAD	114	128	144	132	136	113	132	124	120	136	122	100	139	118	139	112	89	126	111	141
92009	CARLSBAD	162	203	219	209	215	178	181	182	165	196	166	145	205	165	200	154	123	173	157	204
92010	CARLSBAD	116	146	148	144	150	134	127	131	121	134	122	99	144	121	141	119	88	126	125	148
92011	CARLSBAD	154	189	210	193	203	175	170	176	158	183	158	134	191	155	190	152	116	167	161	197
92014	DEL MAR	201	262	315	273	289	240	237	239	217	255	217	185	278	211	271	206	164	228	213	266
92019	EL CAJON	114	134	140	135	139	125	125	124	121	127	122	95	138	121	134	119	89	123	119	142
92020	EL CAJON	82	71	70	74	70	68	86	74	84	84	86	61	81	85	79	82	61	83	75	89
92021	EL CAJON	86	79	75	80	77	76	87	80	86	86	88	64	84	88	83	85	62	85	80	96
92024	ENCINITAS	137	162	181	167	172	146	157	152	144	164	146	122	172	142	170	137	108	151	137	173
92025	ESCONDIDO	89	91	89	90	92	79	98	90	92	99	96	72	98	93	97	88	70	95	82	102
92026	ESCONDIDO	95	96	95	96	98	92	98	96	96	101	98	73	100	95	99	95	69	98	96	110
92027	ESCONDIDO	99	106	104	102	108	93	106	103	99	109	102	80	108	100	108	95	73	104	93	115
92028	FALLBROOK	104	113	124	113	119	109	110	111	107	115	108	83	116	105	117	105	77	111	107	126
92029	ESCONDIDO	137	154	161	157	159	146	145	145	140	152	140	111	157	140	153	137	101	143	139	166
92036	JULIAN	105	84	133	82	92	111	84	106	88	80	87	77	73	84	91	94	58	98	106	123
92037	LA JOLLA	166	187	221	198	202	175	194	180	178	198	181	145	208	174	204	170	134	182	167	207
92040	LAKESIDE	95	98	94	98	97	95	97	95	96	98	97	74	99	97	98	96	68	96	95	111
92054	OCEANSIDE	81	77	79	79	78	71	89	79	85	87	87	65	86	85	86	82	63	86	76	93
92055	CAMP PENDLETON	90	47	35	54	42	40	85	59	80	79	84	58	64	96	61	73	59	75	53	71
92056	OCEANSIDE	105	113	114	111	115	108	106	109	104	112	104	81	111	103	111	103	74	107	107	125
92057	OCEANSIDE	100	116	114	110	119	105	106	109	101	113	102	80	114	100	113	98	73	106	104	120
92058	OCEANSIDE	89	72	63	73	69	64	88	76	84	88	86	64	79	90	78	80	61	83	71	89
92059	PALA	98	115	109	101	120	87	108	110	92	117	95	84	107	92	113	82	69	103	84	114
92061	PAUMA VALLEY	94	87	86	79	86	82	88	91	84	90	86	70	80	86	85	82	60	90	83	103
92064	POWAY	145	180	182	181	185	162	156	160	147	166	149	123	177	150	171	143	109	152	145	181
92065	RAMONA	116	134	127	134	134	121	123	123	116	128	118	96	131	118	130	113	85	120	114	141
92066	RANCHITA	88	71	114	69	78	93	71	90	74	66	73	66	61	70	77	79	49	83	89	104
92067	RANCHO SANTA FE	271	388	477	406	435	365	312	336	293	348	290	252	405	291	375	281	227	307	295	365
92069	SAN MARCOS	99	104	96	101	103	90	103	99	97	107	100	78	104	100	103	93	72	100	90	112
92070	SANTA YSABEL	116	87	131	84	92	119	88	112	95	82	94	83	73	93	90	104	62	103	114	132
92071	SANTEE	103	115	108	113	114	106	106	107	102	109	103	82	111	105	109	101	73	104	102	123
92075	SOLANA BEACH	160	190	223	199	206	169	191	180	172	198	175	147	207	168	207	161	130	180	159	205
92078	SAN MARCOS	109	124	137	120	134	132	112	124	114	121	113	84	124	108	125	117	79	119	135	138
92081	VISTA	107	107	99	109	104	98	111	102	108	112	110	82	112	110	108	106	78	107	101	122
92082	VALLEY CENTER	121	140	153	140	146	136	125	134	119	130	119	101	135	118	138	117	85	126	124	152
92083	VISTA	88	84	76	81	83	71	92	84	86	94	89	67	87	88	87	82	64	88	75	95
92084	VISTA	91	103	103	99	105	92	100	98	95	101	97	75	105	95	104	93	70	98	91	109
92086	WARNER SPRINGS	89	71	114	70	78	94	71	90	75	67	74	66	61	71	77	80	49	83	90	105
92091	RANCHO SANTA FE	241	344	421	359	385	323	278	300	260	311	258	224	358	258	335	249	200	274	264	326
92096	SAN MARCOS	98	94	119	86	104	112	89	105	94	96	92	69	88	86	97	100	62	101	117	120
92101	SAN DIEGO	64	53	61	60	55	54	75	60	74	69	75	51	69	70	68	74	54	70	67	75
92102	SAN DIEGO	59	50	47	49	50	42	64	55	59	64	63	46	58	60	59	55	45	62	49	62
92103	SAN DIEGO	99	87	96	96	88	81	113	92	106	108	110	81	107	105	105	102	79	104	91	113
92104	SAN DIEGO	70	57	58	61	56	51	77	62	73	74	75	55	70	73	69	69	54	72	60	76
92105	SAN DIEGO	58	48	44	47	47	40	62	53	58	61	62	43	56	60	56	55	45	60	48	60
92106	SAN DIEGO	128	162	190	166	178	144	152	151	137	161	138	119	171	133	171	128	102	147	132	168
92107	SAN DIEGO	97	91	98	97	93	83	110	93	102	107	105	80	106	102	105	97	75	102	89	112
92108	SAN DIEGO	98	67	67	77	64	65	103	77	100	96	103	70	88	102	85	97	73	94	79	99
92109	SAN DIEGO	103	86	93	96	87	81	115	92	109	110	112	82	106	109	104	104	80	105	91	114
92110	SAN DIEGO	91	82	86	88	83	78	100	86	96	97	98	72	96	95	95	93	70	95	86	103
92111	SAN DIEGO	84	89	91	88	90	81	95	87	90	93	92	69	96	89	95	88	67	92	85	101
	CALIFORNIA	112	119	122	118	122	107	121	116	114	124	116	92	124	114	124	110	84	118	107	132
	UNITED STATES	100	100	100	100	100	100	100	100	100	100	100	100	100	100	100	100	100	100	100	100

POPULATION CHANGE

ZIP CODE #	POST OFFICE NAME	COUNTY FIPS CODE	POPULATION 2000	POPULATION 2009	POPULATION 2014	2000-2009 ANNUAL RATE % Rate	2000-2009 ANNUAL RATE State Centile	HOUSEHOLDS 2000	HOUSEHOLDS 2009	HOUSEHOLDS 2014	HOUSEHOLDS % Annual Rate 2000-2009	HOUSEHOLDS 2009 Average HH Size	FAMILIES 2000	FAMILIES 2009	FAMILIES % Annual Rate 2000-2009
92113	SAN DIEGO	073	47956	49545	50703	0.4	30	12099	12446	12708	0.3	3.93	9888	10166	0.3
92114	SAN DIEGO	073	65976	67031	68111	0.2	18	17208	17522	17793	0.2	3.82	14671	14895	0.2
92115	SAN DIEGO	073	58770	60204	60950	0.3	23	21818	22018	22251	0.1	2.54	11370	11388	0.0
92116	SAN DIEGO	073	33080	33037	33264	0.0	9	16545	16492	16577	0.0	1.99	6748	6655	-0.1
92117	SAN DIEGO	073	50149	50035	50447	0.0	9	20206	20263	20430	0.0	2.45	12520	12454	-0.1
92118	CORONADO	073	18922	18705	18759	-0.1	5	7682	7635	7671	-0.1	2.24	4892	4823	-0.2
92119	SAN DIEGO	073	23142	23254	23544	0.1	13	9567	9770	9927	0.2	2.37	6503	6590	0.1
92120	SAN DIEGO	073	23946	24313	24703	0.2	18	10229	10471	10645	0.3	2.32	6788	6903	0.2
92121	SAN DIEGO	073	4287	4237	4244	-0.1	5	1830	1823	1829	0.0	2.32	982	972	-0.1
92122	SAN DIEGO	073	34891	39329	41666	1.3	70	16687	19171	20385	1.5	2.05	7761	8587	1.1
92123	SAN DIEGO	073	26532	30498	32162	1.5	75	9791	11628	12345	1.9	2.51	6328	7390	1.7
92124	SAN DIEGO	073	30187	30660	31169	0.2	18	10576	10837	11022	0.3	2.83	7540	7654	0.2
92126	SAN DIEGO	073	67674	68717	69702	0.2	18	22117	22546	22881	0.2	3.03	16153	16351	0.1
92127	SAN DIEGO	073	17124	35123	41824	8.1	97	5957	12033	14312	7.9	2.89	4481	9113	8.0
92128	SAN DIEGO	073	43608	45954	47405	0.6	45	19113	20009	20534	0.5	2.29	12631	13214	0.5
92129	SAN DIEGO	073	50203	57359	60573	1.5	75	15916	17753	18605	1.2	3.23	13375	15051	1.3
92130	SAN DIEGO	073	28273	43985	50505	4.9	95	10584	16185	18525	4.7	2.70	7476	11672	4.9
92131	SAN DIEGO	073	28056	32606	34782	1.6	77	9985	11674	12476	1.7	2.77	7851	9086	1.6
92134	SAN DIEGO	073	1139	1193	1193	0.5	39	0	0	0	0.0	0.00	0	0	0.0
92135	SAN DIEGO	073	5174	5413	5413	0.5	39	51	52	52	0.2	2.77	42	43	0.3
92136	SAN DIEGO	073	9821	10284	10284	0.5	39	8	8	8	0.0	5.25	7	7	0.0
92139	SAN DIEGO	073	36598	37265	37829	0.2	18	10514	10696	10844	0.2	3.46	8905	9040	0.2
92140	SAN DIEGO	073	4279	4481	4481	0.5	39	5	5	5	0.0	2.80	5	5	0.0
92145	SAN DIEGO	073	6470	6721	6773	0.4	30	542	552	563	0.2	4.09	537	547	0.2
92152	SAN DIEGO	073	459	480	480	0.5	39	0	0	0	0.0	0.00	0	0	0.0
92154	SAN DIEGO	073	69028	83103	88324	2.0	83	16760	20432	21820	2.2	3.71	14423	17727	2.3
92173	SAN YSIDRO	073	27861	29331	30273	0.6	45	7183	7571	7802	0.6	3.87	6258	6576	0.5
92182	SAN DIEGO	073	589	629	641	0.7	50	1	1	1	0.0	3.00	0	0	0.0
92201	INDIO	065	50173	68510	79745	3.4	92	14000	19955	23514	3.9	3.38	11230	15688	3.7
92203	INDIO	065	9059	35061	46116	15.8	99	3498	11356	14711	13.6	3.09	2406	8590	14.7
92210	INDIAN WELLS	065	3966	5027	5721	2.6	89	2046	2540	2879	2.4	1.98	1360	1651	2.1
92211	PALM DESERT	065	19306	27230	32112	3.8	93	9455	13323	15736	3.8	2.04	6394	8874	3.6
92220	BANNING	065	25782	32522	36544	2.5	88	9535	12232	13857	2.7	2.57	6671	8370	2.5
92223	BEAUMONT	065	18125	36279	45464	7.8	97	6653	13891	17447	8.3	2.59	4750	9438	7.7
92225	BLYTHE	065	15991	17610	18708	1.0	62	5360	5715	6051	0.7	3.04	3899	4079	0.5
92227	BRAWLEY	025	23321	25487	28292	1.0	62	7052	7790	8694	1.1	3.22	5583	6127	1.0
92230	CABAZON	065	2348	3054	3518	2.9	91	746	944	1086	2.6	3.11	526	654	2.4
92231	CALEXICO	025	27759	38463	43439	3.6	93	6983	10066	11406	4.0	3.81	6122	8727	3.9
92233	CALIPATRIA	025	9316	10734	11406	1.5	75	1677	2051	2264	2.2	3.15	1246	1515	2.1
92234	CATHEDRAL CITY	065	42779	54722	61631	2.7	90	14099	17506	19566	2.4	3.12	9695	11858	2.2
92236	COACHELLA	065	23279	38735	46961	5.7	96	4950	8536	10387	6.1	4.53	4587	7519	5.5
92239	DESERT CENTER	065	9748	10672	10939	1.0	62	455	641	755	3.8	2.34	297	408	3.5
92240	DESERT HOT SPRINGS	065	23484	32855	38238	3.7	93	8339	11325	13150	3.4	2.88	5457	7286	3.2
92241	DESERT HOT SPRINGS	065	5778	7483	8376	2.8	90	2671	3315	3671	2.4	2.25	1659	2008	2.1
92242	EARP	071	1535	1951	2178	2.6	89	730	899	996	2.3	2.17	458	560	2.2
92243	EL CENTRO	025	45309	51610	55422	1.4	72	13327	15358	16463	1.5	3.26	10536	12131	1.5
92249	HEBER	025	3571	5758	6778	5.3	96	869	1398	1670	5.3	3.83	802	1280	5.2
92250	HOLTVILLE	025	8005	8662	9098	0.9	58	2343	2542	2667	0.9	3.34	1977	2137	0.8
92251	IMPERIAL	025	10054	17373	20819	6.1	97	3025	5237	6255	6.1	3.30	2504	4355	6.2
92252	JOSHUA TREE	071	8102	9393	9985	1.6	77	3455	3895	4112	1.3	2.36	2063	2307	1.2
92253	LA QUINTA	065	23739	49521	62232	8.3	98	8458	17544	22080	8.2	2.82	6569	13517	8.1
92254	MECCA	065	8725	13630	16362	4.9	95	1793	2733	3285	4.7	4.89	1596	2416	4.6
92256	MORONGO VALLEY	071	3516	4357	4814	2.3	86	1516	1820	1995	2.0	2.39	884	1053	1.9
92257	NILAND	025	1074	1079	1101	0.1	13	568	580	590	0.2	1.82	321	324	0.1
92259	OCOTILLO	025	441	520	555	1.8	80	219	262	293	2.0	1.57	126	149	1.8
92260	PALM DESERT	065	29466	33060	35543	1.3	70	13942	15543	16658	1.2	2.11	7833	8484	0.9
92262	PALM SPRINGS	065	25278	30857	34878	2.2	85	11218	13246	14714	1.8	2.28	5423	6258	1.6
92264	PALM SPRINGS	065	18120	20737	22447	1.5	75	9535	10817	11693	1.4	1.91	4186	4598	1.0
92267	PARKER DAM	071	123	136	140	1.1	64	46	49	51	0.7	2.78	27	28	0.4
92270	RANCHO MIRAGE	065	13247	18043	20774	3.4	92	6811	9075	10371	3.2	1.97	4009	5263	3.0
92274	THERMAL	025	22411	29355	34437	3.0	91	4385	5944	7133	3.3	4.07	3601	4875	3.3
92276	THOUSAND PALMS	065	5890	8108	9471	3.5	92	2275	2989	3418	3.0	2.71	1486	1910	2.8
92277	TWENTYNINE PALMS	071	25603	28074	29136	1.0	62	7703	8344	8679	0.9	2.67	5331	5747	0.8
92278	TWENTYNINE PALMS	071	5677	5952	6030	0.5	39	518	554	571	0.7	3.74	511	547	0.7
92280	VIDAL	071	47	51	53	0.9	58	20	21	22	0.5	2.43	13	13	0.0
92281	WESTMORLAND	025	2439	3066	3427	2.5	88	724	923	1031	2.7	3.32	584	742	2.6
92282	WHITE WATER	065	813	1312	1673	5.3	96	277	445	572	5.3	2.73	170	264	4.9
92283	WINTERHAVEN	025	4196	4873	5243	1.6	77	1584	1834	1971	1.6	2.56	1034	1185	1.5
92284	YUCCA VALLEY	071	20866	24561	26292	1.8	80	8595	9775	10365	1.4	2.48	5542	6298	1.4
92285	LANDERS	071	2125	2425	2583	1.4	72	1007	1112	1174	1.1	2.18	608	668	1.0
92301	ADELANTO	071	18972	32232	38317	5.9	96	5015	8140	9634	5.4	3.78	4047	6570	5.4
92304	AMBOY	071	18	25	28	3.6	93	8	11	12	3.5	2.27	5	6	2.0
92305	ANGELUS OAKS	071	171	209	230	2.2	85	74	88	96	1.9	2.38	49	58	1.8
92307	APPLE VALLEY	071	30580	36832	39919	2.0	83	10699	12481	13422	1.7	2.94	8278	9619	1.6
92308	APPLE VALLEY	071	29528	38984	43700	3.0	91	10095	13264	14895	3.0	2.92	7644	9828	2.8
92309	BAKER	071	977	1429	1595	4.2	94	245	332	374	3.3	3.58	161	218	3.3
92310	FORT IRWIN	071	9464	10399	10852	1.0	62	2359	2543	2654	0.8	3.51	2202	2376	0.8
92311	BARSTOW	071	30807	32405	33871	0.5	39	10990	11187	11586	0.2	2.85	7834	7941	0.1
92313	GRAND TERRACE	071	11509	12624	13154	1.0	62	4186	4442	4592	0.6	2.79	3020	3194	0.6
92314	BIG BEAR CITY	071	13955	17469	19402	2.5	88	5635	6830	7523	2.1	2.56	3905	4710	2.0
92315	BIG BEAR LAKE	071	4651	5501	5823	1.8	80	1988	2279	2395	1.5	2.40	1269	1447	1.4
92316	BLOOMINGTON	071	26921	29564	30734	1.0	62	7013	7397	7643	0.6	3.96	5827	6133	0.6
92317	BLUE JAY	071	1013	1247	1382	2.3	86	372	444	487	1.9	2.81	304	361	1.9
92320	CALIMESA	065	6789	7939	9175	1.7	78	2785	3369	3943	2.1	2.32	1914	2301	2.0
92321	CEDAR GLEN	071	1212	1495	1654	2.3	86	453	541	594	1.9	2.76	307	365	1.9
92322	CEDARPINES PARK	071	815	1008	1117	2.3	86	321	385	423	2.0	2.62	221	263	1.9
92324	COLTON	071	52074	57318	59615	1.0	62	15891	16673	17177	0.5	3.41	11982	12549	0.5
92325	CRESTLINE	071	8414	10296	11319	2.2	85	3286	3896	4247	1.9	2.64	2266	2672	1.8
92327	DAGGETT	071	513	577	598	1.3	70	212	231	238	0.9	2.50	136	148	0.9
92328	DEATH VALLEY	027	360	343	332	-0.5	1	208	199	194	-0.5	1.72	94	90	-0.5
92332	ESSEX	071	69	91	102	3.0	91	32	41	46	2.7	2.22	20	25	2.4
92335	FONTANA	071	81634	92000	95436	1.3	70	21136	22527	23205	0.7	4.06	17433	18535	0.7
92336	FONTANA	071	53848	86468	100276	5.3	96	13721	21894	25381	5.2	3.94	12158	19414	5.2
92337	FONTANA	071	29583	36466	39360	2.3	86	7744	9209	9890	1.9	3.96	6740	7938	1.8
92338	LUDLOW	071	68	78	82	1.5	75	25	28	30	1.2	2.79	16	18	1.3
	CALIFORNIA					1.2					1.0	2.93			1.1
	UNITED STATES					1.0					1.1	2.59			0.9

ZIP CODE		RACE (%)						% Hispanic Origin		2009 AGE DISTRIBUTION (%)										MEDIAN AGE	% 2009 Males	% 2009 Females
#	POST OFFICE NAME	White		Black		Asian/Pacific																
		2000	2009	2000	2009	2000	2009	2000	2009	0-4	5-9	10-14	15-19	20-24	25-44	45-64	65-84	85+	18+	2009		
92113	SAN DIEGO	31.5	31.1	18.1	15.4	3.4	3.4	74.6	78.4	11.1	10.2	8.7	10.0	10.3	28.3	15.6	5.0	0.7	63.9	24.8	49.4	50.6
92114	SAN DIEGO	21.0	19.2	29.3	26.5	27.0	27.3	29.8	35.1	7.6	7.8	7.8	9.3	8.4	25.8	23.8	8.4	1.0	70.9	31.2	49.0	51.0
92115	SAN DIEGO	57.3	50.5	10.6	10.4	13.1	14.7	24.0	30.6	7.1	5.9	4.8	10.4	14.9	30.9	17.0	7.1	2.0	79.5	28.5	50.5	49.5
92116	SAN DIEGO	65.5	59.0	11.3	11.3	5.1	5.9	25.1	33.0	6.0	5.3	4.7	5.1	8.0	35.8	26.5	7.1	1.5	81.2	36.5	49.6	50.4
92117	SAN DIEGO	77.2	70.3	2.0	2.1	9.1	11.4	16.1	22.6	5.7	5.4	5.5	5.6	6.8	29.4	27.4	12.0	2.3	80.2	39.6	49.9	50.1
92118	CORONADO	90.2	86.5	1.9	2.2	3.2	4.3	8.6	13.0	5.0	5.1	5.5	5.6	6.1	25.8	27.0	15.7	4.3	81.3	42.7	50.2	49.8
92119	SAN DIEGO	86.6	81.6	2.5	2.9	4.4	5.8	9.1	13.6	5.0	5.2	5.7	5.6	5.0	23.8	28.7	17.8	3.3	80.7	44.8	47.5	52.5
92120	SAN DIEGO	85.7	80.3	2.8	3.3	4.6	6.1	9.1	13.7	4.7	5.0	5.4	5.1	4.2	24.6	29.6	18.0	3.4	81.7	45.6	48.6	51.4
92121	SAN DIEGO	58.1	48.9	1.8	1.9	33.9	41.0	6.2	8.3	5.8	5.3	4.8	3.2	17.6	39.3	19.2	4.3	0.5	82.3	31.3	50.8	49.2
92122	SAN DIEGO	73.9	65.6	1.5	1.6	18.6	24.0	6.7	9.7	4.2	3.2	3.0	3.7	10.1	41.2	22.0	10.7	1.9	87.8	34.4	50.3	49.7
92123	SAN DIEGO	66.0	59.9	8.8	8.5	12.2	14.4	14.1	19.4	7.6	6.3	5.6	6.7	8.7	31.0	21.7	10.7	1.9	76.2	33.9	49.6	50.4
92124	SAN DIEGO	70.7	63.2	8.3	8.9	10.8	13.6	10.5	14.9	9.3	9.7	8.4	5.9	5.3	32.4	21.5	6.8	0.7	68.6	31.6	49.2	50.8
92126	SAN DIEGO	44.7	36.4	4.6	4.6	40.5	45.8	10.2	13.1	6.8	6.5	6.1	6.1	6.8	33.9	25.2	7.6	0.9	76.8	35.4	50.6	49.4
92127	SAN DIEGO	77.0	69.6	2.4	2.7	13.5	18.3	7.6	10.5	7.1	6.9	7.1	7.0	6.4	29.0	26.9	7.5	2.1	74.4	36.0	48.5	51.5
92128	SAN DIEGO	78.2	70.8	2.0	2.2	14.8	19.5	6.1	9.1	6.0	6.1	6.1	5.0	3.3	26.1	26.6	16.2	4.5	78.6	43.3	47.0	53.0
92129	SAN DIEGO	63.0	53.7	2.6	2.6	26.5	33.2	8.3	11.0	7.1	8.0	8.5	7.7	4.8	27.5	29.9	5.8	0.6	71.3	36.9	49.5	50.5
92130	SAN DIEGO	80.4	71.8	0.6	0.9	14.1	18.8	5.9	9.8	7.9	8.7	8.8	6.7	3.5	28.6	29.4	5.8	0.7	69.9	37.6	48.9	51.1
92131	SAN DIEGO	78.8	71.7	2.3	2.6	12.8	16.8	6.9	10.2	7.9	8.6	8.6	6.6	3.8	27.6	30.0	6.4	0.5	70.7	38.2	49.0	51.0
92134	SAN DIEGO	55.4	47.4	16.0	16.8	18.9	22.6	12.2	16.7	0.0	0.0	0.0	7.8	27.2	60.2	4.8	0.0	0.0	99.9	27.9	74.4	25.6
92135	SAN DIEGO	63.1	55.2	17.1	18.4	7.0	8.7	14.4	20.5	0.3	0.1	0.2	14.1	54.0	29.4	1.6	0.1	0.0	99.2	23.3	88.8	11.2
92136	SAN DIEGO	60.2	51.9	17.2	18.3	7.8	9.6	16.2	22.9	0.1	0.0	0.0	14.3	56.0	28.5	1.0	0.0	0.0	99.8	23.2	89.9	10.1
92139	SAN DIEGO	29.3	25.7	14.2	12.8	35.6	36.6	28.3	33.4	8.3	7.3	6.8	7.5	8.0	29.2	23.3	8.2	1.2	72.9	32.1	48.6	51.4
92140	SAN DIEGO	67.8	59.0	8.8	9.4	3.2	3.9	23.0	32.3	0.0	0.0	0.0	50.1	38.3	11.2	0.4	0.0	0.0	96.6	20.0	98.5	1.5
92145	SAN DIEGO	62.0	53.0	13.1	13.8	6.0	7.3	20.6	28.7	7.0	5.2	3.1	10.1	53.2	20.7	0.6	0.1	0.0	83.7	22.3	77.6	22.4
92152	SAN DIEGO	71.7	63.5	9.4	10.4	11.1	14.6	8.5	12.5	0.0	0.0	0.4	7.1	31.5	51.0	9.4	0.6	0.0	99.6	28.0	86.9	13.1
92154	SAN DIEGO	43.6	38.4	7.1	8.8	16.0	14.3	55.3	60.3	7.5	7.2	6.8	7.8	8.8	32.6	21.5	7.1	0.7	74.2	31.9	53.6	46.4
92173	SAN YSIDRO	44.5	42.8	2.2	1.7	3.5	3.1	88.9	91.6	9.8	9.1	8.3	10.5	10.7	27.1	17.7	6.1	0.8	66.6	25.9	48.2	51.8
92182	SAN DIEGO	75.9	68.4	6.1	6.8	6.5	7.9	16.0	23.1	0.2	0.0	0.0	48.5	46.3	4.1	0.6	0.3	0.0	99.7	20.1	44.7	55.3
92201	INDIO	48.0	45.9	2.7	2.5	1.6	1.8	76.4	79.6	10.4	9.2	8.1	8.7	8.6	27.9	18.7	7.5	1.1	67.1	28.1	50.6	49.4
92203	INDIO	80.2	56.8	1.6	1.3	2.3	1.8	26.8	61.9	7.1	6.8	6.5	6.8	6.3	21.2	23.2	19.4	2.8	75.7	40.6	48.5	51.5
92210	INDIAN WELLS	91.1	87.3	0.8	1.0	2.2	3.2	10.2	14.5	2.7	2.8	3.4	3.8	2.6	13.5	33.9	33.0	4.3	88.8	59.2	47.0	53.0
92211	PALM DESERT	89.9	85.7	1.0	1.1	2.0	2.6	11.9	18.4	2.8	2.8	3.0	2.9	2.3	11.4	27.8	41.1	5.9	89.6	63.5	45.9	54.1
92220	BANNING	63.2	59.2	8.3	7.8	5.3	6.0	29.7	36.0	6.5	6.2	6.1	6.9	5.9	19.6	21.2	23.5	4.1	77.0	43.7	48.0	52.0
92223	BEAUMONT	76.5	70.2	2.1	2.7	1.5	2.1	27.3	35.4	6.9	6.5	6.3	6.5	6.2	21.9	25.5	17.4	2.8	76.3	41.1	48.4	51.6
92225	BLYTHE	55.5	47.8	7.8	7.5	1.4	1.5	46.5	56.9	9.5	8.8	8.6	8.1	6.2	25.0	23.0	9.4	1.5	67.9	31.7	50.1	49.9
92227	BRAWLEY	53.9	50.5	2.4	2.2	1.5	1.6	72.4	78.3	9.1	9.0	8.6	8.6	7.1	26.8	21.1	8.4	1.2	67.7	30.2	49.5	50.5
92230	CABAZON	67.6	60.6	3.8	4.0	1.2	1.5	28.8	38.5	6.3	7.8	9.2	8.4	7.0	25.7	24.1	10.0	1.4	71.3	35.8	47.5	52.5
92231	CALEXICO	46.7	48.0	0.5	0.5	1.8	1.8	95.0	94.6	8.4	8.3	8.2	9.4	8.5	25.9	21.4	8.7	1.1	69.2	29.4	47.6	52.4
92233	CALIPATRIA	40.8	35.4	16.5	15.2	1.4	1.4	55.0	63.6	5.2	5.1	4.8	5.4	9.4	42.9	19.3	7.1	0.8	81.8	33.4	70.4	29.6
92234	CATHEDRAL CITY	65.2	59.4	2.8	2.8	3.8	4.3	49.9	58.4	9.0	8.3	7.5	7.5	7.0	27.3	20.9	10.7	1.7	70.4	32.2	50.3	49.7
92236	COACHELLA	39.5	41.1	0.5	0.5	0.4	0.5	96.3	92.1	10.8	9.8	8.5	9.3	9.1	26.8	18.5	6.4	0.7	65.2	26.5	50.3	49.7
92239	DESERT CENTER	28.8	24.3	23.2	20.7	1.9	2.0	45.4	53.0	0.9	0.7	0.5	2.0	16.3	61.4	14.0	4.0	0.3	97.5	33.5	93.2	6.8
92240	DESERT HOT SPRINGS	69.7	63.6	4.9	5.1	1.8	2.1	41.0	50.1	8.6	8.0	7.3	7.7	7.2	24.3	22.6	12.4	2.0	71.3	33.6	49.4	50.6
92241	DESERT HOT SPRINGS	83.3	76.4	0.9	1.1	0.6	0.7	27.4	38.8	5.2	5.1	5.3	5.8	4.3	16.5	30.0	23.8	4.0	80.8	50.8	49.2	50.8
92242	EARP	87.2	82.2	2.1	2.5	0.8	1.1	8.2	12.8	4.9	5.0	4.7	4.5	4.2	11.9	29.3	31.2	4.4	82.7	56.9	47.4	52.6
92243	EL CENTRO	48.5	45.9	2.9	2.5	3.4	3.4	72.9	78.3	8.6	8.2	7.8	8.9	8.4	26.7	22.2	8.2	1.0	69.8	30.1	50.3	49.7
92249	HEBER	34.2	31.9	0.9	1.0	0.4	0.4	95.0	95.7	8.4	8.3	8.3	9.4	9.0	27.9	19.8	8.2	0.6	69.5	29.4	51.6	48.4
92250	HOLTVILLE	58.9	53.7	0.6	0.6	1.2	1.2	67.9	76.4	7.9	8.1	8.6	9.1	7.0	23.6	23.5	10.2	2.0	69.4	33.1	49.3	50.7
92251	IMPERIAL	59.9	52.7	2.4	2.1	2.4	2.8	59.0	68.8	9.2	8.9	8.6	7.9	6.4	29.7	22.5	5.9	0.7	68.1	31.1	49.4	50.6
92252	JOSHUA TREE	88.3	83.6	1.7	1.9	1.4	1.9	10.5	15.7	5.5	5.2	5.6	6.7	6.4	21.5	28.6	17.1	3.4	79.3	44.3	48.9	51.1
92253	LA QUINTA	77.1	68.4	1.4	1.3	1.9	2.3	34.0	44.7	6.6	6.5	6.3	6.0	4.2	22.2	28.8	17.6	1.8	76.7	43.5	49.0	51.0
92254	MECCA	32.2	30.1	0.2	0.2	0.7	0.7	94.7	96.4	11.7	10.5	8.7	9.7	10.2	29.1	15.6	4.0	0.5	63.0	24.6	54.4	45.6
92256	MORONGO VALLEY	91.1	87.2	1.0	1.1	0.6	0.9	10.2	15.7	4.9	4.6	5.1	6.5	6.9	20.7	32.6	16.4	2.3	81.0	45.9	48.9	51.1
92257	NILAND	85.3	81.0	7.7	9.0	0.6	0.6	11.0	15.8	1.9	1.5	1.5	1.5	1.9	6.3	24.9	52.2	8.2	94.2	68.5	49.1	50.9
92259	OCOTILLO	66.7	60.8	10.0	9.6	0.5	0.4	29.0	37.7	3.3	3.5	3.8	4.2	8.7	29.2	28.8	16.7	1.7	87.3	42.7	66.2	33.8
92260	PALM DESERT	87.4	83.4	1.0	1.2	2.5	3.3	17.7	23.8	3.8	3.5	3.6	4.3	4.5	17.8	27.3	28.9	6.3	86.6	55.4	46.9	53.1
92262	PALM SPRINGS	74.3	66.3	5.5	6.4	3.5	4.2	27.8	38.1	6.1	5.7	5.5	5.8	5.6	22.9	28.2	16.7	3.5	79.2	43.7	51.6	48.4
92264	PALM SPRINGS	84.8	80.9	1.4	1.8	4.5	5.2	17.8	23.1	3.2	3.2	3.2	3.3	3.0	15.4	33.1	30.4	5.3	88.4	57.9	53.0	47.0
92267	PARKER DAM	64.2	58.1	0.8	0.7	0.0	0.0	17.9	23.5	3.7	6.6	7.4	3.7	1.5	16.2	39.0	18.4	3.7	79.4	50.4	50.0	50.0
92270	RANCHO MIRAGE	92.1	87.8	0.9	1.2	1.5	2.3	10.4	15.5	2.7	2.8	3.1	3.0	2.8	11.9	30.9	36.6	6.2	89.5	61.7	47.6	52.4
92274	THERMAL	38.8	36.2	6.6	5.3	1.0	1.0	75.7	81.2	9.0	7.7	6.4	7.2	10.4	32.5	17.6	8.4	0.9	72.9	29.5	60.7	39.3
92276	THOUSAND PALMS	77.2	70.7	0.7	0.7	1.0	1.2	39.9	50.9	6.4	6.1	5.9	6.5	5.5	19.6	24.2	22.4	3.5	77.6	45.0	49.7	50.3
92277	TWENTYNINE PALMS	72.0	65.0	9.2	9.8	4.5	5.6	15.7	22.0	8.7	6.6	5.6	9.1	19.9	27.6	15.2	6.4	0.9	75.9	25.1	59.7	40.3
92278	TWENTYNINE PALMS	70.2	62.8	10.9	11.5	3.3	4.2	19.1	26.7	7.3	3.2	2.1	13.4	43.5	29.2	1.2	0.0	0.0	86.6	22.8	79.6	20.4
92280	VIDAL	66.0	56.9	0.0	2.0	2.1	2.0	17.0	23.5	3.9	5.9	7.8	3.9	3.9	15.7	37.3	17.6	3.9	78.4	49.5	52.9	47.1
92281	WESTMORLAND	55.9	52.1	1.2	1.1	0.7	0.6	79.6	86.2	9.3	8.2	8.2	9.6	8.2	23.7	22.4	9.2	1.2	68.7	29.6	48.3	51.7
92282	WHITE WATER	72.0	66.2	7.4	7.0	1.5	1.8	33.1	43.8	8.2	7.6	7.9	11.7	5.1	22.7	22.7	12.7	1.3	66.5	33.2	55.6	44.4
92283	WINTERHAVEN	41.7	38.2	3.5	3.4	0.5	0.5	32.2	40.3	8.0	7.6	8.0	6.9	5.3	21.5	26.2	14.9	1.7	72.1	37.7	51.0	49.0
92284	YUCCA VALLEY	87.9	83.3	2.1	2.4	1.5	2.0	11.1	16.4	5.7	5.6	5.7	6.3	5.8	20.3	29.7	17.3	3.5	79.1	45.4	48.3	51.7
92285	LANDERS	91.7	88.4	1.4	1.6	0.7	0.8	9.0	13.7	2.7	2.8	3.2	4.9	4.4	14.6	38.4	26.1	2.9	88.3	55.5	51.5	48.5
92301	ADELANTO	52.0	44.7	12.3	11.4	1.8	2.0	44.5	55.0	10.5	9.7	8.8	9.4	9.0	28.3	18.2	5.5	0.6	65.0	26.6	52.2	47.8
92304	AMBOY	82.4	64.0	0.0	4.0	0.0	0.0	17.6	24.0	4.0	8.0	4.0	8.0	8.0	20.0	32.0	16.0	0.0	76.0	43.8	52.0	48.0
92305	ANGELUS OAKS	92.4	88.0	0.0	0.0	1.2	1.4	5.9	9.1	4.8	5.3	5.7	5.3	2.4	23.9	38.3	12.9	1.4	79.4	46.1	51.2	48.8
92307	APPLE VALLEY	78.4	72.3	7.1	7.6	2.4	3.1	16.6	23.5	7.1	6.7	7.1	7.7	7.0	22.1	27.4	13.4	1.7	74.3	38.6	48.8	51.2
92308	APPLE VALLEY	76.1	70.5	7.7	7.9	2.3	2.9	19.6	26.6	7.0	7.4	7.8	8.0	6.4	22.4	25.2	13.8	2.1	72.6	37.5	48.3	51.7
92309	BAKER	69.1	64.5	5.2	3.6	0.9	1.0	51.5	64.6	10.0	8.3	6.6	8.4	10.1	36.9	15.7	3.7	0.3	70.6	27.8	57.7	42.3
92310	FORT IRWIN	56.6	47.6	17.3	17.7	3.9	4.7	19.0	26.0	15.9	10.7	6.3	5.8	19.9	38.1	3.0	0.4	0.0	64.5	22.9	56.8	43.2
92311	BARSTOW	61.4	54.7	9.7	9.3	3.5	3.9	34.6	44.2	8.3	7.7	7.2	7.7	8.1	25.9	23.2	10.4	1.4	72.2	32.3	50.3	49.7
92313	GRAND TERRACE	73.6	66.8	4.6	4.6	6.1	7.5	25.5	34.2	6.7	6.4	6.4	6.9	6.7	28.2	26.6	10.3	1.8	76.3	36.9	47.1	52.9
92314	BIG BEAR CITY	89.9	85.6	0.6	0.7	0.6	0.8	11.1	16.5	5.3	6.2	6.9	7.1	4.8	23.1	32.3	13.3	1.1	76.8	42.7	49.9	50.1
92315	BIG BEAR LAKE	90.6	86.9	0.8	0.8	0.9	1.2	14.7	21.1	5.0	5.4	5.9	5.9	4.3	20.9	32.8	17.9	2.0	80.1	46.8	51.2	48.8
92316	BLOOMINGTON	51.9	46.6	6.7	5.8	2.0	2.0	61.8	71.2	9.5	9.1	8.4	9.7	8.9	27.2	20.2	6.2	0.8	67.1	27.6	50.3	49.7
92317	BLUE JAY	93.1	90.1	0.2	0.2	1.3	1.8	11.5	17.3	4.6	5.4	6.3	6.2	4.2	19.7	35.9	16.4	1.4	80.0	47.2	48.7	51.3
92320	CALIMESA	88.0	82.9	0.5	0.6	1.4	1.8	16.3	23.9	5.3	5.3	5.6	6.7	5.5	21.9	29.1	16.9	3.5	79.5	44.6	48.0	52.0
92321	CEDAR GLEN	88.1	82.9	0.9	1.1	0.6	0.7	16.9	24.8	5.8	6.2	6.8	7.1	5.2	23.1	31.9	12.6	1.3	76.9	41.7	49.1	50.9
92322	CEDARPINES PARK	89.8	85.2	0.9	0.9	0.7	1.0	10.3	15.4	6.0	6.7	7.5	7.5	5.3	21.4	33.9	10.4	1.2	74.9	41.8	51.2	48.8
92324	COLTON	44.0	39.8	10.4	9.2	5.4	5.9	59.7	66.5	9.8	9.1	8.6	9.1	8.7	28.6	19.2	6.0	0.8	67.0	27.8	49.6	50.4
92325	CRESTLINE	87.7	82.3	0.8	0.9	0.8	1.0	10.9	16.4	5.8	6.2	6.9	7.1	6.1	23.3	32.3	11.3	1.1	76.6	41.0	49.8	50.2
92327	DAGGETT	73.1	66.4	3.7	4.0	1.8	2.3	15.0	21.5	5.0	5.0	6.1	6.6	5.7	23.1	33.4	13.3	1.7	79.5	43.8	50.8	49.2
92328	DEATH VALLEY	81.7	81.0	0.3	0.3	1.9	2.0	6.7	7.0	2.9	4.4	3.5	3.5	2.9	23.9	41.4	15.5	2.0	86.3	48.1	53.1	46.9
92332	ESSEX	75.0	64.8	1.5	2.2	1.5	2.2	17.6	24.2	4.4	5.5	5.5	5.5	5.5	18.7	34.1	15.4	5.5	79.1	48.2	60.4	39.6
92335	FONTANA	47.6	43.1	6.1	5.2	1.7	1.7	68.7	76.7	11.0	10.0	8.6	9.7	9.6	28.1	17.2	5.0	0.7	64.6	25.6	50.6	49.4
92336	FONTANA	44.0	40.4	14.4	13.8	6.4	7.2	51.4	55.4	10.0	9.4	8.9	8.6	7.0	31.1	20.2	4.2	0.5	66.3	28.8	49.4	50.6
92337	FONTANA	41.6	37.6	12.6	10.7	5.7	5.9	58.7	66.3	10.3	9.5	8.9	9.2	7.7	30.8	19.3	4.0	0.4	65.6	27.7	50.3	49.7
92338	LUDLOW	85.3	78.2	1.5	2.6	0.0	1.3	16.2	23.1	5.1	5.1	5.1	5.1	5.1	20.5	34.6	16.7	2.6	80.8	47.5	50.0	50.0
	CALIFORNIA	59.5	54.5	6.7	6.2	11.3	12.5	32.4	38.3	7.5	7.1	6.9	7.5	7.4	28.5	24.2	9.3	1.6	74.1	34.3	49.9	50.1
	UNITED STATES	75.1	72.0	12.3	12.7	3.8	4.6	12.5	15.7	6.8	6.7	6.6	7.1	6.9	27.0	26.0	10.9	1.9	75.7	36.9	49.2	50.8

ZIP CODE #	POST OFFICE NAME	2009 Per Capita Income	2009 HH Income Base	2009 Household Income Distribution (%): Less than $25,000	$25,000 to $49,999	$50,000 to $99,999	$100,000 to $149,999	$150,000 or More	Median Household Income: 2009	2014	2009 National Centile	2009 State Centile	2009 Home Value Base	2009 Home Value Distribution (%): Less than $50,000	$50,000 to $89,999	$90,000 to $174,999	$175,000 to $399,999	$400,000 or More	2009 Median Home Value
92113	SAN DIEGO	9904	12446	42.4	32.8	20.6	2.7	1.5	29045	30129	7	5	3926	1.6	2.3	31.8	60.0	4.2	192566
92114	SAN DIEGO	16921	17522	16.6	24.6	44.5	10.8	3.4	59184	62265	76	57	12028	1.3	0.6	9.5	86.8	1.7	234198
92115	SAN DIEGO	20705	22018	31.6	28.2	29.4	7.7	3.1	40648	43020	35	22	8182	0.6	1.1	7.7	72.9	17.7	277900
92116	SAN DIEGO	29497	16492	24.8	31.6	31.3	6.7	5.5	44623	46565	47	32	4660	0.3	0.6	9.0	48.8	41.4	332888
92117	SAN DIEGO	28616	20263	13.7	25.0	43.7	12.5	5.2	61270	64183	79	60	11529	0.9	0.2	2.7	62.8	33.3	353619
92118	CORONADO	47238	7635	9.2	17.0	35.1	18.9	19.8	80591	82115	92	81	3759	0.3	0.5	0.4	2.5	96.2	958856
92119	SAN DIEGO	35097	9770	11.0	17.2	45.4	17.6	8.8	71194	73673	87	72	7049	0.0	0.4	7.7	58.0	33.9	348575
92120	SAN DIEGO	38187	10471	10.0	19.8	41.7	18.7	9.8	73188	75707	88	74	7647	1.7	1.4	5.6	48.9	42.4	374849
92121	SAN DIEGO	47546	1823	12.1	14.6	30.9	17.0	25.4	84076	84777	94	83	1003	0.5	0.0	1.2	29.5	68.8	507494
92122	SAN DIEGO	44189	19171	16.1	17.7	35.2	16.6	14.5	69631	72837	87	71	6967	0.3	0.2	2.4	27.1	70.0	534720
92123	SAN DIEGO	28088	11628	12.1	25.9	42.8	14.4	4.8	61494	64058	79	61	5792	2.6	1.3	4.9	71.6	19.7	326083
92124	SAN DIEGO	32820	10837	7.7	17.1	44.5	17.3	13.5	74944	77107	89	75	5222	1.1	0.5	0.7	39.1	58.6	449889
92126	SAN DIEGO	27808	22546	7.4	16.7	48.2	20.3	7.5	74338	75885	89	74	13309	1.5	1.1	6.0	69.5	21.9	313800
92127	SAN DIEGO	44056	12033	4.6	13.0	34.4	23.0	25.0	96006	96000	96	90	8642	0.2	0.2	1.5	33.2	65.0	470772
92128	SAN DIEGO	45792	20009	8.3	14.9	36.4	22.4	18.0	84002	86293	93	83	13889	0.5	0.2	2.1	40.4	56.7	437621
92129	SAN DIEGO	36402	17753	5.7	10.3	32.9	26.9	24.3	101908	102333	97	91	12572	0.6	0.1	2.3	24.0	73.1	485185
92130	SAN DIEGO	62236	16185	7.6	6.9	22.0	19.3	44.2	133549	139440	99	97	11966	0.0	0.4	1.5	22.5	75.6	629696
92131	SAN DIEGO	52333	11674	3.7	7.6	30.0	24.6	34.1	120591	120272	99	95	9553	0.3	0.3	0.8	23.5	75.2	578505
92134	SAN DIEGO	20781	0	0.0	0.0	0.0	0.0	0.0	0	0	0	0	0	0.0	0.0	0.0	0.0	0.0	0
92135	SAN DIEGO	22554	52	0.0	0.0	0.0	44.2	55.8	185359	185359	100	99	0	0.0	0.0	0.0	0.0	0.0	0
92136	SAN DIEGO	20696	0	0.0	0.0	0.0	0.0	0.0	0	0	0	0	0	0.0	0.0	0.0	0.0	0.0	0
92139	SAN DIEGO	19971	10696	11.0	24.4	48.8	12.3	3.6	61282	63801	79	60	6397	1.5	0.4	8.9	87.4	1.8	246202
92140	SAN DIEGO	20847	5	0.0	0.0	0.0	100.0	0.0	110087	110087	98	93	0	0.0	0.0	0.0	0.0	0.0	0
92145	SAN DIEGO	18501	552	10.7	39.1	43.1	5.4	1.6	50174	53979	62	43	6	0.0	0.0	0.0	100.0	0.0	270000
92152	SAN DIEGO	20482	0	0.0	0.0	0.0	0.0	0.0	0	0	0	0	0	0.0	0.0	0.0	0.0	0.0	0
92154	SAN DIEGO	19679	20432	15.6	24.7	39.2	14.3	6.1	60627	64655	78	59	13201	6.8	2.4	6.8	71.4	12.6	255209
92173	SAN YSIDRO	10807	7571	38.1	31.2	25.1	4.6	1.0	33347	35411	14	11	2589	7.0	3.6	12.9	72.1	4.4	240119
92182	SAN DIEGO	12311	0	0.0	0.0	0.0	0.0	0.0	0	0	0	0	0	0.0	0.0	0.0	0.0	0.0	0
92201	INDIO	16167	19955	25.2	31.4	34.5	6.2	2.7	44618	47538	47	32	11348	9.0	7.1	47.5	33.4	3.0	151512
92203	INDIO	21307	11356	21.4	30.6	31.0	9.8	7.2	48023	49643	57	39	7780	2.1	3.2	38.5	36.3	19.8	203614
92210	INDIAN WELLS	62381	2540	10.4	19.2	31.9	12.4	26.1	76056	76915	90	76	1978	1.2	1.7	9.6	26.2	61.4	538714
92211	PALM DESERT	43229	13323	13.3	24.5	37.0	12.7	12.5	61843	63573	80	61	10371	1.7	2.6	13.2	46.4	36.1	323864
92220	BANNING	19894	12232	29.0	30.1	33.1	5.3	2.5	40423	44179	34	22	8494	12.4	9.5	36.8	38.4	2.8	156041
92223	BEAUMONT	20916	13891	27.7	31.5	30.8	6.9	3.1	40336	43632	34	22	10192	7.2	4.1	46.3	32.8	9.7	157073
92225	BLYTHE	16393	5715	32.1	27.4	32.3	6.4	1.9	39630	42585	32	21	3061	11.4	12.5	49.8	24.7	1.6	128456
92227	BRAWLEY	15451	7790	33.6	25.9	31.7	6.4	2.3	39325	43330	31	20	3885	13.4	12.6	51.8	19.2	3.0	120715
92230	CABAZON	12450	944	45.8	30.7	18.1	3.7	1.7	27697	29187	5	4	621	37.0	27.2	25.0	10.8	0.0	67889
92231	CALEXICO	12301	10066	35.6	29.8	27.0	4.7	2.9	36066	39733	21	15	5747	5.1	4.4	61.7	26.3	2.5	141919
92233	CALIPATRIA	15919	2051	36.0	33.5	26.0	3.8	0.7	32090	33497	12	9	1232	43.3	22.7	30.2	3.7	0.0	58542
92234	CATHEDRAL CITY	19671	17506	21.7	28.6	36.7	8.3	4.7	49748	51982	60	42	10771	10.9	7.9	32.4	46.7	2.2	172901
92236	COACHELLA	9836	8536	30.8	35.2	29.2	3.9	0.9	35790	38354	20	15	5175	9.0	6.4	63.4	18.8	2.3	131990
92239	DESERT CENTER	20594	641	30.1	31.7	33.4	4.8	0.0	35707	38058	20	15	413	19.1	9.0	59.6	12.1	0.2	116156
92240	DESERT HOT SPRINGS	14920	11325	35.4	33.4	26.7	3.3	1.3	34233	36608	16	12	6160	16.6	19.3	42.0	21.2	1.0	114588
92241	DESERT HOT SPRINGS	19622	3315	35.1	33.7	25.2	4.0	2.0	33788	36147	15	12	2599	36.7	18.1	29.5	15.1	0.6	76682
92242	EARP	16302	899	44.5	35.7	15.8	3.1	0.9	27360	28160	5	4	708	31.5	29.1	31.2	7.6	0.6	73333
92243	EL CENTRO	17293	15358	29.6	25.0	33.6	7.0	4.8	44926	48042	48	33	8131	14.4	11.7	49.2	22.2	2.4	125233
92249	HEBER	12391	1398	31.6	33.3	29.3	3.6	2.1	37194	40545	24	17	985	15.6	13.8	61.5	7.7	1.3	112269
92250	HOLTVILLE	16677	2542	24.5	26.2	37.8	8.3	3.1	49197	51633	59	41	1567	18.4	14.0	45.3	21.4	0.9	116681
92251	IMPERIAL	21330	5237	16.1	17.6	48.4	12.5	5.5	63326	65295	82	64	3812	2.9	5.2	52.0	37.0	2.9	153791
92252	JOSHUA TREE	17090	3895	37.9	32.9	25.1	2.5	1.5	32395	33989	12	9	2608	15.5	31.5	38.7	14.0	0.3	93697
92253	LA QUINTA	30152	17544	15.2	24.8	37.5	11.0	11.6	60963	63387	79	60	13227	4.4	1.7	23.1	40.1	30.6	244722
92254	MECCA	8400	2733	41.4	32.8	22.4	2.5	0.9	29035	29932	7	5	1148	22.0	10.6	56.4	5.9	5.1	108074
92256	MORONGO VALLEY	23051	1820	27.6	30.3	33.0	5.4	3.6	43091	46155	43	29	1307	13.8	28.8	44.8	9.7	2.8	97201
92257	NILAND	20720	580	43.8	34.3	16.7	3.3	1.9	29844	30766	8	6	481	71.9	17.3	7.5	3.3	0.0	32045
92259	OCOTILLO	25286	262	44.7	22.9	27.1	5.3	0.0	31715	33543	11	8	190	23.2	57.9	16.3	2.6	0.0	71250
92260	PALM DESERT	34156	15543	19.4	28.0	35.5	8.5	8.6	53314	57801	69	48	9930	3.8	4.9	22.5	48.0	20.7	220305
92262	PALM SPRINGS	24199	13246	30.1	30.5	28.1	6.7	4.6	39266	41932	31	20	6936	7.7	6.8	28.4	42.5	14.5	190769
92264	PALM SPRINGS	36518	10817	23.1	27.6	32.5	8.7	8.1	49161	51892	59	41	6820	17.9	6.0	20.4	35.3	20.5	191997
92267	PARKER DAM	15784	49	40.8	28.6	26.5	2.0	2.0	31691	36152	11	8	30	10.0	20.0	56.7	13.3	0.0	117857
92270	RANCHO MIRAGE	54324	9075	16.0	21.1	31.4	12.0	19.6	66454	67809	85	68	7198	7.9	5.8	12.1	31.0	43.2	348626
92274	THERMAL	11707	5944	41.6	34.5	19.6	2.9	1.5	29049	30289	7	6	3174	35.9	20.0	23.1	11.1	9.9	78800
92276	THOUSAND PALMS	18968	2989	30.5	32.3	30.5	4.9	1.8	40953	43595	36	23	2327	11.1	26.0	42.8	19.4	0.6	112027
92277	TWENTYNINE PALMS	17335	8344	31.6	35.7	27.5	4.5	0.8	36537	39211	22	16	3540	21.1	26.2	41.6	10.8	0.3	93893
92278	TWENTYNINE PALMS	17722	554	24.0	43.5	28.2	3.6	0.7	36284	40450	28	19	11	18.2	36.4	27.3	18.2	0.0	85000
92280	VIDAL	16912	21	33.3	33.3	28.6	4.8	0.0	36100	40000	21	15	13	0.0	15.4	46.2	38.5	0.0	143750
92281	WESTMORLAND	11831	923	43.3	27.4	24.5	3.7	1.1	30822	32248	9	7	458	11.4	18.6	63.3	6.8	0.0	103571
92282	WHITE WATER	16555	445	38.0	28.3	28.3	2.5	2.9	35219	37866	18	14	286	21.0	28.3	40.9	5.9	3.8	95000
92283	WINTERHAVEN	12551	1834	53.4	29.1	14.9	1.4	1.2	22812	23399	2	2	1136	59.9	20.4	12.7	3.0	4.0	33529
92284	YUCCA VALLEY	18447	9775	34.2	31.4	27.0	5.5	1.9	36854	39862	23	16	6691	14.1	21.0	45.3	17.4	2.4	110840
92285	LANDERS	16864	1112	44.7	33.5	17.0	4.5	0.3	27967	30000	6	4	870	28.2	35.1	28.4	7.5	0.9	70000
92301	ADELANTO	11925	8140	30.0	32.8	33.9	2.9	0.4	40273	44604	34	22	5391	5.1	16.3	68.4	9.4	0.8	117136
92304	AMBOY	23092	11	0.0	45.5	54.5	0.0	0.0	54545	50000	70	51	6	16.7	16.7	33.3	33.3	0.0	112500
92305	ANGELUS OAKS	33765	88	13.6	23.9	43.2	8.0	11.4	67977	68382	86	69	65	3.1	4.6	18.5	63.1	10.8	221667
92307	APPLE VALLEY	21424	12481	20.2	26.7	39.2	10.0	3.8	53139	56570	68	48	8596	4.8	3.5	41.9	45.5	4.4	174748
92308	APPLE VALLEY	19421	13264	25.5	29.1	32.6	9.2	3.6	45737	48239	50	34	9174	7.4	6.3	52.5	31.8	2.1	144824
92309	BAKER	13490	332	30.1	34.9	29.8	4.5	0.6	34280	35610	16	12	154	58.4	1.9	16.9	14.3	8.4	13571
92310	FORT IRWIN	15742	2543	10.4	49.9	33.1	5.4	1.2	43683	45667	44	30	179	40.2	40.8	10.6	8.4	0.0	55469
92311	BARSTOW	19063	11187	26.6	27.4	36.1	7.3	2.6	46683	48720	53	36	6215	15.5	19.4	52.7	11.4	1.0	105500
92313	GRAND TERRACE	26538	4442	11.6	18.3	50.5	15.1	4.5	69201	71099	86	70	2799	5.9	2.0	21.6	67.4	3.0	200698
92314	BIG BEAR CITY	21959	6830	23.8	31.8	33.9	7.3	3.2	44565	47459	47	32	4792	0.6	7.9	39.8	41.9	9.7	179293
92315	BIG BEAR LAKE	23692	2279	29.0	27.7	31.3	7.3	4.7	42150	45473	40	26	1370	12.6	1.0	13.4	49.0	24.0	253629
92316	BLOOMINGTON	13849	7397	24.2	29.9	35.9	7.6	2.4	46847	48609	54	36	5435	13.4	4.1	49.0	31.2	2.4	153214
92317	BLUE JAY	39833	444	9.5	12.2	44.6	15.5	18.2	82129	81893	93	82	351	0.0	0.0	3.4	48.4	48.1	388393
92320	CALIMESA	25551	3369	22.7	27.8	39.4	6.4	3.6	49348	52178	60	41	2656	19.7	2.7	31.5	38.4	7.8	165625
92321	CEDAR GLEN	30357	541	16.6	16.1	36.6	20.3	10.4	72344	73810	88	73	374	0.0	0.0	19.8	52.7	27.5	247333
92322	CEDARPINES PARK	25641	385	19.7	21.8	42.3	10.4	5.7	62538	64317	81	62	296	1.0	2.4	40.9	47.3	8.4	188710
92324	COLTON	15937	16673	25.8	29.7	35.7	6.0	2.8	45566	47776	50	34	8814	6.5	7.1	49.9	33.7	2.9	153540
92325	CRESTLINE	23654	3896	19.6	28.1	36.8	11.3	4.2	51937	53925	66	45	2677	3.7	5.3	40.5	46.9	3.5	175814
92327	DAGGETT	16515	231	48.1	14.7	33.8	3.0	0.4	27338	30000	5	4	127	60.6	12.6	22.0	3.9	0.8	41563
92328	DEATH VALLEY	28242	199	34.7	21.1	35.2	9.0	0.0	44308	47138	46	31	75	49.3	21.3	9.3	10.7	9.3	50625
92332	ESSEX	24810	41	14.6	39.0	39.0	4.9	2.4	47343	50000	55	38	23	17.4	13.0	43.5	26.1	0.0	114583
92335	FONTANA	12614	22527	25.8	32.0	34.7	5.5	2.0	43050	45662	43	29	12109	5.8	3.7	55.4	34.0	1.1	158204
92336	FONTANA	20665	21894	10.5	17.6	45.9	18.3	7.6	74593	76485	89	75	18129	1.1	1.0	25.3	70.4	2.2	212005
92337	FONTANA	18620	9209	10.6	19.9	50.7	13.6	5.1	66010	67474	84	67	7093	2.2	0.6	29.3	65.1	2.8	193205
92338	LUDLOW	17785	28	25.0	25.0	46.4	3.6	0.0	50000	56236	61	43	18	5.6	11.1	55.6	22.2	5.6	120000
	CALIFORNIA	28199		18.5	22.2	33.9	14.0	11.5	61614	64088				3.3	2.6	13.6	41.0	39.5	321752
	UNITED STATES	27277		20.9	24.4	35.3	11.7	7.6	54719	56938				9.3	13.1	31.6	32.6	13.5	162279

ZIP CODE		FINANCIAL SERVICES				THE HOME						ENTERTAINMENT						PERSONAL			
						Home Improvements		Furnishings													
#	POST OFFICE NAME	Auto Loan	Home Loan	Invest-ments	Retire-ment Plans	Home Repair	Lawn & Garden	Comput-ers & Hard-ware-Personal	Major Appli-ances	TV, Radio, Sound Equip-ment	Furni-ture	Dine out/ Carry out	Sports Equip-ment	Fees & Tickets	Toys & Games	Travel	Cable TV	Apparel & Services	Auto Repairs	Health Insur-ance	Pets & Supplies
92113	SAN DIEGO	54	48	41	45	47	38	57	51	53	59	56	42	53	54	53	49	41	56	43	55
92114	SAN DIEGO	85	101	96	93	104	81	95	95	85	100	88	73	99	86	100	80	64	92	79	101
92115	SAN DIEGO	74	60	61	63	60	56	84	66	77	77	80	58	73	78	72	74	57	76	63	80
92116	SAN DIEGO	82	69	72	74	69	62	90	74	85	88	87	64	83	85	83	80	63	85	71	90
92117	SAN DIEGO	87	101	108	101	105	92	101	95	97	99	99	75	108	96	106	96	72	98	93	109
92118	CORONADO	142	165	192	170	180	154	161	159	149	170	150	124	176	145	176	143	110	157	148	179
92119	SAN DIEGO	102	128	138	125	134	122	116	118	113	117	114	87	131	111	128	114	82	116	120	132
92120	SAN DIEGO	110	136	153	136	146	128	125	128	119	130	119	96	140	116	140	117	87	125	122	143
92121	SAN DIEGO	157	155	144	166	151	135	164	145	155	169	159	126	166	162	157	146	115	150	132	172
92122	SAN DIEGO	120	113	126	124	117	107	136	115	129	133	132	98	134	128	131	125	96	126	114	139
92123	SAN DIEGO	100	98	97	99	98	91	104	96	102	103	103	76	104	104	101	100	73	101	94	112
92124	SAN DIEGO	126	128	137	134	133	113	139	125	128	140	132	105	142	133	139	121	96	131	112	144
92126	SAN DIEGO	115	129	133	128	134	105	128	122	113	136	114	100	131	113	133	103	83	121	102	137
92127	SAN DIEGO	177	199	195	205	202	177	183	180	173	198	175	144	201	179	191	165	127	175	163	205
92128	SAN DIEGO	139	167	176	167	176	157	147	155	140	162	140	115	166	139	163	136	101	146	148	172
92129	SAN DIEGO	157	187	182	194	189	164	167	166	157	178	160	133	187	162	178	149	118	160	146	189
92130	SAN DIEGO	216	272	294	285	286	241	240	240	222	259	224	193	279	225	266	209	169	228	208	269
92131	SAN DIEGO	194	236	243	245	245	209	207	209	193	226	195	166	237	198	226	182	144	198	183	235
92134	SAN DIEGO	0	0	0	0	0	0	0	0	0	0	0	0	0	0	0	0	0	0	0	0
92135	SAN DIEGO	426	221	165	256	198	188	400	277	376	372	396	276	304	452	289	346	278	353	250	337
92136	SAN DIEGO	0	0	0	0	0	0	0	0	0	0	0	0	0	0	0	0	0	0	0	0
92139	SAN DIEGO	96	105	99	100	106	86	104	99	94	108	96	78	104	97	104	88	69	99	85	110
92140	SAN DIEGO	207	107	80	124	96	91	194	134	183	181	192	134	147	219	140	168	135	171	121	164
92145	SAN DIEGO	101	52	39	61	47	45	95	66	89	88	94	65	72	107	68	82	66	84	59	80
92152	SAN DIEGO	0	0	0	0	0	0	0	0	0	0	0	0	0	0	0	0	0	0	0	0
92154	SAN DIEGO	100	111	101	103	112	88	108	105	97	114	100	82	109	99	109	90	73	103	86	113
92173	SAN YSIDRO	60	52	44	48	51	42	62	56	58	64	62	44	56	59	57	55	45	61	48	61
92182	SAN DIEGO	0	0	0	0	0	0	0	0	0	0	0	0	0	0	0	0	0	0	0	0
92201	INDIO	79	73	72	70	73	67	79	76	76	80	79	58	75	78	76	74	56	79	70	86
92203	INDIO	96	91	94	83	96	96	88	97	93	98	93	61	89	89	91	96	64	96	105	107
92210	INDIAN WELLS	170	178	233	177	201	206	163	187	170	181	168	120	177	155	184	177	115	180	207	213
92211	PALM DESERT	116	125	161	119	145	151	114	136	122	128	119	82	127	109	134	130	81	130	161	151
92220	BANNING	70	74	78	66	79	77	70	77	71	76	71	50	72	67	75	73	49	75	83	84
92223	BEAUMONT	73	74	80	71	77	79	76	78	77	77	77	55	77	74	78	80	54	78	84	90
92225	BLYTHE	75	74	66	68	72	66	72	72	70	76	71	54	69	72	70	68	50	72	67	82
92227	BRAWLEY	76	71	60	64	69	63	70	71	69	76	71	52	66	71	67	68	50	72	65	79
92230	CABAZON	57	56	47	51	54	49	55	54	53	59	54	41	52	55	52	51	38	54	50	62
92231	CALEXICO	72	67	56	58	66	57	67	68	65	73	67	47	62	66	64	64	47	68	61	74
92233	CALIPATRIA	64	55	58	50	55	58	55	61	57	59	57	44	50	57	54	58	39	59	59	69
92234	CATHEDRAL CITY	88	87	87	82	89	82	88	89	85	93	87	65	86	85	88	83	61	89	85	99
92236	COACHELLA	67	58	56	53	58	52	64	64	62	67	65	49	58	62	61	59	46	66	56	70
92239	DESERT CENTER	62	66	72	63	69	68	63	67	64	65	63	48	66	61	67	65	44	66	69	76
92240	DESERT HOT SPRINGS	63	56	59	55	57	58	61	61	62	62	62	45	57	61	59	62	43	63	62	71
92241	DESERT HOT SPRINGS	64	63	77	58	69	71	60	69	62	65	61	46	59	57	65	64	41	66	74	78
92242	EARP	52	50	63	46	55	59	47	56	50	51	49	36	47	46	51	53	33	53	62	64
92243	EL CENTRO	82	78	69	74	76	70	80	78	79	84	81	59	77	81	77	77	57	80	73	89
92249	HEBER	74	62	48	52	60	57	62	65	65	69	66	42	55	66	56	66	46	66	62	72
92250	HOLTVILLE	81	81	76	73	81	70	81	81	76	85	78	61	78	78	80	73	56	81	71	89
92251	IMPERIAL	104	113	94	106	108	93	103	102	96	111	99	79	104	102	102	91	69	98	89	115
92252	JOSHUA TREE	59	53	61	51	55	63	55	60	58	52	57	43	51	56	55	62	39	59	67	70
92253	LA QUINTA	124	127	140	124	133	131	117	127	118	127	118	89	121	115	123	119	81	122	129	145
92254	MECCA	56	54	43	48	53	39	60	55	53	63	57	45	56	55	58	47	42	59	43	57
92256	MORONGO VALLEY	83	73	80	74	76	85	77	82	80	74	78	61	71	79	76	83	54	81	88	96
92257	NILAND	44	54	70	46	65	69	47	59	52	55	49	31	57	43	60	56	33	56	78	63
92259	OCOTILLO	56	54	68	49	59	64	51	60	54	55	53	39	50	49	56	57	35	58	67	69
92260	PALM DESERT	96	100	119	98	110	112	98	106	101	103	100	71	104	94	106	105	69	105	119	120
92262	PALM SPRINGS	77	73	81	72	75	78	77	78	79	77	79	57	76	75	78	81	55	80	85	91
92264	PALM SPRINGS	97	96	123	94	107	111	94	105	98	100	96	69	97	90	102	102	66	103	116	120
92267	PARKER DAM	64	61	78	56	68	73	58	69	62	63	60	45	58	56	64	65	40	66	77	79
92270	RANCHO MIRAGE	143	151	193	146	171	178	141	162	150	156	147	102	154	135	161	158	100	158	189	183
92274	THERMAL	57	51	54	48	53	49	57	56	55	60	57	43	54	55	56	53	41	59	53	63
92276	THOUSAND PALMS	68	74	84	65	83	81	69	79	71	78	70	49	74	65	78	73	48	76	89	85
92277	TWENTYNINE PALMS	67	53	51	54	52	53	65	58	65	64	66	47	58	67	58	64	45	64	60	70
92278	TWENTYNINE PALMS	79	41	31	47	37	35	74	51	70	69	73	51	56	84	53	64	51	65	46	62
92280	VIDAL	59	58	69	55	63	66	55	63	58	59	57	42	56	54	60	61	39	61	69	72
92281	WESTMORLAND	64	55	45	47	53	50	55	57	56	60	57	38	49	57	50	57	40	58	54	63
92282	WHITE WATER	67	63	71	59	67	70	60	68	63	64	62	46	59	61	62	65	42	66	72	78
92283	WINTERHAVEN	52	40	47	37	41	50	41	48	46	43	45	33	36	45	40	50	30	47	51	56
92284	YUCCA VALLEY	69	62	78	61	67	75	62	71	65	62	64	50	59	62	65	69	43	68	76	82
92285	LANDERS	55	51	68	48	57	62	49	59	52	52	51	39	47	48	53	55	34	56	64	67
92301	ADELANTO	63	61	53	56	59	52	64	61	62	66	63	46	60	63	60	60	45	63	56	69
92304	AMBOY	86	69	108	69	76	90	71	87	74	67	73	64	62	70	76	78	49	82	87	101
92305	ANGELUS OAKS	131	106	169	104	117	139	106	134	111	100	109	97	93	105	115	118	73	124	133	155
92307	APPLE VALLEY	88	91	92	92	91	91	89	90	88	89	89	68	91	88	91	88	62	90	90	105
92308	APPLE VALLEY	81	81	87	78	83	85	79	84	79	81	80	61	79	78	82	81	55	82	86	96
92309	BAKER	64	49	44	48	47	44	64	55	62	64	66	45	56	64	56	59	47	63	51	64
92310	FORT IRWIN	92	48	36	55	43	41	87	60	81	80	86	60	66	98	62	75	60	76	54	73
92311	BARSTOW	75	75	71	74	74	73	78	75	77	76	78	58	77	78	76	78	55	77	76	88
92313	GRAND TERRACE	102	114	109	113	113	103	107	104	102	109	104	81	113	105	110	100	74	104	99	120
92314	BIG BEAR CITY	86	78	107	77	83	92	76	89	78	74	78	65	73	75	82	82	53	85	89	103
92315	BIG BEAR LAKE	89	76	107	75	83	95	77	91	81	75	79	65	71	77	81	85	54	87	94	106
92316	BLOOMINGTON	79	83	73	73	83	66	81	80	74	87	76	60	78	76	80	69	54	79	68	87
92317	BLUE JAY	147	182	187	188	187	173	155	164	149	166	150	122	177	148	174	146	108	155	155	188
92320	CALIMESA	87	85	95	82	87	96	81	90	84	81	83	65	80	82	85	88	57	87	96	105
92321	CEDAR GLEN	105	139	143	136	143	127	116	122	111	120	113	90	135	112	132	111	82	116	115	137
92322	CEDARPINES PARK	88	107	120	102	111	104	93	100	90	92	91	74	102	90	104	91	65	96	96	113
92324	COLTON	79	76	67	72	75	63	81	76	76	85	78	59	76	78	77	72	55	78	67	85
92325	CRESTLINE	86	94	105	92	96	96	86	93	86	85	86	70	91	85	93	88	61	90	92	107
92327	DAGGETT	69	51	72	50	54	72	55	68	61	50	59	50	45	59	54	66	39	63	73	79
92328	DEATH VALLEY	71	68	87	63	76	81	65	77	69	70	67	50	64	63	71	73	45	73	85	87
92332	ESSEX	88	74	110	74	80	93	74	90	77	71	77	66	67	74	80	81	51	84	90	104
92335	FONTANA	73	69	61	63	68	55	77	71	70	80	74	56	71	72	72	65	53	75	60	77
92336	FONTANA	117	132	114	125	129	105	120	119	109	130	112	94	124	114	122	101	81	114	98	131
92337	FONTANA	107	118	101	110	115	94	109	108	100	117	102	84	110	104	109	93	73	104	91	119
92338	LUDLOW	75	69	92	64	76	84	66	79	70	69	68	53	64	64	72	74	46	75	86	91
	CALIFORNIA	112	119	122	118	122	107	121	116	114	124	116	92	124	114	124	110	84	118	107	132
	UNITED STATES	100	100	100	100	100	100	100	100	100	100	100	100	100	100	100	100	100	100	100	100

ZIP CODE			POPULATION			2000-2009 ANNUAL RATE		HOUSEHOLDS					FAMILIES		
#	POST OFFICE NAME	COUNTY FIPS CODE	2000	2009	2014	% Rate	State Centile	2000	2009	2014	% Annual Rate 2000-2009	2009 Average HH Size	2000	2009	% Annual Rate 2000-2009
92339	FOREST FALLS	071	1186	1500	1673	2.6	89	518	635	703	2.2	2.36	320	389	2.1
92342	HELENDALE	071	4846	6050	6723	2.4	87	1923	2330	2570	2.1	2.59	1458	1756	2.0
92344	HESPERIA	071	7714	18342	22843	9.8	98	2477	5663	6993	9.4	3.23	2044	4683	9.4
92345	HESPERIA	071	60807	74184	80819	2.2	85	19385	22899	24756	1.8	3.23	15325	18067	1.8
92346	HIGHLAND	071	46718	54172	57300	1.6	77	15036	16785	17602	1.2	3.13	11525	12951	1.3
92347	HINKLEY	071	2239	2329	2385	0.4	30	779	787	799	0.1	2.95	563	564	0.0
92350	LOMA LINDA	071	6	6	6	0.0	9	4	4	4	0.0	1.50	2	2	0.0
92352	LAKE ARROWHEAD	071	5097	6475	7226	2.6	89	1781	2192	2427	2.3	2.95	1437	1761	2.2
92354	LOMA LINDA	071	18559	21790	22656	1.8	80	7155	8002	8250	1.2	2.65	4461	4987	1.2
92356	LUCERNE VALLEY	071	5309	6417	7005	2.1	84	2050	2407	2610	1.8	2.66	1352	1574	1.7
92358	LYTLE CREEK	071	753	855	898	1.4	72	314	345	360	1.0	2.48	210	230	1.0
92359	MENTONE	071	7310	8155	8537	1.2	68	2580	2784	2888	0.8	2.88	1772	1902	0.8
92363	NEEDLES	071	5469	5726	5821	0.5	39	2240	2276	2296	0.2	2.51	1442	1455	0.1
92364	NIPTON	071	204	257	283	2.5	88	93	113	124	2.1	2.14	46	56	2.1
92365	NEWBERRY SPRINGS	071	4250	4815	5022	1.4	72	1662	1824	1887	1.0	2.63	1158	1272	1.0
92368	ORO GRANDE	071	972	1093	1142	1.3	70	335	365	379	0.9	2.98	227	246	0.9
92371	PHELAN	071	12449	15591	17396	2.5	88	4082	4946	5476	2.1	3.14	3248	3917	2.0
92372	PINON HILLS	071	3996	4703	5077	1.8	80	1412	1601	1710	1.4	2.94	1083	1222	1.3
92373	REDLANDS	071	29696	32686	34042	1.0	62	12637	13497	13957	0.7	2.38	7837	8304	0.6
92374	REDLANDS	071	37748	42163	44349	1.2	68	12498	13535	14136	0.9	3.01	9131	9843	0.8
92376	RIALTO	071	75847	85126	88500	1.3	70	20221	21695	22379	0.8	3.90	16630	17796	0.7
92377	RIALTO	071	18544	21241	22309	1.5	75	5084	5571	5833	1.0	3.76	4448	4893	1.0
92382	RUNNING SPRINGS	071	2454	2934	3207	2.0	83	846	999	1092	1.8	2.65	593	697	1.8
92384	SHOSHONE	027	196	186	181	-0.6	1	105	101	98	-0.4	1.84	48	46	-0.5
92385	SKYFOREST	071	2175	2636	2903	2.1	84	809	950	1038	1.8	2.77	605	708	1.7
92389	TECOPA	027	82	78	76	-0.5	1	37	35	34	-0.6	2.23	17	16	-0.7
92392	VICTORVILLE	071	30758	52452	61995	5.9	96	9283	15220	17859	5.5	3.44	7765	12754	5.5
92394	VICTORVILLE	071	13560	32162	38991	9.8	98	4336	8698	10677	7.8	3.25	3333	6733	7.9
92395	VICTORVILLE	071	31406	39446	43338	2.5	88	11336	13967	15296	2.3	2.80	8015	9853	2.3
92397	WRIGHTWOOD	071	4500	5497	6056	2.2	85	1728	2047	2240	1.8	2.68	1234	1453	1.8
92399	YUCAIPA	071	41633	52490	56951	2.5	88	15354	18783	20294	2.2	2.76	10808	13220	2.2
92401	SAN BERNARDINO	071	1614	1857	1949	1.5	75	542	603	628	1.2	3.03	362	393	0.9
92404	SAN BERNARDINO	071	54823	59685	61542	0.9	58	17683	18337	18765	0.4	3.17	12648	13044	0.3
92405	SAN BERNARDINO	071	24882	27314	27887	1.0	62	7806	8096	8196	0.4	3.34	5660	5844	0.3
92407	SAN BERNARDINO	071	55582	65448	70008	1.8	80	16979	19322	20559	1.4	3.29	12520	14243	1.4
92408	SAN BERNARDINO	071	13854	15653	16339	1.3	70	3935	4268	4439	0.9	3.43	2821	3043	0.8
92410	SAN BERNARDINO	071	43276	49505	51979	1.5	75	11894	12969	13510	0.9	3.76	9084	9885	0.9
92411	SAN BERNARDINO	071	23152	25427	26255	1.0	62	6083	6467	6630	0.7	3.86	4899	5187	0.6
92501	RIVERSIDE	065	18955	22426	24516	1.8	80	6170	7193	7835	1.7	2.90	3844	4410	1.5
92503	RIVERSIDE	065	71666	83331	90938	1.6	77	21375	24661	26876	1.6	3.33	16540	18943	1.5
92504	RIVERSIDE	065	45544	51769	55722	1.4	72	14937	16699	17877	1.2	3.04	10685	11825	1.1
92505	RIVERSIDE	065	38449	45505	49625	1.8	80	11283	13219	14397	1.7	3.37	8690	10063	1.6
92506	RIVERSIDE	065	42773	47349	50350	1.1	64	15191	16621	17607	1.0	2.78	11408	12364	0.9
92507	RIVERSIDE	065	47935	58261	64611	2.1	84	16655	20225	22471	2.1	2.80	9799	11639	1.9
92508	RIVERSIDE	065	17850	33672	42784	7.1	97	5264	9867	12463	7.0	3.40	4557	8443	6.9
92509	RIVERSIDE	065	63792	73773	79553	1.6	77	17256	19501	20906	1.3	3.74	14175	15843	1.2
92518	MARCH AIR RESERVE BA	065	990	1053	1182	0.7	50	523	548	612	0.5	1.92	310	316	0.2
92521	RIVERSIDE	065	885	927	927	0.5	39	9	9	9	0.0	2.11	2	2	0.0
92530	LAKE ELSINORE	065	38790	49070	54958	2.6	89	12184	15110	16838	2.4	3.24	9264	11443	2.3
92532	LAKE ELSINORE	065	4387	11519	14768	11.0	99	1366	3623	4638	11.1	3.18	1105	2905	11.0
92536	AGUANGA	065	2347	3057	3523	2.9	91	863	1109	1271	2.7	2.75	622	780	2.5
92539	ANZA	065	3769	5010	5728	3.1	91	1475	1946	2217	3.0	2.57	998	1286	2.8
92543	HEMET	065	29407	33465	36015	1.4	72	12298	13725	14714	1.2	2.40	7292	7978	1.0
92544	HEMET	065	38785	44374	48080	1.5	75	14188	16143	17471	1.4	2.70	10170	11306	1.2
92545	HEMET	065	24761	34605	41053	3.7	93	11276	14635	17025	2.9	2.30	6941	9130	3.0
92548	HOMELAND	065	4779	5643	6323	1.8	80	1953	2277	2528	1.7	2.48	1271	1453	1.5
92549	IDYLLWILD	065	3679	5066	5923	3.5	92	1672	2295	2675	3.5	2.16	999	1334	3.2
92551	MORENO VALLEY	065	22963	30157	34970	3.0	91	5929	7743	8949	2.9	3.89	5246	6854	2.9
92553	MORENO VALLEY	065	61030	73964	82148	2.1	84	16217	19361	21419	1.9	3.80	13686	16195	1.8
92555	MORENO VALLEY	065	13123	32666	41815	10.4	98	3827	9452	12071	10.3	3.45	3346	8062	10.0
92557	MORENO VALLEY	065	46018	52672	56848	1.5	75	13507	15253	16379	1.3	3.43	11222	12542	1.2
92561	MOUNTAIN CENTER	065	1517	1788	1948	1.8	80	670	780	846	1.7	2.26	410	463	1.3
92562	MURRIETA	065	36361	60516	74025	5.7	96	11989	19409	23509	5.3	3.11	9647	15575	5.3
92563	MURRIETA	065	18135	54853	70821	12.7	99	5784	16863	21642	12.3	3.21	4579	13667	12.5
92567	NUEVO	065	7373	8895	10138	2.0	83	2327	2815	3215	2.1	3.15	1832	2197	2.0
92570	PERRIS	065	36459	46744	52330	2.7	90	10268	13042	14576	2.6	3.56	8226	10302	2.5
92571	PERRIS	065	26175	48312	58624	6.9	97	6817	12300	14903	6.6	3.91	5880	10452	6.4
92582	SAN JACINTO	065	4590	13435	17422	12.3	99	1604	4880	6334	12.8	2.71	1106	3275	12.5
92583	SAN JACINTO	065	21724	28716	33924	3.1	91	7577	9915	11610	3.0	2.85	5198	6646	2.7
92584	MENIFEE	065	14275	36730	48646	10.8	99	4735	12242	16150	10.8	3.00	3854	9654	10.4
92585	SUN CITY	065	9301	14711	18412	5.1	96	3346	5429	6792	5.4	2.69	2342	3641	4.9
92586	SUN CITY	065	17751	21758	24461	2.2	85	8695	10091	11109	1.6	2.12	5131	5955	1.6
92587	SUN CITY	065	13230	19223	22808	4.1	94	4620	6476	7617	3.7	2.97	3736	5189	3.6
92590	TEMECULA	065	3044	3755	4206	2.3	86	1004	1209	1345	2.0	3.11	767	911	1.9
92591	TEMECULA	065	25801	41738	50768	5.3	96	8266	12755	15339	4.8	3.27	6754	10316	4.7
92592	TEMECULA	065	46519	70044	84455	4.5	95	14496	21128	25290	4.2	3.31	12383	17894	4.1
92595	WILDOMAR	065	18819	28205	33524	4.5	95	6086	8961	10619	4.3	3.14	4924	7173	4.2
92596	WINCHESTER	065	4110	20053	26743	18.7	99	1320	6186	8218	18.2	3.21	1098	5189	18.3
92602	IRVINE	059	2431	18943	24179	24.9	99	817	6708	8494	25.6	2.82	710	5542	24.9
92603	IRVINE	059	9790	22955	26761	9.7	98	3291	7831	9079	9.8	2.86	2671	5448	8.0
92604	IRVINE	059	27873	28699	29140	0.3	23	10048	10187	10253	0.1	2.81	7342	7453	0.2
92606	IRVINE	059	17619	20045	21087	1.4	72	6657	7340	7665	1.1	2.73	4534	5052	1.2
92610	FOOTHILL RANCH	059	10953	11789	12502	0.8	54	3830	4088	4330	0.7	2.88	2989	3242	0.9
92612	IRVINE	059	20018	24074	25678	2.0	83	8373	10633	11470	2.6	2.25	4232	4895	1.6
92614	IRVINE	059	22493	23057	23499	0.3	23	8509	8618	8733	0.1	2.68	5830	5911	0.1
92617	IRVINE	059	10841	15386	17228	3.9	93	2192	3966	4752	6.6	2.33	1036	1881	6.7
92618	IRVINE	059	5858	14819	16964	10.6	98	2322	5741	6613	10.3	2.41	1204	3307	11.5
92620	IRVINE	059	26418	39926	45603	4.6	95	9033	13907	15856	4.8	2.87	6978	10234	4.2
92624	CAPISTRANO BEACH	059	7586	7682	7742	0.1	13	2828	2821	2820	0.0	2.69	1912	1908	0.0
92625	CORONA DEL MAR	059	12589	12643	12802	0.0	9	6015	5973	5989	-0.1	2.07	3291	3271	-0.1
92626	COSTA MESA	059	47860	49085	49627	0.3	23	17814	17933	17975	0.1	2.63	10679	10745	0.1
92627	COSTA MESA	059	61548	64450	65149	0.5	39	21703	21797	21848	0.0	2.89	12230	12290	0.1
92629	DANA POINT	059	27716	28337	28682	0.2	18	11704	11840	11901	0.1	2.39	7307	7394	0.1
92630	LAKE FOREST	059	58675	59927	60488	0.2	18	19996	20024	20046	0.0	2.95	14740	14750	0.0
92637	LAGUNA WOODS	059	15419	17398	17783	1.3	70	11016	12233	12418	1.1	1.42	3867	4340	1.3
	CALIFORNIA					1.2					1.0	2.93			1.1
	UNITED STATES					1.0					1.1	2.59			0.9

ZIP CODE #	POST OFFICE NAME	RACE (%) White 2000	White 2009	Black 2000	Black 2009	Asian/Pacific 2000	Asian/Pacific 2009	% Hispanic Origin 2000	% Hispanic Origin 2009	2009 AGE DISTRIBUTION (%) 0-4	5-9	10-14	15-19	20-24	25-44	45-64	65-84	85+	18+	MEDIAN AGE 2009	% 2009 Males	% 2009 Females
92339	FOREST FALLS	79.9	71.9	0.3	0.3	0.5	0.6	9.6	13.9	5.0	4.3	4.6	5.5	8.5	27.4	34.0	9.7	1.0	82.8	40.3	49.4	50.6
92342	HELENDALE	87.9	83.6	2.2	2.4	1.2	1.7	14.6	20.8	5.0	6.2	6.7	5.0	2.6	18.3	33.8	21.4	1.0	78.6	49.3	50.6	49.4
92344	HESPERIA	81.8	74.1	3.1	3.4	1.1	1.5	19.8	30.6	7.3	7.7	8.2	7.8	5.0	26.9	28.6	8.0	0.7	71.7	36.8	49.6	50.4
92345	HESPERIA	74.3	67.1	4.0	4.1	1.3	1.5	29.4	39.4	8.1	8.0	8.1	8.5	6.9	25.7	23.6	9.6	1.4	70.4	32.6	49.2	50.8
92346	HIGHLAND	61.0	55.6	11.9	11.2	6.3	7.6	29.4	36.5	8.2	7.7	7.6	7.9	6.6	27.6	25.2	8.2	1.0	71.5	34.1	49.4	50.6
92347	HINKLEY	76.6	69.6	2.1	2.2	1.3	1.4	26.9	37.0	6.1	6.8	7.8	7.6	5.7	22.5	30.3	11.8	1.4	74.5	39.8	50.5	49.5
92350	LOMA LINDA	80.0	66.7	0.0	0.0	20.0	16.7	20.0	16.7	0.0	0.0	0.0	0.0	33.3	66.7	0.0	0.0	0.0	100.0	26.3	33.3	66.7
92352	LAKE ARROWHEAD	91.8	88.2	0.5	0.5	1.2	1.7	9.3	13.9	5.4	6.6	8.0	8.0	3.7	20.0	34.4	12.8	1.0	74.5	43.7	49.8	50.2
92354	LOMA LINDA	52.1	44.5	6.8	6.4	25.4	29.4	18.9	23.7	6.9	6.4	6.1	6.4	7.7	30.1	22.3	10.8	3.2	76.7	35.3	47.5	52.5
92356	LUCERNE VALLEY	84.4	78.7	2.2	2.5	1.3	1.7	14.5	21.2	5.7	5.8	6.3	7.0	5.3	21.1	31.8	15.2	1.9	77.4	44.1	50.3	49.7
92358	LYTLE CREEK	88.2	83.3	0.8	1.1	2.8	3.9	9.2	14.0	4.2	6.0	6.3	5.6	5.0	20.0	39.2	12.3	1.4	79.4	46.0	50.6	49.4
92359	MENTONE	75.6	68.4	4.1	4.3	2.9	3.8	24.2	33.0	7.5	7.0	6.9	7.6	7.6	27.9	25.6	8.2	1.6	73.7	33.7	48.7	51.3
92363	NEEDLES	76.1	69.9	1.5	1.7	1.5	1.9	18.4	25.5	6.4	6.6	7.0	7.2	5.0	19.6	30.5	15.1	2.5	75.2	43.4	49.7	50.3
92364	NIPTON	80.9	75.1	2.5	1.9	0.5	0.4	19.1	25.3	4.3	4.7	5.1	5.8	7.0	24.9	31.5	14.0	2.7	82.1	43.9	59.9	40.1
92365	NEWBERRY SPRINGS	81.9	75.6	2.5	2.8	2.1	2.7	16.0	23.2	5.3	5.9	6.7	7.7	4.9	20.9	33.3	13.6	1.7	77.0	44.0	52.0	48.0
92368	ORO GRANDE	73.9	67.6	2.6	2.4	0.2	0.3	43.2	55.0	7.9	7.9	9.5	8.0	4.3	21.5	27.0	13.1	0.9	69.2	37.9	54.1	45.9
92371	PHELAN	80.1	73.1	2.2	2.4	1.5	1.9	20.3	29.0	6.3	6.7	6.9	8.0	7.1	23.6	30.4	10.1	0.9	75.2	37.6	51.2	48.8
92372	PINON HILLS	89.0	84.1	0.7	0.8	0.8	1.0	13.6	20.7	5.4	6.5	7.9	8.7	5.6	21.5	31.4	11.9	1.0	74.4	41.5	50.3	49.7
92373	REDLANDS	81.9	76.0	3.1	3.3	6.4	8.6	12.9	18.5	5.4	5.1	5.3	5.8	7.0	26.4	28.4	13.1	3.5	80.6	41.3	47.4	52.6
92374	REDLANDS	66.4	60.1	5.6	5.3	5.1	6.2	32.6	40.2	7.1	7.0	7.4	9.1	8.5	26.6	24.2	8.6	1.4	73.6	32.7	47.8	52.2
92376	RIALTO	37.5	34.2	21.9	19.0	2.7	2.7	54.5	63.0	10.2	9.7	8.8	9.9	9.3	26.6	19.0	5.8	0.7	65.1	26.3	49.0	51.0
92377	RIALTO	45.1	40.0	24.8	22.9	3.6	4.0	37.8	46.9	8.8	8.3	8.0	8.9	7.1	29.5	22.8	6.1	0.5	69.5	30.8	49.8	50.2
92382	RUNNING SPRINGS	87.9	83.2	0.9	1.0	1.2	1.6	12.7	18.7	5.4	5.4	8.8	9.1	5.9	22.5	32.2	9.8	1.0	74.2	39.5	52.1	47.9
92384	SHOSHONE	81.6	81.2	0.5	0.5	1.5	1.6	6.6	7.5	2.7	4.8	3.2	3.8	3.2	23.7	40.9	16.1	1.6	86.6	48.1	52.2	47.8
92385	SKYFOREST	89.7	84.9	0.2	0.3	1.2	1.7	8.4	12.9	5.9	5.9	6.6	7.7	6.3	23.0	31.9	11.7	1.1	76.9	41.2	49.1	50.9
92389	TECOPA	80.7	80.8	0.0	0.0	2.4	2.6	7.2	7.7	2.6	5.1	3.8	3.8	3.8	23.1	37.2	17.9	2.6	84.6	48.8	50.0	50.0
92392	VICTORVILLE	64.9	58.5	10.6	10.3	4.2	4.9	30.4	39.3	9.0	8.3	7.9	8.2	6.9	28.9	22.6	7.5	0.8	69.4	31.2	48.9	51.1
92394	VICTORVILLE	57.9	51.3	15.6	15.9	3.3	4.7	33.6	40.9	7.8	7.3	6.9	7.6	8.0	31.4	22.0	8.0	1.0	73.4	32.7	54.7	45.3
92395	VICTORVILLE	64.9	59.5	8.9	8.6	3.2	4.0	30.7	37.0	7.8	7.7	7.1	7.4	6.6	23.8	24.2	13.2	2.3	72.8	36.3	48.4	51.6
92397	WRIGHTWOOD	90.7	86.6	0.4	0.4	1.1	1.5	8.8	13.4	6.0	6.6	7.3	7.2	5.0	22.6	33.8	10.5	0.9	75.2	41.9	50.9	49.1
92399	YUCAIPA	85.3	80.0	0.9	1.0	1.3	2.0	18.3	24.9	6.5	6.7	7.0	7.5	5.9	23.7	27.7	12.2	2.8	74.8	39.4	48.6	51.4
92401	SAN BERNARDINO	33.3	29.8	17.8	15.2	2.0	1.9	62.3	70.2	13.0	11.7	8.9	8.8	9.5	28.8	14.9	3.9	0.5	61.1	24.0	49.9	50.1
92404	SAN BERNARDINO	53.2	46.9	15.9	15.1	2.9	3.3	38.2	47.6	9.9	8.9	8.2	9.2	8.1	25.5	19.9	8.5	1.7	67.0	28.7	48.7	51.3
92405	SAN BERNARDINO	49.4	43.7	13.1	11.8	1.7	1.8	50.9	60.6	10.9	9.9	8.5	8.7	8.4	27.6	18.7	6.0	1.2	65.5	27.1	49.2	50.8
92407	SAN BERNARDINO	57.2	52.1	12.4	11.5	4.0	4.5	35.7	43.5	8.8	8.3	7.8	9.3	8.8	29.6	20.8	6.0	0.6	69.8	28.9	50.0	50.0
92408	SAN BERNARDINO	37.8	33.3	14.5	12.9	15.2	15.9	44.9	51.9	10.2	8.9	7.8	8.4	9.6	31.0	17.5	5.7	0.9	68.1	27.7	51.7	48.3
92410	SAN BERNARDINO	37.9	34.4	14.5	12.3	4.0	4.1	61.8	69.5	11.9	10.7	8.8	9.7	9.7	26.7	16.2	5.4	0.8	62.7	24.6	49.6	50.4
92411	SAN BERNARDINO	28.4	28.4	24.7	21.1	2.4	2.4	66.8	71.9	10.5	10.5	10.0	9.6	7.7	24.4	18.2	7.8	1.2	63.0	26.2	49.0	51.0
92501	RIVERSIDE	56.8	48.5	9.0	8.9	2.7	3.3	42.9	53.0	8.6	7.6	7.0	8.0	9.1	30.7	20.6	6.3	2.0	72.2	30.4	51.0	49.0
92503	RIVERSIDE	60.3	54.3	5.4	5.2	5.2	6.2	42.8	50.5	8.9	8.5	8.0	8.7	7.7	28.2	22.1	6.9	1.0	69.1	30.2	49.5	50.5
92504	RIVERSIDE	63.7	57.5	6.9	6.8	3.9	4.5	36.1	44.4	7.7	7.1	7.0	8.2	8.3	27.1	23.1	9.4	2.0	73.4	32.7	48.8	51.2
92505	RIVERSIDE	57.2	51.1	5.8	5.6	5.6	5.9	45.1	53.0	8.6	8.1	7.5	9.2	9.2	28.4	21.1	6.9	1.0	70.5	29.4	49.7	50.3
92506	RIVERSIDE	76.2	69.5	5.7	6.1	5.4	7.2	19.0	25.7	5.9	6.1	6.6	7.4	6.2	24.6	29.9	11.1	2.1	76.8	40.0	48.5	51.5
92507	RIVERSIDE	43.9	38.8	11.9	11.3	10.9	12.4	42.9	47.9	8.7	7.2	5.9	9.8	13.7	30.6	17.2	6.1	0.8	74.5	27.1	50.0	50.0
92508	RIVERSIDE	69.9	62.8	8.5	8.9	6.5	8.1	21.9	29.3	8.4	8.3	8.5	7.9	4.6	30.5	25.2	6.0	0.7	69.6	34.4	48.9	51.1
92509	RIVERSIDE	56.8	49.4	5.2	4.9	2.7	3.0	50.1	60.0	8.9	8.5	8.2	9.1	8.3	27.5	22.2	6.4	0.8	68.9	29.3	50.4	49.6
92518	MARCH AIR RESERVE BA	86.4	81.4	7.0	8.5	1.9	2.7	3.9	6.2	2.7	2.9	3.8	2.5	2.2	10.4	6.8	53.7	15.1	88.8	77.9	49.3	50.7
92521	RIVERSIDE	33.4	27.7	11.5	10.7	40.0	43.4	19.4	23.2	0.0	0.2	0.0	88.1	9.9	1.4	0.2	0.1	0.0	98.4	17.8	47.2	52.8
92530	LAKE ELSINORE	69.3	62.4	4.1	4.3	2.0	2.4	36.2	45.2	9.5	8.8	8.1	8.6	7.7	28.2	21.7	6.5	0.9	68.1	29.5	49.7	50.3
92532	LAKE ELSINORE	80.1	72.8	3.4	4.5	2.7	3.8	21.4	30.3	8.3	7.9	7.8	7.5	5.8	28.2	25.0	8.8	0.8	71.1	33.2	49.3	50.7
92536	AGUANGA	85.6	80.8	1.1	1.2	1.4	1.9	18.5	26.2	5.4	6.6	7.1	6.6	3.7	19.0	35.0	15.4	1.2	76.6	45.9	51.2	48.8
92539	ANZA	85.1	80.2	0.6	0.7	0.8	1.1	17.8	25.7	5.1	6.6	7.7	7.1	3.4	19.1	31.9	17.4	1.7	75.4	45.6	50.6	49.4
92543	HEMET	76.7	70.1	2.8	3.1	1.5	1.9	29.7	38.9	7.5	6.9	6.0	6.1	6.6	20.5	19.8	20.3	6.3	76.0	41.3	46.6	53.4
92544	HEMET	82.3	76.3	1.6	1.8	1.6	2.1	20.0	27.7	6.6	6.5	6.7	7.4	6.2	21.8	25.9	15.2	3.7	75.5	40.6	48.2	51.8
92545	HEMET	85.9	79.1	2.2	2.7	1.4	1.9	15.0	23.5	5.0	4.7	4.5	4.9	4.2	16.3	23.6	28.5	8.1	82.6	54.7	46.3	53.7
92548	HOMELAND	79.9	72.4	0.7	0.8	0.7	0.9	28.8	39.9	5.3	5.8	5.7	6.6	4.9	19.5	24.9	23.4	4.0	79.3	46.9	48.4	51.6
92549	IDYLLWILD	90.1	85.6	0.9	1.0	0.7	1.0	9.6	14.4	3.2	3.8	4.8	6.7	3.6	18.9	39.2	18.2	1.7	83.8	50.6	51.0	49.0
92551	MORENO VALLEY	40.7	35.9	23.3	22.5	7.3	8.1	41.5	48.3	10.2	9.2	8.4	8.9	7.9	30.6	19.7	4.8	0.4	66.6	27.8	49.0	51.0
92553	MORENO VALLEY	42.0	36.6	20.5	19.4	6.1	6.8	45.2	53.1	10.1	9.5	9.0	9.7	9.7	27.3	19.3	4.9	0.5	65.5	26.1	49.1	50.9
92555	MORENO VALLEY	61.1	50.3	15.0	16.5	5.4	6.7	27.4	38.2	7.7	8.0	8.4	8.4	6.3	27.6	25.9	7.0	0.7	70.3	33.4	49.6	50.4
92557	MORENO VALLEY	53.1	46.5	18.5	18.2	6.6	7.8	30.6	38.3	7.8	8.1	8.2	8.9	7.0	27.8	25.3	6.2	0.7	70.2	31.8	48.9	51.1
92561	MOUNTAIN CENTER	85.6	81.1	1.1	1.5	1.1	1.4	14.2	20.0	4.5	4.1	5.6	6.1	3.2	19.3	40.2	16.1	1.0	81.7	48.2	52.7	47.3
92562	MURRIETA	82.5	77.2	3.2	3.5	4.1	5.0	17.2	24.6	7.5	8.0	8.2	7.9	4.9	25.1	26.6	10.5	1.3	71.1	37.3	49.0	51.0
92563	MURRIETA	79.3	69.9	3.6	3.8	4.7	5.6	18.1	29.5	8.6	8.1	7.8	7.6	5.6	29.2	24.1	7.9	1.1	71.0	34.0	49.2	50.8
92567	NUEVO	74.0	66.0	2.6	2.7	1.1	1.3	32.9	43.7	7.0	7.0	7.2	7.8	6.1	24.1	28.1	11.3	1.3	73.9	37.8	50.2	49.8
92570	PERRIS	49.8	45.3	13.4	11.7	1.5	1.6	49.4	57.5	8.8	8.6	8.4	9.0	7.4	25.1	22.3	9.3	1.2	68.6	30.6	50.4	49.6
92571	PERRIS	42.4	38.1	16.1	15.0	3.8	4.4	54.7	60.4	11.0	9.9	9.2	9.1	7.5	29.8	18.4	4.6	0.6	64.3	27.1	49.4	50.6
92582	SAN JACINTO	79.9	73.7	2.2	1.7	1.2	1.3	26.1	36.1	6.0	6.1	6.4	6.7	5.3	21.9	28.4	16.2	3.0	77.2	43.2	49.0	51.0
92583	SAN JACINTO	68.9	63.8	2.6	2.6	1.3	1.6	40.4	48.2	8.1	7.6	7.3	7.7	6.7	23.5	23.1	13.3	2.6	72.2	35.6	48.8	51.2
92584	MENIFEE	84.7	80.2	1.5	1.6	2.6	3.2	18.7	25.5	6.5	7.5	7.8	7.2	4.4	24.8	28.3	12.2	1.4	73.7	39.7	49.5	50.5
92585	SUN CITY	73.6	66.5	2.7	2.9	1.7	2.2	32.3	41.8	6.5	6.3	6.5	7.1	5.6	22.4	26.2	16.4	3.0	76.3	41.4	48.2	51.8
92586	SUN CITY	89.6	84.4	2.2	2.6	1.3	1.9	12.5	19.8	4.1	3.9	3.7	4.0	3.5	13.1	19.6	38.0	10.0	85.5	63.5	44.3	55.7
92587	SUN CITY	86.6	79.5	1.3	1.5	2.0	2.7	17.2	27.4	7.2	7.7	7.7	8.1	4.9	25.5	27.1	10.5	1.4	72.3	37.4	49.9	50.1
92590	TEMECULA	70.7	63.6	2.0	2.1	3.1	3.6	39.3	49.6	8.9	9.0	7.1	7.4	7.7	24.7	24.7	9.3	1.1	70.9	32.9	51.1	48.9
92591	TEMECULA	78.9	69.5	3.1	3.4	4.6	5.9	19.8	30.4	8.7	8.1	7.8	7.7	6.9	29.8	23.7	6.5	0.8	70.6	31.8	49.5	50.5
92592	TEMECULA	79.1	72.2	3.8	4.4	5.3	7.1	16.8	23.5	9.3	9.3	9.3	8.2	4.8	28.8	23.8	5.9	0.6	66.6	32.8	48.7	51.3
92595	WILDOMAR	81.4	74.9	1.9	2.3	2.3	3.1	22.4	30.8	7.1	7.5	7.8	7.9	5.5	25.5	27.3	10.1	1.4	72.4	37.0	49.6	50.4
92596	WINCHESTER	78.8	71.4	3.0	4.4	2.8	4.5	24.2	27.4	8.2	8.4	8.2	7.2	4.2	29.5	26.6	7.0	0.7	70.6	35.9	50.1	49.9
92602	IRVINE	47.0	43.4	1.0	1.9	44.5	43.8	8.0	12.4	9.2	8.8	7.7	5.3	4.6	37.0	22.0	4.8	0.6	71.0	34.6	49.5	50.5
92603	IRVINE	74.9	79.7	0.8	0.4	20.1	13.6	3.5	9.5	4.8	5.6	6.7	7.4	4.8	18.5	35.9	14.5	1.8	78.7	46.3	48.5	51.5
92604	IRVINE	68.3	59.5	1.1	1.2	23.5	29.4	8.2	12.2	5.2	5.8	6.5	7.5	6.6	25.4	30.7	10.6	1.7	77.9	40.0	48.5	51.5
92606	IRVINE	49.2	40.0	2.2	2.0	40.0	46.6	7.8	10.9	7.7	7.3	7.2	6.0	6.0	35.3	24.6	5.4	0.5	74.1	34.1	49.0	51.0
92610	FOOTHILL RANCH	74.2	65.7	1.9	2.1	15.1	19.4	11.2	17.0	12.5	10.6	7.9	5.0	3.0	38.5	19.8	2.5	0.2	65.5	33.4	49.7	50.3
92612	IRVINE	60.0	52.1	1.3	1.5	30.4	33.7	7.0	10.4	3.7	3.2	3.1	7.5	15.5	32.1	22.5	9.6	2.6	87.7	32.5	48.9	51.1
92614	IRVINE	61.5	51.9	1.3	1.4	29.0	35.4	7.4	10.8	5.8	5.8	6.4	7.0	7.2	31.9	28.9	6.3	0.6	77.6	36.1	48.6	51.4
92617	IRVINE	44.8	35.2	2.3	2.2	42.6	49.1	10.3	14.3	2.7	1.9	1.7	23.3	34.9	26.4	7.1	1.7	0.2	92.5	22.9	48.7	51.3
92618	IRVINE	61.5	43.4	2.3	2.0	22.3	25.0	14.9	18.4	6.6	5.5	4.9	5.2	8.7	41.0	22.4	5.1	0.5	80.5	33.5	52.4	47.6
92620	IRVINE	65.0	53.3	1.2	2.3	27.6	33.1	6.8	12.2	6.8	6.5	6.4	6.7	8.4	30.8	26.2	7.2	1.1	76.3	34.8	49.3	50.7
92624	CAPISTRANO BEACH	90.1	85.6	0.5	0.6	2.0	2.7	13.5	21.1	5.1	5.3	5.5	5.2	5.3	24.5	31.8	14.3	2.9	80.7	44.3	50.2	49.8
92625	CORONA DEL MAR	93.1	89.9	0.3	0.3	4.2	6.0	3.8	6.4	3.6	4.1	4.7	4.0	3.4	27.4	31.7	17.6	3.4	84.9	46.7	47.6	52.4
92626	COSTA MESA	71.8	63.8	1.8	1.9	12.5	14.9	19.1	26.9	6.0	5.3	5.1	6.2	8.3	34.3	23.8	9.6	1.4	80.5	35.4	50.5	49.5
92627	COSTA MESA	68.0	61.1	1.1	1.1	3.6	4.1	41.2	50.7	8.1	7.0	6.0	6.6	8.2	35.4	21.4	6.0	1.2	74.9	32.4	51.9	48.1
92629	DANA POINT	86.9	81.7	0.9	1.0	2.7	3.7	15.5	22.6	5.4	5.1	5.2	4.8	5.1	27.9	31.3	13.5	1.7	81.3	42.7	49.4	50.6
92630	LAKE FOREST	76.0	68.3	1.8	1.9	9.8	12.2	18.7	27.0	6.9	6.9	7.2	7.0	5.5	28.6	27.6	8.5	1.8	74.8	37.3	49.1	50.9
92637	LAGUNA WOODS	95.0	92.8	0.4	0.5	2.9	4.2	3.2	5.1	0.7	0.7	0.6	0.6	0.6	3.9	14.4	52.7	25.8	97.6	77.0	36.4	63.6
	CALIFORNIA	59.5	54.5	6.7	6.2	11.3	12.5	32.4	38.3	7.5	7.1	6.9	7.5	7.4	28.5	24.2	9.3	1.6	74.1	34.3	49.9	50.1
	UNITED STATES	75.1	72.0	12.3	12.7	3.8	4.6	12.5	15.7	6.8	6.7	6.6	7.1	6.9	27.0	26.0	10.9	1.9	75.7	36.9	49.2	50.8

ZIP CODE #	POST OFFICE NAME	2009 Per Capita Income	2009 HH Income Base	2009 Household Income Distribution (%) Less than $25,000	$25,000 to $49,999	$50,000 to $99,999	$100,000 to $149,999	$150,000 or More	Median Household Income 2009	2014	2009 National Centile	2009 State Centile	2009 Home Value Base	2009 Home Value Distribution (%) Less than $50,000	$50,000 to $89,999	$90,000 to $174,999	$175,000 to $399,999	$400,000 or More	2009 Median Home Value
92339	FOREST FALLS	31142	635	20.9	26.8	31.0	9.9	11.3	55480	60935	72	52	409	0.2	2.2	26.7	61.6	9.3	214320
92342	HELENDALE	25994	2330	14.5	21.5	48.6	11.5	3.9	61312	62561	79	60	1795	2.5	1.7	39.9	49.8	6.1	184953
92344	HESPERIA	24285	5663	7.8	22.0	46.9	17.6	5.7	72671	74616	88	74	4959	4.6	2.9	39.6	46.5	6.4	179779
92345	HESPERIA	17677	22899	21.9	28.5	40.7	6.4	2.5	49582	52177	60	42	15932	3.5	6.8	61.0	27.9	0.9	142252
92346	HIGHLAND	23693	16785	18.7	20.7	38.7	13.7	8.3	61257	64095	79	60	11894	9.8	4.5	26.5	53.5	5.7	193096
92347	HINKLEY	15872	787	26.9	34.9	31.4	5.3	1.4	36776	40394	23	16	540	6.9	33.0	52.4	6.5	1.3	100620
92350	LOMA LINDA	0	0	0.0	0.0	0.0	0.0	0.0	0	65000	0	0	0	0.0	0.0	0.0	0.0	0.0	0
92352	LAKE ARROWHEAD	36076	2192	9.4	13.1	39.6	20.2	17.7	83173	84199	93	82	1738	0.2	0.0	3.6	47.8	48.4	392742
92354	LOMA LINDA	23418	8002	26.2	25.2	32.5	10.0	6.1	48651	50448	58	40	3229	6.4	2.1	19.7	60.5	11.2	236615
92356	LUCERNE VALLEY	16083	2407	41.0	22.9	31.0	4.4	0.8	34972	38250	18	13	1630	15.1	22.2	43.4	17.5	1.8	105300
92358	LYTLE CREEK	21579	345	27.8	25.8	35.7	9.3	1.4	46226	48457	52	35	256	7.8	10.2	49.6	28.9	3.5	146575
92359	MENTONE	21509	2784	21.4	27.2	38.4	8.9	4.1	51226	53762	64	44	1822	9.8	4.1	32.2	48.5	5.4	181907
92363	NEEDLES	17593	2276	41.0	25.4	27.5	4.1	1.8	31995	34849	11	9	1290	23.9	22.2	39.9	11.6	2.4	94673
92364	NIPTON	20437	113	26.5	42.5	25.7	4.4	0.9	40449	41159	34	22	60	46.7	6.7	20.0	13.3	13.3	66667
92365	NEWBERRY SPRINGS	16812	1824	35.3	27.6	31.3	4.6	1.3	38109	41299	27	18	1215	19.6	26.2	37.2	13.2	3.9	94055
92368	ORO GRANDE	13197	365	42.2	32.6	19.5	3.8	1.9	28798	29910	6	5	197	9.6	34.5	39.6	12.7	3.6	104297
92371	PHELAN	18529	4946	21.4	25.9	42.1	7.3	3.4	51834	53803	66	45	3862	4.5	11.0	49.5	32.2	2.8	147760
92372	PINON HILLS	17612	1601	27.2	25.4	40.2	5.6	1.7	46604	50363	53	36	1256	4.1	10.5	38.3	44.6	2.5	169182
92373	REDLANDS	35741	13497	15.7	23.2	35.1	11.7	14.3	61788	63479	80	61	7195	1.8	1.6	13.2	54.2	29.1	289337
92374	REDLANDS	22280	13535	18.4	23.9	40.3	11.9	5.5	57182	60404	74	55	8278	6.7	5.4	27.8	56.4	3.7	190145
92376	RIALTO	13824	21695	23.6	30.6	36.5	7.2	2.0	46529	48600	53	36	13220	9.7	2.8	56.1	31.0	0.4	154595
92377	RIALTO	19723	5571	9.7	22.2	47.4	16.8	3.9	64788	65643	83	65	4871	2.7	1.5	18.5	76.4	0.9	207117
92382	RUNNING SPRINGS	27143	999	15.8	18.7	47.3	10.9	7.2	64655	66342	83	65	736	0.0	0.4	35.3	42.8	21.5	207787
92384	SHOSHONE	26290	101	34.7	20.8	36.6	7.9	0.0	44537	45756	47	32	38	47.4	21.1	10.5	10.5	10.5	52500
92385	SKYFOREST	26775	950	9.5	28.4	40.4	14.7	6.9	66666	68052	85	68	727	0.0	2.8	31.4	64.8	1.1	196389
92389	TECOPA	22092	35	37.1	20.0	34.3	8.6	0.0	43640	50000	44	30	13	53.8	15.4	15.4	7.7	7.7	37500
92392	VICTORVILLE	19457	15220	14.4	24.7	44.5	12.7	3.7	60381	62303	78	59	12173	1.8	2.9	50.5	44.5	0.4	169353
92394	VICTORVILLE	15556	8698	32.8	25.1	36.0	4.4	1.7	41620	46455	38	25	5521	6.8	11.0	66.3	15.0	0.9	128790
92395	VICTORVILLE	18995	13967	29.8	28.8	32.2	5.6	3.5	41717	45270	38	25	8233	7.1	9.0	46.6	32.3	5.0	145701
92397	WRIGHTWOOD	24955	2047	20.4	18.7	46.2	8.1	6.7	60017	61559	77	58	1443	1.2	0.5	20.2	68.7	9.3	226885
92399	YUCAIPA	23812	18783	22.1	26.4	33.3	12.8	5.5	51974	56487	66	46	13865	25.1	2.2	21.5	42.7	8.4	177674
92401	SAN BERNARDINO	8673	603	60.0	28.4	10.3	0.5	0.8	19333	20069	1	2	110	8.2	6.4	80.9	2.7	1.8	105978
92404	SAN BERNARDINO	15406	18337	33.0	29.3	29.8	5.8	2.1	37751	40150	26	18	9230	3.3	3.2	61.5	29.3	2.7	147118
92405	SAN BERNARDINO	13521	8096	35.2	29.5	29.1	4.8	1.4	36073	38141	21	15	4157	1.4	3.9	74.3	19.6	0.8	135496
92407	SAN BERNARDINO	18960	19322	20.6	26.1	39.6	9.7	3.9	52943	55920	68	48	11289	2.6	3.7	43.1	44.9	5.7	175935
92408	SAN BERNARDINO	11876	4268	44.7	27.0	23.7	3.7	1.0	29377	30619	7	6	1557	14.5	9.1	46.2	28.9	1.3	139133
92410	SAN BERNARDINO	10124	12969	43.6	31.8	20.8	2.9	0.9	28774	30196	6	5	5919	29.6	10.8	48.4	9.8	1.4	103325
92411	SAN BERNARDINO	10234	6467	44.4	30.1	20.8	3.2	1.4	27991	29098	6	4	3388	7.4	16.3	67.7	7.9	0.7	114761
92501	RIVERSIDE	17555	7193	30.6	30.6	30.9	5.5	2.4	38871	41852	29	20	2965	2.2	4.0	51.0	40.5	2.3	167047
92503	RIVERSIDE	21201	24661	17.7	25.6	38.6	10.6	7.4	57425	60960	75	55	15319	7.9	2.8	24.0	55.6	9.6	199782
92504	RIVERSIDE	20712	16699	20.9	27.2	38.5	8.6	4.8	51653	54462	65	45	9429	2.4	2.6	34.7	50.5	9.9	190571
92505	RIVERSIDE	18996	13219	16.5	30.5	39.2	9.3	4.6	52649	54678	67	47	6840	3.8	1.0	25.0	67.9	2.3	201255
92506	RIVERSIDE	35078	16621	11.9	19.3	36.1	16.7	16.1	76303	76994	90	77	12078	0.6	0.4	13.0	64.6	21.4	266049
92507	RIVERSIDE	18448	20225	34.8	24.8	29.0	8.0	3.5	38727	42101	29	19	7000	6.4	3.7	33.4	51.9	4.6	187848
92508	RIVERSIDE	29528	9867	6.6	11.9	41.1	25.7	14.7	87915	91771	95	85	8657	1.1	1.4	6.5	80.5	10.5	265569
92509	RIVERSIDE	17544	19501	19.2	23.8	42.4	10.7	3.9	57787	60713	75	55	13565	9.1	3.0	30.4	55.0	2.4	189391
92518	MARCH AIR RESERVE BA	47985	548	10.6	13.5	47.1	17.3	11.5	81199	80421	93	81	82	15.9	4.9	7.3	53.7	18.3	256522
92521	RIVERSIDE	20355	0	0.0	0.0	0.0	0.0	0.0	0	0	0	0	0	0.0	0.0	0.0	0.0	0.0	0
92530	LAKE ELSINORE	18984	15110	23.3	24.9	37.0	10.7	4.1	51989	55661	66	46	9601	5.7	5.7	28.7	56.7	3.2	195374
92532	LAKE ELSINORE	26386	3623	15.1	20.2	37.1	16.0	11.6	68207	70171	86	70	3022	1.9	3.9	28.7	48.1	17.5	223274
92536	AGUANGA	20661	1109	27.9	26.5	34.6	8.0	3.0	46414	48812	53	35	845	6.4	5.6	33.3	45.8	9.0	185658
92539	ANZA	18235	1946	29.5	33.0	31.7	3.8	2.0	36215	40445	21	16	1374	11.8	6.9	40.0	38.5	2.8	162342
92543	HEMET	16718	13725	40.5	33.3	21.8	2.9	1.5	30158	31658	8	7	7709	29.6	21.8	34.5	12.1	2.0	87506
92544	HEMET	20762	16143	27.2	27.4	34.0	7.8	3.7	45268	47933	49	33	11142	14.3	6.6	40.6	32.8	5.6	150231
92545	HEMET	21029	14635	28.6	33.8	31.4	4.7	1.6	39341	42569	31	20	10613	22.7	15.3	31.5	28.6	1.9	124728
92548	HOMELAND	15173	2277	41.5	36.0	18.2	3.6	0.7	28609	29624	6	5	1672	23.2	39.8	21.5	13.6	1.9	74570
92549	IDYLLWILD	25478	2295	28.4	27.8	34.2	5.2	4.4	42879	46901	42	28	1450	5.0	2.9	13.0	64.3	14.8	235215
92551	MORENO VALLEY	17634	7743	12.2	23.9	49.5	10.9	3.4	63786	65861	82	64	5991	4.4	1.2	46.9	47.0	0.6	171947
92553	MORENO VALLEY	14398	19361	23.3	29.0	37.7	7.9	2.1	47858	49949	56	38	11217	2.2	3.3	58.3	34.9	1.3	158138
92555	MORENO VALLEY	21867	9452	13.6	18.7	46.8	15.0	5.8	66968	67522	85	69	7798	2.3	0.8	33.6	59.0	4.3	194745
92557	MORENO VALLEY	21771	15253	10.9	21.0	48.1	14.4	5.6	66863	68242	85	69	10673	2.4	1.1	27.6	66.4	2.4	203221
92561	MOUNTAIN CENTER	26317	780	23.7	26.8	37.1	6.5	5.9	49539	50984	60	41	568	8.1	7.6	22.9	35.0	26.4	211446
92562	MURRIETA	30166	19409	10.1	16.4	41.8	18.1	13.5	76052	78343	90	76	15396	0.6	0.6	6.0	69.8	22.9	288628
92563	MURRIETA	25965	16863	11.4	19.1	44.4	16.3	8.9	71439	74442	88	72	13671	0.3	0.9	12.7	70.1	15.9	256470
92567	NUEVO	19039	2815	20.5	22.5	45.7	8.0	3.3	54810	57366	71	51	2038	2.3	4.7	39.1	48.9	5.1	183299
92570	PERRIS	14550	13042	30.2	29.6	30.6	6.9	2.7	40717	43947	35	23	8775	7.4	15.5	36.6	32.0	8.4	148299
92571	PERRIS	15061	12300	17.7	28.2	42.6	8.9	2.5	52806	55715	68	47	9146	2.2	4.9	52.0	38.0	2.9	161555
92582	SAN JACINTO	16810	4880	30.1	33.5	31.6	4.0	0.7	39243	41421	30	20	3821	10.8	12.9	47.7	27.1	1.4	135609
92583	SAN JACINTO	16383	9915	33.5	29.9	29.7	5.3	1.6	36379	41291	22	16	6723	30.0	12.1	33.4	23.5	1.0	110885
92584	MENIFEE	22886	12242	12.1	25.9	46.6	10.7	4.6	61440	63160	79	60	10302	1.3	2.2	20.6	70.9	5.0	219681
92585	SUN CITY	18391	5429	26.2	32.4	34.3	5.6	1.5	41983	45616	39	26	3893	10.1	4.8	38.3	45.0	1.7	169849
92586	SUN CITY	22428	10091	29.0	34.7	30.1	4.4	1.8	38279	41767	28	19	7992	7.7	7.1	46.6	38.6	0.0	154742
92587	SUN CITY	28648	6476	10.9	17.8	45.5	15.1	10.7	72136	72738	88	73	5278	0.7	3.5	17.4	56.0	22.3	258760
92590	TEMECULA	23130	1209	34.9	26.1	18.4	8.3	12.3	35598	40800	20	14	501	0.0	0.2	4.8	22.6	72.5	700231
92591	TEMECULA	25479	12755	8.9	19.8	44.9	17.8	8.6	71973	74505	88	72	8628	3.5	1.2	4.4	72.6	18.3	277685
92592	TEMECULA	30133	21128	6.8	12.3	43.1	24.2	13.6	84325	85688	94	83	17487	0.7	0.3	4.1	73.2	21.7	290510
92595	WILDOMAR	23191	8961	14.5	21.4	46.7	11.8	5.7	62495	64308	81	62	7583	1.9	3.2	23.8	64.2	6.9	212311
92596	WINCHESTER	30163	6186	6.5	14.8	43.5	21.6	13.6	81054	82379	92	81	5529	0.2	0.8	7.9	60.9	30.3	289763
92602	IRVINE	58691	6708	5.1	4.3	20.1	24.9	45.7	141239	142420	99	98	5119	0.1	0.4	0.8	9.5	89.2	638707
92603	IRVINE	64833	7831	5.0	8.5	18.4	24.9	43.3	136220	137791	99	97	6396	0.3	0.4	4.5	6.6	88.2	944599
92604	IRVINE	38897	10187	8.8	11.5	33.7	25.4	20.6	92934	99032	96	88	6577	2.2	3.1	0.9	29.7	64.1	457844
92606	IRVINE	42332	7340	9.3	9.9	32.1	23.7	24.9	97451	103301	96	90	3784	1.4	1.2	0.7	19.7	76.9	545535
92610	FOOTHILL RANCH	50666	4088	2.4	3.4	29.1	27.0	38.1	130200	129068	99	97	2994	0.4	0.2	0.0	20.8	78.7	540121
92612	IRVINE	42123	10633	16.5	15.0	32.3	19.8	16.4	76270	80752	90	77	4451	0.8	0.5	0.2	29.7	68.8	469183
92614	IRVINE	45927	8618	6.8	9.5	31.9	27.7	24.2	102985	106631	97	92	4803	0.4	1.3	0.3	33.4	64.6	481591
92617	IRVINE	28652	3966	37.8	11.5	25.8	11.6	13.3	50870	50841	63	44	870	9.4	0.8	0.0	45.1	44.7	359649
92618	IRVINE	34488	5741	20.5	11.9	38.2	17.8	11.6	67512	73079	85	69	2636	0.1	0.6	4.1	62.6	32.7	314739
92620	IRVINE	46868	13907	7.6	11.1	28.3	23.7	29.3	106277	106545	97	92	10257	0.3	0.5	1.3	32.5	65.5	498970
92624	CAPISTRANO BEACH	38733	2821	10.4	14.9	39.0	20.3	15.5	80196	84194	92	81	1873	2.3	3.5	4.9	21.4	67.8	508333
92625	CORONA DEL MAR	92996	5973	6.2	7.7	22.8	16.5	46.9	140341	148109	99	98	3819	0.0	0.0	0.4	2.0	97.7	1000001
92626	COSTA MESA	34984	17933	9.7	16.1	42.0	19.3	12.8	77671	80736	91	78	8152	0.1	0.1	0.2	27.3	72.3	466181
92627	COSTA MESA	26901	21797	15.5	22.7	38.0	15.5	8.3	62015	64931	80	62	7563	7.2	2.6	1.4	31.5	57.3	438097
92629	DANA POINT	48482	11840	8.1	12.6	35.4	22.1	21.8	88694	95221	95	86	7047	0.4	0.2	1.7	15.9	81.8	612468
92630	LAKE FOREST	36883	20024	6.7	14.7	35.7	24.5	18.4	87963	93160	95	85	14061	1.7	3.6	4.7	30.8	59.2	440090
92637	LAGUNA WOODS	40586	12233	27.2	29.6	30.2	8.7	4.1	43268	45661	43	29	9783	1.0	2.3	38.5	49.3	8.9	200549
	CALIFORNIA	28199		18.5	22.2	33.9	14.0	11.5	61614	64088				3.3	2.6	13.6	41.0	39.5	321752
	UNITED STATES	27277		20.9	24.4	35.3	11.7	7.6	54719	56938				9.3	13.1	31.6	32.6	13.5	162279

#	POST OFFICE NAME	FINANCIAL SERVICES: Auto Loan	FINANCIAL SERVICES: Home Loan	FINANCIAL SERVICES: Invest-ments	FINANCIAL SERVICES: Retire-ment Plans	THE HOME: Home Improvements: Home Repair	THE HOME: Home Improvements: Lawn & Garden	THE HOME: Furnishings: Comput-ers & Hard-ware-Personal	THE HOME: Furnishings: Major Appli-ances	THE HOME: Furnishings: TV, Radio, Sound Equip-ment	THE HOME: Furnishings: Furni-ture	ENTERTAINMENT: Dine out/ Carry out	ENTERTAINMENT: Sports Equip-ment	ENTERTAINMENT: Fees & Tickets	ENTERTAINMENT: Toys & Games	ENTERTAINMENT: Travel	ENTERTAINMENT: Cable TV	PERSONAL: Apparel & Services	PERSONAL: Auto Repairs	PERSONAL: Health Insur-ance	PERSONAL: Pets & Supplies
92339	FOREST FALLS	106	103	112	104	103	106	105	105	104	104	104	82	103	103	105	105	73	106	106	125
92342	HELENDALE	94	97	131	96	111	115	88	104	93	99	91	66	95	84	101	97	62	99	115	117
92344	HESPERIA	110	130	113	129	125	114	112	114	106	118	108	90	121	111	117	103	77	108	104	131
92345	HESPERIA	81	85	77	82	83	78	81	81	80	83	81	61	82	82	81	79	57	81	78	93
92346	HIGHLAND	105	111	105	109	110	101	107	106	103	112	104	82	109	105	108	100	74	105	98	121
92347	HINKLEY	79	63	81	61	64	81	62	75	67	59	67	56	54	67	62	73	45	70	78	89
92350	LOMA LINDA	0	0	0	0	0	0	0	0	0	0	0	0	0	0	0	0	0	0	0	0
92352	LAKE ARROWHEAD	138	174	182	178	181	164	148	156	141	158	142	116	170	140	167	138	103	148	147	178
92354	LOMA LINDA	86	83	82	85	83	78	91	84	88	92	89	67	90	88	89	86	63	88	83	99
92356	LUCERNE VALLEY	75	55	79	53	58	77	56	71	62	53	61	53	46	61	57	68	40	65	74	84
92358	LYTLE CREEK	88	72	114	71	79	94	72	90	75	68	74	66	63	71	78	79	49	83	89	104
92359	MENTONE	81	91	86	90	90	85	89	86	87	87	87	68	93	87	91	86	62	87	85	100
92363	NEEDLES	62	58	62	56	59	64	62	63	64	61	63	46	59	62	61	67	44	64	70	74
92364	NIPTON	69	62	67	60	62	66	61	66	62	62	62	50	57	63	60	64	42	65	65	78
92365	NEWBERRY SPRINGS	72	59	79	55	62	75	59	70	64	60	62	51	52	62	60	68	42	67	75	83
92368	ORO GRANDE	58	58	50	52	57	48	58	57	54	63	56	42	55	56	56	51	39	57	49	62
92371	PHELAN	89	87	78	85	85	87	81	85	83	84	83	62	80	85	80	84	57	83	85	100
92372	PINON HILLS	85	73	90	71	75	85	71	82	73	70	73	60	64	73	72	77	49	78	82	96
92373	REDLANDS	114	119	128	122	123	113	124	116	119	126	121	91	129	119	127	117	87	121	114	135
92374	REDLANDS	93	100	95	97	100	91	97	95	93	99	94	72	100	94	98	91	67	95	89	108
92376	RIALTO	76	78	71	71	79	64	80	77	73	84	76	60	77	74	79	69	54	78	66	84
92377	RIALTO	104	122	110	116	120	103	107	108	100	113	102	84	114	105	111	96	73	103	95	120
92382	RUNNING SPRINGS	99	115	113	117	115	108	104	105	100	108	102	80	114	101	111	99	73	103	101	122
92384	SHOSHONE	71	68	87	62	75	81	64	76	68	70	67	50	64	62	70	72	45	73	85	87
92385	SKYFOREST	100	115	113	117	116	108	105	105	101	109	103	81	114	102	112	100	73	103	102	123
92389	TECOPA	72	69	88	63	77	82	66	77	69	71	68	51	65	63	72	73	45	74	86	88
92392	VICTORVILLE	101	105	86	101	98	90	97	95	93	103	95	74	97	99	94	90	66	93	87	110
92394	VICTORVILLE	67	68	62	65	66	60	71	66	68	71	69	52	69	69	69	66	49	69	63	76
92395	VICTORVILLE	75	74	76	71	75	74	75	76	75	75	75	57	74	75	75	76	53	77	77	88
92397	WRIGHTWOOD	104	94	127	94	99	109	92	106	93	89	93	79	87	91	98	96	63	101	104	123
92399	YUCAIPA	93	97	103	95	99	100	92	98	92	92	92	73	94	92	96	94	65	94	97	112
92401	SAN BERNARDINO	37	26	23	26	25	22	38	31	37	38	40	26	33	38	33	35	29	38	28	36
92404	SAN BERNARDINO	67	63	59	62	62	58	70	64	69	70	71	51	68	70	67	68	50	69	63	75
92405	SAN BERNARDINO	63	61	54	58	59	52	66	61	63	67	65	48	63	64	63	61	47	65	56	69
92407	SAN BERNARDINO	89	91	81	88	88	80	91	86	87	94	89	67	90	89	88	84	63	88	81	100
92408	SAN BERNARDINO	58	48	42	47	46	42	57	51	56	59	58	41	52	57	51	54	41	56	48	59
92410	SAN BERNARDINO	55	46	41	44	45	41	55	50	53	56	56	39	50	55	50	51	40	55	46	57
92411	SAN BERNARDINO	60	53	43	47	51	49	54	54	56	58	57	37	50	57	50	56	40	56	53	62
92501	RIVERSIDE	72	65	60	64	64	60	74	68	72	75	74	53	69	73	69	70	52	72	66	79
92503	RIVERSIDE	98	105	98	100	105	90	103	100	97	108	99	78	104	98	104	92	71	100	89	112
92504	RIVERSIDE	86	91	86	88	91	80	92	88	87	94	89	69	93	88	92	84	64	89	82	100
92505	RIVERSIDE	89	90	84	86	90	76	95	89	89	97	91	70	92	90	92	85	65	91	80	100
92506	RIVERSIDE	128	155	158	154	160	140	141	141	133	147	134	109	156	133	152	128	98	137	130	159
92507	RIVERSIDE	75	61	57	62	60	56	82	67	76	76	78	56	71	77	69	73	55	75	63	79
92508	RIVERSIDE	140	169	154	172	167	147	142	146	134	155	136	118	160	141	152	127	99	136	127	165
92509	RIVERSIDE	93	102	90	93	101	82	97	96	88	104	91	73	96	91	97	83	65	94	81	104
92518	MARCH AIR RESERVE BA	126	133	181	132	154	157	120	142	127	136	124	88	132	114	139	132	85	135	158	160
92521	RIVERSIDE	0	0	0	0	0	0	0	0	0	0	0	0	0	0	0	0	0	0	0	0
92530	LAKE ELSINORE	90	90	81	87	88	80	90	87	86	93	88	68	88	89	87	83	62	87	80	100
92532	LAKE ELSINORE	130	134	111	129	127	117	121	122	117	130	119	95	121	125	118	113	82	117	111	141
92536	AGUANGA	92	78	119	77	85	98	76	95	79	73	78	70	69	76	83	83	52	88	93	110
92539	ANZA	72	66	76	62	69	74	64	72	67	67	66	51	61	65	66	69	45	70	75	84
92543	HEMET	57	52	55	50	53	56	56	57	58	57	57	41	53	55	55	59	40	58	62	66
92544	HEMET	79	81	85	78	84	83	78	82	79	81	79	59	79	77	81	80	55	81	85	94
92545	HEMET	70	66	82	61	73	81	64	75	69	68	67	49	64	64	70	74	45	72	86	86
92548	HOMELAND	61	50	67	47	53	65	50	61	54	49	53	43	44	52	51	59	35	57	66	71
92549	IDYLLWILD	92	74	119	73	81	98	74	94	77	69	76	69	64	73	80	82	51	87	93	109
92551	MORENO VALLEY	103	110	90	103	104	89	101	100	94	109	97	78	101	100	99	88	68	96	86	112
92553	MORENO VALLEY	80	79	69	73	78	64	82	77	75	86	78	60	77	77	78	71	55	79	67	86
92555	MORENO VALLEY	106	123	109	118	119	105	108	109	102	115	104	84	115	106	112	97	74	105	97	123
92557	MORENO VALLEY	107	118	104	114	114	102	108	107	102	113	104	83	112	106	109	99	74	105	97	122
92561	MOUNTAIN CENTER	98	80	124	78	87	102	80	100	83	76	83	73	70	79	86	88	55	93	98	115
92562	MURRIETA	128	151	154	151	155	138	132	137	126	143	127	103	147	127	143	122	91	130	127	155
92563	MURRIETA	121	135	123	132	132	120	119	122	114	129	116	95	126	119	123	110	82	116	111	139
92567	NUEVO	95	84	89	84	84	96	83	92	86	81	85	69	77	87	82	90	58	88	94	108
92570	PERRIS	77	75	70	70	75	69	74	76	72	78	73	57	71	73	73	70	51	75	69	85
92571	PERRIS	88	92	77	84	88	75	87	86	81	94	83	65	85	85	84	76	58	84	74	95
92582	SAN JACINTO	77	59	81	57	62	79	60	74	66	59	65	54	51	64	61	71	43	69	78	87
92583	SAN JACINTO	68	62	64	59	64	67	65	67	67	66	67	48	62	65	64	69	46	68	71	78
92584	MENIFEE	98	108	98	108	106	103	96	100	95	100	95	76	102	97	100	94	67	96	98	116
92585	SUN CITY	77	67	76	66	70	79	68	76	71	68	70	54	63	70	68	75	48	73	81	89
92586	SUN CITY	60	69	83	62	79	81	62	74	66	70	64	43	70	58	73	70	43	70	90	80
92587	SUN CITY	120	137	125	134	135	120	121	124	115	130	117	94	129	119	127	111	83	119	112	140
92590	TEMECULA	107	97	87	99	94	88	107	96	103	109	105	78	102	107	99	99	73	102	92	115
92591	TEMECULA	118	132	119	131	128	114	120	117	114	126	116	93	128	120	122	109	83	115	106	134
92592	TEMECULA	140	166	148	170	162	140	143	143	133	156	135	117	159	141	150	124	99	134	122	162
92595	WILDOMAR	107	114	107	111	113	109	102	107	101	108	101	80	105	104	105	101	71	103	103	124
92596	WINCHESTER	136	163	148	165	161	140	138	141	129	152	131	113	154	136	147	121	95	132	122	159
92602	IRVINE	228	260	241	270	257	215	244	231	222	260	229	198	262	234	250	204	167	225	194	263
92603	IRVINE	226	314	378	323	350	291	264	281	242	293	239	209	323	234	315	229	181	259	249	307
92604	IRVINE	140	168	187	170	180	150	160	158	145	170	146	123	175	142	175	137	107	154	142	177
92606	IRVINE	165	168	156	177	164	146	170	156	160	177	164	132	174	168	167	151	118	159	140	183
92610	FOOTHILL RANCH	211	244	209	250	235	201	211	209	196	233	199	174	231	211	216	181	145	195	175	236
92612	IRVINE	131	113	123	123	115	106	151	120	138	142	141	105	138	137	135	131	102	135	115	146
92614	IRVINE	164	177	186	188	182	158	181	167	168	186	171	139	190	169	185	159	125	171	151	195
92617	IRVINE	115	65	70	77	64	69	156	89	128	115	131	90	106	126	99	118	94	116	87	115
92618	IRVINE	129	115	101	121	108	102	127	112	123	130	126	94	121	129	116	118	88	119	105	135
92620	IRVINE	191	188	183	199	187	172	196	180	188	204	191	147	201	194	192	181	138	187	169	212
92624	CAPISTRANO BEACH	134	154	184	157	169	143	154	152	140	162	141	119	163	134	167	133	103	150	138	172
92625	CORONA DEL MAR	240	297	360	313	327	279	279	278	259	296	261	215	320	252	313	249	195	269	255	312
92626	COSTA MESA	123	129	142	134	135	115	139	126	128	141	131	104	143	128	142	122	96	132	116	146
92627	COSTA MESA	104	99	106	103	103	86	119	103	109	118	113	87	114	108	116	101	82	112	93	120
92629	DANA POINT	146	175	204	180	190	157	170	166	154	179	155	132	185	149	187	144	114	164	148	188
92630	LAKE FOREST	150	167	163	170	168	151	157	154	149	165	151	122	168	152	164	144	109	152	143	178
92637	LAGUNA WOODS	67	82	106	72	99	103	72	90	79	84	76	48	87	66	91	86	51	85	118	95
	CALIFORNIA	112	119	122	118	122	107	121	116	114	124	116	92	124	114	124	110	84	118	107	132
	UNITED STATES	100	100	100	100	100	100	100	100	100	100	100	100	100	100	100	100	100	100	100	100

#	POST OFFICE NAME	COUNTY FIPS CODE	POPULATION 2000	POPULATION 2009	POPULATION 2014	2000-2009 ANNUAL RATE % Rate	2000-2009 ANNUAL RATE State Centile	HOUSEHOLDS 2000	HOUSEHOLDS 2009	HOUSEHOLDS 2014	HOUSEHOLDS % Annual Rate 2000-2009	HOUSEHOLDS 2009 Average HH Size	FAMILIES 2000	FAMILIES 2009	FAMILIES % Annual Rate 2000-2009
92646	HUNTINGTON BEACH	059	57113	57649	58313	0.1	13	21868	21802	21863	0.0	2.64	15233	15195	0.0
92647	HUNTINGTON BEACH	059	58989	60227	60757	0.2	18	20303	20340	20357	0.0	2.95	14215	14250	0.0
92648	HUNTINGTON BEACH	059	42011	45653	47246	0.9	58	18007	19235	19699	0.7	2.35	10045	10839	0.8
92649	HUNTINGTON BEACH	059	32314	33390	34266	0.4	30	13924	14203	14463	0.2	2.35	8499	8694	0.2
92651	LAGUNA BEACH	059	24761	24564	25166	-0.1	5	11911	11974	12207	0.1	2.04	6087	5939	-0.3
92653	LAGUNA HILLS	059	31861	32136	32698	0.1	13	11187	10463	10528	-0.7	3.03	8116	7909	-0.3
92655	MIDWAY CITY	059	8041	8447	8546	0.5	39	2448	2489	2496	0.2	3.37	1813	1845	0.2
92656	ALISO VIEJO	059	42223	47329	49944	1.2	68	16974	18567	19357	1.0	2.55	10978	12087	1.0
92657	NEWPORT COAST	059	5381	8941	10182	5.6	96	2295	3872	4388	5.8	2.31	1473	2519	6.0
92660	NEWPORT BEACH	059	29839	32667	34150	1.0	62	13414	14430	14936	0.8	2.26	7983	8644	0.9
92661	NEWPORT BEACH	059	4166	4131	4138	-0.1	5	2074	2032	2021	-0.2	2.03	919	903	-0.2
92662	NEWPORT BEACH	059	3120	3008	2988	-0.4	2	1736	1653	1629	-0.5	1.82	765	730	-0.5
92663	NEWPORT BEACH	059	22834	23239	23480	0.2	18	10819	10845	10861	0.0	2.08	4636	4678	0.1
92672	SAN CLEMENTE	073	34310	35211	35599	0.3	23	13859	14020	14070	0.1	2.48	8670	8778	0.1
92673	SAN CLEMENTE	059	15898	30503	35245	7.3	97	5571	9810	11142	6.3	3.10	4457	8199	6.8
92675	SAN JUAN CAPISTRANO	059	34497	36948	39315	0.7	50	11136	11849	12598	0.7	3.08	8415	9010	0.7
92676	SILVERADO	059	1762	1875	1915	0.7	50	734	772	782	0.5	2.42	468	493	0.6
92677	LAGUNA NIGUEL	059	63390	66638	68151	0.5	39	23856	24729	25112	0.4	2.68	17180	17742	0.3
92679	TRABUCO CANYON	059	32246	34894	35900	0.9	58	9927	10389	10572	0.5	3.34	8692	9121	0.5
92683	WESTMINSTER	059	87736	91712	93115	0.5	39	26119	26563	26720	0.2	3.43	20120	20474	0.2
92688	RANCHO SANTA MARGARI	059	41319	43495	44546	0.6	45	14872	15270	15508	0.3	2.85	10837	11124	0.3
92691	MISSION VIEJO	059	46822	48474	49299	0.4	30	15742	16143	16325	0.3	2.94	12375	12675	0.3
92692	MISSION VIEJO	059	46314	48016	48938	0.4	30	16719	16970	17105	0.2	2.82	12861	13029	0.1
92694	LADERA RANCH	059	356	22367	28551	56.5	100	122	7632	9683	56.4	2.93	102	6367	56.3
92697	IRVINE	059	698	886	1006	2.6	89	0	68	84	0.0	2.54	0	29	0.0
92701	SANTA ANA	059	58671	64289	66180	1.0	62	12449	13001	13248	0.5	4.89	10234	10727	0.5
92703	SANTA ANA	059	68869	70794	71082	0.3	23	12471	12362	12333	-0.1	5.48	10955	10864	-0.1
92704	SANTA ANA	059	92287	96368	97142	0.5	39	19978	20005	20016	0.0	4.80	16162	16183	0.0
92705	SANTA ANA	059	44154	46383	46986	0.5	39	14235	14419	14496	0.1	3.19	11175	11332	0.2
92706	SANTA ANA	059	36384	38147	38522	0.5	39	9378	9392	9414	0.0	4.00	7505	7510	0.0
92707	SANTA ANA	059	62965	66252	67547	0.6	45	13307	13445	13607	0.1	4.87	10864	10992	0.1
92708	FOUNTAIN VALLEY	059	54173	56965	58389	0.5	39	17830	18549	18882	0.4	3.04	14073	14650	0.4
92780	TUSTIN	059	55127	58719	59781	0.7	50	18316	18646	18796	0.2	3.13	12695	13030	0.3
92782	TUSTIN	059	17815	20617	21615	1.6	77	7423	8512	8844	1.5	2.42	4699	5291	1.3
92801	ANAHEIM	059	56139	59595	60560	0.6	45	16180	16511	16637	0.2	3.56	12190	12433	0.2
92802	ANAHEIM	059	43817	46446	47109	0.6	45	11761	11873	11941	0.1	3.86	9127	9217	0.1
92804	ANAHEIM	059	85581	90221	91403	0.6	45	25668	25949	26023	0.1	3.40	19299	19516	0.1
92805	ANAHEIM	059	68833	73621	75664	0.7	50	16909	17182	17481	0.2	4.26	13302	13520	0.2
92806	ANAHEIM	059	34350	36267	36913	0.6	45	10734	10881	10982	0.1	3.32	7862	7978	0.2
92807	ANAHEIM	059	36145	37392	38324	0.4	30	12517	12715	12932	0.2	2.92	9879	10071	0.2
92808	ANAHEIM	059	19385	20519	20928	0.6	45	6974	7185	7269	0.3	2.85	5338	5483	0.3
92821	BREA	059	34071	35800	36685	0.5	39	12572	13012	13214	0.4	2.74	8903	9199	0.4
92823	BREA	059	1411	2950	3418	8.3	98	523	1148	1326	8.9	2.57	389	835	8.6
92831	FULLERTON	059	33812	35381	36041	0.5	39	12768	13001	13126	0.2	2.63	7535	7720	0.3
92832	FULLERTON	059	24039	25323	25817	0.6	45	7523	7791	7894	0.4	3.16	4808	4962	0.3
92833	FULLERTON	059	46328	50323	52052	0.9	58	14725	15745	16179	0.7	3.16	11406	12266	0.8
92835	FULLERTON	059	21192	22511	23214	0.7	50	8173	8583	8787	0.5	2.57	5770	6056	0.5
92840	GARDEN GROVE	059	52069	56251	57918	0.8	54	15042	15523	15812	0.3	3.57	11325	11695	0.3
92841	GARDEN GROVE	059	30773	31810	32089	0.4	30	8831	8805	8793	0.0	3.54	6903	6886	0.0
92843	GARDEN GROVE	059	44239	46439	47018	0.5	39	10537	10637	10682	0.1	4.32	8817	8902	0.1
92844	GARDEN GROVE	059	24263	25295	25526	0.5	39	6611	6591	6583	0.0	3.78	5415	5401	0.0
92845	GARDEN GROVE	059	16351	16455	16578	0.1	13	5697	5662	5660	-0.1	2.88	4488	4464	-0.1
92860	NORCO	065	24229	28025	30078	1.6	77	6160	7199	7818	1.7	3.19	5001	5742	1.5
92861	VILLA PARK	059	5927	6033	6088	0.2	18	1922	1931	1933	0.1	3.11	1730	1739	0.1
92862	ORANGE	059	18	19	19	0.6	45	6	6	6	0.0	3.17	5	5	0.0
92865	ORANGE	059	18007	19102	19668	0.6	45	5907	6059	6179	0.3	3.14	4509	4632	0.3
92866	ORANGE	059	15485	15885	16091	0.3	23	5925	5913	5941	0.0	2.64	3606	3607	0.0
92867	ORANGE	059	41240	44675	45879	0.9	58	12566	13469	13730	0.8	3.23	9949	10712	0.8
92868	ORANGE	059	23280	25553	26339	1.0	62	6570	6956	7125	0.6	3.13	4225	4512	0.7
92869	ORANGE	059	37331	38641	39052	0.4	30	11540	11675	11704	0.1	3.28	9203	9311	0.1
92870	PLACENTIA	059	48264	51701	53134	0.7	50	15804	16651	16998	0.6	3.09	12092	12744	0.6
92879	CORONA	065	44547	50383	54033	1.3	70	13442	14905	15889	1.1	3.36	10309	11276	1.0
92880	CORONA	065	16389	56157	72576	14.2	99	4713	14590	18582	13.0	3.84	4015	12075	12.6
92881	CORONA	065	21802	29719	34987	3.4	92	6552	8682	10139	3.1	3.41	5566	7407	3.1
92882	CORONA	065	59962	71265	78156	1.9	81	17813	20684	22544	1.6	3.44	14442	16660	1.6
92883	CORONA	065	12934	26972	35064	8.3	98	4018	8369	10854	8.3	3.22	3384	6914	8.0
92886	YORBA LINDA	059	40456	46332	49344	1.5	75	13537	15440	16364	1.4	2.99	11143	12602	1.3
92887	YORBA LINDA	059	21045	22268	22832	0.6	45	6676	6955	7062	0.4	3.20	5708	5965	0.5
93001	VENTURA	111	32527	34224	34740	0.6	45	12736	13304	13488	0.5	2.51	7408	7711	0.4
93003	VENTURA	111	47077	49743	50735	0.6	45	18263	19345	19759	0.6	2.48	12069	12700	0.6
93004	VENTURA	111	27187	29857	31046	1.0	62	9587	10520	10929	1.0	2.83	7227	7909	1.0
93010	CAMARILLO	111	42763	44812	45490	0.5	39	15046	15840	16113	0.6	2.74	11171	11680	0.5
93012	CAMARILLO	111	24942	32934	36116	3.1	91	9769	12645	13784	2.8	2.59	6934	9067	2.9
93013	CARPINTERIA	083	17143	17381	17499	0.1	13	6141	6316	6350	0.3	2.73	4080	4174	0.2
93015	FILLMORE	111	17433	19276	20020	1.1	64	4820	5285	5484	1.0	3.58	3895	4275	1.0
93021	MOORPARK	111	32939	39042	41638	1.9	81	9456	11027	11712	1.7	3.54	8081	9362	1.6
93022	OAK VIEW	111	6321	6495	6542	0.3	23	2127	2186	2201	0.3	2.90	1557	1595	0.3
93023	OJAI	111	21882	22550	22699	0.3	23	8224	8450	8504	0.3	2.59	5678	5807	0.2
93030	OXNARD	111	46401	59347	64652	2.7	90	11563	14198	15307	2.2	4.11	9252	11571	2.4
93033	OXNARD	111	77887	82171	82877	0.6	45	16736	17176	17316	0.3	4.70	14440	14786	0.3
93035	OXNARD	111	25490	28162	29294	1.1	64	9191	10188	10611	1.1	2.75	6218	6871	1.1
93036	OXNARD	111	33151	36895	38575	1.2	68	9684	10578	11040	1.0	3.44	7714	8435	1.0
93041	PORT HUENEME	111	19413	19634	19720	0.1	13	6771	6809	6845	0.1	2.83	4503	4510	0.0
93042	POINT MUGU NAWC	111	3060	3189	3202	0.4	30	658	653	652	-0.1	3.93	642	637	-0.1
93043	PORT HUENEME CBC BAS	111	3026	3290	3347	0.9	58	628	680	698	0.9	3.38	607	657	0.9
93060	SANTA PAULA	111	32608	33890	34152	0.4	30	9117	9318	9368	0.2	3.53	7198	7337	0.2
93063	SIMI VALLEY	111	49096	55336	58245	1.3	70	16419	18415	19343	1.2	2.98	12991	14620	1.3
93065	SIMI VALLEY	111	64703	72233	75104	1.2	68	20857	23467	24454	1.3	3.06	16596	18638	1.3
93066	SOMIS	111	3132	3645	3861	1.7	78	1005	1173	1245	1.7	3.03	817	953	1.7
93067	SUMMERLAND	083	593	617	630	0.4	30	288	309	316	0.8	2.00	161	171	0.7
93101	SANTA BARBARA	083	31995	32593	32805	0.2	18	12262	12622	12693	0.3	2.53	5842	5973	0.2
93103	SANTA BARBARA	083	19557	19580	19615	0.0	9	6904	7009	7012	0.2	2.74	4075	4116	0.1
93105	SANTA BARBARA	083	26297	26606	26775	0.1	13	11366	11765	11845	0.4	2.18	6413	6605	0.3
93106	SANTA BARBARA	083	1	2731	2731	135.2	100	1	1	1	0.0	1.00	0	0	0.0
93108	SANTA BARBARA	083	14105	14098	14153	0.0	9	5459	5612	5647	0.3	2.33	3514	3593	0.2
	CALIFORNIA					1.2					1.0	2.93			1.1
	UNITED STATES					1.0					1.1	2.59			0.9

#	POST OFFICE NAME	RACE (%) White 2000	White 2009	Black 2000	Black 2009	Asian/Pacific 2000	Asian/Pacific 2009	% Hispanic Origin 2000	% Hispanic Origin 2009	2009 AGE DISTRIBUTION (%) 0-4	5-9	10-14	15-19	20-24	25-44	45-64	65-84	85+	18+	MEDIAN AGE 2009	% 2009 Males	% 2009 Females
92646	HUNTINGTON BEACH	83.1	76.7	0.7	0.8	9.5	12.6	9.4	14.7	5.5	5.6	6.1	5.9	4.9	26.9	29.7	13.4	2.0	79.0	41.9	49.5	50.5
92647	HUNTINGTON BEACH	69.9	62.4	1.2	1.3	12.0	14.7	24.2	31.5	7.5	6.8	6.4	6.8	7.5	31.4	23.5	8.9	1.1	75.2	34.2	50.4	49.6
92648	HUNTINGTON BEACH	82.2	75.2	0.6	0.7	8.2	11.1	12.4	18.6	5.6	5.2	5.2	4.8	6.3	35.0	26.4	9.6	1.9	81.1	37.3	50.2	49.8
92649	HUNTINGTON BEACH	85.0	78.7	0.6	0.7	7.5	10.2	9.7	15.2	5.1	5.2	5.5	5.3	5.0	28.0	30.6	13.8	1.6	81.0	42.5	50.0	50.0
92651	LAGUNA BEACH	92.3	88.3	0.7	0.9	2.1	2.9	6.6	11.0	3.9	4.2	4.7	4.4	3.3	24.6	37.0	15.1	2.7	84.3	47.5	50.3	49.7
92653	LAGUNA HILLS	77.5	69.4	1.4	1.4	10.0	12.9	15.8	23.3	6.1	6.2	7.0	7.0	4.9	24.0	29.8	11.4	3.6	76.5	41.3	48.2	51.8
92655	MIDWAY CITY	43.5	36.3	1.1	1.1	40.4	43.4	22.0	28.2	7.1	6.7	6.5	7.2	6.3	29.5	25.5	9.8	1.5	75.4	36.5	50.1	49.9
92656	ALISO VIEJO	77.7	70.4	2.1	2.3	11.1	14.2	13.0	19.2	9.6	8.2	6.8	5.0	4.9	39.7	21.8	3.6	0.3	72.2	34.0	48.1	51.9
92657	NEWPORT COAST	82.1	76.8	0.4	0.4	13.9	17.3	3.7	7.1	6.8	7.8	8.5	5.1	2.7	24.8	33.2	10.2	0.9	73.5	42.0	48.8	51.2
92660	NEWPORT BEACH	91.2	87.0	0.6	0.7	5.3	7.8	4.2	7.1	5.1	5.6	6.2	5.5	4.0	23.2	32.5	15.5	2.5	79.6	45.3	48.9	51.1
92661	NEWPORT BEACH	94.0	90.9	0.6	0.7	1.5	2.2	5.2	8.9	3.1	3.5	3.8	3.1	6.6	34.9	28.2	14.2	2.6	87.7	41.4	52.3	47.7
92662	NEWPORT BEACH	95.0	92.3	0.4	0.5	2.2	3.3	3.2	5.6	2.7	2.7	3.1	2.9	3.7	27.1	33.3	20.2	4.4	89.7	50.4	43.8	56.2
92663	NEWPORT BEACH	91.5	87.5	0.7	0.8	3.2	4.4	7.2	11.8	3.5	3.4	3.7	4.2	8.1	35.7	26.3	12.1	3.0	87.1	38.9	52.1	47.9
92672	SAN CLEMENTE	86.8	81.9	1.0	1.1	2.5	3.3	18.0	25.7	6.1	5.7	5.6	5.9	6.3	28.8	27.6	11.7	2.3	79.0	39.4	50.9	49.1
92673	SAN CLEMENTE	89.7	86.2	0.7	0.6	3.4	4.1	11.2	17.8	6.8	7.8	8.5	7.5	4.0	24.0	31.7	8.5	1.1	71.9	40.0	50.0	50.0
92675	SAN JUAN CAPISTRANO	78.1	72.8	0.8	0.8	2.3	3.0	33.2	41.1	7.4	7.6	7.7	7.6	5.0	24.6	26.9	10.9	2.3	72.4	38.1	49.4	50.6
92676	SILVERADO	91.7	87.4	0.5	0.6	1.1	1.7	5.2	9.0	4.3	5.7	6.3	5.2	3.8	26.4	41.3	6.3	0.5	80.4	44.0	51.2	48.8
92677	LAGUNA NIGUEL	83.5	77.1	1.3	1.4	7.8	10.5	10.4	16.0	6.5	7.0	7.5	6.7	5.0	25.5	31.4	9.2	1.3	74.8	40.1	48.7	51.3
92679	TRABUCO CANYON	87.5	82.1	1.0	1.2	5.9	8.3	7.8	12.6	9.3	10.5	10.2	8.1	3.2	26.5	28.2	3.7	0.3	64.4	35.4	50.1	49.9
92683	WESTMINSTER	46.2	39.4	1.0	0.9	37.8	40.6	22.3	28.5	7.4	7.1	6.8	7.2	6.6	28.8	24.1	10.6	1.5	74.4	35.9	49.9	50.1
92688	RANCHO SANTA MARGARI	79.7	72.5	2.0	2.2	8.3	10.7	14.4	21.8	10.7	9.9	8.3	6.2	4.7	36.5	20.2	3.3	0.3	67.1	32.1	49.2	50.8
92691	MISSION VIEJO	83.4	77.2	1.1	1.2	7.1	9.1	13.6	20.7	6.4	6.7	7.3	7.0	4.9	25.3	29.6	11.0	1.8	75.1	40.4	49.1	50.9
92692	MISSION VIEJO	82.9	76.6	1.2	1.3	8.9	11.7	10.4	15.9	6.9	7.6	7.9	6.8	4.1	24.3	28.0	11.9	2.4	73.0	40.6	48.5	51.5
92694	LADERA RANCH	92.4	88.7	0.3	0.4	3.9	5.5	7.0	11.9	5.5	6.2	6.6	5.9	3.0	20.0	36.2	14.6	1.9	77.6	46.5	48.5	51.5
92697	IRVINE	38.3	30.0	2.4	2.3	48.4	53.8	11.5	15.0	2.1	0.9	0.7	27.2	35.7	29.1	3.0	0.9	0.3	95.7	22.7	49.7	50.3
92701	SANTA ANA	42.5	40.4	1.3	1.2	3.4	2.9	88.3	91.6	12.3	10.7	8.4	9.4	9.7	31.7	13.6	3.7	0.5	63.2	24.8	52.3	47.7
92703	SANTA ANA	39.3	37.4	2.0	1.6	11.2	10.4	79.7	83.6	10.5	9.8	8.4	9.2	8.7	32.2	16.1	4.5	0.6	65.9	26.8	52.9	47.1
92704	SANTA ANA	39.1	35.8	1.8	1.5	15.3	14.8	68.4	73.9	9.8	9.0	7.9	8.7	8.5	31.9	18.2	5.4	0.5	68.1	28.3	51.2	48.8
92705	SANTA ANA	71.5	65.1	1.5	1.4	6.5	8.2	33.2	40.8	8.0	7.7	7.7	7.2	5.8	25.5	25.0	11.3	1.9	72.2	36.5	49.6	50.4
92706	SANTA ANA	49.1	44.0	1.7	1.5	6.9	6.8	67.4	75.3	10.4	9.5	8.1	8.4	7.9	30.1	17.9	6.3	1.4	67.0	28.5	50.8	49.2
92707	SANTA ANA	45.5	42.4	1.4	1.2	6.8	6.5	78.9	83.7	10.3	9.4	8.1	8.9	9.2	32.0	17.1	4.4	0.6	67.0	27.1	51.5	48.5
92708	FOUNTAIN VALLEY	63.9	55.1	1.1	1.1	26.0	31.3	11.2	16.1	6.0	6.0	6.2	6.2	5.4	26.7	28.3	13.2	1.9	77.8	40.6	48.7	51.3
92780	TUSTIN	58.2	51.0	3.1	2.9	11.5	12.5	41.1	50.7	8.5	7.8	6.9	7.2	7.6	31.2	21.6	7.9	1.3	72.4	32.2	49.2	50.8
92782	TUSTIN	67.7	57.2	1.8	1.9	23.1	29.2	8.6	14.3	7.6	7.1	6.4	4.5	5.3	37.4	25.6	5.6	0.5	76.0	35.9	49.4	50.6
92801	ANAHEIM	47.7	41.4	4.1	3.6	13.3	13.7	51.8	61.0	9.9	8.9	7.5	7.9	8.3	30.2	18.9	6.8	1.5	69.1	29.3	49.6	50.4
92802	ANAHEIM	48.2	42.3	2.3	2.0	11.3	11.8	58.1	66.1	10.2	9.1	7.7	8.1	8.3	30.3	18.3	6.7	1.3	68.2	28.7	50.6	49.4
92804	ANAHEIM	52.1	44.5	3.1	2.8	18.0	19.2	39.1	49.0	8.8	8.1	7.4	8.0	7.9	29.3	21.1	8.1	1.5	71.2	31.4	49.7	50.3
92805	ANAHEIM	48.8	44.2	1.7	1.4	5.1	4.9	74.1	81.4	10.9	9.9	8.5	9.0	8.4	30.6	17.2	4.8	0.8	65.4	27.0	51.6	48.4
92806	ANAHEIM	59.2	51.7	2.5	2.2	10.7	11.7	44.5	55.2	8.6	7.6	6.9	7.1	7.7	31.5	20.9	8.7	1.1	72.7	32.2	50.0	50.0
92807	ANAHEIM	76.2	68.8	1.8	1.9	12.9	16.4	14.3	21.2	5.6	5.8	6.4	6.5	5.1	25.5	31.3	12.2	1.6	78.0	41.7	48.8	51.2
92808	ANAHEIM	68.8	60.1	2.1	2.2	21.3	26.5	11.0	16.4	8.8	8.8	8.1	5.7	3.2	33.8	26.3	5.0	0.3	70.6	36.4	49.1	50.9
92821	BREA	76.7	69.3	1.3	1.4	9.4	11.8	21.1	29.8	6.0	5.9	6.2	6.8	7.0	27.4	27.8	11.2	1.7	77.9	38.3	48.8	51.2
92823	BREA	88.1	81.9	1.1	1.2	5.2	8.7	11.9	17.3	5.8	5.8	6.3	6.3	5.2	22.8	31.3	14.4	2.0	77.8	43.4	48.3	51.7
92831	FULLERTON	65.6	58.1	2.6	2.5	12.0	14.1	29.5	38.0	6.6	5.8	5.3	7.6	11.5	32.6	20.8	8.1	1.6	78.8	31.4	50.1	49.9
92832	FULLERTON	58.2	51.8	2.5	2.2	7.5	8.0	49.8	59.2	8.6	7.6	6.7	7.6	8.3	32.8	19.5	7.4	1.5	72.6	31.0	50.0	50.0
92833	FULLERTON	53.5	46.5	2.4	2.2	25.7	28.9	28.8	35.4	7.2	7.2	7.1	7.6	6.8	27.2	26.2	9.4	1.4	73.8	35.8	49.4	50.6
92835	FULLERTON	78.8	71.5	1.3	1.4	12.5	16.4	11.4	17.1	5.4	5.5	5.9	5.9	5.4	23.3	28.4	15.9	4.3	79.5	43.9	47.7	52.3
92840	GARDEN GROVE	51.0	44.1	1.6	1.5	24.0	25.2	38.0	47.3	8.0	7.6	7.1	7.9	7.7	29.9	22.2	8.1	1.4	72.6	32.5	49.7	50.3
92841	GARDEN GROVE	48.2	40.7	1.4	1.3	32.1	34.6	26.7	34.4	7.7	7.5	7.1	7.4	6.8	28.8	23.5	9.6	1.6	73.2	34.7	49.8	50.2
92843	GARDEN GROVE	37.1	33.4	1.1	1.0	35.1	34.6	44.9	51.7	9.1	8.5	7.7	8.4	8.3	30.2	20.1	6.7	1.0	69.5	29.8	50.6	49.4
92844	GARDEN GROVE	30.9	25.5	1.4	1.2	52.7	54.7	21.8	26.9	7.9	7.7	7.3	7.7	7.3	29.7	23.2	8.4	0.8	72.3	33.8	50.8	49.2
92845	GARDEN GROVE	81.1	74.3	0.9	1.0	11.0	14.4	10.9	16.9	6.1	6.1	6.7	7.0	5.1	23.9	29.2	14.0	2.0	76.7	42.0	48.4	51.6
92860	NORCO	82.1	77.3	6.3	6.2	1.4	1.8	23.1	31.0	5.2	5.6	5.9	6.2	6.4	33.6	28.3	8.1	0.7	79.5	38.1	55.5	44.5
92861	VILLA PARK	82.7	76.3	0.6	0.8	12.7	17.2	6.4	10.2	4.2	5.0	6.3	7.3	3.8	18.8	33.3	19.7	1.7	79.9	47.7	50.3	49.7
92862	ORANGE	63.2	57.9	0.0	0.0	26.3	31.6	10.5	15.8	10.5	10.5	10.5	10.5	0.0	36.8	21.1	0.0	0.0	57.9	32.5	52.6	47.4
92865	ORANGE	72.0	63.5	1.6	1.7	6.4	7.7	30.2	40.8	7.4	7.1	6.9	7.8	6.7	28.5	24.5	9.9	1.3	73.8	35.4	49.4	50.6
92866	ORANGE	73.4	66.0	1.9	1.9	5.2	6.1	33.3	44.4	8.0	7.0	6.2	6.2	8.0	32.7	22.4	7.4	2.1	75.2	33.2	49.1	50.9
92867	ORANGE	72.6	66.0	1.1	1.0	9.5	12.2	30.2	37.1	7.4	7.4	7.2	8.4	7.0	27.0	25.0	9.4	1.2	73.4	34.9	49.7	50.3
92868	ORANGE	61.3	54.6	2.7	2.4	11.9	12.5	44.5	55.9	7.2	6.7	6.2	9.0	9.1	32.3	19.4	8.1	2.0	74.4	31.5	53.5	46.5
92869	ORANGE	71.9	65.4	1.3	1.3	10.7	12.8	31.3	39.0	7.2	7.1	7.1	7.1	5.6	28.3	26.8	9.6	1.1	74.3	37.1	49.5	50.5
92870	PLACENTIA	68.0	61.0	1.8	1.7	11.5	14.4	30.3	37.4	7.5	7.2	6.9	6.8	6.4	30.2	24.4	9.5	1.1	74.3	35.1	49.5	50.5
92879	CORONA	55.1	47.9	7.3	7.3	8.9	10.1	41.7	49.8	10.0	8.8	7.8	7.7	7.6	31.1	19.6	6.2	1.2	68.8	29.6	49.3	50.7
92880	CORONA	68.7	59.5	4.9	4.1	5.2	3.7	34.5	51.3	9.5	9.2	8.6	8.6	7.4	28.6	20.8	6.3	0.8	66.9	29.3	50.5	49.5
92881	CORONA	69.6	61.8	7.4	8.5	6.6	8.4	24.3	31.4	10.1	9.7	8.8	7.2	4.9	31.7	21.4	5.6	0.6	66.7	32.2	48.9	51.1
92882	CORONA	62.7	55.8	4.5	4.9	6.6	8.1	40.1	46.9	9.7	9.3	8.5	8.1	6.5	30.5	21.4	5.4	0.7	67.4	30.5	49.7	50.3
92883	CORONA	74.5	66.9	6.3	7.2	3.9	5.5	24.5	33.1	10.5	9.9	9.2	7.2	4.6	31.9	21.5	4.8	0.4	65.5	31.6	49.2	50.8
92886	YORBA LINDA	84.1	78.1	1.0	1.2	8.4	11.0	11.2	17.4	5.7	6.5	7.3	7.3	4.8	24.2	32.2	10.6	1.3	75.6	41.0	49.0	51.0
92887	YORBA LINDA	77.0	69.1	1.5	1.7	15.8	21.1	8.6	13.2	5.9	7.7	8.6	8.7	4.7	24.6	33.5	5.7	0.6	72.1	38.5	49.3	50.7
93001	VENTURA	74.8	68.3	1.3	1.4	2.0	2.4	32.5	41.3	6.8	6.6	6.0	6.4	7.0	29.9	26.6	9.2	1.4	76.6	36.0	50.8	49.2
93003	VENTURA	80.7	73.9	1.5	1.7	3.8	4.7	19.9	28.4	5.9	5.8	6.1	6.7	6.2	26.0	28.1	12.0	3.1	78.0	40.2	48.8	51.2
93004	VENTURA	79.0	71.8	1.2	1.3	3.1	3.8	24.5	34.1	7.0	7.1	7.6	7.5	5.3	25.6	28.2	10.1	1.6	73.4	38.0	48.6	51.4
93010	CAMARILLO	78.4	70.4	1.9	3.5	7.0	8.5	18.7	26.0	6.5	6.6	6.8	7.2	5.6	25.0	26.9	12.9	2.4	76.4	39.5	48.8	51.2
93012	CAMARILLO	86.4	79.0	0.9	1.4	6.8	8.9	9.2	15.8	6.4	6.7	7.3	6.4	4.6	22.8	28.9	12.5	4.4	75.6	42.2	48.3	51.7
93013	CARPINTERIA	75.9	69.9	0.6	0.5	2.6	2.9	38.8	48.5	5.9	5.7	6.0	6.8	7.0	27.8	28.0	10.8	2.0	78.3	38.2	50.4	49.6
93015	FILLMORE	54.4	47.6	0.3	0.3	1.1	1.2	65.6	75.3	8.7	8.0	7.5	8.6	8.2	26.9	21.5	8.7	2.0	70.7	30.9	50.5	49.5
93021	MOORPARK	74.5	66.4	1.5	1.6	5.7	6.6	27.9	38.9	7.8	8.4	8.7	8.7	6.0	27.1	27.2	5.5	0.6	69.6	33.3	49.7	50.3
93022	OAK VIEW	86.8	80.9	0.6	0.7	1.1	1.5	16.2	24.4	5.7	5.6	6.2	7.2	6.8	24.7	31.4	10.4	2.1	78.0	40.0	48.5	51.5
93023	OJAI	88.1	82.8	0.5	0.6	1.3	1.7	15.8	23.7	5.1	5.2	5.9	7.4	6.9	22.0	31.1	13.1	3.2	79.0	42.8	48.0	52.0
93030	OXNARD	38.9	34.6	3.7	2.9	4.7	4.5	74.1	81.6	9.0	8.8	8.1	8.8	8.3	29.0	19.6	7.1	1.2	68.8	29.2	51.3	48.7
93033	OXNARD	35.5	32.3	3.4	2.7	9.5	8.8	73.9	79.5	9.8	9.2	8.3	9.2	8.6	30.1	18.1	5.9	0.8	67.2	27.8	51.7	48.3
93035	OXNARD	67.0	61.2	4.0	3.7	6.4	7.1	33.4	40.9	6.7	6.6	6.4	6.4	5.9	26.7	28.4	11.6	1.2	76.2	38.8	50.0	50.0
93036	OXNARD	49.1	43.2	4.0	3.6	6.9	7.1	60.8	68.7	9.2	8.7	8.0	8.7	7.8	28.4	20.9	7.4	0.9	69.1	30.0	50.1	49.9
93041	PORT HUENEME	56.8	49.5	5.1	4.9	5.8	6.2	45.8	56.0	8.1	7.5	6.4	6.9	7.7	28.1	22.3	10.8	2.2	74.1	33.5	48.6	51.4
93042	POINT MUGU NAWC	64.2	56.3	10.5	11.0	12.0	14.3	15.3	21.6	14.7	11.4	7.9	6.8	13.9	42.5	2.6	0.2	0.0	62.7	23.3	58.8	41.2
93043	PORT HUENEME CBC BAS	60.9	52.3	11.3	11.9	13.1	15.7	12.7	18.0	13.6	8.1	5.6	9.5	25.1	35.4	2.5	0.3	0.0	70.7	22.6	61.4	38.6
93060	SANTA PAULA	56.0	50.1	0.5	0.5	0.9	0.9	68.5	77.4	8.8	8.4	7.7	8.5	7.9	28.3	20.7	8.2	1.6	70.2	30.7	51.8	48.2
93063	SIMI VALLEY	82.7	76.9	1.2	1.3	6.3	8.1	15.1	21.6	6.7	6.9	7.3	7.4	5.3	26.8	29.4	9.0	1.2	74.4	38.3	49.3	50.7
93065	SIMI VALLEY	80.6	74.4	1.3	1.4	6.4	8.0	17.9	24.8	7.3	7.6	7.6	7.4	5.6	27.9	27.2	8.4	1.0	72.8	36.4	49.5	50.5
93066	SOMIS	72.6	64.1	1.3	1.3	2.8	3.4	34.7	45.9	5.9	6.8	7.8	7.5	4.8	24.0	28.2	13.4	1.6	75.0	40.7	52.1	47.9
93067	SUMMERLAND	90.6	86.2	0.5	0.5	2.2	2.9	10.5	15.1	3.6	3.2	3.9	4.9	5.2	28.0	33.9	15.2	2.1	86.2	45.7	47.8	52.2
93101	SANTA BARBARA	65.7	59.8	1.9	1.8	2.5	2.8	47.8	56.6	6.9	6.0	5.2	5.8	9.0	38.5	20.8	6.3	1.5	78.8	32.4	51.0	49.0
93103	SANTA BARBARA	65.7	61.6	2.4	2.2	1.9	2.2	50.8	57.3	6.3	5.9	5.6	6.6	7.1	31.5	25.3	9.7	1.9	78.3	36.1	50.4	49.6
93105	SANTA BARBARA	87.1	82.8	1.0	1.0	2.9	3.6	15.6	21.6	4.6	4.6	4.7	4.9	4.7	25.4	29.1	15.8	6.0	82.9	45.6	47.1	52.9
93106	SANTA BARBARA	100.0	41.6	0.0	19.2	0.0	4.6	0.0	45.8	1.4	1.4	1.4	8.3	15.7	53.1	13.3	4.2	1.0	94.7	32.6	80.9	19.1
93108	SANTA BARBARA	90.8	87.2	0.7	0.7	1.8	2.3	10.1	14.5	3.8	4.3	5.5	8.6	7.1	19.0	31.4	16.5	3.9	82.5	46.3	46.9	53.1
	CALIFORNIA	59.5	54.5	6.7	6.2	11.3	12.5	32.4	38.3	7.5	7.1	6.9	7.5	7.4	28.5	24.2	9.3	1.6	74.1	34.3	49.9	50.1
	UNITED STATES	75.1	72.0	12.3	12.7	3.8	4.6	12.5	15.7	6.8	6.7	6.6	7.1	6.9	27.0	26.0	10.9	1.9	75.7	36.9	49.2	50.8

ZIP CODE #	POST OFFICE NAME	2009 Per Capita Income	2009 HH Income Base	2009 HOUSEHOLD INCOME DISTRIBUTION (%) Less than $25,000	$25,000 to $49,999	$50,000 to $99,999	$100,000 to $149,999	$150,000 or More	MEDIAN HOUSEHOLD INCOME 2009	2014	2009 National Centile	2009 State Centile	2009 Home Value Base	2009 HOME VALUE DISTRIBUTION (%) Less than $50,000	$50,000 to $89,999	$90,000 to $174,999	$175,000 to $399,999	$400,000 or More	2009 Median Home Value
92646	HUNTINGTON BEACH	40875	21802	7.1	12.9	34.6	26.2	19.2	91724	98001	95	88	15942	1.4	1.9	3.5	22.9	70.3	495335
92647	HUNTINGTON BEACH	30352	20340	9.8	17.7	40.4	21.5	10.7	76757	79599	90	77	10172	1.5	1.9	1.6	23.4	71.6	466677
92648	HUNTINGTON BEACH	49606	19235	10.3	13.7	32.3	19.8	23.9	88109	94624	95	86	10049	1.8	2.0	2.8	14.6	78.8	617959
92649	HUNTINGTON BEACH	51724	14203	7.1	11.2	34.4	24.3	23.0	95008	100973	96	89	8801	2.1	2.4	3.3	22.7	69.5	503477
92651	LAGUNA BEACH	70413	11974	8.3	11.7	27.4	21.8	30.9	105243	110975	97	92	7334	0.4	0.7	1.1	7.1	90.5	920796
92653	LAGUNA HILLS	41445	10463	8.4	11.5	33.4	19.3	27.3	93978	99756	96	89	8048	0.7	0.9	6.6	27.9	63.9	493473
92655	MIDWAY CITY	21895	2489	18.9	18.8	36.8	20.2	5.3	63908	67585	82	65	1304	3.9	1.8	1.9	50.7	41.7	366038
92656	ALISO VIEJO	47204	18567	4.4	9.1	35.6	27.8	23.1	101408	105349	97	91	11642	0.2	0.3	0.8	41.4	57.3	430410
92657	NEWPORT COAST	93159	3872	3.8	4.8	17.6	21.6	52.2	156671	162398	100	99	2922	0.1	0.1	1.6	2.7	95.6	1000001
92660	NEWPORT BEACH	78891	14430	7.2	8.3	22.5	18.4	43.6	134407	138964	99	97	8444	0.7	1.1	1.5	5.5	91.2	927231
92661	NEWPORT BEACH	70233	2032	7.4	9.3	34.4	17.9	31.0	97887	106233	96	90	872	1.8	0.0	0.0	1.1	97.0	1000001
92662	NEWPORT BEACH	83325	1653	7.4	12.5	25.0	22.2	32.8	111342	116594	98	94	751	0.0	0.0	5.6	2.7	91.7	1000001
92663	NEWPORT BEACH	62703	10845	9.0	11.9	31.0	20.8	27.4	96270	103136	96	90	5105	3.9	1.4	0.7	15.0	78.9	724898
92672	SAN CLEMENTE	42051	14020	10.0	17.3	36.1	19.0	17.6	78707	82852	91	79	7424	0.0	0.3	0.6	16.3	82.9	611678
92673	SAN CLEMENTE	49155	9810	4.3	8.0	24.8	25.5	37.4	128047	130594	99	96	8268	0.1	0.1	1.1	22.4	76.3	579980
92675	SAN JUAN CAPISTRANO	38811	11849	8.8	15.8	34.5	18.8	22.1	84283	91048	94	83	9128	1.6	2.3	9.6	33.5	53.0	421791
92676	SILVERADO	50868	772	6.9	7.4	30.4	22.3	33.0	112766	116972	98	94	560	1.3	0.0	0.0	43.0	55.7	436782
92677	LAGUNA NIGUEL	50940	24729	5.4	9.7	31.2	23.9	29.9	108486	112541	98	93	17932	0.0	0.1	0.7	22.5	76.6	581008
92679	TRABUCO CANYON	58891	10389	2.0	4.0	17.0	21.2	55.8	160371	163362	100	99	9364	0.0	0.0	0.4	14.9	84.6	691455
92683	WESTMINSTER	22426	26563	15.9	20.7	37.9	18.2	7.2	64696	68044	83	65	15213	6.6	2.5	1.8	48.4	40.7	368823
92688	RANCHO SANTA MARGARI	41348	15270	4.1	11.5	33.8	27.5	23.0	100858	104726	97	91	10895	0.2	0.1	2.0	39.9	57.8	432507
92691	MISSION VIEJO	38986	16143	5.3	10.5	35.3	26.2	22.7	98154	103117	96	90	12566	0.3	0.3	0.9	25.1	73.4	479417
92692	MISSION VIEJO	47804	16970	5.6	11.2	27.4	24.5	31.3	112439	115636	98	94	13683	0.6	0.3	0.3	24.1	74.8	531340
92694	LADERA RANCH	78040	7632	6.8	4.7	18.1	15.8	54.6	160679	167568	100	99	7122	0.1	0.1	3.9	37.3	58.7	448973
92697	IRVINE	12780	68	48.5	14.7	30.9	2.9	2.9	30000	35000	8	6	5	20.0	0.0	0.0	40.0	40.0	350000
92701	SANTA ANA	11131	13001	25.9	32.4	32.2	6.6	3.0	42722	44580	42	27	3577	0.4	2.3	14.5	72.4	10.5	269688
92703	SANTA ANA	11773	12362	19.9	27.2	38.7	11.2	3.0	52681	54591	67	47	6356	8.9	3.5	6.6	75.4	5.6	264085
92704	SANTA ANA	15544	20005	13.1	22.5	42.4	16.7	5.2	64628	67306	83	65	11234	8.8	2.7	6.1	66.3	16.1	287224
92705	SANTA ANA	37703	14419	8.6	17.6	30.9	16.8	26.1	86145	91069	94	84	9937	1.1	1.1	2.3	19.1	76.4	591532
92706	SANTA ANA	19497	9392	14.7	23.9	35.9	16.7	8.9	60361	63436	78	59	5014	0.2	0.0	3.3	51.7	44.8	382228
92707	SANTA ANA	15396	13445	12.4	24.8	42.2	14.9	5.7	62697	64803	81	63	7307	0.7	0.5	4.6	78.5	15.8	284676
92708	FOUNTAIN VALLEY	34613	18549	6.2	12.2	36.9	27.8	16.8	91342	96239	95	88	13396	1.7	1.2	1.2	20.2	75.7	491479
92780	TUSTIN	24328	18646	12.7	24.1	40.4	15.3	7.5	61784	64015	80	61	8097	3.3	2.5	3.7	41.4	49.0	392434
92782	TUSTIN	57127	8512	4.4	8.4	29.9	27.5	30.0	113738	115410	98	94	5319	0.4	0.8	1.2	29.8	67.8	519696
92801	ANAHEIM	17594	16511	17.2	28.4	41.0	10.3	3.1	53384	54914	69	48	6918	7.4	2.5	4.5	70.6	14.9	295169
92802	ANAHEIM	17091	11873	17.3	27.4	38.2	13.0	4.1	54694	56916	71	51	4971	7.4	1.8	2.4	66.8	21.6	321113
92804	ANAHEIM	19544	25949	17.1	27.7	38.5	12.1	4.5	54889	57073	71	51	11609	3.2	1.5	3.2	71.6	20.6	327299
92805	ANAHEIM	14968	17182	17.6	30.7	36.6	10.8	4.4	51478	53052	65	45	7199	4.4	0.9	2.7	76.9	15.0	306206
92806	ANAHEIM	22800	10881	11.3	23.6	42.3	16.7	6.0	65140	67786	83	66	5473	4.3	2.2	4.0	52.6	36.9	359781
92807	ANAHEIM	42876	12715	6.6	10.9	32.1	23.9	26.5	100648	106095	97	91	9714	1.6	0.9	1.3	26.8	69.3	477348
92808	ANAHEIM	51913	7185	2.4	5.2	28.7	29.3	34.3	127450	128061	99	96	5898	0.1	0.5	0.3	29.4	69.7	525081
92821	BREA	33450	13012	10.7	16.5	38.4	22.4	12.1	77643	81197	91	78	7992	1.4	3.2	5.3	32.0	58.1	431358
92823	BREA	40233	1148	6.9	13.9	40.6	23.0	15.7	84087	88346	94	83	1010	6.2	5.2	7.9	16.5	64.1	453383
92831	FULLERTON	30850	13001	15.6	23.1	35.7	15.1	10.6	61633	64039	80	61	5411	0.6	0.4	1.8	41.8	55.4	424271
92832	FULLERTON	21786	7791	19.2	21.7	41.9	11.9	5.4	57797	59683	75	56	3000	2.6	2.2	2.2	66.8	26.1	331256
92833	FULLERTON	27091	15745	13.4	20.2	37.0	18.9	10.5	70001	74684	87	71	9783	2.9	2.1	1.7	52.6	40.7	363787
92835	FULLERTON	44004	8583	7.9	14.6	34.6	23.9	19.0	87443	93373	94	85	6156	0.0	0.3	1.7	26.6	71.3	508513
92840	GARDEN GROVE	20374	15523	14.3	24.1	41.8	14.3	5.5	61252	63484	79	60	8902	4.9	2.1	3.4	70.1	19.5	318124
92841	GARDEN GROVE	21145	8805	15.1	23.1	39.9	14.1	7.8	62098	64969	80	62	5127	3.1	0.7	2.0	64.4	29.8	347171
92843	GARDEN GROVE	14998	10637	18.3	26.6	38.2	13.3	3.5	54859	57157	71	51	5535	7.4	1.8	2.8	74.9	13.1	296990
92844	GARDEN GROVE	17078	6591	18.3	25.0	41.3	11.9	3.5	55643	58046	72	53	3144	5.5	0.7	3.0	74.3	16.5	284454
92845	GARDEN GROVE	34417	5662	6.6	11.9	38.5	29.9	13.2	89114	94259	95	86	4556	0.4	0.0	0.1	40.2	59.2	422993
92860	NORCO	26941	7199	9.7	16.8	42.5	19.4	11.7	76220	77440	90	77	5693	1.1	0.2	5.1	70.4	23.1	300617
92861	VILLA PARK	62375	1931	3.3	5.6	21.6	18.4	51.1	152113	156331	100	99	1801	0.0	0.1	1.7	2.1	96.2	888867
92862	ORANGE	45395	6	0.0	0.0	16.7	33.3	50.0	150000	150000	100	98	5	0.0	0.0	0.0	0.0	100.0	625000
92865	ORANGE	26702	6059	10.9	19.4	41.2	19.7	8.8	69917	73590	87	71	3824	3.0	1.6	3.2	45.8	46.3	385914
92866	ORANGE	28094	5913	16.0	21.6	40.6	16.1	5.6	61868	64879	80	61	2327	2.8	1.0	4.2	37.1	54.9	414623
92867	ORANGE	34336	13469	9.3	15.1	32.3	22.9	20.4	87594	95083	95	85	9205	2.7	1.3	1.3	27.0	67.7	472058
92868	ORANGE	22240	6956	17.9	21.3	41.4	14.1	5.4	59734	62416	77	58	2806	6.1	1.8	3.5	72.9	15.8	286144
92869	ORANGE	36756	11675	6.3	11.1	34.1	25.3	23.2	97301	102823	96	90	9061	0.6	0.4	1.4	31.8	65.9	477733
92870	PLACENTIA	31243	16651	8.2	15.9	38.0	24.0	13.8	81070	85059	92	81	10797	2.0	1.1	1.7	31.9	63.3	442987
92879	CORONA	22246	14905	13.7	19.8	44.6	15.4	6.5	65487	67097	84	66	8489	5.2	2.3	13.0	69.4	10.0	243611
92880	CORONA	17686	14590	17.5	25.1	38.2	13.9	5.4	57736	58156	75	55	11056	1.5	14.3	14.4	53.7	16.1	283176
92881	CORONA	32286	8682	6.8	10.5	37.0	26.4	19.4	93656	97572	96	88	7103	1.5	0.9	4.6	66.6	26.3	324877
92882	CORONA	24662	20684	11.3	20.2	40.3	17.0	11.1	72190	74303	88	73	13535	3.7	0.8	10.7	64.7	20.1	280145
92883	CORONA	32162	8369	5.1	11.1	43.9	24.7	15.0	87536	87422	94	85	7770	3.1	2.3	13.7	70.0	11.0	251186
92886	YORBA LINDA	42767	15440	4.9	8.5	30.2	29.3	27.1	111941	114776	98	94	12908	0.2	0.5	1.7	21.5	76.1	514877
92887	YORBA LINDA	53697	6955	3.0	6.3	20.2	24.8	45.7	141274	142842	99	98	5666	0.3	0.3	0.4	12.4	86.6	677271
93001	VENTURA	28862	13304	19.8	24.8	33.9	13.4	8.0	55620	58120	72	53	6077	3.7	1.5	6.4	47.8	40.6	339054
93003	VENTURA	33254	19345	12.5	19.3	40.6	18.8	8.8	70878	74669	87	72	11833	1.9	2.7	6.8	48.6	40.0	364063
93004	VENTURA	31995	10520	11.7	16.9	35.9	24.2	11.3	77750	81557	91	79	7368	2.0	2.4	1.5	48.8	45.2	386569
93010	CAMARILLO	36651	15840	10.1	15.7	36.2	23.0	15.0	80906	85142	92	81	10631	1.2	0.8	1.0	40.9	56.1	429344
93012	CAMARILLO	43166	12645	10.2	15.6	29.3	22.4	22.4	88505	96332	95	86	10224	0.5	0.9	2.2	43.4	52.9	418099
93013	CARPINTERIA	32051	6316	13.4	20.9	35.7	18.7	11.4	67279	70958	85	69	3732	2.2	0.6	8.0	20.6	68.6	574899
93015	FILLMORE	19486	5285	19.2	24.0	34.8	16.7	5.3	56679	59195	74	54	3156	6.1	3.3	6.7	69.5	14.3	263653
93021	MOORPARK	31414	11027	6.9	14.0	32.0	28.3	18.7	94425	98568	96	89	8736	0.4	0.5	3.4	38.9	56.8	438969
93022	OAK VIEW	31141	2186	13.4	16.0	35.8	23.4	11.4	75054	79317	89	76	1614	4.2	2.3	2.2	52.4	38.9	360832
93023	OJAI	32759	8450	15.4	22.2	33.6	19.2	9.6	65873	70213	84	67	5660	5.1	3.6	1.9	37.0	52.3	415802
93030	OXNARD	16931	14198	19.9	23.0	35.6	15.8	5.6	56760	59792	74	54	7607	3.9	0.5	3.1	72.2	20.3	289618
93033	OXNARD	14573	17176	16.6	25.2	39.1	14.8	4.3	57422	59512	75	55	9962	9.1	3.2	5.2	79.8	2.9	261576
93035	OXNARD	33717	10188	7.7	16.7	43.0	22.2	10.3	76468	79614	90	77	6067	0.1	0.8	4.5	51.0	43.6	375825
93036	OXNARD	22296	10578	15.1	24.6	34.5	17.5	8.3	62806	65997	81	63	6216	4.5	1.8	4.3	57.1	32.2	319884
93041	PORT HUENEME	22201	6809	18.5	25.7	41.3	11.2	3.2	54824	56803	71	51	3616	0.5	0.3	8.9	83.8	6.5	255166
93042	POINT MUGU NAWC	15722	653	9.5	41.0	41.5	6.0	2.0	49181	50447	59	41	11	0.0	0.0	0.0	54.5	45.5	375000
93043	PORT HUENEME CBC BAS	15405	680	16.9	51.0	26.2	5.9	0.0	38369	39737	28	19	25	24.0	16.0	20.0	40.0	0.0	109375
93060	SANTA PAULA	19163	9318	21.8	25.5	33.1	14.4	5.2	52910	55275	68	47	5249	6.9	3.4	9.6	62.2	17.9	263293
93063	SIMI VALLEY	34252	18415	9.1	12.9	34.0	28.8	15.1	89156	96303	95	86	14320	1.4	1.3	2.8	51.6	42.9	376737
93065	SIMI VALLEY	36977	23467	6.8	11.2	34.3	28.8	18.8	95640	101358	96	89	17733	0.6	0.3	0.9	51.1	47.1	390799
93066	SOMIS	42788	1173	5.9	19.2	33.2	15.6	26.2	83520	90677	93	83	776	1.7	1.2	1.2	20.4	75.6	773952
93067	SUMMERLAND	51918	309	10.0	13.6	43.0	19.4	13.9	72437	76000	88	73	186	0.0	0.0	1.1	19.9	79.0	768293
93101	SANTA BARBARA	26605	12622	23.1	23.5	35.5	11.5	6.4	53990	59572	70	50	3153	1.2	0.4	1.6	7.7	89.1	635165
93103	SANTA BARBARA	34473	7009	14.0	22.3	33.0	15.2	15.5	65892	68598	84	67	3303	1.7	1.9	1.2	5.1	90.2	778324
93105	SANTA BARBARA	47054	11765	11.6	17.3	31.6	21.7	17.7	77977	80539	91	79	6555	1.0	0.2	1.1	4.5	93.2	807608
93106	SANTA BARBARA	20773	0	0.0	0.0	0.0	0.0	0.0	0	0	0	0	0	0.0	0.0	0.0	0.0	0.0	0
93108	SANTA BARBARA	69038	5612	8.6	9.9	23.7	19.7	38.2	122996	127336	99	96	3849	0.2	1.1	1.5	5.1	92.1	1000001
	CALIFORNIA	28199		18.5	22.2	33.9	14.0	11.5	61614	64088				3.3	2.6	13.6	41.0	39.5	321752
	UNITED STATES	27277		20.9	24.4	35.3	11.7	7.6	54719	56938				9.3	13.1	31.6	32.6	13.5	162279

ZIP CODE #	POST OFFICE NAME	FINANCIAL SERVICES: Auto Loan	FINANCIAL SERVICES: Home Loan	FINANCIAL SERVICES: Invest-ments	FINANCIAL SERVICES: Retire-ment Plans	THE HOME: Home Improvements: Home Repair	THE HOME: Home Improvements: Lawn & Garden	THE HOME: Furnishings: Comput-ers & Hard-ware-Personal	THE HOME: Furnishings: Major Appli-ances	THE HOME: Furnishings: TV, Radio, Sound Equip-ment	THE HOME: Furnishings: Furni-ture	ENTERTAINMENT: Dine out/ Carry out	ENTERTAINMENT: Sports Equip-ment	ENTERTAINMENT: Fees & Tickets	ENTERTAINMENT: Toys & Games	ENTERTAINMENT: Travel	ENTERTAINMENT: Cable TV	PERSONAL: Apparel & Services	PERSONAL: Auto Repairs	PERSONAL: Health Insur-ance	PERSONAL: Pets & Supplies
92646	HUNTINGTON BEACH	135	168	190	168	181	157	153	156	144	162	144	118	174	140	172	139	105	152	147	174
92647	HUNTINGTON BEACH	114	129	140	129	135	113	132	123	122	133	124	99	139	121	138	116	91	127	112	139
92648	HUNTINGTON BEACH	149	161	181	171	170	147	173	157	161	174	164	130	181	158	178	154	121	163	147	182
92649	HUNTINGTON BEACH	152	184	207	187	197	168	176	172	162	183	164	135	194	160	193	156	121	170	159	194
92651	LAGUNA BEACH	177	221	262	230	242	201	208	206	190	221	191	162	236	184	234	180	143	200	185	231
92653	LAGUNA HILLS	158	199	219	201	212	188	176	183	168	188	168	137	203	164	199	164	123	175	175	205
92655	MIDWAY CITY	93	115	127	112	125	90	114	110	95	121	97	89	118	92	124	85	72	107	86	120
92656	ALISO VIEJO	174	183	162	190	177	156	176	165	166	187	169	139	183	176	173	156	122	164	146	192
92657	NEWPORT COAST	261	347	412	365	381	321	300	308	279	327	280	238	366	278	346	267	214	290	273	341
92660	NEWPORT BEACH	220	272	325	285	298	251	256	253	236	272	238	198	293	231	285	225	178	246	227	284
92661	NEWPORT BEACH	176	202	240	218	217	185	208	192	193	212	198	158	228	190	222	185	148	195	176	221
92662	NEWPORT BEACH	188	221	261	234	239	198	223	210	203	230	206	171	243	198	241	192	154	209	187	239
92663	NEWPORT BEACH	168	184	216	197	197	169	197	180	181	200	186	148	208	178	206	173	137	185	165	208
92672	SAN CLEMENTE	134	149	169	154	159	133	155	146	142	160	145	118	163	139	163	134	106	149	131	166
92673	SAN CLEMENTE	201	249	260	259	259	224	215	221	201	234	203	173	248	204	238	191	150	208	195	249
92675	SAN JUAN CAPISTRANO	159	188	197	187	198	175	170	176	161	182	162	132	187	159	185	156	117	169	164	196
92676	SILVERADO	151	198	234	202	219	175	180	183	160	196	159	142	205	154	206	148	119	173	157	202
92677	LAGUNA NIGUEL	182	212	225	220	220	191	197	194	184	209	186	154	218	186	211	175	136	189	174	221
92679	TRABUCO CANYON	264	336	332	347	343	291	278	287	258	309	260	229	328	271	305	241	195	263	242	318
92683	WESTMINSTER	100	116	122	112	122	97	115	112	103	120	105	88	118	101	121	96	76	111	96	124
92688	RANCHO SANTA MARGARI	172	184	159	189	176	155	172	164	162	184	165	136	180	173	170	152	118	160	143	189
92691	MISSION VIEJO	148	185	197	187	194	167	165	166	154	173	155	128	187	155	182	148	114	160	151	187
92692	MISSION VIEJO	177	214	225	217	225	201	189	196	180	207	181	147	216	179	209	174	131	187	187	219
92694	LADERA RANCH	274	382	459	392	425	353	320	342	293	358	290	253	391	282	384	278	218	316	305	374
92697	IRVINE	67	28	28	35	26	33	94	46	75	64	76	50	56	73	50	68	54	66	46	63
92701	SANTA ANA	77	65	57	62	64	51	81	71	75	83	80	58	73	77	74	69	58	79	60	78
92703	SANTA ANA	88	89	76	79	89	67	94	89	83	100	88	70	89	85	92	75	64	91	71	94
92704	SANTA ANA	103	106	97	98	107	82	113	105	101	118	105	85	109	102	111	91	76	108	86	114
92705	SANTA ANA	152	182	204	185	195	164	174	171	161	183	163	132	193	159	189	153	121	169	153	190
92706	SANTA ANA	102	110	108	104	113	90	115	108	105	118	110	85	116	106	117	99	81	111	93	118
92707	SANTA ANA	104	104	95	97	106	80	114	105	101	119	106	85	108	102	111	91	77	109	85	113
92708	FOUNTAIN VALLEY	132	166	183	164	177	144	154	152	140	160	141	119	170	139	170	133	104	149	135	169
92780	TUSTIN	99	104	105	104	106	90	112	102	105	111	109	82	114	106	112	101	80	108	94	116
92782	TUSTIN	187	203	208	214	207	178	203	189	189	211	193	157	215	193	207	178	141	190	168	218
92801	ANAHEIM	83	85	80	80	86	69	94	86	86	94	90	69	91	86	91	81	66	90	74	95
92802	ANAHEIM	89	89	86	86	91	73	99	90	90	101	94	73	96	91	97	84	69	95	78	101
92804	ANAHEIM	85	93	92	89	95	77	99	92	91	98	94	73	99	90	99	86	69	95	81	102
92805	ANAHEIM	88	89	80	82	90	68	96	89	86	100	90	71	92	87	94	78	66	93	73	96
92806	ANAHEIM	103	105	104	103	106	92	112	104	105	113	108	83	111	106	111	101	78	108	95	119
92807	ANAHEIM	160	201	219	203	213	180	180	183	166	192	167	141	203	165	200	158	123	175	163	204
92808	ANAHEIM	206	243	226	252	242	207	212	211	197	233	201	173	237	209	223	184	147	199	179	238
92821	BREA	121	135	141	136	139	126	131	128	126	134	128	99	140	126	137	124	92	129	124	147
92823	BREA	126	169	184	166	178	154	145	149	137	148	138	112	169	137	165	135	102	143	140	165
92831	FULLERTON	112	104	109	108	106	95	125	107	117	121	119	89	120	117	117	112	86	117	101	125
92832	FULLERTON	90	90	92	90	92	76	104	92	95	103	99	76	101	95	102	90	72	99	83	105
92833	FULLERTON	111	131	136	126	138	109	127	124	114	134	117	97	133	113	135	107	86	122	106	136
92835	FULLERTON	144	172	192	172	183	163	161	161	156	165	156	120	179	153	176	155	114	160	158	181
92840	GARDEN GROVE	93	106	104	100	109	84	110	103	98	111	102	82	110	98	111	92	75	104	87	112
92841	GARDEN GROVE	96	113	115	107	120	88	115	109	99	119	102	87	116	97	119	90	75	108	88	118
92843	GARDEN GROVE	88	94	86	85	96	71	98	93	86	103	90	74	95	87	98	78	66	94	74	98
92844	GARDEN GROVE	83	97	99	92	102	74	99	94	85	103	87	76	99	84	103	76	64	93	75	101
92845	GARDEN GROVE	117	165	179	158	173	150	137	142	132	137	133	104	164	133	158	133	99	137	137	156
92860	NORCO	117	149	145	148	150	136	126	131	121	131	122	100	143	123	139	119	88	125	122	148
92861	VILLA PARK	231	325	394	335	363	303	271	290	249	302	246	215	335	241	326	237	187	268	259	317
92862	ORANGE	199	246	226	253	245	206	205	209	188	230	191	171	235	201	221	174	141	191	174	233
92865	ORANGE	105	128	133	124	132	113	120	118	113	121	115	90	131	113	129	111	85	117	109	131
92866	ORANGE	96	101	108	103	105	90	111	100	103	110	106	82	112	102	112	99	77	106	93	116
92867	ORANGE	141	175	183	171	182	153	160	159	150	165	153	122	178	151	174	145	113	156	144	176
92868	ORANGE	89	94	92	92	96	80	104	94	98	101	102	75	104	97	102	96	75	99	88	106
92869	ORANGE	155	191	201	190	201	167	174	174	160	184	163	135	194	161	190	152	120	169	153	192
92870	PLACENTIA	128	146	148	145	150	130	140	136	131	144	133	107	149	133	147	126	97	136	124	153
92879	CORONA	108	111	98	107	107	95	109	105	104	113	107	83	109	109	107	99	76	105	94	119
92880	CORONA	100	102	88	94	100	84	100	98	93	107	96	75	97	97	97	88	68	97	85	108
92881	CORONA	156	180	160	183	177	152	159	158	148	173	151	129	173	157	164	139	109	150	136	178
92882	CORONA	119	129	114	127	126	106	124	119	115	131	119	96	128	120	124	107	86	118	102	133
92883	CORONA	154	173	143	171	164	142	150	150	140	165	143	121	159	152	151	131	102	140	128	170
92886	YORBA LINDA	161	212	228	214	223	190	181	187	167	194	169	144	211	168	206	160	125	177	167	208
92887	YORBA LINDA	223	278	294	291	289	252	241	244	227	258	229	192	282	232	266	217	171	232	217	276
93001	VENTURA	96	99	104	99	104	85	110	100	99	112	103	82	108	98	111	93	74	105	89	113
93003	VENTURA	105	123	131	123	128	114	120	116	114	120	116	90	130	113	127	113	84	117	113	132
93004	VENTURA	121	142	143	140	145	132	128	132	123	133	124	100	139	123	138	121	89	128	125	149
93010	CAMARILLO	127	158	170	156	165	144	144	143	138	147	139	109	163	138	158	136	102	142	136	161
93012	CAMARILLO	146	174	187	176	185	167	156	163	150	170	150	121	177	148	173	147	108	156	159	182
93013	CARPINTERIA	110	129	138	130	135	116	128	123	119	130	121	97	137	117	136	115	88	124	114	139
93015	FILLMORE	95	111	106	98	116	86	105	106	91	113	93	81	105	90	110	82	68	102	85	111
93021	MOORPARK	154	181	165	177	179	154	159	161	149	171	152	126	172	154	167	141	110	154	140	181
93022	OAK VIEW	111	147	163	144	158	128	131	133	120	136	120	102	149	118	148	115	89	128	118	147
93023	OJAI	107	132	148	131	142	123	122	125	115	125	115	94	135	112	135	113	84	121	117	139
93030	OXNARD	92	103	96	94	105	80	104	99	92	107	96	78	104	93	105	86	70	100	82	106
93033	OXNARD	94	104	93	92	107	77	103	101	89	111	93	79	101	90	105	80	68	99	78	105
93035	OXNARD	125	141	150	138	149	125	136	136	125	145	127	104	142	123	144	119	91	132	121	151
93036	OXNARD	105	117	109	107	119	93	115	111	103	121	106	87	115	105	117	95	77	110	93	120
93041	PORT HUENEME	81	87	84	84	88	76	92	86	87	92	89	67	93	85	92	84	65	89	82	97
93042	POINT MUGU NAWC	100	52	39	60	46	44	94	65	88	87	93	65	71	106	68	81	65	83	59	79
93043	PORT HUENEME CBC BAS	78	40	30	47	36	34	73	51	69	68	72	50	56	83	53	63	51	65	46	62
93060	SANTA PAULA	95	99	97	90	101	87	98	99	92	101	94	76	96	92	100	88	68	98	88	108
93063	SIMI VALLEY	135	164	159	163	164	146	145	146	138	150	140	113	161	141	156	134	101	142	135	166
93065	SIMI VALLEY	150	181	177	179	184	157	163	162	152	171	155	127	179	156	174	145	113	157	144	182
93066	SOMIS	163	217	249	214	239	193	188	199	169	209	169	148	218	164	218	158	126	185	172	214
93067	SUMMERLAND	129	162	190	165	179	139	154	153	135	166	135	122	169	130	172	124	101	147	128	170
93101	SANTA BARBARA	88	85	91	89	87	75	103	88	95	100	98	76	99	94	100	89	72	97	81	103
93103	SANTA BARBARA	123	134	144	135	141	118	141	132	130	144	133	105	145	128	145	123	98	134	118	148
93105	SANTA BARBARA	130	153	176	158	165	138	154	147	140	159	142	118	166	136	167	133	104	148	135	167
93106	SANTA BARBARA	0	0	0	0	0	0	0	0	0	0	0	0	0	0	0	0	0	0	0	0
93108	SANTA BARBARA	205	278	334	285	309	253	241	252	218	266	217	191	287	211	283	205	163	235	220	276
	CALIFORNIA	112	119	122	118	122	107	121	116	114	124	116	92	124	114	124	110	84	118	107	132
	UNITED STATES	100	100	100	100	100	100	100	100	100	100	100	100	100	100	100	100	100	100	100	100

ZIP CODE #	POST OFFICE NAME	COUNTY FIPS CODE	POPULATION 2000	POPULATION 2009	POPULATION 2014	2000-2009 ANNUAL RATE % Rate	2000-2009 ANNUAL RATE State Centile	HOUSEHOLDS 2000	HOUSEHOLDS 2009	HOUSEHOLDS 2014	HOUSEHOLDS % Annual Rate 2000-2009	HOUSEHOLDS 2009 Average HH Size	FAMILIES 2000	FAMILIES 2009	FAMILIES % Annual Rate 2000-2009
93109	SANTA BARBARA	083	10862	10751	10742	-0.1	5	4525	4611	4617	0.2	2.32	2597	2633	0.1
93110	SANTA BARBARA	083	14668	15065	15234	0.3	23	5727	5962	6019	0.4	2.45	3418	3551	0.4
93111	SANTA BARBARA	083	16996	17542	17806	0.3	23	5953	6307	6414	0.6	2.73	4386	4620	0.6
93117	GOLETA	083	49958	48574	49129	-0.3	3	15488	16092	16250	0.4	2.82	7963	8286	0.4
93202	ARMONA	031	1745	2139	2356	2.2	85	468	562	614	2.0	3.77	400	480	2.0
93203	ARVIN	029	14497	18817	21060	2.9	91	3411	4300	4802	2.5	4.35	2972	3725	2.5
93204	AVENAL	031	14702	17192	17697	1.7	78	1938	2116	2218	1.0	4.36	1650	1800	0.9
93205	BODFISH	029	1934	2336	2593	2.1	84	885	1050	1160	1.9	2.22	573	664	1.6
93206	BUTTONWILLOW	029	1942	2140	2263	1.1	64	527	569	600	0.8	3.73	435	464	0.7
93207	CALIFORNIA HOT SPRIN	107	887	1046	1133	1.8	80	282	324	348	1.5	3.22	216	247	1.5
93210	COALINGA	019	17812	20013	20950	1.3	70	3958	4429	4689	1.2	3.19	2973	3308	1.2
93212	CORCORAN	031	23605	28168	29499	1.9	81	3547	4141	4475	1.7	3.56	2873	3358	1.7
93215	DELANO	029	45054	54163	58639	2.0	83	9660	11279	12255	1.7	4.21	8374	9770	1.7
93219	EARLIMART	107	10226	12284	13357	2.0	83	2411	2802	3029	1.6	4.38	2074	2407	1.6
93221	EXETER	107	13399	15698	16917	1.7	78	4432	5047	5393	1.4	3.09	3490	3965	1.4
93223	FARMERSVILLE	107	8483	9197	9572	0.9	58	2087	2192	2265	0.5	4.14	1804	1893	0.5
93224	FELLOWS	029	615	664	690	0.8	54	212	222	231	0.5	2.51	168	173	0.3
93225	FRAZIER PARK	029	6709	8195	9124	2.2	85	2632	3161	3504	2.0	2.59	1833	2164	1.8
93226	GLENNVILLE	029	247	299	332	2.1	84	103	122	135	1.8	2.45	73	85	1.7
93230	HANFORD	031	54427	64215	69235	1.8	80	18059	21012	22566	1.7	3.01	13647	15897	1.7
93234	HURON	019	8887	10520	11429	1.8	80	1873	2218	2416	1.8	4.41	1634	1925	1.8
93235	IVANHOE	107	4524	4885	5055	0.8	54	1156	1203	1237	0.4	4.06	979	1018	0.4
93238	KERNVILLE	029	943	1146	1268	2.1	84	435	522	582	2.0	1.93	254	297	1.7
93239	KETTLEMAN CITY	031	1807	2148	2334	1.9	81	382	446	484	1.7	4.65	339	396	1.7
93240	LAKE ISABELLA	029	5572	6992	7847	2.5	88	2538	3133	3506	2.3	2.21	1555	1884	2.1
93241	LAMONT	029	15468	16533	17259	0.7	50	3621	3785	3943	0.5	4.37	3133	3249	0.4
93242	LATON	019	2870	3283	3528	1.5	75	852	962	1028	1.3	3.41	702	788	1.3
93243	LEBEC	111	727	872	967	2.0	83	250	294	323	1.8	2.97	186	216	1.6
93244	LEMON COVE	107	134	147	162	1.0	62	54	58	63	0.8	2.53	40	43	0.8
93245	LEMOORE	031	30594	38091	41904	2.4	87	9338	11448	12558	2.2	3.21	7502	9184	2.2
93247	LINDSAY	107	15278	17417	18464	1.4	72	4164	4542	4781	0.9	3.80	3396	3702	0.9
93249	LOST HILLS	029	2667	3274	3625	2.2	85	515	618	683	2.0	5.27	461	551	1.9
93250	MC FARLAND	029	10997	13822	15388	2.5	88	2305	2871	3235	2.4	4.29	2076	2573	2.3
93251	MC KITTRICK	029	438	475	493	0.9	58	145	152	158	0.5	2.57	116	120	0.4
93252	MARICOPA	111	4338	2225	2421	-7.0	0	666	765	831	1.5	2.88	488	555	1.4
93254	NEW CUYAMA	083	690	747	774	0.9	58	245	269	278	1.0	2.78	174	190	1.0
93255	ONYX	029	354	422	465	1.9	81	162	190	210	1.7	2.14	103	118	1.5
93256	PIXLEY	107	4009	4733	5066	1.8	80	1041	1155	1224	1.1	4.08	880	976	1.1
93257	PORTERVILLE	107	64989	75811	81577	1.7	78	19356	21864	23337	1.3	3.39	15077	17066	1.3
93260	POSEY	107	245	287	310	1.7	78	103	117	125	1.4	2.44	71	80	1.3
93262	SEQUOIA NATIONAL PAR	107	35	43	47	2.3	86	19	22	25	1.6	1.95	11	12	0.9
93263	SHAFTER	029	15150	19277	21563	2.6	89	3970	4890	5453	2.3	3.72	3323	4074	2.2
93265	SPRINGVILLE	107	4201	5409	6034	2.8	90	1748	2159	2382	2.3	2.45	1202	1485	2.3
93266	STRATFORD	031	1650	2152	2387	2.9	91	390	483	534	2.3	4.46	339	421	2.4
93267	STRATHMORE	107	5696	6410	6799	1.3	70	1492	1619	1703	0.9	3.95	1234	1338	0.9
93268	TAFT	029	14929	18853	19649	2.6	89	5206	5506	5762	0.6	2.85	3739	3886	0.4
93270	TERRA BELLA	107	6080	7198	7810	1.8	80	1593	1818	1953	1.4	3.95	1355	1547	1.4
93271	THREE RIVERS	107	2272	2652	2893	1.7	78	1006	1143	1234	1.4	2.31	676	763	1.3
93272	TIPTON	107	2824	3349	3642	1.9	81	766	872	939	1.4	3.84	643	731	1.4
93274	TULARE	107	56077	69820	76833	2.4	87	17087	20606	22492	2.0	3.37	13713	16560	2.1
93276	TUPMAN	029	92	101	106	1.0	62	30	32	34	0.7	2.72	24	26	0.9
93277	VISALIA	107	44932	51618	55224	1.5	75	16530	18514	19661	1.2	2.74	11866	13299	1.2
93280	WASCO	029	22518	27119	29543	2.0	83	4328	5152	5746	1.9	3.85	3703	4374	1.8
93283	WELDON	029	2136	2607	2894	2.2	85	933	1119	1238	2.0	2.33	609	716	1.8
93285	WOFFORD HEIGHTS	029	3440	4163	4622	2.1	84	1692	2011	2221	1.9	2.05	1018	1183	1.6
93286	WOODLAKE	107	9321	10532	11217	1.3	70	2695	2955	3120	1.0	3.56	2207	2415	1.0
93287	WOODY	029	127	154	171	2.1	84	53	63	70	1.9	2.44	38	44	1.6
93291	VISALIA	107	36738	48466	54079	3.0	91	10356	13634	15229	3.0	3.44	8110	10849	3.2
93292	VISALIA	107	30507	39453	44115	2.8	90	9992	12677	14095	2.6	3.08	7805	9826	2.5
93301	BAKERSFIELD	029	12844	14019	14727	1.0	62	5021	5326	5590	0.6	2.41	2853	2951	0.4
93304	BAKERSFIELD	029	45762	50401	53385	1.0	62	14995	16115	16987	0.8	3.10	10799	11426	0.6
93305	BAKERSFIELD	029	35661	38269	39966	0.8	54	10445	10871	11304	0.4	3.40	7779	7980	0.3
93306	BAKERSFIELD	029	53462	63244	70208	1.8	80	17631	20513	22770	1.7	3.05	13306	15324	1.5
93307	BAKERSFIELD	029	59443	75704	85511	2.6	89	16182	20120	22641	2.4	3.74	13128	16209	2.3
93308	BAKERSFIELD	029	44848	54068	59705	2.0	83	16129	19079	21038	1.8	2.70	11207	13115	1.7
93309	BAKERSFIELD	029	58488	62066	64746	0.6	45	22395	23317	24243	0.4	2.63	15005	15330	0.2
93311	BAKERSFIELD	029	20295	36622	42829	6.6	97	7318	11785	13588	5.3	3.08	5348	9052	5.9
93312	BAKERSFIELD	029	27713	59019	72951	8.5	98	9048	18415	22589	8.0	3.20	7476	15375	8.1
93313	BAKERSFIELD	029	25476	36982	44195	4.1	94	7597	10614	12626	3.7	3.46	6423	8948	3.6
93314	BAKERSFIELD	029	13151	20867	25176	5.1	96	3987	6221	7476	4.9	3.33	3538	5499	4.9
93401	SAN LUIS OBISPO	079	27041	27613	28064	0.2	18	11739	12519	12810	0.7	2.14	5579	5915	0.6
93402	LOS OSOS	079	14756	14570	14600	-0.1	5	6051	6262	6332	0.4	2.31	3989	4081	0.2
93405	SAN LUIS OBISPO	079	31491	32843	33538	0.5	39	9156	10165	10554	1.1	2.22	3650	4065	1.2
93407	SAN LUIS OBISPO	079	1395	1404	1404	0.1	13	12	12	12	0.0	2.58	1	1	0.0
93420	ARROYO GRANDE	079	25127	28010	29376	1.2	68	9955	11620	12283	1.7	2.39	6975	8101	1.6
93422	ATASCADERO	079	29664	31757	32828	0.7	50	10674	11967	12485	1.2	2.52	7681	8556	1.2
93426	BRADLEY	053	1420	1496	1532	0.6	45	578	631	651	1.0	2.37	415	448	0.8
93427	BUELLTON	083	5589	6464	6825	1.6	77	2035	2378	2504	1.7	2.72	1447	1686	1.7
93428	CAMBRIA	079	6479	6803	6988	0.5	39	2916	3199	3311	1.0	2.12	1947	2113	0.9
93429	CASMALIA	083	1	1	1	0.0	9	0	1	1	0.0	1.00	0	0	0.0
93430	CAYUCOS	079	3216	3212	3232	0.0	9	1509	1575	1600	0.5	2.03	875	901	0.3
93432	CRESTON	079	1131	1255	1328	1.1	64	428	500	535	1.7	2.48	326	378	1.6
93433	GROVER BEACH	079	13002	13228	13391	0.2	18	4984	5262	5371	0.6	2.49	3285	3428	0.5
93434	GUADALUPE	083	5701	6471	6784	1.4	72	1424	1659	1744	1.7	3.90	1224	1424	1.6
93436	LOMPOC	083	52006	54687	55556	0.5	39	17118	18124	18435	0.6	2.78	12455	13176	0.6
93437	LOMPOC	083	6168	5750	5618	-0.8	1	1714	1640	1605	-0.5	3.22	1608	1536	-0.5
93441	LOS OLIVOS	083	1021	1097	1132	0.8	54	373	414	429	1.1	2.64	287	317	1.1
93442	MORRO BAY	079	11060	11285	11464	0.2	18	5259	5624	5764	0.7	1.96	2782	2931	0.6
93444	NIPOMO	079	14929	17796	18929	1.9	81	4912	6063	6498	2.3	2.93	3983	4890	2.2
93445	OCEANO	079	7295	7768	7991	0.7	50	2453	2701	2801	1.0	2.87	1721	1878	0.9
93446	PASO ROBLES	079	37169	44644	47847	2.0	83	13346	16722	18080	2.5	2.61	9720	12148	2.4
93449	PISMO BEACH	079	8551	9393	9773	1.0	62	4230	4869	5116	1.5	1.92	2320	2631	1.4
93450	SAN ARDO	053	873	865	869	-0.1	5	286	290	293	0.2	2.98	209	210	0.1
93451	SAN MIGUEL	053	1809	1999	2085	1.1	64	618	707	742	1.5	2.81	466	530	1.4
93452	SAN SIMEON	079	528	536	541	0.2	18	242	249	251	0.3	2.14	137	138	0.1
	CALIFORNIA					1.2					1.0	2.93			1.1
	UNITED STATES					1.0					1.1	2.59			0.9

#	POST OFFICE NAME	White 2000	White 2009	Black 2000	Black 2009	Asian/Pacific 2000	Asian/Pacific 2009	% Hispanic Origin 2000	% Hispanic Origin 2009	0-4	5-9	10-14	15-19	20-24	25-44	45-64	65-84	85+	18+	MEDIAN AGE 2009	% 2009 Males	% 2009 Females
ZIP CODE		RACE (%)								2009 AGE DISTRIBUTION (%)												
93109	SANTA BARBARA	85.6	80.7	1.3	1.4	3.8	4.9	15.6	22.0	4.6	4.4	4.7	5.3	6.4	28.9	30.3	12.7	2.9	83.6	42.1	49.5	50.5
93110	SANTA BARBARA	82.3	77.2	1.2	1.3	4.2	5.1	19.4	25.9	5.4	5.0	5.4	6.2	5.9	25.6	27.9	14.6	4.0	80.6	42.5	47.9	52.1
93111	SANTA BARBARA	81.5	76.4	1.0	1.0	5.5	6.8	19.5	25.9	5.2	5.4	6.1	6.4	5.1	23.9	30.4	15.1	2.6	79.3	43.6	48.8	51.2
93117	GOLETA	73.2	65.6	1.8	1.7	9.3	11.2	23.4	31.2	4.9	4.5	4.3	12.6	24.7	23.7	17.4	6.7	1.1	83.3	24.8	50.4	49.6
93202	ARMONA	54.4	47.0	4.5	4.1	1.7	1.7	50.9	61.2	9.2	8.6	8.2	9.8	9.2	27.4	20.6	6.3	0.7	68.2	28.0	48.9	51.1
93203	ARVIN	47.6	44.8	1.1	1.0	1.2	1.1	84.6	89.7	11.7	10.8	9.3	9.9	9.4	27.8	15.4	5.0	0.7	62.1	24.4	52.3	47.7
93204	AVENAL	35.9	37.9	12.6	10.4	0.4	2.5	65.8	67.4	6.1	5.6	4.8	8.6	12.2	42.8	15.2	3.8	0.8	80.4	30.1	69.7	30.3
93205	BODFISH	90.8	86.3	0.1	0.1	0.8	1.1	5.6	9.5	3.7	3.9	4.1	5.2	4.7	14.0	34.2	27.0	3.3	85.2	54.6	48.8	51.2
93206	BUTTONWILLOW	43.7	34.4	3.1	2.7	0.3	0.3	59.8	71.4	9.8	9.3	8.6	9.6	9.2	27.5	19.6	5.8	0.7	67.0	27.0	52.3	47.7
93207	CALIFORNIA HOT SPRIN	65.8	58.4	0.7	0.7	0.8	1.0	37.1	45.7	8.2	8.4	8.3	7.6	5.5	23.4	24.4	12.8	1.2	70.0	35.0	51.4	48.6
93210	COALINGA	52.3	45.2	8.3	7.0	1.4	2.7	51.1	58.7	7.6	6.7	6.0	8.7	10.6	35.5	17.6	6.1	1.1	76.0	30.0	59.2	40.8
93212	CORCORAN	32.7	30.0	17.0	14.0	0.6	1.5	56.2	63.2	5.3	5.1	4.6	6.7	11.4	45.7	16.1	4.4	0.7	82.2	31.7	72.6	27.4
93215	DELANO	26.7	26.3	5.1	4.5	14.3	11.9	70.1	73.6	9.8	8.8	7.8	9.2	9.7	30.9	17.1	5.8	1.0	69.2	27.6	56.3	43.7
93219	EARLIMART	25.6	22.8	1.4	1.1	6.4	6.0	80.9	84.9	12.1	11.2	9.6	10.1	8.9	25.7	16.1	5.6	0.6	60.8	23.9	51.4	48.6
93221	EXETER	72.3	64.7	0.6	0.6	1.2	1.6	34.4	44.2	8.3	8.0	7.9	8.1	6.8	25.0	24.5	9.6	1.8	70.8	33.3	48.9	51.1
93223	FARMERSVILLE	42.2	35.7	0.3	0.3	1.0	1.0	72.5	80.9	10.8	9.9	9.0	9.8	8.9	27.5	17.4	6.0	0.8	64.4	25.9	50.6	49.4
93224	FELLOWS	76.5	88.7	9.1	3.6	2.3	1.7	13.5	16.4	5.6	5.1	5.1	6.2	3.9	34.3	29.4	8.9	1.5	82.1	40.1	65.4	34.6
93225	FRAZIER PARK	86.9	80.3	0.5	0.7	1.2	1.6	12.3	19.7	6.1	6.9	7.5	6.7	4.5	22.4	33.2	11.7	0.9	75.1	42.2	50.3	49.7
93226	GLENNVILLE	84.1	76.3	0.8	1.3	1.2	1.7	7.7	12.4	4.7	5.0	5.7	6.0	3.7	18.7	39.1	15.4	1.7	80.6	48.6	53.8	46.2
93230	HANFORD	64.4	59.1	4.7	4.3	2.9	3.3	38.1	45.6	8.6	8.2	7.7	7.8	7.2	27.4	22.7	8.8	1.6	70.8	32.1	49.6	50.4
93234	HURON	24.1	22.8	3.2	3.1	0.7	0.8	90.7	93.0	10.8	9.4	7.4	9.0	10.6	32.1	16.8	3.5	0.3	66.9	26.3	59.6	40.4
93235	IVANHOE	49.2	43.4	0.4	0.4	0.8	0.8	73.6	81.9	10.6	10.0	8.7	9.1	9.3	28.4	18.1	5.1	0.7	65.2	26.2	52.6	47.4
93238	KERNVILLE	85.8	81.2	2.0	2.4	0.8	1.2	9.9	16.1	2.4	2.6	4.0	14.4	2.0	11.8	35.6	24.4	2.7	77.8	54.2	56.5	43.5
93239	KETTLEMAN CITY	31.7	29.4	0.4	0.3	0.3	0.2	92.0	94.6	10.2	9.7	8.1	8.7	11.2	30.8	16.6	4.4	0.2	66.7	26.0	56.0	44.0
93240	LAKE ISABELLA	91.3	87.2	0.4	0.6	0.6	0.9	5.9	9.8	4.3	4.4	4.5	5.0	4.8	15.5	32.3	24.5	4.6	83.6	53.4	48.3	51.7
93241	LAMONT	45.0	42.2	2.5	2.6	1.0	0.9	89.0	93.2	11.8	10.5	8.8	10.2	10.1	27.6	15.7	4.6	0.6	62.7	24.3	52.2	47.8
93242	LATON	57.2	47.9	0.5	0.5	0.7	0.8	54.6	66.2	9.5	9.2	8.5	8.7	7.3	27.2	20.6	7.9	1.1	67.3	29.2	50.7	49.3
93243	LEBEC	79.4	69.6	0.8	0.9	1.1	1.3	19.5	30.3	7.0	7.6	7.7	7.6	5.2	22.5	28.7	13.1	0.8	72.8	39.8	50.1	49.9
93244	LEMON COVE	91.0	85.7	0.0	0.0	0.8	1.4	9.8	14.3	4.1	4.8	6.1	6.1	4.1	17.7	38.8	16.3	2.0	81.0	49.4	49.0	51.0
93245	LEMOORE	60.6	53.8	7.3	7.0	7.7	8.7	28.7	36.3	11.4	9.1	7.4	7.7	10.6	31.1	16.8	5.4	0.6	67.9	26.7	51.5	48.5
93247	LINDSAY	48.2	42.6	0.5	0.4	1.6	1.7	70.7	78.2	10.8	9.9	9.0	9.1	7.4	26.4	18.0	7.9	1.5	64.8	27.5	51.0	49.0
93249	LOST HILLS	25.2	21.7	2.8	2.8	0.5	0.4	89.6	93.8	13.0	11.8	9.7	10.0	8.6	29.7	14.1	2.9	0.3	60.1	23.2	55.0	45.0
93250	MC FARLAND	30.4	25.7	3.4	2.7	1.0	0.9	82.1	88.1	10.0	9.3	7.9	9.2	9.9	32.1	16.4	4.6	0.5	68.5	26.9	56.6	43.4
93251	MC KITTRICK	71.0	88.8	12.1	4.8	2.5	1.7	15.3	17.3	5.5	5.1	4.8	4.8	3.8	40.0	29.5	6.3	0.2	84.2	38.7	71.4	28.6
93252	MARICOPA	77.0	78.0	6.9	0.2	1.7	0.9	17.2	27.8	6.2	6.4	7.0	7.5	5.3	22.8	30.6	12.9	1.4	75.8	41.5	52.2	47.8
93254	NEW CUYAMA	78.1	72.4	0.9	0.8	0.6	0.7	42.4	53.9	6.6	7.0	7.4	8.2	4.8	22.5	30.5	12.2	0.9	74.0	39.7	52.9	47.1
93255	ONYX	87.9	83.2	0.6	0.9	0.3	0.2	6.2	10.2	3.8	3.8	4.3	7.8	5.7	11.4	36.5	23.9	2.8	82.0	53.9	51.9	48.1
93256	PIXLEY	36.7	29.2	4.4	3.4	0.7	0.7	65.5	75.1	11.8	11.0	9.8	9.6	7.8	25.6	17.5	6.1	0.8	61.5	25.0	52.1	47.9
93257	PORTERVILLE	55.1	46.7	0.9	0.9	4.3	4.9	49.6	59.6	9.7	8.8	7.9	8.5	8.0	27.2	20.3	8.1	1.5	68.4	29.2	49.6	50.4
93260	POSEY	92.2	89.5	0.8	0.7	0.4	0.7	6.9	10.5	5.2	5.6	5.9	5.9	3.5	15.7	32.4	23.7	2.1	79.1	51.0	51.2	48.8
93262	SEQUOIA NATIONAL PAR	88.9	86.0	0.0	0.0	2.8	2.3	2.8	7.0	4.7	4.7	4.7	4.7	4.7	18.6	37.2	20.9	0.0	81.4	50.5	46.5	53.5
93263	SHAFTER	45.7	36.5	1.8	1.8	0.6	1.1	66.3	76.7	10.5	9.8	8.9	9.2	8.4	27.9	17.8	6.4	1.2	67.0	27.0	52.0	48.0
93265	SPRINGVILLE	79.8	73.9	1.1	1.1	1.1	1.4	10.8	16.3	4.9	5.5	6.5	6.5	4.4	20.6	33.3	16.4	2.0	78.9	46.1	50.0	50.0
93266	STRATFORD	37.6	32.6	1.2	1.2	1.8	1.6	71.3	77.8	10.4	9.8	9.1	9.9	8.6	27.7	18.9	5.0	0.7	64.8	26.2	50.6	49.4
93267	STRATHMORE	51.5	43.6	0.3	0.3	1.3	1.5	58.7	68.6	9.7	9.5	8.7	9.0	7.7	25.7	20.8	7.9	1.0	66.5	28.3	50.2	49.8
93268	TAFT	83.4	72.6	1.4	3.8	1.7	2.4	16.9	28.7	7.2	6.5	6.4	7.7	8.2	30.5	22.2	9.5	1.6	76.1	33.8	55.4	44.6
93270	TERRA BELLA	42.2	35.8	0.5	0.5	2.6	2.6	67.6	75.5	10.6	10.0	8.5	8.5	8.7	27.5	18.5	6.8	0.8	65.6	27.0	52.7	47.3
93271	THREE RIVERS	89.9	85.0	0.2	0.2	0.8	1.1	7.4	11.4	3.8	5.0	5.9	5.8	3.5	16.9	39.1	17.4	2.7	81.6	49.7	49.5	50.5
93272	TIPTON	39.4	29.8	0.3	0.2	0.8	0.8	61.0	71.0	11.7	10.7	9.4	9.1	7.9	29.2	16.2	5.3	0.6	62.6	25.7	52.5	47.5
93274	TULARE	57.5	50.9	4.1	3.4	1.9	2.1	45.6	54.9	9.4	9.0	8.4	8.5	7.3	26.7	21.0	8.3	1.3	67.9	29.9	49.5	50.5
93276	TUPMAN	70.3	82.2	9.9	4.0	2.2	1.0	20.9	24.8	5.9	5.0	5.0	5.9	5.0	38.6	28.7	5.9	0.0	84.2	37.7	68.3	31.7
93277	VISALIA	80.4	73.2	1.9	3.1	2.8	3.6	25.6	34.8	7.2	6.9	6.8	7.0	6.5	26.8	25.3	11.2	2.4	75.1	36.4	48.1	51.9
93280	WASCO	35.2	28.5	9.8	8.8	0.8	0.8	66.5	75.6	8.2	7.5	6.6	7.7	11.0	38.4	15.7	4.3	0.6	73.5	28.9	63.9	36.1
93283	WELDON	89.4	85.8	0.4	0.5	0.4	0.6	6.4	10.6	4.0	4.0	4.3	5.4	5.5	13.4	33.6	26.5	3.3	84.5	54.6	48.8	51.2
93285	WOFFORD HEIGHTS	93.4	90.1	0.1	0.1	0.8	1.1	5.7	9.5	2.9	3.1	3.6	4.4	3.4	12.5	32.7	32.4	4.9	87.5	58.6	49.9	50.1
93286	WOODLAKE	56.7	52.3	0.4	0.4	0.9	1.0	68.5	75.2	9.3	9.1	8.7	8.6	7.0	26.2	21.8	8.2	1.1	67.5	29.9	51.1	48.9
93287	WOODY	83.5	76.0	0.8	1.3	1.6	1.9	7.9	12.3	4.5	5.2	5.8	5.8	3.9	18.2	39.6	14.9	1.9	80.5	49.2	55.8	44.2
93291	VISALIA	54.6	52.2	2.1	1.7	7.4	7.3	53.7	58.2	9.4	8.8	8.2	8.9	7.8	28.4	20.5	7.0	1.0	68.2	29.3	50.0	50.0
93292	VISALIA	72.6	66.5	1.4	1.4	3.6	3.9	34.0	42.9	8.0	7.8	7.6	7.6	6.8	27.5	24.8	8.6	1.3	71.8	33.5	49.3	50.7
93301	BAKERSFIELD	62.9	54.5	11.2	11.4	2.4	2.8	31.3	42.2	9.5	7.6	6.4	6.7	9.0	30.0	18.5	9.4	2.9	72.9	30.8	50.2	49.8
93304	BAKERSFIELD	48.6	40.4	13.3	12.7	4.6	4.8	42.3	53.7	10.1	9.2	8.2	8.4	8.1	26.5	20.0	8.0	1.4	67.3	28.7	48.6	51.4
93305	BAKERSFIELD	45.7	40.3	5.7	4.9	1.2	1.2	65.8	74.6	11.7	9.9	8.3	9.6	9.2	26.3	16.9	6.6	1.4	64.1	25.7	50.2	49.8
93306	BAKERSFIELD	64.5	57.5	3.6	3.6	2.5	2.9	42.2	52.3	8.5	7.8	7.6	8.1	7.7	25.5	23.3	9.7	1.8	71.1	32.0	49.1	50.9
93307	BAKERSFIELD	40.1	35.1	11.6	9.6	2.4	2.5	60.6	69.5	10.3	9.9	9.0	9.7	8.4	26.4	19.1	6.4	0.8	64.9	26.7	50.6	49.4
93308	BAKERSFIELD	87.2	81.6	1.1	1.3	1.4	2.0	12.2	19.0	7.3	7.0	6.8	7.5	7.6	27.1	25.2	10.0	1.4	74.4	34.9	50.1	49.9
93309	BAKERSFIELD	70.6	62.2	8.6	9.3	3.9	4.8	22.8	32.6	8.0	7.0	6.4	7.1	8.8	28.1	22.6	10.1	1.9	74.3	32.1	47.7	52.3
93311	BAKERSFIELD	74.2	63.9	4.1	4.4	9.6	11.2	16.2	26.5	7.4	7.2	7.3	7.5	6.2	29.2	27.2	7.0	1.0	73.3	34.6	48.7	51.3
93312	BAKERSFIELD	86.1	79.0	1.9	2.5	2.5	3.5	13.0	21.8	9.1	8.7	8.5	7.4	4.9	31.7	23.5	5.4	0.6	68.8	33.1	49.3	50.7
93313	BAKERSFIELD	64.4	53.8	7.8	7.7	6.1	7.1	27.6	40.2	9.7	8.7	8.1	7.8	6.5	31.6	21.3	5.4	0.7	68.9	30.1	48.9	51.1
93314	BAKERSFIELD	84.7	79.1	1.7	2.0	2.2	2.8	14.4	21.4	6.3	8.5	10.2	9.0	4.3	25.9	29.4	5.8	0.6	68.9	36.9	50.1	49.9
93401	SAN LUIS OBISPO	86.5	82.2	1.3	1.5	3.7	4.9	11.3	15.4	4.1	3.8	4.1	6.4	16.3	27.7	23.9	10.7	2.8	84.7	33.8	49.9	50.1
93402	LOS OSOS	88.3	84.3	0.6	0.7	4.6	6.0	9.0	12.3	4.0	4.2	4.7	5.9	5.5	22.7	34.7	15.3	3.1	83.5	47.2	48.1	51.9
93405	SAN LUIS OBISPO	80.5	70.6	7.2	5.7	5.5	7.6	16.7	21.6	2.2	2.1	2.4	15.1	25.4	25.9	16.3	8.4	2.0	91.5	26.6	59.7	40.3
93407	SAN LUIS OBISPO	81.9	76.1	1.0	1.1	9.7	12.7	10.5	14.2	0.2	0.1	0.1	59.4	35.3	4.1	0.5	0.2	0.0	99.1	19.2	59.2	40.8
93420	ARROYO GRANDE	88.8	84.7	0.5	0.6	2.8	3.7	11.2	15.6	5.2	5.5	6.0	6.1	5.2	20.8	32.1	16.2	3.0	79.4	45.8	48.2	51.8
93422	ATASCADERO	89.1	85.8	2.2	2.3	1.3	1.7	10.3	14.1	5.3	5.8	6.5	7.2	6.1	25.6	31.2	10.5	1.9	77.9	40.7	51.1	48.9
93426	BRADLEY	82.3	77.3	1.1	1.1	1.0	1.1	20.0	27.1	5.6	6.0	6.4	6.4	4.6	19.9	31.5	18.0	1.5	77.7	45.7	52.4	47.6
93427	BUELLTON	81.9	75.4	0.5	0.6	1.3	1.5	26.5	36.7	6.8	7.2	7.2	7.2	5.7	24.6	28.9	10.8	1.6	74.2	38.4	49.9	50.1
93428	CAMBRIA	91.1	87.9	0.4	0.4	1.3	1.7	14.0	19.3	3.1	3.6	4.2	4.0	2.9	14.4	39.1	25.4	3.2	86.6	55.9	48.1	51.9
93429	CASMALIA	100.0	100.0	0.0	0.0	0.0	0.0	0.0	0.0	0.0	0.0	0.0	0.0	0.0	100.0	0.0	0.0	0.0	100.0	27.5	100.0	0.0
93430	CAYUCOS	93.7	91.0	0.2	0.3	1.3	1.7	7.5	10.7	3.3	3.6	4.2	4.4	3.3	21.6	40.4	15.7	3.5	86.3	50.8	48.5	51.5
93432	CRESTON	90.1	86.8	0.4	0.5	1.0	1.2	11.9	16.2	5.3	5.8	7.0	7.1	4.6	21.9	35.0	12.2	1.1	77.2	43.9	51.0	49.0
93433	GROVER BEACH	79.8	74.2	1.0	1.2	4.1	5.1	22.4	29.2	7.0	6.5	6.2	6.5	7.6	28.6	26.1	9.9	1.7	76.3	35.8	48.4	51.6
93434	GUADALUPE	45.9	43.9	0.7	0.6	6.0	5.3	84.2	87.7	9.9	9.6	8.1	9.2	8.9	27.9	18.7	6.7	1.0	67.0	27.4	51.1	48.9
93436	LOMPOC	69.5	64.4	6.7	6.7	4.0	4.6	32.4	39.9	7.4	7.0	6.6	7.4	7.4	27.6	24.5	10.6	1.6	74.5	35.3	52.7	47.3
93437	LOMPOC	72.3	65.5	11.7	12.5	4.5	5.9	11.1	15.7	15.3	11.2	8.1	5.4	14.3	43.1	2.3	0.3	0.0	62.4	23.5	52.3	47.7
93441	LOS OLIVOS	91.2	87.6	0.6	0.6	0.4	0.5	13.6	19.4	4.7	5.1	6.3	7.6	6.7	19.1	35.5	13.7	1.4	77.6	45.3	50.1	49.9
93442	MORRO BAY	89.5	85.9	0.7	0.8	1.9	2.5	11.3	15.6	3.5	3.4	3.6	4.1	5.1	23.3	32.2	20.1	4.7	87.3	50.3	47.8	52.2
93444	NIPOMO	77.1	71.5	0.6	0.7	1.6	2.0	32.1	40.2	6.9	7.6	7.8	7.5	5.6	23.8	27.7	11.8	1.5	73.1	38.1	49.5	50.5
93445	OCEANO	69.0	63.9	1.1	1.1	1.9	2.1	44.5	52.0	8.3	7.9	7.3	7.6	7.3	26.7	24.0	9.6	1.3	71.9	32.8	49.1	50.9
93446	PASO ROBLES	80.5	75.5	2.5	2.8	1.6	2.0	21.9	27.8	6.6	6.5	6.7	9.0	6.6	24.0	27.5	11.2	1.9	74.7	37.6	50.2	49.8
93449	PISMO BEACH	91.3	88.0	0.6	0.7	3.0	4.1	6.9	9.8	4.0	3.7	3.9	4.0	5.0	23.8	30.4	21.2	4.0	85.9	49.1	48.0	52.0
93450	SAN ARDO	75.2	66.8	1.4	1.5	1.0	1.3	27.6	38.5	7.2	7.6	8.0	7.6	5.7	23.5	29.1	10.2	1.2	72.3	37.2	52.5	47.5
93451	SAN MIGUEL	75.7	69.2	1.3	1.5	0.7	0.9	24.2	31.5	6.8	7.1	7.3	7.9	6.5	26.8	28.5	8.4	0.8	73.6	35.9	51.4	48.6
93452	SAN SIMEON	80.1	75.2	0.2	0.4	0.9	1.1	37.2	46.3	4.7	4.9	5.4	5.4	2.8	26.9	32.1	15.7	2.2	81.5	45.0	51.7	48.3
	CALIFORNIA	59.5	54.5	6.7	6.2	11.3	12.5	32.4	38.3	7.5	7.1	6.9	7.5	7.4	28.5	24.2	9.3	1.6	74.1	34.3	49.9	50.1
	UNITED STATES	75.1	72.0	12.3	12.7	3.8	4.6	12.5	15.7	6.8	6.7	6.6	7.1	6.9	27.0	26.0	10.9	1.9	75.7	36.9	49.2	50.8

ZIP CODE #	POST OFFICE NAME	2009 Per Capita Income	2009 HH Income Base	2009 HOUSEHOLD INCOME DISTRIBUTION (%) Less than $25,000	$25,000 to $49,999	$50,000 to $99,999	$100,000 to $149,999	$150,000 or More	MEDIAN HOUSEHOLD INCOME 2009	2014	2009 National Centile	2009 State Centile	2009 Home Value Base	2009 HOME VALUE DISTRIBUTION (%) Less than $50,000	$50,000 to $89,999	$90,000 to $174,999	$175,000 to $399,999	$400,000 or More	2009 Median Home Value
93109	SANTA BARBARA	43195	4611	13.8	16.9	31.6	21.4	16.3	77308	80044	91	78	2798	0.3	0.3	1.0	3.3	95.1	796465
93110	SANTA BARBARA	38095	5962	13.0	22.7	34.9	15.0	14.4	66385	70112	84	68	3659	0.2	0.8	11.6	14.9	72.4	651407
93111	SANTA BARBARA	40270	6307	6.4	12.6	35.9	26.0	19.1	91376	93785	95	88	4725	0.1	0.1	0.3	4.5	95.0	724231
93117	GOLETA	24823	16092	25.7	20.2	30.9	15.1	8.1	55761	60484	72	53	6558	0.5	0.9	3.7	9.5	85.3	629339
93202	ARMONA	12766	562	25.4	38.3	32.0	2.3	2.0	42041	44708	39	26	396	3.3	3.5	81.3	10.4	1.5	135556
93203	ARVIN	8846	4300	41.9	34.2	20.5	2.3	1.0	30085	31205	8	7	2173	15.3	10.0	65.2	8.5	1.0	114054
93204	AVENAL	15249	2116	30.8	36.0	28.5	3.3	1.4	36248	38958	21	16	1044	9.3	14.2	70.1	6.4	0.0	119000
93205	BODFISH	15644	1050	48.2	34.6	15.2	1.2	0.8	25859	26581	4	3	779	13.7	40.8	34.3	10.9	0.3	85069
93206	BUTTONWILLOW	11952	569	32.3	37.1	26.2	2.8	1.6	34622	36354	17	13	293	13.3	16.0	52.2	16.4	2.0	120433
93207	CALIFORNIA HOT SPRIN	15424	324	32.1	34.9	25.3	4.0	3.7	34363	35814	16	13	232	11.6	12.5	31.0	32.8	12.1	157353
93210	COALINGA	17885	4429	24.2	29.4	37.3	7.1	2.0	45804	49197	51	34	2389	12.7	9.5	50.7	24.9	2.1	137449
93212	CORCORAN	16071	4141	34.0	34.8	26.8	3.2	1.3	35367	37729	19	14	2269	5.4	9.3	63.2	19.5	2.6	129976
93215	DELANO	11441	11279	38.0	33.3	23.8	3.0	1.8	32794	34833	13	10	6295	6.8	6.9	68.0	16.5	1.9	131480
93219	EARLIMART	8311	2802	44.7	35.5	16.5	1.8	1.6	27272	28109	5	4	1451	12.5	16.7	63.1	6.1	1.6	109390
93221	EXETER	18727	5047	24.9	30.0	32.7	8.1	4.3	45873	48188	51	34	3298	4.8	9.4	36.2	35.1	14.5	174000
93223	FARMERSVILLE	9946	2192	37.0	33.5	26.0	2.3	1.2	32638	35014	13	10	1312	2.9	13.2	69.1	12.0	2.8	121458
93224	FELLOWS	22171	222	24.3	27.5	37.4	8.6	2.3	48452	49226	58	40	136	22.8	22.1	39.0	14.7	1.5	97000
93225	FRAZIER PARK	22389	3161	22.3	32.2	33.4	8.2	3.9	46077	47894	52	35	2252	5.1	4.8	35.0	48.4	6.6	185142
93226	GLENNVILLE	22546	122	35.2	21.3	27.0	11.5	4.9	41311	43834	37	24	87	11.5	16.1	21.8	40.2	10.3	176786
93230	HANFORD	20357	21012	23.3	29.9	34.6	7.6	4.7	46994	49829	54	37	12537	4.3	4.8	38.2	46.4	6.2	179535
93234	HURON	9844	2218	38.9	40.0	18.0	1.9	1.2	32256	33179	12	9	629	11.6	14.8	63.3	9.4	1.0	126019
93235	IVANHOE	10244	1203	33.7	39.7	23.1	1.2	2.2	32831	34387	13	10	732	1.0	13.5	65.6	19.3	0.7	121233
93238	KERNVILLE	24484	522	40.8	27.0	22.4	7.3	2.5	31641	35000	11	8	359	32.9	6.4	21.4	27.6	11.7	120357
93239	KETTLEMAN CITY	8951	446	32.5	33.2	31.4	2.7	0.2	33259	34840	14	11	185	30.8	5.9	54.6	8.6	0.0	101172
93240	LAKE ISABELLA	17036	3133	45.4	32.0	18.7	2.0	1.9	27574	28920	5	4	2167	22.8	24.7	34.4	17.0	1.0	93185
93241	LAMONT	8613	3785	40.6	37.5	18.4	2.1	1.4	30418	31423	9	7	1845	13.7	18.9	60.1	7.2	0.2	107470
93242	LATON	14504	962	28.5	39.2	25.3	4.0	3.1	39667	41482	32	21	531	5.5	8.9	48.4	29.2	8.1	140920
93243	LEBEC	16889	294	21.8	35.4	37.4	5.1	0.3	45200	46886	49	33	202	15.3	7.4	24.8	38.6	13.9	181944
93244	LEMON COVE	29885	58	17.2	20.7	37.9	13.8	10.3	63212	64708	81	63	44	2.3	2.3	6.8	61.4	27.3	309091
93245	LEMOORE	18999	11448	19.5	32.1	34.6	9.9	3.9	48341	50984	57	39	5554	4.7	2.4	32.3	54.0	6.5	189919
93247	LINDSAY	11836	4542	35.3	32.7	25.4	4.4	2.2	33896	35891	15	12	2708	8.0	7.9	56.7	24.9	2.6	135739
93249	LOST HILLS	9077	618	29.4	38.7	26.4	3.7	1.8	37265	39012	24	17	204	40.7	12.7	30.9	12.3	3.4	78889
93250	MC FARLAND	10558	2871	40.7	34.3	21.4	2.5	1.1	30415	31648	9	7	1499	4.7	12.0	73.4	6.8	3.1	115903
93251	MC KITTRICK	21821	152	23.7	27.0	38.8	7.9	2.6	49532	51046	60	41	86	17.4	22.1	41.9	17.4	1.2	103125
93252	MARICOPA	17417	765	31.6	32.8	27.8	5.0	2.7	38634	41136	29	19	502	29.7	26.9	23.1	10.6	9.8	76053
93254	NEW CUYAMA	21328	269	28.3	30.9	29.4	6.7	4.8	43980	46637	45	30	156	2.6	6.4	42.3	15.4	33.3	172059
93255	ONYX	15246	190	57.9	18.9	21.1	1.6	0.5	22164	22919	2	2	140	32.9	33.6	15.7	14.3	3.6	60000
93256	PIXLEY	9824	1155	44.8	27.6	22.5	2.6	2.5	30385	31648	9	7	633	8.5	13.0	60.5	9.8	8.2	123524
93257	PORTERVILLE	14442	21864	31.5	29.9	31.5	4.9	2.3	38571	42291	28	19	12599	7.1	5.8	55.9	27.7	3.5	143007
93260	POSEY	16706	117	38.5	33.3	22.2	4.3	1.7	31763	33459	11	8	95	9.5	22.1	32.6	28.4	7.4	135227
93262	SEQUOIA NATIONAL PAR	31692	22	18.2	31.8	36.4	9.1	4.5	50000	54473	61	43	11	0.0	0.0	9.1	45.5	45.5	350000
93263	SHAFTER	12052	4890	34.2	35.3	25.8	3.4	1.4	34566	36360	17	13	2741	13.5	12.0	57.6	15.1	1.8	116756
93265	SPRINGVILLE	24367	2159	28.3	24.5	33.5	7.9	5.8	47170	50404	55	37	1516	8.0	5.2	20.2	46.4	20.2	243850
93266	STRATFORD	10480	483	29.6	36.4	29.8	3.1	1.0	34295	37014	16	12	334	1.8	15.9	71.0	8.4	3.0	122603
93267	STRATHMORE	10859	1619	32.6	35.9	26.3	3.5	1.7	35016	36559	18	14	976	9.7	14.7	39.2	29.2	7.2	129274
93268	TAFT	16565	5506	34.7	30.0	29.0	4.9	1.3	37910	40145	26	18	3171	14.7	27.8	44.2	12.8	0.4	99235
93270	TERRA BELLA	11384	1818	31.8	34.7	28.2	3.2	2.1	35737	37479	20	15	1108	11.1	9.6	47.5	26.2	5.7	137788
93271	THREE RIVERS	29525	1143	23.4	22.0	37.9	8.6	8.0	55737	60293	72	53	790	5.8	3.9	8.2	53.3	28.7	289669
93272	TIPTON	12040	872	33.1	36.6	24.2	3.2	2.9	33265	35776	14	11	429	4.4	9.6	63.2	13.5	9.3	127639
93274	TULARE	15276	20606	27.5	31.1	33.2	5.7	2.4	41660	45210	38	25	12439	5.2	6.6	51.0	29.7	7.5	151244
93276	TUPMAN	20498	32	25.0	28.1	40.6	6.3	0.0	47356	48176	55	38	18	16.7	22.2	38.9	22.2	0.0	112500
93277	VISALIA	24537	18514	20.2	24.1	38.6	10.2	6.8	55519	59007	72	52	11556	7.6	2.7	32.3	51.0	6.3	189540
93280	WASCO	14109	5152	33.7	33.8	27.9	3.1	1.5	34876	37448	17	13	2786	8.4	8.4	66.8	15.0	1.3	124093
93283	WELDON	16104	1119	53.4	27.1	15.7	1.5	2.2	23477	24073	2	2	860	21.2	39.9	27.7	7.9	3.4	76098
93285	WOFFORD HEIGHTS	20820	2011	39.5	33.2	21.0	4.0	2.3	30507	31598	9	7	1567	15.6	21.6	38.6	18.3	5.9	107475
93286	WOODLAKE	12816	2955	36.9	31.7	25.1	3.3	3.0	32665	34912	13	10	1629	2.1	10.9	53.7	23.0	10.4	141155
93287	WOODY	22525	63	36.5	20.6	27.0	11.1	4.8	40761	43640	35	23	45	11.1	17.8	22.2	40.0	8.9	170833
93291	VISALIA	17970	13634	24.9	29.7	31.6	7.5	6.2	45519	48994	50	34	8390	3.6	4.6	48.8	29.3	13.8	152351
93292	VISALIA	21032	12677	19.8	24.5	40.6	8.8	6.3	56313	60550	73	54	8615	2.4	3.0	36.8	47.2	10.5	193913
93301	BAKERSFIELD	18811	5326	43.2	29.0	20.6	4.1	3.1	30392	31110	9	7	1720	18.8	12.1	31.8	32.3	5.0	143240
93304	BAKERSFIELD	13162	16115	37.5	32.3	26.3	3.1	0.8	34162	36025	16	12	8144	7.6	9.6	73.4	8.6	0.8	119591
93305	BAKERSFIELD	11306	10871	43.8	31.8	20.4	2.9	1.1	28568	29380	6	5	4811	3.2	16.8	65.1	13.1	1.9	118393
93306	BAKERSFIELD	20296	20513	23.0	28.4	33.4	10.0	5.1	48245	51165	57	39	13246	5.4	5.9	51.6	30.6	6.5	146875
93307	BAKERSFIELD	10887	20120	39.0	31.5	25.0	3.6	0.8	32641	34677	13	10	11786	9.3	19.5	57.8	12.1	1.3	114405
93308	BAKERSFIELD	20134	19079	30.4	27.8	29.4	8.8	3.6	40945	43735	36	23	11031	10.9	8.0	39.4	37.0	4.7	148319
93309	BAKERSFIELD	22579	23317	25.6	27.1	35.1	7.6	4.6	47322	49223	55	37	11311	3.1	4.4	46.7	40.2	5.6	166473
93311	BAKERSFIELD	29344	11785	11.0	16.6	44.3	15.7	12.4	72281	72815	88	73	8664	0.7	1.8	26.6	54.5	16.5	213937
93312	BAKERSFIELD	28329	18415	7.1	14.0	47.9	21.4	9.7	77497	79571	91	78	15637	1.5	1.4	33.1	56.6	7.3	197202
93313	BAKERSFIELD	20094	10614	14.9	22.0	44.5	14.4	4.1	62686	64618	81	63	8659	2.9	4.8	47.6	42.7	2.1	166552
93314	BAKERSFIELD	31028	6221	8.8	14.4	36.7	21.1	19.0	83110	85444	93	82	5431	2.4	4.3	21.6	53.5	18.2	245128
93401	SAN LUIS OBISPO	31631	12519	25.9	24.9	30.8	10.3	8.0	48966	51829	59	40	5888	2.8	3.4	6.9	19.7	67.1	509016
93402	LOS OSOS	31700	6262	16.6	24.2	40.0	12.1	7.1	60415	63107	78	59	4243	0.4	1.0	7.3	48.6	42.7	372529
93405	SAN LUIS OBISPO	24871	10165	35.1	22.4	26.5	8.6	7.5	41467	44322	38	25	4150	1.3	1.3	3.9	23.9	69.7	496568
93407	SAN LUIS OBISPO	16624	12	83.3	16.7	0.0	0.0	0.0	15000	16237	1	1	0	0.0	0.0	0.0	0.0	0.0	0
93420	ARROYO GRANDE	33670	11620	15.2	22.9	38.6	13.5	9.8	63738	65566	82	64	8185	2.2	2.1	3.0	30.9	61.8	473891
93422	ATASCADERO	27636	11967	15.6	22.3	44.6	11.8	5.7	62406	64637	80	62	7814	1.9	1.3	3.8	50.0	43.0	367673
93426	BRADLEY	29768	631	22.7	23.1	38.7	8.4	7.1	53960	57812	70	50	428	4.4	3.3	15.2	40.2	36.9	339785
93427	BUELLTON	28209	2378	16.0	23.7	34.3	18.7	7.3	63340	66871	82	64	1617	8.8	7.7	9.7	11.2	62.5	452461
93428	CAMBRIA	37105	3199	15.2	22.8	42.6	8.9	10.5	59984	62466	77	58	2273	0.6	0.9	1.1	19.7	77.7	570274
93429	CASMALIA	0	0	0.0	0.0	0.0	0.0	0.0	0	0	0	0	0	0.0	0.0	0.0	0.0	0.0	0
93430	CAYUCOS	32935	1575	19.4	28.9	38.2	8.1	5.3	51199	53651	64	44	871	3.1	0.5	1.4	19.3	75.8	549061
93432	CRESTON	27977	500	15.0	24.8	46.0	7.4	6.8	60000	61649	77	58	343	2.0	0.9	4.7	35.6	56.9	452222
93433	GROVER BEACH	24129	5262	20.8	29.8	38.6	7.3	3.6	49612	51548	60	42	2613	3.3	0.7	2.3	65.0	28.7	315168
93434	GUADALUPE	14358	1659	28.3	28.9	31.5	7.8	3.4	41057	45922	36	24	938	0.2	0.2	29.7	67.5	2.3	192816
93436	LOMPOC	23551	18124	18.9	26.3	36.1	14.0	4.6	55454	60186	72	52	10364	3.8	1.3	8.9	62.8	23.2	254559
93437	LOMPOC	18976	1640	12.1	34.7	40.1	10.8	2.3	52100	54513	66	46	141	65.2	12.8	5.7	14.2	2.1	34219
93441	LOS OLIVOS	43212	414	11.1	17.6	28.7	20.8	21.7	83753	85099	93	83	289	2.4	0.0	1.4	4.5	91.7	699803
93442	MORRO BAY	27958	5624	27.8	26.0	36.1	6.4	3.8	45769	48801	51	34	3080	5.9	1.8	5.3	31.6	55.5	428499
93444	NIPOMO	25954	6063	13.3	23.1	42.0	14.0	7.6	63543	65810	82	64	4547	0.7	0.5	5.4	47.6	45.9	373562
93445	OCEANO	19697	2701	24.7	28.5	36.7	7.3	2.9	46899	49385	54	37	1415	7.0	5.7	14.5	56.0	16.8	254051
93446	PASO ROBLES	25598	16722	19.1	25.7	40.9	8.8	5.5	54909	58681	71	52	11226	1.2	0.9	4.4	61.6	32.0	314945
93449	PISMO BEACH	41806	4869	19.2	22.9	32.2	14.0	11.8	61912	64204	80	61	2969	5.9	3.2	6.1	23.5	61.4	475222
93450	SAN ARDO	17955	290	26.2	29.0	34.8	7.2	2.8	44167	47553	46	31	167	8.4	6.0	29.3	30.5	25.7	198864
93451	SAN MIGUEL	21878	707	18.8	31.3	38.5	7.4	4.1	49929	51160	61	42	441	1.6	1.6	10.9	63.5	22.4	278797
93452	SAN SIMEON	32824	249	7.6	31.3	52.6	4.4	4.0	55782	58587	72	53	133	14.3	9.8	6.0	33.1	36.8	252273
	CALIFORNIA	28199		18.5	22.2	33.9	14.0	11.5	61614	64088				3.3	2.6	13.6	41.0	39.5	321752
	UNITED STATES	27277		20.9	24.4	35.3	11.7	7.6	54719	56938				9.3	13.1	31.6	32.6	13.5	162279

ZIP CODE #	POST OFFICE NAME	FINANCIAL SERVICES: Auto Loan	Home Loan	Investments	Retirement Plans	THE HOME: Home Improvements: Home Repair	Lawn & Garden	Furnishings: Computers & Hardware-Personal	Major Appliances	TV, Radio, Sound Equipment	Furniture	ENTERTAINMENT: Dine out/ Carry out	Sports Equipment	Fees & Tickets	Toys & Games	Travel	Cable TV	PERSONAL: Apparel & Services	Auto Repairs	Health Insurance	Pets & Supplies
93109	SANTA BARBARA	127	149	173	154	163	132	152	144	134	157	135	116	160	131	161	125	100	143	125	162
93110	SANTA BARBARA	118	139	157	141	150	130	136	134	128	142	128	103	148	122	148	124	93	133	129	152
93111	SANTA BARBARA	135	175	203	177	191	159	159	161	146	169	146	123	182	142	180	139	109	155	146	179
93117	GOLETA	95	86	93	90	89	81	119	92	103	105	105	79	104	102	102	97	76	102	86	109
93202	ARMONA	71	71	61	63	70	58	71	69	66	76	68	52	67	68	68	62	48	69	60	76
93203	ARVIN	55	51	42	45	51	39	57	53	52	60	55	42	53	53	54	47	40	56	43	56
93204	AVENAL	67	60	51	55	59	49	68	62	63	71	67	49	62	65	63	59	48	67	54	68
93205	BODFISH	51	49	62	45	54	58	46	55	49	50	48	36	46	45	51	52	32	53	61	63
93206	BUTTONWILLOW	66	66	56	58	65	54	65	64	61	71	63	48	62	63	63	58	44	64	56	71
93207	CALIFORNIA HOT SPRIN	82	66	89	63	69	81	69	80	69	65	70	62	58	68	70	72	47	76	79	94
93210	COALINGA	78	80	67	75	77	67	78	75	74	82	76	59	77	77	76	70	53	76	67	85
93212	CORCORAN	62	61	52	54	60	49	62	60	57	67	60	46	58	59	60	54	42	61	52	66
93215	DELANO	62	58	50	53	57	48	63	59	59	66	62	46	59	61	60	55	44	62	51	65
93219	EARLIMART	57	47	37	41	46	41	51	51	52	56	54	36	46	53	47	51	38	53	46	55
93221	EXETER	79	86	81	84	85	80	83	83	80	83	81	64	85	81	85	79	58	82	79	95
93223	FARMERSVILLE	63	56	47	50	55	48	58	58	57	63	59	41	53	59	54	56	42	59	52	63
93224	FELLOWS	90	82	75	81	81	87	78	85	81	79	81	62	74	84	76	84	55	81	86	100
93225	FRAZIER PARK	92	80	108	79	85	95	79	93	82	76	81	69	73	80	83	85	55	88	92	108
93226	GLENNVILLE	92	74	119	73	81	97	74	94	77	69	76	69	64	73	80	82	51	87	93	109
93230	HANFORD	91	87	83	84	85	84	88	88	86	89	87	68	84	88	86	86	61	88	85	102
93234	HURON	57	48	40	45	47	37	60	53	55	62	59	43	54	57	55	50	43	59	43	57
93235	IVANHOE	61	60	51	53	59	48	62	60	57	66	59	46	58	58	60	53	42	61	50	64
93238	KERNVILLE	69	68	89	64	77	81	64	75	68	70	66	49	65	61	71	71	45	72	84	86
93239	KETTLEMAN CITY	55	52	42	46	52	39	59	54	53	62	56	44	55	54	56	47	41	58	43	56
93240	LAKE ISABELLA	55	52	67	48	58	63	50	59	53	54	51	39	49	48	55	56	35	57	66	67
93241	LAMONT	54	51	41	45	50	38	56	52	51	59	54	42	52	52	54	46	40	55	42	55
93242	LATON	79	69	76	63	69	72	71	76	69	70	70	59	62	70	69	69	48	74	72	88
93243	LEBEC	81	72	76	70	72	79	69	77	72	70	72	56	64	73	68	74	48	73	76	90
93244	LEMON COVE	106	118	135	120	123	121	104	115	102	108	102	85	112	100	116	102	72	108	110	132
93245	LEMOORE	93	84	73	83	80	75	90	83	87	91	89	68	85	92	84	84	62	87	78	97
93247	LINDSAY	68	63	59	57	62	58	64	66	62	66	64	50	59	63	62	61	45	66	60	73
93249	LOST HILLS	66	64	52	57	63	47	72	66	63	75	68	54	67	65	69	56	50	70	52	68
93250	MC FARLAND	60	54	44	47	53	44	58	56	55	62	58	42	54	56	55	52	42	59	48	60
93251	MC KITTRICK	91	83	74	81	82	85	79	83	82	82	82	61	75	85	75	84	56	81	84	99
93252	MARICOPA	88	64	93	63	67	91	67	84	72	60	71	64	53	72	67	79	47	77	87	100
93254	NEW CUYAMA	106	73	116	73	76	112	81	101	84	66	83	83	59	82	80	92	54	94	106	124
93255	ONYX	47	45	58	42	50	54	43	51	45	47	44	33	43	42	47	48	30	49	56	58
93256	PIXLEY	65	55	42	47	53	49	55	58	57	61	59	38	49	58	51	58	41	58	54	63
93257	PORTERVILLE	71	67	61	64	66	62	70	69	68	72	70	53	66	70	67	67	49	70	65	78
93260	POSEY	69	54	88	54	60	73	55	70	57	51	57	51	47	55	59	61	38	64	69	81
93262	SEQUOIA NATIONAL PAR	103	83	134	81	91	109	83	105	87	78	86	77	72	82	90	92	57	97	104	122
93263	SHAFTER	64	62	53	56	61	54	62	62	60	66	61	45	59	61	60	58	43	62	56	68
93265	SPRINGVILLE	90	87	110	88	92	98	82	94	83	82	83	69	81	81	88	85	57	89	93	109
93266	STRATFORD	71	69	61	61	68	59	68	68	65	73	66	51	64	66	66	62	47	68	60	76
93267	STRATHMORE	68	59	57	54	58	59	60	64	60	61	61	48	54	61	58	61	43	64	61	73
93268	TAFT	65	61	58	61	59	66	64	64	65	60	65	49	61	66	61	68	45	64	67	76
93270	TERRA BELLA	67	62	59	56	62	55	66	66	61	68	64	52	60	63	64	58	45	67	57	72
93271	THREE RIVERS	99	99	135	99	110	116	91	107	94	96	93	73	94	87	102	98	64	101	113	123
93272	TIPTON	69	69	59	61	67	56	68	67	64	74	66	50	65	66	66	60	46	67	58	73
93274	TULARE	77	72	71	68	71	70	74	75	72	75	73	57	68	73	72	71	51	75	71	86
93276	TUPMAN	87	82	72	77	80	79	78	81	79	82	79	59	74	82	75	79	55	79	79	95
93277	VISALIA	94	98	93	99	97	94	96	94	95	98	96	73	99	95	97	94	67	95	94	110
93280	WASCO	66	65	55	57	64	52	67	64	61	71	64	49	63	63	64	57	46	66	55	70
93283	WELDON	55	53	67	48	58	63	50	59	53	54	52	39	49	48	55	56	35	57	66	67
93285	WOFFORD HEIGHTS	62	60	78	57	68	72	57	67	60	62	58	43	58	55	63	63	39	64	74	76
93286	WOODLAKE	72	63	58	58	62	63	63	68	65	66	66	48	58	66	61	65	46	67	65	76
93287	WOODY	92	74	119	72	81	97	74	94	77	69	76	68	64	73	80	82	51	86	92	108
93291	VISALIA	88	90	83	87	89	79	89	87	85	93	87	67	89	87	88	81	62	87	79	98
93292	VISALIA	92	98	91	96	96	89	93	92	90	97	91	71	96	92	94	87	64	91	87	106
93301	BAKERSFIELD	64	53	52	54	52	54	66	59	66	63	67	47	60	66	60	67	47	65	61	71
93304	BAKERSFIELD	59	56	49	52	54	49	60	56	57	61	59	43	56	59	56	56	41	58	52	64
93305	BAKERSFIELD	53	46	40	45	44	41	54	49	53	54	56	39	51	55	50	52	40	54	47	56
93306	BAKERSFIELD	86	92	84	89	91	84	89	88	86	92	87	67	91	87	90	84	62	88	84	100
93307	BAKERSFIELD	62	57	48	51	56	49	59	58	57	63	58	42	54	58	55	55	41	59	52	64
93308	BAKERSFIELD	76	75	71	75	73	75	78	75	78	76	78	58	76	78	75	79	55	77	78	89
93309	BAKERSFIELD	84	79	75	80	78	75	87	80	85	88	86	63	85	86	83	84	61	85	80	94
93311	BAKERSFIELD	135	139	135	139	136	132	130	132	125	133	127	106	131	130	131	122	89	128	123	154
93312	BAKERSFIELD	131	151	132	150	145	129	130	132	122	140	125	106	140	130	135	116	89	124	115	150
93313	BAKERSFIELD	106	111	93	106	104	94	101	101	96	108	98	80	101	103	99	92	68	97	89	115
93314	BAKERSFIELD	137	174	171	178	176	154	145	150	136	156	138	118	169	140	161	130	102	141	132	170
93401	SAN LUIS OBISPO	94	84	89	89	87	83	109	90	100	100	101	75	98	99	97	97	72	99	89	108
93402	LOS OSOS	95	112	132	108	121	112	102	109	99	105	99	78	112	95	115	100	71	105	109	122
93405	SAN LUIS OBISPO	84	65	70	70	66	65	103	75	90	88	91	66	83	88	81	85	65	87	73	92
93407	SAN LUIS OBISPO	29	12	12	15	11	14	40	20	32	27	33	21	24	31	22	29	23	28	20	27
93420	ARROYO GRANDE	111	120	133	120	126	123	113	120	111	115	111	88	119	109	121	112	78	116	119	137
93422	ATASCADERO	97	105	102	106	105	99	101	99	98	103	99	76	105	99	103	97	70	99	97	116
93426	BRADLEY	110	102	114	99	106	113	96	108	100	100	99	76	93	99	98	104	68	103	111	126
93427	BUELLTON	115	113	111	111	112	114	108	113	108	109	108	85	105	110	108	109	75	110	112	132
93428	CAMBRIA	109	114	155	113	130	135	103	122	108	115	106	77	112	98	118	114	73	116	135	138
93429	CASMALIA	0	0	0	0	0	0	0	0	0	0	0	0	0	0	0	0	0	0	0	0
93430	CAYUCOS	112	89	143	87	97	119	90	114	94	83	92	84	77	89	96	100	61	105	113	132
93432	CRESTON	108	98	124	98	101	115	95	109	96	90	96	84	89	95	100	100	65	103	109	129
93433	GROVER BEACH	83	81	77	82	80	78	88	82	86	86	87	65	86	86	85	85	61	85	82	97
93434	GUADALUPE	77	86	76	76	88	62	86	83	73	92	77	66	84	74	87	64	56	82	63	86
93436	LOMPOC	89	94	95	92	95	87	95	92	92	95	94	71	97	92	96	91	67	94	88	105
93437	LOMPOC	106	55	42	64	50	47	100	69	94	93	99	69	76	113	72	87	69	88	63	85
93441	LOS OLIVOS	145	179	215	183	198	162	168	170	149	179	149	134	185	144	189	139	110	162	147	190
93442	MORRO BAY	77	73	86	74	78	83	76	80	79	77	78	57	75	75	78	82	54	80	88	93
93444	NIPOMO	104	119	130	111	125	109	109	116	101	112	103	86	113	101	118	99	74	110	104	127
93445	OCEANO	80	78	80	73	80	76	81	82	79	83	80	60	78	78	80	79	56	82	81	93
93446	PASO ROBLES	97	95	101	93	97	97	95	99	94	94	95	75	93	94	96	95	66	97	97	114
93449	PISMO BEACH	101	119	139	119	131	112	117	117	108	124	108	89	127	103	129	103	78	115	112	131
93450	SAN ARDO	86	79	70	76	77	81	74	79	77	78	77	57	70	80	71	79	53	76	79	94
93451	SAN MIGUEL	90	93	81	90	91	87	88	90	85	91	87	68	87	88	88	84	60	87	85	103
93452	SAN SIMEON	120	92	149	91	100	126	95	120	99	86	98	90	79	95	100	106	65	111	120	141
	CALIFORNIA	112	119	122	118	122	107	121	116	114	124	116	92	124	114	124	110	84	118	107	132
	UNITED STATES	100	100	100	100	100	100	100	100	100	100	100	100	100	100	100	100	100	100	100	100

ZIP CODE #	POST OFFICE NAME	COUNTY FIPS CODE	POPULATION 2000	POPULATION 2009	POPULATION 2014	2000-2009 ANNUAL RATE % Rate	2000-2009 ANNUAL RATE State Centile	HOUSEHOLDS 2000	HOUSEHOLDS 2009	HOUSEHOLDS 2014	HOUSEHOLDS % Annual Rate 2000-2009	HOUSEHOLDS 2009 Average HH Size	FAMILIES 2000	FAMILIES 2009	FAMILIES % Annual Rate 2000-2009
93453	SANTA MARGARITA	079	2373	2944	3164	2.4	87	942	1228	1330	2.9	2.37	637	826	2.8
93454	SANTA MARIA	083	30227	32576	33441	0.8	54	10262	11199	11473	0.9	2.75	7131	7819	1.0
93455	SANTA MARIA	083	37769	40325	41595	0.7	50	13341	14793	15335	1.1	2.70	10331	11399	1.1
93458	SANTA MARIA	083	44028	51385	53724	1.7	78	10665	12063	12568	1.3	4.23	8603	9654	1.3
93460	SANTA YNEZ	083	5766	6036	6165	0.5	39	2125	2286	2340	0.8	2.62	1653	1773	0.8
93461	SHANDON	079	1272	1446	1519	1.4	72	376	441	466	1.7	3.26	315	368	1.7
93463	SOLVANG	083	8060	8178	8245	0.2	18	3184	3308	3339	0.4	2.41	2177	2255	0.4
93465	TEMPLETON	079	7930	9492	10099	2.0	83	2736	3380	3623	2.3	2.79	2126	2613	2.3
93501	MOJAVE	029	4851	5641	6148	1.6	77	1813	2064	2241	1.4	2.72	1212	1355	1.2
93505	CALIFORNIA CITY	029	8269	14881	16845	6.6	97	3020	4243	4933	3.7	2.77	2221	3074	3.6
93510	ACTON	037	7364	8519	9069	1.6	77	2390	2705	2865	1.3	3.07	1878	2138	1.4
93512	BENTON	051	190	196	198	0.3	23	75	82	83	1.0	2.39	54	60	1.1
93513	BIG PINE	027	1793	1806	1790	0.1	13	717	727	720	0.1	2.43	511	517	0.1
93514	BISHOP	051	14454	14650	14549	0.1	13	6091	6235	6207	0.3	2.34	4024	4131	0.3
93516	BORON	029	2025	2163	2275	0.7	50	801	840	878	0.5	2.58	536	551	0.3
93517	BRIDGEPORT	051	379	376	376	-0.1	5	154	166	168	0.8	2.19	103	112	0.9
93518	CALIENTE	029	976	1058	1124	0.9	58	412	438	464	0.7	2.40	287	300	0.5
93519	CANTIL	029	134	155	169	1.6	77	80	91	99	1.4	1.70	43	48	1.2
93523	EDWARDS	029	7872	7087	6950	-1.1	0	2351	2047	2001	-1.5	3.15	2045	1754	-1.6
93524	EDWARDS	029	25	26	27	0.4	30	14	15	16	0.7	1.73	10	11	1.0
93526	INDEPENDENCE	027	779	757	740	-0.3	3	368	360	353	-0.2	2.10	216	210	-0.3
93527	INYOKERN	029	2153	2454	2652	1.4	72	901	1008	1083	1.2	2.43	605	665	1.0
93528	JOHANNESBURG	029	189	218	239	1.6	77	92	104	113	1.3	2.10	49	55	1.3
93529	JUNE LAKE	051	611	621	617	0.2	18	263	284	284	0.8	2.19	169	184	0.9
93531	KEENE	029	277	407	459	4.2	94	104	150	168	4.0	2.71	83	120	4.1
93532	LAKE HUGHES	037	2827	2993	3102	0.6	45	995	1037	1073	0.4	2.66	698	727	0.4
93534	LANCASTER	037	34734	40570	43296	1.7	78	12758	14532	15415	1.4	2.68	7950	9168	1.6
93535	LANCASTER	037	57531	71337	77441	2.4	87	18026	21745	23469	2.0	3.26	13798	16589	2.0
93536	LANCASTER	037	49871	73389	82885	4.3	94	15486	22013	24847	3.9	3.10	11763	16776	3.9
93541	LEE VINING	051	496	520	521	0.5	39	191	208	210	0.9	2.50	130	142	1.0
93543	LITTLEROCK	037	11516	12890	13591	1.2	68	3415	3739	3919	1.0	3.42	2667	2923	1.0
93544	LLANO	037	1256	1380	1446	1.0	62	524	567	592	0.9	2.27	354	383	0.9
93545	LONE PINE	027	2247	2210	2166	-0.2	4	960	943	926	-0.2	2.31	601	590	-0.2
93546	MAMMOTH LAKES	051	7129	7654	7863	0.8	54	2831	3224	3341	1.4	2.33	1527	1750	1.5
93550	PALMDALE	037	65960	73606	77126	1.2	68	19398	21021	21887	0.9	3.50	15513	16819	0.9
93551	PALMDALE	037	34773	51410	59031	4.3	94	10940	15902	18166	4.1	3.23	9066	13171	4.1
93552	PALMDALE	037	26530	36805	41208	3.6	93	7390	9720	10797	3.0	3.78	6238	8239	3.1
93553	PEARBLOSSOM	037	1386	1524	1602	1.0	62	536	578	603	0.8	2.63	361	389	0.8
93554	RANDSBURG	029	51	59	64	1.6	77	28	32	34	1.5	1.84	15	17	1.4
93555	RIDGECREST	071	30101	32333	33954	0.8	54	11919	12530	13096	0.5	2.55	8185	8466	0.4
93560	ROSAMOND	029	14923	18315	20392	2.2	85	5205	6237	6904	2.0	2.94	3763	4436	1.8
93561	TEHACHAPI	029	27051	36064	40663	3.2	91	8335	11062	12646	3.1	2.78	6363	8367	3.0
93562	TRONA	071	1988	2049	2096	0.3	23	785	784	795	0.0	2.61	524	519	-0.1
93563	VALYERMO	037	762	811	835	0.7	50	200	209	215	0.5	3.25	123	129	0.5
93591	PALMDALE	037	6616	6956	7155	0.5	39	1877	1933	1978	0.3	3.59	1520	1565	0.3
93601	AHWAHNEE	039	2066	2480	2793	2.0	83	758	908	1019	2.0	2.71	587	702	2.0
93602	AUBERRY	019	3482	3916	4160	1.3	70	1264	1416	1500	1.2	2.67	962	1065	1.1
93604	BASS LAKE	039	436	494	523	1.4	72	214	240	253	1.2	2.06	148	166	1.2
93608	CANTUA CREEK	019	1927	2141	2260	1.1	64	413	456	481	1.1	4.41	359	394	1.0
93609	CARUTHERS	019	5378	5713	5918	0.7	50	1433	1490	1534	0.4	3.79	1212	1253	0.4
93610	CHOWCHILLA	039	19507	24823	27227	2.6	89	4091	5439	6122	3.1	3.18	3131	4184	3.2
93611	CLOVIS	019	34916	47074	52900	3.3	92	11152	14817	16560	3.1	3.15	9333	12383	3.1
93612	CLOVIS	019	34023	37193	39018	1.0	62	13413	14461	15065	0.8	2.56	8468	9051	0.7
93614	COARSEGOLD	039	9697	12426	13975	2.7	90	3739	4750	5312	2.6	2.61	2943	3735	2.6
93615	CUTLER	107	5381	5905	6222	1.0	62	1158	1233	1299	0.7	4.78	1035	1101	0.7
93616	DEL REY	019	1780	1931	2023	0.9	58	477	514	537	0.8	3.69	405	434	0.8
93618	DINUBA	107	24414	28468	31182	1.7	78	6535	7346	7986	1.3	3.84	5431	6108	1.3
93619	CLOVIS	019	12313	31029	38447	10.5	98	4097	9633	11837	9.7	3.22	3497	8221	9.7
93620	DOS PALOS	047	9666	10518	10926	0.9	58	2900	3155	3274	0.9	3.32	2320	2510	0.9
93621	DUNLAP	019	309	342	359	1.1	64	108	119	124	1.1	2.87	81	89	1.0
93622	FIREBAUGH	019	9591	11191	12055	1.7	78	2385	2730	2923	1.5	4.06	2056	2344	1.4
93623	FISH CAMP	043	262	271	273	0.4	30	119	132	136	1.1	1.53	63	70	1.1
93625	FOWLER	019	5643	6895	7633	2.2	85	1719	2104	2328	2.2	3.22	1343	1634	2.1
93626	FRIANT	039	1205	1443	1572	2.0	83	498	592	641	1.9	2.43	355	421	1.9
93627	HELM	019	63	72	78	1.5	75	14	16	17	1.5	4.31	12	14	1.7
93630	KERMAN	019	14601	18533	20582	2.6	89	4081	5128	5669	2.5	3.60	3361	4200	2.4
93631	KINGSBURG	107	14469	16548	17706	1.5	75	4848	5493	5855	1.4	2.99	3802	4266	1.3
93633	KINGS CANYON NATIONA	019	191	205	215	0.8	54	68	73	77	0.8	2.78	45	48	0.7
93635	LOS BANOS	047	29081	40685	45919	3.7	93	8704	11779	13189	3.3	3.43	7002	9506	3.4
93636	MADERA	039	10179	11981	12959	1.8	80	3316	3864	4152	1.7	3.05	2855	3328	1.7
93637	MADERA	039	28265	36737	41050	2.9	91	8865	11322	12587	2.7	3.22	6916	8840	2.7
93638	MADERA	039	39017	48485	52784	2.4	87	9491	11395	12324	2.0	4.20	7916	9505	2.0
93640	MENDOTA	019	9130	12709	14743	3.6	93	2082	2739	3153	3.0	4.60	1756	2309	3.0
93641	MIRAMONTE	019	594	632	655	0.7	50	232	242	249	0.5	2.52	150	155	0.4
93643	NORTH FORK	039	2708	3117	3292	1.5	75	1060	1217	1280	1.5	2.56	794	909	1.5
93644	OAKHURST	039	8606	9755	10337	1.4	72	3633	4083	4300	1.3	2.36	2560	2871	1.2
93645	O NEALS	039	140	169	183	2.1	84	49	59	63	2.0	2.86	36	43	1.9
93646	ORANGE COVE	107	8490	10542	11551	2.4	87	1918	2359	2570	2.3	4.47	1682	2060	2.2
93647	OROSI	107	9707	11190	11962	1.5	75	2295	2539	2692	1.1	4.40	1992	2203	1.1
93648	PARLIER	019	12378	14197	15239	1.5	75	2765	3150	3372	1.4	4.42	2422	2742	1.4
93650	FRESNO	019	4000	4263	4427	0.7	50	1149	1217	1259	0.6	3.50	767	802	0.5
93651	PRATHER	019	1228	1473	1614	2.0	83	432	515	562	1.9	2.86	357	422	1.8
93652	RAISIN CITY	019	233	242	248	0.4	30	61	63	64	0.3	3.81	53	54	0.2
93653	RAYMOND	043	991	1295	1471	2.9	91	383	501	566	2.9	2.58	296	388	3.0
93654	REEDLEY	019	26290	30195	32323	1.5	75	7474	8446	9000	1.3	3.52	6063	6803	1.3
93656	RIVERDALE	019	5632	6480	6932	1.5	75	1585	1789	1904	1.3	3.60	1322	1484	1.3
93657	SANGER	019	29062	36290	40104	2.4	87	8583	10616	11685	2.3	3.39	6961	8556	2.3
93660	SAN JOAQUIN	019	4213	5138	5624	2.2	85	912	1093	1191	2.0	4.70	832	992	1.9
93662	SELMA	019	26416	30962	33377	1.7	78	7557	8659	9263	1.5	3.54	6185	7053	1.4
93664	SHAVER LAKE	019	973	1089	1157	1.2	68	387	431	456	1.2	2.49	293	322	1.0
93667	TOLLHOUSE	019	2456	2830	3050	1.5	75	816	935	1005	1.5	2.98	673	766	1.4
93668	TRANQUILLITY	019	1453	1600	1685	1.0	62	423	462	484	1.0	3.46	350	379	0.9
93669	WISHON	039	575	625	652	0.9	58	247	266	277	0.8	2.35	184	199	0.9
93675	SQUAW VALLEY	019	3205	3553	3751	1.1	64	1225	1350	1422	1.1	2.57	914	996	0.9
93701	FRESNO	019	13750	14090	14378	0.3	23	3396	3448	3505	0.2	4.06	2546	2557	0.0
	CALIFORNIA					1.2					1.0	2.93			1.1
	UNITED STATES					1.0					1.1	2.59			0.9

#	POST OFFICE NAME	RACE (%) White 2000	White 2009	Black 2000	Black 2009	Asian/Pacific 2000	Asian/Pacific 2009	% Hispanic Origin 2000	% Hispanic Origin 2009	2009 AGE DISTRIBUTION (%) 0-4	5-9	10-14	15-19	20-24	25-44	45-64	65-84	85+	18+	MEDIAN AGE 2009	% 2009 Males	% 2009 Females
93453	SANTA MARGARITA	89.8	85.7	0.3	0.4	0.8	1.1	13.5	19.6	4.9	5.5	6.3	6.9	5.8	21.9	34.6	12.7	1.4	79.1	44.0	50.8	49.2
93454	SANTA MARIA	74.8	69.8	2.2	2.1	4.2	4.9	40.4	49.7	7.2	6.8	6.5	7.3	7.3	26.9	23.4	11.8	2.8	75.3	35.9	50.0	50.0
93455	SANTA MARIA	83.5	78.5	1.4	1.5	3.7	4.9	19.4	26.0	5.8	6.1	6.6	7.5	5.8	21.3	29.6	14.8	2.4	76.6	42.5	48.6	51.4
93458	SANTA MARIA	45.2	42.7	1.7	1.4	5.0	4.9	75.8	80.1	11.3	10.0	8.3	8.9	8.9	29.8	15.5	6.2	1.2	65.2	26.4	51.6	48.4
93460	SANTA YNEZ	86.9	82.6	0.2	0.2	1.4	1.8	15.7	22.3	4.9	5.1	6.1	7.1	5.6	20.3	34.4	14.6	2.0	79.1	45.6	48.0	52.0
93461	SHANDON	75.3	69.7	0.5	0.5	0.6	0.7	39.2	48.3	8.4	8.6	8.2	8.4	7.9	28.6	22.9	6.3	0.7	69.7	29.6	52.4	47.6
93463	SOLVANG	88.2	84.2	0.4	0.5	0.9	1.2	18.1	24.7	5.1	5.3	5.7	6.7	6.0	21.0	30.0	15.9	4.3	79.6	45.1	48.3	51.7
93465	TEMPLETON	90.6	87.2	0.8	1.0	0.9	1.2	10.6	14.6	5.6	6.6	7.5	8.0	5.3	22.0	32.8	10.5	1.8	75.1	41.7	48.8	51.2
93501	MOJAVE	70.5	61.0	4.6	5.1	2.0	2.2	25.7	36.3	8.2	7.1	7.0	7.6	7.3	23.0	26.4	11.9	1.4	73.0	35.8	50.5	49.5
93505	CALIFORNIA CITY	68.1	48.9	12.9	13.4	4.0	9.5	16.9	32.5	5.4	5.1	5.1	7.4	8.2	34.2	24.5	8.9	1.1	80.8	32.7	59.4	40.6
93510	ACTON	88.2	82.6	1.7	1.9	1.2	1.7	11.7	19.1	5.5	6.0	6.9	8.1	6.1	23.1	34.5	9.1	0.8	76.4	40.8	50.8	49.2
93512	BENTON	84.2	80.1	0.0	0.0	0.0	0.0	11.1	15.3	5.1	5.1	7.1	8.2	2.6	21.9	36.2	11.2	2.6	77.0	45.0	50.0	50.0
93513	BIG PINE	71.6	70.9	0.3	0.4	0.4	0.6	7.8	8.0	4.8	5.1	5.5	5.6	3.8	18.4	35.4	17.4	3.9	80.6	48.7	47.9	52.1
93514	BISHOP	82.4	81.6	0.1	0.1	1.0	1.0	11.3	12.0	5.3	5.5	6.0	6.7	5.4	20.1	33.1	15.3	2.6	78.8	45.6	49.3	50.7
93516	BORON	85.0	78.6	2.2	2.8	1.7	2.3	9.0	14.8	7.4	6.3	6.5	6.8	6.4	20.8	29.3	14.7	1.8	75.7	41.4	49.8	50.2
93517	BRIDGEPORT	86.1	83.5	0.8	0.8	1.6	2.1	15.0	20.2	4.8	5.3	6.6	4.0	2.4	23.1	39.1	13.6	1.1	80.6	47.0	54.3	45.7
93518	CALIENTE	85.6	78.8	1.4	1.8	1.2	1.6	8.9	14.8	2.9	3.4	4.2	5.7	4.5	12.4	38.5	26.2	2.3	85.6	55.2	51.6	48.4
93519	CANTIL	84.3	77.4	0.7	1.3	0.7	0.6	8.2	13.5	3.2	3.2	3.9	3.9	3.2	14.8	34.2	30.3	3.2	86.5	57.3	51.6	48.4
93523	EDWARDS	74.2	66.2	9.5	10.9	4.7	5.9	11.2	17.2	13.2	9.3	7.8	6.0	17.2	35.9	7.1	3.1	0.2	66.5	24.0	54.5	45.5
93524	EDWARDS	76.0	69.2	4.0	3.8	4.0	3.8	20.0	30.8	7.7	7.7	7.7	7.7	7.7	30.8	30.8	0.0	0.0	73.1	32.5	50.0	50.0
93526	INDEPENDENCE	81.9	81.2	0.0	0.0	1.2	1.2	9.4	9.8	4.8	4.1	6.5	6.7	3.6	17.8	35.0	18.4	3.2	79.9	48.2	48.0	52.0
93527	INYOKERN	90.3	86.0	0.4	0.5	1.5	2.2	6.2	10.1	4.4	5.1	5.9	6.3	4.9	17.8	37.5	16.5	1.5	80.6	48.1	50.1	49.9
93528	JOHANNESBURG	84.1	77.1	1.1	1.4	0.5	0.9	8.5	14.2	3.2	3.2	3.7	3.7	3.2	14.2	33.5	32.1	3.2	88.1	58.2	50.5	49.5
93529	JUNE LAKE	89.0	85.8	0.0	0.0	0.7	0.8	15.5	20.9	3.5	3.7	4.5	6.1	6.4	24.3	37.4	13.4	0.6	84.5	45.8	50.7	49.3
93531	KEENE	87.4	81.8	1.4	2.0	0.7	1.0	9.0	14.7	4.9	6.1	7.4	5.7	2.0	17.9	36.6	18.2	1.2	77.4	48.8	50.4	49.6
93532	LAKE HUGHES	83.2	76.0	4.0	4.6	1.6	2.1	15.8	24.8	6.1	6.8	8.0	14.1	4.1	22.8	30.0	7.4	0.7	68.4	37.2	54.0	46.0
93534	LANCASTER	64.1	57.3	15.7	15.6	3.5	4.5	24.2	33.5	9.0	7.8	7.2	8.9	8.2	26.6	20.3	10.0	2.1	70.4	30.8	48.8	51.2
93535	LANCASTER	60.7	54.1	16.2	15.8	3.0	3.6	28.2	38.6	9.1	8.5	8.2	9.0	7.9	26.6	22.5	7.4	0.9	68.6	29.8	48.6	51.4
93536	LANCASTER	70.3	63.9	11.6	11.5	4.6	6.3	18.0	24.7	6.5	6.6	6.9	7.6	6.6	28.4	27.7	8.5	1.1	75.1	36.2	52.5	47.5
93541	LEE VINING	73.6	67.9	0.6	0.6	1.0	1.3	24.2	31.5	8.1	5.8	5.2	6.3	5.2	27.7	32.7	7.7	1.3	76.5	40.4	53.8	46.2
93543	LITTLEROCK	64.1	56.4	9.7	9.2	0.9	1.0	37.2	49.7	7.3	8.2	9.0	8.7	5.3	23.5	27.9	9.1	1.1	69.8	36.2	51.5	48.5
93544	LLANO	84.5	79.1	5.6	6.2	0.4	0.5	16.7	25.8	4.3	5.3	6.2	5.7	4.6	22.5	34.9	15.1	1.4	80.5	45.8	54.0	46.0
93545	LONE PINE	79.0	78.5	0.1	0.1	0.9	0.9	23.9	24.5	6.1	5.7	5.8	6.2	6.0	20.0	30.2	16.5	3.4	78.2	45.2	48.7	51.3
93546	MAMMOTH LAKES	83.2	78.8	0.4	0.4	1.4	1.7	22.1	28.4	5.6	5.0	5.2	6.0	8.6	34.9	27.9	6.5	0.3	80.9	35.4	55.3	44.7
93550	PALMDALE	50.9	44.4	14.8	13.4	2.9	3.3	43.7	54.5	10.5	9.8	9.1	9.4	8.5	27.3	19.7	5.1	0.6	64.8	26.6	49.3	50.7
93551	PALMDALE	71.0	63.5	8.8	9.0	5.8	7.5	19.4	27.3	7.0	7.5	8.1	8.6	5.7	24.5	29.9	7.9	0.8	71.9	36.5	48.9	51.1
93552	PALMDALE	51.5	45.5	17.1	15.8	4.0	4.4	41.3	52.3	9.3	9.5	9.2	9.4	7.4	27.4	21.5	5.7	0.6	66.0	28.6	49.2	50.8
93553	PEARBLOSSOM	86.9	81.1	1.2	1.3	0.8	0.9	18.9	29.3	5.2	5.9	7.1	7.8	4.1	21.9	33.0	13.1	1.8	76.8	43.3	50.3	49.7
93554	RANDSBURG	84.3	76.3	0.0	1.7	0.0	0.0	7.8	13.6	3.4	3.4	3.4	3.4	3.4	13.6	33.9	32.2	3.4	86.4	58.5	49.2	50.8
93555	RIDGECREST	83.1	76.2	3.1	3.8	4.0	5.2	11.5	18.1	6.9	7.0	7.0	7.5	6.3	23.6	27.6	12.4	1.5	74.5	38.3	49.9	50.1
93560	ROSAMOND	72.2	63.7	6.4	7.2	3.1	3.7	25.6	36.6	7.9	7.5	7.6	8.2	7.1	28.3	24.8	8.0	0.7	72.0	32.4	50.3	49.7
93561	TEHACHAPI	74.3	68.4	6.3	5.7	1.1	1.5	21.3	29.7	5.5	5.9	6.4	6.8	7.0	29.0	27.0	11.1	1.3	77.8	37.9	57.2	42.8
93562	TRONA	86.6	81.6	1.5	1.7	1.1	1.4	15.5	22.6	7.5	7.0	6.7	7.7	7.5	24.1	26.0	12.3	1.3	74.2	35.1	50.4	49.6
93563	VALYERMO	76.6	69.8	9.7	10.7	3.1	3.9	16.4	25.3	4.6	5.2	5.3	4.7	6.7	30.1	32.7	9.9	1.0	81.9	41.6	59.6	40.4
93591	PALMDALE	61.6	52.6	11.2	11.1	1.5	1.7	32.9	44.9	7.9	9.2	9.2	9.5	7.9	24.2	24.6	6.9	0.5	67.6	29.4	50.7	49.3
93601	AHWAHNEE	88.5	83.5	0.1	0.1	0.7	0.9	8.7	13.3	5.1	5.4	5.9	6.0	4.3	19.3	34.8	17.3	1.9	79.7	47.6	49.1	50.9
93602	AUBERRY	84.3	79.1	0.3	0.5	0.7	1.0	7.2	11.4	4.8	6.2	7.0	6.6	4.2	18.9	36.1	14.1	2.1	77.7	46.2	50.0	50.0
93604	BASS LAKE	89.7	84.4	0.0	0.0	0.2	0.2	7.3	11.5	3.8	4.7	3.2	3.6	3.0	16.2	31.0	30.6	3.8	85.4	56.9	48.2	51.8
93608	CANTUA CREEK	41.3	38.2	0.6	0.7	1.0	0.9	89.4	93.3	9.8	8.7	8.2	10.3	10.8	30.1	18.4	3.5	0.3	67.2	26.2	59.3	40.7
93609	CARUTHERS	52.4	43.9	0.7	0.7	6.8	7.2	54.3	64.9	8.4	8.4	8.0	9.1	8.7	27.1	20.7	8.3	1.3	69.6	29.4	51.7	48.3
93610	CHOWCHILLA	58.7	50.5	12.3	12.1	1.8	2.0	32.6	43.0	5.8	5.6	5.8	6.0	7.0	40.7	20.4	7.5	1.2	79.2	35.0	35.9	64.1
93611	CLOVIS	81.3	74.1	1.3	1.6	6.5	8.7	15.4	22.4	7.2	7.5	7.9	7.7	5.3	26.7	28.7	7.8	1.3	72.6	36.5	48.5	51.5
93612	CLOVIS	70.6	61.8	2.4	2.6	6.6	8.1	25.2	34.4	8.2	7.3	6.9	7.2	8.3	28.8	22.1	9.4	1.8	73.2	32.4	47.8	52.2
93614	COARSEGOLD	92.1	89.1	0.4	0.4	0.9	1.1	7.0	11.2	4.4	5.5	6.4	6.4	3.2	19.4	35.5	17.5	1.7	79.3	47.8	49.5	50.5
93615	CUTLER	38.2	36.7	0.3	0.3	1.3	1.3	91.3	93.5	10.6	9.9	9.3	10.2	9.4	28.9	15.6	5.4	0.6	64.1	25.3	54.2	45.8
93616	DEL REY	45.8	41.5	0.4	0.5	4.8	4.7	78.6	84.4	9.0	8.9	8.6	8.3	6.4	25.6	21.9	10.1	1.3	68.5	31.5	50.3	49.7
93618	DINUBA	54.0	48.8	0.3	0.3	2.6	2.8	71.9	79.3	10.4	9.3	8.4	8.9	8.2	28.8	18.1	6.7	1.2	66.5	27.6	51.5	48.5
93619	CLOVIS	85.7	74.0	0.8	1.5	4.6	9.8	10.5	15.7	7.4	7.7	7.9	7.2	4.0	26.1	30.0	8.8	0.9	72.2	38.5	49.1	50.9
93620	DOS PALOS	63.1	57.2	5.1	4.7	0.6	0.6	53.6	64.3	9.1	9.3	8.7	9.1	7.2	25.5	21.3	8.5	1.2	67.0	29.6	50.7	49.3
93621	DUNLAP	90.6	86.3	2.0	2.3	0.3	0.6	7.5	12.0	5.0	5.0	5.3	5.3	4.7	19.9	37.7	15.8	1.5	81.0	48.0	49.4	50.6
93622	FIREBAUGH	44.2	40.8	1.3	1.1	0.9	0.9	84.8	90.0	10.5	9.8	8.7	10.2	10.2	26.8	18.0	5.3	0.6	64.9	25.4	52.8	47.2
93623	FISH CAMP	82.8	77.1	1.5	1.8	1.1	1.5	16.9	22.1	3.7	3.3	3.0	4.8	16.2	35.1	29.2	4.8	0.0	88.9	35.3	59.8	40.2
93625	FOWLER	50.7	44.0	1.7	1.5	6.6	7.1	62.2	71.6	7.9	7.8	7.8	8.4	7.7	25.9	22.9	9.7	1.9	71.5	32.3	50.2	49.8
93626	FRIANT	87.1	83.0	0.7	0.8	2.0	2.8	7.5	11.8	3.6	4.2	5.7	6.2	3.5	18.6	37.1	18.8	2.5	82.3	49.5	50.7	49.3
93627	HELM	40.6	38.9	1.6	1.4	1.6	1.4	87.5	93.1	9.7	9.7	8.3	9.7	12.5	29.2	19.4	1.4	0.0	66.7	25.0	58.3	41.7
93630	KERMAN	45.1	38.4	0.3	0.3	6.6	6.9	62.8	71.2	9.3	8.9	8.1	9.1	8.3	27.7	20.1	7.3	1.0	68.1	28.6	51.2	48.8
93631	KINGSBURG	69.1	60.1	0.5	0.5	3.2	3.9	38.3	49.5	7.8	7.8	7.4	8.0	6.2	26.5	23.3	10.7	2.3	71.8	34.4	49.6	50.4
93633	KINGS CANYON NATIONA	90.0	84.4	0.5	0.5	0.5	1.0	9.5	15.1	4.9	5.4	6.3	5.4	5.4	22.4	34.1	14.6	1.5	79.5	45.1	50.7	49.3
93635	LOS BANOS	59.0	52.7	3.8	3.6	2.5	3.0	50.4	58.8	9.8	9.0	7.9	8.3	7.5	28.0	20.9	7.5	1.2	67.9	29.6	49.9	50.1
93636	MADERA	82.8	77.0	1.5	1.5	1.6	2.0	21.8	30.7	5.4	6.0	7.0	8.1	5.1	23.3	33.1	10.9	1.1	76.3	41.2	50.1	49.9
93637	MADERA	58.7	52.8	2.8	2.7	2.2	2.4	53.0	61.8	9.2	8.6	8.1	8.2	7.3	27.5	21.1	8.6	1.4	69.0	30.6	50.1	49.9
93638	MADERA	43.8	39.9	4.2	3.5	1.0	1.0	73.4	80.6	10.9	9.5	8.1	9.5	9.5	28.1	17.5	6.0	0.8	65.7	26.3	51.9	48.1
93640	MENDOTA	29.3	28.9	0.6	0.5	0.9	0.8	94.2	96.0	10.3	9.2	7.8	8.7	10.0	31.7	17.0	4.7	0.5	67.4	26.8	55.6	44.4
93641	MIRAMONTE	87.2	81.5	1.5	1.9	0.7	1.1	10.5	17.1	4.0	4.9	6.5	6.0	4.9	22.6	35.8	14.1	1.3	80.5	45.6	51.4	48.6
93643	NORTH FORK	79.4	74.5	0.2	0.2	1.1	1.3	9.3	13.8	4.8	5.1	5.7	5.8	4.0	18.1	35.9	18.4	2.1	80.3	49.2	49.8	50.2
93644	OAKHURST	89.3	84.9	0.3	0.3	1.0	1.3	7.1	11.5	4.1	4.5	4.9	5.6	3.9	19.2	33.0	21.1	3.7	83.1	50.3	48.3	51.7
93645	O NEALS	83.7	81.1	1.4	1.2	1.4	1.2	6.4	10.1	4.1	5.3	8.3	7.7	3.0	20.7	33.7	15.4	1.8	76.3	45.5	49.7	50.3
93646	ORANGE COVE	37.3	34.1	0.3	0.3	1.7	1.6	86.5	90.6	11.5	10.3	8.8	10.2	9.9	28.5	15.1	5.0	0.6	63.2	24.6	51.3	48.7
93647	OROSI	34.9	32.1	0.4	0.4	9.6	9.2	79.6	83.6	10.6	9.7	8.7	9.5	8.7	28.7	16.8	6.3	1.1	65.2	26.6	52.4	47.6
93648	PARLIER	35.6	33.2	0.8	0.8	1.9	1.8	92.0	93.9	10.8	10.0	8.8	9.7	9.6	29.2	16.0	5.1	0.8	65.0	25.6	52.1	47.9
93650	FRESNO	47.6	40.0	4.6	4.5	13.3	14.2	42.9	51.3	9.6	8.0	7.2	8.9	11.0	30.4	17.8	6.3	0.8	69.9	27.5	48.2	51.8
93651	PRATHER	89.4	84.7	0.7	0.9	0.7	1.0	7.3	11.9	5.4	6.2	7.1	7.7	5.1	21.2	34.5	11.7	1.1	76.5	42.8	49.4	50.6
93652	RAISIN CITY	53.2	45.9	0.4	0.4	5.6	5.8	59.2	69.4	9.5	8.7	8.3	8.7	9.1	27.3	19.8	7.4	1.2	68.2	28.2	53.3	46.7
93653	RAYMOND	90.3	86.9	0.5	0.6	0.6	0.8	10.8	17.1	4.7	5.6	6.0	5.9	3.9	19.7	36.4	15.8	1.9	79.8	47.9	48.6	51.4
93654	REEDLEY	54.9	49.1	0.4	0.4	4.4	4.8	62.7	70.5	9.1	8.7	8.0	8.2	7.2	28.0	20.2	8.3	2.1	69.1	30.4	51.2	48.8
93656	RIVERDALE	51.5	43.2	2.9	2.5	1.4	1.5	56.1	66.2	9.2	9.1	9.0	9.5	7.7	25.5	20.5	8.1	1.3	67.0	29.1	51.5	48.5
93657	SANGER	58.2	52.9	0.5	0.5	3.3	3.8	62.6	70.0	8.2	8.1	7.8	8.3	7.3	25.4	23.3	9.9	1.6	70.8	32.4	50.2	49.8
93660	SAN JOAQUIN	35.9	33.6	0.3	0.3	2.8	2.6	90.0	92.9	12.5	10.6	8.8	10.4	11.3	28.4	14.2	3.5	0.4	62.0	23.4	53.3	46.7
93662	SELMA	45.0	38.4	0.8	0.7	4.3	4.5	68.6	77.0	9.4	8.9	8.2	8.7	7.5	27.7	19.4	8.7	1.6	68.2	29.7	50.7	49.3
93664	SHAVER LAKE	94.6	91.9	0.0	0.0	0.2	0.4	9.1	14.4	4.0	5.9	7.7	6.1	3.5	20.7	38.2	13.1	0.8	77.7	46.1	53.3	46.7
93667	TOLLHOUSE	87.3	82.8	0.5	0.7	0.7	1.1	7.8	12.4	5.3	6.6	7.8	8.0	4.2	21.0	35.2	10.8	1.2	74.9	43.0	50.0	50.0
93668	TRANQUILLITY	49.3	41.6	0.6	0.6	2.3	2.4	68.6	78.6	9.6	8.7	8.0	9.2	7.9	24.8	23.4	7.6	0.9	67.3	29.3	53.4	46.6
93669	WISHON	77.0	67.7	0.0	0.0	0.7	0.8	5.9	8.6	3.0	3.5	4.0	5.1	3.7	18.7	37.8	22.2	1.9	86.4	52.5	52.2	47.8
93675	SQUAW VALLEY	86.6	81.5	2.2	2.6	0.7	1.0	11.8	18.4	4.3	5.2	6.3	6.4	4.5	20.8	35.9	15.4	1.3	79.7	46.4	50.8	49.2
93701	FRESNO	28.2	25.8	7.0	5.9	16.8	16.2	64.2	69.5	13.9	10.9	8.4	10.7	12.4	26.3	13.2	3.7	0.6	60.5	22.5	52.9	47.1
	CALIFORNIA	59.5	54.5	6.7	6.2	11.3	12.5	32.4	38.3	7.5	7.1	6.9	7.5	7.4	28.5	24.2	9.3	1.6	74.1	34.3	49.9	50.1
	UNITED STATES	75.1	72.0	12.3	12.7	3.8	4.6	12.5	15.7	6.8	6.7	6.6	7.1	6.9	27.0	26.0	10.9	1.9	75.7	36.9	49.2	50.8

#	ZIP CODE / POST OFFICE NAME	2009 Per Capita Income	2009 HH Income Base	2009 HOUSEHOLD INCOME DISTRIBUTION (%)					MEDIAN HOUSEHOLD INCOME				2009 Home Value Base	2009 HOME VALUE DISTRIBUTION (%)					2009 Median Home Value
				Less than $25,000	$25,000 to $49,999	$50,000 to $99,999	$100,000 to $149,999	$150,000 or More	2009	2014	2009 National Centile	2009 State Centile		Less than $50,000	$50,000 to $89,999	$90,000 to $174,999	$175,000 to $399,999	$400,000 or More	
93453	SANTA MARGARITA	26508	1228	19.5	24.0	43.7	8.6	4.2	55895	58556	73	53	792	8.1	9.5	10.5	39.6	32.3	298256
93454	SANTA MARIA	23122	11199	20.8	27.0	36.8	10.8	4.7	52336	56589	67	46	6580	2.1	1.1	9.7	67.1	19.9	248494
93455	SANTA MARIA	29059	14793	12.0	22.7	38.5	19.9	6.9	66516	69367	85	68	11785	4.9	2.2	8.1	45.8	39.0	339715
93458	SANTA MARIA	11970	12063	25.9	34.0	32.2	5.8	2.0	41783	44379	39	25	6059	6.2	5.0	11.1	72.8	4.9	216258
93460	SANTA YNEZ	44766	2286	10.1	16.6	26.1	23.9	23.4	92929	94473	96	88	1677	0.1	0.6	2.9	5.0	91.5	726823
93461	SHANDON	17517	441	19.0	30.8	42.0	5.4	2.7	50086	52511	61	43	310	0.6	0.0	18.4	64.2	16.8	242143
93463	SOLVANG	37089	3308	13.0	23.5	30.2	19.4	13.8	66573	69230	85	68	2147	0.8	0.7	7.8	9.2	81.5	639095
93465	TEMPLETON	26999	3380	15.1	20.7	43.6	13.8	6.8	64063	65857	82	65	2571	2.9	2.2	5.9	33.2	55.8	436044
93501	MOJAVE	15420	2064	38.0	28.2	28.1	5.0	0.7	35076	37111	18	14	1119	19.0	37.5	34.3	7.4	1.7	81250
93505	CALIFORNIA CITY	22062	4243	24.3	22.3	39.1	11.0	3.2	55020	59044	71	52	2680	8.9	20.3	53.2	17.2	0.4	117586
93510	ACTON	32872	2705	8.7	18.3	39.2	17.4	16.3	74471	75098	89	75	2308	4.4	1.0	2.3	26.6	65.8	481655
93512	BENTON	20406	82	23.2	31.7	41.5	3.7	0.0	43648	49319	44	30	64	0.0	6.3	43.8	37.5	12.5	175000
93513	BIG PINE	20738	727	27.9	28.7	35.9	5.2	2.2	42738	47049	42	28	546	12.8	2.6	26.2	52.4	6.0	192164
93514	BISHOP	26090	6235	23.9	25.5	35.7	10.3	4.6	50594	53690	63	43	4299	17.0	5.7	14.0	43.2	20.0	247177
93516	BORON	19485	840	37.3	14.2	40.7	6.0	1.9	46184	50346	52	35	492	20.9	37.2	38.6	3.3	0.0	80476
93517	BRIDGEPORT	21236	166	18.1	44.6	34.3	3.0	0.0	43580	45478	44	30	105	7.6	9.5	12.4	67.6	2.9	215179
93518	CALIENTE	20438	438	36.8	23.5	33.6	3.0	3.2	35963	39709	20	15	353	8.2	8.5	35.1	38.5	9.6	169758
93519	CANTIL	31236	91	34.1	24.2	35.2	4.4	2.2	35566	37998	19	14	65	30.8	43.1	24.6	1.5	0.0	56579
93523	EDWARDS	18065	2047	14.0	37.1	40.4	6.9	1.6	48994	50549	59	40	459	41.0	30.9	22.9	5.2	0.0	57685
93524	EDWARDS	28986	15	33.3	13.3	46.7	6.7	0.0	51268	52719	64	44	9	11.1	33.3	22.2	33.3	0.0	137500
93526	INDEPENDENCE	24178	360	25.0	30.0	38.1	5.3	1.7	46140	48341	52	35	242	13.6	12.4	44.6	24.8	4.5	133871
93527	INYOKERN	23267	1008	27.3	30.2	27.6	11.4	3.6	41894	43312	39	26	769	14.2	35.1	36.8	13.9	0.0	90948
93528	JOHANNESBURG	25204	104	35.6	24.0	34.6	3.8	1.9	33952	39318	15	12	73	30.1	46.6	21.9	1.4	0.0	56042
93529	JUNE LAKE	32662	284	23.9	17.6	46.5	4.2	7.7	62509	63018	81	62	168	3.6	0.0	9.5	42.3	44.6	371875
93531	KEENE	29423	150	15.3	16.7	46.7	12.7	8.7	69277	69594	86	71	126	2.4	2.4	13.5	56.3	25.4	268421
93532	LAKE HUGHES	27475	1037	12.3	21.4	46.5	14.1	5.7	65591	66765	84	66	784	1.5	0.9	12.0	77.0	8.5	242146
93534	LANCASTER	19579	14532	30.3	28.7	32.0	6.1	2.9	41139	44820	36	24	6346	2.6	1.3	51.8	41.9	2.4	167919
93535	LANCASTER	17684	21745	22.2	28.2	39.5	7.1	3.0	49587	52867	60	42	14960	12.5	2.6	39.8	43.7	1.4	168129
93536	LANCASTER	25800	22013	16.2	17.9	39.9	16.4	9.6	68580	71394	86	70	15702	3.1	1.7	12.0	69.3	13.9	244728
93541	LEE VINING	30321	208	12.5	35.1	40.4	1.4	10.6	51296	51606	64	44	127	3.9	13.4	17.3	52.8	12.6	199375
93543	LITTLEROCK	17995	3739	22.5	24.9	38.9	9.7	4.0	53528	59208	69	49	2867	2.3	1.0	33.3	57.2	6.2	198618
93544	LLANO	28911	567	22.6	21.5	37.0	12.5	6.3	56018	60285	73	53	453	8.2	4.2	19.2	43.9	24.5	237500
93545	LONE PINE	17903	943	41.5	28.4	23.8	4.9	1.5	32647	35757	13	10	573	19.2	14.0	28.4	28.1	10.3	135904
93546	MAMMOTH LAKES	34113	3224	15.4	27.2	37.2	10.0	10.2	60538	61484	78	59	1702	6.2	5.5	2.6	30.8	54.9	437838
93550	PALMDALE	15912	21021	25.4	27.2	37.1	7.8	2.5	47614	50266	56	38	12245	3.4	1.7	39.5	53.0	2.5	185910
93551	PALMDALE	30980	15902	7.5	13.0	42.6	23.0	14.0	83408	85364	93	83	13170	1.7	1.1	4.8	66.0	26.4	289862
93552	PALMDALE	19002	9720	10.8	24.1	46.8	13.8	4.5	64967	66584	83	66	8100	2.2	0.4	22.4	72.4	2.7	212592
93553	PEARBLOSSOM	20452	578	33.4	20.2	35.5	7.8	3.1	44713	50155	47	32	415	4.3	2.2	34.5	43.1	15.9	205208
93554	RANDSBURG	23475	32	37.5	21.9	37.5	3.1	0.0	33141	42500	14	11	23	30.4	47.8	21.7	0.0	0.0	56429
93555	RIDGECREST	24598	12530	23.1	25.1	35.5	11.4	5.0	52147	54467	66	46	7798	19.3	24.6	38.1	16.7	1.3	97868
93560	ROSAMOND	19872	6237	21.4	25.9	41.5	9.7	1.6	52712	57190	67	47	4133	16.3	11.0	49.7	21.4	1.6	128912
93561	TEHACHAPI	22701	11062	22.8	22.1	40.5	10.4	4.1	57034	60595	74	54	7688	2.7	4.3	30.7	49.2	13.1	201567
93562	TRONA	20437	784	26.3	24.4	40.6	7.3	1.5	48931	51791	59	40	515	71.8	21.0	6.4	0.8	0.0	39073
93563	VALYERMO	21368	209	23.4	19.6	39.7	12.0	5.3	56144	59716	73	54	163	14.1	5.5	20.2	35.0	25.2	197917
93591	PALMDALE	15160	1933	19.7	32.9	38.1	7.7	1.7	47345	51130	55	38	1441	1.9	2.6	66.7	25.9	3.0	149798
93601	AHWAHNEE	21559	908	22.2	35.6	29.8	7.7	4.6	44541	46396	47	32	660	1.1	2.9	11.4	61.8	22.9	263830
93602	AUBERRY	21045	1416	23.7	26.3	40.6	7.2	2.3	50090	54946	61	43	1115	14.1	4.3	21.0	50.8	9.9	200635
93604	BASS LAKE	26188	240	24.2	43.3	19.6	8.3	4.6	34326	36277	16	12	182	4.9	7.1	18.1	28.6	41.2	281818
93608	CANTUA CREEK	10433	456	27.0	53.5	17.3	0.9	1.3	34685	35766	17	13	111	28.8	26.1	34.2	9.0	1.8	80833
93609	CARUTHERS	14599	1490	26.8	30.1	33.2	6.6	3.2	44042	46615	45	31	865	5.7	4.5	48.6	32.0	9.2	157024
93610	CHOWCHILLA	17186	5439	33.8	30.5	28.7	4.5	2.5	38825	42072	29	20	3074	3.1	8.7	46.2	32.4	9.7	151711
93611	CLOVIS	28986	14817	8.1	14.9	45.3	20.3	11.3	77530	78896	91	78	12115	0.7	0.4	9.2	75.6	14.1	247407
93612	CLOVIS	17561	14461	31.2	35.9	27.3	4.3	1.3	37456	40056	25	17	5674	10.2	4.4	48.9	34.6	1.9	155657
93614	COARSEGOLD	24113	4750	21.3	25.2	38.9	10.3	4.3	53006	56139	68	48	3802	3.5	3.1	13.8	64.1	15.4	240557
93615	CUTLER	8334	1233	36.7	35.1	24.8	1.2	2.1	31902	34173	11	8	670	0.9	3.4	72.1	15.1	8.5	140837
93616	DEL REY	12008	514	36.2	31.5	25.3	6.0	1.0	34318	36249	16	12	295	3.1	2.0	63.4	20.0	11.5	135451
93618	DINUBA	12810	7346	29.5	32.2	32.0	3.6	2.6	40345	44607	34	22	4312	8.6	6.1	46.8	32.8	5.7	152857
93619	CLOVIS	31977	9633	7.7	17.1	36.6	23.3	15.4	81449	83370	93	81	8601	1.5	0.7	3.9	45.1	48.7	393215
93620	DOS PALOS	14333	3155	35.5	30.7	27.1	4.0	2.7	32573	34713	13	10	1677	4.7	41.0	32.6	16.1	5.7	94265
93621	DUNLAP	20677	119	21.8	31.9	32.8	8.4	5.0	46659	49381	53	36	91	7.7	3.3	27.5	53.8	7.7	198864
93622	FIREBAUGH	10763	2730	32.5	37.2	26.4	2.3	1.6	36173	37995	21	15	1289	5.6	9.6	64.9	18.8	1.2	134570
93623	FISH CAMP	44613	132	6.1	35.6	43.2	9.1	6.1	60000	60698	77	58	46	19.6	6.5	21.7	34.8	17.4	181250
93625	FOWLER	16764	2104	26.4	31.0	33.8	5.6	3.2	44444	46818	47	31	1149	5.4	3.0	45.3	34.7	11.7	166208
93626	FRIANT	21600	592	23.3	37.2	28.7	8.1	2.7	42394	44564	41	27	453	13.7	0.9	39.3	15.9	30.2	165057
93627	HELM	8179	16	31.3	62.5	6.3	0.0	0.0	32248	33564	12	9	4	50.0	0.0	50.0	0.0	0.0	70000
93630	KERMAN	12960	5128	35.4	32.2	24.8	5.4	2.2	35875	38217	20	15	2827	9.3	6.8	38.2	36.9	8.8	167992
93631	KINGSBURG	18737	5493	23.8	29.2	36.9	7.5	2.7	46910	49708	54	37	3473	4.7	5.9	28.4	48.4	12.6	200566
93633	KINGS CANYON NATIONA	18569	73	30.1	30.1	32.9	2.7	4.1	39438	42378	31	21	48	0.0	20.8	20.8	45.8	12.5	189286
93635	LOS BANOS	18519	11779	18.0	27.0	40.9	10.2	4.0	54975	59040	71	52	7919	4.1	9.2	56.4	28.5	1.7	143533
93636	MADERA	26403	3864	10.5	16.4	47.9	17.0	8.3	66898	67471	85	69	3381	0.6	1.4	16.7	72.8	8.5	224392
93637	MADERA	17773	11322	26.3	28.2	35.3	5.8	4.4	46446	49000	53	36	6651	3.2	3.2	39.9	45.4	8.4	180779
93638	MADERA	11056	11395	33.4	31.8	28.8	3.9	2.1	36630	39075	22	16	6702	3.5	6.5	57.9	29.0	3.1	145395
93640	MENDOTA	8091	2739	40.9	37.5	18.9	2.3	0.5	29396	30055	7	6	1118	5.2	7.0	76.0	10.6	1.2	132075
93641	MIRAMONTE	19297	242	29.8	32.6	33.9	2.1	1.7	40000	41813	33	21	170	2.9	18.8	41.8	22.9	13.5	144565
93643	NORTH FORK	21000	1217	28.4	31.6	28.4	6.4	5.1	42157	45000	40	26	897	7.2	6.0	18.6	53.2	14.9	217874
93644	OAKHURST	23978	4083	27.7	27.6	33.7	6.5	4.6	44711	47874	47	32	2812	6.7	5.3	10.2	55.7	22.0	249340
93645	O NEALS	17044	59	35.6	23.7	30.5	6.8	3.4	43662	45361	44	30	45	17.8	0.0	13.3	40.0	28.9	240625
93646	ORANGE COVE	9097	2359	40.2	34.1	20.1	4.1	1.5	29328	30672	7	6	1083	10.4	6.6	63.3	12.6	7.1	133406
93647	OROSI	10045	2539	31.8	30.2	33.9	2.8	1.3	37672	40245	26	18	1520	5.6	8.0	63.5	20.3	2.7	138514
93648	PARLIER	8862	3150	40.1	36.2	19.9	2.3	1.5	30479	31875	9	7	1739	4.9	7.1	73.2	11.0	3.8	137189
93650	FRESNO	12837	1217	35.2	33.7	26.4	3.0	1.7	34628	36292	17	13	331	4.2	12.1	50.5	26.6	6.6	134797
93651	PRATHER	21791	515	16.5	31.5	38.8	9.9	3.3	51926	54252	66	45	397	4.8	1.5	23.4	46.1	24.2	238362
93652	RAISIN CITY	17431	63	25.4	23.8	38.1	7.9	4.8	50852	53598	63	44	31	12.9	9.7	16.1	41.9	19.4	215000
93653	RAYMOND	22783	501	27.7	26.1	34.3	5.6	6.2	45698	48737	50	34	380	1.3	1.6	18.7	53.4	25.0	261321
93654	REEDLEY	15119	8446	27.0	29.8	33.9	6.4	2.9	43036	45670	43	29	5001	5.2	3.8	37.8	46.8	6.4	181434
93656	RIVERDALE	13622	1789	29.9	33.1	30.4	3.3	3.3	36919	40329	23	16	938	9.3	11.1	49.5	23.5	6.7	135081
93657	SANGER	16476	10616	27.3	29.5	32.7	7.0	3.4	43290	46010	43	29	6789	3.9	6.5	41.2	36.3	12.1	171765
93660	SAN JOAQUIN	8340	1093	41.7	34.7	20.4	2.1	1.1	29663	30762	8	6	454	5.3	13.4	67.6	11.7	2.0	135878
93662	SELMA	14848	8659	25.9	32.0	34.4	5.2	2.4	43196	45908	43	29	5040	5.5	8.7	45.9	34.1	5.9	155212
93664	SHAVER LAKE	26714	431	14.2	28.8	42.0	10.7	4.4	59812	61398	77	58	273	3.3	3.7	11.0	39.6	42.5	355435
93667	TOLLHOUSE	22997	935	14.8	25.3	43.5	11.2	5.1	61023	62316	79	60	722	4.7	0.7	18.7	51.1	24.8	253125
93668	TRANQUILLITY	15877	462	21.6	36.8	33.1	5.8	2.6	40147	42349	33	21	238	0.0	9.2	57.6	31.1	2.1	145270
93669	WISHON	22663	266	20.3	26.3	48.1	4.5	0.8	53495	59132	69	49	206	0.0	0.0	18.9	67.0	14.1	234921
93675	SQUAW VALLEY	20283	1350	27.7	30.4	33.3	6.1	2.5	42553	45108	41	27	1079	5.5	4.5	45.3	39.8	4.9	160026
93701	FRESNO	6264	3448	66.2	23.5	8.7	0.9	0.8	16309	16428	1	2	553	2.0	36.9	55.2	3.4	2.5	96833
	CALIFORNIA	28199		18.5	22.2	33.9	14.0	11.5	61614	64088				3.3	2.6	13.6	41.0	39.5	321752
	UNITED STATES	27277		20.9	24.4	35.3	11.7	7.6	54719	56938				9.3	13.1	31.6	32.6	13.5	162279

ZIP CODE #	POST OFFICE NAME	FINANCIAL SERVICES Auto Loan	Home Loan	Investments	Retirement Plans	THE HOME Home Improvements Home Repair	Lawn & Garden	Furnishings Computers & Hardware-Personal	Major Appliances	TV, Radio, Sound Equipment	Furniture	ENTERTAINMENT Dine out/ Carry out	Sports Equipment	Fees & Tickets	Toys & Games	Travel	Cable TV	PERSONAL Apparel & Services	Auto Repairs	Health Insurance	Pets & Supplies
93453	SANTA MARGARITA	95	92	99	91	92	97	88	94	88	88	88	72	86	88	90	89	61	91	94	111
93454	SANTA MARIA	87	93	92	89	95	84	93	91	88	95	90	70	94	88	95	86	64	92	85	102
93455	SANTA MARIA	106	123	136	118	128	119	109	118	106	111	107	87	118	105	120	107	76	113	113	132
93458	SANTA MARIA	71	69	62	63	69	57	75	70	69	78	72	55	71	70	72	64	52	73	61	76
93460	SANTA YNEZ	146	188	225	192	208	170	170	175	153	185	152	135	194	147	195	143	113	166	153	194
93461	SHANDON	83	86	74	80	84	75	83	83	79	88	80	63	81	81	82	76	57	82	75	93
93463	SOLVANG	116	132	148	134	141	124	131	129	123	135	124	99	139	119	140	119	90	128	122	146
93465	TEMPLETON	114	114	119	113	114	116	105	114	105	108	105	85	104	106	108	106	72	108	110	133
93501	MOJAVE	61	57	54	54	56	56	60	59	60	60	60	44	57	60	57	61	42	60	60	69
93505	CALIFORNIA CITY	86	89	86	89	89	88	88	88	87	87	88	67	89	88	89	88	62	88	89	103
93510	ACTON	135	169	160	170	168	147	146	148	135	154	137	117	163	138	159	129	99	141	130	168
93512	BENTON	81	65	105	64	72	86	65	83	68	61	67	60	56	65	71	73	45	76	82	96
93513	BIG PINE	84	67	108	66	74	89	67	85	70	63	69	62	58	67	73	75	46	79	84	99
93514	BISHOP	86	88	97	87	91	93	85	90	86	85	85	66	86	83	89	88	59	88	93	104
93516	BORON	80	63	74	62	64	81	69	77	74	64	72	58	59	74	65	80	49	75	84	91
93517	BRIDGEPORT	77	62	100	61	68	82	62	79	65	58	64	58	54	62	67	69	43	73	78	91
93518	CALIENTE	76	67	95	64	75	84	65	80	69	67	67	55	61	64	71	73	45	75	84	91
93519	CANTIL	78	75	95	69	83	89	71	84	75	77	73	55	70	69	78	79	49	80	93	95
93523	EDWARDS	95	57	48	63	53	54	89	69	86	84	89	63	71	99	69	81	62	82	65	83
93524	EDWARDS	75	69	78	69	73	74	70	73	71	75	71	52	69	71	71	72	49	73	76	84
93526	INDEPENDENCE	85	68	110	67	75	90	68	86	71	64	70	63	59	68	74	76	47	80	85	100
93527	INYOKERN	88	81	100	79	85	96	76	90	79	77	79	65	73	78	80	84	54	84	92	104
93528	JOHANNESBURG	77	74	94	68	82	88	70	83	74	76	73	54	70	68	77	79	49	80	92	95
93529	JUNE LAKE	89	112	131	114	123	96	106	105	93	114	93	84	116	90	119	85	69	101	88	117
93531	KEENE	114	114	159	112	130	137	104	125	110	114	108	81	110	100	119	115	74	118	136	142
93532	LAKE HUGHES	104	122	116	122	119	111	105	109	100	109	102	86	115	103	113	98	72	104	100	126
93534	LANCASTER	75	66	60	67	63	63	77	68	77	76	78	55	72	77	71	76	55	75	70	82
93535	LANCASTER	85	85	74	81	82	76	83	82	81	87	82	62	81	84	80	79	58	82	77	94
93536	LANCASTER	111	128	122	126	127	116	115	116	111	119	112	89	124	113	121	108	80	113	109	133
93541	LEE VINING	126	101	163	99	111	134	101	129	106	95	105	94	88	101	110	113	69	119	127	149
93543	LITTLEROCK	85	98	88	94	98	85	89	91	82	94	84	70	93	84	94	79	60	87	81	101
93544	LLANO	105	95	134	95	102	114	91	109	93	88	92	80	85	89	99	96	62	101	107	126
93545	LONE PINE	65	51	65	50	53	66	56	63	61	53	59	46	49	59	54	66	40	62	69	75
93546	MAMMOTH LAKES	103	117	132	120	125	101	121	113	107	125	109	93	126	105	128	99	80	114	98	129
93550	PALMDALE	82	80	69	75	78	67	82	78	77	87	80	61	78	80	78	73	56	80	69	88
93551	PALMDALE	135	166	153	167	164	145	142	144	134	151	136	114	159	139	152	128	98	137	129	164
93552	PALMDALE	104	116	100	106	114	91	107	106	96	116	99	83	107	100	108	89	71	102	87	116
93553	PEARBLOSSOM	74	85	76	87	83	83	75	79	74	76	74	61	81	75	80	74	52	75	77	92
93554	RANDSBURG	63	61	77	56	67	72	58	68	61	62	59	45	57	56	63	65	40	65	76	78
93555	RIDGECREST	90	89	87	90	89	90	89	89	89	90	90	67	89	89	89	90	62	89	91	105
93560	ROSAMOND	89	86	74	84	82	78	85	82	83	88	84	64	82	87	80	81	58	82	78	97
93561	TEHACHAPI	91	93	107	92	97	100	88	96	89	89	89	70	89	87	94	91	62	93	98	111
93562	TRONA	75	77	60	78	71	80	76	74	77	72	77	59	77	79	74	79	53	75	82	90
93563	VALYERMO	117	93	151	92	103	123	93	119	98	88	97	87	81	93	101	104	64	110	117	138
93591	PALMDALE	82	82	71	75	80	70	79	79	75	85	77	59	76	78	77	72	54	78	71	89
93601	AHWAHNEE	97	78	125	77	86	103	78	99	82	74	81	72	68	77	85	87	54	91	98	114
93602	AUBERRY	89	79	111	79	84	96	76	92	78	73	78	68	71	75	82	82	52	86	90	107
93604	BASS LAKE	90	72	116	71	79	95	72	92	75	68	74	67	62	72	78	80	49	84	90	106
93608	CANTUA CREEK	63	58	46	51	57	45	64	60	59	68	62	46	58	60	60	54	45	63	50	63
93609	CARUTHERS	79	86	77	76	87	66	83	82	73	90	76	63	81	75	84	67	54	80	66	87
93610	CHOWCHILLA	78	68	72	65	68	74	70	74	71	68	71	58	63	72	68	73	49	73	74	87
93611	CLOVIS	124	152	141	152	151	133	129	132	122	138	124	104	146	127	139	117	90	125	118	149
93612	CLOVIS	63	58	55	58	57	56	66	60	65	65	66	48	63	65	62	64	46	64	61	71
93614	COARSEGOLD	96	89	121	89	96	107	84	101	87	83	87	72	82	84	93	92	59	95	103	116
93615	CUTLER	59	56	47	49	56	45	58	57	54	63	57	43	54	55	56	51	41	58	48	60
93616	DEL REY	73	59	62	53	59	64	60	67	62	61	63	48	52	62	58	64	43	66	65	77
93618	DINUBA	74	69	62	63	68	61	71	70	68	75	70	53	66	70	68	66	49	71	64	79
93619	CLOVIS	138	172	165	176	173	153	144	150	136	156	138	118	166	141	158	130	101	140	133	169
93620	DOS PALOS	72	69	63	61	68	60	70	70	65	73	67	53	64	67	67	62	47	70	61	77
93621	DUNLAP	99	79	128	78	87	104	79	101	83	74	82	73	69	79	86	88	54	93	99	117
93622	FIREBAUGH	64	60	51	53	59	48	64	62	59	68	62	48	59	61	61	55	45	64	52	66
93623	FISH CAMP	99	100	97	103	98	97	103	97	101	103	102	77	104	101	101	100	72	100	99	117
93625	FOWLER	74	84	78	76	85	68	79	79	72	84	74	60	80	73	82	68	53	77	68	86
93626	FRIANT	78	75	103	72	83	88	71	84	73	73	71	59	70	68	78	76	49	79	87	96
93627	HELM	45	43	35	38	42	31	48	44	43	51	46	36	45	44	46	38	34	47	35	46
93630	KERMAN	71	64	63	58	65	59	68	70	64	69	66	54	61	64	66	61	47	69	61	76
93631	KINGSBURG	81	81	83	78	81	79	80	82	77	80	78	64	78	78	81	77	55	81	78	95
93633	KINGS CANYON NATIONA	89	67	103	66	72	92	68	87	73	64	72	64	57	71	71	79	48	80	88	102
93635	LOS BANOS	92	96	83	91	93	81	93	91	87	98	90	70	92	91	91	83	64	90	81	102
93636	MADERA	112	132	127	132	130	122	113	119	108	118	110	93	124	111	123	106	78	113	109	137
93637	MADERA	80	81	76	78	80	75	82	80	80	83	82	62	82	81	82	78	58	82	77	92
93638	MADERA	67	60	53	57	59	51	67	63	64	70	67	49	63	66	63	61	48	67	55	70
93640	MENDOTA	52	48	39	43	47	36	55	50	50	58	53	40	51	51	52	45	39	54	40	53
93641	MIRAMONTE	81	65	104	64	71	85	65	82	68	61	67	60	56	64	70	72	44	76	81	95
93643	NORTH FORK	90	72	116	71	79	95	72	91	75	67	74	67	62	71	78	80	49	84	90	106
93644	OAKHURST	86	78	107	76	86	95	76	90	80	77	78	62	72	75	82	84	53	86	95	104
93645	O NEALS	81	65	105	64	72	86	65	83	68	61	67	61	57	65	71	73	45	76	82	96
93646	ORANGE COVE	56	55	46	49	55	41	61	57	54	64	58	46	58	56	59	49	43	60	45	59
93647	OROSI	65	63	53	56	62	51	65	63	61	70	63	48	61	62	63	57	45	64	54	68
93648	PARLIER	57	53	45	47	52	44	56	55	53	59	55	41	51	54	53	50	39	56	47	59
93650	FRESNO	69	55	48	54	53	53	65	59	66	66	67	45	58	67	58	66	47	65	60	71
93651	PRATHER	87	98	84	101	95	96	87	91	86	88	86	71	93	88	92	86	60	87	90	107
93652	RAISIN CITY	90	110	102	96	115	79	102	103	85	112	88	80	103	85	108	74	64	96	76	105
93653	RAYMOND	98	79	127	77	86	104	79	100	82	74	81	73	68	78	85	88	54	92	99	116
93654	REEDLEY	75	77	72	72	77	69	76	76	72	79	75	58	75	73	77	70	53	76	70	85
93656	RIVERDALE	74	71	62	63	70	61	71	71	68	76	70	53	66	70	68	65	49	71	63	79
93657	SANGER	83	80	82	75	81	77	80	84	76	82	78	63	76	77	80	75	55	82	76	93
93660	SAN JOAQUIN	55	50	41	45	49	37	59	53	53	61	57	43	54	55	55	48	42	58	43	56
93662	SELMA	76	80	71	72	79	67	77	77	71	82	73	58	75	73	76	68	52	76	67	85
93664	SHAVER LAKE	98	99	126	98	106	110	90	105	91	93	91	74	92	87	100	94	63	98	105	120
93667	TOLLHOUSE	94	109	108	112	110	107	95	102	93	99	94	77	104	93	104	93	66	97	98	118
93668	TRANQUILLITY	80	78	66	69	77	61	82	78	75	87	79	61	77	77	79	69	56	80	65	84
93669	WISHON	89	71	115	70	78	94	71	90	74	67	74	66	62	71	77	79	49	83	89	105
93675	SQUAW VALLEY	88	69	111	68	76	92	70	88	73	65	72	65	60	70	75	78	48	81	88	103
93701	FRESNO	36	25	23	26	24	22	37	30	36	36	39	25	32	37	32	35	28	36	29	35
	CALIFORNIA	112	119	122	118	122	107	121	116	114	124	116	92	124	114	124	110	84	118	107	132
	UNITED STATES	100	100	100	100	100	100	100	100	100	100	100	100	100	100	100	100	100	100	100	100

93702-94133

ZIP CODE #	POST OFFICE NAME	COUNTY FIPS CODE	POPULATION 2000	POPULATION 2009	POPULATION 2014	2000-2009 ANNUAL RATE % Rate	2000-2009 ANNUAL RATE State Centile	HOUSEHOLDS 2000	HOUSEHOLDS 2009	HOUSEHOLDS 2014	HOUSEHOLDS % Annual Rate 2000-2009	HOUSEHOLDS 2009 Average HH Size	FAMILIES 2000	FAMILIES 2009	FAMILIES % Annual Rate 2000-2009
93702	FRESNO	019	47452	50091	51302	0.6	45	11044	11294	11506	0.2	4.36	9220	9371	0.2
93703	FRESNO	019	32166	34111	34982	0.6	45	9903	10123	10308	0.2	3.31	7197	7283	0.1
93704	FRESNO	019	26248	27578	28403	0.5	39	11016	11420	11702	0.4	2.41	6573	6711	0.2
93705	FRESNO	019	37547	40215	41678	0.7	50	12819	13489	13908	0.6	2.96	8971	9336	0.4
93706	FRESNO	019	35621	38177	39669	0.8	54	9552	10053	10388	0.6	3.72	7424	7756	0.5
93710	FRESNO	019	28755	30524	31576	0.6	45	10695	11251	11615	0.5	2.58	6786	7014	0.4
93711	FRESNO	019	35311	38063	39789	0.8	54	14659	15797	16486	0.8	2.40	10074	10606	0.6
93720	FRESNO	019	37690	46501	51665	2.3	86	14317	17216	18969	2.0	2.69	10169	12298	2.1
93721	FRESNO	019	6813	7335	7452	0.8	54	1618	1666	1701	0.3	2.45	792	809	0.2
93722	FRESNO	019	54171	69131	76907	2.7	90	17637	22060	24413	2.4	3.13	13621	17018	2.4
93723	FRESNO	019	5174	7757	8865	4.5	95	1637	2417	2742	4.3	3.19	1320	1955	4.3
93725	FRESNO	019	21389	23813	25441	1.2	68	5657	6186	6582	1.0	3.79	4652	5046	0.9
93726	FRESNO	019	38540	40573	41734	0.6	45	14069	14505	14829	0.3	2.79	9062	9219	0.2
93727	FRESNO	019	55222	66472	72470	2.0	83	17953	21149	23012	1.8	3.09	12986	15298	1.8
93728	FRESNO	019	16643	17642	18190	0.6	45	5929	6145	6297	0.4	2.84	3438	3503	0.2
93730	FRESNO	019	6899	9503	10674	3.5	92	2399	3473	3901	4.1	2.74	1858	2646	3.9
93741	FRESNO	019	23	25	26	0.9	58	16	17	18	0.7	1.47	8	8	0.0
93901	SALINAS	053	35675	26952	26888	-3.0	0	10126	10186	10189	0.1	2.56	6622	6580	-0.1
93905	SALINAS	053	58584	66058	68727	1.3	70	11608	12925	13492	1.2	5.01	10440	11582	1.1
93906	SALINAS	053	53966	59009	61042	1.0	62	15589	16846	17367	0.8	3.48	12333	13363	0.9
93907	SALINAS	053	21641	22633	23083	0.5	39	7035	7466	7638	0.6	3.01	5404	5693	0.6
93908	SALINAS	053	14765	15924	16617	0.8	54	4942	5329	5550	0.8	2.95	4099	4393	0.8
93920	BIG SUR	053	1000	1423	1448	3.9	93	421	448	458	0.7	2.34	226	237	0.5
93923	CARMEL	053	16593	16600	16748	0.0	9	8158	8315	8409	0.2	1.97	4723	4751	0.1
93924	CARMEL VALLEY	053	6596	6693	6758	0.2	18	2701	2804	2844	0.4	2.37	1802	1848	0.3
93925	CHUALAR	053	71	74	76	0.4	30	22	24	24	0.9	2.83	20	22	1.0
93926	GONZALES	053	8449	8730	8856	0.4	30	1915	1989	2025	0.4	4.19	1687	1745	0.4
93927	GREENFIELD	053	14461	17040	17946	1.8	80	3185	3678	3868	1.6	4.60	2797	3217	1.5
93930	KING CITY	053	14401	15892	17010	1.1	64	3777	4132	4400	1.0	3.79	3096	3366	0.9
93932	LOCKWOOD	053	829	858	873	0.4	30	281	297	304	0.6	2.72	207	217	0.5
93933	MARINA	053	27926	21746	21788	-2.7	0	7863	8042	8082	0.2	2.69	5445	5526	0.2
93940	MONTEREY	053	31943	32562	32757	0.2	18	13626	13992	14085	0.3	2.12	7199	7406	0.3
93943	MONTEREY	053	228	241	241	0.6	45	15	15	15	0.0	4.00	14	14	0.0
93950	PACIFIC GROVE	053	15495	15047	14915	-0.3	3	7302	7258	7218	-0.1	2.05	3968	3879	-0.2
93953	PEBBLE BEACH	053	5140	4942	4870	-0.4	2	2322	2284	2260	-0.2	2.14	1602	1559	-0.3
93955	SEASIDE	053	31957	33740	33758	0.6	45	9913	10035	10051	0.1	3.20	7427	7466	0.1
93960	SOLEDAD	053	13057	29363	30781	9.2	98	2972	3837	4186	2.8	4.35	2641	3401	2.8
94002	BELMONT	081	25416	25490	25672	0.0	9	10560	10633	10697	0.1	2.34	6654	6717	0.1
94005	BRISBANE	081	3615	3752	3866	0.4	30	1626	1701	1755	0.5	2.18	863	901	0.5
94010	BURLINGAME	081	40153	40311	40653	0.0	9	16597	16660	16752	0.0	2.39	10429	10482	0.1
94014	DALY CITY	081	46635	48730	49722	0.5	39	12782	13176	13381	0.3	3.68	9916	10221	0.3
94015	DALY CITY	081	63470	63857	64312	0.1	13	20060	20105	20188	0.0	3.15	14683	14730	0.0
94019	HALF MOON BAY	081	18286	19321	19844	0.6	45	6236	6640	6817	0.7	2.77	4440	4723	0.7
94020	LA HONDA	081	1165	1181	1197	0.1	13	441	451	457	0.2	2.44	287	294	0.3
94021	LOMA MAR	081	426	440	449	0.4	30	186	194	198	0.5	2.10	120	125	0.4
94022	LOS ALTOS	085	18456	18584	18824	0.1	13	6964	7000	7070	0.1	2.60	5262	5305	0.1
94024	LOS ALTOS	085	21983	22164	22461	0.1	13	8029	8076	8157	0.1	2.71	6439	6496	0.1
94025	MENLO PARK	081	40472	41371	41919	0.2	18	15981	16119	16265	0.1	2.50	9459	9570	0.1
94027	ATHERTON	081	7307	7347	7418	0.1	13	2453	2470	2487	0.1	2.84	2005	2019	0.1
94028	PORTOLA VALLEY	081	6653	6694	6756	0.1	13	2511	2538	2560	0.1	2.60	1926	1948	0.1
94030	MILLBRAE	081	21061	21226	21539	0.1	13	8052	8126	8237	0.1	2.57	5583	5642	0.1
94035	MOUNTAIN VIEW	085	313	315	315	0.1	13	10	10	10	0.0	2.60	10	10	0.0
94038	MOSS BEACH	081	5443	5715	5857	0.5	39	1890	1985	2031	0.5	2.82	1392	1462	0.5
94040	MOUNTAIN VIEW	085	30472	32174	33197	0.6	45	13079	13667	14032	0.5	2.33	7132	7481	0.5
94041	MOUNTAIN VIEW	085	13470	13634	13875	0.1	13	6132	6180	6268	0.1	2.20	2900	2938	0.1
94043	MOUNTAIN VIEW	085	27934	28502	29094	0.2	18	12349	12538	12764	0.2	2.25	6221	6345	0.2
94044	PACIFICA	081	38447	38337	38610	0.0	9	14024	14086	14166	0.0	2.71	9671	9721	0.1
94060	PESCADERO	081	1700	1753	1782	0.3	23	465	485	494	0.5	3.09	321	334	0.4
94061	REDWOOD CITY	081	35249	35591	35877	0.1	13	13472	13503	13557	0.0	2.60	8721	8753	0.0
94062	REDWOOD CITY	081	26555	26589	26773	0.0	9	10419	10480	10549	0.1	2.49	7163	7220	0.1
94063	REDWOOD CITY	081	32175	33622	34229	0.5	39	8815	9152	9309	0.4	3.53	6087	6262	0.3
94065	REDWOOD CITY	081	10648	11302	11622	0.6	45	4649	4950	5087	0.7	2.28	2909	3110	0.7
94066	SAN BRUNO	081	39676	41985	43037	0.6	45	14537	15427	15823	0.6	2.71	9809	10285	0.5
94070	SAN CARLOS	081	28177	28599	28916	0.2	18	11611	11820	11938	0.2	2.40	7674	7812	0.2
94074	SAN GREGORIO	081	104	104	105	0.0	9	31	31	31	0.0	3.10	20	20	0.0
94080	SOUTH SAN FRANCISCO	081	60698	64330	65995	0.6	45	19718	20733	21179	0.5	3.08	14670	15470	0.6
94085	SUNNYVALE	085	20341	21175	21733	0.4	30	7322	7525	7684	0.3	2.79	4481	4635	0.4
94086	SUNNYVALE	085	44872	47228	48861	0.6	45	19324	20071	20644	0.4	2.34	10871	11374	0.5
94087	SUNNYVALE	085	50213	51794	53141	0.3	23	19554	20049	20486	0.3	2.56	13382	13791	0.3
94089	SUNNYVALE	085	16970	18544	19315	1.0	62	6681	7221	7514	0.8	2.57	3999	4283	0.7
94102	SAN FRANCISCO	075	30248	32290	32998	0.7	50	16615	17699	18069	0.7	1.70	4033	4352	0.8
94103	SAN FRANCISCO	075	23096	25934	26756	1.3	70	9581	10974	11387	1.5	2.04	2907	3353	1.6
94104	SAN FRANCISCO	075	246	252	253	0.3	23	105	106	105	0.1	2.29	43	43	0.0
94105	SAN FRANCISCO	075	2074	3957	4279	7.2	97	1288	2639	2882	8.1	1.38	293	565	7.4
94107	SAN FRANCISCO	075	17118	21392	22960	2.4	87	8989	11472	12403	2.7	1.80	3050	3895	2.7
94108	SAN FRANCISCO	075	14063	13702	13586	-0.3	3	7895	7766	7705	-0.2	1.75	2806	2774	-0.1
94109	SAN FRANCISCO	075	53481	53487	53495	0.0	9	31805	31988	31988	0.1	1.63	8038	8182	0.2
94110	SAN FRANCISCO	075	74063	73657	73445	-0.1	5	25860	25702	25583	-0.1	2.81	12235	12274	0.0
94111	SAN FRANCISCO	075	3351	3404	3408	0.2	18	2301	2354	2363	0.2	1.44	639	656	0.3
94112	SAN FRANCISCO	075	74091	75244	75328	0.2	18	20466	20426	20361	0.0	3.64	15089	15121	0.0
94114	SAN FRANCISCO	075	31303	30128	29745	-0.4	2	17019	16565	16378	-0.3	1.81	4180	4111	-0.2
94115	SAN FRANCISCO	075	32046	32111	32119	0.0	9	16887	16954	16952	0.0	1.85	5479	5557	0.2
94116	SAN FRANCISCO	075	43044	42716	42564	-0.1	5	15139	15012	14934	-0.1	2.82	10288	10248	0.0
94117	SAN FRANCISCO	075	38743	37824	37484	-0.3	3	18116	17824	17680	-0.2	1.97	4725	4703	-0.1
94118	SAN FRANCISCO	075	38933	38044	37759	-0.2	4	17269	17066	16964	-0.1	2.19	8066	8026	-0.1
94121	SAN FRANCISCO	075	42400	41551	41273	-0.2	4	17295	17119	17024	-0.1	2.41	9552	9516	0.0
94122	SAN FRANCISCO	075	55565	55188	54990	-0.1	5	21569	21414	21309	-0.1	2.55	11828	11835	0.0
94123	SAN FRANCISCO	075	25240	24616	24384	-0.3	3	15638	15397	15277	-0.2	1.59	4238	4216	-0.1
94124	SAN FRANCISCO	075	33193	33239	33228	0.0	9	9296	9090	9038	-0.2	3.60	7115	6967	-0.2
94127	SAN FRANCISCO	075	18462	18101	17955	-0.2	4	7178	7089	7036	-0.1	2.54	4759	4725	-0.1
94129	SAN FRANCISCO	075	2285	2361	2397	0.4	30	821	861	873	0.5	2.73	382	404	0.6
94130	SAN FRANCISCO	075	1453	2368	2731	5.4	96	460	806	942	6.3	2.68	159	281	6.3
94131	SAN FRANCISCO	075	29517	28855	28635	-0.2	4	14103	13922	13830	-0.1	1.97	5747	5726	0.0
94132	SAN FRANCISCO	075	26161	27656	28097	0.6	45	9798	10164	10283	0.4	2.57	5772	6018	0.5
94133	SAN FRANCISCO	075	26666	26048	25862	-0.3	3	13506	13385	13320	-0.1	1.94	5289	5275	0.0
	CALIFORNIA					1.2					1.0	2.93			1.1
	UNITED STATES					1.0					1.1	2.59			0.9

ZIP CODE #	POST OFFICE NAME	RACE (%) White 2000	White 2009	Black 2000	Black 2009	Asian/Pacific 2000	Asian/Pacific 2009	% Hispanic Origin 2000	% Hispanic Origin 2009	2009 AGE DISTRIBUTION (%) 0-4	5-9	10-14	15-19	20-24	25-44	45-64	65-84	85+	18+	MEDIAN AGE 2009	% 2009 Males	% 2009 Females
93702	FRESNO	27.8	25.0	4.6	3.9	17.0	16.3	65.4	70.8	11.9	10.8	9.8	11.1	10.0	25.1	15.4	5.1	0.9	60.8	23.2	50.7	49.3
93703	FRESNO	44.3	37.7	5.2	4.8	14.3	14.6	50.0	58.9	10.9	9.8	8.2	8.8	9.0	26.0	17.1	8.2	2.0	65.8	27.0	49.4	50.6
93704	FRESNO	70.3	62.2	3.9	4.2	5.7	7.0	27.5	36.5	6.8	6.2	6.0	6.2	6.9	26.0	26.3	12.7	3.0	77.2	38.2	47.4	52.6
93705	FRESNO	51.8	44.2	9.4	9.0	7.0	7.7	42.0	51.9	10.4	9.0	7.7	8.3	8.7	26.2	18.9	8.9	2.0	67.9	28.5	48.3	51.7
93706	FRESNO	28.9	26.3	25.3	22.1	9.4	9.6	50.2	57.6	9.8	9.3	8.5	9.6	9.0	24.5	19.2	8.5	1.6	66.4	27.4	51.2	48.8
93710	FRESNO	64.2	55.3	6.3	6.7	10.2	12.3	24.2	32.8	7.0	5.7	5.3	9.0	11.9	26.7	20.9	11.0	2.5	78.3	31.0	48.0	52.0
93711	FRESNO	78.4	70.5	3.6	4.2	7.3	9.7	14.8	21.6	5.2	5.1	5.6	6.2	6.3	25.4	29.4	14.6	2.3	80.3	41.9	48.5	51.5
93720	FRESNO	77.6	69.4	2.6	3.0	10.3	13.9	13.6	20.2	8.0	7.6	7.4	6.8	5.8	30.3	25.6	7.1	1.4	72.9	35.1	48.2	51.8
93721	FRESNO	39.2	34.3	14.4	12.8	2.9	3.0	61.1	69.6	7.6	5.6	4.2	7.0	13.7	36.4	15.0	7.5	3.0	80.2	30.3	64.9	35.1
93722	FRESNO	56.9	49.3	8.2	8.0	10.2	11.8	34.5	43.4	9.6	9.0	8.4	7.9	6.8	30.2	21.5	5.9	0.7	68.1	30.4	49.2	50.8
93723	FRESNO	63.7	58.0	1.8	2.3	5.2	5.8	37.9	47.0	6.1	6.2	6.8	7.1	5.1	24.1	30.7	12.3	1.6	76.5	40.9	50.5	49.5
93725	FRESNO	36.6	31.7	6.6	5.8	8.7	9.2	63.2	70.2	9.1	8.9	8.4	9.4	8.0	26.1	20.9	7.9	1.2	67.7	29.1	51.0	49.0
93726	FRESNO	53.7	44.9	7.6	7.5	11.2	12.7	35.4	45.0	8.7	7.6	6.8	8.0	12.5	26.4	19.0	9.4	1.6	72.6	28.5	48.2	51.8
93727	FRESNO	48.5	43.0	8.1	7.3	13.4	13.9	38.4	46.5	9.6	8.4	7.6	8.5	8.9	26.1	19.9	9.2	1.8	69.5	29.3	48.8	51.2
93728	FRESNO	50.0	41.8	4.6	4.3	7.4	8.0	48.7	59.0	8.3	8.0	7.3	8.1	8.3	30.1	21.1	7.4	1.3	71.4	30.5	51.0	49.0
93730	FRESNO	81.4	73.5	1.8	2.1	8.1	11.4	11.7	18.0	7.6	8.1	8.4	6.9	4.1	28.9	28.1	7.3	0.6	71.4	37.0	48.8	51.2
93741	FRESNO	78.3	72.0	4.3	4.0	4.3	4.0	26.1	36.0	8.0	8.0	8.0	8.0	8.0	32.0	28.0	0.0	0.0	72.0	31.3	48.0	52.0
93901	SALINAS	55.8	54.5	6.8	2.1	5.4	7.1	40.4	50.4	7.3	6.7	6.4	7.1	7.3	28.8	24.3	9.7	2.4	77.0	35.6	50.7	49.3
93905	SALINAS	37.1	35.2	1.2	1.1	3.1	3.2	88.2	90.5	11.8	10.6	8.9	9.6	9.2	31.8	14.3	3.3	0.5	64.1	25.0	53.1	46.9
93906	SALINAS	47.4	41.1	2.8	2.5	10.0	10.7	54.8	62.9	9.6	9.0	8.0	8.2	7.5	30.7	19.8	6.3	0.9	68.9	29.5	49.7	50.3
93907	SALINAS	67.3	60.1	2.2	2.1	6.8	7.5	30.8	39.6	6.2	6.8	7.5	8.0	5.9	25.7	30.4	8.5	1.1	74.8	38.4	50.3	49.7
93908	SALINAS	73.2	67.3	0.8	1.0	5.6	7.0	26.2	32.0	6.6	7.6	8.3	7.8	4.9	22.4	30.2	10.8	1.3	73.6	39.8	50.2	49.8
93920	BIG SUR	89.4	74.1	1.5	6.2	1.7	2.8	8.9	21.6	4.0	3.9	4.2	6.4	8.0	29.0	33.1	10.2	1.3	86.5	41.0	59.4	40.6
93923	CARMEL	93.4	90.1	0.4	0.7	3.0	4.3	3.7	6.3	2.2	2.5	3.2	4.0	3.3	13.4	39.5	26.3	5.7	90.1	57.7	46.1	53.9
93924	CARMEL VALLEY	91.9	88.3	0.3	0.4	2.0	2.8	7.4	11.5	3.5	3.8	4.8	6.2	5.1	17.8	38.8	17.7	2.4	84.2	50.3	48.3	51.7
93925	CHUALAR	38.0	33.8	1.4	2.7	2.8	2.7	74.6	77.0	10.8	9.5	8.1	9.5	9.5	32.4	17.6	2.7	0.0	71.6	26.4	54.1	45.9
93926	GONZALES	35.8	32.5	0.7	1.2	2.4	2.3	82.4	86.4	10.1	9.6	8.6	9.4	9.3	29.9	17.1	5.3	0.7	69.7	26.6	53.2	46.8
93927	GREENFIELD	42.0	39.2	1.0	0.9	1.0	0.9	83.8	88.7	10.7	9.9	8.5	9.4	9.4	30.3	16.5	4.7	0.6	69.0	26.1	52.3	47.7
93930	KING CITY	46.9	41.8	0.6	0.7	2.0	1.9	73.2	80.6	10.0	9.1	7.9	8.8	9.4	30.9	17.6	5.6	0.7	70.4	27.4	53.0	47.0
93932	LOCKWOOD	76.0	67.8	2.4	2.8	3.1	4.2	22.3	31.0	7.8	7.8	7.5	7.2	6.4	25.6	28.6	8.2	0.9	72.0	35.6	52.7	47.3
93933	MARINA	44.9	41.5	14.3	10.1	17.7	24.8	22.7	23.7	7.1	6.6	6.4	6.7	8.3	30.0	24.7	9.5	0.8	76.0	34.0	49.1	50.9
93940	MONTEREY	81.3	75.4	2.4	2.6	7.6	9.7	10.5	15.0	5.3	4.5	4.2	6.5	8.5	30.0	25.8	12.0	3.2	83.7	38.2	49.1	50.9
93943	MONTEREY	79.4	73.0	4.8	5.4	10.5	13.7	7.9	12.0	0.8	2.1	4.1	5.8	14.1	59.3	13.7	0.0	0.0	90.9	32.4	85.1	14.9
93950	PACIFIC GROVE	88.0	83.4	1.1	1.3	4.8	6.3	7.1	10.9	3.5	3.4	4.2	4.9	5.9	23.6	34.8	15.8	3.9	86.1	47.8	46.7	53.3
93953	PEBBLE BEACH	90.8	86.9	0.5	0.5	5.6	7.7	2.6	4.2	2.0	2.4	3.2	3.4	2.5	10.2	37.6	32.9	5.8	90.7	60.9	46.1	53.9
93955	SEASIDE	49.4	44.4	12.5	11.7	11.3	11.7	34.4	41.4	9.6	7.7	6.5	7.4	9.1	33.4	18.6	6.9	0.9	72.1	29.7	52.2	47.8
93960	SOLEDAD	34.1	35.1	1.0	8.8	2.3	3.2	84.1	70.5	6.8	6.4	5.7	8.9	11.8	39.7	15.0	4.6	0.9	77.7	29.7	64.5	35.5
94002	BELMONT	75.2	67.3	1.7	1.8	15.9	20.7	8.4	11.5	5.7	5.6	5.5	5.2	5.0	28.4	30.4	12.1	2.1	80.1	41.9	49.1	50.9
94005	BRISBANE	72.3	63.9	1.0	1.1	14.7	18.8	17.1	22.6	4.4	4.3	3.9	4.7	4.5	31.2	37.1	9.0	1.0	84.4	43.4	50.4	49.6
94010	BURLINGAME	75.7	67.9	0.9	1.0	16.8	22.0	8.4	11.6	5.2	5.4	6.2	5.7	5.4	26.1	30.0	12.9	3.0	79.4	42.4	48.2	51.8
94014	DALY CITY	24.7	21.6	4.7	4.1	46.4	47.7	32.9	35.8	6.3	6.2	6.0	6.6	6.6	29.8	26.1	10.8	1.6	77.8	37.2	49.4	50.6
94015	DALY CITY	28.9	23.2	4.2	3.8	53.5	57.6	14.8	16.8	5.9	5.6	5.3	6.0	6.8	30.5	26.2	11.7	2.0	79.7	37.9	49.1	50.9
94019	HALF MOON BAY	79.3	72.9	2.7	2.7	3.4	4.4	21.8	29.4	5.9	5.9	6.5	6.4	5.9	26.3	32.2	9.8	1.1	77.7	40.5	52.2	47.8
94020	LA HONDA	89.3	85.0	0.8	0.8	2.1	2.8	12.2	17.8	4.3	4.2	4.9	6.9	6.5	25.1	39.0	8.2	0.9	81.7	43.7	53.5	46.5
94021	LOMA MAR	87.8	83.0	0.5	0.5	1.9	2.5	18.1	25.5	4.1	3.9	4.5	6.4	6.8	25.5	38.4	9.5	0.9	83.2	44.1	51.6	48.4
94022	LOS ALTOS	80.3	73.5	0.6	0.6	15.9	21.1	2.9	4.1	4.6	5.6	7.1	6.5	3.3	17.2	34.1	17.6	4.1	78.2	48.2	48.5	51.5
94024	LOS ALTOS	78.5	71.1	0.4	0.4	17.2	22.8	3.2	4.5	5.5	6.8	8.4	6.9	3.1	16.9	34.0	15.3	3.2	74.7	46.3	49.1	50.9
94025	MENLO PARK	72.7	67.2	6.1	5.8	8.1	10.5	17.7	21.7	6.6	6.4	6.5	5.7	5.0	29.2	26.7	11.0	3.0	76.8	39.1	49.5	50.5
94027	ATHERTON	85.5	79.4	0.7	0.8	10.1	14.1	2.9	4.2	5.1	6.3	8.3	8.6	4.9	16.1	30.9	16.1	3.7	75.8	45.4	48.5	51.5
94028	PORTOLA VALLEY	92.6	89.1	0.4	0.5	4.1	6.0	3.8	5.7	4.9	6.2	8.1	6.6	2.9	15.6	34.2	17.6	3.9	76.1	48.1	50.5	49.5
94030	MILLBRAE	63.1	54.1	0.8	0.8	28.2	34.8	11.7	14.9	4.9	4.8	5.1	5.6	5.7	24.7	28.9	15.8	4.6	81.6	44.5	47.5	52.5
94035	MOUNTAIN VIEW	60.5	53.3	10.8	10.8	13.7	15.9	15.9	21.0	10.2	7.9	4.4	2.5	15.2	54.9	4.8	0.0	0.0	75.6	28.1	66.3	33.7
94038	MOSS BEACH	86.5	81.4	0.8	0.9	3.2	4.3	13.2	18.0	5.4	6.4	7.3	6.2	4.7	23.2	36.8	8.5	1.4	76.5	42.9	49.4	50.6
94040	MOUNTAIN VIEW	65.6	57.4	2.0	2.0	20.4	25.0	16.7	21.4	5.9	5.2	5.0	4.9	7.5	34.6	24.7	9.9	2.2	80.7	36.5	51.4	48.6
94041	MOUNTAIN VIEW	65.7	58.3	2.1	2.1	19.1	23.1	20.8	25.9	6.2	4.6	3.9	4.2	6.5	42.4	24.0	6.8	1.3	82.8	36.1	52.2	47.8
94043	MOUNTAIN VIEW	60.5	52.3	3.9	3.7	22.3	27.1	18.4	22.8	6.0	4.6	4.2	4.1	7.3	39.4	24.9	8.3	1.2	82.8	36.3	51.8	48.2
94044	PACIFICA	69.4	62.4	3.3	3.2	16.0	19.2	14.6	19.3	5.5	5.5	5.7	6.1	6.3	27.8	31.4	10.5	1.4	79.5	40.5	49.1	50.9
94060	PESCADERO	76.9	71.9	0.5	0.6	1.2	1.5	46.3	55.7	6.4	5.2	5.5	7.5	9.4	29.8	27.3	7.9	1.0	79.3	35.3	55.3	44.7
94061	REDWOOD CITY	75.6	69.6	2.2	2.2	6.1	7.6	29.0	36.5	7.1	6.4	6.1	5.8	6.5	30.6	25.5	9.3	2.8	76.9	37.1	49.1	50.9
94062	REDWOOD CITY	86.9	81.8	0.8	0.9	5.4	7.5	9.3	13.2	5.4	6.1	7.0	5.5	3.7	23.4	34.4	12.2	2.3	77.9	44.4	49.6	50.4
94063	REDWOOD CITY	50.5	46.4	3.4	3.2	6.3	6.7	64.7	70.4	8.9	7.8	6.8	7.9	9.2	34.1	19.3	5.3	0.8	72.0	29.9	53.9	46.1
94065	REDWOOD CITY	62.7	53.0	1.8	1.8	29.6	37.4	5.9	7.6	8.5	5.5	4.6	3.4	3.7	38.6	28.4	6.6	0.7	79.1	37.3	48.5	51.5
94066	SAN BRUNO	57.6	50.2	2.0	2.0	21.6	25.0	24.1	29.0	6.0	5.9	5.9	6.3	6.8	29.4	27.9	10.0	1.7	78.3	38.4	49.3	50.7
94070	SAN CARLOS	84.7	78.6	0.8	0.9	8.1	11.1	7.6	11.0	6.2	6.7	7.3	5.6	3.9	23.8	32.4	11.5	2.6	76.1	43.1	48.9	51.1
94074	SAN GREGORIO	85.6	80.8	1.0	1.0	1.0	1.9	25.0	31.7	5.8	4.8	5.8	6.7	6.7	28.8	31.7	8.7	1.0	78.8	39.4	52.9	47.1
94080	SOUTH SAN FRANCISCO	44.1	37.8	2.8	2.5	30.6	33.6	31.7	36.1	6.4	6.2	6.1	6.8	6.5	28.5	26.2	11.4	1.9	77.2	37.7	49.5	50.5
94085	SUNNYVALE	45.1	38.9	2.2	2.0	30.8	33.6	32.2	37.5	7.5	6.0	5.4	5.5	8.0	39.7	21.2	5.9	0.8	77.9	32.5	54.1	45.9
94086	SUNNYVALE	48.3	40.5	2.8	2.6	36.8	42.0	15.5	19.0	7.0	5.3	4.3	4.0	6.8	42.2	21.8	7.3	1.3	81.1	34.0	52.6	47.4
94087	SUNNYVALE	60.9	52.2	1.6	1.6	30.8	37.4	7.2	9.4	6.6	6.2	6.4	5.6	4.7	28.8	27.8	11.7	2.2	77.2	40.2	49.9	50.1
94089	SUNNYVALE	51.1	44.8	2.6	2.4	31.6	35.2	18.6	21.6	6.1	5.6	5.2	5.1	5.2	32.2	26.2	12.3	2.2	80.1	39.3	50.1	49.9
94102	SAN FRANCISCO	46.9	40.5	15.8	14.7	25.5	30.2	13.3	16.6	3.2	2.9	2.5	3.6	7.7	38.0	28.3	12.3	1.4	89.5	40.3	59.5	40.5
94103	SAN FRANCISCO	44.9	38.5	11.7	11.5	24.1	28.0	25.6	28.7	3.5	3.0	2.6	3.9	8.3	40.8	25.6	10.3	1.9	88.9	38.3	58.5	41.5
94104	SAN FRANCISCO	32.1	25.0	0.4	0.4	61.8	68.3	6.5	7.1	2.4	2.4	2.0	3.2	5.2	30.6	32.1	19.8	2.4	92.5	48.1	50.8	49.2
94105	SAN FRANCISCO	70.3	56.7	7.4	13.7	16.0	19.1	6.3	11.3	1.7	1.1	0.6	1.1	6.2	54.4	29.0	5.1	0.8	96.0	37.3	59.0	41.0
94107	SAN FRANCISCO	61.9	55.3	13.3	12.4	16.1	20.5	9.6	12.7	3.8	2.6	2.2	2.8	6.9	45.4	24.1	10.4	1.8	89.9	37.4	53.5	46.5
94108	SAN FRANCISCO	36.2	30.3	1.6	1.4	58.1	63.2	4.2	5.2	2.6	2.2	2.0	3.1	6.6	33.6	27.3	18.9	3.7	91.6	44.9	49.3	50.7
94109	SAN FRANCISCO	60.3	52.4	3.3	3.2	28.9	35.0	7.9	10.1	2.5	1.8	1.6	2.4	7.5	43.4	24.8	12.5	3.4	93.0	39.0	51.9	48.1
94110	SAN FRANCISCO	52.6	47.0	4.2	3.7	12.7	14.0	45.9	52.6	5.4	4.6	4.2	4.6	7.3	42.0	23.4	7.3	1.2	83.1	35.1	52.3	47.7
94111	SAN FRANCISCO	65.3	57.2	2.1	2.0	29.5	36.6	3.3	4.4	1.7	1.4	1.0	1.0	3.1	24.6	41.4	21.6	4.1	95.3	53.9	53.5	46.5
94112	SAN FRANCISCO	29.0	24.9	6.3	5.3	45.5	48.3	27.6	30.5	5.6	5.6	5.5	6.0	5.6	30.0	27.1	12.3	2.3	79.8	39.7	49.4	50.6
94114	SAN FRANCISCO	82.8	77.1	2.3	2.4	7.3	9.9	8.9	12.5	2.7	1.8	1.5	1.4	4.1	50.4	29.4	7.2	1.5	93.1	39.1	59.6	40.4
94115	SAN FRANCISCO	60.2	54.0	17.6	17.2	16.0	20.5	5.5	7.3	3.6	2.6	2.3	2.8	8.2	43.1	23.3	11.3	2.8	89.9	36.6	48.5	51.5
94116	SAN FRANCISCO	42.8	34.3	1.1	1.0	51.3	58.8	4.8	5.8	4.3	4.5	4.7	5.1	5.2	29.3	29.9	13.9	3.1	83.4	43.1	48.5	51.5
94117	SAN FRANCISCO	72.0	65.9	11.3	11.6	8.9	11.7	7.4	10.2	2.6	1.7	1.6	3.8	10.2	51.7	20.7	6.1	1.5	93.0	33.2	53.2	46.8
94118	SAN FRANCISCO	56.0	47.4	1.8	1.8	36.9	44.2	4.5	5.7	4.0	3.4	3.3	3.9	7.6	38.3	25.7	11.3	2.5	87.3	38.5	47.1	52.9
94121	SAN FRANCISCO	49.0	40.0	1.5	1.4	44.2	52.0	4.4	5.4	4.0	3.7	3.7	4.1	6.0	34.1	28.6	12.8	2.8	86.0	41.4	48.1	51.9
94122	SAN FRANCISCO	47.3	38.5	1.5	1.3	45.8	53.4	5.0	6.1	4.1	3.8	3.8	4.1	6.6	36.5	27.2	11.6	2.3	85.8	39.5	48.7	51.3
94123	SAN FRANCISCO	86.3	81.0	0.6	0.6	9.8	13.6	3.9	5.5	3.0	1.6	1.4	1.2	4.3	51.7	22.9	10.9	2.9	93.2	36.8	46.6	53.4
94124	SAN FRANCISCO	9.6	9.3	47.9	42.3	28.0	31.0	16.7	20.0	7.4	7.4	7.2	8.2	7.7	27.9	23.7	8.9	1.5	72.9	33.1	47.9	52.1
94127	SAN FRANCISCO	63.8	55.4	3.9	3.7	25.7	32.2	7.5	9.7	4.6	5.1	5.8	4.7	3.2	23.7	34.6	15.0	3.2	81.3	46.4	49.4	50.6
94129	SAN FRANCISCO	76.4	69.8	4.5	4.6	9.4	12.2	9.3	12.8	6.7	4.4	3.2	3.4	18.9	51.2	10.8	1.2	0.1	84.5	27.8	53.9	46.1
94130	SAN FRANCISCO	65.3	57.9	12.2	12.2	12.0	15.6	10.2	13.9	4.7	3.3	2.7	7.5	17.9	47.4	13.9	2.2	0.3	87.2	28.9	55.8	44.2
94131	SAN FRANCISCO	67.7	60.3	5.7	5.5	17.1	21.4	12.0	15.8	3.8	3.1	3.3	3.2	4.0	35.8	31.2	12.7	2.9	87.7	43.3	52.0	48.0
94132	SAN FRANCISCO	41.9	34.3	11.9	10.7	38.2	44.9	7.8	9.7	4.5	4.1	4.0	7.2	9.9	31.3	24.4	11.8	2.9	84.8	37.1	47.7	52.3
94133	SAN FRANCISCO	40.0	33.2	1.4	1.3	54.9	60.9	3.4	4.2	3.0	2.6	2.5	3.3	5.9	33.4	28.4	17.3	3.6	90.0	44.5	49.7	50.3
	CALIFORNIA	59.5	54.5	6.7	6.2	11.3	12.5	32.4	38.3	7.5	7.1	6.9	7.5	7.4	28.5	24.2	9.3	1.6	74.1	34.3	49.9	50.1
	UNITED STATES	75.1	72.0	12.3	12.7	3.8	4.6	12.5	15.7	6.8	6.7	6.6	7.1	6.9	27.0	26.0	10.9	1.9	75.7	36.9	49.2	50.8

ZIP CODE #	POST OFFICE NAME	2009 Per Capita Income	2009 HH Income Base	2009 Household Income Distribution (%) Less than $25,000	$25,000 to $49,999	$50,000 to $99,999	$100,000 to $149,999	$150,000 or More	Median Household Income 2009	2014	2009 National Centile	2009 State Centile	2009 Home Value Base	2009 Home Value Distribution (%) Less than $50,000	$50,000 to $89,999	$90,000 to $174,999	$175,000 to $399,999	$400,000 or More	2009 Median Home Value
93702	FRESNO	8227	11294	47.2	32.6	17.2	2.0	1.0	26332	27089	4	3	4686	2.6	17.4	76.7	3.1	0.2	109054
93703	FRESNO	11374	10123	40.5	36.4	20.1	2.2	0.8	30871	32058	9	7	4361	0.4	6.2	90.4	3.0	0.0	126299
93704	FRESNO	24390	11420	25.7	29.8	32.0	7.7	4.7	44967	47235	48	33	6310	4.2	5.5	37.2	46.2	6.9	183903
93705	FRESNO	15048	13489	34.4	31.7	28.8	3.7	1.4	36855	39131	23	16	6487	6.1	4.9	72.7	15.2	1.1	135569
93706	FRESNO	9913	10053	47.9	30.5	17.7	2.6	1.3	26054	26654	4	3	4392	6.2	21.7	51.4	16.0	4.7	114422
93710	FRESNO	20433	11251	29.4	28.3	31.6	8.0	2.7	41764	43754	39	25	5153	2.2	2.3	27.1	68.1	0.2	193085
93711	FRESNO	37514	15797	12.7	22.9	37.1	13.9	13.3	66833	67635	85	68	9699	0.8	0.8	11.7	58.4	28.3	293829
93720	FRESNO	34794	17216	10.4	17.5	39.7	18.9	13.5	75560	77169	90	76	11646	2.6	1.4	9.5	68.2	18.3	256547
93721	FRESNO	15116	1666	67.2	23.0	8.3	0.7	0.8	15987	16131	1	2	203	3.0	29.1	55.7	10.8	1.5	127371
93722	FRESNO	20116	22060	16.6	25.0	47.0	8.4	3.0	59189	61295	76	57	14963	4.4	2.6	36.7	52.5	3.8	183939
93723	FRESNO	20518	2417	22.9	28.6	33.9	8.0	6.5	48339	50529	57	39	1769	1.9	3.0	32.2	41.2	21.8	219221
93725	FRESNO	12526	6186	34.5	31.0	28.3	4.3	1.9	35556	38554	19	14	3730	10.5	9.9	50.5	22.6	6.5	135254
93726	FRESNO	15127	14505	35.2	33.9	27.0	2.9	1.1	35652	37986	20	15	6332	1.7	3.6	80.2	14.3	0.2	141971
93727	FRESNO	17458	21149	30.4	27.8	32.0	6.6	3.1	42136	45891	40	26	10744	2.9	4.6	42.0	43.1	7.3	175921
93728	FRESNO	13364	6145	40.8	35.1	20.9	2.4	0.7	30973	32470	10	8	2835	16.2	6.0	68.6	6.6	2.5	118310
93730	FRESNO	39073	3473	6.5	12.9	43.8	17.4	19.4	82854	83366	93	82	2764	4.8	3.0	2.8	61.4	28.0	275365
93741	FRESNO	40979	17	23.5	23.5	47.1	5.9	0.0	54626	50000	71	51	10	0.0	0.0	40.0	60.0	0.0	187500
93901	SALINAS	26738	10186	18.3	26.4	36.5	13.4	5.3	57316	61279	74	55	4722	1.5	0.7	4.5	62.6	30.7	338560
93905	SALINAS	11966	12925	21.9	30.5	34.8	9.2	3.6	47920	50914	56	39	6114	4.4	1.5	17.1	70.4	6.6	218184
93906	SALINAS	21975	16846	12.7	21.7	43.0	15.1	7.6	65836	69089	84	67	9752	3.6	0.9	7.0	70.9	17.5	277922
93907	SALINAS	29402	7466	9.7	15.8	43.0	20.5	11.1	74528	76406	89	75	5169	3.3	1.3	7.2	44.2	44.0	368552
93908	SALINAS	43871	5329	6.9	11.2	31.3	21.1	29.5	101234	99264	97	91	4229	0.6	0.2	1.5	18.8	78.8	597371
93920	BIG SUR	30392	448	18.3	25.4	33.7	10.0	12.5	57020	61157	74	54	201	1.5	0.0	0.5	11.4	86.6	831522
93923	CARMEL	57383	8315	12.6	17.3	29.9	18.8	21.4	79781	82327	92	80	5630	0.3	0.2	2.1	7.4	89.9	832154
93924	CARMEL VALLEY	52381	2804	9.4	15.3	30.2	19.3	25.7	87528	89483	94	85	1943	2.0	0.6	1.1	8.7	87.7	752702
93925	CHUALAR	27646	24	8.3	25.0	45.8	16.7	4.2	66458	67840	85	68	18	0.0	0.0	16.7	66.7	16.7	235714
93926	GONZALES	15833	1989	13.7	32.8	39.3	10.7	3.5	52916	56157	68	48	1078	1.1	1.1	19.9	63.4	14.5	224451
93927	GREENFIELD	12265	3678	18.0	33.0	39.4	7.8	1.8	49107	51849	59	41	2083	3.8	1.5	43.4	45.2	6.1	176336
93930	KING CITY	15795	4132	26.1	25.7	34.0	10.7	3.5	47712	50746	56	38	2200	5.3	3.9	34.9	47.8	8.1	184559
93932	LOCKWOOD	19635	297	24.2	30.3	37.0	6.4	2.0	44876	48917	48	32	145	6.2	4.8	23.4	33.8	31.7	260417
93933	MARINA	23984	8042	18.8	26.3	39.1	10.9	4.8	55039	59880	71	52	3072	7.3	2.2	5.8	54.5	30.1	330804
93940	MONTEREY	37915	13992	13.2	19.3	42.0	15.1	10.4	67992	70703	86	70	5715	0.5	0.2	1.8	19.4	78.2	586441
93943	MONTEREY	16987	15	60.0	33.3	6.7	0.0	0.0	17238	17238	1	2	0	0.0	0.0	0.0	0.0	0.0	0
93950	PACIFIC GROVE	40937	7258	11.4	21.7	40.6	16.3	9.9	66804	69237	85	68	3511	0.3	0.3	2.5	12.6	84.4	621866
93953	PEBBLE BEACH	71912	2284	4.5	7.5	26.4	25.0	36.6	125857	126974	99	96	1915	0.0	0.6	1.4	1.9	96.2	914739
93955	SEASIDE	19638	10035	16.4	29.6	40.6	10.0	3.5	54684	60052	71	51	4262	4.2	0.9	4.8	60.1	30.0	321382
93960	SOLEDAD	17307	3837	17.4	27.9	41.0	10.0	3.7	55029	59688	71	52	2472	0.4	1.3	14.4	78.0	5.9	215886
94002	BELMONT	62008	10633	6.3	8.7	28.0	20.3	36.6	114488	119131	98	94	6418	0.1	0.1	0.2	3.1	96.5	832252
94005	BRISBANE	48587	1701	12.2	11.7	31.3	26.1	18.7	86341	94377	94	85	1122	2.6	1.3	0.3	12.7	83.1	596369
94010	BURLINGAME	69405	16660	7.8	10.6	24.7	18.5	38.5	116911	122216	98	95	9708	0.1	0.1	0.6	2.3	96.8	1000001
94014	DALY CITY	24884	13176	10.7	16.2	37.7	23.6	11.7	75928	79856	90	76	8130	2.0	2.2	2.5	22.8	70.5	474497
94015	DALY CITY	30177	20105	11.3	14.9	35.4	24.1	14.3	81027	85007	92	81	11672	0.5	0.9	0.6	14.7	83.3	546296
94019	HALF MOON BAY	53813	6640	8.6	10.5	23.0	22.0	35.9	115399	119917	98	94	4898	1.6	1.7	2.3	4.7	89.7	726218
94020	LA HONDA	60701	451	6.7	10.0	25.5	19.3	38.6	118325	125267	98	95	311	1.3	0.3	0.0	5.1	93.2	720652
94021	LOMA MAR	63145	194	8.2	8.8	30.4	18.6	34.0	105592	112252	97	92	126	1.6	0.0	0.0	4.8	93.7	686275
94022	LOS ALTOS	100227	7000	3.5	6.7	14.7	12.5	62.6	209432	220280	100	100	5796	0.0	0.1	0.6	1.2	98.2	1000001
94024	LOS ALTOS	88860	8076	3.3	6.1	13.7	14.7	62.2	188969	200657	100	99	6998	0.0	0.2	0.5	1.8	97.6	1000001
94025	MENLO PARK	67322	16119	8.0	10.8	22.8	15.7	42.8	123172	129991	99	96	9470	0.3	0.2	0.1	4.0	95.4	941960
94027	ATHERTON	99052	2470	1.7	2.5	10.7	11.9	73.2	228836	236353	100	100	2211	0.0	0.0	0.0	0.1	99.9	1000001
94028	PORTOLA VALLEY	102898	2538	2.7	4.7	9.9	12.8	69.8	217600	224869	100	100	2125	0.3	0.0	0.5	1.2	98.1	1000001
94030	MILLBRAE	43162	8126	10.9	13.9	30.7	23.4	21.2	88116	94829	95	86	5108	0.2	0.7	0.6	2.4	96.1	800703
94035	MOUNTAIN VIEW	12401	10	0.0	10.0	70.0	10.0	10.0	68615	68615	86	70	0	0.0	0.0	0.0	0.0	0.0	0
94038	MOSS BEACH	56422	1985	4.0	5.6	23.9	24.7	41.7	129919	132310	99	97	1598	2.8	2.1	1.8	3.1	90.3	697389
94040	MOUNTAIN VIEW	58385	13667	10.3	13.7	27.7	18.2	30.1	95767	103047	96	89	5950	1.8	0.9	0.4	10.0	86.8	817440
94041	MOUNTAIN VIEW	60217	6180	7.3	11.0	31.5	22.4	27.8	100285	106970	97	91	1984	1.3	2.4	4.6	12.7	78.9	739696
94043	MOUNTAIN VIEW	55090	12538	9.7	12.6	28.7	22.5	26.5	97636	104453	96	90	5425	1.3	2.0	2.6	16.9	77.1	589267
94044	PACIFICA	41158	14086	6.8	10.0	35.4	27.5	20.3	95611	101160	96	89	9477	0.4	0.7	0.2	8.6	90.1	586192
94060	PESCADERO	34524	485	5.8	20.4	31.3	19.0	23.5	83873	91433	93	83	254	0.8	0.0	1.2	5.1	92.9	706044
94061	REDWOOD CITY	43135	13503	9.7	15.0	32.7	20.7	21.9	84999	90979	94	84	6815	0.2	0.3	0.3	2.9	96.3	722854
94062	REDWOOD CITY	73126	10480	5.6	9.4	20.9	17.3	46.8	138862	146483	99	98	7655	0.1	0.1	0.2	3.2	96.4	961286
94063	REDWOOD CITY	21644	9152	15.8	23.7	35.0	17.4	8.0	61599	64703	79	61	3706	10.9	5.8	6.9	14.9	61.5	465344
94065	REDWOOD CITY	84415	4950	4.5	5.2	14.0	23.0	53.3	155281	158581	100	99	3589	0.2	0.4	0.0	1.4	98.0	828831
94066	SAN BRUNO	34781	15427	9.9	16.6	35.9	23.6	14.0	79571	83487	92	80	9670	0.3	0.4	1.4	18.1	79.7	568114
94070	SAN CARLOS	65857	11820	7.1	9.6	23.0	21.2	39.1	123652	126895	99	96	8291	0.2	0.1	0.1	2.7	96.9	853648
94074	SAN GREGORIO	53558	31	3.2	9.7	32.3	12.9	41.9	117902	130538	98	95	21	0.0	0.0	0.0	4.8	95.2	925000
94080	SOUTH SAN FRANCISCO	30123	20733	10.4	16.6	36.1	24.3	12.6	78250	82485	91	79	12937	2.9	0.8	0.3	12.5	83.5	556444
94085	SUNNYVALE	38267	7525	7.9	11.9	36.5	25.1	18.6	88328	92879	95	86	2972	1.9	1.9	1.1	17.8	77.4	512130
94086	SUNNYVALE	52733	20071	8.4	11.8	30.1	23.4	26.3	99295	105483	97	91	6509	2.5	2.2	1.9	10.9	82.4	652618
94087	SUNNYVALE	60100	20049	6.7	9.3	25.2	20.6	38.2	118950	128295	98	95	11564	0.4	0.4	0.4	1.8	97.0	828611
94089	SUNNYVALE	40424	7221	10.8	16.8	31.1	24.8	16.5	84347	87742	94	83	4673	3.1	10.9	35.4	18.2	32.3	178251
94102	SAN FRANCISCO	26278	17699	44.1	25.9	20.0	6.9	3.1	29131	30594	7	6	867	0.0	0.0	1.2	17.0	81.9	620487
94103	SAN FRANCISCO	29786	10974	38.3	18.4	25.7	8.1	9.4	40286	44386	34	22	1482	1.1	0.0	0.5	16.3	82.1	663314
94104	SAN FRANCISCO	20316	106	46.2	24.5	17.0	9.4	2.8	27664	32368	5	4	0	0.0	0.0	0.0	0.0	0.0	0
94105	SAN FRANCISCO	115544	2639	7.4	7.3	23.6	23.9	37.8	128448	131874	99	96	1213	0.0	0.0	0.2	13.0	86.8	636136
94107	SAN FRANCISCO	70112	11472	21.0	14.3	23.6	14.6	26.5	80369	86624	92	81	3729	0.0	0.1	6.0	7.9	85.9	711482
94108	SAN FRANCISCO	43675	7766	34.5	22.6	21.1	10.1	11.6	41608	45039	38	25	768	1.4	0.3	2.5	8.6	87.2	820313
94109	SAN FRANCISCO	58077	31988	22.0	21.9	27.1	13.5	15.6	58819	62792	76	57	4745	0.4	0.5	2.0	15.7	81.3	703309
94110	SAN FRANCISCO	32618	25702	13.9	18.2	34.8	19.7	13.3	74596	78363	89	75	7991	0.7	0.8	0.3	12.9	85.3	615133
94111	SAN FRANCISCO	89884	2354	25.1	13.6	22.3	14.6	24.4	77716	81286	91	79	480	0.0	0.0	0.8	2.7	96.5	829167
94112	SAN FRANCISCO	24441	20426	10.4	18.0	38.2	23.0	10.4	74719	78670	89	75	13859	2.8	1.7	0.3	18.4	76.7	511900
94114	SAN FRANCISCO	82517	16565	8.2	9.4	27.8	22.6	31.9	110226	115908	98	93	5974	0.3	0.1	0.3	3.4	96.0	882362
94115	SAN FRANCISCO	68068	16954	19.6	13.3	26.8	15.6	24.8	79829	85904	92	80	3725	1.4	1.0	0.6	5.9	91.1	911515
94116	SAN FRANCISCO	37198	15012	10.4	16.0	31.8	24.1	17.6	85539	91177	94	84	10227	0.9	3.5	0.2	4.7	90.7	634025
94117	SAN FRANCISCO	59539	17824	11.7	13.2	29.7	21.4	24.0	90343	98278	95	87	4193	0.1	0.2	0.5	5.8	93.3	834171
94118	SAN FRANCISCO	59071	17066	12.7	13.8	28.8	18.0	26.7	88922	96353	95	86	5538	0.3	0.9	1.8	3.1	94.0	907765
94121	SAN FRANCISCO	42568	17119	12.1	16.4	32.3	22.6	16.6	81730	86653	93	82	6881	0.6	1.6	0.7	5.4	91.8	741540
94122	SAN FRANCISCO	39389	21414	12.2	15.8	32.6	22.5	16.9	81487	86900	93	81	9819	1.5	3.1	0.6	4.9	89.9	647730
94123	SAN FRANCISCO	112528	15397	7.0	8.4	25.6	17.9	41.0	126479	131662	99	96	3715	0.1	0.0	0.5	2.4	97.0	1000001
94124	SAN FRANCISCO	18354	9090	28.4	22.3	27.8	14.5	7.1	49037	52826	59	41	4704	4.1	1.0	0.9	41.2	52.8	411158
94127	SAN FRANCISCO	65982	7089	6.5	9.9	21.0	21.2	41.4	132001	135348	99	97	5907	0.3	0.3	0.4	2.8	96.3	803807
94129	SAN FRANCISCO	51921	861	6.7	7.2	33.2	24.3	28.6	105764	111854	97	92	35	0.0	0.0	0.0	0.0	100.0	1000001
94130	SAN FRANCISCO	39666	806	8.8	13.6	28.0	30.8	18.7	98779	104331	97	91	0	0.0	0.0	0.0	0.0	0.0	0
94131	SAN FRANCISCO	68431	13922	8.4	10.1	28.3	23.8	29.4	106700	112285	98	93	7201	0.1	0.6	0.2	7.5	91.6	702132
94132	SAN FRANCISCO	35884	10164	14.4	18.5	32.5	21.0	13.6	74359	78922	89	75	4226	2.4	0.8	0.3	8.6	87.8	623570
94133	SAN FRANCISCO	47327	13385	29.1	17.8	22.9	15.7	14.5	55291	60261	72	52	2262	0.6	0.8	1.2	5.4	92.0	814018
	CALIFORNIA	28199		18.5	22.2	33.9	14.0	11.5	61614	64088				3.3	2.6	13.6	41.0	39.5	321752
	UNITED STATES	27277		20.9	24.4	35.3	11.7	7.6	54719	56938				9.3	13.1	31.6	32.6	13.5	162279

ZIP CODE #	POST OFFICE NAME	FINANCIAL SERVICES: Auto Loan	Home Loan	Invest-ments	Retire-ment Plans	THE HOME: Home Improvements: Home Repair	Lawn & Garden	Furnishings: Comput-ers & Hard-ware-Personal	Major Appli-ances	TV, Radio, Sound Equip-ment	Furni-ture	ENTERTAINMENT: Dine out/ Carry out	Sports Equip-ment	Fees & Tickets	Toys & Games	Travel	Cable TV	PERSONAL: Apparel & Services	Auto Repairs	Health Insur-ance	Pets & Supplies
93702	FRESNO	52	45	38	41	44	38	51	48	49	54	51	36	46	50	47	47	37	51	42	52
93703	FRESNO	54	48	42	45	46	42	55	50	53	56	55	39	51	54	50	51	39	54	47	57
93704	FRESNO	79	82	82	82	83	82	84	82	83	84	83	62	86	82	84	84	59	83	85	95
93705	FRESNO	63	59	54	57	58	54	65	61	63	66	65	47	62	64	62	62	46	64	59	70
93706	FRESNO	54	47	42	43	45	45	51	50	52	53	53	37	47	52	47	52	37	52	49	57
93710	FRESNO	74	67	65	69	66	66	79	69	77	76	78	56	74	77	73	76	55	75	71	83
93711	FRESNO	125	130	136	134	133	124	129	125	125	135	126	96	135	125	132	122	90	127	122	145
93720	FRESNO	132	147	133	152	144	129	135	131	128	144	130	107	145	134	138	121	94	128	118	151
93721	FRESNO	36	25	25	27	25	26	38	31	39	37	40	25	33	38	33	39	28	38	34	38
93722	FRESNO	94	96	81	92	92	81	92	90	87	98	89	71	91	92	90	83	63	89	80	102
93723	FRESNO	92	101	110	101	104	104	91	99	89	91	89	75	96	89	99	90	63	94	96	114
93725	FRESNO	73	67	64	60	67	62	67	70	65	71	67	52	62	66	65	64	47	69	63	78
93726	FRESNO	60	52	48	52	51	50	65	56	62	61	63	45	58	63	57	61	44	61	55	66
93727	FRESNO	75	72	68	71	71	66	78	73	76	79	78	57	76	77	75	74	56	77	70	84
93728	FRESNO	55	50	48	47	49	48	56	53	54	55	55	41	51	55	51	54	39	55	51	61
93730	FRESNO	149	178	169	181	178	156	151	156	142	166	144	123	170	148	162	135	105	145	136	176
93741	FRESNO	84	85	81	87	83	82	87	82	86	87	86	65	88	86	86	85	61	85	83	98
93901	SALINAS	83	98	103	95	101	88	99	93	95	95	97	72	105	93	103	95	72	96	90	105
93905	SALINAS	83	83	69	74	82	62	89	83	79	94	84	67	84	81	86	70	61	86	65	87
93906	SALINAS	101	113	105	108	114	91	114	107	103	116	107	86	116	105	115	97	79	108	91	118
93907	SALINAS	121	142	140	138	145	127	127	133	118	134	120	100	135	119	137	114	86	126	119	147
93908	SALINAS	165	213	233	215	228	188	186	192	169	203	170	148	214	167	211	158	127	181	165	211
93920	BIG SUR	102	121	137	123	131	105	118	115	105	126	105	92	126	103	128	97	77	112	98	129
93923	CARMEL	151	171	222	171	195	185	154	173	153	172	151	116	172	141	178	155	107	165	179	194
93924	CARMEL VALLEY	153	201	238	205	223	179	181	185	161	197	161	143	208	155	208	150	120	175	160	204
93925	CHUALAR	107	132	122	115	138	94	122	123	101	134	105	95	123	102	129	89	77	115	91	126
93926	GONZALES	91	96	83	85	97	70	100	95	86	106	91	75	95	88	99	77	67	96	73	98
93927	GREENFIELD	80	78	65	70	77	60	84	79	76	89	80	63	79	78	81	69	58	82	64	84
93930	KING CITY	85	80	67	75	79	66	88	82	82	91	86	66	83	84	84	76	62	87	71	90
93932	LOCKWOOD	84	75	66	74	73	74	76	75	77	78	78	57	71	80	71	77	53	76	75	90
93933	MARINA	89	83	81	85	82	78	96	86	92	92	94	70	91	93	91	91	67	92	85	102
93940	MONTEREY	108	114	131	121	121	101	127	114	115	128	118	96	129	114	130	107	86	119	102	132
93943	MONTEREY	39	20	15	23	18	17	37	25	34	34	36	25	28	41	26	32	25	32	23	31
93950	PACIFIC GROVE	107	125	144	128	135	113	124	121	113	130	114	96	133	109	135	106	83	120	110	137
93953	PEBBLE BEACH	206	233	307	233	266	259	206	237	209	232	206	155	233	191	240	214	145	224	251	266
93955	SEASIDE	85	82	79	81	82	71	94	83	88	91	91	68	91	92	89	85	67	89	76	94
93960	SOLEDAD	88	95	82	84	96	69	97	93	84	104	89	74	94	85	97	74	65	93	71	96
94002	BELMONT	182	220	258	229	239	197	216	207	196	224	199	166	238	192	236	185	148	205	184	234
94005	BRISBANE	133	167	195	170	184	144	159	157	139	170	139	125	174	134	177	127	103	151	132	175
94010	BURLINGAME	209	245	287	258	265	221	245	232	223	254	227	189	269	220	264	210	169	233	207	264
94014	DALY CITY	116	144	162	140	158	114	141	138	118	151	119	111	147	114	155	105	88	133	109	150
94015	DALY CITY	122	141	154	140	150	114	146	137	127	151	129	111	149	124	153	116	95	137	114	152
94019	HALF MOON BAY	193	245	278	251	266	213	225	225	200	242	201	179	252	196	252	185	149	215	191	251
94020	LA HONDA	193	243	284	248	268	209	231	229	202	248	203	182	253	195	258	185	151	220	192	254
94021	LOMA MAR	174	219	256	223	241	188	208	206	182	223	183	164	228	176	232	167	136	198	173	229
94022	LOS ALTOS	317	432	524	450	481	401	370	387	341	407	340	293	453	334	435	325	259	361	343	425
94024	LOS ALTOS	289	404	491	419	451	376	337	358	311	374	309	268	420	304	402	297	236	331	318	392
94025	MENLO PARK	214	253	292	263	273	228	249	239	229	260	232	191	274	225	269	217	174	237	213	268
94027	ATHERTON	344	491	603	514	550	462	396	426	372	441	369	320	514	370	476	357	288	390	374	463
94028	PORTOLA VALLEY	319	455	558	475	510	428	369	397	345	412	341	297	475	341	444	330	265	363	350	432
94030	MILLBRAE	136	174	194	171	186	156	161	160	149	164	150	123	180	146	179	144	110	157	150	178
94035	MOUNTAIN VIEW	145	75	56	87	67	64	136	94	128	126	135	94	103	154	98	117	94	120	85	115
94038	MOSS BEACH	206	263	286	272	280	236	229	235	210	248	211	183	265	210	258	199	157	222	205	264
94040	MOUNTAIN VIEW	180	178	195	190	184	165	204	178	192	201	197	149	205	191	201	185	143	191	173	212
94041	MOUNTAIN VIEW	169	175	199	188	184	155	202	175	182	198	189	151	203	180	203	171	139	186	159	205
94043	MOUNTAIN VIEW	163	160	178	172	166	140	192	163	173	187	180	143	187	172	188	162	131	177	148	193
94044	PACIFICA	138	176	196	174	189	152	164	162	147	169	149	127	181	145	182	139	110	158	142	179
94060	PESCADERO	142	178	208	181	196	153	170	168	148	182	149	134	186	143	189	136	110	162	141	186
94061	REDWOOD CITY	140	160	181	165	170	140	169	155	152	168	157	128	177	150	178	143	115	160	139	177
94062	REDWOOD CITY	223	294	352	305	325	269	262	267	240	283	240	206	310	235	302	228	182	254	236	296
94063	REDWOOD CITY	104	99	92	97	98	84	115	102	107	114	112	84	109	108	109	101	81	110	92	116
94065	REDWOOD CITY	238	272	322	293	293	247	283	259	260	287	266	215	307	257	300	248	200	263	234	298
94066	SAN BRUNO	120	141	148	139	147	120	140	133	127	142	130	106	147	126	148	120	95	134	118	149
94070	SAN CARLOS	195	248	293	255	273	221	232	231	207	249	208	181	262	201	262	194	155	223	201	257
94074	SAN GREGORIO	217	273	319	278	300	234	259	256	227	278	228	205	284	219	289	208	169	247	215	285
94080	SOUTH SAN FRANCISCO	115	141	153	137	151	117	139	135	123	144	125	106	146	119	150	115	92	133	117	148
94085	SUNNYVALE	149	146	147	151	147	124	163	144	149	165	153	123	159	152	159	139	110	152	128	169
94086	SUNNYVALE	164	166	181	176	171	146	188	164	171	187	177	141	187	171	187	161	128	174	149	193
94087	SUNNYVALE	192	236	273	243	255	210	226	220	205	236	207	175	251	201	249	193	154	216	195	247
94089	SUNNYVALE	143	150	152	151	154	139	152	148	143	155	145	116	154	143	155	139	103	148	140	170
94102	SAN FRANCISCO	57	45	50	51	45	47	67	53	68	60	70	44	60	64	59	70	50	63	62	67
94103	SAN FRANCISCO	78	70	77	77	71	65	96	77	93	87	96	65	90	89	88	93	71	88	79	94
94104	SAN FRANCISCO	50	52	56	55	53	51	66	56	69	56	71	42	66	64	63	73	53	62	63	67
94105	SAN FRANCISCO	213	226	267	249	239	207	253	220	235	249	243	189	266	233	258	226	182	232	205	258
94107	SAN FRANCISCO	164	155	178	172	160	146	194	161	184	185	190	139	190	180	187	179	139	179	161	195
94108	SAN FRANCISCO	96	83	92	92	84	83	113	92	113	104	116	77	107	108	104	115	84	106	102	114
94109	SAN FRANCISCO	126	111	123	124	113	106	145	117	139	136	144	102	139	138	135	137	105	133	120	144
94110	SAN FRANCISCO	116	121	136	128	127	105	140	122	127	137	132	104	140	125	141	120	97	130	110	142
94111	SAN FRANCISCO	159	157	186	174	165	153	190	163	184	183	189	136	192	176	188	183	138	178	169	195
94112	SAN FRANCISCO	111	144	162	140	158	112	138	136	114	148	115	109	145	110	153	101	85	129	106	146
94114	SAN FRANCISCO	186	198	234	219	210	181	222	193	206	218	214	165	233	204	226	199	160	203	179	227
94115	SAN FRANCISCO	162	156	180	172	162	148	190	161	181	183	187	137	190	177	185	177	137	177	161	194
94116	SAN FRANCISCO	132	170	194	167	187	135	162	160	135	175	136	129	173	130	181	119	101	152	125	174
94117	SAN FRANCISCO	157	155	179	172	161	143	184	155	173	179	179	135	186	171	181	166	132	169	148	186
94118	SAN FRANCISCO	165	172	200	187	182	153	198	171	179	194	186	148	202	178	200	169	138	182	155	201
94121	SAN FRANCISCO	129	147	168	151	158	123	157	144	137	160	141	121	162	134	165	126	104	146	122	163
94122	SAN FRANCISCO	127	147	167	150	158	120	156	143	134	160	138	120	160	131	164	122	102	144	118	160
94123	SAN FRANCISCO	223	240	285	265	255	221	265	233	247	262	255	198	281	245	273	238	191	244	216	272
94124	SAN FRANCISCO	83	90	95	90	93	80	97	89	93	96	93	70	98	90	97	92	68	93	85	103
94127	SAN FRANCISCO	204	274	327	280	304	246	242	250	217	265	216	191	283	209	281	203	162	235	217	275
94129	SAN FRANCISCO	177	189	224	208	200	173	210	184	195	207	202	157	222	194	215	188	151	193	171	215
94130	SAN FRANCISCO	182	102	88	118	91	100	174	126	174	167	177	114	137	180	132	168	123	161	132	164
94131	SAN FRANCISCO	174	198	233	211	214	177	207	191	188	211	192	158	221	184	219	178	143	193	171	218
94132	SAN FRANCISCO	122	132	148	136	141	112	147	131	128	147	131	111	146	126	149	118	96	136	113	150
94133	SAN FRANCISCO	110	109	125	119	114	104	135	114	132	125	136	95	135	126	132	132	100	126	118	137
	CALIFORNIA	112	119	122	118	122	107	121	116	114	124	116	92	124	114	124	110	84	118	107	132
	UNITED STATES	100	100	100	100	100	100	100	100	100	100	100	100	100	100	100	100	100	100	100	100

ZIP CODE #	POST OFFICE NAME	COUNTY FIPS CODE	POPULATION 2000	POPULATION 2009	POPULATION 2014	2000-2009 ANNUAL RATE % Rate	2000-2009 ANNUAL RATE State Centile	HOUSEHOLDS 2000	HOUSEHOLDS 2009	HOUSEHOLDS 2014	HOUSEHOLDS % Annual Rate 2000-2009	HOUSEHOLDS 2009 Average HH Size	FAMILIES 2000	FAMILIES 2009	FAMILIES % Annual Rate 2000-2009
94134	SAN FRANCISCO	075	39862	42541	43315	0.7	50	10700	11130	11268	0.4	3.80	8485	8875	0.5
94158	SAN FRANCISCO	075	101	989	1250	28.0	100	21	518	659	41.4	1.81	6	200	46.1
94301	PALO ALTO	085	16186	16228	16395	0.0	9	7655	7714	7795	0.1	2.06	3669	3688	0.1
94303	PALO ALTO	085	43938	47189	48312	0.8	54	12499	12888	13140	0.3	3.64	9300	9654	0.4
94304	PALO ALTO	085	2245	3232	3695	4.0	94	1120	1728	2007	4.8	1.81	499	671	3.3
94305	STANFORD	085	13311	15496	16317	1.7	78	3206	3752	4019	1.7	2.47	1322	1515	1.5
94306	PALO ALTO	085	24338	24402	24669	0.0	9	10453	10420	10490	0.0	2.32	6090	6101	0.0
94401	SAN MATEO	081	31892	33559	34314	0.6	45	12216	12617	12806	0.3	2.61	6764	7043	0.4
94402	SAN MATEO	081	23948	24166	24482	0.1	13	9745	9919	10044	0.2	2.40	6348	6444	0.2
94403	SAN MATEO	081	37762	39736	40741	0.6	45	15179	15935	16286	0.5	2.46	9710	10186	0.5
94404	SAN MATEO	081	31876	32874	33472	0.3	23	13332	13818	14053	0.4	2.37	8644	8981	0.4
94501	ALAMEDA	001	58561	59389	60011	0.2	18	25060	25205	25326	0.1	2.32	14039	14210	0.1
94502	ALAMEDA	001	13698	13727	13836	0.0	9	5166	5177	5201	0.0	2.63	3819	3825	0.0
94503	AMERICAN CANYON	055	10023	15781	17970	5.0	95	3295	5198	5906	5.1	3.01	2526	3912	4.8
94505	DISCOVERY BAY	013	8878	13298	15125	4.5	95	3361	4722	5306	3.7	2.80	2635	3663	3.6
94506	DANVILLE	013	22705	27317	29950	2.0	83	7377	8418	9142	1.4	3.23	6525	7498	1.5
94507	ALAMO	013	14606	15306	15620	0.5	39	5041	5231	5325	0.4	2.89	4210	4350	0.4
94508	ANGWIN	055	3884	4266	4445	1.0	62	1102	1247	1314	1.3	2.62	786	887	1.3
94509	ANTIOCH	013	61970	64719	66789	0.5	39	21065	21606	22197	0.3	2.98	15876	16216	0.2
94510	BENICIA	095	26926	28079	28445	0.5	39	10351	10730	10842	0.4	2.61	7261	7559	0.4
94512	BIRDS LANDING	095	50	54	56	0.8	54	22	24	25	0.9	2.25	18	19	0.6
94513	BRENTWOOD	013	27379	55210	68491	7.9	97	8801	17537	21776	7.7	3.14	7153	14146	7.7
94514	BYRON	013	1313	1265	1349	-0.4	2	435	411	439	-0.6	2.86	318	301	-0.6
94515	CALISTOGA	055	6810	7200	7282	0.6	45	2687	2801	2825	0.5	2.51	1664	1730	0.4
94517	CLAYTON	013	12516	13982	14903	1.2	68	4527	4942	5222	1.0	2.82	3636	3963	0.9
94518	CONCORD	013	27263	28154	28625	0.3	23	10227	10431	10576	0.2	2.65	7140	7205	0.1
94519	CONCORD	013	18982	19604	20112	0.3	23	6868	6996	7151	0.2	2.77	4847	4887	0.1
94520	CONCORD	013	36144	38519	39257	0.7	50	12643	12932	13140	0.2	2.96	7799	7850	0.1
94521	CONCORD	013	40653	42703	43790	0.5	39	14689	15281	15635	0.4	2.77	10893	11234	0.3
94523	PLEASANT HILL	013	33091	33647	33972	0.2	18	13855	13969	14075	0.1	2.38	8535	8482	-0.1
94525	CROCKETT	013	3184	3332	3396	0.5	39	1488	1540	1565	0.4	2.16	844	859	0.2
94526	DANVILLE	013	29194	29970	30409	0.3	23	10808	10998	11137	0.2	2.70	8394	8461	0.1
94528	DIABLO	013	743	750	755	0.1	13	252	252	253	0.0	2.96	218	217	0.0
94530	EL CERRITO	013	23274	23695	23952	0.2	18	10257	10347	10435	0.1	2.27	6004	5966	-0.1
94531	ANTIOCH	013	28948	40317	45975	3.6	93	8397	11544	13130	3.5	3.48	7332	10004	3.4
94533	FAIRFIELD	095	62736	67907	69896	0.9	58	20803	22335	22955	0.8	2.95	15345	16543	0.8
94534	FAIRFIELD	095	27798	34948	38071	2.5	88	9279	11738	12787	2.6	2.95	7621	9642	2.6
94535	TRAVIS AFB	095	9985	9585	9390	-0.4	2	2391	2319	2269	-0.3	3.24	2301	2170	-0.6
94536	FREMONT	001	67075	70312	72040	0.5	39	23749	24646	25137	0.4	2.82	17244	17842	0.4
94538	FREMONT	001	55797	58653	60273	0.5	39	19097	19980	20475	0.5	2.91	13748	14342	0.5
94539	FREMONT	001	46950	48208	49377	0.3	23	14706	15070	15424	0.3	3.18	12577	12870	0.2
94541	HAYWARD	001	58466	61958	63498	0.6	45	19925	20631	21019	0.4	2.92	13104	13527	0.3
94542	HAYWARD	001	12683	13113	13349	0.4	30	4463	4566	4625	0.2	2.73	2986	3088	0.4
94544	HAYWARD	001	71675	75130	76467	0.5	39	21840	22226	22485	0.2	3.36	16415	16679	0.2
94545	HAYWARD	001	27571	28087	28668	0.2	18	8697	8716	8881	0.0	3.20	6554	6625	0.1
94546	CASTRO VALLEY	001	41518	41707	42000	0.0	9	16360	16394	16459	0.0	2.49	10846	10863	0.0
94547	HERCULES	013	19431	22532	23982	1.6	77	6407	7537	8062	1.8	2.99	4974	5711	1.5
94548	KNIGHTSEN	013	161	144	185	-1.2	0	56	56	72	0.0	2.57	41	41	0.0
94549	LAFAYETTE	013	27146	27718	28056	0.2	18	10306	10420	10519	0.1	2.64	7658	7657	0.0
94550	LIVERMORE	001	41245	46402	48802	1.3	70	14922	16728	17544	1.2	2.76	11163	12583	1.3
94551	LIVERMORE	001	34321	37710	39786	1.0	62	12015	13104	13787	0.9	2.87	8971	9738	0.9
94552	CASTRO VALLEY	001	13767	14527	15036	0.6	45	4684	4945	5100	0.6	2.94	3837	4044	0.6
94553	MARTINEZ	013	47359	48936	49799	0.4	30	18708	19136	19427	0.2	2.48	12086	12218	0.1
94555	FREMONT	001	33629	33699	34231	0.0	9	10698	10675	10804	0.0	3.15	8671	8670	0.0
94556	MORAGA	013	16421	16573	16671	0.1	13	5705	5709	5734	0.0	2.63	4372	4340	-0.1
94558	NAPA	055	63110	67075	68790	0.7	50	23166	24719	25347	0.7	2.67	16353	17397	0.7
94559	NAPA	055	27652	28893	29323	0.5	39	10186	10564	10696	0.4	2.58	6273	6499	0.4
94560	NEWARK	001	42471	43302	43837	0.2	18	12992	13134	13231	0.1	3.29	10345	10450	0.1
94561	OAKLEY	013	29193	37416	41562	2.7	90	9449	11804	13072	2.4	3.16	7414	9249	2.4
94563	ORINDA	013	17738	18059	18216	0.2	18	6652	6700	6740	0.1	2.68	5168	5163	0.0
94564	PINOLE	013	17746	18252	18521	0.3	23	6267	6374	6452	0.2	2.85	4738	4776	0.1
94565	PITTSBURG	013	78787	85566	89642	0.9	58	24508	26129	27276	0.7	3.25	18530	19556	0.6
94566	PLEASANTON	001	36160	40039	41556	1.1	64	13375	14656	15126	1.0	2.72	9888	10832	1.0
94567	POPE VALLEY	055	706	800	847	1.4	72	258	295	312	1.5	2.69	175	199	1.4
94568	DUBLIN	001	29949	42683	47093	3.9	93	9310	14120	15780	4.6	2.63	6490	9937	4.7
94569	PORT COSTA	013	232	246	252	0.6	45	108	114	116	0.6	2.16	74	77	0.4
94571	RIO VISTA	095	5416	7924	9520	4.2	94	2169	3219	3903	4.4	2.43	1471	2186	4.4
94572	RODEO	013	8167	8409	8539	0.3	23	2733	2775	2811	0.2	3.01	2056	2069	0.1
94574	SAINT HELENA	055	9358	9843	9974	0.5	39	3712	3867	3905	0.4	2.52	2408	2504	0.4
94576	DEER PARK	055	249	283	296	1.4	72	105	120	126	1.5	2.31	71	82	1.6
94577	SAN LEANDRO	001	42074	43778	44532	0.4	30	16353	16643	16820	0.2	2.59	10362	10524	0.2
94578	SAN LEANDRO	001	37430	38702	39390	0.4	30	14265	14358	14503	0.1	2.62	8918	8969	0.1
94579	SAN LEANDRO	001	19802	20263	20492	0.2	18	6894	6933	6968	0.1	2.92	5116	5150	0.1
94580	SAN LORENZO	001	25878	26636	27026	0.3	23	8844	8938	9020	0.1	2.98	6634	6697	0.1
94582	SAN RAMON	013	13380	30399	35836	9.3	98	5396	11683	13715	8.7	2.58	3538	8705	10.2
94583	SAN RAMON	013	31483	33898	35007	0.8	54	11598	12310	12668	0.6	2.75	8691	9176	0.6
94585	SUISUN CITY	095	26142	28093	28962	0.8	54	8018	8653	8931	0.8	3.24	6468	6986	0.8
94586	SUNOL	001	970	1002	1052	0.4	30	365	376	393	0.3	2.66	281	288	0.3
94587	UNION CITY	001	66969	73516	75994	1.0	62	18672	20223	20870	0.9	3.62	15726	16930	0.8
94588	PLEASANTON	001	28887	30888	32097	0.7	50	10467	11218	11642	0.8	2.74	7900	8416	0.7
94589	VALLEJO	095	32459	31570	31386	-0.3	3	9699	9499	9477	-0.2	3.23	7540	7365	-0.3
94590	VALLEJO	095	37026	38835	39111	0.5	39	14114	14558	14600	0.3	2.65	8763	9004	0.3
94591	VALLEJO	095	50298	55922	57465	1.2	68	16765	18131	18466	0.9	3.05	12635	13762	0.9
94592	VALLEJO	095	149	571	707	15.6	99	36	223	284	21.8	2.26	10	62	21.8
94595	WALNUT CREEK	013	16296	16921	17251	0.4	30	9328	9532	9672	0.2	1.73	4029	4080	0.1
94596	WALNUT CREEK	013	19309	19953	20349	0.4	30	8776	9009	9189	0.3	2.19	4818	4827	0.0
94597	WALNUT CREEK	013	21367	21903	22155	0.3	23	10539	10697	10801	0.2	2.04	5264	5257	0.0
94598	WALNUT CREEK	013	25267	25820	26088	0.2	18	9925	10057	10143	0.1	2.54	7120	7136	0.0
94599	YOUNTVILLE	055	3068	3538	3563	1.6	77	1113	1162	1175	0.5	1.97	597	622	0.4
94601	OAKLAND	001	54077	56597	57717	0.5	39	14773	15225	15457	0.3	3.63	10983	11289	0.3
94602	OAKLAND	001	30400	30820	31146	0.1	13	11919	12043	12134	0.1	2.51	7217	7289	0.1
94603	OAKLAND	001	31497	33139	33985	0.6	45	8797	9010	9179	0.3	3.64	6968	7129	0.2
94605	OAKLAND	001	40638	41439	42061	0.2	18	14546	14717	14881	0.1	2.79	10118	10228	0.1
94606	OAKLAND	001	41112	41590	42016	0.1	13	14679	14841	14952	0.1	2.78	8349	8442	0.1
94607	OAKLAND	001	21066	24183	25766	1.5	75	7558	8824	9455	1.7	2.58	4361	5063	1.6
	CALIFORNIA					1.2					1.0	2.93			1.1
	UNITED STATES					1.0					1.1	2.59			0.9

ZIP CODE #	POST OFFICE NAME	RACE (%) White 2000	White 2009	Black 2000	Black 2009	Asian/Pacific 2000	Asian/Pacific 2009	% Hispanic Origin 2000	% Hispanic Origin 2009	2009 AGE DISTRIBUTION (%) 0-4	5-9	10-14	15-19	20-24	25-44	45-64	65-84	85+	18+	MEDIAN AGE 2009	% 2009 Males	% 2009 Females
94134	SAN FRANCISCO	18.9	15.6	12.8	10.8	52.9	56.2	19.5	21.6	6.3	6.1	5.9	6.6	6.3	28.9	26.0	12.0	1.9	77.7	38.1	48.9	51.1
94158	SAN FRANCISCO	77.0	70.4	6.0	6.5	6.0	8.3	11.0	15.5	2.8	1.8	1.4	2.5	12.5	48.5	21.1	7.5	1.7	93.3	33.8	55.6	44.4
94301	PALO ALTO	84.3	78.5	1.9	2.2	9.6	13.1	3.4	4.9	4.2	4.5	5.5	4.8	3.8	29.1	29.6	13.8	4.7	82.6	43.8	48.8	51.2
94303	PALO ALTO	42.9	38.6	15.6	14.1	14.2	15.8	38.8	44.0	8.7	8.4	8.0	8.4	7.3	28.3	22.0	7.7	1.1	69.9	31.2	50.5	49.5
94304	PALO ALTO	76.6	68.1	1.8	2.0	19.2	26.6	3.3	4.4	3.7	3.2	3.3	4.0	8.3	34.7	26.4	13.1	3.3	86.7	40.1	53.4	46.6
94305	STANFORD	60.4	51.5	4.9	4.7	25.7	32.2	9.0	11.9	2.9	1.5	1.3	19.7	40.1	23.6	6.4	3.7	0.7	92.9	23.1	54.1	45.9
94306	PALO ALTO	72.2	64.3	2.3	2.4	19.6	25.2	6.6	8.9	5.0	4.8	5.3	5.7	5.8	29.0	30.1	11.6	2.7	81.2	41.5	49.1	50.9
94401	SAN MATEO	57.3	50.8	4.4	4.0	15.8	17.8	34.3	41.4	6.3	5.6	5.1	5.9	7.2	32.9	24.1	9.6	3.2	79.3	36.7	50.1	49.9
94402	SAN MATEO	74.5	66.9	1.2	1.3	15.7	20.2	10.7	14.1	5.5	5.7	6.4	6.1	4.1	24.3	30.6	14.3	2.9	78.4	43.7	48.7	51.3
94403	SAN MATEO	68.4	60.1	1.8	1.9	18.6	23.0	14.6	19.1	5.9	5.5	5.5	5.2	5.9	29.7	27.6	11.6	3.0	79.9	40.3	49.4	50.6
94404	SAN MATEO	60.7	51.0	2.1	2.2	31.7	39.4	5.4	7.0	5.5	5.0	5.2	4.9	4.9	31.5	30.2	11.6	1.3	81.1	40.6	48.7	51.3
94501	ALAMEDA	57.7	49.9	7.0	6.9	24.3	28.9	10.3	13.2	5.7	5.1	5.0	5.7	7.7	30.3	27.4	10.7	2.4	80.9	38.6	48.4	51.6
94502	ALAMEDA	53.6	44.2	2.8	2.8	37.1	44.4	5.1	6.4	5.6	6.2	7.1	6.5	4.0	21.5	34.1	12.6	2.3	76.9	44.4	47.6	52.4
94503	AMERICAN CANYON	59.9	57.5	7.3	6.1	17.2	16.6	17.3	21.8	6.2	6.5	7.0	7.4	4.8	24.1	29.9	12.4	1.7	75.6	40.8	49.3	50.7
94505	DISCOVERY BAY	88.3	79.2	1.7	2.2	1.9	2.4	10.4	20.2	7.0	7.2	7.6	6.5	3.8	25.5	30.2	11.4	0.8	73.8	40.7	50.3	49.7
94506	DANVILLE	78.0	70.6	2.0	2.4	16.0	21.2	4.3	6.2	6.9	8.1	9.6	8.1	3.6	20.5	34.7	7.8	0.6	70.0	40.7	49.2	50.8
94507	ALAMO	90.3	86.4	0.5	0.6	6.1	8.5	4.1	6.0	5.5	6.8	8.8	7.4	3.6	15.2	36.1	14.3	2.2	73.5	46.4	49.2	50.8
94508	ANGWIN	78.8	74.7	2.8	2.6	9.0	10.0	11.9	16.4	4.9	4.5	4.5	11.9	15.5	25.1	22.2	9.4	1.9	83.6	31.0	48.9	51.1
94509	ANTIOCH	69.2	62.6	7.4	7.8	5.2	6.4	24.6	31.2	8.2	7.9	7.6	7.7	6.8	27.8	24.5	8.2	1.3	71.5	33.3	49.0	51.0
94510	BENICIA	78.1	71.7	5.0	5.8	8.3	10.8	9.1	12.1	5.5	6.0	7.1	7.3	5.6	24.3	32.5	10.2	1.4	76.7	41.1	48.6	51.4
94512	BIRDS LANDING	86.0	81.5	0.0	0.0	2.0	1.9	14.0	20.4	7.4	7.4	7.4	7.4	7.4	24.1	25.9	13.0	0.0	70.4	35.0	50.0	50.0
94513	BRENTWOOD	70.9	63.2	3.8	4.2	3.9	4.7	28.7	36.7	10.0	9.6	9.0	7.7	5.3	29.5	21.3	6.7	0.8	66.2	31.4	49.3	50.7
94514	BYRON	77.2	71.2	3.4	3.5	2.4	3.0	23.3	30.1	6.8	7.7	7.4	12.1	5.1	26.1	25.2	8.3	1.3	69.0	34.4	53.7	46.3
94515	CALISTOGA	79.7	74.7	0.4	0.4	1.1	1.2	33.2	42.0	6.1	5.9	5.6	5.8	5.9	24.9	27.7	14.7	3.5	78.8	41.6	51.2	48.8
94517	CLAYTON	85.9	80.3	1.6	2.1	6.6	9.0	6.8	9.8	6.3	6.9	7.7	6.5	3.8	22.1	34.7	10.8	1.1	74.8	43.0	48.9	51.1
94518	CONCORD	74.6	67.4	2.4	2.6	10.8	13.6	14.5	19.2	6.1	6.1	6.3	6.2	5.6	26.5	29.4	11.7	2.2	77.7	40.6	48.6	51.4
94519	CONCORD	76.4	69.5	2.4	2.7	8.0	9.9	17.3	23.2	6.8	6.8	6.7	6.5	5.7	27.6	27.8	10.1	2.0	75.6	38.4	49.5	50.5
94520	CONCORD	59.2	53.0	4.5	4.4	9.1	10.3	39.8	46.7	8.5	7.6	6.7	7.1	8.0	32.7	21.0	7.0	1.4	73.0	31.8	51.3	48.7
94521	CONCORD	76.1	69.0	2.3	2.5	11.1	14.1	12.4	16.6	6.2	6.1	6.6	6.9	6.2	25.5	30.1	10.8	1.6	76.9	40.1	48.0	52.0
94523	PLEASANT HILL	82.1	76.1	1.5	1.7	9.5	12.5	8.2	11.4	5.6	5.4	5.7	5.5	5.9	27.2	30.4	11.5	2.6	79.8	41.4	48.5	51.5
94525	CROCKETT	82.1	77.0	5.2	5.7	2.6	3.4	12.8	17.8	5.0	4.8	4.9	5.4	6.6	25.2	33.6	12.2	2.3	82.0	43.6	49.2	50.8
94526	DANVILLE	88.8	84.5	0.8	0.9	6.8	9.3	4.8	6.9	5.7	6.6	8.0	6.9	3.9	19.0	34.6	13.3	1.9	74.8	44.9	48.6	51.4
94528	DIABLO	93.7	91.1	0.4	0.4	3.4	4.7	4.8	7.2	6.0	7.2	8.7	7.2	3.6	16.0	35.3	14.3	1.7	73.2	45.7	49.6	50.4
94530	EL CERRITO	57.8	49.6	9.1	9.5	24.0	29.0	7.9	10.1	4.6	4.5	4.8	4.5	5.0	27.8	30.3	14.5	4.0	83.5	44.3	47.6	52.4
94531	ANTIOCH	62.0	54.0	12.5	13.7	11.8	14.2	16.0	20.8	9.7	9.7	9.6	7.7	4.2	30.1	24.4	4.1	0.4	65.6	32.3	49.2	50.8
94533	FAIRFIELD	51.4	45.2	17.6	17.3	11.4	13.6	22.7	26.8	8.1	7.5	7.0	7.5	7.6	28.1	23.1	9.7	1.4	72.7	33.1	48.8	51.2
94534	FAIRFIELD	67.8	61.2	9.0	9.0	12.4	15.1	11.7	15.5	7.3	7.7	8.1	7.0	4.5	25.1	29.4	9.7	1.3	72.2	38.9	48.7	51.3
94535	TRAVIS AFB	65.0	55.8	11.4	12.6	10.0	13.7	11.1	14.7	12.7	8.9	6.3	7.7	24.4	35.3	3.9	0.7	0.0	69.6	22.9	56.5	43.5
94536	FREMONT	55.8	47.3	3.6	3.5	27.4	32.5	16.2	20.0	6.9	6.5	6.2	6.1	6.2	31.4	26.1	9.2	1.5	76.8	36.9	50.0	50.0
94538	FREMONT	52.2	44.0	3.6	3.5	28.2	32.7	19.4	23.8	7.5	6.7	6.2	6.2	7.3	33.7	23.4	7.8	1.1	75.8	34.0	51.0	49.0
94539	FREMONT	41.9	33.4	1.6	1.5	50.3	57.2	6.0	7.3	6.2	6.9	7.8	7.8	5.1	23.2	33.1	8.8	1.0	74.0	40.5	49.5	50.5
94541	HAYWARD	50.2	44.4	13.1	12.3	11.3	12.7	36.0	42.6	8.1	7.5	6.7	7.0	7.6	30.1	22.9	8.0	2.1	73.4	33.4	50.3	49.7
94542	HAYWARD	55.6	48.1	12.4	12.5	19.8	23.8	15.1	18.7	5.1	4.9	5.0	7.6	8.6	30.8	28.0	8.8	1.0	81.7	36.9	48.6	51.4
94544	HAYWARD	41.3	36.6	10.4	9.3	20.4	22.3	39.1	44.1	8.5	7.9	7.2	7.9	7.7	30.8	21.2	7.5	1.3	71.7	31.7	50.1	49.9
94545	HAYWARD	37.2	31.3	9.4	8.5	31.5	34.6	25.1	29.1	6.9	6.6	6.4	7.0	7.3	28.4	25.3	10.5	1.6	75.8	35.7	48.9	51.1
94546	CASTRO VALLEY	75.8	68.9	3.9	4.2	10.2	13.2	12.7	17.3	5.6	5.5	5.8	6.2	5.9	25.4	29.6	12.2	3.7	79.1	41.8	48.3	51.7
94547	HERCULES	29.3	24.3	18.5	18.5	42.3	45.3	10.7	12.5	5.6	5.7	6.1	7.1	6.9	25.5	32.4	9.8	0.9	78.4	39.9	47.5	52.5
94548	KNIGHTSEN	74.5	68.1	0.6	0.7	0.6	1.4	30.4	40.3	7.6	8.3	8.3	7.6	5.6	27.8	23.6	9.7	1.4	72.2	34.0	49.3	50.7
94549	LAFAYETTE	86.7	81.6	0.7	0.8	8.3	11.2	4.2	6.0	5.0	5.8	7.3	7.3	4.7	18.9	34.8	13.8	2.3	76.9	45.5	48.8	51.2
94550	LIVERMORE	84.7	79.3	1.4	1.6	5.0	6.9	12.1	16.6	6.9	7.0	7.4	7.0	5.2	26.5	29.2	9.5	1.3	74.2	38.7	49.6	50.4
94551	LIVERMORE	79.0	72.0	1.7	1.9	7.2	9.6	16.7	22.1	8.1	8.3	8.1	7.1	5.2	30.0	26.4	6.1	0.7	71.0	35.5	50.1	49.9
94552	CASTRO VALLEY	57.8	48.4	3.7	3.6	31.0	38.0	7.3	9.4	6.3	7.3	8.0	6.2	3.3	26.1	33.1	8.8	0.9	74.3	41.2	48.7	51.3
94553	MARTINEZ	79.7	73.6	3.5	3.8	7.2	9.2	11.5	15.8	5.4	5.4	5.9	6.3	5.8	27.2	31.4	10.8	1.6	79.3	41.0	49.5	50.5
94555	FREMONT	32.0	25.2	3.5	3.1	54.2	59.3	8.6	10.1	8.0	8.0	7.6	6.5	5.4	29.5	27.0	7.2	0.8	72.3	36.5	49.7	50.3
94556	MORAGA	81.5	75.0	1.0	1.1	12.1	16.1	4.8	6.7	3.9	4.9	6.3	10.8	7.9	15.9	32.4	15.5	2.6	80.6	45.2	47.6	52.4
94558	NAPA	82.8	77.0	0.5	1.0	2.0	2.3	21.6	28.9	6.1	6.2	6.5	6.7	5.9	23.7	28.6	13.4	2.9	77.0	41.2	49.4	50.6
94559	NAPA	78.3	73.4	1.4	1.3	1.4	1.6	31.1	39.3	6.6	6.3	6.1	6.7	7.1	30.8	25.2	9.0	2.2	77.0	36.0	52.2	47.8
94560	NEWARK	52.2	44.8	4.0	3.8	22.3	25.5	28.6	34.0	7.2	6.8	6.5	7.3	7.3	29.9	25.1	8.9	1.0	75.2	35.0	50.2	49.8
94561	OAKLEY	75.4	68.7	3.8	4.0	3.5	4.2	23.4	31.1	8.2	8.0	8.1	8.0	5.8	28.8	25.8	6.6	0.7	70.6	33.7	49.9	50.1
94563	ORINDA	86.5	81.3	0.5	0.6	9.2	12.5	3.2	4.6	4.8	5.9	7.6	7.3	3.8	15.3	35.1	17.1	3.1	76.9	48.1	48.0	52.0
94564	PINOLE	54.1	46.4	11.8	12.2	21.6	25.4	14.1	17.7	5.8	5.8	6.2	7.0	6.5	24.9	30.3	11.8	1.7	77.9	40.6	48.0	52.0
94565	PITTSBURG	44.6	39.1	17.2	16.5	12.9	14.5	33.9	39.5	8.8	8.3	7.7	7.8	7.5	29.3	22.2	7.2	1.1	70.4	31.2	49.2	50.8
94566	PLEASANTON	84.0	77.9	1.0	1.2	8.8	12.0	7.8	10.8	6.1	7.1	7.7	6.9	4.7	24.1	32.2	9.5	1.6	74.5	41.0	48.7	51.3
94567	POPE VALLEY	86.0	82.0	0.3	0.3	1.3	1.4	14.6	20.3	4.9	5.6	5.8	6.3	3.8	22.3	36.6	13.4	1.5	79.3	45.8	52.0	48.0
94568	DUBLIN	69.4	63.4	10.1	9.3	10.6	14.0	13.5	16.9	6.7	6.4	6.3	6.0	6.5	37.0	25.3	5.3	0.4	77.2	35.7	51.9	48.1
94569	PORT COSTA	87.1	82.5	2.2	2.8	2.6	3.3	8.6	12.6	3.7	4.1	4.5	5.3	5.7	22.0	36.2	15.9	2.8	84.6	48.0	50.4	49.6
94571	RIO VISTA	83.8	74.4	1.6	2.5	1.8	2.1	16.4	26.8	6.1	6.3	6.5	6.3	5.3	23.2	28.9	15.3	2.1	77.2	42.3	50.5	49.5
94572	RODEO	54.3	47.8	15.0	15.3	15.7	18.1	16.8	21.1	7.3	7.2	7.2	7.3	6.6	25.8	27.2	9.7	1.7	73.7	36.0	48.7	51.3
94574	SAINT HELENA	83.7	79.2	0.5	0.5	1.2	1.4	25.2	33.0	5.7	5.7	6.0	6.2	5.2	23.8	30.0	13.7	3.7	78.6	43.0	47.7	52.3
94576	DEER PARK	90.0	87.6	0.4	0.4	2.8	3.2	10.4	14.5	4.9	4.9	5.7	6.0	5.3	26.1	32.5	11.7	2.8	80.6	42.9	47.3	52.7
94577	SAN LEANDRO	52.4	45.7	11.4	11.2	19.6	22.6	21.9	27.0	6.2	6.1	6.2	6.4	6.0	27.1	27.8	11.2	2.9	77.5	39.7	48.7	51.3
94578	SAN LEANDRO	45.1	39.0	17.8	16.7	18.5	21.4	24.2	29.3	7.3	6.6	6.4	7.6	7.5	29.3	24.3	9.0	2.1	75.0	34.8	49.5	50.5
94579	SAN LEANDRO	51.3	43.6	4.7	4.5	32.1	37.1	16.3	20.0	6.5	6.5	6.3	6.4	5.3	27.2	26.2	13.0	2.6	76.8	39.6	47.9	52.1
94580	SAN LORENZO	58.8	51.1	4.9	4.7	17.8	20.8	24.9	31.1	6.6	6.5	6.6	7.3	6.6	27.3	26.8	10.3	2.1	75.9	37.5	48.7	51.3
94582	SAN RAMON	76.0	67.6	2.0	2.7	16.6	22.4	5.5	7.5	8.2	7.9	7.8	6.2	3.7	30.2	29.8	5.4	0.8	71.9	37.2	49.2	50.8
94583	SAN RAMON	78.4	71.4	1.8	2.0	13.5	17.6	7.8	10.7	6.7	7.3	8.0	6.9	4.8	26.3	31.7	7.4	0.8	73.6	39.4	49.3	50.7
94585	SUISUN CITY	44.7	38.5	19.1	18.4	18.7	21.5	17.9	21.3	7.8	8.3	8.5	8.1	6.2	29.6	24.9	5.9	0.7	70.2	33.0	49.3	50.7
94586	SUNOL	85.8	80.1	0.5	0.6	8.0	11.2	5.0	7.4	5.4	6.7	7.5	6.8	3.5	24.1	35.6	9.2	1.3	75.9	42.7	50.3	49.7
94587	UNION CITY	30.3	25.5	6.7	5.8	44.2	47.6	23.9	26.1	7.3	7.2	6.8	7.2	6.7	30.2	25.0	8.3	1.2	74.3	35.1	49.6	50.4
94588	PLEASANTON	76.2	68.1	1.8	2.1	15.3	20.3	8.0	11.1	6.8	7.4	8.0	7.2	4.5	28.1	30.2	7.3	0.6	73.3	38.7	49.7	50.3
94589	VALLEJO	24.5	21.1	29.8	28.0	30.7	33.1	15.3	17.5	6.8	6.7	6.9	7.8	6.9	26.5	25.7	10.7	1.9	74.7	35.8	48.2	51.8
94590	VALLEJO	42.7	36.9	25.3	24.7	12.4	14.4	22.1	26.6	8.3	7.6	6.9	7.0	7.6	27.9	23.9	8.9	1.9	72.9	33.6	48.8	51.2
94591	VALLEJO	39.2	32.4	18.3	16.8	29.9	35.6	12.6	14.7	6.9	6.8	6.9	7.1	6.1	27.9	27.6	9.1	1.5	74.9	36.6	48.6	51.4
94592	VALLEJO	42.3	34.5	20.1	20.0	20.1	23.6	7.4	9.1	2.8	1.1	0.9	13.0	53.8	21.4	5.1	1.6	0.5	95.3	23.0	53.4	46.6
94595	WALNUT CREEK	92.8	89.6	0.5	0.6	4.4	6.2	2.1	3.2	2.7	3.0	3.5	3.1	2.0	10.6	22.8	34.6	17.8	88.8	66.7	41.5	58.5
94596	WALNUT CREEK	83.3	77.4	1.2	1.4	8.7	11.6	8.2	11.4	5.0	4.6	4.9	5.1	7.7	29.4	28.8	11.8	2.7	82.2	39.9	49.1	50.9
94597	WALNUT CREEK	80.8	74.3	1.5	1.8	10.7	14.1	7.5	10.4	4.8	4.4	4.5	4.4	6.3	31.7	30.0	11.6	2.3	83.6	41.3	48.9	51.1
94598	WALNUT CREEK	82.3	76.0	1.0	1.2	11.8	15.7	4.8	6.7	4.6	5.3	6.4	6.4	4.0	19.8	33.9	16.7	2.9	79.3	46.9	48.2	51.8
94599	YOUNTVILLE	91.7	83.2	1.1	3.2	1.4	2.0	10.5	19.0	2.4	2.4	2.9	3.6	4.3	18.1	26.9	32.4	7.1	90.1	57.7	59.0	41.0
94601	OAKLAND	25.6	25.1	23.6	20.3	16.8	17.2	49.9	54.6	9.6	8.6	7.4	8.5	9.3	32.0	17.9	5.6	1.2	69.4	28.4	50.9	49.1
94602	OAKLAND	43.5	38.1	21.8	20.6	23.6	27.5	12.8	15.4	6.3	6.0	6.2	6.3	6.6	27.8	29.0	9.3	2.4	77.5	39.0	46.6	53.4
94603	OAKLAND	16.9	18.1	53.8	48.3	4.0	4.2	37.9	43.7	9.6	9.2	8.2	9.1	8.5	28.4	19.4	6.5	1.0	67.4	28.2	48.7	51.3
94605	OAKLAND	19.4	17.9	61.3	58.7	4.8	5.7	17.4	21.1	7.4	7.4	7.5	7.8	6.5	26.0	26.2	9.7	1.5	72.9	35.7	46.4	53.6
94606	OAKLAND	19.1	16.7	24.0	21.3	39.4	42.1	20.9	23.5	7.4	6.3	5.5	7.0	9.5	35.0	20.9	7.1	1.1	76.6	31.5	50.1	49.9
94607	OAKLAND	11.1	10.9	51.5	45.7	26.1	30.1	12.7	15.0	7.1	6.8	6.2	6.9	7.9	28.3	23.7	10.9	2.2	75.8	35.3	48.8	51.2
	CALIFORNIA	59.5	54.5	6.7	6.2	11.3	12.5	32.4	38.3	7.5	7.1	6.9	7.5	7.4	28.5	24.2	9.3	1.6	74.1	34.3	49.9	50.1
	UNITED STATES	75.1	72.0	12.3	12.7	3.8	4.6	12.5	15.7	6.8	6.7	6.6	7.1	6.9	27.0	26.0	10.9	1.9	75.7	36.9	49.2	50.8

INCOME

ZIP CODE				2009 HOUSEHOLD INCOME DISTRIBUTION (%)					MEDIAN HOUSEHOLD INCOME					2009 HOME VALUE DISTRIBUTION (%)					
#	POST OFFICE NAME	2009 Per Capita Income	2009 HH Income Base	Less than $25,000	$25,000 to $49,999	$50,000 to $99,999	$100,000 to $149,999	$150,000 or More	2009	2014	2009 National Centile	2009 State Centile	2009 Home Value Base	Less than $50,000	$50,000 to $89,999	$90,000 to $174,999	$175,000 to $399,999	$400,000 or More	2009 Median Home Value
94134	SAN FRANCISCO	20997	11130	15.9	18.8	35.9	21.1	8.2	68212	72937	86	70	7308	5.9	2.6	0.3	24.3	66.9	468046
94158	SAN FRANCISCO	40789	518	21.4	25.3	33.2	12.0	8.1	53055	55336	68	48	256	0.0	0.0	63.3	0.0	36.7	157653
94301	PALO ALTO	95365	7714	9.0	11.9	16.4	14.5	48.2	142231	152823	99	98	3865	0.1	0.3	0.4	3.1	96.2	1000001
94303	PALO ALTO	36440	12888	13.6	16.1	26.3	16.7	27.3	84851	90589	94	84	7683	0.8	0.5	0.9	11.6	86.2	758663
94304	PALO ALTO	75565	1728	13.8	13.2	25.1	17.4	30.6	94372	102862	96	89	312	0.0	0.0	0.0	1.9	98.1	986239
94305	STANFORD	35858	3752	25.0	22.6	21.5	10.2	20.7	53117	55499	68	48	838	0.0	0.0	0.4	7.3	92.4	863454
94306	PALO ALTO	72203	10420	10.4	10.3	23.3	17.2	38.8	115503	128131	98	95	5576	1.8	0.3	0.9	2.8	94.2	883307
94401	SAN MATEO	36146	12617	13.0	18.9	33.9	21.1	13.3	72270	76802	88	73	5665	0.2	0.3	0.5	16.2	82.8	584025
94402	SAN MATEO	65780	9919	6.0	11.0	27.8	18.7	36.4	110924	116158	98	93	6317	0.0	0.3	0.4	2.8	96.5	870633
94403	SAN MATEO	47692	15935	8.7	14.1	31.2	21.4	24.6	90845	97726	95	87	9155	0.3	0.3	0.1	6.5	92.8	700761
94404	SAN MATEO	69109	13818	5.0	5.5	23.1	22.1	44.4	134665	138939	99	97	8241	0.1	0.3	0.4	4.0	95.3	751822
94501	ALAMEDA	37943	25205	13.3	21.4	33.5	19.9	11.9	69707	74193	87	71	9912	1.5	0.8	2.9	29.8	65.0	482980
94502	ALAMEDA	57533	5177	5.4	7.7	23.8	27.4	35.8	123873	125044	99	96	4305	0.5	1.0	0.0	15.1	83.4	577536
94503	AMERICAN CANYON	24411	5198	17.5	17.7	40.7	18.0	6.0	65782	67990	84	67	4398	10.3	4.6	6.7	61.9	16.5	263485
94505	DISCOVERY BAY	50504	4722	5.2	6.8	29.2	25.5	33.4	115790	117236	98	95	4154	0.3	0.3	0.4	20.1	78.9	567860
94506	DANVILLE	78146	8418	1.7	3.8	10.8	14.5	69.1	202276	206563	100	100	7733	0.2	0.6	1.6	1.6	96.0	902925
94507	ALAMO	70925	5231	5.0	7.9	12.8	15.9	58.4	171325	178415	100	99	4677	0.5	0.1	0.4	2.7	96.3	933123
94508	ANGWIN	37442	1247	8.1	16.0	37.9	21.8	16.3	78912	81277	92	80	722	1.1	1.4	1.5	30.5	65.5	573980
94509	ANTIOCH	25506	21606	16.8	21.3	35.3	18.9	7.6	63837	67385	82	64	13253	0.6	0.8	8.7	78.5	11.4	264207
94510	BENICIA	40532	10730	8.9	15.1	33.6	24.1	18.2	85650	87165	94	84	7411	1.2	2.3	7.1	55.1	34.4	320501
94512	BIRDS LANDING	31481	24	12.5	29.2	33.3	20.8	4.2	62986	72662	81	63	15	0.0	0.0	33.3	60.0	6.7	190625
94513	BRENTWOOD	33743	17537	8.3	13.8	32.4	27.9	17.6	91215	95229	95	87	14518	0.8	0.9	2.5	46.5	49.4	397207
94514	BYRON	30997	411	21.4	19.5	27.5	15.6	16.1	62928	71288	81	63	314	8.9	1.3	6.4	29.3	54.1	429545
94515	CALISTOGA	32440	2801	17.0	29.1	31.3	12.0	10.5	54781	59966	71	51	1717	8.6	8.6	4.4	18.3	60.0	460105
94517	CLAYTON	54640	4942	3.5	8.4	23.2	25.8	39.1	128183	130915	99	96	4359	0.6	0.2	2.7	16.2	80.3	585976
94518	CONCORD	36389	10431	10.7	18.1	31.2	25.8	14.3	81282	86222	93	81	7159	5.9	2.6	8.3	30.1	53.1	415627
94519	CONCORD	29559	6996	10.0	18.9	39.1	25.6	6.4	76109	79064	90	77	4805	1.1	0.4	4.9	69.0	24.7	322649
94520	CONCORD	20267	12932	22.1	28.1	36.5	10.2	3.1	49793	51176	61	42	5118	2.4	3.9	14.9	73.5	5.2	243402
94521	CONCORD	36262	15281	8.7	14.4	36.2	25.5	15.2	84259	89321	94	83	10966	0.2	0.2	4.0	44.7	50.9	403674
94523	PLEASANT HILL	44399	13969	9.4	13.7	33.5	25.4	18.0	88753	93815	95	86	8716	0.5	0.0	2.2	31.9	65.4	476497
94525	CROCKETT	34266	1540	19.5	24.0	29.0	20.0	7.5	58416	62260	76	56	826	1.7	0.0	7.6	66.1	24.6	290533
94526	DANVILLE	62942	10998	4.1	7.4	20.0	23.8	44.7	137354	140627	99	98	9120	0.3	0.2	0.2	4.8	94.4	788728
94528	DIABLO	74414	252	3.2	8.3	18.3	12.3	57.9	162797	168275	100	99	229	0.0	0.0	0.0	8.3	91.7	738924
94530	EL CERRITO	42081	10347	11.7	17.8	35.8	19.4	15.3	75701	78812	90	76	6148	1.7	1.4	1.8	25.5	69.6	476121
94531	ANTIOCH	37195	11544	3.7	5.4	28.5	35.6	26.8	117205	118227	98	95	10361	0.9	0.1	1.0	56.7	41.3	377471
94533	FAIRFIELD	22912	22335	16.2	25.0	41.0	13.2	4.6	62191	65047	80	62	12377	3.4	2.8	35.7	54.7	3.3	184947
94534	FAIRFIELD	40314	11738	4.8	9.4	36.2	27.5	22.1	99205	98843	97	91	9968	0.9	0.5	4.7	63.1	30.8	298458
94535	TRAVIS AFB	19058	2319	12.6	35.1	41.5	8.1	2.7	53238	60664	68	48	242	3.3	0.0	31.0	62.0	3.7	196111
94536	FREMONT	38466	24646	7.3	12.3	36.2	26.8	17.4	90299	96026	95	87	14305	1.0	1.1	0.8	22.7	74.4	530413
94538	FREMONT	34862	19980	8.3	11.2	38.4	27.9	14.2	87779	93043	95	85	9907	1.6	1.1	2.5	27.0	67.8	456768
94539	FREMONT	54168	15070	5.2	5.6	22.1	22.7	44.4	136409	138115	99	97	12033	0.6	1.3	1.8	8.1	88.2	790902
94541	HAYWARD	24421	20631	15.9	23.6	38.8	15.6	6.0	61099	63522	79	60	8786	1.1	0.1	3.1	65.6	30.2	333965
94542	HAYWARD	42814	4566	9.6	10.2	29.4	24.6	26.2	101090	105881	97	91	2915	0.0	0.2	1.3	22.2	76.3	537587
94544	HAYWARD	22554	22226	13.6	23.4	38.0	18.1	6.8	63545	66520	82	64	11464	2.3	3.2	8.7	57.6	28.1	332254
94545	HAYWARD	25904	8716	11.2	17.0	41.0	22.6	8.1	74772	78147	89	75	6115	2.1	3.9	4.3	54.0	35.8	351179
94546	CASTRO VALLEY	37728	16394	11.1	16.3	38.2	21.2	13.3	76662	80233	90	77	10370	2.9	0.3	2.0	37.0	57.8	429493
94547	HERCULES	34946	7537	4.9	11.1	38.3	31.9	13.9	93234	97365	96	88	6188	1.1	0.4	3.4	57.4	37.7	339474
94548	KNIGHTSEN	31014	56	14.3	21.4	39.3	19.6	5.4	65286	67800	84	66	44	0.0	0.0	9.1	72.7	18.2	281250
94549	LAFAYETTE	63511	10420	5.3	8.9	22.9	20.5	42.4	131092	134676	99	97	7907	0.2	0.2	0.4	3.8	95.4	799791
94550	LIVERMORE	44611	16728	6.9	11.5	30.2	27.0	24.4	101949	105776	97	92	11732	0.1	0.2	1.0	19.8	78.9	541220
94551	LIVERMORE	41082	13104	6.4	10.9	31.3	29.9	21.5	101561	105100	97	91	9308	0.6	1.1	1.6	34.5	62.2	454476
94552	CASTRO VALLEY	58361	4945	3.6	5.5	16.3	26.3	48.3	146309	149766	100	98	4367	0.6	0.8	0.5	8.6	89.4	656621
94553	MARTINEZ	36730	19136	12.1	16.7	34.3	24.1	12.9	78797	82414	92	79	12896	2.6	1.5	4.1	48.6	43.1	365729
94555	FREMONT	41161	10675	5.0	7.0	28.6	31.1	28.2	113678	115772	98	94	7602	1.6	2.6	1.5	15.0	79.2	540006
94556	MORAGA	59981	5709	5.0	9.0	23.3	21.5	41.2	129770	133257	99	97	4683	0.5	0.7	0.6	7.0	91.2	800140
94558	NAPA	36250	24719	11.0	20.8	35.1	18.8	14.3	71388	74070	88	72	16911	2.6	1.9	2.9	36.6	56.0	441223
94559	NAPA	27887	10564	15.8	27.6	36.5	13.4	6.8	58353	61707	76	56	5288	1.9	1.2	1.3	56.3	39.4	357001
94560	NEWARK	30233	13134	7.9	11.9	37.5	29.8	12.9	87424	92919	94	85	9035	0.7	0.5	0.9	30.0	67.8	463746
94561	OAKLEY	27833	11804	11.0	12.6	41.4	26.2	8.8	80591	83606	92	81	9609	5.3	1.4	5.4	74.9	12.9	282108
94563	ORINDA	72947	6700	6.3	7.8	17.8	19.7	48.5	145861	152600	100	98	5753	0.1	0.4	1.0	3.9	94.7	868196
94564	PINOLE	30966	6374	10.3	15.7	38.9	25.8	9.3	79288	82450	92	80	4625	1.0	0.3	4.3	60.9	33.4	345721
94565	PITTSBURG	21701	26129	17.7	23.3	36.6	17.7	4.7	60419	63157	78	59	15782	4.3	2.8	12.2	72.9	7.8	239692
94566	PLEASANTON	57400	14656	6.1	8.7	25.0	22.4	37.8	121118	123812	99	95	10301	0.6	0.3	2.7	8.8	87.6	706330
94567	POPE VALLEY	39048	295	10.8	20.3	37.3	12.9	18.6	68692	71328	86	70	207	6.3	1.0	2.4	40.1	50.2	405556
94568	DUBLIN	47370	14120	3.1	8.7	30.7	27.7	29.9	112222	116012	98	94	9687	0.1	0.1	0.5	24.8	74.5	496881
94569	PORT COSTA	43369	114	7.0	15.8	35.1	35.1	7.0	86767	90405	94	85	91	0.0	0.0	1.1	61.5	37.4	342500
94571	RIO VISTA	27307	3219	20.8	24.4	38.8	10.5	5.4	60149	61950	78	58	2356	4.9	1.4	26.7	56.4	10.6	195833
94572	RODEO	27071	2775	12.7	20.1	36.1	25.4	5.7	76130	78080	90	77	1760	1.4	0.0	3.4	71.9	23.4	310516
94574	SAINT HELENA	46561	3867	11.6	16.4	32.7	19.4	19.9	78934	81105	92	80	2220	1.2	0.5	1.4	14.7	82.2	724957
94576	DEER PARK	45294	120	7.5	12.5	42.5	21.7	15.8	81835	82978	93	82	67	3.0	0.0	0.0	14.9	82.1	717105
94577	SAN LEANDRO	30878	16643	13.1	21.2	39.1	18.5	8.1	65809	69166	84	67	9559	1.9	0.3	2.2	59.2	36.4	356970
94578	SAN LEANDRO	26597	14358	16.3	25.4	38.6	14.1	5.6	58481	61218	76	56	6348	4.6	0.4	2.1	63.9	29.0	332368
94579	SAN LEANDRO	30015	6933	11.5	20.2	32.7	24.4	11.1	75802	80150	90	76	5364	2.7	3.5	5.2	51.3	37.3	363249
94580	SAN LORENZO	27164	8938	12.2	20.8	38.2	20.9	8.0	70168	74334	87	71	6317	1.6	0.2	1.4	71.5	25.3	342268
94582	SAN RAMON	89391	11683	2.9	5.1	15.6	19.8	56.6	164133	172594	100	99	9195	0.2	0.2	0.9	3.9	94.8	834711
94583	SAN RAMON	53565	12310	4.1	5.9	26.2	27.6	36.2	125372	126642	99	96	8858	0.2	0.3	0.7	9.6	89.2	655554
94585	SUISUN CITY	25449	8653	9.0	15.8	48.5	20.2	6.5	74336	77195	89	74	6245	0.7	0.2	24.6	73.3	1.2	197900
94586	SUNOL	63808	376	4.3	1.3	29.5	29.8	35.1	125000	127039	99	96	304	0.0	0.0	0.3	16.4	83.2	747159
94587	UNION CITY	30211	20223	8.5	11.9	32.6	28.4	18.6	94588	100556	96	89	14191	2.0	2.9	2.6	29.6	62.9	462072
94588	PLEASANTON	57112	11218	3.3	6.0	25.6	27.9	37.1	125584	126736	99	96	7872	0.1	0.3	0.3	11.7	87.7	626607
94589	VALLEJO	22763	9499	13.4	22.1	42.2	16.9	5.5	68010	71786	86	70	6743	5.6	1.4	33.3	58.7	1.0	185683
94590	VALLEJO	20389	14558	27.0	27.7	34.8	8.6	2.0	45308	47943	49	33	6436	8.5	6.8	37.3	43.5	3.8	170243
94591	VALLEJO	29899	18131	8.7	17.2	39.6	23.0	11.5	76693	79824	90	77	12968	1.1	0.7	22.2	67.3	8.7	234185
94592	VALLEJO	17065	223	57.0	19.7	9.0	14.3	0.0	21640	21370	2	2	163	0.0	0.0	0.0	54.0	46.0	392614
94595	WALNUT CREEK	50462	9532	16.3	24.5	28.9	16.5	13.9	63099	67118	81	63	7954	0.1	1.0	16.9	33.7	48.3	375228
94596	WALNUT CREEK	51891	9009	8.9	15.0	33.8	21.1	21.1	86494	90545	94	85	3987	0.7	0.3	2.6	13.3	83.2	668750
94597	WALNUT CREEK	50238	10697	10.2	15.4	33.0	25.4	15.9	84422	89807	94	84	5436	0.5	0.0	3.8	29.7	66.0	504648
94598	WALNUT CREEK	53176	10057	6.3	11.5	26.5	24.6	31.0	110928	114528	98	94	7798	0.4	0.5	2.2	12.5	84.3	660962
94599	YOUNTVILLE	36724	1162	15.4	23.7	37.1	11.0	12.8	62367	66189	80	62	816	12.1	10.7	12.7	16.1	48.4	381690
94601	OAKLAND	14945	15225	28.5	29.7	29.0	9.8	2.9	42056	44824	39	26	5178	1.3	0.7	16.1	75.0	6.9	234460
94602	OAKLAND	37152	12043	14.9	20.4	30.5	18.7	15.5	72062	76615	88	72	6659	2.3	0.2	2.0	37.2	58.4	446074
94603	OAKLAND	14929	9010	30.0	28.0	29.6	9.8	2.6	42690	45464	41	27	4701	1.5	0.6	25.4	69.9	2.6	209233
94605	OAKLAND	28944	14717	20.8	20.3	31.9	15.3	11.7	61996	65235	80	62	9017	1.0	0.3	5.8	57.9	35.0	318262
94606	OAKLAND	20083	14841	28.8	30.2	28.3	8.2	4.5	42241	44611	40	26	2997	6.8	1.3	8.9	65.1	17.9	256272
94607	OAKLAND	17790	8824	47.6	22.8	19.7	6.7	3.3	27273	29773	5	4	2289	3.8	1.6	15.9	66.4	12.3	252945
	CALIFORNIA	28199		18.5	22.2	33.9	14.0	11.5	61614	64088				3.3	2.6	13.6	41.0	39.5	321752
	UNITED STATES	27277		20.9	24.4	35.3	11.7	7.6	54719	56938				9.3	13.1	31.6	32.6	13.5	162279

ZIP CODE #	POST OFFICE NAME	FINANCIAL SERVICES: Auto Loan	FINANCIAL SERVICES: Home Loan	FINANCIAL SERVICES: Invest-ments	FINANCIAL SERVICES: Retire-ment Plans	THE HOME: Home Improvements: Home Repair	THE HOME: Home Improvements: Lawn & Garden	THE HOME: Furnishings: Comput-ers & Hard-ware-Personal	THE HOME: Furnishings: Major Appli-ances	THE HOME: Furnishings: TV, Radio, Sound Equip-ment	THE HOME: Furnishings: Furni-ture	ENTERTAINMENT: Dine out/ Carry out	ENTERTAINMENT: Sports Equip-ment	ENTERTAINMENT: Fees & Tickets	ENTERTAINMENT: Toys & Games	ENTERTAINMENT: Travel	ENTERTAINMENT: Cable TV	PERSONAL: Apparel & Services	PERSONAL: Auto Repairs	PERSONAL: Health Insur-ance	PERSONAL: Pets & Supplies
94134	SAN FRANCISCO	101	126	141	123	138	99	124	121	103	133	104	97	129	100	135	91	77	116	94	131
94158	SAN FRANCISCO	107	79	82	91	76	76	117	88	113	108	117	81	104	114	100	110	84	106	92	113
94301	PALO ALTO	247	290	344	311	314	267	288	271	268	298	272	221	323	266	310	257	205	272	246	310
94303	PALO ALTO	177	197	205	191	208	164	197	191	177	210	182	149	204	177	206	164	134	190	161	208
94304	PALO ALTO	192	165	180	184	166	157	212	172	203	204	209	151	202	203	196	196	150	195	173	214
94305	STANFORD	164	104	114	118	105	109	221	133	181	168	183	129	158	177	146	167	132	167	128	169
94306	PALO ALTO	210	250	294	261	272	222	250	237	224	260	227	193	271	219	271	210	169	236	208	269
94401	SAN MATEO	120	130	142	132	137	112	144	130	130	144	133	108	145	126	148	121	97	136	118	149
94402	SAN MATEO	196	247	292	255	271	221	233	230	209	248	210	181	262	203	261	196	157	223	202	257
94403	SAN MATEO	147	174	199	178	187	152	176	166	157	180	161	135	188	154	190	147	118	167	146	188
94404	SAN MATEO	204	246	285	257	265	218	241	230	218	251	222	187	265	214	262	206	165	228	202	261
94501	ALAMEDA	112	119	132	123	125	103	134	119	122	132	125	100	135	120	136	114	92	126	108	138
94502	ALAMEDA	187	249	288	253	273	218	221	227	196	241	196	176	254	190	254	181	146	213	192	249
94503	AMERICAN CANYON	98	118	124	115	122	113	102	109	99	108	99	81	114	98	113	98	71	104	105	124
94505	DISCOVERY BAY	196	232	223	234	232	211	200	208	190	215	193	158	220	195	216	185	137	196	191	237
94506	DANVILLE	321	430	464	449	455	386	350	368	327	389	328	288	431	335	401	309	250	337	316	406
94507	ALAMO	246	345	418	359	385	321	285	304	264	317	262	229	359	260	340	252	202	280	267	332
94508	ANGWIN	143	173	192	176	185	153	164	162	148	173	149	128	178	145	179	139	109	157	142	183
94509	ANTIOCH	102	114	107	112	113	101	110	105	105	111	107	83	115	108	112	103	77	106	99	120
94510	BENICIA	135	164	171	166	169	150	150	149	143	155	144	116	167	142	163	140	105	147	141	170
94512	BIRDS LANDING	84	119	123	110	123	105	98	102	94	98	95	75	116	95	112	94	70	98	97	112
94513	BRENTWOOD	149	173	153	172	169	143	154	153	142	167	145	124	165	150	159	132	106	145	129	170
94514	BYRON	147	132	152	129	132	149	124	143	128	125	128	109	116	130	126	132	87	133	140	167
94515	CALISTOGA	119	114	143	112	122	124	115	125	114	116	114	94	112	110	121	116	80	121	122	143
94517	CLAYTON	191	254	288	260	275	227	220	228	200	240	200	175	258	197	253	188	150	213	198	251
94518	CONCORD	122	148	159	146	156	134	139	138	131	142	133	106	152	130	151	128	97	137	129	155
94519	CONCORD	102	130	133	124	133	116	116	116	111	115	113	88	130	112	127	111	82	114	111	130
94520	CONCORD	79	77	76	76	77	70	88	78	85	85	88	63	86	85	84	84	63	85	78	91
94521	CONCORD	126	157	163	155	162	143	142	141	136	142	138	108	160	137	154	136	101	139	135	159
94523	PLEASANT HILL	132	157	176	159	167	141	155	148	143	157	145	118	168	141	167	137	107	149	137	168
94525	CROCKETT	90	111	113	107	113	103	104	101	103	99	104	76	115	102	110	105	76	102	102	116
94526	DANVILLE	210	278	331	287	307	259	239	252	222	264	220	189	287	216	279	212	166	236	225	278
94528	DIABLO	263	369	447	378	412	342	310	331	283	346	280	245	379	272	372	269	211	306	296	362
94530	EL CERRITO	119	143	162	146	153	128	141	134	129	144	131	108	153	126	152	122	96	135	122	152
94531	ANTIOCH	183	223	193	229	217	184	185	188	171	207	174	156	210	185	196	157	128	172	155	210
94533	FAIRFIELD	92	97	91	95	96	87	99	93	95	99	97	73	100	96	98	93	69	96	89	108
94534	FAIRFIELD	157	199	196	199	201	177	168	173	159	178	161	133	192	163	185	154	117	163	157	194
94535	TRAVIS AFB	104	61	46	68	55	51	98	71	92	93	97	69	77	110	74	85	68	87	64	86
94536	FREMONT	142	166	177	166	175	138	164	157	145	171	148	127	171	145	173	134	108	155	133	175
94538	FREMONT	136	150	156	151	156	124	154	144	137	160	140	118	156	137	159	127	102	145	123	163
94539	FREMONT	219	285	308	290	302	247	249	253	224	268	226	199	286	225	279	210	169	239	215	280
94541	HAYWARD	92	97	95	95	98	84	106	96	100	103	103	77	106	100	104	97	75	101	90	109
94542	HAYWARD	149	184	208	185	198	159	177	172	158	185	160	137	193	155	194	148	119	169	149	192
94544	HAYWARD	99	107	105	103	109	90	113	105	104	113	107	84	113	104	113	99	78	108	93	117
94545	HAYWARD	108	127	130	120	132	109	121	120	111	124	114	92	127	111	128	107	83	118	107	132
94546	CASTRO VALLEY	119	143	153	142	149	131	136	132	129	136	131	102	148	129	146	127	95	133	127	150
94547	HERCULES	134	166	178	164	176	140	156	154	137	165	138	122	167	135	170	127	101	149	131	172
94548	KNIGHTSEN	108	132	122	116	138	95	123	124	102	134	105	96	123	102	129	89	77	116	91	126
94549	LAFAYETTE	204	269	322	278	298	245	241	246	219	260	219	189	283	213	277	206	165	234	216	272
94550	LIVERMORE	159	197	203	198	203	173	178	177	164	186	166	139	198	166	193	157	122	171	158	199
94551	LIVERMORE	159	187	173	187	185	161	171	167	159	178	163	134	185	164	178	152	118	163	148	190
94552	CASTRO VALLEY	226	289	287	302	295	254	240	247	224	262	227	197	283	232	267	211	169	229	212	278
94553	MARTINEZ	119	141	146	141	145	129	132	131	125	135	127	101	144	125	141	123	92	129	124	149
94555	FREMONT	173	209	216	208	219	170	195	192	170	211	172	156	207	170	210	154	126	183	157	213
94556	MORAGA	202	278	334	285	310	254	238	251	216	264	215	188	287	209	282	204	162	233	221	275
94558	NAPA	127	151	164	149	160	140	139	143	131	146	131	107	152	129	152	127	95	138	133	159
94559	NAPA	92	100	104	99	103	90	107	100	101	105	104	78	109	99	108	98	76	104	95	113
94560	NEWARK	127	155	166	149	166	126	150	147	131	158	133	116	158	128	162	120	97	143	122	159
94561	OAKLEY	127	144	134	138	141	125	127	131	119	135	121	102	132	123	132	113	85	124	115	147
94563	ORINDA	234	327	397	337	365	303	274	292	251	305	249	217	338	244	328	239	189	269	259	319
94564	PINOLE	104	141	149	134	146	127	123	124	119	120	121	92	142	119	137	121	89	122	121	138
94565	PITTSBURG	99	104	93	99	102	88	104	99	98	107	100	77	103	100	102	93	71	100	89	112
94566	PLEASANTON	199	247	271	255	261	223	223	223	207	237	209	175	254	207	247	198	155	216	201	252
94567	POPE VALLEY	152	156	218	157	173	172	146	169	142	149	140	125	149	136	165	143	99	156	158	191
94568	DUBLIN	188	212	202	217	211	183	196	190	183	208	186	154	210	190	202	173	135	185	168	218
94569	PORT COSTA	112	157	163	146	163	139	130	135	124	129	125	99	153	126	148	125	93	130	128	148
94571	RIO VISTA	97	97	122	94	103	107	91	104	92	88	92	76	91	90	99	96	64	99	103	118
94572	RODEO	100	127	128	122	130	112	116	115	110	115	113	88	129	111	126	109	83	114	108	128
94574	SAINT HELENA	151	179	206	182	194	165	172	173	157	180	158	134	186	153	188	150	116	168	155	194
94576	DEER PARK	132	165	194	168	182	142	158	156	138	169	138	124	172	133	176	126	103	150	131	173
94577	SAN LEANDRO	101	119	123	115	124	105	117	113	110	116	112	87	124	108	123	107	82	113	105	126
94578	SAN LEANDRO	90	95	95	93	95	84	103	93	99	99	101	74	104	99	101	97	74	99	89	107
94579	SAN LEANDRO	107	142	147	134	148	126	123	127	117	126	118	94	140	117	138	116	87	122	119	139
94580	SAN LORENZO	101	127	128	119	131	108	117	115	109	117	111	88	127	109	125	106	81	114	104	127
94582	SAN RAMON	316	377	360	392	378	318	336	329	308	365	314	274	374	323	355	285	232	311	277	371
94583	SAN RAMON	194	235	240	243	240	211	209	208	197	219	200	164	236	202	226	190	147	201	188	237
94585	SUISUN CITY	114	132	116	128	127	113	118	117	112	123	115	92	126	117	122	109	82	114	106	134
94586	SUNOL	201	288	327	287	310	265	232	247	220	244	221	183	289	222	275	217	167	231	228	269
94587	UNION CITY	141	177	185	170	188	137	168	165	141	180	144	133	176	140	181	126	106	157	129	178
94588	PLEASANTON	214	251	242	261	252	221	224	221	210	239	214	178	250	219	237	200	156	213	196	253
94589	VALLEJO	96	115	114	109	117	101	106	106	100	109	101	81	113	100	113	97	73	104	99	119
94590	VALLEJO	70	72	70	71	72	66	79	72	77	76	78	57	78	76	77	76	56	76	71	84
94591	VALLEJO	120	145	140	141	146	126	132	130	124	136	125	102	144	126	140	120	91	128	119	147
94592	VALLEJO	58	24	24	30	22	28	81	40	64	55	65	43	48	63	43	59	46	57	40	54
94595	WALNUT CREEK	105	132	166	122	155	150	116	136	119	133	116	83	139	105	143	124	80	129	160	146
94596	WALNUT CREEK	149	154	176	165	163	141	171	153	158	173	161	127	176	156	174	150	118	160	142	179
94597	WALNUT CREEK	134	140	156	148	146	125	155	138	141	155	145	116	157	140	157	133	105	145	126	162
94598	WALNUT CREEK	165	221	258	225	243	201	193	200	176	209	176	152	227	172	224	168	131	189	178	221
94599	YOUNTVILLE	120	132	161	128	146	134	125	135	120	135	119	98	131	113	138	119	84	130	133	152
94601	OAKLAND	70	68	62	65	67	56	80	70	75	78	79	57	77	76	76	72	58	77	63	79
94602	OAKLAND	116	134	146	135	141	115	140	130	127	140	131	105	146	125	146	121	97	133	115	146
94603	OAKLAND	75	73	66	70	72	64	79	74	76	80	79	57	77	77	76	74	56	77	69	84
94605	OAKLAND	99	114	118	113	116	107	114	108	114	110	116	82	122	112	117	117	84	112	110	127
94606	OAKLAND	72	66	66	68	66	57	84	70	79	79	83	60	79	79	79	76	61	79	66	82
94607	OAKLAND	54	50	52	53	49	51	64	54	68	57	69	42	62	64	59	73	50	62	64	68
	CALIFORNIA	112	119	122	118	122	107	121	116	114	124	116	92	124	114	124	110	84	118	107	132
	UNITED STATES	100	100	100	100	100	100	100	100	100	100	100	100	100	100	100	100	100	100	100	100

ZIP CODE #	POST OFFICE NAME	COUNTY FIPS CODE	POPULATION 2000	POPULATION 2009	POPULATION 2014	2000-2009 ANNUAL RATE % Rate	2000-2009 ANNUAL RATE State Centile	HOUSEHOLDS 2000	HOUSEHOLDS 2009	HOUSEHOLDS 2014	HOUSEHOLDS % Annual Rate 2000-2009	HOUSEHOLDS 2009 Average HH Size	FAMILIES 2000	FAMILIES 2009	FAMILIES % Annual Rate 2000-2009
94608	EMERYVILLE	001	24731	28546	30373	1.6	77	10986	12721	13514	1.6	2.22	4894	5594	1.5
94609	OAKLAND	001	20859	21188	21507	0.2	18	9371	9509	9635	0.2	2.17	3979	4033	0.1
94610	OAKLAND	001	29672	29430	29506	-0.1	5	15596	15504	15512	-0.1	1.88	6073	6031	-0.1
94611	OAKLAND	001	36941	37157	37534	0.1	13	17223	17343	17463	0.1	2.13	8913	8988	0.1
94612	OAKLAND	001	13204	13866	14237	0.5	39	7588	7964	8178	0.5	1.65	2147	2238	0.4
94613	OAKLAND	001	113	116	116	0.3	23	41	41	41	0.0	2.56	27	27	0.0
94618	OAKLAND	001	14115	14200	14330	0.1	13	6500	6546	6586	0.1	2.15	3320	3350	0.1
94619	OAKLAND	001	26142	26602	27148	0.2	18	9511	9657	9844	0.2	2.67	6228	6322	0.2
94621	OAKLAND	001	30797	32012	32473	0.4	30	8690	8766	8828	0.1	3.63	6513	6569	0.1
94702	BERKELEY	001	15353	15575	15771	0.2	18	6979	7068	7133	0.1	2.19	3261	3298	0.1
94703	BERKELEY	001	19960	20285	20541	0.2	18	8843	8971	9053	0.2	2.23	3883	3934	0.1
94704	BERKELEY	001	19687	20920	21381	0.7	50	8245	8616	8818	0.5	2.01	1428	1498	0.5
94705	BERKELEY	001	12045	12122	12231	0.1	13	5438	5475	5508	0.1	2.18	2512	2540	0.1
94706	ALBANY	001	15757	15935	16126	0.1	13	6878	6921	6977	0.1	2.30	3954	3972	0.0
94707	BERKELEY	001	12080	12044	12077	0.0	9	5060	5041	5041	0.0	2.39	3357	3331	-0.1
94708	BERKELEY	013	11191	11171	11222	0.0	9	4888	4878	4891	0.0	2.28	3036	3020	-0.1
94709	BERKELEY	001	10269	10443	10545	0.2	18	5078	5134	5177	0.1	1.83	1395	1403	0.1
94710	BERKELEY	001	8289	8265	8322	0.0	9	3293	3282	3296	0.0	2.48	1891	1883	0.0
94720	BERKELEY	001	1000	1054	1060	0.6	45	112	111	112	-0.1	3.04	7	7	0.0
94801	RICHMOND	013	28996	31217	32079	0.8	54	8759	9144	9380	0.5	3.37	6070	6246	0.3
94803	EL SOBRANTE	013	26078	26579	26896	0.2	18	9445	9534	9627	0.1	2.76	6812	6808	0.0
94804	RICHMOND	013	38952	39711	40249	0.2	18	14302	14293	14470	0.0	2.75	9108	8982	-0.2
94805	RICHMOND	013	13732	13930	14038	0.2	18	5241	5205	5224	-0.1	2.67	3463	3395	-0.2
94806	SAN PABLO	013	55920	62641	65489	1.2	68	17683	19500	20388	1.1	3.15	12499	13453	0.8
94901	SAN RAFAEL	041	40152	42133	42918	0.5	39	15512	15950	16233	0.3	2.59	8950	9190	0.3
94903	SAN RAFAEL	041	28615	29801	30514	0.4	30	11687	12279	12603	0.5	2.31	7219	7554	0.5
94904	GREENBRAE	041	12257	12380	12503	0.1	13	5547	5593	5649	0.1	2.18	3238	3269	0.1
94920	BELVEDERE TIBURON	041	12157	12281	12417	0.1	13	5337	5377	5427	0.1	2.26	3384	3409	0.1
94922	BODEGA	097	168	177	181	0.6	45	58	62	64	0.7	2.82	38	41	0.8
94923	BODEGA BAY	097	1749	1793	1816	0.3	23	819	856	870	0.5	2.08	506	528	0.5
94924	BOLINAS	041	1519	1568	1600	0.3	23	593	621	636	0.5	2.29	318	333	0.5
94925	CORTE MADERA	041	9339	9464	9581	0.1	13	3861	3897	3935	0.1	2.43	2498	2519	0.1
94928	ROHNERT PARK	097	41571	42439	42629	0.2	18	15047	15402	15494	0.3	2.66	9541	9736	0.2
94929	DILLON BEACH	041	322	353	366	1.0	62	157	172	179	1.0	2.05	99	108	0.9
94930	FAIRFAX	041	8554	8579	8660	0.0	9	3783	3805	3840	0.1	2.25	2143	2156	0.1
94931	COTATI	097	8425	8762	8870	0.4	30	3363	3546	3603	0.6	2.46	2115	2225	0.5
94933	FOREST KNOLLS	041	913	975	1004	0.7	50	381	403	414	0.6	2.42	240	255	0.7
94937	INVERNESS	041	1378	1438	1476	0.5	39	580	618	637	0.7	2.14	308	328	0.7
94938	LAGUNITAS	041	378	406	418	0.8	54	160	171	176	0.7	2.31	103	111	0.8
94939	LARKSPUR	041	6980	6969	7008	0.0	9	3448	3442	3460	0.0	2.02	1746	1744	0.0
94940	MARSHALL	041	122	126	129	0.3	23	58	60	62	0.4	2.02	38	40	0.6
94941	MILL VALLEY	041	29416	29859	30278	0.2	18	13026	13224	13395	0.2	2.23	7435	7547	0.2
94945	NOVATO	041	16407	17406	17934	0.6	45	6334	6741	6945	0.7	2.57	4448	4735	0.7
94946	NICASIO	041	1014	1051	1076	0.4	30	315	329	337	0.5	2.95	206	215	0.5
94947	NOVATO	041	24738	25341	25822	0.3	23	9323	9590	9770	0.3	2.57	6416	6609	0.3
94949	NOVATO	041	13402	16468	17814	2.3	86	5525	6835	7396	2.3	2.39	3532	4348	2.3
94951	PENNGROVE	097	3979	4022	4063	0.1	13	1550	1578	1595	0.2	2.53	1031	1053	0.2
94952	PETALUMA	041	32217	32687	32912	0.2	18	12379	12731	12861	0.3	2.49	8156	8368	0.3
94954	PETALUMA	097	35248	37983	39009	0.8	54	12194	13120	13472	0.8	2.87	9116	9787	0.8
94956	POINT REYES STATION	041	1359	1415	1450	0.4	30	584	614	630	0.5	2.18	343	360	0.5
94960	SAN ANSELMO	041	16361	16530	16706	0.1	13	6612	6685	6755	0.1	2.43	4286	4341	0.1
94963	SAN GERONIMO	041	752	800	824	0.7	50	291	310	319	0.7	2.45	191	204	0.7
94964	SAN QUENTIN	041	6437	6014	6011	-0.7	1	93	91	90	-0.2	2.41	58	56	-0.4
94965	SAUSALITO	041	10875	10871	10934	0.0	9	5880	5898	5928	0.0	1.83	2497	2505	0.0
94970	STINSON BEACH	041	772	790	809	0.2	18	379	390	399	0.3	2.00	183	188	0.3
94971	TOMALES	041	287	295	301	0.3	23	107	111	113	0.4	2.53	70	72	0.3
94972	VALLEY FORD	097	128	136	140	0.7	50	47	51	52	0.9	2.61	33	36	0.9
94973	WOODACRE	041	1635	1709	1754	0.5	39	644	672	687	0.5	2.45	447	466	0.5
95002	ALVISO	085	2068	2100	2137	0.2	18	489	495	502	0.1	4.15	388	394	0.2
95003	APTOS	087	23470	23037	22851	-0.2	4	9855	9977	9929	0.1	2.29	6270	6337	0.1
95004	AROMAS	053	4204	4305	4315	0.3	23	1353	1398	1402	0.4	3.08	1089	1121	0.3
95005	BEN LOMOND	087	7441	7385	7363	-0.1	5	2786	2866	2869	0.3	2.56	1880	1930	0.3
95006	BOULDER CREEK	087	9549	9525	9521	0.0	9	3824	3954	3969	0.4	2.39	2427	2502	0.3
95008	CAMPBELL	085	44680	45884	46958	0.3	23	18404	18862	19237	0.3	2.41	10848	11177	0.3
95010	CAPITOLA	087	9398	9252	9176	-0.2	4	4478	4511	4487	0.1	2.01	2150	2159	0.0
95012	CASTROVILLE	053	9025	9367	9453	0.4	30	2193	2290	2324	0.5	4.06	1861	1927	0.4
95013	COYOTE	085	175	173	174	-0.1	5	45	44	44	-0.2	3.14	36	35	-0.3
95014	CUPERTINO	085	54418	56673	58303	0.4	30	19605	20253	20753	0.4	2.78	14822	15359	0.4
95017	DAVENPORT	087	444	443	439	0.0	9	146	148	148	0.1	2.78	99	100	0.1
95018	FELTON	087	10244	10157	10062	-0.1	5	3507	3553	3531	0.1	2.44	2301	2326	0.1
95019	FREEDOM	087	8009	8827	9043	1.1	64	2024	2206	2254	0.9	3.99	1533	1666	0.9
95020	GILROY	085	49941	56617	60061	1.4	72	14291	16084	17014	1.3	3.46	11563	13061	1.3
95023	HOLLISTER	069	47381	50625	51507	0.7	50	13911	14541	14696	0.5	3.45	11434	11957	0.5
95030	LOS GATOS	085	12784	13036	13310	0.2	18	5244	5348	5444	0.2	2.40	3348	3428	0.3
95032	LOS GATOS	085	24579	25118	25642	0.2	18	9852	10059	10237	0.2	2.44	6458	6615	0.3
95033	LOS GATOS	087	9229	9267	9331	0.0	9	3515	3601	3629	0.3	2.56	2427	2489	0.3
95035	MILPITAS	085	62955	68919	71753	1.0	62	17222	18776	19528	0.9	3.50	14075	15332	0.9
95037	MORGAN HILL	085	40927	46164	48929	1.3	70	13150	14693	15493	1.2	3.10	10508	11790	1.3
95039	MOSS LANDING	053	1610	1752	1809	0.9	58	482	522	540	0.9	3.26	364	391	0.8
95043	PAICINES	069	745	762	756	0.2	18	282	286	281	0.2	2.48	197	200	0.2
95045	SAN JUAN BAUTISTA	069	3668	4081	4163	1.2	68	1196	1320	1338	1.1	3.07	883	978	1.1
95046	SAN MARTIN	085	6001	6375	6622	0.7	50	1726	1827	1889	0.6	3.45	1420	1507	0.6
95050	SANTA CLARA	085	35608	37622	39028	0.6	45	13956	14565	15057	0.5	2.46	7871	8223	0.5
95051	SANTA CLARA	085	51897	52616	53430	0.1	13	19830	19975	20202	0.1	2.63	13182	13339	0.1
95053	SANTA CLARA	085	776	784	932	0.1	13	0	0	0	0.0	0.00	0	0	0.0
95054	SANTA CLARA	085	13013	19739	22588	4.6	95	4274	7147	8320	5.7	2.71	2792	4238	4.6
95060	SANTA CRUZ	087	44766	45381	45505	0.1	13	17323	18012	18112	0.4	2.43	9154	9491	0.4
95062	SANTA CRUZ	087	36127	35895	35652	-0.1	5	14740	14875	14789	0.1	2.35	7721	7781	0.1
95064	SANTA CRUZ	087	4240	4516	4502	0.7	50	439	438	433	0.0	2.45	268	267	0.0
95065	SANTA CRUZ	087	8122	7974	7908	-0.2	4	3136	3154	3132	0.1	2.50	2054	2068	0.1
95066	SCOTTS VALLEY	087	14271	14452	14464	0.1	13	5390	5570	5590	0.4	2.51	3764	3886	0.3
95070	SARATOGA	085	31453	32679	33601	0.4	30	11013	11409	11684	0.4	2.84	9006	9355	0.4
95073	SOQUEL	087	10565	10409	10317	-0.2	4	4094	4140	4120	0.1	2.50	2663	2687	0.1
95076	WATSONVILLE	087	77400	83299	85026	0.8	54	20635	22199	22644	0.8	3.69	16173	17351	0.8
95110	SAN JOSE	085	18309	20501	21514	1.2	68	4667	5460	5837	1.7	3.40	2991	3400	1.4
	CALIFORNIA					1.2					1.0	2.93			1.1
	UNITED STATES					1.0					1.1	2.59			0.9

ZIP CODE #	POST OFFICE NAME	RACE (%) White 2000	White 2009	Black 2000	Black 2009	Asian/Pacific 2000	Asian/Pacific 2009	% Hispanic Origin 2000	% Hispanic Origin 2009	2009 AGE DISTRIBUTION (%) 0-4	5-9	10-14	15-19	20-24	25-44	45-64	65-84	85+	18+	MEDIAN AGE 2009	% 2009 Males	% 2009 Females
94608	EMERYVILLE	25.3	22.2	52.5	50.1	11.7	14.1	9.9	12.7	5.9	5.7	5.4	6.3	7.9	33.2	25.3	8.6	1.7	79.3	35.5	47.7	52.3
94609	OAKLAND	36.4	31.4	43.5	43.3	8.5	10.3	9.5	12.2	5.4	4.8	4.3	5.4	8.4	38.5	23.8	7.5	1.9	82.5	35.0	47.0	53.0
94610	OAKLAND	53.0	46.3	23.7	24.1	14.8	18.3	7.0	9.1	4.2	3.7	3.8	4.0	7.5	35.2	30.2	9.2	2.2	85.9	39.8	47.6	52.4
94611	OAKLAND	72.7	65.8	9.0	9.4	11.9	15.8	5.0	6.8	4.6	4.9	5.6	4.8	4.8	27.4	33.3	11.8	2.9	82.0	43.8	48.0	52.0
94612	OAKLAND	24.4	21.3	38.6	36.4	25.4	28.5	11.0	12.9	4.4	3.8	3.0	3.9	7.9	30.9	24.1	16.9	5.2	86.8	41.9	51.2	48.8
94613	OAKLAND	60.7	51.7	16.1	17.2	12.5	16.4	8.9	11.2	1.7	2.6	1.7	30.2	39.7	16.4	6.0	1.7	0.0	93.1	21.7	11.2	88.8
94618	OAKLAND	78.8	72.5	7.1	7.7	7.8	10.7	5.0	7.1	5.4	4.8	4.8	4.0	4.4	32.4	31.6	10.7	2.0	82.5	41.8	48.4	51.6
94619	OAKLAND	34.6	29.8	32.3	31.1	20.3	23.4	14.2	16.9	6.1	5.9	6.1	7.3	7.2	27.0	28.6	9.8	2.0	77.9	38.3	46.5	53.5
94621	OAKLAND	15.9	16.7	48.1	42.6	6.0	6.3	41.8	47.3	10.1	9.5	8.3	9.3	8.9	28.8	17.6	6.3	1.1	66.4	27.2	49.1	50.9
94702	BERKELEY	44.2	37.9	31.7	31.7	11.0	13.5	13.3	16.9	5.2	4.7	4.7	5.3	7.1	33.8	28.0	9.2	2.0	82.4	38.1	47.7	52.3
94703	BERKELEY	51.7	45.1	24.0	23.8	12.9	16.3	10.7	13.7	5.4	4.6	4.0	4.6	8.6	39.2	24.3	7.6	1.8	83.5	34.4	49.5	50.5
94704	BERKELEY	50.1	41.0	4.0	5.9	33.9	38.5	10.3	12.4	1.4	1.1	1.0	13.6	39.2	26.4	12.0	4.1	1.2	95.1	24.2	54.4	45.6
94705	BERKELEY	76.3	69.4	6.1	6.6	10.3	13.4	5.6	8.0	3.8	3.8	4.1	4.8	8.5	30.6	31.0	11.4	2.1	85.6	41.2	48.9	51.1
94706	ALBANY	64.2	55.7	4.5	4.6	22.6	28.0	7.5	10.0	4.9	4.6	5.1	5.5	7.1	29.7	31.3	9.7	2.1	82.0	40.5	46.8	53.2
94707	BERKELEY	83.0	76.8	2.1	2.4	9.4	12.8	4.1	5.8	4.8	5.5	6.4	5.1	2.9	20.8	35.1	16.5	2.9	79.9	47.6	47.2	52.8
94708	BERKELEY	83.1	76.9	2.2	2.5	9.3	12.8	3.7	5.2	4.2	5.0	5.6	4.2	2.7	22.3	34.5	18.2	3.2	82.4	48.7	48.4	51.6
94709	BERKELEY	67.6	58.9	3.1	3.2	21.8	27.7	5.7	7.6	2.4	1.6	1.5	6.4	17.7	41.7	20.9	6.6	1.3	93.6	31.3	51.0	49.0
94710	BERKELEY	37.2	31.9	25.4	24.1	15.9	17.8	22.8	27.9	8.2	5.9	4.8	5.0	9.7	38.1	21.0	6.1	1.1	78.2	31.6	49.1	50.9
94720	BERKELEY	50.7	41.5	2.3	2.3	36.6	42.8	9.0	11.0	0.1	0.1	0.2	39.4	40.5	16.9	2.8	0.1	0.0	95.3	21.3	61.6	38.4
94801	RICHMOND	30.5	29.9	33.9	31.3	6.1	6.4	44.8	49.1	10.3	9.4	8.1	8.7	8.7	28.5	18.9	6.4	1.0	67.1	27.8	50.2	49.8
94803	EL SOBRANTE	53.1	45.4	14.8	15.4	19.3	22.9	12.8	16.2	5.5	5.5	6.1	6.6	5.6	24.6	31.6	12.4	2.0	78.6	42.1	48.2	51.8
94804	RICHMOND	26.8	24.2	44.0	42.1	11.7	13.3	22.6	26.3	7.7	7.6	7.2	7.4	7.1	28.2	24.1	9.0	1.6	73.0	34.2	47.6	52.4
94805	RICHMOND	47.9	41.5	19.0	19.1	15.6	18.0	20.6	25.0	6.4	6.2	6.4	6.3	5.8	26.8	29.5	10.4	2.1	77.1	39.8	48.0	52.0
94806	SAN PABLO	33.6	29.0	23.2	23.5	16.4	17.4	35.3	38.9	8.0	7.4	7.0	8.0	8.7	29.2	22.0	8.3	1.4	72.9	31.9	49.3	50.7
94901	SAN RAFAEL	72.8	67.7	2.2	2.3	5.3	6.1	29.2	34.8	6.1	5.9	5.7	5.8	6.1	30.8	27.8	10.0	1.8	79.1	38.5	50.8	49.2
94903	SAN RAFAEL	84.6	79.4	2.0	2.3	6.5	8.3	7.8	11.1	4.4	4.7	5.7	5.7	4.6	21.7	32.0	16.2	5.0	81.3	46.9	47.7	52.3
94904	GREENBRAE	92.9	89.9	0.6	0.7	3.4	4.5	2.9	4.4	4.5	5.2	6.5	5.7	3.7	17.2	34.2	18.1	5.0	79.8	49.3	46.3	53.7
94920	BELVEDERE TIBURON	91.7	88.5	0.8	1.0	4.2	5.7	3.5	5.2	4.9	5.4	6.8	5.7	3.2	17.5	36.3	17.4	2.7	78.6	48.6	47.6	52.4
94922	BODEGA	89.9	86.4	0.6	0.6	1.8	2.3	10.1	14.7	2.3	2.3	3.4	2.8	2.3	14.7	39.0	31.1	2.3	89.8	59.1	51.4	48.6
94923	BODEGA BAY	88.0	84.0	0.4	0.4	1.4	1.8	12.5	17.2	3.0	3.2	3.6	3.5	2.3	17.7	38.8	26.2	1.8	88.1	56.4	51.6	48.4
94924	BOLINAS	91.3	88.0	1.8	2.1	2.0	2.6	6.2	9.2	3.1	2.8	6.0	5.7	5.7	26.1	36.5	12.9	1.2	83.8	45.5	53.1	46.9
94925	CORTE MADERA	87.4	82.8	0.9	1.1	6.3	8.2	5.0	7.2	6.1	6.4	7.2	5.9	4.3	21.8	34.3	12.3	1.8	76.5	44.0	47.2	52.8
94928	ROHNERT PARK	80.6	75.1	2.0	2.1	5.9	7.4	13.2	17.6	6.4	5.7	5.7	8.4	10.0	31.0	24.2	7.2	1.4	78.5	32.3	48.5	51.5
94929	DILLON BEACH	92.6	89.8	0.3	0.3	2.8	3.7	5.3	8.2	2.8	3.4	4.2	4.5	3.1	12.7	47.0	20.1	2.0	87.3	55.6	49.0	51.0
94930	FAIRFAX	91.5	88.1	1.1	1.3	2.3	3.0	5.4	8.1	4.4	4.5	5.2	5.0	5.2	24.0	38.8	11.4	1.5	82.6	45.9	47.8	52.2
94931	COTATI	82.5	77.0	2.1	2.2	3.9	4.9	13.7	18.6	6.3	6.3	6.1	6.5	7.3	31.9	27.1	7.6	1.0	77.4	35.4	49.2	50.8
94933	FOREST KNOLLS	88.9	84.5	1.2	1.4	1.5	2.2	5.5	8.1	5.5	5.5	6.2	5.9	6.1	21.6	41.0	7.4	0.7	79.1	44.3	49.4	50.6
94937	INVERNESS	87.1	83.9	0.6	0.6	1.2	1.5	15.0	18.8	4.2	4.5	4.7	4.2	3.5	19.6	40.5	15.5	3.3	83.9	50.3	48.3	51.7
94938	LAGUNITAS	88.4	83.5	1.6	2.0	1.3	1.7	5.6	8.4	3.7	3.7	4.2	6.2	7.4	22.7	40.9	10.6	0.7	84.2	46.1	47.0	53.0
94939	LARKSPUR	92.3	89.2	0.6	0.7	3.3	4.4	4.3	6.5	4.7	5.1	6.1	4.3	3.4	22.7	37.5	14.1	2.0	81.2	46.8	46.8	53.2
94940	MARSHALL	85.0	77.8	0.0	0.8	0.0	0.0	25.8	34.9	4.8	6.3	6.3	5.6	4.0	24.6	34.9	11.9	1.6	79.4	43.9	55.6	44.4
94941	MILL VALLEY	89.7	86.0	1.1	1.3	5.4	7.1	3.8	5.6	4.8	5.3	6.1	5.3	4.1	21.8	37.1	13.2	2.3	80.3	46.4	47.0	53.0
94945	NOVATO	84.6	79.6	1.8	2.1	5.3	6.8	10.9	15.1	5.3	5.1	5.8	6.4	6.2	23.7	33.3	12.6	1.6	79.6	43.2	49.1	50.9
94946	NICASIO	81.2	74.9	0.8	0.9	2.2	2.8	19.1	25.6	4.9	5.6	5.9	6.7	5.6	22.6	36.4	10.8	1.4	79.4	44.1	52.0	48.0
94947	NOVATO	83.6	78.1	1.8	2.0	5.3	6.7	11.6	16.3	5.5	5.4	6.0	6.1	5.8	24.2	31.7	12.7	2.7	79.0	42.9	47.9	52.1
94949	NOVATO	83.4	77.3	1.8	2.3	4.7	6.1	14.4	20.5	6.4	5.3	5.3	5.2	5.2	28.3	27.8	14.3	2.4	79.7	41.3	48.6	51.4
94951	PENNGROVE	90.1	86.7	0.5	0.5	3.4	4.4	7.1	10.0	4.6	4.7	5.1	5.5	4.7	25.4	34.4	13.9	1.6	82.0	45.0	48.7	51.3
94952	PETALUMA	87.7	83.6	0.8	0.9	1.8	2.3	12.6	17.0	5.6	5.5	5.9	6.5	6.4	26.1	31.4	10.5	2.1	79.1	40.7	49.8	50.2
94954	PETALUMA	82.2	76.9	1.3	1.4	5.2	6.7	15.8	20.7	6.8	7.0	7.4	7.3	5.4	25.9	28.9	9.5	1.8	74.2	38.5	48.8	51.2
94956	POINT REYES STATION	87.8	83.7	0.7	0.7	1.0	1.3	14.3	19.4	4.5	4.5	4.7	5.0	6.0	22.8	35.3	14.8	2.4	83.0	46.7	46.7	53.3
94960	SAN ANSELMO	92.3	89.2	0.9	1.0	2.8	3.8	3.7	5.6	5.1	5.6	6.7	6.5	4.8	20.2	37.5	11.6	2.0	77.9	45.6	47.7	52.3
94963	SAN GERONIMO	88.4	83.8	1.3	1.5	1.6	1.9	6.6	10.0	3.4	3.4	4.0	6.0	7.0	23.0	41.0	11.3	1.0	85.0	46.7	47.6	52.4
94964	SAN QUENTIN	51.2	48.5	39.3	40.3	2.1	2.3	20.7	26.3	0.1	0.2	0.2	1.4	10.6	69.0	17.3	0.9	0.2	99.4	36.1	97.6	2.4
94965	SAUSALITO	78.9	75.1	11.1	11.6	5.0	6.4	4.6	6.4	4.0	2.5	2.5	2.8	4.0	33.3	38.7	10.8	1.3	89.2	45.4	48.7	51.3
94970	STINSON BEACH	95.3	93.4	0.6	0.8	0.8	1.0	3.4	5.1	3.8	3.7	4.6	5.3	4.7	20.5	38.1	17.3	2.0	84.3	49.7	49.2	50.8
94971	TOMALES	89.5	85.8	0.3	0.3	1.0	1.4	11.5	15.9	3.4	4.1	4.7	5.1	5.4	24.7	37.6	13.2	1.7	84.4	46.9	49.5	50.5
94972	VALLEY FORD	86.7	83.8	1.6	1.5	2.3	2.9	9.4	13.2	3.7	3.7	4.4	6.6	6.6	22.8	37.5	13.2	1.5	83.1	46.5	50.7	49.3
94973	WOODACRE	92.7	89.5	0.6	0.7	1.3	1.8	6.1	9.1	3.9	3.9	4.6	6.1	6.3	21.3	40.6	11.9	1.3	83.6	47.3	47.2	52.8
95002	ALVISO	41.7	37.3	0.6	0.5	3.7	3.7	75.4	81.4	8.6	8.6	8.3	10.0	7.3	30.2	20.1	6.3	0.6	68.8	29.2	52.4	47.6
95003	APTOS	89.8	85.7	0.6	0.7	2.6	3.5	8.2	12.3	4.6	4.7	5.3	5.4	5.1	24.9	34.6	13.2	2.3	82.0	45.0	48.4	51.6
95004	AROMAS	77.7	69.9	0.4	0.3	2.6	3.1	24.4	33.6	5.2	5.6	6.4	7.5	5.7	24.7	33.4	10.4	1.1	78.3	41.4	50.0	50.0
95005	BEN LOMOND	90.9	86.9	0.6	0.7	1.6	2.1	6.2	9.5	4.9	4.8	5.4	5.9	6.7	27.9	35.8	7.7	0.9	81.3	41.3	50.3	49.7
95006	BOULDER CREEK	90.4	86.6	0.7	0.8	1.7	2.2	6.1	9.4	4.9	4.7	5.4	6.1	6.3	26.1	38.4	7.2	0.7	81.2	42.6	50.8	49.2
95008	CAMPBELL	73.0	65.7	2.5	2.5	14.4	18.3	12.8	17.1	6.2	5.7	5.6	5.6	7.1	31.9	27.3	9.0	1.5	79.1	37.8	49.9	50.1
95010	CAPITOLA	85.0	79.1	1.1	1.2	3.6	4.7	11.9	17.7	4.5	3.8	4.1	5.2	8.2	29.5	29.9	11.8	2.9	84.4	41.2	48.1	51.9
95012	CASTROVILLE	45.7	42.5	1.1	1.1	3.9	4.0	70.9	75.1	9.3	8.9	8.0	8.4	8.9	27.8	20.7	7.1	0.9	69.3	28.8	50.8	49.2
95013	COYOTE	65.5	59.5	1.1	1.2	14.4	16.8	36.2	42.8	4.6	5.2	7.5	22.0	5.2	22.5	24.9	6.9	1.2	64.7	29.8	60.7	39.3
95014	CUPERTINO	50.2	41.2	0.8	0.8	44.2	52.0	4.3	5.4	5.8	6.4	6.8	7.3	5.6	25.5	31.1	10.0	1.5	76.3	40.5	50.0	50.0
95017	DAVENPORT	84.4	78.1	1.6	1.6	2.3	2.9	14.2	21.0	4.7	4.5	5.0	7.4	7.2	25.3	35.0	9.7	1.1	82.4	41.7	53.0	47.0
95018	FELTON	87.8	82.8	0.7	0.8	3.9	5.1	6.2	9.6	4.4	4.3	4.7	13.0	10.8	23.6	31.3	7.0	1.0	83.0	35.7	49.9	50.1
95019	FREEDOM	39.7	34.8	0.6	0.5	3.2	3.0	77.1	83.7	9.6	9.0	7.8	9.0	9.1	28.7	18.0	7.2	1.4	68.0	28.1	50.2	49.8
95020	GILROY	60.4	54.5	1.6	1.6	4.6	5.5	50.9	57.8	8.8	8.7	8.5	8.1	6.5	28.5	23.1	6.9	0.9	69.1	32.1	49.8	50.2
95023	HOLLISTER	64.3	58.8	1.1	1.1	2.6	2.9	49.3	57.4	9.2	8.9	8.5	7.9	6.3	28.9	22.2	6.9	1.1	68.3	31.4	50.5	49.5
95030	LOS GATOS	88.2	83.4	0.3	0.4	7.7	10.6	3.8	5.5	4.7	5.4	6.5	6.0	3.5	22.7	35.0	13.9	2.4	79.4	45.7	48.6	51.4
95032	LOS GATOS	85.8	80.5	0.8	0.9	8.2	11.2	6.0	8.5	5.3	5.9	6.6	6.1	4.3	23.4	31.8	13.8	2.8	78.0	44.0	48.3	51.7
95033	LOS GATOS	92.1	88.8	0.3	0.4	2.2	3.0	5.2	8.0	5.1	5.7	6.8	6.2	4.2	22.1	38.1	10.9	0.9	78.3	45.0	51.5	48.5
95035	MILPITAS	31.1	26.8	3.6	3.5	52.2	54.6	16.6	20.4	6.9	6.6	6.3	6.5	7.2	32.4	25.4	7.8	0.8	76.4	35.4	52.2	47.8
95037	MORGAN HILL	72.1	64.9	1.6	1.5	6.7	8.2	27.3	34.9	7.5	7.7	7.9	7.6	5.5	26.6	27.7	8.4	1.1	71.9	36.2	49.9	50.1
95039	MOSS LANDING	53.0	48.3	1.3	1.6	4.2	4.7	59.9	64.2	8.2	7.5	7.4	7.8	9.1	28.9	21.5	8.4	1.1	75.3	31.1	52.6	47.4
95043	PAICINES	75.9	69.0	0.3	0.3	1.5	1.6	32.0	42.1	5.9	6.2	6.8	7.3	4.5	26.1	31.8	9.7	1.7	76.8	40.4	54.3	45.7
95045	SAN JUAN BAUTISTA	67.1	60.7	0.8	0.7	2.5	2.7	44.4	52.7	7.2	7.1	7.1	7.5	6.7	25.9	27.1	10.0	1.4	73.9	36.2	50.9	49.1
95046	SAN MARTIN	69.1	62.0	0.8	0.8	6.6	7.8	35.1	43.7	6.2	6.5	7.1	7.4	5.5	25.7	29.4	10.9	1.2	75.6	39.2	50.0	50.0
95050	SANTA CLARA	61.7	54.5	2.5	2.4	21.3	24.7	19.6	24.5	6.1	5.4	4.8	7.5	10.7	33.5	21.6	8.2	2.2	81.1	33.7	50.7	49.3
95051	SANTA CLARA	55.9	47.6	2.0	1.9	30.9	36.3	14.3	17.8	6.5	5.8	5.5	5.2	6.1	33.7	25.7	10.1	1.4	79.0	37.5	50.5	49.5
95053	SANTA CLARA	71.3	63.4	2.2	2.3	12.0	14.9	18.6	24.5	2.4	1.1	1.0	25.1	42.2	16.6	8.3	2.7	0.5	95.0	22.4	50.9	49.1
95054	SANTA CLARA	38.1	31.2	2.5	2.2	47.1	53.0	14.1	15.3	6.0	5.0	4.3	4.8	9.0	39.0	22.8	7.7	1.3	81.9	34.2	52.4	47.6
95060	SANTA CRUZ	80.3	74.0	1.6	1.7	3.9	5.0	17.4	23.9	5.2	4.5	4.3	5.1	9.2	35.0	26.9	8.2	1.6	83.3	35.5	50.9	49.1
95062	SANTA CRUZ	80.6	73.7	1.3	1.3	3.5	4.4	17.6	25.1	5.4	4.7	4.8	5.3	8.1	33.4	27.5	8.2	2.6	82.1	37.3	49.3	50.7
95064	SANTA CRUZ	63.9	54.8	2.5	2.6	16.6	19.7	15.9	21.6	2.4	1.9	1.1	49.7	30.3	11.1	3.0	0.4	0.1	93.8	19.5	45.5	54.5
95065	SANTA CRUZ	85.0	80.2	0.8	0.8	3.2	4.1	14.0	19.2	5.1	5.0	5.1	6.0	6.4	25.4	33.1	11.3	2.5	80.9	42.5	49.1	50.9
95066	SCOTTS VALLEY	89.2	84.7	0.5	0.6	4.3	5.8	6.0	9.3	5.8	5.9	6.7	7.3	6.6	21.7	31.7	10.9	3.4	77.3	42.3	48.8	51.2
95070	SARATOGA	67.3	58.9	0.5	0.5	28.8	36.1	3.5	4.7	5.0	6.1	7.8	7.5	3.8	16.6	35.5	15.2	2.5	76.2	46.6	49.2	50.8
95073	SOQUEL	86.8	81.6	1.0	1.1	3.1	4.0	11.2	16.7	4.9	4.7	5.3	6.4	6.6	25.4	34.4	10.4	1.8	81.0	42.5	48.1	51.9
95076	WATSONVILLE	52.9	47.5	0.7	0.7	3.5	3.5	62.6	70.1	8.7	8.2	7.7	8.5	8.2	28.2	21.7	7.6	1.4	70.6	30.5	50.8	49.2
95110	SAN JOSE	40.4	38.1	3.5	3.0	6.2	7.2	69.9	73.0	8.2	7.3	6.5	8.7	8.8	36.6	18.0	5.2	0.8	72.8	30.2	55.9	44.1
	CALIFORNIA	59.5	54.5	6.7	6.2	11.3	12.5	32.4	38.3	7.5	7.1	6.9	7.5	7.4	28.5	24.2	9.3	1.6	74.1	34.3	49.9	50.1
	UNITED STATES	75.1	72.0	12.3	12.7	3.8	4.6	12.5	15.7	6.8	6.7	6.6	7.1	6.9	27.0	26.0	10.9	1.9	75.7	36.9	49.2	50.8

ZIP CODE #	POST OFFICE NAME	2009 Per Capita Income	2009 HH Income Base	2009 HOUSEHOLD INCOME DISTRIBUTION (%) Less than $25,000	$25,000 to $49,999	$50,000 to $99,999	$100,000 to $149,999	$150,000 or More	MEDIAN HOUSEHOLD INCOME 2009	2014	2009 National Centile	2009 State Centile	2009 Home Value Base	2009 HOME VALUE DISTRIBUTION (%) Less than $50,000	$50,000 to $89,999	$90,000 to $174,999	$175,000 to $399,999	$400,000 or More	2009 Median Home Value
94608	EMERYVILLE	29449	12721	27.0	25.8	28.2	11.8	7.2	46754	49398	53	36	4434	1.2	0.6	12.1	69.0	17.2	256028
94609	OAKLAND	30438	9509	26.4	24.4	28.1	14.2	7.0	49009	51660	59	41	2733	1.4	0.3	4.0	43.9	50.4	401774
94610	OAKLAND	51558	15504	13.5	19.9	35.5	14.9	16.2	68967	72677	86	70	5293	0.9	0.4	5.6	25.7	67.5	557449
94611	OAKLAND	67873	17343	10.1	13.6	25.1	17.2	34.0	102712	108011	97	92	10181	0.5	0.2	1.9	11.0	86.4	717340
94612	OAKLAND	23321	7964	47.7	27.7	17.6	5.0	2.0	26732	28060	4	4	627	5.3	0.6	12.8	56.6	24.7	283242
94613	OAKLAND	36991	41	0.0	63.4	36.6	0.0	0.0	46295	46295	52	35	9	0.0	0.0	0.0	66.7	33.3	350000
94618	OAKLAND	71114	6546	8.3	11.3	25.2	21.2	34.1	110281	115449	98	93	3995	0.0	0.1	0.4	6.9	92.6	748153
94619	OAKLAND	35434	9657	13.5	19.2	31.7	20.0	15.7	74747	79268	89	75	6013	1.9	0.3	2.9	47.6	47.1	387008
94621	OAKLAND	13253	8766	35.6	28.2	27.9	5.5	2.9	37190	39756	24	17	3812	1.4	1.1	24.0	69.9	3.7	211701
94702	BERKELEY	31721	7068	23.3	22.9	31.0	15.5	7.3	54479	58379	70	51	3357	0.6	0.2	3.3	46.5	49.4	397530
94703	BERKELEY	34604	8971	20.0	21.6	31.9	15.2	11.4	60319	63849	78	59	3512	0.4	0.0	2.0	30.9	66.6	465471
94704	BERKELEY	23632	8616	49.9	21.0	17.8	5.8	5.5	25059	26439	3	3	1033	0.0	1.5	2.8	21.3	74.4	568487
94705	BERKELEY	69285	5475	13.8	12.7	22.4	17.3	33.7	101963	108302	97	92	3021	0.2	0.0	0.5	9.7	89.6	793122
94706	ALBANY	41167	6921	11.1	17.2	33.3	24.3	14.1	79723	84758	92	80	3741	0.9	0.2	1.6	32.3	64.9	464942
94707	BERKELEY	75102	5041	4.6	8.9	21.0	20.4	45.1	136073	140716	99	97	4182	0.3	0.5	0.3	4.7	94.1	730590
94708	BERKELEY	77429	4878	5.7	7.5	20.6	20.8	45.3	137839	142798	99	98	3934	0.0	0.1	0.2	6.0	93.7	734130
94709	BERKELEY	42819	5134	26.5	20.0	25.3	14.7	13.5	57363	62442	74	55	1234	0.6	0.0	1.0	20.1	78.3	604278
94710	BERKELEY	24314	3282	26.8	26.0	32.5	10.0	4.7	46233	49245	52	35	1105	0.6	0.5	1.6	49.3	47.9	390562
94720	BERKELEY	17450	111	60.4	26.1	7.2	3.6	2.7	13594	13488	1	1	2	0.0	0.0	0.0	50.0	50.0	700000
94801	RICHMOND	16485	9144	33.2	24.7	28.4	10.1	3.5	41383	43949	37	24	3804	4.2	5.8	25.4	45.6	19.1	205201
94803	EL SOBRANTE	32616	9534	11.7	18.2	34.3	24.5	11.3	77414	81322	91	78	6714	1.3	0.3	4.9	55.6	37.8	351986
94804	RICHMOND	23644	14293	23.3	24.8	33.6	13.1	5.3	52123	54660	66	46	6788	0.8	0.5	12.2	74.0	12.5	248168
94805	RICHMOND	28170	5205	13.2	23.3	40.2	16.4	6.9	62224	64389	80	62	3418	0.5	0.4	5.8	70.0	23.3	285201
94806	SAN PABLO	20275	19500	21.4	24.7	35.6	14.4	3.8	53870	55618	69	49	10540	4.8	1.1	13.2	75.4	5.5	230212
94901	SAN RAFAEL	44410	15950	15.0	19.5	24.9	18.5	22.1	71161	72293	87	72	7856	0.4	0.1	0.4	7.3	91.8	759694
94903	SAN RAFAEL	48032	12279	10.4	14.4	27.4	25.9	21.9	92465	98773	95	88	8429	0.2	1.3	2.2	10.7	85.6	631662
94904	GREENBRAE	78391	5593	8.4	14.2	23.5	18.7	35.2	106746	113776	98	93	3510	0.9	0.4	0.3	4.4	94.0	964177
94920	BELVEDERE TIBURON	95275	5377	9.0	7.4	17.3	17.7	48.7	142995	159118	100	98	3554	0.0	0.1	0.3	1.7	97.8	1000001
94922	BODEGA	42877	62	4.8	11.3	41.9	22.6	19.4	78373	84375	91	79	46	0.0	0.0	0.0	4.3	95.7	694444
94923	BODEGA BAY	48629	856	11.6	16.5	39.3	18.2	14.5	70863	73046	87	72	617	0.6	0.6	1.3	12.8	84.6	638699
94924	BOLINAS	39250	621	15.1	21.1	30.3	17.2	16.3	65292	66760	84	66	381	0.5	0.3	1.3	8.7	89.2	710106
94925	CORTE MADERA	60416	3897	7.6	10.0	27.7	22.4	32.3	106426	111809	97	92	2706	0.6	0.2	0.5	2.7	96.0	817325
94928	ROHNERT PARK	29398	15402	14.2	20.5	38.6	19.5	7.1	66643	69782	85	68	8949	4.2	4.3	6.9	55.4	29.2	317980
94929	DILLON BEACH	41215	172	4.7	41.3	24.4	15.7	14.0	52124	53112	66	46	141	10.6	0.7	0.0	14.2	74.5	586864
94930	FAIRFAX	46770	3805	11.7	14.7	33.4	23.2	17.0	78855	81260	92	80	2425	0.2	0.0	0.1	8.1	91.5	638658
94931	COTATI	31965	3546	11.5	24.3	38.8	19.1	6.4	65716	68565	84	67	2189	3.1	1.8	9.6	56.6	28.8	318078
94933	FOREST KNOLLS	36588	403	17.6	19.4	27.3	19.6	16.1	66174	69241	84	67	268	0.0	0.0	0.0	18.3	81.7	573370
94937	INVERNESS	38486	618	17.0	24.9	22.5	23.5	12.1	58936	62326	76	57	375	0.3	0.0	0.0	8.3	91.5	713926
94938	LAGUNITAS	45242	171	18.7	17.0	23.4	24.6	16.4	72223	75000	88	73	117	0.0	0.0	0.0	6.0	94.0	693627
94939	LARKSPUR	74509	3442	10.0	10.3	29.6	19.9	30.2	100079	103848	97	91	1903	2.9	1.2	0.8	3.3	91.7	861913
94940	MARSHALL	39765	60	28.3	21.7	23.3	15.0	11.7	50000	56352	61	43	29	3.4	0.0	0.0	0.0	96.6	968750
94941	MILL VALLEY	75811	13224	8.8	11.0	22.0	18.6	39.6	117533	128898	98	95	8585	0.1	0.0	0.1	2.2	97.5	896380
94945	NOVATO	44817	6741	10.2	15.9	27.7	23.7	22.5	88586	92831	95	86	4682	1.0	0.2	0.2	9.7	88.9	619076
94946	NICASIO	57951	329	10.9	10.9	29.5	20.7	28.0	97004	105229	96	90	209	0.5	0.5	0.0	1.9	97.1	940574
94947	NOVATO	42896	9590	8.5	13.8	31.3	26.3	20.2	89993	94516	95	87	6608	0.3	0.1	0.1	16.9	82.6	583278
94949	NOVATO	46860	6835	9.5	17.2	29.4	21.5	22.4	80257	80599	92	81	4620	0.9	7.2	9.9	8.9	73.2	593768
94951	PENNGROVE	37463	1578	9.6	24.4	30.9	18.9	16.1	72966	77458	88	74	1109	3.9	1.5	2.3	12.8	79.4	635511
94952	PETALUMA	40037	12731	11.7	17.4	33.9	22.2	14.8	75732	79354	90	76	7643	0.7	0.2	1.1	25.0	73.0	535787
94954	PETALUMA	36420	13120	8.6	13.3	32.5	30.2	15.5	89998	91595	95	87	9838	3.4	2.5	1.4	39.9	52.8	412173
94956	POINT REYES STATION	43038	614	12.5	23.6	30.1	17.4	16.3	65034	67281	83	66	384	0.3	0.0	1.0	7.6	91.1	727642
94960	SAN ANSELMO	56074	6685	9.7	13.1	24.0	23.9	29.2	104309	110265	97	92	4734	0.0	0.0	0.1	2.6	97.3	825660
94963	SAN GERONIMO	40191	310	17.1	19.4	22.6	26.5	14.5	72272	74015	88	73	222	0.9	0.9	0.5	5.4	92.3	672500
94964	SAN QUENTIN	21623	91	4.4	5.5	51.6	12.1	26.4	77412	76755	91	78	15	13.3	13.3	0.0	0.0	73.3	604167
94965	SAUSALITO	96199	5898	11.0	12.4	20.7	20.6	35.4	110338	118591	98	93	2738	2.3	0.3	0.6	6.9	89.8	809865
94970	STINSON BEACH	78313	390	14.1	11.3	13.3	24.6	36.7	120327	129502	98	95	232	0.0	0.0	0.4	3.4	96.1	1000000
94971	TOMALES	30501	111	18.9	25.2	31.5	10.8	13.5	56082	61020	73	54	66	6.1	0.0	4.5	16.7	72.7	539474
94972	VALLEY FORD	57432	51	7.8	7.8	25.5	29.4	29.4	117647	121791	98	95	38	0.0	0.0	0.0	13.2	86.8	704545
94973	WOODACRE	43226	672	11.3	21.1	25.3	26.5	15.8	74770	79382	89	75	518	0.0	0.0	0.4	6.2	93.4	642210
95002	ALVISO	20870	495	6.3	22.4	39.8	17.4	14.1	73206	73367	88	74	266	1.5	3.0	8.3	50.0	37.2	360920
95003	APTOS	49763	9977	9.3	13.2	30.4	24.5	22.6	93607	97376	96	88	7062	1.0	0.6	1.7	10.0	86.6	657866
95004	AROMAS	31569	1398	12.0	12.4	35.6	25.1	14.9	83474	88421	93	83	1088	0.9	0.5	1.0	28.3	69.3	485714
95005	BEN LOMOND	40413	2866	8.4	13.9	34.5	29.1	14.1	88532	90749	95	86	1995	0.2	0.3	0.7	24.5	74.3	533051
95006	BOULDER CREEK	47548	3954	11.1	17.1	26.1	23.8	21.9	90588	94745	95	87	2788	0.8	0.6	0.8	28.6	69.3	512318
95008	CAMPBELL	48920	18862	8.4	12.4	32.0	23.4	23.7	93924	100591	96	88	9566	0.2	0.5	1.4	9.1	88.8	649219
95010	CAPITOLA	39709	4511	16.8	21.9	34.8	17.2	9.3	63516	66040	82	64	2144	1.7	1.6	5.8	24.2	66.7	536676
95012	CASTROVILLE	16129	2290	17.4	27.2	40.4	10.0	5.0	54841	58988	71	51	1277	4.0	2.8	15.7	53.6	23.9	261401
95013	COYOTE	33848	44	9.1	13.6	31.8	34.1	11.4	90077	111520	95	87	24	12.5	4.2	0.0	16.7	66.7	650000
95014	CUPERTINO	63208	20253	6.2	7.3	21.7	19.9	44.9	135477	142944	99	97	12614	0.2	0.7	1.4	2.0	95.7	863846
95017	DAVENPORT	47486	148	8.8	12.8	25.7	23.0	29.7	104579	106626	97	92	100	0.0	0.0	3.0	11.0	86.0	681250
95018	FELTON	40248	3553	8.6	11.1	36.0	27.8	16.4	89279	91348	95	86	2590	0.3	0.4	1.0	25.7	72.5	499829
95019	FREEDOM	14535	2206	24.8	30.1	31.8	10.9	2.4	45740	47729	50	34	1073	1.8	7.0	18.0	45.9	27.4	308144
95020	GILROY	31250	16084	10.2	16.3	31.5	23.1	18.9	84018	88312	94	83	10267	0.9	0.8	0.9	15.3	82.1	558163
95023	HOLLISTER	26427	14541	11.2	19.7	35.0	21.0	13.1	76785	81420	90	77	9986	1.4	1.5	1.2	39.3	56.6	433796
95030	LOS GATOS	94883	5348	5.3	5.7	19.6	13.4	56.0	169790	182474	100	99	3741	0.1	0.1	0.5	1.9	97.4	1000001
95032	LOS GATOS	76650	10059	6.9	8.5	21.5	17.3	45.8	135704	145971	99	97	6936	0.3	0.5	0.6	4.8	93.8	862959
95033	LOS GATOS	72027	3601	5.1	7.9	22.4	17.2	47.4	141125	149005	99	98	2811	1.0	0.1	0.5	8.5	89.8	753065
95035	MILPITAS	37032	18776	5.8	9.9	29.1	25.6	29.7	107412	112828	98	93	12842	1.2	1.9	1.5	12.9	82.6	570907
95037	MORGAN HILL	49410	14693	7.6	12.7	23.1	21.9	34.7	112556	121874	98	94	10593	0.8	1.0	1.4	10.3	86.4	672554
95039	MOSS LANDING	23221	522	13.6	24.1	42.7	12.5	7.1	61873	64900	80	61	276	9.1	6.9	12.7	45.3	26.1	275532
95043	PAICINES	25518	286	23.4	26.6	32.5	10.8	6.6	50000	50182	61	43	153	0.0	2.0	7.8	32.7	57.5	488462
95045	SAN JUAN BAUTISTA	26638	1320	15.9	22.8	35.0	16.1	10.2	64771	71506	83	65	782	3.3	1.0	1.3	31.6	62.8	486957
95046	SAN MARTIN	38811	1827	6.5	13.8	28.5	20.4	30.7	101963	108202	97	92	1311	0.4	0.5	0.4	8.0	90.8	770752
95050	SANTA CLARA	40006	14565	13.9	16.6	31.1	20.6	17.8	78549	80825	91	79	5650	0.3	0.1	0.2	11.0	88.4	595484
95051	SANTA CLARA	45841	19975	7.5	11.4	31.2	26.9	23.0	99852	104564	97	91	10532	0.6	0.6	0.4	12.8	85.7	601993
95053	SANTA CLARA	5986	0	0.0	0.0	0.0	0.0	0.0	0	0	0	0	0	0.0	0.0	0.0	0.0	0.0	0
95054	SANTA CLARA	50180	7147	6.0	7.0	24.5	26.9	35.6	121627	128324	99	95	3661	0.0	0.1	0.0	11.5	88.4	613294
95060	SANTA CRUZ	39427	18012	17.8	17.1	28.6	20.1	16.4	74724	77413	89	75	9116	0.6	0.6	0.9	11.2	86.8	657491
95062	SANTA CRUZ	34023	14875	15.9	23.7	33.9	16.8	9.7	63076	66073	81	63	7326	2.9	3.6	5.5	14.8	73.3	558539
95064	SANTA CRUZ	21884	438	36.1	17.1	24.2	13.7	8.9	45000	49830	48	33	127	14.2	0.0	6.3	44.9	34.6	278125
95065	SANTA CRUZ	40940	3154	13.1	16.0	31.6	23.4	15.8	78935	82072	92	80	2037	0.4	1.5	0.6	7.1	90.4	676497
95066	SCOTTS VALLEY	48692	5570	8.1	14.8	28.9	19.9	28.3	95351	100333	96	89	4127	0.7	0.5	2.6	18.7	77.6	628426
95070	SARATOGA	84380	11409	5.5	5.9	11.8	12.1	64.7	202000	207998	100	100	9758	0.1	0.2	0.7	1.6	97.4	1000001
95073	SOQUEL	44391	4140	13.3	17.8	29.2	19.9	19.8	79098	83059	92	80	2925	1.9	3.9	5.5	12.2	76.4	644702
95076	WATSONVILLE	20658	22199	17.8	24.7	34.3	14.9	8.3	59284	61942	77	57	12763	1.3	1.4	4.7	40.4	52.1	412975
95110	SAN JOSE	22979	5460	19.8	19.7	34.4	15.9	10.3	62244	64816	80	62	1889	0.5	0.3	0.8	32.0	66.4	452185
	CALIFORNIA	28199		18.5	22.2	33.9	14.0	11.5	61614	64088				3.3	2.6	13.6	41.0	39.5	321752
	UNITED STATES	27277		20.9	24.4	35.3	11.7	7.6	54719	56938				9.3	13.1	31.6	32.6	13.5	162279

ZIP CODE #	POST OFFICE NAME	FINANCIAL SERVICES: Auto Loan	Home Loan	Invest-ments	Retire-ment Plans	THE HOME: Home Improvements: Home Repair	Lawn & Garden	Furnishings: Comput-ers & Hard-ware-Personal	Major Appli-ances	TV, Radio, Sound Equip-ment	Furni-ture	ENTERTAINMENT: Dine out/ Carry out	Sports Equip-ment	Fees & Tickets	Toys & Games	Travel	Cable TV	PERSONAL: Apparel & Services	Auto Repairs	Health Insur-ance	Pets & Supplies
94608	EMERYVILLE	82	77	81	82	76	73	96	80	96	87	99	66	94	94	90	98	72	90	84	99
94609	OAKLAND	85	81	89	87	83	73	101	84	94	95	98	73	98	93	97	91	71	94	81	101
94610	OAKLAND	131	118	130	130	120	110	148	122	139	143	144	107	143	139	140	134	104	136	119	149
94611	OAKLAND	183	205	240	219	220	191	212	197	198	217	200	159	230	194	223	189	148	201	184	228
94612	OAKLAND	49	38	42	43	38	42	56	46	59	52	59	37	51	54	50	60	42	55	56	58
94613	OAKLAND	87	56	54	62	55	61	104	71	93	82	93	64	76	93	73	91	66	86	74	90
94618	OAKLAND	189	225	267	239	245	204	225	213	205	233	209	172	248	201	245	195	156	212	191	242
94619	OAKLAND	117	142	152	139	149	123	140	133	130	138	133	104	150	128	148	126	98	134	122	149
94621	OAKLAND	63	61	56	59	60	53	70	63	68	68	71	49	67	68	66	67	51	68	59	72
94702	BERKELEY	85	94	105	97	98	83	104	92	96	99	99	76	107	94	106	93	73	98	87	107
94703	BERKELEY	99	97	110	105	101	85	120	100	108	115	113	89	116	107	118	101	82	110	91	119
94704	BERKELEY	71	42	43	49	40	44	93	55	78	71	80	55	65	77	61	73	57	72	55	72
94705	BERKELEY	190	212	250	228	227	193	226	204	207	227	213	171	242	204	237	197	159	211	186	236
94706	ALBANY	122	135	151	140	143	119	142	131	128	145	131	109	147	126	148	120	95	134	117	151
94707	BERKELEY	216	295	355	303	329	270	254	267	230	281	229	201	305	223	300	217	172	249	234	293
94708	BERKELEY	213	289	347	297	321	265	251	263	228	277	227	198	300	220	296	216	171	246	233	289
94709	BERKELEY	113	91	101	103	92	87	136	100	123	120	127	91	119	122	114	117	92	116	98	124
94710	BERKELEY	80	73	79	78	74	64	93	76	86	88	89	68	88	85	88	81	64	86	72	92
94720	BERKELEY	48	21	20	25	19	24	68	34	54	46	55	36	40	53	36	49	39	48	34	45
94801	RICHMOND	74	69	66	68	69	59	83	73	78	82	81	59	78	78	78	75	59	80	67	83
94803	EL SOBRANTE	110	143	149	139	148	131	126	127	122	125	123	95	144	123	139	123	91	125	124	143
94804	RICHMOND	84	87	85	86	86	81	93	86	94	90	95	66	94	92	91	95	69	91	87	101
94805	RICHMOND	91	116	120	112	119	105	106	104	102	103	104	79	119	103	115	103	76	104	102	117
94806	SAN PABLO	87	88	84	84	89	76	94	88	89	95	91	69	92	89	92	85	65	92	81	99
94901	SAN RAFAEL	148	161	182	167	172	141	174	159	157	177	161	131	180	155	181	146	119	165	141	181
94903	SAN RAFAEL	146	173	195	178	185	158	165	163	153	175	153	128	182	150	181	145	112	160	149	184
94904	GREENBRAE	209	262	306	269	287	257	239	246	231	254	230	182	278	221	271	229	169	239	247	276
94920	BELVEDERE TIBURON	263	339	408	356	373	310	309	308	284	330	286	242	364	280	350	270	217	296	272	343
94922	BODEGA	167	176	239	175	203	208	158	187	167	179	164	117	174	150	183	175	113	178	208	212
94923	BODEGA BAY	148	144	205	142	163	174	134	161	140	143	138	107	138	128	151	147	94	152	171	183
94924	BOLINAS	117	147	172	150	162	127	140	139	123	150	123	111	154	119	157	113	91	134	116	154
94925	CORTE MADERA	181	232	274	237	256	204	215	216	191	232	191	169	242	184	244	177	142	207	185	239
94928	ROHNERT PARK	113	111	103	112	108	103	115	108	112	117	113	85	114	114	111	110	80	111	106	127
94929	DILLON BEACH	141	113	182	111	124	149	113	144	118	106	117	105	98	112	122	126	78	133	142	166
94930	FAIRFAX	131	165	193	168	181	142	157	155	137	168	138	124	172	132	175	126	102	149	130	172
94931	COTATI	113	115	102	115	110	105	114	108	111	117	113	86	115	114	112	108	79	111	105	128
94933	FOREST KNOLLS	110	139	162	141	153	119	132	130	115	141	116	104	144	111	147	106	86	126	109	145
94937	INVERNESS	114	128	164	128	144	135	117	130	115	130	114	89	129	106	134	115	81	124	132	146
94938	LAGUNITAS	132	166	194	169	183	143	158	156	138	169	139	125	173	134	176	127	103	151	131	174
94939	LARKSPUR	186	227	269	238	248	203	220	213	199	231	202	171	246	195	243	188	151	209	187	240
94940	MARSHALL	146	100	160	100	105	154	111	139	116	90	115	115	82	114	111	126	74	129	146	170
94941	MILL VALLEY	210	266	315	275	293	236	249	247	223	267	224	195	281	216	280	208	167	238	214	276
94945	NOVATO	142	176	204	180	191	155	170	165	152	176	154	132	187	149	187	143	114	163	145	185
94946	NICASIO	226	281	330	286	309	243	268	266	235	286	235	212	292	227	299	216	174	256	224	296
94947	NOVATO	137	172	199	175	186	153	163	160	148	170	149	126	182	144	182	139	111	157	142	179
94949	NOVATO	151	167	179	170	176	147	167	160	152	176	154	128	174	152	174	143	111	160	142	183
94951	PENNGROVE	136	142	182	143	153	147	134	148	128	138	128	112	137	125	147	127	91	139	136	168
94952	PETALUMA	130	152	172	155	162	136	149	145	135	154	137	116	159	132	160	128	100	143	129	165
94954	PETALUMA	136	170	171	167	174	152	148	152	140	155	142	116	166	142	162	137	103	145	139	170
94956	POINT REYES STATION	120	151	177	154	166	130	144	142	126	154	126	113	157	121	160	115	94	137	119	158
94960	SAN ANSELMO	169	220	260	224	243	193	201	203	178	218	178	159	228	172	229	165	133	194	174	225
94963	SAN GERONIMO	126	158	185	161	174	136	150	149	132	161	132	119	165	127	168	121	98	143	125	165
94964	SAN QUENTIN	134	156	156	162	156	150	149	144	145	149	148	114	165	146	159	145	107	145	145	168
94965	SAUSALITO	221	237	277	258	251	213	265	232	243	262	251	199	275	240	271	231	186	244	212	271
94970	STINSON BEACH	197	247	289	252	272	213	236	233	206	252	207	186	258	199	263	189	153	224	195	259
94971	TOMALES	112	114	150	115	125	120	113	122	105	113	105	96	111	102	123	103	74	116	112	140
94972	VALLEY FORD	189	238	278	242	262	204	226	223	198	242	198	178	248	191	252	181	147	215	187	249
94973	WOODACRE	135	169	198	172	186	145	161	159	141	172	141	127	176	136	179	129	105	153	133	177
95002	ALVISO	117	144	133	126	150	103	133	134	110	146	114	104	134	111	140	97	84	126	99	137
95003	APTOS	145	180	204	184	194	160	167	167	151	179	151	131	186	147	186	142	112	161	147	187
95004	AROMAS	124	163	158	159	164	144	136	141	129	140	131	107	156	132	151	127	95	134	130	158
95005	BEN LOMOND	129	164	187	166	178	142	153	152	136	163	136	120	169	132	171	126	101	147	130	169
95006	BOULDER CREEK	142	179	209	182	197	154	170	168	149	182	149	134	186	144	190	136	111	162	141	187
95008	CAMPBELL	150	166	187	171	176	142	181	162	160	181	165	137	184	158	187	148	121	169	142	187
95010	CAPITOLA	106	103	112	110	106	96	121	105	114	118	116	88	119	112	118	110	84	114	103	126
95012	CASTROVILLE	91	93	83	87	93	79	96	93	88	99	92	73	94	90	95	83	67	95	81	100
95013	COYOTE	140	195	206	182	204	169	165	170	153	167	155	127	191	154	188	151	115	163	155	186
95014	CUPERTINO	220	280	323	283	307	237	263	261	229	283	230	207	290	223	294	209	171	249	216	287
95017	DAVENPORT	172	216	252	220	237	185	205	203	179	220	180	162	225	173	229	164	134	195	170	225
95018	FELTON	134	168	190	171	182	145	158	156	139	168	140	125	173	136	175	128	103	150	132	174
95019	FREEDOM	85	82	68	72	81	65	85	83	79	92	83	62	79	81	82	74	59	85	70	88
95020	GILROY	146	171	160	164	173	142	159	158	145	168	149	124	168	148	166	136	108	153	135	173
95023	HOLLISTER	126	147	136	139	149	119	135	136	121	146	124	106	140	124	141	112	90	129	112	147
95030	LOS GATOS	278	362	436	380	400	334	327	330	301	352	302	256	386	295	374	287	229	315	294	367
95032	LOS GATOS	233	300	354	310	329	269	275	276	248	296	249	216	315	242	312	233	187	264	241	307
95033	LOS GATOS	228	302	348	311	329	270	265	273	239	289	239	211	309	234	305	224	179	257	236	302
95035	MILPITAS	174	206	219	204	219	165	202	195	174	215	177	158	210	173	215	157	129	189	157	215
95037	MORGAN HILL	203	242	238	243	245	211	222	220	207	233	211	173	243	210	236	197	154	214	195	248
95039	MOSS LANDING	102	105	100	101	107	89	113	106	103	116	108	85	111	103	113	96	78	110	93	116
95043	PAICINES	115	79	126	79	83	121	88	109	91	71	90	90	64	89	87	99	59	102	115	134
95045	SAN JUAN BAUTISTA	106	127	121	122	127	113	117	116	112	119	113	89	126	113	124	110	82	115	110	132
95046	SAN MARTIN	170	222	242	216	240	191	195	203	173	214	174	152	220	170	221	161	129	189	172	218
95050	SANTA CLARA	129	134	145	139	139	116	153	134	139	150	144	114	152	138	153	131	105	143	122	156
95051	SANTA CLARA	154	178	198	180	190	148	184	171	161	189	164	141	190	158	194	147	120	172	145	193
95053	SANTA CLARA	0	0	0	0	0	0	0	0	0	0	0	0	0	0	0	0	0	0	0	0
95054	SANTA CLARA	190	179	187	189	181	155	211	181	193	211	199	156	202	195	202	181	143	195	165	215
95060	SANTA CRUZ	125	136	155	142	146	120	149	135	133	150	135	112	151	130	152	123	99	139	119	155
95062	SANTA CRUZ	105	110	118	115	114	100	121	109	112	120	114	90	122	110	121	107	82	114	103	128
95064	SANTA CRUZ	95	43	43	52	40	49	132	67	106	91	107	72	80	103	73	96	76	94	67	90
95065	SANTA CRUZ	130	150	166	152	160	139	148	145	139	155	140	112	159	134	159	134	102	145	139	164
95066	SCOTTS VALLEY	153	194	221	196	210	178	178	180	165	188	165	138	201	159	200	159	121	174	168	201
95070	SARATOGA	287	400	486	415	447	371	335	355	309	371	306	267	417	303	398	293	235	328	312	388
95073	SOQUEL	140	172	192	174	184	151	164	161	147	172	148	128	178	144	180	139	109	157	142	181
95076	WATSONVILLE	104	116	112	107	120	94	114	113	101	121	104	87	114	101	118	93	76	111	93	120
95110	SAN JOSE	103	102	99	100	103	82	121	105	109	118	115	88	115	109	116	101	84	113	91	118
	CALIFORNIA	112	119	122	118	122	107	121	116	114	124	116	92	124	114	124	110	84	118	107	132
	UNITED STATES	100	100	100	100	100	100	100	100	100	100	100	100	100	100	100	100	100	100	100	100

ZIP CODE			POPULATION			2000-2009 ANNUAL RATE		HOUSEHOLDS					FAMILIES		
#	POST OFFICE NAME	COUNTY FIPS CODE	2000	2009	2014	% Rate	State Centile	2000	2009	2014	% Annual Rate 2000-2009	2009 Average HH Size	2000	2009	% Annual Rate 2000-2009
95111	SAN JOSE	085	57670	63357	65883	1.0	62	14073	14911	15470	0.6	4.25	11631	12287	0.6
95112	SAN JOSE	085	51800	59413	63542	1.5	75	16617	18796	20041	1.3	2.98	9295	10711	1.5
95113	SAN JOSE	085	374	1131	1354	12.7	99	254	729	879	12.1	1.52	56	222	16.1
95116	SAN JOSE	085	54157	58405	60473	0.8	54	12734	13408	13818	0.6	4.32	10208	10779	0.6
95117	SAN JOSE	085	31048	32676	33570	0.6	45	11787	12146	12410	0.3	2.68	7143	7420	0.4
95118	SAN JOSE	085	33225	33793	34425	0.2	18	11796	12025	12223	0.2	2.80	8511	8702	0.2
95119	SAN JOSE	085	10137	10111	10199	0.0	9	3161	3153	3172	0.0	3.20	2577	2579	0.0
95120	SAN JOSE	085	37105	37685	38417	0.2	18	12338	12525	12733	0.2	3.01	10573	10762	0.2
95121	SAN JOSE	085	37246	38713	39750	0.4	30	9018	9201	9430	0.2	4.18	7834	8005	0.2
95122	SAN JOSE	085	60381	63169	64536	0.5	39	12037	12292	12518	0.2	5.12	10537	10769	0.2
95123	SAN JOSE	085	59267	62676	64834	0.6	45	20231	21203	21833	0.5	2.95	15135	15984	0.6
95124	SAN JOSE	085	45279	45635	46422	0.1	13	16332	16456	16692	0.1	2.74	11936	12068	0.1
95125	SAN JOSE	085	46428	50965	53197	1.0	62	19053	20583	21368	0.8	2.46	11870	12922	0.9
95126	SAN JOSE	085	28487	32934	34992	1.6	77	11398	12920	13668	1.4	2.48	5988	6837	1.4
95127	SAN JOSE	085	57879	60850	62387	0.5	39	14693	15120	15444	0.3	3.98	12211	12588	0.3
95128	SAN JOSE	085	30389	32678	33902	0.8	54	11615	12282	12679	0.6	2.59	7082	7529	0.7
95129	SAN JOSE	085	36471	37324	38051	0.3	23	13287	13472	13668	0.1	2.74	9647	9816	0.2
95130	SAN JOSE	085	13079	13445	13751	0.3	23	4733	4845	4931	0.3	2.77	3320	3414	0.3
95131	SAN JOSE	085	26384	28638	29833	0.9	58	8099	8602	8894	0.7	3.31	6148	6567	0.7
95132	SAN JOSE	085	40559	41442	42260	0.2	18	11598	11779	11961	0.2	3.51	9651	9822	0.2
95133	SAN JOSE	085	25915	28142	29407	0.9	58	6989	7494	7790	0.8	3.73	5901	6334	0.8
95134	SAN JOSE	085	9703	15731	18154	5.4	96	4089	6135	6938	4.5	2.48	2283	3590	5.0
95135	SAN JOSE	085	15794	18725	20135	1.9	81	5840	6643	7032	1.4	2.82	4446	5177	1.7
95136	SAN JOSE	085	36771	42173	44906	1.5	75	12724	14715	15663	1.6	2.86	9077	10376	1.5
95138	SAN JOSE	085	14876	18050	19206	2.1	84	4817	5813	6175	2.1	3.10	3886	4734	2.2
95139	SAN JOSE	085	6945	6912	6966	-0.1	5	2276	2266	2275	0.0	3.05	1775	1774	0.0
95140	MOUNT HAMILTON	085	248	260	269	0.5	39	94	98	100	0.5	2.58	75	78	0.4
95148	SAN JOSE	085	44118	47198	48947	0.7	50	10903	11574	11963	0.6	4.07	9746	10364	0.7
95202	STOCKTON	077	6649	6931	7031	0.5	39	2886	3028	3080	0.5	2.19	1211	1234	0.2
95203	STOCKTON	077	16689	17104	17251	0.3	23	5631	5704	5728	0.1	2.93	3654	3635	-0.1
95204	STOCKTON	077	28822	29319	29650	0.2	18	11506	11555	11657	0.0	2.50	7293	7153	-0.2
95205	STOCKTON	077	34221	38045	39443	1.2	68	9816	10626	10974	0.9	3.56	7437	7921	0.7
95206	STOCKTON	077	50038	64884	70863	2.8	90	12927	16767	18322	2.9	3.79	10698	13849	2.8
95207	STOCKTON	077	49926	50472	50676	0.1	13	18405	18447	18479	0.0	2.70	12132	11885	-0.2
95209	STOCKTON	077	30692	41605	46085	3.3	92	9419	12762	14150	3.3	3.22	7782	10516	3.3
95210	STOCKTON	077	40742	44473	45810	1.0	62	11347	12122	12441	0.7	3.63	9157	9675	0.6
95211	STOCKTON	077	1719	1563	1565	-1.0	1	24	26	27	0.9	1.35	4	4	0.0
95212	STOCKTON	077	6868	16768	20502	10.1	98	2559	6388	7825	10.4	2.61	1933	4663	10.0
95215	STOCKTON	077	23479	25748	26697	1.0	62	6478	7157	7446	1.1	3.25	4982	5406	0.9
95219	STOCKTON	077	18721	27639	31123	4.3	94	7831	10894	12116	3.6	2.53	5005	7208	4.0
95220	ACAMPO	077	7199	8081	8437	1.3	70	2523	2802	2914	1.1	2.87	2017	2214	1.0
95222	ANGELS CAMP	009	4772	5974	6562	2.5	88	1895	2454	2714	2.8	2.39	1292	1675	2.8
95223	ARNOLD	009	5914	7145	7747	2.1	84	2613	3260	3561	2.4	2.19	1845	2310	2.5
95228	COPPEROPOLIS	009	2637	2967	3103	1.3	70	1056	1198	1252	1.4	2.45	791	899	1.4
95230	FARMINGTON	099	875	977	1053	1.2	68	305	339	364	1.1	2.88	242	267	1.1
95231	FRENCH CAMP	077	4997	5463	6018	1.0	62	860	1050	1215	2.2	3.21	647	781	2.1
95232	GLENCOE	009	317	382	417	2.0	83	136	169	185	2.4	2.26	91	113	2.4
95236	LINDEN	077	3364	4326	4805	2.8	90	1111	1429	1586	2.8	2.90	898	1142	2.6
95237	LOCKEFORD	077	3275	3674	3829	1.3	70	1132	1258	1308	1.1	2.90	885	969	1.0
95240	LODI	077	45606	48489	49452	0.7	50	15663	16373	16650	0.5	2.89	10874	11205	0.3
95242	LODI	077	23201	27084	29106	1.7	78	8972	10311	11033	1.5	2.61	6461	7310	1.3
95245	MOKELUMNE HILL	009	3058	3674	4015	2.0	83	1325	1633	1794	2.3	2.24	898	1108	2.3
95246	MOUNTAIN RANCH	009	1989	2217	2423	1.2	68	848	956	1052	1.3	2.28	580	655	1.3
95247	MURPHYS	009	3822	4778	5221	2.4	87	1701	2200	2424	2.8	2.13	1167	1511	2.8
95249	SAN ANDREAS	009	3522	4526	4883	2.7	90	1473	1940	2104	3.0	2.26	921	1224	3.1
95251	VALLECITO	009	197	250	271	2.6	89	81	107	118	3.1	2.19	57	76	3.2
95252	VALLEY SPRINGS	009	11770	13891	14899	1.8	80	4271	5148	5554	2.0	2.70	3388	4095	2.1
95255	WEST POINT	009	2014	2464	2696	2.2	85	835	1052	1158	2.5	2.34	549	693	2.6
95257	WILSEYVILLE	009	449	541	591	2.0	83	204	254	279	2.4	2.13	133	166	2.4
95258	WOODBRIDGE	077	3949	4539	4756	1.5	75	1307	1492	1564	1.4	3.03	1080	1221	1.3
95301	ATWATER	047	28151	33557	36081	1.9	81	8746	10400	11184	1.9	3.18	6928	8258	1.9
95303	BALLICO	047	912	926	928	0.2	18	280	285	285	0.2	3.21	217	218	0.0
95304	TRACY	077	11651	14885	16701	2.7	90	2677	3846	4436	4.0	2.94	2040	2902	3.9
95306	CATHEYS VALLEY	043	1071	1186	1239	1.1	64	419	492	519	1.8	2.40	297	347	1.7
95307	CERES	099	35109	45376	49433	2.8	90	10887	13673	14778	2.5	3.31	8646	10861	2.5
95309	CHINESE CAMP	109	24	28	30	1.7	78	11	13	14	1.8	2.15	8	9	1.3
95310	COLUMBIA	109	1474	1549	1571	0.5	39	680	721	734	0.6	2.13	435	460	0.6
95311	COULTERVILLE	043	2003	2293	2442	1.5	75	846	1021	1096	2.1	2.23	592	714	2.0
95313	CROWS LANDING	099	1299	1468	1542	1.3	70	417	463	485	1.1	3.17	326	360	1.1
95315	DELHI	047	9921	12264	13336	2.3	86	2632	3234	3509	2.3	3.76	2253	2757	2.2
95316	DENAIR	099	5696	6862	7362	2.0	83	1857	2212	2367	1.9	3.09	1527	1806	1.8
95317	EL NIDO	047	873	895	898	0.3	23	270	280	281	0.4	3.19	216	223	0.3
95318	EL PORTAL	043	578	592	596	0.3	23	256	282	288	1.1	1.54	138	151	1.0
95320	ESCALON	077	11539	13243	13988	1.5	75	3837	4351	4587	1.4	3.03	3030	3388	1.2
95321	GROVELAND	109	3988	3901	3857	-0.2	4	1793	1789	1777	0.0	2.17	1257	1253	0.0
95322	GUSTINE	047	7859	8670	9197	1.1	64	2719	2986	3162	1.0	2.90	2002	2186	1.0
95323	HICKMAN	099	982	1108	1149	1.3	70	316	351	362	1.1	3.14	245	271	1.1
95324	HILMAR	047	7101	7733	7929	0.9	58	2318	2556	2630	1.1	3.02	1904	2090	1.0
95326	HUGHSON	099	6996	10072	11513	4.0	94	2253	3131	3544	3.6	3.21	1828	2527	3.6
95327	JAMESTOWN	109	9915	10340	10474	0.5	39	2301	2508	2571	0.9	2.45	1582	1722	0.9
95329	LA GRANGE	109	1771	2259	2417	2.7	90	694	903	972	2.9	2.50	539	699	2.8
95330	LATHROP	077	11122	17556	20150	5.1	96	3148	5087	5867	5.3	3.45	2662	4167	5.0
95333	LE GRAND	047	4475	5217	5584	1.7	78	1166	1369	1467	1.8	3.77	1024	1200	1.7
95334	LIVINGSTON	047	12790	16375	18108	2.7	90	3075	3993	4447	2.9	4.09	2688	3481	2.8
95335	LONG BARN	109	625	650	661	0.4	30	201	215	221	0.7	2.60	130	139	0.7
95336	MANTECA	077	36528	42726	47109	1.7	78	12103	14013	15383	1.6	3.02	9343	10683	1.5
95337	MANTECA	077	19928	28695	32572	4.0	94	6605	9474	10738	4.0	3.01	5027	7293	4.1
95338	MARIPOSA	043	10182	10810	11053	0.6	45	4174	4659	4804	1.2	2.27	2858	3188	1.2
95340	MERCED	047	35182	38506	40181	1.0	62	11634	12711	13262	1.0	2.93	8520	9343	1.0
95341	MERCED	047	26887	33575	36670	2.4	87	7091	8916	9774	2.5	3.71	5769	7255	2.5
95345	MIDPINES	043	453	436	430	-0.4	2	194	197	195	0.2	1.99	126	127	0.1
95346	MI WUK VILLAGE	109	1039	1087	1103	0.5	39	448	479	490	0.7	2.12	308	329	0.7
95348	MERCED	047	22537	31653	34747	3.7	93	7927	10827	11886	3.4	2.85	5403	7401	3.5
95350	MODESTO	099	52463	53124	53529	0.1	13	19674	19596	19650	0.0	2.66	13339	13172	-0.1
95351	MODESTO	099	46792	48148	48728	0.3	23	12518	12515	12595	0.0	3.83	10128	10061	-0.1
	CALIFORNIA					1.2					1.0	2.93			1.1
	UNITED STATES					1.0					1.1	2.59			0.9

ZIP CODE #	POST OFFICE NAME	RACE (%) White 2000	White 2009	Black 2000	Black 2009	Asian/Pacific 2000	Asian/Pacific 2009	% Hispanic Origin 2000	% Hispanic Origin 2009	2009 AGE DISTRIBUTION (%) 0-4	5-9	10-14	15-19	20-24	25-44	45-64	65-84	85+	18+	MEDIAN AGE 2009	% 2009 Males	% 2009 Females
95111	SAN JOSE	31.8	28.6	4.1	3.4	30.6	31.6	46.7	50.5	8.9	8.4	7.6	8.0	7.8	31.2	21.1	6.3	0.7	70.3	30.6	50.6	49.4
95112	SAN JOSE	43.6	38.5	4.1	3.5	18.6	19.8	50.1	56.4	7.4	6.5	5.7	8.2	11.2	34.7	19.4	6.0	1.1	77.1	30.3	53.1	46.9
95113	SAN JOSE	47.2	42.7	4.5	5.8	36.5	31.7	17.6	30.3	4.4	2.4	1.5	2.7	10.5	38.9	15.9	20.2	3.4	90.7	35.5	49.0	51.0
95116	SAN JOSE	30.5	28.6	3.1	2.5	21.8	21.6	64.3	67.8	9.8	9.0	7.7	8.5	8.6	32.1	17.6	5.8	0.9	68.5	28.5	51.9	48.1
95117	SAN JOSE	56.9	49.6	4.7	4.4	20.7	24.0	24.3	29.5	7.4	6.4	5.7	5.8	7.6	35.9	22.0	7.6	1.6	77.1	34.2	51.2	48.8
95118	SAN JOSE	72.8	65.6	2.3	2.3	10.5	13.1	18.9	24.5	7.3	7.1	7.0	6.4	5.7	29.2	26.4	9.5	1.4	74.7	37.5	49.2	50.8
95119	SAN JOSE	66.6	59.0	3.4	3.4	15.2	18.5	19.9	25.6	7.2	7.4	7.3	7.1	5.5	28.8	27.7	8.3	0.8	73.7	36.6	51.0	49.0
95120	SAN JOSE	70.7	62.4	0.9	1.0	22.7	28.8	5.4	7.3	5.9	6.9	8.1	7.4	3.6	20.8	33.6	12.7	1.0	74.3	43.4	49.4	50.6
95121	SAN JOSE	27.6	23.7	4.8	4.0	45.9	47.9	29.5	32.6	7.5	7.4	7.1	7.5	6.6	30.7	24.7	7.6	0.8	73.3	34.2	50.4	49.6
95122	SAN JOSE	23.9	22.4	3.0	2.4	31.5	31.3	57.8	60.4	9.0	8.6	7.8	8.4	8.2	32.8	18.8	5.8	0.6	69.5	29.4	52.2	47.8
95123	SAN JOSE	65.3	57.3	4.0	3.9	15.4	19.2	20.4	25.7	7.3	7.1	6.9	6.5	6.0	31.0	25.8	8.1	1.1	74.6	36.2	49.3	50.7
95124	SAN JOSE	79.8	73.3	1.7	1.8	9.1	11.8	12.4	17.0	6.8	6.8	7.2	6.5	5.0	26.7	28.7	10.6	1.7	74.9	40.0	49.9	50.1
95125	SAN JOSE	74.1	66.0	2.5	2.6	8.0	10.9	22.4	28.9	7.1	6.5	6.2	5.4	5.5	29.4	27.2	10.0	2.7	77.0	38.8	48.6	51.4
95126	SAN JOSE	60.7	53.9	4.8	4.4	9.5	10.8	36.2	44.3	7.1	6.0	5.3	6.4	9.1	35.0	22.5	7.0	1.6	78.2	33.6	50.9	49.1
95127	SAN JOSE	43.1	38.8	3.4	3.0	18.4	19.3	52.9	58.3	8.1	7.9	7.4	8.0	7.4	29.8	22.4	7.8	1.1	71.9	32.4	51.0	49.0
95128	SAN JOSE	62.6	55.0	3.9	3.9	13.5	16.1	28.7	35.2	7.3	6.2	5.6	5.5	7.1	34.4	23.3	8.2	2.5	77.8	35.4	50.3	49.7
95129	SAN JOSE	49.8	41.0	1.4	1.3	42.1	49.1	6.7	8.3	6.1	6.2	6.5	6.6	6.0	27.0	29.1	10.7	1.8	77.1	40.0	50.0	50.0
95130	SAN JOSE	66.4	58.0	2.9	3.0	18.6	23.1	13.5	17.6	7.3	6.7	6.7	6.4	6.2	29.7	27.2	8.7	1.3	75.4	37.2	49.8	50.2
95131	SAN JOSE	22.4	18.0	3.5	3.0	63.9	67.0	12.2	14.2	7.8	6.9	6.2	5.7	6.3	34.4	24.8	7.2	0.7	75.6	35.5	50.4	49.6
95132	SAN JOSE	33.5	27.5	3.5	3.1	51.9	56.4	14.7	17.0	6.6	6.3	6.2	6.7	6.4	28.9	27.8	10.2	0.9	76.8	37.9	50.1	49.9
95133	SAN JOSE	25.4	22.2	3.3	2.8	55.2	57.8	24.7	26.1	7.2	7.1	6.6	6.8	7.0	30.5	25.2	8.5	0.9	74.9	35.1	50.7	49.3
95134	SAN JOSE	53.3	50.9	5.5	4.5	28.5	26.7	15.9	23.2	7.5	6.0	5.8	5.6	6.4	39.9	23.3	5.0	0.4	77.2	33.6	51.1	48.9
95135	SAN JOSE	53.4	43.1	2.5	2.4	35.7	44.1	11.4	13.8	7.8	8.0	7.7	5.4	3.4	22.4	26.3	15.9	3.0	72.9	42.1	48.4	51.6
95136	SAN JOSE	56.8	49.0	4.7	4.6	23.3	27.2	18.0	22.8	7.2	6.5	6.2	6.0	6.6	33.5	25.1	8.1	0.9	76.7	35.6	49.4	50.6
95138	SAN JOSE	48.7	40.8	4.3	3.8	32.4	37.9	17.8	21.3	9.3	9.1	8.3	5.8	3.8	34.5	24.3	4.6	0.3	69.5	34.2	49.4	50.6
95139	SAN JOSE	68.8	61.0	3.6	3.6	15.1	18.7	16.9	22.2	7.3	7.4	7.6	7.0	5.3	26.9	29.8	7.9	0.8	73.3	37.7	49.6	50.4
95140	MOUNT HAMILTON	63.5	55.4	2.8	2.7	20.5	24.6	17.3	22.3	5.0	5.8	6.9	5.8	3.5	24.6	34.2	12.7	1.5	78.1	44.1	51.5	48.5
95148	SAN JOSE	28.0	23.9	5.1	4.3	50.5	53.4	23.8	26.3	7.1	6.9	6.7	7.2	7.1	29.5	26.8	7.9	0.8	75.0	35.1	50.4	49.6
95202	STOCKTON	39.1	34.1	15.2	14.0	11.5	12.6	45.1	52.3	9.5	7.4	5.8	6.3	8.5	26.2	21.6	12.6	2.2	74.1	33.2	52.9	47.1
95203	STOCKTON	46.2	40.7	9.1	8.4	12.6	13.4	43.8	50.5	9.6	8.1	7.5	7.9	8.7	27.4	21.1	8.3	1.5	70.1	30.0	51.4	48.6
95204	STOCKTON	64.5	56.4	4.2	4.2	10.2	12.0	27.9	36.0	7.4	6.9	6.8	6.8	6.6	25.3	24.3	12.7	3.1	74.7	37.0	47.4	52.6
95205	STOCKTON	38.1	33.9	8.6	7.2	8.1	8.4	58.2	64.9	10.5	9.7	8.8	9.1	8.2	27.1	18.0	7.4	1.2	65.5	27.2	50.7	49.3
95206	STOCKTON	27.6	26.0	15.8	14.6	18.9	19.6	50.4	51.5	10.2	9.8	8.8	8.7	7.4	29.2	18.9	6.1	0.9	65.9	28.1	50.5	49.5
95207	STOCKTON	52.4	45.8	10.1	9.8	19.2	21.5	23.8	29.4	8.6	7.5	6.7	7.5	8.8	26.5	21.4	10.8	2.1	72.7	31.5	47.8	52.2
95209	STOCKTON	56.1	48.9	8.9	8.2	19.7	23.3	17.7	23.0	7.6	7.6	7.7	8.1	6.4	26.6	26.3	8.1	1.6	71.9	34.8	48.2	51.8
95210	STOCKTON	32.3	27.0	12.2	11.2	36.6	39.5	24.5	28.6	9.1	8.9	8.9	9.7	8.3	25.6	20.6	7.7	1.2	67.1	28.2	48.4	51.6
95211	STOCKTON	61.3	50.0	2.7	2.9	12.4	15.2	8.8	11.9	0.0	0.0	0.1	49.7	45.9	3.5	0.4	0.4	0.0	99.7	20.0	41.5	58.5
95212	STOCKTON	77.1	63.9	1.6	2.6	8.9	13.9	16.5	25.4	6.9	6.8	6.8	6.8	6.2	24.7	27.3	12.7	1.8	75.0	38.6	49.2	50.8
95215	STOCKTON	58.6	51.1	4.4	3.9	4.2	4.8	41.0	50.4	7.1	7.1	7.0	11.4	8.9	25.1	22.0	9.8	1.5	72.9	31.3	52.7	47.3
95219	STOCKTON	66.6	56.8	7.4	7.9	13.1	18.0	15.0	20.4	7.3	6.8	6.6	6.4	6.8	27.4	27.9	9.7	1.1	75.3	37.0	48.6	51.4
95220	ACAMPO	85.4	79.6	0.7	0.8	2.8	3.7	17.7	25.5	6.0	6.5	7.2	6.8	4.5	22.2	30.6	14.4	1.8	75.6	42.4	51.0	49.0
95222	ANGELS CAMP	92.6	90.2	0.6	0.7	0.6	0.8	7.0	9.6	4.6	4.9	5.5	6.2	4.9	21.1	33.4	16.9	2.5	81.0	46.8	49.1	50.9
95223	ARNOLD	94.9	93.1	0.2	0.2	0.6	0.8	3.7	5.2	3.2	3.8	4.8	4.7	3.4	15.6	39.8	23.2	1.7	85.3	53.6	50.6	49.4
95228	COPPEROPOLIS	89.4	85.9	1.0	1.2	2.2	2.9	8.2	11.1	4.6	5.0	5.7	5.9	4.1	18.1	35.6	19.8	1.3	81.1	49.4	49.2	50.8
95230	FARMINGTON	83.2	77.1	0.7	0.8	1.3	1.5	20.0	27.6	5.2	5.5	6.3	7.3	4.9	22.2	32.8	14.3	1.4	78.5	43.9	50.4	49.6
95231	FRENCH CAMP	45.5	39.0	11.6	10.1	6.6	7.6	42.5	50.6	5.9	6.0	6.6	10.8	9.8	34.9	18.2	6.8	0.9	74.9	31.0	60.2	39.8
95232	GLENCOE	92.7	89.8	0.0	0.0	1.3	1.8	7.6	10.5	3.4	4.2	4.5	4.7	4.2	17.0	40.8	19.1	2.1	84.8	52.0	49.0	51.0
95236	LINDEN	77.6	71.4	0.5	0.6	1.3	1.6	27.4	35.2	6.4	6.7	7.1	7.5	5.8	24.6	28.6	11.7	1.5	75.1	39.1	50.2	49.8
95237	LOCKEFORD	77.1	68.3	0.2	0.3	1.6	2.0	25.2	35.5	6.4	6.3	6.4	6.8	6.5	25.9	27.8	12.2	1.7	76.8	38.6	51.1	48.9
95240	LODI	70.1	62.6	0.6	0.7	4.9	6.0	33.6	41.8	8.5	7.7	6.9	7.3	7.6	26.5	21.9	10.7	2.8	72.4	33.1	50.0	50.0
95242	LODI	81.7	74.6	0.6	0.6	4.8	7.1	15.4	21.0	6.0	6.2	6.5	6.8	5.3	23.9	29.2	13.6	2.3	77.0	41.5	48.8	51.2
95245	MOKELUMNE HILL	92.8	90.3	0.6	0.7	0.8	1.0	4.8	6.6	3.8	4.2	4.9	5.5	3.8	17.3	39.4	19.1	1.9	83.5	51.3	50.5	49.5
95246	MOUNTAIN RANCH	92.1	89.2	1.0	1.1	1.0	1.3	5.3	7.5	3.2	3.7	4.6	6.2	3.7	17.2	39.4	19.7	2.5	84.2	51.9	50.1	49.9
95247	MURPHYS	93.0	90.8	1.0	1.1	0.7	1.0	4.8	6.7	3.4	4.2	5.1	5.6	4.1	17.5	37.4	20.1	2.5	83.6	51.3	49.2	50.8
95249	SAN ANDREAS	91.8	89.0	0.3	0.3	0.7	0.9	6.1	8.4	4.8	4.9	6.2	7.0	5.0	18.4	31.0	18.2	4.4	79.3	47.6	47.8	52.2
95251	VALLECITO	91.4	89.2	2.5	2.8	0.5	0.4	4.6	6.0	4.0	4.0	4.8	5.2	4.8	22.8	35.6	16.8	2.0	83.6	47.9	52.0	48.0
95252	VALLEY SPRINGS	88.4	84.6	1.1	1.2	1.2	1.6	10.0	13.7	5.1	5.8	6.9	7.4	4.7	21.1	34.8	13.1	1.1	77.4	44.3	50.1	49.9
95255	WEST POINT	87.6	84.7	0.6	0.6	0.6	0.8	5.9	8.0	4.5	4.9	5.2	6.0	4.4	17.3	36.2	18.8	2.7	81.4	49.5	49.4	50.6
95257	WILSEYVILLE	90.8	88.4	0.2	0.2	0.2	0.4	3.8	5.4	3.7	4.1	4.8	5.2	3.9	16.8	38.1	21.3	2.2	84.1	52.1	50.1	49.9
95258	WOODBRIDGE	80.9	73.7	0.1	0.1	4.6	5.9	21.4	30.1	6.1	7.4	8.3	8.3	4.6	23.9	30.9	9.4	1.0	72.6	39.0	49.9	50.1
95301	ATWATER	59.3	53.7	4.4	4.1	6.0	7.5	39.3	45.3	9.3	8.7	8.3	8.5	6.9	27.1	21.4	8.8	1.1	68.5	30.7	49.2	50.8
95303	BALLICO	58.2	50.6	0.3	0.3	7.7	8.7	44.4	53.5	9.0	7.8	8.4	7.9	6.6	27.9	22.4	9.5	0.6	69.8	33.0	53.6	46.4
95304	TRACY	64.6	58.9	12.7	10.7	2.1	3.5	24.6	33.2	4.9	5.2	5.6	6.3	8.0	33.7	26.7	8.4	1.2	80.7	36.9	62.3	37.7
95306	CATHEYS VALLEY	91.6	89.0	0.0	0.0	0.3	0.3	6.0	8.3	4.6	6.2	6.9	7.7	3.8	20.2	34.3	14.5	1.9	77.3	45.4	49.9	50.1
95307	CERES	67.3	60.3	2.0	1.8	3.9	4.7	36.6	45.5	8.8	8.4	8.1	8.8	7.8	27.4	22.0	7.7	1.1	69.3	30.2	49.8	50.2
95309	CHINESE CAMP	91.7	92.9	0.0	0.0	0.0	0.0	4.2	3.6	7.1	7.1	7.1	7.1	3.6	25.0	32.1	10.7	0.0	71.4	40.0	53.6	46.4
95310	COLUMBIA	93.0	90.4	0.5	0.8	0.8	1.0	4.3	6.2	3.8	4.1	4.4	5.4	4.3	15.2	38.6	21.0	3.2	84.8	53.6	49.5	50.5
95311	COULTERVILLE	91.0	88.3	0.4	0.4	0.8	1.0	7.1	9.7	4.2	5.4	5.9	5.2	2.5	16.5	39.0	19.2	2.1	80.9	50.9	51.4	48.6
95313	CROWS LANDING	69.7	62.9	0.4	0.4	0.9	1.0	44.4	54.4	9.6	9.1	8.7	8.3	6.8	28.0	20.4	8.0	1.1	67.9	30.0	51.7	48.3
95315	DELHI	53.6	46.0	1.5	1.4	3.4	3.7	53.2	62.9	10.1	9.4	8.8	9.7	8.4	28.5	18.7	5.8	0.7	65.9	27.4	50.8	49.2
95316	DENAIR	81.7	75.4	0.2	0.2	1.3	1.7	21.5	28.9	6.2	7.2	7.7	8.4	5.9	23.4	29.6	10.2	1.4	73.6	38.4	50.1	49.9
95317	EL NIDO	66.9	59.6	1.4	1.3	1.7	2.0	45.2	55.4	10.3	9.7	8.3	8.6	7.5	28.0	19.7	6.9	1.0	65.9	28.3	55.3	44.7
95318	EL PORTAL	83.2	78.4	1.6	1.7	1.2	1.4	16.3	21.8	3.7	3.5	3.2	5.2	15.2	34.5	29.6	4.7	0.3	87.3	35.9	59.3	40.7
95320	ESCALON	82.7	76.0	0.4	0.5	1.2	1.5	22.6	31.7	7.0	7.2	7.2	7.8	6.6	25.1	27.1	10.3	1.6	73.6	36.0	50.4	49.6
95321	GROVELAND	92.5	89.7	0.7	0.9	0.8	1.0	4.7	6.8	3.2	3.7	3.9	4.0	3.2	12.9	35.8	31.0	2.4	86.7	57.4	48.2	51.8
95322	GUSTINE	68.2	60.2	0.7	0.7	1.2	1.4	38.4	47.8	8.2	8.3	7.8	7.8	6.4	25.2	23.4	10.9	1.9	70.7	34.0	51.5	48.5
95323	HICKMAN	80.9	74.2	0.6	0.6	0.4	0.5	22.0	29.7	6.4	7.1	7.2	7.5	4.2	24.9	29.5	11.5	1.6	74.3	39.5	51.6	48.4
95324	HILMAR	77.8	69.7	0.3	0.3	2.1	2.7	16.2	21.6	7.2	7.1	7.4	8.1	7.8	26.5	24.4	10.0	1.5	73.5	34.3	50.3	49.7
95326	HUGHSON	74.5	66.7	0.5	0.5	2.3	2.6	29.9	39.8	7.3	7.4	7.4	8.3	7.5	26.2	25.1	9.6	1.3	72.6	33.7	49.1	50.9
95327	JAMESTOWN	74.8	70.5	9.7	10.1	1.2	1.4	17.8	22.5	3.8	3.8	3.8	4.7	10.1	38.8	24.2	9.5	1.5	86.2	37.3	69.6	30.4
95329	LA GRANGE	90.7	87.3	0.7	0.9	0.7	1.0	9.3	13.0	4.8	5.3	5.9	5.6	3.7	17.4	36.7	19.4	1.2	80.5	49.5	50.1	49.9
95330	LATHROP	52.0	45.5	4.3	4.1	13.6	15.3	37.8	43.2	8.7	8.5	8.3	8.7	7.3	27.6	23.3	6.7	0.8	69.0	30.6	50.4	49.6
95333	LE GRAND	41.1	36.7	0.6	0.6	0.9	0.9	76.6	82.0	10.2	9.4	8.5	9.9	9.9	25.3	19.7	6.4	0.8	65.8	26.2	51.5	48.5
95334	LIVINGSTON	40.9	38.4	0.7	0.6	13.3	13.3	66.4	70.4	10.0	9.3	8.4	9.6	9.7	27.5	18.1	6.5	0.9	66.5	26.6	50.5	49.5
95335	LONG BARN	94.2	92.0	0.5	0.6	0.5	0.5	4.5	6.8	3.7	3.8	4.5	3.8	5.4	21.8	37.5	17.8	1.5	85.4	50.2	53.7	46.3
95336	MANTECA	75.0	66.8	2.5	2.7	3.6	4.7	23.8	32.4	7.5	7.4	7.4	8.1	6.7	26.8	25.2	9.4	1.5	72.7	34.6	48.9	51.1
95337	MANTECA	73.8	66.4	3.0	2.8	3.8	4.3	26.7	37.2	7.4	7.8	7.9	8.4	6.2	26.8	25.6	8.3	1.5	71.4	34.7	49.8	50.2
95338	MARIPOSA	89.7	86.9	0.6	0.6	0.8	1.1	5.8	8.0	4.2	4.7	5.7	6.7	4.7	18.3	34.4	18.6	2.6	81.4	48.6	49.2	50.8
95340	MERCED	62.3	56.3	4.0	3.8	7.6	9.0	36.3	43.6	8.2	7.8	7.4	8.1	7.5	26.9	23.0	9.6	1.6	71.6	32.5	49.7	50.3
95341	MERCED	39.9	37.4	5.8	5.1	15.8	15.7	52.9	57.0	10.3	9.7	8.8	10.5	9.9	25.6	18.2	6.2	0.9	64.5	25.5	50.8	49.2
95345	MIDPINES	85.9	82.6	1.5	1.8	1.3	1.6	9.9	13.5	4.1	3.9	6.4	8.5	5.5	22.7	34.2	12.8	1.8	81.2	44.3	51.8	48.2
95346	MI WUK VILLAGE	93.9	91.1	0.3	0.4	0.5	0.7	4.9	7.1	3.8	4.9	6.2	5.6	4.2	20.1	37.6	15.9	1.7	81.3	47.8	52.3	47.7
95348	MERCED	56.8	52.0	6.9	5.7	9.9	10.7	35.7	41.4	9.2	7.9	7.1	7.8	8.4	27.3	21.2	9.1	2.0	71.2	30.8	48.8	51.2
95350	MODESTO	74.8	68.6	3.6	3.7	5.3	6.3	19.5	25.7	7.2	6.7	6.5	6.9	7.0	25.8	24.2	12.8	3.0	75.5	36.6	47.7	52.3
95351	MODESTO	47.6	43.0	4.8	4.3	8.5	8.6	54.0	60.8	10.6	9.8	8.7	9.5	8.8	27.5	18.3	5.9	0.8	65.0	26.5	50.8	49.2
	CALIFORNIA	59.5	54.5	6.7	6.2	11.3	12.5	32.4	38.3	7.5	7.1	6.9	7.5	7.4	28.5	24.2	9.3	1.6	74.1	34.3	49.9	50.1
	UNITED STATES	75.1	72.0	12.3	12.7	3.8	4.6	12.5	15.7	6.8	6.7	6.6	7.1	6.9	27.0	26.0	10.9	1.9	75.7	36.9	49.2	50.8

#	POST OFFICE NAME	2009 Per Capita Income	2009 HH Income Base	2009 HOUSEHOLD INCOME DISTRIBUTION (%) Less than $25,000	$25,000 to $49,999	$50,000 to $99,999	$100,000 to $149,999	$150,000 or More	MEDIAN HOUSEHOLD INCOME 2009	2014	2009 National Centile	2009 State Centile	2009 Home Value Base	2009 HOME VALUE DISTRIBUTION (%) Less than $50,000	$50,000 to $89,999	$90,000 to $174,999	$175,000 to $399,999	$400,000 or More	2009 Median Home Value
95111	SAN JOSE	21670	14911	11.4	19.9	35.6	20.1	13.0	72630	72674	88	73	9658	6.9	3.8	6.7	27.2	55.4	420802
95112	SAN JOSE	24168	18796	23.5	23.3	31.7	12.6	8.9	53613	57056	69	49	6672	5.5	4.8	3.8	24.3	61.6	446848
95113	SAN JOSE	45245	729	41.2	15.6	21.3	6.7	15.2	36193	38611	21	15	111	0.0	0.0	0.0	4.5	95.5	564904
95116	SAN JOSE	17109	13408	17.8	22.7	35.7	15.7	8.1	60100	62294	77	58	5763	4.5	1.2	1.1	44.5	48.7	395427
95117	SAN JOSE	36047	12146	11.8	16.9	34.1	22.2	15.0	77129	78294	91	78	4005	0.2	0.6	0.7	11.8	86.7	608965
95118	SAN JOSE	40175	12025	9.0	13.8	29.0	26.9	21.4	96155	101981	96	90	7549	0.3	0.4	0.1	11.2	88.0	600394
95119	SAN JOSE	39654	3153	6.7	7.5	26.4	30.0	29.3	114104	122492	98	94	2343	0.4	0.5	0.0	7.3	91.7	588913
95120	SAN JOSE	72292	12525	2.8	4.7	14.1	18.8	59.7	167396	172070	100	99	10999	0.1	0.3	0.4	2.6	96.6	860313
95121	SAN JOSE	31450	9201	5.8	9.9	33.9	25.7	24.6	100527	105911	97	91	7007	0.7	1.6	1.9	19.5	76.4	500050
95122	SAN JOSE	17615	12292	13.2	16.5	37.5	21.0	11.8	74530	74156	89	75	6979	0.7	1.6	3.3	36.1	58.4	423274
95123	SAN JOSE	40341	21203	6.2	10.8	32.3	27.3	23.5	101007	106144	97	91	14510	0.9	1.6	1.9	18.6	77.0	540529
95124	SAN JOSE	48641	16456	7.2	12.0	26.8	22.4	31.6	106652	113865	98	92	11786	0.0	0.3	0.1	7.0	92.6	654824
95125	SAN JOSE	50787	20583	11.4	14.1	29.2	18.5	26.7	88778	93457	95	86	13183	1.9	1.0	2.1	7.9	87.1	693917
95126	SAN JOSE	37389	12920	15.8	20.7	33.7	13.7	16.1	64948	66498	83	66	4355	0.3	0.1	0.2	17.1	82.3	594236
95127	SAN JOSE	27628	15120	9.7	16.3	33.0	20.9	20.1	82592	85384	93	82	10873	0.3	0.2	0.4	22.8	76.3	488136
95128	SAN JOSE	36418	12282	11.4	19.0	34.2	20.1	15.3	75231	76214	89	76	5174	0.3	0.6	0.8	11.2	87.2	601114
95129	SAN JOSE	48007	13472	7.5	10.2	28.7	21.6	32.0	106442	114108	97	92	8202	0.6	1.2	0.7	5.5	91.8	800456
95130	SAN JOSE	41917	4845	8.0	12.9	33.3	24.4	21.4	91401	97072	95	88	2747	0.1	0.3	0.2	2.9	96.5	665925
95131	SAN JOSE	39845	8602	6.4	7.6	28.6	26.9	30.5	109877	116195	98	93	5881	4.0	2.9	1.6	15.6	76.0	547084
95132	SAN JOSE	36635	11779	5.9	6.8	31.5	28.5	27.4	107266	113186	98	93	8766	1.1	1.1	0.3	12.5	85.0	568609
95133	SAN JOSE	29134	7494	10.2	14.2	32.2	22.0	21.4	88395	92998	95	86	4548	0.9	1.5	0.7	25.0	71.9	513550
95134	SAN JOSE	52133	6135	8.1	11.8	25.2	26.9	28.0	106737	109204	98	93	3432	3.1	12.1	31.4	10.5	42.9	193910
95135	SAN JOSE	66247	6643	6.8	9.0	20.5	17.1	46.6	139523	149757	99	98	5988	0.1	0.2	0.4	9.6	89.8	718285
95136	SAN JOSE	41050	14715	6.4	11.5	33.4	25.3	23.3	97279	101823	96	90	9370	1.8	4.6	9.5	10.6	73.5	541847
95138	SAN JOSE	67885	5813	2.9	6.2	21.1	23.1	46.6	140812	149817	99	98	4933	1.2	1.6	1.5	10.6	85.1	642282
95139	SAN JOSE	40795	2266	6.5	8.1	25.3	33.0	27.1	113883	122045	98	94	1773	0.5	0.3	0.0	10.9	88.4	571204
95140	MOUNT HAMILTON	79326	98	6.1	8.2	17.3	18.4	50.0	150000	153109	100	98	82	1.2	0.0	0.0	4.9	93.9	844828
95148	SAN JOSE	35251	11574	4.1	6.9	25.9	30.7	32.3	117062	125146	98	95	9526	0.4	0.8	0.7	7.7	90.5	611570
95202	STOCKTON	10550	3028	71.0	21.4	5.7	0.7	1.1	13642	13512	1	1	168	0.0	14.3	56.5	25.0	4.2	123571
95203	STOCKTON	14547	5704	38.1	29.1	27.7	4.0	1.1	32544	34819	12	10	2340	7.4	21.6	60.0	10.2	0.8	106029
95204	STOCKTON	22217	11555	27.0	29.6	33.1	6.6	3.6	44123	46188	46	31	6435	0.9	11.5	70.3	15.2	2.1	126359
95205	STOCKTON	11020	10626	39.8	33.7	23.2	2.2	1.1	31421	33429	10	8	5206	10.7	39.3	46.6	2.4	1.1	90010
95206	STOCKTON	15220	16767	26.9	23.2	39.3	7.0	3.6	49969	53049	61	42	10925	3.6	17.7	50.0	28.0	0.5	137203
95207	STOCKTON	18981	18447	30.8	28.7	31.6	6.2	2.8	40556	43075	35	22	7126	3.9	7.2	62.8	24.2	1.8	139205
95209	STOCKTON	24559	12762	14.7	18.2	41.5	17.1	8.5	69235	71756	86	71	9042	0.6	2.7	55.1	40.6	1.0	166259
95210	STOCKTON	14244	12122	26.2	29.7	36.5	5.8	1.8	44313	46954	46	31	6212	6.8	12.1	69.8	11.0	0.3	124104
95211	STOCKTON	20434	26	100.0	0.0	0.0	0.0	0.0	6842	7500	0	1	0	0.0	0.0	0.0	0.0	0.0	0
95212	STOCKTON	28829	6388	22.6	24.8	29.9	13.2	9.7	53100	53758	68	48	5263	13.6	1.8	22.7	43.4	18.4	213383
95215	STOCKTON	15747	7157	30.1	30.1	32.3	5.1	2.4	40652	43403	35	22	4723	17.2	19.5	39.6	19.4	4.2	107865
95219	STOCKTON	36403	10894	15.2	20.0	34.4	13.6	16.8	69615	71960	87	71	6598	2.1	5.4	30.7	52.1	9.7	194381
95220	ACAMPO	24864	2802	19.2	23.3	42.3	8.6	6.5	57768	60619	75	55	2130	10.5	7.3	20.7	39.5	22.0	215041
95222	ANGELS CAMP	25090	2454	24.7	30.1	31.8	8.5	4.9	45606	48096	50	34	1755	7.5	3.4	9.3	52.0	27.8	286603
95223	ARNOLD	33463	3260	19.9	24.8	37.3	9.5	8.5	54014	55894	70	50	2685	1.1	0.9	5.6	59.8	32.7	330000
95228	COPPEROPOLIS	27446	1198	18.5	31.2	35.4	7.5	7.3	50172	51249	62	43	969	1.0	1.0	10.2	52.6	35.1	330193
95230	FARMINGTON	22329	339	22.4	26.5	35.4	8.3	7.4	50831	52222	63	44	250	5.6	8.4	11.6	48.4	26.0	276316
95231	FRENCH CAMP	16998	1050	33.3	30.8	28.5	5.5	1.9	33350	35280	14	11	583	3.8	19.4	38.4	28.5	9.9	135179
95232	GLENCOE	19687	169	24.3	42.0	27.2	4.1	2.4	29923	38400	8	6	140	0.0	2.1	23.6	63.6	10.7	252174
95236	LINDEN	24407	1429	16.9	21.3	45.1	9.6	7.1	60262	61533	78	59	976	1.2	9.5	20.1	55.7	13.4	221466
95237	LOCKEFORD	21940	1258	26.4	23.2	34.5	11.0	4.9	50611	52594	63	44	928	21.0	4.0	33.7	33.3	8.0	157543
95240	LODI	18749	16373	27.8	29.5	33.0	6.4	3.3	42646	45637	41	27	7877	7.9	7.1	51.6	27.8	5.6	149228
95242	LODI	27523	10311	17.3	23.4	39.7	12.2	7.4	59919	61642	77	58	6416	4.6	0.7	39.2	50.2	5.3	184175
95245	MOKELUMNE HILL	23274	1633	24.8	28.7	36.3	8.1	2.2	46561	49068	53	36	1240	3.3	3.2	12.7	53.9	26.9	290385
95246	MOUNTAIN RANCH	25738	956	30.3	24.7	30.0	11.0	4.0	44440	47403	47	31	752	4.0	4.8	11.7	47.6	31.9	302158
95247	MURPHYS	31261	2200	21.9	26.1	33.5	12.3	6.2	52081	54165	66	46	1680	2.1	3.7	9.5	45.2	39.4	350418
95249	SAN ANDREAS	22601	1940	28.3	29.8	32.9	6.9	2.1	42732	45774	42	28	1259	4.5	10.9	16.1	48.4	20.1	244799
95251	VALLECITO	30224	107	22.4	26.2	33.6	13.1	4.7	52716	55677	67	47	82	0.0	4.9	7.3	47.6	40.2	352941
95252	VALLEY SPRINGS	24333	5148	15.0	25.2	45.3	10.4	4.1	57573	60008	75	55	4342	3.2	1.4	6.2	65.2	24.0	297204
95255	WEST POINT	18791	1052	38.6	31.4	22.8	4.5	2.8	32365	35053	12	9	795	5.2	6.0	27.7	48.7	12.5	210880
95257	WILSEYVILLE	24336	254	35.8	26.0	29.5	3.9	4.7	38053	41835	27	18	201	5.0	5.5	22.9	49.3	17.4	234821
95258	WOODBRIDGE	27032	1492	13.3	21.2	39.7	16.5	9.2	67580	68899	85	69	1119	11.6	1.3	34.6	43.3	9.3	188194
95301	ATWATER	18461	10400	20.9	31.5	37.0	7.3	3.3	47911	50506	56	39	6410	5.9	24.3	52.8	14.8	2.2	107732
95303	BALLICO	18244	285	17.9	36.5	33.7	9.5	2.5	44141	47844	46	31	153	7.2	17.0	17.0	23.5	35.3	242500
95304	TRACY	23782	3846	21.4	24.4	33.2	13.1	7.9	55548	57779	72	53	2863	10.9	16.0	9.3	31.6	32.2	268806
95306	CATHEYS VALLEY	25172	492	36.6	17.7	28.0	11.0	6.7	40938	45384	36	23	356	1.4	3.9	32.3	35.4	27.0	305747
95307	CERES	16647	13673	24.6	28.3	37.7	7.4	2.1	47341	49689	55	38	8589	9.4	6.5	61.8	18.3	4.0	136193
95309	CHINESE CAMP	24821	13	30.8	23.1	30.8	15.4	0.0	47338	50000	55	38	10	0.0	0.0	10.0	70.0	20.0	283333
95310	COLUMBIA	29204	721	19.4	35.1	33.1	6.5	5.8	46988	48594	54	37	525	12.4	14.9	11.8	34.5	26.5	246196
95311	COULTERVILLE	19820	1021	35.6	28.3	30.9	3.6	1.7	33807	37407	15	12	776	7.6	5.4	20.6	56.6	9.8	231557
95313	CROWS LANDING	17269	463	26.8	34.1	32.8	3.9	2.4	40521	43168	34	22	214	10.3	7.9	28.0	31.8	22.0	191667
95315	DELHI	14884	3234	21.9	28.4	42.4	5.4	1.9	49656	51900	60	42	2264	5.4	26.9	58.4	6.7	2.7	103640
95316	DENAIR	21954	2212	17.7	28.7	37.9	10.1	5.7	54235	57800	70	50	1587	8.9	5.5	35.5	32.3	17.8	175412
95317	EL NIDO	16805	280	21.4	38.2	33.6	4.3	2.5	42821	45110	42	28	125	15.2	17.6	20.0	20.0	27.2	162500
95318	EL PORTAL	42497	282	8.2	35.1	41.8	8.9	6.0	57618	60335	75	55	103	17.5	5.8	23.3	36.9	16.5	185938
95320	ESCALON	20796	4351	18.9	27.0	37.7	13.4	3.1	54610	57565	71	51	2881	4.8	6.5	37.9	41.8	9.0	176298
95321	GROVELAND	30999	1789	18.2	30.3	36.8	8.7	6.0	51231	53774	64	44	1400	3.9	2.4	14.8	54.6	24.4	294776
95322	GUSTINE	18889	2986	28.2	25.1	37.8	5.6	3.2	46782	49317	53	36	1837	15.6	14.8	42.9	20.8	5.9	120255
95323	HICKMAN	18660	351	26.2	27.9	36.5	6.6	2.8	44816	48121	48	32	213	4.2	8.0	27.7	20.7	39.4	258333
95324	HILMAR	18626	2556	20.0	30.4	40.6	7.4	1.5	49609	52443	60	42	1750	11.4	10.8	55.4	15.4	7.0	126420
95326	HUGHSON	19499	3131	24.7	22.3	40.3	8.3	4.4	53609	58258	69	49	2287	4.9	5.2	46.9	30.4	12.5	162223
95327	JAMESTOWN	21431	2508	31.5	24.6	33.7	6.0	4.1	42818	46470	42	28	1701	7.9	6.7	18.0	50.6	16.8	235570
95329	LA GRANGE	25278	903	18.4	31.7	39.4	5.8	4.8	49953	52361	61	42	741	2.2	1.8	7.0	72.1	17.0	279294
95330	LATHROP	18964	5087	17.1	22.4	44.9	12.1	3.4	61463	62214	79	61	3767	7.9	7.1	39.3	40.0	5.6	165102
95333	LE GRAND	13405	1369	28.0	36.7	26.7	5.6	3.1	36459	39255	22	16	905	5.4	55.0	22.0	8.3	9.3	83824
95334	LIVINGSTON	12151	3993	22.7	39.0	31.1	5.0	2.2	41442	43872	37	24	2371	4.5	38.9	47.4	7.8	1.3	94086
95335	LONG BARN	20175	215	37.7	25.6	27.4	4.7	4.7	29294	31667	7	6	167	0.0	0.0	26.9	62.9	10.2	223125
95336	MANTECA	21734	14013	15.3	25.3	45.8	9.6	3.9	58475	60549	76	56	8613	5.8	4.1	41.3	46.2	2.6	173340
95337	MANTECA	20684	9474	18.7	28.5	39.3	9.9	3.6	52736	54306	67	47	5888	3.6	7.5	27.4	56.4	5.2	198646
95338	MARIPOSA	22611	4659	30.7	28.4	31.7	6.8	2.3	41104	43090	36	24	3312	1.6	3.2	15.4	62.8	16.9	268839
95340	MERCED	21490	12711	24.9	25.1	35.7	8.7	5.6	50098	54104	61	43	7354	1.7	21.4	51.2	21.5	4.3	124912
95341	MERCED	12271	8916	37.2	31.5	24.1	4.7	2.5	32996	35441	13	10	4397	11.0	37.8	31.8	14.3	5.1	90923
95345	MIDPINES	24903	197	29.9	28.4	30.5	9.6	1.5	43127	44171	43	29	137	5.1	1.5	14.6	55.5	23.4	278750
95346	MI WUK VILLAGE	27871	479	24.0	29.0	35.7	6.1	5.2	45681	50712	50	34	375	1.6	0.5	16.8	68.0	13.1	246131
95348	MERCED	19607	10827	25.6	29.5	33.9	7.5	3.5	45020	48433	48	33	5199	8.2	15.8	62.6	11.8	1.7	117043
95350	MODESTO	22063	19596	24.5	27.2	35.7	8.4	4.3	48430	50226	58	39	10676	3.7	3.5	62.4	27.7	2.7	147817
95351	MODESTO	11916	12515	33.6	31.8	28.5	4.8	1.3	36922	39838	23	17	6694	8.7	17.5	59.9	13.4	0.5	110098
	CALIFORNIA	28199		18.5	22.2	33.9	14.0	11.5	61614	64088				3.3	2.6	13.6	41.0	39.5	321752
	UNITED STATES	27277		20.9	24.4	35.3	11.7	7.6	54719	56938				9.3	13.1	31.6	32.6	13.5	162279

ZIP CODE #	POST OFFICE NAME	FINANCIAL SERVICES: Auto Loan	Home Loan	Investments	Retirement Plans	THE HOME: Home Improvements: Home Repair	Lawn & Garden	Furnishings: Computers & Hardware-Personal	Major Appliances	TV, Radio, Sound Equipment	Furniture	ENTERTAINMENT: Dine out/Carry out	Sports Equipment	Fees & Tickets	Toys & Games	Travel	Cable TV	PERSONAL: Apparel & Services	Auto Repairs	Health Insurance	Pets & Supplies
95111	SAN JOSE	125	137	131	128	141	110	139	133	123	145	127	105	137	124	141	114	92	133	111	145
95112	SAN JOSE	97	91	90	92	92	78	112	95	103	107	107	80	104	102	104	98	77	104	87	110
95113	SAN JOSE	92	68	75	79	67	72	104	80	105	95	107	70	92	100	90	106	76	98	94	104
95116	SAN JOSE	100	100	88	92	100	76	112	102	100	114	106	82	106	101	108	91	78	107	83	109
95117	SAN JOSE	123	126	139	132	131	109	147	128	133	143	138	110	146	131	147	125	101	138	116	149
95118	SAN JOSE	139	175	188	173	184	155	162	159	151	163	153	123	180	150	177	146	113	157	146	178
95119	SAN JOSE	161	210	222	208	221	176	187	188	165	200	166	149	208	164	209	152	123	179	158	208
95120	SAN JOSE	266	364	414	375	394	333	303	320	280	332	280	243	369	277	355	267	211	297	283	353
95121	SAN JOSE	170	214	225	207	229	167	201	199	170	217	172	160	212	168	219	151	127	189	155	214
95122	SAN JOSE	120	138	129	125	143	102	138	133	118	146	123	106	137	118	142	105	90	131	103	140
95123	SAN JOSE	159	182	179	183	184	157	175	168	161	181	164	135	185	164	181	153	119	166	148	191
95124	SAN JOSE	163	214	240	212	229	190	193	193	177	199	178	149	219	174	217	170	132	187	175	215
95125	SAN JOSE	159	185	205	187	196	166	184	177	169	188	171	140	196	166	196	162	126	177	161	199
95126	SAN JOSE	123	120	129	125	124	103	144	124	131	141	135	106	139	130	140	122	99	134	111	144
95127	SAN JOSE	142	175	178	164	186	137	167	165	143	178	147	129	174	142	178	130	108	158	131	175
95128	SAN JOSE	121	129	144	134	135	110	146	129	130	144	135	110	146	128	148	121	99	136	113	149
95129	SAN JOSE	169	208	234	209	226	174	199	195	173	213	174	156	214	169	219	158	129	189	162	216
95130	SAN JOSE	143	178	200	177	191	151	173	166	153	177	156	134	187	151	189	143	115	165	144	185
95131	SAN JOSE	179	202	212	200	212	165	202	193	177	215	179	157	205	176	211	160	129	190	159	216
95132	SAN JOSE	162	209	235	204	229	164	199	196	165	214	166	158	211	159	221	145	123	187	153	212
95133	SAN JOSE	139	169	180	163	181	132	167	162	141	178	144	130	173	138	179	126	107	157	127	174
95134	SAN JOSE	189	189	177	194	184	168	193	179	185	199	190	144	193	191	187	178	135	182	166	211
95135	SAN JOSE	251	290	320	292	308	287	256	275	252	282	251	199	286	245	283	249	179	261	274	310
95136	SAN JOSE	161	175	178	177	179	154	173	165	161	180	163	133	179	163	178	153	117	165	149	189
95138	SAN JOSE	300	357	315	358	350	289	307	308	279	340	284	252	335	298	320	256	207	285	253	343
95139	SAN JOSE	158	206	213	202	214	177	180	183	163	188	165	142	202	164	200	155	121	174	160	203
95140	MOUNT HAMILTON	251	345	416	354	385	317	295	312	268	328	266	233	356	258	351	253	200	290	276	342
95148	SAN JOSE	183	237	260	232	257	186	220	219	183	240	185	177	236	179	245	161	137	206	169	237
95202	STOCKTON	29	21	22	23	21	23	32	26	33	30	34	21	28	31	28	34	24	32	31	32
95203	STOCKTON	59	54	49	52	52	49	61	56	60	61	62	44	58	61	58	59	44	60	55	65
95204	STOCKTON	73	77	75	77	77	74	80	76	79	77	80	59	81	78	80	79	57	79	78	89
95205	STOCKTON	59	55	46	49	54	47	57	56	55	61	56	41	53	56	54	52	40	57	50	61
95206	STOCKTON	86	84	71	78	81	71	84	81	80	89	82	62	80	83	80	76	58	82	72	91
95207	STOCKTON	69	67	65	67	66	64	74	68	73	73	75	54	73	73	72	73	53	73	69	80
95209	STOCKTON	104	129	120	125	128	111	113	113	107	117	109	88	124	109	120	104	79	109	103	127
95210	STOCKTON	74	76	68	70	75	64	76	74	71	79	73	57	74	72	74	67	52	74	66	82
95211	STOCKTON	11	5	4	6	4	5	15	7	12	10	12	8	9	12	8	11	9	10	7	10
95212	STOCKTON	114	110	110	107	110	114	106	111	107	109	107	83	103	109	106	108	74	109	111	131
95215	STOCKTON	75	71	73	65	72	71	70	75	69	72	70	55	65	70	69	70	48	73	72	84
95219	STOCKTON	127	135	136	138	137	125	133	128	128	138	129	100	139	129	136	124	93	129	122	149
95220	ACAMPO	109	104	114	106	106	118	98	111	100	95	99	84	95	100	102	104	68	104	111	130
95222	ANGELS CAMP	96	81	113	81	87	101	82	97	85	78	84	71	74	82	86	89	57	92	98	113
95223	ARNOLD	113	101	152	100	114	128	97	120	102	99	100	82	93	94	108	108	68	112	124	137
95228	COPPEROPOLIS	112	90	145	89	99	119	90	115	94	85	93	83	78	90	98	101	62	106	113	133
95230	FARMINGTON	103	88	110	90	92	110	88	104	91	80	90	79	79	90	91	96	60	96	106	122
95231	FRENCH CAMP	68	69	66	65	69	64	68	68	65	69	66	52	66	67	68	65	47	68	64	78
95232	GLENCOE	74	59	96	58	65	78	59	76	62	56	61	55	52	59	64	66	41	70	75	88
95236	LINDEN	98	111	116	109	113	112	99	107	97	96	97	81	105	98	107	99	69	102	105	122
95237	LOCKEFORD	96	95	91	94	94	95	89	93	90	91	90	70	89	92	89	91	62	90	92	110
95240	LODI	76	73	72	71	73	71	77	75	76	77	78	58	75	77	76	76	55	78	75	87
95242	LODI	98	109	114	109	112	109	100	105	99	102	99	79	107	98	108	99	70	102	104	121
95245	MOKELUMNE HILL	86	70	111	69	77	92	69	88	73	66	72	64	61	69	75	78	48	81	88	102
95246	MOUNTAIN RANCH	88	83	116	80	92	101	78	94	82	81	80	64	77	76	87	86	54	89	99	108
95247	MURPHYS	99	95	130	92	105	114	89	107	93	94	92	72	89	86	99	98	62	101	113	122
95249	SAN ANDREAS	74	65	78	66	70	78	71	76	75	69	73	54	67	71	70	79	50	75	83	88
95251	VALLECITO	113	90	146	89	99	119	90	115	94	85	93	84	78	90	98	101	62	106	113	133
95252	VALLEY SPRINGS	98	98	110	99	100	106	90	102	91	89	91	77	90	90	97	93	62	96	100	118
95255	WEST POINT	72	59	86	57	64	77	58	73	62	57	61	52	52	59	62	67	41	68	75	84
95257	WILSEYVILLE	86	69	112	68	76	91	69	88	72	65	72	64	60	69	75	77	48	81	87	102
95258	WOODBRIDGE	110	136	129	137	135	123	115	120	109	121	111	92	129	111	126	106	79	113	110	137
95301	ATWATER	85	87	83	83	86	80	84	85	81	86	83	65	83	83	84	79	58	84	79	96
95303	BALLICO	88	88	97	80	92	83	87	93	78	87	79	74	80	77	89	74	56	87	79	102
95304	TRACY	109	110	106	107	111	111	101	108	102	106	102	79	102	103	103	104	70	104	108	126
95306	CATHEYS VALLEY	101	81	130	80	89	107	81	103	85	76	84	75	70	80	88	90	56	95	101	119
95307	CERES	80	82	73	76	81	70	80	80	76	85	78	60	78	78	79	73	55	79	71	89
95309	CHINESE CAMP	89	71	115	70	78	94	71	91	75	67	74	66	62	71	77	80	49	84	90	105
95310	COLUMBIA	92	89	106	84	96	101	84	96	88	91	87	64	84	83	89	92	59	92	104	110
95311	COULTERVILLE	68	61	84	57	68	75	59	71	62	61	61	48	56	58	64	66	41	68	76	82
95313	CROWS LANDING	85	79	76	71	79	74	79	82	76	83	78	61	72	78	76	75	54	80	75	92
95315	DELHI	84	82	73	73	81	69	82	81	77	88	79	61	77	79	79	73	56	81	71	90
95316	DENAIR	108	98	117	95	100	110	95	108	94	92	94	83	87	94	97	96	64	101	104	125
95317	EL NIDO	80	80	68	71	78	65	79	78	74	85	76	58	75	76	76	70	54	78	67	85
95318	EL PORTAL	99	98	98	100	97	97	100	97	99	100	100	76	101	99	100	99	70	99	98	116
95320	ESCALON	89	95	99	92	95	96	88	94	87	86	87	72	89	88	92	88	61	90	92	108
95321	GROVELAND	94	95	131	94	108	114	88	104	92	96	91	67	93	84	100	97	62	99	114	118
95322	GUSTINE	81	79	76	75	78	78	78	80	77	79	78	61	75	79	77	78	54	79	78	92
95323	HICKMAN	105	72	115	72	75	110	80	99	83	65	82	82	59	81	79	91	53	93	105	122
95324	HILMAR	91	81	89	75	82	85	81	89	78	81	79	69	71	80	79	79	54	84	82	101
95326	HUGHSON	87	99	101	90	102	88	90	95	84	93	85	72	92	84	96	81	61	90	83	104
95327	JAMESTOWN	83	73	94	71	78	88	73	85	76	72	75	60	68	73	76	80	51	81	89	98
95329	LA GRANGE	106	84	136	83	92	112	85	107	88	79	87	79	73	84	91	94	58	99	106	125
95330	LATHROP	96	105	93	96	105	85	97	98	88	104	90	75	96	91	98	83	64	94	82	107
95333	LE GRAND	76	72	71	65	72	65	74	75	68	76	71	59	67	69	73	65	50	75	66	83
95334	LIVINGSTON	71	71	61	63	71	55	75	71	67	79	70	56	70	68	72	61	51	73	58	76
95335	LONG BARN	87	70	112	68	76	92	70	88	73	65	72	65	60	69	75	78	48	82	87	102
95336	MANTECA	86	101	96	97	101	90	94	93	90	94	91	71	100	91	98	89	66	92	88	105
95337	MANTECA	89	94	90	91	93	86	90	91	86	92	87	70	90	87	91	84	62	89	84	103
95338	MARIPOSA	83	67	102	66	73	87	70	84	73	65	72	62	61	70	73	78	48	79	85	98
95340	MERCED	86	94	88	91	93	85	90	89	87	92	89	67	93	88	92	86	63	89	85	101
95341	MERCED	66	61	55	57	60	53	66	63	63	69	65	49	62	64	63	60	47	66	56	70
95345	MIDPINES	84	68	109	67	74	89	68	86	71	63	70	63	59	67	73	75	46	79	85	100
95346	MI WUK VILLAGE	100	80	130	79	88	106	81	102	84	75	83	75	70	80	87	90	55	94	101	119
95348	MERCED	76	77	75	76	77	70	81	75	78	81	80	59	81	79	80	77	57	79	73	87
95350	MODESTO	78	84	81	83	84	80	84	81	82	83	83	62	87	82	85	82	59	83	82	94
95351	MODESTO	67	64	56	58	63	55	66	65	63	70	65	49	62	65	64	61	47	66	58	71
	CALIFORNIA	112	119	122	118	122	107	121	116	114	124	116	92	124	114	124	110	84	118	107	132
	UNITED STATES	100	100	100	100	100	100	100	100	100	100	100	100	100	100	100	100	100	100	100	100

#	POST OFFICE NAME	COUNTY FIPS CODE	POPULATION 2000	POPULATION 2009	POPULATION 2014	2000-2009 ANNUAL RATE % Rate	2000-2009 ANNUAL RATE State Centile	HOUSEHOLDS 2000	HOUSEHOLDS 2009	HOUSEHOLDS 2014	HOUSEHOLDS % Annual Rate 2000-2009	HOUSEHOLDS 2009 Average HH Size	FAMILIES 2000	FAMILIES 2009	FAMILIES % Annual Rate 2000-2009
95354	MODESTO	099	27208	27393	27576	0.1	13	9398	9294	9302	-0.1	2.86	6396	6272	-0.2
95355	MODESTO	099	47007	59348	63927	2.6	89	17188	21008	22410	2.2	2.78	12372	15394	2.4
95356	MODESTO	099	27385	32596	35067	1.9	81	10123	11812	12623	1.7	2.75	7181	8352	1.6
95357	MODESTO	099	12550	13386	13798	0.7	50	3796	3987	4093	0.5	3.34	3070	3186	0.4
95358	MODESTO	099	31450	34833	36121	1.1	64	8468	8985	9242	0.6	3.74	7055	7447	0.6
95360	NEWMAN	099	8487	12374	14203	4.2	94	2543	3588	4080	3.8	3.43	2055	2885	3.7
95361	OAKDALE	099	25563	30931	33405	2.1	84	9183	10941	11759	1.9	2.81	6888	8133	1.8
95363	PATTERSON	099	16486	29275	34284	6.4	97	4499	7838	9115	6.2	3.68	3721	6460	6.1
95364	PINECREST	109	2	2	2	0.0	9	1	1	1	0.0	2.00	1	1	0.0
95366	RIPON	077	12474	16370	18283	3.0	91	4144	5359	5959	2.8	3.03	3288	4217	2.7
95367	RIVERBANK	099	16575	21185	22936	2.7	90	4829	6204	6727	2.7	3.39	4037	5161	2.7
95368	SALIDA	099	12021	13961	14781	1.6	77	3451	3902	4106	1.3	3.55	2995	3372	1.3
95369	SNELLING	047	1219	1245	1240	0.2	18	420	440	441	0.5	2.81	305	317	0.4
95370	SONORA	109	25475	26513	26735	0.4	30	10767	11364	11518	0.6	2.30	7064	7460	0.6
95372	SOULSBYVILLE	109	1538	1677	1724	0.9	58	588	654	677	1.2	2.56	433	480	1.1
95374	STEVINSON	047	1850	1921	1933	0.4	30	560	588	594	0.5	3.24	438	457	0.5
95376	TRACY	077	47931	52799	55437	1.1	64	15096	16423	17188	0.9	3.20	12049	12967	0.8
95377	TRACY	077	9809	29022	36959	12.4	99	2795	8090	10270	12.2	3.59	2468	7114	12.1
95379	TUOLUMNE	109	3986	4345	4468	0.9	58	1507	1668	1724	1.1	2.59	1078	1193	1.1
95380	TURLOCK	099	40297	42349	43016	0.5	39	12825	13189	13322	0.3	3.12	9483	9686	0.2
95382	TURLOCK	099	24831	35218	39662	3.9	93	8574	12146	13654	3.8	2.81	6289	8838	3.7
95383	TWAIN HARTE	109	5498	5817	5920	0.6	45	2334	2517	2580	0.8	2.31	1661	1791	0.8
95385	VERNALIS	099	194	221	238	1.4	72	64	73	78	1.4	2.97	55	62	1.3
95386	WATERFORD	099	8917	11119	12148	2.4	87	2711	3308	3587	2.2	3.35	2232	2711	2.1
95388	WINTON	047	11571	14047	14733	2.1	84	3219	3696	3893	1.5	3.54	2646	3024	1.5
95389	YOSEMITE NATIONAL PA	043	1537	1588	1601	0.4	30	189	208	213	1.0	4.03	102	112	1.0
95391	TRACY	077	475	9064	11927	37.5	100	144	2772	3646	37.7	3.27	114	2230	37.9
95401	SANTA ROSA	097	36340	37083	37259	0.2	18	12870	13089	13142	0.2	2.73	8132	8248	0.2
95403	SANTA ROSA	097	39818	42624	43587	0.7	50	14660	15684	16050	0.7	2.65	9719	10422	0.8
95404	SANTA ROSA	097	36409	38607	39453	0.6	45	14488	15223	15518	0.5	2.48	8745	9290	0.7
95405	SANTA ROSA	097	21962	21948	21918	0.0	9	8759	8859	8873	0.1	2.42	5687	5737	0.1
95407	SANTA ROSA	097	30293	35276	36977	1.7	78	9268	10541	11016	1.4	3.29	6484	7371	1.4
95409	SANTA ROSA	097	25042	25973	26338	0.4	30	11134	11629	11799	0.5	2.18	6905	7242	0.5
95410	ALBION	045	1024	1087	1113	0.6	45	487	521	534	0.7	2.04	254	271	0.7
95412	ANNAPOLIS	097	343	367	378	0.7	50	132	144	149	0.9	2.49	88	95	0.8
95415	BOONVILLE	045	1363	1428	1452	0.5	39	485	511	522	0.6	2.74	339	357	0.6
95417	BRANSCOMB	045	248	250	249	0.1	13	99	100	100	0.1	2.49	67	68	0.2
95420	CASPAR	045	317	343	352	0.9	58	145	158	163	0.9	2.16	92	100	0.9
95421	CAZADERO	097	2068	2130	2158	0.3	23	920	963	978	0.5	2.17	515	535	0.4
95422	CLEARLAKE	033	13668	15216	15830	1.2	68	5766	6251	6486	0.9	2.41	3441	3724	0.9
95423	CLEARLAKE OAKS	033	3804	4259	4447	1.2	68	1826	1993	2073	1.0	2.13	1054	1149	0.9
95425	CLOVERDALE	097	9215	11147	11917	2.1	84	3379	4135	4429	2.2	2.65	2365	2885	2.2
95427	COMPTCHE	045	441	697	714	5.1	96	191	205	210	0.8	3.23	126	136	0.8
95428	COVELO	045	2441	2510	2536	0.3	23	862	892	901	0.4	2.81	584	605	0.4
95429	DOS RIOS	045	72	77	79	0.7	50	33	35	36	0.6	2.20	19	20	0.6
95432	ELK	045	239	254	260	0.7	50	120	128	132	0.7	1.94	62	66	0.7
95436	FORESTVILLE	097	6482	6613	6682	0.2	18	2600	2693	2728	0.4	2.41	1515	1565	0.4
95437	FORT BRAGG	045	14345	14531	14638	0.1	13	5871	6060	6115	0.3	2.34	3652	3777	0.4
95439	FULTON	097	719	819	853	1.4	72	250	284	295	1.4	2.79	162	185	1.4
95441	GEYSERVILLE	097	2701	2873	2938	0.7	50	839	907	932	0.8	2.90	632	680	0.8
95442	GLEN ELLEN	097	4464	4515	4503	0.1	13	1470	1474	1473	0.0	2.31	906	905	0.0
95443	GLENHAVEN	033	64	74	79	1.6	77	37	42	44	1.4	1.74	23	26	1.3
95444	GRATON	097	841	835	831	-0.1	5	288	290	289	0.1	2.77	197	197	0.0
95445	GUALALA	045	2009	2078	2098	0.4	30	895	927	935	0.4	2.23	539	559	0.4
95446	GUERNEVILLE	097	5370	5966	6193	1.1	64	2494	2820	2942	1.3	2.04	1157	1303	1.3
95448	HEALDSBURG	097	17177	18160	18541	0.6	45	6296	6660	6797	0.6	2.65	4336	4565	0.6
95449	HOPLAND	045	1812	1885	1900	0.4	30	572	586	590	0.3	3.11	404	414	0.3
95450	JENNER	097	254	257	259	0.1	13	121	125	126	0.4	2.01	69	71	0.3
95451	KELSEYVILLE	033	11456	12802	13356	1.2	68	4531	4949	5159	1.0	2.55	3089	3369	0.9
95452	KENWOOD	097	1593	1550	1530	-0.3	3	664	657	651	-0.1	2.33	438	432	-0.1
95453	LAKEPORT	033	11171	12588	13149	1.3	70	4332	4770	4981	1.0	2.51	2845	3133	1.0
95454	LAYTONVILLE	045	2287	2349	2349	0.3	23	917	942	943	0.3	2.49	613	629	0.3
95456	LITTLERIVER	045	1144	1203	1227	0.5	39	583	618	631	0.6	1.91	316	334	0.6
95457	LOWER LAKE	033	3730	4244	4518	1.4	72	1509	1672	1771	1.1	2.53	1047	1158	1.1
95458	LUCERNE	033	2684	2976	3073	1.1	64	1240	1342	1382	0.9	2.21	724	782	0.8
95459	MANCHESTER	045	542	590	608	0.9	58	237	260	269	1.0	2.22	141	155	1.0
95460	MENDOCINO	045	2006	2080	2106	0.4	30	959	997	1012	0.4	2.08	551	575	0.5
95461	MIDDLETOWN	033	3464	3857	4020	1.2	68	1330	1445	1503	0.9	2.56	888	959	0.8
95462	MONTE RIO	097	1525	1594	1623	0.5	39	762	811	829	0.7	1.94	338	359	0.7
95464	NICE	033	2265	2581	2730	1.4	72	1024	1139	1203	1.2	2.25	573	637	1.2
95465	OCCIDENTAL	097	2527	2573	2589	0.2	18	1044	1080	1089	0.4	2.35	621	640	0.3
95466	PHILO	045	1247	1324	1353	0.6	45	418	447	458	0.7	2.87	276	295	0.7
95467	HIDDEN VALLEY LAKE	033	3216	4366	4831	3.4	92	1214	1608	1777	3.1	2.71	934	1231	3.0
95468	POINT ARENA	045	1376	1450	1478	0.6	45	550	583	596	0.6	2.48	339	360	0.7
95469	POTTER VALLEY	045	1766	2099	2192	1.9	81	639	787	824	2.3	2.59	456	557	2.2
95470	REDWOOD VALLEY	045	6011	6311	6425	0.5	39	2095	2216	2264	0.6	2.81	1613	1704	0.6
95472	SEBASTOPOL	097	30363	30001	29828	-0.1	5	11967	12013	11980	0.0	2.45	7868	7873	0.0
95476	SONOMA	097	34297	35333	35633	0.3	23	14121	14497	14618	0.3	2.41	8675	8867	0.2
95480	STEWARTS POINT	097	67	72	74	0.8	54	25	27	28	0.8	2.59	17	18	0.6
95482	UKIAH	045	30743	32033	32375	0.4	30	11324	11769	11901	0.4	2.62	7554	7852	0.4
95485	UPPER LAKE	033	2621	2981	3201	1.4	72	1083	1192	1276	1.0	2.47	699	769	1.0
95488	WESTPORT	045	324	329	327	0.2	18	150	153	152	0.2	2.11	74	76	0.3
95490	WILLITS	045	13744	14194	14320	0.3	23	5281	5479	5531	0.4	2.55	3588	3728	0.4
95492	WINDSOR	097	24845	27977	29119	1.3	70	8102	9139	9516	1.3	2.99	6090	6882	1.3
95493	WITTER SPRINGS	033	88	92	100	0.5	39	36	36	39	0.0	2.50	24	24	0.0
95494	YORKVILLE	045	153	162	165	0.6	45	68	72	74	0.6	2.17	45	48	0.7
95497	THE SEA RANCH	097	1076	1152	1186	0.7	50	536	584	604	0.9	1.92	356	386	0.9
95501	EUREKA	023	22611	22570	22335	0.0	9	9480	9499	9423	0.0	2.22	4971	4977	0.0
95503	EUREKA	023	24516	24795	24641	0.1	13	9778	9976	9958	0.2	2.43	6470	6590	0.2
95511	ALDERPOINT	023	306	308	305	0.1	13	109	109	108	0.0	2.25	68	68	0.0
95514	BLOCKSBURG	023	159	159	158	0.0	9	56	56	56	0.0	2.32	35	35	0.0
95519	MCKINLEYVILLE	023	15910	17217	17587	0.9	58	6187	6774	6952	1.0	2.54	4238	4630	1.0
95521	ARCATA	023	20934	21530	21574	0.3	23	8797	9113	9173	0.4	2.19	3889	4038	0.4
95524	BAYSIDE	023	1382	1425	1426	0.3	23	538	560	564	0.4	2.54	366	380	0.4
95525	BLUE LAKE	023	480	507	513	0.6	45	194	206	210	0.7	2.46	126	134	0.7
	CALIFORNIA					1.2					1.0	2.93			1.1
	UNITED STATES					1.0					1.1	2.59			0.9

ZIP CODE #	POST OFFICE NAME	RACE (%) White 2000	White 2009	Black 2000	Black 2009	Asian/Pacific 2000	Asian/Pacific 2009	% Hispanic Origin 2000	% Hispanic Origin 2009	2009 AGE DISTRIBUTION (%) 0-4	5-9	10-14	15-19	20-24	25-44	45-64	65-84	85+	18+	MEDIAN AGE 2009	% 2009 Males	% 2009 Females
95354	MODESTO	68.9	62.6	3.3	3.3	4.6	5.1	30.2	37.5	8.3	7.9	7.3	7.9	7.7	28.3	23.0	8.1	1.4	71.8	32.2	49.9	50.1
95355	MODESTO	78.5	71.3	3.0	3.1	5.2	7.6	16.1	21.8	7.3	7.0	6.8	7.1	6.6	28.2	25.6	9.6	1.7	74.5	35.2	48.3	51.7
95356	MODESTO	75.9	69.2	3.6	3.9	6.3	7.7	18.2	24.5	7.2	6.9	6.7	6.9	7.2	27.4	26.0	10.1	1.6	74.9	35.2	48.5	51.5
95357	MODESTO	70.4	63.9	2.5	2.4	6.2	7.0	27.9	35.2	7.7	7.4	7.4	8.0	6.5	28.5	24.7	8.5	1.1	72.3	33.6	49.0	51.0
95358	MODESTO	60.4	54.3	3.3	3.2	4.3	4.8	44.6	52.7	9.0	8.6	8.3	9.1	7.8	28.3	21.3	6.7	0.9	68.6	29.6	51.2	48.8
95360	NEWMAN	61.6	54.7	1.2	1.2	1.7	2.0	49.9	59.6	9.1	8.9	8.4	8.8	8.4	27.1	20.9	7.3	1.2	68.3	29.0	50.7	49.3
95361	OAKDALE	85.7	81.2	0.4	0.5	1.2	1.5	17.1	22.8	6.7	6.9	7.2	7.1	5.6	25.1	28.0	11.5	1.9	74.7	38.6	49.2	50.8
95363	PATTERSON	56.0	49.5	1.6	2.2	2.1	2.8	56.9	62.3	9.6	8.9	8.4	8.2	6.8	30.0	21.4	6.0	0.8	68.0	30.1	50.3	49.7
95364	PINECREST	100.0	100.0	0.0	0.0	0.0	0.0	0.0	0.0	0.0	0.0	0.0	0.0	0.0	0.0	100.0	0.0	0.0	100.0	50.0	100.0	0.0
95366	RIPON	83.7	78.0	0.3	0.4	1.7	2.3	19.1	26.3	7.0	7.3	7.7	8.2	5.8	25.5	27.3	9.2	2.0	73.0	36.5	48.6	51.4
95367	RIVERBANK	68.1	64.5	1.5	1.5	1.5	1.9	44.3	48.8	8.6	8.4	8.1	7.9	6.4	27.7	23.8	8.1	1.0	70.0	32.4	49.3	50.7
95368	SALIDA	68.6	61.9	3.2	3.3	4.9	5.7	31.4	39.5	10.7	9.8	9.0	8.2	6.0	31.6	19.2	4.9	0.7	65.4	29.5	49.5	50.5
95369	SNELLING	76.4	70.7	0.3	0.4	1.3	1.5	35.4	44.4	9.2	9.1	8.5	7.8	6.8	24.2	24.0	9.2	1.2	68.2	31.2	50.1	49.9
95370	SONORA	93.1	90.6	0.4	0.6	0.9	1.1	6.5	9.3	4.5	4.7	5.4	6.2	4.9	19.3	32.5	19.2	3.3	81.7	48.4	48.2	51.8
95372	SOULSBYVILLE	93.3	90.8	0.0	0.0	0.5	0.6	7.5	11.0	5.4	6.0	6.8	7.9	5.5	21.2	31.1	14.3	2.0	77.0	42.7	49.8	50.2
95374	STEVINSON	78.4	72.3	2.1	2.1	0.3	0.4	29.5	38.7	7.8	7.7	7.4	7.2	6.7	27.9	25.0	9.2	1.0	72.6	33.6	50.3	49.7
95376	TRACY	65.4	57.2	5.3	5.5	7.7	9.4	29.5	37.8	9.2	9.0	8.7	8.1	6.2	29.6	22.3	5.9	1.1	68.1	31.4	49.8	50.2
95377	TRACY	66.2	56.3	5.8	6.3	13.1	17.4	18.5	24.8	10.8	10.4	9.7	7.4	4.1	32.7	21.3	3.4	0.3	64.4	31.5	50.4	49.6
95379	TUOLUMNE	88.5	86.1	0.2	0.3	0.7	0.9	5.6	7.9	6.1	6.0	6.4	7.4	5.3	23.1	31.6	12.1	1.9	76.8	41.8	49.7	50.3
95380	TURLOCK	67.9	61.5	1.1	1.1	3.7	4.1	38.2	46.4	9.0	8.6	7.9	8.0	7.9	27.7	20.8	8.5	1.7	69.8	30.5	49.5	50.5
95382	TURLOCK	79.9	71.9	1.7	1.9	5.2	7.1	16.4	23.4	7.6	6.6	6.2	6.8	8.5	31.4	21.9	8.8	2.2	75.8	32.6	47.9	52.1
95383	TWAIN HARTE	93.6	91.0	0.1	0.1	1.0	1.3	5.0	7.3	3.7	4.7	6.2	6.6	3.9	17.9	37.8	17.6	1.5	80.9	48.7	50.5	49.5
95385	VERNALIS	47.4	41.6	1.0	0.9	0.5	1.4	66.5	73.8	9.5	9.0	8.1	9.0	8.6	27.1	21.3	6.3	0.9	67.9	28.5	51.6	48.4
95386	WATERFORD	74.7	68.0	0.5	0.5	1.0	1.1	31.7	40.5	8.5	8.4	8.1	8.7	7.3	27.7	22.6	7.6	1.0	69.5	30.8	50.2	49.8
95388	WINTON	50.8	44.4	2.1	1.8	5.6	6.6	54.6	61.9	9.3	9.0	8.4	9.4	8.4	28.7	19.3	6.7	0.8	67.5	28.3	52.9	47.1
95389	YOSEMITE NATIONAL PA	82.6	77.5	1.6	1.8	1.2	1.5	16.8	22.4	3.6	3.3	2.9	5.2	16.7	35.0	29.0	4.1	0.3	88.4	35.1	60.0	40.0
95391	TRACY	74.3	61.6	4.4	5.5	5.1	7.6	18.7	28.6	6.3	7.0	7.7	7.5	4.4	25.9	30.8	9.4	1.0	73.6	39.7	50.3	49.7
95401	SANTA ROSA	74.7	68.7	2.2	2.2	4.7	5.8	21.4	27.2	6.6	6.1	6.0	6.7	7.4	30.1	26.0	9.2	1.9	77.3	35.6	49.5	50.5
95403	SANTA ROSA	77.4	72.6	2.4	2.4	4.8	5.8	18.5	23.0	6.4	6.4	6.4	6.9	6.8	28.2	27.2	9.4	2.2	76.7	36.8	49.8	50.2
95404	SANTA ROSA	82.0	77.5	1.6	1.7	2.7	3.6	17.0	21.4	5.8	5.7	5.7	5.9	6.1	27.2	28.9	12.1	2.5	79.1	40.1	49.1	50.9
95405	SANTA ROSA	88.2	84.4	1.2	1.4	2.9	3.7	9.0	12.2	5.2	5.2	5.8	6.1	5.7	24.6	30.9	13.1	3.4	79.7	43.1	47.3	52.7
95407	SANTA ROSA	59.9	53.3	3.1	3.0	5.0	5.6	39.3	46.5	8.8	8.5	7.9	8.1	7.7	30.3	21.8	5.9	1.0	70.1	30.6	51.1	48.9
95409	SANTA ROSA	89.5	85.8	1.0	1.2	2.5	3.4	7.1	10.0	4.6	4.6	5.0	5.8	5.0	19.0	27.8	21.6	6.8	81.9	49.7	46.5	53.5
95410	ALBION	93.6	90.5	0.3	0.4	1.1	1.6	2.7	3.9	2.3	2.7	5.1	4.8	3.0	15.9	46.4	15.8	4.0	86.5	51.7	47.3	52.7
95412	ANNAPOLIS	84.5	79.3	0.6	0.8	1.2	1.4	14.9	20.4	3.0	3.0	3.5	3.0	3.0	12.5	36.8	33.0	2.2	88.6	59.3	51.0	49.0
95415	BOONVILLE	64.5	56.4	1.1	1.1	1.2	1.4	39.3	48.8	6.5	6.8	7.2	6.7	5.0	25.5	30.5	10.5	1.4	75.3	39.3	53.4	46.6
95417	BRANSCOMB	85.1	81.2	0.8	0.8	0.8	1.2	5.6	8.0	4.8	7.2	8.0	8.0	4.0	20.4	38.8	8.4	0.4	74.0	43.3	53.6	46.4
95420	CASPAR	91.8	89.2	0.6	0.6	0.9	1.2	3.8	5.2	3.5	4.1	5.2	5.8	3.2	20.4	41.4	14.3	2.0	83.1	48.8	50.4	49.6
95421	CAZADERO	87.2	83.1	0.6	0.7	1.4	1.8	8.1	11.2	3.0	4.3	5.7	5.3	3.5	21.1	42.5	13.3	1.3	83.4	48.2	50.8	49.2
95422	CLEARLAKE	82.7	78.5	5.1	5.4	1.3	1.6	10.8	14.7	6.0	6.5	6.5	6.2	5.0	19.3	29.0	18.5	3.1	77.1	45.4	48.3	51.7
95423	CLEARLAKE OAKS	88.4	85.5	3.6	3.9	0.8	1.0	6.8	9.3	4.0	4.2	4.4	4.6	4.0	14.9	33.7	27.0	3.3	84.4	54.7	50.0	50.0
95425	CLOVERDALE	79.2	74.1	0.2	0.2	1.1	1.5	25.1	31.5	6.1	6.2	6.5	7.1	5.3	24.6	29.3	12.4	2.4	76.7	40.7	50.7	49.3
95427	COMPTCHE	85.0	80.1	0.5	1.1	0.9	1.1	18.1	22.5	4.3	5.3	5.3	7.6	4.6	21.8	39.0	10.5	1.6	81.5	45.5	53.2	46.8
95428	COVELO	51.5	48.5	0.8	0.9	0.7	0.8	7.7	9.6	7.2	7.3	7.3	7.6	6.1	21.7	27.6	13.9	1.5	73.7	38.8	49.0	51.0
95429	DOS RIOS	77.5	72.7	1.4	1.3	1.4	1.3	7.0	9.1	3.9	7.8	7.8	6.5	3.9	16.9	39.0	13.0	1.3	76.6	46.4	51.9	48.1
95432	ELK	93.7	90.6	0.4	0.4	1.3	1.6	2.5	3.5	2.4	2.4	5.1	4.3	3.1	16.1	47.2	15.4	3.9	86.6	51.8	47.6	52.4
95436	FORESTVILLE	90.5	87.1	0.7	0.8	1.3	1.7	8.6	11.9	4.1	3.9	4.7	6.2	7.3	23.7	37.4	11.1	1.7	83.4	45.1	49.4	50.6
95437	FORT BRAGG	84.2	79.6	0.6	0.6	0.9	1.2	15.8	21.5	5.3	5.5	5.6	6.2	5.6	23.5	32.9	13.2	2.4	80.6	43.8	49.8	50.2
95439	FULTON	81.4	76.2	1.9	2.2	5.0	6.1	14.3	19.0	6.1	5.9	6.0	6.3	6.3	29.2	28.2	9.9	2.1	78.4	38.3	50.4	49.6
95441	GEYSERVILLE	72.0	65.7	0.3	0.4	0.4	0.5	35.8	44.6	4.9	5.7	6.5	7.2	4.8	27.3	32.3	10.0	1.3	78.4	41.1	55.5	44.5
95442	GLEN ELLEN	89.2	85.8	2.1	2.3	2.4	3.1	9.0	12.5	3.3	3.0	4.5	6.2	6.9	27.5	36.1	11.0	1.5	85.0	44.2	53.0	47.0
95443	GLENHAVEN	89.1	86.5	3.1	4.1	1.6	1.4	6.3	8.1	4.1	5.4	5.4	4.1	2.7	13.5	40.5	21.6	2.7	82.4	54.2	54.1	45.9
95444	GRATON	79.0	72.8	0.5	0.5	1.2	1.4	25.7	33.8	4.9	4.7	5.5	8.0	7.2	26.0	33.5	8.7	1.4	80.0	40.0	50.2	49.8
95445	GUALALA	89.8	86.2	0.2	0.2	1.1	1.4	11.1	15.3	4.0	4.6	5.1	4.5	3.3	17.6	41.0	17.4	2.4	83.3	51.8	49.3	50.7
95446	GUERNEVILLE	87.2	82.8	0.9	1.0	1.2	1.5	11.0	14.9	4.1	3.7	4.8	6.0	6.5	25.9	38.5	9.0	1.5	83.8	44.3	52.3	47.7
95448	HEALDSBURG	81.0	76.3	0.5	0.5	0.9	1.1	26.5	33.7	5.7	5.6	5.9	6.8	6.6	25.7	29.6	11.5	2.5	78.8	39.8	50.6	49.4
95449	HOPLAND	64.1	57.3	0.3	0.4	0.8	1.0	28.6	36.0	7.0	7.3	7.9	8.2	7.4	25.4	27.5	8.4	1.0	72.4	33.7	51.2	48.8
95450	JENNER	85.8	81.3	0.8	0.8	1.2	1.6	8.7	11.7	3.1	4.7	5.8	5.4	3.5	21.0	43.2	12.1	1.2	82.5	47.9	51.4	48.6
95451	KELSEYVILLE	86.6	83.0	0.8	0.9	1.0	1.2	14.4	18.7	4.5	5.1	6.3	6.7	4.2	21.1	33.9	16.0	2.1	79.5	46.2	50.2	49.8
95452	KENWOOD	93.4	90.7	0.3	0.3	1.4	1.9	5.8	8.1	2.3	2.8	4.1	5.4	4.0	15.5	41.7	19.9	4.1	87.4	54.2	48.5	51.5
95453	LAKEPORT	86.3	82.7	0.9	0.9	1.0	1.3	14.2	19.0	5.3	5.2	5.7	6.3	6.2	22.2	30.0	16.1	3.0	79.5	44.3	50.2	49.8
95454	LAYTONVILLE	80.2	76.3	0.5	0.5	1.3	1.6	7.3	9.9	5.2	6.5	6.9	6.6	4.6	22.9	35.2	10.9	1.1	77.4	43.0	50.9	49.1
95456	LITTLERIVER	94.1	91.4	0.3	0.4	1.2	1.7	2.0	3.1	2.7	2.9	4.8	4.9	3.9	17.0	44.4	15.7	3.6	86.0	51.4	47.4	52.6
95457	LOWER LAKE	88.2	84.4	1.2	1.3	1.0	1.3	8.5	11.7	4.7	5.3	6.2	6.6	4.1	20.5	35.3	15.7	1.5	79.3	46.4	50.3	49.7
95458	LUCERNE	87.9	84.5	1.7	1.8	0.5	0.6	8.5	11.8	4.4	4.7	5.0	5.5	3.8	17.1	34.6	22.3	2.5	82.5	51.4	49.7	50.3
95459	MANCHESTER	84.2	81.2	0.9	0.8	0.7	1.0	15.8	21.5	4.1	4.2	4.6	5.6	4.2	19.8	37.1	18.0	2.4	83.1	49.5	51.9	48.1
95460	MENDOCINO	94.6	92.3	0.2	0.2	1.1	1.6	2.4	3.6	2.3	3.2	5.3	4.7	3.1	16.3	43.8	19.0	2.3	85.7	52.8	46.2	53.8
95461	MIDDLETOWN	89.1	85.9	0.4	0.4	1.2	1.4	11.6	15.9	5.2	6.0	6.9	6.5	3.7	22.8	35.6	12.0	1.3	77.2	44.3	51.1	48.9
95462	MONTE RIO	91.1	87.5	0.7	0.9	1.5	2.1	6.2	8.9	4.1	3.9	4.7	4.9	6.5	23.8	39.1	11.7	1.3	84.2	46.1	52.0	48.0
95464	NICE	88.1	85.3	2.3	2.4	0.6	0.8	7.8	10.8	5.1	5.2	5.5	6.0	4.5	17.1	32.6	20.8	3.1	80.2	50.3	48.3	51.7
95465	OCCIDENTAL	89.8	86.5	0.8	0.9	1.3	1.6	8.0	11.2	3.6	3.4	4.2	5.8	6.6	24.7	38.0	12.3	1.4	85.0	46.2	50.0	50.0
95466	PHILO	77.9	71.9	0.6	0.6	0.9	1.1	25.2	32.8	5.1	6.2	6.3	7.5	4.5	21.8	37.6	9.7	1.4	77.2	44.0	53.2	46.8
95467	HIDDEN VALLEY LAKE	92.3	89.5	0.7	0.7	1.0	1.3	7.0	10.0	5.7	6.5	7.4	7.9	4.7	21.7	31.2	13.5	1.4	75.0	42.5	50.1	49.9
95468	POINT ARENA	71.0	66.2	0.6	0.7	0.6	0.8	19.6	25.1	5.9	7.0	7.5	6.0	4.8	23.0	34.1	10.6	1.2	75.4	42.2	51.0	49.0
95469	POTTER VALLEY	83.0	78.0	0.2	0.2	0.5	0.6	14.9	19.7	4.1	5.1	6.2	6.3	6.0	24.8	35.3	10.9	1.2	80.0	43.2	53.4	46.6
95470	REDWOOD VALLEY	84.6	80.4	0.3	0.3	1.1	1.4	12.4	17.0	4.9	5.3	6.2	7.5	5.5	24.3	34.0	10.8	1.4	78.5	42.1	50.4	49.6
95472	SEBASTOPOL	89.4	85.6	0.7	0.7	1.5	2.0	9.1	12.7	4.1	4.2	5.0	6.5	6.6	23.2	35.6	12.4	2.4	82.5	45.2	47.9	52.1
95476	SONOMA	86.8	82.9	0.4	0.4	1.5	1.9	19.8	25.6	5.5	5.5	5.8	5.8	5.3	22.9	29.5	16.0	3.7	79.7	44.3	48.1	51.9
95480	STEWARTS POINT	84.8	79.2	0.0	1.4	1.5	1.4	15.2	20.8	2.8	2.8	2.8	2.8	2.8	11.1	38.9	33.3	2.8	90.3	60.0	51.4	48.6
95482	UKIAH	77.4	71.9	0.8	0.9	2.1	2.6	22.0	28.6	7.2	6.6	6.7	7.3	7.1	26.0	25.7	10.9	2.4	74.9	36.1	49.5	50.5
95485	UPPER LAKE	82.3	79.1	1.3	1.3	0.4	0.5	11.5	15.7	5.5	5.8	6.4	7.0	4.4	20.5	33.1	15.2	2.2	77.5	45.3	49.3	50.7
95488	WESTPORT	86.8	82.4	0.9	0.9	0.3	0.6	4.9	7.0	3.0	4.0	4.0	4.9	3.6	18.8	45.9	14.0	1.8	86.6	52.2	54.7	45.3
95490	WILLITS	86.7	82.8	0.4	0.5	0.8	1.1	11.2	15.3	6.1	6.3	6.8	7.2	5.5	22.4	31.4	12.4	2.0	76.3	41.4	49.0	51.0
95492	WINDSOR	79.3	73.0	0.9	1.0	2.3	2.8	23.4	30.9	7.3	7.6	7.9	7.6	5.3	26.7	27.0	9.0	1.5	72.3	36.9	50.4	49.6
95493	WITTER SPRINGS	87.5	83.7	1.1	1.1	0.0	1.1	6.8	9.8	4.3	4.3	4.3	6.5	4.3	18.5	39.1	16.3	2.2	80.4	50.0	50.0	50.0
95494	YORKVILLE	65.1	58.0	0.7	0.6	0.7	0.6	33.6	42.0	6.2	6.8	7.4	7.4	4.9	22.8	33.3	9.9	1.2	74.1	40.9	52.5	47.5
95497	THE SEA RANCH	84.3	79.4	0.7	0.7	1.2	1.5	14.9	20.6	2.8	3.0	3.5	2.9	2.9	12.1	37.8	32.9	2.3	88.7	59.8	50.3	49.7
95501	EUREKA	83.1	78.9	1.6	1.7	2.9	3.8	8.1	10.8	5.9	5.2	5.1	6.5	8.7	29.8	25.9	10.5	2.4	80.2	36.3	49.7	50.3
95503	EUREKA	86.9	83.1	0.8	0.9	3.0	3.8	5.4	7.3	5.3	5.3	5.8	6.6	6.0	24.3	30.9	13.2	2.7	79.9	42.4	48.7	51.3
95511	ALDERPOINT	86.9	83.8	3.3	3.6	0.7	1.0	6.2	8.8	4.2	4.5	4.9	5.8	7.5	31.8	31.2	9.4	0.6	82.5	39.0	55.8	44.2
95514	BLOCKSBURG	86.9	83.6	3.1	3.1	1.3	1.3	5.6	8.8	3.8	4.4	5.0	6.3	7.5	30.8	32.1	8.8	1.3	83.0	39.4	55.3	44.7
95519	MCKINLEYVILLE	88.0	84.4	0.3	0.4	1.1	1.5	4.2	5.8	6.5	6.3	6.3	6.3	6.3	28.5	28.8	9.5	1.4	77.0	37.4	49.1	50.9
95521	ARCATA	85.3	81.1	1.4	1.5	2.1	2.8	6.5	8.8	4.1	3.5	3.8	9.6	20.3	27.8	21.4	8.0	1.6	85.6	28.8	50.1	49.9
95524	BAYSIDE	91.2	88.4	0.4	0.5	1.2	1.7	2.9	4.2	4.0	3.6	4.3	6.0	7.1	26.0	34.5	12.9	1.7	83.9	44.0	49.5	50.5
95525	BLUE LAKE	87.5	84.6	0.2	0.2	1.0	1.4	3.1	3.9	4.7	6.1	5.7	6.5	5.1	23.5	35.9	10.7	1.8	78.9	43.9	50.3	49.7
	CALIFORNIA	59.5	54.5	6.7	6.2	11.3	12.5	32.4	38.3	7.5	7.1	6.9	7.5	7.4	28.5	24.2	9.3	1.6	74.1	34.3	49.9	50.1
	UNITED STATES	75.1	72.0	12.3	12.7	3.8	4.6	12.5	15.7	6.8	6.7	6.6	7.1	6.9	27.0	26.0	10.9	1.9	75.7	36.9	49.2	50.8

ZIP CODE #	POST OFFICE NAME	2009 Per Capita Income	2009 HH Income Base	2009 Household Income Distribution (%) Less than $25,000	$25,000 to $49,999	$50,000 to $99,999	$100,000 to $149,999	$150,000 or More	Median Household Income 2009	2014	2009 National Centile	2009 State Centile	2009 Home Value Base	2009 Home Value Distribution (%) Less than $50,000	$50,000 to $89,999	$90,000 to $174,999	$175,000 to $399,999	$400,000 or More	2009 Median Home Value
95354	MODESTO	17978	9294	28.7	30.9	32.1	5.7	2.6	41727	44519	38	25	4387	1.9	7.1	70.5	17.9	2.6	128823
95355	MODESTO	26246	21008	15.6	23.9	40.5	12.7	7.2	61212	64305	79	60	13094	4.2	2.7	41.1	47.3	4.8	178049
95356	MODESTO	27828	11812	18.1	26.1	34.7	12.4	8.7	56338	59815	73	54	7233	10.7	2.1	32.2	39.1	15.9	186483
95357	MODESTO	21329	3987	18.7	26.5	34.5	14.0	6.2	55321	58193	72	52	2994	13.5	3.2	38.5	35.5	9.3	162813
95358	MODESTO	16394	8985	21.8	30.0	35.7	8.6	3.8	48334	49964	57	39	6117	2.5	12.6	51.6	23.7	9.8	144569
95360	NEWMAN	17429	3588	21.7	28.3	38.7	8.8	2.6	50024	52599	61	43	2446	3.6	6.9	67.7	17.5	4.3	136081
95361	OAKDALE	24839	10941	18.4	28.0	35.6	12.3	5.7	53701	56710	69	49	7002	6.6	3.8	34.9	40.0	14.7	188499
95363	PATTERSON	18268	7838	18.5	25.9	41.0	9.4	5.2	57860	61653	75	56	5622	3.3	3.0	51.5	35.2	7.1	164986
95364	PINECREST	0	0	0.0	0.0	0.0	0.0	0.0	0	0	0	0	0	0.0	0.0	0.0	0.0	0.0	0
95366	RIPON	24214	5359	12.8	24.0	46.3	12.2	4.7	64182	65427	82	65	3652	0.6	2.1	35.7	55.2	6.4	195298
95367	RIVERBANK	21582	6204	14.1	23.8	43.2	12.5	6.3	60707	63578	78	59	4577	6.7	5.9	49.2	31.4	6.8	153872
95368	SALIDA	22866	3902	9.4	14.4	52.4	17.3	6.5	75350	76492	90	76	3193	0.6	2.1	43.6	50.5	3.2	179280
95369	SNELLING	18854	440	26.1	38.9	26.6	5.0	3.4	38167	40053	27	19	237	13.5	23.2	33.8	20.3	9.3	111859
95370	SONORA	25350	11364	24.4	28.6	34.4	8.3	4.3	46626	49577	53	36	7713	7.1	3.5	10.3	58.3	20.9	266778
95372	SOULSBYVILLE	25495	654	15.7	22.3	49.4	9.5	3.1	57465	60338	75	55	508	1.0	2.0	8.5	77.6	11.0	255674
95374	STEVINSON	14681	588	28.6	37.1	28.1	6.1	0.2	42014	43154	39	26	330	22.4	11.2	28.5	32.4	5.5	142391
95376	TRACY	25807	16423	12.7	18.2	40.7	18.5	9.8	72296	72785	88	73	10761	4.9	2.4	15.7	73.4	3.7	226646
95377	TRACY	30850	8090	6.4	7.5	38.0	29.8	18.3	96917	100610	96	90	7174	1.2	0.6	6.6	71.7	20.0	290836
95379	TUOLUMNE	20800	1668	23.8	29.3	37.6	7.3	2.0	47298	49538	54	37	1129	1.2	0.0	17.7	63.1	18.1	244202
95380	TURLOCK	16950	13189	28.7	30.8	31.6	6.0	2.9	41843	44445	39	25	6491	9.0	8.8	49.4	26.1	6.7	143834
95382	TURLOCK	24274	12146	20.0	23.1	39.6	11.3	6.0	58045	61025	75	56	7753	1.7	1.9	47.0	46.8	2.5	174231
95383	TWAIN HARTE	28448	2517	12.9	27.4	47.1	8.6	4.0	60162	61602	78	58	1962	1.0	0.5	8.3	70.9	19.3	286772
95385	VERNALIS	18278	73	23.3	28.8	42.5	5.5	0.0	48372	49075	57	39	40	10.0	22.5	47.5	15.0	5.0	106250
95386	WATERFORD	17369	3308	22.1	30.8	38.6	6.8	1.7	47745	49325	56	38	2192	9.4	6.1	58.5	16.6	9.4	129795
95388	WINTON	13987	3696	27.6	35.0	31.8	3.1	2.7	40135	42791	33	21	2077	8.7	47.5	28.3	9.4	6.2	86164
95389	YOSEMITE NATIONAL PA	18957	208	7.7	35.1	42.8	8.7	5.8	58079	60338	75	56	76	18.4	6.6	23.7	35.5	15.8	179167
95391	TRACY	24715	2772	13.5	23.4	35.6	19.3	8.2	67044	66256	85	69	2291	0.3	1.7	7.1	58.5	32.4	332071
95401	SANTA ROSA	26776	13089	14.7	22.9	37.7	18.6	6.0	64040	66673	82	65	7642	1.9	2.0	6.0	65.0	25.0	295500
95403	SANTA ROSA	31724	15684	12.7	20.7	35.0	21.7	9.9	69084	73095	86	70	9255	5.0	2.4	4.6	45.9	42.1	364648
95404	SANTA ROSA	37883	15223	15.1	18.4	33.8	18.0	14.7	69499	73045	86	71	8920	2.6	0.6	1.6	39.8	55.4	435630
95405	SANTA ROSA	40226	8859	9.1	17.4	38.2	22.8	12.6	74152	77458	89	74	5560	0.0	0.0	2.6	53.0	44.4	379292
95407	SANTA ROSA	20956	10541	18.6	22.8	40.0	14.0	4.6	61449	63748	79	60	5624	8.2	1.8	4.3	65.0	20.7	281973
95409	SANTA ROSA	42824	11629	12.1	19.7	34.6	20.1	13.6	70480	74069	87	71	8183	3.3	1.5	2.2	39.7	53.3	416252
95410	ALBION	36661	521	20.3	24.8	35.9	9.0	10.0	53750	57519	69	49	354	1.7	0.0	1.7	42.7	54.0	434146
95412	ANNAPOLIS	40941	144	10.4	17.4	35.4	21.5	15.3	75000	78238	89	76	108	0.0	0.0	0.9	23.1	75.9	578125
95415	BOONVILLE	18148	511	29.7	30.7	30.1	7.2	2.2	41160	43481	37	24	276	6.9	1.1	13.8	47.1	31.2	305455
95417	BRANSCOMB	18819	100	34.0	29.0	29.0	6.0	2.0	37689	40000	26	18	69	8.7	5.8	23.2	43.5	18.8	253125
95420	CASPAR	27093	158	23.4	29.7	36.7	5.1	5.1	47575	49397	56	38	115	6.1	0.0	5.2	55.7	33.0	337097
95421	CAZADERO	31490	963	24.8	28.5	30.0	10.4	6.3	46604	49612	53	36	617	1.8	0.8	6.3	46.8	44.2	348551
95422	CLEARLAKE	14413	6251	50.2	30.2	16.1	2.7	0.8	24875	25621	3	3	4001	15.0	18.3	42.4	20.3	4.0	126783
95423	CLEARLAKE OAKS	19912	1993	38.3	32.7	21.4	5.3	2.4	32906	34686	13	10	1476	5.4	9.8	29.8	42.9	12.1	188931
95425	CLOVERDALE	25799	4135	22.5	23.2	34.6	13.6	6.1	59719	62621	77	57	2809	4.0	1.2	6.6	62.3	26.0	298841
95427	COMPTCHE	19366	205	26.8	31.7	26.3	8.8	6.3	41151	45000	37	24	138	4.3	0.0	1.4	38.4	55.8	447059
95428	COVELO	16233	892	34.2	29.0	30.2	4.6	2.0	37298	40664	24	17	567	12.2	12.0	31.7	28.4	15.7	155060
95429	DOS RIOS	18213	35	40.0	25.7	25.7	5.7	2.9	32368	30000	12	9	25	4.0	8.0	16.0	52.0	20.0	275000
95432	ELK	38733	128	20.3	24.2	35.2	9.4	10.9	54150	58322	70	50	87	1.1	0.0	2.3	41.4	55.2	445000
95436	FORESTVILLE	35588	2693	14.7	22.9	33.1	18.6	10.7	66331	69124	84	68	1851	1.6	0.4	5.5	53.2	39.3	329715
95437	FORT BRAGG	22470	6060	27.2	29.6	34.3	5.9	3.0	42808	46196	42	28	3552	6.9	0.7	7.7	55.2	29.5	317104
95439	FULTON	26608	284	13.0	22.5	34.9	24.3	5.3	66423	68852	84	68	181	5.5	1.1	6.6	47.5	39.2	356667
95441	GEYSERVILLE	30334	907	9.3	27.2	35.2	15.1	13.2	66276	69251	84	67	561	2.3	0.9	6.1	30.5	60.2	507102
95442	GLEN ELLEN	38242	1474	9.2	19.2	33.8	22.8	15.0	79211	83420	92	80	885	0.0	0.0	1.9	17.5	80.6	654904
95443	GLENHAVEN	30359	42	23.8	35.7	28.6	7.1	4.8	43187	43191	43	29	32	0.0	0.0	21.9	59.4	18.8	243750
95444	GRATON	30615	290	14.8	16.9	33.1	24.5	10.7	74619	77414	89	75	201	0.0	0.5	6.0	44.3	49.3	394444
95445	GUALALA	30393	927	18.8	26.1	41.3	6.9	6.9	54747	59213	71	51	676	3.3	5.9	6.7	32.1	52.1	413725
95446	GUERNEVILLE	29698	2820	22.7	28.3	35.0	9.5	4.5	49306	56754	60	41	1603	1.7	0.9	10.5	61.1	25.8	275104
95448	HEALDSBURG	33913	6660	13.0	20.6	36.0	18.3	12.1	67610	70412	85	69	4171	0.4	0.2	2.0	38.4	59.1	454552
95449	HOPLAND	19546	586	27.3	28.8	31.9	7.7	4.3	43151	46328	43	29	325	9.5	4.3	10.8	33.5	41.8	345918
95450	JENNER	31364	125	24.8	28.0	32.0	10.4	4.8	46962	49310	54	37	78	1.3	1.3	6.4	43.6	47.4	377778
95451	KELSEYVILLE	23174	4949	25.4	29.3	31.4	9.1	4.8	44891	47957	48	32	3677	6.1	4.1	16.0	53.2	20.6	242281
95452	KENWOOD	47535	657	4.7	12.6	40.5	26.5	15.7	85049	87918	94	84	507	0.0	0.4	3.4	28.6	67.7	537921
95453	LAKEPORT	20855	4770	26.3	31.8	32.5	6.1	3.3	42775	45395	42	28	3235	9.2	3.8	19.2	49.6	18.2	229532
95454	LAYTONVILLE	18909	942	34.8	27.3	31.8	3.7	2.3	39881	42389	32	21	599	4.0	4.8	27.7	51.8	11.7	227813
95456	LITTLERIVER	42106	618	19.7	24.1	35.3	8.4	12.5	54330	57522	70	50	419	1.2	1.2	1.0	34.6	62.1	495283
95457	LOWER LAKE	19973	1672	24.8	30.7	36.5	6.2	1.8	44782	47771	48	32	1316	1.6	8.1	21.6	57.8	10.9	226383
95458	LUCERNE	17601	1342	39.0	35.3	19.4	5.2	1.0	31072	32060	10	8	948	9.4	14.9	38.2	30.0	7.6	150210
95459	MANCHESTER	23723	260	30.4	29.2	32.7	4.2	3.5	43003	46125	42	28	152	0.7	4.6	7.9	34.2	52.6	418182
95460	MENDOCINO	37645	997	20.3	23.6	35.4	10.8	9.9	58072	61977	75	56	686	0.0	2.5	1.2	14.7	81.6	620575
95461	MIDDLETOWN	22405	1445	29.7	23.8	37.0	5.8	3.7	46719	49714	53	36	1018	1.9	4.6	20.2	55.5	17.8	251471
95462	MONTE RIO	33511	811	27.4	22.4	36.3	7.0	6.9	50310	55002	62	43	486	0.2	0.0	10.7	75.3	13.8	255674
95464	NICE	15608	1139	44.1	35.5	15.6	4.3	0.5	28329	29903	6	5	763	10.1	14.7	37.7	28.7	8.8	150387
95465	OCCIDENTAL	36281	1080	16.6	23.7	31.1	18.1	10.5	65759	69119	84	67	754	0.8	0.5	5.3	22.7	70.7	580049
95466	PHILO	20577	447	26.6	32.4	26.4	9.4	5.1	41191	44339	37	24	288	4.9	0.3	0.7	36.5	57.6	464706
95467	HIDDEN VALLEY LAKE	21616	1608	15.8	26.4	47.9	8.4	1.6	55691	58912	72	53	1300	0.0	0.1	7.0	73.5	19.5	282730
95468	POINT ARENA	19467	583	32.4	29.3	29.5	4.6	4.1	36962	39651	23	17	328	2.1	4.9	12.5	38.4	42.1	355932
95469	POTTER VALLEY	23121	787	26.0	24.7	37.6	7.6	4.1	48473	54145	58	40	547	1.8	2.9	9.7	46.4	39.1	326543
95470	REDWOOD VALLEY	23926	2216	17.1	29.2	39.4	9.7	4.6	52979	55574	68	48	1667	3.5	5.8	8.3	48.7	33.8	341196
95472	SEBASTOPOL	38786	12013	14.9	18.1	31.8	21.6	13.7	72265	76590	88	73	8020	1.1	0.3	1.1	21.6	75.9	562301
95476	SONOMA	36644	14497	14.0	22.9	34.1	18.3	10.7	66547	69628	85	68	9350	5.8	1.4	2.7	34.0	56.1	437264
95480	STEWARTS POINT	39541	27	7.4	18.5	37.0	22.2	14.8	77369	75000	91	78	20	0.0	0.0	0.0	20.0	80.0	607143
95482	UKIAH	22648	11769	25.2	27.7	34.4	8.1	4.6	46562	49813	53	36	6586	11.6	3.7	9.6	52.7	22.5	270987
95485	UPPER LAKE	16947	1192	38.8	31.4	24.2	4.4	1.2	32775	35119	13	10	822	7.3	6.7	23.5	45.6	16.9	200781
95488	WESTPORT	29309	153	30.7	24.2	34.6	7.2	3.3	44298	46565	46	31	102	0.0	0.0	20.6	21.6	57.8	480000
95490	WILLITS	20110	5479	28.8	30.1	32.8	5.9	2.4	42314	45451	40	26	3494	7.6	5.8	14.3	59.8	12.4	233639
95492	WINDSOR	31277	9139	10.8	16.0	35.4	26.3	11.5	76696	82755	90	77	7134	3.7	3.1	2.9	45.1	45.2	380493
95493	WITTER SPRINGS	19597	36	25.0	30.6	36.1	8.3	0.0	42357	47402	40	27	26	3.8	7.7	7.7	53.8	26.9	275000
95494	YORKVILLE	25749	72	27.8	31.9	29.2	8.3	2.8	40899	43897	36	23	43	4.7	0.0	4.7	25.6	65.1	552083
95497	THE SEA RANCH	52802	584	9.9	17.3	36.8	21.2	14.7	74153	77583	89	74	436	0.0	0.0	1.1	22.7	76.1	577519
95501	EUREKA	20548	9499	38.8	28.5	26.1	4.3	2.3	33480	36227	14	11	4095	1.9	1.9	23.4	65.6	7.3	217014
95503	EUREKA	23555	9976	23.0	29.5	36.9	6.4	4.1	47420	50622	55	38	6649	5.5	1.4	18.8	61.8	12.5	240737
95511	ALDERPOINT	20299	109	31.2	38.5	24.8	2.8	2.8	34463	36154	16	13	78	0.0	0.0	26.9	55.1	17.9	234615
95514	BLOCKSBURG	17821	56	32.1	37.5	26.8	3.6	0.0	33680	34159	15	12	40	0.0	0.0	25.0	57.5	17.5	233333
95519	MCKINLEYVILLE	23509	6774	23.6	25.1	40.2	7.0	4.1	51041	53806	64	44	4406	3.6	4.3	14.3	59.7	18.0	249828
95521	ARCATA	21090	9113	42.2	24.3	23.7	6.6	3.1	32503	35206	12	10	3871	10.7	5.5	9.5	57.0	17.3	246135
95524	BAYSIDE	31146	560	15.4	27.3	30.9	16.8	9.6	60270	62132	78	59	405	5.7	1.2	3.0	49.1	41.0	362371
95525	BLUE LAKE	23733	206	25.2	27.7	35.4	7.3	4.4	46879	50415	54	37	134	6.0	7.5	17.9	42.5	26.1	244118
	CALIFORNIA	28199		18.5	22.2	33.9	14.0	11.5	61614	64088				3.3	2.6	13.6	41.0	39.5	321752
	UNITED STATES	27277		20.9	24.4	35.3	11.7	7.6	54719	56938				9.3	13.1	31.6	32.6	13.5	162279

ZIP CODE #	POST OFFICE NAME	FINANCIAL SERVICES: Auto Loan	FINANCIAL SERVICES: Home Loan	FINANCIAL SERVICES: Invest-ments	FINANCIAL SERVICES: Retire-ment Plans	THE HOME: Home Improvements: Home Repair	THE HOME: Home Improvements: Lawn & Garden	THE HOME: Furnishings: Comput-ers & Hard-ware-Personal	THE HOME: Furnishings: Major Appli-ances	THE HOME: Furnishings: TV, Radio, Sound Equip-ment	THE HOME: Furnishings: Furni-ture	ENTERTAINMENT: Dine out/ Carry out	ENTERTAINMENT: Sports Equip-ment	ENTERTAINMENT: Fees & Tickets	ENTERTAINMENT: Toys & Games	ENTERTAINMENT: Travel	ENTERTAINMENT: Cable TV	PERSONAL: Apparel & Services	PERSONAL: Auto Repairs	PERSONAL: Health Insur-ance	PERSONAL: Pets & Supplies
95354	MODESTO	68	73	68	70	73	65	74	72	71	75	72	55	75	71	75	69	52	73	69	81
95355	MODESTO	101	112	104	109	110	101	105	103	101	108	103	80	110	104	107	100	73	102	98	119
95356	MODESTO	109	107	108	108	107	105	110	107	108	111	109	83	109	109	109	107	77	109	106	126
95357	MODESTO	108	108	105	104	106	105	101	106	99	104	100	82	99	103	101	99	70	101	99	122
95358	MODESTO	89	92	88	85	91	83	88	90	83	91	85	70	86	85	89	80	60	88	81	101
95360	NEWMAN	86	92	83	82	92	75	88	89	81	95	83	67	86	82	88	76	59	87	75	96
95361	OAKDALE	99	104	104	103	105	103	99	102	97	99	97	78	100	98	102	97	69	100	100	119
95363	PATTERSON	100	106	91	99	102	90	97	98	92	103	94	75	97	96	96	89	66	95	87	110
95364	PINECREST	0	0	0	0	0	0	0	0	0	0	0	0	0	0	0	0	0	0	0	0
95366	RIPON	104	116	106	113	112	106	104	106	101	108	102	82	109	103	107	99	72	103	100	123
95367	RIVERBANK	104	114	108	109	114	101	105	107	100	112	101	81	108	102	108	97	72	104	98	120
95368	SALIDA	118	134	115	127	130	107	119	119	109	130	112	94	123	116	121	101	80	113	100	132
95369	SNELLING	84	75	81	69	76	76	75	81	74	77	75	61	68	75	74	74	52	79	76	92
95370	SONORA	85	81	99	80	86	93	80	89	82	81	82	63	79	79	84	86	56	86	94	103
95372	SOULSBYVILLE	87	102	99	101	100	104	88	95	90	89	91	71	99	90	98	92	63	92	99	110
95374	STEVINSON	84	62	69	60	62	79	64	74	70	64	69	56	53	73	59	75	47	70	76	89
95376	TRACY	115	132	117	127	130	108	121	119	111	129	114	95	127	116	124	104	82	115	101	132
95377	TRACY	159	189	162	193	183	155	159	160	147	177	150	132	177	159	166	135	109	147	133	179
95379	TUOLUMNE	78	74	85	74	76	82	75	81	77	72	76	61	72	75	77	80	53	79	83	94
95380	TURLOCK	78	71	70	68	71	68	76	75	74	77	76	58	71	75	73	73	53	77	72	86
95382	TURLOCK	96	99	94	99	97	90	99	94	96	100	98	74	101	99	98	95	70	96	91	110
95383	TWAIN HARTE	106	89	140	88	99	115	87	110	92	85	90	78	79	86	96	97	60	102	111	127
95385	VERNALIS	83	78	65	69	76	68	77	78	76	84	78	56	72	78	74	74	54	78	71	86
95386	WATERFORD	91	87	82	81	84	81	84	87	81	87	83	66	78	84	81	80	57	84	80	99
95388	WINTON	73	68	67	62	68	64	69	71	66	71	68	55	63	67	68	64	47	71	64	80
95389	YOSEMITE NATIONAL PA	99	98	99	100	97	97	100	97	99	100	100	76	101	99	100	99	70	99	98	116
95391	TRACY	112	127	109	130	123	124	113	118	111	114	112	92	121	114	120	111	78	113	116	138
95401	SANTA ROSA	103	104	101	103	104	96	108	103	104	109	105	80	107	104	106	101	75	105	99	119
95403	SANTA ROSA	116	124	123	125	125	114	123	119	117	126	119	93	127	118	125	114	85	120	113	137
95404	SANTA ROSA	120	140	152	141	147	126	138	134	128	142	130	105	148	126	147	123	95	134	124	151
95405	SANTA ROSA	123	152	161	151	158	137	141	139	132	143	134	108	156	132	154	129	98	137	131	157
95407	SANTA ROSA	97	103	97	95	105	85	103	102	93	108	96	79	101	95	104	87	69	100	85	111
95409	SANTA ROSA	121	139	159	135	152	146	130	139	130	137	128	96	143	123	145	132	90	136	150	156
95410	ALBION	104	109	149	108	126	129	98	116	104	111	102	73	108	93	114	109	70	111	129	132
95412	ANNAPOLIS	141	149	202	148	172	176	134	158	141	152	139	99	147	127	155	148	95	151	176	179
95415	BOONVILLE	89	63	93	61	65	91	66	83	72	59	71	65	51	71	65	79	46	77	87	100
95417	BRANSCOMB	84	59	87	58	62	86	62	79	68	56	67	60	49	67	61	75	44	72	82	94
95420	CASPAR	98	78	126	77	86	103	78	99	82	73	81	73	68	78	85	87	54	92	98	115
95421	CAZADERO	113	92	147	91	102	121	92	116	96	87	95	84	81	91	100	102	63	107	115	134
95422	CLEARLAKE	50	46	55	43	50	54	47	52	50	49	49	36	45	47	48	53	33	52	58	60
95423	CLEARLAKE OAKS	65	59	81	55	65	72	57	68	60	59	58	46	54	55	62	63	39	65	73	78
95425	CLOVERDALE	109	94	109	91	95	109	95	106	98	92	97	81	85	98	94	102	66	102	107	125
95427	COMPTCHE	104	83	134	82	92	110	83	106	87	78	86	77	73	83	90	93	57	98	104	122
95428	COVELO	74	60	78	59	63	76	62	72	66	59	65	53	54	64	62	70	43	69	75	85
95429	DOS RIOS	67	53	86	53	59	71	54	68	56	50	55	50	46	53	58	60	37	63	67	79
95432	ELK	104	110	149	109	127	130	99	117	104	112	102	73	109	94	114	109	70	111	130	132
95436	FORESTVILLE	112	131	142	132	138	118	126	124	116	131	117	98	135	114	136	111	85	122	113	141
95437	FORT BRAGG	81	70	91	70	73	83	73	81	75	69	75	61	67	73	75	79	51	79	84	95
95439	FULTON	104	110	111	111	111	108	107	107	104	107	105	83	109	104	110	104	74	106	106	125
95441	GEYSERVILLE	133	136	139	139	135	146	126	137	125	122	125	108	127	126	133	127	86	130	136	162
95442	GLEN ELLEN	128	149	173	154	162	129	153	144	135	159	137	118	161	131	164	124	101	144	124	163
95443	GLENHAVEN	89	71	115	70	78	94	71	90	74	67	74	66	62	71	77	79	49	83	89	105
95444	GRATON	107	134	157	137	148	115	128	126	112	137	112	101	140	108	143	102	83	122	106	140
95445	GUALALA	113	91	146	89	99	120	91	115	95	85	94	84	79	90	98	101	62	106	114	134
95446	GUERNEVILLE	95	83	109	83	87	98	85	95	86	81	86	71	78	84	87	90	58	92	96	112
95448	HEALDSBURG	116	138	146	137	145	125	131	130	122	135	124	100	142	121	141	119	90	128	121	146
95449	HOPLAND	96	86	104	80	89	91	85	96	84	86	85	70	78	83	87	85	58	92	89	108
95450	JENNER	106	85	137	83	93	112	85	108	89	79	88	79	73	84	92	95	58	99	106	125
95451	KELSEYVILLE	94	83	113	81	88	99	80	96	83	80	82	70	74	80	85	86	56	90	95	110
95452	KENWOOD	147	175	198	178	187	173	154	166	149	167	149	119	172	143	174	147	106	158	162	188
95453	LAKEPORT	79	74	92	72	77	84	71	81	73	71	73	59	69	71	76	76	50	78	83	94
95454	LAYTONVILLE	83	61	90	59	64	85	62	79	68	58	67	59	51	67	63	74	44	73	81	93
95456	LITTLERIVER	109	120	157	120	137	131	110	123	110	123	109	83	121	101	126	111	76	118	128	139
95457	LOWER LAKE	81	70	94	68	74	87	68	82	71	67	70	59	62	69	72	76	47	77	85	95
95458	LUCERNE	57	54	70	50	60	65	52	61	55	56	53	40	51	50	57	58	36	59	68	70
95459	MANCHESTER	88	70	114	69	77	93	70	90	74	66	73	65	61	70	76	79	48	83	88	104
95460	MENDOCINO	107	115	153	114	131	130	104	120	107	117	105	78	114	97	120	110	73	115	128	135
95461	MIDDLETOWN	93	79	119	78	86	100	77	96	80	74	79	70	70	77	84	84	53	89	94	111
95462	MONTE RIO	98	90	109	91	92	99	91	98	92	89	92	74	88	90	94	94	63	96	98	115
95464	NICE	51	49	63	45	54	59	47	55	49	50	48	36	46	45	51	52	32	53	61	63
95465	OCCIDENTAL	113	131	162	133	144	121	126	129	113	132	113	102	133	109	139	107	82	124	112	145
95466	PHILO	100	77	124	76	84	106	80	100	83	72	82	76	66	80	84	89	54	93	101	118
95467	HIDDEN VALLEY LAKE	83	91	82	94	89	91	82	86	81	82	81	67	86	83	87	81	57	83	85	101
95468	POINT ARENA	81	64	104	63	71	85	65	82	68	60	67	60	56	64	70	72	44	76	81	95
95469	POTTER VALLEY	90	88	101	89	90	98	82	93	83	81	83	71	81	83	88	86	57	88	92	109
95470	REDWOOD VALLEY	102	102	100	101	102	104	93	100	94	96	95	74	94	96	95	96	65	96	99	118
95472	SEBASTOPOL	123	146	171	149	159	131	141	141	127	149	127	112	152	123	155	118	93	136	122	158
95476	SONOMA	114	132	145	131	140	128	125	128	121	131	121	95	136	116	136	119	87	126	127	144
95480	STEWARTS POINT	143	150	204	149	173	177	135	160	143	153	140	100	149	128	156	149	96	152	178	181
95482	UKIAH	83	83	82	83	82	81	85	83	84	85	85	64	85	85	85	84	60	85	83	97
95485	UPPER LAKE	70	55	80	53	59	74	55	69	60	53	58	50	48	57	57	64	39	64	72	81
95488	WESTPORT	104	83	134	82	91	110	83	106	87	78	86	77	72	83	90	93	57	97	104	122
95490	WILLITS	78	70	78	71	70	79	72	77	73	68	73	59	68	73	72	76	50	76	78	91
95492	WINDSOR	132	150	146	148	152	135	135	139	127	144	128	107	143	129	143	122	91	132	125	158
95493	WITTER SPRINGS	81	65	105	64	72	86	65	83	68	61	67	61	57	65	71	73	45	76	82	96
95494	YORKVILLE	98	71	114	71	76	104	76	95	79	65	79	76	59	77	78	86	51	89	99	115
95497	THE SEA RANCH	141	149	202	148	172	176	134	158	142	152	139	99	147	127	155	148	95	151	176	179
95501	EUREKA	64	57	55	59	56	59	67	61	67	63	67	48	63	67	62	67	47	65	65	73
95503	EUREKA	78	84	86	84	86	86	80	83	80	80	80	62	84	79	84	81	56	82	85	96
95511	ALDERPOINT	81	56	89	56	58	86	62	77	64	50	64	64	45	63	62	70	41	72	81	95
95514	BLOCKSBURG	70	49	78	49	52	74	54	67	56	44	55	55	40	55	54	61	36	63	71	82
95519	MCKINLEYVILLE	87	87	91	86	88	87	85	88	84	85	84	68	84	84	86	84	59	86	86	102
95521	ARCATA	68	51	50	55	51	54	76	59	71	66	71	51	62	71	61	69	50	68	61	73
95524	BAYSIDE	102	121	139	123	132	109	117	117	105	123	105	92	125	102	128	99	77	113	102	131
95525	BLUE LAKE	86	86	94	87	89	92	81	88	81	82	81	65	82	81	85	83	56	84	88	102
	CALIFORNIA	112	119	122	118	122	107	121	116	114	124	116	92	124	114	124	110	84	118	107	132
	UNITED STATES	100	100	100	100	100	100	100	100	100	100	100	100	100	100	100	100	100	100	100	100

ZIP CODE #	POST OFFICE NAME	COUNTY FIPS CODE	POPULATION 2000	POPULATION 2009	POPULATION 2014	2000-2009 ANNUAL RATE % Rate	2000-2009 ANNUAL RATE State Centile	HOUSEHOLDS 2000	HOUSEHOLDS 2009	HOUSEHOLDS 2014	HOUSEHOLDS % Annual Rate 2000-2009	HOUSEHOLDS 2009 Average HH Size	FAMILIES 2000	FAMILIES 2009	FAMILIES % Annual Rate 2000-2009
95526	BRIDGEVILLE	023	714	731	741	0.3	23	301	311	318	0.4	2.34	207	214	0.4
95527	BURNT RANCH	105	342	372	390	0.9	58	162	177	186	1.0	2.10	105	115	1.0
95528	CARLOTTA	023	918	893	876	-0.3	3	355	349	344	-0.2	2.56	252	247	-0.2
95531	CRESCENT CITY	015	23376	24942	25488	0.7	50	7598	8110	8323	0.7	2.61	5216	5574	0.7
95536	FERNDALE	023	2942	2985	2983	0.2	18	1183	1210	1214	0.2	2.44	787	804	0.2
95540	FORTUNA	023	12403	13474	13765	0.9	58	4931	5380	5518	0.9	2.46	3332	3639	1.0
95542	GARBERVILLE	023	2392	2505	2527	0.5	39	1001	1057	1071	0.6	2.27	593	626	0.6
95543	GASQUET	015	852	986	1045	1.6	77	350	411	437	1.8	2.29	235	275	1.7
95546	HOOPA	023	3150	3302	3343	0.5	39	1033	1083	1098	0.5	3.04	734	769	0.5
95547	HYDESVILLE	023	1218	1262	1269	0.4	30	461	482	488	0.5	2.62	346	361	0.5
95548	KLAMATH	015	1205	1278	1308	0.6	45	432	463	476	0.8	2.37	285	305	0.7
95549	KNEELAND	023	411	413	410	0.1	13	143	146	145	0.2	2.82	102	103	0.1
95550	KORBEL	023	194	208	211	0.8	54	75	81	82	0.8	2.52	50	54	0.8
95551	LOLETA	023	1292	1343	1343	0.4	30	523	541	541	0.4	2.47	324	334	0.3
95552	MAD RIVER	105	17	19	20	1.2	68	6	7	7	1.7	2.71	4	4	0.0
95554	MYERS FLAT	023	2902	3002	3020	0.4	30	1251	1308	1323	0.5	2.20	724	755	0.5
95555	ORICK	023	450	450	444	0.0	9	183	185	183	0.1	2.42	105	106	0.1
95556	ORLEANS	023	520	514	510	-0.1	5	204	204	203	0.0	2.52	124	124	0.0
95558	PETROLIA	023	281	295	298	0.5	39	127	133	135	0.5	2.13	83	87	0.5
95560	REDWAY	023	524	543	547	0.4	30	240	251	255	0.5	2.08	131	137	0.5
95562	RIO DELL	023	3271	3203	3162	-0.2	4	1264	1243	1229	-0.2	2.57	859	842	-0.2
95563	SALYER	023	880	947	968	0.8	54	387	420	431	0.9	2.25	234	254	0.9
95564	SAMOA	023	394	386	381	-0.2	4	158	157	155	-0.1	2.46	87	85	-0.3
95565	SCOTIA	023	1096	1118	1113	0.2	18	357	368	369	0.3	3.04	281	289	0.3
95567	SMITH RIVER	015	2018	2289	2418	1.4	72	766	875	925	1.4	2.62	541	617	1.4
95568	SOMES BAR	093	317	314	310	-0.1	5	143	147	147	0.3	2.14	92	94	0.2
95569	REDCREST	023	698	716	718	0.3	23	251	261	263	0.4	2.59	169	176	0.4
95570	TRINIDAD	023	2382	2518	2544	0.6	45	1104	1179	1194	0.7	2.13	623	664	0.7
95573	WILLOW CREEK	023	1579	1654	1674	0.5	39	704	746	759	0.6	2.22	436	461	0.6
95585	LEGGETT	045	420	434	437	0.4	30	154	158	160	0.3	2.68	91	93	0.2
95587	PIERCY	045	338	349	351	0.3	23	154	158	160	0.3	2.16	89	91	0.2
95589	WHITETHORN	023	767	794	799	0.4	30	359	377	381	0.5	2.10	209	219	0.5
95595	ZENIA	105	454	506	537	1.2	68	187	210	224	1.3	2.40	127	143	1.3
95602	AUBURN	061	17487	18348	18862	0.5	39	6449	7026	7278	0.9	2.49	4881	5233	0.8
95603	AUBURN	061	25433	26275	26942	0.4	30	10558	11327	11729	0.8	2.29	6781	7066	0.4
95605	WEST SACRAMENTO	113	12749	13963	14901	1.0	62	4127	4582	4911	1.1	3.03	2872	3099	0.8
95606	BROOKS	113	277	307	334	1.1	64	115	130	142	1.3	2.36	78	86	1.1
95607	CAPAY	113	312	349	384	1.2	68	121	138	153	1.4	2.53	81	91	1.3
95608	CARMICHAEL	067	58475	59381	60451	0.2	18	24565	24863	25293	0.1	2.33	15425	15336	-0.1
95610	CITRUS HEIGHTS	067	43606	44718	45685	0.3	23	16891	17285	17656	0.2	2.56	10990	11039	0.0
95612	CLARKSBURG	113	1363	1505	1607	1.1	64	437	484	519	1.1	3.00	347	379	1.0
95614	COOL	017	3660	3987	4129	0.9	58	1336	1449	1501	0.9	2.75	1093	1173	0.8
95615	COURTLAND	067	796	861	906	0.9	58	250	271	286	0.9	2.99	184	196	0.7
95616	DAVIS	113	45641	48390	50539	0.6	45	16701	17739	18685	0.7	2.37	7617	7869	0.4
95618	DAVIS	113	22107	26171	28601	1.8	80	8185	9636	10536	1.8	2.68	5107	5884	1.5
95619	DIAMOND SPRINGS	017	3733	4016	4096	0.8	54	1387	1486	1516	0.7	2.69	963	1014	0.6
95620	DIXON	095	18731	20184	20781	0.8	54	5759	6158	6317	0.7	3.23	4674	4992	0.7
95621	CITRUS HEIGHTS	067	42285	43102	43988	0.2	18	16992	17330	17694	0.2	2.47	10927	10929	0.0
95623	EL DORADO	017	4292	4793	4960	1.2	68	1734	1924	1992	1.1	2.49	1297	1422	1.0
95624	ELK GROVE	067	38683	59813	69024	4.8	95	12547	18705	21449	4.4	3.18	10329	15528	4.5
95626	ELVERTA	067	6266	6751	7167	0.8	54	1925	2077	2212	0.8	3.24	1575	1689	0.8
95627	ESPARTO	113	2504	2780	3009	1.1	64	851	964	1049	1.4	2.86	631	703	1.2
95628	FAIR OAKS	067	41140	42284	43265	0.3	23	16124	16531	16910	0.3	2.53	11463	11583	0.1
95629	FIDDLETOWN	005	879	1025	1091	1.7	78	366	431	461	1.8	2.38	268	315	1.8
95630	FOLSOM	067	51884	73863	83938	3.9	93	17196	24889	28441	4.1	2.69	12527	18256	4.2
95631	FORESTHILL	061	5777	6247	6564	0.8	54	2201	2494	2649	1.4	2.50	1670	1850	1.1
95632	GALT	067	24409	29171	31620	1.9	81	7606	9002	9745	1.8	3.21	6209	7345	1.8
95633	GARDEN VALLEY	017	2902	3146	3225	0.9	58	1062	1145	1175	0.8	2.71	803	855	0.7
95634	GEORGETOWN	017	2447	2716	2830	1.1	64	942	1044	1092	1.1	2.53	685	748	1.0
95635	GREENWOOD	017	952	1061	1105	1.2	68	359	400	418	1.2	2.52	263	289	1.0
95636	GRIZZLY FLATS	017	633	728	761	1.5	75	257	294	308	1.5	2.48	191	216	1.3
95637	GUINDA	113	261	290	317	1.1	64	101	115	126	1.4	2.52	68	76	1.2
95638	HERALD	067	1693	1934	2090	1.4	72	564	645	695	1.5	2.97	469	532	1.4
95640	IONE	005	9653	11284	11963	1.7	78	1994	2591	2853	2.9	2.69	1492	1935	2.9
95641	ISLETON	067	1998	2073	2131	0.4	30	869	901	925	0.4	2.29	532	541	0.2
95642	JACKSON	005	6684	7256	7595	0.9	58	2849	3125	3283	1.0	2.23	1888	2076	1.0
95645	KNIGHTS LANDING	101	1675	2005	2221	2.0	83	563	676	748	2.0	2.96	391	462	1.8
95648	LINCOLN	061	15358	49800	62634	13.6	99	5346	18226	23215	14.2	2.73	4276	14867	14.4
95650	LOOMIS	061	11089	11898	12550	0.8	54	3966	4438	4726	1.2	2.67	3139	3442	1.0
95651	LOTUS	017	813	934	981	1.5	75	316	360	378	1.4	2.59	246	277	1.3
95652	MCCLELLAN	067	1015	1245	1344	2.2	85	274	344	377	2.5	2.96	220	269	2.2
95653	MADISON	113	891	1001	1060	1.3	70	160	181	196	1.3	3.99	127	141	1.1
95655	MATHER	067	914	3206	4130	14.5	99	369	1291	1665	14.5	2.48	220	754	14.2
95658	NEWCASTLE	061	5707	6219	6570	0.9	58	2177	2498	2668	1.5	2.49	1659	1860	1.2
95659	NICOLAUS	101	747	806	836	0.8	54	276	293	302	0.6	2.75	199	209	0.5
95660	NORTH HIGHLANDS	067	31167	31304	31723	0.0	9	10279	10244	10373	0.0	3.04	7586	7458	-0.2
95661	ROSEVILLE	061	25248	28308	30211	1.2	68	9709	11767	12812	2.1	2.34	6653	7583	1.4
95662	ORANGEVALE	067	31894	32578	33579	0.2	18	11649	11859	12214	0.2	2.71	8589	8637	0.1
95663	PENRYN	061	2089	2130	2210	0.2	18	763	812	852	0.7	2.62	606	633	0.5
95664	PILOT HILL	017	1154	1179	1178	0.2	18	411	418	419	0.2	2.82	331	333	0.1
95665	PINE GROVE	005	3840	4415	4699	1.5	75	1545	1801	1926	1.7	2.41	1156	1346	1.7
95666	PIONEER	005	5881	6387	6557	0.9	58	2599	2854	2941	1.0	2.24	1872	2056	1.0
95667	PLACERVILLE	017	34246	37018	37964	0.8	54	13444	14450	14843	0.8	2.52	9500	10075	0.6
95668	PLEASANT GROVE	101	857	918	1006	0.7	50	320	338	371	0.6	2.72	247	260	0.6
95669	PLYMOUTH	005	2537	3034	3283	2.0	83	1014	1213	1314	2.0	2.50	731	875	2.0
95670	RANCHO CORDOVA	067	49713	54845	57659	1.1	64	18762	20768	21904	1.1	2.63	12708	13686	0.8
95672	RESCUE	017	4251	5813	6403	3.4	92	1434	1946	2145	3.4	2.99	1197	1660	3.6
95673	RIO LINDA	067	13933	14458	14855	0.4	30	4605	4751	4877	0.3	3.03	3520	3590	0.2
95674	RIO OSO	101	931	1026	1075	1.1	64	323	350	365	0.9	2.93	242	261	0.8
95677	ROCKLIN	061	21457	23651	26124	1.1	64	8208	9404	10434	1.5	2.50	5905	6561	1.1
95678	ROSEVILLE	061	30597	43045	48779	3.8	93	11771	16389	18526	3.6	2.62	7944	11438	4.0
95679	RUMSEY	113	17	19	21	1.2	68	11	13	14	1.8	1.46	7	6	-1.7
95681	SHERIDAN	061	1206	1420	1582	1.8	80	402	492	550	2.2	2.89	324	389	2.0
95682	SHINGLE SPRINGS	017	24787	27524	29068	1.1	64	9089	10069	10652	1.1	2.73	7110	7762	1.0
95683	SLOUGHHOUSE	067	4812	5980	6623	2.4	87	1969	2446	2712	2.4	2.40	1573	1930	2.2
	CALIFORNIA					1.2					1.0	2.93			1.1
	UNITED STATES					1.0					1.1	2.59			0.9

#	POST OFFICE NAME	RACE (%) White 2000	White 2009	Black 2000	Black 2009	Asian/Pacific 2000	Asian/Pacific 2009	% Hispanic Origin 2000	% Hispanic Origin 2009	2009 AGE DISTRIBUTION (%) 0-4	5-9	10-14	15-19	20-24	25-44	45-64	65-84	85+	18+	MEDIAN AGE 2009	% 2009 Males	% 2009 Females
95526	BRIDGEVILLE	87.0	84.1	0.8	0.8	0.6	0.7	1.5	2.1	3.4	5.5	8.9	7.7	3.3	21.3	37.9	11.8	0.3	77.0	45.0	50.1	49.9
95527	BURNT RANCH	87.7	84.7	0.3	0.3	0.6	0.5	1.8	2.7	3.8	5.6	5.9	5.9	3.0	22.3	38.7	14.8	0.0	80.9	46.6	50.0	50.0
95528	CARLOTTA	90.0	86.9	1.1	1.3	0.2	0.3	3.7	5.2	4.9	5.2	8.5	9.0	4.6	21.1	35.9	9.4	1.5	75.1	42.9	51.2	48.8
95531	CRESCENT CITY	80.0	76.6	4.9	5.1	2.6	3.3	13.7	17.9	5.6	5.6	5.9	6.6	7.1	30.7	26.2	10.6	1.7	78.7	37.0	55.7	44.3
95536	FERNDALE	92.0	89.2	0.3	0.3	0.5	0.6	7.4	10.2	5.8	6.1	6.5	6.2	4.8	22.7	31.3	14.7	1.9	77.8	43.3	49.4	50.6
95540	FORTUNA	88.4	85.1	0.4	0.4	1.1	1.4	9.8	13.1	6.6	6.3	6.6	7.3	6.1	22.6	27.8	13.6	3.1	76.2	40.8	48.2	51.8
95542	GARBERVILLE	92.0	89.5	1.3	1.5	0.8	1.2	4.5	6.2	5.0	5.0	5.5	5.6	5.9	24.3	35.9	11.6	1.2	80.9	44.0	51.9	48.1
95543	GASQUET	86.6	82.2	0.5	0.5	0.5	0.6	4.2	6.0	5.7	5.9	7.9	9.6	2.6	21.5	33.6	12.5	0.7	73.5	42.8	52.0	48.0
95546	HOOPA	15.7	14.5	0.1	0.2	0.4	0.5	4.4	5.3	10.0	10.5	9.4	9.4	6.5	23.6	21.7	7.7	1.2	63.6	28.1	49.0	51.0
95547	HYDESVILLE	90.1	87.2	0.1	0.1	0.2	0.2	6.3	8.7	5.4	6.4	7.1	7.8	4.4	22.5	33.8	11.4	1.3	76.3	42.8	50.8	49.2
95548	KLAMATH	63.2	60.3	2.2	2.6	0.6	0.8	9.0	12.0	4.5	5.3	5.0	5.2	6.6	23.4	31.8	16.3	1.9	81.6	45.0	54.4	45.6
95549	KNEELAND	91.5	88.9	0.5	0.7	0.5	0.7	3.4	4.4	4.4	4.6	5.6	7.3	5.1	22.5	37.3	11.9	1.5	80.6	45.4	50.4	49.6
95550	KORBEL	91.3	88.9	0.5	0.5	1.0	1.0	2.6	3.8	3.8	5.8	5.3	8.2	4.8	23.1	38.0	9.6	1.4	80.3	44.3	50.5	49.5
95551	LOLETA	81.8	78.7	0.2	0.1	0.5	0.7	16.0	21.3	7.9	7.3	6.7	6.4	6.9	26.4	26.6	10.3	1.6	74.2	34.9	49.3	50.7
95552	MAD RIVER	88.2	89.5	0.0	0.0	0.0	0.0	0.0	0.0	0.0	0.0	10.5	10.5	0.0	21.1	47.4	10.5	0.0	84.2	48.8	52.6	47.4
95554	MYERS FLAT	89.2	85.8	1.1	1.2	0.7	0.9	4.7	6.4	4.8	5.1	6.7	7.2	5.0	24.7	35.6	9.4	1.4	78.5	42.8	51.7	48.3
95555	ORICK	86.0	82.9	0.4	0.4	0.2	0.2	4.4	6.0	4.0	4.2	4.9	6.7	4.0	20.9	40.7	12.9	1.8	82.4	47.5	50.9	49.1
95556	ORLEANS	64.6	61.1	0.2	0.2	0.6	0.6	3.3	4.1	6.8	5.8	7.6	6.8	4.7	19.6	34.8	11.7	2.1	74.7	43.8	49.0	51.0
95558	PETROLIA	90.4	87.5	0.4	0.3	0.4	0.3	8.2	10.8	5.4	5.8	6.4	6.1	5.1	23.1	33.6	13.2	1.4	78.3	43.6	51.5	48.5
95560	REDWAY	89.9	86.9	1.1	1.1	0.6	0.7	4.2	5.7	4.6	5.2	6.8	7.0	4.8	24.3	36.3	9.8	1.3	78.8	43.3	51.2	48.8
95562	RIO DELL	85.7	81.5	0.2	0.2	0.4	0.5	10.8	14.6	6.9	6.8	6.6	6.8	6.2	24.9	28.0	12.0	1.8	75.5	37.7	50.5	49.5
95563	SALYER	82.8	79.5	0.0	0.0	0.1	0.1	2.3	3.3	3.8	4.2	5.2	6.4	3.9	17.6	39.4	17.5	1.9	82.9	49.8	51.4	48.6
95564	SAMOA	85.0	80.8	0.8	1.0	1.0	1.3	6.1	8.3	4.9	4.4	4.4	6.7	10.4	30.8	29.0	8.0	1.3	82.6	35.6	51.6	48.4
95565	SCOTIA	90.4	87.6	0.2	0.2	1.2	1.5	7.3	10.0	9.0	9.8	9.3	6.9	5.5	29.5	23.5	5.6	0.7	67.0	30.9	52.6	47.4
95567	SMITH RIVER	71.1	65.8	0.1	0.1	1.9	2.2	24.0	30.6	6.8	6.1	5.6	6.7	4.8	19.4	32.1	16.1	2.4	77.3	45.4	49.4	50.6
95568	SOMES BAR	79.4	75.8	0.3	0.3	0.6	0.6	4.4	6.4	3.2	4.8	8.6	6.4	2.9	18.5	43.0	11.5	1.3	78.7	47.4	53.5	46.5
95569	REDCREST	87.5	84.2	1.1	1.3	0.9	1.1	5.9	8.1	5.6	6.0	7.1	7.5	5.7	27.0	31.0	8.7	1.4	76.4	39.2	51.5	48.5
95570	TRINIDAD	87.1	84.1	0.3	0.4	0.6	0.9	4.1	5.5	3.9	4.1	4.6	5.1	4.4	24.0	38.8	13.3	1.7	84.1	47.3	49.7	50.3
95573	WILLOW CREEK	81.7	78.1	0.6	0.6	0.9	1.1	5.4	7.2	4.6	5.0	5.3	4.7	3.9	18.7	37.5	18.1	2.1	82.3	50.3	49.6	50.4
95585	LEGGETT	85.1	80.9	1.4	1.6	1.9	2.3	6.4	9.0	4.6	5.5	6.2	7.1	5.1	22.8	36.4	11.3	0.9	78.6	43.6	53.0	47.0
95587	PIERCY	85.8	80.8	1.2	1.7	1.5	2.3	6.2	8.6	4.3	5.2	6.0	6.9	5.2	22.3	37.8	11.2	1.1	79.7	45.1	54.2	45.8
95589	WHITETHORN	92.6	89.9	0.4	0.5	0.7	0.9	3.3	4.5	4.5	4.5	5.4	5.5	4.0	19.4	42.9	12.7	0.9	81.9	47.7	52.1	47.9
95595	ZENIA	88.4	86.2	0.2	0.2	0.9	1.0	2.9	3.8	3.6	5.1	8.9	6.5	1.8	20.9	41.9	10.1	1.2	77.9	46.1	53.4	46.6
95602	AUBURN	92.9	90.7	0.5	0.5	1.3	1.6	5.6	7.9	4.6	5.1	6.0	6.8	5.0	19.0	33.1	16.9	3.6	80.4	47.2	49.1	50.9
95603	AUBURN	92.7	90.2	0.5	0.4	1.6	1.9	6.5	9.5	5.0	5.3	5.9	6.5	5.3	21.3	31.6	15.5	3.6	79.6	45.4	47.4	52.6
95605	WEST SACRAMENTO	58.8	50.9	3.1	3.0	7.8	8.8	38.1	46.6	7.7	8.4	8.6	9.0	8.0	24.5	21.5	11.0	1.4	69.7	31.7	49.9	50.1
95606	BROOKS	81.2	73.9	1.8	1.6	1.1	1.6	16.7	22.8	5.9	5.9	5.9	5.5	5.2	23.1	32.2	14.3	2.0	79.2	43.8	50.2	49.8
95607	CAPAY	75.3	67.6	2.2	2.3	2.2	2.9	20.2	27.5	5.4	5.7	6.3	6.0	4.3	23.5	31.2	15.5	2.0	78.8	44.0	50.7	49.3
95608	CARMICHAEL	86.1	81.0	2.9	3.4	4.0	5.4	7.0	10.1	5.2	5.2	5.5	6.1	6.5	24.3	28.5	15.4	3.5	80.5	42.9	47.0	53.0
95610	CITRUS HEIGHTS	84.2	78.6	2.8	3.3	3.3	4.5	10.6	14.8	7.1	6.6	6.3	6.8	7.3	29.6	24.7	9.7	1.8	76.0	34.7	48.9	51.1
95612	CLARKSBURG	72.6	66.4	0.7	0.7	5.1	5.6	42.3	51.8	6.6	7.0	7.9	7.6	4.4	23.5	29.8	11.5	1.7	73.5	39.8	50.5	49.5
95614	COOL	95.1	93.1	0.2	0.3	1.0	1.4	4.8	6.9	4.8	6.3	7.4	7.7	3.5	19.7	35.1	14.0	1.4	75.9	45.3	49.3	50.7
95615	COURTLAND	59.0	50.8	0.8	0.9	6.8	7.7	44.5	54.1	5.3	5.9	6.5	7.0	5.1	24.5	30.9	12.7	2.1	77.7	41.6	55.3	44.7
95616	DAVIS	68.2	60.1	2.4	2.5	19.6	24.1	9.9	13.1	3.5	3.5	3.4	17.1	24.5	24.9	16.0	5.7	1.3	87.1	24.6	47.0	53.0
95618	DAVIS	71.8	63.7	2.2	2.3	15.0	19.0	11.2	15.0	6.9	6.7	6.5	7.4	15.5	29.5	21.3	5.4	0.6	76.2	28.9	49.0	51.0
95619	DIAMOND SPRINGS	91.3	88.3	0.1	0.1	0.7	0.9	7.3	10.4	5.1	5.6	5.9	6.8	5.2	21.9	31.0	15.2	3.4	78.9	44.7	47.5	52.5
95620	DIXON	70.5	63.3	1.8	1.8	3.3	4.0	34.3	42.7	8.5	8.4	8.2	7.7	6.2	29.3	23.7	7.1	0.9	70.1	32.5	50.2	49.8
95621	CITRUS HEIGHTS	85.0	79.7	2.9	3.4	3.1	4.2	9.5	13.5	6.8	6.4	6.3	6.5	6.3	28.0	24.5	12.5	2.7	76.6	37.2	47.7	52.3
95623	EL DORADO	93.0	90.4	0.2	0.3	0.8	1.0	5.9	8.4	4.5	5.5	6.3	6.6	4.2	20.7	35.2	15.1	1.9	79.1	46.2	48.8	51.2
95624	ELK GROVE	71.2	62.7	5.0	5.5	10.9	14.9	12.7	16.6	7.4	7.5	7.7	7.3	5.0	27.3	28.4	8.5	1.1	72.7	36.9	48.7	51.3
95626	ELVERTA	81.4	75.3	2.3	2.5	3.4	4.4	12.2	17.0	6.0	6.1	6.5	8.0	7.1	25.5	30.0	9.9	1.1	76.5	37.2	49.2	50.8
95627	ESPARTO	66.3	57.7	0.8	0.7	1.9	2.2	37.1	46.8	6.9	7.8	8.6	8.2	6.2	24.0	25.2	11.4	1.7	71.5	35.8	50.9	49.1
95628	FAIR OAKS	88.2	83.6	1.7	2.1	4.1	5.6	6.4	9.3	5.3	5.6	6.1	6.3	5.1	24.7	30.8	14.1	2.0	79.0	42.9	48.7	51.3
95629	FIDDLETOWN	94.1	91.6	0.2	0.3	0.5	0.7	5.2	7.8	3.7	4.6	5.3	5.5	3.4	17.1	41.5	17.7	1.4	82.6	50.5	49.9	50.1
95630	FOLSOM	77.9	73.2	6.0	5.1	7.4	11.1	9.5	12.0	7.4	7.4	7.3	6.2	5.0	32.9	26.0	6.6	1.1	74.0	36.4	53.3	46.7
95631	FORESTHILL	92.9	90.5	0.5	0.5	0.7	0.8	4.9	7.1	4.4	4.9	6.0	7.5	5.7	21.8	35.2	13.0	1.6	80.2	44.8	50.5	49.5
95632	GALT	73.0	65.8	1.2	1.4	2.7	3.5	30.2	38.1	8.5	8.6	8.4	8.4	6.0	27.7	23.1	8.3	1.1	69.1	32.7	49.7	50.3
95633	GARDEN VALLEY	94.0	91.6	0.7	0.7	0.6	0.8	4.8	6.8	4.5	5.4	6.7	6.8	3.8	21.6	36.0	13.6	1.6	79.0	45.6	51.5	48.5
95634	GEORGETOWN	93.6	91.5	1.2	1.3	0.7	0.9	4.3	6.1	4.1	5.3	6.3	6.7	3.8	20.0	37.1	14.9	1.8	80.1	47.0	52.1	47.9
95635	GREENWOOD	92.4	90.0	2.1	2.4	0.7	1.0	5.1	7.4	4.8	5.5	7.3	7.3	4.1	22.1	35.3	12.0	1.7	78.3	44.4	54.0	46.0
95636	GRIZZLY FLATS	91.9	89.4	0.3	0.4	0.5	0.5	5.7	8.1	5.2	6.0	5.4	5.2	2.5	22.3	38.6	13.7	1.1	79.3	46.7	52.7	47.3
95637	GUINDA	79.0	72.4	1.9	1.7	1.5	1.7	17.6	24.5	5.5	5.5	6.2	5.9	4.8	23.4	31.7	14.8	2.1	79.3	43.9	50.7	49.3
95638	HERALD	90.0	85.9	0.6	0.8	2.2	3.1	10.5	15.4	5.7	6.8	8.0	7.7	4.1	21.8	33.4	11.6	1.0	74.3	42.2	50.7	49.3
95640	IONE	66.4	62.2	13.3	13.6	1.8	2.0	17.2	21.3	4.2	4.2	4.4	11.0	7.2	36.1	24.5	7.5	0.9	80.9	36.1	68.4	31.6
95641	ISLETON	76.7	70.2	1.4	1.5	6.2	7.6	24.1	31.2	4.4	4.6	5.0	5.7	4.3	19.8	38.0	15.4	2.7	82.2	48.6	53.6	46.4
95642	JACKSON	92.7	89.9	0.4	0.6	0.7	1.0	6.2	8.9	4.6	4.9	5.4	5.9	4.0	18.1	33.1	19.3	4.7	81.1	49.6	47.5	52.5
95645	KNIGHTS LANDING	60.3	53.2	1.1	0.9	1.7	1.8	52.4	62.2	7.5	7.0	6.3	7.6	7.2	26.6	25.3	11.2	1.2	74.8	35.3	54.6	45.4
95648	LINCOLN	81.6	81.2	0.5	0.9	1.5	3.4	21.3	17.9	8.6	8.4	8.0	7.2	4.9	28.4	25.5	8.1	1.0	70.5	35.5	49.1	50.9
95650	LOOMIS	90.2	87.2	0.4	0.4	3.1	3.6	6.3	9.1	5.3	5.7	6.5	7.0	5.1	21.0	33.3	14.2	1.9	77.9	44.5	49.5	50.5
95651	LOTUS	94.5	92.4	0.5	0.5	0.9	1.2	3.7	5.4	4.8	5.1	7.5	8.0	4.2	20.2	36.7	11.9	1.5	77.8	45.1	51.1	48.9
95652	MCCLELLAN	59.5	52.3	17.4	17.8	7.8	9.1	16.4	22.5	11.0	8.7	7.6	7.2	18.1	29.8	13.2	4.2	0.3	70.5	24.3	54.5	45.5
95653	MADISON	47.7	41.0	0.7	0.6	0.8	0.8	67.5	75.7	10.2	10.4	7.4	9.7	7.3	24.9	21.9	7.4	0.9	66.7	29.6	50.1	49.9
95655	MATHER	44.0	34.9	12.9	12.8	9.0	10.1	15.2	18.5	8.6	8.5	8.0	8.5	8.6	27.3	22.3	7.2	1.0	69.8	30.3	47.1	52.9
95658	NEWCASTLE	91.4	88.6	0.2	0.3	2.4	2.7	5.1	7.3	4.5	5.3	6.3	6.8	4.1	18.4	35.5	17.0	2.2	79.6	47.6	48.9	51.1
95659	NICOLAUS	86.2	81.5	0.1	0.1	2.0	2.4	15.0	21.2	4.3	5.0	5.7	6.5	4.2	22.5	34.1	16.0	1.7	80.9	46.1	54.3	45.7
95660	NORTH HIGHLANDS	66.0	58.3	12.0	13.0	6.0	7.3	16.6	21.9	8.9	8.4	7.7	8.2	8.4	25.9	21.3	10.0	1.2	70.1	30.5	48.9	51.1
95661	ROSEVILLE	88.5	85.1	1.3	1.2	3.9	4.9	7.9	11.4	6.2	6.0	6.1	6.4	6.9	26.5	27.4	11.2	3.3	77.6	38.9	47.3	52.7
95662	ORANGEVALE	89.4	85.1	1.2	1.5	2.9	3.9	6.8	10.0	5.7	5.9	6.5	7.5	6.3	25.8	30.1	10.6	1.6	77.2	39.5	49.2	50.8
95663	PENRYN	90.7	87.7	0.2	0.2	3.0	3.4	6.4	9.2	4.8	5.4	6.6	6.9	4.5	19.0	35.4	15.3	2.2	78.7	46.5	49.4	50.6
95664	PILOT HILL	92.9	90.2	0.2	0.3	1.9	2.5	5.9	8.4	4.0	7.5	7.6	7.5	2.9	22.4	38.4	9.2	0.5	75.7	44.1	51.7	48.3
95665	PINE GROVE	91.9	88.2	0.5	0.8	1.4	1.9	6.5	9.7	3.8	4.9	5.5	7.4	3.5	15.6	37.6	19.6	2.1	81.5	50.3	51.6	48.4
95666	PIONEER	95.1	92.9	0.2	0.3	0.5	0.8	5.2	7.5	3.5	3.9	4.5	5.0	3.4	14.7	38.1	24.6	2.5	85.0	54.1	49.8	50.2
95667	PLACERVILLE	91.6	88.6	0.4	0.4	0.9	1.2	7.7	10.8	4.8	5.5	6.3	6.6	4.9	21.4	33.3	14.5	2.7	79.1	45.3	49.1	50.9
95668	PLEASANT GROVE	85.1	79.8	1.2	1.2	1.4	1.6	12.7	17.9	5.6	6.1	6.5	6.5	4.8	23.7	31.0	13.9	1.7	77.8	42.7	52.2	47.8
95669	PLYMOUTH	91.6	88.0	0.2	0.4	1.0	1.5	6.2	9.2	4.9	5.6	5.9	5.8	4.4	20.6	35.6	15.3	1.8	79.7	46.5	49.1	50.9
95670	RANCHO CORDOVA	70.8	62.7	8.8	9.8	9.1	12.1	11.4	15.4	7.9	7.2	6.7	7.0	8.1	27.9	23.9	10.1	1.3	74.0	33.8	49.0	51.0
95672	RESCUE	92.5	90.2	0.3	0.4	1.4	1.6	5.1	7.3	5.2	6.3	7.8	7.9	4.0	19.8	36.3	11.3	1.2	75.7	44.2	50.5	49.5
95673	RIO LINDA	82.4	76.1	2.2	2.6	3.3	4.4	11.3	16.0	6.8	6.6	6.7	8.1	7.4	25.7	27.7	9.9	1.2	75.0	35.8	49.2	50.8
95674	RIO OSO	83.6	78.3	0.0	0.0	3.2	4.0	19.3	26.7	4.8	6.3	8.7	8.4	5.8	22.1	27.8	14.5	1.7	75.0	41.3	50.7	49.3
95677	ROCKLIN	89.0	85.8	0.8	0.7	3.8	4.3	7.9	11.2	6.8	7.0	7.2	7.2	5.9	27.5	27.0	9.9	1.5	74.7	37.2	48.4	51.6
95678	ROSEVILLE	82.7	78.7	1.3	1.4	4.1	5.7	17.9	20.8	8.4	8.0	7.6	6.6	5.5	31.4	23.9	7.4	1.2	71.8	35.0	49.2	50.8
95679	RUMSEY	75.0	57.9	0.0	5.3	0.0	5.3	25.0	26.3	5.3	10.5	10.5	10.5	0.0	31.6	31.6	0.0	0.0	63.2	36.3	52.6	47.4
95681	SHERIDAN	85.2	79.6	0.4	0.4	1.0	1.0	13.1	19.5	5.4	6.5	7.3	8.2	5.0	23.4	31.3	11.5	1.5	75.6	41.0	49.8	50.2
95682	SHINGLE SPRINGS	92.5	89.7	0.6	0.7	1.6	2.1	6.4	9.1	5.9	6.3	7.0	7.3	5.4	23.4	31.3	11.7	1.7	76.1	41.1	48.6	51.4
95683	SLOUGHHOUSE	88.5	84.7	2.6	3.0	3.3	4.5	6.3	8.7	4.9	5.8	6.8	7.3	2.4	17.6	33.8	19.3	2.1	77.5	48.1	49.5	50.5
	CALIFORNIA	59.5	54.5	6.7	6.2	11.3	12.5	32.4	38.3	7.5	7.1	6.9	7.5	7.4	28.5	24.2	9.3	1.6	74.1	34.3	49.9	50.1
	UNITED STATES	75.1	72.0	12.3	12.7	3.8	4.6	12.5	15.7	6.8	6.7	6.6	7.1	6.9	27.0	26.0	10.9	1.9	75.7	36.9	49.2	50.8

ZIP CODE #	POST OFFICE NAME	2009 Per Capita Income	2009 HH Income Base	2009 HOUSEHOLD INCOME DISTRIBUTION (%) Less than $25,000	$25,000 to $49,999	$50,000 to $99,999	$100,000 to $149,999	$150,000 or More	MEDIAN HOUSEHOLD INCOME 2009	2014	2009 National Centile	2009 State Centile	2009 Home Value Base	2009 HOME VALUE DISTRIBUTION (%) Less than $50,000	$50,000 to $89,999	$90,000 to $174,999	$175,000 to $399,999	$400,000 or More	2009 Median Home Value
95526	BRIDGEVILLE	16717	311	39.9	29.3	28.0	2.9	0.0	30666	31572	9	7	203	9.9	10.8	39.4	33.0	6.9	157328
95527	BURNT RANCH	20699	177	32.8	35.6	23.7	6.2	1.7	33191	34387	14	11	121	3.3	9.1	43.8	40.5	3.3	165132
95528	CARLOTTA	19269	349	27.5	28.7	37.0	4.9	2.0	43940	47239	45	30	245	3.3	4.5	22.0	60.0	10.2	236538
95531	CRESCENT CITY	18448	8110	36.1	26.5	28.8	6.8	1.8	36115	38667	21	15	5062	10.1	6.0	25.4	47.4	11.0	198195
95536	FERNDALE	25133	1210	20.2	34.1	33.8	6.3	5.6	45609	48608	50	34	740	1.8	2.3	12.2	52.3	31.5	315951
95540	FORTUNA	20548	5380	30.1	30.9	31.5	4.2	3.2	39415	42531	31	21	3414	2.9	5.4	14.9	63.9	12.8	238664
95542	GARBERVILLE	24766	1057	30.8	26.7	36.1	2.8	3.5	42317	45808	40	26	674	2.5	3.0	8.6	50.7	35.2	329577
95543	GASQUET	15916	411	43.8	26.5	26.8	2.9	0.0	27655	29080	5	4	275	13.1	18.9	11.6	48.0	8.4	203646
95546	HOOPA	11968	1083	48.7	25.5	21.3	3.3	1.2	25821	26986	4	3	769	19.4	11.4	29.8	32.9	6.5	143750
95547	HYDESVILLE	21086	482	23.2	29.5	36.5	8.3	2.5	47165	50000	55	37	382	6.5	1.0	17.0	44.2	31.2	286000
95548	KLAMATH	22188	463	32.4	27.0	29.8	3.2	7.6	39422	40875	31	21	338	15.4	10.1	46.7	15.7	12.1	139912
95549	KNEELAND	24487	146	15.8	26.7	40.4	10.3	6.8	58220	60726	75	56	111	1.8	0.0	9.9	56.8	31.5	329310
95550	KORBEL	27038	81	18.5	27.2	35.8	9.9	8.6	53911	58537	69	50	56	0.0	3.6	12.5	48.2	35.7	333333
95551	LOLETA	19972	541	31.1	34.0	26.2	5.5	3.1	38683	40719	29	19	318	9.7	0.0	16.7	55.3	18.2	236607
95552	MAD RIVER	10132	7	71.4	0.0	28.6	0.0	0.0	15855	15855	1	2	5	0.0	0.0	100.0	0.0	0.0	162500
95554	MYERS FLAT	18970	1308	40.8	31.3	22.8	2.5	2.5	31281	33498	10	8	845	3.6	6.6	18.8	49.5	21.5	243990
95555	ORICK	17703	185	40.5	27.6	25.4	4.3	2.2	33099	35554	13	11	109	14.7	8.3	22.0	23.9	31.2	212500
95556	ORLEANS	15137	204	41.2	30.9	23.0	4.9	0.0	31457	32143	10	8	129	20.9	26.4	24.8	21.7	6.2	95833
95558	PETROLIA	27115	133	21.8	40.6	24.8	6.8	6.0	40600	42325	35	22	82	2.4	2.4	19.5	37.8	37.8	300000
95560	REDWAY	21107	251	40.6	31.9	21.9	2.0	3.6	30798	32340	9	7	162	5.6	8.0	14.8	51.9	19.8	243182
95562	RIO DELL	15953	1243	34.2	34.6	29.2	1.0	1.0	35384	38406	19	14	714	2.8	2.7	39.1	49.9	5.6	184198
95563	SALYER	16278	420	35.0	46.2	13.8	4.3	0.7	28130	28473	6	5	292	12.3	2.4	28.1	46.2	11.0	191406
95564	SAMOA	18337	157	29.3	35.0	28.7	6.4	0.6	36266	37906	21	16	60	5.0	8.3	38.3	43.3	5.0	172917
95565	SCOTIA	15394	368	19.8	42.9	33.4	2.7	1.1	42726	44196	42	28	121	6.6	8.3	26.4	33.1	25.6	205769
95567	SMITH RIVER	17235	875	34.5	33.3	24.6	4.8	2.9	37154	37970	24	17	606	13.4	7.8	28.7	35.6	14.5	175641
95568	SOMES BAR	20625	147	43.5	23.1	25.9	4.1	3.4	28187	28360	6	5	100	5.0	6.0	36.0	41.0	12.0	182500
95569	REDCREST	15790	261	35.6	33.3	27.6	3.1	0.4	35868	38037	20	15	146	2.7	6.2	27.4	42.5	21.2	212500
95570	TRINIDAD	25363	1179	29.9	29.7	28.3	8.3	3.8	40035	43539	33	21	769	6.4	2.6	10.8	41.9	38.4	335612
95573	WILLOW CREEK	21316	746	35.3	26.4	31.0	4.6	2.8	34334	40604	16	13	493	9.7	6.9	29.0	44.6	9.7	188110
95585	LEGGETT	13954	158	48.7	27.2	19.6	3.8	0.6	25523	26926	4	3	94	13.8	6.4	33.0	27.7	19.1	165625
95587	PIERCY	18345	158	46.8	27.2	21.5	3.8	0.6	26463	27478	4	3	95	10.5	5.3	30.5	27.4	26.3	203571
95589	WHITETHORN	23412	377	28.1	31.6	33.2	4.8	2.4	43399	46049	44	29	284	1.4	3.2	6.0	45.1	44.4	374194
95595	ZENIA	16853	210	46.2	21.4	26.7	3.8	1.9	27139	27412	5	4	138	10.9	10.1	28.3	34.8	15.9	178125
95602	AUBURN	31926	7026	14.4	26.4	34.4	15.2	9.5	60751	62267	78	59	5126	1.7	6.0	2.9	43.8	45.6	380370
95603	AUBURN	31998	11327	18.4	24.0	34.7	15.7	7.3	58612	60142	76	56	7083	6.6	3.6	6.5	54.8	28.5	288153
95605	WEST SACRAMENTO	13417	4582	39.0	32.7	24.7	2.8	0.8	32191	33683	12	9	1846	9.4	5.1	64.0	21.4	0.0	135452
95606	BROOKS	29112	130	20.8	24.6	32.3	17.7	4.6	57207	58583	74	55	92	1.1	4.3	5.4	43.5	45.7	381818
95607	CAPAY	26236	138	24.6	23.2	34.1	13.8	4.3	53405	56562	69	49	93	3.2	2.2	5.4	37.6	51.6	410714
95608	CARMICHAEL	30744	24863	17.7	26.5	36.6	12.0	7.1	56001	58485	73	53	13211	0.5	0.4	15.0	66.1	17.9	242027
95610	CITRUS HEIGHTS	24920	17285	16.6	27.6	41.3	10.9	3.6	55360	57872	72	52	8384	3.0	1.3	19.2	74.7	1.8	209466
95612	CLARKSBURG	23157	484	28.1	24.2	28.1	11.8	7.9	48033	49341	57	39	256	3.1	0.0	17.6	37.1	42.2	341176
95614	COOL	32807	1449	6.3	16.1	39.7	28.1	9.8	77086	79597	91	78	1274	0.5	0.0	4.7	73.3	21.5	284716
95615	COURTLAND	18339	271	26.6	31.4	32.5	7.0	2.6	41833	44218	39	25	157	7.6	0.0	26.1	42.0	24.2	264773
95616	DAVIS	28003	17739	33.1	21.6	23.9	11.2	10.2	42918	45786	42	28	6145	2.1	0.1	2.4	48.2	47.3	389399
95618	DAVIS	38218	9636	15.0	20.0	29.3	17.6	18.0	75105	76041	89	76	5377	5.1	1.5	4.2	47.1	42.0	358900
95619	DIAMOND SPRINGS	22101	1486	20.5	31.9	34.6	9.8	3.2	48505	49781	58	40	1158	3.1	5.8	26.2	59.4	5.5	203750
95620	DIXON	24964	6158	10.9	20.8	42.3	18.6	7.4	69258	72284	86	71	4162	1.9	1.0	18.2	73.1	5.8	214595
95621	CITRUS HEIGHTS	23789	17330	17.4	30.4	42.6	7.5	2.0	51689	53521	65	45	10070	7.3	5.0	37.0	50.3	0.5	175865
95623	EL DORADO	26828	1924	15.4	30.4	38.7	10.2	5.2	55298	60712	72	52	1562	3.8	2.6	15.0	59.3	19.2	241143
95624	ELK GROVE	30980	18705	6.9	13.6	42.6	22.7	14.2	82002	83358	93	82	15647	0.8	1.5	9.6	65.5	22.5	261369
95626	ELVERTA	20701	2077	14.4	26.3	40.4	15.6	3.3	56650	58693	74	54	1669	2.0	0.4	49.9	41.8	5.9	169612
95627	ESPARTO	19690	964	22.2	26.2	43.0	6.6	1.9	51259	53895	64	44	667	10.6	1.2	23.8	48.0	16.3	197738
95628	FAIR OAKS	35266	16531	11.0	19.7	40.2	17.3	11.8	72298	72560	88	73	10937	0.3	0.4	12.0	64.2	23.1	265976
95629	FIDDLETOWN	28031	431	21.8	24.1	37.1	12.3	4.6	54162	56135	70	50	354	2.3	2.5	11.9	47.7	35.6	322727
95630	FOLSOM	40437	24889	8.4	12.6	33.3	22.7	22.9	92111	96655	95	88	18510	2.1	1.8	2.9	60.6	32.6	346068
95631	FORESTHILL	26427	2494	17.6	27.5	38.7	11.5	4.7	55650	55522	72	53	1950	8.6	3.2	7.7	71.9	8.5	239840
95632	GALT	20160	9002	15.1	28.1	42.6	11.2	3.1	57350	60977	74	55	6864	4.0	2.4	23.9	64.5	5.2	198012
95633	GARDEN VALLEY	25457	1145	14.7	23.8	41.5	15.4	4.6	61487	64416	79	61	981	2.4	1.0	12.9	71.7	11.9	231334
95634	GEORGETOWN	23110	1044	19.3	28.8	40.4	8.6	2.8	51801	55771	66	45	837	2.5	0.6	21.0	67.4	8.5	224167
95635	GREENWOOD	23788	400	21.5	24.8	41.8	8.5	3.5	52679	54958	67	47	321	1.2	0.0	15.0	73.5	10.3	231186
95636	GRIZZLY FLATS	24314	294	20.1	31.0	37.1	7.8	4.1	49131	51240	59	41	246	0.0	0.0	33.7	50.4	15.9	206122
95637	GUINDA	26727	115	22.6	24.3	33.9	15.7	3.5	54620	58386	71	51	80	2.5	3.8	5.0	41.3	47.5	389474
95638	HERALD	28081	645	6.2	20.5	42.3	24.2	6.8	79491	80029	92	80	531	3.0	2.8	8.9	57.4	27.9	286141
95640	IONE	22659	2591	20.9	27.1	35.5	12.4	4.2	52043	53801	66	46	1860	6.7	1.4	7.6	64.6	19.8	267462
95641	ISLETON	24645	901	27.4	28.5	33.7	5.9	4.4	41925	45209	39	26	608	31.4	8.4	27.0	24.5	8.7	127232
95642	JACKSON	31094	3125	23.1	26.3	32.9	10.6	7.1	50609	52845	63	43	2109	3.8	5.0	11.6	54.1	25.6	284280
95645	KNIGHTS LANDING	16542	676	25.1	32.7	36.5	4.4	1.2	43519	45261	44	30	361	11.6	8.0	32.1	38.2	10.0	167935
95648	LINCOLN	38052	18226	10.2	14.6	35.8	21.3	18.1	82587	93238	93	82	15197	0.9	0.4	10.8	60.1	27.8	277328
95650	LOOMIS	39823	4438	10.7	20.3	30.6	20.7	17.7	79744	83344	92	80	3570	5.0	0.6	5.8	45.9	42.7	350286
95651	LOTUS	29412	360	12.5	24.4	36.9	20.0	6.1	64088	67074	82	65	297	0.3	1.3	9.4	67.0	21.9	263587
95652	MCCLELLAN	14477	344	34.0	43.6	18.3	4.1	0.0	39371	40023	31	20	142	0.7	5.6	47.9	33.8	12.0	164286
95653	MADISON	14592	181	35.9	27.6	27.1	7.7	1.7	41280	41662	37	24	121	10.7	0.0	42.1	32.2	14.9	171983
95655	MATHER	4826	1291	85.7	14.3	0.0	0.0	0.0	8965	9059	0	1	1033	0.0	1.5	35.7	53.9	7.8	193984
95658	NEWCASTLE	37865	2498	11.8	18.6	35.7	22.1	11.7	72907	76144	88	74	2094	6.4	2.4	3.4	33.5	54.2	427532
95659	NICOLAUS	25626	293	20.5	27.6	30.7	11.9	9.2	53114	59242	68	48	200	6.5	7.0	17.0	41.0	28.5	261111
95660	NORTH HIGHLANDS	15338	10244	28.0	33.4	34.0	3.6	1.1	40887	43000	36	23	5625	10.9	2.8	72.6	13.4	0.3	133007
95661	ROSEVILLE	37008	11767	13.5	18.6	37.2	20.4	10.3	71636	75766	88	72	7163	0.8	1.2	5.4	66.7	25.9	298287
95662	ORANGEVALE	28407	11859	10.8	21.9	46.4	14.6	6.2	66834	68132	85	68	8188	3.4	2.2	15.3	68.4	10.7	219267
95663	PENRYN	34847	812	10.7	17.6	38.3	23.0	10.3	75387	79325	90	76	673	1.5	1.0	4.6	42.9	49.9	399635
95664	PILOT HILL	34782	418	5.0	13.6	40.4	29.4	11.5	75984	81377	90	76	372	1.9	0.0	6.5	57.8	33.9	340000
95665	PINE GROVE	30770	1801	16.4	24.3	42.6	9.6	7.1	59235	60716	76	57	1486	3.4	0.7	4.7	61.1	30.1	331797
95666	PIONEER	25880	2854	20.5	32.0	35.7	8.9	2.9	47989	49515	57	39	2369	3.3	3.0	8.6	67.1	18.1	271436
95667	PLACERVILLE	27888	14450	19.2	23.5	33.8	17.8	5.6	60075	62967	77	58	10463	3.9	2.5	12.4	62.2	19.0	246314
95668	PLEASANT GROVE	24584	338	20.1	26.0	37.3	10.9	5.6	55529	60297	72	52	249	3.6	4.0	14.1	48.2	30.1	266346
95669	PLYMOUTH	26520	1213	24.6	24.6	34.7	10.6	5.4	50728	52604	63	44	937	2.2	6.4	16.4	38.1	36.8	285855
95670	RANCHO CORDOVA	27325	20768	17.3	25.5	38.4	11.9	6.9	58246	60509	75	56	9979	3.2	2.8	34.8	46.5	12.7	191245
95672	RESCUE	43364	1946	4.8	7.2	30.6	33.4	23.9	108059	110095	98	93	1724	0.5	0.9	3.7	49.1	45.8	383673
95673	RIO LINDA	20074	4751	18.2	28.5	41.7	9.3	2.3	53236	55566	68	48	3312	0.7	4.1	53.3	40.3	1.6	164606
95674	RIO OSO	18223	350	24.6	28.0	38.9	7.7	0.9	47067	49281	54	37	239	0.0	4.2	18.0	45.6	32.2	246023
95677	ROCKLIN	34493	9404	12.9	22.5	34.0	18.7	11.8	69878	75530	87	71	5964	5.2	1.2	5.3	67.7	20.6	274759
95678	ROSEVILLE	32325	16389	12.3	19.4	35.9	23.0	9.4	71334	78720	88	72	10375	0.6	1.9	13.3	65.8	18.3	252836
95679	RUMSEY	35921	13	30.8	23.1	30.8	15.4	0.0	37321	45000	25	17	9	0.0	0.0	0.0	44.4	55.6	450000
95681	SHERIDAN	25324	492	15.9	29.5	34.8	14.2	5.7	54123	54347	70	50	384	2.6	0.3	20.3	31.0	45.8	358974
95682	SHINGLE SPRINGS	34419	10069	10.3	15.4	38.5	26.2	9.7	77283	80246	91	78	7547	3.5	2.1	5.6	61.6	27.3	299191
95683	SLOUGHHOUSE	47353	2446	7.6	11.2	37.0	21.9	22.3	89292	95250	95	87	2115	0.0	0.9	7.0	52.2	39.8	353254
	CALIFORNIA	28199		18.5	22.2	33.9	14.0	11.5	61614	64088				3.3	2.6	13.6	41.0	39.5	321752
	UNITED STATES	27277		20.9	24.4	35.3	11.7	7.6	54719	56938				9.3	13.1	31.6	32.6	13.5	162279

ZIP CODE		FINANCIAL SERVICES				THE HOME						ENTERTAINMENT						PERSONAL			
						Home Improvements		Furnishings													
#	POST OFFICE NAME	Auto Loan	Home Loan	Invest-ments	Retire-ment Plans	Home Repair	Lawn & Garden	Comput-ers & Hard-ware-Personal	Major Appli-ances	TV, Radio, Sound Equip-ment	Furni-ture	Dine out/ Carry out	Sports Equip-ment	Fees & Tickets	Toys & Games	Travel	Cable TV	Apparel & Services	Auto Repairs	Health Insur-ance	Pets & Supplies
95526	BRIDGEVILLE	63	53	80	51	58	68	52	65	55	51	54	46	47	52	57	58	36	61	66	75
95527	BURNT RANCH	73	58	94	57	64	77	58	74	61	54	60	54	50	58	63	65	40	68	73	86
95528	CARLOTTA	82	66	106	65	72	87	66	84	69	62	68	61	57	65	71	73	45	77	83	97
95531	CRESCENT CITY	72	64	74	63	65	74	65	71	68	63	67	53	60	67	65	71	46	69	74	84
95536	FERNDALE	104	77	108	78	81	108	85	99	88	73	87	79	68	87	84	94	57	95	106	121
95540	FORTUNA	78	66	78	66	67	81	70	77	73	65	72	59	63	73	69	78	49	75	82	91
95542	GARBERVILLE	93	73	101	73	77	97	78	91	81	70	80	70	66	79	78	86	53	87	95	109
95543	GASQUET	60	48	77	47	53	63	48	61	50	45	50	45	42	48	52	54	33	56	60	71
95546	HOOPA	57	46	43	47	42	53	50	49	55	49	54	39	46	55	45	57	37	52	55	63
95547	HYDESVILLE	92	74	119	73	81	97	74	94	77	69	76	68	64	73	80	82	51	87	93	109
95548	KLAMATH	78	74	95	68	83	89	71	83	75	76	73	55	70	68	77	79	49	80	93	95
95549	KNEELAND	97	105	124	106	110	107	96	106	93	99	93	80	100	91	106	93	66	100	99	121
95550	KORBEL	93	106	109	109	109	105	95	101	93	99	94	75	103	93	103	93	66	96	98	116
95551	LOLETA	64	72	71	71	72	69	70	69	69	68	70	55	74	69	73	69	50	70	69	81
95552	MAD RIVER	40	39	49	35	43	46	37	43	39	40	38	28	36	35	40	41	25	42	48	49
95554	MYERS FLAT	69	55	88	54	60	73	56	70	58	52	57	52	48	55	60	62	38	65	70	82
95555	ORICK	71	57	92	56	63	75	57	73	60	54	59	53	50	57	62	64	39	67	72	84
95556	ORLEANS	68	49	70	47	51	69	50	64	56	47	55	48	40	55	50	61	36	58	66	76
95558	PETROLIA	104	72	115	72	75	110	80	99	83	65	82	82	58	81	79	90	53	92	105	122
95560	REDWAY	73	58	94	57	64	78	59	74	61	55	61	55	51	58	63	65	40	69	74	86
95562	RIO DELL	68	50	63	50	51	68	57	64	61	50	59	50	46	60	53	66	40	62	70	77
95563	SALYER	61	49	79	48	54	65	49	62	51	46	51	46	43	49	53	55	34	58	62	72
95564	SAMOA	65	56	48	57	53	58	68	59	68	61	67	48	61	69	59	69	47	65	64	73
95565	SCOTIA	73	65	67	68	67	78	65	74	67	58	66	56	59	68	65	71	45	68	76	86
95567	SMITH RIVER	67	65	71	59	68	67	63	69	63	68	63	47	61	60	65	64	43	67	70	77
95568	SOMES BAR	73	59	95	58	65	78	59	75	62	55	61	55	51	58	64	66	40	69	74	87
95569	REDCREST	66	54	78	54	58	70	54	67	57	49	56	50	47	55	57	60	37	62	67	78
95570	TRINIDAD	82	77	110	76	84	87	75	87	74	74	73	66	72	70	82	75	51	82	82	100
95573	WILLOW CREEK	79	63	102	62	69	83	63	80	66	59	65	59	55	63	68	70	43	74	79	93
95585	LEGGETT	66	46	73	45	48	70	51	63	53	41	52	52	37	52	50	57	34	59	66	77
95587	PIERCY	70	49	78	49	52	74	54	67	56	44	55	55	40	55	54	61	36	62	70	82
95589	WHITETHORN	83	65	105	64	71	87	66	84	69	61	68	62	56	66	71	74	45	77	83	97
95595	ZENIA	64	55	81	53	61	70	54	66	57	54	56	46	50	53	59	60	37	62	69	76
95602	AUBURN	108	123	143	123	132	126	111	120	110	119	109	86	122	106	124	110	78	116	120	136
95603	AUBURN	99	108	115	108	112	108	103	106	102	104	102	79	109	100	109	103	72	105	107	122
95605	WEST SACRAMENTO	58	53	49	50	52	48	60	56	58	60	59	43	55	58	56	56	42	59	53	63
95606	BROOKS	95	102	128	103	111	102	100	105	92	101	92	85	101	89	109	88	66	100	95	120
95607	CAPAY	109	88	128	88	93	115	93	108	92	82	91	89	78	90	96	96	62	102	109	130
95608	CARMICHAEL	93	104	108	105	107	100	102	100	100	103	101	76	109	98	107	100	72	101	102	115
95610	CITRUS HEIGHTS	89	89	85	90	88	82	93	86	90	93	92	68	93	92	91	88	65	90	84	101
95612	CLARKSBURG	125	86	137	86	90	131	95	118	99	78	98	98	70	97	95	108	64	110	125	146
95614	COOL	120	145	153	149	150	140	125	133	120	132	121	99	140	119	140	119	87	126	126	153
95615	COURTLAND	97	67	106	67	70	102	74	92	77	60	76	76	54	76	74	84	49	86	97	113
95616	DAVIS	98	76	79	83	76	75	117	86	105	101	106	77	97	104	93	100	76	99	84	106
95618	DAVIS	143	137	142	145	140	126	161	138	147	155	148	117	153	148	149	140	107	146	128	163
95619	DIAMOND SPRINGS	81	88	92	87	90	97	80	89	83	79	83	63	85	82	86	88	57	85	96	102
95620	DIXON	117	128	116	120	126	109	118	119	110	124	112	93	119	114	120	105	80	114	104	133
95621	CITRUS HEIGHTS	80	84	81	83	84	82	83	82	83	83	83	61	85	83	84	84	59	83	85	95
95623	EL DORADO	102	95	127	94	101	113	90	107	93	87	92	78	87	89	98	98	63	100	108	123
95624	ELK GROVE	136	161	148	161	158	143	140	143	133	149	136	111	153	138	148	129	97	136	131	163
95626	ELVERTA	93	107	106	102	107	99	94	98	92	96	93	73	100	94	100	91	66	94	93	111
95627	ESPARTO	81	86	83	78	88	72	84	85	76	89	77	65	81	76	85	70	55	82	71	92
95628	FAIR OAKS	114	142	149	142	147	130	127	129	120	132	121	98	142	120	140	117	88	125	121	146
95629	FIDDLETOWN	104	92	139	90	102	116	88	109	93	88	91	76	83	86	98	98	61	102	113	126
95630	FOLSOM	160	186	172	190	184	161	164	164	153	178	155	133	179	161	171	144	113	155	143	186
95631	FORESTHILL	96	101	96	102	99	102	92	98	92	92	92	75	95	94	96	93	64	94	97	115
95632	GALT	95	102	93	95	101	87	95	97	88	101	90	74	94	91	96	83	63	93	84	107
95633	GARDEN VALLEY	103	103	126	104	107	113	95	108	95	94	95	81	95	93	103	97	65	102	105	125
95634	GEORGETOWN	97	78	126	77	86	103	78	99	82	73	81	73	68	78	85	87	54	92	98	115
95635	GREENWOOD	101	81	130	79	88	106	81	102	84	76	83	75	70	80	87	90	55	95	101	119
95636	GRIZZLY FLATS	100	80	130	79	88	106	80	102	84	75	83	75	70	80	87	90	55	94	101	118
95637	GUINDA	101	95	128	96	102	108	96	106	92	92	91	87	90	89	102	92	63	101	101	125
95638	HERALD	112	138	133	140	138	126	117	122	111	124	113	94	132	113	129	108	81	115	112	140
95640	IONE	98	94	93	93	94	99	89	96	91	90	91	71	87	93	90	93	62	93	96	113
95641	ISLETON	85	78	102	73	86	96	76	90	80	79	78	61	72	74	82	85	52	86	99	103
95642	JACKSON	105	97	129	96	104	115	95	110	99	95	98	78	93	94	102	103	67	105	114	127
95645	KNIGHTS LANDING	77	70	66	64	70	66	71	73	69	74	70	55	64	71	67	68	49	72	67	82
95648	LINCOLN	149	164	161	165	163	148	148	153	140	156	142	122	156	145	154	134	102	144	135	173
95650	LOOMIS	142	167	175	170	174	162	149	157	144	157	144	117	165	143	164	142	103	150	151	178
95651	LOTUS	113	114	145	115	120	126	104	120	104	105	104	89	105	101	115	106	72	112	116	139
95652	MCCLELLAN	55	46	43	48	44	43	58	49	57	56	58	41	53	58	52	55	41	55	49	59
95653	MADISON	73	72	64	64	71	61	72	71	67	76	69	54	67	69	69	64	49	71	63	79
95655	MATHER	12	10	10	11	9	10	17	13	19	13	20	9	15	17	14	21	16	15	15	16
95658	NEWCASTLE	123	151	154	153	156	147	130	138	127	136	127	101	147	126	145	127	91	131	136	157
95659	NICOLAUS	126	87	138	87	91	133	96	120	100	78	99	99	71	98	96	109	64	112	126	147
95660	NORTH HIGHLANDS	65	63	57	62	61	58	68	63	67	67	68	49	66	67	65	66	48	66	62	74
95661	ROSEVILLE	120	127	127	129	128	120	126	121	122	127	123	95	130	124	128	121	88	123	119	141
95662	ORANGEVALE	101	121	120	119	123	112	109	110	105	110	106	84	120	107	117	105	77	108	106	125
95663	PENRYN	122	144	148	147	148	142	126	134	124	133	124	98	140	122	139	124	88	128	132	154
95664	PILOT HILL	129	160	164	164	164	152	136	144	130	145	132	107	155	130	153	128	94	136	136	165
95665	PINE GROVE	116	103	155	101	115	130	98	122	103	100	102	84	94	96	110	109	69	114	126	140
95666	PIONEER	92	79	122	78	88	101	77	96	81	76	79	67	72	75	85	85	53	89	98	110
95667	PLACERVILLE	101	103	116	105	107	110	98	106	98	98	98	78	99	97	104	100	68	102	107	123
95668	PLEASANT GROVE	117	86	128	84	90	121	89	112	96	81	94	86	72	94	90	104	62	103	115	133
95669	PLYMOUTH	106	94	124	92	99	111	90	107	93	89	92	78	83	91	95	97	62	100	105	124
95670	RANCHO CORDOVA	98	97	95	98	97	91	105	96	102	103	104	76	105	103	102	100	74	102	95	112
95672	RESCUE	169	213	219	220	219	199	180	189	171	193	173	143	207	171	202	167	125	178	176	216
95673	RIO LINDA	76	95	91	91	94	87	86	85	83	85	84	65	95	84	92	84	61	85	84	97
95674	RIO OSO	96	66	105	66	69	101	73	91	76	59	75	75	53	74	73	83	49	85	96	112
95677	ROCKLIN	121	131	126	132	131	118	126	123	119	131	120	97	130	122	128	114	86	121	113	142
95678	ROSEVILLE	115	130	119	131	128	115	122	118	116	126	118	95	130	120	125	112	85	117	110	136
95679	RUMSEY	92	66	103	66	69	97	72	88	74	60	73	73	55	73	73	80	48	83	92	108
95681	SHERIDAN	112	106	115	108	105	122	102	113	102	95	102	90	96	103	105	105	69	107	114	135
95682	SHINGLE SPRINGS	124	148	149	150	150	136	133	134	127	139	128	103	147	128	144	124	92	131	127	154
95683	SLOUGHHOUSE	144	187	230	192	208	180	160	174	149	175	147	128	189	143	190	144	109	161	158	192
	CALIFORNIA	112	119	122	118	122	107	121	116	114	124	116	92	124	114	124	110	84	118	107	132
	UNITED STATES	100	100	100	100	100	100	100	100	100	100	100	100	100	100	100	100	100	100	100	100

ZIP CODE			POPULATION			2000-2009 ANNUAL RATE		HOUSEHOLDS					FAMILIES		
#	POST OFFICE NAME	COUNTY FIPS CODE	2000	2009	2014	% Rate	State Centile	2000	2009	2014	% Annual Rate 2000-2009	2009 Average HH Size	2000	2009	% Annual Rate 2000-2009
95684	SOMERSET	017	3089	3544	3732	1.5	75	1176	1344	1416	1.5	2.64	917	1035	1.3
95685	SUTTER CREEK	005	4411	5447	5974	2.3	86	1880	2333	2560	2.4	2.33	1273	1573	2.3
95687	VACAVILLE	095	63236	67166	68717	0.7	50	19315	20684	21203	0.7	2.81	14088	15045	0.7
95688	VACAVILLE	095	32548	34215	34912	0.5	39	11299	11787	11999	0.5	2.89	8866	9262	0.5
95689	VOLCANO	005	1375	1561	1641	1.4	72	579	666	703	1.5	2.34	438	503	1.5
95690	WALNUT GROVE	067	2384	2643	2922	1.1	64	859	936	1024	0.9	2.76	582	623	0.7
95691	WEST SACRAMENTO	113	19020	32420	38440	5.9	96	7334	12479	14786	5.9	2.58	4765	8436	6.4
95692	WHEATLAND	115	3566	4482	5112	2.5	88	1225	1515	1722	2.3	2.96	934	1149	2.3
95693	WILTON	067	5883	7199	7875	2.2	85	1943	2375	2596	2.2	3.01	1631	1979	2.1
95694	WINTERS	113	8502	9330	9975	1.0	62	2686	2976	3183	1.1	3.10	2148	2353	1.0
95695	WOODLAND	113	38185	39641	41443	0.4	30	13571	14258	14958	0.5	2.71	9671	10008	0.4
95698	ZAMORA	113	246	276	299	1.3	70	86	99	107	1.5	2.79	64	73	1.4
95701	ALTA	061	839	1039	1146	2.3	86	308	400	445	2.9	2.59	220	272	2.3
95703	APPLEGATE	061	1242	1507	1662	2.1	84	455	575	643	2.6	2.60	336	414	2.3
95709	CAMINO	017	4928	5335	5475	0.9	58	1966	2118	2177	0.8	2.52	1413	1501	0.7
95713	COLFAX	061	8764	10773	11823	2.3	86	3376	4328	4801	2.7	2.47	2464	3067	2.4
95714	DUTCH FLAT	061	553	682	757	2.3	86	230	296	332	2.8	2.29	164	201	2.2
95715	EMIGRANT GAP	061	38	47	52	2.3	86	12	16	17	3.2	2.94	9	11	2.2
95717	GOLD RUN	061	182	219	239	2.0	83	75	93	103	2.4	2.35	55	65	1.8
95720	KYBURZ	017	183	200	206	1.0	62	86	94	96	1.0	2.11	49	51	0.4
95721	ECHO LAKE	017	60	66	68	1.0	62	5	5	6	0.0	2.60	3	3	0.0
95722	MEADOW VISTA	061	3600	4222	4539	1.7	78	1317	1607	1746	2.2	2.61	1057	1266	2.0
95724	NORDEN	061	134	160	173	1.9	81	63	78	85	2.3	2.05	42	50	1.9
95726	POLLOCK PINES	017	8511	9257	9495	0.9	58	3311	3578	3674	0.8	2.59	2487	2657	0.7
95728	SODA SPRINGS	057	95	106	111	1.2	68	38	43	45	1.3	2.47	22	25	1.4
95742	RANCHO CORDOVA	067	156	4980	6627	45.4	100	80	2459	3249	44.8	2.02	43	1537	47.2
95746	GRANITE BAY	061	20748	23134	24309	1.2	68	6828	7998	8499	1.7	2.89	5893	6684	1.4
95747	ROSEVILLE	061	25453	45105	55331	6.4	97	9908	17300	21147	6.2	2.61	7637	13364	6.2
95757	ELK GROVE	067	2895	32333	42320	29.8	100	608	10859	14256	36.6	2.87	450	8138	36.7
95758	ELK GROVE	067	44349	58850	67271	3.1	91	14879	19844	22712	3.2	2.96	11853	15570	3.0
95762	EL DORADO HILLS	017	21483	34648	39778	5.3	96	7067	11907	13796	5.8	2.91	6225	10388	5.7
95765	ROCKLIN	061	15454	29236	36255	7.1	97	5232	10334	12880	7.6	2.83	4247	8054	7.2
95776	WOODLAND	113	15391	24390	28490	5.1	96	4558	6458	7444	3.8	3.71	3668	5156	3.7
95811	SACRAMENTO	067	6215	6567	6869	0.6	45	3106	3332	3523	0.8	1.67	757	763	0.1
95814	SACRAMENTO	067	9666	10139	10433	0.5	39	5122	5448	5664	0.7	1.43	997	997	0.0
95815	SACRAMENTO	067	25575	26040	26451	0.2	18	9237	9219	9327	0.0	2.81	5431	5319	-0.2
95816	SACRAMENTO	067	16199	16345	16582	0.1	13	9464	9525	9664	0.1	1.66	2589	2513	-0.3
95817	SACRAMENTO	067	15167	15563	15946	0.3	23	6047	6244	6425	0.3	2.44	3115	3122	0.0
95818	SACRAMENTO	067	21676	21777	22098	0.1	13	10113	10137	10280	0.0	2.13	5051	4940	-0.2
95819	SACRAMENTO	067	16025	16171	16383	0.1	13	7588	7630	7729	0.1	2.01	3767	3689	-0.2
95820	SACRAMENTO	067	37058	37810	38470	0.2	18	12674	12778	12978	0.1	2.93	8213	8133	-0.1
95821	SACRAMENTO	067	34648	35241	35851	0.2	18	15309	15395	15628	0.1	2.26	8568	8432	-0.2
95822	SACRAMENTO	067	46272	48252	49750	0.5	39	16520	17027	17486	0.3	2.80	11161	11331	0.2
95823	SACRAMENTO	067	72493	76322	78904	0.6	45	22494	23189	23871	0.3	3.25	16944	17287	0.2
95824	SACRAMENTO	067	30242	32287	33315	0.7	50	8749	9109	9357	0.4	3.51	6574	6769	0.3
95825	SACRAMENTO	067	29608	30342	30939	0.3	23	14860	15107	15397	0.2	1.95	5829	5749	-0.1
95826	SACRAMENTO	067	38320	39149	39904	0.2	18	15739	15998	16292	0.2	2.39	9067	9047	0.0
95827	SACRAMENTO	067	19990	20739	21335	0.4	30	7279	7507	7712	0.3	2.67	4788	4843	0.1
95828	SACRAMENTO	067	54950	59457	61833	0.9	58	16686	17817	18495	0.7	3.32	13126	13857	0.6
95829	SACRAMENTO	067	11364	21641	26032	7.2	97	3662	6957	8359	7.2	3.10	3031	5813	7.3
95830	SACRAMENTO	067	553	755	913	3.4	92	185	247	299	3.2	3.04	157	210	3.2
95831	SACRAMENTO	067	41566	43078	44312	0.4	30	17413	18027	18551	0.4	2.36	11241	11416	0.2
95832	SACRAMENTO	067	8691	11954	13547	3.5	92	1975	2732	3112	3.6	4.27	1657	2272	3.5
95833	SACRAMENTO	067	31510	34712	36372	1.1	64	12200	13453	14138	1.1	2.57	7309	7844	0.8
95834	SACRAMENTO	067	8348	20615	24924	10.3	98	3190	8938	10971	11.8	2.30	1999	5399	11.3
95835	SACRAMENTO	067	878	38156	50453	50.3	100	295	13109	17322	50.7	2.91	220	9333	50.0
95836	SACRAMENTO	067	40	42	44	0.5	39	17	18	18	0.6	2.33	13	13	0.0
95837	SACRAMENTO	067	254	328	418	2.8	90	110	148	190	3.3	2.22	72	91	2.6
95838	SACRAMENTO	067	34879	37776	39338	0.9	58	10190	10843	11267	0.7	3.45	7561	7949	0.5
95841	SACRAMENTO	067	20838	21077	21424	0.1	13	8639	8688	8826	0.1	2.39	5144	5069	-0.2
95842	SACRAMENTO	067	31161	31739	32368	0.2	18	11445	11574	11782	0.1	2.74	7913	7883	0.0
95843	ANTELOPE	067	36492	42706	45971	1.7	78	11679	13541	14549	1.6	3.15	9359	10748	1.5
95864	SACRAMENTO	067	24592	24801	25157	0.1	13	10498	10539	10676	0.0	2.35	6882	6786	-0.2
95901	MARYSVILLE	115	28485	33145	36530	1.7	78	10061	11485	12586	1.4	2.83	6828	7799	1.4
95903	BEALE AFB	115	5399	4255	4234	-2.5	0	1590	1254	1254	-2.5	3.06	1423	1120	-2.6
95910	ALLEGHANY	091	89	85	84	-0.5	1	36	36	36	0.0	2.36	20	20	0.0
95912	ARBUCKLE	011	4444	5514	6107	2.4	87	1349	1640	1810	2.1	3.36	1062	1289	2.1
95914	BANGOR	007	276	290	297	0.5	39	115	124	128	0.8	2.34	80	86	0.8
95915	BELDEN	063	27	27	27	0.0	9	16	17	17	0.7	1.59	10	10	0.0
95916	BERRY CREEK	007	1284	1469	1553	1.5	75	538	633	675	1.8	2.32	363	426	1.7
95917	BIGGS	007	3097	3333	3445	0.8	54	1034	1131	1173	1.0	2.94	800	873	0.9
95918	BROWNS VALLEY	115	1710	2044	2231	1.9	81	672	806	883	2.0	2.54	499	597	2.0
95919	BROWNSVILLE	115	1063	1242	1347	1.7	78	478	561	611	1.7	2.19	317	368	1.6
95920	BUTTE CITY	021	306	338	355	1.1	64	104	114	119	1.0	2.96	78	85	0.9
95922	CAMPTONVILLE	091	628	701	745	1.2	68	293	329	350	1.3	2.13	172	191	1.1
95923	CANYON DAM	063	28	26	25	-0.8	1	17	17	16	0.0	1.53	13	9	-3.9
95925	CHALLENGE	115	341	397	429	1.7	78	139	162	176	1.7	2.42	88	102	1.6
95926	CHICO	007	35314	37435	38069	0.6	45	14265	15079	15395	0.6	2.32	7217	7615	0.6
95928	CHICO	007	33131	37434	39067	1.3	70	12734	14639	15361	1.5	2.46	6706	7814	1.7
95932	COLUSA	011	7351	7935	8203	0.8	54	2636	2802	2887	0.7	2.81	1897	2012	0.6
95934	CRESCENT MILLS	063	225	228	224	0.1	13	100	106	105	0.6	2.15	62	66	0.7
95935	DOBBINS	115	1113	1301	1409	1.7	78	482	565	615	1.7	2.29	323	376	1.7
95936	DOWNIEVILLE	091	191	182	178	-0.5	1	94	93	92	-0.1	1.96	56	56	0.0
95937	DUNNIGAN	113	1207	1388	1543	1.5	75	409	476	531	1.7	2.92	316	363	1.5
95938	DURHAM	007	3536	3792	3931	0.8	54	1287	1420	1481	1.1	2.66	969	1066	1.0
95939	ELK CREEK	021	360	387	396	0.8	54	102	110	113	0.8	2.93	74	80	0.8
95941	FORBESTOWN	007	696	736	759	0.6	45	314	338	350	0.8	2.18	191	205	0.8
95942	FOREST RANCH	007	1324	1368	1449	0.4	30	544	594	635	1.0	2.26	380	416	1.0
95943	GLENN	021	971	1016	1033	0.5	39	330	342	347	0.4	2.85	238	247	0.4
95944	GOODYEARS BAR	091	137	129	126	-0.6	1	67	66	64	-0.2	1.95	38	37	-0.3
95945	GRASS VALLEY	057	23806	25744	26160	0.8	54	10114	11009	11221	0.9	2.30	6338	6922	1.0
95946	PENN VALLEY	057	8662	9295	9516	0.8	54	3585	3870	3970	0.8	2.40	2763	2981	0.8
95947	GREENVILLE	063	2243	2341	2319	0.5	39	937	1022	1017	0.9	2.27	625	684	1.0
95948	GRIDLEY	007	9814	11141	11695	1.4	72	3336	3832	4034	1.5	2.85	2474	2831	1.5
95949	GRASS VALLEY	057	18776	20186	20561	0.8	54	7376	7995	8164	0.9	2.52	5644	6130	0.9
	CALIFORNIA					1.2					1.0	2.93			1.1
	UNITED STATES					1.0					1.1	2.59			0.9

#	POST OFFICE NAME	RACE (%) White 2000	White 2009	Black 2000	Black 2009	Asian/Pacific 2000	Asian/Pacific 2009	% Hispanic Origin 2000	% Hispanic Origin 2009	2009 AGE DISTRIBUTION (%) 0-4	5-9	10-14	15-19	20-24	25-44	45-64	65-84	85+	18+	MEDIAN AGE 2009	% 2009 Males	% 2009 Females
95684	SOMERSET	93.5	91.1	0.3	0.3	0.5	0.6	4.9	7.0	4.5	5.5	6.3	6.6	3.3	19.7	38.4	14.6	1.0	79.3	47.0	50.6	49.4
95685	SUTTER CREEK	92.3	88.9	0.2	0.3	1.1	1.5	5.9	8.8	4.4	4.6	5.2	5.7	4.7	18.4	35.9	18.3	2.9	82.1	49.5	47.8	52.2
95687	VACAVILLE	69.7	63.8	12.3	12.7	5.0	6.3	16.5	21.2	6.3	6.2	6.1	6.5	7.3	33.7	24.7	8.0	1.2	77.3	34.9	55.6	44.4
95688	VACAVILLE	79.6	74.5	4.0	4.2	3.5	4.6	19.5	24.6	7.3	7.3	7.4	7.2	5.5	26.9	28.0	9.3	1.2	73.5	37.0	49.0	51.0
95689	VOLCANO	95.7	93.7	0.2	0.4	0.4	0.6	3.7	5.6	3.1	3.5	4.3	5.2	3.1	13.0	41.1	25.2	1.5	85.7	54.9	49.1	50.9
95690	WALNUT GROVE	64.8	58.1	1.2	1.2	8.0	9.0	39.4	47.9	6.0	6.3	6.6	6.8	5.7	24.1	26.8	15.7	2.1	76.9	41.2	52.4	47.6
95691	WEST SACRAMENTO	69.2	68.3	2.2	1.6	7.8	8.4	24.4	27.7	6.9	7.1	7.4	7.4	5.3	24.8	28.9	10.6	1.5	74.1	38.7	49.0	51.0
95692	WHEATLAND	77.1	70.1	0.8	1.0	4.4	5.2	19.0	25.0	7.1	7.5	9.1	8.6	6.0	23.7	25.3	11.4	1.3	70.7	35.9	48.8	51.2
95693	WILTON	84.1	78.0	2.0	2.4	2.6	3.6	10.9	15.5	4.7	6.1	7.2	7.4	4.2	20.4	36.0	12.7	1.3	77.2	45.0	50.2	49.8
95694	WINTERS	71.1	63.9	0.8	0.8	1.6	1.7	42.6	52.6	7.7	7.7	7.4	8.8	8.3	26.0	25.2	7.7	1.2	72.0	32.0	50.7	49.3
95695	WOODLAND	69.8	62.9	1.2	1.2	3.3	3.7	35.7	44.3	7.2	6.9	6.7	7.7	7.6	26.4	24.8	10.2	2.5	74.5	35.1	49.2	50.8
95698	ZAMORA	71.1	63.4	4.5	4.7	3.3	4.0	28.9	37.3	6.2	6.2	6.2	6.9	6.5	27.5	29.0	10.1	1.4	77.2	37.5	53.3	46.7
95701	ALTA	94.9	92.8	0.1	0.1	0.6	0.7	4.1	6.0	4.7	6.6	6.5	7.2	4.8	22.4	32.6	14.0	1.1	77.3	43.7	52.2	47.8
95703	APPLEGATE	92.7	90.2	0.2	0.2	1.0	1.1	5.9	8.5	3.8	5.2	5.8	6.8	3.8	19.6	36.0	16.4	2.5	81.0	47.4	50.0	50.0
95709	CAMINO	91.5	88.3	0.2	0.3	1.0	1.3	8.2	11.5	5.0	6.1	6.7	6.3	3.7	20.7	33.9	15.7	2.1	78.2	46.0	50.6	49.4
95713	COLFAX	92.9	90.5	0.5	0.4	1.0	1.1	5.6	8.1	4.6	5.6	6.6	7.1	4.4	21.3	35.4	13.2	1.8	78.5	45.2	49.8	50.2
95714	DUTCH FLAT	94.2	92.4	0.4	0.3	0.7	0.9	4.2	6.2	5.4	6.2	7.5	6.9	3.5	20.8	35.3	12.8	1.6	76.5	44.8	48.8	51.2
95715	EMIGRANT GAP	94.7	93.6	0.0	0.0	0.0	0.0	5.3	6.4	4.3	8.5	6.4	6.4	6.4	23.4	34.0	10.6	0.0	76.6	41.9	53.2	46.8
95717	GOLD RUN	95.0	93.6	0.0	0.0	0.6	0.5	5.0	6.8	5.5	6.4	7.8	6.8	3.2	23.7	32.4	12.3	1.8	75.3	43.0	51.1	48.9
95720	KYBURZ	83.0	76.5	0.5	0.5	1.1	1.5	12.1	17.0	3.5	5.5	4.0	4.0	4.5	21.0	42.0	13.0	2.5	84.5	48.8	55.5	44.5
95721	ECHO LAKE	86.9	84.8	3.3	3.0	3.3	3.0	6.6	9.1	3.0	3.0	3.0	9.1	9.1	18.2	34.8	16.7	3.0	90.9	48.0	56.1	43.9
95722	MEADOW VISTA	95.3	93.6	0.2	0.2	0.8	0.9	4.4	6.6	4.3	5.3	6.6	7.9	4.5	18.4	35.5	15.4	2.1	79.0	46.6	49.3	50.7
95724	NORDEN	94.0	91.9	0.0	0.0	0.7	0.6	3.7	5.0	3.8	6.3	5.6	6.9	5.0	23.1	36.9	11.9	0.6	80.0	44.6	53.1	46.9
95726	POLLOCK PINES	93.6	91.2	0.2	0.2	0.9	1.1	5.4	7.6	4.9	5.6	6.4	6.9	5.3	21.1	33.0	15.0	1.8	78.8	44.9	49.3	50.7
95728	SODA SPRINGS	94.6	91.5	0.0	0.0	0.0	0.9	3.2	3.8	2.8	3.8	5.7	6.6	4.7	23.6	46.2	6.6	0.0	84.9	45.8	54.7	45.3
95742	RANCHO CORDOVA	87.7	83.0	0.0	0.0	3.2	3.7	5.2	7.0	4.1	4.3	4.5	4.5	3.6	17.2	31.8	26.6	3.4	84.3	53.9	48.7	51.3
95746	GRANITE BAY	90.7	87.9	0.7	0.7	4.4	5.3	4.8	7.2	6.3	7.5	8.3	7.9	3.7	22.4	32.8	10.1	1.0	72.5	41.5	49.7	50.3
95747	ROSEVILLE	88.1	84.7	1.3	1.3	4.9	5.6	7.5	11.0	8.1	8.0	7.7	6.3	4.1	25.8	23.7	14.6	1.6	72.0	38.6	48.1	51.9
95757	ELK GROVE	60.0	50.6	16.6	10.8	6.1	18.6	23.5	19.8	10.0	9.5	8.4	6.2	3.7	35.7	22.1	4.1	0.4	68.2	33.8	51.1	48.9
95758	ELK GROVE	58.1	49.5	10.0	10.5	18.8	22.7	14.2	18.0	9.5	9.3	9.0	7.2	4.2	31.4	24.1	4.7	0.5	67.4	33.5	48.7	51.3
95762	EL DORADO HILLS	90.4	85.6	0.7	0.6	4.0	5.1	5.1	10.2	7.6	8.8	9.4	7.7	3.3	25.1	30.2	7.3	0.7	69.0	38.3	49.6	50.4
95765	ROCKLIN	88.0	84.3	1.1	0.9	5.0	6.0	7.5	10.4	9.1	8.8	8.4	6.9	4.4	32.0	24.4	5.6	0.5	69.3	33.8	49.0	51.0
95776	WOODLAND	60.3	54.6	1.6	1.9	5.4	7.2	45.6	49.7	9.9	9.1	8.2	7.3	6.9	31.9	20.3	5.5	0.9	68.4	30.2	50.0	50.0
95811	SACRAMENTO	58.4	52.1	14.0	14.6	12.1	13.5	17.9	22.8	4.3	3.6	3.1	4.0	9.0	43.0	25.1	6.9	1.0	87.0	35.6	54.8	45.2
95814	SACRAMENTO	63.9	58.0	13.7	14.4	7.7	9.3	20.6	25.6	2.3	1.8	1.8	3.6	9.1	37.4	26.0	13.8	4.3	92.9	41.1	58.3	41.7
95815	SACRAMENTO	53.7	46.7	9.3	9.4	11.4	12.8	30.2	36.5	9.1	8.0	7.0	7.7	9.5	28.0	21.4	7.9	1.2	71.4	29.9	50.3	49.7
95816	SACRAMENTO	78.2	71.9	5.0	5.7	4.1	5.3	14.3	19.5	3.4	2.9	2.4	3.0	9.2	41.4	25.3	9.2	3.2	89.8	37.6	48.7	51.3
95817	SACRAMENTO	45.4	41.2	23.3	22.2	9.6	10.6	24.4	29.3	8.2	7.5	6.8	7.2	8.6	28.6	22.6	8.8	1.8	73.2	32.5	48.3	51.7
95818	SACRAMENTO	60.7	54.5	8.7	8.7	17.5	20.1	14.2	18.1	6.0	5.4	5.1	5.1	6.6	30.0	28.8	10.3	2.7	80.4	39.6	47.1	52.9
95819	SACRAMENTO	87.6	83.0	1.8	2.1	3.5	4.7	8.7	12.6	4.4	4.3	4.5	6.7	7.0	27.6	29.8	11.7	4.0	84.4	42.4	46.2	53.8
95820	SACRAMENTO	47.5	41.9	12.0	11.4	11.8	12.8	36.1	42.5	8.5	8.1	7.9	8.2	7.7	27.6	22.0	8.3	1.8	70.6	31.4	48.5	51.5
95821	SACRAMENTO	76.9	70.5	6.8	7.6	4.5	5.7	12.6	17.2	6.8	6.1	5.4	6.0	7.5	25.9	25.8	13.6	3.0	78.3	39.0	47.7	52.3
95822	SACRAMENTO	38.9	33.3	19.5	18.8	21.2	23.8	23.5	27.6	7.2	7.1	7.1	8.1	7.3	24.3	23.6	12.6	2.7	73.6	35.4	47.7	52.3
95823	SACRAMENTO	31.6	26.9	25.7	24.7	21.6	23.6	23.8	27.7	9.7	8.8	7.9	8.7	9.1	27.7	19.7	7.3	1.1	68.4	28.3	48.5	51.5
95824	SACRAMENTO	34.9	29.9	10.9	10.2	27.1	28.8	33.9	38.6	10.7	9.5	8.4	9.1	8.9	27.4	17.8	7.0	1.1	65.8	26.9	50.3	49.7
95825	SACRAMENTO	67.7	60.4	9.2	9.9	7.8	9.7	16.3	21.3	6.0	4.6	3.8	5.2	12.4	33.0	21.1	10.5	3.5	83.4	33.0	47.7	52.3
95826	SACRAMENTO	67.7	60.2	9.0	9.8	10.8	13.5	13.4	17.7	6.1	5.5	5.2	7.0	9.5	33.0	22.4	9.9	1.4	79.6	33.9	49.8	50.2
95827	SACRAMENTO	62.9	55.0	13.2	14.2	11.1	13.6	12.5	16.5	7.3	6.6	6.5	7.7	7.6	29.1	23.6	10.2	1.4	74.4	34.2	48.9	51.1
95828	SACRAMENTO	41.1	34.6	16.0	15.7	25.4	28.6	18.0	21.6	8.1	8.0	8.1	8.8	7.1	27.4	22.9	8.4	1.2	70.2	31.8	48.8	51.2
95829	SACRAMENTO	66.5	60.3	6.0	6.3	16.0	19.1	12.9	16.5	7.6	7.8	8.1	7.8	5.2	27.2	28.8	6.6	0.7	71.1	36.2	49.3	50.7
95830	SACRAMENTO	75.9	68.6	3.3	4.2	10.8	14.3	13.4	17.2	6.0	7.0	9.5	7.7	3.4	23.4	31.9	10.1	0.9	72.1	40.9	51.3	48.7
95831	SACRAMENTO	49.3	41.3	11.4	11.9	29.9	34.9	10.4	12.9	5.0	4.8	5.2	5.9	6.2	25.6	30.8	14.0	2.4	81.3	42.9	46.9	53.1
95832	SACRAMENTO	20.0	16.6	23.4	22.8	34.2	34.6	22.9	26.5	9.3	9.9	9.9	12.6	9.1	23.6	18.0	6.9	0.7	62.9	24.6	49.3	50.7
95833	SACRAMENTO	52.4	47.0	14.2	13.6	9.4	10.6	29.7	34.9	7.7	7.1	6.6	7.2	9.0	32.1	23.1	6.4	0.7	74.4	31.6	48.9	51.1
95834	SACRAMENTO	44.0	54.2	19.9	11.1	12.5	14.0	28.7	21.9	7.2	6.6	6.3	6.8	7.3	27.9	24.8	11.3	1.8	75.8	35.9	47.9	52.1
95835	SACRAMENTO	69.6	62.0	4.8	5.0	8.8	10.8	18.9	24.9	9.5	8.4	7.7	6.6	5.2	34.0	22.4	5.6	0.6	70.3	32.4	49.2	50.8
95836	SACRAMENTO	82.5	76.2	0.0	0.0	2.5	2.4	15.0	21.4	4.8	4.8	4.8	4.8	4.8	28.6	35.7	11.9	0.0	81.0	43.8	50.0	50.0
95837	SACRAMENTO	83.0	76.2	1.2	1.2	4.0	5.5	12.6	17.7	5.5	5.5	5.5	5.2	4.6	26.5	32.9	12.2	2.1	80.2	43.2	49.7	50.3
95838	SACRAMENTO	41.8	36.0	22.6	22.4	17.7	19.8	19.1	23.4	9.7	9.5	9.0	9.7	8.2	26.0	20.2	6.8	0.9	65.7	27.4	48.8	51.2
95841	SACRAMENTO	77.5	70.9	6.7	7.6	5.7	7.3	10.1	14.1	7.8	7.2	6.3	6.6	8.5	28.4	22.6	10.7	1.9	74.9	33.5	47.3	52.7
95842	SACRAMENTO	70.3	63.1	11.3	12.5	5.5	6.9	13.5	18.1	9.1	8.0	7.3	7.7	8.4	29.7	21.7	7.4	0.8	71.2	30.4	48.4	51.6
95843	ANTELOPE	65.5	57.8	10.1	10.8	12.4	15.5	10.7	14.1	9.8	9.1	8.4	7.6	6.3	32.7	21.8	4.1	0.3	67.7	30.3	48.5	51.5
95864	SACRAMENTO	86.0	81.0	2.3	2.7	4.9	6.6	7.5	10.6	5.4	5.6	6.1	6.2	5.0	21.9	30.9	15.6	3.4	79.0	44.8	47.5	52.5
95901	MARYSVILLE	69.6	61.5	3.5	4.0	8.9	10.9	17.2	22.1	8.5	7.6	7.1	7.8	8.8	26.3	22.8	9.6	1.5	72.3	31.3	50.3	49.7
95903	BEALE AFB	71.7	65.0	10.6	12.5	5.8	6.5	11.1	14.4	13.6	11.5	7.7	6.3	19.9	38.5	2.3	0.1	0.1	64.1	22.7	54.1	45.9
95910	ALLEGHANY	93.3	91.8	0.0	0.0	0.0	0.0	3.3	4.7	3.5	4.7	5.9	7.1	1.2	20.0	40.0	15.3	2.4	81.2	49.1	51.8	48.2
95912	ARBUCKLE	59.1	53.6	0.2	0.2	1.4	1.4	57.8	65.9	9.1	9.2	8.2	8.4	7.7	26.8	21.5	8.1	1.0	68.5	29.5	51.4	48.6
95914	BANGOR	86.5	81.7	1.1	1.4	1.1	1.7	5.8	8.3	3.4	3.8	7.6	6.6	1.4	17.9	39.3	18.3	1.7	80.0	50.5	50.3	49.7
95915	BELDEN	92.6	88.9	0.0	0.0	0.0	0.0	7.4	7.4	7.4	3.7	7.4	7.4	7.4	22.2	29.6	14.8	0.0	74.1	41.3	48.1	51.9
95916	BERRY CREEK	83.8	78.8	0.5	0.5	0.7	0.9	5.1	7.0	3.7	4.4	5.4	6.2	3.9	16.1	38.3	20.2	1.9	82.6	50.8	51.6	48.4
95917	BIGGS	79.6	73.2	0.4	0.4	0.8	1.0	21.8	28.9	7.0	7.4	8.4	9.1	5.3	25.1	24.5	11.7	1.5	71.0	35.8	49.5	50.5
95918	BROWNS VALLEY	91.6	88.2	0.2	0.2	1.2	1.5	6.0	8.1	4.8	5.2	5.7	4.8	3.7	18.1	38.9	17.5	1.3	81.2	49.3	50.5	49.5
95919	BROWNSVILLE	88.2	84.4	0.9	1.3	1.0	1.3	4.1	5.6	3.9	4.7	5.0	4.5	4.0	16.8	36.8	21.8	2.4	83.3	51.9	48.7	51.3
95920	BUTTE CITY	72.0	66.0	0.0	0.0	0.3	0.3	42.3	52.1	9.8	8.9	9.2	8.0	6.8	24.3	23.4	8.3	1.5	66.6	30.4	53.6	46.4
95922	CAMPTONVILLE	90.3	87.2	0.0	0.0	0.5	0.6	4.1	5.8	4.3	5.0	5.6	5.4	3.1	19.4	38.8	16.5	1.9	81.9	49.7	51.2	48.8
95923	CANYON DAM	100.0	100.0	0.0	0.0	0.0	0.0	3.7	3.8	0.0	0.0	3.8	0.0	0.0	0.0	50.0	46.2	0.0	96.2	64.0	46.2	53.8
95925	CHALLENGE	88.0	84.4	0.6	0.8	0.9	1.0	4.1	5.8	4.0	4.5	4.8	4.8	4.0	18.1	36.5	20.9	2.3	83.6	51.9	49.4	50.6
95926	CHICO	85.3	80.3	2.0	2.4	3.7	4.7	9.8	13.8	5.0	4.6	4.7	10.1	19.1	25.0	20.7	8.6	2.2	82.5	28.7	49.8	50.2
95928	CHICO	81.5	77.2	1.7	1.8	4.5	5.6	13.6	17.1	5.9	5.4	5.3	8.7	18.9	25.7	20.8	7.5	1.8	80.0	28.3	50.4	49.6
95932	COLUSA	69.7	63.7	0.4	0.4	2.0	2.3	37.6	45.7	7.9	7.3	7.6	7.6	6.5	25.6	25.2	10.6	1.7	72.6	35.1	49.8	50.2
95934	CRESCENT MILLS	91.2	88.2	0.0	0.0	0.9	0.9	6.6	9.2	5.3	4.4	6.6	6.1	4.4	20.6	35.1	14.9	2.6	78.9	46.2	50.4	49.6
95935	DOBBINS	88.9	85.4	0.9	1.1	0.9	1.1	4.6	6.3	4.1	5.3	5.9	4.9	3.5	18.9	37.8	17.6	2.0	81.5	48.8	49.2	50.8
95936	DOWNIEVILLE	94.8	93.4	0.0	0.0	0.5	0.5	6.8	8.8	2.2	2.7	3.8	4.4	3.8	18.7	41.2	19.8	3.3	88.5	54.1	49.5	50.5
95937	DUNNIGAN	63.0	56.2	12.8	12.5	0.9	1.1	32.6	41.7	6.6	6.6	7.3	7.6	4.9	24.3	28.0	13.0	1.9	74.7	39.7	51.2	48.8
95938	DURHAM	91.8	88.7	0.1	0.1	0.6	0.8	9.6	13.4	5.9	6.1	6.6	7.5	6.8	23.6	30.8	11.1	1.7	76.6	40.0	49.8	50.2
95939	ELK CREEK	87.8	85.3	5.0	5.2	0.3	0.3	13.6	18.9	4.9	4.9	5.4	6.2	5.9	30.2	25.3	15.2	1.8	81.1	39.8	61.0	39.0
95941	FORBESTOWN	88.2	85.1	1.3	1.5	0.3	0.4	4.9	6.8	3.4	3.9	6.0	5.0	3.0	17.1	37.8	21.9	1.9	83.3	51.8	51.0	49.0
95942	FOREST RANCH	93.6	91.2	0.3	0.4	1.2	1.6	4.1	5.8	4.5	4.9	5.7	5.7	5.0	21.6	39.0	12.6	1.1	81.4	46.4	50.5	49.5
95943	GLENN	82.0	76.4	0.1	0.1	1.9	2.7	21.0	27.2	7.9	8.6	9.3	8.4	4.4	24.9	25.6	9.4	1.7	68.6	35.8	53.5	46.5
95944	GOODYEARS BAR	95.6	94.6	0.0	0.0	0.0	0.0	4.4	4.7	2.3	2.3	3.1	3.9	3.9	17.1	42.6	21.7	3.1	88.4	55.1	52.7	47.3
95945	GRASS VALLEY	93.4	91.1	0.2	0.2	0.9	1.2	5.5	7.6	5.4	5.4	6.0	6.2	6.0	20.7	30.7	15.5	4.2	79.3	45.2	47.6	52.4
95946	PENN VALLEY	95.1	93.1	0.3	0.4	0.8	1.1	3.8	5.3	3.6	4.3	5.4	5.4	2.9	15.2	34.6	25.5	3.1	83.1	53.6	48.4	51.6
95947	GREENVILLE	87.3	84.8	0.0	0.0	0.4	0.6	7.6	10.1	5.0	5.3	6.0	6.4	4.8	18.2	33.6	17.8	2.9	79.8	47.7	50.2	49.8
95948	GRIDLEY	69.8	64.5	0.3	0.2	3.4	4.2	33.7	39.9	7.2	7.1	7.1	8.1	6.8	24.3	24.4	12.5	2.5	73.8	36.0	50.0	50.0
95949	GRASS VALLEY	95.1	93.2	0.3	0.3	0.8	1.0	3.9	5.5	3.7	4.5	5.5	6.4	4.0	17.1	36.9	19.1	2.8	82.2	50.3	49.3	50.7
	CALIFORNIA	59.5	54.5	6.7	6.2	11.3	12.5	32.4	38.3	7.5	7.1	6.9	7.5	7.4	28.5	24.2	9.3	1.6	74.1	34.3	49.9	50.1
	UNITED STATES	75.1	72.0	12.3	12.7	3.8	4.6	12.5	15.7	6.8	6.7	6.6	7.1	6.9	27.0	26.0	10.9	1.9	75.7	36.9	49.2	50.8

#	POST OFFICE NAME	2009 Per Capita Income	2009 HH Income Base	2009 HOUSEHOLD INCOME DISTRIBUTION (%) Less than $25,000	$25,000 to $49,999	$50,000 to $99,999	$100,000 to $149,999	$150,000 or More	MEDIAN HOUSEHOLD INCOME 2009	2014	2009 National Centile	2009 State Centile	2009 Home Value Base	2009 HOME VALUE DISTRIBUTION (%) Less than $50,000	$50,000 to $89,999	$90,000 to $174,999	$175,000 to $399,999	$400,000 or More	2009 Median Home Value
95684	SOMERSET	27435	1344	16.0	27.9	35.9	15.8	4.3	56628	61432	74	54	1124	1.0	0.1	25.3	51.4	22.2	237696
95685	SUTTER CREEK	26763	2333	21.1	27.2	37.8	9.2	4.6	51427	52945	65	45	1589	1.4	2.8	11.3	50.3	34.2	317327
95687	VACAVILLE	27318	20684	11.3	20.2	43.5	17.3	7.7	69564	73685	87	71	13063	3.4	3.5	21.0	68.8	3.3	208235
95688	VACAVILLE	33073	11787	9.9	17.4	37.3	21.4	14.0	78209	80735	91	79	8339	2.6	0.7	16.8	59.6	20.4	260172
95689	VOLCANO	28766	666	13.7	26.3	43.1	13.1	3.9	59488	60678	77	57	575	0.7	1.0	3.7	55.8	38.8	351504
95690	WALNUT GROVE	20347	936	27.7	27.6	33.3	8.2	3.2	46009	47703	51	35	510	16.1	6.7	22.5	36.1	18.6	193182
95691	WEST SACRAMENTO	26226	12479	22.2	23.7	32.9	15.4	5.8	53986	58514	70	50	8149	9.2	1.3	24.9	56.6	8.1	200493
95692	WHEATLAND	18109	1515	28.8	24.8	36.7	6.5	3.1	46249	48836	52	35	912	4.7	6.9	29.5	51.6	7.2	192920
95693	WILTON	34143	2375	6.7	12.4	45.9	17.8	17.3	81609	82194	93	81	1980	0.8	0.7	18.3	42.3	38.0	343333
95694	WINTERS	23094	2976	14.4	22.3	42.9	14.8	5.6	62326	63513	80	62	1878	2.4	2.4	11.6	65.2	18.4	233880
95695	WOODLAND	23569	14258	19.9	25.0	39.9	11.3	3.8	54297	56658	70	50	7522	1.5	0.7	13.8	67.9	16.1	236865
95698	ZAMORA	24321	99	16.2	32.3	40.4	4.0	7.1	50855	51658	63	44	63	4.8	4.8	14.3	25.4	50.8	403846
95701	ALTA	24410	400	20.8	31.8	30.0	14.0	3.5	47594	48960	56	38	292	2.7	3.8	15.4	64.4	13.7	242063
95703	APPLEGATE	29463	575	15.5	26.1	35.3	16.7	6.4	61189	63987	79	60	449	4.0	1.1	11.6	54.1	29.2	309223
95709	CAMINO	23861	2118	19.7	29.4	35.7	11.3	3.8	50599	52018	63	43	1525	8.3	1.2	16.6	56.3	17.6	227006
95713	COLFAX	28535	4328	17.1	26.7	35.2	16.0	5.1	56957	57749	74	54	3082	2.4	1.5	10.4	60.2	25.5	287709
95714	DUTCH FLAT	30836	296	17.6	23.3	32.1	23.0	4.1	64559	68261	83	65	224	1.8	0.0	12.1	70.1	16.1	276923
95715	EMIGRANT GAP	19703	16	25.0	31.3	31.3	12.5	0.0	45000	42353	48	33	12	0.0	0.0	8.3	75.0	16.7	240000
95717	GOLD RUN	24180	93	23.7	31.2	30.1	11.8	3.2	47017	48079	54	37	73	2.7	0.0	19.2	64.4	13.7	235000
95720	KYBURZ	29368	94	20.2	37.2	26.6	8.5	7.4	41532	40751	38	25	68	0.0	0.0	25.0	52.9	22.1	238235
95721	ECHO LAKE	6476	5	20.0	40.0	40.0	0.0	0.0	28290	27675	6	5	4	0.0	0.0	50.0	50.0	0.0	175000
95722	MEADOW VISTA	36162	1607	5.4	17.6	46.0	21.7	9.4	76770	79300	90	77	1315	1.7	1.5	3.5	55.4	37.9	341296
95724	NORDEN	27294	78	24.4	33.3	32.1	7.7	2.6	42362	45451	41	27	54	1.9	5.6	20.4	57.4	14.8	231818
95726	POLLOCK PINES	25046	3578	16.9	23.6	44.7	12.0	2.8	59724	62411	77	58	2882	6.6	1.1	19.8	63.0	9.4	215262
95728	SODA SPRINGS	20571	43	27.9	37.2	27.9	4.7	2.3	35741	43652	20	15	27	0.0	7.4	22.2	51.9	18.5	258333
95742	RANCHO CORDOVA	24390	2459	18.1	22.4	59.4	0.1	0.0	54476	58942	70	50	1863	2.3	0.0	0.8	67.2	29.7	357757
95746	GRANITE BAY	59164	7998	7.0	8.5	22.1	21.4	40.9	124474	123915	99	96	7020	2.0	0.2	0.6	16.5	80.7	621927
95747	ROSEVILLE	38644	17300	8.8	13.4	37.5	26.5	13.9	84980	94140	94	84	14230	0.1	0.7	4.3	69.3	25.6	297847
95757	ELK GROVE	37314	10859	5.8	13.2	36.1	26.0	18.9	91295	97001	95	87	9222	0.5	0.2	4.7	69.6	25.0	269994
95758	ELK GROVE	33405	19844	7.0	11.1	45.2	23.3	13.3	83673	84881	93	83	16136	1.5	0.2	7.9	81.9	8.6	233515
95762	EL DORADO HILLS	49821	11907	3.8	6.6	31.0	28.7	30.0	112604	110580	98	94	10775	0.4	0.1	2.3	45.9	51.2	406241
95765	ROCKLIN	42031	10334	6.5	10.9	31.2	28.0	23.5	101863	106217	97	91	8133	0.0	0.0	3.3	66.8	29.9	326076
95776	WOODLAND	19455	6458	13.4	21.4	45.7	15.3	4.2	64008	67111	82	65	4433	7.7	5.4	9.4	63.5	14.0	229426
95811	SACRAMENTO	21975	3332	44.0	30.7	21.5	2.5	1.4	29650	30986	8	6	336	1.8	6.8	42.6	47.3	1.5	171667
95814	SACRAMENTO	23928	5448	53.4	24.0	17.9	3.4	1.3	22743	23308	2	2	328	1.8	0.0	51.8	39.3	7.0	170385
95815	SACRAMENTO	13849	9219	40.7	31.0	24.5	3.0	0.7	30665	32258	9	7	3279	10.8	11.0	61.5	16.0	0.6	119393
95816	SACRAMENTO	36299	9525	25.6	27.7	34.0	7.6	5.1	46684	48785	53	36	2310	1.3	0.0	14.0	60.4	24.3	266162
95817	SACRAMENTO	18061	6244	40.8	26.7	26.0	4.7	1.8	32384	34491	12	9	2310	1.6	8.1	47.5	42.0	0.9	161863
95818	SACRAMENTO	34243	10137	29.1	19.7	28.4	10.8	11.9	51352	53177	65	45	4774	1.4	1.5	13.7	59.4	23.9	256908
95819	SACRAMENTO	38420	7630	13.7	20.1	43.2	15.2	7.8	67220	68139	85	69	5003	0.4	0.1	8.9	73.1	17.5	256530
95820	SACRAMENTO	15507	12778	33.3	30.3	31.0	4.3	1.2	38875	41244	29	20	6642	2.1	7.5	70.2	20.0	0.3	134035
95821	SACRAMENTO	24103	15395	28.3	29.4	31.6	7.7	3.0	43206	45323	43	29	6566	4.8	0.8	22.6	65.3	6.4	209588
95822	SACRAMENTO	19146	17027	27.2	30.3	33.3	6.3	2.9	43255	45552	43	29	9722	2.4	2.4	52.5	37.9	4.8	157271
95823	SACRAMENTO	15591	23189	27.3	30.5	35.0	6.0	1.2	43783	45951	45	30	11878	9.9	2.1	55.4	32.4	0.3	152814
95824	SACRAMENTO	11586	9109	38.6	32.6	24.8	3.3	0.8	32628	34475	13	10	3920	5.9	6.2	79.7	8.1	0.1	125000
95825	SACRAMENTO	27951	15107	26.2	30.7	32.9	6.7	3.5	43664	45861	44	30	3627	0.0	4.4	35.0	58.2	2.4	195068
95826	SACRAMENTO	24982	15998	17.5	29.3	41.7	8.5	2.9	52663	54830	67	47	7965	3.3	3.3	30.1	63.0	0.4	188671
95827	SACRAMENTO	22422	7507	18.6	28.6	41.5	8.8	2.4	52334	54158	67	46	3878	14.0	4.4	39.4	41.2	1.0	164980
95828	SACRAMENTO	19123	17817	17.7	26.5	42.0	10.6	3.2	55905	59351	73	53	11910	9.3	4.3	43.2	42.7	0.5	165867
95829	SACRAMENTO	33931	6957	4.4	11.5	47.9	21.7	14.5	82342	83548	93	82	6057	0.2	0.0	10.0	64.8	25.0	243360
95830	SACRAMENTO	40695	247	5.3	13.8	34.8	21.9	24.3	89035	97928	95	86	207	1.0	0.0	4.3	34.3	60.4	459722
95831	SACRAMENTO	35055	18027	11.0	21.1	41.8	16.6	9.5	68403	68977	86	70	10194	1.5	0.7	8.8	72.1	16.9	256656
95832	SACRAMENTO	10371	2732	35.4	31.6	27.8	4.4	0.8	34432	37175	16	13	1449	0.8	8.1	84.8	5.5	0.7	124532
95833	SACRAMENTO	24311	13453	17.4	29.1	42.2	7.8	3.5	53652	56819	69	49	5929	2.7	2.3	44.6	47.1	3.3	175620
95834	SACRAMENTO	32019	8938	12.8	22.5	47.4	13.0	4.3	61288	62906	79	60	6182	3.4	2.5	17.1	64.3	12.6	222627
95835	SACRAMENTO	33569	13109	4.3	19.5	39.2	22.2	14.9	82344	82974	93	82	10629	0.0	0.0	9.9	67.7	22.4	276279
95836	SACRAMENTO	27816	18	22.2	27.8	33.3	11.1	5.6	50000	50000	61	43	13	0.0	0.0	15.4	46.2	38.5	325000
95837	SACRAMENTO	46833	148	12.8	18.9	23.6	15.5	29.1	86622	87927	94	85	122	0.8	0.8	0.0	69.7	28.7	298148
95838	SACRAMENTO	13481	10843	31.6	32.3	30.9	3.7	1.5	38593	40949	28	19	5453	5.6	8.1	62.0	23.8	0.5	137544
95841	SACRAMENTO	21020	8688	28.0	32.6	31.3	5.5	2.6	41175	42856	37	24	3257	12.6	5.1	27.2	50.4	4.7	182944
95842	SACRAMENTO	20094	11574	17.1	34.1	41.4	6.3	1.1	48851	50838	59	40	5748	7.8	5.1	47.1	39.9	0.2	162533
95843	ANTELOPE	26481	13541	6.3	18.4	48.8	19.8	6.7	74400	75274	89	75	9382	0.6	0.4	18.7	79.6	0.7	213896
95864	SACRAMENTO	41426	10539	11.9	21.5	36.7	14.6	15.3	68917	69358	86	70	7119	0.9	0.2	13.5	42.1	43.4	344346
95901	MARYSVILLE	16388	11485	34.8	30.8	27.7	4.6	2.0	34861	37924	17	13	5489	9.6	6.2	48.1	31.7	4.3	142528
95903	BEALE AFB	16962	1254	10.0	51.3	34.9	2.6	1.2	44824	46142	48	32	131	67.2	16.8	3.1	13.0	0.0	37188
95910	ALLEGHANY	22526	36	38.9	16.7	33.3	8.3	2.8	38165	60000	27	19	22	0.0	9.1	45.5	40.9	4.5	141667
95912	ARBUCKLE	16550	1640	22.8	31.5	35.8	5.6	4.3	45842	46952	51	34	1003	4.1	2.0	15.7	61.6	16.7	233300
95914	BANGOR	20965	124	41.1	28.2	20.2	8.1	2.4	31090	32525	10	8	95	3.2	6.3	25.3	43.2	22.1	232500
95915	BELDEN	29792	17	41.2	11.8	41.2	5.9	0.0	42353	42353	40	27	12	8.3	0.0	50.0	41.7	0.0	166667
95916	BERRY CREEK	20278	633	36.0	34.8	21.2	4.6	3.5	34712	36252	17	13	496	5.2	3.0	25.0	51.2	15.5	211111
95917	BIGGS	17787	1131	26.3	31.0	34.0	6.5	2.1	43479	46666	44	30	833	1.4	1.9	54.0	31.6	11.0	164885
95918	BROWNS VALLEY	23319	806	23.3	27.9	37.3	6.2	5.2	49166	50884	59	41	607	0.2	3.3	24.2	55.5	16.8	247277
95919	BROWNSVILLE	20288	561	36.9	28.7	28.2	3.7	2.5	33510	36251	14	11	390	11.3	6.4	36.9	40.3	5.1	159483
95920	BUTTE CITY	16043	114	33.3	43.9	14.0	4.4	4.4	32849	33809	13	10	58	6.9	0.0	34.5	32.8	25.9	200000
95922	CAMPTONVILLE	20123	329	35.3	31.0	28.3	3.3	2.1	33550	35221	14	11	219	10.5	16.4	31.1	34.2	7.8	141848
95923	CANYON DAM	34904	17	17.6	29.4	47.1	5.9	0.0	54626	63351	71	51	14	0.0	0.0	7.1	42.9	50.0	400000
95925	CHALLENGE	16202	162	37.7	32.1	26.5	2.5	1.2	31944	33409	11	9	110	10.0	10.0	40.9	33.6	5.5	138889
95926	CHICO	22424	15079	33.5	25.9	29.8	7.0	3.7	38193	41796	27	19	6844	3.5	1.8	6.6	74.3	13.9	250943
95928	CHICO	22086	14639	31.8	27.2	29.5	6.9	4.6	40143	44705	33	21	6568	2.9	2.1	14.2	56.6	24.2	260595
95932	COLUSA	18790	2802	26.2	31.2	34.4	4.7	3.5	42677	44920	41	27	1751	3.1	2.2	19.6	65.6	9.5	234437
95934	CRESCENT MILLS	22109	106	41.5	18.9	28.3	9.4	1.9	32380	37405	12	9	74	14.9	10.8	39.2	28.4	6.8	153846
95935	DOBBINS	21406	565	34.5	24.4	30.6	6.7	3.7	41522	45143	38	25	401	9.5	3.7	33.7	44.4	8.7	185081
95936	DOWNIEVILLE	25453	93	24.7	26.9	46.2	2.2	0.0	48639	49297	58	40	66	0.0	0.0	33.3	57.6	9.1	221429
95937	DUNNIGAN	19466	476	19.7	32.6	38.9	6.5	2.3	47376	51563	55	38	323	6.8	12.4	29.1	34.1	17.6	180729
95938	DURHAM	31054	1420	16.7	22.5	38.4	13.3	9.2	63902	65744	82	65	970	1.1	0.0	9.4	43.8	45.7	359223
95939	ELK CREEK	18312	110	30.0	29.1	34.5	4.5	1.8	41994	44602	39	26	76	2.6	10.5	31.6	36.8	18.4	186111
95941	FORBESTOWN	22250	338	37.3	26.6	28.1	5.0	3.0	37528	40806	25	18	254	11.8	12.6	26.0	36.2	13.4	173529
95942	FOREST RANCH	33596	594	13.8	19.2	41.4	18.7	6.9	67557	68607	85	69	469	4.1	1.5	9.8	44.3	40.3	310784
95943	GLENN	21201	342	25.4	32.2	31.6	6.1	4.7	42451	43459	41	27	208	5.8	0.5	20.2	39.4	34.1	276316
95944	GOODYEARS BAR	25691	66	24.2	36.4	31.8	6.1	1.5	43636	45616	44	30	47	0.0	2.1	34.0	59.6	4.3	221875
95945	GRASS VALLEY	24944	11009	26.3	30.7	32.0	6.7	4.4	42648	46036	41	27	6720	3.0	2.8	7.5	56.2	30.5	304648
95946	PENN VALLEY	32564	3870	12.4	23.4	43.5	12.8	8.0	64859	66693	83	66	3288	2.4	1.0	2.2	46.7	47.7	390194
95947	GREENVILLE	18797	1022	33.7	30.3	31.7	3.5	0.8	35997	38659	21	15	706	12.7	9.2	26.8	37.1	14.2	182258
95948	GRIDLEY	17228	3832	34.1	28.9	29.3	6.0	1.7	36746	40612	23	16	2380	2.9	3.9	33.9	48.0	11.3	197189
95949	GRASS VALLEY	30777	7995	13.4	25.5	39.4	11.9	9.8	62647	64210	81	63	6952	2.7	3.9	7.7	46.3	39.3	352915
	CALIFORNIA	28199		18.5	22.2	33.9	14.0	11.5	61614	64088				3.3	2.6	13.6	41.0	39.5	321752
	UNITED STATES	27277		20.9	24.4	35.3	11.7	7.6	54719	56938				9.3	13.1	31.6	32.6	13.5	162279

# ZIP CODE	POST OFFICE NAME	FINANCIAL SERVICES: Auto Loan	Home Loan	Investments	Retirement Plans	THE HOME: Home Improvements: Home Repair	Lawn & Garden	Furnishings: Computers & Hardware-Personal	Major Appliances	TV, Radio, Sound Equipment	Furniture	ENTERTAINMENT: Dine out/Carry out	Sports Equipment	Fees & Tickets	Toys & Games	Travel	Cable TV	PERSONAL: Apparel & Services	Auto Repairs	Health Insurance	Pets & Supplies
95684	SOMERSET	110	106	141	106	113	121	98	116	99	98	99	85	97	96	108	102	68	108	112	133
95685	SUTTER CREEK	101	84	122	82	91	106	85	102	88	81	87	74	75	84	89	93	58	96	104	119
95687	VACAVILLE	114	121	110	118	118	110	114	113	111	120	112	86	118	114	115	108	79	112	108	130
95688	VACAVILLE	126	151	145	151	151	135	135	136	129	141	132	106	150	132	145	125	96	132	125	154
95689	VOLCANO	98	95	136	94	108	116	88	107	93	95	92	70	91	85	100	98	62	101	115	122
95690	WALNUT GROVE	95	74	99	71	76	94	78	91	79	72	79	72	64	79	77	83	53	86	91	108
95691	WEST SACRAMENTO	92	102	98	102	101	99	96	97	94	96	95	74	101	95	99	95	67	95	96	112
95692	WHEATLAND	84	75	84	70	77	78	76	82	75	77	76	61	69	75	75	76	52	80	79	94
95693	WILTON	136	167	173	172	172	160	143	152	137	152	139	113	162	136	160	135	99	144	144	174
95694	WINTERS	102	113	108	102	116	92	107	109	95	114	97	84	105	96	110	88	70	104	90	117
95695	WOODLAND	85	92	89	89	92	82	93	89	89	92	91	69	95	89	94	87	65	91	84	101
95698	ZAMORA	96	100	121	100	108	99	98	103	92	101	91	81	99	90	105	89	65	98	93	117
95701	ALTA	100	89	128	89	96	108	85	104	87	83	87	76	80	84	93	91	59	96	101	120
95703	APPLEGATE	119	110	153	110	118	130	104	125	106	102	105	92	99	102	114	110	72	116	122	144
95709	CAMINO	93	82	115	82	88	101	81	96	84	78	83	70	76	81	87	89	57	91	98	111
95713	COLFAX	101	108	121	110	111	113	97	108	96	99	96	81	102	95	106	97	67	102	105	125
95714	DUTCH FLAT	97	112	124	114	116	112	98	107	95	102	96	79	107	94	109	95	68	100	102	122
95715	EMIGRANT GAP	97	77	125	76	85	102	77	98	81	72	80	72	67	77	84	86	53	91	97	114
95717	GOLD RUN	90	81	115	80	87	97	77	93	79	75	78	68	72	76	84	82	53	86	91	108
95720	KYBURZ	93	88	126	88	97	99	86	100	84	86	84	75	83	81	95	85	58	93	93	114
95721	ECHO LAKE	71	74	99	75	82	76	72	79	68	74	67	61	73	65	80	66	48	75	71	89
95722	MEADOW VISTA	116	158	170	157	166	147	130	138	124	135	125	102	155	125	151	124	92	130	130	153
95724	NORDEN	93	75	121	74	82	99	75	95	78	70	77	69	65	74	81	83	51	88	94	110
95726	POLLOCK PINES	90	98	119	94	103	103	89	99	89	87	89	73	92	87	98	92	62	95	98	112
95728	SODA SPRINGS	85	68	109	67	74	89	68	86	71	64	70	63	59	67	73	76	47	79	85	100
95742	RANCHO CORDOVA	72	69	88	64	77	83	66	78	70	71	68	51	65	64	72	74	46	75	86	89
95746	GRANITE BAY	223	284	298	293	297	251	243	250	224	268	225	196	282	227	272	210	167	233	217	279
95747	ROSEVILLE	145	160	159	155	162	152	141	152	137	154	138	113	150	140	150	134	96	142	145	170
95757	ELK GROVE	155	186	162	191	182	154	156	158	144	175	147	131	175	156	164	132	108	144	130	176
95758	ELK GROVE	143	167	142	167	160	139	142	143	133	156	135	116	155	143	147	124	97	134	122	162
95762	EL DORADO HILLS	198	247	229	256	246	211	205	210	190	227	193	170	236	201	222	177	143	193	178	236
95765	ROCKLIN	172	203	172	205	195	166	171	172	158	191	162	142	189	172	177	146	117	159	143	193
95776	WOODLAND	107	110	94	104	106	90	107	103	99	114	102	81	105	104	103	93	72	102	89	116
95811	SACRAMENTO	51	39	40	44	38	38	56	43	55	52	57	38	50	55	49	55	41	52	46	56
95814	SACRAMENTO	46	36	39	40	36	39	52	42	54	48	54	34	47	50	46	55	38	50	51	53
95815	SACRAMENTO	56	48	43	47	46	45	57	51	57	56	58	40	53	58	51	56	41	56	51	60
95816	SACRAMENTO	86	70	73	78	69	66	94	75	89	90	92	66	86	90	84	86	66	86	75	93
95817	SACRAMENTO	61	53	49	54	51	51	65	56	65	62	66	45	60	64	58	65	46	62	59	68
95818	SACRAMENTO	93	99	107	102	103	93	106	98	102	105	104	77	110	100	108	101	75	102	97	115
95819	SACRAMENTO	103	119	126	120	123	111	114	112	108	117	109	87	123	107	121	106	79	111	107	128
95820	SACRAMENTO	63	66	59	61	64	58	65	64	63	67	64	48	65	64	65	62	46	65	61	72
95821	SACRAMENTO	73	71	70	72	71	71	79	73	79	76	79	56	78	77	76	79	56	78	77	86
95822	SACRAMENTO	71	76	74	74	76	75	75	74	76	75	76	55	78	75	77	77	54	76	78	86
95823	SACRAMENTO	74	69	61	66	67	61	75	69	72	76	73	54	70	73	70	69	52	72	65	80
95824	SACRAMENTO	60	55	47	50	53	47	59	56	57	61	59	42	55	58	55	56	42	58	52	63
95825	SACRAMENTO	81	59	60	65	58	60	84	67	82	80	84	57	73	83	71	81	59	79	71	84
95826	SACRAMENTO	84	82	77	82	80	76	90	80	86	87	87	64	87	87	84	84	62	85	79	95
95827	SACRAMENTO	85	84	79	84	82	79	87	82	85	88	86	64	86	87	85	84	61	85	81	97
95828	SACRAMENTO	89	99	90	94	98	86	92	92	86	97	88	70	94	88	94	83	63	90	83	103
95829	SACRAMENTO	150	176	157	174	171	149	151	153	141	164	144	121	164	150	157	134	103	144	133	173
95830	SACRAMENTO	159	208	219	215	217	184	175	182	161	190	162	143	205	162	198	152	121	169	156	204
95831	SACRAMENTO	108	124	130	125	129	115	119	117	114	122	115	90	128	113	127	111	82	117	113	134
95832	SACRAMENTO	65	64	56	57	63	53	64	63	60	69	61	47	60	61	61	57	43	63	55	69
95833	SACRAMENTO	93	83	75	83	80	75	94	84	90	94	92	68	87	93	86	87	64	89	80	100
95834	SACRAMENTO	113	95	94	97	95	103	106	104	108	103	107	80	96	109	99	110	74	107	110	124
95835	SACRAMENTO	146	161	135	155	153	132	143	142	133	156	136	113	147	143	142	125	96	135	122	161
95836	SACRAMENTO	114	83	121	82	87	117	87	108	93	79	92	83	70	92	86	102	61	100	112	129
95837	SACRAMENTO	135	159	191	161	174	146	153	155	137	160	137	124	162	132	169	128	100	149	134	175
95838	SACRAMENTO	67	64	55	62	61	59	67	64	66	68	67	49	65	68	63	65	47	66	62	75
95841	SACRAMENTO	72	62	60	64	61	60	74	65	73	72	74	52	69	74	68	72	52	72	67	78
95842	SACRAMENTO	79	76	69	76	74	69	81	74	78	81	80	59	79	81	77	77	56	78	72	88
95843	ANTELOPE	126	132	109	130	124	110	122	118	116	131	118	95	124	124	119	109	83	115	104	136
95864	SACRAMENTO	123	147	162	149	155	139	138	138	132	143	133	105	153	130	151	129	97	136	132	156
95901	MARYSVILLE	68	61	61	60	60	62	66	65	66	65	67	50	62	67	63	67	47	67	65	76
95903	BEALE AFB	89	46	35	54	41	39	84	58	79	78	83	58	64	95	60	72	58	74	52	71
95910	ALLEGHANY	89	71	115	70	78	94	71	90	74	67	73	66	62	71	77	79	49	83	89	105
95912	ARBUCKLE	87	80	80	72	79	76	81	84	77	83	79	64	73	79	78	75	55	82	77	95
95914	BANGOR	72	69	88	63	76	82	65	77	69	71	67	50	65	63	71	73	45	74	86	88
95915	BELDEN	70	66	86	61	73	79	63	75	67	68	65	49	62	61	69	71	44	72	83	85
95916	BERRY CREEK	76	64	97	62	70	82	63	78	66	61	65	56	57	62	68	70	43	73	80	90
95917	BIGGS	84	73	80	67	73	77	75	81	73	74	74	63	65	74	73	73	51	79	76	93
95918	BROWNS VALLEY	98	79	127	78	87	104	79	100	83	74	82	73	69	78	86	88	54	93	99	116
95919	BROWNSVILLE	67	62	83	58	68	75	59	71	63	62	61	48	57	58	65	66	41	68	77	82
95920	BUTTE CITY	71	71	61	63	70	58	70	69	66	76	68	51	66	68	68	62	48	69	60	76
95922	CAMPTONVILLE	72	57	92	56	63	76	57	73	60	54	59	53	50	57	62	64	39	67	72	84
95923	CANYON DAM	73	77	105	77	89	91	69	82	73	79	72	51	76	66	80	77	49	78	91	93
95925	CHALLENGE	61	54	76	51	59	67	52	64	55	53	54	44	49	51	57	58	36	60	67	73
95926	CHICO	74	63	63	66	63	64	84	68	78	75	79	57	74	77	71	76	56	75	70	83
95928	CHICO	79	68	66	70	67	67	87	72	81	80	81	60	76	81	75	78	57	79	71	87
95932	COLUSA	78	76	75	70	76	72	76	78	73	77	75	59	72	75	75	72	52	77	73	88
95934	CRESCENT MILLS	70	67	85	61	74	80	63	75	67	69	65	49	63	61	69	71	44	72	83	85
95935	DOBBINS	78	67	99	64	73	85	65	81	69	65	68	57	60	64	71	73	45	76	83	93
95936	DOWNIEVILLE	83	67	107	65	73	88	67	85	70	62	69	62	58	66	72	74	46	78	84	98
95937	DUNNIGAN	101	72	105	70	75	104	75	95	82	68	81	72	59	82	74	90	53	87	99	114
95938	DURHAM	109	129	128	130	131	120	118	119	112	121	113	92	128	112	127	110	81	116	113	137
95939	ELK CREEK	93	64	102	64	67	98	71	89	74	58	73	73	52	73	71	81	48	83	94	109
95941	FORBESTOWN	73	67	90	63	74	82	65	77	68	68	67	52	62	63	70	72	45	74	84	89
95942	FOREST RANCH	102	122	122	125	124	115	107	111	103	113	104	83	119	103	117	101	74	106	105	128
95943	GLENN	104	78	110	75	80	105	84	99	85	73	85	81	66	85	83	90	56	94	101	120
95944	GOODYEARS BAR	84	67	108	66	74	89	67	85	70	63	69	62	58	67	73	75	46	79	84	99
95945	GRASS VALLEY	83	77	86	78	79	85	81	83	82	79	82	62	78	80	81	85	57	84	88	98
95946	PENN VALLEY	115	111	158	110	125	134	103	124	108	109	106	83	105	99	116	113	72	117	132	142
95947	GREENVILLE	70	55	80	53	59	75	57	70	61	53	60	51	49	59	58	67	40	66	74	82
95948	GRIDLEY	76	68	76	65	69	74	69	75	68	67	69	58	62	68	69	69	47	73	73	87
95949	GRASS VALLEY	112	115	139	115	123	128	105	120	107	109	106	85	109	103	116	110	73	113	123	138
	CALIFORNIA	112	119	122	118	122	107	121	116	114	124	116	92	124	114	124	110	84	118	107	132
	UNITED STATES	100	100	100	100	100	100	100	100	100	100	100	100	100	100	100	100	100	100	100	100

POPULATION CHANGE

ZIP CODE #	POST OFFICE NAME	COUNTY FIPS CODE	POPULATION 2000	POPULATION 2009	POPULATION 2014	2000-2009 ANNUAL RATE % Rate	2000-2009 ANNUAL RATE State Centile	HOUSEHOLDS 2000	HOUSEHOLDS 2009	HOUSEHOLDS 2014	HOUSEHOLDS % Annual Rate 2000-2009	HOUSEHOLDS 2009 Average HH Size	FAMILIES 2000	FAMILIES 2009	FAMILIES % Annual Rate 2000-2009
95951	HAMILTON CITY	021	2153	2423	2564	1.3	70	577	643	678	1.2	3.77	483	538	1.2
95953	LIVE OAK	101	8544	11366	12798	3.1	91	2536	3307	3710	2.9	3.34	1991	2587	2.9
95954	MAGALIA	007	11366	12127	12448	0.7	50	4705	5095	5245	0.9	2.34	3428	3700	0.8
95955	MAXWELL	011	1355	1637	1802	2.1	84	454	539	592	1.9	3.04	345	407	1.8
95956	MEADOW VALLEY	063	81	80	78	-0.1	5	36	38	38	0.6	2.11	23	25	0.9
95957	MERIDIAN	101	785	882	945	1.3	70	288	322	345	1.2	2.60	206	229	1.2
95959	NEVADA CITY	057	18020	19355	19895	0.8	54	7207	7831	8085	0.9	2.42	4969	5389	0.9
95960	NORTH SAN JUAN	057	565	609	633	0.8	54	252	276	288	1.0	2.17	158	173	1.0
95961	OLIVEHURST	115	16552	26053	30733	5.0	95	5045	8194	9756	5.4	3.17	3851	6275	5.4
95962	OREGON HOUSE	115	485	566	611	1.7	78	189	221	240	1.7	2.56	127	148	1.7
95963	ORLAND	021	14352	16084	17060	1.2	68	5137	5663	5978	1.1	2.83	3778	4160	1.0
95965	OROVILLE	007	18956	20340	21253	0.8	54	6660	7444	7800	1.2	2.64	4502	5014	1.2
95966	OROVILLE	007	28572	30672	31586	0.8	54	10908	11900	12303	0.9	2.54	7525	8186	0.9
95968	PALERMO	007	1253	1420	1492	1.4	72	406	460	483	1.4	3.05	299	337	1.3
95969	PARADISE	007	27658	28181	28425	0.2	18	12116	12603	12763	0.4	2.18	7618	7886	0.4
95970	PRINCETON	011	440	510	550	1.6	77	164	188	202	1.5	2.71	123	140	1.4
95971	QUINCY	063	6450	6526	6446	0.1	13	2808	3032	3012	0.8	2.12	1775	1919	0.8
95972	RACKERBY	115	242	281	304	1.6	77	106	123	134	1.6	2.28	68	79	1.6
95973	CHICO	007	27100	32508	35287	2.0	83	10707	12547	13551	1.7	2.56	6890	8110	1.8
95975	ROUGH AND READY	057	1654	1860	1955	1.3	70	670	760	801	1.4	2.45	467	529	1.4
95977	SMARTVILLE	057	1367	1708	1820	2.4	87	504	632	675	2.5	2.70	392	490	2.4
95979	STONYFORD	011	811	907	956	1.2	68	295	332	351	1.3	2.42	202	226	1.2
95981	STRAWBERRY VALLEY	063	158	174	183	1.0	62	76	85	89	1.2	2.05	46	52	1.3
95982	SUTTER	101	3285	3666	3878	1.2	68	1054	1155	1214	1.0	3.17	877	959	1.0
95983	TAYLORSVILLE	063	321	344	342	0.8	54	134	149	150	1.2	2.31	89	100	1.3
95984	TWAIN	063	108	109	107	0.1	13	53	56	55	0.6	1.95	33	35	0.6
95987	WILLIAMS	011	4528	5789	6434	2.7	90	1244	1553	1725	2.4	3.58	981	1221	2.4
95988	WILLOWS	021	8780	9351	9590	0.7	50	3090	3253	3326	0.6	2.80	2217	2334	0.6
95991	YUBA CITY	101	34940	41790	45419	2.0	83	12436	14427	15562	1.6	2.85	8590	10006	1.7
95993	YUBA CITY	101	27834	35718	39988	2.7	90	9483	12001	13389	2.6	2.95	7356	9253	2.5
96001	REDDING	089	32282	35235	36333	1.0	62	12954	14096	14533	0.9	2.46	8557	9334	0.9
96002	REDDING	089	30963	34309	35534	1.1	64	11490	12685	13141	1.1	2.65	8115	8984	1.1
96003	REDDING	089	38912	43385	45120	1.2	68	15620	17407	18124	1.2	2.41	10299	11474	1.2
96006	ADIN	049	209	215	219	0.3	23	92	98	101	0.7	2.17	64	69	0.8
96007	ANDERSON	089	21063	23624	24600	1.2	68	7940	8876	9253	1.2	2.64	5714	6376	1.2
96008	BELLA VISTA	089	1242	1398	1459	1.3	70	481	541	567	1.3	2.58	363	406	1.2
96010	BIG BAR	105	196	203	203	0.4	30	72	75	75	0.4	2.71	49	51	0.4
96013	BURNEY	089	4536	5078	5271	1.2	68	1836	2063	2148	1.3	2.42	1268	1421	1.2
96014	CALLAHAN	093	356	374	381	0.5	39	150	163	168	0.9	2.29	98	106	0.9
96015	CANBY	049	364	369	374	0.1	13	84	89	92	0.6	3.11	60	64	0.7
96016	CASSEL	089	465	532	562	1.5	75	210	240	254	1.5	2.22	154	175	1.4
96019	SHASTA LAKE	089	8838	10416	11042	1.8	80	3322	3902	4137	1.8	2.66	2329	2728	1.7
96020	CHESTER	063	2650	2649	2599	0.0	9	1124	1184	1168	0.6	2.20	772	816	0.6
96021	CORNING	103	14340	16126	16824	1.3	70	5090	5712	5950	1.3	2.79	3629	4067	1.2
96022	COTTONWOOD	103	12569	14856	15873	1.8	80	4544	5392	5769	1.9	2.75	3520	4170	1.8
96023	DORRIS	093	1233	1279	1285	0.4	30	481	508	513	0.6	2.52	348	368	0.6
96024	DOUGLAS CITY	105	839	917	971	1.0	62	365	402	428	1.0	2.28	241	265	1.0
96025	DUNSMUIR	093	2565	2569	2537	0.0	9	1166	1198	1194	0.3	2.13	686	705	0.3
96027	ETNA	093	2212	2273	2285	0.3	23	893	952	966	0.7	2.38	626	667	0.7
96028	FALL RIVER MILLS	089	1930	2184	2296	1.3	70	695	795	841	1.5	2.55	477	543	1.4
96031	FORKS OF SALMON	093	281	282	280	0.0	9	125	130	130	0.4	2.17	82	85	0.4
96032	FORT JONES	093	2501	2595	2632	0.4	30	1039	1122	1150	0.8	2.29	721	778	0.8
96033	FRENCH GULCH	089	369	397	404	0.8	54	158	170	173	0.8	2.34	110	118	0.8
96034	GAZELLE	093	219	228	230	0.4	30	92	98	100	0.7	2.31	64	68	0.7
96035	GERBER	103	3760	4623	5006	2.3	86	1304	1601	1733	2.2	2.89	978	1199	2.2
96038	GRENADA	093	736	762	767	0.4	30	284	301	307	0.6	2.51	200	212	0.6
96039	HAPPY CAMP	093	1277	1254	1231	-0.2	4	544	554	550	0.2	2.26	331	338	0.2
96040	HAT CREEK	089	334	380	400	1.4	72	129	147	155	1.4	2.59	92	105	1.4
96041	HAYFORK	105	2448	2622	2684	0.7	50	1039	1124	1160	0.9	2.33	658	713	0.9
96044	HORNBROOK	093	981	1010	1012	0.3	23	431	457	462	0.6	2.19	282	299	0.6
96046	HYAMPOM	105	256	276	280	0.8	54	130	142	144	1.0	1.94	70	77	1.0
96047	IGO	089	766	875	925	1.4	72	313	358	379	1.5	2.43	240	274	1.4
96048	JUNCTION CITY	105	718	787	833	1.0	62	309	343	366	1.1	2.22	208	231	1.1
96050	KLAMATH RIVER	093	579	586	585	0.1	13	264	277	280	0.5	2.11	176	185	0.5
96051	LAKEHEAD	089	1481	1705	1794	1.5	75	678	780	823	1.5	2.19	461	529	1.5
96052	LEWISTON	105	2503	2734	2876	1.0	62	1025	1135	1203	1.1	2.30	712	788	1.1
96054	LOOKOUT	049	396	408	416	0.3	23	167	179	184	0.8	2.25	116	125	0.8
96055	LOS MOLINOS	103	3729	4309	4561	1.6	77	1425	1658	1756	1.7	2.57	1012	1174	1.6
96056	MCARTHUR	035	2675	2804	2839	0.5	39	1001	1076	1100	0.8	2.40	742	796	0.8
96057	MCCLOUD	093	1588	1598	1590	0.1	13	696	729	733	0.5	2.19	471	493	0.5
96058	MACDOEL	093	748	771	774	0.3	23	282	296	299	0.5	2.60	202	213	0.6
96059	MANTON	089	452	549	580	2.1	84	193	236	251	2.2	2.21	136	167	2.2
96062	MILLVILLE	089	904	1169	1261	2.8	90	316	410	443	2.9	2.85	247	319	2.8
96063	MINERAL	103	188	210	218	1.2	68	90	102	107	1.4	1.90	64	72	1.3
96064	MONTAGUE	093	4580	4815	4904	0.5	39	1813	1979	2036	1.0	2.38	1299	1416	0.9
96065	MONTGOMERY CREEK	089	802	910	960	1.4	72	324	369	390	1.4	2.44	232	263	1.4
96067	MOUNT SHASTA	093	7222	7475	7536	0.4	30	3172	3391	3454	0.7	2.18	1981	2118	0.7
96069	OAK RUN	089	1361	1568	1679	1.5	75	525	607	651	1.6	2.56	383	442	1.6
96071	OLD STATION	089	174	196	205	1.3	70	86	97	102	1.3	2.02	59	66	1.2
96073	PALO CEDRO	089	3665	4075	4216	1.2	68	1290	1446	1500	1.2	2.81	1081	1207	1.2
96075	PAYNES CREEK	103	463	516	537	1.2	68	185	211	221	1.4	2.22	128	146	1.4
96076	PLATINA	105	176	204	219	1.6	77	78	91	99	1.7	2.23	54	63	1.7
96080	RED BLUFF	103	26712	29839	31270	1.2	68	10439	11845	12441	1.4	2.46	7138	8110	1.4
96085	SCOTT BAR	093	13	14	14	0.8	54	7	8	8	1.5	1.75	5	5	0.0
96086	SEIAD VALLEY	093	64	64	64	0.0	9	26	27	27	0.4	2.37	17	18	0.6
96087	SHASTA	089	70	79	83	1.3	70	30	34	36	1.4	2.32	21	24	1.5
96088	SHINGLETOWN	089	4237	5063	5444	1.9	81	1743	2093	2252	2.0	2.42	1327	1587	2.0
96091	TRINITY CENTER	105	447	464	478	0.4	30	214	223	231	0.4	2.08	141	147	0.5
96093	WEAVERVILLE	105	3355	3635	3760	0.9	58	1433	1572	1635	1.0	2.26	911	1000	1.0
96094	WEED	093	5979	6490	6647	0.9	58	2424	2724	2820	1.3	2.33	1669	1876	1.3
96096	WHITMORE	089	805	955	1031	1.9	81	338	396	428	1.7	2.41	261	305	1.7
96097	YREKA	093	9534	9661	9636	0.1	13	4062	4204	4223	0.4	2.23	2548	2633	0.4
96101	ALTURAS	049	5087	5256	5333	0.4	30	2086	2219	2269	0.7	2.26	1383	1472	0.7
96103	BLAIRSDEN-GRAEAGLE	063	1832	1864	1844	0.2	18	878	958	954	0.9	1.95	597	652	1.0
96104	CEDARVILLE	049	849	856	863	0.1	13	376	394	401	0.5	2.15	246	259	0.6
	CALIFORNIA					1.2					1.0	2.93			1.1
	UNITED STATES					1.0					1.1	2.59			0.9

ZIP CODE #	POST OFFICE NAME	RACE (%) White 2000	White 2009	Black 2000	Black 2009	Asian/Pacific 2000	Asian/Pacific 2009	% Hispanic Origin 2000	% Hispanic Origin 2009	2009 AGE DISTRIBUTION (%) 0-4	5-9	10-14	15-19	20-24	25-44	45-64	65-84	85+	18+	MEDIAN AGE 2009	% 2009 Males	% 2009 Females
95951	HAMILTON CITY	39.5	34.9	0.4	0.4	0.3	0.4	77.6	83.5	9.2	8.5	8.0	8.6	8.6	30.6	18.9	6.7	0.7	69.1	28.8	52.0	48.0
95953	LIVE OAK	57.0	49.7	1.2	1.0	9.2	10.1	40.7	48.9	7.8	8.0	7.8	8.9	7.7	26.6	22.2	9.4	1.7	70.8	31.9	49.3	50.7
95954	MAGALIA	94.3	91.1	0.4	1.0	0.8	1.0	4.9	7.8	4.2	4.5	5.3	7.9	4.8	17.0	30.6	22.5	3.1	82.1	49.5	49.0	51.0
95955	MAXWELL	76.7	72.0	0.5	0.5	1.7	2.0	31.0	39.0	7.7	8.1	8.5	8.6	4.4	23.9	25.8	11.4	1.6	70.3	36.6	49.1	50.9
95956	MEADOW VALLEY	95.1	92.5	0.0	0.0	0.0	0.0	3.7	6.3	3.8	3.8	3.8	5.0	3.8	20.0	37.5	20.0	2.5	88.8	50.6	48.8	51.2
95957	MERIDIAN	85.4	81.7	0.0	0.0	0.3	0.2	24.7	31.7	5.7	6.2	5.7	5.9	7.1	26.1	28.6	12.6	2.2	78.8	39.7	53.4	46.6
95959	NEVADA CITY	93.9	91.7	0.4	0.4	0.9	1.2	3.7	5.2	3.6	4.6	6.1	7.2	4.3	19.2	38.6	14.3	2.2	81.1	47.5	50.5	49.5
95960	NORTH SAN JUAN	91.5	88.7	0.4	0.3	0.7	1.0	3.9	5.3	4.3	4.8	6.4	7.6	3.1	19.9	39.1	13.1	1.8	79.1	47.1	51.9	48.1
95961	OLIVEHURST	63.6	60.1	1.7	1.7	9.6	11.0	24.0	26.8	8.6	8.3	8.3	8.5	6.9	26.0	24.0	8.4	1.0	69.3	31.9	50.5	49.5
95962	OREGON HOUSE	90.1	86.7	0.8	1.1	0.8	0.9	5.0	6.5	4.1	5.8	6.7	5.1	2.8	20.0	39.4	14.5	1.6	80.2	47.3	49.5	50.5
95963	ORLAND	74.8	68.2	0.4	0.5	1.3	1.7	28.6	36.8	7.7	7.4	7.5	7.8	6.1	23.8	25.4	12.3	2.0	72.2	36.8	50.1	49.9
95965	OROVILLE	79.0	72.9	2.1	2.3	6.7	8.8	8.9	11.9	7.8	7.2	6.8	7.9	7.2	23.0	25.8	12.4	1.8	73.3	36.4	49.9	50.1
95966	OROVILLE	81.1	76.6	2.3	2.4	5.3	6.7	8.1	10.8	5.8	6.1	6.4	6.9	5.6	20.1	28.8	17.3	3.0	77.3	44.1	49.1	50.9
95968	PALERMO	76.6	70.3	0.8	1.0	3.2	4.2	21.3	27.9	7.0	7.2	7.4	7.5	5.2	24.2	25.6	13.8	2.1	73.9	38.2	50.0	50.0
95969	PARADISE	93.6	91.1	0.2	0.3	1.1	1.5	4.3	6.1	4.2	4.5	5.0	5.5	4.9	18.4	31.7	20.4	5.4	82.8	50.2	46.9	53.1
95970	PRINCETON	80.3	75.1	0.5	0.4	2.0	2.5	25.6	33.5	7.8	8.4	8.4	7.6	4.1	23.3	26.5	12.0	1.8	70.6	37.3	49.6	50.4
95971	QUINCY	92.1	89.9	1.5	1.6	0.8	1.0	3.7	5.1	4.5	4.6	5.3	6.9	6.5	22.1	34.0	14.1	2.1	81.4	45.1	49.8	50.2
95972	RACKERBY	88.8	84.7	1.2	1.4	1.2	1.8	3.3	4.6	3.6	3.9	4.3	4.3	4.3	12.8	37.0	27.4	2.5	85.1	56.4	48.8	51.2
95973	CHICO	86.3	80.9	1.0	1.1	2.4	3.1	10.6	15.4	6.9	6.7	6.8	6.7	6.5	27.2	26.5	10.0	2.6	75.3	37.0	48.8	51.2
95975	ROUGH AND READY	92.8	89.8	0.2	0.3	0.5	0.8	6.1	8.5	3.8	4.7	6.7	7.2	3.5	21.1	34.9	15.6	2.4	79.7	46.6	51.5	48.5
95977	SMARTVILLE	90.8	88.1	0.3	0.3	1.2	1.5	7.8	10.5	4.7	5.3	6.3	6.1	3.9	19.9	37.9	14.5	1.4	79.6	47.2	50.2	49.8
95979	STONYFORD	85.0	81.8	4.1	4.1	0.9	1.1	14.1	18.9	4.0	4.2	7.8	14.4	4.2	16.5	29.2	17.9	1.8	73.5	44.0	55.9	44.1
95981	STRAWBERRY VALLEY	91.7	87.9	0.0	0.0	0.0	0.6	4.5	6.3	4.0	5.2	5.2	5.2	4.0	19.5	37.9	17.2	1.7	82.2	49.6	50.0	50.0
95982	SUTTER	85.2	79.6	0.2	0.3	1.1	1.4	11.4	16.4	7.1	7.4	7.9	9.0	5.9	24.3	27.3	9.9	1.2	72.0	36.3	50.9	49.1
95983	TAYLORSVILLE	90.7	88.4	0.0	0.0	0.6	0.9	6.2	8.7	5.2	4.4	6.4	6.1	4.1	19.2	36.0	16.3	2.3	80.2	47.4	52.0	48.0
95984	TWAIN	91.7	89.0	0.0	0.0	0.0	0.0	6.5	9.2	5.5	4.6	6.4	5.5	3.7	21.1	35.8	14.7	2.8	78.9	46.3	51.4	48.6
95987	WILLIAMS	52.4	47.6	0.4	0.4	1.2	1.3	61.6	68.4	9.0	8.7	8.2	8.4	7.8	28.8	20.0	7.2	1.8	69.2	29.4	51.1	48.9
95988	WILLOWS	73.5	67.4	0.8	0.8	8.1	9.6	20.4	26.1	7.6	7.8	7.8	8.2	6.7	25.0	23.5	11.0	2.2	71.6	33.8	50.4	49.6
95991	YUBA CITY	67.7	61.6	2.6	2.5	7.8	9.4	26.0	31.3	8.4	7.6	7.0	7.4	7.6	27.9	22.0	10.1	2.2	72.5	32.6	48.9	51.1
95993	YUBA CITY	66.6	59.6	1.8	1.8	19.5	22.6	12.8	16.9	7.0	7.0	7.2	7.1	5.4	26.4	26.6	11.9	1.3	74.2	37.7	49.7	50.3
96001	REDDING	89.8	87.0	0.9	1.0	2.1	2.8	5.3	7.2	5.7	6.0	6.6	7.3	6.1	22.5	30.5	13.0	2.3	77.0	42.0	48.9	51.1
96002	REDDING	87.1	83.2	1.0	1.1	4.0	5.3	5.7	7.8	7.1	6.6	6.8	7.5	7.0	23.8	25.8	12.8	2.5	75.0	37.6	48.4	51.6
96003	REDDING	90.6	87.7	0.9	1.0	1.9	2.6	4.7	6.5	5.9	5.8	6.1	7.5	7.3	23.6	27.8	13.5	2.5	78.2	40.1	48.6	51.4
96006	ADIN	91.4	88.4	0.0	0.0	0.0	0.0	8.1	11.6	5.1	5.6	5.6	6.5	5.6	20.0	32.6	17.2	1.9	79.1	46.0	50.7	49.3
96007	ANDERSON	88.8	85.5	0.5	0.5	1.2	1.5	6.6	9.0	6.4	6.2	6.7	7.6	6.3	22.6	28.3	13.7	2.3	75.9	40.4	48.5	51.5
96008	BELLA VISTA	91.8	89.2	0.3	0.4	0.4	0.6	3.9	5.4	3.6	6.1	7.8	7.0	3.2	20.9	37.8	12.1	1.5	77.6	45.7	50.4	49.6
96010	BIG BAR	83.1	78.8	0.0	0.0	2.1	2.5	6.2	7.9	4.4	5.9	8.9	10.3	2.0	18.7	31.5	16.7	1.5	74.9	44.8	50.2	49.8
96013	BURNEY	88.4	85.7	0.2	0.2	0.7	0.9	6.6	9.1	5.3	5.3	5.6	6.4	6.1	21.5	30.8	16.5	2.5	79.6	44.8	48.5	51.5
96014	CALLAHAN	84.8	81.3	0.3	0.3	1.1	1.9	3.7	4.8	2.7	4.8	7.2	7.0	3.2	18.4	39.6	15.2	1.9	80.5	48.4	53.2	46.8
96015	CANBY	92.3	90.5	1.1	1.4	0.5	0.5	5.5	7.3	4.1	4.9	6.2	8.7	7.3	19.5	32.2	15.7	1.4	78.0	44.5	52.8	47.2
96016	CASSEL	88.4	86.8	0.0	0.0	0.4	0.4	3.2	4.3	3.6	4.5	5.3	5.1	3.2	16.0	37.2	22.2	3.0	83.5	53.6	51.9	48.1
96019	SHASTA LAKE	87.7	84.4	0.7	0.8	0.5	0.6	6.2	8.5	7.1	7.0	7.0	7.1	6.9	24.8	26.8	11.4	1.8	74.2	37.2	49.5	50.5
96020	CHESTER	93.1	90.9	0.2	0.2	0.6	0.7	5.8	8.0	4.4	6.1	6.7	6.7	3.8	19.0	34.1	16.5	2.8	77.8	46.9	50.1	49.9
96021	CORNING	77.1	71.1	0.6	0.7	0.7	0.8	25.5	32.7	7.7	7.5	7.2	7.7	6.5	23.8	25.2	12.4	2.0	72.6	36.0	49.9	50.1
96022	COTTONWOOD	89.8	86.5	0.5	0.5	1.2	1.7	6.7	9.3	5.5	6.1	7.1	7.8	5.5	22.6	31.4	12.7	1.3	76.0	41.6	49.4	50.6
96023	DORRIS	79.3	73.6	0.1	0.1	0.8	0.9	22.7	30.5	6.6	6.9	7.3	7.6	5.3	23.6	27.9	13.1	1.7	74.5	39.3	50.3	49.7
96024	DOUGLAS CITY	91.3	88.4	0.2	0.2	0.4	0.5	2.6	3.5	4.1	5.6	6.9	5.1	2.7	18.1	39.5	16.7	1.3	80.0	48.6	50.7	49.3
96025	DUNSMUIR	90.1	87.4	2.1	2.3	0.7	0.9	9.2	13.0	4.2	4.2	4.5	5.3	7.0	19.9	35.1	16.6	3.2	83.9	48.6	50.1	49.9
96027	ETNA	87.8	84.7	0.1	0.1	0.7	0.9	4.3	6.2	4.0	4.4	6.5	8.0	4.1	18.3	36.6	15.6	2.6	79.5	47.5	50.4	49.6
96028	FALL RIVER MILLS	84.7	81.0	0.2	0.1	0.2	0.2	12.2	16.4	6.5	6.1	5.7	7.8	4.4	20.7	30.7	15.4	2.7	75.9	43.9	50.3	49.7
96031	FORKS OF SALMON	83.9	80.1	0.0	0.0	0.4	0.7	5.0	6.7	2.8	3.9	7.1	8.2	3.2	18.4	40.1	14.2	2.1	80.1	47.8	52.8	47.2
96032	FORT JONES	90.0	86.8	0.4	0.5	0.5	0.7	6.0	8.5	4.7	5.2	6.1	6.0	3.5	19.2	37.8	15.2	2.4	79.4	48.3	49.2	50.8
96033	FRENCH GULCH	94.3	92.2	0.0	0.0	0.5	0.8	1.9	2.8	2.8	4.0	8.3	5.3	1.3	20.4	44.8	12.1	1.0	81.4	48.8	53.4	46.6
96034	GAZELLE	90.4	87.7	0.0	0.0	0.5	0.4	4.6	6.1	5.3	5.7	6.6	7.9	4.8	18.9	32.5	16.7	1.8	77.2	45.6	50.4	49.6
96035	GERBER	74.1	67.8	0.5	0.5	0.6	0.7	26.8	33.8	6.5	7.7	8.3	8.2	5.2	24.4	25.3	12.7	1.6	72.1	37.0	51.1	48.9
96038	GRENADA	91.0	88.3	0.1	0.1	0.4	0.7	4.2	6.2	5.1	5.6	6.3	7.1	5.0	19.3	32.3	17.1	2.2	78.1	46.2	50.1	49.9
96039	HAPPY CAMP	71.2	67.3	0.4	0.4	0.6	0.8	4.1	5.5	4.0	5.3	6.6	5.7	4.0	19.0	37.9	15.4	2.2	80.5	47.9	52.4	47.6
96040	HAT CREEK	88.9	86.6	0.0	0.0	0.3	0.5	3.6	5.0	3.9	4.5	5.3	5.3	3.7	17.1	35.8	21.6	2.9	82.9	52.2	51.3	48.7
96041	HAYFORK	85.2	81.9	0.2	0.2	0.2	0.3	4.7	6.2	4.6	5.7	6.1	6.7	4.7	20.1	35.5	15.2	1.4	79.4	46.4	51.6	48.4
96044	HORNBROOK	88.4	84.9	0.3	0.4	0.5	0.8	5.7	8.1	4.6	4.7	4.9	4.5	4.8	16.5	36.3	21.6	2.3	83.2	51.7	48.9	51.1
96046	HYAMPOM	89.8	87.0	0.0	0.0	1.2	1.4	0.8	1.1	0.7	4.3	6.9	5.4	0.4	19.6	43.5	18.8	0.4	83.0	50.1	52.9	47.1
96047	IGO	91.0	88.0	0.3	0.2	0.9	1.3	4.2	5.8	4.1	4.6	6.2	7.0	4.3	18.9	39.5	14.2	1.3	80.7	47.6	50.6	49.4
96048	JUNCTION CITY	90.8	88.1	0.1	0.1	0.3	0.4	4.0	5.5	2.8	4.2	6.6	6.4	3.0	18.2	42.9	14.7	1.1	81.8	49.4	50.1	49.9
96050	KLAMATH RIVER	80.6	76.8	0.5	0.5	0.5	0.9	4.8	6.8	4.4	4.9	5.6	5.5	4.1	17.1	39.6	16.9	1.9	81.2	50.5	50.2	49.8
96051	LAKEHEAD	93.0	91.1	0.1	0.1	0.3	0.5	3.3	4.5	2.8	3.3	4.0	4.5	3.1	15.2	43.6	21.1	2.3	87.1	54.6	50.4	49.6
96052	LEWISTON	90.6	87.6	1.4	1.6	0.6	0.7	5.5	7.5	3.5	5.4	5.4	6.2	3.2	18.8	38.2	17.7	1.6	81.1	49.5	52.7	47.3
96054	LOOKOUT	90.9	88.0	0.3	0.2	0.3	0.2	8.3	11.5	4.9	5.4	5.6	6.4	5.4	18.9	33.6	18.1	1.7	79.7	47.2	50.7	49.3
96055	LOS MOLINOS	88.9	85.3	0.1	0.1	0.3	0.4	17.0	23.1	6.1	6.1	6.4	6.6	4.9	21.5	30.7	15.3	2.3	77.3	43.8	50.1	49.9
96056	MCARTHUR	88.0	85.0	1.4	1.5	0.3	0.3	11.8	16.4	4.8	5.1	6.5	7.7	5.0	21.9	32.8	14.3	1.9	78.2	44.2	53.8	46.2
96057	MCCLOUD	89.9	86.8	1.6	1.8	1.3	1.8	6.0	8.7	4.5	4.9	5.5	5.7	3.8	18.1	35.8	19.2	2.4	81.5	50.4	48.7	51.3
96058	MACDOEL	80.3	74.8	0.3	0.3	0.8	1.0	21.4	28.8	6.6	6.6	7.1	7.4	5.1	23.1	28.4	13.9	1.8	75.4	40.4	50.1	49.9
96059	MANTON	88.7	86.0	1.5	1.5	0.7	0.7	8.2	10.9	3.5	4.0	4.7	6.0	4.7	19.9	36.2	18.9	2.0	84.0	49.6	52.8	47.2
96062	MILLVILLE	92.7	90.2	0.3	0.3	0.6	0.7	4.3	5.8	3.8	5.5	7.4	7.2	2.2	18.9	40.6	12.7	1.8	77.8	47.7	51.4	48.6
96063	MINERAL	87.8	85.2	2.1	1.9	0.5	0.5	10.1	14.3	3.3	4.3	4.8	6.2	4.8	21.0	35.2	18.6	1.9	83.3	48.5	53.8	46.2
96064	MONTAGUE	90.2	87.2	0.5	0.6	0.7	1.0	4.7	6.9	4.4	5.2	6.0	6.0	4.3	19.5	35.4	17.3	1.9	80.6	47.7	49.9	50.1
96065	MONTGOMERY CREEK	86.8	83.3	0.4	0.3	0.5	0.7	3.4	4.6	3.8	6.9	7.9	6.6	2.9	20.9	36.8	12.4	1.8	76.3	45.5	53.4	46.6
96067	MOUNT SHASTA	92.8	90.0	0.9	1.0	1.5	2.0	4.6	6.6	4.2	4.7	5.6	6.3	4.1	20.2	37.3	15.1	2.4	81.3	47.6	48.3	51.7
96069	OAK RUN	90.0	87.2	0.2	0.3	0.7	0.8	3.4	4.6	3.7	6.1	7.0	6.8	2.4	18.6	40.6	13.0	1.7	77.8	47.7	52.2	47.8
96071	OLD STATION	89.1	87.2	0.0	0.0	0.6	0.5	4.6	6.6	4.6	5.1	5.6	5.1	4.1	19.4	32.1	20.9	3.1	81.6	50.0	48.5	51.5
96073	PALO CEDRO	93.6	91.4	0.4	0.4	0.8	1.1	3.4	4.8	3.8	5.4	7.5	8.5	3.5	18.4	36.9	14.4	1.7	77.4	46.6	49.5	50.5
96075	PAYNES CREEK	87.3	83.7	2.6	2.7	0.4	0.6	10.6	14.5	3.3	4.1	4.7	6.2	4.7	22.3	34.5	18.6	1.7	83.9	48.0	54.1	45.9
96076	PLATINA	92.0	90.2	0.0	0.0	0.6	0.5	4.5	6.9	2.9	4.9	6.4	6.4	3.9	18.1	45.1	11.8	0.5	80.9	48.1	54.4	45.6
96080	RED BLUFF	88.4	84.8	0.5	0.6	1.2	1.5	11.1	15.2	6.1	6.6	6.8	7.1	5.9	22.7	27.9	14.2	2.7	75.9	40.9	48.7	51.3
96085	SCOTT BAR	92.3	92.9	0.0	0.0	0.0	0.0	7.7	7.1	0.0	0.0	0.0	0.0	0.0	0.0	100.0	0.0	0.0	100.0	56.3	50.0	50.0
96086	SEIAD VALLEY	76.6	71.9	0.0	0.0	1.6	1.6	4.7	4.7	3.1	4.7	6.3	6.3	3.1	17.2	37.5	18.8	3.1	79.7	50.8	50.0	50.0
96087	SHASTA	90.0	87.3	0.0	0.0	1.4	1.3	2.9	3.8	2.5	5.1	8.9	7.6	3.8	24.1	32.9	13.9	1.3	78.5	43.9	50.6	49.4
96088	SHINGLETOWN	92.8	90.2	0.2	0.3	0.4	0.6	3.9	5.5	3.5	4.5	5.7	6.1	3.5	18.3	37.6	18.9	1.9	82.2	50.3	50.8	49.2
96091	TRINITY CENTER	89.8	86.6	0.2	0.2	1.1	1.5	1.6	2.4	1.5	3.7	4.5	3.0	2.4	11.0	40.9	31.0	1.9	88.8	58.9	51.7	48.3
96093	WEAVERVILLE	91.5	88.7	0.2	0.3	0.8	1.1	4.4	6.2	5.3	5.3	5.7	6.5	6.3	20.5	30.9	16.1	3.4	79.2	45.3	48.2	51.8
96094	WEED	82.7	79.2	5.3	5.3	3.1	3.6	8.8	11.8	5.6	5.4	6.1	7.8	6.2	19.4	31.7	15.2	2.7	78.7	44.6	49.0	51.0
96096	WHITMORE	93.0	90.5	0.4	0.3	0.5	0.7	4.1	5.8	3.7	5.3	7.0	7.1	2.4	18.6	40.6	13.4	1.8	78.3	48.0	51.0	49.0
96097	YREKA	87.6	84.2	0.6	0.7	1.5	2.1	5.1	7.3	5.4	5.2	5.7	6.5	6.6	20.8	29.6	16.8	3.4	79.3	44.8	48.1	51.9
96101	ALTURAS	87.7	84.4	0.7	0.8	0.9	1.2	10.2	13.9	5.5	5.8	6.2	6.6	5.5	20.6	30.7	16.6	2.4	77.8	44.7	49.7	50.3
96103	BLAIRSDEN-GRAEAGLE	96.8	95.7	0.2	0.3	0.5	0.6	2.2	3.1	1.7	2.4	3.1	3.2	2.7	10.6	42.2	31.7	2.5	90.9	59.4	49.7	50.3
96104	CEDARVILLE	86.4	83.9	0.1	0.1	0.2	0.4	7.5	10.5	4.8	5.4	6.0	5.7	3.6	19.4	33.9	18.0	3.3	79.9	48.4	49.5	50.5
	CALIFORNIA	59.5	54.5	6.7	6.2	11.3	12.5	32.4	38.3	7.5	7.1	6.9	7.5	7.4	28.5	24.2	9.3	1.6	74.1	34.3	49.9	50.1
	UNITED STATES	75.1	72.0	12.3	12.7	3.8	4.6	12.5	15.7	6.8	6.7	6.6	7.1	6.9	27.0	26.0	10.9	1.9	75.7	36.9	49.2	50.8

95951-96104

ZIP CODE #	POST OFFICE NAME	2009 Per Capita Income	2009 HH Income Base	2009 HOUSEHOLD INCOME DISTRIBUTION (%) Less than $25,000	$25,000 to $49,999	$50,000 to $99,999	$100,000 to $149,999	$150,000 or More	MEDIAN HOUSEHOLD INCOME 2009	2014	2009 National Centile	2009 State Centile	2009 Home Value Base	2009 HOME VALUE DISTRIBUTION (%) Less than $50,000	$50,000 to $89,999	$90,000 to $174,999	$175,000 to $399,999	$400,000 or More	2009 Median Home Value
95951	HAMILTON CITY	11341	643	27.5	40.9	29.1	2.0	0.5	40094	40360	33	21	385	5.5	11.2	36.6	42.1	4.7	171235
95953	LIVE OAK	14639	3307	37.5	24.9	30.9	3.7	3.0	36149	40056	21	15	2076	5.0	6.2	60.8	18.0	10.1	136885
95954	MAGALIA	20854	5095	30.4	30.2	32.1	5.3	2.0	41209	45211	37	24	4104	2.3	5.6	33.7	51.3	7.1	196192
95955	MAXWELL	18335	539	28.2	30.1	30.1	7.1	4.6	41019	44593	36	23	339	4.4	1.8	32.4	51.3	10.0	196875
95956	MEADOW VALLEY	21713	38	31.6	26.3	36.8	5.3	0.0	41515	42295	38	25	29	0.0	6.9	20.7	65.5	6.9	243750
95957	MERIDIAN	19872	322	32.6	28.9	27.3	7.5	3.7	41032	41963	36	23	181	12.2	18.8	35.4	25.4	8.3	133482
95959	NEVADA CITY	30517	7831	16.6	28.1	36.0	11.1	8.3	56137	59511	73	54	5916	1.6	1.5	7.7	44.6	44.7	373967
95960	NORTH SAN JUAN	22867	276	33.0	28.6	28.3	5.8	4.3	36310	38633	21	16	189	6.3	8.5	25.9	44.4	14.8	210577
95961	OLIVEHURST	14750	8194	29.6	35.4	28.2	4.6	2.2	36714	40664	23	16	5057	12.6	10.9	54.8	18.5	3.2	122752
95962	OREGON HOUSE	21728	221	32.1	20.4	33.5	9.5	4.5	47897	49380	56	39	161	11.2	2.5	23.6	50.9	11.8	207813
95963	ORLAND	17073	5663	30.4	32.7	29.4	5.4	2.2	38791	40769	29	19	3800	7.0	3.4	22.6	54.1	12.9	204135
95965	OROVILLE	15449	7444	41.2	30.3	24.0	2.8	1.7	30768	32702	9	7	4206	13.8	6.1	38.2	32.8	9.1	159650
95966	OROVILLE	19289	11900	31.8	29.5	31.6	5.0	2.1	38910	42439	29	20	8609	7.8	4.3	37.2	40.8	9.9	176809
95968	PALERMO	13576	460	35.0	36.3	23.7	3.3	1.7	36411	37581	22	16	326	14.1	5.8	50.9	27.0	2.1	143254
95969	PARADISE	23707	12603	30.8	27.9	33.0	5.0	3.2	40691	44421	35	23	8796	10.0	3.8	19.5	52.9	13.8	215197
95970	PRINCETON	20397	188	31.4	27.7	29.3	7.4	4.3	39247	45000	30	20	118	5.9	1.7	28.8	47.5	16.1	208333
95971	QUINCY	26866	3032	28.5	24.6	33.7	8.5	4.7	45274	46905	49	33	1973	8.5	3.3	20.0	58.5	9.6	227033
95972	RACKERBY	21574	123	35.8	31.7	29.3	2.4	0.8	32272	32869	12	9	86	20.9	12.8	17.4	45.3	3.5	170000
95973	CHICO	25672	12547	20.1	25.9	39.3	9.3	5.4	53728	57968	69	49	7851	10.4	3.9	5.1	59.3	21.2	251918
95975	ROUGH AND READY	23190	760	25.1	22.9	42.0	6.7	3.3	52189	55833	66	46	603	3.6	1.7	10.1	54.7	29.9	313830
95977	SMARTVILLE	23701	632	21.4	25.6	39.1	9.0	4.9	52486	54300	67	47	518	1.4	0.0	7.3	54.6	36.7	340000
95979	STONYFORD	18516	332	37.3	27.1	26.5	7.2	1.8	31538	32458	10	8	253	12.6	6.3	26.1	43.1	11.9	189205
95981	STRAWBERRY VALLEY	20722	85	34.1	30.6	30.6	4.7	0.0	35445	37346	19	14	60	8.3	13.3	25.0	45.0	8.3	187500
95982	SUTTER	18051	1155	26.1	21.6	43.2	7.7	1.4	51863	54068	66	45	852	2.1	1.5	49.2	30.5	16.7	169915
95983	TAYLORSVILLE	21078	149	34.2	22.8	35.6	6.7	0.7	41804	44384	39	25	113	10.6	7.1	31.0	40.7	10.6	179688
95984	TWAIN	24511	56	41.1	17.9	32.1	8.9	0.0	35000	32381	18	14	39	12.8	7.7	46.2	28.2	5.1	158750
95987	WILLIAMS	15331	1553	23.1	32.5	37.2	5.2	2.0	45265	46181	49	33	969	3.6	1.3	15.6	66.8	12.7	212215
95988	WILLOWS	17135	3253	28.9	31.4	32.4	6.1	1.1	40182	42842	33	22	1914	1.9	3.7	28.0	58.5	7.9	197238
95991	YUBA CITY	19483	14427	27.1	28.8	32.1	8.3	3.6	44249	47373	46	31	7463	5.4	5.3	48.9	37.2	3.3	161752
95993	YUBA CITY	24574	12001	16.3	26.1	38.4	12.6	6.6	58713	61168	76	56	8470	4.4	2.1	25.8	57.9	9.8	204955
96001	REDDING	25578	14096	28.4	26.7	29.6	9.4	5.8	44215	47585	46	31	8768	3.7	1.2	20.5	57.7	16.9	232141
96002	REDDING	19948	12685	26.4	33.2	31.0	6.7	2.7	42615	45274	41	27	7506	10.4	2.7	22.5	52.6	11.8	206862
96003	REDDING	23629	17407	25.3	27.6	35.0	8.4	3.7	47025	49866	54	37	10889	7.7	3.3	17.5	58.8	12.7	221636
96006	ADIN	18708	98	37.8	32.7	24.5	4.1	1.0	31848	34529	11	8	75	8.0	17.3	46.7	18.7	9.3	142045
96007	ANDERSON	17134	8876	33.3	31.4	30.0	3.6	1.9	37346	40538	25	17	5981	7.8	2.8	36.3	46.4	6.7	181439
96008	BELLA VISTA	22579	541	23.5	32.7	29.9	9.2	4.6	45191	47168	49	33	441	3.4	4.3	28.3	38.3	25.6	226818
96010	BIG BAR	12789	75	49.3	29.3	13.3	8.0	0.0	25354	26093	3	3	47	2.1	2.1	42.6	40.4	12.8	184375
96013	BURNEY	19897	2063	33.1	30.4	29.0	6.1	1.4	39365	42433	31	20	1387	8.3	6.8	54.5	24.7	5.7	146595
96014	CALLAHAN	22322	163	30.1	32.5	28.2	5.5	3.7	39455	40000	31	21	123	8.1	4.1	23.6	46.3	17.9	220833
96015	CANBY	17900	89	27.0	30.3	29.2	13.5	0.0	42763	45000	42	28	69	11.6	17.4	26.1	34.8	10.1	145833
96016	CASSEL	25903	240	20.4	31.3	36.3	6.7	5.4	48890	50232	59	40	189	0.0	1.6	29.1	60.8	8.5	220349
96019	SHASTA LAKE	16174	3902	37.1	32.7	26.0	2.8	1.3	32290	35500	12	9	2464	3.3	7.8	48.4	38.9	1.7	162917
96020	CHESTER	22904	1184	23.6	31.8	36.7	5.8	2.0	43966	44767	45	30	768	2.9	1.2	19.7	62.6	13.7	234821
96021	CORNING	15854	5712	38.3	29.7	25.9	4.1	2.0	33993	36908	15	12	3681	8.0	7.7	38.3	40.3	5.8	167754
96022	COTTONWOOD	19032	5392	22.9	33.1	35.9	5.4	2.7	45146	47561	49	33	4186	5.6	4.3	19.6	59.0	11.6	220408
96023	DORRIS	15274	508	41.5	34.1	20.7	2.6	1.2	29616	30838	7	6	337	7.7	22.3	38.3	24.9	6.8	121875
96024	DOUGLAS CITY	22117	402	36.6	26.9	27.6	4.2	4.7	38116	41473	27	19	310	8.7	5.2	32.6	42.3	11.3	186000
96025	DUNSMUIR	19639	1198	42.0	33.0	18.7	3.4	2.9	29400	30761	7	6	697	4.4	3.7	49.1	36.3	6.5	167255
96027	ETNA	21068	952	33.5	30.5	25.9	6.9	3.2	37158	39392	24	17	713	5.8	3.9	24.8	51.2	14.3	218798
96028	FALL RIVER MILLS	19184	795	31.8	31.7	27.8	5.9	2.8	39146	41686	30	20	552	10.5	4.9	35.1	40.2	9.2	174096
96031	FORKS OF SALMON	24613	130	33.8	30.0	24.6	6.9	4.6	38914	41315	29	20	94	8.5	6.4	20.2	48.9	16.0	219231
96032	FORT JONES	21482	1122	36.1	26.5	28.4	6.1	2.9	38329	40838	28	19	814	3.4	2.6	28.1	48.8	17.1	221277
96033	FRENCH GULCH	19298	170	30.0	30.0	35.9	2.4	1.8	37884	44113	26	18	126	8.7	5.6	26.2	42.1	17.5	192647
96034	GAZELLE	17725	98	35.7	32.7	27.6	3.1	1.0	39076	42351	30	20	67	7.5	9.0	37.3	34.3	11.9	169792
96035	GERBER	16736	1601	32.2	35.4	26.5	3.4	2.5	33818	36363	15	12	1094	4.2	7.1	47.8	33.9	6.9	161264
96038	GRENADA	19240	301	33.2	31.6	29.6	3.7	2.0	40763	41671	35	23	209	7.7	8.6	34.9	36.8	12.0	173214
96039	HAPPY CAMP	17100	554	47.8	27.1	19.9	3.4	1.8	26543	28223	4	4	339	11.5	14.5	39.5	26.3	8.3	139387
96040	HAT CREEK	21312	147	23.1	31.3	34.7	6.1	4.8	47125	48342	54	37	113	1.8	4.4	31.9	52.2	9.7	208750
96041	HAYFORK	15796	1124	42.9	39.4	11.4	4.6	1.7	27937	28614	6	4	768	12.2	7.9	46.9	28.4	4.6	141284
96044	HORNBROOK	20567	457	36.8	32.8	22.1	5.7	2.6	32429	33137	12	9	343	7.3	8.2	37.9	37.6	9.0	169773
96046	HYAMPOM	18928	142	59.2	12.7	18.3	7.0	2.8	19584	21328	1	2	105	3.8	25.7	22.9	30.5	17.1	141071
96047	IGO	29756	358	24.3	26.0	32.1	12.0	5.6	49550	52924	60	41	301	5.3	5.0	17.3	33.2	39.2	307143
96048	JUNCTION CITY	21419	343	27.4	32.7	32.9	5.5	1.5	43782	46014	45	30	268	0.7	6.3	30.2	49.6	13.1	224324
96050	KLAMATH RIVER	19890	277	42.2	27.1	23.5	5.8	1.4	30364	31500	9	7	189	5.3	6.9	32.3	40.2	15.3	195192
96051	LAKEHEAD	22557	780	28.1	32.7	30.0	7.3	1.9	41563	44721	38	25	589	3.9	5.1	26.5	44.5	20.0	226176
96052	LEWISTON	21665	1135	27.9	32.8	31.1	5.6	2.6	41042	43403	36	23	872	8.0	3.8	36.2	42.0	10.0	180822
96054	LOOKOUT	18287	179	36.3	32.4	26.8	3.4	1.1	33623	35000	15	11	137	7.3	16.1	46.7	20.4	9.5	144643
96055	LOS MOLINOS	17747	1658	31.7	30.1	32.9	4.2	1.1	38187	41408	27	19	1174	10.1	6.7	28.6	44.0	10.6	186937
96056	MCARTHUR	18500	1076	37.2	30.7	26.4	3.9	1.9	34605	37148	17	13	806	8.4	10.3	29.9	39.7	11.7	179741
96057	MCCLOUD	19927	729	35.9	29.9	28.8	3.4	1.9	35490	36548	19	14	492	2.6	6.3	36.8	46.7	7.5	181402
96058	MACDOEL	15070	296	40.9	33.4	21.6	2.7	1.4	30186	31396	8	7	196	7.7	19.9	37.8	27.6	7.1	133824
96059	MANTON	21136	236	29.7	35.2	30.5	3.4	1.3	38638	42191	29	19	183	4.4	8.7	26.8	42.1	18.0	199342
96062	MILLVILLE	21610	410	22.9	28.5	36.6	7.8	4.1	48464	51715	58	40	332	4.8	1.8	12.0	46.1	35.2	298750
96063	MINERAL	24291	102	32.4	37.3	25.5	3.9	1.0	34419	38633	16	13	78	9.0	10.3	26.9	38.5	15.4	184375
96064	MONTAGUE	18268	1979	35.0	33.8	25.6	3.9	1.7	34693	35776	17	13	1502	3.5	8.3	39.8	38.4	9.9	172222
96065	MONTGOMERY CREEK	18722	369	32.8	31.4	28.5	5.4	1.9	38241	41543	27	19	283	6.7	6.4	26.5	32.9	27.6	215441
96067	MOUNT SHASTA	25045	3391	32.1	27.0	29.9	6.6	4.4	40768	44165	35	23	2225	6.2	3.2	12.8	54.7	23.1	269496
96069	OAK RUN	21383	607	29.3	28.2	32.3	7.2	3.0	43235	46373	43	29	484	6.0	3.9	17.8	36.8	35.5	279268
96071	OLD STATION	25443	97	26.8	33.0	29.9	6.2	4.1	43635	45991	44	30	71	5.6	5.6	33.8	43.7	11.3	192500
96073	PALO CEDRO	28609	1446	11.1	24.6	38.5	17.2	8.8	63217	64787	81	64	1247	1.0	0.9	9.4	58.3	30.5	297500
96075	PAYNES CREEK	20116	211	33.6	39.3	21.8	4.3	0.9	33261	34854	14	11	161	8.1	11.2	29.8	34.8	16.1	177083
96076	PLATINA	20321	91	40.7	16.5	38.5	4.4	0.0	34088	38667	16	12	77	1.3	7.8	58.4	20.8	11.7	122159
96080	RED BLUFF	20904	11845	28.7	31.2	31.5	5.9	2.7	40906	43949	36	23	7583	5.2	4.2	27.5	52.0	11.1	204074
96085	SCOTT BAR	14643	8	75.0	0.0	25.0	0.0	0.0	15000	40000	1	1	6	0.0	0.0	50.0	50.0	0.0	175000
96086	SEIAD VALLEY	16726	27	40.7	25.9	25.9	7.4	0.0	31111	31111	10	8	18	0.0	5.6	38.9	38.9	16.7	200000
96087	SHASTA	24246	34	23.5	26.5	41.2	8.8	0.0	50000	50000	61	43	27	0.0	0.0	25.9	59.3	14.8	220833
96088	SHINGLETOWN	21742	2093	27.5	28.8	37.0	4.2	2.5	43412	47513	44	29	1728	3.4	2.6	21.4	55.6	17.0	233567
96091	TRINITY CENTER	25095	223	25.1	31.4	35.4	5.4	2.7	42823	45957	42	28	180	2.8	3.9	35.0	45.6	12.8	195833
96093	WEAVERVILLE	23137	1572	27.9	33.3	29.6	5.2	4.1	41183	43512	37	24	1013	4.3	3.6	28.0	55.0	9.1	205429
96094	WEED	20364	2724	35.6	26.9	30.6	5.0	2.0	37514	39306	25	18	1843	3.4	5.2	34.1	45.1	12.1	190743
96096	WHITMORE	25649	396	23.7	27.8	36.1	7.8	4.5	48391	51912	58	39	323	5.0	1.9	13.3	45.2	34.7	295395
96097	YREKA	22355	4204	34.9	28.7	28.3	4.6	3.4	35985	37340	21	15	2624	8.3	3.2	33.4	47.1	8.0	186558
96101	ALTURAS	21626	2219	37.7	26.8	26.7	6.5	2.3	33283	34983	14	11	1525	3.1	14.4	55.9	22.8	3.7	134633
96103	BLAIRSDEN-GRAEAGLE	34535	958	16.4	24.3	43.0	12.3	4.0	62436	63131	81	62	792	2.7	2.0	14.3	50.5	30.6	293145
96104	CEDARVILLE	21922	394	34.3	32.2	26.6	3.3	3.6	35000	36620	18	14	255	5.5	9.4	50.2	25.1	9.8	152616
	CALIFORNIA	28199		18.5	22.2	33.9	14.0	11.5	61614	64088				3.3	2.6	13.6	41.0	39.5	321752
	UNITED STATES	27277		20.9	24.4	35.3	11.7	7.6	54719	56938				9.3	13.1	31.6	32.6	13.5	162279

ZIP CODE		FINANCIAL SERVICES				THE HOME						ENTERTAINMENT						PERSONAL			
						Home Improvements		Furnishings													
#	POST OFFICE NAME	Auto Loan	Home Loan	Invest-ments	Retire-ment Plans	Home Repair	Lawn & Garden	Comput-ers & Hard-ware-Personal	Major Appli-ances	TV, Radio, Sound Equip-ment	Furni-ture	Dine out/ Carry out	Sports Equip-ment	Fees & Tickets	Toys & Games	Travel	Cable TV	Apparel & Services	Auto Repairs	Health Insur-ance	Pets & Supplies
95951	HAMILTON CITY	64	64	55	56	63	52	63	62	59	68	61	46	60	61	61	56	43	62	54	68
95953	LIVE OAK	74	70	68	63	69	65	70	72	67	72	68	55	64	68	68	65	48	71	66	81
95954	MAGALIA	72	68	89	63	76	82	65	77	69	70	67	51	64	63	71	73	45	74	85	88
95955	MAXWELL	100	68	109	68	72	105	76	95	79	62	78	78	56	78	76	86	51	88	100	116
95956	MEADOW VALLEY	76	61	99	60	67	81	61	78	64	57	63	57	53	61	66	68	42	72	77	90
95957	MERIDIAN	88	64	91	63	67	91	70	85	75	62	73	66	55	74	68	81	49	80	90	101
95959	NEVADA CITY	108	110	139	111	117	119	102	116	101	104	101	86	105	98	113	102	70	109	112	133
95960	NORTH SAN JUAN	83	66	107	65	73	88	66	84	70	62	69	62	58	66	72	74	46	78	83	98
95961	OLIVEHURST	69	69	60	66	67	64	67	68	66	69	66	51	65	67	66	65	46	67	65	78
95962	OREGON HOUSE	93	74	120	73	82	98	74	95	78	70	77	69	64	74	81	83	51	87	93	110
95963	ORLAND	77	66	75	64	66	76	68	74	69	64	69	58	60	69	67	72	47	72	75	88
95965	OROVILLE	63	51	60	50	52	60	56	59	59	54	58	45	50	58	54	62	40	60	63	71
95966	OROVILLE	72	67	80	64	70	78	67	74	70	67	69	53	64	67	69	73	47	72	80	86
95968	PALERMO	74	52	75	51	54	75	54	69	60	50	59	52	43	60	53	66	39	63	72	82
95969	PARADISE	76	71	88	70	76	84	70	79	74	71	72	56	69	70	74	78	49	77	86	92
95970	PRINCETON	99	68	109	68	71	104	76	94	79	61	78	78	55	77	75	86	50	88	99	116
95971	QUINCY	84	79	89	79	81	86	80	85	81	79	81	63	77	80	81	83	56	83	86	99
95972	RACKERBY	72	69	88	63	76	82	65	77	69	71	67	51	65	63	71	73	45	74	86	88
95973	CHICO	94	96	93	96	95	92	94	93	92	97	93	72	96	93	95	91	65	93	91	109
95975	ROUGH AND READY	95	76	122	75	83	100	76	96	79	71	78	70	66	75	82	85	52	89	95	112
95977	SMARTVILLE	108	85	133	83	92	114	85	108	90	80	89	79	72	87	90	97	59	100	108	126
95979	STONYFORD	66	61	79	57	67	74	59	70	62	62	61	47	57	57	64	66	41	67	77	80
95981	STRAWBERRY VALLEY	71	57	91	56	62	75	57	72	59	53	59	53	49	56	61	63	39	66	71	83
95982	SUTTER	75	93	87	91	93	87	80	83	78	80	78	63	89	79	87	78	56	80	81	95
95983	TAYLORSVILLE	75	67	94	63	74	83	65	79	68	67	67	54	61	63	71	73	45	75	84	91
95984	TWAIN	70	67	85	62	74	80	64	75	67	69	66	49	63	61	69	71	44	72	84	86
95987	WILLIAMS	83	78	76	70	77	72	79	81	75	81	77	61	72	76	76	73	53	80	73	91
95988	WILLOWS	66	66	67	65	65	67	68	68	67	65	68	53	67	67	68	68	48	69	69	79
95991	YUBA CITY	78	78	72	76	76	72	81	77	78	81	80	60	79	80	78	77	56	79	74	89
95993	YUBA CITY	101	109	112	107	110	105	102	106	100	103	101	81	106	101	107	99	72	103	101	121
96001	REDDING	88	89	95	90	90	93	88	91	89	87	89	69	89	88	91	91	62	90	94	107
96002	REDDING	76	71	71	72	71	75	75	75	76	74	76	58	72	76	74	77	53	76	78	89
96003	REDDING	82	79	85	79	80	82	81	82	81	80	81	62	79	80	81	82	56	83	84	97
96006	ADIN	73	52	75	51	54	74	53	68	59	50	58	51	43	59	53	65	39	62	71	81
96007	ANDERSON	72	59	72	58	61	72	62	70	66	59	65	52	55	65	61	69	44	68	73	82
96008	BELLA VISTA	97	78	125	76	85	103	78	99	81	73	80	72	67	77	84	87	53	91	98	115
96010	BIG BAR	58	46	75	45	51	61	46	59	48	43	48	43	40	46	50	52	32	54	58	68
96013	BURNEY	81	60	81	59	62	83	64	78	71	59	69	58	53	70	62	77	46	73	84	92
96014	CALLAHAN	85	68	110	67	75	90	68	87	72	64	71	63	59	68	74	76	47	80	86	101
96015	CANBY	88	70	113	69	77	94	71	90	74	66	73	66	61	70	76	79	48	83	89	104
96016	CASSEL	96	76	121	75	83	101	77	97	81	72	80	71	66	77	82	86	53	90	97	113
96019	SHASTA LAKE	61	60	62	59	61	63	60	62	61	59	61	47	59	61	60	63	42	62	65	73
96020	CHESTER	82	68	108	67	76	89	67	85	71	65	70	61	60	66	74	75	46	79	85	98
96021	CORNING	69	58	68	56	59	68	61	67	64	59	63	50	54	63	59	67	43	65	69	78
96022	COTTONWOOD	83	74	87	73	76	84	72	81	74	71	74	61	67	74	74	77	50	78	81	96
96023	DORRIS	69	49	71	48	51	70	50	64	56	47	55	48	40	56	50	62	36	59	67	76
96024	DOUGLAS CITY	84	67	109	66	74	89	67	86	71	63	70	63	58	67	73	75	46	79	85	99
96025	DUNSMUIR	65	51	70	51	54	66	58	65	62	53	60	48	49	59	56	66	41	63	70	76
96027	ETNA	84	65	102	64	71	88	67	84	71	62	70	62	57	68	70	77	47	78	86	98
96028	FALL RIVER MILLS	77	65	87	64	69	80	67	77	69	63	68	57	60	67	68	73	46	74	79	90
96031	FORKS OF SALMON	89	71	115	70	78	94	71	91	75	67	74	66	62	71	77	80	49	84	90	105
96032	FORT JONES	82	66	106	65	72	87	66	84	69	62	68	61	57	65	71	73	45	77	82	97
96033	FRENCH GULCH	75	60	97	59	66	79	60	77	63	56	62	56	52	60	65	67	41	71	76	89
96034	GAZELLE	73	53	77	51	55	74	54	69	59	50	58	51	44	59	54	65	39	63	71	81
96035	GERBER	81	65	79	61	67	77	66	77	69	66	69	57	57	69	65	72	47	73	76	89
96038	GRENADA	85	62	90	60	65	87	63	81	70	59	69	60	51	69	64	77	45	74	83	96
96039	HAPPY CAMP	60	53	75	50	59	66	52	63	54	53	53	43	48	51	56	58	36	59	66	72
96040	HAT CREEK	92	72	113	71	78	97	74	93	78	68	77	68	63	75	78	84	51	86	94	108
96041	HAYFORK	63	48	68	46	51	65	48	61	53	47	52	44	41	52	49	58	34	56	64	72
96044	HORNBROOK	71	61	84	58	67	77	60	73	64	61	62	50	55	60	64	68	42	69	78	84
96046	HYAMPOM	61	49	79	48	54	65	49	62	51	46	51	46	43	49	53	55	34	58	62	72
96047	IGO	108	107	139	108	114	120	99	115	99	99	99	84	99	96	109	101	68	107	111	132
96048	JUNCTION CITY	79	64	103	63	70	84	64	81	67	60	66	59	55	63	69	71	44	75	80	94
96050	KLAMATH RIVER	69	56	89	55	62	74	56	71	59	54	58	51	49	56	61	63	39	66	71	82
96051	LAKEHEAD	82	66	106	65	72	87	66	84	69	62	68	61	57	65	71	73	45	77	83	97
96052	LEWISTON	75	69	91	65	76	84	67	79	70	70	69	53	65	65	72	74	46	75	86	90
96054	LOOKOUT	73	53	77	51	55	74	54	69	60	50	59	51	44	59	54	65	39	63	71	82
96055	LOS MOLINOS	79	59	90	58	63	82	60	77	65	56	64	57	50	64	62	71	43	71	78	90
96056	MCARTHUR	75	58	90	56	62	78	58	74	62	54	61	55	49	60	61	67	41	68	75	87
96057	MCCLOUD	73	58	94	57	64	77	58	74	61	55	60	54	51	58	63	65	40	68	73	86
96058	MACDOEL	69	51	73	49	53	70	52	66	57	48	56	49	42	56	52	62	37	60	67	77
96059	MANTON	78	62	101	61	68	82	62	79	65	58	65	58	54	62	68	70	43	73	78	92
96062	MILLVILLE	103	82	133	81	90	109	82	105	86	77	85	76	71	82	89	92	57	97	103	121
96063	MINERAL	78	63	101	62	69	83	63	80	65	59	65	58	54	62	68	70	43	73	78	92
96064	MONTAGUE	73	57	90	56	62	77	58	73	61	54	60	54	49	59	61	66	40	68	73	85
96065	MONTGOMERY CREEK	76	61	98	60	67	80	61	77	64	57	63	56	53	60	66	68	42	71	76	90
96067	MOUNT SHASTA	89	73	108	72	79	93	74	90	77	70	76	66	65	74	78	82	51	84	91	105
96069	OAK RUN	91	73	118	72	80	97	73	93	77	69	76	68	64	73	79	82	50	86	92	108
96071	OLD STATION	86	66	99	64	70	91	68	86	74	63	72	63	57	72	70	80	48	80	89	100
96073	PALO CEDRO	113	125	144	127	130	129	110	123	108	114	109	91	118	107	123	109	77	115	118	141
96075	PAYNES CREEK	74	59	96	58	65	78	59	76	62	56	61	55	52	59	64	66	41	70	75	88
96076	PLATINA	75	61	97	60	66	80	61	77	63	57	63	56	53	60	66	68	42	71	76	89
96080	RED BLUFF	75	69	82	68	71	77	72	76	73	70	73	57	69	71	73	76	50	76	79	89
96085	SCOTT BAR	43	34	55	34	38	45	34	43	36	32	35	32	30	34	37	38	24	40	43	50
96086	SEIAD VALLEY	66	53	85	52	58	70	53	67	55	50	55	49	46	53	57	59	36	62	66	78
96087	SHASTA	94	75	121	74	83	99	75	96	79	71	78	70	65	75	82	84	52	88	94	111
96088	SHINGLETOWN	88	70	113	69	77	93	70	89	74	66	73	65	61	70	76	78	48	82	88	103
96091	TRINITY CENTER	77	73	106	73	83	90	69	83	72	73	71	55	70	66	77	76	48	78	89	95
96093	WEAVERVILLE	77	72	74	72	74	80	73	77	76	72	74	56	71	75	73	79	51	76	83	90
96094	WEED	74	61	84	61	65	77	65	74	68	61	67	54	58	65	66	73	45	72	78	87
96096	WHITMORE	103	83	133	81	91	109	83	105	86	77	85	77	72	82	90	92	57	97	104	122
96097	YREKA	74	63	76	64	66	76	69	74	73	66	71	54	64	70	68	77	49	74	81	87
96101	ALTURAS	77	63	84	63	67	78	68	77	71	64	70	56	60	68	68	75	47	74	80	90
96103	BLAIRSDEN-GRAEAGLE	92	98	128	97	111	112	88	102	92	99	91	65	97	84	101	96	63	98	112	116
96104	CEDARVILLE	83	60	96	59	63	87	64	80	67	54	66	64	50	65	65	72	43	74	83	97
	CALIFORNIA	112	119	122	118	122	107	121	116	114	124	116	92	124	114	124	110	84	118	107	132
	UNITED STATES	100	100	100	100	100	100	100	100	100	100	100	100	100	100	100	100	100	100	100	100

ZIP CODE #	POST OFFICE NAME	COUNTY FIPS CODE	POPULATION 2000	POPULATION 2009	POPULATION 2014	2000-2009 ANNUAL RATE % Rate	2000-2009 ANNUAL RATE State Centile	HOUSEHOLDS 2000	HOUSEHOLDS 2009	HOUSEHOLDS 2014	HOUSEHOLDS % Annual Rate 2000-2009	HOUSEHOLDS 2009 Average HH Size	FAMILIES 2000	FAMILIES 2009	FAMILIES % Annual Rate 2000-2009
96105	CHILCOOT	063	532	562	558	0.6	45	215	238	238	1.1	2.36	151	167	1.1
96106	CLIO	063	218	222	219	0.2	18	105	115	114	1.0	1.93	72	79	1.0
96107	COLEVILLE	051	1340	1235	1205	-0.9	1	546	547	539	0.0	2.17	385	387	0.1
96108	DAVIS CREEK	049	429	410	405	-0.5	1	145	145	144	0.0	2.47	103	102	-0.1
96109	DOYLE	035	1364	1422	1412	0.5	39	544	580	581	0.7	2.45	381	406	0.7
96111	FLORISTON	057	106	119	124	1.3	70	41	47	49	1.5	2.51	24	27	1.3
96112	FORT BIDWELL	049	214	214	216	0.0	9	96	101	103	0.6	2.05	61	65	0.7
96113	HERLONG	035	952	2128	2133	9.1	98	389	425	430	1.0	2.38	265	290	1.0
96114	JANESVILLE	063	3142	3307	3296	0.6	45	1139	1225	1229	0.8	2.68	888	955	0.8
96115	LAKE CITY	049	238	238	240	0.0	9	102	107	109	0.5	2.16	65	69	0.6
96116	LIKELY	049	290	304	312	0.5	39	128	139	144	0.9	2.17	88	96	0.9
96117	LITCHFIELD	035	184	193	192	0.5	39	75	81	81	0.8	2.32	56	61	0.9
96118	LOYALTON	091	1423	1369	1341	-0.4	2	559	557	551	0.0	2.42	390	388	-0.1
96119	MADELINE	035	69	65	64	-0.6	1	25	24	24	-0.4	2.54	18	17	-0.6
96120	MARKLEEVILLE	003	1074	1076	1076	0.0	9	415	432	433	0.4	2.49	257	267	0.4
96121	MILFORD	035	460	464	457	0.1	13	185	192	191	0.4	2.42	124	129	0.4
96122	PORTOLA	063	4113	4378	4346	0.7	50	1660	1845	1844	1.1	2.36	1142	1271	1.2
96123	RAVENDALE	035	3800	49	48	-37.5	0	14	14	13	0.0	3.29	10	10	0.0
96124	CALPINE	091	336	329	325	-0.2	4	154	157	156	0.2	2.08	99	101	0.2
96125	SIERRA CITY	091	385	363	355	-0.6	1	190	187	184	-0.2	1.94	110	108	-0.2
96126	SIERRAVILLE	091	747	730	718	-0.2	4	296	300	298	0.1	2.39	205	207	0.1
96128	STANDISH	035	253	265	265	0.5	39	98	106	106	0.9	2.44	74	80	0.8
96130	SUSANVILLE	035	21540	26147	26023	2.1	84	6396	6716	6698	0.5	2.53	4393	4616	0.5
96132	TERMO	035	74	70	68	-0.6	1	37	36	35	-0.3	1.81	26	26	0.0
96133	TOPAZ	051	510	432	412	-1.8	0	178	166	159	-0.8	2.39	132	124	-0.7
96134	TULELAKE	093	2496	2407	2372	-0.4	2	897	878	870	-0.2	2.74	638	625	-0.2
96135	VINTON	063	3	3	3	0.0	9	1	1	1	0.0	3.00	1	1	0.0
96136	WENDEL	035	174	183	182	0.5	39	57	62	62	0.9	2.87	43	46	0.7
96137	WESTWOOD	063	2186	2086	2025	-0.5	1	991	998	975	0.1	2.09	734	741	0.1
96140	CARNELIAN BAY	061	666	837	917	2.5	88	299	392	434	3.0	2.14	172	217	2.5
96141	HOMEWOOD	061	263	338	377	2.7	90	133	180	203	3.3	1.88	59	76	2.8
96142	TAHOMA	061	1454	1742	1853	2.0	83	616	749	803	2.1	2.32	349	413	1.8
96143	KINGS BEACH	061	4567	6154	6911	3.3	92	1641	2222	2506	3.3	2.77	928	1207	2.9
96145	TAHOE CITY	061	6014	7389	8079	2.3	86	2545	3299	3647	2.8	2.18	1329	1647	2.3
96146	OLYMPIC VALLEY	061	263	273	281	0.4	30	105	114	119	0.9	2.39	48	47	-0.2
96148	TAHOE VISTA	061	1138	1530	1713	3.3	92	440	600	675	3.4	2.55	264	346	3.0
96150	SOUTH LAKE TAHOE	017	33082	37027	38673	1.2	68	13097	14518	15175	1.1	2.54	7989	8697	0.9
96161	TRUCKEE	057	15550	18717	20222	2.0	83	5785	7017	7613	2.1	2.66	4014	4856	2.1
96162	TRUCKEE	057	102	116	123	1.4	72	51	59	63	1.6	1.95	30	34	1.4
	CALIFORNIA					1.2					1.0	2.93			1.1
	UNITED STATES					1.0					1.1	2.59			0.9

ZIP CODE #	POST OFFICE NAME	RACE (%) White 2000	White 2009	Black 2000	Black 2009	Asian/Pacific 2000	Asian/Pacific 2009	% Hispanic Origin 2000	% Hispanic Origin 2009	2009 AGE DISTRIBUTION (%) 0-4	5-9	10-14	15-19	20-24	25-44	45-64	65-84	85+	18+	MEDIAN AGE 2009	% 2009 Males	% 2009 Females
96105	CHILCOOT	92.4	89.9	0.2	0.2	0.4	0.5	5.3	7.1	4.3	5.0	8.4	6.9	2.8	21.0	36.7	13.9	1.1	76.9	45.7	51.8	48.2
96106	CLIO	97.7	96.8	0.0	0.5	0.5	0.5	1.8	2.7	1.8	1.8	2.3	2.7	2.7	8.6	42.8	34.7	2.7	93.7	60.9	50.0	50.0
96107	COLEVILLE	82.7	78.8	1.3	1.3	1.3	1.8	10.7	14.7	5.7	5.4	5.3	5.4	5.8	21.4	32.4	16.7	1.8	80.2	45.6	53.0	47.0
96108	DAVIS CREEK	85.3	81.7	3.7	4.1	1.4	2.0	9.8	13.2	2.7	3.4	4.1	5.6	4.6	22.7	36.1	18.8	2.0	85.9	49.4	59.8	40.2
96109	DOYLE	88.9	86.1	1.4	1.7	0.4	0.5	7.4	10.7	5.5	5.6	7.0	6.5	3.2	21.0	35.2	14.9	1.1	77.4	45.7	50.1	49.9
96111	FLORISTON	92.5	90.8	0.0	0.0	0.9	0.8	2.8	3.4	3.4	5.0	5.9	6.7	5.0	22.7	45.4	5.9	0.0	81.5	45.5	54.6	45.4
96112	FORT BIDWELL	79.5	77.6	0.0	0.0	0.9	0.9	7.4	10.7	4.7	5.6	5.6	5.1	3.3	19.6	34.6	17.8	3.7	79.9	50.0	46.7	53.3
96113	HERLONG	77.9	68.5	6.3	8.7	0.7	1.2	10.2	14.1	2.9	3.0	3.0	5.9	12.0	43.1	23.4	6.0	0.7	86.4	35.1	75.6	24.4
96114	JANESVILLE	92.7	90.4	0.5	0.7	0.6	0.8	6.1	9.1	5.7	6.4	8.5	8.2	3.6	23.3	32.5	10.7	1.1	73.6	41.4	51.3	48.7
96115	LAKE CITY	79.8	77.3	0.0	0.0	0.8	1.3	7.6	10.1	5.0	5.0	5.5	5.0	3.4	18.9	36.1	17.2	3.8	79.8	50.6	47.5	52.5
96116	LIKELY	90.0	86.2	0.3	0.3	0.3	0.7	10.0	13.8	4.6	4.6	5.3	6.6	4.3	17.4	33.2	22.0	2.0	80.3	50.0	50.7	49.3
96117	LITCHFIELD	88.0	85.5	0.5	0.5	0.5	0.5	12.0	17.6	6.2	6.7	6.7	7.3	7.3	23.8	30.6	10.4	1.0	76.7	39.3	50.8	49.2
96118	LOYALTON	94.0	92.3	0.4	0.4	0.3	0.3	6.5	9.0	4.9	5.8	6.6	7.2	5.0	19.8	32.9	15.3	2.6	77.6	45.5	49.5	50.5
96119	MADELINE	69.1	67.7	26.5	20.0	0.0	1.5	26.5	56.9	0.0	0.0	0.0	1.5	21.5	69.2	7.7	0.0	0.0	100.0	30.6	98.5	1.5
96120	MARKLEEVILLE	71.3	71.0	0.7	0.7	0.5	0.5	8.2	8.3	5.1	4.6	6.5	8.5	7.9	24.2	33.6	8.3	1.4	78.7	40.9	53.1	46.9
96121	MILFORD	81.1	76.3	5.7	6.7	0.7	0.6	10.0	14.0	5.0	5.4	5.6	5.4	4.1	19.6	38.8	14.4	1.7	80.8	48.1	50.6	49.4
96122	PORTOLA	88.1	84.6	0.5	0.5	0.8	1.0	10.6	14.2	5.3	5.9	6.8	7.9	5.9	21.4	31.8	13.1	1.9	76.4	42.4	50.0	50.0
96123	RAVENDALE	68.0	69.4	26.6	18.4	0.8	0.0	26.7	59.2	0.0	0.0	0.0	2.0	18.4	71.4	8.2	0.0	0.0	100.0	30.8	100.0	0.0
96124	CALPINE	94.3	92.1	0.0	0.0	0.0	0.0	5.4	7.3	4.6	4.6	6.4	4.6	2.7	25.2	35.3	14.6	2.1	81.5	46.2	52.0	48.0
96125	SIERRA CITY	95.1	93.7	0.0	0.0	0.3	0.3	5.2	6.6	2.2	2.5	3.0	4.1	3.6	17.6	42.4	21.2	3.3	89.5	55.1	51.2	48.8
96126	SIERRAVILLE	93.9	92.2	0.3	0.3	0.3	0.3	6.8	9.3	4.4	5.5	6.7	7.1	4.4	20.3	34.2	14.7	2.7	78.1	46.0	49.7	50.3
96128	STANDISH	88.5	84.9	0.4	0.8	0.4	0.8	11.9	17.7	6.4	6.4	6.8	7.9	6.8	24.5	30.6	9.4	1.1	75.5	38.4	51.3	48.7
96130	SUSANVILLE	80.2	72.0	8.2	10.3	1.5	2.3	13.6	22.4	5.0	4.8	4.9	7.0	10.3	37.2	22.1	7.3	1.3	81.8	33.8	64.1	35.9
96132	TERMO	68.5	70.0	27.4	18.6	0.0	1.4	27.4	58.6	0.0	0.0	0.0	1.4	20.0	71.4	7.1	0.0	0.0	100.0	30.7	98.6	1.4
96133	TOPAZ	83.8	79.2	2.0	2.1	1.6	1.9	8.6	11.8	8.6	6.9	5.1	6.5	9.7	23.8	24.1	13.7	1.6	75.9	33.9	52.8	47.2
96134	TULELAKE	74.6	67.8	0.6	0.7	0.3	0.3	34.4	43.3	8.5	8.3	8.4	7.8	4.6	22.8	25.8	11.8	2.1	70.1	36.2	50.8	49.2
96135	VINTON	100.0	100.0	0.0	0.0	0.0	0.0	0.0	0.0	0.0	0.0	0.0	0.0	0.0	0.0	100.0	0.0	0.0	100.0	47.5	33.3	66.7
96136	WENDEL	88.5	84.7	0.6	0.5	0.6	0.5	12.1	16.9	6.6	6.6	7.1	8.2	6.6	23.5	30.6	9.8	1.1	74.3	38.6	51.9	48.1
96137	WESTWOOD	95.8	94.6	0.1	0.1	0.4	0.5	3.6	5.1	2.6	2.9	3.5	3.6	2.4	10.6	35.5	36.1	2.6	88.8	60.6	50.8	49.2
96140	CARNELIAN BAY	94.3	92.5	0.0	0.0	4.4	5.1	2.4	3.7	3.7	3.6	4.3	5.4	4.9	28.8	34.3	13.6	1.4	85.5	44.6	52.3	47.7
96141	HOMEWOOD	95.4	94.1	0.4	0.3	1.5	1.8	3.0	5.0	5.3	4.7	3.8	4.4	5.6	28.7	35.8	10.4	1.2	83.4	43.3	53.8	46.2
96142	TAHOMA	94.3	91.9	0.3	0.3	0.8	1.0	4.3	6.4	5.7	4.6	5.9	5.2	6.4	33.1	29.5	8.8	0.9	80.7	38.5	52.6	47.4
96143	KINGS BEACH	72.6	66.9	0.7	0.6	0.6	0.6	43.7	52.1	8.0	6.9	6.1	7.3	8.8	34.2	23.4	4.9	0.5	74.8	31.5	52.9	47.1
96145	TAHOE CITY	95.5	94.1	0.4	0.3	1.2	1.4	2.9	4.3	3.5	3.7	4.2	4.6	6.9	33.4	32.5	9.8	1.4	85.5	41.0	53.8	46.2
96146	OLYMPIC VALLEY	94.3	92.3	0.4	0.4	1.1	1.5	4.2	5.9	2.2	2.6	4.8	4.8	10.6	37.0	31.9	5.9	0.4	86.8	34.9	60.1	39.9
96148	TAHOE VISTA	84.2	78.4	0.1	0.1	0.9	0.9	22.5	31.0	5.9	5.7	5.5	5.8	6.1	32.0	30.0	8.3	0.7	79.3	37.6	50.9	49.1
96150	SOUTH LAKE TAHOE	80.9	76.6	0.7	0.7	4.8	5.6	20.6	25.4	6.3	6.0	6.0	6.9	7.7	28.8	29.0	8.4	0.9	77.7	36.7	51.3	48.7
96161	TRUCKEE	89.1	85.9	0.2	0.3	1.0	1.3	12.3	16.3	5.7	6.0	6.6	7.0	5.9	29.0	32.4	6.9	0.6	77.3	38.8	52.3	47.7
96162	TRUCKEE	94.1	91.4	0.0	0.0	0.0	0.9	3.0	4.3	3.4	5.2	5.2	6.0	5.2	23.3	43.1	7.8	0.9	82.8	45.6	51.7	48.3
	CALIFORNIA	59.5	54.5	6.7	6.2	11.3	12.5	32.4	38.3	7.5	7.1	6.9	7.5	7.4	28.5	24.2	9.3	1.6	74.1	34.3	49.9	50.1
	UNITED STATES	75.1	72.0	12.3	12.7	3.8	4.6	12.5	15.7	6.8	6.7	6.6	7.1	6.9	27.0	26.0	10.9	1.9	75.7	36.9	49.2	50.8

ZIP CODE #	POST OFFICE NAME	2009 Per Capita Income	2009 HH Income Base	2009 HOUSEHOLD INCOME DISTRIBUTION (%)					MEDIAN HOUSEHOLD INCOME				2009 Home Value Base	2009 HOME VALUE DISTRIBUTION (%)					2009 Median Home Value
				Less than $25,000	$25,000 to $49,999	$50,000 to $99,999	$100,000 to $149,999	$150,000 or More	2009	2014	2009 National Centile	2009 State Centile		Less than $50,000	$50,000 to $89,999	$90,000 to $174,999	$175,000 to $399,999	$400,000 or More	
96105	CHILCOOT	26880	238	28.6	19.3	39.9	8.4	3.8	52996	54646	68	48	183	6.6	3.8	19.1	31.7	38.8	290385
96106	CLIO	34631	115	15.7	24.3	44.3	11.3	4.3	63130	63586	81	63	96	1.0	1.0	12.5	53.1	32.3	315000
96107	COLEVILLE	21869	547	21.0	39.1	35.6	3.1	1.1	42745	45284	42	28	332	19.3	2.7	16.3	51.2	10.5	213768
96108	DAVIS CREEK	19911	145	33.1	14.5	47.6	4.8	0.0	51852	55251	66	45	115	3.5	15.7	45.2	30.4	5.2	136719
96109	DOYLE	17975	580	41.4	25.7	26.9	3.3	2.8	34457	37446	16	13	438	9.8	13.2	34.0	34.5	8.4	156548
96111	FLORISTON	19895	47	25.5	34.0	34.0	4.3	2.1	39074	41158	30	20	30	0.0	6.7	20.0	56.7	16.7	260000
96112	FORT BIDWELL	23902	101	36.6	32.7	21.8	5.0	4.0	33267	34678	14	11	72	9.7	12.5	44.4	25.0	8.3	140909
96113	HERLONG	20801	425	24.7	30.4	37.2	7.3	0.5	44678	47259	47	32	233	9.9	9.0	40.8	32.2	8.2	148438
96114	JANESVILLE	24410	1225	16.8	27.0	40.3	10.6	5.2	55094	58231	71	52	1005	0.8	2.3	14.2	64.7	18.0	270972
96115	LAKE CITY	22864	107	35.5	33.6	22.4	4.7	3.7	34052	34140	16	12	76	9.2	11.8	44.7	26.3	7.9	143750
96116	LIKELY	19449	139	39.6	27.3	26.6	5.8	0.7	35277	36733	19	14	105	3.8	9.5	49.5	24.8	12.4	145313
96117	LITCHFIELD	24064	81	24.7	28.4	37.0	6.2	3.7	47357	50402	55	38	57	3.5	1.8	15.8	66.7	12.3	229167
96118	LOYALTON	21344	557	28.9	31.8	30.2	5.9	3.2	40508	42338	34	22	397	7.1	6.8	42.6	31.5	12.1	165341
96119	MADELINE	14994	24	50.0	16.7	29.2	4.2	0.0	25000	22257	3	3	18	11.1	11.1	16.7	33.3	27.8	216667
96120	MARKLEEVILLE	26034	432	21.8	27.5	38.9	6.9	4.9	50664	52737	63	44	292	5.5	5.8	17.5	38.0	33.2	318333
96121	MILFORD	21112	192	26.6	30.2	33.3	9.4	0.5	44003	47349	45	31	132	10.6	9.1	39.4	32.6	8.3	150000
96122	PORTOLA	20941	1845	32.8	27.5	31.8	5.4	2.4	39908	41944	32	21	1204	6.7	5.2	37.7	39.0	11.4	176099
96123	RAVENDALE	11503	14	42.9	21.4	28.6	7.1	0.0	32500	27290	12	9	11	27.3	9.1	18.2	27.3	18.2	162500
96124	CALPINE	24772	157	25.5	29.9	35.0	6.4	3.2	46326	46822	52	35	118	3.4	7.6	39.8	33.9	15.3	173750
96125	SIERRA CITY	25780	187	23.5	32.6	38.0	4.3	1.6	46049	46662	51	35	133	0.0	2.3	33.8	57.1	6.8	219000
96126	SIERRAVILLE	21161	300	28.0	33.0	29.0	7.0	3.0	41074	42220	36	24	217	6.5	6.0	33.6	37.8	16.1	203750
96128	STANDISH	22969	106	24.5	27.4	38.7	6.6	2.8	48211	51268	57	39	75	4.0	2.7	14.7	66.7	12.0	228125
96130	SUSANVILLE	20920	6716	26.5	27.6	36.3	7.4	2.1	46172	48836	52	35	4360	8.1	4.0	28.7	50.9	8.3	195262
96132	TERMO	20069	36	47.2	22.2	27.8	2.8	0.0	26476	27279	4	3	28	17.9	7.1	14.3	39.3	21.4	208333
96133	TOPAZ	20275	166	24.1	37.3	33.1	2.4	3.0	40628	43109	35	22	88	28.4	0.0	13.6	46.6	11.4	216667
96134	TULELAKE	14726	878	40.4	29.5	24.7	5.1	0.2	32026	33667	11	9	548	15.3	22.8	36.3	19.0	6.6	117411
96135	VINTON	0	0	0.0	0.0	0.0	0.0	0.0	0	0	0	0	0	0.0	0.0	0.0	0.0	0.0	0
96136	WENDEL	19425	62	24.2	27.4	37.1	6.5	4.8	48639	51186	58	40	44	2.3	2.3	15.9	65.9	13.6	230769
96137	WESTWOOD	30971	998	17.1	27.2	41.7	7.2	6.8	55618	57247	72	53	820	2.7	1.3	13.2	42.3	40.5	340458
96140	CARNELIAN BAY	33295	392	15.1	19.6	38.8	21.7	4.8	60301	63743	78	59	266	0.0	0.0	0.0	33.1	66.9	480357
96141	HOMEWOOD	34268	180	5.6	18.9	62.2	12.8	0.6	60438	61696	78	59	99	0.0	0.0	0.0	72.7	27.3	343750
96142	TAHOMA	37099	749	10.4	15.1	42.2	22.4	9.9	77281	80556	91	78	502	1.2	0.0	3.6	55.4	39.8	350485
96143	KINGS BEACH	21361	2222	22.4	33.8	28.6	12.3	2.9	46009	46985	51	35	882	6.3	1.1	10.5	48.1	33.9	297059
96145	TAHOE CITY	45729	3299	11.6	21.6	32.5	19.7	14.5	71752	76006	88	72	2018	0.0	0.2	1.4	23.7	74.7	607258
96146	OLYMPIC VALLEY	61528	114	8.8	13.2	32.5	18.4	27.2	91085	94205	95	87	68	0.0	0.0	2.9	8.8	88.2	856061
96148	TAHOE VISTA	31815	600	16.5	21.3	32.0	19.8	10.3	58804	64904	76	56	348	12.9	1.7	9.8	31.9	43.7	346341
96150	SOUTH LAKE TAHOE	24518	14518	18.3	30.7	35.7	11.4	3.8	50804	52579	63	44	7649	3.9	0.7	13.8	65.1	16.5	235407
96161	TRUCKEE	34976	7017	7.6	19.7	45.7	16.0	11.0	74274	75458	89	74	5219	4.3	1.1	3.2	32.0	59.4	449397
96162	TRUCKEE	23062	59	27.1	39.0	27.1	5.1	1.7	32954	37357	13	10	39	2.6	5.1	35.9	38.5	17.9	195833
	CALIFORNIA	28199		18.5	22.2	33.9	14.0	11.5	61614	64088				3.3	2.6	13.6	41.0	39.5	321752
	UNITED STATES	27277		20.9	24.4	35.3	11.7	7.6	54719	56938				9.3	13.1	31.6	32.6	13.5	162279

ZIP CODE	FINANCIAL SERVICES				THE HOME						ENTERTAINMENT						PERSONAL			
					Home Improvements		Furnishings													
# POST OFFICE NAME	Auto Loan	Home Loan	Invest-ments	Retire-ment Plans	Home Repair	Lawn & Garden	Comput-ers & Hard-ware-Personal	Major Appli-ances	TV, Radio, Sound Equip-ment	Furni-ture	Dine out/ Carry out	Sports Equip-ment	Fees & Tickets	Toys & Games	Travel	Cable TV	Apparel & Services	Auto Repairs	Health Insur-ance	Pets & Supplies
96105 CHILCOOT	106	85	137	83	93	112	85	108	89	79	88	79	74	84	92	95	58	99	106	125
96106 CLIO	92	97	131	96	111	114	87	103	92	98	90	64	96	83	101	96	62	98	114	116
96107 COLEVILLE	77	63	90	63	67	77	66	76	67	63	67	57	58	65	68	70	45	73	75	89
96108 DAVIS CREEK	82	65	105	64	71	87	65	83	68	61	68	61	56	65	70	73	45	77	82	96
96109 DOYLE	66	61	81	57	68	74	59	70	62	62	61	47	57	57	64	66	41	67	77	80
96111 FLORISTON	83	67	108	66	73	88	67	85	70	63	69	62	58	66	72	75	46	78	84	99
96112 FORT BIDWELL	82	66	106	65	72	87	66	84	69	62	68	61	57	65	71	73	45	77	83	97
96113 HERLONG	81	66	96	65	70	81	68	80	70	65	69	60	60	68	71	73	47	76	79	93
96114 JANESVILLE	94	102	100	103	103	100	91	96	90	96	91	71	96	91	96	90	64	92	93	112
96115 LAKE CITY	82	66	107	65	72	87	66	84	69	62	68	61	57	66	72	74	45	77	83	97
96116 LIKELY	70	56	91	55	62	74	56	72	59	53	58	52	49	56	61	63	39	66	71	83
96117 LITCHFIELD	90	83	74	80	81	85	78	83	81	81	81	60	74	84	75	83	55	80	83	98
96118 LOYALTON	87	68	106	66	73	91	69	87	73	64	72	64	59	70	73	79	48	81	88	101
96119 MADELINE	66	47	67	46	49	67	48	61	54	45	53	46	39	53	48	59	35	56	64	73
96120 MARKLEEVILLE	98	95	110	96	97	106	89	101	90	87	90	77	87	89	95	93	61	95	100	118
96121 MILFORD	85	68	110	67	75	90	68	87	71	64	70	63	59	68	74	76	47	80	86	100
96122 PORTOLA	81	65	90	64	69	84	67	80	71	63	70	59	58	69	68	76	47	75	82	94
96123 RAVENDALE	63	45	65	44	47	64	46	59	51	43	51	44	37	51	46	57	33	54	61	70
96124 CALPINE	86	69	111	68	75	91	69	87	72	64	71	64	60	68	75	77	47	81	86	101
96125 SIERRA CITY	83	67	108	66	73	88	67	85	70	63	69	62	58	66	72	75	46	78	84	98
96126 SIERRAVILLE	84	68	109	67	74	89	68	86	71	63	70	63	59	67	73	75	46	79	85	100
96128 STANDISH	90	83	73	80	81	85	78	83	81	81	81	60	74	84	74	83	55	80	83	98
96130 SUSANVILLE	78	77	73	76	76	77	75	76	76	76	76	57	74	76	74	77	52	76	77	90
96132 TERMO	65	46	67	45	48	66	48	61	53	44	52	45	38	52	47	58	34	56	63	72
96133 TOPAZ	75	64	68	64	63	65	70	69	69	70	70	54	64	71	66	69	48	71	67	82
96134 TULELAKE	66	55	64	52	56	61	58	63	56	55	57	50	49	57	56	57	39	61	61	73
96135 VINTON	0	0	0	0	0	0	0	0	0	0	0	0	0	0	0	0	0	0	0	0
96136 WENDEL	90	82	73	80	80	84	78	82	81	81	81	60	74	84	74	83	55	80	82	98
96137 WESTWOOD	91	93	127	92	106	110	85	100	89	94	88	64	91	81	97	93	60	95	110	114
96140 CARNELIAN BAY	89	111	130	113	122	96	106	105	93	114	93	83	116	89	118	85	69	101	88	116
96141 HOMEWOOD	89	94	78	95	89	95	93	89	92	89	91	71	94	93	92	92	64	91	96	108
96142 TAHOMA	110	126	139	130	133	112	128	120	116	131	118	98	135	114	136	109	86	122	108	138
96143 KINGS BEACH	78	76	74	76	76	65	88	78	83	86	86	64	85	83	84	79	63	84	71	89
96145 TAHOE CITY	128	146	173	152	159	131	151	143	135	155	138	116	159	132	161	127	101	143	127	163
96146 OLYMPIC VALLEY	183	195	230	215	206	178	218	190	203	215	210	163	229	201	223	195	157	200	176	223
96148 TAHOE VISTA	111	120	115	122	119	113	116	112	113	118	114	88	122	114	119	111	81	113	111	133
96150 SOUTH LAKE TAHOE	85	86	88	86	86	82	90	86	88	88	89	68	90	88	90	87	64	89	84	101
96161 TRUCKEE	126	144	147	146	147	130	135	134	125	140	128	106	143	126	143	120	91	131	121	154
96162 TRUCKEE	74	61	92	60	66	77	61	75	63	58	63	55	54	60	65	67	42	70	74	87
CALIFORNIA	112	119	122	118	122	107	121	116	114	124	116	92	124	114	124	110	84	118	107	132
UNITED STATES	100	100	100	100	100	100	100	100	100	100	100	100	100	100	100	100	100	100	100	100

POPULATION CHANGE

 80002-80246

ZIP CODE #	POST OFFICE NAME	COUNTY FIPS CODE	POPULATION 2000	POPULATION 2009	POPULATION 2014	2000-2009 ANNUAL RATE % Rate	2000-2009 ANNUAL RATE State Centile	HOUSEHOLDS 2000	HOUSEHOLDS 2009	HOUSEHOLDS 2014	HOUSEHOLDS % Annual Rate 2000-2009	HOUSEHOLDS 2009 Average HH Size	FAMILIES 2000	FAMILIES 2009	FAMILIES % Annual Rate 2000-2009
80002	ARVADA	059	14699	16553	17212	1.3	56	6246	7095	7410	1.4	2.33	3814	4159	0.9
80003	ARVADA	059	34254	33511	33527	-0.2	16	12738	12688	12750	0.0	2.62	8893	8648	-0.3
80004	ARVADA	059	37248	36208	35888	-0.3	13	14431	14248	14205	-0.1	2.51	10185	9869	-0.3
80005	ARVADA	059	24781	25478	25721	0.3	31	9213	9609	9748	0.5	2.64	7017	7223	0.3
80007	ARVADA	059	5849	7271	7993	2.4	78	1952	2394	2637	2.2	3.03	1719	2090	2.1
80010	AURORA	001	45952	49198	50811	0.7	43	13953	14028	14409	0.1	3.28	9417	9030	-0.5
80011	AURORA	005	45740	46894	48401	0.3	31	16850	17305	17901	0.3	2.67	11272	10908	-0.4
80012	AURORA	005	42571	43981	45388	0.4	34	17707	18508	19185	0.5	2.35	10728	10545	-0.2
80013	AURORA	005	57306	67054	71675	1.7	67	19965	23818	25600	1.9	2.82	15183	17544	1.6
80014	AURORA	005	34141	36332	37710	0.7	43	16624	17790	18502	0.7	2.02	8590	8721	0.2
80015	AURORA	005	53682	64551	69988	2.0	73	17877	21512	23317	2.0	2.99	14428	17067	1.8
80016	AURORA	005	7769	36528	47931	18.2	99	2435	11587	15303	18.4	3.15	2189	10369	18.3
80017	AURORA	005	29470	32853	35374	1.2	54	11359	12745	13717	1.3	2.58	7462	7865	0.6
80018	AURORA	005	1426	6278	8296	17.4	98	497	2399	3195	18.6	2.61	403	1761	17.3
80019	AURORA	001	61	1731	2345	43.6	100	17	606	822	47.2	2.82	13	440	46.3
80020	BROOMFIELD	014	46449	50383	54154	0.9	47	16281	17744	19222	0.9	2.83	12467	13237	0.7
80021	BROOMFIELD	059	28305	31839	33024	1.3	56	10687	12232	12790	1.5	2.59	7312	8023	1.0
80022	COMMERCE CITY	001	28138	43301	50137	4.8	93	8982	14123	16397	5.0	3.04	6746	10587	5.0
80023	BROOMFIELD	014	2952	13997	20357	18.3	99	986	4621	6730	18.2	3.03	857	3854	17.6
80026	LAFAYETTE	013	25174	27129	28113	0.8	45	9562	10351	10733	0.9	2.61	6505	6818	0.5
80027	LOUISVILLE	013	28161	30360	31528	0.8	45	10660	11530	11981	0.9	2.63	7293	7568	0.4
80030	WESTMINSTER	001	15912	16276	16984	0.2	28	6097	6251	6525	0.3	2.55	3852	3761	-0.3
80031	WESTMINSTER	001	34710	39503	42979	1.4	58	12967	14792	16036	1.4	2.67	9105	10096	1.1
80033	WHEAT RIDGE	059	26253	25492	25208	-0.3	13	11599	11375	11282	-0.2	2.18	6632	6287	-0.6
80101	AGATE	039	286	375	425	3.0	85	113	146	164	2.8	2.57	80	102	2.7
80102	BENNETT	001	4265	5446	6318	2.7	82	1490	1948	2266	2.9	2.80	1161	1466	2.6
80103	BYERS	001	2051	2448	2736	1.9	70	725	891	1000	2.3	2.75	560	662	1.8
80104	CASTLE ROCK	035	15030	27668	34963	6.8	95	5514	10498	13346	7.2	2.63	4153	7738	7.0
80105	DEER TRAIL	005	1245	1430	1530	1.5	62	459	525	563	1.5	2.72	326	356	1.0
80106	ELBERT	039	3587	3893	4332	0.9	47	1234	1360	1520	1.1	2.86	1042	1123	0.8
80107	ELIZABETH	039	10086	11970	12852	1.9	70	3373	3948	4218	1.7	3.03	2886	3347	1.6
80108	CASTLE ROCK	035	9132	23401	31439	10.7	98	3255	8091	10871	10.3	2.87	2738	6817	10.4
80109	CASTLE ROCK	035	5613	17419	23480	13.0	98	1785	5209	6965	12.3	3.34	1610	4653	12.2
80110	ENGLEWOOD	005	21489	21760	22296	0.1	26	8786	9042	9307	0.3	2.38	5247	5054	-0.4
80111	ENGLEWOOD	005	26170	29645	32643	1.4	58	9503	10961	12121	1.6	2.67	7020	7779	1.1
80112	ENGLEWOOD	005	21503	29670	32001	3.5	89	7764	10826	11770	3.7	2.66	5758	7970	3.6
80113	ENGLEWOOD	005	21619	21480	21816	-0.1	19	9670	9729	9916	0.1	2.13	5226	4951	-0.6
80116	FRANKTOWN	035	4018	4476	5338	1.2	54	1431	1622	1947	1.4	2.76	1237	1380	1.2
80117	KIOWA	039	2547	3150	3438	2.3	76	883	1066	1157	2.1	2.95	716	855	1.9
80118	LARKSPUR	035	3979	5001	5685	2.5	79	1451	1868	2138	2.8	2.64	1233	1554	2.5
80120	LITTLETON	005	29309	28677	28988	-0.2	16	12585	12559	12778	0.0	2.24	7530	7090	-0.6
80121	LITTLETON	005	18171	18365	18822	0.1	26	6711	6932	7146	0.4	2.62	5202	5178	0.0
80122	LITTLETON	005	31761	30981	31189	-0.3	13	11892	11859	12015	0.0	2.59	8958	8582	-0.5
80123	LITTLETON	059	40356	44681	46833	1.1	52	16256	18244	19235	1.3	2.45	10935	11819	0.8
80124	LITTLETON	035	12662	20787	25357	5.5	94	4476	7465	9131	5.7	2.78	3597	6087	5.9
80125	LITTLETON	035	6053	10699	13788	6.4	94	2196	3920	5053	6.5	2.73	1795	3177	6.4
80126	LITTLETON	035	30371	41103	48196	3.3	88	10337	13805	16067	3.2	2.98	8245	10863	3.0
80127	LITTLETON	059	39480	43375	45002	1.0	50	13443	15083	15756	1.3	2.87	11062	12209	1.1
80128	LITTLETON	059	34300	36127	36832	0.6	40	12456	13386	13745	0.8	2.69	9521	10006	0.5
80129	LITTLETON	035	19976	27367	31417	3.5	89	6809	9478	10922	3.6	2.89	5618	7632	3.4
80130	LITTLETON	035	17966	25936	30782	4.0	90	6544	9650	11549	4.3	2.69	5111	7246	3.8
80132	MONUMENT	041	13815	18953	21222	3.5	89	4637	6460	7278	3.6	2.93	3997	5477	3.5
80133	PALMER LAKE	041	2087	2322	2456	1.2	54	828	946	1008	1.5	2.45	622	679	1.0
80134	PARKER	035	30446	58861	73905	7.4	96	9972	19652	24745	7.6	2.99	8589	16636	7.4
80135	SEDALIA	035	3689	4013	4722	0.9	47	1373	1493	1761	0.9	2.68	1099	1178	0.8
80136	STRASBURG	001	2704	4162	5241	4.8	93	934	1442	1827	4.8	2.88	738	1099	4.4
80137	WATKINS	005	2157	2349	2608	0.9	47	765	849	949	1.1	2.76	601	627	0.5
80138	PARKER	035	20114	30324	36284	4.5	92	6844	10332	12387	4.6	2.92	5788	8688	4.5
80202	DENVER	031	4315	8045	9385	7.0	95	2949	5494	6435	7.0	1.39	610	1221	7.8
80203	DENVER	031	18577	19736	20531	0.7	43	12819	13637	14146	0.7	1.39	1883	1886	0.0
80204	DENVER	031	32960	33894	34731	0.3	31	11179	11461	11786	0.3	2.92	6704	6522	-0.3
80205	DENVER	031	29600	32875	34877	1.1	52	10313	11472	12210	1.2	2.77	5985	6449	0.8
80206	DENVER	031	20721	21013	21564	0.2	28	11743	11941	12230	0.2	1.71	3670	3550	-0.4
80207	DENVER	031	21200	21387	21676	0.1	26	7954	7967	8031	0.0	2.64	5424	5279	-0.3
80208	DENVER	031	1966	1890	1865	-0.4	11	379	341	332	-1.1	3.00	77	65	-1.8
80209	DENVER	031	20553	20747	21280	0.1	26	11648	11796	12056	0.1	1.76	4313	4189	-0.3
80210	DENVER	031	30433	30103	30513	-0.1	19	15317	15089	15221	-0.2	1.93	6557	6197	-0.6
80211	DENVER	031	38788	39061	39919	0.1	26	14472	14466	14723	0.0	2.64	8351	8124	-0.3
80212	DENVER	031	18140	18525	19074	0.2	28	8326	8540	8779	0.3	2.13	4279	4215	-0.2
80214	DENVER	059	25992	25325	24992	-0.3	13	11236	10903	10777	-0.3	2.22	5763	5371	-0.8
80215	DENVER	059	19052	18652	18469	-0.2	16	8255	8177	8132	-0.1	2.22	5008	4803	-0.5
80216	DENVER	031	10933	12753	13699	1.7	67	2856	3235	3466	1.4	3.84	2191	2434	1.1
80218	DENVER	031	16474	16433	16765	0.0	22	10252	10217	10379	0.0	1.58	2269	2147	-0.6
80219	DENVER	031	59884	60662	61376	0.1	26	19309	18916	18982	-0.2	3.19	13796	13220	-0.5
80220	DENVER	031	33582	33862	34595	0.1	26	15505	15433	15655	-0.1	2.18	7799	7487	-0.4
80221	DENVER	001	38370	39116	40527	0.2	28	13227	13321	13728	0.1	2.89	9238	8990	-0.3
80222	DENVER	031	19446	19480	19920	0.0	22	9244	9220	9395	0.0	2.04	4487	4304	-0.4
80223	DENVER	031	19402	19277	19462	-0.1	19	7131	6942	6959	-0.3	2.76	4175	3957	-0.6
80224	DENVER	031	17967	18120	18464	0.1	26	8471	8423	8523	-0.1	2.11	4220	4047	-0.5
80226	DENVER	059	29379	29768	29893	0.1	26	11896	12287	12426	0.4	2.36	7296	7267	0.0
80227	DENVER	059	32229	33024	33536	0.3	31	14090	14627	14893	0.4	2.25	8606	8665	0.1
80228	DENVER	059	30977	31348	31686	0.1	26	12865	13124	13281	0.2	2.38	8269	8308	0.1
80229	DENVER	001	40557	48139	53754	1.9	70	14348	17049	18980	1.9	2.81	10166	11781	1.6
80230	DENVER	031	2185	5450	6709	10.4	98	892	2659	3297	12.5	2.05	511	1463	12.0
80231	DENVER	031	28569	29327	30192	0.3	31	15158	15369	15742	0.1	1.90	6448	6036	-0.7
80232	DENVER	059	21294	21113	21007	-0.1	19	8576	8619	8619	0.1	2.42	5756	5647	-0.2
80233	DENVER	001	36000	44862	49848	2.4	78	12560	16236	18176	2.8	2.75	9405	11426	2.1
80234	DENVER	001	21617	26281	29522	2.1	73	8740	10498	11715	2.0	2.50	5683	6589	1.6
80235	DENVER	059	7923	8213	8597	0.4	34	3147	3440	3592	1.0	2.22	1842	2007	0.9
80236	DENVER	031	16431	17018	17551	0.4	34	6105	6226	6396	0.2	2.59	4058	4020	-0.1
80237	DENVER	031	16459	16756	17255	0.2	28	8427	8625	8849	0.3	1.94	4157	4091	-0.2
80238	DENVER	031	0	7108	7473	0.0	22	0	3151	3293	0.0	2.26	0	1463	0.0
80239	DENVER	031	28796	34574	36798	2.0	73	8381	10053	10715	2.0	3.44	6808	7904	1.6
80241	DENVER	001	27414	33878	38237	2.3	76	9369	11792	13348	2.5	2.85	7458	8996	2.0
80246	DENVER	031	13098	13339	13604	0.2	28	7017	7011	7116	0.0	1.90	2521	2351	-0.8
	COLORADO					1.7					1.6	2.55			1.5
	UNITED STATES					1.0					1.1	2.59			0.9

ZIP CODE #	POST OFFICE NAME	RACE (%) White 2000	White 2009	Black 2000	Black 2009	Asian/Pacific 2000	Asian/Pacific 2009	% Hispanic Origin 2000	% Hispanic Origin 2009	2009 AGE DISTRIBUTION (%) 0-4	5-9	10-14	15-19	20-24	25-44	45-64	65-84	85+	18+	MEDIAN AGE 2009	% 2009 Males	% 2009 Females
80002	ARVADA	89.2	87.1	0.9	1.1	1.6	2.0	14.1	17.7	7.8	7.3	6.9	6.4	6.8	28.0	27.1	8.5	1.2	74.5	35.8	50.2	49.8
80003	ARVADA	86.4	83.4	0.8	0.9	4.0	5.1	14.2	18.1	6.4	6.4	6.8	7.0	6.3	28.1	28.1	9.9	1.0	76.1	37.5	49.6	50.4
80004	ARVADA	92.5	91.1	0.6	0.6	1.7	2.1	7.9	10.0	6.1	6.2	6.4	6.6	5.9	24.4	28.9	13.1	2.5	77.1	40.9	48.0	52.0
80005	ARVADA	93.5	92.2	0.6	0.6	1.9	2.5	6.9	8.7	5.3	6.1	6.8	6.8	4.7	24.7	34.3	10.4	0.9	77.5	42.0	49.0	51.0
80007	ARVADA	95.8	95.0	0.4	0.5	1.2	1.5	5.0	6.4	7.1	8.0	8.6	7.4	4.2	24.5	33.1	6.8	0.4	71.4	39.3	49.3	50.7
80010	AURORA	53.7	50.9	16.5	16.1	2.7	2.9	48.8	55.7	10.1	8.9	7.4	7.6	8.6	34.2	17.1	5.2	0.9	69.3	28.9	54.5	45.5
80011	AURORA	61.8	57.7	17.8	18.7	3.7	4.3	24.8	30.5	8.7	7.9	7.1	7.2	8.1	30.0	21.6	8.4	1.0	72.0	31.5	50.2	49.8
80012	AURORA	62.7	59.4	19.3	19.5	5.9	7.0	16.9	21.4	7.3	6.6	6.2	6.6	8.1	30.4	24.4	9.3	1.0	76.1	34.3	48.7	51.3
80013	AURORA	77.7	73.9	8.5	9.0	5.2	6.7	10.8	14.2	8.1	7.9	7.8	7.2	6.4	32.6	25.5	4.4	0.3	71.8	33.1	49.7	50.3
80014	AURORA	80.8	78.6	8.3	8.5	5.1	6.2	6.9	9.1	4.3	4.1	4.4	5.3	6.7	27.2	29.3	14.9	3.9	84.1	43.5	46.7	53.3
80015	AURORA	82.2	78.4	5.7	6.1	6.0	7.7	7.3	10.1	8.4	8.8	8.9	7.7	5.3	31.1	26.2	3.2	0.4	68.9	33.9	49.1	50.9
80016	AURORA	88.7	88.4	2.9	2.2	5.1	4.9	4.3	7.1	6.6	7.7	8.6	8.0	3.9	23.4	34.2	6.9	0.7	71.7	40.3	49.6	50.4
80017	AURORA	69.4	65.9	14.8	15.3	5.0	6.0	13.0	17.2	8.3	7.5	7.1	6.9	7.9	32.8	24.5	4.8	0.3	73.2	32.0	48.8	51.2
80018	AURORA	80.7	83.9	6.5	4.8	5.0	4.0	8.7	9.0	6.7	7.1	7.4	6.6	3.9	26.1	31.7	9.5	1.0	74.7	40.4	49.3	50.7
80019	AURORA	77.0	70.5	3.3	4.0	4.9	6.5	21.3	28.6	6.7	7.5	8.2	8.4	4.8	27.8	29.6	6.3	0.6	72.8	37.2	50.7	49.3
80020	BROOMFIELD	87.9	85.4	0.9	1.0	5.1	6.2	9.1	11.5	7.8	7.8	7.9	7.2	5.6	30.6	26.5	5.9	0.6	72.0	34.9	49.9	50.1
80021	BROOMFIELD	89.6	87.4	1.1	1.1	4.0	5.4	8.7	10.7	6.5	6.4	6.5	6.3	6.3	35.6	26.4	5.2	0.7	76.7	34.8	49.9	50.1
80022	COMMERCE CITY	66.8	67.1	1.9	1.8	0.7	1.2	51.0	51.7	8.2	7.8	7.7	8.0	7.0	27.6	24.3	8.5	1.0	71.6	33.2	51.7	48.3
80023	BROOMFIELD	91.4	88.0	0.7	0.7	2.8	4.8	8.3	11.1	8.9	9.3	9.2	6.8	3.2	30.6	26.9	4.8	0.4	68.2	36.5	49.3	50.7
80026	LAFAYETTE	86.0	83.7	0.9	1.0	3.4	4.1	15.6	18.6	7.4	7.5	7.4	6.3	5.6	31.5	27.5	6.0	0.8	73.7	36.0	49.2	50.8
80027	LOUISVILLE	89.8	87.2	1.0	1.1	4.8	6.5	5.0	6.5	7.2	7.7	7.5	6.6	5.3	33.0	27.6	4.5	0.6	73.3	36.0	50.2	49.8
80030	WESTMINSTER	74.4	69.0	1.1	1.3	8.1	9.9	30.4	38.1	7.8	7.2	6.4	6.5	7.4	29.0	23.1	9.8	2.7	74.9	34.4	50.1	49.9
80031	WESTMINSTER	82.0	77.8	1.4	1.7	5.4	7.1	17.9	22.8	7.0	6.8	6.8	6.8	6.3	30.6	26.4	8.6	0.7	75.4	35.7	49.9	50.1
80033	WHEAT RIDGE	90.0	87.9	0.9	1.0	1.3	1.7	12.3	15.6	5.8	5.4	5.4	5.6	6.2	25.1	27.7	14.5	4.5	79.9	42.4	47.5	52.5
80101	AGATE	93.0	92.3	0.0	0.0	0.0	0.0	7.7	9.1	5.6	6.4	7.2	7.5	4.0	22.9	32.0	12.3	2.1	76.0	42.2	50.4	49.6
80102	BENNETT	93.6	92.0	0.8	1.0	0.6	0.8	5.5	7.7	7.7	8.2	8.2	7.5	5.5	26.5	28.8	6.9	0.7	71.2	35.6	50.5	49.5
80103	BYERS	95.8	94.9	0.3	0.4	0.1	0.2	4.0	5.6	7.3	7.4	7.6	7.6	6.1	25.3	29.2	8.5	1.0	73.0	37.2	51.1	48.9
80104	CASTLE ROCK	94.1	93.7	0.4	0.5	1.1	1.4	5.8	6.4	8.2	7.8	7.4	6.5	5.3	30.1	26.3	7.6	0.9	72.4	35.6	49.2	50.8
80105	DEER TRAIL	95.7	95.0	0.6	0.6	0.6	0.8	3.2	4.3	7.1	7.3	7.3	7.9	5.9	23.5	27.6	11.2	2.2	72.9	38.0	50.8	49.2
80106	ELBERT	94.3	93.5	1.4	1.5	0.4	0.6	4.1	5.2	6.2	7.0	8.0	8.1	4.6	25.3	33.5	6.8	0.4	73.4	39.5	49.6	50.4
80107	ELIZABETH	95.3	94.6	0.4	0.5	0.6	0.7	4.0	5.0	6.3	7.2	7.9	7.8	4.7	24.7	34.2	6.8	0.5	73.7	39.5	49.7	50.3
80108	CASTLE ROCK	94.9	94.6	0.9	0.9	1.3	1.5	4.5	5.3	6.6	7.7	8.7	7.7	4.3	22.6	33.8	7.9	0.8	72.1	40.7	50.3	49.7
80109	CASTLE ROCK	94.8	94.8	0.5	0.5	1.2	1.6	5.3	5.2	9.6	9.8	9.4	7.0	3.5	28.8	26.5	5.1	0.4	66.7	34.9	50.0	50.0
80110	ENGLEWOOD	82.0	78.6	2.0	2.0	2.3	2.7	21.4	26.9	7.0	6.4	5.9	6.4	7.4	29.8	25.7	9.7	1.6	77.0	36.1	50.9	49.1
80111	ENGLEWOOD	89.8	87.6	1.9	2.2	5.1	6.5	5.5	7.2	5.0	6.3	7.7	7.9	5.6	23.9	34.7	8.1	0.9	75.7	40.4	50.2	49.8
80112	ENGLEWOOD	92.9	82.2	1.9	10.4	2.6	3.2	4.8	7.5	5.3	5.9	6.6	7.6	5.9	25.1	33.1	9.7	0.8	77.3	40.7	49.9	50.1
80113	ENGLEWOOD	91.3	89.5	1.3	1.4	1.8	2.3	7.8	10.4	4.9	5.1	5.5	5.6	7.0	27.2	28.8	11.4	4.5	81.0	41.0	48.9	51.1
80116	FRANKTOWN	97.0	96.6	0.2	0.2	0.6	0.8	2.7	3.4	4.3	5.8	7.4	7.1	3.5	18.2	40.8	11.8	1.1	77.7	46.8	49.9	50.1
80117	KIOWA	94.9	94.0	0.7	0.8	0.5	0.7	3.7	4.8	7.0	7.7	8.2	8.0	5.0	24.1	31.9	7.7	0.6	71.7	38.8	50.9	49.1
80118	LARKSPUR	96.7	96.2	0.3	0.2	0.8	1.0	3.3	4.2	5.1	6.3	8.3	7.7	3.4	18.2	38.8	11.4	0.8	75.0	45.4	49.7	50.3
80120	LITTLETON	91.5	89.9	1.2	1.3	1.8	2.2	8.6	11.0	5.4	5.4	5.7	6.2	6.3	24.3	29.6	14.2	2.8	79.7	42.4	48.5	51.5
80121	LITTLETON	94.2	93.1	0.9	1.0	1.7	2.1	4.2	5.7	5.2	6.0	7.3	7.2	4.5	20.5	32.8	14.7	1.8	76.7	44.5	49.0	51.0
80122	LITTLETON	94.9	93.9	0.7	0.8	2.0	2.5	4.0	5.4	5.1	5.8	6.9	7.4	5.0	22.0	34.0	12.2	1.7	77.1	43.6	48.0	52.0
80123	LITTLETON	91.3	89.1	1.0	1.0	2.4	3.1	8.7	11.9	6.2	6.3	6.5	6.3	6.0	29.9	28.3	9.3	1.2	77.0	37.7	48.8	51.2
80124	LITTLETON	91.8	89.9	1.3	1.7	3.6	4.7	4.4	5.4	9.2	9.1	8.8	6.7	3.5	29.4	28.0	5.0	0.3	68.5	35.9	49.4	50.6
80125	LITTLETON	94.4	93.4	0.4	0.3	1.4	1.8	5.2	6.8	8.5	8.6	8.7	6.7	4.2	29.1	28.1	5.8	0.4	70.0	36.3	49.9	50.1
80126	LITTLETON	91.2	89.9	1.2	1.1	3.7	4.8	5.0	6.5	8.7	9.4	9.3	7.4	3.7	29.2	27.7	4.1	0.4	67.6	35.7	49.4	50.6
80127	LITTLETON	93.9	92.6	0.5	0.5	2.0	2.5	6.0	7.8	7.1	8.3	9.0	7.7	4.4	27.9	30.4	4.9	0.4	70.5	37.1	50.1	49.9
80128	LITTLETON	93.6	92.2	0.7	0.8	1.5	2.1	6.5	8.5	6.6	6.9	7.5	7.0	5.0	28.1	30.3	7.9	0.7	74.4	38.2	49.2	50.8
80129	LITTLETON	91.2	83.6	1.2	2.3	3.4	5.6	6.5	10.9	11.9	9.6	7.8	5.2	3.3	37.5	20.2	4.1	0.4	67.2	32.3	49.6	50.4
80130	LITTLETON	89.5	87.1	1.5	1.5	5.4	7.5	5.3	6.5	10.7	8.9	7.8	5.7	3.6	37.6	21.6	3.8	0.3	68.7	32.5	49.5	50.5
80132	MONUMENT	94.6	93.3	0.9	1.0	1.4	1.8	3.7	5.1	6.2	7.6	8.8	8.1	4.3	21.3	34.8	8.2	0.7	72.0	40.9	50.4	49.6
80133	PALMER LAKE	94.2	93.0	0.6	0.6	0.9	1.2	5.4	7.4	5.8	6.8	7.5	6.9	4.7	25.7	33.7	8.1	0.9	74.9	40.5	50.6	49.4
80134	PARKER	93.5	93.0	0.9	0.8	1.9	2.4	4.8	5.7	9.5	9.5	9.0	7.0	3.9	30.3	26.2	4.4	0.3	67.4	34.8	49.7	50.3
80135	SEDALIA	96.4	96.0	0.3	0.3	0.7	0.9	3.8	4.7	4.8	5.9	7.2	6.7	3.3	19.9	39.2	12.2	0.9	77.5	46.1	50.6	49.4
80136	STRASBURG	95.3	94.2	0.8	0.9	0.3	0.4	3.9	5.8	6.5	7.3	7.9	7.6	4.7	24.2	31.6	9.0	1.2	73.4	40.2	50.4	49.6
80137	WATKINS	89.5	86.6	1.8	2.1	1.0	1.4	8.8	12.1	7.9	8.6	8.6	7.0	4.5	26.0	29.3	7.7	0.6	70.6	36.7	50.7	49.3
80138	PARKER	94.5	93.7	0.8	0.8	1.0	1.4	4.7	6.0	8.2	8.2	8.5	7.1	4.2	29.4	27.8	6.1	0.6	70.5	36.1	49.6	50.4
80202	DENVER	79.9	78.3	5.7	5.9	6.4	5.6	10.9	16.0	2.5	1.8	1.5	1.7	6.4	39.2	29.9	14.8	2.2	93.5	42.9	55.0	45.0
80203	DENVER	80.5	77.3	5.4	5.6	2.9	3.6	14.6	20.0	2.2	1.3	1.0	1.6	9.3	53.1	22.5	7.3	1.7	94.9	34.6	57.3	42.7
80204	DENVER	52.0	50.6	4.2	3.6	2.9	2.9	66.4	71.6	10.0	8.7	7.3	7.5	9.1	31.9	17.9	6.4	1.2	69.7	28.6	51.3	48.7
80205	DENVER	32.1	33.7	36.6	31.1	1.0	1.0	43.9	50.9	8.8	7.5	6.6	7.3	9.0	32.2	19.8	7.4	1.3	72.6	30.4	52.1	47.9
80206	DENVER	84.9	83.4	6.8	6.9	2.1	2.6	8.1	11.0	3.7	2.7	2.6	3.1	7.3	39.1	29.9	9.5	2.1	89.2	39.5	50.4	49.6
80207	DENVER	32.0	32.1	55.7	53.3	1.0	1.4	15.7	20.2	7.5	7.6	7.6	7.8	6.2	24.9	26.0	11.0	1.4	72.5	36.9	46.7	53.3
80208	DENVER	78.1	75.1	4.4	4.3	8.3	10.1	8.5	11.6	2.0	1.4	1.1	28.5	28.6	29.5	7.3	1.4	0.2	94.3	23.0	52.6	47.4
80209	DENVER	91.3	89.9	1.3	1.3	1.7	2.1	7.2	9.7	3.9	3.1	3.2	2.8	5.6	38.2	29.9	10.9	2.5	88.2	40.9	50.0	50.0
80210	DENVER	90.6	89.2	1.4	1.4	2.6	3.2	6.4	8.7	4.3	3.8	3.9	5.0	8.2	35.1	26.3	9.6	3.9	85.8	38.3	48.9	51.1
80211	DENVER	59.0	55.8	1.8	1.6	1.3	1.3	60.4	67.7	8.0	7.2	6.4	6.4	7.5	32.9	21.3	8.1	2.3	74.8	33.5	50.8	49.2
80212	DENVER	79.1	75.1	1.0	1.0	1.5	1.7	30.0	37.8	5.7	5.2	5.1	4.9	6.7	30.5	27.7	11.0	3.3	81.2	39.8	48.2	51.8
80214	DENVER	78.2	74.9	2.1	2.2	1.6	1.9	29.2	35.0	7.6	6.2	5.5	5.7	8.6	30.4	23.9	9.4	2.9	77.8	34.9	50.1	49.9
80215	DENVER	90.7	88.9	1.4	1.5	1.7	2.1	9.5	12.2	5.8	5.4	5.5	6.1	6.4	24.0	28.6	15.0	3.3	79.7	42.5	48.2	51.8
80216	DENVER	42.1	42.0	6.0	5.0	0.5	0.5	77.9	82.9	10.3	9.7	8.9	8.5	7.8	31.2	17.0	5.8	0.8	66.0	27.7	53.6	46.4
80218	DENVER	82.4	80.3	6.9	7.0	2.1	2.5	11.3	15.4	3.4	2.5	2.2	2.6	9.4	46.3	24.2	7.9	1.4	90.6	35.8	53.1	46.9
80219	DENVER	57.3	54.2	1.4	1.2	4.1	4.1	62.3	69.3	9.2	8.8	8.1	7.6	7.1	29.7	20.1	8.1	1.3	69.2	30.9	51.0	49.0
80220	DENVER	71.6	69.4	14.6	14.3	2.7	3.2	15.1	19.6	6.5	6.0	5.9	5.7	7.0	32.2	27.1	8.1	1.6	78.3	37.0	49.8	50.2
80221	DENVER	70.6	66.0	1.1	1.3	3.4	4.0	45.8	54.8	7.9	7.3	6.7	7.4	7.4	30.5	22.0	9.6	1.2	74.0	33.0	50.9	49.1
80222	DENVER	83.4	81.5	4.9	4.9	3.7	4.3	11.9	15.6	5.4	4.9	4.9	5.0	6.6	28.9	27.1	13.0	4.3	82.0	41.0	48.9	51.1
80223	DENVER	62.9	60.0	2.6	2.2	2.6	2.7	57.6	64.9	8.3	8.1	7.3	7.1	6.9	32.4	21.4	7.4	1.0	72.1	32.2	52.5	47.5
80224	DENVER	77.9	75.7	9.3	9.3	4.5	5.4	10.5	13.7	5.3	4.9	4.8	4.5	6.2	27.3	26.7	15.9	4.3	82.7	42.7	48.3	51.7
80226	DENVER	86.0	83.5	1.1	1.2	2.9	3.7	19.2	23.5	5.9	5.5	5.4	6.7	7.5	28.7	24.9	12.9	2.6	79.7	37.7	48.8	51.2
80227	DENVER	86.3	83.5	1.2	1.3	3.7	4.6	14.9	18.7	5.8	5.1	5.2	5.6	7.4	30.0	27.3	12.3	1.3	80.6	38.2	48.5	51.5
80228	DENVER	91.2	89.4	1.1	1.2	2.9	3.8	7.1	9.1	5.6	5.8	6.2	6.3	6.8	29.0	29.3	10.1	1.0	78.6	38.2	49.5	50.5
80229	DENVER	75.5	70.2	1.6	1.9	1.8	2.6	32.4	40.3	8.8	8.0	7.3	7.3	7.6	32.4	21.3	6.5	0.7	71.6	31.0	49.7	50.3
80230	DENVER	67.2	54.2	18.9	23.5	2.0	1.8	11.8	20.6	9.3	7.9	7.0	7.1	9.4	32.3	20.2	5.8	1.1	71.7	30.4	49.7	50.3
80231	DENVER	76.0	73.6	10.4	10.4	5.4	6.4	9.9	13.5	5.4	4.2	3.6	3.9	10.3	37.7	24.4	8.9	1.6	84.8	34.4	49.7	50.3
80232	DENVER	87.3	84.7	0.9	1.0	3.6	4.6	15.3	19.1	5.8	5.8	6.0	6.1	6.5	26.0	27.9	13.6	2.2	78.6	40.4	48.4	51.6
80233	DENVER	84.3	80.8	1.2	1.4	2.7	3.8	19.0	23.7	7.7	7.4	7.3	6.8	6.0	30.4	24.2	8.5	1.5	73.3	34.9	49.3	50.7
80234	DENVER	85.1	81.0	1.7	2.1	4.7	6.1	13.4	18.0	7.8	7.0	6.5	5.6	7.2	33.5	24.1	7.7	0.6	75.4	34.1	50.0	50.0
80235	DENVER	81.5	80.5	3.8	3.3	4.0	4.4	17.4	20.7	5.9	5.3	5.4	6.2	6.8	34.8	24.6	10.1	1.0	79.5	36.2	52.5	47.5
80236	DENVER	74.7	70.8	1.8	1.7	4.9	5.5	32.2	39.7	6.5	6.1	6.1	6.7	6.9	29.2	24.1	12.1	2.3	77.1	36.9	50.0	50.0
80237	DENVER	84.8	83.1	6.6	6.5	2.9	3.6	6.6	9.0	4.5	4.2	4.4	4.3	6.9	30.7	27.0	15.2	2.8	84.5	41.4	48.0	52.0
80238	DENVER	0.0	17.7	0.0	16.6	0.0	19.8	0.0	53.1	5.7	5.4	5.5	5.2	4.6	27.1	32.3	12.1	2.2	80.3	42.8	48.4	51.6
80239	DENVER	26.0	29.3	44.8	39.1	3.1	3.3	36.0	40.4	10.1	9.0	8.3	8.4	7.8	31.5	19.6	5.0	0.2	67.5	28.6	50.0	50.0
80241	DENVER	87.9	84.0	1.2	1.6	3.0	4.2	13.2	18.5	9.0	8.5	8.1	6.7	5.7	33.5	23.7	4.1	0.6	70.2	32.8	49.7	50.3
80246	DENVER	73.9	70.9	7.4	7.3	5.2	6.1	20.6	26.1	5.6	4.2	3.7	4.5	11.9	42.0	19.7	7.2	1.2	84.6	31.5	52.9	47.1
	COLORADO	82.8	80.7	3.8	3.8	2.3	2.9	17.1	20.2	6.9	6.7	6.7	6.9	7.0	29.0	26.5	8.8	1.4	75.7	35.9	50.2	49.8
	UNITED STATES	75.1	72.0	12.3	12.7	3.8	4.6	12.5	15.7	6.8	6.7	6.6	7.1	6.9	27.0	26.0	10.9	1.9	75.7	36.9	49.2	50.8

80002-80246

ZIP CODE #	POST OFFICE NAME	2009 Per Capita Income	2009 HH Income Base	2009 Household Income Distribution (%): Less than $25,000	$25,000 to $49,999	$50,000 to $99,999	$100,000 to $149,999	$150,000 or More	Median Household Income: 2009	2014	2009 National Centile	2009 State Centile	2009 Home Value Base	2009 Home Value Distribution (%): Less than $50,000	$50,000 to $89,999	$90,000 to $174,999	$175,000 to $399,999	$400,000 or More	2009 Median Home Value
80002	ARVADA	28645	7095	16.6	28.2	37.8	12.3	5.1	54575	55787	71	60	3896	6.4	1.8	32.8	50.6	8.5	188696
80003	ARVADA	29180	12688	9.0	21.4	43.7	21.1	4.8	67929	72047	86	79	9635	0.4	0.3	28.1	70.0	1.2	202806
80004	ARVADA	30895	14248	13.6	20.6	38.6	20.6	6.5	66479	70738	85	77	10194	0.2	0.3	15.0	78.6	5.9	231001
80005	ARVADA	37906	9609	6.2	13.4	34.7	32.8	12.9	92246	100483	95	93	8307	0.2	0.6	14.5	74.3	10.3	261151
80007	ARVADA	49097	2394	4.9	3.4	24.6	32.2	34.8	126193	125259	99	99	2210	0.0	0.0	1.4	39.8	58.7	426223
80010	AURORA	15684	14028	24.5	32.7	34.2	7.2	1.5	44687	45950	47	37	5949	3.0	5.7	63.0	28.0	0.3	149315
80011	AURORA	21805	17305	18.4	30.1	40.3	9.2	2.0	51016	53045	64	54	9775	14.5	7.4	39.1	38.6	0.5	159234
80012	AURORA	27259	18508	14.9	28.5	39.8	13.9	3.0	54769	58213	71	60	9957	1.3	7.3	38.5	52.6	0.4	179371
80013	AURORA	31481	23818	4.4	14.1	47.0	28.7	5.8	80749	83290	92	88	18746	0.7	1.7	22.6	74.8	0.2	205719
80014	AURORA	35580	17790	13.8	25.4	38.8	16.8	5.2	59427	63019	77	67	11509	0.3	3.5	36.2	57.4	2.5	191862
80015	AURORA	35472	21512	3.4	11.5	35.3	37.0	12.9	99731	100866	97	95	18059	0.6	1.2	15.2	76.7	6.3	238042
80016	AURORA	52207	11587	2.8	4.7	21.7	33.9	37.0	130824	130654	99	100	10323	0.0	0.3	2.5	41.8	55.4	423305
80017	AURORA	28002	12745	8.3	23.8	47.7	16.8	3.3	64330	67820	83	75	8356	0.8	4.2	37.5	57.4	0.1	183229
80018	AURORA	29776	2399	11.9	17.6	43.4	23.5	3.6	76221	77848	90	85	2188	0.6	11.4	13.0	63.4	11.6	239059
80019	AURORA	28975	606	0.0	0.0	86.6	13.4	0.0	77424	78424	91	86	493	0.0	0.0	44.6	55.0	0.4	180019
80020	BROOMFIELD	32984	17744	6.9	15.0	39.4	28.3	10.4	81999	84727	93	89	14044	4.3	4.8	8.1	74.1	8.7	241515
80021	BROOMFIELD	37064	12232	4.6	12.0	44.0	29.3	10.1	84277	90474	94	90	8223	0.0	0.7	16.7	74.5	8.2	235263
80022	COMMERCE CITY	20115	14123	19.2	29.7	38.3	9.1	3.6	50781	54047	63	53	9802	8.8	7.1	48.4	33.3	2.4	152836
80023	BROOMFIELD	38897	4621	4.9	7.9	33.1	35.6	18.5	104346	106264	97	97	4215	5.8	5.4	3.9	53.1	31.8	301980
80026	LAFAYETTE	38276	10351	10.4	17.6	36.4	21.8	13.9	79138	82263	92	86	7759	9.1	3.1	12.9	50.3	24.8	249794
80027	LOUISVILLE	42869	11530	6.7	12.2	33.9	28.3	18.8	94626	98897	96	94	7973	2.3	1.0	3.6	59.2	33.9	338220
80030	WESTMINSTER	22625	6251	19.2	30.2	38.5	10.1	2.0	50484	51930	62	52	3260	1.3	1.7	43.8	53.0	0.3	179553
80031	WESTMINSTER	31696	14792	7.9	20.1	44.5	19.0	8.5	70041	72521	87	81	10094	3.4	1.8	22.3	66.4	6.2	222609
80033	WHEAT RIDGE	28626	11375	19.7	29.8	34.0	12.7	3.8	50519	51931	62	52	6220	1.3	2.5	25.5	63.8	6.8	213703
80101	AGATE	20640	146	13.0	39.7	38.4	8.2	0.7	48033	48172	57	46	112	10.7	17.0	36.6	29.5	6.3	119565
80102	BENNETT	23509	1948	12.2	28.3	45.0	11.8	2.7	58738	62488	76	65	1545	24.5	10.5	24.7	35.7	4.6	148231
80103	BYERS	22054	891	17.2	29.1	39.7	12.1	1.9	52806	55818	68	57	681	12.0	12.3	32.2	41.0	2.5	156762
80104	CASTLE ROCK	39605	10498	6.3	14.2	41.8	21.2	16.0	82582	85238	93	89	8670	0.5	0.1	9.6	76.2	13.7	253780
80105	DEER TRAIL	20237	525	21.7	34.9	31.0	9.9	2.5	44722	45960	47	37	401	19.0	13.5	33.9	24.4	9.2	125305
80106	ELBERT	33620	1360	7.0	15.6	36.0	31.2	10.3	87400	90841	94	91	1202	3.2	1.7	7.1	66.7	21.4	302550
80107	ELIZABETH	32282	3948	3.9	13.2	44.8	26.7	11.4	84689	90299	94	91	3602	1.6	1.1	12.2	62.4	22.7	302673
80108	CASTLE ROCK	73986	8091	1.8	9.5	22.9	17.9	48.0	144461	148751	100	100	6937	0.3	0.0	0.5	33.4	65.7	482329
80109	CASTLE ROCK	46937	5209	2.0	2.7	30.0	27.6	37.7	130755	133443	99	99	4964	2.1	2.1	1.9	70.5	23.5	307525
80110	ENGLEWOOD	23561	9042	21.6	30.3	36.5	9.5	2.2	48541	49516	58	49	4967	9.7	3.3	33.9	52.7	0.4	178738
80111	ENGLEWOOD	50949	10961	4.9	9.0	29.5	29.1	27.5	110159	109531	98	98	7359	0.2	0.6	6.3	49.1	43.9	373796
80112	ENGLEWOOD	44892	10826	5.2	10.5	32.8	30.7	20.7	101758	101523	97	96	8087	0.3	0.4	6.5	76.8	16.0	298260
80113	ENGLEWOOD	41754	9729	16.2	23.2	35.9	12.1	12.6	60770	64916	78	70	5379	0.7	0.3	28.1	46.1	24.8	217909
80116	FRANKTOWN	50102	1622	5.6	11.0	31.3	18.3	33.7	104205	110078	97	97	1526	0.0	0.0	0.2	31.1	68.7	506522
80117	KIOWA	27077	1066	8.1	22.2	45.3	17.6	6.8	68816	73210	86	80	910	5.3	4.0	14.8	52.2	23.7	285000
80118	LARKSPUR	50253	1868	7.0	9.9	31.0	23.1	29.0	103259	109084	97	96	1730	3.0	3.2	10.0	38.3	45.5	379365
80120	LITTLETON	32961	12559	16.4	23.3	35.4	17.9	7.0	60563	63716	78	70	7509	5.4	3.8	13.1	71.3	6.4	227680
80121	LITTLETON	47826	6932	5.9	13.2	32.1	27.3	21.4	97366	93160	96	95	5808	0.2	0.0	7.9	72.2	19.8	253934
80122	LITTLETON	39597	11859	6.5	13.6	37.3	30.4	12.2	87395	86802	94	91	9894	0.5	1.0	13.2	76.5	8.9	252154
80123	LITTLETON	39924	18244	7.7	15.2	39.2	25.2	12.7	80435	82527	92	88	13103	0.4	1.2	16.7	67.6	14.1	238084
80124	LITTLETON	62790	7465	3.5	7.4	25.8	20.3	43.0	135126	142161	99	100	6069	0.1	0.0	1.1	59.6	39.1	364270
80125	LITTLETON	51154	3920	5.1	4.3	41.5	21.4	27.8	98855	104349	97	95	3735	0.1	0.0	1.9	71.2	26.8	289540
80126	LITTLETON	52805	13805	3.2	5.4	31.7	22.6	37.0	125308	128695	99	99	11951	0.8	0.1	3.0	63.8	32.3	346116
80127	LITTLETON	44410	15083	3.1	7.1	31.1	36.1	22.7	109363	111259	98	98	13367	0.1	0.3	6.4	72.7	20.6	283208
80128	LITTLETON	36866	13386	4.1	12.2	41.3	31.9	10.6	87859	94292	95	92	11460	0.2	1.9	16.4	75.2	6.3	241343
80129	LITTLETON	46827	9478	1.9	4.9	32.0	27.5	33.7	124769	127405	99	98	8445	0.1	0.1	0.5	77.8	21.4	333759
80130	LITTLETON	52745	9650	2.8	6.8	28.3	28.1	34.0	125558	128057	99	99	8213	0.3	0.0	1.1	76.4	22.2	327315
80132	MONUMENT	42991	6460	5.4	10.7	32.1	28.3	23.5	102788	106030	97	96	5669	3.7	1.5	4.6	46.4	43.9	375494
80133	PALMER LAKE	33248	946	10.6	21.8	40.4	18.9	8.4	66798	68377	85	78	745	10.6	3.5	11.8	55.0	19.1	247222
80134	PARKER	50720	19652	3.6	5.9	33.0	23.8	33.7	118147	123986	98	98	17437	0.1	0.4	2.8	64.7	32.0	335492
80135	SEDALIA	45877	1493	15.5	8.5	29.9	20.8	25.3	93138	101263	96	94	1367	4.8	3.7	7.3	41.4	42.8	364695
80136	STRASBURG	22142	1442	15.8	24.5	46.7	10.5	2.4	58846	62161	76	66	1149	14.2	9.8	23.3	47.8	4.9	184299
80137	WATKINS	21742	849	12.5	38.0	38.6	9.2	1.6	49561	55802	60	51	750	50.1	13.9	6.8	24.7	4.5	49910
80138	PARKER	45090	10332	4.3	6.0	35.8	24.7	29.3	107132	113721	98	97	9263	0.0	0.6	4.8	68.3	26.4	328695
80202	DENVER	57873	5494	34.8	16.9	23.8	11.1	13.4	47209	56421	55	43	2273	0.8	1.0	10.0	46.5	41.8	353818
80203	DENVER	38519	13637	28.4	27.4	32.8	7.9	3.5	44989	47009	48	38	2522	0.7	5.6	36.0	50.1	7.5	191812
80204	DENVER	17661	11461	33.6	27.7	29.0	6.2	3.5	40240	42408	33	24	4097	0.8	4.6	57.2	32.4	5.0	150864
80205	DENVER	18931	11472	33.3	25.9	30.5	7.0	3.3	41098	43854	36	26	5244	1.6	5.1	47.8	40.2	5.2	164430
80206	DENVER	49718	11941	17.8	24.5	32.3	12.7	12.8	59030	62219	76	67	4740	0.4	1.0	14.5	46.9	37.2	335669
80207	DENVER	26288	7967	20.6	25.8	36.4	9.8	7.5	53712	57085	69	58	5447	0.6	2.7	34.7	51.5	10.4	201895
80208	DENVER	16395	341	32.0	33.1	27.9	5.9	1.2	37514	40211	25	17	31	0.0	0.0	41.9	58.1	0.0	187500
80209	DENVER	58624	11796	13.4	18.4	33.3	17.9	17.0	74009	76912	89	83	6409	0.1	0.3	7.5	55.0	37.0	346191
80210	DENVER	42972	15089	14.0	21.9	38.3	15.6	10.1	65653	67580	84	76	8904	0.1	0.1	12.8	69.8	17.2	264556
80211	DENVER	21950	14466	25.6	26.0	36.1	9.0	3.3	48500	50864	58	48	7467	0.4	2.7	37.2	57.5	2.2	194509
80212	DENVER	29518	8540	16.9	28.3	41.2	10.0	3.5	54086	56888	70	59	5402	5.1	2.3	31.7	58.1	2.7	192296
80214	DENVER	26004	10903	21.1	31.6	34.6	9.7	3.1	48098	48861	57	46	4535	4.0	7.0	37.0	49.7	2.3	178147
80215	DENVER	33988	8177	13.6	24.9	36.9	17.5	7.1	60980	64591	79	71	4887	0.5	1.7	16.7	68.1	13.1	255897
80216	DENVER	13005	3235	29.6	29.5	33.8	5.7	1.4	42755	45440	42	31	1908	4.5	14.7	67.5	11.6	1.8	121553
80218	DENVER	44468	10217	22.8	27.2	31.7	10.1	8.1	49946	52876	61	51	2860	0.1	2.9	20.1	43.5	33.4	282994
80219	DENVER	17406	18916	21.7	30.0	39.4	6.7	2.1	48580	51135	58	49	12332	2.1	3.3	60.3	33.8	0.5	153931
80220	DENVER	38034	15433	17.0	23.7	33.1	15.3	10.9	61899	64035	80	72	8651	0.4	1.9	23.5	50.9	23.3	259754
80221	DENVER	20305	13321	18.3	30.0	40.1	9.4	2.1	51184	53138	64	55	8633	6.9	3.1	43.0	46.2	0.8	170913
80222	DENVER	32612	9220	15.2	27.3	40.6	12.6	4.4	57342	60882	74	64	5131	1.1	4.4	22.2	70.6	1.7	210723
80223	DENVER	20316	6942	24.0	30.6	36.2	5.9	3.3	46058	48471	51	40	3739	3.8	3.9	56.2	35.5	0.7	155909
80224	DENVER	34998	8423	15.8	24.7	39.7	12.7	7.2	60014	62434	77	69	4708	1.0	2.6	29.0	62.1	5.3	215446
80226	DENVER	29579	12287	15.4	24.1	38.9	17.2	4.4	59893	62746	77	68	7531	4.0	2.7	25.4	65.6	2.3	202784
80227	DENVER	35546	14627	9.5	23.4	41.2	18.9	7.1	65305	68068	84	75	9259	0.4	2.5	27.5	60.8	8.9	219781
80228	DENVER	40013	13124	7.3	17.8	38.9	24.0	12.0	78000	83322	91	86	8773	0.3	2.1	15.4	72.3	9.8	247692
80229	DENVER	22531	17049	13.5	25.6	48.1	11.1	1.7	58813	61934	76	66	11596	11.5	6.1	39.4	42.5	0.5	164299
80230	DENVER	43945	2659	14.5	38.6	17.0	14.1	15.7	47672	47504	56	45	1151	0.0	0.0	1.2	54.8	44.0	382754
80231	DENVER	38913	15369	11.8	26.9	40.9	14.0	6.5	59525	62279	77	67	6556	0.6	4.3	30.2	59.4	5.5	213983
80232	DENVER	31662	8619	8.9	23.5	42.0	19.7	5.8	65709	69757	84	76	6317	0.7	2.0	26.4	69.2	1.7	205572
80233	DENVER	27000	16236	9.3	19.3	49.5	18.9	2.9	68877	70821	86	80	11485	1.0	1.3	23.2	73.9	0.5	210987
80234	DENVER	31923	10498	8.9	20.5	45.4	18.4	6.8	69202	72064	86	81	6699	5.2	6.7	16.7	61.9	9.4	231274
80235	DENVER	35807	3440	10.6	28.0	37.1	16.2	8.2	63073	66408	81	74	2026	0.3	10.2	26.9	45.8	16.9	214005
80236	DENVER	25696	6226	14.0	25.5	43.5	13.3	3.7	59265	61768	76	67	3922	3.4	4.6	25.1	64.0	2.9	201525
80237	DENVER	43452	8625	10.9	21.9	41.8	16.0	9.5	67226	69610	85	79	4879	0.5	4.0	29.0	54.0	12.5	247943
80238	DENVER	17327	3151	59.2	23.4	9.2	3.5	4.7	19238	19964	1	2	2232	0.0	3.0	35.6	51.4	10.0	198606
80239	DENVER	20674	10053	11.6	25.3	45.4	12.9	4.8	62469	64836	81	73	6935	0.9	0.5	43.8	54.6	0.3	179934
80241	DENVER	32951	11792	3.2	12.2	50.7	23.8	10.1	82319	82898	93	89	9178	1.1	0.4	8.9	80.4	9.3	263060
80246	DENVER	32799	7011	21.9	31.2	31.7	10.0	5.3	47554	48894	56	44	1714	0.0	0.3	32.9	41.9	24.9	220979
	COLORADO	30807		15.5	22.5	37.5	15.8	8.6	62597	65813				4.4	4.3	23.6	52.9	14.8	220998
	UNITED STATES	27277		20.9	24.4	35.3	11.7	7.6	54719	56938				9.3	13.1	31.6	32.6	13.5	162279

ZIP CODE	FINANCIAL SERVICES				THE HOME						ENTERTAINMENT						PERSONAL			
					Home Improvements		Furnishings													
# POST OFFICE NAME	Auto Loan	Home Loan	Invest-ments	Retire-ment Plans	Home Repair	Lawn & Garden	Computers & Hardware-Personal	Major Appliances	TV, Radio, Sound Equipment	Furniture	Dine out/ Carry out	Sports Equipment	Fees & Tickets	Toys & Games	Travel	Cable TV	Apparel & Services	Auto Repairs	Health Insurance	Pets & Supplies
80002 ARVADA	93	90	83	92	87	85	97	89	95	96	97	72	96	97	94	94	69	95	88	106
80003 ARVADA	107	116	105	116	112	106	110	107	107	112	108	83	115	110	111	105	76	107	103	125
80004 ARVADA	103	117	112	118	116	112	110	109	108	112	109	83	118	108	115	108	77	109	110	127
80005 ARVADA	136	162	152	164	160	146	142	144	135	150	137	112	157	139	152	131	98	138	133	165
80007 ARVADA	203	254	235	264	253	216	210	215	195	233	198	175	244	206	228	181	146	197	180	241
80010 AURORA	74	62	55	61	60	54	75	67	73	76	76	53	69	75	69	70	54	74	62	76
80011 AURORA	86	77	68	78	73	73	85	77	85	85	86	62	81	87	79	83	60	83	78	93
80012 AURORA	94	82	74	85	78	77	95	84	94	94	95	68	90	96	87	92	67	92	84	101
80013 AURORA	131	139	117	138	131	118	129	125	123	137	125	100	132	130	127	117	88	123	112	145
80014 AURORA	99	99	100	101	101	98	103	98	102	106	103	75	106	101	104	101	72	102	102	116
80015 AURORA	153	170	149	172	164	145	154	150	145	166	147	122	164	153	155	136	106	145	131	172
80016 AURORA	211	279	287	290	288	248	229	238	214	250	216	188	275	219	259	203	162	221	206	267
80017 AURORA	110	100	84	101	94	89	107	97	104	110	106	78	101	109	98	100	74	102	92	116
80018 AURORA	107	127	123	129	127	116	110	114	104	118	106	86	121	107	119	101	75	108	105	130
80019 AURORA	111	139	122	139	134	120	116	118	109	122	112	94	131	114	126	105	80	113	106	136
80020 BROOMFIELD	132	149	132	150	145	130	134	133	127	142	130	106	143	134	137	122	93	128	121	152
80021 BROOMFIELD	139	145	129	146	139	127	140	133	134	146	137	108	143	140	138	129	97	133	123	156
80022 COMMERCE CITY	90	91	79	86	89	82	88	88	85	92	87	67	87	87	87	83	61	88	82	100
80023 BROOMFIELD	161	202	187	209	201	171	166	170	154	185	157	139	193	163	181	143	116	157	143	191
80026 LAFAYETTE	143	157	139	158	152	136	145	141	138	153	140	114	153	145	146	131	100	138	127	163
80027 LOUISVILLE	158	177	163	182	173	155	162	158	154	172	156	128	175	160	167	146	113	154	142	182
80030 WESTMINSTER	78	78	73	79	76	74	84	77	82	82	84	62	84	83	82	82	60	82	78	91
80031 WESTMINSTER	120	127	115	128	123	115	122	118	118	127	120	93	126	122	122	114	85	118	112	137
80033 WHEAT RIDGE	83	87	86	88	88	88	89	87	89	88	90	66	92	88	90	91	63	89	93	102
80101 AGATE	95	65	104	65	68	100	72	90	75	59	74	74	53	74	72	82	48	84	95	111
80102 BENNETT	98	103	87	102	98	96	93	95	92	97	93	72	95	96	93	91	64	92	91	112
80103 BYERS	93	91	82	90	89	93	84	89	86	86	86	67	83	89	84	88	59	86	89	106
80104 CASTLE ROCK	145	164	157	166	163	145	150	148	142	159	144	117	162	147	155	136	103	143	134	169
80105 DEER TRAIL	95	74	93	72	75	95	74	89	80	71	79	67	63	80	73	86	53	83	91	106
80106 ELBERT	134	159	138	163	155	142	136	140	129	144	131	112	151	136	144	124	94	131	126	160
80107 ELIZABETH	133	166	145	166	160	142	139	141	130	147	133	113	157	136	149	124	96	133	125	161
80108 CASTLE ROCK	278	344	362	363	358	315	298	303	282	321	285	238	349	287	330	270	212	289	271	345
80109 CASTLE ROCK	217	268	246	276	267	225	224	228	206	250	209	186	256	219	240	190	154	209	190	254
80110 ENGLEWOOD	76	78	74	78	77	75	81	76	80	80	81	60	82	80	80	80	57	80	78	90
80111 ENGLEWOOD	179	211	225	224	219	193	195	190	184	206	186	153	220	186	210	176	138	186	172	219
80112 ENGLEWOOD	162	191	190	195	193	174	172	172	164	180	166	134	191	167	184	160	121	168	160	197
80113 ENGLEWOOD	122	124	125	128	125	119	131	121	128	131	130	97	135	128	130	127	93	127	122	144
80116 FRANKTOWN	173	232	253	241	246	212	192	203	179	211	180	155	232	178	223	171	134	188	180	227
80117 KIOWA	114	127	110	128	123	121	112	116	110	115	111	90	119	114	117	110	78	112	112	136
80118 LARKSPUR	173	224	230	233	231	205	186	194	175	201	177	150	219	177	210	169	131	182	175	221
80120 LITTLETON	99	106	106	107	107	103	105	102	104	106	105	78	111	103	108	104	75	105	105	119
80121 LITTLETON	163	202	209	205	208	191	175	182	169	185	170	136	201	170	194	167	123	174	174	206
80122 LITTLETON	134	164	166	167	168	154	143	147	138	150	140	112	163	139	158	137	101	142	142	168
80123 LITTLETON	135	147	140	151	145	132	141	135	135	147	137	108	149	138	144	130	98	135	126	157
80124 LITTLETON	239	294	272	304	292	252	248	252	231	272	235	204	283	243	266	216	173	234	215	284
80125 LITTLETON	201	232	207	229	225	197	200	203	188	217	192	160	216	199	207	178	137	191	177	230
80126 LITTLETON	217	260	239	269	257	222	224	224	209	244	213	183	252	221	237	196	156	211	192	254
80127 LITTLETON	176	210	194	214	207	182	182	183	171	195	174	146	203	179	193	162	126	173	161	208
80128 LITTLETON	138	160	146	161	156	141	142	142	135	150	137	112	154	140	148	129	98	137	129	163
80129 LITTLETON	194	222	200	228	218	190	193	195	181	214	184	159	212	193	201	170	134	182	168	220
80130 LITTLETON	201	236	207	243	230	196	204	202	189	224	193	168	226	203	211	175	141	189	170	228
80132 MONUMENT	166	210	207	218	213	188	176	181	166	190	168	144	205	171	195	159	124	170	161	206
80133 PALMER LAKE	111	128	120	132	128	123	114	118	111	118	112	91	125	113	123	110	79	114	115	137
80134 PARKER	212	253	232	260	250	215	217	218	202	238	205	177	243	214	229	189	150	204	186	246
80135 SEDALIA	168	195	232	201	208	196	170	187	163	179	163	141	189	161	193	161	118	174	174	212
80136 STRASBURG	89	100	86	103	97	98	89	93	88	90	88	73	95	90	94	88	62	89	92	109
80137 WATKINS	93	91	80	89	88	91	84	88	86	87	86	66	83	89	82	87	59	85	88	104
80138 PARKER	183	219	202	226	217	188	188	189	176	206	179	154	212	186	199	165	131	178	162	214
80202 DENVER	107	90	103	102	92	92	123	100	123	116	125	85	116	116	114	123	90	116	112	125
80203 DENVER	77	57	59	65	55	55	84	63	82	78	85	58	75	82	72	80	60	76	67	82
80204 DENVER	72	61	56	61	59	55	77	65	75	75	77	53	70	75	69	74	55	74	65	78
80205 DENVER	73	64	61	65	63	59	78	68	76	76	78	55	73	76	72	74	56	75	67	80
80206 DENVER	116	103	113	114	104	97	131	107	124	126	128	94	126	124	123	120	93	121	106	132
80207 DENVER	89	100	101	100	101	95	98	95	98	98	99	71	104	96	101	99	71	97	97	112
80208 DENVER	66	45	44	50	43	47	77	54	70	64	71	49	60	71	57	68	50	65	56	69
80209 DENVER	136	139	155	146	145	133	151	139	144	152	146	112	154	141	153	140	105	145	136	163
80210 DENVER	113	118	121	122	119	112	123	114	119	123	120	91	127	118	124	116	86	118	113	135
80211 DENVER	80	76	71	75	75	70	85	78	83	84	85	61	82	83	81	81	60	83	76	90
80212 DENVER	85	88	85	88	87	86	91	86	90	89	91	67	92	90	90	90	64	89	89	102
80214 DENVER	82	71	67	73	69	69	87	75	86	84	87	61	81	86	79	85	61	84	79	91
80215 DENVER	101	107	109	108	109	107	108	105	108	108	108	79	113	106	111	108	76	108	110	123
80216 DENVER	74	71	61	63	70	59	73	71	68	77	71	53	68	70	69	65	50	72	62	78
80218 DENVER	99	79	84	90	78	75	109	85	104	103	108	77	100	105	97	101	77	99	86	107
80219 DENVER	80	80	70	74	79	70	81	79	78	85	79	59	78	79	79	75	56	80	73	88
80220 DENVER	114	111	115	115	112	101	124	111	117	125	120	91	122	117	121	112	86	118	106	131
80221 DENVER	82	85	77	82	83	78	85	82	83	86	84	63	86	84	84	81	59	83	80	94
80222 DENVER	92	89	88	91	88	87	98	89	97	96	98	70	97	96	95	97	69	96	94	107
80223 DENVER	77	75	70	72	74	65	83	76	79	84	81	60	80	79	80	76	58	81	71	87
80224 DENVER	99	101	103	101	103	101	106	101	106	106	106	76	109	104	107	107	75	106	109	119
80226 DENVER	96	97	93	98	96	95	101	95	100	100	101	74	102	100	100	101	71	100	99	112
80227 DENVER	113	111	106	114	110	106	116	108	114	117	115	85	116	115	114	112	81	113	109	129
80228 DENVER	136	132	124	138	129	123	138	127	135	142	137	103	139	138	134	132	97	133	125	152
80229 DENVER	95	89	77	87	84	81	93	87	91	95	92	69	88	94	87	88	64	90	84	103
80230 DENVER	126	119	110	123	116	108	133	118	129	132	131	98	130	132	126	124	94	127	114	140
80231 DENVER	111	87	83	95	83	83	112	92	110	110	112	79	102	112	98	106	79	105	93	114
80232 DENVER	105	112	104	113	110	107	110	106	108	110	109	82	115	110	111	107	77	108	106	124
80233 DENVER	105	113	100	111	109	104	106	104	104	110	105	81	110	107	107	102	74	104	102	121
80234 DENVER	118	111	99	114	106	100	118	107	114	121	116	87	115	119	111	110	82	112	101	127
80235 DENVER	124	108	103	113	106	105	121	111	119	122	121	89	114	122	113	117	84	118	111	133
80236 DENVER	92	95	93	96	95	93	96	93	96	96	97	72	99	96	97	96	68	96	96	110
80237 DENVER	118	111	114	116	112	107	123	111	120	124	122	89	122	121	119	118	86	119	113	133
80238 DENVER	49	61	72	62	67	53	58	58	51	62	51	46	64	49	65	47	38	55	48	64
80239 DENVER	105	104	88	100	99	89	104	99	100	109	102	78	101	104	99	95	72	100	90	114
80241 DENVER	139	147	125	149	140	124	138	132	130	147	133	108	142	139	135	123	94	129	116	152
80246 DENVER	97	65	61	73	61	63	96	74	95	93	97	65	82	97	79	92	68	89	76	94
COLORADO	114	114	111	115	112	109	114	111	111	116	113	88	114	113	113	110	80	112	108	130
UNITED STATES	100	100	100	100	100	100	100	100	100	100	100	100	100	100	100	100	100	100	100	100

80247-80648

ZIP CODE #	POST OFFICE NAME	COUNTY FIPS CODE	POPULATION 2000	POPULATION 2009	POPULATION 2014	2000-2009 ANNUAL RATE % Rate	2000-2009 ANNUAL RATE State Centile	HOUSEHOLDS 2000	HOUSEHOLDS 2009	HOUSEHOLDS 2014	HOUSEHOLDS % Annual Rate 2000-2009	HOUSEHOLDS 2009 Average HH Size	FAMILIES 2000	FAMILIES 2009	FAMILIES % Annual Rate 2000-2009
80247	DENVER	031	23542	26998	28962	1.5	62	12946	14430	15359	1.2	1.87	5054	5271	0.5
80249	DENVER	031	7947	16790	20376	8.4	97	2704	6054	7326	9.1	2.77	2031	4322	8.5
80260	DENVER	001	28487	29930	31639	0.5	37	11418	11861	12454	0.4	2.52	7199	7158	-0.1
80262	DENVER	031	45	44	44	-0.2	16	0	0	0	0.0	0.00	0	0	0.0
80301	BOULDER	013	22605	22402	22958	-0.1	19	9667	9655	9931	0.0	2.26	5250	4984	-0.6
80302	BOULDER	013	26570	26959	27275	0.2	28	12041	12307	12473	0.2	2.02	4141	4058	-0.2
80303	BOULDER	013	23418	23711	24062	0.1	26	10708	10917	11094	0.2	2.14	4858	4690	-0.4
80304	BOULDER	013	23772	24892	25363	0.5	37	10099	10523	10703	0.4	2.35	5514	5513	0.0
80305	BOULDER	013	16624	16289	16264	-0.2	16	6925	6882	6888	-0.1	2.36	3614	3391	-0.7
80309	BOULDER	013	5604	5529	5506	-0.1	19	0	0	0	0.0	0.00	0	0	0.0
80401	GOLDEN	059	38516	38473	38403	0.0	22	15569	15752	15805	0.1	2.35	10003	9842	-0.2
80403	GOLDEN	047	17985	20994	22190	1.7	67	7194	8441	8949	1.7	2.48	4960	5721	1.6
80421	BAILEY	093	8186	9133	9482	1.2	54	3159	3558	3710	1.3	2.57	2367	2638	1.2
80422	BLACK HAWK	047	582	576	574	-0.1	19	290	288	287	-0.1	2.00	135	129	-0.5
80423	BOND	037	169	197	214	1.7	67	72	83	90	1.5	2.37	42	48	1.5
80424	BRECKENRIDGE	117	7449	8456	9067	1.4	58	2998	3419	3669	1.4	2.44	1387	1528	1.1
80428	CLARK	107	673	829	906	2.3	76	263	329	362	2.5	2.52	192	235	2.2
80430	COALMONT	057	132	124	120	-0.7	8	54	51	50	-0.6	2.41	39	36	-0.9
80433	CONIFER	059	8182	8290	8347	0.1	26	3107	3212	3254	0.4	2.58	2467	2511	0.2
80435	DILLON	117	6771	7713	8293	1.4	58	2562	2923	3147	1.4	2.50	1350	1495	1.1
80439	EVERGREEN	059	24533	24585	24557	0.0	22	9497	9670	9710	0.2	2.53	7174	7170	0.0
80440	FAIRPLAY	093	2675	3489	3918	2.9	85	1157	1518	1707	3.0	2.25	719	927	2.8
80442	FRASER	049	2088	2442	2569	1.7	67	945	1117	1181	1.8	2.16	446	510	1.5
80443	FRISCO	117	2974	3476	3748	1.7	67	1260	1476	1589	1.7	2.34	649	737	1.4
80446	GRANBY	049	4680	5418	5715	1.6	64	1806	2121	2252	1.8	2.46	1185	1361	1.5
80447	GRAND LAKE	049	1853	2225	2398	2.0	73	854	1038	1122	2.1	2.13	571	679	1.9
80449	HARTSEL	093	195	260	292	3.2	87	90	124	140	3.5	2.10	65	89	3.5
80451	HOT SULPHUR SPRINGS	049	626	731	779	1.7	67	240	286	308	1.9	2.40	165	192	1.7
80452	IDAHO SPRINGS	019	5775	5647	5527	-0.2	16	2555	2519	2475	-0.2	2.23	1531	1471	-0.4
80455	JAMESTOWN	013	351	367	376	0.5	37	164	174	178	0.6	2.11	90	89	-0.1
80456	JEFFERSON	093	610	878	991	4.0	90	285	412	465	4.1	2.13	196	280	3.9
80459	KREMMLING	049	2164	2474	2588	1.5	62	822	953	1003	1.6	2.53	581	662	1.4
80461	LEADVILLE	065	7554	7884	8065	0.5	37	2861	2937	2989	0.3	2.65	1833	1840	0.0
80463	MC COY	037	110	128	139	1.7	67	48	55	60	1.5	2.33	31	35	1.3
80465	MORRISON	059	15026	15911	16287	0.6	40	5397	5795	5952	0.8	2.70	4223	4467	0.6
80466	NEDERLAND	013	3410	3632	3760	0.7	43	1493	1611	1673	0.8	2.25	881	905	0.3
80467	OAK CREEK	107	1994	2540	2774	2.7	82	841	1086	1196	2.8	2.34	525	656	2.4
80468	PARSHALL	049	372	437	468	1.8	69	139	166	179	1.9	2.52	99	116	1.7
80470	PINE	059	3543	3735	3801	0.6	40	1351	1445	1479	0.7	2.58	1036	1091	0.6
80478	TABERNASH	049	201	235	250	1.7	67	87	104	112	1.9	2.12	59	69	1.7
80479	TOPONAS	107	804	941	1003	1.7	67	330	396	425	2.0	2.38	219	257	1.7
80480	WALDEN	057	1445	1335	1278	-0.9	6	607	568	546	-0.7	2.33	404	371	-0.9
80481	WARD	013	933	993	1027	0.7	43	396	428	445	0.8	2.31	221	225	0.2
80482	WINTER PARK	049	138	156	164	1.3	56	67	78	82	1.7	2.00	30	34	1.4
80487	STEAMBOAT SPRINGS	107	13914	16331	17551	1.7	67	5651	6725	7262	1.9	2.39	3212	3731	1.6
80498	SILVERTHORNE	117	6674	7881	8499	1.8	69	2415	2845	3070	1.8	2.63	1463	1680	1.5
80501	LONGMONT	013	55482	61336	63977	1.1	52	20693	22894	23899	1.1	2.65	14140	15186	0.8
80503	LONGMONT	013	25776	33372	36139	2.8	83	9797	12948	14116	3.1	2.56	7210	9138	2.6
80504	LONGMONT	123	8729	20386	25782	9.6	97	2995	7008	8863	9.6	2.90	2492	5550	9.0
80510	ALLENSPARK	013	306	331	346	0.9	47	152	167	176	1.0	1.93	92	96	0.5
80512	BELLVUE	069	2245	2566	2748	1.5	62	945	1116	1207	1.8	2.30	634	717	1.3
80513	BERTHOUD	069	9759	10732	11558	1.0	50	3514	3929	4250	1.2	2.73	2775	3008	0.9
80514	DACONO	123	3235	4285	4806	3.1	86	1170	1532	1711	3.0	2.80	818	1025	2.5
80515	DRAKE	069	928	1034	1113	1.2	54	434	497	540	1.5	2.01	304	333	1.0
80516	ERIE	123	8139	19529	24617	9.9	97	2909	6911	8696	9.8	2.83	2295	5237	9.3
80517	ESTES PARK	069	9266	11126	12173	2.0	73	4233	5242	5792	2.3	2.10	2722	3202	1.8
80520	FIRESTONE	123	2	2	3	0.0	22	2	2	3	0.0	1.00	2	0	-100.0
80521	FORT COLLINS	069	28943	29903	30711	0.4	34	11779	12402	12808	0.6	2.36	5093	4983	-0.2
80523	FORT COLLINS	069	4408	4447	4471	0.1	26	227	260	279	1.5	1.18	45	46	0.2
80524	FORT COLLINS	069	27251	30815	32795	1.3	56	11082	12507	13321	1.3	2.42	6769	7519	1.1
80525	FORT COLLINS	069	42819	48403	51540	1.3	56	16937	19183	20408	1.4	2.49	10897	11999	1.0
80526	FORT COLLINS	069	41357	45238	47699	1.0	50	15742	17448	18444	1.1	2.58	10248	10979	0.7
80528	FORT COLLINS	069	6133	14529	18070	9.8	97	2234	5409	6780	10.0	2.69	1693	3933	9.5
80530	FREDERICK	123	3504	5826	7014	5.7	94	1151	1926	2315	5.7	3.02	912	1485	5.4
80534	JOHNSTOWN	123	5315	10581	13452	7.7	96	1875	3789	4810	7.9	2.79	1486	2937	7.6
80535	LAPORTE	069	2400	2409	2466	0.0	22	943	971	1000	0.3	2.48	656	644	-0.2
80536	LIVERMORE	069	1425	1819	1996	2.7	82	601	792	879	3.0	2.25	454	572	2.5
80537	LOVELAND	069	33525	38573	41674	1.5	62	12919	15164	16473	1.7	2.51	9190	10404	1.4
80538	LOVELAND	069	34789	43096	46910	2.3	76	13194	16612	18172	2.5	2.58	9923	12295	2.3
80540	LYONS	013	3815	4194	4419	1.0	50	1587	1776	1880	1.2	2.35	1127	1219	0.9
80542	MEAD	123	2089	2756	3281	3.0	85	668	898	1066	3.3	3.07	554	728	3.0
80543	MILLIKEN	123	3304	6455	7839	7.5	96	1009	1940	2350	7.3	3.33	829	1546	7.0
80545	RED FEATHER LAKES	069	827	1047	1172	2.6	81	385	507	573	3.0	2.03	265	335	2.6
80547	TIMNATH	069	44	80	99	6.7	95	19	40	50	8.4	2.00	16	33	8.1
80549	WELLINGTON	069	4689	6566	7355	3.7	89	1675	2467	2782	4.3	2.66	1276	1803	3.8
80550	WINDSOR	123	11827	18880	22735	5.2	93	4238	6724	8073	5.1	2.79	3232	5025	4.9
80601	BRIGHTON	001	22047	33624	39485	4.7	92	7142	11047	12997	4.8	2.92	5376	8004	4.4
80602	BRIGHTON	001	6170	24280	30867	16.0	98	2054	8120	10305	16.0	2.99	1743	6845	15.9
80603	BRIGHTON	001	5891	11830	14737	7.8	96	1943	3995	4985	8.1	2.95	1593	3188	7.8
80610	AULT	123	2424	3141	3573	2.8	83	902	1162	1318	2.8	2.70	664	823	2.3
80611	BRIGGSDALE	123	528	767	894	4.1	91	194	291	339	4.5	2.61	141	204	4.1
80612	CARR	123	244	253	263	0.4	34	95	98	102	0.3	2.58	72	72	0.0
80615	EATON	123	5365	7838	9249	4.2	91	1922	2749	3213	3.9	2.84	1472	2041	3.6
80620	EVANS	123	10055	17215	20644	6.0	94	3454	5969	7158	6.1	2.88	2499	4119	5.6
80621	FORT LUPTON	123	12170	14452	15984	1.9	70	3807	4486	4952	1.8	3.21	3034	3474	1.5
80624	GILL	123	835	987	1126	1.8	69	260	319	363	2.2	3.09	204	243	1.9
80631	GREELEY	123	42658	48342	52092	1.4	58	15247	16831	18044	1.1	2.77	9147	9634	0.6
80634	GREELEY	123	40292	54550	61874	3.3	88	15390	20320	22849	3.0	2.67	10902	14065	2.8
80639	GREELEY	123	3023	3025	3033	0.0	22	121	119	121	-0.2	4.36	20	17	-1.7
80640	HENDERSON	001	2071	9294	12488	17.6	99	676	2965	3988	17.3	3.12	542	2349	17.2
80642	HUDSON	123	2751	3726	4406	3.3	88	905	1225	1445	3.3	3.04	721	946	3.0
80643	KEENESBURG	123	2012	2615	3011	2.9	85	699	904	1038	2.8	2.89	548	687	2.5
80644	KERSEY	123	2979	3666	4016	2.3	76	994	1196	1309	2.0	3.06	819	959	1.7
80645	LA SALLE	123	3759	4339	4678	1.6	64	1290	1475	1585	1.5	2.91	1008	1114	1.1
80648	NUNN	123	779	820	860	0.6	40	275	287	299	0.5	2.86	207	209	0.1
	COLORADO					1.7					1.6	2.55			1.5
	UNITED STATES					1.0					1.1	2.59			0.9

ZIP CODE #	POST OFFICE NAME	RACE (%) White 2000	White 2009	Black 2000	Black 2009	Asian/Pacific 2000	Asian/Pacific 2009	% Hispanic Origin 2000	% Hispanic Origin 2009	2009 AGE DISTRIBUTION (%) 0-4	5-9	10-14	15-19	20-24	25-44	45-64	65-84	85+	18+	MEDIAN AGE 2009	% 2009 Males	% 2009 Females
80247	DENVER	69.4	65.3	13.0	13.8	5.1	5.9	15.1	19.8	6.1	4.4	3.6	4.3	10.2	34.5	20.2	12.8	4.0	83.7	35.3	47.3	52.7
80249	DENVER	51.2	50.6	30.8	28.0	4.6	4.7	16.5	20.5	9.9	9.1	8.3	6.6	5.0	35.7	21.6	3.5	0.2	68.5	32.2	48.9	51.1
80260	DENVER	80.4	75.6	1.8	2.2	4.1	5.2	23.5	31.1	8.7	7.4	6.6	6.9	8.4	29.6	21.8	9.7	1.0	73.2	32.0	49.2	50.8
80262	DENVER	71.1	68.2	8.9	9.1	11.1	13.6	11.1	15.9	4.5	2.3	0.0	2.3	9.1	50.0	20.5	9.1	2.3	90.9	36.0	52.3	47.7
80301	BOULDER	88.0	85.6	1.5	1.7	3.7	4.7	8.7	11.2	5.2	5.1	5.5	6.3	8.5	31.2	29.4	7.8	1.2	80.6	37.2	51.0	49.0
80302	BOULDER	92.2	90.6	0.8	0.9	2.7	3.4	4.3	5.7	2.7	2.5	2.6	9.7	27.7	27.4	19.6	6.4	1.5	90.6	27.4	51.9	48.1
80303	BOULDER	87.3	85.0	1.4	1.5	5.0	6.1	8.7	11.1	3.7	3.2	3.4	5.5	18.0	29.5	22.9	10.8	2.9	87.1	33.2	51.6	48.4
80304	BOULDER	90.5	88.0	0.8	0.8	1.9	2.4	9.9	13.3	5.1	5.0	5.5	5.7	7.2	31.8	31.0	7.6	1.1	80.8	38.3	50.2	49.8
80305	BOULDER	91.7	89.9	0.8	0.9	3.6	4.6	4.5	5.9	3.6	3.2	3.7	4.9	13.5	33.5	26.1	10.1	1.2	86.8	35.7	53.2	46.8
80309	BOULDER	80.9	77.1	2.2	2.4	10.9	13.6	6.2	7.9	2.7	1.0	0.6	61.0	21.5	12.0	1.0	0.1	0.0	95.1	18.7	50.9	49.1
80401	GOLDEN	91.9	90.3	0.9	1.0	2.5	3.2	6.3	8.0	4.9	5.0	5.6	7.8	6.8	25.9	30.9	11.7	1.3	80.6	40.6	52.0	48.0
80403	GOLDEN	94.6	93.7	0.3	0.3	1.4	1.8	4.4	5.8	5.7	5.9	6.7	5.9	4.0	27.8	34.8	8.4	0.8	77.7	41.6	52.0	48.0
80421	BAILEY	95.4	94.7	0.4	0.4	0.5	0.6	4.3	5.4	5.5	6.4	7.4	7.2	4.0	23.5	37.6	7.8	0.5	76.0	42.7	50.6	49.4
80422	BLACK HAWK	91.1	90.1	0.9	1.0	1.7	1.9	8.2	10.2	4.7	4.0	3.6	3.5	8.2	29.0	36.5	9.7	0.9	86.5	42.4	52.1	47.9
80423	BOND	84.1	82.2	0.6	0.5	0.0	0.0	12.9	15.2	6.1	6.6	4.1	6.1	7.6	33.0	26.9	8.6	1.0	80.2	39.0	60.4	39.6
80424	BRECKENRIDGE	95.5	94.8	0.2	0.2	0.7	0.9	4.7	6.0	4.6	3.9	3.5	3.5	10.1	47.5	23.0	3.9	0.1	86.2	33.1	58.9	41.1
80428	CLARK	98.8	98.7	0.1	0.1	0.1	0.1	1.3	1.6	5.3	5.3	5.9	7.2	4.6	29.8	36.8	4.5	0.6	77.3	40.7	52.0	48.0
80430	COALMONT	96.2	96.0	0.0	0.0	0.0	0.0	6.9	7.3	4.8	6.5	6.5	5.6	3.2	20.2	37.1	14.5	1.6	77.4	46.5	52.4	47.6
80433	CONIFER	96.1	95.5	0.4	0.4	0.7	0.9	2.7	3.5	5.3	6.3	7.3	6.9	2.4	27.1	38.7	5.5	0.4	76.1	42.4	51.7	48.3
80435	DILLON	90.4	88.5	0.9	0.9	0.9	1.1	13.3	16.9	5.7	4.2	3.7	4.4	9.8	44.8	22.2	4.9	0.2	84.0	32.0	57.7	42.3
80439	EVERGREEN	97.2	96.8	0.2	0.3	0.6	0.8	2.3	3.0	5.0	6.2	7.3	6.8	3.2	21.7	38.5	10.1	1.1	76.8	44.8	49.8	50.2
80440	FAIRPLAY	94.2	93.5	0.8	0.8	0.3	0.3	4.4	5.4	5.3	6.0	6.0	4.8	3.6	33.7	34.0	6.2	0.3	79.6	40.5	53.4	46.6
80442	FRASER	95.7	95.0	0.4	0.5	0.9	1.1	2.8	3.6	4.0	3.4	3.4	4.3	7.7	42.7	27.2	7.0	0.3	86.8	36.0	55.0	45.0
80443	FRISCO	96.4	95.6	0.2	0.2	1.0	1.3	3.1	4.1	3.7	3.0	2.9	4.4	8.9	43.4	25.9	7.5	0.3	87.9	35.8	57.1	42.9
80446	GRANBY	95.6	94.7	0.7	0.8	0.9	1.2	3.5	4.4	5.5	5.1	5.4	5.7	6.7	31.5	32.0	7.5	0.6	80.0	38.9	51.8	48.2
80447	GRAND LAKE	97.3	96.9	0.3	0.4	0.9	1.1	2.5	3.1	4.2	4.0	4.5	5.0	3.5	23.3	43.0	11.6	0.9	84.2	47.4	53.3	46.7
80449	HARTSEL	95.4	95.0	0.0	0.0	0.0	0.0	4.1	5.4	3.1	3.8	3.8	3.1	2.3	15.0	45.8	22.3	0.8	86.9	55.6	52.7	47.3
80451	HOT SULPHUR SPRINGS	96.2	95.3	1.0	1.1	1.0	1.2	2.6	3.1	5.5	4.8	5.3	5.6	6.6	30.1	33.7	7.8	0.7	80.6	40.6	53.9	46.1
80452	IDAHO SPRINGS	95.7	95.5	0.3	0.3	0.5	0.5	4.8	4.9	5.1	5.5	5.4	6.0	6.0	27.7	35.0	8.5	0.9	80.1	41.3	52.1	47.9
80455	JAMESTOWN	96.3	95.4	0.3	0.3	0.9	1.1	2.0	2.5	4.6	4.4	4.6	5.2	9.0	24.0	40.6	7.4	0.3	83.7	43.7	51.8	48.2
80456	JEFFERSON	93.6	93.1	0.8	0.9	0.5	0.6	6.7	8.2	3.0	4.0	5.1	5.5	1.7	24.0	44.9	11.4	0.5	84.2	48.1	52.1	47.9
80459	KREMMLING	91.2	89.2	0.0	0.0	0.4	0.4	10.4	13.2	8.2	8.2	8.0	6.1	4.9	28.3	28.4	6.5	1.5	71.7	36.3	51.3	48.7
80461	LEADVILLE	77.7	74.5	0.2	0.2	0.4	0.5	36.2	42.1	8.0	6.9	6.1	6.9	9.3	31.3	23.5	7.0	1.0	75.1	31.5	53.2	46.8
80463	MC COY	83.6	81.3	0.0	0.0	0.0	0.0	20.9	25.0	7.0	7.0	5.5	7.0	7.8	33.6	24.2	7.0	0.8	77.3	35.6	57.0	43.0
80465	MORRISON	94.5	93.4	0.6	0.6	1.1	1.4	5.9	7.7	5.7	6.6	7.2	7.2	4.5	26.2	33.7	7.8	1.0	75.6	40.3	51.0	49.0
80466	NEDERLAND	96.4	95.7	0.3	0.3	0.8	1.0	2.0	2.7	5.1	4.9	5.2	5.0	6.0	33.3	33.4	6.4	0.6	81.8	40.1	51.9	48.1
80467	OAK CREEK	95.6	95.0	0.1	0.1	0.7	0.8	3.6	4.4	6.1	6.8	6.6	5.7	5.2	30.1	32.9	5.9	0.8	76.7	38.8	52.0	48.0
80468	PARSHALL	96.8	96.1	0.0	0.0	0.0	0.0	3.5	4.6	6.2	6.9	7.3	5.7	4.3	24.9	34.3	9.4	0.9	76.0	41.9	52.6	47.4
80470	PINE	96.1	95.5	0.3	0.3	0.7	0.9	3.2	4.0	5.5	5.8	7.4	6.5	2.6	27.3	38.4	6.0	0.5	76.4	42.7	52.1	47.9
80478	TABERNASH	96.0	95.3	1.0	1.3	1.0	1.3	2.5	3.0	5.5	4.7	5.5	5.5	6.8	31.1	31.9	8.1	0.9	80.0	39.9	53.2	46.8
80479	TOPONAS	96.9	96.5	0.1	0.1	0.1	0.1	3.9	4.9	5.2	6.2	7.9	7.5	3.9	26.4	33.9	7.9	1.2	75.3	40.8	53.0	47.0
80480	WALDEN	96.2	95.4	0.3	0.3	0.1	0.1	6.5	8.3	5.2	6.0	6.4	7.8	4.1	21.3	33.0	14.5	1.6	76.7	44.4	50.3	49.7
80481	WARD	96.4	95.6	0.4	0.5	0.8	0.9	1.8	2.4	4.1	3.9	4.4	4.9	7.8	24.9	40.6	8.5	0.9	84.8	45.0	52.6	47.4
80482	WINTER PARK	95.0	94.9	0.7	0.6	0.7	1.3	2.9	3.8	3.8	3.2	3.2	3.8	7.7	44.2	27.6	6.4	0.0	88.5	35.7	55.1	44.9
80487	STEAMBOAT SPRINGS	97.1	96.7	0.1	0.2	0.5	0.7	2.8	3.6	4.9	4.9	5.5	6.3	7.7	34.5	31.0	4.7	0.5	81.0	36.7	54.5	45.5
80498	SILVERTHORNE	87.4	85.5	1.2	1.2	1.2	1.4	14.6	17.5	6.3	4.6	4.3	5.4	12.4	38.9	23.7	4.1	0.3	81.8	31.7	56.8	43.2
80501	LONGMONT	82.8	79.9	0.5	0.6	1.5	2.0	22.6	26.7	8.0	7.5	7.0	6.7	6.6	29.9	24.6	8.2	1.6	73.6	34.3	49.4	50.6
80503	LONGMONT	93.2	91.4	0.5	0.5	2.2	2.8	5.5	7.2	5.8	6.1	6.7	6.9	5.4	25.0	33.0	9.8	1.2	76.8	41.0	49.2	50.8
80504	LONGMONT	91.0	86.0	0.2	0.2	1.4	1.6	11.3	19.3	7.0	7.3	7.9	7.4	4.3	26.2	30.7	8.6	0.8	73.0	38.9	50.2	49.8
80510	ALLENSPARK	96.1	95.5	0.3	0.6	1.0	1.2	2.0	2.7	2.4	3.3	3.9	3.9	3.0	22.7	43.2	15.7	1.8	87.6	49.9	52.0	48.0
80512	BELLVUE	95.0	94.3	0.3	0.4	0.5	0.6	3.4	4.4	3.9	4.8	5.3	4.7	5.3	25.8	39.6	9.9	0.9	82.8	45.1	52.5	47.5
80513	BERTHOUD	94.5	93.0	0.2	0.2	0.5	0.7	6.5	8.8	5.7	6.8	7.8	7.9	5.2	25.1	32.8	7.7	0.9	74.5	39.9	50.7	49.3
80514	DACONO	77.7	72.6	0.4	0.6	1.0	1.0	31.3	38.2	8.1	7.5	7.3	7.1	6.6	27.9	25.4	9.1	1.0	72.8	35.0	50.3	49.7
80515	DRAKE	97.3	97.0	0.2	0.3	0.2	0.3	2.2	2.9	2.5	3.6	4.5	6.1	4.2	22.5	41.0	14.0	1.5	86.5	48.1	51.0	49.0
80516	ERIE	90.9	90.1	0.4	0.4	2.0	2.2	9.8	11.1	7.5	8.2	8.4	6.6	3.6	26.0	30.8	8.1	0.8	71.6	39.3	49.9	50.1
80517	ESTES PARK	96.2	95.3	0.3	0.3	0.7	0.9	4.0	5.3	3.5	3.8	4.2	5.0	4.2	20.3	38.0	18.8	2.2	85.3	50.1	49.1	50.9
80520	FIRESTONE	100.0	100.0	0.0	0.0	0.0	0.0	0.0	0.0	0.0	0.0	0.0	0.0	0.0	0.0	100.0	0.0	0.0	100.0	50.0	0.0	100.0
80521	FORT COLLINS	87.8	85.2	1.1	1.3	2.8	3.6	11.4	14.5	4.6	3.8	3.6	7.2	31.3	27.9	14.7	5.8	1.0	85.6	24.9	52.1	47.9
80523	FORT COLLINS	87.5	85.1	2.7	3.0	3.5	4.5	7.1	9.2	0.2	0.2	0.1	75.2	20.2	3.4	0.4	0.1	0.0	99.0	18.3	47.3	52.7
80524	FORT COLLINS	87.5	85.7	0.6	0.6	1.0	1.3	14.4	16.8	5.8	5.7	5.8	6.1	9.0	27.8	27.1	10.9	1.9	79.2	37.3	50.4	49.6
80525	FORT COLLINS	91.6	89.7	0.8	1.0	2.4	3.1	6.7	8.7	6.5	6.4	6.7	6.4	8.0	30.4	25.4	8.3	1.8	76.4	34.9	49.5	50.5
80526	FORT COLLINS	91.3	89.8	0.9	1.0	2.3	2.8	7.1	9.1	6.6	6.2	6.4	7.1	10.9	31.8	24.2	5.8	1.0	76.7	31.6	49.9	50.1
80528	FORT COLLINS	90.5	88.3	0.6	0.8	2.9	3.7	6.5	8.6	9.0	8.5	8.2	6.6	4.7	32.4	25.1	5.2	0.4	70.2	34.2	49.9	50.1
80530	FREDERICK	83.3	80.1	0.5	0.7	0.5	0.7	28.7	35.7	8.4	8.2	8.0	7.4	5.7	29.9	25.0	6.8	0.6	70.8	33.7	49.0	51.0
80534	JOHNSTOWN	86.8	84.4	0.2	0.2	0.3	0.4	22.1	27.0	9.1	8.3	7.9	6.6	4.8	32.2	23.3	7.0	0.7	70.6	33.4	50.1	49.9
80535	LAPORTE	92.7	91.3	0.2	0.2	0.5	0.5	7.5	9.9	5.3	5.7	6.1	6.4	5.6	26.7	34.6	8.8	0.9	79.0	40.5	50.4	49.6
80536	LIVERMORE	96.8	96.4	0.1	0.1	0.4	0.5	2.2	2.8	4.1	4.2	4.6	4.6	2.2	23.3	41.6	14.6	0.9	83.8	48.5	50.4	49.6
80537	LOVELAND	92.8	91.0	0.3	0.4	0.7	0.9	8.8	11.7	6.6	6.6	6.7	6.6	6.1	26.9	28.7	9.9	1.9	76.0	38.3	49.3	50.7
80538	LOVELAND	93.8	92.8	0.3	0.4	0.9	1.1	6.9	8.5	6.8	7.0	7.2	7.0	5.3	25.8	28.7	10.5	1.6	74.5	38.7	49.3	50.7
80540	LYONS	95.4	94.5	0.2	0.3	0.7	0.9	4.6	5.9	4.2	4.7	5.8	6.0	4.3	24.5	39.7	10.0	0.8	81.6	45.2	50.5	49.5
80542	MEAD	93.4	90.9	0.1	0.1	0.6	0.8	12.0	17.6	7.6	7.4	7.5	7.4	5.8	28.3	27.5	7.9	0.7	73.0	35.0	50.7	49.3
80543	MILLIKEN	76.5	78.3	0.3	0.3	0.4	0.4	37.3	35.7	9.5	9.1	8.5	7.6	6.0	30.5	21.8	6.4	0.6	68.2	31.3	49.5	50.5
80545	RED FEATHER LAKES	96.9	96.4	0.0	0.0	0.4	0.4	1.6	2.2	3.0	3.2	3.8	3.6	2.3	17.3	41.6	23.6	1.5	87.4	54.6	49.2	50.8
80547	TIMNATH	95.3	92.5	0.0	0.0	0.0	1.3	4.7	7.5	5.0	7.5	7.5	7.5	2.5	23.8	36.3	10.0	0.0	72.5	43.1	48.8	51.2
80549	WELLINGTON	90.0	88.9	0.3	0.3	0.7	0.9	9.3	10.8	7.5	7.6	7.6	6.9	4.8	29.7	28.0	7.3	0.7	72.9	36.4	49.4	50.6
80550	WINDSOR	92.2	89.8	0.4	0.6	0.5	0.7	10.3	14.8	8.2	7.9	7.6	6.6	5.0	31.4	25.6	6.7	1.0	72.1	34.7	49.6	50.4
80601	BRIGHTON	77.4	75.0	1.0	1.6	1.2	1.8	37.2	40.2	9.0	8.2	7.5	6.9	6.5	31.7	21.5	7.3	1.4	71.3	32.3	51.3	48.7
80602	BRIGHTON	89.4	84.6	1.1	1.3	2.0	2.0	13.5	19.1	8.6	8.6	8.4	7.0	4.1	30.6	27.0	5.2	0.4	69.9	35.5	49.6	50.4
80603	BRIGHTON	80.6	76.5	0.8	1.0	0.7	1.1	26.3	32.4	6.6	7.0	7.4	7.2	5.0	26.6	29.9	9.6	0.8	74.5	38.7	51.3	48.7
80610	AULT	83.2	77.4	0.0	0.1	0.7	0.8	24.1	33.8	7.3	7.5	7.5	6.8	5.7	27.3	27.0	9.6	1.3	73.5	36.5	51.4	48.6
80611	BRIGGSDALE	94.3	92.0	0.2	0.4	0.4	0.4	8.1	12.3	6.0	6.5	7.2	7.4	4.8	22.4	30.4	13.2	2.1	75.2	42.0	52.3	47.7
80612	CARR	90.2	86.6	0.4	0.4	0.4	0.4	12.3	17.8	5.9	6.7	6.7	7.5	5.5	25.7	30.8	10.3	0.8	75.9	39.9	49.8	50.2
80615	EATON	90.0	86.5	0.1	0.1	0.7	0.8	15.2	21.5	6.8	7.3	7.7	7.3	4.8	24.3	30.1	10.2	1.4	73.7	39.1	49.8	50.2
80620	EVANS	70.8	69.4	0.8	0.8	0.7	0.9	40.6	44.4	9.7	8.8	8.0	7.4	7.1	32.1	20.3	5.8	0.7	69.1	30.2	49.7	50.3
80621	FORT LUPTON	73.8	68.0	0.4	0.4	0.9	1.0	41.1	51.2	8.2	8.2	8.0	7.7	6.9	28.2	24.9	7.2	0.7	71.0	32.4	51.8	48.2
80624	GILL	83.1	77.8	0.2	0.3	0.2	0.4	21.2	28.8	6.5	7.0	7.7	8.4	5.0	24.1	29.3	10.7	1.3	73.6	38.9	51.6	48.4
80631	GREELEY	72.9	67.5	0.8	0.9	0.9	1.1	43.2	51.9	8.5	7.6	6.8	8.6	13.7	28.0	17.7	7.4	1.7	72.9	27.8	50.4	49.6
80634	GREELEY	88.5	85.2	0.7	0.8	1.1	1.5	15.7	21.4	7.2	6.9	6.8	6.7	6.2	28.8	26.4	9.4	1.6	75.0	35.9	48.8	51.2
80639	GREELEY	81.8	77.0	3.1	3.7	7.4	9.7	8.2	11.9	0.3	0.1	0.1	63.3	30.7	3.1	0.9	0.7	0.8	99.2	18.9	43.3	56.7
80640	HENDERSON	82.7	79.1	0.9	0.9	1.7	2.1	24.2	31.5	6.4	7.0	7.7	7.3	4.5	26.3	30.7	9.2	1.0	74.3	39.4	50.6	49.4
80642	HUDSON	84.8	79.8	0.4	0.7	0.6	0.8	19.4	26.8	8.2	8.2	8.3	7.5	5.3	27.3	26.9	7.5	0.7	70.5	35.3	51.6	48.4
80643	KEENESBURG	88.9	84.9	0.3	0.4	0.9	1.3	11.8	17.2	7.0	7.5	8.2	8.3	4.7	26.6	27.0	9.6	1.3	71.8	37.6	51.1	48.9
80644	KERSEY	89.3	84.9	0.2	0.2	0.8	1.0	17.4	25.5	7.3	7.4	7.6	8.0	5.9	26.2	27.6	8.9	1.0	72.7	36.3	50.4	49.6
80645	LA SALLE	79.1	72.6	0.3	0.4	0.6	0.7	29.5	39.5	6.4	6.5	7.3	8.3	6.5	26.9	26.9	10.0	1.2	74.7	36.5	51.4	48.6
80648	NUNN	88.7	84.5	0.1	0.1	0.1	0.2	15.0	21.8	6.7	6.7	7.1	7.9	5.9	26.2	28.0	10.4	1.1	74.5	38.3	49.4	50.6
	COLORADO	82.8	80.7	3.8	3.8	2.3	2.9	17.1	20.2	6.9	6.7	6.7	6.9	7.0	29.0	26.5	8.8	1.4	75.7	35.9	50.2	49.8
	UNITED STATES	75.1	72.0	12.3	12.7	3.8	4.6	12.5	15.7	6.8	6.7	6.6	7.1	6.9	27.0	26.0	10.9	1.9	75.7	36.9	49.2	50.8

ZIP CODE #	POST OFFICE NAME	2009 Per Capita Income	2009 HH Income Base	2009 HOUSEHOLD INCOME DISTRIBUTION (%) Less than $25,000	$25,000 to $49,999	$50,000 to $99,999	$100,000 to $149,999	$150,000 or More	MEDIAN HOUSEHOLD INCOME 2009	2014	2009 National Centile	2009 State Centile	2009 Home Value Base	2009 HOME VALUE DISTRIBUTION (%) Less than $50,000	$50,000 to $89,999	$90,000 to $174,999	$175,000 to $399,999	$400,000 or More	2009 Median Home Value
80247	DENVER	32748	14430	20.3	31.2	34.0	10.3	4.1	48826	50361	59	49	5650	1.4	15.5	54.0	26.4	2.7	124400
80249	DENVER	31203	6054	2.6	20.8	47.8	20.5	8.2	76485	78918	90	85	4705	0.0	0.3	21.5	76.4	1.8	209907
80260	DENVER	22618	11861	18.4	30.9	41.7	7.4	1.7	50513	52489	62	52	7658	37.8	25.2	16.6	20.4	0.1	65683
80262	DENVER	414	0	0.0	0.0	0.0	0.0	0.0	0	0	0	0	0	0.0	0.0	0.0	0.0	0.0	0
80301	BOULDER	39942	9655	12.5	20.7	31.8	22.1	13.0	71019	74333	87	82	6328	8.5	1.9	11.0	42.7	36.0	319510
80302	BOULDER	34253	12307	28.8	24.7	23.2	13.5	9.9	46074	48031	52	40	4869	1.0	0.2	4.6	30.0	64.1	472445
80303	BOULDER	35343	10917	24.6	20.9	27.7	17.4	9.4	55522	57900	72	61	5198	2.7	1.2	7.5	45.1	43.6	370515
80304	BOULDER	43226	10523	11.7	19.0	30.4	23.4	15.6	78642	82209	91	86	7107	13.2	2.3	5.7	24.8	54.0	423619
80305	BOULDER	38760	6882	12.5	15.9	34.2	26.2	11.2	80350	82908	92	88	4231	1.0	0.0	1.8	61.8	35.4	352934
80309	BOULDER	13815	0	0.0	0.0	0.0	0.0	0.0	0	0	0	0	0	0.0	0.0	0.0	0.0	0.0	0
80401	GOLDEN	42572	15752	13.0	19.4	30.1	20.5	17.1	75811	81172	90	85	11030	7.2	3.6	10.4	50.0	28.7	278036
80403	GOLDEN	42011	8441	7.2	14.8	33.8	29.3	14.8	89390	94788	95	93	6889	1.2	1.2	12.8	60.3	24.5	286187
80421	BAILEY	29765	3558	8.8	20.1	49.5	16.8	4.7	67040	71036	85	79	3158	2.0	3.8	16.4	64.1	13.7	243750
80422	BLACK HAWK	32006	288	19.1	29.2	39.6	7.6	4.5	51068	52644	64	54	149	5.4	5.4	35.6	50.3	3.4	186458
80423	BOND	26248	83	13.3	38.6	31.3	16.9	0.0	48380	50000	58	47	48	0.0	0.0	0.0	47.9	52.1	410000
80424	BRECKENRIDGE	38154	3419	9.7	22.2	38.0	17.7	12.4	70380	71116	87	82	1971	4.0	0.1	3.1	25.3	67.5	552784
80428	CLARK	31417	329	4.0	26.7	46.5	13.4	9.4	66456	64878	85	77	263	0.8	1.9	1.5	22.4	73.4	613839
80430	COALMONT	22179	51	21.6	37.3	31.4	5.9	3.9	42963	46543	42	31	32	9.4	3.1	34.4	43.8	9.4	183333
80433	CONIFER	43859	3212	4.3	9.0	35.3	37.5	13.9	101697	105550	97	95	2844	0.0	0.6	4.9	72.0	22.5	313193
80435	DILLON	34031	2923	9.3	21.5	41.4	17.4	10.3	69253	69555	86	81	1659	3.9	2.9	13.2	29.4	50.7	403898
80439	EVERGREEN	48618	9670	7.7	12.5	28.6	28.3	22.9	101718	104465	97	96	8081	0.2	0.5	6.5	51.3	41.5	361781
80440	FAIRPLAY	31899	1518	10.8	25.9	45.3	12.5	5.5	61270	66945	79	72	1211	8.3	4.8	22.4	59.2	5.4	207629
80442	FRASER	35206	1117	14.0	24.4	40.1	15.0	6.5	58869	58798	76	66	637	2.4	0.0	5.7	45.1	46.9	385448
80443	FRISCO	40128	1476	8.6	12.6	44.4	23.5	10.8	80060	80832	92	87	834	1.1	0.6	2.2	33.2	62.9	487805
80446	GRANBY	27690	2121	13.4	26.1	44.8	10.7	4.9	58812	59572	76	66	1479	4.4	1.5	10.4	42.7	41.0	344375
80447	GRAND LAKE	33360	1038	13.9	28.7	42.8	7.4	7.2	55995	56792	73	62	746	1.9	0.0	6.3	40.1	51.7	409701
80449	HARTSEL	30211	124	16.9	40.3	30.6	5.6	6.5	44436	46371	47	36	111	1.8	17.1	24.3	46.8	9.9	203261
80451	HOT SULPHUR SPRINGS	29340	286	12.6	23.4	46.5	11.5	5.9	61489	61094	79	72	218	2.3	0.5	4.6	36.7	56.0	430233
80452	IDAHO SPRINGS	29683	2519	16.1	26.3	41.0	12.4	4.2	56085	60853	73	62	1707	12.1	10.0	25.1	47.5	5.3	181151
80455	JAMESTOWN	41456	174	13.2	17.2	32.8	28.2	8.6	77177	79890	91	85	126	0.0	0.8	15.1	56.3	27.8	315152
80456	JEFFERSON	27348	412	21.4	26.7	41.5	6.1	4.4	51354	54563	65	55	374	8.3	14.2	27.3	46.0	4.3	175676
80459	KREMMLING	22932	953	17.5	27.7	45.1	8.7	0.9	53885	55189	69	59	661	11.6	2.6	13.2	58.9	13.8	248864
80461	LEADVILLE	22615	2937	20.1	31.1	38.3	7.3	3.2	49312	50663	60	50	1972	12.6	11.6	40.2	32.9	2.7	145203
80463	MC COY	28328	55	12.7	38.2	32.7	14.5	1.8	49434	61955	60	50	33	12.1	0.0	9.1	33.3	45.5	325000
80465	MORRISON	41527	5795	5.3	7.7	40.2	31.6	15.3	94831	100892	96	94	5024	0.2	0.7	9.5	67.3	22.3	245235
80466	NEDERLAND	43611	1611	11.9	14.0	37.2	21.8	15.1	80090	83158	92	87	1156	1.4	1.6	6.8	51.2	38.9	349206
80467	OAK CREEK	28958	1086	16.3	25.7	42.3	11.7	4.1	56579	57809	73	63	786	5.6	3.8	20.6	39.6	30.4	228632
80468	PARSHALL	25517	166	15.1	25.9	45.8	10.2	3.0	58616	60608	76	65	126	2.4	0.8	6.3	51.6	38.9	362162
80470	PINE	39303	1445	5.0	13.2	32.7	39.3	9.8	98297	101328	96	95	1271	0.0	1.1	6.7	68.7	23.5	291023
80478	TABERNASH	33277	104	13.5	24.0	45.2	11.5	5.8	60541	61215	78	69	80	1.3	0.0	3.8	35.0	60.0	442105
80479	TOPONAS	24098	396	19.7	37.9	33.6	5.3	3.5	43983	47007	45	34	280	4.6	1.8	19.6	37.9	36.1	275000
80480	WALDEN	19923	568	27.6	37.0	28.9	4.8	1.8	37555	39022	25	17	384	22.1	14.6	37.8	19.0	6.5	111458
80481	WARD	33488	428	17.8	18.7	33.9	24.3	5.4	68500	72397	86	80	310	0.0	2.6	13.2	59.0	25.2	300000
80482	WINTER PARK	38375	78	12.8	24.4	43.6	14.1	5.1	60000	57995	77	68	43	0.0	0.0	7.0	48.8	44.2	377273
80487	STEAMBOAT SPRINGS	36333	6725	11.4	16.2	42.9	20.5	9.0	72602	72987	88	82	4524	3.4	3.4	6.7	22.4	64.0	490327
80498	SILVERTHORNE	32990	2845	8.6	17.1	45.3	19.5	9.5	75394	75972	90	84	1794	0.9	0.1	4.0	38.5	56.6	433811
80501	LONGMONT	27672	22894	15.2	22.7	38.1	18.5	5.6	63182	66308	81	74	14472	5.8	1.9	16.0	70.2	6.1	217130
80503	LONGMONT	42054	12948	8.0	17.5	29.7	28.2	16.6	90068	93314	95	93	9522	0.9	0.9	3.4	60.4	34.3	331316
80504	LONGMONT	33314	7008	10.2	18.5	42.4	16.5	12.4	75363	75748	90	84	6226	5.1	5.5	20.0	42.5	26.8	232365
80510	ALLENSPARK	32064	167	24.0	28.1	29.3	15.6	3.0	48524	48888	58	48	126	0.0	2.4	12.7	57.9	27.0	309375
80512	BELLVUE	33510	1116	11.3	18.0	51.5	14.2	4.9	65313	67525	84	76	891	1.5	2.4	18.1	51.3	26.8	251437
80513	BERTHOUD	31930	3929	7.9	18.0	48.2	16.7	9.2	75025	76463	89	83	3246	4.7	3.0	12.5	58.8	20.9	265525
80514	DACONO	20282	1532	15.8	32.4	44.7	5.9	1.2	51218	53566	64	55	1204	3.8	19.3	62.4	13.4	1.2	116740
80515	DRAKE	30169	497	17.1	25.2	49.7	5.2	2.8	55099	58793	71	61	386	1.6	2.6	24.9	49.7	21.2	246825
80516	ERIE	38262	6911	7.8	14.1	35.0	27.3	15.7	88926	88515	95	92	5997	0.9	1.7	14.9	57.1	25.4	291987
80517	ESTES PARK	33078	5242	16.2	26.1	42.8	9.7	5.1	57573	61285	75	64	3407	0.5	0.9	9.3	62.9	26.4	304117
80520	FIRESTONE	80641	2	0.0	0.0	100.0	0.0	0.0	87500	81250	94	92	0	0.0	0.0	0.0	0.0	0.0	0
80521	FORT COLLINS	20978	12402	33.1	27.4	31.3	6.0	2.2	40214	42201	33	23	5079	6.3	2.2	33.6	52.3	5.6	186613
80523	FORT COLLINS	18031	260	69.6	21.2	8.1	1.2	0.0	16154	16180	1	1	10	0.0	0.0	40.0	60.0	0.0	200000
80524	FORT COLLINS	28350	12507	19.4	24.8	37.9	11.7	6.2	55811	60686	72	61	8371	15.2	6.9	17.5	44.4	16.0	211478
80525	FORT COLLINS	33361	19183	13.9	19.6	41.4	15.7	9.4	68236	72288	86	79	12723	6.1	3.5	14.3	65.0	11.2	240570
80526	FORT COLLINS	30552	17448	13.0	20.8	42.8	15.9	7.6	67773	70757	85	79	11728	4.9	2.0	15.8	68.7	8.6	223394
80528	FORT COLLINS	39990	5409	6.0	9.5	44.9	23.2	16.4	86666	87242	94	91	4332	1.6	4.5	20.2	51.9	21.8	262224
80530	FREDERICK	21850	1926	15.8	21.8	49.7	10.2	2.5	63944	65829	82	74	1570	2.0	4.8	46.4	45.2	1.7	169697
80534	JOHNSTOWN	26914	3789	11.6	20.1	49.9	12.5	6.0	66916	68536	85	78	3064	3.7	4.5	34.6	47.7	9.5	187759
80535	LAPORTE	25641	971	12.3	23.5	55.7	7.9	0.6	60729	63890	78	70	666	6.0	7.8	23.6	50.9	11.7	205856
80536	LIVERMORE	29109	792	14.0	24.2	51.0	7.6	3.2	60554	63468	78	70	682	2.9	4.3	12.0	58.2	22.6	251630
80537	LOVELAND	27622	15164	15.5	23.2	44.8	11.5	5.0	60906	63700	79	71	10391	3.1	3.1	26.8	54.5	12.5	210872
80538	LOVELAND	30602	16612	11.8	20.0	44.8	16.3	7.1	69924	74553	87	81	12553	5.1	2.0	13.2	69.6	10.1	228052
80540	LYONS	36842	1776	10.1	19.9	41.3	18.9	9.8	71961	75972	88	82	1422	3.8	3.0	8.5	52.2	32.5	303488
80542	MEAD	32156	898	6.9	16.4	41.6	21.0	14.0	80857	81535	92	88	767	1.3	13.2	23.1	38.9	23.6	218689
80543	MILLIKEN	20491	1940	13.2	23.7	49.3	9.5	4.3	59317	62104	77	67	1590	2.9	5.2	45.2	37.0	9.7	169672
80545	RED FEATHER LAKES	26883	507	24.7	27.6	39.3	6.1	2.4	47740	49273	56	45	423	0.9	4.0	22.9	54.4	17.7	229514
80547	TIMNATH	59008	40	10.0	12.5	30.0	25.0	22.5	95404	100000	96	94	33	6.1	3.0	9.1	42.4	39.4	341667
80549	WELLINGTON	27420	2467	9.2	20.8	54.6	10.7	4.8	64782	66914	83	75	2011	0.8	5.1	26.9	47.7	19.5	226069
80550	WINDSOR	27931	6724	11.7	19.9	45.3	17.2	5.8	68831	70544	86	80	5097	1.3	2.0	36.1	53.8	6.9	189556
80601	BRIGHTON	24043	11047	13.7	25.5	39.9	16.1	4.8	62518	67038	81	73	8293	5.2	3.3	20.8	66.0	4.7	216376
80602	BRIGHTON	38543	8120	6.1	5.7	33.5	39.0	15.7	106567	106725	98	97	7549	0.1	0.3	4.0	79.5	16.1	260706
80603	BRIGHTON	22684	3995	12.9	26.7	46.9	9.8	3.7	57219	60375	74	63	3197	9.3	11.8	31.6	37.4	9.9	166715
80610	AULT	18240	1162	28.2	29.5	35.9	5.1	1.3	41917	44062	39	28	741	18.5	11.2	41.6	23.9	4.9	128370
80611	BRIGGSDALE	18239	291	31.3	32.0	30.2	5.2	1.4	39137	40354	30	21	205	17.6	18.0	36.1	21.5	6.8	115417
80612	CARR	22511	98	21.4	27.6	41.8	6.1	3.1	50564	53663	63	53	71	9.9	19.7	28.2	31.0	11.3	137500
80615	EATON	20989	2749	20.7	27.8	40.6	7.8	3.1	51227	53323	64	55	1982	4.6	8.0	38.0	42.0	7.3	173138
80620	EVANS	21080	5969	18.6	26.9	45.9	5.6	3.0	53384	56939	69	58	3776	14.3	6.9	50.7	25.2	2.8	144177
80621	FORT LUPTON	18737	4486	19.5	28.0	40.7	8.5	3.2	51988	54208	66	57	3053	13.0	6.8	39.9	33.5	6.7	155602
80624	GILL	18021	319	27.6	22.9	40.4	7.8	1.3	49487	50511	60	50	222	12.6	18.5	27.5	32.4	9.0	136364
80631	GREELEY	16187	16831	33.9	32.0	28.5	4.1	1.5	35086	36869	18	11	7478	19.8	10.7	48.9	18.7	1.8	123786
80634	GREELEY	27894	20320	15.3	22.5	41.4	13.9	6.8	61949	65149	80	72	14228	1.5	3.8	39.0	50.4	5.3	183296
80639	GREELEY	15822	119	65.5	25.2	8.4	0.8	0.0	17204	17389	1	2	9	0.0	33.3	44.4	22.2	0.0	137500
80640	HENDERSON	26113	2965	9.4	25.4	39.1	18.2	7.9	63837	65616	82	74	2579	1.7	6.5	34.1	53.1	4.6	190635
80642	HUDSON	20691	1225	14.5	28.2	45.5	9.3	2.4	55790	59000	72	61	910	17.0	8.9	35.3	31.4	7.4	146078
80643	KEENESBURG	19989	904	21.5	27.7	42.1	6.3	2.4	50789	53209	63	54	593	9.3	9.1	34.4	40.0	7.3	168750
80644	KERSEY	18241	1196	18.9	28.5	44.3	7.2	1.1	51386	52605	65	56	891	12.0	10.2	41.1	31.4	5.3	145952
80645	LA SALLE	19489	1475	22.1	27.3	41.4	7.5	1.7	50486	52427	62	52	1030	6.5	6.3	57.3	26.0	3.9	142662
80648	NUNN	19619	287	23.3	28.9	39.0	5.9	2.8	47837	48938	56	45	203	15.3	21.7	31.5	26.1	5.4	112054
	COLORADO	30807		15.5	22.5	37.5	15.8	8.6	62597	65813				4.4	4.3	23.6	52.9	14.8	220998
	UNITED STATES	27277		20.9	24.4	35.3	11.7	7.6	54719	56938				9.3	13.1	31.6	32.6	13.5	162279

ZIP CODE #	POST OFFICE NAME	FINANCIAL SERVICES: Auto Loan	Home Loan	Invest-ments	Retire-ment Plans	THE HOME: Home Improvements: Home Repair	Lawn & Garden	Furnishings: Comput-ers & Hard-ware-Personal	Major Appli-ances	TV, Radio, Sound Equip-ment	Furni-ture	ENTERTAINMENT: Dine out/ Carry out	Sports Equip-ment	Fees & Tickets	Toys & Games	Travel	Cable TV	PERSONAL: Apparel & Services	Auto Repairs	Health Insur-ance	Pets & Supplies
80247	DENVER	91	68	67	71	67	70	91	77	91	91	92	61	82	91	80	90	64	89	84	94
80249	DENVER	130	141	115	136	132	116	127	125	119	136	122	99	129	128	124	113	85	119	109	142
80260	DENVER	86	75	70	74	73	74	83	78	83	84	84	60	77	84	77	83	58	82	80	93
80262	DENVER	0	0	0	0	0	0	0	0	0	0	0	0	0	0	0	0	0	0	0	0
80301	BOULDER	133	122	120	130	121	113	136	121	130	139	132	100	133	134	129	125	94	129	115	145
80302	BOULDER	102	77	82	86	78	75	128	88	110	107	111	82	102	108	98	102	80	104	84	110
80303	BOULDER	105	93	98	99	95	89	125	99	112	113	113	85	111	110	108	106	81	109	95	119
80304	BOULDER	137	145	154	151	149	133	150	139	141	153	143	113	155	141	153	135	103	143	130	163
80305	BOULDER	123	126	135	130	131	118	140	125	129	137	130	102	138	128	136	124	94	130	118	147
80309	BOULDER	0	0	0	0	0	0	0	0	0	0	0	0	0	0	0	0	0	0	0	0
80401	GOLDEN	136	153	156	156	156	144	146	143	141	151	142	111	157	140	153	138	102	143	139	166
80403	GOLDEN	139	166	163	171	168	153	148	149	140	155	142	117	164	142	160	136	103	144	139	172
80421	BAILEY	104	124	110	126	121	115	107	111	103	111	105	87	118	106	115	102	74	106	105	129
80422	BLACK HAWK	89	90	86	92	88	87	92	87	91	93	92	69	94	91	91	90	64	90	88	104
80423	BOND	104	83	132	82	91	109	83	105	87	79	86	77	73	83	90	93	57	97	104	122
80424	BRECKENRIDGE	142	115	106	125	109	105	141	118	137	141	140	102	130	143	125	132	99	131	114	145
80428	CLARK	115	120	121	122	120	126	110	120	109	109	110	92	112	110	117	111	76	114	118	140
80430	COALMONT	96	66	105	66	69	101	73	91	76	59	75	75	54	75	73	83	49	85	96	112
80433	CONIFER	150	187	188	192	190	173	157	166	150	168	152	126	180	151	176	146	110	156	152	189
80435	DILLON	130	109	101	117	104	101	131	111	127	130	130	94	122	131	118	123	92	123	109	136
80439	EVERGREEN	159	200	212	206	209	187	172	180	163	185	164	136	199	162	194	159	120	170	167	204
80440	FAIRPLAY	114	112	112	108	109	107	103	110	101	107	102	84	100	105	103	100	70	104	102	127
80442	FRASER	117	101	95	107	96	94	113	102	110	114	113	85	107	115	105	107	79	108	97	123
80443	FRISCO	142	122	110	130	115	109	141	121	136	142	140	103	133	143	128	131	99	131	116	148
80446	GRANBY	112	96	119	95	99	111	95	108	98	94	98	80	86	98	96	102	66	103	107	127
80447	GRAND LAKE	119	95	153	94	104	126	95	121	100	89	98	88	82	95	103	106	65	112	119	140
80449	HARTSEL	104	85	136	84	94	111	84	107	88	80	87	77	74	84	92	94	58	99	106	124
80451	HOT SULPHUR SPRINGS	118	98	150	97	106	126	97	121	101	91	100	89	86	96	105	107	67	112	119	140
80452	IDAHO SPRINGS	97	94	115	93	97	102	92	101	92	89	93	76	90	91	97	95	64	98	100	117
80455	JAMESTOWN	119	126	124	129	125	119	127	120	123	128	124	95	131	122	127	120	88	123	119	142
80456	JEFFERSON	97	78	126	77	85	103	78	99	81	73	81	72	67	77	84	87	53	91	98	115
80459	KREMMLING	91	87	77	85	85	88	81	86	84	84	84	63	79	87	79	85	57	83	86	102
80461	LEADVILLE	90	78	73	79	76	79	88	83	88	86	88	65	81	89	81	88	61	87	84	99
80463	MC COY	108	91	122	88	95	108	90	106	93	88	93	78	81	91	93	97	62	100	105	124
80465	MORRISON	151	189	181	190	189	167	160	164	150	171	152	128	182	154	175	144	110	155	147	187
80466	NEDERLAND	131	149	151	153	151	137	141	138	134	146	136	109	152	134	148	130	98	137	130	160
80467	OAK CREEK	102	102	94	100	100	100	95	98	96	98	96	73	95	98	95	97	67	96	97	116
80468	PARSHALL	91	102	88	105	99	100	91	95	90	91	90	74	97	92	96	90	63	91	94	112
80470	PINE	135	167	165	170	168	155	142	149	135	150	137	113	160	136	157	132	98	141	139	170
80478	TABERNASH	121	97	156	95	106	128	97	123	101	91	100	90	84	96	105	108	67	114	122	143
80479	TOPONAS	102	70	112	70	74	108	78	97	81	63	80	80	57	80	78	89	52	91	103	120
80480	WALDEN	83	59	88	57	61	86	62	78	67	55	66	61	48	66	62	74	43	72	82	95
80481	WARD	116	107	127	108	109	117	109	115	109	107	110	88	105	107	111	111	76	113	116	136
80482	WINTER PARK	116	101	90	108	95	91	115	100	111	116	113	85	108	117	104	106	80	107	94	121
80487	STEAMBOAT SPRINGS	121	131	133	134	132	119	127	124	120	132	122	99	132	122	131	116	87	123	114	143
80498	SILVERTHORNE	135	119	112	125	113	111	131	119	128	132	130	99	124	133	122	124	91	125	113	143
80501	LONGMONT	104	108	98	107	105	98	107	102	103	109	105	81	108	106	105	101	74	103	98	119
80503	LONGMONT	146	167	165	173	169	154	153	152	147	161	149	119	168	149	162	142	107	149	142	176
80504	LONGMONT	141	154	144	154	153	144	136	142	133	146	134	107	144	137	141	131	94	135	133	164
80510	ALLENSPARK	104	84	135	82	92	110	84	106	88	78	86	78	72	83	91	93	57	98	105	123
80512	BELLVUE	115	112	140	113	117	123	106	119	106	105	106	89	105	104	114	108	73	113	116	138
80513	BERTHOUD	123	140	126	139	136	126	124	126	119	130	121	98	132	124	128	116	86	121	116	145
80514	DACONO	83	85	74	82	81	80	81	81	80	83	81	62	81	83	80	80	56	81	79	95
80515	DRAKE	101	83	131	82	91	108	82	103	86	78	85	75	73	81	89	91	56	96	103	120
80516	ERIE	146	178	170	182	178	160	152	157	144	164	146	122	172	148	165	138	106	148	142	178
80517	ESTES PARK	110	96	146	95	107	122	93	115	97	92	96	80	87	91	102	103	64	107	117	132
80520	FIRESTONE	106	131	135	135	135	124	112	118	107	119	108	88	127	107	126	105	78	112	112	135
80521	FORT COLLINS	73	53	50	57	51	54	86	61	77	71	78	55	67	77	64	74	55	72	62	77
80523	FORT COLLINS	36	15	15	19	14	18	51	25	40	34	41	27	30	39	27	37	29	35	25	34
80524	FORT COLLINS	100	97	92	98	95	95	103	96	99	101	100	76	99	101	97	98	70	99	95	114
80525	FORT COLLINS	118	122	114	125	119	111	121	114	117	125	118	92	125	120	120	113	84	116	108	134
80526	FORT COLLINS	114	114	103	117	110	103	118	108	112	119	113	88	116	115	112	107	81	110	101	127
80528	FORT COLLINS	158	179	153	175	171	149	155	156	146	169	149	124	164	156	158	137	105	147	135	177
80530	FREDERICK	99	107	90	103	101	92	95	96	91	102	93	73	97	96	94	88	65	92	87	110
80534	JOHNSTOWN	113	124	100	120	116	103	109	109	103	117	105	87	112	111	108	98	74	104	96	125
80535	LAPORTE	87	97	90	97	95	95	90	92	88	88	89	71	94	89	94	88	62	90	91	107
80536	LIVERMORE	108	89	137	89	97	115	89	111	92	84	91	81	78	88	96	98	61	102	109	128
80537	LOVELAND	99	104	97	104	102	99	99	99	97	101	98	77	102	99	101	96	69	98	96	116
80538	LOVELAND	109	125	115	124	123	114	112	113	108	117	110	87	121	111	117	106	78	110	108	130
80540	LYONS	118	134	142	136	137	131	121	127	118	125	119	96	131	117	132	117	84	123	123	147
80542	MEAD	147	162	132	157	152	137	143	144	136	153	138	114	147	145	143	130	97	136	128	164
80543	MILLIKEN	101	106	89	100	102	91	99	99	94	106	96	76	99	98	98	90	67	97	89	112
80545	RED FEATHER LAKES	91	73	118	72	80	97	73	93	77	69	76	68	64	73	79	82	50	86	92	108
80547	TIMNATH	151	200	207	210	207	179	163	170	153	178	155	134	198	156	186	145	116	158	148	192
80549	WELLINGTON	106	117	101	116	112	105	104	106	100	110	102	81	108	105	106	98	71	101	98	122
80550	WINDSOR	114	127	107	125	121	110	112	113	107	119	109	89	118	113	114	103	76	108	102	130
80601	BRIGHTON	104	110	93	106	105	95	103	101	98	109	100	79	104	104	102	95	70	99	92	116
80602	BRIGHTON	162	196	170	197	189	164	165	167	153	180	156	135	183	164	173	144	113	155	142	188
80603	BRIGHTON	98	103	89	104	100	102	94	98	94	95	94	75	96	97	95	95	65	94	97	116
80610	AULT	79	71	70	70	70	78	68	74	71	68	70	56	63	73	67	73	48	72	75	89
80611	BRIGGSDALE	85	59	93	58	61	90	65	81	68	53	67	67	48	66	65	74	43	75	85	99
80612	CARR	91	87	76	85	85	88	81	85	83	84	83	63	79	86	79	85	57	83	85	101
80615	EATON	87	89	85	91	87	95	83	89	83	80	83	70	84	85	86	85	57	85	90	106
80620	EVANS	94	88	75	85	84	79	89	85	86	93	88	66	84	91	83	84	61	86	80	100
80621	FORT LUPTON	89	90	79	86	88	83	86	87	84	90	85	65	84	87	85	83	59	86	83	100
80624	GILL	84	82	85	84	81	91	77	85	77	73	77	67	75	78	80	79	53	81	86	101
80631	GREELEY	66	55	51	55	54	54	68	60	66	65	67	48	60	66	60	65	47	65	59	71
80634	GREELEY	106	113	103	113	110	104	107	105	104	111	105	82	110	107	107	102	74	104	101	122
80639	GREELEY	36	15	15	19	14	18	50	25	40	34	41	27	30	39	27	36	29	35	25	34
80640	HENDERSON	115	127	111	131	124	126	114	119	113	115	113	93	121	116	120	113	79	115	118	140
80642	HUDSON	98	93	87	93	91	98	88	94	89	88	89	71	85	92	87	92	61	90	94	111
80643	KEENESBURG	88	84	89	86	84	95	80	88	80	76	80	71	77	81	83	83	55	84	90	106
80644	KERSEY	87	82	76	81	81	87	78	84	80	77	80	63	74	82	76	83	54	80	85	99
80645	LA SALLE	84	81	84	80	81	88	80	85	80	75	80	67	76	81	81	82	55	82	86	100
80648	NUNN	90	83	73	80	81	84	78	83	81	81	81	60	74	84	74	83	55	80	83	98
	COLORADO	114	114	111	115	112	109	114	111	111	116	113	88	114	113	113	110	80	112	108	130
	UNITED STATES	100	100	100	100	100	100	100	100	100	100	100	100	100	100	100	100	100	100	100	100

ZIP CODE #	POST OFFICE NAME	COUNTY FIPS CODE	POPULATION 2000	POPULATION 2009	POPULATION 2014	2000-2009 ANNUAL RATE % Rate	2000-2009 ANNUAL RATE State Centile	HOUSEHOLDS 2000	HOUSEHOLDS 2009	HOUSEHOLDS 2014	HOUSEHOLDS % Annual Rate 2000-2009	HOUSEHOLDS 2009 Average HH Size	FAMILIES 2000	FAMILIES 2009	FAMILIES % Annual Rate 2000-2009
80649	ORCHARD	087	333	408	442	2.2	74	133	161	174	2.1	2.53	98	116	1.8
80650	PIERCE	123	1349	1724	1952	2.7	82	483	611	689	2.6	2.82	384	473	2.3
80651	PLATTEVILLE	123	5236	6139	6817	1.7	67	1709	1978	2185	1.6	3.10	1333	1497	1.3
80652	ROGGEN	123	652	793	875	2.1	73	229	278	307	2.1	2.85	183	216	1.8
80653	WELDONA	087	568	657	690	1.6	64	236	269	281	1.4	2.44	176	197	1.2
80654	WIGGINS	087	2141	2434	2550	1.4	58	709	796	830	1.3	3.06	563	623	1.1
80701	FORT MORGAN	087	15429	16126	16280	0.5	37	5430	5500	5512	0.1	2.88	3958	3948	0.0
80705	LOG LANE VILLAGE	087	1135	1140	1139	0.0	22	338	335	332	-0.1	3.40	276	269	-0.3
80720	AKRON	121	2771	2769	2678	0.0	22	1137	1059	1021	-0.8	2.41	775	707	-1.0
80721	AMHERST	095	190	201	202	0.6	40	68	71	71	0.5	2.83	55	57	0.4
80722	ATWOOD	075	364	381	385	0.5	37	132	137	139	0.4	2.78	101	103	0.2
80723	BRUSH	087	6825	7135	7168	0.5	37	2437	2461	2456	0.1	2.74	1704	1684	-0.1
80726	CROOK	075	420	414	411	-0.2	16	171	168	167	-0.2	2.46	129	125	-0.3
80727	ECKLEY	125	456	481	486	0.6	40	160	169	171	0.6	2.85	115	120	0.5
80728	FLEMING	075	2280	912	902	-9.4	0	356	347	344	-0.3	2.63	270	259	-0.4
80729	GROVER	123	538	617	717	1.5	62	236	271	315	1.5	2.25	172	190	1.1
80731	HAXTUN	095	1658	1716	1712	0.4	34	672	687	684	0.2	2.44	470	472	0.0
80733	HILLROSE	121	525	576	593	1.0	50	184	200	206	0.9	2.88	146	156	0.7
80734	HOLYOKE	095	2817	2902	2897	0.3	31	1112	1131	1123	0.2	2.52	767	765	0.0
80735	IDALIA	125	420	405	399	-0.4	11	166	161	158	-0.3	2.52	128	123	-0.4
80736	ILIFF	075	806	827	831	0.3	31	299	306	307	0.3	2.70	228	230	0.1
80737	JULESBURG	115	1800	1633	1538	-1.0	5	756	680	640	-1.1	2.32	513	452	-1.4
80740	LINDON	121	97	87	83	-1.2	4	40	36	35	-1.1	2.42	30	26	-1.5
80741	MERINO	075	781	832	845	0.7	43	288	304	308	0.6	2.74	223	231	0.4
80742	NEW RAYMER	123	273	319	372	1.7	67	106	122	142	1.5	2.59	77	85	1.1
80743	OTIS	121	1086	1045	1011	-0.4	11	435	420	408	-0.4	2.49	323	307	-0.5
80744	OVID	115	542	458	425	-1.8	0	239	202	188	-1.8	2.27	169	140	-2.0
80745	PADRONI	075	144	147	148	0.2	28	56	57	58	0.2	2.58	43	43	0.0
80747	PEETZ	075	493	487	483	-0.1	19	184	181	180	-0.2	2.69	139	134	-0.4
80749	SEDGWICK	115	405	359	336	-1.3	2	170	151	141	-1.3	2.38	122	107	-1.4
80750	SNYDER	087	520	596	625	1.5	62	183	207	215	1.3	2.88	136	150	1.1
80751	STERLING	075	15094	17310	17353	1.5	62	6015	6127	6141	0.2	2.42	3894	3891	0.0
80754	STONEHAM	123	126	157	183	2.4	78	54	65	76	2.0	2.38	39	46	1.8
80755	VERNON	125	162	156	154	-0.4	11	58	56	55	-0.4	2.79	45	43	-0.5
80757	WOODROW	121	292	264	253	-1.1	4	113	102	98	-1.1	2.59	84	75	-1.2
80758	WRAY	125	3780	3753	3719	-0.1	19	1479	1449	1436	-0.2	2.51	1003	966	-0.4
80759	YUMA	125	4474	4600	4605	0.3	31	1725	1751	1750	0.2	2.57	1186	1179	-0.1
80801	ANTON	121	173	156	149	-1.1	4	71	64	62	-1.1	2.44	52	47	-1.1
80802	ARAPAHOE	017	346	305	284	-1.4	2	123	109	102	-1.3	2.80	84	74	-1.4
80804	ARRIBA	073	399	380	361	-0.5	10	171	164	155	-0.5	2.32	121	113	-0.7
80805	BETHUNE	063	415	389	372	-0.7	8	153	143	138	-0.7	2.71	117	108	-0.9
80807	BURLINGTON	063	4847	5094	4947	0.5	37	1717	1624	1566	-0.6	2.52	1176	1092	-0.8
80808	CALHAN	041	6294	7413	8081	1.8	69	2143	2567	2817	2.0	2.87	1680	1936	1.5
80809	CASCADE	041	2542	2689	2805	0.6	40	1102	1197	1259	0.9	2.21	707	719	0.2
80810	CHEYENNE WELLS	017	1279	1135	1059	-1.3	2	511	457	428	-1.2	2.45	354	310	-1.4
80812	COPE	121	315	286	272	-1.0	5	126	115	110	-1.0	2.49	93	83	-1.2
80813	CRIPPLE CREEK	119	1616	1826	1922	1.3	56	682	783	826	1.5	2.27	435	489	1.3
80814	DIVIDE	119	3247	4185	4501	2.8	83	1219	1596	1724	3.0	2.60	935	1202	2.8
80815	FLAGLER	063	979	917	877	-0.7	8	415	385	369	-0.8	2.34	273	248	-1.0
80816	FLORISSANT	119	4616	5339	5698	1.6	64	1913	2230	2386	1.7	2.39	1358	1559	1.5
80817	FOUNTAIN	041	15994	23196	26531	4.1	91	5326	7689	8822	4.0	3.02	4294	6092	3.9
80818	GENOA	073	395	360	345	-1.0	5	154	130	121	-1.8	1.75	107	89	-2.0
80820	GUFFEY	093	787	962	1047	2.2	74	355	437	476	2.3	2.20	243	295	2.1
80821	HUGO	073	1238	1107	1034	-1.2	4	491	431	400	-1.4	2.41	329	283	-1.6
80822	JOES	125	274	293	297	0.7	43	108	115	117	0.7	2.55	84	89	0.6
80823	KARVAL	073	286	273	260	-0.5	10	117	112	107	-0.5	2.44	88	83	-0.6
80824	KIRK	125	284	298	301	0.5	37	110	116	117	0.6	2.57	86	89	0.4
80825	KIT CARSON	017	606	522	484	-1.6	1	246	213	197	-1.5	2.38	165	140	-1.8
80827	LAKE GEORGE	093	783	1005	1119	2.7	82	350	455	508	2.9	2.21	249	319	2.7
80828	LIMON	073	3636	3234	3068	-1.3	2	1060	909	845	-1.6	2.62	693	582	-1.9
80829	MANITOU SPRINGS	041	5247	5149	5176	-0.2	16	2561	2573	2610	0.1	1.99	1337	1234	-0.9
80830	MATHESON	039	231	267	282	1.6	64	89	102	108	1.5	2.59	66	75	1.4
80831	PEYTON	041	10237	18302	21353	6.5	95	3412	6355	7479	7.0	2.88	2824	5131	6.7
80832	RAMAH	039	713	842	909	1.8	69	260	308	332	1.8	2.71	197	226	1.5
80833	RUSH	073	676	732	761	0.9	47	255	277	288	0.9	2.64	197	209	0.6
80834	SEIBERT	063	287	281	272	-0.2	16	133	130	126	-0.2	2.16	93	90	-0.4
80835	SIMLA	039	878	986	1019	1.3	56	316	350	359	1.1	2.77	237	258	0.9
80836	STRATTON	063	1196	1141	1102	-0.5	10	459	437	422	-0.5	2.59	342	320	-0.7
80840	U S A F ACADEMY	041	7536	6769	6599	-1.2	4	1131	899	859	-2.5	3.50	1115	884	-2.5
80861	VONA	063	287	276	267	-0.4	11	113	109	105	-0.4	2.53	80	76	-0.6
80863	WOODLAND PARK	119	11307	12124	12390	0.8	45	4287	4630	4744	0.8	2.61	3265	3478	0.7
80864	YODER	041	1120	1310	1428	1.7	67	407	482	529	1.8	2.72	322	367	1.4
80903	COLORADO SPRINGS	041	15070	14808	14888	-0.2	16	6456	6371	6437	-0.1	1.96	2675	2396	-1.2
80904	COLORADO SPRINGS	041	20762	20687	21036	0.0	22	9856	10077	10338	0.2	2.03	5406	5098	-0.6
80905	COLORADO SPRINGS	041	17338	17226	17367	-0.1	19	7522	7645	7778	0.2	2.20	4080	3812	-0.7
80906	COLORADO SPRINGS	041	35013	36188	37142	0.4	34	13604	14305	14756	0.5	2.46	9239	9226	0.0
80907	COLORADO SPRINGS	041	26967	25828	25825	-0.5	10	12117	11856	11939	-0.2	2.14	6803	6166	-1.1
80908	COLORADO SPRINGS	041	9467	12348	14174	2.9	85	3259	4354	5046	3.2	2.84	2777	3603	2.9
80909	COLORADO SPRINGS	041	38295	36387	36188	-0.6	9	16148	15650	15679	-0.3	2.29	9700	8766	-1.1
80910	COLORADO SPRINGS	041	27758	29789	31142	0.8	45	10707	11790	12486	1.0	2.44	6757	6919	0.3
80911	COLORADO SPRINGS	041	29147	32677	35285	1.2	54	9746	11097	12031	1.4	2.94	7996	8835	1.1
80913	COLORADO SPRINGS	041	10766	12880	13914	2.0	73	1697	2274	2580	3.2	3.60	1635	2177	3.1
80914	COLORADO SPRINGS	041	366	348	345	-0.5	10	1	1	1	0.0	3.00	1	1	0.0
80915	COLORADO SPRINGS	041	19583	20121	21192	0.3	31	7212	7574	8019	0.5	2.65	5420	5466	0.1
80916	COLORADO SPRINGS	041	31669	34218	35994	0.8	45	11069	12141	12832	1.0	2.79	8183	8527	0.4
80917	COLORADO SPRINGS	041	30084	30202	30693	0.0	22	12104	12406	12697	0.3	2.41	8029	7740	-0.4
80918	COLORADO SPRINGS	041	44621	46476	48187	0.4	34	16981	18085	18891	0.7	2.52	11850	11972	0.1
80919	COLORADO SPRINGS	041	27903	29012	29839	0.4	34	10234	10862	11251	0.6	2.66	7796	7897	0.1
80920	COLORADO SPRINGS	041	31350	36035	39106	1.5	62	10140	11708	12706	1.6	3.07	8407	9519	1.4
80921	COLORADO SPRINGS	041	7611	13641	16728	6.5	95	2627	4854	6005	6.9	2.81	2271	4090	6.6
80922	COLORADO SPRINGS	041	12536	25223	30566	7.9	96	3958	8045	9794	8.0	3.14	3420	6780	7.7
80923	COLORADO SPRINGS	041	5614	26217	33462	18.1	99	1944	9115	11682	18.2	2.88	1595	7367	18.0
80924	COLORADO SPRINGS	041	316	5291	6839	35.6	100	106	1569	2027	33.8	3.37	98	1440	33.7
80925	COLORADO SPRINGS	041	3061	4676	5315	4.7	92	960	1477	1692	4.8	3.17	827	1253	4.6
80926	COLORADO SPRINGS	041	1322	1445	1506	1.0	50	536	596	626	1.2	2.41	412	440	0.7
	COLORADO					1.7					1.6	2.55			1.5
	UNITED STATES					1.0					1.1	2.59			0.9

ZIP CODE #	POST OFFICE NAME	RACE (%) White 2000	White 2009	Black 2000	Black 2009	Asian/Pacific 2000	Asian/Pacific 2009	% Hispanic Origin 2000	% Hispanic Origin 2009	2009 AGE DISTRIBUTION (%) 0-4	5-9	10-14	15-19	20-24	25-44	45-64	65-84	85+	18+	MEDIAN AGE 2009	% 2009 Males	% 2009 Females
80649	ORCHARD	94.0	91.7	0.0	0.0	0.0	0.2	10.5	14.5	5.9	6.4	7.1	6.9	3.9	24.3	30.4	13.5	1.7	76.2	42.1	52.2	47.8
80650	PIERCE	87.9	83.5	0.0	0.0	0.6	0.8	19.2	27.6	6.2	6.7	7.3	7.8	4.8	25.6	30.5	9.9	1.2	74.9	39.5	49.8	50.2
80651	PLATTEVILLE	77.1	69.8	0.1	0.2	0.7	0.8	31.7	42.9	8.0	8.6	8.1	8.9	5.9	28.3	24.2	7.3	0.7	69.6	33.2	51.5	48.5
80652	ROGGEN	88.2	84.0	0.3	0.4	0.8	1.0	10.6	15.8	6.6	7.2	7.7	9.2	5.4	25.6	27.2	9.5	1.6	72.3	37.8	52.5	47.5
80653	WELDONA	93.5	91.8	0.4	0.3	0.0	0.2	11.3	14.5	6.1	6.5	7.0	6.5	4.0	23.6	31.4	13.5	1.4	76.3	42.5	52.7	47.3
80654	WIGGINS	87.1	84.1	0.9	1.1	0.1	0.2	18.4	23.3	7.7	8.5	9.0	7.8	4.8	25.5	27.1	7.8	1.6	69.8	35.7	50.8	49.2
80701	FORT MORGAN	77.1	73.4	0.3	0.3	0.5	0.5	34.9	41.1	8.9	8.3	7.7	7.3	6.2	26.5	23.3	9.8	2.0	70.6	33.5	51.0	49.0
80705	LOG LANE VILLAGE	79.8	76.1	0.4	0.4	0.6	0.7	36.6	44.3	9.4	9.1	8.7	7.4	6.0	26.5	23.2	9.1	0.7	68.2	31.8	50.8	49.2
80720	AKRON	95.2	94.2	0.1	0.1	0.1	0.2	8.8	10.8	6.0	5.6	6.2	6.3	5.5	24.0	27.1	16.1	3.1	77.6	42.3	52.9	47.1
80721	AMHERST	96.3	95.0	0.0	0.0	0.0	0.0	4.2	5.5	7.0	7.5	7.5	6.5	4.5	21.4	31.8	12.9	1.0	73.6	40.8	51.2	48.8
80722	ATWOOD	93.4	90.8	1.9	2.4	0.5	0.8	9.1	13.9	6.0	7.6	7.1	7.9	5.2	27.6	26.8	10.5	1.3	73.0	38.1	53.0	47.0
80723	BRUSH	79.8	75.9	0.4	0.4	0.2	0.2	31.2	37.1	8.2	7.5	6.7	6.7	6.7	24.4	23.5	13.0	3.4	73.4	36.3	49.4	50.6
80726	CROOK	96.7	95.9	0.0	0.0	0.2	0.2	6.2	8.2	6.5	6.8	7.0	6.5	5.1	22.2	30.2	13.8	1.9	75.4	41.6	51.7	48.3
80727	ECKLEY	91.0	89.0	0.2	0.2	0.2	0.2	12.7	16.2	7.7	7.9	8.3	8.1	4.0	24.1	24.5	14.1	1.2	71.1	37.9	50.3	49.7
80728	FLEMING	87.1	92.1	10.6	4.8	0.5	0.2	15.3	10.9	5.6	5.7	5.7	6.0	5.9	27.2	29.6	12.3	2.0	79.4	41.1	55.5	44.5
80729	GROVER	94.2	91.7	0.2	0.3	0.4	0.5	8.4	12.6	6.0	6.5	7.1	7.3	4.9	22.5	30.6	13.1	1.9	75.5	42.1	51.9	48.1
80731	HAXTUN	96.8	96.3	0.6	0.6	0.3	0.4	2.5	3.4	5.8	6.3	6.9	6.8	3.8	21.0	29.0	15.7	4.7	76.8	44.5	48.7	51.3
80733	HILLROSE	96.0	95.3	0.2	0.2	0.2	0.2	8.2	10.9	6.4	6.8	7.5	7.1	4.7	22.6	31.3	12.7	1.0	75.2	41.5	51.2	48.8
80734	HOLYOKE	90.9	89.1	0.0	0.0	0.5	0.6	17.1	21.2	7.1	7.3	7.5	7.1	4.2	22.6	26.7	13.5	3.9	73.2	40.7	48.0	52.0
80735	IDALIA	96.4	95.6	0.0	0.0	0.0	0.0	5.3	6.7	6.2	6.7	6.7	6.9	5.2	23.5	31.4	11.9	1.7	76.3	40.7	50.4	49.6
80736	ILIFF	94.2	92.3	1.6	2.1	0.4	0.4	6.9	11.0	6.4	6.9	7.0	6.8	5.3	25.2	28.9	12.2	1.3	75.3	38.9	54.7	45.3
80737	JULESBURG	89.8	87.5	0.3	0.3	0.7	0.8	12.6	15.6	6.1	6.1	6.2	6.4	4.6	22.5	25.4	17.8	4.9	77.4	43.5	48.6	51.4
80740	LINDON	99.0	98.9	0.0	0.0	0.0	0.0	1.0	1.1	4.6	3.4	8.0	9.2	3.4	23.0	33.3	12.6	2.3	77.0	43.8	55.2	44.8
80741	MERINO	95.4	94.5	0.1	0.1	0.5	0.6	6.1	8.2	6.3	7.9	7.7	8.5	4.2	24.4	27.9	11.8	1.3	71.4	39.4	49.4	50.6
80742	NEW RAYMER	94.1	91.8	0.4	0.3	0.4	0.6	8.1	11.6	6.0	6.6	7.2	7.5	5.0	22.6	29.5	13.5	2.2	75.2	41.6	51.7	48.3
80743	OTIS	98.2	97.9	0.0	0.0	0.1	0.1	3.2	4.1	6.3	6.7	6.9	6.4	4.2	23.6	28.7	14.8	2.3	76.0	41.8	52.3	47.7
80744	OVID	89.3	86.9	1.1	1.3	1.1	1.3	13.1	15.9	4.1	4.8	5.2	5.2	4.1	21.6	32.1	19.7	3.1	82.3	48.4	53.3	46.7
80745	PADRONI	96.5	95.2	0.0	0.0	0.0	0.0	5.6	7.5	6.8	7.5	7.5	7.5	4.8	21.8	29.3	13.6	1.4	73.5	39.7	52.4	47.6
80747	PEETZ	96.8	95.9	0.0	0.0	0.2	0.2	6.3	8.6	6.4	6.8	7.0	6.4	5.1	22.2	30.4	13.8	2.1	76.0	41.8	51.7	48.3
80749	SEDGWICK	95.1	93.9	0.7	0.8	1.5	1.9	4.0	4.7	5.6	6.4	6.4	5.3	3.1	21.2	32.3	17.3	2.5	78.0	46.6	53.5	46.5
80750	SNYDER	92.7	91.4	0.4	0.3	0.2	0.3	5.2	7.2	7.7	8.7	9.4	8.9	4.0	21.1	27.0	11.6	1.5	68.5	38.2	48.7	51.3
80751	STERLING	91.6	88.7	1.0	2.1	0.5	0.6	12.5	16.4	6.8	6.5	6.3	8.0	7.6	26.4	24.4	11.5	2.6	76.9	35.7	51.1	48.9
80754	STONEHAM	95.2	92.4	0.0	0.6	0.0	0.0	8.0	11.5	6.4	6.4	7.0	7.6	4.5	22.3	31.2	12.7	1.9	74.5	42.3	51.0	49.0
80755	VERNON	96.3	95.5	0.0	0.0	0.0	0.0	4.9	6.4	6.4	6.4	7.1	7.1	5.1	23.7	30.8	12.2	1.3	76.3	40.5	51.3	48.7
80757	WOODROW	97.9	97.7	0.0	0.0	0.0	0.0	1.7	2.3	4.5	3.8	7.6	9.1	3.4	24.6	33.0	12.1	1.9	77.7	42.9	53.4	46.6
80758	WRAY	95.8	94.9	0.1	0.1	0.1	0.1	7.9	10.0	6.4	6.6	6.9	7.0	4.7	23.2	28.2	13.4	3.6	75.3	41.0	49.2	50.8
80759	YUMA	92.4	90.9	0.1	0.1	0.1	0.1	19.2	23.3	7.0	7.3	7.2	7.2	5.8	24.1	24.5	13.3	3.7	73.8	38.0	48.3	51.7
80801	ANTON	97.1	96.8	0.0	0.0	0.0	0.0	3.4	4.5	4.5	5.1	6.4	7.7	4.5	23.1	32.1	14.1	2.6	78.8	44.0	52.6	47.4
80802	ARAPAHOE	93.4	91.8	0.3	0.3	0.0	0.0	7.8	9.8	7.9	8.2	7.9	6.9	4.6	23.6	29.5	9.8	1.6	70.8	38.1	51.8	48.2
80804	ARRIBA	95.5	94.2	0.0	0.0	1.8	2.4	3.3	4.5	5.0	5.8	6.6	7.1	3.9	22.9	30.8	15.8	2.1	78.2	43.9	53.4	46.6
80805	BETHUNE	89.4	89.7	0.2	0.3	0.2	0.3	13.0	13.1	6.4	6.9	7.2	7.2	4.4	23.7	29.8	12.6	1.8	74.6	39.9	49.6	50.4
80807	BURLINGTON	82.3	82.0	2.8	2.9	0.5	0.5	18.8	19.1	6.0	6.1	6.0	6.3	6.5	32.4	24.3	10.2	2.3	77.8	37.1	58.4	41.6
80808	CALHAN	90.8	89.1	1.7	1.8	0.7	0.8	6.3	8.4	7.5	7.5	7.7	8.2	6.2	26.4	28.1	7.8	0.7	71.7	35.2	50.2	49.8
80809	CASCADE	94.5	93.4	0.4	0.5	0.6	0.8	4.4	6.0	3.9	4.1	6.1	6.8	3.3	23.2	40.2	11.3	1.0	80.8	46.0	50.7	49.3
80810	CHEYENNE WELLS	92.8	91.2	0.6	0.7	0.2	0.2	8.5	10.6	6.7	7.4	7.2	6.7	4.8	23.3	30.7	10.9	2.3	74.3	40.2	51.2	48.8
80812	COPE	97.5	96.9	0.0	0.0	0.3	0.3	4.5	5.2	4.9	5.6	5.9	6.3	4.5	21.7	35.0	14.0	2.1	79.4	45.7	50.7	49.3
80813	CRIPPLE CREEK	92.9	92.0	0.8	0.8	0.6	0.8	5.0	6.2	4.6	5.6	6.5	5.2	5.6	25.5	37.0	9.4	0.6	80.4	43.1	51.5	48.5
80814	DIVIDE	95.1	94.4	0.6	0.6	0.6	0.7	2.8	3.7	5.2	6.4	6.9	6.5	2.9	26.2	36.7	8.6	0.6	77.0	42.9	51.0	49.0
80815	FLAGLER	97.4	97.4	0.0	0.0	0.0	0.0	2.6	2.6	4.5	4.8	5.3	7.2	5.8	20.3	31.3	16.4	4.5	80.5	46.3	49.7	50.3
80816	FLORISSANT	94.8	94.2	0.6	0.7	0.4	0.5	3.9	4.9	5.5	5.5	6.6	6.3	3.8	24.8	37.5	9.6	0.4	78.2	43.5	50.6	49.4
80817	FOUNTAIN	75.4	71.7	8.4	9.3	2.6	3.5	15.0	18.6	9.5	8.6	7.9	7.7	6.9	31.4	21.9	5.7	0.4	69.4	30.6	49.3	50.7
80818	GENOA	76.5	73.6	10.4	10.6	1.0	1.1	11.4	13.9	3.6	3.9	4.7	5.0	7.2	40.0	25.6	8.9	1.1	84.4	37.9	69.7	30.3
80820	GUFFEY	95.4	94.8	0.4	0.4	0.0	0.0	3.6	4.4	4.0	3.7	4.9	5.2	2.5	19.3	45.0	14.8	0.6	83.5	50.3	50.2	49.8
80821	HUGO	95.8	94.9	0.9	1.1	0.3	0.5	3.9	5.0	5.0	5.3	5.6	7.0	6.0	22.6	28.9	15.9	3.7	79.8	43.8	48.2	51.8
80822	JOES	98.9	98.3	0.0	0.0	0.0	0.0	4.0	5.5	5.8	6.1	6.5	6.8	4.8	22.9	31.1	14.0	2.0	77.5	42.9	50.5	49.5
80823	KARVAL	97.9	97.4	0.4	0.4	0.0	0.0	3.2	4.0	4.4	4.4	5.1	7.3	5.1	19.4	31.5	20.1	2.6	81.3	47.4	49.8	50.2
80824	KIRK	98.2	98.0	0.0	0.0	0.0	0.0	4.2	5.7	5.7	6.0	6.7	7.0	4.7	23.2	31.2	13.4	2.0	77.2	42.4	50.7	49.3
80825	KIT CARSON	92.9	91.2	0.3	0.4	0.0	0.0	7.6	9.4	5.6	5.6	5.6	5.7	5.6	19.3	33.1	13.6	5.9	79.1	46.5	49.0	51.0
80827	LAKE GEORGE	95.1	94.8	0.5	0.5	0.4	0.4	4.5	5.2	3.6	4.4	5.2	5.0	2.3	18.2	43.8	16.6	1.0	83.6	51.2	53.2	46.8
80828	LIMON	81.6	78.7	6.8	7.2	0.6	0.7	11.1	13.8	5.3	5.5	6.1	6.0	7.2	33.7	23.7	9.8	2.7	79.3	37.2	60.8	39.2
80829	MANITOU SPRINGS	93.8	92.6	0.5	0.6	1.1	1.5	3.9	5.3	4.0	3.8	4.2	4.7	7.3	26.9	36.0	11.5	1.6	85.3	44.3	49.3	50.7
80830	MATHESON	95.2	94.0	0.0	0.4	0.0	0.0	4.3	5.2	6.0	6.4	7.1	7.5	4.9	22.5	30.3	12.4	3.0	75.3	41.4	50.2	49.8
80831	PEYTON	91.9	91.3	1.1	1.1	0.7	0.8	5.5	7.1	6.7	7.1	7.8	7.9	5.2	25.9	31.7	7.2	0.5	73.2	38.4	50.4	49.6
80832	RAMAH	93.8	92.8	0.6	0.7	0.4	0.5	4.1	5.3	6.3	6.8	7.2	8.2	6.1	23.4	30.5	10.2	1.3	74.0	38.8	50.2	49.8
80833	RUSH	93.8	92.1	0.9	1.1	0.4	0.5	5.6	7.5	6.8	7.1	7.1	7.8	5.6	23.9	28.6	11.7	1.4	73.6	38.7	50.4	49.6
80834	SEIBERT	99.0	98.9	0.0	0.0	0.0	0.0	1.4	1.4	4.3	5.0	6.0	7.1	4.6	18.9	34.2	17.1	2.8	80.4	47.4	55.2	44.8
80835	SIMLA	95.3	94.7	0.2	0.3	0.1	0.2	3.4	4.1	5.8	6.7	7.1	7.2	5.0	22.6	29.8	12.8	3.0	75.2	41.4	50.5	49.5
80836	STRATTON	94.4	94.5	0.0	0.0	0.3	0.3	6.8	6.8	6.2	6.8	7.2	7.7	4.8	21.5	29.8	13.4	2.5	74.5	41.3	50.5	49.5
80840	U S A F ACADEMY	83.5	80.5	5.7	6.4	3.1	3.9	8.7	11.6	8.1	6.6	4.3	20.2	38.2	20.2	2.2	0.2	0.0	78.8	21.4	68.1	31.9
80861	VONA	94.1	94.2	0.0	0.0	0.3	0.4	7.0	6.9	5.1	5.8	6.5	7.6	4.7	20.3	31.9	16.3	1.8	77.5	45.0	53.3	46.7
80863	WOODLAND PARK	95.2	94.5	0.5	0.5	0.8	1.0	3.3	4.2	5.6	6.3	7.3	7.2	4.7	24.7	35.2	8.3	0.7	75.9	41.5	50.2	49.8
80864	YODER	90.7	88.6	1.4	1.7	0.6	0.9	7.5	10.2	8.3	8.3	8.4	7.9	5.9	26.6	26.8	7.1	0.7	69.2	33.7	50.5	49.5
80903	COLORADO SPRINGS	79.2	75.7	7.7	8.4	1.5	1.9	13.9	18.1	5.1	4.1	3.8	10.0	14.2	30.9	22.3	7.7	1.9	84.3	31.6	50.7	49.3
80904	COLORADO SPRINGS	89.7	87.6	1.6	1.8	1.3	1.7	10.1	13.2	5.0	4.8	4.9	5.4	6.7	26.2	30.8	13.2	3.1	82.0	42.8	48.2	51.8
80905	COLORADO SPRINGS	76.3	73.0	5.8	6.0	2.4	2.8	21.0	25.9	7.1	6.3	6.0	6.6	8.7	29.1	24.1	10.2	1.9	76.6	34.5	49.6	50.4
80906	COLORADO SPRINGS	82.0	79.3	6.2	6.6	3.3	4.1	9.4	12.0	6.6	6.3	6.5	6.6	6.5	26.7	27.6	11.2	2.0	76.6	38.2	49.2	50.8
80907	COLORADO SPRINGS	86.5	83.8	2.4	2.7	2.2	2.7	11.3	14.7	6.1	5.8	5.6	5.5	6.9	29.3	27.6	11.0	2.2	79.3	38.4	49.5	50.5
80908	COLORADO SPRINGS	95.1	94.2	0.8	1.0	0.8	0.9	3.2	4.3	4.9	6.4	8.0	8.3	3.6	21.1	38.2	8.9	0.6	75.1	43.8	50.1	49.9
80909	COLORADO SPRINGS	78.9	75.8	7.2	7.6	1.9	2.3	15.5	19.7	7.4	6.2	5.8	6.3	8.0	26.4	24.2	12.9	2.9	77.1	36.7	48.1	51.9
80910	COLORADO SPRINGS	58.9	54.5	17.0	17.5	3.4	3.9	25.9	31.6	9.3	7.6	6.4	6.8	9.2	30.7	18.8	9.3	2.0	72.7	30.1	49.7	50.3
80911	COLORADO SPRINGS	74.0	69.1	10.6	12.1	3.6	4.6	12.6	16.4	7.3	7.2	7.1	7.6	6.6	28.1	25.4	10.0	0.7	73.7	35.1	49.0	51.0
80913	COLORADO SPRINGS	63.0	58.6	19.8	21.0	2.9	3.4	15.3	19.4	13.7	8.8	4.8	8.3	28.4	34.2	1.7	0.1	0.0	71.3	22.5	64.2	35.8
80914	COLORADO SPRINGS	74.6	71.3	13.1	14.4	3.6	4.0	9.6	12.1	13.8	11.5	6.9	9.2	13.8	39.1	5.5	0.3	0.0	64.9	23.1	56.3	43.7
80915	COLORADO SPRINGS	81.0	78.0	7.0	7.6	2.6	3.2	11.2	14.5	8.4	7.5	7.0	7.0	7.6	28.7	23.5	9.2	1.1	72.9	33.1	49.6	50.4
80916	COLORADO SPRINGS	60.4	56.4	18.3	18.8	4.6	5.3	19.1	24.1	10.5	9.3	8.1	7.4	7.6	34.2	18.3	4.2	0.3	67.8	28.7	49.7	50.3
80917	COLORADO SPRINGS	84.7	82.1	5.3	5.9	2.8	3.4	8.7	11.5	6.7	6.4	6.2	6.3	7.0	29.2	27.0	10.0	1.3	77.0	35.9	48.8	51.2
80918	COLORADO SPRINGS	85.3	82.5	4.0	4.4	3.5	4.4	8.5	11.2	6.9	6.7	6.6	7.1	6.6	29.9	26.5	8.6	1.0	75.8	35.2	49.7	50.3
80919	COLORADO SPRINGS	90.4	88.3	1.7	2.0	3.9	5.0	4.7	6.3	6.0	6.5	7.3	7.2	5.3	27.1	32.2	7.5	0.8	75.3	38.9	49.5	50.5
80920	COLORADO SPRINGS	89.1	87.1	3.0	3.3	3.2	4.1	5.7	7.5	7.8	8.6	8.8	8.6	5.2	29.0	27.0	4.6	0.4	69.1	34.4	49.9	50.1
80921	COLORADO SPRINGS	94.5	93.4	1.1	1.2	1.7	2.3	3.6	4.9	5.5	6.7	8.0	7.7	3.9	19.8	36.3	10.6	1.5	74.7	44.0	49.6	50.4
80922	COLORADO SPRINGS	82.0	79.1	5.5	6.3	4.8	5.9	8.8	11.0	10.9	9.9	8.9	7.0	5.1	34.5	20.5	2.9	0.2	65.8	30.6	49.2	50.8
80923	COLORADO SPRINGS	85.6	82.8	4.3	5.6	3.6	4.4	7.3	8.6	10.2	9.3	8.4	6.6	4.9	35.1	20.8	4.4	0.4	68.1	31.8	49.4	50.6
80924	COLORADO SPRINGS	89.0	86.9	3.2	3.4	2.8	3.7	6.3	8.6	10.3	10.1	9.5	7.2	4.3	30.8	24.4	3.0	0.2	65.5	32.1	49.4	50.6
80925	COLORADO SPRINGS	77.9	73.0	8.6	9.9	2.5	3.6	12.7	16.6	8.7	8.3	8.0	7.6	6.4	31.8	24.3	4.6	0.3	70.3	31.6	49.8	50.2
80926	COLORADO SPRINGS	91.5	89.7	1.9	2.2	2.6	3.3	4.9	6.6	5.2	6.1	7.1	6.3	2.9	23.3	37.6	10.4	1.1	77.1	44.4	49.4	50.6
	COLORADO	82.8	80.7	3.8	3.8	2.3	2.9	17.1	20.2	6.9	6.7	6.7	6.9	7.0	29.0	26.5	8.8	1.4	75.7	35.9	50.2	49.8
	UNITED STATES	75.1	72.0	12.3	12.7	3.8	4.6	12.5	15.7	6.8	6.7	6.6	7.1	6.9	27.0	26.0	10.9	1.9	75.7	36.9	49.2	50.8

ZIP CODE #	POST OFFICE NAME	2009 Per Capita Income	2009 HH Income Base	2009 HOUSEHOLD INCOME DISTRIBUTION (%) Less than $25,000	$25,000 to $49,999	$50,000 to $99,999	$100,000 to $149,999	$150,000 or More	MEDIAN HOUSEHOLD INCOME 2009	2014	2009 National Centile	2009 State Centile	2009 Home Value Base	2009 HOME VALUE DISTRIBUTION (%) Less than $50,000	$50,000 to $89,999	$90,000 to $174,999	$175,000 to $399,999	$400,000 or More	2009 Median Home Value
80649	ORCHARD	19102	161	26.1	36.6	31.1	3.7	2.5	40987	45237	36	26	113	8.8	11.5	42.5	28.3	8.8	143750
80650	PIERCE	18376	611	23.2	30.4	39.8	4.9	1.6	45099	48568	49	38	456	7.7	9.9	60.7	17.3	4.4	131341
80651	PLATTEVILLE	20085	1978	19.0	23.7	46.4	7.5	3.4	55728	58943	72	61	1404	13.2	7.1	43.8	28.8	7.1	144783
80652	ROGGEN	18587	278	24.5	28.4	40.3	5.0	1.8	46561	49416	53	42	182	9.3	11.5	23.6	41.8	13.7	200000
80653	WELDONA	20303	269	25.3	36.8	31.6	4.1	2.2	41242	43873	37	27	192	8.3	10.4	37.0	31.8	12.5	156667
80654	WIGGINS	16745	796	23.7	32.5	36.8	4.4	2.5	43446	46848	44	33	577	6.4	7.1	33.6	42.5	10.4	181875
80701	FORT MORGAN	18131	5500	23.0	33.2	36.1	5.8	2.0	43537	46771	44	33	3721	7.3	5.9	45.6	37.0	4.2	157564
80705	LOG LANE VILLAGE	15842	335	23.0	33.1	37.0	3.6	3.3	44147	47111	46	35	237	8.4	13.5	46.4	27.8	3.8	131510
80720	AKRON	19880	1059	28.6	35.9	28.5	4.7	2.3	37006	38959	24	15	788	17.6	22.0	42.9	13.5	4.1	105331
80721	AMHERST	19807	71	22.5	26.8	39.4	5.6	5.6	50593	51094	63	53	53	11.3	7.5	39.6	39.6	1.9	152500
80722	ATWOOD	19747	137	17.5	38.0	34.3	7.3	2.9	46448	48509	53	41	103	12.6	10.7	34.0	34.0	8.7	148958
80723	BRUSH	18144	2461	26.7	31.8	33.9	5.9	1.7	43159	46185	43	32	1647	8.4	6.6	47.8	32.7	4.5	149038
80726	CROOK	18228	168	26.2	38.7	29.8	3.6	1.8	40251	40378	34	24	124	13.7	24.2	33.1	18.5	10.5	110000
80727	ECKLEY	15538	169	32.0	33.7	29.0	4.1	1.2	37136	37891	24	16	118	11.0	15.3	34.7	26.3	12.7	136111
80728	FLEMING	16909	347	29.7	35.7	28.0	4.9	1.7	37147	38355	24	16	268	13.8	11.2	38.8	33.6	2.6	139894
80729	GROVER	21137	271	31.4	31.7	30.3	5.2	1.5	39080	40939	30	20	191	17.3	18.3	35.6	21.5	7.3	116500
80731	HAXTUN	19049	687	29.0	35.7	30.4	3.3	1.6	39174	40295	30	21	524	12.2	22.1	43.5	21.2	1.0	112955
80733	HILLROSE	17522	200	25.5	35.0	33.0	3.5	3.0	40914	45000	36	25	149	13.4	7.4	36.2	35.6	7.4	148611
80734	HOLYOKE	19867	1131	30.4	31.2	31.4	3.6	3.4	39903	41085	32	22	848	12.4	20.5	45.8	20.5	0.8	115981
80735	IDALIA	20506	161	16.8	36.0	43.5	2.5	1.2	46167	46331	52	40	114	12.3	17.5	27.2	25.4	17.5	147500
80736	ILIFF	19280	306	25.5	33.0	34.0	5.2	2.3	43093	45802	43	32	221	10.0	17.2	31.7	32.6	8.6	150625
80737	JULESBURG	18909	680	32.2	37.4	25.7	2.9	1.8	36450	38271	22	14	490	25.9	31.8	34.3	6.3	1.6	81364
80740	LINDON	16207	36	30.6	41.7	25.0	2.8	0.0	33060	33514	13	7	23	30.4	4.3	34.8	26.1	4.3	137500
80741	MERINO	20006	304	18.1	37.2	34.2	7.6	3.0	46387	47984	52	41	230	8.3	11.3	37.0	34.8	8.7	151563
80742	NEW RAYMER	18384	122	31.1	31.1	31.1	4.9	1.6	40000	41741	33	23	86	18.6	17.4	36.0	20.9	7.0	114583
80743	OTIS	21565	420	22.6	36.2	31.9	6.7	2.6	42646	42773	41	31	323	20.7	27.6	35.9	13.3	2.5	92619
80744	OVID	18691	202	36.6	38.1	20.3	3.0	2.0	31749	32671	11	5	150	37.3	26.0	28.7	6.0	2.0	60909
80745	PADRONI	19620	57	26.3	33.3	33.3	5.3	1.8	42361	45890	41	30	41	4.9	19.5	34.1	29.3	12.2	146875
80747	PEETZ	16740	181	26.5	38.7	29.8	3.3	1.7	40336	40478	34	24	133	12.8	24.1	33.1	18.8	11.3	111250
80749	SEDGWICK	20486	151	31.8	39.7	21.9	4.0	2.6	33980	35919	15	8	111	34.2	22.5	33.3	5.4	4.5	77000
80750	SNYDER	18187	207	21.7	30.0	40.6	4.8	2.9	48539	51492	58	48	151	16.6	11.9	38.4	27.8	5.3	144079
80751	STERLING	20453	6127	30.8	26.9	35.1	4.9	2.3	40939	44164	36	26	4186	8.5	12.9	40.2	35.5	3.0	143814
80754	STONEHAM	19887	65	32.3	30.8	30.8	4.6	1.5	39086	41147	30	21	46	21.7	15.2	34.8	21.7	6.5	112500
80755	VERNON	18601	56	17.9	37.5	41.1	3.6	0.0	43207	42358	43	32	40	12.5	17.5	25.0	27.5	17.5	150000
80757	WOODROW	17338	102	29.4	38.2	25.5	3.9	2.9	34152	35000	16	9	65	26.2	6.2	38.5	23.1	6.2	135938
80758	WRAY	19069	1449	30.0	32.5	31.0	4.8	1.7	39501	40311	31	22	1023	13.4	16.3	40.7	25.3	4.3	125453
80759	YUMA	18089	1751	30.8	31.8	30.8	4.6	1.9	38216	39596	27	19	1244	5.7	17.3	49.0	24.7	3.4	132875
80801	ANTON	21084	64	29.7	40.6	20.3	4.7	4.7	36131	36824	21	13	42	28.6	19.0	33.3	16.7	2.4	95000
80802	ARAPAHOE	18822	109	21.1	33.0	37.6	5.5	2.8	47331	47603	55	44	78	29.5	24.4	38.5	7.7	0.0	84000
80804	ARRIBA	21829	164	31.1	29.9	29.3	6.7	3.0	39134	40281	30	21	124	13.7	24.2	34.7	16.1	11.3	112500
80805	BETHUNE	21068	143	30.1	25.2	31.5	8.4	4.9	44457	47893	47	36	107	15.9	19.6	29.0	28.0	7.5	130682
80807	BURLINGTON	20368	1624	27.7	27.5	35.7	6.5	2.6	43435	46187	44	33	1130	15.9	19.5	44.7	18.6	1.3	108766
80808	CALHAN	19622	2567	19.7	29.5	41.9	7.2	1.7	50564	52616	63	53	2036	12.5	12.1	32.9	37.4	5.2	156675
80809	CASCADE	32182	1197	15.4	28.4	39.5	10.2	6.5	54257	56427	70	59	864	5.4	2.7	19.4	54.2	18.3	224038
80810	CHEYENNE WELLS	20984	457	25.4	29.5	35.9	7.0	2.2	46722	47667	53	42	333	25.5	24.0	39.3	9.6	1.5	90833
80812	COPE	21794	115	27.0	47.0	18.3	4.3	3.5	35274	38758	19	11	79	24.1	22.8	38.0	13.9	1.3	96250
80813	CRIPPLE CREEK	24418	783	14.7	37.9	40.2	5.6	1.5	48485	49934	58	48	528	4.7	7.8	45.3	38.6	3.6	155660
80814	DIVIDE	28448	1596	9.2	26.6	47.2	11.7	5.3	62803	67098	81	73	1384	0.7	5.1	26.2	55.3	12.8	228807
80815	FLAGLER	19847	385	32.2	31.4	28.8	5.7	1.8	36648	38389	22	15	289	21.8	27.3	35.3	13.8	1.7	91316
80816	FLORISSANT	25922	2230	16.8	29.2	44.2	6.2	3.5	52923	56519	68	57	1854	2.4	9.5	33.9	47.4	6.8	183442
80817	FOUNTAIN	22486	7689	11.7	26.0	47.1	11.2	3.9	60102	62708	77	69	5474	3.8	3.8	51.8	39.7	0.9	163557
80818	GENOA	23924	130	27.7	33.8	31.5	5.4	1.5	39376	41150	31	22	96	18.8	26.0	35.4	14.6	5.2	98333
80820	GUFFEY	26619	437	22.0	35.2	32.3	6.4	4.1	45441	47148	50	39	389	6.4	10.3	22.9	51.4	9.0	206013
80821	HUGO	19373	431	30.4	31.6	32.7	3.9	1.4	38979	40372	30	20	296	17.6	27.4	42.9	9.1	3.0	95357
80822	JOES	24970	115	23.5	31.3	29.6	8.7	7.0	47315	47684	55	44	86	5.8	16.3	36.0	29.1	12.8	161538
80823	KARVAL	20179	112	27.7	33.9	33.0	3.6	1.8	35000	37767	18	10	83	21.7	22.9	30.1	18.1	7.2	101786
80824	KIRK	23936	116	22.4	31.9	31.0	8.6	6.0	47326	47099	55	44	86	8.1	15.1	34.9	26.7	15.1	160417
80825	KIT CARSON	19417	213	38.5	25.4	28.6	5.6	1.9	35119	36669	18	11	168	33.9	28.6	29.2	7.1	1.2	70714
80827	LAKE GEORGE	25684	455	20.9	27.7	41.5	7.3	2.6	51777	55078	65	56	400	5.0	5.5	32.3	44.3	13.0	194079
80828	LIMON	19024	909	24.4	35.6	30.4	7.3	2.3	40843	42611	35	25	602	18.1	18.9	45.2	16.1	1.7	107452
80829	MANITOU SPRINGS	31482	2573	23.2	27.4	32.6	11.3	5.4	49255	50488	59	50	1359	0.8	2.5	28.3	55.9	12.4	224197
80830	MATHESON	20631	102	22.5	38.2	28.4	7.8	2.9	41987	44208	39	29	78	7.7	15.4	43.6	25.6	7.7	120833
80831	PEYTON	27714	6355	9.9	19.7	44.9	20.0	5.5	70096	74173	87	81	5584	3.0	2.0	19.8	65.6	9.6	243167
80832	RAMAH	20710	308	21.1	31.8	37.0	7.5	2.6	47219	49723	55	43	243	11.1	12.3	35.0	32.9	8.6	145833
80833	RUSH	18598	277	25.6	34.7	33.6	4.7	1.4	40173	43221	33	23	212	18.9	19.3	33.0	24.5	4.2	119048
80834	SEIBERT	20900	130	34.6	33.1	26.9	2.3	3.1	35557	36724	19	12	100	40.0	11.0	27.0	19.0	3.0	86667
80835	SIMLA	19195	350	26.3	35.7	25.7	8.6	3.7	41217	42339	37	26	266	7.1	15.0	44.4	24.1	9.4	121721
80836	STRATTON	18403	437	27.9	35.7	30.7	3.9	1.8	39210	40214	30	21	321	27.7	15.9	37.1	15.0	4.4	103472
80840	U S A F ACADEMY	18036	899	4.6	34.7	50.8	7.7	2.2	54668	56776	71	60	14	0.0	7.1	28.6	64.3	0.0	233333
80861	VONA	18820	109	27.5	40.4	28.4	1.8	1.8	37553	38221	25	17	81	30.9	14.8	38.3	16.0	0.0	98750
80863	WOODLAND PARK	29516	4630	9.6	23.1	43.1	17.6	6.5	66893	69872	85	78	3689	6.0	0.5	16.9	64.5	12.0	235965
80864	YODER	17973	482	24.3	34.6	35.1	5.2	0.8	43487	45552	44	33	376	16.5	18.1	34.0	29.0	2.4	131250
80903	COLORADO SPRINGS	23034	6371	34.6	30.2	27.5	5.4	2.4	36040	36940	21	13	2523	4.3	6.7	44.2	40.5	4.3	164497
80904	COLORADO SPRINGS	28280	10077	21.2	32.8	34.1	8.6	3.2	46912	47688	54	43	5596	3.4	4.9	37.6	46.7	7.4	184300
80905	COLORADO SPRINGS	22474	7645	27.8	32.5	32.0	5.8	1.9	41794	43438	39	28	3408	4.5	7.5	57.9	25.8	4.2	138666
80906	COLORADO SPRINGS	35929	14305	13.5	22.4	37.1	13.9	13.0	63160	65725	81	74	8881	5.8	3.7	17.7	45.1	27.6	255966
80907	COLORADO SPRINGS	27707	11856	22.5	29.5	35.6	8.6	3.8	48260	49378	57	47	6711	11.2	3.0	36.9	44.2	4.7	173288
80908	COLORADO SPRINGS	37801	4354	6.1	11.2	39.4	27.3	16.1	89144	91641	95	93	3836	1.2	0.3	6.3	58.1	34.1	338008
80909	COLORADO SPRINGS	23022	15650	24.6	31.6	35.0	6.4	2.3	44677	46045	47	36	7645	1.0	2.8	47.7	46.7	1.7	173141
80910	COLORADO SPRINGS	19614	11790	27.0	33.3	33.6	4.7	1.4	41227	42732	37	26	5002	5.5	8.6	73.4	12.4	0.2	138681
80911	COLORADO SPRINGS	22942	11097	11.3	23.8	49.5	12.6	2.8	60946	62882	79	71	8709	0.8	1.2	57.2	40.2	0.5	166218
80913	COLORADO SPRINGS	15307	2274	8.1	53.0	35.2	3.2	0.5	44879	45983	48	37	39	0.0	0.0	59.0	12.8	28.2	165278
80914	COLORADO SPRINGS	3106	0	0.0	0.0	0.0	0.0	0.0	0	0	0	0	0	0.0	0.0	0.0	0.0	0.0	0
80915	COLORADO SPRINGS	25974	7574	10.0	26.7	45.6	14.1	3.6	60986	63067	79	71	5092	9.6	4.1	42.4	41.2	2.8	167507
80916	COLORADO SPRINGS	20662	12141	13.7	32.9	44.8	7.2	1.4	52004	54015	66	57	6768	19.0	9.7	54.2	17.1	0.0	137249
80917	COLORADO SPRINGS	27241	12406	13.9	28.6	41.3	12.8	3.4	56810	60462	74	63	7088	0.1	3.2	32.0	62.7	2.0	193040
80918	COLORADO SPRINGS	30695	18085	10.3	22.8	42.8	18.1	6.1	66279	68557	84	77	11309	2.1	2.1	18.9	71.3	5.6	208952
80919	COLORADO SPRINGS	40404	10862	7.1	13.2	39.1	23.4	17.2	84526	84710	94	90	7923	0.0	0.9	11.8	67.1	20.2	290093
80920	COLORADO SPRINGS	32609	11708	4.0	10.6	44.7	29.4	11.4	87465	88475	94	91	9038	0.3	0.4	9.4	85.0	4.9	250663
80921	COLORADO SPRINGS	41097	4854	2.6	7.8	36.2	38.7	14.7	103826	104952	97	96	3939	0.2	0.2	1.3	68.6	29.8	343956
80922	COLORADO SPRINGS	28873	8045	1.6	10.0	56.8	25.2	6.3	81843	83331	93	88	6962	0.5	0.0	8.9	89.9	0.7	218675
80923	COLORADO SPRINGS	32390	9115	2.6	5.6	58.7	26.7	6.4	83865	83854	93	90	7538	0.4	0.0	6.6	91.7	1.2	216482
80924	COLORADO SPRINGS	36499	1569	5.0	2.7	33.8	40.5	18.0	107578	107453	98	98	1434	0.0	0.0	0.8	95.0	4.2	282302
80925	COLORADO SPRINGS	23761	1477	6.5	19.6	54.0	15.4	4.5	66589	67086	85	77	1159	7.2	1.7	33.0	55.2	2.8	183002
80926	COLORADO SPRINGS	49520	596	8.7	12.9	35.4	21.1	21.8	83833	85509	93	89	452	7.3	3.8	3.1	38.7	47.1	384706
	COLORADO	30807		15.5	22.5	37.5	15.8	8.6	62597	65813				4.4	4.3	23.6	52.9	14.8	220998
	UNITED STATES	27277		20.9	24.4	35.3	11.7	7.6	54719	56938				9.3	13.1	31.6	32.6	13.5	162279

SPENDING POTENTIAL INDICES

ZIP CODE #	POST OFFICE NAME	FINANCIAL SERVICES: Auto Loan	Home Loan	Invest-ments	Retire-ment Plans	THE HOME: Home Improvements: Home Repair	Lawn & Garden	Furnishings: Computers & Hardware-Personal	Major Appliances	TV, Radio, Sound Equipment	Furniture	ENTERTAINMENT: Dine out/Carry out	Sports Equipment	Fees & Tickets	Toys & Games	Travel	Cable TV	PERSONAL: Apparel & Services	Auto Repairs	Health Insurance	Pets & Supplies
80649	ORCHARD	83	63	89	63	64	88	66	80	68	56	68	65	53	68	67	73	45	75	84	98
80650	PIERCE	82	73	76	75	74	87	72	81	74	66	73	63	65	75	72	78	50	76	84	96
80651	PLATTEVILLE	95	94	82	90	92	88	89	91	88	93	89	68	87	91	87	87	61	89	87	105
80652	ROGGEN	92	67	100	67	70	98	73	88	75	61	74	73	56	74	73	81	49	83	93	108
80653	WELDONA	88	62	95	62	64	92	68	83	70	56	70	69	51	69	68	76	45	78	88	102
80654	WIGGINS	88	68	87	67	69	89	70	82	73	64	73	65	58	74	69	78	48	78	85	100
80701	FORT MORGAN	82	73	74	70	72	80	73	79	75	71	74	60	67	76	71	77	51	77	80	92
80705	LOG LANE VILLAGE	87	80	70	77	78	81	75	79	78	78	78	58	71	81	71	80	53	77	80	94
80720	AKRON	85	59	91	59	62	89	65	81	69	55	68	65	49	68	64	76	45	76	86	98
80721	AMHERST	100	69	110	69	72	106	77	95	80	62	79	79	56	78	76	87	51	89	101	117
80722	ATWOOD	98	68	108	67	71	104	75	93	78	61	77	77	55	76	75	85	50	87	98	115
80723	BRUSH	75	65	68	65	65	73	71	73	72	67	71	56	64	72	68	74	49	73	77	86
80726	CROOK	80	55	88	55	58	85	61	76	64	50	63	63	45	63	61	70	41	71	81	94
80727	ECKLEY	79	54	87	54	57	83	60	75	63	49	62	62	44	62	60	69	40	70	79	92
80728	FLEMING	79	55	87	55	57	84	61	75	63	49	62	62	44	62	60	69	40	70	80	93
80729	GROVER	85	59	93	59	62	90	65	81	68	53	67	67	48	67	65	74	44	76	85	100
80731	HAXTUN	83	57	91	57	60	88	64	79	66	52	65	65	47	65	63	72	42	74	83	97
80733	HILLROSE	90	62	99	62	65	95	69	86	72	56	71	71	50	70	69	78	46	80	90	105
80734	HOLYOKE	84	64	87	65	65	89	69	81	72	59	71	66	56	71	69	77	47	77	86	99
80735	IDALIA	92	63	101	63	66	97	70	88	73	57	72	72	52	72	70	80	47	82	92	108
80736	ILIFF	93	64	102	64	67	98	71	88	74	58	73	73	52	73	71	81	47	83	93	109
80737	JULESBURG	75	54	76	52	56	78	59	72	65	51	63	55	46	63	57	71	42	68	79	86
80740	LINDON	70	48	77	48	50	74	53	66	56	43	55	55	39	55	53	61	36	62	70	82
80741	MERINO	98	67	108	67	70	103	75	93	78	61	77	77	55	76	74	85	50	87	98	114
80742	NEW RAYMER	85	59	93	58	61	90	65	81	68	53	67	67	48	66	65	74	43	75	85	99
80743	OTIS	96	66	105	66	69	101	73	91	76	59	75	75	54	75	73	83	49	85	96	112
80744	OVID	76	52	83	52	55	80	58	72	60	47	60	59	42	59	58	66	39	67	76	88
80745	PADRONI	91	62	99	62	65	95	69	86	72	56	71	71	51	70	69	78	46	80	91	106
80747	PEETZ	81	55	88	55	58	85	62	76	64	50	63	63	45	63	61	70	41	71	81	94
80749	SEDGWICK	87	60	96	60	63	92	67	83	69	54	68	68	49	68	66	75	44	77	87	102
80750	SNYDER	93	65	103	64	68	99	72	89	74	58	74	73	53	73	71	81	48	83	94	109
80751	STERLING	76	68	69	69	68	77	72	74	73	68	73	57	66	74	69	76	50	74	79	88
80754	STONEHAM	85	59	93	58	61	90	65	81	68	53	67	67	48	66	65	74	43	75	85	99
80755	VERNON	93	64	102	64	67	98	71	88	74	57	73	73	52	72	70	80	47	82	93	108
80757	WOODROW	80	55	88	55	58	85	61	76	64	50	63	63	45	63	61	70	41	71	80	94
80758	WRAY	86	60	92	59	62	89	65	81	69	55	68	65	49	68	64	75	44	75	85	98
80759	YUMA	78	58	81	58	61	82	64	75	67	55	66	59	51	66	63	72	44	72	81	91
80801	ANTON	92	63	101	63	66	97	70	87	73	57	72	72	51	72	70	80	47	81	92	107
80802	ARAPAHOE	94	65	103	65	68	99	72	89	75	58	74	74	53	73	72	82	48	83	94	110
80804	ARRIBA	90	62	99	62	65	95	69	86	72	56	71	71	51	70	69	78	46	80	91	106
80805	BETHUNE	102	70	112	70	74	108	78	97	81	63	80	80	57	80	78	88	52	91	102	119
80807	BURLINGTON	91	66	90	65	68	90	72	85	77	65	76	66	58	77	70	83	50	81	89	102
80808	CALHAN	90	85	74	82	82	84	79	83	81	83	81	62	76	85	76	82	55	80	81	98
80809	CASCADE	111	103	142	103	110	121	97	116	99	95	98	85	93	95	106	102	67	108	113	134
80810	CHEYENNE WELLS	92	63	101	63	66	97	70	87	73	57	72	72	52	72	70	80	47	82	92	108
80812	COPE	97	67	106	67	70	102	74	92	77	60	76	76	54	76	74	84	49	86	97	113
80813	CRIPPLE CREEK	93	75	120	73	82	99	75	95	78	70	77	69	65	74	81	83	51	88	94	110
80814	DIVIDE	106	114	114	117	114	117	103	112	102	103	102	86	107	103	110	103	71	106	109	130
80815	FLAGLER	80	57	83	56	59	84	62	77	68	54	66	60	49	67	61	75	44	72	83	92
80816	FLORISSANT	95	88	107	89	91	102	85	97	87	82	86	73	81	85	90	90	59	92	97	114
80817	FOUNTAIN	102	106	86	103	99	93	98	97	95	103	97	76	98	101	95	92	67	94	90	112
80818	GENOA	84	60	90	60	62	88	66	80	68	55	67	65	50	67	65	74	44	75	85	98
80820	GUFFEY	98	78	126	77	86	103	78	100	82	73	81	73	68	78	85	87	54	92	98	115
80821	HUGO	81	57	83	56	60	84	63	78	69	55	67	60	49	68	61	76	44	73	84	93
80822	JOES	114	78	125	78	82	120	87	108	90	70	89	89	64	89	86	99	58	101	114	133
80823	KARVAL	88	61	97	60	63	93	67	83	70	54	69	69	49	69	67	76	45	78	88	103
80824	KIRK	110	76	121	75	79	116	84	104	87	68	86	86	62	86	84	95	56	97	110	128
80825	KIT CARSON	83	57	91	57	60	87	63	79	66	51	65	65	46	65	63	72	42	73	83	97
80827	LAKE GEORGE	94	76	120	75	83	100	76	96	79	71	78	70	67	76	82	84	52	88	95	111
80828	LIMON	79	66	76	67	68	81	72	78	74	66	73	59	63	73	69	78	49	76	83	92
80829	MANITOU SPRINGS	87	87	89	90	87	86	90	86	89	90	90	68	91	88	90	88	63	89	88	103
80830	MATHESON	95	66	105	66	69	101	73	91	76	59	75	75	53	74	73	83	49	85	96	112
80831	PEYTON	112	131	113	131	126	117	113	116	108	118	110	91	123	113	119	105	78	110	106	133
80832	RAMAH	93	79	84	77	78	91	78	86	81	76	80	65	69	83	75	84	54	83	88	104
80833	RUSH	82	67	77	66	68	82	68	77	70	64	70	59	58	72	66	74	47	73	79	93
80834	SEIBERT	81	56	89	55	58	85	62	77	64	50	63	63	45	63	61	70	41	72	81	94
80835	SIMLA	95	66	104	66	69	100	73	90	76	59	75	74	54	74	72	82	49	84	95	111
80836	STRATTON	85	59	94	59	61	90	65	81	68	53	67	67	48	66	65	74	43	76	86	100
80840	U S A F ACADEMY	111	58	43	67	52	49	105	72	98	97	104	72	79	118	76	91	73	92	65	88
80861	VONA	85	59	94	58	61	90	65	81	68	53	67	67	48	66	65	74	43	76	85	100
80863	WOODLAND PARK	106	124	115	124	121	111	110	111	105	114	106	87	119	108	116	102	76	107	103	128
80864	YODER	78	72	64	70	70	74	68	72	70	71	70	52	64	73	65	72	48	70	72	85
80903	COLORADO SPRINGS	66	56	55	59	55	58	71	61	70	66	70	50	65	69	63	70	49	67	65	75
80904	COLORADO SPRINGS	79	78	77	79	78	80	82	79	83	81	83	60	82	81	81	84	58	82	84	94
80905	COLORADO SPRINGS	69	61	57	63	59	61	73	64	73	69	74	52	69	73	67	73	52	71	69	79
80906	COLORADO SPRINGS	122	132	135	136	134	124	128	125	124	134	125	98	136	124	133	120	90	125	120	145
80907	COLORADO SPRINGS	85	82	76	83	80	80	87	82	86	86	86	64	85	87	84	85	60	85	84	97
80908	COLORADO SPRINGS	140	178	181	184	183	164	149	156	141	160	143	119	174	142	168	136	104	147	142	178
80909	COLORADO SPRINGS	74	67	65	70	66	68	77	70	77	75	78	55	74	77	73	77	54	76	74	84
80910	COLORADO SPRINGS	70	59	54	61	56	58	71	62	71	69	72	51	65	72	64	70	50	69	65	76
80911	COLORADO SPRINGS	97	105	89	103	100	97	96	96	94	99	96	73	99	98	96	94	66	94	94	112
80913	COLORADO SPRINGS	87	46	34	53	41	39	82	57	77	76	81	57	62	92	59	71	57	72	51	69
80914	COLORADO SPRINGS	0	0	0	0	0	0	0	0	0	0	0	0	0	0	0	0	0	0	0	0
80915	COLORADO SPRINGS	99	100	88	100	96	92	100	95	97	102	99	75	100	101	97	95	69	97	92	112
80916	COLORADO SPRINGS	89	79	66	79	74	71	86	78	83	88	85	63	80	88	78	81	59	82	74	93
80917	COLORADO SPRINGS	94	91	85	93	89	86	96	89	94	97	95	70	94	95	92	92	67	93	88	106
80918	COLORADO SPRINGS	111	116	104	117	112	105	113	108	109	116	111	86	116	112	112	106	78	109	104	127
80919	COLORADO SPRINGS	149	169	159	175	167	150	154	151	146	163	148	122	168	152	160	139	107	147	137	175
80920	COLORADO SPRINGS	143	165	144	167	160	140	144	144	135	156	138	116	156	143	148	128	99	136	125	164
80921	COLORADO SPRINGS	152	189	192	195	194	178	160	169	153	172	155	127	183	153	180	150	111	160	158	193
80922	COLORADO SPRINGS	137	151	122	145	141	122	132	132	124	144	127	105	136	134	131	116	89	124	113	149
80923	COLORADO SPRINGS	142	155	124	148	144	126	136	135	128	148	131	108	139	139	134	120	91	128	117	154
80924	COLORADO SPRINGS	175	212	183	218	206	174	176	178	162	198	165	148	200	176	185	148	122	163	145	199
80925	COLORADO SPRINGS	115	122	99	117	114	102	109	109	104	118	106	85	110	111	107	99	74	104	96	125
80926	COLORADO SPRINGS	155	200	205	208	206	183	166	174	157	179	159	134	196	159	188	151	117	163	157	198
	COLORADO	114	114	111	115	112	109	114	111	111	116	113	88	114	113	113	110	80	112	108	130
	UNITED STATES	100	100	100	100	100	100	100	100	100	100	100	100	100	100	100	100	100	100	100	100

ZIP CODE			POPULATION			2000-2009 ANNUAL RATE		HOUSEHOLDS					FAMILIES		
#	POST OFFICE NAME	COUNTY FIPS CODE	2000	2009	2014	% Rate	State Centile	2000	2009	2014	% Annual Rate 2000-2009	2009 Average HH Size	2000	2009	% Annual Rate 2000-2009
80927	COLORADO SPRINGS	041	224	339	444	4.6	92	82	110	145	3.2	3.08	65	84	2.8
80928	COLORADO SPRINGS	041	722	837	908	1.6	64	238	279	305	1.7	3.00	190	215	1.3
80929	COLORADO SPRINGS	041	574	630	660	1.0	50	212	237	250	1.2	2.66	175	189	0.8
80930	COLORADO SPRINGS	041	687	780	835	1.4	58	241	278	299	1.6	2.81	202	226	1.2
80951	COLORADO SPRINGS	041	38	2524	3177	57.4	100	15	886	1119	55.4	2.85	12	625	53.3
81001	PUEBLO	101	29568	29760	30274	0.1	26	11316	11574	11843	0.2	2.49	7420	7308	-0.2
81003	PUEBLO	101	14270	14813	15350	0.4	34	5299	5611	5850	0.6	2.30	2975	3031	0.2
81004	PUEBLO	101	26090	26124	26511	0.0	22	10877	11066	11302	0.2	2.32	6509	6317	-0.3
81005	PUEBLO	101	27578	30764	32490	1.2	54	10861	12244	12980	1.3	2.48	7902	8670	1.0
81006	PUEBLO	101	13021	13124	13406	0.1	26	4709	4817	4949	0.2	2.71	3632	3621	0.0
81007	PUEBLO	101	17145	27045	31616	5.1	93	6085	9560	11189	5.0	2.82	4914	7603	4.8
81008	PUEBLO	101	6855	10272	11796	4.5	92	2756	4071	4659	4.3	2.52	1961	2828	4.0
81019	COLORADO CITY	101	1197	1379	1487	1.5	62	469	549	594	1.7	2.51	357	405	1.4
81020	AGUILAR	071	1038	1118	1156	0.8	45	436	473	491	0.9	2.36	294	311	0.6
81021	ARLINGTON	061	24	23	22	-0.5	10	10	10	10	0.0	2.30	7	7	0.0
81022	AVONDALE	101	1435	1533	1604	0.7	43	482	521	549	0.8	2.92	381	401	0.6
81023	BEULAH	101	1191	1020	1124	-1.7	1	507	456	504	-1.1	2.24	377	328	-1.5
81025	BOONE	101	1277	1338	1390	0.5	37	498	530	553	0.7	2.50	369	381	0.3
81027	BRANSON	071	169	179	183	0.6	40	74	79	81	0.7	2.27	56	58	0.4
81029	CAMPO	009	456	417	395	-1.0	5	177	161	152	-1.0	2.59	136	122	-1.2
81036	EADS	061	1124	977	913	-1.5	1	462	404	378	-1.4	2.36	303	259	-1.7
81039	FOWLER	101	1978	1962	1934	-0.1	19	807	801	789	-0.1	2.38	556	542	-0.3
81040	GARDNER	055	389	373	366	-0.5	10	171	166	164	-0.3	2.25	110	104	-0.6
81041	GRANADA	099	879	809	769	-0.9	6	268	244	232	-1.0	3.32	200	179	-1.2
81043	HARTMAN	099	115	108	103	-0.7	8	41	38	37	-0.8	2.84	31	28	-1.1
81044	HASTY	011	314	282	264	-1.2	4	129	117	109	-1.0	2.41	94	84	-1.2
81045	HASWELL	061	130	126	122	-0.3	13	51	50	48	-0.2	2.52	37	36	-0.3
81047	HOLLY	099	2028	1895	1811	-0.7	8	736	679	648	-0.9	2.72	534	484	-1.1
81049	KIM	071	301	296	296	-0.2	16	135	134	134	-0.1	2.21	94	91	-0.4
81050	LA JUNTA	089	11440	10707	10293	-0.7	8	4443	4181	4028	-0.7	2.46	3050	2815	-0.9
81052	LAMAR	099	10726	9863	9443	-0.9	6	3994	3646	3479	-1.0	2.64	2765	2477	-1.2
81054	LAS ANIMAS	011	4974	4999	4739	0.1	26	1631	1428	1322	-1.4	2.47	1117	958	-1.6
81055	LA VETA	055	1576	1617	1612	0.3	31	732	763	767	0.4	2.07	459	467	0.2
81057	MC CLAVE	011	603	541	507	-1.2	4	204	184	173	-1.1	2.94	149	132	-1.3
81058	MANZANOLA	089	1078	1070	1039	-0.1	19	408	392	381	-0.4	2.48	286	270	-0.6
81059	MODEL	071	251	261	266	0.4	34	93	97	99	0.5	2.69	69	71	0.3
81062	OLNEY SPRINGS	025	1983	2627	2629	3.1	86	345	341	341	-0.1	3.13	254	247	-0.3
81063	ORDWAY	025	2988	3672	3713	2.3	76	803	824	834	0.3	2.74	550	554	0.1
81064	PRITCHETT	009	160	149	142	-0.8	7	62	57	55	-0.9	2.61	47	43	-1.0
81067	ROCKY FORD	089	6164	5709	5470	-0.8	7	2379	2216	2129	-0.8	2.52	1675	1533	-1.0
81069	RYE	101	1938	2140	2280	1.1	52	764	857	919	1.2	2.50	563	612	0.9
81071	SHERIDAN LAKE	061	337	327	315	-0.3	13	139	137	132	-0.2	2.39	102	98	-0.4
81073	SPRINGFIELD	009	2285	2078	1963	-1.0	5	1009	920	870	-1.0	2.19	636	567	-1.2
81076	SUGAR CITY	025	488	638	638	2.9	85	191	187	187	-0.2	1.73	141	136	-0.4
81081	TRINCHERA	071	72	74	75	0.3	31	31	32	33	0.3	2.31	23	24	0.5
81082	TRINIDAD	071	12383	13345	13548	0.8	45	5013	5264	5363	0.5	2.39	3282	3374	0.3
81084	TWO BUTTES	009	107	99	94	-0.8	7	50	47	44	-0.7	2.11	37	33	-1.2
81087	VILAS	009	145	137	131	-0.6	9	57	54	52	-0.6	2.54	44	41	-0.8
81089	WALSENBURG	055	5784	5835	5755	0.1	26	2136	2078	2053	-0.3	2.26	1319	1255	-0.5
81090	WALSH	009	1378	1197	1120	-1.5	1	555	483	452	-1.5	2.43	372	316	-1.7
81091	WESTON	071	999	1197	1260	2.0	73	393	458	485	1.7	2.41	278	318	1.5
81092	WILEY	099	858	802	767	-0.7	8	314	294	281	-0.7	2.73	232	214	-0.9
81101	ALAMOSA	003	13957	14597	14879	0.5	37	5131	5420	5552	0.6	2.51	3386	3502	0.4
81102	ALAMOSA	003	66	65	64	-0.2	16	2	2	2	0.0	2.50	1	1	0.0
81120	ANTONITO	021	2641	2752	2733	0.4	34	1014	1086	1089	0.7	2.53	725	764	0.6
81121	ARBOLES	007	45	67	77	4.4	91	16	25	29	4.9	2.68	12	19	5.1
81122	BAYFIELD	067	6078	7273	7858	2.0	73	2392	2882	3121	2.0	2.52	1749	2076	1.9
81123	BLANCA	023	835	816	790	-0.2	16	303	302	295	0.0	2.70	222	217	-0.2
81125	CENTER	109	3844	4355	4574	1.4	58	1287	1455	1529	1.3	2.99	990	1108	1.2
81130	CREEDE	079	833	980	1052	1.8	69	378	446	480	1.8	2.20	252	291	1.6
81132	DEL NORTE	105	3249	3218	3194	-0.1	19	1241	1233	1227	-0.1	2.57	900	883	-0.2
81133	FORT GARLAND	023	816	731	694	-1.2	4	332	303	290	-1.0	2.41	248	223	-1.1
81136	HOOPER	003	275	304	317	1.1	52	93	104	108	1.2	2.92	75	82	1.0
81137	IGNACIO	067	5006	5863	6287	1.7	67	1831	2172	2342	1.9	2.68	1369	1603	1.7
81140	LA JARA	021	2681	2724	2692	0.2	28	914	950	945	0.4	2.82	671	687	0.3
81143	MOFFAT	109	1432	1812	1974	2.6	81	695	906	998	2.9	1.98	374	480	2.7
81144	MONTE VISTA	105	7601	7060	6912	-0.8	7	2812	2607	2554	-0.8	2.64	2050	1869	-1.0
81146	MOSCA	003	645	706	733	1.0	50	227	249	260	1.0	2.84	177	192	0.9
81147	PAGOSA SPRINGS	007	9344	12477	14295	3.2	87	3753	5112	5903	3.4	2.42	2700	3615	3.2
81149	SAGUACHE	109	990	1125	1185	1.4	58	428	501	534	1.7	2.21	278	322	1.6
81151	SANFORD	021	3902	3828	3743	-0.2	16	1426	1432	1411	0.0	2.67	1046	1038	-0.1
81152	SAN LUIS	023	1080	967	916	-1.2	4	460	423	406	-0.9	2.29	304	274	-1.1
81154	SOUTH FORK	105	1210	1715	1845	3.8	90	532	755	813	3.9	2.27	380	532	3.7
81155	VILLA GROVE	109	126	135	138	0.7	43	50	55	56	1.0	2.45	37	40	0.8
81201	SALIDA	015	8725	8974	9044	0.3	31	3866	4012	4059	0.4	2.21	2431	2464	0.1
81210	ALMONT	051	247	302	326	2.2	74	108	133	143	2.3	2.26	69	84	2.1
81211	BUENA VISTA	015	6681	7236	7425	0.9	47	2331	2616	2713	1.3	2.31	1641	1799	1.0
81212	CANON CITY	043	29213	30286	30499	0.4	34	9924	10303	10380	0.4	2.38	6570	6691	0.2
81220	CIMARRON	085	128	158	178	2.3	76	58	73	83	2.5	2.11	42	52	2.3
81223	COTOPAXI	043	1170	1523	1653	2.9	85	491	637	691	2.9	2.39	377	478	2.6
81224	CRESTED BUTTE	051	3453	3826	4069	1.1	52	1503	1672	1782	1.2	2.29	665	712	0.7
81226	FLORENCE	043	9563	10152	10292	0.6	40	2451	2632	2678	0.8	2.57	1709	1796	0.5
81228	GRANITE	065	80	99	104	2.3	76	35	43	45	2.3	2.30	25	31	2.4
81230	GUNNISON	051	9324	9883	10281	0.6	40	3647	3984	4175	1.0	2.27	1964	2077	0.6
81231	GUNNISON	051	24	24	25	0.0	22	10	11	12	1.0	1.82	6	6	0.0
81233	HOWARD	043	1515	1648	1681	0.9	47	663	721	734	0.9	2.29	503	534	0.6
81235	LAKE CITY	053	750	809	841	0.8	45	344	369	383	0.8	2.19	237	249	0.5
81236	NATHROP	015	865	1002	1054	1.6	64	398	467	494	1.7	2.15	298	341	1.5
81239	PARLIN	051	120	159	176	3.1	86	50	68	75	3.4	2.34	38	50	3.0
81240	PENROSE	043	4585	4692	4681	0.2	28	1665	1710	1711	0.3	2.71	1313	1323	0.1
81241	PITKIN	051	124	170	188	3.5	89	47	65	72	3.6	2.62	36	49	3.4
81243	POWDERHORN	051	99	131	144	3.1	86	35	47	52	3.2	2.68	25	33	3.0
81251	TWIN LAKES	065	195	208	215	0.7	43	89	95	97	0.7	2.19	63	66	0.5
81252	WESTCLIFFE	027	3032	3616	3880	1.9	70	1293	1563	1688	2.1	2.31	931	1107	1.9
81253	WETMORE	027	431	482	501	1.2	54	171	195	204	1.4	2.40	134	151	1.3
	COLORADO					1.7					1.6	2.55			1.5
	UNITED STATES					1.0					1.1	2.59			0.9

ZIP CODE #	POST OFFICE NAME	RACE (%) White 2000	White 2009	Black 2000	Black 2009	Asian/Pacific 2000	Asian/Pacific 2009	% Hispanic Origin 2000	% Hispanic Origin 2009	2009 AGE DISTRIBUTION (%) 0-4	5-9	10-14	15-19	20-24	25-44	45-64	65-84	85+	18+	MEDIAN AGE 2009	% 2009 Males	% 2009 Females
80927	COLORADO SPRINGS	95.5	94.7	0.0	0.0	0.0	0.0	4.9	6.5	6.2	6.8	7.4	7.4	4.4	26.3	31.6	9.1	0.9	74.6	40.1	50.4	49.6
80928	COLORADO SPRINGS	89.3	87.2	2.2	2.5	0.8	1.1	8.2	10.8	8.4	8.4	8.5	7.9	5.9	27.2	26.4	6.8	0.6	69.1	33.4	50.8	49.2
80929	COLORADO SPRINGS	84.3	81.6	4.7	5.2	1.4	1.7	9.9	13.2	7.6	7.5	7.6	7.3	5.2	28.7	28.6	7.0	0.5	73.0	36.4	50.6	49.4
80930	COLORADO SPRINGS	83.8	80.9	5.1	5.5	1.3	1.7	10.3	13.5	9.2	8.3	8.1	7.4	6.3	33.2	22.8	4.5	0.1	69.5	31.0	50.3	49.7
80951	COLORADO SPRINGS	94.7	78.9	0.0	4.8	0.0	1.9	5.3	19.8	8.2	7.6	7.4	7.8	7.7	27.8	24.7	8.1	0.7	72.2	33.2	49.2	50.8
81001	PUEBLO	73.4	70.4	1.7	1.8	1.3	1.5	49.6	56.8	7.3	6.9	6.8	7.8	7.4	25.8	23.8	11.4	2.8	74.7	34.8	48.1	51.9
81003	PUEBLO	74.9	71.2	3.8	3.8	0.6	0.6	42.9	51.8	6.4	5.9	5.6	7.9	7.7	29.6	23.2	11.4	2.4	77.9	36.1	51.9	48.1
81004	PUEBLO	72.3	68.4	3.0	3.1	0.3	0.3	46.7	54.5	7.3	6.8	6.4	6.5	6.4	26.4	25.0	12.5	2.8	75.7	37.1	48.7	51.3
81005	PUEBLO	84.3	81.7	1.9	2.1	0.4	0.6	35.1	42.5	5.8	6.0	6.3	6.7	5.4	23.1	28.4	15.2	3.1	77.7	42.3	47.6	52.4
81006	PUEBLO	82.2	78.8	0.5	0.5	0.4	0.4	34.2	42.1	5.8	6.6	7.0	7.6	5.4	23.7	29.0	13.0	1.8	75.6	40.4	49.9	50.1
81007	PUEBLO	88.5	86.1	0.8	0.9	1.1	1.3	18.2	23.7	8.3	7.8	7.6	6.8	5.6	28.0	26.1	8.9	0.8	71.7	35.4	49.7	50.3
81008	PUEBLO	82.5	77.7	1.5	2.0	1.3	1.7	32.2	40.8	6.9	6.7	6.9	7.0	5.8	25.6	27.3	12.1	1.6	74.9	38.2	48.4	51.6
81019	COLORADO CITY	93.3	91.4	0.8	0.9	0.3	0.3	8.5	12.0	5.4	6.7	7.5	7.9	4.4	22.9	32.0	12.3	0.9	74.9	41.6	49.3	50.7
81020	AGUILAR	85.8	84.6	0.0	0.0	0.5	0.5	42.5	48.8	4.6	4.6	4.8	5.6	4.3	19.4	33.0	20.9	2.8	82.6	50.7	48.6	51.4
81021	ARLINGTON	100.0	100.0	0.0	0.0	0.0	0.0	4.3	4.3	8.7	8.7	8.7	8.7	0.0	34.8	30.4	0.0	0.0	65.2	33.8	47.8	52.2
81022	AVONDALE	88.6	87.0	0.1	0.1	0.2	0.2	37.6	44.7	6.1	6.3	6.7	6.7	5.7	25.8	28.8	12.7	1.2	76.8	39.0	51.3	48.7
81023	BEULAH	94.2	92.5	0.5	0.6	0.2	0.2	9.6	13.4	4.4	5.2	6.2	6.6	2.4	20.7	39.7	13.3	1.6	79.8	47.4	51.3	48.7
81025	BOONE	90.4	88.3	0.4	0.5	0.5	0.5	27.2	34.2	5.8	6.1	6.4	6.2	5.3	23.5	31.1	14.1	1.6	78.2	42.3	50.0	50.0
81027	BRANSON	93.5	93.3	0.6	0.6	0.0	0.0	11.8	14.5	4.5	5.6	9.5	7.8	3.4	24.0	28.5	14.0	2.8	74.9	42.3	50.3	49.7
81029	CAMPO	96.7	96.4	0.0	0.0	0.2	0.2	2.4	3.1	5.3	6.0	6.5	6.5	5.0	21.1	30.7	16.3	2.6	78.2	44.7	53.5	46.5
81036	EADS	96.1	95.4	0.5	0.6	0.0	0.0	3.2	4.0	6.1	6.2	6.2	6.2	5.2	21.7	29.7	14.6	3.9	77.3	43.1	50.3	49.7
81039	FOWLER	94.6	92.9	0.3	0.4	0.1	0.2	12.6	16.8	6.4	6.5	6.5	5.7	5.0	22.5	26.9	16.5	4.0	77.2	42.8	48.5	51.5
81040	GARDNER	75.5	74.3	0.3	0.3	0.0	0.0	32.0	33.8	2.9	4.3	7.0	8.8	5.4	17.4	44.0	9.1	1.1	80.2	46.7	51.2	48.8
81041	GRANADA	64.5	60.8	0.1	0.1	0.0	0.0	59.8	65.6	8.8	8.0	8.0	8.7	8.7	26.2	22.7	7.8	1.1	69.8	30.7	53.2	46.8
81043	HARTMAN	91.3	88.9	0.0	0.0	0.0	0.0	17.4	22.2	6.5	6.5	8.3	7.4	5.6	23.1	25.9	13.9	2.8	72.2	40.6	53.7	46.3
81044	HASTY	85.4	85.1	0.3	0.4	0.6	0.7	17.5	17.7	7.1	7.8	7.8	7.1	3.9	25.2	27.3	12.4	1.4	73.0	38.6	50.4	49.6
81045	HASWELL	96.2	95.2	0.8	0.8	0.0	0.0	3.1	4.0	6.3	6.3	6.3	6.3	4.0	23.8	31.0	13.5	2.4	77.0	41.7	51.6	48.4
81047	HOLLY	80.4	76.3	0.2	0.2	0.0	0.1	29.8	36.2	8.0	7.4	8.0	7.3	7.5	23.3	24.0	11.0	3.5	71.6	35.4	52.3	47.7
81049	KIM	97.4	97.3	0.7	0.7	0.3	0.3	6.3	8.1	3.7	4.1	5.4	7.4	4.1	19.3	31.8	21.6	2.7	82.1	48.2	52.4	47.6
81050	LA JUNTA	78.2	74.4	1.0	1.3	0.8	0.9	36.3	42.7	6.8	6.3	6.9	8.4	6.7	22.8	25.7	13.8	2.5	75.0	38.1	48.7	51.3
81052	LAMAR	78.6	74.8	0.3	0.4	0.5	0.6	32.6	38.4	8.1	7.8	7.5	8.1	6.9	26.9	23.2	9.7	2.0	72.0	32.9	50.4	49.6
81054	LAS ANIMAS	78.3	77.8	4.4	4.4	0.5	0.5	32.8	33.4	4.9	4.9	4.9	4.8	8.0	31.8	23.4	14.4	2.9	82.2	38.4	62.2	37.8
81055	LA VETA	91.4	91.0	0.3	0.4	0.6	0.6	12.7	13.7	3.9	4.9	5.7	6.2	3.4	18.9	37.3	17.1	2.6	81.0	48.6	50.3	49.7
81057	MC CLAVE	85.6	85.2	0.2	0.2	0.7	0.7	17.4	17.7	7.2	7.8	7.8	6.8	4.1	25.1	27.7	12.4	1.1	72.6	38.6	51.0	49.0
81058	MANZANOLA	81.5	77.8	1.7	2.1	0.6	0.7	30.5	36.7	6.1	6.2	6.3	6.3	5.6	26.1	28.7	13.2	1.7	78.0	39.9	53.9	46.1
81059	MODEL	91.2	90.0	0.4	0.4	0.4	0.4	15.5	18.8	4.6	5.7	8.8	7.7	3.4	23.4	29.9	13.8	2.7	75.1	42.7	49.4	50.6
81062	OLNEY SPRINGS	82.7	81.8	8.4	8.0	1.1	1.3	18.2	22.2	2.9	3.0	3.2	4.0	9.9	48.8	21.1	5.7	1.4	88.4	36.0	79.1	20.9
81063	ORDWAY	83.4	81.7	5.7	6.2	0.6	0.7	26.0	31.0	4.3	4.2	4.4	5.6	8.7	37.9	24.4	8.9	1.7	83.7	37.7	67.8	32.2
81064	PRITCHETT	97.5	97.3	0.0	0.0	0.0	0.0	3.1	3.4	5.4	5.4	6.7	6.7	5.4	20.1	29.5	18.1	2.7	78.5	45.2	52.3	47.7
81067	ROCKY FORD	75.8	72.4	0.4	0.5	1.0	1.3	48.1	54.5	6.3	6.2	6.7	7.8	6.0	22.6	26.7	14.9	3.0	75.8	40.1	50.1	49.9
81069	RYE	93.6	92.1	0.3	0.3	0.2	0.2	9.2	12.6	4.3	5.9	6.8	7.4	3.9	20.6	35.0	14.9	1.2	77.7	45.6	50.7	49.3
81071	SHERIDAN LAKE	96.7	96.0	0.3	0.3	0.0	0.0	3.0	3.7	5.8	6.7	7.0	6.7	3.7	23.9	30.3	14.1	1.8	76.1	41.3	50.2	49.8
81073	SPRINGFIELD	94.2	93.0	0.0	0.0	0.3	0.3	6.3	8.1	6.0	6.1	6.1	5.7	4.9	20.6	27.9	17.9	4.7	78.3	45.4	48.4	51.6
81076	SUGAR CITY	83.2	82.1	8.0	7.5	1.2	1.4	17.2	21.2	3.0	3.1	3.3	4.1	9.7	48.0	21.0	6.3	1.6	87.9	36.0	77.9	22.1
81081	TRINCHERA	94.4	94.6	0.0	0.0	0.0	0.0	16.7	20.3	2.7	4.1	6.8	8.1	1.4	24.3	36.5	13.5	2.7	79.7	46.4	47.3	52.7
81082	TRINIDAD	81.3	79.3	0.5	0.5	0.6	0.7	44.1	50.4	5.7	5.6	5.8	7.4	6.9	22.8	27.9	14.5	3.4	78.7	41.6	49.7	50.3
81084	TWO BUTTES	96.3	96.0	0.0	0.0	0.0	0.0	4.7	5.1	3.0	7.1	8.1	9.1	3.0	17.2	36.4	14.1	2.0	74.7	46.4	51.5	48.5
81087	VILAS	92.4	92.0	0.0	0.0	0.7	0.7	7.6	10.2	5.8	6.6	6.6	5.1	4.4	19.7	32.8	16.8	2.2	78.8	46.4	56.2	43.8
81089	WALSENBURG	78.3	77.9	3.6	3.8	0.4	0.4	41.9	42.7	4.3	4.2	4.6	5.7	7.3	27.0	28.3	15.4	3.2	83.1	42.5	57.5	42.5
81090	WALSH	91.6	89.9	0.1	0.1	0.1	0.2	10.3	12.8	6.3	7.9	8.0	6.4	2.8	20.3	30.2	14.4	3.7	72.8	43.5	51.0	49.0
81091	WESTON	86.1	84.2	0.1	0.1	0.6	0.8	32.6	38.5	4.4	5.3	6.0	5.2	4.2	23.2	36.6	13.5	1.6	80.8	46.0	50.8	49.2
81092	WILEY	88.0	84.9	0.1	0.1	0.2	0.2	16.1	20.3	7.4	7.2	8.2	8.1	6.5	28.2	23.7	8.7	2.0	72.1	34.7	50.4	49.6
81101	ALAMOSA	70.2	66.6	1.0	1.1	1.0	1.1	43.4	49.8	7.1	6.6	6.7	9.5	9.9	26.5	23.8	8.5	1.6	75.3	31.5	50.1	49.9
81102	ALAMOSA	74.6	72.3	3.0	3.1	1.5	1.5	26.9	32.3	10.8	6.2	3.1	12.3	27.7	23.1	13.8	1.5	1.5	80.0	23.2	41.5	58.5
81120	ANTONITO	68.9	67.6	0.3	0.3	0.3	0.4	78.5	81.7	7.4	7.4	7.5	7.2	6.0	22.0	26.6	14.2	1.8	73.3	38.7	50.9	49.1
81121	ARBOLES	73.3	71.6	0.0	0.0	0.0	0.0	26.7	31.3	6.0	7.5	7.5	7.5	3.0	17.9	32.8	17.9	0.0	71.6	45.4	53.7	46.3
81122	BAYFIELD	92.3	91.4	0.2	0.2	0.1	0.2	8.1	10.1	5.3	5.8	6.6	6.6	4.4	25.3	34.9	10.4	0.7	78.0	42.3	50.9	49.1
81123	BLANCA	62.8	61.6	1.0	1.0	2.6	2.8	48.7	45.0	5.5	5.9	7.0	8.3	6.3	22.7	30.3	12.9	1.2	76.8	40.4	51.7	48.3
81125	CENTER	61.8	57.3	0.2	0.2	0.2	0.2	62.6	70.4	9.0	8.9	8.6	8.2	7.2	25.8	23.8	7.4	1.0	68.3	30.0	50.4	49.6
81130	CREEDE	96.9	96.8	0.0	0.0	0.0	0.0	2.0	2.3	4.0	4.5	5.1	5.4	3.5	17.7	39.0	19.2	1.7	82.9	50.4	51.2	48.8
81132	DEL NORTE	73.5	72.3	0.3	0.3	0.3	0.3	43.5	45.3	6.6	6.9	6.9	7.3	5.4	22.9	29.5	12.2	2.2	74.5	40.4	49.8	50.2
81133	FORT GARLAND	62.3	60.2	0.5	0.5	2.1	2.3	56.6	52.8	6.2	6.6	6.8	5.7	4.9	20.4	29.4	18.3	1.6	76.9	44.5	49.7	50.3
81136	HOOPER	84.0	80.3	0.4	0.3	1.1	1.3	17.1	21.1	6.6	7.6	9.2	9.2	4.6	27.6	24.0	10.2	1.0	70.4	36.5	51.6	48.4
81137	IGNACIO	65.8	63.9	0.2	0.2	0.2	0.3	22.0	25.7	6.6	6.6	6.8	7.7	6.7	25.8	29.4	9.5	0.9	75.0	37.0	50.9	49.1
81140	LA JARA	71.2	68.1	0.1	0.1	0.3	0.3	52.7	59.3	8.1	8.2	8.1	7.7	5.6	21.5	26.7	11.5	2.6	70.4	36.0	48.3	51.7
81143	MOFFAT	90.9	89.2	0.1	0.1	0.9	1.2	8.2	11.8	3.5	5.0	5.4	5.5	2.6	19.3	45.0	12.1	1.5	82.7	49.1	51.1	48.9
81144	MONTE VISTA	70.6	68.6	0.4	0.4	0.3	0.3	46.1	48.9	7.4	7.0	7.5	7.5	5.9	23.2	26.4	12.6	2.6	73.2	37.9	48.8	51.2
81146	MOSCA	83.4	79.6	0.6	0.7	1.1	1.4	17.7	22.4	6.4	7.4	8.6	8.8	4.8	26.5	26.1	10.6	0.8	71.7	37.0	51.7	48.3
81147	PAGOSA SPRINGS	89.1	87.2	0.4	0.4	0.3	0.4	16.1	19.7	5.2	5.8	7.1	7.3	4.2	22.6	35.8	11.0	0.9	76.8	43.5	50.7	49.3
81149	SAGUACHE	84.0	80.2	0.0	0.0	0.5	0.5	26.2	35.0	4.9	5.2	6.0	6.8	4.2	20.7	35.8	14.2	2.1	79.1	46.1	51.1	48.9
81151	SANFORD	73.8	70.7	0.3	0.3	0.2	0.2	55.6	59.5	7.9	7.7	8.5	8.2	6.5	22.3	24.8	12.2	2.0	70.7	35.0	49.3	50.7
81152	SAN LUIS	57.8	53.2	1.1	1.2	0.2	0.2	78.5	75.5	5.1	5.8	6.1	6.0	5.2	17.7	33.4	18.4	2.4	79.3	47.9	50.5	49.5
81154	SOUTH FORK	92.1	91.7	0.1	0.1	0.2	0.1	12.9	14.6	4.5	4.8	5.4	5.4	3.6	20.1	35.0	19.8	1.5	81.9	48.8	49.3	50.7
81155	VILLA GROVE	92.1	88.9	0.0	0.0	1.6	2.2	10.3	14.1	4.4	4.4	5.2	8.1	2.2	17.8	48.1	7.4	2.2	80.0	48.1	52.6	47.4
81201	SALIDA	93.7	92.5	0.1	0.1	0.5	0.6	8.6	11.0	5.0	5.0	5.3	6.1	5.1	22.4	32.4	16.0	2.9	80.6	45.7	49.5	50.5
81210	ALMONT	95.9	94.7	0.0	0.3	0.8	1.0	4.9	6.3	6.0	4.6	6.0	5.6	7.0	32.1	28.8	9.3	0.7	79.8	38.2	53.0	47.0
81211	BUENA VISTA	86.7	84.9	3.7	3.9	0.5	0.6	9.3	11.3	3.5	4.3	4.9	4.9	7.8	26.5	33.1	13.7	1.2	84.2	43.6	57.5	42.5
81212	CANON CITY	91.1	90.3	4.2	4.4	0.5	0.7	10.5	12.9	4.9	5.0	5.1	5.7	7.3	29.3	26.6	13.2	2.9	81.4	40.2	55.7	44.3
81220	CIMARRON	90.7	89.9	0.0	0.0	0.8	0.6	4.7	5.7	5.1	6.3	5.7	5.7	4.4	21.5	39.9	11.4	0.0	78.5	45.7	49.4	50.6
81223	COTOPAXI	94.9	94.4	0.2	0.3	0.5	0.7	4.0	5.4	3.5	5.9	6.7	6.5	1.6	20.6	41.2	13.5	0.5	78.9	47.6	51.1	48.9
81224	CRESTED BUTTE	97.3	96.9	0.2	0.2	0.4	0.5	2.7	3.5	4.8	3.7	3.6	3.8	10.0	46.5	24.5	3.1	0.0	85.4	32.7	56.2	43.8
81226	FLORENCE	80.2	78.9	12.4	13.2	0.8	0.9	13.3	16.5	4.6	4.4	4.6	4.6	6.9	38.6	25.1	9.6	1.5	83.6	37.8	65.1	34.9
81228	GRANITE	83.5	82.8	0.0	0.0	0.0	0.0	24.1	23.2	6.1	6.1	7.1	7.1	5.1	23.2	34.3	11.1	0.0	74.7	41.8	53.5	46.5
81230	GUNNISON	94.4	93.3	0.6	0.8	0.6	0.8	5.9	7.5	4.5	4.3	4.7	10.2	16.8	28.0	22.9	7.6	1.0	83.4	30.3	53.7	46.3
81231	GUNNISON	95.8	95.8	0.0	0.0	0.0	0.0	4.2	4.2	4.2	4.2	8.3	8.3	8.3	33.3	33.3	0.0	0.0	83.3	35.0	54.2	45.8
81233	HOWARD	96.9	96.2	0.2	0.2	0.1	0.2	4.3	5.8	3.0	4.4	5.0	4.4	2.9	16.8	41.9	19.8	1.7	84.5	52.0	50.7	49.3
81235	LAKE CITY	97.3	97.4	0.0	0.0	0.3	0.2	1.5	1.5	5.9	4.4	4.7	3.7	3.6	25.2	40.3	11.0	1.1	82.2	46.3	51.8	48.2
81236	NATHROP	96.4	95.7	0.1	0.2	0.7	0.9	3.0	4.0	3.5	3.7	4.5	4.8	2.7	17.4	43.5	18.8	1.2	85.1	51.9	50.6	49.4
81239	PARLIN	95.0	93.7	0.0	0.0	0.8	1.3	6.7	8.2	5.7	4.4	6.3	6.9	5.0	25.2	32.7	12.6	1.3	78.6	43.0	52.8	47.2
81240	PENROSE	95.1	94.3	0.6	0.7	0.4	0.6	7.2	9.4	6.0	6.5	6.9	6.8	5.6	23.8	31.8	11.7	0.8	76.2	41.0	51.0	49.0
81241	PITKIN	95.1	94.1	0.0	0.0	0.8	1.2	7.3	8.2	6.5	4.7	7.1	7.1	4.7	24.1	32.4	12.4	1.2	76.5	42.7	51.2	48.8
81243	POWDERHORN	89.9	88.5	0.0	0.0	1.0	0.8	3.0	3.8	5.3	6.1	5.3	5.3	5.3	21.4	39.7	11.5	0.0	79.4	45.6	51.9	48.1
81251	TWIN LAKES	73.3	68.8	0.5	0.5	0.0	0.0	35.9	42.3	8.2	7.7	8.2	8.7	8.2	28.8	23.6	6.7	0.0	71.2	31.6	56.3	43.7
81252	WESTCLIFFE	95.7	95.4	0.4	0.4	0.3	0.2	2.2	2.7	4.4	5.3	5.9	5.1	3.4	16.2	40.5	18.0	1.2	81.0	50.7	50.9	49.1
81253	WETMORE	96.1	95.9	1.2	1.0	0.2	0.2	4.9	6.0	4.1	5.0	7.1	5.2	3.7	21.6	39.6	13.1	0.6	80.3	46.6	51.0	49.0
	COLORADO	82.8	80.7	3.8	3.8	2.3	2.9	17.1	20.2	6.9	6.7	6.7	6.9	7.0	29.0	26.5	8.8	1.4	75.7	35.9	50.2	49.8
	UNITED STATES	75.1	72.0	12.3	12.7	3.8	4.6	12.5	15.7	6.8	6.7	6.6	7.1	6.9	27.0	26.0	10.9	1.9	75.7	36.9	49.2	50.8

ZIP CODE #	POST OFFICE NAME	2009 Per Capita Income	2009 HH Income Base	2009 HOUSEHOLD INCOME DISTRIBUTION (%) Less than $25,000	$25,000 to $49,999	$50,000 to $99,999	$100,000 to $149,999	$150,000 or More	MEDIAN HOUSEHOLD INCOME 2009	2014	2009 National Centile	2009 State Centile	2009 Home Value Base	2009 HOME VALUE DISTRIBUTION (%) Less than $50,000	$50,000 to $89,999	$90,000 to $174,999	$175,000 to $399,999	$400,000 or More	2009 Median Home Value
80927	COLORADO SPRINGS	23819	110	11.8	22.7	49.1	10.9	5.5	67020	68751	85	78	98	2.0	1.0	30.6	58.2	8.2	228571
80928	COLORADO SPRINGS	17247	279	22.6	33.0	36.9	6.5	1.1	46018	47650	51	39	218	15.6	16.5	33.0	32.1	2.8	139000
80929	COLORADO SPRINGS	23996	237	13.1	26.2	46.8	11.0	3.0	56149	57897	73	63	194	7.7	2.1	29.4	55.7	5.2	191406
80930	COLORADO SPRINGS	24928	278	10.1	19.1	56.1	12.2	2.5	64938	66114	83	75	225	10.2	3.1	28.9	55.1	2.7	183929
80951	COLORADO SPRINGS	23150	886	12.1	27.5	45.1	12.6	2.6	58061	61581	75	65	632	46.4	13.4	33.5	6.0	0.6	58214
81001	PUEBLO	19299	11574	34.2	29.0	28.9	5.4	2.5	35970	37523	20	12	7170	10.0	19.8	55.1	13.9	1.3	115157
81003	PUEBLO	17454	5611	37.9	33.7	24.1	3.0	1.3	31865	32236	11	5	2883	6.9	30.2	57.8	4.8	0.3	100830
81004	PUEBLO	17787	11066	38.8	32.1	24.8	2.7	1.6	32648	33664	13	6	6521	4.6	26.0	64.0	4.7	0.8	104677
81005	PUEBLO	23821	12244	21.9	29.8	35.5	9.4	3.4	48145	50455	57	46	9452	3.1	7.2	63.2	24.0	2.5	138869
81006	PUEBLO	21569	4817	23.3	25.9	40.8	7.1	2.9	50679	52854	63	53	3928	8.1	15.9	41.0	32.7	2.4	139649
81007	PUEBLO	25393	9560	10.3	26.7	46.8	11.1	5.1	62247	64162	80	73	7866	2.0	5.5	45.0	45.0	2.6	170740
81008	PUEBLO	23909	4071	19.5	33.2	33.6	10.2	3.5	47922	49852	56	46	2996	11.3	11.4	58.5	17.2	1.5	128527
81019	COLORADO CITY	22285	549	21.3	26.4	45.0	4.4	2.9	51449	53766	65	56	436	5.3	9.6	51.6	24.8	8.7	142448
81020	AGUILAR	16621	473	42.7	34.0	16.3	5.1	1.9	30688	31012	9	4	372	17.5	16.9	41.9	13.2	10.5	114407
81021	ARLINGTON	15870	10	40.0	30.0	30.0	0.0	0.0	30000	30000	8	4	7	0.0	71.4	28.6	0.0	0.0	72500
81022	AVONDALE	16853	521	25.1	41.1	26.5	5.0	2.3	37135	38845	24	16	399	11.8	22.1	48.6	15.0	2.5	110737
81023	BEULAH	27550	456	14.0	28.9	47.4	6.4	3.3	54422	56648	70	60	388	5.7	2.3	43.0	41.2	7.7	172727
81025	BOONE	19153	530	30.9	37.4	22.5	5.8	3.4	35000	35586	18	10	409	17.4	26.9	39.6	12.7	3.4	96184
81027	BRANSON	19948	79	32.9	27.8	32.9	5.1	1.3	36739	37988	23	15	55	10.9	12.7	47.3	18.2	10.9	137500
81029	CAMPO	16170	161	39.1	34.8	20.5	3.1	2.5	33825	35283	15	8	128	50.0	15.6	21.1	8.6	4.7	50000
81036	EADS	20393	404	32.7	32.9	26.7	4.0	3.7	37976	39745	27	18	295	39.3	32.5	25.1	2.0	1.0	63696
81039	FOWLER	19713	801	32.1	32.3	28.7	5.5	1.4	36038	37556	21	12	586	9.2	29.2	49.1	12.1	0.3	102232
81040	GARDNER	20703	166	39.8	21.7	31.9	4.8	1.8	36573	40000	22	14	113	8.0	21.2	31.0	27.4	12.4	131250
81041	GRANADA	12939	244	35.7	34.0	25.8	2.9	1.6	33416	34180	14	7	156	40.4	26.3	28.2	5.1	0.0	62000
81043	HARTMAN	16930	38	28.9	39.5	26.3	2.6	2.6	36507	37315	22	14	28	35.7	17.9	28.6	17.9	0.0	80000
81044	HASTY	21030	117	28.2	35.9	29.1	5.1	1.7	41254	43294	37	27	81	29.6	22.2	30.9	14.8	2.5	87000
81045	HASWELL	19369	50	40.0	26.0	26.0	6.0	2.0	33179	37313	14	7	34	29.4	26.5	35.3	5.9	2.9	76667
81047	HOLLY	16742	679	36.7	32.7	24.7	2.9	2.9	34645	35784	17	9	479	39.7	29.2	20.3	10.6	0.2	64265
81049	KIM	24777	134	28.4	40.3	25.4	2.2	3.7	40887	41554	36	25	107	32.7	13.1	26.2	11.2	16.8	99000
81050	LA JUNTA	18961	4181	34.2	26.6	32.3	5.2	1.7	38514	40758	28	19	2848	17.7	29.3	40.8	11.8	0.4	94104
81052	LAMAR	17624	3646	29.8	32.5	31.3	4.7	1.7	38514	40448	28	19	2361	24.8	24.4	39.1	10.8	0.9	91039
81054	LAS ANIMAS	17292	1428	37.0	32.0	26.5	3.2	1.3	33048	33763	13	6	969	32.2	32.5	28.7	3.8	2.8	72134
81055	LA VETA	23285	763	33.8	28.4	30.7	4.8	2.2	37707	40333	26	18	545	7.0	9.7	40.2	35.8	7.3	157639
81057	MC CLAVE	17335	184	27.7	35.3	29.9	5.4	1.6	41978	42549	39	29	127	29.9	22.0	31.5	14.2	2.4	86875
81058	MANZANOLA	17013	392	38.3	31.4	25.8	2.8	1.8	33561	35303	14	8	281	21.4	32.0	29.2	17.1	0.4	85476
81059	MODEL	16845	97	33.0	28.9	33.0	4.1	1.0	36378	39315	22	14	68	13.2	16.2	41.2	19.1	10.3	132500
81062	OLNEY SPRINGS	16148	341	35.8	32.8	27.3	2.6	1.5	34858	35705	17	10	262	17.6	22.5	32.8	19.5	7.6	108594
81063	ORDWAY	16729	824	36.0	37.1	20.9	3.6	2.3	31546	32367	11	5	572	25.2	29.2	38.3	6.6	0.7	84186
81064	PRITCHETT	15017	57	38.6	36.8	21.1	1.8	1.8	34074	33642	16	8	46	50.0	15.2	17.4	10.9	6.5	50000
81067	ROCKY FORD	17614	2216	36.1	30.3	27.0	4.5	2.1	35670	37251	20	12	1518	18.5	35.4	36.0	9.7	0.4	85630
81069	RYE	23680	857	22.5	31.0	37.2	5.7	3.5	47264	49155	55	43	715	5.0	9.9	53.4	25.0	6.6	141572
81071	SHERIDAN LAKE	20348	137	35.0	29.2	27.7	6.6	1.5	36301	37303	21	13	92	30.4	23.9	35.9	7.6	2.2	78571
81073	SPRINGFIELD	18115	920	40.0	31.2	24.6	3.2	1.1	31834	33477	11	5	690	38.3	29.6	25.5	5.8	0.9	65600
81076	SUGAR CITY	23301	187	36.4	29.4	30.5	2.7	1.1	35406	36987	19	11	142	17.6	21.8	29.6	22.5	8.5	110000
81081	TRINCHERA	19559	32	40.6	25.0	25.0	9.4	0.0	28543	32366	6	3	21	4.8	9.5	47.6	33.3	4.8	140625
81082	TRINIDAD	19222	5264	36.3	28.1	29.5	4.0	2.1	36013	37789	21	12	3601	9.1	10.7	43.3	30.3	6.6	147126
81084	TWO BUTTES	22465	47	25.5	34.0	34.0	4.3	2.1	41707	45000	38	28	33	21.2	24.2	36.4	15.2	3.0	97500
81087	VILAS	20035	54	29.6	29.6	35.2	3.7	1.9	43143	44044	43	32	41	31.7	26.8	26.8	9.8	4.9	83000
81089	WALSENBURG	18078	2078	40.5	31.4	23.1	3.1	1.9	30570	31498	9	4	1457	13.1	28.6	34.7	17.2	6.4	98368
81090	WALSH	17228	483	36.4	33.3	24.8	3.5	1.9	34675	36150	17	10	363	41.0	25.6	23.4	8.3	1.7	62885
81091	WESTON	17317	458	35.8	36.9	22.9	2.2	2.2	33136	34006	14	7	352	7.1	13.6	41.8	32.7	4.8	147596
81092	WILEY	17563	294	28.6	32.0	34.4	3.4	1.7	43837	45986	45	33	207	17.9	25.1	43.5	13.0	0.5	101136
81101	ALAMOSA	18623	5420	34.7	28.3	29.0	5.7	2.2	36613	38257	22	14	3390	11.0	12.9	41.0	30.3	4.9	142808
81102	ALAMOSA	2587	2	100.0	0.0	0.0	0.0	0.0	5000	5000	0	1	0	0.0	0.0	0.0	0.0	0.0	0
81120	ANTONITO	13859	1086	50.1	27.1	18.7	2.9	1.3	24943	25456	3	2	838	24.5	22.8	36.6	11.7	4.4	93966
81121	ARBOLES	17406	25	32.0	28.0	36.0	4.0	0.0	37367	41132	25	16	21	0.0	14.3	19.0	38.1	28.6	268750
81122	BAYFIELD	23183	2882	21.4	28.1	40.0	7.4	3.1	50323	53031	62	51	2291	5.1	3.0	13.0	52.6	26.4	284301
81123	BLANCA	12453	302	43.4	36.1	18.9	1.3	0.3	28119	28384	6	3	238	39.9	27.3	15.5	12.6	4.6	64286
81125	CENTER	14391	1455	36.9	32.3	24.5	3.8	2.5	33254	34197	14	7	939	22.0	18.6	39.0	15.2	5.1	105877
81130	CREEDE	24125	446	24.4	35.4	32.1	5.6	2.5	41947	43487	39	29	332	11.1	7.2	27.1	36.7	17.8	193750
81132	DEL NORTE	17615	1233	36.4	29.8	28.1	3.8	1.9	34323	36040	16	9	923	18.9	22.6	31.7	20.6	6.2	102083
81133	FORT GARLAND	15721	303	45.5	28.7	21.8	1.7	2.3	28028	28596	6	3	239	22.6	17.6	36.4	23.0	0.4	111742
81136	HOOPER	17324	104	26.0	28.8	35.6	7.7	1.9	44207	46882	46	35	83	13.3	16.9	30.1	28.9	10.8	134722
81137	IGNACIO	20666	2172	24.7	27.2	39.6	6.1	2.3	48250	50739	57	47	1611	8.3	6.5	21.7	40.2	23.4	240079
81140	LA JARA	14329	950	41.1	26.5	27.8	3.6	1.1	32578	34036	13	6	736	23.1	24.0	34.0	17.7	1.2	95385
81143	MOFFAT	19165	906	45.6	28.8	20.8	4.0	0.9	28556	29808	6	4	666	15.2	8.0	29.7	34.2	12.9	165500
81144	MONTE VISTA	17504	2607	31.9	34.0	29.2	2.4	2.6	37262	38568	24	16	1766	14.5	19.9	43.4	19.1	3.1	109906
81146	MOSCA	18290	249	28.5	25.7	35.7	7.6	2.4	44408	48403	47	36	196	9.2	14.3	32.1	35.2	9.2	150000
81147	PAGOSA SPRINGS	24206	5112	22.7	31.2	35.3	7.3	3.5	46842	48455	54	42	3903	4.2	4.2	14.9	43.7	32.9	297703
81149	SAGUACHE	17381	501	40.5	31.7	24.4	2.6	0.8	30840	31023	9	4	367	13.9	19.3	39.8	15.5	11.4	126591
81151	SANFORD	13201	1432	49.5	27.9	17.9	4.1	0.6	25336	25865	3	3	1104	25.8	27.2	34.3	12.0	0.6	85600
81152	SAN LUIS	12438	423	55.8	31.7	10.6	1.9	0.0	21388	21916	2	2	361	33.8	27.4	31.6	6.1	1.1	73261
81154	SOUTH FORK	25622	755	21.3	29.8	39.6	6.2	3.0	48330	51364	57	47	567	9.3	11.3	34.4	37.9	7.1	161557
81155	VILLA GROVE	18757	55	23.6	41.8	30.9	3.6	0.0	34153	37327	16	9	45	8.9	17.8	15.6	22.2	35.6	196875
81201	SALIDA	21782	4012	30.3	33.6	27.4	6.3	2.4	38570	39668	28	19	2810	6.7	4.3	18.5	53.6	16.9	230459
81210	ALMONT	30874	133	12.8	25.6	46.6	8.3	6.8	59621	60219	77	68	92	1.1	1.1	4.3	54.3	39.1	360000
81211	BUENA VISTA	22384	2616	24.3	31.5	36.5	5.4	2.3	44862	47367	48	37	1991	6.7	3.5	17.2	50.5	22.1	247837
81212	CANON CITY	20692	10303	27.7	28.5	35.4	6.6	1.7	44093	46818	46	34	7420	6.2	7.0	41.8	39.5	5.6	165934
81220	CIMARRON	21301	73	23.3	38.4	35.6	2.7	0.0	43427	45270	44	32	54	0.0	7.4	9.3	33.3	50.0	400000
81223	COTOPAXI	20875	637	30.3	29.0	33.6	4.1	3.0	39922	45053	32	23	569	2.6	5.4	39.0	43.1	9.8	181762
81224	CRESTED BUTTE	36298	1672	9.9	27.9	40.9	12.4	8.9	61103	63176	79	72	964	0.8	0.4	5.9	34.5	58.3	458394
81226	FLORENCE	17451	2632	31.8	32.7	30.7	4.0	0.9	36912	39639	23	15	2008	9.2	10.8	53.1	24.3	2.6	139653
81228	GRANITE	26829	43	18.6	23.3	48.8	7.0	2.3	58542	60454	76	65	36	16.7	13.9	13.9	33.3	22.2	216667
81230	GUNNISON	22723	3984	25.8	30.8	34.7	6.3	2.3	42329	44868	40	30	2207	6.3	3.2	10.6	56.6	23.4	262359
81231	GUNNISON	27853	11	27.3	27.3	45.5	0.0	0.0	42313	52500	40	30	5	0.0	0.0	0.0	80.0	20.0	275000
81233	HOWARD	20932	721	30.2	31.2	32.9	4.0	1.7	38996	41463	30	20	601	0.8	1.3	27.5	51.6	18.8	234259
81235	LAKE CITY	27618	369	19.2	36.3	35.2	3.3	6.0	45657	46498	50	39	238	3.4	2.5	12.6	40.8	40.8	357692
81236	NATHROP	40757	467	16.7	20.1	37.5	15.0	10.7	65315	66547	84	76	396	10.4	2.5	6.1	34.3	46.7	384884
81239	PARLIN	27871	68	14.7	27.9	47.1	2.9	7.4	54405	54943	70	60	49	0.0	2.0	4.1	63.3	30.6	336667
81240	PENROSE	18358	1710	23.0	31.8	39.8	4.7	0.8	46009	48206	51	39	1429	6.6	8.0	28.1	51.4	5.9	190738
81241	PITKIN	25064	65	13.8	26.2	49.2	3.1	7.7	55937	56510	73	62	47	0.0	2.1	4.3	63.8	29.8	336667
81243	POWDERHORN	15358	47	27.7	42.6	29.8	0.0	0.0	40897	42620	36	25	34	0.0	2.9	8.8	29.4	58.8	430000
81251	TWIN LAKES	31360	95	10.5	25.3	57.9	4.2	2.1	60299	60753	78	69	78	30.8	24.4	17.9	17.9	9.0	78333
81252	WESTCLIFFE	23043	1563	28.5	29.0	32.4	6.0	4.0	41351	43349	37	27	1222	7.4	5.8	16.6	40.3	29.8	271812
81253	WETMORE	23739	195	16.4	39.5	34.9	5.1	4.1	46052	46110	51	40	165	0.0	0.6	30.3	33.3	35.8	302083
	COLORADO	30807		15.5	22.5	37.5	15.8	8.6	62597	65813				4.4	4.3	23.6	52.9	14.8	220998
	UNITED STATES	27277		20.9	24.4	35.3	11.7	7.6	54719	56938				9.3	13.1	31.6	32.6	13.5	162279

ZIP CODE #	POST OFFICE NAME	FINANCIAL SERVICES: Auto Loan	FINANCIAL SERVICES: Home Loan	FINANCIAL SERVICES: Investments	FINANCIAL SERVICES: Retirement Plans	THE HOME: Home Improvements: Home Repair	THE HOME: Home Improvements: Lawn & Garden	THE HOME: Furnishings: Computers & Hardware-Personal	THE HOME: Furnishings: Major Appliances	THE HOME: Furnishings: TV, Radio, Sound Equipment	THE HOME: Furnishings: Furniture	ENTERTAINMENT: Dine out/Carry out	ENTERTAINMENT: Sports Equipment	ENTERTAINMENT: Fees & Tickets	ENTERTAINMENT: Toys & Games	ENTERTAINMENT: Travel	ENTERTAINMENT: Cable TV	PERSONAL: Apparel & Services	PERSONAL: Auto Repairs	PERSONAL: Health Insurance	PERSONAL: Pets & Supplies
80927	COLORADO SPRINGS	102	115	99	119	112	113	103	107	101	103	102	84	110	104	109	101	71	103	106	126
80928	COLORADO SPRINGS	82	77	68	75	75	77	72	76	74	76	74	56	69	78	69	75	51	73	75	90
80929	COLORADO SPRINGS	93	103	86	102	98	92	92	93	88	96	89	73	95	93	93	85	62	88	86	107
80930	COLORADO SPRINGS	107	116	93	111	108	94	102	102	96	111	98	81	104	104	100	90	69	96	88	115
80951	COLORADO SPRINGS	102	97	82	92	92	93	95	94	95	99	95	72	90	99	89	95	66	95	92	112
81001	PUEBLO	69	63	62	64	63	68	68	67	70	66	70	51	65	70	65	72	49	69	72	80
81003	PUEBLO	57	48	47	49	47	54	57	54	60	53	59	42	51	59	52	63	41	58	61	66
81004	PUEBLO	60	53	51	54	52	60	59	58	61	55	60	44	55	61	55	64	41	60	65	70
81005	PUEBLO	81	86	83	86	85	90	82	85	84	81	84	62	85	83	84	87	58	84	92	99
81006	PUEBLO	84	86	79	87	85	91	81	86	83	79	82	65	82	84	83	85	57	83	89	101
81007	PUEBLO	105	112	96	110	107	101	103	103	99	107	101	81	105	104	103	97	71	100	96	119
81008	PUEBLO	90	88	85	85	88	90	85	89	86	87	85	65	83	86	84	87	58	87	91	103
81019	COLORADO CITY	93	75	121	74	82	99	75	95	78	70	77	69	65	74	81	83	51	88	94	110
81020	AGUILAR	58	55	70	50	61	66	52	62	55	56	54	41	51	51	57	59	36	59	69	71
81021	ARLINGTON	65	45	72	45	47	69	50	62	52	40	51	51	37	51	50	57	33	58	65	76
81022	AVONDALE	85	66	82	64	67	84	66	79	71	63	70	59	56	72	64	77	47	74	81	94
81023	BEULAH	103	82	133	81	90	109	82	105	86	77	85	76	71	82	89	92	57	97	103	121
81025	BOONE	84	63	83	61	65	84	64	78	70	61	69	58	53	70	63	76	46	72	81	93
81027	BRANSON	81	56	89	55	58	85	62	77	64	50	63	63	45	63	61	70	41	72	81	94
81029	CAMPO	75	52	82	51	54	79	57	71	59	46	59	59	42	58	57	65	38	66	75	87
81036	EADS	82	59	84	58	61	86	64	80	71	56	69	61	51	70	63	78	46	74	86	94
81039	FOWLER	79	59	78	57	60	81	63	76	69	57	67	57	51	69	61	76	45	71	82	90
81040	GARDNER	78	62	100	61	68	82	62	79	65	58	64	58	54	62	67	69	43	73	78	92
81041	GRANADA	73	57	50	49	55	59	58	64	62	62	63	42	49	63	53	65	43	64	63	72
81043	HARTMAN	86	59	94	59	62	91	66	82	68	53	68	68	48	67	65	75	44	76	86	101
81044	HASTY	91	62	100	62	65	96	69	86	72	56	71	71	51	71	69	79	46	80	91	106
81045	HASWELL	87	60	96	60	63	92	67	83	69	54	69	69	49	68	66	76	44	77	88	102
81047	HOLLY	75	56	67	56	56	74	64	70	67	56	66	56	52	67	59	72	44	69	76	85
81049	KIM	98	67	107	67	70	103	75	93	78	61	77	77	55	76	74	85	50	87	98	114
81050	LA JUNTA	71	62	67	62	62	73	66	70	68	61	67	53	60	67	64	71	46	69	75	83
81052	LAMAR	71	62	60	61	60	69	65	67	68	62	67	51	59	69	61	71	46	68	71	80
81054	LAS ANIMAS	72	51	74	50	53	75	56	69	62	49	60	53	44	60	55	68	40	65	75	82
81055	LA VETA	81	65	104	64	71	85	65	82	68	61	67	60	56	64	70	72	44	76	81	95
81057	MC CLAVE	91	63	100	63	66	96	70	86	72	56	72	72	51	71	69	79	46	81	91	106
81058	MANZANOLA	75	53	77	52	56	76	55	70	61	51	60	53	44	61	55	67	40	65	73	84
81059	MODEL	81	56	87	56	59	85	62	77	65	51	64	62	46	64	61	71	42	71	81	94
81062	OLNEY SPRINGS	76	52	83	52	54	80	58	72	60	47	59	59	42	59	57	65	38	67	76	88
81063	ORDWAY	75	53	77	52	55	78	58	72	64	51	62	55	46	63	57	71	41	67	78	86
81064	PRITCHETT	70	48	77	48	51	74	54	67	56	43	55	55	39	55	53	61	36	62	70	82
81067	ROCKY FORD	70	59	62	58	59	71	61	68	65	57	64	50	54	65	59	69	43	66	72	79
81069	RYE	99	79	127	78	87	104	79	100	83	74	82	73	68	79	86	88	54	93	99	116
81071	SHERIDAN LAKE	87	60	95	60	63	92	66	82	69	54	68	68	49	68	66	75	44	77	87	101
81073	SPRINGFIELD	68	48	70	47	50	71	53	66	58	46	57	50	42	57	52	64	38	61	71	78
81076	SUGAR CITY	79	54	87	54	57	84	61	75	63	49	62	62	44	62	60	69	40	70	79	93
81081	TRINCHERA	81	56	88	56	58	85	62	77	64	50	64	63	46	63	62	70	41	71	81	94
81082	TRINIDAD	72	58	71	58	60	74	63	71	68	59	66	52	55	66	61	73	45	69	77	83
81084	TWO BUTTES	85	58	93	58	61	89	65	80	67	52	66	66	47	66	64	73	43	75	85	99
81087	VILAS	91	63	100	62	65	96	69	86	72	56	71	71	51	71	69	79	46	81	91	106
81089	WALSENBURG	67	51	72	50	54	70	55	66	60	50	58	49	46	58	55	65	39	63	71	77
81090	WALSH	75	51	82	51	54	79	57	71	59	46	59	59	42	58	57	65	38	66	75	87
81091	WESTON	70	55	88	54	61	74	56	71	59	52	58	52	48	56	60	63	38	65	70	82
81092	WILEY	86	59	94	59	62	90	65	81	68	53	67	67	48	67	65	74	44	76	86	100
81101	ALAMOSA	71	63	59	63	61	65	70	66	68	66	68	52	63	70	63	69	47	68	67	79
81102	ALAMOSA	7	5	5	5	5	5	9	6	8	7	8	6	7	8	6	8	6	7	6	8
81120	ANTONITO	64	43	63	41	43	64	46	57	52	43	51	44	35	53	43	58	34	54	61	70
81121	ARBOLES	78	62	101	61	68	82	62	79	65	58	64	58	54	62	68	70	43	73	78	92
81122	BAYFIELD	91	85	93	85	86	94	80	90	82	80	82	68	77	83	83	85	56	86	90	106
81123	BLANCA	60	43	62	42	45	61	44	56	49	41	48	42	35	49	44	54	32	52	58	67
81125	CENTER	70	59	62	53	59	62	61	66	61	61	61	49	52	61	58	61	42	64	63	75
81130	CREEDE	88	71	114	70	78	93	71	90	74	66	73	66	61	70	77	79	49	83	89	104
81132	DEL NORTE	78	57	86	55	60	81	60	75	66	55	64	56	48	64	60	72	43	70	78	89
81133	FORT GARLAND	68	49	70	47	50	69	50	63	55	46	54	48	40	55	49	61	36	58	66	75
81136	HOOPER	89	64	95	64	66	93	69	84	72	59	71	69	53	71	69	78	47	79	88	103
81137	IGNACIO	89	79	82	77	78	86	77	84	79	77	79	64	71	81	76	81	54	81	84	100
81140	LA JARA	72	51	76	49	53	74	54	68	58	47	57	53	41	58	53	64	38	63	71	82
81143	MOFFAT	65	49	79	49	53	69	51	64	53	46	53	49	42	51	54	57	35	60	65	76
81144	MONTE VISTA	75	60	74	58	62	75	64	72	66	60	66	55	54	66	62	70	44	70	75	85
81146	MOSCA	89	69	87	68	70	89	71	83	74	65	74	65	59	75	70	79	49	79	86	101
81147	PAGOSA SPRINGS	98	78	127	77	86	104	79	100	82	74	81	73	68	78	85	88	54	92	99	116
81149	SAGUACHE	68	49	74	48	52	70	51	65	55	47	54	49	41	54	51	60	36	59	67	77
81151	SANFORD	63	43	63	42	44	64	46	58	52	43	51	45	36	52	45	58	34	54	62	70
81152	SAN LUIS	51	36	52	35	38	51	37	47	41	35	41	36	30	41	37	46	27	44	49	56
81154	SOUTH FORK	97	78	125	76	85	103	78	99	81	73	80	72	67	77	84	87	53	91	98	115
81155	VILLA GROVE	77	61	99	61	68	81	62	78	64	58	64	57	53	61	67	69	42	72	77	91
81201	SALIDA	76	63	84	63	67	78	67	76	69	62	68	56	59	67	67	73	46	73	78	89
81210	ALMONT	114	92	127	93	96	111	97	110	99	92	99	85	86	98	99	102	67	106	108	130
81211	BUENA VISTA	85	73	113	72	82	94	71	89	75	70	74	62	66	70	78	79	49	83	90	102
81212	CANON CITY	75	69	74	69	71	78	71	75	73	69	72	55	68	72	71	76	49	74	81	88
81220	CIMARRON	75	60	97	59	66	79	60	77	63	56	62	56	52	60	65	67	41	71	76	89
81223	COTOPAXI	83	67	108	66	73	88	67	85	70	63	69	62	58	66	72	74	46	78	84	98
81224	CRESTED BUTTE	126	110	97	116	103	98	124	108	120	126	123	92	117	126	113	115	86	116	102	131
81226	FLORENCE	69	60	62	60	61	68	62	66	64	61	63	49	57	65	59	67	43	64	69	78
81228	GRANITE	93	89	99	86	92	96	85	92	87	90	87	65	84	86	87	89	59	90	95	108
81230	GUNNISON	78	65	70	67	64	70	83	72	78	73	78	60	71	78	72	77	55	77	73	88
81231	GUNNISON	85	54	77	57	56	69	90	74	81	71	81	63	64	78	69	80	56	81	74	91
81233	HOWARD	80	64	103	63	70	84	64	81	67	60	66	59	55	64	69	71	44	75	80	94
81235	LAKE CITY	101	81	131	80	89	107	81	103	85	76	84	75	70	80	88	90	56	95	102	119
81236	NATHROP	120	127	172	125	146	149	114	134	120	129	118	84	125	108	132	126	81	128	150	152
81239	PARLIN	109	87	140	86	96	115	87	111	91	82	90	81	75	87	94	97	60	102	109	128
81240	PENROSE	77	75	66	74	73	76	69	73	71	72	71	54	68	74	68	73	49	71	73	87
81241	PITKIN	109	88	141	86	96	116	88	111	92	82	91	81	76	87	95	98	60	103	110	129
81243	POWDERHORN	69	55	89	54	60	72	55	70	57	51	57	51	48	55	59	61	38	64	69	81
81251	TWIN LAKES	107	100	85	95	95	96	99	98	99	103	99	75	93	103	93	99	68	99	96	117
81252	WESTCLIFFE	89	71	115	70	78	94	71	90	74	67	73	66	62	71	77	79	49	83	89	105
81253	WETMORE	96	77	122	76	84	101	77	97	80	72	79	71	67	76	83	85	53	90	96	112
	COLORADO	114	114	111	115	112	109	114	111	111	116	113	88	114	113	113	110	80	112	108	130
	UNITED STATES	100	100	100	100	100	100	100	100	100	100	100	100	100	100	100	100	100	100	100	100

POPULATION CHANGE

ZIP CODE #	POST OFFICE NAME	COUNTY FIPS CODE	POPULATION 2000	POPULATION 2009	POPULATION 2014	2000-2009 ANNUAL RATE % Rate	2000-2009 ANNUAL RATE State Centile	HOUSEHOLDS 2000	HOUSEHOLDS 2009	HOUSEHOLDS 2014	HOUSEHOLDS % Annual Rate 2000-2009	HOUSEHOLDS 2009 Average HH Size	FAMILIES 2000	FAMILIES 2009	FAMILIES % Annual Rate 2000-2009
81301	DURANGO	067	24278	28297	30155	1.7	67	9883	11748	12629	1.9	2.27	5485	6364	1.6
81303	DURANGO	067	7198	7972	8353	1.1	52	2710	3037	3196	1.2	2.60	1909	2085	1.0
81320	CAHONE	033	513	561	594	1.0	50	233	261	279	1.2	2.15	136	148	0.9
81321	CORTEZ	083	13326	13975	14376	0.5	37	5142	5485	5682	0.7	2.50	3571	3743	0.5
81323	DOLORES	083	4348	4879	5152	1.3	56	1760	2016	2149	1.5	2.41	1271	1427	1.3
81324	DOVE CREEK	033	1331	1407	1439	0.6	40	552	597	616	0.9	2.36	406	433	0.7
81325	EGNAR	113	141	147	154	0.5	37	56	60	63	0.7	2.45	37	39	0.6
81326	HESPERUS	067	1812	2078	2208	1.5	62	707	819	874	1.6	2.54	518	591	1.4
81327	LEWIS	083	813	919	973	1.3	56	312	360	384	1.6	2.55	239	270	1.3
81328	MANCOS	083	3515	3965	4191	1.3	56	1402	1621	1731	1.6	2.37	978	1107	1.3
81331	PLEASANT VIEW	083	410	470	499	1.5	62	156	182	195	1.7	2.58	120	138	1.5
81334	TOWAOC	083	1431	1643	1750	1.5	62	434	507	545	1.7	3.22	341	392	1.5
81335	YELLOW JACKET	083	103	118	125	1.5	62	39	46	49	1.8	2.57	30	35	1.7
81401	MONTROSE	085	17106	22223	24918	2.9	85	7002	9047	10147	2.8	2.42	4715	6052	2.7
81403	MONTROSE	085	8758	10397	11529	1.9	70	3286	3945	4389	2.0	2.63	2571	3026	1.8
81410	AUSTIN	029	1544	1716	1804	1.1	52	628	700	739	1.2	2.35	479	525	1.0
81411	BEDROCK	085	218	280	317	2.7	82	87	113	128	2.9	2.47	58	73	2.5
81413	CEDAREDGE	029	4473	4899	5085	1.0	50	1998	2178	2263	0.9	2.24	1410	1511	0.8
81415	CRAWFORD	085	1465	1732	1866	1.8	69	604	715	770	1.8	2.42	450	522	1.6
81416	DELTA	029	11991	13058	13589	0.9	47	4421	4812	5013	0.9	2.58	3192	3410	0.7
81418	ECKERT	029	1642	2087	2304	2.6	81	645	826	917	2.7	2.50	501	632	2.5
81419	HOTCHKISS	029	3429	3880	4108	1.3	56	1386	1567	1659	1.3	2.44	980	1090	1.2
81422	NATURITA	085	560	726	821	2.8	83	231	302	343	2.9	2.40	153	194	2.6
81423	NORWOOD	113	1196	1246	1304	0.4	34	507	539	569	0.7	2.31	337	353	0.5
81424	NUCLA	085	1492	1887	2126	2.6	81	635	807	910	2.6	2.34	429	528	2.3
81425	OLATHE	085	4614	5344	5809	1.6	64	1534	1782	1941	1.6	2.92	1198	1362	1.4
81426	OPHIR	113	300	328	352	1.0	50	145	162	175	1.2	2.02	75	81	0.8
81427	OURAY	091	756	937	1026	2.3	76	351	438	481	2.4	2.12	228	279	2.2
81428	PAONIA	029	3985	4491	4745	1.3	56	1638	1854	1965	1.3	2.37	1138	1264	1.1
81430	PLACERVILLE	113	674	747	797	1.1	52	306	345	372	1.3	2.17	158	172	0.9
81431	REDVALE	085	506	644	725	2.6	81	216	278	313	2.8	2.32	146	183	2.5
81432	RIDGWAY	091	2493	3062	3346	2.2	74	1027	1267	1388	2.3	2.41	728	883	2.1
81433	SILVERTON	111	558	579	585	0.4	34	269	282	288	0.5	2.04	158	162	0.3
81434	SOMERSET	051	197	237	253	2.0	73	84	102	110	2.1	2.32	55	65	1.8
81435	TELLURIDE	113	4224	5082	5523	2.0	73	1975	2426	2660	2.2	2.09	804	970	2.0
81501	GRAND JUNCTION	077	21583	23520	25214	0.9	47	9142	9996	10747	1.0	2.18	4567	4822	0.6
81503	GRAND JUNCTION	077	11000	14044	15588	2.7	82	4245	5505	6149	2.8	2.54	3124	3929	2.5
81504	GRAND JUNCTION	077	22392	27865	31244	2.4	78	8663	10813	12178	2.4	2.55	6401	7808	2.2
81505	GRAND JUNCTION	077	6699	10017	11592	4.4	91	2700	4029	4685	4.4	2.44	1924	2807	4.2
81506	GRAND JUNCTION	077	8906	10953	12289	2.3	76	3890	4767	5356	2.2	2.25	2576	3053	1.9
81507	GRAND JUNCTION	077	12293	15319	17191	2.4	78	4823	6065	6840	2.5	2.52	3827	4717	2.3
81520	CLIFTON	077	11799	13589	14900	1.5	62	4286	4963	5460	1.6	2.72	3157	3551	1.3
81521	FRUITA	077	9034	13922	16601	4.8	93	3383	5347	6430	5.1	2.55	2471	3777	4.7
81522	GATEWAY	077	490	539	580	1.0	50	192	213	230	1.1	2.52	148	160	0.8
81523	GLADE PARK	077	595	655	704	1.0	50	232	257	278	1.1	2.53	179	194	0.9
81524	LOMA	077	1507	1979	2244	3.0	85	534	712	810	3.2	2.78	420	547	2.9
81525	MACK	077	433	539	611	2.4	78	167	209	238	2.5	2.58	131	160	2.2
81526	PALISADE	077	5291	6227	6858	1.8	69	2034	2424	2687	1.9	2.49	1469	1704	1.6
81527	WHITEWATER	077	1121	1345	1495	2.0	73	398	486	543	2.2	2.67	306	365	1.9
81601	GLENWOOD SPRINGS	045	12231	15313	17231	2.5	79	4779	5893	6605	2.3	2.55	3078	3721	2.1
81610	DINOSAUR	081	421	419	419	-0.1	19	163	160	160	-0.2	2.49	109	105	-0.4
81611	ASPEN	097	8939	9411	9589	0.6	40	4255	4480	4570	0.6	2.03	1791	1815	0.1
81615	SNOWMASS VILLAGE	097	1827	1856	1880	0.2	28	865	880	892	0.2	2.10	421	414	-0.2
81620	AVON	037	5919	7731	8774	2.9	85	2029	2636	2988	2.9	2.84	1053	1326	2.5
81621	BASALT	097	5558	6930	7521	2.4	78	2096	2588	2793	2.3	2.67	1305	1594	2.2
81623	CARBONDALE	097	13385	17099	19449	2.7	82	4678	5915	6711	2.6	2.86	3259	4025	2.3
81624	COLLBRAN	077	1527	1915	2142	2.5	79	522	672	763	2.8	2.59	391	491	2.5
81625	CRAIG	081	12180	13028	13498	0.7	43	4610	4978	5179	0.8	2.56	3312	3515	0.6
81630	DE BEQUE	045	905	1256	1436	3.6	89	341	472	541	3.6	2.64	258	348	3.3
81631	EAGLE	037	4729	5981	6826	2.6	81	1652	2046	2325	2.3	2.90	1204	1472	2.2
81632	EDWARDS	037	7470	10168	11594	3.4	88	2542	3371	3825	3.1	3.02	1662	2157	2.9
81633	DINOSAUR	081	5	5	5	0.0	22	2	2	2	0.0	2.50	1	1	0.0
81635	PARACHUTE	045	4975	6746	7840	3.3	88	2032	2743	3182	3.3	2.45	1419	1874	3.1
81637	GYPSUM	037	4806	5995	6811	2.4	78	1548	1904	2153	2.3	3.14	1211	1469	2.1
81638	HAMILTON	081	199	227	241	1.4	58	76	88	94	1.6	2.58	58	66	1.4
81639	HAYDEN	107	2298	2694	2875	1.7	67	865	1039	1118	2.0	2.58	627	737	1.8
81640	MAYBELL	081	343	363	374	0.6	40	118	124	128	0.5	2.88	83	85	0.3
81641	MEEKER	103	3301	3434	3529	0.4	34	1345	1422	1471	0.6	2.36	927	961	0.4
81642	MEREDITH	097	76	80	82	0.6	40	41	43	44	0.5	1.86	18	18	0.0
81643	MESA	077	780	963	1097	2.3	76	308	387	442	2.5	2.46	238	292	2.2
81647	NEW CASTLE	045	4358	6131	7170	3.8	90	1567	2195	2563	3.7	2.79	1199	1651	3.5
81648	RANGELY	103	2543	2840	2985	1.2	54	903	1035	1100	1.5	2.59	679	765	1.3
81650	RIFLE	103	10392	13220	15030	2.6	81	3645	4629	5267	2.6	2.78	2601	3236	2.4
81652	SILT	045	3283	4397	5102	3.2	87	1222	1626	1884	3.1	2.70	928	1209	2.9
81653	SLATER	081	43	50	54	1.6	64	17	20	22	1.8	2.40	15	17	1.4
81654	SNOWMASS	097	1303	1376	1413	0.6	40	553	584	600	0.6	2.34	300	307	0.2
81657	VAIL	037	11118	13924	15670	2.5	79	4706	5830	6526	2.3	2.38	2067	2460	1.9
	COLORADO					1.7					1.6	2.55			1.5
	UNITED STATES					1.0					1.1	2.59			0.9

ZIP CODE #	POST OFFICE NAME	RACE (%) White 2000	White 2009	Black 2000	Black 2009	Asian/Pacific 2000	Asian/Pacific 2009	% Hispanic Origin 2000	% Hispanic Origin 2009	2009 AGE DISTRIBUTION (%) 0-4	5-9	10-14	15-19	20-24	25-44	45-64	65-84	85+	18+	MEDIAN AGE 2009	% 2009 Males	% 2009 Females
81301	DURANGO	89.2	87.6	0.4	0.4	0.7	0.8	9.4	11.6	4.4	4.2	4.7	8.7	12.9	27.0	27.4	9.1	1.6	83.4	34.6	50.9	49.1
81303	DURANGO	89.2	87.3	0.2	0.2	0.3	0.3	9.9	12.5	5.4	5.4	5.9	6.6	6.9	26.5	33.2	9.4	0.8	79.4	40.1	50.7	49.3
81320	CAHONE	93.2	92.9	0.0	0.0	1.4	1.8	3.3	3.7	4.3	3.2	4.1	6.1	4.6	30.5	33.5	12.7	1.1	85.2	43.5	54.4	45.6
81321	CORTEZ	82.8	80.8	0.2	0.2	0.3	0.4	11.5	14.1	7.3	6.8	6.9	7.2	6.0	23.7	27.3	12.7	2.1	74.2	38.4	48.7	51.3
81323	DOLORES	91.0	89.5	0.1	0.1	0.2	0.3	8.1	10.4	5.3	5.8	6.8	6.2	3.6	22.1	35.4	13.4	1.3	77.5	45.1	50.2	49.8
81324	DOVE CREEK	96.1	95.7	0.1	0.1	0.1	0.1	4.1	5.2	5.3	5.5	6.0	6.4	4.9	21.2	31.9	16.3	2.4	79.3	45.5	49.6	50.4
81325	EGNAR	97.2	97.3	0.0	0.0	0.0	0.0	3.5	4.8	4.8	5.4	6.8	7.5	3.4	24.5	37.4	8.8	1.4	77.6	43.8	53.7	46.3
81326	HESPERUS	93.3	92.3	0.3	0.3	0.1	0.1	6.8	8.6	5.7	6.3	7.1	7.5	5.4	23.6	33.4	10.2	0.9	76.3	40.8	51.5	48.5
81327	LEWIS	94.0	92.7	0.0	0.0	0.4	0.4	5.2	6.9	6.3	7.3	7.7	6.1	4.0	21.2	32.5	13.6	1.2	74.6	43.2	50.9	49.1
81328	MANCOS	91.5	89.9	0.1	0.1	0.2	0.3	7.9	10.1	5.0	5.2	6.9	6.7	4.2	21.4	34.5	13.8	2.3	78.3	45.3	49.6	50.4
81331	PLEASANT VIEW	94.1	92.8	0.0	0.0	0.0	0.2	5.6	7.2	6.6	7.7	7.9	6.0	4.0	20.0	31.9	14.5	1.5	74.0	43.5	51.5	48.5
81334	TOWAOC	9.1	8.6	0.1	0.1	0.0	0.0	2.9	3.2	10.1	10.0	9.7	9.9	8.3	27.0	19.3	5.2	0.4	63.5	26.4	49.8	50.2
81335	YELLOW JACKET	94.2	93.2	0.0	0.0	0.0	0.0	5.8	7.6	6.8	7.6	7.6	5.9	4.2	19.5	32.2	14.4	1.7	72.9	43.8	51.7	48.3
81401	MONTROSE	89.7	88.0	0.3	0.4	0.6	0.7	15.7	18.9	6.5	6.4	6.6	6.5	5.5	23.0	28.3	14.4	2.9	76.3	41.4	48.7	51.3
81403	MONTROSE	92.3	90.8	0.2	0.3	0.5	0.7	12.2	15.3	6.5	6.6	7.2	7.2	4.5	22.5	32.4	11.6	1.4	74.8	41.6	49.6	50.4
81410	AUSTIN	93.6	92.2	0.1	0.1	0.6	0.8	9.1	11.7	4.7	5.0	5.8	6.5	5.1	17.7	31.6	18.9	4.8	80.3	48.7	48.8	51.2
81411	BEDROCK	93.6	92.9	0.0	0.0	0.0	0.0	5.5	7.5	6.4	6.4	6.4	7.1	5.4	22.9	28.2	15.7	1.4	75.0	41.8	50.4	49.6
81413	CEDAREDGE	96.3	95.8	0.0	0.0	0.4	0.6	4.9	6.3	4.3	4.6	4.9	4.6	4.0	15.4	35.5	23.6	3.2	83.2	53.5	49.8	50.2
81415	CRAWFORD	95.4	94.7	0.1	0.1	0.1	0.2	4.8	6.1	5.3	5.9	6.8	6.6	3.9	19.0	36.3	14.6	1.6	77.7	46.5	51.3	48.7
81416	DELTA	87.6	85.2	1.2	1.3	0.4	0.5	18.8	23.3	6.7	6.4	6.7	6.9	5.7	23.4	27.4	13.9	2.8	75.7	40.2	50.5	49.5
81418	ECKERT	94.5	93.3	0.1	0.1	0.4	0.6	7.0	9.2	4.0	4.3	4.9	5.6	4.6	18.1	33.7	21.6	3.4	83.1	51.1	48.9	51.1
81419	HOTCHKISS	94.6	93.5	0.0	0.0	0.3	0.4	8.2	10.6	5.0	5.4	5.8	5.8	4.6	20.1	35.8	15.5	2.1	80.2	47.2	50.6	49.4
81422	NATURITA	93.8	92.6	0.0	0.0	0.2	0.1	5.7	7.6	6.5	6.5	6.6	7.2	5.2	23.0	28.0	15.6	1.5	75.2	41.6	50.6	49.4
81423	NORWOOD	97.3	97.0	0.0	0.0	0.2	0.2	3.8	4.8	4.7	5.8	7.0	7.7	3.9	23.9	36.5	8.9	1.5	77.2	43.4	52.5	47.5
81424	NUCLA	95.5	94.8	0.1	0.2	0.1	0.2	2.8	3.8	5.2	5.5	5.9	6.4	5.5	21.8	32.8	15.3	1.7	79.4	44.8	50.2	49.8
81425	OLATHE	84.4	80.7	0.3	0.4	0.3	0.3	22.1	28.3	7.7	7.7	7.9	7.2	5.5	24.0	27.3	10.7	1.9	72.0	36.7	50.7	49.3
81426	OPHIR	96.0	95.7	0.0	0.0	0.7	0.9	2.7	3.4	5.5	4.6	4.3	3.7	3.7	38.1	38.1	1.8	0.3	82.3	39.8	54.9	45.1
81427	OURAY	96.6	96.4	0.1	0.1	0.4	0.4	4.8	6.0	5.0	5.7	6.4	5.8	2.8	25.3	36.1	11.4	1.6	79.1	44.4	50.4	49.6
81428	PAONIA	96.8	96.3	0.1	0.0	0.2	0.2	4.9	6.5	5.3	5.3	5.8	6.0	5.1	19.5	34.5	15.7	2.9	79.3	47.0	50.2	49.8
81430	PLACERVILLE	96.6	96.1	0.0	0.0	0.7	0.9	2.1	2.7	5.5	4.6	4.3	3.6	3.5	38.0	38.7	1.7	0.1	82.6	40.0	55.0	45.0
81431	REDVALE	95.7	95.3	0.2	0.2	0.2	0.2	2.2	3.0	5.0	5.1	5.6	6.4	5.4	21.4	34.0	15.2	1.9	80.6	45.7	50.3	49.7
81432	RIDGWAY	96.2	95.8	0.1	0.1	0.4	0.3	4.1	5.2	4.7	5.7	6.3	5.5	2.3	23.5	39.9	11.1	1.0	79.6	46.0	50.9	49.1
81433	SILVERTON	97.1	97.2	0.0	0.0	0.5	0.5	7.3	7.4	4.5	4.0	5.0	6.7	2.4	24.2	46.1	7.1	0.0	81.5	46.3	52.8	47.2
81434	SOMERSET	94.9	94.1	0.0	0.0	1.0	0.8	4.1	5.1	4.2	4.2	5.5	3.8	2.1	21.5	41.8	15.2	1.7	84.0	49.9	55.7	44.3
81435	TELLURIDE	91.7	90.4	0.4	0.4	1.1	1.3	8.7	10.5	4.1	4.5	3.7	4.1	10.9	42.2	27.4	3.0	0.2	85.4	32.9	55.1	44.9
81501	GRAND JUNCTION	89.6	87.6	0.9	1.1	1.0	1.3	14.1	17.5	6.0	5.4	5.0	8.1	9.1	27.3	23.2	12.6	3.4	80.2	36.0	49.3	50.7
81503	GRAND JUNCTION	93.1	91.0	0.4	1.0	0.4	0.5	10.1	13.0	6.1	6.2	6.6	7.1	6.5	26.6	28.6	10.9	1.4	76.8	38.6	49.5	50.5
81504	GRAND JUNCTION	92.1	90.6	0.4	0.5	0.6	0.7	10.9	13.6	7.4	7.2	7.0	7.1	6.1	26.0	26.2	11.4	1.6	73.9	36.7	48.7	51.3
81505	GRAND JUNCTION	92.9	91.3	0.3	0.3	0.6	0.7	10.4	14.4	5.2	5.8	6.2	6.8	5.6	24.0	30.8	13.9	1.8	78.9	42.4	49.9	50.1
81506	GRAND JUNCTION	95.9	95.0	0.3	0.3	0.8	1.0	4.4	5.7	4.1	4.5	5.3	5.6	4.1	17.4	32.2	21.0	5.9	82.4	50.7	46.4	53.6
81507	GRAND JUNCTION	95.8	95.0	0.2	0.2	0.7	1.0	4.5	5.6	4.3	5.3	6.4	6.2	4.2	18.9	35.5	17.0	2.1	80.0	47.8	49.1	50.9
81520	CLIFTON	88.6	86.3	0.6	0.7	0.4	0.5	13.5	16.8	9.5	8.0	7.2	7.8	8.7	27.5	21.6	8.5	1.2	70.8	30.0	48.7	51.3
81521	FRUITA	91.9	90.9	0.3	0.3	0.3	0.4	10.7	13.0	6.5	6.5	6.7	7.1	6.1	25.0	27.8	11.9	2.4	75.8	39.1	48.7	51.3
81522	GATEWAY	95.5	94.6	0.2	0.2	1.2	1.7	4.3	5.4	5.0	5.9	6.9	6.3	4.3	20.0	37.3	13.2	1.1	77.9	46.0	49.4	50.6
81523	GLADE PARK	95.5	94.4	0.2	0.3	1.3	1.7	4.4	5.6	5.0	5.8	6.9	6.3	4.4	20.3	36.9	13.3	1.1	78.0	45.9	49.5	50.5
81524	LOMA	94.6	93.5	0.1	0.2	0.5	0.7	5.6	7.2	6.1	6.8	7.5	7.3	4.1	22.1	32.7	12.1	1.3	75.0	42.3	52.2	47.8
81525	MACK	94.5	93.5	0.2	0.2	0.5	0.6	5.5	7.2	6.3	6.7	7.6	7.2	4.1	22.1	32.7	12.2	1.1	74.8	42.2	52.1	47.9
81526	PALISADE	93.9	92.6	0.2	0.2	0.7	0.9	7.9	10.0	5.6	5.5	6.1	6.6	5.5	21.4	32.3	14.4	2.6	78.8	44.5	49.1	50.9
81527	WHITEWATER	95.1	94.2	0.3	0.3	0.5	0.7	10.3	13.1	6.2	6.4	7.9	7.8	2.9	23.3	35.2	9.4	1.0	74.3	42.1	51.7	48.3
81601	GLENWOOD SPRINGS	90.5	88.8	0.2	0.2	0.8	1.0	14.3	17.6	5.9	5.6	5.7	6.4	7.5	28.1	30.7	8.9	1.3	79.1	38.2	50.3	49.7
81610	DINOSAUR	93.8	92.8	0.0	0.0	0.0	0.0	13.8	17.7	5.7	6.2	6.7	6.7	5.7	24.6	31.3	12.2	1.0	77.6	40.5	53.0	47.0
81611	ASPEN	95.1	94.1	0.6	0.7	1.4	1.8	5.4	6.8	3.6	3.5	3.7	3.7	7.6	34.2	34.5	8.7	0.6	87.0	41.0	53.2	46.8
81615	SNOWMASS VILLAGE	97.1	96.7	0.2	0.2	0.9	1.1	2.8	3.5	3.7	3.3	4.0	4.0	6.1	33.6	35.2	9.7	0.4	86.5	42.2	54.9	45.1
81620	AVON	76.7	72.8	0.6	0.7	1.0	1.2	32.5	38.6	7.8	5.6	4.2	3.8	9.1	46.5	19.0	3.8	0.1	80.4	31.4	57.4	42.6
81621	BASALT	88.5	86.2	0.3	0.3	1.1	1.4	20.0	25.5	6.8	6.5	6.6	5.9	5.4	34.0	30.1	4.3	0.4	76.2	36.2	52.4	47.6
81623	CARBONDALE	87.1	84.5	0.5	0.6	0.7	0.9	25.2	30.3	7.0	6.5	6.5	6.0	6.0	32.2	28.7	6.2	0.9	76.3	36.0	51.9	48.1
81624	COLLBRAN	93.1	92.1	1.4	1.5	0.2	0.2	7.3	9.2	4.4	6.1	7.3	14.9	4.5	18.6	31.6	10.8	1.8	73.0	40.4	51.7	48.3
81625	CRAIG	93.5	92.3	0.2	0.3	0.4	0.5	9.4	11.8	6.9	6.8	7.2	7.0	6.8	27.0	28.4	8.5	1.4	74.6	36.5	51.8	48.2
81630	DE BEQUE	94.9	93.7	0.1	0.1	0.3	0.5	5.2	7.2	5.8	6.2	7.6	6.9	4.1	21.7	32.8	13.6	1.2	75.6	43.1	51.8	48.2
81631	EAGLE	88.4	86.4	0.3	0.3	0.5	0.6	16.2	19.4	8.2	7.8	7.7	7.1	5.6	32.8	26.7	3.7	0.4	71.5	33.6	51.7	48.3
81632	EDWARDS	81.8	78.7	0.4	0.4	0.8	0.9	28.5	33.8	7.6	5.7	5.4	6.5	10.0	36.1	25.0	3.7	0.1	77.7	32.1	53.7	46.3
81633	DINOSAUR	100.0	100.0	0.0	0.0	0.0	0.0	20.0	20.0	0.0	0.0	0.0	0.0	0.0	0.0	100.0	0.0	0.0	100.0	51.3	80.0	20.0
81635	PARACHUTE	93.4	92.3	0.5	0.5	0.4	0.5	9.3	11.8	7.1	7.1	7.3	6.4	4.0	24.8	25.8	15.7	1.8	74.5	40.6	50.0	50.0
81637	GYPSUM	82.4	79.5	0.2	0.2	0.2	0.3	30.7	36.4	9.0	8.1	7.5	6.8	6.3	35.1	23.6	3.4	0.3	72.0	31.5	51.1	48.9
81638	HAMILTON	95.5	94.7	0.0	0.0	0.5	0.4	4.0	5.7	3.5	4.4	11.5	8.4	3.1	21.1	37.0	11.0	0.0	74.4	43.8	54.6	45.4
81639	HAYDEN	96.2	95.6	0.1	0.1	0.2	0.3	5.6	7.1	6.5	7.3	7.3	8.0	5.0	28.9	29.4	6.7	1.0	73.8	36.7	51.8	48.2
81640	MAYBELL	94.2	93.1	0.0	0.0	0.0	0.0	7.3	9.1	4.7	5.2	6.1	7.4	4.7	21.5	33.3	15.2	1.9	79.3	45.2	52.1	47.9
81641	MEEKER	95.8	95.1	0.1	0.1	0.2	0.3	4.6	5.8	5.9	5.9	6.4	6.1	5.4	22.9	31.8	13.4	2.2	77.7	43.0	50.2	49.8
81642	MEREDITH	91.0	91.3	1.3	1.3	1.3	1.3	6.4	8.8	2.5	3.8	5.0	7.5	3.8	31.3	40.0	5.0	1.3	82.5	42.9	56.3	43.7
81643	MESA	95.9	95.0	0.0	0.0	0.3	0.4	3.6	4.6	5.2	5.7	7.3	6.9	3.7	20.6	34.8	14.5	1.3	76.8	45.3	52.0	48.0
81647	NEW CASTLE	93.2	91.8	0.3	0.3	0.3	0.4	11.6	14.5	8.3	7.8	7.5	6.5	5.6	31.7	26.3	5.9	0.5	72.4	33.8	50.8	49.2
81648	RANGELY	93.9	93.0	0.4	0.4	0.4	0.5	5.4	6.8	5.8	5.8	5.8	10.2	8.7	27.1	27.2	8.6	0.8	77.6	34.0	49.5	50.5
81650	RIFLE	89.7	87.7	0.7	0.9	0.3	0.4	17.0	21.5	8.7	7.8	7.4	7.1	7.7	28.7	24.1	7.1	1.3	71.4	32.3	51.3	48.7
81652	SILT	92.0	90.1	0.3	0.3	0.1	0.1	11.1	14.2	7.1	7.2	7.5	7.2	5.6	27.9	29.4	7.5	0.7	73.8	37.0	52.0	48.0
81653	SLATER	100.0	100.0	0.0	0.0	0.0	0.0	11.9	14.0	4.0	6.0	10.0	6.0	4.0	32.0	34.0	2.0	2.0	76.0	40.7	58.0	42.0
81654	SNOWMASS	93.9	92.9	0.7	0.7	0.6	0.8	8.3	10.4	4.2	4.1	4.9	5.9	5.9	28.3	39.0	7.2	0.5	82.6	43.0	52.8	47.2
81657	VAIL	90.0	88.4	0.4	0.5	1.3	1.6	14.8	17.4	4.7	3.6	2.9	3.5	11.9	45.4	23.1	4.6	0.3	86.9	32.4	56.0	44.0
	COLORADO	82.8	80.7	3.8	3.8	2.3	2.9	17.1	20.2	6.9	6.7	6.7	6.9	7.0	29.0	26.5	8.8	1.4	75.7	35.9	50.2	49.8
	UNITED STATES	75.1	72.0	12.3	12.7	3.8	4.6	12.5	15.7	6.8	6.7	6.6	7.1	6.9	27.0	26.0	10.9	1.9	75.7	36.9	49.2	50.8

#	POST OFFICE NAME	2009 Per Capita Income	2009 HH Income Base	2009 HOUSEHOLD INCOME DISTRIBUTION (%) Less than $25,000	$25,000 to $49,999	$50,000 to $99,999	$100,000 to $149,999	$150,000 or More	MEDIAN HOUSEHOLD INCOME 2009	2014	2009 National Centile	2009 State Centile	2009 Home Value Base	2009 HOME VALUE DISTRIBUTION (%) Less than $50,000	$50,000 to $89,999	$90,000 to $174,999	$175,000 to $399,999	$400,000 or More	2009 Median Home Value
81301	DURANGO	28246	11748	22.5	28.4	34.0	8.9	6.2	49098	52099	59	49	7172	7.8	2.2	6.2	48.3	35.5	331110
81303	DURANGO	25988	3037	18.8	25.0	39.2	11.9	5.1	55998	59658	73	62	2280	7.3	4.6	10.5	42.1	35.4	314653
81320	CAHONE	26151	261	27.2	25.3	37.9	6.5	3.1	47948	47911	56	46	184	9.2	10.3	38.0	37.0	5.4	164063
81321	CORTEZ	19682	5485	28.8	33.2	31.1	4.7	2.1	38839	40292	29	20	3959	9.0	7.5	39.2	35.7	8.6	162878
81323	DOLORES	20795	2016	28.9	32.1	30.8	5.6	2.7	39538	41343	31	22	1580	7.6	6.5	19.7	48.6	17.5	232960
81324	DOVE CREEK	18888	597	34.2	30.8	30.8	2.8	1.3	35432	36551	19	11	472	18.2	26.3	38.8	15.5	1.3	97647
81325	EGNAR	21939	60	21.7	28.3	43.3	6.7	0.0	50000	52159	61	51	42	4.8	0.0	16.7	54.8	23.8	235000
81326	HESPERUS	24209	819	20.6	28.1	36.8	11.5	3.1	51170	54291	64	54	674	2.7	3.7	18.5	43.2	31.9	284848
81327	LEWIS	20849	360	17.8	32.5	42.5	5.3	1.9	49583	50311	60	51	311	1.0	7.1	26.7	45.7	19.6	222024
81328	MANCOS	22777	1621	27.2	29.2	32.5	8.2	2.8	44090	46078	46	34	1235	6.5	4.9	24.0	48.0	16.6	224189
81331	PLEASANT VIEW	20530	182	17.0	29.1	46.2	5.5	2.2	51396	52267	65	56	158	0.0	5.1	27.8	47.5	19.6	227083
81334	TOWAOC	11308	507	50.5	27.2	17.8	2.2	2.4	24708	24839	3	2	315	35.6	17.1	35.2	7.0	5.1	83462
81335	YELLOW JACKET	20443	46	17.4	28.3	50.0	4.3	0.0	51176	52585	64	54	40	0.0	5.0	27.5	47.5	20.0	228571
81401	MONTROSE	21130	9047	26.8	29.7	35.0	6.7	1.8	45127	46948	49	38	6406	7.2	2.9	24.8	53.6	11.6	207473
81403	MONTROSE	21431	3945	21.9	29.5	37.7	8.5	2.5	48886	50599	59	49	3298	9.2	5.7	16.9	46.9	21.3	239845
81410	AUSTIN	20581	700	26.3	33.4	35.1	4.0	1.1	44261	44315	46	35	577	3.3	8.5	27.0	51.0	10.2	200872
81411	BEDROCK	15511	113	38.9	32.7	26.5	1.8	0.0	33053	35000	13	6	86	22.1	20.9	33.7	19.8	3.5	102273
81413	CEDAREDGE	23067	2178	28.2	31.4	32.2	5.8	2.4	41654	43127	38	28	1744	3.2	6.3	26.3	47.4	16.9	224208
81415	CRAWFORD	22357	715	29.1	27.3	33.8	6.0	3.8	45048	46156	48	38	557	5.6	5.2	23.5	44.0	21.7	234766
81416	DELTA	18156	4812	29.9	34.4	28.6	5.6	1.6	37874	38483	26	18	3534	7.8	4.4	40.4	36.0	11.4	171383
81418	ECKERT	19604	826	26.3	33.8	35.5	2.7	1.8	42369	44210	41	30	695	0.7	2.2	29.8	63.5	3.9	204970
81419	HOTCHKISS	20012	1567	31.9	29.2	32.0	4.9	2.0	39972	41294	32	23	1209	7.5	4.6	28.0	40.5	19.3	215848
81422	NATURITA	16022	302	37.7	33.1	26.8	1.7	0.7	34115	35568	16	9	231	21.6	20.3	34.6	19.9	3.5	103629
81423	NORWOOD	23433	539	23.2	28.4	39.7	7.1	1.7	48370	51771	57	47	374	6.7	2.9	20.1	48.1	22.2	226119
81424	NUCLA	19521	807	29.2	34.6	30.9	4.3	1.0	37571	38733	25	17	615	10.6	15.3	33.8	29.6	10.7	149836
81425	OLATHE	14970	1782	31.4	32.9	32.3	2.5	0.8	37643	38516	26	18	1305	6.8	4.7	38.5	38.3	11.7	175111
81426	OPHIR	44882	162	5.6	18.5	45.1	22.2	8.6	72905	74717	88	82	111	0.0	3.6	1.8	25.2	69.4	512931
81427	OURAY	29631	438	20.1	35.6	32.4	6.4	5.5	46096	47491	52	40	311	9.6	2.3	4.8	37.6	45.7	381757
81428	PAONIA	20749	1854	28.0	31.2	33.0	6.3	1.6	40303	41727	34	24	1428	3.7	3.9	30.3	49.6	12.5	207143
81430	PLACERVILLE	41746	345	5.5	18.0	45.8	22.6	8.1	72916	75553	88	83	240	0.0	3.3	1.7	23.8	71.3	525735
81431	REDVALE	20358	278	27.3	34.9	31.7	5.0	1.1	38190	39402	27	18	212	7.5	14.2	34.0	32.1	12.3	161364
81432	RIDGWAY	27348	1267	20.2	27.8	38.1	8.4	5.5	51446	52776	65	56	922	4.7	2.2	5.4	31.5	56.3	441135
81433	SILVERTON	20532	282	34.4	35.5	26.2	1.4	2.5	36166	37121	21	13	190	2.6	2.6	42.6	46.8	5.3	180000
81434	SOMERSET	25912	102	23.5	36.3	29.4	5.9	4.9	40876	41344	36	25	72	0.0	13.9	18.1	33.3	34.7	321429
81435	TELLURIDE	42684	2426	16.3	19.6	37.4	16.6	10.1	65139	65693	83	75	1037	0.4	0.1	2.1	28.1	69.3	737981
81501	GRAND JUNCTION	18544	9996	37.6	32.4	25.7	3.3	1.1	32263	33618	12	5	4946	5.5	4.5	49.3	38.8	1.9	163998
81503	GRAND JUNCTION	21336	5505	18.1	35.0	40.0	5.3	1.6	47393	49900	55	44	4244	3.9	3.9	34.5	52.7	5.0	185579
81504	GRAND JUNCTION	21175	10813	19.1	33.4	39.7	6.2	1.7	47659	50415	56	45	8480	4.5	6.2	30.9	57.0	1.4	186222
81505	GRAND JUNCTION	26467	4029	23.2	30.3	31.8	8.4	6.4	46356	49260	52	41	3046	10.6	4.7	15.6	44.4	24.7	262977
81506	GRAND JUNCTION	32473	4767	16.9	26.3	38.3	11.0	7.5	57337	61050	74	63	3564	1.0	3.1	6.0	70.1	19.8	281961
81507	GRAND JUNCTION	32855	6065	10.6	20.5	44.4	17.0	7.6	66048	68063	84	77	5208	0.8	1.3	7.3	63.9	26.7	302102
81520	CLIFTON	16449	4963	28.5	33.5	34.4	3.1	0.5	41565	43586	38	28	3054	21.8	7.4	38.2	28.9	3.7	146558
81521	FRUITA	19602	5347	26.6	33.9	32.1	5.5	1.9	41968	44455	39	29	4225	3.0	4.4	30.8	50.0	11.8	200581
81522	GATEWAY	24822	213	14.1	31.9	43.2	8.9	1.9	53408	56255	69	58	176	5.7	1.1	8.5	68.8	15.9	286538
81523	GLADE PARK	24682	257	14.0	31.9	42.8	8.9	2.3	53580	57262	69	58	213	5.6	0.9	8.5	69.5	15.5	286719
81524	LOMA	20073	712	25.0	29.8	33.0	8.7	3.5	45251	47912	49	39	590	2.7	1.9	17.6	52.2	25.6	295977
81525	MACK	21569	209	25.8	30.1	31.6	8.6	3.8	44251	47007	46	35	173	3.5	2.3	18.5	50.9	24.9	289423
81526	PALISADE	20802	2424	27.0	32.4	32.0	5.6	3.0	41997	44279	39	30	1743	10.6	4.3	19.8	49.3	16.0	223523
81527	WHITEWATER	19799	486	26.5	27.6	38.5	5.3	2.1	46827	49236	54	42	408	0.0	6.4	20.1	52.7	20.8	275000
81601	GLENWOOD SPRINGS	28518	5893	12.7	28.1	40.2	12.4	6.7	59839	63125	77	68	3714	3.5	2.3	8.9	29.9	55.4	430455
81610	DINOSAUR	16592	160	34.4	35.0	28.8	1.9	0.0	38713	42018	29	19	121	33.1	27.3	34.7	2.5	2.5	74375
81611	ASPEN	51910	4480	10.6	17.3	34.8	22.5	14.8	79861	80435	92	87	2461	0.6	0.3	9.3	20.8	69.0	1000001
81615	SNOWMASS VILLAGE	46944	880	9.7	19.3	33.3	22.6	15.1	75343	77765	90	84	489	0.0	0.0	4.5	14.7	80.8	1000001
81620	AVON	38235	2636	7.9	17.4	33.9	25.6	15.1	82295	82412	93	89	1375	1.2	7.8	5.5	22.6	63.0	540119
81621	BASALT	35039	2588	7.6	16.8	40.4	25.7	9.5	79174	79524	92	86	1750	3.2	5.8	13.6	9.3	68.1	581384
81623	CARBONDALE	30150	5915	10.9	18.1	41.9	20.5	8.7	75378	76275	90	84	3980	3.3	3.9	7.3	19.8	65.7	512174
81624	COLLBRAN	20180	672	24.6	33.6	34.2	4.8	2.8	41543	45290	38	27	509	6.9	1.0	16.9	52.3	23.0	242722
81625	CRAIG	22723	4978	18.4	26.5	45.4	8.5	1.2	54086	56294	70	59	3542	6.0	10.8	37.3	40.7	5.3	166724
81630	DE BEQUE	19379	472	25.6	30.1	36.7	5.7	1.9	44749	47663	47	37	354	11.3	4.0	19.5	42.9	22.3	220588
81631	EAGLE	36070	2046	7.8	10.1	37.8	30.7	13.5	90644	91571	95	93	1401	3.7	1.2	1.2	17.2	76.7	575423
81632	EDWARDS	37221	3371	5.5	12.7	38.1	28.1	15.7	88675	90965	95	92	2343	8.0	3.7	3.4	12.7	72.3	644093
81633	DINOSAUR	0	0	0.0	0.0	0.0	0.0	0.0	0	0	0	0	0	0.0	0.0	0.0	0.0	0.0	0
81635	PARACHUTE	21424	2743	20.4	33.0	40.2	5.3	1.1	46885	49719	54	42	1493	2.8	4.8	15.0	57.9	19.6	256052
81637	GYPSUM	30271	1904	5.3	13.1	46.6	24.6	10.5	79693	79566	92	87	1381	6.7	3.1	5.8	33.5	51.0	404720
81638	HAMILTON	18220	88	25.0	38.6	31.8	4.5	0.0	43860	45348	45	34	71	7.0	7.0	16.9	36.6	32.4	245000
81639	HAYDEN	24213	1039	13.8	28.2	44.9	11.8	1.3	57897	60000	75	65	745	9.4	3.1	14.5	55.8	17.2	228459
81640	MAYBELL	17981	124	34.7	21.8	39.5	0.0	4.0	46225	47658	52	41	93	14.0	21.5	17.2	36.6	10.8	162500
81641	MEEKER	19970	1422	27.4	30.0	38.5	3.4	0.6	42850	45713	42	31	1005	6.2	4.7	33.0	44.6	11.5	188030
81642	MEREDITH	47877	43	9.3	25.6	44.2	9.3	11.6	60685	61928	78	70	23	0.0	8.7	30.4	0.0	60.9	1000001
81643	MESA	20513	387	26.9	29.2	36.7	5.4	1.8	44151	47554	46	35	310	11.6	3.9	18.4	43.2	22.9	223864
81647	NEW CASTLE	28506	2195	6.7	19.5	52.8	15.4	5.6	73131	74262	88	83	1702	6.0	3.4	10.5	52.2	27.9	321174
81648	RANGELY	23214	1035	16.4	29.4	41.1	10.6	2.5	53215	54814	68	58	732	10.4	12.3	50.5	24.6	2.2	128070
81650	RIFLE	22545	4629	14.6	26.2	47.8	9.1	2.3	57854	61050	75	64	2971	8.1	11.3	10.9	52.3	17.4	254281
81652	SILT	24133	1626	13.9	27.2	48.2	8.1	2.6	57630	60892	75	64	1263	2.1	2.1	11.0	55.8	29.0	294375
81653	SLATER	22118	20	15.0	30.0	55.0	0.0	0.0	60000	61928	77	68	17	11.8	0.0	11.8	70.6	5.9	225000
81654	SNOWMASS	40773	584	6.5	21.1	40.9	20.2	11.3	75159	73751	89	84	402	1.0	2.2	9.5	24.6	62.7	647321
81657	VAIL	44116	5830	7.0	17.3	34.7	24.0	16.9	83835	83909	93	90	3080	0.7	0.7	1.4	27.5	69.7	575615
	COLORADO	30807		15.5	22.5	37.5	15.8	8.6	62597	65813				4.4	4.3	23.6	52.9	14.8	220998
	UNITED STATES	27277		20.9	24.4	35.3	11.7	7.6	54719	56938				9.3	13.1	31.6	32.6	13.5	162279

ZIP CODE #	POST OFFICE NAME	FINANCIAL SERVICES: Auto Loan	Home Loan	Invest-ments	Retire-ment Plans	THE HOME: Home Improvements: Home Repair	Lawn & Garden	Furnishings: Comput-ers & Hard-ware-Personal	Major Appli-ances	TV, Radio, Sound Equip-ment	Furni-ture	ENTERTAINMENT: Dine out/ Carry out	Sports Equip-ment	Fees & Tickets	Toys & Games	Travel	Cable TV	PERSONAL: Apparel & Services	Auto Repairs	Health Insur-ance	Pets & Supplies
81301	DURANGO	97	85	86	87	84	87	99	90	96	93	96	72	90	96	90	95	67	94	91	108
81303	DURANGO	98	99	91	100	97	97	98	96	96	98	97	74	97	98	96	96	68	96	95	114
81320	CAHONE	88	76	88	76	76	88	78	84	81	75	81	65	72	81	77	84	55	82	87	101
81321	CORTEZ	77	66	71	66	67	75	69	74	72	66	71	55	63	72	67	74	48	72	76	87
81323	DOLORES	84	67	108	66	74	89	67	85	70	63	69	62	58	67	73	75	46	79	84	99
81324	DOVE CREEK	79	57	82	55	59	81	58	74	65	54	64	56	47	64	58	71	42	68	77	88
81325	EGNAR	90	72	116	71	79	95	72	91	75	67	74	67	62	71	78	80	49	84	90	106
81326	HESPERUS	95	91	82	89	89	91	86	89	88	89	88	66	84	91	84	89	61	87	89	106
81327	LEWIS	93	67	108	67	71	98	72	90	75	61	74	72	56	73	74	82	49	84	94	109
81328	MANCOS	90	73	116	72	80	95	73	92	76	68	75	67	63	72	79	81	50	85	90	106
81331	PLEASANT VIEW	95	65	104	65	68	100	72	90	75	59	74	74	53	74	72	82	48	84	95	111
81334	TOWAOC	58	51	41	44	49	45	50	53	52	56	53	35	46	53	47	52	37	53	49	58
81335	YELLOW JACKET	94	65	103	64	68	99	72	89	74	58	74	74	52	73	71	81	48	83	94	110
81401	MONTROSE	80	69	79	69	71	80	71	78	74	69	73	57	65	73	70	77	50	76	81	91
81403	MONTROSE	92	77	107	75	81	94	77	92	80	74	79	68	68	78	80	83	53	86	91	107
81410	AUSTIN	84	63	89	61	66	87	64	80	70	61	69	59	53	69	64	77	46	74	84	95
81411	BEDROCK	68	49	70	47	51	70	50	64	56	47	55	48	40	55	50	61	36	59	67	76
81413	CEDAREDGE	78	72	99	68	80	88	69	83	72	72	71	56	67	67	76	77	48	79	89	95
81415	CRAWFORD	90	73	111	72	79	94	73	90	76	69	75	66	64	73	77	80	50	84	89	105
81416	DELTA	76	59	77	59	61	78	64	74	68	58	67	56	54	67	63	74	45	71	79	88
81418	ECKERT	82	65	103	64	71	87	65	83	69	62	68	60	57	66	70	74	45	77	83	96
81419	HOTCHKISS	82	64	100	63	69	86	65	82	69	60	68	60	55	66	69	74	45	76	83	96
81422	NATURITA	69	49	70	48	51	70	50	64	56	47	55	48	40	56	50	62	36	59	67	76
81423	NORWOOD	90	72	117	71	79	96	72	92	76	68	75	67	63	72	78	81	50	85	91	107
81424	NUCLA	81	58	84	57	61	83	60	76	66	56	65	57	48	66	59	73	43	70	79	91
81425	OLATHE	74	59	64	58	59	73	60	68	63	57	63	52	51	65	57	68	42	64	71	81
81426	OPHIR	115	140	162	143	153	121	135	132	119	144	120	106	147	116	149	110	89	129	112	148
81427	OURAY	105	84	136	83	93	111	84	107	88	79	87	78	73	84	91	94	58	99	106	124
81428	PAONIA	80	66	94	65	71	83	67	80	70	64	69	59	60	68	70	74	46	76	81	93
81430	PLACERVILLE	113	141	165	144	156	122	135	133	118	144	118	106	147	114	150	108	88	128	112	148
81431	REDVALE	84	60	86	58	63	86	62	79	69	58	67	59	50	68	61	76	45	72	82	94
81432	RIDGWAY	107	89	140	88	98	115	88	111	92	85	91	80	79	87	96	98	61	102	110	128
81433	SILVERTON	70	56	90	55	61	74	56	71	59	52	58	52	48	56	61	62	38	66	70	82
81434	SOMERSET	100	80	130	79	88	106	80	102	84	75	83	75	70	80	87	90	55	94	101	118
81435	TELLURIDE	120	118	127	128	120	107	133	115	125	132	129	98	134	127	130	120	94	122	108	137
81501	GRAND JUNCTION	59	48	49	50	48	54	60	55	61	55	60	43	53	60	53	62	42	59	60	66
81503	GRAND JUNCTION	82	77	78	77	75	83	76	80	77	74	77	61	73	78	76	79	53	78	82	95
81504	GRAND JUNCTION	81	78	73	77	76	79	76	78	77	78	78	59	75	79	75	78	53	77	78	92
81505	GRAND JUNCTION	94	94	102	94	97	102	90	97	91	90	91	71	90	90	94	94	63	94	101	113
81506	GRAND JUNCTION	95	109	117	109	114	115	99	106	102	103	102	74	110	97	110	106	71	104	118	121
81507	GRAND JUNCTION	110	130	131	132	133	128	114	121	113	120	113	88	127	111	126	113	80	116	121	139
81520	CLIFTON	69	61	55	60	58	60	65	62	65	66	65	49	60	67	60	65	45	64	62	75
81521	FRUITA	78	71	68	70	70	75	71	74	72	70	72	55	67	74	68	74	49	72	75	87
81522	GATEWAY	87	98	84	101	95	96	88	91	86	88	87	71	93	88	93	86	61	88	90	107
81523	GLADE PARK	87	98	85	101	95	96	88	91	86	88	87	71	94	89	93	86	61	88	90	107
81524	LOMA	99	69	108	69	72	104	76	94	79	62	78	78	57	78	76	86	51	88	99	116
81525	MACK	99	68	109	68	72	105	76	94	79	62	78	78	56	77	76	86	51	88	100	116
81526	PALISADE	76	73	82	75	76	81	73	78	73	72	73	58	71	72	74	75	50	76	80	91
81527	WHITEWATER	88	71	113	70	78	93	71	90	74	67	73	66	62	71	77	79	49	83	89	104
81601	GLENWOOD SPRINGS	99	105	105	108	106	98	107	101	102	108	103	81	110	101	109	99	73	103	98	119
81610	DINOSAUR	74	53	76	51	55	75	54	69	60	50	59	52	43	60	54	66	39	63	72	82
81611	ASPEN	138	150	168	160	157	138	158	145	148	159	151	119	167	147	163	143	111	149	135	169
81615	SNOWMASS VILLAGE	123	141	166	150	152	126	147	135	133	150	136	112	157	130	156	125	101	137	120	155
81620	AVON	164	140	129	151	133	126	166	141	160	166	164	121	156	167	151	153	116	154	135	172
81621	BASALT	135	143	139	143	142	123	138	134	128	146	130	108	141	133	140	121	93	131	118	153
81623	CARBONDALE	120	129	129	131	130	114	127	122	119	132	121	98	131	121	129	113	87	121	110	141
81624	COLLBRAN	88	70	114	69	77	93	71	90	74	66	73	65	61	70	76	79	48	83	88	104
81625	CRAIG	87	83	76	82	81	84	83	84	84	83	84	64	80	86	80	85	58	84	85	99
81630	DE BEQUE	84	68	103	67	73	86	70	84	72	66	71	62	61	69	73	76	48	79	83	98
81631	EAGLE	157	175	146	170	165	143	153	153	143	167	146	122	160	154	153	134	103	144	130	173
81632	EDWARDS	156	161	166	167	164	141	167	155	155	174	157	127	170	157	168	146	113	158	138	180
81633	DINOSAUR	0	0	0	0	0	0	0	0	0	0	0	0	0	0	0	0	0	0	0	0
81635	PARACHUTE	86	70	102	69	75	86	72	85	74	69	74	63	63	72	75	77	49	81	84	99
81637	GYPSUM	145	156	126	149	145	129	139	138	131	150	134	109	141	142	136	125	94	132	121	158
81638	HAMILTON	84	58	92	58	61	89	64	80	67	52	66	66	47	65	64	73	43	74	84	98
81639	HAYDEN	97	94	84	92	91	93	88	92	88	91	89	69	85	92	86	89	61	89	90	109
81640	MAYBELL	93	64	100	64	67	97	70	88	74	59	73	71	52	73	70	81	48	81	92	107
81641	MEEKER	76	63	77	64	66	79	65	75	68	59	67	57	57	67	66	72	45	71	78	89
81642	MEREDITH	146	120	190	119	132	155	120	150	124	114	123	110	106	118	130	131	82	139	147	173
81643	MESA	84	68	109	66	74	89	68	86	71	63	70	63	59	67	73	75	46	79	85	100
81647	NEW CASTLE	120	129	106	124	121	109	116	115	110	124	112	91	117	118	114	105	78	110	102	132
81648	RANGELY	92	91	80	90	86	90	87	88	86	87	87	69	85	89	85	87	60	87	88	105
81650	RIFLE	91	89	81	89	86	84	92	87	90	91	91	69	90	92	89	89	64	89	86	103
81652	SILT	101	99	87	97	96	97	91	96	92	95	93	71	90	96	89	94	64	92	93	113
81653	SLATER	74	84	72	86	81	82	75	78	73	75	74	61	80	75	79	74	52	75	77	91
81654	SNOWMASS	133	140	166	143	149	133	140	141	130	144	130	112	142	128	148	124	93	138	126	161
81657	VAIL	141	132	141	143	133	116	161	135	148	156	154	119	155	149	154	139	111	148	124	162
	COLORADO	114	114	111	115	112	109	114	111	111	116	113	88	114	113	113	110	80	112	108	130
	UNITED STATES	100	100	100	100	100	100	100	100	100	100	100	100	100	100	100	100	100	100	100	100

#	POST OFFICE NAME	COUNTY FIPS CODE	POPULATION 2000	POPULATION 2009	POPULATION 2014	2000-2009 ANNUAL RATE % Rate	2000-2009 ANNUAL RATE State Centile	HOUSEHOLDS 2000	HOUSEHOLDS 2009	HOUSEHOLDS 2014	HOUSEHOLDS % Annual Rate 2000-2009	HOUSEHOLDS 2009 Average HH Size	FAMILIES 2000	FAMILIES 2009	FAMILIES % Annual Rate 2000-2009
06001	AVON	003	16042	17847	18555	1.2	90	6315	7017	7296	1.1	2.52	4548	5032	1.1
06002	BLOOMFIELD	003	19397	20515	20978	0.6	61	7873	8462	8710	0.8	2.36	5134	5430	0.6
06010	BRISTOL	003	60156	60633	60800	0.1	24	24914	25287	25419	0.2	2.37	16204	16264	0.0
06013	BURLINGTON	003	8364	9228	9557	1.1	87	2907	3232	3360	1.2	2.85	2472	2734	1.1
06016	BROAD BROOK	003	5201	6210	6602	1.9	98	2064	2491	2660	2.1	2.47	1429	1702	1.9
06018	CANAAN	005	2699	2811	2847	0.4	46	1140	1200	1221	0.6	2.26	722	749	0.4
06019	CANTON	003	8807	9988	10441	1.4	92	3501	4017	4217	1.5	2.46	2483	2818	1.4
06021	COLEBROOK	005	351	350	346	0.0	12	139	140	139	0.1	2.50	103	103	0.0
06023	EAST BERLIN	003	1385	1383	1409	0.0	12	492	494	504	0.0	2.76	379	378	0.0
06024	EAST CANAAN	005	651	671	672	0.3	38	203	212	213	0.5	2.90	143	148	0.4
06026	EAST GRANBY	003	4673	4997	5121	0.7	66	1817	1960	2016	0.8	2.55	1334	1425	0.7
06027	EAST HARTLAND	003	1430	1615	1690	1.3	91	498	569	597	1.5	2.82	415	471	1.4
06029	ELLINGTON	013	12934	14290	14869	1.1	87	5199	5806	6071	1.2	2.45	3469	3819	1.0
06031	FALLS VILLAGE	005	1554	1556	1553	0.0	12	661	669	669	0.1	2.28	427	426	0.0
06032	FARMINGTON	003	17581	18939	19435	0.8	74	7163	7753	7984	0.9	2.40	4694	5038	0.8
06033	GLASTONBURY	003	26666	27558	27883	0.4	46	10404	10824	10981	0.4	2.52	7527	7773	0.3
06035	GRANBY	003	7299	7639	7760	0.5	54	2750	2897	2950	0.6	2.60	2093	2185	0.5
06037	BERLIN	003	16856	18238	18720	0.9	79	6315	6867	7060	0.9	2.64	4788	5194	0.9
06039	LAKEVILLE	005	2040	2115	2132	0.4	46	890	929	938	0.5	2.21	545	560	0.3
06040	MANCHESTER	003	33434	33916	34090	0.2	29	13967	14228	14321	0.2	2.32	8368	8432	0.1
06042	MANCHESTER	003	21272	22315	22784	0.5	54	9217	9805	10068	0.7	2.26	5631	5890	0.5
06043	BOLTON	013	5132	5366	5441	0.5	54	1948	2062	2101	0.6	2.60	1477	1546	0.5
06051	NEW BRITAIN	003	28076	28353	28406	0.1	24	11560	11627	11649	0.1	2.41	6469	6413	-0.1
06052	NEW BRITAIN	003	8058	7993	7971	-0.1	5	3276	3268	3266	0.0	2.31	2016	1983	-0.2
06053	NEW BRITAIN	003	35397	35142	35021	-0.1	5	13719	13686	13673	0.0	2.39	8456	8306	-0.2
06057	NEW HARTFORD	005	6082	6341	6416	0.5	54	2227	2340	2376	0.5	2.70	1749	1823	0.4
06058	NORFOLK	005	1791	1907	1940	0.7	66	724	778	796	0.8	2.44	497	529	0.7
06060	NORTH GRANBY	003	2190	2443	2545	1.2	90	731	823	860	1.3	2.97	638	714	1.2
06062	PLAINVILLE	003	17235	17333	17350	0.1	24	7348	7439	7463	0.1	2.30	4614	4611	0.0
06063	BARKHAMSTED	005	3243	3432	3497	0.6	61	1225	1308	1338	0.7	2.62	955	1012	0.6
06065	RIVERTON	005	667	722	744	0.9	79	249	272	282	1.0	2.65	195	211	0.9
06066	VERNON ROCKVILLE	013	28022	29691	30283	0.6	61	12255	13114	13452	0.7	2.23	7264	7689	0.6
06067	ROCKY HILL	003	17963	19355	19878	0.8	74	7557	8145	8368	0.8	2.27	4520	4819	0.7
06068	SALISBURY	005	1492	1542	1554	0.4	46	644	674	682	0.5	2.18	378	389	0.3
06069	SHARON	005	2836	2927	2940	0.3	38	1179	1233	1241	0.5	2.26	732	754	0.3
06070	SIMSBURY	003	15625	15968	16088	0.2	29	5778	5958	6022	0.3	2.65	4444	4541	0.2
06071	SOMERS	013	10704	12421	12876	1.6	95	2983	3382	3562	1.4	2.77	2385	2679	1.3
06073	SOUTH GLASTONBURY	003	5214	5670	5850	0.9	79	1854	2023	2092	0.9	2.80	1453	1577	0.9
06074	SOUTH WINDSOR	003	24411	25447	25954	0.5	54	8904	9360	9568	0.5	2.70	6767	7046	0.4
06076	STAFFORD SPRINGS	013	11612	12655	13127	0.9	79	4547	5012	5229	1.1	2.50	3215	3507	0.9
06078	SUFFIELD	003	10309	10769	10902	0.5	54	3470	3664	3727	0.6	2.48	2423	2533	0.5
06081	TARIFFVILLE	003	1371	1496	1550	0.9	79	618	681	707	1.1	2.20	377	410	0.9
06082	ENFIELD	003	45162	45161	45126	0.0	12	16402	16508	16539	0.1	2.50	11382	11344	0.0
06084	TOLLAND	013	13225	14945	15653	1.3	91	4616	5279	5557	1.5	2.81	3809	4320	1.4
06085	UNIONVILLE	003	5575	5916	6042	0.6	61	2111	2250	2302	0.7	2.63	1492	1570	0.6
06088	EAST WINDSOR	003	4667	5010	5178	0.8	74	2030	2203	2284	0.9	2.18	1144	1221	0.7
06089	WEATOGUE	003	2600	2688	2723	0.4	46	959	997	1012	0.4	2.70	736	759	0.3
06090	WEST GRANBY	003	925	1083	1145	1.7	96	329	390	414	1.9	2.76	282	333	1.8
06091	WEST HARTLAND	003	150	164	169	1.0	84	53	58	61	1.0	2.83	42	47	1.2
06092	WEST SIMSBURY	003	3638	3692	3702	0.2	29	1172	1194	1200	0.2	3.04	1036	1051	0.2
06093	WEST SUFFIELD	003	3248	3424	3494	0.6	61	1191	1266	1295	0.7	2.70	929	980	0.6
06095	WINDSOR	003	28334	29123	29378	0.3	38	10613	10973	11095	0.4	2.60	7624	7817	0.3
06096	WINDSOR LOCKS	003	12043	12377	12497	0.3	38	4935	5115	5176	0.4	2.41	3306	3379	0.2
06098	WINSTED	005	11518	11828	11893	0.3	38	4715	4900	4951	0.4	2.40	3101	3178	0.3
06103	HARTFORD	003	738	1000	1103	3.3	99	361	557	637	4.8	1.53	68	105	4.8
06105	HARTFORD	003	19735	20167	20239	0.2	29	9713	9756	9770	0.0	2.00	4018	3965	-0.1
06106	HARTFORD	003	40143	41249	41511	0.3	38	13791	14006	14084	0.2	2.73	8581	8618	0.0
06107	WEST HARTFORD	003	18408	18657	18767	0.1	24	7454	7614	7684	0.2	2.42	5213	5279	0.1
06108	EAST HARTFORD	003	24111	24187	24142	0.0	12	9585	9562	9548	0.0	2.47	5858	5772	-0.2
06109	WETHERSFIELD	003	26399	26107	26013	-0.1	5	11250	11212	11199	0.0	2.30	7435	7324	-0.2
06110	WEST HARTFORD	003	12225	12283	12273	0.1	24	4994	5009	5014	0.0	2.42	3232	3200	-0.1
06111	NEWINGTON	003	29267	29534	29617	0.1	24	12001	12232	12316	0.2	2.37	8245	8305	0.1
06112	HARTFORD	003	21695	24820	24904	1.5	94	7474	7594	7642	0.2	2.90	5357	5389	0.1
06114	HARTFORD	003	26341	27422	27547	0.4	46	9477	9513	9525	0.0	2.83	6325	6270	-0.1
06117	WEST HARTFORD	003	17407	15110	15184	-1.5	0	5286	5395	5444	0.2	2.51	3830	3879	0.1
06118	EAST HARTFORD	003	25464	25298	25194	-0.1	5	10621	10629	10617	0.0	2.36	6970	6889	-0.1
06119	WEST HARTFORD	003	15167	15251	15269	0.1	24	6677	6718	6732	0.1	2.21	3546	3511	-0.1
06120	HARTFORD	003	13437	13062	12911	-0.3	1	4355	4268	4234	-0.2	2.82	2984	2882	-0.4
06226	WILLIMANTIC	015	18197	19128	19282	0.5	54	6535	6757	6829	0.4	2.46	3786	3856	0.2
06231	AMSTON	013	3888	4103	4193	0.6	61	1385	1478	1518	0.7	2.77	1111	1177	0.6
06232	ANDOVER	013	3083	3349	3455	0.9	79	1166	1284	1334	1.0	2.61	875	953	0.9
06234	BROOKLYN	015	7069	8127	8536	1.5	94	2497	2880	3045	1.6	2.57	1809	2065	1.4
06235	CHAPLIN	015	2115	2190	2210	0.4	46	809	847	858	0.5	2.59	579	599	0.4
06237	COLUMBIA	013	4529	5064	5286	1.2	90	1702	1923	2020	1.3	2.62	1327	1486	1.2
06238	COVENTRY	013	11445	12746	13362	1.2	90	4242	4787	5040	1.3	2.66	3176	3546	1.2
06239	DANIELSON	015	11623	11946	12061	0.3	38	4458	4591	4647	0.3	2.52	2938	2992	0.2
06241	DAYVILLE	015	6068	6880	7229	1.4	92	2351	2684	2831	1.4	2.53	1670	1882	1.3
06242	EASTFORD	015	1278	1407	1471	1.0	84	498	554	582	1.2	2.54	363	399	1.0
06243	EAST KILLINGLY	015	71	71	71	0.0	12	25	25	25	0.0	2.84	18	18	0.0
06247	HAMPTON	015	2529	3281	3564	2.9	99	943	1242	1360	3.0	2.64	701	912	2.9
06248	HEBRON	013	5097	5466	5624	0.8	74	1744	1892	1958	0.9	2.89	1467	1580	0.8
06249	LEBANON	011	6856	7338	7487	0.7	66	2427	2646	2719	0.9	2.71	1920	2080	0.9
06250	MANSFIELD CENTER	013	4400	4727	4843	0.8	74	1720	1860	1917	0.8	2.48	1174	1248	0.7
06254	NORTH FRANKLIN	011	1820	1934	1973	0.7	66	681	739	758	0.9	2.61	523	564	0.8
06255	NORTH GROSVENORDALE	015	4513	4962	5160	1.0	84	1779	1976	2065	1.1	2.51	1255	1377	1.0
06256	NORTH WINDHAM	015	1532	1670	1742	0.9	79	663	731	765	1.1	2.27	463	503	0.9
06259	POMFRET CENTER	015	4110	4507	4688	1.0	84	1532	1687	1760	1.0	2.66	1128	1228	0.9
06260	PUTNAM	015	9003	9400	9523	0.5	54	3684	3866	3933	0.5	2.36	2290	2373	0.4
06262	QUINEBAUG	015	374	403	413	0.8	74	182	198	203	0.9	2.04	124	133	0.8
06264	SCOTLAND	015	132	139	141	0.6	61	50	53	54	0.6	2.62	39	41	0.5
06266	SOUTH WINDHAM	015	377	396	403	0.5	54	138	147	150	0.7	2.69	101	106	0.5
06268	STORRS MANSFIELD	013	13947	16255	16381	1.7	96	3417	3590	3655	0.5	2.36	1865	1925	0.3
06269	STORRS MANSFIELD	013	2137	2771	2771	2.8	99	3	3	3	0.0	2.67	2	2	0.0
06277	THOMPSON	015	3602	3943	4099	1.0	84	1381	1526	1595	1.1	2.58	997	1090	1.0
06278	ASHFORD	015	4092	4400	4525	0.8	74	1578	1710	1764	0.9	2.56	1084	1160	0.7
	CONNECTICUT					0.4					0.4	2.53			0.3
	UNITED STATES					1.0					1.1	2.59			0.9

ZIP CODE #	POST OFFICE NAME	RACE (%) White 2000	White 2009	Black 2000	Black 2009	Asian/Pacific 2000	Asian/Pacific 2009	% Hispanic Origin 2000	% Hispanic Origin 2009	2009 AGE DISTRIBUTION (%) 0-4	5-9	10-14	15-19	20-24	25-44	45-64	65-84	85+	18+	MEDIAN AGE 2009	% 2009 Males	% 2009 Females
06001	AVON	95.0	92.0	1.0	1.4	3.0	5.1	1.6	2.6	5.7	6.6	7.9	7.3	3.9	17.7	33.8	14.5	2.6	75.0	45.5	47.9	52.1
06002	BLOOMFIELD	40.5	34.5	53.6	58.3	1.3	1.8	3.7	4.8	4.8	5.0	5.5	5.9	5.2	19.6	30.3	19.1	4.6	81.0	47.8	44.8	55.2
06010	BRISTOL	91.6	87.6	2.7	3.6	1.5	2.5	5.3	8.3	6.2	6.2	6.3	6.2	5.9	27.1	27.7	11.9	2.5	77.4	40.1	48.6	51.4
06013	BURLINGTON	97.3	95.8	0.6	0.9	0.8	1.5	1.4	2.3	6.3	7.6	8.7	7.3	3.6	21.9	34.4	9.2	0.9	72.5	42.2	50.5	49.5
06016	BROAD BROOK	92.9	89.7	3.5	4.9	1.4	2.3	1.9	3.1	6.4	6.6	6.8	6.7	5.5	25.6	29.3	11.3	1.8	76.0	40.3	49.3	50.7
06018	CANAAN	96.8	95.9	1.2	1.5	0.2	0.4	2.6	3.7	5.5	5.4	5.6	6.4	6.2	24.5	28.5	13.7	4.2	79.5	42.6	48.0	52.0
06019	CANTON	97.1	95.6	0.5	0.8	0.7	1.3	1.3	2.2	5.7	6.5	7.4	6.8	4.2	21.8	33.2	12.0	2.3	75.8	43.5	48.1	51.9
06021	COLEBROOK	97.1	95.7	0.6	0.9	0.6	1.1	2.6	3.1	5.4	6.6	7.7	6.6	3.1	20.3	34.3	13.7	2.3	76.0	45.1	49.4	50.6
06023	EAST BERLIN	96.8	94.9	0.6	0.9	1.8	3.1	1.9	3.0	5.7	6.3	6.7	6.6	5.1	22.0	32.1	13.1	2.4	76.7	43.3	49.9	50.1
06024	EAST CANAAN	97.5	97.0	1.1	1.2	0.0	0.0	1.2	1.6	5.2	5.2	5.7	6.9	6.0	24.7	27.1	14.5	4.8	79.6	42.5	48.4	51.6
06026	EAST GRANBY	95.7	93.4	1.3	1.9	1.0	1.8	1.5	2.6	6.2	7.0	7.6	6.9	4.3	21.3	32.3	12.7	1.7	74.9	43.0	48.7	51.3
06027	EAST HARTLAND	98.4	97.5	0.2	0.3	0.6	1.1	0.3	0.5	4.9	5.9	7.3	7.8	3.9	21.2	36.5	11.1	1.3	76.4	44.3	50.3	49.7
06029	ELLINGTON	96.2	94.8	1.0	1.2	1.3	2.2	1.4	2.0	6.1	6.4	6.6	6.6	5.3	27.8	29.9	10.0	1.3	76.7	39.9	48.7	51.3
06031	FALLS VILLAGE	96.8	96.0	1.4	1.7	0.5	0.7	0.7	1.0	4.6	5.3	6.2	6.1	4.8	20.5	33.2	15.4	3.8	79.7	46.4	47.0	53.0
06032	FARMINGTON	92.4	88.2	1.6	2.2	4.1	6.8	2.2	3.6	5.3	5.2	5.8	6.3	5.9	23.0	31.9	13.4	3.2	79.7	44.0	46.6	53.4
06033	GLASTONBURY	92.5	88.6	1.7	2.3	3.6	6.0	2.8	4.4	6.0	6.8	7.8	7.1	4.2	20.7	32.3	12.3	2.7	74.5	43.3	47.0	53.0
06035	GRANBY	97.6	96.2	0.6	0.8	0.8	1.4	1.2	2.1	6.5	7.3	7.4	6.6	3.2	22.8	32.1	12.2	2.0	74.3	42.8	49.4	50.6
06037	BERLIN	97.0	95.3	0.3	0.5	1.6	2.8	1.4	2.4	5.3	5.9	6.8	6.9	4.9	21.6	32.6	13.3	2.6	77.5	44.0	48.5	51.5
06039	LAKEVILLE	95.6	94.2	1.7	2.0	1.2	2.0	1.6	2.2	4.3	5.0	6.6	6.8	5.6	17.9	34.2	16.4	3.3	79.3	47.4	48.3	51.7
06040	MANCHESTER	81.6	76.0	9.4	11.4	3.0	4.4	7.1	10.3	6.2	5.7	5.8	6.1	7.3	27.5	26.4	11.8	3.1	78.4	39.0	48.1	51.9
06042	MANCHESTER	84.6	77.8	6.9	9.2	3.5	5.8	5.7	8.8	6.2	5.5	5.6	5.5	6.9	29.8	26.8	11.3	2.4	79.3	38.4	47.6	52.4
06043	BOLTON	97.7	96.9	0.7	0.8	0.5	0.9	1.6	2.4	5.5	6.1	7.0	6.8	5.1	19.7	35.0	13.1	1.6	77.2	44.8	48.1	51.9
06051	NEW BRITAIN	63.1	55.2	13.5	14.8	1.5	2.0	35.0	44.8	8.2	7.2	6.3	7.3	8.8	27.9	22.0	10.1	2.2	74.1	32.6	48.2	51.8
06052	NEW BRITAIN	81.7	75.4	7.2	8.9	1.5	2.3	15.2	21.8	5.5	5.3	5.6	6.0	6.3	26.1	27.4	13.6	4.3	79.9	41.9	48.0	52.0
06053	NEW BRITAIN	71.6	63.7	9.7	11.2	3.4	4.8	22.8	30.2	6.3	5.9	5.6	8.4	10.1	27.4	22.2	11.2	2.9	78.7	34.3	48.5	51.5
06057	NEW HARTFORD	97.7	96.8	0.6	0.7	0.8	1.4	1.3	1.8	5.9	6.7	7.9	7.0	3.8	22.7	34.7	9.9	1.2	74.8	42.6	49.8	50.2
06058	NORFOLK	97.3	96.2	0.4	0.6	0.5	0.9	1.0	1.4	5.2	6.3	7.1	6.5	3.3	21.1	35.0	13.6	1.8	77.3	45.3	49.2	50.8
06060	NORTH GRANBY	97.0	95.3	0.6	0.9	0.9	1.6	1.6	2.8	5.4	6.9	8.7	8.4	4.1	18.2	39.3	8.3	0.8	73.5	44.0	51.4	48.6
06062	PLAINVILLE	93.5	90.2	2.3	3.1	1.7	2.8	3.6	5.8	4.8	4.8	5.3	6.2	6.6	26.1	30.2	13.2	2.7	81.3	42.4	48.7	51.3
06063	BARKHAMSTED	98.5	98.0	0.1	0.1	0.4	0.7	0.9	1.2	4.9	5.7	6.9	7.0	3.5	23.7	35.2	11.7	1.3	77.9	44.1	49.6	50.4
06065	RIVERTON	98.1	97.4	0.1	0.1	0.6	1.0	1.5	2.2	5.3	4.8	8.9	8.0	2.5	26.2	31.7	11.4	1.2	75.3	42.1	50.3	49.7
06066	VERNON ROCKVILLE	90.0	87.0	4.0	4.5	2.7	4.4	3.6	4.7	5.9	5.6	5.7	6.0	6.6	26.7	27.7	13.1	2.6	79.1	40.5	48.0	52.0
06067	ROCKY HILL	90.2	85.4	3.4	4.5	4.0	6.6	3.2	5.0	4.7	4.9	5.4	5.3	5.7	25.3	31.7	13.9	3.0	81.5	44.1	49.6	50.4
06068	SALISBURY	95.8	94.6	1.7	2.0	0.6	1.1	1.5	2.0	3.2	4.2	5.7	5.1	2.5	16.9	35.9	19.6	7.0	83.2	52.3	46.2	53.8
06069	SHARON	96.8	95.8	1.0	1.1	0.6	1.0	1.9	2.8	3.7	5.7	5.9	5.8	3.6	19.8	33.3	17.2	5.0	80.4	48.0	48.9	51.1
06070	SIMSBURY	95.2	92.4	1.2	1.7	2.2	3.9	1.6	2.7	6.6	7.6	8.7	7.6	4.0	19.6	31.8	11.8	2.3	72.0	42.4	48.6	51.4
06071	SOMERS	83.4	80.4	9.6	9.3	0.7	3.0	7.9	9.0	4.2	4.9	5.4	11.6	12.8	24.5	25.4	9.6	1.6	81.9	34.7	53.7	46.3
06073	SOUTH GLASTONBURY	96.0	93.5	0.6	0.9	2.3	4.1	1.1	1.9	7.1	8.9	10.2	7.9	3.0	17.8	32.8	10.7	1.6	68.0	42.2	48.8	51.2
06074	SOUTH WINDSOR	91.5	86.9	3.0	4.1	3.7	6.3	2.3	3.6	5.8	6.8	7.6	7.4	4.5	21.9	32.1	12.1	1.8	74.9	42.6	48.1	51.9
06076	STAFFORD SPRINGS	96.9	95.9	0.6	0.7	0.9	1.5	1.6	2.2	6.2	6.5	6.8	6.4	5.1	25.3	31.3	10.2	2.1	76.5	41.0	49.2	50.8
06078	SUFFIELD	85.8	81.4	8.9	10.8	1.1	1.9	5.3	7.6	4.9	5.2	5.8	6.5	8.1	25.6	28.6	12.1	3.1	80.3	40.9	55.2	44.8
06081	TARIFFVILLE	92.4	88.6	2.7	3.8	2.0	3.5	1.0	1.7	6.2	6.3	6.3	5.5	5.6	26.5	30.7	10.9	1.9	77.9	41.1	48.7	51.3
06082	ENFIELD	89.7	86.0	5.6	7.0	1.4	2.3	3.7	5.6	5.5	5.8	6.0	6.1	6.7	28.4	26.7	12.8	2.1	78.9	39.7	52.5	47.5
06084	TOLLAND	96.8	95.6	0.8	0.9	1.2	2.0	1.1	1.5	7.0	7.9	8.5	7.0	4.0	24.6	30.6	9.2	1.1	71.9	40.0	49.6	50.4
06085	UNIONVILLE	94.2	91.0	1.4	1.9	2.7	4.6	2.2	3.5	5.7	6.2	7.0	7.5	5.7	22.2	32.5	11.4	1.9	76.3	42.2	50.0	50.0
06088	EAST WINDSOR	89.9	84.9	4.7	6.5	2.8	4.8	2.3	3.8	5.0	5.1	5.6	5.4	5.4	25.8	29.5	14.9	3.3	80.8	43.5	48.7	51.3
06089	WEATOGUE	95.1	92.2	1.0	1.5	2.8	4.8	1.8	3.0	6.0	7.1	8.2	7.4	3.9	21.7	33.5	10.7	1.4	74.1	42.5	48.2	51.8
06090	WEST GRANBY	97.9	96.7	1.1	1.7	0.4	0.8	1.2	2.0	5.7	7.4	8.4	7.0	3.1	20.8	34.1	12.3	1.2	73.5	43.8	49.5	50.5
06091	WEST HARTLAND	98.0	96.3	0.0	0.0	0.7	1.8	1.3	2.4	5.5	3.7	9.1	8.5	1.8	28.7	30.5	11.0	1.2	75.0	41.8	50.6	49.4
06092	WEST SIMSBURY	97.1	95.4	0.4	0.7	1.3	2.3	1.3	2.3	5.7	7.7	9.6	9.5	4.1	13.9	35.0	12.2	2.3	70.6	44.6	49.0	51.0
06093	WEST SUFFIELD	97.8	96.6	0.8	1.1	0.6	1.1	1.0	1.7	5.1	6.2	6.9	6.8	4.5	23.2	34.4	11.4	1.5	77.4	43.3	49.4	50.6
06095	WINDSOR	64.9	57.2	27.3	32.1	3.2	4.8	5.0	7.0	5.6	6.2	6.8	6.5	4.8	23.3	30.9	13.1	2.8	77.3	42.9	47.5	52.5
06096	WINDSOR LOCKS	92.5	88.6	2.7	3.7	2.6	4.4	2.2	3.6	5.9	6.0	6.3	6.5	5.5	24.6	29.3	13.6	2.4	77.8	41.9	48.7	51.3
06098	WINSTED	94.6	92.9	1.2	1.4	0.9	1.5	3.1	4.3	5.6	5.7	6.0	6.3	6.1	24.4	30.7	12.7	2.5	78.8	42.2	48.9	51.1
06103	HARTFORD	61.5	53.4	14.8	18.0	5.4	8.4	24.7	28.2	2.0	2.1	2.5	2.8	7.6	33.7	36.2	11.6	1.5	91.6	44.6	60.7	39.3
06105	HARTFORD	35.0	30.0	42.7	43.5	2.5	3.3	26.8	31.8	7.7	6.9	5.8	6.2	8.8	32.4	22.3	8.5	1.4	76.4	32.8	47.7	52.3
06106	HARTFORD	35.2	30.0	17.1	16.3	2.6	3.1	57.8	64.8	8.6	7.6	6.6	9.8	11.9	27.0	19.4	7.3	2.0	72.6	28.2	49.1	50.9
06107	WEST HARTFORD	93.2	89.5	1.5	2.1	3.2	5.4	2.8	4.5	5.8	6.5	7.5	6.4	4.3	19.1	31.8	14.8	3.9	76.0	45.3	47.3	52.7
06108	EAST HARTFORD	55.8	46.9	23.3	25.8	5.2	7.0	19.3	25.6	7.2	6.6	6.1	6.7	7.7	27.8	24.7	11.0	2.2	76.0	36.1	48.4	51.6
06109	WETHERSFIELD	93.0	89.6	2.1	2.8	1.6	2.7	4.3	6.9	5.0	5.3	5.8	5.5	4.1	20.9	30.0	18.8	4.6	80.4	47.0	46.8	53.2
06110	WEST HARTFORD	72.9	64.7	10.0	11.4	8.0	11.9	13.2	18.1	5.9	6.1	6.3	6.7	5.7	25.1	27.1	12.9	4.2	77.5	41.1	46.9	53.1
06111	NEWINGTON	92.5	88.5	2.1	2.9	2.9	4.8	3.7	6.0	5.0	5.3	5.7	5.8	4.6	23.7	29.9	16.4	3.6	80.3	45.0	47.1	52.9
06112	HARTFORD	3.8	9.5	86.2	78.5	0.4	1.1	9.3	11.2	8.1	8.1	7.5	10.1	10.2	24.1	21.3	9.5	1.1	71.5	29.4	45.9	54.1
06114	HARTFORD	39.8	33.1	15.5	15.3	1.5	1.8	52.1	60.8	8.8	7.8	7.2	8.0	9.2	29.1	20.4	7.8	1.7	71.5	30.0	48.7	51.3
06117	WEST HARTFORD	90.6	86.5	3.6	4.4	3.6	6.2	2.7	4.3	4.7	5.3	6.4	10.2	6.9	13.7	27.7	17.4	7.7	79.1	47.0	44.8	55.2
06118	EAST HARTFORD	73.1	65.6	14.6	17.2	3.0	4.5	11.4	16.2	5.8	5.9	6.0	6.1	5.4	24.3	27.9	15.8	2.8	78.4	42.4	47.4	52.6
06119	WEST HARTFORD	82.5	75.9	5.8	7.1	5.8	8.8	8.9	13.0	5.7	5.3	5.2	5.5	7.8	29.2	26.2	11.5	3.7	80.4	39.2	46.7	53.3
06120	HARTFORD	9.6	9.4	61.2	58.3	0.4	0.5	36.2	39.8	10.2	9.6	7.8	9.2	9.1	27.3	19.1	6.8	0.9	67.1	27.3	48.9	51.1
06226	WILLIMANTIC	70.5	63.1	5.9	6.3	1.8	2.6	30.6	39.5	6.6	5.9	5.5	11.6	13.4	26.0	20.1	8.7	2.3	78.5	29.4	48.7	51.3
06231	AMSTON	97.5	96.5	0.6	0.7	0.7	1.2	1.2	1.8	7.3	8.4	9.1	6.9	3.8	23.5	32.5	7.6	0.9	70.3	40.3	50.0	50.0
06232	ANDOVER	96.7	95.8	0.9	1.1	0.5	0.8	1.6	2.2	6.6	7.4	8.0	7.0	4.4	24.2	32.8	8.6	1.1	72.8	40.8	51.1	48.9
06234	BROOKLYN	93.1	91.5	3.7	4.2	0.5	0.9	2.6	3.8	5.1	5.4	5.9	6.5	6.3	28.0	28.4	11.8	2.6	79.5	40.6	51.5	48.5
06235	CHAPLIN	97.3	96.1	0.7	0.9	0.3	0.6	2.0	3.2	6.3	6.4	6.7	6.4	5.1	27.8	31.5	8.9	1.0	76.8	39.7	50.3	49.7
06237	COLUMBIA	97.4	96.4	0.4	0.4	0.7	1.2	1.7	2.4	5.9	6.6	7.5	7.5	4.4	21.4	33.6	11.5	1.6	74.8	42.8	48.6	51.4
06238	COVENTRY	96.9	96.1	0.6	0.6	0.6	1.0	1.7	2.4	6.6	7.1	7.8	6.6	4.8	26.7	30.3	9.0	1.1	74.2	39.7	50.6	49.4
06239	DANIELSON	93.7	91.3	1.4	1.7	1.6	2.6	2.8	4.4	6.2	6.0	6.0	6.7	7.0	27.3	26.8	11.3	2.6	77.6	38.5	49.3	50.7
06241	DAYVILLE	94.2	92.0	1.2	1.5	1.4	2.4	1.4	2.3	6.6	6.3	6.4	7.3	7.0	26.4	26.9	11.1	2.1	76.2	38.0	49.2	50.8
06242	EASTFORD	97.8	97.0	0.4	0.5	0.4	0.6	1.3	2.1	5.7	6.5	7.2	7.2	4.0	23.1	33.3	11.2	1.7	76.0	42.7	51.4	48.6
06243	EAST KILLINGLY	95.7	93.0	1.4	1.4	1.4	2.8	1.4	1.4	5.6	5.6	7.0	7.0	5.6	26.8	28.2	12.7	1.4	74.6	40.4	50.7	49.3
06247	HAMPTON	97.0	95.6	0.3	0.3	0.8	1.4	1.9	3.0	5.8	6.6	7.4	7.0	4.4	23.1	34.4	10.0	1.2	75.7	42.3	50.6	49.4
06248	HEBRON	97.8	97.1	0.5	0.6	0.5	0.9	1.0	1.4	7.9	9.3	9.8	7.1	3.7	22.4	32.0	7.1	0.6	68.2	39.5	50.4	49.6
06249	LEBANON	96.9	95.8	0.8	1.0	0.3	0.5	1.6	2.5	5.9	6.8	8.0	8.3	4.1	22.5	33.3	9.9	1.2	73.4	41.6	50.5	49.5
06250	MANSFIELD CENTER	91.1	87.5	1.5	1.7	4.5	7.1	3.2	4.3	5.0	4.8	5.2	6.5	7.8	25.0	30.5	12.4	2.8	80.9	41.5	48.4	51.6
06254	NORTH FRANKLIN	98.0	97.3	0.7	0.9	0.1	0.2	1.2	1.9	5.3	5.8	6.3	6.4	5.1	24.1	32.1	13.3	1.7	78.2	43.1	51.0	49.0
06255	NORTH GROSVENORDALE	98.1	97.5	0.5	0.5	0.2	0.3	1.0	1.6	5.9	6.0	6.1	6.6	5.7	25.2	29.8	12.7	2.0	78.0	41.3	49.7	50.3
06256	NORTH WINDHAM	86.5	82.1	1.7	1.9	0.5	0.8	12.5	17.2	6.2	6.3	6.2	6.1	5.7	24.3	29.6	13.9	1.6	77.6	41.4	47.4	52.6
06259	POMFRET CENTER	97.3	96.1	0.4	0.5	0.7	1.2	1.6	2.5	5.7	6.0	6.5	7.2	5.9	23.4	33.1	10.6	1.8	77.3	41.9	48.7	51.3
06260	PUTNAM	95.3	93.8	1.3	1.7	0.4	0.7	1.9	2.9	6.1	6.0	5.9	5.8	6.2	26.3	27.3	12.3	4.2	78.3	40.4	47.9	52.1
06262	QUINEBAUG	98.4	97.8	1.1	1.5	0.3	0.5	0.0	0.2	5.5	5.7	6.0	6.5	4.7	22.6	28.8	17.1	3.2	78.9	44.4	49.6	50.4
06264	SCOTLAND	97.0	97.1	0.8	0.7	0.8	0.7	2.3	2.9	7.2	7.2	7.9	7.2	5.0	24.5	30.2	9.4	1.4	73.4	40.2	48.9	51.1
06266	SOUTH WINDHAM	94.7	92.4	0.8	1.0	0.3	0.5	5.6	8.6	5.3	5.8	6.3	5.6	3.8	26.0	32.6	13.1	1.5	79.0	42.8	50.5	49.5
06268	STORRS MANSFIELD	82.2	76.0	5.6	6.6	7.8	12.0	4.6	6.1	2.3	2.0	2.2	24.8	31.1	16.8	12.7	6.9	1.2	90.0	23.0	50.4	49.6
06269	STORRS MANSFIELD	81.2	74.8	7.0	8.0	7.8	12.1	4.4	5.9	0.3	0.2	0.1	47.9	45.8	4.8	0.5	0.3	0.0	94.8	20.2	46.9	53.1
06277	THOMPSON	97.7	96.8	0.3	0.4	0.6	1.1	0.6	1.0	6.0	6.5	7.1	6.9	4.3	26.3	31.5	10.0	1.4	76.0	40.6	50.2	49.8
06278	ASHFORD	95.7	94.0	1.0	1.3	1.0	1.8	2.0	3.2	5.7	6.3	6.7	6.2	5.6	28.6	30.3	9.2	1.4	77.4	39.0	50.3	49.7
	CONNECTICUT	81.6	78.0	9.1	9.9	2.5	3.8	9.4	12.0	6.3	6.4	6.7	7.2	6.5	24.9	27.9	11.7	2.5	76.3	39.6	48.6	51.4
	UNITED STATES	75.1	72.0	12.3	12.7	3.8	4.6	12.5	15.7	6.8	6.7	6.6	7.1	6.9	27.0	26.0	10.9	1.9	75.7	36.9	49.2	50.8

06001-06278

ZIP CODE #	POST OFFICE NAME	2009 Per Capita Income	2009 HH Income Base	2009 HOUSEHOLD INCOME DISTRIBUTION (%) Less than $25,000	$25,000 to $49,999	$50,000 to $99,999	$100,000 to $149,999	$150,000 or More	MEDIAN HOUSEHOLD INCOME 2009	2014	2009 National Centile	2009 State Centile	2009 Home Value Base	2009 HOME VALUE DISTRIBUTION (%) Less than $50,000	$50,000 to $89,999	$90,000 to $174,999	$175,000 to $399,999	$400,000 or More	2009 Median Home Value
06001	AVON	66614	7017	5.6	10.2	28.4	18.0	37.8	111266	112575	98	89	5937	0.2	0.8	5.2	40.2	53.7	431250
06002	BLOOMFIELD	35823	8462	15.5	20.8	38.1	13.6	12.0	67118	70496	85	33	6224	0.6	1.8	24.8	62.8	10.0	222521
06010	BRISTOL	28314	25287	17.5	24.2	43.2	11.1	4.1	59510	63265	77	24	15699	1.2	2.6	30.3	61.1	4.9	203068
06013	BURLINGTON	45724	3232	4.0	6.7	43.1	19.6	26.6	95768	100800	96	82	3005	0.3	0.9	4.5	59.3	34.9	342522
06016	BROAD BROOK	29241	2491	10.1	21.3	53.3	10.8	4.4	68246	71354	86	36	1645	1.3	0.6	18.6	64.9	14.5	253852
06018	CANAAN	25416	1200	21.3	29.9	36.8	10.2	1.8	48678	50895	58	12	777	1.2	4.2	28.3	57.7	8.6	216195
06019	CANTON	44517	4017	7.3	15.2	41.5	16.9	19.2	82741	83095	93	65	3189	0.3	0.5	14.4	58.1	26.7	297050
06021	COLEBROOK	39385	140	8.6	15.7	45.7	17.1	12.9	78052	79510	91	54	120	0.0	0.0	5.8	62.5	31.7	324138
06023	EAST BERLIN	34713	494	4.9	14.4	45.1	21.9	13.8	85024	85741	94	71	430	3.3	0.5	4.9	79.3	12.1	269802
06024	EAST CANAAN	21758	212	14.2	26.9	45.8	9.9	3.3	57966	58713	75	21	164	0.0	0.6	28.7	56.1	14.6	235484
06026	EAST GRANBY	38605	1960	5.7	16.2	44.3	20.8	13.0	80887	82432	92	61	1590	0.8	1.1	10.1	67.6	20.4	281513
06027	EAST HARTLAND	33975	569	3.7	8.8	60.3	16.3	10.9	80320	81287	92	60	514	0.0	0.0	11.1	72.6	16.3	278467
06029	ELLINGTON	38837	5806	8.5	14.4	38.0	25.5	13.5	81929	87116	93	63	3964	0.6	2.0	14.4	70.9	12.1	259037
06031	FALLS VILLAGE	42330	669	10.8	24.4	37.1	13.5	14.3	74833	76295	89	45	512	0.8	1.8	8.6	48.8	40.0	332895
06032	FARMINGTON	49371	7753	9.4	15.2	36.9	15.7	22.7	83666	84096	93	67	5800	0.4	1.1	7.9	52.1	38.5	331557
06033	GLASTONBURY	50328	10824	8.0	11.2	35.0	17.7	28.1	93216	93179	96	81	8582	0.1	1.0	7.9	51.0	40.0	358745
06035	GRANBY	43217	2897	6.1	8.2	41.0	22.2	22.5	91830	94904	95	79	2465	0.6	0.3	8.2	71.7	19.2	283375
06037	BERLIN	36506	6867	8.5	14.4	42.5	19.7	15.0	81999	83069	93	63	5995	0.8	0.4	6.7	71.8	20.3	289366
06039	LAKEVILLE	44644	929	13.7	22.3	40.6	8.4	15.1	70286	69755	87	39	627	0.2	0.6	5.9	35.2	58.1	467333
06040	MANCHESTER	30559	14228	17.8	24.0	39.7	11.6	6.9	58822	62510	76	23	7762	0.9	3.7	26.5	59.4	9.5	214630
06042	MANCHESTER	33924	9805	10.4	21.8	47.6	13.9	6.3	67054	69906	85	32	5717	0.4	1.2	32.8	63.0	2.5	194458
06043	BOLTON	41636	2062	6.3	12.7	35.0	27.9	18.1	91616	101515	95	79	1751	0.0	0.0	10.8	67.8	21.4	286387
06051	NEW BRITAIN	18290	11627	37.6	29.9	27.2	4.0	1.4	33911	36434	15	4	3604	2.1	8.8	59.2	29.5	0.4	147511
06052	NEW BRITAIN	30847	3268	18.4	24.2	37.2	14.2	5.9	58636	62532	76	22	1939	2.2	4.1	29.8	58.8	5.2	207100
06053	NEW BRITAIN	22493	13686	24.3	30.1	36.4	6.3	2.9	45258	48247	49	10	6713	1.7	3.8	58.3	34.8	1.5	156937
06057	NEW HARTFORD	41392	2340	5.9	11.8	39.8	20.9	21.6	90263	93021	95	76	2023	0.0	2.5	7.2	63.8	26.5	301553
06058	NORFOLK	40419	778	8.4	22.4	38.4	17.6	13.2	76584	77206	90	49	575	0.3	0.2	12.7	47.8	39.0	332447
06060	NORTH GRANBY	46288	823	1.7	5.8	38.3	17.0	37.2	112753	122392	98	90	776	0.0	0.0	2.3	47.0	50.6	402242
06062	PLAINVILLE	28594	7439	16.4	24.1	43.2	12.8	3.5	59842	63117	77	25	5153	1.2	3.8	29.8	62.8	2.3	200210
06063	BARKHAMSTED	38586	1308	4.8	9.2	48.7	20.8	16.5	86107	87940	94	72	1128	0.0	0.0	3.0	80.0	17.0	286081
06065	RIVERTON	35722	272	5.9	10.7	46.7	25.0	11.8	85097	84992	94	72	239	0.0	0.0	3.8	82.4	13.8	272984
06066	VERNON ROCKVILLE	32628	13114	16.6	22.8	36.5	17.7	6.3	60601	62019	78	25	7461	2.4	4.1	21.2	67.7	4.6	216274
06067	ROCKY HILL	37906	8145	8.7	16.5	47.5	16.7	10.6	76756	77811	90	50	5383	0.8	3.7	15.7	62.7	17.2	265275
06068	SALISBURY	38739	674	18.5	23.1	35.0	9.6	13.6	64410	65481	83	29	479	1.0	2.5	6.1	39.7	50.7	406034
06069	SHARON	41106	1233	13.3	21.4	38.8	14.8	11.6	69841	70768	87	38	939	0.5	0.9	8.2	47.3	43.1	359177
06070	SIMSBURY	52226	5958	5.0	10.3	34.4	17.7	32.5	100577	100766	97	84	4973	0.5	0.1	5.9	46.0	47.5	389984
06071	SOMERS	33546	3382	7.5	11.7	38.5	25.2	17.1	86537	92499	94	72	2924	0.0	0.1	5.3	66.5	28.1	326127
06073	SOUTH GLASTONBURY	64329	2023	6.5	6.0	26.1	17.9	43.5	133465	135324	99	94	1826	0.2	0.0	1.5	40.1	58.2	454982
06074	SOUTH WINDSOR	40986	9360	5.6	11.1	42.0	21.4	19.9	89462	90035	95	75	8227	1.4	2.1	12.3	66.5	17.7	273856
06076	STAFFORD SPRINGS	29733	5012	13.2	19.5	42.5	20.3	4.5	69172	73184	86	36	3742	0.7	1.5	26.3	64.8	6.7	212995
06078	SUFFIELD	35725	3664	12.3	16.2	38.8	18.4	14.3	80118	81148	92	60	2910	0.0	1.2	12.7	60.7	25.4	285986
06081	TARIFFVILLE	39180	681	8.5	21.6	44.1	14.5	11.3	77233	77464	91	52	433	0.0	2.1	13.2	83.4	1.4	231676
06082	ENFIELD	27730	16508	12.2	20.8	50.1	12.3	4.5	67090	70185	85	32	12343	0.3	1.0	24.4	72.2	2.1	203746
06084	TOLLAND	44232	5279	4.3	7.0	32.3	30.3	26.1	110337	112960	98	89	4860	0.0	0.1	7.6	70.1	22.2	279393
06085	UNIONVILLE	36577	2250	13.0	16.6	42.2	14.4	13.7	75100	76036	89	46	1700	0.0	0.2	8.2	69.6	21.9	293297
06088	EAST WINDSOR	32243	2203	13.5	22.7	49.7	9.8	4.3	64504	67470	83	30	1445	7.5	6.4	31.3	51.3	3.5	184291
06089	WEATOGUE	51431	997	2.9	7.1	38.9	25.0	26.1	101432	104999	97	85	788	0.0	0.4	6.9	55.8	36.9	341808
06090	WEST GRANBY	54937	390	3.3	5.6	34.4	21.5	35.1	117585	118718	98	91	361	0.0	0.0	6.1	46.5	47.4	388824
06091	WEST HARTLAND	32962	58	5.2	10.3	50.0	29.3	5.2	84050	84228	94	68	52	0.0	0.0	1.9	82.7	15.4	280000
06092	WEST SIMSBURY	56205	1194	2.9	4.7	29.9	14.7	47.7	141165	143552	99	95	1111	0.5	0.0	0.2	35.8	63.5	465721
06093	WEST SUFFIELD	38190	1266	7.4	12.5	43.3	20.1	16.7	85082	86776	94	71	1109	0.0	0.7	8.2	68.6	22.5	309347
06095	WINDSOR	34726	10973	9.9	15.8	43.9	19.0	11.5	78538	79391	91	56	8693	0.2	2.0	17.5	72.6	7.7	235169
06096	WINDSOR LOCKS	28014	5115	13.5	22.1	49.5	12.0	2.9	61436	65317	79	27	3840	0.0	2.2	27.6	68.2	2.1	198075
06098	WINSTED	29218	4900	17.7	23.4	41.5	12.6	4.9	60595	62600	78	25	3183	0.4	2.4	25.1	60.7	11.4	221826
06103	HARTFORD	56369	557	22.4	22.1	21.9	14.9	18.7	57475	63892	77	24	157	0.0	0.0	31.8	50.3	17.8	227632
06105	HARTFORD	21863	9756	48.2	27.2	17.2	3.2	4.1	26197	28093	4	2	1467	5.3	6.1	19.6	39.2	29.8	264739
06106	HARTFORD	14419	14006	44.8	27.9	22.4	3.6	1.3	29040	31236	7	3	3266	1.8	11.7	58.9	26.8	0.9	145635
06107	WEST HARTFORD	49546	7614	6.4	12.8	39.1	18.7	23.0	88713	89709	95	74	6383	0.3	0.6	3.7	65.4	29.9	333875
06108	EAST HARTFORD	22627	9562	25.5	28.9	34.9	8.5	2.2	46302	48373	52	10	4244	3.4	2.7	45.5	47.2	1.2	173193
06109	WETHERSFIELD	34899	11212	13.8	21.5	41.6	14.2	8.9	67009	70116	85	31	8628	0.9	1.4	13.1	68.1	16.5	264360
06110	WEST HARTFORD	26983	5009	16.7	23.7	44.2	12.4	3.1	58173	61734	75	21	3441	0.7	1.2	29.7	67.8	0.6	198958
06111	NEWINGTON	33980	12232	11.3	18.2	46.2	16.7	7.6	73860	75280	89	42	9738	0.2	1.8	20.6	72.2	5.3	234463
06112	HARTFORD	15945	7594	35.9	29.1	28.4	4.3	2.3	35634	38612	20	5	3013	1.4	5.6	59.0	30.1	4.0	151353
06114	HARTFORD	15494	9513	35.6	29.9	29.6	3.8	1.1	35576	38889	19	4	2972	3.8	7.1	51.6	36.2	1.2	154849
06117	WEST HARTFORD	51047	5395	8.3	11.7	33.9	14.5	31.6	92982	94592	96	80	4589	0.3	0.1	2.2	54.9	42.5	370346
06118	EAST HARTFORD	27602	10629	17.9	26.7	40.0	11.7	3.8	55410	59310	72	18	7347	4.7	3.6	35.9	54.9	0.9	184028
06119	WEST HARTFORD	34766	6718	16.5	21.3	41.8	12.9	7.5	64319	67858	83	29	3243	1.3	3.3	16.5	63.4	15.4	254656
06120	HARTFORD	11410	4268	56.7	25.7	14.0	2.5	1.1	19593	21245	1	1	726	8.8	10.3	45.3	28.1	7.4	143182
06226	WILLIMANTIC	19918	6757	34.9	26.0	31.0	5.8	2.4	37254	41062	24	7	2675	3.9	3.6	54.1	36.6	1.8	159659
06231	AMSTON	44530	1478	4.9	4.3	38.8	25.6	26.4	103546	108587	97	86	1312	0.0	0.2	8.1	69.6	22.2	286229
06232	ANDOVER	41168	1284	5.9	8.8	41.2	29.1	15.0	91588	97948	95	78	1102	0.8	0.5	12.3	75.0	11.3	257353
06234	BROOKLYN	26435	2880	17.3	23.0	40.3	12.8	6.5	62309	64641	80	28	2138	2.5	0.7	20.5	63.5	12.8	225546
06235	CHAPLIN	27974	847	12.4	20.5	51.9	11.9	3.2	67423	69090	85	34	661	0.0	4.5	30.7	59.2	5.6	200727
06237	COLUMBIA	40640	1923	5.8	10.1	36.1	32.5	15.4	96028	101674	96	82	1737	0.9	0.2	7.5	74.0	17.4	269666
06238	COVENTRY	37654	4787	7.4	11.6	40.2	25.6	15.1	84993	89803	94	70	4098	0.2	0.5	17.9	72.4	9.1	240498
06239	DANIELSON	23886	4591	22.5	24.9	40.3	9.0	3.3	52457	55652	67	14	2810	3.0	2.4	40.0	51.5	3.1	181528
06241	DAYVILLE	24927	2684	19.0	31.8	37.9	7.0	4.2	49250	51185	59	13	1888	6.4	3.7	39.6	47.0	3.3	175694
06242	EASTFORD	33737	554	12.6	18.2	44.9	15.5	8.7	74714	76432	89	45	440	1.4	2.0	18.4	65.9	12.3	243103
06243	EAST KILLINGLY	24314	25	16.0	24.0	44.0	12.0	4.0	58032	61445	75	21	19	0.0	0.0	36.8	57.9	5.3	195833
06247	HAMPTON	31146	1242	11.1	17.4	47.1	16.6	7.8	74364	76091	89	43	1083	0.4	1.3	18.8	66.6	12.9	233183
06248	HEBRON	43269	1892	5.3	6.5	32.2	30.5	25.4	109612	113040	98	88	1674	0.5	0.4	5.7	72.1	21.3	284272
06249	LEBANON	31811	2646	4.8	14.4	56.6	16.5	7.7	78158	78586	91	55	2322	0.3	0.6	13.4	71.2	14.5	250402
06250	MANSFIELD CENTER	34106	1860	11.5	18.1	37.5	23.8	9.1	71441	77454	88	40	1385	1.0	0.1	19.6	67.4	11.9	232031
06254	NORTH FRANKLIN	31764	739	9.1	18.9	46.5	18.1	7.3	76965	77277	91	51	656	0.3	0.6	16.3	69.5	13.3	253793
06255	NORTH GROSVENORDALE	23962	1976	22.4	22.5	43.7	8.5	2.9	55766	60086	72	18	1466	0.8	2.0	33.6	56.3	7.2	198804
06256	NORTH WINDHAM	23052	731	26.0	30.2	35.3	6.8	1.6	43606	46893	44	9	571	18.7	19.1	26.4	33.6	2.1	127045
06259	POMFRET CENTER	33307	1687	11.1	17.5	45.2	13.8	12.4	76063	77324	90	47	1232	0.4	3.7	12.3	58.4	25.3	277545
06260	PUTNAM	26048	3866	21.0	24.5	42.0	9.0	3.6	54810	57899	71	18	2138	0.0	2.9	47.6	43.3	6.2	174321
06262	QUINEBAUG	27042	198	29.3	24.7	36.4	7.1	2.5	46992	49551	54	11	179	6.1	13.4	27.4	43.6	9.5	183594
06264	SCOTLAND	30823	53	7.5	11.3	66.0	11.3	3.8	76526	77233	90	49	46	0.0	0.0	17.4	73.9	8.7	229412
06266	SOUTH WINDHAM	31076	147	3.4	17.7	61.9	10.9	6.1	75135	76086	89	46	120	2.5	5.8	34.2	57.5	0.0	188235
06268	STORRS MANSFIELD	26032	3590	25.9	18.2	23.9	18.6	13.4	60644	64573	78	26	1995	7.2	3.7	9.9	68.3	10.9	243029
06269	STORRS MANSFIELD	14723	3	100.0	0.0	0.0	0.0	0.0	7500	7500	0	1	0	0.0	0.0	0.0	0.0	0.0	0
06277	THOMPSON	28065	1526	15.5	20.6	47.6	10.7	5.5	63383	64565	82	28	1293	0.6	1.0	29.2	58.8	10.4	213034
06278	ASHFORD	31992	1710	14.1	17.8	44.8	14.9	8.4	69635	70907	87	37	1242	0.5	3.9	17.6	67.1	10.9	235207
	CONNECTICUT	36066		15.8	19.0	36.4	15.2	13.5	70949	74487				1.1	1.8	16.1	53.4	27.5	273826
	UNITED STATES	27277		20.9	24.4	35.3	11.7	7.6	54719	56938				9.3	13.1	31.6	32.6	13.5	162279

ZIP CODE #	POST OFFICE NAME	FINANCIAL SERVICES: Auto Loan	Home Loan	Invest-ments	Retire-ment Plans	THE HOME: Home Improvements: Home Repair	Lawn & Garden	Furnishings: Comput-ers & Hard-ware-Personal	Major Appli-ances	TV, Radio, Sound Equip-ment	Furni-ture	ENTERTAINMENT: Dine out/ Carry out	Sports Equip-ment	Fees & Tickets	Toys & Games	Travel	Cable TV	PERSONAL: Apparel & Services	Auto Repairs	Health Insur-ance	Pets & Supplies
06001	AVON	215	269	298	277	287	253	236	246	223	254	224	186	271	218	266	217	164	234	230	277
06002	BLOOMFIELD	112	123	127	123	125	131	115	120	121	120	120	85	125	115	123	125	83	121	136	141
06010	BRISTOL	88	97	91	97	95	94	96	93	95	94	96	72	101	95	98	96	68	95	96	109
06013	BURLINGTON	170	215	217	222	220	200	180	189	173	193	175	144	210	174	203	168	127	179	176	216
06016	BROAD BROOK	94	112	103	111	110	105	102	103	100	101	101	80	111	101	109	100	72	101	102	119
06018	CANAAN	83	82	80	83	83	86	83	84	83	80	82	64	82	83	83	85	57	84	87	99
06019	CANTON	146	175	174	179	177	163	155	157	149	163	151	121	173	150	168	145	108	152	149	182
06021	COLEBROOK	129	160	164	165	165	152	136	145	131	146	132	107	156	130	153	129	95	137	137	165
06023	EAST BERLIN	117	161	167	152	167	144	134	140	128	135	129	103	157	130	153	128	95	134	132	154
06024	EAST CANAAN	86	99	89	99	97	94	92	92	90	91	91	72	98	91	96	90	64	91	91	107
06026	EAST GRANBY	128	157	153	159	157	149	136	141	133	141	135	106	154	133	151	132	96	137	139	163
06027	EAST HARTLAND	126	157	160	161	161	148	133	141	128	142	129	105	152	127	150	125	93	133	133	161
06029	ELLINGTON	129	149	137	149	145	135	136	134	131	140	133	105	147	134	142	128	95	133	128	156
06031	FALLS VILLAGE	123	157	177	149	167	150	134	144	131	138	131	103	153	128	153	132	95	138	141	160
06032	FARMINGTON	154	185	201	187	196	169	173	173	161	182	161	134	189	157	189	154	117	169	160	197
06033	GLASTONBURY	160	202	214	206	211	191	176	182	171	184	172	137	204	169	197	169	126	175	177	206
06035	GRANBY	153	181	180	185	183	172	158	166	153	166	154	125	175	154	173	151	110	158	158	190
06037	BERLIN	122	157	159	154	160	146	134	140	130	138	131	104	154	130	150	130	95	135	135	158
06039	LAKEVILLE	144	147	198	148	162	155	142	158	135	145	135	120	143	129	157	134	95	149	145	179
06040	MANCHESTER	99	97	92	100	95	95	104	96	103	102	104	76	104	103	101	103	73	102	100	115
06042	MANCHESTER	104	111	104	112	109	106	110	105	108	110	110	82	114	109	111	108	77	108	107	124
06043	BOLTON	144	172	167	174	173	162	151	156	147	158	148	118	168	148	164	145	106	151	151	180
06051	NEW BRITAIN	59	50	47	52	48	50	65	55	66	60	67	44	60	64	58	67	47	63	61	67
06052	NEW BRITAIN	99	101	96	102	100	103	104	101	106	101	105	76	106	104	103	108	74	104	109	119
06053	NEW BRITAIN	73	72	66	72	70	71	80	72	80	76	81	58	79	80	76	81	58	78	77	87
06057	NEW HARTFORD	148	180	183	185	184	170	156	163	150	165	152	122	176	150	173	147	108	156	155	187
06058	NORFOLK	145	149	183	150	156	162	135	154	135	136	135	114	138	132	149	137	93	145	149	178
06060	NORTH GRANBY	177	231	237	242	238	209	190	199	179	206	181	155	227	182	216	171	135	185	176	225
06062	PLAINVILLE	86	96	90	96	94	92	94	90	93	92	94	70	100	93	97	94	67	93	94	106
06063	BARKHAMSTED	134	166	165	170	168	154	141	148	135	150	136	112	160	135	157	131	98	140	138	169
06065	RIVERTON	126	156	153	159	157	144	132	138	126	141	128	105	150	127	147	123	92	131	128	158
06066	VERNON ROCKVILLE	101	99	96	102	98	98	106	99	105	104	106	78	106	105	104	105	74	104	103	118
06067	ROCKY HILL	121	128	127	132	128	124	126	123	123	128	125	95	131	124	129	122	88	124	123	144
06068	SALISBURY	130	122	178	120	138	150	114	139	120	120	118	94	114	111	129	127	80	131	147	159
06069	SHARON	127	144	145	145	147	148	131	138	133	136	133	99	143	130	142	135	93	135	146	159
06070	SIMSBURY	177	228	238	234	237	209	194	200	184	205	186	154	228	185	218	179	137	190	185	226
06071	SOMERS	138	179	182	175	184	164	152	158	146	156	148	118	175	147	171	145	107	152	151	178
06073	SOUTH GLASTONBURY	231	303	312	317	313	276	249	261	235	270	237	203	299	238	283	225	177	242	232	294
06074	SOUTH WINDSOR	147	178	174	181	179	166	155	159	150	162	151	123	174	152	169	147	109	153	151	183
06076	STAFFORD SPRINGS	98	115	103	116	112	111	104	106	103	104	104	82	114	105	111	104	74	104	107	124
06078	SUFFIELD	125	152	156	151	156	146	135	140	133	139	134	103	152	131	149	134	96	136	142	159
06081	TARIFFVILLE	117	130	125	132	129	121	123	120	119	125	120	94	130	120	127	117	86	120	117	141
06082	ENFIELD	95	109	100	109	106	105	101	100	100	101	102	77	110	101	107	101	72	101	104	118
06084	TOLLAND	168	207	192	210	204	183	176	180	166	188	169	142	199	172	191	160	122	171	163	206
06085	UNIONVILLE	122	151	156	148	155	144	133	138	131	133	132	102	150	131	146	132	95	134	136	155
06088	EAST WINDSOR	91	108	100	105	106	100	102	99	100	100	101	78	110	101	107	100	72	101	100	115
06089	WEATOGUE	178	230	239	238	238	213	192	202	182	206	184	154	226	183	218	177	135	190	185	229
06090	WEST GRANBY	197	255	263	267	264	233	211	221	199	228	201	171	251	202	239	191	149	206	197	250
06091	WEST HARTLAND	123	152	155	156	156	144	129	137	124	138	125	102	147	123	145	122	90	129	129	157
06092	WEST SIMSBURY	218	292	313	305	308	264	240	252	223	263	225	196	291	225	277	212	169	233	220	282
06093	WEST SUFFIELD	132	170	175	169	175	157	143	151	137	150	139	112	165	137	162	136	100	143	142	170
06095	WINDSOR	119	141	134	142	139	135	126	128	126	129	127	97	140	126	136	126	90	127	130	149
06096	WINDSOR LOCKS	88	103	93	103	99	101	94	94	94	93	95	72	103	95	100	96	67	94	99	110
06098	WINSTED	92	103	99	103	102	101	99	98	99	97	99	75	105	98	103	100	70	99	101	115
06103	HARTFORD	135	104	107	117	100	98	149	114	144	139	150	104	134	145	130	140	107	136	117	145
06105	HARTFORD	53	44	46	48	44	45	65	52	68	57	69	41	59	63	56	70	51	60	59	64
06106	HARTFORD	53	43	39	44	41	41	58	48	59	54	60	39	52	58	50	59	43	55	50	58
06107	WEST HARTFORD	147	195	215	193	207	185	166	175	161	171	162	127	197	159	191	162	119	167	171	194
06108	EAST HARTFORD	77	70	65	72	68	70	82	73	83	77	83	59	79	83	76	84	59	80	79	89
06109	WETHERSFIELD	102	120	125	119	124	122	110	114	112	112	112	82	123	108	121	115	79	113	124	131
06110	WEST HARTFORD	84	96	92	95	95	93	92	91	92	91	93	69	99	91	97	93	66	92	95	105
06111	NEWINGTON	105	125	122	124	126	122	112	116	112	114	113	86	125	111	122	113	80	114	119	133
06112	HARTFORD	59	55	53	57	53	57	65	57	70	60	70	43	64	67	60	74	50	64	66	72
06114	HARTFORD	59	52	48	52	50	46	65	56	63	62	66	45	61	64	59	62	48	63	54	65
06117	WEST HARTFORD	166	222	253	221	240	214	189	201	184	198	183	145	226	179	220	184	135	191	199	222
06118	EAST HARTFORD	89	91	88	92	89	96	91	91	94	88	94	68	93	93	92	97	66	92	99	107
06119	WEST HARTFORD	102	106	108	108	107	101	113	104	110	111	112	82	116	110	113	110	80	110	106	122
06120	HARTFORD	42	30	28	33	28	33	45	37	50	41	49	28	39	48	36	53	35	43	44	47
06226	WILLIMANTIC	68	63	60	64	62	64	74	66	75	69	75	52	71	74	69	76	53	72	71	80
06231	AMSTON	164	209	195	213	207	183	174	178	163	185	166	141	201	169	191	156	121	168	158	203
06232	ANDOVER	145	175	158	176	170	155	152	153	145	159	147	121	169	149	162	140	105	148	141	177
06234	BROOKLYN	97	105	100	106	104	105	99	102	99	99	99	77	104	99	103	100	70	100	103	118
06235	CHAPLIN	96	110	99	110	108	104	103	102	100	101	101	80	110	102	107	100	72	101	101	119
06237	COLUMBIA	135	178	177	174	181	160	149	155	142	154	144	116	172	144	167	140	105	148	144	174
06238	COVENTRY	135	163	146	164	158	148	141	143	135	146	138	112	157	140	151	133	98	138	135	166
06239	DANIELSON	82	87	80	87	84	84	87	84	87	85	87	65	90	87	87	87	62	86	86	98
06241	DAYVILLE	83	93	85	93	91	89	90	88	89	88	90	69	95	90	93	89	64	89	89	103
06242	EASTFORD	119	134	116	138	130	132	120	125	118	120	119	98	128	121	127	118	83	120	124	147
06243	EAST KILLINGLY	88	110	98	110	106	108	93	98	95	95	96	73	108	96	104	97	67	96	103	114
06247	HAMPTON	115	129	111	133	125	127	115	120	113	116	114	94	123	116	122	114	80	115	119	141
06248	HEBRON	165	212	199	216	210	186	176	180	164	187	167	143	204	170	194	158	122	170	159	205
06249	LEBANON	119	143	125	145	138	130	123	126	118	127	119	100	136	122	132	115	85	121	118	146
06250	MANSFIELD CENTER	117	128	117	130	124	124	121	120	120	122	121	93	128	121	125	120	85	120	122	142
06254	NORTH FRANKLIN	104	135	128	131	134	127	113	118	112	114	114	88	132	114	127	114	82	115	120	134
06255	NORTH GROSVENORDALE	78	92	84	92	90	89	84	85	83	83	84	65	92	84	89	84	59	84	88	99
06256	NORTH WINDHAM	78	74	64	72	70	73	74	73	76	76	76	55	72	78	71	77	53	74	74	87
06259	POMFRET CENTER	118	140	132	140	139	131	125	127	121	126	123	98	136	123	134	121	87	124	124	147
06260	PUTNAM	81	90	86	90	89	87	89	86	88	86	88	67	93	88	91	88	63	88	88	101
06262	QUINEBAUG	72	82	78	80	82	89	73	80	78	72	77	56	80	76	79	83	53	77	91	91
06264	SCOTLAND	113	127	109	131	123	124	113	118	111	114	112	92	121	114	120	112	78	113	117	139
06266	SOUTH WINDHAM	107	133	119	133	128	131	113	118	115	115	116	89	131	116	126	117	82	116	125	138
06268	STORRS MANSFIELD	120	104	101	110	102	105	139	110	127	122	128	93	121	126	116	123	90	122	111	135
06269	STORRS MANSFIELD	11	7	7	8	7	8	13	9	12	11	12	9	10	12	9	12	8	11	10	12
06277	THOMPSON	95	114	101	114	110	111	99	103	100	100	101	78	112	101	108	101	71	101	106	120
06278	ASHFORD	111	126	117	128	124	120	116	116	113	118	115	90	125	115	122	112	81	115	115	136
	CONNECTICUT	120	136	136	137	137	129	132	128	129	132	130	99	141	128	137	129	94	130	128	149
	UNITED STATES	100	100	100	100	100	100	100	100	100	100	100	100	100	100	100	100	100	100	100	100

ZIP CODE #	POST OFFICE NAME	COUNTY FIPS CODE	POPULATION 2000	POPULATION 2009	POPULATION 2014	2000-2009 ANNUAL RATE % Rate	2000-2009 ANNUAL RATE State Centile	HOUSEHOLDS 2000	HOUSEHOLDS 2009	HOUSEHOLDS 2014	HOUSEHOLDS % Annual Rate 2000-2009	HOUSEHOLDS 2009 Average HH Size	FAMILIES 2000	FAMILIES 2009	FAMILIES % Annual Rate 2000-2009
06279	WILLINGTON	013	5979	6424	6604	0.8	74	2362	2570	2659	0.9	2.48	1444	1545	0.7
06280	WINDHAM	015	3410	3729	3860	1.0	84	1311	1445	1504	1.1	2.50	938	1023	0.9
06281	WOODSTOCK	015	6636	7589	8015	1.5	94	2541	2922	3097	1.5	2.59	1868	2126	1.4
06282	WOODSTOCK VALLEY	015	1131	1257	1315	1.1	87	410	460	484	1.3	2.73	320	356	1.2
06320	NEW LONDON	011	25716	26914	26713	0.5	54	10200	10356	10330	0.2	2.22	5401	5377	0.0
06330	BALTIC	011	3426	3470	3437	0.1	24	1277	1317	1315	0.3	2.59	925	946	0.2
06331	CANTERBURY	015	4688	5049	5214	0.8	74	1713	1861	1927	0.9	2.71	1336	1440	0.8
06333	EAST LYME	011	6943	7440	7579	0.8	74	2088	2265	2328	0.9	3.06	1742	1880	0.8
06334	BOZRAH	011	2599	2790	2849	0.8	74	971	1065	1098	1.0	2.58	737	802	0.9
06335	GALES FERRY	011	6742	6786	6719	0.1	24	2475	2548	2541	0.3	2.66	1906	1948	0.2
06336	GILMAN	011	39	43	44	1.1	87	16	18	19	1.3	2.33	11	13	1.8
06339	LEDYARD	011	7897	8352	8504	0.6	61	2794	3024	3101	0.9	2.76	2184	2349	0.8
06340	GROTON	011	31733	31307	31145	-0.1	5	12236	12614	12681	0.3	2.31	7809	7885	0.1
06349	GROTON	011	1	875	877	108.0	100	0	0	0	0.0	0.00	0	0	0.0
06351	JEWETT CITY	011	14791	15638	15843	0.6	61	5684	6127	6247	0.8	2.53	4049	4336	0.7
06353	MONTVILLE	011	208	231	239	1.1	87	94	106	111	1.3	2.18	61	69	1.3
06354	MOOSUP	015	5759	6064	6203	0.6	61	2177	2311	2371	0.6	2.62	1514	1587	0.5
06355	MYSTIC	011	12172	13125	13350	0.8	74	4964	5438	5570	1.0	2.34	3264	3543	0.9
06357	NIANTIC	011	11079	11757	11842	0.6	61	4187	4392	4452	0.5	2.15	2766	2864	0.4
06359	NORTH STONINGTON	011	4991	5350	5476	0.8	74	1833	2005	2066	1.0	2.65	1424	1547	0.9
06360	NORWICH	011	33818	35440	35717	0.5	54	14160	15063	15285	0.7	2.29	8472	8903	0.5
06365	PRESTON	011	4688	4811	4807	0.3	38	1837	1928	1941	0.5	2.50	1360	1418	0.5
06370	OAKDALE	011	6485	7018	7198	0.9	79	2331	2567	2646	1.0	2.73	1809	1980	1.0
06371	OLD LYME	011	9463	9722	9722	0.3	38	3824	3989	4014	0.5	2.43	2776	2872	0.4
06374	PLAINFIELD	015	8219	8980	9277	1.0	84	3019	3325	3450	1.0	2.64	2216	2416	0.9
06375	QUAKER HILL	011	4155	3839	3884	-0.9	1	1411	1504	1530	0.7	2.50	1031	1087	0.6
06377	STERLING	015	2444	2602	2663	0.7	66	892	959	987	0.8	2.71	670	713	0.7
06378	STONINGTON	011	5312	5499	5536	0.4	46	2344	2440	2465	0.4	2.24	1484	1535	0.4
06379	PAWCATUCK	011	8643	8761	8724	0.1	24	3611	3727	3735	0.3	2.35	2330	2380	0.2
06380	TAFTVILLE	011	2360	2346	2306	-0.1	5	974	991	981	0.2	2.37	624	629	0.1
06382	UNCASVILLE	011	11602	12034	12012	0.4	46	3885	3990	4007	0.3	2.51	2726	2773	0.2
06384	VOLUNTOWN	011	2546	2527	2479	-0.1	5	959	969	957	0.1	2.61	708	710	0.0
06385	WATERFORD	011	14955	15099	15025	0.1	24	6114	6251	6258	0.2	2.34	4173	4228	0.1
06401	ANSONIA	009	18440	18585	18661	0.1	24	7463	7576	7625	0.2	2.44	4946	4963	0.0
06403	BEACON FALLS	009	5246	5669	5831	0.8	74	2032	2199	2264	0.9	2.58	1450	1553	0.7
06405	BRANFORD	009	28670	28744	28784	0.0	12	12540	12652	12702	0.1	2.25	7659	7624	0.0
06409	CENTERBROOK	007	551	651	692	1.8	97	252	304	325	2.0	2.11	168	199	1.8
06410	CHESHIRE	009	28607	29412	29591	0.3	38	9371	9657	9746	0.3	2.71	7270	7431	0.2
06412	CHESTER	007	3743	4008	4129	0.7	66	1510	1654	1718	1.0	2.33	1006	1086	0.8
06413	CLINTON	007	13094	13207	13228	0.1	24	5134	5270	5311	0.3	2.51	3616	3668	0.2
06415	COLCHESTER	011	15343	16341	16552	0.7	66	5541	5917	6010	0.7	2.72	4227	4495	0.7
06416	CROMWELL	007	12866	13602	13880	0.6	61	5210	5612	5769	0.8	2.31	3264	3457	0.6
06417	DEEP RIVER	007	4610	4746	4807	0.3	38	1824	1901	1932	0.4	2.43	1262	1298	0.3
06418	DERBY	009	12480	12510	12505	0.0	12	5285	5328	5338	0.1	2.30	3273	3259	0.0
06419	KILLINGWORTH	007	6010	6458	6657	0.8	74	2193	2390	2477	0.9	2.70	1762	1904	0.8
06420	SALEM	011	3804	3999	4072	0.5	54	1339	1434	1468	0.7	2.78	1061	1129	0.7
06422	DURHAM	007	6726	7522	7877	1.2	90	2308	2640	2786	1.5	2.79	1894	2150	1.4
06423	EAST HADDAM	007	4754	5499	5828	1.6	95	1773	2091	2230	1.8	2.60	1301	1518	1.7
06424	EAST HAMPTON	007	13555	13028	13809	-0.4	1	4214	4986	5312	1.8	2.59	3059	3581	1.7
06426	ESSEX	007	3192	3313	3371	0.4	46	1510	1591	1624	0.6	2.02	860	882	0.3
06437	GUILFORD	009	21388	22282	22632	0.4	46	8151	8525	8677	0.5	2.58	6040	6285	0.4
06438	HADDAM	007	2351	2600	2713	1.1	87	898	1014	1067	1.3	2.55	680	759	1.2
06441	HIGGANUM	007	4494	4990	5210	1.1	87	1677	1901	1998	1.4	2.62	1335	1500	1.3
06442	IVORYTON	007	2762	3228	3424	1.7	96	1049	1242	1324	1.8	2.58	749	870	1.6
06443	MADISON	009	17813	18609	18933	0.5	54	6501	6858	7003	0.6	2.69	5107	5345	0.5
06447	MARLBOROUGH	003	5732	6259	6473	1.0	84	2012	2220	2305	1.1	2.77	1631	1788	1.0
06450	MERIDEN	009	34528	35495	35756	0.3	38	13696	14116	14247	0.3	2.44	8787	8943	0.2
06451	MERIDEN	009	23973	24571	24769	0.3	38	9339	9574	9664	0.3	2.55	6248	6358	0.2
06455	MIDDLEFIELD	007	2983	3211	3306	0.8	74	1155	1264	1309	1.0	2.54	838	908	0.9
06457	MIDDLETOWN	007	43035	46693	47429	0.9	79	18464	19514	19931	0.6	2.19	10364	10800	0.4
06459	MIDDLETOWN	007	147	858	870	21.0	100	92	99	101	0.8	4.55	30	32	0.7
06460	MILFORD	009	38465	38602	38680	0.0	12	15727	15889	15960	0.1	2.40	10270	10244	0.0
06461	MILFORD	009	13843	14684	15019	0.6	61	5182	5510	5639	0.7	2.65	3799	4015	0.6
06468	MONROE	001	19482	20031	20187	0.3	38	6545	6731	6778	0.3	2.97	5405	5533	0.3
06469	MOODUS	007	2848	3365	3578	1.8	97	1107	1341	1440	2.1	2.45	772	923	2.0
06470	NEWTOWN	001	14740	16018	16453	0.9	79	4940	5378	5530	0.9	2.89	4030	4364	0.9
06471	NORTH BRANFORD	009	7319	7271	7258	-0.1	5	2836	2832	2834	0.0	2.55	1983	1959	-0.1
06472	NORTHFORD	009	6496	6922	7112	0.7	66	2261	2429	2502	0.8	2.85	1859	1984	0.7
06473	NORTH HAVEN	009	23184	24081	24434	0.4	46	8637	9030	9191	0.5	2.64	6522	6760	0.4
06475	OLD SAYBROOK	007	10367	10451	10475	0.1	24	4184	4284	4319	0.3	2.37	2922	2956	0.1
06477	ORANGE	009	13276	14227	14622	0.8	74	4753	5175	5352	0.9	2.73	3909	4196	0.8
06478	OXFORD	009	10017	12259	13206	2.2	98	3413	4201	4529	2.3	2.92	2845	3483	2.2
06479	PLANTSVILLE	003	10163	10893	11202	0.8	74	3701	4008	4138	0.9	2.64	2809	3013	0.8
06480	PORTLAND	007	8834	9852	10276	1.2	90	3423	3881	4076	1.4	2.48	2447	2756	1.3
06481	ROCKFALL	007	1181	1275	1319	0.8	74	478	527	550	1.1	2.42	352	383	0.9
06482	SANDY HOOK	001	10343	11470	11873	1.1	87	3405	3781	3921	1.1	2.92	2765	3054	1.1
06483	SEYMOUR	009	15310	15966	16223	0.5	54	6100	6403	6526	0.5	2.47	4169	4329	0.4
06484	SHELTON	001	37834	39074	39390	0.3	38	14098	14574	14720	0.4	2.64	10460	10718	0.3
06488	SOUTHBURY	009	18546	20188	20875	0.9	79	7222	7795	8051	0.8	2.44	4829	5179	0.8
06489	SOUTHINGTON	003	29535	30839	31360	0.5	54	11367	11943	12167	0.5	2.56	8466	8837	0.5
06492	WALLINGFORD	009	42736	43970	44437	0.3	38	16603	17152	17364	0.4	2.51	11498	11778	0.3
06498	WESTBROOK	007	6292	6842	7073	0.9	79	2605	2860	2965	1.0	2.37	1694	1833	0.9
06510	NEW HAVEN	009	3002	3367	3548	1.2	90	1436	1693	1819	1.8	1.55	290	338	1.7
06511	NEW HAVEN	009	52775	54940	55596	0.4	46	20275	21119	21430	0.4	2.24	9756	9994	0.3
06512	EAST HAVEN	009	28696	29225	29422	0.2	29	11749	12005	12107	0.2	2.41	7557	7635	0.1
06513	NEW HAVEN	009	34896	35237	35163	0.1	24	13304	13185	13128	-0.1	2.64	8432	8241	-0.2
06514	HAMDEN	009	24764	24921	24997	0.1	24	9829	9992	10059	0.2	2.39	6308	6316	0.0
06515	NEW HAVEN	009	16435	16260	16178	-0.1	5	6292	6170	6151	-0.2	2.37	3792	3683	-0.3
06516	WEST HAVEN	009	52255	52825	52877	0.1	24	21042	21289	21338	0.1	2.42	13091	13070	0.0
06517	HAMDEN	009	14342	14461	14502	0.1	24	6199	6287	6323	0.2	2.26	3689	3692	0.0
06518	HAMDEN	009	17719	18924	19395	0.7	66	6354	6885	7104	0.9	2.34	4011	4281	0.7
06519	NEW HAVEN	009	16114	16659	16836	0.4	46	5306	5514	5590	0.4	2.90	3552	3661	0.3
06524	BETHANY	009	5058	5515	5702	0.9	79	1761	1931	2001	1.0	2.86	1454	1584	0.9
06525	WOODBRIDGE	009	8965	9355	9505	0.5	54	3097	3242	3300	0.5	2.83	2548	2650	0.4
06604	BRIDGEPORT	001	27882	29078	29344	0.5	54	9582	9875	9947	0.3	2.80	5978	6084	0.2
	CONNECTICUT					0.4					0.4	2.53			0.3
	UNITED STATES					1.0					1.1	2.59			0.9

ZIP CODE #	POST OFFICE NAME	RACE (%) White 2000	White 2009	Black 2000	Black 2009	Asian/Pacific 2000	Asian/Pacific 2009	% Hispanic Origin 2000	% Hispanic Origin 2009	2009 AGE DISTRIBUTION (%) 0-4	5-9	10-14	15-19	20-24	25-44	45-64	65-84	85+	18+	MEDIAN AGE 2009	% 2009 Males	% 2009 Females
06279	WILLINGTON	94.0	91.3	1.0	1.1	3.1	5.3	1.8	2.5	4.5	4.5	4.8	5.3	12.4	31.3	28.1	8.0	1.1	83.0	34.4	50.1	49.9
06280	WINDHAM	88.0	84.6	2.1	2.3	0.9	1.4	11.5	15.5	5.8	6.0	6.2	6.0	4.7	23.3	30.0	14.8	3.2	78.1	43.4	47.5	52.5
06281	WOODSTOCK	97.6	96.7	0.1	0.2	0.4	0.8	0.8	1.3	5.3	5.8	6.6	7.1	4.9	22.9	33.8	11.6	2.0	77.7	43.3	49.7	50.3
06282	WOODSTOCK VALLEY	96.2	95.1	0.4	0.6	0.5	0.8	1.1	1.7	5.6	6.4	7.1	7.2	4.9	25.5	33.9	8.5	1.0	76.5	41.4	49.6	50.4
06320	NEW LONDON	63.5	59.2	18.6	19.4	2.2	3.4	19.7	23.2	6.6	5.7	5.5	10.5	14.0	25.5	20.9	9.1	2.2	78.5	30.3	49.4	50.6
06330	BALTIC	95.7	93.9	0.7	0.8	1.3	2.2	1.2	1.8	5.3	5.3	5.9	7.7	6.0	25.8	31.0	11.4	1.7	78.6	41.3	48.4	51.6
06331	CANTERBURY	97.3	96.4	0.4	0.5	0.3	0.5	1.1	1.8	5.2	6.0	7.0	7.0	4.6	27.3	31.8	9.7	1.3	77.3	40.7	50.5	49.5
06333	EAST LYME	88.0	83.5	3.8	4.4	5.3	8.5	3.3	4.4	5.3	6.5	7.8	7.8	4.9	23.1	32.8	10.7	1.0	75.2	41.8	52.5	47.5
06334	BOZRAH	96.1	94.7	0.7	0.8	0.7	1.1	1.8	2.6	5.1	5.7	6.6	6.7	4.2	23.6	33.2	12.7	2.3	78.3	43.9	49.8	50.2
06335	GALES FERRY	92.2	89.4	2.0	2.5	2.2	3.6	2.6	3.8	5.4	7.5	7.8	7.2	4.6	25.6	31.1	10.0	1.0	74.2	40.3	49.0	51.0
06336	GILMAN	100.0	97.7	0.0	0.0	0.0	0.0	2.6	2.3	4.7	4.7	4.7	4.7	4.7	25.6	34.9	14.0	2.3	83.7	45.6	46.5	53.5
06339	LEDYARD	84.8	80.9	2.9	3.5	2.3	3.7	2.9	4.1	6.5	6.9	7.4	6.9	5.3	24.9	30.5	10.6	1.0	74.8	39.9	48.9	51.1
06340	GROTON	81.3	75.8	8.2	9.6	3.8	6.3	5.8	8.0	8.7	7.1	5.7	7.1	9.9	29.6	19.7	9.7	2.3	75.2	31.4	50.7	49.3
06349	GROTON	100.0	70.1	0.0	14.9	0.0	4.0	0.0	12.3	1.8	1.4	1.4	31.9	34.1	23.5	3.5	1.9	0.5	92.2	22.0	77.6	22.4
06351	JEWETT CITY	94.9	93.3	1.1	1.4	0.8	1.3	1.6	2.3	5.8	6.2	6.6	6.9	5.2	26.8	30.4	10.3	1.7	76.9	40.4	49.4	50.6
06353	MONTVILLE	93.8	91.3	1.4	1.7	1.0	1.7	3.4	4.8	5.6	5.6	5.6	6.5	5.6	23.8	30.3	14.3	2.6	78.4	43.2	50.2	49.8
06354	MOOSUP	96.2	94.5	0.5	0.6	0.7	1.2	2.7	4.3	6.9	6.7	6.8	7.4	6.4	27.6	27.3	9.4	1.5	75.0	37.0	49.5	50.5
06355	MYSTIC	93.7	91.2	1.6	1.9	2.0	3.4	1.7	2.5	4.9	5.2	6.0	6.0	4.5	23.0	32.1	15.1	3.2	79.8	45.2	48.2	51.8
06357	NIANTIC	86.8	83.2	8.0	9.5	1.3	2.1	5.5	7.6	4.0	4.0	4.5	5.5	7.0	32.0	26.8	13.6	2.4	84.4	40.7	44.4	55.6
06359	NORTH STONINGTON	94.3	92.5	0.6	0.7	1.1	1.8	1.4	2.1	5.2	5.9	6.9	6.6	4.4	23.3	34.7	12.0	1.1	77.4	43.5	49.6	50.4
06360	NORWICH	82.8	78.4	7.1	8.2	2.2	3.6	6.1	8.4	6.5	6.0	5.6	6.3	7.4	26.4	26.4	12.4	2.9	78.0	38.7	47.7	52.3
06365	PRESTON	95.6	94.0	0.7	0.9	1.2	1.9	1.4	2.0	4.7	5.0	5.5	6.3	5.1	23.7	32.6	15.3	1.9	81.0	44.8	49.5	50.5
06370	OAKDALE	92.7	90.3	2.0	2.4	1.6	2.6	2.7	4.0	5.8	6.7	7.6	7.1	4.4	26.8	30.9	9.8	0.8	75.2	39.9	50.2	49.8
06371	OLD LYME	97.5	96.3	0.2	0.3	1.2	2.1	1.0	1.5	4.9	5.9	7.1	6.6	3.4	17.1	35.4	17.3	2.5	77.7	47.7	49.4	50.6
06374	PLAINFIELD	96.2	94.9	0.9	1.1	0.6	1.0	2.3	3.7	6.2	6.1	6.3	6.7	5.8	27.1	28.0	11.3	2.4	77.1	39.7	48.9	51.1
06375	QUAKER HILL	90.3	83.8	2.8	6.2	2.9	4.0	2.2	5.3	4.9	5.7	6.1	7.7	8.3	19.1	29.3	15.9	3.0	79.7	43.6	47.5	52.5
06377	STERLING	96.2	95.0	0.2	0.2	0.3	0.6	1.3	2.2	6.9	7.4	7.8	7.2	4.0	29.4	29.4	7.1	0.8	73.3	38.0	52.1	47.9
06378	STONINGTON	97.4	96.3	0.3	0.4	0.9	1.6	1.2	1.8	4.5	4.9	5.7	5.6	3.8	20.6	34.2	18.0	2.6	81.3	47.7	49.0	51.0
06379	PAWCATUCK	94.7	92.7	0.8	1.0	1.5	2.5	1.3	2.0	6.2	6.2	6.4	6.5	5.9	24.2	29.2	13.0	2.3	77.2	41.4	48.6	51.4
06380	TAFTVILLE	88.4	85.0	3.1	3.8	0.6	1.0	6.9	10.0	6.9	6.3	5.8	6.5	8.9	30.0	24.9	9.2	1.6	77.2	34.6	48.7	51.3
06382	UNCASVILLE	82.1	77.7	7.6	8.7	2.1	3.3	7.0	9.5	5.0	5.1	5.3	6.6	8.6	30.5	25.6	11.2	2.0	80.8	37.9	57.4	42.6
06384	VOLUNTOWN	96.6	95.7	0.5	0.7	0.3	0.5	1.2	1.7	6.1	7.6	7.3	7.1	3.2	31.2	28.2	8.3	1.0	74.1	38.5	50.9	49.1
06385	WATERFORD	93.0	90.2	2.1	2.5	2.4	4.0	2.4	3.5	4.7	5.2	6.2	6.2	4.4	20.9	31.5	17.3	3.7	79.7	46.4	48.1	51.9
06401	ANSONIA	85.5	80.9	8.4	10.6	1.1	1.8	7.4	10.9	6.9	6.6	6.4	6.5	6.4	27.3	26.1	11.4	2.5	76.2	38.1	48.2	51.8
06403	BEACON FALLS	97.0	95.5	0.7	1.0	1.1	1.8	2.1	3.4	6.2	6.4	6.6	6.2	5.6	27.4	30.5	9.8	1.3	77.1	40.2	50.5	49.5
06405	BRANFORD	94.0	91.0	1.3	1.8	2.8	4.7	2.6	4.0	5.1	5.2	5.6	5.5	5.5	23.5	31.9	14.5	3.2	80.7	44.7	47.2	52.8
06409	CENTERBROOK	97.1	95.9	0.5	0.8	0.4	0.8	2.4	3.5	6.8	7.5	7.7	6.3	4.6	22.3	30.6	12.1	2.2	73.3	41.7	47.6	52.4
06410	CHESHIRE	89.4	85.8	4.7	5.4	2.6	4.5	3.8	5.4	5.3	6.0	7.0	9.2	5.7	23.3	30.2	10.6	2.5	76.4	40.8	53.5	46.5
06412	CHESTER	96.8	95.6	0.9	1.0	0.9	1.5	1.7	2.5	5.8	6.5	6.7	5.6	4.5	21.9	32.5	12.2	4.3	76.9	44.4	47.6	52.4
06413	CLINTON	95.8	94.2	0.6	0.7	1.2	2.0	4.0	5.7	6.1	6.4	6.9	6.7	4.9	24.9	30.6	11.9	1.7	76.4	41.6	48.5	51.5
06415	COLCHESTER	95.6	94.2	1.3	1.6	0.6	1.0	1.9	2.8	7.8	8.3	8.4	7.3	4.8	25.9	28.0	7.8	1.7	70.6	37.7	48.5	51.5
06416	CROMWELL	93.1	90.7	3.1	3.9	1.2	2.1	3.2	4.5	5.1	5.1	5.7	5.7	5.5	25.3	31.2	12.4	3.9	80.3	43.4	48.3	51.7
06417	DEEP RIVER	94.6	92.8	2.4	2.9	0.9	1.5	3.0	4.1	5.0	5.4	6.8	7.8	4.2	24.6	32.0	12.3	1.9	77.4	42.9	49.5	50.5
06418	DERBY	90.1	86.2	3.6	4.6	1.8	2.9	7.6	11.1	6.1	6.1	6.1	6.2	5.4	27.8	26.7	12.7	3.0	77.7	40.2	48.7	51.3
06419	KILLINGWORTH	97.5	96.5	0.4	0.5	0.8	1.4	1.2	1.7	6.6	8.0	9.1	7.2	2.9	19.9	32.8	12.0	1.5	71.6	43.1	48.9	51.1
06420	SALEM	95.5	93.7	0.8	1.1	1.5	2.5	1.2	1.8	6.1	7.0	7.9	8.3	4.6	23.3	33.6	8.4	0.9	73.8	40.8	49.4	50.6
06422	DURHAM	96.7	95.4	1.1	1.4	0.8	1.5	1.5	2.2	6.1	6.9	8.4	8.3	4.2	21.5	32.8	10.3	1.4	72.4	41.6	50.1	49.9
06423	EAST HADDAM	97.0	96.0	1.1	1.4	0.4	0.7	1.0	1.4	6.5	7.4	7.9	6.7	3.6	24.1	32.5	10.1	1.3	73.2	41.9	49.7	50.3
06424	EAST HAMPTON	93.4	91.4	2.0	2.9	2.4	2.8	1.7	3.0	5.4	5.8	6.1	9.9	9.5	23.2	30.3	8.6	1.2	78.7	37.7	49.2	50.8
06426	ESSEX	98.5	97.9	0.3	0.4	0.4	0.8	1.0	1.4	4.0	4.4	5.2	4.5	2.8	16.6	32.6	21.3	8.7	83.2	52.8	46.0	54.0
06437	GUILFORD	96.0	93.9	0.9	1.3	1.7	2.9	2.1	3.4	5.4	6.4	7.5	6.7	4.0	19.7	34.9	13.3	2.1	76.4	45.2	48.0	52.0
06438	HADDAM	96.3	94.8	1.4	1.7	1.1	1.8	1.1	1.6	5.0	6.0	7.0	6.4	3.7	22.5	35.9	11.9	1.6	77.5	44.7	49.8	50.2
06441	HIGGANUM	97.2	96.2	0.9	1.2	0.6	1.1	1.0	1.5	5.1	6.1	7.2	7.2	3.7	21.2	35.9	12.2	1.2	77.1	44.6	50.9	49.1
06442	IVORYTON	97.0	95.8	0.7	0.9	0.8	1.3	1.7	2.5	7.3	8.1	8.5	6.9	4.2	22.2	31.4	9.7	1.7	71.3	40.5	48.4	51.6
06443	MADISON	96.6	94.7	0.4	0.6	1.7	3.0	1.3	2.2	6.0	7.2	8.6	7.9	3.8	17.3	33.4	13.5	2.3	73.0	44.5	48.6	51.4
06447	MARLBOROUGH	97.5	96.2	0.8	1.1	0.7	1.2	1.0	1.8	6.0	6.9	7.7	7.1	3.7	22.7	35.1	9.0	1.6	74.6	42.6	49.7	50.3
06450	MERIDEN	80.5	75.8	6.7	7.6	1.5	2.3	20.4	26.4	6.9	6.6	6.5	6.5	6.1	26.4	26.6	11.6	2.9	76.0	38.6	48.6	51.4
06451	MERIDEN	80.0	75.1	6.0	6.8	1.2	1.8	21.9	28.3	7.2	7.0	6.8	6.9	6.3	26.2	26.4	11.1	2.2	74.8	37.4	49.0	51.0
06455	MIDDLEFIELD	97.9	97.1	0.5	0.7	0.3	0.6	1.5	2.1	5.5	5.9	6.5	7.2	5.6	21.9	32.0	13.1	2.1	77.6	43.3	49.9	50.1
06457	MIDDLETOWN	80.0	75.1	12.3	14.1	2.7	4.4	5.3	7.2	6.1	5.8	5.8	6.7	8.4	28.5	25.5	10.8	2.4	79.0	37.6	49.1	50.9
06459	MIDDLETOWN	77.7	68.1	10.8	15.0	4.1	6.9	5.4	10.4	3.8	3.0	2.7	14.2	30.2	21.2	13.6	9.2	2.0	89.0	24.3	51.4	48.6
06460	MILFORD	93.6	90.5	1.8	2.5	2.5	4.1	3.4	5.2	5.4	5.6	5.9	5.8	5.1	26.4	30.0	13.0	2.7	79.4	42.4	48.4	51.6
06461	MILFORD	93.8	90.6	2.1	2.8	2.1	3.6	3.3	5.2	6.6	7.1	7.2	5.9	4.2	24.9	29.3	12.5	2.3	75.4	41.7	49.0	51.0
06468	MONROE	95.9	93.7	1.2	1.7	1.5	2.6	2.5	4.0	6.9	7.7	8.5	7.7	4.5	21.0	31.4	10.8	1.5	71.8	41.3	49.2	50.8
06469	MOODUS	97.6	96.7	0.6	0.7	0.4	0.7	0.9	1.3	6.0	6.3	6.9	7.1	5.0	24.3	30.9	10.6	2.8	76.0	41.6	49.3	50.7
06470	NEWTOWN	95.4	93.3	1.7	2.1	1.3	2.3	2.4	3.8	6.6	8.0	9.2	7.5	4.1	20.9	32.5	9.9	1.3	71.2	41.5	51.3	48.7
06471	NORTH BRANFORD	95.9	93.9	1.3	1.8	0.8	1.5	2.2	3.6	6.3	6.5	6.8	7.0	5.5	23.1	28.8	12.3	3.7	76.0	41.8	48.0	52.0
06472	NORTHFORD	97.1	95.6	1.0	1.5	1.1	1.9	1.3	2.1	5.7	6.6	7.4	7.1	4.2	22.9	32.9	12.0	1.3	75.8	42.5	49.2	50.8
06473	NORTH HAVEN	93.0	89.4	2.2	3.0	3.3	5.7	1.9	3.0	5.4	5.8	6.3	6.4	5.0	22.6	30.5	15.0	3.0	78.4	44.0	48.5	51.5
06475	OLD SAYBROOK	95.7	93.8	1.0	1.3	1.8	3.1	1.9	2.6	5.1	5.8	6.7	6.1	3.1	18.1	31.8	19.3	4.1	78.5	48.0	47.4	52.6
06477	ORANGE	94.1	90.6	0.8	1.2	3.8	6.6	1.4	2.4	5.3	5.9	6.8	6.8	4.6	18.6	31.7	16.7	3.7	77.6	46.2	48.5	51.5
06478	OXFORD	97.6	96.4	0.5	0.7	0.8	1.3	1.8	3.0	6.1	6.9	7.8	7.4	4.3	25.0	32.7	8.5	1.2	74.4	41.0	50.2	49.8
06479	PLANTSVILLE	97.1	95.4	0.7	1.0	0.7	1.3	1.7	2.8	6.3	6.5	6.8	6.3	5.1	25.2	29.2	12.2	2.3	76.2	41.3	48.6	51.4
06480	PORTLAND	95.1	93.8	2.4	2.8	0.6	1.0	1.9	2.7	6.4	7.2	7.7	7.1	4.2	23.7	29.2	12.1	2.4	74.0	41.3	48.8	51.2
06481	ROCKFALL	97.5	96.5	1.2	1.5	0.5	0.9	0.9	1.4	4.7	5.3	6.3	6.9	4.9	20.0	33.6	15.8	2.5	79.5	46.1	49.1	50.9
06482	SANDY HOOK	94.8	92.4	1.8	2.3	1.6	2.9	2.3	3.6	8.1	8.9	8.8	6.8	3.7	26.2	28.6	7.3	1.5	69.5	38.1	51.7	48.3
06483	SEYMOUR	94.7	92.1	1.4	1.9	1.8	3.0	3.1	4.8	5.9	6.0	6.1	6.5	6.0	26.1	29.6	11.5	2.4	77.9	40.8	48.5	51.5
06484	SHELTON	94.4	91.6	1.1	1.5	2.1	3.5	3.5	5.5	5.9	6.2	6.6	6.2	4.9	23.7	29.9	13.6	3.0	77.3	42.8	48.3	51.7
06488	SOUTHBURY	97.3	95.8	0.5	0.6	1.2	2.1	1.6	2.6	4.8	5.6	6.8	6.3	3.1	16.7	30.5	18.9	7.3	78.5	49.0	46.4	53.6
06489	SOUTHINGTON	96.2	94.1	0.9	1.3	1.2	2.0	2.1	3.6	5.6	6.0	6.5	6.3	4.8	23.2	30.5	14.7	2.4	77.9	43.4	48.6	51.4
06492	WALLINGFORD	94.8	92.3	1.0	1.4	1.8	2.9	4.5	6.8	5.7	6.1	6.6	6.6	5.1	24.4	30.1	12.2	3.2	77.3	42.1	48.2	51.8
06498	WESTBROOK	95.8	94.0	0.7	0.8	1.7	2.7	2.5	3.5	5.1	5.5	6.0	5.2	4.3	24.4	31.7	15.3	2.6	80.0	44.7	49.3	50.7
06510	NEW HAVEN	56.4	46.6	20.6	23.0	13.6	19.2	11.7	14.6	3.0	1.7	1.3	13.7	30.1	33.5	12.0	4.0	0.7	92.6	25.1	51.8	48.2
06511	NEW HAVEN	37.9	32.1	46.2	48.1	6.4	8.8	11.4	13.7	6.2	5.6	5.2	9.7	15.5	31.2	18.6	6.8	1.3	79.1	28.7	49.5	50.5
06512	EAST HAVEN	92.0	88.9	2.2	2.7	1.8	2.9	6.2	9.1	5.8	5.6	5.7	5.8	6.0	26.4	27.8	13.9	3.1	79.5	41.7	48.1	51.9
06513	NEW HAVEN	56.1	50.9	22.0	23.0	2.2	3.1	31.0	36.5	8.5	7.7	7.0	7.5	8.3	27.6	21.0	10.1	2.4	72.4	32.2	47.0	53.0
06514	HAMDEN	70.3	62.8	21.3	25.3	3.9	6.1	5.2	7.2	5.7	5.6	5.8	6.2	7.7	26.8	25.8	12.6	3.8	79.1	39.6	46.3	53.7
06515	NEW HAVEN	50.1	45.0	41.6	44.2	2.0	2.9	8.6	11.1	7.0	6.6	6.1	10.7	10.5	25.8	22.0	9.1	2.1	76.4	31.1	46.0	54.0
06516	WEST HAVEN	74.1	68.7	16.3	18.6	3.0	4.4	9.1	12.3	6.2	6.0	5.9	6.7	7.6	27.2	26.4	11.5	2.4	78.1	38.1	47.8	52.2
06517	HAMDEN	76.3	70.8	17.2	20.0	2.8	4.5	4.6	6.4	5.7	5.6	6.3	6.5	5.8	22.6	27.8	15.2	4.5	78.1	43.2	46.6	53.4
06518	HAMDEN	88.9	83.8	5.1	6.8	3.7	6.3	2.6	3.9	4.3	4.3	4.6	12.6	10.5	23.1	25.0	12.3	3.3	83.9	37.3	45.3	54.7
06519	NEW HAVEN	25.9	23.9	41.0	39.4	0.5	0.7	45.4	50.4	9.5	8.6	7.7	8.7	9.7	27.1	18.2	7.9	2.6	69.1	28.4	48.1	51.9
06524	BETHANY	95.0	92.5	1.8	2.5	1.6	2.8	2.0	3.2	5.5	6.3	7.7	7.6	4.4	19.1	35.2	12.6	1.7	75.8	44.6	50.1	49.9
06525	WOODBRIDGE	91.3	86.7	1.5	2.0	5.1	8.6	1.5	2.4	5.0	6.2	8.0	7.9	4.0	15.5	35.1	15.0	3.3	75.7	46.8	48.9	51.1
06604	BRIDGEPORT	41.3	36.8	27.3	27.9	6.0	7.8	34.4	39.4	8.7	7.8	6.7	8.4	10.3	29.1	19.4	7.9	1.5	72.3	29.3	49.7	50.3
	CONNECTICUT	81.6	78.0	9.1	9.9	2.5	3.8	9.4	12.0	6.3	6.4	6.7	7.2	6.5	24.9	27.9	11.7	2.5	76.3	39.6	48.6	51.4
	UNITED STATES	75.1	72.0	12.3	12.7	3.8	4.6	12.5	15.7	6.8	6.7	6.6	7.1	6.9	27.0	26.0	10.9	1.9	75.7	36.9	49.2	50.8

ZIP CODE #	POST OFFICE NAME	2009 Per Capita Income	2009 HH Income Base	2009 HOUSEHOLD INCOME DISTRIBUTION (%) Less than $25,000	$25,000 to $49,999	$50,000 to $99,999	$100,000 to $149,999	$150,000 or More	MEDIAN HOUSEHOLD INCOME 2009	2014	2009 National Centile	2009 State Centile	2009 Home Value Base	2009 HOME VALUE DISTRIBUTION (%) Less than $50,000	$50,000 to $89,999	$90,000 to $174,999	$175,000 to $399,999	$400,000 or More	2009 Median Home Value
06279	WILLINGTON	32643	2570	15.8	19.2	35.2	22.1	7.7	65134	69645	83	30	1657	0.0	2.1	14.8	72.5	10.6	237693
06280	WINDHAM	28174	1445	16.0	21.4	45.4	12.5	4.8	62158	63380	80	28	1073	1.4	1.3	19.5	69.5	8.3	221154
06281	WOODSTOCK	32088	2922	12.1	22.0	42.6	13.5	9.9	69682	72828	87	37	2389	0.6	1.3	23.9	58.9	15.3	243248
06282	WOODSTOCK VALLEY	31559	460	12.0	9.8	52.0	15.7	10.7	76353	77700	90	49	411	0.0	0.0	17.0	64.2	18.7	253354
06320	NEW LONDON	21824	10356	29.8	30.7	32.4	4.5	2.5	40542	43624	34	8	3942	1.1	2.5	47.1	42.7	6.6	174096
06330	BALTIC	26036	1317	16.2	27.5	38.7	13.4	4.1	60804	65355	79	27	908	0.3	2.2	21.4	65.3	10.8	231100
06331	CANTERBURY	27613	1861	13.6	18.1	48.2	15.0	5.1	72081	74246	88	40	1595	1.4	1.0	22.3	68.3	6.9	219112
06333	EAST LYME	41605	2265	5.1	8.9	33.9	21.7	30.4	103855	104780	97	87	1997	0.0	0.0	4.7	51.8	43.5	365831
06334	BOZRAH	32944	1065	5.5	17.8	51.5	17.2	7.9	72788	75305	88	41	881	0.0	0.3	13.1	70.5	16.1	250706
06335	GALES FERRY	33911	2548	6.9	13.0	51.3	17.1	11.7	79140	79138	92	58	2103	2.8	3.0	6.8	76.3	11.1	251376
06336	GILMAN	28825	18	11.1	27.8	38.9	16.7	5.6	56087	58413	73	19	14	0.0	0.0	14.3	64.3	21.4	250000
06339	LEDYARD	31911	3024	7.8	18.0	48.0	14.5	11.6	77624	78751	91	53	2457	0.4	0.3	18.8	60.0	20.4	250932
06340	GROTON	27666	12614	15.3	29.4	42.0	9.1	4.3	54315	57282	70	17	5508	6.2	3.2	25.1	49.1	16.4	214090
06349	GROTON	14251	0	0.0	0.0	0.0	0.0	0.0	0	0	0	0	0	0.0	0.0	0.0	0.0	0.0	0
06351	JEWETT CITY	27819	6127	11.8	21.8	51.4	11.2	3.8	67875	71243	85	34	4600	2.8	3.4	24.6	62.6	6.6	212555
06353	MONTVILLE	33201	106	16.0	17.0	49.1	10.4	7.5	67378	70270	85	34	76	3.9	2.6	14.5	71.1	7.9	230000
06354	MOOSUP	22134	2311	19.1	26.2	45.3	7.0	2.3	54098	57364	70	16	1484	0.9	1.3	43.1	50.9	3.8	182372
06355	MYSTIC	41677	5438	7.4	15.1	46.1	15.8	15.6	79733	80275	92	59	4181	3.4	0.3	6.4	54.7	35.3	294969
06357	NIANTIC	35361	4392	10.7	17.7	46.8	15.3	9.4	77729	78189	91	54	3212	0.2	0.4	7.0	72.0	20.4	265716
06359	NORTH STONINGTON	32138	2005	7.8	18.8	49.2	14.7	9.5	75015	75578	89	45	1762	2.2	0.1	7.5	62.6	27.6	286469
06360	NORWICH	25251	15063	25.2	25.8	38.2	7.3	3.5	48775	51479	58	12	7990	4.1	4.4	39.2	46.4	5.9	179905
06365	PRESTON	31537	1928	11.2	18.3	48.3	16.0	6.3	70924	72554	87	39	1589	0.4	0.5	15.9	65.9	17.4	250294
06370	OAKDALE	29287	2567	8.4	19.2	49.4	16.3	6.7	75118	76107	89	46	2137	3.7	1.4	13.8	70.8	10.4	222292
06371	OLD LYME	48264	3989	7.9	12.5	41.5	15.1	23.0	84674	86480	94	69	3352	0.0	0.0	2.0	32.6	65.3	490653
06374	PLAINFIELD	24277	3325	16.8	27.4	43.5	8.8	3.5	55972	59172	73	19	2457	4.9	2.0	43.6	46.1	3.3	174240
06375	QUAKER HILL	33532	1504	8.2	18.5	51.5	12.9	8.9	78203	78993	91	55	1306	0.5	0.6	7.1	73.5	18.2	262313
06377	STERLING	24916	959	12.9	22.3	53.4	8.8	2.6	66839	66831	85	31	785	2.7	3.7	28.2	62.7	2.8	196094
06378	STONINGTON	44222	2440	10.4	17.8	40.2	16.4	15.3	76300	77071	90	48	1879	6.2	1.0	2.8	39.1	51.0	407741
06379	PAWCATUCK	28789	3727	17.2	24.7	44.0	9.2	5.0	58390	62246	76	22	2457	0.4	0.9	11.4	69.1	18.2	250481
06380	TAFTVILLE	24482	991	26.7	28.9	32.7	6.4	5.3	46716	47827	53	11	428	1.9	2.8	40.4	50.0	4.9	183077
06382	UNCASVILLE	26903	3990	12.5	20.8	50.8	9.6	6.2	67106	70510	85	33	2952	3.5	3.3	16.6	70.2	6.4	217610
06384	VOLUNTOWN	30444	969	10.4	16.6	50.1	18.6	4.3	76342	76737	90	48	788	0.6	0.1	22.3	68.0	8.9	221491
06385	WATERFORD	34883	6251	11.4	20.2	45.7	12.1	10.7	69578	72771	87	37	5198	1.0	0.6	15.8	59.6	23.0	265431
06401	ANSONIA	25091	7576	21.7	24.4	41.4	9.4	3.2	53939	58377	70	16	4220	0.5	0.6	9.5	85.9	3.5	240226
06403	BEACON FALLS	30958	2199	8.7	20.4	48.7	14.1	8.0	71381	74229	88	39	1724	6.5	1.2	17.9	63.3	11.1	252133
06405	BRANFORD	39686	12652	11.9	20.4	40.4	15.4	11.9	74327	75819	89	43	8640	1.9	1.7	13.1	52.2	31.1	298666
06409	CENTERBROOK	50610	304	8.6	22.7	35.5	15.5	17.8	78460	80879	91	55	239	1.3	0.0	9.2	56.9	32.6	327193
06410	CHESHIRE	43845	9657	7.5	11.4	33.9	20.5	26.8	95261	96693	96	82	8278	0.2	0.5	5.3	51.7	42.3	369872
06412	CHESTER	45832	1654	8.6	14.3	37.6	19.7	19.8	83027	88087	93	66	1219	0.0	0.0	6.0	63.2	30.8	318007
06413	CLINTON	35678	5270	11.0	16.3	39.9	21.2	11.6	78922	82835	92	57	4167	1.8	2.5	9.6	72.9	13.1	270125
06415	COLCHESTER	35454	5917	9.0	11.9	45.1	19.6	14.4	82254	84419	93	64	4632	0.8	2.5	7.9	70.0	18.8	282244
06416	CROMWELL	39392	5612	8.3	16.8	44.6	18.3	12.0	77377	80427	91	52	4223	0.7	3.4	21.2	61.3	13.4	226759
06417	DEEP RIVER	37176	1901	13.0	21.7	38.0	16.6	10.7	67140	70682	85	33	1417	0.5	0.2	7.1	69.2	23.1	272351
06418	DERBY	27951	5328	19.9	23.4	42.6	10.2	3.8	57276	61593	74	20	3134	0.3	0.3	21.9	72.4	5.2	228632
06419	KILLINGWORTH	44744	2390	6.2	10.2	28.5	26.8	28.5	111529	116447	98	90	2257	2.9	5.5	4.7	38.8	48.0	389886
06420	SALEM	36323	1434	6.6	11.4	45.7	16.9	19.4	83217	84918	93	66	1220	2.3	2.0	3.0	64.2	28.6	325852
06422	DURHAM	41853	2640	4.6	8.8	35.3	31.1	20.3	101991	106162	97	85	2372	0.3	0.6	3.2	65.5	30.4	328746
06423	EAST HADDAM	39371	2091	5.2	11.9	46.8	20.3	15.8	83898	88003	93	67	1808	0.0	0.6	5.1	63.1	31.3	311053
06424	EAST HAMPTON	36895	4986	7.9	15.0	38.2	26.5	12.4	84755	90509	94	69	4037	0.2	2.1	14.1	70.8	12.7	244833
06426	ESSEX	62150	1591	9.2	14.0	29.9	18.5	28.3	92142	100814	95	79	1217	0.0	0.3	1.6	35.9	62.1	531478
06437	GUILFORD	49987	8525	5.9	9.7	38.6	19.7	26.1	94053	94459	96	81	7230	0.0	0.5	3.6	43.1	52.8	415414
06438	HADDAM	42891	1014	4.3	6.2	38.1	34.0	17.4	102065	106367	97	85	820	0.0	0.1	3.4	70.1	26.3	305366
06441	HIGGANUM	42761	1901	7.9	9.0	32.7	31.0	19.4	100529	105880	97	84	1653	0.9	0.4	5.8	70.6	22.3	290663
06442	IVORYTON	46789	1242	5.4	15.9	39.0	22.1	17.6	87765	92030	95	73	1010	0.6	0.0	5.3	60.9	33.2	335361
06443	MADISON	54494	6858	6.0	9.0	29.5	18.7	36.8	111701	112783	98	90	5947	0.1	0.7	0.8	36.0	62.4	462079
06447	MARLBOROUGH	45849	2220	5.7	9.3	35.9	24.0	25.0	98323	100358	96	83	1970	0.9	0.6	4.8	70.9	22.8	303604
06450	MERIDEN	25584	14116	21.2	24.0	39.9	11.5	3.4	54712	58285	71	17	8642	2.1	3.9	29.6	61.2	3.3	200241
06451	MERIDEN	24675	9574	23.0	24.2	37.8	10.8	4.2	52720	55961	67	14	5624	0.7	1.3	33.2	61.0	3.8	199299
06455	MIDDLEFIELD	34039	1264	10.9	16.1	46.0	16.4	10.6	77109	80041	91	52	1047	0.0	1.0	8.1	71.8	19.1	273057
06457	MIDDLETOWN	33357	19514	18.0	21.7	36.6	14.3	9.3	61316	63371	79	27	10130	1.2	2.1	23.0	65.9	7.8	224837
06459	MIDDLETOWN	13318	99	39.4	24.2	24.2	7.1	5.1	36400	37741	22	6	21	0.0	0.0	47.6	47.6	4.8	203571
06460	MILFORD	36046	15889	10.6	15.7	46.7	16.6	10.4	76194	77163	90	47	11606	0.7	0.9	7.1	73.9	17.4	281745
06461	MILFORD	38053	5510	7.9	15.2	38.5	23.1	15.4	84016	84562	94	67	4857	0.7	0.4	6.3	62.8	29.9	320803
06468	MONROE	46836	6731	5.1	7.8	29.0	29.6	28.5	116590	117695	98	91	6200	0.1	0.0	3.5	40.2	56.1	428518
06469	MOODUS	37078	1341	10.3	14.5	42.7	21.3	11.2	79085	82996	92	58	1030	0.0	0.0	6.5	81.0	12.5	266366
06470	NEWTOWN	58759	5378	4.4	7.3	24.4	25.5	38.4	130495	131784	99	93	4894	0.5	0.6	1.0	35.3	62.5	460693
06471	NORTH BRANFORD	36023	2832	8.6	17.3	46.9	15.1	12.0	76888	77686	91	51	2253	0.8	0.7	10.3	67.4	20.9	301426
06472	NORTHFORD	34405	2429	6.4	10.8	51.0	19.5	12.3	82098	83384	93	64	2140	0.0	0.2	4.1	71.8	24.0	320086
06473	NORTH HAVEN	37303	9030	7.9	14.3	45.3	17.8	14.7	80918	81436	92	61	7727	0.2	0.5	2.5	71.6	25.2	314853
06475	OLD SAYBROOK	40997	4284	9.8	13.7	40.3	22.2	13.9	80441	85497	92	61	3542	0.2	0.3	4.1	62.0	33.4	333067
06477	ORANGE	45094	5175	7.9	11.5	36.9	18.6	25.1	90864	92096	95	78	4686	1.0	0.0	1.4	32.4	65.2	450070
06478	OXFORD	37603	4201	6.5	8.3	42.7	22.5	19.9	91078	93704	95	78	3764	0.0	0.7	2.6	54.2	42.5	374776
06479	PLANTSVILLE	32285	4008	6.8	14.0	51.1	18.6	9.6	77740	79002	91	54	3195	0.0	0.2	10.5	75.9	13.4	261525
06480	PORTLAND	38273	3881	12.3	14.4	36.6	23.9	12.9	82276	87405	93	65	3026	0.3	0.3	10.5	74.6	14.2	252094
06481	ROCKFALL	35151	527	10.8	20.5	38.9	19.2	10.6	74296	79434	89	43	451	0.0	0.9	4.9	75.2	19.1	272283
06482	SANDY HOOK	48179	3781	6.0	5.8	27.2	27.8	33.2	122420	122985	99	92	3416	0.4	0.5	1.9	44.3	52.9	417531
06483	SEYMOUR	30749	6403	12.0	21.0	46.4	13.7	6.9	68240	71250	86	35	4554	0.0	1.7	6.7	76.1	15.5	268705
06484	SHELTON	39969	14574	9.2	14.1	33.5	27.4	15.8	89470	94524	95	75	11804	0.6	0.6	6.5	57.4	34.8	348386
06488	SOUTHBURY	42582	7795	9.5	18.1	37.7	14.5	20.2	79870	81536	92	59	6887	0.3	0.4	13.8	43.0	42.5	356377
06489	SOUTHINGTON	34373	11943	10.7	17.6	42.4	17.1	12.2	76722	78165	90	50	9708	2.8	2.2	12.5	64.4	18.2	270185
06492	WALLINGFORD	33165	17152	11.6	19.6	42.1	16.5	10.2	74466	76356	89	44	12438	1.6	2.0	9.6	69.2	17.7	274074
06498	WESTBROOK	36874	2860	14.8	19.5	34.4	19.8	11.6	73475	78586	89	42	2086	6.0	3.0	5.8	57.4	27.8	316245
06510	NEW HAVEN	28150	1693	47.5	22.0	21.9	3.1	5.4	27894	32658	5	3	81	0.0	0.0	0.0	22.2	77.8	575000
06511	NEW HAVEN	21583	21119	36.5	25.4	29.8	5.0	3.4	36534	39718	22	6	4851	1.6	6.2	35.2	41.1	15.8	197014
06512	EAST HAVEN	27127	12005	18.8	23.9	42.4	11.0	3.9	57124	61302	74	19	8305	1.0	1.8	23.7	70.0	3.6	212699
06513	NEW HAVEN	18639	13185	36.8	24.3	29.1	7.3	2.4	37526	41350	25	7	5203	2.1	6.2	45.4	44.5	1.8	168567
06514	HAMDEN	28655	9992	15.2	25.6	43.1	10.4	5.7	59822	63119	77	24	6316	0.6	1.2	25.7	66.8	5.6	209977
06515	NEW HAVEN	26459	6170	28.2	23.9	31.2	9.6	7.1	47773	49642	56	12	2810	0.9	2.2	26.4	59.3	11.2	221117
06516	WEST HAVEN	25727	21289	19.7	26.8	39.9	9.6	3.9	53395	57105	69	15	11752	1.5	2.6	30.0	62.8	3.0	202909
06517	HAMDEN	38158	6287	19.1	16.7	39.2	12.2	12.8	66866	69963	85	31	4220	0.7	2.4	15.8	65.9	15.2	240381
06518	HAMDEN	35076	6885	14.6	17.5	38.6	17.0	12.3	76840	78858	90	51	4862	0.5	0.0	9.3	74.0	16.2	269775
06519	NEW HAVEN	13589	5514	47.4	24.4	22.8	4.2	1.2	27227	30377	5	3	1438	4.9	12.4	55.4	25.5	1.9	135281
06524	BETHANY	40503	1931	3.9	9.2	45.5	18.8	22.6	89145	90397	95	75	1748	2.2	1.2	2.1	46.6	47.9	393571
06525	WOODBRIDGE	57432	3242	4.7	7.4	26.7	17.8	43.3	128562	128802	99	93	2840	0.3	0.4	1.0	20.1	78.2	586331
06604	BRIDGEPORT	18237	9875	37.2	26.0	25.2	7.8	3.8	36220	39004	21	6	3173	9.4	9.7	28.8	48.6	3.5	181070
	CONNECTICUT	36066		15.8	19.0	36.4	15.2	13.5	70949	74487				1.1	1.8	16.1	53.4	27.5	273826
	UNITED STATES	27277		20.9	24.4	35.3	11.7	7.6	54719	56938				9.3	13.1	31.6	32.6	13.5	162279

ZIP CODE #	POST OFFICE NAME	FINANCIAL SERVICES: Auto Loan	Home Loan	Invest-ments	Retire-ment Plans	THE HOME: Home Improvements: Home Repair	Lawn & Garden	Furnishings: Comput-ers & Hard-ware-Personal	Major Appli-ances	TV, Radio, Sound Equip-ment	Furni-ture	ENTERTAINMENT: Dine out/ Carry out	Sports Equip-ment	Fees & Tickets	Toys & Games	Travel	Cable TV	PERSONAL: Apparel & Services	Auto Repairs	Health Insur-ance	Pets & Supplies
06279	WILLINGTON	114	113	104	116	110	109	122	111	117	117	118	90	118	118	115	115	83	115	110	133
06280	WINDHAM	94	106	100	107	105	106	99	100	100	99	100	75	108	100	105	102	71	100	105	117
06281	WOODSTOCK	111	132	123	134	130	126	116	120	113	119	115	92	128	115	126	113	81	116	118	139
06282	WOODSTOCK VALLEY	116	145	127	145	140	126	122	124	115	128	117	99	137	120	132	111	84	118	112	143
06320	NEW LONDON	70	59	55	62	57	59	76	64	76	71	77	52	69	75	67	77	54	72	69	79
06330	BALTIC	87	105	95	104	102	100	95	95	94	94	95	73	105	95	102	95	67	95	97	111
06331	CANTERBURY	101	120	105	121	116	115	104	108	102	106	104	83	115	105	112	103	73	104	107	126
06333	EAST LYME	172	222	228	232	229	203	184	193	174	199	176	149	218	176	209	168	130	181	174	219
06334	BOZRAH	111	138	130	139	136	133	117	123	116	121	118	92	135	117	131	117	83	119	124	142
06335	GALES FERRY	120	148	132	148	143	134	126	129	122	131	124	100	142	125	137	120	88	124	122	149
06336	GILMAN	87	109	97	108	104	107	92	96	94	94	95	72	106	95	102	96	67	94	102	112
06339	LEDYARD	114	139	133	139	138	132	122	126	120	125	121	95	137	120	134	120	86	123	125	145
06340	GROTON	93	84	81	87	83	81	97	87	95	95	97	70	94	98	92	94	68	94	88	103
06349	GROTON	0	0	0	0	0	0	0	0	0	0	0	0	0	0	0	0	0	0	0	0
06351	JEWETT CITY	94	110	98	110	107	103	100	100	97	100	98	78	108	99	105	97	70	98	99	117
06353	MONTVILLE	106	101	101	102	103	109	103	106	104	100	102	80	99	104	101	106	71	105	110	124
06354	MOOSUP	75	85	76	85	82	82	82	79	82	80	83	62	87	82	84	83	59	81	82	93
06355	MYSTIC	129	156	154	158	157	149	139	142	135	144	136	108	155	134	152	134	97	139	141	164
06357	NIANTIC	116	131	128	133	131	126	122	122	119	125	121	93	131	120	129	119	85	121	122	142
06359	NORTH STONINGTON	114	135	119	137	131	133	117	123	118	119	119	93	131	120	128	119	83	119	126	143
06360	NORWICH	80	77	75	78	76	80	84	80	85	80	85	61	82	84	81	87	59	83	86	95
06365	PRESTON	99	125	120	121	125	123	107	113	108	107	108	82	122	108	119	111	77	110	118	128
06370	OAKDALE	104	129	115	129	125	123	110	114	109	113	111	87	126	111	121	110	78	111	115	132
06371	OLD LYME	156	186	208	189	196	187	160	176	157	170	158	129	181	154	182	157	113	165	172	199
06374	PLAINFIELD	86	95	88	96	93	95	90	91	91	89	91	69	96	92	94	93	64	91	95	106
06375	QUAKER HILL	109	133	134	132	136	133	115	124	116	118	116	88	130	114	128	118	82	118	128	140
06377	STERLING	94	106	91	109	103	104	95	98	93	95	94	77	101	96	100	93	66	95	98	116
06378	STONINGTON	129	157	166	160	164	148	140	145	133	149	134	109	156	131	156	130	96	139	138	165
06379	PAWCATUCK	91	99	95	98	98	99	96	96	95	93	95	73	99	96	98	97	67	96	99	112
06380	TAFTVILLE	79	77	69	78	74	76	86	77	85	80	84	62	83	85	80	85	59	82	81	93
06382	UNCASVILLE	98	112	104	111	109	109	103	104	102	102	103	80	111	103	108	103	73	103	106	121
06384	VOLUNTOWN	111	125	107	128	121	122	111	116	109	112	110	90	119	112	118	110	77	111	114	136
06385	WATERFORD	109	128	123	128	128	131	112	120	115	115	115	87	126	114	123	118	81	116	128	138
06401	ANSONIA	80	88	83	86	87	85	88	84	87	84	87	65	91	87	89	88	62	87	87	99
06403	BEACON FALLS	111	123	111	122	119	118	111	113	111	114	112	86	119	114	115	112	79	111	114	133
06405	BRANFORD	117	132	136	134	135	128	127	125	124	129	125	96	137	123	134	123	89	126	126	145
06409	CENTERBROOK	131	178	183	168	184	159	150	155	144	150	146	115	174	146	169	144	107	150	147	171
06410	CHESHIRE	162	214	222	215	222	196	178	187	169	188	171	141	210	171	202	166	126	176	173	208
06412	CHESTER	140	177	179	174	181	162	153	157	147	157	149	118	173	148	169	146	108	152	150	178
06413	CLINTON	117	141	135	141	140	130	126	127	122	129	123	97	139	123	135	120	88	124	123	146
06415	COLCHESTER	132	157	141	158	153	139	139	138	132	145	134	110	152	136	146	127	96	133	127	159
06416	CROMWELL	124	138	135	140	138	133	132	130	130	134	131	100	141	130	138	130	93	131	133	153
06417	DEEP RIVER	121	142	135	143	142	139	128	132	126	130	127	99	140	126	138	127	90	129	134	153
06418	DERBY	82	94	86	93	91	89	92	88	92	89	93	68	98	92	94	93	66	90	91	103
06419	KILLINGWORTH	159	198	211	204	207	187	166	177	159	181	160	135	194	159	188	155	117	166	163	201
06420	SALEM	136	171	150	171	165	148	143	146	135	151	137	116	162	140	155	129	99	139	130	167
06422	DURHAM	154	198	191	199	199	177	166	171	157	174	159	132	191	160	184	152	116	162	156	194
06423	EAST HADDAM	137	170	161	172	169	154	145	149	137	153	140	115	163	140	158	134	100	142	138	172
06424	EAST HAMPTON	128	152	143	153	150	138	136	136	131	141	133	106	149	133	145	128	95	133	129	158
06426	ESSEX	156	197	228	200	215	189	180	186	171	192	170	138	206	163	204	168	124	179	182	208
06437	GUILFORD	166	213	227	219	223	194	183	190	171	197	172	146	212	170	207	164	127	179	170	214
06438	HADDAM	143	179	184	182	184	169	152	161	146	161	147	119	174	145	171	144	106	152	152	183
06441	HIGGANUM	144	185	190	184	190	171	156	164	149	163	151	121	179	149	176	147	109	156	155	185
06442	IVORYTON	155	200	193	194	200	177	171	174	162	174	165	133	194	166	187	160	120	168	162	196
06443	MADISON	186	244	268	253	260	223	207	216	192	225	193	166	244	190	237	183	143	202	192	242
06447	MARLBOROUGH	170	215	206	219	215	193	180	186	170	191	173	144	206	174	199	164	125	176	169	213
06450	MERIDEN	84	89	81	89	86	85	90	85	90	88	91	66	93	90	90	90	65	89	88	100
06451	MERIDEN	81	88	83	88	86	87	89	85	90	86	90	65	93	88	90	91	64	88	91	100
06455	MIDDLEFIELD	107	138	140	132	142	128	120	124	117	120	118	91	137	117	134	118	85	121	122	139
06457	MIDDLETOWN	105	103	98	106	101	99	112	102	110	109	111	82	111	110	108	109	79	108	104	122
06459	MIDDLETOWN	79	51	49	56	50	55	94	64	84	75	84	58	69	85	66	82	59	78	67	82
06460	MILFORD	109	136	137	133	139	126	122	123	118	123	119	93	137	118	134	118	86	121	121	140
06461	MILFORD	129	167	165	164	170	153	140	146	135	146	136	110	162	138	156	134	99	139	139	163
06468	MONROE	173	231	245	232	241	211	193	200	183	201	185	152	229	185	220	180	137	190	185	223
06469	MOODUS	125	143	135	145	141	131	131	130	126	135	128	102	142	128	138	123	91	128	124	151
06470	NEWTOWN	217	294	311	302	307	266	240	251	225	256	228	194	291	229	276	218	171	234	224	280
06471	NORTH BRANFORD	111	145	152	138	151	137	127	131	125	126	126	95	145	123	142	128	91	128	134	146
06472	NORTHFORD	129	161	153	161	161	148	137	142	131	142	133	109	155	134	151	129	95	136	134	163
06473	NORTH HAVEN	121	162	171	156	169	149	137	143	132	139	133	105	160	132	156	133	98	138	138	158
06475	OLD SAYBROOK	130	154	163	155	161	159	133	146	135	142	135	102	151	131	150	137	95	139	152	166
06477	ORANGE	146	202	225	198	216	190	169	178	163	173	164	130	203	162	197	164	121	170	175	196
06478	OXFORD	142	183	181	184	185	165	153	159	145	161	147	122	177	147	171	141	107	151	146	180
06479	PLANTSVILLE	111	133	127	133	132	124	122	122	119	123	120	94	134	119	131	118	86	121	120	141
06480	PORTLAND	124	154	151	152	156	142	135	138	130	139	132	105	152	132	147	129	95	133	133	156
06481	ROCKFALL	109	133	138	131	139	135	115	125	116	119	116	87	131	113	129	119	82	119	131	140
06482	SANDY HOOK	192	246	229	249	244	213	203	208	190	218	193	166	235	199	223	181	142	195	182	235
06483	SEYMOUR	96	119	117	115	120	108	108	107	104	107	105	82	120	105	116	104	76	106	104	122
06484	SHELTON	133	168	175	165	174	156	148	151	144	150	145	113	169	144	164	143	106	148	147	170
06488	SOUTHBURY	134	170	186	167	183	173	145	159	145	158	144	110	171	138	169	146	102	151	168	177
06489	SOUTHINGTON	114	138	139	137	140	131	123	126	120	126	121	95	137	119	134	120	87	123	126	145
06492	WALLINGFORD	110	128	125	128	128	122	118	119	116	119	117	90	129	116	125	116	84	117	119	137
06498	WESTBROOK	126	127	154	129	133	139	120	133	121	121	121	98	123	118	130	124	84	128	134	154
06510	NEW HAVEN	70	50	52	58	48	49	78	57	74	71	77	53	67	75	65	72	55	69	59	73
06511	NEW HAVEN	67	55	56	60	54	55	76	61	76	69	78	51	69	75	66	77	56	71	67	77
06512	EAST HAVEN	85	95	91	94	94	92	93	90	92	91	93	69	98	92	96	94	66	92	94	106
06513	NEW HAVEN	66	59	56	60	58	56	72	63	72	69	74	50	68	71	66	72	53	70	65	75
06514	HAMDEN	90	100	98	100	100	96	99	95	98	97	99	73	105	98	102	99	71	98	98	112
06515	NEW HAVEN	87	86	85	88	85	84	95	86	95	92	95	68	95	93	92	95	68	93	91	104
06516	WEST HAVEN	83	87	83	88	86	85	90	85	89	88	90	66	93	89	90	90	64	89	89	100
06517	HAMDEN	110	126	129	127	128	123	122	120	121	123	122	91	133	119	129	122	87	122	124	140
06518	HAMDEN	118	132	136	133	136	129	126	125	125	129	126	94	136	123	134	125	89	126	130	144
06519	NEW HAVEN	51	43	40	45	40	44	57	47	60	52	60	38	53	58	49	62	43	55	54	59
06524	BETHANY	142	193	208	191	203	179	159	169	152	165	153	124	189	153	184	151	113	160	160	187
06525	WOODBRIDGE	200	271	320	279	299	260	227	244	214	250	212	179	278	208	269	208	159	227	227	269
06604	BRIDGEPORT	67	58	56	59	57	56	75	64	76	70	78	51	70	74	68	77	57	73	68	76
	CONNECTICUT	120	136	136	137	137	129	132	128	129	132	130	99	141	128	137	129	94	130	128	149
	UNITED STATES	100	100	100	100	100	100	100	100	100	100	100	100	100	100	100	100	100	100	100	100

ZIP CODE #	POST OFFICE NAME	COUNTY FIPS CODE	POPULATION 2000	POPULATION 2009	POPULATION 2014	2000-2009 ANNUAL RATE % Rate	2000-2009 ANNUAL RATE State Centile	HOUSEHOLDS 2000	HOUSEHOLDS 2009	HOUSEHOLDS 2014	HOUSEHOLDS % Annual Rate 2000-2009	HOUSEHOLDS 2009 Average HH Size	FAMILIES 2000	FAMILIES 2009	FAMILIES % Annual Rate 2000-2009
06605	BRIDGEPORT	001	23968	24587	24651	0.3	38	8701	8843	8857	0.2	2.75	5291	5311	0.0
06606	BRIDGEPORT	001	44716	46441	46859	0.4	46	16767	17100	17191	0.2	2.65	11182	11336	0.1
06607	BRIDGEPORT	001	7600	7736	7791	0.2	29	2673	2724	2744	0.2	2.83	1864	1883	0.1
06608	BRIDGEPORT	001	13407	13898	14087	0.4	46	4127	4246	4299	0.3	3.24	3141	3198	0.2
06610	BRIDGEPORT	001	21966	22614	22731	0.3	38	8463	8577	8594	0.1	2.56	5282	5301	0.0
06611	TRUMBULL	001	34397	35659	36069	0.4	46	11979	12421	12567	0.4	2.82	9754	10072	0.3
06612	EASTON	001	7177	7485	7551	0.5	54	2430	2533	2555	0.4	2.95	2047	2124	0.4
06614	STRATFORD	001	32034	31963	31862	0.0	12	12814	12760	12715	0.0	2.48	9039	8925	-0.1
06615	STRATFORD	001	17962	18070	18028	0.1	24	7090	7088	7069	0.0	2.55	4599	4554	-0.1
06702	WATERBURY	009	4192	4310	4332	0.3	38	1925	1933	1935	0.0	2.00	686	679	-0.1
06704	WATERBURY	009	24717	24899	24894	0.1	24	9474	9530	9534	0.1	2.59	6298	6262	-0.1
06705	WATERBURY	009	25726	25846	25899	0.1	24	10788	10863	10898	0.1	2.34	6601	6562	-0.1
06706	WATERBURY	009	14028	14513	14678	0.4	46	5269	5449	5513	0.4	2.66	3682	3772	0.3
06708	WATERBURY	009	28422	29140	29348	0.3	38	11524	11836	11942	0.3	2.39	7290	7389	0.1
06710	WATERBURY	009	9843	9965	9959	0.1	24	3528	3539	3535	0.0	2.74	2267	2246	-0.1
06712	PROSPECT	009	8641	9087	9255	0.5	54	3000	3175	3244	0.6	2.82	2439	2563	0.5
06716	WOLCOTT	009	15209	16228	16678	0.7	66	5410	5813	5989	0.8	2.77	4246	4529	0.7
06750	BANTAM	005	1396	1410	1391	0.1	24	586	599	595	0.2	2.35	374	378	0.1
06751	BETHLEHEM	005	3393	3729	3869	1.0	84	1237	1377	1435	1.2	2.66	930	1025	1.1
06752	BRIDGEWATER	005	1851	1943	1976	0.5	54	714	751	765	0.5	2.54	533	555	0.4
06754	CORNWALL BRIDGE	005	1458	1548	1571	0.6	61	589	632	645	0.8	2.45	402	425	0.6
06755	GAYLORDSVILLE	005	1119	1227	1271	1.0	84	387	428	445	1.1	2.86	300	329	1.0
06756	GOSHEN	005	2583	3077	3277	1.9	98	1021	1231	1316	2.0	2.50	780	932	1.9
06757	KENT	005	2158	2459	2578	1.4	92	873	1001	1054	1.5	2.40	566	640	1.3
06758	LAKESIDE	005	295	340	358	1.5	94	107	124	131	1.6	2.74	74	85	1.5
06759	LITCHFIELD	005	5928	6243	6338	0.6	61	2375	2535	2588	0.7	2.38	1643	1732	0.6
06762	MIDDLEBURY	009	6692	7209	7407	0.8	74	2470	2673	2750	0.9	2.67	1891	2031	0.8
06763	MORRIS	005	1993	2250	2353	1.3	91	799	912	958	1.4	2.47	562	634	1.3
06770	NAUGATUCK	009	31063	31772	32022	0.2	29	11858	12194	12321	0.3	2.59	8321	8469	0.2
06776	NEW MILFORD	005	25824	27262	27699	0.6	61	9560	10167	10357	0.7	2.66	6921	7299	0.6
06777	NEW PRESTON MARBLE D	005	1556	1675	1718	0.8	74	613	665	685	0.9	2.50	428	459	0.8
06778	NORTHFIELD	005	1139	1204	1231	0.6	61	408	437	449	0.7	2.73	327	348	0.7
06779	OAKVILLE	005	8397	8606	8633	0.3	38	3209	3326	3354	0.4	2.58	2326	2385	0.3
06782	PLYMOUTH	005	2212	2413	2489	0.9	79	778	860	891	1.1	2.77	584	640	1.0
06783	ROXBURY	005	2095	2211	2239	0.6	61	830	885	901	0.7	2.50	608	642	0.6
06784	SHERMAN	001	3962	4202	4257	0.6	61	1488	1569	1591	0.6	2.68	1134	1187	0.5
06785	SOUTH KENT	005	684	793	835	1.6	95	264	309	327	1.7	2.48	177	204	1.5
06786	TERRYVILLE	005	9437	9824	9937	0.4	46	3682	3873	3927	0.5	2.53	2648	2758	0.4
06787	THOMASTON	005	7456	7812	7914	0.5	54	2895	3064	3118	0.6	2.55	2052	2147	0.5
06790	TORRINGTON	005	35349	35768	35778	0.1	24	14798	15033	15062	0.2	2.32	9176	9240	0.1
06791	HARWINTON	005	5359	5635	5732	0.5	54	1987	2110	2153	0.7	2.67	1569	1654	0.6
06793	WASHINGTON	005	1345	1413	1434	0.5	54	515	552	565	0.8	2.29	331	350	0.6
06794	WASHINGTON DEPOT	005	998	1097	1127	1.0	84	421	466	482	1.1	2.34	288	316	1.0
06795	WATERTOWN	005	13356	13732	13827	0.3	38	4877	5064	5116	0.4	2.68	3695	3810	0.3
06796	WEST CORNWALL	005	1086	1201	1246	1.1	87	460	506	524	1.0	2.36	296	321	0.9
06798	WOODBURY	005	9198	9916	10182	0.8	74	3713	4020	4138	0.9	2.47	2572	2764	0.8
06801	BETHEL	001	18050	18582	18706	0.3	38	6499	6700	6750	0.3	2.76	4841	4953	0.2
06804	BROOKFIELD	001	16040	17041	17427	0.7	66	5698	6054	6189	0.7	2.80	4441	4693	0.6
06807	COS COB	001	6612	6630	6626	0.0	12	2553	2563	2563	0.0	2.58	1896	1891	0.0
06810	DANBURY	001	45077	49338	50566	1.0	84	16463	17780	18212	0.8	2.70	10195	10927	0.8
06811	DANBURY	001	29286	30380	30731	0.4	46	10552	10941	11087	0.4	2.60	7578	7776	0.3
06812	NEW FAIRFIELD	001	14024	14484	14608	0.3	38	4668	4822	4863	0.4	3.00	3929	4039	0.3
06820	DARIEN	001	19943	20295	20355	0.2	29	6775	6815	6819	0.1	2.95	5493	5487	0.0
06824	FAIRFIELD	001	32817	33132	33100	0.1	24	11415	11432	11412	0.0	2.67	8368	8316	-0.1
06825	FAIRFIELD	001	20074	20103	20081	0.0	12	7307	7312	7309	0.0	2.54	5245	5201	-0.1
06830	GREENWICH	001	24609	24818	24833	0.1	24	10001	10058	10058	0.1	2.43	6176	6148	0.0
06831	GREENWICH	001	15138	15306	15328	0.1	24	5401	5452	5461	0.1	2.75	4121	4129	0.0
06840	NEW CANAAN	001	19288	19579	19568	0.2	29	6789	6826	6810	0.1	2.85	5250	5244	0.0
06850	NORWALK	001	17717	17965	17992	0.2	29	7102	7200	7212	0.1	2.46	4549	4563	0.0
06851	NORWALK	001	25543	26287	26515	0.3	38	10296	10582	10678	0.3	2.46	6605	6721	0.2
06853	NORWALK	001	3344	3355	3358	0.0	12	1417	1423	1425	0.0	2.36	947	943	0.0
06854	NORWALK	001	27887	28264	28298	0.1	24	10463	10551	10557	0.1	2.66	6786	6777	0.0
06855	NORWALK	001	7962	7992	7959	0.0	12	3223	3224	3209	0.0	2.43	1924	1903	-0.1
06870	OLD GREENWICH	001	7039	7055	7050	0.0	12	2612	2599	2593	-0.1	2.71	2005	1980	-0.1
06877	RIDGEFIELD	001	23649	24019	24070	0.2	29	8435	8554	8568	0.2	2.79	6611	6666	0.1
06878	RIVERSIDE	001	7757	7741	7717	0.0	12	2684	2666	2657	-0.1	2.90	2064	2036	-0.1
06880	WESTPORT	001	26339	26504	26469	0.1	24	9788	9807	9788	0.0	2.68	7340	7298	-0.1
06883	WESTON	001	9911	10011	9971	0.1	24	3269	3268	3249	0.0	3.06	2773	2759	-0.1
06890	SOUTHPORT	001	4290	4360	4382	0.2	29	1616	1636	1643	0.1	2.61	1145	1148	0.0
06896	REDDING	001	8288	9617	10121	1.6	95	2920	3388	3566	1.6	2.84	2416	2787	1.6
06897	WILTON	001	17575	17725	17680	0.1	24	5906	5914	5893	0.0	2.93	4855	4840	0.0
06901	STAMFORD	001	6372	7098	7327	1.2	90	3184	3476	3572	1.0	1.97	1259	1352	0.8
06902	STAMFORD	001	61665	63044	63357	0.2	29	23339	23692	23782	0.2	2.62	14485	14500	0.0
06903	STAMFORD	001	14512	14468	14440	0.0	12	4981	4968	4958	0.0	2.86	4256	4228	-0.1
06905	STAMFORD	001	18364	18539	18557	0.1	24	7312	7404	7416	0.1	2.49	4827	4819	0.0
06906	STAMFORD	001	7475	7573	7596	0.1	24	3004	3038	3048	0.1	2.46	1747	1746	0.0
06907	STAMFORD	001	8559	8592	8574	0.0	12	3502	3523	3517	0.1	2.44	2335	2324	-0.1
	CONNECTICUT					0.4					0.4	2.53			0.3
	UNITED STATES					1.0					1.1	2.59			0.9

ZIP CODE		RACE (%)						% Hispanic Origin		2009 AGE DISTRIBUTION (%)										MEDIAN AGE		
#	POST OFFICE NAME	White		Black		Asian/Pacific																
		2000	2009	2000	2009	2000	2009	2000	2009	0-4	5-9	10-14	15-19	20-24	25-44	45-64	65-84	85+	18+	2009	% 2009 Males	% 2009 Females
06605	BRIDGEPORT	44.8	41.1	29.1	28.7	4.9	6.2	33.7	38.7	9.9	8.2	7.0	7.1	8.9	29.9	20.1	7.5	1.4	70.8	29.7	49.6	50.4
06606	BRIDGEPORT	54.8	48.7	27.6	30.0	2.6	3.6	21.1	26.7	6.9	6.6	6.4	7.1	7.7	28.1	24.0	10.7	2.5	76.0	35.6	48.0	52.0
06607	BRIDGEPORT	14.2	14.0	69.2	67.8	0.5	0.6	24.8	27.6	9.6	9.3	8.2	8.7	8.3	26.7	20.7	7.6	0.8	67.7	28.8	44.7	55.3
06608	BRIDGEPORT	34.0	33.6	26.0	24.1	2.0	2.3	65.1	68.9	10.3	9.1	7.3	9.5	11.7	27.9	17.7	5.8	0.7	67.8	26.1	48.4	51.6
06610	BRIDGEPORT	47.6	42.2	32.1	33.7	1.7	2.3	30.8	37.1	7.6	7.0	6.6	7.1	7.4	27.4	23.0	11.1	2.8	74.6	35.2	47.4	52.6
06611	TRUMBULL	93.9	90.8	1.9	2.6	2.4	4.1	2.8	4.4	6.5	7.1	7.9	7.0	4.5	20.2	29.6	13.8	3.3	73.8	42.9	48.3	51.7
06612	EASTON	96.7	94.7	0.2	0.3	2.0	3.6	1.8	2.9	6.8	8.3	9.9	7.6	3.1	16.9	33.9	11.7	1.9	70.1	43.4	48.8	51.2
06614	STRATFORD	92.9	89.8	3.2	4.3	1.3	2.2	4.9	7.6	5.6	5.9	6.1	5.9	4.6	22.4	29.1	16.5	3.8	78.7	44.6	47.3	52.7
06615	STRATFORD	70.3	65.2	21.5	24.0	1.6	2.4	10.1	13.9	6.5	6.3	6.5	7.2	7.0	25.7	27.1	11.5	2.4	76.5	38.6	47.6	52.4
06702	WATERBURY	48.0	41.9	21.1	21.6	0.7	0.8	44.4	52.7	7.4	6.7	5.7	5.3	6.3	20.8	21.2	19.9	6.7	76.9	42.8	47.1	52.9
06704	WATERBURY	50.7	45.0	29.7	31.5	1.2	1.7	26.0	31.7	8.9	7.8	7.2	7.5	8.0	25.8	22.4	10.4	2.2	71.6	32.7	47.8	52.2
06705	WATERBURY	75.7	69.5	12.5	14.8	1.9	2.9	13.9	19.0	7.0	6.5	6.1	6.2	6.9	27.6	24.2	12.3	3.2	76.6	37.4	47.0	53.0
06706	WATERBURY	65.6	59.8	9.3	10.1	1.7	2.3	34.7	41.6	8.2	7.6	7.0	7.6	7.9	26.8	23.6	9.2	2.1	72.8	33.0	49.0	51.0
06708	WATERBURY	83.1	78.1	7.5	8.9	1.7	2.7	11.8	16.4	6.9	6.4	6.1	6.5	6.5	26.9	25.5	12.2	2.9	76.8	38.5	47.4	52.6
06710	WATERBURY	49.5	43.9	26.4	27.8	1.3	1.6	33.1	39.5	8.8	7.7	7.4	8.4	8.0	26.8	22.3	8.6	2.1	70.9	31.7	48.8	51.2
06712	PROSPECT	96.3	94.6	1.4	2.0	0.7	1.3	1.9	3.1	6.0	6.7	7.3	6.4	3.8	23.2	31.3	12.9	2.3	75.7	43.0	48.6	51.4
06716	WOLCOTT	96.2	94.4	1.2	1.7	0.8	1.4	1.8	2.9	6.2	6.6	7.1	7.1	5.0	24.3	29.7	12.0	2.0	75.5	41.2	48.7	51.3
06750	BANTAM	97.1	96.2	0.4	0.4	0.4	0.7	1.4	2.1	4.6	4.6	5.4	8.2	7.6	18.5	34.0	14.1	3.0	80.6	45.6	46.3	53.7
06751	BETHLEHEM	97.5	96.5	0.3	0.3	0.8	1.4	0.6	0.9	4.5	5.4	6.8	7.5	3.8	19.0	38.1	13.0	1.9	78.1	46.6	49.3	50.7
06752	BRIDGEWATER	97.5	96.7	0.9	1.1	0.8	1.3	0.5	0.7	3.8	4.8	5.9	6.2	3.8	18.2	37.4	18.1	1.9	81.1	49.0	48.8	51.2
06754	CORNWALL BRIDGE	97.7	97.0	0.2	0.2	0.8	1.4	0.6	0.9	4.8	6.0	7.1	6.1	2.9	22.7	33.3	14.5	2.5	77.8	45.2	51.0	49.0
06755	GAYLORDSVILLE	95.1	93.3	1.2	1.4	1.6	2.7	2.5	3.6	6.9	7.7	8.3	7.6	4.2	23.9	31.1	9.2	1.1	72.0	40.2	48.5	51.5
06756	GOSHEN	98.2	97.5	0.5	0.6	0.7	1.3	1.2	1.8	4.6	5.6	6.7	6.2	3.6	19.3	36.2	15.6	2.1	78.7	47.1	48.7	51.3
06757	KENT	95.9	94.5	0.6	0.7	1.0	1.5	2.6	3.6	5.7	6.0	6.6	6.7	5.2	21.6	30.0	14.8	3.5	77.2	43.7	47.9	52.1
06758	LAKESIDE	97.6	96.5	0.3	0.6	0.7	1.2	1.0	1.5	4.4	5.6	6.5	6.2	3.5	20.6	37.1	13.8	2.4	79.7	46.7	49.7	50.3
06759	LITCHFIELD	96.8	95.8	0.8	1.0	0.5	0.9	1.8	2.4	4.6	5.2	6.6	8.0	4.3	17.9	33.9	16.0	3.4	77.5	46.9	47.9	52.1
06762	MIDDLEBURY	96.9	95.2	0.5	0.6	1.3	2.4	1.3	2.2	5.2	5.9	6.8	6.9	4.4	20.4	32.9	14.5	3.0	77.4	45.2	48.5	51.5
06763	MORRIS	97.4	96.5	0.8	0.8	0.9	1.5	0.9	1.2	5.5	6.1	6.7	6.6	4.8	22.1	33.1	13.2	2.0	77.6	43.9	49.6	50.4
06770	NAUGATUCK	91.8	88.4	2.8	3.8	1.7	2.7	4.5	6.9	6.9	6.8	6.7	6.8	6.4	27.5	27.0	9.8	2.1	75.3	37.5	48.8	51.2
06776	NEW MILFORD	94.3	92.2	1.4	1.6	2.0	3.2	2.8	3.9	6.6	7.0	7.5	7.2	4.9	24.9	30.7	9.6	1.6	74.6	40.4	49.3	50.7
06777	NEW PRESTON MARBLE D	97.4	96.4	0.3	0.4	0.4	0.7	1.3	2.0	4.7	6.0	6.9	6.3	3.5	23.0	32.6	15.1	1.9	80.5	44.7	50.2	49.8
06778	NORTHFIELD	97.6	96.9	0.9	1.0	0.4	0.7	0.9	1.2	4.8	5.9	7.3	7.7	3.4	19.9	36.4	12.9	1.7	75.7	45.5	50.4	49.6
06779	OAKVILLE	95.4	94.0	1.3	1.5	1.2	1.9	2.9	4.0	6.1	6.0	6.1	6.8	6.2	26.0	28.8	11.9	2.1	77.5	40.2	47.6	52.4
06782	PLYMOUTH	97.3	96.4	0.6	0.8	0.4	0.6	0.9	1.3	5.1	5.6	6.4	7.0	5.0	23.4	32.2	13.1	2.2	78.3	43.4	49.3	50.7
06783	ROXBURY	97.2	96.1	0.2	0.3	0.9	1.6	1.3	1.9	4.5	5.5	6.5	5.7	3.4	19.0	37.0	16.5	1.8	79.9	48.0	51.5	48.5
06784	SHERMAN	97.3	95.9	0.6	0.8	0.8	1.4	1.7	2.8	5.5	6.6	8.0	7.5	3.9	16.9	35.1	14.6	2.0	75.1	45.9	49.2	50.8
06785	SOUTH KENT	95.5	93.8	0.6	0.6	1.2	2.0	2.3	3.3	5.9	6.3	6.8	6.6	4.8	21.8	30.0	13.9	3.9	76.3	43.5	47.9	52.1
06786	TERRYVILLE	97.4	96.5	0.8	1.0	0.4	0.7	1.3	1.9	6.2	6.2	6.8	6.8	6.0	26.8	28.7	10.5	2.0	76.4	39.2	50.2	49.8
06787	THOMASTON	97.8	97.1	0.6	0.7	0.5	0.8	1.4	2.0	5.7	5.9	6.2	7.2	6.0	25.5	30.8	10.9	1.9	77.8	41.0	49.4	50.6
06790	TORRINGTON	93.1	90.9	2.1	2.4	1.8	3.0	3.3	4.4	5.9	5.8	6.0	6.3	6.1	24.9	28.5	12.9	3.6	78.3	41.7	48.6	51.4
06791	HARWINTON	98.7	98.1	0.1	0.1	0.6	1.0	0.9	1.3	5.5	6.4	7.2	6.7	4.2	21.0	33.6	13.3	2.0	76.6	44.3	50.3	49.7
06793	WASHINGTON	93.9	91.1	1.3	1.5	3.3	5.3	2.6	3.7	3.6	4.6	7.8	8.3	6.7	19.3	31.8	15.6	2.4	81.5	44.8	50.1	49.9
06794	WASHINGTON DEPOT	95.8	94.0	0.3	0.6	0.9	1.5	2.4	3.6	4.6	5.2	6.7	6.8	3.6	21.8	32.9	16.2	2.2	79.4	45.8	50.6	49.4
06795	WATERTOWN	97.0	95.5	0.5	0.6	1.4	2.4	1.3	1.8	5.6	6.4	6.7	6.5	5.2	23.6	31.7	11.9	2.6	77.1	42.5	48.2	51.8
06796	WEST CORNWALL	97.4	96.6	0.4	0.3	0.6	1.1	1.7	2.2	4.5	6.0	7.6	4.9	2.5	21.9	34.5	15.5	2.7	77.9	46.4	48.8	51.2
06798	WOODBURY	97.2	96.2	0.5	0.6	1.2	2.0	1.7	2.3	5.3	5.9	6.8	6.8	4.7	21.7	34.0	12.9	1.9	77.6	44.2	48.6	51.4
06801	BETHEL	92.4	88.5	1.3	1.7	3.6	6.0	3.7	5.8	6.6	7.0	7.6	7.1	4.9	25.3	30.3	9.6	1.6	74.1	40.0	48.7	51.3
06804	BROOKFIELD	95.1	92.3	0.8	1.1	2.5	4.4	2.4	3.9	6.0	6.7	7.8	7.7	4.1	21.5	32.7	12.0	1.6	74.4	42.7	48.1	51.9
06807	COS COB	90.4	84.9	0.4	0.5	7.3	12.0	4.4	6.7	6.8	7.4	8.0	6.3	3.4	22.3	31.6	12.2	1.9	73.6	42.7	48.2	51.8
06810	DANBURY	71.1	64.2	7.1	8.0	5.8	8.5	21.2	27.3	6.6	6.2	5.7	6.5	7.2	32.6	23.7	9.3	2.1	78.1	35.9	50.3	49.7
06811	DANBURY	83.3	77.2	6.3	7.7	5.0	7.9	7.5	10.7	6.1	6.2	6.4	5.9	6.5	27.6	28.7	11.0	1.6	77.7	39.9	46.7	53.3
06812	NEW FAIRFIELD	96.8	95.0	0.4	0.5	1.3	2.2	2.8	4.5	7.0	8.1	9.1	7.8	3.9	21.9	31.3	9.8	1.1	70.7	40.5	50.1	49.9
06820	DARIEN	95.8	93.3	0.5	0.7	2.5	4.4	2.3	3.6	9.4	10.4	10.6	6.8	2.5	20.1	28.6	10.0	1.8	65.0	39.8	49.7	50.3
06824	FAIRFIELD	95.8	93.5	1.0	1.4	1.8	3.1	2.1	3.3	6.5	7.3	8.3	9.9	6.9	20.2	27.6	10.8	2.5	73.7	38.8	48.5	51.5
06825	FAIRFIELD	94.1	91.0	1.3	1.8	2.5	4.3	3.0	4.7	6.1	6.4	6.8	9.1	5.7	21.2	27.1	12.9	4.7	76.9	41.6	47.2	52.8
06830	GREENWICH	87.3	82.2	3.1	3.8	4.8	7.6	9.7	14.0	5.9	6.0	6.9	6.5	5.1	25.0	28.5	12.8	3.3	77.1	41.6	47.4	52.6
06831	GREENWICH	93.5	89.8	0.7	1.0	3.8	6.5	3.9	6.1	6.3	7.2	8.7	6.8	3.2	19.5	30.8	14.2	3.3	73.2	43.9	48.2	51.8
06840	NEW CANAAN	95.3	92.6	1.0	1.5	2.3	4.0	1.7	2.8	7.2	8.6	9.9	8.0	3.2	17.7	31.9	11.5	2.0	68.8	42.0	47.9	52.1
06850	NORWALK	79.4	73.8	10.8	12.5	4.6	6.9	11.4	15.4	6.4	6.4	6.6	5.6	4.8	28.3	27.7	12.0	2.3	77.2	40.3	49.3	50.7
06851	NORWALK	83.3	78.0	7.9	9.5	3.7	5.8	10.1	14.1	6.1	6.2	6.4	5.6	5.0	27.0	28.7	12.4	2.5	77.8	41.5	48.9	51.1
06853	NORWALK	95.1	92.9	1.2	1.6	1.0	1.8	3.2	5.0	7.9	8.9	9.4	4.9	1.9	21.7	29.5	13.9	1.8	70.4	42.8	47.7	52.3
06854	NORWALK	56.8	51.8	28.7	30.3	2.6	3.6	25.2	30.8	7.1	6.6	6.3	6.9	7.7	31.5	24.1	8.7	1.1	75.8	35.0	49.2	50.8
06855	NORWALK	82.2	77.3	8.7	10.3	2.4	3.6	15.1	20.6	6.1	5.8	5.8	5.6	5.9	30.2	26.6	11.5	2.6	78.8	39.5	49.7	50.3
06870	OLD GREENWICH	91.0	86.2	0.9	1.2	6.1	10.0	3.6	5.5	8.0	9.6	10.9	7.6	2.4	18.9	30.2	10.6	1.8	66.2	41.0	48.0	52.0
06877	RIDGEFIELD	96.1	93.9	0.6	0.8	2.1	3.7	2.0	3.1	6.8	8.2	10.0	8.2	3.9	17.2	33.1	10.9	1.6	69.4	42.4	48.7	51.3
06878	RIVERSIDE	90.4	85.5	0.7	0.9	6.6	10.8	4.2	6.4	7.9	8.9	9.5	7.0	2.9	19.5	30.1	12.3	1.9	68.8	41.6	48.9	51.1
06880	WESTPORT	95.2	92.5	1.2	1.6	2.4	4.2	2.3	3.7	6.4	8.0	10.0	8.0	2.9	16.1	33.3	12.9	2.2	69.9	44.1	47.9	52.1
06883	WESTON	95.7	93.3	0.9	1.2	2.1	3.6	2.0	3.3	6.5	8.5	11.5	9.8	3.3	14.4	35.0	10.2	1.0	67.2	42.5	49.4	50.6
06890	SOUTHPORT	96.7	94.8	0.5	0.7	1.8	3.1	1.4	2.3	7.0	8.0	9.4	6.7	3.7	16.9	29.9	14.7	3.7	70.7	43.9	48.3	51.7
06896	REDDING	96.2	94.0	0.7	1.0	1.8	3.1	1.5	2.4	5.9	7.3	8.7	7.4	3.4	17.4	36.5	11.9	1.4	73.0	45.0	49.8	50.2
06897	WILTON	95.5	92.9	0.6	0.8	2.7	4.6	1.5	2.5	6.7	8.3	10.6	8.5	3.4	15.9	33.0	11.2	2.4	68.5	42.9	48.9	51.1
06901	STAMFORD	54.5	48.5	25.0	25.6	7.6	11.0	23.3	28.1	4.6	3.7	3.3	4.6	9.2	37.7	22.9	12.1	2.0	85.7	36.7	50.7	49.3
06902	STAMFORD	58.9	53.6	22.6	23.5	4.4	6.4	24.0	29.1	6.9	6.3	6.0	6.0	7.3	31.6	23.7	9.9	2.3	77.0	36.1	48.7	51.3
06903	STAMFORD	91.8	87.7	3.0	4.1	3.5	5.9	2.7	4.2	6.8	8.2	9.8	6.6	2.4	18.4	31.9	14.0	1.9	70.6	43.8	49.3	50.7
06905	STAMFORD	82.7	75.9	5.5	6.8	7.4	11.2	7.6	10.9	6.8	6.6	6.7	5.3	4.8	27.1	26.8	12.6	3.2	76.4	40.7	48.7	51.3
06906	STAMFORD	78.2	70.8	3.9	10.8	5.7	8.6	12.1	17.1	6.0	5.3	4.9	4.8	6.8	32.6	25.4	11.5	2.6	80.9	38.8	47.7	52.3
06907	STAMFORD	86.9	81.0	4.2	5.4	4.7	7.6	7.5	11.1	6.5	6.6	6.9	5.6	4.9	28.3	28.5	10.6	2.1	76.6	40.5	47.9	52.1
	CONNECTICUT	81.6	78.0	9.1	9.9	2.5	3.8	9.4	12.0	6.3	6.4	6.7	7.2	6.5	24.9	27.9	11.7	2.5	76.3	39.6	48.6	51.4
	UNITED STATES	75.1	72.0	12.3	12.7	3.8	4.6	12.5	15.7	6.8	6.7	6.6	7.1	6.9	27.0	26.0	10.9	1.9	75.7	36.9	49.2	50.8

#	POST OFFICE NAME	2009 Per Capita Income	2009 HH Income Base	2009 HOUSEHOLD INCOME DISTRIBUTION (%) Less than $25,000	$25,000 to $49,999	$50,000 to $99,999	$100,000 to $149,999	$150,000 or More	MEDIAN HOUSEHOLD INCOME 2009	2014	2009 National Centile	2009 State Centile	2009 Home Value Base	2009 HOME VALUE DISTRIBUTION (%) Less than $50,000	$50,000 to $89,999	$90,000 to $174,999	$175,000 to $399,999	$400,000 or More	2009 Median Home Value
06605	BRIDGEPORT	20449	8843	32.5	27.0	26.7	9.7	4.0	41072	43920	36	9	2791	2.8	7.0	35.1	46.9	8.2	193363
06606	BRIDGEPORT	24288	17100	21.2	24.8	37.4	12.9	3.8	53025	54065	68	15	10353	2.3	3.8	34.2	58.1	1.7	196454
06607	BRIDGEPORT	16156	2724	37.1	30.1	24.6	6.1	2.1	34519	37853	17	4	993	12.9	20.7	47.6	17.2	1.5	131960
06608	BRIDGEPORT	11827	4246	49.8	25.7	19.2	3.9	1.5	25148	26481	3	2	1057	4.0	8.5	55.5	29.0	2.9	155239
06610	BRIDGEPORT	20504	8577	29.6	28.7	31.2	7.9	2.6	43036	45717	43	9	4262	8.4	10.3	42.2	38.0	1.0	161563
06611	TRUMBULL	47868	12421	6.3	9.8	30.4	26.8	26.7	106145	109625	97	88	11131	0.2	0.0	0.7	39.6	59.5	438435
06612	EASTON	69997	2533	4.1	6.2	14.9	21.0	53.8	158880	160837	100	97	2350	0.0	0.0	0.3	3.5	96.3	745959
06614	STRATFORD	38564	12760	11.9	17.1	37.1	21.9	12.1	78729	81159	91	56	11147	1.1	2.9	8.1	74.0	13.9	276131
06615	STRATFORD	29137	7088	17.8	23.9	35.9	15.2	7.1	57778	59172	75	20	4700	0.0	1.7	21.4	68.1	8.8	233968
06702	WATERBURY	11118	1933	72.9	18.7	7.4	0.6	0.4	14248	14767	1	1	112	7.1	4.5	67.9	17.9	2.7	138971
06704	WATERBURY	18684	9530	34.3	28.7	28.8	5.5	2.7	36056	39530	21	5	4498	4.1	10.3	52.3	32.6	0.8	154400
06705	WATERBURY	22934	10863	25.2	29.3	38.0	5.3	2.3	46033	48514	51	10	5008	2.2	6.4	51.5	38.8	1.1	164083
06706	WATERBURY	18833	5449	31.9	28.8	31.2	6.0	2.1	37514	40438	25	7	2687	1.6	6.4	50.4	41.3	0.3	165661
06708	WATERBURY	26502	11836	22.8	23.2	39.3	9.6	5.1	53797	57460	69	16	7024	2.0	3.0	36.7	56.0	2.4	188745
06710	WATERBURY	17701	3539	36.1	26.8	26.8	6.8	3.4	38102	40604	27	8	1343	2.2	7.4	51.8	37.4	1.1	161635
06712	PROSPECT	34285	3175	6.0	11.4	48.4	20.4	13.7	81191	82417	92	62	2903	1.7	0.9	6.1	64.5	26.9	314477
06716	WOLCOTT	31815	5813	8.5	14.1	48.5	18.6	10.4	77666	78458	91	53	5055	0.0	0.3	7.8	79.8	12.0	248754
06750	BANTAM	30150	599	24.5	24.4	33.7	7.7	9.7	51309	54911	64	13	414	0.0	0.5	15.9	61.6	22.0	261905
06751	BETHLEHEM	39738	1377	7.6	8.9	40.2	23.7	19.6	90390	90304	95	77	1171	1.1	0.2	1.9	50.4	46.5	386950
06752	BRIDGEWATER	52978	751	5.3	7.6	35.2	18.8	33.2	105289	100223	97	87	671	0.7	0.0	2.2	27.3	69.7	547068
06754	CORNWALL BRIDGE	41183	632	9.7	15.5	43.0	17.6	14.2	78889	79048	92	57	531	0.0	0.4	4.1	49.2	46.3	383750
06755	GAYLORDSVILLE	40028	428	7.5	10.7	39.3	23.6	18.9	88445	91597	95	74	371	1.6	3.0	5.7	48.2	41.5	365761
06756	GOSHEN	41249	1231	7.5	11.8	44.4	22.1	14.3	82975	83225	93	66	1077	0.6	1.1	4.2	48.6	45.6	379873
06757	KENT	41603	1001	12.9	19.4	38.6	15.8	13.4	72547	71278	88	41	725	0.0	1.2	2.2	57.9	38.6	352312
06758	LAKESIDE	35736	124	5.6	16.1	50.8	14.5	12.9	80375	80665	92	60	98	0.0	0.0	8.2	52.0	39.8	356522
06759	LITCHFIELD	41200	2535	11.5	17.6	36.6	17.2	17.1	79466	79860	92	58	1989	0.8	0.4	5.7	54.3	38.9	343782
06762	MIDDLEBURY	40606	2673	9.0	11.9	42.2	18.9	18.0	81894	83346	93	63	2358	0.8	0.4	2.8	54.2	41.8	365841
06763	MORRIS	36929	912	10.5	18.6	42.2	16.6	12.1	76340	76295	90	48	709	0.0	0.1	9.0	56.4	34.4	325338
06770	NAUGATUCK	28031	12194	13.6	23.0	46.1	12.2	5.2	64872	68317	83	30	8160	2.7	5.0	15.7	72.0	4.6	220467
06776	NEW MILFORD	38846	10167	8.2	13.6	39.0	21.7	17.6	84840	85754	94	70	7851	0.4	2.5	8.8	58.6	29.7	316299
06777	NEW PRESTON MARBLE D	35925	665	14.1	19.8	33.4	24.2	8.4	74396	74143	89	44	522	0.4	1.1	4.0	43.9	50.6	403659
06778	NORTHFIELD	36862	437	5.9	15.3	44.9	20.8	13.0	82182	82770	93	64	387	0.0	1.0	4.1	58.7	36.2	335542
06779	OAKVILLE	26731	3326	14.2	25.5	43.2	13.1	3.9	60671	61827	78	26	2408	1.0	0.2	22.9	73.1	2.8	217436
06782	PLYMOUTH	27283	860	10.7	22.0	47.6	14.4	5.3	71531	73414	88	40	744	1.1	2.4	22.2	66.8	7.5	216341
06783	ROXBURY	58591	885	4.2	10.4	25.5	17.6	42.3	130827	131808	99	94	767	0.0	0.0	0.7	14.9	84.5	698495
06784	SHERMAN	53461	1569	4.3	7.5	35.2	27.2	25.7	104125	107739	97	87	1413	0.0	0.1	1.3	40.5	58.0	440536
06785	SOUTH KENT	42859	309	11.0	12.3	46.3	15.5	14.9	78750	79022	91	57	233	0.0	0.4	0.9	52.8	45.9	384921
06786	TERRYVILLE	29703	3873	11.2	22.9	45.9	14.1	6.0	70257	70716	87	38	2968	0.8	1.7	23.8	69.6	4.2	211714
06787	THOMASTON	30809	3064	13.4	21.5	44.3	12.7	8.1	69006	70478	86	36	2257	0.7	2.8	21.4	67.2	7.9	225845
06790	TORRINGTON	27117	15033	21.1	25.9	37.9	11.2	3.9	53116	55898	68	15	9802	1.1	2.3	36.3	56.7	3.7	193396
06791	HARWINTON	40809	2110	7.8	12.1	40.0	20.9	19.1	86828	88087	94	73	1952	0.0	0.9	6.0	66.3	26.8	284054
06793	WASHINGTON	49777	552	5.4	13.6	30.6	27.4	23.0	101043	105000	97	84	442	0.5	0.0	2.9	27.8	68.8	573232
06794	WASHINGTON DEPOT	50346	466	7.3	11.2	30.7	28.3	22.5	102846	100784	97	86	362	1.4	0.0	3.0	36.7	58.8	491429
06795	WATERTOWN	38177	5064	7.8	13.3	40.3	22.3	16.4	84895	85760	94	70	4228	0.4	1.6	7.8	65.9	24.3	286969
06796	WEST CORNWALL	43182	506	12.1	22.7	35.2	13.8	16.2	68191	68474	86	35	404	0.0	0.5	7.2	38.9	53.5	429167
06798	WOODBURY	47185	4020	7.2	13.4	37.7	20.7	21.0	87343	88352	94	73	3007	0.3	0.6	12.3	35.0	51.7	410096
06801	BETHEL	39719	6700	7.1	12.2	35.6	27.9	17.2	92942	97822	96	80	5109	0.1	0.0	5.9	56.2	37.8	353261
06804	BROOKFIELD	49516	6054	5.1	8.3	31.5	28.0	27.1	108325	111262	98	88	5318	0.2	0.2	5.5	44.0	50.0	400094
06807	COS COB	78207	2563	5.5	8.2	19.4	20.7	46.2	140231	143938	99	94	1910	0.0	0.0	0.5	2.0	97.5	928649
06810	DANBURY	26787	17780	17.0	23.8	37.5	15.2	6.5	58279	59934	75	22	8245	1.9	1.3	16.9	65.6	14.3	261299
06811	DANBURY	41627	10941	9.1	14.4	32.8	25.7	18.0	89764	94810	95	76	8731	0.8	1.1	9.0	60.3	28.7	323830
06812	NEW FAIRFIELD	49004	4822	4.7	8.2	26.1	29.1	31.9	118830	120187	98	91	4439	0.5	0.3	3.1	51.2	45.0	380709
06820	DARIEN	81047	6815	3.9	5.7	16.6	17.6	56.2	177146	186906	100	99	5900	0.2	0.1	0.6	4.2	95.0	991555
06824	FAIRFIELD	58709	11432	6.6	9.5	23.6	22.5	37.8	123311	124510	99	93	9534	0.1	0.1	1.4	22.4	76.0	595324
06825	FAIRFIELD	44761	7312	8.7	14.3	27.4	27.2	22.4	99141	103154	97	83	5841	0.3	0.1	1.9	38.5	59.3	438067
06830	GREENWICH	76225	10058	11.3	12.6	19.7	21.6	34.7	120301	123914	98	92	5510	0.2	0.0	0.3	8.5	91.1	954918
06831	GREENWICH	91256	5452	5.2	6.0	21.8	16.4	50.6	152172	159624	100	96	4280	0.0	0.1	0.3	3.1	96.5	1000001
06840	NEW CANAAN	86274	6826	4.8	5.9	18.0	15.8	55.5	178016	188585	100	100	5593	0.1	0.1	0.2	2.3	97.2	1000001
06850	NORWALK	43618	7200	9.9	16.4	34.1	21.4	18.2	84744	88095	94	69	4775	0.1	0.4	5.3	39.9	54.3	423979
06851	NORWALK	45132	10582	10.7	12.9	32.0	27.0	17.4	90268	95116	95	76	7628	0.9	0.5	3.6	39.5	55.5	422030
06853	NORWALK	90643	1423	6.3	7.4	19.0	16.7	50.7	152455	161133	100	97	1179	0.0	0.0	1.3	5.7	93.0	824314
06854	NORWALK	31702	10551	15.8	24.8	31.8	17.8	9.8	58985	61802	76	23	5051	0.4	0.4	10.9	51.5	36.8	346299
06855	NORWALK	42409	3224	11.9	16.7	30.4	23.0	17.9	84386	89257	94	68	1866	0.2	0.0	6.5	31.4	61.9	457513
06870	OLD GREENWICH	82714	2599	4.0	5.8	17.1	19.9	53.2	160789	167477	100	98	2181	0.0	0.0	0.2	4.3	95.5	944911
06877	RIDGEFIELD	67485	8554	5.5	7.1	22.1	18.4	46.8	141687	145350	99	95	7241	0.1	0.1	2.1	10.0	87.8	707388
06878	RIVERSIDE	72133	2666	6.3	7.8	17.0	18.0	51.0	152698	156680	100	97	2164	0.1	0.0	0.2	3.5	96.1	1000001
06880	WESTPORT	81588	9807	4.5	7.1	19.4	15.5	53.5	161180	167473	100	99	8322	0.3	0.1	0.8	4.0	94.8	915761
06883	WESTON	76207	3268	2.4	5.2	17.3	13.5	61.6	187043	193102	100	100	3002	0.0	0.2	0.2	1.8	97.8	943817
06890	SOUTHPORT	75806	1636	5.5	8.7	17.2	20.0	48.7	145664	149893	100	96	1413	0.0	0.0	0.8	15.8	83.4	706473
06896	REDDING	70339	3388	3.2	6.9	18.0	22.9	49.1	147529	150000	100	96	3015	0.0	0.0	0.4	8.4	91.3	670247
06897	WILTON	76820	5914	3.0	5.4	13.9	19.6	58.0	177181	181715	100	99	5272	0.0	0.0	0.2	4.5	95.3	858775
06901	STAMFORD	35508	3476	30.8	19.5	25.8	17.1	6.8	49674	51202	60	13	472	0.0	1.5	31.1	41.7	25.6	309449
06902	STAMFORD	38053	23692	16.4	19.9	31.2	17.6	14.9	72967	76326	88	42	11214	0.5	0.4	11.7	37.8	49.6	397672
06903	STAMFORD	73374	4968	5.1	7.4	19.5	14.4	53.7	160941	166664	100	98	4670	0.0	0.0	0.4	1.6	97.9	878536
06905	STAMFORD	51502	7404	10.5	12.9	29.6	21.6	25.4	94146	100339	96	81	5314	0.2	0.0	3.0	19.0	77.8	538323
06906	STAMFORD	38236	3038	11.4	17.5	34.4	25.0	11.8	81870	84835	93	62	1799	0.4	0.6	6.1	37.9	55.0	422487
06907	STAMFORD	44659	3523	12.4	14.4	28.3	25.0	19.8	90520	95874	95	77	2554	0.0	0.2	0.9	33.9	64.9	464141
	CONNECTICUT	36066		15.8	19.0	36.4	15.2	13.5	70949	74487				1.1	1.8	16.1	53.4	27.5	273826
	UNITED STATES	27277		20.9	24.4	35.3	11.7	7.6	54719	56938				9.3	13.1	31.6	32.6	13.5	162279

ZIP CODE #	POST OFFICE NAME	FINANCIAL SERVICES: Auto Loan	FINANCIAL SERVICES: Home Loan	FINANCIAL SERVICES: Investments	FINANCIAL SERVICES: Retirement Plans	THE HOME: Home Improvements: Home Repair	THE HOME: Home Improvements: Lawn & Garden	THE HOME: Furnishings: Computers & Hardware-Personal	THE HOME: Furnishings: Major Appliances	THE HOME: Furnishings: TV, Radio, Sound Equipment	THE HOME: Furnishings: Furniture	ENTERTAINMENT: Dine out/Carry out	ENTERTAINMENT: Sports Equipment	ENTERTAINMENT: Fees & Tickets	ENTERTAINMENT: Toys & Games	ENTERTAINMENT: Travel	ENTERTAINMENT: Cable TV	PERSONAL: Apparel & Services	PERSONAL: Auto Repairs	PERSONAL: Health Insurance	PERSONAL: Pets & Supplies
06605	BRIDGEPORT	74	64	63	66	63	60	84	71	82	78	85	58	78	81	76	81	61	80	72	84
06606	BRIDGEPORT	84	89	85	88	88	86	93	87	92	90	93	68	95	91	93	93	67	91	91	102
06607	BRIDGEPORT	58	53	51	56	51	54	65	55	69	58	70	43	63	67	59	73	50	63	63	70
06608	BRIDGEPORT	51	40	36	41	38	36	56	46	56	53	59	37	50	56	49	56	43	54	46	55
06610	BRIDGEPORT	68	65	62	66	64	64	76	68	78	71	78	53	74	76	71	79	56	74	73	81
06611	TRUMBULL	164	230	251	225	244	211	188	199	179	194	180	146	227	180	219	178	134	188	187	218
06612	EASTON	245	346	422	359	388	324	286	306	264	319	261	228	359	258	343	252	200	282	272	334
06614	STRATFORD	119	152	159	145	158	145	132	139	130	134	131	100	150	129	148	133	94	135	140	155
06615	STRATFORD	93	108	105	106	108	101	105	101	104	102	105	78	113	104	109	105	76	103	103	117
06702	WATERBURY	26	19	22	22	20	23	31	25	33	28	33	19	27	29	27	34	23	30	33	32
06704	WATERBURY	66	58	55	59	56	60	70	63	72	66	72	49	66	72	64	74	51	69	68	76
06705	WATERBURY	72	70	67	71	69	70	78	72	78	74	79	56	77	78	75	79	56	76	76	86
06706	WATERBURY	67	64	59	64	62	60	73	65	72	70	74	52	71	72	69	71	53	71	66	77
06708	WATERBURY	85	90	84	89	88	88	91	88	92	89	92	68	94	92	91	93	65	90	91	103
06710	WATERBURY	64	61	54	62	58	59	71	62	72	67	73	50	69	71	66	72	52	69	65	75
06712	PROSPECT	128	160	152	161	158	149	135	141	131	142	132	107	154	132	150	129	94	135	135	162
06716	WOLCOTT	111	146	140	141	146	133	122	127	119	124	120	95	142	121	137	119	87	122	123	143
06750	BANTAM	101	100	104	99	103	107	100	104	101	97	100	77	98	101	101	104	70	103	108	120
06751	BETHLEHEM	140	174	178	179	179	165	148	157	142	158	144	117	169	141	166	139	103	148	148	179
06752	BRIDGEWATER	173	224	245	230	237	211	190	202	179	206	180	150	222	176	218	174	131	189	187	227
06754	CORNWALL BRIDGE	143	155	181	158	162	162	138	154	136	143	137	114	147	134	153	137	96	145	148	178
06755	GAYLORDSVILLE	154	194	171	193	187	167	162	165	152	170	156	131	183	159	175	147	112	157	148	189
06756	GOSHEN	138	166	162	171	168	159	143	151	139	150	140	114	160	139	158	137	99	144	145	174
06757	KENT	130	160	160	157	162	146	143	144	137	144	139	109	159	139	155	137	101	141	138	163
06758	LAKESIDE	129	160	163	164	164	151	136	144	130	145	132	107	155	130	152	128	94	136	136	165
06759	LITCHFIELD	131	158	167	160	165	153	139	148	135	147	135	109	155	132	155	134	97	141	143	168
06762	MIDDLEBURY	133	182	194	178	191	167	151	159	144	155	145	117	179	145	174	143	107	151	150	176
06763	MORRIS	115	151	155	148	155	138	126	133	121	131	122	98	146	121	143	120	89	126	125	149
06770	NAUGATUCK	95	110	101	108	107	101	103	101	101	103	102	79	111	102	108	100	73	102	100	117
06776	NEW MILFORD	136	164	157	164	163	150	147	148	141	150	143	115	162	143	157	139	103	144	140	170
06777	NEW PRESTON MARBLE D	140	129	181	129	138	153	122	147	124	119	123	108	116	120	134	129	84	136	143	169
06778	NORTHFIELD	133	165	168	170	169	156	140	148	134	150	136	110	160	134	157	132	97	140	140	170
06779	OAKVILLE	88	104	97	102	102	100	97	96	96	95	97	74	106	96	103	97	69	97	99	112
06782	PLYMOUTH	97	121	108	121	116	119	103	107	104	105	106	80	119	106	114	107	74	105	114	125
06783	ROXBURY	174	244	296	250	273	226	205	219	187	229	185	162	251	180	246	178	140	202	196	240
06784	SHERMAN	182	236	247	238	245	221	198	209	189	208	191	155	231	189	225	187	139	198	198	236
06785	SOUTH KENT	134	179	181	170	183	159	152	156	145	153	147	116	175	148	170	145	108	151	147	173
06786	TERRYVILLE	96	116	106	115	113	109	105	105	104	105	105	81	117	105	113	104	75	105	106	122
06787	THOMASTON	102	118	110	116	116	111	111	110	109	109	110	85	119	110	116	110	78	110	111	127
06790	TORRINGTON	86	90	85	90	89	90	91	89	91	87	91	68	93	91	91	92	64	90	93	104
06791	HARWINTON	139	180	181	181	184	167	150	158	145	158	146	119	176	146	170	142	106	150	149	179
06793	WASHINGTON	153	199	231	203	218	178	178	183	160	193	160	140	204	155	204	150	119	173	160	203
06794	WASHINGTON DEPOT	149	194	219	199	209	183	165	176	154	180	155	131	194	151	192	149	113	164	161	197
06795	WATERTOWN	129	167	169	162	171	153	143	148	138	145	140	110	164	139	160	138	102	143	143	167
06796	WEST CORNWALL	166	139	213	137	152	179	137	171	143	130	141	124	123	136	149	152	94	158	170	197
06798	WOODBURY	149	187	199	190	196	168	166	169	154	175	155	131	187	153	185	147	114	162	152	191
06801	BETHEL	138	176	180	176	180	161	154	156	147	157	149	119	176	149	170	146	109	151	147	176
06804	BROOKFIELD	176	231	238	232	238	210	193	201	184	202	186	153	227	186	218	180	137	191	186	226
06807	COS COB	244	325	391	338	360	298	286	293	262	311	262	225	342	256	331	248	199	277	259	324
06810	DANBURY	94	99	97	98	99	92	106	98	103	102	106	78	107	103	105	103	76	103	97	114
06811	DANBURY	144	173	174	171	175	158	159	157	154	160	156	121	176	155	170	153	113	156	152	180
06812	NEW FAIRFIELD	185	249	256	253	257	224	204	213	192	216	194	164	244	196	233	186	144	200	191	238
06820	DARIEN	286	401	489	418	449	374	332	353	308	368	306	266	419	304	396	294	236	326	310	386
06824	FAIRFIELD	199	271	315	272	296	246	235	242	217	248	218	184	279	214	272	210	164	230	218	266
06825	FAIRFIELD	138	193	214	186	205	178	165	169	160	163	161	124	197	159	189	162	121	164	165	186
06830	GREENWICH	226	278	323	287	299	255	268	258	252	273	255	204	303	247	293	244	191	258	240	292
06831	GREENWICH	305	422	508	435	469	388	357	375	328	392	326	284	438	322	421	312	249	349	329	411
06840	NEW CANAAN	295	410	498	425	457	378	344	363	316	380	314	275	427	311	407	300	241	336	317	397
06850	NORWALK	133	160	176	160	169	145	156	150	147	156	149	117	170	145	168	143	110	152	141	169
06851	NORWALK	137	168	182	166	176	153	159	156	151	159	154	120	176	150	173	149	113	156	149	175
06853	NORWALK	256	352	425	363	393	323	300	316	274	331	272	239	365	268	354	260	207	294	276	346
06854	NORWALK	105	115	118	114	117	100	124	112	118	119	121	90	127	117	125	115	90	119	105	128
06855	NORWALK	125	150	164	149	158	133	152	142	143	147	146	112	163	140	160	140	108	146	133	161
06870	OLD GREENWICH	266	375	458	390	420	350	309	331	287	344	284	248	390	282	370	273	219	304	291	360
06877	RIDGEFIELD	228	312	373	322	346	286	265	278	243	291	242	212	323	238	312	230	184	259	244	305
06878	RIVERSIDE	250	347	422	360	388	321	291	308	268	323	266	233	361	263	346	254	204	285	270	337
06880	WESTPORT	262	367	448	381	411	342	304	324	281	338	279	243	382	276	363	268	214	299	286	354
06883	WESTON	275	393	483	412	441	371	316	341	297	353	294	256	411	296	381	285	230	312	300	370
06890	SOUTHPORT	246	324	386	333	359	289	290	295	260	315	259	230	338	254	332	242	196	279	252	326
06896	REDDING	241	334	394	344	368	308	279	297	256	310	254	222	341	249	332	243	191	274	264	326
06897	WILTON	272	383	467	399	428	357	315	336	293	350	290	253	399	289	376	279	225	309	294	366
06901	STAMFORD	92	73	78	82	72	73	107	83	107	96	110	71	97	104	93	108	79	99	93	105
06902	STAMFORD	127	133	138	136	135	121	147	132	141	142	145	106	150	139	146	139	106	140	128	154
06903	STAMFORD	252	357	435	370	399	333	294	315	272	328	269	234	370	266	353	259	206	290	279	343
06905	STAMFORD	158	196	221	197	209	179	184	180	173	187	175	139	207	172	202	169	129	179	169	203
06906	STAMFORD	115	127	136	129	130	115	139	124	132	131	137	101	143	130	141	130	100	133	122	144
06907	STAMFORD	130	166	184	164	175	150	155	150	146	152	149	117	175	146	170	144	111	151	142	169
	CONNECTICUT	120	136	136	137	137	129	132	128	129	132	130	99	141	128	137	129	94	130	128	149
	UNITED STATES	100	100	100	100	100	100	100	100	100	100	100	100	100	100	100	100	100	100	100	100

POPULATION CHANGE

19701-19979

ZIP CODE			POPULATION			2000-2009 ANNUAL RATE		HOUSEHOLDS					FAMILIES		
#	POST OFFICE NAME	COUNTY FIPS CODE	2000	2009	2014	% Rate	State Centile	2000	2009	2014	% Annual Rate 2000-2009	2009 Average HH Size	2000	2009	% Annual Rate 2000-2009
19701	BEAR	003	32458	40203	43632	2.3	67	11517	14174	15417	2.3	2.82	8636	10423	2.1
19702	NEWARK	003	44058	49403	51641	1.2	47	16026	17980	18847	1.3	2.74	11401	12429	0.9
19703	CLAYMONT	003	15293	14506	14236	-0.6	3	6425	6129	6043	-0.5	2.36	3961	3595	-1.0
19706	DELAWARE CITY	003	1623	1630	1630	0.0	17	580	585	585	0.1	2.73	406	393	-0.4
19707	HOCKESSIN	003	14317	14734	14835	0.3	31	4861	5022	5079	0.4	2.89	4122	4177	0.1
19709	MIDDLETOWN	003	20148	30343	34596	4.5	95	6710	10244	11761	4.7	2.96	5541	8225	4.4
19711	NEWARK	003	55666	57078	57412	0.3	31	18854	19345	19552	0.3	2.58	11933	11710	-0.2
19713	NEWARK	003	31276	31587	31673	0.1	21	12076	12218	12303	0.1	2.55	7918	7672	-0.3
19716	NEWARK	003	276	281	285	0.2	24	5	5	5	0.0	2.60	2	1	-7.2
19720	NEW CASTLE	003	56343	57943	58407	0.3	31	20802	21478	21750	0.3	2.65	14499	14418	-0.1
19734	TOWNSEND	003	5704	8569	10218	4.5	95	2051	2948	3553	4.0	2.91	1661	2345	3.8
19736	YORKLYN	003	49	50	50	0.2	24	16	16	17	0.0	2.94	12	12	0.0
19801	WILMINGTON	003	14809	15926	16321	0.8	45	5666	6179	6372	0.9	2.42	3206	3294	0.3
19802	WILMINGTON	003	27792	27763	27685	0.0	17	9963	9987	10008	0.0	2.55	6274	5981	-0.5
19803	WILMINGTON	003	21273	21266	21211	0.0	17	8470	8508	8527	0.0	2.46	6268	6099	-0.3
19804	WILMINGTON	003	18069	17783	17588	-0.2	7	7484	7395	7351	-0.1	2.40	4873	4610	-0.6
19805	WILMINGTON	003	40444	42423	42937	0.5	34	15418	16108	16339	0.5	2.58	9712	9676	0.0
19806	WILMINGTON	003	9590	9415	9310	-0.2	7	5517	5441	5409	-0.1	1.67	1880	1719	-1.0
19807	WILMINGTON	003	7686	8103	8265	0.6	36	3260	3469	3558	0.7	2.29	2179	2226	0.2
19808	WILMINGTON	003	39647	39779	39929	0.0	17	16030	16169	16303	0.1	2.41	10797	10447	-0.4
19809	WILMINGTON	003	14602	14567	14461	0.0	17	6345	6359	6348	0.0	2.27	3943	3778	-0.5
19810	WILMINGTON	003	25312	25632	25619	0.1	21	10071	10263	10318	0.2	2.45	7260	7148	-0.2
19901	DOVER	001	31321	33795	36490	0.8	45	12276	13189	14334	0.8	2.47	8399	8690	0.4
19902	DOVER AFB	001	455	389	369	-1.7	2	23	20	19	-1.5	2.55	23	19	-2.0
19904	DOVER	001	27863	34877	37842	2.5	72	9898	12942	14148	2.9	2.53	6669	8454	2.6
19930	BETHANY BEACH	005	2577	3438	3808	3.2	79	1303	1749	1944	3.2	1.97	868	1132	2.9
19931	BETHEL	005	223	241	256	0.8	45	95	103	110	0.9	2.34	68	73	0.8
19933	BRIDGEVILLE	005	6623	8220	9487	2.4	71	2414	3005	3499	2.4	2.73	1789	2172	2.1
19934	CAMDEN WYOMING	001	8702	12617	14318	4.1	88	3181	4702	5382	4.3	2.68	2390	3428	4.0
19938	CLAYTON	001	6010	7943	9343	3.1	76	2143	2879	3406	3.2	2.75	1676	2185	2.9
19939	DAGSBORO	005	4838	6458	7231	3.2	79	1966	2674	3002	3.4	2.41	1435	1912	3.2
19940	DELMAR	005	4684	5538	5964	1.8	57	1786	2135	2306	1.9	2.55	1273	1481	1.6
19941	ELLENDALE	005	2409	2533	2499	0.5	34	854	903	892	0.6	2.80	636	660	0.4
19943	FELTON	001	9352	11537	12706	2.3	67	3471	4333	4803	2.4	2.66	2650	3222	2.1
19944	FENWICK ISLAND	005	633	1089	1206	6.0	100	332	587	653	6.4	1.86	221	380	6.0
19945	FRANKFORD	005	7072	8543	10245	2.1	62	2754	3352	4076	2.1	2.55	1986	2352	1.8
19946	FREDERICA	001	3274	4521	5273	3.6	83	1331	1852	2171	3.6	2.44	922	1242	3.3
19947	GEORGETOWN	005	15152	17630	18514	1.7	55	4717	5529	5870	1.7	2.84	3423	3917	1.5
19950	GREENWOOD	005	5722	7108	7600	2.4	71	2084	2606	2791	2.4	2.71	1574	1921	2.2
19951	HARBESON	005	1199	1188	1415	-0.1	9	473	475	571	0.0	2.50	349	342	-0.2
19952	HARRINGTON	001	8307	9928	10607	1.9	59	3126	3753	4027	2.0	2.65	2290	2681	1.7
19953	HARTLY	001	4369	4908	5210	1.3	48	1556	1774	1892	1.4	2.77	1199	1331	1.1
19954	HOUSTON	001	1621	1665	1898	0.3	31	596	634	727	0.7	2.63	466	484	0.4
19956	LAUREL	005	14055	16112	16591	1.5	52	5352	6163	6341	1.5	2.61	3963	4465	1.3
19958	LEWES	005	13870	18229	20513	3.0	74	6258	8318	9362	3.1	2.16	4142	5350	2.8
19960	LINCOLN	005	4781	5535	5717	1.6	53	1720	1995	2057	1.6	2.77	1292	1465	1.4
19962	MAGNOLIA	001	6151	9539	11769	4.9	97	2119	3298	4078	4.9	2.89	1672	2536	4.6
19963	MILFORD	005	15205	18262	19537	2.0	60	6037	7350	7905	2.2	2.45	4242	5051	1.9
19964	MARYDEL	001	1115	1269	1344	1.4	50	416	482	513	1.6	2.63	315	355	1.3
19966	MILLSBORO	005	17171	20927	24826	2.2	64	7390	9067	10794	2.2	2.29	5148	6161	2.0
19967	MILLVILLE	005	297	427	501	4.0	84	127	184	216	4.1	2.32	87	123	3.8
19968	MILTON	005	6816	9199	10549	3.3	81	2739	3736	4293	3.4	2.46	1917	2544	3.1
19970	OCEAN VIEW	005	3882	6398	7398	5.6	98	1816	3010	3483	5.6	2.13	1280	2060	5.3
19971	DEWEY BEACH	005	10019	14480	16366	4.1	88	4872	7021	7902	4.0	2.05	2751	3893	3.8
19973	SEAFORD	005	21193	22512	22969	0.7	40	8009	8563	8741	0.7	2.56	5720	5985	0.5
19975	SELBYVILLE	005	5786	8458	9473	4.2	91	2544	3826	4309	4.5	2.21	1807	2636	4.2
19977	SMYRNA	001	13795	20232	23751	4.2	91	4576	7135	8569	4.9	2.56	3298	5002	4.6
19979	VIOLA	001	624	667	698	0.7	40	235	256	270	0.9	2.61	170	179	0.6
	DELAWARE					1.3					1.4	2.53			1.1
	UNITED STATES					1.0					1.1	2.59			0.9

ZIP CODE #	POST OFFICE NAME	RACE (%) White 2000	White 2009	Black 2000	Black 2009	Asian/Pacific 2000	Asian/Pacific 2009	% Hispanic Origin 2000	% Hispanic Origin 2009	2009 AGE DISTRIBUTION (%) 0-4	5-9	10-14	15-19	20-24	25-44	45-64	65-84	85+	18+	MEDIAN AGE 2009	% 2009 Males	% 2009 Females
19701	BEAR	76.2	70.6	18.1	21.4	2.5	3.9	3.5	5.2	8.2	7.7	7.6	7.1	6.6	31.6	25.0	5.7	0.5	72.0	33.3	49.1	50.9
19702	NEWARK	70.1	63.6	21.9	25.1	4.0	6.2	4.5	6.4	8.9	8.0	7.5	7.1	7.0	34.3	22.4	4.3	0.4	71.3	31.5	49.4	50.6
19703	CLAYMONT	69.0	62.7	24.9	28.9	2.1	3.4	3.8	5.4	7.2	6.4	6.1	6.7	8.0	27.9	24.5	10.9	2.2	76.1	36.3	47.6	52.4
19706	DELAWARE CITY	87.3	83.1	10.5	13.7	0.2	0.4	1.4	2.3	5.0	5.0	5.5	6.2	6.5	26.1	29.0	15.1	1.6	80.8	41.8	51.7	48.3
19707	HOCKESSIN	89.1	83.1	2.5	3.2	7.1	11.9	2.0	3.2	5.8	7.0	8.3	7.6	3.8	20.0	33.9	11.2	2.4	73.8	43.4	48.9	51.1
19709	MIDDLETOWN	86.7	83.4	10.3	12.3	0.8	1.3	2.7	4.6	8.0	8.0	8.2	7.7	5.4	28.0	26.9	7.0	0.8	70.8	35.0	49.7	50.3
19711	NEWARK	86.2	80.9	5.7	7.0	4.5	7.5	4.5	6.5	4.9	5.0	5.2	13.0	16.2	22.7	22.6	9.0	1.2	81.8	29.6	47.9	52.1
19713	NEWARK	78.0	71.9	14.3	16.9	3.4	5.4	4.7	7.0	6.6	6.3	6.2	6.6	8.0	30.1	24.6	10.2	1.4	77.0	35.6	48.6	51.4
19716	NEWARK	91.7	88.6	2.9	3.9	2.5	3.9	2.9	4.6	0.0	0.0	0.0	44.5	48.0	3.6	2.8	0.7	0.4	100.0	20.6	42.0	58.0
19720	NEW CASTLE	63.3	57.5	30.0	33.4	1.7	2.6	7.2	10.0	6.7	6.6	6.7	6.8	6.4	29.4	25.4	10.6	1.4	75.8	36.6	48.0	52.0
19734	TOWNSEND	91.2	88.2	6.9	9.2	0.3	0.5	1.6	2.3	6.0	6.5	7.2	7.4	4.5	25.9	31.3	10.3	1.0	75.6	40.8	50.4	49.6
19736	YORKLYN	91.8	86.0	2.0	2.0	6.1	10.0	2.0	2.0	4.0	4.0	8.0	4.0	4.0	16.0	36.0	16.0	8.0	80.0	51.3	50.0	50.0
19801	WILMINGTON	12.6	11.9	81.7	81.3	0.6	0.8	6.8	8.1	8.0	8.2	7.4	7.9	7.7	27.1	22.5	9.4	1.7	71.7	33.0	45.7	54.3
19802	WILMINGTON	21.0	18.2	75.0	77.0	0.6	0.9	3.2	4.0	7.0	6.8	6.5	7.4	8.5	28.5	24.6	9.3	1.3	75.4	34.5	49.4	50.6
19803	WILMINGTON	92.4	89.0	3.6	4.6	2.9	5.1	1.5	2.4	5.1	5.6	6.6	6.0	3.6	19.5	32.0	17.5	4.1	78.7	47.1	47.8	52.2
19804	WILMINGTON	88.7	84.8	6.4	7.8	0.9	1.5	5.6	8.9	6.0	6.0	5.9	6.2	6.0	26.6	27.1	13.7	2.5	78.2	40.5	48.6	51.4
19805	WILMINGTON	60.2	55.6	26.6	27.6	0.9	1.2	18.4	23.9	7.5	7.3	7.0	7.1	7.0	27.8	24.1	10.0	2.2	73.9	35.3	48.3	51.7
19806	WILMINGTON	84.0	80.1	12.5	14.8	1.3	2.2	2.9	4.3	3.3	2.6	2.5	3.0	8.4	32.7	24.5	17.6	5.3	89.5	43.0	45.5	54.5
19807	WILMINGTON	89.9	85.9	4.7	5.4	3.8	6.5	2.3	3.6	5.0	5.6	6.3	5.2	3.5	19.6	30.8	17.7	6.3	79.4	48.3	46.7	53.3
19808	WILMINGTON	88.5	83.9	5.4	6.6	3.3	5.5	4.3	6.7	5.8	5.9	6.1	6.1	5.4	25.7	28.5	14.2	2.3	78.5	41.6	48.0	52.0
19809	WILMINGTON	80.5	75.0	14.6	17.8	2.6	4.3	2.3	3.6	5.8	5.8	6.1	6.3	6.0	26.5	29.1	11.8	2.6	78.4	41.0	47.8	52.2
19810	WILMINGTON	87.8	83.0	6.9	8.6	3.9	6.6	1.3	2.0	5.0	5.3	5.9	6.0	4.4	22.3	31.1	16.9	3.1	79.8	45.6	48.1	51.9
19901	DOVER	64.6	58.5	27.4	31.1	2.4	3.7	4.4	5.9	7.8	7.1	6.7	7.0	8.3	27.6	22.9	10.7	1.9	75.3	33.9	48.4	51.6
19902	DOVER AFB	72.7	66.1	16.5	19.3	2.2	3.6	7.3	11.1	15.7	10.3	6.7	7.5	21.6	36.2	2.1	0.0	0.0	64.3	22.3	54.8	45.2
19904	DOVER	63.4	59.4	29.8	31.3	2.7	4.5	3.2	4.4	6.7	6.5	6.4	8.7	7.7	25.8	25.2	10.9	2.1	76.4	35.5	47.6	52.4
19930	BETHANY BEACH	98.1	97.2	0.7	0.8	0.5	0.9	1.1	1.9	1.6	1.8	2.3	2.7	1.9	10.2	35.8	40.8	3.0	92.7	62.7	48.5	51.5
19931	BETHEL	83.9	80.5	13.0	15.4	0.9	1.2	2.2	2.9	7.9	7.9	7.9	6.2	5.0	25.3	27.4	11.2	1.2	71.8	37.3	48.1	51.9
19933	BRIDGEVILLE	66.9	60.1	26.6	30.8	0.6	0.9	6.6	10.0	8.0	7.4	6.7	7.2	6.6	25.6	26.1	11.0	1.3	73.5	36.1	48.4	51.6
19934	CAMDEN WYOMING	79.9	74.0	15.4	19.2	1.8	3.1	2.4	3.6	6.0	6.5	7.2	7.2	5.5	25.3	29.4	11.5	1.3	75.7	39.5	49.1	50.9
19938	CLAYTON	91.4	88.7	6.0	7.6	0.3	0.6	1.8	2.9	6.5	6.7	7.0	7.3	5.7	27.2	28.6	9.9	1.1	75.3	38.2	50.2	49.8
19939	DAGSBORO	86.0	84.1	11.3	12.3	0.7	1.1	2.2	3.2	4.8	4.9	5.2	5.2	3.9	20.3	31.7	21.8	2.0	81.8	48.6	48.2	51.8
19940	DELMAR	84.0	79.1	13.1	16.9	0.7	1.3	1.3	2.2	6.8	6.7	6.7	6.4	5.6	24.7	27.6	13.0	2.4	75.8	39.7	48.0	52.0
19941	ELLENDALE	63.3	56.8	32.2	37.1	0.1	0.2	4.3	6.4	6.8	6.8	7.2	7.3	6.0	26.1	28.4	10.4	0.9	74.5	37.2	48.7	51.3
19943	FELTON	83.3	78.7	12.8	15.8	0.9	1.5	2.1	3.3	6.7	7.0	7.1	7.0	5.6	27.4	28.6	9.7	0.9	74.6	38.0	48.8	51.2
19944	FENWICK ISLAND	98.3	97.2	0.6	0.8	0.5	0.8	1.1	1.9	1.6	1.8	2.2	2.8	1.8	10.3	35.7	40.8	3.0	92.7	62.7	48.5	51.5
19945	FRANKFORD	82.1	79.1	13.3	14.7	0.7	1.0	5.2	7.5	5.2	5.6	6.0	5.8	4.1	23.0	32.3	16.4	1.7	79.7	45.2	49.9	50.1
19946	FREDERICA	81.4	77.2	14.0	16.3	0.9	1.6	2.8	4.3	7.3	7.1	7.0	6.9	6.6	26.1	27.4	10.5	1.3	74.5	37.2	49.0	51.0
19947	GEORGETOWN	68.9	63.1	20.6	23.6	0.4	0.7	14.4	18.9	6.4	5.9	5.5	6.9	8.4	30.5	24.2	10.6	1.5	78.4	35.5	54.6	45.4
19950	GREENWOOD	84.1	78.9	12.9	16.8	0.8	1.3	2.0	3.2	6.9	7.1	7.4	6.9	4.6	25.6	27.6	11.9	1.8	74.2	39.2	49.6	50.4
19951	HARBESON	80.2	75.4	15.9	19.4	0.3	0.5	2.3	3.8	4.4	4.7	5.1	5.9	4.6	19.4	33.3	20.6	1.9	82.1	48.6	48.5	51.5
19952	HARRINGTON	83.2	78.8	13.6	16.8	0.5	0.9	2.1	3.2	7.6	7.4	7.5	6.8	5.6	25.5	26.9	11.4	1.5	73.3	37.5	47.5	52.5
19953	HARTLY	91.1	88.5	5.3	6.8	0.6	1.1	1.4	2.2	7.6	7.8	7.8	7.2	5.5	26.0	27.7	9.5	0.8	72.3	36.7	48.9	51.1
19954	HOUSTON	81.2	76.6	15.9	19.4	0.6	1.1	2.0	3.1	6.8	7.3	7.5	7.1	4.6	26.9	28.4	10.3	1.1	73.9	38.8	48.8	51.2
19956	LAUREL	81.6	77.6	14.9	17.5	1.0	1.7	1.7	2.8	7.4	7.4	7.3	6.7	5.4	25.8	26.8	11.8	1.5	73.9	37.9	48.5	51.5
19958	LEWES	89.9	86.5	7.0	9.1	0.8	1.3	1.4	2.5	4.0	4.4	4.7	4.3	3.2	17.3	34.3	24.6	3.2	84.1	52.7	47.6	52.4
19960	LINCOLN	68.0	60.2	27.4	33.1	0.5	0.8	4.9	7.4	6.3	6.3	6.9	8.0	6.1	24.5	28.9	11.7	1.3	75.6	39.2	48.9	51.1
19962	MAGNOLIA	75.4	69.9	17.9	20.8	1.8	3.1	3.8	5.8	9.4	8.5	7.6	7.7	7.9	28.7	22.4	7.1	0.6	70.0	30.2	48.6	51.4
19963	MILFORD	80.4	77.1	13.9	15.3	0.9	1.5	5.3	7.5	6.0	5.9	6.1	6.7	5.7	23.4	29.0	14.5	2.7	77.6	42.1	48.3	51.7
19964	MARYDEL	93.3	91.3	3.2	4.1	0.4	0.6	1.3	2.0	6.9	7.1	7.2	7.1	5.6	25.6	28.8	10.7	0.9	74.5	38.9	50.0	50.0
19966	MILLSBORO	82.4	79.2	12.3	14.0	0.7	1.1	2.8	4.6	4.7	4.7	4.8	5.2	4.4	19.4	29.9	24.4	2.5	82.5	49.8	47.5	52.5
19967	MILLVILLE	97.3	96.3	1.0	1.4	0.3	0.7	0.7	1.4	4.4	4.9	5.4	4.7	3.0	19.7	33.3	22.7	1.9	82.4	49.8	50.1	49.9
19968	MILTON	79.0	73.8	15.7	18.1	0.5	1.0	5.3	8.3	5.8	6.0	6.3	6.0	4.4	22.9	30.6	16.0	1.9	78.1	43.9	48.1	51.9
19970	OCEAN VIEW	97.8	96.8	0.7	1.1	0.4	0.7	0.9	1.5	3.4	3.8	4.2	3.8	2.5	15.1	34.3	30.7	2.3	86.3	56.5	48.9	51.1
19971	DEWEY BEACH	90.8	87.2	6.1	8.1	1.1	2.0	2.2	3.8	4.0	4.2	4.2	3.8	3.1	17.6	35.7	24.5	2.8	84.8	54.2	49.2	50.8
19973	SEAFORD	71.1	65.1	24.1	28.3	1.2	1.8	3.6	5.4	6.7	6.7	7.0	7.0	5.8	24.6	27.0	12.4	2.8	75.4	39.2	47.8	52.2
19975	SELBYVILLE	83.3	82.4	11.0	10.5	1.3	1.9	9.1	11.3	4.0	4.2	4.5	4.6	3.5	17.3	31.4	28.0	2.5	84.5	53.8	49.6	50.4
19977	SMYRNA	77.3	74.7	19.2	20.4	0.8	1.6	2.3	3.3	6.6	6.5	6.4	6.5	6.8	29.9	25.7	10.0	1.6	76.5	36.9	52.7	47.3
19979	VIOLA	81.6	76.8	14.2	17.4	1.0	1.6	2.9	4.0	5.5	6.7	7.3	7.5	6.3	24.7	28.6	12.0	1.2	75.6	39.8	48.1	51.9
	DELAWARE	74.6	70.5	19.2	21.1	2.1	3.3	4.8	6.6	6.5	6.4	6.4	7.1	6.8	26.1	26.7	12.1	1.8	76.7	38.3	48.6	51.4
	UNITED STATES	75.1	72.0	12.3	12.7	3.8	4.6	12.5	15.7	6.8	6.7	6.6	7.1	6.9	27.0	26.0	10.9	1.9	75.7	36.9	49.2	50.8

ZIP CODE #	POST OFFICE NAME	2009 Per Capita Income	2009 HH Income Base	2009 HOUSEHOLD INCOME DISTRIBUTION (%) Less than $25,000	$25,000 to $49,999	$50,000 to $99,999	$100,000 to $149,999	$150,000 or More	MEDIAN HOUSEHOLD INCOME 2009	2014	2009 National Centile	2009 State Centile	2009 Home Value Base	2009 HOME VALUE DISTRIBUTION (%) Less than $50,000	$50,000 to $89,999	$90,000 to $174,999	$175,000 to $399,999	$400,000 or More	2009 Median Home Value
19701	BEAR	33844	14174	5.9	15.0	40.6	26.9	11.6	82900	85175	93	90	11379	7.2	4.2	16.1	64.4	8.0	246725
19702	NEWARK	31635	17980	7.4	18.2	43.1	22.8	8.5	76520	78929	90	81	12675	7.2	1.5	22.0	64.8	4.5	215895
19703	CLAYMONT	26683	6129	16.4	28.2	40.0	12.4	3.0	54472	58611	70	47	3080	1.4	3.6	26.1	67.9	1.0	198277
19706	DELAWARE CITY	23456	585	16.2	27.2	40.0	13.3	3.2	56085	60669	73	57	449	3.6	4.0	51.7	36.5	4.2	165394
19707	HOCKESSIN	52122	5022	3.9	6.6	21.5	27.1	41.0	132349	134584	99	98	4477	0.7	0.4	1.5	46.8	50.6	402585
19709	MIDDLETOWN	33956	10244	9.0	14.6	33.0	28.6	14.9	88617	90552	95	93	8988	5.3	2.5	13.0	60.5	18.7	300284
19711	NEWARK	34319	19345	14.2	16.7	31.4	20.9	16.8	78586	81035	91	84	12510	0.5	1.9	9.7	66.7	21.3	271531
19713	NEWARK	28793	12218	11.7	22.9	44.8	14.9	5.7	64137	67623	82	76	7778	3.4	2.0	32.3	59.8	2.5	185955
19716	NEWARK	11720	5	60.0	0.0	40.0	0.0	0.0	12000	12000	1	2	2	0.0	0.0	0.0	100.0	0.0	350000
19720	NEW CASTLE	26647	21478	14.3	23.3	42.4	15.0	5.1	62306	66590	80	72	14775	1.6	2.6	47.8	46.6	1.5	172549
19734	TOWNSEND	29813	2948	10.6	13.6	43.6	23.9	8.3	78328	80271	91	83	2597	1.6	1.9	14.9	67.4	14.2	264373
19736	YORKLYN	56166	16	0.0	0.0	18.8	25.0	56.3	156400	164796	100	100	12	0.0	0.0	0.0	25.0	75.0	550000
19801	WILMINGTON	17719	6179	41.2	27.0	23.4	6.3	2.0	31579	33418	11	3	1958	4.4	19.7	56.8	18.2	0.9	123820
19802	WILMINGTON	21922	9987	27.2	25.4	34.3	9.0	4.2	47317	49208	55	9	5411	1.6	8.4	59.4	26.9	3.7	147409
19803	WILMINGTON	50672	8508	4.8	10.9	37.3	23.0	24.0	95050	97753	96	95	7336	0.1	0.3	3.3	63.5	32.9	321079
19804	WILMINGTON	27714	7395	12.4	25.5	46.3	13.3	2.5	60044	63935	77	69	5506	1.2	1.4	42.0	54.5	0.9	180570
19805	WILMINGTON	23278	16108	24.1	27.6	34.8	9.2	4.4	48225	49967	57	16	9663	1.1	7.6	58.4	28.8	4.2	150731
19806	WILMINGTON	52748	5441	15.5	24.4	31.8	14.9	13.3	60139	64539	78	71	2761	0.9	5.3	27.3	45.9	20.5	229575
19807	WILMINGTON	75686	3469	5.7	11.5	25.9	12.6	44.3	127554	134487	99	97	2387	0.0	0.0	2.0	20.8	77.1	636643
19808	WILMINGTON	37472	16169	8.9	17.6	41.3	19.8	12.5	76390	78665	90	79	12779	3.6	2.0	16.4	72.0	6.0	234307
19809	WILMINGTON	35276	6359	12.0	22.9	40.6	15.4	9.1	65323	69491	84	78	4453	1.5	4.4	21.8	65.7	6.7	225056
19810	WILMINGTON	42702	10263	6.9	15.2	36.3	23.1	18.5	85729	88698	94	91	8094	2.9	1.1	5.8	75.6	14.6	293246
19901	DOVER	24851	13189	22.3	26.7	37.1	9.2	4.7	50899	53577	63	33	7717	13.4	4.6	25.1	48.6	8.3	190913
19902	DOVER AFB	4505	20	10.0	35.0	50.0	5.0	0.0	54523	57124	70	48	0	0.0	0.0	0.0	0.0	0.0	0
19904	DOVER	25639	12942	19.0	22.6	43.2	10.0	5.3	57672	61294	75	62	8224	4.5	3.4	22.4	61.9	7.9	215917
19930	BETHANY BEACH	54798	1749	10.5	16.7	35.9	17.7	19.2	79202	82005	92	88	1522	1.6	0.9	0.5	40.0	57.0	454359
19931	BETHEL	24381	103	31.1	21.4	35.0	8.7	3.9	48075	49434	57	14	80	20.0	8.8	12.5	48.8	10.0	192500
19933	BRIDGEVILLE	17691	3005	28.2	32.9	32.6	4.6	1.7	39471	41419	31	5	2269	12.5	8.9	30.9	43.1	4.7	170966
19934	CAMDEN WYOMING	25866	4702	15.5	24.4	43.7	10.6	5.9	59611	62290	77	66	3615	8.0	3.5	25.4	50.3	12.9	207219
19938	CLAYTON	22169	2879	15.8	27.8	45.4	9.0	2.0	56085	60597	73	57	2469	9.0	5.3	24.1	54.8	6.8	196695
19939	DAGSBORO	27640	2674	18.3	26.0	40.4	10.2	5.1	56651	61844	74	60	2260	3.3	2.0	17.7	60.0	17.0	251287
19940	DELMAR	22655	2135	22.7	28.2	39.4	5.8	3.8	49208	50223	59	26	1618	9.5	5.9	30.3	47.0	7.2	181818
19941	ELLENDALE	19475	903	23.4	28.0	41.7	5.0	1.9	48696	50351	58	17	738	17.6	10.7	27.4	40.2	4.1	163710
19943	FELTON	22605	4333	14.6	27.0	48.0	8.7	1.8	55833	59817	72	53	3583	11.6	5.4	24.6	52.6	5.9	192622
19944	FENWICK ISLAND	58062	587	10.6	16.9	35.8	17.7	19.1	78997	81781	92	86	511	1.8	0.8	0.6	39.9	56.9	454615
19945	FRANKFORD	22673	3352	19.6	31.6	39.4	6.8	2.7	48924	51074	59	21	2750	3.6	4.2	24.3	55.1	12.8	212741
19946	FREDERICA	24343	1852	20.7	25.1	44.3	7.5	2.5	53754	58182	69	45	1459	17.5	7.6	31.8	36.5	6.6	158361
19947	GEORGETOWN	20265	5529	21.8	27.1	41.0	6.5	3.6	50822	52107	63	31	4102	8.9	5.0	23.8	52.8	9.4	193302
19950	GREENWOOD	21867	2606	16.6	27.6	46.6	7.1	2.1	53640	56121	69	43	2027	6.2	2.7	29.9	52.2	9.0	197560
19951	HARBESON	22408	475	20.6	28.2	43.4	6.1	1.7	50727	51912	63	29	422	10.0	8.1	22.3	49.1	10.7	201493
19952	HARRINGTON	20606	3753	22.8	28.4	40.8	6.4	1.7	48884	50390	59	19	2861	5.5	9.1	36.2	43.6	5.6	173520
19953	HARTLY	22334	1774	16.7	30.7	41.8	6.4	4.3	52053	53901	66	38	1499	10.9	5.3	27.4	47.1	9.3	188565
19954	HOUSTON	22934	634	16.6	22.9	51.6	7.4	1.6	56379	59369	73	59	532	5.5	5.5	31.2	46.6	11.3	190000
19956	LAUREL	21113	6163	25.2	25.9	39.8	6.2	2.9	49104	50050	59	24	4790	12.9	8.9	23.9	46.3	8.1	184563
19958	LEWES	32877	8318	17.9	23.3	42.1	9.7	7.0	58706	62682	76	64	6963	8.4	5.3	9.3	46.1	30.9	308795
19960	LINCOLN	18933	1995	21.2	31.0	42.5	4.2	1.2	48056	49186	57	12	1645	11.2	6.3	23.6	55.0	3.9	193042
19962	MAGNOLIA	21472	3298	18.9	25.4	43.4	9.1	3.3	54598	58315	71	50	2487	21.1	4.8	13.7	52.6	7.7	212386
19963	MILFORD	24105	7350	22.9	27.5	38.9	7.3	3.5	49593	51395	60	28	5159	4.5	1.8	23.5	59.5	10.8	233939
19964	MARYDEL	21454	482	18.5	29.9	44.4	5.0	2.3	51091	52390	64	34	410	6.3	7.1	30.0	48.8	7.8	188235
19966	MILLSBORO	24674	9067	23.0	29.9	37.8	6.0	3.3	47406	49163	55	10	7641	16.0	13.0	27.7	37.5	5.7	157121
19967	MILLVILLE	26856	184	18.5	28.3	41.8	7.6	3.8	53116	57736	68	40	159	3.8	2.5	11.9	69.2	12.6	267000
19968	MILTON	25243	3736	21.7	25.6	40.2	8.2	4.3	52007	54484	66	36	2956	7.3	3.9	16.1	56.3	16.4	236192
19970	OCEAN VIEW	37470	3010	14.2	23.6	39.2	13.5	9.5	63527	66439	82	74	2648	2.6	1.3	10.0	57.4	28.6	316495
19971	DEWEY BEACH	40647	7021	14.0	26.2	38.1	10.2	11.4	60023	63102	77	67	5711	9.6	8.3	14.1	29.5	38.5	301278
19973	SEAFORD	21037	8563	26.0	28.4	35.9	7.1	2.7	45710	47869	50	7	6232	12.0	5.6	23.9	50.3	8.2	192153
19975	SELBYVILLE	29904	3826	15.2	29.1	41.7	9.2	4.8	55378	59982	72	52	3198	6.6	2.7	16.0	54.2	20.5	263743
19977	SMYRNA	23924	7135	19.7	26.4	40.0	10.1	3.8	53258	56074	68	41	5318	12.7	5.9	23.7	49.1	8.7	192068
19979	VIOLA	19663	256	22.7	28.5	43.4	5.1	0.4	49030	49772	59	22	210	22.4	9.0	21.0	41.4	6.2	166667
	DELAWARE	29883		16.0	22.6	38.7	14.2	8.5	61789	65095				5.8	4.2	23.8	53.6	12.6	217670
	UNITED STATES	27277		20.9	24.4	35.3	11.7	7.6	54719	56938				9.3	13.1	31.6	32.6	13.5	162279

SPENDING POTENTIAL INDICES

DELAWARE

19701-19979 **D**

ZIP CODE #	POST OFFICE NAME	FINANCIAL SERVICES: Auto Loan	FINANCIAL SERVICES: Home Loan	FINANCIAL SERVICES: Invest-ments	FINANCIAL SERVICES: Retire-ment Plans	THE HOME: Home Improvements: Home Repair	THE HOME: Home Improvements: Lawn & Garden	THE HOME: Furnishings: Comput-ers & Hard-ware-Personal	THE HOME: Furnishings: Major Appli-ances	THE HOME: Furnishings: TV, Radio, Sound Equip-ment	THE HOME: Furnishings: Furni-ture	ENTERTAINMENT: Dine out/ Carry out	ENTERTAINMENT: Sports Equip-ment	ENTERTAINMENT: Fees & Tickets	ENTERTAINMENT: Toys & Games	ENTERTAINMENT: Travel	ENTERTAINMENT: Cable TV	PERSONAL: Apparel & Services	PERSONAL: Auto Repairs	PERSONAL: Health Insur-ance	PERSONAL: Pets & Supplies
19701	BEAR	140	146	126	147	139	127	140	133	133	146	136	108	143	140	137	128	96	133	122	156
19702	NEWARK	129	128	109	128	121	112	127	119	122	132	125	97	126	129	121	118	87	121	111	141
19703	CLAYMONT	86	86	79	87	83	84	91	84	91	89	91	67	92	91	89	91	64	89	89	101
19706	DELAWARE CITY	92	92	90	92	92	99	90	94	92	88	91	70	90	92	91	95	63	93	100	110
19707	HOCKESSIN	197	256	264	266	266	230	212	222	198	232	200	173	252	202	240	189	149	206	195	249
19709	MIDDLETOWN	138	162	146	162	159	141	144	143	136	151	138	114	157	143	150	131	100	138	129	163
19711	NEWARK	134	132	128	138	131	127	147	129	137	140	139	106	142	139	137	133	99	135	126	154
19713	NEWARK	104	107	96	108	103	100	107	101	104	107	106	80	108	107	105	103	74	104	101	120
19716	NEWARK	59	36	34	40	34	39	73	47	64	56	64	44	51	64	48	61	45	59	49	60
19720	NEW CASTLE	97	105	95	105	101	101	100	99	100	101	101	76	106	101	102	100	71	100	101	116
19734	TOWNSEND	119	139	121	142	135	132	121	126	118	124	119	98	133	122	130	117	84	121	121	147
19736	YORKLYN	206	288	350	296	323	268	242	259	221	270	219	191	297	213	290	210	165	238	231	282
19801	WILMINGTON	55	51	51	52	50	53	60	53	65	56	65	40	59	63	56	69	47	60	62	66
19802	WILMINGTON	72	79	78	77	79	78	79	76	84	75	84	55	84	82	79	88	60	80	83	90
19803	WILMINGTON	155	205	227	204	219	199	172	185	167	182	167	133	205	164	200	167	122	175	182	205
19804	WILMINGTON	87	99	91	98	96	96	93	93	93	92	94	71	100	94	97	94	66	93	96	108
19805	WILMINGTON	78	84	80	82	82	83	85	81	87	80	88	61	88	87	84	91	63	84	87	96
19806	WILMINGTON	122	107	111	115	107	107	133	113	132	128	134	94	127	129	124	131	95	127	123	139
19807	WILMINGTON	213	276	330	289	303	257	249	252	231	267	231	194	294	226	284	221	175	241	228	281
19808	WILMINGTON	120	139	137	139	140	133	128	129	126	130	127	98	140	127	136	126	91	128	130	149
19809	WILMINGTON	107	117	112	118	116	113	114	112	113	114	114	87	120	113	118	113	80	113	114	131
19810	WILMINGTON	139	164	170	165	170	163	145	154	144	152	145	112	162	142	160	146	103	149	156	175
19901	DOVER	92	86	78	86	84	84	90	86	90	91	91	67	87	93	86	90	63	89	87	102
19902	DOVER AFB	96	50	37	58	44	42	90	62	84	84	89	62	68	101	65	78	62	79	56	76
19904	DOVER	94	96	89	97	94	96	94	94	95	94	95	72	96	96	94	96	66	94	96	111
19930	BETHANY BEACH	148	156	212	154	179	184	140	165	148	159	145	103	154	133	162	155	100	158	184	187
19931	BETHEL	100	76	90	72	75	96	76	89	84	76	83	68	64	86	72	91	56	85	92	108
19933	BRIDGEVILLE	77	66	61	65	64	73	68	71	71	67	70	54	61	73	63	74	48	70	74	85
19934	CAMDEN WYOMING	101	102	100	103	102	109	96	103	98	95	98	77	97	99	98	101	68	99	105	120
19938	CLAYTON	97	91	80	88	88	92	85	90	88	88	88	66	81	91	82	90	60	87	90	107
19939	DAGSBORO	102	92	117	92	99	112	90	105	94	88	93	75	86	91	95	100	63	99	110	122
19940	DELMAR	90	81	78	81	82	88	82	86	84	82	84	63	76	86	78	87	57	84	89	101
19941	ELLENDALE	94	74	78	72	73	90	74	84	80	73	79	64	64	84	69	86	54	80	87	101
19943	FELTON	94	89	80	87	87	92	84	89	86	86	86	66	81	89	82	88	59	86	89	105
19944	FENWICK ISLAND	148	156	212	154	179	184	140	165	148	159	145	103	154	133	162	155	100	158	184	187
19945	FRANKFORD	96	78	106	77	82	100	78	95	82	72	81	71	68	81	80	88	54	88	96	111
19946	FREDERICA	91	87	74	84	83	87	84	85	86	86	86	65	81	89	80	87	59	85	87	102
19947	GEORGETOWN	90	84	80	82	83	88	84	87	85	83	85	65	80	87	81	88	59	86	88	102
19950	GREENWOOD	91	85	83	88	86	98	82	92	85	76	84	70	77	87	83	90	57	86	95	108
19951	HARBESON	92	75	102	71	80	98	74	91	81	74	79	65	65	77	77	87	52	85	98	107
19952	HARRINGTON	83	76	71	77	76	82	77	80	79	75	78	60	73	80	74	81	54	78	82	94
19953	HARTLY	98	92	82	89	90	93	86	91	89	90	89	66	82	92	82	91	61	88	91	108
19954	HOUSTON	90	92	80	92	89	92	84	88	85	86	85	67	85	88	85	86	59	85	88	104
19956	LAUREL	90	76	79	74	75	88	76	84	81	75	80	63	68	83	72	85	54	81	87	100
19958	LEWES	110	99	141	95	110	123	95	116	100	97	98	80	91	93	104	106	66	109	122	133
19960	LINCOLN	88	74	73	72	73	83	72	79	77	73	76	59	65	80	68	81	52	76	81	95
19962	MAGNOLIA	96	91	77	89	86	83	91	88	89	94	90	68	86	93	85	87	62	88	83	103
19963	MILFORD	90	81	93	80	83	93	82	90	85	80	84	66	77	84	83	89	58	88	94	105
19964	MARYDEL	94	81	77	78	79	88	78	85	82	80	82	63	71	86	73	86	56	82	86	101
19966	MILLSBORO	84	78	93	74	83	92	77	87	81	79	79	60	74	77	80	85	54	84	95	101
19967	MILLVILLE	103	83	134	82	92	110	83	105	87	79	86	77	73	83	90	93	57	97	105	122
19968	MILTON	99	85	104	85	88	102	85	98	89	82	88	72	77	88	86	94	59	93	100	114
19970	OCEAN VIEW	120	111	163	110	125	138	105	128	110	109	109	87	104	102	118	116	73	120	135	147
19971	DEWEY BEACH	122	118	159	113	133	142	110	132	117	120	114	86	112	107	123	123	77	126	145	150
19973	SEAFORD	84	75	76	74	75	86	75	81	79	73	78	60	70	80	73	83	54	78	86	96
19975	SELBYVILLE	99	93	123	91	103	111	87	103	92	94	91	69	88	87	95	97	62	98	110	118
19977	SMYRNA	99	93	81	90	90	93	90	92	92	92	92	69	86	96	86	94	63	91	93	110
19979	VIOLA	90	66	91	65	69	92	68	85	75	63	73	64	55	74	67	82	48	78	88	101
	DELAWARE	109	111	110	110	111	112	108	110	109	109	109	83	110	109	109	110	76	109	111	128
	UNITED STATES	100	100	100	100	100	100	100	100	100	100	100	100	100	100	100	100	100	100	100	100

 20001-20064

ZIP CODE			POPULATION			2000-2009 ANNUAL RATE		HOUSEHOLDS					FAMILIES		
#	POST OFFICE NAME	COUNTY FIPS CODE	2000	2009	2014	% Rate	State Centile	2000	2009	2014	% Annual Rate 2000-2009	2009 Average HH Size	2000	2009	% Annual Rate 2000-2009
20001	WASHINGTON	001	33683	38674	40929	1.5	92	12032	15011	16326	2.4	2.24	5774	6743	1.7
20002	WASHINGTON	001	49657	49138	49089	-0.1	13	21179	21234	21318	0.0	2.23	10187	9864	-0.3
20003	WASHINGTON	001	23122	23241	23416	0.1	50	10195	10479	10643	0.3	1.94	4031	3941	-0.2
20004	WASHINGTON	001	901	1060	1127	1.8	100	694	841	902	2.1	1.20	199	168	-1.8
20005	WASHINGTON	001	10610	12367	13103	1.7	96	6266	7227	7655	1.6	1.69	1387	1524	1.0
20006	WASHINGTON	001	1874	1901	1911	0.2	58	669	695	702	0.4	1.28	38	39	0.3
20007	WASHINGTON	001	24004	24470	24751	0.2	58	12368	12784	12988	0.4	1.85	4126	4080	-0.1
20008	WASHINGTON	001	26286	27297	27796	0.4	79	16018	16914	17306	0.6	1.59	4607	4613	0.0
20009	WASHINGTON	001	46506	49681	51108	0.7	83	24971	26807	27657	0.8	1.80	6769	7071	0.5
20010	WASHINGTON	001	28853	29573	30247	0.3	67	10814	11078	11348	0.3	2.61	5417	5378	-0.1
20011	WASHINGTON	001	57753	59982	60560	0.4	79	22936	23566	23874	0.3	2.50	13349	13330	0.0
20012	WASHINGTON	001	13307	13391	13464	0.1	50	5411	5509	5563	0.2	2.29	3252	3219	-0.1
20015	WASHINGTON	001	15824	15136	15330	-0.5	4	6177	6407	6519	0.4	2.29	3678	3704	0.1
20016	WASHINGTON	001	31072	32165	32679	0.4	79	13813	14575	14908	0.6	1.94	6120	6241	0.2
20017	WASHINGTON	001	17302	17355	17434	0.0	29	7024	7144	7215	0.2	2.19	3828	3787	-0.1
20018	WASHINGTON	001	16552	16690	16812	0.1	50	6898	7167	7292	0.4	2.24	3769	3749	-0.1
20019	WASHINGTON	001	53436	53509	53954	0.0	29	21507	21777	22035	0.1	2.43	13152	12995	-0.1
20020	WASHINGTON	001	49142	50586	51366	0.3	67	19140	20017	20440	0.5	2.50	12001	12274	0.2
20024	WASHINGTON	001	11856	11986	12115	0.1	50	6896	7040	7135	0.2	1.66	2272	2222	-0.2
20032	WASHINGTON	001	37036	37448	37969	0.1	50	12965	13283	13533	0.3	2.66	8792	8819	0.0
20036	WASHINGTON	001	3808	3686	3678	-0.4	8	2883	2843	2844	-0.2	1.26	342	322	-0.6
20037	WASHINGTON	001	13255	14941	15648	1.3	88	7416	8704	9237	1.7	1.37	1066	1196	1.3
20057	WASHINGTON	001	4467	4450	4455	0.0	29	28	34	36	2.1	2.74	8	9	1.3
20064	WASHINGTON	001	1753	1759	1766	0.0	29	38	51	56	3.2	1.45	1	2	7.8
	DISTRICT OF COLUMBIA					0.3					0.5	2.13			0.1
	UNITED STATES					1.0					1.1	2.59			0.9

ZIP CODE #	POST OFFICE NAME	RACE (%) White 2000	White 2009	Black 2000	Black 2009	Asian/Pacific 2000	Asian/Pacific 2009	% Hispanic Origin 2000	% Hispanic Origin 2009	2009 AGE DISTRIBUTION (%) 0-4	5-9	10-14	15-19	20-24	25-44	45-64	65-84	85+	18+	MEDIAN AGE 2009	% 2009 Males	% 2009 Females
20001	WASHINGTON	8.9	13.0	81.8	74.4	3.1	4.9	7.4	9.5	5.7	5.7	5.3	9.6	11.8	27.5	22.9	9.6	1.8	79.6	33.1	47.6	52.4
20002	WASHINGTON	18.0	21.3	78.1	73.9	0.9	1.2	2.2	2.7	6.0	5.9	5.4	6.2	7.7	29.5	27.1	10.5	1.9	79.2	37.5	47.4	52.6
20003	WASHINGTON	40.5	46.1	54.7	48.2	1.8	2.3	3.1	3.5	4.5	4.0	3.8	5.2	9.0	36.7	27.9	7.9	1.2	85.3	36.7	54.1	45.9
20004	WASHINGTON	50.4	52.2	13.8	8.9	33.6	36.9	4.2	4.1	2.0	1.4	1.0	2.3	11.7	37.7	28.6	12.5	2.7	94.7	40.8	52.8	47.2
20005	WASHINGTON	44.6	50.4	30.1	21.8	7.3	9.0	25.2	27.1	3.7	2.9	2.0	3.2	11.1	45.6	21.6	7.8	2.1	89.9	33.8	58.7	41.3
20006	WASHINGTON	74.3	75.8	7.3	4.8	14.8	16.0	5.1	4.7	0.2	0.0	0.1	35.9	42.3	13.4	3.9	3.3	1.0	99.5	21.6	45.5	54.5
20007	WASHINGTON	86.5	87.7	3.8	2.4	5.9	6.4	6.0	5.7	3.6	2.2	1.9	4.0	15.0	35.6	26.6	9.0	2.1	90.9	34.9	46.7	53.3
20008	WASHINGTON	84.5	86.3	5.4	3.4	6.0	6.5	6.6	6.2	2.8	2.1	2.3	2.2	7.8	38.6	30.7	10.9	2.8	91.4	40.7	44.3	55.7
20009	WASHINGTON	49.2	53.1	31.1	25.4	4.4	5.2	20.3	22.1	4.5	4.0	3.5	4.3	9.2	44.5	23.1	6.1	1.0	86.0	34.3	52.2	47.8
20010	WASHINGTON	23.7	27.7	47.4	39.7	3.9	4.8	32.1	36.0	6.9	6.4	5.8	6.2	8.0	35.0	22.8	7.5	1.4	77.2	33.8	50.8	49.2
20011	WASHINGTON	7.9	12.0	80.1	73.0	0.7	1.2	13.4	16.6	5.7	6.0	6.0	6.3	5.9	25.7	28.2	13.5	2.7	78.4	41.0	46.6	53.4
20012	WASHINGTON	16.4	22.3	74.5	66.3	1.4	1.9	8.0	9.8	4.4	4.7	4.9	5.2	6.1	25.5	31.0	15.7	2.5	82.8	44.4	46.9	53.1
20015	WASHINGTON	82.5	85.3	9.5	6.2	4.1	4.8	4.8	4.7	5.5	5.7	6.6	4.7	3.8	22.1	32.6	14.6	4.3	78.9	45.9	46.8	53.2
20016	WASHINGTON	83.9	85.8	5.9	3.9	5.1	5.6	6.9	6.6	4.0	3.9	4.2	8.3	9.6	26.7	26.8	13.0	3.5	85.5	40.1	44.1	55.9
20017	WASHINGTON	13.4	19.7	81.8	74.2	1.2	1.7	3.0	3.6	4.5	4.6	5.0	6.6	6.5	23.5	28.7	16.8	3.7	82.3	44.3	46.9	53.1
20018	WASHINGTON	3.0	4.4	93.8	91.1	0.6	0.9	2.2	2.8	5.3	5.4	5.7	6.0	5.8	22.1	28.5	17.4	3.9	79.8	44.8	44.5	55.5
20019	WASHINGTON	0.7	1.1	97.6	96.6	0.2	0.3	0.9	1.1	7.7	8.3	7.5	8.0	6.6	23.7	24.9	11.2	2.0	71.4	35.2	43.8	56.2
20020	WASHINGTON	1.8	2.7	96.6	95.0	0.2	0.3	0.9	1.1	8.9	9.5	8.3	8.4	6.9	24.8	23.1	9.0	1.0	68.2	31.2	43.7	56.3
20024	WASHINGTON	26.3	33.8	64.8	55.3	2.7	3.9	4.4	5.1	4.3	4.5	3.7	3.5	6.9	29.3	32.8	13.2	1.8	85.3	43.4	47.4	52.6
20032	WASHINGTON	9.3	11.6	87.6	84.5	0.8	1.1	1.9	2.1	10.2	10.0	8.2	8.8	8.5	27.7	19.6	6.5	0.6	66.4	27.8	46.1	53.9
20036	WASHINGTON	80.5	82.4	6.8	4.5	7.9	8.6	6.8	6.5	1.2	0.5	0.2	1.5	12.9	50.3	24.7	7.2	1.6	97.9	34.4	52.2	47.8
20037	WASHINGTON	78.6	80.8	6.6	4.2	11.0	11.6	5.8	5.5	1.1	0.7	0.5	13.5	20.0	36.4	16.9	8.9	2.0	97.4	29.4	46.4	53.6
20057	WASHINGTON	87.9	89.5	5.4	3.4	6.7	7.0	1.7	1.6	0.1	0.0	0.0	54.6	42.7	1.1	0.7	0.5	0.3	99.3	19.6	45.3	54.7
20064	WASHINGTON	89.1	90.7	4.6	3.0	3.8	4.2	4.6	4.2	0.0	0.1	0.0	48.9	31.9	9.6	3.8	3.3	2.5	99.5	20.2	50.7	49.3
	DISTRICT OF COLUMBIA	30.8	33.9	60.0	55.4	2.7	3.3	7.9	9.0	5.7	5.6	5.2	7.1	8.9	29.9	25.2	10.3	2.0	80.2	35.8	47.2	52.8
	UNITED STATES	75.1	72.0	12.3	12.7	3.8	4.6	12.5	15.7	6.8	6.7	6.6	7.1	6.9	27.0	26.0	10.9	1.9	75.7	36.9	49.2	50.8

20001-20064

ZIP CODE #	POST OFFICE NAME	2009 Per Capita Income	2009 HH Income Base	2009 HOUSEHOLD INCOME DISTRIBUTION (%) Less than $25,000	$25,000 to $49,999	$50,000 to $99,999	$100,000 to $149,999	$150,000 or More	MEDIAN HOUSEHOLD INCOME 2009	2014	2009 National Centile	2009 State Centile	2009 Home Value Base	2009 HOME VALUE DISTRIBUTION (%) Less than $50,000	$50,000 to $89,999	$90,000 to $174,999	$175,000 to $399,999	$400,000 or More	2009 Median Home Value
20001	WASHINGTON	20685	15011	40.1	24.0	24.9	7.2	3.9	33583	36572	15	21	4766	0.9	0.3	2.8	56.0	39.9	358042
20002	WASHINGTON	28004	21234	27.4	26.4	29.0	10.5	6.8	45412	50117	49	38	10012	0.2	0.2	4.7	59.4	35.5	325013
20003	WASHINGTON	42702	10479	21.0	17.2	29.2	16.4	16.2	66311	68057	84	71	5196	0.8	0.1	1.2	33.5	64.4	520208
20004	WASHINGTON	65117	841	40.2	8.9	24.1	12.0	14.7	51059	55014	64	54	223	0.0	0.0	0.0	39.5	60.5	481034
20005	WASHINGTON	34515	7227	30.6	25.5	30.1	8.6	5.2	42785	48095	42	33	1525	1.5	2.2	13.0	27.9	55.4	433951
20006	WASHINGTON	17445	695	61.7	25.5	9.5	1.9	1.4	13642	16370	1	8	42	0.0	0.0	81.0	0.0	19.0	135000
20007	WASHINGTON	71787	12784	12.5	13.7	27.5	15.7	30.6	90914	93590	95	88	6587	0.1	0.1	2.6	15.5	81.6	958409
20008	WASHINGTON	77323	16914	9.1	14.1	33.9	18.6	24.2	86192	87414	94	83	7092	0.0	0.5	3.1	22.7	73.6	790527
20009	WASHINGTON	42124	26807	21.4	23.3	34.0	10.9	10.4	54975	56522	71	63	8278	0.2	0.5	4.7	29.5	65.1	545597
20010	WASHINGTON	23196	11078	29.1	27.5	27.4	8.9	7.1	42010	47062	39	29	3771	0.7	1.0	2.3	47.2	48.8	394376
20011	WASHINGTON	26157	23566	22.6	27.3	32.6	10.9	6.7	50088	52713	61	50	13214	0.3	0.7	1.8	62.2	34.9	358659
20012	WASHINGTON	40043	5509	15.4	19.9	27.2	20.6	16.9	73134	75216	88	79	3778	0.3	0.1	1.2	22.2	76.3	574694
20015	WASHINGTON	64493	6407	8.9	10.3	21.0	19.7	40.1	126172	128034	99	96	4752	0.2	0.3	0.1	6.9	92.5	957365
20016	WASHINGTON	64422	14575	11.3	12.6	27.1	17.5	31.5	97609	99967	96	92	9047	0.0	0.1	1.2	15.7	83.0	891400
20017	WASHINGTON	28350	7144	20.5	23.7	39.5	11.2	5.1	54815	55862	71	58	4448	0.1	0.2	4.0	67.4	28.2	345316
20018	WASHINGTON	26698	7167	28.6	23.1	31.7	11.3	5.3	47402	51702	55	42	4265	0.4	0.2	2.4	63.1	33.9	347758
20019	WASHINGTON	17877	21777	38.1	29.1	25.9	5.1	1.8	34370	37330	16	25	8968	0.4	0.5	7.5	82.8	8.9	247657
20020	WASHINGTON	17380	20017	39.2	29.9	23.6	5.5	1.7	32727	35117	13	17	6502	0.9	1.5	11.0	65.3	21.4	276835
20024	WASHINGTON	34875	7040	24.4	26.1	38.1	7.0	4.4	49328	52459	60	46	2450	1.6	3.0	18.7	51.6	25.2	273031
20032	WASHINGTON	16666	13283	38.3	31.1	23.3	5.0	2.3	32411	34659	12	13	3216	0.5	1.4	6.0	87.6	4.5	247676
20036	WASHINGTON	72085	2843	13.5	19.3	36.5	17.0	13.6	68031	69361	86	75	1055	0.0	0.9	17.4	37.7	44.0	363714
20037	WASHINGTON	52571	8704	25.8	17.2	30.2	14.2	12.6	57416	59031	75	67	3138	0.0	0.0	10.8	33.1	56.1	456716
20057	WASHINGTON	15257	34	0.0	0.0	32.4	35.3	32.4	127673	127710	99	100	19	0.0	0.0	0.0	52.6	47.4	383333
20064	WASHINGTON	14296	51	82.4	0.0	17.6	0.0	0.0	8500	9032	0	4	0	0.0	0.0	0.0	0.0	0.0	0
	DISTRICT OF COLUMBIA	34644		25.5	23.1	29.2	11.1	11.1	51491	53880				0.4	0.5	4.5	45.8	48.9	393913
	UNITED STATES	27277		20.9	24.4	35.3	11.7	7.6	54719	56938				9.3	13.1	31.6	32.6	13.5	162279

ZIP CODE		FINANCIAL SERVICES				THE HOME						ENTERTAINMENT						PERSONAL			
						Home Improvements		Furnishings													
#	POST OFFICE NAME	Auto Loan	Home Loan	Invest-ments	Retire-ment Plans	Home Repair	Lawn & Garden	Comput-ers & Hard-ware-Personal	Major Appli-ances	TV, Radio, Sound Equip-ment	Furni-ture	Dine out/ Carry out	Sports Equip-ment	Fees & Tickets	Toys & Games	Travel	Cable TV	Apparel & Services	Auto Repairs	Health Insur-ance	Pets & Supplies
20001	WASHINGTON	60	53	56	57	53	54	70	58	73	63	74	46	66	70	63	76	53	67	67	73
20002	WASHINGTON	79	77	81	80	77	76	90	79	94	83	95	61	91	90	86	98	69	87	87	97
20003	WASHINGTON	115	112	123	121	114	107	133	114	131	126	134	94	134	129	128	131	98	124	115	138
20004	WASHINGTON	115	85	88	98	82	82	125	94	121	116	126	87	111	123	108	118	90	114	98	121
20005	WASHINGTON	83	62	65	71	60	60	91	68	87	84	91	63	81	88	78	85	65	82	71	88
20006	WASHINGTON	41	18	17	22	16	20	58	29	46	39	47	31	34	45	31	42	33	40	29	39
20007	WASHINGTON	175	173	199	192	180	162	203	173	192	198	198	149	207	190	200	185	146	187	166	206
20008	WASHINGTON	166	147	163	165	149	138	188	152	179	180	185	135	182	179	176	173	135	172	150	187
20009	WASHINGTON	100	81	85	92	79	77	118	91	116	106	120	79	107	113	103	115	88	106	94	114
20010	WASHINGTON	72	67	69	72	66	63	89	73	92	78	94	58	85	87	80	95	70	82	78	89
20011	WASHINGTON	81	86	87	87	86	85	91	85	96	86	97	63	95	92	91	100	70	90	93	102
20012	WASHINGTON	113	143	160	142	152	136	133	133	130	133	130	98	151	125	147	131	96	132	135	150
20015	WASHINGTON	185	231	276	243	254	210	218	214	199	231	201	170	249	195	244	189	151	208	190	240
20016	WASHINGTON	176	188	217	202	199	178	201	183	191	203	195	149	214	188	208	186	143	190	177	214
20017	WASHINGTON	83	88	89	89	88	90	91	87	94	88	95	64	95	90	92	98	67	91	96	104
20018	WASHINGTON	75	77	79	79	77	81	84	78	89	80	89	57	86	83	83	94	63	84	92	96
20019	WASHINGTON	55	52	51	53	51	54	60	54	66	55	66	40	60	63	56	70	47	60	62	67
20020	WASHINGTON	56	50	49	53	49	52	61	53	66	56	66	40	60	64	56	70	48	60	61	66
20024	WASHINGTON	79	65	69	71	65	69	86	72	87	81	88	59	81	84	79	88	62	82	83	90
20032	WASHINGTON	60	48	46	52	46	49	65	53	68	59	69	43	60	68	56	71	50	62	59	67
20036	WASHINGTON	131	97	101	112	93	94	143	108	139	133	144	99	127	140	123	135	103	130	112	139
20037	WASHINGTON	121	87	90	101	83	85	135	98	128	122	133	91	116	129	112	124	95	120	102	127
20057	WASHINGTON	237	101	99	124	92	117	334	164	265	225	270	178	197	259	179	242	191	234	165	223
20064	WASHINGTON	28	12	12	14	11	14	39	19	31	26	32	21	23	30	21	28	22	27	19	26
	DISTRICT OF COLUMBIA	98	91	96	97	91	89	111	94	112	103	114	76	109	109	104	114	83	105	101	116
	UNITED STATES	100	100	100	100	100	100	100	100	100	100	100	100	100	100	100	100	100	100	100	100

A 32003-32218

ZIP CODE #	POST OFFICE NAME	COUNTY FIPS CODE	POPULATION 2000	POPULATION 2009	POPULATION 2014	2000-2009 ANNUAL RATE % Rate	2000-2009 ANNUAL RATE State Centile	HOUSEHOLDS 2000	HOUSEHOLDS 2009	HOUSEHOLDS 2014	HOUSEHOLDS % Annual Rate 2000-2009	HOUSEHOLDS 2009 Average HH Size	FAMILIES 2000	FAMILIES 2009	FAMILIES % Annual Rate 2000-2009
32003	ORANGE PARK	019	13097	25291	31096	7.4	93	4275	8456	10454	7.7	2.99	3701	7188	7.4
32008	BRANFORD	067	3780	4622	5048	2.2	66	1524	1881	2061	2.3	2.44	1081	1306	2.1
32009	BRYCEVILLE	089	3095	4078	4652	3.0	78	1069	1437	1650	3.2	2.84	898	1182	3.0
32011	CALLAHAN	089	11272	13386	14855	1.9	61	4082	4945	5525	2.1	2.71	3231	3836	1.9
32013	DAY	067	1995	2561	2606	2.7	74	306	343	362	1.2	2.60	225	248	1.1
32024	LAKE CITY	023	16698	21827	24601	2.9	77	6158	8236	9355	3.2	2.65	4802	6304	3.0
32025	LAKE CITY	023	17811	21775	23450	2.2	66	6328	7629	8349	2.0	2.45	4241	4999	1.8
32033	ELKTON	109	2256	4236	5365	7.0	93	877	1689	2160	7.3	2.50	668	1244	7.0
32034	FERNANDINA BEACH	089	24878	31232	34835	2.5	72	10270	13023	14581	2.6	2.38	7288	9148	2.5
32038	FORT WHITE	023	5768	7220	7965	2.5	72	2248	2864	3180	2.7	2.52	1626	2026	2.4
32040	GLEN SAINT MARY	003	6733	8330	9084	2.3	69	2279	2897	3190	2.6	2.75	1848	2315	2.5
32043	GREEN COVE SPRINGS	019	19677	25375	28891	2.8	76	7276	9638	11068	3.1	2.58	5556	7165	2.8
32044	HAMPTON	007	1775	2014	2085	1.4	51	655	759	792	1.6	2.62	480	547	1.4
32046	HILLIARD	089	7760	9987	11336	2.8	76	2724	3585	4100	3.0	2.73	2150	2767	2.8
32052	JASPER	047	8265	9267	9475	1.2	46	2253	2497	2607	1.1	2.50	1600	1741	0.9
32053	JENNINGS	047	3371	3549	3635	0.6	30	1225	1320	1363	0.8	2.67	915	970	0.6
32054	LAKE BUTLER	125	11225	13143	13778	1.7	57	3218	3732	3997	1.6	2.65	2478	2830	1.4
32055	LAKE CITY	023	15730	17880	18969	1.4	51	5978	6801	7282	1.4	2.45	4102	4544	1.1
32058	LAWTEY	007	5559	6350	6441	1.4	51	1219	1388	1429	1.4	2.67	918	1028	1.2
32059	LEE	079	1795	1946	1992	0.9	38	709	791	817	1.2	2.46	514	562	1.0
32060	LIVE OAK	121	17631	20323	21910	1.5	53	6869	8040	8717	1.7	2.47	4930	5662	1.5
32061	LULU	023	354	429	471	2.1	64	137	169	187	2.3	2.54	101	122	2.1
32062	MC ALPIN	121	2107	2439	2622	1.6	55	800	937	1012	1.7	2.60	610	704	1.6
32063	MACCLENNY	003	10738	12453	13157	1.6	55	3560	4205	4488	1.8	2.78	2776	3231	1.7
32064	LIVE OAK	121	6149	6835	7297	1.1	44	2262	2538	2723	1.3	2.62	1567	1724	1.0
32065	ORANGE PARK	019	18965	29701	34120	5.0	88	6586	10260	11825	4.9	2.89	5317	8233	4.8
32066	MAYO	067	4353	4994	5310	1.5	53	1560	1801	1927	1.6	2.67	1158	1314	1.4
32068	MIDDLEBURG	019	35207	49913	58449	3.8	84	12006	17541	20713	4.2	2.84	9913	14158	3.9
32071	O BRIEN	121	2770	3495	3906	2.5	72	1109	1410	1580	2.6	2.48	818	1019	2.4
32073	ORANGE PARK	019	39761	44006	46779	1.1	44	14748	16726	17898	1.4	2.57	10916	12022	1.0
32080	SAINT AUGUSTINE	109	16832	22796	26516	3.3	81	8012	11059	12963	3.5	2.06	4925	6483	3.0
32081	PONTE VEDRA	109	503	2032	2711	16.3	99	172	712	953	16.6	2.85	127	518	16.4
32082	PONTE VEDRA BEACH	109	28185	31606	34434	1.2	46	12063	13715	15021	1.4	2.30	8217	8918	0.9
32083	RAIFORD	125	2560	3100	3117	2.1	64	282	296	305	0.5	2.77	229	237	0.4
32084	SAINT AUGUSTINE	109	22828	29686	34504	2.9	77	9103	12050	14125	3.1	2.36	5483	6883	2.5
32086	SAINT AUGUSTINE	109	19333	25646	29701	3.1	79	7823	10541	12293	3.3	2.39	5434	7027	2.8
32087	SANDERSON	003	4621	5618	6046	2.1	64	1144	1435	1587	2.5	3.03	928	1148	2.3
32091	STARKE	007	15382	16674	16878	0.9	38	5208	5663	5770	0.9	2.62	3779	4027	0.7
32092	SAINT AUGUSTINE	109	6528	22460	29678	14.3	98	2463	8684	11549	14.6	2.58	1848	6220	14.0
32094	WELLBORN	121	2167	2543	2756	1.7	57	848	1010	1101	1.9	2.52	636	746	1.7
32095	SAINT AUGUSTINE	109	4883	7918	9955	5.4	90	1788	3057	3901	6.0	2.50	1246	1982	5.1
32096	WHITE SPRINGS	047	2462	2881	3094	1.7	57	972	1169	1266	2.0	2.46	693	816	1.8
32097	YULEE	089	10546	14494	16617	3.5	82	3797	5366	6216	3.8	2.66	2933	4046	3.5
32102	ASTOR	069	2400	2746	2942	1.5	53	1121	1280	1372	1.4	2.13	770	846	1.0
32110	BUNNELL	035	6732	8977	11770	3.2	80	2599	3748	4997	4.0	2.37	1969	2764	3.7
32112	CRESCENT CITY	107	7871	8063	8067	0.3	18	3071	3086	3087	0.1	2.58	2090	2057	-0.2
32113	CITRA	083	5508	6998	7788	2.6	73	2096	2681	3018	2.7	2.37	1526	1904	2.4
32114	DAYTONA BEACH	127	35264	35580	35634	0.1	12	14480	14609	14700	0.1	2.12	6813	6457	-0.6
32117	DAYTONA BEACH	127	23665	24604	24840	0.4	22	9919	10357	10484	0.5	2.32	5772	5742	-0.1
32118	DAYTONA BEACH	127	19030	19125	19054	0.1	12	10189	10242	10237	0.1	1.86	4810	4591	-0.5
32119	DAYTONA BEACH	127	22146	23422	23912	0.6	30	10332	10978	11262	0.7	2.11	6221	6326	0.2
32124	DAYTONA BEACH	127	4147	5464	5982	3.0	78	430	931	1108	8.7	3.00	315	656	8.3
32127	PORT ORANGE	127	28864	30784	31357	0.7	32	12403	13268	13577	0.7	2.29	8356	8618	0.3
32128	PORT ORANGE	127	8678	17785	21776	8.1	95	3619	7451	9177	8.1	2.39	2858	5732	7.8
32129	PORT ORANGE	127	18109	20344	21104	1.3	48	8235	9256	9622	1.3	2.18	5165	5574	0.8
32130	DE LEON SPRINGS	127	4801	5336	5589	1.1	44	1630	1773	1848	0.9	2.98	1221	1289	0.6
32131	EAST PALATKA	107	5120	5265	5297	0.3	18	1858	1903	1920	0.3	2.55	1337	1343	0.0
32132	EDGEWATER	127	7145	7792	8043	0.9	38	3038	3313	3425	0.9	2.34	2042	2148	0.5
32134	FORT MC COY	083	9344	11814	13300	2.6	73	4024	5082	5715	2.6	2.31	2716	3352	2.3
32136	FLAGLER BEACH	035	6936	9902	11943	3.9	84	3488	5134	6248	4.3	1.93	2204	3090	3.7
32137	PALM COAST	035	21702	41313	52773	7.2	93	9393	18393	23700	7.5	2.23	6953	13261	7.2
32139	GEORGETOWN	107	766	792	791	0.4	22	368	375	374	0.2	2.11	250	248	-0.1
32140	FLORAHOME	107	1561	1701	1751	0.9	38	591	640	661	0.9	2.66	452	482	0.7
32141	EDGEWATER	127	15399	18599	20197	2.1	64	6386	7703	8382	2.0	2.41	4740	5558	1.7
32145	HASTINGS	109	3975	6425	8082	5.3	90	1404	2283	2880	5.4	2.80	1021	1595	4.9
32148	INTERLACHEN	107	12046	13377	13866	1.1	44	4717	5187	5386	1.0	2.58	3353	3614	0.8
32159	LADY LAKE	069	23803	30227	36555	2.6	73	11959	15044	18270	2.5	2.00	8822	10705	2.1
32162	LADY LAKE	119	5386	39236	54633	23.9	100	2727	18853	26360	23.2	2.08	2094	14027	22.8
32164	PALM COAST	035	14134	38292	50627	11.4	97	5695	16022	21370	11.8	2.38	4465	12214	11.5
32168	NEW SMYRNA BEACH	127	20403	24306	25953	1.9	61	9022	10690	11407	1.9	2.27	5824	6660	1.5
32169	NEW SMYRNA BEACH	127	10670	12607	13502	1.8	59	5330	6322	6785	1.9	1.97	3238	3668	1.4
32174	ORMOND BEACH	127	39775	49304	53432	2.3	69	16760	20884	22771	2.4	2.30	11499	13984	2.1
32176	ORMOND BEACH	127	16030	16212	16229	0.1	12	7899	8013	8044	0.2	2.02	4801	4660	-0.3
32177	PALATKA	107	24958	25814	26082	0.4	22	9534	9823	9960	0.3	2.55	6669	6742	0.1
32179	OCKLAWAHA	083	8695	10241	11173	1.8	59	3634	4275	4665	1.8	2.38	2503	2861	1.5
32180	PIERSON	127	4903	5554	5812	1.4	51	1255	1448	1533	1.6	3.09	912	1019	1.2
32181	POMONA PARK	107	2503	2572	2572	0.3	18	1039	1059	1060	0.2	2.41	709	706	0.0
32187	SAN MATEO	107	1486	1715	1809	1.6	55	622	712	751	1.5	2.41	435	488	1.3
32189	SATSUMA	107	5058	5958	6323	1.8	59	2252	2617	2776	1.6	2.28	1550	1762	1.4
32190	SEVILLE	127	1143	1317	1387	1.5	53	390	447	472	1.5	2.89	280	311	1.1
32193	WELAKA	107	979	1018	1029	0.4	22	479	495	503	0.4	2.01	311	314	0.1
32195	WEIRSDALE	083	3619	5084	6161	3.7	83	1394	1960	2386	3.8	2.58	1064	1456	3.4
32202	JACKSONVILLE	031	5122	5652	6022	1.1	44	1413	1961	2210	3.6	1.65	315	373	1.8
32204	JACKSONVILLE	031	7143	8069	8576	1.3	48	3098	3757	4073	2.1	1.95	1257	1410	1.2
32205	JACKSONVILLE	031	29658	30735	31423	0.4	22	13171	13959	14345	0.6	2.19	7286	7421	0.2
32206	JACKSONVILLE	031	21240	21853	22329	0.3	18	8309	8748	8984	0.6	2.43	4730	4790	0.1
32207	JACKSONVILLE	031	35195	36946	37934	0.5	26	15783	16949	17500	0.8	2.16	8882	9107	0.3
32208	JACKSONVILLE	031	33457	34710	35529	0.4	22	12504	13276	13656	0.6	2.60	8622	8908	0.4
32209	JACKSONVILLE	031	39756	40306	40824	0.1	12	15303	15874	16155	0.4	2.52	10081	10123	0.0
32210	JACKSONVILLE	031	55996	60434	63056	0.8	35	21787	24019	25150	1.1	2.51	15020	16144	0.8
32211	JACKSONVILLE	031	32158	33901	34910	0.6	30	12689	13707	14186	0.8	2.45	8184	8614	0.6
32214	JACKSONVILLE	031	2483	2436	2460	-0.2	4	345	360	366	0.5	4.40	310	320	0.3
32216	JACKSONVILLE	031	30721	35803	38080	1.7	57	12541	15097	16188	2.0	2.34	8122	9536	1.8
32217	JACKSONVILLE	031	20212	20621	21128	0.2	15	8494	8842	9080	0.4	2.31	5409	5405	0.0
32218	JACKSONVILLE	031	37946	51307	58013	3.3	81	13825	19126	21768	3.6	2.63	10275	13855	3.3
	FLORIDA					1.9					1.9	2.47			1.7
	UNITED STATES					1.0					1.1	2.59			0.9

ZIP CODE #	POST OFFICE NAME	RACE (%) White 2000	White 2009	Black 2000	Black 2009	Asian/Pacific 2000	Asian/Pacific 2009	% Hispanic Origin 2000	% Hispanic Origin 2009	2009 AGE DISTRIBUTION (%) 0-4	5-9	10-14	15-19	20-24	25-44	45-64	65-84	85+	18+	MEDIAN AGE 2009	% 2009 Males	% 2009 Females
32003	ORANGE PARK	89.5	86.3	4.5	5.6	2.9	4.0	4.3	6.7	6.9	7.7	8.4	8.5	4.7	25.0	30.6	7.5	0.7	71.0	38.3	49.6	50.4
32008	BRANFORD	94.3	92.2	1.9	2.5	0.3	0.5	5.3	8.7	5.5	5.7	6.0	7.1	5.9	22.4	30.4	15.6	1.3	78.3	43.0	50.6	49.4
32009	BRYCEVILLE	97.2	96.2	0.9	1.4	0.4	0.6	0.7	1.3	7.3	7.3	7.4	7.4	5.6	26.6	27.8	9.9	0.7	73.4	37.0	49.9	50.1
32011	CALLAHAN	92.1	89.8	6.0	7.8	0.3	0.4	0.8	1.4	6.8	6.5	6.9	6.8	6.1	26.3	28.5	11.0	1.0	75.5	38.4	49.0	51.0
32013	DAY	59.6	53.6	34.0	37.8	0.4	0.5	9.0	13.0	2.0	2.3	2.8	3.1	13.5	55.4	15.5	4.8	0.6	91.2	33.3	83.1	16.9
32024	LAKE CITY	90.2	86.6	6.2	8.3	0.7	1.2	3.3	5.4	6.5	6.7	6.9	7.1	5.7	24.3	28.8	12.7	1.4	75.7	39.6	49.0	51.0
32025	LAKE CITY	79.5	73.5	17.2	22.3	0.7	1.0	3.1	4.7	5.9	5.5	5.5	6.6	8.1	26.5	24.2	15.0	2.8	79.6	38.9	53.4	46.6
32033	ELKTON	84.7	75.9	12.5	20.1	0.7	1.2	2.3	3.7	5.5	5.6	5.9	6.0	5.1	22.2	28.9	18.5	2.3	78.8	44.8	48.8	51.2
32034	FERNANDINA BEACH	88.1	85.7	9.6	11.1	0.7	1.0	2.1	3.3	5.4	5.5	5.7	5.8	5.1	23.1	31.5	16.0	1.9	79.9	44.6	48.4	51.6
32038	FORT WHITE	87.1	82.2	9.6	13.5	0.2	0.3	2.5	3.9	5.8	6.2	6.6	6.2	5.0	22.9	31.7	14.3	1.3	77.5	42.9	49.6	50.4
32040	GLEN SAINT MARY	88.0	84.5	10.3	13.3	0.2	0.3	1.5	2.4	8.0	7.3	7.2	7.3	6.9	28.7	25.6	8.2	0.7	72.8	34.3	51.3	48.7
32043	GREEN COVE SPRINGS	86.1	83.7	9.7	10.8	0.8	1.1	3.7	5.7	6.3	6.5	6.8	6.7	5.1	24.9	28.8	13.0	1.8	76.1	40.6	49.6	50.4
32044	HAMPTON	92.2	89.4	4.5	5.8	0.3	0.5	2.9	4.7	7.5	6.7	6.6	7.5	6.1	25.0	27.0	12.3	1.3	74.5	38.4	50.5	49.5
32046	HILLIARD	91.6	89.0	6.7	8.9	0.3	0.5	0.8	1.3	7.2	7.2	7.2	6.9	6.0	26.2	26.9	11.1	1.3	73.9	37.4	49.2	50.8
32052	JASPER	55.7	50.3	41.3	45.8	0.2	0.2	5.9	8.7	5.3	5.3	5.3	6.3	9.8	33.8	24.0	8.7	1.6	80.3	35.7	63.6	36.4
32053	JENNINGS	68.5	63.4	25.6	28.4	0.4	0.5	10.5	15.3	7.3	7.1	7.4	7.3	5.3	25.4	26.7	12.2	1.2	73.4	37.9	50.8	49.2
32054	LAKE BUTLER	75.2	70.0	21.5	25.6	0.3	0.4	3.3	5.0	6.4	5.9	5.6	6.2	7.9	35.9	23.5	7.7	0.8	78.3	34.8	61.3	38.7
32055	LAKE CITY	67.1	62.2	30.0	34.2	0.9	1.2	2.1	3.1	6.6	6.8	6.8	6.9	6.5	27.0	26.0	11.8	1.6	75.6	37.3	51.6	48.4
32058	LAWTEY	63.8	57.8	32.1	37.0	0.6	0.7	4.5	6.7	3.7	3.9	4.0	4.8	9.0	41.6	24.4	7.9	0.8	85.7	36.4	70.7	29.3
32059	LEE	91.9	89.1	5.5	7.5	0.1	0.2	3.2	5.5	5.9	6.2	6.4	6.6	5.1	22.9	31.1	14.4	1.5	77.6	42.6	50.3	49.7
32060	LIVE OAK	86.7	82.6	10.0	12.9	0.5	0.7	4.4	7.0	5.9	6.1	6.3	5.9	4.5	23.2	28.2	16.7	3.1	78.0	43.3	48.4	51.6
32061	LULU	92.9	89.7	5.1	7.2	0.0	0.2	1.7	3.0	6.5	6.5	6.5	7.2	5.8	27.7	27.0	11.4	1.2	76.0	38.4	50.3	49.7
32062	MC ALPIN	90.3	86.8	6.6	9.0	0.9	1.3	4.4	7.2	5.7	6.2	6.3	5.9	4.1	22.8	30.2	17.2	1.6	78.1	44.2	49.2	50.8
32063	MACCLENNY	87.3	83.8	10.7	13.5	0.7	1.0	1.6	2.7	7.5	7.0	6.6	6.9	7.3	27.2	25.7	10.4	1.3	74.9	35.6	49.7	50.3
32064	LIVE OAK	64.6	58.2	31.8	37.3	0.7	0.9	6.9	9.8	6.5	6.7	6.9	8.0	6.3	24.9	25.0	13.3	2.3	75.2	37.6	49.7	50.3
32065	ORANGE PARK	83.4	76.1	8.5	12.0	3.2	5.1	5.8	9.2	7.8	7.5	7.2	6.8	5.8	31.0	26.0	7.3	0.6	73.3	34.3	48.8	51.2
32066	MAYO	85.7	81.7	7.6	8.5	0.0	0.0	10.1	15.6	7.0	7.2	7.4	7.1	4.7	25.7	24.9	14.0	2.1	74.2	38.3	52.3	47.7
32068	MIDDLEBURG	91.9	88.5	3.7	5.2	1.2	1.9	3.4	5.7	7.5	7.6	7.8	7.5	5.5	28.9	27.1	7.5	0.6	72.3	35.3	49.6	50.4
32071	O BRIEN	92.2	89.1	4.9	6.9	0.5	0.8	4.1	6.7	5.7	6.0	6.2	5.9	4.7	23.8	29.5	16.6	1.7	78.5	43.3	49.9	50.1
32073	ORANGE PARK	81.6	76.5	10.1	12.3	3.3	4.6	5.7	8.8	6.1	5.9	5.8	6.4	7.2	27.2	27.4	12.1	1.8	78.3	38.0	48.3	51.7
32080	SAINT AUGUSTINE	96.9	95.5	0.5	0.8	1.1	1.7	2.4	4.0	3.2	3.3	3.7	3.9	4.9	20.3	34.7	23.3	2.6	87.5	52.2	48.5	51.5
32081	PONTE VEDRA	98.2	98.1	0.4	0.3	0.4	0.3	1.4	1.7	6.1	7.2	8.3	7.9	3.8	24.0	34.9	7.0	0.7	73.3	41.1	51.5	48.5
32082	PONTE VEDRA BEACH	96.3	94.7	1.0	1.5	1.2	1.8	2.5	4.2	4.5	4.8	5.4	6.1	5.2	21.1	35.3	15.3	2.2	81.3	46.7	47.8	52.2
32083	RAIFORD	66.2	60.3	29.2	33.9	0.5	0.8	4.6	7.0	1.8	1.8	2.5	3.0	3.8	55.3	28.5	3.1	0.3	91.8	39.1	87.1	12.9
32084	SAINT AUGUSTINE	76.3	71.9	20.4	23.8	0.5	0.7	2.9	4.7	5.9	5.7	5.5	7.7	7.7	24.8	28.1	12.3	2.3	79.3	39.0	47.6	52.4
32086	SAINT AUGUSTINE	94.7	92.2	2.5	3.9	1.1	1.5	3.2	5.3	5.1	5.2	5.6	6.0	5.1	22.1	30.4	17.1	3.3	80.3	45.5	47.2	52.8
32087	SANDERSON	70.3	65.7	27.0	30.9	0.2	0.3	3.1	4.5	6.5	5.9	5.4	6.5	9.5	34.8	23.9	6.8	0.7	78.4	33.5	60.3	39.7
32091	STARKE	76.7	71.9	20.7	24.8	0.8	1.1	1.7	2.6	6.1	6.1	6.0	6.0	6.1	29.5	26.0	11.9	2.1	78.0	38.0	52.8	47.2
32092	SAINT AUGUSTINE	94.1	90.3	3.9	7.0	0.4	0.7	1.6	2.5	6.3	6.7	7.2	7.0	4.9	26.0	30.8	10.0	1.1	75.3	39.8	50.4	49.6
32094	WELLBORN	91.0	87.5	6.0	8.2	0.4	0.7	3.4	5.7	6.0	6.4	6.7	6.6	4.6	24.4	29.5	14.4	1.5	76.8	41.5	48.3	51.7
32095	SAINT AUGUSTINE	94.4	92.8	3.2	3.9	0.5	0.8	2.9	4.9	6.3	6.5	6.6	6.7	6.3	28.0	29.5	9.3	0.9	76.6	38.2	51.7	48.3
32096	WHITE SPRINGS	60.8	53.8	37.5	44.3	0.1	0.2	0.6	0.9	6.4	7.0	7.1	7.1	6.0	23.8	29.3	11.9	1.4	74.9	39.7	49.7	50.3
32097	YULEE	89.1	85.2	8.1	11.3	0.5	0.7	1.6	2.7	6.7	6.9	7.2	7.0	5.6	27.7	28.5	9.7	0.7	74.9	37.7	51.3	48.7
32102	ASTOR	92.2	89.3	1.2	1.6	0.1	0.2	14.6	20.5	5.5	5.8	5.8	5.0	4.1	18.1	32.0	21.7	2.2	79.9	50.0	50.7	49.3
32110	BUNNELL	81.3	78.0	14.6	16.6	1.2	1.6	4.5	7.0	6.2	6.3	6.6	6.4	5.3	23.4	29.2	14.7	1.8	76.7	41.9	48.9	51.1
32112	CRESCENT CITY	66.2	57.9	17.4	19.4	1.1	1.4	20.1	28.2	6.8	6.7	6.4	6.3	4.8	19.4	25.3	21.0	3.1	76.2	44.4	49.8	50.2
32113	CITRA	76.3	69.6	20.5	26.0	0.4	0.5	3.7	5.6	5.1	5.6	5.9	6.5	5.8	25.9	30.0	13.4	1.8	79.4	41.5	50.3	49.7
32114	DAYTONA BEACH	48.8	41.7	45.9	51.7	1.8	2.3	3.6	5.2	5.7	5.2	4.9	11.1	14.6	23.7	19.8	12.1	3.0	80.9	30.8	50.4	49.6
32117	DAYTONA BEACH	72.3	65.2	23.7	29.6	1.1	1.5	3.6	5.6	5.5	5.4	5.5	6.0	6.4	23.8	27.6	15.9	3.7	79.9	42.9	47.7	52.3
32118	DAYTONA BEACH	94.4	91.7	1.7	2.8	1.6	2.5	2.8	4.8	3.0	2.8	2.9	3.2	4.6	21.0	31.2	26.1	5.3	89.7	53.7	50.2	49.8
32119	DAYTONA BEACH	89.3	84.4	6.6	9.8	1.8	2.6	3.2	5.3	4.7	4.4	4.4	4.7	5.4	24.0	27.9	20.7	3.8	83.8	46.7	48.4	51.6
32124	DAYTONA BEACH	70.9	59.4	24.7	35.1	0.3	0.4	4.9	7.3	2.8	3.2	4.5	10.1	7.4	41.5	23.6	5.9	0.9	82.4	36.3	69.6	30.4
32127	PORT ORANGE	96.6	94.8	1.1	1.8	0.9	1.4	2.3	4.0	4.0	4.4	5.0	5.1	3.8	18.9	32.2	22.5	4.1	83.3	50.8	47.8	52.2
32128	PORT ORANGE	95.7	93.1	1.2	2.2	1.6	2.5	2.1	3.7	3.3	3.5	4.1	4.1	2.7	14.6	37.5	27.5	2.7	86.5	56.0	48.3	51.7
32129	PORT ORANGE	95.0	92.3	2.0	3.3	1.1	1.8	2.4	4.2	3.9	3.7	3.9	4.9	5.8	21.7	29.0	23.1	4.1	85.6	49.4	47.8	52.2
32130	DE LEON SPRINGS	80.8	72.1	4.0	5.6	0.6	0.7	23.3	34.5	7.0	7.1	6.8	7.5	6.4	24.7	24.7	13.8	2.0	74.6	38.2	50.2	49.8
32131	EAST PALATKA	71.1	63.6	26.7	33.4	0.6	0.9	1.8	2.8	5.1	5.3	5.5	5.7	5.2	25.8	29.7	15.9	1.8	80.8	43.0	53.8	46.2
32132	EDGEWATER	96.5	94.6	1.3	2.2	0.4	0.7	2.1	3.7	5.2	5.2	5.4	5.5	5.0	21.7	29.6	19.3	3.3	80.9	46.5	46.6	53.4
32134	FORT MC COY	95.4	93.6	1.7	2.6	0.3	0.4	1.9	3.2	4.5	5.0	5.5	5.8	4.1	19.0	32.6	21.3	2.3	81.3	49.1	50.7	49.3
32136	FLAGLER BEACH	97.5	96.7	0.7	1.0	0.5	0.7	1.8	3.0	2.2	2.4	2.7	2.8	2.4	13.1	38.8	32.0	3.5	90.9	59.3	48.6	51.4
32137	PALM COAST	88.8	85.2	7.2	9.3	1.1	1.7	5.4	8.3	4.0	4.1	4.4	4.6	3.7	16.6	31.8	27.4	3.5	84.5	54.2	48.0	52.0
32139	GEORGETOWN	79.2	72.2	8.1	9.8	1.2	1.8	13.8	20.1	4.8	5.1	5.2	4.9	3.5	16.4	29.8	27.4	2.9	81.8	53.8	50.0	50.0
32140	FLORAHOME	94.3	92.0	1.9	2.8	0.2	0.4	2.8	4.8	6.6	6.6	6.9	6.4	6.0	23.6	29.2	13.6	1.0	75.8	40.2	49.6	50.4
32141	EDGEWATER	96.7	94.8	1.3	2.2	0.5	0.8	1.7	3.0	4.6	4.8	5.1	5.7	5.1	20.1	29.1	22.7	2.8	81.9	48.2	48.5	51.5
32145	HASTINGS	67.1	63.3	30.0	32.9	0.3	0.3	3.1	5.0	7.6	7.5	7.0	7.4	7.6	25.2	25.5	11.0	1.3	73.4	36.2	49.0	51.0
32148	INTERLACHEN	89.5	84.7	4.0	5.5	0.4	0.7	8.7	14.1	6.2	6.2	6.4	6.6	5.4	22.0	29.5	15.7	1.9	77.1	42.8	49.8	50.2
32159	LADY LAKE	96.3	93.5	2.2	4.2	0.5	0.8	1.7	3.1	2.5	2.4	2.4	2.5	2.2	9.2	19.6	53.1	6.0	91.1	68.4	46.2	53.8
32162	LADY LAKE	94.5	89.7	3.8	6.9	0.5	0.6	2.1	5.2	3.4	3.5	3.7	3.9	3.1	14.3	27.0	37.6	3.5	87.0	60.1	48.0	52.0
32164	PALM COAST	82.7	80.6	12.6	13.5	1.6	2.1	6.6	9.2	4.6	4.9	5.3	5.4	3.8	19.6	31.8	22.1	2.5	81.8	49.4	48.2	51.8
32168	NEW SMYRNA BEACH	89.6	86.9	8.0	9.7	0.6	1.0	1.5	2.6	4.2	4.2	4.4	4.9	4.3	19.0	32.3	22.9	3.7	84.1	51.0	48.0	52.0
32169	NEW SMYRNA BEACH	97.5	96.2	0.6	1.0	0.5	0.7	1.6	2.9	2.0	2.3	2.7	2.8	2.2	14.3	36.3	31.9	5.5	91.2	59.7	47.7	52.3
32174	ORMOND BEACH	93.8	91.4	3.4	4.8	1.2	1.8	2.2	3.7	4.1	4.4	5.0	5.6	4.4	18.6	32.7	21.5	3.8	82.9	50.2	48.0	52.0
32176	ORMOND BEACH	97.0	95.6	0.4	0.7	0.9	1.4	2.6	4.5	2.8	3.0	3.3	3.7	3.2	15.4	33.6	29.7	5.3	88.6	57.4	46.8	53.2
32177	PALATKA	70.6	65.3	26.9	31.2	0.4	0.6	2.7	4.4	7.1	6.7	6.7	6.9	6.1	24.3	26.7	13.5	2.1	75.5	38.7	48.1	51.9
32179	OCKLAWAHA	93.7	90.8	3.2	4.8	0.2	0.4	2.9	4.8	5.1	5.5	5.8	5.4	4.4	19.9	31.2	20.2	2.4	79.9	47.7	49.6	50.4
32180	PIERSON	83.9	78.6	2.7	3.4	0.3	0.4	44.9	58.5	5.8	6.0	6.0	6.5	8.9	30.9	23.1	11.1	1.6	78.4	34.4	55.1	44.9
32181	POMONA PARK	88.3	82.7	6.6	9.1	0.2	0.4	6.2	10.4	4.9	4.7	4.7	5.3	4.4	17.1	30.1	26.1	2.8	82.4	51.9	49.2	50.8
32187	SAN MATEO	87.2	84.7	11.2	13.1	0.2	0.3	1.7	2.9	4.8	6.1	5.2	4.9	4.4	21.0	32.5	19.8	1.2	81.1	47.6	51.4	48.6
32189	SATSUMA	93.3	90.4	3.9	5.6	0.4	0.6	2.6	4.5	4.9	5.3	5.2	4.9	4.0	17.4	30.8	25.3	2.2	81.7	51.7	49.9	50.1
32190	SEVILLE	66.1	56.0	17.1	21.3	0.2	0.3	29.8	39.9	7.1	7.1	7.1	6.8	5.8	23.6	26.9	14.0	1.7	74.5	38.2	52.0	48.0
32193	WELAKA	83.0	75.8	12.3	16.8	0.1	0.1	4.7	8.1	4.7	4.5	4.4	4.5	3.5	14.1	30.5	31.1	2.6	83.2	56.1	47.7	52.3
32195	WEIRSDALE	90.9	86.8	6.9	10.3	0.6	0.8	3.3	5.3	4.9	5.1	5.4	5.9	4.4	20.4	30.5	21.0	2.3	81.1	47.5	49.3	50.7
32202	JACKSONVILLE	30.4	22.8	67.0	74.3	0.5	0.4	2.2	2.8	2.7	2.8	2.5	5.9	9.1	33.3	22.2	16.6	4.9	89.5	41.3	62.0	38.0
32204	JACKSONVILLE	51.2	44.8	44.7	50.7	1.3	1.5	2.5	3.4	4.9	4.5	4.2	5.4	8.0	29.4	22.4	14.8	6.4	83.4	40.2	46.9	53.1
32205	JACKSONVILLE	73.7	65.2	20.6	27.5	2.3	3.0	3.0	4.5	7.0	6.3	6.0	6.0	7.0	29.6	26.1	10.0	2.0	77.1	37.0	47.9	52.1
32206	JACKSONVILLE	15.1	10.1	82.4	87.4	0.5	0.5	1.8	2.1	7.8	7.7	7.3	8.1	7.5	23.1	26.5	10.2	1.8	72.3	35.1	47.9	52.1
32207	JACKSONVILLE	72.7	64.6	21.1	27.6	2.1	2.7	4.8	6.9	6.9	6.3	5.9	6.0	6.9	27.4	26.8	11.4	2.5	77.3	38.3	48.0	52.0
32208	JACKSONVILLE	23.2	16.6	75.3	81.8	0.3	0.3	1.0	1.2	6.8	7.1	7.4	7.8	6.5	23.0	27.2	12.3	1.9	73.8	37.9	45.7	54.3
32209	JACKSONVILLE	1.2	0.8	97.7	98.2	0.1	0.1	0.7	0.8	7.3	7.4	7.5	8.4	6.9	21.8	24.8	13.4	2.5	72.7	37.0	44.9	55.1
32210	JACKSONVILLE	67.7	58.1	24.7	32.4	3.2	4.0	4.2	6.1	7.6	6.9	6.7	7.0	7.7	27.2	24.9	10.3	1.6	74.6	35.0	47.9	52.1
32211	JACKSONVILLE	65.1	54.4	28.8	38.1	1.7	2.2	5.0	7.0	7.7	7.2	6.8	6.9	7.4	28.5	24.0	9.9	1.6	74.3	34.5	48.3	51.7
32214	JACKSONVILLE	63.7	52.4	25.3	33.6	2.9	3.5	11.2	15.6	11.8	9.6	6.4	10.1	22.6	32.1	5.3	2.0	0.1	70.1	22.7	60.8	39.2
32216	JACKSONVILLE	72.5	65.4	20.7	26.2	2.8	3.5	5.6	7.6	6.9	6.2	6.3	6.7	7.8	27.1	26.1	11.0	1.8	76.5	36.7	48.3	51.7
32217	JACKSONVILLE	77.6	70.1	13.7	18.9	3.4	4.4	6.1	9.0	6.1	5.9	6.2	6.1	6.4	26.2	26.4	13.6	3.1	78.2	39.9	47.0	53.0
32218	JACKSONVILLE	57.7	51.7	39.8	45.3	0.5	0.6	1.7	2.3	7.4	7.2	7.1	7.2	6.7	28.3	25.8	9.2	1.1	73.8	35.0	48.5	51.5
	FLORIDA	78.0	74.7	14.6	15.8	1.7	2.3	16.8	21.5	6.0	5.9	5.9	6.3	6.2	25.0	26.8	15.3	2.8	78.6	41.1	48.8	51.2
	UNITED STATES	75.1	72.0	12.3	12.7	3.8	4.6	12.5	15.7	6.8	6.7	6.6	7.1	6.9	27.0	26.0	10.9	1.9	75.7	36.9	49.2	50.8

ZIP CODE #	POST OFFICE NAME	2009 Per Capita Income	2009 HH Income Base	2009 Household Income Distribution (%): Less than $25,000	$25,000 to $49,999	$50,000 to $99,999	$100,000 to $149,999	$150,000 or More	Median Household Income: 2009	2014	2009 National Centile	2009 State Centile	2009 Home Value Base	2009 Home Value Distribution (%): Less than $50,000	$50,000 to $89,999	$90,000 to $174,999	$175,000 to $399,999	$400,000 or More	2009 Median Home Value
32003	ORANGE PARK	34987	8456	4.3	13.7	43.1	25.0	13.8	84597	87505	94	95	7307	0.5	0.7	15.1	62.2	21.4	265233
32008	BRANFORD	16779	1881	37.6	32.6	25.6	2.4	1.8	33435	34069	14	11	1566	17.8	27.0	31.8	18.7	4.7	102941
32009	BRYCEVILLE	22345	1437	16.5	25.0	45.9	10.2	2.5	55574	57651	72	71	1283	5.1	21.3	36.6	34.4	2.7	129790
32011	CALLAHAN	21987	4945	21.7	23.5	42.2	9.5	3.1	53327	55710	69	65	4102	13.0	16.5	37.2	30.2	3.1	132428
32013	DAY	16439	343	32.9	36.4	23.0	6.1	1.5	35274	35681	19	14	287	18.1	34.1	32.1	15.3	0.3	84583
32024	LAKE CITY	18885	8236	27.3	32.1	33.1	5.1	2.5	42739	45261	42	36	6999	8.7	15.4	45.1	27.4	3.4	134522
32025	LAKE CITY	19874	7629	27.7	33.5	29.0	7.3	2.4	41474	43846	38	32	5339	8.6	16.8	48.9	22.2	3.5	128966
32033	ELKTON	26111	1689	16.0	30.0	40.0	10.0	4.0	53357	54632	69	65	1487	4.0	6.7	48.4	33.9	7.0	158147
32034	FERNANDINA BEACH	35529	13023	17.2	21.4	37.1	14.2	10.1	62038	63742	80	80	10138	3.2	5.4	23.7	40.4	27.3	252802
32038	FORT WHITE	18162	2864	30.7	30.7	33.0	4.0	1.6	37962	40507	27	22	2444	10.4	19.8	40.5	24.7	4.5	122670
32040	GLEN SAINT MARY	21275	2897	20.3	26.4	40.7	10.3	2.3	52319	55344	67	63	2403	17.5	20.6	35.7	20.5	5.7	115474
32043	GREEN COVE SPRINGS	25064	9638	20.3	25.0	38.7	11.8	4.2	53968	56277	70	67	7232	7.7	13.7	34.5	34.2	9.9	159094
32044	HAMPTON	22829	759	26.6	29.5	35.6	4.9	3.4	45692	47722	50	45	636	13.5	24.1	41.5	14.6	6.3	112037
32046	HILLIARD	19515	3585	23.9	28.0	39.4	6.4	2.3	48009	51259	57	51	2811	22.3	20.1	34.0	20.5	3.0	107149
32052	JASPER	15773	2497	41.2	30.7	23.6	3.3	1.2	29987	30315	8	5	1833	23.8	29.2	36.8	9.0	1.2	84612
32053	JENNINGS	14495	1320	41.7	27.3	26.5	3.4	1.1	30360	29822	9	5	1066	26.0	29.1	32.0	9.8	3.2	80182
32054	LAKE BUTLER	18654	3732	25.6	32.6	33.9	5.2	2.7	41435	45049	37	32	2837	21.5	22.0	39.3	15.5	1.7	98119
32055	LAKE CITY	17232	6801	39.4	31.2	23.2	4.5	1.6	31663	33276	11	8	4764	19.8	23.7	33.5	16.5	6.7	100610
32058	LAWTEY	17636	1388	28.6	28.7	36.2	4.9	1.6	42163	44094	40	35	1142	11.3	25.3	36.3	25.6	1.6	115252
32059	LEE	19916	791	36.0	25.4	31.4	4.2	3.0	37236	40690	24	20	647	29.4	29.8	21.8	12.8	6.2	74643
32060	LIVE OAK	18292	8040	34.3	30.3	28.6	4.6	2.2	36353	37138	22	17	6457	12.4	22.4	37.7	21.6	6.0	118292
32061	LULU	18005	169	28.4	32.5	33.1	4.1	1.8	40201	42353	33	28	140	17.1	21.4	34.3	19.3	7.9	110526
32062	MC ALPIN	16989	937	31.5	31.9	31.6	3.4	1.6	37930	38219	26	22	837	11.0	22.0	37.3	24.0	5.7	122690
32063	MACCLENNY	20266	4205	24.2	26.6	38.5	7.7	2.9	49011	52087	59	54	3269	13.0	19.9	41.7	21.2	4.2	116852
32064	LIVE OAK	16371	2538	36.4	31.4	26.2	4.8	1.1	34127	34787	16	12	1858	14.5	28.5	41.6	12.4	3.1	102682
32065	ORANGE PARK	25442	10260	9.4	24.4	46.2	15.1	5.0	65777	71890	84	84	8024	1.4	4.8	43.1	47.4	3.3	176301
32066	MAYO	17726	1801	32.8	32.8	28.9	2.6	2.9	36799	38284	23	18	1415	18.8	22.5	36.9	18.0	3.8	105998
32068	MIDDLEBURG	24574	17541	12.1	26.1	45.7	11.5	4.6	61091	63249	79	78	14959	5.6	10.7	45.8	32.4	5.6	152484
32071	O BRIEN	17540	1410	33.9	32.1	27.0	5.7	1.2	34062	34682	16	12	1203	11.6	25.5	36.2	20.0	6.8	107788
32073	ORANGE PARK	28698	16726	12.0	26.3	40.6	14.3	6.8	61519	64091	79	79	10664	1.1	4.8	41.7	46.0	6.4	179913
32080	SAINT AUGUSTINE	40968	11059	17.4	25.4	33.1	13.9	10.2	59283	61539	77	75	7781	1.0	2.7	19.1	50.4	26.7	275428
32081	PONTE VEDRA	46613	712	18.3	11.2	29.1	4.4	37.1	78306	87241	91	93	627	0.0	0.5	16.6	30.1	52.8	420588
32082	PONTE VEDRA BEACH	62469	13715	7.6	14.6	27.6	24.0	26.1	100231	104383	97	98	9744	0.3	0.5	6.6	30.2	62.4	482505
32083	RAIFORD	17056	296	15.9	32.8	43.9	7.1	0.3	50969	48770	63	59	178	21.9	36.5	38.8	2.8	0.0	82105
32084	SAINT AUGUSTINE	23860	12050	28.0	31.2	26.1	10.8	4.0	41633	44769	38	33	7542	13.7	14.8	34.4	22.9	14.1	138091
32086	SAINT AUGUSTINE	26393	10541	20.0	25.3	38.4	12.3	3.9	55365	55655	72	70	8141	3.3	5.8	37.1	47.1	6.6	183926
32087	SANDERSON	17602	1435	25.0	26.8	38.2	7.8	2.2	48180	51878	57	51	1205	22.4	28.0	35.9	12.9	0.8	89274
32091	STARKE	17925	5663	30.4	31.4	31.2	5.5	1.6	38655	40245	29	24	4277	12.6	21.7	43.0	19.1	3.7	118819
32092	SAINT AUGUSTINE	26938	8684	15.1	24.4	39.3	17.7	3.5	61368	63002	79	79	7562	4.0	5.4	37.1	36.0	17.5	185961
32094	WELLBORN	18406	1010	34.5	30.8	27.3	5.4	2.0	35809	35737	20	16	868	11.3	24.2	35.3	18.2	11.1	121560
32095	SAINT AUGUSTINE	23886	3057	15.5	32.4	38.5	11.5	2.0	51971	53158	66	62	2219	8.2	20.1	38.6	25.7	7.4	126389
32096	WHITE SPRINGS	15949	1169	41.4	23.9	31.6	2.8	0.3	30149	33275	8	5	967	25.2	30.9	29.2	11.1	3.6	81849
32097	YULEE	22608	5366	19.0	29.2	40.2	8.4	3.2	51807	56015	66	62	4394	6.9	14.7	46.2	24.4	7.7	137986
32102	ASTOR	20982	1280	30.2	34.6	29.7	4.3	1.2	37274	39676	24	20	1022	15.8	34.6	32.5	13.6	3.5	89452
32110	BUNNELL	22805	3748	23.3	31.6	35.6	7.2	2.2	46014	47476	51	46	3163	4.2	7.9	36.7	44.5	6.7	177633
32112	CRESCENT CITY	17579	3086	37.9	36.0	20.0	3.0	3.0	30908	31928	10	6	2445	16.9	27.0	35.3	15.7	5.2	101262
32113	CITRA	19587	2681	36.8	32.9	21.4	5.9	3.1	35820	36851	20	16	2216	31.7	31.7	20.2	10.4	6.0	66267
32114	DAYTONA BEACH	17910	14609	44.6	32.5	18.3	2.7	1.9	27954	29099	6	3	5030	8.3	34.6	42.6	13.3	1.2	99808
32117	DAYTONA BEACH	18201	10357	34.8	36.1	23.8	3.8	1.5	33211	35156	14	10	6305	12.6	35.1	46.2	5.7	0.4	92220
32118	DAYTONA BEACH	31634	10242	29.7	30.9	26.1	7.4	5.8	39902	42920	32	27	6128	0.7	9.5	48.5	33.6	7.7	152458
32119	DAYTONA BEACH	26160	10978	24.6	34.5	30.9	5.8	4.1	42261	45451	40	35	7536	18.4	9.2	48.2	22.0	2.2	128085
32124	DAYTONA BEACH	21391	931	12.0	25.0	31.9	28.1	2.9	64695	64470	83	83	794	1.6	8.2	44.0	41.2	5.0	160000
32127	PORT ORANGE	29206	13268	19.0	29.1	35.5	10.4	5.9	51775	52637	65	62	10884	14.4	8.3	39.4	31.2	6.7	148604
32128	PORT ORANGE	40349	7451	7.8	21.1	38.1	18.6	14.5	74530	75006	89	91	6902	1.0	2.8	28.4	50.9	17.0	230389
32129	PORT ORANGE	23301	9256	23.7	36.5	32.4	4.7	2.6	41736	44808	38	33	6945	16.8	22.6	49.9	10.4	0.3	110551
32130	DE LEON SPRINGS	17946	1773	21.4	34.3	36.9	4.7	2.6	43830	46189	45	39	1475	8.4	21.4	43.7	23.7	2.7	116432
32131	EAST PALATKA	21251	1903	31.1	27.3	29.0	8.5	4.2	41213	44605	37	31	1556	5.3	17.9	42.0	24.7	10.1	140749
32132	EDGEWATER	21750	3313	26.3	34.3	30.1	6.3	3.0	41210	44961	37	31	2570	14.4	19.5	52.2	11.7	2.3	109699
32134	FORT MC COY	19490	5082	32.7	33.1	28.3	4.5	1.4	36252	37928	21	17	4323	25.7	31.5	28.2	9.6	5.0	79203
32136	FLAGLER BEACH	34305	5134	21.3	31.3	30.5	9.9	7.1	47733	49617	56	50	3754	7.9	11.7	22.5	38.0	19.8	198710
32137	PALM COAST	30607	18393	16.9	31.2	35.6	8.9	7.4	51708	52552	65	61	15966	2.3	4.8	30.9	47.0	15.0	206159
32139	GEORGETOWN	34444	375	31.2	34.4	20.0	5.6	8.8	37135	40000	24	19	327	14.7	27.2	38.8	15.6	3.7	98833
32140	FLORAHOME	20625	640	20.9	42.0	28.8	4.8	3.4	40608	42400	35	29	564	6.9	27.3	44.0	20.2	1.6	114118
32141	EDGEWATER	22622	7703	19.4	36.0	37.1	5.2	2.4	46088	47838	52	46	6589	4.0	14.5	66.4	14.0	1.2	122070
32145	HASTINGS	17912	2283	28.1	26.5	36.1	8.0	1.3	43648	47047	44	39	1818	12.0	32.9	46.6	7.2	1.2	98288
32148	INTERLACHEN	15400	5187	39.5	32.9	22.7	3.7	1.3	30701	32149	9	6	4353	24.3	31.6	31.2	11.2	1.7	79063
32159	LADY LAKE	27633	15044	21.5	35.8	33.4	6.1	3.2	44995	47491	48	42	13422	4.2	17.1	37.9	36.4	4.4	148670
32162	LADY LAKE	25937	18853	22.4	34.6	33.6	6.9	2.6	45458	46882	50	44	17618	2.4	4.0	42.2	45.2	6.2	178007
32164	PALM COAST	26155	16022	16.5	30.7	39.7	10.3	2.7	52272	53062	66	63	13379	1.9	1.6	31.6	59.2	5.8	203957
32168	NEW SMYRNA BEACH	24834	10690	27.4	31.0	30.3	6.8	4.6	41782	44631	39	34	8268	9.4	17.9	39.2	27.9	5.6	133744
32169	NEW SMYRNA BEACH	34901	6322	18.7	28.3	36.2	9.4	7.5	52409	53169	67	64	4714	0.2	4.1	37.7	43.4	14.6	196599
32174	ORMOND BEACH	30808	20884	17.9	29.1	34.5	11.0	7.4	52959	53181	68	65	17202	8.2	11.3	39.2	33.8	7.5	150298
32176	ORMOND BEACH	33854	8013	19.3	31.3	32.5	10.0	6.8	49398	50629	60	55	6369	0.6	6.6	50.2	34.5	8.2	159236
32177	PALATKA	19133	9823	36.0	27.3	27.0	6.5	3.1	35413	37195	19	15	6939	10.9	23.0	43.8	19.6	2.7	114867
32179	OCKLAWAHA	17607	4275	33.9	35.9	25.2	3.3	1.7	34226	35979	16	12	3547	26.1	31.0	26.2	13.6	3.2	79755
32180	PIERSON	15022	1448	26.7	40.3	28.0	3.4	1.6	38033	40619	27	23	1085	12.8	26.6	38.5	19.0	3.0	109547
32181	POMONA PARK	17780	1059	34.6	34.9	25.6	3.3	1.6	32731	33426	13	10	913	14.3	29.1	33.5	19.6	3.4	104702
32187	SAN MATEO	18179	712	31.0	34.4	29.2	4.5	0.8	36583	38681	22	18	602	9.5	22.1	46.5	16.4	5.5	118182
32189	SATSUMA	19610	2617	35.3	31.7	26.4	4.9	1.7	33707	35852	15	12	2257	16.4	26.8	43.1	11.0	2.7	101171
32190	SEVILLE	15655	447	31.1	36.2	26.2	5.4	1.1	39086	45099	30	25	337	19.0	30.6	29.7	12.8	8.0	91154
32193	WELAKA	25001	495	30.5	28.5	33.3	4.6	3.0	40309	44609	34	28	408	10.8	24.8	42.9	16.4	5.1	115000
32195	WEIRSDALE	25220	1960	20.4	25.9	39.6	9.1	4.9	53264	53883	68	65	1725	6.3	12.0	38.1	31.1	12.5	159684
32202	JACKSONVILLE	14274	1961	73.1	20.3	5.6	0.0	0.9	11808	11925	1	0	408	11.0	10.8	48.8	23.5	5.9	129091
32204	JACKSONVILLE	20865	3757	40.5	34.2	19.3	4.3	1.7	31589	32000	11	7	1392	13.9	23.3	29.0	24.7	9.1	117785
32205	JACKSONVILLE	26333	13959	24.8	33.0	31.5	6.2	4.6	44372	46769	46	41	8055	3.2	24.0	50.9	14.9	7.0	113162
32206	JACKSONVILLE	12788	8748	54.6	26.9	15.6	2.3	0.7	21804	22320	2	1	3755	27.5	40.8	26.3	4.5	0.9	69264
32207	JACKSONVILLE	27435	16949	27.0	28.3	31.2	8.5	5.1	45172	48188	49	43	9272	3.7	16.3	47.4	22.5	10.0	131564
32208	JACKSONVILLE	18584	13276	33.0	28.8	30.5	5.8	1.9	39816	42078	32	27	9482	8.7	36.8	49.1	5.1	0.3	93279
32209	JACKSONVILLE	14802	15874	46.3	29.9	18.8	3.5	1.4	27145	27648	5	3	9422	19.1	42.5	35.9	2.3	0.2	80748
32210	JACKSONVILLE	25124	24019	19.0	31.2	36.7	8.3	4.9	49857	52349	61	56	15031	4.2	17.4	54.2	17.3	6.9	118891
32211	JACKSONVILLE	22302	13707	21.9	33.9	35.0	6.7	2.6	45539	48551	50	45	7636	4.4	15.2	63.0	15.4	2.0	120200
32214	JACKSONVILLE	12748	360	17.5	39.7	38.3	2.5	1.9	41956	45849	39	34	69	18.8	23.2	34.8	23.2	0.0	96111
32216	JACKSONVILLE	26220	15097	19.6	28.7	37.1	10.4	4.3	51278	53851	64	60	8969	3.4	11.2	60.5	23.4	1.6	133444
32217	JACKSONVILLE	30374	8842	18.1	32.4	31.5	11.2	6.8	49504	52456	60	55	5046	0.9	5.1	45.2	38.5	10.3	173143
32218	JACKSONVILLE	22281	19126	19.4	30.7	38.2	8.5	3.1	49848	52381	61	56	13355	8.6	17.2	51.1	21.0	2.0	120226
	FLORIDA	27128		21.9	27.6	33.8	9.8	6.8	50413	52516				8.0	14.3	38.7	30.4	8.6	144752
	UNITED STATES	27277		20.9	24.4	35.3	11.7	7.6	54719	56938				9.3	13.1	31.6	32.6	13.5	162279

ZIP CODE		FINANCIAL SERVICES				THE HOME						ENTERTAINMENT						PERSONAL			
						Home Improvements		Furnishings													
#	POST OFFICE NAME	Auto Loan	Home Loan	Invest-ments	Retire-ment Plans	Home Repair	Lawn & Garden	Comput-ers & Hard-ware-Personal	Major Appli-ances	TV, Radio, Sound Equip-ment	Furni-ture	Dine out/ Carry out	Sports Equip-ment	Fees & Tickets	Toys & Games	Travel	Cable TV	Apparel & Services	Auto Repairs	Health Insur-ance	Pets & Supplies
32003	ORANGE PARK	141	177	155	177	171	153	148	151	139	156	142	120	167	145	160	134	102	143	135	173
32008	BRANFORD	69	54	75	51	57	73	54	67	59	53	58	49	46	57	55	64	38	62	71	79
32009	BRYCEVILLE	102	94	83	90	91	96	88	93	92	92	92	68	84	95	84	94	62	91	94	111
32011	CALLAHAN	94	88	78	86	85	90	83	87	86	86	86	65	79	89	80	88	58	85	88	104
32013	DAY	79	55	80	53	57	80	57	73	65	54	63	55	45	65	56	71	42	67	76	88
32024	LAKE CITY	81	69	72	68	69	78	69	76	73	69	72	56	63	74	67	76	49	73	78	90
32025	LAKE CITY	75	68	67	67	68	75	70	73	73	69	72	54	66	73	68	76	50	73	79	86
32033	ELKTON	91	96	91	95	96	105	88	96	93	86	92	69	92	92	93	98	64	93	106	111
32034	FERNANDINA BEACH	122	124	122	124	125	127	118	122	120	122	120	90	120	120	120	122	83	121	126	144
32038	FORT WHITE	79	62	76	60	63	78	61	73	67	59	66	55	52	67	60	72	44	69	76	87
32040	GLEN SAINT MARY	94	86	76	82	83	86	84	86	85	87	85	64	78	89	79	87	59	85	85	102
32043	GREEN COVE SPRINGS	100	95	91	94	94	100	91	96	93	92	93	73	88	95	90	95	64	93	98	114
32044	HAMPTON	94	88	75	83	83	84	86	86	87	90	87	65	81	90	81	87	60	86	84	102
32046	HILLIARD	93	72	78	70	71	89	73	83	79	72	78	63	61	82	67	85	53	79	86	100
32052	JASPER	69	47	65	46	47	68	51	61	58	49	57	47	40	58	48	64	38	59	66	75
32053	JENNINGS	70	49	64	47	49	69	51	62	58	49	56	48	40	59	48	63	38	59	66	76
32054	LAKE BUTLER	83	73	72	70	71	78	72	77	75	73	74	58	66	77	69	77	51	75	78	91
32055	LAKE CITY	71	55	62	53	54	68	57	64	63	57	62	48	49	63	54	67	42	63	68	78
32058	LAWTEY	88	65	84	63	66	87	66	80	73	64	72	60	54	74	64	79	48	75	83	96
32059	LEE	88	63	90	61	65	89	64	82	71	60	70	61	51	71	64	79	46	75	85	97
32060	LIVE OAK	79	59	78	57	61	79	60	73	66	58	65	55	50	66	59	72	43	69	77	87
32061	LULU	73	67	60	65	66	69	64	67	66	66	66	49	60	69	61	68	45	65	68	80
32062	MC ALPIN	79	56	81	55	59	80	58	74	64	54	63	55	46	64	57	71	42	68	77	88
32063	MACCLENNY	89	83	73	81	81	84	81	83	82	83	82	61	77	86	77	84	57	82	83	98
32064	LIVE OAK	71	57	66	55	57	72	58	67	63	56	62	50	51	63	56	68	42	64	71	79
32065	ORANGE PARK	110	118	97	115	111	103	106	107	102	113	104	83	108	108	105	99	72	102	98	123
32066	MAYO	85	60	87	58	62	86	62	79	69	58	68	60	49	69	61	77	45	73	82	94
32068	MIDDLEBURG	106	110	93	107	105	101	99	102	98	104	99	78	100	103	98	97	68	98	96	119
32071	O BRIEN	78	56	80	54	58	79	57	73	63	53	62	54	46	63	56	70	41	67	76	86
32073	ORANGE PARK	108	107	96	108	103	101	108	103	106	110	107	81	108	108	105	104	75	105	101	122
32080	SAINT AUGUSTINE	122	119	154	119	130	138	114	129	118	119	116	89	116	111	124	122	80	124	138	149
32081	PONTE VEDRA	171	224	230	235	231	201	185	192	173	200	175	151	221	176	209	165	131	179	168	217
32082	PONTE VEDRA BEACH	191	219	239	221	230	217	200	207	196	210	197	152	220	192	218	196	140	203	208	238
32083	RAIFORD	88	78	74	75	77	83	74	81	78	76	78	59	69	81	71	81	53	78	81	96
32084	SAINT AUGUSTINE	85	76	78	76	76	83	81	81	83	80	82	61	76	83	77	85	57	83	86	97
32086	SAINT AUGUSTINE	92	92	94	90	93	99	87	94	90	88	90	68	88	89	90	94	62	92	100	110
32087	SANDERSON	87	78	72	74	74	80	77	80	79	80	79	61	71	82	73	81	54	79	79	95
32091	STARKE	78	64	74	62	64	78	65	73	69	63	68	55	57	70	63	74	46	70	77	88
32092	SAINT AUGUSTINE	104	106	93	107	104	106	97	102	98	99	98	77	99	101	98	99	68	98	102	121
32094	WELLBORN	80	63	76	61	63	79	62	74	67	60	67	55	53	68	61	72	44	69	76	88
32095	SAINT AUGUSTINE	96	89	78	86	86	90	84	88	87	88	87	65	80	91	80	89	59	86	88	105
32096	WHITE SPRINGS	72	48	71	46	49	71	51	64	58	48	57	50	39	59	48	65	38	60	68	78
32097	YULEE	96	90	79	87	88	91	84	89	87	87	87	65	81	90	81	89	59	86	89	106
32102	ASTOR	70	61	81	57	66	77	59	72	64	61	62	49	55	60	63	68	42	68	78	83
32110	BUNNELL	88	75	88	73	76	88	74	84	78	73	77	62	67	78	74	82	52	81	86	100
32112	CRESCENT CITY	73	58	78	55	62	76	60	71	66	60	64	51	53	64	61	72	43	69	78	84
32113	CITRA	84	60	85	57	62	85	62	78	69	59	68	58	50	69	61	76	45	72	82	93
32114	DAYTONA BEACH	55	42	41	45	40	46	58	48	59	53	59	39	50	58	49	60	41	55	55	61
32117	DAYTONA BEACH	61	55	55	55	55	62	59	60	62	58	61	44	57	61	57	65	42	61	67	71
32118	DAYTONA BEACH	80	77	87	78	81	85	82	82	84	83	84	59	83	80	83	87	58	85	93	96
32119	DAYTONA BEACH	79	74	83	74	78	82	77	79	79	79	79	57	76	76	79	81	54	81	87	93
32124	DAYTONA BEACH	110	124	107	128	120	122	111	115	109	111	110	90	118	112	117	109	77	111	114	136
32127	PORT ORANGE	92	98	109	97	104	107	91	100	94	96	93	69	96	89	99	97	64	97	108	115
32128	PORT ORANGE	132	140	185	139	159	163	126	147	132	141	130	93	138	120	144	138	89	141	163	167
32129	PORT ORANGE	73	68	78	66	73	78	70	75	73	72	72	53	69	69	72	76	49	75	84	87
32130	DE LEON SPRINGS	77	81	74	77	80	76	76	79	74	80	75	59	76	75	78	73	52	77	75	89
32131	EAST PALATKA	90	74	99	73	78	95	74	89	79	71	78	65	66	78	76	85	52	84	93	105
32132	EDGEWATER	72	73	79	70	76	83	68	77	72	70	71	53	70	69	73	76	49	74	86	88
32134	FORT MC COY	72	61	81	57	66	78	60	73	64	61	63	51	54	61	62	69	42	68	79	84
32136	FLAGLER BEACH	93	95	126	92	108	112	87	102	92	97	90	65	92	83	99	96	61	98	114	116
32137	PALM COAST	99	100	118	97	109	113	91	104	96	100	95	68	95	91	99	100	64	100	114	119
32139	GEORGETOWN	113	99	130	92	108	124	96	115	104	102	101	79	91	97	102	111	68	110	127	134
32140	FLORAHOME	99	71	84	69	71	95	74	87	82	71	80	66	59	85	68	89	54	82	91	105
32141	EDGEWATER	79	79	85	76	82	87	74	82	77	77	76	58	75	75	78	80	52	79	88	95
32145	HASTINGS	76	70	60	68	65	70	71	70	73	73	73	53	68	75	66	75	50	71	72	84
32148	INTERLACHEN	68	51	72	49	54	70	52	65	58	51	57	48	44	57	52	63	38	61	69	77
32159	LADY LAKE	71	78	100	70	92	97	71	87	77	80	74	51	80	67	85	82	50	83	107	95
32162	LADY LAKE	78	75	98	68	84	94	70	86	76	76	74	55	71	69	79	82	49	81	99	97
32164	PALM COAST	93	87	118	86	95	106	83	99	87	83	86	69	82	82	91	92	58	93	105	113
32168	NEW SMYRNA BEACH	82	77	92	74	83	91	76	86	81	77	79	59	75	76	80	85	54	83	96	99
32169	NEW SMYRNA BEACH	96	99	134	98	113	117	90	106	95	100	94	68	97	86	103	100	64	102	118	121
32174	ORMOND BEACH	101	103	118	102	110	115	97	108	100	101	99	75	101	96	105	104	68	104	116	124
32176	ORMOND BEACH	95	96	119	94	106	112	91	103	96	97	94	68	95	89	100	101	65	100	116	118
32177	PALATKA	78	63	72	62	64	77	67	74	72	64	71	55	59	72	64	77	48	72	80	88
32179	OCKLAWAHA	67	57	75	53	61	73	56	68	60	57	59	47	51	57	58	65	39	64	73	79
32180	PIERSON	81	58	84	56	61	83	60	76	66	56	65	57	48	66	59	73	43	70	79	91
32181	POMONA PARK	63	60	77	55	66	72	57	67	61	62	59	44	56	55	62	64	40	65	75	77
32187	SAN MATEO	66	62	73	58	67	71	59	68	62	63	61	46	58	59	62	65	41	65	74	78
32189	SATSUMA	68	61	80	57	67	76	59	71	63	62	62	48	56	59	64	68	41	68	78	82
32190	SEVILLE	81	58	83	56	60	82	59	75	66	55	65	57	47	65	59	72	43	69	78	90
32193	WELAKA	74	71	91	65	79	85	67	80	71	73	70	52	67	65	74	76	47	76	89	91
32195	WEIRSDALE	103	92	110	88	97	106	89	102	93	91	92	72	83	90	91	97	62	97	106	119
32202	JACKSONVILLE	26	19	23	22	20	24	30	25	32	27	32	19	27	28	26	35	22	30	34	32
32204	JACKSONVILLE	56	46	46	49	45	51	60	52	63	56	63	41	55	60	53	65	44	59	62	65
32205	JACKSONVILLE	82	76	69	78	73	79	84	78	85	80	84	61	80	85	78	86	59	82	84	95
32206	JACKSONVILLE	44	35	33	36	33	40	43	39	47	42	46	29	39	46	38	50	32	44	47	50
32207	JACKSONVILLE	83	77	74	79	75	79	86	80	87	83	87	63	83	86	81	88	61	85	86	96
32208	JACKSONVILLE	68	64	59	65	61	70	66	65	71	66	70	48	66	69	64	75	48	68	75	81
32209	JACKSONVILLE	54	46	43	47	44	53	50	50	56	51	55	35	48	54	46	60	38	53	59	62
32210	JACKSONVILLE	90	86	78	87	83	85	91	86	91	90	91	67	89	92	87	91	64	90	89	103
32211	JACKSONVILLE	79	71	63	73	68	74	80	74	80	76	80	59	76	81	74	81	56	78	79	89
32214	JACKSONVILLE	84	44	33	51	39	37	79	55	74	74	78	55	60	89	57	68	55	70	49	67
32216	JACKSONVILLE	89	79	74	82	77	79	90	82	90	88	91	65	86	91	84	89	63	88	85	99
32217	JACKSONVILLE	99	97	94	99	96	95	101	96	100	102	101	74	101	100	100	99	71	100	98	114
32218	JACKSONVILLE	91	85	75	83	81	85	84	85	85	84	85	65	79	88	79	86	58	84	85	101
	FLORIDA	96	94	97	93	96	98	95	97	96	97	96	71	95	94	96	97	67	97	101	113
	UNITED STATES	100	100	100	100	100	100	100	100	100	100	100	100	100	100	100	100	100	100	100	100

POPULATION CHANGE

#	POST OFFICE NAME	COUNTY FIPS CODE	POPULATION 2000	POPULATION 2009	POPULATION 2014	2000-2009 ANNUAL RATE % Rate	2000-2009 ANNUAL RATE State Centile	HOUSEHOLDS 2000	HOUSEHOLDS 2009	HOUSEHOLDS 2014	HOUSEHOLDS % Annual Rate 2000-2009	HOUSEHOLDS 2009 Average HH Size	FAMILIES 2000	FAMILIES 2009	FAMILIES % Annual Rate 2000-2009
32219	JACKSONVILLE	031	9494	11637	12576	2.2	66	3517	4442	4819	2.6	2.61	2551	3152	2.3
32220	JACKSONVILLE	031	10954	12989	14063	1.9	61	3993	4893	5328	2.2	2.65	3046	3652	2.0
32221	JACKSONVILLE	031	18876	25903	29146	3.5	82	6602	9416	10691	3.9	2.72	5167	7129	3.5
32222	JACKSONVILLE	031	5116	7559	8730	4.3	86	1857	2807	3258	4.6	2.69	1422	2092	4.3
32223	JACKSONVILLE	031	25424	26640	27327	0.5	26	9610	10396	10740	0.9	2.56	7408	7886	0.7
32224	JACKSONVILLE	031	30669	37387	40867	2.2	66	11835	15109	16718	2.7	2.39	7711	9531	2.3
32225	JACKSONVILLE	031	45715	56286	61398	2.3	69	16595	20420	22236	2.3	2.75	12640	15395	2.2
32226	JACKSONVILLE	031	8017	13855	16590	6.1	91	2960	5265	6340	6.4	2.62	2315	4034	6.2
32233	ATLANTIC BEACH	031	30648	31211	31938	0.2	15	10432	11075	11416	0.6	2.57	7191	7438	0.4
32234	JACKSONVILLE	031	6113	7001	7505	1.5	53	2192	2582	2790	1.8	2.71	1675	1923	1.5
32244	JACKSONVILLE	031	48391	60909	67245	2.5	72	17894	23138	25724	2.8	2.62	12886	16171	2.5
32246	JACKSONVILLE	031	35604	43423	47508	2.2	66	13102	16203	17775	2.3	2.68	9452	11444	2.1
32250	JACKSONVILLE BEACH	031	25821	28719	30221	1.2	46	11688	13454	14279	1.5	2.12	6581	7266	1.1
32254	JACKSONVILLE	031	15743	16060	16317	0.2	15	5559	5776	5892	0.4	2.77	3951	4001	0.1
32256	JACKSONVILLE	031	29136	46797	55048	5.3	90	14032	21447	24991	4.7	2.17	7053	11482	5.4
32257	JACKSONVILLE	031	36364	40511	42578	1.2	46	14856	16869	17819	1.4	2.39	9714	10668	1.0
32258	JACKSONVILLE	031	12637	25316	30413	7.8	94	4332	9191	11105	8.5	2.74	3500	6855	7.5
32259	SAINT JOHNS	109	17955	35526	46059	7.7	94	5952	11773	15323	7.7	3.01	5164	10008	7.4
32266	NEPTUNE BEACH	031	7270	7489	7631	0.3	18	3282	3456	3539	0.6	2.17	1857	1874	0.1
32277	JACKSONVILLE	031	27754	31861	34101	1.5	53	10816	12797	13786	1.8	2.44	7586	8735	1.5
32301	TALLAHASSEE	073	26098	27137	28158	0.4	22	12136	13376	14047	1.1	1.90	4716	4822	0.2
32303	TALLAHASSEE	073	42208	47730	50774	1.3	48	18264	21358	22923	1.7	2.23	10215	11381	1.2
32304	TALLAHASSEE	073	40309	41593	43068	0.3	18	15911	17607	18497	1.1	2.04	4271	4365	0.2
32305	TALLAHASSEE	073	18391	20776	22178	1.3	48	7049	8263	8913	1.7	2.51	4871	5463	1.2
32306	TALLAHASSEE	073	64	52	52	-2.2	0	0	0	0	0.0	0.00	0	0	0.0
32307	TALLAHASSEE	073	890	724	750	-2.2	0	0	0	0	0.0	0.00	0	0	0.0
32308	TALLAHASSEE	073	19901	21961	23259	1.1	44	8596	9995	10713	1.6	2.10	4960	5423	1.0
32309	TALLAHASSEE	073	27884	31324	33233	1.3	48	10762	12544	13433	1.7	2.49	8083	9131	1.3
32310	TALLAHASSEE	073	16718	17571	18175	0.5	26	6885	7504	7869	0.9	2.24	3988	4116	0.3
32311	TALLAHASSEE	073	10623	15364	17371	4.1	86	3888	6130	7054	5.0	2.33	2606	3918	4.5
32312	TALLAHASSEE	073	26137	32364	35431	2.3	69	9390	11888	13097	2.6	2.72	7611	9469	2.4
32317	TALLAHASSEE	073	10211	14339	16229	3.7	83	3629	5290	6053	4.2	2.71	2978	4201	3.8
32320	APALACHICOLA	037	3834	4514	4932	1.8	59	1493	1800	1993	2.0	2.31	975	1149	1.8
32321	BRISTOL	077	5332	6187	6569	1.6	55	1513	1811	1981	2.0	2.52	1087	1276	1.7
32322	CARRABELLE	037	3916	3474	3926	-1.3	0	1257	1648	1881	3.0	2.08	791	1016	2.7
32324	CHATTAHOOCHEE	039	5157	5778	5879	1.2	46	1761	1876	1936	0.7	2.32	1205	1256	0.4
32327	CRAWFORDVILLE	129	18663	25898	29899	3.6	83	6660	9367	10967	3.8	2.60	4987	6895	3.6
32328	EASTPOINT	037	3002	3878	4427	2.8	76	1188	1598	1848	3.3	2.35	861	1128	3.0
32331	GREENVILLE	079	4608	4917	4987	0.7	32	1751	1915	1962	1.0	2.46	1251	1341	0.8
32332	GRETNA	039	1626	1797	1887	1.1	44	490	561	597	1.5	3.20	375	422	1.3
32333	HAVANA	039	11358	12126	12575	0.7	32	4443	4906	5148	1.1	2.46	3203	3464	0.9
32334	HOSFORD	077	1726	2000	2151	1.6	55	725	870	945	2.0	2.28	479	561	1.7
32336	LAMONT	065	1081	1113	1122	0.3	18	413	441	450	0.7	2.52	298	313	0.5
32340	MADISON	079	12246	12657	12710	0.4	22	4139	4343	4405	0.5	2.53	2908	2994	0.3
32343	MIDWAY	039	1502	1776	1902	1.8	59	505	617	669	2.2	2.88	392	472	2.0
32344	MONTICELLO	065	11335	12928	13073	1.4	51	4084	4512	4632	1.1	2.43	2869	3107	0.9
32346	PANACEA	037	2187	3340	4023	4.7	87	985	1524	1842	4.8	2.19	662	1009	4.7
32347	PERRY	123	7788	8040	8114	0.3	18	3037	3203	3259	0.6	2.46	2206	2285	0.4
32348	PERRY	123	9606	10043	10159	0.5	26	3306	3497	3571	0.6	2.52	2349	2437	0.4
32350	PINETTA	079	1096	1048	1025	-0.5	1	435	428	422	-0.2	2.42	308	295	-0.5
32351	QUINCY	039	18743	20419	20993	0.9	38	6349	6891	7177	0.9	2.66	4530	4818	0.7
32352	QUINCY	039	6707	7593	8028	1.4	51	2322	2708	2894	1.7	2.79	1727	1980	1.5
32355	SAINT MARKS	129	220	302	339	3.5	82	110	156	192	3.8	1.66	74	103	3.6
32356	SALEM	123	198	213	218	0.8	35	82	90	93	1.0	2.37	59	64	0.9
32358	SOPCHOPPY	129	2106	3052	3615	4.1	86	856	1260	1499	4.3	2.42	617	896	4.1
32359	STEINHATCHEE	029	1447	1503	1521	0.4	22	658	700	714	0.7	2.13	437	453	0.4
32401	PANAMA CITY	005	24269	24539	24660	0.1	12	10246	10628	10759	0.4	2.22	6136	6197	0.1
32403	PANAMA CITY	005	2760	2769	2757	0.0	9	665	677	678	0.2	3.47	655	664	0.1
32404	PANAMA CITY	005	34810	37426	38620	0.8	35	13165	14547	15123	1.1	2.48	9463	10316	0.9
32405	PANAMA CITY	005	26110	28670	29878	1.0	40	10554	11909	12489	1.3	2.36	7066	7845	1.1
32407	PANAMA CITY BEACH	005	5532	8671	9954	5.0	88	2399	3855	4455	5.3	2.23	1537	2409	5.0
32408	PANAMA CITY	005	13146	17338	19074	3.0	78	6030	8304	9230	3.5	2.08	3612	4856	3.3
32409	PANAMA CITY	005	7368	8786	9454	1.9	61	2747	3364	3642	2.2	2.61	2120	2563	2.1
32413	PANAMA CITY BEACH	005	9315	13022	14726	3.7	83	4215	6011	6842	3.9	2.17	2676	3737	3.7
32420	ALFORD	063	1916	2325	2496	2.1	64	789	973	1051	2.3	2.39	571	691	2.1
32421	ALTHA	013	4045	4493	4647	1.1	44	1535	1736	1808	1.3	2.58	1122	1245	1.1
32423	BASCOM	063	1246	1386	1451	1.2	46	503	569	600	1.3	2.41	353	391	1.1
32424	BLOUNTSTOWN	013	7680	8019	8138	0.5	26	2404	2565	2627	0.7	2.45	1633	1702	0.4
32425	BONIFAY	059	13564	13940	13869	0.3	18	4871	5093	5092	0.5	2.39	3421	3508	0.3
32426	CAMPBELLTON	063	923	989	1030	0.7	32	364	397	416	0.9	2.48	261	279	0.7
32427	CARYVILLE	133	1186	1278	1316	0.8	35	462	510	529	1.1	2.46	326	353	0.9
32428	CHIPLEY	133	14050	15633	16125	1.2	46	5203	5762	5979	1.1	2.47	3679	3998	0.9
32430	CLARKSVILLE	013	726	907	989	2.4	70	307	387	425	2.5	2.34	216	268	2.4
32431	COTTONDALE	063	4688	5388	5711	1.5	53	1862	2175	2319	1.7	2.48	1330	1521	1.5
32433	DEFUNIAK SPRINGS	131	12906	15929	17630	2.3	69	4642	5755	6437	2.4	2.49	3254	4005	2.3
32435	DEFUNIAK SPRINGS	131	6254	7110	7665	1.4	51	2574	2903	3132	1.3	2.38	1733	1940	1.2
32437	EBRO	133	681	794	844	1.7	57	267	318	341	1.9	2.46	194	226	1.7
32438	FOUNTAIN	005	3059	3201	3266	0.5	26	1153	1240	1276	0.8	2.57	830	872	0.5
32439	FREEPORT	131	6203	7851	8918	2.6	73	2561	3228	3663	2.5	2.43	1748	2183	2.4
32440	GRACEVILLE	063	5531	5857	6023	0.6	30	2168	2335	2420	0.8	2.41	1511	1592	0.6
32442	GRAND RIDGE	063	3631	3979	4161	1.0	40	1400	1566	1651	1.2	2.51	1030	1130	1.0
32443	GREENWOOD	063	2682	3090	3246	1.5	53	1089	1266	1349	1.6	1.94	770	877	1.4
32444	LYNN HAVEN	005	15889	18841	20138	1.9	61	6187	7563	8139	2.2	2.48	4711	5669	2.0
32445	MALONE	063	2697	2958	3033	1.0	40	470	517	547	1.0	2.80	319	343	0.8
32446	MARIANNA	063	11181	11836	12189	0.6	30	3779	4030	4201	0.7	2.42	2595	2707	0.5
32448	MARIANNA	063	8907	9495	9796	0.7	32	3422	3706	3857	0.9	2.38	2320	2466	0.7
32449	WEWAHITCHKA	013	505	617	668	2.2	66	200	249	270	2.4	2.48	142	174	2.2
32455	PONCE DE LEON	131	3721	4156	4421	1.2	46	1529	1701	1811	1.2	2.44	1075	1182	1.0
32456	PORT SAINT JOE	045	8192	10241	11208	2.4	70	3386	4538	5055	3.2	2.22	2366	3053	2.8
32459	SANTA ROSA BEACH	131	6162	11263	14154	6.7	92	2789	5052	6353	6.6	2.22	1748	3146	6.6
32460	SNEADS	063	5045	5487	5668	0.9	38	1442	1579	1663	1.0	2.39	1042	1118	0.8
32462	VERNON	133	3551	4311	4603	2.1	64	1410	1736	1880	2.3	2.23	1019	1230	2.1
32464	WESTVILLE	059	3950	4172	4198	0.6	30	1610	1735	1757	0.8	2.39	1159	1228	0.6
32465	WEWAHITCHKA	045	6154	7925	8569	2.8	76	2069	2667	2957	2.8	2.39	1490	1884	2.6
32466	YOUNGSTOWN	005	5444	6428	6910	1.8	59	1941	2359	2560	2.1	2.70	1489	1783	2.0
	FLORIDA					1.9					1.9	2.47			1.7
	UNITED STATES					1.0					1.1	2.59			0.9

ZIP CODE #	POST OFFICE NAME	RACE (%) White 2000	White 2009	Black 2000	Black 2009	Asian/Pacific 2000	Asian/Pacific 2009	% Hispanic Origin 2000	% Hispanic Origin 2009	2009 AGE DISTRIBUTION (%) 0-4	5-9	10-14	15-19	20-24	25-44	45-64	65-84	85+	18+	MEDIAN AGE 2009	% 2009 Males	% 2009 Females
32219	JACKSONVILLE	56.9	57.9	41.5	40.1	0.2	0.3	1.0	1.5	6.4	6.5	6.7	6.9	6.4	25.3	28.6	12.0	1.2	76.3	39.1	49.2	50.8
32220	JACKSONVILLE	92.3	88.2	4.9	7.8	0.7	1.1	1.8	3.1	7.0	7.1	7.1	6.8	5.8	27.6	28.6	9.3	0.7	74.6	37.4	50.9	49.1
32221	JACKSONVILLE	82.8	76.4	11.5	16.1	2.6	3.4	3.1	5.0	7.7	7.4	7.2	7.0	6.3	27.6	26.4	9.2	1.1	73.4	35.3	48.7	51.3
32222	JACKSONVILLE	79.0	69.9	13.7	20.6	3.0	3.9	4.5	6.9	8.0	7.9	7.7	7.5	6.3	28.1	26.7	7.2	0.6	71.8	34.3	50.1	49.9
32223	JACKSONVILLE	91.8	87.8	4.2	6.6	1.8	2.7	3.5	5.6	5.9	6.3	7.1	7.3	5.3	25.2	33.4	8.6	0.9	75.9	40.8	48.7	51.3
32224	JACKSONVILLE	83.3	76.3	8.0	11.9	4.4	6.1	5.7	8.8	8.4	7.1	6.1	7.3	8.4	35.7	20.3	5.7	1.1	75.4	31.0	48.8	51.2
32225	JACKSONVILLE	74.6	64.5	15.7	22.4	5.3	7.4	5.5	8.4	7.6	7.3	7.1	6.8	6.0	31.4	26.0	7.0	0.8	73.8	34.8	48.5	51.5
32226	JACKSONVILLE	97.1	95.5	1.1	2.1	0.4	0.5	1.7	2.8	5.8	6.2	6.7	6.6	4.8	25.6	32.3	10.9	1.0	77.1	41.3	50.4	49.6
32233	ATLANTIC BEACH	72.4	63.5	18.3	24.8	2.7	3.4	7.0	10.1	8.5	7.4	6.1	7.4	12.3	30.2	19.8	6.8	1.5	74.7	29.2	52.7	47.3
32234	JACKSONVILLE	89.9	86.0	8.1	11.4	0.5	0.6	1.4	2.3	7.2	6.8	7.1	7.2	6.0	26.2	28.7	9.9	0.8	74.4	37.2	49.2	50.8
32244	JACKSONVILLE	68.2	58.2	22.4	29.9	4.4	5.5	5.4	8.0	8.1	7.8	7.4	7.1	7.0	30.4	24.0	7.3	0.9	72.4	32.9	48.5	51.5
32246	JACKSONVILLE	71.6	61.7	16.0	22.1	6.6	9.0	6.5	9.5	8.5	7.6	6.9	6.8	7.9	31.6	23.4	6.7	0.6	72.9	32.2	48.9	51.1
32250	JACKSONVILLE BEACH	90.8	86.3	4.7	7.1	1.9	2.9	3.1	5.1	5.3	5.2	5.1	4.6	5.5	31.2	29.8	11.3	2.0	81.6	40.7	49.9	50.1
32254	JACKSONVILLE	41.5	32.8	55.7	64.1	0.6	0.7	1.6	2.1	8.3	8.4	8.5	8.9	6.9	25.5	23.8	8.7	1.0	69.2	31.9	47.4	52.6
32256	JACKSONVILLE	75.5	69.8	12.5	15.6	7.3	9.2	6.2	8.6	6.8	5.6	5.1	5.1	9.4	34.6	24.0	8.0	1.4	79.5	33.9	49.4	50.6
32257	JACKSONVILLE	84.2	76.9	8.6	13.2	3.7	5.2	5.1	8.1	6.8	6.5	6.4	6.6	7.6	29.1	27.2	8.4	1.5	76.3	35.9	48.0	52.0
32258	JACKSONVILLE	86.2	77.8	6.8	11.1	3.9	6.6	4.0	6.7	7.9	8.0	7.9	6.2	5.1	31.3	27.2	5.5	1.0	72.2	35.7	49.4	50.6
32259	SAINT JOHNS	94.8	92.0	2.1	3.3	1.7	2.6	2.4	4.1	7.3	8.0	8.7	7.9	4.5	24.4	31.7	6.6	1.0	70.8	38.4	50.0	50.0
32266	NEPTUNE BEACH	96.1	94.1	0.7	1.2	1.1	1.6	2.1	3.6	4.1	4.0	4.2	5.1	6.6	30.4	31.9	11.9	1.8	84.8	41.7	50.6	49.4
32277	JACKSONVILLE	63.0	51.6	30.8	40.7	2.4	3.0	4.6	6.5	7.7	6.7	6.3	7.6	9.5	28.8	23.7	8.8	1.0	75.3	32.5	48.0	52.0
32301	TALLAHASSEE	50.5	44.3	44.8	49.6	1.9	2.6	3.6	5.4	5.2	3.9	3.4	9.2	22.3	29.7	18.0	6.7	1.4	85.2	27.4	46.5	53.5
32303	TALLAHASSEE	71.9	64.2	23.6	29.7	1.7	2.5	3.4	5.4	6.5	5.6	5.2	6.4	13.6	31.5	22.3	7.7	1.3	79.7	31.5	47.9	52.1
32304	TALLAHASSEE	57.9	50.0	36.4	42.5	2.2	2.8	6.0	8.9	3.3	2.5	2.1	19.2	42.0	18.3	8.6	3.4	0.6	90.5	22.7	49.5	50.5
32305	TALLAHASSEE	46.8	40.6	50.5	56.1	0.4	0.5	1.9	2.8	7.1	7.0	7.1	7.3	7.3	27.1	27.2	9.0	0.9	74.4	35.3	47.0	53.0
32306	TALLAHASSEE	75.0	69.2	15.6	19.2	4.7	5.8	7.8	11.5	0.0	0.0	0.0	71.2	25.0	3.8	0.0	0.0	0.0	100.0	18.5	51.9	48.1
32307	TALLAHASSEE	4.3	3.3	94.9	95.9	0.1	0.1	2.2	2.8	1.7	1.5	0.7	64.5	21.1	5.4	3.2	1.1	0.8	95.2	18.6	48.1	51.9
32308	TALLAHASSEE	74.9	67.4	20.1	25.7	2.6	3.8	3.0	4.8	5.1	4.8	4.8	5.1	6.6	30.5	26.8	12.4	4.0	82.3	39.5	45.6	54.4
32309	TALLAHASSEE	83.2	77.0	12.6	17.1	2.3	3.3	2.7	4.4	5.4	6.0	6.9	7.0	5.0	24.0	33.3	11.0	1.4	77.2	42.0	48.2	51.8
32310	TALLAHASSEE	45.5	39.8	48.7	53.3	2.9	3.4	2.3	3.3	7.6	7.0	6.5	10.0	10.7	28.4	21.0	7.7	0.9	74.6	29.7	49.6	50.4
32311	TALLAHASSEE	65.3	56.0	31.1	39.9	0.8	1.1	5.6	5.7	6.4	6.5	6.6	6.2	5.6	31.9	28.4	7.5	0.8	76.6	37.4	45.7	54.3
32312	TALLAHASSEE	85.9	81.8	10.5	13.2	2.1	3.2	2.3	3.9	6.6	7.1	7.6	7.3	4.6	25.3	31.6	8.8	1.0	73.9	39.5	48.8	51.2
32317	TALLAHASSEE	80.5	74.9	15.2	18.9	2.4	3.7	2.9	4.9	6.3	7.2	8.2	7.9	4.5	23.2	33.7	8.2	0.9	73.0	40.5	48.6	51.4
32320	APALACHICOLA	72.6	64.4	25.4	33.0	0.3	0.4	1.5	2.5	5.6	5.5	5.3	5.5	5.8	25.3	31.5	13.3	2.2	80.3	42.7	52.7	47.3
32321	BRISTOL	69.5	63.1	24.2	28.8	0.2	0.2	5.7	8.5	5.1	5.2	5.4	6.0	6.8	37.7	23.2	9.5	1.0	80.5	35.9	61.8	38.2
32322	CARRABELLE	77.3	73.3	19.6	22.0	0.3	0.5	4.4	6.1	5.0	5.1	5.2	4.8	5.6	29.3	28.0	15.1	1.9	81.8	41.5	56.1	43.9
32324	CHATTAHOOCHEE	48.9	43.0	48.3	53.3	0.7	1.0	3.2	4.9	5.2	5.3	4.9	5.6	6.0	28.5	28.2	14.1	2.2	81.5	41.7	53.2	46.8
32327	CRAWFORDVILLE	85.3	81.6	12.3	15.3	0.3	0.4	1.9	3.1	6.1	6.3	6.8	6.8	5.8	28.6	29.3	9.3	1.0	76.6	38.5	52.1	47.9
32328	EASTPOINT	95.8	94.0	2.0	3.2	0.1	0.2	1.2	2.1	4.7	5.1	5.2	5.3	4.5	22.9	33.2	17.0	1.9	81.6	46.4	50.5	49.5
32331	GREENVILLE	59.5	52.4	38.7	45.4	0.4	0.6	1.1	1.7	5.6	5.9	7.5	8.8	5.0	22.7	28.8	14.0	1.7	74.9	40.7	50.0	50.0
32332	GRETNA	18.7	16.0	74.5	75.3	0.1	0.1	10.5	13.7	7.2	8.8	9.2	9.6	7.3	25.7	22.8	8.0	1.4	68.7	30.3	48.6	51.4
32333	HAVANA	53.8	46.5	44.6	51.6	0.2	0.2	1.1	1.6	5.9	6.2	6.4	6.3	5.6	24.2	31.7	12.2	1.4	77.6	41.4	47.7	52.3
32334	HOSFORD	98.1	97.2	0.4	0.6	0.1	0.1	0.7	1.3	6.6	6.8	6.5	5.7	4.8	25.6	30.3	12.7	1.3	76.6	40.4	50.5	49.5
32336	LAMONT	54.9	48.8	42.6	48.0	0.5	0.6	2.4	3.5	4.9	5.4	5.8	5.8	5.1	25.1	33.0	12.9	1.9	80.2	43.1	47.3	52.7
32340	MADISON	51.6	45.6	46.1	51.4	0.3	0.5	4.0	5.7	5.8	5.9	6.2	6.6	7.4	29.3	24.3	11.9	2.6	78.3	36.8	53.9	46.1
32343	MIDWAY	14.4	11.0	84.6	88.0	0.2	0.2	0.8	1.1	8.6	9.0	8.5	8.4	7.2	25.4	24.3	7.8	0.8	68.9	30.4	44.9	55.1
32344	MONTICELLO	59.6	53.2	38.0	43.7	0.3	0.5	2.2	3.3	4.8	5.0	5.3	5.9	5.7	29.0	29.0	12.9	2.4	81.2	41.4	54.2	45.8
32346	PANACEA	91.0	88.7	6.9	8.6	0.2	0.2	1.4	2.1	4.7	5.1	5.4	5.5	4.6	21.0	33.7	18.4	1.6	81.4	47.4	50.9	49.1
32347	PERRY	84.7	79.8	11.8	15.8	0.4	0.6	1.5	2.2	6.3	6.3	6.6	6.6	5.6	26.0	28.8	12.2	1.5	76.7	39.3	49.7	50.3
32348	PERRY	68.7	63.6	28.3	32.8	0.5	0.7	1.8	2.7	6.0	5.9	6.4	6.8	6.3	28.7	27.2	10.8	1.9	77.5	37.9	54.0	46.0
32350	PINETTA	79.0	72.4	19.3	25.5	0.2	0.3	1.3	1.9	6.5	6.6	6.5	5.8	4.8	23.4	27.8	15.3	3.4	76.9	42.1	49.6	50.4
32351	QUINCY	36.1	32.1	57.6	59.3	0.3	0.3	10.6	14.7	7.0	7.0	6.8	7.0	7.3	30.3	22.7	9.9	1.9	75.0	34.1	46.8	53.2
32352	QUINCY	23.0	18.5	73.5	77.1	0.3	0.4	4.8	6.4	7.2	7.1	7.4	8.3	7.6	26.0	25.8	9.2	1.3	73.2	33.8	47.9	52.1
32355	SAINT MARKS	68.3	62.9	27.6	32.5	0.0	0.0	5.4	7.6	3.0	3.3	3.6	3.6	7.3	45.4	25.5	7.6	0.7	88.1	38.1	73.8	26.2
32356	SALEM	95.5	94.4	0.0	0.5	1.5	2.3	0.0	0.5	4.7	5.2	5.2	8.0	4.2	22.5	31.5	16.0	2.8	80.3	45.2	49.3	50.7
32358	SOPCHOPPY	91.4	89.3	6.5	8.1	0.4	0.7	1.9	2.8	5.2	5.5	6.1	6.5	4.5	22.4	33.2	14.8	1.8	79.3	44.8	50.6	49.4
32359	STEINHATCHEE	97.2	96.1	1.0	1.4	0.3	0.5	0.7	1.1	3.0	3.1	3.4	4.3	4.2	15.7	33.5	30.1	2.7	87.9	57.1	48.4	51.6
32401	PANAMA CITY	67.6	60.7	26.8	31.9	2.1	3.1	2.3	3.5	6.5	6.2	6.1	6.7	6.4	25.3	25.7	13.8	3.2	77.1	39.1	47.2	52.8
32403	PANAMA CITY	74.8	65.3	14.2	19.5	3.1	4.6	8.3	12.4	13.2	11.8	9.4	9.7	13.0	40.0	2.6	0.3	0.0	61.9	22.3	55.1	44.9
32404	PANAMA CITY	80.3	73.1	12.9	17.9	2.6	3.7	3.0	4.6	6.3	6.1	6.1	6.6	6.3	28.9	27.3	11.5	1.0	77.5	37.9	50.9	49.1
32405	PANAMA CITY	84.7	78.7	10.4	14.5	1.9	3.0	2.5	4.0	6.5	6.2	6.1	6.6	6.6	25.7	26.8	13.4	2.2	77.2	39.0	48.1	51.9
32407	PANAMA CITY BEACH	94.7	92.1	1.5	2.2	1.1	1.8	2.6	4.3	4.9	5.1	5.2	5.1	4.5	26.0	31.2	16.4	1.7	81.8	44.5	50.4	49.6
32408	PANAMA CITY	94.5	91.8	1.2	2.1	1.5	2.4	2.6	4.4	5.0	4.7	4.8	5.5	6.5	27.7	29.5	14.4	1.8	82.2	42.0	49.9	50.1
32409	PANAMA CITY	96.2	94.7	0.5	0.8	0.5	0.8	0.9	1.5	6.4	6.5	6.7	6.8	5.3	27.6	29.4	10.5	0.8	76.2	38.9	49.6	50.4
32413	PANAMA CITY BEACH	95.9	94.0	0.8	1.4	0.8	1.4	1.5	2.7	4.3	4.5	4.9	4.8	3.1	22.7	36.0	18.2	1.5	83.3	48.3	50.4	49.6
32420	ALFORD	93.0	90.5	5.1	6.9	0.2	0.3	1.0	1.8	5.5	5.8	6.1	5.6	4.4	22.9	32.3	15.8	1.5	79.2	44.7	49.5	50.5
32421	ALTHA	93.4	90.6	2.8	3.9	0.4	0.6	3.0	5.1	6.3	6.6	7.2	6.7	5.5	25.2	29.4	11.6	1.4	75.5	39.4	50.0	50.0
32423	BASCOM	66.7	58.9	32.0	39.4	0.1	0.2	1.6	2.6	5.8	6.1	6.5	6.2	4.8	23.1	29.5	15.7	2.2	77.6	42.9	51.5	48.5
32424	BLOUNTSTOWN	70.1	63.1	25.2	31.0	0.7	1.1	4.7	7.0	5.8	5.8	5.6	5.2	7.2	33.4	22.5	12.0	2.5	79.7	36.7	57.0	43.0
32425	BONIFAY	86.9	83.4	9.1	11.4	0.4	0.6	2.1	3.4	5.6	5.7	5.9	6.1	6.7	28.9	25.2	13.6	2.4	79.1	38.8	54.4	45.6
32426	CAMPBELLTON	26.0	20.5	72.8	78.4	0.1	0.1	0.9	1.1	5.9	5.9	6.3	7.2	5.8	23.4	29.9	13.5	2.2	77.8	41.4	47.6	52.4
32427	CARYVILLE	82.5	79.0	13.0	15.1	0.1	0.2	2.4	3.7	5.8	6.1	6.7	6.7	4.9	23.9	27.9	15.6	2.3	76.9	42.1	48.6	51.4
32428	CHIPLEY	82.8	78.8	12.9	15.8	0.5	0.7	2.3	3.7	6.0	5.9	6.0	5.9	5.5	26.7	27.3	14.0	2.7	78.3	40.8	52.4	47.6
32430	CLARKSVILLE	96.4	95.1	0.3	0.3	0.1	0.3	0.8	1.3	6.5	6.5	6.7	6.3	4.7	24.7	28.4	14.2	1.9	76.3	41.4	50.6	49.4
32431	COTTONDALE	75.0	69.4	21.3	26.1	0.4	0.5	1.8	2.7	6.4	6.8	7.3	7.1	5.3	24.1	28.7	12.7	1.7	75.0	39.6	48.1	51.9
32433	DEFUNIAK SPRINGS	82.3	76.5	13.4	18.0	0.4	0.5	2.5	3.8	5.9	6.2	6.2	6.2	6.0	28.5	26.9	12.6	1.5	77.9	38.6	54.2	45.8
32435	DEFUNIAK SPRINGS	85.0	77.4	10.7	16.7	0.4	0.5	2.7	4.4	5.5	5.6	5.9	6.4	5.4	23.3	28.8	16.0	3.2	79.1	43.4	48.6	51.4
32437	EBRO	65.8	59.7	27.8	33.0	0.1	0.3	1.9	2.9	6.2	6.5	6.8	6.0	4.8	24.4	30.4	13.6	1.3	76.4	41.4	49.4	50.6
32438	FOUNTAIN	95.3	93.3	0.6	1.0	0.5	0.8	2.5	4.2	5.9	5.7	5.9	7.7	8.3	23.4	31.5	10.7	1.0	78.2	40.2	51.4	48.6
32439	FREEPORT	92.6	89.2	1.1	2.1	0.6	0.8	2.1	3.7	5.8	6.0	6.4	6.3	4.4	23.1	31.7	15.0	1.3	77.9	43.5	51.3	48.7
32440	GRACEVILLE	82.3	77.9	15.7	19.6	0.1	0.2	1.1	1.9	6.2	6.0	6.2	7.0	5.8	25.2	25.8	14.9	2.9	77.8	39.9	48.6	51.4
32442	GRAND RIDGE	86.8	82.4	10.5	13.9	0.2	0.2	1.8	3.0	6.4	6.7	6.9	5.9	4.3	25.7	28.4	13.9	1.9	76.3	40.8	49.5	50.5
32443	GREENWOOD	51.5	43.7	45.7	53.0	0.2	0.3	3.8	5.1	4.5	4.6	4.9	5.3	5.9	32.3	29.6	11.5	1.4	82.7	40.6	54.1	45.9
32444	LYNN HAVEN	88.1	83.1	7.6	10.9	1.7	2.7	1.6	2.6	5.9	6.1	6.7	6.6	5.2	24.0	31.1	12.7	1.6	77.2	41.8	48.6	51.4
32445	MALONE	54.9	47.0	40.1	46.8	0.1	0.1	5.6	8.1	2.7	3.0	3.2	3.8	7.4	45.6	26.0	7.3	0.9	88.7	37.5	74.9	25.1
32446	MARIANNA	70.7	64.4	25.5	30.5	0.9	1.2	4.3	6.6	5.2	5.1	5.2	5.6	6.1	28.7	26.8	14.2	3.1	81.3	41.0	50.6	49.4
32448	MARIANNA	66.3	62.1	30.8	34.2	0.4	0.5	1.8	2.7	6.3	6.4	6.7	10.1	5.9	24.8	25.9	11.8	1.9	73.9	36.4	50.1	49.9
32449	WEWAHITCHKA	95.0	93.5	1.2	1.8	0.2	0.2	0.8	1.6	4.7	4.9	5.7	7.5	5.2	23.8	30.1	16.7	1.5	80.2	43.8	51.5	48.5
32455	PONCE DE LEON	88.9	82.9	6.2	10.7	0.3	0.5	1.2	1.9	5.7	6.4	6.7	7.2	5.3	23.2	30.4	12.7	2.4	76.7	41.8	51.2	48.8
32456	PORT SAINT JOE	81.7	80.9	15.9	15.8	0.5	1.0	0.8	1.6	4.5	4.6	5.1	5.1	4.2	19.9	33.0	21.0	2.6	82.6	49.5	48.9	51.1
32459	SANTA ROSA BEACH	94.7	92.8	0.5	0.9	0.7	1.0	2.6	4.2	4.3	4.6	5.0	4.8	3.2	22.1	36.6	18.0	1.5	83.2	48.6	49.7	50.3
32460	SNEADS	72.0	65.0	23.6	29.1	0.2	0.4	4.5	6.8	4.2	4.4	4.4	5.3	9.7	35.6	24.4	10.4	1.6	83.9	37.3	64.0	36.0
32462	VERNON	77.9	73.9	16.1	18.8	0.4	0.5	2.6	3.9	5.7	5.8	5.8	5.8	5.3	27.0	29.0	13.9	1.6	78.8	41.3	53.7	46.3
32464	WESTVILLE	96.7	95.4	0.5	0.7	0.3	0.6	1.3	2.0	5.6	5.8	6.3	7.2	4.4	24.3	29.5	15.2	1.8	77.5	42.5	50.1	49.9
32465	WEWAHITCHKA	80.1	74.0	15.7	19.7	0.4	0.8	3.6	8.3	5.3	5.4	5.6	6.3	5.6	27.2	28.4	14.7	1.7	80.1	41.2	54.9	45.1
32466	YOUNGSTOWN	94.3	92.0	1.5	2.4	0.5	0.8	1.4	2.4	6.1	6.2	6.4	7.2	6.1	27.7	29.7	9.9	0.7	77.0	38.5	51.0	49.0
	FLORIDA	78.0	74.7	14.6	15.8	1.7	2.3	16.8	21.5	6.0	5.9	5.9	6.3	6.2	25.0	26.8	15.3	2.8	78.6	41.1	48.8	51.2
	UNITED STATES	75.1	72.0	12.3	12.7	3.8	4.6	12.5	15.7	6.8	6.7	6.6	7.1	6.9	27.0	26.0	10.9	1.9	75.7	36.9	49.2	50.8

ZIP CODE #	POST OFFICE NAME	2009 Per Capita Income	2009 HH Income Base	2009 Household Income Distribution (%): Less than $25,000	$25,000 to $49,999	$50,000 to $99,999	$100,000 to $149,999	$150,000 or More	Median Household Income: 2009	2014	2009 National Centile	2009 State Centile	2009 Home Value Base	2009 Home Value Distribution (%): Less than $50,000	$50,000 to $89,999	$90,000 to $174,999	$175,000 to $399,999	$400,000 or More	2009 Median Home Value
32219	JACKSONVILLE	21237	4442	24.3	28.2	37.0	7.7	2.7	47835	50974	56	50	3499	12.5	19.5	50.0	16.6	1.4	110022
32220	JACKSONVILLE	20531	4893	21.1	30.4	41.1	6.0	1.5	48608	51632	58	52	3999	14.2	23.0	43.3	18.8	0.8	113018
32221	JACKSONVILLE	22317	9416	14.9	33.8	39.4	8.7	3.2	51144	53502	64	60	7516	12.6	10.8	50.4	24.6	1.6	134757
32222	JACKSONVILLE	23531	2807	14.0	32.7	39.8	9.4	4.2	53581	56064	69	66	2129	11.8	8.7	45.2	31.8	2.5	152399
32223	JACKSONVILLE	40306	10396	6.1	15.6	40.8	20.3	17.1	82009	82489	93	94	8352	0.2	1.9	30.4	53.1	14.5	226831
32224	JACKSONVILLE	35573	15109	10.5	21.4	41.6	15.3	11.3	68203	68695	86	87	8656	10.2	4.7	12.8	54.4	17.9	239919
32225	JACKSONVILLE	31451	20420	8.0	19.8	44.4	18.1	9.7	72674	72866	88	91	15326	1.2	2.6	41.4	44.8	9.9	183822
32226	JACKSONVILLE	28488	5265	14.8	24.2	37.5	17.7	5.8	63414	64697	82	82	4635	5.5	9.2	36.9	39.7	8.8	171111
32233	ATLANTIC BEACH	25533	11075	15.8	34.1	33.3	10.8	6.1	50123	52623	61	57	5726	6.3	12.1	35.8	21.4	24.4	156462
32234	JACKSONVILLE	19114	2582	22.7	35.0	34.4	6.0	1.9	43680	46509	44	39	2026	16.2	27.9	41.3	13.2	1.5	97947
32244	JACKSONVILLE	22551	23138	17.0	31.1	40.9	8.4	2.6	51407	53597	65	61	15655	10.4	13.5	61.0	14.6	0.4	126660
32246	JACKSONVILLE	23929	16203	16.3	28.6	40.6	10.7	3.8	54728	57048	71	69	11158	4.9	13.1	51.6	29.7	0.6	136425
32250	JACKSONVILLE BEACH	36301	13454	15.7	22.5	38.0	15.7	8.1	62476	63509	81	80	8149	3.3	2.0	21.8	54.5	18.4	235174
32254	JACKSONVILLE	13905	5776	40.6	32.7	22.5	3.1	1.1	30616	31653	9	6	3541	16.4	48.7	31.3	3.1	0.4	76737
32256	JACKSONVILLE	44170	21447	11.5	25.2	35.2	10.8	17.3	62445	64557	81	80	8961	1.8	3.9	28.5	30.2	35.6	267037
32257	JACKSONVILLE	30377	16869	13.3	27.0	39.2	13.6	6.9	59960	60771	77	76	10628	0.7	2.1	45.0	47.5	4.7	178685
32258	JACKSONVILLE	38825	9191	5.0	14.3	36.7	25.1	18.8	89672	91111	95	96	7068	1.3	2.8	29.3	59.1	7.6	206812
32259	SAINT JOHNS	47897	11773	2.8	8.2	22.0	34.7	32.3	122910	125011	99	99	10778	0.6	1.9	5.6	58.4	33.5	322757
32266	NEPTUNE BEACH	38907	3456	9.2	23.8	40.0	16.8	10.0	69155	69438	86	87	2153	0.5	1.0	19.6	61.2	17.7	260743
32277	JACKSONVILLE	27495	12797	14.9	27.9	40.6	11.8	4.7	56455	58070	73	71	7571	0.6	3.0	57.7	35.1	3.6	157695
32301	TALLAHASSEE	23364	13376	35.5	27.8	30.1	4.7	1.9	36968	40886	23	19	4749	2.9	11.8	60.6	23.6	1.0	134211
32303	TALLAHASSEE	26224	21358	22.6	27.8	37.6	8.6	3.4	49541	51503	60	55	12125	4.9	6.5	55.6	29.0	4.0	146648
32304	TALLAHASSEE	13311	17607	61.9	25.0	11.1	1.5	0.5	17822	18588	1	1	3677	21.0	29.2	40.1	7.7	2.0	89819
32305	TALLAHASSEE	19477	8263	28.2	33.7	30.3	5.5	2.3	38348	41884	28	23	5816	20.8	31.3	39.5	8.1	0.3	88093
32306	TALLAHASSEE	16167	0	0.0	0.0	0.0	0.0	0.0	0	0	0	0	0	0.0	0.0	0.0	0.0	0.0	0
32307	TALLAHASSEE	11147	0	0.0	0.0	0.0	0.0	0.0	0	0	0	0	0	0.0	0.0	0.0	0.0	0.0	0
32308	TALLAHASSEE	35431	9995	15.8	23.7	39.4	12.2	8.9	59983	58543	77	76	5622	1.5	4.2	34.0	50.2	10.1	192999
32309	TALLAHASSEE	38137	12544	8.5	14.8	41.3	22.7	12.6	76480	77442	90	93	9805	2.1	2.8	23.9	58.5	12.7	224278
32310	TALLAHASSEE	17035	7504	44.2	27.0	24.6	2.9	1.2	29987	32481	8	5	3826	22.0	28.1	39.3	9.6	1.0	89878
32311	TALLAHASSEE	26261	6130	13.5	31.2	43.4	9.2	2.8	54073	54105	70	67	4577	6.1	10.8	54.1	27.0	2.0	135692
32312	TALLAHASSEE	46565	11888	6.5	10.0	34.7	22.9	26.0	97729	102544	96	97	9823	1.9	2.6	13.0	55.0	27.5	267303
32317	TALLAHASSEE	37134	5290	4.5	10.6	46.3	25.2	13.4	83793	85238	93	95	4632	2.8	4.8	15.4	70.7	6.2	236772
32320	APALACHICOLA	16383	1800	40.2	33.2	21.5	4.2	0.9	28846	29413	6	4	1359	13.1	21.0	32.4	26.5	7.1	133737
32321	BRISTOL	17846	1811	36.7	32.1	23.6	4.7	2.9	33411	34072	14	11	1470	26.7	24.6	32.4	12.2	4.1	87841
32322	CARRABELLE	18299	1648	43.1	31.3	20.9	3.9	0.8	28357	29537	6	3	1323	15.9	20.9	32.8	24.0	6.3	119577
32324	CHATTAHOOCHEE	19942	1876	31.6	29.2	32.0	5.0	2.3	37671	41275	26	21	1351	20.1	32.6	35.4	9.3	2.7	85852
32327	CRAWFORDVILLE	20297	9367	21.5	33.1	35.6	7.2	2.6	45586	46568	50	45	7945	9.8	18.5	37.4	29.1	5.3	138513
32328	EASTPOINT	23423	1598	25.5	28.6	36.7	4.8	4.4	45861	49224	51	46	1304	11.5	13.3	18.6	25.8	30.8	220588
32331	GREENVILLE	15609	1915	37.3	35.3	23.7	3.2	0.5	32687	33925	13	9	1614	30.5	22.6	30.9	14.3	1.7	83243
32332	GRETNA	12332	561	39.2	33.3	22.1	4.5	0.9	31138	32483	10	7	437	30.9	28.8	29.3	7.6	3.4	75000
32333	HAVANA	21437	4906	29.3	25.9	34.8	6.6	3.5	44535	47617	47	41	3965	16.0	14.4	39.5	26.7	3.3	128399
32334	HOSFORD	24066	870	32.2	27.5	32.4	5.7	2.2	39062	41389	30	25	711	33.3	14.6	30.4	20.4	1.3	99667
32336	LAMONT	20383	441	36.1	21.8	33.3	6.3	2.5	41754	43588	38	33	362	12.2	26.8	39.0	18.8	3.3	111638
32340	MADISON	16215	4343	42.8	26.5	25.1	3.5	2.1	30771	31717	9	6	3229	21.3	26.4	36.6	12.4	3.3	93387
32343	MIDWAY	15513	617	34.8	32.4	26.6	4.2	1.9	34945	38270	17	14	500	22.8	21.0	35.6	18.2	2.4	101087
32344	MONTICELLO	20629	4512	32.4	27.4	29.4	7.6	3.1	39598	41435	32	26	3612	16.9	21.8	34.4	20.1	6.9	113373
32346	PANACEA	20862	1524	35.4	35.6	20.7	6.2	2.1	33282	36484	14	11	1171	14.3	16.1	25.2	33.7	10.8	157661
32347	PERRY	19602	3203	27.6	31.5	32.4	7.1	1.4	42721	46038	42	36	2606	23.8	24.6	40.2	9.8	1.6	93415
32348	PERRY	17135	3497	38.8	31.0	22.9	4.9	2.3	31846	32733	11	8	2637	25.0	23.5	34.4	14.0	3.1	93496
32350	PINETTA	23908	428	24.5	37.1	29.4	2.8	6.1	41247	46278	37	32	358	19.3	19.0	42.5	15.1	4.2	109906
32351	QUINCY	17762	6891	34.2	30.4	27.4	5.6	2.5	37541	40466	25	21	5109	16.4	30.4	37.6	13.2	2.4	94211
32352	QUINCY	16329	2708	32.8	30.6	31.2	3.0	2.4	37811	41338	26	22	2186	23.6	25.2	30.4	14.1	6.8	92593
32355	SAINT MARKS	29744	156	34.0	26.9	33.3	5.1	0.6	38662	43250	29	24	118	11.9	19.5	49.2	16.9	2.5	119444
32356	SALEM	17634	90	32.2	36.7	26.7	2.2	2.2	30896	34439	10	6	80	18.8	35.0	27.5	11.3	7.5	85000
32358	SOPCHOPPY	23004	1260	24.6	31.8	33.7	6.2	3.7	43454	45674	44	38	1068	10.8	20.8	30.6	33.4	4.4	134066
32359	STEINHATCHEE	22138	700	41.6	27.9	17.7	8.6	4.3	31988	34136	11	9	616	26.6	18.0	28.1	23.7	3.6	98684
32401	PANAMA CITY	19804	10628	39.9	27.9	26.1	3.8	2.3	33088	35233	13	10	6286	16.6	26.1	41.6	10.0	5.6	100888
32403	PANAMA CITY	15352	677	7.7	48.0	38.4	3.0	3.0	43776	47981	45	39	15	0.0	26.7	20.0	40.0	13.3	254167
32404	PANAMA CITY	21529	14547	23.8	28.4	39.1	6.4	2.4	47488	50078	55	49	10197	11.7	14.1	47.4	23.1	3.7	133561
32405	PANAMA CITY	25688	11909	21.8	28.1	36.9	8.6	4.6	50036	51203	61	57	7619	7.8	12.7	41.1	31.7	6.8	147335
32407	PANAMA CITY BEACH	27938	3855	17.8	29.6	41.0	6.9	4.7	51983	52456	66	62	2610	6.2	6.4	37.0	38.8	11.6	176113
32408	PANAMA CITY	32060	8304	23.4	27.2	31.6	11.0	6.8	49159	51525	59	54	5015	2.6	7.2	33.7	36.0	20.5	196433
32409	PANAMA CITY	18590	3364	25.4	32.0	37.4	4.1	1.2	43460	45607	44	38	2929	17.5	24.8	38.6	16.9	2.2	102587
32413	PANAMA CITY BEACH	26256	6011	23.2	31.2	34.9	7.1	3.6	44876	47904	48	41	4517	7.2	9.0	37.5	38.1	8.3	166606
32420	ALFORD	19985	973	29.5	32.2	30.3	5.0	3.0	39692	42733	32	27	840	9.0	22.0	40.4	20.8	7.7	127976
32421	ALTHA	17083	1736	34.5	31.8	28.5	3.4	1.8	34688	36257	17	13	1451	28.3	27.2	34.3	9.0	1.2	82639
32423	BASCOM	17472	569	31.8	32.9	31.5	3.0	0.9	39874	44261	32	27	477	19.7	22.6	38.2	16.8	2.7	103906
32424	BLOUNTSTOWN	16101	2565	40.2	31.6	22.1	4.7	1.4	30498	31063	9	5	1930	23.1	23.3	40.7	11.5	1.5	95504
32425	BONIFAY	17645	5093	39.9	30.3	23.9	3.9	2.1	32501	33782	12	9	3999	20.9	23.3	35.7	16.8	3.3	98268
32426	CAMPBELLTON	15664	397	45.1	31.5	16.1	5.0	2.3	28764	30138	6	4	336	20.2	20.2	42.3	14.9	2.4	106897
32427	CARYVILLE	16194	510	40.4	28.8	26.7	2.2	2.0	31404	32785	10	7	435	20.7	23.4	35.2	17.9	2.8	103728
32428	CHIPLEY	18835	5762	35.5	29.6	26.3	5.9	2.7	34638	35887	17	13	4579	11.6	19.4	37.9	27.0	4.1	132671
32430	CLARKSVILLE	18756	387	30.7	33.6	29.7	4.4	1.6	38875	42365	29	25	342	24.9	20.2	42.7	9.1	3.2	105000
32431	COTTONDALE	15843	2175	38.2	32.6	24.3	4.1	0.7	31591	32942	11	7	1719	15.5	24.0	39.8	17.7	3.0	110069
32433	DEFUNIAK SPRINGS	16704	5755	35.2	31.7	28.5	3.7	1.0	35314	36409	19	15	4525	20.4	24.3	37.7	14.9	2.7	98641
32435	DEFUNIAK SPRINGS	17019	2903	35.1	36.2	24.7	3.1	0.9	34607	36036	17	13	2133	19.4	20.6	34.9	18.8	6.2	112188
32437	EBRO	17964	318	42.1	30.2	22.0	3.8	1.9	31940	33059	11	9	273	22.0	16.5	38.8	13.9	8.8	109198
32438	FOUNTAIN	16421	1240	40.2	32.7	23.4	1.8	1.9	33088	35663	13	10	1104	35.2	35.1	25.8	3.2	0.6	59702
32439	FREEPORT	18715	3228	33.3	33.4	27.5	4.3	1.6	37389	38181	25	20	2541	17.6	18.2	36.2	22.2	5.7	120972
32440	GRACEVILLE	18361	2335	37.5	26.9	28.4	5.4	1.8	33320	35198	14	11	1686	16.5	23.3	39.6	19.8	0.8	110787
32442	GRAND RIDGE	18398	1566	31.4	30.8	31.1	5.9	0.8	39223	40730	30	26	1285	12.4	28.9	38.2	15.6	4.9	106250
32443	GREENWOOD	22917	1266	29.6	37.8	26.5	4.2	2.0	37188	38462	24	19	1070	18.3	20.2	41.9	18.0	1.6	115141
32444	LYNN HAVEN	28430	7563	15.2	25.4	39.7	13.4	6.2	60047	57913	77	77	5851	3.4	7.4	38.6	42.0	8.6	177319
32445	MALONE	14854	517	46.2	23.4	25.7	4.1	0.6	28955	31238	7	4	415	17.6	18.6	35.7	28.2	0.0	125291
32446	MARIANNA	22380	4030	26.9	28.7	31.1	9.2	4.2	45402	48611	49	44	3048	10.4	13.8	40.5	31.2	4.1	143367
32448	MARIANNA	16015	3706	38.9	35.6	21.1	3.4	0.9	30858	32518	9	6	2687	14.7	27.7	39.4	14.5	3.7	102548
32449	WEWAHITCHKA	12476	249	52.2	26.1	19.3	2.4	0.0	23496	25412	2	2	220	48.2	19.1	18.2	11.4	3.2	52667
32455	PONCE DE LEON	15778	1701	39.6	30.2	27.9	1.8	0.5	33690	35692	15	11	1447	27.0	27.6	31.3	11.4	2.7	81582
32456	PORT SAINT JOE	22766	4538	29.0	31.3	31.4	5.3	3.0	41113	42767	36	31	3479	4.6	11.0	40.9	33.2	10.3	160674
32459	SANTA ROSA BEACH	29428	5052	21.4	30.2	34.9	7.8	5.7	48307	48023	57	52	3840	6.0	6.5	21.6	38.1	27.9	233407
32460	SNEADS	18398	1579	31.2	31.2	30.7	5.5	1.5	39840	41903	32	27	1282	16.1	29.2	38.4	14.9	1.4	97895
32462	VERNON	17700	1736	40.3	31.9	22.8	3.3	1.6	31282	32593	10	7	1474	19.5	18.0	39.2	19.9	3.4	115158
32464	WESTVILLE	16832	1735	36.6	33.0	26.3	2.7	1.4	33232	35148	14	10	1527	25.1	32.0	28.2	9.3	5.4	79867
32465	WEWAHITCHKA	17894	2667	34.4	31.3	27.5	5.2	1.6	33662	35558	15	11	2233	17.6	25.3	37.8	17.1	2.2	102741
32466	YOUNGSTOWN	18432	2359	23.4	33.7	37.7	3.0	2.2	43266	45395	43	38	2038	18.8	25.4	39.1	14.5	2.2	103108
	FLORIDA	27128		21.9	27.6	33.8	9.8	6.8	50413	52516				8.0	14.3	38.7	30.4	8.6	144752
	UNITED STATES	27277		20.9	24.4	35.3	11.7	7.6	54719	56938				9.3	13.1	31.6	32.6	13.5	162279

ZIP CODE #	POST OFFICE NAME	FINANCIAL SERVICES				THE HOME: Home Improvements		THE HOME: Furnishings				ENTERTAINMENT						PERSONAL			
		Auto Loan	Home Loan	Invest-ments	Retire-ment Plans	Home Repair	Lawn & Garden	Comput-ers & Hard-ware-Personal	Major Appli-ances	TV, Radio, Sound Equip-ment	Furni-ture	Dine out/ Carry out	Sports Equip-ment	Fees & Tickets	Toys & Games	Travel	Cable TV	Apparel & Services	Auto Repairs	Health Insur-ance	Pets & Supplies
32219	JACKSONVILLE	87	78	78	76	76	86	76	82	80	77	80	60	71	81	73	84	54	80	86	98
32220	JACKSONVILLE	88	79	73	77	78	83	76	81	79	78	79	59	71	82	72	82	54	78	82	96
32221	JACKSONVILLE	94	90	79	87	87	89	86	88	87	88	88	66	83	91	83	88	60	86	88	104
32222	JACKSONVILLE	97	95	81	91	91	91	90	91	90	94	91	68	88	94	87	91	63	90	89	108
32223	JACKSONVILLE	144	158	148	161	156	145	148	146	142	154	144	114	156	145	152	138	102	144	138	170
32224	JACKSONVILLE	130	116	102	121	110	104	129	114	125	131	127	95	123	131	118	120	90	121	108	137
32225	JACKSONVILLE	128	136	115	133	128	117	126	123	120	133	122	97	128	127	124	115	86	120	113	142
32226	JACKSONVILLE	110	113	102	114	111	116	104	111	105	104	105	84	105	108	107	107	73	106	112	130
32233	ATLANTIC BEACH	98	92	86	94	90	85	101	92	97	101	98	75	97	100	95	94	69	97	88	109
32234	JACKSONVILLE	88	72	76	69	71	84	70	79	76	71	75	59	62	78	67	80	51	76	81	95
32244	JACKSONVILLE	90	85	72	83	80	79	86	82	85	88	86	64	82	89	80	84	59	84	80	98
32246	JACKSONVILLE	96	89	76	89	84	82	95	87	92	96	93	70	90	96	88	90	65	91	85	104
32250	JACKSONVILLE BEACH	106	109	104	112	107	103	111	104	109	112	110	83	114	109	111	108	78	108	105	124
32254	JACKSONVILLE	59	48	42	49	44	54	54	52	58	52	57	40	49	59	48	61	39	55	58	65
32256	JACKSONVILLE	146	116	111	127	112	108	145	121	141	145	144	103	134	146	128	136	102	136	118	148
32257	JACKSONVILLE	109	103	90	103	99	93	107	100	104	110	105	79	103	108	101	101	73	103	96	118
32258	JACKSONVILLE	152	170	149	173	163	147	154	150	145	163	148	122	164	154	157	138	106	146	134	173
32259	SAINT JOHNS	199	243	225	250	242	211	204	210	191	225	194	168	232	200	220	180	141	195	183	237
32266	NEPTUNE BEACH	113	119	120	123	119	109	124	114	117	124	120	94	127	117	125	113	86	119	109	135
32277	JACKSONVILLE	98	92	81	94	88	87	99	90	97	99	99	73	96	100	94	96	69	96	91	109
32301	TALLAHASSEE	67	48	46	52	46	50	73	56	70	65	70	48	60	70	58	68	49	65	59	70
32303	TALLAHASSEE	86	75	69	77	73	73	91	78	86	85	87	64	81	88	79	85	61	84	78	94
32304	TALLAHASSEE	40	21	20	24	20	24	52	30	44	38	44	30	34	43	31	41	31	39	30	39
32305	TALLAHASSEE	75	67	57	66	63	69	69	67	72	70	72	51	65	74	63	74	49	69	71	82
32306	TALLAHASSEE	0	0	0	0	0	0	0	0	0	0	0	0	0	0	0	0	0	0	0	0
32307	TALLAHASSEE	0	0	0	0	0	0	0	0	0	0	0	0	0	0	0	0	0	0	0	0
32308	TALLAHASSEE	105	108	106	112	108	101	111	104	107	113	108	83	113	108	111	104	77	107	102	123
32309	TALLAHASSEE	133	149	141	151	147	138	134	136	130	141	132	105	144	133	141	127	94	132	128	158
32310	TALLAHASSEE	59	47	41	48	44	48	57	50	58	55	58	40	50	59	49	58	40	55	53	62
32311	TALLAHASSEE	92	93	82	94	90	89	90	89	89	92	90	69	90	92	89	89	62	89	88	106
32312	TALLAHASSEE	174	207	195	211	206	183	180	182	170	194	172	144	200	176	191	162	125	173	163	208
32317	TALLAHASSEE	135	167	152	167	164	150	141	145	134	148	137	113	159	138	154	131	98	138	134	167
32320	APALACHICOLA	65	49	69	47	51	68	49	62	55	48	54	45	42	54	50	60	36	58	66	73
32321	BRISTOL	83	59	77	58	60	82	62	75	69	58	67	57	49	70	58	75	45	70	79	90
32322	CARRABELLE	64	50	69	48	53	67	50	62	55	49	54	45	43	53	51	60	36	58	66	73
32324	CHATTAHOOCHEE	79	61	70	61	60	78	66	74	73	63	71	56	58	73	63	78	48	73	81	89
32327	CRAWFORDVILLE	88	76	82	74	77	85	73	82	77	74	76	60	67	78	72	80	52	78	83	97
32328	EASTPOINT	92	74	104	72	80	99	73	90	79	72	78	64	65	77	76	86	52	84	96	106
32331	GREENVILLE	69	48	70	46	49	70	50	64	56	47	55	48	39	57	49	62	37	59	66	76
32332	GRETNA	73	48	71	45	48	72	51	65	59	49	58	50	38	60	48	66	38	61	68	79
32333	HAVANA	86	74	81	71	72	86	72	81	76	71	76	61	65	78	70	81	52	78	83	97
32334	HOSFORD	100	69	99	66	70	100	72	91	81	68	80	69	56	82	69	90	53	84	95	110
32336	LAMONT	94	64	93	61	65	94	67	85	76	63	75	65	52	77	64	84	49	79	89	103
32340	MADISON	70	51	64	50	51	69	54	63	61	52	60	48	46	61	52	67	40	61	68	77
32343	MIDWAY	67	57	47	59	52	61	62	59	67	62	66	46	59	68	56	69	46	63	65	74
32344	MONTICELLO	89	68	87	66	69	90	70	84	76	66	75	63	58	76	68	83	50	79	88	100
32346	PANACEA	79	60	85	58	63	82	60	76	66	57	65	56	50	65	61	72	43	70	79	89
32347	PERRY	81	65	75	64	66	81	66	76	71	63	69	57	57	71	64	75	47	72	79	90
32348	PERRY	74	54	71	53	56	74	58	68	65	56	63	51	48	64	55	71	42	65	74	82
32350	PINETTA	104	74	106	72	77	105	76	97	85	71	83	73	61	84	75	93	55	89	101	115
32351	QUINCY	73	64	63	64	62	70	66	68	70	66	69	51	62	70	63	72	47	69	72	82
32352	QUINCY	78	61	70	57	59	74	62	70	67	62	66	54	53	69	58	71	45	68	72	85
32355	SAINT MARKS	77	55	79	53	57	78	57	72	63	53	62	54	45	62	56	69	41	66	75	86
32356	SALEM	70	55	76	52	59	74	55	68	60	54	59	49	48	58	57	65	39	64	73	80
32358	SOPCHOPPY	96	73	111	71	78	100	74	94	80	69	78	69	62	77	76	86	52	86	95	110
32359	STEINHATCHEE	72	65	85	60	71	80	63	75	67	66	65	51	60	62	67	71	44	71	82	87
32401	PANAMA CITY	63	56	54	57	55	63	62	61	66	60	65	45	59	64	58	69	45	63	69	73
32403	PANAMA CITY	93	48	37	56	43	41	87	61	82	81	86	60	66	98	63	75	60	77	55	74
32404	PANAMA CITY	84	76	74	75	75	80	76	79	78	77	77	59	72	79	73	79	53	78	80	93
32405	PANAMA CITY	89	84	80	85	84	85	87	85	88	87	88	65	85	89	84	89	61	87	88	101
32407	PANAMA CITY BEACH	100	84	115	83	89	103	86	100	89	82	88	74	77	86	89	93	59	95	101	116
32408	PANAMA CITY	93	91	90	94	91	90	97	91	95	96	96	72	96	95	95	95	67	95	93	109
32409	PANAMA CITY	81	69	71	66	68	78	66	75	70	67	70	55	60	72	64	74	47	71	76	89
32413	PANAMA CITY BEACH	93	76	118	74	84	99	76	95	80	73	79	69	67	76	82	85	52	89	96	110
32420	ALFORD	83	62	94	61	66	86	63	80	68	59	67	60	52	67	65	74	45	74	82	94
32421	ALTHA	79	56	77	55	58	79	58	72	65	55	63	55	46	65	56	71	42	67	76	87
32423	BASCOM	74	54	77	52	56	76	55	70	61	52	60	52	45	61	55	67	40	64	73	83
32424	BLOUNTSTOWN	69	51	65	49	51	68	52	63	58	50	57	48	43	58	50	63	38	59	66	76
32425	BONIFAY	75	54	75	53	56	76	57	70	63	53	61	53	45	62	55	69	41	65	74	84
32426	CAMPBELLTON	72	47	69	45	47	70	51	63	58	48	57	49	38	59	47	65	38	60	67	78
32427	CARYVILLE	72	50	72	48	51	72	52	66	59	49	57	50	41	59	50	65	38	61	69	79
32428	CHIPLEY	79	63	80	61	64	80	63	75	68	61	67	56	55	68	63	74	45	71	79	89
32430	CLARKSVILLE	79	56	81	54	58	80	58	73	64	54	63	55	46	64	57	70	42	67	76	87
32431	COTTONDALE	70	50	70	48	51	70	52	65	57	49	56	49	41	57	50	63	37	60	67	77
32433	DEFUNIAK SPRINGS	69	56	67	53	56	69	56	65	61	55	60	48	49	61	55	65	40	62	68	77
32435	DEFUNIAK SPRINGS	70	51	70	50	53	71	54	66	60	50	58	50	44	59	53	65	39	62	70	78
32437	EBRO	79	57	81	55	59	80	58	74	64	54	63	55	46	64	57	71	42	68	77	88
32438	FOUNTAIN	70	58	60	55	56	65	59	63	61	60	61	48	52	64	55	64	42	62	63	76
32439	FREEPORT	76	63	78	61	65	76	62	73	65	61	65	53	55	65	62	69	43	68	73	85
32440	GRACEVILLE	74	56	74	55	58	75	60	71	65	56	64	53	50	65	58	71	43	67	76	84
32442	GRAND RIDGE	82	60	84	58	62	83	61	77	67	57	66	57	50	67	61	74	44	71	80	91
32443	GREENWOOD	86	61	88	59	64	87	63	80	70	58	69	60	50	69	62	77	45	73	83	95
32444	LYNN HAVEN	100	106	100	106	105	105	99	102	99	102	100	76	103	100	102	100	69	100	102	119
32445	MALONE	69	47	68	45	48	69	49	62	56	46	54	48	38	56	47	62	36	58	65	75
32446	MARIANNA	90	78	85	77	79	90	79	86	83	78	82	64	73	83	77	87	56	84	90	102
32448	MARIANNA	63	48	57	47	48	61	51	57	57	50	56	43	44	56	48	61	37	56	62	70
32449	WEWAHITCHKA	55	40	57	38	41	56	41	52	45	38	44	39	32	45	40	50	29	47	54	61
32455	PONCE DE LEON	69	49	71	48	51	70	51	64	56	47	55	48	40	56	50	62	36	59	67	77
32456	PORT SAINT JOE	77	70	90	68	75	85	68	80	72	68	71	56	65	68	72	76	48	76	85	93
32459	SANTA ROSA BEACH	103	91	125	90	99	111	88	105	92	89	91	74	83	88	94	97	61	99	107	122
32460	SNEADS	81	60	85	58	63	83	61	77	67	58	66	57	50	66	61	74	44	71	81	91
32462	VERNON	69	52	74	50	55	71	52	66	58	50	56	48	44	56	53	63	37	61	69	78
32464	WESTVILLE	72	52	70	50	53	72	53	66	59	50	58	50	43	59	51	65	38	61	69	79
32465	WEWAHITCHKA	70	58	78	55	63	76	58	71	63	58	61	49	52	60	60	68	41	66	77	82
32466	YOUNGSTOWN	81	72	67	70	71	76	69	74	72	71	72	54	64	75	66	74	49	71	75	88
	FLORIDA	96	94	97	93	96	98	95	97	96	97	96	71	95	94	96	97	67	97	101	113
	UNITED STATES	100	100	100	100	100	100	100	100	100	100	100	100	100	100	100	100	100	100	100	100

POPULATION CHANGE

 32501-32759

ZIP CODE #	POST OFFICE NAME	COUNTY FIPS CODE	POPULATION 2000	POPULATION 2009	POPULATION 2014	2000-2009 ANNUAL RATE % Rate	2000-2009 ANNUAL RATE State Centile	HOUSEHOLDS 2000	HOUSEHOLDS 2009	HOUSEHOLDS 2014	HOUSEHOLDS % Annual Rate 2000-2009	HOUSEHOLDS 2009 Average HH Size	FAMILIES 2000	FAMILIES 2009	FAMILIES % Annual Rate 2000-2009
32501	PENSACOLA	033	12384	12256	12130	-0.1	6	4679	4674	4663	0.0	2.22	2498	2389	-0.5
32502	PENSACOLA	033	3856	3818	3779	-0.1	6	1649	1666	1664	0.1	2.07	884	855	-0.4
32503	PENSACOLA	033	34090	34308	34079	0.1	12	13261	13663	13714	0.3	2.20	7947	7912	0.0
32504	PENSACOLA	033	22343	22088	21874	-0.1	6	9856	10084	10089	0.2	2.17	6260	6219	-0.1
32505	PENSACOLA	033	29041	30421	30982	0.5	26	10662	11446	11767	0.8	2.62	7287	7632	0.5
32506	PENSACOLA	033	33316	36223	37391	0.9	38	13219	14592	15154	1.1	2.39	9137	9888	0.9
32507	PENSACOLA	033	28863	32089	33432	1.2	46	11359	12797	13418	1.3	2.43	7329	8115	1.1
32508	PENSACOLA	033	10401	11010	10936	0.6	30	390	328	312	-1.9	3.70	384	322	-1.9
32514	PENSACOLA	033	34907	37354	38353	0.7	32	14442	15995	16635	1.1	2.20	8777	9386	0.7
32526	PENSACOLA	033	31985	36890	38976	1.6	55	12012	14292	15267	1.9	2.52	8996	10478	1.7
32531	BAKER	091	4639	5231	5543	1.3	48	1774	2032	2164	1.5	2.57	1392	1570	1.3
32533	CANTONMENT	033	23909	27094	28658	1.4	51	8568	10049	10742	1.7	2.68	6851	7880	1.5
32534	PENSACOLA	033	12117	13599	14157	1.3	48	4802	5536	5817	1.5	2.44	3364	3787	1.3
32535	CENTURY	033	6630	7129	7304	0.8	35	1973	2177	2270	1.1	2.50	1443	1550	0.8
32536	CRESTVIEW	091	12883	18209	20604	3.8	84	4786	6801	7736	3.9	2.63	3654	5138	3.8
32539	CRESTVIEW	091	19948	24118	26329	2.1	64	6829	8518	9400	2.4	2.66	5239	6428	2.2
32541	DESTIN	091	12488	20862	24819	5.7	91	5505	9404	11245	6.0	2.21	3531	5961	5.8
32542	EGLIN AFB	091	12415	11971	12236	-0.4	2	2916	3126	3209	0.8	3.42	2696	2814	0.5
32544	HURLBURT FIELD	091	233	309	345	3.1	79	74	103	117	3.6	2.74	61	84	3.5
32547	FORT WALTON BEACH	091	29695	32016	33345	0.8	35	12577	13851	14518	1.0	2.26	7685	8263	0.8
32548	FORT WALTON BEACH	091	21996	23610	24776	0.8	35	9570	10559	11177	1.1	2.21	5862	6241	0.7
32550	MIRAMAR BEACH	131	3024	8656	11295	12.0	97	1480	4363	5712	12.4	1.95	911	2654	12.3
32561	GULF BREEZE	033	8095	8551	8716	0.6	30	3590	3756	3840	0.5	2.26	2350	2382	0.1
32563	GULF BREEZE	113	17428	22545	24752	2.8	76	6823	8623	9466	2.6	2.60	5155	6413	2.4
32564	HOLT	113	2360	3010	3338	2.7	74	882	1143	1277	2.8	2.59	673	857	2.6
32565	JAY	113	5272	5974	6284	1.4	51	2042	2261	2381	1.1	2.59	1534	1665	0.9
32566	NAVARRE	113	21505	31521	36307	4.2	86	7961	11326	13038	3.9	2.78	6179	8612	3.7
32567	LAUREL HILL	091	3618	4017	4269	1.1	44	1454	1627	1734	1.2	2.47	1053	1160	1.1
32568	MC DAVID	033	3382	3434	3421	0.2	15	1248	1312	1321	0.5	2.60	975	1004	0.3
32569	MARY ESTHER	091	11380	12498	13130	1.0	40	4463	5002	5283	1.2	2.50	3122	3421	1.0
32570	MILTON	113	24722	29561	31817	2.0	62	9193	10758	11602	1.7	2.68	6860	7902	1.5
32571	MILTON	113	23808	30075	32951	2.6	73	8573	10511	11505	2.2	2.86	6820	8259	2.1
32577	MOLINO	033	4448	4930	5169	1.1	44	1609	1844	1958	1.5	2.67	1286	1445	1.3
32578	NICEVILLE	091	27909	31900	34001	1.5	53	10733	12528	13449	1.7	2.51	8193	9438	1.5
32579	SHALIMAR	091	10110	10687	11070	0.6	30	4283	4583	4790	0.7	2.33	3083	3229	0.5
32580	VALPARAISO	091	3903	4058	4168	0.4	22	1665	1766	1825	0.6	2.28	1121	1160	0.4
32583	MILTON	113	19328	23567	25414	2.2	66	6816	8243	8942	2.1	2.67	5081	6016	1.8
32601	GAINESVILLE	001	19362	20925	21843	0.8	35	8691	9609	10115	1.1	2.04	2488	2488	0.0
32603	GAINESVILLE	001	7372	7549	7627	0.3	18	2219	2294	2351	0.4	1.86	712	674	-0.6
32605	GAINESVILLE	001	23918	26066	27582	0.9	38	9911	11226	11976	1.4	2.29	6254	6754	0.8
32606	GAINESVILLE	001	17196	21198	23140	2.3	69	7023	8837	9697	2.5	2.35	4718	5760	2.2
32607	GAINESVILLE	001	25381	28782	30568	1.4	51	11492	13192	14048	1.5	2.16	4988	5565	1.2
32608	GAINESVILLE	001	33145	38631	41491	1.7	57	14985	17677	19065	1.8	2.16	5826	6893	1.8
32609	GAINESVILLE	001	19198	20744	21618	0.8	35	6866	7603	8014	1.1	2.36	3993	4210	0.6
32611	GAINESVILLE	001	4708	4893	4903	0.4	22	205	214	220	0.5	2.51	113	111	-0.2
32615	ALACHUA	001	12476	15055	16322	2.1	64	4777	5987	6553	2.5	2.51	3565	4310	2.1
32617	ANTHONY	083	3348	4228	4842	2.6	73	1247	1582	1815	2.6	2.66	923	1149	2.4
32618	ARCHER	001	8145	9978	10951	2.2	66	3093	3859	4266	2.4	2.58	2254	2714	2.0
32619	BELL	041	3795	4849	5413	2.7	74	1426	1840	2061	2.8	2.58	1071	1359	2.6
32621	BRONSON	075	4297	4930	5300	1.5	53	1535	1785	1931	1.6	2.67	1114	1272	1.4
32622	BROOKER	007	1696	1720	1711	0.2	15	636	655	658	0.3	2.31	475	480	0.1
32625	CEDAR KEY	075	1625	2006	2216	2.3	69	749	938	1041	2.5	2.14	477	583	2.2
32626	CHIEFLAND	075	8321	9579	10283	1.5	53	3426	3990	4298	1.7	2.38	2396	2733	1.4
32628	CROSS CITY	029	4201	4700	4801	1.2	46	1194	1311	1355	1.0	2.63	861	928	0.8
32631	EARLETON	001	537	600	640	1.2	46	211	244	262	1.6	2.46	145	161	1.1
32640	HAWTHORNE	001	10897	12330	13009	1.3	48	4355	4984	5286	1.5	2.47	3088	3433	1.2
32641	GAINESVILLE	001	12902	13459	13940	0.5	26	4563	4919	5134	0.8	2.73	3296	3417	0.4
32643	HIGH SPRINGS	001	8704	10629	11658	2.2	66	3356	4213	4655	2.5	2.51	2433	2963	2.2
32648	HORSESHOE BEACH	029	416	430	431	0.4	22	172	181	182	0.6	2.34	123	126	0.3
32653	GAINESVILLE	001	11881	12805	13591	0.8	35	4839	5346	5702	1.1	2.39	3371	3568	0.6
32656	KEYSTONE HEIGHTS	019	11892	14979	16667	2.5	72	4626	5932	6641	2.7	2.52	3423	4247	2.4
32666	MELROSE	107	4887	5506	5768	1.3	48	2082	2355	2473	1.3	2.34	1440	1590	1.1
32667	MICANOPY	001	4136	5111	5651	2.3	69	1788	2259	2509	2.6	2.25	1194	1455	2.2
32668	MORRISTON	075	4264	5449	6042	2.7	74	1650	2139	2381	2.8	2.53	1181	1501	2.6
32669	NEWBERRY	001	7259	10245	11397	3.8	84	2747	4000	4487	4.1	2.56	2021	2840	3.7
32680	OLD TOWN	029	8847	10144	10673	1.5	53	3702	4317	4571	1.7	2.33	2577	2948	1.5
32686	REDDICK	083	5753	7014	7768	2.2	66	2194	2688	2987	2.2	2.58	1553	1853	1.9
32693	TRENTON	041	10135	12472	13770	2.3	69	3475	4443	4968	2.7	2.55	2507	3144	2.5
32694	WALDO	001	1733	1996	2139	1.5	53	744	883	952	1.9	2.26	490	557	1.4
32696	WILLISTON	075	9700	11618	12617	2.0	62	3793	4607	5031	2.1	2.49	2688	3199	1.9
32701	ALTAMONTE SPRINGS	117	22563	23052	23160	0.2	15	10016	10434	10544	0.4	2.18	5520	5482	-0.1
32702	ALTOONA	069	2865	3336	3643	1.7	57	1142	1323	1452	1.6	2.48	817	915	1.2
32703	APOPKA	095	43586	46786	48423	0.8	35	15637	17103	17818	1.0	2.71	11171	11815	0.6
32707	CASSELBERRY	117	32161	35082	35920	0.9	38	13229	14624	15043	1.1	2.39	8805	9387	0.7
32708	WINTER SPRINGS	117	40139	43713	45520	0.9	38	14669	16164	16860	1.1	2.70	11064	11980	0.9
32709	CHRISTMAS	095	2292	2591	3062	1.3	48	828	919	1090	1.1	2.82	638	689	0.8
32712	APOPKA	095	28830	38168	43164	3.1	79	10172	13721	15589	3.3	2.78	8097	10543	2.9
32713	DEBARY	127	15730	19581	21278	2.4	70	6628	8185	8910	2.3	2.37	4765	5685	1.9
32714	ALTAMONTE SPRINGS	117	34326	35845	36465	0.5	26	14483	15397	15748	0.7	2.32	8625	8812	0.2
32720	DELAND	127	25224	28399	29770	1.3	48	10110	11435	12044	1.3	2.37	6621	7248	1.0
32724	DELAND	127	26807	31759	33829	1.8	59	10667	12615	13475	1.8	2.39	6872	7889	1.5
32725	DELTONA	127	37901	45089	47930	1.9	61	14362	16975	18050	1.8	2.65	10825	12434	1.5
32726	EUSTIS	069	17602	21017	23350	1.9	61	7332	8896	9958	2.1	2.31	4793	5555	1.6
32730	CASSELBERRY	117	5222	5248	5240	0.1	12	2299	2359	2368	0.3	2.17	1415	1394	-0.2
32732	GENEVA	117	5018	6010	6560	2.0	62	1811	2217	2438	2.2	2.69	1428	1710	2.0
32735	GRAND ISLAND	069	2309	3331	3939	4.0	85	1015	1461	1730	4.0	2.28	766	1062	3.6
32736	EUSTIS	069	7291	9741	11196	3.2	80	2692	3620	4178	3.3	2.68	2053	2681	2.9
32738	DELTONA	127	33636	43253	47633	2.8	76	11317	14506	15994	2.7	2.97	9235	11575	2.5
32744	LAKE HELEN	127	3383	3585	3736	0.6	30	1359	1437	1497	0.6	2.49	979	990	0.1
32746	LAKE MARY	117	30958	37682	39995	2.1	64	11754	14299	15237	2.1	2.59	8520	10170	1.9
32750	LONGWOOD	117	22697	23315	23336	0.3	18	8282	8664	8723	0.5	2.62	6255	6378	0.2
32751	MAITLAND	095	19097	20706	21078	0.9	38	7571	8392	8585	1.1	2.43	5048	5282	0.5
32754	MIMS	009	9944	11185	11799	1.3	48	3919	4447	4709	1.4	2.52	2886	3191	1.1
32757	MOUNT DORA	095	18693	23033	25734	2.3	69	7942	9797	10988	2.3	2.31	5223	6252	2.0
32759	OAK HILL	127	2645	3311	3586	2.5	72	1135	1439	1563	2.6	2.30	812	994	2.2
	FLORIDA					1.9					1.9	2.47			1.7
	UNITED STATES					1.0					1.1	2.59			0.9

ZIP CODE #	POST OFFICE NAME	RACE (%) White 2000	White 2009	Black 2000	Black 2009	Asian/Pacific 2000	Asian/Pacific 2009	% Hispanic Origin 2000	% Hispanic Origin 2009	2009 AGE DISTRIBUTION (%) 0-4	5-9	10-14	15-19	20-24	25-44	45-64	65-84	85+	18+	MEDIAN AGE 2009	% 2009 Males	% 2009 Females
32501	PENSACOLA	34.6	29.3	62.3	67.4	0.8	0.9	1.5	2.0	5.5	5.5	5.4	6.7	7.5	27.6	24.9	13.4	3.4	79.9	39.3	51.3	48.7
32502	PENSACOLA	48.7	39.5	46.2	54.5	2.1	2.7	2.2	3.0	5.2	5.0	4.9	6.2	7.0	24.1	28.1	15.6	4.0	81.2	43.0	49.2	50.8
32503	PENSACOLA	65.4	59.9	30.1	34.3	2.0	2.8	1.8	2.7	5.2	4.9	4.8	10.7	11.8	22.4	24.3	13.4	2.5	82.0	35.9	46.1	53.9
32504	PENSACOLA	83.4	77.9	11.2	14.8	2.3	3.3	2.6	4.0	5.5	5.1	5.2	5.5	6.5	26.2	28.7	14.9	2.4	81.0	41.5	47.4	52.6
32505	PENSACOLA	46.1	37.6	47.5	55.0	2.7	3.4	2.1	2.9	8.1	7.8	7.3	7.9	7.2	24.5	24.4	11.3	1.6	72.0	34.2	47.0	53.0
32506	PENSACOLA	76.2	68.4	13.1	17.3	4.9	7.0	3.7	5.8	7.6	6.9	6.4	6.6	6.9	29.9	22.5	11.5	1.6	75.5	34.6	48.8	51.2
32507	PENSACOLA	77.0	72.3	15.7	18.3	2.8	4.0	3.1	4.7	6.7	6.5	6.1	7.2	6.9	27.1	26.1	11.9	1.5	77.0	36.8	49.8	50.2
32508	PENSACOLA	75.3	67.1	13.1	17.1	2.7	3.8	9.8	14.6	2.1	1.6	1.2	24.8	26.7	41.2	2.4	0.0	0.0	94.4	23.8	84.9	15.1
32514	PENSACOLA	81.7	75.3	12.8	17.3	2.0	2.9	2.7	4.1	5.8	5.3	5.1	6.4	7.3	28.9	24.1	13.8	3.4	80.7	38.2	47.0	53.0
32526	PENSACOLA	81.5	76.7	11.8	14.6	2.7	3.7	2.7	4.2	6.0	6.1	6.3	6.3	5.7	27.3	28.9	12.1	1.3	77.6	39.4	49.2	50.8
32531	BAKER	92.9	90.3	3.2	4.5	0.5	0.7	1.0	1.7	6.0	6.2	6.5	7.0	5.8	25.6	28.6	12.8	1.5	77.0	40.0	50.0	50.0
32533	CANTONMENT	84.7	80.1	11.4	14.6	1.0	1.6	1.5	2.4	6.2	6.5	6.9	7.1	5.4	25.5	29.7	11.5	1.1	75.9	39.7	49.3	50.7
32534	PENSACOLA	72.2	66.9	23.3	27.3	1.3	1.9	1.8	2.8	6.3	6.6	6.8	6.6	5.1	24.8	28.7	13.1	2.0	75.9	40.3	47.8	52.2
32535	CENTURY	63.1	54.9	31.9	39.2	0.4	0.5	3.8	5.5	5.7	5.5	6.0	6.4	7.2	33.4	22.7	11.0	2.2	78.8	35.9	58.6	41.4
32536	CRESTVIEW	77.7	72.3	16.2	18.9	2.1	3.3	3.1	5.4	8.1	7.4	7.0	6.8	6.4	28.2	25.2	9.8	1.2	73.3	35.1	48.8	51.2
32539	CRESTVIEW	85.1	80.2	9.3	12.1	1.7	2.7	2.8	4.8	6.6	6.3	6.2	6.6	6.5	29.8	26.5	10.3	1.3	76.8	36.9	51.1	48.9
32541	DESTIN	96.2	94.8	0.4	0.5	1.1	1.7	2.6	4.4	4.8	4.7	5.0	5.6	5.8	25.4	31.6	15.3	1.8	81.9	44.1	49.2	50.8
32542	EGLIN AFB	72.6	65.4	15.1	17.7	3.0	4.2	11.3	16.5	14.8	10.7	7.4	6.3	16.2	36.4	5.8	2.3	0.2	64.4	23.3	54.2	45.8
32544	HURLBURT FIELD	74.2	66.3	13.7	16.8	3.0	3.9	8.2	12.9	12.0	10.7	9.4	8.1	10.4	33.7	8.4	6.8	0.6	64.1	24.8	50.2	49.8
32547	FORT WALTON BEACH	79.5	72.9	11.2	14.3	3.3	4.8	5.0	8.0	6.2	5.6	5.3	6.5	7.8	29.9	24.7	12.2	1.8	79.0	36.4	49.5	50.5
32548	FORT WALTON BEACH	78.1	72.2	13.8	16.8	3.0	4.3	3.9	6.3	5.6	5.4	5.3	5.8	6.6	27.6	27.3	14.5	1.9	80.3	40.2	49.2	50.8
32550	MIRAMAR BEACH	96.7	95.5	0.6	1.0	0.7	1.0	1.3	2.1	2.9	3.0	3.3	2.9	2.0	16.2	37.9	28.8	3.0	89.0	57.0	48.9	51.1
32561	GULF BREEZE	97.2	96.2	0.4	0.5	0.7	1.1	1.4	2.3	3.4	3.9	5.1	5.7	4.7	20.4	36.2	18.2	2.4	84.0	48.7	48.6	51.4
32563	GULF BREEZE	95.7	93.8	0.7	1.1	1.1	1.7	2.4	3.9	5.4	6.0	6.8	6.8	4.7	24.0	31.8	13.0	1.5	77.4	42.6	48.9	51.1
32564	HOLT	95.0	93.8	1.8	2.0	0.3	0.4	1.5	2.5	5.1	5.3	5.7	6.4	5.8	26.0	32.0	12.5	1.2	79.6	42.0	50.7	49.3
32565	JAY	96.1	95.1	0.9	1.2	0.2	0.2	0.9	1.4	5.9	6.2	6.6	6.4	5.0	24.4	30.5	13.4	1.5	77.1	41.7	50.6	49.4
32566	NAVARRE	89.1	85.6	3.7	4.9	2.4	3.4	4.1	6.4	7.2	7.2	7.4	6.9	5.3	27.4	28.6	9.3	0.7	73.9	38.2	50.1	49.9
32567	LAUREL HILL	89.1	84.9	7.7	11.0	0.3	0.5	0.8	1.2	5.8	6.1	6.4	6.3	4.8	22.3	31.2	15.3	1.8	77.8	43.7	50.0	50.0
32568	MC DAVID	84.7	80.1	9.2	12.8	0.1	0.2	0.7	1.1	6.0	6.2	6.6	6.7	4.8	23.8	30.3	14.2	1.4	77.3	41.8	50.8	49.2
32569	MARY ESTHER	81.0	74.5	8.5	10.7	4.4	6.5	4.9	8.0	6.6	5.9	5.6	6.5	8.6	30.1	26.5	9.5	0.7	78.2	35.0	50.9	49.1
32570	MILTON	85.6	82.2	8.6	10.3	1.8	2.6	2.3	3.5	7.3	7.0	6.9	6.5	5.8	26.4	26.3	12.1	1.6	74.7	37.7	48.7	51.3
32571	MILTON	94.2	92.3	1.3	1.8	1.2	1.8	2.0	3.3	6.6	7.3	7.6	7.2	5.2	27.0	28.8	9.5	0.9	73.9	37.9	49.5	50.5
32577	MOLINO	86.0	81.5	10.1	13.8	0.3	0.4	1.0	1.7	6.6	6.8	7.2	7.4	5.3	23.6	28.9	13.1	1.1	74.8	40.2	49.9	50.1
32578	NICEVILLE	89.8	85.7	3.8	5.1	2.6	3.9	3.5	6.0	5.5	5.9	6.4	6.6	5.5	23.1	31.1	14.4	1.6	78.3	42.8	49.1	50.9
32579	SHALIMAR	84.9	79.9	7.2	9.0	3.1	4.6	4.6	7.4	5.0	5.0	5.4	6.1	5.7	23.9	30.2	16.7	1.8	80.8	44.0	48.5	51.5
32580	VALPARAISO	87.8	82.9	4.1	5.3	3.2	4.9	4.1	6.9	5.5	5.5	5.5	5.8	5.4	23.3	29.8	16.5	2.5	80.0	44.1	48.6	51.4
32583	MILTON	87.1	83.6	8.0	10.2	0.8	1.2	2.5	3.8	6.4	6.4	6.4	6.1	6.6	28.6	28.7	10.1	0.8	77.2	38.0	53.3	46.7
32601	GAINESVILLE	67.3	60.3	21.8	25.0	6.4	8.8	7.4	11.0	2.9	2.4	2.5	12.0	37.6	24.8	11.8	4.7	1.3	90.3	24.0	49.9	50.1
32603	GAINESVILLE	77.4	70.3	7.1	8.8	10.1	13.6	10.3	15.2	2.2	1.2	1.0	32.7	37.0	18.2	5.2	2.0	0.6	95.0	21.8	52.7	47.3
32605	GAINESVILLE	86.7	81.4	7.0	9.5	3.2	4.8	5.6	8.9	4.8	4.5	5.0	6.1	8.1	26.3	29.0	13.8	2.5	82.1	41.2	47.6	52.4
32606	GAINESVILLE	85.5	80.0	6.4	8.5	4.9	7.1	6.3	9.9	6.0	5.9	6.2	6.8	6.6	27.7	27.4	10.9	2.4	77.8	38.6	47.6	52.4
32607	GAINESVILLE	76.1	70.2	14.8	17.6	3.9	5.8	7.6	11.3	4.8	3.9	3.9	8.2	26.5	27.1	17.8	6.5	1.4	84.8	26.1	50.2	49.8
32608	GAINESVILLE	79.1	73.0	10.7	13.2	5.4	7.5	7.6	11.2	4.3	3.7	3.4	9.2	30.7	25.6	16.0	6.1	1.0	86.5	24.8	49.1	50.9
32609	GAINESVILLE	54.1	46.3	41.1	47.9	0.8	1.0	4.1	5.7	5.9	5.7	5.9	8.3	9.7	30.9	24.5	8.1	1.1	77.9	34.0	52.2	47.8
32611	GAINESVILLE	70.7	62.1	12.3	15.2	10.8	14.4	11.3	16.3	1.2	0.6	0.4	60.4	28.3	8.1	0.3	0.7	0.0	97.4	19.0	46.1	53.9
32615	ALACHUA	77.3	72.3	19.7	23.4	0.8	1.4	4.0	6.1	6.2	6.7	7.2	7.1	5.3	23.9	31.7	10.7	1.3	75.4	40.3	48.3	51.7
32617	ANTHONY	82.0	75.4	13.5	18.5	0.3	0.4	4.7	7.3	6.4	6.7	6.9	6.6	5.8	25.8	29.2	11.5	1.1	76.0	39.3	51.0	49.0
32618	ARCHER	79.9	74.2	16.8	21.1	1.2	2.0	3.3	5.3	6.1	6.6	7.2	7.1	5.0	24.9	32.4	9.8	1.1	75.7	40.4	48.9	51.1
32619	BELL	95.4	94.1	2.4	3.0	0.1	0.1	2.2	3.6	5.8	6.0	6.3	6.8	6.9	22.7	29.2	14.8	1.5	77.5	41.3	51.2	48.8
32621	BRONSON	84.6	79.6	10.6	14.2	0.1	0.2	6.3	9.5	6.2	6.2	6.5	6.7	6.1	26.1	28.6	12.2	1.6	77.1	39.2	48.9	51.1
32622	BROOKER	84.5	79.7	13.6	17.8	0.2	0.2	1.8	2.7	4.9	5.1	5.6	5.7	5.6	30.4	28.3	12.8	1.6	81.0	40.6	55.1	44.9
32625	CEDAR KEY	97.7	96.8	0.6	0.8	0.2	0.4	1.2	2.1	4.7	5.3	5.4	4.7	3.1	19.3	35.6	19.8	2.0	81.7	50.1	48.1	51.9
32626	CHIEFLAND	86.7	82.2	10.6	14.2	0.6	0.9	2.5	4.0	6.1	6.0	6.0	6.3	5.2	20.9	28.8	18.5	2.2	77.9	44.6	48.6	51.4
32628	CROSS CITY	72.3	65.6	25.1	31.0	0.5	0.7	2.0	3.0	5.9	6.0	5.6	5.4	7.2	35.2	22.9	10.3	1.5	79.1	36.3	61.1	38.9
32631	EARLETON	91.0	87.2	6.5	9.3	0.2	0.5	1.9	2.8	4.0	4.5	5.0	5.2	4.5	22.8	37.5	14.8	1.7	83.5	47.1	51.3	48.7
32640	HAWTHORNE	78.8	71.8	18.5	24.7	0.1	0.2	2.4	4.0	5.3	5.6	5.9	6.5	5.2	22.3	31.8	15.7	1.8	79.1	44.4	49.6	50.4
32641	GAINESVILLE	22.8	18.2	75.0	79.5	0.2	0.2	1.3	1.7	8.8	8.5	8.2	9.2	8.0	22.7	23.7	9.6	1.3	69.1	30.4	45.4	54.6
32643	HIGH SPRINGS	84.2	79.9	13.2	16.5	0.3	0.4	3.6	5.6	5.7	5.9	6.4	6.6	5.7	24.2	31.4	12.2	1.8	77.8	41.7	48.6	51.4
32648	HORSESHOE BEACH	98.1	97.4	1.0	1.4	0.0	0.0	0.2	0.2	4.9	4.9	5.1	6.5	4.7	22.1	29.8	20.0	2.1	81.2	46.4	49.5	50.5
32653	GAINESVILLE	80.5	74.3	13.5	17.2	3.6	5.1	5.2	7.8	6.4	6.4	6.8	6.3	5.5	24.3	30.5	11.8	2.1	76.5	41.2	46.9	53.1
32656	KEYSTONE HEIGHTS	96.3	95.1	1.4	1.7	0.3	0.5	1.8	2.9	5.6	5.9	6.3	6.9	5.7	22.7	30.6	14.1	2.2	77.9	42.7	49.0	51.0
32666	MELROSE	88.2	85.5	8.7	10.3	0.6	0.9	2.2	3.5	4.7	4.9	5.8	5.7	4.3	20.8	33.9	17.5	2.4	81.0	47.4	50.1	49.9
32667	MICANOPY	79.3	72.0	18.2	24.6	0.3	0.4	3.5	5.6	4.0	4.6	5.6	5.6	4.3	21.1	36.9	15.8	2.3	82.2	47.9	49.7	50.3
32668	MORRISTON	91.6	88.5	5.3	7.0	0.4	0.6	5.7	9.1	5.4	5.4	5.7	6.0	3.8	22.7	33.7	15.5	1.7	79.4	45.6	49.7	50.3
32669	NEWBERRY	84.6	78.9	12.8	17.3	0.6	1.1	2.9	4.7	6.2	6.4	6.7	6.7	5.5	26.1	30.6	10.5	1.2	76.6	39.4	49.7	50.3
32680	OLD TOWN	95.9	94.4	2.0	2.7	0.2	0.3	1.9	3.0	5.4	5.5	5.6	5.4	4.4	20.6	30.5	20.8	1.8	80.2	47.3	50.3	49.7
32686	REDDICK	63.1	54.1	33.7	41.5	0.3	0.4	5.1	7.3	5.8	6.4	6.9	6.5	5.1	22.2	32.1	13.3	1.7	76.6	42.8	49.0	51.0
32693	TRENTON	87.6	84.1	9.7	12.3	0.2	0.3	3.2	5.1	5.8	5.9	6.1	7.4	11.2	21.8	26.1	13.9	1.9	78.3	38.1	52.6	47.4
32694	WALDO	82.9	77.6	13.5	17.8	0.3	0.5	2.0	3.3	5.4	5.6	6.2	6.0	5.0	23.0	33.2	13.9	1.8	79.2	44.2	49.2	50.8
32696	WILLISTON	74.6	70.3	21.9	25.1	0.4	0.6	5.2	7.7	6.2	6.0	6.6	7.0	5.4	23.1	29.2	14.2	2.3	76.8	41.6	48.3	51.7
32701	ALTAMONTE SPRINGS	77.2	71.7	13.5	15.3	2.1	2.8	14.0	21.2	5.9	5.2	4.9	5.5	7.9	29.3	25.8	12.9	2.7	80.7	38.7	48.2	51.8
32702	ALTOONA	94.8	92.6	2.4	3.5	0.2	0.3	2.7	4.1	5.7	6.1	6.3	6.2	4.7	23.0	29.3	16.4	2.4	78.2	43.6	49.8	50.2
32703	APOPKA	71.4	65.5	18.5	20.6	2.0	2.8	16.3	23.8	8.0	7.4	7.0	7.0	7.4	29.0	24.1	8.7	1.4	73.3	33.9	49.2	50.8
32707	CASSELBERRY	86.0	80.9	6.0	7.7	2.3	3.2	12.9	20.2	5.6	5.5	5.7	6.0	6.5	28.3	28.3	12.2	1.8	79.6	39.6	48.9	51.1
32708	WINTER SPRINGS	88.0	83.9	4.5	5.5	2.4	3.5	11.4	17.6	5.8	6.2	6.7	7.3	5.8	25.6	30.9	10.2	1.5	76.6	40.0	48.6	51.4
32709	CHRISTMAS	95.8	93.5	0.5	0.8	0.9	1.4	3.4	6.1	5.5	5.7	6.3	7.3	5.6	24.4	32.6	11.7	1.0	78.1	41.8	50.9	49.1
32712	APOPKA	83.6	78.0	9.0	11.6	1.8	2.4	12.2	18.9	6.9	7.1	7.4	7.1	5.0	25.3	28.9	11.1	1.3	74.2	39.2	49.1	50.9
32713	DEBARY	94.8	91.9	1.9	3.2	1.1	1.8	4.6	7.8	4.5	4.8	5.4	5.6	3.9	19.7	32.6	20.3	3.2	81.6	48.9	47.9	52.1
32714	ALTAMONTE SPRINGS	79.2	73.3	9.2	10.9	3.0	4.1	17.9	26.1	6.3	5.5	5.3	5.9	8.4	34.3	24.4	8.8	1.1	79.5	35.0	48.8	51.2
32720	DELAND	81.1	77.4	14.1	16.0	0.6	1.0	6.6	9.7	5.3	5.5	5.6	6.5	5.8	23.0	28.3	16.1	3.9	79.9	43.7	48.3	51.7
32724	DELAND	87.4	82.9	7.7	10.2	0.9	1.5	7.1	10.7	5.3	5.3	5.5	7.3	7.0	20.6	26.7	18.3	4.1	80.4	44.1	47.1	52.9
32725	DELTONA	85.2	78.8	6.1	9.0	1.1	1.5	18.4	27.5	5.7	5.8	6.2	6.4	5.2	23.8	28.6	15.5	2.8	78.2	42.7	47.8	52.2
32726	EUSTIS	78.9	74.8	17.1	20.1	0.8	1.0	6.0	7.9	5.8	5.5	5.4	5.8	5.4	20.3	25.3	21.5	5.0	79.8	46.4	46.5	53.5
32730	CASSELBERRY	83.5	78.1	8.6	10.6	1.7	2.3	14.6	22.5	6.3	5.8	5.4	5.1	6.3	28.5	24.6	14.8	3.0	79.6	39.3	47.8	52.2
32732	GENEVA	93.5	91.2	3.8	5.2	0.7	1.0	2.8	4.9	5.0	5.8	6.5	7.0	4.7	22.7	35.7	11.2	1.5	78.2	43.9	51.5	48.5
32735	GRAND ISLAND	96.0	94.1	1.7	2.5	0.4	0.6	4.8	7.4	4.7	5.3	5.2	5.1	3.2	18.9	26.3	26.9	4.3	81.2	51.4	48.8	51.2
32736	EUSTIS	95.6	93.8	1.2	1.8	0.5	0.7	4.1	6.3	5.4	5.9	6.5	7.1	4.9	22.3	32.2	14.2	1.5	77.8	43.5	50.7	49.3
32738	DELTONA	83.9	76.7	7.8	11.4	0.8	1.1	17.1	25.8	6.8	7.1	7.3	7.7	6.0	27.1	27.3	9.5	1.2	74.0	36.5	48.8	51.2
32744	LAKE HELEN	88.9	82.9	8.1	12.5	0.4	0.6	5.1	8.4	5.2	5.6	5.9	6.0	4.9	22.3	31.2	16.6	2.2	79.6	45.0	48.4	51.6
32746	LAKE MARY	84.4	78.9	6.0	8.0	4.6	6.2	9.8	14.7	6.5	6.6	7.2	6.9	5.6	28.7	28.6	8.8	1.0	75.3	37.8	49.3	50.7
32750	LONGWOOD	88.4	83.8	3.7	4.7	2.7	4.0	9.3	14.9	5.7	5.9	6.3	6.6	5.0	25.3	29.9	12.7	2.5	77.8	41.8	49.3	50.7
32751	MAITLAND	82.7	76.9	12.4	15.7	1.4	2.3	7.1	11.7	5.8	5.9	6.5	6.6	5.6	23.6	28.7	14.1	3.1	77.6	42.1	47.4	52.6
32754	MIMS	88.2	86.1	9.5	11.0	0.4	0.5	1.2	2.0	4.6	5.5	5.4	6.1	5.0	20.4	31.7	19.5	1.8	80.7	46.8	49.6	50.4
32757	MOUNT DORA	82.0	77.2	14.0	17.4	0.9	1.3	7.5	10.1	5.5	5.5	5.8	5.7	4.6	20.3	28.3	19.7	4.7	79.7	46.9	47.4	52.6
32759	OAK HILL	88.1	83.8	9.7	13.4	0.4	0.6	1.0	1.6	3.9	4.2	4.4	4.2	3.4	17.0	30.0	29.8	3.1	84.9	54.5	49.5	50.5
	FLORIDA	78.0	74.7	14.6	15.8	1.7	2.3	16.8	21.5	6.0	5.9	5.9	6.3	6.2	25.0	26.8	15.3	2.8	78.6	41.1	48.8	51.2
	UNITED STATES	75.1	72.0	12.3	12.7	3.8	4.6	12.5	15.7	6.8	6.7	6.6	7.1	6.9	27.0	26.0	10.9	1.9	75.7	36.9	49.2	50.8

ZIP CODE #	POST OFFICE NAME	2009 Per Capita Income	2009 HH Income Base	2009 Household Income Distribution (%): Less than $25,000	$25,000 to $49,999	$50,000 to $99,999	$100,000 to $149,999	$150,000 or More	Median Household Income: 2009	2014	2009 National Centile	2009 State Centile	2009 Home Value Base	2009 Home Value Distribution (%): Less than $50,000	$50,000 to $89,999	$90,000 to $174,999	$175,000 to $399,999	$400,000 or More	2009 Median Home Value
32501	PENSACOLA	18498	4674	47.1	26.9	19.2	2.9	3.9	26751	27700	4	2	2482	22.2	27.5	28.5	18.7	3.0	90565
32502	PENSACOLA	20161	1666	40.6	31.0	22.4	3.4	2.5	30638	31977	9	6	922	21.0	40.5	23.9	9.1	5.5	76000
32503	PENSACOLA	25296	13663	28.0	28.1	31.2	7.7	5.1	44051	46565	46	40	8763	8.0	19.5	43.8	23.0	5.6	121596
32504	PENSACOLA	29982	10084	18.3	29.4	36.9	9.9	5.5	51866	52637	66	62	6596	2.1	13.4	51.6	27.0	5.9	137305
32505	PENSACOLA	15532	11446	40.0	31.3	23.3	3.8	1.6	31539	33576	11	7	7135	22.6	46.0	23.9	6.6	0.9	73655
32506	PENSACOLA	22761	14592	24.3	29.7	36.0	7.1	2.9	45772	49592	51	46	8951	9.7	23.6	46.2	18.8	1.7	114824
32507	PENSACOLA	24133	12797	25.5	28.4	33.4	8.0	4.8	45565	48360	50	45	8460	9.5	24.2	31.6	25.9	8.7	126766
32508	PENSACOLA	16033	328	7.3	52.4	32.9	5.8	1.5	45678	46703	50	45	24	0.0	75.0	8.3	16.7	0.0	56667
32514	PENSACOLA	27184	15995	20.5	28.7	37.4	9.2	4.2	50681	51836	63	58	9285	4.5	15.5	51.5	25.4	3.1	133617
32526	PENSACOLA	23418	14292	18.1	29.2	42.1	7.4	3.3	52060	52335	66	63	11172	10.2	20.0	49.5	18.0	2.4	114453
32531	BAKER	19009	2032	27.2	32.3	33.2	5.4	1.9	40767	44071	35	30	1694	14.9	25.0	37.5	17.9	4.7	106757
32533	CANTONMENT	23983	10049	19.8	25.4	40.0	9.8	5.0	54296	54321	70	68	8392	8.8	15.8	40.8	31.9	2.7	137163
32534	PENSACOLA	22447	5536	27.6	28.9	33.3	6.6	3.7	43710	46640	44	39	4064	14.1	21.6	37.6	25.2	1.4	115614
32535	CENTURY	15694	2177	42.0	29.9	24.1	3.0	0.9	30199	31338	8	5	1673	39.4	25.2	25.9	8.7	0.8	67500
32536	CRESTVIEW	22410	6801	21.5	29.5	37.0	8.5	3.5	49129	52430	59	54	5057	7.9	16.5	55.4	19.3	0.9	127383
32539	CRESTVIEW	21052	8518	20.8	30.0	38.6	7.7	2.8	49135	51702	59	54	6598	10.5	16.0	52.5	19.9	1.1	118571
32541	DESTIN	40148	9404	11.4	22.5	39.7	16.7	9.7	67172	68268	85	86	6756	1.2	2.2	21.2	48.7	26.8	256423
32542	EGLIN AFB	14856	3126	10.8	51.7	32.1	3.9	1.6	41629	44113	38	33	475	43.4	3.8	9.5	36.4	6.9	119167
32544	HURLBURT FIELD	21554	103	14.6	35.9	36.9	8.7	3.9	49324	51949	60	55	26	3.8	0.0	0.0	84.6	11.5	281818
32547	FORT WALTON BEACH	26175	13851	16.8	33.8	37.6	8.0	3.7	49496	52118	60	55	7782	8.7	12.4	47.2	27.2	4.5	138553
32548	FORT WALTON BEACH	27054	10559	19.3	30.5	37.6	8.8	3.8	50157	52384	62	57	6346	3.2	12.5	56.3	22.7	5.3	135066
32550	MIRAMAR BEACH	38301	4363	17.0	25.9	36.8	11.0	9.1	56940	54626	74	72	3693	0.0	0.6	14.6	50.1	34.7	308225
32561	GULF BREEZE	46094	3756	14.4	19.9	33.8	14.7	17.1	69463	70853	86	88	2925	1.2	0.9	23.1	44.5	30.3	261552
32563	GULF BREEZE	32453	8623	13.2	22.0	38.0	16.2	10.6	65523	66278	84	84	6881	3.8	4.4	30.1	43.0	18.7	205703
32564	HOLT	17529	1143	30.6	27.8	37.0	3.0	1.6	42278	46080	40	35	965	24.5	34.3	25.9	14.7	0.6	75377
32565	JAY	18174	2261	33.6	29.1	29.9	5.7	1.8	37312	40905	25	20	1881	26.2	30.1	31.1	11.3	1.3	80954
32566	NAVARRE	23906	11326	15.2	25.9	45.5	9.1	4.3	56814	58177	74	72	9159	8.1	9.1	40.1	33.9	8.8	156907
32567	LAUREL HILL	15870	1627	41.1	31.3	23.4	2.8	1.4	31636	33480	11	8	1367	24.9	23.0	33.9	16.0	2.2	94318
32568	MC DAVID	18857	1312	26.2	31.8	35.2	4.8	2.0	43896	46560	45	39	1134	27.6	26.7	30.3	11.7	3.2	83194
32569	MARY ESTHER	26519	5002	11.6	29.0	45.7	8.8	4.9	55702	56944	72	71	3372	4.4	8.9	54.5	26.4	5.8	148100
32570	MILTON	20453	10758	26.3	27.2	37.1	6.8	2.6	46393	50397	53	48	7904	11.3	22.2	45.5	18.7	2.4	113917
32571	MILTON	24375	10511	17.9	25.2	37.6	13.9	5.4	56165	58437	73	71	8742	9.2	14.7	41.3	30.0	4.7	138168
32577	MOLINO	22310	1844	17.7	30.0	39.3	10.2	2.7	52056	53556	66	63	1584	13.2	20.5	35.5	27.2	3.6	125935
32578	NICEVILLE	33132	12528	12.7	20.6	38.2	17.3	11.2	67742	68115	85	86	9100	3.5	4.6	33.8	47.8	10.3	194418
32579	SHALIMAR	33172	4583	12.9	21.5	41.8	16.3	7.4	65615	66008	84	84	3112	2.4	2.7	31.4	48.0	15.5	218939
32580	VALPARAISO	25658	1766	20.4	26.3	42.0	8.8	2.4	52919	55324	68	65	1158	2.8	8.0	57.8	25.5	5.9	137430
32583	MILTON	20149	8243	23.3	31.7	35.5	6.3	3.2	45277	49158	49	43	6831	15.9	24.7	37.9	18.0	3.6	102990
32601	GAINESVILLE	15641	9609	54.8	26.7	14.9	2.3	1.3	21882	22413	2	2	2187	8.3	27.6	42.8	18.3	3.0	106309
32603	GAINESVILLE	15644	2294	62.7	24.1	8.4	3.3	1.5	17305	17422	1	1	379	3.4	0.0	28.2	59.6	8.7	207836
32605	GAINESVILLE	34693	11226	17.9	23.3	34.7	14.1	10.0	61507	60059	79	79	7669	0.7	4.2	47.5	41.7	5.9	170377
32606	GAINESVILLE	34118	8837	13.1	23.4	38.4	15.9	9.3	62610	61395	81	81	5709	0.4	2.7	29.8	56.4	10.6	206947
32607	GAINESVILLE	24044	13192	38.4	24.7	23.9	7.4	5.5	34699	38506	17	13	4940	6.9	11.8	33.4	37.5	10.4	170247
32608	GAINESVILLE	23869	17677	42.3	25.0	20.6	6.4	5.7	31334	34404	10	7	6541	12.8	12.2	26.8	33.6	14.7	170048
32609	GAINESVILLE	17449	7603	34.1	35.4	25.7	3.8	0.9	34189	36499	16	12	4267	15.2	28.6	48.1	7.6	0.5	95107
32611	GAINESVILLE	15112	214	88.8	8.4	2.8	0.0	0.0	12904	12848	1	0	0	0.0	0.0	0.0	0.0	0.0	0
32615	ALACHUA	25707	5987	25.1	24.1	35.7	9.1	6.1	50945	51870	63	59	4674	7.4	17.7	36.2	30.2	8.5	143610
32617	ANTHONY	18236	1582	25.1	34.5	32.7	5.6	2.2	40943	45091	36	30	1260	9.6	22.4	32.5	22.5	12.9	130189
32618	ARCHER	24680	3859	21.1	24.5	40.3	9.7	4.4	53500	53759	69	66	3179	8.4	20.1	33.7	31.5	6.3	138308
32619	BELL	17164	1840	34.9	31.2	28.3	3.8	1.8	35565	36604	19	16	1584	14.8	30.2	31.9	21.7	1.3	98061
32621	BRONSON	16490	1785	33.7	37.5	22.1	4.9	1.8	32874	34496	13	10	1547	15.8	32.6	34.5	14.3	2.7	93357
32622	BROOKER	20357	655	22.4	36.3	36.0	4.1	1.1	41854	44371	39	34	550	13.6	23.5	41.3	18.7	2.9	118304
32625	CEDAR KEY	22575	938	31.0	32.7	27.4	6.0	2.9	38282	40730	28	23	771	6.2	13.6	25.7	41.5	13.0	185648
32626	CHIEFLAND	17134	3990	37.1	34.1	23.6	4.2	1.1	31883	32893	11	8	3199	14.8	27.2	35.6	20.1	2.2	104299
32628	CROSS CITY	15134	1311	43.1	30.9	21.3	3.5	1.2	28706	29100	6	4	1014	23.9	26.1	36.7	12.0	1.3	90000
32631	EARLETON	21464	244	23.4	29.1	37.7	7.8	2.0	47862	48500	56	50	192	6.8	14.6	41.7	27.1	9.9	148864
32640	HAWTHORNE	19550	4984	29.9	29.3	33.4	5.8	1.6	41230	43891	37	31	4069	14.7	21.1	36.9	22.4	4.9	114527
32641	GAINESVILLE	13690	4919	43.6	30.0	22.1	3.0	1.3	29262	30364	7	4	2929	12.1	45.1	36.5	4.5	1.8	81824
32643	HIGH SPRINGS	19589	4213	29.5	28.5	35.3	4.8	1.8	42103	44946	40	34	3418	12.6	20.6	44.9	19.8	2.2	115723
32648	HORSESHOE BEACH	22119	181	26.0	29.3	33.1	9.4	2.2	44305	47366	46	40	158	19.0	27.8	27.8	22.8	2.5	100000
32653	GAINESVILLE	31112	5346	14.3	25.0	39.1	14.0	7.7	61295	60917	79	79	4203	3.8	7.8	46.5	36.7	5.3	160989
32656	KEYSTONE HEIGHTS	22588	5932	19.9	31.6	39.3	7.0	2.1	48665	49258	58	53	4968	11.2	22.8	42.4	20.0	3.6	118767
32666	MELROSE	24195	2355	23.8	31.1	34.7	6.2	4.2	45344	47324	49	44	1937	10.3	17.0	34.2	32.7	5.8	141186
32667	MICANOPY	28080	2259	25.5	23.9	34.4	10.5	5.8	50704	52588	63	58	1754	11.5	18.9	27.8	30.4	11.4	143235
32668	MORRISTON	20464	2139	30.4	31.5	29.4	4.9	3.7	37995	40020	27	22	1878	10.4	20.1	36.1	24.6	8.8	129023
32669	NEWBERRY	21345	4000	24.1	29.8	37.0	6.5	2.7	45428	48578	50	44	3232	8.7	21.3	35.1	28.7	6.2	133457
32680	OLD TOWN	18247	4317	40.0	30.5	23.5	3.8	2.1	31700	33067	11	8	3796	20.9	28.0	32.3	13.2	5.6	92028
32686	REDDICK	22555	2688	32.8	26.6	27.3	6.7	6.6	38769	41320	29	25	2140	18.6	21.0	24.5	18.4	17.5	116784
32693	TRENTON	17472	4443	32.5	34.7	26.7	4.3	1.9	34557	35540	17	13	3688	15.5	26.0	39.6	15.5	3.4	105928
32694	WALDO	23904	883	30.4	30.0	29.9	4.9	4.9	41206	44021	37	31	691	16.8	22.3	38.2	13.9	8.8	107901
32696	WILLISTON	19105	4607	33.6	32.7	25.3	6.0	2.4	35868	37144	20	16	3753	12.8	24.1	36.7	21.4	5.0	115809
32701	ALTAMONTE SPRINGS	29255	10434	18.2	30.1	35.5	11.6	4.5	51643	52800	65	61	5601	2.7	13.1	49.7	32.3	2.2	144118
32702	ALTOONA	17858	1323	31.8	31.1	32.0	4.5	0.5	39672	43937	32	26	1018	24.3	23.5	27.2	21.1	3.9	95476
32703	APOPKA	22991	17103	19.1	29.7	37.2	9.7	4.3	50925	52993	63	59	11441	10.2	11.3	49.4	25.6	3.5	136720
32707	CASSELBERRY	28356	14624	16.3	25.5	39.7	13.1	5.4	56997	57970	74	73	10200	6.9	7.1	56.2	28.8	1.0	142902
32708	WINTER SPRINGS	34201	16164	8.7	20.7	37.0	21.0	12.7	69971	75621	87	88	12796	3.6	6.1	34.9	46.5	9.0	186322
32709	CHRISTMAS	22036	919	15.5	37.8	34.4	6.4	6.0	47735	51900	56	50	753	15.8	24.3	27.1	24.4	8.4	112331
32712	APOPKA	27497	13721	14.7	24.2	40.0	12.5	8.6	61569	62380	79	79	11425	9.6	9.5	33.6	42.7	4.6	167192
32713	DEBARY	28607	8185	17.9	28.2	37.9	9.3	6.6	53733	54210	69	67	6965	5.6	17.5	38.5	35.1	3.3	135755
32714	ALTAMONTE SPRINGS	29581	15397	12.7	29.2	39.8	13.2	5.0	56822	57650	74	72	7244	2.0	9.3	48.1	35.7	4.9	156339
32720	DELAND	22292	11435	27.7	30.5	31.3	6.5	3.9	41629	45167	38	33	7998	7.3	19.3	45.0	24.6	3.8	123090
32724	DELAND	23967	12615	23.7	34.8	30.3	7.1	4.1	43014	45753	42	37	9339	10.7	22.3	40.9	22.6	3.5	116880
32725	DELTONA	22176	16975	17.2	33.9	37.9	7.6	3.3	49006	50393	59	53	14222	2.2	15.3	63.0	18.5	1.0	129777
32726	EUSTIS	23178	8896	31.0	28.5	29.4	7.7	3.5	41244	44966	37	32	6114	13.2	17.1	40.7	20.6	8.4	119718
32730	CASSELBERRY	30016	2359	18.2	26.4	37.5	13.0	4.8	55188	56916	71	70	1366	1.1	2.5	51.2	43.7	1.5	167949
32732	GENEVA	29089	2217	11.3	23.6	39.5	16.3	9.3	62869	64592	81	81	1890	4.5	8.6	37.4	36.6	13.0	173519
32735	GRAND ISLAND	24488	1461	24.5	33.5	30.0	8.6	3.3	44118	46429	46	40	1296	27.9	14.7	29.9	23.7	3.9	107470
32736	EUSTIS	24903	3620	23.5	26.2	33.5	11.0	5.8	50337	51660	62	57	3129	11.6	19.5	28.2	31.1	9.6	139138
32738	DELTONA	20406	14506	13.6	32.2	43.9	7.5	2.7	52899	53623	68	64	12570	0.7	10.1	72.3	16.4	0.5	129627
32744	LAKE HELEN	21330	1437	20.7	37.1	34.8	5.8	1.7	45058	46709	48	43	1229	12.7	21.5	46.7	18.3	0.8	114117
32746	LAKE MARY	39383	14299	10.2	17.2	36.8	20.0	15.9	76816	82120	90	93	9910	0.5	3.3	26.7	54.8	14.7	220141
32750	LONGWOOD	31407	8664	9.9	19.7	41.3	20.0	9.0	70749	76250	87	89	6840	0.7	5.1	40.7	49.3	4.2	180769
32751	MAITLAND	36727	8392	16.8	22.3	33.4	14.7	12.9	63217	64897	81	81	5544	0.6	5.9	28.7	44.1	20.7	226058
32754	MIMS	21371	4447	28.9	26.7	34.8	6.9	2.7	44652	48030	47	41	3814	19.2	27.0	29.3	21.6	2.9	95637
32757	MOUNT DORA	26633	9797	24.6	27.1	34.7	8.2	5.4	48533	50768	58	52	7039	9.3	10.5	40.7	27.4	11.9	147284
32759	OAK HILL	20474	1439	31.6	35.0	25.9	5.6	2.0	36548	39661	22	17	1202	14.2	27.6	39.9	15.8	2.4	104310
	FLORIDA	27128		21.9	27.6	33.8	9.8	6.8	50413	52516				8.0	14.3	38.7	30.4	8.6	144752
	UNITED STATES	27277		20.9	24.4	35.3	11.7	7.6	54719	56938				9.3	13.1	31.6	32.6	13.5	162279

ZIP CODE #	POST OFFICE NAME	FINANCIAL SERVICES: Auto Loan	Home Loan	Investments	Retirement Plans	THE HOME: Home Improvements: Home Repair	Lawn & Garden	Furnishings: Computers & Hardware Personal	Major Appliances	TV, Radio, Sound Equipment	Furniture	ENTERTAINMENT: Dine out/ Carry out	Sports Equipment	Fees & Tickets	Toys & Games	Travel	Cable TV	PERSONAL: Apparel & Services	Auto Repairs	Health Insurance	Pets & Supplies
32501	PENSACOLA	61	50	49	52	49	57	59	56	63	57	62	42	55	62	54	67	43	60	65	69
32502	PENSACOLA	62	52	52	53	52	60	61	59	64	57	63	44	55	63	55	68	43	62	67	71
32503	PENSACOLA	83	77	76	79	77	83	82	81	85	81	85	60	80	84	80	88	59	84	88	97
32504	PENSACOLA	90	91	90	92	91	94	93	91	93	92	93	69	94	92	93	95	65	93	97	108
32505	PENSACOLA	59	52	45	53	48	57	57	54	61	55	60	42	54	61	52	64	41	58	62	68
32506	PENSACOLA	81	76	69	76	74	76	79	78	80	78	79	60	75	82	75	80	55	78	80	91
32507	PENSACOLA	89	83	81	82	81	86	84	85	85	84	85	65	80	87	81	87	59	85	88	101
32508	PENSACOLA	95	51	38	58	45	43	90	63	84	84	89	62	69	101	65	78	62	79	56	76
32514	PENSACOLA	86	81	79	82	81	84	88	84	89	86	88	65	85	88	85	90	61	88	91	100
32526	PENSACOLA	90	87	78	86	84	91	83	87	85	83	85	65	81	87	81	88	58	85	90	103
32531	BAKER	83	68	71	66	68	79	67	75	71	67	71	56	59	74	63	76	48	72	77	90
32533	CANTONMENT	95	97	90	96	94	100	89	94	91	90	91	71	90	93	91	93	63	91	96	111
32534	PENSACOLA	83	78	79	77	76	87	75	82	79	74	78	61	72	79	75	82	53	79	86	97
32535	CENTURY	69	48	62	46	47	67	51	61	58	50	57	46	41	59	47	64	38	59	66	75
32536	CRESTVIEW	91	86	81	84	84	87	84	87	85	85	85	67	80	87	81	86	58	85	87	102
32539	CRESTVIEW	88	84	77	82	81	84	81	84	81	81	81	64	77	84	78	82	56	81	83	98
32541	DESTIN	122	132	130	134	132	126	126	124	123	130	125	96	133	124	131	122	88	125	123	146
32542	EGLIN AFB	88	46	34	53	41	39	83	58	78	77	82	57	63	94	60	72	58	73	52	70
32544	HURLBURT FIELD	106	55	41	64	49	47	100	69	94	93	99	69	76	113	72	86	69	88	62	84
32547	FORT WALTON BEACH	85	80	74	81	78	78	87	81	86	85	87	63	84	87	83	86	61	85	84	96
32548	FORT WALTON BEACH	84	82	76	83	80	83	86	82	87	84	87	64	85	87	84	88	61	86	87	98
32550	MIRAMAR BEACH	104	109	148	108	126	129	98	116	104	111	102	72	108	93	114	108	70	111	129	131
32561	GULF BREEZE	137	157	176	157	168	167	141	154	144	150	143	106	157	136	158	147	100	149	166	175
32563	GULF BREEZE	119	131	126	132	131	127	118	123	116	124	117	92	126	118	124	116	83	119	119	143
32564	HOLT	80	59	78	58	61	80	60	74	66	58	65	56	50	67	59	72	43	69	77	88
32565	JAY	83	61	84	60	63	84	62	78	69	59	68	58	51	69	61	75	45	72	81	92
32566	NAVARRE	103	101	88	99	98	99	93	98	94	97	95	73	92	99	91	95	65	94	96	115
32567	LAUREL HILL	70	50	72	49	52	71	51	65	57	48	56	49	41	57	51	63	37	60	68	78
32568	MC DAVID	88	63	90	61	65	89	64	82	71	60	70	61	52	71	64	79	46	75	85	97
32569	MARY ESTHER	100	87	79	89	84	86	98	91	96	97	97	72	90	99	90	95	67	95	91	109
32570	MILTON	83	79	76	78	77	85	76	81	79	76	79	61	75	80	76	82	54	79	84	96
32571	MILTON	108	106	98	103	103	104	98	103	98	102	99	79	96	102	97	98	68	99	99	121
32577	MOLINO	98	82	87	83	83	101	82	94	87	76	85	71	72	89	80	93	58	87	98	111
32578	NICEVILLE	117	126	120	129	125	124	118	120	116	120	117	91	124	118	123	116	83	118	120	140
32579	SHALIMAR	108	113	109	113	113	112	108	110	108	112	109	81	113	109	111	109	76	109	113	127
32580	VALPARAISO	82	84	83	84	85	89	81	85	83	82	83	62	83	82	84	86	57	84	91	98
32583	MILTON	86	79	77	77	78	83	76	81	78	78	78	60	72	80	74	80	53	79	81	96
32601	GAINESVILLE	48	28	26	31	26	30	60	37	52	45	52	35	41	51	39	50	37	47	39	48
32603	GAINESVILLE	43	22	21	25	20	24	57	32	47	41	48	32	37	46	34	44	34	42	32	42
32605	GAINESVILLE	112	111	109	114	112	112	117	111	114	115	115	85	116	114	114	114	81	114	115	130
32606	GAINESVILLE	115	117	109	120	114	108	117	111	114	120	116	88	119	117	116	111	82	113	108	131
32607	GAINESVILLE	78	50	48	56	48	51	94	61	82	76	84	58	70	82	66	77	59	76	61	79
32608	GAINESVILLE	78	51	49	56	48	53	94	62	82	75	83	57	69	81	65	78	58	76	63	79
32609	GAINESVILLE	64	51	50	52	49	56	61	57	62	58	62	45	54	63	54	63	43	60	60	70
32611	GAINESVILLE	24	10	10	13	9	12	34	17	27	23	28	18	20	27	18	25	20	24	17	23
32615	ALACHUA	99	96	89	94	94	98	90	95	92	93	92	70	88	94	88	94	63	92	95	112
32617	ANTHONY	82	68	74	65	68	79	66	76	70	66	70	56	58	72	64	74	47	71	77	90
32618	ARCHER	96	96	87	96	94	98	89	94	90	90	90	71	89	93	90	92	62	91	94	111
32619	BELL	79	57	75	55	58	78	59	72	65	56	64	54	48	66	57	71	43	67	75	86
32621	BRONSON	71	61	70	58	62	71	60	68	63	61	63	50	54	63	60	67	42	66	71	80
32622	BROOKER	86	62	88	60	64	88	63	81	70	59	69	60	51	70	63	77	46	74	84	96
32625	CEDAR KEY	81	64	104	63	71	85	65	82	68	60	67	60	56	64	70	72	44	76	81	95
32626	CHIEFLAND	68	54	73	51	57	72	54	66	59	53	58	48	47	57	55	64	38	62	71	78
32628	CROSS CITY	70	48	69	45	48	70	51	64	58	47	56	49	39	58	48	64	37	60	68	77
32631	EARLETON	86	74	92	72	77	87	72	84	75	71	75	61	65	75	73	78	50	79	83	98
32640	HAWTHORNE	78	65	80	63	68	81	65	76	70	65	69	55	58	68	65	74	46	72	81	89
32641	GAINESVILLE	55	46	41	48	43	51	52	49	56	51	56	38	49	56	47	59	38	53	56	62
32643	HIGH SPRINGS	82	68	75	66	68	80	67	76	71	66	71	56	60	72	65	75	48	72	78	90
32648	HORSESHOE BEACH	93	66	95	64	69	94	68	87	76	63	74	65	54	75	67	83	49	80	90	103
32653	GAINESVILLE	109	107	104	108	107	109	106	108	106	107	105	81	104	106	105	106	73	107	109	126
32656	KEYSTONE HEIGHTS	90	79	93	77	83	92	78	88	81	78	81	63	72	80	79	85	54	84	91	103
32666	MELROSE	90	77	104	75	84	97	75	91	80	76	79	64	70	77	80	85	53	85	95	105
32667	MICANOPY	95	89	115	88	95	106	86	100	89	85	88	71	83	85	92	93	60	95	104	115
32668	MORRISTON	78	73	88	68	79	85	70	80	73	75	72	54	68	69	74	77	49	78	87	93
32669	NEWBERRY	85	81	72	79	78	83	76	80	78	78	78	60	74	81	74	80	54	78	81	95
32680	OLD TOWN	69	57	77	54	61	74	56	69	61	57	60	49	50	58	58	66	40	65	74	81
32686	REDDICK	102	75	111	72	79	105	77	97	85	73	83	72	63	83	77	92	55	90	100	115
32693	TRENTON	73	62	73	59	63	74	61	70	65	61	64	51	54	64	61	68	43	67	73	83
32694	WALDO	94	71	96	69	73	94	72	88	78	69	77	65	61	78	71	84	51	82	90	104
32696	WILLISTON	78	63	82	60	66	81	64	76	69	63	68	55	56	67	64	74	45	72	81	89
32701	ALTAMONTE SPRINGS	91	80	75	83	78	79	95	83	94	92	95	67	89	94	87	93	66	92	89	102
32702	ALTOONA	77	58	80	56	61	79	59	73	64	56	63	54	49	63	59	70	42	68	77	87
32703	APOPKA	92	87	79	87	84	82	90	86	89	93	90	67	87	91	86	88	63	89	85	102
32707	CASSELBERRY	97	98	93	98	96	94	97	95	96	100	97	73	98	97	97	95	67	96	95	112
32708	WINTER SPRINGS	129	143	131	144	140	131	132	131	127	137	129	103	139	130	136	124	91	129	124	153
32709	CHRISTMAS	99	92	82	89	90	94	86	92	89	90	89	67	82	93	83	92	61	89	92	109
32712	APOPKA	111	118	108	116	116	114	107	112	106	111	107	83	110	109	110	107	75	108	110	129
32713	DEBARY	97	98	114	98	104	111	92	103	95	94	94	72	94	91	99	99	65	99	110	119
32714	ALTAMONTE SPRINGS	102	91	81	95	87	84	102	91	99	103	101	74	97	103	94	96	71	97	89	109
32720	DELAND	79	73	82	73	74	83	74	79	77	71	76	59	71	75	75	80	52	78	85	93
32724	DELAND	81	80	85	80	82	88	80	84	83	80	83	61	81	81	82	87	57	84	92	98
32725	DELTONA	81	88	85	87	87	93	80	86	83	79	82	63	85	82	85	86	57	83	93	100
32726	EUSTIS	78	71	77	71	73	82	75	78	78	73	77	57	72	76	74	82	53	79	87	92
32730	CASSELBERRY	86	92	88	91	91	89	93	89	93	92	94	68	97	92	95	94	66	93	96	105
32732	GENEVA	109	123	106	127	119	121	110	114	108	110	109	89	117	111	116	108	76	110	113	135
32735	GRAND ISLAND	82	78	100	72	87	93	74	88	79	80	77	57	74	72	81	83	52	84	98	100
32736	EUSTIS	106	97	103	95	97	108	91	103	95	92	95	76	87	97	92	99	65	97	104	121
32738	DELTONA	88	95	81	93	90	88	86	87	85	89	86	66	88	88	87	84	59	85	85	102
32744	LAKE HELEN	78	78	80	77	79	86	73	81	75	72	74	59	72	75	76	78	51	77	85	94
32746	LAKE MARY	144	156	147	159	154	138	150	144	142	156	144	116	156	146	152	136	103	143	132	167
32750	LONGWOOD	114	131	122	131	129	121	117	119	114	122	115	91	127	115	123	112	82	116	115	138
32751	MAITLAND	117	129	134	131	133	125	127	124	125	130	126	95	136	123	133	125	90	126	127	144
32754	MIMS	86	72	92	69	76	90	72	85	77	72	76	60	65	75	73	83	51	81	91	100
32757	MOUNT DORA	89	88	94	87	91	99	84	92	88	85	87	65	85	86	88	92	60	90	101	107
32759	OAK HILL	76	63	85	60	68	82	62	76	67	63	66	54	56	64	65	73	44	72	82	89
	FLORIDA	96	94	97	93	96	98	95	97	96	97	96	71	95	94	96	97	67	97	101	113
	UNITED STATES	100	100	100	100	100	100	100	100	100	100	100	100	100	100	100	100	100	100	100	100

ZIP CODE #	POST OFFICE NAME	COUNTY FIPS CODE	POPULATION 2000	POPULATION 2009	POPULATION 2014	2000-2009 ANNUAL RATE % Rate	2000-2009 ANNUAL RATE State Centile	HOUSEHOLDS 2000	HOUSEHOLDS 2009	HOUSEHOLDS 2014	HOUSEHOLDS % Annual Rate 2000-2009	HOUSEHOLDS 2009 Average HH Size	FAMILIES 2000	FAMILIES 2009	FAMILIES % Annual Rate 2000-2009
32763	ORANGE CITY	127	15966	20024	21526	2.5	72	6981	8696	9343	2.4	2.28	4421	5337	2.1
32764	OSTEEN	127	3114	3962	4307	2.6	73	1220	1544	1683	2.6	2.56	927	1144	2.3
32765	OVIEDO	117	43687	55039	59877	2.5	72	14822	18791	20576	2.6	2.92	11888	14702	2.3
32766	OVIEDO	117	7195	14660	17898	8.0	94	2411	4921	6026	8.0	2.98	2007	4024	7.8
32767	PAISLEY	069	2355	2872	3182	2.2	66	966	1181	1315	2.2	2.43	693	814	1.8
32771	SANFORD	117	30589	44909	51153	4.2	86	11550	17792	20489	4.8	2.50	7845	11866	4.6
32773	SANFORD	117	23895	29176	31656	2.2	66	8637	10865	11917	2.5	2.63	5888	7168	2.1
32776	SORRENTO	069	7049	11101	13407	5.0	88	2574	4067	4928	5.1	2.73	2006	3085	4.8
32778	TAVARES	069	14289	18491	20789	2.8	76	6529	8621	9777	3.1	2.05	4267	5466	2.7
32779	LONGWOOD	117	28820	31480	32711	1.0	40	10577	11685	12149	1.1	2.69	8359	9138	1.0
32780	TITUSVILLE	009	31005	34385	35755	1.1	44	13606	15171	15839	1.2	2.24	8849	9590	0.9
32784	UMATILLA	069	9464	11750	13106	2.4	70	3669	4590	5142	2.5	2.54	2655	3220	2.1
32789	WINTER PARK	095	25134	25152	25285	0.0	9	11074	11111	11211	0.0	2.13	6109	5818	-0.5
32792	WINTER PARK	117	48220	49011	49467	0.2	15	20841	21473	21789	0.3	2.23	11463	11264	-0.2
32796	TITUSVILLE	009	20130	21450	21891	0.7	32	7850	8449	8667	0.8	2.47	5489	5760	0.5
32798	ZELLWOOD	095	2219	2442	2535	1.0	40	1133	1256	1306	1.1	1.92	716	751	0.5
32801	ORLANDO	095	8212	10176	11061	2.3	69	4734	6004	6608	2.6	1.58	1183	1319	1.2
32803	ORLANDO	095	19068	24604	26731	2.8	76	9054	11261	12154	2.4	2.07	3955	5198	3.0
32804	ORLANDO	095	17913	17724	17810	-0.1	6	8589	8622	8700	0.0	2.04	4509	4251	-0.6
32805	ORLANDO	095	25736	26459	26791	0.3	18	9242	9627	9823	0.4	2.61	5677	5579	-0.2
32806	ORLANDO	095	27169	27298	27340	0.1	12	11696	11842	11911	0.1	2.19	6809	6518	-0.5
32807	ORLANDO	095	31611	33353	34318	0.6	30	11934	12691	13085	0.7	2.60	7566	7683	0.2
32808	ORLANDO	095	49959	53677	55244	0.8	35	16962	18045	18561	0.7	2.95	11959	12173	0.2
32809	ORLANDO	095	21931	24943	26444	1.4	51	7923	8952	9473	1.3	2.79	5753	6293	1.0
32810	ORLANDO	095	31127	34298	36172	1.1	44	11268	12532	13291	1.2	2.71	7755	8278	0.7
32811	ORLANDO	095	32501	36050	38047	1.1	44	12605	14243	15110	1.3	2.52	7261	7691	0.6
32812	ORLANDO	095	32121	33097	33494	0.3	18	13065	13581	13779	0.4	2.43	8287	8210	-0.1
32817	ORLANDO	095	36278	38049	38727	0.5	26	13790	14538	14806	0.6	2.61	7730	7759	0.0
32818	ORLANDO	095	36094	43771	47297	2.1	64	12101	14724	15924	2.1	2.95	9272	11000	1.9
32819	ORLANDO	095	23947	25617	27040	0.7	32	8566	9345	9935	0.9	2.74	6579	6900	0.5
32820	ORLANDO	095	2919	6296	7766	8.7	95	1030	2302	2847	9.1	2.74	746	1625	8.8
32821	ORLANDO	095	11757	15248	17035	2.9	77	5639	7236	8040	2.7	2.08	2864	3458	2.1
32822	ORLANDO	095	49755	53915	57300	0.9	38	20212	22477	24030	1.2	2.39	12605	13223	0.5
32824	ORLANDO	095	19546	32881	39781	5.8	91	6025	10123	12240	5.8	3.25	4963	8141	5.5
32825	ORLANDO	095	46068	62658	70817	3.4	81	15192	20798	23636	3.5	2.88	11357	15241	3.2
32826	ORLANDO	095	18976	22563	24044	1.9	61	6388	7466	7987	1.7	2.64	3872	4478	1.6
32827	ORLANDO	095	1967	5120	6187	10.9	97	693	1815	2206	11.0	2.82	528	1347	10.7
32828	ORLANDO	095	22105	57172	74035	10.8	97	7629	19051	24531	10.4	3.00	5847	14128	10.0
32829	ORLANDO	095	4686	15289	18992	13.6	98	1512	5100	6373	14.0	2.97	1203	3850	13.4
32830	ORLANDO	095	23	18	23	-2.6	0	9	9	12	0.0	2.00	5	5	0.0
32831	ORLANDO	095	57	57	71	0.0	9	22	22	28	0.0	2.27	17	17	0.0
32832	ORLANDO	095	1860	12457	16411	22.8	100	695	4732	6262	23.0	2.63	539	3554	22.6
32833	ORLANDO	095	5096	7774	9156	4.7	87	1832	2810	3317	4.7	2.77	1410	2095	4.4
32835	ORLANDO	095	31315	39408	43912	2.5	72	12565	17022	19341	3.3	2.29	7436	8704	1.7
32836	ORLANDO	095	12052	17135	19816	3.9	84	4196	5977	6928	3.9	2.86	3207	4230	3.0
32837	ORLANDO	095	37028	47386	52443	2.7	74	12442	16245	18119	2.9	2.90	9597	11950	2.4
32839	ORLANDO	095	42135	52253	56716	2.4	70	14179	17458	19089	2.3	2.73	9093	10712	1.8
32901	MELBOURNE	009	22817	26510	28098	1.6	55	9787	11636	12476	1.9	2.04	5214	6005	1.5
32903	INDIALANTIC	009	12439	13274	13560	0.7	32	5512	5965	6131	0.9	2.23	3560	3719	0.5
32904	MELBOURNE	009	17942	25234	28043	3.8	84	7856	11060	12342	3.8	2.23	5116	6839	3.2
32905	PALM BAY	009	22128	24036	24785	0.9	38	9944	10917	11323	1.0	2.17	5731	6010	0.5
32907	PALM BAY	009	33636	41449	45048	2.3	69	12072	14975	16334	2.4	2.77	9540	11623	2.2
32908	PALM BAY	009	5915	9103	10502	4.8	87	2043	3157	3657	4.8	2.88	1589	2403	4.6
32909	PALM BAY	009	18076	27439	31724	4.6	87	6394	9833	11429	4.8	2.79	4982	7527	4.6
32920	CAPE CANAVERAL	009	8677	10803	11807	2.4	70	4981	6252	6848	2.5	1.73	2086	2485	1.9
32922	COCOA	009	14842	15162	15301	0.2	15	6338	6544	6636	0.3	2.30	3711	3683	-0.1
32925	PATRICK AFB	009	2193	2158	2151	-0.2	4	558	533	528	-0.5	3.63	547	521	-0.5
32926	COCOA	009	20333	22347	23432	1.0	40	7935	8814	9286	1.1	2.50	5749	6264	0.9
32927	COCOA	009	26979	32012	34206	1.9	61	8760	10524	11324	2.0	2.79	6689	7945	1.9
32931	COCOA BEACH	009	15101	15276	15318	0.1	12	7893	8060	8124	0.2	1.89	4172	4076	-0.3
32934	MELBOURNE	009	16691	19731	21131	1.8	59	6559	7796	8372	1.9	2.51	4828	5651	1.7
32935	MELBOURNE	009	39258	40788	41184	0.4	22	17312	18172	18448	0.5	2.24	10479	10584	0.1
32937	SATELLITE BEACH	009	26984	27492	27629	0.2	15	11513	11939	12098	0.4	2.30	8063	8069	0.0
32940	MELBOURNE	009	18793	29473	34141	5.0	88	7942	12381	14393	4.9	2.36	5983	9079	4.6
32948	FELLSMERE	061	4931	6621	7644	3.2	80	1268	1761	2066	3.6	3.52	1035	1396	3.3
32949	GRANT	009	1456	1577	1612	0.9	38	617	675	694	1.0	2.34	395	419	0.6
32950	MALABAR	009	4107	4661	4880	1.4	51	1616	1853	1948	1.5	2.51	1214	1359	1.2
32951	MELBOURNE BEACH	009	10818	11496	11834	0.7	32	4989	5333	5512	0.7	2.16	3477	3613	0.4
32952	MERRITT ISLAND	009	20696	22212	22840	0.8	35	8373	9010	9271	0.8	2.43	5903	6213	0.6
32953	MERRITT ISLAND	009	21695	24285	25460	1.2	46	9041	10151	10661	1.3	2.35	6035	6646	1.0
32955	ROCKLEDGE	009	24892	34060	37639	3.4	81	9928	13763	15279	3.6	2.44	7183	9735	3.3
32958	SEBASTIAN	061	20413	26832	30649	3.0	78	8977	12170	14034	3.3	2.20	6273	8264	3.0
32960	VERO BEACH	061	20053	22258	23671	1.1	44	9341	10687	11489	1.5	2.02	5016	5474	0.9
32962	VERO BEACH	061	20319	25368	28258	2.4	70	8786	11190	12540	2.6	2.26	5991	7475	2.4
32963	VERO BEACH	061	14077	16797	18273	1.9	61	7011	8605	9451	2.2	1.95	4924	5919	2.0
32966	VERO BEACH	061	13124	17445	19714	3.1	79	6376	8615	9780	3.3	1.97	4003	5166	2.8
32967	VERO BEACH	061	11873	19175	22563	5.3	90	4517	7727	9291	6.0	2.41	3164	5230	5.6
32968	VERO BEACH	061	8159	12600	15019	4.8	87	2862	4670	5644	5.4	2.68	2303	3680	5.2
32976	SEBASTIAN	009	8956	9429	9534	0.6	30	4958	5284	5375	0.7	1.78	3079	3164	0.3
33004	DANIA	011	15043	15790	15922	0.5	26	6810	7035	7055	0.4	2.19	3620	3553	-0.2
33009	HALLANDALE	011	36364	38967	40058	0.8	35	19206	20147	20609	0.5	1.92	9249	9182	-0.1
33010	HIALEAH	086	46778	47344	47616	0.1	12	15169	15476	15578	0.2	2.96	11419	11390	0.0
33012	HIALEAH	086	73686	72913	72766	-0.1	6	23775	23706	23652	0.0	3.03	19050	18678	-0.2
33013	HIALEAH	086	33595	33584	33588	0.0	9	10056	10140	10139	0.1	3.27	8267	8212	-0.1
33014	HIALEAH	086	38113	39511	40092	0.4	22	13293	13906	14125	0.5	2.83	9989	10209	0.2
33015	HIALEAH	086	49330	60827	65244	2.3	69	16680	20212	21591	2.1	3.00	12714	14983	1.8
33016	HIALEAH	086	43719	47681	49255	0.9	38	13206	14370	14795	0.9	3.26	11468	12406	0.9
33018	HIALEAH	086	37282	44322	47027	1.9	61	10494	12022	12694	1.5	3.67	9556	10842	1.4
33019	HOLLYWOOD	011	15977	16367	16524	0.3	18	8793	8835	8889	0.1	1.84	4031	3844	-0.5
33020	HOLLYWOOD	011	40156	41306	41488	0.3	18	17880	18064	18074	0.1	2.24	8968	8598	-0.5
33021	HOLLYWOOD	011	45944	47342	46867	0.3	18	20242	20527	20231	0.2	2.28	12046	11687	-0.3
33023	HOLLYWOOD	011	61179	64244	64391	0.5	26	19798	20321	20270	0.3	3.16	15265	15247	0.0
33024	HOLLYWOOD	011	58915	64825	66638	1.0	40	20990	22666	23187	0.8	2.86	15384	16133	0.5
33025	HOLLYWOOD	011	46414	58473	63266	2.5	72	16840	20544	22091	2.2	2.82	12046	14303	1.9
33026	HOLLYWOOD	011	29582	30109	29842	0.2	15	11495	11520	11389	0.0	2.61	8253	8034	-0.3
	FLORIDA					1.9					1.9	2.47			1.7
	UNITED STATES					1.0					1.1	2.59			0.9

ZIP CODE #	POST OFFICE NAME	RACE (%) White 2000	White 2009	Black 2000	Black 2009	Asian/Pacific 2000	Asian/Pacific 2009	% Hispanic Origin 2000	% Hispanic Origin 2009	2009 AGE DISTRIBUTION (%) 0-4	5-9	10-14	15-19	20-24	25-44	45-64	65-84	85+	18+	MEDIAN AGE 2009	% 2009 Males	% 2009 Females
32763	ORANGE CITY	94.2	90.7	2.4	3.9	0.6	1.0	5.5	9.5	5.3	5.0	5.1	5.1	4.5	20.1	26.6	22.7	5.6	81.4	48.7	46.8	53.2
32764	OSTEEN	91.6	86.5	5.0	8.2	0.4	0.7	5.8	10.4	5.0	5.9	6.7	6.0	4.3	23.9	32.8	13.6	1.8	78.5	43.8	50.4	49.6
32765	OVIEDO	84.9	80.2	7.5	8.9	2.9	4.2	11.1	17.1	7.6	7.5	7.5	7.0	4.9	31.1	26.5	6.9	1.0	72.9	34.9	48.8	51.2
32766	OVIEDO	91.5	87.1	3.2	4.9	1.4	2.2	8.1	14.6	8.3	8.0	8.0	7.5	5.2	30.2	25.9	6.3	0.6	70.8	34.4	49.2	50.8
32767	PAISLEY	97.1	96.1	0.5	0.7	0.4	0.6	2.8	4.2	4.8	5.0	5.6	7.0	5.4	21.7	32.0	16.7	1.7	80.3	45.3	51.3	48.7
32771	SANFORD	56.0	58.5	38.9	34.8	0.8	1.4	5.7	8.3	6.6	6.6	6.7	6.9	6.6	25.3	28.0	11.6	1.8	75.9	38.8	48.4	51.6
32773	SANFORD	77.1	72.3	13.7	15.3	1.7	2.3	11.9	17.3	7.4	7.1	7.0	7.3	7.1	30.2	24.6	8.0	1.2	74.1	34.1	50.4	49.6
32776	SORRENTO	91.4	87.6	3.7	5.9	1.0	1.5	6.1	8.6	6.3	6.7	7.1	6.8	5.1	24.9	31.0	11.0	1.2	75.8	40.5	50.0	50.0
32778	TAVARES	90.4	87.5	6.7	8.4	0.7	0.9	3.4	5.2	3.4	3.5	3.7	4.4	3.9	16.6	28.6	30.4	5.5	86.7	56.3	47.6	52.4
32779	LONGWOOD	92.9	89.5	2.2	3.1	2.9	4.6	5.1	8.4	4.7	5.7	7.0	7.2	4.5	19.9	37.2	12.1	1.7	77.9	45.5	48.7	51.3
32780	TITUSVILLE	86.1	82.7	10.1	12.2	1.1	1.7	3.7	5.7	5.4	5.2	5.3	5.8	5.5	21.2	28.1	20.2	3.5	80.6	46.1	47.7	52.3
32784	UMATILLA	90.8	86.8	5.1	7.3	0.4	0.5	4.5	7.0	6.3	6.5	6.7	6.4	5.1	22.7	28.8	15.0	2.5	76.5	42.2	49.2	50.8
32789	WINTER PARK	84.8	81.5	11.1	12.8	1.6	2.4	4.6	7.3	5.1	5.1	5.4	7.3	7.4	22.8	28.7	14.3	3.8	81.2	42.8	47.4	52.6
32792	WINTER PARK	83.1	77.0	5.9	7.7	3.1	4.3	15.7	23.6	5.3	4.6	4.5	5.4	9.3	32.6	23.4	11.8	3.1	82.7	35.9	49.1	50.9
32796	TITUSVILLE	85.6	81.7	11.0	13.8	0.9	1.3	2.9	4.5	5.7	5.6	5.9	6.5	5.6	21.5	28.7	17.6	2.9	78.8	44.3	47.8	52.2
32798	ZELLWOOD	93.0	89.3	4.0	5.7	0.0	0.1	7.2	12.0	2.2	2.0	2.0	2.0	1.7	8.9	21.1	48.9	11.3	92.6	69.1	45.6	54.4
32801	ORLANDO	80.0	77.0	13.4	14.3	1.7	2.6	11.6	16.8	3.9	3.2	2.8	2.9	6.3	32.6	21.8	18.3	8.3	88.7	43.9	47.6	52.4
32803	ORLANDO	87.2	82.1	5.8	6.4	2.8	3.8	8.8	14.5	5.0	4.6	4.6	5.3	6.7	32.9	25.5	12.3	3.2	82.9	39.2	49.6	50.4
32804	ORLANDO	92.3	88.8	2.9	4.1	1.9	2.8	4.6	7.9	5.1	4.6	4.6	4.8	6.7	29.2	31.0	11.4	2.5	82.8	42.0	49.0	51.0
32805	ORLANDO	15.7	12.5	78.1	80.9	0.5	0.5	5.0	6.5	8.0	7.8	7.3	7.6	6.7	25.3	25.0	10.5	1.9	72.3	35.2	48.9	51.1
32806	ORLANDO	88.5	83.2	5.0	7.2	1.4	2.1	9.6	15.5	5.4	5.2	5.4	5.5	5.4	27.9	28.8	13.8	2.5	80.5	41.9	49.7	50.3
32807	ORLANDO	72.8	65.1	7.6	9.2	3.1	3.8	37.5	49.9	7.0	6.1	5.7	6.5	9.3	32.6	22.0	9.4	1.5	77.7	32.9	50.2	49.8
32808	ORLANDO	33.6	25.8	53.0	59.0	2.6	2.9	12.4	15.8	9.1	8.5	8.0	8.5	8.5	28.4	21.2	6.8	1.0	69.3	29.5	47.6	52.4
32809	ORLANDO	69.7	63.2	12.3	14.4	3.3	3.8	32.7	43.1	7.4	7.1	6.7	7.0	6.9	27.9	25.4	10.3	1.2	74.6	35.4	50.1	49.9
32810	ORLANDO	63.1	54.0	25.9	31.6	2.9	3.7	14.0	20.1	7.9	7.4	7.0	7.2	7.7	30.3	24.1	7.5	1.0	73.5	32.9	49.3	50.7
32811	ORLANDO	34.6	29.9	52.9	55.6	3.2	3.9	13.3	17.4	7.6	6.4	5.7	6.9	12.2	35.3	18.8	6.3	0.7	76.6	29.3	49.1	50.9
32812	ORLANDO	81.1	74.3	6.8	8.9	2.3	3.0	21.8	31.8	6.4	5.8	5.8	6.7	8.2	30.1	26.0	9.5	1.4	77.9	35.8	48.4	51.6
32817	ORLANDO	78.6	70.8	6.1	8.2	6.0	8.0	19.8	29.3	5.4	5.1	4.9	10.2	20.1	27.8	20.0	5.9	0.6	81.5	27.3	51.2	48.8
32818	ORLANDO	44.4	36.7	42.1	47.3	3.7	4.5	13.7	18.1	7.9	7.5	7.3	7.4	7.2	29.3	24.4	8.2	0.9	73.0	33.1	48.1	51.9
32819	ORLANDO	74.3	68.0	12.8	14.0	7.1	10.2	9.3	14.7	5.4	5.9	6.6	7.0	5.8	27.0	32.0	9.4	0.9	77.7	39.5	49.2	50.8
32820	ORLANDO	93.8	90.7	0.9	1.4	0.4	0.7	8.8	14.3	6.8	6.3	6.3	7.5	7.7	27.3	27.7	9.6	0.8	76.1	35.6	50.7	49.3
32821	ORLANDO	84.4	76.6	4.4	6.6	5.3	7.9	12.1	19.7	3.9	2.7	2.3	4.2	10.1	38.3	21.4	14.9	2.2	88.9	35.9	50.3	49.7
32822	ORLANDO	72.5	65.2	8.3	10.1	2.7	3.3	36.5	48.2	7.0	6.3	5.8	6.4	8.6	32.3	23.3	9.2	1.2	77.2	34.0	49.3	50.7
32824	ORLANDO	67.3	61.4	11.7	13.3	4.3	4.5	43.8	56.1	7.6	7.6	7.6	7.7	6.3	30.1	25.1	7.3	0.6	72.4	33.7	48.8	51.2
32825	ORLANDO	72.5	64.3	8.8	12.5	3.4	4.0	31.4	40.8	7.6	7.0	6.6	6.6	6.5	35.3	22.9	6.7	0.8	74.9	33.5	51.1	48.9
32826	ORLANDO	80.1	72.2	7.0	9.7	3.2	4.3	17.5	26.2	6.1	5.6	5.2	15.1	16.3	25.8	15.9	8.7	1.4	80.3	26.1	50.1	49.9
32827	ORLANDO	73.8	81.4	6.8	5.4	1.0	0.8	50.5	43.1	6.7	7.0	7.2	7.0	5.9	25.3	30.5	9.5	0.9	74.8	39.2	49.0	51.0
32828	ORLANDO	78.8	70.7	7.0	9.3	4.7	6.3	20.5	30.5	9.1	8.1	7.4	6.3	5.1	37.4	21.6	4.7	0.4	71.6	32.4	49.4	50.6
32829	ORLANDO	76.0	68.1	7.0	9.9	2.8	3.3	32.9	44.2	7.1	7.1	7.2	7.2	5.5	29.3	26.7	8.8	1.0	74.1	36.4	49.1	50.9
32830	ORLANDO	65.2	61.1	4.3	5.6	4.3	5.6	34.8	44.4	11.1	0.0	0.0	11.1	33.3	44.4	0.0	0.0	0.0	83.3	24.2	55.6	44.4
32831	ORLANDO	69.0	61.4	17.2	21.1	3.4	3.5	24.1	33.3	7.0	7.0	7.0	7.0	5.3	38.6	24.6	3.5	0.0	75.4	32.5	57.9	42.1
32832	ORLANDO	95.8	93.5	0.8	1.3	0.6	1.0	4.4	7.7	5.2	6.1	7.2	7.0	3.5	22.0	37.0	10.9	1.1	77.1	44.4	49.7	50.3
32833	ORLANDO	87.0	79.6	4.0	6.4	4.4	7.0	8.8	14.8	6.6	6.4	6.2	6.2	6.2	27.6	28.5	11.3	1.0	77.1	38.6	50.0	50.0
32835	ORLANDO	73.1	65.9	11.8	14.7	6.7	8.6	12.8	19.2	6.7	5.8	5.5	6.2	10.6	37.1	22.2	5.2	0.8	78.4	32.0	50.1	49.9
32836	ORLANDO	79.9	69.6	3.3	5.0	8.8	11.5	12.5	23.4	6.9	6.4	6.7	7.1	8.0	30.0	27.4	6.7	0.8	75.5	34.3	49.5	50.5
32837	ORLANDO	70.2	63.3	8.0	9.7	8.4	10.5	27.8	36.2	7.5	7.0	6.5	6.1	7.2	34.4	24.5	6.1	0.7	75.2	33.1	49.0	51.0
32839	ORLANDO	45.2	39.4	34.8	37.7	4.2	4.6	28.0	34.3	8.0	6.8	6.0	7.3	10.7	35.7	19.0	5.8	0.7	75.3	30.2	53.3	46.7
32901	MELBOURNE	73.8	70.0	20.2	22.0	2.0	2.7	5.5	8.3	5.0	4.5	4.8	7.7	7.6	20.5	23.3	20.5	6.0	82.0	44.8	48.4	51.6
32903	INDIALANTIC	96.2	94.4	0.7	1.1	1.3	2.0	3.0	4.9	4.3	4.8	5.4	5.4	4.0	19.8	33.0	20.3	3.2	82.3	48.7	49.1	50.9
32904	MELBOURNE	94.6	91.3	1.4	2.2	1.8	2.8	3.5	6.1	4.4	4.6	5.0	5.3	4.2	20.0	28.5	23.0	4.8	82.5	49.3	47.2	52.8
32905	PALM BAY	79.1	73.2	12.5	15.8	2.2	3.0	9.3	13.6	5.9	5.3	5.0	5.5	7.2	25.6	24.6	17.5	3.4	80.5	41.2	47.9	52.1
32907	PALM BAY	82.6	76.7	10.9	14.5	1.7	2.3	8.4	12.8	6.1	6.4	6.8	7.6	6.1	24.5	28.4	12.6	1.6	75.9	39.6	48.6	51.4
32908	PALM BAY	82.8	78.0	9.8	12.4	1.0	1.5	7.9	11.7	7.8	7.7	7.6	8.1	6.7	28.9	24.9	7.5	0.7	71.1	33.1	48.2	51.8
32909	PALM BAY	82.7	77.0	10.8	14.2	1.5	2.1	8.1	12.0	7.1	7.0	7.1	7.3	5.9	27.8	26.9	10.0	1.0	74.2	36.4	49.0	51.0
32920	CAPE CANAVERAL	94.6	92.4	1.4	2.1	1.7	2.5	3.5	5.6	3.4	3.0	2.9	3.7	7.1	24.5	31.8	20.5	3.0	88.7	48.1	51.6	48.4
32922	COCOA	57.4	51.5	37.5	42.1	0.9	1.2	4.9	6.9	7.3	6.8	6.4	6.9	7.3	25.3	24.9	13.0	2.2	75.4	37.0	47.9	52.1
32925	PATRICK AFB	67.1	58.5	19.2	24.0	3.0	3.8	12.0	17.0	12.4	13.2	8.7	6.6	13.2	41.4	3.3	1.2	0.1	62.2	23.5	53.8	46.2
32926	COCOA	81.7	78.6	14.4	16.1	0.8	1.3	3.4	5.3	5.7	5.9	6.5	7.2	6.0	23.3	29.7	14.4	1.5	77.6	41.8	49.5	50.5
32927	COCOA	87.8	84.0	7.6	9.9	1.0	1.5	3.7	5.7	6.0	6.2	6.5	8.5	8.4	26.8	27.7	9.0	0.9	76.6	36.6	52.0	48.0
32931	COCOA BEACH	96.6	95.2	0.6	0.9	1.1	1.6	2.5	4.1	2.3	2.5	2.8	3.2	3.6	16.2	34.2	30.1	5.2	90.5	56.8	50.1	49.9
32934	MELBOURNE	91.3	88.0	3.3	4.7	2.6	3.6	5.2	8.2	5.8	6.3	6.6	6.4	4.5	22.7	29.8	15.6	2.1	77.1	43.2	48.3	51.7
32935	MELBOURNE	89.7	85.9	4.3	5.9	2.3	3.4	5.4	8.4	5.4	5.2	5.2	5.7	6.3	26.3	28.3	15.1	2.5	80.9	42.0	48.4	51.6
32937	SATELLITE BEACH	93.6	91.5	1.9	2.3	1.8	2.6	3.7	5.8	4.3	4.4	4.9	5.5	5.0	20.8	30.4	21.0	3.6	82.8	48.2	47.9	52.1
32940	MELBOURNE	92.8	89.9	2.6	3.6	2.4	3.4	4.3	6.8	4.4	4.8	5.5	5.4	3.1	16.6	32.4	23.9	3.8	81.5	51.2	47.3	52.7
32948	FELLSMERE	68.2	61.0	4.8	5.9	0.2	0.2	57.8	69.1	9.0	8.7	7.9	7.6	7.7	31.2	20.2	7.1	0.7	70.2	30.2	55.4	44.6
32949	GRANT	97.7	96.6	1.0	1.4	0.5	0.8	1.6	2.6	1.4	1.5	1.6	1.8	1.6	6.8	30.1	46.2	8.8	94.4	66.9	46.3	53.7
32950	MALABAR	93.9	91.5	2.6	3.7	1.2	1.8	2.4	4.0	3.9	5.0	6.1	6.0	3.8	17.7	39.6	16.1	1.7	81.0	48.7	50.8	49.2
32951	MELBOURNE BEACH	97.9	97.1	0.2	0.3	0.9	1.3	2.1	3.5	2.7	3.1	3.7	3.7	2.5	13.3	39.3	28.6	3.1	88.0	56.8	49.8	50.2
32952	MERRITT ISLAND	95.0	93.0	0.8	1.2	1.7	2.6	3.6	5.7	4.3	5.1	6.0	6.3	4.2	19.5	33.1	18.2	3.4	80.7	47.6	49.0	51.0
32953	MERRITT ISLAND	86.6	83.4	8.5	9.9	1.8	2.7	4.2	6.5	5.7	5.5	5.7	5.8	4.8	22.2	30.0	17.3	3.0	79.5	45.1	48.5	51.5
32955	ROCKLEDGE	83.1	79.0	12.8	15.3	1.7	2.6	3.2	5.3	5.1	5.4	5.9	6.0	4.6	21.5	31.7	17.5	2.4	79.8	45.9	48.0	52.0
32958	SEBASTIAN	92.8	89.3	4.0	5.7	0.8	1.3	3.7	6.7	4.0	4.3	4.9	5.3	3.8	17.5	31.4	25.3	3.5	83.5	51.9	47.9	52.1
32960	VERO BEACH	90.8	86.4	4.5	6.5	1.4	2.1	5.8	10.3	4.9	4.5	4.4	5.0	5.8	22.5	26.9	20.5	5.5	83.2	47.1	47.4	52.6
32962	VERO BEACH	87.6	81.8	9.3	13.7	0.7	1.0	3.7	6.6	5.6	5.6	5.6	5.7	4.8	22.3	26.2	20.4	3.9	79.8	45.3	47.4	52.6
32963	VERO BEACH	98.4	97.5	0.3	0.4	0.7	1.2	1.7	3.2	1.8	2.2	2.6	3.1	2.0	7.9	33.6	40.9	5.9	91.3	63.7	47.2	52.8
32966	VERO BEACH	95.6	92.5	2.1	3.6	0.5	0.9	3.2	6.3	3.2	3.6	3.9	5.2	2.6	14.1	24.1	32.4	10.9	86.5	60.1	47.4	52.6
32967	VERO BEACH	53.4	58.1	41.7	35.1	0.3	0.4	7.4	10.9	6.3	6.3	6.2	6.5	5.4	22.6	28.3	16.0	2.5	77.3	42.5	48.9	51.1
32968	VERO BEACH	94.7	92.7	1.8	2.3	0.6	1.0	4.1	7.5	5.9	6.6	7.2	7.5	4.3	24.1	30.8	12.2	1.3	75.8	41.3	50.1	49.9
32976	SEBASTIAN	98.6	97.9	0.4	0.6	0.3	0.4	1.5	2.4	1.3	1.3	1.4	1.7	1.7	7.0	29.6	47.5	8.7	95.1	67.3	47.0	53.0
33004	DANIA	64.7	60.5	30.2	32.7	1.0	1.4	10.5	15.3	5.3	5.0	5.0	4.6	6.4	25.7	29.3	15.6	3.1	81.7	43.4	49.3	50.7
33009	HALLANDALE	77.8	73.5	15.4	17.8	1.0	1.3	18.8	26.1	4.0	3.8	3.7	3.7	3.9	19.0	25.4	27.9	8.5	86.2	54.7	46.2	53.8
33010	HIALEAH	87.7	88.2	3.8	3.1	0.2	0.2	91.6	95.1	5.6	5.5	5.4	5.8	6.0	26.1	25.9	16.7	3.0	79.9	41.6	49.9	50.1
33012	HIALEAH	90.1	90.2	1.5	1.3	0.5	0.4	89.9	94.1	5.4	5.4	5.6	6.0	6.2	25.3	25.4	17.6	3.1	79.8	41.9	47.1	52.9
33013	HIALEAH	91.4	91.3	1.3	1.2	0.3	0.3	90.4	94.6	5.3	5.4	5.4	5.6	5.6	25.9	25.7	18.5	2.6	80.4	42.6	49.2	50.8
33014	HIALEAH	86.5	85.8	3.6	3.9	0.9	1.0	78.0	84.7	6.5	6.3	6.2	7.1	7.9	28.8	24.8	11.1	1.4	76.6	36.0	48.7	51.3
33015	HIALEAH	68.5	71.1	17.9	14.0	2.4	2.3	62.2	73.7	8.6	7.6	6.9	7.1	8.4	32.4	21.7	6.6	0.7	72.7	31.5	48.1	51.9
33016	HIALEAH	84.4	85.3	3.0	2.5	0.8	0.8	88.4	92.6	7.5	7.5	7.4	7.6	6.6	29.6	23.6	8.9	1.3	72.8	34.0	47.9	52.1
33018	HIALEAH	86.6	86.9	2.5	2.2	1.2	1.1	87.3	92.0	7.6	7.7	7.7	8.0	6.8	29.0	24.5	7.9	0.8	71.9	34.0	48.9	51.1
33019	HOLLYWOOD	95.0	93.1	1.5	2.0	1.0	1.4	13.5	20.3	3.8	3.9	4.0	2.9	2.7	22.6	32.0	21.3	6.7	86.5	50.9	48.1	51.9
33020	HOLLYWOOD	66.3	60.7	23.1	26.0	1.5	1.9	21.6	28.7	6.4	5.9	5.4	6.0	7.9	27.4	27.4	11.0	2.6	78.9	38.7	49.7	50.3
33021	HOLLYWOOD	85.7	81.6	6.8	8.5	2.1	2.8	17.7	24.8	5.0	5.0	5.2	5.2	5.0	23.2	27.7	17.7	5.9	81.5	45.9	47.3	52.7
33023	HOLLYWOOD	42.7	38.4	45.1	47.6	1.7	2.0	24.1	29.6	7.8	7.5	7.6	7.9	7.3	28.0	24.4	8.3	1.3	72.3	33.2	47.9	52.1
33024	HOLLYWOOD	76.8	72.2	9.8	11.1	3.3	3.9	30.9	40.8	7.1	7.0	7.0	7.4	7.0	27.9	25.7	9.5	1.4	74.5	35.8	48.6	51.4
33025	HOLLYWOOD	46.3	42.0	40.1	42.8	4.3	4.8	24.1	29.5	8.1	7.3	6.9	6.5	7.0	32.9	21.8	8.0	1.6	73.8	33.1	47.2	52.8
33026	HOLLYWOOD	84.6	80.2	7.0	8.6	3.0	4.1	19.6	27.6	5.2	5.5	6.2	6.9	5.4	24.9	30.6	12.4	2.9	78.7	42.2	45.9	54.1
	FLORIDA	78.0	74.7	14.6	15.8	1.7	2.3	16.8	21.5	6.0	5.9	5.9	6.3	6.2	25.0	26.8	15.3	2.8	78.6	41.1	48.8	51.2
	UNITED STATES	75.1	72.0	12.3	12.7	3.8	4.6	12.5	15.7	6.8	6.7	6.6	7.1	6.9	27.0	26.0	10.9	1.9	75.7	36.9	49.2	50.8

ZIP CODE				2009 HOUSEHOLD INCOME DISTRIBUTION (%)					MEDIAN HOUSEHOLD INCOME					2009 HOME VALUE DISTRIBUTION (%)					
#	POST OFFICE NAME	2009 Per Capita Income	2009 HH Income Base	Less than $25,000	$25,000 to $49,999	$50,000 to $99,999	$100,000 to $149,999	$150,000 or More	2009	2014	2009 National Centile	2009 State Centile	2009 Home Value Base	Less than $50,000	$50,000 to $89,999	$90,000 to $174,999	$175,000 to $399,999	$400,000 or More	2009 Median Home Value
32763	ORANGE CITY	22797	8696	27.6	31.5	31.1	6.7	3.1	40709	43525	35	30	6568	14.2	22.4	43.2	18.1	2.1	107567
32764	OSTEEN	25548	1544	17.4	34.0	32.6	9.1	6.9	49072	49763	59	54	1380	4.8	17.2	37.0	33.0	8.0	147531
32765	OVIEDO	37545	18791	7.8	12.2	36.7	24.5	18.8	87126	91263	94	96	15512	2.1	4.5	25.3	59.4	8.7	215597
32766	OVIEDO	31933	4921	5.4	15.3	43.5	24.8	11.0	77640	82397	91	93	4482	0.0	3.5	36.8	50.6	9.1	192247
32767	PAISLEY	17681	1181	34.7	33.9	26.4	3.9	1.1	35419	37560	19	15	1006	16.8	33.2	31.1	16.1	2.8	90000
32771	SANFORD	27440	17792	23.8	24.9	31.8	11.9	7.6	51280	53958	64	60	11218	6.2	16.9	39.1	27.5	10.3	133100
32773	SANFORD	23140	10865	20.0	30.8	34.0	11.0	4.2	49307	50677	60	55	7350	10.2	14.1	56.6	16.8	2.3	118145
32776	SORRENTO	23838	4067	19.1	24.9	42.8	8.5	4.6	55013	55460	71	70	3499	10.9	16.6	35.3	28.1	9.1	137225
32778	TAVARES	26793	8621	26.6	31.9	30.7	6.7	4.1	43026	46196	42	37	6983	16.2	23.8	35.6	18.9	5.4	106220
32779	LONGWOOD	52935	11685	4.9	10.9	32.2	22.6	29.4	103673	107894	97	98	9403	1.2	0.5	12.9	56.7	28.8	278638
32780	TITUSVILLE	27658	15171	22.0	28.1	34.3	10.4	5.3	49893	52817	61	56	10490	5.5	21.9	48.0	21.6	3.1	117542
32784	UMATILLA	19170	4590	32.0	31.7	29.3	4.5	2.6	39543	42279	31	26	3568	21.2	23.5	33.7	17.0	4.6	98744
32789	WINTER PARK	42787	11111	18.8	23.1	29.4	13.2	15.4	59554	61725	77	76	7041	0.6	6.1	23.8	36.3	33.2	273540
32792	WINTER PARK	27916	21473	19.5	28.2	37.2	10.7	4.3	51627	53618	65	61	10236	1.0	5.0	50.8	40.3	2.8	163568
32796	TITUSVILLE	23489	8449	23.6	27.6	35.1	10.4	3.2	48893	51772	59	53	6366	5.6	25.4	52.2	14.8	2.1	110975
32798	ZELLWOOD	23793	1256	30.7	39.7	23.9	3.8	1.9	36745	39210	23	18	1105	7.1	36.6	51.7	4.7	0.0	95423
32801	ORLANDO	35208	6004	38.9	26.1	23.1	5.7	6.1	34413	35449	16	13	1880	0.2	6.3	25.9	51.6	16.0	223485
32803	ORLANDO	34624	11261	14.7	24.4	41.3	12.1	7.5	57038	59843	74	73	6251	1.2	2.8	33.7	51.3	10.9	196319
32804	ORLANDO	37732	8622	16.2	25.5	36.6	13.0	8.7	57471	59623	75	73	5594	6.6	3.6	31.2	44.0	14.6	196454
32805	ORLANDO	13905	9627	47.9	29.2	18.8	3.2	0.9	26302	26598	4	2	3433	6.3	25.6	54.6	13.1	0.4	111096
32806	ORLANDO	32264	11842	19.0	26.2	37.1	10.5	7.2	54466	57130	70	68	7293	0.9	4.8	41.6	41.8	10.9	179830
32807	ORLANDO	18375	12691	25.5	35.0	33.9	4.3	1.3	41423	43803	37	32	6211	3.0	14.6	69.6	12.2	0.7	121854
32808	ORLANDO	15344	18045	30.6	34.4	29.5	4.3	1.2	37848	40253	26	22	9025	2.1	15.1	72.1	10.1	0.6	121259
32809	ORLANDO	20958	8952	21.9	32.5	34.2	7.9	3.5	45773	49555	51	46	5289	7.6	6.4	60.8	18.5	6.7	133564
32810	ORLANDO	22470	12532	18.1	30.1	39.3	8.9	3.6	51458	54265	65	61	7530	5.4	9.2	60.8	23.7	0.9	136667
32811	ORLANDO	18552	14243	24.3	37.7	33.1	3.7	1.2	41570	44043	38	33	4663	4.7	22.6	70.0	2.5	0.3	108580
32812	ORLANDO	26815	13581	16.7	28.9	38.7	10.9	4.8	53660	56166	69	67	7450	4.2	10.0	39.0	42.3	4.5	167327
32817	ORLANDO	22814	14538	20.9	30.6	34.8	9.3	4.3	48780	51635	58	53	7305	2.5	6.8	43.4	42.9	4.4	170082
32818	ORLANDO	20814	14724	18.7	27.0	40.9	10.5	2.9	53687	56611	69	67	10621	9.0	5.4	53.4	31.3	0.9	147654
32819	ORLANDO	38414	9345	10.7	17.4	33.4	17.7	20.8	78654	78113	91	94	6808	1.0	4.8	14.3	61.7	18.2	252834
32820	ORLANDO	20555	2302	18.8	38.1	34.9	4.5	3.7	46909	48805	54	48	1973	17.9	19.3	38.3	18.4	6.1	105972
32821	ORLANDO	34747	7236	9.2	28.7	44.0	12.5	5.6	61816	63777	80	79	3948	0.0	0.5	39.8	55.9	3.7	188305
32822	ORLANDO	22136	22477	20.5	35.0	37.3	5.3	1.9	45524	49375	50	45	11362	16.4	18.6	49.0	15.6	0.4	114764
32824	ORLANDO	20106	10123	13.0	28.0	46.2	9.6	3.2	57727	59441	75	74	7894	2.9	6.4	47.7	42.6	0.4	163723
32825	ORLANDO	25478	20798	10.9	22.3	44.7	16.7	5.4	64608	66778	83	83	15479	2.6	4.9	49.9	39.1	3.6	163215
32826	ORLANDO	22650	7466	19.4	29.4	38.0	8.9	4.3	51099	55389	64	60	4931	17.8	17.8	32.0	29.7	2.7	130840
32827	ORLANDO	26182	1815	10.4	33.1	45.5	4.8	6.3	54210	56142	70	68	1586	1.1	0.9	73.0	14.3	10.7	143678
32828	ORLANDO	30955	19051	8.4	15.5	41.2	23.3	11.7	78985	81143	92	94	13255	1.4	5.5	38.2	48.7	6.3	185140
32829	ORLANDO	21606	5100	13.4	26.4	47.2	10.3	2.6	58452	60194	76	74	4297	9.7	14.6	46.2	29.1	0.4	142865
32830	ORLANDO	19444	9	22.2	55.6	22.2	0.0	0.0	37278	35000	24	20	3	0.0	0.0	100.0	0.0	0.0	112500
32831	ORLANDO	35891	22	0.0	9.1	59.1	27.3	4.5	82895	84816	93	95	20	0.0	5.0	45.0	50.0	0.0	175000
32832	ORLANDO	45678	4732	4.7	16.3	36.7	24.0	18.2	86931	87654	94	96	4257	0.8	4.6	45.5	38.8	10.4	173019
32833	ORLANDO	23606	2810	20.0	26.9	34.7	14.0	4.5	52684	55414	67	64	2045	11.4	12.5	27.4	46.8	1.9	172274
32835	ORLANDO	33539	17022	13.4	26.4	39.1	11.2	9.9	60303	61207	78	77	7954	0.4	3.1	35.7	47.3	13.4	201243
32836	ORLANDO	42299	5977	14.8	21.0	22.4	13.1	28.6	75829	74418	90	92	3823	5.8	6.3	5.5	39.5	42.9	370066
32837	ORLANDO	29315	16245	8.6	19.8	45.3	16.5	9.7	71340	71958	88	90	10798	0.9	0.9	26.2	66.9	5.0	210325
32839	ORLANDO	16835	17458	29.1	36.8	28.9	3.9	1.3	38275	40558	28	23	5587	13.1	14.4	55.5	14.6	2.4	122302
32901	MELBOURNE	21041	11636	37.3	31.7	24.0	4.2	2.8	32394	35040	12	9	6326	13.3	25.2	49.6	11.6	0.2	105296
32903	INDIALANTIC	43697	5965	13.8	20.0	32.7	17.5	16.0	70326	71264	87	89	4448	1.5	1.2	28.9	50.5	17.9	229630
32904	MELBOURNE	28611	11060	17.5	34.2	33.3	8.7	6.3	48657	51835	58	53	8866	7.3	26.8	37.6	25.8	2.5	116139
32905	PALM BAY	20786	10917	32.6	34.3	26.2	5.1	1.8	35499	38044	19	15	6312	9.5	37.4	39.9	12.8	0.5	93133
32907	PALM BAY	22525	14975	15.2	30.3	42.1	9.3	3.1	53709	55702	69	67	12497	1.6	14.1	70.8	13.2	0.3	121097
32908	PALM BAY	20926	3157	14.3	32.8	45.1	5.3	2.5	52074	54763	66	63	2384	0.3	27.7	66.9	4.0	1.1	105327
32909	PALM BAY	20898	9833	15.1	33.2	42.7	6.5	2.5	51575	54224	65	61	7832	0.8	22.0	67.4	9.7	0.1	114481
32920	CAPE CANAVERAL	29680	6252	29.2	30.2	31.6	5.9	3.2	40118	43413	33	28	3169	18.9	16.5	42.1	20.4	2.1	116886
32922	COCOA	18476	6544	42.5	28.6	21.9	4.2	2.8	30114	31068	8	5	3336	17.0	39.5	29.5	10.4	3.6	82791
32925	PATRICK AFB	14971	533	4.5	43.2	49.2	2.6	0.6	51014	52688	64	59	12	100.0	0.0	0.0	0.0	0.0	33750
32926	COCOA	24682	8814	20.1	27.6	36.7	11.4	4.1	51974	54415	66	62	7228	10.8	21.1	42.5	24.2	1.5	115340
32927	COCOA	22302	10524	13.7	27.0	45.9	10.6	2.9	59283	60371	77	75	8970	5.8	14.9	67.8	11.2	0.3	116945
32931	COCOA BEACH	37763	8060	18.3	26.4	37.0	10.8	7.6	54926	56918	71	70	5603	2.1	5.3	37.8	43.8	11.0	186797
32934	MELBOURNE	31713	7796	16.0	22.8	35.0	14.6	11.6	62531	63938	81	80	6332	15.8	6.0	20.1	51.6	6.5	193221
32935	MELBOURNE	25023	18172	20.4	32.9	36.4	7.4	2.8	47536	50246	56	49	11728	7.7	22.8	54.0	14.1	1.4	111197
32937	SATELLITE BEACH	34021	11939	14.0	23.9	39.7	13.9	8.5	62501	63122	81	80	8963	0.8	3.3	45.3	41.6	9.0	176125
32940	MELBOURNE	40580	12381	7.3	18.6	38.7	22.6	12.8	77287	78110	91	93	10704	1.5	1.6	26.6	63.2	7.0	212985
32948	FELLSMERE	14197	1761	30.3	32.1	29.9	6.2	1.5	40702	43029	35	30	1311	8.0	26.4	38.1	25.3	2.1	116239
32949	GRANT	21930	675	28.6	34.4	29.2	5.0	2.8	37983	41329	27	22	610	9.2	47.4	27.7	13.4	2.3	84203
32950	MALABAR	31203	1853	13.3	21.9	38.4	19.2	7.3	67542	68545	85	86	1654	9.9	8.2	23.3	49.2	9.4	193299
32951	MELBOURNE BEACH	43607	5333	11.6	22.3	36.8	15.0	14.2	68533	69988	86	87	4404	4.7	4.9	18.9	50.2	21.3	244131
32952	MERRITT ISLAND	33677	9010	14.4	24.0	33.4	16.5	11.9	63915	65555	82	82	7261	4.3	6.8	34.1	41.2	13.6	188442
32953	MERRITT ISLAND	30608	10151	18.6	25.6	33.8	13.1	8.9	56003	58470	73	71	7354	6.0	10.6	33.6	41.4	8.4	174172
32955	ROCKLEDGE	28686	13763	12.9	26.0	42.0	13.7	5.4	60572	61637	78	77	11256	3.6	10.7	48.5	33.2	4.0	141431
32958	SEBASTIAN	26067	12170	20.9	29.7	37.8	8.9	2.7	49314	51816	60	55	10167	5.7	7.1	42.5	41.3	3.4	165101
32960	VERO BEACH	25131	10687	29.1	30.8	30.4	7.1	2.6	39719	43581	32	27	6268	6.2	11.9	47.3	27.0	7.6	138449
32962	VERO BEACH	25997	11190	20.4	31.5	37.5	7.4	3.2	48218	51075	57	51	8880	6.1	14.6	50.5	27.1	1.7	132723
32963	VERO BEACH	92356	8605	7.9	13.7	25.1	15.9	37.4	107078	115529	98	98	7706	0.6	0.3	2.6	28.0	68.5	589445
32966	VERO BEACH	30331	8615	20.7	33.4	33.8	7.6	4.5	46106	50064	52	47	6913	22.1	17.4	31.2	22.9	6.3	119840
32967	VERO BEACH	27900	7727	28.1	23.8	31.3	10.7	6.2	48150	52167	57	51	5472	8.5	9.3	28.7	33.0	20.4	188512
32968	VERO BEACH	28977	4670	12.6	23.1	41.9	14.7	7.6	63400	64185	82	82	3979	3.2	3.9	37.8	43.8	11.2	193797
32976	SEBASTIAN	27200	5284	29.7	38.4	25.0	4.3	2.6	36207	38636	21	17	4721	12.6	48.0	28.3	8.5	2.6	81517
33004	DANIA	24625	7035	30.1	27.6	30.5	8.0	3.9	42742	45694	42	36	3758	11.1	17.0	40.5	28.3	3.1	121834
33009	HALLANDALE	25083	20147	36.4	27.5	27.9	5.4	2.9	34867	38269	17	14	13244	14.4	28.5	39.0	13.8	4.3	103045
33010	HIALEAH	13432	15476	44.2	28.7	21.8	4.0	1.3	28381	29807	6	3	4962	7.0	4.7	33.5	54.0	0.8	181653
33012	HIALEAH	15306	23706	34.1	32.1	27.1	4.8	1.8	35124	39109	18	14	12444	3.7	10.0	40.4	44.6	1.3	164711
33013	HIALEAH	15103	10140	29.8	32.9	28.1	6.8	2.4	39807	42729	32	27	6313	1.2	3.3	33.0	61.5	1.0	193990
33014	HIALEAH	22689	13906	24.3	26.5	33.4	10.5	5.3	49219	51495	59	55	7101	0.7	3.6	40.3	48.5	7.0	189965
33015	HIALEAH	22612	20212	15.9	28.5	39.2	11.0	5.4	54913	54218	71	70	10839	0.7	1.4	36.8	57.8	3.4	192977
33016	HIALEAH	18634	14370	25.1	30.7	30.9	8.2	5.1	45581	48673	50	45	8951	1.4	10.3	51.5	27.9	8.9	145791
33018	HIALEAH	18615	12022	13.0	26.0	44.8	11.7	4.5	58457	57918	76	75	9798	6.0	1.9	36.2	52.3	3.6	181928
33019	HOLLYWOOD	44460	8835	18.0	21.2	37.0	11.8	12.0	60698	62877	78	78	5455	0.8	5.4	23.3	47.5	22.9	249555
33020	HOLLYWOOD	20078	18064	34.6	31.4	27.0	5.4	1.6	35943	38666	20	16	8098	10.7	20.1	45.9	21.2	2.1	120431
33021	HOLLYWOOD	29949	20527	20.2	26.1	36.2	11.4	6.1	53454	56777	69	66	13999	11.6	16.6	28.0	38.5	5.3	157715
33023	HOLLYWOOD	17407	20321	22.8	29.4	38.7	7.1	2.0	47863	51230	56	50	14505	2.4	7.9	76.9	12.5	0.3	132315
33024	HOLLYWOOD	21642	22666	18.2	26.2	42.9	9.6	3.1	54426	57141	70	68	16466	2.5	8.2	66.5	21.9	0.8	140070
33025	HOLLYWOOD	24277	20544	13.1	23.7	46.5	12.7	4.0	60902	62748	79	78	12284	2.6	14.8	40.3	40.4	1.9	161217
33026	HOLLYWOOD	33178	11520	11.8	18.4	40.9	18.6	10.2	71693	71979	88	90	9567	0.6	11.0	41.3	42.3	4.7	167203
	FLORIDA	27128		21.9	27.6	33.8	9.8	6.8	50413	52516				8.0	14.3	38.7	30.4	8.6	144752
	UNITED STATES	27277		20.9	24.4	35.3	11.7	7.6	54719	56938				9.3	13.1	31.6	32.6	13.5	162279

ZIP CODE #	POST OFFICE NAME	FINANCIAL SERVICES: Auto Loan	Home Loan	Invest-ments	Retire-ment Plans	THE HOME: Home Improvements: Home Repair	Lawn & Garden	Furnishings: Comput-ers & Hard-ware-Personal	Major Appli-ances	TV, Radio, Sound Equip-ment	Furni-ture	ENTERTAINMENT: Dine out/ Carry out	Sports Equip-ment	Fees & Tickets	Toys & Games	Travel	Cable TV	PERSONAL: Apparel & Services	Auto Repairs	Health Insur-ance	Pets & Supplies
32763	ORANGE CITY	70	74	78	72	78	83	71	77	73	73	72	52	75	70	76	77	49	75	88	87
32764	OSTEEN	103	92	123	90	98	110	88	106	92	87	91	77	82	88	95	96	61	99	107	123
32765	OVIEDO	154	181	160	182	175	156	157	157	148	168	151	126	172	156	164	141	108	150	140	180
32766	OVIEDO	139	159	131	154	150	132	138	138	129	148	132	110	145	138	139	122	93	131	120	157
32767	PAISLEY	70	60	69	57	62	71	58	67	62	59	61	48	53	61	58	66	41	64	70	79
32771	SANFORD	95	95	91	98	94	96	97	94	98	98	99	72	99	97	97	100	69	97	100	113
32773	SANFORD	92	84	72	84	79	80	90	84	89	90	89	67	85	92	83	88	62	87	83	100
32776	SORRENTO	99	98	87	97	95	100	91	96	92	93	92	72	90	96	90	94	64	92	96	114
32778	TAVARES	78	79	101	74	89	94	74	87	78	80	76	56	77	71	83	82	51	83	99	98
32779	LONGWOOD	185	230	240	238	238	215	198	206	190	211	191	157	229	190	221	185	139	196	191	235
32780	TITUSVILLE	85	86	87	86	87	93	86	88	89	85	88	64	88	86	88	93	61	89	99	103
32784	UMATILLA	81	64	82	63	66	84	66	78	71	62	70	58	57	70	65	76	47	73	82	92
32789	WINTER PARK	124	135	143	138	140	134	134	132	132	136	132	100	142	129	140	132	94	133	136	153
32792	WINTER PARK	90	80	76	83	78	79	92	83	92	91	93	66	88	92	86	91	65	89	86	100
32796	TITUSVILLE	80	83	81	83	83	88	80	84	84	80	83	60	83	82	83	87	58	83	91	97
32798	ZELLWOOD	59	64	86	56	76	84	57	73	64	65	61	42	65	55	71	70	40	69	93	79
32801	ORLANDO	73	63	69	68	64	68	83	71	85	78	86	57	79	79	78	88	60	81	85	88
32803	ORLANDO	102	102	98	105	101	98	107	100	105	107	106	79	107	105	105	104	75	104	102	119
32804	ORLANDO	106	109	108	111	109	107	111	107	109	111	110	83	113	109	111	109	77	109	109	127
32805	ORLANDO	51	42	38	44	40	47	50	46	55	49	54	35	47	54	45	58	38	51	53	58
32806	ORLANDO	99	102	99	104	101	102	103	100	103	102	103	77	106	102	104	104	73	103	105	119
32807	ORLANDO	70	61	54	62	58	60	71	64	70	69	71	51	66	72	64	70	49	69	66	77
32808	ORLANDO	68	58	50	58	55	55	66	60	66	67	67	47	61	68	59	65	47	65	60	72
32809	ORLANDO	83	81	74	79	80	76	84	81	83	87	84	62	82	84	82	81	59	84	80	94
32810	ORLANDO	91	86	72	86	80	81	89	83	88	90	89	66	86	91	83	87	62	86	83	100
32811	ORLANDO	73	48	44	53	45	49	70	56	71	69	73	47	60	73	58	70	50	68	60	71
32812	ORLANDO	94	89	81	90	85	83	95	87	93	96	95	70	92	96	90	92	66	92	87	105
32817	ORLANDO	89	72	64	75	68	68	98	77	90	88	91	66	82	91	79	86	64	86	75	94
32818	ORLANDO	93	90	76	89	85	83	89	86	88	92	89	67	87	91	85	86	61	87	83	102
32819	ORLANDO	143	166	157	171	164	150	149	148	143	157	145	117	164	147	157	138	105	144	137	172
32820	ORLANDO	88	82	71	79	79	80	80	81	81	84	81	61	76	85	76	82	56	81	80	96
32821	ORLANDO	100	91	93	95	92	94	105	95	106	104	107	75	103	104	101	106	75	103	103	115
32822	ORLANDO	81	68	59	68	64	65	78	70	78	79	79	56	71	80	70	77	55	76	71	85
32824	ORLANDO	99	103	85	98	97	89	94	94	91	101	93	71	94	96	91	88	64	91	86	109
32825	ORLANDO	112	115	97	112	108	99	109	105	104	115	106	83	109	110	105	100	74	104	96	123
32826	ORLANDO	91	85	79	83	84	82	95	86	90	95	91	66	89	90	87	88	63	89	87	100
32827	ORLANDO	102	112	109	115	112	105	106	105	101	110	103	80	112	103	110	99	73	104	100	122
32828	ORLANDO	141	154	124	147	143	125	136	135	127	148	130	107	139	138	133	120	91	128	116	153
32829	ORLANDO	101	98	84	94	94	93	91	94	92	96	92	70	88	96	87	92	63	91	91	111
32830	ORLANDO	63	38	35	42	35	38	60	46	60	58	61	40	48	62	47	59	42	57	49	59
32831	ORLANDO	134	146	117	140	136	118	129	128	121	140	123	102	131	131	126	114	86	121	110	145
32832	ORLANDO	158	196	201	202	201	186	167	177	160	178	162	131	190	159	187	157	116	167	167	202
32833	ORLANDO	91	98	92	98	96	92	93	91	91	96	92	71	97	93	95	90	65	92	89	108
32835	ORLANDO	120	91	81	99	86	83	117	96	115	117	117	83	105	120	100	110	82	109	93	119
32836	ORLANDO	171	180	175	189	181	156	178	167	166	190	168	139	186	172	179	155	122	167	146	193
32837	ORLANDO	129	122	104	124	114	105	127	115	121	131	124	95	122	128	118	116	87	119	106	137
32839	ORLANDO	70	54	48	56	51	50	69	58	68	69	70	48	61	70	60	66	49	67	58	71
32901	MELBOURNE	60	55	58	55	57	63	62	61	65	60	64	44	60	62	60	68	44	63	71	72
32903	INDIALANTIC	129	145	153	145	150	153	131	141	135	137	135	99	145	130	144	139	94	138	153	162
32904	MELBOURNE	89	91	99	90	95	101	88	95	91	89	90	68	91	88	94	94	62	93	104	110
32905	PALM BAY	63	58	57	58	58	62	64	61	66	62	66	47	62	65	62	68	46	65	68	73
32907	PALM BAY	87	99	86	96	95	91	87	89	86	91	87	67	94	88	91	86	61	87	88	103
32908	PALM BAY	89	92	73	90	85	86	86	85	85	88	86	66	87	89	84	85	59	84	85	101
32909	PALM BAY	84	92	78	90	87	83	83	83	81	87	82	63	86	84	84	79	57	81	79	96
32920	CAPE CANAVERAL	71	62	64	64	63	65	75	67	75	73	75	53	71	73	70	75	52	74	74	82
32922	COCOA	61	51	49	52	50	57	61	57	64	57	63	44	55	63	55	66	44	61	64	69
32925	PATRICK AFB	95	49	37	57	44	42	89	62	84	83	88	61	68	101	64	77	62	79	56	75
32926	COCOA	89	93	90	91	92	94	86	91	87	89	87	67	88	87	89	88	60	88	92	106
32927	COCOA	97	99	83	95	93	89	92	92	90	97	91	70	90	94	89	88	63	89	86	107
32931	COCOA BEACH	93	99	118	99	108	112	95	103	100	101	99	69	103	92	105	105	68	103	119	118
32934	MELBOURNE	109	122	119	121	123	117	112	114	110	117	111	85	120	110	118	110	78	112	115	131
32935	MELBOURNE	77	76	73	77	75	79	79	77	81	77	81	59	79	80	78	83	56	80	84	92
32937	SATELLITE BEACH	104	114	114	114	116	118	107	111	110	109	110	80	115	108	114	112	77	110	121	128
32940	MELBOURNE	130	144	170	143	156	159	127	145	132	138	131	96	141	124	144	137	91	138	157	164
32948	FELLSMERE	80	70	68	64	69	71	70	74	71	73	71	56	63	73	66	71	49	73	71	85
32949	GRANT	61	74	92	66	87	91	65	80	70	75	68	45	78	61	81	76	45	75	102	86
32950	MALABAR	104	127	125	130	129	121	109	115	105	115	106	86	122	105	121	104	76	109	110	132
32951	MELBOURNE BEACH	128	137	181	136	156	159	123	144	129	138	127	91	135	117	141	135	87	137	160	163
32952	MERRITT ISLAND	109	124	129	124	129	130	112	120	114	116	113	86	123	110	123	117	79	116	129	138
32953	MERRITT ISLAND	102	103	104	104	105	110	101	105	103	100	102	77	102	102	103	106	71	104	112	122
32955	ROCKLEDGE	96	104	107	104	106	111	96	103	98	97	98	74	102	97	103	102	68	100	110	119
32958	SEBASTIAN	80	83	97	78	90	95	76	88	80	81	79	58	80	75	84	85	54	84	98	100
32960	VERO BEACH	71	68	74	68	71	76	71	73	74	71	73	53	70	71	72	76	50	74	81	85
32962	VERO BEACH	83	88	91	83	90	93	80	88	82	85	82	61	84	80	86	85	56	85	94	100
32963	VERO BEACH	247	262	355	260	301	307	235	277	247	266	242	174	259	223	272	258	167	264	306	313
32966	VERO BEACH	78	88	100	83	97	101	79	92	84	87	82	58	89	77	92	89	56	88	108	102
32967	VERO BEACH	101	92	100	92	95	104	92	98	99	95	97	70	91	96	93	103	67	98	107	117
32968	VERO BEACH	110	122	107	124	119	119	109	114	107	111	108	88	116	110	115	107	75	109	112	133
32976	SEBASTIAN	61	69	89	61	81	86	62	76	67	71	65	44	70	58	75	73	43	73	96	83
33004	DANIA	73	68	73	69	69	75	76	73	80	73	79	55	75	76	74	83	55	78	84	88
33009	HALLANDALE	61	62	69	61	67	71	65	67	69	66	68	46	68	64	68	73	47	69	81	77
33010	HIALEAH	56	48	42	46	47	41	58	52	55	59	59	42	53	57	54	53	42	58	47	58
33012	HIALEAH	68	64	56	58	63	56	66	65	65	70	67	48	63	65	64	63	47	67	60	72
33013	HIALEAH	74	71	61	63	71	62	70	72	69	76	70	51	67	69	68	67	50	72	65	78
33014	HIALEAH	92	91	81	85	90	76	94	90	89	98	92	69	91	91	92	84	66	92	79	99
33015	HIALEAH	99	89	79	90	85	78	101	89	97	102	100	73	95	101	93	94	71	96	84	106
33016	HIALEAH	89	87	75	81	85	72	90	85	84	95	87	66	86	87	86	79	62	87	74	95
33018	HIALEAH	96	110	98	100	111	85	102	102	90	111	93	79	103	92	105	82	67	98	82	109
33019	HOLLYWOOD	101	118	133	117	126	120	113	116	113	117	113	83	124	106	124	115	80	116	126	132
33020	HOLLYWOOD	63	54	51	56	52	55	66	58	67	64	67	46	62	66	60	67	47	64	63	71
33021	HOLLYWOOD	88	99	107	97	105	101	95	98	95	99	95	70	104	91	103	96	67	97	104	111
33023	HOLLYWOOD	78	80	71	76	78	71	79	77	77	82	79	59	79	79	78	75	55	78	73	88
33024	HOLLYWOOD	89	89	80	87	87	81	90	86	87	92	89	67	89	89	88	85	62	88	83	100
33025	HOLLYWOOD	100	98	86	99	94	88	100	93	97	103	99	75	99	101	96	94	69	96	90	110
33026	HOLLYWOOD	115	130	125	131	130	123	121	121	120	126	121	92	131	119	127	119	86	120	123	140
	FLORIDA	96	94	97	93	96	98	95	97	96	97	96	71	95	94	96	97	67	97	101	113
	UNITED STATES	100	100	100	100	100	100	100	100	100	100	100	100	100	100	100	100	100	100	100	100

ZIP CODE #	POST OFFICE NAME	COUNTY FIPS CODE	POPULATION 2000	POPULATION 2009	POPULATION 2014	2000-2009 ANNUAL RATE % Rate	2000-2009 ANNUAL RATE State Centile	HOUSEHOLDS 2000	HOUSEHOLDS 2009	HOUSEHOLDS 2014	HOUSEHOLDS % Annual Rate 2000-2009	HOUSEHOLDS 2009 Average HH Size	FAMILIES 2000	FAMILIES 2009	FAMILIES % Annual Rate 2000-2009
33027	HOLLYWOOD	011	25470	52387	61333	8.1	95	11810	19794	22443	5.7	2.65	6937	13376	7.4
33028	HOLLYWOOD	011	22133	27608	29867	2.4	70	7033	8663	9344	2.3	3.19	5866	7056	2.0
33029	HOLLYWOOD	011	35309	46323	50895	3.0	78	10726	13350	14655	2.4	3.42	9536	11682	2.2
33030	HOMESTEAD	086	27425	30555	31627	1.2	46	8176	8924	9208	1.0	3.37	6135	6577	0.8
33031	HOMESTEAD	086	5626	6172	6473	1.0	40	1868	2043	2139	1.0	2.98	1532	1646	0.8
33032	HOMESTEAD	086	19535	34606	39795	6.4	91	5492	9188	10488	5.7	3.73	4496	7492	5.7
33033	HOMESTEAD	086	32209	50417	56760	5.0	88	9481	14670	16502	4.8	3.43	7522	11470	4.7
33034	HOMESTEAD	086	15429	18838	20222	2.2	66	3932	4896	5303	2.4	3.34	2980	3670	2.3
33035	HOMESTEAD	086	2769	4490	5177	5.4	90	1094	1984	2334	6.6	2.21	673	1172	6.2
33036	ISLAMORADA	087	3500	3472	3411	-0.1	6	1765	1755	1725	-0.1	1.96	973	928	-0.5
33037	KEY LARGO	087	12949	11837	11270	-1.0	1	5820	5318	5061	-1.0	2.22	3660	3249	-1.3
33039	HOMESTEAD	086	446	460	460	0.3	18	13	13	13	0.0	4.85	12	12	0.0
33040	KEY WEST	087	34230	31214	29798	-1.0	1	14527	13247	12639	-1.0	2.29	7717	6834	-1.3
33042	SUMMERLAND KEY	087	6088	6097	6017	0.0	9	2737	2764	2732	0.1	2.21	1793	1763	-0.2
33043	BIG PINE KEY	087	5168	5062	4946	-0.2	4	2325	2266	2215	-0.3	2.21	1451	1373	-0.6
33050	MARATHON	087	12029	10792	10245	-1.2	1	5505	4955	4696	-1.1	2.14	3288	2881	-1.4
33054	OPA LOCKA	086	29034	29418	29784	0.1	12	8818	9009	9129	0.2	3.12	6550	6569	0.0
33055	OPA LOCKA	086	45105	46008	46278	0.2	15	12368	12626	12671	0.2	3.60	10686	10783	0.1
33056	OPA LOCKA	086	33185	36850	38379	1.1	44	9376	10555	11012	1.3	3.46	7874	8700	1.1
33060	POMPANO BEACH	011	34075	35380	35687	0.4	22	13170	13431	13512	0.2	2.58	7842	7656	-0.3
33062	POMPANO BEACH	011	23990	24495	24680	0.2	15	13636	13687	13734	0.0	1.76	6373	6035	-0.6
33063	POMPANO BEACH	011	49146	51516	52177	0.5	26	21907	22394	22590	0.2	2.29	13268	12987	-0.2
33064	POMPANO BEACH	011	53179	53268	53052	0.0	9	21128	20729	20582	-0.2	2.53	12978	12159	-0.7
33065	POMPANO BEACH	011	52715	54684	54423	0.4	22	18357	18712	18549	0.2	2.90	13417	13293	-0.1
33066	POMPANO BEACH	011	16959	17214	17140	0.2	15	9270	9266	9197	0.0	1.84	4861	4612	-0.6
33067	POMPANO BEACH	011	23778	26526	27835	1.2	46	7851	8569	8929	1.0	3.09	6439	6810	0.6
33068	POMPANO BEACH	011	48492	51235	51568	0.6	30	16049	16598	16628	0.4	3.08	11861	11963	0.1
33069	POMPANO BEACH	011	23345	25098	25763	0.8	35	10576	11065	11259	0.5	2.07	5464	5475	0.0
33070	TAVERNIER	087	5565	5116	4883	-0.9	1	2371	2181	2079	-0.9	2.27	1497	1341	-1.2
33071	POMPANO BEACH	011	37577	40510	41159	0.8	35	12668	13447	13616	0.6	3.01	10436	10911	0.5
33073	POMPANO BEACH	011	20091	26061	28546	2.9	77	7820	9854	10742	2.5	2.64	5397	6575	2.2
33076	POMPANO BEACH	011	18881	29868	33867	5.1	89	5862	9045	10210	4.8	3.30	5222	7989	4.7
33109	MIAMI BEACH	086	467	1118	1373	9.9	96	218	521	648	9.9	2.00	76	163	8.6
33125	MIAMI	086	49686	52259	53354	0.5	26	17493	18396	18739	0.5	2.81	11807	12089	0.3
33126	MIAMI	086	45737	48581	49864	0.7	32	16091	17196	17646	0.7	2.79	11831	12350	0.5
33127	MIAMI	086	27871	29552	30393	0.6	30	8774	9386	9653	0.7	3.05	6138	6409	0.5
33128	MIAMI	086	6393	6594	6697	0.3	18	2590	2734	2796	0.6	2.33	1242	1211	-0.3
33129	MIAMI	086	10985	12057	12546	1.0	40	5476	6133	6410	1.2	1.95	2616	2795	0.7
33130	MIAMI	086	20425	23206	24282	1.4	51	8457	9703	10150	1.5	2.38	4711	5178	1.0
33131	MIAMI	086	4723	8655	9828	6.8	92	2841	4870	5513	6.0	1.74	1070	1845	6.1
33132	MIAMI	086	5265	7076	7899	3.2	80	1941	2972	3445	4.7	1.69	639	929	4.1
33133	MIAMI	086	29883	31424	32072	0.5	26	13057	13864	14156	0.7	2.25	7221	7443	0.3
33134	MIAMI	086	33960	35108	35715	0.4	22	14568	15367	15702	0.6	2.28	8738	8880	0.2
33135	MIAMI	086	35861	36223	36317	0.1	12	13935	14157	14192	0.2	2.54	8898	8769	-0.2
33136	MIAMI	086	13367	15016	16018	1.3	48	4936	5547	5923	1.3	2.54	2648	2870	0.9
33137	MIAMI	086	18112	19556	20143	0.8	35	6797	7516	7804	1.1	2.43	3538	3685	0.4
33138	MIAMI	086	29204	28680	28577	-0.2	4	11672	11525	11475	-0.1	2.47	6532	6212	-0.5
33139	MIAMI BEACH	086	37915	40331	41504	0.7	32	23064	24875	25657	0.8	1.58	6439	6596	0.3
33140	MIAMI BEACH	086	20457	21950	22562	0.8	35	10000	10663	10930	0.7	2.05	4820	4933	0.3
33141	MIAMI BEACH	086	36891	37117	37205	0.1	12	16601	16630	16626	0.0	2.21	8802	8481	-0.4
33142	MIAMI	086	53261	55138	55850	0.4	22	16444	17054	17265	0.4	2.97	11286	11440	0.1
33143	MIAMI	086	30582	31271	31559	0.2	15	12680	12908	12997	0.2	2.41	7484	7367	-0.2
33144	MIAMI	086	23893	23526	23615	-0.2	4	7902	7847	7878	-0.1	2.96	6090	5929	-0.3
33145	MIAMI	086	28161	30304	31209	0.8	35	9911	10751	11077	0.9	2.80	7121	7572	0.7
33146	MIAMI	086	13259	13511	13585	0.2	15	3951	4045	4078	0.3	2.46	2694	2680	-0.1
33147	MIAMI	086	48664	46514	45948	-0.5	1	14337	13709	13524	-0.5	3.36	10973	10299	-0.7
33149	KEY BISCAYNE	086	10513	10981	11141	0.5	26	4262	4449	4504	0.5	2.47	2902	2933	0.1
33150	MIAMI	086	26415	26747	26912	0.1	12	8662	8802	8849	0.2	3.02	5961	5905	-0.1
33154	MIAMI BEACH	086	13427	13995	14251	0.4	22	6803	6899	6961	0.2	2.03	3460	3371	-0.3
33155	MIAMI	086	44067	43613	43530	-0.1	6	14951	14945	14922	0.0	2.88	11334	11087	-0.2
33156	MIAMI	086	30815	31149	31246	0.1	12	10522	10583	10584	0.1	2.93	8149	8058	-0.1
33157	MIAMI	086	61221	64202	65152	0.5	26	19940	21095	21401	0.6	3.02	15535	15997	0.3
33158	MIAMI	086	6855	6845	6871	0.0	9	2246	2275	2286	0.1	3.00	1945	1946	0.0
33160	NORTH MIAMI BEACH	086	31423	35700	37440	1.4	51	16403	18500	19361	1.3	1.91	8083	8718	0.8
33161	MIAMI	086	53518	55672	56107	0.4	22	17438	17500	17520	0.0	3.07	11963	11705	-0.2
33162	MIAMI	086	44614	46218	46398	0.4	22	13646	13558	13519	-0.1	3.38	10181	9893	-0.3
33165	MIAMI	086	56620	56143	56121	-0.1	6	17815	17851	17855	0.0	3.11	14469	14258	-0.2
33166	MIAMI	086	22488	22551	22517	0.0	9	8116	8074	8050	-0.1	2.61	5461	5278	-0.4
33167	MIAMI	086	19332	19826	20004	0.3	18	5596	5736	5779	0.3	3.46	4427	4460	0.1
33168	MIAMI	086	24865	25450	25571	0.3	18	6469	6471	6468	0.0	3.93	5415	5344	-0.1
33169	MIAMI	086	36023	38134	38903	0.6	30	11466	12079	12311	0.6	3.10	8443	8669	0.3
33170	MIAMI	086	7268	9323	10490	2.7	74	2117	2825	3176	3.2	3.26	1699	2200	2.8
33172	MIAMI	086	40090	39944	39916	0.0	9	14398	14411	14396	0.0	2.77	10402	10156	-0.3
33173	MIAMI	086	38007	38189	38290	0.1	12	13564	13696	13711	0.1	2.74	9808	9671	-0.2
33174	MIAMI	086	28109	29378	29792	0.5	26	9206	9784	9958	0.7	3.00	7477	7787	0.4
33175	MIAMI	086	52186	54460	56263	0.5	26	15422	16081	16586	0.5	3.32	13569	14033	0.4
33176	MIAMI	086	47746	47291	47201	-0.1	6	17153	17093	17042	0.0	2.75	12629	12321	-0.3
33177	MIAMI	086	45311	55240	58794	2.2	66	12192	14420	15313	1.8	3.71	10792	12640	1.7
33178	MIAMI	086	18388	36695	43015	7.8	94	5613	12026	14241	8.6	2.77	4171	8960	8.6
33179	MIAMI	086	37834	38795	38933	0.3	18	15513	15637	15626	0.1	2.46	9637	9418	-0.2
33180	MIAMI	086	22873	26872	28616	1.8	59	11397	13581	14497	1.9	1.96	6197	7014	1.3
33181	MIAMI	086	17931	18098	18087	0.1	12	7796	7663	7614	-0.2	2.29	4222	4001	-0.6
33182	MIAMI	086	13317	14070	14301	0.6	30	3682	3933	4005	0.7	3.57	3394	3602	0.6
33183	MIAMI	086	37560	38148	38377	0.2	15	12376	12516	12550	0.1	3.03	9885	9841	0.0
33184	MIAMI	086	19562	21413	22288	1.0	40	5931	6355	6577	0.7	3.32	5130	5462	0.7
33185	MIAMI	086	11051	32963	39502	12.5	98	3303	9737	11716	12.4	3.26	2956	8774	12.5
33186	MIAMI	086	57083	66536	70371	1.7	57	19409	22446	23632	1.6	2.95	15023	17133	1.4
33187	MIAMI	086	14023	15488	16113	1.1	44	4141	4513	4669	0.9	3.42	3613	3887	0.8
33189	MIAMI	086	22051	25735	27659	1.7	57	7392	8614	9265	1.7	2.96	5523	6215	1.3
33190	MIAMI	086	3993	9001	10812	9.2	96	1356	2944	3499	8.7	3.06	1047	2322	9.0
33193	MIAMI	086	38747	44602	47234	1.5	53	11816	13230	13888	1.2	3.37	9928	11047	1.2
33194	MIAMI	086	2012	2124	2609	0.6	30	15	32	40	8.5	2.56	14	29	8.2
33196	MIAMI	086	36150	45077	48036	2.4	70	11289	13469	14230	1.9	3.34	9241	10996	1.9
33199	MIAMI	086	1464	1626	1688	1.1	44	293	339	359	1.6	2.83	20	22	1.0
33301	FORT LAUDERDALE	011	11912	14322	15178	2.0	62	5604	6684	7056	1.9	1.86	2039	2217	0.9
	FLORIDA					1.9					1.9	2.47			1.7
	UNITED STATES					1.0					1.1	2.59			0.9

ZIP CODE #	POST OFFICE NAME	RACE (%) White 2000	White 2009	Black 2000	Black 2009	Asian/Pacific 2000	Asian/Pacific 2009	% Hispanic Origin 2000	% Hispanic Origin 2009	2009 AGE DISTRIBUTION (%) 0-4	5-9	10-14	15-19	20-24	25-44	45-64	65-84	85+	18+	MEDIAN AGE 2009	% 2009 Males	% 2009 Females
33027	HOLLYWOOD	79.9	70.8	11.0	15.6	2.9	3.8	31.3	49.3	8.0	7.6	7.0	5.0	3.1	28.7	20.7	15.3	4.6	74.0	39.2	46.2	53.8
33028	HOLLYWOOD	73.3	69.1	12.6	13.9	5.9	7.0	36.2	45.3	9.1	8.9	8.6	6.5	3.6	34.9	23.3	4.6	0.3	69.1	34.5	48.2	51.8
33029	HOLLYWOOD	74.2	70.2	13.9	15.4	4.1	5.0	36.8	46.4	10.0	9.9	9.3	6.8	3.8	31.8	23.8	4.2	0.3	66.2	33.3	48.2	51.8
33030	HOMESTEAD	63.5	64.6	21.2	18.0	0.8	0.9	49.1	60.3	10.1	9.1	8.0	8.8	8.6	29.2	18.9	6.3	1.0	67.7	28.0	52.9	47.1
33031	HOMESTEAD	91.3	89.5	2.4	2.3	1.6	2.0	32.1	45.7	5.4	6.2	7.0	6.6	3.9	24.8	33.4	11.6	1.1	77.2	42.5	51.7	48.3
33032	HOMESTEAD	53.0	49.5	34.2	36.4	1.7	1.3	42.4	51.2	10.1	9.6	8.6	9.1	8.5	26.3	20.6	6.5	0.8	66.1	27.6	48.3	51.7
33033	HOMESTEAD	64.7	68.0	19.3	14.4	0.9	0.9	59.6	70.6	10.0	9.2	8.1	8.6	8.7	27.6	19.3	7.6	0.9	67.5	28.2	50.0	50.0
33034	HOMESTEAD	49.4	51.1	37.6	33.7	0.7	0.9	39.3	49.4	9.4	8.9	7.7	8.0	8.3	31.4	19.1	6.5	0.7	69.4	29.5	51.2	48.8
33035	HOMESTEAD	79.8	80.0	11.3	10.1	2.4	2.7	26.6	38.0	6.7	6.1	5.7	5.7	6.3	27.3	23.3	15.3	3.5	78.2	39.2	45.4	54.6
33036	ISLAMORADA	97.4	96.3	0.3	0.3	0.4	0.7	6.9	11.6	2.5	2.8	3.3	3.5	2.9	19.3	45.7	18.4	1.6	89.2	52.5	55.0	45.0
33037	KEY LARGO	94.7	93.1	1.9	2.4	0.4	0.6	15.4	23.7	4.2	4.8	5.0	4.8	4.0	22.0	35.8	17.0	2.3	83.0	47.7	51.8	48.2
33039	HOMESTEAD	48.7	53.0	39.5	33.3	0.9	0.9	46.2	58.0	12.2	10.0	7.8	5.2	7.0	35.2	18.5	3.5	0.7	68.0	29.9	51.3	48.7
33040	KEY WEST	85.4	82.0	8.4	9.9	1.3	1.8	19.8	28.8	4.9	4.6	4.3	4.5	5.9	30.9	31.7	11.6	1.6	83.6	41.9	54.1	45.9
33042	SUMMERLAND KEY	95.7	93.9	1.1	1.5	0.7	1.0	6.2	10.6	3.2	3.6	4.3	4.0	2.6	21.1	45.0	14.9	1.2	86.1	49.9	52.6	47.4
33043	BIG PINE KEY	94.9	92.7	1.1	1.6	0.6	0.9	6.7	11.4	3.3	3.9	4.7	4.7	2.3	26.3	39.6	13.8	1.5	84.8	47.1	52.9	47.1
33050	MARATHON	92.2	90.6	4.0	4.4	0.5	0.7	17.9	26.4	3.6	3.7	4.4	4.3	4.2	22.4	37.3	18.0	2.1	85.7	49.0	52.6	47.4
33054	OPA LOCKA	17.8	21.1	76.8	72.6	0.2	0.3	20.8	26.5	8.3	8.3	8.0	10.3	9.0	24.0	21.9	8.9	1.3	69.7	29.5	46.0	54.0
33055	OPA LOCKA	48.3	52.7	40.4	34.5	0.6	0.6	52.6	61.9	7.1	7.2	7.4	8.1	7.3	27.6	24.3	10.2	0.8	73.2	33.9	48.5	51.5
33056	OPA LOCKA	6.8	8.8	88.5	85.2	0.3	0.4	9.3	13.7	7.9	8.1	8.3	9.5	8.3	26.1	23.3	7.8	0.6	69.6	30.1	46.8	53.2
33060	POMPANO BEACH	54.4	50.4	35.5	37.7	0.9	1.2	12.0	16.1	7.3	6.7	6.1	6.5	6.8	25.2	25.6	11.7	4.0	76.0	38.5	49.3	50.7
33062	POMPANO BEACH	96.9	95.5	0.7	1.0	0.5	0.8	5.1	8.2	2.3	2.4	2.6	2.2	2.2	15.6	33.9	31.2	7.7	91.5	59.2	47.8	52.2
33063	POMPANO BEACH	82.6	76.8	8.7	11.3	2.7	3.6	13.8	20.3	5.8	5.4	5.2	5.2	5.5	24.6	26.5	16.2	5.8	80.5	43.9	46.9	53.1
33064	POMPANO BEACH	68.5	63.3	19.8	22.4	1.4	1.8	14.0	19.1	6.4	6.3	6.3	6.3	6.1	26.3	27.0	12.5	3.0	77.3	40.1	49.9	50.1
33065	POMPANO BEACH	74.9	68.8	13.4	16.0	3.6	4.7	19.2	26.5	7.6	7.0	6.9	7.3	8.3	29.2	24.0	7.6	2.0	73.8	32.8	48.5	51.5
33066	POMPANO BEACH	93.4	90.7	3.2	4.4	1.1	1.6	5.7	9.0	2.9	2.8	2.5	2.3	2.8	15.5	19.0	36.6	15.7	90.5	67.0	42.4	57.6
33067	POMPANO BEACH	88.7	84.2	4.4	5.9	3.9	5.5	9.9	15.0	7.3	7.6	8.4	8.1	5.2	28.3	29.9	4.7	0.5	71.3	36.0	48.9	51.1
33068	POMPANO BEACH	54.6	48.1	30.5	34.1	3.3	4.0	22.7	28.9	7.9	7.3	6.9	7.5	7.9	30.8	23.7	6.9	1.1	73.4	32.2	49.1	50.9
33069	POMPANO BEACH	64.3	59.4	30.8	34.3	0.9	1.1	10.6	15.2	4.7	4.5	4.1	4.6	5.8	25.9	22.6	20.5	7.3	84.3	45.3	48.5	51.5
33070	TAVERNIER	96.5	95.0	0.7	1.0	0.8	1.2	11.8	18.7	4.6	4.9	5.1	5.3	3.5	24.5	37.0	13.1	2.0	81.7	46.0	51.3	48.7
33071	POMPANO BEACH	87.6	83.3	5.5	7.1	3.0	4.3	13.2	19.4	5.6	6.1	7.2	7.7	5.9	27.3	32.8	6.7	0.7	76.1	38.4	49.0	51.0
33073	POMPANO BEACH	82.3	76.3	7.5	9.8	3.3	4.6	15.7	22.6	8.4	7.8	6.8	4.7	4.2	36.4	23.4	7.5	0.8	73.9	35.7	50.1	49.9
33076	POMPANO BEACH	86.6	83.3	5.6	6.7	3.9	5.1	11.9	17.0	8.5	8.7	9.0	8.1	4.6	29.2	28.1	3.6	0.2	68.7	33.6	49.2	50.8
33109	MIAMI BEACH	91.2	90.7	3.2	2.9	1.7	1.9	39.0	54.1	3.3	3.0	2.7	3.1	5.5	18.8	25.2	29.1	9.4	88.9	56.7	46.9	53.1
33125	MIAMI	82.5	82.8	4.7	4.0	0.8	0.7	89.3	93.5	6.2	5.6	5.5	5.9	6.6	26.4	24.3	16.3	3.2	79.0	40.1	49.6	50.4
33126	MIAMI	87.3	87.3	2.0	1.7	0.7	0.6	91.2	94.9	5.8	5.6	5.5	6.0	6.4	27.3	25.0	15.2	3.0	79.4	40.1	47.2	52.8
33127	MIAMI	23.5	27.9	65.7	60.0	0.3	0.3	31.8	39.4	8.0	8.1	7.8	8.2	7.4	25.5	23.3	10.4	1.3	71.0	33.0	49.1	50.9
33128	MIAMI	78.2	78.9	6.4	5.6	0.4	0.3	91.0	94.4	6.1	5.8	4.8	5.8	7.0	27.1	23.5	16.6	3.4	80.3	40.1	55.6	44.4
33129	MIAMI	92.7	92.5	1.4	1.2	1.3	1.3	62.7	75.0	3.9	3.2	3.1	3.7	6.1	32.7	28.9	14.9	3.5	87.7	43.2	47.3	52.7
33130	MIAMI	79.0	79.3	4.9	4.3	0.4	0.4	90.5	93.9	6.4	5.6	5.0	5.7	7.2	26.8	24.9	15.5	3.0	80.0	39.8	51.0	49.0
33131	MIAMI	90.3	80.4	2.3	8.3	2.3	2.2	55.2	68.3	4.8	3.2	2.9	3.8	9.3	39.7	25.6	8.9	1.8	87.4	35.7	51.8	48.2
33132	MIAMI	72.7	72.1	19.4	18.3	1.6	1.7	54.1	66.2	3.2	2.6	2.1	3.2	10.0	41.8	24.9	10.1	2.2	90.7	37.8	62.3	37.7
33133	MIAMI	77.8	78.6	16.2	14.4	0.9	1.0	44.9	55.8	5.0	4.6	4.8	4.9	6.2	30.0	28.2	13.4	2.8	82.5	41.3	48.9	51.1
33134	MIAMI	93.3	93.0	0.9	0.8	0.9	0.9	68.6	79.1	4.5	4.4	4.5	4.6	5.3	28.1	27.6	17.2	3.9	83.8	44.1	46.2	53.8
33135	MIAMI	86.6	86.8	2.3	2.0	0.5	0.4	92.7	95.7	5.2	4.7	4.8	5.8	5.9	25.1	26.0	18.3	4.3	81.8	43.8	48.8	51.2
33136	MIAMI	29.6	29.3	61.9	61.3	1.2	1.2	30.3	34.2	8.5	8.2	7.6	8.0	8.2	27.5	21.5	8.9	1.6	71.0	31.5	48.9	51.1
33137	MIAMI	46.5	49.0	38.1	33.6	1.3	1.4	37.3	48.4	6.6	6.0	5.5	6.3	7.4	30.5	25.6	8.6	3.4	78.4	36.2	51.5	48.5
33138	MIAMI	46.4	47.9	40.1	37.3	1.7	2.1	22.2	31.5	6.6	6.3	5.9	6.7	7.0	26.0	29.2	10.6	1.7	77.2	39.0	50.9	49.1
33139	MIAMI BEACH	87.2	86.5	3.9	3.6	1.8	2.0	49.8	63.1	2.6	2.0	1.9	2.5	7.7	39.5	23.4	15.5	4.9	92.2	40.8	54.0	46.0
33140	MIAMI BEACH	93.5	92.6	1.6	1.5	1.1	1.3	41.0	55.0	4.5	4.5	4.7	3.9	4.4	26.4	27.9	18.7	5.0	83.9	46.0	48.9	51.1
33141	MIAMI BEACH	81.6	81.3	5.7	4.8	1.5	1.6	62.6	74.7	5.1	4.5	4.3	5.1	8.0	30.2	27.6	12.7	2.6	83.3	40.3	49.3	50.7
33142	MIAMI	33.7	36.4	54.5	50.6	0.2	0.2	45.3	51.0	7.1	7.2	7.0	7.8	8.1	27.0	22.8	11.3	1.6	74.2	34.3	51.7	48.3
33143	MIAMI	80.3	78.6	11.9	12.5	2.7	2.9	43.0	55.3	5.7	5.6	5.9	5.9	6.7	28.7	28.0	11.6	2.0	79.3	39.3	47.8	52.2
33144	MIAMI	92.9	92.9	1.0	0.9	0.4	0.4	88.3	93.3	4.3	4.2	4.4	5.0	4.9	24.0	26.2	22.4	4.6	84.1	47.3	46.6	53.4
33145	MIAMI	90.7	90.6	1.5	1.4	0.9	0.9	85.2	91.2	4.7	4.6	4.8	5.4	6.0	26.1	27.0	17.7	3.7	82.6	43.8	47.7	52.3
33146	MIAMI	88.6	87.0	5.5	5.8	3.0	3.7	36.8	49.7	4.4	5.0	5.4	17.0	15.2	19.0	22.2	9.7	2.2	82.6	29.6	47.9	52.1
33147	MIAMI	25.9	29.4	66.1	61.2	0.2	0.2	31.6	37.9	7.7	8.7	8.2	8.3	7.1	25.3	22.7	10.8	1.3	70.3	32.4	47.5	52.5
33149	KEY BISCAYNE	95.5	94.8	0.5	0.5	0.9	1.0	49.8	65.2	6.8	7.2	8.2	6.5	3.6	22.2	29.4	13.9	2.2	73.6	42.3	46.5	53.5
33150	MIAMI	16.3	20.3	71.9	66.7	0.5	0.5	18.4	25.6	8.2	8.0	7.9	8.3	7.7	25.2	24.3	9.2	1.2	70.9	32.1	47.7	52.3
33154	MIAMI BEACH	92.9	91.8	1.6	1.5	1.1	1.4	35.2	50.4	4.3	4.1	4.5	4.8	4.5	22.5	28.1	20.6	6.5	84.1	48.2	44.8	55.2
33155	MIAMI	93.0	92.7	1.1	1.0	0.7	0.7	75.8	84.7	5.6	5.5	5.7	5.7	5.1	26.2	26.6	16.5	2.9	79.6	42.3	47.5	52.5
33156	MIAMI	90.6	89.3	2.0	1.8	3.7	4.5	34.8	48.6	5.8	6.4	7.9	8.0	5.1	22.0	32.1	11.2	1.5	74.8	41.5	48.0	52.0
33157	MIAMI	57.8	58.7	31.9	29.1	2.3	2.6	30.8	42.1	7.5	7.6	7.7	7.5	6.3	25.6	26.5	9.6	1.7	72.3	35.7	47.8	52.2
33158	MIAMI	89.7	88.0	3.1	3.1	3.5	4.4	27.0	40.5	6.2	7.0	8.7	8.1	4.4	19.9	33.2	11.2	1.3	72.7	42.1	49.2	50.8
33160	NORTH MIAMI BEACH	87.9	86.9	5.4	5.0	1.6	1.9	31.6	45.4	3.8	3.4	3.5	3.6	4.1	22.9	27.4	23.2	8.1	87.2	51.4	45.5	54.5
33161	MIAMI	31.9	33.9	56.2	52.2	2.0	2.4	21.5	30.3	8.4	7.5	6.8	8.0	8.5	28.3	22.8	7.9	1.9	73.0	31.8	48.0	52.0
33162	MIAMI	37.4	38.8	48.1	44.2	4.0	4.7	25.5	34.9	7.4	7.4	7.3	8.2	8.2	27.5	24.2	8.1	1.7	72.9	32.5	48.2	51.8
33165	MIAMI	92.6	92.5	1.1	1.0	1.0	0.9	82.7	89.5	5.0	5.0	5.2	5.7	5.9	26.2	25.8	18.0	3.2	81.4	42.8	47.1	52.9
33166	MIAMI	84.7	84.4	5.4	5.0	2.1	2.1	62.1	73.7	5.8	5.4	5.5	7.0	7.0	31.5	25.7	10.0	2.2	79.1	37.2	50.3	49.7
33167	MIAMI	18.2	22.2	72.5	66.7	0.5	0.6	20.8	28.5	7.9	8.1	8.0	8.8	8.0	26.2	23.7	8.5	0.9	70.6	31.0	47.2	52.8
33168	MIAMI	22.5	26.2	66.7	61.2	1.3	1.6	21.3	29.6	7.1	7.6	7.9	8.7	8.2	26.2	25.2	8.0	1.0	72.0	31.7	48.6	51.4
33169	MIAMI	13.4	15.0	79.6	76.5	1.1	1.3	11.0	16.3	7.9	7.8	7.6	8.1	8.0	27.7	23.2	8.5	1.2	71.7	31.8	46.4	53.6
33170	MIAMI	35.7	38.9	58.1	52.7	0.6	0.7	19.9	30.1	8.0	8.1	7.8	8.1	6.7	24.0	25.3	10.9	1.2	71.2	34.9	47.4	52.6
33172	MIAMI	85.3	85.6	2.1	1.7	2.2	2.0	85.4	90.8	6.4	6.0	5.5	5.9	7.2	32.3	24.0	11.1	1.5	78.6	36.5	47.4	52.6
33173	MIAMI	88.8	88.5	2.6	2.2	2.3	2.3	65.1	76.9	5.9	5.6	5.6	6.0	6.5	29.6	26.0	12.4	2.5	79.3	38.8	47.2	52.8
33174	MIAMI	89.4	89.6	0.9	0.8	0.5	0.5	90.3	94.3	4.8	5.0	5.2	6.0	6.2	26.2	26.6	16.9	3.1	81.4	42.3	46.6	53.4
33175	MIAMI	89.7	89.7	1.9	1.8	1.1	1.0	83.1	89.6	5.5	5.8	6.1	6.8	5.9	27.9	27.5	12.5	2.0	78.4	39.5	48.5	51.5
33176	MIAMI	73.3	72.7	19.1	18.5	2.7	3.1	37.4	49.3	5.8	6.1	6.7	6.9	6.1	26.1	29.4	11.3	1.6	77.0	39.6	47.3	52.7
33177	MIAMI	67.4	70.6	19.1	14.9	1.9	1.9	63.7	74.2	8.6	8.0	7.5	7.5	6.8	32.5	21.6	6.7	0.8	71.2	31.9	50.4	49.6
33178	MIAMI	77.6	82.7	11.8	6.3	4.1	3.8	60.2	75.3	9.3	8.3	6.7	5.5	5.4	38.3	21.5	4.6	0.4	72.6	33.6	53.6	46.4
33179	MIAMI	57.1	56.5	31.7	30.0	3.2	3.8	25.5	36.4	6.5	6.3	6.4	6.3	6.0	26.6	25.8	12.9	3.3	76.9	39.4	45.5	54.5
33180	MIAMI	92.7	91.6	2.3	2.2	1.5	1.9	21.7	33.9	3.8	3.7	3.9	3.5	3.6	22.7	29.5	23.4	6.0	86.3	51.2	45.9	54.1
33181	MIAMI	57.8	57.0	33.2	32.3	2.3	2.8	26.0	36.7	7.3	5.9	5.2	5.9	9.3	30.4	23.9	10.2	2.0	78.6	34.9	49.0	51.0
33182	MIAMI	87.7	87.7	1.0	0.9	1.0	0.9	87.0	92.4	8.2	7.4	6.9	6.1	5.3	35.4	22.7	7.3	0.7	73.5	33.5	47.9	52.1
33183	MIAMI	86.3	86.6	2.8	2.2	1.9	1.8	74.0	83.3	6.5	6.8	6.7	6.8	6.1	29.8	25.9	10.0	1.5	75.8	36.7	47.6	52.4
33184	MIAMI	89.8	89.6	2.1	2.2	0.5	0.5	87.3	91.9	5.4	6.0	6.3	6.6	5.8	27.9	28.1	12.3	1.6	78.2	39.6	48.6	51.4
33185	MIAMI	88.4	87.2	3.7	4.8	1.5	1.1	77.1	85.5	6.7	6.8	7.0	7.0	5.6	29.8	27.2	8.9	1.1	75.1	37.0	49.9	50.1
33186	MIAMI	81.1	81.6	7.1	5.9	3.4	3.7	58.1	69.7	7.0	6.9	7.0	6.7	5.8	31.9	26.4	7.5	0.9	75.0	35.6	47.6	52.4
33187	MIAMI	81.3	81.6	7.3	6.0	2.3	2.4	59.4	71.6	8.6	8.4	8.2	6.9	4.8	30.7	24.7	7.1	0.6	70.3	34.8	49.6	50.4
33189	MIAMI	61.6	63.9	26.5	22.2	2.0	2.3	41.1	54.1	8.8	8.0	7.3	7.3	7.8	28.9	22.7	8.1	1.0	71.4	31.7	48.1	51.9
33190	MIAMI	66.6	58.5	21.2	28.8	1.8	1.5	46.6	54.1	10.8	9.8	8.5	7.3	7.0	30.4	19.9	5.8	0.6	66.4	29.0	46.8	53.2
33193	MIAMI	81.8	82.6	4.6	3.5	1.9	1.8	79.3	86.8	8.4	7.6	7.0	7.7	8.1	32.9	21.6	6.2	0.6	72.4	31.1	47.9	52.1
33194	MIAMI	82.6	85.1	10.7	7.9	0.7	0.7	75.6	84.3	6.0	6.2	6.4	6.5	6.0	29.5	27.6	10.4	1.4	77.3	38.4	51.9	48.1
33196	MIAMI	78.5	79.3	7.6	6.2	3.1	3.0	64.1	74.8	8.6	7.8	7.6	6.9	7.0	34.3	21.9	5.4	0.5	71.7	31.7	47.7	52.3
33199	MIAMI	47.7	46.2	33.8	31.1	7.9	9.3	26.0	36.2	0.1	0.3	0.1	26.9	61.7	7.7	2.6	0.3	0.1	98.8	21.8	41.0	59.0
33301	FORT LAUDERDALE	83.8	71.8	12.5	21.6	0.7	1.0	6.9	11.4	4.0	3.6	3.3	5.0	8.0	33.9	28.7	11.6	2.1	86.6	40.5	57.8	42.2
	FLORIDA	78.0	74.7	14.6	15.8	1.7	2.3	16.8	21.5	6.0	5.9	5.9	6.3	6.2	25.0	26.8	15.3	2.8	78.6	41.1	48.8	51.2
	UNITED STATES	75.1	72.0	12.3	12.7	3.8	4.6	12.5	15.7	6.8	6.7	6.6	7.1	6.9	27.0	26.0	10.9	1.9	75.7	36.9	49.2	50.8

INCOME

ZIP CODE #	POST OFFICE NAME	2009 Per Capita Income	2009 HH Income Base	2009 Household Income Distribution (%): Less than $25,000	$25,000 to $49,999	$50,000 to $99,999	$100,000 to $149,999	$150,000 or More	Median Household Income: 2009	2014	2009 National Centile	2009 State Centile	2009 Home Value Base	2009 Home Value Distribution (%): Less than $50,000	$50,000 to $89,999	$90,000 to $174,999	$175,000 to $399,999	$400,000 or More	2009 Median Home Value
33027	HOLLYWOOD	33504	19794	19.2	18.8	25.9	19.5	16.6	71555	76376	88	90	17480	3.6	13.8	29.3	46.5	6.8	187087
33028	HOLLYWOOD	41015	8663	4.0	6.3	30.2	28.6	31.0	114808	115458	98	98	6888	0.1	0.1	6.4	79.4	14.0	269282
33029	HOLLYWOOD	39368	13350	4.6	6.9	26.0	28.5	34.0	123297	125634	99	99	12302	0.7	2.1	9.3	76.4	11.5	259787
33030	HOMESTEAD	14148	8924	34.3	29.3	26.8	7.5	2.1	36437	40743	22	17	3987	5.1	8.3	48.1	32.6	5.9	146619
33031	HOMESTEAD	28091	2043	10.8	19.8	40.1	19.9	9.3	70828	70667	87	89	1722	1.9	2.8	7.1	58.1	30.1	294282
33032	HOMESTEAD	13041	9188	31.7	29.4	30.4	6.6	1.9	39465	41820	31	26	5824	6.2	5.0	63.4	22.4	3.0	143762
33033	HOMESTEAD	14188	14670	28.8	33.0	30.4	5.2	2.6	40370	44327	34	29	8281	4.6	6.8	68.3	18.7	1.7	134660
33034	HOMESTEAD	12572	4896	43.4	29.5	21.7	3.1	2.4	29453	31450	7	5	2560	8.7	26.5	47.9	13.5	3.5	108922
33035	HOMESTEAD	24429	1984	24.4	29.2	37.8	4.3	4.3	47044	48699	54	49	1370	0.0	20.9	59.5	18.5	1.1	115576
33036	ISLAMORADA	39686	1755	19.6	32.2	26.6	12.1	9.5	48742	50560	58	53	1195	13.1	2.1	4.6	30.5	49.7	398148
33037	KEY LARGO	37905	5318	18.5	26.0	34.2	12.1	9.1	56083	56143	73	71	3837	5.1	4.1	16.8	45.9	28.2	258107
33039	HOMESTEAD	14286	13	100.0	0.0	0.0	0.0	0.0	14077	14077	1	1	0	0.0	0.0	0.0	0.0	0.0	0
33040	KEY WEST	32609	13247	18.4	24.2	36.9	11.8	8.6	57206	56344	74	73	6713	5.2	5.4	8.8	36.6	44.0	364147
33042	SUMMERLAND KEY	34906	2764	15.8	20.4	42.3	13.0	8.4	63870	62571	82	82	2191	0.6	2.0	12.1	40.7	44.6	376157
33043	BIG PINE KEY	26630	2266	24.2	23.8	40.4	8.7	2.9	51304	51899	64	60	1722	6.1	2.3	15.9	55.6	20.1	275333
33050	MARATHON	30045	4955	26.2	27.4	31.6	7.7	7.1	46393	49425	53	48	3258	15.2	3.1	11.4	39.7	30.6	275621
33054	OPA LOCKA	12679	9009	44.4	28.5	21.5	4.6	0.9	28717	30265	6	4	4693	3.6	22.8	67.9	5.4	0.3	113104
33055	OPA LOCKA	15437	12626	22.4	30.2	38.5	6.4	2.5	47665	50026	56	50	10216	9.6	10.7	59.5	20.2	0.0	137343
33056	OPA LOCKA	16129	10555	22.7	29.8	36.5	8.3	2.8	48131	49767	57	51	7594	0.6	6.3	76.8	14.8	1.5	137893
33060	POMPANO BEACH	21863	13431	28.4	27.7	32.0	7.5	4.4	43183	47119	43	38	7184	7.4	16.3	37.9	31.7	6.6	139149
33062	POMPANO BEACH	43381	13687	20.1	25.3	32.9	11.9	9.8	54576	58269	71	69	9895	0.7	5.3	28.6	45.9	19.5	222738
33063	POMPANO BEACH	26063	22394	21.9	26.8	38.5	9.8	2.9	50985	54166	64	59	16986	16.4	24.4	35.4	23.5	0.4	110899
33064	POMPANO BEACH	23723	20729	23.3	29.5	34.4	8.7	4.1	46691	51107	53	48	14392	11.6	19.2	45.7	13.4	10.1	115973
33065	POMPANO BEACH	22770	18712	18.2	26.9	38.3	11.5	5.1	54300	57628	70	68	10462	4.1	24.4	19.1	48.6	3.8	180166
33066	POMPANO BEACH	31811	9266	21.0	29.1	38.6	8.3	2.9	49834	52671	61	56	7850	1.0	16.6	69.7	11.7	0.9	115159
33067	POMPANO BEACH	42782	8569	5.9	9.7	34.7	19.7	30.0	99395	102771	97	98	6353	0.2	0.2	2.3	63.9	33.4	325566
33068	POMPANO BEACH	18704	16598	19.1	29.0	41.8	8.3	1.8	51307	54470	64	60	11173	7.9	13.9	68.0	10.2	0.0	124739
33069	POMPANO BEACH	25779	11065	24.5	30.3	35.2	7.2	2.7	45054	49187	48	42	7121	5.4	25.8	59.7	8.9	0.3	108785
33070	TAVERNIER	30079	2181	16.4	31.1	36.5	9.1	6.9	52845	52848	68	64	1537	3.5	1.8	12.6	47.2	34.8	309144
33071	POMPANO BEACH	36758	13447	6.3	14.7	39.0	21.6	18.3	83305	84537	93	95	9364	0.1	3.7	9.3	70.2	16.7	265866
33073	POMPANO BEACH	31213	9854	10.7	19.4	42.7	19.7	7.5	72904	73265	88	91	6649	17.3	3.3	9.4	67.9	2.1	217919
33076	POMPANO BEACH	58382	9045	2.6	4.8	19.3	20.9	52.4	154105	157615	100	100	7769	0.3	0.2	3.9	48.0	47.5	386871
33109	MIAMI BEACH	47871	521	55.5	10.7	11.7	8.1	14.0	20694	23200	2	1	345	0.0	0.0	12.2	16.5	71.3	654221
33125	MIAMI	12730	18396	48.2	29.6	18.0	2.8	1.3	25908	26957	4	2	5702	3.6	6.2	39.6	49.1	1.5	176136
33126	MIAMI	15538	17196	34.5	34.7	25.3	3.9	1.5	35215	38346	18	14	6977	1.0	12.8	48.1	37.2	0.9	151518
33127	MIAMI	11036	9386	49.6	29.3	18.8	1.5	0.8	25199	25926	3	2	3589	6.2	26.2	59.0	8.4	0.2	108964
33128	MIAMI	10842	2734	64.0	25.9	8.5	1.0	0.7	15167	15253	1	1	159	10.1	6.9	64.8	17.6	0.6	116595
33129	MIAMI	55801	6133	15.8	19.1	30.1	13.6	21.5	73358	75022	89	91	3446	0.6	1.1	9.6	57.9	30.9	302515
33130	MIAMI	11291	9703	61.7	25.2	10.6	1.8	0.7	17416	18317	1	1	1318	3.7	26.6	43.6	19.3	6.8	118676
33131	MIAMI	57800	4870	24.2	16.0	25.1	15.3	19.4	65278	62027	84	84	1844	0.7	0.2	11.3	50.3	37.5	314179
33132	MIAMI	29829	2972	43.5	19.2	19.7	8.7	8.9	31816	34097	11	8	1078	4.2	10.1	15.2	40.8	29.7	246127
33133	MIAMI	46462	13864	22.4	19.9	28.2	11.1	18.4	59902	59403	77	76	7275	0.2	2.3	14.2	35.8	47.5	375203
33134	MIAMI	41332	15367	17.6	23.2	30.5	14.9	13.8	63457	62251	82	82	8316	1.2	1.1	11.9	47.5	38.3	325173
33135	MIAMI	13611	14157	51.1	27.7	17.2	3.3	0.7	24051	25303	3	2	3601	3.8	8.1	34.5	51.5	2.1	183563
33136	MIAMI	11353	5547	61.3	22.9	11.6	3.7	0.5	17047	17800	1	1	595	19.3	14.3	39.0	22.7	4.7	114978
33137	MIAMI	23561	7516	35.0	26.6	26.2	5.8	6.3	37671	41597	26	21	2172	3.5	11.7	38.2	25.3	21.2	164641
33138	MIAMI	24873	11525	33.7	22.2	27.4	9.4	7.2	42569	46562	41	35	5840	6.6	4.9	24.6	39.6	24.2	229466
33139	MIAMI BEACH	41724	24875	33.2	26.2	25.1	7.5	8.0	39165	44961	30	26	8449	1.0	6.9	35.3	27.1	29.7	197654
33140	MIAMI BEACH	48165	10663	23.8	20.2	26.3	11.6	18.0	59674	58629	77	76	6275	1.5	3.5	12.4	38.6	44.0	345276
33141	MIAMI BEACH	21662	16630	39.6	29.2	22.7	4.6	3.9	31690	34472	11	8	5297	1.8	12.6	39.5	27.4	18.8	163032
33142	MIAMI	11698	17054	53.3	26.7	16.5	2.7	0.8	22489	24062	2	2	6437	11.8	23.7	52.8	11.5	0.1	109464
33143	MIAMI	39779	12908	20.9	23.5	28.0	11.7	15.9	56894	55990	74	72	7463	0.9	6.4	22.4	29.5	40.9	320547
33144	MIAMI	18105	7847	28.6	28.8	31.9	8.1	2.5	42478	45998	41	35	5097	3.9	3.4	25.3	65.6	1.7	208816
33145	MIAMI	20192	10751	28.2	29.3	29.0	8.7	4.8	42970	46626	42	37	5451	1.7	1.0	22.3	70.3	4.6	231642
33146	MIAMI	53863	4045	8.8	8.9	22.7	17.1	42.4	128542	132835	99	100	3149	0.0	0.5	2.2	16.4	81.0	595119
33147	MIAMI	12150	13709	45.6	27.5	21.3	3.7	1.8	27193	28350	5	3	7537	12.3	18.8	59.9	8.5	0.6	115544
33149	KEY BISCAYNE	63871	4449	11.1	9.5	24.1	17.7	37.6	113032	117095	98	98	3083	0.0	0.0	0.8	17.0	82.2	658133
33150	MIAMI	13037	8802	44.8	28.8	20.7	4.0	1.6	27930	29077	6	3	3956	16.5	14.4	52.8	16.4	0.0	120638
33154	MIAMI BEACH	45092	6899	20.7	23.7	30.6	11.9	13.1	57820	57371	75	74	4055	0.1	3.2	22.1	41.1	33.6	288238
33155	MIAMI	24226	14945	18.4	24.6	37.2	13.4	6.5	57675	57324	75	74	10591	0.3	0.5	16.6	74.2	8.3	241104
33156	MIAMI	57684	10583	8.1	14.2	22.9	14.0	40.8	118461	126837	98	99	8063	0.1	1.1	7.6	19.2	72.1	604241
33157	MIAMI	26766	21095	23.4	20.0	30.0	13.9	12.7	58900	58392	76	75	14259	1.2	4.1	33.8	44.8	16.1	195144
33158	MIAMI	57445	2275	7.3	7.2	14.4	16.2	54.9	157080	159772	100	100	1925	1.0	1.5	0.4	27.6	69.6	464359
33160	NORTH MIAMI BEACH	33392	18500	30.4	27.1	29.2	6.7	6.7	42977	46237	42	37	11471	2.1	16.7	38.8	24.4	18.0	150014
33161	MIAMI	15489	17500	34.1	31.8	26.7	5.2	2.2	36275	40694	21	17	8373	9.5	11.4	49.3	27.8	1.9	144318
33162	MIAMI	14562	13558	30.4	29.5	32.8	5.1	2.1	41167	44703	37	31	8397	9.2	9.9	53.8	25.8	1.3	145233
33165	MIAMI	21009	17851	22.0	24.4	36.6	12.0	5.1	53712	54365	69	67	12362	0.2	1.1	19.0	73.5	6.2	230893
33166	MIAMI	26363	8074	17.0	26.2	38.9	11.3	6.6	56045	55220	73	71	4001	2.3	3.2	16.8	67.9	9.7	238858
33167	MIAMI	13082	5736	33.7	32.2	27.6	4.8	1.7	36135	39795	21	16	3612	4.2	11.5	72.4	9.7	2.2	126800
33168	MIAMI	12865	6471	25.9	33.7	31.7	6.8	2.0	41757	45378	39	34	5030	1.2	8.9	70.7	18.0	1.1	137933
33169	MIAMI	17842	12079	26.0	28.9	33.5	8.8	2.8	45583	48218	50	45	6748	4.8	9.6	60.8	24.1	0.7	145391
33170	MIAMI	16086	2825	36.4	26.7	24.0	8.4	4.6	39628	44087	32	26	1860	2.3	10.1	45.2	26.8	15.6	153528
33172	MIAMI	18329	14411	25.0	33.9	33.8	5.3	2.0	43920	46674	45	40	7288	9.7	10.9	63.6	15.1	0.8	126971
33173	MIAMI	27998	13696	15.4	22.0	39.6	15.4	7.7	62399	61004	80	80	9055	0.5	2.7	30.7	55.6	10.4	217867
33174	MIAMI	19408	9784	24.7	29.9	32.5	8.9	4.0	46354	48688	52	47	5891	1.1	5.4	34.2	55.4	4.0	194725
33175	MIAMI	22540	16081	14.5	22.8	40.5	15.5	6.7	62723	61931	81	81	13085	1.4	2.1	31.7	54.8	10.0	213175
33176	MIAMI	37330	17093	15.2	18.6	32.1	15.5	18.6	70041	70660	87	88	12197	0.7	4.0	26.9	41.1	27.3	277637
33177	MIAMI	18354	14420	13.2	24.0	47.7	11.0	4.2	60256	60399	78	77	11737	0.7	2.1	46.8	47.6	2.8	175528
33178	MIAMI	37074	12026	16.1	13.4	29.7	17.6	23.1	82254	83536	93	94	8231	0.5	0.4	9.0	62.8	27.3	273237
33179	MIAMI	24189	15637	25.7	30.0	31.7	7.1	5.5	45420	47632	50	44	11527	12.5	24.9	37.7	20.0	5.0	114888
33180	MIAMI	49150	13581	15.9	23.0	30.2	14.9	16.0	63627	63400	82	82	9957	1.8	6.1	22.2	40.5	29.3	265112
33181	MIAMI	28986	7663	28.8	28.6	26.9	7.7	7.9	43352	46739	43	38	3704	8.4	13.9	30.4	21.8	25.5	165234
33182	MIAMI	25002	3933	7.5	18.0	41.1	23.3	10.1	75723	77417	90	92	3463	0.3	0.2	14.2	77.1	8.1	242437
33183	MIAMI	22794	12516	14.6	28.1	40.9	9.9	6.5	55327	55303	72	70	9204	0.0	4.1	52.1	39.7	4.2	163219
33184	MIAMI	20390	6355	17.4	26.0	38.4	12.7	5.5	55232	55370	72	70	4985	13.1	4.6	26.3	48.3	7.7	191367
33185	MIAMI	27989	9737	8.2	16.4	41.4	22.1	11.9	78363	79051	91	94	8547	0.0	0.2	11.2	79.0	9.5	258333
33186	MIAMI	28440	22446	9.5	20.8	42.2	17.0	10.6	68721	68995	86	87	16224	0.3	0.6	33.4	60.8	4.9	208712
33187	MIAMI	25899	4513	10.5	14.3	44.0	21.1	10.1	76908	77493	91	93	3932	1.1	3.5	12.6	67.5	15.2	249219
33189	MIAMI	20721	8614	23.3	25.4	36.0	10.4	4.9	51147	52553	64	60	4919	0.7	3.4	48.2	46.7	1.1	172384
33190	MIAMI	22387	2944	25.2	22.5	31.9	12.8	7.6	53208	54043	68	65	1796	0.0	2.1	50.7	44.9	2.3	171217
33193	MIAMI	18763	13230	17.3	29.9	37.3	11.3	4.2	52469	53429	67	64	8597	0.3	4.0	41.3	53.7	0.7	185627
33194	MIAMI	2434	32	12.5	18.8	34.4	21.9	12.5	68028	75000	86	87	28	0.0	0.0	7.1	78.6	14.3	271429
33196	MIAMI	24978	13469	9.5	20.2	43.6	17.6	9.1	70870	71658	87	89	9599	0.3	1.1	22.4	71.5	4.8	225873
33199	MIAMI	12491	339	63.4	16.8	17.4	2.4	0.0	13994	14936	1	1	84	19.0	0.0	20.2	39.3	21.4	231250
33301	FORT LAUDERDALE	44886	6684	20.3	21.2	32.5	11.3	14.7	58553	59625	76	75	3440	0.3	2.2	18.6	29.2	49.7	396563
	FLORIDA	27128		21.9	27.6	33.8	9.8	6.8	50413	52516				8.0	14.3	38.7	30.4	8.6	144752
	UNITED STATES	27277		20.9	24.4	35.3	11.7	7.6	54719	56938				9.3	13.1	31.6	32.6	13.5	162279

ZIP CODE		FINANCIAL SERVICES				THE HOME						ENTERTAINMENT						PERSONAL			
						Home Improvements		Furnishings													
#	POST OFFICE NAME	Auto Loan	Home Loan	Invest-ments	Retire-ment Plans	Home Repair	Lawn & Garden	Comput-ers & Hard-ware-Personal	Major Appli-ances	TV, Radio, Sound Equip-ment	Furni-ture	Dine out/ Carry out	Sports Equip-ment	Fees & Tickets	Toys & Games	Travel	Cable TV	Apparel & Services	Auto Repairs	Health Insur-ance	Pets & Supplies
33027	HOLLYWOOD	120	142	140	137	148	137	122	132	120	138	119	94	138	119	135	117	84	123	134	145
33028	HOLLYWOOD	185	225	194	232	219	184	187	189	172	210	175	158	212	187	197	158	129	173	154	211
33029	HOLLYWOOD	195	233	198	237	225	190	195	197	180	218	184	163	217	195	203	166	134	181	162	220
33030	HOMESTEAD	68	58	52	57	56	51	70	62	68	70	71	49	65	69	64	65	51	69	58	71
33031	HOMESTEAD	112	137	133	140	138	128	118	123	113	124	114	94	132	114	129	110	81	117	116	141
33032	HOMESTEAD	71	64	57	62	62	59	70	66	70	73	71	50	66	71	65	69	50	69	64	77
33033	HOMESTEAD	71	65	58	61	64	56	71	67	68	75	71	51	67	70	68	65	50	71	60	75
33034	HOMESTEAD	59	50	44	49	47	49	58	53	60	58	60	41	53	60	52	60	42	57	55	64
33035	HOMESTEAD	75	72	69	72	71	72	77	73	78	77	79	55	77	77	75	79	55	77	80	86
33036	ISLAMORADA	121	108	153	106	119	135	104	125	109	106	108	88	100	102	113	115	72	118	132	145
33037	KEY LARGO	129	120	150	118	127	137	115	132	118	116	117	95	111	115	122	123	80	126	134	153
33039	HOMESTEAD	5	3	3	3	3	3	5	4	5	5	5	3	4	5	4	5	4	5	4	5
33040	KEY WEST	104	103	109	105	106	96	112	104	106	112	108	83	111	107	111	103	78	108	99	121
33042	SUMMERLAND KEY	119	107	156	106	118	132	103	124	107	104	106	87	99	100	113	112	71	117	127	143
33043	BIG PINE KEY	96	80	123	77	88	103	79	99	83	76	82	71	70	78	86	88	54	92	100	114
33050	MARATHON	101	89	124	87	97	109	87	104	91	88	90	73	82	87	93	96	61	98	107	120
33054	OPA LOCKA	56	47	42	48	45	50	54	51	58	55	58	38	51	57	49	60	41	55	56	62
33055	OPA LOCKA	80	83	72	76	81	72	80	80	77	86	79	59	79	78	79	75	55	80	74	90
33056	OPA LOCKA	80	78	68	77	74	77	78	76	80	81	81	57	78	80	76	81	56	79	81	92
33060	POMPANO BEACH	77	74	71	75	73	72	82	75	82	81	83	58	80	81	78	82	58	80	79	90
33062	POMPANO BEACH	100	107	127	108	116	117	104	110	108	110	107	76	112	100	114	111	75	110	124	127
33063	POMPANO BEACH	79	82	83	81	83	83	84	82	85	84	85	61	87	83	86	86	60	85	90	96
33064	POMPANO BEACH	85	83	83	82	83	82	86	84	86	87	86	64	85	85	85	86	61	86	86	99
33065	POMPANO BEACH	94	90	82	92	87	83	98	88	94	97	96	72	95	97	93	92	68	93	86	106
33066	POMPANO BEACH	72	81	94	76	91	94	77	86	82	83	81	54	87	74	88	87	55	85	106	95
33067	POMPANO BEACH	186	218	196	224	214	183	191	189	177	208	180	156	211	188	199	164	131	178	160	214
33068	POMPANO BEACH	83	82	72	81	79	75	84	79	82	85	83	62	83	84	81	80	58	82	77	93
33069	POMPANO BEACH	71	72	75	71	74	80	75	75	80	76	79	53	78	75	77	84	55	78	91	88
33070	TAVERNIER	114	95	140	93	102	119	93	115	97	90	96	83	83	94	99	103	64	107	114	133
33071	POMPANO BEACH	149	179	170	184	178	159	157	157	148	166	151	125	176	153	168	142	110	151	141	180
33073	POMPANO BEACH	124	126	106	125	119	107	121	115	115	128	118	93	121	123	117	110	83	114	104	134
33076	POMPANO BEACH	274	332	287	342	323	272	276	279	254	310	259	233	313	275	290	232	190	255	228	311
33109	MIAMI BEACH	118	87	107	100	91	108	142	115	154	127	153	89	126	132	126	165	106	142	161	149
33125	MIAMI	52	41	37	39	40	37	52	47	52	53	54	36	46	52	47	50	38	52	45	53
33126	MIAMI	61	54	52	52	53	53	62	59	63	61	64	45	58	63	58	63	45	63	60	68
33127	MIAMI	48	38	34	39	36	40	47	42	50	47	50	32	43	49	41	51	35	47	46	51
33128	MIAMI	35	24	23	25	24	22	37	30	36	36	39	25	32	36	32	35	28	36	30	35
33129	MIAMI	134	146	167	155	153	135	160	142	152	155	157	118	169	149	164	149	116	150	137	166
33130	MIAMI	36	26	26	28	26	26	39	32	40	37	41	26	34	38	34	39	29	39	35	38
33131	MIAMI	134	117	129	130	119	111	153	124	148	144	153	107	146	147	142	146	112	141	126	153
33132	MIAMI	83	60	63	68	58	60	90	70	90	84	93	61	79	88	78	89	65	85	77	89
33133	MIAMI	131	140	154	145	146	130	153	139	147	149	150	112	159	144	155	144	110	146	135	162
33134	MIAMI	120	129	141	134	134	122	137	126	131	136	133	100	143	129	140	129	97	131	126	147
33135	MIAMI	48	38	35	38	38	34	51	44	50	49	52	35	45	50	45	48	38	50	42	50
33136	MIAMI	40	28	26	30	26	30	40	33	43	39	43	27	35	42	34	44	30	40	38	42
33137	MIAMI	79	67	67	71	66	62	87	72	86	84	88	61	81	85	79	84	64	83	72	88
33138	MIAMI	82	77	76	78	77	74	89	80	89	86	90	62	87	88	84	89	65	87	82	94
33139	MIAMI BEACH	89	70	77	80	70	72	100	79	100	93	102	68	92	96	89	100	72	94	90	101
33140	MIAMI BEACH	121	133	150	136	142	138	137	134	138	138	138	99	147	129	146	141	98	139	151	156
33141	MIAMI BEACH	63	54	57	57	54	55	70	60	71	67	71	48	65	67	65	71	50	69	67	74
33142	MIAMI	50	38	34	38	37	40	47	44	50	48	51	32	42	49	41	52	35	48	47	52
33143	MIAMI	127	133	138	136	135	128	139	129	135	139	136	102	144	134	140	134	98	135	131	153
33144	MIAMI	71	75	72	71	75	75	74	75	76	75	76	53	76	73	76	78	54	76	81	85
33145	MIAMI	70	76	75	75	76	69	82	75	80	77	82	58	83	79	81	80	60	79	75	86
33146	MIAMI	198	262	314	273	289	242	233	238	216	250	217	182	278	212	268	208	164	226	213	263
33147	MIAMI	60	51	45	50	49	53	56	54	61	58	60	39	52	60	51	63	42	58	60	66
33149	KEY BISCAYNE	194	252	298	258	278	222	229	232	204	248	204	182	262	199	261	189	153	220	197	256
33150	MIAMI	56	47	42	48	45	49	55	50	59	54	59	38	52	59	49	62	42	55	56	62
33154	MIAMI BEACH	114	125	137	127	132	128	128	126	128	130	128	93	136	120	135	130	90	129	138	145
33155	MIAMI	91	109	108	102	111	98	99	100	95	101	97	74	107	96	106	95	70	99	95	111
33156	MIAMI	209	269	312	278	293	248	240	244	223	257	223	188	281	220	271	213	167	233	220	272
33157	MIAMI	104	117	115	117	118	109	114	112	114	115	115	83	121	112	117	114	84	112	110	128
33158	MIAMI	202	292	343	293	320	272	235	251	223	250	222	186	297	223	281	219	170	234	230	273
33160	NORTH MIAMI BEACH	79	85	94	84	91	95	86	88	91	87	90	60	93	84	92	96	63	91	108	101
33161	MIAMI	66	58	54	58	57	53	70	61	69	69	71	49	65	69	64	67	50	68	60	72
33162	MIAMI	69	68	62	64	67	60	72	69	69	74	71	52	69	70	69	67	50	71	64	77
33165	MIAMI	86	98	97	93	101	91	92	94	90	94	91	68	97	89	97	90	65	93	92	105
33166	MIAMI	94	98	96	97	98	90	102	94	100	100	102	74	105	101	102	99	73	100	93	110
33167	MIAMI	67	61	53	59	57	62	62	62	66	65	66	45	60	66	59	68	45	64	67	74
33168	MIAMI	71	74	67	70	73	68	72	72	71	75	72	53	73	70	72	70	50	72	69	82
33169	MIAMI	79	68	64	70	66	68	80	72	81	80	83	56	76	81	74	81	57	79	76	88
33170	MIAMI	72	72	68	73	70	73	72	70	76	73	76	52	75	75	72	78	53	73	76	85
33172	MIAMI	72	67	61	66	66	62	74	68	73	74	74	53	71	74	70	72	53	72	67	80
33173	MIAMI	102	113	114	112	115	104	111	107	107	112	108	83	117	107	115	105	77	109	104	124
33174	MIAMI	77	82	81	78	84	76	83	82	80	84	82	61	84	79	85	79	59	83	81	91
33175	MIAMI	100	121	115	114	123	104	108	110	101	113	103	83	116	102	115	97	74	106	98	121
33176	MIAMI	135	152	157	156	156	142	147	143	141	151	143	112	158	141	154	138	103	144	138	166
33177	MIAMI	101	108	92	100	104	88	100	100	94	108	96	77	100	98	99	88	68	96	86	111
33178	MIAMI	156	173	152	177	168	146	157	153	147	171	150	126	168	157	159	138	109	147	132	174
33179	MIAMI	81	78	79	78	79	79	85	81	87	82	86	61	83	85	82	89	61	85	86	95
33180	MIAMI	125	139	169	139	153	148	132	141	133	142	132	98	144	123	147	135	93	139	152	160
33181	MIAMI	94	80	77	83	78	78	99	86	99	96	100	70	92	98	90	98	71	96	90	104
33182	MIAMI	135	148	120	142	138	121	130	130	122	142	125	103	133	132	129	115	88	123	112	147
33183	MIAMI	96	106	97	101	104	95	99	99	95	102	97	75	103	98	101	94	69	98	93	113
33184	MIAMI	96	105	96	99	105	93	96	98	93	102	94	72	99	95	99	91	67	96	91	110
33185	MIAMI	120	154	147	148	154	135	131	133	124	134	126	102	148	128	143	122	92	128	123	150
33186	MIAMI	119	132	116	132	127	115	121	118	115	127	118	94	128	120	123	111	84	116	109	137
33187	MIAMI	133	142	127	138	136	129	126	131	122	133	124	102	129	129	128	119	86	124	120	151
33189	MIAMI	87	83	75	83	80	76	90	82	88	90	90	65	87	90	85	87	63	87	81	97
33190	MIAMI	103	88	74	90	82	80	101	89	101	103	102	72	93	105	89	99	71	96	88	108
33193	MIAMI	93	88	76	85	84	72	95	86	89	98	92	70	89	92	88	83	65	90	76	98
33194	MIAMI	99	140	145	130	145	124	116	120	111	115	112	88	136	112	132	111	83	116	114	132
33196	MIAMI	127	126	106	125	118	107	123	116	117	129	120	95	121	125	117	111	84	116	105	136
33199	MIAMI	43	18	18	22	17	21	60	30	48	41	49	32	36	47	32	44	35	42	30	40
33301	FORT LAUDERDALE	120	120	134	128	126	110	137	121	128	137	130	101	138	126	136	122	95	129	114	143
	FLORIDA	96	94	97	93	96	98	95	97	96	97	96	71	95	94	96	97	67	97	101	113
	UNITED STATES	100	100	100	100	100	100	100	100	100	100	100	100	100	100	100	100	100	100	100	100

POPULATION CHANGE

#	POST OFFICE NAME	COUNTY FIPS CODE	POPULATION 2000	POPULATION 2009	POPULATION 2014	2000-2009 ANNUAL RATE % Rate	2000-2009 ANNUAL RATE State Centile	HOUSEHOLDS 2000	HOUSEHOLDS 2009	HOUSEHOLDS 2014	HOUSEHOLDS % Annual Rate 2000-2009	HOUSEHOLDS 2009 Average HH Size	FAMILIES 2000	FAMILIES 2009	FAMILIES % Annual Rate 2000-2009
33304	FORT LAUDERDALE	011	18923	18632	18803	-0.2	4	9792	9495	9545	-0.3	1.89	3342	3024	-1.1
33305	FORT LAUDERDALE	011	11726	12061	12235	0.3	18	6122	6197	6267	0.1	1.92	2330	2201	-0.6
33306	FORT LAUDERDALE	011	3802	3985	4077	0.5	26	1992	2058	2099	0.4	1.88	931	903	-0.3
33308	FORT LAUDERDALE	011	29673	30017	30184	0.1	12	16691	16664	16721	0.0	1.78	7398	6945	-0.7
33309	FORT LAUDERDALE	011	35420	36724	36530	0.4	22	13500	13679	13544	0.1	2.57	7837	7600	-0.3
33311	FORT LAUDERDALE	011	66088	70015	70481	0.6	30	21670	22512	22584	0.4	3.05	15098	15160	0.0
33312	FORT LAUDERDALE	011	45827	49088	49765	0.7	32	17368	18582	18887	0.7	2.62	10991	11089	0.1
33313	FORT LAUDERDALE	011	56720	58197	58310	0.3	18	21116	21021	20958	0.0	2.72	13940	13365	-0.5
33314	FORT LAUDERDALE	011	23013	24018	24414	0.5	26	9405	9645	9761	0.3	2.48	5497	5376	-0.2
33315	FORT LAUDERDALE	011	12990	13370	13452	0.3	18	6218	6315	6346	0.2	2.10	2953	2816	-0.5
33316	FORT LAUDERDALE	011	10683	11058	11167	0.4	22	5818	5974	6061	0.3	1.75	2299	2183	-0.6
33317	FORT LAUDERDALE	011	34231	35366	35168	0.4	22	12112	12326	12215	0.2	2.85	8967	8865	-0.1
33319	FORT LAUDERDALE	011	41758	43187	43477	0.4	22	19583	19706	19737	0.1	2.18	10909	10476	-0.4
33321	FORT LAUDERDALE	011	38609	42521	43630	1.0	40	19134	20893	21447	1.0	2.02	11227	11676	0.4
33322	FORT LAUDERDALE	011	39521	40279	40250	0.2	15	18299	18233	18163	0.0	2.21	10709	10216	-0.5
33323	FORT LAUDERDALE	011	17652	18663	18674	0.6	30	5823	6061	6042	0.4	3.08	4728	4827	0.2
33324	FORT LAUDERDALE	011	41353	43480	43717	0.5	26	18674	19225	19263	0.3	2.25	10947	10783	-0.2
33325	FORT LAUDERDALE	011	26722	27024	27218	0.1	12	9300	9251	9277	-0.1	2.91	7158	6942	-0.3
33326	FORT LAUDERDALE	011	30829	32963	33273	0.7	32	10972	11300	11336	0.3	2.92	8589	8656	0.1
33327	FORT LAUDERDALE	011	13031	19773	22936	4.6	87	3995	6031	6957	4.6	3.28	3598	5394	4.5
33328	FORT LAUDERDALE	011	22106	24096	24698	0.9	38	8073	8654	8843	0.8	2.78	6102	6349	0.4
33330	FORT LAUDERDALE	011	11260	14739	15947	3.0	78	3541	4535	4882	2.7	3.25	3082	3901	2.6
33331	FORT LAUDERDALE	011	20844	22692	23362	0.9	38	6432	6865	7049	0.7	3.30	5656	5953	0.6
33332	FORT LAUDERDALE	011	4074	8720	10234	8.6	95	1036	2195	2580	8.5	3.94	929	1956	8.4
33334	FORT LAUDERDALE	011	30778	31416	31463	0.2	15	12877	12904	12876	0.0	2.40	7017	6681	-0.5
33351	FORT LAUDERDALE	011	33562	35631	35965	0.6	30	12241	12763	12824	0.5	2.72	8591	8671	0.1
33401	WEST PALM BEACH	099	20753	24145	25321	1.7	57	9321	11228	11960	2.0	1.98	4152	4450	0.8
33403	WEST PALM BEACH	099	12795	13031	13191	0.2	15	5159	5129	5160	-0.1	2.52	3060	2899	-0.6
33404	WEST PALM BEACH	099	27994	30395	31628	0.9	38	11051	11706	12089	0.6	2.58	7039	7215	0.3
33405	WEST PALM BEACH	099	19802	19712	19753	0.0	9	7809	7634	7637	-0.2	2.57	4804	4456	-0.8
33406	WEST PALM BEACH	099	24650	25635	25624	0.4	22	8773	8883	8869	0.1	2.68	5910	5721	-0.4
33407	WEST PALM BEACH	099	28657	31615	32914	1.1	44	10675	11723	12239	1.0	2.58	6449	6842	0.6
33408	NORTH PALM BEACH	099	17932	18366	18576	0.3	18	9165	9341	9441	0.2	1.96	4930	4723	-0.5
33409	WEST PALM BEACH	099	21578	24088	25041	1.2	46	9336	10293	10725	1.1	2.27	4556	4784	0.5
33410	PALM BEACH GARDENS	099	26919	33142	35832	2.3	69	11758	14345	15499	2.2	2.29	7602	8899	1.7
33411	WEST PALM BEACH	099	41536	65718	75246	5.1	89	15173	24182	27817	5.2	2.67	11241	17536	4.9
33412	WEST PALM BEACH	099	8844	16604	19805	7.0	93	2915	5533	6609	7.2	3.00	2537	4731	7.0
33413	WEST PALM BEACH	099	9425	12706	13968	3.3	81	3587	4720	5181	3.0	2.67	2569	3274	2.7
33414	WEST PALM BEACH	099	38282	53874	58922	3.8	84	12945	18053	19729	3.7	2.98	10691	14672	3.5
33415	WEST PALM BEACH	099	39627	41607	42559	0.5	26	16047	16635	16973	0.4	2.50	10099	10028	-0.1
33417	WEST PALM BEACH	099	28627	29481	29942	0.3	18	14395	14675	14871	0.2	1.99	6996	6719	-0.4
33418	PALM BEACH GARDENS	099	26908	35075	38695	2.9	77	11279	14496	15940	2.7	2.40	8128	10175	2.5
33426	BOYNTON BEACH	099	14557	16339	16998	1.3	48	7058	7930	8268	1.3	2.04	4113	4289	0.5
33428	BOCA RATON	099	37682	38321	38501	0.2	15	14115	14262	14333	0.1	2.68	10405	10131	-0.3
33430	BELLE GLADE	099	21107	21048	21054	0.0	9	6323	6241	6250	-0.1	3.11	4534	4318	-0.5
33431	BOCA RATON	099	16063	16436	16475	0.2	15	6052	6106	6121	0.1	2.31	3839	3690	-0.4
33432	BOCA RATON	099	19225	19456	19711	0.1	12	9802	9914	10074	0.1	1.96	5101	4810	-0.6
33433	BOCA RATON	099	40697	41939	42350	0.3	18	19375	19830	20036	0.3	2.06	11431	11068	-0.3
33434	BOCA RATON	099	20731	20671	20630	0.0	9	10337	10207	10195	-0.1	2.03	6126	5807	-0.6
33435	BOYNTON BEACH	099	30902	32620	33194	0.6	30	12653	13309	13570	0.5	2.40	7467	7454	0.0
33436	BOYNTON BEACH	099	36551	40235	41228	1.0	40	16918	18313	18734	0.9	2.17	10661	11092	0.4
33437	BOYNTON BEACH	099	27540	34894	38548	2.6	73	13514	16983	18777	2.5	2.04	10021	12490	2.4
33438	CANAL POINT	099	861	941	956	1.0	40	296	323	328	0.9	2.79	219	231	0.6
33440	CLEWISTON	051	17673	18994	19899	0.8	35	5642	6039	6306	0.7	3.07	4334	4576	0.6
33441	DEERFIELD BEACH	011	26644	27814	27946	0.5	26	11728	12057	12094	0.3	2.30	6408	6281	-0.2
33442	DEERFIELD BEACH	011	28698	29316	29349	0.2	15	15466	15491	15429	0.0	1.85	7417	7054	-0.5
33444	DELRAY BEACH	099	21436	23233	24040	0.9	38	7793	8435	8727	0.9	2.73	4869	5024	0.3
33445	DELRAY BEACH	099	27999	29512	29838	0.6	30	13257	13697	13842	0.4	2.13	7574	7416	-0.2
33446	DELRAY BEACH	099	15787	21397	23926	3.3	81	9202	11614	12766	2.5	1.83	5321	6906	2.9
33449	LAKE WORTH	099	2676	4757	5561	6.4	91	1137	1903	2231	5.7	2.50	994	1633	5.5
33455	HOBE SOUND	085	17811	20644	21643	1.6	55	8112	9406	9918	1.6	2.16	5390	6154	1.4
33458	JUPITER	099	33970	45765	49717	3.3	81	13111	17721	19294	3.3	2.57	9292	12380	3.2
33460	LAKE WORTH	099	31854	33025	33095	0.4	22	12149	12112	12097	0.0	2.66	6843	6459	-0.6
33461	LAKE WORTH	099	36112	39199	40287	0.9	38	14163	14915	15241	0.6	2.58	8681	8721	0.0
33462	LAKE WORTH	099	27635	29938	30524	0.9	38	11641	12528	12797	0.8	2.35	7236	7403	0.2
33463	LAKE WORTH	099	39893	47949	50802	2.0	62	14906	17476	18419	1.7	2.73	10528	12026	1.4
33467	LAKE WORTH	099	37040	50554	56521	3.4	81	15465	20357	22562	3.0	2.48	10979	14462	3.0
33469	JUPITER	085	14236	14974	15212	0.5	26	6546	6890	7009	0.6	2.16	4390	4429	0.1
33470	LOXAHATCHEE	099	19455	27004	30626	3.6	83	6049	8277	9374	3.4	3.26	5130	6894	3.2
33471	MOORE HAVEN	043	6421	6867	7101	0.7	32	2284	2466	2570	0.8	2.44	1660	1762	0.6
33472	BOYNTON BEACH	099	11461	19023	21230	5.6	90	4656	7587	8444	5.4	2.50	3685	5927	5.3
33473	BOYNTON BEACH	099	155	2029	2578	32.1	100	49	641	825	32.0	2.99	42	544	31.9
33476	PAHOKEE	099	8298	8695	8666	0.5	26	2421	2526	2517	0.5	3.35	1834	1847	0.1
33477	JUPITER	099	11897	12136	12259	0.2	15	6320	6440	6507	0.2	1.88	3950	3817	-0.4
33478	JUPITER	099	11315	13025	13648	1.5	53	3721	4276	4487	1.5	3.04	3201	3599	1.3
33480	PALM BEACH	099	11167	10992	10971	-0.2	4	6242	6075	6062	-0.3	1.81	3220	2936	-1.0
33483	DELRAY BEACH	099	12536	13159	13372	0.5	26	6557	6724	6795	0.3	1.94	3216	3082	-0.5
33484	DELRAY BEACH	099	23734	24738	24887	0.4	22	13433	13929	14024	0.4	1.74	7435	7223	-0.3
33486	BOCA RATON	099	21967	22070	22124	0.1	12	8947	8938	8976	0.0	2.41	5726	5459	-0.5
33487	BOCA RATON	099	16326	16848	16932	0.3	18	7967	8192	8240	0.3	2.03	4837	4694	-0.3
33493	SOUTH BAY	099	4198	4435	4436	0.6	30	903	939	938	0.4	3.54	710	715	0.1
33496	BOCA RATON	099	20673	21533	21689	0.4	22	9011	9362	9438	0.4	2.30	6686	6711	0.0
33498	BOCA RATON	099	14498	15335	15419	0.6	30	5219	5431	5447	0.4	2.81	4490	4578	0.2
33510	BRANDON	057	22405	27922	30578	2.4	70	8214	10611	11767	2.8	2.61	6175	7726	2.5
33511	BRANDON	057	44737	60015	67176	3.2	80	16858	22882	25694	3.4	2.60	12181	15669	2.8
33513	BUSHNELL	119	10761	13765	16495	2.7	74	3829	5179	6419	3.3	2.29	2665	3496	3.0
33514	CENTER HILL	119	1337	2444	3372	6.7	92	446	821	1135	6.8	2.97	334	596	6.5
33523	DADE CITY	101	17420	20131	21848	1.6	55	6225	7127	7771	1.5	2.76	4553	5051	1.1
33525	DADE CITY	101	14274	17832	19929	2.4	70	5317	6612	7420	2.4	2.57	3778	4537	2.0
33527	DOVER	057	12419	16667	18376	3.2	80	3957	5279	5844	3.2	3.14	3141	4061	2.8
33534	GIBSONTON	057	7604	14535	17137	7.3	93	2653	4753	5543	6.5	3.05	1856	3417	6.8
33538	LAKE PANASOFFKEE	119	4473	7162	9480	5.2	89	2095	3435	4585	5.5	2.09	1362	2128	4.9
33540	ZEPHYRHILLS	101	8216	9799	10714	1.9	61	3253	3805	4151	1.7	2.56	2415	2726	1.3
33541	ZEPHYRHILLS	101	14887	18326	20298	2.3	69	6864	8385	9344	2.2	2.10	4615	5349	1.6
33542	ZEPHYRHILLS	101	18846	21797	23767	1.6	55	9143	10438	11420	1.4	2.05	5696	6126	0.8
	FLORIDA					1.9					1.9	2.47			1.7
	UNITED STATES					1.0					1.1	2.59			0.9

ZIP CODE # POST OFFICE NAME	RACE (%) White 2000	White 2009	Black 2000	Black 2009	Asian/Pacific 2000	Asian/Pacific 2009	% Hispanic Origin 2000	% Hispanic Origin 2009	2009 AGE DISTRIBUTION (%) 0-4	5-9	10-14	15-19	20-24	25-44	45-64	65-84	85+	18+	MEDIAN AGE 2009	% 2009 Males	% 2009 Females
33304 FORT LAUDERDALE	72.7	68.5	17.7	20.0	1.5	2.0	9.0	12.8	4.5	4.1	3.5	5.0	6.1	32.5	28.6	12.9	2.9	85.6	41.7	54.4	45.6
33305 FORT LAUDERDALE	85.3	82.2	8.0	9.3	1.4	2.0	7.8	11.7	3.8	3.3	3.3	3.6	4.7	28.5	34.8	15.2	2.7	87.3	46.4	55.4	44.6
33306 FORT LAUDERDALE	96.1	94.4	0.9	1.4	1.2	1.7	5.7	9.2	3.6	3.7	4.0	3.3	3.7	22.7	36.5	17.5	5.0	86.6	50.4	52.2	47.8
33308 FORT LAUDERDALE	96.1	94.3	1.0	1.4	1.1	1.6	6.7	10.6	2.4	2.4	2.7	2.9	3.3	18.2	34.8	27.4	5.9	90.7	56.2	49.0	51.0
33309 FORT LAUDERDALE	57.3	51.0	33.5	37.7	1.6	2.1	13.1	17.7	6.4	5.8	5.4	6.3	7.9	29.9	26.5	9.1	2.8	78.7	37.5	50.7	49.3
33311 FORT LAUDERDALE	11.1	9.0	82.0	84.0	0.5	0.6	3.4	4.2	8.5	8.3	8.0	8.4	7.4	24.5	23.3	10.0	1.7	70.0	32.4	47.4	52.6
33312 FORT LAUDERDALE	58.3	55.0	33.8	35.3	1.3	1.7	15.1	19.9	6.1	6.3	6.5	6.7	6.1	26.6	29.6	10.8	1.4	77.0	39.6	51.0	49.0
33313 FORT LAUDERDALE	25.0	20.9	66.8	70.1	1.6	1.9	7.8	9.8	8.2	7.7	7.2	7.5	8.1	26.9	22.7	8.9	2.7	72.3	32.7	46.4	53.6
33314 FORT LAUDERDALE	84.8	80.3	5.3	6.5	2.8	3.6	22.6	31.6	6.3	5.9	5.8	6.7	8.8	31.7	24.4	9.1	1.3	78.1	34.8	49.5	50.5
33315 FORT LAUDERDALE	85.7	81.0	7.2	9.3	1.7	2.3	16.1	22.7	4.6	4.3	4.4	4.6	5.6	29.6	33.4	11.6	1.9	84.0	43.1	51.9	48.1
33316 FORT LAUDERDALE	90.2	86.8	5.0	6.3	1.7	2.4	9.7	14.3	3.1	2.9	3.0	3.1	4.4	26.9	32.2	19.8	4.6	89.3	49.1	52.7	47.3
33317 FORT LAUDERDALE	70.0	65.2	20.8	23.4	2.5	3.2	17.7	23.4	6.2	6.4	6.7	7.0	6.0	24.9	28.4	12.2	2.0	76.3	39.7	48.9	51.1
33319 FORT LAUDERDALE	58.7	51.8	33.0	38.2	1.9	2.3	11.4	15.0	5.5	4.8	4.5	4.5	5.2	22.0	23.6	22.1	7.8	82.5	47.9	45.1	54.9
33321 FORT LAUDERDALE	86.1	81.9	7.1	9.0	1.5	2.0	14.0	19.9	3.9	3.6	3.7	3.4	3.1	19.1	24.5	29.3	9.4	86.8	56.7	44.2	55.8
33322 FORT LAUDERDALE	83.0	77.9	10.2	12.8	2.4	3.3	11.9	17.3	4.4	4.6	4.7	4.4	3.4	20.3	25.9	23.2	9.0	83.5	51.2	45.4	54.6
33323 FORT LAUDERDALE	80.0	74.6	10.8	13.4	3.5	4.6	18.1	25.2	6.8	7.3	7.6	7.1	5.4	30.4	28.6	6.2	0.6	73.6	36.5	49.7	50.3
33324 FORT LAUDERDALE	86.2	81.7	6.4	8.2	2.9	4.0	14.1	20.7	5.2	5.0	4.8	4.6	5.9	29.2	27.6	14.8	2.8	82.3	41.7	46.8	53.2
33325 FORT LAUDERDALE	88.3	84.2	4.0	5.2	2.2	3.0	17.2	25.1	6.8	7.0	7.1	7.3	6.2	27.5	29.9	7.4	0.7	74.5	37.1	48.8	51.2
33326 FORT LAUDERDALE	88.3	85.1	3.4	4.1	2.8	3.6	29.5	39.3	7.2	7.5	7.9	7.5	4.9	27.5	28.1	8.3	1.2	72.6	38.0	48.0	52.0
33327 FORT LAUDERDALE	88.9	86.3	3.5	4.1	3.0	3.6	27.7	37.7	10.4	10.4	10.0	7.4	3.6	29.4	24.1	4.6	0.2	64.2	32.5	48.7	51.3
33328 FORT LAUDERDALE	91.3	88.0	2.0	2.8	3.2	4.5	12.6	18.9	6.0	6.5	7.2	7.0	5.7	25.0	31.4	9.9	1.3	75.9	40.1	48.4	51.6
33330 FORT LAUDERDALE	89.3	86.7	3.8	4.6	3.3	4.2	18.6	26.1	6.1	7.2	8.4	8.5	4.8	22.9	33.9	7.6	0.7	72.5	40.0	49.1	50.9
33331 FORT LAUDERDALE	85.4	81.6	4.9	5.9	4.3	5.4	27.1	36.8	8.5	9.2	9.4	7.6	3.8	28.3	27.4	5.2	0.5	67.9	35.8	48.9	51.1
33332 FORT LAUDERDALE	89.0	86.9	4.7	4.8	1.6	2.4	24.6	34.9	8.4	9.1	9.6	7.8	4.0	25.1	29.3	6.3	0.5	67.8	36.2	48.9	51.1
33334 FORT LAUDERDALE	76.1	71.0	12.5	14.5	1.9	2.4	21.5	29.0	6.4	5.7	5.4	6.1	8.2	28.6	28.1	9.5	2.1	79.0	38.0	52.2	47.8
33351 FORT LAUDERDALE	68.7	62.0	18.9	22.4	4.0	5.1	19.5	26.3	6.9	6.5	6.5	7.1	7.9	29.9	25.5	7.1	2.4	75.7	35.2	47.7	52.3
33401 WEST PALM BEACH	50.3	44.5	41.7	45.8	1.2	1.4	10.2	14.0	5.9	5.2	4.7	7.0	8.5	25.2	23.1	14.3	6.1	80.9	39.7	47.1	52.9
33403 WEST PALM BEACH	54.8	46.2	36.3	43.3	2.9	3.5	5.7	8.6	6.9	6.4	6.0	6.4	7.3	28.0	25.7	10.7	2.5	77.0	37.2	48.4	51.6
33404 WEST PALM BEACH	26.9	22.0	69.5	74.1	0.5	0.5	3.5	4.7	7.9	7.1	6.6	7.6	8.3	21.7	23.5	15.0	2.5	73.9	36.3	47.1	52.9
33405 WEST PALM BEACH	81.9	77.0	4.8	5.6	1.0	1.2	46.3	59.3	6.1	6.0	5.9	6.3	6.5	28.3	27.0	11.7	2.2	78.3	38.8	51.6	48.4
33406 WEST PALM BEACH	81.9	75.3	7.4	9.5	1.6	2.0	28.8	42.1	6.1	6.0	5.9	6.3	7.0	30.6	25.7	10.7	1.8	78.4	37.4	52.4	47.6
33407 WEST PALM BEACH	31.0	25.0	59.8	64.3	1.4	1.7	9.2	12.0	7.5	6.9	6.9	7.3	7.3	26.8	25.7	9.8	1.8	74.1	35.5	49.0	51.0
33408 NORTH PALM BEACH	96.6	94.5	0.9	1.5	1.1	1.6	3.9	7.2	3.1	3.2	3.6	3.8	3.6	17.1	33.2	27.0	5.6	87.8	55.3	48.4	51.6
33409 WEST PALM BEACH	69.4	61.9	20.2	24.8	2.4	3.2	17.3	23.7	6.2	5.5	5.1	6.1	9.6	33.4	21.8	9.8	2.5	80.0	34.4	49.8	50.2
33410 PALM BEACH GARDENS	92.0	89.0	3.6	4.5	2.1	3.0	6.3	10.8	5.0	5.2	5.5	5.6	4.7	23.0	30.9	17.1	3.0	80.9	45.5	48.3	51.7
33411 WEST PALM BEACH	80.0	74.1	12.9	16.1	2.2	3.1	11.5	17.7	5.8	6.0	6.4	6.9	5.6	24.0	29.2	13.7	2.5	77.8	41.9	48.1	51.9
33412 WEST PALM BEACH	86.9	80.2	7.3	11.0	1.8	2.5	9.9	16.7	8.6	8.8	8.9	7.2	3.9	28.5	26.9	6.7	0.5	69.1	36.2	50.2	49.8
33413 WEST PALM BEACH	79.8	71.1	10.5	14.8	2.3	2.8	19.3	30.0	6.5	6.1	5.9	6.0	6.3	27.9	26.0	13.6	1.5	77.7	38.2	49.6	50.4
33414 WEST PALM BEACH	89.1	84.3	5.2	7.3	2.0	2.6	11.2	18.0	6.1	6.9	7.7	7.9	5.3	23.6	32.0	9.3	1.1	74.3	40.1	48.9	51.1
33415 WEST PALM BEACH	76.4	69.5	11.7	14.4	1.8	2.0	27.3	38.3	6.8	6.4	6.1	6.3	6.9	27.3	24.3	13.2	2.7	77.0	37.6	47.6	52.4
33417 WEST PALM BEACH	75.9	68.2	16.9	22.2	1.9	2.3	11.2	16.6	5.0	4.5	4.2	4.3	5.7	20.3	21.7	25.1	9.2	83.7	50.5	45.8	54.2
33418 PALM BEACH GARDENS	94.1	90.8	1.7	2.8	2.5	3.7	5.4	9.5	4.0	4.5	5.2	5.1	3.5	18.4	36.0	20.8	2.6	82.8	50.9	48.0	52.0
33426 BOYNTON BEACH	87.7	81.6	7.5	11.0	1.4	1.9	7.2	12.7	4.1	4.1	4.2	4.0	3.5	19.8	26.3	25.8	8.2	85.2	52.4	44.8	55.2
33428 BOCA RATON	89.1	84.1	3.5	5.2	3.0	4.0	12.1	20.2	6.4	6.6	6.7	6.3	5.2	25.0	27.2	13.2	3.4	76.2	40.9	48.1	51.9
33430 BELLE GLADE	28.9	26.4	54.3	55.3	0.3	0.3	26.0	31.4	9.1	9.0	8.4	8.5	7.9	27.6	21.6	7.4	0.7	68.3	29.7	53.5	46.5
33431 BOCA RATON	89.2	84.0	5.2	7.6	1.9	2.6	8.1	14.1	3.7	4.0	4.6	11.1	10.0	20.7	28.2	14.8	3.0	84.6	41.8	48.8	51.2
33432 BOCA RATON	88.4	83.9	5.5	7.6	2.1	2.6	9.8	15.8	3.8	3.6	3.7	3.9	4.5	21.7	29.1	24.1	5.6	86.6	51.3	48.3	51.7
33433 BOCA RATON	94.5	91.5	1.3	2.1	1.8	2.6	7.8	13.6	3.9	4.0	4.3	4.4	4.2	20.6	27.5	23.1	8.1	85.2	51.3	45.5	54.5
33434 BOCA RATON	95.6	93.1	1.2	2.0	1.4	2.1	5.1	9.2	3.1	3.6	4.1	4.1	2.7	12.3	25.7	31.9	12.6	86.7	61.3	44.1	55.9
33435 BOYNTON BEACH	57.8	51.7	34.8	39.2	0.8	1.0	10.3	14.4	5.8	5.8	5.8	5.8	5.5	21.9	26.2	17.8	5.4	79.0	44.5	47.6	52.4
33436 BOYNTON BEACH	86.2	80.4	8.5	12.0	2.0	2.6	7.6	12.7	5.0	4.4	4.2	3.7	4.0	21.4	23.9	27.0	6.4	84.1	51.5	46.1	53.9
33437 BOYNTON BEACH	93.3	90.3	3.5	5.0	1.4	2.0	5.0	8.2	2.3	2.2	2.4	2.4	2.3	10.7	21.2	50.2	6.3	91.6	68.0	45.7	54.3
33438 CANAL POINT	26.4	21.3	54.7	55.8	0.2	0.2	28.8	34.4	12.1	9.6	8.2	12.1	11.4	24.3	16.0	5.6	0.6	62.0	23.5	49.4	50.6
33440 CLEWISTON	62.4	59.2	23.0	22.3	0.7	0.9	35.4	46.2	9.1	8.2	7.5	8.3	8.9	27.3	21.3	8.4	0.9	70.0	29.9	52.0	48.0
33441 DEERFIELD BEACH	65.6	61.4	26.7	28.9	1.2	1.7	8.8	12.7	5.6	5.3	5.5	5.5	7.0	25.8	26.3	15.5	3.7	80.5	41.8	48.5	51.5
33442 DEERFIELD BEACH	90.9	87.1	4.1	5.6	1.7	2.4	7.4	11.7	3.5	3.4	3.4	2.8	2.6	19.7	23.6	27.8	13.3	88.1	57.6	44.2	55.8
33444 DELRAY BEACH	42.1	38.1	48.2	51.3	0.9	1.0	9.5	13.0	7.1	7.0	6.7	6.8	6.9	26.8	26.6	10.7	1.5	75.2	36.9	49.5	50.5
33445 DELRAY BEACH	77.6	71.7	17.3	21.6	1.5	2.0	5.8	9.3	4.0	4.0	3.9	3.9	3.6	19.3	25.1	26.9	9.2	85.6	54.2	45.6	54.4
33446 DELRAY BEACH	98.0	95.4	0.7	1.5	0.2	0.4	3.1	8.1	1.7	1.9	2.1	1.9	1.1	7.6	22.8	46.7	14.4	93.2	70.4	44.2	55.8
33449 LAKE WORTH	91.1	86.3	3.2	5.1	2.5	3.6	8.9	15.7	6.2	6.5	7.1	6.5	4.1	20.2	28.8	18.4	2.1	75.7	44.6	49.4	50.6
33455 HOBE SOUND	93.9	90.8	4.0	5.6	0.6	1.0	2.4	4.8	3.3	3.7	4.2	4.7	3.1	14.5	33.0	28.5	4.8	85.6	55.7	48.2	51.8
33458 JUPITER	91.8	87.5	3.5	4.9	1.5	2.3	8.7	13.4	6.8	7.2	7.0	6.3	4.8	28.1	27.9	10.5	1.6	75.0	38.9	49.8	50.2
33460 LAKE WORTH	63.0	55.6	20.0	22.9	0.8	0.9	31.5	41.6	7.5	7.1	6.3	6.3	7.2	29.7	23.6	9.3	2.9	75.4	34.9	52.0	48.0
33461 LAKE WORTH	75.1	66.5	9.5	12.1	1.2	1.4	30.1	43.0	7.7	7.1	6.5	6.8	7.4	28.3	22.3	11.2	2.7	75.1	35.1	50.4	49.6
33462 LAKE WORTH	79.6	72.4	11.6	15.1	1.2	1.6	14.8	22.5	5.7	5.5	5.6	5.6	5.1	23.9	27.5	16.7	4.4	79.7	43.9	48.9	51.1
33463 LAKE WORTH	79.0	70.7	8.7	12.0	2.3	3.2	22.1	31.9	7.1	7.1	7.0	6.6	5.4	26.5	24.9	13.1	2.3	74.8	38.2	48.7	51.3
33467 LAKE WORTH	93.1	88.1	2.9	5.1	1.4	2.4	8.1	13.9	5.7	6.1	6.4	5.5	3.3	20.0	27.8	19.5	5.6	78.2	46.8	47.5	52.5
33469 JUPITER	98.0	96.7	0.4	0.8	0.6	0.9	2.5	4.8	3.9	4.4	4.9	4.8	3.3	14.5	34.2	25.2	4.9	83.7	53.6	47.9	52.1
33470 LOXAHATCHEE	88.3	81.7	6.0	9.5	1.2	1.7	11.3	19.5	8.2	8.3	8.6	7.6	4.1	30.0	26.9	6.0	0.5	70.1	35.6	50.6	49.4
33471 MOORE HAVEN	74.2	68.3	17.0	19.3	0.4	0.5	16.1	23.6	5.4	5.3	5.4	6.0	6.2	27.6	26.0	16.8	1.3	80.2	40.6	56.9	43.1
33472 BOYNTON BEACH	91.3	86.1	3.6	6.0	2.5	3.5	7.5	13.9	6.1	6.7	7.4	7.0	3.9	19.9	30.4	16.2	2.4	75.4	44.4	48.0	52.0
33473 BOYNTON BEACH	81.2	73.7	7.8	9.4	0.6	1.0	35.7	50.3	7.0	8.2	8.9	7.5	3.4	25.5	32.7	6.2	0.6	71.1	39.4	50.9	49.1
33476 PAHOKEE	22.1	18.0	62.5	63.5	0.5	0.5	23.9	28.5	11.2	10.0	8.9	10.5	9.5	24.0	18.1	6.9	0.9	63.0	24.9	47.9	52.1
33477 JUPITER	98.2	97.1	0.2	0.4	0.6	1.0	2.0	3.8	1.7	1.9	2.3	2.0	1.3	10.5	36.5	39.6	4.3	92.7	62.6	47.3	52.7
33478 JUPITER	96.4	94.1	1.0	1.7	0.6	1.0	3.8	7.4	5.4	6.6	7.6	7.8	4.3	23.4	36.1	8.2	0.7	75.3	42.0	50.5	49.5
33480 PALM BEACH	96.2	93.9	2.4	3.9	0.6	0.9	2.5	4.8	2.2	2.3	2.6	2.5	1.9	8.0	28.3	40.4	11.9	91.5	66.0	44.0	56.0
33483 DELRAY BEACH	87.4	82.5	7.1	10.1	1.0	1.4	4.9	8.6	2.9	2.9	3.0	2.9	3.3	19.2	33.9	25.0	6.8	89.4	55.4	48.4	51.6
33484 DELRAY BEACH	95.7	93.0	2.4	3.8	0.6	0.9	3.1	5.6	1.4	1.4	1.4	1.3	1.1	6.9	19.7	47.5	19.3	95.0	73.9	42.1	57.9
33486 BOCA RATON	91.3	87.5	2.4	3.5	2.5	3.4	9.4	15.9	5.1	5.5	5.9	5.5	5.3	25.1	30.9	13.6	3.1	80.1	43.4	48.7	51.3
33487 BOCA RATON	94.0	91.3	2.6	3.7	1.0	1.5	6.5	11.3	3.3	3.3	3.6	3.3	2.6	16.1	33.5	27.9	6.4	87.6	56.5	47.2	52.8
33493 SOUTH BAY	28.1	24.2	61.4	63.5	0.5	0.4	23.1	27.4	7.4	7.1	6.7	7.5	7.9	37.0	19.8	6.0	0.6	74.0	31.7	60.6	39.4
33496 BOCA RATON	95.0	92.5	1.3	2.0	2.0	2.9	6.2	11.1	4.0	4.5	5.4	4.9	3.3	14.8	30.1	29.1	3.9	83.1	54.2	46.3	53.7
33498 BOCA RATON	92.5	88.5	1.8	2.9	3.3	4.6	8.9	15.7	6.0	7.0	8.2	7.1	3.4	18.7	32.3	14.9	2.5	74.2	44.8	48.8	51.2
33510 BRANDON	83.1	75.6	8.9	13.1	2.1	2.8	11.2	18.7	6.6	6.4	6.6	6.9	7.4	27.5	27.4	9.8	1.3	76.1	36.8	48.5	51.5
33511 BRANDON	81.4	73.6	9.5	13.6	2.7	3.5	12.8	20.7	7.4	6.6	6.4	6.4	7.3	32.2	24.6	8.0	1.1	75.7	34.1	48.8	51.2
33513 BUSHNELL	81.9	75.0	14.5	20.2	0.4	0.6	4.0	7.1	4.6	4.8	5.0	5.8	6.4	26.5	28.0	16.7	2.1	82.2	42.5	55.9	44.1
33514 CENTER HILL	84.1	77.8	5.6	8.2	1.4	1.9	18.1	29.5	7.9	7.8	7.9	7.7	5.9	24.5	25.4	11.3	1.5	70.9	35.7	52.1	47.9
33523 DADE CITY	76.6	72.8	11.2	11.5	0.3	0.3	21.1	26.7	7.6	7.2	6.8	7.2	6.8	23.5	25.3	13.1	2.4	74.0	37.1	50.9	49.1
33525 DADE CITY	84.8	81.3	7.5	7.6	0.7	0.8	11.0	16.3	5.7	5.7	6.0	7.4	6.5	21.8	28.2	16.0	2.6	78.2	42.3	49.2	50.8
33527 DOVER	84.6	78.0	1.3	2.9	0.7	1.0	26.3	36.6	7.8	7.9	7.7	7.3	6.1	28.3	25.0	8.9	1.0	72.2	34.3	51.2	48.8
33534 GIBSONTON	88.0	83.7	1.4	1.5	0.7	1.6	19.4	29.2	9.2	8.0	7.2	7.6	7.5	27.8	23.6	8.2	0.8	71.1	31.9	51.0	49.0
33538 LAKE PANASOFFKEE	95.1	92.7	2.5	3.7	0.4	0.6	1.2	2.3	4.6	4.8	4.7	4.5	3.3	17.3	30.6	26.9	3.4	83.2	53.4	48.7	51.3
33540 ZEPHYRHILLS	92.4	89.6	3.2	3.9	0.6	1.0	5.3	8.5	5.7	5.6	5.7	6.0	5.1	20.7	27.7	20.4	2.9	79.0	45.8	48.9	51.1
33541 ZEPHYRHILLS	95.3	93.6	2.0	2.4	0.7	1.0	2.9	4.7	3.3	3.4	3.5	3.7	3.3	15.7	27.4	34.2	5.5	87.6	58.9	48.9	51.1
33542 ZEPHYRHILLS	94.6	92.4	1.6	2.0	1.0	1.3	3.6	6.1	4.1	4.0	3.7	3.7	3.3	15.2	24.0	34.7	7.3	85.9	59.9	46.3	53.7
FLORIDA	78.0	74.7	14.6	15.8	1.7	2.3	16.8	21.5	6.0	5.9	5.9	6.3	6.2	25.0	26.8	15.3	2.8	78.6	41.1	48.8	51.2
UNITED STATES	75.1	72.0	12.3	12.7	3.8	4.6	12.5	15.7	6.8	6.7	6.6	7.1	6.9	27.0	26.0	10.9	1.9	75.7	36.9	49.2	50.8

INCOME

ZIP CODE #	POST OFFICE NAME	2009 Per Capita Income	2009 HH Income Base	2009 HOUSEHOLD INCOME DISTRIBUTION (%) Less than $25,000	$25,000 to $49,999	$50,000 to $99,999	$100,000 to $149,999	$150,000 or More	MEDIAN HOUSEHOLD INCOME 2009	2014	2009 National Centile	2009 State Centile	2009 Home Value Base	2009 HOME VALUE DISTRIBUTION (%) Less than $50,000	$50,000 to $89,999	$90,000 to $174,999	$175,000 to $399,999	$400,000 or More	2009 Median Home Value
33304	FORT LAUDERDALE	32259	9495	27.5	27.4	31.3	7.7	6.0	45043	48942	48	42	4225	1.3	7.1	29.6	37.8	24.2	228102
33305	FORT LAUDERDALE	36288	6197	20.5	25.2	37.4	9.2	7.7	52846	55424	68	64	3691	2.1	7.2	34.6	37.7	18.4	197371
33306	FORT LAUDERDALE	48726	2058	14.7	20.9	35.4	14.8	14.2	66878	68789	85	86	1425	1.3	2.4	10.9	45.3	40.1	309355
33308	FORT LAUDERDALE	46691	16664	18.6	23.3	34.9	12.0	11.0	57713	60917	75	74	11853	1.6	11.6	20.8	41.0	25.0	240250
33309	FORT LAUDERDALE	21808	13679	20.3	28.7	41.7	7.4	1.9	50698	53717	63	58	8773	7.6	15.6	60.2	16.0	0.6	124776
33311	FORT LAUDERDALE	13925	22512	39.5	28.5	26.1	4.6	1.3	32399	34386	12	9	11095	10.0	21.7	58.8	8.7	0.7	109389
33312	FORT LAUDERDALE	22678	18582	24.0	26.6	37.4	8.4	3.6	49313	52914	60	55	12231	7.0	11.6	50.6	25.0	5.7	138839
33313	FORT LAUDERDALE	17335	21021	32.0	32.2	28.6	5.1	2.1	37442	40486	25	21	11784	26.7	22.8	40.4	9.6	0.4	91602
33314	FORT LAUDERDALE	22476	9645	25.4	28.6	34.3	8.8	2.8	46140	50280	52	47	5610	33.0	9.6	39.6	15.5	2.3	103466
33315	FORT LAUDERDALE	30610	6315	20.5	25.0	38.5	11.4	4.6	54176	57643	70	67	3490	4.8	4.7	40.3	42.0	8.2	175361
33316	FORT LAUDERDALE	56910	5974	16.3	24.6	30.7	10.7	17.2	59977	62634	77	76	3298	0.9	4.8	20.7	28.1	45.4	345487
33317	FORT LAUDERDALE	27952	12326	16.0	20.2	38.7	15.7	9.4	64863	66465	83	83	9502	3.9	9.7	31.6	50.7	4.2	191074
33319	FORT LAUDERDALE	23995	19706	27.5	31.0	32.1	6.8	2.6	42695	45455	41	36	14283	17.1	33.3	32.3	15.9	1.4	89549
33321	FORT LAUDERDALE	27181	20893	26.9	28.2	35.1	7.3	2.5	45117	48800	49	43	16899	6.6	15.2	56.9	20.4	0.9	130836
33322	FORT LAUDERDALE	27716	18233	27.8	24.1	32.1	11.2	4.8	47551	51253	56	49	14730	19.5	19.1	34.9	24.5	1.9	118303
33323	FORT LAUDERDALE	30318	6061	5.6	12.2	48.2	25.1	8.8	80520	82383	92	94	4890	0.7	1.2	34.2	55.4	8.4	195294
33324	FORT LAUDERDALE	33826	19225	15.4	23.7	39.9	13.1	7.9	59571	61694	77	76	12566	5.9	11.5	41.8	28.5	12.3	146070
33325	FORT LAUDERDALE	29052	9251	10.4	18.5	43.1	17.8	10.3	69334	70557	86	88	7793	29.3	7.5	15.2	36.7	11.4	165641
33326	FORT LAUDERDALE	36927	11300	11.4	14.7	34.6	20.1	19.2	82051	83595	93	94	8678	0.2	2.3	32.7	50.6	14.3	216161
33327	FORT LAUDERDALE	65043	6031	5.1	4.2	18.7	14.5	57.6	169336	176723	100	100	5523	0.1	0.0	3.8	59.0	37.1	306479
33328	FORT LAUDERDALE	33407	8654	10.7	15.0	39.8	21.2	13.3	77227	76879	91	93	7194	2.7	2.5	27.4	59.5	7.9	212324
33330	FORT LAUDERDALE	39450	4535	5.0	6.9	35.5	26.7	26.0	104591	106934	97	98	4136	0.9	0.1	13.8	46.0	39.2	303254
33331	FORT LAUDERDALE	45450	6865	4.4	5.0	28.4	27.0	35.2	124221	125419	99	99	5921	0.2	0.1	5.7	67.7	26.4	294847
33332	FORT LAUDERDALE	48635	2195	4.6	8.5	20.2	18.4	48.3	145122	151847	100	100	2056	0.4	0.6	1.7	52.2	45.1	372678
33334	FORT LAUDERDALE	22534	12904	24.7	30.4	34.6	7.7	2.6	45489	49353	50	44	6849	4.3	11.8	45.2	36.0	2.7	146165
33351	FORT LAUDERDALE	23392	12763	14.4	26.6	46.1	9.8	3.1	56482	59150	73	72	7842	1.2	16.0	46.4	36.0	0.4	151096
33401	WEST PALM BEACH	27905	11228	33.7	30.2	24.3	6.4	5.3	36798	38086	23	18	5121	6.1	17.2	33.1	24.9	18.7	141150
33403	WEST PALM BEACH	20996	5129	22.7	34.5	35.3	5.6	1.8	43729	45534	45	39	2845	13.5	15.5	58.8	11.7	0.5	116366
33404	WEST PALM BEACH	22193	11706	34.1	29.8	25.2	5.2	5.7	37442	40078	25	21	6615	13.2	22.3	35.4	20.4	8.7	112172
33405	WEST PALM BEACH	26214	7634	24.3	27.8	32.5	8.1	7.4	47958	49378	56	51	4845	2.0	12.9	48.2	23.8	13.1	135646
33406	WEST PALM BEACH	23397	8883	15.9	31.0	39.7	9.2	4.2	53094	54447	68	65	5996	3.9	15.7	51.9	27.0	1.5	126166
33407	WEST PALM BEACH	20489	11723	30.9	28.1	32.2	5.9	2.8	41940	44378	39	34	6739	7.7	19.2	54.8	14.2	4.0	112572
33408	NORTH PALM BEACH	52286	9341	15.0	21.7	34.0	13.9	15.4	67216	75653	85	86	6755	0.7	6.8	28.4	40.3	23.8	225000
33409	WEST PALM BEACH	28446	10293	20.9	27.5	38.0	7.9	5.7	51188	52609	64	60	4627	11.6	18.0	47.3	20.0	3.2	108763
33410	PALM BEACH GARDENS	38685	14345	14.7	22.5	35.8	15.0	12.0	64488	69994	83	83	10704	9.0	5.2	35.3	36.9	13.5	176246
33411	WEST PALM BEACH	32265	24182	11.5	19.2	41.7	17.2	10.4	70075	76932	87	88	19914	3.9	10.8	35.6	42.3	7.4	174364
33412	WEST PALM BEACH	45393	5533	4.1	7.3	32.1	26.1	30.4	109631	110762	98	98	5195	0.3	0.7	20.9	61.6	16.5	229052
33413	WEST PALM BEACH	26879	4720	13.7	28.2	43.8	8.5	5.9	60100	61842	77	77	3061	1.2	7.6	40.2	47.9	3.0	176348
33414	WEST PALM BEACH	38284	18053	6.9	15.1	35.5	23.1	19.4	86629	90674	94	95	14851	0.2	2.1	14.5	63.6	19.5	250179
33415	WEST PALM BEACH	20606	16635	26.0	32.7	34.0	5.1	2.2	42790	45012	42	36	11445	21.5	25.5	46.8	4.9	1.3	93395
33417	WEST PALM BEACH	22280	14675	36.3	33.1	24.3	4.4	1.9	33439	35491	14	11	10055	46.7	19.1	27.2	6.5	0.5	55268
33418	PALM BEACH GARDENS	56199	14496	7.9	14.8	32.2	19.2	25.9	89777	95281	95	96	12620	0.2	3.5	28.4	42.0	25.9	254493
33426	BOYNTON BEACH	28735	7930	20.0	28.3	41.2	8.0	2.5	51992	53749	66	63	6250	2.5	14.0	63.8	18.8	0.9	123358
33428	BOCA RATON	36989	14262	12.8	23.8	33.3	13.8	16.3	65309	69623	84	84	11336	2.2	12.2	31.8	38.7	15.1	184361
33430	BELLE GLADE	12783	6241	47.1	25.5	22.0	3.6	1.8	26950	27392	5	3	2496	23.6	26.6	40.5	8.7	0.6	89712
33431	BOCA RATON	47332	6106	11.3	19.7	34.9	11.4	22.7	71468	78363	88	90	4484	0.5	0.1	21.7	48.9	28.7	246026
33432	BOCA RATON	55434	9914	16.4	26.4	28.9	9.0	19.3	59572	64976	77	76	6498	2.1	10.2	20.9	25.9	41.0	293521
33433	BOCA RATON	46997	19830	11.2	21.0	36.3	16.1	15.3	70261	77059	87	88	14025	0.3	3.8	28.7	50.2	17.0	226100
33434	BOCA RATON	50469	10207	23.4	21.7	25.1	11.2	18.6	58542	62241	76	75	8759	6.9	24.1	20.0	26.2	22.9	169063
33435	BOYNTON BEACH	25828	13309	25.9	30.5	31.4	6.9	5.3	44848	46400	48	41	9677	15.7	24.3	38.3	12.8	8.9	102070
33436	BOYNTON BEACH	35079	18313	14.7	27.4	39.9	9.9	8.1	58239	60713	75	74	13723	12.1	11.3	33.1	35.7	7.9	151662
33437	BOYNTON BEACH	39944	16983	10.6	23.1	43.4	13.4	9.5	65372	72033	84	84	14392	1.7	1.3	27.9	61.1	8.1	215984
33438	CANAL POINT	14379	323	45.5	27.2	21.1	4.3	1.9	27576	28138	5	3	117	23.1	35.9	27.4	13.7	0.0	83824
33440	CLEWISTON	16149	6039	30.4	28.8	32.3	6.5	2.0	41409	45064	37	32	4322	17.6	20.5	45.3	14.3	2.3	108942
33441	DEERFIELD BEACH	24894	12057	26.2	27.9	34.3	8.1	3.5	44885	50128	48	42	7086	4.5	23.2	35.0	28.9	8.4	136461
33442	DEERFIELD BEACH	30749	15491	27.6	28.2	31.3	9.2	3.7	43828	47615	45	39	11980	21.4	23.9	30.1	22.6	1.9	99538
33444	DELRAY BEACH	22272	8435	27.2	26.8	32.7	8.2	5.2	45391	47617	49	44	4460	5.7	19.2	36.1	30.2	8.9	139463
33445	DELRAY BEACH	33973	13697	18.4	27.3	35.6	11.0	7.7	54783	56984	71	69	10494	6.1	30.3	31.8	24.2	7.5	117474
33446	DELRAY BEACH	42471	11614	21.9	26.6	33.8	6.8	10.9	51849	55920	66	62	10705	14.0	17.0	29.7	28.7	10.7	139139
33449	LAKE WORTH	56871	1903	5.1	8.9	29.1	26.6	30.3	113977	115632	98	98	1773	0.6	0.1	3.3	54.4	41.7	365457
33455	HOBE SOUND	35668	9406	16.5	27.2	35.2	12.5	8.5	55052	57993	71	70	8009	10.5	16.5	30.1	31.3	11.6	146043
33458	JUPITER	37931	17721	9.5	19.7	39.8	16.0	15.0	72505	78768	88	91	13383	1.6	3.9	32.9	45.6	15.9	202976
33460	LAKE WORTH	17613	12112	30.6	35.1	27.7	4.7	2.0	37493	40232	25	21	5864	8.9	25.2	47.8	14.3	3.7	108187
33461	LAKE WORTH	18980	14915	26.0	36.7	30.3	5.0	2.0	40524	42116	34	29	8778	22.5	23.1	47.8	6.6	0.1	95304
33462	LAKE WORTH	29412	12528	19.9	31.9	33.5	8.2	6.5	48219	49866	57	52	8768	17.0	13.6	40.9	16.5	12.0	123021
33463	LAKE WORTH	22812	17476	17.9	29.7	39.5	8.2	4.7	52122	53506	66	63	13633	14.1	16.5	47.3	20.0	2.0	120497
33467	LAKE WORTH	38587	20357	12.5	22.1	32.5	17.8	15.1	70700	78723	87	89	18768	2.8	14.2	29.2	45.2	8.6	185634
33469	JUPITER	50183	6890	13.4	19.3	34.1	16.0	17.2	71367	77118	88	90	5910	0.5	8.6	23.1	39.5	28.3	231691
33470	LOXAHATCHEE	31923	8277	5.6	11.0	47.4	20.2	15.8	82633	86235	93	95	7534	0.3	1.5	25.4	62.6	10.2	213773
33471	MOORE HAVEN	20113	2466	31.3	31.0	27.4	7.2	3.1	39017	41054	30	25	1958	17.4	27.4	40.2	12.7	2.3	98211
33472	BOYNTON BEACH	40763	7587	7.6	18.4	37.5	21.2	15.2	78991	84205	92	94	7051	0.2	0.6	29.3	61.4	8.4	212901
33473	BOYNTON BEACH	51502	641	6.2	13.3	23.6	12.6	44.3	120312	123900	98	99	604	0.0	0.7	34.4	36.6	28.3	226316
33476	PAHOKEE	12332	2526	44.5	28.1	21.1	4.3	2.1	28629	29119	6	4	1143	33.2	32.2	26.6	7.3	0.6	74631
33477	JUPITER	66554	6440	11.5	18.7	32.2	14.5	23.2	76016	83195	90	92	5365	1.7	1.6	19.3	50.6	26.9	270946
33478	JUPITER	33512	4276	5.0	10.6	46.4	24.3	13.8	84589	87292	94	95	3980	0.5	2.3	12.0	77.5	7.6	239961
33480	PALM BEACH	97964	6075	13.6	13.8	25.2	11.4	36.0	92836	101351	96	97	4970	0.3	2.6	11.7	25.4	60.0	563338
33483	DELRAY BEACH	56190	6724	15.6	22.3	30.6	12.3	19.2	64591	70385	83	83	4989	2.7	7.1	24.7	29.6	35.7	251820
33484	DELRAY BEACH	30498	13929	27.1	33.6	29.0	6.6	3.7	40831	42850	35	30	12113	13.1	33.4	38.1	13.7	1.8	95908
33486	BOCA RATON	41438	8938	12.2	18.2	34.6	18.2	16.8	74947	80538	89	91	6697	0.5	5.6	13.1	64.3	16.4	246231
33487	BOCA RATON	55283	8192	11.7	20.8	31.5	16.8	19.3	72569	80078	88	91	6823	0.4	2.6	21.8	48.5	26.7	267296
33493	SOUTH BAY	12393	939	40.1	32.6	22.3	3.9	1.1	29782	30570	8	5	536	27.6	29.9	41.0	1.5	0.0	81111
33496	BOCA RATON	63599	9362	10.1	16.3	28.8	12.8	32.0	87334	92989	94	96	7946	0.3	1.0	26.0	28.1	44.5	335935
33498	BOCA RATON	49061	5431	5.7	12.9	32.1	21.4	27.9	98606	101254	96	97	5055	0.0	0.2	10.5	54.9	34.4	312375
33510	BRANDON	27604	10611	11.1	22.6	49.3	12.3	4.7	64536	64594	83	83	7074	0.9	5.5	64.3	27.4	1.9	144657
33511	BRANDON	29743	22882	8.3	24.5	44.7	15.9	6.6	66028	67138	84	85	14434	1.4	4.0	55.2	35.9	3.5	160733
33513	BUSHNELL	18654	5179	35.6	33.8	24.2	4.7	1.7	32959	34622	13	10	3978	23.6	30.6	31.6	11.5	2.6	84099
33514	CENTER HILL	14184	821	39.5	30.8	24.8	3.2	1.7	32302	34276	12	9	609	20.4	36.5	30.2	11.7	1.3	79912
33523	DADE CITY	17699	7127	33.2	32.5	26.6	4.7	3.0	36556	38434	22	18	5018	19.5	31.7	31.9	14.2	2.8	88041
33525	DADE CITY	20304	6612	26.9	33.2	30.1	6.5	3.3	40672	44879	35	29	5098	18.4	19.9	41.9	16.1	3.7	109299
33527	DOVER	20259	5279	20.0	28.8	36.4	9.7	5.2	51007	53688	64	59	4081	12.7	18.1	38.6	26.4	4.1	124530
33534	GIBSONTON	18094	4753	23.4	29.8	39.2	4.9	2.6	46618	50810	53	48	3024	20.1	22.4	41.6	13.4	2.5	105462
33538	LAKE PANASOFFKEE	19819	3435	35.7	40.4	18.2	3.7	2.0	31903	33324	11	8	2739	24.0	37.4	32.7	5.3	0.6	74375
33540	ZEPHYRHILLS	18171	3805	26.1	34.4	35.2	3.6	0.7	40731	44020	35	30	3196	18.8	30.0	41.7	7.9	1.6	91439
33541	ZEPHYRHILLS	20855	8385	29.7	40.3	25.2	2.9	1.9	35271	37086	19	14	7263	28.3	38.8	23.6	7.9	1.4	71182
33542	ZEPHYRHILLS	20196	10438	34.9	38.0	22.9	2.5	1.6	33337	34890	14	11	7934	27.4	33.6	33.7	4.3	0.9	75455
	FLORIDA	27128		21.9	27.6	33.8	9.8	6.8	50413	52516				8.0	14.3	38.7	30.4	8.6	144752
	UNITED STATES	27277		20.9	24.4	35.3	11.7	7.6	54719	56938				9.3	13.1	31.6	32.6	13.5	162279

ZIP CODE #	POST OFFICE NAME	FINANCIAL SERVICES: Auto Loan	Home Loan	Investments	Retirement Plans	THE HOME: Home Improvements: Home Repair	Lawn & Garden	Furnishings: Computers & Hardware-Personal	Major Appliances	TV, Radio, Sound Equipment	Furniture	ENTERTAINMENT: Dine out/Carry out	Sports Equipment	Fees & Tickets	Toys & Games	Travel	Cable TV	PERSONAL: Apparel & Services	Auto Repairs	Health Insurance	Pets & Supplies
33304	FORT LAUDERDALE	84	76	79	80	76	74	91	80	90	89	91	65	88	88	87	88	65	88	84	96
33305	FORT LAUDERDALE	95	91	97	94	93	92	101	94	100	101	101	73	101	97	100	100	71	100	100	112
33306	FORT LAUDERDALE	122	138	162	139	150	135	133	135	127	140	127	100	143	121	145	124	91	134	132	154
33308	FORT LAUDERDALE	109	116	137	116	125	127	113	119	117	119	117	82	121	109	123	121	81	120	135	138
33309	FORT LAUDERDALE	78	73	69	74	71	71	82	75	82	80	83	59	79	82	78	82	58	81	78	90
33311	FORT LAUDERDALE	60	52	48	54	49	56	59	55	64	58	63	42	57	63	54	66	44	60	62	68
33312	FORT LAUDERDALE	86	82	83	82	82	84	84	84	85	85	85	63	83	84	84	85	59	86	86	99
33313	FORT LAUDERDALE	67	57	53	59	55	59	68	61	70	66	70	48	63	70	62	71	49	67	67	75
33314	FORT LAUDERDALE	83	74	66	74	71	70	84	75	81	82	82	61	77	84	76	80	57	80	74	91
33315	FORT LAUDERDALE	84	89	90	90	90	86	93	87	91	92	92	69	95	89	94	91	65	91	91	103
33316	FORT LAUDERDALE	137	140	166	145	151	139	150	144	144	155	145	111	153	138	156	141	104	149	144	168
33317	FORT LAUDERDALE	104	120	121	116	123	112	113	113	110	115	111	84	121	109	119	109	80	112	111	127
33319	FORT LAUDERDALE	68	68	74	66	72	75	71	73	75	74	75	50	74	70	74	78	51	75	86	84
33321	FORT LAUDERDALE	73	75	85	73	82	86	74	81	78	77	77	54	78	73	80	82	53	80	94	92
33322	FORT LAUDERDALE	77	88	98	84	96	96	82	89	85	89	84	59	92	78	93	88	58	88	103	100
33323	FORT LAUDERDALE	130	147	133	151	142	128	134	130	127	141	130	106	145	133	138	121	93	128	117	151
33324	FORT LAUDERDALE	105	106	106	108	107	105	109	105	108	112	109	80	112	107	110	107	76	108	110	123
33325	FORT LAUDERDALE	123	129	116	129	125	118	122	119	118	127	119	94	125	123	121	115	85	118	111	140
33326	FORT LAUDERDALE	146	169	162	174	169	152	153	151	146	162	148	120	168	150	161	140	107	147	140	174
33327	FORT LAUDERDALE	303	367	317	378	357	301	305	309	281	343	286	257	346	305	321	257	211	282	252	344
33328	FORT LAUDERDALE	126	146	134	148	144	130	134	131	127	138	129	105	145	131	139	122	93	128	121	151
33330	FORT LAUDERDALE	171	217	206	221	216	189	180	185	169	194	172	147	208	175	198	161	126	173	162	210
33331	FORT LAUDERDALE	208	257	231	265	253	216	213	217	198	236	201	178	245	211	229	183	148	200	182	244
33332	FORT LAUDERDALE	261	329	310	342	330	282	272	279	252	301	256	226	317	266	297	235	190	256	234	312
33334	FORT LAUDERDALE	78	68	65	70	67	66	80	71	79	79	80	58	75	80	74	78	56	78	72	86
33351	FORT LAUDERDALE	94	90	78	90	85	80	94	87	92	96	93	69	91	95	89	89	65	91	83	103
33401	WEST PALM BEACH	76	68	69	70	68	72	81	74	85	79	84	56	78	80	77	87	59	81	86	90
33403	WEST PALM BEACH	72	73	68	72	71	70	76	72	76	75	77	55	76	76	74	77	54	75	74	85
33404	WEST PALM BEACH	81	70	72	72	70	78	79	76	85	80	84	56	76	82	75	89	58	82	88	93
33405	WEST PALM BEACH	92	99	93	94	99	87	98	95	93	101	95	73	100	94	99	90	68	96	88	107
33406	WEST PALM BEACH	90	93	85	91	91	86	92	90	90	95	91	69	93	91	92	89	64	91	88	104
33407	WEST PALM BEACH	76	70	64	71	67	68	77	71	78	76	78	56	74	78	72	78	55	76	74	86
33408	NORTH PALM BEACH	135	146	175	145	161	162	138	150	142	149	141	101	151	132	153	147	98	148	167	171
33409	WEST PALM BEACH	97	80	74	83	77	75	98	84	96	97	98	69	90	98	88	93	69	93	83	102
33410	PALM BEACH GARDENS	118	133	140	134	137	130	125	127	122	130	123	95	135	121	134	122	87	126	127	146
33411	WEST PALM BEACH	120	131	126	132	131	127	122	124	120	126	121	94	129	121	127	120	85	122	124	144
33412	WEST PALM BEACH	193	232	206	239	228	194	194	198	180	218	183	162	219	193	205	166	134	181	165	221
33413	WEST PALM BEACH	108	102	89	102	98	90	106	99	102	110	104	79	102	107	100	98	73	101	91	116
33414	WEST PALM BEACH	153	186	178	188	185	168	161	164	153	169	155	127	180	157	174	149	112	157	151	188
33415	WEST PALM BEACH	73	72	69	69	73	72	73	73	73	76	73	53	73	73	73	73	51	74	76	84
33417	WEST PALM BEACH	58	58	66	55	64	66	61	63	63	64	62	42	64	59	65	65	43	65	75	72
33418	PALM BEACH GARDENS	183	204	248	206	224	220	182	203	185	200	183	138	202	174	206	188	128	194	213	231
33426	BOYNTON BEACH	75	83	92	80	90	93	79	86	82	83	81	57	86	77	87	86	56	85	101	97
33428	BOCA RATON	134	149	141	149	148	141	139	139	137	145	138	106	149	138	145	136	98	138	141	161
33430	BELLE GLADE	57	48	43	47	46	47	55	51	58	55	58	39	51	58	50	59	41	55	53	61
33431	BOCA RATON	160	179	193	183	187	178	169	171	167	176	167	128	184	163	180	166	119	170	174	198
33432	BOCA RATON	141	148	171	150	159	159	149	152	153	155	152	108	158	143	159	156	106	155	170	177
33433	BOCA RATON	135	141	159	142	150	147	136	141	137	146	137	101	144	132	145	138	96	141	149	163
33434	BOCA RATON	126	153	188	145	175	173	133	156	138	151	135	96	158	125	160	144	94	147	180	170
33435	BOYNTON BEACH	87	87	91	85	89	92	86	89	89	89	88	64	88	86	88	92	61	90	97	104
33436	BOYNTON BEACH	105	107	120	103	115	116	105	111	108	113	107	76	110	102	112	110	73	111	124	127
33437	BOYNTON BEACH	105	116	144	109	133	138	107	124	114	119	111	76	120	101	125	120	75	120	149	137
33438	CANAL POINT	53	46	39	47	42	46	59	49	61	53	61	40	55	60	50	62	44	56	54	61
33440	CLEWISTON	76	68	64	66	66	69	70	71	71	72	72	54	65	73	67	72	50	72	70	84
33441	DEERFIELD BEACH	81	72	72	73	72	74	82	76	84	81	84	58	78	82	77	85	59	82	83	91
33442	DEERFIELD BEACH	70	80	91	76	88	91	76	83	80	81	79	53	85	73	86	85	54	82	101	93
33444	DELRAY BEACH	83	79	77	82	78	80	86	80	88	86	89	62	86	87	83	89	62	86	86	97
33445	DELRAY BEACH	96	103	119	99	112	115	97	107	102	104	101	71	105	95	107	106	69	105	122	121
33446	DELRAY BEACH	98	113	149	106	133	137	99	121	107	115	104	70	116	93	121	113	70	115	146	132
33449	LAKE WORTH	166	240	268	231	257	221	195	206	186	197	187	150	238	187	230	187	140	195	196	224
33455	HOBE SOUND	109	113	141	110	125	129	103	119	107	113	106	79	109	99	116	112	72	114	130	136
33458	JUPITER	134	151	144	152	151	139	139	139	134	145	135	108	148	136	144	131	97	136	133	160
33460	LAKE WORTH	65	61	54	60	58	59	68	62	69	66	69	49	65	68	63	69	49	67	65	74
33461	LAKE WORTH	68	65	62	63	65	64	71	67	70	70	71	51	68	70	68	71	50	70	70	78
33462	LAKE WORTH	96	99	103	97	100	102	97	100	98	98	98	73	99	96	100	101	69	99	106	116
33463	LAKE WORTH	92	93	89	89	94	91	88	92	88	93	88	67	88	88	89	88	61	89	92	105
33467	LAKE WORTH	123	152	164	147	162	153	129	143	129	142	128	98	150	124	149	130	90	135	149	159
33469	JUPITER	150	159	193	160	175	179	145	164	150	157	149	110	157	141	162	156	103	158	177	187
33470	LOXAHATCHEE	148	176	150	175	168	147	149	151	139	162	142	121	164	149	156	131	102	141	130	171
33471	MOORE HAVEN	80	68	83	64	71	84	68	78	73	70	71	56	62	71	69	78	48	76	84	93
33472	BOYNTON BEACH	131	165	172	162	172	160	139	150	137	147	138	107	161	136	158	138	98	142	150	168
33473	BOYNTON BEACH	205	271	280	285	281	244	222	231	207	241	210	182	268	212	253	197	158	215	201	261
33476	PAHOKEE	59	50	41	52	45	53	58	52	62	56	61	41	55	62	51	64	43	57	58	66
33477	JUPITER	168	181	245	176	210	216	162	194	172	185	168	118	181	153	191	181	115	184	222	216
33478	JUPITER	138	171	158	172	167	151	144	148	136	151	138	117	162	140	156	131	99	140	133	170
33480	PALM BEACH	215	261	335	247	305	304	228	270	240	260	233	164	273	213	279	253	162	256	319	294
33483	DELRAY BEACH	150	156	188	155	170	172	148	162	153	160	152	109	157	143	161	157	105	159	176	185
33484	DELRAY BEACH	63	76	97	68	91	95	67	83	74	78	71	46	81	63	84	80	48	79	107	89
33486	BOCA RATON	132	151	161	153	157	142	144	141	139	148	140	109	157	138	154	136	101	142	137	162
33487	BOCA RATON	150	164	207	162	183	184	150	169	156	163	154	110	165	143	170	163	107	164	188	191
33493	SOUTH BAY	59	50	40	51	44	53	55	51	59	55	59	40	53	60	49	62	40	55	57	65
33496	BOCA RATON	186	222	266	223	246	236	196	216	197	214	195	148	228	186	226	201	140	206	229	242
33498	BOCA RATON	182	225	237	231	233	215	190	203	184	205	185	150	219	182	215	180	133	192	193	232
33510	BRANDON	103	104	94	105	100	100	103	100	102	105	104	78	105	105	102	102	73	102	100	118
33511	BRANDON	114	114	100	115	108	101	113	106	109	117	111	86	113	114	109	106	78	108	101	125
33513	BUSHNELL	71	59	79	55	63	76	58	70	63	58	61	50	52	60	60	67	41	66	76	82
33514	CENTER HILL	76	54	66	53	55	73	56	67	63	54	61	51	45	64	52	68	41	63	71	81
33523	DADE CITY	74	66	71	63	67	74	67	73	71	68	70	53	63	70	66	74	48	72	77	85
33525	DADE CITY	82	74	82	72	76	85	72	81	75	72	75	59	68	75	73	79	51	78	84	95
33527	DOVER	97	96	86	92	94	92	90	94	89	94	90	70	88	93	89	89	63	91	89	108
33534	GIBSONTON	87	80	70	76	76	79	79	80	80	82	80	61	73	83	74	81	55	80	79	95
33538	LAKE PANASOFFKEE	61	58	74	53	64	69	55	65	58	59	57	43	54	53	60	62	38	62	72	74
33540	ZEPHYRHILLS	74	65	76	61	68	77	63	73	67	65	66	51	58	65	64	70	44	69	77	85
33541	ZEPHYRHILLS	64	62	79	57	69	74	59	69	62	64	61	45	58	57	64	66	41	67	78	79
33542	ZEPHYRHILLS	58	57	70	53	64	69	55	64	59	59	57	41	57	54	61	63	39	62	74	72
	FLORIDA	96	94	97	93	96	98	95	97	96	97	96	71	95	94	96	97	67	97	101	113
	UNITED STATES	100	100	100	100	100	100	100	100	100	100	100	100	100	100	100	100	100	100	100	100

POPULATION CHANGE

ZIP CODE #	POST OFFICE NAME	COUNTY FIPS CODE	POPULATION 2000	POPULATION 2009	POPULATION 2014	2000-2009 ANNUAL RATE % Rate	2000-2009 ANNUAL RATE State Centile	HOUSEHOLDS 2000	HOUSEHOLDS 2009	HOUSEHOLDS 2014	HOUSEHOLDS % Annual Rate 2000-2009	HOUSEHOLDS 2009 Average HH Size	FAMILIES 2000	FAMILIES 2009	FAMILIES % Annual Rate 2000-2009
33543	WESLEY CHAPEL	101	10824	22313	28636	8.1	95	4218	8552	10963	7.9	2.61	3261	6352	7.5
33544	WESLEY CHAPEL	101	6845	19687	25874	12.1	98	2344	6678	8805	12.0	2.95	1933	5190	11.3
33545	WESLEY CHAPEL	101	2735	11427	15241	16.7	99	1014	4208	5627	16.6	2.71	806	3241	16.2
33547	LITHIA	057	7176	17302	21026	10.0	96	2461	6162	7556	10.4	2.80	2006	4953	10.3
33548	LUTZ	057	5448	5528	5618	0.2	15	1968	2018	2058	0.3	2.73	1590	1591	0.0
33549	LUTZ	057	17143	18871	19694	1.0	40	6742	7473	7838	1.1	2.50	4599	4952	0.8
33556	ODESSA	057	17655	29911	35905	5.9	91	6266	10842	13117	6.1	2.76	5142	8566	5.7
33558	LUTZ	057	14948	19674	22083	3.0	78	6206	7931	8873	2.7	2.47	4125	5167	2.5
33559	LUTZ	057	8568	14108	17266	5.5	90	3234	5319	6527	5.5	2.65	2321	3683	5.1
33563	PLANT CITY	057	22495	25210	26390	1.2	46	8229	9080	9487	1.1	2.75	5717	6102	0.7
33565	PLANT CITY	057	15275	16777	17464	1.0	40	5619	6215	6495	1.1	2.64	4342	4686	0.8
33566	PLANT CITY	057	17694	20096	21297	1.4	51	5943	6915	7365	1.7	2.88	4721	5363	1.4
33567	PLANT CITY	057	8823	10389	11160	1.8	59	2834	3366	3634	1.9	3.04	2264	2622	1.6
33569	RIVERVIEW	057	13128	20637	24080	5.0	88	4803	7769	9130	5.3	2.64	3732	5699	4.7
33570	RUSKIN	057	12870	22388	27500	6.2	91	4926	8027	9763	5.4	2.77	3447	5374	4.9
33572	APOLLO BEACH	057	7551	10441	11944	3.6	83	3147	4383	5029	3.6	2.38	2372	3189	3.3
33573	SUN CITY CENTER	057	16381	21095	23117	2.8	76	9154	12042	13336	3.0	1.63	5443	6815	2.5
33576	SAN ANTONIO	101	2186	4331	5182	7.7	94	890	1680	2024	7.1	2.52	661	1247	7.1
33578	RIVERVIEW	057	14869	28871	35615	7.4	93	5973	11589	14360	7.4	2.49	4129	7847	7.2
33579	RIVERVIEW	057	7527	20677	25922	11.5	97	2328	6898	8759	12.5	2.95	1947	5663	12.2
33584	SEFFNER	057	20384	24735	26995	2.1	64	7408	9223	10162	2.4	2.68	5573	6736	2.1
33585	SUMTERVILLE	119	1117	2052	2785	6.8	92	412	782	1077	7.2	2.54	284	521	6.8
33592	THONOTOSASSA	057	9824	10486	10680	0.7	32	3642	3935	4029	0.8	2.63	2565	2683	0.5
33594	VALRICO	057	20654	29207	33134	3.8	84	7680	10868	12350	3.8	2.69	5921	8146	3.5
33596	VALRICO	057	24584	28840	31136	1.7	57	8059	9602	10425	1.9	3.00	7078	8324	1.8
33597	WEBSTER	119	7006	10055	12480	4.0	85	2635	3841	4802	4.2	2.61	1937	2733	3.8
33598	WIMAUMA	057	9181	11661	16623	2.6	73	2361	3078	4302	2.9	3.72	2001	2567	2.7
33602	TAMPA	057	8873	12787	14139	4.0	85	3582	5683	6451	5.1	2.07	1780	2513	3.8
33603	TAMPA	057	20522	20460	20556	0.0	9	8105	8137	8211	0.0	2.50	4808	4594	-0.5
33604	TAMPA	057	35860	36475	36816	0.2	15	14386	14668	14847	0.2	2.48	8591	8362	-0.3
33605	TAMPA	057	17116	18899	20047	1.1	44	6177	7051	7595	1.4	2.60	3793	4056	0.7
33606	TAMPA	057	14717	14908	15032	0.1	12	7140	7240	7364	0.2	1.85	2837	2709	-0.5
33607	TAMPA	057	22828	23758	24168	0.4	22	9373	9890	10114	0.6	2.40	5580	5592	0.0
33609	TAMPA	057	16697	17523	18004	0.5	26	7856	8435	8743	0.8	2.06	3954	3934	-0.1
33610	TAMPA	057	32715	38739	41444	1.8	59	11883	14351	15484	2.1	2.65	8099	9369	1.6
33611	TAMPA	057	29973	31970	32910	0.7	32	14493	15710	16270	0.9	2.03	7308	7521	0.3
33612	TAMPA	057	42830	44758	45575	0.5	26	17547	18196	18541	0.4	2.39	10095	9998	-0.1
33613	TAMPA	057	29525	31537	32410	0.7	32	13327	14332	14803	0.8	2.11	6185	6231	0.1
33614	TAMPA	057	44725	48968	50715	1.0	40	18398	20175	20995	1.0	2.38	10712	11185	0.5
33615	TAMPA	057	40858	44351	45828	0.9	38	16607	18149	18836	1.0	2.43	10356	10897	0.6
33616	TAMPA	057	12019	13423	14351	1.2	46	4927	5602	6024	1.4	2.39	3057	3323	0.9
33617	TAMPA	057	42725	44571	45553	0.5	26	17683	18484	18946	0.5	2.38	10391	10407	0.0
33618	TAMPA	057	24889	25862	26359	0.4	22	10430	10984	11234	0.6	2.33	6884	6986	0.2
33619	TAMPA	057	29733	35224	37206	1.8	59	9251	11387	12203	2.3	2.82	6755	7886	1.7
33620	TAMPA	057	2532	2935	2935	1.6	55	3	3	3	0.0	6.33	0	0	0.0
33621	TAMPA	057	2692	2517	2456	-0.7	1	608	538	522	-1.3	3.79	599	529	-1.3
33624	TAMPA	057	38859	41016	41937	0.6	30	15150	16319	16791	0.8	2.51	10518	10949	0.4
33625	TAMPA	057	17869	22734	25109	2.6	73	6284	8199	9137	2.9	2.74	4860	6109	2.5
33626	TAMPA	057	11116	22563	27529	8.0	94	4177	8315	10136	7.7	2.71	3208	6249	7.5
33629	TAMPA	057	22377	22070	22143	-0.1	6	10343	10311	10401	0.0	2.13	5892	5622	-0.5
33634	TAMPA	057	19903	21213	21863	0.7	32	7505	8149	8462	0.9	2.60	5198	5417	0.4
33635	TAMPA	057	12282	15137	16435	2.3	69	4986	6309	6938	2.6	2.40	3272	3861	1.8
33637	TAMPA	057	12534	13908	14751	1.1	44	5297	6032	6448	1.4	2.31	3065	3288	0.8
33647	TAMPA	057	25996	49319	59181	7.2	93	10146	18933	22691	7.0	2.60	6784	12409	6.7
33701	SAINT PETERSBURG	103	15252	15274	15093	0.0	9	8096	8129	8036	0.0	1.67	2362	2224	-0.6
33702	SAINT PETERSBURG	103	28989	28236	27627	-0.3	3	13581	13162	12875	-0.3	2.12	7681	7256	-0.6
33703	SAINT PETERSBURG	103	25184	24793	24342	-0.2	4	11142	10913	10712	-0.2	2.26	6916	6596	-0.5
33704	SAINT PETERSBURG	103	16629	16157	15792	-0.3	3	7788	7554	7390	-0.3	2.10	4184	3927	-0.7
33705	SAINT PETERSBURG	103	28091	28310	27974	0.1	12	11712	11643	11472	-0.1	2.36	6643	6437	-0.3
33706	SAINT PETERSBURG	103	17376	17411	17173	0.0	9	9420	9457	9347	0.0	1.81	4785	4635	-0.3
33707	SAINT PETERSBURG	103	26482	25810	25280	-0.3	3	13470	13048	12759	-0.3	1.92	6784	6374	-0.7
33708	SAINT PETERSBURG	103	16657	17108	16988	0.3	18	8997	9211	9147	0.3	1.85	4572	4565	0.0
33709	SAINT PETERSBURG	103	26332	26058	25652	-0.1	6	12310	12140	11945	-0.2	2.09	6891	6597	-0.5
33710	SAINT PETERSBURG	103	33273	32460	31782	-0.3	3	14564	14140	13845	-0.3	2.26	8985	8493	-0.6
33711	SAINT PETERSBURG	103	19867	19258	18835	-0.3	3	7383	7127	6966	-0.4	2.50	4830	4550	-0.6
33712	SAINT PETERSBURG	103	26378	25951	25436	-0.2	4	10615	10394	10196	-0.2	2.46	6652	6356	-0.5
33713	SAINT PETERSBURG	103	31157	30751	30160	-0.1	6	13266	12930	12673	-0.3	2.35	7730	7317	-0.6
33714	SAINT PETERSBURG	103	18874	18964	18738	0.1	12	8644	8651	8552	0.0	2.16	4593	4443	-0.4
33715	SAINT PETERSBURG	103	7403	7468	7386	0.1	12	3890	3919	3883	0.1	1.91	2419	2372	-0.2
33716	SAINT PETERSBURG	103	12007	13245	13404	1.1	44	6793	7512	7616	1.1	1.71	2508	2682	0.7
33755	CLEARWATER	103	25722	25011	24425	-0.3	3	10111	9679	9430	-0.5	2.43	6053	5636	-0.8
33756	CLEARWATER	103	28988	30496	30532	0.5	26	13022	13595	13605	0.5	2.16	7175	7164	0.0
33759	CLEARWATER	103	20454	19520	18952	-0.5	1	8755	8249	7999	-0.6	2.24	4880	4469	-0.9
33760	CLEARWATER	103	16942	17107	16964	0.1	12	6063	6101	6041	0.1	2.27	3556	3479	-0.2
33761	CLEARWATER	103	17529	17232	16925	-0.2	4	8208	8068	7928	-0.2	2.13	5134	4911	-0.5
33762	CLEARWATER	103	5484	6024	6099	1.0	40	2889	3177	3218	1.0	1.88	1317	1378	0.5
33763	CLEARWATER	103	19663	19753	19514	0.0	9	10314	10302	10172	0.0	1.90	5585	5420	-0.3
33764	CLEARWATER	103	27062	26443	25902	-0.2	4	12583	12278	12035	-0.3	2.12	7344	6946	-0.6
33765	CLEARWATER	103	11781	11739	11543	0.0	9	5305	5274	5197	-0.1	2.19	2951	2834	-0.4
33767	CLEARWATER BEACH	103	8750	8770	8649	0.0	9	4841	4865	4808	0.1	1.80	2680	2601	-0.3
33770	LARGO	103	24329	24623	24379	0.1	12	11755	11780	11637	0.0	2.05	6337	6192	-0.2
33771	LARGO	103	24848	25232	24991	0.2	15	12328	12512	12409	0.2	1.96	6675	6565	-0.2
33772	SEMINOLE	103	23811	23609	23230	-0.1	6	11111	11048	10902	-0.1	2.10	6637	6408	-0.4
33773	LARGO	103	18912	19298	19162	0.2	15	8443	8603	8546	0.2	2.19	5244	5210	-0.1
33774	LARGO	103	18936	18694	18370	-0.1	6	8553	8424	8283	-0.2	2.19	5282	5087	-0.4
33776	SEMINOLE	103	12913	12883	12707	0.0	9	5122	5114	5052	0.0	2.50	3801	3730	-0.2
33777	SEMINOLE	103	17195	17565	17445	0.2	15	6867	7049	7016	0.3	2.45	4825	4856	0.1
33778	LARGO	103	13332	13297	13121	0.0	9	5698	5666	5592	-0.1	2.32	3713	3610	-0.3
33781	PINELLAS PARK	103	24473	24531	24236	0.0	9	9906	9918	9802	0.0	2.45	6273	6116	-0.3
33782	PINELLAS PARK	103	19616	20156	20057	0.3	18	8349	8542	8492	0.2	2.30	5331	5323	0.0
33785	INDIAN ROCKS BEACH	103	6777	6830	6743	0.1	12	3689	3726	3686	0.1	1.83	1880	1831	-0.3
33786	BELLEAIR BEACH	103	1751	1680	1646	-0.4	2	825	791	779	-0.5	2.12	522	488	-0.7
33801	LAKELAND	105	31746	32866	33835	0.4	22	13429	14067	14537	0.5	2.28	7961	7986	0.0
33803	LAKELAND	105	26108	28214	29480	0.8	35	11464	12606	13264	1.0	2.13	7039	7459	0.6
33805	LAKELAND	105	19745	22259	23800	1.3	48	7429	8503	9133	1.5	2.55	5006	5562	1.1
	FLORIDA					1.9					1.9	2.47			1.7
	UNITED STATES					1.0					1.1	2.59			0.9

#	POST OFFICE NAME	White 2000	White 2009	Black 2000	Black 2009	Asian/Pacific 2000	Asian/Pacific 2009	% Hispanic Origin 2000	% Hispanic Origin 2009	0-4	5-9	10-14	15-19	20-24	25-44	45-64	65-84	85+	18+	MEDIAN AGE 2009	% 2009 Males	% 2009 Females
33543	WESLEY CHAPEL	87.7	81.9	4.5	6.5	3.5	4.9	8.6	14.4	8.8	8.2	7.6	6.0	4.7	30.2	24.7	9.0	1.0	71.7	35.9	48.5	51.5
33544	WESLEY CHAPEL	92.4	85.2	2.5	5.2	1.9	3.7	8.6	14.5	8.5	8.0	7.6	6.2	4.8	30.9	25.0	8.4	0.7	72.1	35.6	48.8	51.2
33545	WESLEY CHAPEL	93.4	90.7	1.4	1.9	1.8	2.4	6.7	11.0	8.8	8.0	7.5	6.5	5.3	32.4	24.1	6.8	0.6	71.7	33.8	49.2	50.8
33547	LITHIA	94.6	89.1	1.6	3.6	0.5	1.0	5.1	10.9	8.4	8.0	7.8	6.8	5.2	30.9	25.3	6.9	0.6	71.5	34.3	49.4	50.6
33548	LUTZ	95.6	93.3	1.4	2.2	0.9	1.4	7.2	13.0	5.1	6.1	7.3	6.7	3.8	22.7	36.1	11.0	1.3	77.2	44.0	49.1	50.9
33549	LUTZ	88.2	83.9	5.4	7.1	1.7	2.3	10.2	16.5	6.2	6.3	6.7	6.5	6.2	26.6	30.6	9.8	1.2	76.8	39.5	50.0	50.0
33556	ODESSA	91.3	88.2	3.8	5.1	2.2	2.9	8.2	12.8	7.0	7.6	8.0	6.8	3.8	27.1	30.6	8.4	0.8	73.2	39.5	49.9	50.1
33558	LUTZ	88.6	84.2	3.8	5.3	3.7	5.0	11.7	19.4	6.5	6.5	6.7	5.8	5.8	30.2	28.8	8.7	0.9	76.5	37.9	49.4	50.6
33559	LUTZ	88.2	83.9	5.6	7.5	2.4	3.1	11.4	18.0	7.8	7.3	7.0	6.7	7.5	30.4	25.8	6.8	0.7	73.9	33.8	48.5	51.5
33563	PLANT CITY	66.1	59.0	19.6	20.4	0.4	0.5	21.6	32.4	8.7	7.9	7.4	7.2	7.3	26.2	22.3	10.9	2.0	71.8	33.1	48.9	51.1
33565	PLANT CITY	92.4	87.5	1.2	2.0	0.5	0.7	8.7	15.7	6.7	6.9	6.8	6.4	5.0	24.7	27.0	15.1	1.4	76.0	40.3	49.2	50.8
33566	PLANT CITY	84.4	77.5	4.7	6.2	1.3	1.8	15.8	25.1	7.4	7.5	7.2	7.1	6.0	27.2	26.3	10.1	1.1	73.4	36.3	49.7	50.3
33567	PLANT CITY	73.9	65.8	11.7	12.9	0.3	0.4	22.6	34.3	8.1	7.9	7.5	7.4	6.6	28.5	24.0	9.0	1.0	72.1	33.3	50.8	49.2
33569	RIVERVIEW	89.4	84.5	5.3	8.2	1.3	1.7	7.4	12.4	6.6	7.3	7.5	6.4	4.1	25.0	28.4	13.1	1.6	74.8	40.7	49.8	50.2
33570	RUSKIN	84.2	71.4	1.0	1.2	0.6	0.6	32.3	53.6	7.4	7.0	6.7	6.4	5.7	24.2	24.4	16.1	2.2	75.1	38.9	50.1	49.9
33572	APOLLO BEACH	93.3	88.7	0.8	1.2	1.4	2.0	8.3	15.8	4.3	4.7	5.4	5.4	3.8	19.9	35.3	19.0	2.2	82.3	48.9	49.2	50.8
33573	SUN CITY CENTER	98.9	97.9	0.1	0.2	0.5	0.7	1.5	5.0	0.6	0.5	0.5	0.5	0.7	3.0	13.6	62.4	18.3	98.2	75.9	42.3	57.7
33576	SAN ANTONIO	94.3	92.2	1.6	2.1	0.9	1.3	7.4	11.9	5.7	6.4	6.7	6.9	4.7	23.8	30.8	13.8	1.2	77.2	42.2	50.1	49.9
33578	RIVERVIEW	82.5	72.8	10.5	17.7	1.6	2.2	11.1	17.9	8.2	7.3	6.9	6.5	7.0	31.0	24.0	8.1	0.9	73.5	33.7	48.7	51.3
33579	RIVERVIEW	83.8	76.9	5.5	10.7	1.2	1.8	16.4	22.4	8.6	7.9	7.4	8.4	6.1	31.8	23.0	6.3	0.5	71.8	32.0	49.9	50.1
33584	SEFFNER	86.4	80.2	7.3	10.6	1.0	1.3	9.0	15.5	7.0	6.8	6.8	7.1	6.4	27.2	27.6	10.0	1.1	75.0	37.1	49.5	50.5
33585	SUMTERVILLE	89.3	84.5	6.6	9.9	1.0	1.3	5.2	9.3	5.7	5.9	6.3	6.5	5.2	24.7	28.9	15.1	1.8	78.1	41.9	50.4	49.6
33592	THONOTOSASSA	83.3	76.5	11.4	16.2	0.6	0.8	6.4	11.0	6.9	6.8	6.8	7.1	6.2	25.9	27.6	11.3	1.5	75.5	37.8	50.4	49.6
33594	VALRICO	85.9	80.0	6.7	9.0	2.0	2.7	12.7	21.4	6.6	6.5	6.7	6.5	4.8	26.5	28.5	12.5	1.4	76.1	39.9	48.5	51.5
33596	VALRICO	90.0	85.3	5.1	7.7	2.3	3.3	6.6	11.5	6.6	7.3	8.0	7.9	4.9	25.8	31.9	6.9	0.6	72.9	38.2	49.2	50.8
33597	WEBSTER	82.6	74.6	12.3	18.1	0.3	0.4	6.4	11.2	6.6	6.9	7.1	6.8	5.0	23.3	27.6	14.8	1.7	74.7	40.7	49.8	50.2
33598	WIMAUMA	62.9	59.7	3.8	3.7	0.7	0.8	55.1	60.9	10.0	9.6	9.1	9.3	6.4	27.1	20.6	7.1	0.8	65.7	29.1	51.3	48.7
33602	TAMPA	45.6	51.6	46.8	35.5	1.1	1.7	17.2	26.7	6.2	5.4	5.0	6.0	7.7	30.4	25.6	11.4	2.3	80.0	37.3	50.5	49.5
33603	TAMPA	61.0	56.2	28.1	30.4	0.7	0.7	28.7	39.0	7.2	7.2	6.6	6.7	7.8	27.8	24.2	10.3	2.1	74.8	35.6	48.6	51.4
33604	TAMPA	64.4	57.1	24.8	29.3	1.5	1.7	21.0	29.9	7.6	7.0	6.6	7.3	8.3	27.4	25.4	8.9	1.5	74.3	34.4	48.9	51.1
33605	TAMPA	27.4	26.1	62.6	63.2	0.2	0.2	26.0	30.2	7.3	7.5	7.0	7.9	7.0	23.5	24.8	12.5	2.5	73.3	36.5	49.1	50.9
33606	TAMPA	83.8	80.1	11.2	13.0	1.8	2.5	8.0	13.6	4.1	4.0	4.4	8.6	11.4	31.0	25.7	8.9	1.8	84.8	35.6	49.8	50.2
33607	TAMPA	50.3	48.1	38.4	39.7	1.3	1.4	40.9	46.2	6.7	6.7	6.4	6.3	6.3	25.8	23.7	15.1	3.0	76.4	38.0	47.8	52.2
33609	TAMPA	84.5	80.3	7.1	9.0	2.0	2.5	21.3	29.9	5.0	4.9	5.2	5.6	6.6	27.3	29.2	13.0	3.0	81.6	41.6	49.0	51.0
33610	TAMPA	37.7	36.3	56.5	56.6	0.6	0.8	9.1	12.8	7.8	7.7	7.2	7.7	7.0	24.4	25.2	11.3	1.6	72.6	35.2	47.0	53.0
33611	TAMPA	85.1	79.4	6.2	8.7	3.5	4.7	10.5	17.5	5.3	5.0	5.1	5.2	5.9	29.0	28.5	13.5	2.6	81.4	41.7	48.7	51.3
33612	TAMPA	60.1	53.3	29.0	33.3	2.1	2.3	17.8	25.3	8.0	7.0	6.4	7.1	8.4	28.5	22.9	9.6	2.1	74.6	33.2	48.7	51.3
33613	TAMPA	68.7	60.8	18.7	22.9	3.3	4.3	16.8	24.6	6.6	5.3	4.7	6.7	15.5	28.9	19.4	9.4	3.5	80.4	30.0	49.3	50.7
33614	TAMPA	74.4	70.3	9.1	10.3	3.6	3.8	47.0	58.8	6.8	6.0	5.6	6.2	9.1	32.4	22.5	9.9	1.6	78.2	33.9	49.6	50.4
33615	TAMPA	77.8	71.8	8.2	10.0	3.0	3.7	28.6	40.7	6.3	6.0	5.9	6.2	7.0	30.6	25.7	10.9	1.4	78.1	37.1	48.9	51.1
33616	TAMPA	67.1	57.6	17.8	23.7	6.4	7.8	13.5	20.7	6.8	6.6	6.2	7.4	7.9	30.0	25.2	9.1	0.8	75.9	34.8	50.0	50.0
33617	TAMPA	62.4	54.7	27.3	32.6	2.9	3.4	14.0	20.3	6.7	6.1	5.9	7.7	11.0	28.8	23.5	9.1	1.3	77.6	32.4	48.4	51.6
33618	TAMPA	88.4	84.1	4.1	5.7	2.9	3.8	14.5	23.7	5.3	5.3	5.9	6.0	5.8	25.8	31.2	12.8	1.9	79.7	42.1	47.9	52.1
33619	TAMPA	51.9	44.7	38.8	41.2	0.7	1.9	18.0	26.3	7.3	7.0	7.0	8.5	8.5	29.4	23.1	8.4	0.9	73.6	32.2	51.6	48.4
33620	TAMPA	60.5	50.0	31.5	40.3	4.4	5.3	8.1	12.2	0.0	0.0	0.0	58.2	38.5	3.0	0.2	0.0	0.0	99.4	19.3	38.9	61.1
33621	TAMPA	61.8	50.9	24.5	31.6	3.3	3.9	12.0	18.2	13.4	12.7	8.4	8.4	18.8	34.5	3.5	0.2	0.1	61.5	21.9	53.9	46.1
33624	TAMPA	82.7	77.0	6.9	9.0	4.0	5.1	18.5	28.7	6.1	6.2	6.5	6.7	6.4	29.7	29.0	8.4	0.9	77.0	37.5	48.0	52.0
33625	TAMPA	81.1	75.6	7.5	9.3	3.3	4.0	21.7	33.0	7.4	7.4	7.4	6.9	6.1	29.7	26.9	7.2	1.0	73.9	35.7	48.6	51.4
33626	TAMPA	86.9	80.2	5.1	8.6	4.1	5.7	11.9	19.3	10.0	10.2	9.4	5.4	2.6	32.6	23.8	5.5	0.5	66.7	36.1	48.5	51.5
33629	TAMPA	95.4	93.2	1.2	1.8	1.3	1.9	8.4	15.0	5.9	5.9	6.6	5.1	4.3	25.5	30.3	13.0	3.4	78.4	43.1	47.9	52.1
33634	TAMPA	77.0	72.1	8.3	9.9	3.4	3.7	37.1	50.4	6.5	6.3	6.2	6.9	7.3	30.6	25.0	10.1	1.0	76.7	35.8	48.3	51.7
33635	TAMPA	83.5	77.8	5.8	8.2	4.5	5.5	16.3	25.0	7.2	6.9	6.7	6.1	5.4	30.9	26.0	9.8	1.0	75.5	37.3	49.1	50.9
33637	TAMPA	74.8	66.4	16.4	21.8	2.5	3.3	12.1	19.1	7.3	6.7	6.2	6.5	8.3	34.8	22.1	7.2	0.9	76.0	32.3	48.8	51.2
33647	TAMPA	82.7	74.7	6.0	8.9	6.9	9.9	9.3	16.2	8.3	8.0	7.4	5.9	6.1	35.5	23.5	4.9	0.5	72.6	33.2	49.5	50.5
33701	SAINT PETERSBURG	72.9	66.6	21.6	26.6	1.9	2.6	3.8	5.7	4.6	3.5	3.5	4.0	5.9	26.4	28.2	16.6	7.3	86.4	46.4	50.4	49.6
33702	SAINT PETERSBURG	89.4	84.9	2.8	4.3	3.2	4.8	5.2	8.3	4.6	4.5	4.6	5.2	6.0	23.7	30.3	17.2	3.8	83.1	45.8	48.2	51.8
33703	SAINT PETERSBURG	93.8	90.9	1.1	1.8	2.3	3.5	3.9	6.5	5.2	5.5	5.9	5.7	4.7	22.3	31.6	15.7	3.5	79.8	45.4	47.8	52.2
33704	SAINT PETERSBURG	93.5	90.5	1.9	3.0	1.7	2.6	3.9	6.5	5.4	5.2	5.3	5.1	5.7	25.2	33.1	11.8	3.2	80.9	43.7	47.9	52.1
33705	SAINT PETERSBURG	39.5	31.1	55.5	63.4	1.3	1.6	3.2	4.1	6.4	6.8	7.1	7.1	6.1	22.8	26.4	13.3	4.0	75.3	40.1	46.2	53.8
33706	SAINT PETERSBURG	97.6	96.4	0.5	0.8	0.6	0.9	2.4	4.0	2.0	2.2	2.4	2.4	2.0	14.7	41.5	28.3	4.5	91.9	57.9	49.8	50.2
33707	SAINT PETERSBURG	91.4	87.7	5.6	8.2	0.8	1.2	2.8	4.5	3.1	3.3	3.6	3.7	3.9	16.6	30.9	27.5	7.4	87.7	55.9	46.3	53.7
33708	SAINT PETERSBURG	97.3	96.1	0.3	0.6	0.7	1.1	2.6	4.4	2.2	2.4	2.7	2.5	2.4	15.0	38.3	29.3	5.1	91.2	58.0	49.1	50.9
33709	SAINT PETERSBURG	90.7	86.4	2.7	4.1	2.8	4.1	4.5	7.3	4.8	4.8	4.8	4.8	4.2	19.3	29.3	22.5	5.5	82.5	50.0	47.4	52.6
33710	SAINT PETERSBURG	92.4	88.9	2.0	3.0	2.6	4.0	4.6	7.4	5.1	5.4	5.7	5.7	5.1	24.0	30.0	15.3	3.8	80.4	44.4	47.7	52.3
33711	SAINT PETERSBURG	37.0	31.7	59.4	64.4	0.9	1.2	2.5	3.2	6.1	7.0	6.6	9.2	8.8	20.0	25.9	13.4	2.9	76.0	37.4	45.6	54.4
33712	SAINT PETERSBURG	26.1	19.8	69.6	75.7	0.9	1.0	2.9	3.5	7.0	6.8	6.8	7.2	7.5	24.6	25.5	12.5	2.2	75.1	36.7	46.3	53.7
33713	SAINT PETERSBURG	78.4	70.8	9.9	13.4	7.0	9.8	6.0	9.1	6.3	6.1	5.9	6.0	6.5	27.2	29.0	10.5	2.4	78.0	39.5	49.9	50.1
33714	SAINT PETERSBURG	88.1	83.0	2.9	4.5	5.1	7.4	4.4	7.1	5.3	5.1	5.0	5.5	6.0	23.7	29.1	16.9	3.4	81.2	44.6	49.5	50.5
33715	SAINT PETERSBURG	96.6	94.8	1.2	2.0	1.1	1.6	2.9	4.9	2.0	1.9	2.4	2.2	1.5	14.6	38.1	32.8	4.5	92.2	59.3	48.8	51.2
33716	SAINT PETERSBURG	86.5	80.7	5.0	7.5	3.9	5.5	7.4	11.3	4.2	3.5	3.1	3.9	9.4	44.0	21.9	7.6	2.3	87.3	36.1	50.1	49.9
33755	CLEARWATER	66.9	59.6	25.1	30.0	1.0	1.3	11.3	15.9	6.4	6.1	5.9	6.7	7.3	28.2	27.0	10.4	2.0	77.4	37.5	49.6	50.4
33756	CLEARWATER	88.5	84.1	6.3	8.7	0.9	1.4	8.3	12.6	5.5	5.3	5.2	5.5	5.6	22.2	27.5	17.4	5.8	80.6	45.5	47.7	52.3
33759	CLEARWATER	83.2	77.1	9.2	12.7	2.7	3.8	9.3	13.5	6.1	5.7	5.3	6.5	7.8	24.7	24.3	13.7	5.9	79.5	39.9	47.7	52.3
33760	CLEARWATER	76.7	68.7	15.5	20.9	3.3	4.4	7.6	11.0	6.0	5.0	4.7	6.4	8.1	34.7	24.0	9.6	1.6	80.8	36.7	55.1	44.9
33761	CLEARWATER	96.1	94.0	0.8	1.3	1.6	2.5	4.0	6.7	3.7	4.0	4.6	4.6	3.9	19.1	32.3	23.2	4.6	84.8	51.8	45.3	54.7
33762	CLEARWATER	90.7	85.9	3.2	5.0	3.2	4.8	4.3	7.1	3.1	2.8	2.6	2.4	4.0	32.5	25.8	22.1	4.7	90.2	47.1	47.7	52.3
33763	CLEARWATER	93.9	91.1	1.8	2.7	1.6	2.3	6.6	10.3	3.2	3.0	3.0	3.4	4.1	16.5	25.7	32.0	9.2	88.9	59.6	44.8	55.2
33764	CLEARWATER	92.6	89.1	2.8	4.2	1.8	2.7	5.0	8.0	4.4	4.6	4.8	5.0	4.1	22.3	29.3	21.0	4.3	83.0	48.0	48.4	51.6
33765	CLEARWATER	86.8	81.1	5.4	7.8	2.8	4.1	9.7	14.7	5.1	4.8	4.6	5.2	7.2	29.3	27.3	13.6	2.9	82.4	40.6	48.1	51.9
33767	CLEARWATER BEACH	97.7	96.7	0.3	0.4	0.8	1.3	2.6	4.4	1.6	1.9	2.1	1.7	1.5	12.6	38.5	34.9	5.2	93.3	61.3	49.6	50.4
33770	LARGO	93.3	89.9	2.6	4.1	1.4	2.1	3.7	6.0	4.3	4.2	4.5	4.8	4.8	21.6	28.8	20.4	6.5	84.0	48.8	47.4	52.6
33771	LARGO	92.0	88.0	2.6	4.1	2.3	3.4	4.7	7.6	4.4	4.3	4.1	4.1	3.9	21.4	27.8	24.0	6.1	84.8	50.9	46.8	53.2
33772	SEMINOLE	96.2	94.3	0.5	0.9	1.1	1.7	2.9	4.9	3.9	4.3	5.0	5.2	3.9	19.1	31.1	20.5	7.1	83.4	50.2	46.4	53.6
33773	LARGO	92.2	88.5	2.0	3.1	3.2	4.6	3.9	6.3	4.6	4.6	5.0	5.4	4.7	22.2	30.1	19.4	4.0	82.2	47.3	48.0	52.0
33774	LARGO	91.3	87.5	5.7	8.2	1.2	1.8	2.9	4.7	4.3	4.5	5.3	5.1	4.4	19.2	30.4	21.6	5.1	82.6	49.7	46.6	53.4
33776	SEMINOLE	96.9	95.3	0.4	0.6	1.3	2.1	2.3	3.9	3.7	4.5	5.5	6.3	4.3	17.9	34.3	19.7	3.9	81.9	49.8	46.7	53.3
33777	SEMINOLE	93.4	90.0	1.3	2.2	2.9	4.4	3.8	6.3	5.0	5.1	5.7	6.2	5.2	21.7	30.3	17.2	3.6	80.4	45.7	47.0	53.0
33778	LARGO	83.5	79.9	12.9	15.1	1.2	1.7	3.5	5.5	4.8	5.2	5.6	5.9	4.4	21.2	30.2	18.9	3.8	80.5	46.8	47.3	52.7
33781	PINELLAS PARK	89.0	84.0	2.3	3.4	3.9	5.7	7.2	11.3	6.5	6.0	5.9	6.4	6.7	27.1	27.2	12.1	2.3	77.8	39.1	49.0	51.0
33782	PINELLAS PARK	90.0	85.6	1.3	2.1	4.6	6.8	4.7	7.5	4.8	4.7	4.9	5.5	5.0	22.3	27.6	20.6	4.6	81.9	46.9	46.9	53.1
33785	INDIAN ROCKS BEACH	97.5	96.1	0.3	0.6	0.6	0.9	3.1	5.3	2.1	1.9	2.2	2.5	2.2	20.3	41.8	24.6	2.4	92.2	55.1	50.5	49.5
33786	BELLEAIR BEACH	97.5	96.5	0.1	0.1	1.2	1.8	2.7	4.3	1.4	1.6	2.0	1.4	1.2	9.0	41.3	38.5	3.6	94.5	62.7	48.9	51.1
33801	LAKELAND	81.3	75.9	12.5	15.7	1.1	1.5	7.2	10.6	6.9	6.3	5.8	6.7	7.8	26.8	24.2	12.9	2.4	77.4	36.6	48.7	51.3
33803	LAKELAND	89.8	85.4	4.9	7.0	1.5	2.1	7.6	11.7	5.8	5.4	5.4	7.0	7.6	24.6	25.4	15.2	3.6	80.0	40.3	47.0	53.0
33805	LAKELAND	43.7	40.4	50.7	52.8	0.5	0.6	7.5	9.7	8.3	7.8	7.4	7.4	6.6	23.3	23.5	12.9	2.7	72.0	35.8	47.1	52.9
	FLORIDA	78.0	74.7	14.6	15.8	1.7	2.3	16.8	21.5	6.0	5.9	5.9	6.3	6.2	25.0	26.8	15.3	2.8	78.6	41.1	48.8	51.2
	UNITED STATES	75.1	72.0	12.3	12.7	3.8	4.6	12.5	15.7	6.8	6.7	6.6	7.1	6.9	27.0	26.0	10.9	1.9	75.7	36.9	49.2	50.8

INCOME

ZIP CODE				2009 HOUSEHOLD INCOME DISTRIBUTION (%)					MEDIAN HOUSEHOLD INCOME					2009 HOME VALUE DISTRIBUTION (%)					
#	POST OFFICE NAME	2009 Per Capita Income	2009 HH Income Base	Less than $25,000	$25,000 to $49,999	$50,000 to $99,999	$100,000 to $149,999	$150,000 or More	2009	2014	2009 National Centile	2009 State Centile	2009 Home Value Base	Less than $50,000	$50,000 to $89,999	$90,000 to $174,999	$175,000 to $399,999	$400,000 or More	2009 Median Home Value
33543	WESLEY CHAPEL	31643	8552	10.7	22.4	40.3	17.4	9.2	66056	69509	84	85	7658	3.4	11.1	31.7	48.1	5.7	182475
33544	WESLEY CHAPEL	28819	6678	8.1	17.6	46.3	19.3	8.7	70662	72715	87	89	6088	1.0	6.7	33.2	53.4	5.6	191263
33545	WESLEY CHAPEL	28918	4208	11.7	19.7	42.0	20.8	5.8	70095	69881	87	88	3847	0.9	7.5	46.5	43.9	1.2	167971
33547	LITHIA	28939	6162	12.3	19.3	40.8	18.2	9.4	70809	73215	87	89	5462	4.5	13.8	28.4	38.0	15.3	185493
33548	LUTZ	43325	2018	10.3	14.2	32.9	19.3	23.4	88617	91178	95	96	1749	2.8	5.8	23.1	51.6	16.8	251270
33549	LUTZ	29669	7473	15.4	24.2	37.2	15.6	7.5	60640	61548	78	78	5318	6.9	5.6	42.1	41.4	4.1	166954
33556	ODESSA	42597	10842	9.0	15.1	29.9	21.7	24.3	90761	90186	95	96	9830	1.0	4.4	22.2	53.1	19.2	260669
33558	LUTZ	38278	7931	11.9	21.5	35.7	14.6	16.2	69132	70029	86	87	4761	2.2	5.4	19.5	54.3	18.6	255341
33559	LUTZ	27587	5319	11.0	25.6	44.1	13.5	5.9	61071	62236	79	78	4235	3.6	14.9	46.3	33.2	2.1	157427
33563	PLANT CITY	17630	9080	28.2	34.1	31.5	4.4	1.8	40513	42868	34	29	5606	18.2	25.2	46.1	9.4	1.1	99739
33565	PLANT CITY	21851	6215	20.2	29.8	39.7	7.9	2.3	49920	52521	61	56	5105	19.8	22.1	31.4	22.7	4.0	110795
33566	PLANT CITY	26254	6915	16.2	23.3	40.8	12.0	7.7	60908	61298	79	78	5115	6.9	16.4	34.4	37.0	5.3	153881
33567	PLANT CITY	17421	3366	23.9	30.9	37.8	5.9	1.5	46254	49090	52	47	2534	21.5	22.1	34.2	20.7	1.5	104698
33569	RIVERVIEW	27599	7769	13.4	27.3	37.1	15.0	7.3	60165	60662	78	77	6760	12.7	13.1	28.3	41.2	4.7	165148
33570	RUSKIN	16198	8027	29.5	36.8	28.1	4.1	1.6	37129	39735	24	19	6166	22.9	17.4	37.3	18.6	3.8	107877
33572	APOLLO BEACH	37162	4383	13.8	19.9	36.1	17.6	12.5	66549	66747	85	85	3699	4.3	10.8	29.0	41.9	14.1	202347
33573	SUN CITY CENTER	32475	12042	22.5	32.1	36.5	6.3	2.7	46822	49676	54	48	10430	2.4	15.3	51.2	28.3	2.8	137692
33576	SAN ANTONIO	25344	1680	20.0	22.6	39.3	14.6	3.5	56432	56143	73	71	1459	8.1	6.8	37.8	42.7	4.6	170252
33578	RIVERVIEW	26364	11589	20.7	24.3	38.8	11.1	5.1	55673	57740	72	71	7652	7.7	12.1	40.8	35.6	3.7	153044
33579	RIVERVIEW	27692	6898	7.3	15.9	51.2	18.4	7.3	71227	74808	87	90	5973	1.9	7.1	53.3	36.7	1.1	153328
33584	SEFFNER	23051	9223	17.4	28.4	41.5	9.1	3.6	53591	55191	69	66	6839	14.4	11.8	53.7	18.8	1.2	122963
33585	SUMTERVILLE	18429	782	32.6	30.6	30.3	4.9	1.7	36074	40045	21	16	610	22.8	32.5	26.9	14.8	3.1	80588
33592	THONOTOSASSA	20552	3935	22.3	28.6	40.5	6.7	1.9	49036	51662	59	54	2749	27.6	20.6	33.1	15.9	2.8	94760
33594	VALRICO	27313	10868	15.1	23.7	39.6	15.8	5.9	62757	63697	81	81	9252	8.4	10.6	45.2	32.8	2.9	149530
33596	VALRICO	39853	9602	4.9	8.6	37.9	25.4	23.1	97570	99139	96	97	8325	1.5	3.5	22.6	62.2	10.2	226973
33597	WEBSTER	15064	3841	38.0	34.8	22.6	3.2	1.4	31791	33090	11	8	3154	30.0	24.8	34.4	9.9	0.9	83936
33598	WIMAUMA	16623	3078	27.0	25.1	32.7	9.6	5.6	47624	49219	56	50	2258	18.4	17.1	35.5	25.9	3.2	120562
33602	TAMPA	39797	5683	33.3	20.1	22.3	7.3	17.0	46293	51223	52	47	2629	2.6	16.9	40.9	21.4	18.2	142571
33603	TAMPA	18466	8137	31.8	32.4	28.9	5.1	1.8	38038	40824	27	23	4924	5.6	29.5	54.7	8.7	1.5	105197
33604	TAMPA	18411	14668	32.7	31.0	30.6	4.3	1.3	38882	41560	29	25	8639	8.0	30.6	54.7	5.8	0.9	101993
33605	TAMPA	12808	7051	52.9	28.0	15.4	2.5	1.2	22899	23162	2	2	3446	21.7	35.5	36.3	5.2	1.2	84172
33606	TAMPA	53049	7240	14.2	21.6	32.1	13.2	18.9	66431	66729	84	85	3176	1.5	5.4	14.4	36.7	42.1	340566
33607	TAMPA	20743	9890	37.2	27.8	26.0	5.4	3.6	34319	36792	16	13	4935	7.1	28.3	57.6	6.3	0.7	104732
33609	TAMPA	38216	8435	19.3	25.7	34.5	9.9	10.6	54236	55904	70	68	4801	1.5	10.8	39.4	26.3	22.0	169212
33610	TAMPA	16737	14351	34.4	32.8	27.3	3.8	1.7	35308	37839	19	14	8947	22.6	30.4	42.3	4.0	0.6	86979
33611	TAMPA	32632	15710	20.3	30.1	34.7	9.0	5.8	49644	52431	60	56	8718	6.4	15.7	47.7	18.3	11.8	131166
33612	TAMPA	18665	18196	35.1	33.6	25.1	4.5	1.8	34364	36488	16	13	8245	7.3	22.9	57.6	10.2	1.9	109617
33613	TAMPA	21505	14332	36.2	34.2	22.3	4.5	2.8	34281	35593	16	12	4465	24.3	12.7	36.4	21.0	5.6	116838
33614	TAMPA	21010	20175	25.6	35.0	32.1	5.3	2.0	41724	44672	38	33	8490	4.5	21.2	60.1	13.6	0.5	117685
33615	TAMPA	26607	18149	17.9	30.1	38.7	8.6	4.6	51777	54331	65	62	10708	6.3	11.4	58.4	19.6	4.3	127522
33616	TAMPA	21600	5602	24.2	32.3	36.5	5.7	1.2	45129	47463	49	43	2845	13.1	20.9	60.6	4.9	0.5	103420
33617	TAMPA	24205	18484	25.7	30.9	30.6	8.4	4.4	44243	47253	46	40	8629	2.7	17.0	50.4	25.6	4.2	129077
33618	TAMPA	36947	10984	12.1	25.8	37.3	13.5	11.3	62967	63935	81	81	7168	0.4	5.0	32.0	47.1	15.6	210884
33619	TAMPA	16885	11387	29.4	32.1	31.9	5.0	1.6	40942	43690	36	30	7493	11.4	37.1	42.9	7.7	0.9	91420
33620	TAMPA	16143	3	0.0	33.3	66.7	0.0	0.0	52500	52500	67	64	0	0.0	0.0	0.0	0.0	0.0	0
33621	TAMPA	14539	538	7.4	45.5	41.8	3.5	1.7	48410	50638	58	52	13	100.0	0.0	0.0	0.0	0.0	43500
33624	TAMPA	31815	16319	9.0	23.3	45.5	14.9	7.3	66555	66808	85	85	11531	1.2	4.3	52.3	39.9	2.3	163339
33625	TAMPA	27657	8199	9.4	21.3	47.8	15.6	5.9	66623	66322	85	85	6393	4.1	4.2	58.3	31.1	2.3	149497
33626	TAMPA	54159	8315	3.9	9.7	30.4	20.2	35.9	116715	123570	98	99	6835	0.3	5.4	15.0	60.7	18.7	264987
33629	TAMPA	50079	10311	11.5	19.3	34.4	14.8	20.1	76302	76872	90	92	7673	0.2	1.3	20.7	47.1	30.7	281911
33634	TAMPA	23687	8149	15.2	30.9	41.9	8.7	3.3	52984	55016	68	65	5018	1.0	16.7	62.3	16.8	3.2	120185
33635	TAMPA	30538	6309	14.0	21.7	44.5	13.4	6.4	61399	62324	79	79	4732	27.7	9.8	26.1	33.9	2.5	145504
33637	TAMPA	22795	6032	21.8	32.4	37.6	6.4	1.8	47246	49919	55	49	2795	12.2	15.9	57.3	13.8	0.8	115284
33647	TAMPA	46193	18933	9.7	12.5	32.1	22.1	23.6	91837	95246	95	97	12168	0.5	1.8	18.2	59.8	19.7	252069
33701	SAINT PETERSBURG	25200	8129	46.5	26.8	17.8	5.8	3.0	26960	27928	5	3	2438	15.0	16.7	28.8	30.1	9.4	138038
33702	SAINT PETERSBURG	27947	13162	22.7	31.8	32.8	8.1	4.7	46022	48825	51	46	8983	20.5	19.4	39.2	16.8	4.1	104891
33703	SAINT PETERSBURG	33437	10913	17.7	28.0	32.6	12.3	9.5	54648	55709	71	69	8960	8.5	20.2	37.6	23.6	10.1	122422
33704	SAINT PETERSBURG	39585	7554	16.9	24.8	32.8	14.1	11.4	59888	59658	77	76	5142	3.2	11.6	34.2	35.4	15.6	178591
33705	SAINT PETERSBURG	21128	11643	35.2	29.6	25.8	5.7	3.7	35199	38493	18	14	6440	11.0	28.4	44.1	13.9	2.7	101311
33706	SAINT PETERSBURG	46383	9457	17.8	23.7	34.6	10.5	13.4	59538	60293	77	75	6432	0.6	3.8	23.6	44.0	28.0	263055
33707	SAINT PETERSBURG	31100	13048	28.4	31.4	27.5	6.3	6.4	41000	44757	36	30	9220	5.6	25.9	40.5	19.5	8.4	115338
33708	SAINT PETERSBURG	36361	9211	23.9	29.0	30.3	8.9	7.9	46663	50327	53	48	6743	11.6	8.0	32.5	35.5	12.4	167078
33709	SAINT PETERSBURG	23153	12140	29.2	34.9	28.9	4.5	2.5	38081	41057	27	23	9313	25.4	28.1	40.7	5.3	0.5	86272
33710	SAINT PETERSBURG	27547	14140	20.0	29.3	37.8	8.9	4.1	50600	52262	63	58	11133	4.1	19.4	60.0	13.9	2.7	116904
33711	SAINT PETERSBURG	21257	7127	28.7	32.9	27.9	5.6	5.0	40399	43057	34	29	4911	12.9	34.9	30.6	14.8	6.8	92300
33712	SAINT PETERSBURG	18812	10394	31.7	34.1	26.9	5.3	2.0	35525	38529	19	15	5497	12.2	24.7	50.5	11.2	1.4	107564
33713	SAINT PETERSBURG	21993	12930	24.6	34.0	33.0	6.1	2.3	42695	45906	41	36	9054	6.6	35.8	53.0	4.1	0.4	95319
33714	SAINT PETERSBURG	19254	8651	34.7	38.1	22.2	3.6	1.5	33154	34886	14	10	5896	33.2	33.4	31.5	1.3	0.6	70425
33715	SAINT PETERSBURG	63054	3919	9.6	17.7	28.0	22.7	22.0	86837	90710	94	95	3360	0.3	0.8	28.9	42.1	27.9	254157
33716	SAINT PETERSBURG	39592	7512	12.8	32.1	40.8	8.0	6.3	53646	55225	69	66	1567	22.1	27.8	14.0	26.4	9.6	90070
33755	CLEARWATER	21508	9679	25.6	31.3	34.2	6.6	2.3	43854	47051	45	39	5796	4.7	20.0	61.2	11.9	2.2	116542
33756	CLEARWATER	28134	13595	27.5	29.4	29.4	7.6	6.1	43214	46257	43	38	8677	6.2	17.0	48.7	19.0	9.1	128101
33759	CLEARWATER	26438	8249	24.1	30.0	31.3	9.6	4.9	46595	49713	53	48	4737	19.4	16.3	37.7	20.2	6.4	116929
33760	CLEARWATER	24125	6101	22.6	34.1	30.5	8.6	4.2	44920	47939	48	42	3631	20.4	19.4	42.7	16.7	0.8	102423
33761	CLEARWATER	36301	8068	17.6	25.9	34.8	11.3	10.4	57183	57520	74	73	6547	11.1	16.7	30.8	35.3	6.1	140358
33762	CLEARWATER	41860	3177	14.1	27.9	38.6	10.4	9.0	56639	58402	74	72	1693	20.4	12.6	35.0	25.5	6.4	133114
33763	CLEARWATER	27335	10302	24.6	33.7	34.1	5.4	2.3	42972	46046	42	37	8140	10.1	32.7	47.8	9.2	0.2	99124
33764	CLEARWATER	30153	12278	21.4	29.6	34.3	8.9	5.8	48975	51547	59	53	8727	29.6	9.6	31.9	25.6	3.4	120119
33765	CLEARWATER	27627	5274	20.3	33.3	33.2	9.2	4.0	47831	49498	56	50	2818	14.0	12.7	50.3	18.6	4.4	124566
33767	CLEARWATER BEACH	56119	4865	16.5	22.1	31.4	13.2	16.8	63691	63830	82	82	3349	0.3	2.1	13.0	48.4	36.3	284634
33770	LARGO	28665	11780	26.2	31.7	30.9	7.0	4.3	43339	46329	43	38	7827	17.5	15.7	44.9	17.6	4.3	115528
33771	LARGO	24542	12512	25.6	37.1	31.8	3.9	1.6	40157	43703	33	28	8453	36.1	23.7	33.3	6.3	0.6	73138
33772	SEMINOLE	30513	11048	19.4	29.4	35.7	9.9	5.6	51077	52671	64	59	8724	12.1	11.6	45.2	27.5	3.7	132340
33773	LARGO	26697	8603	21.5	30.5	35.1	9.2	3.7	47875	50663	56	51	6511	22.5	23.9	36.1	16.4	1.1	95307
33774	LARGO	28876	8424	20.0	31.0	33.7	10.2	5.1	49084	51304	59	54	6213	5.2	16.0	47.8	26.8	4.2	135164
33776	SEMINOLE	33742	5114	10.8	19.9	39.9	19.9	9.5	71338	70971	88	90	4557	1.4	2.4	35.7	55.5	5.0	192125
33777	SEMINOLE	33537	7049	15.4	27.7	34.6	11.3	11.0	57210	58122	74	73	5915	2.4	22.8	46.4	17.8	10.7	123232
33778	LARGO	25068	5666	19.9	33.3	34.0	9.4	3.3	47140	50177	54	49	4642	20.5	21.1	43.6	13.1	1.7	103162
33781	PINELLAS PARK	21903	9918	22.0	34.3	35.9	5.7	2.1	45570	48126	50	45	6867	16.5	27.7	48.0	5.6	2.2	94234
33782	PINELLAS PARK	24520	8542	21.5	32.9	36.1	6.6	2.9	46297	49355	52	47	7033	13.9	24.1	52.7	8.1	1.2	102884
33785	INDIAN ROCKS BEACH	49628	3726	13.3	22.5	36.9	13.7	13.6	64941	65705	83	83	2463	1.1	1.9	17.9	52.7	26.3	259679
33786	BELLEAIR BEACH	65928	791	10.4	13.4	33.9	17.6	24.8	82588	85486	93	94	659	0.0	0.0	4.9	59.9	35.2	298063
33801	LAKELAND	20113	14067	31.4	34.6	27.0	4.9	2.1	37194	40088	24	19	7865	16.4	32.2	44.7	5.7	1.0	91433
33803	LAKELAND	29459	12606	21.7	29.7	34.4	7.5	6.7	48474	50727	58	52	7961	13.4	14.9	40.2	24.2	7.2	126153
33805	LAKELAND	17218	8503	35.8	31.3	27.1	3.6	2.2	33709	35980	15	12	4755	17.9	33.9	40.4	6.3	1.4	88274
	FLORIDA	27128		21.9	27.6	33.8	9.8	6.8	50413	52516				8.0	14.3	38.7	30.4	8.6	144752
	UNITED STATES	27277		20.9	24.4	35.3	11.7	7.6	54719	56938				9.3	13.1	31.6	32.6	13.5	162279

ZIP CODE #	POST OFFICE NAME	FINANCIAL SERVICES: Auto Loan	Home Loan	Invest-ments	Retire-ment Plans	THE HOME: Home Improvements: Home Repair	Lawn & Garden	Furnishings: Comput-ers & Hard-ware-Personal	Major Appli-ances	TV, Radio, Sound Equip-ment	Furni-ture	ENTERTAINMENT: Dine out/ Carry out	Sports Equip-ment	Fees & Tickets	Toys & Games	Travel	Cable TV	PERSONAL: Apparel & Services	Auto Repairs	Health Insur-ance	Pets & Supplies
33543	WESLEY CHAPEL	125	133	117	126	128	116	119	122	114	129	115	93	120	120	119	110	80	116	112	138
33544	WESLEY CHAPEL	127	138	115	133	131	117	123	123	117	133	119	96	127	125	122	112	83	117	111	140
33545	WESLEY CHAPEL	119	130	105	125	121	106	115	114	108	124	110	91	117	117	113	102	77	108	99	130
33547	LITHIA	123	130	109	126	123	116	117	119	113	123	114	93	118	120	115	110	79	113	109	137
33548	LUTZ	155	196	202	203	201	182	164	173	156	176	158	132	191	157	185	152	115	163	159	198
33549	LUTZ	103	111	102	113	109	104	106	104	103	109	105	82	111	105	109	102	74	105	101	123
33556	ODESSA	167	193	178	196	192	174	165	171	158	179	160	134	182	166	174	152	115	160	154	195
33558	LUTZ	142	137	138	141	135	129	137	134	132	141	135	109	136	137	135	129	95	134	124	157
33559	LUTZ	110	108	92	107	102	94	108	101	103	113	105	81	106	109	103	99	73	103	94	119
33563	PLANT CITY	70	65	58	64	63	65	70	66	70	69	71	51	67	71	66	71	49	70	69	79
33565	PLANT CITY	89	85	84	83	86	91	80	87	83	83	82	63	78	83	80	86	56	84	90	102
33566	PLANT CITY	115	113	104	112	110	110	108	110	107	110	108	85	106	111	106	107	75	108	106	130
33567	PLANT CITY	85	76	72	73	74	80	74	79	76	76	76	59	69	79	71	78	52	77	78	93
33569	RIVERVIEW	108	113	114	108	113	111	102	110	101	109	101	82	104	102	106	101	70	105	107	126
33570	RUSKIN	68	64	70	60	66	70	62	68	64	65	63	48	60	62	63	66	43	66	72	79
33572	APOLLO BEACH	121	137	142	138	141	138	122	130	121	129	121	96	133	119	133	121	85	125	131	151
33573	SUN CITY CENTER	64	79	102	68	95	100	68	87	75	81	72	46	83	63	88	82	48	82	113	91
33576	SAN ANTONIO	91	98	95	97	99	102	88	95	90	91	90	67	93	90	93	93	62	91	99	110
33578	RIVERVIEW	100	94	83	94	90	89	94	91	94	98	95	71	91	98	89	93	66	92	90	109
33579	RIVERVIEW	126	134	108	128	125	111	120	119	114	130	116	94	121	123	117	108	81	114	105	136
33584	SEFFNER	93	90	85	88	86	92	87	90	88	87	88	69	85	91	85	90	61	88	90	106
33585	SUMTERVILLE	84	60	86	58	62	85	62	78	69	58	67	59	49	68	61	75	44	72	82	93
33592	THONOTOSASSA	85	76	71	74	74	79	76	78	79	78	79	59	71	81	72	81	54	78	80	94
33594	VALRICO	108	115	109	111	114	110	103	109	102	110	102	81	106	103	106	101	71	104	106	125
33596	VALRICO	166	200	178	203	195	172	170	172	160	184	162	139	190	168	181	151	118	162	151	196
33597	WEBSTER	70	50	71	49	52	71	52	65	57	48	56	49	41	57	51	63	37	60	68	78
33598	WIMAUMA	95	91	83	85	90	86	86	91	87	92	88	65	83	88	85	87	61	89	86	103
33602	TAMPA	117	100	103	109	99	104	126	108	128	120	129	89	119	125	115	130	92	121	119	134
33603	TAMPA	66	61	54	61	58	61	66	62	68	65	68	48	63	68	62	69	47	66	67	75
33604	TAMPA	65	57	50	59	54	59	66	60	68	63	68	47	62	68	60	69	47	65	66	73
33605	TAMPA	47	38	36	39	37	44	45	43	50	45	49	31	42	48	41	53	34	47	51	53
33606	TAMPA	140	134	149	146	139	127	157	136	150	154	153	114	157	149	153	146	112	147	133	163
33607	TAMPA	72	61	62	62	60	69	69	68	74	67	73	51	65	72	65	77	51	71	76	82
33609	TAMPA	107	107	110	111	109	105	115	107	112	114	113	85	116	111	114	111	80	112	110	127
33610	TAMPA	65	59	52	59	56	63	62	60	65	62	65	45	60	65	58	68	45	63	67	74
33611	TAMPA	92	89	88	90	89	90	95	91	95	94	95	70	94	94	93	95	67	94	95	108
33612	TAMPA	64	54	51	56	52	55	65	58	66	63	67	46	61	66	59	67	47	64	63	71
33613	TAMPA	67	51	49	54	50	52	73	57	69	67	70	49	62	69	60	68	49	67	60	71
33614	TAMPA	74	61	55	63	58	58	75	65	74	74	75	53	68	75	67	73	53	72	66	78
33615	TAMPA	94	89	81	89	86	84	94	88	93	95	94	69	91	95	89	92	66	92	89	105
33616	TAMPA	76	64	55	67	60	64	76	66	76	74	77	54	71	78	68	76	54	74	71	82
33617	TAMPA	84	69	67	73	68	69	86	75	85	84	86	60	79	86	77	84	60	83	77	91
33618	TAMPA	118	129	127	131	130	121	124	121	119	128	121	94	131	120	129	117	86	122	118	141
33619	TAMPA	72	67	59	65	64	65	69	67	69	70	69	52	65	70	65	69	48	69	67	79
33620	TAMPA	81	34	34	42	31	40	114	56	91	77	92	61	67	88	61	83	65	80	56	76
33621	TAMPA	94	49	37	57	44	42	89	61	83	82	88	61	67	100	64	77	62	78	55	75
33624	TAMPA	115	120	107	121	115	107	116	111	111	120	113	88	118	115	115	108	80	112	104	130
33625	TAMPA	115	120	99	116	113	104	110	109	106	117	108	84	111	112	107	103	75	106	100	127
33626	TAMPA	211	250	218	254	243	208	210	213	195	235	199	174	234	210	220	181	145	196	179	239
33629	TAMPA	136	159	172	163	167	155	150	150	146	155	147	114	167	143	162	145	106	149	151	172
33634	TAMPA	91	88	76	86	84	79	90	85	87	93	89	66	87	90	86	85	62	87	81	99
33635	TAMPA	107	111	97	108	106	99	106	103	103	112	104	81	107	107	104	99	73	102	98	120
33637	TAMPA	81	68	58	69	63	62	79	69	77	79	78	56	72	80	70	75	54	75	67	84
33647	TAMPA	175	183	161	191	176	156	176	165	166	187	170	139	183	176	173	156	122	163	146	192
33701	SAINT PETERSBURG	58	49	52	52	49	54	63	55	66	60	65	43	59	61	58	68	46	63	66	68
33702	SAINT PETERSBURG	82	78	79	79	79	83	84	81	86	83	86	61	83	84	83	88	60	85	91	97
33703	SAINT PETERSBURG	102	110	108	110	110	115	105	108	107	105	106	80	110	105	109	110	74	108	118	127
33704	SAINT PETERSBURG	114	120	120	123	121	119	121	118	118	121	118	92	124	117	122	117	83	119	119	138
33705	SAINT PETERSBURG	70	63	59	65	61	69	70	66	75	69	74	50	68	72	66	78	51	71	77	82
33706	SAINT PETERSBURG	112	120	153	120	135	137	112	125	118	122	116	82	123	107	127	122	81	122	141	143
33707	SAINT PETERSBURG	80	82	96	79	90	97	82	89	86	84	84	59	85	80	88	91	58	88	105	101
33708	SAINT PETERSBURG	94	94	120	90	104	111	90	103	94	95	93	68	93	87	99	99	63	100	116	117
33709	SAINT PETERSBURG	69	65	78	62	70	80	65	74	70	66	68	50	64	66	69	75	46	72	85	85
33710	SAINT PETERSBURG	84	90	85	90	89	95	87	88	89	85	89	66	91	88	90	92	62	89	98	104
33711	SAINT PETERSBURG	78	69	71	71	69	77	75	74	79	77	79	54	73	77	72	82	54	78	83	89
33712	SAINT PETERSBURG	68	57	53	59	55	60	65	60	69	66	69	46	62	69	60	71	48	66	67	74
33713	SAINT PETERSBURG	73	70	61	71	67	75	74	71	76	70	75	55	72	76	70	78	52	74	79	86
33714	SAINT PETERSBURG	61	54	56	53	54	63	58	60	61	56	60	45	55	60	56	65	41	61	68	71
33715	SAINT PETERSBURG	163	177	237	176	203	203	157	184	164	178	161	117	175	148	183	170	112	175	201	208
33716	SAINT PETERSBURG	109	75	66	83	69	70	106	83	104	104	106	73	90	109	87	100	74	98	83	105
33755	CLEARWATER	76	70	64	72	68	73	76	72	78	74	77	56	73	78	72	79	54	75	77	87
33756	CLEARWATER	83	80	82	82	81	87	86	84	89	85	89	62	87	86	86	92	62	88	95	100
33759	CLEARWATER	83	75	75	77	75	79	86	80	88	84	89	61	83	86	82	90	62	86	90	96
33760	CLEARWATER	86	72	70	74	71	76	87	79	87	83	87	62	79	87	79	88	60	85	85	96
33761	CLEARWATER	103	111	127	109	119	124	103	114	108	109	107	77	111	101	114	113	74	111	128	131
33762	CLEARWATER	111	107	109	107	110	109	112	109	112	118	113	80	114	111	113	112	78	112	118	127
33763	CLEARWATER	68	72	85	67	81	85	69	78	73	76	72	49	75	67	78	77	48	77	95	87
33764	CLEARWATER	89	91	101	89	96	100	87	95	91	91	90	66	91	86	93	94	62	93	104	109
33765	CLEARWATER	85	79	79	82	79	80	88	82	88	87	89	64	86	87	85	88	62	87	86	98
33767	CLEARWATER BEACH	137	145	192	144	165	170	132	153	140	147	137	97	145	126	151	146	94	147	173	174
33770	LARGO	82	79	83	79	81	87	83	84	85	81	84	61	82	83	83	89	58	85	94	99
33771	LARGO	70	68	82	64	73	78	65	74	69	69	67	50	65	64	70	72	46	72	82	85
33772	SEMINOLE	86	93	99	91	98	102	88	95	91	91	90	65	94	86	95	94	62	93	106	108
33773	LARGO	85	81	88	79	85	89	82	87	84	84	83	62	81	81	84	87	57	86	94	101
33774	LARGO	84	87	96	87	92	96	87	90	90	88	89	63	91	85	91	94	62	91	102	105
33776	SEMINOLE	108	127	131	129	131	129	115	120	116	120	117	87	129	112	127	119	82	118	129	138
33777	SEMINOLE	116	118	116	118	118	126	115	120	118	114	117	88	117	116	118	122	81	119	130	140
33778	LARGO	83	84	94	82	88	93	79	88	82	82	81	61	81	79	84	85	56	85	94	102
33781	PINELLAS PARK	78	72	67	72	70	77	77	75	79	74	78	58	73	79	73	81	53	77	82	90
33782	PINELLAS PARK	77	82	80	80	83	89	78	82	81	79	80	59	82	78	82	83	55	81	93	96
33785	INDIAN ROCKS BEACH	125	132	173	132	150	152	120	138	125	134	123	89	131	114	137	130	85	132	151	157
33786	BELLEAIR BEACH	192	203	275	201	233	239	182	215	192	206	189	134	200	173	211	201	130	205	240	243
33801	LAKELAND	68	57	59	58	57	65	66	65	68	63	67	49	59	68	61	71	46	67	71	78
33803	LAKELAND	91	88	92	87	90	95	90	92	92	90	91	68	88	90	90	95	63	93	99	108
33805	LAKELAND	67	55	54	56	53	64	61	61	66	59	65	47	56	66	56	70	44	63	68	75
	FLORIDA	96	94	97	93	96	98	95	97	96	97	96	71	95	94	96	97	67	97	101	113
	UNITED STATES	100	100	100	100	100	100	100	100	100	100	100	100	100	100	100	100	100	100	100	100

POPULATION CHANGE

ZIP CODE #	POST OFFICE NAME	COUNTY FIPS CODE	POPULATION 2000	POPULATION 2009	POPULATION 2014	2000-2009 ANNUAL RATE % Rate	2000-2009 ANNUAL RATE State Centile	HOUSEHOLDS 2000	HOUSEHOLDS 2009	HOUSEHOLDS 2014	HOUSEHOLDS % Annual Rate 2000-2009	HOUSEHOLDS 2009 Average HH Size	FAMILIES 2000	FAMILIES 2009	FAMILIES % Annual Rate 2000-2009
33809	LAKELAND	105	26167	30305	32738	1.6	55	10072	11945	13010	1.9	2.47	7346	8440	1.5
33810	LAKELAND	105	31047	46710	55159	4.5	86	11907	18345	21789	4.8	2.53	9170	13745	4.5
33811	LAKELAND	105	16135	19365	22020	2.3	69	6202	7874	8749	2.6	2.53	4484	5454	2.1
33812	LAKELAND	105	9335	12597	14856	3.3	81	3180	4342	5122	3.4	2.87	2626	3535	3.3
33813	LAKELAND	105	26330	32917	36174	2.4	70	9683	12166	13383	2.5	2.70	7548	9330	2.3
33815	LAKELAND	105	13980	15446	16454	1.1	44	5633	6296	6742	1.2	2.42	3582	3836	0.7
33823	AUBURNDALE	105	26696	30768	33023	1.5	53	10039	11751	12674	1.7	2.60	7450	8553	1.5
33825	AVON PARK	055	21654	23750	24913	1.0	40	8692	9401	9846	0.9	2.49	6197	6610	0.7
33827	BABSON PARK	105	2423	2966	3280	2.2	66	870	1080	1199	2.4	2.64	620	747	2.0
33830	BARTOW	105	24559	26966	28378	1.0	40	8732	9723	10290	1.2	2.59	6230	6738	0.9
33834	BOWLING GREEN	081	7330	8373	8718	1.4	51	1968	2176	2278	1.1	3.20	1552	1690	0.9
33837	DAVENPORT	105	11471	17997	21279	5.0	88	4348	6867	8155	5.1	2.60	3257	5012	4.8
33838	DUNDEE	105	2900	3704	4204	2.7	74	1079	1390	1581	2.8	2.64	790	989	2.5
33839	EAGLE LAKE	105	2305	3112	3503	3.3	81	890	1186	1334	3.2	2.61	623	806	2.8
33841	FORT MEADE	105	8468	9214	9719	0.9	38	2955	3246	3430	1.0	2.81	2247	2408	0.8
33843	FROSTPROOF	105	10939	12691	13576	1.6	55	3253	3858	4186	1.9	2.72	2376	2736	1.5
33844	HAINES CITY	105	30256	36864	41037	2.2	66	11455	13919	15530	2.1	2.61	8429	10004	1.9
33849	KATHLEEN	105	986	932	1075	-0.6	1	347	335	388	-0.4	2.78	277	262	-0.6
33850	LAKE ALFRED	105	4612	5490	6169	1.9	61	1788	2177	2455	2.2	2.50	1312	1552	1.8
33852	LAKE PLACID	055	19672	24102	26397	2.2	66	8326	9956	10850	2.0	2.40	5788	6791	1.7
33853	LAKE WALES	105	10866	11499	11889	0.6	30	4309	4619	4799	0.8	2.42	2727	2816	0.3
33857	LORIDA	055	1633	1986	2168	2.1	64	712	844	916	1.9	2.35	511	592	1.6
33859	LAKE WALES	105	7803	9550	10511	2.2	66	3114	3924	4360	2.5	2.39	2226	2714	2.2
33860	MULBERRY	105	17364	21155	23525	2.2	66	6235	7743	8662	2.4	2.72	4803	5819	2.1
33865	ONA	049	551	650	689	1.8	59	216	251	266	1.6	2.39	152	174	1.5
33868	POLK CITY	105	11303	13965	16054	2.3	69	3543	4752	5477	3.2	2.82	2837	3703	2.9
33870	SEBRING	055	17249	19234	20309	1.2	46	7284	8033	8485	1.1	2.31	4554	4854	0.7
33872	SEBRING	055	11323	14550	16174	2.7	74	5465	6934	7692	2.6	2.10	3746	4648	2.4
33873	WAUCHULA	049	14323	15079	15262	0.6	30	4454	4522	4556	0.2	3.11	3337	3331	0.0
33875	SEBRING	055	10114	11928	12859	1.8	59	4509	5235	5616	1.6	2.26	3256	3719	1.4
33876	SEBRING	055	4418	5294	5786	2.0	62	1933	2301	2513	1.9	2.28	1386	1619	1.7
33880	WINTER HAVEN	105	35646	40261	43147	1.3	48	13563	15367	16450	1.4	2.61	9325	10289	1.1
33881	WINTER HAVEN	105	27925	30183	31639	0.8	35	12076	13236	13943	1.0	2.23	7708	8174	0.6
33884	WINTER HAVEN	105	19605	24929	27785	2.6	73	8152	10537	11817	2.8	2.32	5893	7363	2.4
33890	ZOLFO SPRINGS	049	5250	5740	5961	1.0	40	1699	1844	1908	0.9	3.09	1351	1445	0.7
33896	DAVENPORT	097	3553	8040	10040	9.2	96	1401	3244	4071	9.5	2.40	1063	2382	9.1
33897	DAVENPORT	105	3992	10978	13800	11.6	97	1855	4879	6288	11.0	2.02	1431	3674	10.7
33898	LAKE WALES	105	15830	18130	19533	1.5	53	6888	8000	8661	1.6	2.24	4883	5506	1.3
33901	FORT MYERS	071	21095	21794	22564	0.4	22	9030	9578	10053	0.6	2.17	4710	4633	-0.2
33903	NORTH FORT MYERS	071	22141	24344	26632	1.0	40	10768	12366	13645	1.5	1.96	6822	7166	0.5
33904	CAPE CORAL	071	32903	34618	36257	0.6	30	15030	16260	17123	0.9	2.12	10062	10362	0.3
33905	FORT MYERS	071	25853	32755	37345	2.6	73	9164	11941	13668	2.9	2.70	6457	8138	2.5
33907	FORT MYERS	071	21472	23836	25602	1.1	44	9732	11474	12570	1.8	2.00	4987	5319	0.7
33908	FORT MYERS	071	24355	38540	46445	5.1	89	11845	18813	22725	5.1	2.01	7569	11436	4.6
33909	CAPE CORAL	071	9410	22520	29075	9.9	96	3346	8371	10899	10.4	2.69	2561	6048	9.7
33912	FORT MYERS	071	10548	17419	21543	5.6	90	4837	7943	9844	5.5	2.19	3538	5540	5.0
33913	FORT MYERS	071	4004	15919	21426	16.1	99	1460	5784	7884	16.0	2.72	1236	4757	15.7
33914	CAPE CORAL	071	25543	42638	52596	5.7	91	9785	16618	20583	5.9	2.57	7690	12759	5.6
33916	FORT MYERS	071	20490	22673	24828	1.1	44	7326	8735	9900	1.9	2.49	4658	4912	0.6
33917	NORTH FORT MYERS	071	28757	32496	35038	1.3	48	13157	15497	16884	1.8	2.09	8645	9592	1.1
33919	FORT MYERS	071	25806	30941	34695	2.0	62	12596	15769	17872	2.5	1.96	7845	9185	1.7
33920	ALVA	071	3950	5407	6414	3.5	82	1513	2158	2582	3.9	2.51	1143	1553	3.4
33921	BOCA GRANDE	071	1087	1469	1679	3.3	81	565	794	915	3.7	1.85	401	535	3.2
33922	BOKEELIA	071	4186	4321	4418	0.3	18	1877	2008	2072	0.7	2.15	1309	1340	0.3
33924	CAPTIVA	071	254	320	353	2.5	72	140	180	200	2.8	1.78	92	111	2.1
33928	ESTERO	071	8740	18478	23221	8.4	95	4226	9077	11488	8.6	2.02	3062	6492	8.5
33931	FORT MYERS BEACH	071	11405	14726	17095	2.8	76	6123	8138	9531	3.1	1.81	3756	4716	2.5
33935	LABELLE	051	19232	22424	24194	1.7	57	5760	6695	7226	1.6	3.18	4218	4816	1.4
33936	LEHIGH ACRES	071	18072	20609	22124	1.4	51	7585	8765	9452	1.6	2.35	5137	5530	0.8
33946	PLACIDA	015	1575	1985	2237	2.5	72	808	1045	1189	2.8	1.90	585	719	2.3
33947	ROTONDA WEST	015	5263	8070	9265	4.7	87	2384	3734	4317	5.0	2.15	1767	2703	4.7
33948	PORT CHARLOTTE	015	14168	16843	17511	1.9	61	5762	7075	7415	2.2	2.35	4256	5027	1.8
33950	PUNTA GORDA	015	19163	21722	22604	1.4	51	9465	10901	11371	1.5	1.96	6586	7430	1.3
33952	PORT CHARLOTTE	015	30710	31047	30918	0.1	12	14013	14173	14158	0.1	2.18	8884	8730	-0.2
33953	PORT CHARLOTTE	015	3462	5317	6147	4.7	87	1552	2418	2809	4.9	2.20	1152	1750	4.6
33954	PORT CHARLOTTE	015	7275	8804	9484	2.1	64	2784	3421	3704	2.3	2.57	2231	2683	2.0
33955	PUNTA GORDA	015	6785	8360	8962	2.3	69	3199	4027	4343	2.5	2.08	2348	2852	2.1
33956	SAINT JAMES CITY	071	4095	4306	4490	0.5	26	2135	2309	2423	0.9	1.86	1419	1447	0.2
33957	SANIBEL	071	6268	8073	9027	2.8	76	3145	4166	4685	3.1	1.94	2197	2739	2.4
33960	VENUS	055	744	784	802	0.6	30	290	302	309	0.4	2.55	204	209	0.3
33966	FORT MYERS	071	3979	9814	13061	10.3	97	1619	4169	5622	10.8	2.34	1198	2943	10.2
33967	FORT MYERS	071	19076	23278	25804	2.2	66	6913	8840	9928	2.7	2.63	5322	6528	2.2
33971	LEHIGH ACRES	071	5221	17522	23317	14.0	98	1731	5951	7997	14.3	2.92	1417	4677	13.8
33972	LEHIGH ACRES	071	4675	9049	11199	7.4	93	1603	3137	3902	7.5	2.88	1257	2402	7.3
33973	LEHIGH ACRES	071	986	4044	5480	16.5	99	359	1520	2079	16.9	2.66	274	1127	16.5
33974	LEHIGH ACRES	071	1188	7151	9332	21.4	99	419	2592	3416	21.8	2.75	344	2029	21.1
33976	LEHIGH ACRES	071	2674	10590	14333	16.0	98	797	3260	4452	16.4	3.25	658	2591	16.0
33980	PORT CHARLOTTE	015	9536	10302	10947	0.8	35	4592	4987	5326	0.9	1.95	2776	2926	0.6
33981	PORT CHARLOTTE	015	7155	9707	11021	3.4	81	3069	4275	4893	3.6	2.27	2291	3088	3.3
33982	PUNTA GORDA	015	8929	9876	10306	1.1	44	3528	3956	4182	1.2	2.19	2440	2679	1.0
33983	PUNTA GORDA	015	10960	14184	15858	2.8	76	4600	5981	6710	2.9	2.35	3462	4404	2.6
33990	CAPE CORAL	071	23222	30484	35588	3.0	78	8788	12029	14202	3.5	2.51	6740	8837	3.0
33991	CAPE CORAL	071	8610	19107	24845	9.0	95	3018	6978	9170	9.5	2.72	2443	5493	9.2
33993	CAPE CORAL	071	4240	20810	28099	18.8	99	1635	7506	10162	17.9	2.77	1218	5783	18.3
34102	NAPLES	021	11794	11591	11583	-0.2	4	5975	5868	5859	-0.2	1.95	3476	3255	-0.7
34103	NAPLES	021	13167	12840	12724	-0.3	3	6556	6458	6427	-0.2	1.97	4168	3912	-0.7
34104	NAPLES	021	18862	25159	27824	3.2	80	8382	11204	12449	3.2	2.25	5661	7302	2.8
34105	NAPLES	021	10037	14427	15868	4.0	85	4791	6771	7435	3.8	2.10	2932	4147	3.8
34108	NAPLES	021	16590	18550	19653	1.2	46	7690	8823	9429	1.5	2.08	5276	5853	1.1
34109	NAPLES	021	17741	24140	27744	3.4	81	7644	10516	12133	3.5	2.28	5230	6903	3.0
34110	NAPLES	021	16177	22207	24572	3.5	82	7580	10619	11815	3.7	2.04	5138	6970	3.4
34112	NAPLES	021	26604	31959	34093	2.0	62	12051	14495	15482	2.0	2.15	7524	8698	1.6
34113	NAPLES	021	14219	17553	19110	2.3	69	5636	6945	7605	2.3	2.50	3833	4726	2.3
34114	NAPLES	021	8610	15916	19377	6.9	92	3559	6555	7984	6.8	2.34	2403	4254	6.4
34116	NAPLES	021	25170	29873	31340	1.9	61	8137	9645	10204	1.9	3.09	6171	6997	1.4
	FLORIDA					1.9					1.9	2.47			1.7
	UNITED STATES					1.0					1.1	2.59			0.9

ZIP CODE #	POST OFFICE NAME	RACE (%) White 2000	White 2009	Black 2000	Black 2009	Asian/Pacific 2000	Asian/Pacific 2009	% Hispanic Origin 2000	% Hispanic Origin 2009	2009 AGE DISTRIBUTION (%) 0-4	5-9	10-14	15-19	20-24	25-44	45-64	65-84	85+	18+	MEDIAN AGE 2009	% 2009 Males	% 2009 Females
33809	LAKELAND	91.0	87.0	4.2	6.2	1.4	2.0	5.1	8.0	5.9	5.9	6.3	6.5	5.3	24.4	27.4	15.0	3.5	77.9	42.0	47.8	52.2
33810	LAKELAND	89.4	85.8	6.9	8.6	0.7	1.1	4.7	7.7	6.6	6.5	6.4	6.1	5.5	23.9	26.0	17.4	1.7	76.8	41.3	49.0	51.0
33811	LAKELAND	88.4	82.7	6.8	9.4	0.6	0.8	6.6	11.1	6.9	6.8	6.9	6.6	6.2	27.3	27.6	10.4	1.3	75.4	37.4	49.3	50.7
33812	LAKELAND	86.2	80.3	6.9	9.7	3.9	5.8	6.2	9.1	6.9	7.4	8.0	8.0	5.2	25.9	28.9	8.4	1.3	72.5	37.9	49.2	50.8
33813	LAKELAND	91.6	87.4	3.7	5.8	2.2	3.4	5.0	7.5	5.8	6.4	7.3	7.3	4.7	23.5	31.0	12.4	1.7	75.7	41.6	48.6	51.4
33815	LAKELAND	65.5	58.3	26.3	30.2	0.5	0.6	10.8	15.7	7.8	7.8	7.2	6.5	5.1	21.5	23.3	17.7	3.2	73.2	39.4	48.6	51.4
33823	AUBURNDALE	85.8	81.3	8.0	10.2	0.6	0.8	7.8	11.1	6.8	6.6	6.5	6.5	5.4	24.1	27.2	15.0	1.8	76.1	40.4	49.2	50.8
33825	AVON PARK	73.5	67.4	16.1	18.2	1.9	2.5	15.8	22.5	5.8	5.5	5.5	5.9	5.3	18.9	25.8	23.5	3.7	79.6	47.6	48.9	51.1
33827	BABSON PARK	89.5	84.4	6.2	9.2	0.7	1.0	5.5	8.7	5.5	5.6	5.8	7.1	6.8	21.2	29.6	16.1	2.4	79.2	43.3	49.1	50.9
33830	BARTOW	69.2	62.7	23.1	26.9	0.7	1.0	11.2	15.5	7.0	6.8	6.9	8.0	6.7	26.5	24.0	12.0	2.0	74.2	36.1	50.2	49.8
33834	BOWLING GREEN	68.4	61.8	12.3	12.8	0.3	0.4	31.9	42.1	6.7	6.3	6.3	6.8	7.2	30.7	21.9	12.6	1.5	76.8	35.6	58.7	41.3
33837	DAVENPORT	84.5	79.6	6.5	8.2	0.7	1.0	16.6	23.0	6.4	6.5	6.4	5.5	4.0	23.2	28.0	18.1	1.9	77.3	43.6	49.4	50.6
33838	DUNDEE	69.0	59.9	23.8	30.3	0.7	0.8	10.7	15.3	6.5	6.5	6.9	7.1	5.0	22.8	26.2	16.2	2.8	75.9	41.2	49.1	50.9
33839	EAGLE LAKE	86.5	79.4	4.4	6.2	0.4	0.5	13.2	21.1	7.4	7.2	6.9	6.8	6.0	24.4	26.2	13.0	2.2	74.6	38.2	49.2	50.8
33841	FORT MEADE	70.9	63.0	15.5	18.2	0.1	0.2	21.6	29.6	7.0	7.2	7.6	8.0	6.5	24.1	24.3	13.4	1.9	73.2	36.4	50.2	49.8
33843	FROSTPROOF	68.3	57.6	14.2	18.7	0.3	0.4	20.6	28.1	5.1	5.5	5.5	7.0	7.7	28.7	23.1	14.9	2.5	80.0	38.3	59.5	40.5
33844	HAINES CITY	69.7	64.0	18.5	20.5	0.4	0.5	20.4	27.1	6.8	6.5	6.1	6.3	5.7	22.0	24.1	19.9	2.5	76.7	41.7	49.6	50.4
33849	KATHLEEN	95.1	92.8	0.8	1.2	0.6	1.0	5.1	8.0	4.7	4.8	4.9	4.9	4.0	16.3	30.3	28.2	1.8	82.6	52.7	49.0	51.0
33850	LAKE ALFRED	79.5	70.8	16.3	23.3	0.7	1.0	5.5	8.1	6.1	6.5	6.4	6.0	4.8	22.0	26.0	19.2	3.0	77.0	43.4	46.7	53.3
33852	LAKE PLACID	85.4	80.1	7.5	9.6	0.5	0.8	16.6	24.5	4.8	4.7	4.8	5.5	4.4	18.7	25.9	26.9	4.2	82.4	51.2	50.1	49.9
33853	LAKE WALES	59.5	53.5	34.1	38.3	0.6	0.8	10.3	14.0	7.5	7.0	6.6	6.9	6.7	23.5	23.2	14.9	3.7	74.5	37.7	47.9	52.1
33857	LORIDA	96.2	94.0	0.5	0.8	0.3	0.5	6.7	11.5	3.8	5.4	5.8	4.4	3.3	18.2	28.3	27.9	2.8	81.9	53.3	51.5	48.5
33859	LAKE WALES	82.4	77.3	10.5	13.2	0.5	0.6	11.4	15.1	5.2	5.2	5.5	6.2	6.2	18.5	26.0	24.8	2.5	80.4	48.0	50.0	50.0
33860	MULBERRY	81.5	75.5	11.6	14.6	0.6	0.8	12.0	17.5	7.7	7.4	7.3	7.4	6.4	27.1	25.5	10.2	1.1	73.1	35.6	50.2	49.8
33865	ONA	76.2	69.1	11.6	12.8	0.4	0.5	17.6	26.9	5.8	5.8	6.2	5.4	4.9	26.5	28.6	14.9	1.8	78.5	41.3	54.8	45.2
33868	POLK CITY	88.7	83.3	6.5	9.7	0.8	1.2	7.0	10.9	5.5	5.5	5.8	6.4	4.7	22.7	28.7	19.0	1.6	79.2	44.5	51.6	48.4
33870	SEBRING	77.2	71.7	14.6	17.0	0.8	1.1	10.8	16.1	5.4	5.2	4.9	5.4	5.4	19.6	24.3	23.9	5.9	81.3	48.7	48.1	51.9
33872	SEBRING	92.2	88.0	3.1	4.6	1.5	2.2	8.7	14.7	3.7	3.5	3.5	3.2	2.7	13.0	27.8	36.0	6.6	87.4	61.1	46.8	53.2
33873	WAUCHULA	69.5	62.9	8.3	8.3	0.3	0.4	37.1	48.8	8.1	7.4	7.0	7.4	7.8	27.7	21.6	11.3	1.7	73.3	33.1	53.5	46.5
33875	SEBRING	94.9	92.1	1.7	2.7	0.9	1.4	4.1	7.2	3.9	4.3	4.5	4.6	3.5	16.2	29.8	28.5	4.7	84.3	54.5	47.5	52.5
33876	SEBRING	91.7	87.3	2.7	3.9	0.4	0.6	8.8	14.6	4.1	4.1	4.2	4.3	3.9	16.5	29.2	29.8	3.9	85.0	55.1	49.1	50.9
33880	WINTER HAVEN	80.1	73.1	10.0	13.5	1.1	1.5	13.2	18.6	7.4	7.1	7.0	6.9	6.4	26.4	25.1	11.6	2.0	74.3	36.5	48.9	51.1
33881	WINTER HAVEN	67.6	62.5	27.1	30.7	0.8	1.0	4.8	6.9	5.5	5.3	5.2	5.5	5.4	18.8	25.2	23.8	5.3	80.7	48.6	47.0	53.0
33884	WINTER HAVEN	93.1	89.6	2.3	3.5	1.8	2.6	4.9	8.5	5.0	5.1	5.5	5.5	4.4	20.3	28.7	21.4	4.0	80.7	47.8	47.0	53.0
33890	ZOLFO SPRINGS	77.9	71.5	2.1	2.1	0.5	0.6	37.4	50.5	8.4	8.1	8.0	7.4	5.8	27.2	22.1	11.5	1.6	71.0	33.8	52.4	47.6
33896	DAVENPORT	84.8	79.3	7.6	9.3	1.1	2.4	13.1	20.1	5.7	5.9	6.1	5.9	3.8	23.7	29.5	17.7	1.6	78.4	44.2	51.1	48.9
33897	DAVENPORT	81.4	74.0	13.4	18.6	1.1	1.4	8.6	12.7	3.8	4.0	4.3	5.8	3.7	21.0	30.2	24.9	2.3	84.0	50.4	54.3	45.7
33898	LAKE WALES	85.9	81.6	10.1	12.6	0.6	0.9	4.5	7.1	4.6	4.8	5.1	5.6	4.8	18.4	27.9	25.4	3.5	82.2	50.4	49.3	50.7
33901	FORT MYERS	68.6	60.4	22.4	28.8	1.3	1.5	10.4	14.5	6.7	5.5	5.4	5.7	6.8	26.1	24.7	13.5	5.6	79.1	40.4	49.1	50.9
33903	NORTH FORT MYERS	94.9	92.1	1.4	2.3	0.9	1.3	4.6	7.8	3.5	3.4	3.4	3.5	3.4	14.0	25.1	37.1	6.7	87.6	61.1	46.8	53.2
33904	CAPE CORAL	94.9	91.4	1.2	2.3	0.8	1.2	6.7	12.2	3.7	3.8	4.2	4.5	3.4	16.7	32.4	26.7	4.6	85.5	54.4	47.8	52.2
33905	FORT MYERS	74.3	68.7	13.5	16.0	0.9	1.2	22.4	27.2	6.7	6.7	6.6	6.6	6.6	25.1	26.4	13.5	1.8	76.0	38.5	50.0	50.0
33907	FORT MYERS	85.5	79.7	6.6	9.3	1.3	2.0	15.3	21.3	5.7	4.9	4.3	4.7	7.6	27.4	22.0	17.3	6.1	82.6	40.8	48.9	51.1
33908	FORT MYERS	95.1	87.3	2.2	6.5	0.5	0.8	5.3	13.1	2.7	2.9	3.1	3.2	2.5	13.7	31.9	34.3	5.7	89.3	60.3	47.4	52.6
33909	CAPE CORAL	90.2	85.4	3.5	5.3	0.7	0.9	10.0	14.3	7.0	6.9	6.7	7.0	6.2	25.6	25.2	13.5	2.0	75.2	38.0	48.4	51.6
33912	FORT MYERS	96.7	94.1	0.7	1.5	1.4	2.5	2.6	5.8	4.2	4.6	4.9	4.6	3.3	16.9	30.7	27.1	3.8	83.4	53.0	47.6	52.4
33913	FORT MYERS	92.3	86.1	2.7	5.0	1.3	2.1	7.9	16.7	7.0	7.0	7.0	6.9	5.1	24.4	28.7	12.5	1.4	75.3	40.2	48.8	51.2
33914	CAPE CORAL	93.9	89.5	1.5	2.7	0.8	1.0	8.1	15.0	6.2	6.2	6.4	6.4	5.0	24.6	30.1	13.7	1.4	77.3	41.7	48.9	51.1
33916	FORT MYERS	29.7	28.0	58.5	58.4	0.7	0.8	17.1	20.7	9.8	8.1	7.0	7.8	10.4	28.2	18.4	8.2	2.2	70.9	28.4	49.5	50.5
33917	NORTH FORT MYERS	97.2	95.5	0.4	0.8	0.4	0.5	2.8	5.2	3.9	3.9	4.1	4.0	3.5	15.6	28.1	32.3	4.5	85.7	56.9	48.3	51.7
33919	FORT MYERS	96.1	93.8	1.2	2.2	1.0	1.5	3.4	6.0	3.3	3.4	3.7	3.6	3.0	15.3	32.5	29.7	5.4	87.4	57.3	46.4	53.6
33920	ALVA	86.0	82.2	9.7	11.4	0.5	0.6	4.5	7.4	5.9	6.4	6.6	6.3	4.6	21.3	30.6	16.5	1.9	77.1	44.2	49.0	51.0
33921	BOCA GRANDE	99.4	99.0	0.3	0.5	0.2	0.3	1.5	2.7	2.0	1.8	1.6	1.9	1.7	7.4	38.6	41.1	3.9	93.5	63.5	46.8	53.2
33922	BOKEELIA	97.5	96.2	0.1	0.2	0.2	0.3	7.1	12.1	3.9	4.0	4.7	4.0	2.8	17.0	33.0	27.7	3.0	84.9	55.0	51.4	48.6
33924	CAPTIVA	97.6	96.6	0.0	0.0	1.6	2.5	1.6	2.8	2.5	1.3	1.3	0.0	1.3	6.3	40.9	43.1	3.4	95.0	64.2	50.3	49.7
33928	ESTERO	97.7	94.6	0.4	1.3	0.4	0.6	4.0	10.2	2.8	2.8	2.9	3.1	2.7	12.0	28.1	40.9	4.7	90.2	62.9	47.8	52.2
33931	FORT MYERS BEACH	98.0	96.9	0.1	0.2	0.3	0.4	2.7	4.7	1.1	1.4	1.4	1.4	1.4	9.4	31.2	46.8	5.8	95.1	65.9	48.8	51.2
33935	LABELLE	71.6	65.3	4.9	5.7	0.3	0.3	43.8	54.9	8.2	7.7	7.1	7.7	8.2	28.3	21.0	10.6	1.2	72.5	31.8	55.6	44.4
33936	LEHIGH ACRES	84.4	75.5	8.6	13.9	0.9	1.2	13.3	21.1	5.7	5.6	5.6	5.9	5.0	20.7	26.8	20.5	4.1	79.5	46.1	47.5	52.5
33946	PLACIDA	98.7	97.8	0.3	0.6	0.2	0.4	0.8	1.6	1.4	1.4	1.6	2.0	1.6	5.9	33.2	47.9	5.1	94.5	66.0	47.3	52.7
33947	ROTONDA WEST	98.4	97.8	0.4	0.6	0.3	0.4	1.3	2.3	2.1	2.1	2.3	2.4	1.9	9.3	31.0	43.9	5.0	92.0	64.6	47.3	52.7
33948	PORT CHARLOTTE	89.9	86.8	6.5	8.2	1.1	1.6	4.2	6.9	4.5	4.7	5.1	5.2	4.4	19.8	30.9	21.8	3.8	82.5	49.7	47.3	52.7
33950	PUNTA GORDA	94.9	93.5	2.9	3.3	0.7	1.1	1.9	3.3	2.2	2.3	2.5	2.7	2.2	10.0	29.8	42.6	5.7	91.4	64.3	47.5	52.5
33952	PORT CHARLOTTE	90.0	86.3	5.5	7.1	1.2	1.8	5.5	9.1	4.5	4.4	4.5	5.0	4.4	18.3	28.1	24.7	6.1	83.5	51.8	46.4	53.6
33953	PORT CHARLOTTE	94.5	92.5	2.9	3.8	0.8	1.2	2.6	4.3	3.6	3.6	3.9	3.8	3.2	14.8	28.4	35.6	3.2	86.6	58.6	47.8	52.2
33954	PORT CHARLOTTE	86.4	82.0	9.3	11.8	1.3	2.0	4.6	7.5	5.3	5.6	6.1	6.5	4.7	21.1	29.6	18.7	2.4	79.0	45.4	47.4	52.6
33955	PUNTA GORDA	97.4	96.1	0.9	1.4	0.6	1.0	1.7	2.8	2.4	2.6	2.7	2.9	2.4	10.9	29.8	41.7	4.6	90.6	63.3	47.6	52.4
33956	SAINT JAMES CITY	99.0	98.3	0.1	0.2	0.3	0.4	0.8	1.6	1.3	1.5	1.8	1.8	1.5	7.1	33.3	46.5	5.2	94.4	65.6	49.1	50.9
33957	SANIBEL	98.0	96.5	0.9	1.9	0.4	0.6	1.3	2.7	1.8	2.2	2.6	2.7	2.0	9.1	34.5	40.5	4.6	91.8	63.2	47.4	52.6
33960	VENUS	92.5	88.8	3.5	5.2	0.4	0.6	9.4	15.4	4.0	5.4	6.1	6.1	4.2	20.2	29.3	23.1	1.7	80.7	48.0	51.3	48.7
33966	FORT MYERS	94.5	90.6	2.2	4.1	1.8	2.7	3.8	6.9	5.7	5.6	6.0	6.2	5.5	26.0	30.3	13.1	1.5	78.4	41.7	48.3	51.7
33967	FORT MYERS	94.3	91.1	1.1	1.9	0.8	1.1	7.5	12.6	7.5	7.4	7.2	6.5	5.3	27.9	26.6	10.3	1.2	73.7	37.2	49.5	50.5
33971	LEHIGH ACRES	82.2	69.8	10.9	19.5	1.2	1.9	15.5	22.2	9.3	8.5	8.0	7.0	5.5	31.2	22.8	6.7	1.0	69.8	32.8	49.0	51.0
33972	LEHIGH ACRES	85.8	78.7	8.0	11.6	0.5	0.9	11.2	18.3	7.8	7.4	7.2	7.1	5.4	28.1	25.5	10.2	1.3	73.2	36.0	49.4	50.6
33973	LEHIGH ACRES	80.5	69.3	10.2	16.2	0.4	0.6	15.4	24.8	7.0	6.3	6.4	7.2	7.4	27.1	24.8	12.2	1.6	76.1	36.7	48.1	51.9
33974	LEHIGH ACRES	86.1	77.0	5.9	8.8	1.3	2.2	13.1	24.4	6.3	6.4	6.6	6.2	4.5	22.6	28.8	16.4	2.1	76.9	42.9	49.5	50.5
33976	LEHIGH ACRES	84.4	76.9	9.6	15.2	0.5	0.5	14.1	21.5	8.8	8.6	8.3	8.1	6.6	30.9	22.6	5.5	0.5	69.3	31.1	49.8	50.2
33980	PORT CHARLOTTE	89.0	84.9	7.8	10.4	1.2	1.9	3.5	5.8	2.9	2.7	2.7	3.3	3.3	12.4	25.2	35.9	11.5	89.8	63.5	44.4	55.6
33981	PORT CHARLOTTE	95.6	94.0	1.6	1.9	0.7	1.0	2.5	4.1	4.5	4.6	4.6	4.6	3.5	16.7	29.2	28.5	3.7	83.4	53.7	48.7	51.3
33982	PUNTA GORDA	91.0	88.5	6.5	8.0	0.4	0.6	3.1	4.9	3.5	3.7	4.1	5.1	4.6	23.8	30.8	21.5	2.9	85.3	48.7	55.4	44.6
33983	PUNTA GORDA	89.7	85.5	6.6	9.1	1.4	2.1	3.3	5.7	3.7	3.9	4.3	4.4	3.3	14.4	31.2	30.4	4.4	85.3	56.2	45.7	54.3
33990	CAPE CORAL	90.9	85.1	2.8	4.9	1.5	2.1	10.5	18.2	5.8	5.8	6.0	6.2	5.5	23.9	29.2	14.8	2.7	78.5	42.6	48.2	51.8
33991	CAPE CORAL	92.4	87.5	2.5	4.3	1.1	1.3	7.4	13.3	7.0	7.0	7.1	7.1	5.4	26.8	27.7	10.4	1.4	74.4	38.0	48.8	51.2
33993	CAPE CORAL	94.5	89.5	1.9	4.3	0.6	0.9	4.6	9.1	7.6	7.3	7.2	6.7	5.1	27.7	27.0	10.3	1.0	73.7	37.1	49.0	51.0
34102	NAPLES	88.0	83.6	8.0	11.0	0.4	0.6	2.0	4.1	3.3	3.7	3.8	4.0	2.6	13.9	33.4	29.4	5.8	86.5	57.5	47.3	52.7
34103	NAPLES	96.4	93.1	0.7	1.2	0.5	0.7	7.8	14.8	2.8	2.9	3.2	3.1	2.5	12.7	28.2	37.4	7.1	89.2	62.2	46.7	53.3
34104	NAPLES	89.8	84.1	3.6	5.6	1.3	1.7	14.4	25.2	5.3	4.8	4.7	4.3	4.3	22.5	25.8	25.6	2.7	82.6	48.3	48.1	51.9
34105	NAPLES	96.2	93.5	0.8	1.4	1.1	1.6	6.3	12.3	3.2	3.2	3.5	3.5	2.9	15.3	30.6	31.9	5.9	87.8	58.2	46.2	53.8
34108	NAPLES	95.9	93.2	0.7	1.1	0.7	1.0	7.9	13.7	2.9	3.2	3.3	3.4	3.0	15.7	30.3	33.6	4.5	88.4	58.8	48.0	52.0
34109	NAPLES	95.5	91.8	1.2	2.3	1.1	1.5	6.6	13.5	4.5	4.9	5.0	5.0	4.2	20.7	31.6	21.1	2.9	82.0	48.6	47.4	52.6
34110	NAPLES	96.9	94.3	0.7	1.4	0.5	0.7	6.2	10.9	3.0	3.2	3.3	3.5	3.0	12.4	30.9	34.5	6.3	88.4	60.6	47.4	52.6
34112	NAPLES	87.7	82.0	5.5	7.4	0.6	0.8	16.6	25.3	4.1	3.9	3.9	3.7	3.5	18.9	27.0	30.5	4.5	86.0	55.3	49.6	50.4
34113	NAPLES	78.0	73.1	7.2	7.9	0.5	0.6	30.8	39.5	5.4	5.0	4.7	4.8	4.6	21.3	26.7	23.7	3.8	82.0	48.7	50.3	49.7
34114	NAPLES	87.6	76.3	1.8	2.9	0.6	0.7	28.0	49.9	4.7	4.8	4.9	5.0	3.8	20.7	27.8	25.6	2.8	82.8	49.9	51.7	48.3
34116	NAPLES	79.7	71.7	8.9	11.2	0.9	1.1	32.4	47.0	8.2	7.7	7.2	7.3	7.7	31.4	22.4	7.2	0.8	72.5	31.9	51.6	48.4
	FLORIDA	78.0	74.7	14.6	15.8	1.7	2.3	16.8	21.5	6.0	5.9	5.9	6.3	6.2	25.0	26.8	15.3	2.8	78.6	41.1	48.8	51.2
	UNITED STATES	75.1	72.0	12.3	12.7	3.8	4.6	12.5	15.7	6.8	6.7	6.6	7.1	6.9	27.0	26.0	10.9	1.9	75.7	36.9	49.2	50.8

#	POST OFFICE NAME	2009 Per Capita Income	2009 HH Income Base	2009 HOUSEHOLD INCOME DISTRIBUTION (%) Less than $25,000	$25,000 to $49,999	$50,000 to $99,999	$100,000 to $149,999	$150,000 or More	MEDIAN HOUSEHOLD INCOME 2009	2014	2009 National Centile	2009 State Centile	2009 Home Value Base	2009 HOME VALUE DISTRIBUTION (%) Less than $50,000	$50,000 to $89,999	$90,000 to $174,999	$175,000 to $399,999	$400,000 or More	2009 Median Home Value
33809	LAKELAND	26573	11945	16.6	26.3	40.8	11.9	4.5	56624	55402	74	72	8803	9.2	14.0	42.8	30.3	3.7	144139
33810	LAKELAND	22525	18345	19.9	31.5	38.2	7.3	3.2	48355	50366	57	52	14805	8.6	19.7	48.1	20.8	2.8	120254
33811	LAKELAND	24862	7874	17.5	27.8	40.5	9.8	4.4	53458	53168	69	66	5436	8.9	12.9	44.9	29.2	4.1	140650
33812	LAKELAND	28387	4342	11.2	19.2	41.0	20.3	8.3	66803	66652	85	86	3666	4.0	4.9	45.9	40.4	4.9	164754
33813	LAKELAND	34429	12166	10.3	20.5	41.0	15.5	12.7	67146	67020	85	86	10072	6.0	6.1	37.0	39.4	11.4	177485
33815	LAKELAND	17290	6296	40.3	35.8	17.6	4.2	2.1	31138	32239	10	7	3955	49.5	24.8	17.6	5.9	2.2	50814
33823	AUBURNDALE	21268	11751	24.6	30.0	34.2	7.8	3.4	44957	48132	48	42	8631	11.7	27.5	38.8	18.1	3.8	106503
33825	AVON PARK	18949	9401	31.4	34.7	25.2	6.1	2.6	36047	40401	21	16	7210	13.1	21.1	43.2	20.7	1.9	119693
33827	BABSON PARK	21171	1080	25.4	27.7	38.4	5.1	3.4	47116	48984	54	49	861	11.6	33.1	36.2	14.4	4.6	98750
33830	BARTOW	21440	9723	26.2	28.3	35.2	6.3	3.9	45046	48408	48	42	6921	11.4	31.2	41.3	14.4	1.7	99375
33834	BOWLING GREEN	15979	2176	29.6	35.3	26.8	5.2	3.1	36806	39636	23	18	1661	23.7	28.4	32.0	14.1	1.9	86546
33837	DAVENPORT	21094	6867	19.8	34.6	37.5	5.2	3.0	45793	48014	51	46	5682	19.0	19.8	38.2	22.2	0.8	113567
33838	DUNDEE	16222	1390	31.7	36.5	26.2	4.7	0.9	35602	37764	20	16	1081	24.6	20.8	46.4	7.7	0.5	97279
33839	EAGLE LAKE	16998	1186	31.5	33.1	29.5	4.8	1.0	36975	39803	24	19	848	20.3	33.4	34.4	9.3	2.6	86125
33841	FORT MEADE	18203	3246	29.2	29.9	32.5	5.5	2.9	41121	45405	36	31	2378	24.7	29.1	36.7	8.7	0.8	85381
33843	FROSTPROOF	17484	3858	31.3	33.8	28.6	3.7	2.7	36623	39337	22	18	2961	24.3	35.1	25.7	13.3	1.6	76516
33844	HAINES CITY	19419	13919	29.1	34.9	27.8	4.6	3.5	38021	40850	27	23	10219	18.7	33.6	32.2	12.9	2.6	87415
33849	KATHLEEN	22588	335	23.3	27.5	34.0	9.0	6.3	49098	50873	59	54	299	6.4	25.4	49.5	16.4	2.3	108686
33850	LAKE ALFRED	21478	2177	25.8	27.0	38.3	5.8	3.0	46518	49387	53	48	1591	12.8	27.7	44.8	14.1	0.6	100349
33852	LAKE PLACID	20354	9956	29.1	38.0	25.3	5.1	2.5	37445	41007	25	21	8134	8.7	16.7	43.4	25.5	5.6	134340
33853	LAKE WALES	20107	4619	37.0	30.7	22.7	5.3	4.3	33509	35578	14	11	2535	10.3	32.1	45.2	9.8	2.6	100828
33857	LORIDA	16852	844	38.7	37.6	18.4	1.2	4.1	31327	33061	10	7	677	24.5	17.9	21.3	28.8	7.5	113750
33859	LAKE WALES	20584	3924	32.1	34.0	26.3	3.7	3.9	37658	40244	26	21	3170	22.4	36.2	27.9	7.9	5.6	77537
33860	MULBERRY	22694	7743	15.7	31.4	42.0	7.3	3.6	52218	53087	66	63	5899	11.0	24.0	45.0	17.6	2.4	113569
33865	ONA	20617	251	31.1	30.3	31.5	5.2	2.0	40311	41743	34	28	181	10.5	25.4	39.2	17.1	7.7	118452
33868	POLK CITY	19862	4752	19.1	33.8	37.4	6.9	2.8	47430	49442	55	49	4160	8.5	23.7	43.4	21.5	2.9	114496
33870	SEBRING	18971	8033	38.4	32.5	22.2	4.4	2.4	32100	33634	12	9	5569	20.3	26.5	38.6	11.6	3.0	94747
33872	SEBRING	24855	6934	24.9	36.0	30.5	5.4	3.1	41263	44649	37	32	5702	6.6	19.4	51.9	20.4	1.8	119430
33873	WAUCHULA	15491	4522	32.0	33.0	27.3	5.2	2.4	36837	40149	23	18	3222	17.8	27.3	36.3	17.0	1.7	97843
33875	SEBRING	24841	5235	21.9	32.5	35.9	6.5	3.2	45626	49983	50	45	4574	9.1	16.5	43.2	28.1	3.1	136851
33876	SEBRING	22431	2301	22.5	38.0	31.8	4.8	2.9	42082	46051	40	34	1969	10.1	15.6	43.4	26.7	4.2	136002
33880	WINTER HAVEN	20051	15367	26.3	30.5	35.0	6.0	2.3	43156	45886	43	37	10217	10.7	29.5	44.4	12.9	2.6	101209
33881	WINTER HAVEN	22213	13236	31.4	31.8	27.9	6.2	2.7	38382	41224	28	24	8948	17.4	30.5	36.3	13.4	2.3	92600
33884	WINTER HAVEN	32646	10537	14.4	28.6	38.0	11.0	8.0	56493	56618	73	72	8608	8.2	10.2	46.9	27.2	7.6	148073
33890	ZOLFO SPRINGS	15085	1844	32.1	33.0	28.1	4.8	2.0	38607	41412	28	24	1411	20.1	30.1	32.9	13.2	3.7	89643
33896	DAVENPORT	26393	3244	14.3	32.9	39.9	8.8	4.1	52405	52750	67	63	2676	9.1	12.7	40.9	31.7	5.6	151703
33897	DAVENPORT	28980	4879	12.1	37.1	38.2	9.9	2.7	50695	51499	63	58	4511	2.5	12.6	48.9	34.2	1.8	151882
33898	LAKE WALES	22413	8000	28.9	35.7	26.8	5.5	3.2	38012	40796	27	23	6094	17.8	28.7	30.9	19.4	3.2	95902
33901	FORT MYERS	25622	9578	32.1	31.5	23.9	6.7	5.8	36606	38775	22	18	4147	10.3	25.7	39.4	18.3	6.3	109955
33903	NORTH FORT MYERS	26709	12366	26.4	34.3	30.4	5.7	3.2	40977	43846	36	30	9882	26.1	38.7	25.1	8.5	1.5	72584
33904	CAPE CORAL	29320	16260	19.4	29.7	38.6	7.4	4.9	50688	52735	63	58	12639	1.6	10.7	54.8	29.4	3.4	137322
33905	FORT MYERS	21065	11941	25.4	31.4	31.1	8.6	3.5	45153	48996	49	43	9009	14.9	33.7	31.6	17.1	2.6	91782
33907	FORT MYERS	24920	11474	24.5	36.1	32.4	5.0	2.2	42600	45095	41	35	5103	8.9	32.0	51.1	7.5	0.4	101097
33908	FORT MYERS	36244	18813	20.3	31.7	29.5	9.5	9.1	48184	50866	57	51	14253	10.0	21.6	32.6	24.9	10.9	129010
33909	CAPE CORAL	20832	8371	18.1	33.4	39.7	6.3	2.5	48627	51058	58	53	6253	2.4	33.1	54.9	8.4	1.1	101681
33912	FORT MYERS	42889	7943	11.0	21.3	39.0	14.9	13.8	67650	68171	85	86	6517	10.1	5.8	19.1	47.0	18.0	223364
33913	FORT MYERS	42697	5784	7.2	10.8	33.7	29.2	19.2	97036	99411	96	97	5358	0.0	0.5	20.3	67.2	12.0	231561
33914	CAPE CORAL	30530	16618	11.3	22.3	46.1	12.0	8.3	64244	65608	83	83	13239	1.3	5.6	50.1	34.5	8.5	155824
33916	FORT MYERS	15208	8735	41.4	33.9	20.1	3.4	1.2	30038	31065	8	5	2784	34.3	41.6	20.5	2.6	1.0	63745
33917	NORTH FORT MYERS	24172	15497	27.0	33.9	31.1	5.4	2.6	41748	44377	38	33	12907	34.6	31.5	20.9	11.6	1.3	65852
33919	FORT MYERS	37206	15769	16.9	29.6	35.0	9.8	8.6	53635	55795	69	66	12785	2.2	17.3	46.4	29.2	4.9	139615
33920	ALVA	27471	2158	18.4	26.6	40.9	7.0	7.1	53584	55639	69	66	1860	10.9	24.8	32.8	25.2	6.2	114317
33921	BOCA GRANDE	100071	794	11.8	12.1	21.2	8.9	46.0	126292	137306	99	99	637	0.0	1.9	0.8	15.9	81.5	793367
33922	BOKEELIA	28144	2008	26.7	27.6	31.9	7.9	5.8	46055	48953	51	46	1582	14.7	22.6	30.8	28.3	3.7	117005
33924	CAPTIVA	79875	180	5.6	20.0	43.3	8.3	22.8	68393	66895	86	87	142	0.0	0.0	0.0	11.3	88.7	693750
33928	ESTERO	39028	9077	15.7	30.0	34.1	9.6	10.7	54252	56723	70	68	7985	15.5	17.5	23.8	33.8	9.3	150772
33931	FORT MYERS BEACH	37896	8138	21.4	28.3	34.1	9.0	7.2	50247	52634	62	57	6553	21.5	10.8	17.4	36.5	13.8	176054
33935	LABELLE	16595	6695	29.1	30.7	31.4	5.8	2.9	41110	44043	36	30	4832	11.5	24.7	40.4	18.6	4.7	115324
33936	LEHIGH ACRES	21090	8765	23.9	35.5	34.9	4.1	1.6	42654	45414	41	36	6953	6.0	42.2	44.8	6.7	0.4	92039
33946	PLACIDA	64442	1045	15.2	26.6	27.2	11.5	19.5	60530	58866	78	77	903	2.3	8.2	24.1	18.5	46.8	350862
33947	ROTONDA WEST	27089	3734	18.7	30.5	38.8	8.5	3.5	50477	51673	62	58	3206	2.9	11.7	50.4	34.3	0.7	144843
33948	PORT CHARLOTTE	24226	7075	19.3	31.9	37.8	8.3	2.7	49014	50564	59	54	5861	1.0	28.0	56.9	13.3	0.7	110270
33950	PUNTA GORDA	38236	10901	19.4	26.0	35.2	9.8	9.6	54805	54752	71	69	9192	11.4	14.1	20.3	40.1	14.2	195869
33952	PORT CHARLOTTE	23398	14173	27.6	34.1	29.4	5.8	3.2	40557	43616	35	29	11052	5.3	40.4	44.0	9.3	1.0	95521
33953	PORT CHARLOTTE	30866	2418	19.4	29.9	34.0	9.8	6.9	50775	51678	63	58	2077	3.9	28.4	37.6	23.4	6.7	120574
33954	PORT CHARLOTTE	27230	3421	12.1	28.0	43.1	12.7	4.1	60562	59286	78	77	3011	0.9	18.7	51.7	28.4	0.3	128690
33955	PUNTA GORDA	33925	4027	19.3	28.0	37.6	7.3	7.7	51873	52582	66	62	3653	20.5	22.6	23.5	27.3	6.1	112416
33956	SAINT JAMES CITY	31297	2309	27.4	27.9	33.8	6.1	4.8	44137	47820	46	40	2061	7.6	21.3	44.3	23.7	3.0	117252
33957	SANIBEL	72563	4166	10.2	15.5	28.0	15.7	30.6	91167	90704	95	96	3429	0.9	2.9	4.7	22.6	68.9	534834
33960	VENUS	17644	302	35.4	38.7	21.2	1.3	3.3	30613	32891	9	6	252	38.1	12.3	19.0	29.0	1.6	89167
33966	FORT MYERS	34620	4169	9.6	20.6	46.3	17.2	6.4	69178	69457	86	87	3001	0.0	6.4	44.7	40.4	8.4	172191
33967	FORT MYERS	28042	8840	10.7	24.5	46.3	11.6	6.9	62310	64207	80	80	6841	3.7	8.3	65.3	20.4	2.3	134238
33971	LEHIGH ACRES	23327	5951	10.3	22.6	53.5	10.4	3.3	61966	63760	80	80	5324	0.9	20.4	54.9	21.5	2.2	125250
33972	LEHIGH ACRES	21060	3137	14.3	30.6	43.9	8.6	2.5	54407	57337	70	68	2674	1.5	27.3	58.1	12.3	0.9	110950
33973	LEHIGH ACRES	22574	1520	11.5	38.8	39.9	5.1	4.7	49871	51358	61	56	892	0.9	23.7	58.6	16.8	0.0	109187
33974	LEHIGH ACRES	23659	2592	12.2	33.6	43.9	5.9	4.4	53155	54352	68	65	2349	0.9	13.4	64.9	18.9	1.9	119860
33976	LEHIGH ACRES	19431	3260	11.5	33.1	43.7	9.5	2.1	54262	55623	70	68	2981	1.9	44.3	48.9	4.8	0.0	92053
33980	PORT CHARLOTTE	27078	4987	27.5	32.9	29.5	6.3	4.0	42300	45396	40	35	3871	12.8	37.7	39.9	8.5	1.0	89523
33981	PORT CHARLOTTE	23564	4275	19.3	34.6	37.8	6.5	1.7	46411	48501	53	48	3697	4.0	29.3	45.1	20.0	1.5	110473
33982	PUNTA GORDA	24556	3956	23.4	35.6	30.7	6.0	4.3	42010	44940	39	34	3353	23.3	29.4	26.2	16.8	4.4	85960
33983	PUNTA GORDA	27433	5981	12.7	31.4	41.8	9.6	4.4	54562	55662	71	69	5023	3.6	14.5	55.8	25.4	0.6	137881
33990	CAPE CORAL	23102	12029	15.7	32.1	42.9	7.2	2.2	51608	53489	65	61	9061	0.6	9.4	66.6	22.4	1.0	131151
33991	CAPE CORAL	26300	6978	12.0	27.3	43.2	11.1	6.5	60186	60254	78	77	5777	1.8	6.6	62.9	27.5	1.3	133961
33993	CAPE CORAL	26985	7506	7.6	28.0	46.4	13.7	4.2	62597	63729	81	81	6254	1.9	13.8	59.3	22.3	2.7	123169
34102	NAPLES	59233	5868	13.8	20.6	27.2	15.2	23.2	75221	81743	89	92	4140	0.6	1.9	14.0	28.0	55.5	468675
34103	NAPLES	65000	6458	10.5	21.1	30.7	13.8	23.9	74745	81581	89	91	5328	1.5	2.1	21.5	24.5	50.5	404310
34104	NAPLES	30822	11204	13.0	28.8	41.5	11.4	5.2	58047	58625	75	74	7692	8.3	8.5	39.8	39.4	4.0	159722
34105	NAPLES	51192	6771	14.0	19.1	32.4	16.4	18.2	71384	79226	88	90	4991	0.4	6.0	25.9	39.6	28.2	250156
34108	NAPLES	69440	8823	10.1	18.5	29.7	15.6	26.2	77926	88822	91	93	7217	0.7	0.4	16.2	30.5	52.1	419308
34109	NAPLES	45680	10516	9.3	23.0	34.3	16.9	16.6	69963	76182	87	88	7229	0.6	1.6	20.4	52.1	25.2	257611
34110	NAPLES	52272	10619	12.3	21.2	30.2	17.9	18.5	71834	79539	88	91	8484	5.4	6.1	19.1	42.1	27.4	241412
34112	NAPLES	30513	14495	17.1	34.5	32.4	9.8	6.2	48545	50288	58	52	10782	9.2	18.9	43.0	23.9	4.9	118898
34113	NAPLES	29882	6945	19.9	25.0	36.3	11.3	7.5	57202	59947	74	73	4961	7.4	14.7	44.8	23.3	9.8	123336
34114	NAPLES	23778	6555	22.8	34.4	32.1	7.2	3.4	45174	46699	49	43	5157	13.2	28.2	36.4	16.6	5.5	101448
34116	NAPLES	21069	9645	15.2	30.8	39.9	9.9	4.1	53513	54065	69	66	5727	1.1	8.6	65.3	23.2	1.8	131199
	FLORIDA	27128		21.9	27.6	33.8	9.8	6.8	50413	52516				8.0	14.3	38.7	30.4	8.6	144752
	UNITED STATES	27277		20.9	24.4	35.3	11.7	7.6	54719	56938				9.3	13.1	31.6	32.6	13.5	162279

ZIP CODE #	POST OFFICE NAME	FINANCIAL SERVICES: Auto Loan	Home Loan	Investments	Retirement Plans	THE HOME: Home Improvements: Home Repair	Lawn & Garden	Furnishings: Computers & Hardware Personal	Major Appliances	TV, Radio, Sound Equipment	Furniture	ENTERTAINMENT: Dine out/ Carry out	Sports Equipment	Fees & Tickets	Toys & Games	Travel	Cable TV	PERSONAL: Apparel & Services	Auto Repairs	Health Insurance	Pets & Supplies
33809	LAKELAND	98	94	90	95	94	101	93	98	95	92	94	73	90	96	92	98	65	96	101	115
33810	LAKELAND	88	83	84	78	84	88	79	86	82	83	81	61	76	82	78	84	55	83	89	100
33811	LAKELAND	93	91	81	91	88	90	89	89	90	90	90	68	88	92	88	90	62	89	91	105
33812	LAKELAND	118	132	117	131	128	121	115	119	112	121	114	92	123	117	120	111	80	114	111	138
33813	LAKELAND	132	143	139	144	144	140	130	136	129	135	129	102	137	130	136	129	91	131	132	158
33815	LAKELAND	64	56	67	53	59	67	57	64	61	58	59	45	53	58	57	64	40	63	70	75
33823	AUBURNDALE	82	78	81	76	79	86	77	82	79	78	78	59	74	78	77	82	54	80	87	96
33825	AVON PARK	69	63	78	60	69	77	63	73	68	65	66	49	62	64	67	72	45	71	82	84
33827	BABSON PARK	92	75	102	71	81	99	75	92	81	74	79	65	66	78	77	88	53	86	98	107
33830	BARTOW	82	80	74	79	77	84	79	81	82	78	81	60	78	82	77	84	56	81	86	96
33834	BOWLING GREEN	83	69	85	66	71	84	69	80	73	69	72	59	62	72	69	77	49	76	83	94
33837	DAVENPORT	89	75	105	72	80	93	74	89	77	73	77	64	66	74	78	82	51	84	90	104
33838	DUNDEE	74	56	77	54	58	76	57	71	62	54	61	52	47	61	57	68	40	65	74	84
33839	EAGLE LAKE	74	56	65	55	56	72	61	68	66	57	64	52	51	66	57	71	43	66	73	82
33841	FORT MEADE	82	71	76	68	71	82	70	78	74	71	73	57	64	75	68	78	50	75	82	92
33843	FROSTPROOF	76	65	75	62	67	78	66	74	70	67	69	54	60	69	65	74	47	72	79	87
33844	HAINES CITY	76	68	78	64	72	79	69	77	73	71	72	52	65	70	70	77	49	75	84	88
33849	KATHLEEN	92	88	112	81	98	105	84	99	89	91	86	65	83	81	91	94	58	95	110	113
33850	LAKE ALFRED	81	73	82	71	75	89	73	82	78	72	76	59	70	76	74	82	51	79	91	96
33852	LAKE PLACID	73	67	87	63	73	82	65	77	70	68	68	52	63	65	70	74	46	74	85	89
33853	LAKE WALES	73	60	62	61	61	71	69	70	73	66	71	51	62	72	64	77	49	71	78	83
33857	LORIDA	58	56	71	51	62	66	53	62	56	57	54	41	52	51	58	59	37	60	69	71
33859	LAKE WALES	76	68	87	63	74	84	66	78	70	69	69	53	62	66	69	75	46	75	86	90
33860	MULBERRY	100	88	82	85	85	93	86	91	90	88	90	68	80	93	81	93	61	89	92	109
33865	ONA	90	64	92	62	67	91	66	84	73	61	72	63	53	73	65	80	47	77	87	100
33868	POLK CITY	86	80	93	76	85	91	76	87	80	81	79	60	74	77	79	84	53	84	93	101
33870	SEBRING	64	54	66	53	57	67	60	64	65	59	63	46	55	61	59	69	43	65	74	76
33872	SEBRING	69	74	97	68	86	91	67	82	72	76	70	49	74	64	79	77	47	78	97	90
33873	WAUCHULA	83	62	72	59	62	79	65	75	71	63	70	55	54	72	60	77	47	72	79	89
33875	SEBRING	83	79	102	75	87	95	75	89	79	80	77	59	74	73	82	84	52	85	97	102
33876	SEBRING	77	71	92	66	78	86	68	81	73	73	71	54	66	67	74	77	48	78	90	93
33880	WINTER HAVEN	80	70	67	69	68	76	74	75	77	72	76	57	68	77	70	79	52	76	79	90
33881	WINTER HAVEN	70	64	73	62	68	78	68	73	73	68	71	50	66	68	69	78	48	73	86	85
33884	WINTER HAVEN	110	109	121	108	115	123	104	115	108	106	107	81	105	104	110	113	73	111	124	133
33890	ZOLFO SPRINGS	84	60	70	59	60	80	63	73	70	61	68	56	50	73	57	76	46	69	77	89
33896	DAVENPORT	98	90	120	88	97	106	88	102	89	88	88	74	83	85	94	93	60	97	104	118
33897	DAVENPORT	90	86	110	79	96	103	82	97	87	89	85	63	81	79	90	92	57	93	108	111
33898	LAKE WALES	77	69	89	65	75	85	67	80	71	69	70	55	64	67	72	76	47	76	87	92
33901	FORT MYERS	77	69	72	71	71	74	81	75	83	79	82	57	78	80	78	84	57	81	84	90
33903	NORTH FORT MYERS	69	72	88	67	81	88	69	80	74	73	72	51	74	67	78	79	48	77	96	89
33904	CAPE CORAL	84	90	105	88	97	101	83	93	87	88	86	62	89	81	92	91	59	90	104	106
33905	FORT MYERS	82	82	82	79	82	85	79	83	81	81	81	61	79	80	80	83	56	82	86	96
33907	FORT MYERS	73	61	63	62	62	65	73	67	74	73	74	51	68	72	68	75	51	73	74	81
33908	FORT MYERS	103	104	139	98	119	127	96	116	102	106	100	72	102	92	110	109	67	110	132	130
33909	CAPE CORAL	79	83	78	79	83	80	79	81	79	83	79	59	81	79	80	78	55	80	82	92
33912	FORT MYERS	125	141	162	140	152	148	127	138	128	138	128	95	141	122	142	131	89	134	147	157
33913	FORT MYERS	144	190	205	184	200	176	162	169	156	164	157	124	189	158	183	157	116	162	161	186
33914	CAPE CORAL	109	120	120	119	122	117	110	114	108	115	108	85	117	108	116	107	76	110	113	131
33916	FORT MYERS	57	40	37	43	38	44	55	47	58	53	58	37	48	58	46	60	40	54	53	59
33917	NORTH FORT MYERS	69	73	86	67	81	85	67	78	71	73	69	50	71	65	75	75	47	75	90	87
33919	FORT MYERS	97	105	128	101	117	121	96	110	101	105	99	71	105	92	110	106	68	106	126	124
33920	ALVA	105	99	112	98	101	109	95	105	97	96	96	77	92	96	98	99	66	101	106	123
33921	BOCA GRANDE	242	283	370	287	323	308	244	280	248	275	244	186	286	231	287	252	175	263	290	312
33922	BOKEELIA	90	84	115	80	94	103	80	96	85	85	83	64	79	78	88	89	56	91	104	110
33924	CAPTIVA	195	205	279	204	237	242	185	218	195	209	191	136	203	175	214	204	131	208	243	247
33928	ESTERO	106	112	146	106	129	133	104	122	110	116	107	75	113	98	119	116	73	117	140	136
33931	FORT MYERS BEACH	89	98	130	92	114	119	88	106	94	100	92	63	99	83	105	101	62	101	127	117
33935	LABELLE	84	74	73	69	73	78	73	79	76	76	76	57	67	76	71	78	52	77	79	91
33936	LEHIGH ACRES	69	69	74	67	71	78	67	73	71	68	70	51	68	67	70	75	48	72	83	85
33946	PLACIDA	157	176	236	165	208	215	156	190	168	180	163	111	179	146	189	179	110	180	228	209
33947	ROTONDA WEST	76	84	113	79	99	102	75	91	80	86	78	53	85	70	90	85	53	86	108	100
33948	PORT CHARLOTTE	83	81	97	79	85	95	77	88	81	77	80	62	77	77	82	85	54	84	95	101
33950	PUNTA GORDA	106	107	142	103	122	128	99	117	105	110	103	74	105	95	112	111	70	112	132	132
33952	PORT CHARLOTTE	72	67	82	65	73	80	69	76	73	70	72	53	67	68	72	78	49	75	86	88
33953	PORT CHARLOTTE	88	97	113	91	109	115	89	103	95	97	92	64	99	86	102	100	63	99	123	114
33954	PORT CHARLOTTE	94	106	103	105	107	111	95	102	98	97	98	73	103	97	102	101	68	99	110	117
33955	PUNTA GORDA	98	100	132	95	114	120	92	110	98	103	95	69	98	88	105	103	65	105	124	124
33956	SAINT JAMES CITY	78	83	114	77	97	103	75	93	80	83	78	56	83	70	90	86	52	87	110	102
33957	SANIBEL	193	203	273	198	233	240	183	217	194	207	190	135	200	174	211	203	130	207	244	245
33960	VENUS	66	63	80	58	70	75	60	71	64	65	62	46	59	58	65	67	42	68	79	81
33966	FORT MYERS	110	123	118	125	121	114	116	113	112	118	114	88	123	113	120	110	81	113	110	133
33967	FORT MYERS	105	116	105	113	113	104	105	106	102	111	103	81	110	105	107	100	73	103	100	122
33971	LEHIGH ACRES	102	109	91	105	104	94	99	99	94	106	96	78	100	100	98	90	67	95	90	113
33972	LEHIGH ACRES	91	93	82	91	90	88	86	89	85	90	86	67	86	88	85	85	59	86	86	103
33973	LEHIGH ACRES	90	80	78	81	80	85	87	86	87	85	87	65	80	88	82	89	60	87	89	101
33974	LEHIGH ACRES	96	96	103	93	99	104	89	99	91	93	91	71	90	89	94	94	62	95	103	114
33976	LEHIGH ACRES	95	99	82	94	94	85	92	91	88	98	89	70	91	92	89	84	62	88	82	104
33980	PORT CHARLOTTE	69	74	87	69	83	90	71	81	77	75	74	50	77	69	80	83	50	79	100	90
33981	PORT CHARLOTTE	77	74	100	70	83	92	71	85	75	73	73	56	71	69	79	80	49	81	96	97
33982	PUNTA GORDA	88	77	111	73	85	97	75	92	79	76	78	64	70	74	82	84	52	87	97	106
33983	PUNTA GORDA	86	95	116	92	106	111	84	100	89	91	88	64	94	82	98	94	60	94	113	111
33990	CAPE CORAL	81	84	92	83	86	88	81	86	81	79	81	64	83	80	85	83	57	84	87	99
33991	CAPE CORAL	104	113	104	111	111	103	102	104	99	109	100	78	106	102	104	97	70	100	98	120
33993	CAPE CORAL	110	118	109	115	116	109	105	109	103	114	105	81	110	106	108	102	73	105	105	126
34102	NAPLES	148	173	219	169	195	189	155	174	159	170	156	114	177	146	179	164	111	167	189	194
34103	NAPLES	168	185	228	180	206	211	170	192	178	185	176	124	188	163	194	187	121	186	219	216
34104	NAPLES	98	95	113	94	103	106	94	102	98	100	97	70	97	93	100	101	67	101	111	117
34105	NAPLES	145	153	193	150	172	179	143	163	151	156	148	104	155	137	161	159	102	158	188	185
34108	NAPLES	202	210	272	207	233	239	194	222	201	208	199	149	206	187	218	209	137	213	238	253
34109	NAPLES	142	149	181	151	163	159	144	152	144	154	144	107	152	136	156	146	101	151	160	176
34110	NAPLES	147	159	208	156	181	184	142	166	148	160	146	105	157	135	164	155	100	158	184	187
34112	NAPLES	89	91	113	87	103	108	88	100	93	95	91	64	94	85	98	98	62	98	116	112
34113	NAPLES	104	105	132	101	117	119	100	113	104	111	103	73	105	96	111	108	71	111	124	127
34114	NAPLES	84	78	109	73	87	97	74	91	79	77	77	61	72	72	83	84	51	86	100	104
34116	NAPLES	96	92	83	87	90	81	96	91	92	100	94	70	91	94	92	89	66	94	85	104
	FLORIDA	96	94	97	93	96	98	95	97	96	97	96	71	95	94	96	97	67	97	101	113
	UNITED STATES	100	100	100	100	100	100	100	100	100	100	100	100	100	100	100	100	100	100	100	100

POPULATION CHANGE

ZIP CODE #	POST OFFICE NAME	COUNTY FIPS CODE	POPULATION 2000	POPULATION 2009	POPULATION 2014	2000-2009 ANNUAL RATE % Rate	2000-2009 ANNUAL RATE State Centile	HOUSEHOLDS 2000	HOUSEHOLDS 2009	HOUSEHOLDS 2014	HOUSEHOLDS % Annual Rate 2000-2009	HOUSEHOLDS 2009 Average HH Size	FAMILIES 2000	FAMILIES 2009	FAMILIES % Annual Rate 2000-2009
34117	NAPLES	021	10236	13962	15659	3.4	81	3229	4429	4978	3.5	3.15	2727	3656	3.2
34119	NAPLES	021	9674	22321	28455	9.8	96	3932	9441	11815	9.9	2.42	3150	7389	9.7
34120	NAPLES	021	12131	24338	30494	7.8	94	3825	7615	9532	7.7	3.18	3236	6320	7.5
34134	BONITA SPRINGS	071	11621	15974	18695	3.5	82	5956	8485	10019	3.9	1.88	4066	5526	3.4
34135	BONITA SPRINGS	071	25125	40046	49062	5.2	89	10398	17841	22222	6.0	2.24	7299	12492	6.0
34140	GOODLAND	021	320	307	328	-0.4	2	186	186	199	0.0	1.65	121	115	-0.5
34141	OCHOPEE	021	1252	1583	1695	2.6	73	576	739	797	2.7	2.10	388	475	2.2
34142	IMMOKALEE	021	23655	26084	27236	1.1	44	5352	5970	6276	1.2	3.96	4173	4525	0.9
34145	MARCO ISLAND	021	14893	17339	18215	1.7	57	7141	8365	8799	1.7	2.07	5176	5847	1.3
34201	BRADENTON	081	1127	2763	3255	10.2	96	589	1459	1724	10.3	1.89	384	898	9.6
34202	BRADENTON	081	7970	20752	25760	10.9	97	2850	7959	9951	11.7	2.61	2448	6520	11.2
34203	BRADENTON	081	26529	37519	41785	3.8	84	10660	15298	17110	4.0	2.42	7618	10627	3.7
34205	BRADENTON	081	31819	31695	31838	0.0	9	13832	13831	13976	0.0	2.23	7761	7234	-0.8
34207	BRADENTON	081	31084	32285	32551	0.4	22	15118	15962	16196	0.6	2.02	8204	8027	-0.2
34208	BRADENTON	081	30677	32917	34238	0.8	35	11029	11978	12533	0.9	2.71	7876	8117	0.3
34209	BRADENTON	081	33229	34513	35443	0.4	22	14578	15290	15759	0.5	2.21	9763	9714	-0.1
34210	BRADENTON	081	12993	15405	16579	1.9	61	6737	8050	8674	1.9	1.91	3965	4427	1.2
34211	BRADENTON	081	1884	2794	3276	4.4	86	713	1070	1259	4.5	2.61	619	908	4.2
34212	BRADENTON	081	5511	15410	19602	11.8	97	1926	5598	7143	12.2	2.73	1604	4533	11.9
34215	CORTEZ	081	564	607	617	0.8	35	284	310	317	1.0	1.96	175	179	0.2
34217	BRADENTON BEACH	081	8262	9247	9598	1.2	46	4238	4805	5004	1.4	1.92	2445	2583	0.6
34219	PARRISH	081	6000	14154	17945	9.7	96	2354	5689	7259	10.0	2.47	1916	4483	9.6
34221	PALMETTO	081	32610	37932	40723	1.6	55	12130	14341	15479	1.8	2.48	8492	9644	1.4
34222	ELLENTON	081	8118	10065	10769	2.4	70	4337	5311	5690	2.2	1.89	2741	3115	1.4
34223	ENGLEWOOD	115	17664	18601	19003	0.6	30	8843	9520	9788	0.8	1.94	5677	5841	0.3
34224	ENGLEWOOD	115	15052	17937	19060	1.9	61	7245	8723	9287	2.0	2.05	4945	5798	1.7
34228	LONGBOAT KEY	115	7603	7843	7926	0.3	18	4280	4528	4617	0.6	1.73	2845	2858	0.0
34229	OSPREY	115	4882	7694	8936	5.0	88	2332	3641	4221	4.9	2.11	1642	2450	4.4
34231	SARASOTA	115	32639	32640	32802	0.0	9	15776	16200	16417	0.3	1.97	8649	8308	-0.4
34232	SARASOTA	115	32032	32058	32410	0.0	9	13313	13669	13934	0.3	2.32	8812	8642	-0.2
34233	SARASOTA	115	14717	16629	17610	1.3	48	6538	7595	8127	1.6	2.16	4254	4682	1.0
34234	SARASOTA	115	19811	19368	19493	-0.2	4	8303	8316	8418	0.0	2.20	4778	4503	-0.6
34235	SARASOTA	115	13333	14509	14926	0.9	38	6192	6917	7183	1.2	2.07	4048	4300	0.7
34236	SARASOTA	115	11982	13609	14425	1.4	51	6218	7438	8039	2.0	1.68	2567	2785	0.9
34237	SARASOTA	115	16995	17041	17219	0.0	9	7134	7294	7418	0.2	2.21	3852	3684	-0.5
34238	SARASOTA	115	13415	21349	24809	5.2	89	6508	10184	11815	5.0	2.08	4334	6446	4.4
34239	SARASOTA	115	15456	14936	14890	-0.4	2	7318	7260	7300	-0.1	2.02	4081	3789	-0.8
34240	SARASOTA	115	7250	10471	12123	4.1	86	2556	3826	4477	4.5	2.72	2151	3148	4.2
34241	SARASOTA	115	11617	14621	16165	2.5	72	4409	5699	6353	2.8	2.56	3544	4454	2.5
34242	SARASOTA	115	9581	10176	10475	0.7	32	5019	5501	5711	1.0	1.85	3035	3134	0.3
34243	SARASOTA	081	21604	24800	27031	1.5	53	9504	11166	12285	1.8	2.21	6496	7274	1.2
34251	MYAKKA CITY	081	4202	5486	6079	2.9	77	1257	1653	1849	3.0	3.03	1044	1341	2.7
34266	ARCADIA	027	28342	30644	31546	0.8	35	8920	9566	9819	0.8	2.88	6343	6675	0.6
34269	ARCADIA	027	3867	4465	4733	1.6	55	1826	2105	2225	1.5	2.09	1333	1506	1.3
34275	NOKOMIS	115	14935	15753	16186	0.6	30	7153	7681	7932	0.8	2.05	4819	4991	0.4
34285	VENICE	115	18186	20146	21071	1.1	44	9932	11380	12034	1.5	1.70	5417	5777	0.7
34286	NORTH PORT	115	5242	18266	23386	14.4	98	1847	6607	8524	14.8	2.76	1521	5319	14.5
34287	NORTH PORT	115	19094	24935	27976	2.9	77	8877	11551	12936	2.9	2.15	5969	7503	2.5
34288	NORTH PORT	115	1497	12179	15901	25.4	100	508	4257	5592	25.8	2.86	431	3521	25.5
34289	NORTH PORT	115	0	1513	1975	0.0	9	0	522	685	0.0	2.90	0	432	0.0
34291	NORTH PORT	115	1822	5599	6959	12.9	98	623	2021	2526	13.6	2.75	491	1513	12.9
34292	VENICE	115	7433	11544	13920	4.9	88	3652	5815	7066	5.2	1.96	2540	3848	4.6
34293	VENICE	115	31029	34070	37052	1.0	40	14334	16180	17822	1.3	2.11	10068	10887	0.8
34420	BELLEVIEW	083	13698	15237	16311	1.2	46	5697	6329	6775	1.1	2.39	3908	4180	0.7
34428	CRYSTAL RIVER	017	8891	10719	11783	2.0	62	3702	4483	4942	2.1	2.36	2563	3008	1.7
34429	CRYSTAL RIVER	017	8900	10048	10873	1.3	48	4017	4578	4990	1.4	2.13	2726	3010	1.1
34431	DUNNELLON	083	6658	8009	8731	2.0	62	3012	3622	3954	2.0	2.17	2060	2415	1.7
34432	DUNNELLON	083	9772	11856	13190	2.1	64	4251	5218	5802	2.2	2.25	3099	3708	2.0
34433	DUNNELLON	017	4254	6410	7382	4.5	86	1731	2632	3033	4.6	2.43	1281	1901	4.4
34434	DUNNELLON	017	4927	7595	9007	4.8	87	2187	3338	3963	4.7	2.26	1577	2352	4.4
34436	FLORAL CITY	017	8432	9695	10360	1.5	53	3711	4286	4595	1.6	2.24	2571	2887	1.3
34442	HERNANDO	017	10272	13551	15001	3.0	78	4681	6101	6768	2.9	2.19	3329	4286	2.8
34446	HOMOSASSA	017	12379	16270	18559	3.0	78	5616	7502	8612	3.2	2.16	4151	5439	3.0
34448	HOMOSASSA	017	8941	10509	11384	1.8	59	4017	4728	5130	1.8	2.22	2688	3074	1.5
34449	INGLIS	075	3883	4661	5076	2.0	62	1725	2113	2317	2.2	2.18	1136	1359	2.0
34450	INVERNESS	017	10043	11101	11673	1.1	44	4836	5343	5623	1.1	2.07	3156	3385	0.8
34452	INVERNESS	017	10391	11831	12572	1.4	51	4530	5190	5538	1.5	2.18	3044	3384	1.2
34453	INVERNESS	017	7936	10415	11702	3.0	78	3445	4543	5115	3.0	2.25	2299	2963	2.8
34461	LECANTO	017	9601	11919	13358	2.4	70	3659	4721	5315	2.8	2.48	2786	3492	2.5
34465	BEVERLY HILLS	017	12571	15635	16999	2.4	70	6256	7535	8171	2.0	2.03	3993	4766	1.9
34470	OCALA	083	18590	20758	22007	1.2	46	8422	9464	10090	1.3	2.16	5190	5604	0.8
34471	OCALA	083	23927	28579	31287	1.9	61	9300	11052	12149	1.9	2.46	6206	7138	1.5
34472	OCALA	083	18514	25204	29079	3.4	81	7475	10022	11497	3.2	2.51	5421	7086	2.9
34473	OCALA	083	8555	14567	17294	5.9	91	3234	5568	6593	6.0	2.62	2418	4071	5.8
34474	OCALA	083	9521	13844	16003	4.1	86	4313	6276	7345	4.1	1.97	2609	3741	4.0
34475	OCALA	083	12696	14958	15863	1.8	59	3759	4371	4694	1.6	2.83	2456	2797	1.4
34476	OCALA	083	12180	17141	19909	3.8	84	5724	8117	9471	3.8	2.11	4244	5916	3.7
34479	OCALA	083	11913	13593	14552	1.4	51	4551	5232	5619	1.5	2.56	3310	3705	1.2
34480	OCALA	083	14297	18908	21069	3.1	79	5312	7012	7827	3.0	2.68	4047	5222	2.8
34481	OCALA	083	13631	16874	19064	2.3	69	7044	8663	9845	2.3	1.92	4898	5827	1.9
34482	OCALA	083	16183	20499	23035	2.6	73	6243	8015	9113	2.7	2.46	4450	5572	2.5
34484	OXFORD	119	2366	3164	4145	3.2	80	890	1252	1667	3.8	2.53	665	899	3.3
34488	SILVER SPRINGS	083	8891	9913	10493	1.2	46	3892	4337	4599	1.2	2.25	2660	2874	0.8
34491	SUMMERFIELD	083	17066	29804	36595	6.2	91	7157	12694	15724	6.4	2.34	5400	9333	6.1
34498	YANKEETOWN	075	599	676	743	1.3	48	298	336	372	1.3	1.97	191	211	1.1
34601	BROOKSVILLE	053	21043	23304	24833	1.1	44	8795	9725	10408	1.1	2.35	5792	6210	0.8
34602	BROOKSVILLE	053	5883	7035	7733	2.0	62	2271	2739	3038	2.0	2.57	1705	1992	1.7
34604	BROOKSVILLE	053	6427	9236	10882	4.1	86	2148	3238	3863	4.5	2.60	1601	2350	4.2
34606	SPRING HILL	053	23994	27922	30391	1.7	57	11030	12748	13908	1.6	2.18	7724	8652	1.2
34607	SPRING HILL	053	7037	8908	10076	2.6	73	3154	3973	4506	2.5	2.24	2350	2894	2.3
34608	SPRING HILL	053	23207	30796	35446	3.1	79	9793	13014	15048	3.1	2.34	7242	9381	2.8
34609	SPRING HILL	053	21848	35722	43515	5.5	90	8650	14095	17225	5.4	2.53	6863	10992	5.2
34610	SPRING HILL	101	10644	12997	15002	2.2	66	3846	4626	5341	2.0	2.81	2894	3354	1.6
34613	BROOKSVILLE	053	13674	19345	22619	3.8	84	6526	9057	10594	3.6	2.13	4507	6109	3.3
34614	BROOKSVILLE	053	2921	5456	6845	7.0	93	1096	2073	2613	7.1	2.63	833	1547	6.9
	FLORIDA					1.9					1.9	2.47			1.7
	UNITED STATES					1.0					1.1	2.59			0.9

POPULATION COMPOSITION

ZIP CODE #	POST OFFICE NAME	RACE (%) White 2000	White 2009	Black 2000	Black 2009	Asian/Pacific 2000	Asian/Pacific 2009	% Hispanic Origin 2000	% Hispanic Origin 2009	2009 AGE DISTRIBUTION (%) 0-4	5-9	10-14	15-19	20-24	25-44	45-64	65-84	85+	18+	MEDIAN AGE 2009	% 2009 Males	% 2009 Females
34117	NAPLES	89.4	80.3	1.8	2.8	0.6	0.8	20.4	38.3	7.8	7.6	7.5	7.2	5.5	30.3	26.9	6.7	0.5	72.6	35.1	51.2	48.8
34119	NAPLES	97.1	94.7	0.6	0.9	0.6	1.2	4.6	9.6	3.4	3.7	4.3	4.3	2.7	13.9	35.8	29.3	2.7	85.9	56.4	47.7	52.3
34120	NAPLES	88.7	79.9	3.0	4.6	0.4	0.5	22.5	42.1	8.7	8.4	8.1	7.4	5.5	29.9	24.4	7.2	0.5	70.0	33.3	50.6	49.4
34134	BONITA SPRINGS	97.9	96.5	0.4	0.7	0.5	0.7	2.6	4.6	1.9	2.0	2.2	1.9	1.5	10.3	32.9	43.9	3.4	92.7	64.0	48.5	51.5
34135	BONITA SPRINGS	85.9	83.7	0.4	0.6	0.4	0.5	26.4	29.8	5.0	4.7	4.7	4.7	4.1	20.3	28.1	25.7	2.8	82.8	50.5	50.8	49.2
34140	GOODLAND	97.8	95.1	0.3	1.0	0.6	1.0	4.7	10.1	2.9	2.9	3.3	2.6	3.3	12.4	38.8	31.3	2.6	89.6	57.7	49.2	50.8
34141	OCHOPEE	95.5	91.7	1.4	2.6	0.2	0.4	3.8	8.7	3.2	3.2	3.5	3.9	3.3	17.8	32.6	29.9	2.6	87.6	56.2	51.5	48.5
34142	IMMOKALEE	41.3	36.3	17.7	16.0	0.4	0.3	68.1	75.6	10.7	9.2	7.4	9.5	11.5	31.9	15.5	4.1	0.3	67.7	25.8	57.6	42.4
34145	MARCO ISLAND	98.1	96.5	0.3	0.5	0.6	0.9	4.0	8.6	2.2	2.6	2.7	2.5	1.8	11.0	31.6	41.6	4.0	90.9	63.1	48.6	51.4
34201	BRADENTON	95.8	92.6	1.3	2.7	1.6	2.4	2.3	5.1	1.7	1.8	2.0	1.7	1.0	16.0	33.9	38.8	3.2	93.4	62.0	47.6	52.4
34202	BRADENTON	95.5	91.8	1.4	2.6	1.7	2.6	3.5	6.5	6.5	6.8	6.9	5.9	3.2	22.3	30.9	16.2	1.4	76.1	44.0	48.5	51.5
34203	BRADENTON	84.5	81.8	8.6	9.7	1.1	1.6	12.2	15.3	6.2	5.9	5.7	5.4	4.8	19.9	26.5	21.8	3.9	78.9	46.6	48.9	51.1
34205	BRADENTON	84.8	77.9	8.2	11.4	0.9	1.2	12.3	20.6	6.0	5.7	5.4	5.8	6.0	24.7	24.9	15.7	5.7	79.3	42.2	48.2	51.8
34207	BRADENTON	89.2	83.0	5.1	8.0	1.3	1.7	7.9	14.5	5.4	4.5	4.3	4.6	6.0	21.3	24.2	24.6	5.3	83.1	48.5	47.1	52.9
34208	BRADENTON	65.9	58.6	25.7	30.3	0.6	0.8	15.1	21.3	8.0	7.5	7.2	7.4	7.5	24.9	23.4	12.0	2.2	72.7	34.6	49.3	50.7
34209	BRADENTON	96.6	94.1	0.9	1.8	1.0	1.4	2.5	5.6	3.5	3.9	4.3	4.8	4.0	16.6	31.6	24.6	6.7	85.3	54.1	46.2	53.8
34210	BRADENTON	94.9	91.1	1.7	3.3	1.6	2.5	3.4	7.4	3.2	3.0	3.1	3.5	4.5	18.8	27.4	31.8	4.8	88.8	56.9	47.6	52.4
34211	BRADENTON	96.4	93.5	0.8	1.6	0.9	1.4	2.9	6.3	3.7	4.2	5.6	5.9	2.8	18.4	34.0	23.8	1.5	82.7	51.7	50.2	49.8
34212	BRADENTON	94.5	88.5	1.8	3.2	1.0	1.3	5.1	12.5	6.7	7.3	7.7	6.6	4.0	23.3	31.6	11.4	1.4	73.8	41.6	49.6	50.4
34215	CORTEZ	98.4	97.5	0.4	0.8	0.9	1.3	1.4	3.1	1.2	1.5	1.8	2.0	1.5	9.4	37.4	39.7	5.6	94.2	63.3	50.1	49.9
34217	BRADENTON BEACH	98.5	97.5	0.2	0.4	0.3	0.5	1.8	4.0	1.9	2.2	2.7	3.3	2.3	13.1	41.0	29.3	4.2	91.1	58.4	48.7	51.3
34219	PARRISH	94.0	89.3	3.0	5.6	0.4	0.6	5.0	10.2	4.8	5.1	5.6	5.3	3.7	19.1	32.7	21.8	1.9	81.2	49.0	49.0	51.0
34221	PALMETTO	74.9	69.3	16.8	19.4	0.4	0.5	17.7	24.7	6.2	6.4	6.0	6.3	5.7	21.6	26.1	18.8	3.0	77.8	43.3	50.0	50.0
34222	ELLENTON	95.9	92.9	1.6	2.8	0.3	0.4	5.3	10.2	3.3	3.1	3.0	2.6	2.4	11.1	23.3	43.0	8.1	88.9	65.5	45.6	54.4
34223	ENGLEWOOD	98.4	97.5	0.2	0.3	0.5	0.7	1.5	2.8	2.0	2.1	2.4	2.8	2.4	10.5	30.9	39.4	7.5	91.8	63.5	47.1	52.9
34224	ENGLEWOOD	98.3	97.6	0.3	0.4	0.3	0.5	1.3	2.3	3.0	3.0	3.2	3.5	3.3	12.9	31.2	35.0	5.0	88.7	60.0	47.8	52.2
34228	LONGBOAT KEY	99.2	98.8	0.1	0.1	0.4	0.7	0.7	1.4	0.5	0.7	0.8	0.7	0.5	3.5	27.4	56.9	9.0	97.5	69.9	45.6	54.4
34229	OSPREY	97.7	95.9	0.2	0.4	1.0	1.6	1.4	3.1	3.4	3.8	4.5	4.3	2.6	14.5	34.8	28.3	3.8	85.5	56.1	48.0	52.0
34231	SARASOTA	96.5	94.3	0.6	1.1	0.9	1.4	3.5	6.6	3.5	3.4	3.7	4.2	4.7	19.7	31.2	23.3	6.4	86.9	52.4	47.1	52.9
34232	SARASOTA	94.7	91.3	1.4	2.5	0.9	1.4	5.4	9.8	5.1	5.2	5.6	5.9	5.0	23.6	30.0	15.8	3.8	80.3	44.6	47.8	52.2
34233	SARASOTA	96.7	94.7	0.7	1.3	1.1	1.6	3.1	5.7	3.6	4.0	4.6	5.3	4.0	15.9	31.4	24.3	6.8	84.2	53.3	46.1	53.9
34234	SARASOTA	54.8	47.1	40.0	46.3	0.7	0.9	6.7	9.7	6.2	6.1	5.8	7.3	7.5	23.0	25.1	15.9	3.1	78.4	39.4	47.5	52.5
34235	SARASOTA	92.5	88.1	3.5	5.7	1.1	1.8	5.1	9.1	4.0	4.2	4.6	4.0	3.0	18.5	28.1	27.3	6.1	84.6	53.6	45.9	54.1
34236	SARASOTA	79.3	73.5	12.1	16.3	0.9	1.1	14.2	16.9	3.5	3.2	2.9	3.4	4.8	20.1	26.5	27.1	8.4	88.5	55.0	49.3	50.7
34237	SARASOTA	86.0	79.5	5.7	8.3	1.1	1.4	18.1	27.7	5.9	5.0	4.7	5.4	8.0	28.4	23.9	14.6	4.2	81.3	39.5	49.8	50.2
34238	SARASOTA	97.0	95.0	0.9	1.9	1.3	2.1	2.4	4.9	2.7	2.9	3.2	3.3	2.7	13.4	33.1	33.5	5.0	88.8	59.5	46.5	53.5
34239	SARASOTA	95.5	92.8	0.9	1.5	1.3	2.0	5.2	9.5	4.2	4.3	4.7	4.7	4.4	21.1	31.5	19.8	5.2	83.9	49.1	47.0	53.0
34240	SARASOTA	97.6	96.3	0.6	1.1	0.6	1.0	2.8	5.2	4.8	5.7	7.5	6.9	3.6	21.0	35.9	13.1	1.6	77.5	45.3	49.3	50.7
34241	SARASOTA	97.1	95.5	0.5	0.9	0.7	1.1	2.8	5.1	4.1	4.6	5.4	6.3	4.5	17.9	35.6	19.6	2.1	81.7	49.4	49.0	51.0
34242	SARASOTA	98.5	97.6	0.1	0.3	0.5	0.9	1.5	2.9	1.8	2.1	2.6	2.6	2.0	11.0	34.1	38.2	5.7	92.0	62.4	47.9	52.1
34243	SARASOTA	91.9	87.0	4.0	6.6	1.7	2.3	4.9	9.4	4.6	4.8	5.0	4.5	3.5	20.5	31.7	22.1	3.2	83.0	49.6	47.9	52.1
34251	MYAKKA CITY	96.1	93.6	0.7	1.3	0.7	0.9	16.3	26.4	7.8	7.8	8.2	7.3	5.7	29.1	26.6	6.8	0.7	71.7	35.1	50.9	49.1
34266	ARCADIA	70.6	64.0	14.1	15.1	0.5	0.6	27.7	38.4	6.4	5.9	6.2	7.4	8.4	27.0	22.1	14.4	2.1	77.3	35.7	56.7	43.3
34269	ARCADIA	93.4	90.3	2.9	4.1	0.2	0.3	4.6	7.5	3.5	3.5	3.9	4.0	3.4	14.9	27.4	35.4	3.9	86.4	59.2	49.5	50.5
34275	NOKOMIS	96.8	95.3	1.3	2.0	0.6	1.0	1.3	2.5	2.4	2.8	3.2	3.6	2.8	12.2	35.1	32.9	5.2	89.4	59.6	48.5	51.5
34285	VENICE	98.2	97.2	0.5	0.9	0.4	0.7	1.1	2.1	1.2	1.2	1.3	1.7	1.6	6.3	25.2	47.1	14.5	95.4	69.6	43.5	56.5
34286	NORTH PORT	94.0	89.8	3.5	6.3	0.4	0.6	2.9	5.5	9.2	8.3	7.7	6.6	5.1	32.4	22.5	7.6	0.6	70.7	33.3	49.3	50.7
34287	NORTH PORT	93.8	89.9	3.5	6.2	0.5	0.7	2.7	5.1	4.3	4.3	4.5	4.9	3.9	17.3	24.1	30.5	6.1	83.7	54.0	46.3	53.7
34288	NORTH PORT	95.0	92.3	1.2	2.2	0.7	1.1	4.2	7.9	9.7	8.6	7.9	6.9	5.3	34.0	21.0	6.0	0.5	69.4	32.0	49.3	50.7
34289	NORTH PORT	0.0	92.3	0.0	2.2	0.0	1.1	0.0	7.8	9.7	8.6	7.9	6.9	5.3	34.1	21.0	5.9	0.5	69.5	32.1	49.1	50.9
34291	NORTH PORT	91.8	87.1	5.2	8.6	0.4	0.7	3.0	5.3	7.5	6.9	6.8	6.5	5.3	27.5	24.7	12.4	2.3	74.5	37.8	48.3	51.7
34292	VENICE	98.2	97.1	0.5	0.9	0.5	0.8	1.4	2.8	1.7	1.8	2.1	2.4	1.9	9.6	30.4	44.0	6.1	92.8	65.0	46.1	53.9
34293	VENICE	97.8	96.5	0.4	0.7	0.7	1.1	1.5	2.9	3.0	3.2	3.5	3.9	3.3	14.4	29.6	33.8	5.4	88.0	59.0	46.8	53.2
34420	BELLEVIEW	91.8	88.2	4.0	5.7	0.4	0.6	6.2	10.2	5.5	5.4	5.5	5.8	5.2	21.5	29.0	19.2	2.9	79.9	45.7	48.3	51.7
34428	CRYSTAL RIVER	92.8	90.8	3.8	4.6	1.0	1.5	2.8	4.4	4.3	4.5	5.0	5.5	4.3	18.9	32.8	22.0	2.7	82.3	50.3	48.4	51.6
34429	CRYSTAL RIVER	92.6	90.3	4.6	6.0	1.1	1.7	2.2	3.5	3.3	3.8	4.6	4.5	3.2	16.0	33.5	26.9	4.2	85.3	55.3	48.2	51.8
34431	DUNNELLON	92.6	89.5	4.5	6.2	0.6	0.9	3.9	6.5	3.8	3.8	4.1	4.9	4.3	17.1	30.7	26.9	4.4	85.3	53.6	47.7	52.3
34432	DUNNELLON	90.9	87.4	6.0	8.2	0.5	0.7	4.5	7.1	3.1	3.3	3.5	3.8	3.0	13.3	26.9	38.0	5.1	87.7	61.1	47.1	52.9
34433	DUNNELLON	95.6	93.9	2.0	2.6	0.6	0.9	2.5	4.6	4.2	4.2	4.5	5.3	4.2	17.5	32.9	24.4	2.8	83.7	52.1	48.6	51.4
34434	DUNNELLON	90.5	88.5	5.9	6.5	0.6	0.9	4.4	6.9	4.3	4.1	4.1	4.7	3.8	16.1	29.5	29.2	4.3	84.6	55.5	47.9	52.1
34436	FLORAL CITY	97.1	96.2	1.0	1.3	0.2	0.3	2.6	4.2	3.8	3.9	4.0	4.8	4.8	15.8	32.8	26.7	3.4	85.3	53.9	48.7	51.3
34442	HERNANDO	94.9	92.9	2.2	2.9	1.2	2.1	1.9	3.3	3.2	3.4	3.7	4.3	3.3	13.9	31.4	32.7	4.1	87.0	58.3	48.6	51.4
34446	HOMOSASSA	97.6	96.9	0.6	0.8	0.6	0.9	1.6	2.6	2.9	2.9	3.1	3.5	3.3	12.6	28.9	37.8	4.9	89.0	61.6	47.8	52.2
34448	HOMOSASSA	96.7	95.8	0.9	1.2	0.5	0.8	1.6	2.6	4.0	4.2	4.4	4.9	3.9	17.1	31.5	27.0	3.1	84.2	53.2	49.6	50.4
34449	INGLIS	97.1	96.1	1.2	1.6	0.3	0.5	1.5	2.5	3.6	3.7	4.2	5.2	4.1	16.9	34.6	25.0	2.6	85.1	53.9	49.9	50.1
34450	INVERNESS	95.2	93.9	2.5	3.1	0.4	0.7	2.4	3.8	3.5	3.7	3.9	4.3	3.8	14.6	31.7	30.1	4.4	86.3	56.8	47.4	52.6
34452	INVERNESS	94.9	93.4	2.4	3.0	0.6	0.8	4.8	7.6	4.1	4.2	4.5	5.3	4.6	18.1	28.9	25.4	4.8	83.8	51.8	47.5	52.5
34453	INVERNESS	94.4	92.5	3.2	4.1	0.9	1.3	2.3	3.7	4.4	4.5	4.7	5.0	3.8	17.5	30.4	25.6	4.2	83.1	52.8	47.9	52.1
34461	LECANTO	95.0	93.5	2.0	2.5	1.3	1.8	2.6	4.2	3.5	3.9	4.7	5.2	3.7	16.3	32.1	27.4	3.2	84.5	54.3	48.8	51.2
34465	BEVERLY HILLS	95.4	93.7	2.0	2.7	0.9	1.4	3.5	5.4	2.9	2.7	2.7	2.7	2.7	11.0	26.2	40.3	8.9	89.9	64.6	45.3	54.7
34470	OCALA	86.2	80.9	10.0	13.7	0.8	1.2	5.0	8.1	6.4	6.0	5.7	5.8	5.4	22.7	25.9	18.2	3.9	78.4	43.2	46.5	53.5
34471	OCALA	81.1	76.4	14.1	16.6	1.7	2.5	5.2	8.3	6.3	5.8	5.9	6.8	7.3	22.9	26.5	14.6	3.9	78.1	40.9	47.4	52.6
34472	OCALA	74.0	67.4	18.8	22.7	0.8	1.1	10.5	15.6	6.8	6.6	6.6	6.8	5.7	24.2	23.9	16.6	2.7	75.5	39.7	47.2	52.8
34473	OCALA	76.3	71.5	11.8	13.5	0.7	0.9	26.1	33.4	5.5	5.6	6.4	6.0	4.4	20.1	25.8	23.7	2.6	78.6	46.7	47.6	52.4
34474	OCALA	84.2	80.3	9.9	12.0	1.9	2.5	6.6	10.1	3.9	3.8	4.1	6.1	5.7	22.4	26.9	23.3	3.7	85.0	48.2	51.4	48.6
34475	OCALA	46.4	41.7	49.1	52.8	0.5	0.7	5.3	7.2	6.3	5.9	5.8	8.7	7.9	29.0	23.8	10.5	2.0	77.3	36.0	51.0	49.0
34476	OCALA	93.9	91.1	3.2	4.5	0.9	1.5	4.2	6.8	2.6	2.7	2.9	2.9	2.2	10.4	26.1	45.3	4.9	90.0	65.1	46.2	53.8
34479	OCALA	85.9	80.1	10.5	14.7	0.7	1.1	4.7	7.5	6.7	6.8	6.9	6.7	5.2	25.3	27.6	12.8	1.9	75.4	39.9	48.4	51.6
34480	OCALA	88.5	83.1	7.4	10.7	1.2	1.8	4.8	8.2	6.2	6.2	6.5	6.7	6.0	22.8	29.4	13.9	2.2	76.8	41.6	48.2	51.8
34481	OCALA	95.2	92.9	2.9	4.3	0.4	0.7	2.8	4.8	2.0	2.0	2.1	2.1	1.7	8.2	24.1	48.6	9.3	92.7	68.5	45.2	54.8
34482	OCALA	77.5	70.6	17.0	21.9	0.5	0.8	8.8	12.7	5.4	5.4	5.8	6.0	5.0	24.1	28.9	17.6	1.9	79.7	43.7	50.0	50.0
34484	OXFORD	76.0	62.7	21.0	33.5	0.3	0.4	3.6	6.0	6.7	6.7	7.0	7.2	5.6	25.0	27.6	12.7	1.5	75.0	38.9	49.1	50.9
34488	SILVER SPRINGS	94.6	92.4	3.0	4.2	0.3	0.5	2.2	3.7	4.9	5.2	6.0	6.2	4.1	21.0	29.1	20.6	2.9	79.8	46.9	49.8	50.2
34491	SUMMERFIELD	92.4	89.7	4.1	5.9	0.3	0.4	6.3	8.8	4.7	4.8	4.9	5.1	4.3	18.8	29.0	25.4	3.0	82.5	50.6	48.5	51.5
34498	YANKEETOWN	97.7	97.0	0.5	0.6	0.3	0.4	0.8	1.5	2.7	3.0	3.3	6.2	4.3	13.8	34.6	29.4	2.8	86.7	56.9	51.5	48.5
34601	BROOKSVILLE	85.0	81.9	11.6	13.7	0.7	1.0	3.0	4.6	5.8	5.6	5.7	5.9	5.1	20.6	28.3	19.0	3.9	79.0	45.9	47.5	52.5
34602	BROOKSVILLE	88.7	85.4	8.6	11.2	0.4	0.5	4.2	6.3	5.7	5.9	6.3	6.2	5.1	20.8	31.6	16.2	2.2	78.2	45.0	49.0	51.0
34604	BROOKSVILLE	89.2	84.8	7.1	10.2	0.6	0.8	5.2	8.1	5.3	5.6	6.3	7.1	7.0	25.3	28.6	13.2	1.6	78.5	40.2	49.2	50.8
34606	SPRING HILL	95.0	92.8	1.8	2.7	0.5	0.8	5.7	8.9	4.1	4.0	4.0	4.1	3.5	15.4	22.8	35.7	6.4	85.3	59.0	46.4	53.6
34607	SPRING HILL	95.3	93.2	1.7	2.6	1.3	2.1	2.7	4.4	2.4	2.7	3.1	3.5	2.8	11.3	38.3	32.6	3.2	89.7	59.9	48.5	51.5
34608	SPRING HILL	94.4	91.9	2.4	3.5	0.7	1.1	7.0	11.0	4.2	4.3	4.4	4.7	4.3	17.5	29.9	26.0	4.6	84.1	53.0	47.0	53.0
34609	SPRING HILL	94.0	91.4	2.8	4.0	0.8	1.3	6.8	10.1	4.5	4.6	5.0	5.3	4.4	18.4	30.7	24.1	3.1	82.5	50.6	47.4	52.6
34610	SPRING HILL	96.6	95.4	0.8	1.0	0.2	0.3	3.8	6.1	6.1	6.3	6.5	6.6	5.8	23.9	30.7	12.7	1.4	77.0	41.2	49.6	50.4
34613	BROOKSVILLE	97.6	96.3	0.6	0.9	0.5	0.7	2.8	5.0	2.8	2.9	3.0	3.2	2.6	11.3	27.0	40.4	6.7	89.3	63.5	46.9	53.1
34614	BROOKSVILLE	95.8	93.9	0.6	0.8	0.4	0.4	5.0	8.5	5.4	5.7	6.0	6.4	4.4	20.2	30.0	19.9	2.1	78.9	46.5	49.8	50.2
	FLORIDA	78.0	74.7	14.6	15.8	1.7	2.3	16.8	21.5	6.0	5.9	5.9	6.3	6.2	25.0	26.8	15.3	2.8	78.6	41.1	48.8	51.2
	UNITED STATES	75.1	72.0	12.3	12.7	3.8	4.6	12.5	15.7	6.8	6.7	6.6	7.1	6.9	27.0	26.0	10.9	1.9	75.7	36.9	49.2	50.8

ZIP CODE #	POST OFFICE NAME	2009 Per Capita Income	2009 HH Income Base	2009 HOUSEHOLD INCOME DISTRIBUTION (%) Less than $25,000	$25,000 to $49,999	$50,000 to $99,999	$100,000 to $149,999	$150,000 or More	MEDIAN HOUSEHOLD INCOME 2009	2014	2009 National Centile	2009 State Centile	2009 Home Value Base	2009 HOME VALUE DISTRIBUTION (%) Less than $50,000	$50,000 to $89,999	$90,000 to $174,999	$175,000 to $399,999	$400,000 or More	2009 Median Home Value
34117	NAPLES	26096	4429	8.0	14.9	50.8	19.3	7.0	71523	76103	88	90	4024	1.1	3.7	46.9	45.9	2.4	172352
34119	NAPLES	52665	9441	6.9	10.2	36.6	22.2	24.0	92593	95620	96	97	8235	0.5	0.8	14.7	52.9	31.1	288664
34120	NAPLES	26238	7615	7.3	19.5	48.4	17.6	7.3	69538	73914	87	88	7068	1.4	4.9	50.3	42.9	0.4	165192
34134	BONITA SPRINGS	65400	8485	9.1	22.3	32.8	13.5	22.3	75350	76249	90	92	6955	3.9	4.9	17.0	37.0	37.3	279470
34135	BONITA SPRINGS	40315	17841	14.6	27.0	33.0	10.6	14.7	57552	59770	75	74	14549	10.5	14.7	28.2	37.1	9.6	164486
34140	GOODLAND	52301	186	17.2	23.1	32.8	17.2	9.7	64889	71220	83	83	157	1.3	2.5	8.3	40.1	47.8	384091
34141	OCHOPEE	27215	739	14.9	40.6	34.4	4.9	5.3	46426	47244	53	48	586	24.1	22.2	30.0	18.8	4.9	100746
34142	IMMOKALEE	10428	5970	42.2	32.0	21.3	3.2	1.3	30603	31547	9	6	2628	38.9	28.1	26.5	6.1	0.4	68786
34145	MARCO ISLAND	54325	8365	11.4	19.9	32.8	16.2	19.7	73709	80361	89	91	7140	0.7	1.4	9.8	41.8	46.3	377759
34201	BRADENTON	54929	1459	10.5	14.7	40.1	18.8	16.0	75201	73785	89	92	944	0.0	2.2	23.5	46.3	28.0	283333
34202	BRADENTON	53689	7959	7.0	11.2	23.2	23.6	35.1	120724	123299	99	99	6771	1.5	0.0	7.3	51.4	39.9	345581
34203	BRADENTON	25518	15298	19.8	29.4	36.3	10.5	4.0	50772	54172	63	58	12328	14.3	16.7	36.2	32.0	0.8	134423
34205	BRADENTON	21009	13831	30.4	34.4	28.4	5.2	1.5	37181	39514	24	19	8143	13.9	29.3	50.6	5.4	0.9	100105
34207	BRADENTON	21205	15962	31.0	38.4	26.5	3.0	1.1	34866	36606	17	13	9975	38.4	23.9	34.8	2.6	0.3	67178
34208	BRADENTON	20035	11978	24.6	33.3	32.4	6.2	3.4	43622	46482	44	38	6951	12.6	23.6	42.5	18.8	2.6	109241
34209	BRADENTON	32559	15290	13.9	29.3	39.5	11.4	5.8	54910	55939	71	69	12130	2.7	12.5	52.6	28.0	4.2	142242
34210	BRADENTON	31946	8050	18.2	31.9	38.1	8.5	3.2	49899	52473	61	56	5225	5.2	13.7	52.3	26.6	2.2	129969
34211	BRADENTON	36923	1070	6.3	20.0	35.8	26.1	11.9	82845	83351	93	95	985	2.5	0.9	18.1	62.8	15.6	247326
34212	BRADENTON	30925	5598	9.9	15.8	44.3	22.3	7.7	75237	73582	89	92	4793	2.6	3.3	21.8	67.9	4.4	230363
34215	CORTEZ	34439	310	24.2	28.1	28.4	14.8	4.5	48518	50373	58	52	259	8.1	15.8	30.5	42.5	3.1	155833
34217	BRADENTON BEACH	34281	4805	20.9	29.0	36.1	7.3	6.6	50027	52554	61	57	3226	5.6	2.6	17.0	54.1	20.7	260495
34219	PARRISH	30467	5689	14.2	27.8	39.3	10.6	8.0	58766	59445	76	75	5152	1.2	19.8	38.0	29.9	11.0	141758
34221	PALMETTO	21528	14341	24.4	32.1	34.5	6.2	2.8	44512	47670	47	41	11303	25.3	23.7	39.1	10.7	1.2	91684
34222	ELLENTON	24848	5311	28.1	36.0	29.7	4.7	1.4	38678	41522	29	25	4609	43.5	27.0	22.1	6.6	0.8	57104
34223	ENGLEWOOD	32008	9520	20.9	34.3	32.1	7.1	5.5	45312	48753	49	44	8001	6.1	23.0	40.5	23.1	7.3	118784
34224	ENGLEWOOD	27129	8723	25.4	31.9	32.5	6.6	3.5	43131	46055	43	37	7320	5.2	27.7	47.9	15.4	3.8	109120
34228	LONGBOAT KEY	95598	4528	10.1	13.7	25.8	16.7	33.7	101153	106695	97	98	4053	0.6	0.7	5.9	32.9	59.9	523649
34229	OSPREY	55965	3641	15.8	18.6	31.0	15.1	19.5	70367	73277	87	89	3288	7.7	7.3	15.4	33.6	36.0	294493
34231	SARASOTA	36392	16200	17.5	31.4	34.1	8.8	8.2	51144	55032	64	60	11409	5.8	8.8	48.1	27.7	9.6	142681
34232	SARASOTA	30085	13669	14.2	28.9	41.5	9.3	6.0	57078	60148	74	73	10654	2.0	10.5	59.5	26.0	1.9	134686
34233	SARASOTA	34123	7595	14.3	26.6	38.6	12.0	8.5	60390	61914	78	77	6396	8.6	12.9	36.5	38.7	3.3	149316
34234	SARASOTA	21359	8316	35.9	29.0	27.9	4.4	2.8	37375	40017	25	20	5097	19.8	36.0	29.5	10.1	4.6	84466
34235	SARASOTA	38205	6917	12.6	22.7	42.5	13.5	8.7	62115	63281	80	80	5557	0.9	7.4	53.1	35.7	2.9	149620
34236	SARASOTA	42780	7438	28.9	25.4	26.9	7.5	11.4	44814	48697	48	41	3880	3.5	4.6	17.9	39.0	35.0	293079
34237	SARASOTA	21496	7294	25.6	38.2	30.5	4.3	1.3	40125	42023	33	28	3824	5.4	29.1	61.7	3.5	0.4	101491
34238	SARASOTA	47904	10184	12.3	18.9	35.9	15.8	17.1	70822	72090	87	89	7850	5.5	3.8	10.9	56.3	23.6	280696
34239	SARASOTA	33781	7260	17.9	29.6	35.3	10.9	6.3	52229	55174	66	63	5412	6.2	8.5	50.3	25.9	9.1	144083
34240	SARASOTA	45920	3826	5.4	9.6	38.0	22.4	24.6	94529	96821	96	97	3537	0.0	1.0	9.1	59.6	30.2	294103
34241	SARASOTA	41451	5699	6.5	21.0	37.7	18.3	16.5	75810	77546	90	92	5041	2.7	6.0	25.2	42.5	23.7	229844
34242	SARASOTA	70378	5501	9.5	19.6	29.3	17.2	24.4	82760	86428	93	95	4435	0.0	0.2	5.5	36.2	58.1	464183
34243	SARASOTA	36017	11166	12.2	21.7	43.2	15.1	7.8	65002	65324	83	84	8578	1.9	3.6	42.2	47.5	4.7	178739
34251	MYAKKA CITY	26927	1653	9.4	19.9	49.8	11.9	8.9	69223	69812	86	88	1393	6.3	8.9	35.2	40.1	9.5	174038
34266	ARCADIA	16272	9566	31.7	35.1	26.5	4.5	2.2	36202	39415	21	16	6899	14.0	27.9	36.7	16.7	4.7	104336
34269	ARCADIA	27435	2105	26.0	23.3	41.4	6.5	2.8	50372	50458	62	57	1810	13.0	12.5	36.2	30.3	8.1	139915
34275	NOKOMIS	40557	7681	18.3	26.8	33.5	9.3	12.1	54494	58002	70	69	6576	14.1	9.9	27.9	32.1	16.0	167671
34285	VENICE	34758	11380	21.4	35.0	30.5	8.0	5.2	45120	47539	49	43	9007	19.6	21.0	29.7	23.5	6.2	106874
34286	NORTH PORT	26431	6607	7.7	25.6	48.0	13.8	5.0	64224	66671	83	82	5952	0.0	6.1	66.0	26.5	1.4	136140
34287	NORTH PORT	23480	11551	25.5	33.4	34.0	4.4	2.6	42323	45824	40	35	9932	9.0	37.6	47.4	5.9	0.1	93145
34288	NORTH PORT	24797	4257	6.7	25.6	53.3	10.1	4.3	62533	62942	81	81	3752	0.2	4.1	66.9	26.9	1.9	138411
34289	NORTH PORT	24579	522	6.5	25.3	53.6	10.3	4.2	62915	63340	81	81	460	0.2	4.1	66.7	27.0	2.0	138564
34291	NORTH PORT	24188	2021	16.2	25.7	41.3	11.9	4.8	56955	61392	74	73	1762	0.2	25.4	54.7	17.6	2.0	116924
34292	VENICE	42172	5815	11.1	28.4	37.0	10.3	13.2	60577	62675	78	78	4713	3.4	7.3	30.7	47.1	11.6	203369
34293	VENICE	29416	16180	14.7	33.3	41.1	6.5	4.4	51417	54322	65	61	14106	2.8	12.1	56.2	27.3	1.7	128475
34420	BELLEVIEW	19338	6329	29.7	34.9	29.4	4.7	1.3	38272	41044	27	23	4935	18.5	27.8	40.8	10.5	2.5	95567
34428	CRYSTAL RIVER	23325	4483	27.1	34.0	26.1	9.2	3.6	39793	43161	32	27	3523	8.1	15.3	37.1	34.0	5.5	144972
34429	CRYSTAL RIVER	28092	4578	25.7	30.8	29.0	9.3	5.2	42896	46440	42	36	3703	6.1	12.2	40.9	32.3	8.5	155798
34431	DUNNELLON	21776	3622	30.6	33.5	29.2	4.1	2.5	37222	39523	24	19	3081	8.2	20.5	48.8	17.9	4.6	121445
34432	DUNNELLON	23616	5218	22.7	34.5	33.0	7.4	2.5	44074	46788	46	40	4615	8.3	19.1	39.3	29.8	3.5	134312
34433	DUNNELLON	20244	2632	29.1	35.5	27.3	5.0	3.0	37707	39964	26	22	2340	6.6	18.7	43.6	27.7	3.4	138019
34434	DUNNELLON	21550	3338	26.6	38.3	28.3	4.1	2.6	38427	40927	28	24	3001	2.8	15.8	53.1	26.4	1.9	140430
34436	FLORAL CITY	20068	4286	32.3	35.4	25.7	5.1	1.5	35461	38024	19	15	3815	15.5	18.6	42.1	21.0	2.8	118019
34442	HERNANDO	25712	6101	24.5	33.0	31.6	6.9	4.0	45273	47654	49	43	5207	9.8	16.6	27.1	38.5	8.1	163954
34446	HOMOSASSA	25078	7502	22.5	32.3	35.3	7.4	2.5	46006	49120	51	46	6649	6.7	16.2	32.1	41.9	3.1	161951
34448	HOMOSASSA	19836	4728	32.5	35.6	25.7	4.0	2.2	35490	37736	19	15	3867	17.7	24.8	32.3	19.0	6.2	100431
34449	INGLIS	20168	2113	39.2	30.0	24.3	4.3	2.3	32502	34060	12	9	1772	16.9	24.1	29.2	24.1	5.8	110180
34450	INVERNESS	24719	5343	31.4	33.9	25.0	6.6	3.1	37531	40953	25	21	4353	9.6	14.6	46.5	25.3	4.0	139598
34452	INVERNESS	21379	5190	28.6	40.0	24.5	5.3	1.6	35544	37816	19	15	4343	4.1	15.6	58.1	20.9	1.2	129954
34453	INVERNESS	20997	4543	31.6	34.4	26.0	5.7	2.4	37433	40605	25	20	3807	11.0	20.6	42.6	22.2	3.6	117774
34461	LECANTO	23245	4721	22.9	29.7	35.8	7.5	4.1	47560	50292	56	49	4123	8.8	14.2	32.6	37.5	6.9	161960
34465	BEVERLY HILLS	24820	7535	30.0	35.4	26.1	5.2	3.2	37990	41627	27	22	6607	2.9	24.5	43.5	25.0	4.1	127892
34470	OCALA	22044	9464	31.3	30.8	30.9	4.9	2.1	38062	40864	27	23	6103	19.3	19.6	49.9	10.1	1.0	107409
34471	OCALA	28782	11052	22.1	27.8	30.1	10.5	9.4	50043	51371	61	57	6887	4.6	11.3	37.6	34.2	12.3	166377
34472	OCALA	19276	10022	26.2	34.4	32.8	4.2	2.4	40093	44626	33	28	7924	9.7	27.1	50.1	12.1	1.0	107968
34473	OCALA	18527	5568	24.3	37.4	32.1	4.1	2.2	40080	43498	33	28	4510	6.7	25.2	52.2	14.1	1.8	113863
34474	OCALA	26982	6276	28.0	33.4	27.4	6.9	4.3	39435	41946	31	26	4229	25.1	20.7	23.1	21.5	9.6	101060
34475	OCALA	14354	4371	44.4	30.1	21.2	2.4	1.9	29063	30395	7	4	2603	22.6	31.2	34.4	9.0	2.8	85267
34476	OCALA	26211	8117	20.5	36.0	34.7	6.1	2.7	45021	47639	48	42	7249	6.6	13.8	43.9	31.2	4.6	151660
34479	OCALA	20466	5232	25.5	32.0	34.6	5.4	2.5	43299	46164	43	38	4131	10.9	21.9	50.2	14.1	2.9	110304
34480	OCALA	25529	7012	20.1	26.9	35.1	10.9	7.0	52633	54015	67	64	5502	11.0	8.6	38.6	31.2	10.7	156789
34481	OCALA	24888	8663	25.1	37.9	31.1	4.4	1.5	39611	43143	32	26	7976	3.2	23.8	53.4	17.8	1.6	117796
34482	OCALA	20492	8015	27.2	36.5	28.7	4.3	3.3	38726	41561	29	25	5980	16.0	23.2	29.4	24.0	7.3	111968
34484	OXFORD	17718	1252	30.7	35.6	27.7	5.4	0.6	38438	40356	28	24	1050	13.0	20.1	34.4	27.3	5.2	125943
34488	SILVER SPRINGS	19321	4337	34.0	34.3	26.4	3.4	1.8	34882	36732	17	14	3547	37.5	25.9	27.5	7.4	1.8	68249
34491	SUMMERFIELD	21892	12694	27.0	36.0	29.2	5.7	2.1	39796	43082	32	27	11495	7.9	16.3	53.0	19.6	3.1	128865
34498	YANKEETOWN	23762	336	36.3	28.9	27.4	5.4	2.1	36956	38204	23	19	287	12.2	21.6	34.1	27.5	4.5	117378
34601	BROOKSVILLE	20002	9725	32.4	32.1	29.0	4.2	2.3	36455	39735	22	17	7448	28.6	21.7	28.2	18.4	3.0	89271
34602	BROOKSVILLE	20106	2739	25.0	33.2	34.2	5.4	2.2	44081	46446	46	40	2419	8.7	29.8	32.6	21.0	7.9	108346
34604	BROOKSVILLE	18836	3238	24.3	35.9	33.5	4.3	2.0	43166	46323	43	38	2718	18.4	22.8	32.5	23.5	2.8	103817
34606	SPRING HILL	23614	12748	26.7	34.6	31.1	4.9	2.7	40343	43079	34	29	10707	2.5	16.6	51.8	28.0	1.1	135108
34607	SPRING HILL	31545	3973	20.1	29.0	32.6	9.4	8.9	51015	52374	64	59	3572	5.7	9.3	27.8	49.5	7.7	196217
34608	SPRING HILL	22113	13014	24.9	33.5	34.4	5.1	2.1	42120	45653	40	34	11115	0.6	12.9	63.5	22.9	0.1	131546
34609	SPRING HILL	22878	14095	16.3	36.6	36.5	7.6	3.0	47653	50418	56	50	12554	1.5	10.1	53.2	33.4	1.8	144943
34610	SPRING HILL	16630	4626	27.9	34.6	31.2	4.8	1.4	38579	40752	28	24	3870	11.9	23.4	45.2	16.7	2.8	108374
34613	BROOKSVILLE	23415	9057	29.2	39.1	22.6	5.6	3.5	36242	38433	21	17	8241	10.5	38.1	31.8	15.3	4.3	92334
34614	BROOKSVILLE	22170	2073	27.0	29.4	32.3	5.1	6.2	42450	46310	41	35	1866	12.5	20.6	40.0	23.6	3.4	121443
	FLORIDA	27128		21.9	27.6	33.8	9.8	6.8	50413	52516				8.0	14.3	38.7	30.4	8.6	144752
	UNITED STATES	27277		20.9	24.4	35.3	11.7	7.6	54719	56938				9.3	13.1	31.6	32.6	13.5	162279

ZIP CODE #	POST OFFICE NAME	FINANCIAL SERVICES: Auto Loan	Home Loan	Invest-ments	Retire-ment Plans	THE HOME: Home Improvements: Home Repair	Lawn & Garden	Furnishings: Comput-ers & Hard-ware-Personal	Major Appli-ances	TV, Radio, Sound Equip-ment	Furni-ture	ENTERTAINMENT: Dine out/ Carry out	Sports Equip-ment	Fees & Tickets	Toys & Games	Travel	Cable TV	PERSONAL: Apparel & Services	Auto Repairs	Health Insur-ance	Pets & Supplies
34117	NAPLES	119	137	117	132	130	115	119	120	112	127	114	94	125	119	121	107	81	113	105	136
34119	NAPLES	175	189	242	188	212	214	168	195	175	188	172	126	186	161	193	181	119	185	211	221
34120	NAPLES	123	137	113	132	129	115	121	121	114	129	117	96	125	121	122	109	82	116	108	138
34134	BONITA SPRINGS	170	177	241	173	203	211	160	191	169	179	166	120	174	152	185	178	113	181	213	215
34135	BONITA SPRINGS	129	129	157	124	141	143	122	137	126	132	125	92	125	118	133	129	86	133	146	156
34140	GOODLAND	118	125	170	124	144	147	112	133	119	127	116	83	123	107	130	124	80	127	148	150
34141	OCHOPEE	84	81	103	74	90	96	77	91	81	83	79	59	76	74	84	86	53	87	101	104
34142	IMMOKALEE	58	47	42	44	46	40	57	52	55	59	58	41	51	57	52	52	42	57	46	58
34145	MARCO ISLAND	155	161	222	157	186	195	146	176	155	163	152	110	159	139	170	163	103	167	198	198
34201	BRADENTON	143	151	204	149	173	178	135	160	143	153	140	100	149	128	156	149	96	152	178	181
34202	BRADENTON	195	225	236	227	234	215	192	208	188	216	188	154	215	188	211	183	134	194	198	234
34203	BRADENTON	86	88	97	86	93	96	84	91	87	89	87	63	88	83	90	90	60	90	99	104
34205	BRADENTON	65	61	62	61	61	66	66	65	69	64	68	48	64	67	64	72	47	68	73	77
34207	BRADENTON	60	57	66	54	61	66	58	63	61	60	60	43	58	58	61	64	41	63	72	73
34208	BRADENTON	79	71	71	70	71	74	78	76	79	77	79	58	74	78	74	80	55	79	79	90
34209	BRADENTON	96	107	122	102	116	118	97	109	100	105	99	72	107	93	110	104	68	105	122	123
34210	BRADENTON	85	81	92	79	86	89	85	87	87	89	86	61	85	83	88	89	59	89	97	101
34211	BRADENTON	137	146	170	143	157	153	130	146	132	146	132	99	140	127	143	134	91	138	151	165
34212	BRADENTON	132	128	158	128	132	137	117	135	116	119	116	104	115	116	125	116	80	124	124	154
34215	CORTEZ	93	98	132	97	112	115	88	104	93	99	91	65	96	83	101	97	62	99	115	117
34217	BRADENTON BEACH	96	93	133	92	106	114	86	105	91	93	90	69	89	83	98	96	61	99	112	119
34219	PARRISH	114	107	139	105	116	127	101	120	105	104	104	84	99	100	111	110	70	113	125	138
34221	PALMETTO	79	76	84	72	78	84	74	81	78	76	77	57	73	75	76	81	52	79	87	94
34222	ELLENTON	61	67	85	60	77	81	61	73	65	68	63	44	68	57	72	70	43	70	89	81
34223	ENGLEWOOD	84	88	115	83	102	107	81	97	86	91	84	59	88	77	94	92	57	92	114	108
34224	ENGLEWOOD	76	78	100	72	89	95	73	87	78	80	75	54	77	70	83	83	51	83	101	97
34228	LONGBOAT KEY	223	239	323	233	277	285	214	255	227	244	222	156	239	202	251	239	152	243	291	286
34229	OSPREY	159	176	211	176	193	197	156	178	162	170	161	117	174	151	178	169	111	170	196	202
34231	SARASOTA	100	99	114	98	106	112	99	106	103	102	102	73	101	97	104	107	70	105	119	122
34232	SARASOTA	93	105	102	104	106	104	98	100	98	100	98	74	105	97	103	99	69	99	104	115
34233	SARASOTA	103	107	122	105	114	119	100	111	104	105	103	75	105	98	108	108	71	107	121	127
34234	SARASOTA	69	62	62	62	62	67	67	66	70	68	69	49	64	68	64	72	48	69	73	79
34235	SARASOTA	102	121	128	117	127	129	106	117	110	113	109	79	121	104	121	114	75	113	131	132
34236	SARASOTA	101	98	116	98	106	110	104	106	108	107	108	74	106	100	108	112	75	110	122	123
34237	SARASOTA	68	60	60	62	60	63	70	64	70	68	70	50	66	69	66	71	49	69	70	78
34238	SARASOTA	134	142	185	141	161	166	131	150	139	144	136	96	143	125	149	146	94	145	171	171
34239	SARASOTA	93	98	104	98	102	102	96	99	97	97	96	73	100	94	101	98	67	98	105	115
34240	SARASOTA	162	205	218	211	215	194	174	185	166	188	167	138	202	164	199	162	121	174	173	210
34241	SARASOTA	147	165	183	164	174	168	144	158	145	158	145	110	158	140	160	146	101	151	161	181
34242	SARASOTA	174	194	254	194	221	213	174	198	176	195	174	131	194	161	201	179	122	189	208	223
34243	SARASOTA	109	119	129	119	124	124	109	116	110	115	110	82	118	107	118	112	77	114	122	134
34251	MYAKKA CITY	125	138	114	136	130	120	122	123	116	129	118	97	127	123	123	112	83	117	112	142
34266	ARCADIA	74	62	72	60	64	75	64	71	68	64	67	52	58	67	63	72	45	70	77	85
34269	ARCADIA	85	81	103	74	89	97	77	91	82	83	79	60	76	75	84	86	53	87	101	104
34275	NOKOMIS	118	118	158	113	134	142	109	130	116	119	113	83	114	105	123	122	77	124	145	147
34285	VENICE	73	86	111	78	102	107	76	94	83	88	80	52	90	71	94	90	54	89	119	101
34286	NORTH PORT	111	121	98	116	113	99	107	106	100	115	103	84	109	108	105	95	72	100	93	120
34287	NORTH PORT	67	72	81	68	78	84	66	76	71	69	70	50	71	66	74	76	47	74	90	86
34288	NORTH PORT	108	118	94	113	110	96	104	103	97	113	100	82	106	106	102	92	70	97	89	117
34289	NORTH PORT	109	118	95	113	110	96	104	104	98	113	100	82	106	106	102	92	70	98	89	117
34291	NORTH PORT	97	102	92	100	99	98	94	97	94	97	94	74	96	96	95	94	65	94	96	112
34292	VENICE	106	121	159	114	141	146	106	129	114	122	111	76	123	100	129	121	75	122	154	142
34293	VENICE	80	89	104	82	99	106	80	95	87	87	84	59	89	79	93	93	57	91	114	105
34420	BELLEVIEW	72	62	77	59	66	77	62	73	67	63	65	51	57	64	64	71	44	69	79	84
34428	CRYSTAL RIVER	86	75	101	73	82	94	73	88	79	74	77	61	69	75	78	84	52	83	94	102
34429	CRYSTAL RIVER	88	85	116	81	96	104	80	96	85	86	83	62	81	77	90	89	56	91	106	109
34431	DUNNELLON	71	66	87	61	73	80	63	75	67	67	65	50	62	61	69	71	44	72	83	86
34432	DUNNELLON	75	75	98	71	85	93	69	84	74	76	73	53	73	68	79	80	49	79	96	94
34433	DUNNELLON	75	68	88	63	74	84	65	78	70	69	68	53	62	65	70	74	46	74	86	90
34434	DUNNELLON	73	68	88	63	75	82	65	77	69	70	67	51	63	64	70	73	45	74	85	88
34436	FLORAL CITY	67	63	81	58	70	76	60	71	64	65	62	47	59	58	65	67	42	68	79	81
34442	HERNANDO	82	79	105	76	89	96	74	88	79	81	77	57	76	72	83	84	52	84	98	101
34446	HOMOSASSA	75	75	98	68	86	94	70	86	76	77	74	53	74	68	81	82	49	82	101	96
34448	HOMOSASSA	67	61	80	57	67	75	58	70	62	62	61	47	56	58	63	66	41	66	77	81
34449	INGLIS	65	62	79	57	68	74	59	69	62	63	61	45	58	57	64	66	41	67	77	79
34450	INVERNESS	74	72	91	67	80	85	68	80	72	74	70	53	68	66	75	76	47	77	89	92
34452	INVERNESS	68	66	85	60	74	80	62	74	66	68	65	48	62	60	69	71	43	71	84	85
34453	INVERNESS	71	66	87	62	73	81	63	75	67	67	66	50	61	62	68	71	44	72	83	86
34461	LECANTO	87	80	108	77	89	99	76	92	81	81	80	61	75	76	83	87	54	87	100	105
34465	BEVERLY HILLS	69	71	94	66	82	89	65	80	71	72	68	49	71	63	76	76	46	76	95	89
34470	OCALA	67	64	67	63	66	72	66	69	69	65	68	50	65	67	67	73	47	69	77	81
34471	OCALA	104	99	100	101	100	105	102	103	104	101	103	78	100	103	101	106	72	104	108	121
34472	OCALA	72	70	69	67	70	74	67	72	69	69	69	51	65	69	67	71	47	70	75	84
34473	OCALA	71	69	81	64	75	80	65	75	68	70	67	49	65	64	70	72	45	72	84	86
34474	OCALA	80	77	91	73	83	87	76	83	79	80	78	58	76	74	80	82	53	82	91	97
34475	OCALA	60	50	48	50	49	57	55	55	59	54	58	41	51	59	51	62	40	57	61	67
34476	OCALA	73	79	103	74	92	96	71	86	76	81	74	51	79	68	84	81	50	82	102	95
34479	OCALA	82	75	73	74	75	83	73	80	76	71	75	59	68	77	72	79	51	76	82	94
34480	OCALA	105	94	100	94	95	109	95	104	99	92	97	77	89	99	94	103	67	100	109	122
34481	OCALA	60	68	90	60	81	87	60	76	66	69	64	43	70	57	75	72	42	72	97	82
34482	OCALA	77	70	87	67	75	83	68	79	72	71	71	54	66	69	72	76	48	76	84	91
34484	OXFORD	76	61	73	59	62	76	60	71	65	59	64	53	52	66	59	70	43	67	73	85
34488	SILVER SPRINGS	66	61	75	57	66	73	58	68	62	62	61	46	56	58	62	65	41	65	74	79
34491	SUMMERFIELD	78	71	88	67	77	86	69	81	73	73	71	55	66	69	73	77	48	77	88	93
34498	YANKEETOWN	69	66	84	61	73	79	63	74	66	68	65	49	62	61	69	70	44	71	83	85
34601	BROOKSVILLE	73	62	79	60	66	77	64	73	68	63	67	52	59	65	65	73	45	71	79	85
34602	BROOKSVILLE	88	68	92	66	72	90	69	84	75	67	73	61	59	74	69	81	49	78	87	99
34604	BROOKSVILLE	78	70	82	69	72	80	68	77	70	68	70	56	64	70	69	73	48	73	78	90
34606	SPRING HILL	72	71	90	65	80	86	67	81	73	72	71	51	69	66	76	78	47	77	95	91
34607	SPRING HILL	100	101	139	99	116	121	92	110	98	102	96	70	99	88	106	102	65	105	121	125
34608	SPRING HILL	76	72	89	67	79	86	69	81	74	73	72	54	68	68	74	78	48	78	90	93
34609	SPRING HILL	79	84	95	82	90	96	76	87	81	80	80	58	82	77	85	86	55	84	98	99
34610	SPRING HILL	74	67	67	65	67	73	64	70	67	67	67	51	60	68	63	70	45	68	72	83
34613	BROOKSVILLE	64	71	91	63	83	87	64	78	69	73	67	45	72	60	77	74	45	74	97	85
34614	BROOKSVILLE	86	82	97	76	89	94	79	90	83	85	81	60	78	78	84	86	55	87	98	103
	FLORIDA	96	94	97	93	96	98	95	97	96	97	96	71	95	94	96	97	67	97	101	113
	UNITED STATES	100	100	100	100	100	100	100	100	100	100	100	100	100	100	100	100	100	100	100	100

POPULATION CHANGE

ZIP CODE #	POST OFFICE NAME	COUNTY FIPS CODE	POPULATION 2000	POPULATION 2009	POPULATION 2014	2000-2009 ANNUAL RATE % Rate	2000-2009 ANNUAL RATE State Centile	HOUSEHOLDS 2000	HOUSEHOLDS 2009	HOUSEHOLDS 2014	HOUSEHOLDS % Annual Rate 2000-2009	HOUSEHOLDS 2009 Average HH Size	FAMILIES 2000	FAMILIES 2009	FAMILIES % Annual Rate 2000-2009
34637	LAND O LAKES	101	369	5547	7412	34.0	100	147	2078	2781	33.2	2.67	108	1489	32.8
34638	LAND O LAKES	101	3528	17325	23259	18.8	99	1334	6602	8896	18.9	2.60	958	4566	18.4
34639	LAND O LAKES	101	13803	26912	33740	7.5	93	4830	9278	11658	7.3	2.90	3895	7271	7.0
34652	NEW PORT RICHEY	101	24331	25579	26534	0.5	26	11612	12098	12596	0.4	2.08	6737	6578	-0.3
34653	NEW PORT RICHEY	101	30750	33445	35043	0.9	38	13572	14560	15317	0.8	2.21	8510	8645	0.2
34654	NEW PORT RICHEY	101	16374	20760	23548	2.6	73	6446	8132	9282	2.5	2.54	4700	5714	2.1
34655	NEW PORT RICHEY	101	24423	38233	45151	5.0	88	10473	16121	19038	4.8	2.37	7745	11525	4.4
34667	HUDSON	101	30104	34668	37507	1.5	53	13889	15625	16878	1.3	2.17	9068	9752	0.8
34668	PORT RICHEY	101	42435	44188	45699	0.4	22	19792	20333	21067	0.3	2.15	12071	11680	-0.4
34669	HUDSON	101	10556	12933	14421	2.2	66	4113	4998	5592	2.1	2.57	3012	3516	1.7
34677	OLDSMAR	103	20044	21440	21556	0.7	32	8066	8576	8611	0.7	2.49	5658	5876	0.4
34683	PALM HARBOR	103	34688	35526	35304	0.3	18	14113	14515	14460	0.3	2.44	9765	9816	0.1
34684	PALM HARBOR	103	26593	26301	25885	-0.1	6	12253	12023	11817	-0.2	2.10	7606	7271	-0.5
34685	PALM HARBOR	103	17037	18829	19075	1.1	44	6673	7194	7253	0.8	2.62	5233	5567	0.7
34688	TARPON SPRINGS	103	5367	6455	6653	2.0	62	2105	2522	2601	2.0	2.54	1637	1940	1.9
34689	TARPON SPRINGS	103	23485	25360	25590	0.8	35	10207	10928	11012	0.7	2.28	6649	6968	0.5
34690	HOLIDAY	101	12799	14940	16308	1.7	57	5914	6822	7475	1.6	2.15	3570	3867	0.9
34691	HOLIDAY	101	18915	20518	21648	0.9	38	8885	9490	10014	0.7	2.16	5423	5466	0.1
34695	SAFETY HARBOR	103	18164	18159	17924	0.0	9	7553	7542	7448	0.0	2.35	5098	4981	-0.3
34698	DUNEDIN	103	36880	37038	36577	0.0	9	17587	17723	17538	0.1	2.03	9962	9735	-0.2
34705	ASTATULA	069	2173	2633	3001	2.1	64	831	954	1082	1.5	2.76	631	702	1.2
34711	CLERMONT	069	23220	51922	66457	9.1	95	8953	19803	25434	9.0	2.60	6685	14611	8.8
34714	CLERMONT	069	6301	14391	18711	9.3	96	2492	5758	7529	9.5	2.50	1925	4311	9.1
34715	CLERMONT	069	9008	14912	18826	5.6	90	2860	4910	6238	6.0	2.98	2255	3768	5.7
34731	FRUITLAND PARK	069	9785	11590	12720	1.8	59	4129	4922	5424	1.9	2.35	3013	3468	1.5
34734	GOTHA	095	3732	4330	4886	1.6	55	1349	1561	1769	1.6	2.71	896	1019	1.4
34736	GROVELAND	069	8364	12348	14865	4.3	86	3079	4668	5705	4.6	2.52	2384	3490	4.2
34737	HOWEY IN THE HILLS	069	1939	2789	3364	4.0	85	731	1117	1354	4.7	2.50	570	839	4.3
34739	KENANSVILLE	097	817	975	1071	1.9	61	323	392	432	2.1	2.48	238	280	1.8
34741	KISSIMMEE	097	35274	46687	53476	3.1	79	13246	17563	20090	3.1	2.63	8483	10921	2.8
34743	KISSIMMEE	097	26358	37374	43736	3.8	84	8229	11760	13774	3.9	3.18	6826	9564	3.7
34744	KISSIMMEE	097	28653	41768	49333	4.2	86	9660	14770	17658	4.7	2.74	7480	11044	4.3
34746	KISSIMMEE	097	18008	33121	41355	6.8	92	6947	12309	15204	6.4	2.68	4789	8504	6.4
34747	KISSIMMEE	097	5227	15986	21322	12.8	98	1869	5678	7560	12.8	2.81	1387	3920	11.9
34748	LEESBURG	069	30212	40751	46819	3.3	81	13766	18731	21711	3.4	2.14	9283	12411	3.2
34753	MASCOTTE	069	2725	5179	6353	7.2	93	820	1605	1984	7.5	3.22	655	1247	7.2
34756	MONTVERDE	069	2420	2775	3012	1.5	53	916	1061	1158	1.6	2.60	738	833	1.3
34758	KISSIMMEE	097	13505	31340	41204	9.5	96	4374	10141	13339	9.5	3.09	3622	8196	9.2
34759	KISSIMMEE	105	7464	29476	38717	16.0	98	2521	10301	13516	16.4	2.86	2008	7883	15.9
34761	OCOEE	095	26248	34546	38273	3.0	78	8798	11699	13006	3.1	2.94	7151	9182	2.7
34762	OKAHUMPKA	069	822	937	1082	1.4	51	381	436	505	1.5	2.15	279	304	0.9
34769	SAINT CLOUD	097	18428	24640	29052	3.2	80	7219	9846	11637	3.4	2.46	5074	6725	3.1
34771	SAINT CLOUD	097	9864	16369	20098	5.6	90	3615	6076	7474	5.8	2.69	2830	4649	5.5
34772	SAINT CLOUD	097	11033	20481	25669	6.9	92	3766	7103	8920	7.1	2.87	2961	5466	6.9
34773	SAINT CLOUD	097	1657	2553	3262	5.2	89	554	909	1121	5.5	2.91	420	665	5.1
34785	WILDWOOD	119	15374	21229	23832	3.6	83	4764	5799	6974	2.1	2.26	3226	3793	1.8
34786	WINDERMERE	095	9189	20548	24722	9.1	95	3050	7003	8440	9.4	2.93	2604	5723	8.9
34787	WINTER GARDEN	095	22219	43983	53384	7.7	94	8147	16044	19538	7.6	2.70	5747	11673	8.0
34788	LEESBURG	069	15639	18359	20105	1.7	57	7482	8802	9677	1.8	2.09	5063	5716	1.3
34797	YALAHA	069	974	1124	1358	1.6	55	442	553	672	2.5	2.03	343	413	2.0
34945	FORT PIERCE	111	4087	4288	4709	0.5	26	1285	1397	1563	0.9	2.66	948	986	0.4
34946	FORT PIERCE	111	6600	7288	7769	1.1	44	2527	2842	3061	1.3	2.55	1721	1832	0.7
34947	FORT PIERCE	111	10299	12366	13384	2.0	62	3303	4035	4406	2.2	2.96	2429	2829	1.7
34949	FORT PIERCE	111	6601	8677	9926	3.0	78	3531	4700	5395	3.1	1.84	2140	2701	2.5
34950	FORT PIERCE	111	18018	18815	19457	0.5	26	6424	6645	6879	0.4	2.79	3899	3789	-0.3
34951	FORT PIERCE	111	12940	15873	17335	2.2	66	5845	7314	8040	2.5	2.16	4125	4924	1.9
34952	PORT SAINT LUCIE	111	31008	38586	43206	2.4	70	13668	17117	19228	2.5	2.22	8952	10636	1.9
34953	PORT SAINT LUCIE	111	25714	57732	76123	9.1	95	8912	20366	26978	9.3	2.83	7131	15749	8.9
34956	INDIANTOWN	085	9168	10126	10454	1.1	44	2300	2519	2619	1.0	3.45	1776	1904	0.8
34957	JENSEN BEACH	085	19050	22972	24408	2.0	62	9447	11257	11986	1.9	2.04	5704	6532	1.5
34972	OKEECHOBEE	093	17813	20218	21484	1.4	51	5250	6009	6455	1.5	2.97	3908	4402	1.3
34974	OKEECHOBEE	043	21744	24618	26222	1.4	51	8954	10219	10918	1.4	2.40	6214	6938	1.2
34981	FORT PIERCE	111	3684	5252	6251	3.9	84	1324	1860	2220	3.7	2.75	929	1249	3.3
34982	FORT PIERCE	111	23110	25567	27450	1.1	44	9345	10372	11164	1.1	2.44	6307	6656	0.6
34983	PORT SAINT LUCIE	111	26851	37637	43138	3.7	83	10119	14514	16750	4.0	2.57	7676	10531	3.5
34984	PORT SAINT LUCIE	111	9739	13341	15165	3.5	82	3574	4978	5683	3.6	2.68	2860	3855	3.3
34986	PORT SAINT LUCIE	111	6114	24939	33960	16.4	99	2927	11401	15593	15.8	2.19	2306	8679	15.4
34987	PORT SAINT LUCIE	111	1122	6172	8180	20.2	99	378	2421	3234	22.2	2.55	310	1861	21.4
34988	PORT SAINT LUCIE	111	70	96	107	3.5	82	25	37	41	4.3	2.59	21	30	3.9
34990	PALM CITY	085	23737	27210	28642	1.5	53	9897	11285	11901	1.4	2.39	7476	8349	1.2
34994	STUART	085	14764	15129	15568	0.3	18	7058	7243	7484	0.3	1.96	3679	3627	-0.2
34996	STUART	085	10976	11439	11607	0.4	22	5500	5681	5767	0.4	1.98	3209	3207	0.0
34997	STUART	085	31965	36941	38986	1.6	55	13973	16132	17099	1.6	2.27	9510	10724	1.3
	FLORIDA					1.9					1.9	2.47			1.7
	UNITED STATES					1.0					1.1	2.59			0.9

# ZIP CODE	POST OFFICE NAME	RACE (%) White 2000	White 2009	Black 2000	Black 2009	Asian/Pacific 2000	Asian/Pacific 2009	% Hispanic Origin 2000	% Hispanic Origin 2009	2009 AGE DISTRIBUTION (%) 0-4	5-9	10-14	15-19	20-24	25-44	45-64	65-84	85+	18+	MEDIAN AGE 2009	% 2009 Males	% 2009 Females
34637	LAND O LAKES	95.7	94.4	0.8	0.3	0.3	0.2	6.5	8.0	6.5	6.6	7.0	7.2	5.6	26.2	29.8	10.1	1.0	75.4	38.8	50.2	49.8
34638	LAND O LAKES	95.5	93.6	1.1	2.1	0.7	1.3	4.5	7.7	6.3	6.4	6.6	6.7	5.1	24.7	28.4	14.2	1.7	76.2	40.9	49.4	50.6
34639	LAND O LAKES	93.9	91.9	1.8	2.3	1.2	1.5	9.1	13.6	7.1	6.9	7.1	7.1	5.8	28.6	28.4	8.1	0.8	74.5	36.3	48.9	51.1
34652	NEW PORT RICHEY	95.4	93.7	0.7	0.9	1.0	1.3	4.1	6.5	4.4	4.3	4.3	4.4	4.2	18.8	29.2	24.7	5.6	84.3	52.4	47.6	52.4
34653	NEW PORT RICHEY	95.0	93.2	1.0	1.3	1.1	1.4	4.7	7.5	5.3	5.0	5.0	5.1	4.9	20.9	26.3	21.3	6.2	81.4	47.7	46.6	53.4
34654	NEW PORT RICHEY	96.7	95.6	0.6	0.8	0.8	1.1	2.5	4.1	5.2	5.2	5.5	6.0	5.4	20.3	31.4	18.1	2.9	80.1	46.5	49.4	50.6
34655	NEW PORT RICHEY	96.4	95.1	0.9	1.1	1.1	1.4	3.1	5.2	4.9	5.2	5.7	5.6	4.1	18.4	30.9	21.6	3.6	80.6	48.8	48.0	52.0
34667	HUDSON	96.7	95.5	0.5	0.6	0.8	1.1	2.8	4.6	3.6	3.8	3.9	4.1	3.7	15.7	29.8	29.5	6.1	86.2	56.6	48.1	51.9
34668	PORT RICHEY	95.5	93.8	1.1	1.4	0.9	1.1	4.9	7.7	4.7	4.6	4.5	4.6	4.2	18.9	26.7	25.2	6.6	83.4	51.8	46.8	53.2
34669	HUDSON	96.8	95.8	0.5	0.7	0.5	0.7	2.6	4.2	5.0	5.1	5.3	5.6	4.7	20.5	32.4	19.2	2.2	81.0	47.6	49.8	50.2
34677	OLDSMAR	91.6	87.6	2.5	3.9	2.6	4.0	6.0	9.6	5.8	6.0	6.4	6.3	5.3	25.8	28.6	13.7	2.1	77.9	41.5	47.8	52.2
34683	PALM HARBOR	96.2	94.4	0.8	1.3	1.1	1.7	3.4	5.7	4.6	5.2	6.2	6.3	4.6	23.7	32.3	14.6	2.5	79.8	44.6	48.0	52.0
34684	PALM HARBOR	95.4	93.0	1.1	1.8	1.5	2.3	3.5	5.8	4.1	4.0	4.3	4.4	3.7	18.6	27.8	24.6	8.4	84.8	52.7	45.2	54.8
34685	PALM HARBOR	94.9	92.2	1.1	1.7	2.4	3.6	3.7	6.0	5.3	6.2	7.2	7.5	4.5	19.1	34.1	14.2	2.0	76.6	45.1	48.7	51.3
34688	TARPON SPRINGS	95.1	92.5	1.0	1.6	2.4	3.7	3.2	5.3	4.5	5.0	5.6	6.4	4.6	17.0	34.8	19.6	2.4	80.8	49.0	47.8	52.2
34689	TARPON SPRINGS	90.3	87.2	5.9	7.4	1.1	1.7	4.2	6.7	5.0	5.0	5.2	5.0	4.4	19.6	30.9	21.4	3.7	82.0	49.0	48.0	52.0
34690	HOLIDAY	95.8	94.3	0.8	1.1	0.9	1.1	4.4	6.9	5.1	5.1	4.9	4.5	3.6	19.5	26.7	24.3	6.3	82.1	50.7	46.9	53.1
34691	HOLIDAY	94.8	92.8	1.6	2.2	1.0	1.3	3.7	5.8	4.7	4.6	4.5	4.6	3.9	19.4	26.6	26.3	5.5	83.3	51.6	47.0	53.0
34695	SAFETY HARBOR	92.2	88.5	4.2	6.4	1.6	2.4	3.5	5.7	4.5	4.9	5.6	5.9	4.9	19.6	34.5	16.4	3.8	81.1	47.5	47.7	52.3
34698	DUNEDIN	94.9	92.5	2.0	3.1	1.1	1.7	3.3	5.4	3.7	3.6	4.0	4.4	4.3	19.6	29.7	23.7	7.0	85.9	52.2	45.6	54.4
34705	ASTATULA	88.1	83.6	1.1	1.7	0.2	0.3	14.3	20.1	5.7	6.2	6.8	6.5	4.1	22.4	31.8	14.7	1.9	77.3	43.9	48.9	51.1
34711	CLERMONT	86.4	83.0	7.7	8.6	1.3	1.8	9.0	13.6	7.7	7.2	6.9	6.1	5.0	29.6	25.9	10.4	1.3	74.5	37.2	49.1	50.9
34714	CLERMONT	91.0	86.8	2.5	3.9	1.3	1.7	9.9	14.9	6.9	6.8	6.7	5.6	3.9	28.2	28.1	12.6	1.1	76.0	39.9	49.1	50.9
34715	CLERMONT	88.1	84.0	5.6	7.2	1.3	1.8	9.7	14.2	7.8	7.6	7.3	6.5	5.1	30.2	25.5	9.0	1.0	73.2	36.0	49.9	50.1
34731	FRUITLAND PARK	91.8	87.5	5.3	8.7	1.0	1.3	2.1	3.1	4.8	4.8	5.1	5.5	4.8	19.2	29.2	23.4	3.1	81.9	49.2	48.5	51.5
34734	GOTHA	80.3	73.0	9.8	13.0	2.9	4.4	13.2	19.7	7.7	7.0	6.6	6.7	8.3	31.8	23.6	6.8	1.7	74.9	33.6	48.0	52.0
34736	GROVELAND	84.1	78.9	8.5	11.9	0.5	0.7	11.1	14.3	5.2	5.2	5.4	5.5	4.8	23.2	28.4	20.4	2.0	81.0	45.5	52.5	47.5
34737	HOWEY IN THE HILLS	93.9	91.4	2.8	4.0	0.8	1.2	4.0	6.0	4.2	4.5	4.9	4.9	3.6	16.9	30.5	27.3	3.1	83.2	52.5	48.4	51.6
34739	KENANSVILLE	95.0	91.9	0.1	0.3	0.1	0.2	8.4	15.4	4.2	4.7	5.1	6.9	6.8	23.4	28.3	19.3	1.3	81.4	44.2	52.9	47.1
34741	KISSIMMEE	69.1	60.9	8.3	8.9	3.6	4.6	40.0	54.9	8.5	6.7	5.8	7.1	12.1	32.7	19.3	6.8	1.0	75.1	29.1	49.8	50.2
34743	KISSIMMEE	61.8	56.8	11.2	10.6	2.7	2.9	57.8	70.5	7.4	7.8	7.6	7.9	7.2	28.7	23.4	9.0	1.0	72.4	32.9	48.6	51.4
34744	KISSIMMEE	77.3	72.4	9.7	9.4	1.9	2.5	24.6	36.2	6.3	6.5	6.8	7.1	6.4	27.5	27.7	10.5	1.2	76.1	37.5	50.0	50.0
34746	KISSIMMEE	84.1	76.9	3.1	4.6	3.5	4.4	20.6	33.2	6.3	6.3	6.5	6.3	5.3	26.0	28.1	12.8	2.4	77.1	40.4	49.3	50.7
34747	KISSIMMEE	88.0	85.1	2.9	3.4	4.2	5.3	11.6	18.0	6.0	5.9	6.3	6.4	5.2	26.7	31.6	10.6	1.4	77.2	40.8	49.2	50.8
34748	LEESBURG	78.4	75.0	18.3	20.8	1.0	1.2	3.3	4.5	4.6	4.5	4.4	4.7	4.1	16.4	23.9	32.0	5.6	83.8	55.6	46.8	53.2
34753	MASCOTTE	70.2	67.1	8.1	10.1	0.3	0.4	33.4	35.8	8.1	7.9	7.3	7.5	6.6	25.8	22.5	13.1	1.1	71.8	34.3	52.5	47.5
34756	MONTVERDE	94.7	91.8	0.9	1.5	0.6	0.8	5.5	8.7	5.3	6.1	6.8	6.7	4.4	23.3	34.1	12.0	1.3	77.5	43.3	49.6	50.4
34758	KISSIMMEE	68.1	61.7	15.9	16.9	1.2	1.5	34.7	48.7	7.9	7.8	7.6	8.1	7.3	25.8	24.0	10.3	1.2	71.8	33.2	49.5	50.5
34759	KISSIMMEE	69.5	64.6	13.9	15.2	1.2	1.2	37.2	45.5	8.5	8.2	7.7	7.4	6.3	28.1	23.1	9.6	1.1	71.0	33.1	49.6	50.4
34761	OCOEE	81.4	73.8	6.6	9.3	2.7	3.9	15.0	21.8	8.0	8.0	7.8	7.1	5.8	29.3	25.8	7.2	0.9	71.9	34.6	49.5	50.5
34762	OKAHUMPKA	87.6	82.1	9.9	14.7	0.2	0.3	1.6	2.1	4.2	3.9	3.8	3.4	3.1	12.8	26.8	37.7	4.3	85.9	60.6	47.0	53.0
34769	SAINT CLOUD	92.2	87.7	1.9	2.8	0.9	1.5	10.0	17.5	6.4	6.1	6.1	6.3	5.9	24.9	26.8	14.8	2.6	77.5	40.8	48.5	51.5
34771	SAINT CLOUD	95.2	92.6	1.5	2.2	0.7	1.2	5.4	10.1	6.0	6.3	6.7	6.7	4.9	24.3	32.2	11.9	1.1	76.8	41.8	50.1	49.9
34772	SAINT CLOUD	90.8	84.9	2.7	3.9	0.9	1.4	12.6	23.4	7.5	7.0	7.1	7.1	6.2	27.0	25.8	10.7	1.5	73.9	36.4	48.5	51.5
34773	SAINT CLOUD	94.0	90.2	0.8	1.2	0.1	0.2	6.3	12.1	6.0	5.6	5.6	7.4	8.9	27.4	27.8	10.4	0.9	78.5	36.8	51.1	48.9
34785	WILDWOOD	69.5	59.4	25.8	33.8	0.4	0.5	12.5	20.8	3.1	3.3	3.2	3.6	5.3	35.2	26.5	17.0	2.7	88.3	42.6	62.7	37.3
34786	WINDERMERE	90.1	85.0	2.9	4.2	4.3	6.4	5.1	9.6	6.7	7.6	8.4	7.1	3.6	22.6	32.1	10.8	1.1	72.7	41.4	49.5	50.5
34787	WINTER GARDEN	76.1	69.1	15.2	20.1	1.0	1.6	14.6	18.1	7.1	7.1	7.2	6.8	5.4	26.3	27.6	10.7	1.8	74.4	38.4	49.2	50.8
34788	LEESBURG	95.1	92.8	2.3	3.5	1.0	1.4	2.2	3.3	3.1	3.2	3.3	3.4	2.8	12.8	27.3	39.0	5.1	88.3	61.9	47.4	52.6
34797	YALAHA	91.8	88.3	4.9	7.2	0.6	0.9	3.5	5.2	3.0	3.2	3.5	3.7	3.0	13.1	27.8	39.2	3.4	87.8	60.6	48.4	51.6
34945	FORT PIERCE	86.9	76.4	9.5	17.4	0.5	0.6	6.3	11.3	3.1	3.2	3.4	4.7	6.2	22.2	28.4	25.9	3.0	88.0	50.9	54.5	45.5
34946	FORT PIERCE	44.8	36.5	51.6	59.3	0.3	0.4	3.6	4.7	5.8	6.4	7.0	7.3	6.2	20.6	28.4	16.1	2.1	76.1	42.0	48.4	51.6
34947	FORT PIERCE	30.1	26.7	61.8	64.0	0.7	0.8	11.5	14.4	8.7	8.5	7.8	9.0	8.3	24.8	22.4	9.0	1.5	69.9	30.1	48.9	51.1
34949	FORT PIERCE	97.6	96.1	0.7	1.4	0.8	1.1	2.2	4.2	1.7	1.8	2.0	2.1	2.2	11.6	30.1	42.4	6.1	93.4	64.2	47.4	52.6
34950	FORT PIERCE	32.4	24.6	55.9	61.3	0.5	0.5	18.3	22.4	8.4	7.7	7.1	7.6	8.3	25.9	22.7	10.3	2.0	72.3	32.5	50.4	49.6
34951	FORT PIERCE	92.5	87.5	4.7	8.2	0.7	0.8	2.9	5.4	4.5	4.6	4.8	4.8	3.9	17.6	27.6	27.1	5.0	83.1	52.2	48.2	51.8
34952	PORT SAINT LUCIE	88.1	79.9	6.8	12.4	1.3	1.6	7.4	12.6	4.8	4.6	4.6	5.0	5.1	18.5	26.5	25.4	5.6	83.0	50.9	46.9	53.1
34953	PORT SAINT LUCIE	88.1	80.2	7.0	12.5	1.2	1.7	7.2	12.2	6.3	6.6	6.9	6.8	4.7	24.9	29.0	13.2	1.5	75.9	41.1	48.7	51.3
34956	INDIANTOWN	50.6	41.5	21.9	23.3	0.8	0.9	40.6	50.4	8.2	7.3	6.4	7.2	8.5	32.3	18.7	10.2	1.2	73.9	32.1	60.1	39.9
34957	JENSEN BEACH	96.4	93.4	1.8	3.6	0.4	0.7	2.5	5.1	3.4	3.7	4.0	4.3	3.5	15.6	31.7	28.9	4.9	86.1	55.4	48.4	51.6
34972	OKEECHOBEE	68.8	61.7	14.3	15.7	0.3	0.4	25.6	35.2	7.1	7.0	6.9	9.1	7.2	29.8	22.3	9.3	1.3	73.4	33.0	56.7	43.3
34974	OKEECHOBEE	88.1	83.3	1.7	2.2	1.0	1.4	10.6	17.3	6.0	5.6	5.4	5.4	5.2	21.0	26.9	22.0	2.6	79.9	46.2	50.5	49.5
34981	FORT PIERCE	82.8	74.5	11.1	17.1	1.4	1.8	11.7	17.2	6.4	6.4	6.7	7.9	6.8	25.7	26.8	11.4	1.9	76.6	37.5	50.0	50.0
34982	FORT PIERCE	85.5	76.6	7.9	13.5	1.2	1.4	10.8	17.0	6.0	5.6	5.6	5.8	5.5	21.8	25.8	20.6	3.2	79.2	44.7	48.3	51.7
34983	PORT SAINT LUCIE	89.1	80.9	6.1	11.7	1.1	1.5	6.8	11.8	5.4	5.5	6.0	6.6	5.4	22.9	30.3	15.1	2.9	78.9	43.7	48.4	51.6
34984	PORT SAINT LUCIE	90.4	82.6	5.9	11.5	1.0	1.3	7.0	12.6	5.2	5.6	6.3	6.1	4.1	21.7	31.7	17.6	1.8	79.0	45.6	48.9	51.1
34986	PORT SAINT LUCIE	90.9	83.8	4.7	9.4	1.7	2.3	5.9	10.6	4.8	5.2	5.9	5.8	3.5	19.9	31.6	20.6	2.7	80.4	47.9	47.4	52.6
34987	PORT SAINT LUCIE	92.5	84.4	2.4	8.4	0.9	2.0	10.1	12.3	5.0	5.4	6.0	5.8	3.7	20.7	31.9	19.1	2.4	80.0	47.0	48.2	51.8
34988	PORT SAINT LUCIE	94.2	87.5	1.4	2.1	0.0	1.0	13.0	22.9	5.2	5.2	7.3	5.2	4.2	28.1	33.3	10.4	1.0	78.1	41.4	54.2	45.8
34990	PALM CITY	96.3	93.8	1.3	2.2	1.0	1.4	3.2	6.4	4.1	4.9	5.6	5.9	3.6	17.0	33.9	21.2	3.8	81.7	50.4	48.1	51.9
34994	STUART	84.2	79.3	12.0	14.5	0.7	1.0	6.4	11.6	4.2	4.1	4.1	4.9	5.2	21.3	28.4	22.0	5.8	84.5	49.6	48.2	51.8
34996	STUART	94.5	91.4	2.0	2.6	0.5	0.8	5.0	9.0	2.6	2.9	3.2	3.5	3.0	13.9	28.2	34.5	8.1	89.1	61.0	46.7	53.3
34997	STUART	91.5	87.9	4.3	5.3	0.7	1.0	8.1	13.5	4.7	4.5	4.7	5.0	4.6	18.2	31.2	23.3	3.9	83.0	50.9	48.6	51.4
	FLORIDA	78.0	74.7	14.6	15.8	1.7	2.3	16.8	21.5	6.0	5.9	5.9	6.3	6.2	25.0	26.8	15.3	2.8	78.6	41.1	48.8	51.2
	UNITED STATES	75.1	72.0	12.3	12.7	3.8	4.6	12.5	15.7	6.8	6.7	6.6	7.1	6.9	27.0	26.0	10.9	1.9	75.7	36.9	49.2	50.8

ZIP CODE #	POST OFFICE NAME	2009 Per Capita Income	2009 HH Income Base	2009 Household Income Distribution (%): Less than $25,000	$25,000 to $49,999	$50,000 to $99,999	$100,000 to $149,999	$150,000 or More	Median Household Income: 2009	2014	2009 National Centile	2009 State Centile	2009 Home Value Base	2009 Home Value Distribution (%): Less than $50,000	$50,000 to $89,999	$90,000 to $174,999	$175,000 to $399,999	$400,000 or More	2009 Median Home Value
34637	LAND O LAKES	21557	2078	23.0	27.6	36.4	8.4	4.6	48962	49466	59	53	1942	4.1	11.0	40.2	29.6	15.0	155597
34638	LAND O LAKES	21388	6602	20.6	36.4	33.4	6.5	3.0	44462	46447	47	41	5921	3.0	9.7	48.4	31.0	8.0	147283
34639	LAND O LAKES	26997	9278	9.9	18.0	47.3	17.5	7.2	67926	67912	86	87	8263	4.1	6.1	39.4	46.0	4.3	175642
34652	NEW PORT RICHEY	21544	12098	33.5	36.8	24.0	3.1	2.6	34251	35565	16	12	8798	12.2	39.2	33.4	11.6	3.5	88430
34653	NEW PORT RICHEY	20601	14560	30.4	35.3	29.3	3.3	1.7	37265	39148	24	20	10515	15.8	26.7	47.6	9.7	0.2	98882
34654	NEW PORT RICHEY	21405	8132	23.7	32.2	35.3	5.8	3.0	45055	47536	48	42	7047	18.8	22.2	36.0	18.5	4.6	111201
34655	NEW PORT RICHEY	29060	16121	16.4	29.3	37.6	9.9	6.8	53587	52648	69	66	14289	2.0	13.9	37.5	41.6	5.0	165910
34667	HUDSON	21510	15625	29.5	34.6	30.1	3.7	2.0	37664	39753	26	21	12637	15.1	22.7	44.7	16.2	1.2	105721
34668	PORT RICHEY	18644	20333	34.1	37.3	25.3	2.3	1.0	33895	35677	15	12	15447	8.0	34.3	54.3	3.1	0.3	95744
34669	HUDSON	17768	4998	25.1	40.4	28.7	4.6	1.2	37833	39776	26	22	4119	8.6	27.4	51.9	10.7	1.5	108238
34677	OLDSMAR	32675	8576	11.6	23.9	42.0	12.0	10.5	65288	65831	84	84	6473	0.8	15.0	45.1	32.0	7.1	143990
34683	PALM HARBOR	36021	14515	13.0	23.5	35.9	16.0	11.6	65609	65962	84	84	11461	6.2	7.4	31.8	45.0	9.5	185968
34684	PALM HARBOR	30661	12023	16.4	31.8	36.1	9.6	6.1	51385	52706	65	61	8946	2.4	13.5	50.6	29.7	3.8	142332
34685	PALM HARBOR	48021	7194	8.4	13.3	30.4	20.7	27.3	95647	100720	96	97	6088	0.5	4.8	14.8	49.9	30.0	286984
34688	TARPON SPRINGS	47050	2522	9.3	16.4	28.6	21.9	23.8	90240	94589	95	96	2191	0.5	7.2	10.1	50.3	31.9	283744
34689	TARPON SPRINGS	27193	10928	22.9	28.8	34.4	9.3	4.6	48402	51023	58	52	8523	15.0	12.4	39.1	28.1	5.4	135780
34690	HOLIDAY	20277	6822	31.3	40.1	24.2	3.1	1.3	35429	36991	19	15	5492	7.4	49.9	39.6	2.8	0.2	84774
34691	HOLIDAY	19807	9490	31.3	37.5	27.5	2.5	1.1	34744	36419	17	13	7701	9.0	45.4	40.2	4.8	0.6	86356
34695	SAFETY HARBOR	35441	7542	14.0	22.5	36.5	16.0	11.1	64008	64201	82	82	6346	7.7	13.3	32.3	38.0	8.7	161761
34698	DUNEDIN	29120	17723	24.5	29.8	32.6	8.6	4.5	45426	48950	50	44	13178	12.8	15.6	47.4	20.6	3.6	123336
34705	ASTATULA	17971	954	22.5	41.5	28.8	5.1	2.0	39680	44420	32	27	817	9.1	26.3	41.9	18.1	4.7	111650
34711	CLERMONT	29020	19803	11.3	26.3	40.7	14.8	6.9	61705	62825	80	79	16486	2.9	3.8	32.2	51.3	9.8	195841
34714	CLERMONT	30031	5758	8.7	28.0	43.2	14.2	5.9	61711	61799	80	79	5079	1.9	3.0	25.5	58.1	11.4	216751
34715	CLERMONT	26494	4910	9.7	23.0	42.4	17.3	7.7	66096	67210	84	85	4236	2.7	4.4	41.4	45.6	5.9	177797
34731	FRUITLAND PARK	23853	4922	24.0	33.8	32.4	6.5	3.3	44627	46947	47	41	4120	23.5	22.3	34.5	17.6	2.0	98878
34734	GOTHA	26249	1561	11.1	29.1	41.9	11.8	6.1	58261	60245	75	74	789	3.9	2.0	35.7	43.6	14.7	198063
34736	GROVELAND	22850	4668	23.4	27.1	37.9	7.6	4.0	49636	50878	60	56	3813	14.9	17.9	29.2	31.8	6.3	130244
34737	HOWEY IN THE HILLS	27388	1117	14.1	28.7	39.0	12.4	5.7	57305	57018	74	73	978	2.5	3.6	37.5	49.1	7.4	186581
34739	KENANSVILLE	20965	392	30.4	29.3	31.1	7.4	1.8	44308	46462	46	40	304	11.8	21.7	37.8	22.4	6.3	110606
34741	KISSIMMEE	17412	17563	27.0	38.8	29.4	3.3	1.5	38618	40949	28	24	6149	11.7	12.8	48.1	24.8	2.5	131775
34743	KISSIMMEE	16649	11760	22.4	31.6	38.2	5.6	2.1	46180	48802	52	47	8364	0.9	6.7	50.6	41.5	0.3	163968
34744	KISSIMMEE	24143	14770	18.0	26.2	38.8	11.4	5.6	55290	55752	72	70	10862	10.1	4.3	30.4	46.4	8.7	185456
34746	KISSIMMEE	23597	12309	19.7	30.2	34.6	10.6	4.9	50057	52087	61	57	9247	15.1	12.0	28.5	39.2	5.1	161077
34747	KISSIMMEE	33659	5678	11.3	20.4	40.2	16.0	12.2	66129	65696	84	85	3238	0.6	1.7	20.9	37.8	38.9	290230
34748	LEESBURG	24466	18731	28.1	32.1	30.8	5.4	3.6	41364	44651	37	32	14130	14.0	22.8	37.6	22.3	3.3	115404
34753	MASCOTTE	16157	1605	25.3	33.6	32.2	6.4	2.6	43089	45936	43	37	1258	12.0	18.0	45.9	19.2	4.8	118919
34756	MONTVERDE	31041	1061	11.4	22.8	42.8	14.1	8.9	66786	67269	85	86	923	4.6	22.1	26.5	32.2	14.6	163993
34758	KISSIMMEE	15701	10141	25.8	32.2	36.2	5.0	0.9	42641	45457	41	36	8401	0.8	4.9	60.4	32.6	1.4	154759
34759	KISSIMMEE	18359	10301	18.3	30.6	44.9	5.7	0.5	50908	51524	63	59	9029	0.4	4.2	74.7	19.1	1.5	139423
34761	OCOEE	28985	11699	12.5	20.7	41.1	14.9	10.7	65734	68409	84	84	9377	2.0	7.1	42.3	39.6	9.0	171021
34762	OKAHUMPKA	24387	436	19.0	45.0	27.5	6.0	2.5	41119	44494	36	31	381	38.8	20.7	25.5	13.9	1.0	69500
34769	SAINT CLOUD	21193	9846	23.8	30.1	38.2	5.8	2.1	46323	49163	52	47	7042	8.3	10.6	49.5	29.8	1.8	143364
34771	SAINT CLOUD	22206	6076	17.2	29.1	40.8	9.7	3.2	52788	53325	68	64	5147	13.1	8.1	27.2	42.4	9.2	178606
34772	SAINT CLOUD	21507	7103	18.7	25.1	44.3	8.5	3.4	53794	53871	69	67	5197	2.5	5.2	36.8	51.7	3.9	182616
34773	SAINT CLOUD	15965	909	35.1	30.8	26.8	5.7	1.5	37244	40320	24	20	676	15.2	37.7	22.2	20.9	4.0	85652
34785	WILDWOOD	16917	5799	36.2	37.5	22.6	3.2	0.5	32617	34746	13	9	4556	28.0	28.9	31.8	9.7	1.7	79405
34786	WINDERMERE	53191	7003	6.9	14.0	22.8	17.0	39.3	116584	119746	98	99	6070	1.9	4.0	10.1	37.3	46.7	375845
34787	WINTER GARDEN	29938	16044	15.8	23.8	36.4	12.0	11.9	60866	64805	79	78	11945	5.3	12.1	22.9	38.3	21.5	215174
34788	LEESBURG	24218	8802	27.1	35.9	28.7	5.3	3.0	40584	42950	35	29	7761	26.7	25.9	28.9	16.3	2.2	85025
34797	YALAHA	26845	553	19.0	37.1	34.7	7.1	2.2	44371	47475	46	41	500	2.8	7.2	38.8	47.2	4.0	176765
34945	FORT PIERCE	21644	1397	23.2	35.8	27.8	7.9	5.2	41743	43457	38	33	1185	27.5	32.7	17.2	19.0	3.5	73190
34946	FORT PIERCE	16900	2842	37.1	33.2	23.2	4.4	2.1	33112	34740	13	10	2066	41.7	26.0	22.8	5.7	3.8	64561
34947	FORT PIERCE	13636	4035	44.4	29.4	20.9	3.5	1.8	28605	29983	6	4	2112	19.4	40.8	31.5	8.2	0.1	78864
34949	FORT PIERCE	37465	4700	21.1	29.4	31.8	9.8	7.9	49458	49956	60	55	3581	5.5	5.4	24.5	46.4	18.1	221179
34950	FORT PIERCE	13182	6645	51.9	25.9	17.5	2.5	2.2	23773	24097	3	2	2682	19.5	46.6	30.7	2.3	0.9	75558
34951	FORT PIERCE	25007	7314	26.5	31.4	32.8	5.6	3.6	43041	45194	43	37	6132	25.9	22.6	37.5	11.6	2.4	93158
34952	PORT SAINT LUCIE	24129	17117	25.2	34.0	30.1	6.7	3.9	41998	44916	39	34	12903	19.7	11.6	39.9	25.1	3.7	123969
34953	PORT SAINT LUCIE	22613	20366	13.2	27.6	46.3	9.4	3.4	56473	57094	73	72	16828	0.5	8.0	62.0	26.8	2.8	141634
34956	INDIANTOWN	14127	2519	29.9	29.1	35.2	4.3	1.6	38656	42526	29	24	1631	22.3	26.1	36.1	11.5	4.0	93232
34957	JENSEN BEACH	33612	11257	22.3	26.5	35.1	8.9	7.2	50995	52610	64	59	9122	10.7	17.6	32.9	30.5	8.3	135448
34972	OKEECHOBEE	15894	6009	31.3	34.1	28.1	4.6	1.9	36418	40007	22	17	4173	12.3	19.2	44.9	21.5	2.2	118930
34974	OKEECHOBEE	20729	10219	30.4	32.8	27.2	6.9	2.7	38937	41365	30	25	8094	10.6	20.0	43.8	21.8	3.7	122237
34981	FORT PIERCE	22044	1860	25.1	33.7	27.5	8.2	5.6	41506	44252	38	32	1119	3.8	24.6	37.5	31.0	3.1	133690
34982	FORT PIERCE	21266	10372	27.7	33.6	30.2	4.8	3.7	40310	42464	34	28	7888	16.5	24.9	40.6	16.2	1.9	103625
34983	PORT SAINT LUCIE	23026	14514	18.8	33.0	36.8	7.4	4.0	48173	49153	57	51	12002	0.9	11.6	65.6	20.6	1.5	133822
34984	PORT SAINT LUCIE	28855	4978	13.3	27.8	40.8	11.2	6.8	58510	55775	76	75	4260	1.2	4.9	56.9	27.0	9.9	152321
34986	PORT SAINT LUCIE	33190	11401	11.0	25.1	45.5	12.4	6.0	61179	61245	79	78	10130	0.1	4.9	53.6	34.5	6.9	155119
34987	PORT SAINT LUCIE	29268	2421	10.2	24.0	46.8	12.6	6.3	61967	61925	80	80	2095	0.1	4.9	49.2	38.3	7.6	164653
34988	PORT SAINT LUCIE	34682	37	5.4	16.2	56.8	13.5	8.1	66169	66073	84	85	26	0.0	3.8	7.7	76.9	11.5	272222
34990	PALM CITY	44657	11285	8.4	16.5	38.1	18.8	18.2	78218	79349	91	93	9637	0.5	2.4	24.9	53.7	18.4	247724
34994	STUART	29123	7243	26.1	30.7	30.4	7.6	5.3	41176	45602	37	31	4516	10.5	34.8	30.3	16.5	8.0	98724
34996	STUART	44868	5681	21.2	23.7	32.1	9.0	14.0	54735	57541	71	69	4600	6.2	22.8	27.0	21.0	23.0	143249
34997	STUART	35573	16132	16.2	26.9	36.5	10.2	10.1	55216	57530	72	70	12986	6.8	17.5	32.7	31.1	11.9	143059
	FLORIDA	27128		21.9	27.6	33.8	9.8	6.8	50413	52516				8.0	14.3	38.7	30.4	8.6	144752
	UNITED STATES	27277		20.9	24.4	35.3	11.7	7.6	54719	56938				9.3	13.1	31.6	32.6	13.5	162279

ZIP CODE		FINANCIAL SERVICES				THE HOME						ENTERTAINMENT						PERSONAL			
						Home Improvements		Furnishings													
#	POST OFFICE NAME	Auto Loan	Home Loan	Invest-ments	Retire-ment Plans	Home Repair	Lawn & Garden	Comput-ers & Hard-ware-Personal	Major Appli-ances	TV, Radio, Sound Equip-ment	Furni-ture	Dine out/ Carry out	Sports Equip-ment	Fees & Tickets	Toys & Games	Travel	Cable TV	Apparel & Services	Auto Repairs	Health Insur-ance	Pets & Supplies
34637	LAND O LAKES	91	85	75	83	83	87	80	85	83	83	83	62	77	86	77	85	56	82	85	101
34638	LAND O LAKES	88	81	80	78	82	87	77	84	80	80	80	60	74	81	76	83	54	81	86	99
34639	LAND O LAKES	116	125	103	123	118	110	113	113	108	119	110	89	116	115	113	105	77	109	104	131
34652	NEW PORT RICHEY	65	60	75	58	66	74	61	69	65	62	63	47	59	60	64	69	43	67	79	79
34653	NEW PORT RICHEY	68	62	71	61	65	73	63	69	66	63	65	49	60	64	64	69	44	68	76	81
34654	NEW PORT RICHEY	81	78	88	75	82	88	74	83	77	77	76	58	73	75	77	80	52	80	88	96
34655	NEW PORT RICHEY	96	101	113	100	108	110	93	103	96	99	95	71	99	92	101	99	65	99	111	118
34667	HUDSON	68	66	83	61	73	79	62	73	66	67	64	48	63	61	69	70	43	71	83	84
34668	PORT RICHEY	58	54	66	51	59	66	54	62	58	56	56	41	53	53	57	61	38	60	70	71
34669	HUDSON	71	63	81	59	68	77	61	73	65	64	63	49	57	61	65	69	42	69	79	84
34677	OLDSMAR	110	123	117	125	122	120	114	115	113	116	114	88	123	114	120	113	80	114	116	135
34683	PALM HARBOR	121	132	131	134	133	134	122	128	122	124	122	95	129	121	129	124	86	125	131	148
34684	PALM HARBOR	87	93	109	91	102	106	87	98	91	93	90	65	95	85	98	96	62	95	111	110
34685	PALM HARBOR	165	201	203	207	205	190	175	181	168	185	170	137	198	169	193	165	123	173	172	208
34688	TARPON SPRINGS	163	180	198	183	189	183	166	174	165	176	165	126	179	160	179	165	116	170	177	201
34689	TARPON SPRINGS	91	87	101	85	92	100	85	95	89	86	87	67	84	85	89	93	59	92	102	110
34690	HOLIDAY	65	60	76	56	66	73	58	69	62	61	61	46	56	58	62	66	41	66	76	79
34691	HOLIDAY	64	59	74	55	63	72	57	67	61	59	60	46	55	57	61	65	40	64	75	77
34695	SAFETY HARBOR	115	126	130	126	129	127	117	122	117	121	117	90	125	115	125	118	82	119	125	141
34698	DUNEDIN	80	81	90	79	85	91	81	86	86	82	85	60	83	80	85	90	58	86	99	100
34705	ASTATULA	87	64	93	63	67	89	65	83	72	61	70	62	54	71	66	78	47	76	85	98
34711	CLERMONT	118	115	116	111	112	111	108	114	106	112	107	88	104	110	108	104	74	109	106	131
34714	CLERMONT	119	113	127	109	113	116	105	117	104	108	105	89	100	106	108	104	72	110	109	135
34715	CLERMONT	120	130	106	125	122	110	115	116	110	123	112	91	118	117	114	105	78	110	104	132
34731	FRUITLAND PARK	80	81	88	77	84	90	76	84	79	79	78	59	78	76	81	83	53	82	93	98
34734	GOTHA	107	98	87	100	94	88	107	96	103	109	105	79	102	107	99	99	73	102	91	115
34736	GROVELAND	90	82	97	76	87	95	79	91	83	83	82	63	75	80	82	87	55	87	97	105
34737	HOWEY IN THE HILLS	94	101	114	98	108	112	91	103	95	97	94	70	98	90	101	99	64	99	113	118
34739	KENANSVILLE	79	74	84	69	79	83	71	80	74	75	73	54	69	71	73	77	49	77	86	92
34741	KISSIMMEE	71	50	46	53	48	49	70	57	69	68	70	48	59	71	58	67	49	67	58	71
34743	KISSIMMEE	79	80	68	72	78	66	78	77	73	84	75	57	74	76	75	69	53	76	67	85
34744	KISSIMMEE	95	101	91	99	98	94	95	95	94	98	95	72	98	96	96	93	66	94	93	111
34746	KISSIMMEE	93	94	87	92	93	95	89	92	89	92	89	68	89	91	90	91	62	91	95	108
34747	KISSIMMEE	123	147	157	150	155	132	139	138	126	146	127	110	150	124	151	119	92	134	123	157
34748	LEESBURG	72	72	84	67	79	86	70	79	75	74	73	51	72	69	76	80	50	78	93	90
34753	MASCOTTE	77	76	73	68	77	69	75	77	72	81	73	56	72	72	74	70	51	76	72	85
34756	MONTVERDE	113	127	109	131	123	125	114	118	112	114	112	92	121	115	120	112	78	113	117	139
34758	KISSIMMEE	72	72	67	65	72	65	70	71	67	75	68	52	67	68	69	66	48	70	67	80
34759	KISSIMMEE	79	79	75	73	78	72	75	78	73	79	74	58	73	74	75	71	52	76	72	88
34761	OCOEE	124	134	116	130	129	116	124	122	118	131	120	95	127	123	123	113	85	119	110	140
34762	OKAHUMPKA	72	74	95	67	85	90	68	82	73	76	71	51	72	65	79	78	47	79	97	92
34769	SAINT CLOUD	78	73	71	72	73	79	73	76	76	74	75	56	71	75	72	78	51	76	82	90
34771	SAINT CLOUD	94	88	90	86	88	94	83	91	85	83	85	67	79	86	83	87	58	87	91	107
34772	SAINT CLOUD	96	88	78	87	85	87	88	88	89	91	90	67	83	92	83	90	61	88	88	105
34773	SAINT CLOUD	73	68	62	64	65	67	66	68	67	68	67	51	62	69	63	68	46	67	67	80
34785	WILDWOOD	58	53	68	49	58	67	51	61	56	54	54	40	51	52	55	60	36	59	71	70
34786	WINDERMERE	209	256	267	263	266	238	216	229	206	237	207	176	249	208	241	199	152	214	208	259
34787	WINTER GARDEN	118	122	112	122	120	118	116	117	114	119	115	91	118	117	117	113	80	115	114	137
34788	LEESBURG	69	72	90	66	81	86	66	79	70	73	69	49	70	63	76	75	46	75	91	88
34797	YALAHA	80	76	97	70	85	91	73	86	77	79	75	56	72	70	79	81	50	82	95	98
34945	FORT PIERCE	87	85	105	79	93	99	80	94	84	86	82	62	80	78	87	89	55	90	103	107
34946	FORT PIERCE	63	61	68	59	63	69	58	64	61	61	61	44	58	58	61	64	41	63	71	76
34947	FORT PIERCE	59	50	46	51	48	54	56	53	60	56	59	41	53	59	52	62	41	57	59	66
34949	FORT PIERCE	86	95	115	92	106	111	90	100	97	97	95	64	100	86	102	103	65	99	123	113
34950	FORT PIERCE	52	42	39	43	40	46	52	48	56	50	55	36	47	55	46	58	38	53	54	58
34951	FORT PIERCE	73	79	88	75	84	89	72	82	76	76	74	55	78	71	80	80	51	79	92	93
34952	PORT SAINT LUCIE	73	75	84	72	80	83	73	79	76	76	75	54	77	72	79	79	52	78	88	90
34953	PORT SAINT LUCIE	90	100	91	100	98	97	89	93	89	92	89	70	95	90	94	89	62	90	94	108
34956	INDIANTOWN	69	66	66	61	68	64	68	70	66	72	67	51	65	65	68	66	47	70	68	78
34957	JENSEN BEACH	93	99	120	95	109	111	92	104	95	99	93	70	98	88	103	99	64	100	114	118
34972	OKEECHOBEE	73	67	65	63	67	68	67	70	67	69	67	51	62	68	64	68	46	69	68	81
34974	OKEECHOBEE	75	70	81	66	74	81	68	77	71	71	70	53	65	68	70	74	47	74	83	89
34981	FORT PIERCE	91	81	78	85	81	87	87	87	88	83	88	68	82	90	84	90	61	88	90	104
34982	FORT PIERCE	73	73	78	71	77	80	72	77	74	74	73	54	72	71	75	76	50	76	83	89
34983	PORT SAINT LUCIE	82	88	86	88	87	93	82	86	84	81	83	64	86	83	86	86	58	85	92	101
34984	PORT SAINT LUCIE	103	120	120	120	121	123	104	113	106	109	106	81	117	105	116	109	74	109	119	130
34986	PORT SAINT LUCIE	95	112	115	112	116	118	97	107	100	102	100	74	109	96	109	103	69	102	115	121
34987	PORT SAINT LUCIE	98	115	116	116	119	120	100	110	102	105	103	77	112	100	112	105	72	105	117	125
34988	PORT SAINT LUCIE	125	141	122	145	137	139	126	131	124	126	125	102	135	127	133	124	87	126	130	154
34990	PALM CITY	146	162	187	164	174	173	145	160	147	157	146	111	159	139	162	149	102	154	167	183
34994	STUART	80	77	86	75	82	89	80	85	85	82	83	58	81	80	83	89	57	86	98	98
34996	STUART	116	132	164	126	149	149	119	137	123	132	120	87	134	112	138	128	83	131	154	152
34997	STUART	118	112	143	110	122	131	110	124	114	114	113	86	110	108	118	119	77	120	133	143
	FLORIDA	96	94	97	93	96	98	95	97	96	97	96	71	95	94	96	97	67	97	101	113
	UNITED STATES	100	100	100	100	100	100	100	100	100	100	100	100	100	100	100	100	100	100	100	100

ZIP CODE #	POST OFFICE NAME	COUNTY FIPS CODE	POPULATION 2000	POPULATION 2009	POPULATION 2014	2000-2009 ANNUAL RATE % Rate	2000-2009 ANNUAL RATE State Centile	HOUSEHOLDS 2000	HOUSEHOLDS 2009	HOUSEHOLDS 2014	HOUSEHOLDS % Annual Rate 2000-2009	HOUSEHOLDS 2009 Average HH Size	FAMILIES 2000	FAMILIES 2009	FAMILIES % Annual Rate 2000-2009
30002	AVONDALE ESTATES	089	7484	8025	8351	0.8	41	3095	3293	3417	0.7	2.43	1776	1769	0.0
30004	ALPHARETTA	121	29053	50106	62333	6.1	97	10456	18194	22620	6.2	2.75	8078	13465	5.7
30005	ALPHARETTA	121	26990	34456	39160	2.7	79	9397	11691	13235	2.4	2.95	7232	8730	2.1
30008	MARIETTA	067	31784	35678	37112	1.3	54	10546	11300	11801	0.7	2.78	7048	7175	0.2
30009	ALPHARETTA	121	12307	16688	19190	3.3	86	5255	7033	8084	3.2	2.36	3156	3899	2.3
30011	AUBURN	013	12067	18057	21304	4.5	93	4054	6043	7117	4.4	2.98	3279	4781	4.2
30012	CONYERS	247	23869	28635	30770	2.0	70	8085	9677	10431	2.0	2.85	5857	6755	1.6
30013	CONYERS	247	18483	24041	27002	2.9	82	6624	8633	9701	2.9	2.78	5127	6532	2.7
30014	COVINGTON	217	26672	37170	43703	3.7	89	9607	13323	15754	3.6	2.72	7367	9956	3.3
30016	COVINGTON	217	26273	52883	67303	7.9	99	9337	19034	24275	8.0	2.78	7252	14345	7.7
30017	GRAYSON	135	9620	19280	23951	7.8	99	3081	6282	7790	8.0	3.07	2699	5355	7.7
30019	DACULA	135	18321	38530	48827	8.4	99	6159	12851	16239	8.3	2.98	5305	10719	7.9
30021	CLARKSTON	089	22445	24462	25445	0.9	45	7712	8189	8469	0.7	2.99	5051	5100	0.1
30022	ALPHARETTA	121	54440	70270	79904	2.8	80	19084	24310	27599	2.7	2.89	14456	17730	2.2
30024	SUWANEE	135	37977	64207	79186	5.8	96	12403	20959	25773	5.8	3.05	10580	17294	5.5
30025	SOCIAL CIRCLE	297	7097	10325	11903	4.1	91	2476	3602	4160	4.1	2.82	1970	2801	3.9
30028	CUMMING	117	12474	19604	25257	5.1	95	4411	6870	8725	4.9	2.88	3596	5447	4.6
30030	DECATUR	089	24786	26671	27819	0.8	41	11354	12470	13098	1.0	2.03	5297	5311	0.0
30032	DECATUR	089	58316	59873	61156	0.3	25	18947	19668	20155	0.4	2.87	13482	13368	-0.1
30033	DECATUR	089	26590	27576	28363	0.4	28	12805	13530	13970	0.6	1.95	6053	5910	-0.3
30034	DECATUR	089	43928	50434	53669	1.5	60	14554	17094	18288	1.8	2.90	11172	12616	1.3
30035	DECATUR	089	19145	22440	24080	1.7	66	6572	7807	8393	1.9	2.87	4778	5413	1.4
30038	LITHONIA	089	23697	38199	44941	5.3	95	8202	13513	15956	5.5	2.83	6268	9974	5.2
30039	SNELLVILLE	135	28384	40672	47426	4.0	91	9325	13327	15497	3.9	3.03	7690	10639	3.6
30040	CUMMING	117	30027	56959	74202	7.2	98	10399	19610	25524	7.1	2.86	8367	15364	6.8
30041	CUMMING	117	32171	55721	71452	6.1	97	11568	19663	25056	5.9	2.83	9249	15417	5.7
30043	LAWRENCEVILLE	135	62053	83405	94512	3.2	85	19491	26051	29497	3.2	3.10	16259	21000	2.8
30044	LAWRENCEVILLE	135	66840	87013	98246	2.9	82	23145	29740	33364	2.7	2.91	17142	20974	2.2
30045	LAWRENCEVILLE	135	38386	65085	78237	5.9	96	13208	21860	26101	5.6	2.95	10075	16279	5.3
30047	LILBURN	135	54606	60752	64331	1.2	52	18438	20272	21373	1.0	2.98	14805	15656	0.6
30052	LOGANVILLE	297	35100	60831	74648	6.1	97	11869	20453	25077	6.1	2.97	9940	16648	5.7
30054	OXFORD	217	9215	12618	14523	3.5	88	3067	4201	4883	3.5	2.88	2526	3392	3.2
30055	MANSFIELD	217	2521	3268	3696	2.8	80	953	1220	1381	2.7	2.66	779	974	2.4
30056	NEWBORN	159	2084	2768	3128	3.1	85	680	921	1047	3.3	3.00	555	736	3.1
30058	LITHONIA	089	43950	57883	64346	3.0	83	14771	19499	21667	3.0	2.95	11185	14209	2.6
30060	MARIETTA	067	35870	39242	40520	1.0	47	13051	13743	14155	0.6	2.72	8081	8059	0.0
30062	MARIETTA	067	60122	64631	67053	0.8	41	21509	23030	23877	0.7	2.79	16735	17275	0.3
30064	MARIETTA	067	42000	48671	52357	1.6	63	15257	17443	18716	1.5	2.76	11573	12930	1.2
30066	MARIETTA	067	50388	55010	57724	1.0	47	17625	19267	20281	1.0	2.84	13934	14653	0.5
30067	MARIETTA	067	47022	50760	52483	0.8	41	20015	20845	21440	0.4	2.39	10733	10500	-0.2
30068	MARIETTA	067	31812	33313	34204	0.5	31	11931	12439	12743	0.5	2.67	9203	9241	0.0
30069	MARIETTA	067	27	39	39	4.1	91	6	7	7	1.7	1.00	6	0	-100.0
30071	NORCROSS	135	23526	27563	29375	1.7	66	7213	8104	8612	1.3	3.29	4995	5259	0.6
30075	ROSWELL	121	48055	57270	62810	1.9	68	17105	20265	22220	1.8	2.80	13281	15179	1.5
30076	ROSWELL	121	41101	49102	54091	1.9	68	15546	18094	19897	1.7	2.70	10532	11630	1.1
30078	SNELLVILLE	135	30171	36629	40424	2.1	72	9979	12011	13195	2.0	3.02	8323	9696	1.7
30079	SCOTTDALE	089	3107	3283	3434	0.6	34	1146	1225	1281	0.7	2.66	664	675	0.2
30080	SMYRNA	067	42890	50009	53378	1.7	66	19932	22951	24447	1.5	2.17	9161	9606	0.5
30082	SMYRNA	067	23475	26424	28068	1.3	54	9391	10491	11183	1.2	2.47	6048	6350	0.5
30083	STONE MOUNTAIN	089	56647	60689	63265	0.7	37	20274	21613	22482	0.7	2.79	13518	13634	0.1
30084	TUCKER	089	38272	44016	46735	1.5	60	14581	16558	17564	1.4	2.64	9506	10225	0.8
30087	STONE MOUNTAIN	089	31699	36853	40242	1.6	63	10984	12750	13866	1.6	2.88	8769	9817	1.2
30088	STONE MOUNTAIN	089	28165	29254	30054	0.4	28	9775	10275	10567	0.5	2.84	7126	7178	0.1
30092	NORCROSS	135	32727	37467	39996	1.5	60	12891	14362	15222	1.2	2.60	8274	8665	0.5
30093	NORCROSS	135	44629	52249	56187	1.7	66	15885	17912	19171	1.3	2.91	9985	10376	0.4
30094	CONYERS	247	26495	31994	34992	2.1	72	8960	10985	12064	2.2	2.90	7529	9027	2.0
30096	DULUTH	135	50291	60963	67091	2.1	72	19757	23310	25458	1.8	2.61	12538	13625	0.9
30097	DULUTH	121	25006	43187	51739	6.1	97	8464	14365	17131	5.9	3.00	7191	11850	5.5
30101	ACWORTH	067	38357	56883	66091	4.4	93	13472	19787	22908	4.2	2.87	10725	15450	4.0
30102	ACWORTH	057	32200	38061	41653	1.8	66	10812	12796	13988	1.8	2.97	8450	9684	1.5
30103	ADAIRSVILLE	015	10700	13996	15641	2.9	82	3922	5175	5790	3.0	2.70	3082	3956	2.7
30104	ARAGON	233	3967	4424	4589	1.2	52	1451	1632	1697	1.3	2.71	1159	1270	1.0
30105	ARMUCHEE	115	2695	2980	3103	1.1	49	1008	1124	1175	1.2	2.65	809	879	0.9
30106	AUSTELL	067	15620	20428	22549	2.9	82	5794	7481	8254	2.8	2.68	4207	5169	2.3
30107	BALL GROUND	057	8323	13342	16362	5.2	95	2975	4835	5942	5.4	2.76	2387	3788	5.1
30108	BOWDON	045	7621	8718	9230	1.5	60	3036	3516	3740	1.6	2.48	2224	2478	1.2
30110	BREMEN	143	10617	12707	13586	2.0	70	4067	4896	5261	2.0	2.53	2979	3473	1.7
30113	BUCHANAN	143	6277	7083	7427	1.3	54	2360	2673	2814	1.4	2.59	1759	1932	1.0
30114	CANTON	057	21767	48692	62860	9.1	100	7693	17279	22368	9.1	2.79	5849	13031	9.0
30115	CANTON	057	19784	34084	42728	6.1	97	6901	11968	14993	6.1	2.83	5625	9521	5.9
30116	CARROLLTON	045	18511	24322	27242	3.0	83	6531	8708	9811	3.2	2.74	5055	6535	2.8
30117	CARROLLTON	045	30491	37111	40101	2.1	72	11612	14171	15419	2.2	2.49	7654	8890	1.6
30118	CARROLLTON	045	2135	2511	2661	1.8	66	13	16	18	2.3	2.56	5	6	2.0
30120	CARTERSVILLE	015	29207	37000	40581	2.6	78	10535	13287	14558	2.5	2.76	8037	9878	2.3
30121	CARTERSVILLE	015	15820	21942	24902	3.6	88	5592	7912	9036	3.8	2.69	4253	5809	3.4
30122	LITHIA SPRINGS	097	17297	22359	25378	2.8	80	6688	8958	10274	3.2	2.50	4651	5835	2.5
30124	CAVE SPRING	115	2693	3003	3142	1.2	52	1040	1170	1227	1.3	2.56	804	875	0.9
30125	CEDARTOWN	233	22470	24293	25028	0.8	41	8148	8809	9078	0.8	2.68	5942	6225	0.5
30126	MABLETON	067	24071	32587	36775	3.3	86	8884	11990	13520	3.3	2.71	6583	8472	2.8
30127	POWDER SPRINGS	067	47896	61927	69321	2.8	80	15566	19893	22225	2.7	3.09	13184	16494	2.5
30132	DALLAS	223	16293	29392	37614	6.6	98	5879	10630	13653	6.6	2.72	4552	8105	6.4
30134	DOUGLASVILLE	097	30802	45008	53201	4.2	92	10708	15771	18710	4.3	2.81	8282	11895	4.0
30135	DOUGLASVILLE	097	43464	61976	72846	3.9	90	14804	21486	25432	4.1	2.87	12011	16987	3.8
30137	EMERSON	015	1490	1999	2294	3.2	85	512	685	786	3.2	2.92	412	535	2.9
30139	FAIRMOUNT	129	3620	4414	4804	2.2	73	1378	1711	1874	2.4	2.58	1063	1277	2.0
30141	HIRAM	223	12395	21666	26887	6.2	97	4234	7605	9443	6.5	2.85	3463	6059	6.2
30143	JASPER	227	17086	22898	26396	3.2	85	6869	9360	10865	3.4	2.42	5178	6857	3.1
30144	KENNESAW	067	38719	46235	50123	1.9	68	14688	17607	19069	2.0	2.62	10173	11520	1.4
30145	KINGSTON	015	6093	7858	8844	2.8	80	2094	2682	3018	2.7	2.93	1714	2151	2.5
30147	LINDALE	115	4803	5261	5456	1.0	47	1843	2031	2110	1.1	2.58	1395	1490	0.7
30148	MARBLE HILL	085	825	1150	1334	3.7	89	318	450	526	3.8	2.55	253	350	3.6
30149	MOUNT BERRY	115	1230	1318	1318	0.7	37	34	34	34	0.0	2.56	16	14	-1.4
30152	KENNESAW	067	26635	41098	47400	4.8	94	8767	13756	15923	5.0	2.96	7284	11018	4.6
30153	ROCKMART	233	14153	18756	21262	3.1	85	5324	7081	8018	3.1	2.63	3972	5160	2.9
30157	DALLAS	223	30146	49141	60590	5.4	95	10173	16900	20893	5.6	2.89	8323	13427	5.3
	GEORGIA					2.1					2.1	2.65			1.8
	UNITED STATES					1.0					1.1	2.59			0.9

ZIP CODE #	POST OFFICE NAME	RACE (%) White 2000	White 2009	Black 2000	Black 2009	Asian/Pacific 2000	Asian/Pacific 2009	% Hispanic Origin 2000	% Hispanic Origin 2009	2009 AGE DISTRIBUTION (%) 0-4	5-9	10-14	15-19	20-24	25-44	45-64	65-84	85+	18+	MEDIAN AGE 2009	% 2009 Males	% 2009 Females
30002	AVONDALE ESTATES	40.7	34.0	50.7	55.3	1.9	2.3	2.0	2.8	8.5	7.0	5.9	6.3	9.8	30.6	23.8	6.9	1.3	75.4	32.0	47.4	52.6
30004	ALPHARETTA	91.6	85.3	3.1	6.2	2.4	3.6	4.0	6.7	7.7	8.3	8.5	6.6	3.4	29.6	28.3	6.8	0.7	71.1	37.7	49.8	50.2
30005	ALPHARETTA	83.1	74.0	5.3	9.6	8.8	11.9	3.5	5.9	10.4	10.4	9.4	6.1	3.8	34.0	22.6	3.1	0.2	65.6	32.9	49.6	50.4
30008	MARIETTA	51.8	43.8	36.0	39.6	2.5	3.1	14.5	19.6	7.8	6.9	6.2	6.7	8.4	36.7	19.9	6.3	1.2	75.4	32.3	52.6	47.4
30009	ALPHARETTA	84.5	73.7	7.2	13.2	4.1	5.5	5.7	10.6	7.6	7.1	6.6	5.1	5.0	37.7	23.8	6.2	0.8	75.7	35.4	50.6	49.4
30011	AUBURN	90.4	86.5	3.3	4.7	3.0	4.1	3.2	5.2	9.7	8.7	8.0	6.7	5.2	34.9	21.0	5.2	0.5	69.4	32.2	50.4	49.6
30012	CONYERS	69.2	63.7	21.7	23.2	1.3	1.7	12.4	17.5	7.0	6.6	6.4	7.0	7.5	29.2	24.6	10.0	1.7	76.0	35.1	50.8	49.2
30013	CONYERS	72.6	66.2	21.4	25.2	3.4	4.6	3.9	6.0	6.8	6.9	7.4	7.5	6.2	27.6	28.1	8.7	0.8	74.2	36.6	49.2	50.8
30014	COVINGTON	70.8	64.9	26.9	32.1	0.7	0.9	1.9	2.7	7.3	7.0	6.9	7.6	6.7	27.2	25.2	10.5	1.7	74.5	36.0	48.9	51.1
30016	COVINGTON	78.9	73.0	18.4	23.2	0.7	1.0	2.0	3.0	8.5	8.0	7.5	6.5	5.6	31.5	22.9	8.4	1.0	71.9	34.5	49.1	50.9
30017	GRAYSON	91.4	85.8	4.5	6.6	1.8	3.0	3.0	6.1	8.1	7.7	7.7	7.2	5.8	29.8	26.7	6.5	0.6	71.5	34.4	49.2	50.8
30019	DACULA	91.8	85.9	4.6	7.6	1.6	2.7	2.9	5.9	9.0	8.5	8.1	6.7	5.2	32.0	24.4	5.6	0.5	70.1	33.3	49.4	50.6
30021	CLARKSTON	21.3	16.8	60.6	61.4	10.1	12.2	4.3	5.9	9.4	7.8	6.8	7.5	10.8	35.4	17.7	4.2	0.4	71.8	28.3	49.4	50.6
30022	ALPHARETTA	81.1	70.7	7.1	12.4	8.5	11.6	4.2	7.0	7.7	8.2	8.8	7.5	4.4	29.2	29.2	4.7	0.4	70.3	36.3	48.8	51.2
30024	SUWANEE	84.3	76.7	6.3	8.2	6.6	10.3	4.1	7.3	10.1	10.3	9.8	6.5	3.3	32.1	24.0	3.6	0.3	65.3	33.8	49.6	50.4
30025	SOCIAL CIRCLE	75.8	68.6	22.6	29.3	0.5	0.7	1.1	1.5	7.3	7.3	7.5	6.6	5.1	26.9	26.4	11.0	1.8	73.7	37.7	49.6	50.4
30028	CUMMING	97.0	95.6	0.2	0.2	0.4	0.5	3.2	4.8	9.3	8.8	8.0	5.9	4.6	32.4	23.4	7.0	0.6	70.2	34.0	50.1	49.9
30030	DECATUR	64.3	58.5	30.6	34.1	2.6	3.9	1.8	3.0	5.5	4.6	4.5	6.0	8.7	31.1	25.4	10.7	3.6	82.4	38.5	43.4	56.6
30032	DECATUR	7.1	5.6	88.7	89.1	0.9	1.0	2.6	3.6	6.9	6.9	6.8	8.1	8.9	29.8	24.6	7.1	0.8	74.6	32.5	48.8	51.2
30033	DECATUR	78.7	72.1	10.5	12.5	7.8	10.9	3.6	5.9	4.5	3.9	3.9	5.0	9.2	30.7	25.2	13.5	3.9	85.4	39.9	46.3	53.7
30034	DECATUR	4.1	2.9	94.1	94.9	0.2	0.2	1.1	1.3	7.1	6.9	7.1	7.6	7.4	30.0	26.8	6.5	0.6	74.1	33.7	46.9	53.1
30035	DECATUR	7.0	5.1	89.8	90.9	1.1	1.4	1.7	2.2	7.9	7.6	7.3	7.9	8.9	30.0	24.6	5.3	0.5	72.5	31.3	45.9	54.1
30038	LITHONIA	9.2	9.2	88.6	87.9	0.2	0.2	1.3	1.8	8.0	7.7	7.6	7.3	6.6	31.3	25.2	5.8	0.6	72.1	33.5	47.2	52.8
30039	SNELLVILLE	77.2	68.1	17.2	22.9	2.0	3.0	4.1	7.3	6.3	6.7	7.3	7.6	5.6	28.6	30.8	6.3	0.8	74.8	37.1	49.6	50.4
30040	CUMMING	93.9	90.7	1.1	1.3	0.5	0.8	8.0	12.1	8.6	8.3	8.0	6.2	4.6	31.7	24.0	7.5	1.1	71.1	35.2	50.6	49.4
30041	CUMMING	95.2	92.7	0.5	0.6	0.8	1.1	5.3	8.4	8.4	8.7	8.6	6.3	3.8	29.3	27.0	7.3	0.6	70.2	36.6	50.9	49.1
30043	LAWRENCEVILLE	79.4	69.4	10.1	13.5	6.9	10.8	5.2	9.5	8.8	8.6	8.4	7.2	4.9	32.8	24.8	4.1	0.4	69.5	33.1	50.3	49.7
30044	LAWRENCEVILLE	67.5	56.3	16.6	20.1	9.2	12.8	10.3	16.7	8.3	7.7	7.3	6.5	6.7	33.9	24.3	4.8	0.5	72.6	32.8	49.5	50.5
30045	LAWRENCEVILLE	78.9	70.6	11.8	14.6	3.4	5.1	9.7	15.6	8.8	8.0	7.4	6.7	6.4	32.2	23.1	6.6	0.9	71.7	32.8	49.5	50.5
30047	LILBURN	78.1	69.6	9.2	11.2	7.8	11.5	7.7	12.3	5.8	6.2	6.8	7.0	5.6	26.1	32.2	9.2	1.0	76.8	39.7	49.4	50.6
30052	LOGANVILLE	93.4	89.2	3.3	5.0	1.0	1.8	2.8	5.3	8.6	8.1	7.7	6.7	5.1	31.1	25.0	7.1	0.7	71.4	34.6	49.1	50.9
30054	OXFORD	82.8	79.1	14.7	17.7	0.9	1.2	1.3	1.9	6.5	6.7	7.0	8.6	5.1	26.7	27.1	11.0	1.2	75.8	38.2	49.6	50.4
30055	MANSFIELD	87.7	83.3	11.0	14.7	0.4	0.5	1.1	1.6	6.9	7.0	7.6	7.1	4.8	27.6	27.7	10.2	1.1	74.0	38.2	49.7	50.3
30056	NEWBORN	76.4	70.2	21.2	26.8	0.2	0.2	2.4	3.2	7.9	7.8	7.8	7.0	5.7	26.7	26.7	9.3	1.0	72.2	35.8	50.6	49.4
30058	LITHONIA	9.2	7.1	87.6	89.0	0.6	0.7	2.2	2.8	8.7	8.3	8.1	7.7	7.0	32.8	22.7	4.1	0.5	70.1	30.9	46.7	53.3
30060	MARIETTA	51.8	44.2	31.1	32.0	2.6	3.1	21.4	29.3	8.1	6.8	6.1	7.5	10.4	31.8	19.4	8.2	1.7	75.3	30.8	51.9	48.1
30062	MARIETTA	83.8	77.9	8.1	10.1	4.8	6.8	4.6	7.4	6.0	6.5	7.2	7.1	5.4	26.3	32.7	7.9	0.9	75.7	39.5	49.8	50.2
30064	MARIETTA	79.5	74.5	15.1	17.3	1.6	2.3	5.9	8.7	6.6	6.8	7.2	7.3	5.4	27.0	29.6	8.8	1.3	74.7	38.0	49.4	50.6
30066	MARIETTA	86.1	80.5	7.0	9.1	3.6	5.3	3.8	6.5	6.2	6.7	7.2	7.1	5.5	27.8	31.1	7.6	0.8	75.4	38.3	49.5	50.5
30067	MARIETTA	60.3	53.8	26.3	28.2	5.3	6.9	10.6	15.0	6.6	5.4	5.2	6.0	12.1	37.1	20.8	6.1	0.8	79.3	31.0	50.8	49.2
30068	MARIETTA	89.3	84.9	4.1	5.3	4.3	6.4	2.6	4.3	4.8	5.7	6.9	6.8	4.9	22.5	35.2	12.0	1.2	78.0	43.8	48.9	51.1
30069	MARIETTA	59.3	51.3	33.3	35.9	0.0	0.0	11.1	15.4	5.1	2.6	0.0	7.7	46.2	35.9	2.6	0.0	0.0	92.3	23.8	84.6	15.4
30071	NORCROSS	51.3	43.7	21.9	21.4	8.4	10.1	36.2	45.9	8.1	6.9	6.3	6.5	9.3	37.9	19.6	4.8	0.6	75.0	30.8	54.8	45.2
30075	ROSWELL	88.5	81.2	5.6	9.3	2.7	3.9	5.5	9.1	6.4	7.0	7.6	6.7	4.3	26.5	32.0	8.1	1.3	74.8	40.0	49.9	50.1
30076	ROSWELL	77.5	66.9	9.4	14.3	4.0	5.0	16.1	22.7	7.0	6.3	6.3	6.6	8.6	32.5	24.7	6.9	1.2	76.6	33.8	51.6	48.4
30078	SNELLVILLE	86.2	78.6	7.0	9.5	3.2	5.7	4.6	8.5	6.6	6.8	7.3	7.3	5.4	27.1	29.8	8.4	1.3	74.5	37.6	48.9	51.1
30079	SCOTTDALE	32.6	26.6	58.3	61.6	5.1	6.6	3.4	4.8	8.7	8.2	6.7	6.8	7.7	31.2	21.0	8.0	1.8	72.4	32.0	45.6	54.4
30080	SMYRNA	58.7	50.2	27.5	30.8	3.6	4.5	14.8	20.6	6.3	4.9	4.3	4.9	12.0	40.7	20.1	5.8	0.9	81.8	31.4	50.6	49.4
30082	SMYRNA	62.4	55.5	26.9	29.9	3.2	4.1	11.1	15.0	7.2	6.5	6.0	5.2	5.9	34.2	23.7	9.5	1.6	77.1	36.1	48.6	51.4
30083	STONE MOUNTAIN	17.9	14.0	72.7	74.1	4.4	5.3	4.6	6.5	8.4	7.7	6.9	6.7	8.9	33.7	21.1	5.8	0.8	73.1	30.4	47.5	52.5
30084	TUCKER	59.6	52.3	21.7	22.4	9.0	11.6	16.3	22.6	7.0	6.5	6.1	5.5	6.6	32.2	24.1	10.3	1.6	77.1	36.3	50.1	49.9
30087	STONE MOUNTAIN	41.4	33.5	51.3	56.5	3.9	5.3	3.4	4.9	6.9	7.1	7.4	7.0	4.9	28.4	29.0	8.5	0.9	74.2	37.5	48.2	51.8
30088	STONE MOUNTAIN	8.4	6.4	87.5	88.6	1.3	1.5	2.2	2.9	7.3	7.2	7.2	7.5	7.5	31.9	25.9	5.1	0.4	73.8	32.4	46.5	53.5
30092	NORCROSS	64.9	56.0	19.7	21.3	8.8	12.9	9.5	14.2	7.7	7.4	7.3	6.2	7.6	32.9	25.2	5.4	0.5	74.0	33.2	50.3	49.7
30093	NORCROSS	44.6	36.4	26.4	26.3	13.7	16.1	27.2	36.1	8.4	6.9	5.9	6.5	10.8	37.5	19.4	4.2	0.3	75.1	29.7	51.9	48.1
30094	CONYERS	82.4	77.2	14.1	17.4	1.6	2.3	2.0	3.7	6.1	6.5	7.0	7.5	5.5	26.0	31.2	9.3	0.9	75.7	39.2	49.0	51.0
30096	DULUTH	65.3	54.3	13.8	15.7	12.5	16.9	12.7	19.7	7.1	6.2	6.0	5.9	8.3	36.6	24.0	5.3	0.5	77.3	33.1	50.5	49.5
30097	DULUTH	77.7	69.1	6.2	9.1	13.2	17.2	3.4	5.7	9.2	9.6	9.2	6.9	3.2	31.3	26.3	4.0	0.3	67.0	35.3	49.3	50.7
30101	ACWORTH	87.5	83.9	7.5	8.8	1.7	2.3	3.7	5.7	9.1	9.0	8.7	6.9	4.5	31.9	23.8	5.5	0.5	68.7	34.0	49.4	50.6
30102	ACWORTH	87.4	81.9	6.0	7.6	2.0	2.8	5.4	9.2	8.0	7.8	7.6	6.7	5.5	31.8	26.3	5.8	0.4	72.4	34.4	50.3	49.7
30103	ADAIRSVILLE	90.1	86.9	7.2	9.2	0.7	0.9	1.5	2.6	7.7	7.5	7.4	6.7	5.6	28.3	25.9	9.9	1.1	73.2	36.6	49.3	50.7
30104	ARAGON	90.9	87.7	7.7	10.0	0.2	0.2	1.5	2.7	7.8	7.8	7.6	6.2	5.3	27.6	26.9	9.9	0.9	73.0	36.7	50.2	49.8
30105	ARMUCHEE	96.5	94.9	1.9	2.8	0.4	0.6	0.6	1.1	6.0	6.4	6.9	6.6	4.7	24.9	30.9	12.2	1.3	76.5	41.3	50.4	49.6
30106	AUSTELL	61.8	54.2	32.3	37.5	1.6	2.0	4.3	7.0	7.7	7.1	6.6	6.1	6.5	30.9	24.1	9.2	1.8	74.8	35.5	48.1	51.9
30107	BALL GROUND	97.5	96.4	1.0	1.3	0.1	0.2	1.2	2.1	6.9	7.2	7.4	6.6	4.7	27.7	28.8	9.7	1.0	74.4	38.6	50.0	50.0
30108	BOWDON	85.6	81.6	12.4	15.5	0.1	0.2	1.5	2.7	6.7	6.7	6.9	6.7	5.3	25.8	27.7	12.6	1.6	75.6	39.4	49.9	50.1
30110	BREMEN	90.9	88.5	7.5	9.2	0.4	0.6	0.6	0.9	6.9	6.8	6.9	6.6	5.7	26.7	26.5	11.8	1.9	75.2	38.3	49.3	50.7
30113	BUCHANAN	96.0	94.8	3.0	3.7	0.1	0.2	0.5	0.8	6.5	6.6	6.8	6.4	5.2	26.2	27.2	13.2	2.0	76.2	40.0	49.9	50.1
30114	CANTON	88.5	86.2	3.6	3.7	0.6	0.8	10.1	12.5	7.7	7.7	7.6	6.8	5.4	29.4	25.6	8.5	1.3	73.0	36.0	49.7	50.3
30115	CANTON	95.5	93.2	1.0	1.1	0.3	0.5	4.3	7.1	7.2	7.6	7.8	6.8	4.6	28.4	28.4	8.3	0.9	73.1	37.5	50.2	49.8
30116	CARROLLTON	80.4	75.4	16.7	20.4	0.8	1.1	1.5	2.5	7.5	7.4	7.3	6.9	5.9	29.1	25.9	8.8	1.2	73.5	35.5	49.6	50.4
30117	CARROLLTON	73.0	67.3	22.7	26.5	0.8	1.0	4.3	6.5	6.7	6.4	6.1	8.6	10.5	27.4	22.5	9.7	2.0	76.8	32.7	48.6	51.4
30118	CARROLLTON	60.0	50.5	31.8	36.6	0.9	1.2	7.8	12.7	1.4	1.2	1.2	40.5	37.6	9.4	6.6	1.9	0.2	93.5	20.8	42.4	57.6
30120	CARTERSVILLE	83.4	79.6	12.3	14.2	0.5	0.6	4.7	6.9	7.8	7.7	7.3	6.6	5.6	28.8	25.0	9.7	1.5	73.0	35.8	49.0	51.0
30121	CARTERSVILLE	87.2	82.6	8.9	11.3	0.7	1.0	3.6	5.9	7.7	7.4	7.2	6.7	6.1	30.8	24.3	8.5	1.2	73.6	35.1	49.5	50.5
30122	LITHIA SPRINGS	70.9	65.5	24.3	27.7	1.4	1.9	3.5	5.2	7.1	6.9	6.7	6.4	6.3	30.4	25.1	9.9	1.2	75.4	36.0	48.7	51.3
30124	CAVE SPRING	92.8	88.8	4.8	7.4	0.5	0.7	1.5	2.8	5.8	6.3	6.6	6.4	4.7	23.4	31.3	13.9	1.6	77.4	42.9	49.8	50.2
30125	CEDARTOWN	77.6	70.7	13.2	14.6	0.4	0.5	12.1	18.7	7.1	6.7	6.6	7.1	7.1	26.4	24.8	12.2	1.9	75.3	36.5	50.8	49.2
30126	MABLETON	63.9	54.9	28.6	34.7	1.6	2.3	7.4	10.5	7.3	7.4	7.2	6.3	5.1	30.1	26.5	8.9	1.1	74.0	37.2	48.7	51.3
30127	POWDER SPRINGS	74.4	69.2	21.6	25.1	1.0	1.5	3.1	4.7	8.0	8.3	8.3	7.6	5.0	30.4	25.8	5.8	0.7	70.3	34.9	49.2	50.8
30132	DALLAS	92.6	90.5	5.0	6.0	0.4	0.7	1.6	2.6	9.0	8.5	8.2	7.0	5.1	32.1	22.1	7.0	0.9	69.8	33.5	49.8	50.2
30134	DOUGLASVILLE	75.5	70.1	20.6	24.6	0.7	0.9	3.0	4.4	9.3	8.6	7.9	7.2	6.6	31.8	21.3	6.6	0.7	69.9	32.2	49.7	50.3
30135	DOUGLASVILLE	83.0	77.9	13.2	16.6	1.4	2.0	2.3	3.5	7.1	7.0	7.0	7.1	6.0	30.0	27.5	7.5	0.8	74.6	35.5	48.5	51.5
30137	EMERSON	90.6	87.3	6.9	9.0	0.3	0.4	1.9	3.2	6.8	7.1	7.5	7.0	5.3	26.4	29.5	9.6	0.9	74.3	38.3	50.0	50.0
30139	FAIRMOUNT	97.7	96.6	1.1	1.5	0.1	0.1	1.2	1.9	6.8	6.7	6.9	6.8	5.6	27.4	28.0	10.7	1.2	75.5	38.5	50.1	49.9
30141	HIRAM	89.4	85.9	7.9	10.3	0.3	0.4	2.0	3.0	8.9	8.3	8.0	6.9	5.0	32.7	23.3	6.4	0.6	70.5	33.8	49.5	50.5
30143	JASPER	96.1	94.5	1.4	1.7	0.3	0.5	2.1	3.4	5.9	6.0	6.1	5.8	4.7	24.7	29.4	15.8	1.6	78.5	42.8	48.7	51.3
30144	KENNESAW	81.7	74.5	10.1	13.1	3.6	5.2	5.3	8.7	8.3	7.6	6.9	5.8	6.2	37.3	21.9	5.3	0.5	73.6	33.0	49.6	50.4
30145	KINGSTON	92.6	89.7	5.5	7.3	0.2	0.4	1.4	2.5	8.7	8.1	7.8	6.9	5.5	30.8	23.8	7.6	0.8	71.0	34.0	49.5	50.5
30147	LINDALE	95.7	93.2	2.0	3.1	0.4	0.6	1.6	2.9	6.2	6.4	6.5	6.5	5.4	26.2	28.4	12.6	1.7	76.9	39.7	50.0	50.0
30148	MARBLE HILL	98.4	97.7	0.1	0.2	0.1	0.2	0.5	0.8	5.8	6.0	6.3	5.9	4.5	22.5	31.4	16.5	1.0	78.4	44.3	49.8	50.2
30149	MOUNT BERRY	88.3	81.7	4.5	6.6	2.0	2.7	5.4	9.6	2.0	1.6	0.5	32.5	46.7	7.5	4.3	3.0	1.8	95.4	21.4	39.8	60.2
30152	KENNESAW	87.8	81.4	6.1	7.8	2.4	3.5	4.5	9.1	8.1	8.0	7.9	7.1	4.6	31.5	26.5	5.6	0.6	71.2	34.7	49.8	50.2
30153	ROCKMART	84.7	81.8	13.6	15.7	0.4	0.5	1.2	2.0	7.2	7.1	7.0	6.8	5.7	27.0	26.5	11.3	1.5	74.4	37.4	49.7	50.3
30157	DALLAS	92.2	89.0	5.3	7.4	0.4	0.6	1.6	2.5	8.7	8.3	7.9	7.0	5.5	32.3	23.3	6.4	0.7	70.7	33.6	49.7	50.3
	GEORGIA	65.1	61.1	28.7	30.1	2.2	2.9	5.3	7.7	7.3	7.0	6.9	7.1	7.1	29.3	25.1	8.9	1.3	74.7	35.0	49.4	50.6
	UNITED STATES	75.1	72.0	12.3	12.7	3.8	4.6	12.5	15.7	6.8	6.7	6.6	7.1	6.9	27.0	26.0	10.9	1.9	75.7	36.9	49.2	50.8

ZIP CODE #	POST OFFICE NAME	2009 Per Capita Income	2009 HH Income Base	2009 Household Income Distribution (%): Less than $25,000	$25,000 to $49,999	$50,000 to $99,999	$100,000 to $149,999	$150,000 or More	Median Household Income: 2009	2014	2009 National Centile	2009 State Centile	2009 Home Value Base	2009 Home Value Distribution (%): Less than $50,000	$50,000 to $89,999	$90,000 to $174,999	$175,000 to $399,999	$400,000 or More	2009 Median Home Value
30002	AVONDALE ESTATES	28677	3293	22.2	26.5	30.1	13.8	7.4	51982	57363	66	71	1465	5.0	8.9	37.7	44.4	4.0	170712
30004	ALPHARETTA	53897	18194	6.5	10.5	25.7	28.8	28.6	110551	114648	98	99	15410	1.4	3.8	30.1	38.8	25.9	232467
30005	ALPHARETTA	59895	11691	5.6	6.2	26.7	22.3	39.2	128221	130823	99	100	8772	1.3	1.9	21.2	56.2	19.5	252078
30008	MARIETTA	25347	11300	13.0	22.6	45.1	13.2	6.0	61272	60469	79	81	7029	15.3	13.8	55.5	15.1	0.3	113066
30009	ALPHARETTA	44728	7033	6.7	14.2	43.7	21.2	14.1	79802	81696	92	93	3640	1.1	5.2	55.4	30.0	8.4	143980
30011	AUBURN	27408	6043	8.2	15.6	55.4	14.6	6.2	73845	75656	89	90	4928	5.0	10.0	53.2	26.8	5.0	147647
30012	CONYERS	20371	9677	22.7	29.1	36.2	7.9	4.1	48063	53034	57	65	5806	18.6	22.3	41.9	13.8	3.4	100208
30013	CONYERS	31749	8633	9.0	21.1	39.6	17.3	13.1	71215	76131	87	89	6041	4.7	8.0	47.1	36.0	4.2	150632
30014	COVINGTON	21513	13323	22.6	26.5	39.8	7.4	3.7	50656	54723	63	69	9250	11.6	22.5	40.5	21.4	4.0	114283
30016	COVINGTON	25613	19034	12.0	21.3	50.8	10.9	5.1	63299	66926	82	83	15145	10.0	14.1	54.6	19.5	1.8	129127
30017	GRAYSON	36023	6282	3.7	7.9	42.6	28.3	17.4	93738	101323	96	97	5663	1.8	2.6	35.7	52.5	7.4	189770
30019	DACULA	38132	12851	5.2	8.4	39.5	27.7	19.3	95179	101729	96	97	11723	3.6	5.1	34.4	48.6	8.4	187554
30021	CLARKSTON	19218	8189	20.8	29.3	39.2	8.3	2.5	49923	53023	61	68	2424	9.6	15.7	70.2	4.5	0.0	111986
30022	ALPHARETTA	54535	24310	4.8	8.2	29.8	23.9	33.2	116232	119975	98	99	18364	0.7	1.6	32.0	43.1	22.6	232933
30024	SUWANEE	50853	20959	3.1	5.6	26.6	26.9	37.8	127661	129639	99	100	17826	2.6	2.9	15.1	65.6	13.9	243252
30025	SOCIAL CIRCLE	22990	3602	18.9	26.6	41.1	9.2	4.2	54633	58293	71	76	2803	12.3	21.7	31.3	28.9	5.8	130974
30028	CUMMING	33120	6870	8.2	13.2	41.3	24.7	12.6	83288	85811	93	94	5878	13.5	14.2	33.7	28.4	10.2	152149
30030	DECATUR	40207	12470	16.1	20.6	35.5	16.8	10.9	65073	68828	83	85	6831	1.3	6.0	31.0	54.7	7.0	204180
30032	DECATUR	19010	19668	22.4	30.7	36.5	8.1	2.3	46839	50800	54	63	10453	6.3	50.3	40.9	1.9	0.6	86214
30033	DECATUR	44074	13530	13.1	18.5	39.2	17.4	11.8	69733	75050	87	88	7861	1.2	4.0	36.6	53.5	4.7	190897
30034	DECATUR	25688	17094	11.4	23.3	41.0	19.3	5.0	65602	68995	84	85	11901	1.9	15.6	70.7	11.1	0.7	117658
30035	DECATUR	22476	7807	13.1	23.9	49.8	10.4	2.8	60386	61449	78	80	4636	1.4	27.0	67.7	3.0	0.9	105138
30038	LITHONIA	29095	13513	8.5	17.0	52.6	14.8	7.2	69511	73444	86	88	10588	1.5	14.7	71.2	9.7	3.0	119071
30039	SNELLVILLE	32402	13327	5.3	11.5	44.9	24.7	13.6	83922	90405	93	95	11551	9.0	2.5	44.1	39.1	5.4	164729
30040	CUMMING	37612	19610	11.2	15.3	31.1	22.4	20.0	86572	90970	94	96	16436	10.5	9.6	28.9	37.9	13.2	178571
30041	CUMMING	45176	19663	7.7	10.6	32.0	21.5	28.1	99329	103965	97	98	17343	6.5	5.8	20.6	51.5	15.6	232046
30043	LAWRENCEVILLE	37110	26051	4.3	8.2	36.4	29.5	21.5	101469	106334	97	98	21420	4.8	1.4	29.8	60.5	3.5	199533
30044	LAWRENCEVILLE	31322	29740	6.4	14.0	47.6	21.3	10.7	79307	82409	92	93	20502	3.1	3.0	49.9	43.0	1.1	167688
30045	LAWRENCEVILLE	29777	21860	10.5	14.2	45.4	20.1	9.8	76359	79480	90	92	16124	7.9	4.3	48.2	36.3	3.3	158593
30047	LILBURN	33685	20272	6.6	12.4	41.8	25.0	14.1	85443	90402	94	95	16197	3.5	1.9	37.3	54.4	3.0	187300
30052	LOGANVILLE	28921	20453	7.8	17.6	47.3	18.2	9.2	76748	79221	90	92	17811	12.0	5.5	43.6	34.5	4.4	156197
30054	OXFORD	23931	4201	12.6	25.1	47.1	10.2	5.0	60748	63993	78	80	3558	13.4	16.2	31.7	31.3	7.5	137154
30055	MANSFIELD	22973	1220	18.9	29.3	39.6	8.4	3.8	51529	54596	65	71	1034	11.5	14.3	42.7	26.1	5.3	121059
30056	NEWBORN	17490	921	21.3	36.0	36.7	3.8	2.2	45782	48409	51	60	747	21.8	20.5	38.2	15.9	3.6	100268
30058	LITHONIA	25655	19499	10.4	21.2	46.1	16.8	5.4	65666	68422	84	85	14535	3.4	16.1	68.5	11.3	0.7	116009
30060	MARIETTA	22043	13743	22.3	28.5	36.8	8.2	4.2	49073	51619	59	66	5904	10.9	22.0	55.8	9.9	1.4	104467
30062	MARIETTA	43105	23030	5.5	10.3	35.7	25.9	22.7	97260	103347	96	98	18484	1.7	2.1	33.8	54.9	7.4	194516
30064	MARIETTA	39011	17443	8.1	11.4	38.4	24.8	17.5	87184	95269	94	96	13970	4.7	4.7	37.6	46.8	6.3	181402
30066	MARIETTA	38300	19267	5.5	11.7	39.8	25.6	17.5	89312	95468	95	97	15721	0.6	3.1	52.2	40.1	4.0	165390
30067	MARIETTA	37093	20845	12.0	22.0	41.0	13.0	12.0	64123	63741	82	84	7867	2.6	7.9	35.4	32.4	21.6	188694
30068	MARIETTA	55861	12439	5.4	9.1	28.7	25.5	31.3	113911	117428	98	99	10629	1.3	1.3	17.1	66.2	14.1	244323
30069	MARIETTA	26004	7	0.0	0.0	100.0	0.0	0.0	87500	87500	94	96	0	0.0	0.0	0.0	0.0	0.0	0
30071	NORCROSS	21839	8104	13.1	22.2	45.0	14.5	5.2	63060	63257	81	83	4127	4.6	10.0	58.1	25.6	1.8	143495
30075	ROSWELL	48224	20265	6.6	12.0	30.1	21.7	29.6	102448	104383	97	99	16378	0.9	4.2	28.7	52.1	14.1	224252
30076	ROSWELL	41186	18094	8.0	14.7	38.5	21.6	17.2	82691	84610	93	94	10584	1.1	5.0	41.6	40.3	12.0	179967
30078	SNELLVILLE	34402	12011	5.3	13.6	41.6	23.8	15.6	85768	91011	94	96	9835	1.3	1.2	44.9	44.1	8.4	179522
30079	SCOTTDALE	19983	1225	31.2	28.1	28.2	9.3	3.3	41456	43317	38	48	487	14.8	24.4	46.4	14.2	0.2	110167
30080	SMYRNA	34858	22951	13.4	23.4	42.8	13.7	6.7	60735	59281	78	80	8411	3.9	15.2	49.1	23.3	8.4	122384
30082	SMYRNA	33291	10491	10.0	18.3	44.1	19.3	8.3	69153	71017	86	88	6605	9.3	7.9	49.6	31.7	1.5	137344
30083	STONE MOUNTAIN	23444	21613	12.6	28.7	44.3	10.8	3.6	58684	60531	76	79	10944	1.8	21.5	71.0	5.2	0.4	111157
30084	TUCKER	30837	16558	9.9	21.6	42.0	17.7	8.7	67437	70846	85	87	9483	5.4	6.7	54.3	31.9	1.7	151852
30087	STONE MOUNTAIN	34972	12750	6.9	12.3	42.5	25.0	13.2	83284	86687	93	94	11146	5.4	2.9	48.3	39.6	3.8	164561
30088	STONE MOUNTAIN	26484	10275	8.2	23.6	47.4	15.8	5.1	66230	70204	84	86	7193	0.2	16.1	76.5	7.0	0.2	116511
30092	NORCROSS	44441	14362	8.8	18.8	33.1	15.9	23.4	80566	84311	92	93	7272	1.9	4.8	13.9	55.6	23.8	289248
30093	NORCROSS	23684	17912	11.7	26.8	45.1	12.1	4.2	59825	59087	77	80	6976	10.6	6.4	61.8	20.5	0.7	133203
30094	CONYERS	30979	10985	7.4	16.2	45.4	21.6	9.3	77638	79316	91	92	9607	3.5	9.4	57.8	26.8	2.5	135876
30096	DULUTH	33844	23310	7.8	18.6	44.6	18.5	10.4	74920	77857	89	91	11108	6.1	3.3	37.8	47.6	5.1	179458
30097	DULUTH	61248	14365	3.6	5.7	21.9	24.5	44.3	137447	140709	99	100	12261	6.3	2.1	11.1	55.1	25.5	249923
30101	ACWORTH	37359	19787	7.5	13.3	35.7	25.8	17.7	89320	95412	95	97	16971	3.9	5.2	39.9	46.6	4.3	176608
30102	ACWORTH	29265	12796	8.4	16.4	44.2	22.1	8.9	77044	80363	91	92	10525	10.7	10.0	54.4	24.0	0.9	139808
30103	ADAIRSVILLE	19319	5175	23.7	30.8	39.2	4.2	2.2	45811	50168	51	61	3916	16.0	29.5	36.5	15.1	2.9	96705
30104	ARAGON	17825	1632	26.7	31.1	35.4	5.6	1.2	42939	47887	42	53	1311	18.6	32.3	32.9	14.3	1.9	89161
30105	ARMUCHEE	20790	1124	23.8	26.0	41.9	7.2	1.1	50215	52526	62	69	937	13.2	27.5	37.6	17.0	4.7	103693
30106	AUSTELL	27256	7481	11.9	20.9	48.4	13.9	4.9	63386	62863	82	83	5229	3.7	20.1	65.3	10.1	0.7	113833
30107	BALL GROUND	24810	4835	14.1	21.4	49.8	10.9	3.7	61379	61696	79	81	4104	12.1	14.9	35.3	29.1	8.7	144506
30108	BOWDON	19748	3516	31.1	28.6	34.0	4.4	1.8	40766	44722	35	45	2658	27.4	28.1	31.9	10.6	2.0	78909
30110	BREMEN	18405	4896	32.2	30.7	31.3	4.1	1.7	36937	39881	23	33	3563	20.7	32.5	38.7	7.5	0.6	85290
30113	BUCHANAN	17632	2673	32.4	31.3	30.7	3.7	1.9	38144	40556	27	37	2111	26.0	36.0	28.7	7.5	1.8	76233
30114	CANTON	30815	17279	13.7	16.7	41.0	18.5	10.1	71500	76311	88	89	13741	5.2	13.0	31.6	41.3	8.9	175634
30115	CANTON	30866	11968	10.3	17.3	40.7	22.4	9.3	76623	80914	90	92	10226	7.0	9.0	31.3	40.5	12.2	181954
30116	CARROLLTON	22903	8708	21.9	22.1	43.9	7.6	4.5	55638	57210	72	76	6536	17.8	22.9	40.7	14.5	4.0	99557
30117	CARROLLTON	21401	14171	31.6	24.5	33.4	6.7	3.8	41764	47936	39	49	7990	17.5	25.5	40.8	13.8	2.4	97890
30118	CARROLLTON	8324	16	37.5	43.8	12.5	6.3	0.0	30000	32265	8	8	4	100.0	0.0	0.0	0.0	0.0	5000
30120	CARTERSVILLE	23135	13287	18.7	25.2	43.4	8.2	4.5	55712	59007	72	76	9525	12.7	24.7	44.5	16.4	1.7	106897
30121	CARTERSVILLE	22665	7912	16.4	26.8	46.5	7.1	3.1	55924	59125	73	76	5411	16.8	21.6	47.3	13.3	1.1	103449
30122	LITHIA SPRINGS	25378	8958	17.3	26.5	44.6	8.1	3.4	55689	59103	72	76	5361	18.8	16.0	48.6	15.7	0.8	110925
30124	CAVE SPRING	20983	1170	23.8	28.2	40.5	5.2	2.3	47960	51355	56	64	967	18.3	32.7	32.3	11.7	5.1	88643
30125	CEDARTOWN	17869	8809	32.3	30.6	30.6	4.4	2.1	38839	41678	29	40	6005	11.6	22.5	48.8	15.6	1.5	110361
30126	MABLETON	30411	11990	12.6	18.0	40.4	21.1	7.9	69877	75333	87	89	9596	8.5	19.3	48.7	20.0	3.5	112953
30127	POWDER SPRINGS	32097	19893	6.8	12.3	42.2	25.9	12.7	83964	88744	93	95	17924	3.7	7.3	54.2	31.9	2.9	145010
30132	DALLAS	25867	10630	12.7	19.6	48.7	15.1	3.9	64670	67007	83	85	8245	13.7	11.5	44.8	28.3	1.7	136780
30134	DOUGLASVILLE	24457	15771	15.3	21.4	45.6	13.3	4.4	62376	65142	80	82	11832	12.0	10.2	55.1	22.1	0.5	133886
30135	DOUGLASVILLE	29145	21486	7.4	16.8	51.0	16.2	8.5	74417	76875	89	91	17708	5.6	6.8	57.8	25.6	4.2	137986
30137	EMERSON	21593	685	17.5	29.1	42.6	8.2	2.6	53032	57264	68	72	561	21.6	26.2	34.4	14.4	3.4	92907
30139	FAIRMOUNT	19815	1711	22.6	31.3	40.4	4.3	1.4	46422	47751	53	62	1418	23.3	19.3	34.4	16.5	6.4	104310
30141	HIRAM	26563	7605	10.6	18.1	49.3	17.3	4.8	68828	72520	86	88	6619	9.9	11.7	54.4	21.2	2.8	136061
30143	JASPER	25856	9360	19.8	26.2	41.9	7.3	4.7	53608	56428	69	74	7535	14.2	23.3	36.7	19.7	6.0	109370
30144	KENNESAW	34672	17607	6.9	14.3	48.0	20.3	10.5	77814	81337	91	92	11919	6.1	5.6	52.3	34.6	1.4	149784
30145	KINGSTON	21757	2682	17.0	24.6	46.5	8.5	3.3	59216	60871	76	79	2247	15.2	24.3	44.7	13.3	2.5	103650
30147	LINDALE	20884	2031	21.9	32.6	37.1	5.7	2.7	46435	49791	53	62	1543	15.4	35.9	38.3	8.6	1.8	88968
30148	MARBLE HILL	25215	450	16.9	28.9	42.2	6.4	5.6	54303	57228	70	75	395	21.3	20.8	31.1	17.5	9.4	97683
30149	MOUNT BERRY	11256	34	41.2	32.4	26.5	0.0	0.0	35000	42353	18	25	5	0.0	40.0	60.0	0.0	0.0	95000
30152	KENNESAW	42676	13756	4.4	7.6	37.6	26.9	23.5	100589	106365	97	98	11752	11.7	2.3	37.3	41.0	7.7	171488
30153	ROCKMART	19332	7081	26.1	30.6	36.4	5.3	1.5	44487	48962	47	57	5531	11.7	23.5	44.5	16.9	3.3	112583
30157	DALLAS	26019	16900	11.0	19.6	46.9	17.7	4.8	67531	70917	85	87	14221	9.9	12.7	52.0	23.4	2.0	137431
	GEORGIA	26980		20.7	23.1	36.8	11.7	7.7	56761	58593				13.2	17.9	39.1	24.2	5.5	121444
	UNITED STATES	27277		20.9	24.4	35.3	11.7	7.6	54719	56938				9.3	13.1	31.6	32.6	13.5	162279

ZIP CODE		FINANCIAL SERVICES				THE HOME						ENTERTAINMENT						PERSONAL			
						Home Improvements		Furnishings													
#	POST OFFICE NAME	Auto Loan	Home Loan	Invest-ments	Retire-ment Plans	Home Repair	Lawn & Garden	Comput-ers & Hard-ware-Personal	Major Appli-ances	TV, Radio, Sound Equip-ment	Furni-ture	Dine out/ Carry out	Sports Equip-ment	Fees & Tickets	Toys & Games	Travel	Cable TV	Apparel & Services	Auto Repairs	Health Insur-ance	Pets & Supplies
30002	AVONDALE ESTATES	101	86	80	90	82	84	102	90	102	101	104	73	96	103	93	101	72	99	93	110
30004	ALPHARETTA	204	249	230	255	247	215	210	214	197	230	200	172	238	207	225	185	146	200	185	242
30005	ALPHARETTA	255	287	249	297	278	239	255	249	238	280	243	208	277	256	259	220	177	236	211	283
30008	MARIETTA	113	102	88	102	96	91	111	101	108	113	110	82	104	113	101	104	76	106	96	120
30009	ALPHARETTA	155	158	140	165	152	137	155	144	147	164	150	121	159	156	151	139	108	145	129	169
30011	AUBURN	125	135	109	129	126	111	120	119	112	130	115	94	122	122	117	106	80	113	103	135
30012	CONYERS	88	82	72	82	78	82	85	83	85	83	85	64	80	88	80	86	59	84	84	99
30013	CONYERS	127	132	119	135	128	121	127	123	123	132	125	98	131	128	127	120	89	123	116	144
30014	COVINGTON	88	83	74	83	80	87	84	84	86	81	85	65	80	88	80	88	59	84	89	101
30016	COVINGTON	102	109	95	106	105	99	102	101	100	105	101	79	104	104	102	98	71	99	97	117
30017	GRAYSON	164	184	151	178	172	152	161	160	151	173	154	127	167	162	161	143	108	152	140	182
30019	DACULA	172	191	155	185	179	155	166	166	156	182	159	133	173	169	165	146	112	156	142	188
30021	CLARKSTON	88	62	55	66	58	58	87	70	86	86	88	60	75	88	73	83	62	83	70	87
30022	ALPHARETTA	219	259	241	269	257	222	225	224	210	246	213	183	253	222	237	196	157	211	192	254
30024	SUWANEE	224	266	227	271	257	218	224	225	207	250	211	186	249	224	232	190	154	207	186	252
30025	SOCIAL CIRCLE	101	98	86	97	96	99	91	96	93	94	93	71	89	96	90	95	64	93	96	114
30028	CUMMING	144	158	127	152	147	130	139	139	131	150	134	110	142	141	137	124	94	131	121	158
30030	DECATUR	115	112	113	117	112	110	123	112	121	122	122	89	123	119	120	120	86	119	116	135
30032	DECATUR	81	71	62	73	66	74	78	72	82	79	82	56	76	82	72	83	57	78	80	90
30033	DECATUR	119	117	122	123	118	113	129	116	126	128	128	94	131	125	127	124	91	124	119	139
30034	DECATUR	108	111	95	111	105	101	108	103	106	111	108	81	110	110	106	104	75	105	101	122
30035	DECATUR	95	87	75	88	81	84	93	86	94	94	95	68	90	96	87	93	66	91	89	105
30038	LITHONIA	120	127	108	125	120	111	119	116	114	125	117	91	122	120	118	110	82	114	107	135
30039	SNELLVILLE	138	162	140	161	155	140	141	141	133	149	136	112	153	140	147	128	97	136	127	163
30040	CUMMING	156	175	149	174	167	151	157	156	149	166	151	125	165	157	159	142	107	149	140	178
30041	CUMMING	184	212	181	210	203	182	183	186	173	196	176	147	197	184	189	166	125	175	165	212
30043	LAWRENCEVILLE	172	198	165	196	188	162	170	170	158	186	162	138	182	171	173	148	116	159	144	192
30044	LAWRENCEVILLE	137	138	116	138	130	119	134	127	128	141	131	103	134	136	129	122	92	127	115	148
30045	LAWRENCEVILLE	131	138	115	133	130	117	129	125	123	137	125	99	130	130	126	117	88	123	113	144
30047	LILBURN	138	159	147	161	156	144	143	143	137	149	139	112	155	141	150	133	99	140	134	166
30052	LOGANVILLE	127	141	117	137	133	121	124	125	118	132	120	99	129	126	125	113	84	119	113	143
30054	OXFORD	104	105	95	107	104	109	98	104	99	97	99	80	98	101	100	101	68	100	105	122
30055	MANSFIELD	96	91	81	90	89	94	85	91	88	87	88	67	82	91	83	90	60	87	91	108
30056	NEWBORN	89	72	74	71	71	86	72	81	77	71	76	61	62	80	67	82	52	77	84	97
30058	LITHONIA	116	117	95	113	109	100	111	107	107	118	109	85	109	113	106	102	76	106	98	125
30060	MARIETTA	87	77	68	78	73	75	91	79	90	86	91	64	84	91	81	90	64	87	83	97
30062	MARIETTA	163	190	183	196	190	172	171	170	163	180	166	135	189	167	181	158	120	166	156	197
30064	MARIETTA	150	170	156	171	166	153	155	154	148	161	151	120	166	153	160	144	107	150	144	178
30066	MARIETTA	151	172	157	176	168	153	156	153	149	163	151	123	169	154	162	143	108	150	141	178
30067	MARIETTA	137	103	95	113	98	98	135	110	133	134	136	95	122	138	116	129	95	127	111	137
30068	MARIETTA	200	238	238	247	241	218	211	212	200	223	203	166	236	204	228	194	148	205	195	245
30069	MARIETTA	143	74	55	86	66	63	134	93	126	125	133	93	102	152	97	116	93	119	84	113
30071	NORCROSS	109	98	85	98	94	87	108	98	104	110	107	79	101	108	99	100	75	104	92	115
30075	ROSWELL	186	215	208	223	215	193	193	191	183	205	186	153	214	189	204	176	135	186	173	221
30076	ROSWELL	161	152	146	161	150	141	163	148	158	167	161	121	163	163	157	153	115	155	141	176
30078	SNELLVILLE	144	171	150	171	165	151	148	149	142	156	144	118	163	148	156	137	103	143	138	172
30079	SCOTTDALE	76	61	55	65	57	64	77	66	81	74	81	53	71	80	67	83	56	75	74	84
30080	SMYRNA	117	85	76	93	79	81	115	93	114	113	116	80	101	118	97	110	81	108	94	116
30082	SMYRNA	121	118	107	119	114	108	121	113	118	124	120	90	120	122	117	115	84	117	110	134
30083	STONE MOUNTAIN	102	84	71	86	78	77	98	85	96	99	98	70	89	100	86	93	68	93	83	104
30084	TUCKER	116	115	108	118	113	108	119	111	115	121	117	88	119	118	116	113	82	115	109	132
30087	STONE MOUNTAIN	142	165	149	164	161	144	144	146	136	155	139	114	156	142	151	131	99	139	131	167
30088	STONE MOUNTAIN	114	109	91	108	102	96	111	103	107	115	109	82	107	112	103	104	76	106	97	122
30092	NORCROSS	171	155	145	166	151	141	171	151	165	175	168	127	168	172	160	158	120	161	142	181
30093	NORCROSS	108	82	71	87	76	76	105	87	103	104	105	73	92	107	89	99	73	99	86	108
30094	CONYERS	126	144	126	144	139	132	127	130	123	131	125	101	136	127	133	121	88	125	123	151
30096	DULUTH	133	120	104	125	113	106	131	116	127	134	130	97	126	133	121	122	91	124	109	140
30097	DULUTH	258	316	279	326	310	263	262	266	242	293	247	220	299	260	279	223	182	244	220	298
30101	ACWORTH	159	175	146	172	166	147	156	155	147	168	150	124	162	157	155	139	106	147	136	176
30102	ACWORTH	132	138	115	134	130	121	126	126	121	134	123	98	126	129	123	117	86	121	115	145
30103	ADAIRSVILLE	87	71	71	70	70	83	72	79	77	70	76	60	63	80	67	82	51	76	83	95
30104	ARAGON	85	65	70	63	64	80	66	75	72	65	71	57	55	75	60	77	48	71	78	90
30105	ARMUCHEE	90	76	81	77	77	92	76	87	80	71	79	65	68	81	74	85	53	81	89	102
30106	AUSTELL	108	108	94	106	102	100	107	103	105	108	106	82	105	109	103	103	74	104	101	121
30107	BALL GROUND	104	103	93	104	101	107	96	102	97	96	97	78	95	100	96	99	67	97	102	120
30108	BOWDON	88	62	77	60	62	85	65	78	73	63	71	60	52	75	60	80	48	74	83	94
30110	BREMEN	82	61	67	59	60	78	64	72	70	62	69	55	52	73	58	76	46	69	77	88
30113	BUCHANAN	83	59	68	58	59	79	62	72	69	60	67	55	50	71	56	75	45	68	76	87
30114	CANTON	125	132	117	131	128	125	123	124	121	125	122	96	126	125	123	120	85	121	120	145
30115	CANTON	123	139	122	140	135	130	124	127	120	128	122	99	132	124	130	119	86	122	121	148
30116	CARROLLTON	97	92	83	90	90	93	89	92	91	90	91	68	86	94	86	93	63	90	92	109
30117	CARROLLTON	82	70	66	70	68	74	80	75	80	76	80	59	71	82	71	82	55	78	78	91
30118	CARROLLTON	61	39	38	43	38	42	72	49	65	57	65	45	53	65	51	63	46	60	52	63
30120	CARTERSVILLE	97	93	83	92	90	94	91	92	92	91	92	71	88	95	88	94	64	91	93	109
30121	CARTERSVILLE	96	89	78	88	86	87	88	88	88	91	89	68	84	92	84	88	61	88	86	105
30122	LITHIA SPRINGS	93	90	82	90	88	88	91	89	90	91	91	69	89	93	88	91	63	90	90	105
30124	CAVE SPRING	90	72	88	72	74	94	72	87	78	66	76	66	62	78	72	84	51	80	91	103
30125	CEDARTOWN	82	61	69	60	61	79	66	74	72	63	70	56	55	73	61	78	48	71	79	89
30126	MABLETON	118	129	110	128	123	118	117	117	115	122	116	91	123	119	118	113	81	114	113	136
30127	POWDER SPRINGS	145	164	138	161	156	140	143	144	136	154	138	114	151	144	145	130	98	137	129	165
30132	DALLAS	109	109	92	106	104	101	101	103	100	106	101	79	100	106	98	99	70	99	98	120
30134	DOUGLASVILLE	105	103	88	100	98	94	101	99	98	105	99	77	97	103	96	96	69	98	93	115
30135	DOUGLASVILLE	124	133	111	131	126	116	121	120	116	128	118	93	124	122	120	112	83	116	110	139
30137	EMERSON	104	90	85	87	88	98	87	94	92	89	91	70	79	96	82	96	62	91	96	113
30139	FAIRMOUNT	91	68	75	66	67	86	69	79	76	68	75	61	57	79	63	82	50	75	83	96
30141	HIRAM	116	120	100	117	114	108	108	111	106	115	107	85	109	112	107	103	74	106	102	128
30143	JASPER	100	89	96	87	91	101	86	96	91	88	90	69	81	91	85	95	61	92	100	113
30144	KENNESAW	137	136	115	137	128	116	134	125	128	141	130	103	133	136	128	121	92	126	113	147
30145	KINGSTON	103	96	88	93	92	96	90	96	91	93	91	74	85	96	86	92	62	91	92	112
30147	LINDALE	84	75	75	75	73	87	75	81	78	71	77	62	69	80	73	82	53	79	86	97
30148	MARBLE HILL	110	85	112	84	89	111	86	103	93	85	92	76	74	93	85	101	62	97	107	122
30149	MOUNT BERRY	54	35	33	38	34	38	64	44	57	51	57	40	47	58	45	56	40	53	46	56
30152	KENNESAW	188	213	177	209	202	175	184	185	172	202	176	148	195	186	186	161	125	173	158	209
30153	ROCKMART	85	68	70	67	67	82	71	77	75	68	74	59	61	78	65	80	50	75	81	93
30157	DALLAS	116	118	99	114	112	107	108	109	106	114	107	84	107	112	105	104	74	105	103	127
	GEORGIA	110	101	97	102	98	103	103	103	104	104	104	80	99	107	99	105	73	103	103	122
	UNITED STATES	100	100	100	100	100	100	100	100	100	100	100	100	100	100	100	100	100	100	100	100

30161-30336

ZIP CODE #	POST OFFICE NAME	COUNTY FIPS CODE	POPULATION 2000	POPULATION 2009	POPULATION 2014	2000-2009 ANNUAL RATE % Rate	2000-2009 ANNUAL RATE State Centile	HOUSEHOLDS 2000	HOUSEHOLDS 2009	HOUSEHOLDS 2014	HOUSEHOLDS % Annual Rate 2000-2009	HOUSEHOLDS 2009 Average HH Size	FAMILIES 2000	FAMILIES 2009	FAMILIES % Annual Rate 2000-2009
30161	ROME	115	34007	34953	35275	0.3	25	13010	13372	13510	0.3	2.50	8938	8845	-0.1
30165	ROME	115	35973	39062	40187	0.9	45	13766	14839	15267	0.8	2.53	9562	9926	0.4
30168	AUSTELL	067	23011	26712	28560	1.6	63	8525	9699	10339	1.4	2.75	5566	5992	0.8
30170	ROOPVILLE	149	2732	3106	3274	1.4	57	1003	1152	1217	1.5	2.70	776	866	1.2
30171	RYDAL	015	2029	2464	2681	2.1	72	714	873	951	2.2	2.82	576	688	1.9
30173	SILVER CREEK	115	6425	6990	7214	0.9	45	2318	2539	2624	1.0	2.75	1881	2008	0.7
30175	TALKING ROCK	227	4801	6840	7849	3.9	90	1798	2617	3026	4.1	2.60	1384	1948	3.8
30176	TALLAPOOSA	143	6515	7065	7270	0.9	45	2578	2806	2891	0.9	2.51	1853	1953	0.6
30177	TATE	227	318	371	416	1.7	66	129	156	176	2.1	2.38	100	118	1.8
30178	TAYLORSVILLE	015	2920	3678	4072	2.5	77	1002	1264	1401	2.5	2.91	829	1023	2.3
30179	TEMPLE	045	9755	14950	17611	4.7	94	3515	5482	6490	4.9	2.73	2783	4224	4.6
30180	VILLA RICA	045	17924	34130	41808	7.2	98	6536	12540	15411	7.3	2.72	5096	9493	7.0
30182	WACO	045	2360	2653	2810	1.3	54	873	994	1056	1.4	2.67	650	716	1.1
30183	WALESKA	057	3971	5701	6739	4.0	91	1387	2032	2438	4.2	2.61	1110	1588	3.9
30184	WHITE	015	5815	7936	9126	3.4	87	2080	2878	3317	3.6	2.75	1699	2292	3.3
30185	WHITESBURG	045	3860	4613	4995	1.9	68	1386	1676	1825	2.1	2.75	1081	1269	1.7
30187	WINSTON	097	6062	8528	10154	3.8	90	2127	3055	3661	4.0	2.79	1764	2464	3.7
30188	WOODSTOCK	057	36594	57507	69489	5.0	94	12878	20629	25051	5.2	2.77	10034	15629	4.9
30189	WOODSTOCK	057	35007	43990	49697	2.5	77	11991	15023	16961	2.5	2.93	9745	11942	2.2
30204	BARNESVILLE	171	11733	12730	13061	0.9	45	4169	4615	4768	1.1	2.58	3055	3273	0.7
30205	BROOKS	113	2658	3215	3478	2.1	72	928	1133	1231	2.2	2.84	791	947	2.0
30206	CONCORD	231	2304	3135	3561	3.4	87	771	1057	1206	3.5	2.95	627	840	3.2
30213	FAIRBURN	121	16266	29375	36136	6.6	98	5615	10418	12864	6.9	2.80	4144	7333	6.4
30214	FAYETTEVILLE	113	21252	24167	25514	1.4	57	7658	8844	9388	1.6	2.71	6179	6941	1.3
30215	FAYETTEVILLE	113	27040	35357	39633	2.9	82	9047	11846	13309	3.0	2.97	7693	9891	2.8
30216	FLOVILLA	035	2212	2582	2864	1.7	66	726	867	971	1.9	2.98	581	676	1.7
30217	FRANKLIN	149	8763	9420	9583	0.8	41	3232	3502	3572	0.9	2.65	2417	2543	0.6
30218	GAY	199	2033	2321	2463	1.4	57	693	822	883	1.9	2.82	548	633	1.6
30220	GRANTVILLE	077	3166	4202	4802	3.1	85	1162	1572	1807	3.3	2.67	874	1149	3.0
30222	GREENVILLE	199	4452	4884	5091	1.0	47	1558	1768	1866	1.4	2.66	1141	1250	1.0
30223	GRIFFIN	255	34582	37168	38241	0.8	41	12510	13587	14037	0.9	2.72	9192	9689	0.6
30224	GRIFFIN	255	21566	24849	26325	1.5	60	8207	9576	10201	1.7	2.52	5989	6758	1.3
30228	HAMPTON	151	20588	37123	45142	6.6	98	6700	12288	15020	6.8	2.91	5397	9616	6.4
30230	HOGANSVILLE	285	8146	8850	9163	0.9	45	3029	3329	3463	1.0	2.62	2231	2373	0.7
30233	JACKSON	035	18264	23578	26115	2.8	80	6118	8091	9114	3.1	2.62	4618	5946	2.8
30234	JENKINSBURG	035	1458	1795	1980	2.3	74	495	628	701	2.6	2.85	374	461	2.3
30236	JONESBORO	063	45023	54429	58606	2.1	72	16320	19233	20597	1.8	2.79	11821	13452	1.4
30238	JONESBORO	063	32721	38161	40445	1.7	66	10839	12364	13027	1.4	3.09	8601	9508	1.1
30240	LAGRANGE	285	25929	29379	30566	1.4	57	9694	10925	11420	1.3	2.57	6877	7496	0.9
30241	LAGRANGE	285	20213	22337	23160	1.1	49	7470	8239	8591	1.1	2.58	5276	5609	0.7
30248	LOCUST GROVE	151	11160	22246	28264	7.7	98	3753	7618	9712	8.0	2.92	3142	6202	7.6
30251	LUTHERSVILLE	199	1968	2274	2417	1.6	63	691	825	888	1.9	2.76	540	626	1.6
30252	MCDONOUGH	151	18652	39029	49982	8.3	99	6335	13215	16922	8.3	2.95	5474	11115	8.0
30253	MCDONOUGH	151	25929	48983	60884	7.1	98	8930	16850	21018	7.1	2.87	6956	12882	6.9
30256	MEANSVILLE	231	2244	3181	3589	3.8	90	807	1145	1293	3.9	2.74	637	878	3.5
30257	MILNER	171	3730	4468	4784	2.0	70	1363	1653	1778	2.1	2.70	1088	1286	1.8
30258	MOLENA	231	2270	2864	3238	2.5	77	772	1005	1145	2.9	2.77	620	789	2.6
30259	MORELAND	077	2486	3093	3479	2.4	75	870	1084	1221	2.4	2.85	696	854	2.2
30260	MORROW	063	22399	24204	24694	0.8	41	7912	8406	8564	0.7	2.84	5495	5544	0.1
30263	NEWNAN	077	41825	55309	63250	3.1	85	14844	19764	22641	3.1	2.76	11164	14405	2.8
30265	NEWNAN	077	17821	31387	38043	6.3	97	6301	11099	13464	6.3	2.83	5076	8679	6.0
30268	PALMETTO	121	7115	10714	12678	4.5	93	2567	3842	4542	4.5	2.77	1900	2765	4.1
30269	PEACHTREE CITY	113	32282	37634	39793	1.7	66	11172	13104	13877	1.7	2.86	9056	10364	1.5
30273	REX	063	12636	16008	18055	2.6	78	4256	5302	5951	2.4	3.02	3362	4035	2.0
30274	RIVERDALE	063	28850	32732	34106	1.4	57	9960	11122	11540	1.2	2.92	7153	7662	0.7
30276	SENOIA	077	8976	13356	15848	4.4	93	3095	4638	5522	4.5	2.88	2518	3708	4.3
30277	SHARPSBURG	077	15427	19630	22381	2.6	78	5299	6701	7637	2.6	2.93	4517	5609	2.4
30281	STOCKBRIDGE	151	46669	63601	72261	3.4	87	16634	22727	25899	3.4	2.78	13046	17344	3.1
30285	THE ROCK	293	674	765	816	1.4	57	252	294	316	1.7	2.60	201	229	1.4
30286	THOMASTON	293	23973	24112	23984	0.1	19	9375	9535	9523	0.2	2.48	6626	6496	-0.2
30288	CONLEY	089	6840	8153	8891	1.9	68	2225	2661	2903	2.0	3.06	1690	1945	1.5
30290	TYRONE	113	5260	7390	8457	3.7	89	1820	2596	2987	3.9	2.85	1563	2179	3.7
30291	UNION CITY	121	12027	20132	24114	5.7	95	5114	8299	9913	5.4	2.42	3252	5074	4.9
30292	WILLIAMSON	231	4619	6036	6848	2.9	82	1593	2130	2429	3.2	2.77	1238	1613	2.9
30293	WOODBURY	199	3479	3442	3398	-0.1	14	1277	1311	1309	0.3	2.62	923	913	-0.1
30294	ELLENWOOD	089	26422	39072	44530	4.3	92	8569	12790	14644	4.4	3.00	6912	9955	4.0
30295	ZEBULON	231	3308	4384	4952	3.1	85	1208	1606	1825	3.1	2.64	941	1218	2.8
30296	RIVERDALE	063	22532	30555	33855	3.3	86	7756	10311	11383	3.1	2.95	5687	7185	2.6
30297	FOREST PARK	063	32263	34383	35200	0.7	37	10360	10614	10746	0.3	3.19	7410	7270	-0.2
30303	ATLANTA	121	4050	4674	5072	1.6	63	1143	1423	1622	2.4	1.98	285	319	1.2
30305	ATLANTA	121	20633	24183	26557	1.7	66	11319	13145	14418	1.6	1.82	4288	4555	0.7
30306	ATLANTA	121	21058	23071	24512	1.0	47	11266	12410	13218	1.1	1.82	3661	3624	-0.1
30307	ATLANTA	089	16875	19508	21121	1.6	63	7556	8853	9651	1.7	2.13	3282	3558	0.9
30308	ATLANTA	121	12044	16549	18845	3.5	88	6804	9702	11175	3.9	1.56	1351	1688	2.4
30309	ATLANTA	121	18536	22897	25893	2.3	74	11333	14216	16174	2.5	1.53	2463	2686	0.9
30310	ATLANTA	121	34018	35899	37828	0.6	34	12006	12668	13416	0.6	2.70	7172	7090	-0.1
30311	ATLANTA	121	34127	38154	41392	1.2	52	13259	14874	16169	1.3	2.56	8647	9135	0.6
30312	ATLANTA	121	19880	26173	29816	3.0	83	8711	11630	13343	3.2	2.15	3567	4241	1.9
30313	ATLANTA	121	8234	9818	10543	1.9	68	1626	2314	2650	3.9	1.84	471	612	2.9
30314	ATLANTA	121	26668	28156	29588	0.6	34	9236	9847	10422	0.7	2.52	5007	4832	-0.4
30315	ATLANTA	121	39569	45989	49902	1.6	63	11566	13341	14559	1.6	3.19	8026	8774	1.0
30316	ATLANTA	089	32392	37572	40725	1.6	63	11601	13744	14982	1.8	2.66	7462	8189	1.0
30317	ATLANTA	089	13956	14418	14898	0.4	28	5085	5462	5701	0.8	2.62	3107	3127	0.1
30318	ATLANTA	121	56078	69486	77196	2.3	74	19127	24019	27038	2.5	2.55	10891	12798	1.8
30319	ATLANTA	089	38527	42361	44619	1.0	47	16872	18508	19546	1.0	2.24	8450	8654	0.3
30322	ATLANTA	089	1731	1920	1926	1.1	49	6	6	7	0.0	2.50	1	1	0.0
30324	ATLANTA	121	21144	25233	27523	1.9	68	11034	12590	13617	1.4	2.00	3360	3514	0.5
30326	ATLANTA	121	2169	4472	5221	8.1	99	1343	2633	3093	7.5	1.58	405	837	8.2
30327	ATLANTA	121	20999	25089	27675	1.9	68	8775	10419	11479	1.9	2.40	5607	6349	1.4
30328	ATLANTA	121	28742	33385	36642	1.6	63	13338	15412	16913	1.6	2.16	7130	7755	0.9
30329	ATLANTA	089	22808	24154	25063	0.6	34	9731	10186	10575	0.5	2.20	3457	3280	-0.6
30330	ATLANTA	121	294	309	321	0.5	31	68	72	76	0.6	3.04	65	68	0.5
30331	ATLANTA	121	43038	54850	61992	2.7	79	15747	20304	23020	2.8	2.69	11098	13676	2.3
30334	ATLANTA	121	90	98	102	0.9	45	21	25	28	1.9	1.48	7	7	0.0
30336	ATLANTA	121	1371	2325	2647	5.9	96	441	641	714	4.1	3.54	295	433	4.2
	GEORGIA					2.1					2.1	2.65			1.8
	UNITED STATES					1.0					1.1	2.59			0.9

ZIP CODE #	POST OFFICE NAME	RACE (%) White 2000	White 2009	Black 2000	Black 2009	Asian/Pacific 2000	Asian/Pacific 2009	% Hispanic Origin 2000	% Hispanic Origin 2009	2009 AGE DISTRIBUTION (%) 0-4	5-9	10-14	15-19	20-24	25-44	45-64	65-84	85+	18+	MEDIAN AGE 2009	% 2009 Males	% 2009 Females
30161	ROME	72.1	66.6	23.6	27.1	0.6	0.8	5.1	7.3	6.3	6.5	6.5	6.4	6.3	26.4	26.1	13.0	2.5	76.9	38.8	49.1	50.9
30165	ROME	82.3	75.6	9.6	12.2	1.8	2.4	8.2	12.7	6.9	6.7	6.8	7.5	6.9	26.2	24.2	12.7	2.2	75.6	36.9	47.8	52.2
30168	AUSTELL	35.7	29.6	54.0	56.2	0.9	1.0	13.4	18.1	8.7	7.7	7.1	7.3	9.0	34.1	20.0	5.3	0.7	72.2	30.0	49.2	50.8
30170	ROOPVILLE	92.6	89.7	6.3	8.6	0.1	0.2	0.8	1.3	8.0	8.0	8.1	7.1	5.2	27.3	25.6	9.4	1.1	71.3	35.7	50.3	49.7
30171	RYDAL	97.6	96.5	1.1	1.5	0.1	0.2	1.2	2.2	7.0	7.1	7.4	6.8	4.8	28.6	27.6	9.7	1.0	74.1	37.8	50.5	49.5
30173	SILVER CREEK	95.4	93.0	3.0	4.5	0.4	0.6	1.2	2.1	6.4	6.4	6.6	6.8	6.1	27.5	28.9	10.4	1.0	76.6	38.2	50.2	49.8
30175	TALKING ROCK	96.0	93.7	0.3	0.5	0.2	0.3	3.6	5.8	7.3	7.3	7.2	6.2	5.1	28.4	26.7	10.6	1.3	74.5	37.6	50.3	49.7
30176	TALLAPOOSA	94.4	92.8	3.4	4.2	0.5	0.7	0.6	0.9	7.1	6.9	7.1	7.0	5.4	25.9	26.1	12.8	1.7	74.6	38.5	48.4	51.6
30177	TATE	96.2	94.6	2.2	3.0	0.3	0.5	0.6	1.1	6.2	6.5	6.7	6.7	5.4	26.7	28.0	12.4	1.3	76.3	39.1	51.8	48.2
30178	TAYLORSVILLE	94.8	92.6	3.5	4.7	0.2	0.4	1.6	2.7	8.2	7.7	7.4	7.0	5.6	31.2	25.1	7.2	0.5	72.2	34.8	50.3	49.7
30179	TEMPLE	91.2	87.5	7.1	10.0	0.3	0.5	0.9	1.5	7.3	7.4	7.4	6.9	5.2	29.1	26.3	9.6	0.9	73.6	36.8	49.4	50.6
30180	VILLA RICA	86.7	81.2	10.7	14.7	0.7	0.9	1.6	3.0	7.4	7.4	7.4	6.9	5.4	28.0	26.7	9.8	1.0	73.5	36.9	49.5	50.5
30182	WACO	89.4	86.5	8.5	10.5	0.5	0.6	1.0	1.5	7.2	7.2	7.2	7.3	6.0	27.1	26.6	10.3	1.2	74.1	36.9	50.1	49.9
30183	WALESKA	97.2	96.1	0.8	0.9	0.5	0.6	1.5	2.4	5.2	5.9	5.9	8.5	7.8	24.5	31.0	10.3	0.8	79.6	39.5	50.0	50.0
30184	WHITE	95.8	94.1	1.6	1.9	0.4	0.6	1.7	3.0	6.8	6.9	7.2	6.8	5.5	28.0	29.0	9.1	0.8	74.6	38.1	50.0	50.0
30185	WHITESBURG	92.4	89.8	6.6	8.7	0.1	0.1	0.5	0.8	7.0	7.1	7.2	6.9	5.7	27.1	28.6	9.3	1.1	74.4	37.6	51.3	48.7
30187	WINSTON	89.6	86.9	8.0	9.7	0.4	0.6	1.6	2.5	6.9	7.3	7.7	6.9	4.4	26.4	30.2	9.5	0.8	73.7	39.1	49.1	50.9
30188	WOODSTOCK	92.6	89.0	2.8	3.6	1.0	1.5	4.7	7.3	7.8	7.8	7.8	6.7	5.0	31.3	26.5	6.3	0.8	72.4	35.6	49.3	50.7
30189	WOODSTOCK	91.6	87.4	3.0	3.9	1.3	2.0	4.9	8.3	9.3	9.3	8.8	6.9	3.9	31.7	25.1	4.6	0.4	68.1	34.4	49.7	50.3
30204	BARNESVILLE	63.0	56.6	35.1	41.0	0.4	0.5	1.2	1.7	6.2	6.3	6.3	9.4	6.9	25.5	26.1	11.5	1.8	77.3	37.1	47.6	52.4
30205	BROOKS	96.1	94.7	1.8	2.4	0.4	0.6	1.4	2.2	5.3	7.2	8.1	7.9	3.8	25.8	31.1	9.9	0.8	74.0	40.0	50.5	49.5
30206	CONCORD	74.4	69.5	24.2	28.5	0.0	0.1	1.1	1.7	7.2	7.3	7.5	7.1	5.5	26.9	26.8	10.2	1.3	73.4	36.9	49.4	50.6
30213	FAIRBURN	49.3	37.4	44.9	55.1	0.8	1.0	6.3	8.5	6.4	6.5	6.7	6.8	5.8	25.9	28.4	11.6	1.8	76.0	39.0	48.2	51.8
30214	FAYETTEVILLE	77.7	73.3	17.8	20.4	2.4	3.4	2.3	3.3	4.9	5.5	6.7	6.9	4.6	22.1	34.5	13.1	1.8	78.5	44.6	48.3	51.7
30215	FAYETTEVILLE	84.8	80.8	11.8	14.1	1.7	2.6	2.3	3.5	6.2	7.3	8.3	7.8	4.5	25.1	31.9	8.1	1.0	73.1	39.7	49.4	50.6
30216	FLOVILLA	66.3	59.7	32.1	38.3	0.2	0.2	1.1	1.5	6.1	6.3	6.6	6.5	5.3	26.4	30.2	11.4	1.1	77.0	39.8	50.0	50.0
30217	FRANKLIN	85.7	82.2	12.6	15.4	0.2	0.3	1.1	1.7	7.6	7.6	7.8	7.3	5.5	26.3	26.1	10.3	1.5	72.4	37.0	49.4	50.6
30218	GAY	57.3	49.6	41.8	49.2	0.0	0.0	0.4	0.5	7.2	7.2	7.4	6.5	5.2	27.6	27.2	10.4	1.2	74.1	37.6	50.5	49.5
30220	GRANTVILLE	68.4	64.1	29.8	33.7	0.3	0.4	1.4	1.9	7.5	7.6	7.7	7.0	5.4	26.4	26.9	10.2	1.2	72.8	37.1	48.8	51.2
30222	GREENVILLE	43.7	37.2	54.9	61.0	0.1	0.1	1.1	1.5	6.6	6.7	6.9	7.0	6.1	24.5	27.5	12.3	2.4	75.9	39.2	47.9	52.1
30223	GRIFFIN	60.1	54.4	37.2	42.0	0.6	0.9	1.9	2.7	7.8	7.6	7.3	7.3	6.4	26.9	25.1	10.1	1.5	73.0	35.3	48.1	51.9
30224	GRIFFIN	74.9	68.6	23.0	28.5	0.8	1.0	1.1	1.7	6.9	6.5	6.5	6.8	6.3	26.1	26.4	12.2	2.2	76.0	38.1	48.9	51.1
30228	HAMPTON	77.7	70.8	19.0	24.2	1.2	1.8	2.2	3.4	7.6	7.5	7.5	7.2	5.7	31.0	25.3	7.3	0.7	72.9	35.1	51.0	49.0
30230	HOGANSVILLE	75.0	68.0	23.2	29.5	0.3	0.4	1.0	1.5	7.2	7.3	7.5	7.2	5.8	25.5	27.0	11.0	1.7	73.6	37.5	49.0	51.0
30233	JACKSON	73.4	68.5	24.6	28.8	0.3	0.4	1.5	2.2	6.5	6.3	6.3	6.2	6.4	30.8	25.8	10.3	1.4	77.4	37.4	53.7	46.3
30234	JENKINSBURG	54.4	47.9	43.2	48.9	0.3	0.4	1.4	2.1	6.6	6.9	7.5	7.4	5.5	26.5	29.1	9.8	0.9	74.7	37.7	48.0	52.0
30236	JONESBORO	52.3	45.2	37.7	41.1	3.8	5.1	8.4	11.6	7.7	7.1	6.7	6.9	7.9	30.1	24.6	8.1	0.9	74.3	33.4	49.4	50.6
30238	JONESBORO	39.7	33.3	54.0	58.2	2.2	3.0	4.0	5.7	8.8	8.2	7.8	7.7	6.8	32.2	23.0	5.0	0.4	70.4	31.3	47.2	52.8
30240	LAGRANGE	73.0	66.9	24.5	29.6	0.8	1.1	1.9	2.7	6.9	7.0	7.0	7.7	7.0	24.9	26.0	11.2	2.3	74.5	36.9	46.9	53.1
30241	LAGRANGE	54.8	49.2	42.5	47.0	0.7	0.9	2.0	2.9	7.4	7.2	7.1	7.1	7.1	27.7	24.6	10.1	1.7	73.9	35.0	49.4	50.6
30248	LOCUST GROVE	86.8	82.5	10.8	14.1	0.3	0.4	1.9	2.8	8.1	8.1	8.1	7.1	4.8	29.7	25.7	7.7	0.7	71.3	35.8	50.2	49.8
30251	LUTHERSVILLE	63.5	57.3	34.2	39.8	0.1	0.1	0.9	1.2	7.6	7.3	7.5	7.2	6.2	26.4	27.4	9.3	1.1	73.1	36.1	48.6	51.4
30252	MCDONOUGH	92.1	87.7	6.0	9.5	0.6	0.9	1.2	2.0	7.6	7.5	7.8	7.1	4.7	28.7	27.3	8.4	0.8	72.6	37.1	49.6	50.4
30253	MCDONOUGH	75.5	71.8	19.9	21.7	2.0	2.7	3.0	4.5	8.5	8.0	7.7	7.1	6.3	31.4	23.5	6.7	0.8	71.5	33.2	48.7	51.3
30256	MEANSVILLE	89.7	85.8	8.6	11.4	0.3	0.5	1.4	2.3	6.3	6.8	8.0	6.5	5.4	25.3	28.0	12.2	1.5	74.7	39.0	51.3	48.7
30257	MILNER	83.5	79.5	14.8	18.2	0.3	0.5	0.7	0.9	6.4	6.6	7.0	6.6	5.0	26.7	29.2	11.4	1.1	75.9	39.6	49.1	50.9
30258	MOLENA	84.2	79.3	14.3	18.6	0.2	0.3	1.1	1.7	6.7	6.8	7.0	6.7	5.6	26.9	27.6	10.9	1.7	75.0	38.4	49.8	50.2
30259	MORELAND	87.3	83.0	11.3	15.2	0.1	0.2	0.7	1.0	7.0	7.4	8.0	7.6	4.0	27.5	27.6	9.7	1.1	72.8	37.9	50.3	49.7
30260	MORROW	44.4	35.7	40.4	43.9	8.9	11.6	6.6	9.8	7.5	6.7	6.5	7.7	9.7	30.5	21.3	8.8	1.3	75.0	31.2	48.5	51.5
30263	NEWNAN	70.4	65.9	26.7	30.4	0.5	0.7	3.1	3.9	7.6	7.4	7.3	7.1	6.2	27.7	25.7	9.5	1.5	73.4	35.9	49.0	51.0
30265	NEWNAN	85.6	78.7	10.2	14.3	1.3	1.6	3.7	7.2	8.6	8.0	7.6	6.6	5.3	32.2	24.6	6.5	0.6	71.6	34.4	49.9	50.1
30268	PALMETTO	66.8	51.9	27.6	40.4	0.4	0.5	7.1	9.8	7.5	7.4	7.5	7.3	5.6	27.0	26.6	9.9	1.2	72.8	36.5	49.0	51.0
30269	PEACHTREE CITY	88.1	82.6	5.8	8.6	3.6	5.1	3.7	5.6	6.3	6.8	7.7	8.0	5.5	25.2	31.0	8.1	1.3	73.8	38.2	48.6	51.4
30273	REX	48.8	40.6	44.3	49.7	2.8	3.7	4.1	6.3	8.1	8.0	7.9	7.7	6.0	30.8	24.8	6.2	0.5	71.2	33.3	47.9	52.1
30274	RIVERDALE	27.3	21.7	61.4	63.7	6.0	7.5	5.8	8.0	8.8	7.7	7.2	8.1	10.1	31.0	21.0	5.5	0.6	71.5	29.2	47.6	52.4
30276	SENOIA	84.2	79.2	13.4	17.5	0.4	0.6	1.4	1.9	8.3	8.6	8.4	7.1	4.7	30.5	23.8	7.8	0.7	70.1	35.0	49.7	50.3
30277	SHARPSBURG	89.4	85.3	7.2	9.8	0.9	1.2	3.3	4.9	8.6	8.4	8.0	6.5	4.0	30.9	26.0	7.0	0.5	70.8	35.7	50.0	50.0
30281	STOCKBRIDGE	80.6	73.6	14.4	18.6	2.5	4.3	2.7	4.1	7.4	7.4	7.4	7.0	5.8	28.7	27.4	7.8	0.9	73.2	36.2	49.3	50.7
30285	THE ROCK	85.6	80.8	13.1	17.4	0.1	0.4	0.9	1.2	6.3	6.5	7.3	6.9	5.8	25.4	28.2	12.2	1.4	75.7	39.1	50.2	49.8
30286	THOMASTON	69.7	64.0	28.7	33.9	0.4	0.6	1.3	1.8	6.5	6.5	6.6	6.8	5.9	25.3	26.7	13.1	2.6	76.3	39.3	47.6	52.4
30288	CONLEY	27.4	22.7	62.9	65.3	3.6	4.3	7.4	9.6	7.8	8.0	7.9	8.3	7.4	29.5	23.5	7.0	0.6	71.5	31.7	47.9	52.1
30290	TYRONE	90.1	88.0	7.2	8.1	1.2	1.7	1.7	2.6	5.6	6.4	7.4	7.4	4.4	24.2	34.0	9.8	0.9	76.0	41.3	49.3	50.7
30291	UNION CITY	23.0	15.2	71.1	77.8	1.0	0.9	6.2	7.8	7.9	7.7	7.5	7.5	7.8	30.5	22.6	7.2	1.3	72.2	31.4	46.7	53.3
30292	WILLIAMSON	81.7	77.7	16.7	20.1	0.4	0.5	1.2	1.7	7.1	7.0	7.1	6.7	6.1	27.3	27.2	10.2	1.2	74.7	37.2	49.4	50.6
30293	WOODBURY	50.5	44.2	48.2	54.1	0.1	0.2	0.8	1.1	6.4	6.6	6.7	6.7	5.4	24.3	28.6	13.7	1.7	76.3	40.0	48.3	51.7
30294	ELLENWOOD	29.4	25.2	66.6	69.5	1.7	2.0	2.2	3.2	7.6	7.5	7.4	7.4	7.2	31.4	25.1	5.9	0.5	72.9	33.0	48.4	51.6
30295	ZEBULON	82.3	77.6	15.8	19.7	0.6	0.9	1.4	2.1	6.6	6.7	7.2	7.1	6.1	26.8	27.6	10.7	1.3	75.2	38.0	50.6	49.4
30296	RIVERDALE	21.7	16.9	70.4	72.9	2.9	3.3	5.2	7.4	7.4	7.1	7.1	7.5	7.5	28.8	26.1	7.4	1.1	73.8	33.8	47.8	52.2
30297	FOREST PARK	41.8	36.2	40.6	40.2	6.6	8.7	18.1	23.8	9.0	7.9	7.1	7.6	9.2	31.3	19.7	7.4	0.9	71.7	29.7	50.3	49.7
30303	ATLANTA	22.7	13.6	70.3	78.3	1.2	1.0	7.7	9.1	5.3	3.5	3.2	5.3	12.5	49.6	17.6	2.6	0.4	85.6	31.8	62.5	37.5
30305	ATLANTA	91.8	85.4	3.7	7.0	2.1	3.0	4.9	9.0	4.6	3.6	3.7	3.1	5.7	37.2	25.4	12.7	4.1	86.1	39.8	48.7	51.3
30306	ATLANTA	90.1	83.5	5.6	9.6	1.9	2.8	3.4	6.0	4.1	2.9	3.2	2.6	7.4	47.0	25.0	6.1	1.7	87.9	35.1	52.0	48.0
30307	ATLANTA	69.7	61.9	24.7	30.3	2.5	3.5	2.3	3.7	5.8	4.8	4.5	5.6	9.4	38.0	24.9	5.7	1.2	82.0	34.3	49.2	50.8
30308	ATLANTA	51.3	42.1	43.5	51.1	1.8	2.6	3.7	4.8	3.5	2.6	2.3	4.0	10.5	47.5	21.5	6.8	1.4	90.3	34.4	55.6	44.4
30309	ATLANTA	78.6	65.6	15.5	26.0	3.2	4.0	3.4	5.7	3.0	1.9	1.5	2.1	10.1	50.5	23.7	5.8	1.3	92.5	34.8	54.7	45.3
30310	ATLANTA	3.8	2.0	93.1	95.2	1.5	1.2	1.3	1.3	6.9	7.3	7.0	9.7	8.3	24.9	25.1	9.5	1.4	74.3	33.9	49.0	51.0
30311	ATLANTA	2.8	1.9	95.5	96.4	0.1	0.1	2.1	2.2	7.5	7.4	7.0	7.1	7.0	25.7	24.8	12.1	1.4	73.7	35.7	44.7	55.3
30312	ATLANTA	24.1	17.3	70.8	76.4	1.0	0.9	4.4	6.2	7.7	7.1	5.8	6.0	7.9	34.1	21.9	8.0	1.6	76.3	33.1	48.5	51.5
30313	ATLANTA	49.6	36.1	35.6	47.1	12.7	14.3	3.0	3.9	3.1	2.1	1.3	26.5	32.9	21.3	8.8	3.2	0.6	92.4	22.6	55.3	44.7
30314	ATLANTA	1.4	0.7	97.0	97.8	0.2	0.2	1.0	1.0	6.3	6.4	5.9	13.1	12.4	21.8	21.1	10.1	2.9	77.6	29.7	44.1	55.9
30315	ATLANTA	13.1	9.3	78.0	80.7	2.9	2.7	9.6	11.1	9.3	8.8	7.7	8.0	8.2	29.6	20.2	7.3	1.1	69.5	29.7	50.7	49.3
30316	ATLANTA	17.8	14.8	78.8	80.6	0.4	0.5	3.3	4.8	7.1	6.9	6.7	7.1	8.0	30.6	24.5	8.1	0.9	75.0	33.5	47.3	52.7
30317	ATLANTA	11.8	9.6	85.7	87.3	0.3	0.3	3.6	4.5	6.4	6.7	6.4	6.7	6.4	28.6	25.4	11.7	1.8	76.7	37.4	48.1	51.9
30318	ATLANTA	26.2	21.6	67.3	70.3	3.4	4.1	4.2	5.5	7.0	6.8	5.8	8.6	13.5	29.9	19.2	7.9	1.3	76.8	29.3	50.5	49.5
30319	ATLANTA	70.1	63.0	13.9	15.0	4.5	5.6	18.2	25.0	5.8	4.8	4.4	4.9	8.7	38.5	22.8	8.4	1.7	82.6	34.7	52.4	47.6
30322	ATLANTA	75.1	66.0	7.5	9.1	14.1	20.1	3.2	5.3	0.1	0.0	0.0	56.6	31.8	1.0	0.5	3.8	6.3	99.3	19.4	47.1	52.9
30324	ATLANTA	70.2	58.1	9.7	14.0	4.4	5.2	20.0	28.2	3.9	2.5	2.1	3.5	13.0	45.3	20.4	7.6	1.7	89.8	33.0	56.1	43.9
30326	ATLANTA	87.3	79.5	7.7	13.4	2.6	3.3	4.1	6.1	3.4	3.0	2.5	2.9	5.1	28.2	23.2	16.9	15.0	90.0	49.5	44.0	56.0
30327	ATLANTA	93.3	88.4	3.2	6.0	2.0	3.0	2.1	3.7	5.1	6.0	7.2	6.1	4.5	23.6	33.2	11.8	2.4	77.6	43.3	49.1	50.9
30328	ATLANTA	83.0	73.6	10.5	17.1	3.1	4.0	6.2	9.6	5.2	4.8	4.8	4.4	6.8	33.2	25.2	12.4	3.1	82.5	39.0	48.0	52.0
30329	ATLANTA	69.5	62.9	14.0	14.5	6.9	9.2	18.2	23.7	4.6	3.1	2.6	4.3	13.4	44.1	16.0	7.9	3.9	87.9	31.9	52.5	47.5
30330	ATLANTA	50.7	33.7	40.8	55.0	1.0	1.0	9.2	12.3	10.7	8.1	3.2	4.5	17.8	41.7	13.9	0.0	0.0	75.1	26.7	58.3	41.7
30331	ATLANTA	2.7	2.9	95.1	95.2	0.4	0.3	1.8	1.6	7.4	7.7	7.4	7.2	6.5	26.5	25.6	10.6	1.1	73.1	35.4	45.5	54.5
30334	ATLANTA	18.9	11.2	76.7	84.7	1.1	1.0	5.6	6.1	4.1	3.1	3.1	6.1	12.2	55.1	16.3	0.0	0.0	85.7	33.1	69.4	30.6
30336	ATLANTA	2.5	1.5	91.6	94.4	0.7	0.4	6.2	4.2	8.0	8.3	8.6	8.8	7.2	28.4	24.2	6.2	0.5	69.8	32.1	47.7	52.3
	GEORGIA	65.1	61.1	28.7	30.1	2.2	2.9	5.3	7.7	7.3	7.0	6.9	7.1	7.1	29.3	25.1	8.9	1.3	74.7	35.0	49.4	50.6
	UNITED STATES	75.1	72.0	12.3	12.7	3.8	4.6	12.5	15.7	6.8	6.7	6.6	7.1	6.9	27.0	26.0	10.9	1.9	75.7	36.9	49.2	50.8

30161-30336

#	POST OFFICE NAME	2009 Per Capita Income	2009 HH Income Base	2009 Household Income Distribution (%) Less than $25,000	$25,000 to $49,999	$50,000 to $99,999	$100,000 to $149,999	$150,000 or More	Median Household Income 2009	2014	2009 National Centile	2009 State Centile	2009 Home Value Base	2009 Home Value Distribution (%) Less than $50,000	$50,000 to $89,999	$90,000 to $174,999	$175,000 to $399,999	$400,000 or More	2009 Median Home Value
30161	ROME	20299	13372	32.0	26.6	33.0	5.3	3.1	40794	45355	35	45	8437	19.6	32.2	35.9	10.4	1.8	87705
30165	ROME	21425	14839	25.7	29.5	35.3	6.0	3.6	44605	48957	47	57	9332	15.7	30.1	41.7	10.6	1.9	94146
30168	AUSTELL	21394	9699	18.5	27.9	44.0	7.1	2.5	52427	53535	67	72	4804	20.7	26.2	48.2	4.6	0.3	93072
30170	ROOPVILLE	19682	1152	23.7	31.3	38.0	4.9	2.2	44340	48423	46	56	944	26.1	29.3	29.3	13.3	1.9	80556
30171	RYDAL	20377	873	21.6	26.8	42.6	6.4	2.5	51292	54428	64	70	753	21.5	23.8	36.0	11.3	7.4	96574
30173	SILVER CREEK	19419	2539	23.2	27.9	42.9	4.4	1.6	49040	51496	59	66	1965	15.8	33.4	40.8	8.9	1.1	90764
30175	TALKING ROCK	21156	2617	20.1	34.1	38.2	4.9	2.6	46505	50590	53	62	2147	26.5	17.9	33.1	18.6	3.9	99409
30176	TALLAPOOSA	19054	2806	29.8	31.0	32.5	4.7	2.0	41172	43272	37	47	2046	25.6	32.7	36.0	4.3	1.4	78947
30177	TATE	20252	156	23.7	34.0	38.5	3.8	0.0	45000	47584	48	59	128	11.7	43.0	38.3	7.0	0.0	83333
30178	TAYLORSVILLE	22325	1264	11.7	27.2	47.1	10.4	3.6	58014	59868	75	78	1087	14.3	20.8	47.4	16.1	1.5	107080
30179	TEMPLE	19732	5482	22.4	28.7	40.7	6.4	1.8	48858	51846	59	66	4574	20.4	28.8	40.5	9.2	1.1	90764
30180	VILLA RICA	21790	12540	20.9	24.5	43.5	8.6	2.4	53460	55314	69	73	9916	12.1	21.9	45.8	18.5	1.7	109541
30182	WACO	17637	994	29.3	31.8	34.5	3.0	1.4	41151	44464	37	46	766	29.8	31.7	29.2	7.7	1.6	73000
30183	WALESKA	27848	2032	14.0	16.9	46.5	16.9	5.6	64484	63709	83	84	1711	17.1	10.1	26.2	34.0	12.6	165378
30184	WHITE	24434	2878	16.1	24.6	44.0	11.5	3.9	60054	61857	77	80	2465	12.3	16.8	39.1	26.6	5.3	128019
30185	WHITESBURG	21774	1676	25.6	28.3	35.0	6.6	4.5	45134	49969	49	59	1371	23.6	27.9	32.5	13.1	2.8	86091
30187	WINSTON	25178	3055	11.8	26.3	47.5	10.5	3.9	62387	67007	80	82	2740	9.2	15.1	47.7	24.5	3.5	125854
30188	WOODSTOCK	36362	20629	5.2	11.6	44.6	24.9	13.7	84554	90622	94	95	17441	3.3	4.3	45.5	41.8	5.1	170672
30189	WOODSTOCK	43661	15023	5.2	8.9	33.3	28.0	24.5	103969	108317	97	99	12469	6.1	1.6	26.9	59.0	6.4	205717
30204	BARNESVILLE	19168	4615	26.5	30.4	35.9	4.8	2.5	43316	46388	43	54	3127	19.0	35.1	35.5	8.6	1.8	85584
30205	BROOKS	28173	1133	11.4	20.6	41.0	18.9	8.2	69476	72976	86	88	1031	4.3	11.4	41.1	32.3	10.9	156250
30206	CONCORD	19733	1057	21.6	25.3	43.9	6.6	2.6	52459	56080	67	72	877	18.5	24.9	37.9	15.8	3.0	101810
30213	FAIRBURN	26181	10418	14.6	24.0	43.3	11.3	6.7	63911	66624	82	84	7612	10.9	23.5	52.4	9.3	4.0	99282
30214	FAYETTEVILLE	40055	8844	7.9	13.5	36.7	24.2	17.7	88749	93332	95	96	7773	12.5	4.0	33.0	42.8	7.7	176001
30215	FAYETTEVILLE	38799	11846	5.1	11.1	40.8	21.4	21.6	89867	93359	95	97	10474	4.0	2.3	29.8	54.6	9.2	202337
30216	FLOVILLA	18686	867	20.2	35.2	35.2	5.3	4.2	46440	48421	53	62	686	15.0	26.4	42.0	10.9	5.7	102022
30217	FRANKLIN	17667	3502	30.8	28.3	35.8	4.0	1.1	41391	43975	37	47	2651	30.4	32.2	31.5	5.4	0.5	74558
30218	GAY	20267	822	22.1	33.7	35.6	5.4	3.2	45344	47425	49	60	683	18.4	25.0	43.0	9.7	3.8	99271
30220	GRANTVILLE	19146	1572	28.1	28.9	34.7	5.3	2.9	42835	46374	42	52	1205	32.0	29.9	28.2	8.4	1.5	72773
30222	GREENVILLE	17510	1768	36.7	25.8	31.0	4.0	2.5	36342	39670	22	31	1299	33.2	29.4	27.7	8.7	1.0	73351
30223	GRIFFIN	18304	13587	28.6	29.3	35.2	5.0	1.9	42127	46850	40	50	7967	20.8	34.9	35.7	7.2	1.5	82732
30224	GRIFFIN	24647	9576	21.1	25.8	39.1	8.9	5.1	53070	55372	68	73	6482	7.5	20.4	55.4	15.1	1.6	111264
30228	HAMPTON	25199	12288	11.9	19.4	48.2	13.9	6.5	65691	67047	84	86	10801	12.4	13.6	43.6	28.7	1.7	137019
30230	HOGANSVILLE	17627	3329	32.2	29.7	32.9	3.6	1.6	40725	41355	35	45	2497	18.8	28.9	36.3	14.1	1.9	92883
30233	JACKSON	20559	8091	23.0	27.6	39.8	6.8	2.8	49320	51388	60	67	6272	15.4	21.4	49.1	12.4	1.6	106619
30234	JENKINSBURG	18746	628	21.8	28.0	43.8	3.8	2.5	50137	51030	61	69	478	19.2	31.0	38.3	11.3	0.2	89667
30236	JONESBORO	25129	19233	14.2	26.1	42.8	10.4	6.5	60654	62881	78	80	11329	8.2	10.9	53.1	25.1	2.8	125292
30238	JONESBORO	21371	12364	12.7	25.6	49.4	8.7	3.6	60310	61956	78	80	9719	10.1	16.7	65.0	7.8	0.4	109638
30240	LAGRANGE	23400	10925	25.3	26.4	35.3	7.2	5.7	47976	47735	57	65	6979	7.8	14.5	39.7	32.2	5.9	141370
30241	LAGRANGE	17448	8239	33.9	28.5	31.1	5.1	1.5	38870	40539	29	40	4914	14.4	21.5	48.0	14.1	2.0	109478
30248	LOCUST GROVE	24921	7618	9.5	23.7	49.9	12.1	4.7	62920	60688	81	83	6841	14.0	18.2	42.2	22.6	3.0	126992
30251	LUTHERSVILLE	17400	825	28.6	29.5	36.0	5.0	1.0	42249	45751	40	50	582	28.2	27.5	31.6	12.2	0.5	79318
30252	MCDONOUGH	30394	13215	6.5	11.2	51.4	21.6	9.3	78599	82621	91	93	12302	2.5	6.3	36.7	49.9	4.6	183965
30253	MCDONOUGH	30088	16850	8.1	16.7	45.2	20.5	9.5	76308	79577	90	91	13074	6.3	11.1	41.0	35.9	5.7	159770
30256	MEANSVILLE	20174	1145	22.9	27.6	39.4	7.3	2.8	49378	52494	60	67	976	26.6	22.8	29.6	18.2	2.7	91020
30257	MILNER	20875	1653	19.6	30.7	41.0	6.6	2.1	49683	51081	60	68	1373	18.4	28.0	41.9	10.0	1.7	93486
30258	MOLENA	19632	1005	21.7	25.7	45.8	5.4	1.5	51689	54772	65	71	832	23.4	23.2	31.3	18.3	3.8	94828
30259	MORELAND	22460	1084	18.6	26.4	40.9	9.8	4.3	56205	60093	73	77	933	11.9	12.3	36.2	34.8	4.7	150379
30260	MORROW	20233	8406	18.4	28.9	44.8	5.9	2.0	52147	55433	66	72	4270	3.2	18.6	73.2	4.8	0.2	107472
30263	NEWNAN	24513	19764	20.5	24.2	36.4	12.9	6.0	56051	59587	73	77	13179	13.0	19.9	40.4	21.5	5.2	113693
30265	NEWNAN	33239	11099	7.7	13.2	44.3	23.7	11.1	80676	82009	92	93	9119	4.1	6.5	51.9	33.6	3.9	153166
30268	PALMETTO	22660	3842	18.9	28.4	41.0	8.7	2.9	53446	57749	69	73	2755	17.6	27.3	46.5	5.4	3.1	93337
30269	PEACHTREE CITY	45085	13104	5.9	10.2	33.2	22.5	28.2	101235	105500	97	98	10496	2.4	1.8	24.0	59.6	12.1	223241
30273	REX	22405	5302	11.3	21.2	54.9	9.4	3.2	62052	63013	80	82	4438	7.7	9.4	74.5	8.2	0.2	116342
30274	RIVERDALE	19388	11122	16.7	31.9	43.2	6.4	1.8	51020	54338	64	70	5984	2.7	23.4	71.0	2.8	0.2	104857
30276	SENOIA	25556	4638	9.0	26.4	46.7	12.4	5.6	64047	67179	82	84	4004	11.6	13.1	51.0	20.4	3.9	121022
30277	SHARPSBURG	32962	6701	4.5	10.8	48.3	25.4	11.0	84545	85545	94	95	6212	4.7	5.2	47.1	41.0	2.0	164236
30281	STOCKBRIDGE	28931	22727	8.4	17.8	48.3	18.2	7.2	71964	76022	88	90	18086	9.4	9.8	42.6	35.7	2.5	152035
30285	THE ROCK	19139	294	24.5	28.9	41.8	3.1	1.7	47349	50000	55	64	247	18.6	28.3	37.2	14.2	1.6	93571
30286	THOMASTON	18976	9535	33.5	29.8	30.5	4.1	2.1	37172	39712	24	33	6400	15.5	32.7	38.5	12.1	1.3	92575
30288	CONLEY	18702	2661	21.5	29.7	38.0	8.1	2.7	48227	52918	57	65	1662	6.8	36.7	54.2	2.3	0.0	93375
30290	TYRONE	36519	2596	6.1	13.0	42.9	22.3	15.6	82947	85291	93	94	2289	2.3	11.4	30.8	48.0	7.4	187706
30291	UNION CITY	24126	8299	19.5	29.0	41.7	7.8	2.1	52295	57036	66	72	3896	11.9	42.4	44.1	0.3	1.2	86288
30292	WILLIAMSON	22889	2130	19.2	25.5	42.1	7.9	5.3	55379	58702	72	76	1580	11.0	20.9	42.0	22.7	3.4	114206
30293	WOODBURY	17472	1311	34.8	30.2	29.1	4.4	1.5	37279	39894	24	34	1020	35.4	34.6	24.3	5.0	0.7	65658
30294	ELLENWOOD	25041	12790	9.6	17.8	51.8	16.0	4.8	66853	68390	85	86	10862	6.5	16.0	60.8	15.7	1.0	119579
30295	ZEBULON	23289	1606	22.0	26.7	39.5	6.4	5.5	51051	54800	64	70	1230	19.3	24.6	34.1	18.3	3.7	101613
30296	RIVERDALE	23017	10311	11.9	28.4	43.7	11.4	4.5	59680	61559	77	79	7077	10.4	7.8	67.7	12.9	1.1	118361
30297	FOREST PARK	16143	10614	23.3	34.7	35.3	4.5	2.2	42518	47403	41	51	5379	10.1	45.4	42.8	1.4	0.3	86164
30303	ATLANTA	20321	1423	40.9	23.0	26.4	6.5	3.2	33766	36775	15	21	225	1.8	26.2	49.8	16.9	5.3	110991
30305	ATLANTA	77891	13145	13.9	17.2	27.1	18.1	23.8	84390	88075	94	95	6494	0.1	0.9	12.9	24.2	61.9	553390
30306	ATLANTA	63388	12410	10.7	15.3	34.6	19.1	20.3	82308	85437	93	94	5764	2.3	2.0	7.3	52.6	35.8	350092
30307	ATLANTA	46510	8853	16.0	18.2	31.2	17.0	17.6	71173	75912	87	89	4336	3.2	4.8	16.4	54.7	20.9	270401
30308	ATLANTA	41119	9702	26.9	20.8	33.6	12.9	5.8	54325	59765	70	75	2451	2.4	9.0	43.7	33.1	11.7	156786
30309	ATLANTA	62963	14216	16.2	22.5	32.4	15.3	13.6	66552	71704	85	86	4938	0.2	3.0	34.8	25.7	36.2	243924
30310	ATLANTA	15265	12668	42.0	29.9	23.0	3.5	1.6	30529	31667	9	10	5226	19.1	60.4	18.4	1.5	0.6	70938
30311	ATLANTA	20211	14874	35.7	27.3	26.0	7.9	3.0	35714	38472	20	27	6575	7.2	38.3	49.4	4.6	0.5	92436
30312	ATLANTA	22257	11630	45.2	21.3	20.8	8.3	4.4	30271	33110	9	9	3342	7.5	16.6	41.1	30.3	4.5	135054
30313	ATLANTA	16017	2314	60.4	16.1	17.3	3.9	2.3	17796	18585	1	1	263	6.1	9.9	39.5	33.5	11.0	159239
30314	ATLANTA	13149	9847	53.3	27.9	15.0	2.8	0.9	23101	23961	2	1	3190	26.8	56.4	14.1	1.5	1.1	66941
30315	ATLANTA	12091	13341	48.5	25.3	20.5	4.2	1.4	26104	27612	4	2	4665	25.4	53.6	13.4	6.7	0.9	66444
30316	ATLANTA	20264	13744	27.2	28.5	34.0	7.8	2.5	44587	48675	47	57	7494	6.6	38.0	45.2	10.0	0.2	94308
30317	ATLANTA	20126	5462	33.2	26.8	30.0	6.6	3.5	39784	42205	32	43	2831	8.7	28.5	43.6	17.6	1.5	106152
30318	ATLANTA	21913	24019	37.5	24.0	24.5	8.5	5.5	37056	39336	24	33	9627	15.9	33.3	24.1	16.9	9.8	91193
30319	ATLANTA	50668	18508	10.5	16.8	34.3	19.5	18.9	78789	82947	91	93	8455	1.3	1.5	16.2	54.6	26.4	282826
30322	ATLANTA	12395	6	66.7	0.0	33.3	0.0	0.0	20000	22183	1	1	0	0.0	0.0	0.0	0.0	0.0	0
30324	ATLANTA	48882	12590	11.6	19.7	37.0	18.4	13.3	73666	77436	89	90	4343	3.0	0.8	21.9	52.2	22.2	242104
30326	ATLANTA	93982	2633	15.5	11.5	26.8	21.2	25.0	92744	96003	96	97	1331	0.0	0.0	16.8	24.5	58.8	462973
30327	ATLANTA	80692	10419	8.1	8.7	24.9	16.2	42.0	129785	135038	99	100	7578	0.2	0.9	7.4	13.3	78.2	658347
30328	ATLANTA	55739	15412	10.9	14.2	35.0	21.1	18.8	83546	85867	93	95	8120	1.5	5.9	23.1	42.0	27.5	281898
30329	ATLANTA	35387	10186	15.7	21.3	37.8	15.9	9.3	63860	67670	82	84	2747	0.1	0.1	22.8	66.3	10.7	230951
30330	ATLANTA	24518	72	0.0	0.0	87.5	8.3	4.2	78052	79160	91	93	0	0.0	0.0	0.0	0.0	0.0	0
30331	ATLANTA	24348	20304	23.9	26.7	32.4	11.6	5.4	49231	56157	59	67	11584	4.6	32.5	50.5	8.7	3.6	98828
30334	ATLANTA	26216	25	28.0	12.0	44.0	12.0	4.0	63534	67947	82	83	6	0.0	16.7	33.3	33.3	16.7	175000
30336	ATLANTA	20635	641	25.4	19.7	31.5	15.3	8.1	61300	65753	79	81	314	1.6	16.6	53.2	18.2	10.5	127717
	GEORGIA	26980		20.7	23.1	36.8	11.7	7.7	56761	58593				13.2	17.9	39.1	24.2	5.5	121444
	UNITED STATES	27277		20.9	24.4	35.3	11.7	7.6	54719	56938				9.3	13.1	31.6	32.6	13.5	162279

ZIP CODE #	POST OFFICE NAME	FINANCIAL SERVICES				THE HOME						ENTERTAINMENT						PERSONAL			
						Home Improvements		Furnishings													
		Auto Loan	Home Loan	Invest-ments	Retire-ment Plans	Home Repair	Lawn & Garden	Comput-ers & Hard-ware-Personal	Major Appli-ances	TV, Radio, Sound Equip-ment	Furni-ture	Dine out/ Carry out	Sports Equip-ment	Fees & Tickets	Toys & Games	Travel	Cable TV	Apparel & Services	Auto Repairs	Health Insur-ance	Pets & Supplies
30161	ROME	78	69	70	69	68	79	71	75	75	69	74	56	66	75	68	79	51	74	81	89
30165	ROME	82	74	74	74	75	81	78	80	80	76	79	60	72	80	74	82	55	79	83	94
30168	AUSTELL	90	75	64	77	70	71	87	77	86	87	88	63	80	90	78	85	61	84	77	94
30170	ROOPVILLE	88	76	72	74	75	83	73	79	77	75	77	59	67	80	69	81	52	76	81	95
30171	RYDAL	93	84	76	81	82	88	80	85	83	83	83	62	75	87	76	86	56	82	86	101
30173	SILVER CREEK	83	74	70	74	73	82	75	79	78	72	77	60	69	80	71	81	53	77	82	94
30175	TALKING ROCK	93	76	79	74	76	89	76	84	80	75	80	63	66	83	71	85	54	80	86	101
30176	TALLAPOOSA	82	62	74	60	62	82	64	76	71	61	69	57	53	72	61	78	47	71	81	90
30177	TATE	87	62	72	61	62	82	65	75	72	63	71	58	52	75	59	78	47	72	80	92
30178	TAYLORSVILLE	103	100	86	96	96	94	92	96	92	97	93	72	89	97	89	92	64	92	91	112
30179	TEMPLE	87	78	72	76	76	83	74	80	78	76	78	59	69	81	71	81	53	77	82	96
30180	VILLA RICA	91	86	75	85	83	89	84	86	86	84	85	65	80	88	80	88	59	85	88	103
30182	WACO	84	62	69	60	62	79	64	73	70	63	69	56	52	73	58	76	46	70	77	89
30183	WALESKA	124	106	133	103	110	124	103	120	107	101	106	88	93	106	105	112	71	113	120	141
30184	WHITE	108	98	92	95	97	102	93	100	97	96	97	73	88	100	90	100	66	97	100	119
30185	WHITESBURG	100	85	82	82	83	95	82	90	87	84	87	67	74	91	78	92	59	87	92	108
30187	WINSTON	101	110	94	111	106	107	99	102	98	100	98	79	103	101	102	98	68	99	101	120
30188	WOODSTOCK	148	165	139	162	157	140	146	145	138	156	141	115	153	147	147	131	100	139	129	166
30189	WOODSTOCK	186	213	181	213	205	179	184	185	172	201	176	149	198	185	188	162	126	173	159	209
30204	BARNESVILLE	81	67	69	67	66	80	69	75	74	67	73	57	62	76	65	79	50	74	81	91
30205	BROOKS	114	122	115	127	122	126	112	120	111	110	111	91	116	113	117	113	77	113	119	139
30206	CONCORD	94	86	76	83	84	88	81	86	84	84	84	63	77	88	77	86	57	83	86	102
30213	FAIRBURN	102	111	100	110	108	109	103	104	103	104	104	79	108	104	106	104	72	104	107	122
30214	FAYETTEVILLE	148	172	173	176	175	167	152	159	148	159	149	119	167	148	165	147	106	152	154	183
30215	FAYETTEVILLE	154	189	178	191	188	170	163	167	155	171	157	129	183	158	177	150	113	159	154	191
30216	FLOVILLA	97	73	90	72	74	97	75	90	82	70	80	68	62	83	72	89	54	83	94	107
30217	FRANKLIN	84	61	71	59	61	80	63	74	70	62	69	56	51	73	58	76	46	70	77	90
30218	GAY	98	79	81	76	78	93	78	87	84	79	83	66	68	88	73	90	56	84	90	105
30220	GRANTVILLE	90	68	76	66	67	86	69	80	76	68	75	61	57	79	64	82	50	76	83	97
30222	GREENVILLE	87	58	82	55	58	85	61	76	70	59	69	59	47	71	57	78	45	72	80	93
30223	GRIFFIN	77	66	61	66	64	74	70	71	74	68	73	54	64	75	65	77	50	71	76	86
30224	GRIFFIN	90	88	80	88	85	91	89	88	91	87	91	67	88	92	86	93	63	89	93	105
30228	HAMPTON	111	119	102	116	113	108	106	109	103	112	105	85	109	109	107	101	73	104	101	126
30230	HOGANSVILLE	79	60	66	59	59	76	63	71	69	61	68	54	53	71	58	75	46	68	76	86
30233	JACKSON	90	77	77	76	76	87	77	84	82	76	81	63	70	84	73	86	55	81	87	100
30234	JENKINSBURG	96	70	79	68	69	91	72	84	80	70	78	64	58	83	66	87	53	79	88	102
30236	JONESBORO	103	97	87	99	93	89	104	95	101	105	103	76	100	104	98	98	72	100	91	113
30238	JONESBORO	99	103	84	100	96	89	96	94	92	101	94	74	96	98	92	89	65	92	87	109
30240	LAGRANGE	89	85	79	87	83	88	87	86	88	86	88	67	85	90	84	90	61	87	89	103
30241	LAGRANGE	72	59	58	59	57	68	64	65	68	62	67	50	57	69	59	71	46	66	70	79
30248	LOCUST GROVE	111	111	97	110	108	109	102	107	103	105	103	81	102	107	101	104	71	103	105	126
30251	LUTHERSVILLE	86	62	73	60	62	82	65	75	71	63	70	58	52	74	59	78	47	71	79	91
30252	MCDONOUGH	127	146	124	145	139	130	128	130	122	134	124	102	137	128	132	119	88	124	121	150
30253	MCDONOUGH	128	134	113	132	127	116	127	122	121	133	123	97	128	128	124	116	86	121	113	142
30256	MEANSVILLE	93	76	87	75	77	94	75	88	80	72	79	66	66	82	74	86	53	82	91	104
30257	MILNER	93	80	77	78	79	89	78	85	82	79	82	63	71	85	74	86	55	81	86	101
30258	MOLENA	90	79	74	76	77	85	76	82	80	78	79	61	69	83	72	83	54	79	83	98
30259	MORELAND	91	100	87	102	97	99	90	94	89	90	89	73	95	91	94	89	62	90	93	110
30260	MORROW	85	75	65	77	70	71	85	75	84	84	85	61	80	87	78	83	59	82	77	92
30263	NEWNAN	100	96	86	97	93	98	96	96	98	96	98	73	94	100	93	100	68	96	99	115
30265	NEWNAN	139	151	128	146	143	129	136	135	130	145	132	106	140	137	135	125	93	130	122	155
30268	PALMETTO	96	92	80	91	89	94	89	91	91	90	90	69	86	94	86	93	62	90	93	109
30269	PEACHTREE CITY	179	212	195	216	210	186	184	186	173	198	176	149	204	181	195	165	127	176	165	212
30273	REX	103	107	87	103	100	92	98	97	94	104	96	74	97	100	94	91	67	94	89	113
30274	RIVERDALE	87	75	64	76	70	68	85	75	83	86	84	61	78	86	76	80	58	81	73	91
30276	SENOIA	113	114	96	111	109	106	104	107	104	110	105	80	103	109	102	103	72	103	102	125
30277	SHARPSBURG	141	161	134	157	152	135	140	140	131	149	134	111	147	140	142	125	95	133	123	160
30281	STOCKBRIDGE	118	123	105	124	118	112	117	114	113	120	114	90	118	118	116	110	80	113	108	134
30285	THE ROCK	89	64	78	62	65	86	67	79	74	64	72	60	53	76	62	81	48	74	83	96
30286	THOMASTON	77	61	66	60	60	76	65	71	70	62	69	54	56	71	60	76	47	70	77	86
30288	CONLEY	84	81	66	80	76	77	83	78	82	84	83	61	80	85	78	82	58	81	79	94
30290	TYRONE	141	170	154	174	167	157	146	151	140	152	142	118	162	144	157	137	101	143	140	174
30291	UNION CITY	86	74	67	74	71	71	85	77	85	86	86	61	79	86	78	84	60	84	79	93
30292	WILLIAMSON	101	91	85	89	88	97	89	94	93	89	92	70	83	96	85	96	63	92	96	112
30293	WOODBURY	83	57	80	54	58	82	60	74	68	57	67	57	47	69	57	75	44	70	78	90
30294	ELLENWOOD	114	120	99	116	113	104	109	108	105	117	107	84	110	111	107	102	75	105	99	126
30295	ZEBULON	104	87	92	84	86	101	85	95	90	85	90	71	76	93	82	95	61	91	97	114
30296	RIVERDALE	100	98	85	98	93	90	99	94	97	102	98	73	97	100	95	95	68	96	91	111
30297	FOREST PARK	74	64	54	66	60	64	76	67	76	73	77	54	71	77	68	76	54	74	71	82
30303	ATLANTA	70	49	50	56	47	48	75	56	73	70	76	51	65	74	63	72	54	69	59	73
30305	ATLANTA	183	189	215	204	198	182	208	187	200	207	204	152	218	196	211	196	149	197	187	221
30306	ATLANTA	153	147	167	163	152	136	176	149	165	172	171	129	176	165	171	159	125	162	142	179
30307	ATLANTA	135	125	137	137	128	118	152	128	145	148	148	110	149	144	145	141	108	141	126	155
30308	ATLANTA	97	71	72	81	68	69	106	79	102	98	106	72	93	103	90	99	75	96	83	102
30309	ATLANTA	138	111	120	127	110	106	153	119	147	144	153	108	142	148	137	142	110	139	121	150
30310	ATLANTA	59	50	46	52	47	56	57	53	62	57	62	40	54	60	52	66	42	58	63	67
30311	ATLANTA	73	63	58	66	60	68	72	66	77	72	77	50	70	76	67	81	53	73	76	83
30312	ATLANTA	67	54	53	58	53	56	71	60	73	68	73	49	66	72	63	74	52	69	67	75
30313	ATLANTA	46	32	35	37	31	34	54	39	53	47	54	35	45	50	44	53	38	49	46	51
30314	ATLANTA	48	35	33	37	34	41	47	41	51	45	50	32	41	49	40	54	35	47	49	53
30315	ATLANTA	55	42	37	44	39	46	54	47	58	52	58	37	49	57	46	61	40	54	55	60
30316	ATLANTA	78	70	64	72	67	73	77	72	80	77	80	56	74	79	72	81	55	77	79	89
30317	ATLANTA	72	67	63	69	64	73	72	69	78	71	78	50	72	75	69	83	54	74	81	86
30318	ATLANTA	84	67	65	72	65	72	85	74	88	82	88	59	78	87	75	91	62	83	82	93
30319	ATLANTA	155	152	160	161	154	139	171	150	162	169	166	126	172	164	167	156	120	161	144	179
30322	ATLANTA	35	26	32	30	27	32	43	34	46	38	46	27	38	40	38	49	32	42	48	45
30324	ATLANTA	133	116	125	128	116	107	149	121	141	143	146	107	141	142	138	135	106	136	117	148
30326	ATLANTA	211	186	207	209	188	174	239	193	227	228	236	171	230	228	223	220	171	218	190	237
30327	ATLANTA	236	301	363	319	331	282	273	273	255	292	256	213	326	253	308	245	196	263	246	305
30328	ATLANTA	162	165	173	173	169	157	174	161	169	177	171	129	180	168	175	166	123	168	161	190
30329	ATLANTA	116	88	90	99	85	86	124	97	121	117	125	85	111	122	108	119	88	115	103	123
30330	ATLANTA	154	80	60	93	72	68	145	100	136	135	144	100	110	164	105	125	101	128	91	122
30331	ATLANTA	94	90	80	92	85	90	92	88	95	93	95	68	93	96	89	96	66	92	94	107
30334	ATLANTA	98	72	75	83	69	70	107	80	103	99	107	74	95	104	92	100	76	97	84	103
30336	ATLANTA	106	100	88	103	95	92	107	97	105	108	107	80	106	108	102	102	76	104	94	117
	GEORGIA	110	101	97	102	98	103	103	103	104	104	104	80	99	107	99	105	73	103	103	122
	UNITED STATES	100	100	100	100	100	100	100	100	100	100	100	100	100	100	100	100	100	100	100	100

ZIP CODE			POPULATION			2000-2009 ANNUAL RATE		HOUSEHOLDS					FAMILIES		
#	POST OFFICE NAME	COUNTY FIPS CODE	2000	2009	2014	% Rate	State Centile	2000	2009	2014	% Annual Rate 2000-2009	2009 Average HH Size	2000	2009	% Annual Rate 2000-2009
30337	ATLANTA	121	16654	17076	17670	0.3	25	6580	6646	6857	0.1	2.55	3909	3715	-0.5
30338	ATLANTA	089	28622	32174	34256	1.3	54	11843	13826	14885	1.7	2.29	7859	8555	0.9
30339	ATLANTA	067	16850	18210	18896	0.8	41	9522	10234	10593	0.8	1.77	3228	3125	-0.3
30340	ATLANTA	089	27004	30042	31493	1.2	52	9988	10855	11345	0.9	2.76	5907	6013	0.2
30341	ATLANTA	089	32396	37120	39241	1.5	60	12021	13622	14441	1.4	2.71	6949	7379	0.7
30342	ATLANTA	121	26626	30946	33807	1.6	63	11892	13449	14649	1.3	2.27	5372	5587	0.4
30344	ATLANTA	121	39104	43806	47015	1.2	52	14530	16043	17200	1.1	2.70	9358	9799	0.5
30345	ATLANTA	089	22182	25030	26573	1.3	54	8463	9410	9986	1.2	2.64	5338	5658	0.6
30346	ATLANTA	089	1452	2750	3204	7.1	98	827	1599	1882	7.4	1.67	284	536	7.1
30349	ATLANTA	121	53909	74392	85273	3.5	88	20443	27551	31365	3.3	2.69	13213	17551	3.1
30350	ATLANTA	121	31485	36065	39146	1.5	60	15365	17425	18890	1.4	2.07	7030	7347	0.5
30354	ATLANTA	121	17993	19864	21273	1.1	49	6204	6791	7271	1.0	2.91	4356	4565	0.5
30360	ATLANTA	089	16520	17595	18343	0.7	37	6523	6908	7136	0.6	2.56	3851	3827	-0.1
30363	ATLANTA	121	0	2297	2992	0.0	17	0	1195	1554	0.0	1.91	0	377	0.0
30401	SWAINSBORO	107	13266	14002	14301	0.6	34	4926	5292	5439	0.8	2.56	3500	3635	0.4
30410	AILEY	209	1238	1407	1480	1.4	57	471	538	569	1.4	2.52	337	371	1.0
30411	ALAMO	309	3970	4555	4689	1.7	66	1158	1212	1236	0.5	2.48	826	837	0.1
30413	BARTOW	163	1760	1718	1670	-0.3	11	648	647	635	0.0	2.61	479	463	-0.4
30415	BROOKLET	031	5831	7001	7691	2.0	70	2093	2550	2817	2.2	2.75	1592	1842	1.6
30417	CLAXTON	109	10582	11387	12608	1.3	54	3821	4339	4625	1.4	2.60	2710	2972	1.0
30420	COBBTOWN	267	1666	1688	1705	0.1	19	668	676	684	0.1	2.50	460	449	-0.3
30421	COLLINS	267	1699	1711	1735	0.1	19	699	708	718	0.1	2.42	467	455	-0.3
30425	GARFIELD	107	1180	1263	1298	0.7	37	454	496	514	1.0	2.55	341	362	0.6
30426	GIRARD	033	1070	1103	1107	0.3	25	395	416	421	0.6	2.65	280	285	0.2
30427	GLENNVILLE	267	9800	11033	11643	1.3	54	3219	3762	4008	1.7	2.60	2256	2540	1.3
30428	GLENWOOD	309	2677	2795	2829	0.5	31	1044	1095	1118	0.5	2.44	709	717	0.1
30434	LOUISVILLE	163	6354	6117	5935	-0.4	9	2263	2196	2140	-0.3	2.59	1591	1490	-0.7
30436	LYONS	279	11244	11898	12291	0.6	34	4172	4502	4678	0.8	2.61	2902	3018	0.4
30438	MANASSAS	267	918	935	947	0.2	22	338	342	346	0.1	2.72	237	231	-0.3
30439	METTER	043	9378	10777	11485	1.5	60	3298	3734	3974	1.4	2.77	2369	2596	1.0
30441	MIDVILLE	107	1843	1807	1783	-0.2	13	693	694	691	0.0	2.60	493	476	-0.4
30442	MILLEN	165	7688	7728	7675	0.1	19	2875	2948	2947	0.3	2.58	2017	1998	-0.1
30445	MOUNT VERNON	209	3315	3652	3716	1.1	49	998	1090	1122	1.0	2.56	679	713	0.5
30446	NEWINGTON	251	1515	1635	1676	0.8	41	588	645	666	1.0	2.53	437	465	0.7
30450	PORTAL	031	2840	3543	3946	2.4	75	1024	1316	1479	2.7	2.69	767	935	2.2
30452	REGISTER	031	1612	1924	2160	1.9	68	567	697	785	2.3	2.76	431	505	1.7
30453	REIDSVILLE	267	8091	8085	8205	0.0	17	2073	2125	2164	0.3	2.69	1410	1390	-0.2
30454	ROCKLEDGE	175	641	723	757	1.3	54	272	312	329	1.5	2.32	204	226	1.1
30455	ROCKY FORD	251	761	785	784	0.3	25	293	306	308	0.5	2.51	217	220	0.1
30456	SARDIS	033	2040	2001	1980	-0.2	13	722	719	714	0.0	2.77	517	497	-0.4
30457	SOPERTON	283	6852	6774	6750	-0.1	14	2533	2555	2571	0.1	2.48	1826	1782	-0.3
30458	STATESBORO	031	32342	37892	40519	1.7	66	12057	14189	15406	1.8	2.35	5924	6620	1.2
30461	STATESBORO	031	10212	12924	14303	2.6	78	3882	5037	5626	2.9	2.54	2757	3341	2.1
30467	SYLVANIA	251	13228	13304	13206	0.1	19	4969	5019	5007	0.1	2.56	3490	3401	-0.3
30470	TARRYTOWN	209	812	1165	1257	4.0	91	336	496	539	4.3	2.35	236	339	4.0
30471	TWIN CITY	107	4581	4725	4774	0.3	25	1561	1635	1664	0.5	2.68	1120	1134	0.1
30473	UVALDA	209	2969	3061	3115	0.3	25	1120	1176	1204	0.5	2.60	829	843	0.2
30474	VIDALIA	279	15596	16798	17519	0.8	41	6031	6615	6935	1.0	2.50	4140	4378	0.6
30477	WADLEY	163	3153	2948	2834	-0.7	3	1171	1117	1083	-0.5	2.55	814	749	-0.9
30501	GAINESVILLE	139	29356	34327	37244	1.7	66	9419	10534	11375	1.2	3.13	6212	6622	0.7
30504	GAINESVILLE	139	15592	23739	28037	4.6	93	5235	7656	8984	4.2	3.08	3801	5298	3.7
30506	GAINESVILLE	139	31925	44551	52522	3.7	89	11536	15863	18641	3.5	2.80	9129	12166	3.2
30507	GAINESVILLE	139	21199	28399	32827	3.2	85	6666	8730	10020	3.0	3.20	5338	6804	2.7
30510	ALTO	011	6868	8106	8645	1.8	66	2149	2505	2713	1.7	2.63	1635	1852	1.4
30511	BALDWIN	011	3323	3735	3916	1.3	54	1177	1299	1357	1.1	2.81	874	935	0.7
30512	BLAIRSVILLE	291	15813	20638	23035	2.9	82	6531	8795	9925	3.3	2.29	4747	6190	2.9
30513	BLUE RIDGE	111	9346	12835	14326	3.5	88	3981	5621	6334	3.8	2.26	2825	3854	3.4
30516	BOWERSVILLE	147	1817	1982	2042	0.9	45	714	792	821	1.1	2.50	539	580	0.8
30517	BRASELTON	157	5188	11145	13995	8.6	100	1835	3938	4965	8.6	2.77	1485	3121	8.4
30518	BUFORD	135	29470	42193	49923	4.0	91	10694	15160	17857	3.8	2.77	7960	10799	3.4
30519	BUFORD	135	19372	40902	52357	8.4	99	6111	13207	16894	8.7	3.05	5111	10707	8.3
30520	CANON	119	3778	4311	4526	1.4	57	1494	1737	1836	1.6	2.47	1091	1222	1.2
30521	CARNESVILLE	119	4510	5047	5256	1.2	52	1714	1939	2028	1.3	2.57	1295	1422	1.0
30522	CHERRYLOG	123	1117	1565	1766	3.7	89	485	683	774	3.8	2.27	358	491	3.5
30523	CLARKESVILLE	137	10873	13691	15217	2.5	77	4316	5476	6103	2.6	2.47	3241	3980	2.2
30525	CLAYTON	241	8247	9240	9726	1.2	52	3492	3944	4181	1.3	2.30	2372	2574	0.9
30527	CLERMONT	139	3134	4165	4792	3.1	85	1129	1477	1690	2.9	2.82	932	1188	2.7
30528	CLEVELAND	311	16589	21781	24609	3.0	83	6273	8330	9453	3.1	2.56	4745	6126	2.8
30529	COMMERCE	157	9006	11622	13554	2.8	80	3450	4489	5275	2.9	2.51	2495	3131	2.5
30530	COMMERCE	011	5038	6179	6761	2.2	73	1825	2261	2489	2.3	2.71	1398	1675	2.0
30531	CORNELIA	137	9207	11367	12433	2.3	74	3491	4310	4724	2.3	2.59	2497	2980	1.9
30533	DAHLONEGA	187	18237	24358	27508	3.2	85	6849	9270	10573	3.3	2.50	4866	6360	2.9
30534	DAWSONVILLE	085	16822	24236	28409	4.0	91	6323	9299	11017	4.3	2.56	4852	6940	3.9
30535	DEMOREST	137	6165	7734	8568	2.5	77	2346	2973	3319	2.6	2.46	1742	2145	2.3
30536	ELLIJAY	123	6324	7840	8515	2.4	75	2543	3179	3469	2.4	2.43	1890	2286	2.1
30537	DILLARD	241	689	1466	1633	8.5	99	320	688	779	8.6	1.94	227	473	8.3
30538	EASTANOLLEE	257	1505	1495	1489	-0.1	14	583	585	584	0.0	2.56	454	442	-0.3
30539	EAST ELLIJAY	123	51	61	65	2.0	70	20	24	26	2.0	2.42	15	17	1.4
30540	ELLIJAY	123	14411	19701	22230	3.4	87	5443	7493	8474	3.5	2.62	3984	5319	3.2
30541	EPWORTH	111	1433	1698	1827	1.9	68	580	702	760	2.1	2.42	446	524	1.8
30542	FLOWERY BRANCH	139	20333	29990	35713	4.3	92	7193	10367	12240	4.0	2.88	5725	8037	3.7
30543	GILLSVILLE	139	3181	4435	5076	3.7	89	1127	1511	1719	3.2	2.94	905	1185	3.0
30545	HELEN	311	684	974	1129	3.9	90	330	467	541	3.8	2.09	217	294	3.3
30546	HIAWASSEE	281	6154	7896	8805	2.7	79	2762	3592	4025	2.9	2.15	1920	2412	2.5
30547	HOMER	011	2430	2746	2891	1.3	54	940	1069	1126	1.4	2.57	726	802	1.1
30548	HOSCHTON	157	6153	13891	17738	9.2	100	2190	4918	6295	9.1	2.79	1767	3880	8.9
30549	JEFFERSON	157	12442	21929	27501	6.3	97	4341	7804	9869	6.5	2.73	3306	5764	6.2
30552	LAKEMONT	241	1633	1788	1843	1.0	47	706	788	819	1.2	2.26	511	552	0.8
30553	LAVONIA	119	6777	7181	7348	0.6	34	2811	3026	3112	0.8	2.37	2030	2113	0.4
30554	LULA	139	6145	7733	8568	2.5	77	2226	2778	3068	2.4	2.78	1777	2161	2.1
30555	MC CAYSVILLE	111	1818	2223	2352	2.2	73	813	1016	1082	2.4	2.19	547	656	2.0
30557	MARTIN	119	4917	5443	5597	1.1	49	1904	2148	2222	1.3	2.53	1426	1555	0.9
30558	MAYSVILLE	011	4936	6125	6957	2.4	75	1782	2249	2564	2.5	2.71	1397	1718	2.3
30559	MINERAL BLUFF	111	3445	4318	4736	2.5	77	1414	1830	2030	2.8	2.35	1029	1289	2.5
30560	MORGANTON	111	3668	4463	4839	2.1	72	1529	1909	2089	2.4	2.33	1138	1381	2.1
	GEORGIA					2.1					2.1	2.65			1.8
	UNITED STATES					1.0					1.1	2.59			0.9

ZIP CODE #	POST OFFICE NAME	RACE (%) White 2000	White 2009	Black 2000	Black 2009	Asian/Pacific 2000	Asian/Pacific 2009	% Hispanic Origin 2000	% Hispanic Origin 2009	2009 AGE DISTRIBUTION (%) 0-4	5-9	10-14	15-19	20-24	25-44	45-64	65-84	85+	18+	MEDIAN AGE 2009	% 2009 Males	% 2009 Females
30337	ATLANTA	14.4	9.4	80.2	84.4	0.6	0.5	6.6	7.6	8.6	7.5	6.6	7.9	10.3	31.6	21.0	5.5	0.9	72.8	29.5	48.7	51.3
30338	ATLANTA	84.9	78.4	4.5	5.7	7.8	11.4	4.9	8.0	6.0	6.0	6.4	5.0	5.2	29.5	27.0	13.1	1.7	78.5	40.3	49.3	50.7
30339	ATLANTA	77.5	70.0	13.4	16.7	5.9	8.1	3.9	6.5	3.6	2.3	2.3	2.9	15.1	48.8	19.4	5.0	0.5	90.1	29.8	50.4	49.6
30340	ATLANTA	50.4	44.2	22.1	21.2	12.5	14.3	26.8	35.2	7.0	6.0	5.6	6.5	10.5	34.2	21.6	7.8	0.9	77.9	32.3	52.4	47.6
30341	ATLANTA	58.1	50.3	9.7	10.0	12.1	13.3	32.8	40.9	6.7	5.2	4.4	5.8	9.8	37.4	20.7	8.7	1.2	80.5	32.6	55.1	44.9
30342	ATLANTA	78.6	68.4	6.9	10.6	2.3	3.0	16.7	23.9	6.1	4.9	4.4	4.0	10.0	40.5	21.2	7.3	1.6	82.2	32.8	52.1	47.9
30344	ATLANTA	16.6	10.2	77.5	83.3	0.7	0.7	7.6	8.4	8.5	7.5	7.1	7.9	8.8	27.7	23.3	7.8	1.3	72.3	31.3	47.1	52.9
30345	ATLANTA	68.7	61.7	11.7	11.4	5.1	6.7	24.0	31.8	6.3	5.5	5.1	6.2	8.5	31.1	24.2	11.0	2.2	79.8	36.1	54.1	45.9
30346	ATLANTA	78.0	69.9	8.5	10.5	10.6	15.3	3.5	5.7	3.5	2.3	1.8	3.5	13.9	48.3	19.2	5.9	1.7	91.2	33.0	51.4	48.6
30349	ATLANTA	8.6	7.5	86.4	87.3	2.1	2.0	2.3	2.6	7.8	6.9	6.6	7.1	9.0	31.6	23.4	6.8	0.8	74.5	31.7	47.2	52.8
30350	ATLANTA	72.1	60.3	17.6	25.8	4.5	5.6	7.2	10.4	5.3	4.6	4.4	4.6	10.6	39.7	22.8	6.9	1.2	83.1	33.6	49.5	50.5
30354	ATLANTA	21.1	15.7	70.0	73.5	3.2	3.4	10.1	12.4	9.3	8.4	7.5	8.1	9.2	28.6	21.7	6.4	0.9	70.1	29.3	47.4	52.6
30360	ATLANTA	55.5	48.1	21.9	21.2	6.0	7.3	25.3	34.4	6.7	5.7	5.2	4.8	8.1	40.0	21.7	7.3	0.7	79.8	33.3	53.3	46.7
30363	ATLANTA	0.0	74.0	0.0	19.3	0.0	3.7	0.0	3.5	3.8	2.6	2.4	2.7	7.1	42.1	28.1	9.3	2.0	89.6	38.1	51.6	48.4
30401	SWAINSBORO	61.0	55.2	36.2	40.7	0.3	0.4	3.2	4.7	7.2	6.8	7.3	8.2	6.6	23.5	26.3	12.0	2.2	73.5	36.7	47.0	53.0
30410	AILEY	73.3	67.4	24.3	28.9	0.1	0.1	1.9	3.3	7.3	7.0	6.7	7.0	7.3	26.9	26.7	9.9	1.1	74.9	36.1	49.4	50.6
30411	ALAMO	60.9	55.4	38.0	43.0	0.1	0.0	2.2	3.1	4.6	4.6	4.8	5.4	9.5	38.6	23.5	7.7	1.3	83.2	36.1	66.5	33.5
30413	BARTOW	43.1	37.2	55.4	60.8	0.2	0.2	1.8	2.2	7.1	7.2	7.0	6.8	5.9	24.3	27.7	12.1	1.9	74.7	38.7	47.1	52.9
30415	BROOKLET	85.0	80.2	13.8	18.1	0.2	0.3	1.1	1.6	6.9	6.9	7.0	6.9	5.8	27.5	28.2	9.7	1.0	74.9	37.2	49.4	50.6
30417	CLAXTON	61.6	54.9	33.0	37.1	0.3	0.4	6.0	8.9	6.9	6.9	6.9	7.2	6.8	27.6	25.1	10.7	1.9	74.8	35.9	49.1	50.9
30420	COBBTOWN	77.0	68.3	11.6	13.6	0.1	0.1	12.8	20.2	6.9	7.0	6.6	5.6	4.7	26.4	25.9	14.9	1.9	76.1	39.9	50.4	49.6
30421	COLLINS	66.8	58.9	28.5	33.5	0.1	0.1	4.4	7.4	7.1	7.2	7.2	6.4	5.1	24.4	26.5	14.3	1.9	74.7	39.4	49.4	50.6
30425	GARFIELD	73.0	68.1	25.5	29.8	0.1	0.1	1.9	2.7	6.9	6.7	7.1	7.9	6.3	24.1	26.2	13.1	1.6	74.3	37.9	49.1	50.9
30426	GIRARD	44.4	37.4	54.2	60.8	0.6	0.7	1.5	2.0	7.4	8.0	8.3	7.5	5.4	25.1	26.7	10.2	1.4	71.6	36.6	49.3	50.7
30427	GLENNVILLE	63.9	57.7	29.6	32.5	0.6	1.0	6.8	9.8	6.4	6.4	6.2	6.9	8.1	30.0	23.6	10.6	1.9	77.2	35.2	52.8	47.2
30428	GLENWOOD	73.4	67.9	22.6	26.0	0.1	0.2	5.4	8.3	6.8	7.0	6.8	5.8	5.2	24.1	28.2	12.9	3.0	75.4	40.4	48.8	51.2
30434	LOUISVILLE	36.3	30.4	62.6	68.2	0.2	0.3	1.0	1.2	6.7	6.8	7.0	7.5	6.8	25.6	25.8	11.3	2.4	74.9	36.9	47.4	52.6
30436	LYONS	71.7	64.2	19.0	21.7	0.2	0.3	14.0	20.3	8.3	7.7	7.2	7.1	7.2	27.0	23.8	10.2	1.4	72.5	33.5	49.7	50.3
30438	MANASSAS	61.4	50.3	26.9	31.6	0.1	0.1	11.6	18.1	7.4	7.2	6.8	6.1	6.0	29.4	25.2	10.8	1.1	74.8	36.0	51.8	48.2
30439	METTER	65.4	58.3	27.3	30.9	0.3	0.4	9.0	13.1	7.1	7.1	7.0	6.9	7.4	23.7	26.1	12.3	2.6	74.7	37.4	50.5	49.5
30441	MIDVILLE	45.5	39.6	53.0	58.6	0.1	0.1	1.1	1.4	6.2	7.0	7.7	7.4	5.8	23.2	28.3	12.0	2.4	74.5	38.8	47.9	52.1
30442	MILLEN	54.4	51.7	42.6	45.3	0.3	0.3	3.1	3.1	7.1	7.4	7.4	7.6	6.4	23.7	26.6	12.0	1.9	73.7	37.1	48.4	51.6
30445	MOUNT VERNON	57.1	50.3	40.9	46.8	0.5	0.7	1.9	2.9	6.2	5.8	5.6	9.2	12.6	30.1	20.7	8.7	1.2	78.7	31.4	55.0	45.0
30446	NEWINGTON	51.7	45.1	46.4	52.5	0.5	0.4	1.7	2.0	7.0	6.7	7.2	7.6	5.9	24.0	28.1	12.0	1.5	74.5	38.6	48.7	51.3
30450	PORTAL	63.7	56.4	34.1	40.6	0.1	0.2	4.5	6.3	7.7	7.1	7.8	7.6	8.3	24.6	25.1	10.6	1.2	73.0	34.3	50.5	49.5
30452	REGISTER	64.8	57.1	32.3	38.8	0.2	0.3	2.7	3.9	8.0	7.5	7.1	7.9	8.1	27.4	24.4	8.6	1.0	72.9	32.7	49.4	50.6
30453	REIDSVILLE	51.5	42.4	38.9	42.8	0.3	0.3	10.1	15.5	5.7	5.4	5.3	5.8	9.9	39.1	21.0	6.8	1.0	80.5	33.1	64.4	35.6
30454	ROCKLEDGE	92.4	89.1	6.9	9.7	0.0	0.0	0.8	1.2	6.1	6.2	6.2	5.9	4.8	26.8	27.5	14.7	1.7	77.7	40.5	49.2	50.8
30455	ROCKY FORD	61.6	55.4	37.6	43.7	0.1	0.1	0.8	1.0	6.0	5.9	6.4	6.4	6.4	26.0	29.8	11.3	1.9	78.1	39.6	49.6	50.4
30456	SARDIS	51.6	44.4	47.8	54.8	0.0	0.0	0.8	1.0	9.0	8.3	7.6	7.7	6.2	23.3	25.7	10.7	1.4	70.4	34.2	47.0	53.0
30457	SOPERTON	65.7	63.2	33.1	35.5	0.3	0.3	1.2	1.2	6.9	7.2	7.1	8.0	7.0	24.8	25.4	11.6	1.9	74.6	36.3	50.3	49.7
30458	STATESBORO	62.0	56.2	34.8	39.3	1.2	1.6	2.2	3.1	4.8	4.3	4.5	16.8	24.3	19.4	16.7	7.8	1.4	83.4	24.0	48.7	51.3
30461	STATESBORO	76.6	70.2	21.4	26.8	0.7	1.1	1.1	1.8	7.4	6.6	6.4	6.8	8.0	29.6	24.4	9.4	1.3	75.6	34.0	49.0	51.0
30467	SYLVANIA	53.5	47.5	45.4	51.0	0.3	0.4	0.9	1.2	6.4	6.7	7.1	7.4	6.4	24.0	27.3	12.4	2.3	75.3	38.7	48.3	51.7
30470	TARRYTOWN	86.7	82.5	10.8	14.3	0.0	0.1	4.2	5.2	6.5	6.9	7.0	6.4	4.5	25.5	30.6	11.0	1.5	75.6	40.0	51.8	48.2
30471	TWIN CITY	61.4	54.4	35.6	41.2	0.2	0.3	3.5	5.1	6.0	6.0	6.4	8.0	8.7	24.7	27.0	11.6	1.5	77.0	37.0	52.3	47.7
30473	UVALDA	80.1	72.4	12.9	15.9	0.1	0.1	7.5	12.5	7.2	7.3	7.4	6.7	4.9	25.0	27.6	12.7	1.2	74.0	38.7	50.6	49.4
30474	VIDALIA	67.0	61.4	28.7	32.1	0.7	0.9	4.7	7.1	7.4	7.0	7.0	6.9	6.7	25.5	25.6	11.7	2.2	74.3	36.8	47.0	53.0
30477	WADLEY	31.0	25.9	66.8	70.9	0.1	0.1	2.3	3.3	7.1	6.9	7.1	7.9	6.5	23.2	26.0	12.0	3.2	74.7	36.9	46.2	53.8
30501	GAINESVILLE	66.7	59.7	12.5	12.6	1.7	2.0	39.9	50.5	8.7	7.3	6.1	7.3	9.1	31.0	18.8	9.6	2.1	74.0	31.0	51.7	48.3
30504	GAINESVILLE	70.6	59.3	5.3	5.9	4.8	5.7	34.8	49.4	8.7	7.8	7.0	6.9	7.9	32.2	20.8	7.7	1.1	72.5	31.4	51.8	48.2
30506	GAINESVILLE	94.5	91.3	1.0	1.3	0.5	0.7	6.7	11.3	7.0	7.3	7.4	6.3	4.5	27.5	28.3	10.6	1.2	74.5	38.6	50.2	49.8
30507	GAINESVILLE	70.4	61.5	15.6	17.1	1.4	1.8	22.0	33.3	9.0	8.9	8.3	7.1	6.0	30.6	21.8	7.4	0.9	69.4	32.3	50.9	49.1
30510	ALTO	80.0	73.8	13.7	16.7	1.7	2.5	6.5	9.9	6.3	6.4	6.3	10.3	10.1	29.2	22.5	7.8	1.0	75.9	32.6	59.6	40.4
30511	BALDWIN	91.7	87.7	2.0	2.3	1.4	2.1	12.3	18.6	7.1	6.5	6.4	6.7	6.2	26.6	26.5	11.6	2.4	76.2	37.5	50.7	49.3
30512	BLAIRSVILLE	97.9	97.1	0.6	0.7	0.2	0.4	0.9	1.4	4.8	5.1	5.4	5.4	4.0	21.2	31.7	19.7	2.7	81.4	47.8	49.5	50.5
30513	BLUE RIDGE	98.3	97.7	0.2	0.2	0.2	0.4	0.8	1.2	5.3	5.5	5.8	5.4	4.2	22.8	31.0	17.6	2.5	80.1	45.8	48.5	51.5
30516	BOWERSVILLE	90.0	86.9	8.1	10.6	0.3	0.4	0.8	1.3	7.2	7.3	7.5	6.7	4.8	26.2	27.2	11.7	1.4	73.9	38.9	49.5	50.5
30517	BRASELTON	93.2	87.8	2.9	6.0	1.5	2.1	3.4	5.5	8.1	7.7	7.5	6.6	5.5	31.2	25.0	7.6	0.7	72.6	35.2	51.6	48.4
30518	BUFORD	85.5	79.3	7.1	8.2	1.4	2.3	9.7	16.4	8.3	8.0	7.6	6.3	5.0	31.5	24.7	7.5	1.0	72.1	35.2	50.0	50.0
30519	BUFORD	89.7	84.3	5.7	7.5	1.4	2.5	4.8	9.0	8.7	8.1	7.7	6.7	5.6	32.5	24.1	6.2	0.5	71.3	33.4	50.2	49.8
30520	CANON	87.1	83.9	10.9	13.4	0.3	0.4	1.0	1.5	6.8	7.0	7.2	6.8	5.0	25.9	27.6	12.2	1.5	74.7	38.8	49.9	50.1
30521	CARNESVILLE	91.0	87.9	7.9	10.4	0.2	0.3	0.8	1.3	6.5	6.7	6.8	6.6	5.2	26.5	27.8	12.3	1.5	76.0	39.4	51.1	48.9
30522	CHERRYLOG	97.0	95.8	0.3	0.3	0.1	0.1	1.8	2.9	4.8	5.2	5.5	4.7	3.2	21.4	35.3	18.5	1.4	81.5	48.5	50.4	49.6
30523	CLARKESVILLE	95.5	93.2	1.3	1.8	0.3	0.5	3.5	6.0	5.8	5.8	5.9	6.0	5.4	23.6	29.9	15.7	1.9	78.9	43.2	49.1	50.9
30525	CLAYTON	94.1	91.1	0.8	0.9	0.5	0.6	5.4	8.5	5.5	5.7	6.1	5.9	4.1	23.4	29.7	17.5	2.2	79.1	44.5	50.2	49.8
30527	CLERMONT	97.1	95.2	0.5	0.7	0.3	0.5	2.2	4.2	6.9	7.2	7.5	7.1	4.7	26.5	28.3	10.7	1.2	74.0	38.4	49.9	50.1
30528	CLEVELAND	95.6	94.1	1.8	2.3	0.4	0.5	1.7	2.6	6.7	6.7	6.8	7.2	5.8	26.4	27.4	11.6	1.5	75.8	38.2	49.9	50.1
30529	COMMERCE	87.1	83.0	10.6	13.6	0.5	0.7	1.8	2.6	6.8	6.8	6.8	6.2	4.7	27.3	25.5	12.9	3.0	75.6	39.0	48.1	51.9
30530	COMMERCE	92.6	90.0	4.8	6.2	0.6	0.8	1.8	2.8	7.2	7.3	7.4	6.8	5.2	27.6	27.2	10.3	1.2	74.1	37.3	49.5	50.5
30531	CORNELIA	83.0	77.1	4.9	5.7	4.1	5.5	14.9	21.7	6.8	6.6	6.5	7.2	6.3	27.0	25.5	12.1	2.1	76.2	37.2	50.6	49.4
30533	DAHLONEGA	93.8	91.6	1.5	1.9	0.4	0.6	3.7	5.9	6.5	6.4	6.6	8.3	6.9	28.6	25.6	9.8	1.3	76.4	35.5	49.8	50.2
30534	DAWSONVILLE	97.1	95.9	0.4	0.5	0.4	0.5	1.7	2.7	6.7	7.0	7.2	6.8	4.7	27.6	28.8	10.3	0.8	75.1	38.8	50.4	49.6
30535	DEMOREST	95.0	92.6	1.3	1.8	1.5	2.2	2.8	4.6	5.7	5.9	6.2	8.0	7.3	24.0	28.1	12.7	2.0	78.4	39.6	49.3	50.7
30536	ELLIJAY	95.0	92.2	0.2	0.2	0.3	0.5	5.1	8.2	6.0	6.0	6.4	5.7	4.4	24.6	29.9	15.3	1.7	78.2	42.8	50.8	49.2
30537	DILLARD	94.1	93.1	1.6	1.7	0.9	0.8	4.3	5.9	4.8	5.0	6.0	8.5	4.0	20.9	28.9	18.7	3.3	78.2	45.6	48.6	51.4
30538	EASTANOLLEE	94.8	92.9	3.7	4.8	0.1	0.3	0.7	1.1	7.0	7.0	7.4	7.2	5.6	26.2	27.3	10.8	1.5	74.2	38.1	51.0	49.0
30539	EAST ELLIJAY	88.0	78.7	0.0	0.0	2.0	1.6	14.0	21.3	6.6	6.6	6.6	6.6	3.3	29.5	24.6	13.1	3.3	77.0	38.1	49.2	50.8
30540	ELLIJAY	92.6	88.8	0.3	0.4	0.6	0.8	9.5	14.5	7.2	7.4	7.4	6.2	4.7	26.9	26.8	12.0	1.3	74.1	38.0	50.7	49.3
30541	EPWORTH	97.7	96.9	0.1	0.2	0.1	0.1	0.6	0.9	5.3	5.7	6.1	5.5	4.1	24.8	30.7	15.8	2.1	79.4	44.0	50.4	49.6
30542	FLOWERY BRANCH	90.1	85.0	5.2	7.0	0.8	1.2	6.5	11.6	8.7	8.0	7.7	6.4	5.2	31.9	24.7	6.7	0.6	71.6	34.8	50.1	49.9
30543	GILLSVILLE	85.9	77.9	6.2	7.8	0.7	1.0	11.6	21.8	8.3	8.3	7.9	7.0	6.3	28.3	24.5	8.6	0.8	71.2	34.2	50.5	49.5
30545	HELEN	88.3	85.4	7.2	8.2	3.5	5.0	1.2	1.5	4.4	4.8	5.1	4.8	3.0	20.1	36.1	19.5	2.1	82.5	49.6	49.8	50.2
30546	HIAWASSEE	98.8	98.3	0.0	0.0	0.3	0.5	0.9	1.3	4.2	4.5	4.8	4.4	3.1	18.9	30.9	25.3	3.9	83.8	52.8	48.5	51.5
30547	HOMER	92.7	90.3	4.8	5.9	0.2	0.3	2.0	3.2	6.9	7.1	7.3	6.4	5.3	26.8	28.3	10.9	1.1	74.7	37.8	51.9	48.1
30548	HOSCHTON	93.2	89.3	2.9	4.6	1.4	1.9	3.9	6.7	8.0	7.7	7.6	6.8	5.4	30.5	25.4	7.8	0.7	72.4	35.4	51.3	48.7
30549	JEFFERSON	85.2	81.7	11.7	13.8	1.1	1.6	2.9	4.4	7.0	7.0	7.2	7.0	5.7	28.7	26.8	9.5	1.1	74.5	37.0	51.0	49.0
30552	LAKEMONT	97.1	95.2	0.3	0.3	0.0	0.1	2.8	4.8	5.8	6.2	6.4	5.4	4.2	23.3	31.5	15.8	1.5	78.2	44.0	50.4	49.6
30553	LAVONIA	85.8	82.7	12.3	14.5	0.2	0.3	1.1	1.7	5.7	5.5	5.9	5.9	4.6	22.7	31.2	16.8	1.7	79.3	44.8	47.8	52.2
30554	LULA	95.3	93.1	2.5	3.3	0.5	0.7	2.2	4.0	7.2	7.3	7.3	6.5	5.3	28.7	26.1	10.4	1.1	74.1	37.1	49.4	50.6
30555	MC CAYSVILLE	97.4	96.4	0.1	0.0	0.3	0.5	0.9	1.6	6.3	6.2	6.4	6.3	5.2	23.4	26.7	16.8	2.7	77.2	42.1	47.7	52.3
30557	MARTIN	88.7	85.6	10.0	12.5	0.3	0.5	0.9	1.3	5.9	6.1	6.4	6.4	5.3	25.5	30.0	13.0	1.4	77.7	41.2	50.1	49.9
30558	MAYSVILLE	93.2	90.7	3.5	4.3	0.5	0.6	2.6	4.0	7.2	7.2	7.2	6.7	5.5	27.8	27.0	10.3	1.1	74.2	37.3	50.2	49.8
30559	MINERAL BLUFF	97.4	96.6	0.1	0.1	0.1	0.2	0.5	0.7	5.2	5.4	5.7	5.7	4.4	23.9	30.5	17.3	1.8	79.9	44.7	49.3	50.7
30560	MORGANTON	98.2	97.6	0.2	0.2	0.3	0.4	0.5	0.7	4.9	5.4	5.7	5.3	3.9	21.4	33.9	17.7	1.9	80.6	47.1	48.9	51.1
	GEORGIA	65.1	61.1	28.7	30.1	2.2	2.9	5.3	7.7	7.3	7.0	6.9	7.1	7.1	29.3	25.1	8.9	1.3	74.7	35.0	49.4	50.6
	UNITED STATES	75.1	72.0	12.3	12.7	3.8	4.6	12.5	15.7	6.8	6.7	6.6	7.1	6.9	27.0	26.0	10.9	1.9	75.7	36.9	49.2	50.8

INCOME

#	POST OFFICE NAME	2009 Per Capita Income	2009 HH Income Base	2009 HOUSEHOLD INCOME DISTRIBUTION (%) Less than $25,000	$25,000 to $49,999	$50,000 to $99,999	$100,000 to $149,999	$150,000 or More	MEDIAN HOUSEHOLD INCOME 2009	2014	2009 National Centile	2009 State Centile	2009 Home Value Base	2009 HOME VALUE DISTRIBUTION (%) Less than $50,000	$50,000 to $89,999	$90,000 to $174,999	$175,000 to $399,999	$400,000 or More	2009 Median Home Value
30337	ATLANTA	19389	6646	29.7	31.9	30.6	5.7	2.1	38729	41360	29	40	1621	7.1	33.7	52.7	6.4	0.2	96889
30338	ATLANTA	57532	13826	6.5	10.3	30.1	24.0	29.1	105346	103293	97	99	8733	0.8	0.9	9.3	75.5	13.5	284696
30339	ATLANTA	60473	10234	8.5	13.8	45.0	18.1	14.6	76062	81232	90	91	2237	2.6	2.8	15.4	39.2	39.9	330521
30340	ATLANTA	24772	10855	15.0	26.9	41.5	11.5	5.1	57133	58788	74	78	4999	3.1	17.8	55.1	23.1	0.9	128738
30341	ATLANTA	31830	13622	12.1	20.9	38.7	17.0	11.3	67743	72204	85	87	6136	1.9	6.9	35.4	52.2	3.6	184319
30342	ATLANTA	56487	13449	8.2	11.3	38.8	21.3	20.5	86793	89998	94	96	6542	0.7	4.2	15.7	37.0	42.5	356537
30344	ATLANTA	18774	16043	28.1	32.1	32.0	5.8	1.9	40551	43352	35	44	7097	7.3	46.7	43.6	2.0	0.4	86937
30345	ATLANTA	40424	9410	7.3	15.6	37.5	20.4	19.2	82637	85410	93	94	5918	1.1	1.5	18.5	69.7	9.2	239944
30346	ATLANTA	64484	1599	9.0	9.8	38.8	24.3	18.2	86979	87717	94	96	195	0.0	3.1	1.5	80.5	14.9	302143
30349	ATLANTA	23070	27551	16.1	30.4	40.9	9.7	2.8	54210	59308	70	75	13741	3.1	26.2	66.2	3.0	1.5	100822
30350	ATLANTA	46879	17425	9.7	21.0	44.0	12.1	13.2	70600	75064	87	89	5506	1.0	9.3	25.3	19.5	45.0	357121
30354	ATLANTA	15315	6791	32.0	34.7	28.1	4.2	1.0	35792	37584	20	28	2510	12.0	62.0	25.0	1.0	0.0	72738
30360	ATLANTA	32755	6908	11.5	24.1	39.0	14.7	10.7	66162	70162	84	86	2719	0.2	7.7	31.7	52.7	7.6	201949
30363	ATLANTA	88472	1195	11.5	9.0	19.8	27.4	32.3	113935	119973	98	99	653	0.3	2.6	9.0	17.6	70.4	544859
30401	SWAINSBORO	16187	5292	44.9	25.9	22.6	4.6	2.0	29029	29804	7	5	3450	26.2	33.5	28.8	10.8	0.8	75836
30410	AILEY	17339	538	33.3	29.6	31.8	4.5	0.9	37682	39086	26	36	426	36.2	20.0	28.4	12.9	2.6	80370
30411	ALAMO	15833	1212	39.9	30.6	23.1	4.3	2.1	32042	33314	11	14	949	37.3	26.6	27.2	7.1	1.9	70890
30413	BARTOW	15356	647	39.3	29.1	28.0	2.6	1.1	32163	33375	12	14	518	36.9	28.4	24.1	8.7	1.9	61351
30415	BROOKLET	19328	2550	20.2	35.8	37.2	4.9	2.0	45593	50023	50	60	1984	20.3	20.6	37.7	18.9	2.6	105066
30417	CLAXTON	14773	4339	42.2	31.1	23.0	2.6	1.2	30740	31426	9	11	3097	30.4	23.8	31.5	12.0	2.3	81957
30420	COBBTOWN	15134	676	41.6	32.5	21.9	3.3	0.7	30208	30888	8	9	514	35.2	29.2	26.1	8.6	1.0	71750
30421	COLLINS	14561	708	47.6	29.5	19.6	2.5	0.7	27486	29298	5	3	550	40.4	29.8	23.3	6.4	0.2	63333
30425	GARFIELD	16521	496	43.1	25.0	25.8	3.0	3.0	29530	31902	7	6	396	30.6	24.5	28.5	11.1	5.3	82857
30426	GIRARD	13756	416	43.0	29.6	24.8	2.6	0.0	30269	32544	9	9	360	50.6	25.0	17.2	2.8	4.4	49636
30427	GLENNVILLE	17147	3762	35.9	25.4	32.9	3.7	2.1	37583	38748	25	35	2622	26.3	22.1	36.4	14.8	0.5	93007
30428	GLENWOOD	15756	1095	44.9	26.5	25.3	1.9	1.4	27770	28854	5	4	839	37.4	31.3	24.6	6.2	0.5	61328
30434	LOUISVILLE	16318	2196	45.0	23.6	26.3	2.7	2.4	31536	33801	11	13	1521	43.5	20.2	29.9	5.5	0.9	60929
30436	LYONS	15168	4502	43.2	27.2	24.6	3.6	1.5	30272	30348	9	9	3081	36.0	30.2	20.5	11.7	1.7	67171
30438	MANASSAS	15999	342	33.9	34.8	25.7	4.1	1.5	37699	38142	26	36	260	31.2	33.1	23.8	7.3	4.6	72778
30439	METTER	14110	3734	42.6	28.3	24.7	3.5	0.9	29937	30659	8	8	2719	29.0	29.9	24.8	14.0	2.3	75945
30441	MIDVILLE	14180	694	45.0	33.0	17.9	2.4	1.7	28950	29031	7	5	540	38.9	31.1	22.6	4.8	2.6	62558
30442	MILLEN	15494	2948	45.1	26.1	22.5	4.9	1.4	28251	28985	6	4	2135	36.6	32.2	21.0	8.5	1.7	61455
30445	MOUNT VERNON	17075	1090	38.0	25.0	29.6	4.1	3.2	36061	37444	21	29	737	36.6	23.7	30.0	7.3	2.3	74767
30446	NEWINGTON	15409	645	38.8	27.6	30.5	2.8	0.3	33516	37368	14	19	525	33.7	27.2	26.1	10.5	2.5	74432
30450	PORTAL	16170	1316	36.7	31.5	25.7	4.8	1.1	34881	35337	17	24	970	31.5	22.9	30.6	9.4	5.6	80851
30452	REGISTER	15867	697	31.6	31.3	32.6	3.3	1.3	36076	38864	21	29	534	26.8	23.2	33.1	15.9	0.9	90000
30453	REIDSVILLE	14871	2125	40.0	27.2	28.2	3.5	1.1	32250	33926	12	15	1409	30.7	28.2	31.4	8.7	1.1	77752
30454	ROCKLEDGE	19094	312	35.9	36.9	21.8	3.2	2.2	36018	37762	21	29	271	29.5	30.3	32.1	3.0	5.2	76333
30455	ROCKY FORD	17555	306	31.7	31.0	33.0	3.3	1.0	38214	40767	27	37	254	42.1	26.4	26.4	5.1	0.0	61667
30456	SARDIS	14240	719	40.6	27.0	29.1	2.6	0.7	32753	34154	13	16	584	45.9	34.9	17.5	1.2	0.5	54615
30457	SOPERTON	15928	2555	42.9	28.2	24.7	2.5	1.8	29627	30663	7	7	1898	46.5	20.3	25.0	7.4	0.8	59054
30458	STATESBORO	18170	14189	42.3	26.4	23.4	4.9	3.1	30919	32271	10	11	6377	17.2	13.0	37.7	27.3	4.9	133844
30461	STATESBORO	21495	5037	28.0	27.9	34.0	6.9	3.2	44433	49257	47	57	3431	11.8	14.9	39.1	30.8	3.4	135516
30467	SYLVANIA	16965	5019	35.6	31.6	28.1	2.8	1.9	35948	36785	20	28	3826	33.2	27.2	30.3	8.4	0.9	72103
30470	TARRYTOWN	18986	496	31.7	33.9	28.0	5.6	0.8	37589	37368	25	35	393	35.9	11.2	30.5	17.0	5.3	98846
30471	TWIN CITY	14720	1635	40.9	30.5	23.7	3.9	0.9	29980	30566	8	8	1295	35.5	29.2	25.4	7.6	2.3	67151
30473	UVALDA	16127	1176	37.2	31.5	26.7	2.7	1.8	33544	33926	14	19	1002	37.9	26.2	25.7	10.1	0.0	63770
30474	VIDALIA	18209	6615	36.8	27.7	28.7	4.9	1.9	34912	36656	17	24	4173	23.7	20.3	41.0	13.4	1.6	99047
30477	WADLEY	14245	1117	49.3	26.9	20.8	1.6	1.3	25367	26654	3	2	795	50.8	26.0	14.5	8.2	0.5	49404
30501	GAINESVILLE	19024	10534	27.8	25.0	35.0	6.8	5.5	45000	51999	48	59	4735	12.2	19.0	41.5	21.0	6.2	119378
30504	GAINESVILLE	20886	7656	21.7	23.5	40.6	8.3	5.9	53971	56625	70	74	4038	11.2	21.4	45.0	16.0	6.3	113148
30506	GAINESVILLE	26972	15863	14.8	22.2	44.7	11.1	7.2	62157	63577	80	82	12796	11.7	13.5	36.4	27.7	10.7	141089
30507	GAINESVILLE	18658	8730	19.4	26.1	45.1	6.3	3.1	52876	55730	68	72	6583	23.6	20.0	40.9	13.7	1.8	96755
30510	ALTO	18368	2505	25.2	33.7	35.8	3.8	1.4	43578	45079	44	54	1938	17.7	19.0	37.8	22.3	3.1	114875
30511	BALDWIN	17907	1299	25.9	29.3	39.2	2.8	2.8	45755	46400	51	60	958	15.1	21.6	35.4	24.1	3.8	117460
30512	BLAIRSVILLE	20523	8795	30.7	31.3	32.1	4.0	2.0	38700	40294	29	39	7158	6.6	9.5	36.0	37.8	10.0	170098
30513	BLUE RIDGE	19698	5621	33.1	32.4	29.3	3.5	1.7	38287	39621	28	38	4455	10.5	15.6	37.9	28.9	7.1	136219
30516	BOWERSVILLE	17404	792	32.8	32.6	30.4	2.8	1.4	36638	38004	22	32	660	15.9	20.8	37.3	21.4	4.7	110241
30517	BRASELTON	29109	3938	14.1	17.9	43.3	15.7	8.9	68646	69665	86	88	3404	9.0	7.0	34.4	39.5	10.1	174242
30518	BUFORD	30167	15160	13.0	18.5	41.8	17.7	9.0	70528	74847	87	89	11558	20.3	8.2	32.1	35.2	4.2	152898
30519	BUFORD	35856	13207	5.6	9.4	40.5	27.9	16.6	92150	99281	95	97	11577	6.4	3.3	32.4	51.6	6.3	186287
30520	CANON	17237	1737	36.5	30.3	28.2	3.5	1.5	33673	35958	15	20	1374	22.3	22.8	35.9	14.8	4.2	98933
30521	CARNESVILLE	18689	1939	27.3	30.5	38.0	2.3	1.9	42997	44527	42	53	1626	13.1	25.5	36.5	17.4	7.5	108960
30522	CHERRYLOG	22861	683	25.5	31.2	35.9	5.9	1.6	44019	46962	45	55	605	6.6	14.7	29.4	41.8	7.4	172606
30523	CLARKESVILLE	21509	5476	27.7	28.0	35.8	5.3	3.1	43619	43881	44	55	4382	6.4	11.9	36.3	37.1	8.2	161920
30525	CLAYTON	22800	3944	26.3	31.9	34.2	4.5	3.1	42596	44479	41	51	3017	12.2	13.0	35.4	28.5	10.8	144375
30527	CLERMONT	22034	1477	17.2	27.0	45.0	6.4	4.5	53680	56142	69	74	1232	13.4	15.7	37.7	24.8	8.3	129664
30528	CLEVELAND	19089	8330	24.7	33.7	36.1	4.2	1.4	42808	43953	42	52	6537	8.6	9.4	37.2	38.6	6.1	162066
30529	COMMERCE	21064	4489	29.4	29.2	32.6	5.1	3.7	42260	45323	40	51	3078	13.3	16.0	38.8	25.2	6.7	132867
30530	COMMERCE	18366	2261	27.8	29.5	36.3	4.3	2.1	43578	45487	44	54	1787	15.3	21.4	38.4	19.4	5.5	113238
30531	CORNELIA	19494	4310	29.0	30.0	33.7	4.5	2.8	42232	43356	40	50	2927	15.2	15.6	38.2	24.7	6.4	130957
30533	DAHLONEGA	21563	9270	25.7	27.7	37.5	5.9	3.2	46438	47420	53	62	6649	9.3	9.9	34.4	36.2	10.1	166752
30534	DAWSONVILLE	25866	9299	16.5	25.3	43.9	9.9	4.5	59355	62323	77	79	7460	13.6	17.7	35.0	24.8	8.9	123222
30535	DEMOREST	20345	2973	26.0	30.0	36.5	5.5	2.0	44460	44219	47	57	2234	11.8	18.8	37.2	27.8	4.4	129965
30536	ELLIJAY	21373	3179	25.8	31.2	36.1	4.1	2.8	44260	46456	46	56	2642	11.3	16.5	33.8	32.5	6.0	143588
30537	DILLARD	25782	688	28.5	35.0	29.1	3.6	3.8	39184	39884	30	41	544	11.2	11.9	36.9	32.2	7.7	150877
30538	EASTANOLLEE	16701	585	32.8	33.8	28.7	3.6	1.0	35835	36277	20	28	491	24.8	27.5	32.8	12.2	2.6	87326
30539	EAST ELLIJAY	20283	24	20.8	29.2	45.8	4.2	0.0	50000	50000	61	68	17	0.0	11.8	52.9	29.4	5.9	146875
30540	ELLIJAY	18248	7493	29.9	32.3	31.5	4.4	2.0	41058	42367	36	46	5575	15.6	18.0	35.0	26.8	4.6	130544
30541	EPWORTH	19601	702	22.4	35.9	36.5	4.0	1.3	44130	49544	46	56	611	9.5	18.3	36.3	27.0	8.8	133686
30542	FLOWERY BRANCH	27120	10367	10.3	17.6	50.4	14.6	7.0	67886	70877	86	87	8618	13.4	11.2	49.7	21.8	4.0	127197
30543	GILLSVILLE	20150	1511	18.6	23.2	50.3	5.4	2.6	54517	55715	70	75	1264	18.9	27.8	34.7	14.4	4.1	93832
30545	HELEN	26104	467	29.3	29.6	32.5	4.3	4.3	42263	43494	40	51	343	1.5	11.1	28.3	43.1	16.0	211735
30546	HIAWASSEE	22759	3592	32.7	28.7	30.2	4.9	3.5	38416	39904	28	39	3002	13.1	8.7	28.7	37.7	11.8	172713
30547	HOMER	20057	1069	27.4	30.3	34.6	5.2	2.4	44035	45790	45	56	832	13.7	19.1	33.4	27.6	6.1	122292
30548	HOSCHTON	27026	4918	15.6	20.8	43.2	13.3	7.2	63856	63909	82	83	4154	10.1	6.8	34.8	37.9	10.4	171535
30549	JEFFERSON	20358	7804	26.2	24.5	40.1	6.4	2.8	49245	48789	59	67	5973	6.5	11.7	35.9	34.7	11.1	164643
30552	LAKEMONT	22637	788	23.7	39.3	31.1	2.5	3.3	38113	39198	27	37	665	15.9	15.5	31.1	23.6	13.8	133402
30553	LAVONIA	19985	3026	31.7	29.9	32.4	3.8	2.3	38943	39863	30	41	2327	15.4	16.2	35.8	26.1	6.4	124730
30554	LULA	20531	2778	20.4	25.8	46.3	4.9	2.7	52552	54307	67	72	2220	23.2	20.3	31.3	18.8	6.4	102511
30555	MC CAYSVILLE	16667	1016	41.9	31.4	23.9	2.3	0.5	30473	32106	9	10	769	11.8	23.0	42.8	18.7	3.6	108420
30557	MARTIN	18184	2148	31.0	33.0	30.0	4.7	1.3	38308	39140	28	38	1795	15.2	24.9	36.5	18.4	5.0	108745
30558	MAYSVILLE	19961	2249	24.5	30.1	37.3	5.3	2.8	46085	47108	52	61	1801	11.1	15.5	41.6	23.4	8.3	134838
30559	MINERAL BLUFF	17199	1830	36.2	36.0	23.7	2.5	1.7	33114	34571	13	17	1574	17.5	18.1	38.7	21.9	3.8	120455
30560	MORGANTON	18991	1909	31.1	32.0	32.7	3.5	0.7	38660	40709	29	39	1642	13.5	12.3	40.4	26.5	7.3	135842
	GEORGIA	26980		20.7	23.1	36.8	11.7	7.7	56761	58593				13.2	17.9	39.1	24.2	5.5	121444
	UNITED STATES	27277		20.9	24.4	35.3	11.7	7.6	54719	56938				9.3	13.1	31.6	32.6	13.5	162279

ZIP CODE		FINANCIAL SERVICES				THE HOME						ENTERTAINMENT						PERSONAL			
						Home Improvements		Furnishings													
#	POST OFFICE NAME	Auto Loan	Home Loan	Invest-ments	Retire-ment Plans	Home Repair	Lawn & Garden	Comput-ers & Hard-ware-Personal	Major Appli-ances	TV, Radio, Sound Equip-ment	Furni-ture	Dine out/ Carry out	Sports Equip-ment	Fees & Tickets	Toys & Games	Travel	Cable TV	Apparel & Services	Auto Repairs	Health Insur-ance	Pets & Supplies
30337	ATLANTA	71	56	52	59	54	55	74	61	74	70	75	51	67	75	64	74	53	71	64	76
30338	ATLANTA	176	195	213	205	204	180	193	183	182	201	184	146	209	183	202	175	135	184	171	212
30339	ATLANTA	153	122	126	137	120	115	164	130	158	158	163	115	151	160	146	152	116	150	130	162
30340	ATLANTA	101	87	80	90	84	82	102	89	100	101	101	73	95	102	93	97	71	97	89	108
30341	ATLANTA	120	109	108	114	108	102	128	112	124	127	127	93	123	124	121	120	90	123	110	134
30342	ATLANTA	176	158	176	176	162	149	194	162	185	190	190	140	191	186	183	179	139	179	157	196
30344	ATLANTA	72	61	55	63	57	63	73	65	76	71	76	51	69	76	66	77	53	72	71	80
30345	ATLANTA	133	156	171	158	164	140	156	148	145	156	148	118	169	144	166	140	109	150	136	167
30346	ATLANTA	156	115	120	133	111	111	170	128	165	158	171	118	151	166	146	160	122	154	133	165
30349	ATLANTA	92	81	71	83	76	77	91	81	91	92	92	65	86	93	84	89	64	88	83	99
30350	ATLANTA	145	111	110	123	108	105	147	119	143	145	146	103	134	148	128	138	104	137	118	147
30354	ATLANTA	65	51	45	53	47	54	65	56	68	62	67	45	58	68	56	70	47	63	63	71
30360	ATLANTA	122	107	104	114	105	100	125	109	121	126	123	90	119	124	116	117	87	118	107	132
30363	ATLANTA	211	225	265	248	238	206	252	219	234	247	242	188	264	232	257	225	181	230	203	257
30401	SWAINSBORO	70	51	61	50	51	67	56	63	62	54	61	48	47	63	51	68	41	62	68	76
30410	AILEY	73	60	64	58	59	69	61	67	64	61	64	51	54	66	58	67	43	65	68	80
30411	ALAMO	76	53	70	51	53	74	56	68	62	53	61	52	44	64	52	69	41	63	71	82
30413	BARTOW	75	49	72	46	48	73	52	66	60	49	59	51	39	61	49	67	39	62	69	81
30415	BROOKLET	89	74	77	72	73	86	72	81	77	73	77	60	64	80	69	82	52	78	83	97
30417	CLAXTON	68	50	61	48	49	65	52	60	57	50	56	46	42	58	48	62	38	58	63	73
30420	COBBTOWN	69	47	69	45	48	69	49	62	56	46	55	48	38	56	48	62	36	58	65	75
30421	COLLINS	64	44	63	42	44	64	46	58	52	43	51	44	35	53	44	58	34	54	61	70
30425	GARFIELD	77	52	73	50	53	75	55	68	63	53	61	53	43	64	52	69	41	64	72	83
30426	GIRARD	68	44	65	42	44	67	47	60	55	45	53	46	35	56	44	61	35	56	63	73
30427	GLENNVILLE	75	61	66	60	61	73	63	70	67	61	66	53	55	68	59	71	45	67	73	83
30428	GLENWOOD	72	47	69	44	47	70	50	63	58	48	57	49	38	59	47	65	37	59	67	78
30434	LOUISVILLE	77	52	70	50	52	75	56	68	64	54	63	52	44	65	52	71	42	65	73	83
30436	LYONS	65	51	54	50	50	61	55	58	59	54	58	45	47	60	50	62	40	58	61	71
30438	MANASSAS	76	58	63	56	57	72	59	67	65	58	64	52	49	67	55	69	43	64	70	81
30439	METTER	68	51	63	49	51	66	52	61	58	51	57	47	44	59	50	62	38	59	64	74
30441	MIDVILLE	68	45	67	43	46	67	48	61	55	45	54	47	37	55	46	61	35	57	64	74
30442	MILLEN	73	49	69	47	49	72	52	65	60	50	58	50	40	61	49	66	39	61	69	79
30445	MOUNT VERNON	78	58	74	57	59	77	63	72	68	60	67	55	52	68	59	74	45	69	77	87
30446	NEWINGTON	72	48	70	45	48	71	51	64	58	48	57	50	38	59	48	65	38	60	68	78
30450	PORTAL	81	53	78	50	53	79	57	71	65	54	64	55	43	66	53	72	42	67	75	87
30452	REGISTER	69	64	56	61	61	63	62	63	63	65	63	48	58	66	59	64	43	63	63	75
30453	REIDSVILLE	69	56	60	53	55	66	57	63	60	56	60	48	49	62	53	64	40	61	65	75
30454	ROCKLEDGE	82	55	75	52	55	79	58	71	66	56	65	55	45	68	54	73	43	67	75	88
30455	ROCKY FORD	80	57	66	56	57	76	60	70	66	58	65	53	48	69	54	72	44	66	73	85
30456	SARDIS	74	48	71	45	48	72	51	65	59	49	58	50	38	60	48	66	38	61	68	79
30457	SOPERTON	74	48	71	45	48	73	52	65	60	49	58	51	39	61	48	66	39	61	69	80
30458	STATESBORO	67	52	50	53	50	55	71	58	67	63	67	48	58	67	57	66	47	64	60	72
30461	STATESBORO	84	76	72	76	74	77	78	78	79	79	79	60	74	81	74	80	55	78	78	93
30467	SYLVANIA	78	55	72	52	54	76	58	69	65	56	64	53	46	66	54	72	43	66	74	85
30470	TARRYTOWN	80	57	73	56	58	78	59	72	66	57	65	55	48	67	56	72	43	67	75	87
30471	TWIN CITY	74	48	71	46	48	72	52	65	59	49	58	50	39	60	48	66	38	61	68	80
30473	UVALDA	76	53	71	51	53	75	55	68	62	53	61	52	43	63	52	69	41	64	71	82
30474	VIDALIA	68	62	58	62	60	67	64	65	67	63	66	49	61	68	61	69	46	66	69	78
30477	WADLEY	64	44	59	42	43	63	47	57	55	46	53	43	37	55	44	61	36	55	62	70
30501	GAINESVILLE	85	76	72	76	75	74	87	81	87	86	88	63	82	87	81	87	62	86	83	95
30504	GAINESVILLE	97	84	75	83	82	79	95	88	93	95	95	70	87	95	87	91	66	93	85	104
30506	GAINESVILLE	110	116	103	117	113	114	106	110	106	108	106	84	109	109	108	106	74	106	109	129
30507	GAINESVILLE	92	89	79	84	87	83	86	88	84	90	85	66	82	87	83	84	59	86	83	101
30510	ALTO	91	67	75	65	66	87	69	80	76	67	75	61	56	79	63	83	50	76	84	97
30511	BALDWIN	89	67	73	65	66	84	69	78	75	68	74	60	57	78	63	81	50	75	81	95
30512	BLAIRSVILLE	79	63	97	61	69	84	63	80	67	60	66	58	55	64	67	72	44	74	81	93
30513	BLUE RIDGE	77	58	82	57	61	79	59	74	65	55	63	55	49	64	60	70	42	68	76	87
30516	BOWERSVILLE	76	58	64	57	58	74	59	68	64	57	63	52	49	67	55	70	43	64	72	82
30517	BRASELTON	128	127	107	122	121	117	116	119	115	123	116	90	113	122	112	114	80	115	113	139
30518	BUFORD	126	130	110	126	123	118	121	121	118	126	119	94	120	124	118	115	83	117	114	141
30519	BUFORD	168	181	146	173	169	149	161	160	152	175	155	127	163	164	158	144	109	152	139	182
30520	CANON	77	54	70	52	54	75	56	68	63	54	62	53	44	65	53	70	41	64	72	83
30521	CARNESVILLE	87	62	78	60	63	84	64	77	71	62	70	59	52	73	60	78	47	72	81	93
30522	CHERRYLOG	88	69	108	68	75	92	70	88	73	65	72	65	60	70	74	79	48	81	88	102
30523	CLARKESVILLE	87	70	87	70	73	89	73	84	78	68	76	63	64	77	72	83	51	80	88	99
30525	CLAYTON	89	70	93	68	73	90	71	85	76	68	75	63	61	75	71	82	50	80	88	100
30527	CLERMONT	96	90	86	92	90	100	86	95	89	83	88	72	82	91	86	92	60	89	96	111
30528	CLEVELAND	79	71	72	69	71	76	68	74	71	70	70	55	63	72	67	73	48	72	74	88
30529	COMMERCE	89	73	78	71	73	87	73	82	78	72	77	61	64	80	69	83	52	78	86	98
30530	COMMERCE	87	68	71	66	67	82	68	77	74	68	73	58	58	77	63	79	49	73	80	93
30531	CORNELIA	84	69	72	67	68	81	70	77	75	69	74	58	62	77	66	79	50	74	80	92
30533	DAHLONEGA	86	79	72	78	78	82	77	80	79	79	79	59	73	82	74	81	54	79	81	95
30534	DAWSONVILLE	102	100	96	99	99	103	93	100	94	94	94	75	91	96	94	96	65	96	99	118
30535	DEMOREST	88	67	78	66	68	85	69	80	75	67	74	60	58	77	65	81	50	76	83	96
30536	ELLIJAY	92	68	94	66	70	92	70	86	76	65	75	65	57	76	69	82	50	80	89	102
30537	DILLARD	90	69	99	68	73	91	70	86	75	67	74	64	59	74	71	81	49	80	87	102
30538	EASTANOLLEE	77	55	64	54	55	73	58	67	64	56	63	51	46	66	52	70	42	63	71	81
30539	EAST ELLIJAY	90	65	74	63	64	86	67	78	75	65	73	60	54	78	61	81	49	74	83	95
30540	ELLIJAY	83	64	71	63	64	80	65	75	71	63	69	57	55	73	61	76	47	71	78	90
30541	EPWORTH	76	65	76	67	68	81	65	76	68	59	67	57	58	68	66	72	45	70	78	89
30542	FLOWERY BRANCH	116	124	109	122	120	113	112	114	108	118	110	88	115	113	113	106	77	109	107	132
30543	GILLSVILLE	97	83	81	78	82	88	83	89	85	86	85	67	74	88	78	87	59	86	87	104
30545	HELEN	91	73	117	72	80	96	73	92	76	68	75	68	63	72	79	81	50	85	91	107
30546	HIAWASSEE	79	67	97	65	74	86	65	81	70	66	68	57	60	66	70	74	46	75	85	93
30547	HOMER	93	67	77	65	66	88	69	81	77	68	75	62	56	80	63	84	51	76	85	98
30548	HOSCHTON	120	116	100	112	112	111	107	111	108	113	109	83	104	114	103	108	74	107	107	130
30549	JEFFERSON	92	80	75	78	79	86	78	83	82	80	81	61	72	85	73	85	55	81	84	99
30552	LAKEMONT	89	67	88	66	70	89	69	82	75	67	73	62	58	75	67	81	49	77	85	98
30553	LAVONIA	79	60	86	59	64	81	64	77	69	60	67	57	54	67	64	74	45	72	80	90
30554	LULA	97	79	80	77	78	92	78	87	84	79	83	65	69	87	73	89	56	83	90	105
30555	MC CAYSVILLE	63	46	59	44	47	64	49	59	54	45	53	44	39	55	46	60	35	55	63	70
30557	MARTIN	82	59	77	58	61	81	61	74	68	59	67	57	49	69	58	74	44	70	78	90
30558	MAYSVILLE	92	76	75	73	74	87	74	82	80	75	79	61	66	83	70	84	53	79	84	99
30559	MINERAL BLUFF	72	52	74	50	54	73	53	68	59	49	58	51	43	59	53	65	38	62	70	80
30560	MORGANTON	77	58	88	57	62	79	59	75	63	55	62	55	49	62	61	69	41	69	76	88
	GEORGIA	110	101	97	102	98	103	103	103	104	104	104	80	99	107	99	105	73	103	103	122
	UNITED STATES	100	100	100	100	100	100	100	100	100	100	100	100	100	100	100	100	100	100	100	100

POPULATION CHANGE

 30563-30818

ZIP CODE #	POST OFFICE NAME	COUNTY FIPS CODE	POPULATION 2000	POPULATION 2009	POPULATION 2014	2000-2009 ANNUAL RATE % Rate	2000-2009 ANNUAL RATE State Centile	HOUSEHOLDS 2000	HOUSEHOLDS 2009	HOUSEHOLDS 2014	HOUSEHOLDS % Annual Rate 2000-2009	HOUSEHOLDS 2009 Average HH Size	FAMILIES 2000	FAMILIES 2009	FAMILIES % Annual Rate 2000-2009
30563	MOUNT AIRY	137	4037	5292	5921	3.0	83	1531	2016	2260	3.0	2.62	1190	1527	2.7
30564	MURRAYVILLE	139	3477	4601	5254	3.1	85	1267	1671	1907	3.0	2.75	993	1266	2.7
30565	NICHOLSON	157	4211	5569	6497	3.1	85	1520	2006	2340	3.0	2.78	1187	1524	2.7
30566	OAKWOOD	139	6896	9138	10507	3.1	85	2418	3140	3590	2.9	2.90	1846	2326	2.5
30567	PENDERGRASS	157	2554	3554	4379	3.6	88	905	1259	1558	3.6	2.82	724	981	3.3
30568	RABUN GAP	241	2108	2614	2832	2.4	75	792	966	1058	2.2	2.50	561	660	1.8
30571	SAUTEE NACOOCHEE	311	2594	3740	4328	4.0	91	1104	1614	1878	4.2	2.27	803	1136	3.8
30572	SUCHES	291	1134	1598	1828	3.8	90	498	721	831	4.1	2.22	352	492	3.7
30575	TALMO	157	1377	1883	2344	3.4	87	455	623	778	3.5	3.01	365	486	3.1
30576	TIGER	241	2222	2414	2497	0.9	45	887	983	1025	1.1	2.44	625	669	0.7
30577	TOCCOA	257	22257	22281	22292	0.0	17	8698	8826	8865	0.2	2.42	6137	6017	-0.2
30582	YOUNG HARRIS	281	3564	4042	4208	1.4	57	1406	1605	1689	1.4	2.25	1032	1143	1.1
30597	DAHLONEGA	187	1035	1292	1457	2.4	75	0	0	0	0.0	0.00	0	0	0.0
30601	ATHENS	059	17880	20249	21467	1.4	57	7102	7998	8483	1.3	2.52	3896	4162	0.7
30602	ATHENS	059	1400	1523	1534	0.9	45	4	4	4	0.0	2.50	1	1	0.0
30605	ATHENS	059	38834	43381	45491	1.2	52	14694	16560	17580	1.3	2.21	6171	6423	0.4
30606	ATHENS	059	34849	40261	43157	1.6	63	14708	16971	18208	1.6	2.30	7611	8478	1.2
30607	ATHENS	157	9307	11669	13152	2.5	77	3296	4133	4686	2.5	2.79	2324	2779	2.0
30609	ATHENS	059	112	136	147	2.1	72	43	52	56	2.1	2.62	7	8	1.5
30619	ARNOLDSVILLE	221	1195	1400	1500	1.7	66	473	564	608	1.9	2.48	339	391	1.6
30620	BETHLEHEM	013	5476	11762	15196	8.6	100	1831	3911	5046	8.6	3.01	1508	3134	8.2
30621	BISHOP	219	3518	4830	5515	3.5	88	1212	1657	1898	3.4	2.86	965	1290	3.2
30622	BOGART	219	7290	9280	10282	2.6	78	2630	3383	3756	2.8	2.73	2029	2537	2.4
30624	BOWMAN	105	2984	3167	3219	0.6	34	1163	1260	1290	0.9	2.50	853	893	0.5
30625	BUCKHEAD	211	2006	2667	2984	3.1	85	774	1041	1173	3.3	2.55	611	802	3.0
30627	CARLTON	221	1960	2109	2199	0.8	41	767	844	887	1.0	2.47	555	591	0.7
30628	COLBERT	195	5967	6994	7442	1.7	66	2230	2645	2829	1.9	2.64	1669	1922	1.5
30629	COMER	195	4316	5134	5450	1.9	68	1618	1957	2092	2.1	2.55	1181	1383	1.7
30630	CRAWFORD	221	2008	2330	2497	1.6	63	778	924	999	1.9	2.46	553	635	1.5
30631	CRAWFORDVILLE	265	2166	2002	1918	-0.8	2	894	861	835	-0.4	2.30	579	535	-0.9
30633	DANIELSVILLE	195	7935	8975	9431	1.3	54	3031	3479	3672	1.5	2.57	2294	2558	1.2
30634	DEWY ROSE	105	1532	1715	1771	1.2	52	495	560	584	1.3	2.83	373	409	1.0
30635	ELBERTON	105	16949	17092	17003	0.1	19	6614	6767	6762	0.2	2.49	4749	4698	-0.1
30641	GOOD HOPE	297	1382	1838	2147	3.1	85	523	700	823	3.2	2.62	416	542	2.9
30642	GREENSBORO	133	9157	11029	11729	2.0	70	3514	4421	4771	2.5	2.47	2658	3235	2.1
30643	HARTWELL	147	15064	15903	16119	0.6	34	6096	6540	6685	0.8	2.35	4358	4519	0.4
30646	HULL	195	5847	6377	6594	0.9	45	2222	2466	2565	1.1	2.59	1672	1798	0.8
30648	LEXINGTON	221	2682	3232	3510	2.0	70	1012	1249	1364	2.3	2.57	748	895	2.0
30650	MADISON	211	10189	12461	13470	2.2	73	3625	4523	4928	2.4	2.71	2754	3339	2.1
30655	MONROE	297	17647	24702	28361	3.7	89	6512	9055	10435	3.6	2.67	4844	6540	3.3
30656	MONROE	297	10534	17092	20679	5.4	95	3680	5974	7253	5.4	2.83	2960	4682	5.1
30660	RAYLE	317	1208	1232	1229	0.2	22	471	491	495	0.5	2.49	331	334	0.1
30662	ROYSTON	119	8058	8454	8606	0.5	31	3062	3256	3332	0.7	2.43	2134	2191	0.3
30663	RUTLEDGE	211	2549	2931	3135	1.5	60	912	1073	1154	1.8	2.73	728	837	1.5
30666	STATHAM	013	5457	8306	10395	4.6	93	1952	2948	3693	4.6	2.79	1511	2199	4.1
30667	STEPHENS	221	1019	1143	1195	1.2	52	373	428	452	1.5	2.64	272	302	1.1
30668	TIGNALL	317	2073	1936	1869	-0.7	3	869	836	814	-0.4	2.30	600	556	-0.8
30669	UNION POINT	133	3442	3295	3228	-0.5	7	1304	1275	1260	-0.2	2.49	879	820	-0.7
30673	WASHINGTON	317	8093	7869	7667	-0.3	11	3256	3244	3188	0.0	2.38	2242	2154	-0.4
30677	WATKINSVILLE	219	13869	16865	18615	2.1	72	4854	5940	6560	2.2	2.83	3924	4696	2.0
30678	WHITE PLAINS	133	1293	1444	1519	1.2	52	481	555	590	1.6	2.60	370	414	1.2
30680	WINDER	013	25327	39535	48028	4.9	94	9222	14435	17548	5.0	2.70	6839	10402	4.6
30683	WINTERVILLE	221	5317	6032	6389	1.4	57	2079	2411	2572	1.6	2.47	1449	1595	1.0
30701	CALHOUN	129	29846	37664	41292	2.5	77	10898	13773	15125	2.6	2.70	8125	9974	2.2
30705	CHATSWORTH	213	30806	35365	37234	1.5	60	11158	12908	13621	1.6	2.72	8611	9695	1.3
30707	CHICKAMAUGA	295	13956	15473	16224	1.1	49	5295	5986	6321	1.3	2.58	4128	4531	1.0
30708	CISCO	213	664	821	899	2.3	74	263	329	362	2.5	2.50	199	241	2.1
30710	COHUTTA	313	5389	6257	6740	1.6	63	1910	2186	2337	1.5	2.86	1581	1772	1.2
30711	CRANDALL	213	3420	4056	4360	1.9	68	1285	1538	1659	2.0	2.64	1003	1168	1.7
30720	DALTON	313	24342	27201	28368	1.2	52	8964	9691	10044	0.8	2.72	6241	6494	0.4
30721	DALTON	313	41464	49624	53206	2.0	70	14044	16307	17377	1.6	3.03	10760	12134	1.3
30725	FLINTSTONE	295	3566	4150	4412	1.7	66	1391	1648	1763	1.8	2.52	1039	1192	1.5
30728	LA FAYETTE	295	17195	18696	19339	0.9	45	6648	7309	7615	1.0	2.47	4857	5171	0.7
30730	LYERLY	055	1811	1857	1889	0.3	25	708	745	763	0.6	2.49	531	542	0.2
30731	MENLO	055	2373	2496	2561	0.5	31	1023	1103	1141	0.8	2.26	755	789	0.5
30733	PLAINVILLE	129	1839	2147	2290	1.7	66	688	809	863	1.8	2.65	534	611	1.5
30734	RANGER	129	3097	3982	4472	2.8	80	1123	1471	1660	3.0	2.69	881	1125	2.7
30735	RESACA	129	5212	5721	5950	1.0	47	1869	2057	2142	1.0	2.78	1465	1570	0.8
30736	RINGGOLD	047	34446	42004	46030	2.2	73	12706	15679	17261	2.3	2.66	10054	12117	2.0
30738	RISING FAWN	083	3401	3693	3818	0.9	45	1316	1462	1523	1.1	2.50	1030	1113	0.8
30739	ROCK SPRING	295	3574	4581	4945	2.7	79	1220	1609	1757	3.0	2.67	959	1234	2.8
30740	ROCKY FACE	313	7478	8624	9198	1.6	63	2742	3121	3310	1.4	2.76	2154	2380	1.1
30741	ROSSVILLE	295	28080	30193	31260	0.8	41	11518	12572	13100	1.0	2.37	8064	8449	0.5
30742	FORT OGLETHORPE	047	5627	7094	7778	2.5	77	2298	2974	3302	2.8	2.29	1496	1853	2.3
30746	SUGAR VALLEY	129	956	1099	1191	1.5	60	353	411	447	1.7	2.67	276	314	1.4
30747	SUMMERVILLE	055	16212	17177	17583	0.6	34	5814	6289	6493	0.9	2.46	4170	4361	0.5
30750	LOOKOUT MOUNTAIN	083	4088	4270	4281	0.5	31	1308	1361	1376	0.4	2.60	982	989	0.1
30751	TENNGA	213	70	90	99	2.8	80	27	35	39	2.8	2.57	20	25	2.4
30752	TRENTON	083	8759	9584	9943	1.0	47	3365	3766	3940	1.2	2.51	2542	2762	0.9
30753	TRION	055	6595	6897	7056	0.5	31	2611	2790	2873	0.7	2.47	1833	1889	0.3
30755	TUNNEL HILL	313	8086	9247	9838	1.5	60	2966	3378	3591	1.4	2.74	2360	2621	1.1
30757	WILDWOOD	083	1778	1828	1842	0.3	25	720	743	753	0.3	2.43	516	515	0.0
30802	APPLING	073	5257	5978	6380	1.4	57	1774	2087	2258	1.8	2.75	1401	1576	1.3
30803	AVERA	163	679	703	699	0.4	28	291	309	310	0.7	2.27	207	212	0.3
30805	BLYTHE	245	2953	3289	3340	1.2	52	1000	1133	1157	1.4	2.87	779	856	1.0
30807	CAMAK	301	107	82	75	-2.8	0	51	40	37	-2.6	2.05	37	29	-2.6
30808	DEARING	189	4264	4597	4714	0.8	41	1535	1689	1744	1.0	2.71	1184	1266	0.7
30809	EVANS	073	24680	37652	44489	4.7	94	8232	12722	15147	4.8	2.94	7068	10792	4.7
30810	GIBSON	125	1775	1894	1936	0.7	37	689	755	780	1.0	2.38	485	513	0.6
30813	GROVETOWN	073	16304	24729	28246	4.6	93	5371	8683	10029	5.3	2.82	4201	6640	5.1
30814	HARLEM	073	6975	8172	8848	1.7	66	2533	3067	3356	2.1	2.66	1974	2314	1.7
30815	HEPHZIBAH	245	34809	36169	36145	0.4	28	11443	12198	12269	0.7	2.95	9416	9794	0.4
30816	KEYSVILLE	033	1309	1378	1402	0.6	34	478	514	527	0.8	2.67	368	384	0.5
30817	LINCOLNTON	181	7918	7906	7900	0.0	17	3070	3164	3194	0.3	2.48	2250	2244	0.0
30818	MATTHEWS	163	568	566	557	0.0	17	196	199	197	0.2	2.84	148	145	-0.2
	GEORGIA					2.1					2.1	2.65			1.8
	UNITED STATES					1.0					1.1	2.59			0.9

ZIP CODE #	POST OFFICE NAME	RACE (%) White 2000	White 2009	Black 2000	Black 2009	Asian/Pacific 2000	Asian/Pacific 2009	% Hispanic Origin 2000	% Hispanic Origin 2009	2009 AGE DISTRIBUTION (%) 0-4	5-9	10-14	15-19	20-24	25-44	45-64	65-84	85+	18+	MEDIAN AGE 2009	% 2009 Males	% 2009 Females
30563	MOUNT AIRY	92.5	87.9	1.0	1.3	2.0	3.2	5.3	9.2	6.5	6.7	6.9	6.3	4.6	26.8	28.2	12.6	1.4	75.9	39.7	50.7	49.3
30564	MURRAYVILLE	96.8	94.7	0.6	1.0	0.4	0.5	2.2	4.1	6.9	7.1	7.3	7.0	5.0	27.6	27.5	10.6	1.0	74.4	38.1	50.3	49.7
30565	NICHOLSON	93.5	90.9	3.2	4.1	0.2	0.3	3.6	5.3	8.0	8.0	7.8	6.8	5.4	28.8	25.6	8.7	0.9	72.0	35.6	51.1	48.9
30566	OAKWOOD	82.7	74.1	5.7	6.9	2.2	2.8	15.9	26.2	7.3	7.0	6.8	6.9	7.0	29.9	25.6	8.5	1.0	74.8	34.8	50.8	49.2
30567	PENDERGRASS	93.4	90.6	2.3	3.1	1.1	1.4	4.9	6.9	7.6	7.6	7.6	7.0	5.4	28.8	26.1	9.1	0.9	72.8	36.2	50.6	49.4
30568	RABUN GAP	93.5	90.0	1.3	1.7	0.7	1.1	5.0	8.5	5.4	5.5	6.4	9.1	4.9	21.5	27.5	17.2	2.5	76.4	42.8	49.3	50.7
30571	SAUTEE NACOOCHEE	94.1	92.8	3.0	3.3	1.5	2.1	0.8	1.0	4.5	4.8	5.3	6.2	4.5	20.2	34.2	18.4	1.8	82.2	47.8	50.1	49.9
30572	SUCHES	98.0	97.1	0.4	0.5	0.4	0.6	0.5	0.8	3.8	4.0	4.6	4.9	3.4	19.5	36.5	21.1	2.2	84.5	51.1	49.6	50.4
30575	TALMO	87.3	81.4	3.3	4.1	1.7	2.2	14.6	22.6	8.5	8.4	8.2	7.2	5.5	30.6	23.6	7.3	0.7	70.5	33.8	51.5	48.5
30576	TIGER	97.3	95.8	0.4	0.5	0.1	0.2	2.6	4.2	5.0	5.3	5.6	5.2	3.6	21.3	33.9	17.9	2.0	80.7	47.6	50.0	50.0
30577	TOCCOA	85.6	82.1	12.1	14.6	0.7	1.0	1.0	1.5	5.9	6.0	6.1	7.3	6.8	24.1	27.1	14.1	2.5	78.1	40.1	48.3	51.7
30582	YOUNG HARRIS	98.7	98.3	0.3	0.4	0.3	0.4	0.4	0.6	3.9	3.9	4.1	11.8	6.6	16.5	28.8	22.1	2.3	85.7	47.8	45.9	54.1
30597	DAHLONEGA	95.0	93.4	1.4	1.9	0.7	0.9	2.6	4.1	5.0	4.5	5.1	19.6	18.8	19.5	21.0	5.6	1.0	82.7	24.2	43.7	56.3
30601	ATHENS	40.0	34.8	53.3	55.9	0.7	0.8	10.2	13.5	7.6	6.9	5.9	7.5	14.1	30.0	19.6	7.4	1.0	75.7	28.8	49.0	51.0
30602	ATHENS	71.3	62.8	12.5	15.1	13.4	18.1	2.9	4.1	1.6	0.9	0.5	50.6	32.2	11.9	1.6	0.5	0.1	96.7	19.6	45.2	54.8
30605	ATHENS	74.8	68.3	17.2	20.8	5.0	6.7	3.1	4.5	4.1	3.6	3.1	15.5	30.5	22.8	14.4	5.3	0.7	87.3	23.9	48.8	51.2
30606	ATHENS	70.8	65.1	22.5	25.2	2.5	3.4	5.5	8.3	5.2	4.7	4.6	6.8	18.5	27.2	20.9	9.8	2.2	82.3	30.6	48.5	51.5
30607	ATHENS	57.0	50.1	29.7	31.4	1.0	1.2	17.4	23.9	8.3	7.4	6.8	7.6	8.4	33.2	20.1	7.0	1.1	73.0	30.5	51.3	48.7
30609	ATHENS	85.8	81.6	9.7	12.5	1.8	2.9	2.7	4.4	1.5	1.5	0.0	10.3	71.3	9.6	5.1	0.7	0.0	97.1	22.6	46.3	53.7
30619	ARNOLDSVILLE	77.3	72.8	21.2	24.9	0.1	0.1	1.0	1.4	7.0	7.4	7.4	6.4	4.8	24.6	29.6	11.4	1.5	74.0	39.5	48.4	51.6
30620	BETHLEHEM	82.7	77.2	10.0	12.3	3.2	4.3	5.4	8.2	8.3	7.8	7.6	6.8	5.3	32.1	23.8	7.5	0.8	72.1	34.3	50.6	49.4
30621	BISHOP	89.5	87.0	8.8	10.5	0.5	0.6	2.0	3.0	6.2	6.5	7.2	7.9	5.4	25.8	29.8	9.3	1.9	74.9	39.2	49.6	50.4
30622	BOGART	80.9	77.8	14.9	16.0	2.2	3.1	3.0	4.6	6.5	7.1	7.6	7.2	5.2	26.6	28.9	9.7	1.2	74.1	38.4	48.9	51.1
30624	BOWMAN	80.2	74.6	17.9	22.7	0.1	0.2	1.0	1.6	6.8	6.9	7.0	6.5	5.4	26.6	28.1	11.3	1.4	75.3	38.6	49.3	50.7
30625	BUCKHEAD	80.0	74.5	18.0	22.9	0.3	0.4	2.0	2.6	5.8	6.3	6.6	6.4	4.6	24.4	31.7	13.0	1.2	76.9	41.9	49.8	50.2
30627	CARLTON	71.2	65.6	26.8	31.7	0.6	0.9	1.3	1.8	5.8	6.3	7.2	6.8	4.9	25.2	29.0	12.6	2.1	76.3	40.8	48.9	51.1
30628	COLBERT	87.6	84.0	9.9	12.2	0.2	0.3	2.0	3.1	8.0	7.9	7.9	7.0	4.9	28.1	26.1	9.2	0.9	71.8	36.3	49.5	50.5
30629	COMER	82.7	78.5	15.6	19.3	0.5	0.7	0.9	1.3	7.1	7.2	7.2	6.6	5.4	24.9	27.0	12.2	2.4	74.0	38.9	48.2	51.8
30630	CRAWFORD	81.2	77.0	16.9	20.3	0.2	0.3	1.3	2.0	6.9	7.3	7.2	5.9	4.4	24.6	28.3	12.8	2.6	74.7	40.3	47.9	52.1
30631	CRAWFORDVILLE	40.6	34.9	57.7	63.1	0.0	0.1	1.3	1.6	6.7	6.7	6.4	5.3	5.6	23.3	27.3	16.1	2.6	76.9	42.0	49.1	50.9
30633	DANIELSVILLE	96.0	94.5	2.2	2.8	0.2	0.2	1.7	2.6	6.4	6.6	6.9	6.8	5.4	27.3	28.6	10.7	1.2	75.8	38.8	49.5	50.5
30634	DEWY ROSE	73.1	66.9	25.5	31.0	0.1	0.2	0.8	1.1	6.5	6.8	6.9	5.9	6.0	29.2	26.9	10.6	1.2	75.9	38.0	53.6	46.4
30635	ELBERTON	63.9	57.9	33.8	38.9	0.3	0.4	2.7	3.9	6.3	6.4	6.4	6.6	5.8	25.1	27.3	13.7	2.3	76.7	39.9	48.2	51.8
30641	GOOD HOPE	87.0	82.4	11.2	15.1	0.4	0.5	0.9	1.4	6.1	6.3	6.7	6.3	5.1	25.8	29.9	12.1	1.6	77.0	40.7	51.1	48.9
30642	GREENSBORO	53.1	48.4	44.0	47.6	0.3	0.4	3.4	4.6	6.0	6.1	6.4	6.2	4.9	21.0	34.9	13.0	1.5	77.7	44.5	48.7	51.3
30643	HARTWELL	77.1	72.4	21.2	25.3	0.7	0.9	0.9	1.3	5.9	5.9	6.0	5.8	5.1	23.5	28.6	16.6	2.7	78.7	43.4	49.1	50.9
30646	HULL	85.1	80.9	11.3	13.4	0.3	0.4	3.0	4.9	6.7	6.8	7.0	6.8	5.4	28.4	27.6	10.3	0.9	75.3	37.5	49.5	50.5
30648	LEXINGTON	68.8	63.0	29.4	34.6	0.3	0.5	1.0	1.4	6.3	6.5	7.1	6.9	5.4	25.2	29.1	11.9	1.7	75.8	40.2	49.0	51.0
30650	MADISON	64.1	58.5	33.7	38.5	0.4	0.6	1.9	2.6	6.4	6.6	7.0	7.4	5.0	25.7	28.0	11.9	2.1	75.4	39.4	49.2	50.8
30655	MONROE	71.0	65.9	26.5	30.8	0.5	0.6	2.0	2.7	7.9	7.6	7.1	6.8	6.0	28.3	25.1	9.7	1.5	73.4	35.6	48.3	51.7
30656	MONROE	77.8	72.5	18.4	22.1	1.6	2.2	2.0	3.0	8.1	7.7	7.5	6.8	5.5	28.7	25.5	8.9	1.4	72.5	35.6	48.7	51.3
30660	RAYLE	68.4	61.9	28.1	33.0	0.2	0.3	4.0	5.8	6.3	6.5	6.5	6.3	5.0	25.6	28.2	13.6	2.0	76.8	40.9	50.7	49.3
30662	ROYSTON	88.3	85.0	9.6	12.1	0.6	0.8	1.1	1.6	6.0	6.0	6.3	8.1	7.3	24.3	25.5	13.5	2.9	77.7	38.6	48.4	51.6
30663	RUTLEDGE	79.0	73.0	19.9	25.5	0.3	0.4	0.9	1.1	7.2	7.3	7.5	6.9	5.0	25.9	27.9	11.2	1.2	73.8	38.5	48.4	51.6
30666	STATHAM	84.4	79.5	12.8	16.4	1.0	1.4	1.5	2.2	7.3	7.4	7.5	6.8	5.1	27.7	26.6	10.2	1.5	73.4	37.5	49.5	50.5
30667	STEPHENS	69.6	63.4	27.7	32.3	0.3	0.4	2.5	3.9	6.1	6.5	6.6	6.9	5.1	25.6	27.4	14.1	1.7	76.6	40.0	49.6	50.4
30668	TIGNALL	61.7	55.6	36.6	42.0	0.1	0.2	2.2	2.9	5.6	6.0	6.3	6.3	4.3	22.5	29.5	16.7	2.8	78.4	44.2	50.7	49.3
30669	UNION POINT	49.1	39.4	48.9	57.8	0.3	0.5	1.7	2.5	7.5	7.4	7.0	6.3	5.9	22.7	26.6	13.4	3.2	74.4	39.5	48.1	51.9
30673	WASHINGTON	52.6	47.0	45.8	51.0	0.3	0.4	1.6	2.2	5.9	6.0	6.0	6.2	5.2	24.6	28.2	15.0	2.9	78.3	42.0	47.4	52.6
30677	WATKINSVILLE	90.0	87.5	6.5	7.5	1.4	1.9	2.5	3.6	6.2	6.7	7.4	7.5	5.0	25.6	31.4	9.0	1.1	74.6	39.6	49.8	50.2
30678	WHITE PLAINS	53.6	44.5	45.0	53.3	0.3	0.4	2.2	3.2	5.9	6.1	6.0	5.5	4.4	23.8	29.9	16.8	1.5	78.7	43.6	49.0	51.0
30680	WINDER	83.5	79.7	11.6	13.2	1.9	2.6	2.9	4.4	7.7	7.3	7.1	6.8	6.0	30.4	24.3	8.8	1.4	73.6	35.3	49.7	50.3
30683	WINTERVILLE	81.9	76.0	14.5	18.4	0.6	0.8	3.0	5.0	6.5	6.3	6.6	6.9	9.7	28.1	25.8	8.8	1.3	76.2	35.1	49.6	50.4
30701	CALHOUN	86.7	81.0	4.5	5.3	0.7	1.0	9.7	15.1	7.2	6.8	6.9	6.7	6.3	28.8	25.5	10.5	1.4	75.0	36.5	49.7	50.3
30705	CHATSWORTH	95.0	92.2	0.7	0.8	0.3	0.4	6.0	9.5	7.9	7.7	7.4	6.8	6.0	29.5	25.7	8.3	0.8	72.8	35.0	50.1	49.9
30707	CHICKAMAUGA	94.1	92.4	4.5	5.6	0.2	0.3	0.5	0.8	6.3	6.4	6.8	6.5	5.3	27.5	28.8	11.2	1.2	76.5	38.7	49.7	50.3
30708	CISCO	97.6	96.1	0.2	0.2	0.2	0.2	2.4	3.8	6.9	6.9	7.3	7.2	5.1	28.0	27.5	10.0	1.0	74.3	37.7	51.0	49.0
30710	COHUTTA	95.6	92.9	1.4	2.0	0.2	0.3	2.2	4.3	6.8	7.2	7.5	7.0	5.0	27.0	30.0	8.7	0.8	74.1	38.3	49.6	50.4
30711	CRANDALL	98.0	97.0	0.3	0.4	0.1	0.2	1.4	2.3	7.4	7.4	7.4	6.8	5.3	27.6	27.4	9.9	0.9	73.6	37.3	50.2	49.8
30720	DALTON	79.7	71.2	3.9	4.5	2.0	2.6	23.2	33.8	7.8	7.0	6.7	6.4	6.8	29.0	23.2	10.8	2.3	74.7	35.0	50.5	49.5
30721	DALTON	75.7	67.0	4.7	4.8	0.5	0.6	29.6	40.8	8.6	8.3	7.8	7.0	5.9	29.1	22.9	9.2	1.1	70.9	33.5	51.0	49.0
30725	FLINTSTONE	94.9	93.3	3.2	4.0	0.5	0.7	0.7	1.1	6.4	6.4	6.6	5.9	5.5	26.6	27.8	13.2	1.6	76.9	39.3	49.5	50.5
30728	LA FAYETTE	93.6	91.7	4.7	5.8	0.3	0.5	1.1	1.7	6.6	6.5	6.6	6.3	5.9	26.5	27.1	12.5	2.0	76.4	38.8	49.3	50.7
30730	LYERLY	88.6	84.9	9.3	12.1	0.0	0.0	0.4	0.6	7.0	7.0	7.0	6.1	5.4	26.2	28.1	12.1	1.1	75.3	39.1	50.0	50.0
30731	MENLO	96.6	95.1	1.9	2.5	0.2	0.2	0.8	1.5	5.5	5.8	6.2	5.5	4.4	25.0	31.6	14.4	1.6	79.0	43.1	50.0	50.0
30733	PLAINVILLE	95.3	93.0	1.2	1.5	0.1	0.1	4.5	7.3	6.6	6.8	7.1	6.4	4.7	29.2	27.7	10.3	1.2	75.4	38.1	50.4	49.6
30734	RANGER	98.3	97.4	0.2	0.3	0.2	0.2	1.0	1.6	6.8	6.8	7.0	6.3	5.1	27.7	28.1	10.9	1.3	75.7	38.8	51.1	48.9
30735	RESACA	94.9	91.6	0.8	1.1	0.4	0.6	4.0	7.1	7.8	7.7	7.7	6.9	5.5	28.7	25.2	9.7	0.9	72.6	36.1	50.8	49.2
30736	RINGGOLD	96.7	95.4	1.3	1.6	0.5	0.7	1.2	1.9	7.1	7.2	7.2	6.8	5.2	28.6	27.0	10.1	1.0	74.3	37.3	49.3	50.7
30738	RISING FAWN	98.7	98.2	0.2	0.3	0.2	0.3	0.6	0.9	6.1	6.3	6.5	6.3	5.3	24.9	31.2	12.0	1.4	77.4	40.8	50.4	49.6
30739	ROCK SPRING	94.5	92.8	4.2	5.4	0.3	0.4	0.6	0.9	5.7	6.0	6.3	5.9	5.0	28.6	28.6	12.6	1.3	78.3	40.3	52.4	47.6
30740	ROCKY FACE	94.3	90.9	1.6	2.2	0.9	1.2	3.4	6.3	7.1	7.3	7.4	6.6	5.2	27.3	28.0	10.2	0.9	74.1	37.9	49.7	50.3
30741	ROSSVILLE	95.4	93.9	2.1	2.4	0.7	1.0	1.1	1.7	6.4	6.3	6.3	6.2	5.6	26.1	26.5	14.4	2.3	77.2	39.9	48.0	52.0
30742	FORT OGLETHORPE	92.7	91.0	3.4	3.7	1.6	2.2	1.4	2.1	6.4	5.6	5.5	5.7	6.1	22.5	26.0	18.1	4.2	79.1	43.4	45.0	55.0
30746	SUGAR VALLEY	92.6	88.9	2.8	3.6	0.3	0.4	4.1	6.8	6.3	6.2	6.8	6.8	5.6	27.8	29.0	10.5	0.9	76.4	39.2	51.0	49.0
30747	SUMMERVILLE	82.5	78.6	15.8	18.9	0.1	0.2	1.2	1.8	6.4	6.3	6.3	6.0	7.1	28.5	25.3	12.3	2.0	77.7	37.8	53.1	46.9
30750	LOOKOUT MOUNTAIN	97.9	97.0	0.3	0.4	0.4	0.6	1.2	1.9	5.4	5.7	6.0	13.8	12.8	21.2	24.4	9.2	1.4	78.3	31.6	47.4	52.6
30751	TENNGA	98.6	96.7	0.0	0.0	0.0	0.0	1.4	2.2	6.7	6.7	7.8	7.8	5.6	27.8	25.6	11.1	1.1	74.4	37.1	50.0	50.0
30752	TRENTON	97.9	97.1	0.3	0.4	0.3	0.5	0.9	1.4	6.2	6.3	6.8	6.7	5.4	26.7	27.9	12.5	1.6	76.6	39.5	50.0	50.0
30753	TRION	95.2	93.0	1.8	2.4	0.2	0.3	5.1	7.6	6.7	6.8	6.9	6.4	5.4	27.4	26.2	12.3	1.9	75.6	38.2	49.9	50.1
30755	TUNNEL HILL	95.9	93.5	1.5	2.1	0.4	0.6	2.6	4.9	6.6	7.7	7.3	6.6	5.5	28.5	27.8	9.2	0.9	74.9	36.5	50.0	50.0
30757	WILDWOOD	94.5	92.5	3.3	4.3	0.7	1.1	0.5	0.9	5.4	5.7	6.2	6.8	4.6	28.4	29.4	12.1	1.3	78.2	39.9	50.3	49.7
30802	APPLING	79.7	75.4	17.6	20.8	0.7	1.0	1.0	1.6	6.1	6.4	7.0	7.3	5.4	23.9	30.5	11.2	2.3	76.2	40.7	49.7	50.3
30803	AVERA	68.9	62.2	30.5	37.0	0.1	0.1	0.9	1.4	5.3	5.8	6.3	6.1	5.0	25.7	30.7	13.4	1.7	78.9	42.2	51.5	48.5
30805	BLYTHE	69.7	61.7	26.2	32.7	1.2	1.5	2.3	3.3	7.2	7.0	6.9	7.8	7.0	27.2	26.8	9.2	0.9	73.8	35.4	49.7	50.3
30807	CAMAK	39.3	42.7	58.9	54.9	0.0	0.0	0.9	1.2	6.1	6.1	7.3	7.3	4.9	23.2	31.7	12.2	1.2	76.8	41.0	50.0	50.0
30808	DEARING	75.0	69.3	22.8	27.5	0.4	0.5	2.1	3.0	7.4	6.8	6.8	7.2	7.2	26.3	27.1	10.1	1.2	74.5	36.5	49.0	51.0
30809	EVANS	85.1	80.6	9.0	11.1	3.7	5.3	2.1	3.0	7.7	7.9	8.3	7.5	4.9	27.7	28.8	6.5	0.7	71.2	35.5	48.8	51.2
30810	GIBSON	91.7	89.8	7.5	9.3	0.0	0.0	0.5	0.6	6.7	6.8	6.7	5.9	4.8	23.7	25.8	16.2	3.6	76.2	41.6	47.4	52.6
30813	GROVETOWN	76.2	72.6	17.7	18.8	1.7	2.6	4.7	6.5	7.7	7.5	7.3	7.2	6.4	29.9	26.0	7.2	0.7	72.9	34.3	49.7	50.3
30814	HARLEM	78.9	73.8	17.8	21.5	0.7	1.1	2.1	3.2	6.9	6.9	7.0	7.0	5.7	28.4	27.0	10.1	1.0	74.9	36.9	49.4	50.6
30815	HEPHZIBAH	41.6	35.4	52.6	57.6	2.0	2.3	3.1	4.0	7.5	7.5	7.7	8.3	7.3	27.9	27.1	6.3	0.5	71.9	32.8	48.0	52.0
30816	KEYSVILLE	51.3	44.1	45.6	51.7	0.5	0.7	2.0	2.8	6.9	7.2	7.3	7.3	6.2	24.4	28.4	11.0	1.4	73.9	37.5	48.0	52.0
30817	LINCOLNTON	64.1	61.6	34.6	37.1	0.2	0.2	0.9	0.9	5.3	5.7	6.2	6.5	5.2	24.4	31.0	14.2	1.4	78.7	42.5	48.7	51.3
30818	MATTHEWS	66.0	59.5	31.0	36.0	0.2	0.2	3.0	4.6	7.2	7.1	7.4	6.9	4.9	28.8	25.4	10.8	1.4	74.0	37.0	50.0	50.0
	GEORGIA	65.1	61.1	28.7	30.1	2.2	2.9	5.3	7.7	7.3	7.0	6.9	7.1	7.1	29.3	25.1	8.9	1.3	74.7	35.0	49.4	50.6
	UNITED STATES	75.1	72.0	12.3	12.7	3.8	4.6	12.5	15.7	6.8	6.7	6.6	7.1	6.9	27.0	26.0	10.9	1.9	75.7	36.9	49.2	50.8

ZIP CODE #	POST OFFICE NAME	2009 Per Capita Income	2009 HH Income Base	2009 Household Income Distribution (%): Less than $25,000	$25,000 to $49,999	$50,000 to $99,999	$100,000 to $149,999	$150,000 or More	Median Household Income: 2009	2014	2009 National Centile	2009 State Centile	2009 Home Value Base	2009 Home Value Distribution (%): Less than $50,000	$50,000 to $89,999	$90,000 to $174,999	$175,000 to $399,999	$400,000 or More	2009 Median Home Value
30563	MOUNT AIRY	20835	2016	25.3	29.2	37.4	5.5	2.7	46117	45232	52	61	1643	11.1	12.2	36.0	34.6	6.0	145761
30564	MURRAYVILLE	22303	1671	19.2	27.4	43.6	5.7	4.2	53975	56469	70	74	1339	12.8	13.6	35.2	27.4	11.1	139773
30565	NICHOLSON	20121	2006	21.8	29.3	40.2	6.4	2.2	48911	48470	59	66	1558	13.0	16.8	37.4	28.2	4.7	128833
30566	OAKWOOD	23172	3140	15.5	21.5	47.8	12.0	3.3	61714	62931	80	81	2062	5.4	11.2	61.6	18.9	2.9	123965
30567	PENDERGRASS	20753	1259	23.0	27.6	39.4	7.1	2.9	49378	49615	60	67	966	12.7	11.1	34.6	31.5	10.1	154950
30568	RABUN GAP	19251	966	26.7	37.0	30.2	3.2	2.9	39710	40261	32	43	757	11.6	13.1	38.6	30.4	6.3	140665
30571	SAUTEE NACOOCHEE	23792	1614	22.1	32.2	38.0	4.4	3.3	46071	46416	52	61	1318	1.7	8.4	27.8	49.4	12.7	213089
30572	SUCHES	29283	721	28.6	26.5	36.2	6.5	2.2	42764	47597	42	52	617	10.4	12.6	30.5	29.5	17.0	162784
30575	TALMO	19488	623	22.6	26.6	41.4	6.7	2.6	50662	51170	63	69	445	19.6	10.3	29.4	32.8	7.9	137829
30576	TIGER	21491	983	23.4	37.7	31.4	3.5	4.0	39266	40557	31	42	822	11.8	12.0	34.1	25.1	17.0	144375
30577	TOCCOA	18754	8826	32.7	33.0	28.4	3.6	2.2	36277	36921	21	30	6214	14.5	24.0	41.6	16.8	3.2	108219
30582	YOUNG HARRIS	22138	1605	25.9	34.1	32.3	4.4	3.3	42710	44413	42	51	1389	13.8	12.5	27.7	35.3	10.7	160395
30597	DAHLONEGA	3731	0	0.0	0.0	0.0	0.0	0.0	0	0	0	0	0	0.0	0.0	0.0	0.0	0.0	0
30601	ATHENS	14550	7998	45.9	29.2	21.5	2.4	1.0	27940	30041	6	4	3171	51.7	22.2	19.0	6.9	0.3	48723
30602	ATHENS	9736	4	100.0	0.0	0.0	0.0	0.0	6667	6667	0	0	0	0.0	0.0	0.0	0.0	0.0	0
30605	ATHENS	19467	16560	43.8	22.8	24.4	5.1	4.0	31032	34428	10	12	6031	11.7	14.4	52.6	19.1	2.2	120394
30606	ATHENS	26341	16971	31.6	25.8	27.8	7.7	7.1	41989	46564	39	49	7805	9.2	14.1	39.4	29.8	7.5	143408
30607	ATHENS	19419	4133	26.6	29.0	36.9	3.9	3.5	44223	48537	46	56	2121	10.0	24.8	39.7	19.6	5.8	112737
30609	ATHENS	10505	52	63.5	21.2	11.5	3.8	0.0	19203	18472	1	1	5	40.0	40.0	20.0	0.0	0.0	75000
30619	ARNOLDSVILLE	19814	564	33.3	27.0	32.8	4.8	2.1	42010	44560	39	49	435	29.0	22.1	29.7	16.3	3.0	87750
30620	BETHLEHEM	23290	3911	12.7	20.4	52.1	10.4	4.3	63942	65303	82	84	3552	6.2	14.0	52.4	25.2	2.3	146504
30621	BISHOP	23999	1657	15.6	24.9	41.5	12.9	5.2	60751	61394	78	81	1423	16.4	16.4	30.4	28.6	8.2	125288
30622	BOGART	28737	3383	14.5	20.1	42.7	14.4	8.4	65586	68113	84	85	2541	10.1	12.7	38.1	32.9	6.2	146887
30624	BOWMAN	17701	1260	34.0	32.7	28.5	3.4	1.4	36913	38004	23	33	1034	24.1	29.1	34.5	10.6	1.6	85147
30625	BUCKHEAD	24382	1041	19.0	26.7	41.4	8.1	4.8	53111	51980	68	73	865	8.9	11.3	37.8	31.1	10.9	150179
30627	CARLTON	20958	844	31.0	32.8	28.9	3.4	3.8	40850	43264	35	45	720	32.8	20.8	33.5	11.9	1.0	82973
30628	COLBERT	19554	2645	25.8	29.8	36.1	6.5	1.8	45075	46749	48	59	2106	21.4	27.3	37.7	11.3	2.4	91530
30629	COMER	18908	1957	31.1	30.5	32.1	3.9	2.5	39281	41571	31	42	1575	29.0	27.7	31.9	9.0	2.4	81492
30630	CRAWFORD	19433	924	33.9	29.2	30.3	4.2	2.4	40334	42452	34	44	693	28.6	21.5	36.5	12.3	1.2	89848
30631	CRAWFORDVILLE	17839	861	42.5	30.9	20.6	3.6	2.4	29542	30949	7	6	660	36.7	32.0	23.3	7.9	0.2	62051
30633	DANIELSVILLE	19355	3479	24.7	30.2	39.7	4.4	1.0	45421	46821	50	60	2859	24.7	24.4	36.8	11.5	2.6	90825
30634	DEWY ROSE	16614	560	25.9	34.1	34.3	4.3	1.4	41880	43943	39	49	487	22.2	25.3	31.2	19.1	2.3	94630
30635	ELBERTON	16972	6767	37.9	29.5	27.8	3.5	1.3	33868	34943	15	21	4964	23.5	26.6	33.4	14.1	2.4	89563
30641	GOOD HOPE	23437	700	18.4	24.4	48.4	5.9	2.9	57358	59435	74	78	596	8.2	19.0	39.1	21.5	12.2	128879
30642	GREENSBORO	28142	4421	31.9	24.5	28.3	7.4	7.7	43201	44056	43	53	3342	17.0	19.0	25.2	11.0	27.7	121084
30643	HARTWELL	20513	6540	31.3	29.6	32.1	4.8	2.3	39622	40137	32	42	5187	11.0	25.0	35.0	22.1	6.9	112998
30646	HULL	20018	2466	23.8	32.6	35.7	6.0	1.9	44526	46650	47	57	1852	21.9	30.4	37.3	8.3	2.2	88073
30648	LEXINGTON	20190	1249	28.1	31.9	32.3	5.0	2.7	40620	42204	35	45	1043	31.4	26.2	29.2	11.1	2.0	79717
30650	MADISON	21258	4523	27.0	26.8	36.2	6.3	3.6	46218	47715	52	62	3368	12.1	16.7	30.9	25.8	14.4	139899
30655	MONROE	21120	9055	26.6	27.7	34.7	6.9	4.1	44812	50129	48	58	5753	15.7	23.8	37.4	18.6	4.5	108168
30656	MONROE	22323	5974	19.4	26.3	40.6	9.3	4.4	54621	57863	71	76	4610	13.0	15.6	43.6	23.3	4.5	119586
30660	RAYLE	17293	491	36.0	32.2	27.9	2.0	1.8	36349	36447	22	31	408	33.1	27.7	26.5	11.8	1.0	79167
30662	ROYSTON	18794	3256	33.0	29.2	32.5	3.7	1.6	38432	40000	28	39	2438	23.0	26.3	33.0	14.7	3.1	91377
30663	RUTLEDGE	21001	1073	23.2	31.1	34.3	8.7	2.7	46548	47245	53	62	865	4.6	11.1	38.6	37.8	7.9	156250
30666	STATHAM	20073	2948	23.8	26.8	39.8	6.4	3.3	49229	52712	59	67	2444	16.0	22.2	37.5	20.3	4.1	109121
30667	STEPHENS	17925	428	32.7	24.5	38.8	2.8	1.2	43493	45379	44	54	367	34.1	27.5	28.9	7.4	2.2	75625
30668	TIGNALL	17171	836	38.4	32.2	25.2	4.2	0.0	32499	33217	12	15	671	35.8	34.3	21.0	7.7	1.2	63197
30669	UNION POINT	16431	1275	37.5	34.0	23.8	3.5	1.2	33931	35917	15	21	918	35.4	26.5	30.9	6.1	1.1	70816
30673	WASHINGTON	18643	3244	36.8	26.2	31.1	4.2	1.8	35524	36914	19	27	2384	23.1	31.9	31.5	11.7	1.7	82899
30677	WATKINSVILLE	29044	5940	11.7	21.2	41.3	17.3	8.5	67540	71840	85	87	4902	11.0	11.0	34.8	33.5	9.6	155613
30678	WHITE PLAINS	19273	555	31.7	25.6	34.1	6.7	2.0	40916	42416	44	54	461	32.5	16.5	27.1	12.8	11.1	91957
30680	WINDER	22034	14435	21.2	24.2	43.8	8.0	2.8	54074	57934	70	75	9798	15.3	17.3	43.9	21.2	2.3	120257
30683	WINTERVILLE	21804	2411	21.2	33.1	37.1	6.1	2.4	46601	49243	53	63	1771	22.7	23.3	40.4	10.6	3.0	94897
30701	CALHOUN	20577	13773	24.7	27.0	39.8	5.8	2.8	47999	48721	57	65	9244	9.6	12.1	48.2	26.0	4.2	131770
30705	CHATSWORTH	18615	12908	25.4	30.4	38.5	3.9	1.8	44894	46700	48	58	9445	32.6	28.7	31.3	6.8	0.6	74785
30707	CHICKAMAUGA	19719	5986	25.5	31.1	37.7	4.1	1.7	44329	48979	46	56	4770	19.8	30.4	41.8	7.1	0.8	89792
30708	CISCO	18113	329	30.1	31.9	33.1	4.3	0.6	37609	39272	26	36	255	50.6	23.1	20.8	3.9	1.6	49063
30710	COHUTTA	22942	2186	16.1	24.6	46.5	9.4	3.5	58716	59027	76	79	1855	20.3	22.4	40.6	16.0	0.7	96964
30711	CRANDALL	17881	1538	26.2	36.2	31.7	4.9	1.0	40974	42565	36	46	1179	44.3	20.8	30.7	2.0	2.3	58438
30720	DALTON	26242	9691	20.1	28.4	35.2	7.8	8.5	51547	54676	65	71	5525	13.1	22.0	41.0	19.2	4.7	109582
30721	DALTON	17018	16307	24.4	31.3	37.6	4.7	2.0	43731	49860	45	55	10794	23.9	30.3	40.5	3.9	1.3	84772
30725	FLINTSTONE	20312	1648	20.7	33.3	41.0	4.3	0.7	44872	50741	48	58	1254	13.2	32.1	48.4	6.0	0.2	92624
30728	LA FAYETTE	18079	7309	32.6	28.4	34.9	2.8	1.3	38918	43657	29	40	5383	24.4	32.0	36.7	5.6	1.4	82581
30730	LYERLY	19392	745	22.7	34.8	37.4	3.9	1.2	43898	46330	45	55	575	18.3	23.1	38.3	17.9	2.4	105540
30731	MENLO	20921	1103	27.4	33.7	33.5	3.6	1.7	41551	43353	38	48	913	19.5	24.9	37.1	15.8	2.7	98443
30733	PLAINVILLE	17868	809	26.5	30.7	38.4	3.6	0.9	43147	45498	43	53	623	10.9	19.7	49.8	16.7	2.9	114073
30734	RANGER	19017	1471	19.9	35.8	39.4	3.4	1.5	45320	47083	49	59	1239	22.7	22.4	34.6	15.5	4.8	101466
30735	RESACA	18153	2057	23.8	32.1	38.3	3.9	1.9	44719	46593	47	58	1643	26.4	17.5	34.7	17.7	3.8	103713
30736	RINGGOLD	23324	15679	17.4	26.1	44.2	9.0	3.4	55959	58039	73	77	12723	12.8	18.1	49.7	16.9	2.5	112066
30738	RISING FAWN	18650	1462	28.6	33.2	33.4	3.6	1.2	41000	43344	36	46	1214	27.0	27.4	33.8	10.3	1.5	81563
30739	ROCK SPRING	18935	1609	23.4	29.1	40.4	5.8	1.3	47430	51359	55	64	1388	16.7	26.8	45.5	10.4	0.6	95056
30740	ROCKY FACE	22104	3121	21.1	25.1	40.8	9.5	3.6	54220	56529	70	75	2477	19.1	26.1	42.6	9.4	2.8	94979
30741	ROSSVILLE	18871	12572	30.2	32.5	32.9	3.1	1.2	38877	42232	29	40	9016	25.5	38.5	32.9	3.0	0.1	74734
30742	FORT OGLETHORPE	19675	2974	33.4	29.4	31.0	4.0	2.2	37943	41473	27	37	1767	9.3	37.1	47.3	6.4	0.0	92560
30746	SUGAR VALLEY	20277	411	26.3	29.4	36.0	4.6	3.6	45723	46956	50	60	330	18.2	16.7	36.1	21.2	7.9	119886
30747	SUMMERVILLE	17446	6289	32.5	31.4	31.5	3.5	1.0	37476	39298	25	34	4633	24.1	25.8	35.5	13.2	1.5	90215
30750	LOOKOUT MOUNTAIN	27011	1361	15.7	24.1	40.3	12.9	7.1	61893	60942	80	82	1125	14.0	12.7	30.1	31.4	11.7	156548
30751	TENNGA	16922	35	34.3	31.4	28.6	5.7	0.0	33622	38637	15	20	28	50.0	25.0	17.9	7.1	0.0	50000
30752	TRENTON	18474	3766	30.7	30.7	33.9	2.9	1.6	40763	43844	35	45	2973	30.9	31.3	31.4	5.0	1.4	71124
30753	TRION	17725	2790	31.9	33.8	29.6	3.4	1.4	36136	38387	21	30	2120	25.0	35.9	30.2	6.4	2.5	77906
30755	TUNNEL HILL	20248	3378	21.0	27.7	43.6	5.9	1.7	51120	54415	64	70	2713	20.5	33.9	36.3	7.7	1.7	84240
30757	WILDWOOD	23253	743	21.1	31.5	38.5	5.4	3.5	47784	48745	56	64	581	28.7	31.0	28.7	11.2	0.3	78929
30802	APPLING	22144	2087	15.2	30.3	42.1	9.7	2.7	53854	54847	69	74	1791	24.5	31.6	24.2	14.3	5.3	74702
30803	AVERA	19848	309	31.7	31.7	30.7	3.6	2.3	35623	39542	20	27	265	34.3	30.9	20.4	10.6	3.8	68333
30805	BLYTHE	16758	1133	30.1	30.2	33.3	4.7	1.8	40980	44687	36	46	914	35.2	18.8	40.8	4.8	0.3	81591
30807	CAMAK	23310	40	32.5	22.5	42.5	2.5	0.0	45000	42393	48	59	35	34.3	28.6	22.9	8.6	5.7	75000
30808	DEARING	16930	1689	29.7	38.1	26.8	3.9	1.6	37516	39913	25	35	1383	27.8	36.4	29.2	5.2	1.3	72438
30809	EVANS	38050	12722	5.1	8.1	38.5	28.9	19.3	97208	104286	96	98	11127	2.7	3.3	39.4	47.6	7.1	185669
30810	GIBSON	17372	755	38.0	29.8	27.0	4.5	0.7	37491	38157	25	34	583	31.6	29.7	27.1	8.2	3.4	75000
30813	GROVETOWN	22570	8683	16.6	24.7	45.2	10.8	2.7	59150	58038	76	79	6531	25.9	18.8	40.4	13.0	1.8	98802
30814	HARLEM	20300	3067	23.5	30.0	38.1	6.4	2.0	46205	50196	52	61	2463	28.5	31.8	31.1	7.8	0.9	71423
30815	HEPHZIBAH	17734	12198	21.3	31.2	40.1	6.0	1.4	47568	51310	56	64	9189	17.6	23.8	53.0	5.2	0.3	96246
30816	KEYSVILLE	15235	514	41.6	26.7	26.8	3.3	1.6	31912	33467	11	14	414	35.0	32.6	25.8	5.6	1.0	66857
30817	LINCOLNTON	18380	3164	33.1	29.7	31.3	4.5	1.4	38403	39509	28	38	2553	24.4	25.7	28.1	17.9	4.0	89881
30818	MATTHEWS	16018	199	28.6	32.7	34.2	2.5	2.0	36812	41167	23	32	147	35.4	22.4	29.9	10.9	1.4	79000
	GEORGIA	26980		20.7	23.1	36.8	11.7	7.7	56761	58593				13.2	17.9	39.1	24.2	5.5	121444
	UNITED STATES	27277		20.9	24.4	35.3	11.7	7.6	54719	56938				9.3	13.1	31.6	32.6	13.5	162279

ZIP CODE #	POST OFFICE NAME	FINANCIAL SERVICES: Auto Loan	Home Loan	Invest-ments	Retire-ment Plans	THE HOME: Home Improvements: Home Repair	Lawn & Garden	Furnishings: Comput-ers & Hard-ware-Personal	Major Appli-ances	TV, Radio, Sound Equip-ment	Furni-ture	ENTERTAINMENT: Dine out/ Carry out	Sports Equip-ment	Fees & Tickets	Toys & Games	Travel	Cable TV	PERSONAL: Apparel & Services	Auto Repairs	Health Insur-ance	Pets & Supplies
30563	MOUNT AIRY	91	74	82	75	75	92	75	86	80	70	78	65	65	81	72	85	53	80	90	102
30564	MURRAYVILLE	95	91	81	90	89	94	86	91	88	87	88	67	83	91	84	90	60	87	91	107
30565	NICHOLSON	94	78	77	76	77	89	77	84	82	78	81	63	68	85	72	86	55	81	87	101
30566	OAKWOOD	97	99	89	99	96	89	98	94	94	101	96	74	98	97	96	91	67	95	88	110
30567	PENDERGRASS	94	86	76	83	84	88	81	86	84	85	84	63	77	88	78	87	57	84	86	102
30568	RABUN GAP	87	64	87	62	66	86	66	80	72	62	70	60	54	72	64	78	47	75	83	96
30571	SAUTEE NACOOCHEE	91	73	117	72	80	96	73	92	76	68	75	67	63	72	79	81	50	85	91	107
30572	SUCHES	108	87	140	85	95	114	87	110	91	81	90	80	75	86	94	97	60	102	109	128
30575	TALMO	93	87	76	83	85	85	82	86	84	86	84	63	78	87	79	85	58	84	85	101
30576	TIGER	87	70	102	69	76	91	70	86	75	68	74	63	62	72	74	80	49	81	88	101
30577	TOCCOA	75	59	69	59	60	76	63	71	68	58	66	54	54	68	60	73	45	68	76	85
30582	YOUNG HARRIS	78	72	94	67	80	88	69	83	74	74	72	55	67	68	75	78	48	79	91	95
30597	DAHLONEGA	0	0	0	0	0	0	0	0	0	0	0	0	0	0	0	0	0	0	0	0
30601	ATHENS	56	41	37	43	39	44	56	47	56	52	56	38	47	57	45	57	39	53	50	59
30602	ATHENS	11	4	4	5	4	5	15	7	12	10	12	8	9	12	8	11	8	10	7	10
30605	ATHENS	67	47	45	51	45	49	80	56	71	65	71	50	60	71	58	68	50	66	57	70
30606	ATHENS	89	75	71	78	72	74	97	79	92	89	93	66	85	92	82	90	65	88	81	97
30607	ATHENS	83	73	65	72	70	69	80	75	79	81	80	58	73	81	73	77	55	78	72	89
30609	ATHENS	42	18	18	22	16	21	59	29	47	40	48	32	35	46	32	43	34	41	29	40
30619	ARNOLDSVILLE	85	66	78	63	65	83	66	77	72	65	71	58	56	74	63	77	48	73	79	93
30620	BETHLEHEM	110	108	92	104	103	102	99	103	99	104	100	77	96	105	96	100	69	99	99	120
30621	BISHOP	102	106	92	107	103	106	97	101	97	98	97	77	99	100	98	98	67	98	101	120
30622	BOGART	113	120	114	120	120	118	110	114	110	114	110	85	114	111	113	110	77	111	113	134
30624	BOWMAN	81	56	72	54	56	78	59	71	66	56	65	55	46	68	54	73	43	67	75	86
30625	BUCKHEAD	97	88	88	91	90	103	87	98	89	80	88	74	80	91	87	94	60	91	100	114
30627	CARLTON	94	67	82	65	67	90	70	83	77	67	76	63	56	80	65	84	51	78	87	100
30628	COLBERT	83	76	68	74	74	78	72	76	75	75	75	55	68	78	68	77	51	74	76	91
30629	COMER	86	65	71	63	64	81	66	75	72	65	71	57	55	75	60	78	48	72	79	91
30630	CRAWFORD	84	64	80	61	64	83	64	77	71	62	70	58	53	72	62	76	46	72	80	92
30631	CRAWFORDVILLE	76	50	73	47	50	75	53	67	62	51	60	52	40	63	50	69	40	63	71	82
30633	DANIELSVILLE	86	67	72	66	67	83	68	77	74	67	72	58	58	76	63	79	49	73	80	93
30634	DEWY ROSE	82	63	71	63	64	81	65	75	70	61	69	57	54	72	61	76	46	70	79	90
30635	ELBERTON	72	54	64	52	54	71	57	65	63	55	62	49	48	64	53	69	42	63	71	79
30641	GOOD HOPE	94	89	84	91	89	98	85	93	88	82	87	70	82	90	85	92	60	88	96	109
30642	GREENSBORO	111	93	126	91	99	120	92	109	100	94	98	77	86	96	95	108	66	104	118	129
30643	HARTWELL	82	63	83	62	65	82	66	78	71	62	70	58	55	71	65	77	47	74	81	92
30646	HULL	87	73	71	71	72	82	71	78	76	72	75	58	64	79	67	79	51	75	80	94
30648	LEXINGTON	92	69	81	67	69	89	70	82	77	68	76	62	58	79	65	83	51	78	86	99
30650	MADISON	96	80	87	79	80	96	79	90	84	77	83	67	70	86	77	89	56	85	93	107
30655	MONROE	88	79	77	78	76	86	80	83	82	78	82	65	74	85	76	85	56	82	85	99
30656	MONROE	96	94	83	94	91	96	89	93	90	89	90	71	87	93	88	92	62	90	94	110
30660	RAYLE	78	54	75	52	55	77	57	70	64	54	63	54	44	65	54	71	42	66	74	85
30662	ROYSTON	81	59	73	58	60	80	62	73	69	59	67	56	51	70	58	75	45	70	78	88
30663	RUTLEDGE	91	83	77	83	83	90	80	87	83	79	82	64	75	85	78	86	56	82	88	102
30666	STATHAM	91	81	79	79	80	89	77	84	81	79	81	62	72	84	74	85	55	81	86	100
30667	STEPHENS	85	61	87	59	63	86	62	79	69	58	68	59	50	69	62	76	45	73	82	94
30668	TIGNALL	73	49	71	46	49	72	51	65	59	49	58	50	39	60	49	65	38	61	68	79
30669	UNION POINT	76	50	74	47	50	75	53	67	61	51	60	52	40	62	50	69	40	63	71	83
30673	WASHINGTON	76	57	75	55	58	79	59	72	66	55	64	54	49	66	57	72	43	67	77	86
30677	WATKINSVILLE	115	129	117	132	127	126	115	120	113	117	114	92	123	115	122	113	80	115	118	140
30678	WHITE PLAINS	86	65	103	63	70	89	66	84	72	63	70	63	55	69	69	77	47	78	85	99
30680	WINDER	92	87	77	85	85	86	85	86	86	86	86	65	82	89	81	87	59	85	86	102
30683	WINTERVILLE	87	78	74	76	77	82	76	80	78	77	78	59	70	81	72	81	53	78	80	95
30701	CALHOUN	92	76	77	74	75	87	77	83	82	77	81	63	69	84	72	86	55	81	87	100
30705	CHATSWORTH	87	69	71	67	68	82	70	77	75	70	74	59	60	78	65	79	50	74	80	93
30707	CHICKAMAUGA	86	68	73	68	68	85	70	79	75	67	74	61	60	78	65	81	50	75	83	95
30708	CISCO	82	59	67	57	58	77	61	71	68	59	66	54	49	70	55	74	45	67	75	86
30710	COHUTTA	103	95	92	96	94	106	91	99	94	89	93	77	86	97	90	98	64	95	101	118
30711	CRANDALL	85	61	70	59	61	81	64	74	71	62	69	57	51	73	58	77	46	70	78	90
30720	DALTON	105	99	92	100	96	97	104	100	104	103	105	78	101	106	99	104	74	103	101	118
30721	DALTON	83	70	68	67	69	76	72	77	75	72	75	58	64	77	68	77	52	75	76	90
30725	FLINTSTONE	82	71	74	71	72	84	70	80	74	66	73	60	63	75	69	79	49	75	83	94
30728	LA FAYETTE	75	58	62	58	57	73	62	68	67	59	66	52	53	69	57	72	45	66	73	82
30730	LYERLY	87	63	72	61	62	83	65	76	72	63	71	58	52	75	59	79	48	72	80	92
30731	MENLO	85	61	79	59	62	84	63	77	70	60	69	58	50	71	60	77	46	71	80	92
30733	PLAINVILLE	83	64	69	62	63	79	64	73	70	64	69	55	54	73	60	75	47	70	76	89
30734	RANGER	93	66	76	65	66	88	69	80	77	67	75	62	55	80	63	84	51	76	85	98
30735	RESACA	89	67	73	65	66	84	69	78	75	68	74	59	57	78	63	80	50	74	81	94
30736	RINGGOLD	98	93	85	91	90	94	87	93	89	89	89	70	84	92	85	90	61	89	91	109
30738	RISING FAWN	82	62	73	61	63	79	63	74	69	61	68	56	53	70	60	74	45	70	77	89
30739	ROCK SPRING	84	71	73	72	71	85	71	80	75	67	74	60	63	77	68	80	50	75	82	95
30740	ROCKY FACE	96	89	86	88	88	94	85	91	87	86	87	69	81	90	83	90	60	87	91	108
30741	ROSSVILLE	72	59	64	58	59	72	62	68	66	59	65	52	54	67	59	70	44	66	73	81
30742	FORT OGLETHORPE	67	57	63	58	59	69	63	67	67	59	66	49	58	66	61	71	45	67	74	78
30746	SUGAR VALLEY	98	70	81	68	70	93	73	85	81	71	79	65	59	85	66	88	53	81	90	103
30747	SUMMERVILLE	77	56	66	54	55	74	59	69	66	56	64	53	48	67	54	72	43	66	73	83
30750	LOOKOUT MOUNTAIN	111	120	120	120	123	118	107	114	106	115	106	84	114	108	113	106	75	109	110	132
30751	TENNGA	79	56	65	55	56	75	59	68	65	57	64	52	47	68	53	71	43	65	72	83
30752	TRENTON	83	61	69	59	60	79	63	73	69	61	68	56	51	72	57	75	46	69	76	88
30753	TRION	78	56	68	54	56	76	59	70	65	56	64	53	47	67	54	72	43	66	74	84
30755	TUNNEL HILL	93	76	79	76	76	91	76	86	81	74	80	66	67	84	72	86	54	81	88	102
30757	WILDWOOD	92	83	75	81	81	86	79	84	82	82	82	61	74	85	75	85	56	81	84	100
30802	APPLING	101	88	94	86	88	98	85	95	89	86	89	69	78	91	83	93	60	90	95	112
30803	AVERA	82	58	68	56	58	78	61	71	67	59	66	55	48	70	55	74	44	67	75	86
30805	BLYTHE	78	69	65	66	67	73	67	71	70	69	70	53	62	73	64	72	48	70	71	85
30807	CAMAK	89	58	86	55	58	87	62	78	72	59	70	61	46	73	58	80	46	73	83	96
30808	DEARING	77	63	62	61	61	71	64	69	68	65	67	52	56	70	59	70	46	67	70	83
30809	EVANS	159	190	167	192	184	160	160	163	150	176	153	131	179	160	169	141	111	151	140	183
30810	GIBSON	73	52	67	51	53	73	56	67	62	52	60	51	45	63	53	68	40	63	72	80
30813	GROVETOWN	100	97	83	93	93	91	91	93	91	96	92	70	88	96	87	91	63	90	89	109
30814	HARLEM	87	80	70	77	78	81	75	80	78	78	78	58	71	81	72	80	53	77	80	95
30815	HEPHZIBAH	80	78	68	76	75	76	73	75	75	77	75	55	72	77	71	76	52	74	76	89
30816	KEYSVILLE	71	52	64	49	50	68	54	63	61	53	59	49	45	62	51	66	40	61	66	77
30817	LINCOLNTON	81	59	79	56	60	81	60	74	67	58	66	56	49	67	59	73	44	69	78	89
30818	MATTHEWS	77	63	68	60	62	74	62	70	67	62	66	52	54	69	58	71	45	67	71	84
	GEORGIA	110	101	97	102	98	103	103	103	104	104	104	80	99	107	99	105	73	103	103	122
	UNITED STATES	100	100	100	100	100	100	100	100	100	100	100	100	100	100	100	100	100	100	100	100

ZIP CODE #	POST OFFICE NAME	COUNTY FIPS CODE	POPULATION 2000	POPULATION 2009	POPULATION 2014	2000-2009 ANNUAL RATE % Rate	2000-2009 ANNUAL RATE State Centile	HOUSEHOLDS 2000	HOUSEHOLDS 2009	HOUSEHOLDS 2014	HOUSEHOLDS % Annual Rate 2000-2009	HOUSEHOLDS 2009 Average HH Size	FAMILIES 2000	FAMILIES 2009	FAMILIES % Annual Rate 2000-2009
30820	MITCHELL	125	844	910	940	0.8	41	346	384	400	1.1	2.35	253	271	0.7
30821	NORWOOD	301	1105	1033	996	-0.7	3	439	426	416	-0.3	2.42	297	278	-0.7
30822	PERKINS	165	616	637	638	0.4	28	237	249	251	0.5	2.56	175	178	0.2
30823	STAPLETON	163	1331	1371	1363	0.3	25	478	501	501	0.5	2.71	364	371	0.2
30824	THOMSON	189	16783	16959	16981	0.1	19	6362	6530	6577	0.3	2.54	4618	4583	-0.1
30828	WARRENTON	301	4337	3977	3797	-0.9	2	1621	1547	1493	-0.5	2.51	1119	1028	-0.9
30830	WAYNESBORO	033	13513	14101	14284	0.5	31	4820	5112	5213	0.6	2.71	3495	3582	0.3
30833	WRENS	163	4309	4094	3967	-0.6	4	1624	1571	1531	-0.4	2.61	1181	1107	-0.7
30901	AUGUSTA	245	21549	19339	18559	-1.2	1	8559	7863	7568	-0.9	2.32	4782	4182	-1.4
30904	AUGUSTA	245	29299	27069	26194	-0.9	2	12524	11910	11581	-0.5	2.17	6962	6225	-1.2
30905	AUGUSTA	245	7827	7406	7382	-0.6	4	885	927	927	0.5	3.59	860	898	0.5
30906	AUGUSTA	245	61546	59194	57948	-0.4	9	21387	21171	20820	-0.1	2.72	15940	15242	-0.5
30907	AUGUSTA	073	46591	50468	53657	0.9	45	17403	19395	20743	1.2	2.57	13177	14264	0.9
30909	AUGUSTA	245	34642	37827	38331	1.0	47	15115	17022	17372	1.3	2.15	9216	9823	0.7
31001	ABBEVILLE	315	3388	3643	3645	0.8	41	808	821	829	0.2	2.45	570	559	-0.2
31002	ADRIAN	167	2846	2895	2861	0.2	22	1112	1103	1097	-0.1	2.44	799	768	-0.4
31003	ALLENTOWN	319	14	14	13	0.0	17	7	7	7	0.0	2.00	5	5	0.0
31005	BONAIRE	153	10451	14718	17015	3.8	90	3584	5231	6119	4.2	2.81	3117	4403	3.8
31006	BUTLER	269	5308	5309	5259	0.0	17	1914	1958	1955	0.2	2.54	1348	1331	-0.1
31007	BYROMVILLE	093	1126	1139	1120	0.1	19	366	367	362	0.0	2.81	270	263	-0.3
31008	BYRON	225	13175	19418	22153	4.3	92	4771	7172	8252	4.5	2.70	3719	5408	4.1
31009	CADWELL	175	1197	1299	1349	0.9	45	473	526	550	1.2	2.47	346	371	0.8
31011	CHAUNCEY	091	1018	992	984	-0.3	11	369	370	370	0.0	2.65	274	267	-0.3
31012	CHESTER	091	2324	2429	2420	0.5	31	523	522	521	0.0	2.46	383	371	-0.3
31014	COCHRAN	023	12669	13641	13679	0.8	41	4743	4993	5036	0.6	2.50	3388	3449	0.2
31015	CORDELE	081	20867	21185	21217	0.2	22	7900	8106	8164	0.3	2.54	5557	5504	-0.1
31016	CULLODEN	207	1523	1866	1996	2.2	73	552	684	737	2.3	2.71	415	495	1.9
31017	DANVILLE	319	2231	2157	2107	-0.4	9	873	869	857	0.0	2.48	632	609	-0.4
31018	DAVISBORO	303	2506	2782	2782	1.1	49	464	498	500	0.8	2.99	349	363	0.4
31019	DEXTER	175	2112	2248	2316	0.7	37	842	916	951	0.9	2.45	609	639	0.5
31020	DRY BRANCH	289	2970	2834	2770	-0.5	7	1089	1068	1054	-0.2	2.65	827	787	-0.5
31021	DUBLIN	175	27044	28711	29400	0.6	34	10253	10987	11338	0.8	2.47	7100	7346	0.4
31022	DUDLEY	175	1113	1296	1373	1.7	66	430	514	549	1.9	2.52	324	376	1.6
31023	EASTMAN	091	13211	13771	14008	0.4	28	5137	5443	5581	0.6	2.40	3479	3547	0.2
31024	EATONTON	237	17833	20345	21582	1.4	57	6980	8227	8799	1.8	2.46	5159	5894	1.5
31025	ELKO	153	1450	1617	1775	1.2	52	515	595	661	1.6	2.72	406	447	1.0
31027	EAST DUBLIN	175	9442	10070	10354	0.7	37	3520	3828	3963	0.9	2.63	2621	2756	0.5
31028	CENTERVILLE	153	3922	5406	5942	3.5	88	1452	2137	2388	4.3	2.52	1146	1605	3.7
31029	FORSYTH	207	13417	15852	16475	1.8	66	4716	5419	5669	1.5	2.70	3552	3958	1.2
31030	FORT VALLEY	225	17529	18226	18627	0.4	28	6109	6464	6658	0.6	2.65	4226	4293	0.2
31031	GORDON	319	6231	6283	6226	0.1	19	2362	2442	2439	0.4	2.56	1732	1734	0.0
31032	GRAY	169	9807	12504	13646	2.7	79	3509	4568	5028	2.9	2.66	2738	3470	2.6
31033	HADDOCK	169	2220	2698	2943	2.1	72	846	1054	1158	2.4	2.56	627	757	2.1
31035	HARRISON	303	1435	1375	1337	-0.5	7	520	505	494	-0.3	2.71	400	378	-0.6
31036	HAWKINSVILLE	235	10984	11946	12248	0.9	45	3907	4294	4435	1.0	2.50	2728	2901	0.7
31037	HELENA	271	2754	3312	3283	2.0	70	668	663	657	-0.1	2.52	466	447	-0.4
31038	HILLSBORO	169	637	728	760	1.5	60	243	280	294	1.5	2.60	179	199	1.2
31041	IDEAL	193	1072	1036	1000	-0.4	9	390	388	378	-0.1	2.44	284	273	-0.4
31042	IRWINTON	319	1915	1830	1780	-0.5	7	685	671	657	-0.2	2.69	513	487	-0.6
31044	JEFFERSONVILLE	289	3472	3372	3307	-0.3	11	1211	1207	1195	0.0	2.67	898	868	-0.4
31045	JEWELL	301	540	507	483	-0.7	3	216	211	203	-0.3	2.40	161	153	-0.5
31046	JULIETTE	207	2815	3294	3530	1.7	66	1029	1223	1317	1.9	2.69	843	981	1.7
31047	KATHLEEN	153	5806	9216	10715	5.1	95	1967	3227	3793	5.5	2.82	1617	2548	5.0
31049	KITE	167	1534	1479	1451	-0.4	9	614	605	599	-0.2	2.39	453	434	-0.5
31050	KNOXVILLE	079	1519	1637	1717	0.8	41	515	563	593	1.0	2.91	409	436	0.7
31052	LIZELLA	021	7519	8573	9030	1.4	57	2762	3185	3371	1.6	2.67	2180	2424	1.2
31054	MC INTYRE	319	1601	1638	1618	0.2	22	583	615	614	0.6	2.66	428	437	0.2
31055	MC RAE	271	5028	6291	6235	2.5	77	1927	1981	1977	0.3	2.44	1347	1334	-0.1
31057	MARSHALLVILLE	193	1925	1870	1831	-0.3	11	719	725	717	0.1	2.48	505	491	-0.3
31058	MAUK	269	1774	2045	2086	1.5	60	669	786	807	1.8	2.58	500	569	1.4
31060	MILAN	271	2576	2463	2416	-0.5	7	961	933	922	-0.3	2.32	694	653	-0.7
31061	MILLEDGEVILLE	009	43812	46418	47236	0.6	34	14446	15636	16108	0.9	2.43	9606	9994	0.4
31063	MONTEZUMA	193	6052	5876	5707	-0.3	11	2131	2126	2086	0.0	2.71	1551	1497	-0.4
31064	MONTICELLO	159	7754	9889	10763	2.7	79	2889	3719	4063	2.8	2.64	2107	2627	2.4
31065	MONTROSE	175	921	974	1002	0.6	34	340	366	379	0.8	2.65	264	277	0.5
31066	MUSELLA	079	1219	1306	1340	0.7	37	460	504	519	1.0	2.57	339	359	0.6
31068	OGLETHORPE	193	4405	4240	4134	-0.4	9	1375	1317	1289	-0.5	2.66	982	909	-0.8
31069	PERRY	153	15228	15832	16256	0.4	28	5696	6109	6332	0.8	2.55	4219	4225	0.0
31070	PINEHURST	093	815	769	739	-0.6	4	341	329	319	-0.4	2.33	235	219	-0.8
31071	PINEVIEW	315	808	792	784	-0.2	13	287	282	281	-0.2	2.62	209	199	-0.5
31072	PITTS	315	1351	1352	1358	0.0	17	533	546	553	0.3	2.39	372	368	-0.1
31075	RENTZ	175	1791	1827	1868	0.2	22	705	739	761	0.5	2.47	525	532	0.1
31076	REYNOLDS	269	2964	2921	2889	-0.2	13	1152	1170	1168	0.2	2.42	780	762	-0.3
31077	RHINE	091	799	783	786	-0.2	13	336	337	340	0.0	2.32	235	227	-0.4
31078	ROBERTA	079	2924	3120	3200	0.7	37	1093	1184	1221	0.9	2.55	820	862	0.5
31079	ROCHELLE	315	3157	3044	3009	-0.4	9	1204	1185	1180	-0.2	2.53	860	818	-0.5
31081	RUPERT	269	204	219	223	0.8	41	90	98	101	0.9	2.23	64	68	0.7
31082	SANDERSVILLE	303	10495	10289	10079	-0.2	13	3981	3990	3940	0.0	2.51	2849	2761	-0.3
31085	SHADY DALE	159	994	1208	1363	2.1	72	327	405	459	2.3	2.98	262	316	2.0
31087	SPARTA	141	10039	9694	9310	-0.4	9	3224	3184	3074	-0.1	2.55	2302	2197	-0.5
31088	WARNER ROBINS	153	37164	48719	54026	3.0	83	14313	18802	20853	3.0	2.58	10252	13245	2.8
31089	TENNILLE	303	4939	4928	4844	0.0	17	1798	1817	1797	0.1	2.66	1293	1261	-0.3
31090	TOOMSBORO	319	1170	1177	1158	0.1	19	422	428	424	0.2	2.60	308	303	-0.2
31091	UNADILLA	093	3849	4029	3973	0.5	31	1076	1074	1059	0.0	2.46	750	721	-0.4
31092	VIENNA	093	5806	5691	5556	-0.2	13	2158	2149	2109	0.0	2.63	1536	1477	-0.4
31093	WARNER ROBINS	153	27504	27420	27644	0.0	17	10932	11271	11483	0.3	2.39	7349	7102	-0.4
31094	WARTHEN	303	1272	1233	1207	-0.3	11	485	482	475	-0.1	2.54	352	339	-0.4
31096	WRIGHTSVILLE	167	6152	7161	7119	1.7	66	2170	2241	2246	0.3	2.50	1551	1549	0.0
31097	YATESVILLE	293	1185	1299	1335	1.0	47	448	499	516	1.2	2.60	358	388	0.9
31098	WARNER ROBINS	153	5582	5667	5730	0.2	22	1142	1147	1179	0.0	3.47	1070	1025	-0.5
31201	MACON	021	10912	10450	10240	-0.5	7	4179	3927	3848	-0.7	2.09	1878	1621	-1.6
31204	MACON	021	34114	33016	32675	-0.4	9	14291	13971	13889	-0.2	2.33	8889	8243	-0.8
31206	MACON	021	30307	29050	28636	-0.5	7	11132	10695	10571	-0.4	2.67	7674	7054	-0.9
31210	MACON	021	27601	30362	31469	1.0	47	11018	12162	12629	1.1	2.46	7673	8169	0.7
31211	MACON	169	15956	17008	17372	0.7	37	6602	7078	7257	0.8	2.39	4380	4536	0.4
	GEORGIA					2.1					2.1	2.65			1.8
	UNITED STATES					1.0					1.1	2.59			0.9

ZIP CODE #	POST OFFICE NAME	RACE (%) White 2000	White 2009	Black 2000	Black 2009	Asian/Pacific 2000	Asian/Pacific 2009	% Hispanic Origin 2000	% Hispanic Origin 2009	2009 AGE DISTRIBUTION (%) 0-4	5-9	10-14	15-19	20-24	25-44	45-64	65-84	85+	18+	MEDIAN AGE 2009	% 2009 Males	% 2009 Females
30820	MITCHELL	76.4	75.4	21.8	22.4	0.0	0.0	0.6	0.7	5.5	6.2	6.4	5.8	4.0	24.7	31.8	13.5	2.2	78.2	43.2	49.5	50.5
30821	NORWOOD	35.7	38.6	63.3	60.2	0.1	0.1	0.4	0.4	6.4	6.9	7.0	6.3	4.8	23.6	31.0	11.9	2.1	75.9	41.2	47.0	53.0
30822	PERKINS	65.5	63.7	29.2	31.1	0.5	0.5	5.7	5.5	7.1	7.4	7.5	8.0	5.8	25.7	26.4	11.0	1.1	73.2	36.4	49.8	50.2
30823	STAPLETON	59.4	54.0	39.6	44.7	0.0	0.0	0.6	0.7	6.9	7.1	7.3	6.9	5.6	24.9	28.1	11.2	2.0	74.2	38.6	50.0	50.0
30824	THOMSON	56.8	50.4	41.6	47.6	0.4	0.5	1.1	1.5	7.1	7.1	7.1	7.3	6.4	25.3	26.9	11.0	1.9	74.2	37.4	47.2	52.8
30828	WARRENTON	40.3	43.9	58.6	54.7	0.1	0.2	0.9	1.1	6.8	7.0	7.2	6.8	5.3	23.4	27.1	13.5	2.9	74.8	39.4	46.9	53.1
30830	WAYNESBORO	43.1	37.3	55.0	60.2	0.2	0.2	1.4	1.8	8.2	8.3	7.8	8.0	6.8	24.6	25.1	9.4	1.8	70.4	33.3	47.1	52.9
30833	WRENS	47.0	40.5	50.8	56.5	0.1	0.1	1.6	2.3	7.8	7.8	7.8	7.7	5.7	25.2	25.2	10.9	1.7	71.4	35.7	46.8	53.2
30901	AUGUSTA	10.1	8.3	87.9	89.5	0.5	0.6	1.1	1.2	8.5	7.9	6.8	7.3	7.8	23.1	22.7	13.1	2.8	72.4	34.3	47.1	52.9
30904	AUGUSTA	53.3	47.4	42.9	47.4	1.4	2.0	1.9	2.7	6.6	6.4	5.9	6.4	7.9	27.3	23.9	13.0	2.7	77.8	36.8	46.6	53.4
30905	AUGUSTA	55.7	46.9	33.3	38.8	2.6	3.1	10.6	14.3	7.9	6.7	5.1	22.5	26.3	29.3	2.0	0.1	0.1	78.4	21.5	67.1	32.9
30906	AUGUSTA	42.7	35.7	53.1	59.0	1.3	1.6	2.6	3.5	7.3	7.2	7.3	8.2	7.1	26.7	25.4	9.8	1.0	73.1	34.4	47.2	52.8
30907	AUGUSTA	82.6	77.5	10.4	12.6	4.6	6.5	2.3	3.5	6.2	6.4	6.8	7.1	5.8	27.3	29.3	9.9	1.4	76.3	38.2	48.0	52.0
30909	AUGUSTA	59.4	51.2	35.7	42.2	1.9	2.5	2.8	3.8	6.9	6.2	5.8	5.9	8.3	31.0	23.4	10.7	1.8	77.8	34.9	48.6	51.4
31001	ABBEVILLE	52.7	45.3	46.3	53.5	0.2	0.2	1.0	1.3	3.9	4.1	4.2	4.3	8.8	40.2	24.5	8.8	1.3	85.5	37.2	69.9	30.1
31002	ADRIAN	84.2	79.1	12.7	16.2	0.0	0.0	2.8	4.5	6.1	6.2	6.4	7.8	5.5	25.2	26.3	13.8	2.7	76.0	39.9	51.2	48.8
31003	ALLENTOWN	78.6	78.6	21.4	21.4	0.0	0.0	0.0	0.0	0.0	0.0	0.0	0.0	0.0	14.3	85.7	0.0	0.0	100.0	53.3	57.1	42.9
31005	BONAIRE	85.2	78.2	10.6	15.6	1.9	2.6	2.8	4.2	6.4	6.7	7.3	7.7	5.4	26.1	31.3	8.6	0.5	74.8	38.2	50.0	50.0
31006	BUTLER	52.6	49.8	44.9	47.7	0.1	0.1	2.5	2.5	7.4	7.6	7.6	7.0	5.7	26.1	25.2	11.4	2.0	73.1	36.8	49.7	50.3
31007	BYROMVILLE	40.7	38.5	51.9	54.2	1.0	1.0	9.2	9.2	7.4	7.4	7.1	6.5	5.4	23.4	24.5	14.7	3.7	73.4	39.1	45.7	54.3
31008	BYRON	85.2	76.7	12.2	18.9	0.6	1.1	1.9	3.4	7.9	7.6	7.5	6.9	5.3	30.0	25.7	8.5	0.7	72.8	35.7	49.0	51.0
31009	CADWELL	79.8	72.9	19.6	26.3	0.1	0.2	0.8	1.2	5.9	6.2	6.5	6.1	5.2	26.2	30.9	11.2	1.8	77.6	39.7	50.3	49.7
31011	CHAUNCEY	70.5	64.8	28.8	34.3	0.0	0.0	0.7	1.1	6.8	6.8	7.1	6.7	5.4	26.5	27.7	11.5	1.6	75.2	39.3	49.1	50.9
31012	CHESTER	59.7	53.8	39.1	44.6	0.1	0.1	1.1	1.5	3.0	3.4	3.5	4.6	9.4	45.3	23.0	7.2	0.6	87.9	37.0	73.3	26.7
31014	COCHRAN	73.0	67.7	24.9	29.5	0.9	1.2	0.9	1.3	6.2	6.2	6.5	11.4	7.3	23.4	24.8	12.3	1.8	75.5	36.1	48.8	51.2
31015	CORDELE	52.7	46.6	44.7	49.9	0.7	0.9	1.8	2.6	7.8	7.6	7.3	7.2	6.4	24.7	25.3	11.5	2.2	72.9	36.0	47.2	52.8
31016	CULLODEN	50.7	45.5	48.6	53.7	0.1	0.1	0.8	1.0	5.1	5.7	6.8	6.5	5.1	25.3	32.2	11.9	1.4	78.5	41.9	49.8	50.2
31017	DANVILLE	62.1	56.3	36.7	42.3	0.1	0.1	0.6	0.8	6.2	6.3	6.5	6.8	5.4	25.9	28.3	12.8	1.8	76.9	40.5	48.0	52.0
31018	DAVISBORO	44.7	41.6	53.8	57.1	0.2	0.2	1.0	1.0	4.1	4.1	4.1	5.6	9.5	45.3	21.0	5.4	0.8	84.8	35.2	30.4	69.6
31019	DEXTER	90.1	86.2	9.2	12.9	0.1	0.2	0.2	0.4	6.8	6.9	7.0	6.0	5.2	26.6	29.3	10.9	1.4	75.6	38.6	50.0	50.0
31020	DRY BRANCH	58.5	51.9	39.8	45.8	0.1	0.2	1.0	1.4	6.7	7.2	7.1	7.1	5.9	25.3	28.6	11.2	1.0	74.7	38.2	48.4	51.6
31021	DUBLIN	56.7	51.2	40.9	45.6	1.3	1.7	1.1	1.5	6.9	6.8	6.7	6.8	5.9	25.4	26.1	12.7	2.6	75.4	38.6	48.6	51.4
31022	DUDLEY	71.0	63.9	27.9	34.7	0.1	0.2	0.4	0.6	6.0	6.6	6.9	6.7	4.8	26.5	29.6	11.1	1.8	76.3	40.2	48.1	51.9
31023	EASTMAN	68.6	62.9	29.5	34.2	0.3	0.5	1.5	2.3	6.6	6.8	7.1	9.2	5.6	24.5	25.7	12.3	2.2	73.1	37.6	48.8	51.2
31024	EATONTON	66.6	60.9	30.8	35.5	0.7	0.9	2.1	3.1	6.0	6.1	6.1	5.6	4.8	23.8	30.5	15.8	1.4	78.5	43.2	49.3	50.7
31025	ELKO	59.1	49.3	39.7	49.1	0.3	0.4	1.4	2.0	6.4	6.3	6.5	7.4	6.8	24.7	29.7	11.1	1.1	76.5	39.7	48.1	51.9
31027	EAST DUBLIN	68.4	61.0	30.0	36.8	0.2	0.2	1.6	2.3	7.0	7.2	6.9	7.9	6.5	26.2	26.5	10.5	1.2	74.1	36.1	48.1	51.9
31028	CENTERVILLE	83.2	76.0	12.7	18.0	1.3	1.9	2.7	4.4	8.1	7.6	7.3	6.8	5.6	30.1	24.5	9.1	0.8	72.7	34.9	48.5	51.5
31029	FORSYTH	62.8	57.0	35.4	40.7	0.4	0.5	1.4	1.8	6.1	6.2	6.5	7.0	7.4	27.7	26.9	10.5	1.8	77.8	37.1	51.5	48.5
31030	FORT VALLEY	37.1	30.0	58.4	63.9	0.3	0.4	5.8	8.1	6.4	6.4	6.6	9.1	12.1	24.8	23.8	9.5	1.4	76.3	32.1	48.4	51.6
31031	GORDON	68.8	65.4	29.9	33.2	0.1	0.2	0.6	0.8	7.5	7.3	7.2	6.4	5.7	26.8	26.7	11.2	1.2	74.1	37.3	48.5	51.5
31032	GRAY	75.0	69.6	23.4	28.2	0.5	0.6	0.8	1.1	6.1	6.5	7.0	7.1	5.1	26.5	29.1	10.9	1.7	76.7	39.4	49.4	50.6
31033	HADDOCK	67.0	60.2	30.6	36.7	0.4	0.5	1.6	2.1	6.5	6.4	7.4	7.4	5.7	27.4	28.3	9.6	1.2	75.1	37.4	49.8	50.2
31035	HARRISON	55.1	51.6	44.2	47.6	0.1	0.1	1.0	1.0	6.3	6.5	6.8	7.1	5.7	23.7	30.8	11.7	1.5	76.2	40.6	50.5	49.5
31036	HAWKINSVILLE	64.9	58.7	32.5	37.8	0.4	0.6	2.7	3.7	6.0	6.1	6.2	6.5	6.1	28.9	26.5	11.9	1.9	77.9	38.5	44.2	55.8
31037	HELENA	45.9	42.5	51.4	53.8	0.3	0.4	2.8	3.8	3.6	3.8	3.9	5.2	12.2	43.4	20.1	6.5	1.3	86.0	33.7	71.0	29.0
31038	HILLSBORO	66.0	58.4	32.9	40.2	0.2	0.3	0.6	1.0	6.6	6.6	7.3	6.3	6.0	25.4	29.4	11.0	1.4	75.8	38.7	49.9	50.1
31041	IDEAL	44.6	37.7	54.3	61.0	0.1	0.1	0.5	0.5	6.2	6.3	6.7	6.7	5.3	21.4	27.4	16.0	4.1	76.5	43.1	44.9	55.1
31042	IRWINTON	33.2	30.0	64.8	68.0	0.0	0.0	2.4	2.3	7.0	7.3	7.1	8.6	6.7	25.0	26.2	10.7	1.5	73.0	36.6	48.1	51.9
31044	JEFFERSONVILLE	41.2	34.9	57.8	63.8	0.1	0.1	1.3	1.6	6.1	6.4	6.3	6.6	5.7	25.7	28.7	12.5	1.8	77.1	39.8	47.3	52.7
31045	JEWELL	38.0	41.2	61.0	57.4	0.2	0.2	0.9	1.4	6.1	6.1	6.3	6.9	5.9	25.0	28.2	13.8	1.6	77.3	40.5	46.4	53.6
31046	JULIETTE	82.0	76.9	16.7	21.3	0.2	0.4	0.8	1.2	6.6	7.0	7.3	6.8	4.7	26.2	30.7	9.7	0.9	74.8	39.1	49.4	50.6
31047	KATHLEEN	81.3	74.7	15.7	20.8	1.0	1.6	1.8	2.8	6.5	6.7	7.1	7.5	5.6	27.8	30.1	7.8	0.9	74.8	37.3	49.9	50.1
31049	KITE	88.1	84.9	11.4	14.1	0.0	0.0	1.3	2.0	7.5	7.5	7.6	7.2	4.8	23.5	26.6	13.3	2.0	72.3	38.6	47.5	52.5
31050	KNOXVILLE	87.7	83.5	10.4	13.6	0.1	0.2	1.1	1.6	7.0	7.0	7.2	7.6	5.8	27.4	28.2	9.0	0.7	74.0	37.3	50.5	49.5
31052	LIZELLA	82.0	74.0	16.4	23.7	0.6	0.8	0.9	1.4	6.0	6.5	6.8	6.0	4.5	26.7	31.1	11.5	0.9	76.9	40.9	50.5	49.5
31054	MC INTYRE	61.4	59.6	36.9	38.8	0.2	0.2	1.1	1.1	7.8	8.0	7.6	6.3	5.3	25.8	26.6	11.4	1.3	72.5	37.3	47.6	52.4
31055	MC RAE	61.0	55.9	37.2	41.6	0.3	0.3	1.6	2.3	5.2	5.3	5.3	6.0	8.1	32.9	24.1	10.8	2.3	80.3	36.9	57.6	42.4
31057	MARSHALLVILLE	28.7	23.3	70.6	75.9	0.1	0.1	0.3	0.4	6.7	6.7	7.0	6.8	5.5	22.5	28.9	12.4	3.6	75.7	39.7	44.1	55.9
31058	MAUK	85.5	80.7	11.2	14.9	0.3	0.3	1.5	2.6	6.2	6.1	6.5	7.3	6.5	24.4	30.6	11.0	1.4	76.6	39.4	50.2	49.8
31060	MILAN	77.3	70.7	21.5	27.4	0.0	0.0	1.0	1.7	5.4	5.7	5.6	6.3	7.2	27.2	27.6	13.0	1.8	79.9	39.7	56.6	43.4
31061	MILLEDGEVILLE	54.0	47.8	43.6	49.0	1.0	1.3	1.3	1.7	5.0	5.1	5.1	8.5	9.5	29.5	25.2	10.6	1.4	80.7	36.0	54.3	45.7
31063	MONTEZUMA	35.2	30.0	61.5	65.4	0.6	0.8	2.7	3.7	8.1	8.2	8.0	7.4	5.7	23.2	25.9	11.7	1.9	71.1	35.7	46.5	53.5
31064	MONTICELLO	67.6	62.3	30.7	35.2	0.2	0.3	2.1	2.9	6.6	6.7	7.0	6.9	5.1	24.8	28.7	12.4	1.7	75.4	40.0	49.3	50.7
31065	MONTROSE	48.8	40.7	49.1	57.0	0.5	0.7	0.7	0.9	6.2	6.3	6.7	7.3	6.2	26.3	29.0	10.6	1.6	76.4	39.0	47.3	52.7
31066	MUSELLA	60.0	52.4	37.6	44.5	0.2	0.4	1.2	1.7	5.7	6.2	6.6	6.4	5.5	24.0	30.9	12.9	1.8	77.6	41.4	49.5	50.5
31068	OGLETHORPE	41.4	35.5	54.2	58.5	1.0	1.3	3.9	5.4	5.5	5.6	5.8	6.5	7.4	31.7	26.8	9.4	1.2	79.0	37.1	57.9	42.1
31069	PERRY	66.9	59.4	30.3	36.6	1.0	1.4	1.5	2.2	6.8	6.8	6.7	7.0	6.5	26.1	27.7	10.7	1.8	75.4	37.7	48.5	51.5
31070	PINEHURST	56.3	53.7	40.1	42.7	0.4	0.4	3.6	3.8	5.5	5.3	5.6	6.4	6.4	24.7	29.9	14.0	2.1	79.7	42.2	48.2	51.8
31071	PINEVIEW	67.6	60.9	30.8	37.1	0.1	0.1	1.7	2.4	6.7	6.9	6.9	6.6	5.6	21.6	26.1	14.6	4.9	75.8	41.3	46.3	53.7
31072	PITTS	87.9	84.2	10.7	13.7	0.1	0.1	3.7	5.5	6.2	6.5	6.5	6.4	5.4	24.2	29.6	13.3	1.8	76.7	41.5	51.0	49.0
31075	RENTZ	83.5	77.8	15.1	20.0	0.2	0.3	1.2	1.9	6.8	6.8	6.8	6.2	5.4	28.0	27.0	11.7	1.3	75.7	38.5	49.6	50.4
31076	REYNOLDS	53.0	49.6	46.0	49.4	0.4	0.4	0.7	0.8	6.0	6.1	7.3	8.5	5.2	23.6	28.5	12.9	2.1	74.7	40.4	48.6	51.4
31077	RHINE	77.7	72.9	21.5	25.9	0.0	0.0	1.3	1.7	5.9	6.0	6.4	6.3	4.9	23.5	30.3	14.6	2.3	77.9	43.1	48.5	51.5
31078	ROBERTA	45.4	37.6	51.6	58.7	0.2	0.2	1.9	2.5	5.6	6.0	6.3	6.7	5.6	24.0	30.2	13.5	2.1	77.8	41.7	49.0	51.0
31079	ROCHELLE	62.1	58.3	36.6	39.8	0.3	0.3	1.4	2.0	7.5	7.5	7.6	6.9	5.4	23.6	27.1	12.3	2.2	73.2	37.9	47.1	52.9
31081	RUPERT	80.8	79.0	17.2	19.2	0.0	0.0	1.0	0.9	5.9	5.9	6.4	6.4	3.7	24.2	31.5	14.6	1.4	77.2	43.0	51.6	48.4
31082	SANDERSVILLE	45.9	43.8	53.0	55.2	0.5	0.5	0.3	0.3	6.2	7.1	7.5	7.5	5.6	24.1	27.2	12.2	2.4	74.4	38.9	46.0	54.0
31085	SHADY DALE	77.0	71.4	20.7	25.6	0.1	0.1	2.5	3.6	7.7	7.5	7.6	7.3	6.1	26.3	27.5	9.0	1.0	72.8	36.0	50.3	49.7
31087	SPARTA	21.7	22.8	77.5	76.2	0.1	0.1	0.5	0.6	5.5	5.9	6.4	6.7	7.5	28.9	25.8	11.7	1.7	78.1	37.1	54.4	45.6
31088	WARNER ROBINS	74.0	67.4	20.6	25.0	2.0	2.8	3.9	5.4	7.4	6.9	6.8	7.2	7.5	29.7	25.8	7.9	0.9	74.3	34.1	49.2	50.8
31089	TENNILLE	40.6	37.8	58.2	61.0	0.1	0.1	0.9	0.9	7.1	7.7	7.7	8.1	6.0	25.2	25.1	10.6	2.5	72.6	36.1	47.3	52.7
31090	TOOMSBORO	55.3	51.2	43.8	47.8	0.0	0.0	0.9	0.8	6.5	6.6	6.5	6.2	5.2	23.6	26.4	15.3	3.7	76.2	41.7	46.2	53.8
31091	UNADILLA	42.1	39.6	54.0	56.5	0.4	0.4	3.7	3.6	4.8	5.0	4.8	5.2	8.4	37.6	24.5	8.4	1.3	82.6	37.0	64.8	35.2
31092	VIENNA	48.5	45.9	47.1	49.7	0.6	0.6	4.5	4.5	7.7	7.5	7.2	7.0	6.7	25.7	26.2	10.5	1.5	73.3	35.3	48.4	51.6
31093	WARNER ROBINS	60.0	52.5	35.4	41.3	1.5	2.0	2.8	3.9	7.4	7.0	6.7	7.1	6.8	28.1	24.5	11.1	1.4	74.5	35.3	47.8	52.2
31094	WARTHEN	54.9	51.7	44.8	47.9	0.1	0.1	0.5	0.5	5.6	6.0	6.5	7.1	5.5	24.9	30.3	12.0	2.0	77.5	41.2	48.0	52.0
31096	WRIGHTSVILLE	52.2	47.1	47.1	52.1	0.2	0.2	0.9	1.1	6.0	6.0	8.0	20.4	5.0	20.3	21.1	11.0	2.1	63.6	29.6	56.3	43.7
31097	YATESVILLE	76.6	71.6	22.2	26.7	0.2	0.2	1.2	1.8	5.5	5.8	6.2	6.9	5.9	25.7	30.7	12.0	1.3	78.4	40.7	50.2	49.8
31098	WARNER ROBINS	59.4	49.2	31.0	38.7	2.7	3.3	5.3	7.6	10.5	9.7	7.0	14.7	19.7	32.9	4.4	0.8	0.1	69.3	22.0	56.0	44.0
31201	MACON	30.2	24.9	67.3	72.0	1.1	1.4	1.2	1.4	7.3	5.6	4.4	13.1	14.8	23.4	18.6	10.0	2.8	80.2	28.1	41.4	58.6
31204	MACON	38.9	33.3	59.3	64.4	0.6	0.7	1.1	1.3	7.5	7.3	6.8	6.7	6.4	24.3	25.5	12.6	3.0	74.5	38.0	44.6	55.4
31206	MACON	33.5	23.4	64.3	73.9	0.5	0.6	1.5	1.9	8.9	8.2	7.6	8.2	7.5	25.8	22.4	9.7	1.7	70.2	31.6	45.5	54.5
31210	MACON	78.7	70.9	16.6	23.0	3.2	4.1	1.5	2.3	6.4	6.6	6.8	7.2	7.1	26.5	27.6	10.2	1.5	75.9	37.2	46.8	53.2
31211	MACON	51.2	45.3	47.0	52.4	0.6	0.8	0.9	1.2	6.5	6.8	6.7	6.7	6.1	27.1	27.1	11.1	1.9	75.9	38.1	46.6	53.4
	GEORGIA	65.1	61.1	28.7	30.1	2.2	2.9	5.3	7.7	7.3	7.0	6.9	7.1	7.1	29.3	25.1	8.9	1.3	74.7	35.0	49.4	50.6
	UNITED STATES	75.1	72.0	12.3	12.7	3.8	4.6	12.5	15.7	6.8	6.7	6.6	7.1	6.9	27.0	26.0	10.9	1.9	75.7	36.9	49.2	50.8

#	POST OFFICE NAME	2009 Per Capita Income	2009 HH Income Base	2009 Household Income Distribution (%): Less than $25,000	$25,000 to $49,999	$50,000 to $99,999	$100,000 to $149,999	$150,000 or More	Median Household Income: 2009	2014	2009 National Centile	2009 State Centile	2009 Home Value Base	2009 Home Value Distribution (%): Less than $50,000	$50,000 to $89,999	$90,000 to $174,999	$175,000 to $399,999	$400,000 or More	2009 Median Home Value
30820	MITCHELL	18821	384	37.2	29.9	26.8	3.9	2.1	33692	34203	15	20	318	35.5	34.3	19.8	10.1	0.3	70294
30821	NORWOOD	17445	426	40.1	27.7	27.0	2.8	2.3	33185	33270	14	17	363	52.6	24.5	17.6	4.7	0.6	48304
30822	PERKINS	14908	249	41.4	28.9	28.1	1.6	0.0	30913	33122	10	11	193	46.1	24.4	19.7	8.3	1.6	54167
30823	STAPLETON	16077	501	34.7	34.9	24.8	4.0	1.6	36338	38034	22	30	408	34.1	31.9	27.0	7.1	0.0	68966
30824	THOMSON	19463	6530	35.2	25.4	31.6	5.1	2.7	39507	43185	31	42	4409	21.2	34.1	32.4	10.6	1.6	82982
30828	WARRENTON	16121	1547	43.2	26.6	26.0	2.6	1.6	32383	32739	12	15	1110	36.7	29.4	25.6	7.4	1.0	68158
30830	WAYNESBORO	15716	5112	41.5	25.2	27.5	4.4	1.4	32942	34730	13	16	3586	30.0	34.5	30.3	4.9	0.4	71806
30833	WRENS	15384	1571	41.1	29.3	26.0	2.1	1.6	31324	31912	10	13	1065	37.4	24.9	32.0	5.4	0.4	72988
30901	AUGUSTA	12293	7863	63.7	22.4	11.1	1.8	1.1	17389	18140	1	1	2420	53.3	34.4	6.9	4.5	0.8	48228
30904	AUGUSTA	21793	11910	37.5	28.7	26.5	4.2	3.0	34598	37708	17	23	5963	17.2	33.3	39.6	7.1	2.9	89424
30905	AUGUSTA	14356	927	9.9	43.3	42.6	3.7	0.5	48059	51309	57	65	35	2.9	20.0	77.1	0.0	0.0	97308
30906	AUGUSTA	17372	21171	28.6	31.1	34.9	4.3	1.1	41434	45163	37	48	14246	15.1	43.5	39.7	1.2	0.4	82334
30907	AUGUSTA	32643	19395	9.2	19.2	47.1	15.4	9.1	70082	74405	87	89	14606	4.3	12.6	55.9	22.1	5.1	126421
30909	AUGUSTA	29112	17022	24.0	28.4	33.7	7.9	6.0	47217	51449	55	63	8872	8.9	16.3	51.1	20.6	3.0	120101
31001	ABBEVILLE	15742	821	36.8	29.7	28.9	3.4	1.2	34285	35212	16	22	651	41.0	34.1	20.9	4.0	0.0	58125
31002	ADRIAN	15564	1103	44.8	25.6	24.9	3.9	0.8	28071	29182	6	4	881	38.1	30.5	24.9	6.2	0.2	61382
31003	ALLENTOWN	23786	7	28.6	42.9	28.6	0.0	0.0	42248	42248	40	50	6	0.0	66.7	33.3	0.0	0.0	77500
31005	BONAIRE	30488	5231	6.0	15.6	52.7	15.7	10.1	74469	76240	89	91	4523	7.4	15.7	51.6	23.8	1.5	121900
31006	BUTLER	15124	1958	42.4	29.0	24.3	3.3	1.1	29563	30422	7	6	1447	34.7	32.1	24.6	7.9	0.7	66176
31007	BYROMVILLE	19406	367	40.6	26.7	24.0	1.1	7.6	31979	34088	11	14	272	27.6	44.5	22.1	5.5	0.4	66522
31008	BYRON	23218	7172	16.7	24.7	45.6	9.8	3.2	56721	58388	74	77	5713	13.8	24.9	42.9	17.0	1.4	105363
31009	CADWELL	17674	526	33.3	32.3	29.5	3.8	1.1	37693	39369	26	36	408	27.0	34.1	25.5	9.1	4.4	74615
31011	CHAUNCEY	15178	370	37.8	35.1	22.2	3.2	1.6	31304	31440	10	12	308	41.9	30.2	21.4	5.2	1.3	58621
31012	CHESTER	16246	522	34.5	30.3	30.7	2.7	1.9	34353	36191	16	23	425	32.0	33.9	26.4	6.6	1.2	71548
31014	COCHRAN	18841	4993	32.8	28.6	31.2	5.5	1.9	39143	39936	30	41	3811	31.5	24.0	34.4	8.9	1.2	81880
31015	CORDELE	16941	8106	42.3	25.3	25.3	4.9	2.1	31968	32972	11	14	4791	22.8	24.1	35.4	14.9	2.8	95476
31016	CULLODEN	20246	684	26.9	32.6	32.0	4.7	3.8	41662	45173	38	48	553	29.1	26.0	33.3	9.8	1.8	82083
31017	DANVILLE	18512	869	33.5	29.2	31.0	4.5	1.8	38680	39617	29	39	739	33.6	34.4	24.6	4.7	2.7	68443
31018	DAVISBORO	14815	498	34.9	27.9	30.3	3.8	3.0	37606	39474	26	36	398	26.9	34.4	28.9	8.5	1.3	80816
31019	DEXTER	20972	916	31.7	28.7	30.8	5.8	3.1	39176	41207	30	41	768	22.3	33.2	29.8	12.4	2.3	81064
31020	DRY BRANCH	18451	1068	29.9	27.6	35.1	6.0	1.4	42905	45882	42	52	880	39.0	35.8	22.7	2.4	0.1	62299
31021	DUBLIN	20166	10987	33.5	27.0	30.5	6.1	3.0	39403	41832	31	42	7147	17.9	21.2	40.3	18.2	2.4	106657
31022	DUDLEY	21808	514	26.1	21.8	43.8	6.2	2.1	51323	52454	64	71	437	13.3	22.0	41.4	21.3	2.1	107008
31023	EASTMAN	17985	5443	37.9	31.7	24.4	4.2	1.9	33088	33471	13	17	3769	35.1	25.5	26.4	10.7	2.3	72131
31024	EATONTON	22517	8227	27.9	29.4	32.8	6.3	3.6	42979	43162	42	53	6461	15.2	19.6	32.8	21.7	10.6	121928
31025	ELKO	18918	595	27.1	36.3	30.9	2.7	3.0	40149	42164	33	43	490	38.6	33.7	21.2	6.1	0.4	65102
31027	EAST DUBLIN	15850	3828	37.7	30.3	27.9	2.8	1.4	34948	37394	17	24	2877	33.4	29.3	30.3	6.3	0.7	71201
31028	CENTERVILLE	24790	2137	13.0	32.1	44.2	7.5	3.2	54033	57785	70	74	1598	11.8	44.6	39.1	4.1	0.4	86357
31029	FORSYTH	19936	5419	26.5	27.2	36.8	6.4	3.1	45999	50919	51	61	3957	27.1	32.2	31.3	8.5	1.0	78343
31030	FORT VALLEY	16606	6464	38.1	28.5	25.9	5.4	2.1	33656	36516	15	20	4095	18.4	26.1	41.8	13.0	0.7	97609
31031	GORDON	18627	2442	30.1	29.2	34.9	4.1	1.6	42760	44003	42	52	2010	31.1	30.4	30.2	7.2	1.1	74074
31032	GRAY	22580	4568	22.1	22.9	42.7	8.8	3.5	53679	55864	69	74	3882	22.8	24.5	38.3	13.4	0.9	93100
31033	HADDOCK	19724	1054	29.9	27.2	34.5	6.4	2.0	42014	46235	39	50	904	33.5	30.1	27.9	8.0	0.6	72963
31035	HARRISON	16852	505	37.0	24.2	31.9	5.5	1.4	36594	37603	22	32	412	36.7	28.2	26.5	7.5	1.2	66563
31036	HAWKINSVILLE	19397	4294	33.2	28.8	31.2	4.1	2.8	39701	41389	32	42	3211	23.5	24.1	35.6	15.1	1.7	93984
31037	HELENA	14523	663	42.4	31.8	21.1	3.2	1.5	29831	29550	8	7	501	44.9	31.9	18.8	3.8	0.6	53493
31038	HILLSBORO	21045	280	33.9	21.4	33.6	7.9	3.2	43400	48930	44	54	237	41.4	32.5	19.0	7.2	0.0	61250
31041	IDEAL	17644	388	44.3	20.6	27.8	2.8	4.4	29523	32004	7	6	318	47.2	24.2	24.5	3.5	0.6	52045
31042	IRWINTON	15913	671	39.2	27.9	27.0	4.2	1.8	32821	35748	13	16	521	35.9	30.1	26.5	6.3	1.2	69857
31044	JEFFERSONVILLE	16367	1207	40.9	23.9	27.5	5.5	2.2	33751	36629	15	20	957	38.9	33.6	23.8	3.0	0.6	63454
31045	JEWELL	20750	211	34.1	33.2	29.4	0.5	2.8	37727	38120	26	36	182	32.4	31.3	25.8	8.8	1.6	73125
31046	JULIETTE	26855	1223	14.5	19.4	47.8	12.8	5.6	66580	68291	85	86	1057	19.5	18.9	35.4	22.9	3.3	104709
31047	KATHLEEN	24749	3227	13.8	23.1	46.5	11.6	5.0	61693	62957	80	81	2865	12.2	28.5	41.5	16.0	1.8	99318
31049	KITE	17010	605	45.1	23.3	27.3	2.3	2.0	28532	29324	6	5	493	46.2	23.9	26.0	3.7	0.2	53776
31050	KNOXVILLE	18627	563	23.3	26.5	42.5	5.7	2.1	50119	50637	61	69	494	30.2	26.1	38.7	4.9	0.2	79756
31052	LIZELLA	23803	3185	17.5	24.5	44.0	11.4	2.6	57522	57212	75	78	2769	13.5	28.0	48.2	9.1	1.1	97663
31054	MC INTYRE	16404	615	35.6	27.5	32.8	3.3	0.8	34199	37140	16	22	498	33.1	26.9	29.7	10.2	0.0	75581
31055	MC RAE	16680	1981	38.2	29.8	25.7	4.2	2.0	33426	34023	14	18	1523	40.6	33.4	19.9	5.1	1.1	58295
31057	MARSHALLVILLE	15020	725	44.3	27.2	24.8	2.3	1.4	29554	33301	7	6	536	31.2	39.4	17.7	10.4	1.3	71571
31058	MAUK	16824	786	33.0	31.2	30.3	4.2	1.4	37423	40236	25	34	680	39.1	26.0	28.7	4.4	1.8	70185
31060	MILAN	17480	933	41.4	28.0	25.3	3.2	2.1	32736	34288	13	16	779	34.9	32.1	27.3	3.2	2.4	65732
31061	MILLEDGEVILLE	20649	15636	28.8	28.5	33.3	5.6	3.8	42775	43091	42	52	10205	18.0	21.1	38.4	19.2	3.3	107042
31063	MONTEZUMA	14090	2126	44.0	26.2	25.3	4.0	0.5	27795	28474	5	4	1436	29.5	35.3	28.3	5.7	1.1	74014
31064	MONTICELLO	22386	3719	24.4	25.4	40.8	6.5	2.9	50177	52987	62	69	2877	22.1	21.8	40.1	13.5	2.5	96698
31065	MONTROSE	18489	366	27.3	29.8	36.9	4.6	1.4	43682	46187	44	55	306	23.2	26.5	35.9	13.4	1.0	90714
31066	MUSELLA	19893	504	29.0	24.4	37.9	6.3	2.4	46614	48414	53	63	384	33.1	31.8	29.2	6.0	0.0	72308
31068	OGLETHORPE	14863	1317	42.6	27.6	24.8	3.3	1.7	30430	31980	9	10	978	45.8	25.7	24.7	3.1	0.7	54881
31069	PERRY	19846	6109	29.4	26.9	36.4	4.9	2.4	43104	47357	43	53	3998	21.0	29.8	38.6	9.7	0.9	88925
31070	PINEHURST	18997	329	37.1	22.5	37.1	2.1	1.2	36986	39550	24	33	252	34.1	27.8	29.0	7.9	1.2	71500
31071	PINEVIEW	17016	282	38.3	27.0	30.1	2.1	2.5	33893	34833	15	21	238	36.6	25.2	28.2	10.1	0.0	77778
31072	PITTS	17344	546	35.7	34.6	22.9	6.0	0.7	33566	33483	15	19	448	38.2	36.8	15.8	9.2	0.0	59298
31075	RENTZ	18422	739	30.7	33.3	31.3	3.5	1.2	39181	41303	30	41	621	27.5	33.5	28.8	9.5	0.6	76277
31076	REYNOLDS	16126	1170	43.0	28.9	22.7	4.0	1.4	30420	31143	9	9	920	29.9	28.7	34.8	5.5	1.1	74773
31077	RHINE	19009	337	42.7	24.3	26.7	4.5	1.8	30990	33207	10	12	283	42.4	24.4	26.9	6.4	0.0	58958
31078	ROBERTA	16782	1184	38.1	27.7	28.1	4.5	1.6	35219	38861	18	26	919	39.9	33.0	21.1	5.0	1.0	62403
31079	ROCHELLE	17327	1185	40.8	25.9	27.3	3.3	2.7	32951	34579	13	17	904	43.0	25.7	25.0	6.1	0.2	63111
31081	RUPERT	18442	98	39.8	25.5	28.6	3.1	3.1	34286	36170	16	23	84	46.4	20.2	25.0	4.8	3.6	70000
31082	SANDERSVILLE	18978	3990	35.6	26.3	29.5	6.5	2.2	36482	37165	22	31	2858	28.7	27.1	27.8	14.9	1.6	79954
31085	SHADY DALE	17260	405	20.2	36.0	38.8	3.2	1.7	46966	49581	54	63	324	19.1	25.0	44.8	9.9	1.2	94872
31087	SPARTA	13968	3184	47.3	29.8	19.6	2.5	0.8	26473	26973	4	3	2385	39.6	31.1	22.1	6.2	1.0	64524
31088	WARNER ROBINS	26614	18802	13.6	23.4	47.2	11.0	4.8	61925	63926	80	82	12801	10.3	24.9	55.3	9.1	0.4	101078
31089	TENNILLE	15744	1817	43.7	24.8	25.9	3.6	2.0	30480	33657	9	10	1267	42.2	23.4	24.3	9.4	0.7	59949
31090	TOOMSBORO	16089	428	39.5	23.6	32.5	3.7	0.7	33944	37046	15	22	337	40.9	31.8	25.2	1.8	0.3	66905
31091	UNADILLA	15066	1074	43.9	30.2	21.9	3.0	1.0	30362	30979	9	9	758	30.6	35.4	28.9	5.0	0.1	66914
31092	VIENNA	17507	2149	36.1	28.1	30.0	3.9	2.0	35809	36934	20	28	1497	27.5	30.2	30.9	10.3	1.2	75786
31093	WARNER ROBINS	20594	11271	28.0	29.2	36.5	4.4	1.8	42046	47375	39	50	6309	19.3	47.1	31.1	2.2	0.3	75786
31094	WARTHEN	17685	482	38.0	22.8	33.0	5.8	0.4	36821	37600	23	32	391	35.5	19.7	28.9	15.3	0.5	77188
31096	WRIGHTSVILLE	14684	2241	45.2	27.3	23.0	3.6	0.8	27896	28326	5	4	1721	44.0	27.1	22.0	6.3	0.6	55535
31097	YATESVILLE	19527	499	27.1	25.7	42.3	3.2	1.8	47748	49725	56	64	419	17.4	25.8	40.3	14.8	1.7	100174
31098	WARNER ROBINS	14356	1147	14.4	42.5	39.1	3.2	0.8	44913	49746	48	58	79	30.4	39.2	30.4	0.0	0.0	72083
31201	MACON	13104	3927	64.0	22.9	10.3	1.9	0.9	16643	17472	1	0	839	52.1	26.0	12.6	8.5	0.8	48577
31204	MACON	20276	13971	38.2	25.8	27.8	4.8	3.4	33982	37556	15	22	7180	21.5	41.2	32.1	4.5	0.7	77199
31206	MACON	14388	10695	42.0	29.8	25.3	2.2	0.7	30618	32890	9	10	5446	39.6	52.1	8.0	0.1	0.1	56272
31210	MACON	34910	12162	12.8	19.6	42.7	13.2	11.7	68755	70514	86	88	7964	3.1	14.4	49.5	26.8	6.2	133211
31211	MACON	24795	7078	24.3	26.6	37.6	6.9	4.7	49191	52382	59	67	4551	19.4	36.4	34.8	8.3	1.1	84266
	GEORGIA	26980		20.7	23.1	36.8	11.7	7.7	56761	58593				13.2	17.9	39.1	24.2	5.5	121444
	UNITED STATES	27277		20.9	24.4	35.3	11.7	7.6	54719	56938				9.3	13.1	31.6	32.6	13.5	162279

ZIP CODE #	POST OFFICE NAME	FINANCIAL SERVICES: Auto Loan	Home Loan	Invest-ments	Retire-ment Plans	THE HOME: Home Improvements: Home Repair	Lawn & Garden	Furnishings: Comput-ers & Hard-ware-Personal	Major Appli-ances	TV, Radio, Sound Equip-ment	Furni-ture	ENTERTAINMENT: Dine out/ Carry out	Sports Equip-ment	Fees & Tickets	Toys & Games	Travel	Cable TV	PERSONAL: Apparel & Services	Auto Repairs	Health Insur-ance	Pets & Supplies
30820	MITCHELL	80	56	81	54	58	81	58	74	65	54	64	56	46	65	57	72	42	68	77	88
30821	NORWOOD	79	51	76	48	51	77	55	69	63	52	62	54	41	64	51	71	41	65	73	85
30822	PERKINS	69	49	60	47	48	67	51	60	57	49	56	47	40	59	47	63	37	57	64	74
30823	STAPLETON	80	54	74	51	54	78	57	70	65	55	64	55	44	67	53	72	42	66	74	86
30824	THOMSON	83	64	70	63	63	79	68	74	74	66	73	56	59	75	63	79	49	73	80	90
30828	WARRENTON	75	50	70	47	50	73	53	66	61	51	59	51	40	62	49	67	39	62	69	81
30830	WAYNESBORO	67	54	55	55	52	64	58	60	64	58	63	46	53	64	54	68	43	61	66	74
30833	WRENS	67	52	58	50	50	65	54	60	60	53	59	46	47	60	51	64	39	59	65	74
30901	AUGUSTA	40	30	29	32	29	36	39	35	44	38	43	27	35	42	34	47	30	40	43	45
30904	AUGUSTA	68	60	57	62	59	65	68	64	71	66	71	49	65	70	63	74	49	68	71	78
30905	AUGUSTA	93	50	37	57	44	43	88	61	83	82	87	61	67	99	64	76	61	78	56	75
30906	AUGUSTA	70	66	57	66	62	68	66	66	69	67	69	50	65	70	63	71	47	67	71	80
30907	AUGUSTA	119	129	116	131	125	119	121	119	117	125	119	93	127	121	123	115	84	117	114	139
30909	AUGUSTA	96	80	75	83	78	81	93	85	94	92	94	67	86	95	85	94	65	91	88	103
31001	ABBEVILLE	78	51	76	48	51	77	55	69	63	52	62	54	41	64	51	70	41	65	73	85
31002	ADRIAN	70	47	69	45	48	70	50	63	57	47	56	48	38	57	48	63	37	59	66	77
31003	ALLENTOWN	85	61	87	59	63	86	62	79	69	58	68	60	50	69	62	76	45	73	83	94
31005	BONAIRE	124	140	121	139	135	124	122	125	117	130	119	98	130	123	126	113	84	118	113	143
31006	BUTLER	71	48	70	46	49	70	50	64	57	47	56	49	39	57	48	63	37	59	67	77
31007	BYROMVILLE	105	68	101	64	68	103	73	92	84	69	82	72	55	86	68	94	54	86	97	113
31008	BYRON	99	96	83	93	92	92	89	92	89	93	90	69	86	94	86	89	62	89	89	108
31009	CADWELL	78	56	72	55	57	77	58	71	64	55	63	54	47	66	55	71	42	66	74	85
31011	CHAUNCEY	75	49	70	47	49	73	52	65	60	50	59	51	40	61	49	67	39	62	69	80
31012	CHESTER	83	56	78	53	56	81	59	73	67	56	66	57	45	68	55	74	44	69	77	89
31014	COCHRAN	83	63	75	61	63	82	65	75	71	63	70	57	54	73	61	77	47	72	79	91
31015	CORDELE	70	54	61	54	54	67	59	64	65	57	63	48	51	64	55	69	43	64	69	77
31016	CULLODEN	97	72	95	69	73	97	73	89	81	70	79	67	60	81	70	88	53	83	93	107
31017	DANVILLE	84	57	80	54	57	83	60	75	68	57	67	58	46	70	56	76	44	70	79	91
31018	DAVISBORO	87	56	84	53	56	85	60	76	70	57	68	59	45	71	56	78	45	72	80	94
31019	DEXTER	92	66	84	64	67	90	69	83	76	66	75	63	55	78	65	83	50	77	87	100
31020	DRY BRANCH	85	64	77	61	63	83	65	76	73	64	71	58	54	74	61	79	48	73	81	93
31021	DUBLIN	78	68	67	68	68	77	70	73	74	70	73	54	66	75	67	78	50	73	78	88
31022	DUDLEY	87	77	79	79	78	92	76	86	79	70	78	65	69	81	75	84	53	80	89	101
31023	EASTMAN	76	54	66	53	54	74	58	68	66	56	64	52	47	66	54	72	43	65	73	82
31024	EATONTON	93	73	103	71	77	95	74	90	80	71	78	67	64	78	76	85	52	85	92	106
31025	ELKO	92	66	80	64	66	89	69	81	77	67	75	62	55	79	63	84	50	77	85	99
31027	EAST DUBLIN	74	53	67	50	52	71	56	65	62	54	61	51	45	64	52	67	41	63	69	80
31028	CENTERVILLE	95	97	80	94	92	89	90	90	88	94	89	69	89	93	87	87	62	88	86	106
31029	FORSYTH	87	79	74	77	77	84	76	81	80	78	80	59	72	82	73	83	54	79	84	97
31030	FORT VALLEY	70	58	60	57	56	68	60	64	66	60	65	48	55	66	57	70	44	64	70	78
31031	GORDON	84	62	76	60	62	82	64	75	71	62	69	57	52	72	60	77	46	72	79	91
31032	GRAY	95	88	84	88	87	96	84	92	87	83	87	69	80	90	83	91	59	87	93	109
31033	HADDOCK	85	70	74	67	69	82	68	77	74	69	73	58	60	76	65	78	49	74	79	93
31035	HARRISON	85	55	82	52	55	83	59	75	68	56	67	58	44	70	55	76	44	70	79	92
31036	HAWKINSVILLE	84	65	77	64	65	84	67	78	74	64	72	59	57	74	64	80	48	74	84	94
31037	HELENA	70	46	68	44	46	69	50	62	57	47	55	48	37	58	46	63	37	58	66	76
31038	HILLSBORO	99	70	86	67	70	95	73	87	82	71	80	67	58	84	67	89	54	82	91	106
31041	IDEAL	82	53	79	50	53	80	57	72	66	54	64	56	43	67	53	73	42	67	76	88
31042	IRWINTON	80	52	77	49	52	78	56	70	64	53	63	55	42	65	52	71	41	66	74	86
31044	JEFFERSONVILLE	82	53	79	50	53	80	57	72	66	54	64	56	43	67	53	73	43	68	76	88
31045	JEWELL	93	60	89	57	60	91	65	81	75	61	73	64	48	76	60	83	48	77	86	100
31046	JULIETTE	108	114	100	112	110	107	101	105	101	106	102	80	104	105	103	101	71	101	101	124
31047	KATHLEEN	104	110	94	109	106	104	99	102	98	103	99	79	101	102	100	97	68	98	98	120
31049	KITE	76	50	73	47	50	74	53	67	61	50	59	52	40	62	50	68	39	63	71	82
31050	KNOXVILLE	87	80	71	77	78	82	75	80	78	78	78	58	71	81	72	80	53	77	80	95
31052	LIZELLA	93	96	87	97	95	100	88	94	90	88	90	71	90	92	91	92	62	90	96	110
31054	MC INTYRE	78	56	78	54	57	78	57	72	64	54	63	54	46	64	56	70	42	67	75	86
31055	MC RAE	77	52	75	49	53	77	56	70	64	52	62	54	43	64	53	71	41	66	75	85
31057	MARSHALLVILLE	69	45	67	43	45	68	48	61	56	46	55	48	36	57	45	62	36	57	64	75
31058	MAUK	74	59	65	57	58	70	60	67	63	59	63	51	52	65	56	67	42	64	68	80
31060	MILAN	77	51	75	49	52	76	54	69	62	51	61	53	42	63	52	69	40	64	72	84
31061	MILLEDGEVILLE	82	71	71	71	70	78	77	77	79	74	79	59	70	80	71	82	54	78	80	92
31063	MONTEZUMA	64	47	56	46	46	63	50	58	58	49	56	43	43	57	47	63	38	57	64	70
31064	MONTICELLO	98	79	90	79	80	101	81	94	86	75	85	71	70	88	78	93	57	88	98	111
31065	MONTROSE	86	65	77	62	64	82	66	77	72	65	71	58	55	74	62	78	48	73	79	93
31066	MUSELLA	91	66	89	64	67	90	68	83	75	65	74	63	55	75	66	82	49	78	87	100
31068	OGLETHORPE	72	48	67	46	48	70	52	63	60	50	59	49	41	61	48	67	39	61	69	78
31069	PERRY	74	72	64	73	70	73	72	72	73	72	73	55	71	74	70	75	51	72	74	85
31070	PINEHURST	82	54	77	51	54	80	58	72	66	55	65	56	44	68	54	74	43	68	76	88
31071	PINEVIEW	84	55	81	52	55	82	59	74	68	56	66	58	44	69	55	75	44	70	78	91
31072	PITTS	76	52	76	50	53	76	55	69	62	51	60	53	42	62	53	68	40	64	72	83
31075	RENTZ	82	59	68	57	59	78	61	71	68	60	67	55	49	71	56	74	45	68	75	87
31076	REYNOLDS	73	48	70	45	48	71	51	64	58	48	57	50	38	59	48	65	38	60	68	79
31077	RHINE	80	55	80	53	57	80	58	73	65	54	64	56	45	65	56	72	42	68	77	88
31078	ROBERTA	78	54	75	51	54	77	56	70	64	54	63	54	44	65	53	71	42	66	73	85
31079	ROCHELLE	80	55	79	52	56	80	57	72	65	54	64	55	44	65	55	72	42	67	76	88
31081	RUPERT	74	53	76	51	55	75	54	69	60	50	59	52	43	60	54	66	39	63	72	82
31082	SANDERSVILLE	79	61	72	60	61	79	64	73	71	63	70	54	55	71	60	77	47	71	79	88
31085	SHADY DALE	90	69	74	67	68	85	70	79	76	69	75	60	59	79	64	82	51	76	83	96
31087	SPARTA	61	43	55	42	43	60	47	55	54	46	52	41	39	53	44	59	35	53	60	67
31088	WARNER ROBINS	102	101	86	101	96	92	100	96	98	103	99	76	99	102	96	95	69	96	92	112
31089	TENNILLE	77	51	73	48	50	75	54	68	63	52	61	53	41	64	51	70	41	64	72	83
31090	TOOMSBORO	78	51	76	48	51	77	55	69	63	52	61	54	41	64	51	70	41	65	73	85
31091	UNADILLA	72	47	69	44	47	70	50	63	58	47	56	49	37	59	47	64	37	59	67	77
31092	VIENNA	82	58	71	56	57	79	62	72	69	59	67	56	49	71	56	76	45	69	77	88
31093	WARNER ROBINS	73	69	58	69	65	68	71	68	72	71	72	53	69	74	67	73	50	70	71	82
31094	WARTHEN	82	56	77	53	56	80	59	72	67	57	66	56	46	68	55	74	44	68	76	89
31096	WRIGHTSVILLE	69	45	67	43	45	68	48	61	56	46	55	48	36	57	45	62	36	57	64	75
31097	YATESVILLE	92	66	77	64	65	87	68	80	76	67	74	61	55	79	62	83	50	76	84	97
31098	WARNER ROBINS	87	49	38	55	45	43	82	59	78	77	81	57	64	92	61	72	57	73	54	72
31201	MACON	38	27	27	30	26	32	39	33	42	37	41	26	34	40	32	44	29	38	39	42
31204	MACON	67	59	57	61	58	65	65	63	71	66	70	47	63	69	62	74	48	67	72	77
31206	MACON	56	48	42	49	45	52	54	50	58	53	57	38	51	57	49	60	39	54	57	63
31210	MACON	122	125	120	129	123	118	125	119	121	127	123	94	128	123	124	119	87	121	115	140
31211	MACON	88	79	80	80	78	87	83	84	86	81	86	64	79	86	80	90	59	85	91	102
	GEORGIA	110	101	97	102	98	103	103	103	104	104	104	80	99	107	99	105	73	103	103	122
	UNITED STATES	100	100	100	100	100	100	100	100	100	100	100	100	100	100	100	100	100	100	100	100

POPULATION CHANGE

ZIP CODE #	POST OFFICE NAME	COUNTY FIPS CODE	POPULATION 2000	POPULATION 2009	POPULATION 2014	2000-2009 ANNUAL RATE % Rate	2000-2009 ANNUAL RATE State Centile	HOUSEHOLDS 2000	HOUSEHOLDS 2009	HOUSEHOLDS 2014	HOUSEHOLDS % Annual Rate 2000-2009	HOUSEHOLDS 2009 Average HH Size	FAMILIES 2000	FAMILIES 2009	FAMILIES % Annual Rate 2000-2009
31216	MACON	021	14656	16886	17731	1.5	60	5196	6070	6416	1.7	2.58	4055	4592	1.4
31217	MACON	289	20391	19681	19407	-0.4	9	7194	6995	6925	-0.3	2.73	5298	4987	-0.7
31220	MACON	021	11153	12105	12506	0.9	45	4144	4560	4738	1.0	2.63	3172	3376	0.7
31301	ALLENHURST	179	4651	5341	5618	1.5	60	1617	1867	1969	1.6	2.84	1157	1289	1.2
31302	BLOOMINGDALE	051	8437	10147	11343	2.0	70	3090	3799	4275	2.3	2.67	2390	2852	1.9
31303	CLYO	103	1976	2347	2679	1.9	68	695	852	979	2.2	2.75	540	643	1.9
31304	CRESCENT	191	1896	1962	1989	0.4	28	717	757	773	0.6	2.59	508	518	0.2
31305	DARIEN	191	4485	4685	4814	0.5	31	1691	1815	1875	0.8	2.52	1202	1244	0.4
31308	ELLABELL	029	6282	8058	8925	2.7	79	2222	2913	3257	3.0	2.75	1736	2205	2.6
31309	FLEMING	179	754	768	824	0.2	22	271	290	314	0.7	2.51	201	208	0.4
31312	GUYTON	103	11374	17054	20409	4.5	93	3938	6005	7216	4.7	2.83	3165	4712	4.4
31313	HINESVILLE	179	35851	37020	37667	0.3	25	12398	12875	13114	0.4	2.87	9456	9538	0.1
31314	FORT STEWART	179	3700	3585	3652	-0.3	11	184	197	203	0.7	2.55	176	188	0.7
31315	FORT STEWART	179	9576	9277	9446	-0.3	11	2262	2425	2504	0.8	2.75	2194	2343	0.7
31316	LUDOWICI	183	8662	9972	10668	1.5	60	3018	3403	3626	1.3	2.91	2276	2494	1.0
31319	MERIDIAN	191	198	213	221	0.8	41	76	84	87	1.1	2.54	56	59	0.6
31320	MIDWAY	179	7143	7538	7835	0.6	34	2649	2853	2979	0.8	2.60	1947	2027	0.4
31321	PEMBROKE	029	5727	7487	8506	2.9	82	2026	2706	3095	3.2	2.76	1566	2023	2.8
31322	POOLER	051	6475	12486	14687	7.4	98	2333	4614	5510	7.7	2.60	1851	3482	7.1
31323	RICEBORO	179	1582	1624	1677	0.3	25	560	587	609	0.5	2.77	417	422	0.1
31324	RICHMOND HILL	029	14502	21099	24794	4.1	91	4940	7335	8682	4.4	2.87	4064	5900	4.1
31326	RINCON	103	12277	18819	22680	4.7	94	4313	6669	8079	4.8	2.82	3473	5242	4.6
31328	TYBEE ISLAND	051	3696	4093	4302	1.1	49	1704	1926	2049	1.3	2.02	1003	1062	0.6
31329	SPRINGFIELD	103	6925	9095	10681	3.0	83	2397	3220	3812	3.2	2.77	1881	2459	2.9
31331	TOWNSEND	191	4268	5177	5569	2.1	72	1718	2157	2346	2.5	2.39	1248	1517	2.1
31401	SAVANNAH	051	21769	22477	22975	0.3	25	9026	9508	9823	0.6	2.14	4044	3953	-0.2
31404	SAVANNAH	051	32048	32765	33326	0.2	22	11977	12347	12634	0.3	2.58	7912	7724	-0.3
31405	SAVANNAH	051	31454	35587	37060	1.3	54	11871	13172	13831	1.1	2.42	7671	8252	0.8
31406	SAVANNAH	051	34463	35256	35855	0.2	22	13433	13848	14195	0.3	2.44	9189	9043	-0.2
31407	SAVANNAH	051	3306	3509	3782	0.6	34	1298	1420	1585	1.0	2.14	907	944	0.4
31408	SAVANNAH	051	10346	11838	12389	1.5	60	3607	4085	4268	1.4	2.68	2430	2615	0.8
31409	SAVANNAH	051	1308	716	730	-6.3	0	161	10	11	-25.9	2.60	157	10	-25.7
31410	SAVANNAH	051	22165	24411	25687	1.0	47	8721	9832	10432	1.3	2.48	6316	6817	0.8
31411	SAVANNAH	051	6958	7963	8492	1.5	60	3207	3788	4076	1.8	2.10	2714	3127	1.5
31415	SAVANNAH	051	13506	14008	14134	0.4	28	5036	5130	5214	0.2	2.68	3416	3306	-0.4
31419	SAVANNAH	051	40953	47282	50351	1.6	63	16149	18925	20269	1.7	2.47	10817	12208	1.3
31501	WAYCROSS	299	14546	14280	14177	-0.2	13	6031	6033	6030	0.0	2.28	3869	3703	-0.5
31503	WAYCROSS	299	20878	21542	21758	0.3	25	7444	7819	7966	0.5	2.51	5403	5480	0.2
31510	ALMA	005	8725	9218	9390	0.6	34	3313	3514	3609	0.6	2.53	2430	2497	0.3
31512	AMBROSE	069	2322	2625	2756	1.3	54	875	1004	1059	1.5	2.61	659	734	1.2
31513	BAXLEY	001	15380	15921	16166	0.4	28	5799	6058	6176	0.5	2.58	4263	4315	0.1
31516	BLACKSHEAR	229	11964	13634	14613	1.4	57	4575	5343	5773	1.7	2.53	3400	3851	1.4
31518	BRISTOL	001	704	751	789	0.7	37	285	311	329	0.9	2.41	213	226	0.6
31519	BROXTON	069	3588	4050	4244	1.3	54	1361	1558	1642	1.5	2.59	997	1105	1.1
31520	BRUNSWICK	127	21796	22031	22391	0.1	19	8576	8682	8865	0.1	2.45	5431	5192	-0.5
31522	SAINT SIMONS ISLAND	127	14366	16427	17709	1.5	60	6579	7489	8080	1.4	2.18	4130	4473	0.9
31523	BRUNSWICK	127	8798	11605	13014	3.0	83	3334	4416	4973	3.1	2.63	2621	3336	2.6
31525	BRUNSWICK	127	21390	26678	29457	2.4	75	8077	10112	11215	2.5	2.59	5784	6986	2.1
31527	JEKYLL ISLAND	127	950	960	988	0.1	19	488	496	511	0.2	1.94	327	310	-0.6
31532	DENTON	161	680	690	701	0.2	22	249	259	265	0.4	2.66	189	191	0.1
31533	DOUGLAS	069	14957	15869	16122	0.6	34	5527	5855	5961	0.6	2.63	3884	3974	0.2
31535	DOUGLAS	069	10225	10685	10815	0.5	31	3621	3799	3861	0.5	2.76	2759	2807	0.2
31537	FOLKSTON	049	8183	8592	8671	0.5	31	2572	2703	2752	0.5	2.68	1909	1944	0.2
31539	HAZLEHURST	161	12183	12731	13024	0.5	31	4644	4955	5104	0.7	2.55	3451	3570	0.4
31542	HOBOKEN	025	2566	2603	2595	0.2	22	956	1002	1009	0.5	2.60	754	772	0.3
31543	HORTENSE	305	2654	2881	2986	0.9	45	982	1105	1160	1.3	2.60	745	815	1.0
31544	JACKSONVILLE	271	782	726	704	-0.8	2	322	309	303	-0.4	2.35	224	207	-0.8
31545	JESUP	305	14248	15576	16343	1.0	47	5311	5910	6245	1.2	2.60	3984	4298	0.8
31546	JESUP	305	7009	7773	7961	1.1	49	2049	2203	2295	0.8	2.51	1469	1528	0.4
31547	KINGS BAY	039	1329	1310	1277	-0.2	13	239	208	199	-1.5	3.16	237	206	-1.5
31548	KINGSLAND	039	15051	19769	21453	3.0	83	5223	6855	7464	3.0	2.88	4015	5150	2.7
31549	LUMBER CITY	271	1799	1667	1616	-0.8	2	706	672	657	-0.5	2.36	468	428	-1.0
31550	MANOR	299	808	903	938	1.2	52	313	356	373	1.4	2.48	244	269	1.1
31551	MERSHON	229	1025	1100	1155	0.8	41	363	397	422	1.0	2.72	277	296	0.7
31552	MILLWOOD	299	829	837	841	0.1	19	303	314	318	0.4	2.65	240	242	0.1
31553	NAHUNTA	025	3638	4555	4964	2.5	77	1361	1779	1964	2.9	2.52	1015	1289	2.6
31554	NICHOLLS	069	5835	7030	7293	2.0	70	1814	2067	2176	1.4	2.62	1363	1507	1.1
31555	ODUM	305	2680	2879	3004	0.8	41	949	1043	1097	1.0	2.58	722	769	0.7
31557	PATTERSON	229	2661	3355	3705	2.5	77	1018	1317	1468	2.8	2.54	752	942	2.5
31558	SAINT MARYS	039	19345	21270	22533	1.0	47	6336	7019	7469	1.1	2.84	4949	5339	0.8
31560	SCREVEN	305	2307	3417	3961	4.3	92	892	1353	1578	4.6	2.52	672	992	4.3
31561	SEA ISLAND	127	319	341	359	0.7	37	174	187	198	0.8	1.82	124	124	0.0
31562	SAINT GEORGE	049	2287	2398	2444	0.5	31	835	892	915	0.7	2.69	642	667	0.4
31563	SURRENCY	001	1179	1187	1206	0.1	19	468	478	488	0.2	2.46	343	338	-0.2
31565	WAVERLY	039	1505	1903	2095	2.6	78	599	774	857	2.8	2.46	435	542	2.4
31566	WAYNESVILLE	025	4291	4656	4789	0.9	45	1548	1726	1794	1.2	2.70	1195	1298	0.9
31567	WEST GREEN	069	866	977	1025	1.3	54	325	373	392	1.5	2.62	244	273	1.2
31568	WHITE OAK	039	1182	1385	1495	1.7	66	426	505	548	1.9	2.73	323	372	1.5
31569	WOODBINE	039	4945	4844	4814	-0.2	13	1776	1763	1760	-0.1	2.68	1334	1281	-0.4
31601	VALDOSTA	185	31038	31810	32510	0.3	25	11461	12202	12606	0.7	2.55	7514	7608	0.1
31602	VALDOSTA	185	29010	32543	34242	1.3	54	10659	12226	13007	1.5	2.38	6691	7360	1.0
31605	VALDOSTA	185	14639	13499	20381	2.6	78	5249	6900	7707	3.0	2.51	4040	5106	2.6
31606	VALDOSTA	185	3454	3840	4055	1.2	52	1253	1467	1570	1.7	2.61	983	1106	1.3
31620	ADEL	075	10312	10560	10683	0.3	25	3841	4005	4075	0.5	2.58	2782	2802	0.1
31622	ALAPAHA	019	1528	1584	1601	0.4	28	604	643	655	0.7	2.46	450	464	0.3
31623	ARGYLE	065	151	148	145	-0.2	13	49	49	49	0.0	2.82	38	38	0.0
31624	AXSON	003	1310	1449	1513	1.1	49	467	521	545	1.2	2.78	363	393	0.9
31625	BARNEY	027	1124	1112	1099	-0.1	14	423	431	430	0.2	2.52	322	318	-0.1
31626	BOSTON	275	3292	3502	3575	0.7	37	1270	1385	1425	0.9	2.51	913	961	0.6
31629	DIXIE	027	1126	1166	1171	0.4	28	406	433	438	0.7	2.69	298	307	0.3
31630	DU PONT	065	658	626	604	-0.5	7	242	237	231	-0.2	2.59	190	182	-0.5
31631	FARGO	065	527	505	488	-0.5	7	205	202	197	-0.2	2.50	151	144	-0.5
31632	HAHIRA	185	6749	8651	9500	2.7	79	2462	3204	3551	2.9	2.69	1873	2316	2.3
31634	HOMERVILLE	065	5544	5502	5383	-0.1	14	2017	2056	2028	0.2	2.51	1444	1425	-0.1
31635	LAKELAND	173	4971	5404	5679	0.9	45	1799	1998	2116	1.1	2.57	1313	1409	0.8
	GEORGIA					2.1					2.1	2.65			1.8
	UNITED STATES					1.0					1.1	2.59			0.9

ZIP CODE		RACE (%)						% Hispanic Origin		2009 AGE DISTRIBUTION (%)										MEDIAN AGE		
#	POST OFFICE NAME	White 2000	White 2009	Black 2000	Black 2009	Asian/Pacific 2000	Asian/Pacific 2009	2000	2009	0-4	5-9	10-14	15-19	20-24	25-44	45-64	65-84	85+	18+	2009	% 2009 Males	% 2009 Females
31216	MACON	85.4	77.9	12.4	18.7	0.5	0.7	1.5	2.4	5.8	6.1	6.4	6.1	4.7	28.0	29.1	12.3	1.4	77.8	40.5	52.5	47.5
31217	MACON	36.5	32.3	62.0	65.9	0.3	0.4	1.0	1.1	7.6	7.4	7.5	8.1	6.6	23.9	26.0	10.9	2.0	72.5	35.9	46.4	53.6
31220	MACON	82.3	73.6	14.9	22.6	1.4	1.9	1.2	1.9	7.1	7.3	7.4	6.1	4.5	28.7	28.7	8.8	1.3	74.1	38.0	47.9	52.1
31301	ALLENHURST	48.4	42.4	45.6	49.5	1.1	1.3	4.8	6.6	12.0	9.6	7.5	7.2	11.9	31.8	15.7	3.9	0.4	66.8	25.9	49.8	50.2
31302	BLOOMINGDALE	92.6	89.3	5.2	7.4	0.4	0.5	1.1	1.7	6.9	7.1	7.1	6.7	5.4	27.2	29.1	9.6	0.9	74.8	37.9	50.7	49.3
31303	CLYO	71.3	65.1	26.6	32.0	0.3	0.4	0.8	1.0	6.9	7.0	7.0	6.9	5.7	27.1	28.8	9.5	1.1	74.8	37.0	49.3	50.7
31304	CRESCENT	45.4	37.9	52.6	59.7	0.3	0.3	0.6	0.7	6.8	7.0	7.3	7.6	6.1	23.2	29.1	11.6	1.2	74.3	38.4	49.0	51.0
31305	DARIEN	64.5	57.2	33.5	40.2	0.5	0.6	1.2	1.5	6.9	7.7	7.2	8.9	6.0	25.1	26.5	10.2	1.5	72.0	35.4	49.4	50.6
31308	ELLABELL	83.3	78.4	15.0	19.3	0.2	0.3	0.8	1.1	7.3	7.1	7.0	7.1	6.8	27.4	27.4	9.1	0.8	74.3	35.5	50.4	49.6
31309	FLEMING	42.3	35.3	52.3	57.8	1.1	1.3	4.0	5.3	7.8	7.0	6.4	7.6	9.5	28.6	23.7	8.1	1.3	73.8	32.2	49.2	50.8
31312	GUYTON	88.4	85.4	9.5	11.8	0.3	0.4	1.3	1.9	7.7	7.9	8.0	6.9	5.4	29.0	26.7	7.7	0.8	72.1	35.6	50.2	49.8
31313	HINESVILLE	43.8	37.4	44.4	47.0	2.7	3.3	8.6	11.9	11.0	9.0	7.4	7.6	11.0	33.0	17.0	3.6	0.3	68.3	26.7	49.6	50.4
31314	FORT STEWART	50.0	42.4	36.8	39.4	2.2	2.8	12.0	16.8	14.4	9.5	6.0	9.3	26.4	32.6	1.5	0.2	0.0	68.1	22.0	61.6	38.4
31315	FORT STEWART	49.6	42.2	37.0	39.5	2.2	2.8	12.1	17.0	14.5	9.5	6.0	9.3	26.6	32.6	1.3	0.1	0.0	68.0	22.0	61.7	38.3
31316	LUDOWICI	68.9	63.3	23.3	26.2	0.9	1.1	9.4	12.7	10.9	10.0	8.4	7.1	7.0	31.4	19.2	5.5	0.5	66.9	28.6	50.9	49.1
31319	MERIDIAN	63.6	55.9	34.3	41.3	0.5	0.5	1.5	1.9	7.0	8.5	6.6	7.5	5.6	26.3	29.1	8.0	1.4	73.2	35.2	48.8	51.2
31320	MIDWAY	66.4	60.6	30.4	35.1	0.7	1.0	1.6	2.4	6.3	6.2	6.2	6.8	6.6	26.1	29.3	11.3	1.2	77.0	39.4	49.9	50.1
31321	PEMBROKE	77.8	72.4	20.5	25.1	0.3	0.5	1.0	1.5	7.6	7.1	6.8	7.2	8.0	26.8	26.2	9.2	1.0	74.3	34.2	49.0	51.0
31322	POOLER	88.1	79.0	7.9	15.4	1.8	2.2	1.3	2.4	7.3	7.1	7.0	6.9	5.3	30.9	25.3	8.9	1.1	74.2	35.8	50.2	49.8
31323	RICEBORO	12.5	9.9	87.0	89.5	0.1	0.1	0.8	0.8	6.2	7.0	7.8	7.6	6.9	23.3	28.5	11.3	1.6	74.8	39.0	49.0	51.0
31324	RICHMOND HILL	85.6	81.8	10.6	12.9	1.2	1.6	2.6	3.8	7.7	8.0	8.2	7.6	5.9	28.4	26.0	7.0	1.1	71.1	34.8	49.4	50.6
31326	RINCON	86.1	81.7	10.7	13.8	0.9	1.2	2.0	3.0	8.4	7.8	7.5	6.9	5.8	31.2	24.8	7.0	0.7	72.0	33.5	49.2	50.8
31328	TYBEE ISLAND	96.2	93.9	1.7	3.0	0.8	1.2	1.4	2.2	2.6	3.0	3.5	3.4	3.0	20.0	41.6	20.0	2.9	88.7	52.9	48.6	51.4
31329	SPRINGFIELD	73.9	68.3	24.4	29.5	0.2	0.2	1.2	1.6	7.5	7.5	7.3	7.5	5.9	27.2	26.4	9.2	1.5	72.9	35.7	48.9	51.1
31331	TOWNSEND	65.0	60.3	33.4	37.6	0.2	0.3	0.8	1.2	5.5	6.0	6.4	6.5	4.3	21.4	33.1	15.3	1.4	77.9	44.9	49.8	50.2
31401	SAVANNAH	32.1	26.4	64.7	69.4	1.4	1.9	1.5	2.0	6.5	6.3	5.7	9.2	13.5	26.7	20.9	9.5	1.8	78.0	29.8	48.5	51.5
31404	SAVANNAH	30.0	22.1	66.4	73.7	2.0	2.3	1.0	1.2	7.5	7.5	7.2	8.3	8.2	25.9	23.6	9.8	2.0	73.4	33.2	46.2	53.8
31405	SAVANNAH	46.1	40.1	50.9	55.7	0.7	1.1	2.1	3.3	6.4	6.1	6.0	7.4	8.9	28.1	23.7	10.9	2.6	77.3	35.5	50.6	49.4
31406	SAVANNAH	65.4	55.6	29.9	38.4	2.1	2.6	2.6	3.5	6.5	6.4	6.6	7.2	7.0	26.9	25.4	11.4	2.6	76.4	36.9	47.7	52.3
31407	SAVANNAH	75.4	68.9	21.1	26.1	1.2	1.8	2.5	3.6	5.6	5.2	5.1	6.1	6.4	30.8	24.9	13.5	2.5	80.7	39.0	54.4	45.6
31408	SAVANNAH	48.5	40.2	45.7	52.7	1.1	1.5	6.2	7.2	7.2	7.0	6.5	6.6	7.3	30.8	23.2	9.9	1.5	75.5	34.8	52.6	47.4
31409	SAVANNAH	53.9	41.5	37.2	46.8	1.9	2.4	10.5	13.5	7.3	4.5	2.8	10.9	30.7	36.2	2.8	2.1	2.8	81.6	24.0	71.9	28.1
31410	SAVANNAH	89.0	83.1	6.0	9.4	3.3	4.9	1.6	2.6	6.2	6.5	6.6	6.3	4.8	28.4	29.9	10.0	1.4	76.7	39.4	48.8	51.2
31411	SAVANNAH	97.6	95.9	0.5	0.9	1.4	2.2	0.8	1.3	1.6	1.8	2.2	2.6	2.2	6.6	32.6	46.7	3.6	92.5	65.1	47.8	52.2
31415	SAVANNAH	3.6	3.3	95.1	95.2	0.1	0.1	0.8	1.1	8.0	7.9	7.6	8.5	7.3	21.2	23.2	13.8	2.5	71.4	35.0	45.4	54.6
31419	SAVANNAH	65.6	54.2	27.8	37.1	2.7	3.3	4.0	5.5	7.4	6.5	6.2	6.6	8.3	32.1	23.4	8.3	1.2	76.2	33.2	48.3	51.7
31501	WAYCROSS	56.4	51.2	41.4	45.9	0.8	1.1	1.1	1.6	6.3	6.3	6.4	6.4	5.8	23.4	26.9	15.3	3.2	77.1	41.3	47.0	53.0
31503	WAYCROSS	79.3	73.2	18.5	23.6	0.3	0.4	2.2	3.3	6.4	6.5	6.7	6.5	7.0	28.2	25.3	11.2	2.1	76.4	36.9	51.7	48.3
31510	ALMA	80.1	75.5	17.1	20.3	0.3	0.5	3.3	4.9	7.3	7.1	7.0	6.4	6.1	27.2	25.5	11.9	1.5	74.6	37.2	49.6	50.4
31512	AMBROSE	74.2	66.8	19.0	22.7	0.3	0.4	8.7	13.1	7.4	7.4	7.5	7.0	5.4	28.7	26.7	8.7	1.0	73.3	35.4	49.4	50.6
31513	BAXLEY	76.1	70.7	20.1	23.5	0.3	0.4	4.8	7.3	7.5	7.4	7.3	6.9	5.8	26.8	26.2	10.7	1.6	73.6	36.2	49.8	50.2
31516	BLACKSHEAR	87.3	84.8	10.9	12.5	0.2	0.2	1.6	2.6	6.9	6.7	6.6	6.8	6.5	26.3	27.4	11.4	1.4	75.7	37.9	49.4	50.6
31518	BRISTOL	91.2	87.5	6.2	8.5	0.6	0.9	6.7	10.1	5.9	6.3	6.5	6.0	4.3	25.3	30.0	14.2	1.6	77.9	41.6	51.8	48.2
31519	BROXTON	73.1	66.7	22.5	26.4	0.2	0.3	4.6	7.1	7.7	7.8	7.7	6.8	5.7	26.0	26.3	10.6	1.3	72.6	36.6	48.4	51.6
31520	BRUNSWICK	44.5	37.4	52.1	57.9	0.4	0.5	5.2	7.0	7.6	7.2	6.7	7.3	7.0	25.4	23.9	12.2	2.7	74.2	35.9	48.0	52.0
31522	SAINT SIMONS ISLAND	94.2	90.4	3.9	6.6	0.9	1.3	1.8	3.1	4.1	4.5	5.2	5.2	4.0	19.8	34.2	19.5	3.6	82.8	49.6	47.0	53.0
31523	BRUNSWICK	88.1	81.1	9.9	16.0	0.3	0.5	1.1	2.0	6.2	6.5	6.9	6.6	5.1	26.0	30.7	10.9	1.1	76.2	40.0	49.5	50.5
31525	BRUNSWICK	72.9	64.4	23.7	30.9	0.9	1.1	2.4	3.8	7.2	6.8	6.8	8.1	7.4	26.3	27.0	9.5	1.0	74.4	35.2	48.7	51.3
31527	JEKYLL ISLAND	97.4	95.3	1.5	2.5	0.4	0.7	1.1	2.1	1.4	1.4	1.5	1.3	1.9	12.3	34.1	39.0	7.4	95.2	63.7	48.3	51.7
31532	DENTON	89.0	84.3	8.1	10.6	0.0	0.1	2.9	5.2	7.4	7.4	7.1	5.4	6.1	25.7	28.6	11.2	1.3	74.6	38.9	49.0	51.0
31533	DOUGLAS	65.3	59.2	27.3	29.8	0.9	1.3	8.5	12.5	7.6	7.4	7.4	7.2	6.7	27.6	23.6	10.5	1.9	73.5	34.5	48.3	51.7
31535	DOUGLAS	68.3	61.7	26.5	30.4	0.6	0.8	5.5	8.3	8.5	8.0	7.6	8.2	7.4	28.8	23.3	7.3	0.9	71.4	31.7	48.4	51.6
31537	FOLKSTON	61.2	54.6	36.7	42.9	0.3	0.4	0.8	1.0	6.3	6.2	6.3	8.1	9.1	28.5	24.5	9.6	1.5	76.8	35.4	54.4	45.6
31539	HAZLEHURST	80.8	76.1	15.5	18.3	0.5	0.7	5.2	7.8	7.7	7.5	7.3	6.5	6.0	26.2	26.3	11.1	1.4	73.5	36.5	49.6	50.4
31542	HOBOKEN	94.1	92.8	3.6	3.9	0.1	0.1	1.3	2.0	6.0	6.9	7.5	7.4	5.2	26.9	28.4	11.0	0.6	74.6	37.0	51.1	48.9
31543	HORTENSE	96.5	94.0	1.9	3.6	0.1	0.1	1.0	1.7	7.5	7.2	7.3	7.3	6.6	26.0	26.5	10.6	1.1	73.9	36.2	50.0	50.0
31544	JACKSONVILLE	75.6	67.9	23.3	30.2	0.0	0.0	0.9	1.7	7.3	7.2	6.9	6.1	5.1	24.4	28.5	12.0	2.6	74.9	39.4	47.5	52.5
31545	JESUP	77.2	72.7	19.2	22.0	0.5	0.7	3.6	5.5	7.7	7.3	7.2	7.1	6.6	26.9	25.6	10.3	1.2	73.5	35.4	48.8	51.2
31546	JESUP	67.8	63.5	29.6	32.7	0.6	0.8	6.1	8.7	4.7	4.9	4.9	5.1	6.0	36.2	27.1	9.8	1.3	82.5	38.5	62.1	37.9
31547	KINGS BAY	73.6	66.9	18.1	21.1	1.0	1.2	8.9	13.1	11.6	5.4	2.7	10.3	43.1	25.8	1.1	0.1	0.0	79.2	22.3	73.4	26.6
31548	KINGSLAND	76.2	71.3	19.2	22.2	1.1	1.6	3.0	4.7	9.3	8.4	7.9	7.5	6.7	33.6	21.6	4.6	0.4	69.5	31.2	50.3	49.7
31549	LUMBER CITY	56.9	47.5	41.7	50.3	0.0	0.0	2.0	3.1	7.3	7.3	7.2	5.7	4.6	22.4	28.0	13.9	3.7	74.6	41.3	47.7	52.3
31550	MANOR	93.0	88.8	2.7	4.2	0.1	0.2	4.9	8.2	6.3	6.6	7.4	7.1	4.9	25.1	26.4	14.8	1.3	75.7	40.4	50.6	49.4
31551	MERSHON	88.7	84.1	6.8	9.0	0.4	0.5	7.2	11.1	7.4	7.5	7.5	6.2	5.0	28.3	26.8	10.2	1.3	74.0	36.6	52.7	47.3
31552	MILLWOOD	91.2	86.3	3.3	4.8	0.1	0.1	6.4	10.3	7.3	7.4	7.5	6.9	5.3	28.3	25.7	10.4	1.2	73.8	37.2	50.4	49.6
31553	NAHUNTA	92.7	90.1	5.9	7.9	0.2	0.2	0.9	1.4	7.1	7.0	6.9	6.8	6.4	25.9	26.4	11.4	1.9	74.4	37.0	49.9	50.1
31554	NICHOLLS	71.9	64.8	25.0	30.6	0.1	0.2	4.5	6.8	6.1	5.9	5.7	6.0	9.4	36.1	22.5	7.7	0.7	79.0	34.5	60.6	39.4
31555	ODUM	89.4	86.1	8.1	10.2	0.2	0.3	1.6	2.7	6.5	6.6	7.1	6.9	4.9	29.3	26.5	10.9	1.2	75.4	38.2	53.7	46.3
31557	PATTERSON	84.5	78.0	12.7	17.8	0.3	0.4	2.2	3.5	7.0	6.9	6.9	6.9	5.7	26.0	26.6	12.4	1.5	75.1	37.9	50.1	49.9
31558	SAINT MARYS	76.4	70.8	17.7	21.0	1.4	1.8	4.7	6.9	9.7	7.8	6.7	7.4	11.3	34.4	17.6	4.6	0.5	71.6	28.6	52.5	47.5
31560	SCREVEN	82.5	71.5	16.2	26.3	0.0	0.1	1.1	2.1	6.5	6.7	6.9	6.9	5.4	24.6	28.5	12.9	1.7	75.7	39.9	49.9	50.1
31561	SEA ISLAND	95.0	91.8	3.8	6.2	0.9	1.8	0.6	1.2	1.8	1.8	2.3	2.9	2.9	9.1	35.8	37.2	6.2	92.4	62.5	45.7	54.3
31562	SAINT GEORGE	95.1	93.4	2.2	2.9	0.7	1.0	1.0	1.5	7.9	7.8	7.8	7.1	6.0	25.5	26.0	11.1	0.8	72.1	36.8	51.5	48.5
31563	SURRENCY	76.1	70.7	21.5	25.6	0.2	0.3	2.3	3.7	6.2	6.6	6.7	6.2	5.4	24.3	30.4	12.4	1.7	76.6	40.3	50.1	49.9
31565	WAVERLY	69.2	63.1	28.7	34.4	0.2	0.2	0.3	0.5	5.7	6.2	6.5	6.4	5.0	23.3	31.5	13.8	1.5	77.6	42.6	48.2	51.8
31566	WAYNESVILLE	92.3	90.7	6.1	6.9	0.1	0.1	0.7	1.1	8.3	7.2	7.2	7.8	7.1	27.7	25.8	8.5	0.5	72.6	34.4	51.2	48.8
31567	WEST GREEN	90.8	87.0	6.4	8.2	0.0	0.0	5.0	8.0	8.0	7.8	7.7	6.3	5.5	28.8	24.0	10.8	1.1	72.7	36.2	50.6	49.4
31568	WHITE OAK	68.3	62.0	30.4	36.2	0.0	0.1	0.8	1.2	5.5	6.8	7.9	8.3	5.3	24.0	30.2	10.6	1.4	73.9	39.8	48.9	51.1
31569	WOODBINE	70.2	64.3	27.2	32.3	0.6	0.8	1.7	2.4	6.1	6.3	6.7	8.3	7.0	24.9	30.5	9.4	0.9	75.3	38.7	48.8	51.2
31601	VALDOSTA	38.8	33.2	58.3	63.1	0.6	0.7	2.5	3.3	8.4	7.6	7.2	8.1	11.0	26.6	21.9	8.2	1.1	72.3	29.6	47.7	52.3
31602	VALDOSTA	70.1	62.5	25.9	32.2	1.6	2.1	2.1	2.8	6.3	5.8	5.6	8.4	12.4	29.5	21.0	9.0	1.9	79.1	31.6	49.6	50.4
31605	VALDOSTA	72.3	62.8	21.4	28.6	2.5	3.3	3.5	5.0	7.8	7.4	6.8	6.9	9.1	34.7	20.3	6.4	0.6	73.8	31.0	51.2	48.8
31606	VALDOSTA	84.0	76.9	13.8	19.7	0.2	0.3	1.8	2.9	7.4	7.3	8.0	7.0	5.7	26.7	26.9	10.3	0.7	72.9	36.8	49.1	50.9
31620	ADEL	63.9	58.2	33.1	37.5	0.5	0.7	3.3	4.8	8.0	7.7	7.2	6.7	6.5	25.9	23.9	12.2	2.0	73.0	35.9	47.4	52.6
31622	ALAPAHA	70.2	64.8	28.9	34.0	0.1	0.1	0.3	0.5	7.2	7.3	7.4	6.1	4.4	25.1	27.0	13.9	1.7	74.2	39.7	49.6	50.4
31623	ARGYLE	90.7	89.9	7.3	8.1	0.0	0.0	1.3	1.4	7.4	6.1	7.4	5.4	5.4	27.0	27.0	12.2	2.0	75.7	38.1	50.0	50.0
31624	AXSON	86.2	79.2	4.2	5.1	0.0	0.0	13.1	20.6	9.4	9.2	8.6	6.6	5.9	27.1	23.9	8.5	0.9	68.8	33.0	50.1	49.9
31625	BARNEY	65.0	62.1	29.4	32.2	0.2	0.2	6.5	6.5	5.6	6.3	6.1	6.6	5.8	25.4	28.8	13.5	2.0	78.0	40.4	51.3	48.7
31626	BOSTON	47.6	39.2	50.5	58.4	0.1	0.1	2.5	3.2	6.9	6.8	7.0	7.3	5.9	24.0	28.1	12.3	1.8	74.5	39.5	48.2	51.8
31629	DIXIE	42.9	39.9	56.4	59.4	0.2	0.2	0.8	0.9	5.7	5.8	6.3	8.1	6.0	23.8	28.8	13.2	2.2	77.1	40.2	50.1	49.9
31630	DU PONT	62.5	59.4	36.2	39.1	0.0	0.0	1.5	1.6	7.8	6.5	8.6	8.3	7.2	27.3	25.9	7.5	0.8	71.7	33.8	49.5	50.5
31631	FARGO	84.1	82.4	13.7	15.2	0.0	0.0	0.4	0.4	6.5	6.5	6.7	6.5	6.3	24.8	29.3	12.1	1.2	76.2	40.1	50.5	49.5
31632	HAHIRA	82.4	75.3	14.5	20.1	0.4	0.5	2.4	3.8	7.4	7.2	7.2	7.4	6.4	27.4	27.2	8.9	1.0	73.7	35.9	49.4	50.6
31634	HOMERVILLE	67.7	65.4	30.8	33.1	0.1	0.1	0.7	0.7	7.2	7.3	7.4	7.1	5.7	26.4	25.7	11.7	1.6	73.4	36.9	49.9	50.1
31635	LAKELAND	66.2	60.1	31.1	36.3	0.4	0.6	1.9	2.6	6.9	7.2	6.5	7.4	7.3	27.7	25.2	10.1	1.6	74.8	35.3	51.2	48.8
	GEORGIA	65.1	61.1	28.7	30.1	2.2	2.9	5.3	7.7	7.3	7.0	6.9	7.1	7.1	29.3	25.1	8.9	1.3	74.7	35.0	49.4	50.6
	UNITED STATES	75.1	72.0	12.3	12.7	3.8	4.6	12.5	15.7	6.8	6.7	6.6	7.1	6.9	27.0	26.0	10.9	1.9	75.7	36.9	49.2	50.8

31216-31635

ZIP CODE				2009 HOUSEHOLD INCOME DISTRIBUTION (%)					MEDIAN HOUSEHOLD INCOME					2009 HOME VALUE DISTRIBUTION (%)					
#	POST OFFICE NAME	2009 Per Capita Income	2009 HH Income Base	Less than $25,000	$25,000 to $49,999	$50,000 to $99,999	$100,000 to $149,999	$150,000 or More	2009	2014	2009 National Centile	2009 State Centile	2009 Home Value Base	Less than $50,000	$50,000 to $89,999	$90,000 to $174,999	$175,000 to $399,999	$400,000 or More	2009 Median Home Value
31216	MACON	24896	6070	16.6	21.4	49.1	9.9	3.0	62900	63384	81	83	5153	13.2	21.1	58.6	6.6	0.6	102138
31217	MACON	15768	6995	37.2	27.9	30.2	3.3	1.5	34919	38650	17	24	4568	38.9	42.5	16.6	1.9	0.2	58959
31220	MACON	28679	4560	8.4	23.4	50.0	12.8	5.4	66359	66878	84	86	3666	6.6	28.6	50.6	12.3	1.9	99023
31301	ALLENHURST	15136	1867	31.1	34.7	30.4	3.2	0.6	36847	39859	23	32	969	37.6	15.8	42.0	4.0	0.6	79375
31302	BLOOMINGDALE	21264	3799	19.0	30.9	43.0	4.8	2.3	50047	53123	61	68	3101	25.2	27.7	32.7	11.7	2.7	84741
31303	CLYO	19868	852	25.8	24.3	42.6	6.1	1.2	49819	54937	61	68	745	24.0	27.1	33.0	13.6	2.3	88300
31304	CRESCENT	15214	757	38.3	28.8	29.2	3.2	0.5	33315	35533	14	18	609	55.8	19.5	16.7	4.6	3.3	45563
31305	DARIEN	16018	1815	36.3	32.6	27.5	2.4	1.3	35129	36185	18	26	1394	45.4	27.7	21.0	2.9	2.9	55766
31308	ELLABELL	19130	2913	27.3	30.6	31.1	8.5	2.4	41419	44633	37	48	2467	40.7	27.0	19.6	10.7	2.1	59893
31309	FLEMING	18393	290	29.7	33.8	29.7	5.9	1.0	39075	43105	30	41	213	31.5	21.6	43.7	3.3	0.0	85357
31312	GUYTON	22511	6005	16.1	27.6	44.2	7.9	4.2	55934	59392	73	77	5175	21.8	23.6	32.2	20.4	2.0	95475
31313	HINESVILLE	18225	12875	23.2	32.7	37.1	4.7	2.4	44669	50004	47	57	6424	11.0	24.2	57.2	6.8	0.7	101565
31314	FORT STEWART	6485	197	16.2	49.2	31.5	2.5	0.5	41372	43536	37	47	18	55.6	11.1	22.2	11.1	0.0	40000
31315	FORT STEWART	15961	2425	15.8	51.1	30.5	2.1	0.6	40899	43272	36	46	112	59.8	18.8	14.3	3.6	3.6	39286
31316	LUDOWICI	13862	3403	33.4	36.4	27.2	2.4	0.7	35821	37627	20	28	2275	36.0	27.8	31.8	3.9	0.5	69974
31319	MERIDIAN	15846	84	34.5	34.5	27.4	2.4	1.2	35000	35950	18	25	64	35.9	25.0	32.8	6.3	0.0	67500
31320	MIDWAY	19327	2853	26.4	34.0	30.5	6.9	2.2	39893	43787	32	43	2306	28.8	17.6	33.2	19.0	1.3	96029
31321	PEMBROKE	18614	2706	29.1	27.6	33.8	7.5	2.0	42976	46602	42	53	2102	33.5	28.4	27.1	10.0	1.0	67828
31322	POOLER	24424	4614	15.8	24.2	46.4	10.3	3.2	57757	58196	75	78	3852	10.7	22.8	54.3	11.4	0.8	108895
31323	RICEBORO	14354	587	44.3	24.7	27.3	2.0	1.7	29602	33011	7	7	512	51.8	20.5	23.0	4.7	0.0	48714
31324	RICHMOND HILL	29738	7335	13.3	17.8	39.7	18.3	10.9	72600	76661	88	90	5509	6.9	13.1	45.9	30.9	3.2	142446
31326	RINCON	26308	6669	12.6	21.0	49.4	10.4	6.7	67609	71681	85	87	5222	9.4	17.2	42.4	27.7	3.2	127302
31328	TYBEE ISLAND	33300	1926	21.5	21.5	42.1	8.7	6.2	58566	59086	76	78	1318	5.2	2.4	31.0	44.3	17.1	208173
31329	SPRINGFIELD	20740	3220	23.1	25.3	41.6	7.0	3.0	51349	55236	64	71	2528	19.8	26.7	33.4	16.9	3.2	94055
31331	TOWNSEND	19081	2157	31.8	34.0	28.2	4.5	1.4	38287	39864	28	38	1908	33.5	26.2	24.7	11.6	4.0	70894
31401	SAVANNAH	17622	9508	53.8	25.4	15.8	2.7	2.4	22588	24276	2	1	2448	22.5	23.3	19.6	15.0	19.6	99189
31404	SAVANNAH	17741	12347	35.6	28.8	30.0	3.6	2.0	35210	37972	18	26	6468	15.3	49.4	31.3	3.5	0.5	76513
31405	SAVANNAH	21571	13172	27.6	31.7	32.0	5.1	3.6	40613	46566	35	44	8181	17.0	21.7	42.8	15.3	3.2	104926
31406	SAVANNAH	26608	13848	20.0	26.6	39.0	8.5	5.9	53380	55717	69	73	8757	5.6	18.7	51.4	18.8	5.4	118719
31407	SAVANNAH	27073	1420	17.0	24.5	47.5	9.1	2.0	58342	59540	76	78	1039	11.7	52.3	31.7	4.3	0.0	78285
31408	SAVANNAH	17121	4085	29.0	33.7	32.2	3.6	1.5	37574	41604	25	35	2053	35.5	26.7	32.2	4.9	0.7	73629
31409	SAVANNAH	9285	10	30.0	30.0	40.0	0.0	0.0	35000	37303	18	25	0	0.0	0.0	0.0	0.0	0.0	0
31410	SAVANNAH	35680	9832	8.9	17.7	46.7	15.8	11.0	73330	74985	89	90	7225	0.5	3.0	56.1	32.8	7.6	162178
31411	SAVANNAH	70556	3788	5.9	8.3	35.7	17.6	32.6	100352	98998	97	98	3624	0.0	0.0	5.0	48.4	46.6	382006
31415	SAVANNAH	13273	5130	51.8	25.9	18.7	2.3	1.2	23711	25346	3	2	2676	42.1	37.0	18.9	1.4	0.6	59550
31419	SAVANNAH	25411	18925	18.0	26.2	43.4	8.3	4.1	54577	56021	71	75	10975	10.8	13.9	56.1	16.5	2.6	117366
31501	WAYCROSS	19544	6033	38.4	26.5	28.5	4.5	2.0	34461	36104	16	23	3817	22.2	28.8	37.1	10.9	1.0	88969
31503	WAYCROSS	16884	7819	34.8	32.4	28.0	3.5	1.3	35016	36288	18	25	5830	33.2	29.5	27.7	7.7	1.9	72861
31510	ALMA	16046	3514	41.7	28.0	25.9	2.6	1.8	31132	31903	10	12	2583	29.9	30.9	28.4	9.1	1.7	71514
31512	AMBROSE	17728	1004	33.2	29.5	31.3	3.9	2.2	36067	39089	21	29	807	31.2	28.6	26.6	9.9	3.6	73900
31513	BAXLEY	17696	6058	36.5	27.9	28.8	4.8	2.0	35918	36970	20	28	4680	29.8	28.3	30.1	10.6	1.3	77069
31516	BLACKSHEAR	16378	5343	35.9	31.7	27.6	3.9	0.9	35007	35665	18	25	4205	30.5	24.9	29.3	13.4	1.9	80679
31518	BRISTOL	18140	311	36.3	33.4	21.2	6.8	2.3	33286	34443	14	17	257	20.2	16.7	42.4	19.1	1.6	106786
31519	BROXTON	19432	1558	34.0	32.3	26.7	4.1	2.9	35992	38240	21	29	1257	32.5	25.4	25.5	15.6	1.0	79795
31520	BRUNSWICK	16081	8682	43.6	27.9	23.8	2.7	2.0	29857	31592	8	8	4241	36.4	38.2	22.1	3.1	0.2	63669
31522	SAINT SIMONS ISLAND	42885	7489	10.7	18.6	39.9	16.3	14.6	72668	74318	88	90	5533	1.6	3.0	27.5	46.1	21.7	229354
31523	BRUNSWICK	22220	4416	20.4	28.9	41.3	7.1	2.3	50821	54318	63	70	3726	20.6	29.2	36.6	11.8	1.8	90292
31525	BRUNSWICK	21456	10112	24.6	26.8	39.1	7.1	2.3	48191	52063	57	65	6416	22.5	37.5	32.2	7.0	0.8	80545
31527	JEKYLL ISLAND	41771	496	6.7	16.7	54.4	15.3	6.9	74271	76339	89	90	364	0.0	4.9	23.9	70.3	0.8	218750
31532	DENTON	16277	259	42.9	31.7	19.3	3.5	2.7	29564	29060	7	6	228	41.7	23.7	24.1	10.5	0.0	63125
31533	DOUGLAS	17867	5855	34.1	31.7	27.5	4.3	2.5	36153	37985	21	30	3840	25.7	26.4	35.4	10.9	1.7	86802
31535	DOUGLAS	16991	3799	31.0	31.6	32.0	3.4	2.0	38499	41144	28	39	2979	35.0	26.0	27.3	10.2	1.6	72703
31537	FOLKSTON	15213	2703	38.8	28.0	28.3	3.8	1.2	33595	34352	15	19	2081	32.8	25.1	30.8	10.3	1.0	76027
31539	HAZLEHURST	16440	4955	37.6	32.6	24.8	3.1	2.0	32680	33507	13	16	3770	33.4	27.6	30.5	7.6	0.8	73648
31542	HOBOKEN	17188	1002	35.2	28.6	32.2	2.5	1.4	35571	37038	19	27	904	45.8	30.4	18.1	4.0	1.7	53423
31543	HORTENSE	16425	1105	32.1	32.1	32.3	2.5	0.9	36207	38615	21	30	968	37.6	34.4	22.0	4.9	1.1	64091
31544	JACKSONVILLE	18034	309	42.1	29.4	25.2	2.3	1.0	30558	31003	9	10	276	54.0	21.4	21.7	2.9	0.0	44500
31545	JESUP	18112	5910	34.7	27.9	30.3	5.0	2.1	38074	41424	27	37	4349	26.4	24.2	32.6	14.7	2.0	88617
31546	JESUP	18608	2203	32.2	25.2	32.7	7.4	2.5	42059	45842	39	50	1588	27.8	25.2	27.8	16.6	2.6	85766
31547	KINGS BAY	14395	208	13.5	48.1	38.0	0.5	0.0	43928	47010	45	55	0	0.0	0.0	0.0	0.0	0.0	0
31548	KINGSLAND	20457	6855	18.1	27.8	44.5	7.1	2.5	53362	54884	69	73	4478	14.4	17.5	49.0	17.2	1.9	116687
31549	LUMBER CITY	17056	672	47.2	26.2	21.0	2.7	3.0	27316	28484	5	3	486	48.6	26.3	17.7	7.4	0.0	53182
31550	MANOR	16147	356	27.2	52.0	16.6	3.9	0.3	36869	36767	23	32	292	54.5	14.7	12.7	14.4	3.8	40000
31551	MERSHON	15561	397	38.0	33.8	21.4	5.8	1.0	31364	32000	10	13	325	23.4	23.4	36.3	13.5	3.4	94038
31552	MILLWOOD	16202	314	26.1	37.3	34.4	1.9	0.3	40701	43508	35	45	262	33.2	29.0	29.0	6.9	1.9	81795
31553	NAHUNTA	16516	1779	35.6	32.9	27.1	3.0	1.3	34981	36988	18	24	1491	41.9	32.7	19.0	5.4	0.9	58741
31554	NICHOLLS	15221	2067	36.9	31.7	27.5	2.4	1.5	34665	36495	17	23	1625	39.8	26.7	24.2	7.9	1.4	59569
31555	ODUM	18990	1043	29.7	26.7	36.1	5.0	2.4	43383	48539	44	54	884	30.1	23.2	28.5	15.2	3.1	83409
31557	PATTERSON	15927	1317	33.8	33.0	29.7	3.0	0.5	37222	38692	24	34	1099	26.6	28.4	31.7	13.0	0.4	81349
31558	SAINT MARYS	22175	7019	15.3	27.2	43.8	10.0	3.8	56681	58574	74	77	3726	5.3	10.3	56.4	23.8	4.2	132303
31560	SCREVEN	17998	1353	31.6	34.9	28.5	3.4	1.7	37202	39785	24	34	1117	22.5	26.7	39.1	8.9	2.9	91159
31561	SEA ISLAND	59662	187	14.4	23.5	25.7	13.9	22.5	77827	80329	91	92	174	0.0	1.1	8.0	47.1	43.7	321429
31562	SAINT GEORGE	16071	892	31.7	33.1	31.2	2.9	1.1	34334	34060	16	23	792	31.6	23.2	28.4	16.3	0.5	82400
31563	SURRENCY	18254	478	35.8	28.2	31.2	3.8	1.0	37967	37808	27	37	406	31.8	26.6	30.8	9.9	1.0	78667
31565	WAVERLY	20237	774	33.3	24.5	35.0	4.1	3.0	41506	45994	38	48	647	21.5	19.2	29.5	23.5	6.3	122545
31566	WAYNESVILLE	15677	1726	29.1	36.5	31.9	2.2	0.3	37865	39896	26	37	1531	48.0	30.4	16.5	5.0	0.1	52542
31567	WEST GREEN	16919	373	28.7	41.8	25.5	2.9	1.1	37545	39815	25	35	311	31.5	35.0	24.8	6.4	2.3	66250
31568	WHITE OAK	17293	505	34.9	22.0	37.4	3.4	2.4	41904	46591	39	49	457	33.5	21.9	23.0	19.7	2.0	83553
31569	WOODBINE	19943	1763	25.2	23.5	45.4	4.4	1.5	51028	52556	64	70	1379	18.9	20.4	35.4	23.7	1.6	115074
31601	VALDOSTA	14046	12202	47.6	27.0	22.4	2.1	0.9	27022	29478	5	3	6039	43.2	34.1	19.4	2.8	0.5	56450
31602	VALDOSTA	24727	12226	23.3	27.5	35.5	8.1	5.6	49023	51859	59	66	7284	10.0	24.7	45.9	18.3	1.0	107627
31605	VALDOSTA	25444	6900	16.6	25.2	46.4	7.1	4.7	57100	56670	74	77	4372	13.9	19.5	50.9	10.1	5.6	106039
31606	VALDOSTA	18230	1467	28.8	29.9	35.7	4.5	1.2	39843	44298	32	43	1237	28.4	37.0	27.2	6.1	1.2	72008
31620	ADEL	15637	4005	38.0	32.2	25.2	3.9	0.7	32409	33006	12	15	2842	23.9	30.9	29.5	14.4	1.4	83026
31622	ALAPAHA	16703	643	33.6	34.1	27.4	3.9	1.1	33696	34072	15	20	519	35.5	25.6	28.9	6.6	3.5	69821
31623	ARGYLE	12640	49	38.8	42.9	14.3	4.1	0.0	35346	32327	19	26	41	31.7	34.1	26.8	2.4	4.9	61667
31624	AXSON	12748	521	38.4	38.0	21.7	1.9	0.0	31637	32190	11	13	438	52.1	27.2	14.4	5.3	1.1	48696
31625	BARNEY	17752	431	30.6	28.1	38.1	2.6	0.7	41174	46689	37	47	362	42.5	29.8	20.4	4.7	2.5	59643
31626	BOSTON	15630	1385	43.9	29.4	22.7	2.0	1.9	29708	32445	8	7	1044	24.8	30.2	29.3	12.8	2.9	82239
31629	DIXIE	15114	433	38.6	25.6	31.6	4.2	0.0	37101	42525	24	33	363	42.4	27.3	20.7	8.5	1.1	60172
31630	DU PONT	17624	237	28.3	30.4	38.0	1.3	2.1	42752	50233	42	51	195	41.0	28.2	22.6	4.6	3.6	64583
31631	FARGO	15198	202	40.1	35.6	21.8	2.0	0.5	33360	32914	14	18	161	59.6	31.1	8.1	1.2	0.0	34861
31632	HAHIRA	18874	3204	26.5	29.7	36.3	6.0	1.4	41105	45744	36	46	2475	24.5	26.5	36.5	10.5	1.9	88101
31634	HOMERVILLE	15408	2056	44.2	26.9	24.4	2.7	1.8	30862	31378	9	11	1443	35.8	32.7	23.5	5.3	2.6	63929
31635	LAKELAND	16803	1998	33.6	32.7	28.7	3.4	1.6	35920	38191	20	28	1429	36.9	32.5	23.2	7.0	0.3	64049
	GEORGIA	26980		20.7	23.1	36.8	11.7	7.7	56761	58593				13.2	17.9	39.1	24.2	5.5	121444
	UNITED STATES	27277		20.9	24.4	35.3	11.7	7.6	54719	56938				9.3	13.1	31.6	32.6	13.5	162279

ZIP CODE #	POST OFFICE NAME	FINANCIAL SERVICES: Auto Loan	FINANCIAL SERVICES: Home Loan	FINANCIAL SERVICES: Invest-ments	FINANCIAL SERVICES: Retire-ment Plans	THE HOME: Home Improvements: Home Repair	THE HOME: Home Improvements: Lawn & Garden	THE HOME: Furnishings: Comput-ers & Hard-ware-Personal	THE HOME: Furnishings: Major Appli-ances	THE HOME: Furnishings: TV, Radio, Sound Equip-ment	THE HOME: Furnishings: Furni-ture	ENTERTAINMENT: Dine out/ Carry out	ENTERTAINMENT: Sports Equip-ment	ENTERTAINMENT: Fees & Tickets	ENTERTAINMENT: Toys & Games	ENTERTAINMENT: Travel	ENTERTAINMENT: Cable TV	PERSONAL: Apparel & Services	PERSONAL: Auto Repairs	PERSONAL: Health Insur-ance	PERSONAL: Pets & Supplies
31216	MACON	94	102	92	102	99	102	92	97	93	93	93	73	97	95	96	94	65	94	98	113
31217	MACON	66	57	54	56	54	64	59	60	64	60	63	45	55	64	55	68	43	62	67	74
31220	MACON	109	122	104	120	116	111	107	110	104	112	106	85	113	109	110	102	74	105	103	127
31301	ALLENHURST	67	63	53	60	60	60	62	61	62	65	62	47	58	65	58	62	43	62	60	73
31302	BLOOMINGDALE	96	79	79	77	78	91	78	86	83	79	83	64	69	87	73	88	56	83	88	104
31303	CLYO	89	79	76	76	78	85	75	82	79	77	79	60	70	82	72	82	53	79	83	98
31304	CRESCENT	73	48	71	45	48	72	51	64	59	49	58	50	38	60	48	66	38	61	68	79
31305	DARIEN	71	53	65	50	52	68	55	64	60	53	59	49	45	61	52	64	39	61	66	77
31308	ELLABELL	84	77	67	74	75	77	74	77	76	77	76	57	70	79	70	77	52	75	76	91
31309	FLEMING	73	68	58	65	65	65	67	67	68	70	68	51	64	71	63	68	47	67	65	80
31312	GUYTON	102	96	84	92	93	95	89	94	91	94	92	69	85	96	86	93	63	91	92	111
31313	HINESVILLE	80	66	57	68	63	61	79	68	77	79	78	57	71	80	69	74	54	75	67	83
31314	FORT STEWART	82	44	34	50	40	38	77	54	72	72	76	53	59	86	56	67	53	68	49	66
31315	FORT STEWART	81	42	31	49	38	36	76	53	72	71	75	53	58	86	55	66	53	67	48	64
31316	LUDOWICI	64	58	52	55	55	58	58	58	58	60	58	44	53	61	54	59	40	58	58	70
31319	MERIDIAN	75	49	72	46	49	73	52	66	60	50	59	51	39	61	49	67	39	62	69	81
31320	MIDWAY	81	73	71	70	71	76	71	75	73	73	73	56	66	75	68	74	49	73	74	89
31321	PEMBROKE	82	72	65	69	69	75	73	75	75	74	75	57	66	78	67	77	51	74	76	89
31322	POOLER	100	99	87	97	95	96	91	95	91	94	92	73	90	96	90	92	63	91	92	111
31323	RICEBORO	74	48	71	45	48	72	52	65	59	49	58	51	39	60	48	66	38	61	69	80
31324	RICHMOND HILL	122	130	113	130	124	114	125	118	118	128	121	96	128	124	123	114	85	119	109	139
31326	RINCON	116	117	98	112	111	105	106	109	104	113	106	83	105	111	103	102	73	104	100	126
31328	TYBEE ISLAND	115	92	149	91	102	122	93	118	97	87	96	86	80	92	100	103	64	109	116	136
31329	SPRINGFIELD	92	85	76	82	83	87	80	85	83	83	83	62	76	87	77	86	57	83	86	101
31331	TOWNSEND	81	58	89	56	61	82	60	76	66	57	65	57	49	65	60	72	43	71	78	91
31401	SAVANNAH	55	41	40	44	39	46	58	48	60	53	59	38	50	58	48	61	41	55	55	60
31404	SAVANNAH	66	58	52	60	55	63	65	61	69	64	68	47	62	68	60	71	47	65	69	75
31405	SAVANNAH	79	74	69	74	72	78	76	75	79	77	79	56	75	79	73	81	54	77	81	90
31406	SAVANNAH	94	92	85	94	90	92	94	91	95	94	95	70	94	96	92	95	66	94	95	109
31407	SAVANNAH	93	87	86	87	85	100	86	92	90	82	89	70	83	90	85	94	61	90	100	110
31408	SAVANNAH	68	59	56	60	57	64	65	63	69	64	69	48	61	69	61	71	47	67	69	77
31409	SAVANNAH	77	40	30	46	36	34	72	50	68	67	72	50	55	82	52	63	50	64	45	61
31410	SAVANNAH	122	137	130	139	136	124	127	125	121	133	123	98	135	124	132	117	87	123	118	145
31411	SAVANNAH	204	215	291	213	247	253	193	228	204	218	200	142	212	183	223	213	137	217	254	258
31415	SAVANNAH	52	42	39	44	41	49	48	47	54	49	53	34	45	53	44	58	36	50	55	58
31419	SAVANNAH	96	84	77	86	81	83	92	86	92	92	92	68	86	95	85	91	64	90	86	103
31501	WAYCROSS	70	57	64	57	58	71	61	67	67	59	65	49	55	66	59	72	44	66	74	80
31503	WAYCROSS	73	56	66	54	56	72	58	67	64	56	63	50	49	65	55	69	42	64	72	81
31510	ALMA	74	51	64	50	51	71	55	65	61	52	60	50	43	63	50	67	40	61	68	79
31512	AMBROSE	82	62	67	60	61	78	63	72	69	62	68	55	52	72	58	74	46	68	75	87
31513	BAXLEY	78	61	66	59	60	74	63	70	68	62	67	53	54	70	58	72	45	68	73	84
31516	BLACKSHEAR	69	56	59	54	55	66	57	63	61	57	60	47	50	63	53	65	41	61	65	75
31518	BRISTOL	79	56	74	55	57	78	58	71	64	55	63	54	47	65	56	71	42	66	75	86
31519	BROXTON	91	64	79	62	64	88	67	80	75	65	74	61	53	78	61	83	49	75	84	97
31520	BRUNSWICK	58	50	47	51	48	56	55	54	59	54	58	41	52	59	51	62	40	57	61	66
31522	SAINT SIMONS ISLAND	123	144	160	146	153	145	129	137	127	138	127	99	144	123	144	127	90	132	139	156
31523	BRUNSWICK	91	86	77	85	85	89	81	86	84	83	84	64	78	87	79	86	57	83	87	102
31525	BRUNSWICK	85	77	69	77	75	77	80	78	81	81	81	60	76	83	75	82	56	80	79	94
31527	JEKYLL ISLAND	111	117	159	116	135	138	105	124	111	119	109	78	116	100	122	116	75	118	138	141
31532	DENTON	79	55	68	53	55	76	58	69	65	56	63	53	46	67	53	71	43	65	73	84
31533	DOUGLAS	79	62	65	61	61	75	65	71	70	64	69	54	56	72	60	75	47	69	75	86
31535	DOUGLAS	77	66	62	64	64	71	66	70	69	67	68	53	59	72	61	71	47	68	70	83
31537	FOLKSTON	76	52	70	49	51	74	55	67	62	52	61	52	42	64	50	69	40	63	70	82
31539	HAZLEHURST	73	54	62	52	53	69	57	65	62	56	61	50	47	64	53	67	41	62	68	78
31542	HOBOKEN	80	57	77	56	59	80	59	73	66	56	64	55	47	66	57	72	43	68	76	88
31543	HORTENSE	74	57	61	55	56	69	59	65	63	58	62	50	50	66	54	67	42	63	67	79
31544	JACKSONVILLE	79	51	76	48	51	77	55	69	63	52	62	54	41	64	51	71	41	65	73	85
31545	JESUP	74	66	62	64	64	70	66	69	69	66	68	51	61	70	63	71	47	68	71	82
31546	JESUP	84	69	80	67	69	85	69	80	75	67	74	59	61	75	67	81	50	76	85	95
31547	KINGS BAY	83	43	32	50	38	36	78	54	73	72	77	54	59	88	56	67	54	69	48	65
31548	KINGSLAND	92	90	77	86	86	83	84	86	84	89	84	65	82	88	81	83	58	83	82	100
31549	LUMBER CITY	76	49	73	46	49	74	53	66	61	50	59	52	39	62	49	68	39	62	70	82
31550	MANOR	72	51	72	50	53	73	53	67	59	49	58	50	42	59	52	64	38	61	70	80
31551	MERSHON	77	55	63	53	55	73	57	67	63	56	62	51	46	66	52	69	42	63	70	81
31552	MILLWOOD	77	56	64	54	55	74	58	67	64	56	63	52	46	67	53	70	42	64	71	82
31553	NAHUNTA	73	55	65	52	53	69	56	65	62	56	61	50	47	63	53	66	41	62	67	79
31554	NICHOLLS	71	55	60	52	53	66	56	63	60	56	60	48	47	63	52	64	40	61	64	76
31555	ODUM	84	70	76	67	70	82	68	78	72	68	72	57	60	74	66	77	48	74	79	92
31557	PATTERSON	73	53	60	51	52	69	55	63	61	53	59	49	44	63	50	66	40	60	67	77
31558	SAINT MARYS	99	98	81	96	92	85	94	91	91	99	93	72	93	97	90	87	64	90	84	106
31560	SCREVEN	83	57	82	54	57	83	59	75	67	56	66	57	46	68	57	74	43	70	79	91
31561	SEA ISLAND	149	157	214	156	181	186	141	167	149	160	147	104	156	134	164	156	101	159	186	189
31562	SAINT GEORGE	78	56	64	54	56	74	58	68	65	57	63	52	47	67	53	70	43	64	71	82
31563	SURRENCY	82	56	78	54	57	81	59	73	67	56	66	56	46	68	56	74	44	69	77	89
31565	WAVERLY	89	64	91	61	66	90	65	83	73	61	71	62	52	72	64	80	47	76	86	99
31566	WAYNESVILLE	66	61	53	58	58	60	61	61	61	63	61	46	57	64	57	61	42	61	59	72
31567	WEST GREEN	78	58	64	57	58	74	60	68	66	59	65	53	50	69	55	71	44	65	72	83
31568	WHITE OAK	87	58	85	55	58	86	61	78	70	58	69	60	47	71	58	78	46	73	82	95
31569	WOODBINE	89	76	78	73	75	86	74	82	78	74	78	60	67	80	71	82	52	79	84	98
31601	VALDOSTA	55	42	40	43	41	46	52	47	54	51	54	37	46	54	45	56	37	52	51	59
31602	VALDOSTA	91	83	77	85	81	82	92	84	90	90	90	67	86	91	84	89	63	88	85	101
31605	VALDOSTA	99	95	83	95	90	86	96	91	94	100	95	72	94	98	91	91	66	93	86	107
31606	VALDOSTA	81	65	69	63	65	78	65	73	70	65	69	55	56	72	61	74	47	70	75	88
31620	ADEL	66	53	52	52	51	62	56	59	61	55	59	44	49	62	51	64	40	59	64	72
31622	ALAPAHA	75	51	74	48	52	75	54	68	61	51	60	52	41	61	51	68	39	63	71	82
31623	ARGYLE	64	46	53	45	46	61	48	55	53	46	52	43	38	55	43	58	35	53	59	68
31624	AXSON	64	46	53	45	46	61	48	56	53	47	52	43	38	55	43	58	35	53	59	68
31625	BARNEY	84	54	81	51	54	82	58	73	67	55	66	57	44	68	54	75	43	69	78	90
31626	BOSTON	73	48	69	45	48	71	51	64	59	49	57	50	39	60	48	65	38	60	68	78
31629	DIXIE	76	49	73	46	49	74	53	66	61	50	59	52	40	62	49	68	39	63	70	82
31630	DU PONT	85	56	82	52	55	83	59	75	68	56	67	58	44	70	55	76	44	70	79	92
31631	FARGO	71	46	68	43	46	69	49	62	57	47	56	48	37	58	46	63	37	58	66	76
31632	HAHIRA	80	74	65	72	71	76	71	74	74	73	73	55	68	76	68	75	50	73	75	88
31634	HOMERVILLE	72	48	68	45	47	70	51	63	58	48	57	49	38	59	47	65	38	60	67	78
31635	LAKELAND	74	57	65	55	56	71	60	67	64	57	63	51	50	66	56	69	43	65	70	81
	GEORGIA	110	101	97	102	98	103	103	103	104	104	104	80	99	107	99	105	73	103	103	122
	UNITED STATES	100	100	100	100	100	100	100	100	100	100	100	100	100	100	100	100	100	100	100	100

ZIP CODE #	POST OFFICE NAME	COUNTY FIPS CODE	POPULATION 2000	POPULATION 2009	POPULATION 2014	2000-2009 ANNUAL RATE % Rate	2000-2009 ANNUAL RATE State Centile	HOUSEHOLDS 2000	HOUSEHOLDS 2009	HOUSEHOLDS 2014	HOUSEHOLDS % Annual Rate 2000-2009	HOUSEHOLDS 2009 Average HH Size	FAMILIES 2000	FAMILIES 2009	FAMILIES % Annual Rate 2000-2009
31636	LAKE PARK	101	8077	9332	9986	1.6	63	3017	3554	3821	1.8	2.61	2176	2452	1.3
31637	LENOX	075	2158	2301	2362	0.7	37	854	932	964	0.9	2.46	615	649	0.6
31638	MORVEN	027	965	1015	1024	0.5	31	343	372	380	0.9	2.67	239	250	0.5
31639	NASHVILLE	019	9316	9616	9661	0.3	25	3638	3844	3890	0.6	2.46	2576	2629	0.2
31641	NAYLOR	185	780	1369	1637	6.3	97	277	504	609	6.7	2.71	224	393	6.3
31642	PEARSON	003	4341	4703	4931	0.9	45	1531	1662	1744	0.9	2.82	1101	1155	0.5
31643	QUITMAN	027	9221	9254	9181	0.0	17	3417	3519	3522	0.3	2.55	2391	2378	-0.1
31645	RAY CITY	019	3638	4444	4700	2.2	73	1325	1639	1744	2.3	2.70	989	1193	2.0
31647	SPARKS	075	3095	3595	3776	1.6	63	1112	1297	1366	1.7	2.75	824	935	1.4
31648	STATENVILLE	101	1174	1213	1209	0.4	28	410	420	417	0.3	2.89	312	311	0.0
31649	STOCKTON	173	1581	1947	2128	2.3	74	571	721	793	2.6	2.70	440	540	2.2
31650	WILLACOOCHEE	003	3125	3397	3528	0.9	45	1151	1262	1313	1.0	2.67	857	910	0.7
31699	MOODY A F B	185	3163	3461	3504	1.0	47	21	23	24	1.0	2.57	16	17	0.7
31701	ALBANY	095	22693	23214	23414	0.2	22	8338	8674	8796	0.4	2.53	5324	5399	0.2
31704	ALBANY	095	987	907	877	-0.9	2	232	213	207	-0.9	3.34	221	202	-1.0
31705	ALBANY	095	37475	36603	36051	-0.3	11	12343	12240	12130	-0.1	2.73	9041	8671	-0.5
31707	ALBANY	095	22095	22301	22441	0.1	19	9470	9912	10063	0.5	2.25	6002	6020	0.0
31709	AMERICUS	261	15930	15814	15604	-0.1	14	6023	5991	5937	-0.1	2.46	3941	3756	-0.5
31711	ANDERSONVILLE	261	1051	1058	1049	0.1	19	380	387	387	0.2	2.48	291	287	-0.1
31712	ARABI	081	1051	1139	1171	0.9	45	410	455	472	1.1	2.50	295	317	0.8
31714	ASHBURN	287	6999	6714	6541	-0.4	9	2560	2506	2456	-0.2	2.64	1852	1752	-0.6
31716	BACONTON	205	3105	3210	3227	0.4	28	1102	1181	1201	0.8	2.71	857	894	0.5
31719	AMERICUS	261	10860	10725	10591	-0.1	14	3686	3664	3638	-0.1	2.76	2844	2748	-0.4
31721	ALBANY	095	18712	19694	20293	0.6	34	7236	7925	8226	1.0	2.47	5420	5763	0.7
31730	CAMILLA	205	10311	10356	10275	0.0	17	3586	3683	3687	0.3	2.56	2661	2649	0.0
31733	CHULA	277	1476	1581	1627	0.7	37	557	610	633	1.0	2.52	444	474	0.7
31735	COBB	261	870	982	1003	1.3	54	366	422	434	1.6	2.33	262	293	1.2
31738	COOLIDGE	275	1918	2021	2060	0.6	34	763	825	848	0.8	2.45	539	561	0.4
31743	DE SOTO	177	591	649	667	1.0	47	198	224	233	1.3	2.90	149	164	1.0
31744	DOERUN	071	2870	2952	3000	0.3	25	1129	1190	1219	0.6	2.48	828	842	0.2
31749	ENIGMA	019	3285	3504	3572	0.7	37	1214	1318	1351	0.9	2.66	938	990	0.6
31750	FITZGERALD	017	18163	18355	18444	0.1	19	6936	7120	7195	0.3	2.52	4824	4775	-0.1
31756	HARTSFIELD	071	976	1047	1089	0.8	41	373	408	426	1.0	2.57	299	319	0.7
31757	THOMASVILLE	275	9452	10801	11320	1.5	60	3454	4034	4268	1.7	2.62	2576	2916	1.3
31760	IRWINVILLE	155	313	326	327	0.4	28	125	132	132	0.6	2.47	93	95	0.2
31763	LEESBURG	177	19762	27084	31283	3.5	88	6558	9168	10689	3.7	2.85	5378	7362	3.5
31764	LESLIE	261	1552	1545	1549	0.0	17	535	545	550	0.2	2.83	411	408	-0.1
31765	MEIGS	205	2619	2734	2797	0.5	31	973	1041	1074	0.7	2.61	711	734	0.3
31768	MOULTRIE	071	22213	23333	23979	0.5	31	8621	9162	9457	0.7	2.51	5894	6036	0.3
31771	NORMAN PARK	071	5116	5815	6141	1.4	57	1720	1994	2128	1.6	2.74	1309	1472	1.3
31772	OAKFIELD	321	568	580	575	0.2	22	209	220	220	0.6	2.64	160	163	0.2
31773	OCHLOCKNEE	275	3244	3532	3619	0.9	45	1257	1396	1441	1.1	2.53	931	1001	0.8
31774	OCILLA	155	6954	7063	6983	0.2	22	2497	2506	2486	0.0	2.60	1842	1791	-0.3
31775	OMEGA	071	3023	3410	3597	1.3	54	986	1115	1179	1.3	2.97	750	822	1.0
31778	PAVO	027	3654	3783	3776	0.4	28	1412	1499	1508	0.6	2.51	1003	1027	0.3
31779	PELHAM	205	9597	9646	9592	0.1	19	3042	3132	3148	0.3	2.70	2163	2151	-0.1
31780	PLAINS	261	2511	2475	2446	-0.2	13	894	893	888	0.0	2.62	648	626	-0.4
31781	POULAN	321	1721	1789	1776	0.4	28	639	683	684	0.7	2.61	492	511	0.4
31783	REBECCA	287	1273	1310	1305	0.3	25	478	494	494	0.4	2.65	361	362	0.0
31784	SALE CITY	205	637	636	630	0.0	17	249	257	257	0.3	2.47	191	192	0.1
31787	SMITHVILLE	177	1982	2572	3106	3.3	86	684	937	1095	3.5	2.85	532	712	3.2
31788	MOULTRIE	071	10107	11214	11754	1.1	49	3375	3740	3933	1.1	2.82	2537	2713	0.7
31789	SUMNER	321	1736	1786	1770	0.3	25	655	694	693	0.6	2.57	501	516	0.3
31790	SYCAMORE	287	1873	1947	1938	0.4	28	642	670	669	0.5	2.80	507	515	0.2
31791	SYLVESTER	321	12898	12354	11948	-0.5	7	4667	4565	4444	-0.2	2.66	3496	3317	-0.6
31792	THOMASVILLE	275	22874	23954	24105	0.5	31	8851	9342	9465	0.6	2.43	6001	6082	0.1
31793	TIFTON	277	6904	7622	8001	1.1	49	2321	2614	2769	1.3	2.71	1757	1915	0.9
31794	TIFTON	277	26578	28445	29488	0.7	37	9871	10749	11219	0.9	2.56	7004	7366	0.5
31795	TY TY	321	1957	2115	2197	0.8	41	728	806	843	1.1	2.62	559	602	0.8
31796	WARWICK	321	1236	1205	1170	-0.3	11	499	500	491	0.0	2.41	364	352	-0.4
31798	WRAY	155	940	901	884	-0.5	7	359	351	346	-0.2	2.57	266	252	-0.6
31801	BOX SPRINGS	263	2524	2609	2622	0.4	28	945	1010	1027	0.7	2.54	721	749	0.4
31803	BUENA VISTA	197	4919	4778	4676	-0.3	11	1849	1842	1818	0.0	2.57	1283	1230	-0.5
31804	CATAULA	145	4320	5475	6167	2.6	78	1561	2003	2268	2.7	2.73	1313	1644	2.5
31805	CUSSETA	053	2798	2656	2637	-0.6	4	1051	1060	1076	0.1	2.50	783	697	-1.2
31806	ELLAVILLE	249	3731	4253	4534	1.4	57	1418	1644	1764	1.6	2.58	1029	1155	1.3
31807	ELLERSLIE	145	1179	1746	2113	4.3	92	422	651	791	4.8	2.68	353	531	4.5
31808	FORTSON	145	4846	6137	6862	2.6	78	1760	2274	2560	2.8	2.70	1453	1832	2.5
31811	HAMILTON	145	3220	4316	4948	3.2	85	1202	1632	1880	3.4	2.61	909	1201	3.1
31812	JUNCTION CITY	263	378	371	361	-0.2	13	151	154	152	0.2	2.41	103	100	-0.3
31815	LUMPKIN	259	2025	1725	1600	-1.7	1	800	714	671	-1.2	2.36	543	466	-1.6
31816	MANCHESTER	199	5751	5574	5500	-0.3	11	2289	2266	2257	-0.1	2.46	1587	1510	-0.5
31820	MIDLAND	215	5224	7139	7836	3.4	87	1839	2584	2855	3.7	2.76	1412	1953	3.6
31821	OMAHA	259	840	717	666	-1.7	1	334	299	281	-1.2	2.40	224	193	-1.6
31822	PINE MOUNTAIN	145	4640	5790	6421	2.4	75	1735	2206	2461	2.6	2.62	1329	1639	2.3
31823	PINE MOUNTAIN VALLEY	145	1044	1385	1596	3.1	85	404	541	632	3.2	2.40	314	409	2.9
31824	PRESTON	307	1910	1831	1796	-0.5	7	725	718	712	-0.1	2.55	535	514	-0.4
31825	RICHLAND	259	2389	2239	2142	-0.7	3	874	858	828	-0.2	2.36	583	550	-0.6
31826	SHILOH	145	1814	2241	2456	2.3	74	660	816	899	2.3	2.73	512	616	2.0
31827	TALBOTTON	263	2507	2576	2589	0.3	25	974	1034	1051	0.6	2.47	684	700	0.3
31829	UPATOI	215	754	834	862	1.1	49	258	287	298	1.2	2.91	227	248	1.0
31830	WARM SPRINGS	199	3036	2955	2928	-0.3	11	1121	1124	1125	0.0	2.39	787	759	-0.4
31831	WAVERLY HALL	145	2335	2701	2913	1.6	63	876	1008	1089	1.5	2.56	662	737	1.2
31832	WESTON	307	478	455	446	-0.5	7	185	182	180	-0.2	2.50	139	132	-0.6
31833	WEST POINT	145	6566	7116	7371	0.9	45	2542	2795	2909	1.0	2.54	1831	1947	0.7
31836	WOODLAND	263	1713	1757	1763	0.3	25	670	712	723	0.7	2.47	491	505	0.3
31901	COLUMBUS	215	8273	7707	7613	-0.8	2	3593	3520	3498	-0.2	1.93	1569	1411	-1.1
31903	COLUMBUS	215	22501	22070	21898	-0.2	13	8529	8452	8417	-0.1	2.61	5565	5237	-0.7
31904	COLUMBUS	215	29996	31925	32743	0.7	37	12052	13094	13480	0.9	2.40	8003	8442	0.6
31905	FORT BENNING	053	23455	24231	25631	0.4	28	3914	4485	4938	1.5	3.45	3743	4272	1.4
31906	COLUMBUS	215	24375	23300	22927	-0.5	7	10369	10123	10022	-0.3	2.30	6285	5803	-0.9
31907	COLUMBUS	215	56125	55581	55669	-0.1	14	20416	20847	20994	0.2	2.58	14761	14510	-0.2
31909	COLUMBUS	215	28036	31434	32912	1.2	52	10866	12543	13226	1.6	2.49	8063	8999	1.2
39813	ARLINGTON	037	1806	1724	1667	-0.5	7	663	646	630	-0.3	2.67	456	429	-0.7
39815	ATTAPULGUS	087	2375	2550	2609	0.8	41	753	825	852	1.0	3.05	592	632	0.7
	GEORGIA					2.1					2.1	2.65			1.8
	UNITED STATES					1.0					1.1	2.59			0.9

#	POST OFFICE NAME	White 2000	White 2009	Black 2000	Black 2009	Asian/Pacific 2000	Asian/Pacific 2009	% Hispanic Origin 2000	% Hispanic Origin 2009	0-4	5-9	10-14	15-19	20-24	25-44	45-64	65-84	85+	18+	MEDIAN AGE 2009	% 2009 Males	% 2009 Females
31636	LAKE PARK	82.6	75.3	8.8	11.6	0.4	0.6	10.0	15.1	7.3	7.0	6.7	6.4	6.4	29.3	25.3	10.3	1.2	75.2	35.6	51.0	49.0
31637	LENOX	79.7	73.4	16.7	21.0	0.1	0.2	3.4	5.3	6.9	6.9	6.9	6.1	5.1	25.2	27.9	13.3	1.7	75.5	39.6	50.5	49.5
31638	MORVEN	59.3	56.1	36.1	39.3	0.3	0.3	4.5	4.3	6.1	6.3	6.4	7.1	6.5	25.3	28.3	12.0	2.0	76.7	39.2	49.2	50.8
31639	NASHVILLE	85.4	81.3	11.8	14.6	0.3	0.4	2.1	3.4	6.5	6.8	6.8	6.9	5.4	25.6	27.2	12.7	2.2	75.7	38.9	48.8	51.2
31641	NAYLOR	72.1	63.7	26.1	34.1	0.1	0.3	0.8	1.1	7.5	7.0	7.6	7.2	6.7	26.0	26.9	10.2	0.9	73.6	36.4	50.3	49.7
31642	PEARSON	63.7	55.0	19.9	21.2	0.1	0.1	19.1	27.3	9.7	9.1	8.3	7.3	7.0	28.1	21.8	7.8	1.0	68.8	30.3	49.8	50.2
31643	QUITMAN	49.8	47.7	47.7	49.9	0.3	0.3	2.2	2.1	7.1	6.9	6.9	7.5	6.4	24.5	25.2	12.5	3.0	74.5	37.6	46.7	53.3
31645	RAY CITY	87.4	82.1	9.5	13.3	1.0	1.6	1.6	2.7	8.8	8.4	7.9	7.1	7.3	28.8	22.9	7.8	0.9	70.6	31.9	50.3	49.7
31647	SPARKS	74.1	67.1	22.8	28.6	0.5	0.7	2.7	4.0	8.2	7.6	7.2	7.4	7.1	26.7	24.2	10.1	1.4	72.5	34.5	48.7	51.3
31648	STATENVILLE	78.3	71.7	11.8	14.0	0.1	0.1	9.0	13.4	8.4	7.7	7.0	7.2	8.2	27.4	23.4	9.6	1.1	72.7	32.3	50.7	49.3
31649	STOCKTON	84.3	79.5	13.2	17.1	0.2	0.3	1.1	1.7	7.8	7.5	7.2	7.2	6.3	28.4	25.8	9.1	0.9	73.2	34.4	50.9	49.1
31650	WILLACOOCHEE	66.1	58.4	24.8	28.0	0.4	0.5	12.3	17.8	9.1	8.3	8.3	7.8	6.2	27.7	22.8	8.7	1.1	69.6	32.3	49.5	50.5
31699	MOODY A F B	70.6	59.9	22.6	30.8	1.8	2.2	5.7	8.4	2.9	2.6	2.4	5.2	22.8	53.9	7.7	2.3	0.1	90.6	29.0	73.2	26.8
31701	ALBANY	23.2	23.9	75.4	74.2	0.4	0.6	0.7	0.9	8.3	8.0	7.3	7.0	6.9	24.9	23.5	11.2	2.9	72.3	34.8	46.0	54.0
31704	ALBANY	54.9	44.4	38.8	47.7	1.7	2.0	7.0	8.9	15.8	8.8	5.2	6.8	19.6	37.9	5.2	0.7	0.0	67.5	23.4	59.9	40.1
31705	ALBANY	31.1	24.8	66.8	72.7	0.3	0.4	1.7	2.0	8.3	7.8	7.3	11.1	10.2	25.6	20.8	8.0	0.8	71.1	28.4	47.3	52.7
31707	ALBANY	56.8	50.6	41.0	46.3	0.9	1.2	1.3	1.9	6.2	6.0	6.4	6.6	6.7	26.5	25.9	13.5	2.2	77.5	38.5	46.6	53.4
31709	AMERICUS	52.2	45.5	44.1	49.5	1.0	1.4	3.3	4.5	7.6	6.9	6.4	7.9	9.6	27.3	21.5	10.0	2.7	75.3	32.4	46.4	53.6
31711	ANDERSONVILLE	60.3	52.9	36.3	42.2	0.6	0.7	4.0	5.7	7.4	7.4	6.9	6.2	6.1	30.0	26.0	9.1	0.9	74.4	36.0	54.6	45.4
31712	ARABI	80.6	71.2	17.7	26.7	0.8	1.0	0.1	0.1	6.0	6.0	6.4	6.8	6.3	24.8	30.0	12.1	1.6	77.5	40.5	51.7	48.3
31714	ASHBURN	47.6	41.6	49.9	54.9	0.4	0.5	2.5	3.5	8.1	7.3	7.6	8.2	6.8	24.1	24.2	11.6	2.1	72.4	34.5	47.2	52.8
31716	BACONTON	65.6	62.5	31.3	34.5	0.1	0.2	1.8	1.8	7.3	7.4	7.4	6.5	5.6	27.9	26.8	10.3	0.8	73.7	36.5	50.8	49.2
31719	AMERICUS	36.7	31.8	62.0	66.5	0.2	0.3	1.5	1.9	8.5	8.5	8.3	8.1	7.1	25.8	23.1	8.9	1.6	69.9	32.2	49.0	51.0
31721	ALBANY	60.3	52.8	37.5	44.3	1.1	1.5	1.2	1.6	6.3	6.5	6.8	6.6	5.7	27.9	28.8	10.4	1.0	76.4	38.1	47.6	52.4
31730	CAMILLA	40.2	37.4	57.2	60.0	0.4	0.4	2.2	2.2	7.3	7.4	7.0	7.2	7.3	29.4	23.3	9.3	1.7	74.0	33.9	50.6	49.4
31733	CHULA	87.5	81.3	7.4	10.6	0.3	0.4	5.4	8.8	6.5	6.8	7.0	5.9	4.9	26.1	30.4	11.4	1.0	76.3	39.7	51.3	48.7
31735	COBB	73.3	65.5	19.3	23.4	0.0	0.0	7.2	11.0	5.4	5.6	6.0	5.6	3.4	22.0	35.7	14.9	1.4	79.4	46.3	50.2	49.8
31738	COOLIDGE	71.4	63.1	25.8	32.8	0.7	0.9	2.2	3.3	6.1	6.4	6.7	7.0	5.3	23.9	30.2	12.4	1.9	76.4	41.1	48.2	51.8
31743	DE SOTO	55.2	49.3	41.8	45.9	0.0	0.0	3.6	5.1	5.7	6.0	6.5	6.8	4.9	24.2	31.9	12.3	1.7	77.7	41.6	48.7	51.3
31744	DOERUN	77.7	70.7	20.2	26.5	0.3	0.4	1.8	2.6	6.6	6.6	6.6	6.1	5.6	25.7	28.1	13.2	1.5	76.5	39.9	50.4	49.6
31749	ENIGMA	89.8	85.5	4.9	6.3	0.6	0.7	4.8	7.7	8.0	7.4	7.0	6.5	5.8	28.7	26.0	9.8	0.7	73.3	35.1	49.6	50.4
31750	FITZGERALD	64.2	58.0	31.7	36.0	0.3	0.4	4.5	6.6	7.2	7.0	6.8	6.7	6.3	25.5	26.0	12.2	2.3	74.8	37.4	48.2	51.8
31756	HARTSFIELD	91.4	87.6	5.2	7.2	0.2	0.3	4.2	6.5	6.7	6.6	7.0	7.4	6.3	26.3	27.0	11.6	1.1	75.4	38.3	52.7	47.3
31757	THOMASVILLE	73.4	66.2	24.4	30.9	0.4	0.6	1.6	2.3	6.9	6.8	6.7	7.1	6.9	27.1	26.7	10.3	1.5	75.2	37.0	47.9	52.1
31760	IRWINVILLE	95.8	95.7	2.2	2.5	0.0	0.0	2.2	2.1	7.1	7.1	7.1	6.4	5.2	27.6	25.2	12.9	1.5	74.8	38.1	49.4	50.6
31763	LEESBURG	83.7	79.7	13.9	16.9	0.8	1.2	1.2	1.9	7.1	7.4	7.6	7.5	6.4	30.5	26.3	6.5	0.6	73.1	34.4	50.6	49.4
31764	LESLIE	52.9	45.2	44.7	51.3	0.4	0.5	2.1	3.0	6.6	6.7	7.1	7.3	5.8	25.4	29.4	10.2	1.4	75.1	38.3	48.5	51.5
31765	MEIGS	60.1	53.6	35.4	40.6	0.8	0.8	5.0	6.5	6.9	7.6	7.1	7.7	6.1	24.3	26.7	11.8	1.7	73.6	37.1	47.7	52.3
31768	MOULTRIE	61.3	55.6	32.6	35.3	0.3	0.4	7.9	11.6	7.7	7.4	7.2	7.0	6.6	25.6	24.3	12.0	2.2	73.4	35.8	48.7	51.3
31771	NORMAN PARK	76.4	67.1	10.4	13.5	0.2	0.3	15.6	22.7	7.4	7.1	7.1	7.0	6.8	30.5	23.2	9.6	1.3	74.3	34.6	51.6	48.4
31772	OAKFIELD	80.0	74.5	18.1	23.3	0.2	0.2	0.5	0.9	6.4	6.4	6.7	6.6	6.2	25.9	29.5	11.7	0.7	76.4	39.4	50.5	49.5
31773	OCHLOCKNEE	88.4	84.4	9.2	12.2	0.4	0.6	1.4	2.2	6.4	6.6	6.8	6.4	5.1	26.5	29.3	11.5	1.4	76.2	39.7	49.0	51.0
31774	OCILLA	64.9	62.5	33.2	35.5	0.4	0.4	1.8	1.8	7.0	6.9	7.4	11.0	6.1	24.3	23.0	11.8	2.6	70.7	34.5	49.8	50.2
31775	OMEGA	68.2	55.7	11.3	13.7	0.2	0.2	24.7	36.0	8.5	8.3	8.0	7.0	6.2	28.2	23.3	9.3	1.2	71.0	33.7	51.2	48.8
31778	PAVO	72.9	67.6	20.9	25.1	0.5	0.6	6.1	7.4	6.1	6.3	6.5	6.2	5.2	24.6	30.0	13.2	2.0	77.4	41.6	49.7	50.3
31779	PELHAM	52.5	50.3	45.4	47.4	0.3	0.2	1.7	1.8	6.8	6.9	8.1	6.3	6.6	27.6	24.2	11.3	2.1	74.5	36.0	52.7	47.3
31780	PLAINS	54.6	48.2	43.6	49.4	0.1	0.1	2.8	3.8	7.0	6.8	7.3	6.7	6.6	22.2	25.8	14.2	3.4	74.7	39.2	47.8	52.2
31781	POULAN	76.5	70.0	22.0	27.9	0.1	0.1	1.0	1.5	7.0	7.2	7.3	7.1	5.9	25.0	28.5	10.7	1.3	74.1	37.2	48.9	51.1
31783	REBECCA	88.2	83.1	8.7	13.0	0.3	0.4	2.7	3.6	6.5	6.5	6.8	6.6	5.9	26.4	27.1	12.4	1.8	76.0	38.8	49.0	51.0
31784	SALE CITY	78.8	76.1	17.1	19.7	0.3	0.3	3.0	3.3	6.9	7.1	6.9	6.4	4.1	25.0	28.5	13.5	1.6	75.2	40.2	52.2	47.8
31787	SMITHVILLE	50.4	43.1	48.5	55.6	0.2	0.2	1.0	1.3	9.0	9.0	8.3	6.6	5.8	24.7	26.4	8.8	1.3	69.5	34.0	47.8	52.2
31788	MOULTRIE	71.6	62.1	14.4	17.4	0.3	0.4	17.2	24.7	8.5	8.1	7.6	7.1	6.7	29.9	21.8	8.8	1.4	71.8	32.4	51.5	48.5
31789	SUMNER	78.5	72.2	19.1	24.4	0.1	0.1	2.0	3.1	7.1	7.1	7.2	7.1	6.0	25.4	28.0	10.9	1.3	74.2	37.0	49.2	50.8
31790	SYCAMORE	79.4	70.0	17.6	25.5	0.1	0.2	2.6	4.1	7.6	7.1	7.4	7.4	6.5	25.6	25.5	11.0	1.8	73.4	35.8	52.3	47.7
31791	SYLVESTER	62.4	56.8	36.2	41.3	0.3	0.4	0.8	1.1	7.3	7.3	7.3	7.3	6.4	25.0	26.4	11.2	1.7	73.3	36.8	47.1	52.9
31792	THOMASVILLE	50.3	44.7	47.7	52.7	0.5	0.6	1.4	1.9	6.8	6.7	6.7	6.9	6.3	24.6	26.5	12.7	2.9	75.4	38.7	46.7	53.3
31793	TIFTON	76.8	67.3	14.4	19.1	1.1	1.5	10.6	16.3	7.0	6.9	6.6	8.6	7.6	29.4	23.6	9.4	0.9	75.8	33.6	51.5	48.5
31794	TIFTON	60.6	55.4	34.4	37.6	1.1	1.4	5.5	7.7	7.9	7.5	7.0	7.3	7.3	26.4	23.9	10.8	1.9	73.5	34.3	48.2	51.8
31795	TY TY	80.1	71.2	16.4	23.3	0.2	0.3	3.0	4.8	7.1	7.2	7.4	7.0	5.5	27.3	26.9	10.5	1.2	73.9	36.7	49.9	50.1
31796	WARWICK	67.5	60.0	30.1	36.6	0.2	0.3	1.1	1.7	6.1	6.3	6.9	7.3	5.1	21.4	30.4	14.9	1.7	76.3	42.4	48.5	51.5
31798	WRAY	77.4	73.3	18.4	21.8	0.4	0.4	4.2	5.1	6.5	6.4	6.5	5.9	5.2	24.5	28.7	14.2	1.9	76.8	41.1	49.5	50.5
31801	BOX SPRINGS	66.9	64.8	30.6	31.7	0.2	0.3	1.5	2.4	5.7	5.9	6.3	7.1	6.2	23.8	30.9	12.5	1.5	77.6	41.0	48.9	51.1
31803	BUENA VISTA	48.6	40.6	45.6	51.3	0.4	0.4	7.6	10.7	6.6	6.7	6.4	8.1	7.0	25.3	27.3	10.9	1.7	75.4	37.3	49.5	50.5
31804	CATAULA	85.6	81.3	12.5	16.0	0.5	0.7	0.9	1.3	6.0	6.7	7.4	7.0	4.0	25.4	32.3	10.3	0.9	75.5	41.1	49.3	50.7
31805	CUSSETA	63.3	57.8	33.1	37.9	1.2	1.4	1.5	2.1	7.9	7.5	6.7	7.2	8.0	27.8	25.1	9.1	0.8	73.6	33.6	48.5	51.5
31806	ELLAVILLE	65.5	59.6	31.5	36.3	0.2	0.3	2.4	3.4	8.6	8.3	8.1	6.9	5.9	25.5	24.6	10.9	1.2	70.6	35.4	47.9	52.1
31807	ELLERSLIE	83.6	78.9	14.1	17.8	0.8	1.1	1.9	2.7	6.0	6.6	7.5	7.5	4.1	24.9	32.4	10.0	1.1	75.2	41.1	50.5	49.5
31808	FORTSON	90.5	87.3	6.9	9.0	0.8	1.1	1.2	1.9	5.6	7.5	7.5	7.1	3.7	28.1	31.8	8.0	0.7	74.9	39.3	50.4	49.6
31811	HAMILTON	74.6	70.0	23.5	27.4	0.4	0.6	0.8	1.1	5.8	6.2	6.6	6.4	4.9	24.4	31.9	12.5	1.3	77.2	42.1	50.6	49.4
31812	JUNCTION CITY	35.3	36.9	63.7	61.5	0.3	0.5	1.3	1.3	5.9	6.5	7.0	6.5	4.0	21.8	30.7	15.4	2.2	76.5	43.6	48.5	51.5
31815	LUMPKIN	34.2	29.2	65.2	70.1	0.0	0.0	0.6	0.6	6.4	7.4	7.9	6.7	5.1	23.5	26.8	13.6	2.6	74.5	38.9	47.9	52.1
31816	MANCHESTER	61.9	58.4	36.3	39.1	0.8	1.0	0.8	1.1	7.1	6.9	6.9	7.3	6.2	23.5	26.6	13.1	2.4	74.7	38.4	47.3	52.7
31820	MIDLAND	79.1	72.4	15.7	20.8	2.7	3.4	2.9	4.1	6.1	6.2	6.5	6.7	5.9	29.3	29.7	8.8	0.8	77.2	37.7	50.1	49.9
31821	OMAHA	38.5	32.5	60.6	66.4	0.0	0.0	0.8	1.0	5.3	5.6	5.9	6.6	5.6	24.1	30.5	13.8	2.6	79.2	42.6	49.8	50.2
31822	PINE MOUNTAIN	72.1	65.1	26.4	32.8	0.1	0.1	1.1	1.6	6.5	6.9	7.0	6.6	4.8	24.5	29.4	12.5	1.8	75.4	40.6	48.5	51.5
31823	PINE MOUNTAIN VALLEY	87.1	83.2	10.6	13.6	0.0	0.0	1.2	1.9	5.6	6.1	6.6	6.9	5.6	25.1	30.0	12.4	1.7	77.5	41.0	53.6	46.4
31824	PRESTON	51.1	44.8	46.4	51.5	0.0	0.0	2.6	3.8	6.7	7.0	7.4	6.4	4.9	24.5	28.5	12.8	1.9	75.2	40.3	50.7	49.3
31825	RICHLAND	39.1	33.3	58.8	64.0	0.4	0.4	2.5	3.2	6.0	6.4	6.9	6.7	4.3	22.2	27.2	15.8	4.6	76.6	43.2	47.3	52.7
31826	SHILOH	67.1	62.9	30.6	33.9	0.2	0.2	1.2	1.7	6.1	6.2	6.7	7.5	6.4	24.4	30.3	11.2	1.2	76.5	39.2	48.4	51.6
31827	TALBOTTON	27.2	28.5	70.5	68.6	0.7	0.9	1.7	2.1	5.9	6.2	6.6	6.9	5.3	22.8	31.8	12.6	1.8	77.3	42.0	46.4	53.6
31829	UPATOI	83.3	75.1	14.2	21.3	1.2	1.6	0.9	1.6	4.8	5.5	6.7	8.2	5.0	22.2	35.7	10.9	1.0	78.1	43.2	49.3	50.7
31830	WARM SPRINGS	68.2	62.5	29.8	34.9	0.5	0.7	0.7	0.9	5.0	5.7	6.2	8.6	6.8	22.6	27.9	14.3	3.0	78.9	41.5	48.6	51.4
31831	WAVERLY HALL	71.3	65.6	26.6	31.6	0.6	0.9	1.2	1.6	5.0	5.3	5.9	7.0	4.5	23.2	31.2	15.0	2.9	79.0	44.4	49.0	51.0
31832	WESTON	48.0	42.0	49.7	54.7	0.0	0.0	3.3	5.1	6.2	6.8	6.8	6.4	4.8	24.4	30.8	11.9	2.0	76.0	41.0	51.9	48.1
31833	WEST POINT	56.6	51.2	42.1	47.1	0.6	0.8	0.7	0.9	6.4	7.1	7.2	7.1	5.2	23.0	28.6	13.4	2.1	74.6	40.7	47.2	52.8
31836	WOODLAND	41.0	42.6	57.9	56.1	0.0	0.0	1.1	1.3	5.9	5.9	6.4	6.9	5.2	23.4	30.6	14.1	1.6	77.6	42.2	46.9	53.1
31901	COLUMBUS	41.6	34.8	55.8	61.6	0.3	0.4	2.1	3.0	7.0	6.5	5.6	6.2	7.3	29.2	23.7	11.4	3.1	77.6	36.8	48.7	51.3
31903	COLUMBUS	21.5	15.4	70.4	74.4	1.6	1.7	7.6	9.8	8.6	8.5	7.8	8.5	7.8	25.8	21.8	10.0	1.2	69.9	31.0	46.9	53.1
31904	COLUMBUS	75.3	68.5	20.3	24.8	1.6	2.2	3.1	4.9	7.3	7.1	6.9	6.5	5.7	25.4	26.3	12.3	2.6	74.7	38.5	47.5	52.5
31905	FORT BENNING	57.3	48.3	27.7	31.9	2.5	2.9	13.7	18.8	11.1	8.8	6.3	13.6	24.7	32.9	2.3	0.2	0.0	71.1	22.1	65.9	34.1
31906	COLUMBUS	30.8	26.4	66.4	70.1	0.6	0.7	2.4	3.2	7.1	6.9	6.6	6.8	7.5	26.3	24.6	12.0	2.3	75.3	36.0	45.8	54.2
31907	COLUMBUS	38.0	29.9	56.6	63.2	1.6	1.8	3.8	5.2	6.5	6.3	6.4	7.5	8.0	28.4	25.0	10.3	1.5	76.3	34.6	47.6	52.4
31909	COLUMBUS	82.6	74.2	11.4	16.9	2.8	4.0	3.4	5.6	7.0	6.9	6.7	6.4	5.5	30.3	25.8	10.0	1.3	75.3	36.5	48.2	51.8
39813	ARLINGTON	34.8	29.2	64.2	69.5	0.3	0.3	1.1	1.4	8.0	7.8	7.9	8.2	5.9	22.6	25.6	11.9	2.0	71.4	36.5	46.8	53.2
39815	ATTAPULGUS	26.0	20.3	68.5	72.1	0.0	0.0	5.7	7.9	7.5	7.6	7.6	7.5	6.4	25.1	26.6	10.1	1.6	72.7	35.7	48.9	51.1
	GEORGIA	65.1	61.1	28.7	30.1	2.2	2.9	5.3	7.7	7.3	7.0	6.9	7.1	7.1	29.3	25.1	8.9	1.3	74.7	35.0	49.4	50.6
	UNITED STATES	75.1	72.0	12.3	12.7	3.8	4.6	12.5	15.7	6.8	6.7	6.6	7.1	6.9	27.0	26.0	10.9	1.9	75.7	36.9	49.2	50.8

ZIP CODE #	POST OFFICE NAME	2009 Per Capita Income	2009 HH Income Base	2009 HOUSEHOLD INCOME DISTRIBUTION (%) Less than $25,000	$25,000 to $49,999	$50,000 to $99,999	$100,000 to $149,999	$150,000 or More	MEDIAN HOUSEHOLD INCOME 2009	2014	2009 National Centile	2009 State Centile	2009 Home Value Base	2009 HOME VALUE DISTRIBUTION (%) Less than $50,000	$50,000 to $89,999	$90,000 to $174,999	$175,000 to $399,999	$400,000 or More	2009 Median Home Value
31636	LAKE PARK	18720	3554	33.8	24.1	34.4	5.5	2.1	40168	44422	33	44	2583	25.1	26.6	36.2	11.3	0.7	87331
31637	LENOX	17302	932	38.2	26.7	30.9	2.0	2.1	33775	35721	15	21	762	31.1	31.4	27.3	7.0	3.3	73115
31638	MORVEN	14551	372	39.5	33.6	23.9	1.6	1.3	30604	31121	9	10	307	48.5	25.4	18.9	5.5	1.6	52045
31639	NASHVILLE	18346	3844	34.4	31.1	29.8	2.8	1.9	36192	37381	21	30	2773	28.1	24.0	33.8	12.6	1.5	84387
31641	NAYLOR	17481	504	35.1	25.0	33.5	5.4	1.0	36414	40127	22	31	436	29.6	52.8	9.2	7.6	0.9	64375
31642	PEARSON	14873	1662	39.9	27.0	28.3	3.0	1.8	32956	35655	13	17	1186	50.1	23.1	17.7	7.9	1.2	49928
31643	QUITMAN	15620	3519	41.3	30.0	23.8	3.2	1.7	29595	30761	7	7	2449	37.0	34.0	22.8	5.4	0.8	63543
31645	RAY CITY	15390	1639	30.8	39.0	26.7	2.7	0.7	36991	37751	24	33	1209	26.9	26.7	33.3	10.2	2.9	81471
31647	SPARKS	15221	1297	32.8	37.8	24.7	3.5	1.2	34856	35327	17	24	1006	28.3	28.1	33.9	9.3	0.3	79146
31648	STATENVILLE	16534	420	36.4	41.4	16.4	3.1	2.6	30366	30682	9	9	347	46.4	34.6	16.1	2.9	0.0	54808
31649	STOCKTON	14042	721	37.6	33.0	26.2	3.2	0.0	32206	33948	12	15	619	49.4	25.7	22.6	1.1	1.1	50673
31650	WILLACOOCHEE	15337	1262	38.0	32.1	25.2	3.1	1.7	33390	34755	14	18	975	44.2	24.6	21.2	9.0	0.9	55650
31699	MOODY A F B	9864	23	34.8	26.1	39.1	0.0	0.0	36108	40000	21	29	16	31.3	12.5	56.3	0.0	0.0	95000
31701	ALBANY	14891	8674	48.7	22.7	24.1	3.1	1.5	26309	30510	4	3	3657	26.8	41.9	27.8	2.5	1.0	70757
31704	ALBANY	17041	213	6.1	42.7	41.3	8.5	1.4	50947	53457	63	70	29	48.3	51.7	0.0	0.0	0.0	62500
31705	ALBANY	15093	12240	39.9	28.3	27.3	3.4	1.0	32717	35417	13	16	6831	33.9	44.6	19.7	1.6	0.2	64518
31707	ALBANY	24805	9912	27.5	27.4	34.5	6.8	3.9	44989	50168	48	58	5577	8.8	43.3	42.1	5.5	0.3	88187
31709	AMERICUS	19233	5991	32.2	32.7	27.6	4.6	2.9	37570	39867	25	35	3339	19.6	32.1	36.1	11.3	0.9	87300
31711	ANDERSONVILLE	21222	387	30.5	24.5	35.4	4.7	4.9	42897	50375	42	52	314	29.3	28.3	28.7	8.0	5.7	82258
31712	ARABI	17031	455	37.4	26.2	32.5	2.6	1.3	33311	34582	14	18	369	29.5	32.2	24.7	12.2	1.4	67979
31714	ASHBURN	14765	2506	46.2	25.9	22.8	4.1	1.1	27291	28478	5	3	1676	39.3	30.1	22.2	6.8	1.7	64409
31716	BACONTON	17202	1181	29.3	31.9	33.9	3.8	1.1	40400	45046	34	44	975	24.7	28.3	35.2	10.8	1.0	85530
31719	AMERICUS	15494	3664	35.4	32.0	27.3	3.8	1.5	34687	36822	17	23	2384	22.8	33.9	31.6	11.0	0.6	81744
31721	ALBANY	33374	7925	14.6	19.6	42.2	12.5	11.0	65231	66828	83	85	5456	8.6	20.2	48.7	19.5	2.9	114587
31730	CAMILLA	16289	3683	43.3	25.2	24.8	4.0	2.7	29784	29924	8	7	2492	25.0	30.2	29.4	14.0	1.4	79621
31733	CHULA	23606	610	22.3	25.4	41.0	6.9	4.4	51736	53540	65	71	501	17.4	27.1	21.6	28.5	5.4	102926
31735	COBB	21407	422	21.1	29.9	42.9	5.5	0.7	49089	51447	59	66	339	21.8	22.1	35.1	17.7	3.2	108929
31738	COOLIDGE	16556	825	39.9	29.5	26.7	3.2	0.8	32190	34014	12	14	664	30.6	23.6	30.0	14.8	1.1	84043
31743	DE SOTO	15936	224	30.8	29.9	32.1	5.4	1.8	37537	39402	25	35	175	30.9	31.4	26.9	9.7	1.1	73929
31744	DOERUN	18467	1190	34.9	29.1	30.3	3.9	1.8	35000	37924	18	25	929	24.0	29.7	32.4	11.6	2.3	84435
31749	ENIGMA	17638	1318	34.1	31.8	28.1	4.2	1.8	36386	38041	22	31	1070	36.4	23.4	30.3	8.7	1.2	72568
31750	FITZGERALD	17480	7120	39.4	27.0	26.4	5.4	1.9	33512	34216	14	19	4769	31.0	32.0	27.6	8.7	0.7	72453
31756	HARTSFIELD	21906	408	20.6	30.6	42.4	3.4	2.9	48714	52250	58	66	349	27.2	24.4	31.8	11.7	4.9	86765
31757	THOMASVILLE	19221	4034	30.1	28.0	34.4	5.4	2.1	41688	45134	38	48	3039	21.0	19.3	36.2	21.2	2.3	110359
31760	IRWINVILLE	20256	132	28.8	33.3	31.8	3.8	2.3	41224	40647	37	47	111	25.2	33.3	30.6	9.9	0.9	77857
31763	LEESBURG	23358	9168	15.8	24.3	44.7	10.1	5.1	59074	61383	76	79	7005	23.5	20.1	40.2	15.2	1.0	100643
31764	LESLIE	16482	545	35.8	27.0	29.0	6.4	1.8	35699	37427	20	27	433	29.1	33.7	24.7	11.1	1.4	75595
31765	MEIGS	15208	1041	45.4	27.0	22.3	3.7	1.5	28983	30615	7	5	764	33.5	29.2	24.0	11.6	1.7	69286
31768	MOULTRIE	16947	9162	39.6	29.9	25.0	3.4	2.0	32946	32798	13	17	5572	22.9	29.5	33.2	11.7	2.8	86667
31771	NORMAN PARK	15963	1994	31.7	33.3	30.7	3.1	1.2	35759	36214	20	27	1533	35.5	22.8	32.1	8.5	1.1	74257
31772	OAKFIELD	17598	220	39.5	31.8	21.4	4.5	2.7	33523	36279	14	19	192	39.1	36.5	22.9	1.6	0.0	66667
31773	OCHLOCKNEE	19007	1396	28.5	26.5	39.7	4.5	0.8	43953	48472	45	55	1117	19.1	23.6	38.7	15.9	2.7	104514
31774	OCILLA	16582	2506	35.6	29.7	29.1	3.5	2.1	34911	35818	17	24	1821	30.3	39.2	20.3	9.9	0.4	67244
31775	OMEGA	14126	1115	35.4	30.5	29.9	3.4	0.8	35512	38451	19	26	821	37.1	30.5	23.3	6.7	2.4	66644
31778	PAVO	16135	1499	40.7	29.6	25.3	3.1	1.3	32626	35046	13	15	1240	33.1	28.1	25.2	11.5	2.0	74091
31779	PELHAM	14763	3132	42.1	30.3	23.2	2.6	1.8	30943	31697	10	12	2182	24.6	30.5	30.6	12.7	2.1	83267
31780	PLAINS	16823	893	31.8	32.8	30.3	4.3	0.8	36881	38819	23	32	696	35.3	30.5	25.0	8.6	0.6	64493
31781	POULAN	17299	683	34.3	28.6	32.1	3.4	1.8	38832	40669	29	40	505	36.6	37.4	20.8	4.8	0.4	66630
31783	REBECCA	16645	494	30.6	37.4	28.1	2.6	1.2	37778	39181	26	36	413	30.3	32.4	26.9	9.0	1.5	68875
31784	SALE CITY	20351	257	35.0	23.7	30.7	8.9	1.6	40619	43144	35	44	205	26.8	21.0	32.7	14.1	5.4	94091
31787	SMITHVILLE	17608	937	24.7	27.3	42.9	3.8	1.3	47385	51663	55	64	765	43.8	27.3	18.8	7.8	2.2	57422
31788	MOULTRIE	15761	3740	36.3	27.9	29.9	4.6	1.3	35087	35397	18	25	2525	27.6	25.9	28.0	16.3	2.2	85370
31789	SUMNER	17129	694	33.6	30.8	31.7	2.4	1.4	38336	40059	28	38	526	36.5	37.1	21.1	5.1	0.2	67636
31790	SYCAMORE	17699	670	34.0	29.7	27.5	5.8	3.0	38350	39692	28	38	542	29.2	32.3	27.5	10.5	0.6	75849
31791	SYLVESTER	18335	4565	33.9	26.8	32.0	4.4	2.9	39655	41699	32	42	3284	26.2	39.6	29.3	4.4	0.4	71637
31792	THOMASVILLE	19808	9342	33.9	27.9	30.2	4.8	3.2	38896	40845	29	40	5875	15.3	25.7	34.0	19.9	5.0	104990
31793	TIFTON	20409	2614	25.6	27.9	36.0	6.7	3.9	46038	49303	51	61	1914	22.3	18.8	31.1	23.1	4.8	109045
31794	TIFTON	19475	10749	34.6	27.6	29.2	5.9	2.8	39158	41481	30	41	6735	24.7	19.0	37.1	16.2	3.1	99030
31795	TY TY	20074	806	30.0	31.5	30.6	3.5	4.3	40080	41390	33	43	654	28.6	27.4	20.5	17.4	6.1	81875
31796	WARWICK	19676	500	30.4	30.2	34.2	4.0	1.2	41925	43460	39	49	394	28.4	35.3	32.0	4.3	0.0	77447
31798	WRAY	18471	351	31.9	33.3	27.4	6.0	1.4	35421	35891	19	26	293	43.7	24.2	17.4	11.9	2.7	59250
31801	BOX SPRINGS	17859	1010	29.9	31.5	32.8	5.0	0.9	39906	42780	32	43	839	35.8	27.7	27.8	7.7	1.1	70077
31803	BUENA VISTA	15508	1842	42.0	26.0	27.1	3.7	1.1	31844	33739	11	13	1337	38.2	28.0	26.6	5.6	1.6	66708
31804	CATAULA	26581	2003	12.9	20.6	47.6	12.9	6.0	65660	70857	84	85	1817	14.3	18.1	34.1	29.3	4.3	127885
31805	CUSSETA	15206	1060	38.0	34.1	25.2	2.2	0.6	31189	32867	10	12	884	29.9	29.4	34.8	4.3	1.6	76000
31806	ELLAVILLE	17304	1644	34.7	29.8	29.9	4.0	1.6	38255	39340	27	38	1248	29.4	31.7	26.8	9.9	2.2	72892
31807	ELLERSLIE	27299	651	12.3	16.6	54.5	11.8	4.8	64060	67043	82	84	586	11.6	18.6	43.5	23.7	2.6	113095
31808	FORTSON	30309	2274	9.5	15.0	49.8	18.6	7.1	74789	76852	89	91	2107	9.8	16.3	38.2	33.4	2.4	139565
31811	HAMILTON	25832	1632	23.5	23.5	33.2	11.6	8.1	53137	56976	68	73	1384	13.8	25.4	24.6	25.2	11.0	110685
31812	JUNCTION CITY	14751	154	46.8	29.2	20.1	2.6	1.3	28429	27632	6	5	131	54.2	18.3	19.1	7.6	0.8	45769
31815	LUMPKIN	17317	714	44.0	30.3	22.5	1.3	2.0	29869	30606	8	8	504	49.8	27.8	15.9	5.8	0.8	50189
31816	MANCHESTER	18753	2266	35.3	29.0	28.2	5.4	2.0	36436	38536	22	31	1519	38.6	34.5	23.0	3.6	0.3	63349
31820	MIDLAND	29756	2584	10.1	20.9	42.9	17.6	8.4	67927	70654	86	87	1886	5.2	10.9	36.3	43.7	3.8	166725
31821	OMAHA	15393	299	36.8	43.5	15.1	4.7	0.0	29376	28919	7	5	241	44.0	24.5	17.4	5.8	8.3	57632
31822	PINE MOUNTAIN	22861	2206	25.0	25.4	36.4	8.0	5.3	49550	51665	60	68	1595	19.7	17.7	28.4	25.8	8.3	115417
31823	PINE MOUNTAIN VALLEY	24291	541	24.6	25.7	37.0	8.1	4.6	49732	54147	60	68	437	20.1	55.1	16.2	8.5	0.0	73257
31824	PRESTON	17253	718	36.4	31.1	27.4	2.8	2.4	34190	34293	16	22	578	44.8	27.0	22.1	4.5	1.6	60256
31825	RICHLAND	20206	858	42.9	29.0	22.0	3.5	2.6	30069	31548	8	8	614	46.6	25.9	24.6	2.9	0.0	53889
31826	SHILOH	18095	816	30.4	21.9	41.4	5.0	1.2	47241	51089	55	63	661	31.5	39.2	18.9	6.7	3.8	68239
31827	TALBOTTON	17168	1034	43.6	21.1	30.2	3.2	1.9	31304	32957	10	12	815	40.9	22.9	26.1	8.2	1.8	63088
31829	UPATOI	29710	287	5.6	19.5	47.4	18.8	8.7	75125	76749	89	91	268	4.5	6.0	35.4	48.9	5.2	186000
31830	WARM SPRINGS	20272	1124	34.8	24.4	31.4	7.7	1.7	41915	44776	39	49	824	30.8	30.6	31.8	5.2	1.6	78148
31831	WAVERLY HALL	19936	1008	28.2	23.3	41.2	5.2	2.2	47312	52232	55	63	850	32.2	27.8	24.8	14.2	0.9	71087
31832	WESTON	18634	182	33.5	37.4	24.2	1.6	3.3	33652	34257	15	20	147	47.6	20.4	23.8	6.8	1.4	54375
31833	WEST POINT	20521	2795	31.5	28.6	30.0	6.0	3.9	41235	43050	37	47	1980	19.2	26.1	37.9	13.2	3.6	95222
31836	WOODLAND	17237	712	44.4	22.6	26.5	5.5	1.0	29600	29346	7	7	591	33.2	28.8	25.4	12.7	0.0	67614
31901	COLUMBUS	16252	3520	56.0	25.7	13.9	2.6	1.8	19753	21104	1	1	819	25.5	24.4	38.2	10.3	1.6	90075
31903	COLUMBUS	13538	8452	47.1	29.5	21.0	1.5	0.9	27093	29308	5	3	3352	29.0	51.5	19.0	0.3	0.1	66852
31904	COLUMBUS	25671	13094	29.5	24.7	32.0	6.4	7.3	44829	50616	48	58	7830	9.5	25.0	45.1	15.0	5.5	105015
31905	FORT BENNING	15071	4485	13.0	42.8	38.1	4.8	1.3	45092	50510	49	59	166	29.5	27.7	33.7	7.2	1.8	79167
31906	COLUMBUS	21314	10123	35.8	31.7	24.2	4.0	4.4	34248	36907	16	22	4831	17.9	28.1	38.1	13.4	2.5	94035
31907	COLUMBUS	21653	20847	19.7	31.8	40.1	6.2	2.1	48614	52116	58	65	13348	7.4	38.3	48.9	5.2	0.2	92664
31909	COLUMBUS	27404	12543	13.2	22.8	49.4	10.3	4.3	61827	61644	80	82	8853	2.8	18.8	63.3	14.6	0.6	113231
39813	ARLINGTON	14709	646	41.8	30.3	22.6	4.2	1.1	30757	30955	9	11	471	50.3	25.7	18.5	5.5	0.0	49732
39815	ATTAPULGUS	14835	825	39.0	30.2	25.1	3.5	2.2	32461	33624	12	15	658	36.2	38.1	14.6	9.3	1.8	58273
	GEORGIA	26980		20.7	23.1	36.8	11.7	7.7	56761	58593				13.2	17.9	39.1	24.2	5.5	121444
	UNITED STATES	27277		20.9	24.4	35.3	11.7	7.6	54719	56938				9.3	13.1	31.6	32.6	13.5	162279

ZIP CODE #	POST OFFICE NAME	FINANCIAL SERVICES: Auto Loan	FINANCIAL SERVICES: Home Loan	FINANCIAL SERVICES: Invest-ments	FINANCIAL SERVICES: Retire-ment Plans	THE HOME: Home Improvements: Home Repair	THE HOME: Home Improvements: Lawn & Garden	THE HOME: Furnishings: Comput-ers & Hard-ware-Personal	THE HOME: Furnishings: Major Appli-ances	THE HOME: Furnishings: TV, Radio, Sound Equip-ment	THE HOME: Furnishings: Furni-ture	ENTERTAINMENT: Dine out/ Carry out	ENTERTAINMENT: Sports Equip-ment	ENTERTAINMENT: Fees & Tickets	ENTERTAINMENT: Toys & Games	ENTERTAINMENT: Travel	ENTERTAINMENT: Cable TV	PERSONAL: Apparel & Services	PERSONAL: Auto Repairs	PERSONAL: Health Insur-ance	PERSONAL: Pets & Supplies
31636	LAKE PARK	78	70	64	68	69	73	69	72	71	70	71	53	64	73	65	73	48	71	73	85
31637	LENOX	78	53	76	51	54	77	56	70	63	53	62	54	43	64	53	70	41	65	73	85
31638	MORVEN	71	48	67	46	48	69	51	63	58	49	57	49	39	59	48	64	38	59	66	77
31639	NASHVILLE	80	57	75	55	58	79	60	73	67	57	66	55	48	68	57	74	44	69	77	88
31641	NAYLOR	86	61	73	60	61	82	64	75	71	62	69	58	51	73	59	77	46	71	79	91
31642	PEARSON	72	56	62	53	55	68	57	64	62	57	61	49	48	64	53	66	41	62	66	78
31643	QUITMAN	69	50	62	48	49	67	54	62	60	51	58	47	44	60	50	65	39	60	66	75
31645	RAY CITY	66	60	52	57	57	59	59	60	60	61	60	46	55	63	56	61	41	60	59	71
31647	SPARKS	71	57	61	54	56	67	58	64	62	58	61	49	50	64	54	65	41	62	65	77
31648	STATENVILLE	74	70	59	66	66	67	69	68	69	72	69	52	65	72	64	69	48	69	67	81
31649	STOCKTON	64	52	52	50	50	60	53	57	56	53	55	44	46	58	49	59	38	56	58	69
31650	WILLACOOCHEE	72	53	66	50	52	69	55	64	61	54	60	50	45	62	52	66	40	62	67	78
31699	MOODY A F B	73	68	58	65	65	65	67	67	67	70	68	51	63	70	63	67	47	67	65	79
31701	ALBANY	55	46	42	47	44	50	53	50	57	53	56	37	49	56	47	60	39	54	56	61
31704	ALBANY	105	55	41	63	49	46	99	68	93	92	98	68	75	112	71	85	69	87	62	83
31705	ALBANY	64	51	48	52	49	58	58	57	62	57	62	44	52	63	52	65	42	60	62	70
31707	ALBANY	79	75	73	76	74	81	78	78	81	77	80	58	77	80	76	84	56	80	86	93
31709	AMERICUS	72	61	57	61	58	65	71	66	72	67	71	52	64	73	63	74	49	70	70	80
31711	ANDERSONVILLE	91	76	78	73	75	87	74	83	79	76	79	61	67	82	71	84	53	79	84	99
31712	ARABI	77	55	65	54	55	74	57	67	64	56	62	52	46	66	53	69	42	64	71	82
31714	ASHBURN	65	48	60	48	48	64	53	60	58	50	57	45	44	58	49	63	38	58	64	72
31716	BACONTON	80	64	66	62	63	75	64	71	69	64	68	53	56	71	59	73	46	68	73	86
31719	AMERICUS	70	55	59	55	53	68	58	63	64	57	63	48	51	65	54	69	43	63	69	77
31721	ALBANY	120	124	117	126	122	118	117	117	115	122	117	90	120	118	118	114	82	116	114	138
31730	CAMILLA	71	53	60	52	51	66	57	62	63	56	62	48	49	64	53	67	42	62	67	77
31733	CHULA	93	89	83	89	87	95	83	90	86	83	85	69	81	89	83	88	59	86	91	107
31735	COBB	83	67	107	65	73	88	67	85	70	62	69	62	58	66	72	74	46	78	84	98
31738	COOLIDGE	74	51	68	49	51	72	54	65	60	51	59	50	42	62	50	66	39	61	69	80
31743	DE SOTO	81	60	84	57	61	81	61	75	67	59	66	57	50	67	60	73	44	71	77	90
31744	DOERUN	82	59	75	58	60	80	61	74	68	58	66	56	49	69	58	74	44	69	77	89
31749	ENIGMA	75	68	60	65	66	69	66	68	68	69	68	51	62	71	62	69	46	67	68	82
31750	FITZGERALD	74	56	66	55	56	73	60	68	66	57	64	52	51	67	56	71	44	66	73	82
31756	HARTSFIELD	101	73	84	71	72	96	76	88	84	74	82	68	61	88	69	92	55	84	93	107
31757	THOMASVILLE	81	74	66	71	71	75	71	74	73	74	73	55	67	76	67	75	50	73	74	88
31760	IRWINVILLE	90	65	75	63	64	86	67	78	75	66	73	60	54	78	61	82	49	74	83	95
31763	LEESBURG	106	103	91	101	100	101	95	99	96	100	96	74	93	100	92	97	66	95	96	117
31764	LESLIE	84	60	74	58	60	81	62	74	69	61	68	57	50	72	58	76	46	70	77	90
31765	MEIGS	73	49	70	47	49	72	52	65	59	49	58	50	40	60	49	65	38	61	68	79
31768	MOULTRIE	68	53	58	53	53	66	59	62	64	56	62	47	51	64	54	68	43	62	68	76
31771	NORMAN PARK	79	57	65	56	57	75	60	69	66	58	65	53	48	69	54	72	43	65	73	84
31772	OAKFIELD	84	60	69	58	60	80	63	73	69	61	68	56	50	72	57	76	46	69	77	89
31773	OCHLOCKNEE	81	66	75	64	67	80	65	75	70	64	69	56	57	71	63	74	46	71	77	90
31774	OCILLA	76	55	64	54	55	73	59	67	65	57	64	51	48	67	54	71	43	65	73	82
31775	OMEGA	77	53	69	50	52	74	56	67	63	53	62	52	43	65	51	69	41	64	71	82
31778	PAVO	73	51	69	49	52	72	53	66	60	51	59	50	42	61	51	66	39	61	69	80
31779	PELHAM	66	50	59	49	49	65	54	61	60	52	59	46	46	60	50	65	40	60	67	74
31780	PLAINS	81	56	77	53	56	80	59	72	66	56	65	56	46	67	55	73	43	68	76	88
31781	POULAN	81	59	67	58	59	77	61	71	67	59	66	54	50	70	56	73	44	67	75	86
31783	REBECCA	80	57	66	56	57	76	59	69	66	58	65	53	48	69	54	72	43	66	73	84
31784	SALE CITY	92	62	95	60	63	93	67	84	73	59	72	68	50	73	65	81	47	79	89	103
31787	SMITHVILLE	93	61	88	58	61	91	65	82	75	62	73	64	49	77	61	84	49	77	86	100
31788	MOULTRIE	74	63	61	61	61	70	62	67	65	62	65	51	55	68	58	68	44	65	69	81
31789	SUMNER	80	57	66	55	57	76	59	69	66	58	65	53	48	69	54	72	43	65	73	84
31790	SYCAMORE	90	63	91	60	64	91	65	83	73	61	72	63	51	73	63	81	48	77	87	99
31791	SYLVESTER	80	63	68	63	62	77	67	73	73	65	71	55	59	74	62	77	48	72	78	88
31792	THOMASVILLE	72	66	64	66	64	73	67	69	71	67	71	51	65	71	65	75	49	70	75	83
31793	TIFTON	93	79	75	77	77	85	79	83	83	81	82	63	72	86	74	85	56	82	84	100
31794	TIFTON	75	65	61	66	63	70	71	70	75	70	74	53	66	75	66	77	51	72	75	84
31795	TY TY	92	71	76	69	70	87	72	81	78	71	77	62	60	81	66	84	52	77	85	98
31796	WARWICK	85	61	83	59	63	85	63	78	69	59	68	59	50	70	61	76	45	72	82	93
31798	WRAY	85	61	83	59	63	85	63	78	69	59	68	59	50	70	61	76	45	72	82	93
31801	BOX SPRINGS	81	58	73	56	57	77	61	71	67	59	66	56	50	70	57	73	45	68	74	87
31803	BUENA VISTA	73	50	65	48	50	70	53	64	60	51	58	49	41	61	49	66	39	60	67	78
31804	CATAULA	101	114	98	117	111	112	102	106	100	102	101	83	109	103	108	100	70	102	105	125
31805	CUSSETA	59	55	47	53	53	53	55	54	55	57	55	41	51	57	51	55	38	55	53	65
31806	ELLAVILLE	81	58	66	56	57	76	60	70	67	59	65	54	48	70	55	73	44	66	74	85
31807	ELLERSLIE	102	115	99	118	111	113	103	107	101	103	101	83	109	104	108	101	71	103	106	126
31808	FORTSON	113	129	115	133	127	125	115	119	112	116	113	92	123	115	122	112	79	114	116	140
31811	HAMILTON	107	98	106	98	99	110	93	104	96	93	96	78	88	98	94	100	65	98	105	123
31812	JUNCTION CITY	66	43	64	41	43	65	46	58	53	44	52	45	35	54	43	59	34	55	61	71
31815	LUMPKIN	76	50	74	47	50	75	53	67	62	51	60	52	40	63	50	69	40	63	71	83
31816	MANCHESTER	75	57	65	57	57	74	63	69	69	60	67	52	54	69	58	75	45	68	77	83
31820	MIDLAND	116	128	114	131	124	116	118	116	113	122	115	93	125	117	121	110	81	114	108	136
31821	OMAHA	69	45	66	42	45	67	48	60	55	45	54	47	36	56	45	62	36	57	64	74
31822	PINE MOUNTAIN	94	83	99	83	86	97	83	93	85	80	85	69	76	85	84	89	57	89	95	109
31823	PINE MOUNTAIN VALLEY	93	84	84	88	86	100	83	94	86	75	84	71	77	88	83	91	58	87	97	109
31824	PRESTON	82	53	79	50	53	80	57	72	66	54	64	56	43	67	53	73	43	68	76	88
31825	RICHLAND	92	60	88	56	60	90	64	81	74	61	72	63	48	75	60	82	48	76	85	99
31826	SHILOH	89	64	76	62	64	86	66	78	74	64	72	60	53	77	61	81	49	74	82	95
31827	TALBOTTON	79	52	76	49	51	78	55	69	64	52	62	54	41	65	51	71	41	65	73	86
31829	UPATOI	116	146	128	146	141	126	122	124	115	129	117	99	138	120	132	110	84	118	111	143
31830	WARM SPRINGS	91	62	90	59	63	91	65	82	74	61	72	63	51	74	63	82	48	77	87	100
31831	WAVERLY HALL	83	72	83	70	70	88	69	79	74	68	74	61	64	76	70	80	50	76	83	95
31832	WESTON	87	56	84	53	56	85	60	76	70	57	68	59	45	71	56	78	45	72	80	94
31833	WEST POINT	83	68	77	67	68	85	70	78	77	69	75	58	63	76	68	83	51	76	86	94
31836	WOODLAND	79	52	76	49	51	78	55	69	64	52	62	54	41	65	51	71	41	65	73	86
31901	COLUMBUS	45	35	34	37	34	39	46	40	49	44	48	31	41	47	40	51	34	45	47	51
31903	COLUMBUS	52	43	38	44	41	47	49	46	53	49	53	35	46	53	44	56	36	50	53	58
31904	COLUMBUS	86	87	83	88	85	89	88	86	89	87	88	66	89	89	87	91	62	87	90	102
31905	FORT BENNING	95	50	37	57	44	42	89	62	84	83	89	62	68	101	65	77	62	79	56	75
31906	COLUMBUS	71	62	58	63	60	66	69	65	73	69	72	49	66	72	64	75	50	70	72	80
31907	COLUMBUS	80	79	69	80	75	80	80	77	81	80	82	59	80	82	78	83	57	80	83	93
31909	COLUMBUS	98	105	90	104	100	97	97	97	96	101	97	75	101	99	97	95	68	95	95	113
39813	ARLINGTON	73	48	70	45	47	72	51	64	59	48	57	50	38	60	48	66	38	60	68	79
39815	ATTAPULGUS	84	55	81	52	55	82	59	74	68	56	66	58	44	69	55	76	44	70	78	91
	GEORGIA	110	101	97	102	98	103	103	103	104	104	104	80	99	107	99	105	73	103	103	122
	UNITED STATES	100	100	100	100	100	100	100	100	100	100	100	100	100	100	100	100	100	100	100	100

ZIP CODE			POPULATION			2000-2009 ANNUAL RATE		HOUSEHOLDS					FAMILIES		
#	POST OFFICE NAME	COUNTY FIPS CODE	2000	2009	2014	% Rate	State Centile	2000	2009	2014	% Annual Rate 2000-2009	2009 Average HH Size	2000	2009	% Annual Rate 2000-2009
39817	BAINBRIDGE	087	11127	11827	12028	0.7	37	4008	4301	4399	0.8	2.63	2929	3042	0.4
39819	BAINBRIDGE	087	10601	11087	11195	0.5	31	4049	4271	4341	0.6	2.51	2808	2854	0.2
39823	BLAKELY	099	8627	8368	8140	-0.3	11	3228	3221	3157	0.0	2.53	2265	2183	-0.4
39824	BLUFFTON	061	720	664	649	-0.9	2	274	266	264	-0.3	2.50	199	187	-0.7
39825	BRINSON	087	1485	1532	1547	0.3	25	572	603	613	0.6	2.54	442	454	0.3
39826	BRONWOOD	273	906	863	832	-0.5	7	317	306	298	-0.4	2.74	228	212	-0.8
39827	CAIRO	131	3458	3732	3853	0.8	41	1266	1381	1432	0.9	2.69	968	1023	0.6
39828	CAIRO	131	14534	15258	15605	0.5	31	5394	5713	5860	0.6	2.65	3937	4039	0.3
39834	CLIMAX	087	2357	2449	2474	0.4	28	883	935	951	0.6	2.62	685	705	0.3
39836	COLEMAN	243	338	308	293	-1.0	1	141	132	127	-0.7	2.33	98	88	-1.2
39837	COLQUITT	201	6178	5937	5797	-0.4	9	2383	2328	2289	-0.3	2.48	1693	1598	-0.6
39840	CUTHBERT	243	5782	5510	5329	-0.5	7	2165	2083	2026	-0.4	2.47	1447	1339	-0.8
39841	DAMASCUS	099	1263	1180	1136	-0.7	3	489	467	452	-0.5	2.52	344	317	-0.9
39842	DAWSON	273	9686	9534	9280	-0.2	13	3527	3476	3401	-0.2	2.64	2568	2453	-0.5
39845	DONALSONVILLE	253	8479	8430	8312	-0.1	14	3257	3295	3270	0.1	2.45	2357	2306	-0.2
39846	EDISON	037	1957	1816	1729	-0.8	2	738	702	673	-0.5	2.47	501	459	-0.9
39851	FORT GAINES	061	2638	2548	2513	-0.4	9	1073	1078	1077	0.1	2.32	729	705	-0.4
39854	GEORGETOWN	239	1571	1511	1497	-0.4	9	623	612	610	-0.2	2.47	447	425	-0.5
39859	IRON CITY	253	1258	1269	1257	0.1	19	483	500	500	0.4	2.53	359	360	0.0
39861	JAKIN	099	2060	1947	1871	-0.6	4	847	820	796	-0.3	2.37	589	550	-0.7
39862	LEARY	037	987	879	828	-1.2	1	381	352	335	-0.9	2.50	268	239	-1.2
39866	MORGAN	037	2001	1999	1958	0.0	17	322	294	279	-1.0	2.30	226	199	-1.4
39867	MORRIS	239	1027	1043	1061	0.2	22	424	434	443	0.3	2.40	309	306	-0.1
39870	NEWTON	007	3956	3953	3960	0.0	17	1473	1496	1506	0.2	2.64	1065	1046	-0.2
39877	PARROTT	273	349	332	321	-0.5	7	147	144	140	-0.2	2.31	108	102	-0.6
39886	SHELLMAN	243	1674	1545	1480	-0.9	2	604	572	552	-0.6	2.70	427	390	-1.0
39897	WHIGHAM	131	3734	4157	4360	1.2	52	1377	1567	1652	1.4	2.59	1040	1150	1.1
	GEORGIA					2.1					2.1	2.65			1.8
	UNITED STATES					1.0					1.1	2.59			0.9

#	POST OFFICE NAME	RACE (%) White 2000	White 2009	Black 2000	Black 2009	Asian/Pacific 2000	Asian/Pacific 2009	% Hispanic Origin 2000	% Hispanic Origin 2009	2009 AGE DISTRIBUTION (%) 0-4	5-9	10-14	15-19	20-24	25-44	45-64	65-84	85+	18+	MEDIAN AGE 2009	% 2009 Males	% 2009 Females
39817	BAINBRIDGE	55.1	48.8	43.2	48.9	0.1	0.1	1.8	2.6	8.1	7.8	7.3	7.1	7.2	26.7	24.5	10.0	1.4	72.4	34.4	49.0	51.0
39819	BAINBRIDGE	61.1	55.5	34.8	38.5	0.8	1.1	4.5	6.6	6.9	7.0	7.0	6.7	5.5	24.6	25.9	13.4	3.0	74.8	39.2	46.9	53.1
39823	BLAKELY	47.6	41.6	50.7	56.2	0.3	0.4	1.3	1.6	7.4	7.5	8.0	7.6	6.0	22.7	25.4	12.4	2.9	72.2	37.3	46.8	53.2
39824	BLUFFTON	50.6	44.4	48.3	54.2	1.1	1.4	0.1	0.2	4.1	4.4	5.0	7.2	6.9	22.3	33.1	14.5	2.6	82.2	45.1	48.8	51.2
39825	BRINSON	77.2	70.5	21.0	26.6	0.0	0.0	2.0	3.1	6.9	6.8	6.8	6.1	6.2	26.0	28.3	11.6	1.3	75.4	38.6	50.3	49.7
39826	BRONWOOD	47.3	40.3	51.9	58.6	0.2	0.3	1.7	1.9	7.2	7.1	7.4	7.5	5.7	21.3	28.3	13.0	2.5	73.3	39.3	48.6	51.4
39827	CAIRO	84.3	77.2	9.7	13.4	0.1	0.2	6.4	10.2	7.4	7.4	7.2	6.2	5.3	27.7	26.3	10.9	1.6	74.0	37.2	49.4	50.6
39828	CAIRO	54.8	48.5	39.6	43.5	0.4	0.6	6.0	8.7	7.2	7.5	7.5	7.2	5.9	25.8	25.8	11.2	1.9	73.3	36.2	47.3	52.7
39834	CLIMAX	65.2	57.5	32.4	39.1	0.2	0.2	2.2	3.3	7.3	7.1	7.3	7.2	6.0	24.1	27.8	11.7	1.4	73.9	38.1	47.8	52.2
39836	COLEMAN	27.9	22.4	70.6	75.3	0.0	0.0	1.2	1.9	6.8	6.8	7.1	7.1	6.2	23.7	31.2	9.4	1.6	74.7	39.1	50.0	50.0
39837	COLQUITT	69.6	64.2	29.5	34.6	0.1	0.1	0.8	1.2	6.2	6.3	6.5	6.8	5.5	23.4	27.7	14.4	3.1	76.5	41.4	47.6	52.4
39840	CUTHBERT	37.6	32.3	60.6	65.5	0.4	0.4	1.4	1.9	6.6	6.5	6.4	9.6	6.8	21.6	26.3	13.0	3.2	75.9	38.3	46.7	53.3
39841	DAMASCUS	39.8	33.6	58.9	64.8	0.2	0.2	1.3	1.9	7.0	6.8	6.7	7.4	5.8	23.9	27.8	12.8	1.8	75.0	39.6	47.0	53.0
39842	DAWSON	36.0	30.8	62.6	67.5	0.4	0.5	1.2	1.4	7.7	7.5	7.2	7.4	6.6	23.6	25.3	12.4	2.3	73.3	37.1	47.4	52.6
39845	DONALSONVILLE	61.9	59.4	34.3	36.7	0.2	0.2	3.9	3.9	6.8	7.0	6.8	7.0	5.7	23.1	27.3	14.0	2.3	75.1	39.8	48.7	51.3
39846	EDISON	39.1	34.0	59.6	64.3	0.0	0.0	1.6	2.1	7.3	7.4	7.3	6.8	5.6	22.4	26.7	12.6	4.0	73.7	39.0	45.4	54.6
39851	FORT GAINES	35.1	29.9	63.8	68.8	0.1	0.2	1.2	1.4	7.4	7.7	7.2	6.6	5.0	20.0	26.8	16.4	2.9	73.6	41.4	44.7	55.3
39854	GEORGETOWN	46.6	43.7	52.9	55.7	0.1	0.1	0.2	0.2	6.2	6.3	6.6	6.9	5.5	21.6	28.8	15.8	2.4	76.8	42.7	46.6	53.4
39859	IRON CITY	67.1	63.3	31.8	35.7	0.1	0.1	1.3	1.2	7.9	8.0	7.9	6.3	4.6	24.0	26.2	13.3	1.7	72.3	38.2	47.3	52.7
39861	JAKIN	70.6	64.3	28.1	33.9	0.0	0.0	0.8	1.1	5.9	6.1	6.3	6.4	4.9	23.1	29.3	15.9	2.2	77.8	43.0	47.8	52.2
39862	LEARY	38.5	32.5	59.4	64.5	0.0	0.0	2.0	2.7	7.1	7.3	7.2	6.1	5.3	23.3	31.9	10.7	1.1	74.6	39.4	46.4	53.6
39866	MORGAN	40.7	35.3	58.7	63.9	0.0	0.1	6.2	6.8	1.8	1.8	1.8	2.9	13.5	52.1	20.6	4.9	0.9	93.4	35.6	82.8	17.2
39867	MORRIS	60.6	57.8	37.7	40.6	0.0	0.0	1.0	1.0	6.5	6.7	6.7	6.2	4.3	20.6	29.6	17.1	2.2	76.2	44.0	48.4	51.6
39870	NEWTON	47.4	44.8	50.5	53.0	0.0	0.0	2.7	2.7	7.2	7.6	7.8	6.9	5.8	25.0	25.7	11.9	2.0	73.4	37.0	46.0	54.0
39877	PARROTT	67.3	60.2	30.9	37.0	0.6	0.9	2.0	2.7	6.6	6.9	6.6	5.1	4.5	22.9	30.1	15.7	1.5	76.5	43.1	48.8	51.2
39886	SHELLMAN	45.8	39.2	53.2	59.7	0.1	0.1	0.2	0.3	8.2	7.3	7.2	7.8	6.0	21.8	27.2	12.5	2.0	72.2	38.0	47.6	52.4
39897	WHIGHAM	74.2	66.2	21.4	28.2	0.2	0.2	2.1	3.3	6.5	6.5	6.7	6.2	5.1	24.2	29.0	13.3	2.4	76.3	40.9	48.3	51.7
	GEORGIA	65.1	61.1	28.7	30.1	2.2	2.9	5.3	7.7	7.3	7.0	6.9	7.1	7.1	29.3	25.1	8.9	1.3	74.7	35.0	49.4	50.6
	UNITED STATES	75.1	72.0	12.3	12.7	3.8	4.6	12.5	15.7	6.8	6.7	6.6	7.1	6.9	27.0	26.0	10.9	1.9	75.7	36.9	49.2	50.8

#	POST OFFICE NAME	2009 Per Capita Income	2009 HH Income Base	2009 Household Income Distribution (%): Less than $25,000	$25,000 to $49,999	$50,000 to $99,999	$100,000 to $149,999	$150,000 or More	Median Household Income: 2009	2014	2009 National Centile	2009 State Centile	2009 Home Value Base	2009 Home Value Distribution (%): Less than $50,000	$50,000 to $89,999	$90,000 to $174,999	$175,000 to $399,999	$400,000 or More	2009 Median Home Value
39817	BAINBRIDGE	15183	4301	41.3	30.4	23.9	3.4	1.0	30863	31959	9	11	2926	24.5	26.7	37.1	10.4	1.3	88087
39819	BAINBRIDGE	20433	4271	33.2	25.7	31.8	6.0	3.3	41282	44237	37	47	2976	13.0	24.3	39.0	20.7	3.0	109843
39823	BLAKELY	15955	3221	45.4	27.0	21.0	4.9	1.7	29261	29649	7	5	2209	34.4	31.8	25.7	7.2	0.9	66133
39824	BLUFFTON	17377	266	37.6	29.7	27.1	3.0	2.6	38448	40441	28	39	213	48.4	19.2	24.4	6.1	1.9	52917
39825	BRINSON	16595	603	33.7	34.5	27.9	2.7	1.3	33949	35283	15	22	498	24.7	35.5	23.7	12.9	3.2	82817
39826	BRONWOOD	12835	306	50.7	29.7	15.0	2.9	1.6	24542	26925	3	2	228	40.8	38.2	14.9	6.1	0.0	59545
39827	CAIRO	18683	1381	31.9	25.6	34.6	6.2	1.7	42705	49402	42	51	1054	20.0	19.8	30.9	23.2	6.0	112389
39828	CAIRO	15390	5713	41.7	29.0	23.9	3.6	1.9	31504	33194	11	13	3952	21.7	29.0	32.1	13.9	3.2	88824
39834	CLIMAX	16931	935	35.1	27.5	31.9	4.5	1.1	37492	38929	25	34	789	23.8	29.3	28.6	14.8	3.4	85917
39836	COLEMAN	18701	132	39.4	29.5	25.8	3.8	1.5	33475	33460	14	18	103	47.6	32.0	11.7	8.7	0.0	53125
39837	COLQUITT	17008	2328	40.3	30.7	22.9	3.9	2.3	31886	32444	11	14	1773	34.3	30.9	24.3	9.4	1.2	66849
39840	CUTHBERT	14707	2083	48.8	25.2	21.8	2.7	1.5	25803	26982	4	2	1407	43.6	31.6	18.9	5.0	0.9	59050
39841	DAMASCUS	19383	467	42.2	23.8	25.5	5.6	3.0	36089	39709	21	29	361	31.3	32.1	26.3	10.2	0.0	68939
39842	DAWSON	16155	3476	38.8	30.4	25.8	2.7	2.3	33503	36176	14	18	2236	31.4	37.6	26.6	3.6	0.8	70041
39845	DONALSONVILLE	18183	3295	38.0	28.4	27.0	4.4	2.1	33902	34721	15	21	2616	27.6	34.2	29.5	7.7	0.9	74864
39846	EDISON	14063	702	47.6	28.5	20.5	2.4	1.0	26010	26794	4	2	468	40.4	32.5	23.1	4.1	0.0	64242
39851	FORT GAINES	16300	1078	50.0	27.5	18.1	1.9	2.5	25000	25741	3	2	781	43.9	29.4	17.2	7.2	2.3	58190
39854	GEORGETOWN	15521	612	41.2	33.3	21.6	2.9	1.0	29892	30129	8	8	471	42.9	32.3	18.5	6.4	0.0	59571
39859	IRON CITY	16726	500	39.8	29.4	23.8	5.2	1.8	30717	31222	9	11	410	46.3	23.4	20.2	10.0	0.0	58333
39861	JAKIN	19062	820	44.9	23.2	26.1	3.0	2.8	31370	32598	10	13	662	45.6	21.5	26.9	4.2	1.8	58286
39862	LEARY	17719	352	38.4	27.3	29.5	2.8	2.0	33918	36211	15	21	267	36.7	25.1	27.3	8.2	2.6	67250
39866	MORGAN	15745	294	31.6	33.0	29.9	3.1	2.4	35746	39020	20	27	235	31.5	45.1	15.3	8.1	0.0	67581
39867	MORRIS	17980	434	34.3	36.4	24.4	3.2	1.6	32913	34392	13	16	366	33.9	32.8	28.1	5.2	0.0	66410
39870	NEWTON	17836	1496	36.2	29.4	28.3	4.3	1.8	36265	38054	21	30	1156	43.2	27.9	25.7	3.1	0.1	59518
39877	PARROTT	28808	144	25.7	27.8	36.1	2.1	8.3	45769	51398	51	60	118	22.9	22.0	45.8	5.9	3.4	95455
39886	SHELLMAN	14125	572	42.5	32.2	20.1	4.4	0.9	28020	29202	6	4	399	50.9	22.1	18.0	7.3	1.8	48600
39897	WHIGHAM	15759	1567	34.5	32.5	29.2	3.3	0.6	35378	36762	19	26	1255	25.3	22.9	35.3	13.7	2.8	94592
	GEORGIA	26980		20.7	23.1	36.8	11.7	7.7	56761	58593				13.2	17.9	39.1	24.2	5.5	121444
	UNITED STATES	27277		20.9	24.4	35.3	11.7	7.6	54719	56938				9.3	13.1	31.6	32.6	13.5	162279

ZIP CODE	FINANCIAL SERVICES				THE HOME						ENTERTAINMENT						PERSONAL			
					Home Improvements		Furnishings													
# POST OFFICE NAME	Auto Loan	Home Loan	Invest-ments	Retire-ment Plans	Home Repair	Lawn & Garden	Comput-ers & Hard-ware-Personal	Major Appli-ances	TV, Radio, Sound Equip-ment	Furni-ture	Dine out/ Carry out	Sports Equip-ment	Fees & Tickets	Toys & Games	Travel	Cable TV	Apparel & Services	Auto Repairs	Health Insur-ance	Pets & Supplies
39817 BAINBRIDGE	68	50	59	49	49	65	54	60	60	52	59	47	45	61	50	65	40	59	66	74
39819 BAINBRIDGE	81	69	78	68	70	83	72	78	76	70	74	58	65	75	69	80	51	76	83	93
39823 BLAKELY	73	49	69	47	49	72	53	65	61	51	59	50	41	61	49	67	39	62	69	79
39824 BLUFFTON	81	53	78	50	52	79	56	71	65	53	63	55	42	66	52	72	42	67	75	87
39825 BRINSON	76	55	63	53	54	72	57	66	63	55	62	51	45	66	52	69	41	63	70	80
39826 BRONWOOD	65	43	63	40	42	64	46	57	53	43	51	45	34	53	42	59	34	54	61	71
39827 CAIRO	85	70	72	68	70	81	69	77	73	69	73	57	61	76	65	77	49	73	78	92
39828 CAIRO	68	51	60	50	51	67	54	62	61	53	60	46	46	61	51	66	40	60	67	75
39834 CLIMAX	80	57	70	55	57	77	59	71	66	57	65	54	47	68	55	72	43	67	74	86
39836 COLEMAN	81	53	78	50	53	80	57	71	65	54	64	56	42	66	53	73	42	67	75	88
39837 COLQUITT	77	53	76	51	54	77	55	70	63	52	61	54	43	63	53	69	41	65	73	85
39840 CUTHBERT	64	44	61	42	44	64	48	58	55	45	53	44	38	55	45	61	35	55	63	70
39841 DAMASCUS	91	59	88	56	59	89	63	80	73	60	71	62	48	74	59	82	47	75	84	98
39842 DAWSON	72	53	64	52	52	69	57	65	64	56	63	49	48	64	53	70	42	64	70	79
39845 DONALSONVILLE	80	57	81	54	58	81	59	74	66	56	65	55	47	66	57	73	43	69	78	89
39846 EDISON	65	42	62	40	42	63	45	57	52	43	51	44	34	53	42	58	34	53	60	70
39851 FORT GAINES	70	46	68	43	46	69	49	62	57	47	55	48	37	57	46	63	37	58	66	76
39854 GEORGETOWN	71	46	69	44	46	70	50	63	57	47	56	49	37	58	46	64	37	59	66	77
39859 IRON CITY	78	52	76	49	52	77	55	69	63	52	62	54	42	64	52	70	41	65	73	85
39861 JAKIN	83	56	82	54	57	82	59	75	67	56	66	57	46	67	57	74	43	69	78	90
39862 LEARY	82	54	79	51	53	81	57	72	66	55	65	56	43	67	54	74	43	68	76	89
39866 MORGAN	82	54	80	51	54	81	58	72	66	55	65	57	43	67	54	74	43	68	77	89
39867 MORRIS	80	52	78	49	52	79	56	71	65	53	63	55	42	66	52	72	42	66	75	87
39870 NEWTON	87	58	82	55	58	85	61	76	70	59	69	59	47	72	57	78	46	72	81	94
39877 PARROTT	119	85	122	82	88	120	87	111	97	81	95	83	70	96	86	106	63	102	115	132
39886 SHELLMAN	71	46	68	43	46	69	49	62	57	47	56	49	37	58	46	64	37	59	66	77
39897 WHIGHAM	73	52	70	51	54	73	54	67	60	51	59	51	43	61	52	66	39	62	70	80
GEORGIA	110	101	97	102	98	103	103	103	104	104	104	80	99	107	99	105	73	103	103	122
UNITED STATES	100	100	100	100	100	100	100	100	100	100	100	100	100	100	100	100	100	100	100	100

POPULATION CHANGE

96701-96863

ZIP CODE #	POST OFFICE NAME	COUNTY FIPS CODE	POPULATION 2000	POPULATION 2009	POPULATION 2014	2000-2009 ANNUAL RATE % Rate	2000-2009 ANNUAL RATE State Centile	HOUSEHOLDS 2000	HOUSEHOLDS 2009	HOUSEHOLDS 2014	HOUSEHOLDS % Annual Rate 2000-2009	HOUSEHOLDS 2009 Average HH Size	FAMILIES 2000	FAMILIES 2009	FAMILIES % Annual Rate 2000-2009
96701	AIEA	003	41277	41365	41577	0.0	19	13671	14070	14230	0.3	2.86	10152	10139	0.0
96704	CAPTAIN COOK	001	7727	9924	11134	2.7	86	2808	3705	4189	3.0	2.68	1930	2465	2.7
96705	ELEELE	007	2176	2389	2484	1.0	49	679	772	814	1.4	3.09	535	595	1.2
96706	EWA BEACH	003	43571	54805	59048	2.5	82	11710	15116	16424	2.8	3.60	9809	12475	2.6
96707	KAPOLEI	003	25180	32357	34684	2.7	86	7239	9529	10246	3.0	3.39	6203	7890	2.6
96708	HAIKU	009	8256	10026	10892	2.1	72	2930	3679	4034	2.5	2.69	1911	2326	2.1
96710	HAKALAU	001	268	305	323	1.4	55	100	117	125	1.7	2.61	69	78	1.3
96712	HALEIWA	003	7858	8067	8164	0.3	30	2688	2824	2878	0.5	2.84	1828	1840	0.1
96713	HANA	009	1855	2167	2322	1.7	63	592	701	755	1.8	3.09	406	467	1.5
96716	HANAPEPE	007	2664	3097	3253	1.6	57	869	1039	1106	2.0	2.97	660	771	1.7
96717	HAUULA	003	5063	5197	5224	0.3	30	1341	1366	1376	0.2	3.70	1041	1032	-0.1
96718	HAWAII NATIONAL PARK	001	132	161	179	2.2	74	59	75	84	2.6	2.12	43	53	2.3
96719	HAWI	001	2732	3219	3541	1.8	64	638	798	903	2.4	3.24	477	582	2.2
96720	HILO	001	42992	46957	48788	1.0	49	15366	17115	17914	1.2	2.66	10689	11578	0.9
96722	PRINCEVILLE	007	3369	3706	3879	1.0	49	1419	1648	1750	1.6	2.23	901	1007	1.2
96725	HOLUALOA	001	2639	3351	3715	2.6	84	986	1283	1433	2.9	2.61	666	838	2.5
96726	HONAUNAU	001	4	4	4	0.0	19	2	2	2	0.0	2.00	1	1	0.0
96727	HONOKAA	001	5021	6387	7127	2.6	84	1715	2251	2539	3.0	2.78	1253	1603	2.7
96728	HONOMU	001	572	756	853	3.1	92	204	274	311	3.2	2.76	151	197	2.9
96729	HOOLEHUA	009	1079	1282	1385	1.9	65	288	354	385	2.3	3.62	234	283	2.1
96730	KAAAWA	003	1422	1539	1599	0.9	45	503	551	574	1.0	2.79	347	364	0.5
96731	KAHUKU	003	3178	3117	3094	-0.2	7	855	849	845	-0.1	3.51	654	631	-0.4
96732	KAHULUI	009	20625	22287	23004	0.8	42	6014	6584	6833	1.0	3.25	4501	4824	0.8
96734	KAILUA	003	49448	48948	48816	-0.1	11	15428	15553	15590	0.1	2.95	12244	12062	-0.2
96738	WAIKOLOA	001	4861	6392	7382	3.0	91	1780	2335	2697	3.0	2.73	1251	1593	2.6
96740	KAILUA KONA	001	25329	31659	35015	2.4	78	9342	11848	13181	2.6	2.66	6422	7889	2.2
96741	KALAHEO	007	5290	5682	5858	0.8	42	1922	2176	2276	1.4	2.61	1405	1546	1.0
96742	KALAUPAPA	005	146	146	146	0.0	19	114	119	120	0.5	1.23	22	21	-0.5
96743	KAMUELA	001	8610	12074	13625	3.7	100	3010	4347	4954	4.1	2.72	2203	3082	3.7
96744	KANEOHE	003	54488	54395	54559	0.0	19	16941	17368	17531	0.3	3.10	13670	13674	0.0
96746	KAPAA	007	17772	18853	19286	0.6	35	5999	6686	6947	1.2	2.79	4354	4715	0.9
96747	KAUMAKANI	007	542	557	559	0.3	30	183	196	200	0.7	2.84	144	150	0.4
96748	KAUNAKAKAI	009	4688	5488	5899	1.7	63	1527	1828	1976	2.0	2.99	1129	1320	1.7
96749	KEAAU	001	8663	11886	13535	3.5	99	2957	4150	4762	3.7	2.86	2144	2925	3.4
96750	KEALAKEKUA	001	1433	1681	1820	1.7	63	497	601	656	2.1	2.76	360	426	1.8
96752	KEKAHA	007	3231	3323	3341	0.3	30	1088	1183	1207	0.9	2.80	803	849	0.6
96753	KIHEI	009	21836	26181	28269	2.0	70	8448	10240	11077	2.1	2.55	5190	6084	1.7
96754	KILAUEA	007	2979	3316	3480	1.2	50	1017	1190	1266	1.7	2.77	722	820	1.4
96755	KAPAAU	001	2966	3843	4313	2.8	89	971	1288	1459	3.1	2.94	711	917	2.8
96756	KOLOA	007	5394	5406	5421	0.0	19	1977	2079	2113	0.5	2.57	1427	1457	0.2
96757	KUALAPUU	009	862	1032	1119	2.0	70	279	345	376	2.3	2.99	228	278	2.2
96760	KURTISTOWN	001	5302	7164	8131	3.3	97	1754	2416	2761	3.5	2.96	1261	1687	3.2
96761	LAHAINA	009	17927	23182	25501	2.8	89	6017	7712	8473	2.7	3.00	3779	4702	2.4
96762	LAIE	003	4883	5325	5447	0.9	45	983	1064	1092	0.9	4.57	796	841	0.6
96763	LANAI CITY	009	3193	3843	4166	2.0	70	1161	1442	1577	2.4	2.66	805	973	2.1
96764	LAUPAHOEHOE	001	1029	1292	1443	2.5	82	357	459	516	2.8	2.81	278	350	2.5
96766	LIHUE	007	12775	14349	15002	1.3	52	4263	4978	5264	1.7	2.82	3040	3479	1.5
96768	MAKAWAO	009	15976	17153	17777	0.8	42	5361	5936	6203	1.1	2.89	4015	4352	0.9
96769	MAKAWELI	007	608	591	583	-0.3	3	176	176	176	0.0	3.36	145	143	-0.2
96770	MAUNALOA	009	629	732	786	1.7	63	212	255	276	2.0	2.87	170	200	1.8
96771	MOUNTAIN VIEW	001	4979	6658	7532	3.2	93	1817	2492	2844	3.5	2.64	1228	1629	3.1
96772	NAALEHU	001	4201	5650	6429	3.3	97	1654	2291	2624	3.6	2.47	1037	1385	3.2
96773	NINOLE	001	62	84	95	3.3	97	27	37	42	3.5	2.27	20	27	3.3
96774	OOKALA	001	413	566	640	3.5	99	133	184	209	3.6	3.08	99	134	3.3
96776	PAAUILO	001	1087	1360	1523	2.5	82	368	472	533	2.7	2.88	279	349	2.4
96777	PAHALA	001	1467	1819	2017	2.4	78	481	614	688	2.7	2.93	348	433	2.4
96778	PAHOA	001	8597	10345	11329	2.0	70	3115	3817	4199	2.2	2.71	2073	2455	1.8
96779	PAIA	009	2817	3197	3377	1.4	55	902	1049	1117	1.6	2.97	630	712	1.3
96780	PAPAALOA	001	216	270	305	2.4	78	80	103	117	2.8	2.62	60	75	2.4
96781	PAPAIKOU	001	1664	2027	2235	2.2	74	569	712	792	2.5	2.85	431	525	2.2
96782	PEARL CITY	003	37879	37345	37392	-0.2	7	11092	11251	11335	0.2	3.09	9020	8962	-0.1
96783	PEPEEKEO	001	1890	2230	2479	2.0	70	689	851	932	2.3	2.68	504	608	2.0
96785	VOLCANO	001	3821	5004	5634	3.0	91	1506	2045	2330	3.4	2.38	916	1196	2.9
96786	WAHIAWA	003	40984	42054	42673	0.3	30	11059	11711	12000	0.6	3.19	9405	9796	0.4
96789	MILILANI	003	45123	50866	53324	1.3	52	14902	17519	18583	1.8	2.90	12078	13738	1.4
96790	KULA	009	7282	7865	8159	0.8	42	2776	3089	3232	1.2	2.46	1872	2024	0.8
96791	WAIALUA	003	7908	8233	8484	0.5	34	2405	2612	2703	0.9	3.10	1763	1848	0.5
96792	WAIANAE	003	42259	44029	44862	0.4	33	10535	11189	11464	0.7	3.89	8809	9189	0.5
96793	WAILUKU	009	21070	24141	25669	1.5	56	7001	8266	8859	1.8	2.92	5028	5763	1.5
96795	WAIMANALO	003	10161	10384	10532	0.2	22	2442	2559	2612	0.5	3.97	2072	2128	0.3
96796	WAIMEA	007	1663	1723	1731	0.4	33	591	643	656	0.9	2.61	436	462	0.6
96797	WAIPAHU	003	64125	68204	70080	0.7	38	17421	18871	19501	0.9	3.53	14090	14940	0.6
96813	HONOLULU	003	24933	24736	24758	-0.1	11	10673	10932	11031	0.3	2.09	5228	5047	-0.4
96814	HONOLULU	003	16574	19439	20652	1.7	63	8948	10542	11189	1.8	1.81	3696	4128	1.2
96815	HONOLULU	003	27648	28368	28808	0.3	30	14717	15438	15753	0.5	1.83	5982	5805	-0.3
96816	HONOLULU	003	48453	47541	47296	-0.2	7	17412	17558	17585	0.1	2.66	12041	11682	-0.3
96817	HONOLULU	003	49878	50015	50030	0.0	19	17538	17806	17908	0.2	2.73	11608	11267	-0.3
96818	HONOLULU	003	46289	47268	47862	0.2	22	14718	15194	15429	0.3	3.06	11726	11887	0.1
96819	HONOLULU	003	48319	47962	47949	-0.1	11	11647	11659	11694	0.0	3.90	9792	9602	-0.2
96821	HONOLULU	003	19068	19761	20120	0.4	33	6518	6954	7131	0.7	2.82	5228	5444	0.4
96822	HONOLULU	003	42784	42910	43114	0.0	19	17654	18152	18343	0.3	2.18	9763	9528	-0.3
96825	HONOLULU	003	27657	30109	31307	0.9	45	9666	10941	11491	1.3	2.75	7796	8620	1.1
96826	HONOLULU	003	27003	26802	26749	-0.1	11	13117	13290	13337	0.1	2.00	6269	5944	-0.6
96853	HICKAM AFB	003	6736	7156	7114	0.7	38	1848	1844	1845	0.0	3.33	1802	1793	-0.1
96858	FORT SHAFTER	003	253	214	204	-1.8	1	77	64	60	-2.0	2.75	75	62	-2.0
96860	PEARL HARBOR	003	1653	2065	2116	2.4	78	66	188	205	12.0	5.03	61	180	12.4
96861	CAMP H M SMITH	003	199	205	208	0.3	30	5	6	6	2.0	2.50	5	5	0.0
96863	M C B H KANEOHE BAY	003	3897	3594	3513	-0.9	2	630	560	539	-1.3	3.17	618	548	-1.3
	HAWAII					0.8					1.1	2.85			0.8
	UNITED STATES					1.0					1.1	2.59			0.9

#	POST OFFICE NAME	White 2000	White 2009	Black 2000	Black 2009	Asian/Pacific 2000	Asian/Pacific 2009	% Hispanic Origin 2000	% Hispanic Origin 2009	0-4	5-9	10-14	15-19	20-24	25-44	45-64	65-84	85+	18+	MEDIAN AGE 2009	% 2009 Males	% 2009 Females
96701	AIEA	16.5	17.7	2.0	2.7	61.0	59.0	6.1	6.9	5.6	5.5	5.5	5.7	6.4	28.7	27.8	12.8	2.0	79.9	39.7	50.6	49.4
96704	CAPTAIN COOK	35.0	35.3	0.4	0.5	35.5	34.6	6.9	7.7	5.4	5.4	6.8	7.4	4.9	21.5	34.7	12.1	1.9	77.6	44.0	50.5	49.5
96705	ELEELE	11.2	12.1	0.3	0.3	64.8	63.4	8.3	9.4	7.2	7.2	7.3	7.9	6.3	24.7	25.7	11.2	2.5	73.4	37.2	48.0	52.0
96706	EWA BEACH	16.5	15.8	2.2	2.6	56.9	57.1	8.8	9.0	9.4	9.0	8.0	7.1	5.5	32.7	20.9	6.6	0.8	69.1	32.2	50.2	49.8
96707	KAPOLEI	21.8	22.2	2.5	3.1	47.9	44.7	9.4	10.3	9.0	8.3	8.0	7.6	6.4	30.5	23.3	6.4	0.5	69.9	32.2	49.8	50.2
96708	HAIKU	57.9	58.7	0.6	0.7	15.9	14.8	8.1	9.4	6.4	6.1	6.5	6.4	6.1	27.4	32.6	7.5	0.9	76.9	38.9	50.4	49.6
96710	HAKALAU	24.6	24.6	0.4	0.3	45.9	45.9	8.2	8.5	6.2	6.2	6.6	6.2	5.6	22.0	27.9	16.1	3.3	77.4	42.0	48.2	51.8
96712	HALEIWA	45.8	47.7	1.6	2.4	25.8	23.7	9.2	10.8	7.4	5.7	6.0	6.1	7.6	31.0	27.1	7.8	1.2	77.4	35.6	52.3	47.7
96713	HANA	26.3	27.4	0.1	0.1	41.6	39.0	5.1	5.6	6.9	6.6	9.0	7.8	5.4	22.7	30.8	9.3	1.5	72.3	38.1	47.9	52.1
96716	HANAPEPE	14.9	16.0	0.1	0.1	58.4	56.8	8.2	8.9	6.6	7.5	7.1	8.1	6.5	24.8	27.1	10.0	2.4	73.7	37.6	50.5	49.5
96717	HAUULA	21.2	22.8	0.6	0.9	40.6	38.0	8.1	8.8	9.0	8.6	7.7	8.1	7.6	27.0	22.2	8.4	1.4	69.8	30.4	48.6	51.4
96718	HAWAII NATIONAL PARK	15.0	14.9	0.0	0.0	53.4	52.2	6.0	6.2	5.0	5.0	6.2	6.2	5.6	23.6	31.7	14.3	2.5	79.5	43.6	50.9	49.1
96719	HAWI	40.4	40.3	1.0	1.2	31.0	30.3	9.0	10.3	4.6	4.9	5.6	7.0	7.7	26.5	29.6	12.1	1.9	81.1	39.8	51.4	48.6
96720	HILO	17.4	17.8	0.4	0.6	51.3	50.3	8.8	9.4	5.7	5.8	6.0	7.6	7.0	23.5	27.5	14.1	2.8	78.2	40.4	48.8	51.2
96722	PRINCEVILLE	73.3	74.4	0.2	0.3	13.5	12.5	4.1	5.1	5.4	5.3	6.0	5.6	5.7	22.4	34.7	13.2	1.7	79.8	44.7	49.8	50.2
96725	HOLUALOA	47.1	47.5	0.3	0.4	27.8	27.0	8.2	9.5	5.2	5.0	5.6	5.8	5.7	24.8	33.6	12.4	1.9	80.8	43.3	50.0	50.0
96726	HONAUNAU	50.0	50.0	0.0	0.0	25.0	25.0	0.0	0.0	0.0	0.0	0.0	0.0	0.0	0.0	100.0	0.0	0.0	100.0	50.0	50.0	50.0
96727	HONOKAA	30.7	31.3	0.1	0.1	39.1	38.2	9.3	10.4	5.9	6.6	6.9	7.3	5.1	23.1	29.0	13.4	2.8	75.9	41.5	49.4	50.6
96728	HONOMU	23.5	23.9	0.0	0.0	35.7	34.9	12.1	12.8	5.6	5.6	6.2	7.1	5.3	22.5	28.4	16.3	3.0	78.3	43.2	47.2	52.8
96729	HOOLEHUA	12.0	12.5	0.2	0.2	56.7	54.3	4.5	4.8	8.0	8.0	8.3	8.7	5.7	22.4	25.8	11.6	1.6	70.1	35.5	50.6	49.4
96730	KAAAWA	35.2	37.7	0.4	0.6	31.8	29.2	8.1	9.7	7.2	6.9	6.8	6.4	6.0	24.9	29.9	10.2	1.6	75.0	37.7	48.2	51.8
96731	KAHUKU	18.9	20.4	0.6	0.7	51.1	48.8	7.7	8.3	8.2	7.6	7.2	9.2	8.9	26.5	21.6	8.9	1.9	71.2	29.5	50.8	49.2
96732	KAHULUI	10.3	11.4	0.2	0.3	63.4	61.3	8.7	9.8	7.5	6.5	6.1	6.8	7.0	26.7	23.0	13.4	3.0	75.8	36.6	49.0	51.0
96734	KAILUA	46.8	48.1	2.6	3.3	26.3	24.6	7.4	8.7	6.6	6.0	6.0	7.3	9.9	26.6	25.3	10.7	1.6	77.5	35.9	51.5	48.5
96738	WAIKOLOA	45.9	46.4	0.4	0.6	26.3	25.4	8.8	9.9	7.1	6.8	7.2	7.8	6.4	25.5	29.8	8.4	0.9	73.4	37.4	49.8	50.2
96740	KAILUA KONA	47.0	47.7	0.5	0.6	27.0	25.9	8.0	9.2	6.1	6.0	6.2	6.3	5.7	24.6	31.7	11.9	1.5	77.8	41.3	49.5	50.5
96741	KALAHEO	40.2	42.0	0.3	0.3	33.0	31.3	11.7	13.1	5.1	5.5	6.2	6.9	5.0	24.7	32.2	12.4	2.1	79.0	42.5	50.0	50.0
96742	KALAUPAPA	25.9	26.0	0.0	0.0	65.3	65.1	4.1	4.1	1.4	0.0	0.0	2.1	0.0	9.6	39.0	45.2	2.7	97.3	64.3	46.6	53.4
96743	KAMUELA	35.2	36.8	0.4	0.5	33.3	31.6	7.5	8.6	6.1	6.0	6.8	7.0	6.2	25.9	30.0	10.6	1.3	76.5	39.0	48.9	51.1
96744	KANEOHE	21.6	23.0	0.8	1.0	48.0	46.2	7.1	7.9	6.0	5.9	6.1	6.8	6.2	26.0	28.4	12.7	1.9	77.6	39.9	49.2	50.8
96746	KAPAA	29.4	31.0	0.4	0.5	41.0	38.9	9.0	9.9	6.5	6.6	7.1	7.4	6.1	24.9	29.4	10.3	1.8	74.9	38.5	49.3	50.7
96747	KAUMAKANI	3.9	4.3	0.0	0.0	79.7	78.8	5.4	5.6	3.8	6.8	7.5	9.5	2.5	24.6	24.4	17.4	3.4	75.9	42.4	50.1	49.9
96748	KAUNAKAKAI	14.4	15.1	0.1	0.1	52.8	50.5	5.2	5.6	7.1	7.2	9.7	8.5	5.4	19.6	27.8	12.3	2.4	70.7	38.4	48.1	51.9
96749	KEAAU	30.4	31.3	0.5	0.5	36.0	34.6	13.1	14.2	6.9	6.8	7.0	7.8	7.3	25.3	27.6	9.9	1.4	73.9	36.0	50.5	49.5
96750	KEALAKEKUA	37.8	36.7	0.3	0.4	35.7	35.9	7.4	8.5	4.7	5.1	5.7	5.2	3.5	20.1	37.1	16.4	2.2	81.1	48.7	49.8	50.2
96752	KEKAHA	17.1	18.5	0.2	0.3	55.2	53.3	8.7	9.6	5.6	5.1	6.2	7.1	5.3	23.0	30.5	14.3	2.9	78.6	43.3	49.7	50.3
96753	KIHEI	54.1	53.7	0.8	1.0	28.0	27.7	7.0	8.5	6.3	5.9	5.6	6.2	6.9	28.9	30.2	9.0	1.0	78.5	38.5	50.0	50.0
96754	KILAUEA	53.6	55.1	0.6	0.7	28.6	26.9	6.0	7.4	6.1	5.7	6.2	7.5	8.2	25.2	31.6	8.0	1.3	77.4	37.6	51.0	49.0
96755	KAPAAU	23.7	25.3	0.1	0.2	37.7	36.1	18.4	20.1	7.1	6.8	7.0	8.4	6.1	23.2	27.8	11.5	2.1	73.5	38.4	48.9	51.1
96756	KOLOA	37.1	37.9	0.2	0.3	38.9	37.6	9.8	11.0	5.5	5.8	6.1	6.5	5.9	22.5	30.9	13.6	3.2	78.2	43.2	50.5	49.5
96757	KUALAPUU	7.7	8.0	0.0	0.0	58.7	56.5	5.5	5.6	7.6	7.4	7.8	8.9	5.8	22.7	26.3	11.8	1.7	71.8	36.6	52.0	48.0
96760	KURTISTOWN	31.8	32.9	0.7	0.9	31.6	30.2	15.3	16.7	7.9	8.0	8.0	7.7	6.3	27.1	26.0	8.1	0.8	71.2	33.2	50.9	49.1
96761	LAHAINA	41.7	43.4	0.5	0.6	39.3	37.4	8.6	10.3	6.6	6.1	5.9	5.6	6.5	29.6	28.2	10.1	1.5	78.1	38.3	50.4	49.6
96762	LAIE	25.8	27.6	0.5	0.6	47.1	44.5	3.8	4.5	9.2	7.8	7.2	9.8	14.0	30.5	15.6	5.2	0.6	71.2	25.7	47.5	52.5
96763	LANAI CITY	13.6	14.1	0.1	0.2	64.8	63.8	7.7	7.9	7.0	6.8	6.3	7.2	6.9	25.4	24.2	13.2	3.0	74.7	37.0	50.0	50.0
96764	LAUPAHOEHOE	26.1	26.6	0.3	0.5	42.7	41.8	9.6	10.8	6.0	6.6	7.0	6.4	4.5	24.9	28.0	14.1	2.5	76.5	40.1	50.5	49.5
96766	LIHUE	18.3	19.2	0.3	0.4	58.1	56.5	6.9	7.6	6.5	6.1	6.1	6.6	6.2	26.6	25.8	13.2	2.8	76.9	38.6	48.6	51.4
96768	MAKAWAO	38.5	39.5	0.3	0.4	31.1	29.8	9.8	11.0	6.4	6.7	7.0	7.0	5.6	26.7	30.1	9.2	1.2	75.4	38.2	49.6	50.4
96769	MAKAWELI	9.2	9.8	0.2	0.2	69.2	67.9	5.6	5.6	7.8	5.8	7.8	8.0	6.8	26.1	23.0	13.0	1.9	73.6	36.3	51.9	48.1
96770	MAUNALOA	20.3	21.4	0.5	0.7	52.8	49.9	2.9	3.1	9.0	9.3	9.2	8.1	5.3	21.6	24.7	11.5	1.4	66.4	33.3	48.0	52.0
96771	MOUNTAIN VIEW	33.9	34.7	0.7	1.0	33.1	31.9	11.7	12.8	5.8	7.3	8.1	7.7	4.6	25.1	30.8	9.4	1.1	73.4	40.1	51.8	48.2
96772	NAALEHU	42.7	43.6	1.1	1.5	28.5	26.8	7.2	8.1	5.9	6.4	6.3	6.6	3.6	21.4	35.2	13.3	1.2	76.9	44.8	52.1	47.9
96773	NINOLE	31.1	31.0	0.0	0.0	36.1	35.7	9.8	10.7	4.8	4.8	7.1	7.1	4.8	21.4	34.5	13.1	2.4	78.6	45.0	52.4	47.6
96774	OOKALA	31.2	31.4	0.2	0.2	36.1	35.7	9.4	9.9	5.3	5.7	6.4	7.4	5.3	23.5	31.3	12.9	2.3	78.1	42.3	50.5	49.5
96776	PAAUILO	26.2	26.8	0.1	0.1	38.7	37.9	12.1	12.9	6.0	6.7	7.4	7.9	5.1	21.8	29.6	13.5	1.9	75.0	41.1	50.2	49.8
96777	PAHALA	14.9	14.9	0.2	0.3	53.1	52.6	6.3	6.4	5.4	5.6	5.8	6.2	5.6	23.3	31.3	14.0	2.7	78.7	43.2	50.1	49.9
96778	PAHOA	38.0	38.2	0.8	1.0	30.6	29.4	12.3	13.7	6.2	6.7	7.4	7.3	5.2	22.7	32.0	11.0	1.5	75.0	40.7	51.0	49.0
96779	PAIA	38.9	41.3	0.3	0.3	32.8	30.7	10.3	11.3	6.8	6.9	6.9	7.8	6.4	26.6	28.5	8.6	1.4	75.1	36.9	50.3	49.7
96780	PAPAALOA	31.5	31.5	0.0	0.4	36.1	35.9	9.3	10.4	5.2	5.9	6.7	7.4	5.2	24.1	30.0	13.0	2.6	77.8	41.7	50.4	49.6
96781	PAPAIKOU	16.5	16.6	0.5	0.6	54.1	53.6	7.0	7.4	6.1	6.1	6.2	6.2	5.4	22.7	27.4	16.8	3.1	77.8	42.7	49.3	50.7
96782	PEARL CITY	16.7	17.5	2.5	3.2	59.8	58.1	7.4	8.1	5.6	5.0	4.8	6.0	10.0	27.5	23.6	15.5	2.1	81.4	38.0	52.4	47.6
96783	PEPEEKEO	20.0	19.7	0.2	0.3	55.1	55.6	8.0	8.4	5.7	5.6	5.9	6.0	4.8	21.7	28.3	18.6	3.4	79.2	45.3	48.5	51.5
96785	VOLCANO	39.6	40.3	0.4	0.6	25.8	24.6	12.7	13.8	5.9	7.5	7.3	6.8	4.6	26.3	31.6	9.0	1.0	74.8	40.5	51.2	48.8
96786	WAHIAWA	32.4	31.9	11.3	13.5	33.1	31.5	13.0	14.3	11.3	7.8	6.0	7.2	15.2	30.3	13.5	7.2	1.5	71.7	26.0	53.2	46.8
96789	MILILANI	18.6	19.2	3.0	3.7	53.0	51.7	7.6	8.1	7.5	7.4	7.4	7.1	5.8	28.8	27.6	7.6	0.8	73.2	36.0	49.9	50.1
96790	KULA	58.3	58.8	0.2	0.3	23.4	22.5	5.2	6.3	4.2	4.2	5.1	5.7	6.1	21.6	37.3	13.1	2.8	82.7	47.0	48.1	51.9
96791	WAIALUA	24.7	26.7	1.0	1.4	46.6	44.4	7.0	8.0	6.7	6.3	6.1	6.9	8.4	28.3	23.9	11.5	1.9	76.7	35.1	51.7	48.3
96792	WAIANAE	11.2	12.8	1.1	1.6	45.5	42.8	13.9	14.8	9.3	8.8	8.3	8.7	8.3	27.1	21.0	7.6	0.8	68.1	28.9	49.8	50.2
96793	WAILUKU	18.1	19.2	0.3	0.3	54.9	53.1	7.5	8.5	6.5	6.5	6.5	7.1	7.3	25.3	28.1	10.8	1.8	76.0	37.9	50.0	50.0
96795	WAIMANALO	14.0	15.4	0.3	0.5	50.8	48.5	8.2	9.0	7.3	7.2	7.1	8.5	7.7	26.8	24.3	9.6	1.4	73.3	33.7	50.5	49.5
96796	WAIMEA	13.8	14.6	0.1	0.1	55.0	53.3	7.0	7.8	5.7	5.7	7.2	6.9	6.2	21.9	28.6	12.5	5.2	76.2	41.9	49.1	50.9
96797	WAIPAHU	8.5	9.4	1.6	2.1	70.9	69.1	6.3	6.7	7.4	7.3	6.9	6.9	6.2	29.8	24.3	9.7	1.5	74.1	35.5	49.8	50.2
96813	HONOLULU	21.0	22.4	1.0	1.4	59.9	58.1	4.2	4.8	4.4	3.9	4.0	4.8	6.2	29.6	29.2	14.7	3.2	85.1	43.0	49.7	50.3
96814	HONOLULU	17.1	18.6	1.2	1.7	68.4	66.0	3.7	4.4	4.0	3.7	3.5	4.2	6.0	30.6	28.7	16.0	3.4	86.6	43.7	47.9	52.1
96815	HONOLULU	38.9	40.5	1.7	2.2	46.9	44.7	4.1	5.0	3.5	3.0	3.0	3.2	5.9	29.2	31.4	17.0	3.9	88.8	46.4	50.9	49.1
96816	HONOLULU	17.0	18.3	0.3	0.5	65.4	63.9	3.5	4.0	4.2	4.3	4.5	5.8	6.0	25.7	29.8	15.2	4.5	83.7	44.6	48.9	51.1
96817	HONOLULU	8.8	9.7	0.6	0.8	75.5	74.1	4.2	4.7	4.9	5.0	5.1	6.1	5.9	24.5	27.9	16.7	3.9	81.2	43.8	48.0	52.0
96818	HONOLULU	27.6	28.2	7.2	9.5	49.2	46.5	6.9	8.0	9.2	8.2	7.0	5.8	7.6	34.4	18.7	8.1	1.0	72.0	31.6	49.5	50.5
96819	HONOLULU	8.5	8.9	1.6	1.9	73.7	72.7	5.3	5.8	7.1	6.5	6.0	6.7	7.4	28.2	22.6	12.9	2.4	76.5	36.2	50.7	49.3
96821	HONOLULU	24.7	26.3	0.1	0.2	59.6	58.0	2.6	3.0	4.1	4.7	5.6	5.7	3.8	21.4	34.0	17.1	3.7	81.8	47.9	49.3	50.7
96822	HONOLULU	22.2	23.6	0.9	1.2	60.8	59.0	3.9	4.5	4.0	3.7	3.8	6.2	8.5	28.2	28.4	13.7	3.5	86.0	41.7	48.1	51.9
96825	HONOLULU	31.1	33.1	0.4	0.6	51.2	49.1	3.4	4.1	5.0	5.3	5.9	5.7	4.4	24.5	32.2	15.3	1.8	80.1	44.5	48.9	51.1
96826	HONOLULU	14.5	15.7	1.0	1.4	67.0	65.2	4.5	5.1	4.6	4.0	3.9	4.9	7.5	31.5	28.0	12.8	2.7	84.8	40.4	49.3	50.7
96853	HICKAM AFB	66.6	64.9	11.7	14.7	8.9	7.9	8.5	10.1	12.2	11.4	9.3	6.4	14.3	40.1	6.0	0.3	0.0	63.8	23.7	52.7	47.3
96858	FORT SHAFTER	59.8	57.9	19.7	23.4	7.9	7.0	10.6	12.6	14.5	8.9	5.6	6.1	15.0	40.2	9.8	0.0	0.0	68.7	25.0	53.7	46.3
96860	PEARL HARBOR	63.4	62.0	15.5	18.5	11.5	9.8	6.6	8.6	5.5	3.8	3.1	9.1	30.6	39.0	8.1	0.7	0.1	86.2	24.7	71.1	28.9
96861	CAMP H M SMITH	33.7	35.6	6.0	7.8	28.6	25.4	14.1	16.6	3.9	3.4	2.9	3.4	16.6	59.0	10.2	0.5	0.0	88.8	31.9	85.9	14.1
96863	M C B H KANEOHE BAY	67.4	65.9	12.3	14.8	5.9	5.1	15.2	17.8	8.7	5.2	3.7	10.8	45.7	24.5	1.3	0.1	0.0	81.0	22.4	73.8	26.2
	HAWAII	24.3	25.5	1.8	2.3	51.0	48.8	7.2	8.2	6.6	6.2	6.1	6.6	7.1	27.5	26.3	11.4	2.0	77.1	37.5	50.0	50.0
	UNITED STATES	75.1	72.0	12.3	12.7	3.8	4.6	12.5	15.7	6.8	6.7	6.6	7.1	6.9	27.0	26.0	10.9	1.9	75.7	36.9	49.2	50.8

#	POST OFFICE NAME	2009 Per Capita Income	2009 HH Income Base	2009 HOUSEHOLD INCOME DISTRIBUTION (%) Less than $25,000	$25,000 to $49,999	$50,000 to $99,999	$100,000 to $149,999	$150,000 or More	MEDIAN HOUSEHOLD INCOME 2009	2014	2009 National Centile	2009 State Centile	2009 Home Value Base	2009 HOME VALUE DISTRIBUTION (%) Less than $50,000	$50,000 to $89,999	$90,000 to $174,999	$175,000 to $399,999	$400,000 or More	2009 Median Home Value
96701	AIEA	31561	14070	9.8	20.0	36.9	19.4	13.9	75832	77496	90	90	8734	0.4	0.6	3.6	17.8	77.6	663866
96704	CAPTAIN COOK	25560	3705	21.5	26.6	34.1	10.8	7.0	52355	53364	67	48	2310	0.9	1.4	2.0	21.9	73.7	616692
96705	ELEELE	21192	772	22.9	21.5	40.3	10.2	5.1	57862	60222	75	60	566	0.9	0.2	0.9	48.1	50.0	400000
96706	EWA BEACH	24472	15116	7.1	15.3	45.8	24.1	7.7	79092	80959	92	94	10953	0.1	0.3	2.4	25.1	72.0	515165
96707	KAPOLEI	25365	9529	11.0	14.7	43.6	22.5	8.2	78008	79693	91	93	6939	0.6	0.6	1.1	29.7	67.9	521427
96708	HAIKU	27541	3679	19.0	23.9	41.7	7.6	7.9	56650	57712	74	57	2232	0.0	0.0	0.0	12.5	87.5	774784
96710	HAKALAU	25176	117	32.5	20.5	26.5	12.0	8.5	46401	48972	53	27	79	0.0	0.0	3.8	41.8	54.4	429167
96712	HALEIWA	27067	2824	19.5	23.9	32.2	13.5	10.9	58048	61726	75	61	1312	1.1	0.5	0.4	8.1	90.0	696429
96713	HANA	20877	701	23.7	29.1	32.2	8.6	6.4	47088	48492	54	33	447	1.8	2.2	2.5	21.9	71.6	638274
96716	HANAPEPE	20919	1039	19.4	22.2	46.2	8.6	3.6	57212	59415	74	58	659	0.0	0.0	0.3	44.6	55.1	422789
96717	HAUULA	16908	1366	21.5	30.7	33.4	8.9	5.5	48124	49042	57	35	626	1.9	1.8	5.6	16.1	74.6	535545
96718	HAWAII NATIONAL PARK	20330	75	34.7	33.3	26.7	4.0	1.3	35442	37848	19	8	55	3.6	0.0	30.9	56.4	9.1	210294
96719	HAWI	23604	798	18.0	21.8	39.1	12.2	8.9	65380	66223	84	80	555	0.7	0.0	0.5	25.6	73.2	595930
96720	HILO	23989	17115	25.9	24.8	31.5	12.2	5.5	49123	50867	59	38	10529	0.6	0.8	4.6	48.1	45.8	382687
96722	PRINCEVILLE	39534	1648	20.3	23.5	29.1	13.3	13.7	58781	59714	76	64	1015	0.0	0.0	1.6	19.1	79.3	864540
96725	HOLUALOA	30105	1283	18.7	24.2	34.3	12.5	10.3	58597	59657	76	63	737	0.1	0.4	1.2	9.6	88.6	830598
96726	HONAUNAU	0	0	0.0	0.0	0.0	0.0	0.0	0	0	0	0	0	0.0	0.0	0.0	0.0	0.0	0
96727	HONOKAA	24338	2251	20.3	30.4	33.8	9.1	6.5	49270	51360	59	39	1576	0.1	1.1	8.0	35.6	55.1	434468
96728	HONOMU	22242	274	29.9	28.8	25.5	6.6	9.1	41542	44803	38	20	201	0.0	0.0	22.9	45.3	31.8	251563
96729	HOOLEHUA	15857	354	25.4	31.9	33.9	4.8	4.0	42712	46011	42	23	241	4.6	5.4	14.5	48.5	27.0	284259
96730	KAAAWA	25429	551	15.4	23.8	43.2	11.4	6.2	61237	64483	79	75	311	0.3	0.6	2.9	6.1	90.0	687500
96731	KAHUKU	18265	849	23.6	25.8	35.7	10.6	4.4	50698	52911	63	42	477	1.7	0.2	1.3	31.4	65.4	469340
96732	KAHULUI	22207	6584	20.6	20.6	39.8	12.3	6.7	59700	60486	77	69	3545	1.0	1.6	1.0	18.5	77.9	515165
96734	KAILUA	34788	15553	8.8	17.1	36.8	18.2	19.2	80750	82677	92	95	9654	0.1	0.3	0.1	5.8	93.7	810995
96738	WAIKOLOA	26560	2335	12.6	28.0	38.3	16.1	5.0	59267	58773	77	67	1256	0.0	0.0	0.0	20.4	79.6	563765
96740	KAILUA KONA	29953	11848	14.9	26.0	36.1	13.0	10.0	60056	60748	77	72	7051	0.3	0.1	1.0	19.9	78.7	630854
96741	KALAHEO	30364	2176	13.0	22.2	36.3	21.9	6.7	67364	67218	85	84	1451	1.2	1.9	1.4	28.7	66.8	538391
96742	KALAUPAPA	12510	119	67.2	32.8	0.0	0.0	0.0	9015	10000	0	2	0	0.0	0.0	0.0	0.0	0.0	0
96743	KAMUELA	29485	4347	11.5	25.5	41.5	14.3	7.1	64506	65154	83	78	2739	1.2	1.1	1.4	23.7	72.6	597507
96744	KANEOHE	31770	17368	8.3	13.4	40.1	25.2	13.0	83737	85064	93	97	11963	0.1	0.1	0.7	10.7	88.4	667215
96746	KAPAA	23395	6686	21.7	25.2	39.7	7.5	5.9	52339	53222	67	47	3947	0.7	0.7	3.1	30.5	65.1	488370
96747	KAUMAKANI	16269	196	33.2	33.7	26.5	5.1	1.5	38628	41940	29	14	4	0.0	0.0	100.0	0.0	0.0	158333
96748	KAUNAKAKAI	16978	1828	32.1	28.4	31.2	6.1	2.2	39772	44343	32	16	1137	2.6	1.8	4.6	52.7	38.3	362034
96749	KEAAU	20248	4150	26.2	29.7	31.1	8.5	4.4	45424	47612	50	25	2996	1.2	1.5	9.4	64.8	23.1	302300
96750	KEALAKEKUA	26482	601	17.6	31.1	36.6	6.7	8.0	51517	52887	65	44	372	0.0	0.0	3.5	18.3	78.2	592857
96752	KEKAHA	22242	1183	22.2	26.8	38.3	7.3	5.4	51339	53816	64	43	748	0.0	0.0	11.6	48.8	39.6	359585
96753	KIHEI	29566	10240	17.3	25.6	36.4	11.3	9.4	56551	56251	73	56	5211	0.2	0.0	1.1	31.6	67.1	555916
96754	KILAUEA	24789	1190	23.6	27.7	32.2	9.6	6.9	48723	50000	58	36	761	0.4	0.1	0.8	25.2	73.5	584478
96755	KAPAAU	22337	1288	18.2	22.1	44.9	11.2	3.6	60369	62389	78	74	901	0.2	1.7	1.8	41.3	55.0	426149
96756	KOLOA	28950	2079	20.5	22.3	37.8	11.5	7.9	58910	60661	76	65	1180	0.3	0.1	0.6	25.3	73.7	596990
96757	KUALAPUU	19690	345	21.2	31.0	40.0	4.1	3.8	47668	49600	56	34	257	5.1	5.4	13.2	52.5	23.7	283036
96760	KURTISTOWN	16488	2416	40.4	21.3	27.9	6.5	3.9	36191	41411	21	10	1659	2.4	4.2	17.5	58.0	17.8	234131
96761	LAHAINA	28759	7712	15.3	20.0	37.9	14.2	12.7	65897	63956	84	82	4104	0.6	0.1	2.5	14.0	82.8	669830
96762	LAIE	15088	1064	20.8	23.8	38.7	11.7	5.0	55538	60000	72	53	458	0.7	0.7	0.7	8.3	89.7	667112
96763	LANAI CITY	24541	1442	19.3	21.9	47.1	7.4	4.3	55510	56974	72	52	725	0.8	0.3	8.0	61.1	29.8	329227
96764	LAUPAHOEHOE	17409	459	29.8	27.7	35.9	4.4	2.2	41346	46773	37	19	354	0.0	3.1	11.9	62.1	22.9	275000
96766	LIHUE	26081	4978	16.4	20.4	43.4	12.8	7.0	62951	63351	81	76	3135	0.3	0.2	2.9	33.4	63.2	483199
96768	MAKAWAO	28056	5936	14.8	18.3	43.4	16.0	7.4	69417	67794	86	85	3655	0.4	0.2	0.9	12.4	86.1	628269
96769	MAKAWELI	13324	176	34.1	30.7	29.5	4.5	1.1	31139	33132	10	3	43	0.0	0.0	0.0	62.8	37.2	371053
96770	MAUNALOA	18912	255	33.7	33.3	21.6	6.7	4.7	36806	38886	23	11	139	4.3	3.6	19.4	38.1	34.5	277941
96771	MOUNTAIN VIEW	19331	2492	34.5	26.8	27.3	7.7	3.7	38685	42363	29	15	1888	5.1	6.4	13.0	47.1	28.3	269635
96772	NAALEHU	18871	2291	38.8	27.7	24.6	5.1	3.8	35570	39258	19	9	1706	8.0	7.4	19.6	50.5	14.4	224825
96773	NINOLE	30198	37	16.2	29.7	35.1	13.5	5.4	57222	56300	74	59	29	0.0	0.0	20.7	34.5	44.8	362500
96774	OOKALA	22287	184	15.2	28.3	37.5	14.7	4.3	60000	60391	77	70	147	0.0	0.0	19.7	33.3	46.9	379545
96776	PAAUILO	20117	472	20.8	33.5	33.1	8.5	4.2	45763	48217	51	26	374	1.6	5.1	28.6	31.8	32.9	238298
96777	PAHALA	14799	614	35.7	32.7	25.6	5.0	1.0	35000	37460	18	6	447	6.5	1.3	31.3	53.2	7.6	202600
96778	PAHOA	16036	3817	39.8	29.1	24.2	5.4	1.5	34710	37365	17	5	2602	1.6	7.2	22.9	55.5	12.9	216417
96779	PAIA	29874	1049	14.7	17.2	45.6	11.5	11.1	73343	72243	89	89	694	0.0	0.0	0.7	23.2	76.1	554734
96780	PAPAALOA	26153	103	16.5	29.1	34.0	15.5	4.9	56059	58093	73	55	82	0.0	0.0	19.5	32.9	47.6	383333
96781	PAPAIKOU	19507	712	28.8	25.1	35.3	7.4	3.4	46467	48662	53	28	522	0.0	1.3	12.1	55.6	31.0	308333
96782	PEARL CITY	28082	11251	10.5	17.4	38.9	22.5	10.7	76677	78457	90	92	7456	0.1	0.6	3.7	13.6	82.0	608241
96783	PEPEEKEO	24041	851	28.9	21.5	31.1	12.5	6.0	49598	51449	60	40	634	0.9	1.1	3.3	53.3	41.3	366463
96785	VOLCANO	19107	2045	35.8	32.4	24.3	5.2	2.2	35091	38432	18	7	1477	4.7	3.4	16.5	52.7	22.6	248102
96786	WAHIAWA	18395	11711	21.1	32.5	33.7	9.5	3.2	46881	48043	54	31	3508	1.4	0.8	1.0	15.3	81.6	563445
96789	MILILANI	32732	17519	5.9	13.3	41.2	28.5	11.1	85040	87653	94	98	13315	0.1	0.5	3.1	25.9	70.5	567040
96790	KULA	37082	3089	14.8	19.7	35.3	16.6	13.6	70007	70871	87	86	1855	0.0	0.0	0.6	4.7	94.6	941190
96791	WAIALUA	23115	2612	16.8	24.7	39.2	12.2	7.1	59692	63077	77	68	1284	0.0	1.3	3.5	19.1	76.1	549266
96792	WAIANAE	16401	11189	24.6	23.4	36.0	9.9	6.0	51872	54711	66	45	6475	1.7	1.8	8.4	47.9	40.1	361485
96793	WAILUKU	27443	8266	16.4	19.6	40.2	14.6	9.2	65695	65569	84	81	5403	0.5	0.3	1.4	28.0	69.7	516966
96795	WAIMANALO	20531	2559	12.7	23.1	36.7	19.2	8.4	66111	69908	84	83	1730	1.0	1.4	5.7	25.0	66.9	511628
96796	WAIMEA	25864	643	17.9	23.3	42.5	12.6	3.7	60219	60810	78	73	345	0.6	0.0	2.9	33.0	63.5	487736
96797	WAIPAHU	24413	18871	10.1	17.7	41.4	20.8	10.0	76140	78022	90	91	12039	0.3	0.3	2.8	18.3	78.2	565231
96813	HONOLULU	30576	10932	26.1	28.5	27.1	11.0	7.3	44908	46971	48	24	4504	0.9	0.7	2.3	25.1	71.0	580422
96814	HONOLULU	29008	10542	34.7	29.3	26.5	5.3	4.2	37393	39832	25	13	3385	1.7	1.5	4.7	30.6	61.5	471284
96815	HONOLULU	31976	15438	28.6	31.6	26.5	7.6	5.7	40947	43714	36	18	5995	1.5	2.3	4.5	30.5	61.2	481968
96816	HONOLULU	35583	17558	12.7	20.1	34.9	18.3	13.9	72249	75350	88	88	10520	0.2	0.6	0.9	7.0	91.4	838736
96817	HONOLULU	25004	17806	29.0	23.1	29.0	10.0	8.9	46803	48724	54	30	6975	1.2	1.2	2.1	19.4	76.1	676903
96818	HONOLULU	24413	15194	9.3	29.2	41.2	12.5	7.8	59036	61617	76	66	5795	2.4	1.1	3.8	29.9	62.8	523797
96819	HONOLULU	20173	11659	17.7	20.8	36.0	16.1	9.5	63610	66683	82	77	5454	0.2	0.7	2.5	6.6	89.9	725607
96821	HONOLULU	53635	6954	5.2	10.2	29.9	21.6	33.1	108468	109612	98	100	5617	0.1	0.4	0.5	1.1	98.0	1000001
96822	HONOLULU	36415	18152	18.7	26.0	32.3	10.6	12.4	54681	57171	71	51	8673	1.4	0.7	1.0	21.4	75.3	785270
96825	HONOLULU	43803	10941	6.7	9.2	35.1	25.7	23.3	98229	100940	96	99	8409	0.2	0.7	0.7	3.3	95.2	803048
96826	HONOLULU	25239	13290	27.8	33.0	30.6	6.4	2.2	41730	44025	38	22	3906	1.8	2.5	5.7	40.1	49.9	399497
96853	HICKAM AFB	19633	1844	7.9	35.9	42.4	9.4	4.4	53474	54929	69	49	17	29.4	0.0	0.0	41.2	29.4	312500
96858	FORT SHAFTER	24886	64	6.3	37.5	37.5	12.5	6.3	54460	54523	70	50	1	0.0	0.0	0.0	0.0	100.0	875000
96860	PEARL HARBOR	17384	188	11.7	40.4	36.2	8.5	3.2	47033	49184	54	32	13	7.7	0.0	7.7	23.1	61.5	575000
96861	CAMP H M SMITH	18086	6	0.0	50.0	33.3	16.7	0.0	50000	50000	61	41	0	0.0	0.0	0.0	0.0	0.0	0
96863	M C B H KANEOHE BAY	18902	560	19.5	45.2	28.0	6.6	0.7	40348	41389	34	17	14	0.0	0.0	0.0	100.0	0.0	322222
	HAWAII	27398		17.4	22.5	35.8	14.8	9.4	61537	63474				0.8	0.9	3.3	23.8	71.3	581441
	UNITED STATES	27277		20.9	24.4	35.3	11.7	7.6	54719	56938				9.3	13.1	31.6	32.6	13.5	162279

ZIP CODE #	POST OFFICE NAME	FINANCIAL SERVICES				THE HOME						ENTERTAINMENT						PERSONAL			
						Home Improvements		Furnishings													
		Auto Loan	Home Loan	Investments	Retirement Plans	Home Repair	Lawn & Garden	Computers & Hardware-Personal	Major Appliances	TV, Radio, Sound Equipment	Furniture	Dine out/ Carry out	Sports Equipment	Fees & Tickets	Toys & Games	Travel	Cable TV	Apparel & Services	Auto Repairs	Health Insurance	Pets & Supplies
96701	AIEA	116	136	145	136	143	119	135	129	123	138	124	102	142	121	143	117	90	129	117	147
96704	CAPTAIN COOK	103	98	134	97	107	108	98	110	92	96	92	87	92	89	106	92	64	104	101	127
96705	ELEELE	79	109	113	102	113	98	91	95	87	90	88	69	106	88	103	88	65	91	91	104
96706	EWA BEACH	125	142	128	137	141	115	131	128	119	139	121	102	136	125	133	111	87	123	108	142
96707	KAPOLEI	122	136	122	133	132	114	127	123	117	133	120	98	131	123	128	111	85	120	108	140
96708	HAIKU	93	115	129	116	124	100	110	108	98	115	98	86	120	95	121	91	73	105	94	121
96710	HAKALAU	98	87	90	88	89	99	93	97	96	89	94	72	86	95	90	100	64	96	104	113
96712	HALEIWA	98	115	128	115	123	99	114	109	103	117	105	87	121	103	122	97	77	109	95	122
96713	HANA	96	95	129	91	102	107	88	103	88	84	88	75	87	86	97	92	61	97	100	117
96716	HANAPEPE	76	101	103	95	104	89	88	89	83	88	84	67	100	84	98	82	62	87	84	99
96717	HAUULA	80	98	92	90	100	78	92	91	83	95	85	70	96	83	97	78	62	88	77	98
96718	HAWAII NATIONAL PARK	77	55	79	53	57	78	57	72	63	53	62	54	45	62	56	69	41	66	75	86
96719	HAWI	94	126	138	122	134	110	111	113	102	115	103	86	126	101	126	98	76	109	101	124
96720	HILO	85	93	95	92	95	93	91	91	90	89	90	68	94	89	94	91	63	91	93	105
96722	PRINCEVILLE	110	139	162	141	153	119	132	130	115	141	116	104	144	111	147	106	86	126	109	145
96725	HOLUALOA	98	123	144	125	135	106	117	116	102	125	103	92	128	99	130	94	76	111	97	129
96726	HONAUNAU	0	0	0	0	0	0	0	0	0	0	0	0	0	0	0	0	0	0	0	0
96727	HONOKAA	106	94	130	91	99	116	92	110	95	84	94	83	83	93	97	101	64	103	111	128
96728	HONOMU	103	75	103	73	78	108	82	100	91	73	88	75	66	89	79	100	59	94	109	118
96729	HOOLEHUA	97	74	97	73	77	98	77	92	84	73	82	69	65	83	76	90	55	87	97	109
96730	KAAAWA	96	107	103	108	106	100	101	99	98	103	99	77	107	99	105	96	70	99	96	116
96731	KAHUKU	86	101	95	94	104	80	95	94	84	101	86	73	97	84	99	77	62	91	78	102
96732	KAHULUI	90	106	113	103	112	90	108	103	97	109	99	81	111	94	114	92	72	103	92	114
96734	KAILUA	134	159	175	160	169	141	153	148	141	156	143	116	167	143	165	135	106	148	134	165
96738	WAIKOLOA	98	110	106	112	109	102	104	101	100	106	101	79	110	101	108	98	72	101	98	119
96740	KAILUA KONA	112	116	125	118	120	117	113	116	111	115	111	88	116	110	118	111	78	114	115	135
96741	KALAHEO	102	129	131	127	133	116	113	117	105	118	106	89	125	105	126	102	77	112	107	131
96742	KALAUPAPA	18	13	16	15	14	17	22	18	24	19	23	14	19	20	19	25	16	22	25	23
96743	KAMUELA	105	127	132	129	131	112	117	116	108	123	109	92	128	107	127	102	79	113	104	132
96744	KANEOHE	125	160	176	157	172	132	148	147	128	157	129	116	161	126	164	118	95	141	123	162
96746	KAPAA	85	100	108	97	105	93	93	95	89	93	89	72	99	88	100	88	65	93	90	107
96747	KAUMAKANI	69	69	59	61	68	56	68	67	64	74	66	50	65	66	66	60	46	67	58	74
96748	KAUNAKAKAI	78	70	86	67	73	78	70	79	72	70	71	57	65	70	72	74	49	76	78	90
96749	KEAAU	79	83	88	81	83	84	82	84	81	78	82	65	83	81	85	83	58	83	84	97
96750	KEALAKEKUA	122	98	158	96	108	129	98	124	102	92	101	91	85	97	106	109	67	115	123	144
96752	KEKAHA	92	90	100	88	89	104	83	94	88	81	88	70	83	88	87	94	60	90	101	111
96753	KIHEI	107	102	102	105	102	94	112	102	107	113	108	83	109	108	108	103	77	107	98	121
96754	KILAUEA	79	103	113	100	108	93	97	94	94	93	95	71	109	91	106	94	71	95	91	106
96755	KAPAAU	91	101	125	96	107	104	90	102	89	88	89	75	95	88	101	91	63	96	97	114
96756	KOLOA	95	112	133	108	121	108	105	110	101	106	102	81	113	97	116	101	74	107	106	123
96757	KUALAPUU	105	75	108	73	78	107	77	98	86	72	84	74	62	85	77	94	56	90	102	117
96760	KURTISTOWN	75	74	71	72	71	71	69	72	68	71	69	55	67	70	69	68	48	70	69	84
96761	LAHAINA	110	125	136	127	132	106	131	121	116	133	119	100	134	114	137	108	87	123	106	138
96762	LAIE	76	92	98	90	95	83	94	87	91	87	94	68	101	90	98	93	70	91	86	99
96763	LANAI CITY	82	97	91	94	95	89	93	90	91	91	92	71	100	91	97	90	66	91	89	104
96764	LAUPAHOEHOE	73	71	69	73	71	81	68	76	70	63	69	57	65	71	69	73	47	70	78	88
96766	LIHUE	97	116	119	113	120	100	108	108	99	114	100	83	115	98	116	94	72	104	98	120
96768	MAKAWAO	111	131	125	129	131	114	117	118	109	124	111	91	125	111	124	104	79	113	106	134
96769	MAKAWELI	56	73	73	67	75	64	63	65	60	64	61	48	71	61	69	59	44	63	60	71
96770	MAUNALOA	81	72	75	73	74	82	77	80	79	74	78	59	71	78	74	82	53	80	86	94
96771	MOUNTAIN VIEW	86	67	109	66	74	90	68	86	71	63	70	64	58	68	73	76	47	80	86	101
96772	NAALEHU	75	63	94	62	68	81	62	77	65	59	64	56	56	62	67	69	43	72	78	89
96773	NINOLE	88	109	97	109	105	107	93	97	94	94	95	73	107	95	103	96	67	95	102	113
96774	OOKALA	88	109	97	109	105	107	93	97	94	94	95	73	107	95	103	96	67	95	102	113
96776	PAAUILO	91	78	94	78	77	99	78	89	83	73	82	68	71	80	79	88	55	86	97	109
96777	PAHALA	77	55	79	53	57	78	57	72	63	53	62	54	45	62	56	69	41	66	75	86
96778	PAHOA	76	56	83	55	59	78	57	73	63	53	62	54	47	61	58	68	41	67	75	86
96779	PAIA	108	146	158	140	155	128	127	130	118	131	119	98	146	117	144	115	88	125	117	143
96780	PAPAALOA	88	109	97	109	105	107	93	97	94	94	95	73	107	95	103	96	67	95	102	113
96781	PAPAIKOU	74	82	79	80	82	89	74	81	79	73	78	57	80	77	80	84	54	78	92	93
96782	PEARL CITY	114	135	146	133	144	115	132	128	117	137	118	101	139	116	141	109	86	126	111	142
96783	PEPEEKEO	91	91	94	92	94	100	89	95	92	89	91	68	89	90	92	95	63	93	102	110
96785	VOLCANO	75	60	97	59	66	80	60	77	63	57	62	56	52	60	65	67	42	71	76	89
96786	WAHIAWA	84	70	68	73	70	61	88	75	83	86	85	64	81	88	80	78	61	82	69	87
96789	MILILANI	131	154	145	150	154	126	141	139	127	150	129	111	148	131	147	118	93	133	118	156
96790	KULA	115	145	169	147	159	124	138	136	120	147	121	108	151	116	154	110	90	131	114	151
96791	WAIALUA	99	109	106	104	113	86	110	105	96	117	98	84	109	97	112	87	71	104	85	115
96792	WAIANAE	86	96	90	90	97	80	94	91	87	97	89	70	95	87	95	83	64	90	81	101
96793	WAILUKU	103	123	128	118	130	103	120	117	107	125	108	92	124	104	128	100	78	115	102	130
96795	WAIMANALO	102	135	139	125	143	109	120	122	105	126	107	93	131	105	133	98	79	116	101	130
96796	WAIMEA	87	109	127	106	120	88	104	105	87	112	87	84	109	83	116	77	64	99	82	114
96797	WAIPAHU	118	136	133	133	139	110	130	126	115	139	117	101	134	117	135	106	85	123	105	141
96813	HONOLULU	84	84	90	87	87	79	97	86	92	95	94	70	95	89	96	90	67	93	87	102
96814	HONOLULU	64	61	67	65	63	61	76	66	77	71	78	52	75	72	74	78	56	74	74	80
96815	HONOLULU	77	75	80	78	78	74	86	78	83	85	84	62	85	80	85	83	59	83	82	93
96816	HONOLULU	120	151	171	149	166	123	146	143	123	156	124	115	155	119	161	110	91	137	116	156
96817	HONOLULU	79	89	98	91	94	81	100	91	96	94	98	70	102	90	101	97	73	95	90	105
96818	HONOLULU	111	97	91	101	96	85	115	99	107	114	110	85	107	115	106	100	78	107	90	115
96819	HONOLULU	96	117	129	115	126	94	119	113	104	122	105	90	123	100	127	96	78	111	94	124
96821	HONOLULU	183	252	300	255	280	224	218	229	194	242	193	173	258	187	257	181	145	213	197	249
96822	HONOLULU	105	112	122	116	118	107	120	112	114	120	115	88	124	111	123	111	83	116	111	130
96825	HONOLULU	149	196	224	198	214	170	175	178	156	189	156	139	200	152	200	145	116	169	152	197
96826	HONOLULU	64	61	62	64	60	59	74	64	74	69	75	51	71	71	70	75	54	71	69	78
96853	HICKAM AFB	112	58	44	68	52	50	106	73	99	98	104	73	80	119	76	91	73	93	66	89
96858	FORT SHAFTER	123	64	48	74	57	54	115	80	109	107	114	80	88	130	83	100	80	102	72	97
96860	PEARL HARBOR	102	53	39	61	47	45	96	66	90	89	95	66	73	108	69	83	66	84	60	81
96861	CAMP H M SMITH	116	60	45	70	54	51	109	75	102	101	108	75	82	123	78	94	75	96	68	92
96863	M C B H KANEOHE BAY	86	44	33	52	40	38	80	56	76	75	80	55	61	91	58	70	56	71	50	68
	HAWAII	105	115	122	114	119	103	115	112	107	117	109	88	119	107	120	103	78	112	103	127
	UNITED STATES	100	100	100	100	100	100	100	100	100	100	100	100	100	100	100	100	100	100	100	100

ZIP CODE			POPULATION			2000-2009 ANNUAL RATE		HOUSEHOLDS					FAMILIES		
#	POST OFFICE NAME	COUNTY FIPS CODE	2000	2009	2014	% Rate	State Centile	2000	2009	2014	% Annual Rate 2000-2009	2009 Average HH Size	2000	2009	% Annual Rate 2000-2009
83201	POCATELLO	005	36011	37404	38320	0.4	33	13119	13962	14402	0.7	2.59	8981	9398	0.5
83202	POCATELLO	005	16692	19637	21047	1.8	75	5541	6731	7274	2.1	2.91	4367	5202	1.9
83203	FORT HALL	005	132	144	152	0.9	53	40	45	48	1.3	3.20	33	37	1.2
83204	POCATELLO	077	17540	17954	18315	0.3	28	6645	7002	7200	0.6	2.45	4399	4554	0.4
83209	POCATELLO	005	1	28	28	43.4	100	1	0	0	-100.0	0.00	1	0	-100.0
83210	ABERDEEN	011	3538	3915	4103	1.1	61	1125	1246	1309	1.1	3.13	870	952	1.0
83211	AMERICAN FALLS	077	5956	6157	6270	0.4	33	2028	2128	2175	0.5	2.87	1547	1604	0.4
83212	ARBON	077	95	98	98	0.3	28	38	40	40	0.6	2.45	30	31	0.4
83213	ARCO	023	1817	1770	1740	-0.3	11	714	724	721	0.2	2.42	489	491	0.0
83214	ARIMO	005	604	692	739	1.5	71	176	211	227	2.0	3.28	144	169	1.7
83217	BANCROFT	029	835	800	776	-0.5	8	289	290	285	0.0	2.76	219	218	0.0
83220	BERN	007	222	231	233	0.4	33	72	78	80	0.9	2.96	57	61	0.7
83221	BLACKFOOT	011	23349	24966	25840	0.7	45	7618	8369	8728	1.0	2.95	6062	6595	0.9
83226	CHALLIS	037	2527	2456	2429	-0.3	11	1030	1049	1051	0.2	2.33	716	718	0.0
83227	CLAYTON	037	3	3	3	0.0	18	1	1	1	0.0	3.00	1	1	0.0
83228	CLIFTON	041	431	464	480	0.8	49	124	136	141	1.0	3.41	105	115	1.0
83232	DAYTON	041	715	796	835	1.2	64	208	237	250	1.4	3.36	178	201	1.3
83234	DOWNEY	005	1268	1344	1399	0.6	40	454	502	528	1.1	2.64	344	372	0.8
83235	ELLIS	059	278	287	290	0.3	28	132	141	144	0.7	2.04	89	94	0.6
83236	FIRTH	011	4355	4790	5028	1.0	58	1350	1539	1632	1.4	3.09	1108	1252	1.3
83237	FRANKLIN	041	1119	1350	1454	2.0	80	330	400	431	2.1	3.38	281	339	2.0
83238	GENEVA	007	118	113	111	-0.5	8	36	36	35	0.0	3.06	27	26	-0.4
83241	GRACE	029	2017	2020	1985	0.0	18	706	742	739	0.5	2.72	558	580	0.4
83243	HOLBROOK	071	202	218	225	0.8	49	60	67	70	1.2	3.25	51	56	1.0
83244	HOWE	023	206	187	180	-1.0	2	69	65	64	-0.6	2.88	57	54	-0.6
83245	INKOM	005	1874	1994	2078	0.7	45	623	691	728	1.1	2.89	519	568	1.0
83246	LAVA HOT SPRINGS	005	1061	1151	1209	0.9	53	420	475	504	1.3	2.40	274	301	1.0
83250	MCCAMMON	005	1630	1783	1872	1.0	58	565	644	683	1.4	2.76	464	520	1.2
83251	MACKAY	037	1240	1215	1201	-0.2	13	505	517	518	0.3	2.29	339	341	0.1
83252	MALAD CITY	071	3923	3997	3998	0.2	25	1370	1435	1447	0.5	2.75	1042	1080	0.4
83253	MAY	059	212	220	222	0.4	33	92	99	101	0.8	2.22	62	65	0.5
83254	MONTPELIER	007	4738	4647	4582	-0.2	13	1649	1671	1665	0.1	2.75	1240	1240	0.0
83255	MOORE	023	911	846	819	-0.8	2	317	308	302	-0.3	2.74	263	253	-0.4
83261	PARIS	007	877	924	937	0.6	40	313	346	355	1.1	2.67	244	266	0.9
83262	PINGREE	011	1301	1286	1287	-0.1	15	401	408	413	0.2	3.15	326	328	0.1
83263	PRESTON	041	8062	9079	9535	1.3	66	2522	2878	3029	1.4	3.13	2057	2326	1.3
83271	ROCKLAND	077	573	589	592	0.3	28	177	186	188	0.5	3.17	139	145	0.5
83272	SAINT CHARLES	007	200	212	214	0.6	40	78	86	88	1.1	2.45	58	63	0.9
83274	SHELLEY	019	8909	9893	10442	1.1	61	2763	3182	3390	1.5	3.09	2300	2625	1.4
83276	SODA SPRINGS	029	4491	4233	4088	-0.6	5	1576	1544	1510	-0.2	2.70	1210	1172	-0.3
83278	STANLEY	037	540	534	526	-0.1	15	223	228	228	0.2	2.21	135	136	0.1
83283	THATCHER	041	115	134	143	1.7	73	39	46	50	1.8	2.91	32	38	1.9
83285	WAYAN	019	119	124	129	0.4	33	46	50	53	0.9	2.48	35	37	0.6
83286	WESTON	041	879	1055	1140	2.0	80	249	305	331	2.2	3.46	216	262	2.1
83287	FISH HAVEN	007	183	196	199	0.7	45	87	98	101	1.3	2.00	65	72	1.1
83301	TWIN FALLS	083	42157	49663	53931	1.8	75	15954	19270	21042	2.1	2.51	11020	13129	1.9
83302	ROGERSON	083	133	136	140	0.2	25	55	58	61	0.6	2.28	41	43	0.5
83313	BELLEVUE	013	3104	3732	3976	2.0	80	1155	1419	1521	2.3	2.63	845	1019	2.0
83314	BLISS	047	915	915	914	0.0	18	331	327	325	-0.1	2.80	240	233	-0.3
83316	BUHL	083	9444	10331	10923	1.0	58	3526	3932	4171	1.2	2.62	2599	2862	1.0
83318	BURLEY	031	16064	16216	16201	0.1	22	5346	5482	5494	0.3	2.90	4105	4165	0.2
83320	CAREY	013	952	1092	1139	1.5	71	311	365	383	1.7	2.99	243	281	1.6
83321	CASTLEFORD	083	378	398	413	0.6	40	144	155	162	0.8	2.57	105	112	0.7
83322	CORRAL	025	55	63	67	1.5	71	18	21	23	1.7	3.00	13	15	1.6
83323	DECLO	031	1313	1330	1336	0.1	22	393	408	412	0.4	3.26	322	331	0.3
83324	DIETRICH	063	540	613	643	1.4	68	172	198	208	1.5	3.10	133	152	1.5
83325	EDEN	053	1050	1116	1159	0.7	45	389	414	430	0.7	2.70	298	313	0.5
83327	FAIRFIELD	025	936	1071	1138	1.5	71	378	448	481	1.9	2.38	274	320	1.7
83328	FILER	083	4434	5577	6243	2.5	87	1591	2039	2288	2.7	2.72	1181	1491	2.6
83330	GOODING	047	5916	6166	6262	0.4	33	2156	2204	2224	0.2	2.73	1547	1559	0.1
83332	HAGERMAN	083	2206	2440	2547	1.1	61	877	968	1006	1.1	2.52	606	660	0.9
83333	HAILEY	013	9923	11796	12680	1.9	77	3894	4720	5097	2.1	2.47	2616	3110	1.9
83334	HANSEN	031	1971	2157	2319	1.0	58	664	740	799	1.2	2.90	514	563	1.0
83335	HAZELTON	053	1677	1847	1946	1.0	58	563	618	650	1.0	2.99	440	477	0.9
83336	HEYBURN	067	5175	5165	5101	0.0	18	1788	1851	1844	0.4	2.79	1402	1434	0.2
83338	JEROME	053	15481	17752	19031	1.5	71	5310	6058	6478	1.4	2.91	4040	4558	1.3
83340	KETCHUM	013	5006	5695	5906	1.4	68	2417	2809	2932	1.6	1.96	1135	1280	1.3
83341	KIMBERLY	083	4776	6023	6673	2.5	87	1607	2054	2285	2.7	2.91	1264	1595	2.5
83342	MALTA	031	2292	2281	2268	-0.1	15	777	796	797	0.3	2.87	631	639	0.1
83343	MINIDOKA	067	77	74	72	-0.4	10	19	18	18	-0.6	4.00	16	16	0.0
83344	MURTAUGH	083	1076	1173	1235	0.9	53	329	365	386	1.1	3.13	269	295	1.0
83346	OAKLEY	031	1414	1465	1477	0.4	33	449	473	479	0.6	3.08	352	367	0.5
83347	PAUL	067	3102	2867	2772	-0.8	2	1114	1058	1025	-0.6	2.71	836	784	-0.7
83348	PICABO	013	6	7	7	1.7	73	3	4	4	3.2	1.75	2	3	4.5
83349	RICHFIELD	063	876	1079	1162	2.3	84	310	387	417	2.4	2.79	230	283	2.3
83350	RUPERT	067	12208	11607	11221	-0.5	8	4156	4026	3912	-0.3	2.85	3190	3051	-0.5
83352	SHOSHONE	063	2501	2786	2901	1.2	64	934	1047	1089	1.2	2.63	663	732	1.1
83355	WENDELL	047	5213	5657	5808	0.9	53	1718	1850	1892	0.8	3.03	1343	1430	0.7
83401	IDAHO FALLS	019	30134	36330	40370	2.0	80	10261	12780	14331	2.4	2.80	7666	9424	2.3
83402	IDAHO FALLS	019	24562	26365	27856	0.8	49	8981	9954	10622	1.1	2.62	6298	6770	0.8
83404	IDAHO FALLS	019	18267	21831	23897	1.9	77	6582	8133	9001	2.3	2.66	5028	6107	2.1
83406	IDAHO FALLS	019	8452	15099	18340	6.5	99	2510	4791	5919	7.2	3.12	2150	3994	6.9
83420	ASHTON	043	2706	2929	3051	0.9	53	939	1043	1097	1.1	2.77	717	789	1.0
83422	DRIGGS	081	2110	3256	3915	4.8	96	720	1135	1376	5.0	2.86	500	773	4.8
83423	DUBOIS	033	947	1046	1096	1.1	61	309	334	348	0.8	3.13	235	251	0.7
83424	FELT	081	169	292	361	6.1	98	45	85	106	7.1	3.44	34	63	6.9
83425	HAMER	051	588	593	610	0.1	22	163	169	175	0.4	3.51	135	139	0.3
83428	IRWIN	019	184	199	214	0.9	53	77	88	96	1.5	2.26	57	63	1.1
83429	ISLAND PARK	043	826	1038	1114	2.5	87	372	484	526	2.9	2.14	266	342	2.8
83431	LEWISVILLE	051	800	990	1120	2.3	84	260	333	380	2.7	2.97	219	279	2.7
83434	MENAN	051	1546	1864	2119	2.0	80	471	590	677	2.5	3.16	405	503	2.4
83435	MONTEVIEW	051	463	469	483	0.1	22	139	145	150	0.5	3.23	115	119	0.4
83436	NEWDALE	065	79	84	88	0.7	45	21	23	24	1.0	3.65	17	19	1.2
83440	REXBURG	065	25440	35799	41362	3.8	93	6677	9877	11553	4.3	3.52	4461	6484	4.1
83442	RIGBY	051	12957	17265	19859	3.2	90	4073	5581	6471	3.5	3.08	3341	4544	3.4
	IDAHO					2.1					2.2	2.65			2.1
	UNITED STATES					1.0					1.1	2.59			0.9

ZIP CODE #	POST OFFICE NAME	RACE (%) White 2000	White 2009	Black 2000	Black 2009	Asian/Pacific 2000	Asian/Pacific 2009	% Hispanic Origin 2000	% Hispanic Origin 2009	2009 AGE DISTRIBUTION (%) 0-4	5-9	10-14	15-19	20-24	25-44	45-64	65-84	85+	18+	MEDIAN AGE 2009	% 2009 Males	% 2009 Females
83201	POCATELLO	92.4	91.2	0.7	0.9	1.6	2.0	4.7	5.7	8.3	7.2	6.7	7.7	10.3	28.4	20.9	9.0	1.7	74.2	30.4	49.0	51.0
83202	POCATELLO	84.8	84.1	0.3	0.4	0.9	1.0	5.4	6.5	9.3	8.8	8.1	7.4	6.1	28.8	22.4	8.0	1.1	69.3	31.1	48.8	51.2
83203	FORT HALL	34.1	31.9	0.0	0.0	0.8	0.7	3.0	3.5	8.3	8.3	8.3	6.9	6.9	29.2	22.9	7.6	1.4	70.8	31.8	49.3	50.7
83204	POCATELLO	91.3	90.0	0.7	0.9	0.8	1.1	5.3	6.4	7.6	6.9	6.7	7.5	9.0	28.6	24.7	7.9	1.1	74.8	32.5	50.5	49.5
83209	POCATELLO	100.0	96.4	0.0	0.0	0.0	3.6	0.0	0.0	7.1	7.1	7.1	14.3	14.3	28.6	21.4	0.0	0.0	78.6	25.0	46.4	53.6
83210	ABERDEEN	76.8	72.2	0.1	0.1	0.4	0.5	28.7	34.2	9.9	9.7	9.4	8.0	5.2	22.3	22.9	10.3	2.2	65.5	31.9	49.8	50.2
83211	AMERICAN FALLS	84.1	81.1	0.1	0.1	0.3	0.4	25.8	30.2	8.8	7.8	9.2	8.8	6.3	23.2	25.1	9.2	1.6	68.2	32.6	50.2	49.8
83212	ARBON	96.8	95.9	0.0	0.0	0.0	0.0	3.2	4.1	8.2	8.2	9.2	9.2	6.1	19.4	26.5	11.2	2.0	68.4	33.8	50.0	50.0
83213	ARCO	94.4	93.6	0.4	0.5	0.2	0.2	4.3	5.3	5.9	6.3	7.0	7.6	5.1	20.6	29.8	15.7	1.9	75.9	42.8	48.6	51.4
83214	ARIMO	97.4	97.0	0.0	0.0	0.5	0.6	0.7	0.9	8.4	9.0	9.0	8.1	5.5	21.0	29.0	8.2	1.9	68.5	33.5	50.6	49.4
83217	BANCROFT	97.0	96.5	0.1	0.1	0.1	0.1	2.6	3.4	8.5	8.9	9.5	9.1	4.4	20.8	25.3	11.1	2.5	67.3	35.0	50.3	49.7
83220	BERN	98.6	98.7	0.5	0.4	0.0	0.0	0.9	0.9	8.2	7.8	7.4	7.8	6.5	19.9	26.0	14.3	2.2	71.4	36.3	48.1	51.9
83221	BLACKFOOT	86.3	83.9	0.2	0.3	0.8	1.0	13.3	16.0	9.0	8.4	8.4	8.3	6.8	25.0	23.4	9.3	1.4	68.9	31.4	50.2	49.8
83226	CHALLIS	97.7	97.3	0.0	0.0	0.1	0.1	4.8	5.8	5.1	5.6	6.1	6.5	5.2	20.3	34.6	14.7	1.9	78.8	45.7	50.6	49.4
83227	CLAYTON	100.0	100.0	0.0	0.0	0.0	0.0	0.0	0.0	0.0	0.0	0.0	0.0	0.0	0.0	100.0	0.0	0.0	100.0	51.3	100.0	0.0
83228	CLIFTON	95.4	94.4	0.2	0.2	0.0	0.0	4.6	5.8	10.8	11.0	10.1	8.6	4.7	24.6	21.1	8.0	1.1	62.5	28.8	51.5	48.5
83232	DAYTON	95.9	95.4	0.1	0.1	0.1	0.1	4.3	5.3	10.3	10.3	10.3	9.3	5.2	24.0	21.4	8.0	1.3	62.6	28.5	51.5	48.5
83234	DOWNEY	97.1	96.6	0.2	0.3	0.5	0.6	1.4	1.8	7.1	7.4	7.7	8.2	4.9	21.3	26.9	12.9	3.6	71.7	39.5	50.1	49.9
83235	ELLIS	95.0	94.4	0.0	0.0	0.4	0.3	2.9	3.5	4.2	4.2	3.8	5.2	4.9	12.5	35.5	27.2	2.4	84.3	57.0	53.0	47.0
83236	FIRTH	50.2	48.8	0.2	0.3	0.1	0.1	9.4	10.5	8.7	8.6	8.9	9.2	6.8	25.1	23.3	8.2	1.2	67.7	30.7	49.6	50.4
83237	FRANKLIN	90.0	87.7	0.0	0.0	0.1	0.1	10.2	12.6	11.3	10.5	10.2	9.4	6.0	23.6	20.3	7.5	1.2	62.1	27.2	50.3	49.7
83238	GENEVA	98.3	98.2	0.0	0.0	0.0	0.0	2.6	1.8	6.2	6.2	6.2	6.2	5.3	23.0	30.1	13.3	3.5	76.1	41.5	52.2	47.8
83241	GRACE	94.6	93.4	0.1	0.1	0.1	0.1	6.7	8.2	8.2	8.3	8.4	7.4	4.4	23.2	26.1	11.9	2.1	70.5	36.8	51.6	48.4
83243	HOLBROOK	96.5	96.8	0.0	0.0	0.0	0.0	3.0	3.2	7.8	8.3	7.8	7.3	5.5	23.9	27.5	10.6	1.4	71.1	35.8	54.6	45.4
83244	HOWE	94.7	93.6	0.0	0.0	0.5	0.5	4.9	5.9	9.1	8.0	9.6	7.5	2.7	25.1	24.1	12.8	1.1	67.9	36.0	50.3	49.7
83245	INKOM	96.5	95.9	0.4	0.6	0.3	0.4	2.0	2.5	6.1	6.3	6.8	7.6	6.3	23.5	31.3	11.1	1.1	76.2	39.3	50.4	49.6
83246	LAVA HOT SPRINGS	97.4	97.0	0.0	0.0	0.2	0.2	2.2	2.6	5.7	6.3	6.4	6.4	6.5	18.5	33.8	14.2	2.1	76.9	45.1	50.4	49.6
83250	MCCAMMON	96.6	96.2	0.3	0.4	0.4	0.4	1.7	2.0	5.8	6.1	6.7	7.8	5.9	23.3	30.3	12.9	1.2	76.7	39.5	50.2	49.8
83251	MACKAY	96.0	95.3	0.0	0.0	0.0	0.0	4.3	5.4	5.2	5.5	5.7	6.1	4.2	20.2	35.1	16.1	1.9	79.1	46.8	49.1	50.9
83252	MALAD CITY	97.6	97.5	0.1	0.1	0.2	0.2	2.3	2.3	7.8	8.0	7.7	7.2	5.4	22.5	26.3	12.4	2.8	71.9	37.0	50.4	49.6
83253	MAY	95.3	95.0	0.0	0.0	0.0	0.0	2.8	3.2	4.1	3.6	3.6	4.5	5.0	11.8	36.4	28.2	2.7	85.5	58.4	52.3	47.7
83254	MONTPELIER	97.3	97.2	0.1	0.1	0.1	0.2	2.8	2.9	7.5	7.5	7.3	7.6	6.4	22.9	25.8	12.5	2.4	72.7	36.2	49.1	50.9
83255	MOORE	95.2	94.4	0.0	0.0	0.2	0.2	3.6	4.5	6.1	6.9	7.2	7.9	5.0	21.3	29.9	14.2	1.5	74.8	41.2	49.5	50.5
83261	PARIS	99.0	98.9	0.2	0.2	0.0	0.0	0.9	1.0	7.4	7.5	7.4	7.7	6.1	18.6	28.6	14.7	2.2	72.9	40.1	49.5	50.5
83262	PINGREE	85.2	81.8	0.2	0.2	0.8	1.1	15.7	19.3	8.5	8.3	8.4	8.6	7.4	25.5	24.2	7.9	1.2	69.6	30.7	50.5	49.5
83263	PRESTON	95.4	94.5	0.1	0.2	0.2	0.2	4.8	6.0	10.1	9.6	9.1	8.6	6.6	23.3	20.7	9.8	2.2	65.6	29.5	49.7	50.3
83271	ROCKLAND	96.0	95.2	0.0	0.0	0.2	0.2	3.7	4.6	8.3	8.5	8.5	8.7	5.3	19.7	27.7	11.7	1.7	69.3	35.9	49.7	50.3
83272	SAINT CHARLES	99.0	98.6	0.0	0.0	0.0	0.0	1.5	1.4	7.1	7.1	7.1	7.1	5.2	17.0	31.1	15.6	2.8	74.1	44.5	51.4	48.6
83274	SHELLEY	92.0	90.4	0.1	0.1	0.4	0.5	8.7	10.7	9.5	9.2	9.0	8.4	6.2	25.4	22.6	8.6	1.2	66.9	30.1	50.2	49.8
83276	SODA SPRINGS	96.7	96.1	0.0	0.0	0.3	0.3	2.9	3.5	7.4	7.4	7.5	7.2	6.4	24.6	26.4	11.4	1.7	73.0	35.7	49.1	50.9
83278	STANLEY	98.3	98.3	0.0	0.0	0.0	0.0	1.1	1.1	6.0	6.0	5.2	4.9	2.4	24.5	43.6	7.1	0.2	79.8	45.4	53.6	46.4
83283	THATCHER	97.4	95.5	0.0	0.0	0.9	0.7	4.4	6.0	7.5	9.0	8.2	9.7	5.2	18.7	28.4	11.9	1.5	68.7	35.8	53.0	47.0
83285	WAYAN	96.6	96.0	0.0	0.0	0.0	0.0	3.4	4.0	4.8	5.6	8.1	6.5	4.0	16.9	34.7	16.9	2.4	78.2	48.1	51.6	48.4
83286	WESTON	97.6	97.3	0.0	0.0	0.3	0.4	3.3	4.0	9.5	8.5	11.3	11.2	6.0	22.2	21.7	8.2	1.4	62.7	27.5	50.8	49.2
83287	FISH HAVEN	98.9	98.5	0.0	0.0	0.0	0.0	1.6	1.0	6.6	7.1	7.1	7.1	5.6	16.3	31.6	15.8	2.6	74.0	45.0	51.0	49.0
83301	TWIN FALLS	92.4	91.0	0.2	0.3	1.1	1.4	8.4	10.2	7.7	7.1	6.8	7.0	6.9	26.2	24.6	11.1	2.5	74.3	35.2	48.8	51.2
83302	ROGERSON	93.9	91.9	0.0	0.0	0.0	0.0	11.4	13.2	4.4	6.6	8.1	11.0	5.1	25.0	29.4	8.8	1.5	72.1	37.8	53.7	46.3
83313	BELLEVUE	88.8	86.4	0.1	0.1	0.9	1.1	14.5	17.4	6.3	6.6	6.9	6.4	5.2	28.6	31.6	7.7	0.9	76.3	38.8	53.2	46.8
83314	BLISS	84.9	81.3	1.1	1.7	0.0	0.0	19.0	23.1	9.3	10.1	9.2	5.8	3.8	23.6	26.2	10.6	1.4	67.7	34.5	51.9	48.1
83316	BUHL	90.7	89.0	0.1	0.1	0.4	0.5	12.5	15.0	7.0	7.1	7.2	7.0	5.1	23.9	26.8	13.4	2.4	74.2	38.8	50.8	49.2
83318	BURLEY	83.3	80.1	0.2	0.2	0.5	0.6	20.3	24.0	9.0	8.7	8.6	8.5	6.0	24.2	22.7	10.0	2.2	68.2	32.2	49.9	50.1
83320	CAREY	88.6	86.5	0.1	0.1	0.3	0.4	13.6	16.3	8.3	8.6	9.0	7.9	4.6	24.5	26.6	9.1	1.6	69.0	34.0	52.6	47.4
83321	CASTLEFORD	91.0	89.2	0.0	0.3	0.5	0.5	20.2	23.9	6.0	6.5	7.0	8.0	4.8	25.4	29.1	11.6	1.5	75.4	39.4	49.5	50.5
83322	CORRAL	96.3	95.2	1.9	1.6	0.0	0.0	5.6	6.3	3.2	4.8	7.9	7.9	3.2	23.8	33.3	14.3	1.6	76.2	44.4	55.6	44.4
83323	DECLO	85.6	82.0	0.2	0.2	0.3	0.3	16.4	20.5	9.7	9.7	9.4	8.6	5.1	23.8	24.4	8.2	1.1	65.6	31.6	50.8	49.2
83324	DIETRICH	83.9	80.9	0.9	1.1	0.2	0.2	15.4	18.8	8.6	8.2	8.5	7.8	6.5	26.1	25.3	8.3	0.7	70.0	32.2	53.2	46.8
83325	EDEN	86.4	83.5	0.1	0.1	0.9	1.1	15.5	18.8	7.8	8.1	8.1	7.1	4.6	24.6	27.6	10.6	1.7	71.6	37.2	51.9	48.1
83327	FAIRFIELD	95.1	95.1	1.2	1.0	0.2	0.2	5.5	6.2	4.3	4.9	8.0	7.6	4.4	24.4	33.1	11.4	2.0	77.4	42.6	51.4	48.6
83328	FILER	95.6	94.8	0.2	0.3	0.2	0.2	7.6	9.4	7.2	7.4	7.8	7.7	5.9	25.3	26.6	10.3	1.8	72.6	36.2	51.0	49.0
83330	GOODING	90.4	88.6	0.1	0.1	0.3	0.3	14.0	16.9	7.0	7.1	7.6	7.8	5.3	23.2	25.8	13.3	3.0	74.0	38.5	50.8	49.2
83332	HAGERMAN	91.5	89.9	0.2	0.4	0.4	0.4	11.0	13.2	6.1	6.7	6.7	5.8	4.2	21.4	30.3	16.2	2.5	76.8	44.2	52.4	47.6
83333	HAILEY	90.2	88.2	0.2	0.2	0.8	1.0	11.3	13.7	6.3	6.6	7.1	6.6	5.4	27.4	31.7	8.0	0.9	75.9	38.9	50.7	49.3
83334	HANSEN	93.2	92.1	0.3	0.4	0.3	0.3	10.8	12.9	7.6	8.2	8.6	8.8	6.0	24.8	25.8	9.2	1.0	69.4	34.1	50.6	49.4
83335	HAZELTON	84.7	81.5	0.2	0.4	0.4	0.4	21.1	25.3	8.1	8.2	8.2	8.1	5.0	24.9	25.8	10.0	1.7	70.4	35.2	50.9	49.1
83336	HEYBURN	79.2	74.9	0.3	0.3	0.5	0.6	23.1	27.7	8.8	8.4	8.2	7.8	6.0	25.2	23.9	10.3	1.3	69.8	33.0	49.5	50.5
83338	JEROME	87.3	84.9	0.2	0.3	0.3	0.3	16.8	20.1	8.6	8.4	8.0	7.4	6.1	26.1	24.1	9.7	1.6	70.2	33.2	50.7	49.3
83340	KETCHUM	93.4	92.3	0.1	0.1	0.7	0.9	6.5	7.9	3.0	2.8	3.4	4.6	7.4	29.4	34.9	13.5	0.9	88.4	44.5	52.5	47.5
83341	KIMBERLY	95.3	94.5	0.1	0.1	0.4	0.4	7.2	8.8	7.3	7.7	7.9	8.1	5.7	25.1	26.5	10.0	1.7	72.0	35.9	49.8	50.2
83342	MALTA	90.1	87.5	0.2	0.2	0.1	0.1	13.0	16.3	8.8	9.0	9.1	8.4	5.1	22.3	24.9	10.9	1.4	67.5	33.4	52.8	47.2
83343	MINIDOKA	64.9	59.5	0.0	0.0	1.3	1.4	37.7	43.2	10.8	10.8	9.5	6.8	6.8	27.0	20.3	8.1	0.0	63.5	28.3	51.4	48.6
83344	MURTAUGH	81.7	78.2	0.3	0.4	0.1	0.2	29.1	34.2	8.7	9.3	9.4	8.5	5.0	26.4	24.1	7.2	1.3	66.8	32.3	51.2	48.8
83346	OAKLEY	90.1	87.4	0.0	0.0	0.1	0.1	12.5	15.8	9.0	9.3	9.5	8.6	5.2	22.9	23.3	10.4	1.9	66.4	32.2	51.9	48.1
83347	PAUL	81.2	77.2	0.1	0.2	0.5	0.6	19.1	23.2	7.4	7.7	7.6	7.0	4.8	25.3	26.5	11.8	1.9	72.9	37.1	51.6	48.4
83348	PICABO	83.3	85.7	0.0	0.0	0.0	0.0	16.7	14.3	0.0	0.0	0.0	0.0	0.0	14.3	85.7	0.0	0.0	100.0	51.9	71.4	28.6
83349	RICHFIELD	91.4	89.9	0.8	1.0	0.1	0.2	9.6	11.8	7.9	8.3	9.1	8.5	5.7	22.9	27.2	9.2	1.1	70.0	34.7	52.2	47.8
83350	RUPERT	77.1	73.0	0.3	0.4	0.4	0.4	27.8	32.3	8.6	8.6	8.3	7.8	5.7	24.0	24.1	11.1	1.8	69.5	33.4	50.3	49.7
83352	SHOSHONE	85.4	82.7	0.2	0.3	0.7	0.9	14.2	17.3	7.3	7.3	7.5	7.3	4.9	25.2	26.2	12.1	2.3	73.5	37.7	50.9	49.1
83355	WENDELL	83.8	81.1	0.2	0.3	0.3	0.4	22.9	26.9	9.1	8.9	8.6	7.4	5.3	27.3	22.2	9.7	1.5	68.7	32.8	51.2	48.8
83401	IDAHO FALLS	92.4	90.3	0.5	0.7	0.6	0.8	7.8	10.2	9.0	8.4	8.0	7.9	7.4	27.0	22.6	8.2	1.6	69.8	31.0	50.0	50.0
83402	IDAHO FALLS	90.4	88.4	0.5	0.6	1.0	1.2	10.1	12.4	8.6	8.2	7.6	7.5	7.0	27.6	23.8	8.7	1.1	70.9	32.6	50.7	49.3
83404	IDAHO FALLS	94.9	93.8	0.6	0.7	1.3	1.7	3.4	4.3	7.1	7.6	8.1	7.6	5.1	24.1	27.8	10.9	1.6	72.1	37.6	48.9	51.1
83406	IDAHO FALLS	96.0	95.1	0.2	0.4	0.7	0.8	3.1	4.0	10.3	9.3	9.1	8.3	5.9	28.4	21.5	6.4	0.9	65.9	29.4	49.0	51.0
83420	ASHTON	89.5	87.3	0.3	0.3	0.2	0.3	11.2	13.8	8.1	8.0	8.0	7.2	4.7	22.9	25.8	12.7	2.5	71.2	37.6	50.1	49.9
83422	DRIGGS	89.2	86.5	0.0	0.1	0.6	0.7	14.5	18.0	7.6	7.8	9.8	8.5	6.6	30.3	21.2	7.1	1.0	68.9	31.0	52.5	47.5
83423	DUBOIS	73.0	73.1	0.1	0.1	0.3	0.3	35.9	35.9	9.7	9.1	8.9	8.6	6.5	25.8	21.8	8.8	0.9	67.1	29.9	51.7	48.3
83424	FELT	92.3	89.7	0.0	0.3	0.6	0.3	14.3	17.5	9.2	8.9	8.9	7.5	5.8	26.7	24.7	7.5	0.7	68.2	32.4	54.1	45.9
83425	HAMER	85.2	80.4	0.2	0.2	0.5	0.7	15.0	19.9	9.9	8.8	12.0	10.1	7.4	21.2	21.4	7.9	1.2	62.1	26.5	54.6	45.4
83428	IRWIN	96.8	96.5	0.0	0.0	1.1	1.0	1.1	1.5	4.5	5.0	5.5	5.0	3.5	17.1	39.2	18.1	2.0	81.9	51.3	50.8	49.2
83429	ISLAND PARK	95.9	95.1	0.0	0.0	0.5	0.6	3.3	4.0	4.6	5.2	5.4	4.5	2.9	18.8	34.2	23.2	1.2	82.2	50.7	52.2	47.8
83431	LEWISVILLE	92.7	90.3	0.1	0.2	0.0	0.1	7.5	10.1	7.3	8.1	9.7	9.6	6.3	22.0	25.3	10.1	1.7	68.4	34.4	50.7	49.3
83434	MENAN	91.3	88.6	0.1	0.2	0.1	0.1	9.3	12.3	9.1	9.1	9.3	9.1	6.4	23.6	23.0	9.1	1.2	66.7	30.3	50.3	49.7
83435	MONTEVIEW	84.4	79.5	0.2	0.2	0.4	0.6	16.2	21.3	10.0	9.0	11.3	10.0	8.5	21.7	20.5	7.9	1.1	62.7	26.0	55.2	44.8
83436	NEWDALE	91.0	89.3	0.0	0.0	0.0	0.0	11.5	13.1	9.5	7.1	9.5	11.9	8.3	20.2	26.2	7.1	0.0	65.5	28.0	54.8	45.2
83440	REXBURG	95.4	94.6	0.2	0.3	0.8	0.9	4.1	4.9	7.4	6.2	6.4	21.2	20.0	17.9	14.6	5.3	0.9	74.9	22.2	47.9	52.1
83442	RIGBY	94.3	92.8	0.2	0.3	0.3	0.4	6.3	8.1	9.3	9.0	8.8	8.5	6.2	25.1	23.5	8.4	1.1	67.3	31.0	50.1	49.9
	IDAHO	91.0	89.5	0.4	0.5	1.0	1.3	7.9	9.5	7.7	7.4	7.3	7.7	7.0	26.7	25.0	9.6	1.6	73.1	34.4	50.1	49.9
	UNITED STATES	75.1	72.0	12.3	12.7	3.8	4.6	12.5	15.7	6.8	6.7	6.6	7.1	6.9	27.0	26.0	10.9	1.9	75.7	36.9	49.2	50.8

INCOME

83201-83442

#	POST OFFICE NAME	2009 Per Capita Income	2009 HH Income Base	2009 HOUSEHOLD INCOME DISTRIBUTION (%) Less than $25,000	$25,000 to $49,999	$50,000 to $99,999	$100,000 to $149,999	$150,000 or More	MEDIAN HOUSEHOLD INCOME 2009	2014	2009 National Centile	2009 State Centile	2009 Home Value Base	2009 HOME VALUE DISTRIBUTION (%) Less than $50,000	$50,000 to $89,999	$90,000 to $174,999	$175,000 to $399,999	$400,000 or More	2009 Median Home Value
83201	POCATELLO	23386	13962	23.2	26.4	37.6	7.8	5.0	50292	52712	62	85	9165	4.7	9.5	66.7	17.7	1.4	130044
83202	POCATELLO	20826	6731	18.2	27.3	43.2	8.2	3.0	53315	55219	69	91	5258	11.6	9.8	56.7	20.7	1.2	134375
83203	FORT HALL	14942	45	31.1	35.6	28.9	4.4	0.0	39288	43197	31	36	38	5.3	18.4	63.2	13.2	0.0	127778
83204	POCATELLO	24426	7002	26.4	25.3	33.9	9.2	5.1	47979	51767	57	78	4721	9.8	11.4	51.6	23.8	3.3	132675
83209	POCATELLO	7007	0	0.0	0.0	0.0	0.0	0.0	0	0	0	0	0	0.0	0.0	0.0	0.0	0.0	0
83210	ABERDEEN	15209	1246	27.8	42.9	23.4	4.0	2.0	38112	40195	27	27	960	14.5	18.6	46.3	14.8	5.8	118000
83211	AMERICAN FALLS	19571	2128	25.0	34.3	31.3	5.6	3.9	42865	46451	42	57	1546	12.9	18.2	49.5	17.0	2.3	122004
83212	ARBON	18583	40	35.0	25.0	35.0	5.0	0.0	42364	46526	41	55	33	15.2	24.2	54.5	6.1	0.0	106250
83213	ARCO	18992	724	34.7	27.1	32.0	4.1	2.1	36480	38603	22	18	545	13.9	27.0	44.6	12.1	2.4	102724
83214	ARIMO	18432	211	21.8	29.9	38.9	5.2	4.3	48795	51308	58	81	182	3.8	19.8	51.6	23.1	1.6	126613
83217	BANCROFT	17629	290	33.8	28.3	31.4	5.2	1.4	36655	39749	23	19	231	18.2	26.0	35.9	16.9	3.0	99643
83220	BERN	15656	78	25.6	34.6	35.9	3.8	0.0	42362	41149	41	54	68	7.4	20.6	58.8	13.2	0.0	115278
83221	BLACKFOOT	19050	8369	21.2	32.5	37.0	6.8	2.4	46990	50343	54	76	6548	6.7	10.4	52.2	27.9	2.8	140179
83226	CHALLIS	18754	1049	33.4	30.4	31.3	4.2	0.8	38452	39957	28	29	806	11.2	12.4	45.3	21.8	9.3	136290
83227	CLAYTON	0	0	0.0	0.0	0.0	0.0	0.0	0	0	0	0	0	0.0	0.0	0.0	0.0	0.0	0
83228	CLIFTON	14816	136	20.6	44.9	27.9	4.4	2.2	41374	43418	37	49	109	7.3	11.0	59.6	16.5	5.5	132813
83232	DAYTON	15365	237	18.6	43.9	31.6	3.8	2.1	42622	44598	41	56	193	4.7	10.4	62.7	18.1	4.1	134593
83234	DOWNEY	16242	502	33.5	31.5	32.3	0.8	2.0	38171	40812	27	28	423	9.7	20.1	55.8	14.4	0.0	121235
83235	ELLIS	16868	141	44.7	34.0	18.4	1.4	1.4	27253	27282	5	3	120	14.2	8.3	52.5	22.5	2.5	130208
83236	FIRTH	15059	1539	28.7	33.5	30.9	5.7	1.3	41459	44942	38	49	1202	17.1	16.6	42.6	21.0	2.7	115323
83237	FRANKLIN	14581	400	17.8	48.3	27.0	5.3	1.8	40304	42185	34	43	322	7.1	7.1	60.9	22.4	2.5	141949
83238	GENEVA	15350	36	27.8	33.3	30.6	5.6	2.8	38581	42391	28	29	29	0.0	13.8	65.5	17.2	3.4	123611
83241	GRACE	16034	742	27.5	37.7	30.7	3.6	0.4	40169	42608	33	41	592	10.0	21.8	46.1	16.9	5.2	114815
83243	HOLBROOK	15251	67	23.9	35.8	37.3	1.5	1.5	45306	45000	49	68	57	15.8	7.0	35.1	40.4	1.8	160938
83244	HOWE	14879	65	32.3	29.2	35.4	3.1	0.0	34664	35000	17	9	50	2.0	14.0	60.0	16.0	8.0	135000
83245	INKOM	20918	691	15.5	30.4	43.3	8.0	2.9	53050	54932	68	90	620	6.6	10.8	57.9	21.8	2.9	138346
83246	LAVA HOT SPRINGS	18796	475	31.6	33.5	29.9	3.8	1.3	37881	39445	26	24	348	10.1	7.8	60.6	19.5	2.0	131395
83250	MCCAMMON	20615	644	19.4	29.7	42.5	6.1	2.3	50488	52572	62	85	568	5.1	12.0	59.3	20.8	2.8	133000
83251	MACKAY	21132	517	31.1	30.6	30.9	4.6	2.7	37595	39045	26	22	398	9.8	14.6	47.5	21.6	6.5	132328
83252	MALAD CITY	17621	1435	24.5	34.8	36.5	3.0	1.3	43177	44712	43	60	1178	8.3	10.4	51.4	27.1	2.8	140821
83253	MAY	15098	99	46.5	34.3	17.2	1.0	1.0	26375	27275	4	3	85	11.8	8.2	54.1	23.5	2.4	131618
83254	MONTPELIER	17273	1671	25.0	35.4	34.4	4.7	0.5	40315	41198	34	43	1349	6.4	18.2	59.7	13.3	2.4	119011
83255	MOORE	17485	308	22.4	39.0	31.2	5.5	1.9	39576	39411	31	39	254	7.5	22.8	51.2	16.1	2.4	122917
83261	PARIS	17440	346	26.3	35.0	33.8	4.0	0.9	41545	42527	38	50	306	7.2	15.0	55.9	19.6	2.3	122333
83262	PINGREE	15306	408	18.6	40.0	37.7	2.9	0.7	42353	47052	40	54	333	9.6	7.2	44.1	35.1	3.9	159267
83263	PRESTON	17769	2878	18.9	34.6	38.6	5.6	2.3	47590	49662	56	77	2309	3.7	10.2	58.9	25.6	1.6	136974
83271	ROCKLAND	14402	186	32.3	26.9	36.0	4.3	0.5	42645	46942	41	57	153	12.4	23.5	55.6	6.5	2.0	110096
83272	SAINT CHARLES	19143	86	25.6	34.9	34.9	3.5	1.2	40000	40000	33	41	75	5.3	8.0	49.3	30.7	6.7	144792
83274	SHELLEY	17422	3182	20.1	30.0	42.2	5.7	1.9	49863	51575	61	84	2628	6.7	8.1	56.6	27.1	1.5	141735
83276	SODA SPRINGS	20829	1544	20.3	27.3	42.7	7.3	2.3	51230	52038	64	87	1226	10.2	11.3	55.6	20.6	2.2	127370
83278	STANLEY	22726	228	21.1	31.6	41.7	3.5	2.2	47717	47857	56	78	152	9.9	8.6	36.8	28.3	16.4	165476
83283	THATCHER	15840	46	21.7	34.8	39.1	4.3	0.0	43194	45000	43	60	38	2.6	10.5	47.4	39.5	0.0	155000
83285	WAYAN	23219	50	30.0	22.0	36.0	6.0	6.0	47384	50839	55	76	41	12.2	14.6	34.1	29.3	9.8	146875
83286	WESTON	15622	305	16.7	41.0	36.7	2.6	3.0	44623	47141	47	65	254	2.4	7.9	64.6	23.6	1.6	138679
83287	FISH HAVEN	23544	98	24.5	36.7	35.7	2.0	1.0	40914	41760	36	47	87	5.7	8.0	49.4	31.0	5.7	143269
83301	TWIN FALLS	22444	19270	24.6	30.9	35.0	6.0	3.4	45805	48781	51	71	12828	6.0	7.8	42.5	38.2	5.6	163789
83302	ROGERSON	17947	58	27.6	46.6	22.4	1.7	1.7	35880	39301	20	16	43	7.0	14.0	55.8	20.9	2.3	136458
83313	BELLEVUE	28339	1419	12.5	25.7	42.1	13.5	6.1	62425	62210	81	94	1002	2.8	4.0	13.4	49.0	30.8	288655
83314	BLISS	18338	327	27.2	38.8	26.9	1.8	5.2	37679	37890	26	23	231	21.2	11.7	29.9	27.7	9.5	142262
83316	BUHL	20016	3932	26.4	30.1	36.9	3.5	3.1	44010	47700	45	63	2864	8.3	8.3	46.8	28.2	8.4	143820
83318	BURLEY	16955	5482	28.6	31.8	32.8	5.1	1.7	41865	45139	39	51	3958	8.8	11.8	56.9	18.4	4.0	130060
83320	CAREY	18748	365	26.3	31.8	35.3	4.1	2.5	41007	45676	36	47	263	4.6	18.6	47.1	23.6	6.1	133681
83321	CASTLEFORD	18807	155	32.9	29.7	32.3	3.2	1.9	39235	41856	30	35	108	14.8	6.5	33.3	33.3	12.0	162500
83322	CORRAL	15675	21	23.8	33.3	38.1	4.8	0.0	42367	48618	41	55	16	0.0	12.5	50.0	25.0	12.5	150000
83323	DECLO	15124	408	31.1	31.9	30.9	3.7	2.5	38062	40648	27	26	318	17.9	5.7	42.5	25.5	8.5	133696
83324	DIETRICH	15140	198	21.2	41.4	33.3	3.5	0.5	42176	42882	40	53	148	4.7	14.9	57.4	19.6	3.4	126923
83325	EDEN	17796	414	31.2	36.7	23.9	6.0	2.2	38867	41502	29	31	268	7.1	11.2	45.5	30.6	5.6	145909
83327	FAIRFIELD	23397	448	25.4	32.1	34.2	4.7	3.6	42875	44408	42	58	350	2.9	18.9	39.7	26.3	12.3	151190
83328	FILER	18710	2039	24.5	32.8	36.4	3.9	2.5	43587	46962	44	61	1493	5.2	9.8	47.1	30.3	7.6	146843
83330	GOODING	18199	2204	27.0	31.2	34.5	4.4	2.9	41078	42231	36	48	1619	5.3	20.3	49.8	19.8	4.9	127269
83332	HAGERMAN	18603	968	30.0	31.7	33.2	3.2	2.0	40264	41622	34	42	719	5.6	5.1	46.2	33.1	10.0	157321
83333	HAILEY	38530	4720	10.3	20.3	37.0	20.3	12.1	73325	73817	89	98	3372	5.4	1.7	5.3	38.3	49.4	396360
83334	HANSEN	17828	740	24.5	34.6	33.1	5.1	2.7	43056	46794	43	59	543	18.0	9.8	45.7	20.4	6.1	122649
83335	HAZELTON	14447	618	34.0	35.1	25.4	4.2	1.3	35946	38101	20	16	392	9.7	13.3	40.8	25.0	11.2	135185
83336	HEYBURN	17563	1851	25.0	32.1	37.1	4.3	1.5	43057	47317	43	59	1468	9.2	15.5	56.1	17.4	1.8	117174
83338	JEROME	18523	6058	21.7	32.9	37.2	5.9	2.3	46104	48610	52	72	4344	6.9	11.3	44.8	31.1	6.0	143053
83340	KETCHUM	53680	2809	14.0	23.1	30.5	15.0	17.4	67499	68561	85	96	1806	2.7	1.2	3.4	17.4	75.4	765015
83341	KIMBERLY	19020	2054	22.6	32.6	36.7	5.4	2.8	45949	49387	51	71	1575	5.5	4.6	48.3	34.6	7.1	161950
83342	MALTA	18966	796	20.4	36.3	36.8	3.0	3.5	45646	47326	50	70	585	16.1	9.9	42.6	25.0	6.5	134691
83343	MINIDOKA	10823	18	27.8	38.9	33.3	0.0	0.0	37278	37278	24	21	11	9.1	0.0	63.6	18.2	9.1	137500
83344	MURTAUGH	13957	365	32.6	34.2	28.5	3.3	1.4	36424	38512	22	17	206	12.6	12.1	41.7	28.2	5.3	131250
83346	OAKLEY	16044	473	25.6	33.6	35.5	3.4	1.9	40634	44487	35	45	362	9.1	14.4	50.8	21.3	4.4	126630
83347	PAUL	18156	1058	29.0	35.5	30.2	3.3	2.0	38899	41645	29	31	807	6.9	10.9	57.9	22.4	1.9	129536
83348	PICABO	35207	4	0.0	0.0	100.0	0.0	0.0	65000	60000	83	96	0	0.0	0.0	0.0	0.0	0.0	0
83349	RICHFIELD	15629	387	28.2	34.6	33.3	3.9	0.0	39554	40600	31	38	302	12.9	15.6	43.4	20.9	7.3	127857
83350	RUPERT	17017	4026	31.2	32.9	30.2	3.1	2.6	39049	41697	30	32	3053	10.0	16.7	53.7	16.6	3.0	119081
83352	SHOSHONE	18747	1047	27.5	35.7	30.2	4.4	2.2	39064	40102	30	33	781	4.9	11.4	58.0	23.7	2.0	135133
83355	WENDELL	16492	1850	26.4	37.2	30.5	4.0	1.9	39511	40523	31	38	1320	9.6	10.1	53.3	20.8	6.2	133144
83401	IDAHO FALLS	21137	12780	21.1	27.9	41.1	7.1	2.9	50874	53969	63	87	9392	9.0	13.4	56.9	18.6	2.1	130706
83402	IDAHO FALLS	22961	9954	20.9	28.1	38.9	9.3	2.8	50860	53846	63	86	6796	5.6	9.9	59.4	23.4	1.6	141449
83404	IDAHO FALLS	33587	8133	14.2	16.1	41.3	16.5	11.9	72000	73000	88	98	6615	1.2	5.5	42.2	44.4	6.7	177992
83406	IDAHO FALLS	25311	4791	14.0	15.7	47.3	16.8	6.3	70213	71208	87	97	3740	1.3	4.3	51.4	38.3	4.7	162848
83420	ASHTON	16341	1043	28.9	35.8	30.8	3.4	1.2	37936	38703	26	24	879	14.7	18.3	42.4	22.0	2.6	128533
83422	DRIGGS	20094	1135	18.4	28.9	46.6	3.9	2.2	51447	53043	65	89	794	16.6	3.1	9.1	48.1	23.0	258333
83423	DUBOIS	12432	334	30.2	41.3	26.6	1.2	0.6	38168	39286	27	28	230	22.2	20.0	50.9	5.2	1.7	105556
83424	FELT	16238	85	17.6	29.4	45.9	5.9	1.2	51418	52848	65	88	65	4.6	6.2	18.5	55.4	15.4	262500
83425	HAMER	12650	169	30.8	35.5	28.4	3.6	1.8	36023	39654	21	16	129	21.7	10.1	41.9	20.9	5.4	118452
83428	IRWIN	27195	88	25.0	28.4	35.2	5.7	5.7	46159	50000	52	73	74	10.8	13.5	33.8	29.7	12.2	160000
83429	ISLAND PARK	26830	484	22.7	37.8	33.7	1.2	4.5	44429	45735	46	63	406	5.2	9.4	33.5	41.6	10.3	180882
83431	LEWISVILLE	17849	333	17.4	34.8	39.9	6.0	1.8	48235	50292	57	79	290	6.2	12.1	48.6	27.9	5.2	142308
83434	MENAN	17218	590	19.3	29.2	45.8	3.9	1.9	50600	51053	63	86	513	9.7	10.3	54.6	21.6	3.7	137861
83435	MONTEVIEW	13598	145	31.0	35.2	29.0	3.4	1.4	36262	40000	21	17	111	21.6	9.9	41.4	21.6	5.4	118750
83436	NEWDALE	16645	23	13.0	39.1	39.1	0.0	8.7	49038	50000	59	82	20	0.0	5.0	45.0	40.0	10.0	175000
83440	REXBURG	14273	9877	28.8	32.9	31.6	4.2	2.4	40183	42539	33	42	5658	9.5	6.8	22.2	51.9	9.5	201456
83442	RIGBY	17722	5581	21.2	32.2	38.1	6.3	2.2	46847	48972	54	75	4735	7.5	10.5	45.9	31.8	4.4	148699
	IDAHO	23160		20.9	28.6	37.9	8.3	4.4	50374	53004				6.9	7.8	39.2	38.3	7.9	167282
	UNITED STATES	27277		20.9	24.4	35.3	11.7	7.6	54719	56938				9.3	13.1	31.6	32.6	13.5	162279

ZIP CODE #	POST OFFICE NAME	FINANCIAL SERVICES: Auto Loan	Home Loan	Investments	Retirement Plans	THE HOME: Home Improvements: Home Repair	Lawn & Garden	Furnishings: Computers & Hardware-Personal	Major Appliances	TV, Radio, Sound Equipment	Furniture	ENTERTAINMENT: Dine out/Carry out	Sports Equipment	Fees & Tickets	Toys & Games	Travel	Cable TV	PERSONAL: Apparel & Services	Auto Repairs	Health Insurance	Pets & Supplies
83201	POCATELLO	88	82	74	84	79	82	91	83	89	86	89	67	86	90	84	89	62	87	86	100
83202	POCATELLO	91	90	79	88	86	87	86	88	86	88	86	67	84	89	84	86	60	86	86	103
83203	FORT HALL	77	71	62	68	69	72	66	70	69	69	69	51	63	72	63	71	47	68	71	84
83204	POCATELLO	89	82	75	83	80	82	91	84	89	87	88	66	84	90	83	88	62	87	85	100
83209	POCATELLO	0	0	0	0	0	0	0	0	0	0	0	0	0	0	0	0	0	0	0	0
83210	ABERDEEN	81	59	72	59	59	80	66	74	71	59	69	59	53	71	61	76	46	72	79	90
83211	AMERICAN FALLS	90	79	83	77	78	88	79	85	81	77	80	66	71	82	76	83	55	83	86	102
83212	ARBON	81	56	89	56	59	86	62	77	65	50	64	64	46	63	62	71	41	72	82	95
83213	ARCO	82	58	85	57	61	84	61	77	67	56	66	58	48	66	60	73	43	71	80	92
83214	ARIMO	108	74	119	74	78	114	83	103	86	67	85	85	60	84	82	94	55	96	108	126
83217	BANCROFT	87	60	95	60	63	92	66	83	69	54	68	68	49	68	66	75	44	77	87	102
83220	BERN	83	59	85	57	61	84	61	77	68	57	66	58	49	67	60	74	44	71	81	92
83221	BLACKFOOT	89	79	79	78	78	88	79	85	81	77	80	64	72	82	76	84	55	82	87	100
83226	CHALLIS	78	55	84	54	57	81	59	74	63	51	62	58	45	62	59	69	41	68	77	89
83227	CLAYTON	0	0	0	0	0	0	0	0	0	0	0	0	0	0	0	0	0	0	0	0
83228	CLIFTON	90	62	99	62	65	95	69	86	72	56	71	71	51	70	69	78	46	80	91	106
83232	DAYTON	92	63	101	63	66	97	70	88	73	57	72	72	52	72	70	80	47	82	93	108
83234	DOWNEY	77	53	84	53	55	81	58	73	61	47	60	60	43	60	58	66	39	68	77	89
83235	ELLIS	51	48	62	44	53	58	46	54	48	49	47	36	44	45	50	51	32	52	60	62
83236	FIRTH	75	63	64	63	61	72	64	68	68	63	67	53	58	69	61	71	46	68	72	84
83237	FRANKLIN	77	70	68	72	71	80	68	76	71	64	70	57	63	72	68	74	48	71	78	89
83238	GENEVA	82	58	88	58	61	86	63	78	66	52	65	64	48	65	63	72	43	73	82	96
83241	GRACE	78	54	86	54	56	82	60	74	62	48	61	61	44	61	59	68	40	69	78	91
83243	HOLBROOK	89	61	97	61	64	94	68	84	70	55	70	70	50	69	67	77	45	79	89	104
83244	HOWE	77	53	84	53	55	81	58	73	61	47	60	60	43	60	58	66	39	68	77	89
83245	INKOM	91	87	86	91	89	99	84	94	86	78	85	71	80	87	85	90	58	87	95	109
83246	LAVA HOT SPRINGS	81	58	83	56	60	82	59	76	66	55	65	57	47	65	59	72	43	69	79	90
83250	MCCAMMON	91	79	85	81	81	97	79	91	82	70	80	70	70	83	79	87	54	84	94	106
83251	MACKAY	81	65	105	64	71	86	65	82	68	61	67	60	56	64	70	72	45	76	81	96
83252	MALAD CITY	79	64	86	63	66	87	66	78	69	57	68	62	56	67	67	74	45	74	85	94
83253	MAY	49	47	60	43	52	56	45	53	47	48	46	35	44	43	49	50	31	51	59	60
83254	MONTPELIER	79	61	78	62	63	83	64	77	69	57	67	59	54	69	64	75	45	72	82	91
83255	MOORE	85	59	94	59	62	90	65	81	68	54	67	66	49	67	65	74	44	76	85	99
83261	PARIS	81	60	91	59	64	84	61	78	67	57	66	58	51	65	63	73	44	72	80	92
83262	PINGREE	80	67	73	66	67	78	67	74	69	65	69	57	59	71	64	72	46	71	76	89
83263	PRESTON	87	76	81	77	76	91	78	86	80	71	79	66	70	81	76	84	53	82	90	102
83271	ROCKLAND	82	56	90	56	59	86	62	77	65	50	64	64	46	64	62	71	42	72	82	95
83272	SAINT CHARLES	79	62	100	61	68	84	63	80	66	58	65	59	53	63	67	70	43	74	80	93
83274	SHELLEY	85	76	76	76	75	87	75	82	78	71	77	63	69	79	73	81	52	78	85	98
83276	SODA SPRINGS	90	79	81	78	79	90	78	86	81	76	81	64	71	83	76	85	55	82	89	102
83278	STANLEY	85	68	109	67	74	90	68	86	71	64	71	63	59	68	73	76	47	80	86	100
83283	THATCHER	83	57	91	57	59	87	63	78	66	51	65	65	46	64	63	71	42	73	83	96
83285	WAYAN	98	75	120	74	81	104	78	98	81	69	80	75	64	78	82	87	53	91	99	116
83286	WESTON	97	66	106	66	70	102	74	92	77	60	76	76	54	75	73	84	49	86	97	113
83287	FISH HAVEN	79	63	102	62	69	83	63	80	66	59	65	58	55	63	68	70	43	74	79	93
83301	TWIN FALLS	82	79	72	80	76	82	81	80	82	78	81	62	78	83	78	83	56	81	84	95
83302	ROGERSON	73	51	81	50	53	78	56	70	58	45	58	58	41	57	56	64	37	65	74	86
83313	BELLEVUE	110	108	114	108	107	116	105	112	104	100	104	89	102	105	107	106	72	108	111	132
83314	BLISS	92	63	101	63	66	97	70	87	73	57	72	72	51	71	70	80	47	81	92	107
83316	BUHL	90	65	93	65	67	94	71	86	76	61	74	68	56	75	70	82	49	81	92	104
83318	BURLEY	80	66	71	64	66	77	68	75	71	65	71	56	59	72	65	75	48	73	78	89
83320	CAREY	100	69	110	69	72	105	77	95	80	63	79	78	57	78	76	87	51	89	100	117
83321	CASTLEFORD	86	59	95	59	62	91	66	82	69	53	68	68	48	67	66	75	44	77	87	101
83322	CORRAL	78	63	101	62	69	83	63	80	66	59	65	58	54	62	68	70	43	74	79	93
83323	DECLO	88	61	97	61	63	93	67	84	70	55	69	69	49	69	67	76	45	78	88	103
83324	DIETRICH	76	68	64	66	67	72	65	70	68	67	68	51	61	70	62	70	46	67	70	83
83325	EDEN	86	59	94	59	62	91	66	81	68	53	67	67	48	67	65	74	44	76	86	100
83327	FAIRFIELD	93	75	120	73	82	98	75	95	78	70	77	69	65	74	81	83	51	87	94	110
83328	FILER	84	68	81	67	68	86	70	80	74	64	73	62	60	74	68	78	49	77	85	97
83330	GOODING	84	61	87	61	64	88	67	81	72	59	71	63	53	71	66	79	47	76	87	97
83332	HAGERMAN	81	60	96	60	65	85	63	79	66	56	65	62	51	64	66	71	43	74	81	95
83333	HAILEY	130	153	150	154	154	136	137	138	129	145	130	108	150	131	146	123	94	133	125	157
83334	HANSEN	83	73	75	71	71	80	73	78	74	71	74	61	66	76	71	76	50	76	78	94
83335	HAZELTON	77	53	85	53	56	81	59	73	61	48	61	61	43	60	59	67	39	68	77	90
83336	HEYBURN	80	66	70	66	65	82	68	75	71	63	70	59	59	73	65	76	48	72	80	91
83338	JEROME	83	76	72	75	73	82	76	79	78	74	77	61	71	80	73	80	53	78	82	95
83340	KETCHUM	140	149	176	155	161	138	160	150	147	164	149	121	164	142	167	139	108	154	138	173
83341	KIMBERLY	89	77	84	76	77	91	76	86	80	73	79	65	69	80	75	84	53	82	89	102
83342	MALTA	97	67	107	67	70	103	74	92	77	60	76	76	54	76	74	84	50	86	97	114
83343	MINIDOKA	70	58	69	54	58	66	60	67	59	57	60	53	51	60	59	61	41	64	65	78
83344	MURTAUGH	78	53	85	53	56	82	59	74	62	48	61	61	43	60	59	67	40	69	78	91
83346	OAKLEY	89	61	97	61	64	93	68	84	70	55	69	69	49	69	67	77	45	78	89	103
83347	PAUL	88	62	92	61	65	90	66	83	71	58	70	65	51	70	65	77	46	76	86	100
83348	PICABO	110	76	121	76	79	116	84	105	88	68	87	86	62	86	84	95	56	98	110	129
83349	RICHFIELD	78	54	86	53	56	82	60	74	62	48	61	61	44	61	59	68	40	69	78	91
83350	RUPERT	84	61	83	59	62	85	66	79	71	59	69	62	52	70	63	77	46	74	83	95
83352	SHOSHONE	86	64	88	63	66	88	67	81	71	60	70	63	53	71	66	77	46	76	84	98
83355	WENDELL	84	69	77	67	70	82	68	78	73	67	72	58	60	74	66	77	48	74	80	93
83401	IDAHO FALLS	87	84	75	84	81	84	85	84	85	84	85	65	82	87	82	86	59	84	85	100
83402	IDAHO FALLS	88	86	76	86	82	84	87	84	86	86	87	66	85	89	83	87	60	86	86	101
83404	IDAHO FALLS	124	137	129	140	136	133	127	129	124	131	125	98	134	126	132	123	88	126	128	150
83406	IDAHO FALLS	116	128	105	126	121	112	114	115	109	120	111	91	119	116	115	105	78	110	105	132
83420	ASHTON	80	57	87	56	59	84	62	76	64	52	64	62	47	63	62	70	42	71	80	93
83422	DRIGGS	94	83	83	80	81	91	80	87	83	80	82	66	73	85	77	85	56	84	88	104
83423	DUBOIS	70	50	58	49	50	67	52	61	58	51	57	47	42	61	48	63	38	58	64	74
83424	FELT	90	82	73	80	80	84	78	82	81	81	81	60	73	84	74	83	55	80	82	98
83425	HAMER	79	55	87	54	57	84	61	75	63	49	62	62	44	62	60	69	40	70	80	93
83428	IRWIN	103	82	133	81	90	108	82	104	86	77	85	76	71	82	89	92	56	96	103	121
83429	ISLAND PARK	96	77	124	76	84	101	77	98	80	72	79	71	67	76	83	86	53	90	96	113
83431	LEWISVILLE	95	65	104	65	68	100	72	90	75	59	75	74	53	74	72	82	48	84	95	111
83434	MENAN	90	76	82	75	76	88	75	84	78	73	78	64	67	80	73	82	52	80	85	101
83435	MONTEVIEW	78	54	86	54	56	83	60	74	62	48	62	61	44	61	60	68	40	69	79	91
83436	NEWDALE	109	76	107	75	78	110	83	100	88	73	87	80	63	89	79	96	57	94	105	122
83440	REXBURG	77	61	59	62	59	65	81	68	75	70	76	57	66	76	65	74	52	73	68	83
83442	RIGBY	85	80	76	78	78	85	76	81	78	76	78	61	73	80	75	81	53	78	83	96
	IDAHO	94	87	87	87	86	92	88	90	88	86	88	70	83	90	85	90	61	89	91	107
	UNITED STATES	100	100	100	100	100	100	100	100	100	100	100	100	100	100	100	100	100	100	100	100

POPULATION CHANGE

83443-83703

ZIP CODE #	POST OFFICE NAME	COUNTY FIPS CODE	POPULATION 2000	POPULATION 2009	POPULATION 2014	2000-2009 ANNUAL RATE % Rate	2000-2009 ANNUAL RATE State Centile	HOUSEHOLDS 2000	HOUSEHOLDS 2009	HOUSEHOLDS 2014	HOUSEHOLDS % Annual Rate 2000-2009	HOUSEHOLDS 2009 Average HH Size	FAMILIES 2000	FAMILIES 2009	FAMILIES % Annual Rate 2000-2009
83443	RIRIE	019	643	825	921	2.7	88	210	278	314	3.1	2.97	172	222	2.8
83444	ROBERTS	051	1456	1675	1815	1.5	71	398	464	505	1.7	3.61	338	391	1.6
83445	SAINT ANTHONY	043	6696	7097	7275	0.6	40	2095	2249	2326	0.8	2.98	1652	1760	0.7
83446	SPENCER	033	75	74	74	-0.1	15	31	30	30	-0.4	2.47	22	21	-0.5
83448	SUGAR CITY	065	1987	2864	3399	4.0	94	547	816	976	4.4	3.51	476	710	4.4
83449	SWAN VALLEY	019	408	443	479	0.9	53	171	196	215	1.5	2.26	127	140	1.1
83450	TERRETON	051	1184	1219	1264	0.3	28	340	358	373	0.6	3.35	281	293	0.5
83451	TETON	043	1108	1227	1290	1.1	61	342	392	416	1.5	3.13	276	313	1.4
83452	TETONIA	081	1216	1914	2352	5.0	97	425	689	854	5.4	2.78	318	512	5.3
83455	VICTOR	081	2504	4233	5273	5.8	98	888	1566	1975	6.3	2.69	613	1067	6.2
83460	REXBURG	065	375	399	426	0.7	45	0	0	0	0.0	0.00	0	0	0.0
83462	CARMEN	059	271	288	293	0.7	45	110	120	123	0.9	2.38	71	76	0.7
83463	GIBBONSVILLE	059	152	170	177	1.2	64	69	79	83	1.5	2.13	46	52	1.3
83464	LEADORE	059	638	633	623	-0.1	15	235	240	238	0.2	2.63	170	171	0.1
83466	NORTH FORK	059	495	520	527	0.5	36	220	237	242	0.8	2.19	141	149	0.6
83467	SALMON	059	5702	6031	6155	0.6	40	2387	2592	2665	0.9	2.32	1623	1734	0.7
83469	SHOUP	059	55	56	56	0.2	25	30	31	31	0.4	1.81	16	16	0.0
83501	LEWISTON	069	32659	34180	34946	0.5	36	13480	14272	14642	0.6	2.34	8793	9155	0.4
83520	AHSAHKA	035	86	93	95	0.8	49	32	35	36	1.0	2.66	25	27	0.8
83522	COTTONWOOD	049	1691	1707	1688	0.1	22	615	612	608	-0.1	2.28	441	433	-0.2
83523	CRAIGMONT	061	859	866	865	0.1	22	345	360	364	0.5	2.40	249	256	0.3
83524	CULDESAC	069	1087	1127	1150	0.4	33	417	442	454	0.6	2.55	314	328	0.5
83525	ELK CITY	049	585	551	537	-0.6	5	260	252	248	-0.3	2.14	174	166	-0.5
83526	FERDINAND	049	738	745	735	0.1	22	160	158	156	-0.1	3.79	124	121	-0.3
83530	GRANGEVILLE	049	5104	5454	5544	0.7	45	2019	2208	2265	1.0	2.41	1400	1508	0.8
83533	GREENCREEK	049	270	259	254	-0.4	10	94	93	92	-0.1	2.75	74	72	-0.3
83535	JULIAETTA	069	932	1021	1056	1.0	58	382	423	439	1.1	2.41	271	297	1.0
83536	KAMIAH	049	3687	3604	3538	-0.2	13	1515	1529	1516	0.1	2.34	1043	1037	-0.1
83537	KENDRICK	057	1194	1287	1328	0.8	49	489	536	556	1.0	2.40	360	390	0.9
83539	KOOSKIA	049	2698	2676	2653	-0.1	15	1085	1105	1104	0.2	2.38	788	792	0.1
83540	LAPWAI	069	2073	2181	2240	0.6	40	702	755	779	0.8	2.89	540	573	0.6
83541	LENORE	035	1115	1190	1217	0.7	45	465	508	523	1.0	2.34	346	373	0.8
83542	LUCILE	049	252	241	237	-0.5	8	101	100	99	-0.1	2.40	62	60	-0.4
83543	NEZPERCE	061	742	763	771	0.3	28	284	298	303	0.5	2.53	215	222	0.3
83544	OROFINO	035	6094	6150	6127	0.1	22	2327	2393	2400	0.3	2.30	1612	1635	0.2
83545	PECK	069	471	503	518	0.7	45	210	229	237	0.9	2.20	156	168	0.8
83546	PIERCE	035	754	721	708	-0.5	8	313	311	308	-0.1	2.31	236	231	-0.2
83547	POLLOCK	049	417	404	400	-0.3	11	184	185	184	0.1	2.18	114	112	-0.2
83548	REUBENS	069	134	139	141	0.4	33	50	53	55	0.6	2.60	35	37	0.6
83549	RIGGINS	049	752	719	707	-0.5	8	361	358	355	-0.1	2.00	220	214	-0.3
83552	STITES	049	273	275	274	0.1	22	105	109	110	0.4	2.50	80	82	0.3
83553	WEIPPE	035	1213	1215	1211	0.0	18	470	484	486	0.3	2.51	367	373	0.2
83554	WHITE BIRD	049	659	646	636	-0.2	13	285	286	285	0.0	2.25	207	206	-0.1
83555	WINCHESTER	061	375	381	384	0.2	25	164	173	176	0.6	2.17	112	116	0.4
83601	ATLANTA	039	134	147	149	1.0	58	69	76	78	1.1	1.93	43	48	1.2
83602	BANKS	015	0	19	21	0.0	18	0	8	9	0.0	2.38	0	6	0.0
83604	BRUNEAU	073	731	775	778	0.6	40	296	321	324	0.9	2.40	189	201	0.7
83605	CALDWELL	027	26091	32644	36553	2.5	87	9080	11535	12964	2.6	2.75	6386	7993	2.5
83607	CALDWELL	027	16746	27358	32739	5.4	98	5553	9321	11207	5.8	2.93	4542	7359	5.4
83610	CAMBRIDGE	087	977	1024	1051	0.5	36	392	417	429	0.7	2.46	283	297	0.5
83611	CASCADE	085	2330	2898	3241	2.4	86	989	1283	1454	2.9	2.24	723	925	2.7
83612	COUNCIL	003	1882	2072	2151	1.0	58	774	894	941	1.6	2.28	556	633	1.4
83615	DONNELLY	085	561	668	752	1.9	77	248	307	350	2.3	2.18	184	225	2.2
83616	EAGLE	001	15162	22848	27310	4.5	95	5201	8031	9663	4.8	2.84	4187	6267	4.5
83617	EMMETT	045	14182	16250	17265	1.5	71	5186	5947	6314	1.5	2.70	3898	4416	1.4
83619	FRUITLAND	075	6047	7180	7823	1.9	77	2183	2586	2812	1.8	2.78	1683	1970	1.7
83622	GARDEN VALLEY	015	1787	1954	2025	1.0	58	715	799	833	1.2	2.41	514	567	1.1
83623	GLENNS FERRY	039	2140	2241	2241	0.5	36	797	836	836	0.5	2.67	578	608	0.5
83624	GRAND VIEW	073	1572	1597	1582	0.2	25	554	573	569	0.4	2.78	420	430	0.3
83626	GREENLEAF	027	1301	1568	1728	2.0	80	408	498	549	2.2	3.15	332	397	2.0
83627	HAMMETT	039	446	466	466	0.5	36	139	147	148	0.6	3.12	108	115	0.7
83628	HOMEDALE	073	3980	4446	4597	1.2	64	1338	1486	1532	1.1	2.97	990	1086	1.0
83629	HORSESHOE BEND	015	1622	1986	2171	2.2	83	606	760	838	2.5	2.56	443	548	2.3
83631	IDAHO CITY	015	1018	1351	1489	3.1	90	408	556	616	3.4	2.42	279	375	3.2
83632	INDIAN VALLEY	003	202	228	240	1.3	66	88	104	111	1.8	2.19	67	78	1.7
83633	KING HILL	039	331	347	349	0.5	36	113	120	122	0.7	2.85	89	95	0.7
83634	KUNA	001	12899	20901	24496	5.4	98	3347	5884	7133	6.3	3.02	2739	4677	6.0
83636	LETHA	045	50	61	67	2.2	83	20	24	26	2.0	2.54	16	19	1.9
83637	LOWMAN	015	225	247	255	1.0	58	101	113	118	1.2	2.15	73	80	1.0
83638	MCCALL	085	4771	5899	6470	2.3	84	1974	2528	2803	2.7	2.31	1348	1702	2.6
83639	MARSING	073	2850	3052	3129	0.7	45	975	1062	1092	0.9	2.87	744	801	0.8
83641	MELBA	027	1794	2532	2912	3.8	93	607	854	983	3.8	2.88	466	642	3.5
83642	MERIDIAN	001	23634	36176	43519	4.7	96	7959	12393	15010	4.9	2.90	6425	9811	4.7
83643	MESA	003	122	128	128	0.5	36	55	61	62	1.1	2.10	42	46	1.0
83644	MIDDLETON	027	6194	9210	10956	4.4	95	2114	3191	3801	4.6	2.89	1665	2472	4.4
83645	MIDVALE	087	690	823	880	1.9	77	273	328	351	2.0	2.51	200	238	1.9
83646	MERIDIAN	001	21460	44453	54840	8.2	99	7283	15614	19454	8.6	2.84	5946	12423	8.3
83647	MOUNTAIN HOME	039	16825	18560	18915	1.1	61	6387	7076	7216	1.1	2.60	4489	4997	1.2
83648	MOUNTAIN HOME A F B	039	9202	7722	7416	-1.9	1	1566	1230	1146	-2.6	3.34	1524	1196	-2.6
83650	MURPHY	073	1487	1608	1668	0.8	49	536	594	619	1.1	2.67	405	443	1.0
83651	NAMPA	027	20762	29037	33733	3.7	92	7736	10875	12664	3.8	2.63	5313	7362	3.6
83654	NEW MEADOWS	003	1210	1397	1459	1.6	73	481	571	602	1.9	2.45	348	407	1.7
83655	NEW PLYMOUTH	075	3798	4597	5078	2.1	82	1318	1612	1780	2.2	2.84	1030	1244	2.1
83657	OLA	045	151	181	196	2.0	80	63	76	83	2.0	2.36	49	59	2.0
83660	PARMA	027	5404	6984	7904	2.8	88	1889	2440	2757	2.8	2.86	1474	1867	2.6
83661	PAYETTE	075	9605	10625	11248	1.1	61	3512	3877	4099	1.1	2.72	2575	2801	0.9
83669	STAR	001	2957	6363	8081	8.6	100	1052	2328	2976	9.0	2.73	834	1803	8.7
83670	SWEET	045	485	581	630	2.0	80	164	199	216	2.1	2.89	128	153	1.9
83672	WEISER	087	8310	8585	8720	0.4	33	3097	3218	3267	0.4	2.62	2253	2311	0.3
83676	WILDER	027	3808	4966	5684	2.9	89	1209	1554	1768	2.8	3.20	983	1242	2.6
83677	YELLOW PINE	085	25	29	32	1.6	73	11	13	15	1.8	2.23	6	7	1.7
83686	NAMPA	027	30921	45081	53421	4.2	94	10342	15195	18026	4.2	2.91	8096	11840	4.2
83687	NAMPA	027	19116	29798	35840	4.9	96	6309	9957	12026	5.1	2.94	4870	7582	4.9
83702	BOISE	001	21313	23136	24798	0.9	53	10114	11501	12492	1.4	1.95	4809	5010	0.4
83703	BOISE	001	17102	19225	20692	1.3	66	6863	7989	8673	1.7	2.36	4380	4839	1.1
	IDAHO					2.1					2.2	2.65			2.1
	UNITED STATES					1.0					1.1	2.59			0.9

ZIP CODE #	POST OFFICE NAME	RACE (%) White 2000	White 2009	Black 2000	Black 2009	Asian/Pacific 2000	Asian/Pacific 2009	% Hispanic Origin 2000	% Hispanic Origin 2009	2009 AGE DISTRIBUTION (%) 0-4	5-9	10-14	15-19	20-24	25-44	45-64	65-84	85+	18+	MEDIAN AGE 2009	% 2009 Males	% 2009 Females
83443	RIRIE	96.0	94.8	0.3	0.5	0.0	0.0	3.0	4.2	9.5	8.7	9.0	8.8	5.1	23.6	23.9	9.9	1.5	67.0	32.9	49.1	50.9
83444	ROBERTS	73.1	66.0	1.3	2.1	0.3	0.4	30.2	38.0	9.5	8.8	8.4	9.1	8.2	26.0	22.4	6.9	0.8	67.8	28.5	53.6	46.4
83445	SAINT ANTHONY	92.8	91.4	0.1	0.2	0.6	0.7	9.2	11.2	9.1	8.8	7.9	10.3	5.7	25.0	22.0	9.8	1.3	67.2	31.0	52.3	47.7
83446	SPENCER	89.2	87.8	0.0	0.0	0.0	0.0	13.5	13.5	5.4	5.4	5.4	6.8	1.4	14.9	32.4	27.0	1.4	78.4	50.0	52.7	47.3
83448	SUGAR CITY	94.1	93.2	0.2	0.2	0.7	0.8	6.2	7.7	8.7	9.6	9.9	13.0	7.3	21.1	22.1	7.5	0.9	63.2	26.3	50.2	49.8
83449	SWAN VALLEY	97.3	96.8	0.0	0.0	0.5	0.7	1.2	1.6	4.7	5.2	5.9	4.7	3.6	17.4	38.6	17.6	2.3	81.3	50.9	50.3	49.7
83450	TERRETON	80.6	75.1	0.1	0.1	0.5	0.6	20.8	26.9	10.0	10.0	9.7	9.6	9.3	24.0	18.7	7.9	0.9	63.8	26.2	53.9	46.1
83451	TETON	86.6	83.7	0.2	0.2	0.1	0.1	17.8	21.5	9.9	9.4	8.7	7.6	6.8	26.6	21.4	8.3	1.2	67.3	29.2	50.0	50.0
83452	TETONIA	91.4	89.8	0.2	0.2	0.5	0.5	14.3	17.2	9.1	8.8	8.8	7.6	5.9	27.3	24.1	7.5	0.7	68.4	32.2	53.5	46.5
83455	VICTOR	93.0	91.7	0.3	0.3	0.3	0.3	8.1	9.8	9.0	8.3	7.8	6.3	5.1	34.6	23.4	4.9	0.7	70.9	32.8	51.5	48.5
83460	REXBURG	97.6	96.7	0.3	0.5	0.8	1.3	1.9	2.0	0.5	0.0	0.0	56.1	37.6	1.3	0.0	1.8	2.8	98.7	19.4	39.3	60.7
83462	CARMEN	97.4	96.9	0.0	0.0	0.0	0.3	1.9	2.1	5.6	5.6	5.6	5.2	4.2	19.8	36.1	16.0	2.1	79.5	48.0	51.0	49.0
83463	GIBBONSVILLE	96.7	95.9	0.0	0.0	0.0	0.0	2.0	2.4	4.7	4.7	5.9	5.9	4.1	18.2	39.4	15.3	1.8	80.6	49.2	50.6	49.4
83464	LEADORE	95.0	94.0	0.0	0.0	0.3	0.3	4.9	6.2	5.8	6.5	7.1	8.5	4.9	19.7	33.6	12.5	1.3	72.8	42.5	50.6	49.4
83466	NORTH FORK	97.2	97.1	0.0	0.0	0.2	0.2	1.6	2.1	5.4	5.8	5.8	5.2	3.8	19.8	36.2	15.8	2.3	79.4	48.1	51.0	49.0
83467	SALMON	96.9	96.6	0.1	0.2	0.2	0.3	1.9	2.3	5.0	5.3	5.9	6.7	4.9	19.4	34.6	16.0	2.2	79.5	46.8	49.5	50.5
83469	SHOUP	98.2	98.2	0.0	0.0	0.0	0.0	0.0	0.0	3.6	1.8	3.6	3.6	3.6	10.7	55.4	17.9	0.0	89.3	55.7	53.6	46.4
83501	LEWISTON	95.1	94.4	0.3	0.4	0.8	1.0	1.9	2.2	5.9	5.8	5.9	6.7	6.4	25.8	26.5	13.8	3.1	78.6	39.7	48.8	51.2
83520	AHSAHKA	91.8	91.4	0.0	0.0	0.0	0.0	1.2	1.1	6.5	6.5	7.5	5.4	2.2	20.4	38.7	12.9	0.0	74.2	45.7	52.7	47.3
83522	COTTONWOOD	96.2	95.3	0.3	0.4	0.3	0.5	2.1	2.6	5.0	5.4	6.8	9.3	8.7	23.2	25.5	12.7	3.5	77.7	38.3	55.3	44.7
83523	CRAIGMONT	96.3	96.2	0.0	0.0	0.2	0.2	0.8	0.7	4.7	5.7	5.7	6.1	5.0	21.4	34.1	15.6	1.8	80.0	45.8	53.0	47.0
83524	CULDESAC	68.3	66.6	0.2	0.3	0.2	0.2	2.1	2.2	7.1	7.2	7.3	6.6	5.2	22.0	29.2	13.8	1.6	74.4	40.7	49.6	50.4
83525	ELK CITY	96.4	96.2	0.0	0.0	0.2	0.2	1.5	2.0	5.3	4.0	5.4	3.8	3.1	21.1	45.4	11.3	0.7	82.2	48.6	55.9	44.1
83526	FERDINAND	94.6	93.8	0.3	0.4	0.3	0.4	2.3	3.0	5.0	5.5	6.0	9.5	9.7	24.6	25.4	12.3	2.0	78.3	37.1	55.7	44.3
83530	GRANGEVILLE	96.3	96.0	0.1	0.1	0.3	0.3	1.5	1.9	5.7	6.0	6.6	6.5	4.5	19.4	32.7	15.3	3.3	77.5	45.8	48.4	51.6
83533	GREENCREEK	95.2	95.0	0.0	0.0	0.0	0.0	0.7	0.8	6.6	6.9	6.9	8.1	4.2	21.6	29.7	14.3	1.5	73.4	42.0	48.3	51.7
83535	JULIAETTA	88.4	88.0	0.1	0.1	0.1	0.1	1.4	1.7	6.0	6.1	6.4	6.3	5.5	22.9	30.6	14.2	2.2	77.9	42.5	51.3	48.7
83536	KAMIAH	86.7	85.7	0.2	0.2	0.4	0.4	2.4	2.6	5.0	5.4	6.2	7.4	4.7	20.3	30.7	17.9	2.4	78.3	45.6	49.1	50.9
83537	KENDRICK	97.2	96.7	0.2	0.2	0.0	0.0	1.6	2.0	5.2	5.7	6.1	6.1	4.2	21.5	32.3	16.6	2.4	79.3	45.8	52.2	47.8
83539	KOOSKIA	93.0	92.5	0.0	0.0	0.3	0.3	1.2	1.4	4.8	5.1	5.8	7.0	4.3	20.2	34.3	16.8	1.8	79.6	46.8	51.9	48.1
83540	LAPWAI	50.5	48.1	0.3	0.4	0.2	0.2	3.1	3.2	9.2	8.8	8.5	7.0	5.5	24.1	25.3	10.5	1.1	69.1	34.6	49.3	50.7
83541	LENORE	92.0	91.7	0.0	0.0	0.4	0.3	1.7	1.8	4.9	5.5	6.0	4.8	3.0	18.7	38.5	17.1	1.5	80.2	49.3	52.3	47.7
83542	LUCILE	98.4	98.3	0.0	0.0	0.0	0.0	1.2	1.7	2.9	4.6	5.4	5.8	2.1	16.6	40.7	19.1	2.9	82.6	51.8	51.9	48.1
83543	NEZPERCE	92.0	92.0	0.9	0.9	0.9	0.9	0.5	0.5	5.0	5.6	6.4	8.8	5.2	18.2	32.4	16.0	2.4	77.6	45.4	53.7	46.3
83544	OROFINO	94.3	94.1	0.2	0.2	0.5	0.5	2.2	2.2	4.6	5.0	5.4	5.7	5.0	23.9	32.7	15.4	2.4	81.2	45.3	54.9	45.1
83545	PECK	94.9	94.6	0.0	0.0	0.0	0.0	0.4	0.6	4.4	5.2	5.6	5.6	4.2	20.9	33.8	17.7	2.8	81.5	47.3	49.9	50.1
83546	PIERCE	96.3	96.1	0.0	0.0	0.0	0.0	1.2	1.2	4.9	5.0	5.4	6.5	4.7	22.6	34.4	15.8	0.7	79.6	45.6	50.6	49.4
83547	POLLOCK	98.1	97.8	0.0	0.0	0.0	0.0	1.4	2.0	3.0	5.0	5.4	5.9	2.2	16.3	40.8	18.1	3.2	82.4	51.6	52.0	48.0
83548	REUBENS	94.0	93.5	0.0	0.0	0.0	0.0	0.8	0.7	4.3	4.3	5.8	5.0	4.3	19.4	35.3	19.4	2.2	82.7	49.3	51.8	48.2
83549	RIGGINS	98.0	97.9	0.0	0.0	0.0	0.0	1.3	1.8	2.9	4.7	5.4	6.1	2.1	16.3	40.5	18.8	3.2	82.5	51.7	51.5	48.5
83552	STITES	96.3	96.0	0.0	0.0	0.0	0.0	0.7	1.1	4.4	5.1	6.5	7.6	3.3	18.5	37.8	15.3	1.5	79.3	47.4	52.7	47.3
83553	WEIPPE	98.1	98.1	0.1	0.1	0.0	0.0	0.8	0.8	5.3	6.3	7.4	6.7	4.7	19.9	32.8	14.5	2.2	76.6	44.6	50.3	49.7
83554	WHITE BIRD	96.1	95.5	0.2	0.2	0.5	0.6	2.3	2.9	5.3	5.6	6.7	6.3	3.7	18.6	37.2	14.7	2.0	77.9	47.2	50.5	49.5
83555	WINCHESTER	92.0	91.9	0.0	0.0	0.5	0.5	1.1	1.0	3.9	4.5	4.7	5.5	3.4	18.4	38.3	19.7	1.6	82.9	51.7	52.5	47.5
83601	ATLANTA	94.8	93.2	0.0	0.0	0.0	0.0	5.2	7.5	2.0	2.7	4.1	6.8	0.7	14.3	48.3	19.0	2.0	85.7	51.7	53.7	46.3
83602	BANKS	0.0	94.7	0.0	0.0	0.0	0.0	0.0	10.5	10.5	10.5	10.5	10.5	5.3	21.1	31.6	0.0	0.0	57.9	36.3	52.6	47.4
83604	BRUNEAU	87.3	85.0	0.0	0.0	0.0	0.0	20.5	24.1	4.9	5.4	5.7	6.1	5.5	27.2	30.1	13.3	1.8	79.4	41.5	56.5	43.5
83605	CALDWELL	76.3	71.6	0.4	0.6	1.0	1.2	26.2	31.4	9.3	8.3	7.7	7.9	7.4	27.2	21.2	9.0	2.0	70.2	31.2	49.1	50.9
83607	CALDWELL	83.8	80.7	0.2	0.3	0.7	0.9	18.3	22.4	7.7	7.7	7.7	7.7	5.7	25.7	26.7	9.9	1.2	72.1	35.6	50.4	49.6
83610	CAMBRIDGE	97.7	97.7	0.4	0.4	0.2	0.3	0.6	0.8	6.0	6.7	6.8	6.2	4.5	19.4	31.1	16.8	2.5	76.7	45.3	52.4	47.6
83611	CASCADE	96.3	95.8	0.0	0.1	0.5	0.6	1.6	1.9	3.9	4.2	4.9	5.7	4.5	17.1	37.1	20.8	1.9	82.5	50.6	50.5	49.5
83612	COUNCIL	96.3	96.1	0.0	0.0	0.3	0.3	1.5	1.7	3.9	4.5	5.3	5.8	4.9	15.4	39.6	18.7	2.0	82.3	50.6	51.3	48.7
83615	DONNELLY	95.9	95.4	0.0	0.1	0.4	0.3	1.8	2.1	4.3	6.1	6.4	6.3	2.4	22.5	40.3	10.9	0.7	78.6	45.9	53.4	46.6
83616	EAGLE	96.1	95.3	0.3	0.4	0.9	1.2	2.6	3.2	7.8	8.2	8.9	7.8	5.0	25.2	28.6	7.7	0.9	69.9	36.6	49.5	50.5
83617	EMMETT	93.7	92.6	0.1	0.1	0.4	0.5	7.1	8.6	7.2	7.2	7.2	7.1	5.5	23.6	26.9	12.8	2.5	73.9	38.6	49.3	50.7
83619	FRUITLAND	89.5	87.6	0.0	0.1	1.2	1.5	13.3	16.1	8.3	8.1	8.3	7.8	5.1	24.2	25.3	11.4	1.6	70.3	35.7	49.3	50.7
83622	GARDEN VALLEY	96.9	96.4	0.2	0.3	0.3	0.4	3.2	3.9	5.4	5.4	7.0	7.0	2.5	18.1	38.2	15.1	1.4	76.9	47.3	52.7	47.3
83623	GLENNS FERRY	84.5	82.0	0.0	0.1	0.3	0.4	27.6	31.4	7.3	7.5	7.7	7.5	6.0	21.6	27.8	12.8	1.8	72.7	38.7	51.0	49.0
83624	GRAND VIEW	76.3	74.2	0.2	0.2	0.4	0.5	14.2	16.2	7.4	8.8	8.3	9.3	5.6	25.4	24.2	9.6	1.4	69.3	33.1	52.1	47.9
83626	GREENLEAF	83.2	78.1	0.3	0.4	0.6	0.8	16.6	22.1	7.0	7.1	7.3	8.1	6.4	24.5	28.5	9.9	1.2	73.7	36.4	51.1	48.9
83627	HAMMETT	82.7	79.8	0.4	0.9	0.4	0.4	28.7	32.8	6.4	6.9	6.4	7.1	6.4	25.1	29.8	10.3	1.5	75.5	38.2	51.3	48.7
83628	HOMEDALE	71.3	66.1	0.2	0.2	0.9	1.0	30.4	36.2	9.5	9.2	8.8	8.3	5.6	23.7	21.8	10.7	2.4	67.1	32.4	50.2	49.8
83629	HORSESHOE BEND	94.3	93.7	0.0	0.0	0.1	0.1	5.5	6.6	6.1	6.6	7.4	7.0	4.9	22.8	31.9	11.7	1.5	74.6	40.8	51.4	48.6
83631	IDAHO CITY	94.2	93.7	0.1	0.1	0.5	0.7	3.4	4.1	5.8	6.0	8.3	7.0	3.2	23.9	36.2	9.0	0.6	74.3	42.4	51.1	48.9
83632	INDIAN VALLEY	97.5	97.8	0.0	0.0	0.5	0.4	0.5	0.0	2.6	3.1	3.9	5.7	5.3	12.3	40.8	24.1	2.2	86.8	55.8	51.3	48.7
83633	KING HILL	81.9	79.3	0.3	0.3	0.3	0.3	31.3	35.7	5.8	6.6	6.6	6.9	5.5	23.6	32.0	11.2	1.7	76.1	41.2	49.9	50.1
83634	KUNA	94.4	93.4	0.5	0.5	0.4	0.7	6.7	7.4	8.3	7.5	6.9	6.4	7.4	36.3	21.7	5.1	0.5	73.5	32.4	57.2	42.8
83636	LETHA	98.0	95.1	0.0	0.0	0.0	0.0	4.1	4.9	6.6	6.6	6.6	6.6	8.2	26.2	29.5	9.8	0.0	75.4	36.9	49.2	50.8
83637	LOWMAN	96.9	96.4	0.0	0.4	0.4	0.4	3.1	3.6	5.7	5.3	6.9	6.9	2.4	18.2	38.5	15.0	1.2	76.9	47.3	52.2	47.8
83638	MCCALL	96.6	96.1	0.0	0.1	0.3	0.3	2.2	2.7	4.3	5.3	6.8	7.1	3.0	22.3	37.2	12.5	1.4	78.3	45.5	52.1	47.9
83639	MARSING	77.2	74.2	0.2	0.2	0.2	0.2	24.3	27.6	8.5	8.4	8.2	7.7	4.9	26.9	24.1	10.0	1.2	70.0	34.0	53.3	46.7
83641	MELBA	81.4	75.8	0.3	0.4	0.4	0.5	18.6	24.8	8.0	7.7	7.7	7.5	6.1	28.6	24.8	8.6	1.0	72.0	33.9	53.8	46.2
83642	MERIDIAN	94.1	92.9	0.5	0.6	1.4	1.9	3.7	4.5	9.7	9.2	8.7	7.2	5.0	29.8	22.7	6.6	1.0	67.7	32.7	48.8	51.2
83643	MESA	96.7	96.9	0.0	0.0	0.0	0.0	1.6	2.3	2.3	3.9	5.5	5.5	3.1	10.9	47.7	19.5	1.6	83.6	54.2	53.1	46.9
83644	MIDDLETON	93.6	92.0	0.2	0.2	0.5	0.6	7.3	9.6	8.1	8.0	8.2	7.8	5.7	26.7	26.2	8.4	0.9	70.8	35.0	50.4	49.6
83645	MIDVALE	94.8	94.2	0.0	0.0	0.0	0.0	2.5	3.2	5.6	6.3	6.7	6.6	4.0	17.9	31.8	18.6	2.6	77.4	46.9	49.5	50.5
83646	MERIDIAN	94.6	93.5	0.5	0.6	1.3	1.7	3.5	4.4	10.3	9.4	8.8	7.1	4.9	31.8	21.5	5.7	0.7	66.6	31.7	49.4	50.6
83647	MOUNTAIN HOME	86.7	84.0	1.9	2.7	1.7	2.1	11.9	13.8	8.4	7.5	6.8	6.9	8.1	28.3	23.9	9.0	1.2	73.2	32.5	50.6	49.4
83648	MOUNTAIN HOME A F B	83.2	79.3	6.7	9.0	2.7	3.2	7.1	8.3	9.7	7.1	3.9	4.9	22.4	48.9	2.7	0.4	0.1	77.6	25.6	65.5	34.5
83650	MURPHY	86.6	84.5	0.1	0.1	0.6	0.8	12.0	14.6	5.0	5.6	6.3	7.6	5.3	22.1	32.4	14.4	1.4	78.3	43.5	54.8	45.2
83651	NAMPA	83.6	80.2	0.3	0.4	1.2	1.4	16.8	20.8	8.9	8.1	7.4	7.0	6.7	28.0	21.6	10.0	2.3	71.3	33.0	49.1	50.9
83654	NEW MEADOWS	96.0	95.7	0.2	0.1	0.0	0.0	1.8	2.3	4.7	5.7	7.4	7.9	4.2	22.4	34.8	11.5	1.5	77.2	43.6	51.3	48.7
83655	NEW PLYMOUTH	93.4	92.2	0.2	0.3	0.3	0.5	7.8	9.5	7.2	7.4	7.7	7.9	5.1	24.3	27.2	11.5	1.7	72.6	37.4	49.8	50.2
83657	OLA	95.4	95.0	0.0	0.0	0.0	0.0	4.0	5.0	5.5	6.6	7.2	7.2	4.4	19.9	30.9	16.0	2.2	75.7	44.3	52.5	47.5
83660	PARMA	87.5	84.0	0.1	0.2	1.3	1.5	18.5	23.8	7.5	7.7	7.9	7.7	5.3	23.7	27.4	11.1	1.6	72.1	37.5	50.8	49.2
83661	PAYETTE	89.1	87.3	0.1	0.1	0.8	1.0	13.5	16.1	7.7	7.3	7.2	7.9	6.7	25.2	24.5	11.5	2.1	72.9	35.5	49.2	50.8
83669	STAR	95.0	94.2	0.2	0.2	0.4	0.5	3.8	4.8	9.6	8.9	8.2	6.4	4.9	31.0	23.4	6.8	0.8	69.1	32.7	49.6	50.4
83670	SWEET	95.3	94.3	0.0	0.0	0.0	0.2	3.9	5.0	5.5	6.2	6.9	7.2	4.5	19.6	32.0	16.0	2.1	76.2	45.1	52.7	47.3
83672	WEISER	85.8	83.0	0.1	0.1	1.3	1.6	16.2	19.7	7.1	7.1	7.3	7.3	5.4	22.6	26.7	13.8	2.7	73.9	38.9	49.4	50.6
83676	WILDER	65.3	57.1	0.2	0.2	0.9	0.9	39.5	48.6	8.7	8.5	8.2	8.3	6.5	24.7	23.6	10.3	1.2	69.4	32.7	50.1	49.9
83677	YELLOW PINE	84.6	86.2	0.0	0.0	3.8	3.4	0.0	0.0	0.0	10.3	3.4	3.4	3.4	13.8	48.3	17.2	0.0	86.2	48.8	51.7	48.3
83686	NAMPA	88.3	85.5	0.4	0.5	0.9	1.1	12.3	15.8	9.9	8.8	8.0	7.7	7.0	29.3	20.6	7.4	1.4	68.8	30.6	49.3	50.7
83687	NAMPA	82.2	80.4	0.3	0.4	1.0	1.3	19.8	21.3	10.9	9.8	8.5	7.2	5.6	33.1	18.3	5.8	0.7	66.4	30.4	50.7	49.3
83702	BOISE	93.9	92.7	0.6	0.9	1.4	1.7	3.6	4.6	5.6	4.8	4.6	5.1	8.3	33.8	27.0	8.8	1.9	82.4	36.7	51.2	48.8
83703	BOISE	93.3	92.1	0.6	0.9	1.2	1.5	4.8	6.0	6.6	6.4	6.1	6.2	7.7	28.8	28.1	8.3	1.7	77.2	36.3	49.7	50.3
	IDAHO	91.0	89.5	0.4	0.5	1.0	1.3	7.9	9.5	7.7	7.4	7.3	7.7	7.0	26.7	25.0	9.6	1.6	73.1	34.4	50.1	49.9
	UNITED STATES	75.1	72.0	12.3	12.7	3.8	4.6	12.5	15.7	6.8	6.7	6.6	7.1	6.9	27.0	26.0	10.9	1.9	75.7	36.9	49.2	50.8

INCOME

ZIP CODE #	POST OFFICE NAME	2009 Per Capita Income	2009 HH Income Base	2009 Household Income Distribution (%) Less than $25,000	$25,000 to $49,999	$50,000 to $99,999	$100,000 to $149,999	$150,000 or More	Median Household Income 2009	2014	2009 National Centile	2009 State Centile	2009 Home Value Base	2009 Home Value Distribution (%) Less than $50,000	$50,000 to $89,999	$90,000 to $174,999	$175,000 to $399,999	$400,000 or More	2009 Median Home Value
83443	RIRIE	16695	278	21.6	40.3	31.7	5.8	0.7	40420	42462	34	45	225	10.7	14.7	52.0	19.6	3.1	128526
83444	ROBERTS	15561	464	23.5	29.1	40.7	4.3	2.4	48140	48820	57	79	392	14.8	13.5	56.9	12.2	2.6	123214
83445	SAINT ANTHONY	16323	2249	25.2	36.4	31.8	4.8	1.8	41291	42582	37	48	1858	11.4	16.0	48.4	21.5	2.6	124923
83446	SPENCER	20332	30	26.7	20.0	46.7	6.7	0.0	51268	51268	64	88	18	22.2	22.2	38.9	16.7	0.0	100000
83448	SUGAR CITY	17153	816	13.5	29.7	48.0	6.9	2.0	55132	56189	71	92	704	7.8	3.6	28.6	57.7	2.4	192929
83449	SWAN VALLEY	26960	196	24.5	29.1	35.7	5.1	5.6	46027	50901	51	72	165	10.9	13.3	37.6	27.3	10.9	151786
83450	TERRETON	12631	358	31.6	36.6	27.4	2.8	1.7	36453	40290	22	18	279	22.6	14.3	38.4	21.5	3.2	110662
83451	TETON	14905	392	23.0	42.6	28.6	5.1	0.8	43067	43893	43	59	347	13.5	18.4	50.4	16.1	1.4	120833
83452	TETONIA	20189	689	17.1	29.6	46.6	5.1	1.6	51509	52970	65	89	526	7.0	5.7	16.7	52.3	18.3	262162
83455	VICTOR	29059	1566	8.9	17.4	54.9	14.4	4.4	70124	70614	87	96	1199	3.3	6.4	7.6	57.1	25.5	305929
83460	REXBURG	2909	0	0.0	0.0	0.0	0.0	0.0	0	0	0	0	0	0.0	0.0	0.0	0.0	0.0	0
83462	CARMEN	17804	120	32.5	35.0	27.5	3.3	1.7	35000	38640	18	12	84	8.3	7.1	45.2	32.1	7.1	152500
83463	GIBBONSVILLE	22314	79	34.2	31.6	26.6	3.8	3.8	37986	41751	27	25	60	6.7	10.0	50.0	26.7	6.7	141667
83464	LEADORE	16116	240	39.6	35.4	19.2	4.2	1.7	33162	33328	14	6	172	19.2	19.2	25.0	22.1	14.5	138636
83466	NORTH FORK	18706	237	31.2	36.3	28.7	3.8	0.0	35186	38523	18	12	162	8.6	6.8	43.8	33.3	7.4	155263
83467	SALMON	20456	2592	31.9	31.6	29.7	4.6	2.2	40368	41955	34	43	2003	7.8	14.2	43.6	27.5	6.9	142863
83469	SHOUP	10450	31	74.2	25.8	0.0	0.0	0.0	12430	12430	1	2	26	30.8	0.0	0.0	3.8	65.4	466667
83501	LEWISTON	24919	14272	22.5	28.1	38.8	7.3	3.2	49398	52423	60	82	9658	5.5	5.5	43.0	42.9	3.1	167931
83520	AHSAHKA	20408	35	20.0	25.7	51.4	2.9	0.0	51391	50000	65	88	29	20.7	3.4	27.6	34.5	13.8	170833
83522	COTTONWOOD	22138	612	20.9	35.1	36.4	4.9	2.6	43976	48877	45	62	495	7.7	10.9	58.6	19.4	3.4	131189
83523	CRAIGMONT	19984	360	33.1	31.7	28.1	5.6	1.7	38515	40266	28	29	288	8.0	14.9	55.2	21.2	0.7	124167
83524	CULDESAC	18024	442	29.4	32.4	33.3	3.8	1.1	39230	43736	30	34	337	13.4	14.2	38.9	27.3	6.2	130592
83525	ELK CITY	17166	252	31.0	50.8	16.7	1.6	0.0	33011	32559	13	6	194	18.6	13.9	49.0	15.5	3.1	126351
83526	FERDINAND	13833	158	24.7	39.9	28.5	3.8	3.2	40679	41853	35	46	130	9.2	13.1	37.7	30.0	10.0	155882
83530	GRANGEVILLE	18753	2208	30.5	31.7	32.0	5.1	0.8	40402	42298	34	44	1673	9.6	10.9	47.6	25.6	6.2	139198
83533	GREENCREEK	17262	93	26.9	40.9	26.9	2.2	3.2	39444	40749	31	37	77	7.8	11.7	35.1	33.8	11.7	167045
83535	JULIAETTA	20122	423	28.6	33.6	32.9	3.3	1.7	38831	43948	29	30	327	17.4	13.1	44.6	21.7	3.1	119531
83536	KAMIAH	18595	1529	36.0	31.2	27.7	3.3	1.8	34457	35978	16	9	1134	12.3	9.0	43.9	28.0	6.8	142647
83537	KENDRICK	22236	536	21.1	37.3	34.9	4.5	2.2	45094	47077	49	67	421	9.7	9.7	38.5	30.9	11.2	151736
83539	KOOSKIA	16004	1105	37.7	36.7	22.0	2.9	0.7	31413	31995	10	4	855	16.0	13.1	34.5	25.5	10.9	136596
83540	LAPWAI	16146	755	29.4	31.9	33.8	3.8	1.1	39605	44365	32	39	569	13.9	10.4	39.7	27.6	8.4	137664
83541	LENORE	21758	508	25.0	31.5	36.6	5.3	1.6	45586	47469	50	69	417	10.3	6.2	30.2	40.0	13.2	187054
83542	LUCILE	18956	100	33.0	32.0	31.0	3.0	1.0	36861	39446	23	20	73	11.0	12.3	46.6	17.8	12.3	133654
83543	NEZPERCE	20478	298	25.2	32.6	35.2	4.4	2.7	45351	47230	49	68	245	6.5	22.0	55.1	12.7	3.7	122635
83544	OROFINO	20095	2393	28.5	34.2	31.6	4.4	1.3	39631	40586	32	40	1831	13.4	15.2	42.8	25.2	3.3	127679
83545	PECK	21072	229	28.8	34.5	30.1	5.7	0.9	38713	42572	29	30	179	10.6	13.4	32.4	31.3	12.3	151042
83546	PIERCE	19444	311	30.9	33.1	33.8	1.3	1.0	39263	40323	31	35	259	28.2	35.5	27.4	7.7	1.2	74310
83547	POLLOCK	20896	185	31.9	32.4	30.3	3.8	1.6	37600	39386	26	22	135	9.6	11.9	45.9	20.7	11.9	137500
83548	REUBENS	18553	53	28.3	35.8	30.2	5.7	0.0	39295	44086	31	36	43	4.7	16.3	51.2	23.3	4.7	121250
83549	RIGGINS	22699	358	32.4	32.7	29.3	3.9	1.7	37219	39234	24	20	260	10.4	12.3	46.5	19.2	11.5	134375
83552	STITES	17233	109	33.0	33.9	27.5	5.5	0.0	38003	38652	27	25	88	13.6	9.1	31.8	30.7	14.8	162500
83553	WEIPPE	17291	484	30.0	36.6	30.2	2.5	0.8	35696	36802	20	14	393	22.6	23.4	33.6	17.3	3.1	95962
83554	WHITE BIRD	19687	286	32.9	32.2	29.4	5.6	0.0	39213	40371	30	34	220	5.9	10.5	45.0	29.1	9.5	150000
83555	WINCHESTER	22839	173	25.4	31.8	34.7	7.5	0.6	45169	46686	49	67	143	5.6	14.7	54.5	20.3	4.9	121181
83601	ATLANTA	21583	76	19.7	52.6	27.6	0.0	0.0	41692	43420	38	51	59	18.6	27.1	10.2	35.6	8.5	137500
83602	BANKS	16579	8	37.5	25.0	37.5	0.0	0.0	30000	27247	8	4	7	0.0	0.0	100.0	0.0	0.0	121875
83604	BRUNEAU	22103	321	38.0	37.7	15.9	2.2	6.2	32532	34230	12	6	175	21.7	9.1	38.9	18.3	12.0	127976
83605	CALDWELL	18373	11535	25.7	33.8	33.3	4.9	2.2	42256	45737	40	53	7511	7.6	12.0	52.0	26.2	2.2	140520
83607	CALDWELL	18563	9321	20.2	33.9	38.7	5.0	2.2	46637	50229	53	73	7341	6.9	6.3	41.8	38.0	7.1	165188
83610	CAMBRIDGE	16861	417	36.9	35.0	22.8	3.4	1.9	31516	32791	11	5	321	9.3	9.7	48.3	25.5	7.2	142026
83611	CASCADE	22966	1283	23.7	37.2	32.3	4.3	2.6	42127	44332	40	53	1063	6.8	8.7	34.6	41.0	8.8	174375
83612	COUNCIL	17509	894	34.7	37.6	23.7	3.1	0.9	29461	31722	7	4	718	7.9	14.6	40.9	26.2	10.3	136735
83615	DONNELLY	26002	307	23.1	29.3	39.4	6.2	2.0	47661	48857	56	77	264	3.0	4.5	25.4	45.5	21.6	248333
83616	EAGLE	34809	8031	9.6	19.6	35.8	19.2	15.8	77251	80839	91	100	6659	7.3	4.8	11.2	50.7	26.0	268845
83617	EMMETT	18781	5947	27.6	29.2	34.9	6.4	1.9	44144	48333	46	63	4706	5.7	6.7	52.4	30.9	4.3	151391
83619	FRUITLAND	18358	2586	26.0	35.3	32.8	3.2	2.7	41455	42367	38	49	2007	8.9	8.2	47.6	32.9	2.4	150621
83622	GARDEN VALLEY	23824	799	25.4	28.0	35.5	7.6	3.4	46750	49746	53	74	662	6.3	9.8	33.5	39.4	10.9	176020
83623	GLENNS FERRY	16761	836	32.1	32.9	30.4	2.9	1.8	35803	37686	20	15	529	13.2	22.9	40.3	19.7	4.0	112500
83624	GRAND VIEW	16254	573	36.0	31.1	27.7	2.3	3.0	33653	34562	15	8	337	21.1	15.4	44.8	15.4	3.3	110880
83626	GREENLEAF	17197	498	21.3	33.5	39.2	5.2	0.8	45000	49672	48	67	388	10.1	6.4	44.1	35.1	4.4	156696
83627	HAMMETT	17137	147	23.8	34.0	35.4	4.8	2.0	42534	44489	41	56	91	14.3	16.5	26.4	35.2	7.7	151786
83628	HOMEDALE	15042	1486	34.2	33.9	25.7	4.2	2.0	33211	34745	14	7	1097	11.9	14.2	57.5	13.6	2.8	115792
83629	HORSESHOE BEND	17855	760	29.6	30.8	34.3	5.0	0.3	39707	44340	32	40	628	17.8	15.6	38.4	19.1	9.1	121181
83631	IDAHO CITY	18436	556	27.5	34.0	34.0	4.0	0.5	40797	45089	35	46	425	17.2	17.6	35.1	24.5	5.6	130523
83632	INDIAN VALLEY	20867	104	26.9	35.6	28.8	5.8	2.9	38161	41765	27	27	96	3.1	6.3	35.4	36.5	18.8	200000
83633	KING HILL	18748	120	25.0	34.2	34.2	4.2	2.5	41830	43185	39	51	74	14.9	17.6	24.3	35.1	8.1	145833
83634	KUNA	21867	5884	12.4	23.9	48.7	12.3	2.7	62280	65440	80	94	4979	2.1	1.7	46.7	38.1	11.3	174354
83636	LETHA	23590	24	20.8	33.3	37.5	4.2	4.2	47330	47338	55	76	20	0.0	0.0	35.0	55.0	10.0	220000
83637	LOWMAN	26743	113	24.8	28.3	36.3	7.1	3.5	46955	50000	54	75	94	5.3	9.6	34.0	39.4	11.7	178571
83638	MCCALL	23506	2528	22.7	30.9	37.9	6.3	2.3	46834	47892	54	74	1937	3.3	2.6	22.2	49.1	22.8	259710
83639	MARSING	16397	1062	24.1	41.8	27.6	4.7	1.8	37782	41038	26	24	789	8.0	13.9	50.8	20.5	6.7	136884
83641	MELBA	17298	854	26.2	33.1	34.1	3.9	2.7	41973	44862	39	52	574	7.0	13.6	32.9	36.6	9.9	165000
83642	MERIDIAN	29356	12393	9.9	18.0	45.8	17.9	8.5	73641	76983	89	98	9938	1.9	2.1	25.3	60.4	10.3	217220
83643	MESA	19888	61	31.1	36.1	26.2	4.9	1.6	35554	36540	19	13	54	0.0	7.4	35.2	38.9	18.5	210000
83644	MIDDLETON	18920	3191	16.9	34.0	43.8	3.7	1.6	49351	51596	60	82	2652	4.4	8.4	40.2	41.0	6.0	168080
83645	MIDVALE	19822	328	33.8	30.5	27.7	2.7	5.2	36563	38301	22	18	258	8.9	10.9	33.3	28.3	18.6	165909
83646	MERIDIAN	30808	15614	7.4	16.1	48.2	19.9	8.4	76683	79024	90	99	13045	4.5	1.5	24.0	63.3	6.8	207177
83647	MOUNTAIN HOME	20992	7076	19.2	32.3	40.0	6.5	1.9	48657	50784	58	80	4700	10.8	8.6	48.9	29.9	1.8	145204
83648	MOUNTAIN HOME A F B	15686	1230	13.3	54.1	29.5	2.4	0.7	40407	42437	34	44	59	18.6	10.2	22.0	49.2	0.0	172500
83650	MURPHY	16999	594	31.5	31.8	30.1	4.4	2.2	34801	38759	17	10	439	12.8	10.7	31.9	29.4	15.3	163915
83651	NAMPA	19481	10875	25.0	30.3	38.1	5.0	1.6	44872	49661	48	66	7549	11.7	5.9	54.5	26.7	1.2	142695
83654	NEW MEADOWS	18033	571	28.4	36.8	29.8	3.9	1.2	37429	40189	25	21	425	11.1	5.6	39.5	30.6	13.2	160904
83655	NEW PLYMOUTH	17028	1612	26.6	36.4	29.7	5.0	2.3	41021	42027	36	47	1238	10.2	7.8	38.4	35.0	8.6	161395
83657	OLA	21179	76	31.6	28.9	31.6	5.3	2.6	39063	41751	30	33	64	1.6	4.7	32.8	45.3	15.6	214286
83660	PARMA	16631	2440	29.7	34.3	31.1	2.4	2.5	38079	40498	27	26	1735	8.8	21.4	36.0	30.2	3.6	134110
83661	PAYETTE	18013	3877	30.6	28.4	35.8	2.6	2.6	40145	41130	33	41	2728	3.2	12.6	54.3	26.8	3.0	145234
83669	STAR	28487	2328	10.7	25.9	39.9	14.9	8.5	64604	68143	83	95	2018	0.6	5.9	23.7	43.9	25.8	224571
83670	SWEET	17206	199	31.2	29.1	32.7	4.5	2.5	39467	42369	31	37	169	2.4	4.7	33.7	44.4	14.8	209722
83672	WEISER	18652	3218	29.0	34.7	30.1	3.4	2.7	39284	40713	31	35	2361	5.1	10.3	52.3	28.6	3.7	147735
83676	WILDER	14125	1554	30.9	37.0	26.6	3.5	1.9	35540	35864	19	13	1029	9.5	16.9	38.1	29.8	5.6	130875
83677	YELLOW PINE	15357	13	46.2	30.8	15.4	7.7	0.0	26024	22278	4	2	10	20.0	0.0	60.0	20.0	0.0	112500
83686	NAMPA	22828	15195	14.0	27.4	45.1	8.9	4.7	56249	57819	73	92	11579	1.4	2.8	42.9	48.2	4.7	180069
83687	NAMPA	20766	9957	15.5	27.9	47.1	6.9	2.6	54854	58153	71	91	7700	6.1	9.8	43.9	34.0	6.2	162821
83702	BOISE	35946	11501	24.5	26.8	31.2	7.9	9.7	48538	51688	58	80	5545	1.3	2.5	26.0	51.0	19.2	232901
83703	BOISE	31383	7989	17.5	24.4	39.5	10.2	8.4	58580	61861	76	93	4988	3.2	2.2	38.3	47.2	9.2	187889
	IDAHO	23160		20.9	28.6	37.9	8.3	4.4	50374	53004				6.9	7.8	39.2	38.3	7.9	167282
	UNITED STATES	27277		20.9	24.4	35.3	11.7	7.6	54719	56938				9.3	13.1	31.6	32.6	13.5	162279

ZIP CODE	FINANCIAL SERVICES				THE HOME						ENTERTAINMENT						PERSONAL			
					Home Improvements		Furnishings													
# POST OFFICE NAME	Auto Loan	Home Loan	Invest-ments	Retire-ment Plans	Home Repair	Lawn & Garden	Comput-ers & Hard-ware-Personal	Major Appli-ances	TV, Radio, Sound Equip-ment	Furni-ture	Dine out/ Carry out	Sports Equip-ment	Fees & Tickets	Toys & Games	Travel	Cable TV	Apparel & Services	Auto Repairs	Health Insur-ance	Pets & Supplies
83443 RIRIE	84	65	84	66	67	87	68	80	71	60	70	64	56	71	67	76	46	75	84	97
83444 ROBERTS	90	83	74	80	81	85	78	83	81	81	81	61	74	84	75	83	55	80	83	99
83445 SAINT ANTHONY	81	64	75	63	64	81	66	75	71	62	70	58	57	71	64	76	47	72	80	91
83446 SPENCER	84	67	107	66	73	88	67	85	70	63	69	62	58	67	72	75	46	78	84	99
83448 SUGAR CITY	91	94	80	92	89	87	85	87	84	89	85	66	86	88	84	83	59	85	83	103
83449 SWAN VALLEY	102	81	131	80	89	108	82	103	85	76	84	76	70	81	88	91	56	96	102	120
83450 TERRETON	75	52	83	52	54	79	57	71	60	47	59	59	42	59	57	65	38	67	75	88
83451 TETON	84	60	70	59	60	80	63	73	70	61	68	56	50	73	57	76	46	69	77	89
83452 TETONIA	90	82	75	79	80	85	78	83	81	80	81	61	73	84	74	83	55	80	84	99
83455 VICTOR	120	130	105	124	121	106	115	114	107	124	110	91	116	116	112	101	77	108	99	129
83460 REXBURG	0	0	0	0	0	0	0	0	0	0	0	0	0	0	0	0	0	0	0	0
83462 CARMEN	71	57	92	56	62	75	57	72	59	53	59	53	49	56	62	63	39	67	71	84
83463 GIBBONSVILLE	80	64	103	63	70	84	64	81	67	60	66	59	55	63	69	71	44	75	80	94
83464 LEADORE	76	52	83	52	55	80	58	72	60	47	59	59	42	59	58	66	39	67	76	88
83466 NORTH FORK	68	55	88	54	60	72	55	69	57	51	56	51	47	54	59	61	37	64	68	80
83467 SALMON	79	62	91	62	66	84	64	79	67	58	66	59	54	66	66	73	44	73	81	93
83469 SHOUP	31	25	41	25	28	33	25	32	26	24	26	23	22	25	27	28	17	30	32	37
83501 LEWISTON	86	79	80	80	79	87	84	85	85	79	84	64	79	85	81	88	58	85	90	100
83520 AHSAHKA	90	72	117	71	80	96	72	92	76	68	75	67	63	72	79	81	50	85	91	107
83522 COTTONWOOD	85	68	85	68	70	88	73	82	76	66	75	64	62	75	72	81	50	80	88	99
83523 CRAIGMONT	86	60	94	59	62	90	65	81	68	54	67	66	49	67	65	74	44	76	85	99
83524 CULDESAC	79	62	78	60	63	79	62	74	66	59	65	56	53	66	61	71	44	69	76	88
83525 ELK CITY	61	49	79	48	54	65	49	63	51	46	51	46	43	49	53	55	34	58	62	72
83526 FERDINAND	85	60	92	60	63	90	67	81	69	55	69	67	51	68	66	75	45	76	86	100
83530 GRANGEVILLE	73	60	84	59	63	79	60	74	64	55	63	55	53	62	63	70	42	69	78	86
83533 GREENCREEK	85	59	93	58	61	90	65	81	68	53	67	67	48	66	65	74	43	75	85	99
83535 JULIAETTA	85	64	85	62	66	85	65	79	71	61	70	59	53	71	64	77	46	74	82	95
83536 KAMIAH	76	55	78	53	57	78	58	72	64	52	62	54	46	63	57	70	41	67	77	85
83537 KENDRICK	95	66	105	66	69	100	73	91	76	60	75	74	54	74	72	83	49	84	95	111
83539 KOOSKIA	65	49	73	48	52	68	50	64	55	46	54	47	42	53	51	60	36	59	66	74
83540 LAPWAI	77	67	67	64	66	74	64	71	67	65	67	52	58	69	62	71	45	68	72	84
83541 LENORE	85	68	109	67	74	90	68	87	71	63	70	64	59	68	74	76	47	80	86	101
83542 LUCILE	67	64	81	59	71	76	61	72	64	66	63	47	60	59	66	68	42	69	80	82
83543 NEZPERCE	93	64	102	64	67	98	71	88	74	57	73	73	52	72	71	80	47	82	93	109
83544 OROFINO	79	61	90	59	65	83	62	78	67	59	66	57	53	65	64	73	44	72	81	91
83545 PECK	82	58	92	57	61	87	63	79	66	52	65	64	47	64	63	71	42	73	82	96
83546 PIERCE	80	58	83	56	60	81	59	75	65	55	64	56	47	65	59	72	42	69	78	89
83547 POLLOCK	67	64	82	59	71	76	61	72	64	65	63	47	59	59	66	68	42	69	79	82
83548 REUBENS	83	62	100	62	67	88	65	82	68	57	67	63	53	66	68	73	44	76	83	98
83549 RIGGINS	67	64	81	59	71	76	61	71	64	66	62	47	60	59	66	68	42	69	80	82
83552 STITES	74	57	88	56	61	77	58	73	61	53	61	54	48	59	60	66	40	67	74	86
83553 WEIPPE	77	56	74	54	57	77	58	71	64	55	63	53	47	64	56	70	42	66	74	85
83554 WHITE BIRD	74	59	95	58	65	78	59	75	62	55	61	55	51	59	64	66	41	69	74	87
83555 WINCHESTER	83	66	107	65	73	88	67	85	70	62	69	62	58	66	72	74	46	78	83	98
83601 ATLANTA	61	58	75	54	65	70	56	66	59	60	57	43	55	54	61	62	39	63	73	75
83602 BANKS	70	51	74	49	53	71	52	66	57	48	56	49	42	56	52	63	37	60	68	78
83604 BRUNEAU	95	65	104	65	68	100	72	90	75	59	74	74	53	74	72	82	48	84	95	111
83605 CALDWELL	77	69	62	68	67	72	72	72	74	70	73	54	67	75	67	76	51	73	75	86
83607 CALDWELL	86	79	74	78	78	83	76	81	78	77	78	61	72	81	74	80	53	78	81	96
83610 CAMBRIDGE	74	51	81	51	53	78	57	70	59	46	58	58	41	58	56	64	38	66	74	86
83611 CASCADE	86	69	111	68	76	91	69	88	72	65	71	64	60	68	75	77	47	81	86	102
83612 COUNCIL	69	52	79	51	56	71	53	67	57	49	56	50	44	55	55	62	37	62	68	79
83615 DONNELLY	94	76	122	74	83	100	76	96	79	71	78	70	66	75	82	84	52	89	95	111
83616 EAGLE	138	161	144	161	156	142	141	142	134	149	136	112	153	140	148	129	97	136	130	164
83617 EMMETT	82	68	75	68	68	84	70	79	74	64	72	60	61	75	68	79	49	75	84	94
83619 FRUITLAND	89	68	82	66	68	88	69	81	75	66	74	62	57	76	66	80	49	76	84	98
83622 GARDEN VALLEY	96	77	124	76	84	102	77	98	81	72	80	72	67	77	83	86	53	90	97	113
83623 GLENNS FERRY	80	57	83	55	59	82	59	75	65	53	64	58	46	64	59	71	42	69	78	90
83624 GRAND VIEW	79	57	71	57	57	77	61	71	67	57	66	56	49	68	57	72	44	68	75	87
83626 GREENLEAF	86	79	72	78	78	83	75	81	78	77	78	59	71	81	72	81	53	77	81	95
83627 HAMMETT	94	67	100	67	70	98	73	89	76	61	75	73	56	75	72	82	49	84	94	109
83628 HOMEDALE	76	56	66	55	55	74	62	69	66	56	65	54	50	67	57	71	43	67	74	84
83629 HORSESHOE BEND	82	59	84	57	61	83	60	76	67	56	65	57	48	66	59	73	43	70	80	91
83631 IDAHO CITY	75	59	95	58	65	79	60	76	63	56	62	55	51	60	64	67	41	70	75	88
83632 INDIAN VALLEY	76	61	99	60	67	81	61	78	64	57	63	57	53	61	66	68	42	72	77	90
83633 KING HILL	95	66	105	65	69	101	73	91	76	59	75	75	53	74	72	83	49	85	96	111
83634 KUNA	103	109	91	107	104	97	98	99	95	104	96	78	100	100	97	92	67	95	92	115
83636 LETHA	96	88	78	86	86	90	83	88	87	87	87	64	79	90	80	89	59	86	89	105
83637 LOWMAN	97	77	125	76	85	102	77	98	81	73	80	72	67	77	84	86	53	91	97	114
83638 MCCALL	91	73	117	72	80	96	73	92	76	68	75	67	63	72	79	81	50	85	91	107
83639 MARSING	85	59	82	59	61	85	64	77	69	57	68	62	49	69	61	75	45	73	81	95
83641 MELBA	79	74	65	72	72	75	69	73	72	72	72	54	66	74	67	73	49	71	73	87
83642 MERIDIAN	124	136	114	134	129	118	123	122	117	129	120	97	128	124	124	113	84	118	111	141
83643 MESA	70	56	90	55	61	74	56	71	58	52	58	52	48	55	60	62	38	65	70	82
83644 MIDDLETON	82	82	71	82	80	82	77	80	77	79	78	60	76	80	76	78	54	77	79	94
83645 MIDVALE	89	61	98	61	64	94	68	84	71	55	70	70	50	69	68	77	45	79	89	104
83646 MERIDIAN	131	144	118	140	136	121	127	127	120	136	122	101	131	129	127	114	86	120	112	145
83647 MOUNTAIN HOME	82	78	69	77	75	78	78	77	79	79	79	59	75	81	75	79	54	78	78	92
83648 MOUNTAIN HOME A F B	80	44	33	50	39	38	75	53	71	70	74	52	58	84	55	66	52	67	49	65
83650 MURPHY	81	56	89	56	58	85	62	77	64	50	64	64	45	63	62	70	41	72	81	95
83651 NAMPA	77	72	67	70	70	73	73	73	74	73	74	55	70	75	70	75	51	74	75	87
83654 NEW MEADOWS	76	58	82	57	61	77	59	72	64	56	63	54	50	63	60	68	42	68	74	86
83655 NEW PLYMOUTH	85	63	86	62	65	86	65	79	70	59	69	61	53	70	64	75	46	74	82	95
83657 OLA	90	62	98	61	64	94	68	85	71	55	70	70	50	70	68	78	46	79	90	105
83660 PARMA	84	61	83	59	63	84	64	78	69	59	68	60	51	69	62	75	45	73	81	94
83661 PAYETTE	74	67	65	67	67	75	69	73	71	65	70	56	64	72	67	74	48	71	76	86
83669 STAR	119	125	103	121	118	109	112	113	108	120	110	88	113	115	110	105	76	108	103	130
83670 SWEET	89	61	98	61	64	94	68	84	71	55	70	70	50	69	68	77	45	79	89	104
83672 WEISER	80	65	76	66	66	82	67	77	71	62	70	58	59	72	65	76	47	73	80	91
83676 WILDER	75	61	58	58	61	69	61	69	66	62	65	49	54	67	58	69	45	66	70	79
83677 YELLOW PINE	50	48	61	44	53	57	46	54	48	49	47	35	45	44	50	51	32	52	60	62
83686 NAMPA	100	101	85	99	95	91	97	95	94	100	95	75	96	99	93	92	66	93	89	111
83687 NAMPA	94	93	79	89	88	84	89	88	87	92	88	68	86	91	84	85	61	86	83	102
83702 BOISE	98	94	93	98	93	91	106	94	102	103	103	76	103	102	100	101	73	101	96	114
83703 BOISE	107	106	94	107	102	100	109	102	107	109	108	81	108	110	104	105	76	105	101	122
IDAHO	94	87	87	87	86	92	88	90	88	86	88	70	83	90	85	90	61	89	91	107
UNITED STATES	100	100	100	100	100	100	100	100	100	100	100	100	100	100	100	100	100	100	100	100

POPULATION CHANGE

ZIP CODE #	POST OFFICE NAME	COUNTY FIPS CODE	POPULATION 2000	POPULATION 2009	POPULATION 2014	2000-2009 ANNUAL RATE % Rate	2000-2009 ANNUAL RATE State Centile	HOUSEHOLDS 2000	HOUSEHOLDS 2009	HOUSEHOLDS 2014	HOUSEHOLDS % Annual Rate 2000-2009	HOUSEHOLDS 2009 Average HH Size	FAMILIES 2000	FAMILIES 2009	FAMILIES % Annual Rate 2000-2009
83704	BOISE	001	38953	42334	45070	0.9	53	14561	16469	17771	1.3	2.46	9905	10603	0.7
83705	BOISE	001	26282	28227	30007	0.8	49	11252	12525	13441	1.2	2.24	6563	6853	0.5
83706	BOISE	001	29082	31304	33205	0.8	49	12550	14024	15056	1.2	2.13	6947	7265	0.5
83709	BOISE	001	35039	47125	54045	3.3	91	12177	17146	19822	3.8	2.73	9657	13390	3.6
83712	BOISE	001	7577	8514	9205	1.3	66	3374	3888	4224	1.5	2.16	1977	2135	0.8
83713	BOISE	001	22537	27447	31274	2.2	83	7657	9747	11201	2.6	2.81	6021	7406	2.3
83714	GARDEN CITY	001	16927	21076	23754	2.4	86	6688	8667	9847	2.8	2.42	4474	5560	2.4
83716	BOISE	001	12032	14646	16137	2.1	82	4378	5444	6067	2.4	2.69	3306	3968	2.0
83725	BOISE	001	780	880	910	1.3	66	0	0	0	0.0	0.00	0	0	0.0
83801	ATHOL	055	4573	6482	7493	3.8	93	1662	2391	2768	4.0	2.71	1269	1798	3.8
83802	AVERY	079	105	99	96	-0.6	5	46	45	44	-0.2	2.16	30	29	-0.4
83803	BAYVIEW	055	325	423	496	2.9	89	168	224	262	3.2	1.89	108	141	2.9
83804	BLANCHARD	017	1065	1363	1483	2.7	88	416	545	599	3.0	2.50	307	396	2.8
83805	BONNERS FERRY	021	5947	6735	7181	1.4	68	2241	2640	2851	1.8	2.50	1608	1868	1.6
83809	CAREYWOOD	017	568	690	750	2.1	82	217	271	297	2.4	2.55	168	206	2.2
83810	CATALDO	055	1394	1556	1649	1.2	64	554	631	671	1.4	2.45	410	456	1.2
83811	CLARK FORK	017	1175	1365	1460	1.6	73	494	588	634	1.9	2.32	329	385	1.7
83812	CLARKIA	079	103	97	94	-0.6	5	38	37	36	-0.3	2.59	25	24	-0.4
83813	COCOLALLA	017	1013	1147	1224	1.4	68	389	456	491	1.7	2.52	295	340	1.5
83814	COEUR D ALENE	055	22409	25527	27290	1.4	68	9239	10548	11287	1.4	2.33	5679	6362	1.2
83815	COEUR D ALENE	055	22044	30066	34264	3.4	91	8609	11884	13586	3.5	2.50	6077	8236	3.3
83821	COOLIN	017	197	160	150	-2.2	0	97	81	77	-1.9	1.95	62	51	-2.1
83822	OLDTOWN	017	2215	2617	2822	1.8	75	842	1014	1099	2.0	2.58	594	703	1.8
83823	DEARY	057	1635	1666	1675	0.2	25	632	655	661	0.4	2.54	472	484	0.3
83824	DESMET	009	258	272	278	0.6	40	88	94	97	0.7	2.88	66	70	0.6
83827	ELK RIVER	035	137	133	131	-0.3	11	62	62	61	0.0	2.15	47	47	0.0
83830	FERNWOOD	009	443	458	469	0.4	33	175	188	194	0.8	2.44	126	133	0.6
83832	GENESEE	057	1455	1496	1500	0.3	28	551	574	577	0.4	2.61	421	433	0.3
83833	HARRISON	055	1499	1558	1623	0.4	33	646	682	712	0.6	2.28	460	474	0.3
83834	HARVARD	057	148	160	165	0.8	49	61	68	70	1.2	2.35	47	52	1.1
83835	HAYDEN	055	15599	21464	24611	3.5	92	5791	8036	9225	3.6	2.66	4505	6148	3.4
83836	HOPE	017	1090	1194	1257	1.0	58	479	534	565	1.2	2.24	346	380	1.0
83837	KELLOGG	079	4421	4219	4094	-0.5	8	1927	1880	1839	-0.3	2.20	1192	1142	-0.5
83839	KINGSTON	079	1013	972	946	-0.4	10	411	411	405	0.0	2.36	293	290	-0.1
83842	MEDIMONT	055	84	92	97	1.0	58	35	39	41	1.2	2.33	26	28	0.8
83843	MOSCOW	057	24862	26090	26423	0.5	36	9125	9697	9903	0.7	2.24	4856	5046	0.4
83845	MOYIE SPRINGS	021	2179	2505	2683	1.5	71	820	971	1051	1.8	2.57	608	711	1.7
83846	MULLAN	079	926	867	833	-0.7	3	399	385	374	-0.4	2.25	254	240	-0.6
83847	NAPLES	021	1645	1865	1997	1.4	68	608	724	785	1.9	2.48	451	531	1.8
83848	NORDMAN	017	266	233	223	-1.4	1	133	120	116	-1.1	1.84	84	74	-1.4
83850	PINEHURST	079	2143	2033	1970	-0.6	5	919	910	891	-0.1	2.23	645	630	-0.3
83851	PLUMMER	009	1573	1700	1754	0.8	49	543	600	624	1.1	2.82	416	451	0.9
83852	PONDERAY	017	622	695	737	1.2	64	258	300	322	1.6	2.21	174	199	1.5
83853	PORTHILL	021	100	112	119	1.2	64	38	44	47	1.6	2.55	31	36	1.6
83854	POST FALLS	055	27073	35627	40501	3.0	90	9889	13163	14988	3.1	2.70	7373	9590	2.9
83855	POTLATCH	057	2118	2131	2135	0.1	22	838	858	864	0.3	2.48	591	597	0.1
83856	PRIEST RIVER	017	6354	6833	7149	0.8	49	2490	2745	2893	1.1	2.49	1778	1926	0.9
83857	PRINCETON	057	863	935	962	0.9	53	320	354	368	1.1	2.64	249	272	1.0
83858	RATHDRUM	055	10346	14706	16903	3.9	94	3536	5070	5820	4.0	2.89	2848	4015	3.8
83860	SAGLE	017	5137	6238	6767	2.1	82	1992	2477	2709	2.4	2.52	1510	1850	2.2
83861	SAINT MARIES	009	6759	6861	6942	0.2	25	2722	2852	2912	0.5	2.36	1886	1947	0.3
83864	SANDPOINT	017	15870	17575	18625	1.1	61	6421	7327	7825	1.4	2.36	4267	4798	1.3
83868	SMELTERVILLE	079	263	253	247	-0.4	10	112	111	110	-0.1	2.28	68	66	-0.3
83869	SPIRIT LAKE	055	3204	3983	4500	2.4	86	1149	1409	1591	2.2	2.82	884	1064	2.0
83870	TENSED	009	464	489	499	0.6	40	176	188	193	0.7	2.59	132	139	0.6
83871	TROY	057	1808	1811	1794	0.0	18	702	719	718	0.3	2.52	522	529	0.1
83872	VIOLA	057	617	655	671	0.6	40	243	264	272	0.9	2.48	186	199	0.7
83873	WALLACE	079	4560	4377	4248	-0.4	10	1959	1937	1895	-0.1	2.20	1282	1247	-0.3
83876	WORLEY	055	1303	1547	1706	1.9	77	462	549	607	1.9	2.82	355	412	1.6
	IDAHO					2.1					2.2	2.65			2.1
	UNITED STATES					1.0					1.1	2.59			0.9

POPULATION COMPOSITION

ZIP CODE #	POST OFFICE NAME	RACE (%) White 2000	White 2009	Black 2000	Black 2009	Asian/Pacific 2000	Asian/Pacific 2009	% Hispanic Origin 2000	% Hispanic Origin 2009	2009 AGE DISTRIBUTION (%) 0-4	5-9	10-14	15-19	20-24	25-44	45-64	65-84	85+	18+	MEDIAN AGE 2009	% 2009 Males	% 2009 Females
83704	BOISE	92.1	90.2	0.7	0.9	2.4	3.2	4.5	5.7	6.8	6.3	6.4	7.2	7.7	28.5	24.6	9.9	2.6	76.2	34.7	49.1	50.9
83705	BOISE	90.7	88.7	0.9	1.3	1.9	2.4	6.3	7.9	7.2	6.4	5.9	6.2	8.3	31.5	22.4	9.6	2.6	77.0	33.8	49.4	50.6
83706	BOISE	91.4	89.6	1.0	1.4	2.5	3.2	4.6	5.6	5.9	5.0	4.7	7.7	12.1	30.7	24.3	7.9	1.8	81.0	32.5	50.0	50.0
83709	BOISE	92.9	91.6	0.5	0.6	2.5	3.1	4.0	4.9	7.0	7.1	7.4	7.2	5.6	27.8	27.9	8.9	1.1	73.9	36.5	49.4	50.6
83712	BOISE	94.3	93.2	0.6	0.9	1.7	2.2	2.7	3.5	5.0	5.2	5.5	5.5	5.3	30.3	30.8	10.4	2.1	80.7	40.5	48.0	52.0
83713	BOISE	92.7	91.1	0.7	0.9	2.6	3.5	3.7	4.6	9.1	8.9	8.6	7.5	5.1	29.9	24.3	6.0	0.7	68.4	33.0	49.4	50.6
83714	GARDEN CITY	91.4	90.3	0.4	0.6	1.3	1.7	7.4	8.7	8.0	7.6	7.1	6.3	5.9	29.8	24.8	9.3	1.3	73.5	35.2	50.0	50.0
83716	BOISE	92.0	90.5	1.0	1.4	2.7	3.3	3.9	4.9	9.1	8.7	8.4	6.7	4.6	32.5	24.3	5.4	0.4	69.6	34.2	50.8	49.2
83725	BOISE	84.5	81.3	1.9	2.5	4.1	5.2	7.9	10.0	4.7	1.9	1.3	31.6	36.8	17.2	4.9	1.3	0.5	91.1	21.4	48.3	51.7
83801	ATHOL	96.2	95.9	0.1	0.1	0.2	0.2	1.9	2.3	5.6	5.8	6.3	7.0	5.7	23.7	32.3	12.6	1.1	77.9	42.2	51.1	48.9
83802	AVERY	94.3	91.9	0.0	0.0	1.9	3.0	1.0	2.0	5.1	6.1	6.1	6.1	4.0	20.2	33.3	18.2	1.0	78.8	46.6	54.5	45.5
83803	BAYVIEW	95.7	95.0	0.3	0.2	0.0	0.5	1.2	1.7	2.8	3.3	3.3	4.0	3.3	13.7	37.6	29.3	2.6	88.2	57.6	52.0	48.0
83804	BLANCHARD	95.8	95.5	0.0	0.0	0.0	0.0	0.9	1.2	4.3	4.8	8.3	8.0	3.8	21.3	37.0	11.7	0.8	77.3	44.6	52.6	47.4
83805	BONNERS FERRY	94.6	93.9	0.2	0.2	0.7	0.9	3.6	4.3	6.7	6.9	7.0	6.6	6.0	22.3	29.3	13.0	2.1	74.9	39.9	49.8	50.2
83809	CAREYWOOD	95.6	95.4	0.0	0.0	0.2	0.3	2.1	2.5	4.9	5.4	7.5	6.2	3.2	22.3	39.3	10.6	0.6	77.7	45.2	51.3	48.7
83810	CATALDO	96.4	96.0	0.2	0.3	0.4	0.4	1.3	1.5	5.0	4.4	6.8	7.3	3.8	21.1	36.4	13.2	1.9	78.8	45.7	52.1	47.9
83811	CLARK FORK	95.5	95.0	0.3	0.5	0.3	0.3	1.3	1.7	4.2	4.8	5.5	6.0	3.7	18.5	38.8	16.8	1.8	81.5	49.9	50.3	49.7
83812	CLARKIA	94.2	91.8	0.0	0.0	1.9	3.1	1.0	2.1	5.2	6.2	6.2	6.2	4.1	20.6	33.0	17.5	1.0	77.3	45.9	54.6	45.4
83813	COCOLALLA	96.4	96.3	0.1	0.1	0.3	0.3	1.5	1.7	4.3	6.1	8.0	6.7	3.9	20.5	39.4	9.9	1.2	76.5	45.2	51.4	48.6
83814	COEUR D ALENE	95.9	95.4	0.2	0.3	0.6	0.8	2.5	3.0	6.1	5.8	5.8	6.6	7.1	26.8	26.8	12.0	2.8	78.5	38.0	49.4	50.6
83815	COEUR D ALENE	96.4	95.9	0.2	0.2	0.6	0.8	2.5	3.1	6.6	6.7	6.9	6.9	5.3	25.2	27.5	12.4	2.5	75.7	39.3	48.6	51.4
83821	COOLIN	96.9	97.5	0.0	0.0	0.0	0.0	1.0	0.6	2.5	5.6	3.8	5.0	3.1	18.8	44.4	16.3	0.6	84.4	51.7	53.8	46.2
83822	OLDTOWN	96.3	95.7	0.1	0.2	0.3	0.4	1.4	1.7	6.5	6.8	6.8	6.0	5.5	21.9	31.3	13.9	1.2	76.1	41.9	50.1	49.9
83823	DEARY	96.1	95.7	0.0	0.0	0.6	0.7	2.0	2.4	5.8	7.0	8.3	6.5	3.5	23.9	31.6	12.1	1.3	75.0	41.2	51.3	48.7
83824	DESMET	62.8	61.4	0.0	0.0	0.4	0.4	3.1	3.3	8.5	8.1	8.5	7.0	5.1	20.6	27.6	13.2	1.5	69.1	38.8	49.6	50.4
83827	ELK RIVER	97.1	97.0	0.0	0.0	0.0	0.0	0.7	0.8	3.8	4.5	4.5	3.8	3.8	12.8	40.6	24.8	1.5	83.5	55.7	55.6	44.4
83830	FERNWOOD	96.8	96.5	0.0	0.0	0.2	0.4	0.7	0.7	5.0	5.5	6.1	6.6	5.0	20.3	34.1	16.2	1.3	79.5	45.9	51.1	48.9
83832	GENESEE	96.7	96.4	0.1	0.1	0.6	0.8	0.9	1.0	7.4	7.6	8.1	7.4	4.9	24.9	28.3	10.1	1.2	72.3	38.7	51.7	48.3
83833	HARRISON	95.2	94.8	0.1	0.1	0.6	0.8	1.3	1.5	4.0	4.9	5.8	5.4	2.7	16.8	37.0	21.9	1.5	81.8	52.1	52.2	47.8
83834	HARVARD	97.3	96.9	0.0	0.6	0.7	0.6	2.0	2.5	5.0	5.6	5.6	6.3	5.6	23.1	33.8	13.8	1.3	80.6	43.8	50.6	49.4
83835	HAYDEN	96.9	96.3	0.1	0.2	0.6	0.7	2.1	2.4	6.2	6.7	7.3	7.2	5.1	24.5	30.1	11.5	1.5	75.2	40.1	49.8	50.2
83836	HOPE	97.6	97.2	0.5	0.6	0.4	0.5	2.0	2.5	3.5	4.1	4.9	5.4	3.5	16.2	41.3	18.8	2.3	84.2	52.5	50.0	50.0
83837	KELLOGG	95.3	94.5	0.1	0.1	0.4	0.5	1.9	2.3	6.2	5.8	6.1	6.6	5.6	22.8	28.5	15.4	3.1	77.8	42.4	49.1	50.9
83839	KINGSTON	96.2	95.5	0.1	0.2	0.2	0.3	1.5	1.9	4.8	5.1	5.8	5.6	3.9	20.0	36.4	16.7	1.7	80.7	47.7	51.9	48.1
83842	MEDIMONT	92.9	93.5	0.0	0.0	1.2	1.1	1.2	2.2	5.4	4.3	7.6	7.6	2.2	19.6	39.1	12.0	2.2	77.2	46.5	50.0	50.0
83843	MOSCOW	92.8	91.6	0.8	1.0	2.9	3.6	2.3	2.8	5.1	4.2	4.0	13.1	21.6	25.8	18.1	6.4	1.8	84.0	26.0	52.3	47.7
83845	MOYIE SPRINGS	97.3	97.0	0.0	0.1	0.4	0.6	1.4	1.7	6.0	6.4	7.5	7.8	5.2	22.4	32.9	11.0	0.7	74.9	41.1	49.9	50.1
83846	MULLAN	96.3	95.6	0.0	0.0	0.3	0.5	2.7	3.3	4.5	4.6	5.1	6.7	6.1	21.8	31.8	16.4	3.0	81.9	45.8	50.6	49.4
83847	NAPLES	94.8	94.0	0.2	0.2	0.7	0.9	5.4	6.4	7.2	7.7	7.8	6.9	5.7	22.5	30.0	11.2	1.0	72.8	38.0	52.5	47.5
83848	NORDMAN	97.4	97.0	0.4	0.4	0.0	0.0	1.5	1.3	1.7	2.1	2.1	3.4	3.0	16.3	45.9	23.6	1.7	91.8	55.2	52.8	47.2
83850	PINEHURST	96.7	96.1	0.0	0.1	0.2	0.3	1.5	1.8	5.9	6.1	6.1	5.9	4.3	21.9	30.6	16.9	2.3	78.5	44.8	48.6	51.4
83851	PLUMMER	68.5	67.4	0.5	0.7	0.3	0.4	2.5	2.8	8.5	8.8	8.5	7.4	5.2	24.8	24.7	11.0	1.1	69.5	34.0	49.7	50.3
83852	PONDERAY	97.1	96.8	0.2	0.1	0.5	0.6	1.4	1.7	6.8	7.2	7.2	6.0	5.3	25.3	29.8	10.8	1.6	75.0	38.9	50.4	49.6
83853	PORTHILL	96.0	96.4	0.0	0.0	1.0	0.9	2.0	1.8	7.1	7.1	8.0	8.0	3.6	21.4	31.3	11.6	1.8	72.3	40.0	48.2	51.8
83854	POST FALLS	96.2	95.7	0.2	0.2	0.6	0.7	2.3	2.8	8.3	8.1	8.0	7.3	5.4	28.6	24.8	8.6	1.1	71.0	34.5	49.6	50.4
83855	POTLATCH	96.6	95.9	0.0	0.1	0.3	0.4	2.5	3.1	5.9	5.9	6.3	7.6	5.9	24.2	29.7	12.5	2.0	77.2	40.8	50.2	49.8
83856	PRIEST RIVER	96.5	96.2	0.0	0.0	0.2	0.2	1.3	1.6	5.9	6.2	7.3	6.8	4.7	21.9	34.0	12.1	1.1	76.1	42.8	50.8	49.2
83857	PRINCETON	97.8	97.4	0.3	0.4	0.5	0.6	1.7	2.1	4.9	5.5	6.0	6.2	5.2	22.7	34.8	12.9	1.8	79.8	44.5	51.1	48.9
83858	RATHDRUM	96.1	95.6	0.2	0.2	0.4	0.5	2.6	3.1	7.5	7.5	7.8	7.7	5.9	26.7	28.1	8.2	0.7	72.4	36.1	50.5	49.5
83860	SAGLE	97.1	96.9	0.1	0.1	0.5	0.6	1.6	2.0	4.9	6.0	7.6	7.3	4.1	20.9	36.1	12.0	1.2	76.2	44.5	50.0	50.0
83861	SAINT MARIES	95.7	95.4	0.0	0.0	0.2	0.3	1.3	1.5	5.5	6.0	6.7	6.9	4.4	22.1	31.9	14.2	2.1	77.1	43.7	51.7	48.3
83864	SANDPOINT	96.6	96.3	0.1	0.2	0.4	0.5	1.9	2.2	5.7	5.9	6.6	6.8	5.6	22.4	33.3	11.4	2.1	77.4	42.7	49.4	50.6
83868	SMELTERVILLE	96.6	96.4	0.0	0.0	0.4	0.4	1.5	2.0	6.3	6.3	6.3	5.9	4.3	22.9	28.5	16.6	2.8	77.5	43.4	49.4	50.6
83869	SPIRIT LAKE	96.1	95.6	0.1	0.2	0.3	0.5	2.0	2.4	6.2	6.1	7.0	7.4	5.2	24.4	32.4	10.6	0.8	75.9	41.0	50.4	49.6
83870	TENSED	62.9	61.3	0.0	0.0	0.2	0.2	3.0	3.3	8.6	7.2	8.6	7.0	5.3	20.2	27.8	13.7	1.6	70.1	39.4	50.5	49.5
83871	TROY	97.0	96.7	0.1	0.1	0.4	0.5	0.9	1.0	6.2	7.0	7.6	7.2	4.0	24.3	30.8	11.7	1.3	74.6	41.2	51.4	48.6
83872	VIOLA	95.3	95.0	0.0	0.0	0.5	0.6	3.1	3.7	5.5	5.8	7.2	7.8	4.3	22.3	34.8	11.0	1.4	76.5	42.9	51.3	48.7
83873	WALLACE	95.8	95.2	0.2	0.2	0.2	0.2	2.2	2.6	4.7	4.9	5.3	5.7	5.9	19.9	33.6	17.3	2.7	81.2	47.2	49.9	50.1
83876	WORLEY	63.8	62.8	0.2	0.3	0.4	0.5	1.5	1.7	7.8	7.8	7.9	7.0	4.5	22.0	28.3	13.4	1.2	72.0	39.3	50.6	49.4
	IDAHO	91.0	89.5	0.4	0.5	1.0	1.3	7.9	9.5	7.7	7.4	7.3	7.7	7.0	26.7	25.0	9.6	1.6	73.1	34.4	50.1	49.9
	UNITED STATES	75.1	72.0	12.3	12.7	3.8	4.6	12.5	15.7	6.8	6.7	6.6	7.1	6.9	27.0	26.0	10.9	1.9	75.7	36.9	49.2	50.8

INCOME

ZIP CODE #	POST OFFICE NAME	2009 Per Capita Income	2009 HH Income Base	2009 Household Income Distribution (%): Less than $25,000	$25,000 to $49,999	$50,000 to $99,999	$100,000 to $149,999	$150,000 or More	Median Household Income: 2009	2014	2009 National Centile	2009 State Centile	2009 Home Value Base	2009 Home Value Distribution (%): Less than $50,000	$50,000 to $89,999	$90,000 to $174,999	$175,000 to $399,999	$400,000 or More	2009 Median Home Value
83704	BOISE	26208	16469	14.7	28.8	43.1	9.4	4.0	55409	57986	72	92	10809	7.1	6.5	35.8	47.3	3.3	176138
83705	BOISE	25030	12525	20.9	31.7	39.2	5.8	2.6	47943	50934	56	78	7002	3.9	3.8	58.0	31.5	2.7	154229
83706	BOISE	32254	14024	19.3	30.5	33.6	8.9	7.8	50232	53672	62	84	7474	4.5	1.8	34.8	46.6	12.3	199925
83709	BOISE	28874	17146	8.9	21.2	47.1	16.2	6.6	70296	75268	87	97	14276	1.9	1.5	28.9	61.9	5.8	209648
83712	BOISE	39113	3888	17.0	22.4	33.9	14.4	12.3	63079	67121	81	95	2393	0.0	0.9	11.1	67.3	20.7	285192
83713	BOISE	32221	9747	8.7	17.1	46.4	16.6	11.2	74395	77193	89	99	7770	6.0	5.8	20.5	57.4	10.4	215970
83714	GARDEN CITY	31673	8667	13.1	25.5	40.1	13.4	7.9	60924	63833	79	93	6108	13.1	9.8	24.3	42.7	10.1	181884
83716	BOISE	34692	5444	6.9	15.7	45.2	21.1	11.1	77557	79832	91	100	4486	8.3	6.0	25.1	51.3	9.4	194408
83725	BOISE	7215	0	0.0	0.0	0.0	0.0	0.0	0	0	0	0	0	0.0	0.0	0.0	0.0	0.0	0
83801	ATHOL	19150	2391	25.7	32.4	35.0	4.5	2.5	43389	47148	44	61	2028	9.0	9.7	29.7	41.3	10.2	180000
83802	AVERY	19242	45	33.3	37.8	22.2	6.7	0.0	35743	35000	20	15	30	26.7	16.7	20.0	33.3	3.3	125000
83803	BAYVIEW	30872	224	27.2	23.2	39.7	6.7	3.1	49629	52759	60	83	181	13.3	5.0	23.8	38.1	19.9	208333
83804	BLANCHARD	16238	545	32.1	33.8	31.6	1.5	1.1	37463	38821	25	22	465	6.5	19.1	40.9	30.5	3.0	141211
83805	BONNERS FERRY	18348	2640	34.0	32.5	28.4	3.1	2.0	34921	36644	17	10	1995	9.4	5.4	40.3	35.5	9.5	165030
83809	CAREYWOOD	22239	271	22.5	35.1	34.7	3.3	4.4	44385	46393	46	64	230	0.0	3.9	35.2	40.0	20.9	220000
83810	CATALDO	19378	631	27.1	30.4	35.7	6.5	0.3	42369	46991	41	55	527	12.3	10.4	33.4	25.4	18.4	155183
83811	CLARK FORK	17936	588	37.6	27.6	30.3	2.6	2.0	32174	35701	12	5	456	10.3	16.4	37.7	26.3	9.2	128431
83812	CLARKIA	16269	37	35.1	35.1	24.3	5.4	0.0	35733	36502	20	14	25	16.0	16.0	36.0	32.0	0.0	117500
83813	COCOLALLA	19694	456	24.1	31.8	38.8	3.7	1.5	44459	48531	47	65	385	3.6	4.9	32.5	46.5	12.5	202232
83814	COEUR D ALENE	23491	10548	26.2	31.0	34.0	5.2	3.7	44467	48362	47	65	6457	2.4	2.6	36.0	42.3	16.7	198186
83815	COEUR D ALENE	23446	11884	21.3	29.9	37.3	7.5	4.0	48946	51943	59	81	8653	6.8	9.1	19.8	55.4	8.9	204347
83821	COOLIN	28488	81	28.4	27.2	34.6	4.9	4.9	42997	46177	42	58	65	0.0	9.2	33.8	44.6	12.3	202778
83822	OLDTOWN	15408	1014	35.3	36.7	24.1	3.6	0.4	35000	36062	18	12	828	14.9	9.4	38.0	30.6	7.1	142241
83823	DEARY	20697	655	22.6	32.1	36.3	7.8	1.2	45901	48866	51	71	526	17.3	18.3	28.9	27.6	8.0	128804
83824	DESMET	14095	94	34.0	35.1	26.6	3.2	1.1	33850	34132	15	8	69	13.0	14.5	37.7	21.7	13.0	133750
83827	ELK RIVER	18654	62	29.0	50.0	19.4	1.6	0.0	35000	38593	18	12	51	15.7	13.7	33.3	33.3	3.9	140278
83830	FERNWOOD	17507	188	30.9	32.4	34.6	1.1	1.1	34440	36378	16	8	159	23.3	17.0	34.0	23.9	1.9	113125
83832	GENESEE	24300	574	17.9	28.7	43.2	5.7	4.4	51966	52689	66	90	452	12.2	8.2	38.1	36.7	4.9	157075
83833	HARRISON	22737	682	20.5	36.1	36.2	4.4	2.8	45444	48989	50	69	576	5.9	6.1	15.3	38.2	34.5	309184
83834	HARVARD	17953	68	29.4	32.4	36.8	1.5	0.0	39057	42843	30	32	57	14.0	12.3	42.1	31.6	0.0	130357
83835	HAYDEN	23417	8036	20.0	28.9	38.8	8.0	4.4	50854	53233	63	86	6590	5.8	3.7	17.3	57.8	15.3	227295
83836	HOPE	22803	534	34.1	29.4	26.8	5.4	4.3	39158	40509	30	33	443	1.8	4.7	24.8	43.8	24.8	262981
83837	KELLOGG	20877	1880	33.5	30.5	30.9	3.5	1.6	36591	37856	22	19	1222	15.4	21.8	51.9	9.6	1.4	107748
83839	KINGSTON	19601	411	30.9	28.7	34.5	4.1	1.7	39452	43290	31	37	333	15.3	15.6	47.7	18.9	2.4	124167
83842	MEDIMONT	19862	39	25.6	30.8	38.5	5.1	0.0	45745	50341	51	70	33	15.2	15.2	18.2	33.3	18.2	181250
83843	MOSCOW	23150	9697	31.2	26.2	30.9	8.3	3.5	41595	45117	38	50	4838	14.0	4.1	20.8	53.9	7.2	202543
83845	MOYIE SPRINGS	19458	971	25.0	32.4	38.3	2.4	1.9	42770	45505	42	57	806	7.3	5.6	37.3	40.7	9.1	174490
83846	MULLAN	21736	385	25.2	31.4	37.4	5.7	0.3	43792	48238	45	62	298	16.1	30.2	49.0	4.4	0.3	95000
83847	NAPLES	19169	724	26.1	33.6	36.0	3.5	0.8	41934	44208	39	52	590	10.0	5.8	35.6	39.0	9.7	172674
83848	NORDMAN	30223	120	30.8	28.3	30.8	6.7	3.3	37602	39371	26	23	99	4.0	5.1	26.3	42.4	22.2	260714
83850	PINEHURST	20617	910	33.6	27.0	33.1	4.6	1.6	38115	40793	27	27	703	11.2	15.5	56.0	16.6	0.6	119750
83851	PLUMMER	14982	600	31.3	33.8	31.3	2.7	0.8	35000	36854	18	12	449	14.7	18.7	38.5	20.5	7.6	120772
83852	PONDERAY	19381	300	31.3	34.7	30.3	2.3	1.3	35667	36883	20	14	224	8.9	9.4	40.6	34.4	6.7	152273
83853	PORTHILL	19464	44	31.8	27.3	34.1	2.3	4.5	45000	47354	48	67	37	8.1	2.7	35.1	29.7	24.3	193750
83854	POST FALLS	21364	13163	18.4	31.8	40.8	6.3	2.7	49808	52159	61	84	9987	9.2	7.5	27.2	47.7	8.4	186968
83855	POTLATCH	22141	858	20.9	30.8	40.8	5.6	2.0	48487	50471	58	80	650	17.2	14.0	37.4	27.5	3.8	121875
83856	PRIEST RIVER	17984	2745	30.7	32.9	32.2	3.0	1.2	39564	41033	31	39	2219	7.1	12.5	40.0	33.5	6.9	154877
83857	PRINCETON	18663	354	28.2	33.9	35.0	1.1	1.7	38997	42442	30	31	299	14.4	10.7	40.1	33.1	1.7	137500
83858	RATHDRUM	18584	5070	19.2	31.1	42.5	5.3	1.9	49701	52045	60	83	4194	6.2	5.9	33.6	45.5	8.8	185456
83860	SAGLE	19956	2477	27.1	29.8	34.5	7.3	1.3	44441	47202	47	64	2078	7.9	4.7	22.3	44.1	21.0	232414
83861	SAINT MARIES	20083	2852	29.3	32.5	31.8	4.9	1.6	40492	42182	34	45	2281	17.2	14.5	36.4	25.8	6.1	127696
83864	SANDPOINT	22353	7327	27.9	28.9	35.2	5.1	2.9	43764	46545	45	61	5281	5.6	5.8	35.2	41.7	11.7	185417
83868	SMELTERVILLE	19412	111	36.0	30.6	28.8	2.7	1.8	34679	35000	17	10	81	21.0	23.5	48.1	7.4	0.0	97500
83869	SPIRIT LAKE	17474	1409	25.8	31.7	36.8	3.5	2.1	45462	48294	50	69	1168	5.6	9.6	30.0	45.4	9.5	194000
83870	TENSED	15670	188	35.6	35.1	26.1	2.7	0.5	33226	34852	14	7	139	14.4	15.1	37.4	20.9	12.2	129605
83871	TROY	23117	719	15.7	32.5	41.9	8.3	1.5	51568	52518	65	90	554	2.9	4.5	35.4	51.3	6.0	197727
83872	VIOLA	25235	264	14.0	26.9	49.2	8.0	1.9	61002	60484	79	94	221	13.1	0.9	27.6	50.7	7.7	197024
83873	WALLACE	20748	1937	30.8	34.3	28.3	4.8	1.8	36735	38076	23	20	1452	13.3	23.5	48.6	13.6	1.0	108750
83876	WORLEY	19984	549	27.1	27.7	34.8	7.3	3.1	46624	49290	53	73	417	5.5	5.0	24.2	35.0	30.2	262234
	IDAHO	23160		20.9	28.6	37.9	8.3	4.4	50374	53004				6.9	7.8	39.2	38.3	7.9	167282
	UNITED STATES	27277		20.9	24.4	35.3	11.7	7.6	54719	56938				9.3	13.1	31.6	32.6	13.5	162279

ZIP CODE		FINANCIAL SERVICES				THE HOME						ENTERTAINMENT						PERSONAL			
						Home Improvements		Furnishings													
#	POST OFFICE NAME	Auto Loan	Home Loan	Invest-ments	Retire-ment Plans	Home Repair	Lawn & Garden	Comput-ers & Hard-ware-Personal	Major Appli-ances	TV, Radio, Sound Equip-ment	Furni-ture	Dine out/ Carry out	Sports Equip-ment	Fees & Tickets	Toys & Games	Travel	Cable TV	Apparel & Services	Auto Repairs	Health Insur-ance	Pets & Supplies
83704	BOISE	94	92	84	93	89	88	95	90	93	96	94	71	94	95	92	92	66	93	90	107
83705	BOISE	81	74	68	75	72	74	82	76	82	80	82	60	78	83	77	82	57	80	79	92
83706	BOISE	103	89	82	92	86	86	108	92	103	103	104	76	98	105	95	101	73	100	92	112
83709	BOISE	115	123	110	122	119	113	113	114	110	118	111	88	116	113	114	107	77	111	108	133
83712	BOISE	114	122	121	127	122	115	122	115	118	124	120	92	128	119	124	116	86	119	114	137
83713	BOISE	134	146	125	145	141	129	129	131	125	139	126	103	135	132	130	120	89	125	119	151
83714	GARDEN CITY	116	118	101	115	112	104	112	109	108	118	109	86	112	114	109	104	76	108	100	127
83716	BOISE	138	152	131	148	145	132	134	137	128	143	130	107	139	135	136	123	91	129	123	156
83725	BOISE	0	0	0	0	0	0	0	0	0	0	0	0	0	0	0	0	0	0	0	0
83801	ATHOL	83	75	75	72	75	81	71	79	75	74	74	56	67	76	70	78	50	75	81	93
83802	AVERY	74	53	76	52	55	76	55	70	61	51	60	52	44	60	54	67	39	64	72	83
83803	BAYVIEW	85	82	104	75	91	97	78	92	82	84	80	60	77	75	85	87	54	88	102	105
83804	BLANCHARD	73	52	74	50	54	74	53	68	59	50	58	51	43	59	53	65	38	62	71	81
83805	BONNERS FERRY	79	58	77	57	59	79	62	73	67	57	66	56	50	67	60	73	44	70	78	88
83809	CAREYWOOD	94	76	122	74	83	100	76	96	79	71	78	70	66	75	82	84	52	89	95	111
83810	CATALDO	80	63	100	62	69	84	63	80	67	59	66	59	54	64	68	72	44	74	80	94
83811	CLARK FORK	69	56	90	55	61	73	56	71	58	52	57	52	48	55	60	62	38	65	70	82
83812	CLARKIA	75	54	77	52	56	76	55	70	61	51	60	53	44	61	54	67	40	64	73	83
83813	COCOLALLA	83	66	107	65	73	87	66	84	69	62	68	61	57	66	72	74	45	78	83	97
83814	COEUR D ALENE	78	74	71	76	74	76	80	76	80	78	79	59	77	80	77	80	55	79	79	91
83815	COEUR D ALENE	86	84	80	84	84	86	82	84	84	83	84	63	81	84	81	86	58	83	87	100
83821	COOLIN	93	75	120	73	82	99	75	95	78	70	77	69	65	74	81	83	51	88	94	110
83822	OLDTOWN	71	51	73	49	53	72	52	66	58	49	57	50	42	58	52	64	38	61	69	79
83823	DEARY	88	71	85	71	73	91	71	85	76	65	75	64	62	77	71	82	50	78	88	100
83824	DESMET	72	52	74	50	54	73	53	68	59	50	58	51	43	59	53	65	38	62	70	80
83827	ELK RIVER	67	53	86	53	59	71	53	68	56	50	55	50	46	53	58	60	37	63	67	79
83830	FERNWOOD	76	55	78	53	57	77	56	71	62	52	61	53	45	62	55	68	40	65	74	85
83832	GENESEE	102	92	85	89	91	97	88	94	91	91	91	69	82	95	84	94	62	91	95	112
83833	HARRISON	87	69	111	68	76	91	69	88	73	65	72	64	60	69	75	77	48	81	87	102
83834	HARVARD	75	54	77	52	56	77	55	71	62	52	60	53	44	61	55	68	40	65	73	84
83835	HAYDEN	95	94	88	93	94	96	86	92	88	90	88	67	87	90	87	90	61	89	92	108
83836	HOPE	85	68	110	67	75	90	68	87	71	64	70	63	59	68	74	76	47	80	85	100
83837	KELLOGG	73	57	73	56	59	76	62	72	68	58	66	53	53	66	60	74	45	69	79	85
83839	KINGSTON	80	60	85	58	64	83	61	77	67	59	66	56	51	66	62	73	44	71	81	90
83842	MEDIMONT	77	62	100	61	68	82	62	79	65	58	64	58	54	62	67	69	43	73	78	91
83843	MOSCOW	79	63	59	66	61	63	91	69	82	78	83	60	75	83	72	80	59	78	69	85
83845	MOYIE SPRINGS	81	71	83	70	73	81	69	78	71	68	71	57	63	71	69	74	48	74	78	92
83846	MULLAN	83	60	83	58	62	86	65	80	73	58	70	60	52	71	63	80	47	75	88	94
83847	NAPLES	76	69	67	68	68	76	66	72	69	66	68	55	62	71	64	71	47	69	73	86
83848	NORDMAN	95	76	122	75	83	100	76	96	79	71	78	70	66	75	82	85	52	89	95	112
83850	PINEHURST	76	60	78	59	62	81	61	74	67	57	66	55	53	66	61	73	44	69	80	87
83851	PLUMMER	73	57	69	55	58	72	57	68	61	55	61	50	48	62	55	66	40	63	69	80
83852	PONDERAY	74	58	71	56	59	73	58	69	62	56	62	51	49	63	56	67	41	64	71	82
83853	PORTHILL	89	61	97	61	64	93	68	84	70	55	70	70	50	69	67	77	45	79	89	103
83854	POST FALLS	90	87	78	85	84	84	82	85	82	85	82	64	79	85	79	82	57	82	82	99
83855	POTLATCH	89	73	86	73	74	94	75	88	80	68	78	66	65	80	74	86	53	82	93	103
83856	PRIEST RIVER	77	60	81	58	62	77	60	73	64	57	64	54	51	64	60	69	42	68	74	86
83857	PRINCETON	88	63	90	61	65	89	65	82	72	60	71	62	52	71	64	79	47	76	86	98
83858	RATHDRUM	85	79	73	77	78	82	75	80	77	77	77	59	71	80	73	79	53	77	80	95
83860	SAGLE	79	71	91	71	74	85	68	81	70	65	70	60	64	69	73	74	47	75	81	94
83861	SAINT MARIES	81	62	85	61	65	84	63	78	69	58	67	59	53	68	64	75	45	72	81	92
83864	SANDPOINT	83	71	87	71	73	84	74	81	76	70	75	61	67	75	73	80	51	79	83	96
83868	SMELTERVILLE	71	56	73	55	58	77	59	71	65	54	63	52	51	64	58	71	42	67	78	83
83869	SPIRIT LAKE	82	69	83	67	71	81	67	78	71	66	70	57	60	71	67	74	47	74	78	92
83870	TENSED	72	52	74	50	54	73	53	68	59	50	58	51	43	59	53	65	38	62	70	80
83871	TROY	82	90	80	93	88	91	82	86	80	81	81	67	86	82	86	81	56	82	85	101
83872	VIOLA	87	98	85	101	95	97	88	91	86	88	87	71	93	89	93	87	61	88	90	107
83873	WALLACE	71	59	74	58	62	76	62	71	67	59	65	51	56	65	62	72	44	68	78	83
83876	WORLEY	92	80	93	78	82	91	77	88	80	77	80	64	71	81	78	84	54	84	88	104
	IDAHO	94	87	87	87	86	92	88	90	88	86	88	70	83	90	85	90	61	89	91	107
	UNITED STATES	100	100	100	100	100	100	100	100	100	100	100	100	100	100	100	100	100	100	100	100

ZIP CODE #	POST OFFICE NAME	COUNTY FIPS CODE	POPULATION 2000	POPULATION 2009	POPULATION 2014	2000-2009 ANNUAL RATE % Rate	2000-2009 ANNUAL RATE State Centile	HOUSEHOLDS 2000	HOUSEHOLDS 2009	HOUSEHOLDS 2014	HOUSEHOLDS % Annual Rate 2000-2009	HOUSEHOLDS 2009 Average HH Size	FAMILIES 2000	FAMILIES 2009	FAMILIES % Annual Rate 2000-2009
60002	ANTIOCH	097	19539	25112	28053	2.7	94	7414	9413	10474	2.6	2.67	5365	6688	2.4
60004	ARLINGTON HEIGHTS	031	52384	51084	50390	-0.3	32	20191	19803	19525	-0.2	2.55	14178	13654	-0.4
60005	ARLINGTON HEIGHTS	031	29210	28989	28730	-0.1	45	12664	12634	12524	0.0	2.27	7743	7568	-0.2
60007	ELK GROVE VILLAGE	031	35531	34451	33851	-0.3	32	13556	13296	13071	-0.2	2.58	9467	9119	-0.4
60008	ROLLING MEADOWS	031	23426	23217	22902	-0.1	45	8492	8395	8270	-0.1	2.73	5821	5657	-0.3
60010	BARRINGTON	031	41144	43909	45132	0.7	78	14450	15380	15760	0.7	2.85	11884	12495	0.5
60012	CRYSTAL LAKE	111	9858	12537	13481	2.6	93	3183	4062	4381	2.7	3.06	2636	3284	2.4
60013	CARY	111	24032	29415	31961	2.2	92	7765	9411	10189	2.1	3.12	6351	7586	1.9
60014	CRYSTAL LAKE	111	44685	51047	54199	1.4	88	15206	17313	18326	1.4	2.94	11690	13054	1.2
60015	DEERFIELD	097	26367	26947	27209	0.2	61	8903	9099	9172	0.2	2.87	7162	7203	0.1
60016	DES PLAINES	031	58539	59542	59337	0.2	61	23479	23950	23874	0.2	2.46	15038	14848	-0.1
60018	DES PLAINES	031	29738	30554	30715	0.3	65	10326	10472	10496	0.2	2.86	7232	7219	0.0
60020	FOX LAKE	097	7219	10124	11127	3.7	96	3273	4399	4781	3.2	2.30	1906	2664	3.7
60021	FOX RIVER GROVE	111	5832	6278	6413	0.8	79	2035	2211	2266	0.9	2.83	1562	1659	0.7
60022	GLENCOE	031	8529	8164	7982	-0.5	18	2989	2859	2790	-0.5	2.86	2484	2351	-0.6
60025	GLENVIEW	031	39932	38917	38325	-0.3	32	15294	14916	14662	-0.3	2.57	11124	10667	-0.5
60026	GLENVIEW	031	10269	13561	14261	3.1	95	3488	4665	4915	3.2	2.84	2888	3850	3.2
60029	GOLF	031	67	65	64	-0.3	32	23	22	22	-0.5	2.95	19	18	-0.6
60030	GRAYSLAKE	097	31940	41392	44998	2.8	94	11433	14583	15813	2.7	2.84	8777	10955	2.4
60031	GURNEE	097	36146	40215	41708	1.2	85	13271	14371	14810	0.9	2.80	9809	10456	0.7
60033	HARVARD	111	13111	14747	15905	1.3	87	4394	4898	5278	1.2	3.00	3300	3594	0.9
60034	HEBRON	111	1914	2424	2811	2.6	93	702	900	1046	2.7	2.69	520	636	2.2
60035	HIGHLAND PARK	097	30805	30829	31209	0.0	50	11376	11513	11609	0.1	2.66	8797	8730	-0.1
60037	FORT SHERIDAN	097	849	1202	1311	3.8	96	225	324	352	4.0	3.71	200	284	3.9
60040	HIGHWOOD	097	4082	6116	6382	4.5	98	1535	1885	1936	2.2	3.20	921	1109	2.0
60041	INGLESIDE	097	8714	9093	9537	0.5	72	3166	3320	3479	0.5	2.74	2339	2406	0.3
60042	ISLAND LAKE	111	8684	9054	9183	0.5	72	3020	3154	3196	0.5	2.86	2273	2313	0.2
60043	KENILWORTH	031	2610	2523	2476	-0.4	25	830	799	782	-0.4	3.16	722	689	-0.5
60044	LAKE BLUFF	097	10853	10916	11048	0.1	56	4332	4318	4349	0.0	2.49	2977	2898	-0.3
60045	LAKE FOREST	097	21853	22620	23095	0.4	69	7276	7488	7623	0.3	2.83	5821	5931	0.2
60046	LAKE VILLA	097	29800	34005	36012	1.4	88	10208	11510	12125	1.3	2.93	8157	9065	1.1
60047	LAKE ZURICH	097	36733	43672	46588	1.9	91	11429	13544	14421	1.9	3.19	9921	11609	1.7
60048	LIBERTYVILLE	097	29344	31004	31820	0.6	75	10039	10638	10893	0.6	2.85	7634	7978	0.5
60050	MCHENRY	111	26529	33596	37044	2.6	93	9672	12247	13497	2.6	2.72	6962	8707	2.4
60051	MCHENRY	111	21304	29357	32928	3.5	96	7488	10381	11657	3.6	2.83	5834	7877	3.3
60053	MORTON GROVE	031	22099	22612	22549	0.2	61	7945	8209	8187	0.4	2.74	6177	6251	0.1
60056	MOUNT PROSPECT	031	56842	56684	56112	0.0	50	21701	21534	21264	-0.1	2.63	15217	14845	-0.3
60060	MUNDELEIN	097	36344	40122	42051	1.1	85	11632	12608	13148	0.9	3.17	9077	9693	0.7
60061	VERNON HILLS	097	20461	25014	26503	2.2	92	7654	9252	9804	2.1	2.70	5466	6548	2.0
60062	NORTHBROOK	031	40689	40588	40385	0.0	50	15128	15224	15163	0.1	2.60	11667	11564	-0.1
60064	NORTH CHICAGO	097	15080	15852	16064	0.5	72	4670	4796	4835	0.3	3.27	3348	3386	0.1
60067	PALATINE	031	36734	38159	38305	0.4	69	14514	15246	15321	0.5	2.47	9759	10072	0.3
60068	PARK RIDGE	031	37593	36488	35968	-0.3	32	14186	13852	13650	-0.3	2.60	10469	10058	-0.4
60069	LINCOLNSHIRE	097	7363	8554	9102	1.6	89	2627	3027	3211	1.5	2.80	2240	2554	1.4
60070	PROSPECT HEIGHTS	031	17188	16830	16603	-0.2	38	6468	6237	6122	-0.4	2.70	4044	3807	-0.7
60071	RICHMOND	111	3086	4451	5113	4.0	97	1101	1607	1847	4.2	2.77	845	1220	4.1
60072	RINGWOOD	111	563	824	924	4.2	97	202	289	325	3.9	2.85	172	243	3.8
60073	ROUND LAKE	097	39988	56807	62967	3.9	97	12072	17469	19453	4.1	3.24	9528	13507	3.8
60074	PALATINE	031	39067	39421	39068	0.1	56	14762	14666	14503	-0.1	2.68	9759	9505	-0.3
60076	SKOKIE	031	33957	33128	32585	-0.3	32	11602	11223	10993	-0.4	2.87	9051	8634	-0.5
60077	SKOKIE	031	24776	27631	28115	1.2	85	9933	10990	11135	1.1	2.49	6693	7224	0.8
60081	SPRING GROVE	111	7622	9944	11152	2.9	94	2566	3301	3690	2.8	3.01	1984	2542	2.7
60082	TECHNY	031	46	50	50	0.9	81	15	16	17	0.7	3.06	13	14	0.8
60083	WADSWORTH	097	5622	7209	7940	2.7	94	1970	2575	2834	2.9	2.80	1493	1948	2.9
60084	WAUCONDA	097	12942	15859	17993	2.2	92	4844	5816	6534	2.0	2.70	3386	4012	1.9
60085	WAUKEGAN	097	73067	75535	75936	0.4	69	23086	22960	23024	-0.1	3.22	15611	15138	-0.3
60087	WAUKEGAN	097	24279	27784	29133	1.5	88	8306	9341	9744	1.3	2.96	6168	6800	1.1
60088	GREAT LAKES	097	19284	16468	16165	-1.7	1	2039	1751	1662	-1.6	3.57	1915	1637	-1.7
60089	BUFFALO GROVE	097	43822	45229	45613	0.3	65	16028	16411	16485	0.3	2.74	12082	12204	0.1
60090	WHEELING	031	35899	38077	38341	0.6	75	13926	14611	14656	0.5	2.58	9141	9370	0.3
60091	WILMETTE	031	27700	26829	26376	-0.3	32	10053	9737	9556	-0.3	2.73	7726	7376	-0.5
60093	WINNETKA	031	19634	18962	18606	-0.4	25	6961	6709	6566	-0.4	2.83	5493	5228	-0.5
60096	WINTHROP HARBOR	097	6900	7290	7335	0.6	75	2451	2566	2573	0.5	2.84	1921	1980	0.3
60097	WONDER LAKE	111	10160	11690	12933	1.5	88	3581	4157	4601	1.6	2.81	2771	3113	1.3
60098	WOODSTOCK	111	27515	33549	36527	2.2	92	9802	12004	13072	2.2	2.73	6936	8350	2.0
60099	ZION	097	29929	32905	34147	1.0	83	10177	11157	11556	1.0	2.91	7536	8105	0.8
60101	ADDISON	043	37950	39507	39954	0.4	69	12335	12774	12907	0.4	3.08	9558	9765	0.2
60102	ALGONQUIN	111	25486	33879	37586	3.1	95	8529	10810	11914	2.6	3.13	6938	8697	2.5
60103	BARTLETT	043	36874	40479	41281	1.0	83	12206	13416	13697	1.0	3.01	10000	10881	0.9
60104	BELLWOOD	031	20535	19584	19173	-0.5	18	6440	6171	6030	-0.5	3.16	5100	4824	-0.6
60106	BENSENVILLE	043	22686	22950	22814	0.1	56	7569	7569	7514	0.0	2.98	5216	5137	-0.2
60107	STREAMWOOD	031	36475	37578	37528	0.3	65	12093	12611	12604	0.5	2.96	9247	9482	0.3
60108	BLOOMINGDALE	043	22480	23300	23498	0.4	69	8459	8846	8950	0.5	2.55	5935	6095	0.3
60110	CARPENTERSVILLE	089	32148	42577	46766	3.1	95	9326	12463	13721	3.2	3.42	7745	10133	2.9
60111	CLARE	037	261	285	296	1.0	83	93	102	107	1.0	2.79	72	78	0.9
60112	CORTLAND	037	2354	2967	3655	2.5	93	824	1001	1234	2.1	2.96	613	708	1.6
60115	DEKALB	037	41557	48893	52308	1.8	91	14209	16820	18189	1.8	2.43	7158	8162	1.4
60118	DUNDEE	089	14651	19321	21409	3.0	95	5393	6994	7655	2.9	2.76	4050	5196	2.7
60119	ELBURN	089	7416	11183	13133	4.5	98	2598	3814	4444	4.2	2.93	2109	2989	3.8
60120	ELGIN	031	48897	52239	53200	0.7	78	15554	16385	16647	0.6	3.17	11314	11626	0.3
60123	ELGIN	089	46035	48846	51534	0.6	75	16327	17105	18043	0.5	2.76	11367	11487	0.1
60124	ELGIN	089	9024	19297	23837	8.6	99	2901	6151	7510	8.5	3.13	2465	5048	8.1
60126	ELMHURST	043	45196	45138	44957	0.0	50	16477	16551	16515	0.0	2.64	11966	11827	-0.1
60129	ESMOND	141	401	434	449	0.9	81	140	153	160	1.0	2.84	107	115	0.8
60130	FOREST PARK	031	15634	15258	15077	-0.3	32	7608	7439	7345	-0.2	2.02	3466	3269	-0.6
60131	FRANKLIN PARK	031	19201	18821	18522	-0.2	38	6424	6237	6113	-0.3	2.99	4696	4480	-0.5
60133	HANOVER PARK	043	38078	39444	39580	0.4	69	11030	11331	11350	0.3	3.48	8966	9128	0.2
60134	GENEVA	089	21846	30975	35044	3.8	96	7402	10032	11171	3.3	3.03	5649	7626	3.3
60135	GENOA	037	6228	7045	7486	1.3	87	2258	2557	2718	1.4	2.76	1713	1894	1.1
60136	GILBERTS	089	1606	5445	9063	14.1	100	503	1440	2363	12.0	3.78	442	1238	11.8
60137	GLEN ELLYN	043	38544	39392	39585	0.2	61	14292	14617	14681	0.2	2.69	10263	10355	0.1
60139	GLENDALE HEIGHTS	043	31949	33021	33263	0.4	69	10844	11222	11316	0.4	2.94	7759	7881	0.2
60140	HAMPSHIRE	089	7471	12990	17257	6.2	98	2565	4713	6387	6.8	2.75	2085	3791	6.7
60141	HINES	031	301	292	286	-0.3	32	32	31	31	-0.3	2.55	16	15	-0.7
60142	HUNTLEY	111	7490	26584	33621	14.7	100	2904	10051	12725	14.4	2.64	2318	8001	14.3
	ILLINOIS					0.6					0.6	2.64			0.4
	UNITED STATES					1.0					1.1	2.59			0.9

ZIP CODE #	POST OFFICE NAME	RACE (%) White 2000	White 2009	Black 2000	Black 2009	Asian/Pacific 2000	Asian/Pacific 2009	% Hispanic Origin 2000	% Hispanic Origin 2009	2009 AGE DISTRIBUTION (%) 0-4	5-9	10-14	15-19	20-24	25-44	45-64	65-84	85+	18+	MEDIAN AGE 2009	% 2009 Males	% 2009 Females
60002	ANTIOCH	96.4	94.2	0.7	1.3	0.8	1.2	3.0	5.7	6.6	6.7	7.0	6.7	5.1	26.5	29.8	10.2	1.3	75.5	39.1	49.9	50.1
60004	ARLINGTON HEIGHTS	90.1	85.7	1.2	1.9	5.2	7.2	6.3	9.6	6.0	6.2	6.6	6.3	5.4	25.0	28.4	13.1	2.9	77.6	41.3	48.3	51.7
60005	ARLINGTON HEIGHTS	86.8	82.4	1.3	1.7	7.8	10.3	6.7	10.0	5.7	5.7	6.1	5.9	5.7	26.2	26.6	14.2	3.9	78.7	41.4	48.3	51.7
60007	ELK GROVE VILLAGE	86.2	80.4	1.5	2.0	8.6	11.9	6.3	10.4	5.7	5.9	6.3	6.5	5.6	26.6	29.8	11.8	1.6	78.0	40.3	48.9	51.1
60008	ROLLING MEADOWS	82.6	78.0	2.7	3.1	6.3	8.0	19.8	24.7	6.7	6.7	6.5	6.4	6.1	30.0	25.6	10.4	1.5	76.0	36.7	50.4	49.6
60010	BARRINGTON	93.5	90.6	0.6	0.9	4.4	6.3	2.1	3.7	5.7	6.8	8.5	7.8	3.9	18.4	34.9	12.6	1.4	74.0	44.2	49.3	50.7
60012	CRYSTAL LAKE	95.3	93.3	0.4	0.5	1.4	1.9	5.5	8.9	6.2	7.4	8.2	8.0	4.8	24.4	31.4	8.0	1.5	72.8	39.0	50.2	49.8
60013	CARY	95.9	94.4	0.4	0.4	1.1	1.5	5.8	8.6	8.1	9.5	9.2	7.5	3.9	28.2	26.5	6.5	0.8	68.4	36.2	50.3	49.7
60014	CRYSTAL LAKE	94.3	92.3	0.6	0.7	1.9	2.5	6.3	9.0	8.1	8.2	8.1	7.2	5.2	28.0	26.5	7.7	1.1	71.0	35.5	49.6	50.4
60015	DEERFIELD	94.0	91.1	0.7	1.0	3.7	5.3	2.3	4.0	6.6	7.8	9.2	8.3	4.7	19.3	31.5	11.0	1.6	71.7	41.2	49.3	50.7
60016	DES PLAINES	75.3	69.0	2.6	3.1	15.8	19.1	10.3	15.9	5.9	5.6	5.6	5.6	5.9	28.2	26.7	13.3	3.3	79.6	40.3	47.9	52.1
60018	DES PLAINES	80.2	73.8	1.0	1.1	7.3	9.4	24.0	33.0	6.2	6.3	6.3	6.8	6.5	26.2	25.9	12.1	3.5	77.0	38.7	49.8	50.2
60020	FOX LAKE	95.5	92.4	0.6	1.0	0.8	1.6	6.0	10.5	6.7	6.5	6.5	6.2	5.8	28.1	28.1	10.1	2.1	76.5	38.8	50.1	49.9
60021	FOX RIVER GROVE	95.6	94.0	0.5	0.7	1.7	2.3	3.7	5.7	6.6	7.1	7.7	7.4	4.8	25.4	31.7	8.4	1.0	73.6	39.7	51.1	48.9
60022	GLENCOE	95.0	92.7	2.0	3.0	1.7	2.6	1.3	2.2	6.4	8.3	11.0	9.5	3.4	13.5	33.1	12.7	2.2	68.1	43.5	49.2	50.8
60025	GLENVIEW	86.0	80.8	0.8	1.1	10.3	13.9	5.0	7.9	5.9	6.4	7.1	6.5	4.8	21.2	30.0	15.1	3.0	76.4	43.6	48.3	51.7
60026	GLENVIEW	75.1	63.2	4.9	13.0	16.6	18.4	5.5	9.0	9.3	7.6	6.8	5.6	7.2	28.3	22.4	10.7	2.0	72.8	33.2	48.4	51.6
60029	GOLF	95.6	93.8	0.0	0.0	2.9	4.6	1.5	1.5	6.2	6.2	9.2	7.7	3.1	15.4	33.8	15.4	3.1	70.8	46.3	49.2	50.8
60030	GRAYSLAKE	92.0	88.3	1.3	2.0	3.6	4.9	4.7	8.4	9.7	8.8	7.9	6.3	4.3	30.2	24.6	7.3	0.9	69.5	34.9	49.2	50.8
60031	GURNEE	82.6	75.7	5.1	7.3	7.5	10.1	6.2	10.0	9.1	8.7	8.4	6.7	4.2	30.0	25.6	6.4	0.8	69.4	35.3	48.8	51.2
60033	HARVARD	84.2	79.1	0.6	0.7	1.2	1.5	25.4	34.0	8.1	7.9	7.5	6.8	6.2	29.2	24.1	8.8	1.4	72.4	33.6	52.2	47.8
60034	HEBRON	98.0	97.2	0.3	0.3	0.1	0.2	3.7	5.7	6.8	6.8	6.8	7.0	6.8	25.0	28.8	10.3	1.6	75.3	37.9	50.5	49.5
60035	HIGHLAND PARK	91.4	86.2	1.5	4.0	2.2	3.0	9.3	13.2	6.8	7.6	8.6	6.9	4.8	18.9	30.3	14.1	2.2	73.1	42.6	48.5	51.5
60037	FORT SHERIDAN	79.6	70.0	12.0	18.3	3.1	4.3	4.5	8.2	9.9	12.6	11.4	7.8	5.5	38.4	11.9	2.1	0.4	65.1	26.6	50.4	49.6
60040	HIGHWOOD	74.5	64.2	2.2	8.4	2.2	3.6	36.2	40.6	6.4	5.2	4.9	10.1	12.7	29.2	20.0	8.9	2.6	81.0	31.2	51.9	48.1
60041	INGLESIDE	96.2	94.0	0.4	0.6	0.7	1.0	4.8	8.7	6.8	7.2	7.5	6.8	4.6	27.4	29.8	9.0	0.9	74.1	38.9	50.3	49.7
60042	ISLAND LAKE	93.8	90.8	0.6	0.9	1.5	2.0	8.2	13.0	8.9	8.8	8.6	7.6	4.6	30.6	25.2	5.3	0.5	68.8	34.7	49.7	50.3
60043	KENILWORTH	97.0	95.5	0.2	0.2	2.3	3.5	1.4	2.5	6.6	8.4	11.3	10.4	4.0	13.2	31.7	13.0	1.3	67.1	41.3	47.0	53.0
60044	LAKE BLUFF	90.9	86.7	2.1	3.2	4.9	6.9	2.8	4.8	6.9	7.1	7.8	6.8	5.3	23.7	29.7	11.2	1.5	73.6	39.2	48.8	51.2
60045	LAKE FOREST	93.6	90.4	1.4	2.1	3.6	5.3	2.1	3.7	5.5	6.6	8.5	9.6	6.5	14.8	32.4	13.4	2.6	74.0	43.7	48.0	52.0
60046	LAKE VILLA	92.2	88.2	2.0	3.1	2.5	3.6	4.5	7.9	9.0	8.5	8.2	6.9	4.5	30.6	25.2	6.3	0.9	69.6	34.8	49.5	50.5
60047	LAKE ZURICH	92.9	89.2	0.8	1.2	4.0	5.7	4.1	7.3	6.9	8.3	9.3	8.5	4.0	21.4	33.0	7.4	1.0	69.8	39.8	49.9	50.1
60048	LIBERTYVILLE	91.6	87.5	1.2	1.9	5.1	7.3	2.8	4.9	6.4	7.1	8.1	7.4	4.6	22.1	31.6	10.7	2.0	73.2	41.3	48.9	51.1
60050	MCHENRY	94.8	93.1	0.3	0.3	0.8	1.1	6.4	9.1	6.9	7.2	7.3	7.4	5.8	28.1	27.1	8.7	1.6	74.1	36.7	49.3	50.7
60051	MCHENRY	97.0	95.7	0.3	0.3	0.6	0.8	3.7	6.2	6.4	7.0	7.5	7.4	4.9	27.5	29.7	8.6	1.0	74.4	38.5	50.8	49.2
60053	MORTON GROVE	73.8	66.0	0.7	0.9	22.2	28.6	4.6	7.3	4.9	5.1	5.7	6.1	4.9	22.7	29.7	17.6	3.4	80.5	45.4	47.6	52.4
60056	MOUNT PROSPECT	80.5	75.1	1.9	2.2	11.4	14.2	12.1	16.8	6.4	6.3	6.3	6.1	6.1	27.6	26.0	13.0	2.2	77.1	38.8	49.9	50.1
60060	MUNDELEIN	79.9	72.9	1.6	2.1	6.2	8.1	22.2	30.8	8.4	8.5	8.4	7.4	5.4	29.5	25.4	6.2	0.7	69.9	33.7	50.7	49.3
60061	VERNON HILLS	82.4	76.6	1.7	2.2	10.8	14.4	8.5	11.7	7.6	8.2	8.2	7.0	5.2	29.8	27.3	5.8	1.0	71.2	35.8	49.3	50.7
60062	NORTHBROOK	87.3	82.3	0.7	1.0	10.3	14.3	2.2	3.6	5.1	5.8	6.8	6.4	4.0	18.0	32.1	18.0	3.7	77.9	47.4	48.3	51.7
60064	NORTH CHICAGO	22.6	20.0	58.9	59.6	0.9	0.8	29.2	32.7	10.1	9.7	8.4	8.2	7.6	27.6	19.9	7.7	0.9	67.0	28.9	50.0	50.0
60067	PALATINE	88.9	83.9	1.3	1.8	6.8	9.5	4.9	8.4	5.8	6.0	6.6	6.3	5.4	26.8	30.5	11.0	1.5	77.5	40.4	49.3	50.7
60068	PARK RIDGE	95.1	92.9	0.3	0.4	3.1	4.4	2.8	4.7	5.5	6.0	7.0	7.0	4.7	19.7	30.5	16.0	3.7	77.1	45.2	47.6	52.4
60069	LINCOLNSHIRE	91.1	87.6	0.6	1.0	6.8	9.2	2.9	5.1	6.5	8.3	9.8	7.7	3.1	19.8	32.3	11.4	1.1	70.1	41.8	49.0	51.0
60070	PROSPECT HEIGHTS	77.5	71.1	2.1	2.4	5.8	7.3	24.8	33.0	6.8	6.3	5.9	5.6	6.2	30.1	24.7	12.5	1.9	77.7	37.7	49.6	50.4
60071	RICHMOND	98.1	97.3	0.3	0.3	0.4	0.6	3.0	4.4	6.6	6.7	7.0	7.1	6.3	24.4	30.4	10.2	1.3	75.3	38.7	49.0	51.0
60072	RINGWOOD	98.0	97.7	0.2	0.1	0.4	0.5	2.7	3.6	5.8	6.4	7.0	7.4	5.1	27.5	31.4	8.5	0.7	76.2	39.1	50.5	49.5
60073	ROUND LAKE	77.4	72.5	2.5	2.9	1.6	2.2	28.4	35.0	9.8	9.3	8.5	7.4	5.5	31.7	21.8	5.4	0.6	67.7	31.4	50.6	49.4
60074	PALATINE	78.7	72.6	2.9	3.5	8.2	10.2	20.8	28.2	7.7	7.2	6.8	6.1	6.5	32.6	23.5	8.4	1.1	74.5	34.4	50.2	49.8
60076	SKOKIE	67.1	58.1	4.8	6.1	22.3	28.2	6.0	8.9	5.3	5.7	6.6	6.9	5.4	23.3	29.1	14.2	3.5	78.0	42.5	48.1	51.9
60077	SKOKIE	69.8	60.5	2.8	3.3	22.6	29.7	5.6	8.6	4.8	4.8	5.1	5.9	5.6	23.9	27.9	17.3	4.7	81.5	44.9	46.5	53.5
60081	SPRING GROVE	97.5	96.5	0.2	0.3	0.6	0.9	2.3	3.7	7.3	7.7	8.4	8.1	4.5	25.4	29.4	8.2	1.1	71.6	37.9	50.6	49.4
60082	TECHNY	91.3	88.0	0.0	0.0	6.5	10.0	0.0	0.0	4.0	8.0	8.0	8.0	4.0	14.0	30.0	20.0	4.0	72.0	48.3	46.0	54.0
60083	WADSWORTH	87.4	82.7	5.2	6.7	2.5	3.1	5.3	8.6	6.1	6.4	7.1	6.9	5.3	25.3	31.8	10.2	0.8	76.1	40.0	50.0	50.0
60084	WAUCONDA	91.7	87.4	0.4	0.7	1.5	2.2	10.5	16.4	6.8	7.2	7.4	6.6	4.4	27.4	28.8	9.7	1.6	74.6	39.0	50.5	49.5
60085	WAUKEGAN	48.2	42.5	19.2	19.7	3.7	4.1	48.7	56.9	10.0	8.9	7.7	7.8	8.1	32.2	18.5	5.8	1.0	68.9	29.2	51.1	48.9
60087	WAUKEGAN	64.5	56.6	13.2	14.9	3.6	3.9	29.1	38.8	8.1	7.7	7.6	7.2	6.3	28.4	24.4	9.1	1.2	72.2	34.3	49.5	50.5
60088	GREAT LAKES	65.1	55.3	20.8	27.0	5.3	6.4	10.7	15.8	7.3	5.2	3.4	29.0	27.2	24.0	2.1	1.4	0.2	82.1	20.9	70.2	29.8
60089	BUFFALO GROVE	89.1	84.2	0.8	1.2	8.0	11.5	3.4	5.6	6.0	7.0	7.7	7.2	4.9	24.8	31.7	9.2	1.4	75.3	40.4	48.4	51.6
60090	WHEELING	76.2	68.4	2.4	3.0	8.8	11.0	22.2	31.3	6.5	6.3	5.9	6.2	6.7	30.7	25.7	10.2	1.8	77.6	36.6	49.5	50.5
60091	WILMETTE	89.6	85.4	0.6	0.8	8.2	11.4	2.1	3.6	6.4	7.7	8.9	7.6	3.8	15.9	32.2	14.3	3.1	71.8	44.7	47.9	52.1
60093	WINNETKA	94.1	91.3	0.4	0.6	3.6	5.2	3.0	4.8	7.0	7.9	9.5	8.3	3.7	15.9	31.5	14.0	2.1	69.7	43.1	48.7	51.3
60096	WINTHROP HARBOR	91.9	87.9	1.9	2.8	1.9	2.7	5.2	9.1	6.2	6.5	7.0	7.1	5.3	27.0	30.3	9.5	0.9	75.7	38.6	49.5	50.5
60097	WONDER LAKE	96.4	95.1	0.2	0.3	0.6	0.8	4.8	7.1	7.2	7.2	7.1	7.1	5.8	29.1	27.5	8.2	0.9	74.1	36.4	51.1	48.9
60098	WOODSTOCK	90.0	86.6	0.8	0.9	1.7	2.1	14.9	21.0	7.2	7.0	7.0	7.1	6.5	28.2	26.4	9.0	1.7	74.3	35.9	50.6	49.4
60099	ZION	64.9	58.0	22.3	25.3	1.9	2.3	14.1	20.0	8.3	7.8	7.6	7.8	6.9	27.7	24.4	8.3	1.2	71.3	33.0	48.8	51.2
60101	ADDISON	76.9	72.3	2.4	2.4	7.4	9.3	27.0	33.4	7.7	7.1	6.7	6.7	6.8	30.5	23.7	9.8	1.1	74.4	34.3	50.3	49.7
60102	ALGONQUIN	94.2	91.4	0.9	1.1	2.4	3.5	4.2	7.5	9.7	9.3	8.3	6.4	3.8	31.7	24.6	5.6	0.5	68.5	35.1	49.6	50.4
60103	BARTLETT	86.6	81.2	2.2	2.8	7.9	10.8	5.8	9.7	10.0	8.9	8.3	6.7	4.1	30.6	25.2	5.6	0.7	68.4	34.3	49.5	50.5
60104	BELLWOOD	11.7	9.4	81.7	83.0	1.0	1.0	7.9	9.6	7.2	7.7	8.1	8.3	6.2	26.2	26.8	8.4	1.0	71.9	34.7	46.5	53.5
60106	BENSENVILLE	72.9	68.6	2.6	2.5	6.0	6.5	33.9	41.8	7.4	6.9	6.5	6.3	7.4	30.4	23.1	9.9	2.1	75.5	34.7	51.0	49.0
60107	STREAMWOOD	77.9	70.4	3.7	4.6	8.6	11.1	16.9	24.4	8.4	8.2	7.7	6.3	4.8	32.8	23.9	7.0	0.8	71.7	34.9	49.9	50.1
60108	BLOOMINGDALE	85.2	80.5	2.6	2.8	9.0	12.3	5.2	7.5	5.4	5.4	5.8	5.9	5.5	29.2	28.4	12.1	2.3	79.8	40.0	48.4	51.6
60110	CARPENTERSVILLE	68.2	61.5	5.5	5.6	1.9	2.2	39.5	50.6	10.5	10.0	9.1	8.1	6.5	31.6	19.1	4.8	0.4	65.4	28.8	51.1	48.9
60111	CLARE	95.8	94.0	0.4	0.4	0.0	0.4	1.9	2.8	7.0	8.1	7.7	6.3	4.2	26.7	28.8	9.8	1.4	73.0	39.3	50.9	49.1
60112	CORTLAND	95.5	93.1	0.9	1.7	1.1	1.5	5.2	8.2	8.7	7.9	7.7	8.1	6.3	30.1	23.0	7.2	1.1	70.8	32.6	48.7	51.3
60115	DEKALB	80.2	75.4	8.7	9.8	4.6	6.3	8.7	11.9	5.7	4.9	4.5	10.5	24.9	24.9	16.4	6.7	1.5	81.8	24.9	50.3	49.7
60118	DUNDEE	92.9	87.9	1.0	1.7	2.2	3.4	4.5	9.6	7.2	7.5	7.6	6.6	4.5	27.0	29.3	9.2	1.1	73.6	38.7	49.3	50.7
60119	ELBURN	97.4	95.3	0.2	0.2	0.7	1.1	2.5	5.8	8.3	8.4	8.7	7.4	4.1	27.6	27.6	7.0	0.8	69.7	35.7	48.9	51.1
60120	ELGIN	64.7	57.6	6.6	6.7	4.7	5.2	44.0	55.8	9.9	9.1	7.9	7.3	7.1	31.2	20.7	5.8	1.0	68.6	30.3	50.7	49.3
60123	ELGIN	78.0	68.8	6.2	7.6	3.3	3.9	22.6	36.3	8.0	7.4	7.0	6.7	6.6	29.6	23.4	9.3	2.0	73.8	34.6	49.1	50.9
60124	ELGIN	91.9	85.1	1.9	3.4	3.0	4.8	5.9	13.8	8.7	9.0	8.4	6.6	3.8	30.5	25.9	6.4	0.6	69.8	35.8	50.0	50.0
60126	ELMHURST	93.1	90.7	1.0	1.1	3.9	5.3	4.1	6.2	6.5	6.9	7.3	7.3	5.8	22.2	28.4	12.8	2.9	75.0	41.0	48.4	51.6
60129	ESMOND	96.3	95.2	0.2	0.5	0.2	0.2	2.0	3.0	6.9	7.6	7.6	6.9	4.6	25.8	29.5	9.7	1.4	73.5	39.4	52.1	47.9
60130	FOREST PARK	56.2	46.8	31.2	37.3	6.9	8.3	7.8	11.2	6.2	5.3	5.1	5.2	7.8	31.5	26.8	9.8	2.3	80.5	38.3	47.4	52.6
60131	FRANKLIN PARK	79.5	73.2	0.8	0.9	2.4	2.9	38.0	49.7	7.3	6.9	6.4	6.5	6.7	29.6	23.9	10.6	2.2	75.6	35.7	50.1	49.9
60133	HANOVER PARK	69.6	62.5	5.6	6.4	11.9	14.9	25.3	31.8	8.6	8.4	8.0	7.6	6.4	32.1	23.0	5.4	0.5	70.3	31.9	51.1	48.9
60134	GENEVA	96.2	93.8	1.2	1.6	1.2	1.8	3.0	6.6	7.8	8.5	8.8	8.5	4.7	24.9	28.3	7.1	1.5	69.5	35.9	49.6	50.4
60135	GENOA	96.0	94.4	0.2	0.2	0.3	0.4	8.5	12.5	8.5	8.1	7.8	7.1	5.6	29.2	24.0	8.6	1.1	71.3	34.1	50.3	49.7
60136	GILBERTS	95.5	91.8	0.4	0.5	1.6	2.2	2.9	8.1	6.4	7.3	8.1	8.0	4.5	26.0	31.8	7.2	0.7	73.2	38.5	49.8	50.2
60137	GLEN ELLYN	88.1	84.8	2.6	2.8	5.3	7.1	5.5	7.8	6.9	7.3	8.0	7.3	5.5	24.2	29.2	10.2	1.4	73.3	38.8	49.1	50.9
60139	GLENDALE HEIGHTS	65.9	58.7	4.5	4.6	19.0	23.3	17.3	22.5	8.0	7.5	6.8	6.5	7.6	34.3	23.0	5.8	0.5	74.0	32.1	51.0	49.0
60140	HAMPSHIRE	97.9	95.9	0.1	0.2	0.4	0.8	2.9	7.0	6.1	6.5	7.0	7.0	5.2	24.0	30.7	12.2	1.3	76.0	41.1	49.2	50.8
60141	HINES	32.5	25.3	61.9	68.5	1.7	1.7	5.6	7.2	5.1	5.1	5.5	5.8	6.2	27.1	28.1	14.7	2.4	80.8	42.1	51.7	48.3
60142	HUNTLEY	95.4	93.6	0.5	0.7	1.8	2.6	4.3	6.5	7.8	7.2	6.5	5.5	3.7	27.3	26.6	14.1	1.3	75.0	39.4	49.1	50.9
	ILLINOIS	73.5	70.6	15.1	15.3	3.4	4.4	12.3	15.7	7.1	6.9	6.8	7.1	6.9	27.5	25.4	10.3	1.9	75.0	36.1	49.1	50.9
	UNITED STATES	75.1	72.0	12.3	12.7	3.8	4.6	12.5	15.7	6.8	6.7	6.6	7.1	6.9	27.0	26.0	10.9	1.9	75.7	36.9	49.2	50.8

INCOME

#	POST OFFICE NAME	2009 Per Capita Income	2009 HH Income Base	2009 HOUSEHOLD INCOME DISTRIBUTION (%): Less than $25,000	$25,000 to $49,999	$50,000 to $99,999	$100,000 to $149,999	$150,000 or More	MEDIAN HOUSEHOLD INCOME: 2009	2014	2009 National Centile	2009 State Centile	2009 Home Value Base	2009 HOME VALUE DISTRIBUTION (%): Less than $50,000	$50,000 to $89,999	$90,000 to $174,999	$175,000 to $399,999	$400,000 or More	2009 Median Home Value
60002	ANTIOCH	32958	9413	10.9	19.5	41.6	18.3	9.7	76455	79309	90	88	7084	1.1	0.9	23.6	60.1	14.2	232502
60004	ARLINGTON HEIGHTS	38148	19803	8.3	16.9	41.1	18.9	14.8	79757	80578	92	92	14930	0.2	0.8	12.3	60.9	25.8	309385
60005	ARLINGTON HEIGHTS	39500	12634	10.8	22.2	39.8	13.9	13.3	70060	72291	87	80	8475	2.9	0.3	20.4	52.3	24.1	289866
60007	ELK GROVE VILLAGE	33269	13296	9.1	16.0	49.7	16.4	8.8	75725	76434	90	87	9842	1.0	0.2	15.0	74.5	9.3	250696
60008	ROLLING MEADOWS	30045	8395	8.4	20.5	48.5	13.6	9.1	72878	74802	88	83	6340	1.1	1.5	23.8	63.0	10.5	223223
60010	BARRINGTON	63840	15380	6.9	9.3	23.8	17.9	42.1	129685	131951	99	99	13759	0.6	0.3	2.3	29.5	67.3	530217
60012	CRYSTAL LAKE	42684	4062	8.1	11.9	25.6	23.5	30.9	106009	107950	97	98	3378	1.1	0.3	4.5	47.6	46.5	383333
60013	CARY	38047	9411	5.6	10.2	33.4	29.3	21.4	100779	105154	97	98	8450	0.6	0.7	9.5	63.6	25.6	298047
60014	CRYSTAL LAKE	34760	17313	7.1	14.0	37.5	26.3	15.1	86331	92885	94	95	14288	0.9	0.5	12.0	71.4	15.3	268890
60015	DEERFIELD	56827	9099	6.1	8.2	25.4	22.0	38.3	127144	128637	99	99	7941	0.4	0.1	2.9	33.9	62.7	474428
60016	DES PLAINES	28986	23950	13.4	22.9	47.1	11.6	4.9	63765	66124	82	71	16176	1.8	2.4	28.3	61.1	6.5	219588
60018	DES PLAINES	24441	10472	15.4	22.3	45.4	12.7	4.3	62678	65413	81	69	7682	16.1	2.8	10.0	65.9	5.3	226310
60020	FOX LAKE	32681	4399	14.7	21.2	42.5	15.4	6.1	67446	71722	85	77	3039	1.1	6.1	37.1	44.6	11.2	192650
60021	FOX RIVER GROVE	36868	2211	9.5	14.2	37.4	25.8	13.1	82766	86923	93	93	1840	0.0	1.1	8.3	63.8	26.7	289124
60022	GLENCOE	78711	2859	4.7	6.1	20.1	12.2	56.9	194083	196802	100	100	2526	0.0	0.2	2.4	8.3	89.2	890052
60025	GLENVIEW	46788	14916	8.0	15.9	38.3	15.9	21.9	83025	83823	93	93	11961	1.7	0.8	10.0	43.6	43.9	371114
60026	GLENVIEW	40037	4665	5.7	21.0	38.1	15.8	19.4	78287	77272	91	91	3428	0.8	0.5	10.2	32.9	55.6	437945
60029	GOLF	50193	22	9.1	4.5	54.5	9.1	22.7	81055	86438	92	92	20	0.0	0.0	0.0	25.0	75.0	750000
60030	GRAYSLAKE	36979	14583	7.6	12.9	37.7	26.0	15.7	87839	95383	95	95	12146	0.8	0.5	15.4	70.5	12.8	242815
60031	GURNEE	39675	14371	8.4	11.6	34.3	26.4	19.3	92912	102036	96	96	11400	0.6	0.8	17.6	62.8	18.2	264499
60033	HARVARD	24773	4898	13.5	22.7	42.7	15.7	5.4	63897	65833	82	72	3164	2.7	1.2	26.7	56.0	13.4	220924
60034	HEBRON	27207	900	10.2	26.6	41.0	18.2	4.0	64749	66577	83	74	648	2.2	1.9	18.5	56.9	20.5	236826
60035	HIGHLAND PARK	60884	11513	7.7	12.6	22.2	21.3	36.2	119332	123134	98	99	9321	0.4	0.3	2.4	29.6	67.3	530699
60037	FORT SHERIDAN	26570	324	3.4	26.2	50.6	6.5	13.3	68784	69358	86	79	71	0.0	0.0	0.0	29.6	70.4	552083
60040	HIGHWOOD	26056	1885	10.8	28.4	43.1	9.1	8.5	60513	63183	78	65	776	0.0	0.0	6.4	51.8	41.8	352941
60041	INGLESIDE	30210	3320	10.6	15.5	49.8	17.5	6.5	78147	80420	91	90	2684	0.6	2.5	34.4	52.5	10.1	206260
60042	ISLAND LAKE	31343	3154	6.5	12.0	50.9	21.9	8.7	79290	82148	92	91	2810	0.0	2.0	24.8	67.8	5.4	213315
60043	KENILWORTH	84700	799	3.6	4.8	11.9	9.5	70.2	220016	225095	100	100	717	0.0	0.0	0.0	2.8	97.2	1000001
60044	LAKE BLUFF	56320	4318	9.6	14.0	28.7	20.0	27.7	95011	104778	96	97	3206	1.2	3.9	2.9	28.5	63.4	489212
60045	LAKE FOREST	70015	7488	5.9	10.5	17.5	15.8	50.3	151605	159857	100	100	6454	0.0	0.0	1.1	9.7	89.2	902725
60046	LAKE VILLA	33967	11510	6.3	11.0	44.8	25.9	12.0	86196	93540	94	95	9946	0.4	1.0	18.4	71.6	8.5	227880
60047	LAKE ZURICH	51768	13544	4.6	8.3	27.4	21.6	38.2	123702	124784	99	99	12362	0.5	0.3	3.5	42.3	53.3	421641
60048	LIBERTYVILLE	53116	10638	6.2	10.4	28.0	21.7	33.7	111799	117987	98	98	8743	0.3	0.4	6.3	45.2	47.7	389716
60050	MCHENRY	31211	12247	10.7	19.4	39.6	21.0	9.3	73982	77225	89	84	9690	0.4	1.0	19.4	68.6	10.6	234507
60051	MCHENRY	30615	10381	8.6	14.6	45.5	24.6	6.7	78376	81386	91	91	8913	1.2	1.8	16.6	67.3	13.0	235044
60053	MORTON GROVE	31465	8209	9.3	16.7	46.1	18.8	9.1	76607	77238	90	88	7294	1.2	0.4	5.8	79.0	13.7	291638
60056	MOUNT PROSPECT	31245	21534	11.1	19.3	45.7	15.5	8.4	71015	73280	87	81	14708	0.5	1.3	14.8	68.8	14.6	285755
60060	MUNDELEIN	34008	12608	6.8	13.7	39.8	22.5	17.2	86888	93171	94	95	10232	1.5	0.6	20.5	62.0	15.5	229154
60061	VERNON HILLS	42665	9252	7.5	14.0	35.1	21.9	21.4	90010	98327	95	96	7175	0.9	1.2	23.6	50.0	24.4	275798
60062	NORTHBROOK	52038	15224	7.5	14.5	31.6	17.1	29.2	92649	92874	96	96	12670	0.9	0.5	3.6	33.0	62.0	469490
60064	NORTH CHICAGO	16400	4796	27.4	29.3	34.1	6.4	2.8	41414	44804	37	20	2333	3.1	12.5	66.2	17.5	0.7	133614
60067	PALATINE	47196	15246	7.7	15.0	38.2	18.2	20.9	85077	85317	94	94	11308	0.7	1.0	11.7	50.9	35.6	323360
60068	PARK RIDGE	41410	13852	8.0	15.7	39.8	19.4	17.1	82763	83403	93	93	11609	0.4	0.2	4.5	45.3	49.6	398473
60069	LINCOLNSHIRE	61015	3027	5.8	7.8	19.3	21.7	45.4	139868	142079	99	99	2769	0.9	0.2	1.9	23.9	73.1	548913
60070	PROSPECT HEIGHTS	29218	6237	12.4	23.0	46.5	9.9	8.2	63996	66332	82	72	4152	1.0	4.0	35.9	43.6	15.5	228825
60071	RICHMOND	33821	1607	9.8	16.7	37.6	23.0	12.9	76611	79854	90	89	1305	0.4	0.2	9.6	56.9	33.0	332165
60072	RINGWOOD	31994	289	5.5	10.7	49.1	26.0	8.7	80291	83868	92	92	253	0.0	0.0	9.1	59.7	31.2	318103
60073	ROUND LAKE	25635	17469	9.8	17.0	47.7	18.3	7.2	76828	79455	90	89	14218	7.2	2.6	41.2	41.7	7.2	173104
60074	PALATINE	31912	14666	10.0	17.8	47.9	14.7	9.6	74467	75338	89	85	9259	0.7	3.5	25.7	59.4	10.6	237627
60076	SKOKIE	32237	11223	9.9	18.1	41.0	17.9	13.0	76883	78038	91	89	8663	1.3	0.3	5.9	76.1	16.3	294939
60077	SKOKIE	30023	10990	16.5	20.0	44.5	12.3	6.6	63718	66795	82	71	7338	1.8	1.1	14.5	70.8	11.8	269918
60081	SPRING GROVE	31866	3301	10.0	13.6	36.7	25.4	14.2	84275	88795	94	94	2918	0.4	3.4	13.6	51.9	30.7	323401
60082	TECHNY	73347	16	6.3	0.0	12.5	6.3	75.0	186242	191580	100	100	15	0.0	0.0	0.0	0.0	100.0	1000001
60083	WADSWORTH	40422	2575	6.0	13.2	35.4	27.7	17.7	93198	101730	96	97	2064	0.0	0.7	10.0	59.3	30.0	323660
60084	WAUCONDA	32471	5816	11.6	17.5	44.7	16.5	9.8	76083	78474	90	88	4791	3.6	3.8	22.1	56.0	14.4	220926
60085	WAUKEGAN	18425	22960	22.0	28.5	38.9	7.9	2.7	49518	49809	60	42	11856	11.4	5.6	53.7	27.9	1.4	145298
60087	WAUKEGAN	24775	9341	11.8	22.8	44.7	17.0	3.7	68290	71462	86	79	6990	5.1	1.4	46.0	45.2	2.2	171411
60088	GREAT LAKES	16233	1751	9.1	41.7	42.5	4.2	2.4	49395	49311	60	41	81	59.3	17.3	23.5	0.0	0.0	40625
60089	BUFFALO GROVE	46577	16411	5.1	12.1	33.5	25.3	24.1	98714	104153	96	98	14210	0.3	1.1	11.5	62.6	24.5	295759
60090	WHEELING	31278	14611	10.5	18.4	50.2	13.2	7.6	69420	71006	86	80	9755	4.1	3.2	24.8	59.8	8.2	211840
60091	WILMETTE	58767	9737	6.4	10.5	27.6	16.1	39.5	114679	115877	98	99	8115	0.5	1.1	2.8	20.0	75.6	611900
60093	WINNETKA	73831	6709	6.1	9.8	20.8	11.5	51.8	157369	160474	100	100	5841	2.0	0.7	1.9	10.9	84.5	869139
60096	WINTHROP HARBOR	29110	2566	10.0	15.2	46.5	21.7	6.5	77665	81219	91	90	2067	3.3	0.0	34.0	58.5	4.2	197786
60097	WONDER LAKE	28061	4157	8.4	22.7	42.1	21.7	5.1	71445	74983	88	82	3603	0.6	0.9	26.2	61.7	10.7	216408
60098	WOODSTOCK	31336	12004	13.9	20.8	37.4	17.3	10.5	68444	70724	86	79	8117	0.3	0.8	15.8	61.0	22.1	253520
60099	ZION	24269	11157	16.7	22.7	42.1	14.2	4.4	62718	65894	81	69	7336	6.0	4.0	45.3	41.4	3.3	166745
60101	ADDISON	26476	12774	11.2	21.8	42.3	16.7	8.0	70955	73273	87	81	9061	0.8	2.2	13.2	74.9	8.9	236384
60102	ALGONQUIN	37527	10810	3.9	8.6	36.9	29.4	21.1	100649	104547	97	98	9995	0.4	0.2	4.4	72.0	23.0	308748
60103	BARTLETT	37885	13416	4.4	10.9	37.7	27.7	19.3	95657	100822	96	97	12110	2.0	0.9	11.6	70.4	15.1	272441
60104	BELLWOOD	23523	6171	13.5	19.4	49.9	12.5	4.7	67751	70214	85	78	4589	0.7	2.7	63.1	33.1	0.4	158099
60106	BENSENVILLE	25699	7569	11.4	20.4	47.0	15.5	5.7	71087	73335	87	81	4562	0.0	0.7	20.6	72.5	6.1	227225
60107	STREAMWOOD	29914	12611	5.1	13.7	55.5	17.2	8.5	78844	79651	92	91	10774	1.2	1.0	29.7	64.1	4.0	199233
60108	BLOOMINGDALE	38742	8846	6.9	15.6	40.9	22.9	13.8	83275	87859	93	93	6512	0.4	0.0	13.7	65.6	20.2	289869
60110	CARPENTERSVILLE	23237	12463	10.5	19.2	49.0	14.1	7.2	70013	73883	87	80	9722	0.9	0.7	37.1	51.9	9.4	191295
60111	CLARE	26396	102	9.8	18.6	57.8	8.8	4.9	72383	75714	88	83	69	4.3	0.0	18.8	68.1	8.7	229000
60112	CORTLAND	22746	1001	12.6	19.7	55.8	8.4	3.5	64879	67296	83	74	738	13.7	2.4	23.7	57.6	2.6	197321
60115	DEKALB	22041	16820	30.4	23.0	34.5	8.4	3.7	45333	48566	49	30	7213	1.2	2.8	25.4	63.4	7.2	216896
60118	DUNDEE	35667	6994	8.6	16.4	38.0	23.4	13.7	81838	91178	93	92	5650	0.8	0.6	6.7	64.5	27.4	306730
60119	ELBURN	39200	3814	6.0	11.6	34.8	25.8	21.8	95499	105686	96	97	3330	0.2	1.0	5.8	57.7	35.4	349218
60120	ELGIN	23930	16385	12.0	21.8	47.2	12.8	6.2	65306	67225	84	75	11038	3.3	1.6	31.0	57.9	6.3	197326
60123	ELGIN	26396	17105	13.6	20.7	46.4	14.3	5.0	65319	68456	84	75	11676	2.3	2.5	20.3	70.0	4.9	222040
60124	ELGIN	33712	6151	3.1	8.9	48.0	25.9	14.2	88923	99451	95	96	5683	0.4	0.1	7.8	66.3	25.4	293777
60126	ELMHURST	39311	16551	8.8	14.6	37.4	22.1	17.1	84342	90188	94	94	13656	1.2	0.9	6.1	65.6	26.2	295851
60129	ESMOND	25683	153	11.1	20.9	52.3	9.8	5.9	68022	69662	86	78	107	2.8	1.9	29.0	54.2	12.1	219167
60130	FOREST PARK	33258	7439	14.5	26.4	46.8	7.6	4.6	58636	61828	76	62	3392	0.4	12.0	36.5	48.9	2.3	177075
60131	FRANKLIN PARK	21763	6237	15.8	24.1	47.9	9.4	2.8	61031	63801	79	66	4380	0.3	1.0	24.9	73.2	0.7	201169
60133	HANOVER PARK	25008	11331	7.2	17.2	47.9	19.5	8.2	77892	79592	91	90	9242	0.5	0.7	31.8	64.1	2.9	202970
60134	GENEVA	36832	10032	7.1	11.4	39.4	20.5	21.7	88402	101745	95	96	8269	0.1	0.8	3.8	61.4	33.9	346360
60135	GENOA	26136	2557	11.1	18.3	55.0	10.8	4.8	68258	72772	86	79	1907	7.3	3.1	20.8	62.7	6.1	207265
60136	GILBERTS	27568	1440	4.7	10.0	49.6	21.2	14.5	85467	90357	94	94	1351	0.1	0.2	3.4	50.6	45.7	383750
60137	GLEN ELLYN	42380	14617	8.1	16.8	33.4	20.8	20.8	86024	92442	94	94	11285	0.0	0.7	10.9	54.7	33.7	324837
60139	GLENDALE HEIGHTS	27703	11222	7.6	19.6	48.7	17.2	6.9	74949	76304	89	85	7977	0.6	2.3	27.0	68.6	1.6	205101
60140	HAMPSHIRE	31577	4713	8.6	16.4	48.2	18.6	8.2	77545	81923	91	89	4131	0.8	0.4	6.4	60.8	31.5	315167
60141	HINES	10234	31	12.9	22.6	48.4	12.9	3.2	61496	66479	79	67	22	4.5	4.5	63.6	27.3	0.0	131250
60142	HUNTLEY	35084	10051	6.8	16.3	43.7	22.5	10.6	79555	83009	92	92	8936	0.4	0.0	5.8	73.1	20.7	305313
	ILLINOIS	28587		18.2	22.2	39.3	12.1	8.2	60823	63631				6.3	10.0	30.9	40.6	12.3	185324
	UNITED STATES	27277		20.9	24.4	35.3	11.7	7.6	54719	56938				9.3	13.1	31.6	32.6	13.5	162279

ZIP CODE		FINANCIAL SERVICES				THE HOME						ENTERTAINMENT						PERSONAL			
						Home Improvements		Furnishings													
#	POST OFFICE NAME	Auto Loan	Home Loan	Invest-ments	Retire-ment Plans	Home Repair	Lawn & Garden	Comput-ers & Hard-ware-Personal	Major Appli-ances	TV, Radio, Sound Equip-ment	Furni-ture	Dine out/ Carry out	Sports Equip-ment	Fees & Tickets	Toys & Games	Travel	Cable TV	Apparel & Services	Auto Repairs	Health Insur-ance	Pets & Supplies
60002	ANTIOCH	123	138	124	139	135	128	124	126	121	129	122	97	133	124	130	118	86	122	120	146
60004	ARLINGTON HEIGHTS	126	152	157	152	156	142	137	138	133	140	134	105	154	134	149	132	97	136	134	157
60005	ARLINGTON HEIGHTS	118	128	133	129	131	122	128	122	126	128	127	94	136	125	132	126	91	126	125	141
60007	ELK GROVE VILLAGE	113	134	129	132	133	122	122	121	118	123	119	93	133	120	129	116	86	120	116	138
60008	ROLLING MEADOWS	111	122	116	122	120	112	117	113	114	120	117	88	124	117	121	112	84	116	110	131
60010	BARRINGTON	229	299	338	311	322	280	251	266	237	275	238	201	303	236	289	229	178	248	240	296
60012	CRYSTAL LAKE	174	215	211	221	217	194	184	188	175	197	177	147	210	178	201	168	129	179	171	215
60013	CARY	164	199	178	201	194	173	169	172	159	182	161	137	189	167	180	151	117	161	152	195
60014	CRYSTAL LAKE	142	165	148	164	160	145	146	146	139	154	141	115	158	144	152	134	101	141	134	168
60015	DEERFIELD	205	277	314	286	299	255	231	243	216	252	216	185	282	215	268	207	163	226	216	269
60016	DES PLAINES	93	103	103	102	104	97	102	98	100	101	101	75	107	99	105	100	72	100	101	113
60018	DES PLAINES	90	105	104	100	107	97	99	98	97	99	99	73	106	97	104	98	71	99	98	111
60020	FOX LAKE	101	109	105	108	108	106	107	106	106	105	106	82	110	106	109	107	75	106	108	123
60021	FOX RIVER GROVE	143	167	150	170	163	154	148	150	142	152	144	118	161	146	157	140	102	145	142	175
60022	GLENCOE	265	378	464	395	424	356	306	329	286	341	283	246	395	284	368	274	221	301	290	358
60025	GLENVIEW	149	193	212	192	205	179	170	174	162	177	162	131	197	160	192	159	119	168	166	195
60026	GLENVIEW	164	157	168	164	164	141	174	156	161	177	164	129	174	171	170	151	119	164	140	178
60029	GOLF	177	247	299	254	276	229	208	222	190	232	188	164	254	182	250	180	141	205	198	243
60030	GRAYSLAKE	145	169	157	172	167	150	149	150	142	160	144	119	164	147	157	135	104	143	136	171
60031	GURNEE	154	182	162	185	177	156	159	158	149	170	152	128	175	157	166	142	110	151	140	180
60033	HARVARD	100	113	102	109	110	103	106	105	103	107	104	81	112	104	110	102	74	105	102	121
60034	HEBRON	95	110	101	110	108	103	104	103	102	102	103	81	112	103	109	102	73	103	102	120
60035	HIGHLAND PARK	199	260	306	267	285	245	227	237	213	245	213	177	270	209	261	207	159	224	219	262
60037	FORT SHERIDAN	173	90	67	104	80	77	163	113	153	152	161	112	124	184	118	141	113	144	102	137
60040	HIGHWOOD	100	112	119	112	115	100	122	109	117	114	121	88	127	115	124	116	89	117	106	126
60041	INGLESIDE	112	130	114	132	126	124	116	119	114	117	115	93	125	116	123	114	81	116	117	139
60042	ISLAND LAKE	130	148	124	144	140	124	130	130	122	138	125	103	137	130	132	116	88	123	115	148
60043	KENILWORTH	316	449	551	470	503	421	364	391	341	405	338	294	470	339	437	326	263	358	343	425
60044	LAKE BLUFF	183	225	241	230	236	200	204	204	188	228	189	161	228	188	224	178	139	196	181	231
60045	LAKE FOREST	248	342	414	355	381	324	285	304	269	314	266	227	357	263	338	260	204	282	276	333
60046	LAKE VILLA	143	163	140	163	156	140	144	143	136	154	138	115	154	144	147	129	98	137	128	164
60047	LAKE ZURICH	215	278	282	288	285	250	232	240	218	250	220	188	275	223	260	208	164	225	212	271
60048	LIBERTYVILLE	199	250	260	258	259	226	217	222	203	232	205	173	249	204	241	194	151	211	199	252
60050	MCHENRY	117	133	118	131	128	120	122	120	118	125	119	94	129	121	125	115	85	118	115	139
60051	MCHENRY	118	139	123	140	134	129	122	124	118	125	120	97	133	122	129	116	85	120	120	145
60053	MORTON GROVE	101	141	152	134	148	130	119	123	115	118	116	90	141	115	136	117	86	119	121	136
60056	MOUNT PROSPECT	105	123	127	121	127	115	116	114	113	116	114	86	127	113	123	113	83	115	114	129
60060	MUNDELEIN	148	171	154	171	167	150	154	153	147	162	150	122	167	152	160	141	108	148	139	174
60061	VERNON HILLS	159	172	165	179	170	155	166	158	159	172	161	128	176	163	169	153	116	159	147	185
60062	NORTHBROOK	173	218	256	222	238	214	189	202	182	206	181	147	222	176	218	179	133	192	195	226
60064	NORTH CHICAGO	75	68	60	69	65	69	76	70	79	75	79	54	74	79	71	80	56	76	75	85
60067	PALATINE	157	177	180	183	180	162	168	163	161	175	163	129	183	163	177	156	118	163	153	189
60068	PARK RIDGE	131	177	196	173	188	166	149	157	144	154	144	115	177	142	172	144	106	150	153	173
60069	LINCOLNSHIRE	213	290	329	302	314	264	238	252	221	265	221	193	295	222	278	210	168	231	220	277
60070	PROSPECT HEIGHTS	110	110	111	110	111	105	113	108	111	116	113	83	114	112	113	110	79	112	108	127
60071	RICHMOND	127	150	137	151	146	135	133	133	127	138	129	105	145	130	141	124	92	130	125	155
60072	RINGWOOD	124	153	134	152	147	132	130	131	122	136	124	104	145	127	139	117	89	125	117	151
60073	ROUND LAKE	121	131	112	127	126	112	121	120	114	129	117	93	123	120	121	109	82	116	107	136
60074	PALATINE	120	124	117	125	122	113	124	117	120	126	122	93	127	123	123	118	87	120	114	137
60076	SKOKIE	112	151	163	146	159	138	130	134	125	131	126	99	152	125	148	125	93	130	129	148
60077	SKOKIE	91	106	113	105	111	102	105	103	104	104	105	77	114	100	112	106	76	105	108	117
60081	SPRING GROVE	134	155	140	157	152	140	136	139	130	143	132	110	148	135	143	126	94	132	127	159
60082	TECHNY	270	386	474	404	432	363	310	334	291	346	288	250	403	290	373	279	225	305	294	363
60083	WADSWORTH	155	177	174	184	177	162	160	160	153	170	156	125	175	156	170	148	112	156	148	185
60084	WAUCONDA	117	141	130	142	138	127	125	125	119	129	121	98	138	123	133	117	87	121	117	144
60085	WAUKEGAN	86	78	69	76	76	68	88	80	84	89	87	64	83	87	82	81	62	85	74	92
60087	WAUKEGAN	101	109	98	107	106	101	104	103	102	107	104	79	109	104	107	100	73	104	100	118
60088	GREAT LAKES	97	51	38	59	45	43	91	63	86	85	91	63	69	103	66	79	64	81	57	77
60089	BUFFALO GROVE	168	205	203	211	208	187	180	182	172	190	173	142	204	174	195	166	127	175	169	208
60090	WHEELING	110	116	108	116	114	104	118	110	113	118	116	88	120	115	117	110	83	114	105	128
60091	WILMETTE	193	269	320	275	297	248	225	238	208	246	206	179	276	204	267	199	157	221	212	260
60093	WINNETKA	250	348	417	359	386	325	287	306	268	316	266	229	359	266	340	258	204	283	272	334
60096	WINTHROP HARBOR	108	132	118	131	128	123	115	117	113	117	115	90	129	115	124	113	81	114	116	135
60097	WONDER LAKE	110	126	108	124	121	113	112	113	108	115	110	89	120	113	116	106	78	110	107	131
60098	WOODSTOCK	117	128	119	129	126	118	124	120	120	125	122	95	130	122	127	118	87	121	116	140
60099	ZION	103	104	92	102	100	97	102	100	100	104	101	77	102	103	100	99	71	100	97	117
60101	ADDISON	107	119	114	117	119	105	118	113	112	119	115	89	123	113	121	109	83	115	105	128
60102	ALGONQUIN	165	198	172	201	192	168	168	170	157	183	160	138	187	167	177	147	116	159	146	192
60103	BARTLETT	161	187	164	188	181	159	164	163	154	177	157	132	178	163	170	145	113	155	143	186
60104	BELLWOOD	99	111	101	110	107	111	101	104	104	104	105	76	110	103	107	107	73	104	111	123
60106	BENSENVILLE	104	107	101	107	105	98	112	104	109	111	111	83	113	110	110	107	79	108	101	121
60107	STREAMWOOD	128	144	122	140	137	122	129	128	121	137	124	101	134	128	130	116	87	123	114	146
60108	BLOOMINGDALE	140	151	144	155	149	138	145	140	139	150	141	111	152	143	148	135	101	140	132	164
60110	CARPENTERSVILLE	115	124	106	117	120	103	116	114	109	124	111	89	117	114	115	103	79	111	100	127
60111	CLARE	103	116	100	120	113	113	103	107	101	104	102	84	111	104	109	101	72	103	106	126
60112	CORTLAND	99	109	91	105	103	91	98	97	93	104	95	77	101	99	98	89	67	93	86	110
60115	DEKALB	81	66	63	69	64	65	95	72	85	82	86	62	79	85	75	81	61	81	71	88
60118	DUNDEE	131	157	148	159	156	143	139	140	133	145	135	110	154	136	148	130	97	135	131	160
60119	ELBURN	159	191	173	196	188	164	164	165	153	178	156	134	183	161	173	144	113	155	143	187
60120	ELGIN	105	110	98	106	108	93	111	105	105	114	108	84	112	107	110	100	78	108	95	118
60123	ELGIN	101	108	99	106	106	99	106	102	103	107	105	79	109	105	106	102	74	104	101	118
60124	ELGIN	151	177	154	175	171	149	152	153	142	164	145	122	165	151	157	134	104	144	133	173
60126	ELMHURST	129	171	181	166	178	158	146	151	141	149	142	112	171	141	165	142	104	146	147	169
60129	ESMOND	105	111	99	115	109	115	102	108	102	100	101	84	105	104	106	103	70	103	109	127
60130	FOREST PARK	88	87	88	89	87	85	99	89	97	95	98	71	98	95	97	97	70	96	94	106
60131	FRANKLIN PARK	85	95	88	93	93	89	93	90	91	92	93	70	98	92	96	91	66	92	90	104
60133	HANOVER PARK	125	134	116	131	129	115	126	123	120	133	123	97	129	125	126	114	87	121	110	141
60134	GENEVA	153	186	172	187	184	162	160	162	151	172	153	129	179	157	171	144	111	154	145	183
60135	GENOA	100	113	99	111	109	100	104	102	99	106	101	81	109	103	106	97	71	100	96	118
60136	GILBERTS	140	176	157	177	171	153	147	150	138	155	141	119	167	144	160	133	102	142	134	172
60137	GLEN ELLYN	146	177	186	180	184	165	160	162	153	168	155	124	180	152	175	150	113	158	155	184
60139	GLENDALE HEIGHTS	120	120	103	118	115	101	121	113	114	126	116	91	119	119	116	108	82	115	101	131
60140	HAMPSHIRE	116	138	131	139	137	129	122	125	118	126	119	96	135	119	132	116	85	121	120	144
60141	HINES	94	90	86	93	88	90	101	91	101	98	102	73	100	100	98	101	72	99	99	111
60142	HUNTLEY	130	147	149	146	150	139	129	137	126	141	127	101	140	127	139	124	89	130	132	155
	ILLINOIS	106	108	105	108	107	106	109	106	108	107	109	83	110	108	108	108	77	108	107	125
	UNITED STATES	100	100	100	100	100	100	100	100	100	100	100	100	100	100	100	100	100	100	100	100

POPULATION CHANGE

ZIP CODE #	POST OFFICE NAME	COUNTY FIPS CODE	POPULATION 2000	POPULATION 2009	POPULATION 2014	2000-2009 ANNUAL RATE % Rate	2000-2009 ANNUAL RATE State Centile	HOUSEHOLDS 2000	HOUSEHOLDS 2009	HOUSEHOLDS 2014	HOUSEHOLDS % Annual Rate 2000-2009	HOUSEHOLDS 2009 Average HH Size	FAMILIES 2000	FAMILIES 2009	FAMILIES % Annual Rate 2000-2009
60143	ITASCA	043	9456	10205	10483	0.8	79	3604	3931	4050	0.9	2.56	2673	2871	0.8
60145	KINGSTON	037	2294	2590	2739	1.3	87	774	882	936	1.4	2.92	636	710	1.2
60146	KIRKLAND	037	2199	2429	2584	1.1	85	805	893	953	1.1	2.72	613	663	0.9
60148	LOMBARD	043	51146	53101	53663	0.4	69	19549	20464	20717	0.5	2.53	13145	13481	0.3
60150	MALTA	037	1659	1936	2278	1.7	90	621	732	862	1.8	2.64	451	517	1.5
60151	MAPLE PARK	089	3685	5217	5765	3.8	96	1276	1825	2021	3.9	2.86	1021	1418	3.6
60152	MARENGO	111	10959	13595	14801	2.4	93	3949	4923	5368	2.4	2.75	3020	3684	2.2
60153	MAYWOOD	031	27058	24877	24101	-0.9	4	7967	7297	7053	-0.9	3.38	6167	5591	-1.1
60154	WESTCHESTER	031	16817	16212	15917	-0.4	25	7011	6825	6699	-0.3	2.36	4887	4665	-0.5
60155	BROADVIEW	031	8200	7802	7741	-0.5	18	3166	3027	3007	-0.5	2.51	2114	1979	-0.7
60156	LAKE IN THE HILLS	111	23097	30430	33894	3.0	95	7636	9912	10990	2.9	3.07	6388	8219	2.8
60157	MEDINAH	043	2938	3035	3073	0.4	69	993	1034	1050	0.4	2.87	688	705	0.3
60160	MELROSE PARK	031	23098	24521	24589	0.6	75	7596	7911	7903	0.4	3.09	5422	5575	0.3
60162	HILLSIDE	031	8326	8087	7947	-0.3	32	3061	2963	2904	-0.4	2.64	2125	2017	-0.6
60163	BERKELEY	031	5240	5108	5020	-0.3	32	1876	1828	1792	-0.3	2.68	1383	1327	-0.4
60164	MELROSE PARK	031	21869	21365	21025	-0.3	32	7008	6764	6624	-0.4	3.12	5155	4892	-0.6
60165	STONE PARK	031	5127	5029	4926	-0.2	38	1265	1193	1160	-0.6	4.22	1060	992	-0.7
60169	HOFFMAN ESTATES	031	32999	32277	31784	-0.2	38	11680	11362	11156	-0.3	2.81	8063	7681	-0.5
60171	RIVER GROVE	031	10699	10822	10746	0.1	56	4381	4388	4337	0.0	2.45	2772	2725	-0.2
60172	ROSELLE	043	25050	25378	25334	0.1	56	9111	9268	9255	0.2	2.73	6810	6842	0.1
60173	SCHAUMBURG	031	11684	11293	11145	-0.4	25	5701	5457	5368	-0.5	2.07	2633	2445	-0.8
60174	SAINT CHARLES	089	30509	34936	36817	1.5	88	11195	12688	13324	1.4	2.66	8116	8951	1.1
60175	SAINT CHARLES	089	18228	25354	29136	3.6	96	5568	7908	9065	3.9	3.20	4951	6744	3.4
60176	SCHILLER PARK	031	11713	11910	12027	0.2	61	4195	4252	4280	0.1	2.80	3008	2996	0.0
60177	SOUTH ELGIN	089	16719	21353	23776	2.7	94	5787	7312	8113	2.6	2.89	4538	5635	2.4
60178	SYCAMORE	037	16327	21194	23536	2.9	94	6236	8094	8997	2.9	2.60	4389	5656	2.8
60180	UNION	111	1643	2008	2298	2.2	92	560	688	791	2.3	2.92	465	560	2.0
60181	VILLA PARK	043	29555	30833	31028	0.5	72	10995	11388	11460	0.4	2.69	7518	7659	0.2
60184	WAYNE	043	2180	2398	2708	1.0	83	733	793	892	0.9	3.01	644	686	0.7
60185	WEST CHICAGO	043	33249	37705	38863	1.4	88	9716	10812	11148	1.2	3.45	7869	8690	1.1
60187	WHEATON	043	29894	29967	30014	0.0	50	9597	9656	9699	0.1	2.72	6958	6896	-0.1
60188	CAROL STREAM	043	43518	45411	45950	0.5	72	14780	15229	15374	0.3	2.98	10986	11168	0.2
60189	WHEATON	043	31855	31750	31646	0.0	50	11661	11688	11654	0.0	2.69	8550	8458	-0.1
60190	WINFIELD	043	10720	11297	11517	0.6	75	3574	3832	3924	0.8	2.88	2956	3115	0.6
60191	WOOD DALE	043	14015	14542	14671	0.4	69	5289	5532	5600	0.5	2.63	3870	3987	0.3
60192	HOFFMAN ESTATES	031	12910	14412	14563	1.2	85	4008	4530	4572	1.3	3.18	3472	3857	1.1
60193	SCHAUMBURG	031	40530	39368	38764	-0.3	32	16269	15987	15750	-0.2	2.45	11238	10822	-0.4
60194	SCHAUMBURG	031	21810	20841	20438	-0.5	18	8708	8278	8102	-0.5	2.49	5925	5555	-0.7
60195	SCHAUMBURG	031	4473	4314	4238	-0.4	25	2285	2211	2167	-0.4	1.95	1012	940	-0.8
60201	EVANSTON	031	40258	40395	40289	0.0	50	15965	16164	16149	0.1	2.19	8195	7947	-0.3
60202	EVANSTON	031	32208	31050	30533	-0.4	25	13704	13220	12995	-0.4	2.30	7781	7305	-0.7
60203	EVANSTON	031	4589	4400	4307	-0.5	18	1679	1617	1580	-0.4	2.72	1310	1246	-0.5
60208	EVANSTON	031	1857	1908	1901	0.3	65	9	9	8	0.0	2.56	4	4	0.0
60301	OAK PARK	031	2357	2497	2533	0.6	75	1493	1599	1622	0.7	1.56	460	479	0.4
60302	OAK PARK	031	32285	31151	30587	-0.4	25	14680	14299	14043	-0.3	2.15	7895	7499	-0.6
60304	OAK PARK	031	17882	17262	17052	-0.4	25	6906	6723	6631	-0.3	2.56	4625	4410	-0.5
60305	RIVER FOREST	031	11635	11326	11144	-0.3	32	4092	3986	3913	-0.3	2.60	2909	2784	-0.5
60401	BEECHER	197	5384	8265	9800	4.7	98	2122	3133	3688	4.3	2.61	1598	2286	3.9
60402	BERWYN	031	60373	59947	59059	-0.1	45	22225	21335	20885	-0.4	2.78	14637	13774	-0.7
60403	CREST HILL	197	10558	20128	24023	7.2	99	4418	7860	9371	6.4	2.52	2885	4851	5.8
60404	SHOREWOOD	197	9722	21109	26849	8.7	99	3237	6716	8522	8.2	3.14	2729	5510	7.9
60406	BLUE ISLAND	031	25280	24864	25123	-0.2	38	9061	8833	8870	-0.3	2.81	5931	5661	-0.5
60407	BRACEVILLE	063	1739	1959	2204	1.3	87	622	703	795	1.3	2.78	462	508	1.0
60408	BRAIDWOOD	197	4996	6424	7153	2.8	94	1705	2141	2387	2.5	2.99	1340	1633	2.2
60409	CALUMET CITY	031	38642	37904	37341	-0.2	38	14893	14537	14282	-0.3	2.61	9907	9467	-0.5
60410	CHANNAHON	197	7776	12954	15561	5.7	98	2440	4159	5037	5.9	3.11	2092	3408	5.4
60411	CHICAGO HEIGHTS	031	60074	57626	56832	-0.4	25	20075	19355	19103	-0.4	2.94	14799	14039	-0.6
60415	CHICAGO RIDGE	031	14086	13612	13470	-0.4	25	5650	5491	5426	-0.3	2.41	3461	3284	-0.6
60416	COAL CITY	063	7316	8612	9739	1.8	91	2838	3413	3886	2.0	2.52	2043	2383	1.7
60417	CRETE	197	15122	17491	18639	1.6	89	5416	6200	6632	1.5	2.79	4276	4734	1.1
60419	DOLTON	031	25156	24123	23675	-0.5	18	8352	7924	7743	-0.6	3.03	6344	5932	-0.7
60420	DWIGHT	105	6299	6240	6177	-0.1	45	1997	2024	2006	0.1	2.67	1358	1351	-0.1
60421	ELWOOD	197	3471	4051	4572	1.7	90	1274	1463	1648	1.5	2.77	992	1101	1.1
60422	FLOSSMOOR	031	9598	9581	9493	0.0	50	3434	3461	3426	0.1	2.77	2684	2659	-0.1
60423	FRANKFORT	197	22532	32688	38876	4.1	97	7222	10324	12304	3.9	3.15	6191	8687	3.7
60424	GARDNER	063	2941	3308	3601	1.3	87	1157	1329	1456	1.5	2.49	807	898	1.2
60425	GLENWOOD	031	9125	8833	8751	-0.4	25	3421	3335	3300	-0.3	2.65	2532	2432	-0.4
60426	HARVEY	031	34950	32133	31189	-0.9	4	10537	9645	9337	-1.0	3.29	7897	7131	-1.1
60428	MARKHAM	031	12411	12793	12856	0.3	65	3791	3945	3967	0.4	3.24	3074	3160	0.3
60429	HAZEL CREST	031	16222	15869	15635	-0.2	38	5593	5501	5414	-0.2	2.86	4169	4038	-0.3
60430	HOMEWOOD	031	20403	19909	19672	-0.3	32	7852	7686	7584	-0.2	2.55	5525	5312	-0.4
60431	JOLIET	197	13325	22938	27270	6.0	98	4551	7812	9345	6.0	2.90	3475	5975	6.0
60432	JOLIET	197	21159	23110	23907	1.0	83	5652	6307	6593	1.2	3.42	4377	4769	0.9
60433	JOLIET	197	17844	18673	19295	0.5	72	5805	6034	6253	0.4	2.96	4185	4178	0.0
60435	JOLIET	197	42007	49119	52581	1.7	90	16632	19034	20353	1.5	2.53	10554	11646	1.1
60436	JOLIET	197	16850	18712	19573	1.1	85	6368	7003	7327	1.0	2.62	4069	4259	0.5
60437	KINSMAN	063	204	221	235	0.9	81	82	90	97	1.0	2.46	66	72	0.9
60438	LANSING	031	28916	28100	28008	-0.3	32	11630	11372	11319	-0.2	2.47	7934	7608	-0.5
60439	LEMONT	031	19736	21597	22284	1.0	83	6516	7139	7359	1.0	2.94	5216	5639	0.8
60440	BOLINGBROOK	197	46887	57132	62253	2.2	92	14604	17526	19120	2.0	3.25	11609	13657	1.8
60441	LOCKPORT	197	28419	38557	44421	3.4	95	8889	12522	14523	3.8	2.89	6682	9249	3.6
60442	MANHATTAN	197	6261	10629	12991	5.9	98	2029	3443	4224	5.9	3.09	1662	2731	5.5
60443	MATTESON	031	15062	18706	19934	2.4	93	5539	6833	7236	2.3	2.71	4139	5112	2.3
60444	MAZON	063	1559	1878	2140	2.0	91	576	714	819	2.3	2.63	452	547	2.1
60445	MIDLOTHIAN	031	26006	26214	26145	0.1	56	9995	10196	10175	0.2	2.50	6645	6588	-0.1
60446	ROMEOVILLE	197	20302	36047	42936	6.4	99	6777	12504	15094	6.8	2.82	5285	9307	6.3
60447	MINOOKA	093	7174	14423	18324	7.8	99	2432	4959	6334	8.0	2.91	1985	3904	7.6
60448	MOKENA	197	19534	26235	29811	3.2	95	6280	8169	9258	2.9	3.21	5298	6758	2.7
60449	MONEE	197	6060	8148	9194	3.3	95	2245	2949	3324	3.0	2.76	1740	2237	2.8
60450	MORRIS	063	19002	20633	22225	0.9	81	7319	8177	8876	1.2	2.48	5097	5525	0.9
60451	NEW LENOX	197	26990	36027	41690	3.2	95	8760	11540	13369	3.0	3.12	7360	9438	2.7
60452	OAK FOREST	031	27796	27838	27706	0.0	50	9704	9762	9707	0.1	2.80	7285	7229	-0.1
60453	OAK LAWN	031	55392	54519	53894	-0.2	38	22292	22088	21830	-0.1	2.45	14573	14173	-0.3
60455	BRIDGEVIEW	031	15203	15597	15582	0.3	65	5581	5719	5704	0.3	2.66	3780	3788	0.0
60456	HOMETOWN	031	4467	4316	4237	-0.4	25	1895	1848	1813	-0.3	2.34	1172	1116	-0.5
	ILLINOIS					0.6					0.6	2.64			0.4
	UNITED STATES					1.0					1.1	2.59			0.9

ZIP CODE #	POST OFFICE NAME	RACE (%) White 2000	White 2009	Black 2000	Black 2009	Asian/Pacific 2000	Asian/Pacific 2009	% Hispanic Origin 2000	% Hispanic Origin 2009	2009 AGE DISTRIBUTION (%) 0-4	5-9	10-14	15-19	20-24	25-44	45-64	65-84	85+	18+	MEDIAN AGE 2009	% 2009 Males	% 2009 Females
60143	ITASCA	89.6	86.4	1.1	1.2	5.1	6.9	5.9	8.4	6.0	6.0	6.3	5.9	5.3	26.5	28.9	13.0	2.1	78.0	41.5	48.6	51.4
60145	KINGSTON	96.4	94.9	0.4	0.5	0.3	0.3	4.6	7.2	8.1	7.8	7.6	7.1	5.4	28.9	26.9	7.3	0.7	71.9	34.9	49.3	50.7
60146	KIRKLAND	97.4	96.4	0.4	0.5	0.1	0.2	2.3	3.5	7.1	7.0	6.9	6.6	6.6	26.5	28.4	9.5	1.4	75.0	37.3	50.8	49.2
60148	LOMBARD	86.5	82.3	2.9	3.2	6.9	9.4	6.2	8.7	6.2	6.1	6.2	6.3	6.4	27.9	26.5	11.4	3.0	77.6	39.0	48.8	51.2
60150	MALTA	96.6	95.5	0.7	0.8	0.2	0.3	1.6	2.5	6.8	7.1	7.4	6.8	4.6	25.9	27.6	11.9	1.9	74.5	39.0	49.6	50.4
60151	MAPLE PARK	98.0	96.5	0.3	0.5	0.3	0.5	2.2	4.9	6.1	6.4	7.0	7.7	5.3	25.8	30.9	9.6	1.2	75.7	38.9	51.4	48.6
60152	MARENGO	94.1	92.1	0.3	0.3	0.4	0.5	9.1	13.1	6.8	7.0	7.3	7.3	5.5	26.0	27.8	10.8	1.5	74.3	37.9	50.0	50.0
60153	MAYWOOD	9.7	8.4	82.7	82.9	0.3	0.3	10.5	12.3	8.1	8.3	8.0	8.7	7.1	26.0	22.8	9.8	1.2	70.1	32.2	46.3	53.7
60154	WESTCHESTER	85.0	79.2	7.9	10.5	3.8	5.3	5.8	9.4	5.2	5.7	6.2	5.2	3.3	22.1	29.1	18.7	4.6	79.5	46.5	46.7	53.3
60155	BROADVIEW	23.7	18.6	71.5	76.0	1.4	1.5	3.8	5.0	6.2	6.5	6.9	6.8	5.4	26.7	28.4	11.6	1.7	76.2	39.3	46.8	53.2
60156	LAKE IN THE HILLS	92.2	89.7	1.4	1.5	3.2	4.2	6.1	8.6	12.4	10.9	8.7	5.7	3.4	36.5	18.5	3.6	0.3	64.2	31.3	49.9	50.1
60157	MEDINAH	89.0	85.9	2.8	3.1	4.6	6.1	6.3	9.0	6.2	5.8	6.1	5.8	6.4	27.0	27.9	13.3	1.4	78.2	39.8	50.4	49.6
60160	MELROSE PARK	71.6	66.3	2.9	3.3	2.0	2.2	53.8	63.8	8.9	8.2	7.1	7.1	7.5	30.5	20.5	8.6	1.6	71.6	31.7	50.2	49.8
60162	HILLSIDE	52.3	43.9	34.9	39.9	4.4	5.2	12.7	17.5	6.4	6.3	6.3	7.0	6.3	26.5	26.1	12.3	2.8	76.8	38.7	48.0	52.0
60163	BERKELEY	60.8	51.6	26.8	31.8	3.7	4.5	14.8	21.1	6.1	6.6	7.0	7.1	4.6	24.8	27.5	12.3	3.9	75.9	41.0	48.9	51.1
60164	MELROSE PARK	74.7	67.6	3.0	3.3	4.1	4.6	35.3	47.8	6.9	6.8	6.9	7.3	6.6	28.0	24.7	10.2	2.6	74.9	35.7	50.3	49.7
60165	STONE PARK	54.3	50.2	1.8	1.7	2.1	1.9	78.6	85.9	10.9	10.2	8.5	8.4	8.2	31.7	16.7	4.9	0.5	65.4	27.1	53.3	46.7
60169	HOFFMAN ESTATES	71.5	64.0	6.0	7.2	14.6	18.0	13.8	19.7	6.9	6.5	6.4	6.9	7.6	30.2	25.8	8.1	1.5	75.9	35.2	49.5	50.5
60171	RIVER GROVE	91.8	87.2	0.3	0.5	2.1	3.1	10.4	17.3	5.7	5.3	5.4	6.0	7.3	27.7	26.7	13.2	2.8	80.1	39.2	48.2	51.8
60172	ROSELLE	87.6	83.2	1.7	2.1	7.1	9.8	5.8	8.7	6.6	6.5	6.8	6.7	5.9	28.5	29.1	8.8	1.2	76.0	37.9	48.9	51.1
60173	SCHAUMBURG	66.1	57.0	5.3	6.5	24.6	31.2	5.6	8.3	5.2	4.3	4.0	4.7	10.3	38.4	25.2	7.0	0.8	83.6	35.5	50.6	49.4
60174	SAINT CHARLES	93.3	89.3	2.1	2.9	1.8	2.7	5.5	10.8	5.9	6.4	7.3	8.8	5.1	24.8	30.3	9.8	1.7	74.3	39.4	50.4	49.6
60175	SAINT CHARLES	96.1	93.0	0.8	1.4	1.6	2.5	2.5	6.1	7.5	8.3	9.4	8.5	4.4	23.8	31.3	6.4	0.5	69.2	37.2	50.5	49.5
60176	SCHILLER PARK	80.9	73.5	2.0	2.5	5.2	6.6	22.0	32.6	6.8	6.4	6.0	6.3	6.9	32.6	24.2	9.6	1.2	77.0	35.3	50.7	49.3
60177	SOUTH ELGIN	85.6	78.4	3.8	5.2	4.6	5.8	10.9	20.9	9.5	8.9	8.3	6.3	4.8	31.9	22.7	6.5	1.0	69.4	33.6	49.5	50.5
60178	SYCAMORE	94.2	92.6	2.2	2.5	0.8	1.1	3.9	6.1	6.8	6.7	6.9	7.1	6.4	26.5	28.1	9.9	1.6	75.3	37.5	49.1	50.9
60180	UNION	97.5	96.5	0.1	0.1	0.5	0.7	4.5	6.7	5.9	6.5	7.2	7.3	4.4	24.4	32.2	10.7	1.3	75.6	40.8	48.9	51.1
60181	VILLA PARK	85.7	82.3	2.8	2.8	5.7	7.4	13.2	17.4	6.7	6.4	6.3	6.7	6.6	28.9	26.1	10.4	1.9	76.5	37.1	49.9	50.1
60184	WAYNE	92.3	88.6	1.1	1.3	4.1	5.6	4.2	7.7	8.8	8.7	8.4	6.2	2.8	26.5	29.4	8.3	0.9	69.9	38.6	48.5	51.5
60185	WEST CHICAGO	82.0	78.8	1.6	1.5	2.0	2.7	35.6	42.1	8.8	8.5	8.0	7.0	5.9	30.7	23.4	7.0	0.8	70.4	32.4	51.7	48.3
60187	WHEATON	90.9	88.2	2.8	3.2	3.6	4.9	3.8	5.6	6.2	6.5	7.0	9.2	10.2	23.4	25.3	9.6	2.6	75.9	35.7	49.3	50.7
60188	CAROL STREAM	79.2	73.8	4.0	4.1	11.0	14.4	9.6	13.2	8.0	8.0	7.9	7.6	6.3	31.5	24.9	4.9	0.9	71.3	32.9	49.6	50.4
60189	WHEATON	90.0	86.9	2.4	2.7	5.5	7.6	3.7	5.3	6.0	6.8	7.6	7.3	5.7	24.6	30.3	10.0	1.6	74.8	39.5	48.7	51.3
60190	WINFIELD	92.4	89.7	1.5	1.6	3.0	4.2	6.1	9.6	7.0	7.6	7.8	7.4	4.5	25.2	30.5	9.0	1.1	72.6	39.0	50.0	50.0
60191	WOOD DALE	87.7	83.8	0.6	0.7	3.6	4.8	15.5	21.5	5.9	6.1	6.1	6.0	5.2	26.3	28.5	14.2	1.7	78.2	41.1	49.6	50.4
60192	HOFFMAN ESTATES	81.5	73.9	1.3	2.0	14.3	19.1	4.0	7.7	7.1	8.3	9.0	7.5	4.1	25.6	31.6	6.3	0.5	70.7	38.0	49.5	50.5
60193	SCHAUMBURG	85.6	79.7	2.0	2.8	9.2	12.7	5.3	8.6	5.9	5.9	5.9	5.7	5.4	28.9	29.1	11.5	1.7	78.7	39.9	48.4	51.6
60194	SCHAUMBURG	75.1	67.5	4.5	5.6	15.5	20.1	7.4	11.1	6.6	6.5	6.8	6.8	6.5	29.4	27.2	7.5	2.6	75.7	36.5	48.3	51.7
60195	SCHAUMBURG	67.0	58.0	4.5	5.7	24.7	31.2	4.3	6.5	6.3	4.9	4.0	4.1	8.9	47.3	18.4	5.3	0.7	82.5	32.5	53.9	46.1
60201	EVANSTON	69.5	64.1	18.7	20.1	7.4	10.1	4.3	6.4	5.0	5.0	5.0	10.5	13.8	25.0	22.2	10.0	3.3	81.9	32.3	47.7	52.3
60202	EVANSTON	59.6	52.5	28.2	32.1	4.0	5.0	8.4	11.6	6.3	5.6	5.4	5.6	7.7	32.6	27.1	8.2	1.4	79.1	36.3	46.9	53.1
60203	EVANSTON	77.2	70.0	11.6	15.1	7.9	10.5	3.9	6.1	6.9	7.8	9.0	7.4	4.2	17.9	29.7	14.5	2.7	71.6	42.6	48.1	51.9
60208	EVANSTON	71.5	62.3	5.5	7.2	18.7	24.5	4.6	7.1	0.5	0.4	0.5	51.0	36.8	3.9	3.7	2.7	0.5	98.2	19.8	46.9	53.1
60301	OAK PARK	72.5	63.7	16.1	21.1	7.9	10.5	4.2	6.6	3.6	2.0	2.1	2.4	6.5	37.8	24.6	13.7	7.2	90.5	42.1	41.3	58.7
60302	OAK PARK	68.7	60.2	23.2	29.2	3.9	5.1	4.1	6.2	5.9	5.6	6.1	5.7	7.3	29.2	29.2	8.9	2.0	78.7	38.2	46.8	53.2
60304	OAK PARK	68.4	60.2	21.8	26.9	4.1	5.3	5.4	8.3	7.6	7.2	7.3	6.6	6.4	28.2	28.0	7.5	1.0	73.5	36.0	47.6	52.4
60305	RIVER FOREST	89.4	84.6	4.8	6.8	3.2	4.5	4.0	6.7	5.6	6.4	7.8	10.8	8.7	17.2	29.6	11.6	2.3	75.3	39.4	46.1	53.9
60401	BEECHER	97.4	96.2	0.5	0.7	0.2	0.3	2.3	4.2	5.2	5.5	6.0	6.4	4.8	23.0	31.5	15.2	2.5	79.5	44.5	48.4	51.6
60402	BERWYN	75.3	67.2	1.2	1.4	2.5	2.8	36.1	49.2	7.8	7.3	6.9	6.9	6.6	29.1	23.2	10.0	2.3	73.9	34.9	49.2	50.8
60403	CREST HILL	88.7	83.1	5.4	8.6	1.6	1.5	7.7	11.7	6.5	6.2	6.2	6.3	6.6	29.7	26.2	10.8	1.6	77.3	37.3	50.2	49.8
60404	SHOREWOOD	93.0	89.0	2.2	3.6	1.4	1.9	4.3	7.9	7.2	7.5	7.9	7.6	4.8	27.5	29.3	7.6	0.7	72.7	36.9	49.4	50.6
60406	BLUE ISLAND	52.8	46.1	26.0	27.3	0.4	0.4	35.6	44.9	8.9	8.4	7.5	7.6	7.5	29.7	21.5	7.4	1.4	70.4	31.0	49.3	50.7
60407	BRACEVILLE	97.9	97.0	0.1	0.2	0.2	0.3	2.3	3.7	8.0	7.8	7.6	7.3	6.0	28.0	24.9	9.6	1.0	72.1	34.7	49.3	50.7
60408	BRAIDWOOD	97.6	96.0	0.3	0.5	0.3	0.4	2.9	5.4	7.2	7.3	8.2	8.3	6.0	28.3	25.3	8.3	1.1	72.0	34.9	50.2	49.8
60409	CALUMET CITY	39.1	31.8	52.5	57.5	0.6	0.6	11.0	14.5	7.8	7.7	7.2	7.2	6.9	27.4	23.9	10.2	1.8	72.9	34.3	46.9	53.1
60410	CHANNAHON	97.3	95.7	0.4	0.6	0.3	0.5	3.6	6.2	7.8	7.8	7.9	7.4	5.3	28.4	27.8	7.0	0.6	71.9	35.1	50.7	49.3
60411	CHICAGO HEIGHTS	49.9	44.2	37.6	40.3	0.7	0.8	17.1	21.9	8.8	8.5	8.1	8.0	6.6	26.8	22.5	9.4	1.4	69.6	32.3	48.9	51.1
60415	CHICAGO RIDGE	89.3	84.9	2.6	3.5	1.4	1.9	6.3	10.4	7.8	7.2	6.6	5.8	6.0	31.4	22.0	10.6	2.5	74.9	35.7	48.5	51.5
60416	COAL CITY	98.1	97.3	0.1	0.1	0.1	0.1	2.3	3.7	6.9	6.4	6.4	6.9	6.6	27.9	27.4	10.1	1.5	76.1	37.4	49.0	51.0
60417	CRETE	84.8	77.3	11.9	17.8	0.7	1.0	4.0	6.6	5.1	5.8	6.8	6.6	4.1	21.7	32.9	14.9	2.2	78.3	45.0	48.9	51.1
60419	DOLTON	14.5	10.5	82.1	85.7	0.6	0.6	3.2	3.9	7.1	7.9	8.2	8.6	6.5	25.2	26.9	8.4	1.4	71.6	34.4	46.4	53.6
60420	DWIGHT	90.0	88.3	7.7	8.5	0.3	0.4	3.0	4.2	6.1	5.9	6.0	6.7	6.5	30.8	25.6	10.2	2.3	78.0	36.9	43.6	56.4
60421	ELWOOD	96.5	94.6	1.3	2.2	0.5	0.7	3.5	6.2	7.0	7.5	7.9	6.4	3.8	26.3	28.2	11.7	1.2	73.5	39.3	49.6	50.4
60422	FLOSSMOOR	66.0	56.9	27.8	35.1	3.7	4.7	2.5	3.7	5.1	5.9	7.3	7.6	5.3	18.6	33.1	14.9	2.2	76.9	45.1	47.8	52.2
60423	FRANKFORT	94.6	91.4	1.8	3.1	1.8	2.5	3.1	5.4	7.2	8.0	8.6	8.0	4.4	23.9	30.7	8.2	1.0	70.8	38.4	48.9	51.1
60424	GARDNER	98.0	96.9	0.1	0.1	0.2	0.4	2.7	4.2	7.0	6.8	6.7	6.6	5.6	26.9	26.0	12.3	2.1	75.2	38.3	49.5	50.5
60425	GLENWOOD	52.0	44.0	43.7	50.1	0.6	0.8	5.1	7.5	5.7	5.8	6.4	7.3	5.4	24.7	29.7	13.2	1.9	77.7	41.0	46.8	53.2
60426	HARVEY	10.7	9.1	79.7	79.4	0.4	0.4	12.0	14.8	9.4	9.7	9.0	8.8	7.0	24.9	21.3	8.9	1.1	66.5	29.4	47.8	52.2
60428	MARKHAM	18.1	13.7	78.0	81.8	0.6	0.7	3.1	4.1	7.4	7.9	8.2	8.9	6.8	23.1	24.7	11.6	1.4	71.1	34.4	45.9	54.1
60429	HAZEL CREST	27.8	21.0	67.6	73.7	1.1	1.2	3.9	5.0	6.9	7.3	7.7	8.0	6.2	24.8	27.8	9.6	1.7	73.1	36.4	45.8	54.2
60430	HOMEWOOD	73.4	66.2	22.3	27.8	1.6	2.1	3.0	4.7	5.4	5.8	6.8	7.5	5.4	21.2	31.3	13.4	3.2	77.1	43.4	46.2	53.8
60431	JOLIET	88.5	83.4	6.0	8.6	1.8	2.0	6.4	10.6	9.0	8.1	7.5	7.6	5.4	31.9	21.9	7.2	1.4	70.5	32.6	49.2	50.8
60432	JOLIET	42.4	40.0	30.4	30.6	0.3	0.4	46.6	49.5	10.2	9.4	8.1	8.4	8.8	31.8	16.9	5.6	0.7	67.5	27.6	53.7	46.3
60433	JOLIET	48.6	41.3	42.6	47.4	0.2	0.2	14.9	19.1	7.8	7.9	7.8	8.8	7.1	25.3	22.4	10.2	2.8	71.3	33.1	47.6	52.4
60435	JOLIET	80.1	73.3	10.2	12.8	1.4	1.8	12.4	18.6	7.8	7.1	6.6	6.5	6.8	28.4	23.3	11.0	2.5	74.9	35.7	48.1	51.9
60436	JOLIET	66.0	57.2	22.8	27.1	0.7	0.9	14.6	21.1	7.9	7.4	6.7	6.9	6.5	28.2	22.8	11.1	2.5	73.9	35.0	49.3	50.7
60437	KINSMAN	98.0	97.3	0.0	0.0	0.0	0.0	4.9	7.7	6.3	7.2	7.2	8.1	5.4	22.2	29.9	12.2	1.4	74.7	40.2	49.8	50.2
60438	LANSING	85.3	80.8	11.2	14.1	0.7	1.0	5.7	9.3	6.3	6.4	6.6	6.4	5.5	25.9	27.7	12.9	2.3	76.8	39.8	47.8	52.2
60439	LEMONT	97.1	95.3	0.3	0.5	1.1	1.6	2.9	5.3	6.2	7.1	7.9	7.5	4.2	22.0	30.7	11.3	3.1	73.8	41.7	48.3	51.7
60440	BOLINGBROOK	64.1	53.7	20.8	27.2	5.9	6.7	14.0	19.3	8.7	8.5	8.1	7.4	5.9	30.8	24.2	5.8	0.6	70.2	32.7	49.7	50.3
60441	LOCKPORT	81.9	80.1	13.6	13.8	0.8	1.0	6.2	9.4	7.4	7.2	7.0	6.7	6.4	31.5	24.6	8.1	1.1	74.5	34.8	52.2	47.8
60442	MANHATTAN	97.6	95.7	0.3	0.5	0.2	0.2	2.3	5.0	8.0	8.0	8.2	7.4	5.2	28.7	27.1	6.6	0.9	71.2	34.6	50.7	49.3
60443	MATTESON	39.4	33.1	56.3	61.3	1.5	1.6	3.2	5.0	5.8	6.2	6.8	7.1	5.2	24.1	30.2	12.9	1.8	76.7	41.1	46.7	53.3
60444	MAZON	96.6	95.3	0.2	0.2	0.1	0.2	2.8	4.4	6.3	6.7	7.3	7.2	4.7	26.9	28.4	10.8	1.6	75.1	38.6	50.9	49.1
60445	MIDLOTHIAN	90.3	86.7	5.3	6.7	1.2	1.7	5.4	8.9	6.6	6.5	6.5	6.5	5.6	27.1	26.3	12.4	2.5	76.4	39.0	48.0	52.0
60446	ROMEOVILLE	86.8	77.3	4.3	9.1	2.1	3.2	11.8	17.6	8.6	8.0	7.4	6.9	6.0	32.2	20.5	9.3	1.0	72.6	34.4	49.4	50.6
60447	MINOOKA	97.8	97.0	0.3	0.3	0.3	0.4	3.0	4.8	7.4	7.6	7.8	7.5	5.3	28.2	27.6	7.9	0.8	72.6	36.0	50.2	49.8
60448	MOKENA	96.7	94.7	0.6	0.9	1.3	1.8	3.0	5.5	7.3	7.8	8.1	7.6	4.8	27.5	28.8	7.3	0.7	71.9	36.9	50.0	50.0
60449	MONEE	90.6	88.4	5.8	6.1	0.5	0.7	3.3	5.8	6.8	7.3	7.6	6.6	4.0	26.5	28.8	11.1	1.3	74.1	39.6	50.4	49.6
60450	MORRIS	96.3	94.6	0.3	0.3	0.5	0.7	5.5	7.9	6.4	6.4	6.3	6.5	6.1	26.3	28.0	11.4	2.6	76.8	38.9	49.5	50.5
60451	NEW LENOX	97.6	95.9	0.4	0.6	0.4	0.6	3.1	5.7	8.0	8.0	8.0	7.6	4.9	27.3	27.9	7.5	0.8	71.0	36.1	49.1	50.9
60452	OAK FOREST	90.3	86.4	3.7	4.7	2.7	3.7	5.9	9.8	6.5	6.6	6.8	6.6	5.4	28.6	28.1	10.2	1.3	76.1	38.1	49.6	50.4
60453	OAK LAWN	93.3	90.1	1.2	1.7	1.7	2.5	5.3	9.1	5.5	5.5	5.8	5.9	5.2	23.8	27.0	17.1	4.2	79.6	43.7	47.0	53.0
60455	BRIDGEVIEW	87.2	81.5	0.9	1.3	2.2	3.0	9.3	15.2	7.0	6.7	6.3	6.1	5.5	26.9	26.0	13.2	2.3	76.3	38.9	49.5	50.5
60456	HOMETOWN	97.3	95.7	0.0	0.0	0.3	0.4	3.8	6.8	6.0	6.1	6.1	5.9	5.5	26.1	25.1	16.1	3.0	78.1	41.0	45.8	54.2
	ILLINOIS	73.5	70.6	15.1	15.3	3.4	4.4	12.3	15.7	7.1	6.9	6.8	7.1	6.9	27.5	25.4	10.3	1.9	75.0	36.1	49.1	50.9
	UNITED STATES	75.1	72.0	12.3	12.7	3.8	4.6	12.5	15.7	6.8	6.7	6.6	7.1	6.9	27.0	26.0	10.9	1.9	75.7	36.9	49.2	50.8

ZIP CODE				2009 HOUSEHOLD INCOME DISTRIBUTION (%)					MEDIAN HOUSEHOLD INCOME					2009 HOME VALUE DISTRIBUTION (%)					
#	POST OFFICE NAME	2009 Per Capita Income	2009 HH Income Base	Less than $25,000	$25,000 to $49,999	$50,000 to $99,999	$100,000 to $149,999	$150,000 or More	2009	2014	2009 National Centile	2009 State Centile	2009 Home Value Base	Less than $50,000	$50,000 to $89,999	$90,000 to $174,999	$175,000 to $399,999	$400,000 or More	2009 Median Home Value
60143	ITASCA	42254	3931	7.1	12.4	38.0	28.0	14.5	88546	97461	95	96	3177	1.3	1.5	7.0	68.8	21.4	299301
60145	KINGSTON	27248	882	8.0	13.0	57.8	14.6	6.5	74739	75862	89	85	716	1.7	2.1	25.8	56.7	13.7	220536
60146	KIRKLAND	26549	893	12.2	18.5	53.5	10.5	5.3	66994	69692	85	77	686	0.9	1.5	35.7	51.9	10.1	202744
60148	LOMBARD	34414	20464	9.3	18.3	42.8	20.1	9.5	77225	79785	91	89	15603	0.4	1.4	17.5	73.2	7.5	232135
60150	MALTA	27037	732	10.2	19.9	55.5	9.6	4.8	67476	71747	85	77	515	0.6	2.3	34.2	53.8	9.1	199094
60151	MAPLE PARK	28665	1825	10.1	12.5	55.7	15.1	6.5	74965	76595	89	86	1460	2.5	0.9	12.3	67.4	17.0	260246
60152	MARENGO	32493	4923	9.1	19.9	39.0	19.9	12.0	75726	78484	90	87	3633	0.9	0.1	14.0	62.8	22.1	262911
60153	MAYWOOD	18484	7297	21.0	24.4	41.3	8.8	4.5	54444	58495	70	55	4580	1.2	4.8	66.4	27.2	0.3	146628
60154	WESTCHESTER	34085	6825	9.1	21.6	43.9	18.9	6.5	72107	72619	88	82	5953	0.7	0.1	11.5	79.6	8.1	237236
60155	BROADVIEW	26937	3027	16.3	23.1	46.5	10.3	3.8	61186	64302	79	67	2026	4.4	2.6	53.6	39.0	0.4	163544
60156	LAKE IN THE HILLS	38239	9912	3.6	7.8	36.7	31.8	20.1	101751	106168	97	98	9122	0.2	0.3	8.4	75.7	15.5	283900
60157	MEDINAH	32759	1034	11.2	15.7	41.2	21.1	10.8	77660	81434	91	90	729	0.5	3.3	15.2	54.2	26.7	304237
60160	MELROSE PARK	20422	7911	20.5	25.0	41.5	9.2	3.9	54128	57971	70	54	4399	7.6	1.5	21.0	68.0	1.9	215594
60162	HILLSIDE	26807	2963	12.5	21.9	50.9	10.6	4.2	67520	70204	85	78	2151	0.5	2.6	32.5	64.0	0.4	189120
60163	BERKELEY	29324	1828	11.8	20.0	42.5	20.3	5.5	72806	74834	88	83	1513	0.9	0.2	33.6	64.7	0.6	190600
60164	MELROSE PARK	21654	6764	14.2	19.3	53.6	10.1	2.8	65204	67636	83	75	5091	0.8	3.9	31.0	63.5	0.7	189527
60165	STONE PARK	14931	1193	21.7	26.7	41.1	7.5	3.0	51070	52957	64	46	720	13.8	0.1	45.8	38.9	1.4	165278
60169	HOFFMAN ESTATES	28499	11362	8.2	19.1	50.3	15.0	7.4	71844	73761	88	82	7765	1.0	5.6	29.3	59.6	4.5	209090
60171	RIVER GROVE	25108	4388	17.8	28.7	43.3	7.5	2.6	53260	56952	68	52	2598	0.7	1.2	32.1	63.2	2.8	200687
60172	ROSELLE	34510	9268	6.1	15.6	46.5	21.9	10.0	79316	82130	92	91	7480	0.6	0.1	15.2	74.4	9.8	238619
60173	SCHAUMBURG	43971	5457	9.3	16.1	51.1	12.8	10.7	74032	74157	89	85	2352	0.4	1.1	39.8	34.5	24.1	212050
60174	SAINT CHARLES	39588	12688	8.8	15.3	39.6	19.7	16.6	81174	89388	92	92	9300	0.7	0.2	5.9	62.9	30.3	302194
60175	SAINT CHARLES	47401	7908	4.9	8.4	29.1	23.7	33.9	111386	114806	98	98	7165	0.1	0.3	3.5	40.2	55.9	431534
60176	SCHILLER PARK	22614	4252	15.8	27.7	44.2	9.1	3.2	55266	58489	72	57	2251	1.9	0.8	19.6	74.0	3.7	223031
60177	SOUTH ELGIN	35091	7312	8.0	11.1	46.6	21.7	12.6	82844	90787	93	93	6041	0.8	0.1	13.9	69.8	15.5	247547
60178	SYCAMORE	29764	8094	10.3	18.8	51.7	13.0	6.1	72868	75586	88	83	5888	5.0	1.1	19.9	62.1	11.9	228236
60180	UNION	32413	688	8.7	13.7	38.7	29.2	9.7	82468	88704	93	93	581	0.0	1.2	13.6	55.2	29.9	302101
60181	VILLA PARK	29572	11388	10.0	21.7	46.1	16.0	6.3	71717	74954	88	82	8395	0.4	0.6	23.0	70.8	5.1	215858
60184	WAYNE	54691	793	4.0	5.2	22.6	28.5	39.7	133055	134943	99	99	744	0.1	0.0	3.4	34.1	62.4	501938
60185	WEST CHICAGO	29385	10812	8.8	14.8	38.0	22.8	15.6	84059	90280	94	94	8499	1.2	1.4	14.4	60.0	23.0	245508
60187	WHEATON	37345	9656	7.4	13.1	37.4	25.4	16.7	87820	95009	95	95	7224	0.1	0.4	5.3	70.3	24.0	290357
60188	CAROL STREAM	32210	15229	8.4	14.7	41.6	22.6	12.7	82010	86075	93	93	11005	0.7	1.7	16.2	71.2	10.1	235860
60189	WHEATON	51148	11688	5.4	13.2	33.0	20.4	27.9	96965	104238	96	97	9097	0.4	0.4	12.9	50.2	36.0	334779
60190	WINFIELD	42193	3832	3.8	9.7	39.5	26.2	20.8	95437	102363	96	97	3478	0.1	0.0	7.8	71.0	21.0	283133
60191	WOOD DALE	31683	5532	9.0	19.8	44.3	19.4	7.5	75644	77263	90	87	4521	1.2	1.0	13.0	73.2	11.5	236151
60192	HOFFMAN ESTATES	40591	4530	3.3	8.4	37.3	24.7	26.4	101306	103029	97	98	4080	1.3	0.2	4.2	72.7	21.7	292767
60193	SCHAUMBURG	35219	15987	8.0	16.9	49.3	17.3	8.5	76176	76645	90	88	12903	0.4	1.1	26.8	64.3	7.4	228335
60194	SCHAUMBURG	34450	8278	8.6	16.3	49.6	16.2	9.4	75746	76396	90	87	5981	0.3	1.5	28.7	60.8	8.7	224980
60195	SCHAUMBURG	41571	2211	7.7	14.6	56.4	14.7	6.7	76939	77005	91	89	408	0.0	1.2	3.7	87.5	7.6	265254
60201	EVANSTON	44625	16164	20.0	16.6	29.9	13.3	20.2	71383	74665	88	82	8248	0.4	2.6	11.7	36.2	49.2	394326
60202	EVANSTON	40210	13220	11.1	17.8	44.1	14.1	12.9	73140	75040	88	83	7011	0.6	1.3	20.0	55.1	23.0	263901
60203	EVANSTON	45743	1617	8.3	11.7	32.8	21.3	25.8	93552	93462	96	97	1428	0.9	0.0	4.6	50.5	44.0	377212
60208	EVANSTON	14442	9	22.2	0.0	22.2	0.0	55.6	171824	125000	100	100	6	0.0	0.0	0.0	33.3	66.7	750000
60301	OAK PARK	54813	1599	13.4	19.8	47.3	11.2	8.3	68978	70567	86	79	533	3.0	3.4	50.3	34.7	8.6	164435
60302	OAK PARK	47827	14299	12.2	18.4	38.8	12.3	18.3	75482	76292	90	86	7759	1.4	2.9	15.0	45.1	35.6	317199
60304	OAK PARK	34146	6723	10.6	18.9	41.8	18.2	10.5	75368	76263	90	86	4333	0.9	1.1	10.3	74.0	13.7	264958
60305	RIVER FOREST	53237	3986	9.0	15.9	27.6	12.1	35.4	94554	96103	96	97	3329	0.0	2.5	13.1	23.2	61.2	476020
60401	BEECHER	26986	3133	14.7	21.6	42.7	17.7	3.4	64813	67710	83	74	2658	7.9	7.3	17.6	54.2	13.0	227419
60402	BERWYN	23263	21335	16.2	26.7	44.8	8.4	3.9	57551	61319	75	60	13418	1.3	1.7	35.9	60.3	0.8	188911
60403	CREST HILL	26423	7860	14.2	25.7	46.9	9.8	3.4	58847	58552	76	62	5571	0.3	2.2	48.4	47.3	1.8	173925
60404	SHOREWOOD	33676	6716	6.7	10.9	41.4	26.5	14.4	87660	93100	95	95	6268	3.8	0.8	8.2	73.0	14.2	271973
60406	BLUE ISLAND	19132	8833	24.2	31.2	36.7	6.1	1.8	45247	47690	49	30	5033	14.6	8.6	54.4	21.5	0.8	135501
60407	BRACEVILLE	22591	703	15.5	23.6	49.8	8.8	2.3	60156	62869	78	64	544	10.5	9.9	41.2	34.9	3.5	158245
60408	BRAIDWOOD	23037	2141	16.3	21.3	45.4	13.5	3.5	64621	65938	83	73	1759	3.1	4.8	46.9	43.8	1.4	170388
60409	CALUMET CITY	22590	14537	20.6	27.5	41.2	8.1	2.6	51640	54485	65	48	9205	4.9	12.9	69.1	12.3	0.7	123398
60410	CHANNAHON	27695	4159	6.2	12.6	52.0	21.4	7.8	78961	81171	92	91	3650	2.0	1.5	15.6	69.9	11.0	245392
60411	CHICAGO HEIGHTS	20808	19355	23.2	23.9	40.5	8.9	3.6	52880	56622	68	51	13305	11.3	13.5	56.8	17.3	1.1	122263
60415	CHICAGO RIDGE	26141	5491	16.9	23.6	47.7	9.2	2.5	59081	62240	76	63	2881	0.8	4.2	50.3	43.4	1.3	165320
60416	COAL CITY	28899	3413	14.4	19.7	45.8	14.4	5.7	66163	69789	84	75	2453	13.7	1.4	26.6	49.7	8.6	194126
60417	CRETE	32402	6200	8.5	15.9	43.4	21.9	10.3	78245	80806	91	90	5439	6.0	2.5	17.2	57.0	17.3	259970
60419	DOLTON	22139	7924	14.2	23.6	48.5	10.6	3.1	61824	64545	80	68	6225	0.9	11.1	75.9	11.5	0.5	128713
60420	DWIGHT	23143	2024	18.0	28.3	39.6	9.6	4.5	52335	54145	67	49	1477	8.7	9.7	56.2	23.5	1.8	135777
60421	ELWOOD	28295	1463	12.2	18.6	41.4	22.6	5.2	75883	79684	90	87	1224	4.2	2.7	17.1	66.9	9.1	224011
60422	FLOSSMOOR	47889	3461	8.0	11.7	32.6	20.7	26.9	95579	94607	96	97	3122	0.1	1.2	17.7	58.7	22.2	274115
60423	FRANKFORT	33705	10324	6.3	12.7	38.9	27.6	14.6	88676	97814	95	96	9513	0.1	0.8	8.7	57.0	33.4	332516
60424	GARDNER	25356	1329	17.7	26.3	44.1	8.2	3.7	54717	57902	71	55	1013	11.7	6.5	48.4	30.6	2.8	154748
60425	GLENWOOD	29409	3335	9.9	21.1	46.7	15.3	7.0	69028	70825	86	80	2727	0.7	9.0	49.9	39.5	0.9	157751
60426	HARVEY	14886	9645	31.7	30.0	31.1	5.3	2.0	39652	42425	32	15	5694	15.1	30.9	50.0	3.5	0.5	93455
60428	MARKHAM	18521	3945	21.3	24.2	43.5	7.8	3.1	53458	56588	69	52	3220	2.4	29.8	63.1	4.4	0.4	103347
60429	HAZEL CREST	25012	5501	11.9	22.6	49.2	11.5	4.9	64142	66440	82	72	4297	1.3	9.0	64.4	23.5	1.8	137060
60430	HOMEWOOD	31332	7686	12.2	18.1	45.6	16.5	7.5	71208	73177	87	81	6338	0.8	3.7	43.8	49.4	2.3	177612
60431	JOLIET	29890	7812	8.7	14.1	48.0	21.9	7.2	79301	82131	92	91	6809	0.5	1.1	12.8	77.7	7.9	237096
60432	JOLIET	15184	6307	26.9	29.5	35.2	6.5	2.0	43487	45333	44	25	3346	6.6	17.9	55.8	14.6	5.1	122871
60433	JOLIET	19768	6034	22.3	27.9	37.5	8.9	3.4	49779	49716	61	43	3760	3.2	15.4	62.2	18.1	1.1	132592
60435	JOLIET	25069	19034	19.2	24.9	40.6	12.1	3.2	55751	56730	72	57	12343	0.7	2.1	45.1	50.7	1.4	178785
60436	JOLIET	21803	7003	25.1	26.2	37.0	9.1	2.6	48310	49446	57	39	4388	1.6	6.4	68.0	22.9	1.2	149477
60437	KINSMAN	29570	90	13.3	13.3	62.2	4.4	6.7	70166	73396	87	80	67	3.0	4.5	28.4	49.3	14.9	225000
60438	LANSING	27826	11372	14.5	23.5	48.0	10.0	3.9	62324	65280	80	69	8359	1.0	5.6	56.8	35.5	1.1	155802
60439	LEMONT	38781	7139	7.8	11.6	39.0	21.3	20.3	88253	89749	95	95	5985	0.1	0.7	8.3	54.1	36.9	347563
60440	BOLINGBROOK	27336	17526	7.7	13.9	47.6	22.3	8.5	78607	81741	91	91	14134	0.9	1.2	23.8	67.9	6.3	215044
60441	LOCKPORT	27444	12522	10.3	18.3	47.5	16.7	7.1	72966	75872	88	83	9979	1.7	2.5	22.8	56.6	16.3	239343
60442	MANHATTAN	27563	3443	9.2	15.0	45.5	22.1	8.1	76822	78920	90	89	2958	0.0	0.6	12.7	61.1	25.6	299373
60443	MATTESON	29925	6833	12.4	18.2	47.1	14.5	7.8	69662	72851	87	80	5620	5.4	8.9	39.5	43.1	3.1	168293
60444	MAZON	27664	714	11.5	17.8	56.6	11.2	2.9	75235	76184	89	86	526	3.0	3.2	33.5	52.5	7.8	192089
60445	MIDLOTHIAN	26990	10196	13.9	22.0	48.9	11.5	3.6	62512	64795	81	69	8043	0.3	3.0	56.5	38.4	1.7	161364
60446	ROMEOVILLE	28030	12504	6.2	18.0	52.2	18.9	4.7	75650	77567	90	87	10590	0.7	0.5	31.6	63.3	4.0	208023
60447	MINOOKA	27405	4959	10.3	16.7	49.0	17.0	7.0	74023	75881	89	85	4291	3.4	2.8	14.1	67.4	12.2	251594
60448	MOKENA	31959	8169	4.3	11.9	43.6	27.0	13.2	86823	92922	94	95	7147	0.4	1.3	9.5	58.3	30.5	325480
60449	MONEE	32094	2949	10.2	17.0	40.9	22.7	9.2	78718	82611	91	91	2463	0.1	4.1	25.5	45.2	25.0	252201
60450	MORRIS	29453	8177	15.0	20.0	46.3	13.0	5.6	67487	71395	85	78	5208	2.4	1.1	22.0	59.5	15.0	230919
60451	NEW LENOX	30336	11540	6.3	13.3	44.9	25.8	9.8	83118	87179	93	93	10193	0.0	0.2	10.5	69.5	19.8	293105
60452	OAK FOREST	28456	9762	10.3	18.5	49.3	15.5	6.3	74562	75703	89	85	7724	1.2	0.8	26.2	68.8	3.0	203902
60453	OAK LAWN	28453	22088	15.3	24.9	43.3	12.0	4.6	60497	63519	78	65	17660	1.6	2.2	31.4	61.9	2.9	203888
60455	BRIDGEVIEW	23321	5719	18.6	25.0	44.0	9.3	3.1	56228	60355	73	58	4267	18.1	3.6	28.5	48.8	1.0	174704
60456	HOMETOWN	24298	1848	20.8	27.6	40.8	8.1	2.7	51067	52586	64	46	1396	4.1	1.9	87.2	6.5	0.3	136769
	ILLINOIS	28587		18.2	22.2	39.3	12.1	8.2	60823	63631				6.3	10.0	30.9	40.6	12.3	185324
	UNITED STATES	27277		20.9	24.4	35.3	11.7	7.6	54719	56938				9.3	13.1	31.6	32.6	13.5	162279

ZIP CODE		FINANCIAL SERVICES				THE HOME						ENTERTAINMENT						PERSONAL			
						Home Improvements		Furnishings													
#	POST OFFICE NAME	Auto Loan	Home Loan	Invest-ments	Retire-ment Plans	Home Repair	Lawn & Garden	Comput-ers & Hard-ware-Personal	Major Appli-ances	TV, Radio, Sound Equip-ment	Furni-ture	Dine out/ Carry out	Sports Equip-ment	Fees & Tickets	Toys & Games	Travel	Cable TV	Apparel & Services	Auto Repairs	Health Insur-ance	Pets & Supplies
60143	ITASCA	145	171	171	172	173	157	154	155	148	159	150	118	170	150	165	145	108	151	147	178
60145	KINGSTON	117	130	107	128	123	114	115	116	109	121	111	92	119	116	116	106	78	110	106	133
60146	KIRKLAND	95	110	99	110	107	104	102	102	100	101	101	80	110	102	107	100	72	101	101	119
60148	LOMBARD	115	135	133	133	135	123	125	123	121	126	123	95	136	122	132	120	88	123	119	141
60150	MALTA	96	112	101	113	109	112	98	103	98	99	99	79	108	100	106	100	69	100	106	121
60151	MAPLE PARK	111	133	118	132	129	118	116	118	111	120	113	93	127	115	123	108	80	113	109	136
60152	MARENGO	119	141	128	139	138	126	128	127	122	130	124	99	138	126	134	120	89	124	120	146
60153	MAYWOOD	86	85	77	85	82	86	87	84	90	87	91	63	88	89	85	93	63	88	91	102
60154	WESTCHESTER	104	126	127	124	129	127	109	117	110	113	111	83	124	108	122	113	78	113	123	133
60155	BROADVIEW	87	100	93	100	97	99	94	93	97	92	98	69	102	96	98	100	69	95	100	111
60156	LAKE IN THE HILLS	171	199	167	199	190	163	169	170	157	187	161	139	184	170	174	146	116	158	143	191
60157	MEDINAH	125	146	149	146	149	133	135	132	130	137	132	102	148	133	143	128	95	132	126	151
60160	MELROSE PARK	83	88	81	84	87	75	93	86	87	92	90	68	93	88	92	84	66	90	79	96
60162	HILLSIDE	91	108	104	106	108	100	102	100	99	100	100	77	111	100	108	99	72	100	99	115
60163	BERKELEY	99	131	126	126	131	122	110	114	108	110	109	85	128	109	123	110	79	111	114	129
60164	MELROSE PARK	89	104	95	99	103	92	98	97	92	100	94	74	103	93	102	90	67	96	92	109
60165	STONE PARK	88	85	69	75	84	62	95	87	84	100	91	71	89	86	91	75	66	93	68	91
60169	HOFFMAN ESTATES	113	114	106	115	111	104	117	109	113	118	116	87	118	116	115	111	82	113	105	128
60171	RIVER GROVE	80	86	83	86	85	82	89	83	87	86	88	65	92	87	89	87	63	87	86	98
60172	ROSELLE	127	147	139	147	145	132	135	132	129	138	131	104	146	132	141	126	94	131	124	152
60173	SCHAUMBURG	139	109	98	118	103	101	137	114	134	136	137	97	124	140	119	130	96	129	112	141
60174	SAINT CHARLES	143	169	166	172	170	155	152	153	145	159	147	119	169	147	163	141	106	149	143	176
60175	SAINT CHARLES	205	255	243	263	256	222	214	219	200	234	203	175	247	209	233	189	150	204	189	247
60176	SCHILLER PARK	80	89	84	88	88	80	92	86	89	89	91	68	96	89	93	87	66	89	83	99
60177	SOUTH ELGIN	147	162	138	159	154	137	148	145	140	157	143	116	154	149	148	134	101	140	130	166
60178	SYCAMORE	104	119	107	119	115	111	110	109	107	111	109	85	118	109	115	106	77	108	107	127
60180	UNION	129	152	135	155	148	143	133	137	128	136	130	107	145	132	142	127	92	131	131	160
60181	VILLA PARK	101	124	122	119	125	112	113	112	109	112	110	85	124	110	121	109	80	111	110	127
60184	WAYNE	217	282	287	292	292	246	231	240	215	258	216	191	278	224	258	201	163	220	203	265
60185	WEST CHICAGO	139	159	147	158	157	138	147	145	138	154	141	114	156	142	152	132	102	142	130	164
60187	WHEATON	144	169	167	172	170	155	156	153	149	159	151	120	171	151	165	146	110	151	145	176
60188	CAROL STREAM	136	145	128	148	139	127	139	132	133	145	135	108	145	139	139	127	97	132	121	154
60189	WHEATON	185	215	213	222	217	197	196	194	188	205	190	153	217	190	208	182	138	190	181	224
60190	WINFIELD	166	205	186	206	200	180	174	177	165	184	168	140	196	170	188	159	121	169	161	203
60191	WOOD DALE	107	128	128	125	131	122	116	119	114	118	115	88	128	113	126	114	82	117	119	135
60192	HOFFMAN ESTATES	172	220	208	226	219	191	181	186	169	197	172	149	212	176	200	160	127	174	161	211
60193	SCHAUMBURG	118	133	126	134	131	121	123	121	119	127	121	95	132	121	128	116	86	120	115	141
60194	SCHAUMBURG	122	128	118	129	125	117	124	120	120	129	122	94	128	123	125	117	86	121	115	140
60195	SCHAUMBURG	113	92	95	103	90	88	123	98	119	117	123	87	114	120	110	116	88	113	100	123
60201	EVANSTON	138	139	155	150	144	132	157	138	150	154	153	114	160	148	155	147	112	147	135	165
60202	EVANSTON	119	127	137	132	130	116	137	123	130	134	134	101	142	130	139	128	98	130	119	144
60203	EVANSTON	148	210	234	205	225	191	172	182	162	179	163	134	209	162	202	160	122	171	169	198
60208	EVANSTON	232	220	246	235	233	220	272	226	248	249	247	188	258	248	243	240	182	242	218	267
60301	OAK PARK	121	89	93	103	86	86	132	99	128	123	133	91	117	129	113	124	94	120	104	128
60302	OAK PARK	136	139	151	147	143	129	154	137	145	152	148	114	157	144	154	139	107	145	132	162
60304	OAK PARK	115	131	130	131	131	121	125	121	121	125	123	94	134	123	130	120	88	122	118	140
60305	RIVER FOREST	180	236	274	243	259	216	209	216	192	227	191	165	244	186	240	182	143	204	193	239
60401	BEECHER	96	108	104	107	108	109	97	103	98	99	98	77	105	97	105	100	68	100	106	120
60402	BERWYN	84	94	87	91	93	86	93	89	91	92	92	70	97	91	95	90	66	91	88	103
60403	CREST HILL	92	96	89	97	93	94	95	92	95	94	96	72	98	96	96	95	67	94	95	109
60404	SHOREWOOD	145	176	152	174	168	154	150	152	143	158	146	120	166	149	159	138	103	145	140	175
60406	BLUE ISLAND	75	76	68	72	74	67	78	75	76	80	77	58	77	77	76	74	55	77	70	85
60407	BRACEVILLE	92	91	76	91	86	93	89	89	91	88	90	68	88	93	86	92	62	89	93	107
60408	BRAIDWOOD	103	107	92	104	102	101	97	100	97	101	98	74	99	101	97	97	68	97	98	117
60409	CALUMET CITY	82	78	69	79	74	79	84	78	86	82	86	61	83	86	80	87	60	83	85	95
60410	CHANNAHON	125	141	121	138	135	124	123	125	118	130	120	98	130	124	126	114	84	119	113	144
60411	CHICAGO HEIGHTS	86	87	75	86	83	84	87	84	88	87	88	64	87	89	85	89	62	86	87	100
60415	CHICAGO RIDGE	88	88	80	89	85	84	92	85	91	91	92	68	93	92	90	90	65	90	87	102
60416	COAL CITY	98	109	97	107	105	104	104	102	102	103	103	79	109	104	106	103	73	103	103	120
60417	CRETE	123	144	139	145	144	140	125	132	124	131	125	98	139	124	137	124	88	127	131	153
60419	DOLTON	93	99	88	98	95	97	93	93	95	96	96	69	97	95	94	97	66	94	98	111
60420	DWIGHT	97	87	87	89	86	100	92	95	94	84	92	74	84	94	88	97	63	94	101	114
60421	ELWOOD	104	124	109	125	120	122	108	112	108	109	109	86	120	110	117	109	76	109	115	131
60422	FLOSSMOOR	161	221	240	218	233	206	182	192	174	188	175	142	219	175	211	174	130	182	183	213
60423	FRANKFORT	144	177	168	179	176	158	150	155	142	160	144	120	169	146	163	137	104	146	140	176
60424	GARDNER	88	92	79	92	88	96	88	89	90	86	90	68	90	91	89	93	62	89	97	106
60425	GLENWOOD	104	120	109	118	116	114	108	110	108	110	109	82	117	109	114	109	77	108	113	127
60426	HARVEY	71	65	56	65	61	69	67	66	72	69	72	48	66	71	64	74	49	69	73	81
60428	MARKHAM	83	86	77	87	82	92	80	83	86	83	86	59	85	84	82	90	59	84	94	101
60429	HAZEL CREST	98	107	98	108	104	106	99	100	101	102	101	74	106	101	102	102	71	100	105	119
60430	HOMEWOOD	105	122	119	123	122	121	111	114	111	114	112	85	123	110	120	112	79	112	118	132
60431	JOLIET	129	141	117	135	133	119	126	125	120	135	122	98	129	127	125	115	86	120	114	143
60432	JOLIET	73	69	58	66	66	60	76	69	73	77	75	55	72	74	71	70	54	74	65	80
60433	JOLIET	83	80	68	82	75	84	82	79	86	81	86	61	83	86	79	89	59	83	88	97
60435	JOLIET	89	89	81	89	86	87	91	87	91	91	92	67	91	92	89	92	64	90	91	103
60436	JOLIET	78	80	72	80	78	82	80	79	82	80	82	59	82	81	80	84	57	81	86	93
60437	KINSMAN	103	112	99	116	110	113	102	107	101	101	101	83	106	103	107	102	70	102	106	126
60438	LANSING	92	102	93	102	99	100	97	96	97	95	97	73	103	97	100	98	68	96	100	113
60439	LEMONT	147	190	195	192	196	174	161	167	154	168	155	127	187	155	181	151	114	159	155	189
60440	BOLINGBROOK	129	139	120	138	133	121	128	126	123	135	125	99	133	129	128	118	88	123	115	145
60441	LOCKPORT	115	127	112	124	121	117	115	116	113	119	115	90	121	117	118	112	80	113	113	135
60442	MANHATTAN	122	140	117	138	133	122	122	123	116	128	118	98	130	122	126	112	83	117	112	142
60443	MATTESON	110	128	122	126	127	121	114	117	111	118	112	89	124	112	122	111	80	114	115	136
60444	MAZON	97	115	101	116	111	112	100	104	100	101	101	80	111	102	109	101	71	101	106	122
60445	MIDLOTHIAN	91	101	92	101	98	100	96	96	96	94	96	73	102	97	99	98	68	96	101	112
60446	ROMEOVILLE	113	121	106	122	116	111	114	111	111	118	113	88	119	116	115	109	80	110	108	130
60447	MINOOKA	119	126	110	123	122	118	112	116	111	118	112	88	115	116	113	110	78	111	110	136
60448	MOKENA	143	171	151	173	166	146	146	147	137	158	140	119	163	145	154	130	101	139	129	168
60449	MONEE	123	141	122	144	136	134	125	128	121	127	123	101	134	125	132	120	86	124	124	150
60450	MORRIS	99	110	101	110	108	105	105	103	103	104	104	81	110	104	108	103	73	103	103	121
60451	NEW LENOX	128	156	140	157	152	137	134	135	127	142	129	108	150	132	143	122	93	129	123	155
60452	OAK FOREST	107	124	112	124	120	115	113	112	110	115	112	87	123	113	119	109	80	112	111	131
60453	OAK LAWN	88	104	102	102	105	104	95	98	97	96	97	71	106	95	103	100	69	98	106	113
60455	BRIDGEVIEW	85	92	84	90	89	90	88	88	88	88	89	67	91	89	90	89	62	88	90	103
60456	HOMETOWN	78	78	72	79	76	84	79	79	82	75	81	60	80	82	79	86	56	81	89	94
	ILLINOIS	106	108	105	108	107	106	109	106	108	107	109	83	110	108	108	108	77	108	107	125
	UNITED STATES	100	100	100	100	100	100	100	100	100	100	100	100	100	100	100	100	100	100	100	100

ZIP CODE			POPULATION			2000-2009 ANNUAL RATE		HOUSEHOLDS					FAMILIES		
#	POST OFFICE NAME	COUNTY FIPS CODE	2000	2009	2014	% Rate	State Centile	2000	2009	2014	% Annual Rate 2000-2009	2009 Average HH Size	2000	2009	% Annual Rate 2000-2009
60457	HICKORY HILLS	031	13181	12936	12853	-0.2	38	4907	4839	4802	-0.2	2.66	3507	3401	-0.3
60458	JUSTICE	031	14028	14016	13911	0.0	50	5161	5137	5083	-0.1	2.72	3541	3460	-0.2
60459	BURBANK	031	27875	27471	27125	-0.2	38	9316	9225	9096	-0.1	2.96	7289	7123	-0.2
60460	ODELL	105	1665	1681	1673	0.1	56	652	678	676	0.4	2.21	478	488	0.2
60461	OLYMPIA FIELDS	031	4715	4919	5109	0.5	72	1688	1781	1852	0.6	2.73	1360	1417	0.4
60462	ORLAND PARK	031	38365	38678	38434	0.1	56	14335	14546	14440	0.2	2.64	10861	10898	0.0
60463	PALOS HEIGHTS	031	13054	13660	13709	0.5	72	4830	5090	5104	0.6	2.55	3606	3750	0.4
60464	PALOS PARK	031	9941	10639	10718	0.7	78	3654	3898	3912	0.7	2.67	2698	2827	0.5
60465	PALOS HILLS	031	18413	18226	18138	-0.1	45	7630	7607	7557	0.0	2.37	4977	4868	-0.2
60466	PARK FOREST	197	30090	31157	31684	0.4	69	11386	11712	11870	0.3	2.63	7930	7992	0.1
60467	ORLAND PARK	031	21012	25354	26312	2.1	92	6888	8398	8715	2.2	3.00	5845	7041	2.0
60468	PEOTONE	197	5215	7138	8120	3.5	96	1870	2528	2881	3.3	2.82	1423	1857	2.9
60469	POSEN	031	4701	4987	5013	0.6	75	1620	1702	1707	0.5	2.93	1177	1217	0.4
60470	RANSOM	099	670	695	704	0.4	69	238	255	260	0.7	2.59	186	195	0.5
60471	RICHTON PARK	031	12825	13524	13632	0.6	75	4686	4925	4947	0.5	2.68	3290	3423	0.4
60472	ROBBINS	031	6642	6463	6537	-0.3	32	1991	1953	1978	-0.2	3.08	1487	1433	-0.4
60473	SOUTH HOLLAND	031	23341	22576	22291	-0.4	25	8168	7910	7795	-0.3	2.77	6325	6053	-0.5
60475	STEGER	031	10182	10658	10809	0.5	72	4044	4203	4269	0.4	2.54	2619	2615	0.0
60476	THORNTON	031	2596	2457	2397	-0.6	13	1013	968	944	-0.5	2.54	690	646	-0.7
60477	TINLEY PARK	031	37765	39369	39401	0.5	72	14271	15086	15132	0.6	2.56	10035	10443	0.4
60478	COUNTRY CLUB HILLS	031	16518	16624	16610	0.1	56	5403	5508	5508	0.2	2.99	4202	4257	0.1
60479	VERONA	063	676	770	844	1.4	88	229	268	296	1.7	2.87	186	213	1.5
60480	WILLOW SPRINGS	031	4719	5234	5467	1.1	85	1817	2018	2097	1.1	2.59	1333	1456	1.0
60481	WILMINGTON	197	11683	13649	14724	1.7	90	4398	5106	5522	1.6	2.61	3146	3515	1.2
60482	WORTH	031	10983	10721	10551	-0.3	32	4411	4342	4273	-0.2	2.47	2818	2714	-0.4
60487	TINLEY PARK	031	19148	26387	28437	3.5	96	5986	8262	8893	3.5	3.18	5020	6879	3.5
60490	BOLINGBROOK	197	9148	18541	23120	7.9	99	2739	5459	6836	7.7	3.40	2492	4883	7.5
60491	HOMER GLEN	197	21128	29792	34529	3.8	96	6397	8861	10287	3.6	3.36	5688	7735	3.4
60501	SUMMIT ARGO	031	11199	11368	11316	0.2	61	3561	3578	3546	0.1	3.17	2576	2544	-0.1
60502	AURORA	043	12707	20113	23142	5.1	98	4351	6730	7685	4.8	2.98	3312	5081	4.7
60503	AURORA	197	3725	14695	19858	16.0	100	1355	5163	7015	15.6	2.85	1105	4137	15.3
60504	AURORA	043	27902	36731	40670	3.0	95	10249	13480	14904	3.0	2.72	7376	9566	2.9
60505	AURORA	089	57324	64707	67251	1.3	87	16318	17891	18559	1.0	3.58	12240	13030	0.7
60506	AURORA	089	50350	57216	60294	1.4	88	17308	19321	20270	1.2	2.90	12519	13666	1.0
60510	BATAVIA	089	26518	33086	35660	2.4	93	9385	11407	12184	2.1	2.85	7107	8480	1.9
60511	BIG ROCK	089	1895	2035	2079	0.8	79	661	703	714	0.7	2.89	550	576	0.5
60512	BRISTOL	093	875	1119	1644	2.7	94	301	420	619	3.7	2.66	251	334	3.1
60513	BROOKFIELD	031	19119	18386	18087	-0.4	25	7552	7302	7176	-0.4	2.48	5042	4776	-0.6
60514	CLARENDON HILLS	043	9125	9571	9629	0.5	72	3510	3646	3658	0.4	2.59	2441	2501	0.3
60515	DOWNERS GROVE	043	27302	27053	26878	-0.1	45	11095	11047	10990	0.0	2.40	7149	6970	-0.3
60516	DOWNERS GROVE	043	32931	33057	32920	0.0	50	12290	12414	12373	0.1	2.66	9171	9153	0.0
60517	WOODRIDGE	043	29034	32570	33779	1.3	87	10507	11895	12369	1.4	2.73	7483	8309	1.1
60518	EARLVILLE	099	3701	4109	4248	1.1	85	1364	1534	1592	1.3	2.68	1046	1157	1.1
60520	HINCKLEY	037	2774	3034	3169	1.0	83	1000	1106	1162	1.1	2.74	771	834	0.9
60521	HINSDALE	043	18531	18226	18305	-0.2	38	6431	6265	6300	-0.3	2.88	5066	4876	-0.4
60523	OAK BROOK	043	9707	9833	9863	0.1	56	3606	3658	3668	0.2	2.55	2629	2632	0.0
60525	LA GRANGE	031	31619	30572	30280	-0.4	25	12466	12108	11999	-0.3	2.46	8425	8005	-0.6
60526	LA GRANGE PARK	031	13302	12815	12573	-0.4	25	5436	5230	5115	-0.4	2.38	3599	3393	-0.6
60527	WILLOWBROOK	043	27789	28729	28857	0.4	69	10941	11304	11356	0.4	2.50	7342	7472	0.2
60530	LEE	103	617	634	641	0.3	65	219	229	233	0.5	2.76	169	172	0.2
60531	LELAND	099	1936	2044	2084	0.6	75	700	750	768	0.7	2.73	537	564	0.5
60532	LISLE	043	27460	32400	34128	1.8	91	11548	14073	15006	2.2	2.26	6475	7425	1.5
60534	LYONS	031	10130	9974	9862	-0.2	38	3975	3914	3866	-0.2	2.55	2549	2452	-0.4
60537	MILLINGTON	099	406	450	545	1.1	85	128	142	170	1.1	2.51	104	114	1.0
60538	MONTGOMERY	089	14113	25115	31257	6.4	99	5195	8974	11086	6.1	2.79	3935	6812	6.1
60539	MOOSEHEART	089	0	94	113	0.0	50	0	31	37	0.0	3.03	0	25	0.0
60540	NAPERVILLE	043	42948	43431	43649	0.1	56	15126	15340	15419	0.2	2.76	11460	11501	0.0
60541	NEWARK	093	2808	4062	5165	4.1	97	962	1381	1761	4.0	2.94	776	1092	3.8
60542	NORTH AURORA	089	10907	16296	18533	4.4	97	4143	6029	6790	4.1	2.68	2977	4279	4.0
60543	OSWEGO	093	18647	35347	47778	7.2	99	6337	11996	16259	7.1	2.94	5062	9466	7.0
60544	PLAINFIELD	197	18130	26132	30836	4.0	97	6970	9643	11395	3.6	2.71	5431	7305	3.3
60545	PLANO	093	7647	14209	19273	6.9	99	2585	4809	6550	6.9	2.95	2013	3703	6.8
60546	RIVERSIDE	031	15809	15111	14828	-0.5	18	6574	6306	6182	-0.4	2.32	4236	3974	-0.7
60548	SANDWICH	037	11002	12635	13387	1.5	88	3977	4593	4886	1.6	2.71	2981	3374	1.3
60549	SERENA	099	496	543	560	1.0	83	181	201	208	1.1	2.70	143	156	0.9
60550	SHABBONA	037	1338	1503	1595	1.3	87	475	537	573	1.3	2.67	341	374	1.0
60551	SHERIDAN	099	4808	4972	5053	0.4	69	1097	1210	1245	1.1	2.98	862	934	0.9
60552	SOMONAUK	037	3912	4326	4516	1.1	85	1392	1562	1640	1.3	2.77	1096	1208	1.1
60553	STEWARD	103	766	753	744	-0.2	38	265	266	264	0.0	2.83	211	209	-0.1
60554	SUGAR GROVE	089	5378	11258	13782	8.3	99	1805	3658	4424	7.9	3.08	1472	2896	7.6
60555	WARRENVILLE	043	13979	14096	13949	0.1	56	5152	5199	5141	0.1	2.70	3620	3571	-0.1
60556	WATERMAN	037	1814	2081	2390	1.5	88	666	772	890	1.6	2.70	504	568	1.3
60558	WESTERN SPRINGS	031	12350	12198	12271	-0.1	45	4262	4203	4225	-0.2	2.90	3488	3404	-0.3
60559	WESTMONT	043	26097	26976	27268	0.4	69	10459	10879	11019	0.4	2.40	6657	6786	0.2
60560	YORKVILLE	093	11125	20080	27193	6.6	99	3899	7011	9504	6.5	2.85	3093	5470	6.4
60561	DARIEN	043	23565	23905	23974	0.2	61	8942	9133	9173	0.2	2.59	6562	6580	0.0
60563	NAPERVILLE	043	30882	34443	35795	1.2	85	12680	14298	14908	1.3	2.35	7944	8697	1.0
60564	NAPERVILLE	197	32084	45058	52738	3.7	96	9523	13234	15517	3.6	3.40	8423	11564	3.5
60565	NAPERVILLE	043	41307	43311	43989	0.5	72	13052	13607	13803	0.5	3.17	11074	11455	0.4
60585	PLAINFIELD	197	5617	21299	28179	15.5	100	1727	6577	8709	15.6	3.24	1570	5948	15.5
60586	PLAINFIELD	197	20455	45269	58245	9.0	99	6294	13538	17402	8.6	3.34	5491	11542	8.4
60601	CHICAGO	031	5620	7308	8314	2.9	94	3512	4529	5148	2.8	1.60	1339	1667	2.4
60602	CHICAGO	031	67	556	691	25.7	100	21	316	378	34.1	1.75	8	113	33.1
60603	CHICAGO	031	380	432	569	1.4	88	14	25	35	6.5	6.88	7	13	6.9
60604	CHICAGO	031	85	336	402	16.0	100	36	137	193	15.5	2.28	22	76	14.3
60605	CHICAGO	031	12639	17917	21468	3.8	96	6773	9900	12094	4.2	1.62	2258	3178	3.8
60606	CHICAGO	031	1372	2407	3305	6.3	98	837	1361	1819	5.4	1.71	320	486	4.6
60607	CHICAGO	031	15592	22215	23554	3.9	97	7072	9537	10216	3.3	2.04	2866	3735	2.9
60608	CHICAGO	031	82808	84424	83964	0.2	61	24690	25349	25172	0.3	3.28	17750	17890	0.1
60609	CHICAGO	031	78897	76431	75678	-0.3	32	22658	21906	21641	-0.4	3.47	16884	16045	-0.5
60610	CHICAGO	031	40593	40993	41084	0.1	56	23757	23877	23745	0.1	1.65	7147	7085	-0.1
60611	CHICAGO	031	25721	27148	28830	0.6	75	17067	18096	19274	0.6	1.47	5338	5402	0.1
60612	CHICAGO	031	38609	39539	40503	0.3	65	12511	13275	13553	0.6	2.77	7481	7794	0.4
60613	CHICAGO	031	49819	49099	48476	-0.2	38	28866	28666	28296	-0.1	1.69	7961	7586	-0.5
60614	CHICAGO	031	64637	62933	62243	-0.3	32	35975	35035	34641	-0.3	1.70	10458	9792	-0.7
	ILLINOIS					0.6					0.6	2.64			0.4
	UNITED STATES					1.0					1.1	2.59			0.9

ZIP CODE #	POST OFFICE NAME	RACE (%) White 2000	White 2009	Black 2000	Black 2009	Asian/Pacific 2000	Asian/Pacific 2009	% Hispanic Origin 2000	% Hispanic Origin 2009	2009 AGE DISTRIBUTION (%) 0-4	5-9	10-14	15-19	20-24	25-44	45-64	65-84	85+	18+	MEDIAN AGE 2009	% 2009 Males	% 2009 Females
60457	HICKORY HILLS	86.3	81.4	6.0	7.4	2.1	3.0	7.6	12.6	6.6	6.4	6.3	6.3	6.2	28.0	26.0	12.5	1.6	76.8	37.9	49.3	50.7
60458	JUSTICE	79.4	73.5	12.3	14.6	1.6	2.1	7.6	12.1	8.0	7.3	6.8	7.1	7.9	29.5	24.7	7.7	1.0	73.6	33.1	49.4	50.6
60459	BURBANK	90.3	85.5	0.3	0.4	1.8	2.5	11.7	19.2	6.2	6.2	6.3	6.7	5.7	27.8	26.6	12.7	1.9	77.2	38.4	48.9	51.1
60460	ODELL	90.0	88.9	8.0	8.6	0.3	0.4	2.0	2.7	6.0	6.1	6.2	6.8	7.4	29.0	25.2	11.7	1.6	77.9	37.2	43.5	56.5
60461	OLYMPIA FIELDS	41.9	33.2	53.5	61.4	2.8	3.3	2.2	2.8	5.2	5.8	6.8	6.4	4.0	18.5	31.2	19.3	2.7	78.3	47.3	46.7	53.3
60462	ORLAND PARK	93.3	90.0	0.6	0.9	3.6	5.2	3.9	6.7	4.9	5.2	6.0	6.4	4.9	23.4	31.1	15.4	2.9	80.0	44.4	47.7	52.3
60463	PALOS HEIGHTS	96.3	94.5	0.6	0.8	1.7	2.6	1.7	3.0	4.5	4.8	5.6	7.3	5.7	17.8	29.1	21.4	3.8	81.4	48.1	47.4	52.6
60464	PALOS PARK	95.9	93.6	0.3	0.5	2.5	3.9	2.4	4.3	4.1	4.7	5.9	6.6	4.3	19.1	33.8	17.5	3.9	80.9	48.8	48.0	52.0
60465	PALOS HILLS	87.2	82.3	5.4	7.0	2.7	3.7	5.1	8.5	4.9	4.8	4.9	4.9	5.1	26.9	27.7	17.7	3.2	82.4	43.8	46.6	53.4
60466	PARK FOREST	48.2	38.1	46.8	56.0	0.8	0.9	4.4	6.1	7.3	7.2	7.2	7.3	6.5	27.2	25.8	10.0	1.4	73.7	35.7	46.9	53.1
60467	ORLAND PARK	94.8	92.3	0.8	1.3	2.9	4.2	3.1	5.3	6.2	6.7	7.8	7.7	4.5	21.4	31.2	12.8	1.7	74.2	41.8	48.6	51.4
60468	PEOTONE	97.2	95.4	0.9	1.5	0.4	0.6	1.8	3.4	6.1	6.4	6.9	7.3	5.6	25.1	30.4	10.5	1.5	76.1	39.4	48.7	51.3
60469	POSEN	74.5	67.3	13.1	14.9	0.3	0.4	21.8	32.1	8.3	8.1	7.7	7.6	6.8	27.9	23.6	8.9	1.3	71.4	33.1	50.2	49.8
60470	RANSOM	98.5	98.1	0.3	0.3	0.3	0.4	1.6	2.4	5.8	6.0	6.6	6.9	5.0	22.9	28.9	14.0	3.9	76.8	42.6	50.1	49.9
60471	RICHTON PARK	38.6	29.7	56.1	64.0	1.5	1.7	4.1	5.5	7.3	6.9	7.1	7.2	6.4	29.3	25.9	8.6	1.4	74.1	34.7	45.6	54.4
60472	ROBBINS	7.9	6.7	87.9	88.8	0.2	0.1	7.4	8.0	8.4	8.6	8.1	8.2	6.5	25.0	22.9	10.4	1.8	69.5	33.3	46.9	53.1
60473	SOUTH HOLLAND	42.7	33.8	53.0	60.8	0.9	1.0	3.9	5.3	5.9	6.4	6.9	7.0	4.7	22.3	27.3	15.8	3.6	76.4	42.5	47.0	53.0
60475	STEGER	84.8	77.4	8.8	12.9	0.6	0.8	8.2	13.5	7.3	7.0	6.7	6.4	6.3	30.2	24.8	9.9	1.4	75.1	35.5	49.7	50.3
60476	THORNTON	93.2	90.1	4.0	5.5	0.5	0.7	3.9	6.8	5.2	5.3	5.7	5.9	4.8	21.7	29.2	18.6	3.6	80.2	45.9	46.2	53.8
60477	TINLEY PARK	92.1	86.7	3.2	6.4	2.0	2.8	4.4	7.4	6.3	6.5	6.7	6.5	5.0	27.8	28.5	10.8	1.8	76.4	39.0	48.6	51.4
60478	COUNTRY CLUB HILLS	19.0	14.9	77.4	81.2	1.0	1.1	1.8	2.4	6.3	7.1	7.5	7.9	5.8	25.1	29.1	9.9	1.4	74.2	37.8	45.8	54.2
60479	VERONA	97.0	95.8	0.0	0.0	0.3	0.4	5.0	7.8	6.1	6.9	7.4	7.4	5.3	22.1	32.6	10.9	1.3	75.2	40.1	51.6	48.4
60480	WILLOW SPRINGS	91.8	88.7	3.0	3.4	1.8	2.6	5.1	8.8	5.4	6.1	6.9	6.9	4.7	22.7	33.4	12.5	1.5	77.3	43.1	49.9	50.1
60481	WILMINGTON	96.2	93.9	1.6	2.6	0.2	0.4	2.0	3.8	6.2	6.5	7.0	6.6	5.5	26.9	29.3	10.3	1.7	75.9	38.9	49.3	50.7
60482	WORTH	92.7	88.9	1.4	1.9	1.2	1.8	6.0	10.3	6.6	6.5	6.1	6.3	6.0	29.0	26.2	11.7	1.6	77.0	37.6	49.2	50.8
60487	TINLEY PARK	91.6	88.7	2.3	3.0	3.1	4.2	4.0	6.7	7.8	7.6	7.7	7.8	5.6	29.2	27.7	5.9	0.7	71.8	33.7	49.3	50.7
60490	BOLINGBROOK	71.6	62.1	15.7	21.8	7.8	9.0	6.9	10.9	11.4	11.3	10.2	6.6	3.0	33.9	21.0	2.5	0.2	62.7	32.4	50.1	49.9
60491	HOMER GLEN	96.5	94.5	0.4	0.7	1.6	2.2	3.3	6.1	6.8	7.5	8.2	7.8	4.5	26.0	31.1	7.4	0.8	72.4	37.9	50.1	49.9
60501	SUMMIT ARGO	65.1	59.8	11.4	11.2	1.4	1.5	46.3	57.6	8.8	8.2	7.5	7.8	7.2	30.0	20.5	8.4	1.5	70.9	31.1	51.4	48.6
60502	AURORA	83.2	78.3	5.9	6.6	6.8	9.1	6.5	10.9	10.2	10.1	9.4	6.4	3.6	32.8	23.5	3.5	0.4	66.0	33.7	49.5	50.5
60503	AURORA	82.4	76.4	5.2	7.3	8.3	10.0	5.7	9.9	11.0	10.6	9.7	6.4	3.3	35.9	20.0	2.9	0.2	64.6	32.6	49.5	50.5
60504	AURORA	79.2	71.6	8.0	9.9	7.0	8.6	8.0	14.8	10.9	9.9	8.8	6.2	4.8	37.7	18.9	2.5	0.2	66.3	31.1	49.5	50.5
60505	AURORA	57.9	51.9	10.3	9.9	0.7	0.6	60.0	72.5	10.8	9.9	8.5	7.9	7.8	31.5	17.0	5.7	1.0	66.1	27.8	51.7	48.3
60506	AURORA	72.0	64.7	13.3	14.7	1.4	1.6	23.7	34.9	8.5	8.1	7.9	7.4	6.4	27.9	23.8	8.2	1.7	71.0	33.5	49.6	50.4
60510	BATAVIA	92.8	88.2	2.6	4.0	1.5	2.2	5.3	10.8	7.8	8.1	8.2	7.6	4.6	25.9	28.8	7.5	1.4	70.8	37.0	49.5	50.5
60511	BIG ROCK	96.6	94.1	0.7	1.1	0.2	0.3	2.7	5.9	4.6	6.5	7.2	7.6	5.5	23.7	35.3	8.1	1.4	77.0	41.8	50.6	49.4
60512	BRISTOL	96.2	95.1	0.7	0.6	0.8	0.9	3.7	6.0	6.4	7.1	7.7	7.2	4.4	26.3	30.6	9.3	1.0	74.1	39.5	50.6	49.4
60513	BROOKFIELD	93.5	89.9	0.9	1.3	1.3	1.8	8.1	13.7	6.3	6.5	6.5	6.2	5.6	26.5	28.5	11.1	3.0	77.0	40.3	47.8	52.2
60514	CLARENDON HILLS	93.4	91.1	0.9	1.0	3.9	5.4	2.7	4.1	7.8	8.3	8.9	7.3	4.8	22.6	28.1	9.9	2.3	69.8	39.1	47.6	52.4
60515	DOWNERS GROVE	93.7	91.5	1.3	1.5	3.2	4.5	3.0	4.6	5.8	6.2	6.7	6.2	5.4	23.0	30.0	13.0	3.7	77.2	42.8	47.4	52.6
60516	DOWNERS GROVE	83.4	79.1	3.1	3.2	10.3	13.6	5.1	7.0	6.2	6.5	7.0	6.7	5.3	26.4	30.6	10.0	1.3	76.1	39.7	49.6	50.4
60517	WOODRIDGE	77.6	73.0	7.8	7.8	9.3	12.6	8.8	11.6	7.2	6.6	6.5	6.4	6.9	31.3	27.1	7.2	0.7	75.6	35.2	49.6	50.4
60518	EARLVILLE	97.2	96.4	0.1	0.1	0.4	0.5	2.6	3.8	7.3	7.2	7.9	7.2	5.1	24.6	27.5	11.7	1.5	73.2	38.9	50.5	49.5
60520	HINCKLEY	97.5	96.5	0.3	0.4	0.1	0.2	2.6	4.1	6.0	6.9	7.4	7.6	4.5	26.0	31.7	8.7	1.3	75.0	40.1	50.6	49.4
60521	HINSDALE	92.5	89.8	0.8	0.9	5.2	7.3	2.4	3.7	7.6	8.8	9.1	7.5	3.9	19.4	30.6	10.6	2.5	69.4	40.6	48.2	51.8
60523	OAK BROOK	80.1	74.1	1.7	1.8	16.2	21.7	2.8	3.9	3.5	3.8	4.7	4.9	3.7	18.2	29.7	25.0	6.5	84.9	54.0	45.4	54.6
60525	LA GRANGE	91.9	88.8	3.6	4.4	1.2	1.8	6.9	10.6	6.4	6.4	6.8	6.1	4.4	22.7	30.0	14.4	2.8	76.4	43.1	48.8	51.2
60526	LA GRANGE PARK	93.2	90.1	3.1	4.4	1.7	2.5	3.6	6.2	6.7	6.8	7.2	6.0	4.5	22.2	26.9	14.3	5.4	75.3	42.6	46.3	53.7
60527	WILLOWBROOK	82.0	76.9	4.7	5.0	10.3	14.0	4.1	6.0	5.1	5.4	6.3	6.3	5.0	23.9	31.1	14.3	2.7	79.2	43.6	47.8	52.2
60530	LEE	98.2	97.5	0.2	0.3	0.2	0.2	3.1	4.4	6.8	7.7	8.5	7.7	4.7	25.6	27.3	10.3	1.4	71.9	38.2	51.9	48.1
60531	LELAND	97.6	96.5	0.1	0.1	0.1	0.2	3.0	4.5	6.8	6.9	7.6	7.3	5.3	25.0	29.2	10.5	1.3	74.1	39.9	50.5	49.5
60532	LISLE	83.6	79.2	3.5	3.8	9.6	12.6	5.1	7.2	6.0	5.6	5.7	6.5	8.8	32.1	26.6	7.3	1.5	79.2	34.9	50.9	49.1
60534	LYONS	87.1	80.8	1.0	1.3	1.4	1.9	15.9	25.4	7.5	7.1	6.7	6.1	5.8	28.8	25.5	10.4	1.9	74.8	36.6	49.8	50.2
60537	MILLINGTON	81.2	80.2	14.6	14.4	0.2	0.4	4.0	4.9	5.6	6.0	6.4	7.3	8.2	32.7	25.6	7.3	0.9	78.2	34.7	62.0	38.0
60538	MONTGOMERY	89.7	88.0	2.9	2.5	0.9	1.0	10.9	14.6	7.4	7.6	7.8	7.0	4.9	27.5	27.4	9.3	1.2	72.9	37.2	49.6	50.4
60539	MOOSEHEART	0.0	88.3	0.0	3.2	0.0	2.1	0.0	13.8	7.4	8.5	8.5	8.5	4.3	25.5	30.9	6.4	0.0	69.1	37.1	50.0	50.0
60540	NAPERVILLE	87.5	83.3	2.0	2.2	8.3	11.5	3.5	5.1	7.1	7.5	8.1	8.2	5.7	24.8	28.7	8.5	1.3	72.5	37.5	49.2	50.8
60541	NEWARK	98.4	97.7	0.2	0.2	0.2	0.3	1.5	2.3	6.2	6.8	7.4	7.3	4.4	26.3	30.4	9.7	1.5	74.9	39.0	51.6	48.4
60542	NORTH AURORA	87.2	82.2	4.7	5.6	2.6	2.9	10.3	18.4	8.2	7.8	7.5	6.4	4.6	28.7	26.1	9.0	1.7	72.4	37.0	49.5	50.5
60543	OSWEGO	92.8	89.4	2.0	2.4	1.3	2.0	6.0	10.3	8.6	8.4	8.2	6.9	4.5	31.1	24.9	6.6	0.8	70.5	35.0	49.3	50.7
60544	PLAINFIELD	90.1	86.8	2.8	3.6	2.8	3.3	7.6	11.7	9.3	9.1	8.6	6.7	4.4	30.0	22.4	8.5	1.0	68.7	35.4	49.3	50.7
60545	PLANO	86.0	83.6	0.4	0.3	0.4	0.4	20.3	24.0	7.3	7.6	7.9	7.7	5.3	26.8	27.3	9.1	1.0	72.4	36.4	49.8	50.2
60546	RIVERSIDE	92.7	89.0	1.8	2.5	2.0	2.9	7.0	11.9	5.4	5.6	6.0	5.5	4.8	22.8	29.8	15.8	4.3	79.6	45.0	48.1	51.9
60548	SANDWICH	96.4	95.1	0.2	0.3	0.3	0.4	5.9	8.3	6.8	6.8	7.1	7.2	5.5	26.1	27.5	10.9	2.1	74.6	38.4	49.3	50.7
60549	SERENA	98.0	97.4	0.0	0.0	0.4	0.6	2.0	2.9	7.6	7.9	8.1	6.4	4.1	25.4	29.5	9.9	1.1	72.2	38.1	52.1	47.9
60550	SHABBONA	98.4	97.8	0.2	0.3	0.1	0.1	1.1	1.7	6.6	6.9	7.1	7.5	5.5	21.3	26.5	14.1	4.5	74.5	41.4	45.4	54.6
60551	SHERIDAN	77.1	74.6	17.6	18.5	0.2	0.3	5.6	7.4	5.8	6.1	6.1	6.5	9.5	36.0	22.6	6.6	0.8	78.8	33.6	63.8	36.2
60552	SOMONAUK	97.4	96.4	0.1	0.2	0.4	0.6	1.9	2.9	7.1	7.3	7.5	7.4	5.8	25.3	28.5	9.8	1.4	73.6	37.6	49.5	50.5
60553	STEWARD	97.8	96.9	0.1	0.1	0.0	0.0	3.5	5.4	7.2	7.8	8.5	7.4	4.5	26.4	26.7	10.1	1.3	71.7	37.9	52.9	47.1
60554	SUGAR GROVE	95.1	90.8	1.7	3.1	0.6	1.2	4.2	9.6	7.1	7.6	8.1	7.1	4.1	26.4	29.9	9.0	0.8	72.7	39.0	50.1	49.9
60555	WARRENVILLE	88.7	85.2	2.5	2.7	3.5	4.8	11.2	15.8	7.3	7.3	7.5	6.9	5.2	31.4	27.1	6.3	1.0	73.4	35.7	49.2	50.8
60556	WATERMAN	98.3	97.8	0.4	0.5	0.1	0.1	1.4	2.1	7.2	7.9	8.2	7.9	4.8	24.5	28.5	9.0	2.1	71.7	37.6	49.2	50.8
60558	WESTERN SPRINGS	98.4	97.5	0.2	0.3	0.7	1.0	1.7	3.0	7.1	8.2	9.4	8.5	3.7	17.0	30.6	12.8	2.8	69.8	42.3	47.9	52.1
60559	WESTMONT	80.1	74.4	4.4	4.7	11.4	15.5	6.2	8.8	6.6	5.9	5.9	5.8	6.6	29.0	25.4	11.3	3.6	78.2	38.2	47.6	52.4
60560	YORKVILLE	97.0	95.8	0.5	0.5	0.5	0.6	3.0	4.7	7.5	7.8	7.7	7.1	4.9	28.6	26.8	8.4	1.1	72.5	36.0	49.9	50.1
60561	DARIEN	84.2	79.2	2.2	2.4	11.1	15.0	4.1	5.9	5.2	5.6	6.1	6.1	4.7	24.0	31.7	14.3	2.3	79.1	43.7	48.4	51.6
60563	NAPERVILLE	82.7	77.4	4.4	5.3	10.2	13.7	4.3	6.4	6.7	6.4	6.5	5.8	6.0	33.6	25.0	7.9	2.0	76.6	36.1	48.6	51.4
60564	NAPERVILLE	84.7	78.3	4.8	7.3	7.6	10.0	4.2	7.1	11.3	11.6	10.4	7.0	2.7	33.7	20.8	2.3	0.2	61.8	32.3	49.7	50.3
60565	NAPERVILLE	85.5	80.3	2.5	3.1	10.3	14.2	2.5	3.8	7.1	8.4	9.6	9.0	4.6	21.8	32.9	6.0	0.6	69.0	37.7	49.2	50.8
60585	PLAINFIELD	92.8	89.1	1.8	3.0	3.0	4.0	3.9	6.9	11.3	11.1	10.5	7.6	3.3	30.5	22.5	2.8	0.2	62.0	31.1	49.6	50.4
60586	PLAINFIELD	92.7	88.3	1.9	3.2	1.5	2.0	6.7	11.6	11.7	10.9	9.8	7.0	3.9	33.9	19.1	3.5	0.3	63.1	30.8	50.0	50.0
60601	CHICAGO	74.5	64.0	11.1	15.8	10.6	14.5	5.7	9.6	3.2	1.5	1.4	1.7	4.8	30.4	41.3	13.9	1.8	93.1	48.9	47.5	52.5
60602	CHICAGO	62.7	61.7	4.5	0.5	25.4	14.0	20.9	53.6	4.1	3.1	2.7	2.7	6.1	39.9	28.4	11.0	2.0	89.0	39.0	50.5	49.5
60603	CHICAGO	65.0	55.6	8.4	10.2	17.9	22.7	13.4	19.7	2.8	1.2	1.6	27.3	28.9	19.4	16.0	2.8	0.0	93.1	23.0	48.4	51.6
60604	CHICAGO	43.5	33.9	12.9	13.7	31.8	41.1	18.8	22.6	5.1	6.3	7.1	8.3	4.8	22.9	33.6	10.4	1.5	79.2	42.6	49.7	50.3
60605	CHICAGO	53.7	39.0	33.8	45.9	7.8	9.0	4.9	6.6	3.9	3.7	3.5	5.0	8.9	41.1	24.9	7.6	1.4	87.2	35.5	51.4	48.6
60606	CHICAGO	72.7	59.6	5.8	7.1	16.5	20.7	8.2	22.5	4.1	3.1	2.8	4.2	7.9	46.4	24.4	6.4	0.8	88.3	34.0	51.6	48.4
60607	CHICAGO	47.3	39.2	33.6	41.3	13.6	12.8	8.2	10.5	4.5	3.8	3.4	5.3	13.2	40.0	21.1	7.5	1.2	86.0	32.5	51.3	48.7
60608	CHICAGO	37.8	33.6	12.0	13.8	5.6	5.9	68.5	71.5	10.4	9.2	7.7	8.4	9.2	31.4	17.1	5.8	0.8	67.8	27.6	51.7	48.3
60609	CHICAGO	34.6	33.3	39.2	36.6	1.3	1.5	43.1	49.2	11.4	10.5	8.6	9.1	9.1	28.0	17.1	5.5	0.7	64.1	25.8	49.3	50.7
60610	CHICAGO	64.1	59.2	29.2	31.8	4.0	5.3	3.6	6.7	5.0	4.2	3.4	4.4	10.6	35.9	24.8	10.1	1.6	85.1	35.1	46.3	53.7
60611	CHICAGO	82.7	76.0	5.1	7.1	9.5	12.9	3.6	5.9	2.2	1.3	1.0	1.2	7.4	37.7	32.7	14.1	2.3	94.8	44.3	46.9	53.1
60612	CHICAGO	19.3	15.7	65.1	67.6	5.8	4.7	14.1	17.6	8.3	7.9	7.3	10.2	10.1	27.1	19.7	8.2	1.2	70.6	28.7	47.8	52.2
60613	CHICAGO	76.9	69.3	8.7	10.9	5.8	7.5	13.1	19.6	3.7	2.2	2.0	2.5	11.7	48.4	20.3	7.8	1.5	90.7	33.7	51.8	48.2
60614	CHICAGO	87.6	82.3	4.8	6.5	3.7	5.2	5.4	9.0	4.2	2.2	1.9	4.2	12.9	47.9	19.5	5.8	1.4	90.4	31.4	49.1	50.9
	ILLINOIS	73.5	70.6	15.1	15.3	3.4	4.4	12.3	15.7	7.1	6.9	6.8	7.1	6.9	27.5	25.4	10.3	1.9	75.0	36.1	49.1	50.9
	UNITED STATES	75.1	72.0	12.3	12.7	3.8	4.6	12.5	15.7	6.8	6.7	6.6	7.1	6.9	27.0	26.0	10.9	1.9	75.7	36.9	49.2	50.8

60457-60614

#	POST OFFICE NAME	2009 Per Capita Income	2009 HH Income Base	2009 Household Income Distribution (%): Less than $25,000	$25,000 to $49,999	$50,000 to $99,999	$100,000 to $149,999	$150,000 or More	Median Household Income: 2009	2014	2009 National Centile	2009 State Centile	2009 Home Value Base	2009 Home Value Distribution (%): Less than $50,000	$50,000 to $89,999	$90,000 to $174,999	$175,000 to $399,999	$400,000 or More	2009 Median Home Value
60457	HICKORY HILLS	28822	4839	11.7	19.9	48.4	14.4	5.6	68769	70608	86	79	3294	0.6	0.8	19.4	73.0	6.2	224360
60458	JUSTICE	25037	5137	15.3	21.8	50.1	9.1	3.8	62682	65372	81	69	3175	20.8	4.3	22.8	49.7	2.4	178940
60459	BURBANK	23262	9225	13.8	21.6	49.4	11.8	3.5	64035	66736	82	72	7412	0.4	1.1	38.4	57.8	2.3	187934
60460	ODELL	27173	678	16.5	27.4	43.4	10.9	1.8	56084	59179	73	58	535	7.9	18.1	54.0	17.2	2.8	125619
60461	OLYMPIA FIELDS	45034	1781	9.1	10.3	35.3	21.5	23.8	91541	92443	95	96	1525	0.5	0.5	9.6	63.0	26.4	304894
60462	ORLAND PARK	35047	14546	8.3	17.0	44.2	18.6	11.9	77857	78493	91	90	12471	0.6	0.4	16.4	71.8	10.9	260853
60463	PALOS HEIGHTS	36276	5090	11.5	18.1	41.3	16.8	12.4	76586	77253	90	88	4516	0.1	0.8	7.4	74.9	16.7	286456
60464	PALOS PARK	41675	3898	8.1	17.2	35.2	20.0	19.5	82837	83880	93	93	3435	1.3	0.3	5.3	50.5	42.5	371405
60465	PALOS HILLS	29895	7607	11.3	23.7	48.9	12.3	3.9	64960	67138	83	74	5709	1.3	1.3	30.6	60.2	6.5	212067
60466	PARK FOREST	25977	11712	14.7	22.9	46.4	12.1	3.9	61625	63648	80	67	8164	17.4	9.6	59.7	12.5	0.8	121376
60467	ORLAND PARK	39555	8398	5.8	9.8	41.3	23.5	19.5	90564	91560	95	96	7775	0.3	0.0	3.1	68.4	28.1	332946
60468	PEOTONE	28493	2528	8.8	17.0	47.5	22.2	4.4	73161	77051	88	84	1797	1.0	3.0	12.1	68.3	15.5	263345
60469	POSEN	22161	1702	13.7	22.2	51.9	10.1	2.0	63144	65811	81	70	1331	4.4	6.5	72.0	16.8	0.3	127440
60470	RANSOM	25556	255	15.3	22.4	47.8	10.2	4.3	63615	64198	82	71	212	10.8	17.5	43.9	24.5	3.3	126852
60471	RICHTON PARK	27035	4925	11.6	24.6	44.4	14.3	5.1	62436	64936	81	69	3254	2.0	9.4	45.5	39.8	3.3	159741
60472	ROBBINS	13021	1953	41.8	26.7	27.4	3.4	0.7	32317	35399	12	3	1158	21.8	43.8	26.9	6.6	0.9	74834
60473	SOUTH HOLLAND	28919	7910	11.3	19.9	44.9	17.0	7.0	73371	75118	89	84	6792	0.9	2.0	43.2	51.3	2.6	180539
60475	STEGER	24236	4203	23.2	23.4	38.7	11.7	3.0	54200	56865	70	54	2545	1.3	4.3	65.5	27.4	1.4	146146
60476	THORNTON	28010	968	14.3	28.8	42.1	9.8	5.0	58502	61575	76	62	822	1.0	2.9	80.9	14.6	0.6	143091
60477	TINLEY PARK	30417	15086	10.2	19.1	49.3	15.5	6.0	73542	74366	89	84	11986	0.2	0.8	25.4	68.8	4.7	213423
60478	COUNTRY CLUB HILLS	25285	5508	8.8	22.5	47.3	16.2	5.1	70334	71643	87	80	4770	0.4	6.6	62.8	28.6	1.6	148062
60479	VERONA	23371	268	10.1	26.5	53.4	7.1	3.0	66268	68022	84	76	203	5.9	13.8	26.6	36.5	17.2	183929
60480	WILLOW SPRINGS	36548	2018	11.3	16.3	48.1	13.1	11.1	76927	77376	91	89	1635	0.2	0.2	13.1	62.7	23.7	297201
60481	WILMINGTON	26527	5106	14.2	23.9	44.5	13.0	4.4	62988	64030	81	70	3796	2.7	7.0	43.3	41.6	5.4	170934
60482	WORTH	25294	4342	18.9	23.7	46.2	8.5	2.7	56129	60110	73	58	2955	8.5	2.4	37.2	49.7	2.2	178044
60487	TINLEY PARK	29012	8262	5.3	10.9	53.6	19.9	10.3	81094	83068	92	92	7350	0.4	0.2	11.2	76.7	11.5	257708
60490	BOLINGBROOK	39667	5459	2.9	5.3	20.0	44.9	26.9	125643	126886	99	99	5268	0.0	0.8	1.8	69.6	27.8	336620
60491	HOMER GLEN	33632	8861	5.0	8.8	41.3	26.5	18.3	92621	99023	96	96	8413	1.5	0.2	2.0	54.7	41.5	375927
60501	SUMMIT ARGO	17578	3578	25.7	25.4	38.7	7.2	3.0	48938	50929	59	40	1966	0.7	3.8	59.1	35.4	1.0	157732
60502	AURORA	44758	6730	4.3	8.7	35.9	24.8	26.3	101820	107301	97	98	5545	0.6	1.0	17.8	47.7	32.9	310444
60503	AURORA	49740	5163	3.3	7.9	32.8	26.8	29.2	108809	111839	98	98	4697	1.0	0.6	1.1	48.9	48.4	393616
60504	AURORA	40115	13480	4.9	13.2	35.5	28.7	17.6	93750	101069	96	97	9988	0.4	1.8	23.1	62.2	12.5	233088
60505	AURORA	15570	17891	21.0	29.0	41.6	6.5	1.8	49932	49653	61	43	10809	3.3	4.9	61.6	29.9	0.4	147650
60506	AURORA	25601	19321	14.8	21.2	44.8	12.0	7.2	63482	66149	82	71	13136	0.7	3.3	29.2	59.5	7.2	209707
60510	BATAVIA	34236	11407	9.4	13.2	41.6	20.0	15.7	81650	89753	93	92	8926	0.9	0.3	5.3	67.3	26.1	313031
60511	BIG ROCK	32191	703	6.4	11.1	52.6	20.1	9.8	79384	85104	92	91	584	0.0	0.0	7.0	68.2	24.8	306369
60512	BRISTOL	36457	420	6.2	13.8	40.5	29.0	10.5	85663	90972	94	94	378	0.0	0.5	1.3	66.4	31.7	352740
60513	BROOKFIELD	29802	7302	10.9	21.5	47.6	15.4	4.6	67335	69552	85	77	5305	0.5	0.3	18.0	79.0	2.2	216646
60514	CLARENDON HILLS	50332	3646	4.6	15.7	32.1	21.5	26.1	95537	103373	96	97	2859	0.0	0.6	5.0	43.0	51.5	409002
60515	DOWNERS GROVE	38798	11047	14.1	17.9	34.5	20.2	13.2	75671	79227	90	87	8730	0.5	3.4	15.9	59.4	20.8	268404
60516	DOWNERS GROVE	39059	12414	6.5	14.4	38.3	25.5	15.2	86578	92899	94	95	9856	0.5	0.2	13.3	69.0	17.0	285689
60517	WOODRIDGE	35144	11895	7.2	17.8	41.0	21.6	12.5	80022	84122	92	92	8527	0.6	5.6	18.3	64.1	11.4	230446
60518	EARLVILLE	24206	1534	16.9	23.7	46.5	9.8	3.1	60514	61720	78	65	1124	8.5	8.8	45.7	33.5	3.6	150503
60520	HINCKLEY	27972	1106	8.5	13.9	61.2	12.6	3.8	76426	76988	90	88	817	0.0	0.5	14.8	76.5	8.2	242199
60521	HINSDALE	62798	6265	8.0	12.0	20.7	17.0	42.3	127241	129189	99	99	5254	0.6	0.4	1.4	21.2	76.4	686204
60523	OAK BROOK	62370	3658	10.8	11.6	20.9	16.1	40.7	119698	124238	98	99	3165	0.8	1.0	4.0	24.9	69.4	658076
60525	LA GRANGE	39011	12108	12.5	19.8	36.4	16.2	15.0	75760	76774	90	87	9434	6.9	2.6	11.4	49.8	29.3	289773
60526	LA GRANGE PARK	37491	5230	11.5	21.6	39.4	16.9	10.7	73513	75435	89	84	3725	0.2	0.5	7.1	70.1	22.1	288422
60527	WILLOWBROOK	46592	11304	7.3	18.3	36.7	16.2	21.5	81863	85463	93	92	8668	0.2	4.0	17.3	37.3	41.2	321178
60530	LEE	24868	229	14.0	19.7	54.1	7.9	4.4	67056	68756	85	77	168	1.8	5.4	36.3	40.5	16.1	194643
60531	LELAND	24267	750	14.0	23.1	52.0	7.6	3.3	63125	64153	81	70	564	1.4	4.6	42.4	44.3	7.3	178516
60532	LISLE	44308	14073	9.2	15.8	41.1	18.2	15.7	77676	80707	91	90	7454	0.8	1.4	18.7	58.3	20.8	269670
60534	LYONS	26051	3914	14.4	23.1	50.7	8.2	3.7	59544	62309	77	63	2378	0.3	1.5	45.6	47.6	5.0	178890
60537	MILLINGTON	26026	142	12.7	16.2	49.3	17.6	4.2	65830	67814	84	75	109	0.0	6.4	33.0	38.5	22.0	201667
60538	MONTGOMERY	30554	8974	8.6	16.3	45.5	22.3	7.3	77287	80965	91	89	7421	0.5	1.2	8.4	72.6	17.3	274190
60539	MOOSEHEART	37076	31	3.2	12.9	48.4	19.4	16.1	83484	90212	93	93	27	0.0	0.0	0.0	74.1	25.9	282143
60540	NAPERVILLE	48417	15340	6.3	9.5	27.6	25.9	30.7	112787	116520	98	98	12092	1.4	0.4	3.2	63.4	31.6	343482
60541	NEWARK	27593	1381	8.3	14.6	46.6	25.9	4.6	76102	79081	90	88	1053	0.7	3.8	9.9	59.4	26.2	281514
60542	NORTH AURORA	33233	6029	7.8	17.3	46.8	17.0	11.1	76843	81622	90	89	4760	0.2	0.9	13.3	65.8	19.7	249385
60543	OSWEGO	34050	11996	6.8	13.3	38.1	28.7	13.0	87819	93594	95	95	10142	0.2	0.5	4.6	59.7	35.0	351077
60544	PLAINFIELD	31679	9643	6.9	15.3	49.3	21.0	7.5	78112	81083	91	90	8221	0.3	0.8	10.4	78.5	9.9	266385
60545	PLANO	25253	4809	10.4	23.6	46.4	14.7	4.8	66807	69900	85	76	3686	0.0	1.3	6.5	76.4	15.8	262458
60546	RIVERSIDE	35927	6306	12.0	21.2	44.7	11.7	10.3	68336	70800	86	79	4617	0.4	0.4	11.2	65.9	22.1	251002
60548	SANDWICH	25081	4593	13.3	21.2	52.5	10.3	2.7	67799	71589	85	78	3472	4.4	4.8	23.8	63.0	4.0	213622
60549	SERENA	27185	201	13.4	18.4	52.7	11.9	3.5	68433	70066	86	79	151	5.3	9.3	33.8	43.7	7.9	181944
60550	SHABBONA	26524	537	14.0	18.6	54.2	9.1	4.1	67385	71423	85	77	376	1.1	0.3	38.6	54.3	5.9	189615
60551	SHERIDAN	21695	1210	12.6	20.2	51.8	11.7	3.6	66740	68558	85	76	964	2.7	10.5	41.3	41.3	4.3	165733
60552	SOMONAUK	25636	1562	8.0	21.5	58.7	9.3	2.4	71516	74546	88	82	1235	1.1	3.2	21.9	69.1	4.5	219853
60553	STEWARD	24366	266	11.3	22.9	53.8	8.3	3.8	66853	66935	85	77	204	2.0	7.8	40.7	40.7	8.8	173958
60554	SUGAR GROVE	39387	3658	6.5	11.0	37.6	23.3	21.7	92772	102346	96	96	3201	0.0	0.4	6.0	61.5	32.1	327462
60555	WARRENVILLE	34884	5199	5.2	14.2	51.4	20.5	8.8	78275	81064	91	91	4179	0.3	1.1	28.5	62.5	7.6	210791
60556	WATERMAN	25735	772	15.4	19.3	54.9	6.0	4.4	66722	69284	85	76	552	3.1	1.8	26.1	60.0	9.1	212258
60558	WESTERN SPRINGS	54072	4203	4.5	11.3	25.5	21.8	36.9	114667	115848	98	98	3745	0.3	0.5	1.5	35.4	62.3	458842
60559	WESTMONT	36665	10879	13.2	18.9	39.3	17.0	11.6	73470	76640	89	84	6711	0.1	1.5	16.9	63.2	18.3	244303
60560	YORKVILLE	31915	7011	8.4	14.3	40.3	27.5	9.5	81086	86451	92	92	5664	1.5	0.3	2.4	62.7	33.1	348134
60561	DARIEN	40798	9133	8.1	12.9	39.0	24.0	16.0	85755	92082	94	94	7636	0.8	0.2	8.4	73.4	17.2	298282
60563	NAPERVILLE	44923	14298	7.8	15.3	35.8	24.2	16.8	86030	92729	94	95	8625	0.7	1.3	15.6	60.2	22.2	272683
60564	NAPERVILLE	46801	13234	2.3	5.1	24.0	28.6	40.0	132680	134153	99	99	12556	1.2	0.5	2.4	42.7	53.3	421535
60565	NAPERVILLE	46102	13607	4.3	8.4	24.9	28.1	34.3	125854	127389	99	99	12318	0.7	0.8	5.6	50.5	42.4	373183
60585	PLAINFIELD	44147	6577	2.2	3.5	27.5	31.0	35.7	126557	128397	99	99	6346	0.0	0.2	1.8	42.1	55.9	431853
60586	PLAINFIELD	30670	13538	2.8	7.3	48.1	30.8	11.0	90255	96011	95	96	12823	0.1	0.3	4.3	82.2	13.1	281933
60601	CHICAGO	99096	4529	5.1	13.4	31.9	19.0	30.5	98610	97360	96	97	2327	1.4	0.0	10.8	43.9	43.8	364035
60602	CHICAGO	29404	316	47.8	30.7	10.1	3.8	7.6	25843	26881	4	1	164	0.0	0.0	10.4	45.1	44.5	367857
60603	CHICAGO	17833	25	4.0	8.0	40.0	0.0	48.0	98081	89519	96	97	10	0.0	0.0	30.0	70.0	0.0	212500
60604	CHICAGO	74446	137	2.9	5.8	0.0	0.0	91.2	185194	182657	100	100	42	0.0	0.0	7.1	92.9	0.0	223611
60605	CHICAGO	51492	9900	26.4	14.3	32.7	11.8	14.8	64149	68434	82	72	3926	0.2	0.6	4.3	61.8	33.0	324005
60606	CHICAGO	67599	1361	2.6	1.2	57.4	15.7	23.1	86657	80436	94	95	914	0.0	0.2	7.3	64.8	27.7	312446
60607	CHICAGO	38799	9537	29.6	14.2	32.1	9.2	14.9	60835	64645	79	66	3947	1.8	1.1	6.5	51.9	38.7	342348
60608	CHICAGO	14112	25349	35.7	30.6	26.9	4.7	2.1	35646	37904	20	7	8417	4.7	4.9	43.2	42.7	4.4	169415
60609	CHICAGO	13328	21906	40.1	26.6	26.2	4.8	2.3	33613	35913	15	5	7902	6.4	17.0	48.5	25.6	2.6	128955
60610	CHICAGO	59383	23877	23.4	15.1	35.5	10.3	15.7	67103	69621	85	77	8907	0.5	1.3	15.6	36.6	46.1	370161
60611	CHICAGO	92694	18096	11.9	12.6	34.1	15.1	26.2	86044	87025	94	95	8749	0.5	1.2	12.3	37.6	48.3	385341
60612	CHICAGO	17624	13275	42.5	22.5	25.7	4.9	4.3	33804	35671	15	5	3562	4.9	6.7	30.9	42.4	15.1	209855
60613	CHICAGO	48371	28666	16.5	19.5	42.8	11.5	9.8	64252	66854	83	73	9624	0.6	3.6	22.4	41.2	32.3	283022
60614	CHICAGO	78525	35035	12.5	12.9	33.4	14.9	26.2	85458	86000	94	94	14497	0.1	0.7	6.8	31.3	61.0	497234
	ILLINOIS	28587		18.2	22.2	39.3	12.1	8.2	60823	63631				6.3	10.0	30.9	40.6	12.3	185324
	UNITED STATES	27277		20.9	24.4	35.3	11.7	7.6	54719	56938				9.3	13.1	31.6	32.6	13.5	162279

ZIP CODE		FINANCIAL SERVICES				THE HOME						ENTERTAINMENT						PERSONAL			
						Home Improvements		Furnishings													
#	POST OFFICE NAME	Auto Loan	Home Loan	Invest-ments	Retire-ment Plans	Home Repair	Lawn & Garden	Comput-ers & Hard-ware-Personal	Major Appli-ances	TV, Radio, Sound Equip-ment	Furni-ture	Dine out/ Carry out	Sports Equip-ment	Fees & Tickets	Toys & Games	Travel	Cable TV	Apparel & Services	Auto Repairs	Health Insur-ance	Pets & Supplies
60457	HICKORY HILLS	99	118	113	114	117	109	109	107	106	108	107	82	118	107	115	106	77	108	106	123
60458	JUSTICE	102	96	83	96	91	90	100	94	98	101	99	75	96	102	94	96	69	97	92	112
60459	BURBANK	88	108	98	106	105	103	96	97	95	96	96	74	107	96	104	96	68	96	100	112
60460	ODELL	95	87	85	88	83	101	89	93	90	81	90	74	83	91	87	94	61	92	101	113
60461	OLYMPIA FIELDS	157	197	213	199	208	194	170	182	166	182	165	131	197	161	194	165	119	173	181	205
60462	ORLAND PARK	121	145	146	146	148	140	128	133	126	134	127	99	144	125	141	126	91	129	133	152
60463	PALOS HEIGHTS	122	148	166	146	158	151	129	140	129	134	129	98	147	126	146	132	92	134	144	157
60464	PALOS PARK	143	181	201	181	193	180	153	166	151	163	150	118	179	147	176	151	109	157	166	186
60465	PALOS HILLS	93	103	101	102	104	103	99	99	100	99	100	73	106	98	104	102	70	100	107	115
60466	PARK FOREST	96	98	85	99	93	96	97	94	98	97	99	73	99	99	96	99	69	96	99	112
60467	ORLAND PARK	146	202	214	199	211	182	165	172	156	171	157	130	198	158	190	153	117	163	159	191
60468	PEOTONE	107	125	111	125	121	120	112	114	111	112	112	89	122	113	120	112	79	112	115	134
60469	POSEN	90	95	81	92	91	89	93	91	91	94	92	70	94	93	92	91	65	92	91	106
60470	RANSOM	105	96	93	99	97	111	94	105	97	87	95	79	87	99	93	102	65	97	108	122
60471	RICHTON PARK	109	105	90	104	100	95	107	101	104	110	106	78	103	107	101	102	73	103	98	120
60472	ROBBINS	57	51	46	52	48	57	53	53	58	54	58	38	52	57	50	62	39	55	61	66
60473	SOUTH HOLLAND	105	127	119	127	125	126	110	115	112	113	113	85	125	111	122	114	79	113	122	134
60475	STEGER	89	86	74	87	82	85	89	85	89	87	89	67	87	91	85	89	61	87	88	102
60476	THORNTON	92	103	101	101	104	113	94	102	101	93	100	71	103	97	102	107	69	100	118	117
60477	TINLEY PARK	104	123	113	122	120	114	111	111	108	113	109	86	121	110	117	107	78	109	108	129
60478	COUNTRY CLUB HILLS	106	118	104	115	113	111	105	107	106	109	107	79	112	108	108	107	75	105	108	125
60479	VERONA	102	97	93	100	98	110	94	104	96	86	94	79	89	98	94	100	65	97	107	121
60480	WILLOW SPRINGS	127	148	141	151	148	141	133	136	129	137	131	105	145	131	143	128	93	132	132	158
60481	WILMINGTON	96	105	93	106	102	104	98	99	98	97	98	77	103	100	101	99	69	98	102	117
60482	WORTH	81	91	85	90	89	86	89	86	87	87	89	67	95	88	92	87	63	88	87	100
60487	TINLEY PARK	133	155	130	151	147	129	133	134	125	143	128	107	143	133	137	119	91	127	117	153
60490	BOLINGBROOK	190	232	200	238	225	191	193	195	178	215	181	162	218	192	203	163	133	178	160	218
60491	HOMER GLEN	153	190	174	192	186	166	160	163	150	170	153	129	181	156	173	144	111	154	146	187
60501	SUMMIT ARGO	78	81	72	75	79	69	82	78	77	84	79	60	80	79	80	74	57	80	71	88
60502	AURORA	191	219	190	225	212	184	192	190	180	210	183	157	211	192	198	167	133	179	162	215
60503	AURORA	206	241	204	243	231	197	204	205	189	227	193	169	224	205	210	175	140	189	171	230
60504	AURORA	160	170	148	176	163	144	159	151	150	171	153	127	167	160	158	140	110	148	132	175
60505	AURORA	81	77	66	72	75	65	83	77	78	86	81	61	78	80	78	73	57	81	69	86
60506	AURORA	103	112	103	110	110	102	107	105	104	110	105	81	111	105	109	102	75	105	101	121
60510	BATAVIA	131	160	151	162	159	143	139	141	132	146	134	110	156	136	149	128	97	135	130	160
60511	BIG ROCK	119	153	158	152	158	142	129	136	124	135	125	101	149	124	146	123	91	129	129	154
60512	BRISTOL	135	154	133	158	149	148	136	141	133	137	134	111	146	137	144	133	94	136	138	166
60513	BROOKFIELD	95	116	112	112	116	107	104	105	102	104	103	79	116	103	112	102	74	104	104	120
60514	CLARENDON HILLS	170	213	217	217	218	193	184	187	175	193	177	145	212	178	203	170	130	180	171	212
60515	DOWNERS GROVE	118	146	151	144	150	138	131	133	128	134	129	99	147	126	144	128	93	131	134	151
60516	DOWNERS GROVE	140	161	155	163	160	146	148	145	142	153	144	114	161	145	155	138	104	144	137	168
60517	WOODRIDGE	136	141	130	145	137	127	139	131	134	143	136	106	144	138	139	130	97	134	124	155
60518	EARLVILLE	96	93	87	96	92	104	91	98	93	84	92	75	88	94	91	97	63	93	102	115
60520	HINCKLEY	109	119	106	122	116	120	107	113	106	107	106	89	112	108	113	107	74	108	112	133
60521	HINSDALE	221	301	355	312	332	275	255	267	234	280	234	205	311	231	298	222	178	249	232	294
60523	OAK BROOK	198	262	307	267	287	253	227	239	218	243	217	175	273	211	263	216	161	227	233	264
60525	LA GRANGE	126	148	162	148	155	146	135	140	133	140	133	103	150	130	148	133	96	136	140	159
60526	LA GRANGE PARK	108	142	150	138	147	133	124	127	123	123	124	93	144	121	139	125	91	125	129	142
60527	WILLOWBROOK	156	178	187	183	184	169	166	166	161	174	161	127	183	161	177	157	117	163	160	190
60530	LEE	104	100	107	102	99	114	95	105	96	90	96	84	92	97	99	99	65	100	107	126
60531	LELAND	102	94	95	98	95	110	92	103	94	84	93	79	86	96	93	99	63	96	106	121
60532	LISLE	146	134	128	141	131	125	148	132	145	150	147	108	146	149	140	141	105	142	131	159
60534	LYONS	84	98	93	96	97	90	95	91	92	92	94	72	102	93	99	92	67	93	91	106
60537	MILLINGTON	104	108	98	111	106	114	100	107	100	96	100	83	101	102	103	103	69	102	108	126
60538	MONTGOMERY	118	135	116	135	129	126	120	122	118	123	119	95	129	122	125	117	84	119	119	142
60539	MOOSEHEART	151	190	167	190	183	164	159	162	149	167	153	129	180	156	172	144	110	154	145	186
60540	NAPERVILLE	180	220	218	226	223	197	191	193	181	204	183	153	218	186	208	174	135	184	175	219
60541	NEWARK	113	127	110	131	124	125	114	118	112	114	112	92	121	115	120	112	79	114	117	139
60542	NORTH AURORA	123	139	126	139	136	126	127	126	123	132	125	100	136	127	132	120	89	124	120	146
60543	OSWEGO	144	167	143	165	160	141	144	145	135	155	138	116	155	144	149	129	98	137	128	165
60544	PLAINFIELD	117	137	122	135	133	122	122	122	117	126	119	96	132	122	127	115	85	119	115	140
60545	PLANO	106	115	98	114	111	109	106	108	103	108	104	84	109	106	109	102	73	105	105	126
60546	RIVERSIDE	107	129	132	127	132	127	117	120	117	117	117	88	131	115	127	119	84	118	125	136
60548	SANDWICH	91	106	96	106	103	102	96	97	94	96	95	75	104	96	101	95	67	95	98	113
60549	SERENA	104	113	100	117	111	114	103	108	102	102	102	84	107	104	108	103	71	103	108	127
60550	SHABBONA	95	113	105	113	109	114	98	103	99	98	100	78	110	100	108	102	70	101	109	121
60551	SHERIDAN	101	107	96	111	105	111	98	105	98	96	98	81	101	100	102	100	68	99	105	123
60552	SOMONAUK	96	110	99	110	107	105	100	102	98	100	99	80	107	100	106	98	70	99	100	119
60553	STEWARD	102	103	102	106	102	111	96	104	96	92	96	82	96	97	100	98	66	99	105	124
60554	SUGAR GROVE	165	200	188	204	199	181	170	176	162	181	164	138	191	167	184	157	118	166	160	201
60555	WARRENVILLE	132	151	133	150	145	133	135	134	129	141	131	105	144	134	139	125	93	131	124	156
60556	WATERMAN	101	105	100	108	103	111	97	104	96	94	96	82	98	98	101	98	67	99	104	123
60558	WESTERN SPRINGS	192	262	290	267	280	241	217	228	204	232	205	172	263	203	253	198	153	214	208	253
60559	WESTMONT	118	131	129	131	131	121	128	122	125	127	126	95	136	126	131	124	91	125	121	142
60560	YORKVILLE	128	149	127	147	142	130	131	131	124	137	126	104	140	130	135	120	90	126	120	151
60561	DARIEN	137	170	174	169	174	159	148	152	143	153	144	114	167	143	163	142	104	148	147	173
60563	NAPERVILLE	152	158	149	165	155	141	156	146	149	162	152	120	162	155	155	142	109	148	135	172
60564	NAPERVILLE	226	274	237	282	267	225	228	231	210	256	214	192	258	227	240	192	157	211	188	257
60565	NAPERVILLE	191	243	244	252	248	218	205	210	193	220	195	166	240	198	227	185	145	198	187	238
60585	PLAINFIELD	203	246	212	253	240	202	205	207	188	230	192	172	232	204	215	172	141	189	169	231
60586	PLAINFIELD	149	174	147	174	167	143	148	149	137	163	140	121	161	148	152	127	101	138	125	167
60601	CHICAGO	202	209	243	230	220	194	236	206	222	231	229	175	245	220	238	215	170	218	195	243
60602	CHICAGO	65	67	79	74	71	63	76	67	71	75	74	57	79	71	77	69	55	70	63	78
60603	CHICAGO	174	208	229	216	219	199	190	190	183	200	183	147	218	182	206	178	135	185	180	218
60604	CHICAGO	212	294	355	308	327	278	241	257	228	267	226	194	308	227	286	219	175	238	229	282
60605	CHICAGO	121	103	107	114	101	99	134	108	133	125	137	93	127	132	121	132	99	124	113	136
60606	CHICAGO	158	149	154	160	148	140	177	150	170	169	175	128	174	171	168	166	126	165	150	182
60607	CHICAGO	114	97	104	106	97	94	133	105	126	120	129	91	121	125	117	124	93	120	107	130
60608	CHICAGO	63	55	49	54	54	46	69	59	66	68	69	48	63	66	63	63	50	67	54	67
60609	CHICAGO	64	54	49	54	52	50	67	58	68	66	70	47	62	68	61	67	50	66	59	69
60610	CHICAGO	134	113	124	128	114	110	151	122	148	143	152	106	143	146	138	146	110	139	127	152
60611	CHICAGO	184	165	184	185	167	154	209	170	199	200	206	150	203	199	197	192	150	191	167	208
60612	CHICAGO	62	54	55	58	54	55	71	59	73	65	74	48	67	70	64	76	53	68	66	74
60613	CHICAGO	113	93	99	105	92	87	126	99	120	119	125	90	117	121	114	116	90	115	100	125
60614	CHICAGO	184	165	185	185	168	155	210	171	200	201	207	151	204	199	198	194	151	192	169	210
	ILLINOIS	106	108	105	108	107	106	109	106	108	107	109	83	110	108	108	108	77	108	107	125
	UNITED STATES	100	100	100	100	100	100	100	100	100	100	100	100	100	100	100	100	100	100	100	100

ZIP CODE #	POST OFFICE NAME	COUNTY FIPS CODE	POPULATION 2000	POPULATION 2009	POPULATION 2014	2000-2009 ANNUAL RATE % Rate	2000-2009 ANNUAL RATE State Centile	HOUSEHOLDS 2000	HOUSEHOLDS 2009	HOUSEHOLDS 2014	HOUSEHOLDS % Annual Rate 2000-2009	HOUSEHOLDS 2009 Average HH Size	FAMILIES 2000	FAMILIES 2009	FAMILIES % Annual Rate 2000-2009
60615	CHICAGO	031	45077	43178	42405	-0.5	18	21330	20402	19969	-0.5	2.02	9260	8593	-0.8
60616	CHICAGO	031	47561	50232	51575	0.6	75	19459	21073	21769	0.9	2.24	10182	10513	0.3
60617	CHICAGO	031	96549	92679	90821	-0.4	25	31697	30437	29770	-0.4	3.04	23618	22335	-0.6
60618	CHICAGO	031	99028	102013	101956	0.3	65	35257	35784	35654	0.2	2.84	22145	21948	-0.1
60619	CHICAGO	031	74868	71358	69921	-0.5	18	29824	28584	27974	-0.5	2.49	18623	17461	-0.7
60620	CHICAGO	031	82505	78071	76250	-0.6	13	27355	26043	25410	-0.5	2.98	20200	18933	-0.7
60621	CHICAGO	031	47604	44734	43936	-0.7	9	14993	14152	13888	-0.6	3.10	10308	9549	-0.8
60622	CHICAGO	031	56304	59006	59232	0.5	72	22708	24095	24202	0.6	2.42	11284	11593	0.3
60623	CHICAGO	031	117211	116577	115328	-0.1	45	27641	27484	27129	-0.1	3.83	22543	22143	-0.2
60624	CHICAGO	031	45650	44003	43392	-0.4	25	13744	13227	13015	-0.4	3.25	9907	9407	-0.6
60625	CHICAGO	031	91260	88783	87524	-0.3	32	30547	29417	28875	-0.4	2.95	19739	18636	-0.6
60626	CHICAGO	031	60494	58360	57345	-0.4	25	24386	23274	22782	-0.5	2.39	11687	10805	-0.8
60628	CHICAGO	031	87487	81243	79027	-0.8	6	26920	25216	24524	-0.7	3.19	20476	18906	-0.9
60629	CHICAGO	031	114229	116123	114682	0.2	61	32540	31393	30807	-0.4	3.69	25172	23945	-0.5
60630	CHICAGO	031	54618	53624	52876	-0.2	38	21468	20885	20512	-0.3	2.56	13879	13222	-0.5
60631	CHICAGO	031	28767	28159	27804	-0.2	38	11898	11731	11576	-0.2	2.34	7531	7259	-0.4
60632	CHICAGO	031	88040	92737	92175	0.6	75	24625	24204	23903	-0.2	3.83	19108	18532	-0.3
60633	CHICAGO	031	13103	12359	12049	-0.6	13	5026	4757	4634	-0.6	2.53	3280	3039	-0.8
60634	CHICAGO	031	74965	74953	74210	0.0	50	26422	25956	25577	-0.2	2.86	18921	18246	-0.4
60636	CHICAGO	031	51073	48080	46839	-0.7	9	13907	13154	12801	-0.6	3.62	10982	10260	-0.7
60637	CHICAGO	031	57346	54862	54115	-0.5	18	21811	20718	20393	-0.6	2.51	12317	11373	-0.9
60638	CHICAGO	031	55831	54010	53226	-0.4	25	20769	20208	19900	-0.3	2.67	14452	13772	-0.5
60639	CHICAGO	031	91999	92997	91738	0.1	56	25155	24396	23929	-0.3	3.80	20143	19301	-0.5
60640	CHICAGO	031	75896	75113	74756	-0.1	45	36210	35962	35708	-0.1	1.98	13935	13365	-0.5
60641	CHICAGO	031	73507	75045	74318	0.2	61	25241	24800	24397	-0.2	3.00	17014	16408	-0.4
60642	CHICAGO	031	19502	21335	21875	1.0	83	8194	9038	9298	1.1	2.34	3704	3975	0.8
60643	CHICAGO	031	55838	53581	52772	-0.4	25	18669	18084	17808	-0.3	2.94	14163	13519	-0.5
60644	CHICAGO	031	59210	58686	58004	-0.1	45	17946	17791	17553	-0.1	3.21	13051	12737	-0.3
60645	CHICAGO	031	43516	42020	41144	-0.4	25	15948	15094	14697	-0.6	2.72	10208	9453	-0.8
60646	CHICAGO	031	26151	25694	25381	-0.2	38	10401	10264	10129	-0.1	2.50	7236	7004	-0.4
60647	CHICAGO	031	97584	98967	98656	0.2	61	32989	33590	33479	0.2	2.92	20173	20093	0.0
60649	CHICAGO	031	54520	51861	50701	-0.5	18	23411	22405	21887	-0.5	2.28	12745	11876	-0.8
60651	CHICAGO	031	78000	77462	76631	-0.1	45	21305	21211	20950	0.0	3.64	17308	17033	-0.2
60652	CHICAGO	031	39212	38567	37993	-0.2	38	12901	12528	12287	-0.3	3.08	10127	9704	-0.5
60653	CHICAGO	031	34503	33951	33730	-0.2	38	12898	12611	12522	-0.2	2.60	7553	7147	-0.6
60654	CHICAGO	031	6617	12152	13285	6.8	99	4735	8130	8864	6.0	1.49	1067	1943	6.7
60655	CHICAGO	031	29063	28702	28341	-0.1	45	10728	10668	10527	-0.1	2.65	7448	7283	-0.2
60656	CHICAGO	031	27575	26755	26266	-0.3	32	12273	11922	11691	-0.3	2.24	7439	7068	-0.6
60657	CHICAGO	031	68742	67959	67285	-0.1	45	40985	40713	40241	-0.1	1.64	10234	9779	-0.5
60659	CHICAGO	031	39700	38922	38511	-0.2	38	13276	12843	12640	-0.4	2.99	9384	8921	-0.5
60660	CHICAGO	031	46822	45390	44807	-0.3	32	22115	21335	21018	-0.4	2.03	9116	8503	-0.7
60661	CHICAGO	031	4276	6957	7605	5.4	98	2874	3910	4186	3.4	1.78	798	1127	3.8
60706	HARWOOD HEIGHTS	031	22263	21851	21526	-0.2	38	9017	8893	8755	-0.1	2.41	6007	5806	-0.4
60707	ELMWOOD PARK	031	42586	43105	42822	0.1	56	15820	15717	15537	-0.1	2.73	10786	10515	-0.3
60712	LINCOLNWOOD	031	12359	11851	11666	-0.5	18	4482	4315	4238	-0.4	2.74	3446	3270	-0.6
60714	NILES	031	30186	29835	29478	-0.1	45	11763	11715	11580	0.0	2.40	7993	7782	-0.3
60803	ALSIP	031	23286	22843	22513	-0.2	38	9096	8980	8848	-0.1	2.53	5909	5719	-0.4
60804	CICERO	031	86096	88319	86985	0.3	65	23117	22139	21653	-0.5	3.97	18110	17116	-0.6
60805	EVERGREEN PARK	031	20911	20192	19801	-0.4	25	7503	7253	7101	-0.4	2.73	5328	5059	-0.6
60827	RIVERDALE	031	33243	30670	29897	-0.9	4	10784	9867	9593	-1.0	3.10	8123	7287	-1.2
60901	KANKAKEE	091	37213	37770	38231	0.2	61	13662	13874	14086	0.2	2.60	9090	9020	-0.1
60911	ASHKUM	075	1484	1439	1404	-0.3	32	580	571	561	-0.2	2.46	430	416	-0.4
60912	BEAVERVILLE	075	647	602	579	-0.8	6	253	237	229	-0.7	2.54	174	160	-0.9
60913	BONFIELD	091	1692	1953	2076	1.6	89	588	692	741	1.8	2.82	492	571	1.6
60914	BOURBONNAIS	091	22075	25495	27022	1.6	89	8062	9423	10048	1.7	2.54	5756	6603	1.5
60915	BRADLEY	091	10692	10844	11122	0.2	61	4175	4311	4436	0.3	2.46	2787	2798	0.0
60917	BUCKINGHAM	091	461	480	489	0.4	69	154	163	168	0.6	2.94	126	131	0.4
60918	BUCKLEY	075	953	949	929	0.0	50	398	400	394	0.1	2.37	292	288	-0.1
60919	CABERY	053	526	531	531	0.1	56	203	204	204	0.1	2.60	147	146	-0.1
60921	CHATSWORTH	105	1733	1650	1597	-0.5	18	692	670	652	-0.3	2.46	473	447	-0.6
60922	CHEBANSE	075	2424	2506	2526	0.4	69	893	941	953	0.6	2.65	668	690	0.4
60924	CISSNA PARK	075	1891	1866	1834	-0.1	45	743	741	731	0.0	2.50	528	516	-0.2
60927	CLIFTON	075	2330	2195	2122	-0.6	13	872	835	812	-0.5	2.56	648	609	-0.7
60928	CRESCENT CITY	075	807	778	757	-0.4	25	324	315	307	-0.3	2.47	242	231	-0.5
60929	CULLOM	105	750	701	676	-0.7	9	321	305	296	-0.6	2.30	206	191	-0.8
60930	DANFORTH	075	909	931	927	0.3	65	319	332	332	0.4	2.58	233	238	0.2
60931	DONOVAN	075	699	664	643	-0.6	13	258	246	239	-0.5	2.70	188	176	-0.7
60934	EMINGTON	105	322	326	325	0.1	56	126	130	130	0.3	2.51	98	99	0.1
60935	ESSEX	091	847	939	989	1.1	85	303	342	361	1.3	2.75	244	271	1.1
60936	GIBSON CITY	053	4532	4499	4472	-0.1	45	1909	1913	1907	0.0	2.30	1276	1253	-0.2
60938	GILMAN	075	2064	1980	1926	-0.4	25	856	826	803	-0.4	2.33	585	552	-0.6
60940	GRANT PARK	091	3271	3698	3901	1.3	87	1155	1332	1416	1.6	2.70	913	1035	1.4
60941	HERSCHER	091	2105	2309	2409	1.0	83	733	819	860	1.2	2.82	603	663	1.0
60942	HOOPESTON	183	6828	6416	6199	-0.7	9	2626	2478	2397	-0.6	2.44	1754	1616	-0.9
60946	KEMPTON	053	404	403	401	0.0	50	140	139	138	-0.1	2.89	101	99	-0.2
60948	LODA	075	1440	1476	1463	0.3	65	588	608	604	0.4	2.43	440	448	0.2
60949	LUDLOW	019	753	764	774	0.2	61	309	326	334	0.6	2.34	211	215	0.2
60950	MANTENO	091	8832	11090	12096	2.5	93	3402	4335	4751	2.7	2.51	2440	3037	2.4
60951	MARTINTON	075	926	899	883	-0.3	32	343	333	327	-0.3	2.65	270	258	-0.5
60952	MELVIN	053	714	725	724	0.2	61	281	287	287	0.2	2.53	199	200	0.1
60953	MILFORD	075	2657	2442	2351	-0.9	4	1118	1040	1004	-0.8	2.35	788	721	-1.0
60954	MOMENCE	091	7041	7274	7408	0.4	69	2522	2623	2676	0.4	2.68	1785	1811	0.2
60955	ONARGA	075	2169	2101	2048	-0.3	32	696	672	655	-0.4	2.93	500	473	-0.6
60957	PAXTON	053	5640	5631	5625	0.0	50	2175	2194	2196	0.1	2.47	1503	1486	-0.1
60959	PIPER CITY	053	1090	1083	1073	-0.1	45	410	405	402	-0.1	2.52	296	287	-0.3
60960	RANKIN	183	1237	1180	1146	-0.5	18	471	453	441	-0.4	2.55	331	311	-0.7
60961	REDDICK	091	861	918	947	0.7	78	318	346	359	0.9	2.65	255	273	0.7
60962	ROBERTS	053	650	673	674	0.4	69	270	280	281	0.4	2.39	191	194	0.2
60963	ROSSVILLE	183	1930	1853	1809	-0.4	25	807	782	765	-0.3	2.37	554	526	-0.6
60964	SAINT ANNE	091	7829	8057	8182	0.3	65	2752	2877	2937	0.5	2.68	2008	2063	0.3
60966	SHELDON	075	1925	1857	1807	-0.4	25	736	714	696	-0.3	2.55	535	509	-0.5
60968	THAWVILLE	075	335	331	323	-0.1	45	134	134	132	0.0	2.47	98	96	-0.2
60970	WATSEKA	075	7920	7751	7596	-0.2	38	3196	3164	3107	-0.1	2.37	2142	2075	-0.3
60973	WELLINGTON	075	483	452	436	-0.7	9	200	190	184	-0.6	2.38	151	142	-0.7
61001	APPLE RIVER	085	1059	1087	1101	0.3	65	469	499	512	0.7	2.18	337	352	0.5
	ILLINOIS					0.6					0.6	2.64			0.4
	UNITED STATES					1.0					1.1	2.59			0.9

ZIP CODE #	POST OFFICE NAME	RACE (%) White 2000	White 2009	Black 2000	Black 2009	Asian/Pacific 2000	Asian/Pacific 2009	% Hispanic Origin 2000	% Hispanic Origin 2009	2009 AGE DISTRIBUTION (%) 0-4	5-9	10-14	15-19	20-24	25-44	45-64	65-84	85+	18+	MEDIAN AGE 2009	% 2009 Males	% 2009 Females
60615	CHICAGO	23.1	17.7	67.5	71.6	5.8	6.6	2.9	3.7	6.0	5.0	4.6	6.4	10.4	31.8	24.2	9.9	1.7	81.3	33.8	46.1	53.9
60616	CHICAGO	26.7	22.5	37.6	38.8	29.2	30.7	9.6	12.5	6.1	5.6	4.8	6.7	10.0	29.9	23.3	11.5	2.1	80.3	35.4	48.5	51.5
60617	CHICAGO	23.6	21.7	54.7	53.5	0.2	0.2	34.2	39.1	8.3	8.3	7.8	8.0	6.8	25.5	22.6	11.4	1.3	70.6	33.1	46.7	53.3
60618	CHICAGO	59.3	52.2	3.1	3.3	5.1	5.4	49.1	60.0	8.0	7.0	6.1	6.8	8.5	34.4	21.3	6.8	1.0	74.8	31.6	50.3	49.7
60619	CHICAGO	0.6	0.4	98.1	98.2	0.1	0.1	0.7	0.8	6.7	7.2	7.1	7.3	5.9	23.2	26.5	13.5	2.5	74.6	39.2	43.9	56.1
60620	CHICAGO	0.6	0.4	98.3	98.5	0.1	0.1	0.6	0.7	7.2	7.8	7.7	7.8	6.1	23.4	25.2	13.3	1.5	72.5	36.9	44.7	55.3
60621	CHICAGO	0.6	0.5	98.2	98.3	0.1	0.1	0.8	0.9	9.6	9.8	8.5	8.8	7.5	23.1	20.5	10.2	1.9	66.6	29.5	45.2	54.8
60622	CHICAGO	59.0	52.9	10.2	10.0	1.9	2.2	45.6	55.0	7.1	5.8	5.0	5.9	9.8	40.7	18.4	6.1	1.1	78.7	31.2	51.3	48.7
60623	CHICAGO	20.8	19.5	38.2	39.0	0.2	0.2	58.9	59.3	10.2	9.5	7.9	9.4	10.0	31.9	15.6	4.8	0.6	67.2	26.5	53.6	46.4
60624	CHICAGO	0.8	0.6	98.1	98.2	0.1	0.1	1.0	1.1	9.6	9.5	8.7	9.6	8.3	24.6	20.0	8.7	1.1	66.3	28.1	45.7	54.3
60625	CHICAGO	55.5	49.5	3.9	4.1	17.3	18.6	37.7	46.3	7.9	6.9	6.0	7.1	8.7	34.3	20.7	7.1	1.3	75.2	31.8	51.0	49.0
60626	CHICAGO	46.8	40.7	28.9	31.0	7.8	8.5	27.2	33.6	7.8	6.5	5.5	7.1	10.8	35.1	20.1	5.9	1.2	76.7	30.4	51.2	48.8
60628	CHICAGO	2.6	2.2	94.8	94.9	0.1	0.1	3.1	3.5	7.6	7.9	8.0	8.7	6.6	24.0	23.7	12.3	1.3	71.2	34.6	45.4	54.6
60629	CHICAGO	43.0	38.8	26.2	24.8	0.8	0.8	48.3	57.1	9.7	9.2	8.3	8.7	8.3	29.1	19.2	6.2	1.3	67.5	28.4	49.0	51.0
60630	CHICAGO	81.4	74.7	0.5	0.6	7.5	9.5	16.6	24.9	6.3	6.1	6.1	6.0	5.6	28.2	27.5	11.7	2.5	78.0	39.6	48.7	51.3
60631	CHICAGO	94.6	91.8	1.0	1.5	2.2	3.1	5.1	8.8	5.6	5.8	6.0	5.4	4.3	23.4	28.9	16.1	4.7	79.3	44.8	46.8	53.2
60632	CHICAGO	54.7	49.1	1.2	1.1	2.0	1.9	70.6	79.7	10.6	9.8	8.3	8.2	8.1	30.4	17.4	6.1	1.1	66.3	27.8	51.2	48.8
60633	CHICAGO	66.7	59.6	18.0	19.1	0.6	0.7	23.0	33.3	6.5	6.7	6.8	6.8	5.0	24.8	27.0	13.8	2.4	75.7	40.5	48.4	51.6
60634	CHICAGO	83.8	77.1	0.7	0.9	3.8	4.9	19.5	29.2	6.0	5.9	5.9	5.9	5.7	28.3	27.1	12.4	2.7	78.6	39.7	48.5	51.5
60636	CHICAGO	0.8	0.7	97.8	97.9	0.1	0.1	1.2	1.3	8.7	9.1	8.7	9.2	7.5	24.2	21.7	9.8	1.1	67.9	29.9	46.2	53.8
60637	CHICAGO	12.6	10.6	82.3	83.3	3.2	3.9	1.3	1.7	8.2	7.9	7.2	9.2	9.3	24.7	21.1	10.2	2.2	72.2	30.5	45.1	54.9
60638	CHICAGO	82.8	78.6	8.0	7.2	0.8	1.0	15.3	24.2	6.3	6.3	6.4	6.2	5.2	26.7	26.6	13.6	2.8	77.2	40.1	48.4	51.6
60639	CHICAGO	42.0	39.1	18.0	16.9	1.4	1.3	66.5	73.0	9.7	9.2	8.1	8.6	8.7	30.2	19.1	5.6	0.8	68.0	28.2	49.7	50.3
60640	CHICAGO	52.9	45.0	19.2	21.4	13.5	15.4	21.1	28.0	5.4	4.7	4.1	4.7	7.7	37.5	23.8	9.8	2.2	83.2	36.8	51.1	48.9
60641	CHICAGO	70.9	63.2	1.4	1.6	4.0	4.6	39.0	51.2	7.3	6.7	6.2	6.6	7.8	30.2	25.1	8.7	1.3	75.9	34.5	49.8	50.2
60642	CHICAGO	58.6	52.2	13.1	14.1	2.1	2.3	44.1	54.0	6.8	5.4	4.5	5.1	9.6	43.5	18.4	5.9	0.8	80.4	31.9	53.3	46.7
60643	CHICAGO	23.0	19.8	74.6	77.4	0.3	0.4	1.9	2.5	6.1	6.6	7.2	7.7	6.0	23.0	28.0	13.4	2.0	75.3	39.7	46.0	54.0
60644	CHICAGO	2.5	2.0	95.3	95.6	0.3	0.4	2.2	2.6	9.4	9.2	8.2	8.7	7.9	25.4	21.5	8.9	1.0	68.1	29.5	45.6	54.4
60645	CHICAGO	61.0	53.9	10.6	11.6	16.2	19.1	15.5	21.0	7.3	6.7	6.5	6.6	7.2	26.3	24.4	11.5	3.5	75.3	36.7	49.0	51.0
60646	CHICAGO	89.8	85.3	0.4	0.5	6.1	8.5	6.6	11.1	6.3	6.6	7.0	5.8	4.4	22.8	29.6	14.3	3.2	76.5	43.2	48.3	51.7
60647	CHICAGO	45.7	40.4	6.6	6.3	1.4	1.4	67.7	75.6	9.1	7.8	6.6	7.7	9.4	36.0	17.6	5.1	0.7	71.9	29.1	51.0	49.0
60649	CHICAGO	1.4	1.0	96.8	97.2	0.2	0.2	1.1	1.3	7.8	7.7	7.0	7.2	6.7	26.9	24.9	10.3	1.5	73.2	35.2	43.6	56.4
60651	CHICAGO	11.1	10.8	70.0	68.4	0.5	0.5	27.3	30.0	9.6	9.3	8.5	9.3	8.9	27.3	20.4	6.2	0.5	67.0	27.6	46.7	53.3
60652	CHICAGO	44.5	37.7	41.8	44.3	1.1	1.3	17.4	23.6	7.4	7.6	7.8	8.1	5.9	26.9	25.4	9.1	1.8	72.3	35.2	47.6	52.4
60653	CHICAGO	0.8	0.8	97.9	97.9	0.1	0.2	0.8	1.0	9.6	9.7	8.3	8.6	7.1	23.3	20.3	10.1	3.0	67.3	30.3	43.9	56.1
60654	CHICAGO	76.2	68.1	12.5	19.3	7.2	8.0	6.3	11.0	3.1	2.3	1.9	2.2	6.8	46.9	27.8	7.8	1.2	91.7	38.2	52.3	47.7
60655	CHICAGO	91.9	88.7	5.5	7.3	0.5	0.6	3.6	6.3	6.8	7.0	7.3	7.4	5.9	26.1	27.1	10.2	2.3	74.7	38.0	49.0	51.0
60656	CHICAGO	89.6	85.0	1.1	1.5	5.6	7.8	6.6	11.0	5.2	4.8	4.6	4.4	5.6	28.8	27.4	15.9	3.3	82.8	42.4	48.1	51.9
60657	CHICAGO	86.1	80.1	3.4	4.7	5.2	7.2	8.0	13.0	3.4	1.7	1.3	1.5	13.1	54.0	16.5	6.2	2.2	92.8	31.5	50.1	49.9
60659	CHICAGO	54.4	47.0	5.0	5.3	27.1	31.2	16.0	21.3	7.5	6.7	6.3	6.7	7.6	28.9	23.9	10.1	2.3	75.4	35.0	49.2	50.8
60660	CHICAGO	54.1	45.8	18.1	20.8	12.6	14.4	20.9	27.5	5.8	4.7	4.0	6.0	8.4	36.1	23.6	9.4	1.9	82.9	35.1	50.5	49.5
60661	CHICAGO	63.0	47.3	16.1	30.8	17.0	15.6	4.8	6.4	3.0	1.6	1.3	1.9	10.2	55.9	21.5	3.9	0.6	93.2	33.1	51.9	48.1
60706	HARWOOD HEIGHTS	93.7	90.4	0.2	0.3	3.5	5.0	4.6	7.9	4.2	4.3	4.5	4.9	4.8	24.8	28.4	19.4	4.7	84.0	46.7	46.6	53.4
60707	ELMWOOD PARK	79.7	73.1	6.8	7.9	2.6	3.2	19.0	28.0	6.3	6.2	6.2	6.6	6.3	27.7	26.8	11.5	2.5	77.4	38.6	48.5	51.5
60712	LINCOLNWOOD	74.5	66.2	0.4	0.5	21.1	27.8	4.2	6.6	5.4	5.6	6.4	6.3	4.8	19.5	28.3	18.9	4.7	78.6	46.4	46.9	53.1
60714	NILES	82.5	76.4	0.6	0.8	12.9	17.0	5.4	8.5	4.1	4.1	4.3	4.8	5.0	23.1	26.9	21.1	6.5	84.5	48.3	46.7	53.3
60803	ALSIP	83.0	76.9	9.2	11.9	1.8	2.5	8.4	13.3	7.0	6.5	6.2	6.8	7.5	28.3	25.4	10.7	1.8	76.3	36.2	48.6	51.4
60804	CICERO	48.5	43.3	1.1	1.0	1.0	0.9	77.2	85.2	11.3	10.3	8.6	8.5	8.4	30.3	16.3	5.2	1.1	64.7	26.6	51.5	48.5
60805	EVERGREEN PARK	88.4	83.6	7.9	10.8	1.2	1.7	4.0	6.7	6.7	7.0	7.5	7.3	5.5	24.9	26.2	11.8	3.2	74.2	38.8	47.7	52.3
60827	RIVERDALE	8.3	6.7	88.6	89.7	0.2	0.2	3.5	4.5	9.7	10.4	9.5	9.3	7.2	25.7	21.0	6.2	0.9	64.4	27.8	45.1	54.9
60901	KANKAKEE	62.1	55.9	31.5	36.4	0.3	0.4	7.2	9.0	7.5	7.4	7.1	7.4	6.6	25.8	24.7	11.0	2.5	73.4	36.0	48.3	51.7
60911	ASHKUM	98.4	97.7	0.1	0.1	0.0	0.1	1.0	1.6	5.5	5.9	6.4	5.9	4.2	23.9	30.7	13.9	3.6	78.4	43.6	50.1	49.9
60912	BEAVERVILLE	87.6	85.4	10.7	12.8	0.2	0.2	0.3	0.5	6.8	7.5	7.8	7.0	4.3	22.9	25.7	15.6	2.3	73.4	39.5	50.5	49.5
60913	BONFIELD	98.8	98.2	0.0	0.1	0.2	0.2	0.8	1.3	6.1	6.6	7.1	7.0	4.8	25.8	30.7	10.9	1.2	75.9	40.2	51.2	48.8
60914	BOURBONNAIS	92.2	88.7	3.5	5.3	2.0	2.6	2.5	4.0	7.0	6.6	6.5	8.2	8.4	27.7	24.9	9.4	1.3	75.9	34.0	48.0	52.0
60915	BRADLEY	95.5	93.1	1.3	2.1	0.7	0.9	3.9	6.2	7.8	7.3	6.9	6.8	6.3	29.7	22.8	10.1	2.3	74.3	34.7	48.2	51.8
60917	BUCKINGHAM	97.0	95.2	0.0	0.2	0.0	0.0	0.9	1.7	6.7	7.1	7.5	7.5	4.8	24.4	27.9	12.7	1.5	74.0	38.6	50.0	50.0
60918	BUCKLEY	98.0	97.0	0.2	0.2	0.2	0.3	2.8	4.3	6.0	6.3	6.7	6.3	4.0	21.6	30.2	16.4	2.3	77.0	44.3	50.9	49.1
60919	CABERY	97.5	97.4	0.0	0.0	0.2	0.2	1.9	2.3	7.9	7.7	7.9	7.9	6.0	24.5	25.0	11.5	1.5	71.6	35.7	51.0	49.0
60921	CHATSWORTH	98.5	97.9	0.3	0.4	0.1	0.2	1.6	2.3	6.4	6.3	6.8	7.9	6.2	21.8	28.0	14.2	2.4	75.6	40.5	50.2	49.8
60922	CHEBANSE	94.5	91.6	3.4	5.4	0.5	0.6	2.0	3.1	6.2	6.4	7.4	7.3	5.7	25.1	28.1	12.3	1.6	75.0	39.0	49.4	50.6
60924	CISSNA PARK	99.0	98.6	0.2	0.2	0.3	0.5	1.0	1.4	6.1	6.4	6.8	7.2	5.2	20.4	29.4	15.1	3.4	75.8	43.2	49.2	50.8
60927	CLIFTON	99.1	98.8	0.0	0.0	0.3	0.4	0.8	1.1	6.2	6.7	7.0	6.9	4.4	24.3	28.5	12.8	3.3	75.6	41.4	48.8	51.2
60928	CRESCENT CITY	97.8	96.7	0.0	0.1	0.6	0.9	1.5	2.4	6.7	7.2	7.6	6.4	4.0	24.4	27.0	14.1	2.6	74.4	40.8	52.6	47.4
60929	CULLOM	98.8	98.3	0.5	0.7	0.1	0.3	0.3	0.4	6.3	6.7	7.0	6.8	4.1	23.7	27.5	15.1	2.7	75.6	42.0	49.2	50.8
60930	DANFORTH	98.2	97.4	0.2	0.3	0.2	0.3	1.2	1.9	5.6	6.0	6.3	5.7	3.9	22.2	30.0	13.7	6.6	77.9	45.2	49.2	50.8
60931	DONOVAN	95.7	94.6	2.6	3.2	0.1	0.2	1.6	2.4	6.0	6.8	7.4	7.2	4.2	22.6	31.2	12.5	2.1	75.3	41.7	50.0	50.0
60934	EMINGTON	98.5	98.2	0.0	0.0	0.3	0.3	0.6	1.2	6.1	6.7	7.4	8.0	4.3	22.7	31.0	12.0	1.8	74.8	41.0	53.4	46.6
60935	ESSEX	97.5	96.5	0.1	0.1	0.1	0.1	0.6	1.0	6.0	6.4	6.7	6.7	5.1	26.0	30.2	11.6	1.3	76.8	39.9	51.8	48.2
60936	GIBSON CITY	98.3	98.2	0.5	0.5	0.4	0.4	0.7	0.7	5.9	6.0	6.2	6.2	5.2	22.4	27.9	16.1	4.2	77.8	43.5	47.9	52.1
60938	GILMAN	92.9	89.6	0.3	0.4	0.3	0.4	8.5	12.5	5.5	5.6	6.3	7.1	5.1	24.1	26.8	15.8	3.8	78.3	42.2	48.9	51.1
60940	GRANT PARK	97.2	95.6	0.2	0.4	0.3	0.4	2.6	4.3	5.9	6.4	6.9	7.1	4.5	26.3	30.9	10.7	1.3	76.3	40.3	50.8	49.2
60941	HERSCHER	97.5	96.3	0.3	0.5	0.5	0.7	1.2	2.0	7.0	7.4	7.6	6.8	5.2	26.4	28.2	9.9	1.7	73.8	37.1	50.1	49.9
60942	HOOPESTON	92.4	89.2	0.7	1.0	0.3	0.4	7.6	11.3	6.9	6.8	6.6	6.2	5.1	22.2	26.3	16.6	3.3	75.7	41.8	50.5	49.5
60946	KEMPTON	98.3	98.3	0.0	0.0	0.2	0.2	1.7	1.7	7.9	7.7	7.7	7.9	5.7	23.6	25.8	11.9	1.7	72.0	36.3	51.4	48.6
60948	LODA	97.4	96.7	0.8	0.9	0.3	0.4	1.9	2.7	4.7	5.3	5.5	5.5	3.8	19.9	34.3	19.0	1.9	81.2	48.0	50.4	49.6
60949	LUDLOW	94.0	91.6	1.7	2.2	0.3	0.5	4.0	5.9	8.6	8.8	8.6	6.0	5.2	24.9	26.7	9.9	1.2	70.4	35.9	48.3	51.7
60950	MANTENO	96.1	93.4	1.6	2.9	0.3	0.4	2.9	4.8	6.8	7.1	7.1	8.1	4.8	26.2	26.3	12.3	1.4	74.2	38.0	50.0	50.0
60951	MARTINTON	97.8	97.1	0.9	1.1	0.1	0.1	1.3	2.0	7.1	7.5	7.6	7.0	4.7	24.2	27.9	11.7	2.3	73.3	39.2	49.4	50.6
60952	MELVIN	99.2	99.2	0.0	0.0	0.0	0.0	1.3	1.2	8.3	8.6	8.3	6.6	3.6	24.3	25.5	12.8	2.1	70.8	38.2	49.9	50.1
60953	MILFORD	98.1	97.3	0.2	0.3	0.1	0.2	2.6	4.0	5.0	5.3	5.6	5.7	4.8	23.6	31.0	16.3	2.8	80.5	45.0	50.4	49.6
60954	MOMENCE	81.3	76.4	13.8	16.3	0.1	0.2	7.6	11.6	6.6	6.6	6.7	6.7	5.8	25.1	26.5	13.2	2.8	75.9	39.3	49.5	50.5
60955	ONARGA	79.7	73.9	1.5	1.6	0.2	0.2	25.2	32.9	6.6	6.6	8.1	10.6	5.8	22.5	25.1	12.2	2.6	71.9	36.4	51.8	48.2
60957	PAXTON	98.0	97.7	0.2	0.3	0.3	0.4	1.5	1.7	6.6	6.3	6.4	6.8	5.9	24.2	26.0	13.7	4.1	76.7	40.5	48.3	51.7
60959	PIPER CITY	97.6	97.6	0.1	0.1	0.6	0.6	1.2	1.2	5.7	5.9	5.8	6.1	6.1	19.4	28.3	18.0	4.7	78.9	45.7	47.9	52.1
60960	RANKIN	95.4	93.6	0.5	0.6	0.4	0.6	3.6	5.3	6.5	6.8	7.1	7.4	4.3	22.5	28.1	14.4	3.0	74.8	41.3	50.2	49.8
60961	REDDICK	97.4	96.2	0.1	0.1	0.1	0.1	0.8	1.3	6.3	6.8	7.1	7.2	4.9	24.9	29.0	12.3	1.5	75.5	39.4	51.1	48.9
60962	ROBERTS	99.4	99.4	0.0	0.0	0.0	0.0	0.6	0.6	6.7	7.3	7.7	6.8	3.7	20.2	31.4	14.0	2.2	73.8	42.8	47.4	52.6
60963	ROSSVILLE	97.9	97.2	0.2	0.3	0.2	0.2	1.7	2.5	6.0	6.2	6.3	6.6	4.7	23.8	28.1	16.1	2.2	77.4	41.9	48.7	51.3
60964	SAINT ANNE	66.9	64.0	28.4	29.5	0.4	0.4	4.7	7.3	6.5	6.7	7.2	7.2	5.6	21.9	27.1	15.8	2.1	75.1	40.6	52.0	48.0
60966	SHELDON	97.2	96.2	0.4	0.5	0.5	0.8	1.7	2.5	7.3	7.5	7.7	6.4	4.8	22.2	27.8	13.5	2.8	73.3	40.2	49.4	50.6
60968	THAWVILLE	97.9	97.3	0.0	0.0	0.3	0.3	3.3	4.5	6.3	6.3	6.9	6.6	3.9	22.7	28.7	16.0	2.4	76.1	43.0	50.5	49.5
60970	WATSEKA	96.9	95.8	0.6	0.7	0.5	0.7	2.3	3.5	6.3	6.3	6.5	6.4	5.1	22.6	27.2	15.7	4.0	77.0	42.4	48.3	51.7
60973	WELLINGTON	98.8	98.5	0.2	0.2	0.0	0.0	1.9	2.7	7.3	7.7	7.7	5.5	3.5	22.3	30.1	13.5	2.2	73.7	42.4	52.0	48.0
61001	APPLE RIVER	99.3	98.9	0.2	0.3	0.2	0.3	0.7	1.1	5.5	6.1	6.3	6.7	4.0	20.6	28.4	19.9	2.4	77.8	45.5	51.1	48.9
	ILLINOIS	73.5	70.6	15.1	15.3	3.4	4.4	12.3	15.7	7.1	6.9	6.8	7.1	6.9	27.5	25.4	10.3	1.9	75.0	36.1	49.1	50.9
	UNITED STATES	75.1	72.0	12.3	12.7	3.8	4.6	12.5	15.7	6.8	6.7	6.6	7.1	6.9	27.0	26.0	10.9	1.9	75.7	36.9	49.2	50.8

ZIP CODE #	POST OFFICE NAME	2009 Per Capita Income	2009 HH Income Base	2009 Household Income Distribution (%) Less than $25,000	$25,000 to $49,999	$50,000 to $99,999	$100,000 to $149,999	$150,000 or More	Median Household Income 2009	2014	2009 National Centile	2009 State Centile	2009 Home Value Base	2009 Home Value Distribution (%) Less than $50,000	$50,000 to $89,999	$90,000 to $174,999	$175,000 to $399,999	$400,000 or More	2009 Median Home Value
60615	CHICAGO	29501	20402	33.3	22.5	32.1	6.1	6.0	43023	46703	42	24	5554	4.7	8.2	27.9	41.0	18.1	204873
60616	CHICAGO	24794	21073	33.5	21.8	33.1	6.7	4.9	43686	47380	44	26	6494	5.4	3.1	20.9	57.3	13.3	236220
60617	CHICAGO	18410	30437	28.2	26.0	35.8	6.9	3.1	45529	48210	50	30	18473	3.3	13.9	66.5	15.6	0.8	124351
60618	CHICAGO	24494	35784	17.8	25.0	41.9	9.1	6.2	56913	60862	74	59	14264	0.4	1.5	11.8	64.7	21.5	279146
60619	CHICAGO	21934	28584	27.4	27.3	35.6	6.6	3.1	45441	48010	50	30	13542	2.3	11.1	59.6	25.1	1.9	135477
60620	CHICAGO	18865	26043	27.4	25.6	36.7	6.9	3.2	46360	49274	52	33	13953	1.6	9.8	72.0	15.8	0.8	129762
60621	CHICAGO	11885	14152	50.4	24.9	20.4	2.9	1.5	24650	25784	3	1	4465	12.5	32.5	46.2	8.2	0.6	94746
60622	CHICAGO	29367	24095	25.7	20.7	35.2	9.6	8.8	54075	58720	70	54	6767	0.9	2.1	9.9	41.9	45.1	376752
60623	CHICAGO	12393	27484	36.5	28.1	28.9	4.5	2.0	36735	39409	23	9	9427	4.4	9.1	50.5	34.8	1.3	152258
60624	CHICAGO	13181	13227	43.8	25.3	24.8	4.0	2.2	30566	33160	9	3	4060	3.6	11.7	51.7	30.9	2.2	138217
60625	CHICAGO	22576	29417	20.2	24.4	41.3	8.7	5.5	55153	59299	71	56	9696	1.6	1.5	17.7	58.0	21.1	275556
60626	CHICAGO	21345	23274	30.0	30.6	31.6	4.5	3.3	40651	45564	35	18	4524	3.2	11.8	29.8	42.2	13.0	195848
60628	CHICAGO	18107	25216	25.3	25.1	38.4	8.1	3.1	49568	51985	60	42	16308	4.1	16.6	67.5	11.0	0.9	118120
60629	CHICAGO	16034	31393	21.4	26.5	41.2	7.8	3.0	51851	54989	66	48	19876	1.1	4.5	61.1	32.4	1.0	154126
60630	CHICAGO	27335	20885	16.4	22.3	44.2	11.7	5.3	62232	65267	80	68	13166	1.0	0.6	15.0	74.9	8.5	251151
60631	CHICAGO	33492	11731	12.6	21.6	41.8	16.6	7.5	68087	70275	86	78	8978	0.5	0.3	12.1	72.4	14.7	288542
60632	CHICAGO	14848	24204	22.9	28.8	38.8	7.1	2.4	48338	50504	57	39	14080	0.9	4.0	48.9	45.1	1.1	169540
60633	CHICAGO	23963	4757	20.1	26.5	42.0	8.5	2.9	53168	56785	68	51	3571	8.1	11.4	69.6	10.1	0.9	126399
60634	CHICAGO	24576	25956	14.5	21.9	46.6	12.6	4.4	64022	66530	82	72	18957	0.5	0.8	16.3	78.5	3.9	230236
60636	CHICAGO	12491	13154	38.3	25.9	28.7	5.7	1.4	35380	37798	19	7	7217	6.6	29.2	57.7	5.7	0.7	101789
60637	CHICAGO	19757	20718	43.1	23.0	24.8	4.6	4.5	32277	35194	12	3	4958	5.1	12.0	43.1	27.9	11.9	144363
60638	CHICAGO	24339	20208	20.4	21.2	43.1	11.4	3.8	58616	62061	76	62	15411	0.8	2.5	35.6	59.4	1.6	189501
60639	CHICAGO	16232	24396	20.3	26.4	41.7	7.6	4.0	52637	55489	67	50	12176	1.1	1.2	27.8	67.4	2.6	207927
60640	CHICAGO	29819	35962	30.2	22.9	34.2	7.1	5.6	46689	49363	53	34	8959	1.8	5.8	22.8	43.7	25.9	251783
60641	CHICAGO	21963	24800	17.4	25.5	43.5	8.8	4.9	56202	60218	73	58	12189	0.7	0.6	16.0	72.6	10.1	241837
60642	CHICAGO	31890	9038	21.5	21.6	39.1	8.9	8.9	58662	62812	76	62	2566	1.4	0.2	5.9	56.9	35.6	346288
60643	CHICAGO	27003	18084	16.3	20.7	40.0	13.8	9.1	65393	67902	84	75	13957	1.6	7.4	48.0	36.1	6.9	157100
60644	CHICAGO	15958	17791	36.5	24.2	31.4	4.8	3.1	38000	41723	27	12	5693	2.7	9.2	52.7	31.1	4.2	147546
60645	CHICAGO	24138	15094	21.4	24.6	39.8	8.3	5.8	53593	57002	69	53	7534	1.6	6.2	26.2	53.7	12.2	231511
60646	CHICAGO	37305	10264	11.1	18.3	42.6	14.3	13.6	75848	76603	90	87	8012	0.9	0.3	3.8	59.0	36.0	346150
60647	CHICAGO	21311	33590	25.8	25.9	35.3	7.4	5.6	48290	50258	57	39	11136	1.7	2.2	19.6	53.2	23.3	255692
60649	CHICAGO	21177	22405	34.1	28.5	29.6	5.0	2.8	38000	41059	27	12	5278	3.4	15.7	43.8	29.7	7.3	145429
60651	CHICAGO	15253	21211	29.0	25.5	35.9	6.2	3.5	44646	48070	47	28	9404	1.7	5.3	60.3	30.6	2.1	147670
60652	CHICAGO	23259	12528	12.9	20.0	51.2	12.1	3.8	68524	70506	86	79	10908	1.2	2.0	60.6	35.1	1.1	160802
60653	CHICAGO	14514	12611	56.9	18.3	18.3	3.4	3.1	19031	20458	1	0	1922	2.5	10.0	15.9	50.6	21.0	243883
60654	CHICAGO	78647	8130	8.5	10.5	42.7	16.6	21.7	83611	85411	93	94	3753	0.7	1.7	6.0	54.4	37.1	342390
60655	CHICAGO	30687	10668	11.2	14.5	51.3	17.4	5.6	75713	76190	90	87	8986	0.5	1.4	37.6	58.1	2.4	189824
60656	CHICAGO	31131	11922	16.4	21.5	45.9	11.6	4.7	61114	63785	79	66	7524	0.7	0.9	19.2	70.0	9.1	256213
60657	CHICAGO	60894	40713	12.3	18.0	40.1	14.7	14.9	74093	75701	89	85	12920	0.8	1.3	9.3	39.8	48.8	392929
60659	CHICAGO	23252	12843	20.8	22.1	41.2	9.6	6.3	57629	61531	75	60	5802	1.7	4.5	17.0	59.9	16.8	274667
60660	CHICAGO	27982	21335	26.2	26.9	36.8	6.1	3.9	47139	49238	54	35	7100	3.8	11.9	31.5	38.3	14.5	185944
60661	CHICAGO	51948	3910	13.1	15.5	40.9	15.0	15.5	74398	75793	89	85	1419	0.0	0.0	0.0	65.4	34.6	345238
60706	HARWOOD HEIGHTS	27824	8893	16.0	25.1	44.8	10.2	3.9	59573	62474	77	64	6469	0.5	0.4	7.0	84.2	7.9	274366
60707	ELMWOOD PARK	25307	15717	15.4	23.9	43.3	12.9	4.4	61253	63838	79	67	10698	0.6	1.4	18.7	74.0	5.4	232367
60712	LINCOLNWOOD	42471	4315	9.1	15.0	39.8	15.3	20.8	82027	82917	93	93	3746	0.9	0.7	1.7	45.7	51.1	405384
60714	NILES	28459	11715	15.1	22.2	46.4	11.2	5.0	62340	65151	80	69	8828	0.8	0.5	8.6	77.5	12.6	277756
60803	ALSIP	26087	8980	15.9	23.4	46.9	10.3	3.4	59683	62651	77	64	6004	5.6	5.0	37.6	50.8	1.0	177798
60804	CICERO	14241	22139	20.5	30.3	40.9	6.1	2.2	49126	51240	59	41	12266	1.5	2.8	56.4	38.7	0.6	162238
60805	EVERGREEN PARK	27907	7253	14.1	19.2	45.2	15.3	6.1	68478	70903	86	79	5960	0.5	1.2	39.7	57.4	1.1	185274
60827	RIVERDALE	16404	9867	30.3	24.9	36.8	6.1	1.9	43738	47108	45	26	4970	3.2	17.0	74.6	5.1	0.2	116349
60901	KANKAKEE	21229	13874	28.3	26.1	35.7	6.6	3.4	46201	48256	52	32	8677	7.9	18.2	51.1	20.1	2.7	122566
60911	ASHKUM	24438	571	23.5	27.0	36.6	8.2	4.7	49476	49930	60	42	448	5.1	12.1	55.4	23.0	4.5	135613
60912	BEAVERVILLE	19980	237	24.5	30.8	36.7	6.8	1.3	45173	47201	49	29	190	10.5	28.9	48.9	8.4	3.2	106897
60913	BONFIELD	26975	692	8.2	24.3	50.6	12.0	4.9	74537	75185	89	85	586	2.4	8.5	35.7	44.9	8.5	184615
60914	BOURBONNAIS	27138	9423	14.7	24.8	44.6	10.7	5.2	61404	63735	79	67	6708	11.7	7.1	37.1	40.1	4.0	165515
60915	BRADLEY	23968	4311	20.2	30.5	38.6	7.4	3.3	49397	51576	60	41	2799	2.0	11.4	71.0	15.0	0.6	129889
60917	BUCKINGHAM	24785	163	11.0	22.7	52.1	11.0	3.1	73314	75386	88	84	138	5.1	9.4	60.1	23.9	1.4	132955
60918	BUCKLEY	24692	400	16.3	32.3	43.5	5.3	2.8	50805	51284	63	46	326	6.4	22.1	48.5	19.6	3.4	116667
60919	CABERY	25529	204	14.2	30.4	40.7	11.8	2.9	54503	58077	70	55	158	11.4	16.5	50.6	20.9	0.6	124038
60921	CHATSWORTH	19827	670	27.6	27.2	39.1	5.4	0.7	43977	47712	45	27	472	14.0	39.8	36.7	8.9	0.6	86949
60922	CHEBANSE	21683	941	18.3	27.8	44.5	8.2	1.2	53198	53741	68	52	754	24.5	5.0	42.6	26.4	1.5	134643
60924	CISSNA PARK	21020	741	23.1	29.0	42.5	3.5	1.9	47214	49067	55	36	600	7.0	24.7	48.2	19.3	0.8	117677
60927	CLIFTON	24829	835	17.7	22.9	48.5	8.6	2.3	59356	59169	77	63	657	3.2	7.8	54.5	30.7	3.8	146058
60928	CRESCENT CITY	23962	315	14.3	28.6	49.2	6.0	1.9	55406	55234	72	57	253	4.3	18.6	56.1	19.8	1.2	123843
60929	CULLOM	20485	305	25.2	33.8	36.4	3.9	0.7	42205	46076	40	21	232	16.8	25.9	46.6	10.8	0.0	101829
60930	DANFORTH	20126	332	22.9	31.3	38.6	5.4	1.8	45808	47689	51	32	249	7.6	16.1	52.6	13.7	10.0	124722
60931	DONOVAN	21508	246	19.1	35.4	37.4	5.7	2.4	46437	47837	53	33	191	12.6	28.8	44.0	11.0	3.7	104741
60934	EMINGTON	24195	130	11.5	33.1	46.9	6.2	2.3	53348	55342	69	52	97	9.3	20.6	36.1	29.9	4.1	139773
60935	ESSEX	23627	342	14.6	21.9	53.2	7.3	2.9	62730	62779	81	69	296	14.2	15.9	37.5	29.4	3.0	141667
60936	GIBSON CITY	22836	1913	23.8	30.9	37.3	5.8	2.2	43853	48196	45	26	1352	11.5	21.3	50.8	15.7	0.7	113578
60938	GILMAN	23036	826	21.2	30.5	42.3	3.6	2.4	47941	49415	56	38	622	10.9	19.1	53.5	14.6	1.8	118202
60940	GRANT PARK	26053	1332	12.8	21.1	50.8	12.2	3.2	70555	72734	87	81	1050	5.5	5.5	30.1	53.4	5.4	193023
60941	HERSCHER	23432	819	13.6	21.6	54.5	8.7	1.7	64444	64960	83	73	626	0.3	6.1	49.7	40.3	3.7	165206
60942	HOOPESTON	19107	2478	29.4	33.1	31.3	4.8	1.5	39142	42900	30	14	1702	19.4	46.8	29.7	3.6	0.5	73261
60946	KEMPTON	22652	139	13.7	32.4	38.8	12.2	2.9	52979	56743	68	51	104	10.6	14.4	53.8	21.2	0.0	126250
60948	LODA	28582	608	11.7	23.2	55.1	6.6	3.5	59480	59623	77	63	518	8.9	16.4	42.7	31.7	0.4	135714
60949	LUDLOW	23283	326	19.3	36.8	36.5	5.5	1.8	45000	47509	48	29	237	42.2	15.2	23.6	18.1	0.8	73125
60950	MANTENO	26778	4335	16.1	25.1	44.7	8.7	5.4	60820	61965	79	66	3157	13.9	6.2	32.9	42.7	4.2	164672
60951	MARTINTON	22809	333	17.7	25.8	47.4	6.3	2.7	54996	54950	71	56	262	6.9	16.4	50.4	20.6	5.7	131250
60952	MELVIN	20238	287	23.7	27.9	41.5	6.3	0.7	46698	50814	53	34	231	26.8	38.1	31.2	3.9	0.0	76579
60953	MILFORD	21501	1040	27.9	31.2	35.0	3.9	2.0	41244	44254	37	19	796	17.6	27.1	39.9	13.4	1.9	98235
60954	MOMENCE	22562	2623	19.6	28.8	41.4	6.4	3.8	51764	53442	65	48	1885	7.7	15.6	45.6	29.1	2.0	139576
60955	ONARGA	17261	672	23.4	31.8	38.7	4.0	2.1	43898	46524	45	26	518	14.1	26.1	46.3	11.0	2.5	101163
60957	PAXTON	22745	2194	18.0	30.9	41.6	7.5	2.0	50776	53466	63	45	1724	7.1	23.0	55.9	13.6	0.4	109976
60959	PIPER CITY	22046	405	19.8	36.3	35.6	4.9	3.5	43725	47124	45	26	311	8.7	20.6	58.2	11.9	0.6	117736
60960	RANKIN	18432	453	29.4	36.0	30.5	3.3	0.9	39012	41835	30	14	359	29.2	26.5	34.8	7.8	1.7	80238
60961	REDDICK	25305	346	13.0	23.7	51.4	8.7	3.2	63898	64822	82	72	291	10.3	13.7	46.7	27.1	2.1	137202
60962	ROBERTS	23043	280	17.9	30.4	44.3	6.4	1.1	51300	53837	64	47	225	17.3	19.1	48.0	14.7	0.9	108864
60963	ROSSVILLE	20755	782	25.3	29.8	40.7	2.9	1.3	46243	48631	52	33	597	21.1	33.3	38.2	6.9	0.5	83690
60964	SAINT ANNE	21284	2877	25.6	25.1	37.8	8.8	2.7	49365	50587	60	41	2190	13.7	15.9	41.0	26.2	3.2	127316
60966	SHELDON	20051	714	24.4	32.6	36.4	5.0	1.5	43684	45813	44	26	528	14.4	27.5	47.0	9.5	1.7	98431
60968	THAWVILLE	22793	134	17.2	33.6	41.0	5.2	3.0	49220	50000	59	41	108	5.6	24.1	49.1	16.7	4.6	113750
60970	WATSEKA	21956	3164	27.9	29.6	34.5	4.7	3.2	40928	43506	36	19	2242	10.8	27.1	45.5	15.0	1.6	103546
60973	WELLINGTON	24923	190	20.0	42.1	26.8	5.3	5.8	41510	42443	38	20	148	23.0	29.7	38.5	8.8	0.0	86000
61001	APPLE RIVER	27799	499	15.8	32.7	41.9	6.2	3.4	51323	52321	64	47	389	10.0	16.5	33.9	30.8	8.7	140682
	ILLINOIS	28587		18.2	22.2	39.3	12.1	8.2	60823	63631				6.3	10.0	30.9	40.6	12.3	185324
	UNITED STATES	27277		20.9	24.4	35.3	11.7	7.6	54719	56938				9.3	13.1	31.6	32.6	13.5	162279

ZIP CODE #	POST OFFICE NAME	FINANCIAL SERVICES: Auto Loan	Home Loan	Invest-ments	Retire-ment Plans	THE HOME: Home Improvements: Home Repair	Lawn & Garden	Furnishings: Computers & Hardware-Personal	Major Appli-ances	TV, Radio, Sound Equip-ment	Furni-ture	ENTERTAINMENT: Dine out/ Carry out	Sports Equip-ment	Fees & Tickets	Toys & Games	Travel	Cable TV	PERSONAL: Apparel & Services	Auto Repairs	Health Insur-ance	Pets & Supplies
60615	CHICAGO	81	66	69	73	65	66	91	72	91	84	93	62	84	89	81	91	66	85	78	92
60616	CHICAGO	69	63	66	67	63	63	82	69	84	74	86	54	79	80	76	87	63	78	77	84
60617	CHICAGO	77	75	68	75	73	75	78	75	81	79	82	56	78	80	75	83	57	79	81	90
60618	CHICAGO	88	87	86	88	87	74	105	90	98	99	102	75	101	98	100	94	75	99	83	104
60619	CHICAGO	71	71	68	72	69	75	74	71	80	72	81	52	76	78	73	85	57	76	81	88
60620	CHICAGO	74	76	71	77	73	80	76	74	82	75	83	53	79	79	75	87	58	78	85	91
60621	CHICAGO	51	37	35	40	35	43	51	44	57	49	56	34	46	55	43	61	40	51	53	57
60622	CHICAGO	90	86	91	91	87	75	109	91	101	103	106	78	104	100	103	97	77	101	85	107
60623	CHICAGO	63	55	48	53	54	48	67	59	65	66	68	47	62	65	61	63	49	66	55	67
60624	CHICAGO	54	47	47	50	46	49	60	51	65	54	65	39	58	62	54	69	47	58	59	64
60625	CHICAGO	84	83	84	84	83	71	100	86	94	94	99	72	97	94	96	91	73	95	80	99
60626	CHICAGO	75	54	52	58	52	51	79	62	77	75	79	54	68	78	67	74	56	74	63	77
60628	CHICAGO	78	78	72	79	75	83	78	77	84	78	85	56	81	82	77	89	59	80	88	95
60629	CHICAGO	81	81	73	76	80	69	87	81	83	88	86	63	84	84	84	80	61	85	74	91
60630	CHICAGO	82	103	107	99	105	95	98	95	97	91	99	70	108	96	104	101	73	96	97	107
60631	CHICAGO	95	124	130	118	128	118	109	112	108	108	108	81	125	106	121	111	79	110	117	125
60632	CHICAGO	80	79	67	71	78	61	85	80	77	89	81	63	81	79	82	70	59	83	66	85
60633	CHICAGO	85	88	84	87	86	98	82	88	88	80	87	64	85	86	85	93	59	87	100	104
60634	CHICAGO	87	107	105	102	108	97	100	98	97	97	99	74	109	97	106	98	72	98	97	111
60636	CHICAGO	63	56	51	58	53	62	61	58	68	61	67	43	60	66	57	72	46	63	68	73
60637	CHICAGO	65	53	54	58	52	56	72	59	76	66	77	47	67	73	63	80	55	69	69	75
60638	CHICAGO	84	97	91	95	96	96	90	91	91	89	91	68	98	90	95	93	64	91	97	106
60639	CHICAGO	83	82	72	76	81	65	92	83	85	92	90	67	88	86	88	80	66	89	72	91
60640	CHICAGO	76	68	73	74	69	64	91	74	88	83	91	62	86	85	84	88	67	84	76	90
60641	CHICAGO	81	87	86	85	87	77	96	86	93	90	97	68	98	92	95	93	71	92	84	99
60642	CHICAGO	96	90	96	95	92	79	114	95	106	108	110	82	108	104	109	100	80	107	90	113
60643	CHICAGO	105	119	116	118	118	119	109	111	111	111	112	81	119	109	115	114	79	111	118	131
60644	CHICAGO	63	58	58	61	57	59	72	61	77	64	78	47	71	75	66	82	57	70	70	77
60645	CHICAGO	83	88	90	87	89	82	95	87	94	91	96	68	98	92	95	94	70	93	89	101
60646	CHICAGO	109	149	161	143	156	138	128	131	125	126	127	96	151	125	145	128	94	128	130	146
60647	CHICAGO	82	77	74	76	77	63	94	81	87	92	92	68	89	87	89	82	67	90	72	91
60649	CHICAGO	63	56	55	59	54	57	69	59	73	63	73	46	66	71	63	76	52	67	67	74
60651	CHICAGO	71	70	66	70	69	66	79	71	80	75	82	55	79	78	75	82	60	77	73	84
60652	CHICAGO	97	112	99	109	108	106	100	102	99	102	100	76	108	100	105	99	70	100	103	118
60653	CHICAGO	47	37	37	41	36	40	53	44	59	48	58	34	49	55	46	62	42	52	53	56
60654	CHICAGO	160	135	147	152	135	127	179	142	171	170	177	127	169	171	163	165	128	163	142	177
60655	CHICAGO	103	130	122	127	128	123	113	116	112	113	113	87	129	113	124	113	81	114	117	133
60656	CHICAGO	89	99	100	97	100	97	98	95	98	95	99	72	104	97	102	100	70	98	101	111
60657	CHICAGO	138	114	125	130	114	108	154	122	147	146	153	109	144	148	140	142	110	140	122	152
60659	CHICAGO	83	93	95	91	94	84	100	91	98	93	101	71	104	96	101	99	75	97	91	104
60660	CHICAGO	76	67	70	72	67	64	87	72	84	81	87	61	82	82	81	83	62	82	75	88
60661	CHICAGO	128	100	107	115	98	96	142	109	136	133	141	99	129	137	125	132	101	129	112	138
60706	HARWOOD HEIGHTS	84	102	102	98	104	103	91	96	94	90	94	69	102	92	100	98	67	94	105	109
60707	ELMWOOD PARK	86	103	103	99	105	95	98	96	95	95	97	72	106	95	103	96	71	97	95	108
60712	LINCOLNWOOD	137	192	215	186	206	180	159	168	154	163	154	122	193	152	187	155	114	161	165	184
60714	NILES	86	104	109	101	108	101	97	98	96	96	97	72	107	93	105	99	69	98	104	111
60803	ALSIP	89	92	88	92	91	88	95	90	94	93	95	71	97	95	95	94	67	94	92	106
60804	CICERO	80	78	65	70	77	59	85	79	76	89	81	63	80	78	81	70	59	83	64	84
60805	EVERGREEN PARK	98	120	113	117	119	115	106	109	105	106	106	81	119	106	115	107	76	107	111	125
60827	RIVERDALE	73	64	55	66	59	69	70	66	76	70	76	50	68	75	64	80	52	71	76	83
60901	KANKAKEE	78	74	66	75	71	78	78	76	82	75	81	58	77	82	75	85	57	79	84	92
60911	ASHKUM	98	82	94	85	85	104	84	97	87	74	85	76	73	87	84	92	57	90	101	115
60912	BEAVERVILLE	79	72	71	75	73	84	71	80	73	64	72	60	65	74	71	77	49	74	82	93
60913	BONFIELD	107	119	103	123	116	118	107	111	105	107	106	87	113	108	112	106	74	107	110	131
60914	BOURBONNAIS	106	105	97	104	101	99	101	101	99	104	101	79	100	103	99	98	70	100	97	119
60915	BRADLEY	83	86	69	87	80	88	85	82	85	82	85	65	86	87	83	87	59	83	90	99
60917	BUCKINGHAM	94	116	104	116	112	114	99	103	100	100	101	77	114	101	110	102	71	101	109	120
60918	BUCKLEY	103	73	116	73	77	109	80	99	83	66	82	81	60	81	80	90	53	93	104	121
60919	CABERY	93	97	84	98	91	102	93	94	95	89	95	74	95	96	94	97	65	94	103	113
60921	CHATSWORTH	83	60	84	58	62	87	65	80	72	57	70	61	52	71	63	79	46	75	87	95
60922	CHEBANSE	90	82	79	82	81	91	81	88	83	77	82	67	75	85	79	86	56	83	89	103
60924	CISSNA PARK	80	72	87	71	74	92	71	82	75	64	74	63	66	73	74	80	50	78	90	97
60927	CLIFTON	98	93	98	95	93	106	89	99	90	83	89	78	85	91	92	93	61	94	100	118
60928	CRESCENT CITY	93	82	86	86	84	100	82	94	85	74	83	71	74	86	82	90	57	86	97	109
60929	CULLOM	84	58	92	58	61	89	64	80	67	52	66	66	47	66	64	73	43	75	84	98
60930	DANFORTH	94	65	104	65	68	100	72	90	75	58	74	74	53	74	72	82	48	84	95	110
60931	DONOVAN	100	74	106	75	77	106	80	97	83	66	82	78	62	82	79	89	54	90	102	117
60934	EMINGTON	109	75	119	74	78	114	83	103	86	67	85	85	61	85	82	94	55	96	109	127
60935	ESSEX	100	92	90	96	94	107	90	101	93	82	91	77	84	95	91	98	62	94	104	118
60936	GIBSON CITY	77	74	79	73	75	87	71	80	76	68	75	59	70	75	74	80	51	77	88	93
60938	GILMAN	76	79	77	79	79	89	73	81	77	69	76	59	75	76	77	82	52	77	89	94
60940	GRANT PARK	99	111	96	114	108	110	100	104	98	100	98	81	106	101	105	98	69	100	103	122
60941	HERSCHER	89	104	91	106	101	103	91	95	91	92	92	73	100	93	98	92	64	92	97	112
60942	HOOPESTON	77	61	72	60	61	80	64	74	69	59	67	55	54	69	61	75	46	70	80	87
60946	KEMPTON	98	90	88	92	86	105	93	96	94	84	94	77	87	95	90	98	63	95	105	117
60948	LODA	119	89	143	89	96	126	94	118	98	82	97	91	75	94	98	105	64	109	120	140
60949	LUDLOW	97	71	82	70	71	93	74	86	81	71	79	66	60	84	68	88	53	81	90	104
60950	MANTENO	101	102	96	98	101	101	95	100	96	99	96	74	94	97	95	97	66	97	100	116
60951	MARTINTON	98	83	93	86	85	104	84	97	87	74	85	75	74	88	84	93	58	90	101	115
60952	MELVIN	91	63	100	63	66	96	70	87	73	57	72	72	51	71	69	79	47	81	92	107
60953	MILFORD	87	62	91	61	64	92	68	84	74	58	72	65	53	72	66	81	47	78	90	100
60954	MOMENCE	87	87	79	88	85	94	85	88	88	81	87	67	84	88	85	91	60	87	95	105
60955	ONARGA	87	67	80	67	68	88	69	81	74	64	73	63	57	76	66	80	49	76	85	97
60957	PAXTON	86	77	77	78	74	91	79	83	82	73	81	66	74	83	77	86	55	83	92	101
60959	PIPER CITY	97	69	100	68	72	102	76	94	83	66	80	72	59	81	74	91	53	87	101	111
60960	RANKIN	81	58	85	57	60	85	63	78	69	54	67	61	49	67	62	75	44	73	84	94
60961	REDDICK	98	98	99	100	98	111	92	102	94	87	94	78	92	96	96	99	65	97	107	119
60962	ROBERTS	99	68	109	68	71	104	75	94	78	61	78	78	55	77	75	86	50	88	99	115
60963	ROSSVILLE	81	63	79	63	65	85	66	80	72	59	70	60	56	72	65	78	47	74	85	93
60964	SAINT ANNE	84	81	76	82	79	90	79	83	83	77	82	64	78	84	79	87	56	82	90	100
60966	SHELDON	92	65	87	64	67	91	69	83	75	64	74	65	54	76	65	82	49	78	88	101
60968	THAWVILLE	100	70	111	69	73	106	77	96	80	63	79	78	57	78	77	87	51	89	100	117
60970	WATSEKA	81	70	78	71	71	87	72	81	76	66	75	61	65	76	71	82	51	77	88	95
60973	WELLINGTON	106	73	116	73	76	112	81	101	84	66	83	83	59	83	81	92	54	94	106	124
61001	APPLE RIVER	98	82	111	83	88	105	82	100	86	76	84	74	73	84	86	91	57	92	100	116
	ILLINOIS	106	108	105	108	107	106	109	106	108	107	109	83	110	108	108	108	77	108	107	125
	UNITED STATES	100	100	100	100	100	100	100	100	100	100	100	100	100	100	100	100	100	100	100	100

ZIP CODE			POPULATION			2000-2009 ANNUAL RATE		HOUSEHOLDS					FAMILIES		
#	POST OFFICE NAME	COUNTY FIPS CODE	2000	2009	2014	% Rate	State Centile	2000	2009	2014	% Annual Rate 2000-2009	2009 Average HH Size	2000	2009	% Annual Rate 2000-2009
61006	ASHTON	103	1833	1858	1856	0.1	56	685	705	708	0.3	2.61	517	524	0.1
61007	BAILEYVILLE	141	563	608	628	0.8	79	202	221	230	1.0	2.75	168	182	0.9
61008	BELVIDERE	007	28142	35328	39403	2.5	93	10064	12580	14012	2.4	2.79	7486	9157	2.2
61010	BYRON	141	7079	8091	8743	1.5	88	2443	2806	3032	1.5	2.85	1924	2171	1.3
61011	CALEDONIA	007	2602	3531	4027	3.4	95	914	1277	1457	3.7	2.77	774	1074	3.6
61012	CAPRON	007	1981	2517	2833	2.6	93	681	871	981	2.7	2.89	534	662	2.4
61014	CHADWICK	015	1193	1119	1084	-0.7	9	464	444	433	-0.5	2.52	352	332	-0.6
61015	CHANA	141	1081	1185	1226	1.0	83	392	436	454	1.2	2.72	321	351	1.0
61016	CHERRY VALLEY	201	4166	5071	5510	2.1	92	1538	1879	2053	2.2	2.70	1236	1478	2.0
61018	DAKOTA	177	1118	1029	990	-0.9	4	420	394	381	-0.7	2.61	324	298	-0.9
61019	DAVIS	177	3409	3734	3840	1.0	83	1313	1460	1508	1.2	2.55	1052	1150	1.0
61020	DAVIS JUNCTION	141	1683	2714	3254	5.3	98	567	918	1104	5.3	2.96	470	746	5.1
61021	DIXON	103	23349	23163	23097	-0.1	45	8570	8748	8766	0.2	2.37	5712	5713	0.0
61024	DURAND	201	2596	2816	2941	0.9	81	950	1035	1085	0.9	2.61	712	756	0.7
61025	EAST DUBUQUE	085	4832	4933	4995	0.2	61	1887	1988	2030	0.6	2.48	1336	1381	0.4
61028	ELIZABETH	085	2007	1998	2025	0.0	50	849	872	892	0.3	2.24	560	558	0.0
61030	FORRESTON	141	2339	2595	2696	1.1	85	922	1031	1075	1.2	2.52	686	753	1.0
61031	FRANKLIN GROVE	103	1871	1874	1869	0.0	50	657	676	679	0.3	2.60	473	478	0.1
61032	FREEPORT	177	33093	30995	29994	-0.7	9	13814	13078	12698	-0.6	2.31	8909	8232	-0.9
61036	GALENA	085	6268	6720	6864	0.8	79	2670	2965	3068	1.1	2.24	1746	1911	1.0
61038	GARDEN PRAIRIE	007	1325	1457	1625	1.0	83	476	526	589	1.1	2.75	388	414	0.7
61039	GERMAN VALLEY	177	867	836	819	-0.4	25	319	314	309	-0.2	2.66	252	244	-0.3
61041	HANOVER	085	1322	1396	1426	0.6	75	601	654	675	0.9	2.13	386	408	0.6
61042	HARMON	103	523	509	502	-0.3	32	195	194	193	-0.1	2.62	153	151	-0.1
61044	KENT	177	206	205	204	-0.1	45	70	71	71	0.2	2.68	53	53	0.0
61046	LANARK	015	2872	2810	2761	-0.2	38	1174	1162	1146	-0.1	2.40	854	829	-0.3
61047	LEAF RIVER	141	1740	1934	2025	1.1	85	664	746	786	1.3	2.59	516	570	1.1
61048	LENA	177	4516	4458	4394	-0.1	45	1707	1717	1703	0.1	2.57	1257	1239	-0.2
61049	LINDENWOOD	141	447	458	498	0.3	65	168	177	192	0.6	2.59	128	132	0.3
61050	MC CONNELL	177	453	436	423	-0.4	25	176	173	169	-0.2	2.52	140	135	-0.4
61051	MILLEDGEVILLE	015	1623	1512	1460	-0.8	6	663	626	608	-0.6	2.41	478	443	-0.8
61052	MONROE CENTER	141	1335	1394	1527	0.5	72	482	516	567	0.7	2.70	383	401	0.5
61053	MOUNT CARROLL	015	3179	3017	2935	-0.6	13	1265	1209	1179	-0.5	2.41	879	823	-0.7
61054	MOUNT MORRIS	141	4128	4219	4235	0.2	61	1709	1769	1786	0.4	2.35	1157	1169	0.1
61060	ORANGEVILLE	177	1483	1382	1334	-0.8	6	573	542	526	-0.6	2.55	425	394	-0.8
61061	OREGON	141	7612	8112	8301	0.7	78	3028	3266	3359	0.8	2.40	2137	2257	0.6
61062	PEARL CITY	177	2058	2014	1986	-0.2	38	748	745	738	0.0	2.66	595	583	-0.2
61063	PECATONICA	201	4075	4352	4653	0.7	78	1579	1699	1824	0.8	2.56	1211	1269	0.5
61064	POLO	141	3980	4069	4081	0.2	61	1567	1625	1640	0.4	2.46	1098	1112	0.1
61065	POPLAR GROVE	007	7188	10755	13327	4.5	98	2261	3404	4235	4.5	3.15	1908	2824	4.3
61067	RIDOTT	177	897	838	812	-0.7	9	347	330	322	-0.5	2.54	269	252	-0.7
61068	ROCHELLE	141	14698	15442	15694	0.5	72	5501	5836	5959	0.6	2.62	3883	4024	0.4
61070	ROCK CITY	177	1119	1116	1106	0.0	50	406	411	409	0.1	2.72	312	310	-0.1
61071	ROCK FALLS	195	14895	14482	14224	-0.3	32	5936	5886	5818	-0.1	2.44	4157	4043	-0.3
61072	ROCKTON	201	8918	11185	12243	2.5	93	3198	3952	4319	2.3	2.81	2515	3053	2.1
61073	ROSCOE	201	15782	21262	23603	3.3	95	5384	7108	7900	3.0	2.99	4566	5924	2.9
61074	SAVANNA	015	4982	4685	4550	-0.7	9	2119	2023	1974	-0.5	2.27	1313	1224	-0.8
61075	SCALES MOUND	085	1003	1015	1026	0.1	56	383	402	411	0.5	2.52	292	302	0.4
61078	SHANNON	015	1394	1378	1359	-0.1	45	526	528	522	0.0	2.55	389	383	-0.2
61080	SOUTH BELOIT	201	8527	10180	11566	1.9	91	3372	3973	4526	1.8	2.55	2343	2654	1.4
61081	STERLING	195	23002	22413	22039	-0.3	32	8958	8838	8728	-0.1	2.48	6178	5970	-0.4
61084	STILLMAN VALLEY	141	2942	3355	3527	1.4	88	1057	1222	1293	1.6	2.74	849	963	1.4
61085	STOCKTON	085	3608	3582	3559	-0.1	45	1478	1507	1511	0.2	2.33	1029	1029	0.0
61087	WARREN	085	1876	1872	1861	0.0	50	779	802	807	0.3	2.33	524	529	0.1
61088	WINNEBAGO	201	4837	6026	6525	2.4	93	1680	2106	2286	2.5	2.86	1383	1694	2.2
61089	WINSLOW	177	920	897	878	-0.3	32	327	324	318	-0.1	2.77	249	242	-0.3
61101	ROCKFORD	201	23927	24462	24835	0.2	61	8305	8496	8669	0.2	2.73	5769	5745	0.0
61102	ROCKFORD	201	20192	20386	20784	0.1	56	6886	6913	7057	0.0	2.90	5035	4931	-0.2
61103	ROCKFORD	201	24119	23912	24256	-0.1	45	10182	10215	10400	0.0	2.25	5867	5698	-0.3
61104	ROCKFORD	201	19759	19606	19672	-0.1	45	7983	7817	7852	-0.2	2.49	4357	4094	-0.7
61107	ROCKFORD	201	30793	33077	34267	0.8	79	12741	13563	14068	0.7	2.37	8217	8503	0.4
61108	ROCKFORD	201	27572	28613	29333	0.4	69	11472	11901	12237	0.4	2.36	7542	7590	0.1
61109	ROCKFORD	201	26262	28198	29354	0.8	79	10526	11294	11795	0.8	2.49	7069	7380	0.5
61111	LOVES PARK	201	20277	24517	26199	2.1	92	8257	9810	10484	1.9	2.49	5486	6464	1.8
61112	ROCKFORD	201	13	311	358	40.9	100	4	109	126	42.9	2.85	3	74	41.4
61114	ROCKFORD	201	15076	16712	17557	1.1	85	5841	6438	6774	1.1	2.52	4225	4511	0.7
61115	MACHESNEY PARK	201	20737	22871	23981	1.1	85	7758	8598	9048	1.1	2.65	5863	6361	0.9
61201	ROCK ISLAND	161	39886	38475	38005	-0.4	25	16225	15794	15648	-0.3	2.28	9583	9070	-0.6
61230	ALBANY	195	1205	1223	1217	0.2	61	469	487	489	0.4	2.51	357	364	0.2
61231	ALEDO	131	5717	5581	5491	-0.3	32	2263	2238	2208	-0.1	2.40	1600	1555	-0.3
61232	ANDALUSIA	161	862	841	835	-0.3	32	343	340	340	-0.1	2.47	273	267	-0.2
61234	ANNAWAN	073	1265	1239	1216	-0.2	38	504	500	493	-0.1	2.42	362	352	-0.3
61235	ATKINSON	073	1439	1423	1409	-0.1	45	597	601	598	0.1	2.31	415	409	-0.2
61238	CAMBRIDGE	073	3507	3392	3322	-0.4	25	1362	1340	1319	-0.2	2.46	1003	968	-0.4
61240	COAL VALLEY	161	5976	6147	6209	0.3	65	2155	2256	2290	0.5	2.66	1701	1753	0.3
61241	COLONA	073	7183	7075	6974	-0.2	38	2699	2713	2689	0.1	2.61	2086	2065	-0.1
61242	CORDOVA	161	1191	1329	1381	1.2	85	457	519	542	1.4	2.53	342	380	1.1
61243	DEER GROVE	195	266	268	268	0.1	56	93	96	96	0.3	2.79	77	79	0.3
61244	EAST MOLINE	161	23969	25089	25139	0.5	72	9949	10013	10045	0.1	2.41	6362	6259	-0.2
61250	ERIE	195	2676	2854	2867	0.7	78	998	1090	1103	1.0	2.62	766	823	0.8
61251	FENTON	195	377	382	381	0.1	56	137	143	143	0.5	2.67	110	112	0.2
61252	FULTON	195	5772	5758	5703	0.0	50	2280	2317	2305	0.2	2.43	1635	1631	0.0
61254	GENESEO	073	11270	11211	11093	-0.1	45	4314	4344	4312	0.1	2.54	3197	3171	-0.1
61256	HAMPTON	161	1618	1901	1974	1.8	91	622	742	790	1.9	1.95	480	560	1.7
61257	HILLSDALE	161	1323	1452	1502	1.0	83	489	544	565	1.2	2.64	368	403	1.0
61259	ILLINOIS CITY	161	1387	1289	1258	-0.8	6	501	469	459	-0.7	2.75	415	384	-0.8
61260	JOY	131	840	831	818	-0.1	45	337	336	333	0.0	2.47	253	248	-0.2
61261	LYNDON	195	880	936	939	0.7	78	344	370	374	0.8	2.53	260	276	0.6
61262	LYNN CENTER	073	1209	1203	1188	-0.1	45	419	426	423	0.2	2.82	345	347	0.1
61263	MATHERVILLE	131	784	788	783	0.1	56	293	295	293	0.1	2.67	221	219	-0.1
61264	MILAN	161	12171	10859	10782	-1.2	2	4591	4566	4559	-0.1	2.36	3198	3124	-0.3
61265	MOLINE	161	45237	44457	44220	-0.2	38	19102	18941	18901	-0.1	2.33	12025	11588	-0.4
61270	MORRISON	195	7729	7640	7547	-0.1	45	2986	3005	2984	0.1	2.42	2153	2127	-0.1
61272	NEW BOSTON	131	1508	1694	1727	1.3	87	616	698	714	1.4	2.43	434	486	1.2
61273	ORION	073	3252	3320	3302	0.2	61	1250	1302	1303	0.4	2.52	957	980	0.3
	ILLINOIS					0.6					0.6	2.64			0.4
	UNITED STATES					1.0					1.1	2.59			0.9

# ZIP CODE	POST OFFICE NAME	RACE (%) White 2000	White 2009	Black 2000	Black 2009	Asian/Pacific 2000	Asian/Pacific 2009	% Hispanic Origin 2000	% Hispanic Origin 2009	2009 AGE DISTRIBUTION (%) 0-4	5-9	10-14	15-19	20-24	25-44	45-64	65-84	85+	18+	MEDIAN AGE 2009	% 2009 Males	% 2009 Females
61006	ASHTON	97.6	96.7	0.8	1.1	0.5	0.7	2.7	4.0	6.4	7.5	7.5	7.9	5.7	25.3	25.8	12.4	1.5	73.6	38.0	49.2	50.8
61007	BAILEYVILLE	98.4	97.9	0.2	0.2	0.4	0.5	0.9	1.3	5.3	5.8	6.1	6.9	4.9	23.2	32.2	14.1	1.5	78.6	43.6	50.5	49.5
61008	BELVIDERE	87.6	83.3	1.0	1.1	0.5	0.7	15.9	22.0	7.7	7.4	7.4	7.5	6.0	26.4	25.7	10.3	1.6	72.9	36.1	49.7	50.3
61010	BYRON	97.9	97.2	0.3	0.4	0.4	0.6	1.1	1.8	6.7	7.5	8.6	8.9	5.8	25.6	26.7	8.4	1.7	70.9	36.6	49.4	50.6
61011	CALEDONIA	94.6	92.2	1.4	1.8	1.3	1.7	4.1	6.9	7.9	7.7	7.9	7.8	5.4	27.3	27.7	7.7	0.7	71.7	35.2	50.3	49.7
61012	CAPRON	91.7	87.4	0.5	0.6	0.3	0.4	12.7	19.9	7.7	7.9	7.9	7.0	4.8	27.0	26.3	10.5	0.9	72.1	36.2	50.3	49.7
61014	CHADWICK	98.2	97.7	0.1	0.1	0.4	0.5	1.6	2.3	6.2	6.6	6.6	6.4	4.0	24.8	29.4	13.8	2.2	76.5	41.7	51.8	48.2
61015	CHANA	98.3	97.7	0.3	0.3	0.4	0.7	1.2	1.8	5.4	6.3	7.3	6.9	4.2	23.6	34.1	11.1	1.0	76.5	42.4	51.9	48.1
61016	CHERRY VALLEY	96.0	93.9	1.2	1.8	1.6	2.4	2.1	3.5	5.1	5.7	6.4	6.7	4.8	24.8	35.0	10.6	0.9	78.6	42.5	49.9	50.1
61018	DAKOTA	98.4	97.7	0.3	0.4	0.4	0.6	0.4	0.8	5.5	6.0	6.6	7.3	5.0	25.2	31.5	11.2	1.7	77.4	41.1	49.8	50.2
61019	DAVIS	98.7	98.0	0.3	0.5	0.2	0.3	0.7	1.3	5.3	5.8	6.3	6.8	4.4	20.8	29.2	19.7	1.8	78.4	45.4	48.6	51.4
61020	DAVIS JUNCTION	96.0	94.0	0.1	0.2	0.3	0.4	4.2	6.5	7.1	7.4	8.0	8.0	4.5	26.8	28.7	8.5	0.9	72.4	37.7	48.6	51.4
61021	DIXON	89.9	87.9	7.3	8.3	0.7	1.0	3.6	5.0	5.1	5.2	5.4	6.1	6.5	28.5	28.6	12.2	2.5	80.6	40.4	51.6	48.4
61024	DURAND	97.6	96.3	0.7	1.1	0.1	0.2	1.1	1.8	5.6	5.9	6.7	7.7	5.6	22.4	30.2	12.9	3.0	76.5	41.9	49.5	50.5
61025	EAST DUBUQUE	98.9	98.5	0.2	0.2	0.2	0.3	0.8	1.2	6.3	6.7	6.9	7.0	5.3	24.1	30.8	12.0	1.1	76.0	40.4	51.2	48.8
61028	ELIZABETH	98.5	97.9	0.2	0.3	0.1	0.2	1.1	1.7	4.9	5.2	5.6	5.5	3.7	20.0	31.3	19.2	4.7	80.7	48.8	49.7	50.3
61030	FORRESTON	98.9	98.6	0.0	0.0	0.3	0.4	1.0	1.6	6.6	6.8	7.3	7.6	4.8	23.8	28.3	12.6	2.0	74.3	40.5	49.3	50.7
61031	FRANKLIN GROVE	98.1	97.4	0.5	0.7	0.3	0.5	1.4	2.0	6.2	6.2	6.4	7.1	6.4	24.3	26.1	12.4	5.0	76.7	40.0	48.4	51.6
61032	FREEPORT	84.8	81.7	11.3	13.1	1.0	1.3	1.8	2.5	6.4	6.1	5.9	6.3	6.0	24.5	27.3	14.2	3.3	77.8	40.9	47.4	52.6
61036	GALENA	98.1	97.6	0.3	0.3	0.2	0.3	3.2	4.4	5.0	5.4	5.6	5.4	4.8	21.4	32.2	17.3	2.9	80.6	46.6	49.7	50.3
61038	GARDEN PRAIRIE	96.2	94.2	0.5	0.6	0.5	0.7	4.2	7.0	5.8	6.3	6.9	7.1	4.7	23.7	31.4	12.4	1.6	76.5	41.9	49.8	50.2
61039	GERMAN VALLEY	99.2	99.0	0.0	0.0	0.5	0.6	1.2	1.7	4.4	6.9	8.0	7.7	5.0	25.8	27.3	12.2	2.6	75.4	40.1	50.1	49.9
61041	HANOVER	98.0	97.6	0.2	0.1	0.2	0.2	1.3	1.9	5.7	5.7	5.7	5.4	4.9	21.8	30.2	18.3	2.4	79.6	45.6	50.0	50.0
61042	HARMON	97.7	97.1	0.4	0.4	0.0	0.0	3.3	4.7	5.5	5.9	6.5	7.1	4.5	22.2	33.0	13.8	1.6	78.0	43.8	50.7	49.3
61044	KENT	99.5	98.5	0.0	0.5	0.0	0.0	1.0	1.5	5.4	6.3	6.8	6.8	3.9	22.4	28.3	13.7	6.3	76.6	43.7	49.8	50.2
61046	LANARK	97.9	97.3	0.1	0.1	0.7	1.0	0.6	0.8	4.8	5.6	6.2	6.7	4.5	22.6	30.3	16.9	2.5	79.1	44.8	51.1	48.9
61047	LEAF RIVER	98.4	97.8	0.6	0.7	0.1	0.3	0.9	1.4	5.6	6.0	6.7	7.1	5.0	23.8	31.3	13.1	1.3	77.3	42.1	50.4	49.6
61048	LENA	98.8	98.3	0.2	0.2	0.1	0.1	1.1	1.6	5.7	6.0	6.3	7.1	5.8	23.5	28.7	14.0	2.9	77.7	41.7	49.5	50.5
61049	LINDENWOOD	96.9	95.6	0.2	0.4	0.2	0.2	2.9	4.6	6.6	7.0	7.4	7.9	4.8	24.9	30.3	9.6	1.5	74.0	39.5	52.2	47.8
61050	MC CONNELL	98.9	98.6	0.0	0.0	0.2	0.2	0.9	1.4	5.5	5.5	6.4	6.9	4.6	24.3	31.9	13.3	1.6	78.4	42.4	51.8	48.2
61051	MILLEDGEVILLE	97.6	96.8	0.1	0.1	0.3	0.5	1.5	2.3	5.8	6.0	6.3	6.6	5.0	25.6	28.9	13.5	2.3	77.8	41.0	49.1	50.9
61052	MONROE CENTER	97.4	96.1	0.1	0.1	0.1	0.1	3.1	4.7	7.0	7.2	7.6	7.7	4.4	27.8	27.7	9.3	1.2	73.4	38.0	51.0	49.0
61053	MOUNT CARROLL	98.0	97.4	0.2	0.2	0.2	0.4	1.4	1.9	6.3	6.6	7.0	6.7	4.2	22.5	27.2	15.8	3.7	76.1	42.3	49.4	50.6
61054	MOUNT MORRIS	97.3	96.2	0.1	0.2	0.4	0.6	2.4	3.7	6.7	6.7	6.8	6.3	4.8	24.4	27.1	13.8	3.4	75.8	40.9	48.8	51.2
61060	ORANGEVILLE	98.8	98.4	0.3	0.4	0.1	0.1	0.8	1.1	4.9	8.2	7.3	6.9	4.3	25.3	29.7	11.6	1.8	75.1	39.8	50.3	49.7
61061	OREGON	97.0	96.0	0.6	0.7	0.5	0.6	1.8	2.9	5.3	5.6	6.0	6.4	5.4	23.3	30.2	14.9	2.8	79.0	43.4	49.6	50.4
61062	PEARL CITY	98.6	98.1	0.3	0.4	0.1	0.1	0.5	0.9	6.6	7.1	7.3	6.9	4.2	24.1	29.9	11.5	2.4	74.6	40.7	49.6	50.4
61063	PECATONICA	98.4	97.5	0.2	0.4	0.1	0.2	0.8	1.4	6.2	6.5	6.9	6.8	5.1	24.2	30.4	12.0	1.8	76.0	40.9	49.3	50.7
61064	POLO	98.4	97.8	0.1	0.0	0.3	0.4	1.6	2.6	5.7	5.8	6.0	7.0	6.1	23.4	29.1	13.5	3.3	78.2	41.8	49.4	50.6
61065	POPLAR GROVE	95.7	94.4	0.9	0.9	0.4	0.6	4.6	6.6	8.5	8.1	8.0	7.6	5.9	27.4	25.3	8.2	1.0	70.5	33.8	50.2	49.8
61067	RIDOTT	98.1	97.4	0.3	0.4	0.3	0.5	0.9	1.3	5.3	5.7	6.6	7.6	4.8	23.4	31.6	13.4	1.7	77.7	42.5	50.8	49.2
61068	ROCHELLE	89.4	85.7	0.9	1.0	0.7	0.9	16.8	23.6	7.6	7.3	7.2	7.3	6.5	27.1	24.6	10.6	1.9	73.4	35.2	50.0	50.0
61070	ROCK CITY	98.0	97.1	0.2	0.3	0.6	1.0	0.6	0.9	5.8	6.9	8.2	8.2	3.3	25.0	28.2	12.1	2.2	73.5	39.7	50.3	49.7
61071	ROCK FALLS	93.0	90.3	0.8	0.9	0.2	0.3	9.7	14.1	6.8	6.3	6.2	6.3	6.1	24.8	27.3	14.3	1.9	76.9	39.9	48.5	51.5
61072	ROCKTON	97.0	95.4	0.8	1.1	0.7	1.1	1.9	3.2	6.7	6.8	7.3	7.8	5.8	25.8	29.5	9.1	1.1	74.0	37.9	49.8	50.2
61073	ROSCOE	96.4	94.5	1.1	1.8	1.0	1.3	1.8	3.1	6.7	7.2	7.9	7.5	4.9	25.8	31.4	8.1	0.6	73.4	38.4	50.3	49.7
61074	SAVANNA	95.0	93.5	1.3	1.5	0.3	0.4	4.3	6.0	5.7	5.6	5.9	6.4	5.4	22.3	28.6	16.1	4.1	78.6	44.0	48.6	51.4
61075	SCALES MOUND	98.6	98.2	0.3	0.3	0.3	0.4	1.2	1.9	4.4	5.2	6.2	7.7	4.1	20.0	31.4	18.9	2.0	79.3	46.4	52.6	47.4
61078	SHANNON	97.3	96.5	0.3	0.4	1.1	1.5	1.0	1.4	4.6	5.0	5.7	5.9	4.5	19.4	33.4	18.5	3.0	80.6	48.0	50.7	49.3
61080	SOUTH BELOIT	89.9	86.1	3.5	4.7	0.8	1.2	7.0	10.2	7.3	7.0	6.9	6.9	5.9	28.6	26.2	9.9	1.3	74.6	36.4	50.3	49.7
61081	STERLING	87.4	83.6	1.8	2.0	0.8	1.1	15.6	21.2	6.7	6.6	6.5	6.6	6.3	25.2	26.7	12.7	2.7	76.4	38.7	48.8	51.2
61084	STILLMAN VALLEY	97.7	97.0	0.3	0.3	0.4	0.6	0.8	1.3	5.1	7.2	8.4	7.3	4.8	24.3	30.8	10.8	1.4	74.3	39.8	50.3	49.7
61085	STOCKTON	99.1	98.9	0.1	0.1	0.1	0.1	0.6	0.9	5.9	5.7	6.3	6.6	5.2	22.1	28.7	16.7	2.8	77.6	43.6	48.9	51.1
61087	WARREN	99.4	99.2	0.2	0.2	0.0	0.0	1.1	1.6	5.3	5.5	5.8	6.4	5.0	24.2	29.0	15.7	3.0	79.5	43.2	49.4	50.6
61088	WINNEBAGO	97.8	96.8	1.1	1.5	0.4	0.5	1.4	2.3	6.5	7.2	7.6	7.6	4.7	25.7	29.9	9.7	1.1	73.9	39.2	50.2	49.8
61089	WINSLOW	98.4	97.5	0.1	0.2	0.2	0.3	1.3	1.9	6.0	6.6	9.3	7.5	4.7	26.4	27.0	11.4	1.2	72.7	38.1	50.7	49.3
61101	ROCKFORD	56.7	51.6	35.2	38.3	0.4	0.4	9.2	11.9	8.0	7.7	7.4	8.1	7.8	26.0	23.1	10.1	1.9	72.0	33.0	48.3	51.7
61102	ROCKFORD	48.1	45.1	37.8	39.0	0.4	0.5	18.9	21.3	8.7	8.5	7.9	7.9	6.9	25.9	23.2	9.6	1.3	70.1	32.8	49.8	50.2
61103	ROCKFORD	79.8	73.4	14.0	17.9	0.8	1.1	6.3	9.5	7.1	6.5	6.2	6.7	7.1	26.7	24.9	11.5	3.3	76.0	37.2	47.5	52.5
61104	ROCKFORD	70.0	62.8	14.2	16.7	4.2	4.8	16.5	23.0	9.7	8.3	7.0	7.1	8.1	30.1	21.4	7.1	1.2	70.8	31.1	50.6	49.4
61107	ROCKFORD	89.5	85.4	4.4	6.0	2.4	3.2	5.7	8.7	5.9	5.8	5.9	6.3	5.9	24.2	28.0	14.7	3.4	78.7	42.0	48.4	51.6
61108	ROCKFORD	87.6	82.5	5.2	7.2	2.4	3.2	6.5	10.2	6.4	6.3	6.2	5.6	5.5	25.4	27.1	14.3	3.1	77.6	41.2	48.4	51.6
61109	ROCKFORD	83.4	77.6	8.0	10.2	3.1	4.2	7.5	11.3	7.5	7.0	6.6	6.3	6.7	29.1	25.7	10.2	0.9	75.2	35.6	49.9	50.1
61111	LOVES PARK	93.2	89.3	2.2	3.6	1.7	2.9	3.2	5.4	7.4	6.8	6.5	6.5	6.5	30.4	25.0	9.5	1.3	75.3	35.5	48.8	51.2
61112	ROCKFORD	100.0	90.7	0.0	2.3	0.0	3.2	8.3	7.1	6.8	6.8	6.4	5.1	4.8	28.0	30.2	10.9	1.0	76.5	39.2	49.8	50.2
61114	ROCKFORD	88.9	84.1	4.8	6.8	3.8	5.3	2.7	4.4	5.7	5.7	6.3	6.3	4.7	21.8	30.7	14.8	3.9	78.1	44.5	47.2	52.8
61115	MACHESNEY PARK	95.3	93.0	1.4	2.1	1.0	1.4	2.8	4.7	6.5	6.6	6.9	6.8	5.7	27.2	28.8	10.5	1.0	75.8	38.4	49.6	50.4
61201	ROCK ISLAND	76.8	73.1	17.5	19.3	0.8	1.2	5.9	8.2	6.3	5.7	5.5	8.1	8.8	24.0	25.4	12.9	3.2	79.0	37.8	47.6	52.4
61230	ALBANY	98.6	98.2	0.5	0.7	0.1	0.1	0.8	1.4	6.5	6.7	7.0	7.0	4.8	23.5	29.7	13.3	1.6	75.6	41.9	49.6	50.4
61231	ALEDO	98.3	98.2	0.4	0.4	0.3	0.3	0.9	0.9	5.6	5.7	5.9	6.1	5.0	22.4	29.0	15.7	4.6	79.0	44.5	48.1	51.9
61232	ANDALUSIA	97.2	96.1	0.8	1.2	0.1	0.1	1.6	2.4	4.4	5.2	5.9	7.3	4.5	23.8	34.5	13.1	1.3	79.9	44.2	49.6	50.4
61234	ANNAWAN	99.4	99.2	0.1	0.1	0.0	0.1	1.3	1.9	6.5	6.1	6.5	6.5	4.4	22.2	27.0	16.5	4.4	76.4	43.3	47.5	52.5
61235	ATKINSON	98.6	98.2	0.3	0.4	0.1	0.1	1.2	1.6	5.5	5.8	6.3	6.4	5.1	22.4	28.7	16.0	3.9	78.4	43.9	48.8	51.2
61238	CAMBRIDGE	98.4	97.9	0.5	0.6	0.3	0.4	0.6	0.9	5.5	5.7	6.1	6.8	6.5	25.5	28.8	12.8	2.2	78.6	40.2	51.0	49.0
61240	COAL VALLEY	97.0	95.8	1.0	1.3	0.4	0.6	2.5	3.9	5.5	6.2	6.7	7.1	4.5	24.5	31.5	12.4	1.6	76.8	41.6	50.6	49.4
61241	COLONA	97.0	96.0	0.3	0.4	0.2	0.3	3.6	5.2	6.2	6.4	6.3	6.8	5.8	27.1	29.7	10.8	0.8	76.9	38.7	50.1	49.9
61242	CORDOVA	97.1	96.2	0.3	0.3	0.3	0.5	2.0	3.1	5.1	5.6	6.4	6.6	5.0	22.0	32.3	15.5	1.5	78.0	44.4	51.8	48.2
61243	DEER GROVE	96.6	95.1	0.4	0.4	0.0	0.0	3.4	5.2	9.3	8.6	9.3	7.1	3.7	26.1	23.5	11.2	1.1	68.3	34.8	48.5	51.5
61244	EAST MOLINE	82.3	78.1	6.6	7.6	1.9	2.6	13.4	17.8	6.9	6.3	6.0	6.5	7.0	25.6	25.5	13.6	2.7	77.3	38.1	48.6	51.4
61250	ERIE	98.4	97.7	0.2	0.2	0.1	0.1	1.0	1.6	5.9	6.3	6.7	6.9	4.8	24.3	30.5	12.9	1.8	76.8	41.5	48.7	51.3
61251	FENTON	98.7	98.2	0.3	0.3	0.0	0.0	1.1	1.3	5.8	6.0	6.8	7.6	4.5	23.6	31.7	12.6	1.6	76.7	41.9	48.7	51.3
61252	FULTON	98.1	97.4	0.5	0.6	0.4	0.7	1.1	1.8	5.9	6.0	6.0	5.9	5.4	23.6	29.5	14.3	3.5	78.4	42.8	50.1	49.9
61254	GENESEO	98.6	98.1	0.2	0.3	0.3	0.4	1.2	1.7	5.5	6.0	6.8	6.9	4.9	21.7	30.5	14.4	3.2	77.3	43.6	48.9	51.1
61256	HAMPTON	94.9	85.6	0.6	6.2	0.1	1.8	5.3	8.5	4.8	5.2	5.7	9.0	9.1	24.4	27.4	13.0	1.3	81.4	38.6	50.2	49.8
61257	HILLSDALE	96.1	94.7	0.6	0.7	0.4	0.6	2.2	3.3	6.0	6.2	6.5	7.0	5.8	25.9	30.5	11.0	1.2	77.1	40.1	49.2	50.8
61259	ILLINOIS CITY	98.4	97.8	0.1	0.2	0.1	0.2	1.6	2.5	5.7	6.2	7.0	7.2	4.6	22.7	32.3	13.0	1.5	76.4	42.8	50.6	49.4
61260	JOY	99.0	99.0	0.0	0.0	0.1	0.1	0.7	0.7	6.3	6.6	6.9	6.5	3.6	27.0	28.0	13.5	1.7	76.2	40.2	50.3	49.7
61261	LYNDON	96.5	95.2	0.1	0.1	0.3	0.4	1.5	2.4	5.8	6.3	7.1	6.7	4.4	23.1	32.3	13.0	1.4	76.5	42.6	51.2	48.8
61262	LYNN CENTER	98.3	97.8	0.2	0.2	0.4	0.7	1.2	1.7	4.7	6.1	7.7	7.4	4.5	21.6	31.8	14.6	1.7	77.1	43.6	50.8	49.2
61263	MATHERVILLE	98.3	98.2	0.0	0.0	0.3	0.4	0.9	1.0	9.8	6.7	7.5	7.6	4.6	27.5	24.2	9.9	2.2	70.4	34.7	48.9	51.1
61264	MILAN	89.5	88.2	7.5	7.2	0.3	1.4	3.0	3.8	5.8	5.9	5.9	6.5	6.1	26.1	28.6	13.2	1.8	79.0	40.2	50.0	50.0
61265	MOLINE	88.6	85.1	3.0	3.7	1.4	1.9	11.7	15.6	6.4	6.1	6.0	6.0	5.9	26.1	27.4	13.4	2.6	77.9	39.9	47.9	52.1
61270	MORRISON	98.1	97.4	0.5	0.5	0.1	0.2	1.9	2.9	5.3	5.6	6.2	7.7	5.6	23.3	29.0	13.7	3.6	78.6	42.1	49.7	50.3
61272	NEW BOSTON	99.1	99.1	0.1	0.1	0.0	0.0	0.8	0.8	5.9	6.0	6.0	5.7	5.4	24.7	30.0	14.6	1.7	78.6	41.8	51.1	48.9
61273	ORION	98.9	98.3	0.2	0.3	0.1	0.2	1.4	2.2	5.5	5.7	6.0	6.4	5.6	23.1	31.2	14.2	2.3	78.9	43.3	50.1	49.9
	ILLINOIS	73.5	70.6	15.1	15.3	3.4	4.4	12.3	15.7	7.1	6.9	6.8	7.1	6.9	27.5	25.4	10.3	1.9	75.0	36.1	49.1	50.9
	UNITED STATES	75.1	72.0	12.3	12.7	3.8	4.6	12.5	15.7	6.8	6.7	6.6	7.1	6.9	27.0	26.0	10.9	1.9	75.7	36.9	49.2	50.8

ZIP CODE #	POST OFFICE NAME	2009 Per Capita Income	2009 HH Income Base	2009 Household Income Distribution (%) Less than $25,000	$25,000 to $49,999	$50,000 to $99,999	$100,000 to $149,999	$150,000 or More	Median Household Income 2009	2014	2009 National Centile	2009 State Centile	2009 Home Value Base	2009 Home Value Distribution (%) Less than $50,000	$50,000 to $89,999	$90,000 to $174,999	$175,000 to $399,999	$400,000 or More	2009 Median Home Value
61006	ASHTON	25661	705	13.2	29.6	44.4	8.9	3.8	56712	58723	74	59	522	3.4	15.5	55.6	23.4	2.1	133850
61007	BAILEYVILLE	26287	221	15.4	20.8	50.7	8.6	4.5	62049	62416	80	68	168	4.2	11.3	40.5	37.5	6.5	161842
61008	BELVIDERE	25866	12580	16.7	23.0	45.0	9.5	5.8	61849	65662	80	68	9158	9.3	4.5	39.9	38.3	8.1	169225
61010	BYRON	26263	2806	14.2	19.4	45.6	14.1	6.7	67314	68881	85	77	2183	3.3	2.5	28.9	60.1	5.2	213588
61011	CALEDONIA	38135	1277	6.3	11.7	48.6	20.0	13.4	82458	82704	93	93	1144	4.6	2.6	21.9	55.4	15.4	219118
61012	CAPRON	24500	871	13.8	19.7	52.5	10.1	3.9	64880	67147	83	74	703	7.8	3.8	34.1	45.4	8.8	183477
61014	CHADWICK	23226	444	20.0	26.1	45.0	5.6	3.2	52697	53627	67	50	332	9.3	29.8	37.0	15.1	8.7	104688
61015	CHANA	30335	436	5.5	11.5	59.4	19.7	3.9	76886	77474	91	89	360	0.8	6.9	26.9	51.7	13.6	218382
61016	CHERRY VALLEY	30676	1879	7.3	16.6	51.8	18.3	6.0	77760	77326	91	90	1615	2.5	3.7	44.1	48.1	1.5	174551
61018	DAKOTA	23817	394	12.9	31.0	45.7	6.6	3.8	55377	58887	72	57	307	10.7	19.2	43.6	22.5	3.9	118008
61019	DAVIS	28844	1460	10.0	19.1	56.0	11.4	3.5	70613	72639	87	81	1312	1.8	5.0	49.0	40.2	4.0	164840
61020	DAVIS JUNCTION	25492	918	5.3	18.2	63.5	9.8	3.2	74591	75897	89	85	801	9.5	8.6	28.0	47.7	6.2	185642
61021	DIXON	24929	8748	19.8	29.2	38.9	8.6	3.6	51165	53864	64	47	6381	6.3	16.4	53.3	20.9	3.1	122753
61024	DURAND	28520	1035	12.9	19.3	52.1	10.3	5.3	68783	68589	86	79	805	1.9	8.6	45.7	40.1	3.7	157065
61025	EAST DUBUQUE	25409	1988	17.3	29.4	43.8	6.7	2.8	52967	54704	68	51	1585	8.1	17.9	41.5	28.3	4.2	135841
61028	ELIZABETH	23227	872	24.0	39.8	28.6	3.3	4.4	42383	45610	41	22	661	8.3	12.4	37.7	25.9	15.7	148346
61030	FORRESTON	22077	1031	23.0	28.1	40.9	6.1	1.8	48866	50781	59	40	788	8.4	12.4	56.0	18.8	4.4	129856
61031	FRANKLIN GROVE	24074	676	15.4	26.0	46.7	7.1	4.7	57612	60097	75	60	483	4.8	13.5	57.1	22.4	2.3	131807
61032	FREEPORT	24624	13078	23.5	28.0	38.3	7.3	3.0	48173	50603	58	40	9323	16.1	23.8	43.5	15.3	1.2	104776
61036	GALENA	28242	2965	20.1	27.3	40.8	5.9	5.9	52301	52462	66	49	2224	3.6	10.4	37.1	38.4	10.5	172490
61038	GARDEN PRAIRIE	28053	526	9.1	20.0	49.8	14.8	6.3	73358	75612	89	84	440	0.0	0.9	20.0	68.0	11.1	231008
61039	GERMAN VALLEY	25354	314	14.6	28.0	45.2	8.6	3.5	58288	60592	76	61	254	4.7	14.6	46.5	28.7	5.5	132500
61041	HANOVER	25032	654	25.5	35.9	31.0	4.1	3.4	44099	45917	46	27	478	9.4	25.5	42.5	14.6	7.9	111218
61042	HARMON	24416	194	7.7	40.7	41.2	6.7	3.6	51022	51815	64	46	149	3.4	24.8	47.7	22.1	2.0	125543
61044	KENT	20524	71	19.7	32.4	39.4	5.6	2.8	47996	48620	57	38	52	9.6	17.3	40.4	25.0	7.7	137500
61046	LANARK	26201	1162	18.0	27.8	44.1	7.1	3.0	53653	55040	69	53	942	8.7	27.6	42.0	16.0	5.6	106731
61047	LEAF RIVER	25801	746	13.5	25.2	44.8	13.4	3.1	57197	58193	74	59	592	2.4	6.8	39.4	36.5	15.0	178879
61048	LENA	23135	1717	18.7	28.4	41.9	8.5	2.5	52934	56284	68	51	1345	3.6	16.7	52.3	26.2	1.2	131307
61049	LINDENWOOD	27395	177	9.0	24.3	53.1	9.6	4.0	64198	65385	83	73	135	5.9	8.1	38.5	37.8	9.6	169853
61050	MC CONNELL	22086	173	28.3	26.0	38.2	5.2	2.3	46148	47338	52	32	141	6.4	27.0	41.1	20.6	5.0	120395
61051	MILLEDGEVILLE	25156	626	14.7	34.2	43.6	4.0	3.5	50981	52394	64	46	496	10.7	31.7	49.4	6.5	1.8	96909
61052	MONROE CENTER	27889	516	10.9	17.6	56.6	10.7	4.3	71484	72834	88	82	425	7.3	4.7	30.8	46.8	10.4	196181
61053	MOUNT CARROLL	21566	1209	23.1	32.1	37.9	4.6	2.3	44241	46752	46	27	921	13.8	24.9	42.5	15.6	3.3	105565
61054	MOUNT MORRIS	25596	1769	21.7	24.5	42.8	6.9	4.0	52214	53368	66	49	1295	10.0	8.4	54.6	25.0	1.9	137386
61060	ORANGEVILLE	22108	542	18.1	30.6	44.3	6.3	0.7	50965	52513	63	46	422	5.9	22.7	47.4	20.9	3.1	115625
61061	OREGON	26850	3266	21.6	24.4	37.9	10.2	5.9	53602	55798	69	53	2403	2.3	7.2	48.5	36.3	5.7	161738
61062	PEARL CITY	23027	745	15.6	26.7	48.6	7.2	1.9	57552	59825	75	60	591	12.9	13.2	47.2	24.0	2.7	127793
61063	PECATONICA	27269	1699	11.9	20.0	57.4	8.1	2.6	69517	70394	86	80	1367	2.9	9.9	52.2	31.2	3.9	145010
61064	POLO	24332	1625	19.5	23.7	45.8	8.4	2.6	54385	55468	70	55	1202	3.5	11.6	58.5	21.7	4.7	133333
61065	POPLAR GROVE	25125	3404	7.7	18.2	52.2	16.8	5.1	75390	75857	90	86	3031	5.0	2.8	27.9	58.5	5.8	205353
61067	RIDOTT	26768	330	13.0	23.0	51.8	9.7	2.4	66207	68175	84	75	264	9.5	14.8	39.8	28.0	8.0	136429
61068	ROCHELLE	23109	5836	19.0	27.1	42.6	8.2	3.1	53019	54601	68	51	3877	6.0	6.3	50.3	35.4	2.0	157529
61070	ROCK CITY	24145	411	17.8	25.5	42.3	9.0	5.4	57553	60528	75	60	334	6.9	9.9	48.8	31.4	3.0	138793
61071	ROCK FALLS	23048	5886	21.0	29.3	41.5	5.8	2.4	49721	52127	60	43	4238	8.1	29.0	50.5	11.7	0.7	103237
61072	ROCKTON	27882	3952	8.8	19.2	51.9	12.9	7.2	71206	72978	87	81	3244	0.6	3.6	46.0	47.2	2.6	174674
61073	ROSCOE	31794	7108	6.0	12.1	53.7	17.0	11.3	80085	80535	92	92	6090	1.1	1.9	36.3	53.3	7.5	192524
61074	SAVANNA	20819	2023	31.7	30.8	31.2	4.3	1.9	39613	42442	32	15	1459	28.6	33.4	26.2	9.9	1.9	74167
61075	SCALES MOUND	24602	402	14.9	32.1	43.3	5.7	4.0	52607	53357	67	50	340	3.2	10.6	38.5	35.6	12.1	167857
61078	SHANNON	26719	528	14.6	26.5	46.0	8.3	4.5	57949	59327	75	61	430	7.0	22.1	42.6	21.4	7.0	120565
61080	SOUTH BELOIT	24844	3973	19.4	28.3	39.8	8.4	4.1	52467	55190	67	50	2893	11.9	15.8	44.4	24.7	3.2	134976
61081	STERLING	24810	8838	19.9	28.2	40.2	8.3	3.5	51925	54867	66	48	6150	5.1	20.5	52.5	20.2	1.7	116334
61084	STILLMAN VALLEY	29327	1222	11.3	18.6	48.2	16.0	5.9	72577	72010	88	83	1003	2.8	0.7	29.7	57.4	9.4	208838
61085	STOCKTON	23649	1507	20.6	34.2	37.7	4.8	2.7	47537	47521	56	37	1146	9.0	16.1	47.9	19.5	7.4	124631
61087	WARREN	24718	802	22.3	30.4	39.0	6.1	2.1	48104	48968	57	38	640	12.0	25.9	48.6	10.8	2.7	109200
61088	WINNEBAGO	27027	2106	10.2	16.9	51.7	17.9	3.3	76158	76763	90	88	1768	2.3	5.5	45.9	42.8	3.6	168868
61089	WINSLOW	19714	324	19.8	23.1	51.5	4.6	0.9	53323	55417	69	52	249	4.0	26.1	47.4	16.9	5.6	115365
61101	ROCKFORD	18337	8496	29.8	29.3	33.7	5.2	2.0	41817	45393	39	21	5049	14.2	38.8	35.0	11.4	0.6	86982
61102	ROCKFORD	18268	6913	28.8	29.4	32.8	6.5	2.5	42955	46269	42	24	4718	24.6	35.0	25.4	13.7	1.2	76366
61103	ROCKFORD	25204	10215	26.3	26.8	36.7	6.6	3.6	47581	49221	56	37	5990	3.4	22.2	60.2	12.6	1.7	108788
61104	ROCKFORD	17320	7817	35.8	30.3	30.1	2.6	1.2	34975	36995	18	6	3174	7.0	54.0	37.9	0.9	0.1	83676
61107	ROCKFORD	33226	13563	15.4	24.3	40.6	9.8	9.9	60690	62210	78	66	9596	1.0	5.7	60.6	28.9	3.7	143350
61108	ROCKFORD	26804	11901	14.8	27.9	45.3	8.8	3.3	56958	59428	74	59	8647	0.8	6.5	73.4	19.1	0.2	127319
61109	ROCKFORD	24688	11294	18.3	27.5	42.2	8.5	3.5	53626	55652	69	53	7404	10.8	15.3	58.4	15.0	0.5	122985
61111	LOVES PARK	26857	9810	14.7	23.0	48.9	9.7	3.6	61722	63252	80	67	6945	8.7	9.0	55.1	26.1	1.0	132150
61112	ROCKFORD	26725	109	5.5	20.2	50.5	22.9	0.9	75767	76180	90	87	69	2.9	2.9	44.9	44.9	4.3	174107
61114	ROCKFORD	38009	6438	10.7	17.9	40.0	18.0	13.5	75912	75929	90	88	4807	0.5	1.4	44.1	48.7	5.3	182058
61115	MACHESNEY PARK	25578	8598	12.1	23.2	54.2	8.1	2.4	64083	65188	82	72	6978	1.7	16.4	63.1	17.9	0.9	127852
61201	ROCK ISLAND	23875	15794	26.4	29.2	35.0	6.4	3.1	45617	47878	50	31	10251	12.9	28.9	46.5	10.8	0.8	100603
61230	ALBANY	26293	487	14.6	27.3	43.9	10.3	3.9	60233	61809	78	65	420	12.6	16.2	56.7	14.5	0.0	117473
61231	ALEDO	21428	2238	25.2	32.0	35.4	5.4	1.9	45648	47811	50	31	1675	8.7	29.3	43.8	15.6	2.7	106332
61232	ANDALUSIA	30342	340	10.0	25.9	42.9	17.1	4.1	67525	68698	85	78	295	4.4	13.9	54.9	23.7	3.1	131360
61234	ANNAWAN	24680	500	19.2	27.8	42.6	7.0	3.4	52937	56418	68	51	385	7.5	31.2	47.5	12.5	1.3	105871
61235	ATKINSON	22676	601	25.6	28.0	39.6	5.3	1.5	46798	49154	54	34	448	14.1	28.8	44.6	11.4	1.1	98205
61238	CAMBRIDGE	23958	1340	19.0	28.1	43.7	6.3	3.0	53155	57718	68	51	1058	10.7	24.4	51.2	12.0	1.7	107407
61240	COAL VALLEY	26296	2256	14.4	23.9	45.1	10.5	6.0	63775	66048	82	71	2042	16.7	10.6	40.0	29.1	3.5	134189
61241	COLONA	23911	2713	16.8	26.5	44.8	7.9	3.9	56355	59923	73	58	2267	13.1	23.0	45.7	16.8	1.5	110836
61242	CORDOVA	30441	519	11.4	22.0	50.9	7.7	8.1	69339	69442	86	80	425	4.9	16.0	43.3	28.5	7.3	145833
61243	DEER GROVE	21911	96	11.5	32.3	46.9	5.2	4.2	54943	55528	71	56	69	5.8	15.9	43.5	27.5	7.2	136250
61244	EAST MOLINE	22803	10013	23.9	30.6	35.3	7.3	2.9	47152	48890	54	36	6677	11.1	24.8	50.8	12.7	0.5	108798
61250	ERIE	25626	1090	13.9	26.2	45.6	10.1	4.2	58390	60602	76	62	868	6.0	18.0	57.9	16.4	1.7	125127
61251	FENTON	27397	143	11.9	25.2	44.8	10.5	7.7	62311	62559	80	68	118	0.8	12.7	67.8	17.8	0.8	126000
61252	FULTON	24823	2317	16.6	32.4	40.7	6.4	3.9	50730	52126	63	45	1821	7.0	22.1	50.0	17.9	2.9	116725
61254	GENESEO	25994	4344	15.1	25.4	45.0	10.2	4.2	60858	62493	79	66	3453	2.8	12.6	48.0	33.6	3.0	147944
61256	HAMPTON	32864	742	16.7	20.6	46.2	10.2	6.2	64461	65867	83	73	638	2.4	21.0	55.5	16.8	4.4	125000
61257	HILLSDALE	25517	544	13.4	25.4	50.9	5.5	4.8	60231	62438	78	65	432	13.7	17.4	40.0	25.9	3.0	124554
61259	ILLINOIS CITY	25964	469	12.8	21.7	49.0	12.2	4.3	65893	66265	84	75	391	8.2	9.5	40.9	40.7	0.8	152365
61260	JOY	21863	336	18.5	37.2	37.8	3.6	3.0	46937	48610	54	34	248	23.4	25.4	37.1	11.7	2.4	91667
61261	LYNDON	20514	370	21.1	33.0	40.3	5.4	0.3	47068	49062	54	35	314	18.5	26.1	48.1	7.3	0.0	95484
61262	LYNN CENTER	23965	426	11.5	22.1	53.8	10.3	2.3	64659	65319	83	74	368	5.7	15.8	51.1	25.5	1.9	134649
61263	MATHERVILLE	20265	295	25.1	24.4	42.0	6.8	1.7	50272	50576	62	44	224	11.6	37.5	44.6	5.8	0.4	91333
61264	MILAN	25799	4566	21.0	26.9	39.9	8.9	3.2	53401	59975	69	52	3459	19.2	18.2	40.2	20.5	1.9	108905
61265	MOLINE	26251	18941	21.1	29.0	38.4	7.4	4.1	49919	53128	61	43	12700	5.5	24.9	50.1	16.8	2.7	112804
61270	MORRISON	26895	3005	14.5	27.7	46.1	7.0	4.7	58852	60736	76	63	2417	3.6	20.9	52.8	20.9	1.8	121964
61272	NEW BOSTON	19656	698	25.4	33.8	35.8	4.2	0.9	44140	47041	46	27	551	35.6	22.3	24.5	9.4	8.2	80543
61273	ORION	27636	1302	11.3	21.1	54.3	9.1	4.1	66268	66765	84	76	1079	2.3	10.2	54.0	30.1	3.3	143944
	ILLINOIS	28587		18.2	22.2	39.3	12.1	8.2	60823	63631				6.3	10.0	30.9	40.6	12.3	185324
	UNITED STATES	27277		20.9	24.4	35.3	11.7	7.6	54719	56938				9.3	13.1	31.6	32.6	13.5	162279

ZIP CODE #	POST OFFICE NAME	FINANCIAL SERVICES: Auto Loan	Home Loan	Invest-ments	Retire-ment Plans	THE HOME: Home Improvements: Home Repair	Lawn & Garden	Furnishings: Comput-ers & Hard-ware-Personal	Major Appli-ances	TV, Radio, Sound Equip-ment	Furni-ture	ENTERTAINMENT: Dine out/ Carry out	Sports Equip-ment	Fees & Tickets	Toys & Games	Travel	Cable TV	PERSONAL: Apparel & Services	Auto Repairs	Health Insur-ance	Pets & Supplies
61006	ASHTON	99	94	90	95	90	106	95	98	97	88	96	78	91	97	93	100	65	98	106	119
61007	BAILEYVILLE	113	102	109	105	104	122	100	114	103	91	101	87	92	104	101	109	69	106	117	134
61008	BELVIDERE	108	103	98	103	102	107	102	105	103	102	103	81	100	105	101	104	71	103	106	123
61010	BYRON	101	115	103	115	112	106	108	105	104	107	105	84	115	107	111	103	75	105	102	123
61011	CALEDONIA	152	175	152	173	168	149	151	153	143	163	145	121	162	151	156	136	103	144	135	174
61012	CAPRON	109	106	93	105	104	107	99	104	101	102	101	77	97	104	97	103	69	100	104	123
61014	CHADWICK	102	74	109	74	77	108	80	98	83	66	82	80	61	82	80	90	54	91	103	120
61015	CHANA	116	128	113	132	125	128	115	121	114	115	114	94	121	117	121	115	80	116	120	142
61016	CHERRY VALLEY	111	135	120	135	130	123	116	119	112	120	114	93	129	115	125	110	81	114	113	138
61018	DAKOTA	100	85	95	88	87	107	86	99	89	76	88	77	76	90	86	95	59	92	103	117
61019	DAVIS	102	114	107	116	113	117	102	109	102	103	102	82	109	102	109	103	71	104	111	126
61020	DAVIS JUNCTION	105	118	102	122	115	116	106	110	104	106	104	86	113	107	112	104	73	106	109	129
61021	DIXON	89	86	81	87	84	94	86	89	88	82	88	68	84	89	85	92	60	88	96	106
61024	DURAND	106	114	94	117	108	115	107	107	107	105	107	85	111	109	109	108	74	106	113	129
61025	EAST DUBUQUE	96	88	88	90	87	103	87	96	91	81	89	74	82	92	87	96	61	92	102	113
61028	ELIZABETH	87	67	97	65	71	93	70	86	75	64	74	64	59	73	71	82	49	80	92	101
61030	FORRESTON	92	75	85	76	76	95	76	88	80	70	79	68	66	82	75	86	53	82	92	105
61031	FRANKLIN GROVE	93	91	80	93	87	99	90	92	92	85	91	72	88	93	89	95	62	91	100	111
61032	FREEPORT	82	78	75	79	77	85	81	82	83	77	83	62	78	83	79	87	57	82	89	97
61036	GALENA	89	90	102	89	93	102	85	95	90	85	89	67	87	86	91	95	61	92	104	110
61038	GARDEN PRAIRIE	114	116	109	119	116	123	108	117	109	104	108	90	108	111	111	112	75	110	118	137
61039	GERMAN VALLEY	104	96	94	100	98	112	94	106	97	86	95	80	88	99	94	102	65	98	109	123
61041	HANOVER	87	70	87	70	72	92	72	87	78	65	76	65	62	77	72	84	51	80	91	101
61042	HARMON	106	86	104	88	88	112	88	104	92	77	90	82	75	92	88	98	60	96	108	124
61044	KENT	99	68	109	68	72	105	76	94	79	62	78	78	56	77	76	86	51	88	100	116
61046	LANARK	102	86	108	88	90	109	87	103	90	78	88	78	76	89	89	96	59	95	105	120
61047	LEAF RIVER	99	99	92	102	98	108	93	102	94	88	94	78	91	97	95	98	65	96	104	119
61048	LENA	89	84	86	85	83	99	82	91	85	76	84	69	78	86	83	90	57	87	98	107
61049	LINDENWOOD	106	104	98	108	104	115	99	108	100	93	99	83	96	102	101	104	68	102	110	127
61050	MC CONNELL	100	68	109	68	72	105	76	94	79	62	78	78	56	78	76	86	51	88	100	116
61051	MILLEDGEVILLE	94	85	86	89	87	101	84	96	87	76	86	73	77	89	84	92	58	88	99	111
61052	MONROE CENTER	105	118	102	122	115	116	106	110	104	106	104	86	113	107	112	104	73	106	109	129
61053	MOUNT CARROLL	86	69	87	69	71	91	71	85	76	64	74	64	61	76	71	82	50	79	90	100
61054	MOUNT MORRIS	95	82	88	83	82	101	83	94	88	76	86	72	75	88	82	94	58	89	100	111
61060	ORANGEVILLE	91	77	87	79	79	97	78	90	81	69	79	70	68	81	78	86	53	84	94	107
61061	OREGON	96	91	92	92	92	102	91	98	94	86	93	73	87	94	91	98	64	95	103	114
61062	PEARL CITY	97	86	102	88	87	105	85	97	86	77	86	78	77	86	87	90	58	92	99	117
61063	PECATONICA	95	108	92	109	103	107	97	99	97	96	98	77	105	99	102	99	68	98	104	118
61064	POLO	88	86	76	88	82	94	85	87	87	79	86	69	83	88	84	89	59	86	94	105
61065	POPLAR GROVE	119	126	105	124	120	113	113	116	110	120	112	90	115	117	113	107	78	110	107	134
61067	RIDOTT	104	100	100	102	98	110	94	103	96	91	95	81	92	98	96	99	66	98	104	123
61068	ROCHELLE	86	87	81	85	86	87	86	87	87	85	87	65	86	87	85	88	60	87	89	101
61070	ROCK CITY	111	86	117	87	88	118	90	107	93	77	92	87	74	92	91	99	61	101	112	130
61071	ROCK FALLS	83	77	72	78	74	86	79	81	82	75	81	63	76	83	77	86	56	81	89	97
61072	ROCKTON	113	125	109	123	120	114	112	114	108	116	110	89	117	113	114	107	77	110	108	131
61073	ROSCOE	133	155	137	155	150	139	134	138	129	142	131	107	146	134	141	126	93	131	128	158
61074	SAVANNA	75	60	71	60	61	77	65	73	70	59	68	55	56	69	62	75	46	71	79	86
61075	SCALES MOUND	99	86	111	87	91	106	84	101	88	79	86	74	77	86	88	93	58	94	103	117
61078	SHANNON	109	95	119	97	100	117	94	111	97	87	96	83	85	96	98	103	65	103	112	129
61080	SOUTH BELOIT	96	91	80	90	86	91	91	90	92	90	91	71	87	95	86	92	63	90	91	107
61081	STERLING	87	85	79	87	83	92	88	87	90	83	89	67	86	90	86	93	62	88	95	104
61084	STILLMAN VALLEY	118	120	110	124	119	129	112	122	113	107	112	94	112	116	115	117	78	115	123	142
61085	STOCKTON	89	73	87	73	73	95	76	87	80	68	79	68	66	80	75	86	53	83	94	104
61087	WARREN	88	78	92	76	79	99	77	90	83	71	82	67	71	82	79	90	55	85	100	106
61088	WINNEBAGO	108	122	105	126	119	118	109	113	106	110	107	88	116	109	115	106	75	108	110	132
61089	WINSLOW	96	68	104	68	71	102	75	92	78	61	77	75	56	76	74	84	50	86	97	112
61101	ROCKFORD	71	66	56	68	62	70	71	67	74	68	74	53	70	75	67	77	51	71	75	82
61102	ROCKFORD	80	71	61	70	67	74	74	73	78	75	78	55	70	79	69	81	54	75	78	88
61103	ROCKFORD	80	75	66	77	72	78	83	77	85	78	84	61	80	84	78	87	59	82	85	94
61104	ROCKFORD	58	50	44	52	47	52	63	54	66	57	65	44	58	64	55	68	46	61	62	67
61107	ROCKFORD	108	111	108	113	111	114	112	110	114	111	114	83	115	112	113	116	80	113	117	130
61108	ROCKFORD	87	90	81	91	87	94	90	89	92	87	91	68	91	91	89	94	63	90	97	105
61109	ROCKFORD	92	80	72	83	77	84	89	84	91	86	90	67	83	93	82	92	63	88	88	102
61111	LOVES PARK	98	98	82	97	92	93	97	94	96	98	96	74	96	99	93	95	67	94	94	111
61112	ROCKFORD	103	115	111	117	114	107	109	106	105	111	107	83	116	106	113	103	76	106	104	125
61114	ROCKFORD	134	150	144	151	149	143	137	140	134	142	135	106	146	135	144	133	96	136	137	162
61115	MACHESNEY PARK	96	101	86	103	97	102	96	97	96	95	96	75	98	98	96	97	67	96	101	115
61201	ROCK ISLAND	77	74	69	75	73	81	78	77	81	75	80	58	77	80	76	85	56	79	86	92
61230	ALBANY	102	93	92	97	95	110	92	104	95	83	93	78	85	97	92	100	63	96	107	120
61231	ALEDO	85	66	87	65	68	91	70	84	75	62	74	63	59	74	69	82	49	78	91	99
61232	ANDALUSIA	112	110	104	114	110	122	105	115	106	98	105	88	102	108	107	110	72	108	117	134
61234	ANNAWAN	90	83	81	84	79	96	85	88	87	77	86	71	79	87	83	90	58	88	96	108
61235	ATKINSON	91	64	94	63	67	95	71	87	77	61	75	68	55	76	69	85	49	82	94	104
61238	CAMBRIDGE	87	84	82	84	81	96	83	88	85	76	85	68	80	85	83	89	58	86	97	105
61240	COAL VALLEY	97	111	102	111	108	107	98	102	97	101	98	77	106	99	104	97	69	99	101	119
61241	COLONA	95	90	84	90	87	98	87	92	90	85	89	71	84	91	85	93	61	90	96	110
61242	CORDOVA	118	111	108	116	113	127	108	120	110	99	109	91	102	113	109	116	75	112	123	140
61243	DEER GROVE	109	75	120	75	79	115	84	104	87	68	86	86	61	85	83	95	56	97	110	128
61244	EAST MOLINE	77	76	70	76	74	82	78	78	81	74	80	59	77	80	76	84	55	79	87	92
61250	ERIE	104	94	94	98	96	112	93	105	96	84	94	80	86	98	93	102	64	97	109	122
61251	FENTON	113	103	102	108	105	122	102	115	105	92	103	87	94	107	102	111	70	106	119	134
61252	FULTON	86	88	80	90	87	96	84	89	87	81	86	67	85	87	86	90	59	86	96	105
61254	GENESEO	94	100	99	100	100	106	91	99	93	89	92	75	94	93	96	96	64	95	103	115
61256	HAMPTON	97	114	104	113	112	118	99	106	103	99	103	77	111	103	109	107	72	103	116	123
61257	HILLSDALE	104	101	90	100	99	104	94	100	96	95	96	75	92	99	93	99	66	96	100	118
61259	ILLINOIS CITY	97	112	98	115	109	110	99	103	98	100	99	79	108	100	106	99	69	100	104	121
61260	JOY	90	72	90	73	74	95	75	88	77	64	76	70	62	77	74	83	51	82	92	105
61261	LYNDON	92	67	94	65	69	94	68	87	76	63	74	65	55	75	68	83	49	79	90	103
61262	LYNN CENTER	97	101	95	103	100	110	93	102	95	89	95	77	95	97	97	99	65	96	106	118
61263	MATHERVILLE	76	78	61	79	72	81	77	74	78	73	78	60	78	80	75	80	54	76	83	91
61264	MILAN	88	86	83	87	84	95	85	89	88	81	87	68	83	88	85	91	60	88	96	106
61265	MOLINE	85	85	80	85	84	92	85	87	89	82	88	65	86	88	85	92	61	87	96	102
61270	MORRISON	97	95	90	97	95	107	91	99	95	86	94	75	90	96	93	100	64	95	107	116
61272	NEW BOSTON	85	62	79	60	63	84	64	77	70	60	69	59	51	72	60	77	46	72	81	93
61273	ORION	97	104	97	105	103	109	96	102	98	95	98	76	101	99	101	102	68	99	108	119
	ILLINOIS	106	108	105	108	107	106	109	106	108	107	109	83	110	108	108	108	77	108	107	125
	UNITED STATES	100	100	100	100	100	100	100	100	100	100	100	100	100	100	100	100	100	100	100	100

ZIP CODE #	POST OFFICE NAME	COUNTY FIPS CODE	POPULATION 2000	POPULATION 2009	POPULATION 2014	2000-2009 ANNUAL RATE % Rate	2000-2009 ANNUAL RATE State Centile	HOUSEHOLDS 2000	HOUSEHOLDS 2009	HOUSEHOLDS 2014	HOUSEHOLDS % Annual Rate 2000-2009	HOUSEHOLDS 2009 Average HH Size	FAMILIES 2000	FAMILIES 2009	FAMILIES % Annual Rate 2000-2009
61274	OSCO	073	410	404	399	-0.2	38	151	152	151	0.1	2.66	123	122	-0.1
61275	PORT BYRON	161	4671	4881	5003	0.5	72	1802	1914	1969	0.7	2.54	1359	1418	0.5
61277	PROPHETSTOWN	195	3744	3570	3489	-0.5	18	1439	1390	1364	-0.4	2.46	1044	990	-0.6
61279	REYNOLDS	131	1018	1006	1002	-0.1	45	408	410	410	0.1	2.45	316	312	-0.1
61281	SHERRARD	131	2611	2551	2507	-0.3	32	956	949	938	-0.1	2.69	774	760	-0.2
61282	SILVIS	161	8365	8679	8814	0.4	69	3447	3632	3706	0.6	2.37	2245	2310	0.3
61283	TAMPICO	011	1674	1630	1603	-0.3	32	590	583	576	-0.1	2.79	445	432	-0.3
61284	TAYLOR RIDGE	161	2740	2719	2719	-0.1	45	1012	1021	1025	0.1	2.66	816	811	-0.1
61285	THOMSON	015	1729	1720	1705	-0.1	45	703	714	712	0.2	2.41	512	510	0.0
61301	LA SALLE	099	10577	10524	10485	-0.1	45	4476	4512	4509	0.1	2.30	2734	2674	-0.2
61310	AMBOY	103	4241	4213	4175	-0.1	45	1608	1624	1615	0.1	2.53	1141	1131	-0.1
61311	ANCONA	105	207	209	208	0.1	56	80	83	82	0.4	2.52	61	62	0.2
61312	ARLINGTON	011	1108	1075	1047	-0.3	32	430	424	415	-0.2	2.53	318	308	-0.3
61313	BLACKSTONE	105	214	202	195	-0.6	13	84	81	79	-0.4	2.41	68	65	-0.5
61314	BUDA	011	926	1039	1056	1.3	87	359	406	414	1.3	2.56	269	299	1.1
61318	COMPTON	103	700	696	690	-0.1	45	266	269	268	0.1	2.59	206	205	-0.1
61319	CORNELL	105	807	781	759	-0.4	25	308	304	298	-0.1	2.57	227	220	-0.3
61320	DALZELL	011	949	922	897	-0.3	32	369	365	357	-0.1	2.50	271	263	-0.3
61321	DANA	099	357	350	344	-0.2	38	129	129	127	0.0	2.71	94	92	-0.2
61325	GRAND RIDGE	099	987	1005	1003	0.2	61	367	383	384	0.5	2.62	283	290	0.3
61326	GRANVILLE	155	2978	3089	3104	0.4	69	1193	1248	1257	0.5	2.47	834	856	0.3
61327	HENNEPIN	155	1202	1250	1264	0.4	69	469	498	507	0.7	2.50	339	355	0.5
61329	LADD	011	1231	1187	1154	-0.4	25	527	517	505	-0.2	2.29	349	335	-0.4
61330	LA MOILLE	011	1617	1572	1539	-0.3	32	612	607	597	-0.1	2.59	470	459	-0.3
61333	LONG POINT	105	476	463	451	-0.3	32	175	172	169	-0.2	2.67	140	136	-0.3
61334	LOSTANT	099	721	716	710	-0.1	45	289	294	293	0.2	2.43	204	202	-0.1
61335	MC NABB	155	686	658	643	-0.4	25	272	266	261	-0.2	2.47	208	201	-0.4
61336	MAGNOLIA	155	525	503	491	-0.5	18	193	189	186	-0.2	2.66	149	144	-0.4
61337	MALDEN	011	703	674	652	-0.5	18	249	243	236	-0.3	2.77	199	191	-0.4
61341	MARSEILLES	099	7993	8442	8575	0.6	75	3052	3280	3345	0.8	2.55	2213	2335	0.6
61342	MENDOTA	099	9285	9497	9528	0.2	61	3483	3615	3641	0.4	2.56	2467	2506	0.2
61344	MINERAL	011	440	437	431	-0.1	45	176	178	177	0.1	2.46	129	128	-0.1
61345	NEPONSET	011	785	786	776	0.0	50	310	316	314	0.2	2.49	228	228	0.0
61346	NEW BEDFORD	011	156	159	158	0.2	61	64	66	66	0.3	2.32	47	48	0.2
61348	OGLESBY	099	4508	4537	4524	0.1	56	1946	2002	2007	0.3	2.26	1260	1263	0.0
61349	OHIO	011	1201	1153	1122	-0.4	25	463	454	445	-0.2	2.54	347	335	-0.4
61350	OTTAWA	099	24234	24703	25024	0.2	61	9738	10075	10232	0.4	2.41	6556	6639	0.1
61353	PAW PAW	103	1270	1256	1241	-0.1	45	493	495	492	0.0	2.54	346	341	-0.2
61354	PERU	099	10717	10882	10928	0.2	61	4483	4660	4702	0.4	2.28	2924	2958	0.1
61356	PRINCETON	011	13187	12723	12394	-0.4	25	5416	5306	5192	-0.2	2.35	3568	3420	-0.5
61358	RUTLAND	123	514	492	479	-0.5	18	207	203	198	-0.2	2.42	153	146	-0.5
61360	SENECA	099	3119	3286	3352	0.6	75	1132	1215	1248	0.8	2.70	878	925	0.6
61361	SHEFFIELD	011	2036	2046	2024	0.1	56	818	832	826	0.2	2.46	581	579	0.0
61362	SPRING VALLEY	011	5722	5602	5463	-0.2	38	2287	2258	2208	-0.1	2.41	1565	1512	-0.4
61364	STREATOR	099	21121	20338	19977	-0.4	25	8528	8353	8237	-0.2	2.41	5679	5432	-0.5
61367	SUBLETTE	103	865	854	843	-0.1	45	340	342	340	0.1	2.50	247	244	-0.1
61368	TISKILWA	011	1499	1384	1330	-0.9	4	581	549	531	-0.6	2.52	441	411	-0.8
61369	TOLUCA	123	1741	1706	1679	-0.2	38	731	727	718	-0.1	2.23	463	450	-0.3
61370	TONICA	099	1255	1270	1266	0.1	56	536	555	556	0.4	2.29	365	369	0.1
61373	UTICA	099	1848	1947	1976	0.6	75	725	775	787	0.7	2.43	506	529	0.5
61375	VARNA	123	1477	1469	1448	-0.1	45	599	607	601	0.1	2.42	478	477	0.0
61376	WALNUT	011	2108	2078	2040	-0.2	38	812	811	800	0.0	2.50	584	572	-0.2
61377	WENONA	123	1441	1450	1433	0.1	56	584	597	594	0.2	2.43	377	375	-0.1
61378	WEST BROOKLYN	103	545	568	568	0.4	69	208	219	221	0.6	2.59	155	160	0.3
61379	WYANET	011	1386	1481	1485	0.7	78	546	596	601	1.0	2.48	391	420	0.8
61401	GALESBURG	095	36922	34591	33263	-0.7	9	14604	13814	13280	-0.6	2.21	8962	8275	-0.9
61410	ABINGDON	095	4139	3864	3697	-0.7	9	1638	1558	1497	-0.5	2.44	1144	1064	-0.8
61411	ADAIR	109	461	421	402	-1.0	3	191	178	172	-0.8	2.37	144	133	-0.9
61412	ALEXIS	131	1559	1498	1460	-0.4	25	641	624	611	-0.3	2.40	469	448	-0.5
61413	ALPHA	073	1122	1089	1069	-0.3	32	445	437	430	-0.2	2.49	335	323	-0.4
61414	ALTONA	095	957	852	804	-1.2	2	360	323	305	-1.2	2.64	280	247	-1.3
61415	AVON	057	2027	1977	1930	-0.3	32	806	799	783	-0.1	2.43	604	588	-0.3
61417	BERWICK	187	311	305	297	-0.2	38	127	126	123	-0.1	2.42	99	97	-0.2
61418	BIGGSVILLE	071	586	622	625	0.6	75	246	266	269	0.8	2.34	176	187	0.7
61420	BLANDINSVILLE	109	1243	1120	1066	-1.1	2	520	472	450	-1.0	2.37	365	327	-1.2
61421	BRADFORD	175	1884	1836	1815	-0.3	32	728	721	716	-0.1	2.55	534	519	-0.3
61422	BUSHNELL	109	3633	3369	3228	-0.8	6	1487	1382	1327	-0.8	2.43	1012	925	-1.0
61423	CAMERON	187	717	705	693	-0.2	38	274	273	269	0.0	2.58	221	217	-0.2
61425	CARMAN	071	377	350	339	-0.8	6	165	155	150	-0.7	2.26	120	111	-0.8
61427	CUBA	057	2456	2415	2368	-0.2	38	970	967	953	0.0	2.45	709	694	-0.2
61428	DAHINDA	095	823	770	738	-0.7	9	366	350	337	-0.5	2.19	289	273	-0.6
61430	EAST GALESBURG	095	851	906	906	0.7	78	348	379	382	0.9	2.39	217	231	0.7
61431	ELLISVILLE	057	404	401	396	-0.1	45	169	170	169	0.1	2.36	130	128	-0.2
61432	FAIRVIEW	057	609	651	654	0.7	78	244	263	265	0.8	2.48	180	191	0.6
61433	FIATT	057	77	82	83	0.7	78	31	34	34	1.0	2.41	23	24	0.5
61434	GALVA	073	3692	3571	3497	-0.4	25	1538	1501	1475	-0.3	2.37	1021	974	-0.5
61435	GERLAW	187	160	152	147	-0.6	13	67	65	63	-0.3	2.34	54	51	-0.6
61436	GILSON	095	1065	996	952	-0.7	9	403	385	370	-0.5	2.58	312	293	-0.7
61437	GLADSTONE	071	1158	1078	1042	-0.8	6	488	461	448	-0.6	2.34	349	324	-0.8
61438	GOOD HOPE	109	732	711	689	-0.3	32	302	297	289	-0.2	2.39	220	212	-0.4
61440	INDUSTRY	109	884	823	790	-0.8	6	340	323	312	-0.6	2.55	264	248	-0.7
61441	IPAVA	057	1016	1001	986	-0.2	38	425	425	421	0.0	2.35	303	297	-0.2
61442	KEITHSBURG	131	857	846	836	-0.1	45	345	344	341	0.0	2.46	252	247	-0.2
61443	KEWANEE	073	14377	14027	13798	-0.3	32	5893	5803	5726	-0.2	2.38	3794	3644	-0.4
61447	KIRKWOOD	187	1014	948	916	-0.7	9	387	367	355	-0.6	2.58	298	278	-0.7
61448	KNOXVILLE	095	4074	3907	3767	-0.5	18	1545	1505	1456	-0.3	2.49	1148	1099	-0.5
61449	LA FAYETTE	175	520	510	505	-0.2	38	204	203	201	-0.1	2.51	152	149	-0.2
61450	LA HARPE	067	1835	1768	1714	-0.4	25	725	699	677	-0.4	2.47	510	482	-0.6
61451	LAURA	143	415	447	461	0.8	79	151	167	173	1.1	2.68	113	122	0.8
61452	LITTLETON	169	372	351	339	-0.6	13	140	135	131	-0.4	2.60	107	101	-0.6
61453	LITTLE YORK	187	493	501	499	0.2	61	195	200	199	0.3	2.51	147	148	0.1
61454	LOMAX	071	992	945	922	-0.5	18	397	383	375	-0.4	2.39	277	262	-0.6
61455	MACOMB	109	21670	21863	21507	0.1	56	7836	7893	7764	0.1	2.13	3883	3804	-0.2
61458	MAQUON	095	869	785	745	-1.1	2	373	344	328	-0.9	2.28	258	234	-1.0
61459	MARIETTA	057	403	421	421	0.5	72	156	165	166	0.6	2.55	116	121	0.5
	ILLINOIS					0.6					0.6	2.64			0.4
	UNITED STATES					1.0					1.1	2.59			0.9

ZIP CODE #	POST OFFICE NAME	RACE (%) White 2000	White 2009	Black 2000	Black 2009	Asian/Pacific 2000	Asian/Pacific 2009	% Hispanic Origin 2000	% Hispanic Origin 2009	2009 AGE DISTRIBUTION (%) 0-4	5-9	10-14	15-19	20-24	25-44	45-64	65-84	85+	18+	MEDIAN AGE 2009	% 2009 Males	% 2009 Females
61274	OSCO	98.5	98.3	0.0	0.0	0.2	0.2	0.7	0.7	5.2	6.2	6.4	5.9	4.2	23.0	33.4	14.1	1.5	78.5	44.1	52.7	47.3
61275	PORT BYRON	97.5	96.3	0.3	0.4	0.2	0.3	2.0	3.2	5.4	6.1	6.4	6.0	4.8	23.7	33.5	12.6	1.5	78.2	43.2	51.4	48.6
61277	PROPHETSTOWN	98.1	97.5	0.5	0.6	0.1	0.1	1.4	2.2	5.8	6.2	6.2	5.7	4.8	22.9	28.9	15.8	3.6	78.1	43.6	49.7	50.3
61279	REYNOLDS	98.8	98.5	0.2	0.3	0.2	0.2	1.2	1.7	5.8	6.2	6.7	6.6	4.4	23.8	30.8	13.9	2.0	77.3	42.5	50.1	49.9
61281	SHERRARD	98.4	98.3	0.3	0.4	0.2	0.2	1.5	1.6	4.9	6.0	7.1	7.9	5.0	24.8	33.2	9.9	1.3	77.2	41.3	50.2	49.8
61282	SILVIS	86.4	82.1	3.5	4.2	0.8	1.1	13.7	18.8	7.0	6.4	6.1	6.3	6.9	24.7	26.6	13.3	2.7	76.5	38.6	48.3	51.7
61283	TAMPICO	98.3	97.6	0.4	0.5	0.2	0.3	1.9	2.9	8.0	7.9	7.7	7.4	5.8	23.8	25.9	11.7	1.7	71.9	36.3	50.3	49.7
61284	TAYLOR RIDGE	98.0	97.2	0.6	0.8	0.2	0.3	1.3	2.1	4.9	5.5	6.2	6.6	4.6	22.3	34.0	14.5	1.4	79.2	44.9	50.2	49.8
61285	THOMSON	97.1	96.3	0.8	1.0	0.5	0.7	1.2	1.7	5.8	6.3	6.3	6.2	4.8	22.8	29.5	16.3	1.9	77.7	43.1	50.8	49.2
61301	LA SALLE	94.0	91.7	1.2	1.5	0.6	0.8	7.8	11.1	6.8	6.5	6.1	5.8	6.3	26.4	26.2	12.9	2.9	77.2	38.6	49.9	50.1
61310	AMBOY	98.1	97.3	0.6	0.8	0.1	0.1	2.1	3.2	6.5	6.3	6.4	7.3	5.9	23.8	27.4	13.9	2.5	76.3	40.1	49.5	50.5
61311	ANCONA	98.6	98.1	0.0	0.0	0.0	0.0	1.9	2.9	5.3	6.2	5.7	5.7	4.3	23.4	34.0	13.9	1.4	78.9	44.4	50.7	49.3
61312	ARLINGTON	97.4	96.3	0.2	0.2	0.4	0.5	2.3	3.6	6.6	7.0	7.2	6.4	4.4	23.5	30.7	11.9	2.3	75.0	41.6	49.5	50.5
61313	BLACKSTONE	94.9	94.1	3.3	4.0	0.0	0.0	1.9	3.0	5.4	5.4	6.4	7.4	5.9	24.8	27.7	15.3	1.5	78.7	41.6	48.5	51.5
61314	BUDA	98.9	98.4	0.0	0.0	0.5	0.8	1.0	1.5	6.7	6.8	6.7	7.7	6.5	24.8	25.8	13.0	1.8	75.2	37.4	47.4	52.6
61318	COMPTON	98.6	97.7	0.0	0.0	0.6	0.9	1.6	2.3	7.3	7.5	8.0	7.6	5.0	22.7	28.2	12.4	1.3	72.4	39.7	49.6	50.4
61319	CORNELL	98.8	98.1	0.4	0.5	0.1	0.1	1.2	2.0	6.0	6.5	7.3	7.3	4.5	23.7	31.4	11.7	1.7	75.4	40.8	49.9	50.1
61320	DALZELL	97.9	97.1	0.2	0.3	0.2	0.2	3.2	5.1	6.0	6.2	6.6	6.5	4.8	24.8	28.5	13.8	2.8	76.6	41.9	48.2	51.8
61321	DANA	99.4	99.4	0.0	0.0	0.0	0.0	1.4	1.7	6.9	6.9	6.3	6.3	6.3	26.0	27.4	12.3	1.7	75.7	39.1	50.6	49.4
61325	GRAND RIDGE	99.3	99.1	0.2	0.2	0.1	0.1	2.0	3.1	7.8	8.0	7.8	6.5	4.9	22.0	28.2	13.0	2.0	72.4	39.8	49.3	50.7
61326	GRANVILLE	98.0	97.3	0.2	0.3	0.2	0.3	3.8	5.3	6.5	6.5	6.8	7.1	5.7	23.6	28.6	12.7	2.5	75.8	40.7	47.7	52.3
61327	HENNEPIN	97.4	96.9	0.9	1.1	0.4	0.6	2.7	3.8	5.6	6.2	6.3	5.7	4.8	23.5	31.4	14.3	2.2	78.5	43.4	51.8	48.2
61329	LADD	97.6	96.4	0.2	0.2	0.0	0.0	3.2	5.3	6.7	6.7	6.7	5.8	4.5	27.3	25.3	13.6	3.5	76.2	40.2	48.9	51.1
61330	LA MOILLE	98.2	97.4	0.2	0.2	0.0	0.0	2.9	4.7	6.9	7.2	7.4	6.8	4.3	24.9	28.3	12.6	1.7	74.3	39.8	51.0	49.0
61333	LONG POINT	97.7	97.0	0.6	0.9	0.6	0.9	0.4	0.6	5.0	5.6	6.0	7.1	5.4	22.0	33.0	13.8	1.9	78.8	44.2	49.2	50.8
61334	LOSTANT	98.5	97.9	0.3	0.4	0.1	0.1	1.0	1.4	6.1	6.6	6.8	6.3	4.5	25.6	29.5	12.0	2.7	76.5	40.6	48.9	51.1
61335	MC NABB	97.5	96.8	1.3	1.5	0.1	0.3	0.6	0.8	6.1	6.7	6.8	6.7	5.2	24.3	29.5	12.9	1.8	76.1	40.8	50.6	49.4
61336	MAGNOLIA	97.1	96.6	1.3	1.6	0.2	0.4	0.4	0.6	6.2	6.8	7.0	6.8	5.2	24.1	29.2	13.3	1.6	75.7	40.5	50.9	49.1
61337	MALDEN	97.4	96.3	0.1	0.1	0.4	0.6	2.0	3.3	6.8	7.3	7.6	6.4	4.6	23.6	29.2	12.9	1.6	74.3	40.6	52.5	47.5
61341	MARSEILLES	98.0	97.3	0.2	0.2	0.2	0.3	1.6	2.4	6.4	6.7	6.9	6.6	5.1	24.9	29.2	12.2	1.9	75.8	39.9	49.3	50.7
61342	MENDOTA	90.5	87.4	0.3	0.4	0.7	1.0	15.1	20.6	7.0	6.6	6.7	7.3	5.9	23.4	26.1	13.4	3.5	75.3	39.3	48.6	51.4
61344	MINERAL	98.0	97.0	0.5	0.7	0.2	0.2	1.1	2.1	6.2	6.9	6.9	5.7	3.9	24.3	27.7	16.7	1.8	76.2	42.3	51.7	48.3
61345	NEPONSET	98.3	97.7	0.4	0.4	0.9	1.3	1.8	3.1	3.8	4.1	4.6	6.1	5.2	24.6	32.6	16.5	2.5	84.1	46.0	49.7	50.3
61346	NEW BEDFORD	98.7	98.1	0.6	0.6	0.0	0.0	1.3	2.5	6.9	7.5	7.5	6.9	5.0	23.3	24.5	14.5	3.8	73.6	40.2	50.9	49.1
61348	OGLESBY	98.2	97.6	0.4	0.5	0.3	0.4	2.7	3.9	5.7	5.8	6.1	6.3	5.1	24.6	28.0	15.2	3.2	78.6	42.3	48.6	51.4
61349	OHIO	98.8	98.4	0.3	0.4	0.1	0.1	1.7	2.7	6.2	6.6	6.9	6.6	5.0	23.8	28.4	14.6	2.0	76.3	41.8	49.6	50.4
61350	OTTAWA	95.9	94.6	1.1	1.4	0.8	1.1	4.5	6.5	6.3	6.4	6.2	6.3	6.0	24.8	27.7	13.5	2.9	77.2	40.5	48.4	51.6
61353	PAW PAW	98.7	98.3	0.0	0.0	0.6	0.7	1.1	1.7	6.4	7.0	7.3	7.6	5.1	21.3	30.7	12.8	1.7	74.6	41.5	50.6	49.4
61354	PERU	96.5	95.1	0.3	0.4	1.1	1.6	3.9	5.8	5.6	5.4	5.4	5.7	6.1	24.2	27.7	15.6	4.2	80.2	43.1	47.5	52.5
61356	PRINCETON	95.4	94.0	0.3	0.3	0.9	1.2	8.2	10.9	5.7	5.5	5.6	6.1	5.7	23.4	28.9	15.2	3.9	79.2	43.4	48.6	51.4
61358	RUTLAND	98.6	98.6	0.2	0.2	0.2	0.2	1.4	2.0	6.5	6.5	6.3	6.3	5.7	26.4	28.5	12.2	1.6	76.4	40.0	51.8	48.2
61360	SENECA	98.5	97.8	0.1	0.2	0.1	0.1	1.7	2.6	6.4	6.9	7.8	7.6	5.4	24.6	28.8	11.3	1.3	73.7	39.0	49.7	50.3
61361	SHEFFIELD	98.1	97.3	0.3	0.4	0.3	0.5	1.4	2.3	6.0	6.2	6.5	7.1	5.1	23.7	28.6	14.3	2.6	76.7	41.4	48.6	51.4
61362	SPRING VALLEY	95.9	94.3	0.7	0.8	0.5	0.7	6.5	10.2	6.1	5.9	5.8	6.2	5.8	25.7	26.9	13.9	3.8	78.5	40.7	48.4	51.6
61364	STREATOR	95.5	94.0	1.4	1.8	0.4	0.5	5.3	7.6	6.3	6.3	6.4	6.6	5.6	23.8	26.6	15.2	3.1	76.7	41.0	48.7	51.3
61367	SUBLETTE	98.2	97.5	0.5	0.6	0.0	0.0	3.0	4.3	5.7	6.0	6.3	7.0	4.8	24.4	29.3	14.5	2.0	77.8	42.0	51.8	48.2
61368	TISKILWA	97.8	97.0	0.2	0.2	0.5	0.8	0.9	1.5	6.1	6.8	6.9	6.7	4.2	22.9	29.3	14.7	2.4	76.1	42.1	48.8	51.2
61369	TOLUCA	97.9	97.1	0.1	0.1	0.3	0.5	1.4	2.1	5.3	5.5	5.8	6.3	4.4	22.7	27.4	17.6	5.0	79.5	45.0	47.2	52.8
61370	TONICA	98.5	98.0	0.2	0.2	0.4	0.6	2.9	4.3	5.9	6.1	6.6	6.5	4.2	23.0	28.8	15.6	3.3	77.6	43.3	48.7	51.3
61373	UTICA	97.7	97.0	0.2	0.3	0.4	0.6	2.3	3.4	6.4	6.8	7.0	6.5	4.2	23.1	29.6	12.9	3.5	75.8	42.5	47.6	52.4
61375	VARNA	98.7	98.3	0.1	0.1	0.1	0.2	1.2	1.8	5.2	5.7	6.3	6.3	3.6	23.1	32.1	16.1	1.7	78.8	44.9	49.6	50.4
61376	WALNUT	98.8	98.5	0.3	0.3	0.1	0.1	1.0	1.7	6.5	6.6	6.8	6.8	5.5	22.0	26.3	15.4	3.8	75.8	41.7	49.4	50.6
61377	WENONA	98.0	97.4	0.3	0.4	0.1	0.2	1.2	1.6	6.3	6.2	6.3	6.7	5.7	22.8	27.2	15.9	2.9	77.1	41.6	48.2	51.8
61378	WEST BROOKLYN	97.2	96.1	0.2	0.2	0.6	0.9	2.8	3.9	6.2	6.7	7.4	7.9	4.8	24.1	29.4	12.0	1.6	74.8	40.5	48.2	51.8
61379	WYANET	99.0	98.6	0.0	0.0	0.4	0.5	0.7	1.2	6.4	6.2	6.4	7.4	6.3	26.7	26.6	12.4	1.7	76.6	38.0	50.0	50.0
61401	GALESBURG	85.4	82.3	9.4	10.7	1.0	1.4	4.6	6.4	5.5	5.3	5.5	6.9	8.2	25.1	25.7	14.3	3.6	80.1	39.7	50.4	49.6
61410	ABINGDON	98.2	97.7	0.5	0.6	0.1	0.2	1.0	1.5	6.2	6.7	6.3	6.5	5.6	25.0	27.2	13.8	2.7	76.6	40.1	48.6	51.4
61411	ADAIR	98.9	98.6	0.4	0.5	0.2	0.5	0.9	1.2	5.0	5.2	5.7	5.5	3.8	22.3	32.5	17.6	2.4	80.8	46.3	48.9	51.1
61412	ALEXIS	99.2	99.2	0.1	0.1	0.1	0.1	1.3	1.5	5.1	5.5	5.7	5.2	5.1	22.9	32.6	15.6	2.3	80.6	45.3	50.9	49.1
61413	ALPHA	98.2	97.6	0.2	0.2	0.2	0.3	1.2	1.8	5.2	5.8	6.3	7.4	4.6	23.9	31.1	13.0	2.6	77.9	42.8	51.1	48.9
61414	ALTONA	99.3	99.1	0.0	0.0	0.1	0.1	0.7	1.1	6.5	6.9	7.5	6.8	4.2	22.3	31.1	13.0	1.6	74.6	41.7	49.5	50.5
61415	AVON	99.0	98.5	0.0	0.1	0.1	0.3	0.4	0.7	5.2	5.5	5.8	5.6	4.2	22.9	29.7	17.6	3.6	80.3	45.6	49.9	50.1
61417	BERWICK	99.4	99.3	0.0	0.0	0.3	0.3	0.6	0.7	5.9	6.6	6.9	6.2	3.9	24.3	29.5	15.1	1.6	76.7	42.4	48.9	51.1
61418	BIGGSVILLE	98.5	97.9	0.7	0.8	0.2	0.3	1.0	1.4	5.3	5.6	5.6	4.8	4.0	25.6	31.2	15.4	2.4	80.7	44.2	50.6	49.4
61420	BLANDINSVILLE	99.0	98.7	0.0	0.0	0.1	0.1	0.6	0.8	5.2	5.6	6.0	6.3	4.7	23.5	30.7	15.1	2.9	79.3	44.0	49.1	50.9
61421	BRADFORD	98.6	98.5	0.2	0.2	0.3	0.3	0.8	0.9	6.7	7.2	7.7	6.7	3.8	23.3	28.8	13.6	2.2	74.1	41.1	50.0	50.0
61422	BUSHNELL	98.8	98.5	0.1	0.1	0.1	0.2	0.6	0.9	6.3	6.4	6.5	7.0	5.5	26.1	26.7	13.1	2.5	76.4	38.7	48.3	51.7
61423	CAMERON	99.2	99.0	0.0	0.0	0.6	0.7	0.6	0.7	4.0	4.4	5.2	6.7	5.4	23.3	32.9	16.6	1.6	82.3	45.7	51.8	48.2
61425	CARMAN	98.7	98.3	0.0	0.0	0.0	0.0	1.3	1.4	4.3	4.9	5.1	4.3	3.7	20.9	36.0	19.1	1.7	82.6	48.8	49.4	50.6
61427	CUBA	98.5	97.8	0.2	0.3	0.2	0.5	0.5	0.9	5.8	5.8	6.0	5.9	5.1	23.6	29.1	15.0	3.7	78.6	43.3	48.6	51.4
61428	DAHINDA	98.4	97.9	0.6	0.6	0.4	0.5	1.3	1.9	3.8	4.3	4.5	3.9	3.2	17.8	37.9	23.0	1.6	84.9	53.3	53.5	46.5
61430	EAST GALESBURG	97.5	96.6	0.6	0.7	0.2	0.3	1.6	2.5	4.9	4.7	5.3	5.1	5.4	24.0	31.6	16.0	3.1	82.1	45.5	48.7	51.3
61431	ELLISVILLE	99.5	99.0	0.0	0.0	0.0	0.0	0.5	0.5	4.7	5.5	5.7	6.0	3.5	22.7	32.2	17.2	2.5	80.0	46.0	52.9	47.1
61432	FAIRVIEW	99.2	98.9	0.2	0.2	0.2	0.3	0.2	0.2	4.8	5.4	5.8	6.8	4.5	24.6	32.0	13.8	2.5	79.7	43.3	52.7	47.3
61433	FIATT	100.0	100.0	0.0	0.0	0.0	0.0	0.0	0.0	4.9	6.1	6.1	7.3	4.9	24.4	30.5	13.4	2.4	78.0	41.3	50.0	50.0
61434	GALVA	98.2	97.7	0.5	0.5	0.1	0.2	1.8	2.6	5.9	6.0	6.2	6.6	5.3	23.2	28.7	14.9	3.1	77.7	42.6	48.4	51.6
61435	GERLAW	98.8	98.7	0.0	0.0	0.0	0.0	1.3	1.3	4.6	5.3	5.3	6.6	5.3	23.0	31.6	16.4	2.0	80.9	45.0	50.0	50.0
61436	GILSON	98.9	98.4	0.0	0.1	0.1	0.1	0.9	1.4	4.9	5.5	5.9	6.0	3.8	22.8	32.6	16.7	1.7	79.8	45.6	51.6	48.4
61437	GLADSTONE	98.4	98.0	0.2	0.2	0.2	0.3	0.8	1.1	4.4	4.9	5.3	5.6	4.6	22.5	34.9	16.3	1.5	82.0	46.7	50.3	49.7
61438	GOOD HOPE	99.3	99.2	0.0	0.0	0.3	0.4	0.3	0.3	6.3	6.8	7.3	5.9	3.4	23.8	29.7	15.2	1.7	75.8	42.4	51.6	48.4
61440	INDUSTRY	98.2	97.7	0.1	0.1	0.8	1.1	0.8	1.1	6.0	6.4	6.7	6.1	4.1	22.8	31.3	14.0	2.6	77.2	43.3	48.6	51.4
61441	IPAVA	98.8	98.2	0.0	0.0	0.1	0.3	0.9	1.2	5.6	6.0	6.5	6.1	4.2	23.6	30.2	14.7	3.2	78.0	43.5	50.7	49.3
61442	KEITHSBURG	98.1	98.1	0.4	0.4	0.0	0.0	0.4	0.4	6.6	6.7	7.1	7.9	5.1	24.9	25.3	14.2	2.1	74.8	39.3	50.7	49.3
61443	KEWANEE	90.9	88.2	3.3	3.9	0.4	0.5	5.8	8.2	6.9	6.7	6.3	6.3	5.8	23.8	25.5	14.9	3.8	76.3	40.2	47.9	52.1
61447	KIRKWOOD	98.1	97.3	0.1	0.2	0.2	0.3	1.6	2.3	6.8	7.0	6.8	5.1	4.7	23.1	31.1	13.8	1.7	76.6	42.6	48.2	51.8
61448	KNOXVILLE	98.3	97.7	0.4	0.5	0.1	0.1	0.9	1.3	5.8	6.0	6.1	5.9	5.2	21.8	28.9	15.8	4.6	78.4	44.3	47.7	52.3
61449	LA FAYETTE	98.7	98.6	0.0	0.0	0.2	0.2	1.0	1.0	5.5	5.9	6.1	6.7	4.7	24.3	31.8	12.9	2.2	78.2	42.5	50.6	49.4
61450	LA HARPE	99.3	99.1	0.0	0.0	0.0	0.0	0.1	0.2	5.3	5.7	6.2	7.2	4.9	21.9	28.6	16.0	4.4	78.1	44.1	48.0	52.0
61451	LAURA	97.1	95.5	0.0	0.0	0.0	0.2	2.7	4.0	6.7	7.2	7.2	6.7	4.3	24.6	28.2	13.2	2.0	74.9	40.2	49.9	50.1
61452	LITTLETON	98.4	97.7	0.8	1.1	0.0	0.0	0.5	0.9	6.0	6.6	6.8	6.0	3.7	23.1	31.9	14.0	2.0	76.9	43.6	51.0	49.0
61453	LITTLE YORK	99.0	98.4	0.0	0.0	0.2	0.4	0.8	1.4	5.4	6.0	6.6	7.8	4.6	23.8	31.5	12.0	1.8	77.4	41.2	50.3	49.7
61454	LOMAX	98.9	98.5	0.1	0.1	0.2	0.3	0.9	1.4	6.3	6.2	6.6	6.6	4.8	22.8	27.7	14.7	4.3	76.5	42.4	47.4	52.6
61455	MACOMB	89.8	85.7	5.2	7.3	3.0	4.1	1.9	3.4	3.8	3.8	3.9	12.1	23.9	20.3	18.9	10.5	2.9	85.4	26.9	49.8	50.2
61458	MAQUON	99.1	98.5	0.0	0.0	0.3	0.5	1.4	2.2	6.8	7.0	6.8	5.4	4.5	23.7	28.9	14.4	2.7	76.1	42.1	47.6	52.4
61459	MARIETTA	98.8	98.3	0.0	0.0	0.0	0.0	1.0	1.2	5.2	5.5	6.2	6.7	4.0	25.9	29.7	15.4	1.4	78.9	42.8	51.1	48.9
	ILLINOIS	73.5	70.6	15.1	15.3	3.4	4.4	12.3	15.7	7.1	6.9	6.8	7.1	6.9	27.5	25.4	10.3	1.9	75.0	36.1	49.1	50.9
	UNITED STATES	75.1	72.0	12.3	12.7	3.8	4.6	12.5	15.7	6.8	6.7	6.6	7.1	6.9	27.0	26.0	10.9	1.9	75.7	36.9	49.2	50.8

INCOME

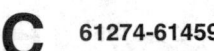

#	POST OFFICE NAME	2009 Per Capita Income	2009 HH Income Base	2009 Household Income Distribution (%): Less than $25,000	$25,000 to $49,999	$50,000 to $99,999	$100,000 to $149,999	$150,000 or More	Median Household Income: 2009	2014	2009 National Centile	2009 State Centile	2009 Home Value Base	2009 Home Value Distribution (%): Less than $50,000	$50,000 to $89,999	$90,000 to $174,999	$175,000 to $399,999	$400,000 or More	2009 Median Home Value
61274	OSCO	23716	152	23.0	23.0	47.4	3.3	3.3	54575	60133	71	55	105	1.9	20.0	34.3	26.7	17.1	151786
61275	PORT BYRON	30754	1914	14.2	22.4	42.8	11.2	9.4	65819	66776	84	75	1616	8.5	11.3	43.2	31.9	5.0	143293
61277	PROPHETSTOWN	24170	1390	17.5	34.0	36.3	8.6	3.6	48951	50329	59	40	1060	6.6	22.0	52.5	16.6	2.4	114335
61279	REYNOLDS	25942	410	19.5	22.4	45.6	9.3	3.2	58211	60359	75	61	329	5.5	21.6	44.4	23.4	5.2	130163
61281	SHERRARD	28409	949	7.8	16.3	60.6	11.8	3.5	71631	73077	88	82	835	6.7	17.7	43.7	30.4	1.4	138796
61282	SILVIS	21759	3632	23.3	35.4	33.1	6.1	2.2	45545	47161	50	30	2272	8.2	26.5	58.0	7.1	0.2	105672
61283	TAMPICO	20080	583	19.4	30.5	41.9	5.8	2.4	50055	51920	61	44	433	6.0	29.8	49.2	10.6	4.4	106057
61284	TAYLOR RIDGE	28553	1021	12.5	21.3	43.5	19.0	3.7	74728	73694	89	85	888	4.6	13.6	43.8	34.5	3.5	146212
61285	THOMSON	24224	714	17.4	34.2	38.8	6.6	3.1	48362	49380	57	39	548	13.3	24.1	46.7	11.3	4.6	109593
61301	LA SALLE	23820	4512	27.9	27.1	36.5	5.8	2.7	45244	47817	49	30	3014	7.1	22.2	51.0	17.5	2.2	114018
61310	AMBOY	22756	1624	19.3	33.7	38.4	5.7	2.9	48390	49456	58	39	1226	15.6	11.0	54.6	14.4	4.3	120940
61311	ANCONA	27132	83	10.8	22.9	47.0	16.9	2.4	63552	64046	82	71	71	8.5	15.5	54.9	19.7	1.4	117763
61312	ARLINGTON	23809	424	14.6	29.0	47.6	6.6	2.1	54658	56434	71	55	344	6.1	29.9	42.7	17.2	4.1	111818
61313	BLACKSTONE	28785	81	12.3	19.8	59.3	6.2	2.5	67652	66371	85	78	65	7.7	20.0	52.3	13.8	6.2	122115
61314	BUDA	21605	406	20.7	32.8	38.4	6.9	1.2	47938	49307	56	38	327	20.8	29.7	41.0	4.9	3.7	89400
61318	COMPTON	23627	269	17.8	22.7	50.2	8.2	1.1	62048	63637	80	68	213	8.9	10.3	41.3	31.0	8.5	149583
61319	CORNELL	24147	304	18.1	21.4	50.7	6.9	3.0	60363	61845	78	65	236	21.6	26.7	41.5	7.2	3.0	93077
61320	DALZELL	26329	365	13.2	26.0	49.6	8.5	2.7	61509	62402	79	67	301	4.7	19.6	52.5	21.9	1.3	129953
61321	DANA	18304	129	31.0	32.6	27.9	7.0	1.6	40746	43305	35	18	103	29.1	26.2	34.0	8.7	1.9	83889
61325	GRAND RIDGE	24893	383	16.2	28.2	43.1	7.8	4.7	56564	60176	73	58	308	8.1	14.3	43.2	27.6	6.8	137179
61326	GRANVILLE	23085	1248	18.8	28.4	43.6	7.9	1.4	52237	53554	66	49	1022	11.6	18.9	50.8	18.1	0.6	119833
61327	HENNEPIN	27078	498	14.3	27.5	42.8	10.0	5.4	60448	61335	78	65	403	5.0	11.4	44.2	37.2	2.2	153750
61329	LADD	27967	517	16.4	28.4	44.3	8.1	2.7	54326	56580	70	54	404	3.0	25.2	58.7	12.6	0.5	113352
61330	LA MOILLE	23437	607	17.5	33.3	39.5	6.8	3.0	49464	52282	60	42	447	3.8	23.3	46.3	23.9	2.7	125933
61333	LONG POINT	24484	172	16.9	23.8	48.3	7.0	4.1	57660	60709	75	60	143	17.5	21.0	38.5	17.5	5.6	122115
61334	LOSTANT	25514	294	14.3	30.6	43.5	9.5	2.0	55102	57395	71	56	243	10.7	19.8	53.9	12.3	3.3	117733
61335	MC NABB	27031	266	12.4	24.1	51.5	9.8	2.3	64080	63651	82	72	214	13.1	19.2	44.9	22.4	0.5	129605
61336	MAGNOLIA	25415	189	12.2	24.3	50.8	10.6	2.1	64170	64148	82	73	152	10.5	17.8	46.1	25.0	0.7	135345
61337	MALDEN	23303	243	15.2	20.6	53.9	8.6	1.6	62312	63603	80	69	196	8.7	24.0	46.9	17.9	2.6	116912
61341	MARSEILLES	24639	3280	18.3	25.7	43.8	9.5	2.8	57681	60868	75	60	2553	7.8	12.5	47.5	28.9	3.4	138725
61342	MENDOTA	23853	3615	18.3	27.1	42.7	8.1	3.8	53795	55742	69	53	2697	5.2	10.3	58.3	24.2	2.0	137312
61344	MINERAL	26364	178	14.0	34.8	38.8	9.0	3.4	51771	54645	65	48	133	15.8	25.6	34.6	17.3	6.8	106250
61345	NEPONSET	24110	316	19.9	30.4	38.0	10.1	1.6	49722	51997	60	43	257	21.4	30.4	36.2	9.7	2.3	87955
61346	NEW BEDFORD	27984	66	21.2	25.8	40.9	6.1	6.1	53604	53604	69	53	50	16.0	20.0	50.0	10.0	4.0	106250
61348	OGLESBY	24670	2002	27.2	26.0	36.8	7.4	2.6	47102	49329	54	35	1568	7.7	21.4	51.3	17.5	2.0	116418
61349	OHIO	23786	454	13.7	30.8	44.3	8.4	2.9	53777	55482	69	53	346	10.1	24.9	50.6	12.1	2.3	108427
61350	OTTAWA	24867	10075	23.7	27.0	36.6	8.9	3.8	49396	51319	60	41	7130	3.9	12.4	53.0	28.2	2.6	138614
61353	PAW PAW	23302	495	17.8	31.3	43.2	5.9	1.8	51414	55919	65	47	401	2.5	9.7	54.1	30.7	3.0	146701
61354	PERU	26247	4660	21.8	28.9	38.6	6.7	4.0	49439	51013	60	42	3469	3.5	16.6	57.7	20.1	2.1	129720
61356	PRINCETON	25284	5306	23.5	25.1	41.3	6.9	3.2	51356	54155	65	47	3911	9.8	17.4	48.6	21.9	2.3	125879
61358	RUTLAND	20983	203	27.6	33.0	31.0	6.4	2.0	43252	45618	43	25	163	27.6	25.2	33.1	11.0	3.1	86538
61360	SENECA	24745	1215	15.2	21.1	51.3	9.2	3.2	64346	65806	83	73	995	8.2	8.2	42.7	36.7	4.1	159750
61361	SHEFFIELD	22689	832	17.9	36.5	36.5	8.1	1.0	47290	48692	55	36	640	13.8	34.4	39.7	7.8	4.4	92553
61362	SPRING VALLEY	24993	2258	23.0	26.4	37.5	9.3	3.8	50850	54683	63	46	1671	5.4	23.7	52.2	18.4	0.3	114739
61364	STREATOR	21884	8353	26.6	28.4	37.0	6.3	1.7	46110	48141	52	32	6287	17.6	32.2	40.1	9.5	0.6	90402
61367	SUBLETTE	28149	342	14.6	26.9	39.8	14.0	4.7	61777	62546	80	67	262	9.9	9.9	49.2	29.8	1.1	138776
61368	TISKILWA	24694	549	17.1	30.2	43.7	5.3	3.6	53079	56969	68	51	438	6.6	19.6	44.1	24.7	5.0	126531
61369	TOLUCA	23245	727	22.8	33.4	37.8	4.3	1.7	46401	48333	53	33	565	19.3	32.2	34.7	12.9	0.9	88191
61370	TONICA	27275	555	17.8	27.4	44.5	7.6	2.7	55080	57831	71	56	439	7.3	18.0	56.3	14.8	3.6	122270
61373	UTICA	27694	775	15.1	26.6	48.3	6.3	3.7	59560	62231	77	63	624	13.5	13.8	35.6	32.4	4.8	145139
61375	VARNA	24757	607	13.2	32.5	45.1	5.8	3.5	54108	54878	70	54	507	7.7	16.6	47.3	26.2	2.2	130132
61376	WALNUT	24597	811	22.4	28.1	37.6	7.5	4.3	49537	51702	60	42	627	8.3	26.6	52.3	10.0	2.7	106031
61377	WENONA	21593	597	29.5	27.0	37.0	4.5	2.0	45371	47919	49	30	471	15.1	31.4	47.3	5.5	0.6	93113
61378	WEST BROOKLYN	26116	219	14.6	20.1	52.5	10.0	2.7	64431	65791	83	73	163	6.1	11.7	46.0	29.4	6.7	139674
61379	WYANET	24058	596	16.4	29.0	46.8	5.9	1.8	53484	55477	69	52	466	5.2	28.8	53.9	10.5	1.7	106992
61401	GALESBURG	22741	13814	27.6	30.5	34.0	5.3	2.6	41446	45547	38	20	9148	15.6	35.4	38.7	9.6	0.8	89006
61410	ABINGDON	20447	1558	22.2	33.1	39.7	4.4	0.6	46177	48831	52	32	1231	22.4	40.3	34.4	2.8	0.1	75236
61411	ADAIR	23379	178	24.2	28.1	39.3	6.2	2.2	48048	50000	57	38	141	23.4	38.3	27.0	9.2	2.1	76429
61412	ALEXIS	22834	624	18.3	30.8	44.4	5.0	1.6	50692	53307	63	45	487	18.5	35.3	34.9	8.0	3.3	85889
61413	ALPHA	22822	437	14.9	34.1	45.3	3.7	2.1	51035	54277	64	46	369	17.9	30.9	40.9	7.6	2.7	91216
61414	ALTONA	18407	323	17.6	39.9	38.7	3.1	0.6	43503	46622	44	25	264	20.1	36.7	36.7	2.7	3.8	84000
61415	AVON	21805	799	22.5	32.8	36.4	5.0	3.3	44549	46910	47	28	625	24.5	29.0	33.9	10.1	2.6	85000
61417	BERWICK	23103	126	21.4	28.6	38.9	7.9	3.2	50000	50960	61	44	92	15.2	26.1	42.4	13.0	3.3	105769
61418	BIGGSVILLE	22569	266	21.1	32.0	42.1	3.0	1.9	47502	47767	55	37	207	32.9	31.9	24.2	10.6	0.5	65526
61420	BLANDINSVILLE	19785	472	27.5	31.8	36.7	3.0	1.1	41221	45680	37	19	362	29.0	37.6	26.0	6.4	1.1	70333
61421	BRADFORD	20663	721	21.6	32.6	38.7	4.9	2.2	46414	47205	53	33	571	13.7	29.9	39.9	12.8	3.7	99125
61422	BUSHNELL	19886	1382	28.1	33.7	33.3	3.0	2.0	40275	43551	34	17	1029	40.6	37.0	18.6	3.3	0.5	57366
61423	CAMERON	25099	273	11.4	26.4	48.0	12.1	2.2	60295	61308	78	65	226	11.1	31.0	40.7	15.9	1.3	104286
61425	CARMAN	23443	155	16.1	35.5	43.2	3.9	1.3	49061	48850	59	40	124	37.1	35.5	23.4	4.0	0.0	60769
61427	CUBA	20380	967	25.1	36.0	32.5	4.3	2.1	39971	43738	32	16	781	22.0	28.0	36.0	13.1	0.9	89833
61428	DAHINDA	31113	350	12.6	25.1	49.7	8.3	4.3	61474	62728	79	67	310	6.8	21.6	36.1	28.1	7.4	133750
61430	EAST GALESBURG	29687	379	16.9	25.1	43.8	5.5	8.7	56853	60642	74	59	235	15.7	29.4	32.3	18.7	3.8	97188
61431	ELLISVILLE	20785	170	24.1	38.8	31.8	4.1	1.2	39658	42718	32	15	136	18.4	22.8	46.3	9.6	2.9	96000
61432	FAIRVIEW	20082	263	22.8	35.7	35.4	5.7	0.4	43336	45501	43	25	209	15.8	34.9	44.5	4.8	0.0	89063
61433	FIATT	20180	34	23.5	35.3	38.2	2.9	0.0	42353	45000	40	22	27	11.1	33.3	51.9	3.7	0.0	97500
61434	GALVA	21216	1501	27.2	30.6	35.4	5.0	1.8	43652	47076	44	25	1143	16.2	36.0	36.1	9.4	2.4	87278
61435	GERLAW	22449	65	21.5	35.4	38.5	4.6	0.0	42732	47375	42	23	50	12.0	18.0	50.0	18.0	2.0	112500
61436	GILSON	23234	385	13.0	33.5	44.2	7.0	2.3	53797	58360	69	53	313	10.2	27.2	41.9	16.3	4.5	110417
61437	GLADSTONE	21613	461	21.3	34.7	38.2	5.0	0.9	46887	47458	54	34	376	29.0	34.0	30.6	5.1	1.3	72800
61438	GOOD HOPE	21628	297	18.9	31.3	46.8	1.7	1.3	49894	50937	61	43	224	22.3	29.9	34.8	9.8	3.1	87368
61440	INDUSTRY	20422	323	22.9	27.9	42.7	5.6	0.9	49311	50535	60	41	252	20.6	35.7	26.2	15.1	2.4	82381
61441	IPAVA	20074	425	26.8	32.2	36.2	2.6	2.1	39902	45697	32	16	349	31.8	39.8	17.5	9.2	1.7	65303
61442	KEITHSBURG	18250	344	27.3	38.4	31.4	1.5	1.5	37902	41499	26	11	278	41.0	30.2	22.7	6.1	0.0	58065
61443	KEWANEE	19683	5803	31.1	33.0	29.7	3.9	2.2	38109	41643	27	12	4277	29.7	40.2	21.9	7.4	0.7	68323
61447	KIRKWOOD	18682	367	20.2	37.6	39.0	2.2	1.1	42600	45538	41	22	293	33.1	29.0	32.1	4.4	1.4	72895
61448	KNOXVILLE	25155	1505	14.0	21.6	53.2	7.8	3.5	59128	61218	76	63	1259	9.9	25.8	48.7	14.2	1.4	108498
61449	LA FAYETTE	20485	203	21.7	32.5	40.4	3.4	2.0	47330	47080	55	36	152	17.8	43.4	25.0	12.5	1.3	81053
61450	LA HARPE	19048	699	24.5	40.6	29.5	3.7	1.7	39152	41674	30	14	569	27.8	38.1	27.6	6.3	0.2	75565
61451	LAURA	24561	167	15.6	26.9	44.3	8.4	4.8	58074	60511	75	61	129	5.4	31.0	36.4	22.5	4.7	115625
61452	LITTLETON	22452	135	20.7	25.9	44.4	4.4	4.4	51472	52896	65	47	109	26.6	20.2	26.6	21.1	5.5	95833
61453	LITTLE YORK	21041	200	25.5	25.0	42.0	4.0	3.5	49500	50850	60	42	149	28.2	29.5	28.2	8.1	6.0	76111
61454	LOMAX	20194	383	24.8	32.4	37.1	4.4	1.3	40191	43943	33	16	300	27.3	37.0	27.0	8.0	0.7	70417
61455	MACOMB	20542	7893	38.2	24.4	29.9	5.2	2.2	36702	39864	23	9	4284	17.4	26.8	42.1	12.4	1.3	97545
61458	MAQUON	21598	344	18.6	41.6	34.3	4.9	0.6	42689	45657	41	23	268	22.4	34.0	33.2	9.0	1.5	83200
61459	MARIETTA	21609	165	17.6	37.0	38.2	4.8	2.4	45760	47764	51	32	137	29.9	22.6	34.3	11.7	1.5	79286
	ILLINOIS	28587		18.2	22.2	39.3	12.1	8.2	60823	63631				6.3	10.0	30.9	40.6	12.3	185324
	UNITED STATES	27277		20.9	24.4	35.3	11.7	7.6	54719	56938				9.3	13.1	31.6	32.6	13.5	162279

#	POST OFFICE NAME	FINANCIAL SERVICES: Auto Loan	Home Loan	Invest-ments	Retire-ment Plans	THE HOME: Home Improvements: Home Repair	Lawn & Garden	Furnishings: Comput-ers & Hard-ware-Personal	Major Appli-ances	TV, Radio, Sound Equip-ment	Furni-ture	ENTERTAINMENT: Dine out/ Carry out	Sports Equip-ment	Fees & Tickets	Toys & Games	Travel	Cable TV	PERSONAL: Apparel & Services	Auto Repairs	Health Insur-ance	Pets & Supplies
61274	OSCO	113	78	124	77	81	119	86	107	90	70	89	88	63	88	86	98	57	100	113	132
61275	PORT BYRON	120	111	109	116	113	129	109	122	112	99	110	93	102	114	109	118	75	113	125	142
61277	PROPHETSTOWN	91	84	94	84	86	103	82	94	86	75	85	71	77	85	84	92	57	88	101	110
61279	REYNOLDS	90	96	99	95	94	105	86	94	88	83	89	73	91	89	93	91	61	91	100	112
61281	SHERRARD	107	117	98	120	112	117	108	109	107	106	107	86	113	109	111	108	74	107	112	130
61282	SILVIS	74	67	60	68	64	74	74	71	77	69	75	56	69	77	68	80	52	74	80	86
61283	TAMPICO	88	75	84	76	74	94	78	85	80	70	80	69	70	81	77	85	53	83	92	105
61284	TAYLOR RIDGE	104	118	106	120	115	119	105	110	105	104	106	84	114	107	112	107	74	106	113	129
61285	THOMSON	92	81	85	84	83	98	81	92	84	73	82	71	73	85	81	89	56	85	95	108
61301	LA SALLE	77	75	67	76	73	80	78	76	80	74	79	59	77	81	75	83	55	78	84	91
61310	AMBOY	90	80	81	82	79	95	81	88	84	74	83	68	75	85	79	88	56	85	94	105
61311	ANCONA	108	95	100	99	97	115	95	108	98	85	96	83	86	99	95	104	65	100	112	127
61312	ARLINGTON	97	82	95	84	84	104	83	97	86	73	85	75	73	87	83	92	57	90	101	115
61313	BLACKSTONE	110	98	101	102	100	118	98	111	101	88	99	84	89	102	97	107	67	102	114	129
61314	BUDA	78	79	64	81	74	84	79	77	80	74	79	62	78	81	77	82	55	78	85	94
61318	COMPTON	96	86	88	89	87	103	85	97	88	76	86	73	77	89	85	93	59	89	100	113
61319	CORNELL	98	86	91	89	88	105	86	98	89	77	87	75	77	90	86	94	59	91	102	115
61320	DALZELL	88	103	94	102	99	104	90	94	92	90	92	71	100	93	98	94	64	93	101	111
61321	DANA	90	64	74	63	64	85	67	78	74	65	73	60	54	77	61	81	49	74	82	95
61325	GRAND RIDGE	100	94	90	97	95	106	91	100	93	86	92	76	86	96	91	97	63	94	103	117
61326	GRANVILLE	93	77	81	78	78	94	79	88	83	74	82	67	69	85	76	89	56	84	93	105
61327	HENNEPIN	103	98	96	101	99	111	94	105	97	87	95	80	90	98	96	101	65	98	108	123
61329	LADD	87	96	79	97	90	97	90	89	91	87	91	70	95	93	92	93	63	90	97	107
61330	LA MOILLE	100	81	99	83	83	107	84	99	87	73	85	78	71	87	83	93	57	91	103	118
61333	LONG POINT	117	81	129	81	84	124	90	111	93	73	92	92	66	91	89	102	60	104	118	137
61334	LOSTANT	96	88	87	91	89	103	86	98	89	78	88	74	80	91	86	94	60	90	101	113
61335	MC NABB	100	98	92	101	98	109	93	103	95	87	94	78	90	97	95	99	64	96	105	120
61336	MAGNOLIA	101	100	93	103	100	109	94	103	96	89	95	79	92	98	96	99	65	97	105	121
61337	MALDEN	106	87	105	89	89	113	89	105	92	77	91	82	76	93	89	99	61	97	109	125
61341	MARSEILLES	92	92	82	94	89	98	88	92	90	85	89	71	88	91	89	92	61	90	96	109
61342	MENDOTA	89	88	80	88	86	93	87	90	88	84	88	68	85	89	86	91	60	88	95	105
61344	MINERAL	102	90	96	93	92	110	90	103	93	80	91	79	80	94	90	99	62	95	106	121
61345	NEPONSET	93	85	84	88	86	100	83	94	86	75	84	71	77	88	83	91	58	87	97	109
61346	NEW BEDFORD	104	92	96	95	94	111	91	104	94	82	93	80	82	96	91	100	63	96	108	122
61348	OGLESBY	83	78	82	77	76	91	76	84	80	72	79	64	73	80	77	85	54	81	91	99
61349	OHIO	96	84	89	87	86	102	84	96	87	75	85	73	75	88	83	92	58	89	99	112
61350	OTTAWA	85	85	81	85	84	91	84	87	87	81	86	66	84	87	84	90	60	86	93	102
61353	PAW PAW	92	83	83	87	85	98	82	93	85	74	83	70	76	86	82	90	57	86	96	108
61354	PERU	86	84	80	84	83	93	84	87	87	80	86	65	83	87	84	91	59	87	96	103
61356	PRINCETON	87	83	85	84	83	94	83	88	86	80	85	66	81	85	83	90	58	86	95	104
61358	RUTLAND	92	65	80	64	65	89	69	81	75	65	74	63	54	78	64	82	49	76	85	99
61360	SENECA	92	105	92	105	101	104	92	96	93	93	94	72	100	95	98	94	65	93	99	113
61361	SHEFFIELD	85	77	91	76	78	96	75	87	79	68	78	66	70	78	78	85	53	83	95	103
61362	SPRING VALLEY	83	86	78	86	84	92	84	86	88	81	87	64	87	87	85	92	60	86	96	101
61364	STREATOR	80	70	73	71	70	85	73	79	77	67	76	60	67	77	71	82	52	77	87	94
61367	SUBLETTE	113	97	105	100	99	119	97	112	101	88	99	85	86	103	96	108	67	103	116	131
61368	TISKILWA	98	87	94	89	88	105	86	98	89	77	87	76	78	90	87	94	59	92	102	116
61369	TOLUCA	90	64	91	63	67	94	70	87	78	62	75	66	56	76	68	85	50	81	94	103
61370	TONICA	86	93	88	93	93	101	84	92	88	82	88	67	89	88	90	93	60	88	101	106
61373	UTICA	106	99	105	99	98	113	93	105	96	90	96	81	89	98	96	101	65	99	107	125
61375	VARNA	97	82	105	83	86	103	82	98	85	74	84	74	72	84	85	90	56	90	99	114
61376	WALNUT	90	89	89	90	90	103	84	95	88	79	87	70	83	88	88	94	60	89	102	109
61377	WENONA	88	66	86	65	68	91	70	85	77	63	75	64	58	77	68	85	50	79	92	100
61378	WEST BROOKLYN	107	94	99	98	96	114	94	107	97	84	95	82	85	99	94	103	65	99	111	126
61379	WYANET	86	85	74	86	80	92	85	85	86	79	85	68	83	87	83	89	59	85	93	103
61401	GALESBURG	75	68	69	69	68	79	72	75	76	68	75	56	68	75	70	80	52	75	84	89
61410	ABINGDON	79	66	68	67	65	81	70	76	74	64	72	58	62	75	66	79	49	74	82	90
61411	ADAIR	99	68	109	68	71	104	76	94	79	61	78	78	55	77	75	86	50	88	99	116
61412	ALEXIS	94	72	94	72	74	97	74	90	79	66	78	69	61	79	73	86	52	83	94	107
61413	ALPHA	88	80	79	84	82	95	79	89	82	72	80	68	73	83	79	86	55	82	92	104
61414	ALTONA	87	60	95	60	63	92	66	82	69	54	68	68	49	68	66	75	44	77	87	101
61415	AVON	90	68	91	68	70	95	72	87	77	63	75	68	58	76	71	84	50	81	93	104
61417	BERWICK	96	72	101	72	74	102	77	93	80	64	79	75	60	79	76	86	52	87	98	113
61418	BIGGSVILLE	94	68	97	65	70	96	69	88	77	64	76	66	55	76	69	85	50	81	92	105
61420	BLANDINSVILLE	81	57	84	56	60	85	63	78	69	54	67	60	49	67	62	75	44	73	84	93
61421	BRADFORD	92	66	99	67	69	97	72	88	75	59	74	72	55	74	72	81	48	82	93	108
61422	BUSHNELL	77	63	71	63	62	80	67	74	71	61	70	57	58	71	64	76	47	72	81	89
61423	CAMERON	100	91	91	95	93	108	90	102	93	82	91	77	83	95	90	98	62	94	105	118
61425	CARMAN	91	70	90	69	72	94	71	87	77	65	75	65	59	77	70	84	50	80	90	103
61427	CUBA	80	65	84	64	68	87	67	80	73	62	71	59	59	71	67	79	48	75	87	94
61428	DAHINDA	112	92	137	92	100	119	92	114	96	86	95	84	81	93	98	102	63	106	114	133
61430	EAST GALESBURG	104	98	102	100	101	108	100	105	102	98	100	77	97	101	100	105	69	103	110	122
61431	ELLISVILLE	88	60	96	60	63	92	67	83	70	54	69	69	49	68	67	76	45	78	88	102
61432	FAIRVIEW	89	64	91	62	66	90	65	83	72	61	71	62	52	72	65	80	47	76	86	99
61433	FIATT	87	62	89	60	65	88	64	81	71	59	70	61	51	70	63	78	46	75	85	97
61434	GALVA	81	65	84	64	67	88	67	80	73	61	71	60	59	72	67	80	48	76	88	95
61435	GERLAW	83	73	76	76	75	88	73	83	75	66	74	63	66	77	72	80	50	77	86	97
61436	GILSON	97	82	93	85	85	103	83	96	86	74	85	74	73	87	83	92	57	89	100	113
61437	GLADSTONE	91	65	81	63	66	88	68	81	75	65	73	62	54	77	63	82	49	76	85	98
61438	GOOD HOPE	92	64	102	64	67	98	71	88	74	57	73	73	52	72	70	80	47	82	93	108
61440	INDUSTRY	93	64	102	64	67	98	71	88	74	58	73	73	52	72	71	81	47	82	93	109
61441	IPAVA	81	58	83	57	60	85	63	78	69	55	67	60	50	68	62	76	44	73	84	93
61442	KEITHSBURG	81	58	71	56	58	78	61	71	66	57	65	56	48	69	56	72	44	67	75	87
61443	KEWANEE	73	60	68	60	60	76	64	71	69	59	67	54	57	69	62	74	46	69	79	85
61447	KIRKWOOD	86	61	90	60	63	89	64	81	70	57	69	63	50	69	64	77	45	75	85	97
61448	KNOXVILLE	97	88	89	90	87	103	88	96	92	82	90	74	83	92	87	97	62	92	103	114
61449	LA FAYETTE	92	63	101	63	66	97	70	87	73	57	72	72	51	72	70	80	47	82	92	107
61450	LA HARPE	81	58	83	56	60	85	63	78	69	55	67	60	49	68	61	76	44	73	84	93
61451	LAURA	103	92	94	96	94	110	91	104	94	82	93	79	83	96	91	100	63	96	107	121
61452	LITTLETON	104	72	115	72	75	110	80	99	83	65	82	82	58	81	79	90	53	93	105	122
61453	LITTLE YORK	94	65	103	65	68	99	72	89	75	58	74	74	53	73	72	82	48	84	94	110
61454	LOMAX	86	63	87	61	65	87	64	81	71	59	69	61	52	70	63	77	46	74	84	96
61455	MACOMB	68	53	56	55	53	60	74	62	70	63	70	51	61	69	61	70	49	68	66	76
61458	MAQUON	83	62	84	61	64	87	66	81	72	58	70	62	54	71	65	79	47	75	87	96
61459	MARIETTA	88	76	84	78	78	94	76	88	79	68	78	68	67	80	76	84	52	82	91	104
	ILLINOIS	106	108	105	108	107	106	109	106	108	107	109	83	110	108	108	108	77	108	107	125
	UNITED STATES	100	100	100	100	100	100	100	100	100	100	100	100	100	100	100	100	100	100	100	100

ZIP CODE			POPULATION			2000-2009 ANNUAL RATE		HOUSEHOLDS					FAMILIES		
#	POST OFFICE NAME	COUNTY FIPS CODE	2000	2009	2014	% Rate	State Centile	2000	2009	2014	% Annual Rate 2000-2009	2009 Average HH Size	2000	2009	% Annual Rate 2000-2009
61460	MEDIA	071	468	443	429	-0.6	13	180	172	168	-0.5	2.58	140	132	-0.6
61462	MONMOUTH	187	12036	11490	11127	-0.5	18	4521	4315	4174	-0.5	2.40	2970	2769	-0.8
61465	NEW WINDSOR	131	1153	1138	1122	-0.1	45	466	467	462	0.0	2.44	341	336	-0.2
61466	NORTH HENDERSON	131	338	332	327	-0.2	38	134	134	132	0.0	2.48	104	102	-0.2
61467	ONEIDA	095	1278	1165	1103	-1.0	3	502	464	443	-0.8	2.51	384	349	-1.0
61469	OQUAWKA	071	2640	2518	2455	-0.5	18	1098	1059	1036	-0.4	2.36	732	693	-0.6
61470	PRAIRIE CITY	109	595	593	585	0.0	50	204	205	202	0.1	2.76	161	159	-0.1
61471	RARITAN	071	322	304	294	-0.6	13	124	118	115	-0.5	2.58	97	91	-0.7
61472	RIO	095	619	594	571	-0.4	25	245	239	232	-0.3	2.49	188	181	-0.4
61473	ROSEVILLE	187	1787	1700	1648	-0.5	18	709	680	660	-0.5	2.39	509	478	-0.7
61474	SAINT AUGUSTINE	095	344	314	298	-1.0	3	138	128	123	-0.8	2.45	100	92	-0.9
61475	SCIOTA	109	243	240	234	-0.1	45	90	89	87	-0.1	2.70	69	68	-0.2
61476	SEATON	071	729	689	670	-0.6	13	288	275	268	-0.5	2.51	221	208	-0.7
61477	SMITHFIELD	057	599	605	599	0.1	56	242	249	248	0.3	2.43	184	186	0.1
61478	SMITHSHIRE	187	327	319	310	-0.3	32	129	128	125	-0.1	2.49	100	97	-0.3
61479	SPEER	175	504	496	493	-0.2	38	185	186	186	0.1	2.67	144	142	-0.2
61480	STRONGHURST	071	1164	1111	1084	-0.5	18	448	433	424	-0.4	2.52	326	310	-0.5
61482	TABLE GROVE	057	607	606	600	0.0	50	245	248	247	0.1	2.44	177	176	-0.1
61483	TOULON	175	2317	2281	2267	-0.2	38	910	911	910	0.0	2.38	620	607	-0.2
61484	VERMONT	057	958	933	912	-0.3	32	376	370	362	-0.2	2.52	268	258	-0.4
61485	VICTORIA	095	634	595	569	-0.7	9	234	221	212	-0.6	2.69	181	168	-0.8
61486	VIOLA	131	1566	1660	1667	0.6	75	609	650	654	0.7	2.55	459	482	0.5
61488	WATAGA	095	1237	1124	1066	-1.0	3	485	451	430	-0.8	2.49	377	344	-1.0
61489	WILLIAMSFIELD	095	1006	895	844	-1.3	2	390	352	333	-1.1	2.53	286	253	-1.3
61490	WOODHULL	073	1122	1095	1075	-0.3	32	469	465	459	-0.1	2.35	334	324	-0.3
61491	WYOMING	175	1592	1560	1539	-0.2	38	691	691	686	0.0	2.26	466	457	-0.2
61501	ASTORIA	057	2022	2030	1996	0.0	50	829	846	836	0.2	2.35	586	586	0.0
61516	BENSON	203	686	748	770	0.9	81	267	295	304	1.1	2.53	194	210	0.9
61517	BRIMFIELD	143	3192	3269	3309	0.3	65	1159	1217	1240	0.5	2.68	923	949	0.3
61519	BRYANT	057	10	10	10	0.0	50	6	6	6	0.0	1.67	4	4	0.0
61520	CANTON	057	19335	18685	18230	-0.4	25	7259	7055	6884	-0.3	2.32	4823	4587	-0.5
61523	CHILLICOTHE	143	11025	10991	10999	0.0	50	4369	4443	4473	0.2	2.45	3183	3165	-0.1
61524	DUNFERMLINE	057	21	21	20	0.0	50	11	11	11	0.0	1.91	8	8	0.0
61525	DUNLAP	143	5371	7331	7817	3.4	95	1879	2782	2998	4.3	2.64	1538	2170	3.8
61526	EDELSTEIN	143	1065	1137	1165	0.7	78	357	386	397	0.8	2.95	292	310	0.6
61528	EDWARDS	143	1644	2003	2118	2.2	92	600	754	801	2.5	2.65	467	569	2.2
61529	ELMWOOD	143	2677	2846	2921	0.7	78	1050	1144	1183	0.9	2.46	784	835	0.7
61530	EUREKA	203	6112	6456	6572	0.6	75	2135	2302	2362	0.8	2.52	1492	1570	0.6
61531	FARMINGTON	057	3485	3426	3352	-0.2	38	1389	1374	1347	-0.1	2.43	985	956	-0.3
61532	FOREST CITY	125	631	607	591	-0.4	25	228	223	218	-0.2	2.72	175	169	-0.4
61533	GLASFORD	143	2221	2196	2192	-0.1	45	848	858	861	0.1	2.56	661	657	-0.1
61534	GREEN VALLEY	179	1765	1884	1948	0.7	78	632	689	718	0.9	2.72	503	539	0.8
61535	GROVELAND	179	1520	1663	1732	1.0	83	569	641	673	1.3	2.59	454	504	1.1
61536	HANNA CITY	143	2955	3454	3645	1.7	90	1049	1272	1356	2.1	2.52	829	988	1.9
61537	HENRY	123	3217	3149	3093	-0.2	38	1269	1264	1248	0.0	2.43	863	839	-0.3
61540	LACON	123	2792	2734	2688	-0.2	38	1112	1108	1094	0.0	2.37	797	779	-0.2
61542	LEWISTOWN	057	3983	3915	3834	-0.2	38	1641	1628	1599	-0.1	2.35	1097	1065	-0.3
61543	LIVERPOOL	057	171	168	167	-0.2	38	70	70	70	0.0	2.40	53	52	-0.2
61544	LONDON MILLS	057	765	743	725	-0.3	32	285	281	276	-0.2	2.64	220	214	-0.3
61545	LOWPOINT	203	776	855	893	1.1	85	281	317	334	1.3	2.70	226	251	1.1
61546	MANITO	179	4493	4671	4712	0.4	69	1723	1831	1860	0.7	2.55	1337	1399	0.5
61547	MAPLETON	143	3865	4176	4302	0.8	79	1360	1502	1558	1.1	2.77	1144	1249	1.0
61548	METAMORA	203	9517	11109	11813	1.7	90	3389	4044	4334	1.9	2.71	2728	3214	1.8
61550	MORTON	179	16852	17672	18096	0.5	72	6630	7110	7330	0.8	2.42	4776	5026	0.6
61552	MOSSVILLE	143	157	165	169	0.5	72	65	70	72	0.8	2.36	54	57	0.6
61554	PEKIN	179	44680	45565	46190	0.2	61	17399	18132	18511	0.4	2.39	11991	12250	0.2
61559	PRINCEVILLE	143	3003	3357	3501	1.2	85	1146	1307	1369	1.4	2.57	867	965	1.2
61560	PUTNAM	155	814	854	866	0.5	72	341	365	373	0.7	2.34	263	276	0.5
61561	ROANOKE	203	2962	3255	3388	1.0	83	1050	1174	1227	1.2	2.71	806	884	1.0
61563	SAINT DAVID	057	14	13	13	-0.8	6	5	5	5	0.0	2.60	4	4	0.0
61565	SPARLAND	123	1665	1768	1770	0.7	78	605	656	662	0.9	2.70	485	519	0.7
61567	TOPEKA	125	1003	965	936	-0.4	25	390	380	370	-0.3	2.54	289	277	-0.5
61568	TREMONT	179	4266	4520	4664	0.6	75	1541	1670	1737	0.9	2.69	1209	1286	0.7
61569	TRIVOLI	143	1174	1207	1216	0.3	65	450	473	481	0.5	2.52	370	384	0.4
61570	WASHBURN	203	1875	1941	1963	0.4	69	703	740	753	0.6	2.62	530	546	0.3
61571	WASHINGTON	179	19639	21569	22475	1.0	83	7715	8663	9090	1.3	2.47	5599	6165	1.0
61572	YATES CITY	095	1163	1166	1151	0.0	50	476	486	483	0.2	2.40	347	347	0.0
61602	PEORIA	143	728	723	721	-0.1	45	340	326	323	-0.5	1.73	140	126	-1.1
61603	PEORIA	143	18975	17707	17277	-0.7	9	7226	6782	6640	-0.7	2.51	4291	3881	-1.1
61604	PEORIA	143	32988	32007	31680	-0.3	32	13249	13005	12933	-0.2	2.34	8311	7898	-0.5
61605	PEORIA	143	18576	17489	17061	-0.6	13	6932	6646	6518	-0.5	2.60	4432	4052	-1.0
61606	PEORIA	143	7898	7531	7400	-0.5	18	2853	2678	2621	-0.7	2.36	1289	1153	-1.2
61607	PEORIA	143	10180	10166	10171	0.0	50	4105	4194	4222	0.2	2.42	2991	2988	0.0
61610	CREVE COEUR	179	5455	5390	5400	-0.1	45	2221	2249	2270	0.1	2.40	1493	1475	-0.1
61611	EAST PEORIA	179	24674	25300	25732	0.3	65	10122	10620	10886	0.5	2.35	7085	7288	0.3
61614	PEORIA	143	28055	27193	26871	-0.3	32	12521	12365	12296	-0.1	2.13	7491	7147	-0.5
61615	PEORIA	143	19567	22895	24473	1.7	90	8279	9690	10377	1.7	2.31	5456	6280	1.5
61616	PEORIA HEIGHTS	143	6161	5827	5720	-0.6	13	2811	2697	2659	-0.4	2.14	1559	1440	-0.9
61625	PEORIA	143	1751	1761	1746	0.1	56	6	5	5	-2.0	2.60	3	3	0.0
61635	PEORIA	179	92	183	198	7.7	99	4	65	71	35.2	2.75	3	50	35.5
61701	BLOOMINGTON	113	37149	37033	37175	0.0	50	16191	16399	16589	0.1	2.11	8388	8056	-0.4
61704	BLOOMINGTON	113	27917	34962	38646	2.5	93	10695	13395	14818	2.5	2.60	7389	9080	2.3
61705	BLOOMINGTON	113	7660	10556	11639	3.5	96	2613	3651	4053	3.7	2.88	2238	3039	3.4
61720	ANCHOR	113	356	369	377	0.4	69	117	124	128	0.6	2.90	88	91	0.4
61721	ARMINGTON	179	658	673	682	0.2	61	238	245	249	0.3	2.75	193	196	0.2
61722	ARROWSMITH	113	724	769	799	0.7	78	245	266	280	0.9	2.86	195	206	0.6
61723	ATLANTA	107	2462	2366	2299	-0.4	25	968	944	921	-0.3	2.33	703	673	-0.5
61724	BELLFLOWER	113	659	689	713	0.5	72	250	268	280	0.8	2.57	190	197	0.4
61725	CARLOCK	113	1114	1156	1183	0.4	69	424	451	465	0.7	2.56	344	358	0.4
61726	CHENOA	113	2966	2918	2918	-0.2	38	1105	1110	1118	0.0	2.56	828	804	-0.3
61727	CLINTON	039	10425	10182	9960	-0.3	32	4226	4171	4095	-0.1	2.39	2839	2747	-0.4
61728	COLFAX	113	1482	1572	1625	0.6	75	571	613	638	0.8	2.48	394	408	0.4
61729	CONGERVILLE	203	1139	1287	1358	1.3	87	392	453	481	1.6	2.84	334	381	1.4
61730	COOKSVILLE	113	439	456	466	0.4	69	183	194	200	0.6	2.29	139	143	0.3
61731	CROPSEY	113	236	270	289	1.5	88	80	94	101	1.8	2.87	65	75	1.6
	ILLINOIS					0.6					0.6	2.64			0.4
	UNITED STATES					1.0					1.1	2.59			0.9

ZIP CODE		RACE (%)						% Hispanic Origin		2009 AGE DISTRIBUTION (%)										MEDIAN AGE		
#	POST OFFICE NAME	White		Black		Asian/Pacific																
		2000	2009	2000	2009	2000	2009	2000	2009	0-4	5-9	10-14	15-19	20-24	25-44	45-64	65-84	85+	18+	2009	% 2009 Males	% 2009 Females
61460	MEDIA	97.0	96.2	1.1	1.4	0.0	0.0	0.9	1.1	5.6	6.3	6.3	5.9	4.5	23.0	31.2	15.1	2.0	77.7	43.6	50.3	49.7
61462	MONMOUTH	93.6	91.9	2.4	2.8	0.6	0.7	3.8	5.4	5.9	5.7	5.6	9.2	10.4	22.7	25.2	12.3	2.9	79.1	36.1	48.1	51.9
61465	NEW WINDSOR	98.6	98.5	0.1	0.1	0.2	0.2	2.3	2.5	5.4	5.5	5.9	6.2	5.1	22.6	29.5	17.0	2.8	79.5	44.5	50.0	50.0
61466	NORTH HENDERSON	99.1	99.1	0.0	0.0	0.0	0.0	2.1	2.1	5.4	5.7	5.7	4.8	5.1	24.4	30.7	16.0	2.1	80.4	44.0	50.0	50.0
61467	ONEIDA	98.7	98.2	0.1	0.1	0.4	0.5	1.1	1.6	6.0	6.4	6.6	6.4	4.1	24.4	28.8	15.1	2.3	77.2	42.5	50.0	50.0
61469	OQUAWKA	98.4	97.9	0.1	0.2	0.1	0.2	0.9	1.3	6.2	6.4	6.5	5.8	4.2	23.6	29.2	16.2	2.1	77.6	43.0	50.4	49.6
61470	PRAIRIE CITY	98.2	97.5	0.0	0.0	0.7	1.0	0.7	1.0	4.6	7.4	7.4	6.1	6.2	21.6	27.0	13.5	6.2	76.4	42.4	49.6	50.4
61471	RARITAN	96.9	96.4	1.2	1.3	0.0	0.0	0.6	1.0	5.9	6.3	6.3	5.9	4.3	23.0	31.3	15.5	1.6	78.0	43.7	50.3	49.7
61472	RIO	99.2	98.8	0.0	0.0	0.0	0.2	1.1	1.9	5.6	5.9	6.6	6.6	4.2	21.9	32.8	14.6	1.9	77.9	44.5	50.2	49.8
61473	ROSEVILLE	99.6	99.5	0.1	0.1	0.1	0.1	0.4	0.6	5.1	5.5	5.9	6.2	4.2	22.9	26.6	18.0	5.6	79.6	45.2	47.2	52.8
61474	SAINT AUGUSTINE	98.8	98.4	0.0	0.0	0.0	0.0	0.6	0.6	6.4	6.7	6.7	6.4	4.5	24.8	27.1	16.2	1.3	76.4	40.5	49.7	50.3
61475	SCIOTA	98.8	98.8	0.4	0.4	0.4	0.4	0.4	0.4	5.8	6.3	6.7	6.3	4.6	21.3	31.7	15.4	2.1	77.1	44.4	49.6	50.4
61476	SEATON	98.4	98.1	1.1	1.2	0.0	0.0	0.3	0.3	6.7	7.0	7.1	6.8	4.2	24.1	29.3	13.2	1.6	74.7	41.3	51.1	48.9
61477	SMITHFIELD	98.7	98.2	0.0	0.0	0.0	0.2	0.8	1.3	5.0	5.5	6.4	6.8	3.6	25.6	30.4	14.9	1.8	78.8	43.1	53.2	46.8
61478	SMITHSHIRE	99.7	99.7	0.0	0.0	0.0	0.0	0.6	0.6	6.9	7.2	7.5	6.0	3.4	23.8	30.4	13.2	1.6	74.6	41.3	48.9	51.1
61479	SPEER	98.2	98.2	0.0	0.0	0.0	0.0	2.6	2.6	6.5	7.3	7.5	6.5	3.6	23.4	29.4	13.7	2.2	74.6	41.6	52.8	47.2
61480	STRONGHURST	99.1	98.9	0.1	0.1	0.2	0.2	0.9	1.3	5.9	6.0	6.2	5.9	4.8	21.9	30.3	15.7	3.2	78.0	44.4	48.5	51.5
61482	TABLE GROVE	99.5	99.5	0.0	0.0	0.2	0.2	0.2	0.0	5.1	5.4	6.1	7.1	4.1	22.8	31.8	14.7	2.8	78.9	44.4	52.5	47.5
61483	TOULON	98.4	98.4	0.1	0.1	0.1	0.1	0.9	0.9	6.0	6.0	6.1	6.3	5.0	23.1	27.0	15.0	5.5	77.9	43.1	47.0	53.0
61484	VERMONT	97.9	97.1	0.0	0.0	0.3	0.4	0.9	1.4	6.9	6.5	6.8	7.4	5.8	23.0	28.0	13.6	2.0	75.3	40.4	52.3	47.7
61485	VICTORIA	99.2	99.2	0.0	0.0	0.0	0.0	0.6	0.8	6.2	6.7	7.2	5.9	4.0	21.7	32.3	14.3	1.7	76.0	43.5	52.6	47.4
61486	VIOLA	97.3	97.1	0.4	0.4	0.1	0.1	2.9	3.1	6.4	6.3	6.5	7.1	6.0	24.2	28.5	13.4	1.7	76.6	40.8	49.1	50.9
61488	WATAGA	98.1	97.6	0.4	0.5	0.2	0.2	1.2	1.7	6.0	6.1	6.3	6.0	5.4	24.7	30.7	13.3	1.4	77.9	41.1	47.4	52.6
61489	WILLIAMSFIELD	99.1	98.7	0.0	0.0	0.0	0.0	0.8	1.1	6.5	6.8	6.8	5.9	3.9	25.6	28.8	13.7	1.9	76.0	41.1	51.2	48.8
61490	WOODHULL	98.8	98.5	0.4	0.5	0.2	0.2	1.2	1.9	5.0	5.1	5.7	7.4	5.4	23.7	30.0	15.1	2.6	79.5	43.4	51.1	48.9
61491	WYOMING	98.9	98.8	0.1	0.1	0.2	0.2	0.2	0.2	6.3	6.4	7.0	6.5	4.7	23.5	27.4	15.3	2.8	76.2	41.3	48.0	52.0
61501	ASTORIA	98.6	98.0	0.0	0.0	0.2	0.3	1.0	1.5	5.1	5.3	5.7	7.0	4.9	24.2	27.4	16.7	3.7	79.6	43.3	49.3	50.7
61516	BENSON	99.0	98.8	0.1	0.1	0.1	0.3	0.3	0.5	7.2	8.0	7.9	7.0	4.5	23.1	26.7	13.2	2.3	72.3	38.6	51.3	48.7
61517	BRIMFIELD	98.0	97.2	0.3	0.4	0.1	0.2	1.3	2.0	6.0	6.6	7.4	7.1	4.1	22.9	32.0	12.4	1.4	75.1	42.1	51.4	48.6
61519	BRYANT	100.0	100.0	0.0	0.0	0.0	0.0	0.0	0.0	0.0	0.0	0.0	0.0	0.0	60.0	40.0	0.0	0.0	100.0	43.3	40.0	60.0
61520	CANTON	91.5	89.0	7.0	7.4	0.4	1.5	1.8	2.7	5.5	5.4	5.4	7.7	8.0	26.3	24.7	14.0	3.1	80.6	38.5	51.1	48.9
61523	CHILLICOTHE	97.7	96.7	0.3	0.4	0.4	0.5	2.3	3.5	5.9	6.1	6.3	6.6	5.4	24.5	29.9	13.1	2.1	77.6	41.4	48.8	51.2
61524	DUNFERMLINE	100.0	100.0	0.0	0.0	0.0	0.0	0.0	0.0	4.8	4.8	9.5	4.8	4.8	33.3	38.1	0.0	0.0	76.2	38.8	52.4	47.6
61525	DUNLAP	96.2	93.8	0.7	1.5	2.0	3.0	0.9	1.5	5.9	6.5	7.2	7.1	5.0	22.3	32.9	11.8	1.2	75.7	42.0	49.8	50.2
61526	EDELSTEIN	98.4	97.8	0.4	0.4	0.4	0.6	0.8	1.3	5.7	6.2	6.9	7.0	4.8	22.3	34.1	11.4	1.4	76.6	42.7	50.2	49.8
61528	EDWARDS	94.8	92.0	2.7	4.1	1.5	2.4	1.2	2.0	6.9	6.9	7.1	6.2	4.7	23.5	32.0	11.0	1.6	74.9	41.3	50.7	49.3
61529	ELMWOOD	98.0	97.2	0.7	0.9	0.1	0.2	0.9	1.4	7.0	7.1	6.9	6.6	5.5	24.8	26.3	13.0	2.7	74.8	39.1	48.7	51.3
61530	EUREKA	97.9	97.3	0.5	0.7	0.4	0.6	1.0	1.4	6.4	6.6	6.5	9.3	8.9	22.4	21.5	12.8	5.7	76.3	35.6	47.3	52.7
61531	FARMINGTON	98.8	98.3	0.1	0.2	0.1	0.2	0.8	1.1	6.3	6.5	6.5	6.0	4.5	24.1	26.8	15.1	4.2	76.9	41.9	48.5	51.5
61532	FOREST CITY	98.9	98.7	0.2	0.2	0.0	0.0	0.6	0.8	6.8	7.1	7.6	7.1	5.1	23.7	28.7	12.2	1.8	74.1	39.6	49.8	50.2
61533	GLASFORD	98.9	98.4	0.0	0.0	0.0	0.0	0.7	1.0	5.1	5.2	5.6	6.6	5.5	27.4	31.3	11.6	1.7	80.1	41.1	49.0	51.0
61534	GREEN VALLEY	99.2	98.9	0.1	0.2	0.1	0.2	0.6	1.0	6.8	6.9	7.3	7.2	6.1	25.2	29.7	9.4	1.5	74.6	38.2	48.9	51.1
61535	GROVELAND	98.2	97.7	0.1	0.1	0.6	0.9	1.0	1.5	4.4	6.0	6.8	6.2	3.2	21.4	39.0	11.4	1.6	78.4	46.0	50.0	50.0
61536	HANNA CITY	91.6	88.0	6.3	8.9	0.6	0.9	1.1	1.8	5.7	6.3	6.7	6.1	5.2	27.1	28.8	12.2	1.9	77.3	40.1	52.1	47.9
61537	HENRY	97.6	97.0	0.6	0.7	0.3	0.5	0.7	1.0	5.8	6.0	6.0	6.8	4.6	22.8	27.6	16.1	4.4	78.0	43.4	48.2	51.8
61540	LACON	99.2	98.9	0.1	0.1	0.2	0.3	0.9	1.3	5.0	5.3	5.6	6.2	4.6	22.5	28.3	17.6	4.9	80.3	45.5	48.4	51.6
61542	LEWISTOWN	99.0	98.6	0.1	0.2	0.2	0.2	0.9	1.3	5.2	5.2	5.4	5.7	5.7	23.5	28.8	16.4	3.8	80.5	44.2	48.6	51.4
61543	LIVERPOOL	99.4	98.2	0.0	0.0	0.0	0.6	0.6	1.8	4.2	5.4	5.4	5.4	5.4	23.8	32.7	16.1	1.8	81.5	45.4	50.6	49.4
61544	LONDON MILLS	99.3	99.2	0.1	0.1	0.0	0.0	0.4	0.5	7.5	7.8	6.9	5.0	5.5	21.9	29.1	14.0	2.3	74.7	41.3	47.6	52.4
61545	LOWPOINT	97.6	96.5	0.5	0.6	0.6	0.9	1.3	2.0	5.3	6.0	6.4	6.4	5.4	23.9	32.5	12.3	1.9	78.4	42.3	51.7	48.3
61546	MANITO	98.6	98.1	0.2	0.3	0.3	0.4	0.4	0.7	5.9	6.2	6.6	6.2	4.6	24.9	31.3	12.7	1.6	77.6	41.9	51.6	48.4
61547	MAPLETON	97.6	96.6	0.6	0.9	0.4	0.5	0.9	1.5	6.2	6.7	7.0	6.1	4.2	25.7	32.0	11.2	1.0	76.4	41.3	50.4	49.6
61548	METAMORA	98.5	98.0	0.3	0.3	0.4	0.6	0.6	0.9	6.1	6.9	7.6	7.4	4.3	22.8	30.0	12.4	2.4	74.6	41.4	48.3	51.7
61550	MORTON	97.9	97.1	0.1	0.2	1.1	1.6	0.8	1.1	5.6	6.2	6.5	6.3	4.8	23.8	29.6	14.0	3.1	77.6	42.6	48.6	51.4
61552	MOSSVILLE	95.5	93.3	0.6	1.2	2.6	3.6	1.3	1.8	4.8	6.1	7.3	7.3	4.8	20.0	35.8	12.7	1.2	77.0	44.8	49.1	50.9
61554	PEKIN	96.4	95.7	2.0	2.3	0.4	0.6	1.2	1.7	6.5	6.1	6.0	6.2	6.2	27.8	26.5	12.5	2.2	77.7	38.6	49.4	50.6
61559	PRINCEVILLE	97.8	96.7	0.1	0.1	0.2	0.2	1.9	2.9	7.2	7.6	7.7	6.8	4.4	23.6	28.2	12.5	1.9	72.9	39.6	49.7	50.3
61560	PUTNAM	96.9	95.9	0.5	0.6	0.1	0.2	2.6	3.5	4.8	5.3	5.5	4.3	3.0	19.2	36.9	19.3	1.6	81.9	49.8	53.4	46.6
61561	ROANOKE	99.2	99.0	0.1	0.2	0.0	0.1	0.2	0.2	6.9	7.1	7.4	7.0	4.8	23.3	26.1	13.9	3.7	74.1	40.0	48.8	51.2
61563	SAINT DAVID	100.0	100.0	0.0	0.0	0.0	0.0	0.0	0.0	0.0	0.0	0.0	0.0	0.0	0.0	76.9	23.1	0.0	100.0	59.2	38.5	61.5
61565	SPARLAND	98.2	97.8	0.7	0.8	0.2	0.3	1.3	1.9	5.3	5.8	6.4	6.7	4.4	25.5	32.8	11.8	1.2	78.3	42.0	51.6	48.4
61567	TOPEKA	98.7	98.4	0.1	0.1	0.1	0.1	0.5	0.7	5.3	6.0	6.3	6.6	5.0	25.1	32.4	11.7	1.6	78.2	42.1	51.4	48.6
61568	TREMONT	99.1	98.9	0.1	0.2	0.2	0.3	0.7	1.1	6.4	6.7	7.2	6.9	5.4	24.2	29.6	11.4	2.0	75.4	39.6	49.6	50.4
61569	TRIVOLI	97.0	95.4	0.9	1.7	0.2	0.2	1.0	1.6	4.8	5.4	6.2	6.6	4.6	24.1	31.5	14.9	1.9	79.5	43.8	51.1	48.9
61570	WASHBURN	97.4	96.5	0.2	0.3	0.2	0.3	0.9	1.3	6.1	6.1	6.5	7.3	5.6	26.5	28.4	11.3	2.1	76.8	38.8	51.3	48.7
61571	WASHINGTON	98.2	97.6	0.3	0.4	0.4	0.6	0.7	1.0	6.3	6.4	6.7	6.6	5.1	26.1	28.0	12.7	2.1	76.5	39.7	48.6	51.4
61572	YATES CITY	98.9	98.6	0.3	0.3	0.0	0.0	0.4	0.6	5.7	6.1	6.6	6.4	4.4	26.1	28.0	14.8	2.1	77.5	41.8	51.1	48.9
61602	PEORIA	48.4	39.8	40.1	45.5	1.9	2.2	9.7	13.0	6.2	5.8	5.1	6.5	8.3	30.4	24.1	11.5	2.1	79.7	36.4	54.8	45.2
61603	PEORIA	61.0	54.1	32.2	37.4	1.0	1.2	4.7	6.2	8.5	7.7	7.1	8.1	7.4	28.1	23.0	8.4	1.6	71.7	32.6	48.7	51.3
61604	PEORIA	76.8	71.1	18.9	23.4	1.2	1.5	1.7	2.4	7.2	6.8	6.5	6.4	6.1	25.3	25.1	13.1	3.5	75.7	38.7	47.0	53.0
61605	PEORIA	37.7	31.7	57.6	62.8	0.2	0.3	3.2	4.0	10.2	9.6	8.2	8.3	7.3	22.3	21.5	10.8	1.8	67.1	30.1	46.3	53.7
61606	PEORIA	71.5	65.5	21.3	25.2	2.9	3.7	2.3	3.3	5.2	4.0	3.7	13.4	29.8	21.5	16.1	5.4	0.8	84.7	24.0	49.7	50.3
61607	PEORIA	97.7	96.7	0.6	0.9	0.5	0.7	1.0	1.6	5.4	5.7	6.1	6.2	4.7	24.9	30.6	14.5	1.9	78.9	42.8	48.7	51.3
61610	CREVE COEUR	97.2	96.3	0.4	0.5	0.2	0.3	1.9	2.8	6.8	6.6	6.4	6.5	5.8	28.1	26.4	11.8	1.5	76.2	37.3	49.2	50.8
61611	EAST PEORIA	97.5	96.7	0.4	0.6	0.7	0.9	1.3	1.9	5.5	5.6	5.9	6.0	5.1	24.7	30.3	14.6	2.4	79.4	43.1	48.9	51.1
61614	PEORIA	87.9	83.6	6.2	8.4	4.2	5.7	1.3	2.0	5.2	4.9	5.1	5.2	6.1	25.0	27.2	16.7	4.7	81.6	43.9	47.2	52.8
61615	PEORIA	83.9	79.5	10.3	12.7	3.4	4.6	1.6	2.4	6.7	6.1	6.0	6.2	6.6	26.4	28.5	11.6	1.9	77.0	39.1	48.4	51.6
61616	PEORIA HEIGHTS	93.0	90.3	3.5	4.8	1.0	1.4	1.9	2.8	5.8	5.7	5.5	5.5	5.5	28.9	27.0	13.4	2.7	79.7	39.9	47.7	52.3
61625	PEORIA	88.7	84.4	5.7	7.7	2.8	3.8	2.8	4.2	1.0	0.8	1.0	47.0	41.2	4.4	3.5	1.0	0.1	96.5	20.0	47.5	52.5
61635	PEORIA	98.9	96.7	0.0	0.5	0.0	0.5	1.1	1.1	5.5	6.6	6.6	7.1	4.4	24.6	31.1	12.0	2.2	77.0	42.0	50.3	49.7
61701	BLOOMINGTON	84.8	81.5	9.9	11.5	1.5	2.0	3.7	5.3	6.4	5.7	5.4	8.1	10.4	28.7	22.3	10.4	2.7	79.1	34.2	48.1	51.9
61704	BLOOMINGTON	85.3	82.4	6.7	7.6	5.0	6.3	2.9	3.8	8.1	7.8	7.8	7.1	6.7	30.4	25.6	5.9	0.7	71.8	33.1	49.4	50.6
61705	BLOOMINGTON	96.0	93.3	1.4	2.7	0.9	1.6	2.8	3.8	7.4	7.9	8.5	7.5	4.5	24.6	30.8	8.1	0.7	71.4	38.4	49.7	50.3
61720	ANCHOR	98.6	98.1	0.3	0.3	0.0	0.0	0.0	0.3	4.9	5.4	6.0	7.0	7.0	22.5	33.6	11.9	1.6	79.4	42.5	47.2	52.8
61721	ARMINGTON	99.1	98.8	0.3	0.4	0.3	0.3	1.2	1.8	6.4	7.0	7.7	7.9	4.2	21.5	31.4	12.6	1.3	74.1	41.3	52.9	47.1
61722	ARROWSMITH	97.5	96.9	0.6	0.7	0.1	0.3	0.6	1.0	6.8	7.4	7.5	6.6	4.7	25.6	30.0	9.4	2.0	73.9	39.6	49.2	50.8
61723	ATLANTA	98.6	98.2	0.6	0.8	0.2	0.2	0.6	0.8	5.7	5.8	6.0	8.6	8.0	25.4	26.8	11.7	1.9	78.7	37.2	48.4	51.6
61724	BELLFLOWER	96.4	95.4	2.4	3.0	0.2	0.1	0.2	0.3	5.1	5.4	5.8	6.7	6.1	25.8	31.3	11.8	2.0	79.7	41.4	50.7	49.3
61725	CARLOCK	98.4	97.8	0.3	0.3	0.8	1.1	0.5	1.0	5.2	5.9	6.9	8.0	4.2	24.9	35.3	8.2	1.4	77.0	42.1	50.9	49.1
61726	CHENOA	97.8	97.0	0.3	0.4	0.3	0.4	2.1	3.1	7.1	7.0	7.1	6.9	5.8	23.5	26.9	12.7	3.2	74.6	39.2	49.5	50.5
61727	CLINTON	97.2	96.4	0.7	0.8	0.4	0.5	1.7	2.5	6.4	6.6	6.3	6.4	5.8	25.8	26.8	13.2	2.7	76.8	39.5	48.1	51.9
61728	COLFAX	98.8	98.4	0.1	0.2	0.1	0.1	1.2	1.8	5.6	5.6	5.8	6.9	7.6	24.3	27.4	13.1	3.8	78.2	40.8	49.2	50.8
61729	CONGERVILLE	98.4	97.8	0.0	0.0	0.4	0.5	0.2	0.3	6.4	7.1	7.5	6.9	3.8	25.6	32.6	9.0	1.1	74.6	39.5	51.4	48.6
61730	COOKSVILLE	98.4	97.8	0.2	0.4	0.0	0.0	0.2	0.2	5.0	5.5	6.1	7.0	6.6	22.8	34.0	11.4	1.5	78.7	42.4	46.9	53.1
61731	CROPSEY	97.9	97.8	0.4	0.7	0.4	0.4	1.3	1.9	5.9	6.3	6.7	7.4	4.4	23.0	32.2	12.6	1.5	76.3	41.9	51.1	48.9
	ILLINOIS	73.5	70.6	15.1	15.3	3.4	4.4	12.3	15.7	7.1	6.9	6.8	7.1	6.9	27.5	25.4	10.3	1.9	75.0	36.1	49.1	50.9
	UNITED STATES	75.1	72.0	12.3	12.7	3.8	4.6	12.5	15.7	6.8	6.7	6.6	7.1	6.9	27.0	26.0	10.9	1.9	75.7	36.9	49.2	50.8

#	POST OFFICE NAME	2009 Per Capita Income	2009 HH Income Base	2009 Household Income Distribution (%): Less than $25,000	$25,000 to $49,999	$50,000 to $99,999	$100,000 to $149,999	$150,000 or More	Median Household Income: 2009	2014	2009 National Centile	2009 State Centile	2009 Home Value Base	2009 Home Value Distribution (%): Less than $50,000	$50,000 to $89,999	$90,000 to $174,999	$175,000 to $399,999	$400,000 or More	2009 Median Home Value
61460	MEDIA	19510	172	17.4	43.0	32.0	3.5	4.1	39286	41395	31	14	131	26.0	26.0	45.8	1.5	0.8	87727
61462	MONMOUTH	21380	4315	25.7	28.9	37.6	5.4	2.3	44545	47917	47	28	3094	23.2	35.1	33.7	7.3	0.7	78820
61465	NEW WINDSOR	22778	467	18.2	29.8	45.8	5.4	0.9	52471	56461	67	50	375	12.3	36.3	38.7	8.5	4.3	91719
61466	NORTH HENDERSON	22974	134	15.7	30.6	44.8	6.7	2.2	53406	56733	69	52	114	15.8	41.2	31.6	7.0	4.4	82000
61467	ONEIDA	23289	464	17.2	29.5	45.9	5.2	2.2	52714	56038	67	50	363	13.2	31.4	47.4	6.3	1.7	96724
61469	OQUAWKA	19896	1059	28.8	33.3	31.6	5.1	1.1	38215	41351	27	12	829	26.3	34.5	29.0	9.5	0.7	77088
61470	PRAIRIE CITY	20086	205	22.0	25.9	42.9	5.4	3.9	51205	53430	64	47	173	49.7	20.8	22.0	2.9	4.6	50417
61471	RARITAN	19458	118	17.8	42.4	32.2	4.2	3.4	38970	40740	30	14	90	25.6	25.6	46.7	1.1	1.1	88571
61472	RIO	24298	239	7.5	35.1	51.5	3.8	2.1	54731	58304	71	55	194	9.8	17.5	61.3	9.8	1.5	114151
61473	ROSEVILLE	21324	680	25.3	29.4	37.6	5.4	2.2	43878	47753	45	26	525	21.7	35.2	33.3	9.0	0.8	82396
61474	SAINT AUGUSTINE	18901	128	20.3	39.1	37.5	3.1	0.0	43162	46013	43	24	104	25.0	43.3	25.0	6.7	0.0	70000
61475	SCIOTA	21848	89	15.7	33.7	40.4	6.7	3.4	50459	51862	62	44	64	17.2	23.4	35.9	18.8	4.7	105556
61476	SEATON	21844	275	24.0	34.2	33.1	5.1	3.6	43698	46663	44	26	211	20.9	28.0	41.2	10.0	0.0	92083
61477	SMITHFIELD	21646	249	21.3	34.9	36.9	4.0	2.8	42829	46865	42	23	201	22.9	22.9	35.3	16.4	2.5	95313
61478	SMITHSHIRE	20982	128	24.2	31.3	35.2	6.3	3.1	42718	47384	42	23	89	18.0	23.6	43.8	11.2	3.4	105208
61479	SPEER	20443	186	14.5	38.2	39.8	7.0	0.5	48184	47983	57	39	139	2.9	28.1	44.6	20.9	3.6	115500
61480	STRONGHURST	20473	433	21.9	31.2	40.6	4.8	1.4	46938	47513	54	35	344	25.3	34.9	30.8	8.1	0.9	76786
61482	TABLE GROVE	22530	248	21.4	25.4	46.0	4.4	2.8	52351	54138	67	49	207	36.2	31.9	27.5	4.3	0.0	63864
61483	TOULON	20821	911	24.1	34.2	35.1	4.9	1.5	42440	44504	41	22	683	15.8	35.3	36.6	10.8	1.5	88810
61484	VERMONT	16027	370	35.1	34.6	27.0	2.4	0.8	36076	38568	21	8	305	48.5	23.6	23.0	4.3	0.7	51875
61485	VICTORIA	17449	221	21.3	42.1	31.7	4.1	0.9	37954	39135	27	12	173	16.8	25.4	35.8	12.7	9.2	108203
61486	VIOLA	22263	650	18.6	30.2	43.1	6.5	1.7	51295	53888	64	47	530	11.3	35.8	37.9	14.0	0.9	94167
61488	WATAGA	24332	451	17.1	29.0	45.9	3.8	4.2	52461	54969	67	50	366	14.2	31.7	42.9	8.2	3.0	95172
61489	WILLIAMSFIELD	22170	352	17.3	29.3	46.3	5.1	2.0	52820	55521	68	50	289	15.9	33.6	37.0	9.7	3.8	90750
61490	WOODHULL	20782	465	27.5	32.3	36.1	2.8	1.3	43879	46472	45	26	351	14.2	31.1	44.4	9.4	0.9	93837
61491	WYOMING	20553	691	30.0	30.8	34.3	3.9	1.0	38433	41417	28	12	536	15.5	27.1	50.4	6.2	0.9	95797
61501	ASTORIA	18206	846	29.7	34.5	32.7	2.8	0.2	36364	38651	22	8	657	38.1	36.2	20.5	4.1	1.1	60789
61516	BENSON	24220	295	11.5	29.5	48.8	9.2	1.0	58628	62543	76	62	246	6.5	23.6	43.5	26.0	0.4	117188
61517	BRIMFIELD	28458	1217	9.6	20.2	50.3	13.8	6.1	70362	72390	87	81	1035	6.2	14.1	41.8	34.3	3.6	147194
61519	BRYANT	26914	6	33.3	0.0	66.7	0.0	0.0	60000	60000	77	64	5	0.0	40.0	60.0	0.0	0.0	112500
61520	CANTON	21547	7055	28.5	30.1	33.4	5.3	2.7	41865	45317	39	21	5106	14.1	34.0	41.3	9.9	0.7	92474
61523	CHILLICOTHE	27862	4443	14.6	26.0	43.0	12.3	4.1	60168	62240	78	64	3534	9.4	19.2	52.4	16.8	2.2	115510
61524	DUNFERMLINE	30445	11	27.3	9.1	45.5	18.2	0.0	61704	66056	80	67	9	22.2	44.4	33.3	0.0	0.0	75000
61525	DUNLAP	36621	2782	9.2	17.1	44.0	16.0	13.6	77988	78270	91	90	2343	8.4	7.7	27.2	43.4	13.2	196597
61526	EDELSTEIN	26322	386	8.5	21.2	44.0	20.7	5.4	70577	70475	87	81	338	10.7	14.8	34.9	35.8	3.8	146053
61528	EDWARDS	33883	754	10.9	20.4	40.3	17.1	11.3	73397	72870	89	84	610	7.0	8.0	27.9	43.6	13.4	198370
61529	ELMWOOD	26629	1144	13.6	24.9	50.4	8.5	2.5	62032	63425	80	68	919	6.6	24.7	53.3	13.7	1.6	111480
61530	EUREKA	25337	2302	16.5	25.9	45.8	6.9	4.9	57216	61057	74	59	1687	5.4	12.0	58.1	22.2	2.3	137590
61531	FARMINGTON	22892	1374	22.7	30.7	38.9	6.1	1.5	46893	48537	54	34	1098	14.7	25.5	52.5	6.6	0.8	99000
61532	FOREST CITY	20389	223	15.2	38.1	39.5	4.9	2.2	47635	49285	56	37	179	28.5	19.6	38.5	12.8	0.6	95000
61533	GLASFORD	24836	858	14.0	31.4	41.8	10.4	2.4	57416	60794	75	59	706	8.5	23.9	47.5	19.0	1.1	115164
61534	GREEN VALLEY	24634	689	12.3	21.5	52.0	12.0	2.2	66425	68467	84	76	582	5.8	16.3	50.3	25.9	1.5	125291
61535	GROVELAND	34585	641	6.6	19.2	49.8	14.0	10.5	75938	77087	90	88	602	8.6	5.1	26.1	55.6	4.5	193598
61536	HANNA CITY	28120	1272	11.9	24.6	47.1	10.8	5.6	66886	67635	85	77	1075	6.3	17.8	43.3	28.7	4.0	134864
61537	HENRY	23681	1264	20.3	29.1	41.2	7.0	2.5	50687	52797	63	45	981	11.0	28.7	49.3	9.2	1.7	102566
61540	LACON	24002	1108	14.0	31.7	46.2	6.1	2.0	54068	56063	70	54	889	8.9	23.7	52.8	14.2	0.4	114101
61542	LEWISTOWN	21019	1628	26.0	30.6	37.2	4.3	1.9	43836	46320	45	26	1186	19.2	30.9	40.0	9.4	0.5	89765
61543	LIVERPOOL	24199	70	24.3	25.7	40.0	8.6	1.4	50000	50000	61	44	57	17.5	38.6	33.3	10.5	0.0	81250
61544	LONDON MILLS	20588	281	22.8	32.7	36.7	3.9	3.9	45626	47535	50	31	237	26.2	31.6	26.6	10.1	5.5	82292
61545	LOWPOINT	23603	317	14.8	19.2	56.8	7.9	1.3	63863	66160	82	72	269	9.3	16.7	36.4	34.2	3.3	143750
61546	MANITO	26297	1831	14.9	26.0	47.1	7.7	4.3	58653	61473	76	62	1513	8.6	24.1	55.9	10.4	1.0	110101
61547	MAPLETON	29046	1502	6.7	17.2	57.5	12.8	5.9	75618	75669	90	86	1349	3.1	9.1	46.2	39.5	2.1	160596
61548	METAMORA	29344	4044	10.0	15.7	53.0	14.0	7.3	74507	76549	89	85	3509	5.4	5.5	39.0	43.4	6.7	175105
61550	MORTON	32448	7110	11.4	20.1	46.7	13.6	8.2	67491	68301	85	78	5516	6.5	3.4	40.0	45.7	4.4	175242
61552	MOSSVILLE	49826	70	5.7	14.3	41.4	15.7	22.9	85824	87035	94	94	59	3.4	5.1	23.7	44.1	23.7	225000
61554	PEKIN	25191	18132	20.8	25.3	42.8	7.1	3.9	52706	54630	67	50	12914	6.5	25.2	53.4	14.1	0.9	108642
61559	PRINCEVILLE	26881	1307	13.5	24.1	47.4	9.8	5.1	62098	62704	80	68	1037	5.9	22.9	44.7	22.5	4.1	130669
61560	PUTNAM	27178	365	6.8	33.2	48.8	7.9	3.3	58448	60325	76	62	313	2.6	9.3	38.0	45.0	5.1	175338
61561	ROANOKE	25297	1174	15.4	25.0	47.2	8.1	4.3	60352	64743	78	65	977	5.2	15.1	50.5	27.0	2.1	133149
61563	SAINT DAVID	28077	5	0.0	0.0	100.0	0.0	0.0	69801	66333	87	80	4	0.0	0.0	50.0	50.0	0.0	187500
61565	SPARLAND	22145	656	16.5	31.7	39.0	11.0	1.8	52762	54816	67	50	537	7.4	18.2	47.5	24.2	2.6	122801
61567	TOPEKA	21928	380	19.5	33.2	38.7	7.1	1.6	47857	49690	56	37	301	30.6	17.9	37.2	14.0	0.3	91957
61568	TREMONT	27541	1670	8.7	20.5	55.8	11.3	3.7	72961	74561	88	83	1353	1.3	7.6	50.4	37.5	3.2	155391
61569	TRIVOLI	29482	473	8.5	20.3	56.9	10.6	3.8	73265	75432	88	84	403	4.5	13.9	47.1	27.8	6.7	138657
61570	WASHBURN	23731	740	13.4	27.8	47.7	8.5	2.6	57813	60616	75	60	591	9.5	21.5	48.7	18.8	1.5	113832
61571	WASHINGTON	28567	8663	14.3	20.6	48.1	12.1	4.9	62647	64416	81	69	6614	3.6	11.0	56.1	27.2	2.1	136643
61572	YATES CITY	22572	486	18.5	34.6	38.7	6.4	1.9	47762	49817	56	37	401	13.0	29.2	48.1	7.7	2.0	96848
61602	PEORIA	17807	326	54.0	26.1	17.8	1.5	0.6	22714	23062	2	1	96	36.5	34.4	20.8	4.2	4.2	60833
61603	PEORIA	18289	6782	33.2	30.1	31.3	3.9	1.5	38065	41437	27	12	3779	23.0	42.9	32.0	1.1	1.0	73058
61604	PEORIA	22828	13005	25.0	30.0	36.6	5.7	2.7	45603	47984	50	31	8923	10.9	28.3	52.5	8.0	0.2	99127
61605	PEORIA	11682	6646	55.1	28.0	15.0	1.4	0.6	21807	22596	2	1	2942	55.7	33.5	9.1	1.1	0.5	46877
61606	PEORIA	19552	2678	39.5	27.0	24.9	4.9	3.6	34173	35675	16	5	1098	10.5	27.6	43.4	16.0	2.5	105822
61607	PEORIA	27212	4194	13.2	27.5	48.3	7.8	3.2	58148	60426	75	61	3401	5.4	23.1	57.6	13.3	0.6	114164
61610	CREVE COEUR	22562	2249	19.5	29.7	45.3	4.4	1.0	50446	51832	62	44	1678	11.7	43.1	42.7	2.4	0.0	85846
61611	EAST PEORIA	27243	10620	17.9	22.9	46.7	8.8	3.7	57803	60949	75	60	8225	7.8	13.8	51.2	25.5	1.7	132473
61614	PEORIA	34979	12365	14.4	24.3	43.2	10.1	8.0	62085	63430	80	68	7910	2.0	9.1	53.5	31.5	4.0	149568
61615	PEORIA	33856	9690	16.4	22.2	39.5	13.1	8.8	62868	64285	81	70	6771	8.8	12.0	37.8	33.7	7.6	148908
61616	PEORIA HEIGHTS	25544	2697	21.6	35.3	36.9	3.7	2.4	43422	46400	44	25	1708	14.6	42.9	36.2	3.6	2.6	83756
61625	PEORIA	14063	5	0.0	0.0	60.0	40.0	0.0	91155	91155	95	96	3	0.0	0.0	100.0	0.0	0.0	137500
61635	PEORIA	27084	65	13.8	15.4	47.7	16.9	6.2	71215	71161	87	82	56	10.7	5.4	35.7	46.4	1.8	170833
61701	BLOOMINGTON	26185	16399	25.5	26.5	39.2	5.7	3.1	48185	49683	57	39	8964	9.9	19.1	54.7	14.9	1.4	116087
61704	BLOOMINGTON	36670	13395	9.9	17.8	40.1	16.8	15.4	78737	80124	91	91	9826	11.9	2.6	27.5	51.8	6.4	197642
61705	BLOOMINGTON	34698	3651	5.9	10.6	50.3	18.7	14.5	84264	84882	94	94	3175	6.0	1.9	29.6	52.4	10.1	194233
61720	ANCHOR	22513	124	12.1	25.0	52.4	7.3	3.2	63655	63460	82	71	94	11.7	21.3	52.1	14.9	0.0	120313
61721	ARMINGTON	23989	245	11.4	31.8	44.9	9.8	2.0	55629	57981	72	57	204	12.7	25.0	35.3	17.2	9.8	115385
61722	ARROWSMITH	26503	266	7.9	18.4	60.9	9.4	3.4	74571	74327	89	85	209	5.3	20.6	49.3	21.1	3.8	120380
61723	ATLANTA	26797	944	18.2	25.8	41.3	11.2	3.4	56721	60037	74	59	731	8.9	16.0	59.5	14.2	1.4	116690
61724	BELLFLOWER	24632	268	16.4	20.9	53.0	7.5	2.2	59322	62233	77	63	207	22.7	30.4	38.2	8.7	0.0	87174
61725	CARLOCK	29645	451	8.0	18.2	58.1	10.9	4.9	75123	75340	89	86	384	0.5	11.2	43.0	39.8	5.5	165426
61726	CHENOA	25130	1110	15.9	24.0	48.6	8.1	3.4	59210	61540	76	63	847	13.0	27.7	44.4	12.9	2.0	103446
61727	CLINTON	25867	4171	23.2	25.3	37.7	8.7	5.1	51871	53955	66	48	2980	11.0	21.3	49.2	16.0	2.4	112158
61728	COLFAX	24284	613	17.0	23.7	51.2	6.5	1.6	59897	61742	77	64	483	15.3	29.0	46.8	7.7	1.2	98594
61729	CONGERVILLE	28962	453	4.2	18.8	57.0	13.2	6.8	75155	75914	89	86	390	1.5	3.1	36.7	51.3	7.4	197368
61730	COOKSVILLE	28862	194	11.9	25.3	52.1	7.7	3.1	63678	63945	82	71	147	9.5	21.8	53.1	15.6	0.0	121635
61731	CROPSEY	23157	94	20.2	22.3	46.8	7.4	3.2	56578	59346	73	58	68	13.2	25.0	39.7	13.2	8.8	106250
	ILLINOIS	28587		18.2	22.2	39.3	12.1	8.2	60823	63631				6.3	10.0	30.9	40.6	12.3	185324
	UNITED STATES	27277		20.9	24.4	35.3	11.7	7.6	54719	56938				9.3	13.1	31.6	32.6	13.5	162279

ZIP CODE #	POST OFFICE NAME	FINANCIAL SERVICES				THE HOME						ENTERTAINMENT						PERSONAL			
						Home Improvements		Furnishings													
		Auto Loan	Home Loan	Investments	Retirement Plans	Home Repair	Lawn & Garden	Computers & Hardware-Personal	Major Appliances	TV, Radio, Sound Equipment	Furniture	Dine out/ Carry out	Sports Equipment	Fees & Tickets	Toys & Games	Travel	Cable TV	Apparel & Services	Auto Repairs	Health Insurance	Pets & Supplies
61460	MEDIA	90	62	98	62	65	95	69	85	71	56	71	70	50	70	68	78	46	80	90	105
61462	MONMOUTH	78	69	68	70	68	80	75	76	77	69	76	58	69	77	71	81	52	76	83	91
61465	NEW WINDSOR	76	82	79	81	82	91	74	82	79	72	78	59	78	78	79	84	54	79	92	95
61466	NORTH HENDERSON	89	80	80	83	82	95	79	90	82	71	80	68	73	83	79	86	55	83	92	104
61467	ONEIDA	95	79	92	81	81	101	81	94	84	71	82	74	70	84	81	89	55	87	98	112
61469	OQUAWKA	83	59	85	57	61	85	62	78	69	56	67	60	49	68	61	75	44	72	83	93
61470	PRAIRIE CITY	100	69	109	68	72	105	76	95	79	62	78	78	56	78	76	86	51	88	100	116
61471	RARITAN	90	62	98	62	65	95	68	85	71	55	70	70	50	70	68	78	46	79	90	105
61472	RIO	105	77	111	77	80	111	83	101	86	69	85	82	64	85	82	93	56	94	106	123
61473	ROSEVILLE	81	68	85	67	70	89	69	81	74	62	73	61	62	73	70	80	49	77	89	96
61474	SAINT AUGUSTINE	84	59	73	58	60	81	63	74	69	59	67	58	49	71	58	75	45	70	78	90
61475	SCIOTA	100	77	112	77	80	107	81	97	83	69	82	79	65	81	82	89	54	91	101	118
61476	SEATON	98	68	106	68	71	103	75	93	78	61	77	76	55	76	74	85	50	86	98	114
61477	SMITHFIELD	88	69	90	70	71	94	72	86	75	62	74	69	59	75	72	81	49	80	90	104
61478	SMITHSHIRE	94	64	102	64	67	98	71	89	74	58	73	73	52	73	71	81	48	83	94	109
61479	SPEER	96	68	102	69	71	101	75	91	78	62	77	75	57	77	74	84	50	85	96	112
61480	STRONGHURST	87	69	84	69	71	90	70	84	75	64	74	63	60	76	69	81	49	77	87	99
61482	TABLE GROVE	98	68	108	68	71	104	75	93	78	61	77	77	55	77	75	85	50	87	99	115
61483	TOULON	82	64	81	64	64	86	69	79	73	60	71	63	58	72	67	78	47	76	86	96
61484	VERMONT	69	49	69	48	51	72	54	66	60	48	58	50	43	59	52	66	38	62	72	78
61485	VICTORIA	83	58	92	58	61	88	64	80	67	53	66	65	48	65	64	73	43	74	84	97
61486	VIOLA	85	80	74	83	78	91	80	85	82	73	81	66	76	83	79	85	55	82	90	101
61488	WATAGA	92	84	83	85	80	97	86	89	87	78	87	72	80	88	84	91	59	89	97	109
61489	WILLIAMSFIELD	89	78	83	80	80	95	78	89	80	69	79	68	70	81	78	85	54	82	92	105
61490	WOODHULL	83	60	83	59	63	87	65	80	72	58	70	61	53	71	64	79	46	75	87	95
61491	WYOMING	77	59	75	59	61	81	62	75	68	56	66	56	52	68	61	74	44	70	81	88
61501	ASTORIA	71	54	69	54	56	75	58	70	63	52	61	52	48	63	56	69	41	65	75	81
61516	BENSON	95	87	87	91	89	102	85	96	88	78	86	73	80	89	86	92	59	89	99	112
61517	BRIMFIELD	110	116	112	120	117	122	106	115	106	104	106	88	109	108	112	108	74	108	115	134
61519	BRYANT	80	57	82	56	60	81	59	75	65	55	64	56	47	65	58	72	42	69	78	89
61520	CANTON	78	68	72	69	68	82	72	77	76	67	74	58	66	75	69	80	51	75	84	91
61523	CHILLICOTHE	95	102	88	104	99	106	96	98	97	93	96	75	100	98	98	99	67	96	104	116
61524	DUNFERMLINE	90	82	81	85	84	97	81	91	83	73	82	69	75	85	81	88	56	84	94	106
61525	DUNLAP	129	152	145	155	151	145	135	139	131	140	133	106	148	133	146	130	94	134	135	161
61526	EDELSTEIN	112	118	109	121	116	123	108	116	108	106	108	90	111	110	113	109	75	110	116	136
61528	EDWARDS	124	139	135	144	139	130	127	128	123	133	124	99	137	125	134	120	89	125	121	149
61529	ELMWOOD	91	98	82	99	92	101	92	93	94	89	93	73	96	95	94	96	65	93	100	111
61530	EUREKA	94	96	87	95	94	98	92	94	95	92	95	69	94	95	92	98	65	94	101	110
61531	FARMINGTON	84	78	86	76	79	95	74	86	81	71	79	63	72	79	77	87	54	82	95	100
61532	FOREST CITY	86	78	78	81	80	93	77	87	80	70	78	66	71	81	77	84	53	81	90	102
61533	GLASFORD	89	94	77	97	89	96	90	90	90	87	90	71	93	92	90	92	62	90	95	108
61534	GREEN VALLEY	95	100	84	103	96	103	95	96	95	92	94	76	97	97	96	96	65	95	100	115
61535	GROVELAND	120	144	149	147	148	140	124	133	120	132	121	98	139	119	138	119	86	126	128	152
61536	HANNA CITY	108	108	103	112	109	118	102	112	103	97	102	85	100	105	105	106	70	104	113	130
61537	HENRY	88	78	88	78	78	97	79	89	84	72	82	67	73	83	79	89	56	85	98	105
61540	LACON	77	85	85	84	86	94	76	85	81	75	81	60	82	80	83	86	56	82	95	97
61542	LEWISTOWN	77	63	78	62	64	82	67	77	73	61	71	57	59	71	66	79	48	74	85	90
61543	LIVERPOOL	91	81	84	84	83	98	81	92	83	72	82	70	73	85	81	88	56	85	95	107
61544	LONDON MILLS	97	69	100	67	72	99	72	91	79	66	78	69	57	79	71	87	51	84	95	108
61545	LOWPOINT	102	87	97	90	89	109	88	102	91	78	90	79	77	92	88	97	60	94	106	120
61546	MANITO	102	95	90	98	95	110	94	103	96	85	95	79	88	98	93	101	65	97	108	121
61547	MAPLETON	109	130	114	131	125	122	113	116	110	115	111	90	125	113	121	109	79	112	113	135
61548	METAMORA	110	126	115	127	124	124	111	117	110	111	110	90	120	112	119	111	78	112	117	136
61550	MORTON	112	117	117	118	119	123	111	117	112	111	111	87	114	111	115	114	77	114	121	136
61552	MOSSVILLE	154	191	196	197	196	181	163	172	156	174	158	128	186	155	183	153	113	163	163	197
61554	PEKIN	88	85	78	86	82	92	87	87	89	83	88	67	85	89	85	92	61	88	94	104
61559	PRINCEVILLE	105	99	99	103	101	114	96	108	98	88	97	81	91	100	97	103	66	100	110	125
61560	PUTNAM	107	84	135	83	92	113	85	108	89	78	88	80	72	85	91	95	58	100	107	126
61561	ROANOKE	98	101	103	101	100	113	93	103	98	90	97	77	96	98	99	103	67	99	111	120
61563	SAINT DAVID	95	112	116	112	117	118	97	107	100	103	100	74	110	97	110	104	70	103	116	122
61565	SPARLAND	96	81	92	84	84	103	83	96	85	73	84	74	72	86	82	91	57	89	99	113
61567	TOPEKA	86	79	78	82	80	93	77	87	80	70	78	66	71	81	77	85	54	81	90	102
61568	TREMONT	105	112	101	115	110	114	104	109	104	104	104	84	108	106	108	105	72	105	110	128
61569	TRIVOLI	101	117	104	119	114	117	103	108	103	103	104	83	113	105	111	105	73	105	111	127
61570	WASHBURN	97	85	93	86	83	104	87	95	89	78	88	77	79	89	86	93	59	92	101	115
61571	WASHINGTON	96	107	96	108	104	106	99	100	99	99	99	77	106	100	103	100	70	99	104	118
61572	YATES CITY	84	76	76	80	78	90	75	85	78	68	76	64	69	79	75	82	52	79	88	99
61602	PEORIA	42	33	37	34	33	40	44	40	48	41	47	30	39	44	40	51	33	45	51	50
61603	PEORIA	65	58	52	60	55	64	66	62	69	62	68	48	62	68	60	72	47	66	70	76
61604	PEORIA	78	73	68	73	70	80	76	76	79	73	78	58	73	79	73	82	54	78	84	91
61605	PEORIA	44	33	33	34	32	40	41	39	47	40	45	29	37	45	36	50	31	43	48	49
61606	PEORIA	69	53	50	56	52	56	78	60	73	67	73	51	64	73	62	72	51	69	64	75
61607	PEORIA	88	99	89	99	96	104	90	94	93	88	93	69	97	93	95	97	64	92	104	110
61610	CREVE COEUR	76	78	61	79	71	81	77	74	78	73	78	59	78	80	75	80	54	76	83	91
61611	EAST PEORIA	89	94	91	94	94	101	89	94	91	87	90	69	92	90	92	94	63	92	101	109
61614	PEORIA	102	106	106	108	107	108	107	105	107	107	107	79	110	105	109	109	75	107	112	124
61615	PEORIA	110	112	108	115	111	108	114	109	111	114	113	85	116	112	113	110	79	111	109	129
61616	PEORIA HEIGHTS	77	75	66	77	72	80	78	76	79	75	79	59	77	80	76	81	55	78	84	91
61625	PEORIA	140	90	87	99	88	98	166	113	149	132	149	103	121	150	116	145	105	138	119	144
61635	PEORIA	105	118	102	122	115	116	105	110	104	106	104	86	112	106	111	104	73	105	108	129
61701	BLOOMINGTON	79	74	67	76	71	75	83	75	83	79	83	60	79	83	77	84	58	80	81	91
61704	BLOOMINGTON	139	142	127	147	137	125	139	131	133	146	135	108	143	140	136	127	97	132	119	153
61705	BLOOMINGTON	138	163	151	165	161	147	142	145	135	150	137	113	156	139	151	131	98	138	133	167
61720	ANCHOR	102	93	92	97	95	109	91	103	94	83	93	78	84	96	91	100	63	95	106	120
61721	ARMINGTON	118	81	129	81	85	124	90	112	94	73	93	92	66	92	90	102	60	104	118	138
61722	ARROWSMITH	107	119	104	122	115	118	107	112	105	106	106	87	113	108	112	106	74	107	111	131
61723	ATLANTA	91	93	83	94	91	102	89	94	92	84	91	71	89	93	90	96	63	91	103	110
61724	BELLFLOWER	98	90	88	93	91	105	88	99	91	80	89	75	81	93	88	96	61	92	102	115
61725	CARLOCK	104	121	110	124	119	117	106	111	104	108	104	85	115	105	114	103	74	106	108	130
61726	CHENOA	99	89	91	90	86	105	91	96	93	83	92	78	84	94	90	97	63	95	105	118
61727	CLINTON	92	85	81	86	83	96	88	91	91	82	89	70	83	91	85	95	61	90	98	108
61728	COLFAX	90	85	79	87	81	96	86	88	88	80	87	71	82	89	84	91	59	88	96	107
61729	CONGERVILLE	113	130	118	134	129	127	115	120	112	117	113	93	125	114	123	112	80	115	117	140
61730	COOKSVILLE	103	95	93	99	97	110	93	104	96	85	94	79	87	98	94	101	64	97	107	121
61731	CROPSEY	119	82	131	82	86	126	91	113	94	74	93	93	67	93	90	103	61	105	119	139
	ILLINOIS	106	108	105	108	107	106	109	106	108	107	109	83	110	108	108	108	77	108	107	125
	UNITED STATES	100	100	100	100	100	100	100	100	100	100	100	100	100	100	100	100	100	100	100	100

POPULATION CHANGE

#	POST OFFICE NAME	COUNTY FIPS CODE	POPULATION 2000	POPULATION 2009	POPULATION 2014	2000-2009 ANNUAL RATE % Rate	2000-2009 ANNUAL RATE State Centile	HOUSEHOLDS 2000	HOUSEHOLDS 2009	HOUSEHOLDS 2014	HOUSEHOLDS % Annual Rate 2000-2009	HOUSEHOLDS 2009 Average HH Size	FAMILIES 2000	FAMILIES 2009	FAMILIES % Annual Rate 2000-2009
61732	DANVERS	113	2105	2090	2105	-0.1	45	753	767	779	0.2	2.72	597	592	-0.1
61733	DEER CREEK	179	1190	1407	1503	1.8	91	436	527	566	2.1	2.67	340	402	1.8
61734	DELAVAN	179	2887	3083	3193	0.7	78	1078	1160	1206	0.8	2.65	831	877	0.6
61735	DEWITT	039	465	466	462	0.0	50	179	182	181	0.2	2.56	137	137	0.0
61736	DOWNS	113	1671	2389	2713	3.9	97	588	859	983	4.2	2.78	488	692	3.8
61737	ELLSWORTH	113	560	587	607	0.5	72	193	207	217	0.8	2.84	156	163	0.5
61738	EL PASO	203	3843	3959	4001	0.3	65	1395	1458	1481	0.5	2.60	1038	1062	0.2
61739	FAIRBURY	105	4840	4621	4503	-0.5	18	1815	1765	1724	-0.3	2.55	1276	1217	-0.5
61740	FLANAGAN	105	1578	1499	1457	-0.6	13	596	581	568	-0.3	2.40	413	396	-0.5
61741	FORREST	105	1811	1742	1691	-0.4	25	644	621	604	-0.4	2.81	494	470	-0.5
61742	GOODFIELD	203	906	1032	1091	1.4	88	306	352	374	1.5	2.93	255	289	1.4
61743	GRAYMONT	105	240	219	211	-1.0	3	88	81	79	-0.9	2.70	71	65	-0.9
61744	GRIDLEY	113	2147	2322	2429	0.9	81	801	884	932	1.1	2.60	595	623	0.5
61745	HEYWORTH	113	3717	3954	4094	0.7	78	1367	1478	1540	0.8	2.68	1078	1131	0.5
61747	HOPEDALE	179	1501	1576	1617	0.5	72	530	567	586	0.7	2.63	424	447	0.6
61748	HUDSON	113	2583	2968	3161	1.5	88	953	1130	1218	1.9	2.63	769	867	1.3
61749	KENNEY	039	797	794	783	0.0	50	331	335	333	0.1	2.37	244	243	0.0
61752	LE ROY	113	4049	4186	4279	0.4	69	1565	1651	1702	0.6	2.50	1143	1166	0.2
61753	LEXINGTON	113	2889	2869	2887	-0.1	45	1124	1138	1153	0.1	2.49	835	813	-0.3
61754	MC LEAN	113	1331	1456	1531	1.0	83	497	557	590	1.2	2.58	388	422	0.9
61755	MACKINAW	179	3933	4364	4577	1.1	85	1415	1601	1689	1.3	2.72	1128	1260	1.2
61756	MAROA	115	1968	1915	1862	-0.3	32	779	785	771	0.1	2.44	578	570	-0.2
61759	MINIER	179	1550	1625	1664	0.5	72	616	659	680	0.7	2.47	458	480	0.5
61760	MINONK	203	2620	2612	2597	0.0	50	1015	1020	1018	0.1	2.50	719	705	-0.2
61761	NORMAL	113	43730	49540	51828	1.4	88	14687	16952	17984	1.6	2.39	8015	9008	1.3
61764	PONTIAC	105	14678	14227	13979	-0.3	32	5193	5160	5077	-0.1	2.38	3423	3332	-0.3
61769	SAUNEMIN	105	669	643	622	-0.4	25	237	226	218	-0.5	2.85	189	177	-0.7
61770	SAYBROOK	113	1132	1249	1316	1.1	85	458	518	552	1.3	2.41	328	358	1.0
61771	SECOR	203	1006	1108	1151	1.0	83	351	393	410	1.2	2.82	285	314	1.1
61772	SHIRLEY	113	378	429	454	1.4	88	143	167	179	1.7	2.49	111	125	1.3
61773	SIBLEY	053	594	589	586	-0.1	45	221	220	219	0.0	2.68	172	169	-0.2
61774	STANFORD	113	1085	1121	1145	0.4	69	387	409	422	0.6	2.73	309	318	0.3
61775	STRAWN	105	242	241	238	0.0	50	87	88	88	0.1	2.74	71	71	0.0
61776	TOWANDA	113	1211	1279	1339	0.6	75	464	498	525	0.8	2.57	371	381	0.3
61777	WAPELLA	039	1004	1025	1018	0.2	61	391	408	407	0.5	2.47	289	295	0.2
61778	WAYNESVILLE	039	687	659	641	-0.4	25	271	265	259	-0.2	2.48	197	189	-0.4
61790	NORMAL	113	1932	1942	1935	0.1	56	576	575	576	0.0	2.99	261	222	-1.7
61801	URBANA	019	29235	30778	30907	0.6	75	11147	11563	11741	0.4	2.08	4516	4325	-0.5
61802	URBANA	019	16804	18591	19310	1.1	85	7257	8152	8531	1.3	2.20	4304	4639	0.8
61810	ALLERTON	183	372	382	382	0.3	65	142	147	148	0.4	2.60	113	115	0.2
61811	ALVIN	183	747	753	750	0.1	56	260	265	265	0.2	2.84	205	206	0.1
61812	ARMSTRONG	183	309	298	289	-0.4	25	123	120	117	-0.3	2.45	94	90	-0.5
61813	BEMENT	147	2066	1969	1928	-0.5	18	795	772	759	-0.3	2.46	566	539	-0.5
61814	BISMARCK	183	1100	1109	1103	0.1	56	414	422	422	0.2	2.62	332	334	0.1
61816	BROADLANDS	019	455	459	461	0.1	56	180	186	189	0.4	2.47	140	141	0.1
61817	CATLIN	183	2932	2950	2911	0.1	56	1085	1102	1091	0.2	2.65	821	819	0.0
61818	CERRO GORDO	147	2019	2063	2058	0.2	61	782	811	813	0.4	2.54	589	600	0.2
61820	CHAMPAIGN	019	33715	35380	35648	0.5	72	12673	13139	13331	0.4	2.08	3585	3462	-0.4
61821	CHAMPAIGN	019	30560	30196	30280	-0.1	45	13012	13239	13386	0.2	2.26	7923	7753	-0.2
61822	CHAMPAIGN	019	13723	20163	22716	4.2	97	5488	8096	9170	4.3	2.48	3928	5604	3.9
61830	CISCO	147	482	462	451	-0.5	18	188	184	180	-0.2	2.51	151	146	-0.4
61831	COLLISON	183	200	196	193	-0.2	38	79	78	77	-0.1	2.51	63	61	-0.3
61832	DANVILLE	183	38186	36541	35504	-0.5	18	15862	15267	14874	-0.4	2.34	9989	9381	-0.7
61833	TILTON	183	2590	2450	2368	-0.6	13	1153	1100	1068	-0.5	2.16	717	666	-0.8
61834	DANVILLE	183	8740	8606	8482	-0.2	38	2792	2766	2727	-0.1	2.46	1944	1891	-0.3
61839	DE LAND	147	717	761	774	0.6	75	278	299	306	0.8	2.55	222	235	0.6
61840	DEWEY	019	666	714	738	0.8	79	247	272	284	1.0	2.63	190	204	0.8
61841	FAIRMOUNT	183	1342	1331	1314	-0.1	45	537	537	530	0.0	2.48	407	400	-0.2
61842	FARMER CITY	039	2913	2886	2847	-0.1	45	1159	1161	1147	0.0	2.44	817	801	-0.2
61843	FISHER	019	2079	2151	2195	0.4	69	789	839	863	0.7	2.56	603	622	0.3
61844	FITHIAN	183	1179	1163	1141	-0.1	45	463	462	455	0.0	2.52	348	341	-0.2
61845	FOOSLAND	019	1842	379	384	-15.7	0	145	152	156	0.5	2.49	111	113	0.2
61846	GEORGETOWN	183	5133	5003	4891	-0.3	32	2061	2027	1989	-0.2	2.47	1450	1398	-0.4
61847	GIFFORD	019	1188	1194	1198	0.1	56	437	449	456	0.3	2.47	330	330	0.0
61849	HOMER	019	1731	1734	1733	0.0	50	692	712	719	0.3	2.44	501	501	0.0
61850	INDIANOLA	183	520	518	507	0.0	50	198	198	195	0.0	2.62	153	151	-0.1
61851	IVESDALE	019	502	506	508	0.1	56	200	208	211	0.4	2.43	150	152	0.1
61852	LONGVIEW	019	312	332	340	0.7	78	114	124	128	0.9	2.68	90	95	0.6
61853	MAHOMET	019	10548	12136	12819	1.5	88	3704	4365	4647	1.8	2.78	2973	3422	1.5
61854	MANSFIELD	147	1498	1753	1823	1.7	90	613	729	760	1.9	2.40	469	551	1.8
61855	MILMINE	147	163	157	155	-0.4	25	60	59	58	-0.2	2.66	45	44	-0.2
61856	MONTICELLO	147	6707	6939	7003	0.4	69	2707	2843	2888	0.5	2.40	1900	1955	0.3
61858	OAKWOOD	183	2852	2936	2923	0.3	65	1167	1213	1212	0.4	2.42	862	880	0.2
61859	OGDEN	019	1422	1482	1515	0.4	69	545	581	599	0.7	2.55	416	434	0.5
61862	PENFIELD	019	500	476	469	-0.5	18	175	172	171	-0.2	2.77	138	132	-0.5
61863	PESOTUM	019	778	856	894	1.0	83	310	354	373	1.4	2.42	233	261	1.2
61864	PHILO	019	1592	1682	1723	0.6	75	571	620	642	0.9	2.71	461	493	0.7
61865	POTOMAC	183	1395	1419	1408	0.2	61	510	520	517	0.2	2.71	390	391	0.0
61866	RANTOUL	019	14218	13165	12810	-0.8	6	5858	5585	5488	-0.5	2.34	3734	3428	-0.9
61870	RIDGE FARM	183	1443	1395	1360	-0.4	25	575	562	550	-0.2	2.47	420	402	-0.5
61872	SADORUS	019	735	749	757	0.2	61	277	291	297	0.5	2.57	207	213	0.3
61873	SAINT JOSEPH	019	5001	5213	5327	0.4	69	1879	2019	2084	0.8	2.58	1453	1524	0.5
61874	SAVOY	019	4070	5375	5895	3.1	95	1771	2444	2710	3.5	2.16	1121	1472	3.0
61875	SEYMOUR	019	788	901	947	1.5	88	275	317	334	1.5	2.84	217	246	1.4
61876	SIDELL	183	807	788	768	-0.3	32	306	297	290	-0.3	2.65	234	223	-0.5
61877	SIDNEY	019	1560	1697	1754	0.9	81	602	673	703	1.2	2.52	445	485	0.9
61878	THOMASBORO	019	1496	1584	1632	0.6	75	603	657	684	0.9	2.41	415	436	0.5
61880	TOLONO	019	3347	3895	4092	1.7	90	1325	1598	1697	2.0	2.43	906	1054	1.6
61882	WELDON	039	579	568	556	-0.2	38	237	237	232	0.0	2.40	178	174	-0.2
61883	WESTVILLE	183	4454	4207	4072	-0.6	13	1910	1823	1771	-0.5	2.31	1234	1148	-0.8
61884	WHITE HEATH	147	1198	1358	1420	1.4	88	416	475	498	1.4	2.86	341	384	1.3
61910	ARCOLA	041	4307	4255	4183	-0.1	45	1470	1453	1431	-0.1	2.87	1121	1095	-0.3
61911	ARTHUR	139	4394	4427	4410	0.1	56	1473	1489	1484	0.1	2.93	1099	1093	-0.1
61912	ASHMORE	029	1426	1385	1351	-0.3	32	553	545	535	-0.2	2.54	407	393	-0.4
61913	ATWOOD	041	1896	1892	1864	0.0	50	756	768	760	0.2	2.46	548	544	-0.1
	ILLINOIS					0.6					0.6	2.64			0.4
	UNITED STATES					1.0					1.1	2.59			0.9

ZIP CODE #	POST OFFICE NAME	RACE (%) White 2000	White 2009	Black 2000	Black 2009	Asian/Pacific 2000	Asian/Pacific 2009	% Hispanic Origin 2000	% Hispanic Origin 2009	2009 AGE DISTRIBUTION (%) 0-4	5-9	10-14	15-19	20-24	25-44	45-64	65-84	85+	18+	MEDIAN AGE 2009	% 2009 Males	% 2009 Females
61732	DANVERS	98.1	97.7	0.6	0.7	0.1	0.2	0.7	1.0	7.1	7.4	7.6	8.0	5.6	25.9	27.8	9.5	1.1	73.0	37.0	48.4	51.6
61733	DEER CREEK	98.1	97.4	0.3	0.3	0.4	0.6	0.2	0.4	7.2	7.6	8.0	6.5	4.3	25.5	28.4	11.4	1.1	73.1	38.6	51.0	49.0
61734	DELAVAN	98.4	98.0	0.4	0.5	0.1	0.2	0.3	0.6	6.9	7.1	7.3	6.9	5.1	24.2	27.8	12.8	1.8	74.4	39.0	49.7	50.3
61735	DEWITT	98.5	98.3	0.2	0.2	0.2	0.2	0.4	0.9	6.0	6.4	6.9	6.0	4.1	26.4	29.0	13.5	1.7	77.0	41.3	50.6	49.4
61736	DOWNS	98.4	97.9	0.5	0.7	0.2	0.2	0.6	1.0	6.5	7.2	7.9	7.9	4.5	25.1	30.8	9.4	0.7	73.4	39.6	50.3	49.7
61737	ELLSWORTH	97.1	96.4	0.4	0.5	0.2	0.3	0.5	0.9	7.0	7.8	7.8	6.6	4.8	25.7	30.0	8.9	1.4	73.3	38.6	49.1	50.9
61738	EL PASO	98.8	98.4	0.2	0.3	0.2	0.3	0.7	1.1	7.3	7.6	7.4	6.2	5.0	25.5	27.2	11.3	2.6	73.7	38.6	49.4	50.6
61739	FAIRBURY	96.8	95.6	0.5	0.6	0.4	0.6	2.4	3.6	7.0	7.0	6.8	6.8	6.1	23.3	26.0	12.7	4.3	74.5	38.9	49.0	51.0
61740	FLANAGAN	98.5	97.9	0.4	0.6	0.1	0.2	0.6	0.9	5.2	5.5	6.6	6.5	4.5	21.2	28.6	15.4	6.5	77.7	45.4	46.6	53.4
61741	FORREST	96.5	95.3	0.6	0.7	0.2	0.3	2.2	3.2	7.6	7.5	8.0	8.0	5.9	23.5	26.3	11.4	1.8	71.8	36.8	50.1	49.9
61742	GOODFIELD	98.6	98.1	0.1	0.1	0.1	0.2	0.0	0.0	9.4	10.1	9.7	7.3	3.8	26.6	24.1	8.0	1.0	66.1	33.6	51.2	48.8
61743	GRAYMONT	99.6	99.1	0.0	0.0	0.0	0.0	0.8	0.9	8.2	9.1	9.1	6.8	4.6	21.5	30.6	9.1	0.9	68.9	36.3	49.3	50.7
61744	GRIDLEY	97.9	97.2	0.4	0.5	0.4	0.5	0.8	1.1	6.8	7.4	7.9	7.7	5.2	22.6	29.0	11.2	2.3	73.0	38.7	50.6	49.4
61745	HEYWORTH	98.1	97.5	0.2	0.2	0.3	0.4	0.6	1.1	8.4	8.4	8.4	7.0	4.6	27.0	26.0	9.3	1.1	70.4	36.2	49.5	50.5
61747	HOPEDALE	99.4	99.2	0.1	0.1	0.1	0.1	0.4	0.6	6.7	7.2	7.5	6.2	4.1	24.7	25.8	12.4	5.4	74.9	40.8	48.6	51.4
61748	HUDSON	98.7	98.2	0.1	0.1	0.5	0.6	0.7	1.1	7.4	7.1	6.9	6.5	3.6	27.5	28.1	11.4	1.5	74.1	39.1	49.2	50.8
61749	KENNEY	98.9	98.5	0.3	0.4	0.4	0.5	0.8	1.0	4.4	5.0	5.7	5.8	3.9	26.6	34.1	12.8	1.6	81.2	43.9	51.0	49.0
61752	LE ROY	98.8	98.4	0.3	0.4	0.1	0.1	1.2	1.8	7.0	7.0	7.2	6.9	4.9	26.8	26.1	11.6	2.5	74.2	38.8	48.8	51.2
61753	LEXINGTON	98.6	98.2	0.3	0.3	0.1	0.1	0.6	1.0	6.0	6.5	6.9	6.9	4.6	24.4	30.6	11.5	2.5	76.3	41.2	49.7	50.3
61754	MC LEAN	98.2	97.7	0.5	0.5	0.7	0.9	0.1	0.1	6.2	6.3	6.3	6.2	6.3	24.6	29.7	11.8	2.7	77.4	40.9	49.9	50.1
61755	MACKINAW	97.3	96.3	0.6	0.8	0.5	0.7	0.8	1.3	7.5	7.8	7.8	6.8	5.0	27.7	26.9	9.5	1.0	72.7	37.3	50.1	49.9
61756	MAROA	99.0	98.9	0.2	0.2	0.2	0.3	0.7	1.0	5.8	6.5	6.7	6.8	5.5	24.1	31.2	11.5	1.8	76.7	40.6	51.1	48.9
61759	MINIER	98.8	98.3	0.3	0.4	0.1	0.2	1.0	1.5	6.2	6.7	7.1	6.6	4.6	24.6	28.4	13.6	2.2	75.9	41.0	49.7	50.3
61760	MINONK	99.0	98.6	0.1	0.1	0.0	0.1	1.0	1.5	6.5	6.9	7.2	6.9	4.8	23.1	27.6	12.9	4.2	75.2	41.0	48.3	51.7
61761	NORMAL	88.4	85.4	7.1	8.3	2.1	3.1	2.5	3.6	4.9	4.6	4.5	14.1	25.2	21.8	16.7	6.8	1.4	83.1	24.3	47.3	52.7
61764	PONTIAC	87.3	84.6	9.3	10.8	0.4	0.6	3.8	5.3	6.0	6.0	6.0	6.3	7.6	28.7	25.4	11.3	2.7	78.5	37.3	53.3	46.7
61769	SAUNEMIN	98.8	98.6	0.1	0.2	0.0	0.0	1.5	2.2	6.4	7.2	8.1	9.2	5.8	23.8	28.0	10.6	1.1	72.6	37.4	54.0	46.0
61770	SAYBROOK	98.9	98.5	0.2	0.2	0.1	0.2	0.3	0.4	5.8	6.2	6.7	6.8	3.8	24.6	30.0	14.1	1.8	76.8	42.2	50.0	50.0
61771	SECOR	99.2	99.1	0.1	0.1	0.1	0.2	0.3	0.5	7.1	7.6	7.3	5.7	4.0	24.2	31.8	10.9	1.4	74.4	40.8	50.5	49.5
61772	SHIRLEY	98.9	98.4	0.0	0.0	0.3	0.5	0.5	0.7	4.9	5.6	6.5	6.3	4.7	24.7	31.0	13.3	3.0	79.3	43.4	52.4	47.6
61773	SIBLEY	97.1	96.9	0.0	0.0	0.0	0.0	2.5	2.7	7.1	8.0	8.0	6.3	4.4	24.3	28.0	11.5	2.4	73.0	38.1	52.5	47.5
61774	STANFORD	98.4	98.1	0.0	0.0	0.2	0.2	1.0	1.5	7.5	7.3	7.0	6.9	7.4	24.9	28.4	9.3	1.4	74.0	35.4	48.9	51.1
61775	STRAWN	97.5	96.7	1.2	1.7	0.4	0.4	0.4	0.4	8.3	8.3	8.3	8.3	4.6	24.5	25.7	11.2	0.8	70.1	35.2	50.6	49.4
61776	TOWANDA	97.9	97.1	0.7	0.9	0.7	0.9	0.7	0.9	6.6	7.1	7.7	5.9	4.1	24.9	31.7	10.8	1.3	74.7	41.4	48.9	51.1
61777	WAPELLA	98.4	98.0	0.1	0.1	0.3	0.4	0.6	1.0	6.0	7.2	6.8	6.0	3.8	26.9	28.8	12.1	2.3	76.1	39.4	50.6	49.4
61778	WAYNESVILLE	98.5	98.2	0.4	0.5	0.0	0.0	0.9	1.2	6.4	6.8	7.1	6.8	4.1	24.0	29.0	14.0	1.8	75.4	39.9	49.2	50.8
61790	NORMAL	70.1	64.6	19.9	22.6	5.7	7.3	4.6	6.3	7.9	5.8	4.4	6.2	30.9	28.8	9.0	4.3	2.6	79.2	24.2	45.2	54.8
61801	URBANA	66.6	59.9	12.9	14.4	16.0	20.2	3.8	5.2	3.4	3.2	3.1	17.5	28.1	22.4	13.8	6.8	1.6	87.3	24.1	54.7	45.3
61802	URBANA	78.7	73.4	13.0	15.4	4.9	6.8	2.1	2.9	6.8	6.0	6.1	6.2	8.2	29.5	24.1	10.5	2.6	77.6	35.7	47.9	52.1
61810	ALLERTON	99.2	99.0	0.0	0.0	0.0	0.0	0.5	1.0	5.2	5.8	6.3	6.3	4.5	22.3	34.3	13.4	2.1	78.5	44.8	50.0	50.0
61811	ALVIN	98.9	98.5	0.1	0.1	0.1	0.3	0.3	0.4	6.1	6.2	6.6	7.7	4.6	25.9	29.3	12.2	1.2	76.2	40.4	49.8	50.2
61812	ARMSTRONG	96.4	95.3	1.3	1.7	0.3	0.7	1.0	1.3	5.7	6.0	6.4	6.7	3.7	23.5	33.6	12.1	2.3	77.9	43.5	52.7	47.3
61813	BEMENT	98.4	97.9	0.7	0.9	0.2	0.4	0.3	0.5	5.8	6.1	6.3	6.5	5.1	26.1	27.8	13.5	2.8	77.8	40.5	49.4	50.6
61814	BISMARCK	98.0	97.4	0.3	0.4	0.2	0.2	0.8	1.3	6.4	6.9	7.0	7.0	5.0	23.6	31.5	11.3	1.3	75.2	40.9	48.3	51.7
61816	BROADLANDS	98.2	98.0	0.4	0.4	0.0	0.0	0.2	0.2	6.1	7.0	7.4	6.3	4.6	20.3	33.8	13.1	1.5	75.4	43.7	49.2	50.8
61817	CATLIN	99.0	98.7	0.1	0.1	0.1	0.1	0.5	0.7	6.4	6.3	6.2	6.4	5.7	24.3	28.3	14.6	1.8	77.0	40.8	48.2	51.8
61818	CERRO GORDO	99.3	99.0	0.2	0.3	0.0	0.1	0.4	0.7	6.4	7.2	7.2	7.4	5.8	23.9	28.6	11.8	1.7	74.6	38.9	48.6	51.4
61820	CHAMPAIGN	69.2	63.6	16.3	17.4	9.1	12.3	5.5	7.4	2.9	2.6	2.5	19.1	38.0	19.2	10.3	4.2	1.2	89.7	23.0	53.2	46.8
61821	CHAMPAIGN	76.0	70.9	16.3	18.6	4.3	6.1	2.6	3.5	6.5	6.0	6.0	6.6	8.0	29.7	25.0	10.6	1.7	78.2	35.5	48.7	51.3
61822	CHAMPAIGN	85.3	78.1	6.1	9.1	6.1	9.0	1.7	3.1	7.3	7.3	7.3	6.6	5.6	28.9	27.7	8.4	1.0	74.0	36.3	49.5	50.5
61830	CISCO	97.9	97.2	0.0	0.2	0.0	0.0	0.8	1.1	6.7	7.6	7.1	4.8	3.0	24.7	30.3	14.1	1.7	75.5	42.0	49.1	50.9
61831	COLLISON	97.5	96.4	1.0	1.0	0.0	0.5	0.5	0.5	5.6	5.6	6.1	6.6	4.6	23.0	33.7	12.8	2.0	78.1	43.9	51.5	48.5
61832	DANVILLE	76.5	72.2	18.8	21.6	1.0	1.4	3.7	5.0	7.3	6.8	6.5	6.6	6.3	23.6	25.9	14.1	2.9	75.5	38.9	47.5	52.5
61833	TILTON	98.1	97.3	0.3	0.4	0.2	0.3	1.2	1.8	5.8	5.8	5.9	5.6	4.6	22.9	28.1	17.8	3.5	79.0	44.5	47.2	52.8
61834	DANVILLE	79.6	76.8	17.1	18.7	0.9	1.3	3.3	4.4	4.6	4.8	5.0	5.4	7.9	31.8	26.4	12.4	1.8	82.7	38.5	59.1	40.9
61839	DE LAND	98.2	98.0	0.3	0.3	0.3	0.3	0.7	1.1	5.8	6.2	7.0	7.1	4.5	24.0	32.9	11.0	1.6	76.7	41.4	49.7	50.3
61840	DEWEY	97.9	96.9	0.3	0.4	0.2	0.4	1.4	2.0	6.0	6.4	7.0	7.3	5.2	24.2	31.2	11.1	1.5	76.2	40.8	49.2	50.8
61841	FAIRMOUNT	99.0	98.4	0.1	0.2	0.1	0.1	0.6	1.0	5.6	6.1	6.4	6.2	4.6	23.9	31.3	13.8	2.0	78.0	43.0	49.4	50.6
61842	FARMER CITY	99.2	99.0	0.2	0.2	0.0	0.0	0.4	0.5	5.9	6.1	6.1	6.3	5.7	24.5	28.5	13.7	3.3	78.0	41.6	49.5	50.5
61843	FISHER	90.1	83.6	4.6	9.3	2.7	2.8	2.1	5.4	4.0	4.5	6.0	19.2	12.4	18.8	20.6	10.2	4.4	81.6	28.9	46.0	54.0
61844	FITHIAN	98.9	98.5	0.3	0.3	0.0	0.1	0.4	0.6	6.0	6.2	6.7	7.5	5.2	25.8	30.5	10.6	1.5	76.4	40.2	52.5	47.5
61845	FOOSLAND	84.8	77.6	7.5	13.5	4.5	4.0	2.6	7.1	2.9	3.4	5.3	24.8	16.9	16.9	14.5	9.5	5.8	84.7	24.0	44.9	55.1
61846	GEORGETOWN	96.1	94.9	2.2	2.9	0.1	0.1	1.1	1.6	6.8	6.7	6.7	6.9	6.0	24.9	27.2	12.9	1.9	75.6	38.6	48.9	51.1
61847	GIFFORD	97.5	96.7	1.1	1.3	0.4	0.6	0.8	1.1	5.7	6.4	6.6	5.7	4.2	23.3	28.0	14.2	5.9	77.2	43.5	47.7	52.3
61849	HOMER	99.0	98.4	0.1	0.1	0.3	0.5	0.3	0.5	6.3	6.8	7.2	6.6	4.7	24.0	29.2	13.3	1.9	75.7	41.2	50.3	49.7
61850	INDIANOLA	98.7	97.9	0.2	0.6	0.6	0.8	0.4	0.6	5.2	5.6	6.2	6.9	4.8	23.2	31.5	15.1	1.5	78.6	43.5	49.6	50.4
61851	IVESDALE	97.8	97.2	0.2	0.2	0.0	0.0	0.2	0.2	5.3	6.5	6.3	6.5	4.5	27.3	30.2	11.5	1.8	77.9	40.9	52.6	47.4
61852	LONGVIEW	98.4	97.3	0.3	0.3	0.3	0.6	1.0	1.5	6.6	7.5	8.1	7.2	4.5	23.2	30.1	11.7	0.9	73.2	39.8	52.7	47.3
61853	MAHOMET	97.8	96.9	0.4	0.5	0.6	0.9	0.9	1.4	7.5	7.9	8.4	7.9	5.1	27.2	28.5	6.9	0.6	71.2	35.4	48.9	51.1
61854	MANSFIELD	98.7	98.3	0.1	0.2	0.3	0.5	0.7	1.0	6.2	6.5	6.8	6.6	5.1	23.7	30.6	13.3	1.2	76.3	40.8	50.1	49.9
61855	MILMINE	98.1	97.5	0.6	0.6	0.0	0.0	0.0	0.0	6.4	7.6	7.0	5.1	3.8	20.4	35.7	12.1	1.9	75.2	44.7	51.0	49.0
61856	MONTICELLO	99.0	98.7	0.1	0.1	0.1	0.2	0.8	1.0	5.9	6.1	6.5	6.3	4.9	21.6	30.1	15.3	3.4	77.5	44.0	48.1	51.9
61858	OAKWOOD	99.3	99.0	0.1	0.1	0.0	0.0	0.4	0.6	6.3	6.4	6.5	6.7	5.6	26.0	28.5	12.7	1.4	76.8	39.8	49.6	50.4
61859	OGDEN	98.2	97.6	0.2	0.3	0.4	0.6	0.6	0.9	6.6	6.7	6.9	7.8	5.8	25.3	27.8	11.5	1.6	75.1	38.3	48.9	51.1
61862	PENFIELD	96.8	95.4	0.8	1.1	0.4	0.6	1.8	2.5	5.9	8.2	7.1	7.8	3.4	21.8	31.9	12.2	1.7	73.7	41.2	50.2	49.8
61863	PESOTUM	99.1	98.6	0.0	0.0	0.4	0.7	0.3	0.4	5.1	5.5	6.1	6.3	5.0	24.5	31.4	13.9	2.1	79.3	43.1	50.5	49.5
61864	PHILO	99.2	98.8	0.3	0.4	0.0	0.1	0.3	0.5	6.7	7.1	7.6	7.1	4.9	25.2	28.1	11.6	1.7	74.0	39.1	51.2	48.8
61865	POTOMAC	97.3	96.1	0.4	0.6	0.3	0.5	1.5	2.4	6.3	6.8	7.1	7.1	4.7	24.7	29.2	12.1	2.0	75.3	39.9	50.6	49.4
61866	RANTOUL	77.8	73.2	15.7	18.4	1.8	2.6	2.8	3.9	8.6	7.8	7.1	7.1	7.6	28.4	22.6	9.5	1.3	73.4	33.0	47.8	52.2
61870	RIDGE FARM	99.4	99.3	0.0	0.0	0.1	0.1	0.6	0.9	6.3	6.4	6.5	7.0	5.4	23.4	28.9	14.1	2.0	76.6	41.5	50.0	50.0
61872	SADORUS	97.8	97.3	0.1	0.1	0.1	0.1	0.1	0.3	5.2	6.4	6.4	6.7	4.7	26.6	31.0	11.3	1.7	77.8	40.8	52.3	47.7
61873	SAINT JOSEPH	98.9	98.5	0.1	0.2	0.2	0.3	0.8	1.3	7.0	7.1	7.3	6.9	5.2	27.3	28.9	9.1	1.3	74.0	37.6	48.8	51.2
61874	SAVOY	83.5	76.4	4.1	5.4	9.5	14.1	2.1	3.3	7.5	6.7	6.3	5.5	6.4	29.6	24.3	10.8	3.0	76.1	36.2	46.7	53.3
61875	SEYMOUR	97.1	96.0	0.3	0.2	0.5	1.0	1.0	1.7	7.4	7.9	8.4	7.7	4.8	24.3	29.1	9.3	1.1	71.4	37.2	48.3	51.7
61876	SIDELL	99.5	99.4	0.1	0.1	0.0	0.0	0.6	0.9	6.1	6.2	6.5	7.1	5.2	23.6	30.2	13.3	1.8	76.6	42.0	51.3	48.7
61877	SIDNEY	97.8	97.1	0.3	0.3	0.6	1.1	0.3	0.5	7.1	7.6	8.0	6.7	4.9	23.7	29.2	10.9	1.8	73.1	39.4	49.1	50.9
61878	THOMASBORO	95.7	94.0	1.3	1.6	0.8	1.3	1.1	1.6	6.8	6.6	6.8	6.7	6.5	27.2	27.0	10.9	1.6	75.8	37.6	49.0	51.0
61880	TOLONO	97.2	96.1	0.8	1.1	0.4	0.8	0.9	1.3	7.0	6.6	6.7	5.8	6.6	28.3	27.7	10.3	1.0	76.2	37.4	51.3	48.7
61882	WELDON	97.4	97.0	0.0	0.0	0.5	0.7	0.2	0.2	6.2	7.2	7.2	6.0	3.9	24.6	28.5	14.4	1.9	75.7	41.8	51.8	48.2
61883	WESTVILLE	98.2	97.5	0.3	0.4	0.0	0.0	0.8	1.2	6.2	5.9	6.0	6.3	6.0	24.8	27.4	14.9	2.4	78.0	41.1	48.4	51.6
61884	WHITE HEATH	99.1	98.7	0.1	0.1	0.1	0.1	0.8	1.1	5.9	6.6	7.5	6.9	4.4	23.0	33.7	11.0	1.0	75.6	41.9	50.5	49.5
61910	ARCOLA	92.5	89.8	0.3	0.3	0.5	0.7	13.0	18.2	8.4	8.4	8.1	6.8	5.0	25.3	25.2	11.1	1.7	70.8	35.8	49.7	50.3
61911	ARTHUR	99.5	99.3	0.0	0.0	0.0	0.1	0.5	0.7	8.5	8.4	8.1	7.6	6.1	23.8	23.0	11.6	2.8	69.9	34.0	48.4	51.6
61912	ASHMORE	97.8	97.0	0.4	0.5	0.9	1.3	0.5	0.7	5.9	6.2	6.4	6.6	5.8	26.3	29.8	11.4	1.4	77.5	39.6	48.5	51.5
61913	ATWOOD	99.1	98.8	0.2	0.3	0.1	0.1	0.9	1.5	7.0	7.0	7.1	6.8	5.7	23.4	28.0	13.1	1.8	74.6	40.1	48.8	51.2
	ILLINOIS	73.5	70.6	15.1	15.3	3.4	4.4	12.3	15.7	7.1	6.9	6.8	7.1	6.9	27.5	25.4	10.3	1.9	75.0	36.1	49.1	50.9
	UNITED STATES	75.1	72.0	12.3	12.7	3.8	4.6	12.5	15.7	6.8	6.7	6.6	7.1	6.9	27.0	26.0	10.9	1.9	75.7	36.9	49.2	50.8

ZIP CODE #	POST OFFICE NAME	2009 Per Capita Income	2009 HH Income Base	2009 Household Income Distribution (%) Less than $25,000	$25,000 to $49,999	$50,000 to $99,999	$100,000 to $149,999	$150,000 or More	Median Household Income 2009	2014	2009 National Centile	2009 State Centile	2009 Home Value Base	2009 Home Value Distribution (%) Less than $50,000	$50,000 to $89,999	$90,000 to $174,999	$175,000 to $399,999	$400,000 or More	2009 Median Home Value
61732	DANVERS	25717	767	10.4	20.7	57.0	8.9	3.0	70734	71046	87	81	628	1.4	15.6	56.2	25.5	1.3	138034
61733	DEER CREEK	28025	527	10.6	21.6	52.6	9.7	5.5	65170	66028	83	74	437	3.7	7.3	53.3	29.3	6.4	146695
61734	DELAVAN	24636	1160	13.7	25.9	49.6	6.9	3.9	58524	61509	76	62	931	8.8	21.9	47.5	18.4	3.4	111358
61735	DEWITT	28876	182	12.6	19.2	48.9	13.2	6.0	67859	68398	85	78	147	9.5	19.0	37.4	27.9	6.1	136184
61736	DOWNS	29661	859	6.1	14.7	57.0	16.8	5.5	76290	77436	90	88	744	4.2	9.9	43.5	38.6	3.8	153077
61737	ELLSWORTH	27366	207	6.8	18.8	60.9	10.1	3.4	73272	73216	88	84	164	2.4	22.6	52.4	17.7	4.9	118125
61738	EL PASO	25707	1458	13.2	23.7	50.0	9.5	3.6	60871	63832	79	66	1131	6.8	14.5	53.1	20.4	5.1	128701
61739	FAIRBURY	24311	1765	17.5	23.5	47.9	7.9	3.2	56560	59530	73	58	1270	4.7	12.4	55.2	25.8	1.9	131345
61740	FLANAGAN	24785	581	16.9	28.2	44.6	8.3	2.1	54267	57529	70	54	436	3.4	21.8	58.7	14.9	1.1	119059
61741	FORREST	22416	621	13.8	28.3	47.7	6.4	3.7	55792	59109	72	57	469	7.9	21.7	55.9	13.4	1.1	112612
61742	GOODFIELD	25520	352	8.8	19.9	54.5	12.8	4.0	73688	75195	89	84	292	8.6	9.2	40.4	37.0	4.8	155000
61743	GRAYMONT	30463	81	11.1	17.3	53.1	12.3	6.2	71213	73268	87	81	62	4.8	27.4	37.1	29.0	1.6	130556
61744	GRIDLEY	24381	884	12.8	26.2	49.0	10.0	2.0	59191	61308	76	63	676	6.2	18.9	54.7	18.9	1.2	122651
61745	HEYWORTH	27902	1478	11.7	18.8	51.0	13.7	4.8	67804	68642	85	78	1226	11.0	10.8	50.2	25.3	2.7	131545
61747	HOPEDALE	26571	567	13.6	20.8	52.9	8.5	4.2	66298	66554	84	76	454	4.4	11.9	49.8	30.4	3.5	141558
61748	HUDSON	30853	1130	7.3	14.9	55.2	17.8	4.8	70888	71938	87	81	983	3.1	8.5	45.5	33.5	9.5	162409
61749	KENNEY	29043	335	15.2	27.8	43.0	8.7	5.4	60122	61017	77	64	270	24.1	17.0	29.3	24.4	5.2	108654
61752	LE ROY	27064	1651	12.1	21.9	54.4	9.0	2.7	66339	67611	84	76	1263	6.4	14.3	56.3	22.3	0.7	129720
61753	LEXINGTON	27301	1138	14.9	25.7	44.9	9.5	4.9	60945	62624	79	66	881	9.5	13.5	48.6	23.8	4.5	129611
61754	MC LEAN	26718	557	10.4	23.2	55.3	7.9	3.2	66828	67608	85	76	445	7.2	24.9	56.6	11.2	0.0	107981
61755	MACKINAW	27593	1601	10.9	20.3	47.8	15.4	5.6	70367	70130	87	81	1367	4.8	7.2	49.8	35.4	2.8	148634
61756	MAROA	26371	785	16.7	27.4	42.9	8.3	4.7	54975	58404	71	56	592	21.5	29.6	35.8	9.6	3.5	88537
61759	MINIER	24312	659	17.1	25.2	48.7	5.3	3.6	54185	55634	70	54	501	12.4	13.0	60.3	14.4	0.0	119112
61760	MINONK	23000	1020	20.6	25.5	45.0	6.9	2.1	54108	60058	70	54	796	8.3	25.6	50.4	15.3	0.4	107714
61761	NORMAL	24795	16952	22.7	24.4	38.0	10.0	4.8	53240	56540	68	52	9623	6.4	5.2	49.9	37.2	1.2	157796
61764	PONTIAC	23483	5160	21.0	26.5	41.7	7.3	3.4	51622	53384	65	48	3615	14.6	17.7	49.1	17.8	0.8	111633
61769	SAUNEMIN	23909	226	10.2	22.1	55.3	10.2	2.2	64930	66143	83	74	183	13.1	26.2	43.7	12.6	4.4	104167
61770	SAYBROOK	20933	518	22.6	27.6	46.9	2.9	0.0	49788	51739	61	43	384	17.2	31.5	38.5	12.8	0.0	92000
61771	SECOR	25167	393	14.0	26.2	43.5	8.9	7.4	59552	61636	77	63	324	4.9	20.4	41.4	26.2	7.1	135625
61772	SHIRLEY	29901	167	9.0	22.2	54.5	9.0	5.4	72624	73836	88	83	120	7.5	15.0	48.3	29.2	0.0	122222
61773	SIBLEY	22199	220	26.4	20.0	42.3	5.0	6.4	52230	54993	66	49	167	25.7	35.9	25.7	8.4	4.2	68929
61774	STANFORD	25851	409	12.2	21.5	54.5	6.8	4.9	63913	64883	82	72	320	8.4	26.6	52.2	7.5	5.3	107278
61775	STRAWN	25314	88	8.0	25.0	54.5	9.1	3.4	63475	61304	82	71	68	7.4	17.6	48.5	22.1	4.4	132143
61776	TOWANDA	31150	498	7.2	21.9	52.6	12.4	5.8	75086	74385	89	86	414	6.8	8.7	44.9	32.9	6.8	149138
61777	WAPELLA	27311	408	14.0	27.9	44.6	8.3	5.1	56583	57801	73	59	336	14.3	20.2	42.0	18.5	5.1	107917
61778	WAYNESVILLE	23737	265	17.0	29.4	43.4	6.8	3.4	52206	53644	66	49	229	20.1	28.8	36.2	13.1	1.7	91471
61790	NORMAL	10824	575	50.1	31.8	17.2	0.7	0.2	24943	25628	3	1	114	67.5	16.7	15.8	0.0	0.0	20500
61801	URBANA	20849	11563	41.1	25.7	25.3	4.3	3.5	31618	33437	11	3	4029	4.0	15.5	51.1	27.2	2.2	136144
61802	URBANA	24966	8152	23.1	32.3	35.8	5.2	3.6	45099	47973	49	29	4836	23.3	16.0	39.7	17.9	3.0	107102
61810	ALLERTON	22632	147	15.6	30.6	43.5	7.5	2.7	53489	59030	69	53	119	12.6	34.5	35.3	17.6	0.0	95000
61811	ALVIN	20125	265	16.2	28.7	49.1	3.4	2.6	53022	55196	68	51	206	22.3	32.0	34.0	11.2	0.5	83571
61812	ARMSTRONG	22204	120	18.3	36.7	38.3	5.8	0.8	46838	48910	54	34	91	12.1	22.0	47.3	12.1	6.6	115441
61813	BEMENT	24137	772	14.8	30.2	46.6	5.8	2.6	53636	56738	69	53	619	13.2	31.3	46.7	8.4	0.3	97614
61814	BISMARCK	24939	422	15.9	19.4	49.3	12.1	3.3	62089	63205	80	68	343	12.2	25.9	38.8	21.0	2.0	109949
61816	BROADLANDS	21633	186	16.1	42.5	34.4	3.2	3.8	44680	46599	47	28	148	16.2	25.0	36.5	22.3	0.0	99286
61817	CATLIN	23233	1102	15.2	28.1	45.6	8.2	3.0	57962	61157	75	61	878	8.0	28.0	52.7	10.6	0.7	104673
61818	CERRO GORDO	22448	811	20.0	25.2	44.6	9.1	1.1	53568	56434	69	53	653	8.4	29.1	53.9	6.9	1.7	103967
61820	CHAMPAIGN	17052	13139	51.7	24.5	19.4	2.7	1.7	23955	24725	3	1	3358	13.7	24.0	44.8	16.0	1.5	108634
61821	CHAMPAIGN	30428	13239	17.0	25.0	43.6	9.1	5.3	57176	60156	74	59	8333	2.1	18.0	53.1	24.4	2.5	129157
61822	CHAMPAIGN	38823	8096	8.9	19.6	43.6	13.7	14.2	75323	75808	90	86	5982	4.4	6.5	30.5	48.7	9.8	197059
61830	CISCO	23870	184	13.6	27.2	51.6	6.0	1.6	54839	55999	71	56	139	6.5	23.0	41.7	24.5	4.3	119397
61831	COLLISON	23419	78	15.4	30.8	44.9	6.4	2.6	53302	56006	69	52	61	8.2	21.3	52.5	14.8	3.3	117708
61832	DANVILLE	20648	15267	31.4	30.2	31.6	4.8	2.0	39250	42916	30	14	9884	28.5	32.8	28.6	9.4	0.8	74493
61833	TILTON	18820	1100	31.9	35.6	29.8	2.2	0.5	36615	38448	22	9	840	29.6	45.2	23.7	1.4	0.0	67789
61834	DANVILLE	21443	2766	23.5	25.8	40.6	7.3	2.7	50623	54483	63	45	2074	17.8	23.3	39.6	17.9	1.3	105743
61839	DE LAND	26986	299	17.7	17.1	52.8	6.7	5.7	60094	62240	77	64	231	5.6	21.6	38.5	23.8	10.4	119408
61840	DEWEY	29310	272	10.3	15.8	59.6	9.2	5.1	69698	69752	87	80	211	4.3	10.0	46.9	34.6	4.3	158214
61841	FAIRMOUNT	22439	537	18.6	27.6	46.2	5.6	2.0	52856	57029	68	51	444	18.7	34.0	35.8	11.3	0.2	87143
61842	FARMER CITY	27254	1161	16.4	25.4	42.9	10.2	5.1	57414	58521	74	59	889	8.4	26.2	50.3	14.4	0.7	113024
61843	FISHER	26630	839	11.1	23.6	54.7	7.5	3.1	61098	62589	79	66	657	12.2	14.6	50.1	20.5	2.6	122256
61844	FITHIAN	23834	462	11.9	29.7	50.6	6.5	1.3	60833	61766	79	66	361	18.3	26.6	42.1	11.9	1.1	98409
61845	FOOSLAND	25085	152	11.8	28.9	51.3	6.6	1.3	55225	57828	72	56	119	14.3	17.6	52.9	14.3	0.8	111500
61846	GEORGETOWN	18644	2027	26.5	34.0	34.6	3.8	1.1	41255	44654	37	19	1542	24.3	40.4	30.9	4.0	0.5	71077
61847	GIFFORD	25636	449	10.9	27.2	53.2	5.8	2.9	60208	61567	78	64	363	6.1	17.9	60.1	15.4	0.6	121983
61849	HOMER	24087	712	15.2	35.8	41.7	5.3	2.0	49490	50150	60	42	594	10.8	29.5	46.0	11.4	2.4	102459
61850	INDIANOLA	19991	198	21.7	32.8	37.9	5.6	2.0	47024	49289	54	35	162	38.3	13.6	38.3	6.8	3.1	86667
61851	IVESDALE	29913	208	8.2	26.9	51.4	9.6	3.8	66009	65750	84	75	167	14.4	22.8	45.5	14.4	3.0	101103
61852	LONGVIEW	25417	124	7.3	24.2	63.7	3.2	1.6	66660	69290	85	76	98	10.2	23.5	28.6	37.8	0.0	132143
61853	MAHOMET	28181	4365	10.6	21.4	47.9	14.2	5.9	68782	69877	86	79	3582	11.9	3.9	42.8	36.5	4.8	161031
61854	MANSFIELD	29183	729	10.6	21.8	55.1	9.1	3.4	63342	65654	82	70	585	7.0	19.5	51.1	22.4	0.0	122831
61855	MILMINE	19496	59	22.0	28.8	44.1	5.1	0.0	48668	51006	58	40	48	14.6	29.2	35.4	14.6	6.3	100000
61856	MONTICELLO	29222	2843	14.4	24.9	46.3	9.5	5.0	60553	63516	78	66	2254	8.6	8.9	45.5	34.5	2.6	142941
61858	OAKWOOD	24634	1213	14.9	27.7	48.6	5.7	3.1	55962	60131	73	57	1006	22.4	26.1	39.3	11.7	0.5	92143
61859	OGDEN	27013	581	9.1	27.7	53.4	7.1	2.8	62702	63758	81	69	491	2.6	13.8	60.9	20.6	2.0	128343
61862	PENFIELD	24764	172	9.3	30.2	47.7	9.3	3.5	57435	59139	75	59	131	13.0	20.6	43.5	22.9	0.0	121875
61863	PESOTUM	27883	354	8.8	20.9	61.9	8.5	0.0	66910	67399	85	77	307	5.5	22.5	59.0	9.4	3.6	111058
61864	PHILO	28459	620	5.6	16.6	63.5	10.8	3.4	75931	76406	90	88	527	2.3	7.0	58.8	31.7	0.2	144716
61865	POTOMAC	20306	520	18.7	31.0	43.5	5.0	1.9	50259	52929	62	44	417	20.4	36.9	33.3	7.9	1.4	80161
61866	RANTOUL	23401	5585	20.0	33.8	37.9	5.9	2.4	47317	49026	55	36	2933	17.6	20.8	48.8	12.1	0.8	104621
61870	RIDGE FARM	19914	562	21.5	35.1	37.5	5.0	0.9	46231	47926	52	33	454	30.8	34.8	32.8	1.1	0.4	75319
61872	SADORUS	28859	291	7.2	25.8	53.6	10.0	3.4	67436	67318	85	77	234	13.2	22.6	46.6	14.1	3.4	102604
61873	SAINT JOSEPH	28643	2019	14.1	16.3	54.3	11.2	4.1	71477	72428	88	82	1614	1.5	5.9	57.4	33.3	1.8	154437
61874	SAVOY	36284	2444	18.5	19.9	41.1	11.6	8.9	62903	63632	81	70	1332	4.4	2.6	23.4	61.6	7.9	216356
61875	SEYMOUR	31151	317	7.6	15.8	46.1	20.2	10.4	77945	78488	91	90	248	4.4	9.3	37.5	40.7	8.1	171429
61876	SIDELL	17746	297	26.9	36.4	32.0	3.4	1.3	40664	45127	35	18	240	32.9	33.8	24.2	8.3	0.8	67619
61877	SIDNEY	27879	673	13.7	18.9	54.1	10.0	3.4	67543	68611	85	78	534	8.4	9.7	54.5	24.3	3.0	133333
61878	THOMASBORO	25086	657	14.3	28.9	48.1	7.0	1.7	55702	58003	72	57	483	6.0	28.2	53.6	11.0	1.2	107845
61880	TOLONO	26825	1598	12.6	25.4	50.9	8.0	3.1	61353	62521	79	67	1146	9.6	14.7	56.2	17.4	2.2	119300
61882	WELDON	29343	237	12.2	29.5	43.5	8.4	6.3	61366	62266	79	67	190	15.3	24.7	42.1	14.7	3.2	100862
61883	WESTVILLE	20992	1823	27.0	32.3	36.4	3.3	1.0	42227	46395	40	22	1426	20.3	43.5	31.0	5.2	0.0	76918
61884	WHITE HEATH	27869	475	6.7	18.3	58.9	11.6	4.4	73546	74774	89	84	405	4.7	9.6	38.3	46.7	0.7	168269
61910	ARCOLA	20894	1453	19.5	34.4	34.6	8.5	3.0	47294	49078	55	36	1114	13.7	24.1	42.5	18.2	1.4	109132
61911	ARTHUR	19523	1489	18.5	35.7	36.6	6.6	2.6	47209	48857	55	36	1124	8.1	24.1	48.6	17.4	1.8	112037
61912	ASHMORE	21009	545	17.8	29.4	48.4	2.8	1.7	51506	51925	65	48	448	18.8	30.8	42.4	6.9	1.1	90909
61913	ATWOOD	21638	768	25.8	30.7	36.2	4.9	2.3	44791	47212	48	29	617	15.2	26.9	43.8	13.3	0.8	99898
	ILLINOIS	28587		18.2	22.2	39.3	12.1	8.2	60823	63631				6.3	10.0	30.9	40.6	12.3	185324
	UNITED STATES	27277		20.9	24.4	35.3	11.7	7.6	54719	56938				9.3	13.1	31.6	32.6	13.5	162279

ZIP CODE #	POST OFFICE NAME	FINANCIAL SERVICES Auto Loan	Home Loan	Investments	Retirement Plans	THE HOME Home Improvements Home Repair	Lawn & Garden	Furnishings Computers & Hardware-Personal	Major Appliances	TV, Radio, Sound Equipment	Furniture	ENTERTAINMENT Dine out/ Carry out	Sports Equipment	Fees & Tickets	Toys & Games	Travel	Cable TV	PERSONAL Apparel & Services	Auto Repairs	Health Insurance	Pets & Supplies
61732	DANVERS	104	110	92	109	105	100	100	101	97	105	99	77	102	102	100	96	68	98	96	118
61733	DEER CREEK	113	108	104	113	109	122	104	115	106	97	105	88	100	109	106	111	72	108	118	135
61734	DELAVAN	93	96	87	98	94	104	91	96	93	87	92	73	92	94	93	96	64	93	102	113
61735	DEWITT	106	112	101	116	111	117	103	110	103	101	103	85	106	106	107	105	71	105	111	129
61736	DOWNS	114	131	113	134	127	126	116	120	113	117	114	94	124	116	123	113	80	115	117	141
61737	ELLSWORTH	108	122	105	125	118	120	109	113	107	109	108	88	116	110	115	107	75	109	112	133
61738	EL PASO	99	100	95	100	97	107	94	99	96	92	96	76	95	98	96	99	66	97	105	118
61739	FAIRBURY	96	85	89	87	87	100	88	96	90	81	89	72	80	90	86	95	60	92	100	112
61740	FLANAGAN	85	89	91	88	89	101	81	91	86	78	86	66	85	85	87	92	59	87	101	106
61741	FORREST	96	87	87	89	86	103	88	95	90	80	89	75	81	91	87	95	61	92	102	114
61742	GOODFIELD	105	116	101	120	113	116	105	110	103	104	104	86	111	106	110	104	72	105	109	129
61743	GRAYMONT	115	129	112	133	125	127	115	120	114	115	114	94	123	116	122	114	80	116	119	142
61744	GRIDLEY	97	90	87	93	90	104	89	97	91	81	90	75	83	93	89	96	61	92	102	115
61745	HEYWORTH	111	117	101	117	113	111	106	111	104	108	105	87	107	109	107	103	73	105	105	128
61747	HOPEDALE	100	111	97	115	108	110	100	104	99	100	99	82	106	101	105	99	69	100	104	123
61748	HUDSON	116	130	116	127	126	118	114	118	111	122	113	89	121	115	119	109	79	113	113	135
61749	KENNEY	104	100	95	103	100	113	96	106	98	89	97	81	92	100	97	102	66	99	109	124
61752	LE ROY	92	105	89	106	100	104	95	97	95	94	95	75	102	97	99	96	66	95	101	114
61753	LEXINGTON	107	96	102	99	97	115	95	108	97	86	96	83	86	98	96	102	65	100	111	127
61754	MC LEAN	101	99	84	102	94	108	98	100	100	91	99	78	96	102	96	103	68	99	108	120
61755	MACKINAW	105	114	94	117	108	114	106	107	106	104	106	84	111	108	108	107	74	106	111	128
61756	MAROA	97	91	84	94	90	104	90	97	93	83	91	75	86	94	89	97	62	93	102	115
61759	MINIER	93	85	84	88	86	100	83	94	86	75	84	71	77	88	83	91	58	87	97	109
61760	MINONK	92	78	87	80	80	98	79	92	84	71	82	70	70	84	79	90	55	85	97	108
61761	NORMAL	93	80	73	83	77	77	102	83	94	93	95	70	90	96	86	91	67	91	82	101
61764	PONTIAC	88	80	79	81	79	91	82	86	85	78	84	66	77	85	80	88	57	85	92	103
61769	SAUNEMIN	107	94	100	98	97	115	94	108	97	84	96	83	85	99	94	104	65	100	112	126
61770	SAYBROOK	90	62	98	62	65	95	69	85	72	56	71	70	51	70	69	78	46	80	90	105
61771	SECOR	120	93	133	94	97	128	97	117	100	84	99	95	80	98	99	106	65	109	121	142
61772	SHIRLEY	114	108	106	112	110	125	105	117	108	96	106	88	99	110	106	114	73	109	122	136
61773	SIBLEY	106	73	117	73	77	112	81	101	84	66	83	83	59	83	81	92	54	94	107	124
61774	STANFORD	100	101	82	104	95	107	101	99	102	95	101	79	100	104	98	105	70	100	109	120
61775	STRAWN	124	85	136	85	89	131	95	118	98	77	97	97	69	97	94	107	63	110	124	145
61776	TOWANDA	106	127	112	128	122	123	110	114	110	112	111	87	123	112	119	111	78	111	116	133
61777	WAPELLA	109	93	104	96	95	116	94	109	97	83	96	84	83	98	94	104	64	101	113	128
61778	WAYNESVILLE	92	83	83	86	85	98	82	93	85	74	83	70	75	86	82	90	57	86	96	108
61790	NORMAL	45	29	28	32	28	31	53	36	48	42	48	33	39	48	37	47	34	44	38	46
61801	URBANA	66	47	46	51	46	50	79	56	72	65	72	50	62	70	59	69	51	67	59	71
61802	URBANA	81	74	67	75	71	74	81	75	81	80	81	59	77	82	76	81	56	79	79	91
61810	ALLERTON	105	72	115	72	76	111	80	100	84	65	83	83	59	82	80	91	54	93	105	123
61811	ALVIN	89	81	80	84	82	95	80	90	82	72	81	68	73	84	79	87	55	83	93	104
61812	ARMSTRONG	98	67	107	67	70	103	75	93	78	60	77	77	55	76	74	85	50	87	98	114
61813	BEMENT	89	85	77	87	82	95	85	89	87	78	86	69	81	88	83	90	59	86	95	106
61814	BISMARCK	98	96	90	99	96	106	91	100	93	85	92	77	88	95	93	96	63	94	102	117
61816	BROADLANDS	93	68	100	68	70	98	73	89	76	61	75	73	57	75	73	81	49	83	93	109
61817	CATLIN	91	87	79	89	84	97	87	90	89	81	88	71	84	91	86	93	60	89	98	109
61818	CERRO GORDO	84	80	73	81	75	90	81	82	82	75	82	66	77	83	79	85	56	82	90	100
61820	CHAMPAIGN	53	34	32	38	32	37	64	43	57	51	57	39	47	56	44	55	40	52	45	55
61821	CHAMPAIGN	99	93	86	96	90	92	100	93	99	100	100	73	98	101	95	99	70	98	96	112
61822	CHAMPAIGN	140	145	130	148	141	129	140	134	134	147	136	108	144	140	138	129	97	133	123	156
61830	CISCO	105	76	113	76	79	111	82	100	85	68	84	82	63	84	82	92	55	94	106	123
61831	COLLISON	98	78	98	80	80	104	81	96	84	70	83	76	68	84	81	90	55	89	100	115
61832	DANVILLE	71	62	63	62	61	72	68	69	72	64	71	52	63	71	64	76	49	70	78	83
61833	TILTON	69	50	69	48	52	72	54	67	61	48	58	50	44	60	52	67	39	62	73	79
61834	DANVILLE	85	76	81	77	77	90	77	85	81	73	79	63	72	81	76	85	54	81	90	100
61839	DE LAND	106	98	96	102	99	114	96	107	98	87	97	81	89	100	96	104	66	99	110	125
61840	DEWEY	114	115	106	118	114	122	108	117	108	104	108	90	106	111	110	111	74	110	116	136
61841	FAIRMOUNT	98	71	102	70	74	101	75	93	80	66	79	73	59	79	74	87	52	86	97	112
61842	FARMER CITY	98	96	85	99	93	106	94	99	96	88	95	77	92	98	93	100	65	96	105	117
61843	FISHER	103	99	95	103	100	112	95	105	97	88	96	80	91	99	96	102	66	98	108	123
61844	FITHIAN	89	84	78	86	82	96	85	89	86	78	85	70	80	88	83	90	58	87	95	106
61845	FOOSLAND	96	89	87	93	90	103	87	98	89	79	88	74	81	91	87	94	60	90	100	114
61846	GEORGETOWN	76	59	66	58	59	76	63	71	69	58	67	54	53	70	59	74	45	68	77	85
61847	GIFFORD	102	91	94	94	93	110	90	103	93	81	92	79	82	95	90	99	62	95	106	120
61849	HOMER	95	78	92	79	80	101	80	94	85	72	83	72	70	85	79	91	56	87	99	110
61850	INDIANOLA	93	67	96	65	69	95	69	87	76	64	75	66	55	76	68	84	49	80	91	104
61851	IVESDALE	110	105	101	109	106	119	101	113	104	94	102	86	96	106	102	108	70	105	115	131
61852	LONGVIEW	97	105	95	108	103	106	95	100	94	95	95	78	99	96	100	95	66	96	100	118
61853	MAHOMET	116	125	106	122	119	110	112	113	108	119	110	87	115	114	112	105	77	109	104	131
61854	MANSFIELD	98	105	86	108	99	106	99	99	99	97	99	78	103	102	100	100	69	99	104	119
61855	MILMINE	93	64	102	64	67	98	71	88	74	57	73	73	52	72	70	80	47	82	93	108
61856	MONTICELLO	98	103	102	104	105	112	97	104	99	96	99	76	101	98	102	103	68	101	111	120
61858	OAKWOOD	90	85	76	86	83	91	85	88	86	81	85	67	80	88	82	88	59	86	91	104
61859	OGDEN	99	109	92	106	103	100	97	98	96	102	97	74	102	99	99	95	67	96	96	115
61862	PENFIELD	120	86	128	87	90	127	94	115	98	78	96	94	72	96	93	106	63	107	121	140
61863	PESOTUM	87	107	95	107	103	106	91	96	93	93	94	72	105	94	101	94	66	93	101	112
61864	PHILO	102	122	108	123	118	120	106	111	106	107	107	84	118	108	115	108	75	107	114	129
61865	POTOMAC	89	75	86	77	77	95	76	89	79	67	77	69	66	79	76	84	52	82	92	105
61866	RANTOUL	81	73	64	74	70	75	80	75	81	77	80	60	75	82	74	82	56	79	79	91
61870	RIDGE FARM	81	63	79	63	65	85	66	80	72	60	70	60	56	72	65	79	47	74	85	93
61872	SADORUS	110	109	103	112	109	121	103	114	105	97	104	86	101	107	106	110	72	106	116	132
61873	SAINT JOSEPH	106	120	103	117	114	107	105	107	101	111	103	82	111	106	108	99	72	102	100	123
61874	SAVOY	111	109	106	112	108	107	113	108	113	114	114	84	113	113	111	113	80	111	112	127
61875	SEYMOUR	130	139	131	140	139	134	123	129	122	130	123	98	130	126	127	122	87	123	123	151
61876	SIDELL	84	60	87	58	62	86	62	79	68	57	67	60	49	68	61	75	44	72	82	94
61877	SIDNEY	102	101	96	104	101	107	99	103	100	97	99	78	98	101	100	102	69	101	106	121
61878	THOMASBORO	85	88	70	90	82	91	86	84	87	82	86	67	87	89	85	88	60	85	92	102
61880	TOLONO	95	91	85	93	90	100	92	95	94	88	93	73	89	95	91	97	64	94	102	113
61882	WELDON	109	99	98	104	101	117	98	110	101	89	99	84	91	103	98	107	68	102	114	128
61883	WESTVILLE	77	63	73	62	62	81	66	75	71	60	69	57	58	71	64	77	47	72	82	89
61884	WHITE HEATH	111	125	108	128	121	123	112	116	110	112	110	91	119	113	118	110	77	112	115	137
61910	ARCOLA	101	81	91	82	82	103	82	96	88	76	86	73	71	90	79	95	58	89	100	114
61911	ARTHUR	97	76	87	77	77	99	78	91	84	72	82	70	66	86	75	90	55	85	95	109
61912	ASHMORE	79	76	68	78	74	84	75	79	77	70	76	61	72	78	74	80	52	76	84	94
61913	ATWOOD	93	70	87	69	71	93	71	86	78	67	77	65	59	79	69	85	51	80	90	103
	ILLINOIS	106	108	105	108	107	106	109	106	108	107	109	83	110	108	108	108	77	108	107	125
	UNITED STATES	100	100	100	100	100	100	100	100	100	100	100	100	100	100	100	100	100	100	100	100

ZIP CODE #	POST OFFICE NAME	COUNTY FIPS CODE	POPULATION 2000	POPULATION 2009	POPULATION 2014	2000-2009 ANNUAL RATE % Rate	2000-2009 ANNUAL RATE State Centile	HOUSEHOLDS 2000	HOUSEHOLDS 2009	HOUSEHOLDS 2014	HOUSEHOLDS % Annual Rate 2000-2009	HOUSEHOLDS 2009 Average HH Size	FAMILIES 2000	FAMILIES 2009	FAMILIES % Annual Rate 2000-2009
61914	BETHANY	139	1898	1933	1938	0.2	61	769	798	802	0.4	2.42	579	589	0.2
61917	BROCTON	045	632	619	606	-0.2	38	260	259	254	0.0	2.39	185	181	-0.2
61919	CAMARGO	041	760	837	849	1.0	83	302	337	343	1.2	2.48	238	262	1.0
61920	CHARLESTON	029	24428	23404	23043	-0.5	18	8979	8973	8865	0.0	2.23	4350	4195	-0.4
61924	CHRISMAN	045	2496	2363	2287	-0.6	13	950	904	877	-0.5	2.41	657	613	-0.7
61925	DALTON CITY	115	1036	1035	1022	0.0	50	370	377	375	0.2	2.75	300	302	0.1
61928	GAYS	139	893	1045	1098	1.7	90	359	422	445	1.8	2.48	272	316	1.6
61929	HAMMOND	147	933	905	891	-0.3	32	391	384	379	-0.2	2.35	279	268	-0.4
61930	HINDSBORO	041	567	545	532	-0.4	25	214	210	206	-0.2	2.54	160	153	-0.5
61931	HUMBOLDT	029	1347	1410	1411	0.5	72	497	530	533	0.7	2.66	377	394	0.5
61932	HUME	045	527	564	568	0.7	78	234	254	257	0.9	2.22	171	182	0.7
61933	KANSAS	045	1187	1121	1088	-0.6	13	464	439	426	-0.6	2.55	320	296	-0.8
61937	LOVINGTON	139	2006	2025	2002	0.1	56	782	801	795	0.3	2.51	576	578	0.0
61938	MATTOON	029	22324	21333	20806	-0.5	18	9649	9438	9265	-0.2	2.22	5929	5660	-0.5
61940	METCALF	045	355	380	383	0.7	78	135	147	149	0.9	2.59	98	105	0.7
61942	NEWMAN	041	1369	1376	1363	0.1	56	558	566	562	0.2	2.33	382	380	-0.1
61943	OAKLAND	029	1898	1706	1665	-1.1	2	715	694	681	-0.3	2.43	522	497	-0.5
61944	PARIS	045	14153	13618	13255	-0.4	25	5694	5521	5383	-0.3	2.36	3790	3595	-0.6
61951	SULLIVAN	139	7285	7314	7296	0.0	50	2809	2848	2850	0.1	2.43	1999	1989	-0.1
61953	TUSCOLA	041	6391	6392	6324	0.0	50	2541	2581	2563	0.2	2.43	1777	1770	0.0
61956	VILLA GROVE	041	2986	2836	2759	-0.6	13	1185	1148	1123	-0.3	2.46	853	809	-0.6
61957	WINDSOR	173	2036	1908	1833	-0.7	9	800	755	728	-0.6	2.49	584	542	-0.8
62001	ALHAMBRA	119	1602	1704	1754	0.7	78	568	624	650	1.0	2.53	441	475	0.8
62002	ALTON	119	34722	33651	33292	-0.3	32	14108	14051	14014	0.0	2.32	8959	8677	-0.3
62006	BATCHTOWN	013	677	706	720	0.5	72	249	262	268	0.6	2.69	183	189	0.3
62009	BENLD	117	1857	1791	1755	-0.4	25	795	777	764	-0.2	2.30	509	485	-0.5
62010	BETHALTO	119	10785	11194	11374	0.4	69	4168	4477	4592	0.8	2.48	3050	3202	0.5
62011	BINGHAM	051	500	489	481	-0.2	38	196	196	194	0.0	2.49	141	138	-0.2
62012	BRIGHTON	083	6733	7104	7218	0.6	75	2432	2619	2678	0.8	2.69	1956	2080	0.7
62013	BRUSSELS	013	1225	1263	1277	0.3	65	481	505	514	0.5	2.50	349	359	0.3
62014	BUNKER HILL	117	3997	4049	4028	0.1	56	1498	1545	1545	0.3	2.59	1142	1159	0.2
62015	BUTLER	135	551	558	555	0.1	56	220	228	228	0.4	2.45	173	177	0.2
62016	CARROLLTON	061	3151	3025	2931	-0.4	25	1262	1222	1187	-0.3	2.42	886	842	-0.5
62017	COFFEEN	135	1289	1190	1173	-0.9	4	527	496	492	-0.7	2.20	379	349	-0.9
62018	COTTAGE HILLS	119	4306	4181	4136	-0.3	32	1610	1609	1604	0.0	2.51	1172	1145	-0.3
62019	DONNELLSON	005	669	679	681	0.2	61	284	295	298	0.4	1.85	202	206	0.2
62021	DORSEY	119	832	910	943	1.0	83	316	357	373	1.3	2.55	261	292	1.2
62022	DOW	083	1058	1074	1081	0.2	61	388	401	406	0.4	2.57	304	310	0.2
62024	EAST ALTON	119	10915	10420	10240	-0.5	18	4600	4504	4463	-0.2	2.31	2994	2851	-0.5
62025	EDWARDSVILLE	119	31126	34338	35572	1.1	85	11130	12603	13166	1.4	2.49	7669	8495	1.1
62027	ELDRED	061	758	698	667	-0.9	4	296	276	264	-0.8	2.53	212	195	-0.9
62028	ELSAH	083	1581	1675	1707	0.6	75	420	461	477	1.0	2.91	309	335	0.9
62030	FIDELITY	083	137	151	157	1.1	85	55	62	65	1.3	2.44	43	47	1.0
62031	FIELDON	083	1292	1398	1448	0.9	81	487	536	559	1.0	2.60	372	405	0.9
62032	FILLMORE	135	801	869	879	0.9	81	310	339	343	1.0	2.50	228	244	0.7
62033	GILLESPIE	117	5865	5703	5626	-0.3	32	2407	2383	2363	-0.1	2.35	1629	1578	-0.3
62034	GLEN CARBON	119	11599	13418	14359	1.6	89	4483	5338	5760	1.9	2.49	3222	3743	1.6
62035	GODFREY	119	14390	15013	15302	0.5	72	5758	6203	6388	0.8	2.36	4201	4423	0.6
62036	GOLDEN EAGLE	013	249	256	259	0.3	65	106	111	113	0.5	2.31	77	79	0.3
62037	GRAFTON	083	2022	2113	2153	0.5	72	745	794	814	0.7	2.58	552	583	0.6
62040	GRANITE CITY	119	45883	44145	43539	-0.4	25	18364	18103	18002	-0.2	2.42	12556	12067	-0.4
62044	GREENFIELD	061	1761	1726	1684	-0.2	38	713	705	688	-0.1	2.45	502	488	-0.3
62045	HAMBURG	013	393	406	412	0.4	69	161	169	173	0.5	2.40	117	121	0.4
62047	HARDIN	013	1133	1160	1172	0.3	65	453	473	481	0.5	2.34	297	304	0.3
62048	HARTFORD	119	1529	1502	1490	-0.2	38	645	652	654	0.1	2.30	431	425	-0.2
62049	HILLSBORO	135	7085	8910	8816	2.5	93	2862	2836	2810	-0.1	2.46	1954	1893	-0.3
62050	HILLVIEW	061	644	584	556	-1.1	2	233	214	205	-0.9	2.73	184	166	-1.1
62051	IRVING	135	2871	883	875	-12.0	0	337	345	345	0.3	2.52	255	256	0.0
62052	JERSEYVILLE	083	11677	12478	12759	0.7	78	4585	4998	5145	0.9	2.43	3151	3360	0.7
62053	KAMPSVILLE	013	545	586	603	0.8	79	236	260	270	1.1	2.25	161	174	0.8
62054	KANE	061	1131	1114	1093	-0.2	38	419	417	411	-0.1	2.67	324	318	-0.2
62056	LITCHFIELD	135	8963	8737	8607	-0.3	32	3564	3527	3493	-0.1	2.40	2415	2348	-0.3
62060	MADISON	119	5853	5471	5353	-0.7	9	2409	2280	2244	-0.6	2.40	1488	1360	-1.0
62061	MARINE	119	1337	1485	1522	1.1	85	525	596	616	1.4	2.49	392	436	1.2
62062	MARYVILLE	119	4958	7101	7647	4.0	97	1851	2780	3025	4.5	2.49	1406	2098	4.4
62063	MEDORA	083	1326	1380	1400	0.4	69	471	495	505	0.5	2.79	354	366	0.4
62065	MICHAEL	013	325	352	364	0.9	81	130	144	150	1.1	2.44	88	96	0.9
62067	MORO	119	2223	2628	2792	1.8	91	962	1171	1260	2.1	2.24	640	757	1.8
62069	MOUNT OLIVE	117	3793	3779	3747	0.0	50	1551	1561	1554	0.1	2.42	1086	1070	-0.2
62070	MOZIER	013	236	242	244	0.3	65	99	104	106	0.5	2.33	72	74	0.3
62074	NEW DOUGLAS	119	1725	1802	1839	0.5	72	705	755	775	0.7	2.39	504	527	0.5
62075	NOKOMIS	135	3810	3678	3594	-0.4	25	1563	1536	1508	-0.2	2.32	1025	989	-0.4
62079	PIASA	117	270	273	272	0.1	56	98	101	101	0.3	2.70	75	77	0.3
62080	RAMSEY	051	3063	4462	4421	4.2	97	1212	1223	1213	0.1	2.49	886	878	-0.1
62081	ROCKBRIDGE	061	706	680	659	-0.4	25	273	265	258	-0.3	2.56	202	192	-0.5
62082	ROODHOUSE	061	3112	2905	2793	-0.7	9	1165	1087	1045	-0.7	2.52	823	754	-0.9
62083	ROSAMOND	021	173	177	177	0.2	61	68	71	71	0.5	2.11	49	50	0.2
62084	ROXANA	119	1458	1454	1449	0.0	50	622	638	641	0.3	2.28	407	406	0.0
62086	SORENTO	005	1713	1881	1948	1.0	83	664	741	771	1.2	2.54	497	544	1.0
62087	SOUTH ROXANA	119	1961	1991	2002	0.2	61	738	769	780	0.4	2.59	540	550	0.2
62088	STAUNTON	117	6814	6899	6886	0.1	56	2733	2799	2805	0.3	2.43	1894	1899	0.0
62090	VENICE	119	1586	1260	1184	-2.5	0	572	468	444	-2.1	2.69	411	328	-2.4
62091	WALSHVILLE	135	409	397	391	-0.3	32	153	152	151	-0.1	2.61	117	115	-0.2
62092	WHITE HALL	061	3611	3410	3298	-0.6	13	1444	1375	1332	-0.5	2.40	981	915	-0.8
62094	WITT	135	1266	1273	1264	0.1	56	542	555	554	0.3	2.29	342	342	0.0
62095	WOOD RIVER	119	11811	11677	11634	-0.1	45	4953	5002	5016	0.1	2.31	3221	3179	-0.1
62097	WORDEN	119	2624	2852	2951	0.9	81	1010	1129	1176	1.2	2.52	777	853	1.0
62201	EAST SAINT LOUIS	163	9242	8967	8952	-0.3	32	3421	3365	3378	-0.2	2.64	2192	2066	-0.6
62203	EAST SAINT LOUIS	163	10083	9426	9197	-0.7	9	3171	3064	3013	-0.4	2.87	2341	2214	-0.6
62204	EAST SAINT LOUIS	163	10724	9520	9146	-1.3	2	3431	3130	3032	-1.0	3.03	2478	2215	-1.2
62205	EAST SAINT LOUIS	163	10193	9571	9378	-0.7	9	3766	3643	3600	-0.4	2.60	2471	2321	-0.7
62206	EAST SAINT LOUIS	163	18315	17619	17338	-0.4	25	6299	6156	6094	-0.2	2.83	4690	4485	-0.5
62207	EAST SAINT LOUIS	163	9908	9361	9186	-0.6	13	3558	3459	3424	-0.3	2.69	2483	2367	-0.5
62208	FAIRVIEW HEIGHTS	163	14681	15826	16210	0.8	79	5929	6585	6804	1.1	2.39	4076	4402	0.8
62214	ADDIEVILLE	189	1287	1315	1302	0.2	61	474	491	488	0.4	2.68	369	377	0.2
	ILLINOIS					0.6					0.6	2.64			0.4
	UNITED STATES					1.0					1.1	2.59			0.9

ZIP CODE #	POST OFFICE NAME	RACE (%) White 2000	White 2009	Black 2000	Black 2009	Asian/Pacific 2000	Asian/Pacific 2009	% Hispanic Origin 2000	% Hispanic Origin 2009	2009 AGE DISTRIBUTION (%) 0-4	5-9	10-14	15-19	20-24	25-44	45-64	65-84	85+	18+	MEDIAN AGE 2009	% 2009 Males	% 2009 Females
61914	BETHANY	98.8	98.6	0.1	0.1	0.0	0.0	0.5	0.7	5.4	5.7	6.2	6.4	4.5	23.7	30.8	15.1	2.2	78.7	43.6	50.0	50.0
61917	BROCTON	99.1	99.0	0.0	0.0	0.2	0.2	0.5	0.8	5.3	6.0	6.3	6.8	4.4	22.0	33.1	13.7	2.4	78.0	44.4	49.8	50.2
61919	CAMARGO	98.7	98.4	0.4	0.4	0.0	0.0	0.3	0.4	5.3	6.1	6.6	6.5	4.8	23.8	31.9	13.6	1.6	78.0	42.9	50.7	49.3
61920	CHARLESTON	93.2	88.5	3.7	6.0	1.3	2.6	1.7	3.5	4.3	4.2	4.3	9.8	23.4	23.2	20.1	8.9	1.7	84.1	27.6	49.1	50.9
61924	CHRISMAN	99.0	98.7	0.4	0.6	0.2	0.2	0.2	0.3	5.1	6.3	6.1	6.1	4.4	21.8	26.4	16.6	7.2	78.5	45.1	48.5	51.5
61925	DALTON CITY	98.5	98.2	0.6	0.7	0.2	0.2	0.9	1.4	6.5	6.8	7.2	7.2	4.9	23.9	32.3	10.2	1.0	75.1	40.4	49.5	50.5
61928	GAYS	97.8	97.1	0.8	0.9	0.7	1.0	0.4	0.6	5.8	6.2	6.6	6.1	4.7	25.2	30.0	13.6	1.7	77.7	41.4	51.0	49.0
61929	HAMMOND	98.6	98.3	0.4	0.6	0.1	0.1	0.3	0.4	6.2	6.7	7.1	7.4	4.9	23.9	29.7	12.0	2.1	75.5	40.5	51.4	48.6
61930	HINDSBORO	99.3	99.3	0.0	0.0	0.2	0.2	1.4	2.2	6.2	7.3	7.2	5.7	3.5	21.8	30.3	15.2	2.8	75.6	43.5	49.7	50.3
61931	HUMBOLDT	99.1	98.5	0.0	0.0	0.0	0.0	1.7	2.6	8.7	8.8	8.5	6.7	4.6	26.5	24.1	10.6	1.5	69.8	35.7	49.1	50.9
61932	HUME	99.6	99.3	0.0	0.0	0.0	0.0	0.9	1.8	5.7	6.2	6.4	5.9	3.9	23.9	31.0	14.5	2.5	78.2	43.5	50.5	49.5
61933	KANSAS	98.7	98.6	0.3	0.3	0.2	0.3	1.3	1.8	5.7	5.7	6.2	7.7	6.2	23.6	27.5	14.8	2.6	77.8	41.2	47.5	52.5
61937	LOVINGTON	98.9	98.5	0.2	0.3	0.2	0.3	0.4	0.7	6.2	6.6	6.8	7.2	4.8	26.2	29.1	11.4	1.7	76.0	39.5	50.5	49.5
61938	MATTOON	97.0	96.1	1.2	1.5	0.4	0.6	1.2	1.7	6.5	6.2	5.9	5.8	5.6	27.0	26.1	13.9	3.0	77.9	39.4	48.2	51.8
61940	METCALF	99.4	99.5	0.0	0.0	0.0	0.0	0.8	1.6	5.8	6.3	6.6	6.1	3.9	24.2	29.7	15.0	2.4	77.4	42.8	50.5	49.5
61942	NEWMAN	98.0	97.5	0.9	1.1	0.1	0.1	0.4	0.5	5.6	6.0	6.0	5.4	5.2	21.7	28.3	17.1	4.8	79.1	45.2	47.3	52.7
61943	OAKLAND	98.2	89.9	0.6	7.1	0.1	2.2	1.0	2.7	5.5	5.9	5.8	6.5	5.7	23.3	29.4	15.7	2.2	80.2	42.2	48.9	51.1
61944	PARIS	96.4	95.6	2.5	2.9	0.2	0.3	0.8	1.2	5.9	5.8	6.1	6.2	6.0	25.4	27.3	14.2	3.1	78.4	40.6	49.2	50.8
61951	SULLIVAN	99.0	98.7	0.2	0.2	0.1	0.2	0.4	0.6	6.2	6.5	6.5	6.1	5.0	23.6	26.6	14.8	4.7	76.9	41.8	48.4	51.6
61953	TUSCOLA	98.2	97.6	0.3	0.4	0.4	0.6	1.1	1.7	6.5	6.5	6.4	6.1	5.8	25.2	27.5	13.3	2.8	76.8	40.1	48.7	51.3
61956	VILLA GROVE	98.1	97.5	0.4	0.4	0.1	0.1	0.8	1.3	6.5	6.7	6.5	6.4	5.9	25.6	27.9	12.4	2.0	76.2	38.9	49.2	50.8
61957	WINDSOR	99.3	99.0	0.0	0.0	0.0	0.0	0.3	0.4	5.8	6.0	6.5	7.4	4.6	23.3	29.1	13.9	3.4	77.0	42.2	48.7	51.3
62001	ALHAMBRA	98.8	98.3	0.0	0.1	0.1	0.2	0.7	1.1	4.6	5.2	5.6	6.2	4.5	21.5	30.9	16.4	5.1	83.0	46.4	49.2	50.8
62002	ALTON	75.9	72.0	21.4	24.8	0.4	0.5	1.4	1.9	6.8	6.6	6.6	6.5	6.0	25.9	25.6	13.0	3.0	76.7	38.6	47.8	52.2
62006	BATCHTOWN	98.8	98.7	0.1	0.1	0.0	0.0	0.7	0.8	7.2	7.6	7.5	5.9	3.5	25.2	27.6	13.0	2.3	73.7	39.8	52.8	47.2
62009	BENLD	98.1	97.7	0.5	0.7	0.0	0.0	1.0	1.3	6.8	6.7	6.5	6.6	5.0	25.8	25.7	13.2	3.6	75.8	39.9	49.4	50.6
62010	BETHALTO	97.8	97.1	0.8	1.0	0.4	0.5	0.9	1.4	6.2	6.1	6.2	6.7	6.2	26.8	27.6	12.1	2.0	77.6	39.1	48.8	51.2
62011	BINGHAM	98.8	98.4	0.2	0.2	0.2	0.4	0.2	0.4	6.3	6.7	7.0	6.7	4.5	23.3	29.4	13.9	2.0	75.5	41.1	51.1	48.9
62012	BRIGHTON	98.0	97.3	0.7	0.9	0.4	0.5	0.8	1.2	6.1	6.7	7.0	6.8	4.9	25.8	29.0	12.2	1.5	75.8	40.3	49.5	50.5
62013	BRUSSELS	99.1	98.8	0.0	0.0	0.1	0.2	0.5	0.7	5.1	5.4	5.7	5.9	4.7	24.9	29.8	16.0	2.4	80.0	43.8	50.4	49.6
62014	BUNKER HILL	97.1	96.3	1.9	2.2	0.1	0.2	0.4	0.7	6.1	6.3	6.6	6.6	5.2	25.0	28.6	13.9	1.7	76.9	40.8	48.5	51.5
62015	BUTLER	99.1	98.6	0.2	0.4	0.4	0.5	0.4	0.5	4.8	5.2	5.6	5.9	4.3	24.7	32.3	15.1	2.2	80.6	44.6	51.4	48.6
62016	CARROLLTON	98.7	98.4	0.0	0.0	0.3	0.4	0.4	0.5	6.6	6.5	6.4	6.0	5.9	23.4	26.4	14.7	4.0	76.5	40.8	48.2	51.8
62017	COFFEEN	98.6	96.1	0.0	1.8	0.5	0.8	0.6	5.4	5.5	5.5	5.8	8.1	7.1	22.1	27.7	15.4	2.9	79.3	42.2	49.2	50.8
62018	COTTAGE HILLS	93.8	91.6	4.0	5.5	0.3	0.4	1.0	1.6	6.6	6.9	6.9	7.1	6.2	29.4	25.3	10.5	1.1	75.4	36.0	51.0	49.0
62019	DONNELLSON	97.8	90.6	0.9	5.3	0.1	1.5	0.4	2.5	5.0	5.6	5.7	8.7	8.0	23.9	28.9	12.7	1.6	80.1	39.8	52.6	47.4
62021	DORSEY	97.7	96.7	1.0	1.3	0.4	0.4	0.6	1.0	4.8	5.5	6.0	6.7	4.7	22.7	34.4	13.6	1.4	79.5	44.6	50.2	49.8
62022	DOW	98.1	97.6	0.5	0.6	0.2	0.3	0.7	0.9	5.5	5.9	6.1	7.7	7.2	23.6	30.6	12.5	0.9	78.6	40.6	49.6	50.4
62024	EAST ALTON	97.2	96.3	0.8	1.1	0.4	0.5	1.0	1.4	6.4	6.1	6.1	6.5	5.9	25.8	26.4	14.4	2.4	77.5	39.6	48.1	51.9
62025	EDWARDSVILLE	89.5	86.0	7.4	10.0	1.3	1.8	0.9	1.3	5.6	5.4	5.7	8.8	9.9	26.3	26.1	10.4	1.8	79.4	35.8	47.7	52.3
62027	ELDRED	99.1	98.7	0.0	0.0	0.3	0.3	0.3	0.3	4.2	5.3	6.7	6.3	4.6	22.8	32.5	15.9	1.7	79.5	45.1	49.9	50.1
62028	ELSAH	95.9	94.9	1.3	1.6	0.5	0.7	1.3	1.9	5.4	5.5	5.5	12.3	15.5	19.0	26.3	9.8	0.7	80.1	31.3	49.4	50.6
62030	FIDELITY	99.3	98.0	0.0	0.0	0.0	0.7	0.7	1.3	5.3	6.6	7.9	7.9	5.3	25.2	27.8	11.9	2.0	74.8	40.5	50.3	49.7
62031	FIELDON	98.6	98.1	0.2	0.1	0.6	0.9	0.9	1.2	6.5	6.2	7.2	6.8	5.2	25.6	30.2	11.1	1.3	75.7	40.0	51.6	48.4
62032	FILLMORE	98.0	96.2	0.6	1.5	0.1	0.5	0.7	1.4	6.4	6.7	6.4	6.9	6.0	23.7	28.1	13.7	2.1	76.6	40.5	51.7	48.3
62033	GILLESPIE	98.2	97.8	0.3	0.4	0.1	0.2	0.7	1.0	5.8	5.9	5.8	5.6	5.1	24.9	28.9	14.4	3.6	79.0	42.5	48.1	51.9
62034	GLEN CARBON	90.6	86.9	5.9	8.2	1.9	2.7	1.4	2.0	6.8	6.2	6.2	6.4	6.5	28.7	27.6	10.0	1.7	76.8	36.9	49.1	50.9
62035	GODFREY	93.7	91.4	4.3	6.0	0.7	0.9	1.0	1.5	5.4	5.6	6.1	6.1	5.3	22.0	29.8	17.2	2.6	79.6	44.7	48.2	51.8
62036	GOLDEN EAGLE	99.2	99.2	0.0	0.0	0.0	0.0	0.4	0.8	4.7	4.7	5.1	6.3	4.7	24.6	31.3	16.4	2.3	81.6	45.0	50.4	49.6
62037	GRAFTON	96.4	95.7	2.2	2.6	0.1	0.2	1.0	1.4	5.5	5.7	6.6	8.8	5.3	24.8	29.0	12.9	1.3	75.7	40.0	50.7	49.3
62040	GRANITE CITY	94.0	92.2	2.9	3.7	0.5	0.7	2.4	3.5	6.4	6.1	6.0	6.4	6.4	26.3	27.2	13.1	2.1	77.6	39.1	48.6	51.4
62044	GREENFIELD	99.0	98.9	0.1	0.1	0.1	0.1	0.3	0.5	6.1	6.3	6.1	5.9	5.6	25.7	27.8	13.8	2.7	77.9	40.5	48.6	51.4
62045	HAMBURG	98.7	98.5	0.0	0.0	0.3	0.2	0.5	0.5	5.4	5.9	5.7	5.7	4.2	20.7	33.0	17.2	2.2	79.3	46.3	51.0	49.0
62047	HARDIN	99.4	99.2	0.0	0.0	0.2	0.3	0.7	0.9	5.9	5.9	5.8	6.0	5.3	25.3	24.3	16.9	4.7	78.9	42.2	48.3	51.7
62048	HARTFORD	98.4	97.8	0.1	0.1	0.4	0.5	0.7	1.1	6.1	5.9	5.9	6.3	5.7	24.8	27.4	15.6	2.3	78.2	41.4	50.5	49.5
62049	HILLSBORO	97.5	90.2	1.1	5.5	0.3	1.8	1.0	3.3	5.7	5.7	5.8	8.9	9.1	24.6	24.5	12.5	3.2	79.3	37.0	50.0	50.0
62050	HILLVIEW	98.3	97.8	0.0	0.0	0.0	0.0	1.1	1.5	5.3	5.7	7.0	8.0	5.0	23.3	29.3	14.6	1.9	77.1	42.3	49.7	50.3
62051	IRVING	63.0	41.0	33.4	51.1	0.0	4.3	4.6	5.8	2.4	0.8	1.4	9.7	13.9	49.9	16.3	4.6	0.9	93.9	32.1	76.4	23.6
62052	JERSEYVILLE	98.8	98.5	0.1	0.1	0.2	0.3	0.5	0.8	6.2	6.2	6.4	6.5	5.5	24.6	27.2	13.9	3.4	77.2	40.9	47.6	52.4
62053	KAMPSVILLE	97.8	97.4	0.0	0.0	0.4	0.5	0.9	1.0	5.6	5.5	5.8	6.1	5.5	21.5	28.7	18.8	2.6	79.5	45.0	49.1	50.9
62054	KANE	98.8	98.5	0.1	0.1	0.1	0.1	0.2	0.2	6.1	6.9	7.9	6.7	4.7	24.7	28.7	12.7	1.6	74.8	40.4	50.8	49.2
62056	LITCHFIELD	98.4	97.8	0.3	0.4	0.3	0.4	0.9	1.2	6.3	6.3	6.5	6.7	5.4	23.4	27.4	14.4	3.7	76.7	41.4	47.8	52.2
62060	MADISON	46.2	40.7	51.2	56.0	0.2	0.2	2.4	3.1	7.5	7.9	7.0	7.6	6.9	24.4	24.5	11.9	2.2	72.9	35.8	48.5	51.5
62061	MARINE	98.1	97.3	0.2	0.5	0.1	0.1	0.7	1.0	6.5	6.5	6.3	6.1	6.4	26.9	28.7	11.1	1.5	77.1	38.1	49.6	50.4
62062	MARYVILLE	95.2	93.4	2.4	3.5	0.7	1.0	1.7	2.5	6.6	6.8	7.0	6.8	4.8	26.4	27.9	11.4	2.3	75.0	39.2	48.2	51.8
62063	MEDORA	98.1	97.5	0.2	0.1	0.2	0.2	0.8	1.0	5.3	7.0	8.6	8.3	5.4	24.0	26.3	13.2	2.0	73.9	39.1	50.1	49.9
62065	MICHAEL	97.8	97.4	0.0	0.0	0.3	0.6	0.9	1.4	5.7	5.7	6.0	6.3	5.7	21.3	28.4	18.2	2.8	78.4	44.5	49.4	50.6
62067	MORO	97.9	97.2	0.5	0.7	0.1	0.2	0.7	1.1	5.4	5.0	5.3	6.8	7.6	22.6	28.8	15.3	3.2	80.3	43.0	48.3	51.7
62069	MOUNT OLIVE	98.7	98.4	0.0	0.1	0.1	0.2	0.6	0.8	5.4	6.0	6.6	6.4	5.5	25.2	27.3	14.5	3.1	78.2	41.3	49.8	50.2
62070	MOZIER	98.3	98.3	0.0	0.0	0.4	0.4	0.4	0.4	4.5	4.5	5.0	5.4	4.5	19.0	35.5	19.0	2.5	82.6	48.5	48.8	51.2
62074	NEW DOUGLAS	98.6	98.1	0.1	0.1	0.1	0.2	1.0	1.5	5.5	5.7	6.0	6.7	5.0	24.0	29.4	15.1	2.7	78.8	42.9	50.3	49.7
62075	NOKOMIS	98.5	97.2	0.6	1.3	0.1	0.4	0.3	0.7	5.8	6.2	6.6	6.9	5.1	23.2	26.9	14.7	4.5	77.8	41.9	48.8	51.2
62079	PIASA	98.1	97.1	0.7	1.1	0.4	0.4	0.7	1.1	5.5	6.2	6.2	7.0	5.1	25.3	30.8	12.1	1.8	77.7	41.4	52.0	48.0
62080	RAMSEY	98.8	72.8	0.2	25.7	0.1	0.1	0.4	2.3	4.6	4.4	4.4	6.9	10.1	36.2	22.1	9.5	1.8	83.3	34.9	65.9	34.1
62081	ROCKBRIDGE	98.9	98.7	0.0	0.0	0.1	0.1	0.3	0.3	7.1	7.1	7.4	6.5	5.1	24.3	27.5	13.1	2.1	74.4	39.5	50.3	49.7
62082	ROODHOUSE	95.6	94.6	3.2	3.9	0.1	0.1	0.5	0.7	6.7	6.5	6.9	9.0	8.0	24.5	24.5	11.8	2.0	75.4	35.5	52.0	48.0
62083	ROSAMOND	89.0	87.0	8.7	9.6	0.6	0.6	2.3	3.4	5.1	5.6	6.2	6.2	5.6	27.7	28.2	13.0	2.3	79.7	40.6	57.1	42.9
62084	ROXANA	98.5	98.0	0.1	0.1	0.2	0.3	0.7	1.0	6.7	6.3	6.3	6.3	5.6	27.5	25.0	14.0	2.3	76.8	39.1	47.3	52.7
62086	SORENTO	98.1	97.6	0.1	0.1	0.4	0.4	0.6	1.0	6.3	6.7	6.8	5.9	4.6	24.1	30.8	13.2	1.6	76.5	41.6	49.7	50.3
62087	SOUTH ROXANA	97.8	97.0	0.3	0.5	0.3	0.4	0.8	1.3	6.8	6.2	6.2	7.7	7.4	27.4	26.2	11.1	1.0	76.1	36.2	49.4	50.6
62088	STAUNTON	98.7	98.4	0.1	0.1	0.3	0.4	0.7	0.9	5.9	5.9	6.7	6.8	6.1	24.7	26.6	13.7	3.6	77.4	40.6	48.8	51.2
62090	VENICE	8.1	6.0	91.2	93.3	0.0	0.0	0.7	0.9	10.6	10.3	8.9	9.1	8.3	23.4	21.7	6.7	0.9	64.5	26.9	42.6	57.4
62091	WALSHVILLE	98.8	98.5	0.2	0.5	0.2	0.3	0.2	0.3	4.8	6.0	8.1	6.8	4.8	24.7	30.7	12.1	2.0	77.1	41.3	51.4	48.6
62092	WHITE HALL	98.7	98.3	0.1	0.2	0.0	0.0	0.8	1.2	6.1	6.2	6.5	6.5	5.0	23.5	25.9	16.0	4.4	77.2	42.1	48.1	51.9
62094	WITT	96.9	94.7	2.6	4.2	0.1	0.5	0.6	0.9	6.2	6.0	6.4	6.6	5.7	24.9	27.1	14.5	2.7	77.7	40.6	50.6	49.4
62095	WOOD RIVER	97.9	97.3	0.4	0.6	0.4	0.5	1.2	1.7	6.5	6.0	5.9	6.3	6.0	26.7	25.4	14.1	3.2	77.9	39.1	47.8	52.2
62097	WORDEN	98.5	98.0	0.4	0.6	0.3	0.4	0.6	1.0	5.6	6.0	6.4	6.4	4.3	24.2	32.3	13.2	1.6	78.1	43.0	49.7	50.3
62201	EAST SAINT LOUIS	19.8	19.7	71.0	68.9	0.1	0.1	15.2	19.1	11.6	11.1	8.8	8.1	6.9	23.4	18.7	9.5	1.9	63.6	27.7	45.7	54.3
62203	EAST SAINT LOUIS	5.7	3.9	92.8	94.7	0.1	0.1	1.0	1.0	6.5	7.1	7.5	8.8	8.3	26.0	25.3	9.5	0.9	73.5	33.3	49.3	50.7
62204	EAST SAINT LOUIS	3.6	2.2	94.8	96.2	0.1	0.2	1.6	1.6	9.5	9.5	9.5	10.0	7.7	23.2	21.9	8.0	0.8	65.3	27.9	45.6	54.4
62205	EAST SAINT LOUIS	1.1	0.8	98.0	98.3	0.0	0.0	0.6	0.6	6.5	7.0	7.0	8.1	6.2	22.2	25.9	14.4	2.7	74.6	39.1	46.3	53.7
62206	EAST SAINT LOUIS	55.9	44.3	41.1	52.4	0.4	0.5	2.1	2.5	8.3	8.5	8.1	9.0	7.9	26.1	22.2	8.6	1.4	69.7	30.6	46.7	53.3
62207	EAST SAINT LOUIS	2.0	1.3	96.8	97.7	0.1	0.1	0.5	0.5	9.1	9.4	8.9	8.7	6.6	22.7	22.3	10.4	1.8	67.1	31.2	45.1	54.9
62208	FAIRVIEW HEIGHTS	78.6	69.7	16.9	24.7	2.0	2.5	2.1	2.9	5.6	5.6	5.9	5.9	5.3	25.4	28.9	14.7	2.6	79.2	42.3	47.8	52.2
62214	ADDIEVILLE	99.1	99.2	0.0	0.0	0.1	0.1	0.7	0.8	4.9	6.1	6.9	7.0	5.2	24.2	31.0	13.2	1.4	77.7	42.2	52.0	48.0
	ILLINOIS	73.5	70.6	15.1	15.3	3.4	4.4	12.3	15.7	7.1	6.9	6.8	7.1	6.9	27.5	25.4	10.3	1.9	75.0	36.1	49.1	50.9
	UNITED STATES	75.1	72.0	12.3	12.7	3.8	4.6	12.5	15.7	6.8	6.7	6.6	7.1	6.9	27.0	26.0	10.9	1.9	75.7	36.9	49.2	50.8

#	POST OFFICE NAME	2009 Per Capita Income	2009 HH Income Base	2009 Household Income Distribution (%): Less than $25,000	$25,000 to $49,999	$50,000 to $99,999	$100,000 to $149,999	$150,000 or More	Median Household Income: 2009	2014	2009 National Centile	2009 State Centile	2009 Home Value Base	2009 Home Value Distribution (%): Less than $50,000	$50,000 to $89,999	$90,000 to $174,999	$175,000 to $399,999	$400,000 or More	2009 Median Home Value
61914	BETHANY	23385	798	18.0	30.1	43.4	6.5	2.0	51614	54203	65	48	668	8.8	26.9	47.5	16.2	0.6	111364
61917	BROCTON	21232	259	29.7	32.4	32.8	3.1	1.9	39874	42093	32	16	205	40.0	38.5	18.0	2.9	0.5	61500
61919	CAMARGO	27773	337	12.5	22.3	55.5	7.1	2.7	63833	64890	82	71	281	12.5	12.1	43.4	29.2	2.8	134295
61920	CHARLESTON	20481	8973	39.8	24.2	26.7	6.4	2.9	35068	38913	18	7	4605	13.4	16.9	47.6	18.6	3.5	118328
61924	CHRISMAN	21061	904	23.0	33.3	37.1	4.5	2.1	45983	46817	51	32	682	25.2	28.4	31.1	13.5	1.8	85370
61925	DALTON CITY	25690	377	10.6	22.5	50.7	13.3	2.9	65376	66220	84	75	311	8.0	18.6	50.8	21.9	0.6	118664
61928	GAYS	25290	422	12.8	31.3	46.0	7.1	2.8	55065	56765	71	56	343	16.9	24.8	46.9	11.1	0.3	102218
61929	HAMMOND	25337	384	17.4	25.0	47.7	7.6	2.3	54688	57283	71	55	287	13.9	21.3	52.6	11.1	1.0	105784
61930	HINDSBORO	20629	210	25.7	31.9	33.8	6.2	2.4	43203	46850	43	24	173	17.3	31.2	34.7	11.6	5.2	92273
61931	HUMBOLDT	20826	530	22.1	34.2	35.1	6.8	1.9	46273	47964	52	33	417	17.0	23.5	44.4	13.7	1.4	100893
61932	HUME	24066	254	24.4	34.6	31.5	6.3	3.1	43479	44110	44	25	192	37.5	26.0	25.5	8.3	2.6	66154
61933	KANSAS	16967	439	33.5	33.9	28.7	2.3	1.6	35894	37732	20	8	320	27.8	38.8	30.9	2.5	0.0	70741
61937	LOVINGTON	24096	801	17.5	31.8	40.3	6.4	4.0	50672	54095	63	45	602	16.1	25.4	46.5	11.8	0.2	102976
61938	MATTOON	24071	9438	25.7	28.8	38.0	4.6	2.9	45630	47472	50	31	6210	11.3	32.0	42.1	13.1	1.5	99311
61940	METCALF	20652	147	23.8	34.0	32.7	6.1	3.4	44167	43827	46	27	111	36.9	26.1	25.2	8.1	3.6	66875
61942	NEWMAN	22521	566	27.7	33.9	31.1	4.4	2.8	39813	43555	32	16	449	27.8	35.6	28.1	8.0	0.4	73519
61943	OAKLAND	19362	694	27.8	35.4	32.1	2.9	1.7	40573	42897	35	17	551	23.8	33.0	31.8	8.7	2.7	82188
61944	PARIS	22094	5521	25.4	33.1	34.5	4.3	2.6	43339	45438	43	25	4049	21.7	35.9	32.5	9.0	1.0	79515
61951	SULLIVAN	23007	2848	20.1	30.8	39.4	6.6	3.0	49085	51494	59	40	2194	10.8	18.8	49.4	19.0	2.0	117148
61953	TUSCOLA	23862	2581	15.1	33.9	42.9	5.3	2.8	50776	53208	63	45	1935	12.5	20.5	49.3	16.8	1.0	115163
61956	VILLA GROVE	22393	1148	20.8	30.4	41.0	6.2	1.6	49046	50365	59	40	882	11.8	32.8	46.4	9.1	0.0	95783
61957	WINDSOR	20654	755	21.5	29.5	42.8	4.6	1.6	48572	49748	58	39	630	17.9	33.8	39.8	7.9	0.5	88103
62001	ALHAMBRA	23788	624	15.2	28.4	45.5	8.3	2.6	57543	60769	75	60	527	4.9	16.1	43.8	26.8	8.3	137167
62002	ALTON	22682	14051	29.9	26.9	35.4	5.4	2.5	45295	47297	49	30	9586	13.1	33.3	41.6	10.3	1.8	94618
62006	BATCHTOWN	19607	262	23.7	28.2	40.5	6.1	1.5	47955	47878	56	38	224	9.4	17.0	49.6	21.0	3.1	120930
62009	BENLD	18180	777	34.5	31.4	29.7	3.7	0.6	36618	38389	22	9	632	26.6	38.9	27.4	6.0	1.1	71667
62010	BETHALTO	24894	4477	18.4	26.6	43.5	9.1	2.3	56089	60215	73	58	3319	5.2	17.0	58.5	17.5	1.8	121899
62011	BINGHAM	17511	196	26.5	36.2	34.7	2.6	0.0	40000	41406	33	16	161	24.8	28.6	35.4	9.9	1.2	83889
62012	BRIGHTON	24080	2619	15.4	26.0	45.6	9.6	3.4	58480	61084	76	62	2252	4.3	15.9	49.9	25.7	4.2	128976
62013	BRUSSELS	20297	505	23.8	29.7	40.0	5.0	1.6	46394	46702	53	33	413	9.9	17.4	51.1	19.1	2.4	125528
62014	BUNKER HILL	23126	1545	19.3	24.1	45.9	8.0	2.7	56019	60254	73	58	1249	10.5	21.9	45.6	20.5	1.6	115807
62015	BUTLER	22268	228	17.5	36.8	38.6	5.3	1.8	46536	46732	53	33	195	26.7	25.6	32.8	13.3	1.5	87632
62016	CARROLLTON	21133	1222	26.9	32.9	32.8	4.3	3.0	40895	42777	36	18	924	19.9	30.2	37.7	11.9	0.3	89853
62017	COFFEEN	19679	496	32.5	27.2	36.9	3.2	0.2	41143	43142	36	19	407	38.8	25.6	29.2	5.4	1.0	63387
62018	COTTAGE HILLS	20391	1609	23.6	32.2	38.1	4.8	1.2	46462	48246	53	33	1247	32.7	27.7	30.6	7.6	1.4	75915
62019	DONNELLSON	25826	295	23.4	33.9	36.3	4.4	2.0	44304	45906	46	27	254	32.3	23.2	31.1	10.6	2.8	74444
62021	DORSEY	30650	357	6.7	19.3	54.9	12.9	6.2	75062	75380	89	86	330	2.1	9.1	40.6	42.1	6.1	170714
62022	DOW	24828	401	16.2	23.9	49.4	5.7	4.7	59032	60696	76	63	344	7.6	16.9	42.7	27.3	5.5	139189
62024	EAST ALTON	22280	4504	28.1	27.6	37.9	4.4	2.0	44662	47520	47	28	2940	9.8	34.3	48.9	6.4	0.6	96179
62025	EDWARDSVILLE	29859	12603	15.0	22.5	42.5	12.0	8.0	64581	66521	83	73	9410	4.0	11.3	42.1	36.1	6.6	154597
62027	ELDRED	19619	276	23.9	32.2	36.2	7.2	0.4	43008	44671	42	24	212	30.7	21.2	30.2	11.3	6.6	87500
62028	ELSAH	22556	461	13.4	26.7	47.5	6.1	6.3	57628	59686	75	60	371	8.9	8.1	50.9	26.7	5.4	137897
62030	FIDELITY	20717	62	21.0	32.3	41.9	3.2	1.6	46555	50387	53	33	50	20.0	2.0	40.0	26.0	12.0	141667
62031	FIELDON	21148	536	20.1	28.5	43.8	6.0	1.5	51065	53392	64	46	431	10.9	21.3	36.0	24.6	7.2	131944
62032	FILLMORE	18376	339	33.3	23.3	39.2	2.9	1.2	44372	45885	46	28	287	22.3	37.3	30.7	9.4	0.3	69828
62033	GILLESPIE	21835	2383	27.6	32.5	31.6	6.5	1.8	41815	44809	39	20	1883	20.7	33.7	31.6	12.7	1.3	84970
62034	GLEN CARBON	32629	5338	12.6	22.0	39.2	16.2	10.0	69724	69269	87	80	3976	4.3	3.9	33.3	50.8	7.8	195286
62035	GODFREY	31100	6203	14.2	21.7	47.1	11.0	6.1	63959	65848	82	72	5164	1.8	10.8	52.9	29.2	5.3	141136
62036	GOLDEN EAGLE	21893	111	24.3	29.7	40.5	4.5	0.9	46151	46788	52	32	90	8.9	17.8	53.3	17.8	2.2	126471
62037	GRAFTON	24313	794	21.2	28.2	39.4	7.7	3.5	50724	54755	63	45	631	15.4	12.2	49.4	18.2	4.8	123623
62040	GRANITE CITY	22994	18103	22.7	30.5	38.9	5.3	2.6	47919	49523	56	38	13145	16.0	34.3	43.9	5.5	0.4	89776
62044	GREENFIELD	19267	705	28.1	34.0	33.2	3.4	1.3	39666	41056	32	15	524	24.6	44.3	25.4	4.2	1.5	72540
62045	HAMBURG	19751	169	27.8	27.2	40.8	3.0	1.2	43660	45513	44	25	144	15.3	20.8	39.6	20.8	3.5	111458
62047	HARDIN	20770	473	32.6	32.3	29.8	4.0	1.3	37459	39543	25	10	342	15.5	32.2	43.9	7.3	1.2	92581
62048	HARTFORD	21241	652	28.1	29.3	36.8	4.4	1.4	44315	47239	46	28	500	25.4	48.8	24.8	1.0	0.0	67937
62049	HILLSBORO	19634	2836	28.0	30.2	35.2	4.6	2.0	41875	42975	39	21	2110	24.1	32.6	33.5	9.3	0.5	81013
62050	HILLVIEW	15850	214	30.8	34.1	32.2	2.8	0.0	38517	41227	28	13	174	44.8	39.1	12.1	3.4	0.6	53600
62051	IRVING	17748	345	29.0	32.8	33.9	3.8	0.6	37724	38674	26	11	283	33.2	23.7	28.3	14.8	0.0	80714
62052	JERSEYVILLE	23932	4998	26.9	23.5	39.1	6.6	3.9	49626	52804	60	42	3629	6.2	17.3	50.8	22.2	3.6	126962
62053	KAMPSVILLE	18872	260	35.8	29.2	31.9	1.9	1.2	36118	37460	21	8	204	20.1	23.5	41.7	13.2	1.5	96500
62054	KANE	18964	417	23.3	30.7	39.6	5.8	0.7	45603	48785	50	31	328	23.5	26.5	32.3	12.5	5.2	90000
62056	LITCHFIELD	20440	3527	28.9	31.7	31.6	5.3	2.4	40593	41846	35	18	2676	22.1	30.6	32.1	13.6	1.5	86712
62060	MADISON	16095	2280	43.7	27.8	24.8	2.8	1.0	29457	31404	7	2	1338	39.5	47.3	10.5	2.2	0.6	57663
62061	MARINE	27223	596	18.0	26.5	39.6	10.1	5.9	56348	60131	73	58	465	6.0	8.6	56.3	27.5	1.5	134583
62062	MARYVILLE	33006	2780	9.4	18.5	48.1	17.1	6.9	75492	74982	90	86	2354	4.3	6.7	43.2	43.3	2.5	168470
62063	MEDORA	18257	495	22.8	33.3	38.2	3.4	2.2	44758	48213	48	28	401	20.7	20.0	34.4	15.5	9.5	106731
62065	MICHAEL	17285	144	36.8	29.9	30.6	1.4	1.4	35397	36658	19	7	112	20.5	23.2	42.9	12.5	0.9	95833
62067	MORO	23235	1171	24.4	29.5	39.5	4.8	1.7	47110	48642	54	35	843	4.4	23.6	49.6	21.1	1.3	121160
62069	MOUNT OLIVE	20366	1561	26.5	31.4	37.1	3.4	1.6	42603	45954	41	23	1307	21.4	35.3	32.2	10.6	0.5	81881
62070	MOZIER	19385	104	29.8	27.9	40.4	1.0	1.0	40916	43204	36	18	88	18.2	22.7	35.2	21.6	2.3	105769
62074	NEW DOUGLAS	22800	755	23.0	29.0	40.4	6.4	1.2	48409	50275	58	39	617	16.0	31.8	37.4	13.1	1.6	93553
62075	NOKOMIS	19337	1536	31.0	33.4	31.0	3.5	1.1	37865	39155	26	11	1242	29.2	39.4	26.1	4.5	0.8	69111
62079	PIASA	22198	101	16.8	30.7	43.6	6.9	2.0	52152	57858	66	49	84	10.7	25.0	35.7	26.2	2.4	115909
62080	RAMSEY	17957	1223	27.7	38.1	29.1	3.6	1.5	38279	40434	28	12	1003	27.1	27.6	32.8	11.6	0.9	80865
62081	ROCKBRIDGE	17512	265	28.7	33.6	33.6	3.0	1.1	38864	40560	29	13	206	27.2	35.9	27.7	6.8	2.4	74211
62082	ROODHOUSE	16902	1087	28.4	38.2	30.4	2.5	0.6	37760	39766	26	11	823	37.5	37.2	21.7	2.6	1.0	60050
62083	ROSAMOND	24993	71	26.8	31.0	31.0	7.0	4.2	42338	47996	40	22	56	14.3	21.4	39.3	23.2	1.8	117857
62084	ROXANA	24416	638	20.2	34.0	35.7	7.8	2.2	47414	48960	55	37	447	11.9	48.1	38.5	0.7	0.9	82193
62086	SORENTO	20321	741	23.2	32.5	38.1	4.5	1.8	44167	47252	46	27	640	27.0	26.9	28.1	14.7	3.3	80385
62087	SOUTH ROXANA	20196	769	25.7	31.2	36.7	4.7	1.7	45728	47738	50	32	566	17.3	53.4	26.9	2.5	0.0	71125
62088	STAUNTON	22349	2799	22.8	29.7	40.0	4.6	2.9	47661	49959	56	37	2171	12.4	25.0	49.9	12.0	0.7	106003
62090	VENICE	13446	468	52.6	25.4	15.8	3.6	2.6	21668	25000	2	0	200	51.5	40.5	7.5	0.5	0.0	49268
62091	WALSHVILLE	22288	152	23.7	27.6	38.2	7.2	3.3	48791	49692	58	40	132	21.2	27.3	37.1	9.8	4.5	91818
62092	WHITE HALL	17058	1375	36.4	34.1	24.9	3.0	1.7	32038	33065	11	3	1013	40.7	32.5	19.2	6.1	1.5	60245
62094	WITT	17977	555	37.5	30.8	28.3	2.2	1.3	33776	35427	15	5	441	39.9	29.5	22.2	7.9	0.5	59889
62095	WOOD RIVER	23952	5002	22.9	31.4	36.8	6.0	3.0	46814	48892	54	34	3517	7.3	36.7	48.3	7.2	0.5	95919
62097	WORDEN	25397	1129	18.8	21.2	48.9	7.8	3.4	60113	62185	77	64	961	9.8	20.0	36.9	27.6	5.7	124748
62201	EAST SAINT LOUIS	10492	3365	62.4	22.8	13.0	1.2	0.6	16341	17275	1	0	1325	45.5	38.2	13.6	2.6	0.1	53993
62203	EAST SAINT LOUIS	16041	3064	33.2	30.5	31.2	3.9	1.1	37467	40428	25	11	2137	22.1	48.4	26.0	3.5	0.0	70682
62204	EAST SAINT LOUIS	11048	3130	53.6	27.2	15.9	2.4	0.8	22112	23202	2	1	1572	45.2	39.6	14.9	0.4	0.0	53128
62205	EAST SAINT LOUIS	15479	3643	41.7	30.8	21.4	4.9	1.3	29913	31319	8	2	2268	36.7	38.1	22.4	2.2	0.5	61239
62206	EAST SAINT LOUIS	16936	6156	32.7	30.7	30.9	4.4	1.3	38186	41798	27	12	3994	36.9	46.8	15.3	0.6	0.4	57153
62207	EAST SAINT LOUIS	11548	3459	53.3	27.4	17.0	1.6	0.7	22539	23748	2	1	1690	43.5	36.3	17.1	3.1	0.0	56322
62208	FAIRVIEW HEIGHTS	27244	6585	15.4	26.7	44.6	9.5	3.8	57926	60836	75	61	4915	6.3	16.0	57.9	18.5	1.3	122587
62214	ADDIEVILLE	21829	491	22.0	26.1	42.4	7.5	2.0	52129	53087	66	49	416	8.4	23.8	38.9	22.8	6.0	131164
	ILLINOIS	28587		18.2	22.2	39.3	12.1	8.2	60823	63631				6.3	10.0	30.9	40.6	12.3	185324
	UNITED STATES	27277		20.9	24.4	35.3	11.7	7.6	54719	56938				9.3	13.1	31.6	32.6	13.5	162279

ZIP CODE #	POST OFFICE NAME	FINANCIAL SERVICES: Auto Loan	FINANCIAL SERVICES: Home Loan	FINANCIAL SERVICES: Invest-ments	FINANCIAL SERVICES: Retire-ment Plans	THE HOME: Home Improvements: Home Repair	THE HOME: Home Improvements: Lawn & Garden	THE HOME: Furnishings: Comput-ers & Hard-ware-Personal	THE HOME: Furnishings: Major Appli-ances	THE HOME: Furnishings: TV, Radio, Sound Equip-ment	THE HOME: Furnishings: Furni-ture	ENTERTAINMENT: Dine out/ Carry out	ENTERTAINMENT: Sports Equip-ment	ENTERTAINMENT: Fees & Tickets	ENTERTAINMENT: Toys & Games	ENTERTAINMENT: Travel	ENTERTAINMENT: Cable TV	PERSONAL: Apparel & Services	PERSONAL: Auto Repairs	PERSONAL: Health Insur-ance	PERSONAL: Pets & Supplies
61914	BETHANY	91	76	86	77	77	96	77	90	82	70	80	68	68	82	76	88	54	84	95	105
61917	BROCTON	91	62	100	62	65	96	69	86	72	56	71	71	51	71	69	79	46	80	91	106
61919	CAMARGO	99	106	98	108	103	109	96	102	96	95	96	80	99	98	101	97	67	98	102	121
61920	CHARLESTON	70	54	53	57	53	59	77	62	72	66	72	52	63	72	62	71	50	69	65	76
61924	CHRISMAN	85	67	82	67	69	89	70	83	76	63	73	63	60	75	69	82	49	78	89	98
61925	DALTON CITY	106	103	97	107	103	114	98	108	100	92	99	83	95	102	100	104	68	101	110	126
61928	GAYS	98	89	87	91	90	103	87	97	90	81	89	73	80	92	86	95	60	91	100	114
61929	HAMMOND	96	81	92	84	84	103	83	96	85	73	84	74	72	86	82	91	57	89	99	113
61930	HINDSBORO	94	65	103	65	68	99	72	89	75	58	74	74	53	73	72	82	48	83	94	110
61931	HUMBOLDT	93	75	80	76	76	93	76	87	81	71	80	66	66	84	73	87	54	81	91	103
61932	HUME	96	66	105	66	69	101	73	91	76	59	75	75	53	74	73	83	49	85	96	112
61933	KANSAS	73	53	74	52	55	77	58	71	64	51	62	53	46	63	56	70	41	66	77	84
61937	LOVINGTON	95	85	87	88	87	102	84	96	87	76	85	73	77	88	84	92	58	88	99	112
61938	MATTOON	77	73	69	74	71	80	76	76	78	72	77	58	73	78	73	81	53	77	84	91
61940	METCALF	95	66	105	66	69	101	73	91	76	59	75	75	53	74	73	83	49	85	96	112
61942	NEWMAN	92	66	93	64	68	95	70	88	78	63	76	66	56	77	69	86	50	81	94	104
61943	OAKLAND	82	59	84	57	61	85	62	78	69	56	67	59	50	68	61	76	45	72	83	93
61944	PARIS	84	68	75	69	69	85	73	81	78	67	76	61	64	78	70	83	51	78	87	96
61951	SULLIVAN	89	76	83	77	76	94	78	88	82	72	81	67	71	83	77	88	55	84	94	104
61953	TUSCOLA	90	81	81	81	79	92	81	87	84	77	83	66	75	85	79	88	57	85	92	104
61956	VILLA GROVE	81	79	70	81	76	87	78	81	79	72	79	63	75	81	77	82	54	79	87	97
61957	WINDSOR	82	70	77	71	71	88	71	82	75	64	73	62	63	75	70	80	50	76	86	96
62001	ALHAMBRA	96	87	88	90	88	103	85	97	88	78	87	73	79	90	85	94	59	90	100	113
62002	ALTON	76	71	64	72	68	78	75	74	78	72	77	57	73	78	71	81	53	76	82	89
62006	BATCHTOWN	94	65	103	65	68	99	72	89	75	59	74	73	53	74	71	82	48	83	94	110
62009	BENLD	71	51	71	50	53	74	56	69	62	50	60	51	45	61	54	68	40	64	75	81
62010	BETHALTO	86	92	79	92	87	91	87	87	88	86	88	66	90	89	88	89	61	87	92	103
62011	BINGHAM	74	58	72	58	60	76	59	71	63	54	62	54	50	64	58	68	42	65	74	84
62012	BRIGHTON	97	93	88	97	93	105	91	99	93	84	91	76	87	94	91	97	63	93	102	116
62013	BRUSSELS	91	65	94	63	67	93	67	85	74	61	72	65	53	73	66	81	48	78	89	102
62014	BUNKER HILL	92	85	82	87	85	98	84	92	86	77	85	70	78	88	83	91	58	87	97	108
62015	BUTLER	97	67	106	67	70	103	74	92	77	61	77	76	55	76	74	84	50	86	97	113
62016	CARROLLTON	83	65	81	65	67	86	70	81	76	65	74	60	60	75	68	81	50	77	87	95
62017	COFFEEN	73	55	74	53	57	77	58	71	65	53	63	53	48	64	57	71	42	67	78	83
62018	COTTAGE HILLS	77	74	74	72	72	81	70	77	74	70	73	57	69	74	71	77	50	74	81	90
62019	DONNELLSON	85	70	87	69	72	91	69	83	75	65	74	62	61	75	70	81	50	77	88	98
62021	DORSEY	108	121	108	123	118	123	108	114	108	107	109	87	116	110	115	110	76	110	117	133
62022	DOW	100	93	95	95	94	106	90	101	92	84	91	76	84	93	91	96	62	94	103	118
62024	EAST ALTON	72	70	66	70	69	78	71	73	75	68	74	54	71	75	70	79	51	74	83	86
62025	EDWARDSVILLE	107	114	102	117	110	112	110	108	109	109	110	85	114	110	111	109	77	109	111	129
62027	ELDRED	86	64	87	64	67	89	66	82	72	60	71	63	54	72	66	78	47	76	85	98
62028	ELSAH	114	99	115	97	101	112	96	109	100	96	99	80	88	100	96	104	67	104	109	128
62030	FIDELITY	88	64	96	64	66	94	69	84	71	57	71	70	53	70	69	77	46	79	89	104
62031	FIELDON	90	75	86	76	77	95	75	89	79	68	78	67	65	80	74	85	53	82	92	104
62032	FILLMORE	81	59	84	58	62	83	60	77	67	56	66	57	49	67	60	74	44	70	80	91
62033	GILLESPIE	83	66	83	66	68	87	70	82	75	64	73	61	60	74	69	81	49	78	88	96
62034	GLEN CARBON	115	121	113	122	119	117	116	115	115	118	116	88	120	116	117	115	81	115	115	136
62035	GODFREY	103	108	109	109	110	117	102	109	104	102	104	79	106	103	107	108	72	106	117	126
62036	GOLDEN EAGLE	90	65	93	63	67	92	66	84	74	62	72	63	53	73	66	81	48	77	88	100
62037	GRAFTON	102	88	91	87	88	103	87	98	92	84	91	73	78	94	84	97	61	93	101	115
62040	GRANITE CITY	80	77	70	77	75	84	78	79	81	75	80	60	77	82	76	85	56	80	87	94
62044	GREENFIELD	81	58	85	57	60	85	63	78	69	55	67	61	49	68	62	76	44	73	84	94
62045	HAMBURG	85	60	89	58	62	87	63	80	69	56	68	62	49	68	62	75	44	73	83	96
62047	HARDIN	83	60	84	58	62	87	65	81	73	58	70	60	52	71	63	80	47	75	88	95
62048	HARTFORD	69	68	63	67	67	76	67	70	72	64	70	51	67	71	67	76	48	70	79	82
62049	HILLSBORO	79	66	77	65	67	83	69	78	73	64	72	58	62	73	68	79	49	75	84	91
62050	HILLVIEW	77	55	80	54	57	79	57	72	63	52	62	55	45	62	56	69	41	66	75	86
62051	IRVING	80	57	82	56	60	81	59	75	65	55	64	56	47	65	58	72	42	69	78	89
62052	JERSEYVILLE	90	80	88	80	80	96	80	90	85	75	83	68	74	85	80	90	57	86	96	106
62053	KAMPSVILLE	73	52	73	51	54	75	56	70	63	51	61	52	45	62	55	69	40	65	76	82
62054	KANE	85	68	84	68	70	88	68	82	73	64	72	62	59	73	68	79	48	76	85	97
62056	LITCHFIELD	77	66	70	66	65	80	68	75	72	63	71	58	62	72	66	77	48	73	81	89
62060	MADISON	60	45	47	46	44	57	54	55	59	50	57	41	46	58	48	63	39	56	62	67
62061	MARINE	94	101	81	103	94	101	97	95	97	93	96	75	99	99	96	98	67	95	101	114
62062	MARYVILLE	116	132	117	131	127	119	118	118	114	123	116	91	126	118	122	112	82	115	113	137
62063	MEDORA	91	64	95	63	67	94	68	85	73	60	72	67	53	73	67	81	47	79	89	103
62065	MICHAEL	72	52	72	50	54	75	56	69	63	50	60	52	45	61	54	69	40	65	75	82
62067	MORO	71	68	69	69	68	75	73	73	76	69	75	54	71	75	71	80	52	75	81	86
62069	MOUNT OLIVE	80	64	82	62	66	86	65	79	72	60	70	58	57	71	65	79	47	74	86	92
62070	MOZIER	80	58	83	56	60	82	59	75	66	55	65	57	47	65	59	72	43	69	78	89
62074	NEW DOUGLAS	92	70	91	69	72	96	73	89	80	66	78	67	61	79	72	87	52	82	94	105
62075	NOKOMIS	78	55	80	54	57	81	60	75	66	53	64	58	47	65	59	73	42	70	81	89
62079	PIASA	100	82	100	81	83	104	81	96	86	76	85	73	71	86	81	92	57	89	99	114
62080	RAMSEY	80	61	72	61	62	80	62	74	68	59	67	56	52	69	60	74	45	69	77	88
62081	ROCKBRIDGE	78	57	79	56	60	79	60	73	65	56	64	55	49	65	59	71	43	68	77	87
62082	ROODHOUSE	71	53	60	54	53	69	60	65	64	54	62	51	49	65	55	68	42	64	70	79
62083	ROSAMOND	97	73	96	73	76	99	75	92	81	69	80	69	62	81	74	89	53	85	96	109
62084	ROXANA	86	74	78	73	72	90	77	84	82	71	80	65	70	82	74	87	54	82	92	100
62086	SORENTO	90	67	91	66	69	92	68	85	75	63	74	64	56	75	68	82	49	78	89	101
62087	SOUTH ROXANA	78	68	58	70	64	76	76	72	78	70	76	57	69	80	68	81	53	75	81	89
62088	STAUNTON	83	73	73	74	71	87	76	81	80	70	78	63	70	80	73	84	53	79	88	97
62090	VENICE	53	38	32	42	35	43	51	43	57	50	56	35	46	56	42	59	39	51	51	57
62091	WALSHVILLE	95	80	90	81	82	100	80	93	84	72	82	71	70	85	79	90	56	86	97	110
62092	WHITE HALL	70	50	72	49	52	73	55	68	60	48	58	51	43	59	53	66	39	63	73	80
62094	WITT	71	51	72	50	53	74	54	68	61	49	59	51	44	60	53	67	39	63	73	81
62095	WOOD RIVER	76	78	68	79	75	83	78	77	80	74	80	59	79	80	77	83	55	79	86	92
62097	WORDEN	103	89	100	90	90	109	87	102	92	81	90	77	79	93	88	98	61	94	105	120
62201	EAST SAINT LOUIS	42	31	27	31	29	34	38	35	42	39	42	26	34	42	33	45	29	39	40	44
62203	EAST SAINT LOUIS	65	62	57	63	59	68	61	62	67	64	67	44	63	65	60	71	45	64	72	77
62204	EAST SAINT LOUIS	49	39	36	40	37	46	45	44	51	46	50	31	42	49	40	55	34	47	52	55
62205	EAST SAINT LOUIS	58	51	48	52	49	59	53	54	60	55	59	38	52	58	51	65	40	57	64	67
62206	EAST SAINT LOUIS	71	61	52	63	57	68	68	64	72	65	71	50	63	73	61	75	49	68	73	80
62207	EAST SAINT LOUIS	46	35	33	36	33	42	42	40	48	42	47	29	38	47	37	52	32	44	49	51
62208	FAIRVIEW HEIGHTS	89	96	93	96	96	102	89	94	92	88	92	69	94	91	94	96	64	92	102	109
62214	ADDIEVILLE	96	78	95	80	81	102	81	95	84	70	82	74	69	84	81	89	55	88	99	113
	ILLINOIS	106	108	105	108	107	106	109	106	108	107	109	83	110	108	108	108	77	108	107	125
	UNITED STATES	100	100	100	100	100	100	100	100	100	100	100	100	100	100	100	100	100	100	100	100

ZIP CODE #	POST OFFICE NAME	COUNTY FIPS CODE	POPULATION 2000	POPULATION 2009	POPULATION 2014	2000-2009 ANNUAL RATE % Rate	2000-2009 ANNUAL RATE State Centile	HOUSEHOLDS 2000	HOUSEHOLDS 2009	HOUSEHOLDS 2014	HOUSEHOLDS % Annual Rate 2000-2009	HOUSEHOLDS 2009 Average HH Size	FAMILIES 2000	FAMILIES 2009	FAMILIES % Annual Rate 2000-2009
62215	ALBERS	027	991	1108	1157	1.2	85	321	372	393	1.6	2.94	245	278	1.4
62217	BALDWIN	157	4109	892	876	-15.2	0	352	351	347	0.0	2.54	253	248	-0.2
62218	BARTELSO	027	1498	1641	1702	1.0	83	495	560	588	1.3	2.93	408	455	1.2
62220	BELLEVILLE	163	18554	19061	19210	0.3	65	7376	7694	7806	0.5	2.40	4659	4781	0.3
62221	BELLEVILLE	163	22518	25991	27012	1.6	89	9082	10528	10985	1.6	2.45	6255	7166	1.5
62223	BELLEVILLE	163	17544	17541	17473	0.0	50	7397	7651	7697	0.4	2.26	4882	4900	0.0
62225	SCOTT AIR FORCE BASE	163	5684	5138	5289	-1.1	2	1444	1283	1331	-1.3	3.87	1366	1203	-1.4
62226	BELLEVILLE	163	28536	29060	29342	0.2	61	11762	12178	12382	0.4	2.30	7317	7474	0.2
62230	BREESE	027	5933	6390	6549	0.8	79	2140	2348	2424	1.0	2.68	1582	1710	0.8
62231	CARLYLE	027	8656	8903	9005	0.3	65	3348	3543	3618	0.6	2.47	2375	2459	0.4
62232	CASEYVILLE	163	7156	7151	7146	0.0	50	2785	2857	2880	0.3	2.45	1967	1975	0.0
62233	CHESTER	157	6642	9372	9258	3.8	96	2595	2559	2520	-0.2	2.36	1707	1644	-0.4
62234	COLLINSVILLE	119	31920	33485	34243	0.5	72	13113	14029	14456	0.7	2.38	8732	9097	0.4
62236	COLUMBIA	133	10335	12081	12855	1.7	90	3949	4682	4997	1.9	2.55	2920	3403	1.7
62237	COULTERVILLE	145	2909	2984	2968	0.3	65	1163	1218	1219	0.5	2.45	852	876	0.3
62238	CUTLER	145	817	810	804	-0.1	45	298	299	298	0.0	2.71	227	223	-0.2
62239	DUPO	163	4886	4955	4980	0.2	61	1933	2003	2030	0.4	2.47	1334	1347	0.1
62240	EAST CARONDELET	163	1801	1790	1778	-0.1	45	650	661	662	0.2	2.71	470	467	-0.1
62241	ELLIS GROVE	157	1116	1127	1120	0.1	56	423	438	438	0.4	2.53	319	325	0.2
62242	EVANSVILLE	157	1602	1634	1629	0.2	61	631	661	663	0.5	2.43	443	455	0.3
62243	FREEBURG	163	5461	5823	5989	0.7	78	1970	2142	2218	0.9	2.65	1539	1642	0.7
62244	FULTS	133	1155	1278	1316	1.1	85	403	455	472	1.3	2.81	327	364	1.2
62245	GERMANTOWN	027	2091	2253	2328	0.8	79	758	845	882	1.2	2.66	581	636	1.0
62246	GREENVILLE	005	10069	10333	10350	0.3	65	3179	3290	3305	0.4	2.39	2172	2203	0.2
62248	HECKER	133	475	535	557	1.3	87	188	216	225	1.5	2.48	146	165	1.3
62249	HIGHLAND	119	13593	15245	15923	1.2	85	5174	5932	6242	1.5	2.54	3737	4206	1.3
62253	KEYESPORT	005	734	780	801	0.7	78	319	347	359	0.9	2.25	226	241	0.7
62254	LEBANON	163	6011	6903	7252	1.5	88	2155	2554	2708	1.9	2.53	1516	1782	1.8
62255	LENZBURG	163	1233	1286	1303	0.5	72	440	471	482	0.7	2.73	341	357	0.5
62257	MARISSA	163	3718	3517	3443	-0.6	13	1478	1435	1416	-0.3	2.45	1058	1000	-0.6
62258	MASCOUTAH	163	7340	8234	8603	1.3	87	2740	3172	3348	1.6	2.55	2037	2307	1.4
62260	MILLSTADT	163	6149	7233	7624	1.8	91	2340	2806	2978	2.0	2.57	1760	2073	1.8
62261	MODOC	157	202	200	199	-0.1	45	84	86	85	0.3	2.22	62	62	0.0
62262	MULBERRY GROVE	005	2091	2157	2179	0.3	65	839	881	894	0.5	2.45	601	617	0.3
62263	NASHVILLE	189	5151	5014	4896	-0.3	32	2088	2042	1998	-0.2	2.44	1475	1418	-0.4
62264	NEW ATHENS	163	3344	3392	3458	0.2	61	1275	1326	1362	0.4	2.52	945	949	0.0
62265	NEW BADEN	027	4560	4806	4901	0.6	75	1681	1830	1886	0.9	2.58	1237	1323	0.7
62268	OAKDALE	189	881	886	874	0.1	56	326	331	328	0.2	2.68	261	261	0.0
62269	O FALLON	163	24976	30074	32166	2.0	91	9507	11571	12407	2.1	2.58	6918	8281	2.0
62271	OKAWVILLE	189	2008	2125	2124	0.6	75	818	878	882	0.8	2.42	566	595	0.5
62272	PERCY	157	2269	2223	2191	-0.2	38	898	894	885	0.0	2.47	631	616	-0.3
62274	PINCKNEYVILLE	145	8343	8361	8308	0.0	50	2576	2618	2612	0.2	2.54	1772	1764	0.0
62275	POCAHONTAS	005	3697	4013	4135	0.9	81	1403	1547	1603	1.1	2.59	1044	1134	0.9
62277	PRAIRIE DU ROCHER	157	1425	1444	1440	0.1	56	552	572	574	0.4	2.51	402	411	0.2
62278	RED BUD	133	6479	6763	6802	0.5	72	2420	2576	2606	0.7	2.57	1759	1843	0.5
62280	ROCKWOOD	077	428	398	397	-0.8	6	162	170	171	0.5	2.34	124	127	0.3
62281	SAINT JACOB	119	1694	1885	1968	1.2	85	619	703	739	1.4	2.68	492	549	1.2
62284	SMITHBORO	005	641	684	696	0.7	78	244	264	270	0.9	2.59	188	199	0.6
62285	SMITHTON	163	3060	3710	3859	2.1	92	1062	1310	1369	2.3	2.76	829	1012	2.2
62286	SPARTA	157	7252	6776	6578	-0.7	9	2872	2740	2675	-0.5	2.42	1974	1849	-0.7
62288	STEELEVILLE	157	2928	2821	2756	-0.4	25	1209	1191	1172	-0.2	2.35	823	793	-0.4
62293	TRENTON	027	5646	5934	6006	0.5	72	2140	2319	2370	0.9	2.52	1620	1725	0.7
62294	TROY	119	11938	13832	14651	1.6	89	4252	5035	5366	1.8	2.73	3323	3892	1.7
62295	VALMEYER	133	940	1381	1561	4.2	97	335	496	563	4.3	2.78	259	373	4.0
62297	WALSH	157	400	398	394	-0.1	45	159	162	161	0.2	2.46	120	120	0.0
62298	WATERLOO	133	13900	16638	17952	2.0	91	5105	6166	6680	2.1	2.66	3910	4654	1.9
62301	QUINCY	001	34985	33859	33266	-0.4	25	14357	14127	13923	-0.2	2.24	8689	8338	-0.4
62305	QUINCY	001	17266	17750	17748	0.3	65	6599	6998	7047	0.6	2.52	4870	5041	0.4
62311	AUGUSTA	067	906	843	810	-0.8	6	364	340	326	-0.7	2.47	234	211	-1.1
62312	BARRY	149	2453	2465	2464	0.1	56	970	989	993	0.2	2.41	686	686	0.0
62313	BASCO	067	375	366	355	-0.3	32	153	151	147	-0.1	2.42	116	112	-0.4
62314	BAYLIS	149	574	562	556	-0.2	38	213	209	207	-0.2	2.68	156	151	-0.4
62316	BOWEN	067	727	621	589	-1.7	1	277	237	225	-1.7	2.57	194	163	-1.9
62319	CAMDEN	169	270	253	244	-0.7	9	111	106	103	-0.5	2.39	81	76	-0.7
62320	CAMP POINT	001	2264	1992	1899	-1.4	1	829	735	702	-1.3	2.59	606	528	-1.5
62321	CARTHAGE	067	4469	4151	3963	-0.8	6	1848	1725	1651	-0.7	2.35	1220	1116	-1.0
62323	CHAMBERSBURG	149	200	196	193	-0.2	38	82	81	80	-0.1	2.42	55	53	-0.4
62324	CLAYTON	001	1604	1583	1564	-0.1	45	560	558	553	0.0	2.57	384	373	-0.3
62325	COATSBURG	001	537	536	533	0.0	50	206	212	211	0.3	2.52	151	152	0.1
62326	COLCHESTER	109	2808	2701	2628	-0.4	25	1145	1114	1089	-0.3	2.40	798	766	-0.4
62330	DALLAS CITY	067	2014	2090	2086	0.4	69	835	879	880	0.6	2.36	593	612	0.3
62334	ELVASTON	067	151	144	138	-0.5	18	66	64	62	-0.3	2.25	53	50	-0.6
62338	FOWLER	001	1455	1312	1274	-1.1	2	529	494	483	-0.7	2.66	421	385	-1.0
62339	GOLDEN	001	916	909	897	-0.1	45	355	356	353	0.0	2.48	264	260	-0.2
62340	GRIGGSVILLE	149	1587	1525	1503	-0.4	25	623	602	595	-0.4	2.52	457	435	-0.5
62341	HAMILTON	067	3627	3419	3285	-0.6	13	1437	1371	1321	-0.5	2.42	986	921	-0.7
62343	HULL	149	665	619	606	-0.8	6	272	257	252	-0.6	2.41	186	172	-0.8
62344	HUNTSVILLE	169	160	149	144	-0.8	6	70	67	64	-0.5	2.22	50	47	-0.7
62345	KINDERHOOK	149	370	360	356	-0.3	32	151	149	148	-0.1	2.42	110	107	-0.3
62346	LA PRAIRIE	001	168	168	166	0.0	50	63	63	63	0.0	2.67	47	47	0.0
62347	LIBERTY	001	2210	2189	2169	-0.1	45	824	841	839	0.2	2.60	655	658	0.0
62348	LIMA	001	37	35	35	-0.6	13	19	19	18	0.0	1.84	14	13	-0.8
62349	LORAINE	001	703	733	733	0.5	72	262	281	284	0.8	2.59	203	213	0.5
62351	MENDON	001	1796	1785	1771	-0.1	45	640	654	652	0.2	2.55	468	468	0.0
62352	MILTON	149	541	551	552	0.2	61	212	217	218	0.3	2.51	157	158	0.1
62353	MOUNT STERLING	009	5186	5020	4920	-0.4	25	1408	1353	1316	-0.4	2.25	889	835	-0.7
62354	NAUVOO	067	1588	1511	1462	-0.5	18	623	599	580	-0.4	2.42	448	424	-0.6
62355	NEBO	013	938	924	920	-0.2	38	380	380	379	0.0	2.43	272	267	-0.2
62356	NEW CANTON	149	673	678	679	0.1	56	274	279	280	0.2	2.43	208	207	-0.1
62357	NEW SALEM	149	300	297	295	-0.1	45	113	112	111	-0.1	2.64	84	82	-0.3
62358	NIOTA	067	652	659	653	0.1	56	252	259	258	0.3	2.50	185	186	0.1
62359	PALOMA	001	157	156	155	-0.1	45	65	66	66	0.2	2.36	47	47	0.0
62360	PAYSON	001	1936	1944	1932	0.0	50	700	723	724	0.4	2.69	537	545	0.2
62361	PEARL	149	355	384	390	0.9	81	149	163	166	1.0	2.36	105	112	0.7
62362	PERRY	149	636	618	610	-0.3	32	276	271	268	-0.2	2.28	190	183	-0.4
	ILLINOIS					0.6					0.6	2.64			0.4
	UNITED STATES					1.0					1.1	2.59			0.9

ZIP CODE #	POST OFFICE NAME	RACE (%) White 2000	White 2009	Black 2000	Black 2009	Asian/Pacific 2000	Asian/Pacific 2009	% Hispanic Origin 2000	% Hispanic Origin 2009	2009 AGE DISTRIBUTION (%) 0-4	5-9	10-14	15-19	20-24	25-44	45-64	65-84	85+	18+	MEDIAN AGE 2009	% 2009 Males	% 2009 Females
62215	ALBERS	94.5	92.0	0.3	0.5	0.2	0.4	5.3	7.8	6.9	7.0	7.0	6.9	4.9	29.6	27.4	9.3	1.0	74.6	37.1	51.1	48.9
62217	BALDWIN	47.3	28.8	47.1	61.7	0.2	3.1	6.3	8.2	1.7	1.7	1.7	8.6	15.8	54.9	12.9	2.2	0.4	93.9	30.0	79.5	20.5
62218	BARTELSO	98.6	98.1	0.3	0.4	0.2	0.3	0.8	1.2	7.4	7.9	7.9	7.5	4.8	27.3	26.9	9.4	1.0	72.1	36.4	51.6	48.4
62220	BELLEVILLE	84.8	78.4	11.9	17.2	0.9	1.1	1.9	2.7	6.8	6.5	6.2	6.6	7.4	27.1	25.5	10.9	2.9	76.4	36.9	48.2	51.8
62221	BELLEVILLE	78.3	68.4	17.0	25.6	1.9	2.4	2.5	3.5	7.8	7.1	6.9	6.6	6.9	29.9	25.3	8.5	1.2	74.2	34.5	48.2	51.8
62223	BELLEVILLE	84.4	79.3	13.6	18.3	0.5	0.7	1.1	1.5	5.1	5.2	5.7	6.1	5.2	23.2	30.0	16.3	3.2	80.2	44.6	47.2	52.8
62225	SCOTT AIR FORCE BASE	80.1	71.6	12.3	18.5	2.5	3.1	4.6	6.5	11.9	11.9	11.1	8.1	6.1	34.9	13.3	2.5	0.2	59.6	25.7	49.5	50.5
62226	BELLEVILLE	82.3	74.7	14.6	21.5	1.2	1.6	1.5	2.1	6.1	5.9	5.9	6.2	6.5	26.4	27.2	12.5	3.2	78.3	39.7	47.4	52.6
62230	BREESE	98.7	98.2	0.1	0.1	0.3	0.5	1.1	1.6	7.2	7.3	7.5	7.2	5.3	26.2	25.5	11.6	2.3	73.5	37.2	49.5	50.5
62231	CARLYLE	96.6	95.5	2.2	2.9	0.4	0.5	0.9	1.3	6.1	6.3	6.5	6.4	5.7	24.9	27.2	14.0	3.0	77.2	40.5	49.7	50.3
62232	CASEYVILLE	90.0	85.1	6.7	10.4	0.6	0.8	3.0	4.4	6.0	6.1	6.2	6.4	5.3	25.8	28.2	13.5	2.5	77.7	40.6	48.9	51.1
62233	CHESTER	95.9	84.9	2.8	9.3	0.2	2.4	0.7	4.0	5.0	5.1	5.2	10.0	10.9	26.2	23.5	11.4	2.8	81.5	35.7	53.1	46.9
62234	COLLINSVILLE	92.5	89.9	4.8	6.6	0.6	0.8	2.5	3.5	6.2	6.1	6.2	6.3	6.2	27.6	27.5	12.0	2.1	77.8	38.8	49.0	51.0
62236	COLUMBIA	98.6	98.2	0.1	0.1	0.3	0.4	0.9	1.2	6.3	6.9	7.3	6.9	4.8	24.2	29.5	11.8	2.2	75.0	40.8	48.6	51.4
62237	COULTERVILLE	97.3	96.3	1.0	1.3	0.3	0.4	0.6	1.0	5.8	6.0	6.3	6.8	5.4	23.9	30.8	13.2	1.7	77.7	41.9	50.0	50.0
62238	CUTLER	98.3	97.8	0.1	0.2	0.1	0.1	0.7	1.0	7.9	7.8	8.1	6.7	5.2	26.8	26.0	10.1	1.4	72.0	35.3	49.6	50.4
62239	DUPO	97.4	96.0	1.1	1.9	0.2	0.3	0.8	1.2	6.4	6.2	6.8	6.6	6.2	29.0	26.9	10.5	1.4	76.7	36.9	49.2	50.8
62240	EAST CARONDELET	96.8	95.3	1.4	2.5	0.1	0.2	0.4	0.6	6.9	6.5	7.6	7.6	7.4	27.2	25.9	9.9	1.2	74.5	35.5	49.6	50.4
62241	ELLIS GROVE	98.7	98.0	0.4	0.4	0.1	0.3	0.3	0.4	6.7	7.2	7.4	7.4	5.4	23.7	28.7	12.1	1.4	74.4	39.1	49.0	51.0
62242	EVANSVILLE	94.1	92.2	4.6	5.8	0.2	0.7	1.2	1.6	5.8	6.0	6.2	6.1	5.9	26.3	27.4	13.4	3.0	78.5	40.8	51.8	48.2
62243	FREEBURG	97.2	95.7	1.0	1.7	0.4	0.6	1.6	2.4	6.0	6.3	6.7	7.3	5.7	24.7	29.6	10.8	2.9	76.4	40.3	48.7	51.3
62244	FULTS	99.0	98.6	0.0	0.0	0.3	0.5	0.4	0.7	6.7	7.3	7.3	7.0	4.8	24.2	32.1	9.6	1.2	74.3	40.1	51.8	48.2
62245	GERMANTOWN	98.9	98.5	0.1	0.2	0.1	0.2	0.8	1.2	6.6	7.0	7.2	6.7	4.4	27.3	28.3	10.9	1.5	74.9	39.1	50.6	49.4
62246	GREENVILLE	87.0	84.7	11.1	12.9	0.4	0.5	1.9	2.7	4.9	4.9	5.1	7.5	9.2	30.1	24.0	11.5	2.7	81.7	36.5	56.8	43.2
62248	HECKER	99.4	99.1	0.0	0.0	0.0	0.2	0.2	0.2	6.7	7.3	7.3	6.2	4.1	27.3	27.5	12.7	0.9	74.8	39.0	50.8	49.2
62249	HIGHLAND	98.8	98.3	0.1	0.2	0.4	0.5	1.0	1.4	6.4	6.6	6.8	6.8	5.8	25.2	27.7	12.2	2.5	76.0	39.6	48.7	51.3
62253	KEYESPORT	98.6	98.2	0.4	0.5	0.1	0.3	0.4	0.8	5.4	5.8	6.2	5.9	4.0	23.5	30.1	17.2	2.1	79.0	44.5	49.9	50.1
62254	LEBANON	83.8	76.4	13.0	19.5	0.7	1.1	1.4	2.1	5.9	6.0	6.3	9.6	9.1	22.7	26.8	11.4	2.1	77.1	37.2	48.0	52.0
62255	LENZBURG	98.9	98.4	0.3	0.5	0.1	0.1	0.6	0.9	6.9	7.1	6.9	6.8	5.9	25.4	27.4	12.2	1.3	75.0	38.8	50.5	49.5
62257	MARISSA	98.7	98.1	0.3	0.6	0.2	0.3	0.7	0.9	6.1	6.2	6.3	6.4	5.3	25.1	28.1	14.3	2.0	77.4	40.8	48.5	51.5
62258	MASCOUTAH	93.2	90.0	3.3	5.4	0.9	1.1	1.6	2.3	5.6	5.9	6.2	7.0	5.8	26.3	28.6	12.0	2.6	77.7	39.8	48.8	51.2
62260	MILLSTADT	98.1	97.3	0.5	0.8	0.2	0.3	0.7	1.1	5.9	6.4	7.0	6.7	4.3	24.3	31.1	12.2	2.1	76.4	41.8	49.4	50.6
62261	MODOC	98.5	98.5	0.0	0.0	0.5	0.5	0.5	0.5	6.0	6.5	6.5	5.0	4.5	22.0	31.0	15.0	3.5	78.0	44.6	50.5	49.5
62262	MULBERRY GROVE	91.0	88.6	7.6	9.5	0.2	0.3	0.6	0.9	6.6	6.7	6.9	6.6	5.5	23.3	27.7	14.7	2.1	75.8	40.7	50.2	49.8
62263	NASHVILLE	98.8	98.8	0.2	0.2	0.3	0.3	0.8	0.9	5.9	6.0	6.3	6.8	5.5	24.9	28.8	13.3	2.6	77.6	41.3	48.3	51.7
62264	NEW ATHENS	98.4	97.7	0.4	0.8	0.4	0.5	0.6	0.9	6.3	6.4	6.4	6.1	5.8	25.1	28.9	12.4	2.6	77.3	40.3	48.7	51.3
62265	NEW BADEN	95.7	93.7	1.3	1.8	0.7	1.0	2.3	3.7	6.6	6.6	6.8	7.0	5.8	27.0	27.7	10.8	1.6	75.6	38.2	49.5	50.5
62268	OAKDALE	98.6	98.5	0.0	0.0	0.2	0.2	0.6	0.6	6.5	6.8	6.5	5.9	5.0	23.6	30.0	14.0	1.7	76.5	41.9	50.6	49.4
62269	O FALLON	83.8	76.6	11.1	16.8	2.4	3.1	2.3	3.3	6.5	6.5	6.6	6.8	6.6	27.5	29.5	8.8	1.2	76.3	37.6	48.8	51.2
62271	OKAWVILLE	98.6	98.4	0.3	0.3	0.1	0.2	0.5	0.6	6.4	6.4	6.6	6.6	5.8	25.9	26.6	13.2	2.5	76.6	39.9	50.3	49.7
62272	PERCY	99.4	99.2	0.1	0.1	0.0	0.0	1.1	1.5	7.1	7.4	7.2	6.1	5.0	26.4	25.9	12.8	2.2	74.7	38.1	48.9	51.1
62274	PINCKNEYVILLE	84.2	81.7	12.9	14.4	0.3	0.5	2.7	3.7	4.3	4.7	5.0	6.1	8.5	31.6	25.6	11.7	2.5	82.7	38.3	58.6	41.4
62275	POCAHONTAS	97.8	97.2	0.3	0.3	0.2	0.3	1.0	1.6	6.7	7.0	7.3	6.6	5.4	26.2	28.8	10.8	1.3	75.1	38.8	51.4	48.6
62277	PRAIRIE DU ROCHER	98.6	98.2	0.0	0.0	0.1	0.1	0.5	0.8	7.3	7.3	7.3	6.4	5.3	25.7	28.5	10.6	1.7	74.1	38.2	49.2	50.8
62278	RED BUD	98.6	98.1	0.2	0.2	0.3	0.4	0.6	0.9	6.2	6.5	6.6	6.0	4.9	25.4	28.2	13.5	2.9	77.0	40.9	49.6	50.4
62280	ROCKWOOD	99.1	98.0	0.0	0.0	0.2	0.5	0.2	1.0	6.5	7.0	6.8	6.0	5.0	23.9	29.4	13.1	2.3	76.1	41.0	51.5	48.5
62281	SAINT JACOB	98.3	97.8	0.1	0.2	0.2	0.3	1.6	2.3	6.0	6.2	6.7	6.6	4.9	26.6	29.8	12.0	1.2	77.0	40.8	50.7	49.3
62284	SMITHBORO	96.9	96.1	1.7	2.2	0.0	0.1	0.8	0.9	6.0	6.4	7.2	7.5	4.2	23.5	30.6	12.9	1.8	75.6	41.4	51.0	49.0
62285	SMITHTON	97.7	96.9	0.6	0.8	0.6	0.7	0.5	0.8	6.5	7.0	7.3	6.8	4.9	25.5	30.1	10.4	1.4	75.1	39.7	49.4	50.6
62286	SPARTA	86.0	82.8	11.7	14.3	0.4	0.6	1.4	1.8	6.0	5.9	6.3	6.7	6.0	23.7	28.1	14.1	3.2	77.8	41.3	48.7	51.3
62288	STEELEVILLE	98.8	98.3	0.1	0.2	0.4	0.6	0.8	1.1	5.4	5.7	6.1	6.4	4.6	24.7	28.7	15.1	3.3	79.0	42.7	48.7	51.3
62293	TRENTON	98.3	97.7	0.4	0.7	0.5	0.7	1.1	1.6	6.1	6.2	6.6	6.9	5.2	25.7	28.3	12.7	2.4	76.7	40.6	49.4	50.6
62294	TROY	96.0	94.6	1.4	1.9	0.6	0.8	1.4	2.1	6.9	6.8	7.1	7.5	6.9	27.8	27.5	8.3	1.2	74.3	35.6	49.1	50.9
62295	VALMEYER	98.6	98.3	0.2	0.2	0.4	0.5	0.6	0.9	7.0	7.7	7.7	6.5	4.4	25.1	30.8	9.2	1.4	73.3	38.4	49.4	50.6
62297	WALSH	84.7	79.4	13.3	17.1	0.0	1.0	2.3	2.5	4.5	5.0	5.0	6.5	8.0	31.9	25.9	11.6	1.5	82.4	37.8	59.0	41.0
62298	WATERLOO	98.8	98.4	0.0	0.0	0.3	0.5	0.7	1.0	6.4	6.7	7.1	6.9	4.9	25.9	28.4	11.6	2.1	75.5	39.9	49.2	50.8
62301	QUINCY	92.7	91.2	5.0	5.8	0.5	0.7	0.9	1.2	6.2	5.8	5.7	7.2	7.1	24.7	24.5	14.4	4.3	78.4	39.3	47.7	52.3
62305	QUINCY	97.0	96.1	1.2	1.5	0.6	0.8	0.8	1.2	6.2	6.2	6.5	6.5	5.2	22.6	29.6	15.1	2.2	77.0	42.6	48.3	51.7
62311	AUGUSTA	99.6	99.5	0.0	0.0	0.1	0.1	0.7	0.9	5.3	5.6	5.7	6.2	4.9	24.0	29.1	16.0	3.3	79.5	43.5	46.4	53.6
62312	BARRY	99.0	98.7	0.0	0.0	0.3	0.5	0.7	1.0	6.0	6.5	6.7	6.2	4.5	22.7	27.4	15.3	4.6	77.1	42.9	48.2	51.8
62313	BASCO	99.7	99.5	0.0	0.0	0.0	0.0	0.3	0.5	5.7	6.0	6.6	6.6	4.1	25.7	29.8	13.9	1.6	77.3	42.1	51.9	48.1
62314	BAYLIS	98.6	98.2	0.0	0.0	0.3	0.5	0.3	0.5	6.2	7.8	8.2	7.1	4.4	23.5	27.6	12.5	2.7	73.3	39.6	51.2	48.8
62316	BOWEN	98.6	98.1	0.1	0.2	0.3	0.5	0.3	0.3	6.6	7.7	7.7	7.2	4.7	25.4	25.0	13.5	2.1	72.8	38.4	50.4	49.6
62319	CAMDEN	98.9	98.4	0.4	0.4	0.0	0.0	0.7	0.8	6.7	7.1	7.1	5.1	3.2	24.9	29.2	14.6	2.0	75.5	41.5	53.8	46.2
62320	CAMP POINT	98.9	98.5	0.0	0.1	0.1	0.2	0.4	0.6	6.1	6.4	7.0	7.4	5.5	23.6	26.2	13.6	4.1	75.4	40.3	48.4	51.6
62321	CARTHAGE	98.6	98.2	0.3	0.4	0.4	0.6	0.4	0.5	5.9	5.9	6.1	6.6	5.9	23.1	27.7	15.2	3.6	78.0	42.3	48.3	51.7
62323	CHAMBERSBURG	99.0	98.5	0.0	0.0	0.0	0.0	0.0	0.0	6.6	6.6	6.6	5.6	4.6	23.0	26.0	17.3	3.6	76.5	42.5	46.9	53.1
62324	CLAYTON	91.3	89.3	7.1	8.7	0.0	0.0	1.6	2.1	6.6	6.8	6.7	6.3	5.4	27.0	25.2	13.5	2.7	75.7	38.9	53.5	46.5
62325	COATSBURG	99.3	98.9	0.0	0.0	0.0	0.0	0.7	1.1	6.9	6.9	7.3	6.9	4.1	24.3	29.1	12.9	1.7	74.4	40.8	49.4	50.6
62326	COLCHESTER	99.0	98.8	0.1	0.1	0.1	0.1	0.6	0.9	5.3	5.7	5.9	5.9	4.9	23.8	30.5	15.6	2.4	79.6	43.8	48.8	51.2
62330	DALLAS CITY	98.5	98.0	0.0	0.0	0.1	0.1	0.5	0.7	5.3	5.8	6.4	6.7	4.3	22.3	31.4	15.1	2.6	78.5	44.3	48.8	51.2
62334	ELVASTON	100.0	99.3	0.0	0.0	0.0	0.7	0.7	0.7	4.9	6.3	6.3	5.6	4.2	25.0	31.9	13.9	2.1	78.5	43.5	50.7	49.3
62338	FOWLER	98.1	97.4	0.7	0.9	0.1	0.2	0.4	0.5	6.6	7.2	7.5	6.8	4.7	23.5	29.6	13.0	1.1	74.3	41.0	49.6	50.4
62339	GOLDEN	99.1	98.8	0.0	0.0	0.1	0.2	1.0	1.3	7.2	7.4	7.5	7.3	4.7	21.7	26.6	13.8	4.0	73.9	41.3	48.6	51.4
62340	GRIGGSVILLE	99.3	99.1	0.1	0.1	0.1	0.1	0.2	0.3	6.6	6.7	7.1	6.7	5.5	23.8	27.8	13.6	2.2	75.5	40.2	47.8	52.2
62341	HAMILTON	98.4	98.0	0.5	0.6	0.4	0.6	0.7	1.0	4.9	5.2	5.8	6.5	4.9	25.3	29.8	14.2	3.5	80.1	43.2	48.4	51.6
62343	HULL	98.3	98.1	0.0	0.0	0.3	0.5	0.5	0.6	5.7	6.0	6.3	5.7	4.2	25.8	31.2	12.8	2.4	78.5	42.4	50.7	49.3
62344	HUNTSVILLE	99.4	99.3	0.0	0.0	0.0	0.0	0.6	0.7	6.7	6.7	7.4	5.4	3.4	25.5	27.5	15.4	2.0	75.8	40.3	53.7	46.3
62345	KINDERHOOK	98.4	98.1	0.3	0.3	0.0	0.0	1.1	1.4	5.6	5.8	6.4	5.8	5.0	25.8	31.7	12.5	1.4	78.6	41.7	51.4	48.6
62346	LA PRAIRIE	100.0	100.0	0.0	0.0	0.0	0.0	0.6	0.6	7.7	8.3	7.7	7.7	4.2	21.4	28.0	12.5	2.4	70.8	40.4	50.6	49.4
62347	LIBERTY	99.0	98.8	0.0	0.0	0.0	0.1	0.4	0.5	6.1	6.7	7.4	6.9	4.2	25.5	29.8	11.9	1.4	75.4	40.0	51.3	48.7
62348	LIMA	100.0	100.0	0.0	0.0	0.0	0.0	0.0	0.0	8.6	8.6	5.7	5.7	5.7	22.9	28.6	14.3	0.0	71.4	38.8	45.7	54.3
62349	LORAINE	99.6	99.3	0.0	0.0	0.0	0.0	0.3	0.4	6.3	6.7	7.4	7.4	4.5	23.9	29.3	12.8	1.8	75.2	40.8	50.5	49.5
62351	MENDON	99.6	99.4	0.1	0.2	0.0	0.0	0.4	0.6	7.1	7.5	7.3	5.9	4.3	23.2	26.2	13.1	5.6	74.8	40.9	47.5	52.5
62352	MILTON	99.3	99.1	0.0	0.0	0.0	0.0	0.4	0.4	7.8	7.8	7.8	6.7	4.2	24.0	25.2	13.8	2.7	72.6	39.2	49.7	50.3
62353	MOUNT STERLING	73.9	71.1	24.4	27.0	0.2	0.3	5.1	6.6	3.7	3.3	3.2	5.6	11.8	40.4	20.2	9.5	2.2	86.8	34.6	68.6	31.4
62354	NAUVOO	98.2	97.6	0.2	0.2	0.1	0.3	1.1	1.6	5.8	6.4	6.7	5.9	4.0	21.5	29.7	17.0	3.0	79.5	44.8	49.7	50.3
62355	NEBO	98.6	98.4	0.0	0.0	0.1	0.1	0.9	1.1	5.6	6.0	6.2	6.3	5.3	22.1	32.7	14.2	1.7	78.2	43.8	52.3	47.7
62356	NEW CANTON	99.7	99.4	0.0	0.0	0.0	0.0	0.1	0.3	5.0	5.3	5.5	6.2	5.9	24.3	30.1	15.3	2.4	80.4	43.5	48.7	51.3
62357	NEW SALEM	98.3	98.0	0.0	0.0	0.3	0.3	0.3	0.7	6.1	8.1	8.8	7.1	4.7	23.6	27.6	11.4	2.7	72.7	39.0	51.2	48.8
62358	NIOTA	98.8	98.3	0.0	0.0	0.2	0.3	0.5	0.5	5.9	6.4	6.5	5.8	4.2	22.6	30.7	15.6	2.3	78.9	43.9	50.4	49.6
62359	PALOMA	99.4	99.4	0.0	0.0	0.0	0.0	0.6	0.6	7.1	7.1	7.7	6.4	3.8	25.0	28.8	12.8	1.3	74.4	40.4	50.0	50.0
62360	PAYSON	98.6	98.1	0.4	0.5	0.1	0.1	0.4	0.6	6.6	6.7	6.7	7.5	6.4	26.2	27.8	10.5	1.4	75.4	37.2	50.4	49.6
62361	PEARL	98.0	97.7	0.0	0.0	0.3	0.3	0.3	0.3	6.5	6.5	6.8	6.8	4.4	21.9	28.6	15.9	2.6	75.8	42.8	49.7	50.3
62362	PERRY	98.9	98.7	0.0	0.0	0.3	0.3	0.0	0.0	6.5	6.6	6.8	6.5	4.2	23.5	27.0	15.9	3.1	76.1	41.6	49.5	50.5
	ILLINOIS	73.5	70.6	15.1	15.3	3.4	4.4	12.3	15.7	7.1	6.9	6.8	7.1	6.9	27.5	25.4	10.3	1.9	75.0	36.1	49.1	50.9
	UNITED STATES	75.1	72.0	12.3	12.7	3.8	4.6	12.5	15.7	6.8	6.7	6.6	7.1	6.9	27.0	26.0	10.9	1.9	75.7	36.9	49.2	50.8

ZIP CODE #	POST OFFICE NAME	2009 Per Capita Income	2009 HH Income Base	2009 HOUSEHOLD INCOME DISTRIBUTION (%) Less than $25,000	$25,000 to $49,999	$50,000 to $99,999	$100,000 to $149,999	$150,000 or More	MEDIAN HOUSEHOLD INCOME 2009	2014	2009 National Centile	2009 State Centile	2009 Home Value Base	2009 HOME VALUE DISTRIBUTION (%) Less than $50,000	$50,000 to $89,999	$90,000 to $174,999	$175,000 to $399,999	$400,000 or More	2009 Median Home Value
62215	ALBERS	23947	372	15.3	21.0	47.0	12.6	4.0	65300	66367	84	75	297	8.1	11.1	48.1	31.3	1.3	139224
62217	BALDWIN	18052	351	26.2	37.9	30.5	4.0	1.4	40443	42623	34	17	298	28.5	32.2	31.5	7.4	0.3	75500
62218	BARTELSO	25217	560	9.3	19.8	57.1	9.6	4.1	72557	73492	88	83	490	6.3	11.6	46.5	30.2	5.3	150000
62220	BELLEVILLE	22956	7694	23.0	30.3	37.1	6.9	2.8	47503	49672	55	37	4715	9.5	26.5	45.7	17.3	1.0	108518
62221	BELLEVILLE	28585	10528	17.0	26.6	40.4	9.7	6.2	57929	61308	75	61	6338	5.1	12.0	46.2	29.5	7.2	151628
62223	BELLEVILLE	31414	7651	16.7	26.5	41.3	8.9	6.5	58407	61347	76	62	5782	7.1	15.4	54.3	19.6	3.6	126540
62225	SCOTT AIR FORCE BASE	19275	1283	4.8	33.9	46.1	9.5	5.7	61148	62201	79	66	355	15.5	10.1	16.3	38.6	19.4	225893
62226	BELLEVILLE	26476	12178	21.5	28.6	37.8	8.0	4.0	49898	52385	61	43	7877	9.2	21.0	45.5	21.7	2.7	119326
62230	BREESE	25886	2348	10.6	24.1	51.6	8.8	4.9	64203	64850	83	73	1872	3.8	13.6	48.3	31.0	3.3	147449
62231	CARLYLE	23030	3543	23.1	27.7	39.0	8.0	2.3	49439	51131	60	42	2832	18.6	24.2	39.4	15.4	2.4	102764
62232	CASEYVILLE	22178	2857	19.4	34.7	37.9	6.0	2.0	47072	49289	54	35	2335	13.4	26.8	45.7	12.0	2.0	102663
62233	CHESTER	21992	2559	23.0	26.5	41.6	5.5	3.4	50410	52546	62	44	1994	18.4	32.0	38.0	11.1	0.5	89512
62234	COLLINSVILLE	26553	14029	19.5	25.2	42.0	9.7	3.7	55556	59453	72	57	9850	7.3	15.3	54.3	20.8	2.4	125708
62236	COLUMBIA	32412	4682	9.8	15.8	49.1	18.0	7.2	75835	77179	90	87	3726	1.2	2.1	36.2	52.6	7.9	203212
62237	COULTERVILLE	21811	1218	25.6	29.8	36.7	5.9	2.0	45432	46950	50	30	1010	28.0	28.8	32.9	10.1	0.2	81375
62238	CUTLER	19604	299	26.8	34.8	33.1	2.3	3.0	39580	40000	31	15	239	49.8	31.4	15.1	2.9	0.8	50313
62239	DUPO	26102	2003	14.5	27.2	46.9	8.0	3.4	57965	60941	75	61	1480	17.1	28.5	42.6	11.2	0.6	96842
62240	EAST CARONDELET	21762	661	18.0	30.9	42.7	6.5	2.0	51020	55206	64	46	520	25.0	34.6	28.7	10.4	1.3	79024
62241	ELLIS GROVE	24226	438	17.4	24.2	48.2	6.4	3.9	54743	57607	71	56	372	17.5	30.6	38.7	12.4	0.8	93889
62242	EVANSVILLE	20697	661	25.3	32.7	36.6	3.9	1.5	43346	45916	43	25	542	22.1	34.7	34.1	7.4	1.7	82128
62243	FREEBURG	25932	2142	14.8	22.5	49.2	9.2	4.3	64529	66452	83	73	1663	11.0	6.9	41.1	36.5	4.6	153289
62244	FULTS	22554	455	13.6	22.9	53.2	9.2	1.1	62764	66432	81	70	397	9.3	11.6	35.3	37.8	6.0	162750
62245	GERMANTOWN	26248	845	15.1	23.6	45.7	11.6	4.0	65149	65303	83	74	713	7.7	13.3	48.2	28.9	1.8	137367
62246	GREENVILLE	21905	3290	24.6	26.2	39.0	7.3	2.9	49050	51584	59	40	2451	11.9	21.9	46.6	17.9	1.8	112763
62248	HECKER	31450	216	12.5	18.5	52.3	11.1	5.6	72562	76480	88	83	181	5.0	8.8	38.1	40.9	7.2	172083
62249	HIGHLAND	27477	5932	15.9	24.5	45.3	9.1	5.3	63620	65505	82	71	4565	1.2	9.8	52.3	33.2	3.5	148896
62253	KEYESPORT	20147	347	32.9	26.5	36.6	3.7	0.3	40837	44846	35	18	275	24.7	21.8	33.1	14.2	6.2	95000
62254	LEBANON	26174	2554	19.2	25.1	39.4	9.8	6.6	55394	59060	72	57	1809	10.3	14.3	42.9	28.0	4.5	132925
62255	LENZBURG	19789	471	21.7	32.9	38.0	6.4	1.1	47476	49181	55	37	380	23.4	21.8	32.9	20.8	1.1	99000
62257	MARISSA	21634	1435	23.9	31.1	37.6	6.4	1.0	46164	48394	52	32	1122	22.3	30.0	33.6	12.8	1.2	87045
62258	MASCOUTAH	26551	3172	14.7	23.4	50.3	7.9	3.7	62151	65092	80	68	2319	6.1	18.6	52.8	18.8	3.8	121909
62260	MILLSTADT	28256	2806	12.0	23.8	46.1	13.5	4.6	68057	68936	86	78	2234	4.2	8.6	40.9	39.4	6.9	168881
62261	MODOC	24320	86	20.9	31.4	38.4	7.0	2.3	48433	48451	58	39	72	22.2	16.7	41.7	15.3	4.2	106818
62262	MULBERRY GROVE	20365	881	25.0	30.4	39.8	3.4	1.4	43852	47154	45	26	710	23.4	29.2	31.3	14.5	1.7	87049
62263	NASHVILLE	25668	2042	17.3	30.0	41.1	7.6	3.9	52698	53411	67	50	1584	7.4	25.6	46.8	17.9	2.4	116034
62264	NEW ATHENS	24928	1326	18.1	26.5	45.0	6.9	3.5	54737	58098	71	55	1086	10.2	22.2	47.1	17.6	2.9	114268
62265	NEW BADEN	25039	1830	16.3	24.3	46.8	9.4	3.1	61873	63321	80	68	1408	9.2	14.7	49.4	25.6	1.1	129167
62268	OAKDALE	24826	331	12.4	31.1	44.1	8.8	3.6	54994	55669	71	56	283	9.2	19.8	42.4	25.4	3.2	136648
62269	O FALLON	30145	11571	11.9	23.7	42.1	13.5	8.8	66988	68037	85	77	8095	8.2	11.1	37.8	39.0	3.9	156481
62271	OKAWVILLE	23444	878	24.5	26.1	40.5	6.8	2.1	49379	50767	60	41	690	14.3	25.5	43.6	14.6	1.9	107826
62272	PERCY	18551	894	29.0	36.6	30.8	2.3	1.3	37843	40295	26	11	703	34.0	35.1	28.6	2.3	0.0	66397
62274	PINCKNEYVILLE	18535	2618	27.3	31.0	36.5	3.5	1.7	43646	45113	44	25	2049	17.9	31.8	39.3	10.1	1.0	90457
62275	POCAHONTAS	21516	1547	21.1	28.3	42.9	5.9	1.8	50416	53169	62	44	1326	17.9	19.3	41.3	19.4	2.1	111264
62277	PRAIRIE DU ROCHER	21829	572	18.4	30.9	44.4	4.9	1.4	50775	55451	63	45	454	18.5	24.9	38.3	14.1	4.2	98571
62278	RED BUD	23304	2576	19.4	24.1	46.4	7.5	2.6	56199	60591	73	58	2063	10.6	14.5	43.8	27.2	3.9	134094
62280	ROCKWOOD	22478	170	17.1	34.1	45.3	2.9	0.6	49145	51327	59	41	149	23.5	25.5	38.3	12.1	0.7	91500
62281	SAINT JACOB	27949	703	10.2	24.9	46.5	10.5	7.8	64781	65486	83	74	592	4.7	14.5	44.3	30.7	5.7	146134
62284	SMITHBORO	24683	264	21.2	23.5	40.9	9.1	5.3	54702	59508	71	55	215	11.6	16.7	34.9	30.7	6.0	141071
62285	SMITHTON	24123	1310	17.0	20.6	51.2	7.7	3.4	62802	64808	81	70	1139	5.6	13.3	47.8	29.1	4.1	146578
62286	SPARTA	19840	2740	26.8	30.6	36.7	4.2	1.6	42192	44833	40	21	2061	25.1	33.4	34.0	6.6	1.0	80412
62288	STEELEVILLE	22676	1191	23.6	32.0	36.4	6.0	2.0	45853	47539	51	32	960	17.4	27.1	47.9	7.5	0.1	95955
62293	TRENTON	27559	2319	14.9	21.1	48.6	11.0	4.4	65197	65853	83	74	1893	4.8	10.1	50.0	30.4	4.7	149187
62294	TROY	29449	5035	9.4	20.8	48.4	13.5	7.8	75035	75545	89	86	3952	2.6	7.1	45.4	41.5	3.3	165893
62295	VALMEYER	23856	496	15.1	23.4	48.2	10.7	2.6	65612	72017	84	75	413	5.1	8.2	35.4	47.5	3.9	178819
62297	WALSH	20739	162	19.1	34.6	41.4	3.7	1.2	46547	48117	53	33	140	21.4	29.3	39.3	9.3	0.7	89000
62298	WATERLOO	27445	6166	12.5	20.1	50.6	11.8	5.0	68915	75023	86	79	4917	1.9	6.0	35.3	51.4	5.4	197842
62301	QUINCY	21742	14127	29.6	31.6	32.4	3.9	2.5	38442	41999	28	13	9115	11.4	30.5	44.4	12.4	1.3	99395
62305	QUINCY	24248	6998	19.6	29.0	40.4	6.8	4.3	51402	53200	65	47	5863	15.6	9.5	43.7	27.1	4.1	137283
62311	AUGUSTA	18265	340	32.9	33.5	28.5	3.8	1.2	39016	41391	30	14	279	51.6	25.1	17.9	3.6	1.8	48714
62312	BARRY	18885	989	35.1	29.2	30.4	3.1	2.1	34617	35881	17	6	757	30.8	30.5	30.9	6.9	0.9	76532
62313	BASCO	20695	151	17.2	37.1	41.7	4.0	0.0	44780	44487	48	29	129	34.1	36.4	25.6	3.9	0.0	64333
62314	BAYLIS	17933	209	27.8	33.0	35.4	2.4	1.4	41466	43254	38	20	154	37.7	22.1	33.1	5.8	1.3	73333
62316	BOWEN	16954	237	29.1	35.9	35.4	1.3	1.3	39092	41551	30	14	189	45.5	31.2	16.4	2.6	4.2	54250
62319	CAMDEN	19483	106	28.3	35.8	31.1	3.8	0.9	41874	43068	39	21	84	36.9	25.0	22.6	13.1	2.4	68571
62320	CAMP POINT	19297	735	28.3	30.5	34.7	4.8	1.8	41860	45767	39	21	574	19.2	30.7	37.1	12.0	1.0	90345
62321	CARTHAGE	22547	1725	23.0	29.0	40.1	6.3	1.6	47101	46981	54	35	1284	18.6	35.6	38.9	6.2	0.7	85537
62323	CHAMBERSBURG	17950	81	37.0	28.4	30.9	2.5	1.2	33606	35000	15	5	63	34.9	34.9	20.6	9.5	0.0	62500
62324	CLAYTON	17573	558	35.1	29.2	29.4	4.1	2.2	35843	37796	20	8	437	40.0	32.0	19.2	5.7	3.2	59063
62325	COATSBURG	18980	212	25.5	32.5	36.3	4.2	1.4	45242	46781	49	30	173	16.8	28.3	32.4	16.8	5.8	103125
62326	COLCHESTER	21139	1114	26.1	30.7	36.7	4.1	2.3	42980	46075	42	24	868	30.8	32.7	26.5	9.0	1.0	69886
62330	DALLAS CITY	20317	879	25.4	33.0	36.4	4.3	0.9	41885	43559	39	21	692	26.4	33.2	30.5	9.5	0.3	77619
62334	ELVASTON	25364	64	15.6	28.1	51.6	4.7	0.0	54460	53790	70	55	55	23.6	23.6	38.2	10.9	3.6	95000
62338	FOWLER	22120	494	17.2	23.7	52.8	4.5	1.8	60069	60481	77	64	431	8.8	22.0	43.4	24.6	1.2	122070
62339	GOLDEN	19966	356	20.8	35.4	36.5	6.7	0.6	43982	47246	45	27	285	17.5	31.6	31.6	16.5	2.8	92083
62340	GRIGGSVILLE	18427	602	26.7	33.6	34.9	3.7	1.2	41076	40945	36	19	454	26.7	34.4	35.0	3.3	0.7	75172
62341	HAMILTON	23838	1371	20.7	25.1	46.7	5.0	2.5	53121	52528	68	51	1121	17.0	33.7	37.0	11.3	0.9	89325
62343	HULL	18883	257	28.0	37.4	30.4	4.3	0.0	38649	38739	29	13	199	30.7	36.7	24.1	5.5	3.0	68478
62344	HUNTSVILLE	17725	67	32.8	40.3	22.4	4.5	0.0	33338	33873	14	4	52	38.5	25.0	25.0	11.5	0.0	67500
62345	KINDERHOOK	21768	149	23.5	34.2	36.9	3.4	2.0	45182	46126	49	29	120	33.3	40.0	21.7	3.3	1.7	62500
62346	LA PRAIRIE	17243	63	23.8	34.9	39.7	1.6	0.0	42367	46363	41	22	50	18.0	46.0	26.0	8.0	2.0	82222
62347	LIBERTY	22158	841	17.5	30.9	44.4	4.8	2.5	50985	51890	64	46	696	17.5	22.6	40.4	16.4	3.2	110976
62348	LIMA	28872	19	15.8	26.3	52.6	5.3	0.0	54378	56087	70	55	15	6.7	40.0	40.0	13.3	0.0	95000
62349	LORAINE	22927	281	14.2	31.7	45.9	6.4	1.8	53245	55442	68	52	230	26.1	28.3	30.0	14.3	1.3	83333
62351	MENDON	19555	654	25.2	31.0	37.9	3.7	2.1	44621	47528	47	28	519	14.1	29.9	43.5	10.0	2.5	96848
62352	MILTON	18922	217	26.7	35.5	33.6	1.8	2.3	38710	39532	29	13	181	32.0	27.1	27.6	9.9	3.3	76818
62353	MOUNT STERLING	18721	1353	33.0	28.6	33.6	3.3	1.6	37830	40896	26	11	964	30.0	35.7	26.8	6.1	1.5	72532
62354	NAUVOO	22937	599	19.4	28.2	44.2	6.5	1.7	51998	51598	66	49	492	14.4	29.1	41.7	13.0	1.8	100000
62355	NEBO	18768	380	31.3	32.1	32.6	2.9	1.1	39086	39601	30	14	320	39.4	26.3	20.9	10.3	3.1	62368
62356	NEW CANTON	16752	279	38.0	30.5	28.3	2.2	1.1	32983	35000	13	4	218	45.0	35.8	14.7	4.1	0.5	54400
62357	NEW SALEM	18838	112	26.8	32.1	37.5	2.7	0.9	42605	43961	41	23	83	39.8	18.1	37.3	3.6	1.2	73750
62358	NIOTA	20886	259	20.8	31.7	40.9	5.4	1.2	46647	46545	53	34	215	18.6	36.7	33.5	10.2	0.9	83611
62359	PALOMA	19131	66	28.8	31.8	34.8	3.0	1.5	43216	45000	43	25	53	15.1	30.2	30.2	17.0	7.5	102083
62360	PAYSON	20375	723	21.2	27.2	44.1	5.1	2.4	51101	52167	64	47	597	13.2	31.0	40.0	14.6	1.2	98214
62361	PEARL	20409	163	35.6	30.7	27.6	2.5	3.7	34422	34688	16	5	135	45.9	24.4	12.6	5.9	11.1	55000
62362	PERRY	19374	271	34.3	30.3	30.6	2.6	2.2	35988	37333	21	8	208	33.7	35.1	22.6	8.2	0.5	64444
	ILLINOIS	28587		18.2	22.2	39.3	12.1	8.2	60823	63631				6.3	10.0	30.9	40.6	12.3	185324
	UNITED STATES	27277		20.9	24.4	35.3	11.7	7.6	54719	56938				9.3	13.1	31.6	32.6	13.5	162279

ZIP CODE #	POST OFFICE NAME	FINANCIAL SERVICES: Auto Loan	Home Loan	Invest-ments	Retire-ment Plans	THE HOME: Home Improvements: Home Repair	Lawn & Garden	Furnishings: Comput-ers & Hard-ware-Personal	Major Appli-ances	TV, Radio, Sound Equip-ment	Furni-ture	ENTERTAINMENT: Dine out/ Carry out	Sports Equip-ment	Fees & Tickets	Toys & Games	Travel	Cable TV	PERSONAL: Apparel & Services	Auto Repairs	Health Insur-ance	Pets & Supplies
62215	ALBERS	108	104	96	105	103	112	98	107	101	96	100	80	95	103	98	104	69	101	108	125
62217	BALDWIN	82	59	84	57	61	83	60	77	67	56	66	57	48	66	60	73	43	70	80	91
62218	BARTELSO	107	112	101	116	111	117	103	110	103	100	103	85	105	106	107	105	71	105	111	129
62220	BELLEVILLE	79	75	67	76	73	79	80	77	81	76	81	59	77	82	75	83	56	79	83	92
62221	BELLEVILLE	104	100	87	100	96	97	102	98	101	102	101	77	98	104	97	100	70	100	98	117
62223	BELLEVILLE	98	104	101	103	104	112	98	104	101	97	101	75	102	100	102	106	70	102	114	120
62225	SCOTT AIR FORCE BASE	121	101	80	102	93	83	116	99	108	118	112	86	104	123	100	101	79	106	87	116
62226	BELLEVILLE	88	85	78	85	83	88	88	86	90	85	89	66	86	90	85	92	62	88	92	103
62230	BREESE	101	105	94	106	102	108	98	103	98	96	98	79	99	101	99	100	68	99	104	120
62231	CARLYLE	88	78	84	78	78	94	79	87	82	73	81	66	72	82	78	87	55	84	94	103
62232	CASEYVILLE	83	77	77	76	76	86	75	82	79	73	78	61	72	80	75	82	53	79	86	96
62233	CHESTER	88	81	86	81	81	96	81	89	85	76	84	66	77	85	81	90	57	86	97	104
62234	COLLINSVILLE	90	90	82	90	87	94	89	90	91	87	90	68	89	92	88	93	63	90	96	106
62236	COLUMBIA	108	134	119	134	129	128	114	118	113	116	115	90	130	116	125	115	81	115	121	137
62237	COULTERVILLE	92	70	88	69	71	94	71	87	78	66	77	66	59	79	70	85	51	80	90	103
62238	CUTLER	95	69	81	67	69	92	71	84	79	69	77	64	58	82	66	86	52	79	88	102
62239	DUPO	91	94	75	95	87	96	92	89	93	89	93	71	93	95	90	95	64	91	98	108
62240	EAST CARONDELET	87	88	74	85	83	85	84	84	84	86	85	64	83	87	82	85	58	84	84	99
62241	ELLIS GROVE	98	86	91	88	88	104	85	98	89	77	87	74	77	90	85	94	59	90	101	114
62242	EVANSVILLE	85	64	84	63	66	88	67	82	74	61	72	62	56	73	66	81	48	76	88	97
62243	FREEBURG	96	109	96	108	105	106	95	100	96	98	97	75	104	99	101	98	68	97	102	116
62244	FULTS	94	94	87	97	93	102	88	97	89	84	89	74	87	91	90	93	61	91	98	113
62245	GERMANTOWN	106	101	96	105	102	113	97	107	99	91	98	81	93	102	98	104	67	100	109	125
62246	GREENVILLE	86	75	80	76	75	89	79	85	82	73	80	65	71	82	76	86	55	83	90	100
62248	HECKER	109	122	105	126	119	120	109	114	107	109	108	89	116	110	115	108	75	109	112	134
62249	HIGHLAND	97	104	94	105	102	105	99	100	99	97	99	77	102	100	101	100	69	99	103	118
62253	KEYESPORT	81	58	83	56	60	82	59	76	66	55	65	57	48	66	59	73	43	69	79	90
62254	LEBANON	101	95	93	97	96	102	96	100	97	95	96	75	93	98	95	99	67	98	103	117
62255	LENZBURG	92	73	79	73	73	91	74	85	79	70	78	65	63	82	70	86	53	79	89	101
62257	MARISSA	85	71	83	70	72	91	71	83	77	66	76	63	64	77	71	84	51	78	89	98
62258	MASCOUTAH	95	103	89	103	99	103	95	97	96	95	96	73	99	98	97	98	67	96	101	114
62260	MILLSTADT	100	112	101	114	110	114	100	106	101	99	101	81	107	102	107	103	70	102	109	124
62261	MODOC	87	76	81	79	78	93	76	87	79	69	77	66	68	80	75	84	53	80	90	102
62262	MULBERRY GROVE	83	64	80	65	66	87	68	81	73	60	71	61	57	73	66	79	48	75	86	95
62263	NASHVILLE	96	86	93	87	86	103	87	96	90	80	89	74	80	90	87	95	60	92	102	114
62264	NEW ATHENS	90	92	82	93	89	99	87	91	90	85	90	69	89	91	89	93	62	89	99	108
62265	NEW BADEN	91	97	86	98	94	98	91	93	92	89	92	71	94	94	93	94	64	91	97	109
62268	OAKDALE	103	94	93	98	96	111	92	104	95	84	94	79	85	97	92	101	64	96	108	121
62269	O FALLON	113	116	108	117	115	113	110	111	109	113	110	85	113	112	111	109	77	110	109	130
62271	OKAWVILLE	90	77	85	77	75	94	78	87	82	72	81	68	70	82	77	87	55	84	93	105
62272	PERCY	81	59	70	58	59	79	62	72	68	59	67	55	50	71	57	75	45	68	77	87
62274	PINCKNEYVILLE	81	62	80	61	64	85	65	79	71	58	69	59	54	70	63	77	46	73	84	93
62275	POCAHONTAS	96	74	84	74	75	95	76	88	82	72	81	68	64	84	72	88	54	83	92	106
62277	PRAIRIE DU ROCHER	93	74	80	74	74	93	75	86	81	71	79	66	64	83	71	87	54	81	90	103
62278	RED BUD	92	87	84	87	87	97	83	91	86	80	85	68	80	88	83	90	58	87	95	107
62280	ROCKWOOD	86	71	83	71	73	91	71	85	76	65	75	64	62	77	71	82	50	78	88	99
62281	SAINT JACOB	111	111	105	114	111	121	104	114	106	98	105	87	103	108	107	110	72	107	116	133
62284	SMITHBORO	102	89	105	90	90	109	88	101	90	81	90	80	79	90	90	95	60	95	104	121
62285	SMITHTON	102	101	89	101	99	102	94	99	95	96	95	74	93	99	93	97	66	95	98	117
62286	SPARTA	77	63	70	63	64	79	66	74	71	62	69	55	58	71	63	76	47	71	80	87
62288	STEELEVILLE	81	74	78	75	76	89	73	83	77	67	75	62	68	77	74	82	51	78	89	96
62293	TRENTON	98	104	97	105	102	108	97	102	99	96	98	76	100	99	101	101	68	99	106	119
62294	TROY	114	123	108	122	118	113	116	113	112	119	114	89	120	116	116	110	80	113	110	132
62295	VALMEYER	94	103	90	106	100	104	93	98	92	92	92	76	97	94	97	93	64	94	98	115
62297	WALSH	87	68	85	67	70	90	68	83	74	63	72	63	58	74	68	80	48	77	86	98
62298	WATERLOO	102	115	98	116	110	111	103	106	102	104	103	82	110	105	107	102	72	102	106	124
62301	QUINCY	70	66	63	67	64	72	70	69	72	66	72	53	68	72	67	75	50	71	76	83
62305	QUINCY	92	90	85	89	89	95	85	91	87	85	87	68	84	89	85	90	60	88	93	107
62311	AUGUSTA	77	55	78	54	57	80	60	74	67	53	64	56	48	65	58	73	43	69	81	87
62312	BARRY	80	57	82	56	59	82	61	76	67	54	65	58	48	66	60	73	43	70	80	90
62313	BASCO	90	62	98	62	65	95	69	85	71	56	70	70	50	70	68	78	46	79	90	105
62314	BAYLIS	86	60	92	59	63	89	65	81	69	56	68	64	49	68	64	76	45	75	85	98
62316	BOWEN	78	54	85	53	56	82	59	74	62	48	61	61	44	61	59	67	40	69	78	91
62319	CAMDEN	83	57	91	57	60	88	64	79	66	51	65	65	47	65	63	72	42	74	83	97
62320	CAMP POINT	83	65	81	65	67	87	68	81	74	61	71	61	57	73	67	80	48	76	87	95
62321	CARTHAGE	85	70	82	70	71	87	75	82	77	68	76	64	65	76	73	81	51	80	88	99
62323	CHAMBERSBURG	77	55	79	54	58	79	57	73	63	53	62	54	46	63	56	70	41	67	76	86
62324	CLAYTON	78	55	81	54	58	82	61	75	66	52	64	58	47	65	59	73	43	70	81	90
62325	COATSBURG	83	61	88	61	63	88	66	80	68	55	67	65	51	67	65	74	44	74	84	97
62326	COLCHESTER	86	64	88	63	66	90	68	83	74	60	72	64	56	73	67	81	48	78	89	99
62330	DALLAS CITY	85	61	89	60	64	88	64	80	70	58	68	62	50	69	63	76	45	74	84	96
62334	ELVASTON	102	70	112	70	73	108	78	97	81	63	80	80	57	79	78	88	52	90	102	119
62338	FOWLER	88	86	82	89	86	96	82	90	83	77	82	69	79	85	83	87	57	84	92	105
62339	GOLDEN	83	66	83	68	68	88	69	81	71	59	70	64	57	71	68	76	47	75	85	97
62340	GRIGGSVILLE	76	61	73	61	62	80	63	75	68	56	66	56	54	68	62	73	44	69	79	87
62341	HAMILTON	93	80	81	81	79	96	81	89	84	75	83	69	72	86	78	90	56	85	94	107
62343	HULL	81	57	87	56	59	85	61	77	65	52	64	61	46	64	61	71	42	71	81	93
62344	HUNTSVILLE	71	48	77	48	51	74	54	67	56	44	55	55	39	55	54	61	36	62	71	82
62345	KINDERHOOK	94	67	96	65	70	95	69	88	77	64	75	66	55	76	68	84	50	81	91	104
62346	LA PRAIRIE	82	57	90	56	59	87	63	78	65	51	65	65	46	64	62	71	42	73	82	96
62347	LIBERTY	91	80	85	83	82	98	80	92	83	71	81	70	72	84	80	88	55	85	95	107
62348	LIMA	82	75	74	78	77	88	74	84	76	67	75	63	68	78	74	81	51	77	86	97
62349	LORAINE	94	83	87	86	85	101	83	94	85	74	84	72	75	87	83	91	57	87	98	110
62351	MENDON	89	64	92	63	67	92	67	84	73	60	72	65	53	72	67	80	47	78	88	101
62352	MILTON	85	60	89	59	63	87	63	80	69	56	68	62	49	68	63	76	44	74	84	96
62353	MOUNT STERLING	75	55	75	54	57	77	61	72	67	55	65	54	50	66	58	73	44	69	79	85
62354	NAUVOO	91	77	87	79	79	97	78	90	80	68	79	70	68	81	78	86	53	83	93	106
62355	NEBO	82	58	84	56	60	83	60	76	66	55	65	58	48	66	60	73	43	70	80	91
62356	NEW CANTON	73	52	75	50	54	74	53	68	59	50	58	51	43	59	53	65	38	62	71	81
62357	NEW SALEM	89	63	93	62	66	91	66	83	72	59	71	64	52	71	65	79	47	77	87	100
62358	NIOTA	89	69	89	70	72	93	71	86	76	64	74	66	59	76	71	82	50	79	89	102
62359	PALOMA	81	56	89	55	58	85	62	77	64	50	64	63	45	63	61	70	41	72	81	94
62360	PAYSON	82	77	73	78	74	87	77	81	79	71	78	64	73	80	76	82	53	79	87	98
62361	PEARL	86	59	94	59	62	90	65	81	68	54	68	67	48	67	65	75	44	76	86	100
62362	PERRY	79	56	83	55	58	81	59	74	64	52	63	58	46	63	58	70	41	69	78	89
	ILLINOIS	106	108	105	108	107	106	109	106	108	107	109	83	110	108	108	108	77	108	107	125
	UNITED STATES	100	100	100	100	100	100	100	100	100	100	100	100	100	100	100	100	100	100	100	100

ZIP CODE #	POST OFFICE NAME	COUNTY FIPS CODE	POPULATION 2000	POPULATION 2009	POPULATION 2014	2000-2009 ANNUAL RATE % Rate	2000-2009 ANNUAL RATE State Centile	HOUSEHOLDS 2000	HOUSEHOLDS 2009	HOUSEHOLDS 2014	HOUSEHOLDS % Annual Rate 2000-2009	HOUSEHOLDS 2009 Average HH Size	FAMILIES 2000	FAMILIES 2009	FAMILIES % Annual Rate 2000-2009
62363	PITTSFIELD	149	6457	6253	6186	-0.3	32	2514	2456	2435	-0.3	2.31	1665	1593	-0.5
62365	PLAINVILLE	001	746	866	888	1.6	89	271	324	335	1.9	2.67	216	254	1.8
62366	PLEASANT HILL	149	1456	1420	1408	-0.3	32	602	593	590	-0.2	2.36	415	400	-0.4
62367	PLYMOUTH	169	1473	1303	1250	-1.3	2	571	501	481	-1.4	2.56	406	352	-1.5
62370	ROCKPORT	149	655	651	650	-0.1	45	243	243	243	0.0	2.68	182	179	-0.2
62373	SUTTER	067	421	415	405	-0.2	38	146	145	142	-0.1	2.86	116	113	-0.3
62374	TENNESSEE	067	280	241	225	-1.6	1	121	106	100	-1.4	2.27	87	75	-1.6
62375	TIMEWELL	009	530	484	463	-1.0	3	200	186	179	-0.8	2.60	143	131	-0.9
62376	URSA	001	1284	1235	1213	-0.4	25	505	500	495	-0.1	2.47	369	358	-0.3
62378	VERSAILLES	009	1134	1053	1019	-0.8	6	462	438	427	-0.6	2.40	321	298	-0.8
62379	WARSAW	067	2288	2176	2091	-0.5	18	920	887	856	-0.4	2.45	652	617	-0.6
62380	WEST POINT	067	512	484	465	-0.6	13	193	184	177	-0.5	2.63	144	134	-0.8
62401	EFFINGHAM	049	19584	19304	19072	-0.2	38	7843	7896	7855	0.1	2.40	5245	5179	-0.1
62410	ALLENDALE	185	1085	1021	981	-0.7	9	399	381	368	-0.5	2.63	307	289	-0.7
62411	ALTAMONT	049	3956	4042	4045	0.2	61	1485	1548	1560	0.5	2.55	1077	1095	0.2
62413	ANNAPOLIS	033	468	448	438	-0.5	18	174	169	167	-0.3	2.65	136	130	-0.5
62414	BEECHER CITY	051	1857	1853	1835	0.0	50	738	750	746	0.2	2.47	548	545	-0.1
62417	BRIDGEPORT	101	3156	2992	2882	-0.6	13	1289	1212	1170	-0.7	2.39	886	817	-0.9
62418	BROWNSTOWN	051	2533	2646	2637	0.5	72	998	1044	1044	0.5	2.53	707	725	0.3
62419	CALHOUN	159	465	450	444	-0.4	25	180	178	177	-0.1	2.53	136	133	-0.2
62420	CASEY	023	4944	4697	4602	-0.6	13	2039	1943	1906	-0.5	2.35	1353	1259	-0.8
62421	CLAREMONT	159	839	850	851	0.1	56	313	323	325	0.3	2.63	250	254	0.2
62422	COWDEN	051	1518	1453	1412	-0.5	18	576	557	542	-0.4	2.61	422	402	-0.5
62423	DENNISON	023	699	737	742	0.6	75	271	290	292	0.7	2.54	203	213	0.5
62424	DIETERICH	049	2122	2168	2163	0.2	61	692	720	723	0.4	3.01	565	578	0.2
62425	DUNDAS	159	634	624	620	-0.2	38	233	235	235	0.1	2.63	178	176	-0.1
62426	EDGEWOOD	025	769	783	784	0.2	61	321	336	338	0.5	2.33	242	248	0.3
62427	FLAT ROCK	033	2223	2251	2229	0.1	56	849	867	862	0.2	2.58	650	654	0.1
62428	GREENUP	035	3113	3038	2973	-0.3	32	1312	1300	1277	-0.1	2.29	860	835	-0.3
62431	HERRICK	173	687	691	682	0.1	56	262	267	265	0.2	2.59	188	188	0.0
62432	HIDALGO	079	559	556	554	-0.1	45	228	232	233	0.2	2.38	164	162	-0.1
62433	HUTSONVILLE	033	1057	994	968	-0.7	9	400	380	371	-0.6	2.38	286	267	-0.7
62434	INGRAHAM	025	755	706	681	-0.7	9	236	224	217	-0.6	2.92	183	172	-0.7
62436	JEWETT	035	538	549	545	0.2	61	202	210	209	0.4	2.60	149	152	0.2
62438	LAKEWOOD	173	409	385	371	-0.7	9	161	154	149	-0.5	2.50	125	118	-0.6
62439	LAWRENCEVILLE	101	7456	7743	7557	0.4	69	3144	3067	2995	-0.3	2.21	2006	1913	-0.5
62440	LERNA	029	1379	1465	1469	0.7	78	526	571	576	0.9	2.56	407	434	0.7
62441	MARSHALL	023	7426	7373	7322	-0.1	45	3057	3074	3065	0.1	2.36	2100	2072	-0.1
62442	MARTINSVILLE	023	2515	2625	2640	0.5	72	1030	1084	1094	0.6	2.42	753	774	0.3
62443	MASON	049	1899	1957	1967	0.3	65	652	689	697	0.6	2.84	506	524	0.4
62445	MONTROSE	035	1244	1275	1271	0.3	65	418	440	442	0.6	2.90	328	339	0.4
62446	MOUNT ERIE	191	419	387	375	-0.9	4	169	159	155	-0.7	2.42	131	121	-0.9
62447	NEOGA	035	3772	3663	3562	-0.3	32	1397	1378	1348	-0.1	2.62	1032	1001	-0.3
62448	NEWTON	079	6036	5785	5695	-0.5	18	2394	2330	2306	-0.3	2.45	1664	1591	-0.5
62449	OBLONG	033	3217	3065	2990	-0.5	18	1289	1239	1213	-0.4	2.41	919	865	-0.7
62450	OLNEY	159	11925	11623	11495	-0.3	32	5035	4983	4953	-0.1	2.30	3306	3202	-0.3
62451	PALESTINE	033	2169	2021	1966	-0.8	6	946	891	869	-0.6	2.02	637	586	-0.9
62452	PARKERSBURG	159	436	423	418	-0.3	32	188	187	186	-0.1	2.26	143	139	-0.3
62454	ROBINSON	033	11874	11486	11304	-0.4	25	4418	4297	4231	-0.3	2.40	2996	2856	-0.5
62458	SAINT ELMO	051	1964	1898	1859	-0.4	25	755	741	729	-0.2	2.50	547	527	-0.4
62460	SAINT FRANCISVILLE	101	1739	1682	1636	-0.4	25	690	679	664	-0.2	2.48	505	488	-0.4
62461	SHUMWAY	049	564	577	578	0.2	61	204	214	216	0.5	2.70	156	159	0.2
62462	SIGEL	173	1255	1214	1181	-0.4	25	405	398	389	-0.2	3.05	314	305	-0.3
62463	STEWARDSON	173	1267	1400	1410	1.1	85	501	560	566	1.2	2.50	354	388	1.0
62465	STRASBURG	173	901	853	822	-0.6	13	315	300	289	-0.5	2.60	228	214	-0.7
62466	SUMNER	101	2419	2501	2436	0.4	69	905	874	851	-0.4	2.49	642	608	-0.6
62467	TEUTOPOLIS	049	3198	3316	3334	0.4	69	1026	1096	1112	0.7	3.02	796	834	0.5
62468	TOLEDO	035	2557	2586	2550	0.1	56	1025	1053	1044	0.3	2.44	721	727	0.1
62469	TRILLA	035	573	563	551	-0.2	38	202	201	198	-0.1	2.76	142	139	-0.2
62471	VANDALIA	051	10209	8651	8529	-1.8	1	3570	3570	3532	0.0	2.35	2352	2307	-0.2
62473	WATSON	049	1232	1247	1242	0.1	56	426	444	447	0.4	2.81	340	349	0.3
62474	WESTFIELD	023	1017	991	979	-0.3	32	405	400	396	-0.1	2.48	292	283	-0.3
62475	WEST LIBERTY	079	374	373	372	0.0	50	129	132	132	0.2	2.83	98	99	0.1
62476	WEST SALEM	047	2060	2006	1969	-0.3	32	833	824	811	-0.1	2.40	598	581	-0.3
62477	WEST UNION	023	1144	1106	1088	-0.4	25	460	449	443	-0.3	2.46	326	312	-0.5
62478	WEST YORK	033	428	416	409	-0.3	32	166	164	162	-0.1	2.54	123	120	-0.3
62479	WHEELER	079	863	896	900	0.4	69	310	329	333	0.6	2.72	249	260	0.5
62480	WILLOW HILL	079	1159	1144	1138	-0.1	45	450	453	453	0.1	2.53	345	341	-0.1
62481	YALE	079	428	399	390	-0.8	6	157	149	147	-0.6	2.68	122	114	-0.7
62501	ARGENTA	115	2623	2597	2540	-0.1	45	1013	1038	1025	0.3	2.50	800	803	0.0
62510	ASSUMPTION	021	1854	1766	1714	-0.5	18	770	743	725	-0.4	2.38	535	505	-0.6
62512	BEASON	107	546	541	530	-0.1	45	186	186	183	0.0	2.91	153	151	-0.1
62513	BLUE MOUND	115	1746	1700	1664	-0.3	32	688	695	687	0.1	2.45	517	511	-0.1
62514	BOODY	115	159	150	144	-0.6	13	59	58	56	-0.2	2.59	47	45	-0.5
62515	BUFFALO	167	942	979	992	0.4	69	360	385	394	0.7	2.54	274	285	0.4
62517	BULPITT	021	206	200	196	-0.3	32	96	95	93	-0.1	2.11	66	63	-0.5
62518	CHESTNUT	107	466	469	465	0.1	56	185	187	186	0.1	2.51	147	147	0.0
62520	DAWSON	167	1376	1436	1457	0.5	72	542	580	593	0.7	2.47	426	444	0.4
62521	DECATUR	115	37527	35947	34861	-0.5	18	15387	15154	14809	-0.2	2.35	10771	10376	-0.4
62522	DECATUR	115	18902	17589	16880	-0.8	6	7287	6853	6592	-0.7	2.29	4258	3883	-1.0
62523	DECATUR	115	548	543	531	-0.1	45	135	129	123	-0.5	1.71	36	33	-0.9
62526	DECATUR	115	36928	34618	33365	-0.7	9	15856	15258	14808	-0.4	2.20	9777	9161	-0.7
62530	DIVERNON	167	1519	1530	1538	0.1	56	607	628	636	0.4	2.44	451	453	0.0
62531	EDINBURG	021	2005	2037	2025	0.2	61	807	837	838	0.4	2.43	577	586	0.2
62533	FARMERSVILLE	135	1076	1062	1054	-0.1	45	432	436	434	0.1	2.44	305	300	-0.2
62534	FINDLAY	173	1358	1278	1230	-0.7	9	568	544	527	-0.5	2.35	415	391	-0.6
62535	FORSYTH	115	2297	2484	2497	0.8	79	846	953	965	1.3	2.59	660	728	1.1
62536	GLENARM	167	958	1013	1033	0.6	75	324	351	361	0.9	2.89	277	294	0.6
62538	HARVEL	135	452	456	453	0.1	56	175	180	180	0.3	2.53	133	134	0.1
62539	ILLIOPOLIS	167	1288	1299	1302	0.1	56	502	518	523	0.3	2.51	372	373	0.0
62543	LATHAM	107	501	484	470	-0.4	25	203	200	195	-0.2	2.42	155	150	-0.4
62544	MACON	115	1764	1803	1778	0.2	61	678	719	717	0.6	2.45	511	529	0.4
62545	MECHANICSBURG	167	1097	1106	1107	0.1	56	425	439	442	0.4	2.52	318	320	0.1
62546	MORRISONVILLE	021	1673	1624	1590	-0.3	32	657	649	640	-0.1	2.50	479	462	-0.4
62547	MOUNT AUBURN	021	744	713	696	-0.5	18	319	312	306	-0.2	2.29	240	231	-0.4
	ILLINOIS					0.6					0.6	2.64			0.4
	UNITED STATES					1.0					1.1	2.59			0.9

ZIP CODE #	POST OFFICE NAME	RACE (%) White 2000	White 2009	Black 2000	Black 2009	Asian/Pacific 2000	Asian/Pacific 2009	% Hispanic Origin 2000	% Hispanic Origin 2009	2009 AGE DISTRIBUTION (%) 0-4	5-9	10-14	15-19	20-24	25-44	45-64	65-84	85+	18+	MEDIAN AGE 2009	% 2009 Males	% 2009 Females
62363	PITTSFIELD	94.7	93.7	4.0	4.7	0.4	0.5	0.6	0.8	5.2	5.1	5.7	6.3	6.1	24.4	25.9	16.0	5.2	80.6	42.8	50.7	49.3
62365	PLAINVILLE	98.9	98.5	0.0	0.0	0.0	0.0	0.1	0.2	6.5	6.7	6.9	6.9	5.0	25.1	29.1	12.2	1.6	75.5	40.3	51.4	48.6
62366	PLEASANT HILL	98.8	98.4	0.0	0.0	0.1	0.2	0.5	0.8	6.8	6.8	6.9	6.6	4.6	24.3	25.6	15.1	3.3	74.9	41.0	51.7	48.3
62367	PLYMOUTH	98.4	98.0	0.1	0.2	0.3	0.5	0.6	1.0	7.2	7.4	7.4	6.3	4.1	24.3	27.9	13.3	2.0	73.6	39.8	51.0	49.0
62370	ROCKPORT	99.4	99.2	0.2	0.2	0.0	0.0	0.6	0.9	5.5	6.0	6.5	6.8	4.9	24.1	33.2	11.2	1.8	77.9	41.4	50.4	49.6
62373	SUTTER	99.3	99.0	0.0	0.0	0.2	0.2	0.5	0.7	7.0	7.5	7.7	7.0	3.9	20.2	30.4	14.0	2.4	73.5	42.7	50.4	49.6
62374	TENNESSEE	98.9	98.8	0.0	0.0	0.0	0.0	0.0	0.0	5.0	5.4	6.2	6.2	3.7	23.7	33.2	14.5	2.1	78.8	44.9	51.0	49.0
62375	TIMEWELL	98.3	97.9	0.2	0.2	0.2	0.4	1.1	1.7	5.2	5.6	5.8	7.0	4.8	25.6	30.4	14.0	1.7	78.9	42.2	53.9	46.1
62376	URSA	99.1	98.9	0.0	0.0	0.2	0.2	1.1	1.4	7.0	7.3	7.0	6.2	5.2	24.0	29.0	12.4	1.9	74.9	40.5	47.3	52.7
62378	VERSAILLES	99.5	99.4	0.1	0.1	0.2	0.2	0.2	0.3	5.1	5.6	6.1	6.6	4.4	24.3	31.8	13.8	2.4	79.0	43.0	50.6	49.4
62379	WARSAW	98.8	98.5	0.1	0.1	0.2	0.2	0.8	1.1	5.5	5.8	6.1	6.6	5.5	23.2	31.5	13.6	2.3	78.6	42.8	50.0	50.0
62380	WEST POINT	99.4	99.2	0.2	0.2	0.0	0.0	0.0	0.0	5.8	7.9	7.6	7.9	4.8	24.0	26.4	13.8	1.9	73.3	39.1	51.2	48.8
62401	EFFINGHAM	98.1	97.5	0.3	0.3	0.5	0.7	1.0	1.4	7.1	6.9	6.8	7.0	6.1	24.8	26.7	12.1	2.5	75.0	38.3	49.7	50.3
62410	ALLENDALE	98.3	97.8	0.5	0.5	0.1	0.1	0.7	1.1	4.8	6.6	7.5	9.2	5.0	21.8	31.3	12.0	1.7	75.7	41.7	51.2	48.8
62411	ALTAMONT	99.4	99.2	0.1	0.1	0.0	0.0	0.4	0.5	6.6	6.7	6.9	6.9	5.6	24.3	27.5	12.0	3.5	75.3	39.0	49.1	50.9
62413	ANNAPOLIS	97.6	97.1	0.2	0.2	0.2	0.2	1.1	1.6	6.3	6.7	6.7	5.8	4.9	23.0	32.8	12.3	1.6	76.6	42.2	50.9	49.1
62414	BEECHER CITY	99.5	99.4	0.0	0.0	0.0	0.0	0.3	0.5	6.7	6.8	6.9	6.3	5.5	24.2	28.8	13.0	1.8	75.7	40.1	49.9	50.1
62417	BRIDGEPORT	98.5	98.1	0.3	0.4	0.0	0.0	0.6	0.9	5.9	5.9	6.4	6.8	4.9	24.6	26.9	14.9	3.7	77.6	41.8	48.2	51.8
62418	BROWNSTOWN	98.9	98.4	0.2	0.5	0.1	0.2	0.4	0.7	6.3	6.3	6.7	7.1	5.2	24.1	29.1	12.9	2.3	76.2	40.8	48.0	52.0
62419	CALHOUN	98.7	98.0	0.0	0.0	0.9	1.3	0.0	0.0	5.8	6.0	6.4	6.4	5.6	26.7	28.2	13.3	1.6	78.0	40.7	50.9	49.1
62420	CASEY	98.9	98.5	0.3	0.3	0.0	0.0	0.3	0.4	5.9	6.6	6.6	6.8	4.8	23.7	26.4	15.3	4.1	76.6	41.6	47.5	52.5
62421	CLAREMONT	98.4	97.8	0.0	0.0	0.7	1.1	0.4	0.6	6.0	5.8	8.0	7.1	4.0	24.5	29.3	13.3	2.1	75.3	41.1	50.7	49.3
62422	COWDEN	99.0	98.7	0.2	0.3	0.0	0.0	0.1	0.2	6.8	6.9	7.0	7.6	5.9	24.8	26.4	13.1	1.4	74.5	37.6	50.0	50.0
62423	DENNISON	99.3	98.9	0.0	0.0	0.0	0.1	0.3	0.4	5.4	6.0	6.4	6.9	4.3	24.3	31.8	13.2	1.8	78.0	42.6	51.6	48.4
62424	DIETERICH	99.3	99.1	0.1	0.1	0.1	0.2	0.2	0.3	8.6	8.7	8.7	8.4	5.8	25.6	24.5	8.8	1.0	68.7	33.2	52.5	47.5
62425	DUNDAS	99.2	99.0	0.0	0.0	0.3	0.5	1.4	2.1	5.9	6.4	6.9	7.1	4.6	23.6	29.6	12.7	3.2	76.0	41.9	48.4	51.6
62426	EDGEWOOD	99.2	98.7	0.0	0.0	0.1	0.3	0.8	1.1	7.2	7.2	7.3	7.4	5.5	26.7	26.8	10.7	1.3	73.8	37.3	50.8	49.2
62427	FLAT ROCK	97.0	96.2	1.2	1.5	0.3	0.4	0.4	0.4	5.5	5.9	6.4	6.9	4.9	23.2	30.8	14.9	1.5	77.7	42.9	49.5	50.5
62428	GREENUP	99.1	98.9	0.1	0.1	0.2	0.2	0.3	0.5	5.8	6.2	6.0	5.7	5.0	24.1	28.2	15.0	4.1	78.7	42.9	49.0	51.0
62431	HERRICK	99.6	99.3	0.0	0.0	0.0	0.1	0.4	0.6	9.3	8.7	8.4	6.9	6.1	24.9	21.4	12.0	2.3	69.0	34.5	54.1	45.9
62432	HIDALGO	99.1	99.1	0.0	0.0	0.2	0.2	0.2	0.4	5.0	5.2	5.8	6.5	4.9	25.2	30.9	13.5	3.1	79.3	43.1	50.9	49.1
62433	HUTSONVILLE	98.2	97.6	0.9	1.1	0.1	0.1	0.8	1.1	4.5	4.7	5.1	7.0	4.9	23.8	31.0	16.1	2.7	81.6	44.9	52.1	47.9
62434	INGRAHAM	99.2	99.0	0.1	0.1	0.1	0.3	0.3	0.3	6.1	6.4	6.4	5.5	4.4	23.5	27.3	13.9	6.5	77.8	43.2	50.0	50.0
62436	JEWETT	99.3	98.7	0.0	0.2	0.0	0.0	0.4	0.7	6.2	6.4	6.4	7.3	5.8	27.5	28.1	10.6	1.8	76.0	37.7	48.6	51.4
62438	LAKEWOOD	99.0	98.7	0.5	0.8	0.0	0.0	0.5	0.5	5.2	5.7	6.2	7.5	4.9	24.4	29.9	14.3	1.8	78.2	42.4	52.5	47.5
62439	LAWRENCEVILLE	97.8	97.3	0.9	1.1	0.2	0.3	1.3	1.8	5.2	5.0	5.1	5.8	6.0	24.6	26.2	16.6	5.5	81.5	43.7	50.3	49.7
62440	LERNA	98.1	97.4	0.4	0.5	0.5	0.8	0.8	1.3	5.5	6.9	7.0	6.8	4.4	25.5	31.9	10.7	1.2	76.0	41.0	51.4	48.6
62441	MARSHALL	98.6	98.3	0.2	0.2	0.3	0.4	0.5	0.6	6.2	6.1	6.4	6.7	5.5	24.1	27.6	14.3	3.2	77.3	41.3	48.2	51.8
62442	MARTINSVILLE	99.2	99.0	0.1	0.2	0.1	0.2	0.2	0.2	6.4	6.7	6.7	6.4	5.2	23.4	28.2	14.6	2.4	76.3	41.1	48.6	51.4
62443	MASON	99.2	98.9	0.0	0.0	0.2	0.3	0.6	0.9	7.1	7.2	7.6	8.0	5.5	26.5	26.9	9.9	1.3	73.0	37.0	50.8	49.2
62445	MONTROSE	99.4	99.1	0.0	0.0	0.1	0.2	0.5	0.7	7.9	8.1	7.8	7.5	5.0	26.2	26.5	9.6	1.4	71.5	35.7	50.8	49.2
62446	MOUNT ERIE	98.1	97.7	0.2	0.3	0.5	0.5	0.7	1.0	5.4	5.7	5.7	5.2	4.9	24.8	31.5	14.5	2.3	79.8	43.8	54.3	45.7
62447	NEOGA	98.5	98.0	0.2	0.2	0.2	0.3	0.8	1.1	7.5	7.6	7.5	6.7	4.8	25.3	25.4	13.1	2.0	73.1	38.4	50.1	49.9
62448	NEWTON	99.1	98.9	0.1	0.1	0.2	0.3	0.5	0.6	5.9	6.2	6.4	6.8	5.2	24.5	28.0	13.9	3.2	77.3	41.2	48.6	51.4
62449	OBLONG	98.6	98.2	0.5	0.7	0.1	0.1	0.4	0.7	5.8	5.7	6.2	6.2	5.6	23.8	28.8	14.6	3.2	77.9	42.5	49.3	50.7
62450	OLNEY	97.9	97.3	0.4	0.4	0.7	0.9	0.8	1.2	6.2	6.1	6.2	6.1	5.3	24.3	27.0	15.5	3.2	77.8	41.4	47.9	52.1
62451	PALESTINE	91.8	90.0	6.8	8.1	0.3	0.4	2.0	2.9	5.6	5.7	6.0	5.7	6.5	27.8	26.4	14.0	2.3	79.4	39.2	54.6	45.4
62452	PARKERSBURG	98.6	98.1	0.0	0.0	0.9	1.2	0.0	0.0	5.7	6.1	6.4	6.4	5.4	26.0	28.4	13.9	1.7	77.8	41.0	51.3	48.7
62454	ROBINSON	91.4	89.7	6.2	7.1	0.5	0.7	2.3	3.2	5.5	5.5	5.6	6.0	6.6	27.8	26.3	13.9	2.8	79.8	39.9	52.9	47.1
62458	SAINT ELMO	98.9	98.6	0.1	0.1	0.2	0.2	0.1	0.1	7.6	7.5	7.4	6.3	5.0	22.7	26.1	14.5	2.8	73.4	40.0	47.9	52.1
62460	SAINT FRANCISVILLE	98.8	98.5	0.1	0.1	0.1	0.1	0.3	0.4	5.5	5.6	5.9	6.6	4.6	25.1	31.5	12.9	2.3	79.0	42.2	49.5	50.5
62461	SHUMWAY	98.4	97.9	0.2	0.3	0.2	0.3	0.2	0.2	7.1	7.6	8.0	7.6	4.5	22.9	29.6	11.1	1.6	72.4	38.4	51.8	48.2
62462	SIGEL	98.9	98.4	0.0	0.0	0.3	0.5	0.8	1.2	7.2	8.6	9.0	8.8	5.0	25.7	23.4	11.1	1.1	69.5	34.9	51.2	48.8
62463	STEWARDSON	99.4	99.3	0.0	0.0	0.1	0.1	0.2	0.2	6.7	6.9	6.8	6.1	5.0	24.8	27.1	14.1	2.5	75.9	39.4	50.1	49.9
62465	STRASBURG	99.3	99.2	0.2	0.2	0.1	0.1	0.1	0.1	4.3	5.3	6.1	6.9	4.7	21.6	28.4	16.2	6.6	79.8	45.8	47.0	53.0
62466	SUMNER	98.1	97.6	1.0	1.2	0.0	0.0	0.5	0.7	4.9	5.5	6.0	5.8	4.5	24.3	30.9	15.3	3.0	80.1	44.4	48.9	51.1
62467	TEUTOPOLIS	99.7	99.6	0.0	0.0	0.1	0.1	0.5	0.7	7.8	7.8	7.8	8.1	6.2	25.4	25.8	9.5	1.6	71.3	35.0	51.9	48.1
62468	TOLEDO	99.1	98.8	0.0	0.1	0.0	0.1	0.5	0.7	5.8	6.1	6.7	7.7	5.6	25.7	27.3	12.9	2.2	76.3	39.5	48.8	51.2
62469	TRILLA	97.6	96.6	1.4	1.8	0.5	1.1	0.9	1.1	6.7	6.7	6.0	5.5	5.0	31.6	24.9	11.5	2.0	77.1	36.6	50.8	49.2
62471	VANDALIA	88.4	97.7	10.3	0.7	0.2	0.4	1.4	1.3	6.7	6.5	6.4	6.3	5.5	24.1	26.7	14.6	3.2	76.6	40.6	48.5	51.5
62473	WATSON	98.9	98.4	0.0	0.0	0.2	0.5	0.5	0.7	7.4	7.5	7.6	7.5	5.4	27.9	26.9	8.8	1.0	72.9	35.9	50.5	49.5
62474	WESTFIELD	98.0	97.6	0.4	0.4	0.3	0.5	0.3	0.6	6.2	6.6	6.9	7.1	4.6	23.4	30.0	13.7	1.6	76.0	41.7	50.1	49.9
62475	WEST LIBERTY	100.0	100.0	0.0	0.0	0.0	0.0	0.3	0.5	5.9	6.7	6.7	7.8	5.1	24.4	28.2	12.3	2.9	76.1	40.5	49.3	50.7
62476	WEST SALEM	98.6	98.2	0.3	0.3	0.3	0.4	0.3	0.5	5.3	5.9	6.5	6.6	4.6	25.1	29.9	13.8	2.3	78.3	41.8	50.3	49.7
62477	WEST UNION	99.1	98.9	0.1	0.1	0.0	0.0	0.1	0.1	5.2	6.1	6.3	6.5	4.8	23.9	30.7	14.2	2.4	78.4	43.0	52.2	47.8
62478	WEST YORK	98.1	97.8	0.5	0.5	0.2	0.5	0.9	1.4	4.6	5.0	6.0	7.2	4.8	25.0	33.7	11.8	1.9	79.6	43.0	52.6	47.4
62479	WHEELER	99.4	99.2	0.0	0.1	0.1	0.1	0.5	0.7	6.4	6.7	6.8	6.7	5.2	26.0	28.7	12.2	1.3	76.0	39.1	51.9	48.1
62480	WILLOW HILL	98.8	98.4	0.0	0.0	0.5	0.8	0.4	0.5	6.0	6.1	7.1	7.0	6.1	23.9	28.8	12.8	2.2	76.4	40.4	50.5	49.5
62481	YALE	98.6	98.5	0.2	0.3	0.0	0.0	1.2	1.8	4.8	5.0	8.8	7.8	5.8	25.3	28.3	12.0	2.3	76.2	40.7	51.1	48.9
62501	ARGENTA	98.3	97.7	0.5	0.7	0.2	0.3	0.3	0.5	5.2	5.9	7.1	6.9	5.2	23.2	32.1	13.3	1.1	77.4	42.6	49.9	50.1
62510	ASSUMPTION	99.6	99.4	0.1	0.1	0.2	0.2	0.2	0.2	6.5	6.2	6.6	7.0	5.8	24.3	27.1	13.6	2.8	76.4	40.0	48.1	51.9
62512	BEASON	99.5	99.4	0.2	0.2	0.0	0.0	0.4	0.6	5.9	6.3	7.0	8.1	5.0	23.1	30.7	12.4	1.5	75.4	41.3	50.3	49.7
62513	BLUE MOUND	99.5	99.4	0.1	0.1	0.0	0.0	0.2	0.4	6.2	6.5	6.9	6.6	4.0	26.3	29.1	12.2	2.1	76.1	40.8	48.8	51.2
62514	BOODY	100.0	99.3	0.0	0.0	0.0	0.0	0.6	1.3	4.7	5.3	6.7	7.3	4.0	23.3	34.7	12.7	1.3	78.7	44.1	50.7	49.3
62515	BUFFALO	98.0	97.1	0.4	0.6	0.2	0.3	0.5	0.8	5.7	6.3	6.6	6.3	4.5	25.3	32.7	11.2	1.2	77.2	41.7	48.9	51.1
62517	BULPITT	100.0	99.5	0.0	0.5	0.0	0.0	0.0	0.0	7.0	7.0	8.0	6.5	4.0	21.5	28.0	16.0	2.0	73.5	41.7	50.5	49.5
62518	CHESTNUT	98.5	98.1	0.4	0.6	0.0	0.0	0.4	0.6	5.5	6.2	6.8	7.2	4.5	22.8	30.9	14.3	1.7	77.0	42.9	51.0	49.0
62520	DAWSON	98.0	97.1	0.4	0.7	0.2	0.3	0.6	0.9	5.4	5.9	6.4	6.3	4.5	23.8	34.5	11.8	1.3	78.3	43.3	48.9	51.1
62521	DECATUR	83.0	80.9	14.6	16.1	0.6	0.8	0.9	1.2	6.2	6.1	6.4	6.5	5.6	23.1	29.4	14.5	2.3	77.2	41.9	48.0	52.0
62522	DECATUR	73.3	69.0	23.8	27.2	0.5	0.7	1.0	1.4	5.9	5.7	5.7	11.1	13.7	21.7	23.6	10.4	2.2	79.3	32.3	46.8	53.2
62523	DECATUR	42.4	35.0	54.3	61.1	0.2	0.2	1.6	2.2	4.1	4.1	1.8	7.9	12.3	36.6	18.0	12.3	2.8	85.8	34.0	67.4	32.6
62526	DECATUR	81.4	77.2	15.6	18.9	0.7	1.0	1.3	1.8	6.6	6.3	6.2	6.1	6.3	24.0	26.5	14.7	3.3	77.2	40.1	46.5	53.5
62530	DIVERNON	98.7	98.1	0.3	0.5	0.1	0.2	1.4	2.2	6.4	6.7	6.8	6.6	5.1	26.9	28.8	11.4	1.4	76.1	39.2	49.0	51.0
62531	EDINBURG	99.0	98.5	0.1	0.3	0.1	0.2	0.5	0.9	5.9	6.7	7.2	6.5	4.3	23.7	30.1	13.9	1.8	76.1	42.0	50.0	50.0
62533	FARMERSVILLE	97.8	96.9	0.7	0.8	0.9	1.4	0.5	0.7	7.3	7.7	7.8	6.2	3.8	26.0	28.5	10.9	1.8	73.3	38.9	49.2	50.8
62534	FINDLAY	98.7	98.3	0.4	0.5	0.2	0.4	0.7	1.0	5.3	5.7	6.2	6.7	4.9	23.6	29.3	16.3	2.1	78.8	43.2	48.8	51.2
62535	FORSYTH	96.5	95.2	1.7	2.3	1.3	1.8	0.8	1.2	5.4	6.1	7.6	8.2	3.9	19.0	33.6	14.5	1.9	75.2	44.9	49.2	50.8
62536	GLENARM	98.6	98.1	0.4	0.6	0.1	0.2	0.9	1.3	6.1	5.6	7.9	7.2	3.8	24.6	37.6	6.3	0.9	75.9	41.8	52.2	47.8
62538	HARVEL	98.9	98.2	0.2	0.4	0.2	0.4	0.7	0.7	5.3	5.7	6.1	6.6	4.6	23.2	32.7	14.0	1.8	78.9	43.8	50.9	49.1
62539	ILLIOPOLIS	98.6	98.2	0.5	0.6	0.0	0.0	0.2	0.3	6.2	6.3	6.3	6.5	5.2	27.4	28.6	12.3	1.2	77.0	39.0	48.7	51.3
62543	LATHAM	99.6	99.4	0.0	0.0	0.2	0.4	0.2	0.2	5.2	5.4	6.2	7.2	4.8	24.8	30.8	13.8	1.9	78.5	42.6	50.2	49.8
62544	MACON	99.0	98.6	0.2	0.3	0.3	0.4	0.5	0.8	5.5	5.8	6.3	6.9	5.3	23.7	30.1	12.8	3.7	77.9	42.7	49.0	51.0
62545	MECHANICSBURG	98.4	97.8	0.5	0.6	0.3	0.4	0.4	0.5	6.2	6.7	7.0	6.5	5.2	25.5	30.2	11.6	1.2	76.0	39.9	50.9	49.1
62546	MORRISONVILLE	98.6	98.1	0.2	0.2	0.5	0.7	0.8	1.2	5.5	6.0	6.3	7.0	5.5	22.7	30.0	14.9	2.1	78.0	42.6	50.2	49.8
62547	MOUNT AUBURN	98.8	98.5	0.0	0.0	0.3	0.3	0.3	0.3	4.2	4.6	5.3	6.6	4.3	25.2	33.1	14.9	1.7	82.0	44.8	48.8	51.2
	ILLINOIS	73.5	70.6	15.1	15.3	3.4	4.4	12.3	15.7	7.1	6.9	6.8	7.1	6.9	27.5	25.4	10.3	1.9	75.0	36.1	49.1	50.9
	UNITED STATES	75.1	72.0	12.3	12.7	3.8	4.6	12.5	15.7	6.8	6.7	6.6	7.1	6.9	27.0	26.0	10.9	1.9	75.7	36.9	49.2	50.8

ZIP CODE #	POST OFFICE NAME	2009 Per Capita Income	2009 HH Income Base	2009 Household Income Distribution (%): Less than $25,000	$25,000 to $49,999	$50,000 to $99,999	$100,000 to $149,999	$150,000 or More	Median Household Income: 2009	2014	2009 National Centile	2009 State Centile	2009 Home Value Base	2009 Home Value Distribution (%): Less than $50,000	$50,000 to $89,999	$90,000 to $174,999	$175,000 to $399,999	$400,000 or More	2009 Median Home Value
62363	PITTSFIELD	19077	2456	33.1	26.8	36.4	2.8	0.8	38201	39908	27	12	1827	15.7	32.6	38.5	11.9	1.3	92114
62365	PLAINVILLE	19466	324	17.0	35.8	42.0	4.6	0.6	47895	49183	56	38	274	18.6	23.4	38.0	19.3	0.7	104545
62366	PLEASANT HILL	16219	593	37.6	32.9	26.6	2.9	0.0	31638	32280	11	3	472	30.9	37.1	24.8	6.8	0.4	68913
62367	PLYMOUTH	18959	501	26.9	32.5	35.5	2.8	2.2	42269	44424	40	22	398	42.2	21.6	24.4	10.6	1.3	63226
62370	ROCKPORT	16536	243	30.0	33.7	31.3	4.5	0.4	39180	39785	30	14	202	29.2	23.8	32.2	14.9	0.0	86000
62373	SUTTER	18315	145	19.3	34.5	38.6	6.2	1.4	45988	46669	51	32	119	15.1	31.9	37.8	12.6	2.5	97000
62374	TENNESSEE	20754	106	24.5	34.0	39.6	1.9	0.0	44300	47309	46	27	90	31.1	28.9	22.2	12.2	5.6	65000
62375	TIMEWELL	20174	186	14.0	41.4	38.7	3.2	2.7	47300	47157	55	36	139	25.9	35.3	26.6	12.2	0.0	78684
62376	URSA	21271	500	20.6	28.6	44.6	4.2	2.0	50467	51980	62	45	393	15.0	29.8	39.4	13.5	2.3	96833
62378	VERSAILLES	21115	438	24.4	29.0	40.6	4.1	1.8	48000	47469	57	38	351	35.3	32.8	23.9	7.1	0.9	65000
62379	WARSAW	21691	887	22.2	34.6	36.6	4.4	2.1	43412	45560	44	25	725	20.6	35.7	37.2	5.7	0.8	84091
62380	WEST POINT	17619	184	24.5	33.2	39.7	2.2	0.5	42580	43703	41	22	152	30.9	36.2	25.0	2.0	5.9	65789
62401	EFFINGHAM	24200	7896	22.5	28.0	39.7	6.3	3.5	49507	52507	60	42	5654	8.7	13.5	48.7	24.5	4.6	132774
62410	ALLENDALE	18745	381	24.9	33.1	37.5	3.4	1.0	44241	44622	46	27	322	28.3	34.8	31.1	5.6	0.3	73667
62411	ALTAMONT	21538	1548	22.3	32.8	38.9	4.3	1.7	46884	48729	54	34	1210	12.5	25.0	47.0	14.5	1.1	106875
62413	ANNAPOLIS	18441	169	27.2	32.0	34.9	5.3	0.6	43028	45472	42	24	147	38.8	28.6	26.5	6.1	0.0	61250
62414	BEECHER CITY	18678	750	26.5	37.9	31.3	2.9	1.3	40830	43503	35	18	607	28.2	22.1	30.8	15.3	3.6	89559
62417	BRIDGEPORT	17374	1212	34.4	34.3	28.4	1.8	1.1	34932	36204	17	6	940	35.1	38.1	23.7	1.7	1.4	62676
62418	BROWNSTOWN	18628	1044	29.2	39.1	26.3	3.0	2.4	34893	36497	17	6	864	23.0	31.7	31.8	11.9	1.5	82679
62419	CALHOUN	17879	178	32.0	29.2	33.7	4.5	0.6	40000	39654	33	16	151	35.1	28.5	29.1	7.3	0.0	63182
62420	CASEY	20035	1943	29.9	30.9	32.8	5.4	1.0	40578	43890	35	17	1482	23.2	29.6	40.1	7.1	0.0	86306
62421	CLAREMONT	16017	323	29.4	37.5	30.3	2.5	0.3	37359	38446	25	10	281	27.8	19.9	36.3	15.3	0.7	95417
62422	COWDEN	16072	557	35.7	30.5	29.6	3.4	0.7	34768	37264	17	6	465	38.5	30.1	26.9	4.5	0.0	62788
62423	DENNISON	21679	290	14.1	36.6	42.4	4.8	2.1	49272	50321	59	41	249	15.7	18.5	39.0	24.5	2.4	119097
62424	DIETERICH	19463	720	13.8	30.3	47.2	7.2	1.5	54131	56673	70	54	600	12.3	20.5	46.5	20.2	0.5	116827
62425	DUNDAS	14624	235	35.3	40.0	21.7	3.0	0.0	30539	33021	9	3	204	27.5	34.8	28.9	5.4	3.4	78000
62426	EDGEWOOD	18731	336	28.9	33.9	33.6	2.4	1.2	38946	43940	30	14	279	39.4	22.9	25.8	9.7	2.2	65357
62427	FLAT ROCK	18605	867	27.8	32.5	34.0	3.2	2.4	40525	42794	34	17	759	30.2	33.7	28.9	6.3	0.9	72761
62428	GREENUP	19902	1300	29.4	35.8	30.9	2.2	1.7	37461	40512	25	10	1049	18.8	32.6	40.7	7.5	0.4	88739
62431	HERRICK	18655	267	31.5	34.1	29.2	2.2	3.0	36539	38622	22	9	220	36.4	32.7	24.1	5.0	1.8	65833
62432	HIDALGO	19697	232	19.8	41.8	34.9	1.7	1.7	39655	40345	32	15	199	30.2	24.1	34.7	9.5	1.5	83462
62433	HUTSONVILLE	20775	380	26.3	32.6	33.4	5.8	1.8	41212	42484	37	19	308	29.5	32.8	32.5	4.5	0.6	68000
62434	INGRAHAM	18459	224	20.1	31.3	39.3	8.0	1.3	48903	49842	59	40	200	29.5	20.0	35.5	14.5	0.5	91000
62436	JEWETT	18525	210	25.7	31.4	37.1	4.8	1.0	39333	42693	31	15	170	18.8	31.8	36.5	10.6	2.4	89167
62438	LAKEWOOD	22754	154	18.2	29.2	43.5	6.5	2.6	51871	51732	66	48	132	22.7	25.0	37.1	14.4	0.8	93000
62439	LAWRENCEVILLE	22043	3067	33.4	29.4	29.9	4.2	3.1	37074	39190	24	10	2218	30.5	36.1	26.1	6.5	0.8	65897
62440	LERNA	27114	571	14.7	22.1	48.9	9.3	5.1	62070	62510	80	68	500	16.6	11.6	37.0	29.2	5.6	132895
62441	MARSHALL	23531	3074	24.4	27.8	39.4	5.3	3.1	48141	49371	57	38	2292	16.1	26.3	42.5	13.9	1.2	101542
62442	MARTINSVILLE	19129	1084	27.7	34.0	32.5	4.9	0.9	40872	43136	36	18	871	30.5	28.8	31.2	9.3	0.1	78333
62443	MASON	17394	689	23.2	32.1	39.8	3.6	1.3	46358	48225	52	33	569	27.8	19.2	36.6	14.6	1.9	96034
62445	MONTROSE	19386	440	21.6	26.8	43.6	5.0	3.0	51217	51208	64	47	370	11.9	24.9	34.3	24.9	4.1	115179
62446	MOUNT ERIE	17356	159	32.7	29.6	34.6	3.1	0.0	34792	34825	17	6	128	32.0	28.1	24.2	10.9	4.7	79167
62447	NEOGA	21795	1378	17.0	29.5	45.4	6.1	2.0	52102	52869	66	49	1143	15.4	22.7	45.6	15.2	1.0	107969
62448	NEWTON	19485	2330	28.5	29.3	36.2	4.9	1.1	39924	41657	32	16	1855	19.7	30.1	40.8	8.7	0.6	90184
62449	OBLONG	18222	1239	30.3	34.7	30.3	4.0	0.7	37114	38951	24	10	1024	29.0	34.1	31.5	4.3	1.1	71951
62450	OLNEY	21104	4983	31.5	28.9	32.5	4.9	2.1	38745	40590	29	13	3674	22.4	28.4	35.9	11.3	2.0	88982
62451	PALESTINE	20605	891	32.8	33.4	29.1	3.7	1.0	36768	38694	23	9	704	32.0	36.9	27.1	3.1	0.9	66866
62452	PARKERSBURG	20509	187	31.0	28.3	35.8	4.3	0.5	41676	42373	38	20	159	34.0	25.8	31.4	8.8	0.0	66818
62454	ROBINSON	20300	4297	28.2	31.3	33.1	4.7	2.6	39331	40897	31	15	3311	20.5	36.1	34.1	8.2	1.1	81705
62458	SAINT ELMO	17371	741	33.6	31.7	31.7	1.9	1.1	37180	39706	24	10	597	32.7	31.5	27.8	7.7	0.3	69909
62460	SAINT FRANCISVILLE	17854	679	29.0	38.1	28.0	3.1	1.8	35860	36753	20	8	553	41.8	31.8	22.6	3.4	0.4	58922
62461	SHUMWAY	21571	214	22.9	34.6	35.0	3.3	4.2	45258	46768	49	30	181	14.9	17.1	29.8	25.4	12.7	131250
62462	SIGEL	17838	398	19.8	33.4	38.4	6.0	2.3	47525	47695	55	37	329	12.2	22.5	39.2	20.1	6.1	116406
62463	STEWARDSON	19446	560	22.7	33.4	38.8	3.4	1.8	43805	46049	45	26	448	21.2	32.4	34.6	10.5	1.3	85429
62465	STRASBURG	21480	300	19.0	26.7	46.3	5.7	2.3	52536	53495	67	50	267	9.4	22.1	55.4	12.4	0.7	109821
62466	SUMNER	17014	874	31.6	33.4	31.2	2.6	1.1	37393	39129	25	10	712	34.8	38.5	21.5	4.1	1.1	63600
62467	TEUTOPOLIS	23442	1096	17.2	21.4	47.6	7.4	6.4	60289	61563	78	65	891	5.7	13.1	50.3	28.1	2.8	137303
62468	TOLEDO	20655	1053	22.8	32.1	39.9	3.9	1.3	45043	46289	48	29	841	19.9	26.3	40.4	12.2	1.2	95909
62469	TRILLA	20096	201	21.9	28.9	42.8	3.5	3.0	49312	50590	60	41	155	17.4	27.7	31.6	21.9	1.3	101786
62471	VANDALIA	19921	3570	30.1	32.9	31.4	3.5	2.1	39731	41482	32	15	2655	17.2	31.6	41.3	9.0	0.8	91142
62473	WATSON	19241	444	16.0	34.0	44.6	3.6	1.8	50000	52419	61	44	381	12.3	21.3	49.1	14.4	2.9	110192
62474	WESTFIELD	18777	400	23.0	38.3	33.8	3.8	1.3	42162	44276	40	21	320	26.3	30.0	34.4	8.4	0.9	78235
62475	WEST LIBERTY	16580	132	21.2	40.9	32.6	4.5	0.8	42720	42838	42	23	115	20.9	28.7	35.7	13.9	0.9	90714
62476	WEST SALEM	19190	824	24.3	37.9	33.1	3.6	1.1	40501	41979	34	17	691	36.5	33.7	24.5	3.8	1.6	65000
62477	WEST UNION	19393	449	27.6	28.3	39.2	4.2	0.7	41014	47245	36	19	374	37.2	26.7	32.6	3.5	0.0	67222
62478	WEST YORK	25843	164	20.1	24.4	40.9	10.4	4.3	54223	56967	70	54	143	22.4	26.6	38.5	11.2	1.4	91250
62479	WHEELER	19884	329	21.6	24.6	45.0	7.6	1.2	52329	53413	67	49	280	20.0	18.9	39.6	20.0	1.4	109444
62480	WILLOW HILL	19935	453	26.5	37.3	30.9	3.1	2.2	40294	41969	34	17	393	28.2	23.2	34.1	13.2	1.3	88226
62481	YALE	19569	149	22.8	37.6	34.9	1.3	3.4	41158	42912	37	19	132	28.8	25.8	38.6	6.8	0.0	83333
62501	ARGENTA	27641	1038	12.0	20.3	54.3	9.6	3.7	64758	66132	83	74	881	6.9	24.7	44.0	21.6	2.7	111884
62510	ASSUMPTION	24246	743	22.9	29.5	40.4	4.6	2.7	48077	49955	57	38	576	18.1	44.6	31.4	5.4	0.5	76182
62512	BEASON	22021	186	12.4	28.5	46.8	10.8	1.6	60000	62046	77	64	139	12.2	20.1	45.3	16.5	5.8	108173
62513	BLUE MOUND	26150	695	15.3	23.7	49.9	7.2	3.9	60451	61628	78	65	548	19.5	32.8	38.3	8.4	0.9	87347
62514	BOODY	27333	58	13.8	15.5	58.6	8.6	3.4	71299	70604	87	82	49	18.4	14.3	34.7	24.5	8.2	122917
62515	BUFFALO	26356	385	15.6	19.5	52.2	9.6	3.1	66268	67074	84	76	302	18.9	21.2	38.4	19.5	2.0	104412
62517	BULPITT	21674	95	30.5	29.5	35.8	4.2	0.0	40371	42359	34	17	78	25.6	33.3	33.3	7.7	0.0	81250
62518	CHESTNUT	27216	187	12.8	21.4	52.4	9.6	3.7	64164	65169	82	73	144	9.7	23.6	50.7	11.1	4.9	111905
62520	DAWSON	29262	580	11.9	18.6	53.4	12.4	3.6	71303	71847	88	82	466	16.3	16.3	36.9	28.8	1.7	120956
62521	DECATUR	26264	15154	21.5	26.3	40.9	7.3	4.0	52018	55167	66	49	11608	16.9	29.2	40.6	11.5	1.9	94590
62522	DECATUR	21807	6853	33.2	25.1	33.1	6.1	2.6	39759	42641	32	15	4049	19.9	34.8	37.2	6.8	1.2	82134
62523	DECATUR	14346	129	72.1	23.3	4.7	0.0	0.0	13850	14081	1	0	17	11.8	88.2	0.0	0.0	0.0	56500
62526	DECATUR	24196	15258	28.5	29.6	31.9	6.2	3.7	41317	44474	37	20	10066	26.0	27.9	36.6	8.8	0.6	83542
62530	DIVERNON	28442	628	9.7	23.4	54.9	6.8	5.1	62878	63714	81	70	484	9.7	22.1	53.1	13.2	1.9	108471
62531	EDINBURG	23290	837	17.7	31.7	43.0	5.3	2.4	50460	53122	62	44	662	15.4	24.0	45.5	14.2	0.9	105983
62533	FARMERSVILLE	22840	436	18.6	33.7	37.8	8.0	1.8	47599	48365	56	37	335	12.5	34.0	42.7	10.1	0.6	93286
62534	FINDLAY	21787	544	23.7	32.4	36.9	5.3	1.7	42958	45225	42	24	429	22.6	30.3	39.2	6.1	1.9	85968
62535	FORSYTH	38597	953	10.4	20.9	35.4	15.7	17.6	77153	77455	91	89	805	0.6	6.3	40.0	44.1	8.9	185381
62536	GLENARM	29842	351	5.1	11.7	60.7	13.7	8.8	78201	77915	91	90	313	1.0	4.2	53.4	37.7	3.8	161480
62538	HARVEL	20036	180	18.9	44.4	28.3	7.2	1.1	38791	39356	29	13	145	19.3	18.6	43.4	16.6	2.1	110938
62539	ILLIOPOLIS	28178	518	9.7	25.1	52.5	8.1	4.6	64269	65645	83	73	389	10.8	38.8	42.7	6.9	0.8	90417
62543	LATHAM	28470	200	16.5	20.0	46.0	14.0	3.5	65122	66333	83	74	152	7.2	27.6	55.9	7.9	1.3	100000
62544	MACON	26661	719	17.1	25.5	45.1	8.6	3.8	57959	60816	75	61	574	12.7	34.7	41.6	9.4	1.6	92542
62545	MECHANICSBURG	23662	439	18.9	24.1	47.4	6.6	3.0	55885	60000	72	57	360	19.4	23.1	41.4	15.6	0.6	99643
62546	MORRISONVILLE	22706	649	21.3	30.2	40.7	4.9	2.9	48536	50518	58	39	521	13.2	32.8	44.9	7.1	1.9	95694
62547	MOUNT AUBURN	25411	312	10.6	32.7	49.7	5.8	1.3	54702	58268	71	55	257	18.3	31.9	35.0	13.6	1.2	89722
	ILLINOIS	28587		18.2	22.2	39.3	12.1	8.2	60823	63631				6.3	10.0	30.9	40.6	12.3	185324
	UNITED STATES	27277		20.9	24.4	35.3	11.7	7.6	54719	56938				9.3	13.1	31.6	32.6	13.5	162279

ZIP CODE #	POST OFFICE NAME	FINANCIAL SERVICES: Auto Loan	Home Loan	Invest-ments	Retire-ment Plans	THE HOME: Home Improvements: Home Repair	Lawn & Garden	Furnishings: Comput-ers & Hard-ware-Personal	Major Appli-ances	TV, Radio, Sound Equip-ment	Furni-ture	ENTERTAINMENT: Dine out/ Carry out	Sports Equip-ment	Fees & Tickets	Toys & Games	Travel	Cable TV	PERSONAL: Apparel & Services	Auto Repairs	Health Insur-ance	Pets & Supplies
62363	PITTSFIELD	71	58	75	57	60	77	59	71	64	54	63	53	52	63	60	70	42	67	78	84
62365	PLAINVILLE	81	73	73	76	75	87	72	82	75	65	73	62	67	76	72	79	50	75	84	95
62366	PLEASANT HILL	66	47	69	46	49	70	51	64	56	44	54	50	40	55	50	61	36	59	68	76
62367	PLYMOUTH	87	60	95	60	63	92	66	82	69	54	68	68	49	68	66	75	44	77	87	101
62370	ROCKPORT	79	54	87	54	57	84	60	75	63	49	62	62	44	62	60	69	40	70	79	93
62373	SUTTER	92	66	98	66	69	97	72	88	75	59	74	72	55	74	71	81	48	82	92	107
62374	TENNESSEE	84	58	93	58	61	89	64	80	67	52	66	66	47	66	64	73	43	75	85	99
62375	TIMEWELL	94	65	103	64	68	99	72	89	75	58	74	74	53	73	71	81	48	83	94	110
62376	URSA	84	72	80	74	74	90	73	84	75	64	74	65	64	76	73	80	50	78	87	99
62378	VERSAILLES	91	65	94	63	67	92	67	85	74	62	73	64	53	73	66	81	48	78	88	101
62379	WARSAW	87	69	85	70	71	92	72	86	77	64	75	65	61	77	71	84	51	80	91	101
62380	WEST POINT	83	57	91	57	60	87	63	79	66	51	65	65	46	65	63	72	42	73	83	97
62401	EFFINGHAM	86	79	78	81	80	87	83	85	85	79	84	64	78	85	80	87	58	84	90	101
62410	ALLENDALE	85	65	85	64	67	88	66	81	72	61	70	61	55	72	65	78	47	75	84	96
62411	ALTAMONT	85	77	79	78	76	91	76	85	80	71	78	65	71	81	76	84	53	81	90	100
62413	ANNAPOLIS	86	63	87	62	66	88	65	81	71	60	70	61	53	71	64	78	46	74	84	96
62414	BEECHER CITY	80	61	73	60	62	80	62	74	68	59	67	56	52	69	59	74	45	69	77	88
62417	BRIDGEPORT	72	52	74	50	54	75	55	69	61	49	59	52	44	60	54	67	39	64	74	82
62418	BROWNSTOWN	83	59	83	57	61	85	63	78	69	56	67	60	49	68	61	76	45	72	83	93
62419	CALHOUN	82	59	67	57	58	77	61	71	68	59	66	54	49	70	55	74	45	67	75	86
62420	CASEY	77	62	73	62	62	80	64	75	69	58	67	57	55	69	63	75	45	71	80	88
62421	CLAREMONT	75	52	83	52	54	79	57	71	60	47	59	59	42	59	57	65	38	67	75	88
62422	COWDEN	75	55	63	53	54	72	57	66	63	55	61	51	46	65	52	68	41	62	69	80
62423	DENNISON	86	78	76	81	79	91	77	86	79	71	78	65	71	81	76	83	53	80	88	100
62424	DIETERICH	91	83	82	86	84	97	82	92	84	74	83	70	75	86	81	89	56	85	95	107
62425	DUNDAS	67	48	72	48	50	71	52	64	55	43	54	53	40	54	52	59	35	60	68	79
62426	EDGEWOOD	78	57	65	56	57	75	59	68	65	57	64	52	48	68	54	71	43	65	72	83
62427	FLAT ROCK	85	62	86	61	64	86	64	80	70	59	69	60	52	70	63	77	46	73	83	95
62428	GREENUP	78	58	78	57	60	81	61	75	67	55	65	56	50	67	59	74	44	70	80	89
62431	HERRICK	86	63	72	61	63	83	65	76	72	63	71	58	53	75	60	78	47	72	80	92
62432	HIDALGO	84	60	86	58	62	85	62	78	68	57	67	59	49	68	61	75	44	72	82	93
62433	HUTSONVILLE	83	64	82	64	66	88	68	82	74	61	72	61	57	74	66	81	48	76	88	96
62434	INGRAHAM	85	76	76	79	77	90	75	85	78	68	77	65	69	80	75	83	52	79	88	99
62436	JEWETT	87	61	78	60	62	85	65	77	71	61	70	61	51	73	61	78	47	73	82	94
62438	LAKEWOOD	89	80	80	83	82	95	79	89	82	72	80	68	73	83	79	87	55	83	92	104
62439	LAWRENCEVILLE	76	66	73	66	67	80	70	76	74	64	72	57	63	73	68	79	49	74	83	89
62440	LERNA	100	106	95	110	104	109	97	103	97	96	97	80	100	99	101	98	67	98	103	121
62441	MARSHALL	86	74	77	75	75	88	78	85	82	72	80	63	70	82	75	87	55	82	90	99
62442	MARTINSVILLE	78	61	70	61	62	79	63	74	68	58	66	56	53	69	60	74	45	69	78	87
62443	MASON	82	68	71	68	67	82	67	76	72	66	71	58	60	75	65	77	48	72	79	91
62445	MONTROSE	95	73	97	74	76	101	77	92	80	66	79	74	63	80	77	87	52	86	96	111
62446	MOUNT ERIE	75	54	77	52	56	76	55	70	61	51	60	53	44	61	55	67	40	64	73	83
62447	NEOGA	90	81	81	82	81	94	80	89	82	74	81	68	73	84	79	87	55	84	92	105
62448	NEWTON	80	61	79	61	63	84	65	78	70	57	68	59	54	69	63	76	45	72	83	92
62449	OBLONG	75	56	71	55	58	77	59	71	65	55	63	54	49	65	57	71	42	66	76	84
62450	OLNEY	77	65	73	65	66	81	67	76	71	62	69	57	60	71	66	76	47	72	82	89
62451	PALESTINE	75	54	70	52	55	75	57	69	63	53	61	52	45	64	54	69	41	64	73	82
62452	PARKERSBURG	82	61	69	59	61	79	63	73	69	61	68	56	51	72	58	75	46	69	77	88
62454	ROBINSON	80	65	77	65	66	84	67	78	73	62	71	59	59	72	66	78	48	74	84	92
62458	SAINT ELMO	76	54	77	53	56	78	57	72	64	52	62	54	46	63	56	70	41	67	76	85
62460	SAINT FRANCISVILLE	77	55	78	54	58	79	58	73	65	53	63	55	47	64	57	71	42	68	78	87
62461	SHUMWAY	104	72	111	72	75	108	79	98	83	66	82	80	59	82	78	91	54	91	103	120
62462	SIGEL	97	67	106	67	70	102	74	92	77	60	76	76	55	76	74	84	50	86	97	113
62463	STEWARDSON	81	61	80	60	63	85	65	79	71	58	69	59	54	71	64	78	46	74	85	93
62465	STRASBURG	88	80	80	83	82	95	79	90	82	72	80	68	73	83	79	87	55	83	92	104
62466	SUMNER	74	53	77	52	55	77	56	71	62	51	60	54	45	61	56	68	40	65	75	84
62467	TEUTOPOLIS	110	99	100	103	102	118	99	111	102	89	100	84	90	103	98	108	68	103	115	130
62468	TOLEDO	84	68	74	69	69	86	69	80	74	64	72	61	60	75	67	79	49	74	83	95
62469	TRILLA	87	81	75	81	80	88	77	84	80	76	79	63	73	82	76	83	54	80	85	99
62471	VANDALIA	75	62	70	61	63	78	64	73	69	59	67	54	57	69	62	75	46	70	79	86
62473	WATSON	85	80	71	78	78	82	75	80	78	78	78	58	72	81	73	80	53	77	80	95
62474	WESTFIELD	80	61	79	61	63	82	62	76	67	57	66	57	52	68	62	73	44	70	79	90
62475	WEST LIBERTY	84	59	89	58	61	87	63	79	67	55	66	62	48	67	62	74	43	73	83	95
62476	WEST SALEM	81	60	74	59	61	81	62	74	68	58	67	56	51	69	59	74	45	69	78	89
62477	WEST UNION	81	63	80	63	65	84	64	78	69	59	68	59	54	69	64	75	45	72	81	92
62478	WEST YORK	102	92	92	96	94	109	91	103	94	82	92	78	84	96	91	100	63	95	106	120
62479	WHEELER	87	74	83	76	76	93	75	87	78	66	76	67	66	78	75	83	51	80	90	102
62480	WILLOW HILL	84	67	83	68	69	88	68	82	73	61	71	63	58	73	68	78	48	76	85	97
62481	YALE	93	65	101	65	68	98	72	89	74	59	74	73	53	73	71	81	48	83	93	109
62501	ARGENTA	103	102	95	106	102	112	97	106	98	91	97	81	95	100	99	101	67	99	107	123
62510	ASSUMPTION	89	78	80	79	77	94	80	87	84	73	82	67	73	84	78	89	56	84	95	104
62512	BEASON	99	90	89	94	92	107	89	101	92	81	90	76	82	94	89	97	62	93	104	117
62513	BLUE MOUND	99	91	89	94	92	106	89	100	92	81	90	76	83	93	89	97	62	93	103	116
62514	BOODY	98	111	96	114	108	109	99	103	97	99	98	81	106	100	105	98	68	99	102	121
62515	BUFFALO	99	100	91	103	99	106	93	101	94	91	94	77	93	97	95	97	65	95	101	118
62517	BULPITT	77	56	77	54	58	80	61	75	68	54	65	56	49	66	59	75	44	70	82	88
62518	CHESTNUT	106	96	95	100	98	114	95	107	98	86	96	81	88	100	95	104	66	99	111	125
62520	DAWSON	105	109	99	112	108	115	101	109	101	97	101	83	102	104	104	104	70	103	110	127
62521	DECATUR	89	86	82	87	85	95	86	89	90	83	88	66	85	89	85	94	61	89	97	105
62522	DECATUR	75	66	63	67	64	74	75	72	76	69	75	56	68	76	68	79	52	74	79	86
62523	DECATUR	22	17	20	19	17	21	27	22	29	24	29	17	24	25	24	31	20	27	30	28
62526	DECATUR	78	70	68	71	69	78	76	75	79	72	78	57	72	78	72	82	54	77	83	90
62530	DIVERNON	97	103	85	106	98	105	98	98	98	95	98	77	101	100	99	99	68	97	103	117
62531	EDINBURG	89	79	82	81	81	95	78	90	82	71	80	68	71	83	78	87	54	83	93	104
62533	FARMERSVILLE	89	77	83	79	79	95	77	89	80	69	78	68	69	81	77	85	53	82	92	104
62534	FINDLAY	83	66	81	66	68	88	69	82	75	62	73	62	59	74	68	81	49	77	88	96
62535	FORSYTH	132	164	167	168	168	155	139	147	133	149	135	110	159	133	156	131	97	139	139	169
62536	GLENARM	115	141	134	144	141	131	120	126	115	126	117	96	135	117	132	113	83	119	118	145
62538	HARVEL	85	66	93	65	68	93	69	83	72	59	71	66	56	71	70	78	47	78	89	101
62539	ILLIOPOLIS	104	101	88	104	97	111	100	104	102	92	101	81	96	104	98	106	69	101	111	124
62543	LATHAM	107	97	96	101	99	115	96	108	99	87	97	82	88	101	96	105	66	100	112	126
62544	MACON	97	94	85	98	93	105	93	98	94	86	93	76	90	96	92	98	64	94	104	116
62545	MECHANICSBURG	91	89	80	88	87	93	83	89	85	83	85	66	81	88	82	87	58	85	90	104
62546	MORRISONVILLE	87	78	95	77	79	99	76	89	81	69	80	68	71	79	80	87	54	84	98	105
62547	MOUNT AUBURN	90	82	81	85	84	97	81	91	83	73	82	69	74	85	81	88	56	84	94	106
	ILLINOIS	106	108	105	108	107	106	109	106	108	107	109	83	110	108	108	108	77	108	107	125
	UNITED STATES	100	100	100	100	100	100	100	100	100	100	100	100	100	100	100	100	100	100	100	100

ZIP CODE #	POST OFFICE NAME	COUNTY FIPS CODE	POPULATION 2000	POPULATION 2009	POPULATION 2014	2000-2009 ANNUAL RATE % Rate	2000-2009 ANNUAL RATE State Centile	HOUSEHOLDS 2000	HOUSEHOLDS 2009	HOUSEHOLDS 2014	HOUSEHOLDS % Annual Rate 2000-2009	HOUSEHOLDS 2009 Average HH Size	FAMILIES 2000	FAMILIES 2009	FAMILIES % Annual Rate 2000-2009
62548	MOUNT PULASKI	107	2484	2353	2273	-0.6	13	995	953	924	-0.5	2.34	704	661	-0.7
62549	MT ZION	115	5594	5791	5744	0.4	69	2101	2253	2260	0.8	2.54	1649	1735	0.6
62550	MOWEAQUA	173	3189	3051	2958	-0.5	18	1222	1187	1155	-0.3	2.50	913	872	-0.5
62551	NIANTIC	115	896	844	815	-0.6	13	328	320	311	-0.3	2.64	245	233	-0.5
62553	OCONEE	173	687	657	636	-0.5	18	248	241	235	-0.3	2.73	204	196	-0.4
62554	OREANA	115	1598	1623	1597	0.2	61	583	613	607	0.5	2.65	470	481	0.3
62555	OWANECO	021	559	553	552	-0.1	45	206	213	213	0.4	1.79	165	168	0.2
62556	PALMER	021	458	456	451	0.0	50	161	163	162	0.1	2.80	126	125	-0.1
62557	PANA	021	7445	7315	7194	-0.2	38	3009	3007	2971	0.0	2.33	1978	1929	-0.3
62558	PAWNEE	167	3661	3841	3911	0.5	72	1400	1498	1535	0.7	2.56	1034	1073	0.4
62560	RAYMOND	135	1489	1529	1523	0.3	65	589	608	607	0.3	2.50	428	433	0.1
62561	RIVERTON	167	4645	4918	5035	0.6	75	1796	1945	2002	0.9	2.53	1304	1367	0.5
62563	ROCHESTER	167	4747	5332	5569	1.3	87	1765	2016	2123	1.4	2.64	1448	1621	1.2
62565	SHELBYVILLE	173	7565	7411	7253	-0.2	38	3159	3137	3083	-0.1	2.33	2123	2064	-0.3
62567	STONINGTON	021	1239	1210	1192	-0.3	32	495	494	489	0.0	2.45	370	362	-0.2
62568	TAYLORVILLE	021	18289	17827	17484	-0.3	32	7056	6957	6839	-0.2	2.40	4693	4542	-0.4
62571	TOWER HILL	173	1575	1482	1425	-0.7	9	604	578	560	-0.5	2.56	457	431	-0.6
62572	WAGGONER	135	430	502	517	1.7	90	161	192	198	1.9	2.61	126	148	1.8
62573	WARRENSBURG	115	1837	1687	1615	-0.9	4	705	669	645	-0.6	2.51	537	499	-0.8
62601	ALEXANDER	137	471	477	472	0.1	56	184	190	188	0.3	2.51	142	143	0.1
62611	ARENZVILLE	017	1104	1141	1153	0.4	69	428	447	454	0.5	2.52	316	323	0.2
62612	ASHLAND	017	2013	2079	2104	0.3	65	798	830	841	0.4	2.50	580	592	0.2
62613	ATHENS	129	3396	3768	3901	1.1	85	1307	1483	1549	1.4	2.54	967	1076	1.2
62615	AUBURN	167	5880	6110	6221	0.4	69	2181	2315	2376	0.6	2.61	1636	1685	0.3
62617	BATH	125	954	905	876	-0.6	13	413	397	385	-0.4	2.28	292	276	-0.6
62618	BEARDSTOWN	017	7622	7790	7819	0.2	61	2890	2943	2952	0.2	2.60	1985	1979	0.0
62621	BLUFFS	171	1241	1172	1117	-0.6	13	497	477	457	-0.4	2.46	351	330	-0.7
62624	BROWNING	169	628	579	555	-0.9	4	264	249	241	-0.6	2.33	191	177	-0.8
62625	CANTRALL	167	920	1018	1057	1.1	85	321	362	378	1.3	2.81	263	290	1.1
62626	CARLINVILLE	117	8156	7963	7841	-0.3	32	3062	2992	2953	-0.2	2.44	2122	2032	-0.5
62627	CHANDLERVILLE	017	1157	1190	1202	0.3	65	472	490	497	0.4	2.43	332	338	0.2
62628	CHAPIN	137	1005	954	923	-0.6	13	378	367	358	-0.3	2.60	292	279	-0.5
62629	CHATHAM	167	9589	11647	12473	2.1	92	3461	4283	4620	2.3	2.72	2778	3358	2.1
62630	CHESTERFIELD	117	604	593	586	-0.2	38	236	234	232	-0.1	2.53	177	173	-0.2
62631	CONCORD	137	286	273	266	-0.5	18	107	105	102	-0.2	2.59	86	83	-0.4
62633	EASTON	125	908	852	818	-0.7	9	360	343	332	-0.5	2.48	277	261	-0.6
62634	ELKHART	107	1032	980	952	-0.6	13	403	388	378	-0.4	2.05	297	281	-0.6
62635	EMDEN	107	828	786	759	-0.6	13	320	305	295	-0.5	2.58	236	221	-0.7
62638	FRANKLIN	137	1199	1229	1222	0.3	65	448	471	472	0.5	2.61	339	348	0.3
62639	FREDERICK	169	731	705	688	-0.4	25	300	295	290	-0.2	2.39	229	223	-0.3
62640	GIRARD	117	4095	3987	3929	-0.3	32	1601	1586	1571	-0.1	2.48	1145	1112	-0.3
62642	GREENVIEW	129	1593	1606	1587	0.1	56	630	647	643	0.3	2.48	466	471	0.1
62643	HARTSBURG	107	580	561	544	-0.4	25	210	205	200	-0.3	2.74	164	158	-0.4
62644	HAVANA	125	5506	5270	5101	-0.5	18	2219	2138	2074	-0.4	2.40	1550	1464	-0.6
62649	HETTICK	117	471	457	450	-0.3	32	186	184	182	-0.1	2.48	134	130	-0.3
62650	JACKSONVILLE	137	28108	27362	26776	-0.3	32	10701	10541	10329	-0.2	2.28	6796	6544	-0.4
62655	KILBOURNE	125	607	578	559	-0.5	18	240	233	226	-0.3	2.48	171	163	-0.5
62656	LINCOLN	107	20695	20071	19581	-0.3	32	7055	6845	6661	-0.3	2.37	4576	4346	-0.6
62661	LOAMI	167	1319	1329	1334	0.1	56	508	525	530	0.4	2.53	393	395	0.1
62664	MASON CITY	125	3180	2990	2873	-0.7	9	1269	1203	1160	-0.6	2.42	861	799	-0.8
62665	MEREDOSIA	137	1720	1724	1699	0.0	50	717	733	726	0.2	2.35	496	495	0.0
62666	MIDDLETOWN	107	655	636	621	-0.3	32	242	238	233	-0.2	2.67	185	179	-0.4
62667	MODESTO	117	550	514	497	-0.7	9	210	199	194	-0.6	2.58	161	150	-0.8
62668	MURRAYVILLE	137	1591	1514	1465	-0.5	18	594	579	564	-0.3	2.61	466	447	-0.4
62670	NEW BERLIN	167	2675	2791	2876	0.5	72	1050	1121	1163	0.7	2.49	787	816	0.4
62671	NEW HOLLAND	107	622	584	562	-0.7	9	237	224	217	-0.6	2.61	182	170	-0.7
62672	NILWOOD	117	340	325	318	-0.5	18	136	131	129	-0.4	2.35	103	98	-0.5
62673	OAKFORD	129	550	553	545	0.1	56	216	221	219	0.2	2.50	156	157	0.1
62674	PALMYRA	117	1545	1468	1433	-0.6	13	676	654	643	-0.4	2.24	477	453	-0.6
62675	PETERSBURG	129	5315	5306	5253	0.0	50	2119	2141	2126	0.1	2.39	1493	1481	-0.1
62677	PLEASANT PLAINS	167	2562	2680	2721	0.5	72	950	1015	1039	0.7	2.64	767	801	0.5
62681	RUSHVILLE	169	4658	4627	4558	-0.1	45	1943	1953	1930	0.1	2.32	1305	1284	-0.2
62682	SAN JOSE	125	993	947	915	-0.5	18	371	356	345	-0.4	2.66	282	267	-0.6
62683	SCOTTVILLE	117	204	186	178	-1.0	3	75	69	66	-0.9	2.70	57	52	-1.0
62684	SHERMAN	167	3500	4307	4604	2.3	92	1257	1569	1688	2.4	2.64	1016	1241	2.2
62685	SHIPMAN	117	2122	2170	2163	0.2	61	805	837	839	0.4	2.59	613	627	0.2
62688	TALLULA	129	1624	1638	1642	0.1	56	603	616	621	0.2	2.66	470	473	0.1
62690	VIRDEN	117	4195	4210	4190	0.0	50	1714	1749	1752	0.2	2.31	1133	1129	0.0
62691	VIRGINIA	017	2480	2440	2434	-0.2	38	1021	1014	1013	-0.1	2.34	681	662	-0.3
62692	WAVERLY	137	2191	2044	1969	-0.7	9	890	843	817	-0.6	2.42	606	559	-0.9
62693	WILLIAMSVILLE	167	1700	1748	1765	0.3	65	627	659	672	0.5	2.65	491	502	0.2
62694	WINCHESTER	171	3871	3652	3481	-0.6	13	1570	1503	1438	-0.5	2.39	1099	1033	-0.7
62701	SPRINGFIELD	167	1159	1111	1094	-0.5	18	696	672	663	-0.4	1.24	107	93	-1.5
62702	SPRINGFIELD	167	38921	37499	36712	-0.4	25	17067	16684	16428	-0.2	2.21	9734	9146	-0.7
62703	SPRINGFIELD	167	31001	29269	28759	-0.6	13	12769	12210	12069	-0.5	2.33	7698	7076	-0.9
62704	SPRINGFIELD	167	41420	40542	40190	-0.2	38	19544	19483	19431	0.0	2.05	10456	9939	-0.5
62707	SPRINGFIELD	167	8816	8683	8761	-0.2	38	3254	3276	3329	0.1	2.56	2378	2324	-0.2
62711	SPRINGFIELD	167	11291	14548	15734	2.8	94	4358	5744	6259	3.0	2.50	3166	4051	2.7
62712	SPRINGFIELD	167	7920	9713	10283	2.2	92	2944	3765	4028	2.7	2.53	2303	2843	2.3
62801	CENTRALIA	121	24322	23109	22392	-0.6	13	9220	8827	8564	-0.5	2.35	6066	5677	-0.7
62803	HOYLETON	189	1110	1102	1080	-0.1	45	394	394	387	0.0	2.64	291	287	-0.1
62806	ALBION	047	2939	2836	2775	-0.4	25	1252	1220	1197	-0.3	2.29	835	797	-0.5
62807	ALMA	121	892	945	947	0.6	75	361	389	392	0.8	2.43	267	281	0.6
62808	ASHLEY	189	1423	1448	1436	0.2	61	548	559	555	0.2	2.57	388	388	0.0
62809	BARNHILL	191	179	170	166	-0.6	13	76	73	72	-0.4	2.33	58	56	-0.4
62810	BELLE RIVE	081	1128	1163	1177	0.3	65	406	424	430	0.5	2.74	323	332	0.3
62812	BENTON	055	11934	12259	12361	0.3	65	4970	5158	5220	0.4	2.32	3314	3363	0.2
62814	BLUFORD	081	2113	2167	2185	0.3	65	782	817	828	0.5	2.65	615	633	0.3
62815	BONE GAP	047	492	473	461	-0.4	25	178	173	169	-0.3	2.73	149	143	-0.4
62816	BONNIE	081	1321	1280	1262	-0.3	32	524	513	508	-0.2	2.36	391	376	-0.4
62817	BROUGHTON	065	655	593	566	-1.1	2	262	238	227	-1.0	2.49	197	176	-1.2
62818	BROWNS	047	374	359	351	-0.4	25	153	149	146	-0.3	2.41	116	112	-0.4
62819	BUCKNER	055	467	513	533	1.0	83	213	238	248	1.2	2.16	137	149	0.9
62820	BURNT PRAIRIE	193	205	199	194	-0.3	32	89	88	86	-0.1	2.25	62	60	-0.4
62821	CARMI	193	8218	7748	7499	-0.6	13	3531	3365	3265	-0.5	2.21	2299	2142	-0.8
	ILLINOIS					0.6					0.6	2.64			0.4
	UNITED STATES					1.0					1.1	2.59			0.9

ZIP CODE #	POST OFFICE NAME	RACE (%) White 2000	White 2009	Black 2000	Black 2009	Asian/Pacific 2000	Asian/Pacific 2009	% Hispanic Origin 2000	% Hispanic Origin 2009	2009 AGE DISTRIBUTION (%) 0-4	5-9	10-14	15-19	20-24	25-44	45-64	65-84	85+	18+	MEDIAN AGE 2009	% 2009 Males	% 2009 Females
62548	MOUNT PULASKI	98.4	98.2	1.0	1.2	0.0	0.0	0.5	0.7	5.8	6.0	6.3	6.2	5.1	23.0	26.3	16.0	5.2	77.7	43.1	47.9	52.1
62549	MT ZION	98.2	97.4	0.2	0.3	0.7	1.1	0.3	0.5	5.5	5.9	6.6	7.1	4.7	25.1	32.4	11.1	1.5	77.3	41.5	50.5	49.5
62550	MOWEAQUA	98.7	98.4	0.2	0.2	0.2	0.4	0.5	0.6	6.0	6.2	6.7	6.7	4.8	23.4	28.4	14.0	3.8	77.1	42.0	47.7	52.3
62551	NIANTIC	99.1	98.7	0.3	0.5	0.0	0.0	0.4	0.6	7.6	6.9	8.1	7.2	5.0	25.5	25.5	12.1	2.3	73.0	38.1	49.2	50.8
62553	OCONEE	98.5	97.9	0.1	0.3	0.9	1.2	0.4	0.8	5.8	6.2	6.8	7.6	4.7	23.9	28.9	14.2	1.8	76.6	41.2	50.5	49.5
62554	OREANA	98.5	97.8	0.3	0.5	0.3	0.3	0.4	0.7	5.4	6.2	6.7	6.4	4.4	23.4	33.1	13.1	1.2	77.6	43.2	50.8	49.2
62555	OWANECO	66.5	60.4	28.0	31.8	0.4	0.5	7.0	9.4	3.1	3.3	3.4	5.6	8.7	45.6	23.0	6.3	1.1	87.9	37.2	75.6	24.4
62556	PALMER	97.8	96.9	0.2	0.4	0.7	0.9	0.4	0.4	5.9	6.8	7.2	7.0	4.6	23.9	29.8	12.9	1.8	75.7	41.7	50.7	49.3
62557	PANA	98.5	98.0	0.6	0.7	0.3	0.5	0.6	0.9	6.5	6.2	6.2	6.5	5.6	22.9	25.8	16.2	4.1	76.8	41.6	48.3	51.7
62558	PAWNEE	98.5	97.9	0.3	0.4	0.2	0.3	0.4	0.5	6.6	6.7	7.0	7.1	5.9	26.8	28.3	10.1	1.4	75.2	38.5	49.0	51.0
62560	RAYMOND	99.3	99.3	0.2	0.2	0.1	0.1	0.2	0.3	6.6	7.0	7.5	6.5	4.6	24.9	28.5	11.9	2.5	75.0	40.1	49.4	50.6
62561	RIVERTON	98.7	98.0	0.3	0.4	0.1	0.1	0.8	1.3	6.1	6.9	7.0	6.9	5.8	26.8	30.1	9.2	1.2	75.6	38.6	49.7	50.3
62563	ROCHESTER	98.1	97.4	0.6	0.8	0.4	0.5	0.5	0.6	4.5	5.8	7.5	8.2	4.6	22.3	35.6	10.2	1.2	76.8	43.2	49.9	50.1
62565	SHELBYVILLE	98.8	98.4	0.2	0.2	0.3	0.5	0.7	1.0	5.7	6.0	6.2	6.1	5.4	23.9	27.5	16.2	3.1	78.5	42.4	49.0	51.0
62567	STONINGTON	99.3	99.0	0.2	0.2	0.1	0.1	0.6	0.9	7.9	7.8	7.8	6.7	5.1	21.7	26.2	14.3	2.6	72.5	39.4	49.1	50.9
62568	TAYLORVILLE	95.2	94.1	2.9	3.4	0.5	0.7	1.2	1.6	5.9	6.0	6.3	6.3	5.7	26.0	27.1	13.4	3.3	77.9	40.5	51.0	49.0
62571	TOWER HILL	99.0	98.9	0.1	0.1	0.1	0.1	0.3	0.3	6.5	6.5	6.7	7.0	5.3	24.8	27.7	13.9	1.6	76.0	40.4	50.3	49.7
62572	WAGGONER	99.5	99.2	0.0	0.0	0.0	0.0	0.0	0.0	7.6	7.8	7.8	6.6	4.8	27.1	27.1	10.0	1.4	72.7	35.9	52.6	47.4
62573	WARRENSBURG	97.9	97.0	0.7	0.9	0.2	0.3	0.4	0.7	6.6	6.8	7.2	6.4	4.9	26.6	30.7	9.8	1.1	75.3	40.1	50.3	49.7
62601	ALEXANDER	98.1	97.5	0.4	0.6	0.0	0.0	0.9	1.3	4.8	6.5	7.5	8.8	4.8	24.9	28.7	11.5	2.3	75.5	40.6	50.3	49.7
62611	ARENZVILLE	99.2	98.9	0.2	0.2	0.0	0.0	1.0	1.7	5.8	6.5	6.9	6.3	4.3	22.5	30.9	14.2	2.6	76.8	43.2	50.8	49.2
62612	ASHLAND	98.7	98.3	0.2	0.3	0.1	0.2	0.2	0.3	6.0	6.3	6.8	6.7	4.9	26.0	29.3	12.6	1.6	76.8	41.1	50.0	50.0
62613	ATHENS	98.5	98.1	0.3	0.3	0.2	0.3	1.1	1.5	6.6	7.1	7.6	7.2	5.2	25.7	29.8	9.7	1.1	74.3	38.3	49.2	50.8
62615	AUBURN	98.6	97.9	0.2	0.4	0.2	0.4	0.7	1.2	8.1	7.8	7.7	7.3	6.2	27.6	24.9	8.5	2.0	71.8	35.0	48.4	51.6
62617	BATH	98.1	97.7	0.1	0.1	0.0	0.0	0.4	0.6	6.0	6.1	6.5	6.3	4.2	24.3	28.5	16.2	1.9	77.5	42.7	49.3	50.7
62618	BEARDSTOWN	92.2	89.6	0.7	0.8	0.4	0.5	14.5	20.2	7.4	6.8	6.4	6.4	6.0	26.7	24.9	12.7	2.6	75.3	37.2	49.9	50.1
62621	BLUFFS	99.4	99.2	0.0	0.0	0.2	0.3	0.2	0.3	6.7	7.3	6.9	5.8	4.4	26.8	29.4	11.1	1.8	75.5	39.5	49.1	50.9
62624	BROWNING	98.6	98.3	0.0	0.0	0.0	0.0	0.8	1.2	5.4	6.2	6.6	5.4	3.3	23.8	33.2	13.5	2.8	78.8	44.6	52.8	47.2
62625	CANTRALL	98.4	98.0	0.1	0.2	0.4	0.6	0.3	0.5	5.8	6.5	7.7	7.3	4.6	22.8	34.2	10.3	0.9	75.6	42.1	49.7	50.3
62626	CARLINVILLE	97.2	96.6	1.4	1.6	0.3	0.5	0.7	1.0	5.5	5.4	5.6	7.9	7.7	22.3	27.1	14.5	4.0	79.5	41.2	48.5	51.5
62627	CHANDLERVILLE	97.3	96.6	0.2	0.3	0.4	0.7	1.0	1.5	6.1	6.4	6.6	6.6	4.5	25.4	28.9	13.4	2.1	76.7	41.3	50.0	50.0
62628	CHAPIN	99.1	98.8	0.0	0.0	0.0	0.0	0.5	0.7	6.7	7.0	7.2	6.9	4.8	23.4	28.6	13.7	1.6	74.5	40.5	53.0	47.0
62629	CHATHAM	97.3	96.1	0.9	1.3	0.9	1.3	0.8	1.2	6.9	7.0	7.3	7.8	6.0	27.5	29.4	7.2	0.9	73.9	35.7	49.0	51.0
62630	CHESTERFIELD	97.7	97.1	1.0	1.0	0.0	0.0	0.5	0.7	5.2	6.9	7.9	7.4	5.7	23.9	27.8	13.0	2.0	75.0	39.7	49.4	50.6
62631	CONCORD	99.7	99.6	0.0	0.0	0.0	0.0	0.3	0.4	5.1	5.5	6.2	5.9	4.4	22.7	32.2	15.8	2.2	78.8	45.1	52.7	47.3
62633	EASTON	99.2	99.1	0.0	0.0	0.1	0.1	0.1	0.1	4.5	5.9	6.2	7.5	4.2	22.7	32.4	13.7	2.9	79.3	44.4	50.8	49.2
62634	ELKHART	87.1	85.0	11.9	13.8	0.1	0.2	2.2	2.9	4.3	5.6	6.7	6.5	6.6	33.3	25.4	9.9	1.6	79.0	37.6	53.5	46.5
62635	EMDEN	98.7	98.2	0.0	0.0	0.5	0.8	0.6	0.9	6.9	7.4	7.4	6.5	4.5	23.3	27.5	14.1	2.5	74.4	40.3	47.2	52.8
62638	FRANKLIN	98.6	98.0	0.3	0.3	0.0	0.0	1.1	1.6	5.5	6.4	6.8	7.6	5.5	24.2	29.7	12.6	1.8	76.6	40.9	50.6	49.4
62639	FREDERICK	98.8	98.6	0.1	0.1	0.4	0.6	0.5	0.7	5.7	6.0	6.4	6.1	4.5	23.0	34.0	13.2	1.1	78.3	44.0	50.8	49.2
62640	GIRARD	98.7	98.4	0.2	0.3	0.3	0.4	0.8	1.2	5.9	6.0	6.8	7.1	5.3	23.8	27.3	14.5	3.2	76.9	41.3	49.4	50.6
62642	GREENVIEW	99.1	98.9	0.3	0.4	0.2	0.2	0.6	0.9	6.0	7.1	8.1	6.7	4.9	27.8	26.4	11.5	1.6	74.6	37.8	51.2	48.8
62643	HARTSBURG	98.1	97.7	0.0	0.0	0.2	0.2	1.4	1.8	7.0	7.7	7.7	6.1	4.8	23.5	30.7	11.1	1.6	74.0	39.1	51.2	48.8
62644	HAVANA	98.8	98.4	0.1	0.1	0.4	0.5	0.5	0.7	5.7	5.7	6.2	6.5	5.0	23.9	28.1	15.5	3.5	78.6	42.7	47.6	52.4
62649	HETTICK	98.9	98.9	0.6	0.7	0.0	0.0	0.2	0.2	5.5	6.1	6.3	5.7	4.6	24.1	31.5	14.2	2.0	78.3	43.2	51.9	48.1
62650	JACKSONVILLE	90.3	88.2	6.9	7.7	0.6	1.2	1.6	2.5	5.5	5.3	5.5	8.6	8.5	24.5	25.8	13.3	3.0	80.0	38.6	49.2	50.8
62655	KILBOURNE	98.4	98.3	0.2	0.2	0.2	0.2	0.5	0.5	5.2	5.5	5.7	6.9	4.8	24.2	29.1	16.4	2.1	79.1	43.2	52.8	47.2
62656	LINCOLN	88.7	86.7	9.1	10.4	0.8	1.1	2.0	2.7	5.1	5.1	5.1	7.7	8.5	29.5	24.4	12.2	2.6	81.4	37.0	50.8	49.2
62661	LOAMI	98.2	97.7	0.4	0.6	0.9	1.1	1.5	2.2	6.5	6.9	7.0	6.8	4.7	26.0	31.1	10.0	1.1	75.4	40.0	48.7	51.3
62664	MASON CITY	99.1	98.8	0.1	0.1	0.2	0.2	0.5	0.8	5.9	5.9	6.0	6.8	5.7	22.9	27.3	15.3	4.3	77.9	42.5	48.2	51.8
62665	MEREDOSIA	99.4	99.2	0.2	0.3	0.0	0.0	0.2	0.2	5.7	5.9	6.0	7.0	4.9	24.1	29.4	14.8	2.1	78.1	42.7	48.8	51.2
62666	MIDDLETOWN	98.5	98.0	0.2	0.2	0.2	0.3	0.8	1.3	5.8	7.1	7.4	6.8	5.3	24.7	30.3	11.3	1.3	75.5	40.5	51.4	48.6
62667	MODESTO	99.8	99.6	0.0	0.0	0.2	0.4	0.4	0.4	4.7	4.9	7.0	8.6	4.5	23.3	29.6	14.8	2.7	77.2	43.0	50.0	50.0
62668	MURRAYVILLE	98.8	98.6	0.2	0.2	0.1	0.1	0.1	0.1	5.8	6.2	6.7	6.9	5.0	25.1	31.0	12.0	1.3	76.9	41.0	50.8	49.2
62670	NEW BERLIN	98.5	97.9	0.4	0.6	0.3	0.4	0.7	1.1	6.7	6.9	7.1	6.8	5.3	24.7	30.0	11.1	1.4	75.0	40.1	49.8	50.2
62671	NEW HOLLAND	98.7	98.1	0.2	0.2	0.0	0.0	0.8	1.2	7.4	8.0	7.7	6.5	5.3	22.9	28.9	11.3	1.9	72.8	38.8	50.2	49.8
62672	NILWOOD	98.5	98.2	0.6	0.6	0.3	0.3	0.9	1.2	6.5	6.8	7.1	8.3	5.8	24.0	27.1	12.6	1.8	75.4	38.6	51.4	48.6
62673	OAKFORD	98.7	98.6	0.2	0.2	0.2	0.2	0.7	1.1	6.1	5.1	8.7	7.6	4.3	26.9	28.8	11.4	1.1	74.7	38.7	50.8	49.2
62674	PALMYRA	99.2	99.0	0.2	0.2	0.3	0.3	0.4	0.7	5.2	5.3	6.2	6.5	4.3	23.4	30.2	15.9	2.9	79.1	44.3	50.3	49.7
62675	PETERSBURG	98.4	98.1	0.5	0.6	0.2	0.3	0.7	1.0	5.4	5.6	6.2	6.8	5.3	22.6	29.7	14.9	3.4	78.6	43.6	48.4	51.6
62677	PLEASANT PLAINS	97.8	96.8	1.0	1.4	0.2	0.3	0.7	1.1	6.0	6.9	7.3	6.7	4.7	22.8	32.9	11.3	1.4	75.5	41.9	49.4	50.6
62681	RUSHVILLE	98.9	98.6	0.2	0.2	0.1	0.1	0.5	0.7	5.6	5.7	5.9	6.0	4.8	23.4	28.1	16.3	4.1	79.0	43.8	49.0	51.0
62682	SAN JOSE	98.3	98.0	0.2	0.2	0.1	0.1	1.2	1.6	7.7	7.8	7.7	7.2	4.3	24.5	26.1	12.6	2.1	72.2	38.2	48.7	51.3
62683	SCOTTVILLE	99.5	99.5	0.0	0.0	0.5	0.5	0.5	1.1	4.8	4.8	8.6	10.8	4.3	23.7	25.8	14.0	3.2	73.1	40.9	50.0	50.0
62684	SHERMAN	98.0	97.2	0.4	0.5	0.7	1.0	0.5	0.7	5.6	6.4	7.1	7.4	4.6	23.3	31.4	10.7	3.5	76.1	42.1	48.9	51.1
62685	SHIPMAN	93.0	91.7	5.6	6.5	0.1	0.2	0.6	1.0	5.7	6.0	6.4	6.8	5.0	24.4	30.2	13.8	1.7	77.8	42.0	50.8	49.2
62688	TALLULA	98.6	98.3	0.2	0.3	0.1	0.1	0.4	0.5	5.3	6.6	7.6	7.6	4.7	25.9	31.4	9.8	1.1	75.3	41.2	51.7	48.3
62690	VIRDEN	99.0	98.9	0.1	0.2	0.1	0.1	0.4	0.5	6.3	5.9	5.8	6.3	5.4	24.4	25.7	15.2	5.0	77.8	41.7	47.9	52.1
62691	VIRGINIA	98.1	97.4	0.1	0.2	0.3	0.4	1.1	1.7	5.5	5.7	5.9	5.8	5.1	23.1	29.6	15.1	4.1	78.8	44.1	48.1	51.9
62692	WAVERLY	99.4	99.3	0.0	0.0	0.0	0.0	0.5	0.8	6.0	6.1	6.3	6.5	5.2	24.0	30.1	13.4	2.4	77.6	42.0	49.3	50.7
62693	WILLIAMSVILLE	98.3	97.8	0.5	0.7	0.2	0.2	0.7	1.1	6.1	6.6	7.2	7.8	5.0	24.5	28.7	12.2	1.9	75.3	40.5	47.4	52.6
62694	WINCHESTER	99.5	99.3	0.1	0.1	0.1	0.2	0.2	0.3	6.3	6.4	6.5	6.4	5.1	22.9	28.1	15.0	3.3	76.6	42.1	48.1	51.9
62701	SPRINGFIELD	72.7	64.8	22.9	29.7	2.1	2.6	1.3	1.6	2.1	1.6	1.5	3.7	7.6	36.1	26.9	17.0	3.5	93.7	43.5	61.7	38.3
62702	SPRINGFIELD	87.0	83.0	9.8	12.9	0.8	1.1	1.2	1.7	6.5	6.3	6.2	6.4	6.1	26.7	26.4	12.9	2.6	77.1	38.9	47.7	52.3
62703	SPRINGFIELD	63.6	58.8	32.8	36.7	0.9	1.3	1.2	1.6	7.4	7.2	6.8	7.1	7.5	26.4	24.7	10.8	2.0	74.2	35.4	46.9	53.1
62704	SPRINGFIELD	88.6	84.7	7.3	9.8	2.1	2.9	1.3	1.8	5.7	5.2	5.2	5.5	7.2	26.6	27.6	13.7	3.3	80.7	40.8	47.0	53.0
62707	SPRINGFIELD	95.9	94.3	2.2	3.1	0.5	0.7	0.8	1.1	5.9	6.3	6.5	6.0	5.1	25.1	31.9	11.0	2.0	77.5	41.6	49.2	50.8
62711	SPRINGFIELD	94.2	91.7	2.5	3.6	2.3	3.3	0.9	1.4	6.2	6.7	7.5	7.0	4.5	24.1	32.1	10.0	1.9	75.0	41.1	47.4	52.6
62712	SPRINGFIELD	94.2	91.2	3.0	4.7	1.5	2.3	0.9	1.4	5.2	5.7	6.8	6.7	6.0	22.5	33.9	11.9	1.2	77.9	42.9	49.0	51.0
62801	CENTRALIA	86.2	83.3	10.8	12.8	0.6	0.8	1.6	2.2	6.0	5.8	6.0	6.6	6.8	27.1	26.2	12.7	2.9	78.4	38.9	51.5	48.5
62803	HOYLETON	97.0	96.9	2.0	2.1	0.3	0.3	0.7	0.7	6.4	6.9	7.9	8.7	4.0	24.7	27.1	11.1	3.2	73.7	38.6	48.9	51.1
62806	ALBION	98.9	98.7	0.1	0.1	0.5	0.6	0.5	0.6	5.8	5.9	6.1	6.1	4.8	23.5	27.7	16.3	3.9	78.4	43.4	47.7	52.3
62807	ALMA	99.2	98.8	0.2	0.3	0.0	0.0	0.4	0.6	5.8	6.2	6.5	6.5	4.7	24.8	30.4	13.1	2.1	77.5	41.8	51.0	49.0
62808	ASHLEY	98.7	98.6	0.1	0.2	0.1	0.1	0.7	0.8	5.0	6.8	7.1	7.5	5.6	24.5	27.8	12.7	3.0	76.2	40.4	50.6	49.4
62809	BARNHILL	100.0	99.4	0.0	0.0	0.0	0.0	0.6	0.6	5.3	5.3	5.9	5.9	5.9	25.9	31.2	13.5	1.2	80.0	42.1	50.6	49.4
62810	BELLE RIVE	98.1	97.5	0.8	1.1	0.0	0.0	0.2	0.2	5.6	5.6	6.0	6.6	5.7	23.9	32.0	12.8	1.8	78.8	42.1	51.3	48.7
62812	BENTON	98.6	97.9	0.2	0.4	0.2	0.4	0.6	0.8	5.3	5.6	5.9	6.4	5.3	23.5	28.5	15.8	3.7	79.4	43.4	48.5	51.5
62814	BLUFORD	98.9	98.5	0.0	0.1	0.1	0.1	0.9	1.5	6.0	7.2	7.9	6.9	5.4	25.4	27.3	12.0	1.8	74.9	37.9	50.7	49.3
62815	BONE GAP	99.4	99.2	0.0	0.0	0.2	0.2	0.2	0.2	6.8	7.2	7.4	5.9	4.7	25.4	28.8	12.5	1.5	74.8	38.6	50.5	49.5
62816	BONNIE	94.8	93.4	3.3	4.1	0.2	0.3	1.1	1.6	5.4	5.7	6.1	6.0	4.7	29.0	29.8	11.7	1.6	79.1	40.7	53.1	46.9
62817	BROUGHTON	98.9	98.8	0.2	0.2	0.2	0.2	0.5	0.7	5.4	5.7	6.2	6.1	4.4	22.6	31.4	16.0	2.2	78.8	44.7	50.4	49.6
62818	BROWNS	99.2	99.2	0.0	0.0	0.5	0.6	0.5	0.8	4.5	4.7	5.3	6.1	4.7	26.2	32.0	14.5	1.9	81.6	43.9	50.4	49.6
62819	BUCKNER	98.5	98.4	0.0	0.0	0.0	0.0	1.1	1.4	4.9	4.9	5.3	6.4	6.0	25.0	27.5	17.0	3.1	81.3	43.4	50.9	49.1
62820	BURNT PRAIRIE	99.0	99.0	0.0	0.0	0.5	0.5	0.5	0.5	5.0	6.0	5.5	5.0	4.0	24.1	30.7	17.6	2.0	80.4	45.2	50.8	49.2
62821	CARMI	97.9	97.4	0.4	0.5	0.2	0.2	0.8	1.2	5.1	5.1	5.5	6.0	4.9	23.0	28.6	17.0	4.8	80.6	45.3	47.9	52.1
	ILLINOIS	73.5	70.6	15.1	15.3	3.4	4.4	12.3	15.7	7.1	6.9	6.8	7.1	6.9	27.5	25.4	10.3	1.9	75.0	36.1	49.1	50.9
	UNITED STATES	75.1	72.0	12.3	12.7	3.8	4.6	12.5	15.7	6.8	6.7	6.6	7.1	6.9	27.0	26.0	10.9	1.9	75.7	36.9	49.2	50.8

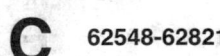

#	POST OFFICE NAME	2009 Per Capita Income	2009 HH Income Base	2009 Household Income Distribution (%): Less than $25,000	$25,000 to $49,999	$50,000 to $99,999	$100,000 to $149,999	$150,000 or More	Median Household Income: 2009	2014	2009 National Centile	2009 State Centile	2009 Home Value Base	2009 Home Value Distribution (%): Less than $50,000	$50,000 to $89,999	$90,000 to $174,999	$175,000 to $399,999	$400,000 or More	2009 Median Home Value
62548	MOUNT PULASKI	24289	953	19.1	30.0	41.1	8.1	1.7	50782	52554	63	45	744	7.0	22.6	59.0	10.6	0.8	109746
62549	MT ZION	28608	2253	13.6	16.6	53.6	12.6	3.6	72892	75371	88	83	1762	2.0	10.6	67.9	17.8	1.7	123298
62550	MOWEAQUA	24169	1187	15.0	27.1	46.4	8.8	2.6	58258	59506	75	61	942	14.2	23.8	47.6	11.5	3.0	106325
62551	NIANTIC	25081	320	14.1	24.7	50.6	8.1	2.5	58291	60905	76	61	257	13.6	28.0	46.7	10.5	1.2	97414
62553	OCONEE	19441	241	17.0	33.6	47.7	0.8	0.8	49480	49880	60	42	211	18.0	29.4	34.6	16.1	1.9	92750
62554	OREANA	27062	613	12.6	19.1	53.3	10.0	5.1	66808	67592	85	76	541	6.1	24.0	50.8	17.4	1.7	109324
62555	OWANECO	32632	213	14.1	25.4	49.8	8.5	2.3	60225	61793	78	65	176	17.0	25.0	38.6	16.5	2.8	106579
62556	PALMER	22696	163	22.1	25.8	42.9	4.3	4.9	51296	53205	64	47	127	15.7	28.3	38.6	12.6	4.7	101293
62557	PANA	19284	3007	31.5	36.3	26.9	3.5	1.8	37791	40440	26	11	2225	24.7	34.6	32.0	8.1	0.5	78107
62558	PAWNEE	27040	1498	13.4	23.2	49.8	9.0	4.6	63812	64751	82	71	1218	9.9	23.7	53.9	11.7	0.7	106902
62560	RAYMOND	20932	608	19.6	33.7	39.1	5.6	2.0	47008	47160	54	35	472	23.3	33.7	33.1	9.5	0.4	82500
62561	RIVERTON	26901	1945	14.1	24.4	46.9	9.0	5.6	60694	62193	78	66	1513	14.1	16.2	54.5	14.7	0.5	114164
62563	ROCHESTER	32337	2016	8.7	18.7	46.7	15.9	10.1	76390	76874	90	88	1784	1.8	5.9	48.2	39.2	4.9	161816
62565	SHELBYVILLE	23480	3137	21.9	31.3	38.3	5.7	2.8	45938	47941	51	32	2404	16.3	26.3	43.9	12.0	1.5	99271
62567	STONINGTON	23004	494	21.1	26.9	42.7	7.3	2.0	51328	53778	64	47	395	18.7	30.6	40.8	6.8	3.0	91316
62568	TAYLORVILLE	21852	6957	24.7	29.0	37.8	6.4	2.0	46589	49229	53	34	5157	13.3	32.6	42.6	10.8	0.8	94920
62571	TOWER HILL	18752	578	25.3	33.6	36.0	4.3	0.9	41622	44129	38	20	482	35.7	27.6	29.9	6.4	0.4	70588
62572	WAGGONER	18452	192	20.3	37.5	38.5	3.6	0.0	45000	45553	48	29	153	39.2	36.6	20.9	2.6	0.7	64091
62573	WARRENSBURG	27487	669	10.3	22.4	54.1	9.0	4.2	63591	64373	82	71	510	6.5	25.7	47.6	17.8	2.4	110204
62601	ALEXANDER	21675	190	22.6	26.8	42.6	5.8	2.1	50350	51916	62	44	143	10.5	25.2	42.7	14.7	7.0	112500
62611	ARENZVILLE	21839	447	16.8	32.9	43.2	5.8	1.3	50173	49709	62	44	360	15.0	25.8	41.1	13.9	4.2	105435
62612	ASHLAND	22703	830	19.3	29.8	43.5	4.8	2.7	50621	49713	63	45	647	11.6	26.1	48.8	11.4	2.0	107283
62613	ATHENS	25715	1483	14.7	21.9	50.3	10.5	2.6	59383	61412	77	63	1194	6.1	18.0	49.7	25.0	1.2	131077
62615	AUBURN	24684	2315	16.4	25.6	47.8	6.4	3.9	58364	60467	76	62	1770	5.4	27.4	55.5	10.5	1.2	106343
62617	BATH	20573	397	29.7	32.2	33.8	2.8	1.5	40065	41528	33	16	326	38.7	25.5	29.1	5.8	0.9	65806
62618	BEARDSTOWN	17861	2943	29.5	31.5	33.8	4.4	0.8	38796	41402	29	13	2120	26.0	37.0	30.3	6.4	0.3	74596
62621	BLUFFS	21869	477	25.2	28.1	37.5	6.3	2.9	47273	48155	55	36	373	27.6	31.4	25.2	12.9	2.9	77045
62624	BROWNING	20043	249	25.3	35.3	35.7	2.8	0.8	38745	42359	29	13	212	50.9	18.4	23.1	4.7	2.8	49130
62625	CANTRALL	24855	362	9.9	21.8	50.0	14.6	3.6	63400	63582	82	70	315	8.3	14.0	44.4	30.5	2.9	131071
62626	CARLINVILLE	22166	2992	25.3	29.5	35.4	6.0	3.8	45210	48169	49	29	2169	8.3	25.4	44.2	20.9	1.2	113963
62627	CHANDLERVILLE	19191	490	31.6	27.1	35.7	5.1	0.4	39479	42174	31	15	394	31.2	29.9	33.8	4.3	0.8	71176
62628	CHAPIN	22345	367	18.0	25.1	49.9	5.2	1.9	54039	56291	70	53	311	11.9	31.8	44.4	10.3	1.6	97500
62629	CHATHAM	30223	4283	9.0	16.9	52.2	14.8	7.1	76682	76614	90	89	3580	6.5	5.5	53.7	32.2	2.1	143778
62630	CHESTERFIELD	23609	234	21.8	28.6	39.7	5.1	4.7	49576	51633	60	42	190	14.2	22.6	38.9	17.9	6.3	112097
62631	CONCORD	21337	105	25.7	25.7	41.9	4.8	1.9	47398	50750	55	36	87	14.9	18.4	43.7	18.4	4.6	114844
62633	EASTON	19134	343	29.4	26.5	38.8	4.1	1.2	42525	45504	41	22	281	16.0	35.6	35.6	10.0	2.8	88393
62634	ELKHART	29441	388	13.4	25.3	47.9	10.6	2.8	60184	61854	78	64	296	11.8	24.7	44.3	16.6	2.7	110294
62635	EMDEN	20911	305	21.6	36.4	32.1	7.9	2.0	45680	47339	50	31	225	5.8	27.6	57.3	9.3	0.0	104167
62638	FRANKLIN	23423	471	18.7	24.0	45.6	8.7	3.0	56179	58585	73	58	368	10.6	24.5	40.5	18.2	6.3	116204
62639	FREDERICK	25000	295	19.0	30.5	44.1	3.4	3.1	50324	51835	62	44	253	27.3	16.6	47.0	9.1	0.0	101250
62640	GIRARD	21139	1586	24.6	30.5	37.3	5.7	1.9	44703	48287	47	28	1225	13.5	26.8	40.2	17.6	1.9	106651
62642	GREENVIEW	25935	647	15.5	26.9	45.6	9.1	2.9	55206	57717	72	56	501	11.8	28.9	42.5	14.4	2.4	106076
62643	HARTSBURG	25411	205	12.7	26.3	47.8	8.3	4.9	61470	62496	79	67	157	7.0	21.0	53.5	18.5	0.0	120109
62644	HAVANA	20627	2138	26.1	34.3	32.9	4.6	2.1	41269	43138	37	20	1558	21.8	40.9	30.6	6.2	0.4	76127
62649	HETTICK	23010	184	21.7	32.1	36.4	5.4	4.3	47339	49060	55	36	148	20.9	14.2	37.8	14.9	12.2	127381
62650	JACKSONVILLE	23355	10541	23.6	29.6	38.1	5.5	3.2	45162	49306	49	29	7011	11.6	20.6	48.8	17.0	2.0	113714
62655	KILBOURNE	20780	233	24.5	30.9	36.9	4.3	3.4	42155	45000	40	21	188	31.9	42.6	21.8	2.1	1.6	69375
62656	LINCOLN	22669	6845	22.9	29.7	37.1	6.9	3.4	48000	49800	57	38	4663	12.1	21.2	51.1	14.5	1.1	109478
62661	LOAMI	24263	525	11.8	31.6	49.7	5.3	1.5	53608	54329	69	53	443	27.1	23.5	39.5	9.5	0.5	89138
62664	MASON CITY	22663	1203	23.4	29.3	40.0	4.9	2.3	47435	49563	55	37	921	19.3	35.8	39.1	5.6	0.1	85602
62665	MEREDOSIA	21120	733	26.1	33.4	37.2	2.0	1.2	40946	44751	36	19	586	27.8	41.1	27.3	3.4	0.3	69677
62666	MIDDLETOWN	23339	238	14.3	24.4	52.1	5.9	3.4	57550	60684	75	60	180	13.9	32.2	36.7	16.7	0.6	97778
62667	MODESTO	23564	199	17.6	25.6	48.2	6.5	2.0	53474	55882	69	52	163	19.6	19.0	39.9	17.8	3.7	112500
62668	MURRAYVILLE	21635	579	15.5	27.8	50.1	5.2	1.4	54117	56595	70	54	481	12.1	30.8	43.5	11.9	1.9	101017
62670	NEW BERLIN	28041	1121	13.4	22.7	51.1	9.2	3.7	62628	63568	81	69	908	5.7	16.9	52.2	21.3	4.0	121919
62671	NEW HOLLAND	24972	224	14.3	29.5	42.9	9.4	4.0	55621	60119	72	57	170	11.8	24.1	52.4	10.6	1.2	106081
62672	NILWOOD	23252	131	23.7	35.1	32.8	5.3	3.1	43984	46705	45	27	110	20.9	23.6	31.8	20.9	2.7	102273
62673	OAKFORD	21404	221	22.6	29.4	43.0	2.7	2.3	46690	49100	53	34	172	18.0	46.5	29.7	5.8	0.0	73043
62674	PALMYRA	20720	654	30.1	32.0	32.6	4.1	1.2	40882	44462	36	18	499	30.5	24.2	31.5	9.2	4.6	79423
62675	PETERSBURG	27698	2141	19.0	21.7	44.8	9.5	5.0	56780	60030	74	59	1627	6.8	18.5	43.1	30.9	0.7	127705
62677	PLEASANT PLAINS	30628	1015	10.0	17.2	52.3	13.0	7.4	72166	74346	88	82	867	7.5	12.6	51.6	23.9	4.5	130585
62681	RUSHVILLE	19910	1953	30.1	32.1	32.6	3.0	2.3	39755	41565	32	15	1483	29.7	30.0	32.4	7.1	0.7	74550
62682	SAN JOSE	21989	356	19.1	26.7	43.8	8.4	2.0	53013	55330	68	51	269	23.0	29.4	43.1	4.5	0.0	86905
62683	SCOTTVILLE	17083	69	24.6	33.3	37.7	4.3	0.0	44310	47321	46	27	55	27.3	23.6	36.4	7.3	5.5	88333
62684	SHERMAN	31606	1569	4.6	14.5	55.3	19.4	6.2	77584	77672	91	90	1311	2.3	6.6	51.7	36.7	2.7	155548
62685	SHIPMAN	19918	837	22.2	29.5	42.9	3.9	1.4	48197	50771	57	39	685	14.6	22.3	40.0	20.7	2.3	111690
62688	TALLULA	25671	616	15.6	19.0	55.0	6.5	3.9	62957	65340	81	70	516	16.1	21.7	39.7	20.2	2.3	110390
62690	VIRDEN	22313	1749	25.7	27.8	39.5	5.2	1.8	45662	49365	50	31	1307	13.2	27.9	50.7	7.7	0.5	100050
62691	VIRGINIA	21676	1014	27.0	28.2	37.9	5.2	1.7	45656	45896	50	31	752	18.6	29.3	39.1	12.2	0.8	92667
62692	WAVERLY	22566	843	22.2	29.7	41.3	4.9	2.0	47943	50338	56	38	685	14.6	35.3	37.2	11.4	1.5	90111
62693	WILLIAMSVILLE	24805	659	11.8	25.6	50.2	9.9	2.4	62825	63290	81	70	517	2.1	20.7	54.2	22.1	1.0	123467
62694	WINCHESTER	19679	1503	28.3	29.7	37.3	3.5	1.2	40752	45666	35	18	1153	23.2	34.3	33.5	7.8	1.2	81436
62701	SPRINGFIELD	23433	672	62.1	17.7	16.7	1.6	1.9	18504	19734	1	0	32	6.3	25.0	50.0	0.0	18.8	112500
62702	SPRINGFIELD	22876	16684	27.6	30.9	35.1	4.6	1.8	43101	45881	43	24	10966	25.3	34.6	35.1	4.6	0.4	80341
62703	SPRINGFIELD	20717	12210	30.3	29.3	34.6	4.4	1.3	41039	44498	36	19	7331	17.8	39.7	38.4	3.7	0.4	83962
62704	SPRINGFIELD	33319	19483	18.3	28.0	38.6	8.7	6.3	53379	55192	69	52	11622	2.7	16.6	53.9	23.4	3.3	129611
62707	SPRINGFIELD	26032	3276	11.0	23.8	51.2	11.2	2.8	62843	64730	81	70	2764	21.6	13.7	48.3	15.3	1.0	108725
62711	SPRINGFIELD	42044	5744	4.4	16.0	44.6	18.1	17.0	82295	82469	93	93	4598	2.2	3.7	31.2	52.7	10.3	210795
62712	SPRINGFIELD	39113	3765	4.9	16.6	47.6	17.1	13.8	80544	81030	92	92	3113	1.4	2.1	38.1	48.8	9.6	193109
62801	CENTRALIA	21708	8827	28.2	30.2	33.5	5.1	2.9	42617	46470	41	23	6432	28.6	34.0	28.9	7.7	0.7	75513
62803	HOYLETON	21665	394	20.8	30.2	41.9	4.8	2.3	49152	50102	59	41	318	10.1	39.9	38.7	7.5	3.8	90000
62806	ALBION	18645	1220	31.5	36.4	28.3	2.3	1.6	34708	37085	17	6	950	37.7	30.1	25.3	5.8	1.2	65102
62807	ALMA	21344	389	26.5	35.5	28.3	6.2	3.6	38565	42619	28	13	330	23.3	20.6	47.3	8.5	0.3	96452
62808	ASHLEY	19714	559	25.4	32.9	34.5	4.7	2.5	45046	46771	48	29	468	27.4	30.6	28.8	12.2	1.1	80263
62809	BARNHILL	23399	73	20.5	31.5	41.1	5.5	1.4	48622	51316	58	40	63	30.2	27.0	38.1	4.8	0.0	81000
62810	BELLE RIVE	16844	424	27.6	30.4	38.9	2.4	0.7	45561	45839	50	31	358	32.1	27.4	25.4	15.1	0.0	81282
62812	BENTON	18539	5158	35.3	33.9	25.4	3.9	1.6	34742	35688	17	6	3910	24.8	35.5	31.0	8.0	0.6	78000
62814	BLUFORD	19404	817	21.4	32.8	39.7	4.5	1.6	47142	47459	54	36	722	26.5	32.1	30.9	9.0	1.5	79184
62815	BONE GAP	21515	173	20.8	29.5	45.1	1.2	3.5	49784	48779	61	43	149	32.9	24.2	38.3	4.7	0.0	65000
62816	BONNIE	19990	513	25.0	31.0	40.0	3.9	0.2	45576	46156	50	31	431	27.1	31.6	34.1	6.7	0.5	80132
62817	BROUGHTON	14003	238	42.4	34.5	21.4	1.3	0.4	30857	31985	9	3	207	45.4	30.0	17.4	6.3	1.0	60938
62818	BROWNS	22941	149	17.4	32.9	42.3	3.4	4.0	49765	50968	60	43	133	31.6	22.6	36.1	9.0	0.8	85417
62819	BUCKNER	17592	238	38.7	38.2	20.2	0.4	2.5	29066	30789	7	2	194	57.7	24.7	9.8	7.7	0.0	40625
62820	BURNT PRAIRIE	19025	88	33.0	33.0	29.5	4.5	0.0	34063	35000	16	5	73	45.2	28.8	16.4	9.6	0.0	55833
62821	CARMI	19265	3365	36.7	31.0	27.5	3.6	1.3	33357	34186	14	4	2474	34.4	33.5	26.0	5.7	0.4	64292
	ILLINOIS	28587		18.2	22.2	39.3	12.1	8.2	60823	63631				6.3	10.0	30.9	40.6	12.3	185324
	UNITED STATES	27277		20.9	24.4	35.3	11.7	7.6	54719	56938				9.3	13.1	31.6	32.6	13.5	162279

ZIP CODE		FINANCIAL SERVICES				THE HOME						ENTERTAINMENT						PERSONAL			
						Home Improvements		Furnishings													
#	POST OFFICE NAME	Auto Loan	Home Loan	Invest-ments	Retire-ment Plans	Home Repair	Lawn & Garden	Comput-ers & Hard-ware-Personal	Major Appli-ances	TV, Radio, Sound Equip-ment	Furni-ture	Dine out/ Carry out	Sports Equip-ment	Fees & Tickets	Toys & Games	Travel	Cable TV	Apparel & Services	Auto Repairs	Health Insur-ance	Pets & Supplies
62548	MOUNT PULASKI	88	79	90	78	80	98	77	90	83	72	82	66	72	82	79	90	55	85	99	105
62549	MT ZION	103	113	99	117	111	114	102	107	101	102	102	84	108	104	107	102	71	103	107	126
62550	MOWEAQUA	91	87	84	90	88	96	85	92	87	81	86	70	82	88	86	90	59	88	95	107
62551	NIANTIC	92	97	78	100	91	100	94	92	94	91	94	73	96	96	93	96	65	93	100	112
62553	OCONEE	83	74	76	77	76	89	74	84	76	66	75	64	67	77	74	81	51	77	86	97
62554	OREANA	106	106	99	110	106	116	100	109	101	94	100	84	98	103	102	105	69	102	111	127
62555	OWANECO	99	87	92	90	89	106	87	99	90	78	88	76	78	91	87	95	60	92	103	116
62556	PALMER	114	78	124	78	82	119	86	108	90	71	89	88	64	89	86	99	58	100	113	132
62557	PANA	75	56	72	55	57	76	61	72	67	55	65	54	51	66	58	73	44	68	78	85
62558	PAWNEE	98	103	87	105	97	106	98	99	98	95	98	78	100	101	98	100	68	98	105	119
62560	RAYMOND	83	73	77	75	74	87	73	82	75	67	74	63	66	76	72	79	50	77	85	97
62561	RIVERTON	99	103	87	102	98	102	96	97	96	96	97	75	97	99	95	98	67	96	100	116
62563	ROCHESTER	113	137	129	140	136	132	118	124	116	122	117	94	133	117	130	116	83	119	122	143
62565	SHELBYVILLE	84	74	80	75	75	90	75	84	80	70	78	63	69	80	75	85	53	80	91	99
62567	STONINGTON	91	73	91	73	75	96	76	90	82	70	80	68	66	81	75	89	54	84	96	106
62568	TAYLORVILLE	79	72	76	72	72	85	73	80	77	69	76	60	69	77	73	82	52	77	87	94
62571	TOWER HILL	80	65	69	66	66	81	66	75	70	62	69	58	57	73	63	76	47	71	79	90
62572	WAGGONER	79	70	67	68	69	75	67	72	70	68	69	54	62	72	64	72	47	70	73	87
62573	WARRENSBURG	104	101	96	104	101	113	96	106	98	90	97	81	93	100	98	102	67	99	109	124
62601	ALEXANDER	97	67	107	67	70	103	74	92	77	60	76	76	54	76	74	84	50	86	98	114
62611	ARENZVILLE	96	70	101	71	73	101	76	92	79	63	78	75	59	78	75	85	51	86	97	112
62612	ASHLAND	96	77	92	76	78	96	78	90	81	73	81	70	66	82	76	86	54	85	93	109
62613	ATHENS	98	96	84	96	92	100	92	95	93	90	93	73	90	96	90	96	64	93	99	114
62615	AUBURN	93	93	76	95	88	98	92	91	93	88	93	72	91	95	89	96	64	92	99	110
62617	BATH	84	60	86	58	62	85	62	78	68	57	67	59	49	68	61	75	44	72	81	93
62618	BEARDSTOWN	73	60	63	60	59	74	65	70	69	59	67	54	57	69	61	74	46	69	76	84
62621	BLUFFS	96	67	99	67	69	99	73	89	77	62	76	73	55	77	71	84	50	84	94	110
62624	BROWNING	83	60	86	58	62	85	61	78	68	57	67	59	49	67	61	75	44	71	81	93
62625	CANTRALL	103	105	97	108	104	111	98	105	98	95	98	80	98	100	100	101	68	99	106	123
62626	CARLINVILLE	84	73	83	73	75	90	76	84	80	71	79	63	70	79	75	85	54	81	91	99
62627	CHANDLERVILLE	83	59	85	58	62	84	61	78	68	57	67	59	49	67	61	75	44	71	81	92
62628	CHAPIN	92	80	87	83	82	99	81	92	83	72	82	71	72	84	81	88	55	86	96	109
62629	CHATHAM	121	134	115	131	128	115	118	119	112	127	115	92	123	119	119	108	81	113	106	136
62630	CHESTERFIELD	102	79	100	79	82	105	80	98	87	74	85	74	68	87	80	94	57	90	101	115
62631	CONCORD	99	68	109	68	71	104	76	94	79	61	78	78	55	77	75	86	50	88	99	116
62633	EASTON	83	60	90	60	62	88	65	80	68	54	67	65	49	67	65	73	44	74	84	98
62634	ELKHART	113	86	117	88	89	120	91	110	95	77	93	88	73	94	91	102	62	102	115	132
62635	EMDEN	95	67	103	68	70	100	74	91	77	61	76	74	56	75	73	83	49	85	96	111
62638	FRANKLIN	101	81	100	83	84	108	84	99	87	73	86	78	71	88	84	94	57	92	104	118
62639	FREDERICK	99	80	96	81	83	104	81	97	86	74	85	73	70	87	80	93	57	89	100	114
62640	GIRARD	80	71	79	71	71	87	71	80	76	67	75	60	66	75	72	81	51	77	88	95
62642	GREENVIEW	98	88	91	90	85	105	91	96	92	82	92	77	84	93	89	96	62	94	104	117
62643	HARTSBURG	110	96	103	100	98	118	96	111	100	86	98	85	86	101	96	106	66	102	114	130
62644	HAVANA	82	64	79	64	66	85	67	80	73	61	71	60	57	73	66	79	48	75	86	94
62649	HETTICK	99	75	99	74	77	102	76	94	83	70	81	71	63	83	75	90	54	86	98	111
62650	JACKSONVILLE	80	75	74	76	74	83	78	79	81	75	80	60	75	80	76	84	55	80	86	94
62655	KILBOURNE	92	66	95	64	68	94	68	86	75	63	74	65	54	75	67	83	49	79	90	102
62656	LINCOLN	83	78	76	78	78	88	80	83	83	76	82	62	76	83	78	87	56	83	92	98
62661	LOAMI	100	88	87	86	87	96	85	93	88	86	88	69	78	91	82	91	60	89	93	111
62664	MASON CITY	85	74	83	74	74	92	75	84	80	69	78	65	69	79	75	85	53	81	93	100
62665	MEREDOSIA	87	63	87	61	65	89	66	82	73	60	71	62	53	72	64	80	47	76	87	97
62666	MIDDLETOWN	98	87	89	91	89	105	87	98	89	78	88	75	79	91	87	95	60	91	102	115
62667	MODESTO	101	81	100	83	84	107	84	99	87	73	86	78	71	87	84	93	57	92	103	118
62668	MURRAYVILLE	89	80	80	82	81	94	78	89	81	72	80	67	72	83	78	86	54	82	91	103
62670	NEW BERLIN	101	104	88	105	99	105	99	100	99	98	99	78	100	102	98	100	68	99	103	119
62671	NEW HOLLAND	101	91	92	95	93	109	91	103	93	82	92	78	83	95	90	99	63	95	106	119
62672	NILWOOD	94	74	97	72	76	98	73	90	80	70	79	67	64	80	74	87	53	83	94	106
62673	OAKFORD	96	66	104	66	69	101	73	91	76	60	75	74	54	75	72	83	49	85	96	111
62674	PALMYRA	80	58	81	57	60	83	62	77	68	55	66	59	50	67	61	74	44	71	82	91
62675	PETERSBURG	98	96	97	97	97	104	93	99	96	92	95	74	93	95	95	99	66	96	103	116
62677	PLEASANT PLAINS	111	128	117	132	127	125	113	118	110	115	111	91	123	112	121	110	78	113	115	138
62681	RUSHVILLE	79	57	80	56	59	82	62	76	68	55	66	58	49	67	60	75	44	71	82	90
62682	SAN JOSE	91	82	83	86	84	98	81	92	84	73	82	70	75	85	81	89	56	85	95	107
62683	SCOTTVILLE	82	57	90	57	59	87	63	78	65	51	65	65	46	64	63	71	42	73	83	96
62684	SHERMAN	114	138	126	139	136	129	118	123	115	123	116	95	132	117	129	114	83	118	119	142
62685	SHIPMAN	89	68	89	67	70	92	69	85	75	64	74	64	57	75	68	82	49	78	88	100
62688	TALLULA	106	99	106	100	98	113	93	106	96	91	96	81	89	97	96	101	65	99	107	125
62690	VIRDEN	80	70	74	70	69	85	72	79	76	66	75	60	66	76	70	81	51	77	86	94
62691	VIRGINIA	86	64	85	63	66	90	68	84	75	61	73	63	56	74	67	83	49	78	90	98
62692	WAVERLY	87	74	91	73	76	95	73	87	78	68	77	65	66	78	75	85	52	81	93	102
62693	WILLIAMSVILLE	87	103	94	103	100	104	89	94	91	90	91	71	100	92	98	93	64	92	99	110
62694	WINCHESTER	80	60	77	59	61	82	63	77	69	57	68	58	52	69	61	76	45	71	82	90
62701	SPRINGFIELD	40	28	33	32	29	34	46	37	49	42	49	29	40	43	40	51	34	45	49	47
62702	SPRINGFIELD	73	68	64	68	66	73	72	71	74	69	73	54	68	74	68	77	51	73	78	85
62703	SPRINGFIELD	70	63	56	64	60	67	69	65	72	67	71	51	66	72	64	74	49	69	72	80
62704	SPRINGFIELD	96	91	87	94	90	93	99	93	99	97	100	72	97	99	95	100	70	98	99	111
62707	SPRINGFIELD	98	104	92	103	101	100	95	98	94	98	95	74	98	97	96	95	66	95	96	115
62711	SPRINGFIELD	145	171	162	175	170	154	150	152	143	160	145	119	166	147	160	138	104	146	140	175
62712	SPRINGFIELD	135	158	156	163	160	147	141	144	135	149	137	110	156	137	152	132	98	139	135	166
62801	CENTRALIA	80	69	69	69	68	81	73	77	77	69	76	58	66	78	69	82	52	76	84	92
62803	HOYLETON	104	71	114	71	75	109	79	98	82	64	81	81	58	81	79	90	53	92	104	121
62806	ALBION	72	53	72	53	55	75	57	70	63	51	61	53	47	62	56	69	41	65	76	82
62807	ALMA	88	69	86	69	71	91	70	85	75	64	74	64	59	75	69	81	49	78	88	100
62808	ASHLEY	86	64	86	63	66	90	68	83	74	60	72	63	55	74	66	81	48	77	89	98
62809	BARNHILL	88	75	78	77	76	91	75	86	79	69	78	65	67	81	73	85	53	80	89	101
62810	BELLE RIVE	82	60	83	58	62	83	61	76	67	57	66	58	49	67	60	73	44	70	79	91
62812	BENTON	71	55	71	54	57	74	58	69	63	53	62	51	49	62	57	69	41	65	74	81
62814	BLUFORD	90	68	88	66	70	89	69	84	75	66	74	62	57	75	67	81	49	78	86	99
62815	BONE GAP	91	83	82	86	85	98	82	92	84	74	83	70	75	86	82	89	57	85	95	107
62816	BONNIE	84	62	85	60	64	85	63	79	69	59	68	59	51	69	62	76	45	73	82	94
62817	BROUGHTON	62	45	64	43	46	63	46	58	51	43	50	44	37	50	45	56	33	53	61	69
62818	BROWNS	88	76	82	79	78	94	76	88	79	68	78	67	68	80	76	84	53	81	91	103
62819	BUCKNER	64	46	64	45	48	67	50	62	56	45	54	46	40	55	49	62	36	58	68	73
62820	BURNT PRAIRIE	77	55	79	53	57	78	56	72	62	52	61	54	45	62	56	69	40	66	75	85
62821	CARMI	71	54	70	53	55	74	58	69	63	52	61	52	48	62	56	69	41	65	74	81
	ILLINOIS	106	108	105	108	107	106	109	106	108	107	109	83	110	108	108	108	77	108	107	125
	UNITED STATES	100	100	100	100	100	100	100	100	100	100	100	100	100	100	100	100	100	100	100	100

ZIP CODE			POPULATION			2000-2009 ANNUAL RATE		HOUSEHOLDS					FAMILIES		
#	POST OFFICE NAME	COUNTY FIPS CODE	2000	2009	2014	% Rate	State Centile	2000	2009	2014	% Annual Rate 2000-2009	2009 Average HH Size	2000	2009	% Annual Rate 2000-2009
62822	CHRISTOPHER	055	3079	2986	2958	-0.3	32	1390	1367	1359	-0.2	2.18	888	849	-0.5
62823	CISNE	191	1413	1338	1304	-0.6	13	576	551	539	-0.5	2.38	403	378	-0.7
62824	CLAY CITY	025	1973	1800	1713	-1.0	3	816	755	723	-0.8	2.38	568	511	-1.1
62827	CROSSVILLE	193	1331	1359	1351	0.2	61	567	591	591	0.4	2.30	394	401	0.2
62828	DAHLGREN	065	1512	1429	1377	-0.6	13	592	561	541	-0.6	2.54	447	418	-0.7
62829	DALE	065	549	506	484	-0.9	4	208	192	184	-0.9	2.62	163	149	-1.0
62830	DIX	081	1567	1677	1715	0.7	78	664	724	745	0.9	2.32	443	470	0.6
62831	DU BOIS	189	994	1017	1011	0.2	61	329	342	340	0.4	2.51	229	233	0.2
62832	DU QUOIN	145	9722	9327	9157	-0.4	25	3989	3913	3867	-0.2	2.28	2628	2523	-0.4
62833	ELLERY	047	158	151	147	-0.5	18	64	62	61	-0.3	2.44	49	47	-0.4
62835	ENFIELD	193	1199	1197	1183	0.0	50	493	500	497	0.2	2.31	345	343	-0.1
62836	EWING	055	699	752	772	0.8	79	255	274	282	0.8	2.74	193	204	0.6
62837	FAIRFIELD	191	8714	8577	8463	-0.2	38	3756	3762	3733	0.0	2.23	2461	2413	-0.2
62838	FARINA	051	979	924	897	-0.6	13	402	387	377	-0.4	2.34	271	255	-0.7
62839	FLORA	025	6880	6653	6452	-0.4	25	2848	2774	2694	-0.3	2.31	1841	1756	-0.5
62842	GEFF	191	697	667	653	-0.5	18	279	269	264	-0.4	2.48	205	195	-0.5
62843	GOLDEN GATE	191	696	652	634	-0.7	9	281	268	263	-0.5	2.43	215	202	-0.7
62844	GRAYVILLE	193	2343	2293	2242	-0.2	38	986	978	961	-0.1	2.28	665	646	-0.3
62846	INA	081	2687	2662	2658	-0.1	45	285	284	283	0.0	2.77	210	204	-0.3
62849	IUKA	121	2237	2299	2281	0.3	65	846	877	872	0.4	2.62	663	676	0.2
62850	JOHNSONVILLE	191	1251	1176	1143	-0.7	9	491	470	459	-0.5	2.50	380	358	-0.6
62851	KEENES	191	1062	1011	988	-0.5	18	388	374	366	-0.4	2.70	308	293	-0.5
62853	KELL	121	1005	1004	988	0.0	50	377	380	376	0.1	2.64	305	303	-0.1
62854	KINMUNDY	121	1818	1776	1732	-0.3	32	717	711	695	-0.1	2.50	524	510	-0.3
62855	LANCASTER	185	69	70	69	0.2	61	26	27	27	0.4	2.59	20	20	0.0
62858	LOUISVILLE	025	3836	3401	3219	-1.3	2	1489	1331	1261	-1.2	2.42	1073	945	-1.4
62859	MC LEANSBORO	065	4514	4439	4352	-0.2	38	1882	1835	1792	-0.3	2.32	1228	1172	-0.5
62860	MACEDONIA	065	1382	1339	1315	-0.3	32	516	502	492	-0.3	2.63	397	381	-0.4
62862	MILL SHOALS	193	367	356	347	-0.3	32	166	164	161	-0.1	2.16	115	111	-0.4
62863	MOUNT CARMEL	185	11612	11005	10622	-0.6	13	4704	4538	4404	-0.4	2.39	3214	3039	-0.6
62864	MOUNT VERNON	081	24596	24374	24270	-0.1	45	10221	10262	10263	0.0	2.32	6651	6526	-0.2
62865	MULKEYTOWN	055	1820	1972	2034	0.9	81	746	822	853	1.1	2.39	534	578	0.9
62866	NASON	081	11	11	11	0.0	50	6	6	6	0.0	1.83	4	4	0.0
62867	NEW HAVEN	059	622	598	585	-0.4	25	267	261	256	-0.2	2.29	179	172	-0.4
62868	NOBLE	159	1803	1740	1717	-0.4	25	701	691	687	-0.2	2.52	514	497	-0.4
62869	NORRIS CITY	193	2522	2558	2537	0.2	61	1059	1093	1090	0.3	2.34	735	742	0.1
62870	ODIN	121	2086	2095	2069	0.0	50	785	801	795	0.2	2.52	567	566	0.0
62871	OMAHA	059	715	685	669	-0.5	18	302	292	286	-0.4	2.33	205	193	-0.6
62872	OPDYKE	081	1062	1107	1124	0.4	69	359	380	387	0.6	2.88	294	306	0.4
62875	PATOKA	121	1039	1018	990	-0.2	38	432	428	418	-0.1	2.38	294	283	-0.4
62877	RICHVIEW	189	1018	1045	1038	0.3	65	389	405	403	0.4	2.58	291	298	0.3
62878	RINARD	191	362	342	334	-0.6	13	153	147	144	-0.4	2.33	114	108	-0.6
62880	SAINT PETER	051	702	674	658	-0.4	25	289	283	277	-0.2	2.38	208	200	-0.4
62881	SALEM	121	11777	11397	11102	-0.4	25	4676	4586	4479	-0.2	2.40	3185	3054	-0.5
62882	SANDOVAL	121	2738	2556	2451	-0.7	9	1059	1002	966	-0.6	2.55	789	732	-0.8
62883	SCHELLER	081	700	696	693	-0.1	45	270	273	273	0.1	2.53	190	188	-0.1
62884	SESSER	055	3035	3086	3112	0.2	61	1279	1321	1339	0.3	2.31	868	876	0.1
62885	SHOBONIER	051	220	212	207	-0.4	25	77	76	74	-0.1	2.79	54	52	-0.4
62886	SIMS	191	816	765	743	-0.7	9	316	301	293	-0.5	2.54	238	224	-0.7
62887	SPRINGERTON	065	511	487	471	-0.5	18	206	199	194	-0.4	2.42	149	141	-0.6
62888	TAMAROA	145	2203	2237	2230	0.2	61	871	908	913	0.5	2.11	633	646	0.2
62889	TEXICO	081	1098	1182	1210	0.8	79	426	467	480	1.0	2.53	324	349	0.8
62890	THOMPSONVILLE	055	2475	2567	2611	0.4	69	939	989	1013	0.6	2.60	731	759	0.4
62892	VERNON	121	318	308	299	-0.3	32	131	129	125	-0.2	2.39	98	95	-0.3
62893	WALNUT HILL	081	1118	1163	1168	0.4	69	425	449	454	0.6	2.59	340	354	0.4
62894	WALTONVILLE	081	1049	1037	1028	-0.1	45	407	408	406	0.0	2.54	298	293	-0.2
62895	WAYNE CITY	191	1468	1377	1337	-0.7	9	623	590	574	-0.6	2.33	433	402	-0.8
62896	WEST FRANKFORT	055	12915	12757	12771	-0.1	45	5464	5458	5482	0.0	2.30	3620	3545	-0.2
62897	WHITTINGTON	055	421	486	512	1.6	89	176	206	218	1.7	2.36	128	147	1.5
62898	WOODLAWN	081	2351	2525	2580	0.8	79	867	947	973	1.0	2.66	687	737	0.8
62899	XENIA	025	1229	1486	1519	2.1	92	490	600	616	2.2	2.47	371	443	1.9
62901	CARBONDALE	077	22287	25871	25683	1.6	89	10692	10674	10639	0.0	1.98	3915	3788	-0.4
62902	CARBONDALE	199	3882	3895	3897	0.0	50	1714	1741	1751	0.2	2.17	991	956	-0.4
62903	CARBONDALE	077	3403	3883	4100	1.4	88	1436	1603	1689	1.2	2.42	857	921	0.8
62905	ALTO PASS	181	687	691	683	0.1	56	281	289	287	0.3	2.38	211	212	0.1
62906	ANNA	181	7817	7592	7484	-0.3	32	3176	3092	3051	-0.3	2.23	1990	1889	-0.6
62907	AVA	077	2010	1991	1981	-0.1	45	781	796	799	0.2	2.50	573	569	-0.1
62908	BELKNAP	127	378	395	397	0.5	72	147	156	158	0.6	2.53	114	119	0.5
62910	BROOKPORT	127	2354	2395	2394	0.2	61	976	1014	1020	0.4	2.36	713	721	0.1
62912	BUNCOMBE	087	1005	1056	1066	0.5	72	390	414	419	0.6	2.54	301	314	0.5
62914	CAIRO	003	4050	3277	2965	-2.3	1	1756	1445	1313	-2.1	2.20	1013	805	-2.5
62916	CAMPBELL HILL	077	915	897	886	-0.2	38	343	343	342	0.0	2.62	259	253	-0.3
62917	CARRIER MILLS	165	2851	2971	3022	0.4	69	1152	1212	1236	0.6	2.37	788	812	0.3
62918	CARTERVILLE	199	9519	10084	10390	0.6	75	4010	4326	4484	0.8	2.32	2612	2747	0.5
62919	CAVE IN ROCK	069	1860	1736	1678	-0.7	9	727	702	681	-0.4	2.32	523	496	-0.6
62920	COBDEN	181	3032	3095	3095	0.2	61	1183	1230	1235	0.4	2.45	849	864	0.2
62922	CREAL SPRINGS	199	2832	3015	3111	0.7	78	1164	1266	1316	0.9	2.36	872	931	0.7
62923	CYPRESS	087	458	468	463	0.2	61	196	202	201	0.3	2.32	143	145	0.2
62924	DE SOTO	077	3332	3541	3625	0.7	78	1379	1501	1545	0.9	2.36	917	971	0.6
62926	DONGOLA	181	2356	2411	2409	0.2	61	947	981	983	0.4	2.43	681	691	0.2
62928	EDDYVILLE	151	721	704	689	-0.3	32	310	304	299	-0.2	2.05	225	216	-0.4
62930	ELDORADO	165	6726	6599	6563	-0.2	38	2846	2816	2809	-0.1	2.26	1813	1749	-0.4
62931	ELIZABETHTOWN	069	772	721	693	-0.7	9	366	350	340	-0.5	1.99	233	218	-0.7
62932	ELKVILLE	077	2052	1935	1894	-0.6	13	831	811	802	-0.3	2.39	598	568	-0.6
62933	ENERGY	199	1153	1189	1216	0.3	65	453	479	494	0.6	2.27	313	324	0.4
62934	EQUALITY	059	1283	1233	1206	-0.4	25	533	521	512	-0.2	2.36	384	369	-0.4
62935	GALATIA	165	2042	2119	2149	0.4	69	827	871	888	0.6	2.36	577	593	0.3
62938	GOLCONDA	151	2867	2771	2709	-0.4	25	1201	1176	1156	-0.2	2.26	808	774	-0.5
62939	GOREVILLE	087	2831	3167	3295	1.2	85	1162	1300	1360	1.2	2.37	869	957	1.0
62940	GORHAM	077	519	553	564	0.7	78	207	227	234	1.0	2.44	151	161	0.7
62941	GRAND CHAIN	153	817	820	809	0.0	50	319	324	321	0.2	2.53	224	223	0.0
62942	GRAND TOWER	077	735	747	749	0.2	61	308	324	329	0.5	2.31	216	221	0.2
62943	GRANTSBURG	087	3261	3058	3062	-0.7	9	246	261	264	0.6	4.83	185	193	0.5
62946	HARRISBURG	165	13880	13607	13536	-0.2	38	5678	5606	5589	-0.1	2.29	3696	3569	-0.4
62947	HEROD	151	1117	1098	1074	-0.2	38	361	355	349	-0.2	2.70	270	262	-0.3
	ILLINOIS					0.6					0.6	2.64			0.4
	UNITED STATES					1.0					1.1	2.59			0.9

ZIP CODE #	POST OFFICE NAME	RACE (%) White 2000	White 2009	Black 2000	Black 2009	Asian/Pacific 2000	Asian/Pacific 2009	% Hispanic Origin 2000	% Hispanic Origin 2009	2009 AGE DISTRIBUTION (%) 0-4	5-9	10-14	15-19	20-24	25-44	45-64	65-84	85+	18+	MEDIAN AGE 2009	% 2009 Males	% 2009 Females
62822	CHRISTOPHER	98.4	98.0	0.1	0.1	0.3	0.4	0.6	0.8	5.8	5.5	5.6	5.6	5.7	23.6	28.1	16.7	3.5	79.9	43.5	47.1	52.9
62823	CISNE	99.0	98.7	0.2	0.2	0.2	0.4	0.6	0.9	6.1	6.1	6.0	6.3	5.0	24.1	26.0	16.7	3.8	77.7	42.4	49.9	50.1
62824	CLAY CITY	98.8	98.6	0.1	0.1	0.3	0.3	0.3	0.4	5.6	5.8	6.1	6.6	5.1	25.2	29.2	14.2	2.3	78.4	42.1	49.4	50.6
62827	CROSSVILLE	98.3	98.2	0.0	0.0	0.0	0.0	0.9	1.3	5.1	5.6	5.9	6.0	4.1	22.4	32.3	15.9	2.7	79.7	45.5	50.8	49.2
62828	DAHLGREN	98.9	98.7	0.1	0.1	0.1	0.1	1.1	1.4	6.0	6.3	6.6	6.2	4.2	24.7	30.2	13.5	2.2	77.0	42.0	51.4	48.6
62829	DALE	98.5	98.2	0.4	0.4	0.2	0.2	0.9	1.2	4.9	5.3	5.9	6.1	4.2	23.5	33.0	15.4	1.6	80.2	45.0	49.2	50.8
62830	DIX	96.9	95.8	0.8	1.0	0.7	1.0	0.9	1.4	5.4	5.4	6.0	7.0	5.8	23.7	29.8	14.4	2.5	79.0	42.8	48.8	51.2
62831	DU BOIS	98.6	98.4	0.6	0.7	0.0	0.0	0.9	1.2	5.2	5.5	5.8	5.8	4.1	19.6	27.1	17.8	9.0	79.4	47.5	50.1	49.9
62832	DU QUOIN	92.0	90.0	5.7	7.0	0.4	0.5	1.2	1.7	5.8	5.8	5.9	7.0	6.4	23.5	27.2	15.0	3.5	78.5	41.2	49.5	50.5
62833	ELLERY	99.4	99.3	0.0	0.0	0.6	0.7	0.6	0.7	4.6	5.3	5.3	6.0	4.6	25.8	32.5	13.9	2.0	80.8	43.8	49.7	50.3
62835	ENFIELD	99.0	98.8	0.1	0.1	0.1	0.1	0.3	0.4	5.3	5.9	6.3	6.0	4.5	21.4	30.7	16.1	3.6	78.3	45.3	48.4	51.6
62836	EWING	99.3	98.8	0.0	0.0	0.0	0.0	1.0	1.7	7.3	7.8	7.7	6.9	5.5	23.9	26.7	12.0	2.1	72.6	38.6	48.1	51.9
62837	FAIRFIELD	98.7	98.2	0.1	0.1	0.5	0.7	0.5	0.8	5.9	5.9	6.0	5.6	5.1	23.6	27.2	16.6	4.0	78.8	43.3	47.7	52.3
62838	FARINA	99.2	99.0	0.0	0.0	0.0	0.0	0.1	0.2	3.8	5.2	7.0	7.9	4.3	21.4	30.3	15.4	4.7	78.5	45.2	47.9	52.1
62839	FLORA	97.9	97.3	0.1	0.2	1.0	1.4	0.7	1.0	5.9	5.8	6.0	6.5	5.4	24.4	26.5	15.5	4.0	78.3	41.9	47.2	52.8
62842	GEFF	98.4	98.1	0.6	0.6	0.1	0.3	1.3	1.6	7.8	7.8	7.9	6.9	6.0	23.2	26.5	11.8	1.9	72.0	37.3	49.8	50.2
62843	GOLDEN GATE	99.3	99.2	0.0	0.0	0.1	0.2	1.3	2.0	5.5	5.5	5.8	6.6	6.6	25.3	31.6	11.7	1.4	79.3	41.4	54.4	45.6
62844	GRAYVILLE	98.5	98.1	0.1	0.1	0.3	0.5	0.4	0.5	5.5	5.5	5.5	5.2	4.5	23.3	28.8	17.7	4.0	80.1	45.3	47.3	52.7
62846	INA	60.4	53.0	36.8	43.3	0.2	0.2	5.8	7.7	2.1	2.3	2.3	5.0	13.4	51.4	18.1	4.7	0.8	91.9	34.1	85.2	14.8
62849	IUKA	98.9	98.5	0.0	0.0	0.2	0.3	0.6	0.8	6.9	7.0	7.2	7.0	5.6	24.3	28.1	12.3	1.7	74.6	40.0	49.8	50.2
62850	JOHNSONVILLE	98.1	97.4	0.2	0.3	0.5	0.7	0.7	1.1	5.7	6.1	6.5	6.5	4.0	24.5	31.0	13.9	1.7	77.6	42.6	50.6	49.4
62851	KEENES	98.5	98.1	0.3	0.3	0.1	0.1	0.1	0.1	7.0	7.0	7.0	6.4	4.6	24.6	28.4	13.5	1.4	74.9	40.0	47.7	52.3
62853	KELL	99.4	99.3	0.0	0.0	0.1	0.1	0.3	0.5	6.7	7.2	7.2	6.7	4.8	22.7	30.6	12.5	1.7	74.9	41.2	49.8	50.2
62854	KINMUNDY	98.6	98.3	0.2	0.3	0.0	0.0	0.6	0.9	6.0	6.1	6.2	7.0	5.3	24.3	27.9	14.9	2.3	77.6	41.1	49.3	50.7
62855	LANCASTER	100.0	98.6	0.0	0.0	0.0	0.0	0.0	0.0	5.7	5.7	5.7	7.1	5.7	25.7	27.1	14.3	2.9	77.1	41.7	52.9	47.1
62858	LOUISVILLE	99.2	98.9	0.1	0.1	0.1	0.2	0.3	0.3	6.6	6.7	6.8	5.9	4.5	24.4	26.8	13.9	4.3	76.3	41.1	49.9	50.1
62859	MC LEANSBORO	98.3	97.8	0.6	0.7	0.2	0.3	0.5	0.7	6.2	6.2	6.3	6.1	4.9	23.2	26.1	16.6	4.6	77.7	42.8	47.4	52.6
62860	MACEDONIA	96.9	96.5	2.0	2.2	0.1	0.1	0.7	1.0	6.6	6.6	7.2	6.4	4.9	23.2	30.5	12.7	1.9	75.3	40.6	49.0	51.0
62862	MILL SHOALS	98.9	98.6	0.0	0.0	0.8	0.8	0.3	0.3	5.1	5.6	5.3	5.1	3.9	23.6	30.6	18.3	2.5	80.6	45.9	50.3	49.7
62863	MOUNT CARMEL	97.8	97.2	0.4	0.5	0.5	0.8	0.7	1.1	6.1	6.2	6.0	6.1	5.3	25.3	28.5	13.4	3.0	77.9	40.9	48.8	51.2
62864	MOUNT VERNON	88.8	86.6	8.4	9.7	0.7	0.9	1.2	1.7	6.2	6.1	6.3	6.6	5.7	23.7	27.8	14.5	3.2	77.4	41.3	48.0	52.0
62865	MULKEYTOWN	98.9	98.7	0.1	0.1	0.1	0.1	0.7	0.9	4.6	4.8	5.1	6.0	4.5	24.4	32.7	15.8	2.0	81.9	45.3	48.7	51.3
62866	NASON	100.0	100.0	0.0	0.0	0.0	0.0	0.0	0.0	0.0	0.0	0.0	0.0	0.0	27.3	72.7	0.0	0.0	100.0	51.3	54.5	45.5
62867	NEW HAVEN	99.2	99.0	0.2	0.2	0.0	0.0	0.6	1.0	5.4	5.7	6.2	5.9	4.0	23.6	28.6	17.7	3.0	79.3	44.4	50.0	50.0
62868	NOBLE	99.2	98.9	0.1	0.1	0.1	0.2	0.6	0.9	6.8	6.7	6.9	6.6	5.6	27.0	27.1	11.6	1.8	75.5	38.4	51.9	48.1
62869	NORRIS CITY	98.5	98.1	0.1	0.1	0.2	0.2	0.5	0.8	5.7	5.9	6.7	6.3	4.6	24.7	29.3	14.4	2.4	77.7	42.3	48.1	51.9
62870	ODIN	97.8	97.0	0.9	1.2	0.2	0.3	1.2	1.9	6.5	6.5	6.7	6.6	5.6	23.7	27.2	13.3	3.9	76.4	40.6	48.2	51.8
62871	OMAHA	99.3	99.0	0.0	0.0	0.3	0.4	0.0	0.0	5.0	4.7	5.8	9.3	3.9	25.1	26.3	16.6	3.2	79.1	42.4	50.5	49.5
62872	OPDYKE	98.5	98.0	0.4	0.5	0.0	0.1	0.8	1.2	7.2	7.2	7.0	6.7	6.1	25.1	27.0	11.7	1.9	74.4	37.8	49.1	50.9
62875	PATOKA	98.7	98.3	0.2	0.2	0.4	0.5	1.1	1.6	5.6	5.8	6.2	7.0	5.3	23.1	29.1	15.3	2.7	78.1	42.8	49.8	50.2
62877	RICHVIEW	97.6	97.5	0.4	0.5	0.4	0.4	0.8	0.9	6.4	6.6	6.9	7.4	5.7	26.1	29.6	9.7	1.6	75.6	38.1	51.7	48.3
62878	RINARD	100.0	100.0	0.0	0.0	0.0	0.0	1.4	2.0	5.8	5.8	6.1	6.4	5.8	23.7	29.8	14.6	1.8	78.1	42.3	50.3	49.7
62880	SAINT PETER	99.3	99.1	0.0	0.0	0.1	0.1	0.1	0.3	5.6	6.2	6.7	6.4	4.3	23.6	30.1	14.5	2.5	77.4	42.9	51.3	48.7
62881	SALEM	97.6	96.8	0.5	0.7	0.8	1.2	0.6	0.9	6.3	6.4	6.3	6.4	5.5	25.1	26.7	14.3	3.1	77.1	40.3	48.4	51.6
62882	SANDOVAL	98.3	97.7	0.4	0.5	0.3	0.4	0.7	1.1	6.6	7.4	7.7	7.6	5.4	23.9	28.6	11.2	1.5	73.6	37.6	49.6	50.4
62883	SCHELLER	99.0	98.6	0.1	0.3	0.1	0.1	0.4	0.6	6.6	6.8	6.8	5.9	4.6	25.3	27.9	13.9	2.3	76.1	40.4	50.7	49.3
62884	SESSER	98.6	98.3	0.1	0.1	0.1	0.1	0.9	1.2	6.9	6.9	6.8	6.1	4.6	24.7	26.5	15.0	2.5	75.5	40.4	47.9	52.1
62885	SHOBONIER	98.2	96.7	0.0	0.5	0.5	0.5	0.9	1.9	5.7	5.7	6.6	7.5	5.7	22.2	31.6	13.2	1.9	76.4	42.3	50.9	49.1
62886	SIMS	98.8	98.6	0.4	0.4	0.1	0.1	0.6	0.8	6.0	6.3	6.5	6.9	5.0	26.4	28.0	12.8	2.1	76.9	39.9	50.5	49.5
62887	SPRINGERTON	98.8	98.6	0.0	0.0	0.2	0.2	0.6	0.6	6.2	6.4	6.4	6.0	4.9	22.6	29.0	16.2	2.5	77.2	42.9	48.0	52.0
62888	TAMAROA	87.4	85.6	9.8	10.8	0.3	0.4	1.8	2.5	5.3	5.5	5.6	5.6	7.2	31.5	26.3	11.0	1.9	80.4	37.9	57.5	42.5
62889	TEXICO	98.8	98.1	0.3	0.4	0.1	0.2	0.5	0.8	5.3	5.7	6.2	6.9	5.4	23.9	32.1	12.8	1.7	78.6	42.6	51.3	48.7
62890	THOMPSONVILLE	98.4	97.5	0.2	0.5	0.0	0.2	0.6	1.1	6.2	6.5	7.0	5.9	4.8	26.3	29.7	12.0	1.6	76.7	40.1	49.9	50.1
62892	VERNON	98.1	97.1	0.0	0.0	1.3	1.9	1.3	1.3	5.5	6.2	6.5	5.2	4.5	24.7	32.5	13.3	1.6	78.2	42.5	53.9	46.1
62893	WALNUT HILL	98.0	97.2	0.6	0.9	0.2	0.3	0.2	0.3	5.4	5.8	6.4	7.2	5.2	24.8	31.7	12.1	1.4	78.0	41.8	49.7	50.3
62894	WALTONVILLE	99.1	98.8	0.1	0.2	0.1	0.2	0.5	0.9	6.2	6.8	7.1	7.0	4.2	26.1	28.4	12.2	1.9	75.5	40.1	50.1	49.9
62895	WAYNE CITY	99.0	98.8	0.1	0.1	0.1	0.1	0.5	0.6	7.0	6.2	6.3	6.5	6.4	22.6	25.6	15.5	3.8	76.3	40.6	47.2	52.8
62896	WEST FRANKFORT	98.5	97.7	0.2	0.3	0.3	0.6	0.7	1.0	5.8	5.9	6.0	5.9	5.6	24.1	27.9	15.7	3.1	78.8	42.3	48.4	51.6
62897	WHITTINGTON	100.0	99.6	0.0	0.0	0.0	0.0	0.2	0.6	5.6	6.0	6.0	6.0	5.1	22.2	29.6	17.1	2.5	78.8	44.4	49.8	50.2
62898	WOODLAWN	98.7	98.2	0.3	0.4	0.1	0.2	0.4	0.7	6.3	6.9	7.0	7.7	5.5	27.0	27.8	10.4	1.4	75.1	38.6	50.3	49.7
62899	XENIA	98.7	98.3	0.0	0.0	0.2	0.3	1.5	2.2	5.5	5.7	6.7	7.3	4.5	23.8	31.4	13.5	1.7	77.1	42.8	50.1	49.9
62901	CARBONDALE	69.2	64.6	21.4	22.8	5.4	7.2	3.2	5.4	4.6	4.0	3.7	8.9	27.6	26.8	15.5	7.3	1.7	85.3	25.6	52.3	47.7
62902	CARBONDALE	90.1	88.9	5.1	5.9	2.6	2.5	2.2	3.3	5.0	5.0	5.5	6.0	12.7	28.7	26.5	9.7	0.9	81.3	35.2	51.8	48.2
62903	CARBONDALE	75.4	67.6	11.5	14.4	8.3	12.0	3.3	4.7	9.0	7.1	5.1	5.8	17.0	30.6	19.0	5.8	0.6	76.3	27.5	51.7	48.3
62905	ALTO PASS	95.6	93.9	0.1	0.1	0.0	0.1	5.5	8.0	5.2	5.4	5.6	5.8	5.2	24.9	32.1	14.0	1.7	80.0	43.6	51.1	48.9
62906	ANNA	96.3	95.4	1.4	1.7	0.3	0.4	1.6	2.3	4.9	5.0	5.1	5.6	5.2	24.1	28.4	17.3	4.5	81.6	45.1	48.1	51.9
62907	AVA	98.5	97.6	0.5	0.6	0.1	0.5	0.6	1.2	6.5	6.8	6.6	6.2	5.3	24.0	30.3	12.5	1.8	76.8	40.8	51.0	49.0
62908	BELKNAP	97.1	95.7	0.8	1.5	0.3	0.3	0.5	0.8	6.3	7.1	7.1	6.1	3.8	25.8	28.4	13.7	1.8	75.4	41.2	50.9	49.1
62910	BROOKPORT	91.1	89.3	6.8	8.1	0.3	0.3	1.1	1.6	6.5	6.8	6.8	6.4	5.2	25.8	27.6	13.2	1.7	76.0	39.6	49.8	50.2
62912	BUNCOMBE	98.6	98.1	0.2	0.4	0.0	0.0	0.5	0.7	6.5	6.9	6.9	5.8	4.4	24.9	29.2	13.8	1.6	75.9	41.2	50.3	49.7
62914	CAIRO	37.9	31.9	59.8	65.3	0.7	0.9	0.7	0.8	7.7	8.1	6.9	6.9	6.0	20.8	26.3	13.6	3.8	73.0	39.0	45.2	54.8
62916	CAMPBELL HILL	98.4	97.9	1.1	1.4	0.2	0.2	0.2	0.3	6.4	6.8	6.9	6.2	5.4	23.9	30.4	12.2	1.9	76.3	40.2	50.3	49.7
62917	CARRIER MILLS	90.3	88.7	8.0	9.2	0.1	0.2	0.8	1.3	5.9	6.2	6.5	6.1	4.6	23.3	28.1	15.1	4.2	77.7	43.1	47.8	52.2
62918	CARTERVILLE	94.7	93.6	3.1	3.5	0.5	0.8	0.9	1.3	6.7	6.4	6.2	6.0	6.4	27.1	27.1	12.2	1.8	77.1	38.0	48.2	51.8
62919	CAVE IN ROCK	92.7	91.5	5.1	5.9	0.5	0.6	1.2	1.6	5.2	5.7	5.7	5.1	4.2	25.9	30.9	15.4	1.9	80.4	43.7	52.1	47.9
62920	COBDEN	94.0	92.0	0.7	0.8	0.2	0.4	7.1	9.9	5.2	5.3	5.7	6.2	5.2	23.3	31.4	15.5	2.2	79.9	44.3	49.1	50.9
62922	CREAL SPRINGS	98.1	97.3	0.3	0.5	0.1	0.2	1.3	1.8	4.8	5.0	5.4	5.6	4.2	22.5	32.0	18.4	2.1	81.3	46.6	50.0	50.0
62923	CYPRESS	96.5	94.7	1.5	2.6	0.0	0.0	0.2	0.4	7.3	7.5	7.7	6.0	3.6	26.3	26.7	13.0	1.9	73.9	40.4	50.9	49.1
62924	DE SOTO	97.0	96.0	1.0	1.3	0.5	0.8	1.4	2.1	6.8	6.8	6.6	6.0	5.4	28.8	26.8	11.2	1.6	75.8	37.6	48.6	51.4
62926	DONGOLA	93.5	92.5	3.9	4.3	0.3	0.3	0.5	0.7	6.6	6.7	6.7	6.9	5.2	23.9	28.3	13.6	2.1	75.8	40.2	50.0	50.0
62928	EDDYVILLE	90.4	88.6	6.4	7.4	0.4	0.4	1.3	1.7	4.0	4.1	4.1	13.1	7.8	20.2	30.8	14.2	1.7	81.1	42.3	54.4	45.6
62930	ELDORADO	98.2	97.8	0.3	0.4	0.1	0.1	0.9	1.3	5.3	5.7	5.8	6.5	5.4	21.9	27.6	17.8	4.1	79.2	44.6	47.3	52.7
62931	ELIZABETHTOWN	95.7	94.9	3.6	4.3	0.0	0.0	0.8	1.0	4.3	4.0	4.2	6.1	4.2	21.4	33.8	18.4	3.6	83.8	49.2	50.6	49.4
62932	ELKVILLE	96.4	95.6	1.6	2.0	0.0	0.1	1.1	1.7	6.4	6.4	6.4	6.5	4.9	26.2	26.3	14.6	2.3	76.9	40.1	49.0	51.0
62933	ENERGY	97.4	96.6	0.9	1.0	0.8	1.1	1.0	1.3	5.6	5.1	5.0	4.7	5.4	23.5	26.9	19.9	3.8	81.4	45.5	46.4	53.6
62934	EQUALITY	98.8	98.6	0.2	0.2	0.0	0.0	0.9	1.2	5.3	5.4	5.8	6.4	4.9	24.1	29.4	16.3	2.6	79.7	43.7	49.8	50.2
62935	GALATIA	98.7	98.4	0.1	0.1	0.0	0.1	0.5	0.7	6.4	6.7	6.5	5.6	4.3	23.5	27.0	15.9	4.0	77.0	42.4	46.4	53.6
62938	GOLCONDA	96.0	95.2	1.4	1.6	0.2	0.2	0.6	0.8	5.2	5.4	5.7	6.5	5.2	22.1	28.7	17.4	3.9	79.9	45.0	49.4	50.6
62939	GOREVILLE	97.8	96.7	0.8	1.3	0.1	0.3	1.1	1.9	5.4	5.7	5.9	5.7	4.2	23.7	29.7	17.9	1.8	79.5	44.5	51.5	48.5
62940	GORHAM	98.3	94.9	0.2	0.2	0.0	0.0	0.4	3.8	6.3	6.3	6.3	6.1	6.0	26.2	27.1	13.2	2.4	77.2	39.8	50.5	49.5
62941	GRAND CHAIN	88.7	86.0	9.6	11.7	0.1	0.1	1.2	1.7	6.7	6.6	6.7	6.7	5.9	22.7	27.7	14.5	2.6	75.9	40.6	48.5	51.5
62942	GRAND TOWER	97.4	96.9	0.1	0.1	0.0	0.0	0.7	0.9	6.2	6.2	6.0	6.2	6.6	26.1	29.0	12.6	1.2	78.2	39.5	47.8	52.2
62943	GRANTSBURG	54.2	43.3	42.6	52.9	0.2	0.1	6.2	7.8	2.2	2.4	2.5	6.0	14.7	47.1	18.1	6.5	0.7	91.3	33.2	78.5	21.5
62946	HARRISBURG	92.0	90.3	5.8	6.8	0.3	0.5	1.1	1.6	5.8	5.8	5.8	9.3	5.5	22.4	27.3	15.3	2.9	76.7	41.2	49.6	50.4
62947	HEROD	89.2	87.5	7.2	8.2	0.7	0.7	1.3	1.7	4.1	4.5	4.4	13.8	8.0	19.6	30.6	13.8	1.4	79.9	41.5	53.7	46.3
	ILLINOIS	73.5	70.6	15.1	15.3	3.4	4.4	12.3	15.7	7.1	6.9	6.8	7.1	6.9	27.5	25.4	10.3	1.9	75.0	36.1	49.1	50.9
	UNITED STATES	75.1	72.0	12.3	12.7	3.8	4.6	12.5	15.7	6.8	6.7	6.6	7.1	6.9	27.0	26.0	10.9	1.9	75.7	36.9	49.2	50.8

#	POST OFFICE NAME	2009 Per Capita Income	2009 HH Income Base	2009 Household Income Distribution (%): Less than $25,000	$25,000 to $49,999	$50,000 to $99,999	$100,000 to $149,999	$150,000 or More	Median Household Income: 2009	2014	2009 National Centile	2009 State Centile	2009 Home Value Base	2009 Home Value Distribution (%): Less than $50,000	$50,000 to $89,999	$90,000 to $174,999	$175,000 to $399,999	$400,000 or More	2009 Median Home Value
62822	CHRISTOPHER	17837	1367	40.0	30.4	26.0	2.5	1.0	29360	31469	7	2	1013	40.7	35.6	18.7	5.0	0.0	57560
62823	CISNE	16991	551	36.7	31.8	28.9	2.0	0.7	32810	33745	13	4	452	35.8	33.0	25.2	5.1	0.9	62500
62824	CLAY CITY	17561	755	34.4	32.2	30.3	2.0	1.1	35587	37285	19	7	609	39.2	31.9	22.5	4.9	1.5	62813
62827	CROSSVILLE	20225	591	29.6	33.3	32.3	3.0	1.7	40249	41685	34	17	472	38.8	34.1	20.3	6.8	0.0	61500
62828	DAHLGREN	20607	561	23.4	38.5	29.8	4.3	4.1	42775	45039	42	23	489	36.6	22.9	29.2	9.6	1.6	71500
62829	DALE	18283	192	22.4	34.4	39.6	3.6	0.0	43215	45827	43	24	169	36.1	20.7	33.1	10.1	0.0	75500
62830	DIX	19456	724	38.4	22.7	33.1	4.8	1.0	38149	40825	27	12	527	20.1	22.6	41.6	13.7	2.1	102196
62831	DU BOIS	19910	342	25.1	28.4	41.8	2.6	2.0	47242	48844	55	36	304	24.0	33.6	28.3	12.8	1.3	82069
62832	DU QUOIN	19369	3913	33.1	32.5	28.9	4.4	1.0	37463	38476	25	10	2941	26.6	36.8	31.0	5.0	0.5	74845
62833	ELLERY	22972	62	14.5	33.9	43.5	3.2	4.8	50884	53105	63	46	56	30.4	23.2	37.5	8.9	0.0	86000
62835	ENFIELD	20796	500	30.0	38.6	23.8	4.2	3.4	37074	37837	24	10	425	36.0	36.5	18.6	7.8	1.2	67308
62836	EWING	16248	274	34.7	25.2	35.0	4.0	1.1	38645	41567	29	13	230	21.7	28.3	37.0	12.2	0.9	90000
62837	FAIRFIELD	19792	3762	33.9	31.4	29.5	3.3	1.8	35161	36420	18	7	2817	32.0	33.4	28.6	5.4	0.6	69533
62838	FARINA	18906	387	30.2	33.6	30.2	5.4	0.5	37152	38567	24	10	335	40.0	29.0	29.3	1.8	0.0	62115
62839	FLORA	19178	2774	33.3	35.3	26.5	3.2	1.8	34541	35631	17	6	2057	29.3	35.2	28.6	6.1	0.8	71690
62842	GEFF	16626	269	28.6	41.6	25.3	3.7	0.7	33716	34195	15	5	225	46.2	28.4	18.2	6.2	0.9	54250
62843	GOLDEN GATE	17535	268	28.0	40.3	27.2	3.7	0.7	40179	41067	33	16	226	40.7	23.9	26.5	6.6	2.2	62308
62844	GRAYVILLE	19098	978	33.5	34.5	26.8	3.6	1.6	36330	37478	22	8	755	39.2	32.3	23.3	4.6	0.5	57913
62846	INA	16527	284	34.9	28.9	32.0	3.5	0.7	36654	40997	23	9	223	29.1	33.2	26.9	9.4	1.3	72333
62849	IUKA	18676	877	25.0	32.7	37.3	4.1	0.9	41538	46479	38	20	756	27.0	31.3	29.9	10.3	1.5	81000
62850	JOHNSONVILLE	18394	470	22.8	35.3	37.9	3.4	0.6	42257	43950	40	22	420	31.0	37.9	23.6	6.7	1.0	72245
62851	KEENES	16094	374	32.6	27.0	38.0	1.9	0.5	41084	43845	36	19	323	41.5	22.6	26.9	5.9	3.1	62647
62853	KELL	22552	380	16.8	26.8	47.4	6.6	2.4	55218	58698	72	56	336	19.6	21.7	42.0	14.3	2.4	101415
62854	KINMUNDY	18918	711	26.6	32.3	36.3	3.9	0.8	40109	45605	33	16	574	35.2	30.1	27.0	7.5	0.2	63902
62855	LANCASTER	23053	27	18.5	25.9	51.9	0.0	3.7	51552	51394	65	48	24	20.8	41.7	33.3	0.0	4.2	70000
62858	LOUISVILLE	17868	1331	29.8	36.7	28.5	4.1	0.8	37378	39584	25	10	1118	35.2	29.8	28.2	6.4	0.4	69759
62859	MC LEANSBORO	17880	1835	40.3	28.9	25.3	3.9	1.6	30815	32804	9	3	1382	38.4	27.9	28.1	5.5	0.1	65124
62860	MACEDONIA	17706	502	25.5	32.1	38.0	4.0	0.4	42786	45705	42	23	436	29.1	27.5	33.9	9.2	0.2	77826
62862	MILL SHOALS	19253	164	33.5	32.9	29.3	3.7	0.6	33981	34777	15	5	136	46.3	29.4	14.7	9.6	0.0	54167
62863	MOUNT CARMEL	20896	4538	28.0	29.4	35.6	4.7	2.3	42651	45285	41	23	3347	29.2	32.4	28.8	8.6	1.0	70110
62864	MOUNT VERNON	20963	10262	32.0	30.2	30.5	4.9	2.4	38286	40814	28	12	7081	25.9	23.8	36.4	12.0	1.9	90440
62865	MULKEYTOWN	19591	822	31.3	29.8	32.5	3.4	3.0	37512	40276	25	11	700	30.1	28.0	31.4	8.6	1.9	82692
62866	NASON	18864	6	50.0	16.7	33.3	0.0	0.0	25000	35000	3	1	5	0.0	0.0	100.0	0.0	0.0	112500
62867	NEW HAVEN	20104	261	33.3	31.8	30.7	1.9	2.3	36474	39320	22	9	215	35.3	32.1	27.4	5.1	0.0	66136
62868	NOBLE	18632	691	29.2	30.8	34.3	4.8	0.9	40532	41796	34	17	554	27.4	30.3	32.9	7.9	1.4	78378
62869	NORRIS CITY	18167	1093	37.1	28.1	29.7	4.1	0.9	32966	34246	13	4	897	39.2	29.7	25.3	5.2	0.6	62315
62870	ODIN	20281	801	26.6	30.2	36.8	4.6	1.7	42945	47006	42	23	655	28.7	33.7	29.0	6.4	2.1	71170
62871	OMAHA	17418	292	37.0	32.9	24.7	4.5	1.0	32370	35000	12	4	239	39.7	19.7	27.6	13.0	0.0	78438
62872	OPDYKE	17912	380	20.0	35.0	38.2	5.3	1.6	47106	47124	54	35	341	20.8	29.6	39.3	8.5	1.8	89444
62875	PATOKA	18811	428	32.5	31.1	32.0	3.7	0.7	37169	39163	24	10	353	29.7	32.3	30.0	7.6	0.3	74259
62877	RICHVIEW	19388	405	21.5	35.3	39.0	2.7	1.5	45369	47241	49	30	316	24.7	30.1	40.8	4.4	0.0	84444
62878	RINARD	18357	147	29.3	34.0	32.7	4.1	0.0	37374	37877	25	10	129	33.3	30.2	28.7	7.0	0.8	71500
62880	SAINT PETER	18639	283	31.1	35.3	26.5	4.2	2.8	36762	38369	23	9	244	29.9	31.1	33.2	4.5	1.2	76316
62881	SALEM	21312	4586	26.6	29.5	36.4	5.3	2.2	45215	47725	49	30	3403	19.8	31.1	39.9	8.5	0.8	89056
62882	SANDOVAL	18564	1002	32.3	26.3	36.9	3.1	1.3	40870	46308	36	18	776	40.5	29.1	25.6	4.8	0.0	60000
62883	SCHELLER	18159	273	34.1	28.6	31.1	4.0	2.2	40661	43057	35	18	224	22.3	20.5	44.6	9.8	2.7	96667
62884	SESSER	18653	1321	34.2	33.5	26.6	3.9	1.7	33073	34669	13	4	1064	28.8	34.1	32.7	4.4	0.0	72527
62885	SHOBONIER	16397	76	31.6	30.3	34.2	2.6	1.3	40000	43643	33	16	62	21.0	24.2	45.2	9.7	0.0	94286
62886	SIMS	16337	301	31.9	34.9	29.9	2.7	0.7	33802	34676	15	5	250	38.4	31.6	20.8	6.8	2.4	64211
62887	SPRINGERTON	21283	199	29.1	35.2	27.6	4.0	4.0	37550	40000	25	11	167	33.5	33.5	29.3	3.6	0.0	75000
62888	TAMAROA	21104	908	28.0	31.9	35.6	3.9	0.7	42113	44413	40	21	764	31.0	29.8	30.4	7.9	0.9	73778
62889	TEXICO	22222	467	22.1	27.4	42.4	5.8	2.4	50345	50844	62	44	404	19.8	26.2	37.9	14.6	1.5	99412
62890	THOMPSONVILLE	18879	989	27.5	28.6	38.9	3.5	1.4	44653	46843	47	28	834	20.0	25.5	42.2	10.8	1.4	96727
62892	VERNON	23489	129	21.7	27.1	44.2	5.4	1.6	51649	57603	65	48	113	29.2	26.5	27.4	15.9	0.9	81875
62893	WALNUT HILL	26947	449	14.3	24.3	49.4	7.3	4.7	57671	58792	75	60	400	13.3	25.3	43.0	16.5	2.0	106250
62894	WALTONVILLE	18934	408	25.2	31.1	37.3	5.1	1.2	45721	46129	50	31	331	23.0	26.6	37.2	12.4	0.9	90600
62895	WAYNE CITY	17497	590	35.8	29.7	31.2	2.9	0.5	34325	34891	16	5	453	40.4	30.7	24.1	4.4	0.4	63542
62896	WEST FRANKFORT	18507	5458	35.6	30.1	29.3	3.6	1.4	35579	37270	19	7	4091	28.2	34.9	28.8	6.8	1.3	73812
62897	WHITTINGTON	24902	206	24.3	27.2	37.4	6.3	4.9	48742	51465	58	40	167	9.6	22.2	38.9	26.3	3.0	128804
62898	WOODLAWN	21642	947	19.6	31.2	41.1	5.9	2.2	49478	49325	60	42	806	16.1	22.6	41.8	18.9	0.6	106000
62899	XENIA	20799	600	21.7	40.7	32.0	3.0	2.7	41574	44644	38	20	514	21.0	35.0	32.5	10.7	0.8	81389
62901	CARBONDALE	17861	10674	54.0	20.7	20.0	3.5	1.9	22033	23211	2	1	3540	15.9	20.7	45.1	16.5	1.9	110749
62902	CARBONDALE	25829	1741	30.9	24.5	33.3	7.1	4.2	44206	47309	46	27	1144	29.5	9.2	33.7	24.5	3.2	116489
62903	CARBONDALE	18231	1603	47.7	22.7	21.1	4.2	4.2	26361	27614	4	2	701	30.1	12.7	27.8	26.7	2.7	112326
62905	ALTO PASS	21219	289	26.6	32.5	35.3	3.5	2.1	43143	44844	43	24	240	26.7	19.6	34.6	16.7	2.5	98182
62906	ANNA	19394	3092	37.9	28.4	27.8	4.1	1.8	33382	34375	14	4	2093	18.7	29.2	36.1	14.7	1.2	92742
62907	AVA	19762	796	28.1	29.9	35.8	3.8	2.4	43885	47053	45	26	657	22.2	27.9	31.1	17.0	1.8	89861
62908	BELKNAP	19210	156	22.4	37.8	35.3	3.2	1.3	42852	44444	42	23	135	34.1	17.8	35.6	10.4	2.2	83750
62910	BROOKPORT	17783	1014	35.2	32.1	28.4	3.3	1.0	35769	37053	20	7	837	25.3	31.1	32.5	9.9	1.2	79052
62912	BUNCOMBE	18220	414	25.8	36.0	33.8	3.9	0.5	41843	42687	39	21	359	27.3	22.6	35.4	11.7	3.1	90227
62914	CAIRO	17835	1445	50.4	28.7	16.7	2.1	2.2	24695	26766	3	1	828	74.8	19.1	3.5	1.0	1.7	35476
62916	CAMPBELL HILL	19123	343	20.7	32.7	42.0	4.7	0.0	46990	49569	54	35	297	27.3	29.6	24.9	15.2	3.0	79375
62917	CARRIER MILLS	18053	1212	31.7	36.1	26.9	4.4	1.0	35257	36086	19	7	970	35.8	27.6	28.7	7.3	0.6	66709
62918	CARTERVILLE	21045	4326	31.9	25.6	34.5	6.0	1.9	41547	45257	38	20	3007	18.5	27.0	38.6	15.0	0.9	97036
62919	CAVE IN ROCK	17720	702	36.2	32.6	27.2	3.4	0.6	31860	32626	11	3	572	29.9	35.3	28.3	6.5	0.0	70000
62920	COBDEN	19784	1230	27.9	32.7	32.8	4.7	1.9	40411	41384	34	17	1007	23.3	27.2	32.7	14.8	2.0	89267
62922	CREAL SPRINGS	22006	1266	29.9	31.5	31.1	4.6	2.8	38499	41072	28	13	1099	24.7	19.9	33.9	17.8	3.5	99750
62923	CYPRESS	19027	202	29.7	34.7	33.2	1.5	1.0	39596	40170	31	15	174	46.6	23.6	20.7	7.5	1.7	55000
62924	DE SOTO	18924	1501	32.1	30.2	33.2	3.5	0.9	38882	42170	29	14	1060	32.8	35.3	27.2	4.2	0.6	69571
62926	DONGOLA	18236	981	35.2	31.6	27.3	4.2	1.7	35376	36690	19	7	774	26.5	29.7	30.4	11.8	1.7	78571
62928	EDDYVILLE	21484	304	28.0	37.8	29.9	3.0	1.3	36579	37870	22	9	264	21.2	25.0	37.9	12.9	3.0	94545
62930	ELDORADO	17190	2816	38.9	30.6	27.0	3.0	0.5	29587	31841	7	2	2118	39.9	33.1	22.6	3.9	0.4	57918
62931	ELIZABETHTOWN	19725	350	42.0	28.0	26.3	3.1	0.6	30572	31157	9	3	269	35.7	29.0	27.9	7.4	0.0	67500
62932	ELKVILLE	17377	811	30.8	37.0	28.5	2.5	1.2	34214	35611	16	5	619	38.1	28.9	26.2	6.5	0.3	61182
62933	ENERGY	24905	479	24.4	25.1	40.9	6.5	3.1	50474	52007	62	45	336	6.0	16.4	52.7	21.7	3.3	130909
62934	EQUALITY	17280	521	38.6	31.5	26.7	1.9	1.3	31659	32666	11	3	425	39.1	27.3	25.6	5.2	2.8	66042
62935	GALATIA	17570	871	36.7	29.6	28.9	3.8	0.9	33685	35818	15	5	683	25.3	37.9	28.3	8.3	0.1	73551
62938	GOLCONDA	18528	1176	36.1	32.1	27.5	2.6	1.6	33242	34504	14	4	926	30.8	28.1	30.0	8.3	2.8	75806
62939	GOREVILLE	22491	1300	29.1	28.0	35.2	5.6	2.2	44650	45324	47	28	1089	14.2	24.7	38.6	18.4	4.1	112500
62940	GORHAM	18165	227	33.5	29.1	31.7	4.4	1.3	36746	38537	23	9	183	41.5	27.9	26.2	4.4	0.0	58611
62941	GRAND CHAIN	16475	324	38.6	30.6	26.5	4.0	0.3	34686	36148	17	6	257	38.1	36.2	21.8	3.1	0.8	59242
62942	GRAND TOWER	18093	324	31.2	37.0	27.5	3.7	0.6	35690	37063	20	7	251	52.6	29.5	17.9	0.0	0.0	47500
62943	GRANTSBURG	13809	261	27.2	32.2	34.5	4.6	1.5	42538	43204	41	22	233	19.7	21.5	44.6	13.3	0.9	102679
62946	HARRISBURG	19785	5606	34.7	31.6	27.5	3.9	2.4	35678	37510	20	7	4138	33.8	28.3	29.6	6.8	1.5	71894
62947	HEROD	17061	355	24.8	40.6	28.5	4.8	1.4	36666	37822	23	9	315	25.7	24.8	34.9	12.4	2.2	89118
	ILLINOIS	28587		18.2	22.2	39.3	12.1	8.2	60823	63631				6.3	10.0	30.9	40.6	12.3	185324
	UNITED STATES	27277		20.9	24.4	35.3	11.7	7.6	54719	56938				9.3	13.1	31.6	32.6	13.5	162279

ZIP CODE #	POST OFFICE NAME	FINANCIAL SERVICES: Auto Loan	Home Loan	Invest-ments	Retire-ment Plans	THE HOME: Home Improvements: Home Repair	Lawn & Garden	Furnishings: Comput-ers & Hard-ware-Personal	Major Appli-ances	TV, Radio, Sound Equip-ment	Furni-ture	ENTERTAINMENT: Dine out/ Carry out	Sports Equip-ment	Fees & Tickets	Toys & Games	Travel	Cable TV	PERSONAL: Apparel & Services	Auto Repairs	Health Insur-ance	Pets & Supplies
62822	CHRISTOPHER	64	47	63	46	49	66	52	62	58	47	56	46	43	57	50	63	38	59	68	73
62823	CISNE	69	51	67	49	52	71	54	66	60	49	58	49	44	59	52	66	39	61	71	78
62824	CLAY CITY	75	54	74	52	55	75	55	69	61	52	60	52	44	61	54	67	40	64	72	82
62827	CROSSVILLE	83	58	88	57	61	86	62	78	67	54	66	62	48	66	62	73	43	72	82	95
62828	DAHLGREN	94	66	100	65	68	97	70	88	75	61	74	70	54	74	70	83	49	82	93	107
62829	DALE	86	61	88	59	64	87	63	80	70	59	69	60	50	69	62	77	45	73	83	95
62830	DIX	75	59	70	58	60	75	61	71	66	58	65	53	52	66	59	71	43	67	75	84
62831	DU BOIS	92	65	95	64	68	94	68	86	75	62	73	66	54	74	67	82	48	79	90	103
62832	DU QUOIN	73	56	70	55	57	75	60	70	66	55	64	52	51	65	58	72	43	67	76	83
62833	ELLERY	88	78	82	80	79	95	78	89	80	69	79	68	70	81	78	85	53	82	92	104
62835	ENFIELD	85	61	86	59	63	87	64	80	71	58	69	60	51	70	63	78	46	74	85	95
62836	EWING	80	57	82	55	59	81	59	74	65	54	64	56	47	65	58	71	42	68	77	89
62837	FAIRFIELD	74	56	72	55	57	77	59	72	65	54	63	54	49	65	57	72	42	67	78	85
62838	FARINA	79	57	81	55	59	81	59	74	64	54	63	56	47	64	58	71	42	68	77	88
62839	FLORA	74	56	72	55	58	76	60	71	66	55	64	53	50	65	58	71	43	67	77	84
62842	GEFF	74	53	61	52	53	71	56	65	62	54	60	50	45	64	51	67	41	61	68	79
62843	GOLDEN GATE	74	57	63	56	57	73	58	67	63	55	62	51	48	65	54	68	42	63	70	81
62844	GRAYVILLE	75	53	77	52	55	78	58	72	64	51	62	55	46	63	57	70	41	67	78	86
62846	INA	80	58	82	56	60	82	59	75	66	55	64	56	47	65	58	72	42	69	78	89
62849	IUKA	84	65	75	65	66	84	66	78	72	62	70	59	56	74	64	78	47	73	81	93
62850	JOHNSONVILLE	82	59	82	57	61	83	61	76	67	56	66	58	48	67	59	74	44	70	80	91
62851	KEENES	78	55	81	54	57	80	58	73	63	51	62	57	45	62	57	69	41	67	76	88
62853	KELL	92	84	83	88	86	99	83	94	86	75	84	71	76	87	83	90	57	86	96	109
62854	KINMUNDY	77	61	75	61	63	81	64	76	69	57	67	57	54	69	63	75	45	71	81	89
62855	LANCASTER	93	84	83	88	86	99	83	94	86	75	84	71	77	87	83	91	57	87	97	109
62858	LOUISVILLE	74	56	68	56	57	75	59	70	64	54	62	53	49	65	56	70	42	65	74	82
62859	MC LEANSBORO	71	51	72	50	53	74	55	69	61	50	60	51	44	60	54	68	40	64	74	81
62860	MACEDONIA	83	60	85	58	62	84	61	78	68	57	67	58	49	67	60	75	44	71	81	92
62862	MILL SHOALS	75	53	77	52	55	76	55	70	61	51	60	52	44	60	54	67	39	64	73	83
62863	MOUNT CARMEL	79	67	71	68	67	80	70	76	73	65	72	58	63	74	67	77	49	74	81	90
62864	MOUNT VERNON	76	63	70	63	64	77	67	73	72	64	70	54	61	71	65	77	48	72	80	87
62865	MULKEYTOWN	82	59	84	57	61	84	62	77	69	57	67	58	50	68	61	75	45	72	81	92
62866	NASON	62	44	63	43	46	63	45	58	50	42	49	43	36	50	45	55	33	53	60	69
62867	NEW HAVEN	78	56	79	55	59	82	61	76	68	55	66	57	49	67	59	75	44	70	82	89
62868	NOBLE	81	62	68	62	63	80	64	74	69	61	68	56	54	72	60	75	46	69	77	88
62869	NORRIS CITY	74	53	75	52	55	76	56	70	62	51	61	53	45	62	55	69	40	65	75	83
62870	ODIN	88	66	81	65	67	89	69	83	76	64	74	62	57	77	66	83	50	77	88	98
62871	OMAHA	73	50	79	50	52	76	55	69	58	45	57	57	41	57	55	63	37	64	73	85
62872	OPDYKE	85	74	73	71	73	81	71	78	75	72	74	57	65	77	68	78	50	75	79	93
62875	PATOKA	74	57	73	56	58	78	60	73	66	54	64	54	50	65	59	72	43	68	78	85
62877	RICHVIEW	86	69	73	67	68	82	68	77	73	68	73	58	59	76	64	78	49	73	79	93
62878	RINARD	77	55	65	54	55	73	57	67	64	56	62	52	46	66	53	70	42	64	71	82
62880	SAINT PETER	79	55	86	55	57	83	61	75	63	50	63	62	45	62	60	69	41	70	79	92
62881	SALEM	78	70	73	70	70	83	71	78	75	67	74	58	66	75	69	80	50	75	84	91
62882	SANDOVAL	84	60	77	58	60	83	63	76	70	59	69	58	50	72	59	77	46	71	81	92
62883	SCHELLER	82	59	81	57	61	82	61	76	67	57	66	57	49	68	59	74	44	70	79	91
62884	SESSER	75	54	72	52	55	76	57	70	64	53	62	53	46	64	55	70	42	66	75	83
62885	SHOBONIER	80	59	81	58	61	82	61	76	66	56	65	57	50	66	60	73	43	70	79	90
62886	SIMS	75	53	69	52	53	74	56	67	61	51	60	53	44	62	53	66	40	63	71	82
62887	SPRINGERTON	90	65	92	63	67	92	68	86	76	62	74	64	55	75	67	83	49	79	91	101
62888	TAMAROA	82	60	78	58	61	82	61	75	68	58	66	57	50	68	59	74	44	70	78	90
62889	TEXICO	90	77	85	79	79	96	77	90	81	70	80	68	69	82	77	87	54	83	93	105
62890	THOMPSONVILLE	85	66	82	64	67	84	65	79	71	63	70	59	55	72	64	77	47	74	81	94
62892	VERNON	87	79	78	82	81	93	78	88	80	71	79	67	72	82	78	85	54	81	91	102
62893	WALNUT HILL	108	99	97	102	100	115	97	109	100	88	98	82	90	102	97	106	67	101	112	127
62894	WALTONVILLE	84	62	85	61	65	86	64	80	70	59	69	60	52	70	63	77	46	73	83	94
62895	WAYNE CITY	71	51	67	50	52	72	54	66	61	50	59	50	44	61	52	67	39	62	71	79
62896	WEST FRANKFORT	70	54	66	54	55	72	58	67	63	53	61	51	49	63	55	68	41	64	72	80
62897	WHITTINGTON	92	81	85	83	83	96	82	92	85	75	83	69	74	86	81	90	57	86	95	107
62898	WOODLAWN	91	83	78	83	83	91	80	88	83	78	82	65	75	86	78	87	56	83	89	103
62899	XENIA	92	66	94	64	68	93	68	86	75	63	74	64	54	74	67	82	49	79	89	102
62901	CARBONDALE	53	36	35	39	35	39	64	44	57	51	57	39	48	56	45	55	40	53	46	56
62902	CARBONDALE	82	69	67	73	68	72	90	75	85	80	85	62	78	85	76	84	60	82	77	91
62903	CARBONDALE	65	49	46	52	47	51	74	56	68	63	68	48	59	69	57	67	48	64	58	70
62905	ALTO PASS	90	65	89	63	67	90	67	83	74	63	73	63	54	74	65	81	48	77	87	99
62906	ANNA	69	56	71	55	58	74	58	69	64	54	63	51	51	62	58	70	42	66	76	81
62907	AVA	88	63	91	61	66	90	65	83	72	60	71	62	52	72	64	79	47	76	86	98
62908	BELKNAP	87	61	92	60	64	90	65	82	70	57	69	64	50	69	64	77	45	76	86	99
62910	BROOKPORT	73	53	66	52	54	73	56	67	62	53	61	51	46	63	53	68	41	63	72	80
62912	BUNCOMBE	82	60	83	58	62	83	61	77	67	57	66	58	49	67	60	74	44	71	80	91
62914	CAIRO	63	45	52	46	45	60	52	57	60	51	58	42	45	59	48	65	39	58	65	69
62916	CAMPBELL HILL	88	65	88	63	67	90	66	83	73	61	72	62	54	73	65	80	47	76	86	98
62917	CARRIER MILLS	76	54	76	52	55	77	56	71	63	52	62	54	45	63	55	70	41	66	75	85
62918	CARTERVILLE	77	64	69	64	64	75	69	73	72	65	71	55	61	72	65	75	48	72	77	87
62919	CAVE IN ROCK	72	52	73	50	54	74	55	69	61	50	59	51	44	60	53	67	39	63	73	81
62920	COBDEN	83	63	83	62	65	86	65	80	71	59	69	60	54	71	64	77	46	74	84	94
62922	CREAL SPRINGS	89	68	97	66	72	92	69	86	75	66	73	63	58	73	70	81	49	80	90	101
62923	CYPRESS	78	56	80	54	58	80	58	74	64	54	63	55	46	64	57	71	42	68	77	87
62924	DE SOTO	67	61	59	61	58	70	62	65	65	58	64	51	59	65	60	68	44	65	72	78
62926	DONGOLA	78	55	78	53	57	79	58	73	65	53	64	55	46	65	57	72	42	68	78	87
62928	EDDYVILLE	81	58	83	56	60	82	59	76	66	55	65	57	48	66	59	73	43	69	79	90
62930	ELDORADO	63	48	59	48	49	64	53	60	58	48	56	45	44	57	50	63	38	58	66	72
62931	ELIZABETHTOWN	60	54	71	50	59	67	52	63	56	55	55	42	50	52	56	60	37	60	69	72
62932	ELKVILLE	70	51	70	49	52	73	55	68	61	49	59	51	44	60	53	68	40	63	74	80
62933	ENERGY	87	77	80	78	79	88	83	86	85	79	83	64	76	84	80	88	57	85	92	101
62934	EQUALITY	68	51	68	50	53	71	54	67	60	49	58	50	45	59	53	66	39	62	72	78
62935	GALATIA	72	52	74	50	54	74	55	69	61	50	59	52	44	60	54	67	39	64	73	81
62938	GOLCONDA	73	53	75	51	55	75	55	70	62	51	60	52	44	61	54	68	40	64	74	82
62939	GOREVILLE	86	73	88	72	77	92	72	86	77	70	75	62	66	76	74	82	51	80	91	100
62940	GORHAM	75	56	74	55	57	77	59	72	65	54	63	54	48	65	57	71	42	67	77	85
62941	GRAND CHAIN	72	52	68	50	53	73	56	68	62	51	60	51	45	62	53	68	40	63	73	80
62942	GRAND TOWER	75	54	62	53	54	72	56	65	62	55	61	50	45	65	51	68	41	62	69	80
62943	GRANTSBURG	84	60	88	58	62	86	62	79	69	57	67	61	49	68	62	75	44	73	83	95
62946	HARRISBURG	74	57	72	57	59	76	62	72	67	57	65	54	53	66	60	73	44	69	78	85
62947	HEROD	82	60	83	58	62	83	61	77	67	57	66	58	49	67	60	74	44	71	80	91
	ILLINOIS	106	108	105	108	107	106	109	106	108	107	109	83	110	108	108	108	77	108	107	125
	UNITED STATES	100	100	100	100	100	100	100	100	100	100	100	100	100	100	100	100	100	100	100	100

POPULATION CHANGE

62948-62999

ZIP CODE #	POST OFFICE NAME	COUNTY FIPS CODE	POPULATION 2000	POPULATION 2009	POPULATION 2014	2000-2009 ANNUAL RATE % Rate	2000-2009 ANNUAL RATE State Centile	HOUSEHOLDS 2000	HOUSEHOLDS 2009	HOUSEHOLDS 2014	HOUSEHOLDS % Annual Rate 2000-2009	HOUSEHOLDS 2009 Average HH Size	FAMILIES 2000	FAMILIES 2009	FAMILIES % Annual Rate 2000-2009
62948	HERRIN	199	11947	12205	12357	0.2	61	5109	5294	5390	0.4	2.24	3227	3270	0.1
62950	JACOB	077	242	260	266	0.8	79	97	107	110	1.1	2.43	70	75	0.7
62951	JOHNSTON CITY	199	5379	5462	5543	0.2	61	2270	2349	2396	0.4	2.33	1556	1574	0.1
62952	JONESBORO	181	3532	3725	3782	0.6	75	1374	1472	1500	0.7	2.45	975	1020	0.5
62954	JUNCTION	059	614	583	566	-0.6	13	245	237	231	-0.4	2.43	161	153	-0.5
62955	KARBERS RIDGE	069	640	593	570	-0.8	6	269	256	248	-0.5	2.19	179	167	-0.7
62956	KARNAK	127	1003	975	945	-0.3	32	407	397	385	-0.3	2.46	293	280	-0.5
62957	MC CLURE	003	1221	1112	1033	-1.0	3	506	473	443	-0.7	2.35	351	321	-1.0
62958	MAKANDA	181	1970	2030	2051	0.3	65	829	878	894	0.6	2.31	573	589	0.3
62959	MARION	199	24499	26673	27481	0.9	81	9946	10817	11217	0.9	2.32	6739	7185	0.7
62960	METROPOLIS	127	12098	12107	12053	0.0	50	5022	5088	5085	0.1	2.31	3395	3376	-0.1
62961	MILLCREEK	181	38	45	47	1.8	91	14	17	18	2.1	2.65	11	13	1.8
62962	MILLER CITY	003	103	82	74	-2.4	0	45	37	34	-2.1	2.22	29	23	-2.5
62963	MOUND CITY	153	730	591	544	-2.3	1	297	244	225	-2.1	2.42	187	150	-2.4
62964	MOUNDS	153	1787	1565	1474	-1.4	1	672	594	561	-1.3	2.55	455	395	-1.5
62966	MURPHYSBORO	077	20514	15353	15169	-3.1	0	6678	6666	6646	0.0	2.23	4165	4017	-0.4
62967	NEW BURNSIDE	087	448	490	509	1.0	83	169	187	195	1.1	2.62	132	144	0.9
62970	OLMSTED	153	695	689	674	-0.1	45	302	303	298	0.0	2.27	207	203	-0.2
62972	OZARK	087	1081	1163	1206	0.8	79	436	482	501	1.1	2.21	334	363	0.9
62974	PITTSBURG	199	1117	1214	1262	0.9	81	427	475	497	1.2	2.56	329	359	0.9
62975	POMONA	077	337	338	338	0.0	50	126	131	132	0.4	2.58	91	92	0.1
62976	PULASKI	153	451	450	444	0.0	50	186	190	188	0.2	1.81	120	120	0.0
62977	RALEIGH	165	712	721	725	0.1	56	286	294	297	0.3	2.45	206	207	0.1
62979	RIDGWAY	059	1381	1319	1289	-0.5	18	594	576	564	-0.3	2.22	396	376	-0.6
62982	ROSICLARE	069	1283	1181	1128	-0.9	4	533	503	484	-0.6	2.27	360	332	-0.9
62983	ROYALTON	055	1550	1559	1563	0.1	56	684	698	704	0.2	2.23	437	434	-0.1
62984	SHAWNEETOWN	059	2060	1945	1884	-0.6	13	876	840	820	-0.5	2.30	585	550	-0.7
62985	SIMPSON	087	575	565	575	-0.2	38	226	243	247	0.8	1.74	171	181	0.6
62987	STONEFORT	165	737	805	835	1.0	83	287	317	330	1.1	2.54	215	233	0.9
62988	TAMMS	003	2417	2341	2268	-0.3	32	765	754	730	-0.2	2.47	549	527	-0.4
62990	THEBES	003	1823	1578	1444	-1.5	1	745	656	604	-1.4	2.41	540	464	-1.6
62992	ULLIN	153	1111	1059	1020	-0.5	18	391	375	361	-0.5	2.50	245	229	-0.7
62994	VERGENNES	077	876	774	791	-1.3	2	278	308	318	1.1	2.51	209	225	0.8
62995	VIENNA	087	3117	3334	3433	0.7	78	1301	1424	1471	1.0	2.17	882	946	0.8
62996	VILLA RIDGE	153	838	826	809	-0.2	38	325	326	321	0.0	2.53	237	234	-0.1
62997	WILLISVILLE	145	29	30	30	0.4	69	10	11	11	1.0	2.73	8	8	0.0
62998	WOLF LAKE	181	518	565	579	0.9	81	200	222	229	1.1	2.55	150	163	0.9
62999	ZEIGLER	055	1672	1704	1718	0.2	61	713	736	747	0.3	2.26	447	448	0.0
	ILLINOIS					0.6					0.6	2.64			0.4
	UNITED STATES					1.0					1.1	2.59			0.9

ZIP CODE		RACE (%)						% Hispanic Origin		2009 AGE DISTRIBUTION (%)										MEDIAN AGE	% 2009 Males	% 2009 Females
#	POST OFFICE NAME	White		Black		Asian/Pacific																
		2000	2009	2000	2009	2000	2009	2000	2009	0-4	5-9	10-14	15-19	20-24	25-44	45-64	65-84	85+	18+	2009		
62948	HERRIN	96.7	95.9	0.9	1.0	0.7	1.0	1.0	1.3	6.3	6.2	6.1	5.7	5.2	25.1	26.7	15.3	3.4	78.0	41.5	46.6	53.4
62950	JACOB	98.8	94.2	0.0	0.0	0.0	0.0	0.4	5.0	6.9	6.2	6.2	6.2	6.2	26.9	24.6	14.2	2.7	77.3	39.3	50.0	50.0
62951	JOHNSTON CITY	98.8	98.4	0.2	0.2	0.1	0.2	1.0	1.4	5.6	5.8	5.8	6.5	5.0	24.6	28.7	15.1	2.9	78.9	42.4	47.7	52.3
62952	JONESBORO	97.1	96.1	0.4	0.5	0.4	0.6	2.0	2.9	5.5	5.6	5.9	6.7	5.2	24.1	29.2	15.2	2.5	78.9	42.8	48.8	51.2
62954	JUNCTION	96.9	96.6	0.5	0.5	0.0	0.0	1.8	2.2	5.5	5.5	5.7	6.2	5.1	24.2	28.1	16.8	2.9	79.8	43.1	49.2	50.8
62955	KARBERS RIDGE	98.3	98.1	0.2	0.2	0.6	0.7	1.2	1.7	5.4	5.4	5.2	4.7	4.2	22.9	29.0	19.1	4.0	81.3	46.4	49.2	50.8
62956	KARNAK	94.0	92.2	5.1	6.4	0.1	0.2	2.2	3.1	8.2	8.1	7.6	6.4	5.2	22.3	25.2	14.4	2.7	72.1	38.8	47.9	52.1
62957	MC CLURE	97.5	96.6	0.7	0.9	0.4	0.6	1.1	1.5	5.0	5.3	5.7	6.4	4.6	24.1	30.9	16.3	1.7	79.9	44.3	49.8	50.2
62958	MAKANDA	94.4	92.6	1.5	1.9	1.6	2.2	1.4	2.0	4.9	5.6	6.4	6.5	6.6	24.9	33.0	11.2	1.1	78.9	41.7	51.7	48.3
62959	MARION	93.7	92.3	4.0	4.6	0.7	0.9	1.5	2.2	5.5	5.4	5.6	5.9	5.6	25.9	27.9	15.0	3.0	79.7	41.8	50.2	49.8
62960	METROPOLIS	92.7	91.3	5.4	6.2	0.3	0.4	0.7	1.0	6.0	6.2	6.1	5.9	5.0	24.5	27.4	15.3	3.6	78.1	42.0	47.6	52.4
62961	MILLCREEK	100.0	100.0	0.0	0.0	0.0	0.0	2.7	0.0	4.4	4.4	6.7	6.7	4.4	26.7	35.6	11.1	0.0	77.8	42.5	51.1	48.9
62962	MILLER CITY	80.4	75.6	17.6	22.0	0.0	0.0	1.0	1.2	3.7	4.9	4.9	6.1	4.9	22.0	31.7	19.5	2.4	82.9	47.5	47.6	52.4
62963	MOUND CITY	50.8	44.5	48.2	54.3	0.1	0.2	1.1	1.4	7.6	7.6	7.3	8.1	7.3	23.9	25.2	11.0	2.0	72.8	34.9	44.5	55.5
62964	MOUNDS	48.9	44.2	48.8	53.2	0.2	0.2	0.8	0.9	6.7	7.1	8.7	8.1	5.6	20.8	25.8	13.5	3.8	72.7	38.9	48.5	51.5
62966	MURPHYSBORO	85.0	85.1	11.2	10.6	1.0	1.1	2.2	2.7	5.3	5.3	5.3	7.7	7.3	27.0	26.2	13.2	2.6	80.6	38.8	49.6	50.4
62967	NEW BURNSIDE	96.9	95.7	0.7	1.6	0.4	0.6	0.9	1.4	5.7	5.9	6.7	6.5	4.9	24.9	29.6	13.9	1.8	77.8	41.7	51.4	48.6
62970	OLMSTED	83.2	79.5	15.1	18.6	0.3	0.3	0.7	1.2	5.5	5.5	6.0	6.8	5.4	23.5	30.0	15.1	2.2	78.8	43.0	46.9	53.1
62972	OZARK	90.4	88.8	7.4	8.5	0.4	0.5	1.9	2.8	4.6	5.0	5.3	6.1	5.8	25.6	29.8	16.3	1.5	81.4	43.2	55.5	44.5
62974	PITTSBURG	98.5	97.9	0.6	0.7	0.1	0.2	0.5	0.9	5.6	5.4	6.5	7.1	5.7	26.1	30.6	11.9	1.2	77.9	40.2	50.3	49.7
62975	POMONA	97.6	96.4	0.3	0.6	0.0	0.0	1.2	1.8	6.5	6.5	6.2	6.2	5.9	27.5	29.0	11.2	0.9	76.9	38.7	49.7	50.3
62976	PULASKI	49.9	43.6	41.0	44.9	7.1	8.9	5.3	6.7	4.9	6.0	5.3	5.1	7.3	29.8	25.6	13.3	2.7	80.4	39.1	57.1	42.9
62977	RALEIGH	99.2	98.6	0.1	0.1	0.1	0.4	0.1	0.4	6.0	6.5	6.9	6.1	4.4	22.9	31.5	13.7	1.9	76.8	42.9	50.8	49.2
62979	RIDGWAY	99.1	98.9	0.4	0.5	0.1	0.1	0.5	0.8	5.3	5.5	6.0	6.4	3.9	23.4	27.0	18.4	4.2	79.4	44.7	49.1	50.9
62982	ROSICLARE	97.7	97.3	0.5	0.6	1.0	1.1	1.2	1.7	5.7	5.8	5.8	5.2	4.7	23.3	27.9	17.9	3.8	79.5	44.7	47.2	52.8
62983	ROYALTON	99.4	99.2	0.0	0.1	0.1	0.1	0.3	0.4	6.2	6.0	6.5	6.9	4.4	22.8	26.5	17.7	3.0	77.2	43.0	48.1	51.9
62984	SHAWNEETOWN	97.4	97.1	0.3	0.3	0.1	0.2	1.1	1.4	5.5	5.3	5.4	6.5	5.7	24.4	27.9	16.7	2.5	80.0	42.5	47.6	52.4
62985	SIMPSON	64.8	58.1	32.2	38.2	0.3	0.4	5.4	7.1	2.8	3.4	3.5	6.2	11.5	40.4	23.0	8.1	1.1	87.6	35.1	70.8	29.2
62987	STONEFORT	96.2	95.3	3.0	3.7	0.0	0.0	1.2	1.4	5.8	6.1	6.5	7.0	5.0	22.1	30.9	14.8	1.9	77.5	43.2	48.7	51.3
62988	TAMMS	70.1	63.1	27.4	33.8	0.1	0.2	3.6	4.5	4.6	4.8	5.0	5.4	6.5	34.1	25.2	12.5	1.9	82.1	38.3	57.8	42.2
62990	THEBES	85.8	82.5	12.6	15.5	0.1	0.1	0.5	0.6	6.5	6.7	6.8	6.8	5.8	22.8	28.7	13.8	2.2	75.9	40.7	48.8	51.2
62992	ULLIN	61.9	56.0	33.6	38.3	2.5	3.3	2.1	2.6	5.2	6.2	6.0	6.7	6.9	24.5	27.5	13.7	3.3	78.2	40.6	50.5	49.5
62994	VERGENNES	87.8	78.0	9.7	9.7	0.2	5.7	1.9	5.8	4.8	5.9	5.2	18.1	12.9	21.1	21.1	9.6	1.4	81.0	29.1	63.2	36.8
62995	VIENNA	92.6	91.0	4.9	5.4	0.2	0.2	2.5	4.3	5.8	5.6	5.5	5.9	6.7	25.9	27.2	14.0	3.3	79.7	40.6	51.6	48.4
62996	VILLA RIDGE	77.1	72.3	21.7	26.2	0.1	0.2	0.5	0.7	5.6	5.8	6.3	6.8	4.8	24.3	30.4	14.2	1.8	78.3	42.2	49.2	50.8
62997	WILLISVILLE	100.0	100.0	0.0	0.0	0.0	0.0	3.6	3.3	6.7	6.7	6.7	6.7	6.7	23.3	33.3	10.0	0.0	73.3	40.0	53.3	46.7
62998	WOLF LAKE	97.7	96.6	0.2	0.4	0.2	0.2	1.9	3.0	5.7	5.7	6.2	7.4	6.4	26.5	28.7	12.0	1.4	77.9	39.4	50.1	49.9
62999	ZEIGLER	98.9	98.2	0.1	0.3	0.2	0.3	0.5	0.7	6.0	5.9	5.9	5.7	5.1	25.8	27.6	15.1	2.8	78.5	41.5	48.7	51.3
	ILLINOIS	73.5	70.6	15.1	15.3	3.4	4.4	12.3	15.7	7.1	6.9	6.8	7.1	6.9	27.5	25.4	10.3	1.9	75.0	36.1	49.1	50.9
	UNITED STATES	75.1	72.0	12.3	12.7	3.8	4.6	12.5	15.7	6.8	6.7	6.6	7.1	6.9	27.0	26.0	10.9	1.9	75.7	36.9	49.2	50.8

ZIP CODE #	POST OFFICE NAME	2009 Per Capita Income	2009 HH Income Base	2009 HOUSEHOLD INCOME DISTRIBUTION (%) Less than $25,000	$25,000 to $49,999	$50,000 to $99,999	$100,000 to $149,999	$150,000 or More	MEDIAN HOUSEHOLD INCOME 2009	2014	2009 National Centile	2009 State Centile	2009 Home Value Base	2009 HOME VALUE DISTRIBUTION (%) Less than $50,000	$50,000 to $89,999	$90,000 to $174,999	$175,000 to $399,999	$400,000 or More	2009 Median Home Value
62948	HERRIN	20100	5294	35.7	28.4	29.6	4.7	1.6	36378	39493	22	8	3768	20.8	38.6	32.2	7.4	1.0	78216
62950	JACOB	16748	107	40.2	28.0	27.1	4.7	0.0	31923	33185	11	3	85	48.2	27.1	22.4	2.4	0.0	51875
62951	JOHNSTON CITY	17245	2349	38.1	32.0	26.9	2.0	1.0	35439	36571	19	7	1840	31.1	33.9	28.7	5.8	0.5	64144
62952	JONESBORO	18526	1472	31.7	30.5	32.5	3.4	1.8	38283	39901	28	12	1151	23.1	29.7	34.4	11.6	1.2	85548
62954	JUNCTION	16268	237	44.3	27.8	24.5	1.3	2.1	28180	29274	6	2	186	46.2	29.6	19.4	3.8	1.1	54667
62955	KARBERS RIDGE	19748	256	37.1	34.0	23.0	4.3	1.6	32695	33059	13	4	197	34.5	37.1	20.3	6.1	2.0	59242
62956	KARNAK	18064	397	36.0	32.5	26.4	3.3	1.8	36083	37477	21	8	314	37.9	32.2	22.3	6.4	1.3	59500
62957	MC CLURE	19254	473	36.2	34.2	24.3	3.6	1.7	36354	38156	22	8	386	44.8	32.6	17.6	3.4	1.6	54167
62958	MAKANDA	26960	878	21.4	26.2	39.5	6.7	6.2	51789	54515	65	48	669	17.8	15.7	32.4	29.3	4.8	129107
62959	MARION	23068	10817	27.8	30.3	32.6	5.9	3.4	42445	45512	41	22	7789	15.1	22.8	39.3	18.9	4.0	110828
62960	METROPOLIS	19571	5088	34.8	28.5	30.2	5.3	1.1	37623	39224	26	11	3885	19.9	28.3	39.0	11.8	1.0	93438
62961	MILLCREEK	15800	17	35.3	35.3	23.5	5.9	0.0	32330	32265	12	4	15	26.7	20.0	40.0	13.3	0.0	95000
62962	MILLER CITY	22828	37	24.3	35.1	35.1	2.7	2.7	41146	47361	36	19	31	45.2	22.6	25.8	6.5	0.0	62500
62963	MOUND CITY	12308	244	60.7	19.3	15.2	4.9	0.0	18531	19837	1	0	140	63.6	27.9	8.6	0.0	0.0	40000
62964	MOUNDS	14081	594	50.7	23.7	22.4	2.7	0.5	24658	25711	3	1	420	62.9	25.0	10.2	1.9	0.0	39828
62966	MURPHYSBORO	22143	6666	32.1	28.1	32.3	5.0	2.5	39782	44194	32	16	4413	23.8	28.7	34.2	11.3	2.0	85760
62967	NEW BURNSIDE	19051	187	25.1	36.9	29.9	4.8	3.2	37599	38779	26	11	165	32.7	17.0	38.2	7.9	4.2	90417
62970	OLMSTED	17581	303	38.6	26.1	31.4	3.3	0.7	32799	32826	13	4	238	39.5	34.0	21.0	5.5	0.0	57353
62972	OZARK	23898	482	28.6	33.4	29.0	5.2	3.7	38959	40372	30	14	428	22.0	20.3	36.7	16.6	4.4	103750
62974	PITTSBURG	22871	475	24.2	30.1	36.2	3.8	5.7	46563	48077	53	34	420	21.4	26.9	38.8	11.4	1.4	93182
62975	POMONA	22019	131	28.2	28.2	35.1	3.8	4.6	43019	48198	42	24	103	31.1	18.4	31.1	14.6	4.9	91667
62976	PULASKI	20156	190	47.9	23.7	24.2	2.1	2.1	30000	31121	8	2	155	51.6	19.4	24.5	3.9	0.6	47727
62977	RALEIGH	19538	294	28.6	31.0	34.7	4.1	1.7	40564	44260	35	17	250	23.6	31.2	32.0	11.6	1.6	78947
62979	RIDGWAY	20434	576	34.5	30.0	29.9	3.0	2.6	36300	39558	21	8	461	36.2	31.2	27.1	5.4	0.0	67703
62982	ROSICLARE	17210	503	42.1	32.2	21.5	2.6	1.6	29075	29747	7	2	395	41.8	41.0	13.2	3.3	0.8	53779
62983	ROYALTON	16805	698	42.0	33.8	20.6	2.7	0.9	28185	29656	6	2	555	37.8	35.9	22.2	3.4	0.7	60341
62984	SHAWNEETOWN	17913	840	45.5	26.0	23.5	2.0	3.1	27920	29423	6	2	664	45.9	31.8	19.3	2.3	0.8	54737
62985	SIMPSON	28871	243	30.0	30.9	31.7	5.3	2.1	41923	42704	39	21	214	16.4	21.5	41.1	19.2	1.9	109821
62987	STONEFORT	19364	317	23.3	32.5	39.1	4.7	0.3	44872	47641	48	29	269	30.1	24.9	34.6	8.6	1.9	78214
62988	TAMMS	17519	754	37.9	32.0	25.7	2.4	2.0	34638	36840	17	6	626	45.7	27.3	22.5	4.0	0.5	57941
62990	THEBES	20175	656	35.7	33.8	26.1	2.6	1.8	35000	37453	18	6	528	47.7	24.4	23.7	4.0	0.2	54800
62992	ULLIN	14596	375	48.8	24.0	24.0	2.9	0.3	26274	27320	4	1	282	50.4	27.7	17.0	3.2	1.8	49583
62994	VERGENNES	18504	308	23.4	37.0	36.0	2.6	1.0	45000	46815	48	29	253	30.4	27.7	33.6	7.9	0.4	71000
62995	VIENNA	20400	1424	34.6	31.2	28.1	3.9	2.2	36093	37843	21	8	1103	21.7	24.5	38.1	15.4	0.4	96071
62996	VILLA RIDGE	15767	326	38.0	28.8	30.1	3.1	0.0	33403	33808	14	4	263	41.1	34.6	18.6	5.7	0.0	58393
62997	WILLISVILLE	18250	11	0.0	63.6	36.4	0.0	0.0	47090	47090	54	35	9	22.2	22.2	22.2	33.3	0.0	95000
62998	WOLF LAKE	18526	222	30.2	35.1	29.7	2.7	2.3	37499	38454	25	11	167	26.3	18.6	40.7	13.8	0.6	93864
62999	ZEIGLER	15785	736	42.3	33.4	21.1	3.1	0.1	28079	29555	6	2	578	49.3	32.5	15.2	2.2	0.7	50615
	ILLINOIS	28587		18.2	22.2	39.3	12.1	8.2	60823	63631				6.3	10.0	30.9	40.6	12.3	185324
	UNITED STATES	27277		20.9	24.4	35.3	11.7	7.6	54719	56938				9.3	13.1	31.6	32.6	13.5	162279

ZIP CODE	FINANCIAL SERVICES				THE HOME						ENTERTAINMENT						PERSONAL			
					Home Improvements		Furnishings													
# POST OFFICE NAME	Auto Loan	Home Loan	Investments	Retirement Plans	Home Repair	Lawn & Garden	Computers & Hardware-Personal	Major Appliances	TV, Radio, Sound Equipment	Furniture	Dine out/ Carry out	Sports Equipment	Fees & Tickets	Toys & Games	Travel	Cable TV	Apparel & Services	Auto Repairs	Health Insurance	Pets & Supplies
62948 HERRIN	72	58	66	57	58	73	62	69	67	58	65	52	54	67	59	72	44	67	75	82
62950 JACOB	69	50	69	48	52	72	54	67	60	48	58	50	43	59	52	66	39	62	73	79
62951 JOHNSTON CITY	67	51	65	50	52	69	54	65	59	49	57	48	45	59	52	64	38	61	70	76
62952 JONESBORO	78	57	78	55	58	81	60	75	67	55	65	56	48	66	58	74	43	69	80	88
62954 JUNCTION	67	48	67	47	50	70	52	65	59	47	57	48	42	58	51	65	38	60	71	76
62955 KARBERS RIDGE	73	54	75	52	57	77	58	71	64	53	62	53	48	63	57	71	41	67	78	84
62956 KARNAK	76	54	76	53	56	79	59	73	65	53	63	55	47	65	57	72	42	68	79	86
62957 MC CLURE	81	58	83	56	60	82	59	76	66	55	65	57	48	66	59	73	43	69	79	90
62958 MAKANDA	89	90	90	92	89	90	88	88	87	89	88	69	90	88	90	88	62	88	88	105
62959 MARION	83	72	78	72	72	85	76	81	80	72	78	61	70	79	74	84	53	80	87	96
62960 METROPOLIS	72	60	66	59	60	73	62	69	67	59	65	52	55	67	60	71	44	67	75	82
62961 MILLCREEK	75	54	77	52	56	76	55	70	61	51	60	52	44	61	54	67	40	64	73	83
62962 MILLER CITY	90	65	93	63	67	92	66	85	74	62	72	63	53	73	66	81	48	78	88	100
62963 MOUND CITY	44	35	34	35	34	43	39	40	46	41	44	28	36	44	36	50	30	43	49	50
62964 MOUNDS	60	43	54	42	43	59	47	54	54	46	52	40	39	53	44	59	35	53	60	66
62966 MURPHYSBORO	77	65	70	65	65	76	71	74	73	66	72	56	63	73	66	77	49	73	78	88
62967 NEW BURNSIDE	89	64	92	62	66	91	66	83	73	61	71	63	52	72	65	80	47	76	87	99
62970 OLMSTED	71	51	73	49	53	72	52	67	58	49	57	50	42	58	52	64	38	61	70	79
62972 OZARK	92	71	99	68	76	96	72	89	78	70	77	64	61	76	73	85	51	83	95	105
62974 PITTSBURG	102	78	99	75	79	101	78	95	85	75	84	70	65	85	76	92	56	88	98	113
62975 POMONA	97	79	79	76	78	91	78	86	83	79	83	65	68	87	73	88	56	83	89	104
62976 PULASKI	71	47	69	44	47	70	50	63	57	47	56	49	38	58	47	64	37	59	66	77
62977 RALEIGH	83	63	82	62	65	85	64	79	70	59	68	59	53	70	63	76	45	72	82	93
62979 RIDGWAY	79	57	81	55	59	82	60	76	67	54	65	57	48	66	59	74	43	70	81	89
62982 ROSICLARE	66	48	66	46	49	69	52	64	58	46	56	48	42	57	50	64	37	60	70	75
62983 ROYALTON	64	46	64	44	47	66	50	62	55	44	54	46	40	54	48	61	36	57	67	72
62984 SHAWNEETOWN	72	50	71	48	51	73	54	68	61	49	59	51	43	61	52	68	39	63	73	80
62985 SIMPSON	90	65	93	63	67	92	66	85	74	62	73	64	53	73	66	81	48	78	88	101
62987 STONEFORT	88	63	90	61	65	89	65	82	72	60	70	62	52	71	64	79	46	75	85	98
62988 TAMMS	80	54	79	52	55	80	57	72	65	54	63	55	44	65	55	72	42	67	76	87
62990 THEBES	88	61	88	58	62	88	63	80	72	60	70	61	49	72	61	79	46	74	84	97
62992 ULLIN	66	43	64	41	43	65	47	58	53	44	52	45	35	54	44	60	35	55	62	72
62994 VERGENNES	83	59	85	57	62	84	61	78	68	57	67	58	49	67	60	75	44	71	81	92
62995 VIENNA	74	55	73	54	57	75	61	71	67	56	65	53	50	65	58	73	44	68	77	84
62996 VILLA RIDGE	71	51	73	49	53	72	52	67	58	49	57	50	42	58	52	64	38	61	69	79
62997 WILLISVILLE	89	64	91	62	66	90	65	83	73	61	71	62	52	72	65	80	47	76	86	99
62998 WOLF LAKE	85	61	70	59	61	81	64	74	70	62	69	57	51	73	58	77	46	70	78	90
62999 ZEIGLER	60	43	61	42	45	63	47	59	53	42	51	44	38	52	46	58	34	55	64	69
ILLINOIS	106	108	105	108	107	106	109	106	108	107	109	83	110	108	108	108	77	108	107	125
UNITED STATES	100	100	100	100	100	100	100	100	100	100	100	100	100	100	100	100	100	100	100	100

POPULATION CHANGE

A 46001-46202

ZIP CODE #	POST OFFICE NAME	COUNTY FIPS CODE	POPULATION 2000	POPULATION 2009	POPULATION 2014	2000-2009 ANNUAL RATE % Rate	2000-2009 ANNUAL RATE State Centile	HOUSEHOLDS 2000	HOUSEHOLDS 2009	HOUSEHOLDS 2014	HOUSEHOLDS % Annual Rate 2000-2009	HOUSEHOLDS 2009 Average HH Size	FAMILIES 2000	FAMILIES 2009	FAMILIES % Annual Rate 2000-2009
46001	ALEXANDRIA	095	12356	11871	11668	-0.4	18	4809	4704	4652	-0.2	2.49	3473	3261	-0.7
46011	ANDERSON	095	17438	17026	16802	-0.3	22	6947	6902	6857	-0.1	2.40	5107	4874	-0.5
46012	ANDERSON	095	21014	20505	20217	-0.3	22	8472	8300	8220	-0.2	2.29	5735	5387	-0.7
46013	ANDERSON	095	17442	17479	17422	0.0	37	8087	8229	8249	0.2	2.12	4896	4725	-0.4
46016	ANDERSON	095	21705	20098	19550	-0.8	4	8898	8296	8103	-0.8	2.35	5261	4612	-1.4
46017	ANDERSON	095	6212	6072	5994	-0.2	27	2510	2500	2486	0.0	2.38	1791	1713	-0.5
46030	ARCADIA	057	3317	4252	4900	2.7	95	1154	1521	1772	3.0	2.69	889	1112	2.4
46031	ATLANTA	057	2120	2472	2709	1.7	92	759	901	991	1.9	2.70	607	692	1.4
46032	CARMEL	057	34085	44166	51810	2.8	96	12467	16192	18976	2.9	2.70	9234	11310	2.2
46033	CARMEL	057	28863	37726	43596	2.9	96	9469	12638	14667	3.2	2.98	8359	10912	2.9
46034	CICERO	057	6246	8140	9404	2.9	96	2423	3225	3748	3.1	2.52	1832	2318	2.6
46035	COLFAX	023	1108	1088	1082	-0.2	27	416	418	416	0.1	2.60	306	296	-0.4
46036	ELWOOD	095	13065	12565	12357	-0.4	18	5170	5052	4995	-0.2	2.46	3681	3442	-0.7
46037	FISHERS	057	14705	35248	46005	9.9	100	5170	12304	16111	9.8	2.86	4055	9583	9.7
46038	FISHERS	057	26887	36081	41776	3.2	97	10119	13506	15618	3.2	2.67	7350	9389	2.7
46039	FOREST	023	778	776	775	0.0	37	292	298	298	0.2	2.60	229	227	-0.1
46040	FORTVILLE	059	6338	9710	11256	4.7	99	2460	3681	4254	4.5	2.64	1838	2716	4.3
46041	FRANKFORT	023	24681	24169	23914	-0.2	27	9210	9089	9001	-0.1	2.59	6531	6199	-0.6
46044	FRANKTON	095	2901	2921	2910	0.1	43	1135	1166	1168	0.3	2.51	868	859	-0.1
46048	INGALLS	095	1168	1309	1333	1.2	86	420	476	487	1.4	2.75	336	369	1.0
46049	KEMPTON	159	935	900	878	-0.4	18	340	338	333	-0.1	2.66	264	255	-0.4
46050	KIRKLIN	023	1774	1925	1963	0.9	79	660	731	750	1.1	2.63	501	536	0.7
46051	LAPEL	095	2574	2523	2497	-0.2	27	1009	1004	1000	-0.1	2.51	737	703	-0.5
46052	LEBANON	011	21174	22858	23888	0.8	76	8254	9131	9618	1.1	2.45	5774	6067	0.5
46055	MC CORDSVILLE	059	3595	7111	8801	7.7	100	1199	2516	3126	8.3	2.82	1020	2076	8.0
46056	MARKLEVILLE	095	2218	2327	2343	0.5	66	828	886	897	0.7	2.63	662	688	0.4
46057	MICHIGANTOWN	023	1075	1055	1047	-0.2	27	387	389	387	0.1	2.71	306	298	-0.3
46058	MULBERRY	023	2266	2307	2310	0.2	49	812	842	848	0.4	2.57	605	605	0.0
46060	NOBLESVILLE	057	21086	34571	41347	5.5	99	7967	12931	15471	5.4	2.64	5860	9550	5.4
46062	NOBLESVILLE	057	18894	30317	37569	5.2	99	6782	11183	13950	5.6	2.69	5457	8569	5.0
46064	PENDLETON	095	13112	15064	15375	1.5	91	3945	4585	4737	1.6	2.59	3043	3427	1.3
46065	ROSSVILLE	023	3335	3776	3887	1.4	89	1160	1344	1392	1.6	2.75	906	1017	1.3
46068	SHARPSVILLE	159	2957	2941	2894	-0.1	31	1067	1088	1079	0.2	2.70	877	871	-0.1
46069	SHERIDAN	057	6828	7715	8492	1.3	87	2431	2796	3094	1.5	2.71	1859	2009	0.8
46070	SUMMITVILLE	095	2530	2507	2486	-0.1	31	951	957	955	0.1	2.58	729	707	-0.3
46071	THORNTOWN	011	3320	3523	3655	0.6	70	1225	1333	1393	0.9	2.64	965	1009	0.5
46072	TIPTON	159	9662	9409	9202	-0.3	22	3893	3891	3834	0.0	2.37	2705	2595	-0.4
46074	WESTFIELD	057	11165	22636	28344	7.9	100	3921	8019	10087	8.0	2.81	2946	5934	7.9
46075	WHITESTOWN	011	1683	2436	2837	4.1	98	630	944	1110	4.5	2.58	493	709	4.0
46076	WINDFALL	159	1864	1871	1849	0.0	37	715	734	730	0.3	2.55	547	545	0.0
46077	ZIONSVILLE	011	16116	23401	27065	4.1	98	5582	8239	9584	4.3	2.78	4474	6431	4.0
46104	ARLINGTON	139	1161	1119	1100	-0.4	18	403	399	394	-0.1	2.80	323	311	-0.4
46105	BAINBRIDGE	133	1949	2011	2068	0.3	56	734	778	805	0.6	2.58	583	598	0.3
46106	BARGERSVILLE	081	4558	5555	6201	2.2	94	1639	2084	2354	2.6	2.66	1311	1622	2.3
46107	BEECH GROVE	097	13579	13072	12932	-0.4	18	5511	5416	5392	-0.2	2.33	3554	3271	-0.9
46110	BOGGSTOWN	145	411	426	432	0.4	60	155	166	170	0.7	2.57	123	128	0.4
46112	BROWNSBURG	063	25223	33507	37925	3.1	97	9032	12480	14268	3.6	2.66	7161	9646	3.3
46113	CAMBY	109	6225	11741	13401	7.1	99	2217	4310	4961	7.5	2.70	1842	3480	7.1
46115	CARTHAGE	139	1956	1970	1962	0.1	43	753	778	782	0.4	2.53	577	578	0.0
46117	CHARLOTTESVILLE	059	564	645	687	1.5	91	198	234	252	1.8	2.76	167	192	1.5
46118	CLAYTON	063	4343	5115	5577	1.8	93	1596	1960	2157	2.2	2.61	1307	1555	1.9
46120	CLOVERDALE	133	6660	7039	7131	0.6	70	1962	2116	2166	0.8	2.78	1468	1526	0.4
46121	COATESVILLE	063	4964	5917	6251	1.9	93	1828	2247	2395	2.3	2.63	1480	1765	1.9
46122	DANVILLE	063	12342	15840	17688	2.7	95	4410	5850	6612	3.1	2.63	3405	4337	2.7
46123	AVON	063	19579	28999	34085	4.3	98	6862	10460	12413	4.7	2.76	5707	8466	4.4
46124	EDINBURGH	145	7837	7962	8186	0.2	49	3008	3148	3264	0.5	2.50	2131	2133	0.0
46126	FAIRLAND	145	4838	4971	5028	0.3	56	1685	1782	1817	0.6	2.79	1375	1418	0.3
46127	FALMOUTH	139	382	400	402	0.5	66	153	166	168	0.9	2.41	118	124	0.5
46128	FILLMORE	133	1570	1673	1716	0.7	73	568	620	640	1.0	2.69	455	482	0.6
46130	FOUNTAINTOWN	145	2322	2452	2516	0.6	70	833	899	928	0.8	2.72	692	728	0.5
46131	FRANKLIN	081	26964	31386	34268	1.7	92	9410	11492	12770	2.2	2.53	6993	8234	1.8
46133	GLENWOOD	139	965	936	919	-0.3	22	351	352	348	0.0	2.66	272	264	-0.3
46135	GREENCASTLE	133	18064	18384	18307	0.2	49	6203	6349	6347	0.3	2.35	4347	4271	-0.2
46140	GREENFIELD	059	33039	40437	44789	2.2	94	12606	15894	17778	2.5	2.52	9677	11850	2.2
46142	GREENWOOD	081	30973	33564	35826	0.9	79	11674	13103	14094	1.3	2.53	8671	9411	0.9
46143	GREENWOOD	081	31745	46894	54516	4.3	98	12369	18392	21439	4.4	2.54	8868	12815	4.1
46147	JAMESTOWN	011	3090	3410	3608	1.1	84	1128	1282	1366	1.4	2.66	882	965	1.0
46148	KNIGHTSTOWN	065	4921	4906	4835	0.0	37	1954	1989	1972	0.2	2.46	1433	1405	-0.2
46149	LIZTON	063	1837	1998	2064	0.9	79	690	783	818	1.4	2.55	540	589	0.9
46150	MANILLA	139	889	860	845	-0.4	18	331	329	325	-0.1	2.61	258	249	-0.4
46151	MARTINSVILLE	109	31654	33340	33852	0.6	70	11746	12388	12610	0.6	2.65	8952	9151	0.2
46156	MILROY	139	1641	1597	1568	-0.3	22	549	550	545	0.0	2.89	431	419	-0.3
46157	MONROVIA	109	2860	3241	3405	1.4	89	1023	1162	1224	1.4	2.79	828	914	1.1
46158	MOORESVILLE	109	24411	25278	25660	0.4	60	8887	9216	9375	0.4	2.73	7020	7061	0.1
46160	MORGANTOWN	013	6232	6675	6924	0.7	73	2299	2510	2618	1.0	2.64	1813	1919	0.6
46161	MORRISTOWN	145	2598	2710	2763	0.5	66	943	1002	1027	0.7	2.66	720	741	0.3
46162	NEEDHAM	145	301	320	335	0.7	73	122	133	140	0.9	2.41	99	104	0.5
46163	NEW PALESTINE	059	9366	12048	13360	2.8	96	3248	4342	4875	3.2	2.76	2680	3465	2.8
46164	NINEVEH	013	4981	5488	5754	1.1	84	1702	1948	2069	1.5	2.49	1327	1472	1.1
46165	NORTH SALEM	063	1539	1650	1701	0.8	76	574	634	658	1.1	2.60	444	471	0.6
46166	PARAGON	109	2235	2318	2370	0.4	60	775	806	827	0.4	2.88	615	618	0.1
46167	PITTSBORO	063	4850	6362	7346	3.0	97	1709	2320	2704	3.4	2.74	1424	1874	3.0
46168	PLAINFIELD	063	23354	28978	31545	2.4	95	8347	10667	11798	2.7	2.44	5999	7423	2.3
46171	REELSVILLE	133	1878	2012	2061	0.7	73	701	766	788	1.0	2.52	568	603	0.6
46172	ROACHDALE	133	2593	2714	2749	0.5	66	962	1019	1034	0.6	2.66	720	733	0.2
46173	RUSHVILLE	139	11400	10948	10732	-0.4	18	4422	4345	4291	-0.2	2.45	3101	2928	-0.6
46175	RUSSELLVILLE	133	662	530	500	-2.4	0	261	211	199	-2.3	2.51	182	140	-2.8
46176	SHELBYVILLE	145	27410	28006	28250	0.2	49	10806	11313	11507	0.5	2.42	7447	7485	0.1
46180	STILESVILLE	109	1126	1261	1321	1.2	86	437	503	530	1.5	2.51	344	382	1.1
46181	TRAFALGAR	081	4018	4598	4957	1.5	91	1424	1687	1838	1.8	2.72	1174	1352	1.5
46182	WALDRON	145	1904	1948	1972	0.2	49	691	726	741	0.5	2.57	534	543	0.2
46184	WHITELAND	081	9345	11497	13013	2.3	95	3195	4110	4699	2.8	2.79	2646	3313	2.5
46186	WILKINSON	059	1679	1851	1945	1.1	84	625	710	754	1.4	2.61	496	547	1.1
46201	INDIANAPOLIS	097	38851	34862	33665	-1.2	1	14969	13625	13225	-1.0	2.51	8626	7269	-1.8
46202	INDIANAPOLIS	097	15224	15294	15393	0.0	37	7846	8154	8317	0.4	1.69	2452	2223	-1.1
	INDIANA					0.7					0.8	2.49			0.4
	UNITED STATES					1.0					1.1	2.59			0.9

ZIP CODE #	POST OFFICE NAME	RACE (%) White 2000	White 2009	Black 2000	Black 2009	Asian/Pacific 2000	Asian/Pacific 2009	% Hispanic Origin 2000	% Hispanic Origin 2009	2009 AGE DISTRIBUTION (%) 0-4	5-9	10-14	15-19	20-24	25-44	45-64	65-84	85+	18+	MEDIAN AGE 2009	% 2009 Males	% 2009 Females
46001	ALEXANDRIA	98.3	97.7	0.5	0.6	0.2	0.2	0.9	1.4	6.6	6.4	6.4	6.7	6.0	24.8	27.4	13.5	2.1	76.5	39.5	49.0	51.0
46011	ANDERSON	86.5	84.2	11.7	13.6	0.3	0.5	1.0	1.5	5.7	5.8	6.2	6.3	5.1	23.5	29.0	15.6	2.9	78.3	43.1	47.9	52.1
46012	ANDERSON	93.6	91.7	4.2	5.3	0.6	0.8	1.2	1.8	5.4	5.1	5.3	8.5	9.3	22.2	27.0	14.7	2.6	80.9	40.0	47.7	52.3
46013	ANDERSON	92.6	90.6	5.0	6.3	0.7	1.1	1.3	2.0	6.3	6.1	6.1	5.6	4.8	25.0	26.5	16.6	3.0	78.0	42.1	47.4	52.6
46016	ANDERSON	71.1	67.5	24.8	27.5	0.2	0.3	3.4	4.9	7.8	7.6	7.0	6.8	6.6	28.6	23.6	10.0	2.0	73.6	34.9	49.6	50.4
46017	ANDERSON	96.8	95.7	1.8	2.3	0.3	0.5	1.1	1.7	6.0	6.2	6.8	6.7	4.6	24.4	28.4	14.8	2.0	76.5	41.4	48.1	51.9
46030	ARCADIA	97.5	96.8	0.5	0.5	0.2	0.3	0.8	1.3	6.7	6.8	7.0	7.1	5.6	26.8	28.3	10.4	1.2	74.9	38.6	50.3	49.7
46031	ATLANTA	97.5	96.4	0.3	0.3	0.2	0.4	1.2	2.0	6.5	6.8	7.0	7.3	5.3	26.3	30.1	9.4	1.3	74.6	39.3	50.8	49.2
46032	CARMEL	92.6	90.0	1.6	1.7	4.0	6.2	1.8	2.7	8.0	8.1	8.4	7.3	5.4	25.0	28.0	7.9	1.9	70.8	36.8	48.9	51.1
46033	CARMEL	93.4	90.4	1.3	1.4	4.0	6.5	1.6	2.3	8.1	8.7	9.1	7.8	3.1	23.1	31.1	8.2	0.7	68.5	38.8	49.6	50.4
46034	CICERO	98.0	97.1	0.3	0.3	0.3	0.5	1.0	1.8	6.1	6.6	7.1	6.8	4.6	26.4	31.7	9.8	1.1	76.0	40.2	49.5	50.5
46035	COLFAX	99.2	99.1	0.0	0.0	0.1	0.1	2.1	2.3	8.0	8.0	8.1	7.6	5.1	25.6	25.1	11.4	1.1	71.1	37.0	50.4	49.6
46036	ELWOOD	98.4	97.8	0.1	0.1	0.3	0.4	1.5	2.4	6.3	6.1	6.1	6.6	6.7	24.7	28.0	13.2	2.4	77.6	40.0	49.1	50.9
46037	FISHERS	92.2	91.1	3.5	3.6	2.8	3.7	1.5	2.0	11.1	10.9	9.9	6.4	3.0	34.1	21.0	3.5	0.2	63.8	32.9	48.7	51.3
46038	FISHERS	93.0	90.6	2.4	2.8	2.9	4.4	2.1	3.0	10.4	9.9	8.7	6.1	4.7	34.9	21.0	4.0	0.3	66.9	32.4	48.8	51.2
46039	FOREST	98.8	98.8	0.4	0.4	0.0	0.0	1.0	1.2	6.3	6.4	7.1	7.6	4.9	25.6	27.4	13.1	1.4	75.5	39.8	48.7	51.3
46040	FORTVILLE	98.1	96.8	0.4	1.0	0.3	0.8	1.2	1.7	7.9	8.2	8.0	7.0	4.7	28.9	26.1	8.1	1.2	71.3	36.3	49.6	50.4
46041	FRANKFORT	92.8	92.4	0.3	0.4	0.2	0.2	9.7	10.2	7.3	7.0	6.7	6.8	6.3	26.4	25.2	11.9	2.5	75.1	36.9	49.8	50.2
46044	FRANKTON	98.0	97.1	0.1	0.2	0.3	0.4	1.3	2.1	6.4	6.4	6.5	6.6	5.3	27.2	26.5	13.4	1.5	76.5	39.1	48.6	51.4
46048	INGALLS	97.7	97.2	0.3	0.4	0.3	0.3	0.9	1.4	8.5	8.3	7.9	7.0	5.2	28.6	24.1	9.5	0.8	70.9	35.3	50.6	49.4
46049	KEMPTON	98.7	98.3	0.0	0.0	0.1	0.2	1.0	1.3	5.8	6.2	6.8	6.9	5.2	25.6	29.1	12.7	1.8	76.9	41.4	50.6	49.4
46050	KIRKLIN	97.4	97.1	0.3	0.4	0.3	0.3	1.5	1.8	6.8	7.3	7.8	6.7	5.2	24.9	29.6	10.4	1.3	73.9	39.0	51.5	48.5
46051	LAPEL	98.8	98.5	0.2	0.2	0.1	0.1	0.4	0.6	6.8	7.1	7.0	7.0	6.0	26.3	27.4	10.8	1.7	74.9	38.1	48.8	51.2
46052	LEBANON	97.9	97.3	0.3	0.3	0.3	0.5	1.4	2.1	7.4	7.3	7.3	6.8	5.8	26.7	25.8	10.9	2.1	73.7	37.2	48.8	51.2
46055	MC CORDSVILLE	97.2	96.4	1.0	1.2	0.5	0.9	0.8	1.3	7.2	7.8	8.1	6.9	4.0	25.6	30.5	9.0	0.9	72.4	39.2	49.1	50.9
46056	MARKLEVILLE	98.9	98.5	0.1	0.2	0.1	0.2	0.5	0.8	5.4	7.2	6.5	7.3	4.1	24.9	32.1	11.3	1.2	76.0	40.8	50.2	49.8
46057	MICHIGANTOWN	98.8	98.8	0.0	0.0	0.1	0.1	0.8	0.9	6.4	6.9	7.0	7.6	4.6	26.1	28.9	10.6	1.8	74.9	39.3	50.9	49.1
46058	MULBERRY	99.0	99.0	0.1	0.1	0.2	0.2	0.6	0.6	5.6	5.9	6.0	6.5	5.3	26.1	26.9	12.7	4.9	78.5	41.2	47.7	52.3
46060	NOBLESVILLE	96.6	95.6	1.1	1.3	0.6	1.2	1.4	2.0	8.3	8.1	7.9	7.0	5.1	28.7	25.8	8.0	1.0	70.9	35.7	49.1	50.9
46062	NOBLESVILLE	96.9	95.9	0.8	0.9	1.0	1.6	1.1	1.9	9.4	8.9	8.4	6.6	4.7	31.6	23.0	6.5	0.8	69.0	33.3	48.5	51.5
46064	PENDLETON	89.2	86.2	8.7	10.1	0.4	1.5	1.2	1.8	5.2	5.6	6.0	6.4	7.6	32.0	26.9	8.7	1.4	79.7	37.6	58.1	41.9
46065	ROSSVILLE	98.6	98.4	0.2	0.3	0.2	0.2	0.9	1.3	7.1	7.7	8.2	7.3	4.7	26.0	26.0	10.5	2.6	72.2	37.8	47.7	52.3
46068	SHARPSVILLE	98.5	98.0	0.2	0.2	0.3	0.5	1.2	1.8	6.0	6.5	6.9	6.9	5.3	25.6	31.0	10.6	1.2	76.4	40.0	50.5	49.5
46069	SHERIDAN	97.8	97.3	0.5	0.5	0.3	0.4	1.0	1.5	6.6	6.8	7.1	7.4	5.5	26.2	28.4	10.0	1.9	74.8	38.3	49.1	50.9
46070	SUMMITVILLE	99.2	98.9	0.2	0.3	0.1	0.2	0.6	0.9	6.3	6.5	7.1	7.5	4.9	25.2	26.8	13.2	2.6	75.1	40.6	48.9	51.1
46071	THORNTOWN	98.3	97.6	0.1	0.1	0.2	0.2	1.1	1.8	6.6	7.1	7.6	7.6	5.0	23.7	29.7	11.3	1.4	74.0	40.2	49.1	50.9
46072	TIPTON	98.3	97.7	0.2	0.2	0.4	0.6	1.2	1.8	6.2	6.4	6.4	6.1	5.1	25.3	27.8	13.5	3.1	77.1	41.0	48.9	51.1
46074	WESTFIELD	95.1	92.8	0.9	0.9	1.7	3.3	2.1	3.1	9.6	9.2	8.8	7.1	4.9	30.8	23.6	5.2	0.7	67.8	32.2	49.4	50.6
46075	WHITESTOWN	98.2	97.9	0.5	0.4	0.4	0.6	0.6	0.8	5.9	6.4	6.9	7.4	4.7	24.2	32.1	11.2	1.2	76.2	41.5	51.1	48.9
46076	WINDFALL	98.7	98.3	0.1	0.1	0.1	0.1	0.8	1.2	6.4	6.6	6.9	6.6	5.0	25.9	29.1	11.9	1.5	75.8	40.4	50.6	49.4
46077	ZIONSVILLE	97.3	96.4	0.7	0.9	1.0	1.5	1.0	1.5	6.9	7.6	8.5	7.9	4.5	22.1	31.0	9.4	2.2	72.1	40.0	48.7	51.3
46104	ARLINGTON	98.5	98.0	0.1	0.1	0.2	0.4	0.4	0.6	5.9	7.0	8.0	7.5	4.8	26.5	27.6	11.3	1.5	74.1	38.9	51.1	48.9
46105	BAINBRIDGE	98.7	98.3	0.3	0.3	0.2	0.3	0.7	1.0	6.8	7.1	7.4	6.6	5.1	24.8	29.6	11.6	1.2	74.7	40.1	50.0	50.0
46106	BARGERSVILLE	98.9	98.6	0.1	0.1	0.3	0.4	0.6	0.9	6.8	7.2	7.5	7.2	4.9	26.3	29.1	9.9	1.1	73.9	38.2	50.3	49.7
46107	BEECH GROVE	96.1	94.3	1.0	1.5	0.8	1.2	2.1	3.6	6.9	6.5	6.1	6.1	6.6	26.8	25.0	12.5	3.5	76.7	38.1	47.3	52.7
46110	BOGGSTOWN	99.0	98.6	0.0	0.0	0.0	0.0	0.7	0.7	6.3	7.5	8.0	6.8	4.7	23.9	31.5	10.6	0.7	73.7	40.2	50.0	50.0
46112	BROWNSBURG	97.5	96.8	0.3	0.4	0.8	1.2	1.0	1.4	7.7	7.5	7.5	7.3	5.5	27.1	27.1	9.0	1.4	72.7	36.6	48.8	51.2
46113	CAMBY	97.6	96.6	0.4	0.6	0.5	0.8	0.9	1.5	7.5	7.9	8.1	7.4	4.9	27.7	26.9	8.7	1.0	71.7	36.5	49.4	50.6
46115	CARTHAGE	98.1	97.4	0.0	0.0	0.0	0.0	0.9	1.5	6.3	6.9	7.2	6.8	4.3	26.3	29.4	11.4	1.5	75.3	40.2	51.3	48.7
46117	CHARLOTTESVILLE	98.2	97.7	0.2	0.3	0.2	0.2	1.1	1.4	6.8	7.3	7.4	5.6	4.2	26.2	30.2	11.0	1.2	74.9	40.2	51.2	48.8
46118	CLAYTON	98.8	98.6	0.0	0.1	0.1	0.2	0.7	1.0	5.7	6.2	6.9	7.5	4.7	23.9	31.7	12.5	1.1	76.7	41.8	49.5	50.5
46120	CLOVERDALE	91.7	90.4	6.0	6.8	0.2	0.3	1.4	2.0	5.8	5.8	6.0	6.7	8.0	30.3	25.7	10.6	1.1	78.7	37.0	57.2	42.8
46121	COATESVILLE	98.6	98.3	0.3	0.4	0.1	0.2	0.6	0.9	7.0	7.5	7.8	6.8	4.2	24.7	29.0	11.9	1.1	73.4	39.8	50.8	49.2
46122	DANVILLE	98.5	98.3	0.3	0.3	0.2	0.3	0.9	1.3	6.7	6.9	7.2	7.1	5.5	25.7	28.9	10.3	1.7	74.6	38.6	50.5	49.5
46123	AVON	97.0	96.1	0.3	0.4	1.0	1.5	1.3	2.0	8.5	8.3	8.3	7.0	5.1	27.8	26.9	7.3	0.8	70.5	35.3	49.5	50.5
46124	EDINBURGH	98.6	98.1	0.5	0.8	0.1	0.1	1.0	1.6	6.9	6.7	6.7	6.8	6.5	27.4	27.4	10.5	1.1	75.6	37.4	49.6	50.4
46126	FAIRLAND	98.4	98.0	0.1	0.1	0.1	0.2	0.8	1.2	6.2	7.6	7.9	7.1	5.2	24.7	30.5	10.1	0.9	73.7	39.5	50.5	49.5
46127	FALMOUTH	99.5	99.3	0.3	0.3	0.0	0.0	0.0	0.3	7.0	7.5	8.0	6.8	4.5	26.3	28.0	10.5	1.5	73.0	38.4	51.3	48.7
46128	FILLMORE	98.3	97.7	0.3	0.4	0.1	0.3	0.9	1.2	6.7	6.9	7.4	7.8	4.5	24.8	27.7	12.9	1.1	73.8	40.4	49.5	50.5
46130	FOUNTAINTOWN	98.7	98.3	0.1	0.1	0.3	0.4	1.0	1.5	7.1	7.7	7.9	6.7	4.2	25.6	30.7	9.2	1.0	73.0	39.0	50.2	49.8
46131	FRANKLIN	97.0	95.8	1.1	1.5	0.5	0.8	1.2	1.9	7.7	7.1	6.8	7.5	7.3	26.4	23.1	11.0	3.1	74.3	35.7	48.6	51.4
46133	GLENWOOD	98.9	98.6	0.3	0.4	0.0	0.0	0.2	0.2	6.2	6.8	7.4	7.6	4.7	23.6	30.8	11.2	1.7	74.8	40.2	50.3	49.7
46135	GREENCASTLE	94.0	92.4	3.3	3.8	0.9	1.5	1.4	2.0	5.7	5.4	5.7	10.3	12.7	23.5	22.6	11.5	2.7	79.4	34.2	50.9	49.1
46140	GREENFIELD	98.4	98.0	0.1	0.1	0.5	0.7	1.1	1.6	6.8	6.9	7.0	6.5	5.2	26.4	28.4	11.3	1.6	75.3	39.1	49.5	50.5
46142	GREENWOOD	96.9	95.6	0.3	0.4	1.3	2.0	2.0	2.9	7.4	7.3	7.3	6.9	6.0	27.0	26.4	10.1	1.6	73.7	36.4	48.9	51.1
46143	GREENWOOD	97.2	96.3	0.3	0.4	1.2	1.7	1.2	1.9	7.9	7.1	6.9	6.3	6.0	28.8	26.0	9.6	1.4	74.1	35.9	48.5	51.5
46147	JAMESTOWN	98.9	98.5	0.1	0.1	0.1	0.1	1.0	1.5	6.6	7.0	7.3	7.0	4.8	25.4	30.1	10.5	1.2	74.8	39.9	49.3	50.7
46148	KNIGHTSTOWN	99.1	99.0	0.3	0.4	0.1	0.2	0.3	0.4	6.7	6.5	6.7	6.4	5.3	25.0	28.5	13.2	1.6	76.1	40.1	48.8	51.2
46149	LIZTON	98.6	98.1	0.1	0.1	0.3	0.5	0.7	1.0	6.2	6.4	7.0	7.3	4.7	26.0	31.2	10.3	1.1	75.9	40.5	48.6	51.4
46150	MANILLA	98.7	98.3	0.1	0.1	0.4	0.7	0.7	1.0	7.7	7.2	7.1	6.5	5.1	24.1	28.7	11.7	1.9	73.8	39.2	50.2	49.8
46151	MARTINSVILLE	98.7	98.3	0.1	0.1	0.3	0.4	0.8	1.2	6.6	6.8	7.0	6.6	5.1	26.4	28.7	11.3	1.5	75.5	39.3	50.5	49.5
46156	MILROY	98.0	97.3	0.1	0.1	0.4	0.6	1.1	1.6	8.0	7.9	7.8	6.9	4.6	25.6	26.0	11.7	1.6	72.0	37.7	49.7	50.3
46157	MONROVIA	98.9	98.6	0.0	0.0	0.2	0.3	0.5	0.7	6.0	6.5	7.1	7.1	5.0	25.2	31.1	10.7	1.3	75.9	40.7	50.0	50.0
46158	MOORESVILLE	98.4	98.1	0.1	0.1	0.3	0.5	0.7	1.0	7.6	7.5	7.4	6.7	5.7	27.0	27.3	9.7	1.1	73.3	37.0	49.2	50.8
46160	MORGANTOWN	98.7	98.4	0.1	0.1	0.1	0.1	0.9	1.3	5.8	6.6	7.0	6.7	4.8	24.5	31.6	11.4	1.8	76.5	41.5	50.5	49.5
46161	MORRISTOWN	98.9	98.5	0.1	0.1	0.2	0.3	0.8	1.3	6.9	7.6	7.8	7.3	5.2	26.2	26.2	10.8	2.0	73.2	37.3	49.0	51.0
46162	NEEDHAM	99.0	98.8	0.0	0.0	0.0	0.3	0.7	1.3	6.6	7.2	7.8	6.6	4.4	22.5	32.2	11.9	0.9	74.4	41.7	50.9	49.1
46163	NEW PALESTINE	98.7	98.3	0.1	0.1	0.4	0.6	0.6	0.8	6.1	6.8	7.5	7.3	4.6	22.3	32.9	11.4	1.2	74.9	42.0	49.2	50.8
46164	NINEVEH	89.9	89.5	7.7	7.7	0.2	0.3	2.0	2.6	4.7	5.2	5.8	12.0	7.6	22.8	31.5	9.8	0.7	77.3	39.1	53.7	46.3
46165	NORTH SALEM	98.4	98.0	0.1	0.1	0.5	0.6	0.5	0.8	6.8	6.8	7.0	7.1	5.6	25.2	28.2	11.9	1.4	75.0	39.5	48.6	51.4
46166	PARAGON	99.0	98.7	0.0	0.0	0.1	0.2	0.5	0.8	7.3	7.4	7.7	7.6	5.2	24.9	27.6	11.2	1.1	72.9	38.6	50.0	50.0
46167	PITTSBORO	98.4	98.1	0.1	0.1	0.3	0.4	0.6	0.9	7.7	7.9	7.9	7.0	4.5	26.7	28.1	9.3	1.0	72.2	37.1	48.9	51.1
46168	PLAINFIELD	93.6	92.1	3.8	4.5	0.8	1.2	1.4	2.1	6.2	6.2	6.3	8.0	6.3	28.8	26.2	10.2	1.7	76.0	37.3	52.9	47.1
46171	REELSVILLE	96.5	95.8	2.2	2.5	0.0	0.0	0.6	0.8	5.4	6.0	6.4	6.7	5.3	25.0	31.6	12.8	0.9	78.3	41.9	51.0	49.0
46172	ROACHDALE	98.7	98.4	0.2	0.3	0.1	0.2	0.3	0.5	6.7	7.5	7.5	6.9	4.7	25.3	27.5	12.2	1.7	73.7	39.1	50.3	49.7
46173	RUSHVILLE	97.3	96.6	0.9	1.1	0.7	1.1	0.4	0.6	6.7	6.6	6.7	6.9	5.8	25.1	26.5	12.9	2.8	75.6	39.2	48.9	51.1
46175	RUSSELLVILLE	98.0	97.7	0.0	0.0	0.3	0.4	1.2	1.9	7.2	7.0	7.4	7.5	6.0	24.7	26.0	12.8	1.3	74.0	39.7	49.6	50.4
46176	SHELBYVILLE	96.4	95.3	1.1	1.3	0.9	1.4	1.4	2.1	6.9	6.8	6.7	6.6	6.1	26.9	26.8	11.1	2.0	75.5	37.7	49.6	50.4
46180	STILESVILLE	98.6	98.3	0.1	0.1	0.1	0.1	0.5	0.7	6.3	7.0	7.1	5.8	4.2	24.4	30.1	13.6	1.6	76.1	41.9	50.0	50.0
46181	TRAFALGAR	98.7	98.3	0.2	0.3	0.2	0.4	0.6	0.9	6.0	6.4	6.9	7.1	5.0	25.2	31.3	11.1	1.1	76.1	40.6	50.9	49.1
46182	WALDRON	98.7	98.7	0.2	0.2	0.1	0.1	0.4	0.6	5.6	6.1	6.2	6.6	4.8	25.0	29.4	12.8	3.6	77.8	42.1	49.0	51.0
46184	WHITELAND	98.6	98.1	0.1	0.1	0.3	0.5	1.0	1.8	8.5	8.0	7.8	7.3	6.0	30.6	23.6	7.5	0.7	71.1	33.3	48.9	51.1
46186	WILKINSON	99.0	98.9	0.0	0.1	0.1	0.2	0.6	0.9	6.6	7.2	7.2	6.2	4.3	26.7	28.4	12.2	1.1	75.0	39.8	50.7	49.3
46201	INDIANAPOLIS	72.5	65.3	18.9	23.0	0.4	0.5	9.2	13.3	8.6	7.7	7.0	7.3	7.8	30.0	23.0	7.5	1.1	72.3	32.5	49.7	50.3
46202	INDIANAPOLIS	43.2	37.6	50.9	54.9	2.5	3.5	2.9	4.2	5.0	3.9	3.3	5.4	12.2	34.9	22.9	10.3	2.0	85.5	34.4	52.4	47.6
	INDIANA	87.5	85.6	8.4	8.9	1.0	1.5	3.5	5.0	6.9	6.8	6.8	7.2	6.9	26.5	26.2	10.8	1.9	75.4	36.8	49.3	50.7
	UNITED STATES	75.1	72.0	12.3	12.7	3.8	4.6	12.5	15.7	6.8	6.7	6.6	7.1	6.9	27.0	26.0	10.9	1.9	75.7	36.9	49.2	50.8

ZIP CODE #	POST OFFICE NAME	2009 Per Capita Income	2009 HH Income Base	2009 Household Income Distribution (%): Less than $25,000	$25,000 to $49,999	$50,000 to $99,999	$100,000 to $149,999	$150,000 or More	Median Household Income: 2009	2014	2009 National Centile	2009 State Centile	2009 Home Value Base	2009 Home Value Distribution (%): Less than $50,000	$50,000 to $89,999	$90,000 to $174,999	$175,000 to $399,999	$400,000 or More	2009 Median Home Value
46001	ALEXANDRIA	23442	4704	18.4	29.9	42.2	6.9	2.5	51357	53289	65	55	3575	12.8	42.5	37.0	6.8	0.9	87063
46011	ANDERSON	30160	6902	12.9	24.1	43.8	12.9	6.3	62786	62853	81	87	5693	5.8	32.8	50.7	9.7	1.0	101153
46012	ANDERSON	28573	8300	15.6	27.0	40.9	11.0	5.4	56911	58071	74	75	6183	7.9	37.5	47.1	7.3	0.2	95191
46013	ANDERSON	26797	8229	20.6	31.5	37.7	7.6	2.5	47683	51013	56	34	5931	13.9	39.1	44.1	2.5	0.4	87558
46016	ANDERSON	18186	8296	37.3	32.6	24.0	4.3	1.8	32181	33582	12	3	4311	43.4	45.8	9.7	1.0	0.1	54709
46017	ANDERSON	29343	2500	12.2	24.2	45.6	12.6	5.3	61071	61307	79	84	2117	11.0	35.3	48.6	4.8	0.3	92601
46030	ARCADIA	24097	1521	15.1	24.9	41.1	15.6	3.4	61584	61376	79	85	1149	10.3	30.3	42.5	12.4	4.6	100635
46031	ATLANTA	22827	901	19.2	27.2	37.1	14.4	2.1	54029	54508	70	67	727	12.4	27.4	39.9	15.0	5.4	102519
46032	CARMEL	47881	16192	6.9	15.9	27.6	24.4	25.2	98729	102353	96	99	11956	1.8	2.1	24.8	46.2	25.1	248635
46033	CARMEL	55273	12638	3.9	6.3	21.1	28.8	40.0	132318	135819	99	100	11799	2.2	0.7	9.3	64.7	23.1	279080
46034	CICERO	28594	3225	12.4	24.0	43.4	15.6	4.7	64252	64057	83	90	2525	8.4	17.7	45.7	22.3	5.9	127264
46035	COLFAX	20713	418	23.2	27.8	41.9	6.0	1.2	49155	51607	59	42	329	18.5	28.0	43.5	9.4	0.6	92447
46036	ELWOOD	21904	5052	24.5	31.8	33.0	7.9	2.8	43745	46782	45	18	3840	16.1	46.7	32.9	4.0	0.3	79219
46037	FISHERS	47322	12304	4.7	9.0	25.3	36.0	25.1	110038	111785	98	100	10693	0.7	2.0	21.4	57.5	18.4	241736
46038	FISHERS	43795	13506	3.6	10.5	32.3	35.8	17.8	102857	105234	97	100	10238	1.6	1.1	35.9	54.4	7.0	192703
46039	FOREST	23993	298	20.1	29.5	37.2	8.4	4.7	52308	60996	67	60	255	10.2	15.7	63.9	5.5	4.7	110601
46040	FORTVILLE	32534	3681	14.0	19.2	37.5	18.5	10.8	73284	77181	88	95	2973	9.6	9.6	42.9	28.0	10.0	147600
46041	FRANKFORT	21445	9089	23.3	28.0	38.1	8.6	2.1	48522	51683	58	38	6327	9.5	24.9	54.3	10.4	0.8	105463
46044	FRANKTON	23229	1166	19.5	28.0	41.9	8.1	2.6	51975	53880	66	58	1006	16.0	32.5	45.4	5.2	0.9	90987
46048	INGALLS	20629	476	15.3	34.2	42.2	6.7	1.5	50360	52906	62	48	392	9.2	45.7	43.4	1.8	0.0	87532
46049	KEMPTON	25159	338	17.5	24.6	45.6	7.7	4.7	57121	60267	74	76	285	20.0	28.1	43.2	8.4	0.4	91222
46050	KIRKLIN	23709	731	19.0	28.6	39.1	8.8	4.5	51518	53129	65	55	595	11.3	27.4	49.4	8.6	3.4	103676
46051	LAPEL	25767	1004	13.1	30.7	42.6	9.4	4.2	55428	56630	72	71	790	4.4	34.7	52.9	7.7	0.3	96880
46052	LEBANON	24050	9131	19.5	27.0	43.9	7.6	2.0	54193	58222	70	67	6613	10.0	17.9	55.3	15.3	1.5	114032
46055	MC CORDSVILLE	34338	2516	7.2	16.4	37.8	26.0	12.6	83679	85748	93	98	2304	3.1	4.6	34.3	48.5	9.5	190776
46056	MARKLEVILLE	24645	886	13.8	26.9	44.5	13.3	1.6	60061	59841	77	82	795	9.4	24.0	49.7	15.5	1.4	104602
46057	MICHIGANTOWN	24617	389	19.0	29.3	35.7	9.8	6.2	51961	54144	66	58	304	8.9	25.0	49.3	12.2	4.6	107653
46058	MULBERRY	26823	842	12.9	19.4	50.1	12.2	5.3	67035	67036	85	92	677	3.0	13.4	60.1	21.3	2.2	128102
46060	NOBLESVILLE	34043	12931	12.5	19.7	34.9	22.2	10.7	69316	71476	86	94	10039	8.8	13.0	33.6	37.9	6.8	163813
46062	NOBLESVILLE	39925	11183	6.6	12.4	34.2	32.5	14.3	93669	100133	96	99	9133	7.0	5.0	34.0	45.6	8.5	182717
46064	PENDLETON	25291	4585	12.9	25.3	41.9	14.0	5.9	62964	62601	81	88	3830	7.7	11.9	58.1	20.8	1.5	124785
46065	ROSSVILLE	21633	1344	14.1	29.2	46.7	8.4	1.5	55851	57008	72	72	1123	9.1	12.7	60.4	16.9	0.9	126177
46068	SHARPSVILLE	28570	1088	9.4	17.5	49.8	18.1	5.2	69150	73874	86	93	961	11.3	24.6	54.1	9.7	0.3	103469
46069	SHERIDAN	23268	2796	18.7	23.3	38.0	17.6	2.4	56527	57662	73	74	2166	19.3	12.0	44.6	21.9	2.3	121484
46070	SUMMITVILLE	20592	957	22.5	28.6	40.4	6.7	1.8	48716	51432	58	39	782	20.2	33.2	44.2	2.3	0.0	87033
46071	THORNTOWN	22733	1333	14.6	33.0	42.9	7.4	2.1	52523	56345	67	61	1101	15.3	16.5	52.7	12.6	2.9	113873
46072	TIPTON	26242	3891	19.3	23.8	41.1	12.8	2.9	56915	60589	74	75	2958	11.9	33.2	45.2	9.3	0.3	93945
46074	WESTFIELD	35396	8019	10.5	16.5	29.4	29.5	14.2	83825	90091	93	98	6374	13.4	6.5	26.0	45.0	9.0	185769
46075	WHITESTOWN	25898	944	10.6	29.7	47.9	9.2	2.6	61040	62829	79	84	796	3.6	13.2	58.2	21.7	3.3	133275
46076	WINDFALL	24113	734	18.0	30.0	37.6	11.4	3.0	51808	55168	66	57	612	22.4	30.9	38.4	7.2	1.1	86923
46077	ZIONSVILLE	41763	8239	12.0	16.0	29.6	20.2	22.2	85487	87590	94	98	6929	7.6	1.5	29.1	41.7	20.1	206806
46104	ARLINGTON	18668	399	20.6	32.8	37.3	9.3	0.0	46666	48273	53	30	332	7.8	36.1	43.4	12.7	0.0	97692
46105	BAINBRIDGE	21171	778	16.6	35.3	40.2	5.1	2.7	48561	50885	58	38	655	11.1	20.8	46.0	20.2	2.0	113923
46106	BARGERSVILLE	33709	2084	8.6	15.9	40.0	27.1	8.4	76874	79199	91	97	1732	5.0	7.7	50.3	31.6	5.4	140364
46107	BEECH GROVE	26751	5416	15.6	26.7	45.8	7.8	4.1	57290	58976	74	76	3513	0.3	38.2	57.5	3.5	0.4	94927
46110	BOGGSTOWN	24693	166	10.8	34.3	41.0	10.8	3.0	54881	60000	71	69	144	5.6	15.3	41.7	35.4	2.1	140625
46112	BROWNSBURG	33854	12480	7.4	16.8	40.1	25.3	10.3	77770	81658	91	97	10585	5.5	3.6	44.1	41.9	4.9	170216
46113	CAMBY	26554	4310	11.3	19.2	52.7	12.7	4.1	65725	67710	84	91	3807	4.8	11.6	62.1	19.6	1.9	126857
46115	CARTHAGE	23375	778	21.1	26.6	38.4	11.6	2.3	52005	52986	66	58	605	8.4	22.3	51.1	16.0	2.1	119176
46117	CHARLOTTESVILLE	28698	234	12.4	17.5	49.1	15.0	6.0	67104	68595	85	92	202	0.0	10.9	44.1	41.1	4.0	166667
46118	CLAYTON	25503	1960	13.4	25.7	44.9	13.4	2.5	58525	59357	76	79	1695	5.7	21.6	35.0	32.5	5.2	141943
46120	CLOVERDALE	18550	2116	20.3	31.0	40.0	7.1	1.6	49047	51100	59	41	1681	12.8	29.1	46.2	10.8	1.1	100310
46121	COATESVILLE	23877	2247	14.5	28.2	43.7	10.9	2.7	56628	56909	74	75	1986	8.2	16.4	41.6	30.9	2.9	140164
46122	DANVILLE	28019	5850	11.8	23.9	39.9	18.5	6.0	65927	69392	84	92	4566	3.3	13.4	40.7	38.7	3.9	163994
46123	AVON	35243	10460	6.0	10.8	41.0	30.1	12.1	87332	89898	94	99	9363	4.5	1.6	34.7	53.7	5.6	192518
46124	EDINBURGH	22194	3148	22.6	28.3	39.7	6.9	2.5	48942	51649	59	41	2311	26.8	14.3	45.1	12.1	1.6	101314
46126	FAIRLAND	26164	1782	14.1	22.6	40.9	17.1	5.4	61402	62906	79	85	1567	2.9	21.1	51.6	22.7	1.7	124615
46127	FALMOUTH	23723	166	15.7	30.1	45.2	7.2	1.8	53025	53634	68	64	131	9.2	22.9	47.3	16.0	4.6	115972
46128	FILLMORE	21279	620	19.7	32.1	38.9	6.5	2.9	48761	50901	58	40	540	10.4	19.6	48.3	18.9	2.8	116737
46130	FOUNTAINTOWN	28410	899	9.6	23.4	45.3	17.1	4.7	68045	69104	86	93	782	0.3	7.4	60.6	29.5	2.2	145395
46131	FRANKLIN	26860	11492	14.7	22.6	41.0	18.1	3.7	64031	66868	82	89	8247	17.4	8.4	51.9	20.7	1.6	127332
46133	GLENWOOD	20234	352	23.3	27.3	41.8	6.0	1.7	49450	50955	60	43	291	10.7	27.1	49.5	11.7	1.0	99342
46135	GREENCASTLE	21224	6349	24.2	31.4	34.7	6.2	3.5	44080	47370	46	19	4517	13.9	23.5	48.2	13.0	1.5	104004
46140	GREENFIELD	31215	15894	10.2	23.6	42.6	17.4	6.2	68833	72416	86	93	12489	4.7	10.3	46.2	35.0	3.7	157198
46142	GREENWOOD	34083	13103	10.0	16.7	38.8	25.6	8.9	73629	79165	89	95	9976	7.0	3.6	50.1	38.2	1.1	160573
46143	GREENWOOD	36967	18392	11.1	18.7	33.3	23.5	13.4	76746	80896	90	97	13805	7.6	5.9	43.8	37.0	5.8	162381
46147	JAMESTOWN	25245	1282	12.5	26.5	45.6	12.0	3.4	60624	62166	78	83	1044	11.7	14.5	59.1	12.2	2.6	116228
46148	KNIGHTSTOWN	25085	1989	19.8	28.6	38.8	9.9	3.0	52251	54854	66	59	1530	5.7	24.8	51.1	16.7	1.8	110066
46149	LIZTON	27037	783	17.1	25.5	41.3	10.1	6.0	59155	60604	76	80	630	3.8	11.6	43.3	35.9	5.4	156164
46150	MANILLA	21269	329	16.1	35.0	38.3	10.3	0.3	48884	50416	59	40	272	10.7	20.6	44.1	21.7	2.9	119444
46151	MARTINSVILLE	24359	12388	18.9	24.3	43.3	9.7	3.7	57882	61423	75	78	9429	12.4	14.5	47.1	22.6	3.4	124707
46156	MILROY	19945	550	20.5	26.9	40.4	11.8	0.4	52387	52992	67	60	441	11.1	23.1	49.9	11.6	4.3	101067
46157	MONROVIA	24255	1162	19.1	21.9	43.5	12.0	3.4	60572	63468	78	83	988	10.8	16.1	51.9	19.8	1.3	115593
46158	MOORESVILLE	27180	9216	13.7	23.1	42.2	15.7	5.2	64164	68324	82	90	7533	13.7	8.5	52.7	22.0	3.2	130443
46160	MORGANTOWN	22153	2510	23.9	26.8	36.7	9.5	3.1	49057	53341	59	42	2106	15.0	14.7	41.6	25.5	3.1	123204
46161	MORRISTOWN	24893	1002	16.1	24.2	43.9	13.1	2.8	57613	60025	75	77	802	12.1	24.8	45.6	15.5	2.0	106655
46162	NEEDHAM	28557	133	9.0	27.1	47.4	13.5	3.0	62947	64105	81	87	115	7.0	12.2	43.5	33.0	4.3	142361
46163	NEW PALESTINE	32356	4342	10.2	21.7	36.9	20.9	10.3	76278	77961	90	97	3781	4.8	3.8	33.5	53.5	4.4	188523
46164	NINEVEH	24442	1948	13.8	27.6	44.0	10.8	3.9	56814	58571	74	75	1777	3.7	13.8	55.1	25.9	1.5	140008
46165	NORTH SALEM	30111	634	14.0	20.8	41.6	15.8	7.7	65888	68519	84	91	535	7.5	31.8	36.8	18.3	5.6	108726
46166	PARAGON	18968	806	20.6	30.1	41.3	7.2	0.7	49496	51302	60	43	655	26.4	19.2	37.7	13.3	3.4	97917
46167	PITTSBORO	29419	2320	9.2	19.5	44.1	20.4	6.8	70175	73682	87	94	2010	1.6	4.9	39.4	48.6	5.5	185904
46168	PLAINFIELD	28716	10667	14.4	21.4	39.9	18.3	6.0	65217	68753	83	91	7842	10.6	4.3	44.3	39.2	1.7	161364
46171	REELSVILLE	20989	766	21.3	28.7	41.4	6.9	1.7	50000	51164	61	46	692	8.4	26.0	47.0	17.3	1.3	110606
46172	ROACHDALE	21382	1019	18.6	32.4	38.8	6.8	3.4	49171	51398	59	42	838	9.5	35.6	37.7	15.8	1.4	94659
46173	RUSHVILLE	21351	4345	24.7	31.6	35.0	6.1	2.6	45008	47027	48	23	3078	9.4	30.6	50.0	8.3	1.6	99217
46175	RUSSELLVILLE	17347	211	26.1	37.9	32.2	2.8	0.9	39306	42408	31	8	177	22.6	37.3	33.9	6.2	0.0	72917
46176	SHELBYVILLE	25315	11313	20.0	26.7	40.5	9.4	3.4	53079	56465	68	64	7586	8.1	24.5	54.6	11.3	1.5	108459
46180	STILESVILLE	24678	503	13.9	33.2	37.6	13.5	1.8	52574	54604	67	62	420	10.0	15.7	47.6	26.4	0.2	124684
46181	TRAFALGAR	26990	1687	12.1	23.9	43.2	15.1	5.8	63562	65332	82	89	1478	5.2	8.5	44.2	36.2	5.9	158750
46182	WALDRON	22193	726	21.1	29.1	38.8	8.1	2.9	49843	53925	61	45	602	7.0	23.9	53.7	12.8	2.7	107885
46184	WHITELAND	29484	4110	5.1	16.4	48.3	25.4	4.8	73876	76387	89	95	3482	0.0	6.7	75.6	15.2	2.5	123179
46186	WILKINSON	27612	710	13.7	21.5	48.6	13.1	3.1	65606	67532	84	91	599	3.2	13.9	51.1	30.1	1.8	149144
46201	INDIANAPOLIS	16971	13625	33.9	33.6	28.4	3.0	1.0	35362	37130	19	5	6409	32.5	58.4	7.4	1.3	0.3	60759
46202	INDIANAPOLIS	27003	8154	42.6	24.6	22.9	5.0	4.9	30478	31349	9	2	2143	22.4	28.8	23.0	22.6	3.2	88237
	INDIANA	26003		19.5	26.3	38.6	10.5	5.1	54105	56493				12.2	24.1	44.1	17.2	2.4	108938
	UNITED STATES	27277		20.9	24.4	35.3	11.7	7.6	54719	56938				9.3	13.1	31.6	32.6	13.5	162279

ZIP CODE		FINANCIAL SERVICES				THE HOME						ENTERTAINMENT						PERSONAL			
						Home Improvements		Furnishings													
#	POST OFFICE NAME	Auto Loan	Home Loan	Invest-ments	Retire-ment Plans	Home Repair	Lawn & Garden	Comput-ers & Hard-ware-Personal	Major Appli-ances	TV, Radio, Sound Equip-ment	Furni-ture	Dine out/ Carry out	Sports Equip-ment	Fees & Tickets	Toys & Games	Travel	Cable TV	Apparel & Services	Auto Repairs	Health Insur-ance	Pets & Supplies
46001	ALEXANDRIA	86	83	74	85	81	90	83	85	85	79	84	65	81	86	81	88	58	84	91	101
46011	ANDERSON	101	109	100	110	107	115	102	106	104	98	104	80	106	105	106	107	72	104	113	124
46012	ANDERSON	97	95	94	97	95	104	97	98	98	92	97	74	95	98	96	101	67	98	105	116
46013	ANDERSON	85	75	84	75	76	92	77	86	83	72	81	63	72	82	77	89	55	83	95	100
46016	ANDERSON	66	53	51	54	51	63	61	61	65	57	63	47	54	66	54	69	44	63	68	74
46017	ANDERSON	96	104	90	105	100	109	98	100	101	94	100	76	103	101	100	104	69	99	111	118
46030	ARCADIA	96	95	83	98	92	103	93	96	95	88	94	75	92	97	92	98	64	94	102	115
46031	ATLANTA	97	90	84	91	90	99	86	94	89	84	88	71	82	91	85	93	60	89	96	111
46032	CARMEL	179	200	192	207	200	182	186	183	178	196	180	146	201	183	192	171	130	178	169	211
46033	CARMEL	223	279	267	288	281	243	232	240	217	256	220	191	269	226	254	204	162	221	207	269
46034	CICERO	100	111	98	113	109	109	102	104	100	101	101	81	108	102	106	100	71	101	104	122
46035	COLFAX	96	71	80	69	70	92	73	84	80	70	79	65	60	83	67	87	53	80	89	102
46036	ELWOOD	81	74	67	75	71	83	76	78	79	72	78	61	72	80	73	83	53	78	85	94
46037	FISHERS	194	232	199	237	225	190	195	196	180	218	183	163	218	195	203	165	134	180	161	219
46038	FISHERS	173	184	157	188	176	154	171	164	161	184	164	136	178	172	168	150	117	159	142	188
46039	FOREST	97	88	87	92	90	104	87	98	90	79	88	74	80	91	87	95	60	91	101	114
46040	FORTVILLE	120	134	112	137	128	128	121	122	119	124	120	97	130	124	124	118	84	119	121	143
46041	FRANKFORT	82	77	70	78	75	85	79	80	82	75	81	62	76	82	76	85	56	80	87	96
46044	FRANKTON	92	81	79	82	79	95	81	88	85	76	83	68	74	87	78	90	57	84	93	105
46048	INGALLS	91	84	74	81	82	85	79	84	82	82	82	61	75	85	75	84	56	81	84	99
46049	KEMPTON	104	94	94	98	96	111	93	105	96	84	94	80	86	98	93	102	64	97	108	122
46050	KIRKLIN	105	85	90	85	85	105	85	97	91	82	90	74	74	95	81	98	61	92	101	116
46051	LAPEL	90	95	76	97	89	97	92	90	93	89	92	72	94	95	91	94	64	91	98	109
46052	LEBANON	88	83	75	85	81	88	85	85	86	82	85	66	82	88	82	88	59	85	89	102
46055	MC CORDSVILLE	136	156	134	160	151	146	137	141	132	141	133	112	148	137	144	130	94	134	134	164
46056	MARKLEVILLE	100	92	90	96	93	107	90	101	93	82	91	77	84	95	90	98	62	94	104	118
46057	MICHIGANTOWN	102	96	93	100	97	110	93	104	95	86	94	79	88	97	94	100	64	96	106	121
46058	MULBERRY	100	107	88	109	101	108	101	101	101	98	101	80	104	103	102	102	70	100	106	121
46060	NOBLESVILLE	131	139	122	140	135	130	130	130	126	133	127	102	133	131	130	124	89	126	125	151
46062	NOBLESVILLE	160	178	149	174	169	148	157	156	147	170	150	125	164	158	157	139	106	148	136	177
46064	PENDLETON	105	112	100	115	109	116	103	109	103	100	103	84	106	105	107	105	71	104	111	128
46065	ROSSVILLE	93	85	84	88	86	100	83	94	86	76	84	71	77	88	84	91	58	87	97	109
46068	SHARPSVILLE	116	116	104	117	114	120	108	115	109	107	109	87	107	112	109	111	75	110	115	135
46069	SHERIDAN	91	97	82	98	93	96	90	92	89	89	89	72	92	92	91	90	62	89	93	109
46070	SUMMITVILLE	90	72	77	72	72	90	73	84	78	69	77	64	63	81	69	84	52	79	88	100
46071	THORNTOWN	88	89	84	91	88	98	83	91	85	78	84	69	83	86	86	89	58	86	94	106
46072	TIPTON	97	87	86	89	86	101	87	95	91	82	89	72	81	92	86	95	61	91	101	113
46074	WESTFIELD	148	167	138	164	158	137	144	145	135	159	138	117	153	146	145	127	98	135	123	164
46075	WHITESTOWN	102	97	94	100	98	109	93	104	95	86	94	79	89	97	94	99	64	96	105	120
46076	WINDFALL	103	84	89	84	84	103	84	96	90	80	88	73	73	93	80	96	60	90	100	114
46077	ZIONSVILLE	160	192	182	198	193	175	165	170	158	177	160	134	187	163	179	152	115	160	156	194
46104	ARLINGTON	81	74	73	77	75	87	73	82	75	66	74	62	67	77	73	80	50	76	85	96
46105	BAINBRIDGE	91	76	82	75	75	92	75	85	79	72	78	65	66	82	72	85	53	80	88	102
46106	BARGERSVILLE	126	139	121	141	134	134	127	129	125	129	126	99	134	128	131	124	88	126	128	151
46107	BEECH GROVE	89	90	77	91	85	91	90	88	91	88	91	68	91	93	88	93	63	90	94	105
46110	BOGGSTOWN	95	93	88	96	93	103	88	97	90	83	89	74	86	92	90	93	61	91	99	113
46112	BROWNSBURG	130	141	124	139	136	127	130	129	125	135	127	101	135	131	131	123	90	126	122	150
46113	CAMBY	106	113	95	112	108	106	102	104	100	106	102	80	105	104	103	100	70	101	101	122
46115	CARTHAGE	88	87	82	90	87	96	83	91	84	78	83	69	80	86	84	87	57	85	92	106
46117	CHARLOTTESVILLE	110	124	107	128	120	122	111	115	109	111	110	90	118	112	117	109	77	111	114	136
46118	CLAYTON	100	97	92	101	98	108	93	102	94	87	93	78	90	96	95	98	64	95	104	119
46120	CLOVERDALE	89	73	78	74	74	89	75	84	80	71	78	64	66	81	72	85	53	80	88	100
46121	COATESVILLE	93	94	86	97	93	101	88	95	88	84	88	73	87	90	90	91	61	90	96	111
46122	DANVILLE	103	116	103	117	113	113	104	108	104	105	105	83	112	106	110	105	73	105	108	126
46123	AVON	144	159	135	156	151	135	141	141	133	152	136	112	147	142	142	127	96	134	125	161
46124	EDINBURGH	84	79	70	79	75	84	79	80	81	77	80	63	75	83	76	83	55	80	84	97
46126	FAIRLAND	107	109	100	113	108	117	102	110	103	97	102	85	102	105	105	106	70	104	111	129
46127	FALMOUTH	89	80	81	83	82	96	79	90	82	71	81	69	73	83	79	87	55	83	93	105
46128	FILLMORE	87	82	80	85	83	94	80	89	82	73	81	68	75	83	80	86	55	83	91	103
46130	FOUNTAINTOWN	108	121	105	125	118	119	109	113	107	109	107	88	116	110	115	107	75	109	112	133
46131	FRANKLIN	101	102	89	102	98	100	101	99	101	100	101	77	101	103	99	101	71	100	101	117
46133	GLENWOOD	85	74	80	77	76	91	75	86	77	66	76	66	66	78	74	82	51	79	89	100
46135	GREENCASTLE	84	72	73	73	72	84	76	81	80	70	78	61	69	80	72	84	54	79	86	96
46140	GREENFIELD	111	119	103	121	115	117	112	113	111	112	111	88	116	113	114	111	78	111	114	133
46142	GREENWOOD	128	131	114	130	125	119	125	122	122	130	124	96	126	127	123	119	86	122	117	143
46143	GREENWOOD	137	139	122	140	133	126	137	130	132	141	134	104	138	138	133	128	94	131	124	153
46147	JAMESTOWN	100	97	89	100	96	108	94	101	96	88	95	78	91	98	94	100	65	96	105	119
46148	KNIGHTSTOWN	90	90	78	92	87	97	87	90	88	82	88	70	86	90	87	91	60	88	96	107
46149	LIZTON	104	105	92	104	102	105	96	101	98	99	98	76	96	101	96	99	67	98	101	120
46150	MANILLA	86	79	78	82	80	92	77	87	80	71	78	66	72	81	77	84	54	81	89	101
46151	MARTINSVILLE	93	95	83	97	92	99	92	94	93	89	92	73	92	94	92	95	64	92	98	112
46156	MILROY	91	80	84	83	82	97	80	91	83	72	81	70	72	84	80	88	55	85	95	107
46157	MONROVIA	105	96	94	100	97	112	94	106	97	85	95	80	87	99	94	103	65	98	109	123
46158	MOORESVILLE	106	113	99	113	109	111	105	108	104	105	105	83	108	107	107	105	73	105	108	126
46160	MORGANTOWN	91	83	84	85	83	96	81	90	84	77	83	69	77	85	81	88	57	85	93	106
46161	MORRISTOWN	96	98	84	101	94	104	94	97	95	90	94	76	94	97	94	98	65	95	102	115
46162	NEEDHAM	102	102	95	105	101	110	96	104	97	91	96	80	95	99	98	100	66	98	106	122
46163	NEW PALESTINE	121	145	127	147	140	136	125	129	122	128	123	100	139	125	135	121	87	124	125	150
46164	NINEVEH	102	90	110	91	94	108	88	103	91	83	90	77	81	90	91	96	61	96	104	120
46165	NORTH SALEM	109	118	97	121	112	119	111	111	111	108	110	88	115	113	112	112	77	110	116	133
46166	PARAGON	91	74	78	75	75	92	75	86	80	70	78	65	65	82	72	85	53	80	89	102
46167	PITTSBORO	115	130	110	130	124	118	115	117	110	119	112	92	121	116	119	108	79	112	110	136
46168	PLAINFIELD	104	111	100	110	108	110	104	106	105	105	105	80	108	107	106	107	74	105	109	124
46171	REELSVILLE	83	76	75	79	77	89	75	84	77	68	76	64	69	79	75	82	52	78	87	98
46172	ROACHDALE	91	77	85	78	78	97	78	91	83	70	81	68	69	83	77	89	55	84	95	106
46173	RUSHVILLE	83	69	73	70	68	85	74	80	78	68	76	61	65	79	70	83	52	78	86	96
46175	RUSSELLVILLE	79	56	67	55	56	75	59	69	65	57	64	53	47	67	54	71	43	65	72	84
46176	SHELBYVILLE	91	85	77	87	83	92	88	89	90	83	89	69	84	91	85	93	62	89	94	106
46180	STILESVILLE	96	87	86	91	89	103	86	97	89	78	87	74	79	90	86	94	59	90	100	113
46181	TRAFALGAR	107	114	98	115	110	111	104	108	102	105	103	83	106	106	106	102	71	103	105	126
46182	WALDRON	90	82	81	85	83	97	81	91	83	73	82	69	74	85	81	88	56	84	94	106
46184	WHITELAND	123	130	105	127	121	115	119	118	115	125	117	92	121	122	116	112	81	114	111	137
46186	WILKINSON	105	107	98	111	106	115	101	108	101	96	101	84	100	104	103	104	70	103	110	127
46201	INDIANAPOLIS	61	52	45	54	49	56	63	56	65	58	64	45	58	65	55	66	45	61	62	69
46202	INDIANAPOLIS	67	51	51	56	49	54	73	58	73	67	74	49	64	71	62	74	52	68	65	74
	INDIANA	97	91	86	93	89	96	93	94	95	91	94	73	90	96	90	97	65	94	97	112
	UNITED STATES	100	100	100	100	100	100	100	100	100	100	100	100	100	100	100	100	100	100	100	100

POPULATION CHANGE

ZIP CODE #	POST OFFICE NAME	COUNTY FIPS CODE	POPULATION 2000	POPULATION 2009	POPULATION 2014	2000-2009 ANNUAL RATE % Rate	2000-2009 ANNUAL RATE State Centile	HOUSEHOLDS 2000	HOUSEHOLDS 2009	HOUSEHOLDS 2014	HOUSEHOLDS % Annual Rate 2000-2009	HOUSEHOLDS 2009 Average HH Size	FAMILIES 2000	FAMILIES 2009	FAMILIES % Annual Rate 2000-2009
46203	INDIANAPOLIS	097	41649	39908	39606	-0.5	13	16073	15845	15866	-0.2	2.48	10346	9598	-0.8
46204	INDIANAPOLIS	097	6490	7813	8046	2.0	93	1701	2393	2532	3.8	1.56	265	329	2.4
46205	INDIANAPOLIS	097	30674	29137	28715	-0.6	8	12759	12408	12321	-0.3	2.32	6908	6192	-1.2
46208	INDIANAPOLIS	097	24479	22581	21990	-0.9	3	9902	9270	9071	-0.7	2.19	5228	4506	-1.6
46214	INDIANAPOLIS	097	22210	22157	22161	0.0	37	10400	10570	10650	0.2	2.06	5258	4950	-0.7
46216	INDIANAPOLIS	097	385	1639	2033	17.0	100	171	807	1016	18.3	2.03	96	432	17.7
46217	INDIANAPOLIS	097	19223	29737	33587	4.8	99	7306	11392	12928	4.9	2.61	5513	8424	4.7
46218	INDIANAPOLIS	097	34908	31695	30737	-1.0	2	13487	12567	12283	-0.8	2.48	8875	7789	-1.4
46219	INDIANAPOLIS	097	36291	34062	33322	-0.7	5	15824	15216	15005	-0.4	2.19	9281	8312	-1.2
46220	INDIANAPOLIS	097	35189	34094	33688	-0.3	22	16580	16424	16350	-0.1	2.06	8557	7822	-1.0
46221	INDIANAPOLIS	097	24263	26117	27506	0.8	76	9003	9788	10330	0.9	2.65	6442	6740	0.5
46222	INDIANAPOLIS	097	36336	32883	31869	-1.1	1	13816	12685	12352	-0.9	2.50	8433	7243	-1.6
46224	INDIANAPOLIS	097	34766	33923	33581	-0.3	22	15278	15015	14928	-0.2	2.23	8470	7676	-1.1
46225	INDIANAPOLIS	097	8140	7511	7327	-0.9	3	3048	2867	2811	-0.7	2.48	1782	1562	-1.4
46226	INDIANAPOLIS	097	44759	42717	42052	-0.5	13	17841	17367	17204	-0.3	2.46	11660	10682	-0.9
46227	INDIANAPOLIS	097	52817	52766	52839	0.0	37	22506	22927	23097	0.2	2.23	13231	12616	-0.5
46228	INDIANAPOLIS	097	14929	14760	14700	-0.1	31	5829	5858	5863	0.1	2.50	4093	3909	-0.5
46229	INDIANAPOLIS	097	24147	25905	26625	0.8	76	9350	10259	10612	1.0	2.52	6587	6921	0.5
46231	INDIANAPOLIS	063	4952	8897	10523	6.5	99	1759	3269	3908	6.9	2.69	1402	2502	6.5
46234	INDIANAPOLIS	063	18860	23295	25342	2.3	95	7246	9187	10067	2.6	2.50	5015	6189	2.3
46235	INDIANAPOLIS	097	23745	27104	28313	1.4	89	8979	10366	10880	1.6	2.60	6181	6768	1.0
46236	INDIANAPOLIS	097	26881	29284	30325	0.9	79	9367	10218	10592	0.9	2.86	7440	7890	0.6
46237	INDIANAPOLIS	097	28237	35991	39128	2.7	95	10726	13898	15200	2.8	2.58	7678	9659	2.5
46239	INDIANAPOLIS	097	12603	18762	21229	4.4	99	4694	7115	8108	4.6	2.63	3601	5255	4.2
46240	INDIANAPOLIS	097	18093	17869	17870	-0.1	31	9125	9244	9315	0.1	1.91	4364	4034	-0.8
46241	INDIANAPOLIS	097	30584	29993	29901	-0.2	27	11938	11982	12027	0.0	2.50	8108	7712	-0.5
46250	INDIANAPOLIS	097	17621	17957	18124	0.2	49	8694	9107	9281	0.5	1.94	4020	3885	-0.4
46254	INDIANAPOLIS	097	34834	36446	37047	0.5	66	15296	15960	16241	0.5	2.28	8460	8150	-0.4
46256	INDIANAPOLIS	097	24371	24382	24746	0.0	37	9634	9817	10004	0.2	2.46	6550	6414	-0.2
46259	INDIANAPOLIS	097	6605	9469	10617	4.0	98	2188	3139	3521	4.0	3.02	1887	2672	3.8
46260	INDIANAPOLIS	097	31792	31174	30959	-0.2	27	13566	13517	13513	0.0	2.24	7945	7375	-0.8
46268	INDIANAPOLIS	097	22629	24026	24564	0.6	70	10163	10838	11102	0.7	2.15	5307	5272	-0.1
46278	INDIANAPOLIS	097	7008	8164	8617	1.7	92	2495	2992	3186	2.0	2.72	1967	2276	1.6
46280	INDIANAPOLIS	057	6507	7944	8962	2.2	94	2549	3171	3601	2.4	2.50	1832	2150	1.7
46290	INDIANAPOLIS	057	189	198	214	0.5	66	86	92	100	0.7	2.14	64	65	0.2
46303	CEDAR LAKE	089	11598	13387	14938	1.6	91	4194	4961	5579	1.8	2.69	3182	3620	1.4
46304	CHESTERTON	127	21759	24945	26440	1.5	91	8163	9581	10236	1.7	2.58	5848	6578	1.3
46307	CROWN POINT	089	49084	57486	60752	1.7	92	17587	21127	22497	2.0	2.62	13180	15319	1.6
46310	DEMOTTE	073	12337	13326	13883	0.8	76	4347	4855	5110	1.2	2.71	3469	3748	0.8
46311	DYER	089	16268	18944	19934	1.7	92	5610	6721	7128	2.0	2.77	4521	5260	1.7
46312	EAST CHICAGO	089	32385	31363	30846	-0.3	22	11692	11458	11325	-0.2	2.72	7931	7376	-0.8
46319	GRIFFITH	089	19211	19330	19262	0.1	43	7479	7624	7637	0.2	2.53	5295	5162	-0.3
46320	HAMMOND	089	16480	15892	15597	-0.4	18	6018	5855	5771	-0.3	2.69	3740	3441	-0.9
46321	MUNSTER	089	21558	23116	23623	0.8	76	8109	8851	9091	1.0	2.57	6156	6494	0.6
46322	HIGHLAND	089	23445	23626	23707	0.1	43	9593	9918	10032	0.4	2.38	6655	6539	-0.2
46323	HAMMOND	089	23669	23373	23148	-0.1	31	9284	9296	9264	0.0	2.51	6146	5829	-0.6
46324	HAMMOND	089	23472	22425	21966	-0.5	13	9184	8931	8803	-0.3	2.51	6166	5683	-0.9
46327	HAMMOND	089	12060	11575	11327	-0.4	18	4396	4218	4139	-0.4	2.72	2934	2667	-1.0
46340	HANNA	091	1097	1220	1271	1.2	86	399	457	480	1.5	2.67	297	328	1.1
46341	HEBRON	127	9348	10260	10766	1.0	81	3434	3886	4110	1.3	2.64	2626	2865	0.9
46342	HOBART	089	29441	31554	32382	0.8	76	11458	12552	12971	1.0	2.50	8017	8401	0.5
46347	KOUTS	127	3863	4411	4683	1.4	89	1401	1651	1775	1.8	2.63	1102	1259	1.5
46348	LA CROSSE	091	1054	1106	1130	0.5	66	412	447	460	0.9	2.47	297	309	0.4
46349	LAKE VILLAGE	111	3457	3492	3445	0.1	43	1216	1266	1259	0.4	2.76	949	955	0.1
46350	LA PORTE	091	42523	43346	43738	0.2	49	16407	17088	17355	0.4	2.50	11576	11613	0.0
46356	LOWELL	089	15243	16629	17324	0.9	79	5415	6038	6333	1.2	2.73	4206	4524	0.8
46360	MICHIGAN CITY	091	46557	46627	46804	0.0	37	18002	18517	18726	0.3	2.38	11917	11705	-0.2
46365	MILL CREEK	091	978	1007	1020	0.3	56	338	356	364	0.6	2.83	282	290	0.3
46366	NORTH JUDSON	149	6128	6068	6039	-0.1	31	2231	2261	2266	0.1	2.68	1659	1625	-0.2
46368	PORTAGE	127	35311	40116	42704	1.4	89	13484	15717	16894	1.7	2.53	9667	10828	1.2
46371	ROLLING PRAIRIE	091	3243	3472	3569	0.7	73	1196	1310	1355	1.0	2.65	930	985	0.6
46373	SAINT JOHN	089	8729	12223	13581	3.7	97	2929	4193	4694	4.0	2.91	2506	3496	3.7
46374	SAN PIERRE	149	1086	1125	1141	0.4	60	365	390	400	0.7	2.55	257	263	0.2
46375	SCHERERVILLE	089	19114	23239	24815	2.1	94	7359	9034	9683	2.2	2.56	5312	6295	1.9
46382	UNION MILLS	091	3389	3516	3563	0.4	60	1189	1264	1291	0.7	2.78	923	948	0.3
46383	VALPARAISO	127	35876	39374	41555	1.0	81	13635	15399	16420	1.3	2.39	9025	9791	0.9
46385	VALPARAISO	127	33534	38442	41034	1.5	91	11868	14004	15089	1.8	2.72	9334	10711	1.5
46390	WANATAH	091	2438	2546	2590	0.5	66	921	988	1012	0.8	2.58	729	759	0.4
46391	WESTVILLE	091	7880	8099	8279	0.3	56	1833	2021	2107	1.1	2.55	1352	1445	0.7
46392	WHEATFIELD	073	6678	8458	9111	2.6	95	2251	2924	3171	2.9	2.87	1852	2348	2.6
46394	WHITING	089	12533	12141	11943	-0.3	22	5250	5147	5092	-0.2	2.35	3201	2949	-0.9
46402	GARY	089	8972	8115	7800	-1.1	1	3477	3190	3086	-0.9	2.48	2044	1759	-1.6
46403	GARY	089	14620	13966	13713	-0.5	13	5872	5757	5702	-0.2	2.42	3792	3506	-0.8
46404	GARY	089	20818	19257	18716	-0.8	4	7825	7409	7255	-0.6	2.58	5464	4926	-1.1
46405	LAKE STATION	089	13123	12645	12429	-0.4	18	4675	4606	4561	-0.2	2.72	3339	3139	-0.7
46406	GARY	089	12308	11480	11160	-0.8	4	4354	4154	4064	-0.5	2.74	3112	2836	-1.0
46407	GARY	089	18045	15658	14851	-1.5	1	7089	6251	5966	-1.4	2.48	4388	3648	-2.0
46408	GARY	089	20337	18736	18132	-0.9	3	7364	6888	6702	-0.7	2.70	5085	4528	-1.2
46409	GARY	089	12740	11547	11107	-1.1	1	4105	3784	3662	-0.9	3.04	3022	2666	-1.3
46410	MERRILLVILLE	089	32791	36045	37101	1.0	81	12561	14072	14587	1.2	2.51	8701	9303	0.7
46501	ARGOS	099	3740	3782	3786	0.1	43	1358	1403	1412	0.4	2.69	1047	1048	0.0
46504	BOURBON	099	3300	3424	3477	0.4	60	1189	1257	1283	0.6	2.72	884	901	0.2
46506	BREMEN	099	10061	10401	10540	0.4	60	3560	3733	3792	0.5	2.75	2718	2754	0.1
46507	BRISTOL	039	9058	9924	10454	1.0	81	3319	3674	3874	1.1	2.69	2558	2736	0.7
46508	BURKET	085	195	203	203	0.4	60	76	81	82	0.7	2.51	60	63	0.5
46510	CLAYPOOL	085	3481	3612	3623	0.4	60	1235	1322	1337	0.7	2.73	964	1001	0.4
46511	CULVER	099	4233	4368	4423	0.3	56	1655	1738	1769	0.5	2.46	1166	1176	0.1
46514	ELKHART	039	38728	42832	44838	1.1	84	15336	17117	17937	1.2	2.49	10633	11341	0.7
46516	ELKHART	039	35258	36688	37351	0.4	60	12827	13356	13594	0.4	2.73	8674	8649	0.0
46517	ELKHART	039	20507	22863	23978	1.2	86	7665	8599	9017	1.3	2.61	5308	5715	0.8
46524	ETNA GREEN	085	1986	2006	1980	0.1	43	616	631	625	0.3	3.16	475	471	-0.1
46526	GOSHEN	039	27537	30803	32315	1.2	86	9917	11268	11846	1.4	2.62	6906	7520	0.9
46528	GOSHEN	039	21645	25378	27171	1.7	92	7006	8235	8816	1.8	3.07	5573	6396	1.5
46530	GRANGER	141	26932	29755	30845	1.1	84	8786	9862	10274	1.3	3.01	7712	8483	1.0
46531	GROVERTOWN	149	1285	1340	1362	0.5	66	456	487	499	0.7	2.75	365	379	0.4
	INDIANA					0.7					0.8	2.49			0.4
	UNITED STATES					1.0					1.1	2.59			0.9

ZIP CODE #	POST OFFICE NAME	RACE (%) White 2000	White 2009	Black 2000	Black 2009	Asian/Pacific 2000	Asian/Pacific 2009	% Hispanic Origin 2000	% Hispanic Origin 2009	2009 AGE DISTRIBUTION (%) 0-4	5-9	10-14	15-19	20-24	25-44	45-64	65-84	85+	18+	MEDIAN AGE 2009	% 2009 Males	% 2009 Females
46203	INDIANAPOLIS	85.2	81.1	9.6	11.7	0.5	0.7	5.2	7.9	8.1	7.5	7.1	7.1	6.6	27.5	24.6	10.1	1.4	73.0	35.2	49.9	50.1
46204	INDIANAPOLIS	48.0	40.6	47.8	53.7	1.4	2.2	2.5	4.1	1.6	1.2	1.0	5.2	14.8	50.4	18.7	6.0	1.2	95.2	33.9	71.8	28.2
46205	INDIANAPOLIS	28.3	23.1	68.6	73.6	0.4	0.5	1.5	1.9	7.8	6.9	6.4	7.2	8.4	27.6	24.9	9.5	1.3	74.6	34.2	47.1	52.9
46208	INDIANAPOLIS	29.4	27.0	68.3	70.3	0.6	0.8	0.9	1.2	5.9	5.8	5.8	11.0	11.1	22.6	23.8	11.7	2.4	79.0	34.7	45.6	54.4
46214	INDIANAPOLIS	81.3	74.7	12.8	17.1	2.4	3.5	2.7	4.2	6.3	5.3	5.2	6.5	10.3	32.7	22.2	9.4	2.1	79.4	33.5	47.9	52.1
46216	INDIANAPOLIS	72.7	62.0	20.3	30.9	2.3	3.8	1.3	1.4	5.9	6.0	5.8	5.9	5.8	28.4	31.0	9.6	1.6	78.8	39.8	46.9	53.1
46217	INDIANAPOLIS	97.1	95.5	0.4	0.6	1.1	1.8	1.3	2.6	6.2	6.7	7.2	6.8	4.5	25.9	30.4	11.1	1.2	75.6	40.3	49.4	50.6
46218	INDIANAPOLIS	23.7	20.6	73.5	76.1	0.2	0.3	2.1	2.8	7.4	7.6	7.4	8.1	6.6	24.1	24.3	12.5	2.0	72.5	36.1	46.4	53.6
46219	INDIANAPOLIS	85.0	81.0	11.4	14.0	0.7	1.1	2.4	3.8	6.6	6.5	6.3	6.0	5.7	25.5	26.5	13.6	3.2	76.9	40.4	47.4	52.6
46220	INDIANAPOLIS	85.3	80.4	10.9	14.3	1.3	2.0	2.2	3.4	5.6	4.7	4.8	4.5	7.4	33.4	26.3	10.8	2.5	82.1	37.5	48.6	51.4
46221	INDIANAPOLIS	94.7	92.6	1.9	2.5	0.4	0.7	3.9	5.9	8.0	7.7	7.3	7.2	6.5	29.3	24.2	8.8	1.0	72.5	33.9	49.7	50.3
46222	INDIANAPOLIS	53.6	46.5	38.4	43.5	1.6	1.8	7.4	10.3	7.6	7.2	7.0	8.5	8.6	28.7	23.0	8.2	1.3	73.5	32.3	49.6	50.4
46224	INDIANAPOLIS	66.6	59.1	23.0	27.4	2.5	3.5	8.8	11.7	7.8	6.6	5.9	6.4	9.1	31.5	21.3	9.5	1.9	76.3	32.8	48.9	51.1
46225	INDIANAPOLIS	84.9	79.0	8.6	11.3	0.2	0.3	7.0	11.1	8.0	7.2	6.4	6.6	7.8	30.0	23.7	8.6	1.7	74.6	34.0	52.4	47.6
46226	INDIANAPOLIS	43.5	37.0	51.7	57.2	1.1	1.4	3.8	5.3	7.4	6.9	6.7	7.4	8.3	26.4	25.3	10.3	1.2	74.5	34.2	47.3	52.7
46227	INDIANAPOLIS	93.5	90.6	2.4	3.3	1.1	1.7	3.3	5.4	7.1	6.1	5.7	7.2	9.0	27.8	23.2	11.2	2.6	77.4	34.5	48.0	52.0
46228	INDIANAPOLIS	50.5	41.3	44.1	52.3	2.0	2.7	1.7	2.3	6.1	6.1	6.4	6.6	5.8	26.3	28.5	12.5	1.8	77.2	39.7	47.5	52.5
46229	INDIANAPOLIS	75.1	68.5	19.5	24.3	1.8	2.6	2.8	4.2	7.7	7.4	7.1	7.4	7.1	28.2	25.0	9.2	1.1	73.2	34.4	47.6	52.4
46231	INDIANAPOLIS	92.9	90.1	3.4	4.8	2.0	3.1	1.4	2.0	6.9	7.2	7.5	7.7	5.7	27.1	28.1	8.6	1.2	73.5	36.4	48.8	51.2
46234	INDIANAPOLIS	92.8	90.7	3.6	4.6	1.4	2.0	1.9	2.7	7.0	6.8	6.6	6.5	6.1	29.2	27.1	9.2	1.5	75.5	37.1	48.2	51.8
46235	INDIANAPOLIS	39.2	34.9	55.2	58.8	1.0	1.2	4.4	5.5	11.0	9.5	8.3	7.9	8.5	28.3	19.5	6.0	1.1	66.5	27.8	45.7	54.3
46236	INDIANAPOLIS	86.1	80.2	9.5	13.6	2.2	3.3	2.1	3.3	9.0	9.4	9.4	7.5	4.6	27.3	26.9	5.2	0.6	67.4	34.7	49.5	50.5
46237	INDIANAPOLIS	95.6	93.4	0.9	1.3	1.7	2.8	1.8	2.8	8.3	7.6	7.1	6.5	6.6	32.2	24.0	6.9	0.9	73.1	33.1	49.5	50.5
46239	INDIANAPOLIS	93.9	92.0	3.5	4.4	1.1	1.6	1.0	1.7	6.5	6.9	7.3	7.0	4.9	25.4	29.5	11.3	1.2	74.6	39.7	48.7	51.3
46240	INDIANAPOLIS	91.3	87.3	3.9	5.6	1.9	3.0	2.6	4.4	4.4	4.4	4.9	5.1	7.9	28.8	27.3	14.1	3.1	83.1	41.0	48.3	51.7
46241	INDIANAPOLIS	92.3	89.0	4.0	5.6	0.6	1.0	2.8	4.6	7.8	7.3	6.9	7.1	6.9	28.2	25.4	9.3	1.1	73.6	35.0	49.3	50.7
46250	INDIANAPOLIS	86.3	80.9	7.8	10.5	2.7	4.0	3.4	5.5	5.1	4.4	4.4	5.0	12.1	33.1	22.9	10.6	2.4	83.2	34.2	48.2	51.8
46254	INDIANAPOLIS	49.4	41.0	38.9	44.5	3.9	4.9	7.7	10.2	8.9	7.7	6.7	6.1	8.9	36.5	20.1	4.6	0.5	73.1	30.6	47.6	52.4
46256	INDIANAPOLIS	85.0	79.8	8.8	11.8	2.8	4.1	2.8	4.3	6.7	6.9	7.4	7.2	6.2	26.9	28.8	8.9	1.1	74.4	37.4	49.2	50.8
46259	INDIANAPOLIS	98.2	97.1	0.2	0.3	0.6	1.1	0.8	1.4	8.8	8.1	8.3	7.8	4.0	28.7	26.4	7.3	0.6	69.4	35.4	50.0	50.0
46260	INDIANAPOLIS	64.7	57.4	27.8	32.8	1.9	2.6	6.7	9.3	6.6	5.6	5.5	6.0	9.1	28.4	24.3	11.9	2.6	78.7	36.1	47.4	52.6
46268	INDIANAPOLIS	64.3	55.3	28.1	34.9	3.4	4.6	4.2	6.1	6.9	6.1	5.6	5.7	9.1	31.6	22.4	8.2	4.3	77.6	35.1	46.8	53.2
46278	INDIANAPOLIS	78.7	71.6	14.8	19.5	4.5	6.4	1.8	2.8	6.9	7.6	8.6	7.3	4.0	23.7	32.0	8.4	1.7	72.2	40.0	49.5	50.5
46280	INDIANAPOLIS	94.6	92.8	1.0	1.1	2.1	3.2	1.7	2.6	7.2	7.6	7.7	6.1	4.0	25.8	28.0	12.1	1.4	73.5	39.9	47.7	52.3
46290	INDIANAPOLIS	93.7	92.4	2.1	2.0	2.6	4.0	1.1	1.5	6.6	7.6	8.1	6.6	3.0	22.2	29.8	14.6	1.5	73.2	42.6	47.0	53.0
46303	CEDAR LAKE	97.5	95.7	0.1	0.3	0.2	0.3	3.3	6.5	6.8	7.1	7.5	7.2	5.3	27.7	28.2	9.1	1.0	74.1	37.0	50.6	49.4
46304	CHESTERTON	96.4	95.3	0.5	0.6	0.9	1.4	3.7	5.5	6.7	6.9	7.0	6.6	5.8	25.7	29.4	10.5	1.4	75.4	38.7	49.1	50.9
46307	CROWN POINT	94.1	89.5	2.0	4.3	1.1	1.5	4.9	8.7	5.9	6.1	6.4	7.0	6.2	26.0	29.3	11.2	2.0	77.8	39.6	49.0	51.0
46310	DEMOTTE	98.2	97.8	0.1	0.1	0.2	0.3	2.2	3.0	6.9	7.2	7.5	7.2	4.7	25.9	27.6	11.3	1.7	73.9	38.7	49.7	50.3
46311	DYER	95.7	93.0	0.6	1.2	1.5	2.0	4.8	9.1	5.9	6.3	6.8	6.9	5.0	24.7	30.8	11.7	1.9	76.6	40.8	49.2	50.8
46312	EAST CHICAGO	36.5	30.0	36.1	40.1	0.3	0.3	51.6	53.8	9.2	8.8	7.5	7.8	7.5	25.2	21.4	10.7	1.7	69.8	31.5	47.9	52.1
46319	GRIFFITH	85.0	77.5	9.3	13.8	0.9	1.0	8.3	14.1	6.5	6.7	6.9	7.0	5.8	28.5	26.8	10.5	1.3	75.6	37.4	48.4	51.6
46320	HAMMOND	43.3	30.8	39.9	48.5	0.4	0.4	23.9	29.7	9.8	9.0	7.9	8.0	7.8	25.9	21.4	9.1	1.1	68.5	30.3	48.7	51.3
46321	MUNSTER	92.3	87.2	1.0	2.5	4.5	6.6	4.9	8.9	4.8	5.4	6.3	6.8	4.6	20.2	31.7	16.7	3.5	79.2	46.2	47.9	52.1
46322	HIGHLAND	94.5	90.1	1.2	2.7	1.1	1.5	6.6	12.3	5.3	5.4	5.6	5.7	5.0	26.7	28.4	15.4	2.4	80.1	42.3	48.0	52.0
46323	HAMMOND	79.7	69.4	11.2	16.5	0.7	0.8	16.6	26.3	7.9	7.4	6.8	6.5	6.3	28.5	24.7	10.3	1.6	74.0	35.2	49.2	50.8
46324	HAMMOND	79.6	68.6	10.3	16.2	0.6	0.7	16.8	26.1	7.9	7.4	6.9	6.8	6.2	27.7	25.6	9.6	1.9	73.7	35.8	48.6	51.4
46327	HAMMOND	72.0	59.5	3.8	6.0	0.6	0.7	37.4	52.3	8.2	7.9	7.5	7.6	7.0	28.0	23.0	8.7	2.0	71.9	32.7	50.7	49.3
46340	HANNA	98.2	97.5	0.5	0.7	0.5	0.7	0.4	0.6	6.1	6.6	6.6	5.7	4.5	25.7	31.0	12.4	1.6	77.3	41.4	51.3	48.7
46341	HEBRON	97.3	96.3	0.4	0.5	0.3	0.4	3.0	4.6	6.6	6.8	7.0	6.9	5.5	26.3	29.3	10.5	1.2	75.4	38.6	49.3	50.7
46342	HOBART	92.9	87.4	1.3	2.9	0.5	0.7	9.3	16.5	6.4	6.4	6.4	6.2	5.5	27.7	27.1	12.1	2.1	76.8	38.8	48.6	51.4
46347	KOUTS	98.6	98.2	0.3	0.3	0.2	0.2	1.2	1.9	7.1	7.3	7.9	6.8	5.3	26.3	27.6	10.6	1.3	73.2	37.7	50.4	49.6
46348	LA CROSSE	97.9	97.3	0.3	0.4	0.6	0.9	1.5	2.2	5.8	6.0	6.2	6.1	5.1	25.7	30.9	12.3	1.9	78.3	41.9	50.0	50.0
46349	LAKE VILLAGE	96.4	96.3	0.1	0.1	0.2	0.2	2.4	2.5	6.2	6.4	6.6	6.8	5.3	26.9	29.8	11.1	0.9	76.6	39.4	51.0	49.0
46350	LA PORTE	94.7	92.8	1.5	1.9	0.4	0.7	4.1	6.1	6.4	6.3	6.5	6.7	5.6	25.5	28.5	12.3	2.2	76.6	39.9	49.2	50.8
46356	LOWELL	97.4	95.5	0.1	0.3	0.3	0.4	3.0	5.9	6.5	6.8	7.0	7.1	5.5	26.5	28.7	10.5	1.4	75.3	38.5	50.2	49.8
46360	MICHIGAN CITY	77.0	73.6	19.2	21.6	0.6	0.9	2.7	3.8	6.6	6.4	6.2	6.2	6.3	26.1	27.0	13.0	2.3	77.1	39.1	50.3	49.7
46365	MILL CREEK	96.6	95.6	0.9	1.1	0.1	0.2	1.5	2.4	6.8	7.2	7.4	7.6	4.5	25.5	29.6	10.2	1.1	73.8	39.6	51.8	48.2
46366	NORTH JUDSON	97.8	97.0	0.1	0.1	0.1	0.1	3.4	5.0	6.9	7.1	7.5	7.9	5.4	25.8	26.1	11.8	1.5	73.5	37.2	49.0	51.0
46368	PORTAGE	92.9	90.6	1.4	1.6	0.7	0.9	9.4	13.5	7.1	6.9	6.7	6.4	6.0	27.2	26.8	11.4	1.7	75.5	37.2	48.5	51.5
46371	ROLLING PRAIRIE	97.3	96.2	0.3	0.4	0.2	0.3	2.7	4.2	6.3	6.7	7.0	6.6	4.8	25.3	30.9	11.3	1.2	75.9	40.5	51.1	48.9
46373	SAINT JOHN	97.5	95.4	0.1	0.4	0.5	0.9	4.0	7.8	5.6	6.4	7.1	7.4	4.5	24.6	33.2	10.2	1.0	76.2	41.3	50.1	49.9
46374	SAN PIERRE	98.6	98.1	0.2	0.2	0.0	0.0	0.9	1.4	4.6	5.0	5.2	5.2	4.3	22.0	30.0	18.9	4.9	81.9	47.6	51.0	49.0
46375	SCHERERVILLE	93.0	87.8	1.4	3.1	2.4	3.6	5.5	10.2	6.0	6.0	6.2	6.3	5.6	28.0	29.5	11.2	1.3	77.9	38.9	49.1	50.9
46382	UNION MILLS	90.5	87.1	6.7	8.8	0.4	1.0	1.4	2.0	6.2	6.5	6.7	7.7	7.4	27.4	27.6	9.4	1.2	76.1	36.9	53.4	46.6
46383	VALPARAISO	95.5	94.3	1.2	1.4	1.2	1.7	2.9	4.3	5.6	5.7	5.9	8.1	9.6	24.9	27.1	10.9	2.1	79.0	37.2	48.7	51.3
46385	VALPARAISO	95.7	94.2	0.7	0.8	1.3	2.0	4.0	5.8	6.1	6.4	6.9	7.0	5.7	26.4	30.4	10.1	1.1	76.2	38.8	49.2	50.8
46390	WANATAH	87.4	80.0	10.0	14.8	0.2	2.0	1.8	2.8	4.1	5.2	5.2	5.9	9.3	32.3	27.9	9.1	1.0	82.7	38.1	59.8	40.2
46391	WESTVILLE	83.0	81.5	13.6	12.3	0.3	2.9	2.5	3.3	4.7	4.9	5.1	7.7	10.7	32.7	24.8	8.6	0.9	82.4	35.2	59.0	41.0
46392	WHEATFIELD	97.9	97.3	0.4	0.4	0.1	0.1	2.8	4.2	7.4	7.6	7.8	7.2	5.0	27.2	27.1	9.8	0.9	72.4	36.5	50.3	49.7
46394	WHITING	89.7	82.6	0.4	0.7	0.5	0.7	19.8	32.6	6.0	6.1	6.1	6.1	5.5	26.5	27.0	13.6	3.2	78.0	40.3	48.3	51.7
46402	GARY	5.6	3.3	89.0	92.1	0.1	0.1	6.6	6.2	7.6	8.0	7.2	7.3	6.3	21.5	25.1	14.3	2.5	72.9	37.4	45.8	54.2
46403	GARY	20.7	11.4	73.8	83.6	0.3	0.2	5.8	5.9	8.1	7.6	7.2	7.0	7.0	25.1	27.4	9.8	0.9	72.8	34.7	46.1	53.9
46404	GARY	1.8	1.1	96.4	97.5	0.1	0.1	1.5	1.6	8.0	7.9	7.2	7.2	6.8	21.3	24.5	15.2	1.9	72.5	37.1	44.1	55.9
46405	LAKE STATION	84.0	75.0	2.8	3.6	0.4	0.5	20.6	33.6	7.6	7.3	6.9	6.7	6.3	28.8	25.5	9.7	1.3	74.2	34.9	49.8	50.2
46406	GARY	30.6	26.4	63.1	66.2	0.1	0.2	11.4	14.1	7.9	8.1	8.0	7.8	6.5	24.2	24.1	12.1	1.2	71.2	34.6	46.5	53.5
46407	GARY	1.2	0.6	97.2	98.1	0.1	0.1	1.3	1.4	8.8	8.5	7.6	7.9	6.7	21.2	23.4	13.3	2.7	70.4	34.8	44.6	55.4
46408	GARY	38.8	32.4	55.7	61.4	0.3	0.3	7.5	10.0	7.7	7.7	7.7	7.9	7.0	25.3	25.6	9.8	1.2	72.0	34.0	47.0	53.0
46409	GARY	10.3	5.7	84.9	90.0	0.1	0.2	5.5	5.4	9.0	9.5	9.0	9.3	7.2	25.2	23.0	7.1	0.8	66.8	28.9	45.5	54.5
46410	MERRILLVILLE	67.7	55.0	24.9	35.6	1.4	1.6	9.5	13.7	6.7	6.5	6.4	6.3	6.2	27.9	26.0	11.6	2.4	76.4	37.7	48.4	51.6
46501	ARGOS	98.8	98.4	0.2	0.3	0.1	0.2	1.2	1.9	7.5	7.4	7.5	7.6	6.0	26.4	25.9	10.1	1.6	72.9	36.0	50.8	49.2
46504	BOURBON	97.0	95.7	0.3	0.4	0.4	0.6	3.7	5.8	8.6	8.5	8.0	7.2	5.8	26.8	24.4	9.5	1.3	70.5	33.9	49.6	50.4
46506	BREMEN	95.0	92.8	0.1	0.1	0.3	0.5	6.4	9.6	7.6	7.8	8.1	7.0	5.5	25.1	26.1	10.8	2.1	71.9	36.5	50.1	49.9
46507	BRISTOL	93.6	90.6	1.1	1.6	1.1	1.8	4.0	6.6	7.8	8.0	8.1	6.8	4.8	26.8	27.6	9.3	0.9	71.9	36.8	50.4	49.6
46508	BURKET	97.9	97.5	0.5	0.5	0.0	0.0	1.5	2.5	7.4	7.9	7.4	6.9	4.9	28.1	26.1	9.9	1.5	72.9	37.8	51.2	48.8
46510	CLAYPOOL	98.0	97.3	0.2	0.2	0.1	0.1	1.4	2.0	7.2	7.3	7.4	7.0	5.3	27.1	27.0	10.5	1.2	73.7	37.5	51.5	48.5
46511	CULVER	95.9	94.9	1.1	1.3	0.4	0.6	2.4	3.7	6.2	6.2	6.4	6.5	4.9	23.1	29.1	14.6	3.0	77.0	42.4	49.3	50.7
46514	ELKHART	90.9	87.2	3.7	4.9	1.2	1.8	4.3	7.1	7.4	7.1	7.0	6.5	5.9	26.9	26.2	11.2	1.7	74.5	37.4	48.6	51.4
46516	ELKHART	71.7	66.7	15.5	16.5	0.9	1.3	14.2	19.1	8.8	8.0	7.4	7.2	6.9	28.9	23.3	8.4	1.1	71.5	32.8	50.1	49.9
46517	ELKHART	79.7	74.9	9.4	10.6	1.0	1.3	11.2	15.7	7.3	7.0	7.0	6.8	6.1	27.5	26.2	10.1	1.9	74.4	36.5	49.2	50.8
46524	ETNA GREEN	96.8	95.5	0.2	0.2	0.3	0.5	3.5	5.2	9.6	9.4	9.5	8.7	6.5	25.9	22.3	7.2	0.9	65.6	29.9	52.2	47.8
46526	GOSHEN	88.7	83.9	1.4	1.6	1.1	1.5	12.5	18.7	7.3	7.0	6.9	7.2	6.7	27.1	22.9	11.5	3.3	74.7	35.8	49.7	50.3
46528	GOSHEN	87.9	83.4	0.8	0.9	0.9	1.5	13.4	18.5	8.7	8.4	8.5	8.0	6.3	27.7	24.2	7.3	0.8	69.4	32.7	51.5	48.5
46530	GRANGER	94.0	91.5	1.7	2.4	2.7	3.9	1.3	2.3	7.0	7.8	8.4	8.1	4.3	23.3	31.8	8.3	0.8	71.4	38.9	49.3	50.7
46531	GROVERTOWN	98.0	97.2	0.2	0.1	0.2	0.3	2.6	4.0	6.5	7.2	7.3	7.6	5.4	25.4	27.8	11.6	1.2	74.3	38.7	51.0	49.0
	INDIANA	87.5	85.6	8.4	8.9	1.0	1.5	3.5	5.0	6.9	6.8	6.8	7.2	6.9	26.5	26.2	10.8	1.9	75.4	36.8	49.3	50.7
	UNITED STATES	75.1	72.0	12.3	12.7	3.8	4.6	12.5	15.7	6.8	6.7	6.6	7.1	6.9	27.0	26.0	10.9	1.9	75.7	36.9	49.2	50.8

INDIANA

C 46203-46531

ZIP CODE #	POST OFFICE NAME	2009 Per Capita Income	2009 HH Income Base	2009 Household Income Distribution (%): Less than $25,000	$25,000 to $49,999	$50,000 to $99,999	$100,000 to $149,999	$150,000 or More	Median Household Income: 2009	2014	2009 National Centile	2009 State Centile	2009 Home Value Base	2009 Home Value Distribution (%): Less than $50,000	$50,000 to $89,999	$90,000 to $174,999	$175,000 to $399,999	$400,000 or More	2009 Median Home Value
46203	INDIANAPOLIS	19776	15845	28.6	32.3	32.8	4.5	1.8	41182	43474	37	11	9914	24.7	52.4	20.0	2.5	0.4	68449
46204	INDIANAPOLIS	25422	2393	38.4	19.1	27.4	8.1	6.9	36041	39918	21	5	472	1.9	4.9	37.7	40.9	14.6	183784
46205	INDIANAPOLIS	21904	12408	31.9	29.0	30.3	5.4	3.5	40006	41915	33	9	5566	13.4	45.1	27.8	12.5	1.3	81876
46208	INDIANAPOLIS	22404	9270	36.4	27.6	25.6	6.1	4.4	35051	37126	18	4	4762	23.6	35.6	23.0	15.9	1.9	77396
46214	INDIANAPOLIS	30331	10570	15.3	27.6	45.0	8.6	3.4	55857	57079	72	72	5011	1.5	18.2	70.2	9.6	0.5	116961
46216	INDIANAPOLIS	50998	807	11.3	12.1	41.6	16.9	18.1	80618	81280	92	98	410	1.5	0.5	50.7	47.3	0.0	170635
46217	INDIANAPOLIS	30817	11392	7.7	20.7	47.8	16.9	7.0	70235	68537	87	94	9309	0.8	14.8	64.9	18.4	1.2	128694
46218	INDIANAPOLIS	17095	12567	36.7	32.7	26.4	3.0	1.2	33652	35170	15	3	7594	31.6	62.0	6.0	0.3	0.1	59227
46219	INDIANAPOLIS	26597	15216	20.4	29.2	40.0	7.3	3.0	50296	52732	62	48	9907	9.1	41.6	46.5	2.6	0.2	89527
46220	INDIANAPOLIS	41498	16424	11.3	22.1	42.1	13.5	11.1	68736	68360	86	93	10419	0.6	9.1	56.0	30.5	3.7	149627
46221	INDIANAPOLIS	22949	9788	20.6	24.8	42.9	8.4	3.2	54371	58159	70	68	6895	12.6	34.9	47.4	4.5	0.6	91886
46222	INDIANAPOLIS	18953	12685	27.8	35.2	31.2	3.9	1.8	40516	42558	34	10	6709	30.9	58.1	10.5	0.4	0.1	61882
46224	INDIANAPOLIS	23851	15015	21.2	34.3	36.7	5.7	2.1	45538	48528	50	25	5993	5.1	46.1	46.6	2.1	0.1	89397
46225	INDIANAPOLIS	16495	2867	34.7	34.6	27.6	2.7	0.3	35253	37253	19	5	1411	31.7	57.1	10.8	0.5	0.0	61345
46226	INDIANAPOLIS	23740	17367	19.4	32.7	37.6	7.0	3.4	48281	51247	57	37	10331	10.6	58.0	27.6	3.2	0.5	78862
46227	INDIANAPOLIS	26020	22927	20.7	30.9	37.7	7.2	3.5	48403	51593	58	37	11654	6.3	24.3	62.6	6.2	0.5	106149
46228	INDIANAPOLIS	32374	5858	13.8	20.6	39.7	16.2	9.7	68588	68986	86	93	4838	1.9	13.6	61.1	20.5	2.9	129617
46229	INDIANAPOLIS	27057	10259	12.6	28.4	44.4	10.2	4.5	60055	61146	77	81	6296	1.7	21.0	66.6	10.1	0.6	112558
46231	INDIANAPOLIS	28019	3269	8.5	22.1	48.3	15.8	5.3	66771	66822	85	92	2798	9.4	16.4	53.3	19.9	1.0	116819
46234	INDIANAPOLIS	31979	9187	10.4	19.4	46.0	16.5	7.7	69561	71504	87	94	7687	20.8	9.3	48.0	20.4	1.5	121465
46235	INDIANAPOLIS	19768	10366	28.0	29.8	34.5	5.6	2.1	43101	46104	43	15	5069	21.7	35.7	37.8	4.1	0.6	83797
46236	INDIANAPOLIS	42100	10218	6.2	12.7	39.1	18.1	23.8	88541	89764	95	99	9485	10.7	4.2	46.3	31.2	7.6	150609
46237	INDIANAPOLIS	31304	13898	8.2	18.2	51.5	15.6	6.6	72966	73945	88	95	10241	2.4	14.2	70.5	12.0	0.9	119651
46239	INDIANAPOLIS	28895	7115	10.5	20.6	48.5	15.1	5.4	68672	68517	86	93	6178	8.1	9.5	64.3	17.3	0.7	130190
46240	INDIANAPOLIS	40891	9244	15.4	27.7	36.1	10.9	9.9	57795	58373	75	77	4569	1.3	7.7	49.5	33.4	8.0	161231
46241	INDIANAPOLIS	21639	11982	22.3	31.2	39.1	5.4	2.1	47171	50549	55	32	8297	22.3	49.1	26.9	1.3	0.3	74646
46250	INDIANAPOLIS	37825	9107	9.7	27.5	43.2	13.2	6.4	61647	62086	80	85	3954	0.2	5.1	61.3	30.4	3.1	151168
46254	INDIANAPOLIS	28859	15960	15.0	28.3	43.0	9.1	4.6	56077	58287	73	73	7646	1.2	22.0	67.4	8.0	1.5	114158
46256	INDIANAPOLIS	39038	9817	11.8	14.6	40.7	17.2	15.7	75722	76198	90	96	7136	0.1	4.6	53.8	36.4	5.2	160291
46259	INDIANAPOLIS	32602	3139	5.4	12.8	43.8	25.1	12.8	85419	86866	94	98	2938	3.3	7.2	48.9	38.6	2.0	161983
46260	INDIANAPOLIS	35248	13517	14.5	27.9	36.8	10.8	9.9	58366	59694	76	78	6431	1.2	10.7	53.1	29.4	5.6	148851
46268	INDIANAPOLIS	30894	10838	17.4	26.4	39.7	10.3	6.2	56740	58092	74	75	5904	1.6	13.3	70.9	14.2	0.0	129378
46278	INDIANAPOLIS	46401	2992	3.2	15.9	30.8	20.9	29.1	100065	101155	97	99	2782	0.3	7.1	34.5	48.5	9.6	188554
46280	INDIANAPOLIS	38347	3171	6.0	15.4	39.4	27.8	11.4	80609	83328	92	98	2574	3.1	5.6	51.0	35.7	4.5	161596
46290	INDIANAPOLIS	54699	92	3.3	20.7	40.2	18.5	17.4	72411	78646	88	95	81	0.0	6.2	43.2	27.2	23.5	177083
46303	CEDAR LAKE	24516	4961	14.9	25.9	44.1	11.8	3.4	60717	61490	78	84	3865	5.0	20.6	46.5	25.6	2.3	125359
46304	CHESTERTON	30286	9581	12.5	22.5	42.1	15.9	7.0	66253	70195	84	92	7259	12.5	6.9	39.5	34.8	6.3	158768
46307	CROWN POINT	30445	21127	10.7	19.9	44.5	17.3	7.7	72353	73042	88	95	16832	2.2	6.6	51.6	36.5	3.1	159327
46310	DEMOTTE	22977	4855	16.6	28.4	43.6	8.2	3.2	54818	57051	71	69	4039	8.6	10.9	51.1	28.0	1.4	141948
46311	DYER	31129	6721	9.1	18.5	43.7	20.8	7.8	75143	75346	89	96	6100	1.2	5.7	50.8	38.0	4.2	163803
46312	EAST CHICAGO	16605	11458	38.2	28.3	26.3	4.7	2.5	33146	34328	14	3	4917	15.7	54.0	28.3	1.8	0.1	76336
46319	GRIFFITH	27451	7624	13.9	23.2	46.6	12.4	3.9	63380	64106	82	88	5152	1.6	11.6	72.7	13.7	0.3	122609
46320	HAMMOND	15497	5855	39.8	27.8	27.9	2.9	1.6	32467	33782	12	3	2349	24.4	57.3	16.5	1.7	0.2	65670
46321	MUNSTER	37587	8851	10.6	18.1	38.4	15.6	17.3	76264	75951	90	97	7808	1.3	4.6	36.5	50.8	6.8	187747
46322	HIGHLAND	30590	9918	12.4	20.5	49.5	12.8	4.8	65458	66070	84	91	7657	1.6	8.1	70.5	19.1	0.7	137788
46323	HAMMOND	23272	9296	20.6	26.0	43.4	7.5	2.5	52676	54959	67	62	5988	3.5	48.3	46.3	1.7	0.2	89071
46324	HAMMOND	23060	8931	22.6	27.0	41.1	6.7	2.6	50420	53553	62	49	6200	4.2	46.6	45.2	3.7	0.2	89469
46327	HAMMOND	17730	4218	29.5	31.3	33.0	4.3	1.7	40442	42543	34	9	2814	19.3	55.9	24.0	0.7	0.0	73305
46340	HANNA	21300	457	13.1	36.3	44.4	4.4	1.8	50438	53745	62	49	388	6.7	15.5	57.0	19.1	1.8	116758
46341	HEBRON	26679	3886	13.7	19.8	48.3	14.9	3.3	65103	67987	83	90	3204	12.7	6.3	48.3	29.4	3.2	144654
46342	HOBART	26449	12552	15.9	23.6	47.3	9.8	3.4	61316	62713	79	85	10018	10.0	22.0	56.2	11.4	0.4	107799
46347	KOUTS	27009	1651	10.6	21.6	51.7	13.4	2.7	67107	71148	85	92	1389	2.1	7.7	49.8	38.4	2.0	160798
46348	LA CROSSE	22322	447	15.9	34.0	44.1	4.5	1.6	50083	53216	61	47	380	9.2	21.6	55.3	12.9	1.1	104762
46349	LAKE VILLAGE	19532	1266	19.2	30.1	44.1	5.2	1.4	50494	52559	62	49	1082	8.0	18.2	54.8	17.9	1.0	119189
46350	LA PORTE	24943	17088	19.1	25.2	42.7	9.4	3.6	56125	58349	73	73	12937	7.4	15.3	56.7	19.5	1.2	122080
46356	LOWELL	26080	6038	12.7	21.5	49.7	11.7	4.3	65374	65993	84	91	4991	3.6	10.0	58.8	26.0	1.7	137363
46360	MICHIGAN CITY	24886	18517	22.0	28.5	37.0	8.7	3.9	49584	52726	60	44	12847	10.0	24.3	45.9	17.0	2.8	106924
46365	MILL CREEK	24470	356	10.1	28.7	46.6	11.2	3.4	60200	60539	78	82	321	10.0	16.2	54.2	15.9	3.7	120766
46366	NORTH JUDSON	18714	2261	25.5	32.3	35.1	5.9	1.3	43683	45486	44	17	1778	13.6	25.9	50.1	9.5	0.9	103571
46368	PORTAGE	27561	15717	15.6	22.3	44.4	13.6	4.1	63696	67373	82	89	11493	18.7	8.9	54.2	17.0	1.3	129462
46371	ROLLING PRAIRIE	23203	1310	16.9	27.4	42.1	11.5	2.1	55498	57834	72	71	1172	13.1	12.6	52.4	18.9	3.0	123222
46373	SAINT JOHN	31130	4193	6.7	18.2	42.2	21.4	11.5	79334	79518	92	97	3877	1.1	2.9	33.0	60.1	2.8	193731
46374	SAN PIERRE	19301	390	21.5	31.0	39.7	7.4	0.3	47242	48768	55	32	323	18.9	28.8	47.4	5.0	0.0	92778
46375	SCHERERVILLE	35459	9034	8.8	18.8	44.0	17.4	11.1	74541	75160	89	96	7013	1.1	5.3	42.3	46.3	4.9	177199
46382	UNION MILLS	19718	1264	17.3	35.7	38.9	5.9	2.1	46816	51137	54	31	1053	13.5	30.3	44.2	10.6	1.4	95848
46383	VALPARAISO	29509	15399	17.2	22.2	39.8	14.5	6.3	63142	66794	81	88	10286	9.3	5.3	44.5	35.9	5.0	160165
46385	VALPARAISO	33399	14004	9.1	15.3	44.2	21.4	9.9	78450	81395	91	97	11968	4.5	7.3	40.5	41.5	6.1	169480
46390	WANATAH	25168	988	14.7	24.6	48.2	10.7	1.8	61842	62823	80	86	860	1.5	12.0	67.2	17.8	1.5	127322
46391	WESTVILLE	22547	2021	15.9	20.8	44.4	13.9	5.0	63982	65367	82	89	1725	23.4	8.6	31.8	30.1	6.1	133574
46392	WHEATFIELD	22299	2924	12.9	26.5	48.8	10.0	1.9	60498	61104	78	83	2445	8.8	16.3	47.9	24.5	2.5	132559
46394	WHITING	24336	5147	23.9	26.5	39.1	7.3	3.2	49602	52979	60	44	3116	5.5	27.8	61.5	5.1	0.2	102717
46402	GARY	14547	3190	51.6	22.1	22.1	3.2	0.9	23606	24160	3	1	1350	49.9	39.4	9.8	0.5	0.4	50053
46403	GARY	23732	5757	26.2	28.3	32.8	8.5	4.1	45532	48892	50	25	3136	19.5	38.0	32.5	8.8	1.1	79741
46404	GARY	17842	7409	39.2	26.6	25.3	6.3	2.7	33191	34488	14	3	4436	34.0	47.4	17.5	1.0	0.2	59174
46405	LAKE STATION	20134	4606	24.3	28.4	38.4	6.6	2.4	47862	50995	56	35	3541	18.7	50.7	28.9	1.6	0.1	76670
46406	GARY	16031	4154	38.7	28.0	26.7	4.5	2.0	33549	35296	14	3	2497	46.0	44.9	7.8	1.4	0.0	53111
46407	GARY	14911	6251	51.6	25.2	18.3	2.8	2.0	23640	24037	3	2	2762	53.1	37.3	9.3	0.2	0.1	47803
46408	GARY	19937	6888	27.8	26.1	35.4	8.3	2.5	45838	50019	51	26	4485	32.6	47.3	19.3	0.8	0.0	66318
46409	GARY	14827	3784	36.5	29.8	26.7	5.0	2.0	33695	35054	15	4	1996	45.4	46.5	8.1	0.0	0.0	52758
46410	MERRILLVILLE	27753	14072	13.0	24.4	46.1	12.7	3.8	63684	64755	82	89	9641	2.1	19.4	68.9	9.3	0.3	114652
46501	ARGOS	21760	1403	18.1	30.4	42.7	6.8	2.1	51154	52966	64	53	1114	11.0	26.6	50.3	10.1	2.1	104206
46504	BOURBON	22951	1257	15.9	25.6	46.5	9.3	2.6	57896	58367	75	78	970	11.9	24.3	51.4	11.8	0.6	104502
46506	BREMEN	23304	3733	12.8	27.4	48.4	8.3	3.1	58233	58474	75	78	2968	4.1	17.3	55.2	20.6	2.8	121667
46507	BRISTOL	27802	3674	15.5	22.0	44.9	10.5	7.2	61917	63200	80	86	3039	18.4	11.4	38.0	27.8	4.4	129920
46508	BURKET	23456	81	18.5	35.8	39.5	3.7	2.5	46381	50729	52	29	70	18.6	22.9	44.3	12.9	1.4	103846
46510	CLAYPOOL	21742	1322	16.6	33.3	39.6	7.6	3.0	50130	52358	61	47	1123	18.9	22.7	46.7	10.2	1.4	98514
46511	CULVER	23573	1738	20.9	29.1	40.8	5.9	3.3	50000	51854	61	46	1384	12.4	26.7	46.4	11.8	2.7	101489
46514	ELKHART	28164	17117	15.1	25.8	42.8	10.7	5.6	59245	61162	76	80	12606	14.3	20.9	49.2	13.6	1.9	110031
46516	ELKHART	21249	13356	22.6	30.8	36.0	6.7	3.8	46023	50592	51	27	7972	12.0	32.5	44.6	9.8	1.2	95344
46517	ELKHART	23870	8599	19.2	26.8	41.6	8.5	3.9	53492	56415	69	66	5736	9.4	24.7	51.5	13.7	0.7	106891
46524	ETNA GREEN	17446	631	15.1	36.8	41.7	4.6	1.9	48909	51228	59	40	532	22.9	23.7	40.6	12.6	0.2	93673
46526	GOSHEN	24317	11268	17.9	27.3	42.9	7.6	4.4	54351	57595	70	68	7908	12.4	16.4	53.0	16.7	1.5	119297
46528	GOSHEN	22423	8235	12.4	27.2	46.5	9.5	4.5	59189	60995	76	80	6504	11.8	13.7	48.6	23.4	2.5	130155
46530	GRANGER	38731	9862	4.3	10.0	39.9	24.0	21.8	93291	93724	96	99	9309	3.1	4.2	45.1	42.9	4.7	170809
46531	GROVERTOWN	19958	487	21.8	28.1	41.5	6.8	1.8	50058	50903	61	46	419	10.7	16.2	59.7	13.1	0.2	112633
	INDIANA	26003		19.5	26.3	38.6	10.5	5.1	54105	56493				12.2	24.1	44.1	17.2	2.4	108938
	UNITED STATES	27277		20.9	24.4	35.3	11.7	7.6	54719	56938				9.3	13.1	31.6	32.6	13.5	162279

ZIP CODE #	POST OFFICE NAME	FINANCIAL SERVICES: Auto Loan	Home Loan	Invest-ments	Retire-ment Plans	THE HOME: Home Improvements: Home Repair	Lawn & Garden	Furnishings: Comput-ers & Hard-ware-Personal	Major Appli-ances	TV, Radio, Sound Equip-ment	Furni-ture	ENTERTAINMENT: Dine out/ Carry out	Sports Equip-ment	Fees & Tickets	Toys & Games	Travel	Cable TV	PERSONAL: Apparel & Services	Auto Repairs	Health Insur-ance	Pets & Supplies
46203	INDIANAPOLIS	74	63	56	64	60	70	71	68	74	67	73	53	64	75	64	77	50	71	75	83
46204	INDIANAPOLIS	84	64	66	73	62	63	92	71	91	86	93	63	82	90	80	89	66	85	78	91
46205	INDIANAPOLIS	73	62	56	65	59	65	73	66	76	71	76	51	69	76	66	78	53	72	73	82
46208	INDIANAPOLIS	74	63	61	64	62	71	70	69	77	71	76	51	67	75	66	81	52	73	79	84
46214	INDIANAPOLIS	96	75	67	79	71	73	94	80	94	93	95	66	85	96	82	92	66	90	83	98
46216	INDIANAPOLIS	140	156	152	159	155	146	148	144	143	151	145	113	158	144	153	140	103	144	140	169
46217	INDIANAPOLIS	111	126	112	127	123	123	112	117	111	114	112	89	120	113	118	112	78	113	117	136
46218	INDIANAPOLIS	62	54	48	55	51	60	58	57	64	58	63	42	56	63	54	67	43	60	66	71
46219	INDIANAPOLIS	82	80	72	80	77	86	83	81	86	79	85	62	82	85	80	90	59	84	92	98
46220	INDIANAPOLIS	117	118	118	122	118	116	123	116	122	124	123	91	126	121	123	121	87	121	119	138
46221	INDIANAPOLIS	91	86	72	85	81	86	88	85	89	87	88	66	83	91	82	90	61	87	88	102
46222	INDIANAPOLIS	70	59	51	60	55	64	70	63	72	65	71	50	63	73	61	75	50	69	71	79
46224	INDIANAPOLIS	79	62	56	66	59	62	79	67	80	76	81	56	72	81	70	79	56	77	72	84
46225	INDIANAPOLIS	59	49	44	51	46	53	60	54	62	55	61	43	54	62	53	64	43	59	60	66
46226	INDIANAPOLIS	84	76	67	78	72	79	83	78	86	82	86	61	80	86	78	87	59	83	85	95
46227	INDIANAPOLIS	86	74	69	77	72	76	86	79	87	83	87	62	80	87	79	88	60	85	84	95
46228	INDIANAPOLIS	115	123	111	122	119	117	115	115	114	119	115	88	119	116	116	114	80	114	116	135
46229	INDIANAPOLIS	98	97	85	97	93	93	99	94	98	98	98	74	98	100	95	97	69	96	95	112
46231	INDIANAPOLIS	118	117	98	113	111	108	108	110	107	114	109	82	105	112	104	106	74	107	105	129
46234	INDIANAPOLIS	118	122	109	121	118	111	116	114	113	122	114	89	117	117	115	110	80	113	108	134
46235	INDIANAPOLIS	76	66	56	68	62	66	76	68	76	73	76	55	71	78	68	76	53	73	71	83
46236	INDIANAPOLIS	173	199	176	198	193	171	173	174	163	187	166	139	187	173	178	155	119	164	153	198
46237	INDIANAPOLIS	120	125	105	123	118	110	117	114	113	123	115	90	119	119	115	109	80	113	106	133
46239	INDIANAPOLIS	107	118	103	117	114	116	106	110	106	108	107	83	112	109	110	107	74	107	111	128
46240	INDIANAPOLIS	111	103	101	108	102	103	114	105	114	114	114	82	112	113	110	113	80	112	110	126
46241	INDIANAPOLIS	80	73	65	73	70	77	78	76	79	75	78	59	73	81	72	81	54	78	80	91
46250	INDIANAPOLIS	109	90	85	95	88	88	110	95	109	109	110	77	102	110	99	107	77	106	99	116
46254	INDIANAPOLIS	101	84	74	87	80	76	99	86	96	100	98	71	90	100	88	92	68	94	82	104
46256	INDIANAPOLIS	137	143	131	148	139	130	140	133	134	144	137	107	145	139	140	130	97	134	125	156
46259	INDIANAPOLIS	140	160	138	163	155	145	139	143	134	148	135	114	151	141	145	129	96	135	131	164
46260	INDIANAPOLIS	116	104	100	109	102	102	117	107	116	117	118	85	113	117	110	115	82	114	109	128
46268	INDIANAPOLIS	101	84	76	88	80	78	101	87	99	101	101	72	93	102	90	96	70	96	87	106
46278	INDIANAPOLIS	174	210	194	216	208	184	179	183	168	195	171	146	201	176	192	159	124	171	161	207
46280	INDIANAPOLIS	130	155	139	153	150	145	133	138	131	139	133	104	148	135	143	130	94	133	136	159
46290	INDIANAPOLIS	153	185	191	188	192	188	158	172	159	168	160	123	182	156	179	162	113	164	178	195
46303	CEDAR LAKE	96	100	85	101	96	100	94	96	93	93	93	74	95	96	94	94	65	93	97	113
46304	CHESTERTON	110	119	108	119	117	115	111	113	110	112	110	87	115	112	114	110	77	110	112	132
46307	CROWN POINT	109	127	117	128	125	120	115	115	112	117	113	89	125	114	121	111	80	113	114	134
46310	DEMOTTE	94	94	85	95	92	98	87	94	89	86	88	71	87	91	89	91	61	89	94	110
46311	DYER	118	137	121	139	132	130	122	124	120	124	121	97	133	123	129	119	85	121	123	145
46312	EAST CHICAGO	63	54	48	55	51	57	64	58	68	61	68	44	61	67	57	71	48	64	65	71
46319	GRIFFITH	95	105	91	105	100	100	98	97	97	99	99	76	104	100	101	97	69	97	99	114
46320	HAMMOND	58	50	47	51	48	53	60	54	62	57	62	42	55	61	54	64	43	59	62	67
46321	MUNSTER	126	152	152	153	155	150	133	140	133	139	134	103	151	131	147	134	95	136	145	160
46322	HIGHLAND	94	111	102	110	109	109	101	103	101	100	102	77	111	101	108	103	72	102	108	119
46323	HAMMOND	82	80	67	82	75	83	84	79	85	80	85	63	83	86	80	86	59	83	87	96
46324	HAMMOND	80	81	66	82	76	84	82	79	84	78	84	62	83	85	80	86	58	81	87	96
46327	HAMMOND	72	64	58	63	61	68	70	68	71	66	70	53	64	72	64	73	49	70	72	81
46340	HANNA	88	80	79	84	82	95	79	89	82	72	80	68	73	83	79	86	55	82	92	104
46341	HEBRON	96	108	97	108	105	104	99	100	98	99	99	77	105	100	103	98	69	99	101	118
46342	HOBART	91	98	85	98	93	99	93	93	94	92	94	71	97	96	94	96	65	93	99	110
46347	KOUTS	100	107	88	110	101	108	102	101	101	99	101	80	105	104	102	103	70	101	107	121
46348	LA CROSSE	85	78	77	81	80	92	77	87	79	70	78	66	71	81	77	84	53	80	89	101
46349	LAKE VILLAGE	84	77	74	78	77	88	75	83	77	70	76	62	69	79	74	81	52	78	85	97
46350	LA PORTE	89	90	80	92	87	94	88	90	90	86	89	69	89	91	88	92	62	89	95	107
46356	LOWELL	100	110	97	110	107	105	101	103	100	101	101	79	106	102	104	100	70	100	102	120
46360	MICHIGAN CITY	87	83	79	84	81	90	85	86	88	83	88	65	84	88	84	91	61	87	93	102
46365	MILL CREEK	101	104	95	107	103	110	97	104	97	93	97	80	97	99	100	100	67	98	105	122
46366	NORTH JUDSON	82	68	70	69	68	83	69	77	73	65	72	59	61	76	66	78	49	73	81	92
46368	PORTAGE	101	105	91	103	101	101	99	99	99	101	100	75	101	102	99	100	69	99	100	117
46371	ROLLING PRAIRIE	92	91	84	93	90	98	86	93	87	83	87	71	84	89	87	90	60	88	94	109
46373	SAINT JOHN	123	149	134	151	146	136	128	131	122	133	124	103	142	125	138	119	88	125	122	152
46374	SAN PIERRE	81	72	72	75	73	86	71	81	74	65	73	61	65	75	71	78	49	75	83	94
46375	SCHERERVILLE	127	141	128	141	137	127	130	128	126	135	128	101	138	130	134	122	91	126	121	149
46382	UNION MILLS	85	74	71	76	74	87	78	83	80	70	79	63	70	82	74	85	54	80	88	98
46383	VALPARAISO	101	103	96	106	101	102	106	101	104	104	105	79	107	105	104	104	74	103	104	120
46385	VALPARAISO	128	143	128	143	139	133	130	131	126	134	128	101	137	130	134	125	90	128	127	152
46390	WANATAH	100	91	91	95	93	108	90	102	93	82	91	77	83	95	90	98	62	94	105	118
46391	WESTVILLE	106	109	96	108	106	107	100	104	100	103	101	79	101	104	100	101	70	101	102	122
46392	WHEATFIELD	98	94	85	95	92	100	90	96	92	87	91	72	87	94	89	95	63	92	98	113
46394	WHITING	78	81	72	81	78	86	80	80	83	76	82	60	81	82	80	86	57	81	90	95
46402	GARY	50	39	39	42	38	47	49	46	55	49	54	34	46	52	44	59	37	51	57	58
46403	GARY	82	77	68	78	72	80	81	77	84	80	84	59	80	84	77	86	58	81	84	94
46404	GARY	66	60	54	62	57	66	62	61	68	64	68	45	62	67	59	72	46	65	71	77
46405	LAKE STATION	82	74	64	76	70	82	79	77	81	74	80	61	74	83	73	84	55	79	85	94
46406	GARY	64	58	51	59	54	64	61	60	65	60	64	44	59	65	57	68	44	62	68	74
46407	GARY	53	42	40	44	41	50	50	48	57	50	55	35	47	54	45	60	38	52	58	60
46408	GARY	78	74	63	75	69	79	75	74	79	75	79	55	74	79	72	82	54	76	82	90
46409	GARY	67	58	47	59	52	62	62	59	68	63	67	45	60	68	57	70	46	63	67	75
46410	MERRILLVILLE	95	103	92	103	99	100	100	97	99	99	100	75	104	101	101	100	70	99	101	115
46501	ARGOS	87	83	75	86	81	93	83	87	84	76	83	67	79	86	81	88	57	84	93	103
46504	BOURBON	90	91	77	93	87	96	88	90	89	84	89	71	88	91	88	92	61	89	96	108
46506	BREMEN	95	94	85	96	91	102	91	96	92	85	91	75	89	94	91	95	63	92	100	114
46507	BRISTOL	117	109	103	109	106	118	104	111	107	104	107	86	100	111	102	111	74	107	113	132
46508	BURKET	91	83	82	86	85	98	82	92	84	74	83	70	75	86	82	89	57	85	95	107
46510	CLAYPOOL	95	82	84	85	84	99	82	93	86	75	84	71	74	88	81	92	57	87	97	109
46511	CULVER	98	77	97	76	79	102	79	94	85	74	84	70	67	85	77	93	56	88	100	111
46514	ELKHART	103	100	91	101	98	104	100	101	101	98	101	77	97	103	97	103	70	100	104	119
46516	ELKHART	85	77	70	77	74	82	83	81	86	79	85	63	77	86	77	88	59	83	86	97
46517	ELKHART	92	87	79	89	84	93	90	90	91	84	90	71	86	92	86	93	63	90	94	107
46524	ETNA GREEN	100	72	82	70	71	95	74	87	83	72	81	67	60	86	68	90	54	82	91	105
46526	GOSHEN	94	87	82	89	86	94	92	92	94	88	94	70	88	94	88	98	65	93	99	110
46528	GOSHEN	102	101	89	101	99	102	98	101	98	97	98	77	96	100	97	98	68	98	100	118
46530	GRANGER	160	192	181	196	191	172	165	169	156	176	158	133	184	161	177	150	114	160	152	193
46531	GROVERTOWN	87	79	74	79	79	87	76	84	79	74	78	62	71	81	75	82	53	79	85	98
	INDIANA	97	91	86	93	89	96	93	94	95	91	94	73	90	96	90	97	65	94	97	112
	UNITED STATES	100	100	100	100	100	100	100	100	100	100	100	100	100	100	100	100	100	100	100	100

POPULATION CHANGE

# ZIP CODE	POST OFFICE NAME	COUNTY FIPS CODE	POPULATION 2000	POPULATION 2009	POPULATION 2014	2000-2009 ANNUAL RATE % Rate	2000-2009 ANNUAL RATE State Centile	HOUSEHOLDS 2000	HOUSEHOLDS 2009	HOUSEHOLDS 2014	HOUSEHOLDS % Annual Rate 2000-2009	HOUSEHOLDS 2009 Average HH Size	FAMILIES 2000	FAMILIES 2009	FAMILIES % Annual Rate 2000-2009
46532	HAMLET	149	2023	2058	2065	0.2	49	762	798	807	0.5	2.58	589	597	0.1
46534	KNOX	149	11157	11384	11471	0.2	49	4165	4342	4401	0.5	2.58	3052	3077	0.1
46536	LAKEVILLE	141	2945	3093	3149	0.5	66	1115	1187	1212	0.7	2.61	836	858	0.3
46538	LEESBURG	085	4367	4408	4389	0.1	43	1733	1818	1825	0.5	2.42	1287	1302	0.1
46539	MENTONE	085	2233	2426	2500	0.9	79	813	902	935	1.1	2.69	596	636	0.7
46540	MIDDLEBURY	039	10083	11600	12357	1.5	91	3180	3710	3961	1.7	3.12	2646	3009	1.4
46542	MILFORD	085	3894	4223	4393	0.9	79	1385	1569	1647	1.4	2.66	1055	1156	1.0
46543	MILLERSBURG	039	2693	3182	3432	1.8	93	786	939	1015	1.9	3.39	669	783	1.7
46544	MISHAWAKA	141	30080	31850	32288	0.6	70	12031	13103	13340	0.9	2.39	7845	8003	0.2
46545	MISHAWAKA	141	25998	26324	26449	0.1	43	11541	11849	11958	0.3	2.14	6448	6196	-0.4
46550	NAPPANEE	039	12168	13061	13498	0.8	76	4056	4417	4576	0.9	2.95	3120	3285	0.6
46552	NEW CARLISLE	141	6026	6360	6501	0.6	70	2246	2418	2484	0.8	2.52	1591	1638	0.3
46553	NEW PARIS	039	2948	3382	3652	1.5	91	996	1153	1248	1.6	2.93	818	920	1.3
46554	NORTH LIBERTY	141	4070	4161	4181	0.2	49	1553	1617	1632	0.4	2.57	1186	1191	0.0
46555	NORTH WEBSTER	085	2678	2678	2651	0.0	37	1090	1138	1137	0.5	2.33	769	770	0.0
46556	NOTRE DAME	141	7048	8263	8259	1.7	92	14	15	15	0.7	2.53	5	5	0.0
46561	OSCEOLA	141	10092	11471	12044	1.4	89	3541	4102	4324	1.6	2.79	2842	3195	1.3
46562	PIERCETON	085	4043	4264	4316	0.6	70	1494	1627	1661	0.9	2.62	1136	1196	0.6
46563	PLYMOUTH	099	22979	24498	25152	0.7	73	8497	9212	9499	0.9	2.61	6176	6478	0.5
46565	SHIPSHEWANA	087	6897	7932	8430	1.5	91	1967	2295	2454	1.7	3.46	1632	1858	1.4
46567	SYRACUSE	085	9580	9853	9888	0.3	56	3806	4033	4073	0.6	2.43	2708	2761	0.2
46570	TIPPECANOE	099	1065	1116	1145	0.5	66	386	415	429	0.8	2.69	298	310	0.4
46571	TOPEKA	087	5349	6189	6624	1.6	91	1460	1734	1870	1.9	3.57	1224	1419	1.6
46573	WAKARUSA	039	3320	3712	3921	1.2	86	1162	1331	1413	1.5	2.71	909	1004	1.1
46574	WALKERTON	091	8381	8541	8610	0.2	49	3154	3259	3297	0.4	2.59	2331	2318	-0.1
46580	WARSAW	085	21339	22052	22319	0.4	60	7838	8358	8521	0.7	2.52	5553	5711	0.3
46582	WARSAW	085	10539	12059	12645	1.5	91	3889	4531	4766	1.7	2.65	2894	3257	1.3
46590	WINONA LAKE	085	3883	4107	4213	0.6	70	1338	1460	1507	0.9	2.67	948	996	0.5
46601	SOUTH BEND	141	5784	5482	5378	-0.6	8	2492	2368	2331	-0.6	1.96	994	855	-1.6
46613	SOUTH BEND	141	11657	11159	10981	-0.5	13	4259	4061	3990	-0.5	2.73	2750	2483	-1.1
46614	SOUTH BEND	141	29960	30627	31125	0.2	49	12323	12744	13041	0.4	2.35	8292	8200	-0.1
46615	SOUTH BEND	141	15709	15221	15029	-0.3	22	6824	6662	6590	-0.3	2.26	3910	3583	-0.9
46616	SOUTH BEND	141	7336	6664	6460	-1.0	2	2846	2599	2525	-1.0	2.55	1704	1462	-1.6
46617	SOUTH BEND	141	10995	10691	10557	-0.3	22	4261	4162	4115	-0.3	2.36	2535	2342	-0.9
46619	SOUTH BEND	141	21007	20993	20921	0.0	37	7569	7566	7558	0.0	2.75	5394	5175	-0.4
46628	SOUTH BEND	141	26883	26562	26523	-0.1	31	10508	10506	10525	0.0	2.51	7092	6778	-0.5
46635	SOUTH BEND	141	6887	6711	6639	-0.3	22	2604	2583	2567	-0.1	2.46	1879	1783	-0.6
46637	SOUTH BEND	141	15675	14837	14957	-0.6	8	6140	6370	6444	0.4	2.29	3702	3633	-0.2
46701	ALBION	113	7566	7944	8069	0.5	66	2752	2938	2998	0.7	2.62	2048	2116	0.4
46702	ANDREWS	069	2324	2291	2260	-0.2	27	858	864	859	0.1	2.59	672	655	-0.3
46703	ANGOLA	151	17950	18360	18242	0.2	49	6839	7132	7121	0.5	2.45	4584	4574	0.0
46705	ASHLEY	033	1735	1795	1803	0.4	60	674	716	726	0.7	2.51	468	477	0.2
46706	AUBURN	033	17185	18222	18680	0.6	70	6670	7263	7501	0.9	2.47	4647	4878	0.5
46710	AVILLA	113	4125	4643	4870	1.3	87	1511	1753	1856	1.6	2.57	1099	1229	1.2
46711	BERNE	001	7500	7479	7450	0.0	37	2535	2557	2556	0.1	2.86	1888	1847	-0.2
46714	BLUFFTON	179	14586	14842	14818	0.2	49	5681	5921	5951	0.4	2.45	3946	3949	0.0
46721	BUTLER	033	5142	5107	5089	-0.1	31	1840	1871	1878	0.2	2.68	1369	1343	-0.2
46723	CHURUBUSCO	183	7036	7488	7798	0.7	73	2571	2834	2977	1.1	2.63	1965	2090	0.7
46725	COLUMBIA CITY	183	20686	22785	23766	1.1	84	8014	9094	9573	1.4	2.46	5835	6392	1.0
46730	CORUNNA	033	1433	1536	1584	0.8	76	487	539	562	1.1	2.84	387	415	0.8
46731	CRAIGVILLE	179	635	680	690	0.7	73	219	239	245	0.9	2.85	180	192	0.7
46732	CROMWELL	113	3425	3632	3698	0.6	70	1145	1241	1272	0.9	2.93	893	938	0.5
46733	DECATUR	001	19182	19143	19069	0.0	37	7260	7490	7532	0.3	2.53	5203	5169	-0.1
46737	FREMONT	151	6436	6629	6624	0.3	56	2534	2683	2699	0.6	2.47	1845	1887	0.2
46738	GARRETT	033	7564	7894	8031	0.5	66	2859	3063	3142	0.7	2.56	2006	2059	0.3
46740	GENEVA	001	3869	3979	4007	0.3	56	1217	1298	1322	0.7	3.03	887	909	0.3
46741	GRABILL	003	4199	4574	4764	0.9	79	1205	1347	1417	1.2	3.39	992	1063	0.8
46742	HAMILTON	151	3488	3667	3700	0.5	66	1315	1421	1446	0.8	2.58	989	1033	0.5
46743	HARLAN	003	1924	2294	2465	1.9	93	652	795	860	2.2	2.89	538	634	1.8
46745	HOAGLAND	003	1567	1675	1740	0.7	73	547	603	633	1.1	2.78	430	454	0.6
46746	HOWE	087	4445	4814	5020	0.9	79	1554	1721	1807	1.1	2.80	1222	1311	0.8
46747	HUDSON	151	2676	2836	2865	0.6	70	1049	1140	1161	0.9	2.49	782	821	0.5
46748	HUNTERTOWN	003	3191	4347	4848	3.4	97	1126	1538	1725	3.4	2.83	932	1233	3.1
46750	HUNTINGTON	069	27933	27645	27279	-0.1	31	10496	10611	10539	0.1	2.50	7487	7299	-0.3
46755	KENDALLVILLE	113	15200	15515	15650	0.2	49	5907	6176	6263	0.5	2.48	4064	4077	0.0
46759	KEYSTONE	179	783	740	722	-0.6	8	296	288	283	-0.3	2.57	231	218	-0.6
46760	KIMMELL	113	1604	1663	1686	0.4	60	585	619	631	0.6	2.69	448	459	0.3
46761	LAGRANGE	087	10799	11679	12207	0.9	79	3556	3944	4148	1.1	2.91	2668	2862	0.8
46763	LAOTTO	113	1725	1852	1916	0.8	76	627	692	720	1.1	2.68	497	534	0.8
46764	LARWILL	183	1639	1784	1845	0.9	79	563	630	658	1.2	2.81	454	492	0.9
46765	LEO	003	3924	4738	5071	2.1	94	1307	1590	1709	2.1	2.96	1110	1310	1.8
46766	LIBERTY CENTER	179	653	670	674	0.3	56	227	238	241	0.5	2.82	183	187	0.2
46767	LIGONIER	113	8524	9391	9715	1.1	84	2606	2839	2932	0.9	3.28	2012	2127	0.6
46770	MARKLE	179	2289	2401	2431	0.5	66	847	906	923	0.7	2.63	653	680	0.4
46772	MONROE	001	2833	3002	3046	0.6	70	743	792	807	0.7	3.79	633	661	0.5
46773	MONROEVILLE	003	3687	3794	3857	0.3	56	1307	1380	1414	0.6	2.75	1004	1012	0.1
46774	NEW HAVEN	003	14785	16216	16927	1.0	81	5457	6185	6525	1.4	2.60	4032	4342	0.8
46776	ORLAND	151	1483	1461	1448	-0.2	27	587	594	592	0.1	2.46	424	413	-0.3
46777	OSSIAN	179	6389	6564	6594	0.3	56	2348	2468	2497	0.5	2.63	1779	1810	0.2
46779	PLEASANT LAKE	151	1855	1861	1822	0.0	37	719	737	726	0.3	2.53	533	529	-0.1
46781	PONETO	179	719	688	673	-0.5	13	254	248	245	-0.3	2.77	200	190	-0.6
46783	ROANOKE	069	5245	5723	5864	0.9	79	1933	2168	2241	1.2	2.62	1492	1619	0.9
46784	ROME CITY	113	2488	2499	2489	0.0	37	926	954	956	0.3	2.62	728	728	0.0
46785	SAINT JOE	033	1371	1498	1555	1.0	81	468	526	551	1.3	2.85	382	418	1.0
46787	SOUTH WHITLEY	183	3838	3887	3903	0.1	43	1457	1509	1526	0.4	2.57	1063	1062	0.0
46788	SPENCERVILLE	033	3000	3274	3392	0.9	79	935	1048	1095	1.2	3.10	782	849	0.9
46791	UNIONDALE	179	930	1031	1063	1.1	84	335	381	395	1.4	2.70	263	290	1.1
46792	WARREN	069	4142	4210	4185	0.2	49	1466	1519	1521	0.4	2.52	1099	1097	0.0
46793	WATERLOO	033	4143	4487	4636	0.9	79	1532	1710	1783	1.2	2.62	1172	1264	0.8
46794	WAWAKA	113	1509	1562	1575	0.4	60	540	569	576	0.6	2.75	434	445	0.3
46795	WOLCOTTVILLE	087	6006	6155	6283	0.3	56	2267	2384	2449	0.5	2.58	1755	1788	0.2
46797	WOODBURN	003	3866	3970	4038	0.3	56	1364	1439	1475	0.6	2.75	1116	1132	0.2
46798	YODER	003	2078	2138	2172	0.3	56	786	832	852	0.6	2.57	615	623	0.1
46802	FORT WAYNE	003	11270	10629	10448	-0.6	8	4850	4648	4595	-0.5	2.08	1991	1714	-1.6
46803	FORT WAYNE	003	10492	10174	10105	-0.3	22	3903	3886	3895	0.0	2.53	2425	2240	-0.9
	INDIANA					0.7					0.8	2.49			0.4
	UNITED STATES					1.0					1.1	2.59			0.9

ZIP CODE #	POST OFFICE NAME	RACE (%) White 2000	White 2009	Black 2000	Black 2009	Asian/Pacific 2000	Asian/Pacific 2009	% Hispanic Origin 2000	% Hispanic Origin 2009	2009 AGE DISTRIBUTION (%) 0-4	5-9	10-14	15-19	20-24	25-44	45-64	65-84	85+	18+	MEDIAN AGE 2009	% 2009 Males	% 2009 Females
46532	HAMLET	97.3	96.5	0.9	1.1	0.4	0.7	1.1	1.7	6.7	7.7	7.5	7.2	5.0	26.6	27.0	11.0	1.3	73.6	37.9	51.2	48.8
46534	KNOX	97.3	96.5	0.2	0.2	0.3	0.5	1.8	2.7	6.5	6.6	6.8	7.0	5.7	25.4	27.3	13.0	1.8	75.9	39.0	49.8	50.2
46536	LAKEVILLE	98.3	97.5	0.1	0.1	0.1	0.2	1.3	2.3	5.1	5.6	6.1	6.8	5.4	24.4	30.4	14.5	1.6	79.0	42.4	49.4	50.6
46538	LEESBURG	96.7	95.5	0.1	0.1	0.7	1.1	2.5	3.7	6.3	6.5	6.7	5.9	4.6	23.8	30.6	14.1	1.4	76.7	42.3	50.4	49.6
46539	MENTONE	95.9	94.1	0.2	0.2	0.1	0.1	4.5	6.8	8.0	7.6	7.3	7.3	6.5	27.6	24.5	9.8	1.5	72.7	34.6	50.5	49.5
46540	MIDDLEBURY	97.7	96.7	0.2	0.3	0.6	0.9	0.9	1.5	8.3	8.2	8.7	8.7	6.1	25.3	25.9	7.9	0.9	69.3	33.4	50.6	49.4
46542	MILFORD	94.9	92.9	0.5	0.5	0.2	0.3	7.3	10.8	7.4	7.3	7.3	7.4	6.0	25.9	26.0	10.8	1.8	73.1	36.9	50.1	49.9
46543	MILLERSBURG	98.9	98.3	0.1	0.1	0.0	0.1	1.4	2.4	11.1	10.7	10.0	8.4	5.9	26.1	20.8	6.3	0.7	63.0	28.4	52.4	47.6
46544	MISHAWAKA	95.6	93.6	1.6	2.4	0.4	0.7	1.9	3.3	6.9	6.6	6.6	6.9	6.7	26.6	25.6	11.3	2.7	75.6	37.2	48.4	51.6
46545	MISHAWAKA	89.0	84.9	4.7	6.2	2.4	3.6	3.2	5.2	6.8	6.0	5.7	6.6	8.7	30.6	22.6	10.4	2.6	78.4	34.2	48.0	52.0
46550	NAPPANEE	96.5	94.6	0.2	0.3	0.4	0.7	3.5	5.8	9.5	9.0	8.7	8.0	6.6	26.7	21.7	8.5	1.3	67.7	31.1	50.0	50.0
46552	NEW CARLISLE	97.2	96.1	1.0	1.4	0.2	0.3	1.3	2.2	4.9	5.8	6.5	6.9	4.9	24.2	29.5	12.9	4.5	78.2	42.8	48.3	51.7
46553	NEW PARIS	98.3	97.5	0.1	0.1	0.1	0.2	1.4	2.5	7.2	7.4	7.7	8.2	5.8	24.6	27.4	10.3	1.3	72.6	37.1	49.6	50.4
46554	NORTH LIBERTY	97.8	96.7	0.3	0.5	0.3	0.5	1.0	1.8	6.2	6.4	6.8	6.6	5.5	23.5	31.4	11.9	1.7	76.5	41.0	50.8	49.2
46555	NORTH WEBSTER	97.9	97.1	0.1	0.1	0.4	0.6	1.5	2.2	6.3	6.6	6.9	6.1	4.2	26.4	29.4	12.4	1.8	76.4	40.3	49.1	50.9
46556	NOTRE DAME	89.6	81.2	2.9	7.5	2.4	3.9	6.6	10.0	0.4	0.3	0.3	39.1	42.4	7.8	3.8	4.3	1.5	93.2	21.2	54.7	45.3
46561	OSCEOLA	96.7	95.2	0.8	1.2	1.1	1.8	1.0	1.8	6.8	7.1	7.2	7.1	5.1	25.9	29.0	10.5	1.2	74.4	38.7	49.6	50.4
46562	PIERCETON	95.4	93.7	0.4	0.5	0.5	0.8	3.8	5.5	7.4	7.4	7.7	7.4	5.7	26.3	27.7	9.5	1.1	73.3	36.6	51.3	48.7
46563	PLYMOUTH	94.7	92.8	0.3	0.4	0.4	0.5	7.6	10.8	7.1	7.1	7.1	6.8	5.7	26.4	26.7	11.2	2.1	74.6	37.3	50.1	49.9
46565	SHIPSHEWANA	98.3	97.8	0.2	0.2	0.2	0.3	1.5	2.3	12.2	11.3	10.3	8.8	6.7	26.5	17.2	6.2	0.7	60.7	25.4	51.7	48.3
46567	SYRACUSE	96.0	94.6	0.5	0.5	0.4	0.5	3.1	4.6	6.1	6.3	6.7	6.5	5.0	24.7	29.5	13.1	2.0	76.8	41.0	51.1	48.9
46570	TIPPECANOE	98.9	98.6	0.4	0.4	0.2	0.4	1.0	1.6	6.9	7.5	7.6	6.8	5.2	22.8	31.2	10.5	1.5	73.8	40.3	50.9	49.1
46571	TOPEKA	98.6	98.2	0.0	0.1	0.2	0.3	1.1	1.7	12.5	11.2	10.8	9.6	6.8	25.1	17.2	5.9	0.8	59.5	24.3	51.0	49.0
46573	WAKARUSA	97.5	96.3	0.3	0.5	0.5	0.8	1.3	2.4	7.3	7.4	7.9	7.6	4.9	24.3	26.1	11.4	3.0	72.9	38.3	48.1	51.9
46574	WALKERTON	96.7	95.3	0.3	0.3	0.2	0.3	2.7	4.3	6.0	6.3	6.6	6.9	5.1	25.0	28.2	13.5	2.4	76.8	40.8	49.5	50.5
46580	WARSAW	92.6	90.1	1.0	1.2	0.8	1.1	7.0	10.1	7.2	7.0	6.9	6.6	6.0	26.8	25.7	11.4	2.4	74.8	36.9	49.5	50.5
46582	WARSAW	93.1	90.2	0.7	0.8	1.0	1.4	6.1	9.1	8.3	8.2	8.0	6.8	5.2	27.7	25.6	9.1	1.0	71.5	35.4	50.4	49.6
46590	WINONA LAKE	91.2	87.6	0.7	0.8	0.8	1.1	8.5	12.4	8.1	7.9	7.4	7.3	6.4	28.2	22.5	8.4	3.8	71.9	33.3	48.8	51.2
46601	SOUTH BEND	43.1	36.0	48.5	53.9	0.8	0.9	7.6	10.2	8.1	6.7	5.8	7.0	9.4	29.3	20.4	10.3	2.9	75.2	33.5	49.3	50.7
46613	SOUTH BEND	63.5	54.8	22.7	26.2	0.8	1.0	14.3	20.9	9.5	8.9	8.0	8.2	7.4	28.9	21.2	6.7	1.2	68.6	30.3	49.7	50.3
46614	SOUTH BEND	91.3	88.0	4.9	6.5	0.9	1.3	2.4	4.1	6.5	6.3	6.6	6.5	5.3	23.9	27.5	13.9	3.4	76.5	41.2	47.9	52.1
46615	SOUTH BEND	82.9	77.2	9.4	12.2	2.8	3.9	4.1	6.7	7.3	6.7	6.5	6.5	7.9	28.1	23.1	10.9	2.9	75.8	35.5	47.4	52.6
46616	SOUTH BEND	65.5	59.7	25.7	29.0	1.1	1.5	6.8	9.8	8.7	7.8	7.0	6.9	8.1	29.8	22.6	7.6	1.5	72.3	32.1	48.5	51.5
46617	SOUTH BEND	66.4	60.1	27.3	31.6	1.9	2.6	3.9	5.7	6.8	6.8	6.5	8.1	11.7	23.5	21.8	11.9	3.0	75.7	33.5	49.9	50.1
46619	SOUTH BEND	60.3	55.0	24.4	25.7	0.3	0.5	18.3	23.6	8.2	7.9	7.6	7.3	6.3	24.9	23.5	12.0	2.3	71.9	35.2	49.1	50.9
46628	SOUTH BEND	63.3	60.3	31.0	32.6	0.7	1.0	4.6	6.3	8.2	7.8	7.3	7.1	6.1	26.2	25.2	10.4	1.7	72.3	35.9	48.2	51.8
46635	SOUTH BEND	90.5	86.7	4.5	6.2	2.4	3.5	2.4	4.0	5.5	5.8	6.4	6.2	5.6	19.8	28.7	18.0	4.2	78.3	45.5	46.4	53.6
46637	SOUTH BEND	89.0	83.9	5.5	8.5	2.2	3.2	2.6	4.0	5.3	5.1	5.2	6.6	11.4	25.4	25.3	13.1	2.5	80.9	37.1	47.8	52.2
46701	ALBION	98.0	97.0	0.4	0.7	0.1	0.3	1.1	1.8	6.9	7.0	7.2	7.3	5.8	27.3	27.3	9.8	1.3	75.0	37.3	52.5	47.5
46702	ANDREWS	97.5	97.5	0.1	0.1	0.2	0.2	1.4	1.4	6.6	6.8	7.1	6.9	5.0	25.1	28.6	11.4	2.4	74.9	40.0	50.7	49.3
46703	ANGOLA	96.2	95.0	0.6	0.6	0.7	1.0	2.7	4.0	6.9	6.5	6.4	8.2	7.7	26.9	25.8	9.8	1.9	76.1	35.3	50.7	49.3
46705	ASHLEY	97.5	96.8	0.2	0.3	0.5	0.7	1.5	2.2	7.7	7.9	7.9	7.0	5.1	27.3	26.6	9.4	1.2	72.3	36.3	51.1	48.9
46706	AUBURN	97.8	97.1	0.3	0.4	0.5	0.7	1.5	2.3	7.4	7.3	7.3	6.8	5.7	26.4	26.9	10.1	2.0	73.8	37.0	49.4	50.6
46710	AVILLA	97.2	95.5	0.7	0.4	0.3	2.0	0.8	1.3	6.5	7.5	7.7	6.5	5.6	27.1	25.4	11.1	2.6	74.3	37.3	50.1	49.9
46711	BERNE	98.1	97.4	0.1	0.1	0.2	0.3	1.5	2.2	9.9	9.2	8.9	8.4	5.9	23.4	19.9	10.6	3.9	66.7	31.3	49.0	51.0
46714	BLUFFTON	98.0	97.5	0.2	0.3	0.3	0.4	1.9	2.8	6.8	6.7	6.8	6.7	6.0	25.1	26.3	12.8	2.8	75.6	38.3	49.0	51.0
46721	BUTLER	97.8	97.2	0.1	0.2	0.1	0.2	1.9	2.8	7.7	8.0	8.2	7.8	5.4	27.3	25.5	8.6	1.5	71.2	35.0	50.7	49.3
46723	CHURUBUSCO	98.4	97.6	0.2	0.3	0.2	0.6	0.8	1.2	6.4	6.6	6.8	7.1	5.6	26.3	29.7	10.3	1.3	76.0	38.6	50.1	49.9
46725	COLUMBIA CITY	98.3	97.9	0.2	0.2	0.2	0.3	0.9	1.4	6.6	6.7	7.0	6.5	5.4	25.4	28.8	11.7	2.0	75.7	39.6	49.6	50.4
46730	CORUNNA	98.6	98.3	0.1	0.1	0.0	0.0	2.0	3.1	6.8	7.4	7.7	7.2	4.8	24.0	30.5	10.7	1.0	73.6	39.2	50.5	49.5
46731	CRAIGVILLE	98.9	98.5	0.0	0.0	0.0	0.1	0.9	1.3	6.2	6.9	7.4	7.1	5.4	24.3	31.8	9.6	1.5	75.1	39.2	51.2	48.8
46732	CROMWELL	92.0	89.0	0.3	0.3	0.3	0.4	16.5	23.0	9.0	8.9	8.9	7.4	5.4	28.6	24.4	6.5	0.7	68.5	32.6	51.7	48.3
46733	DECATUR	96.5	95.0	0.2	0.2	0.3	0.4	4.9	7.3	6.9	7.1	7.3	7.3	5.6	25.7	26.5	11.2	2.4	74.1	37.4	49.9	50.1
46737	FREMONT	98.5	98.1	0.2	0.2	0.1	0.2	1.3	1.9	5.9	6.2	6.7	6.6	5.1	24.8	31.4	12.0	1.3	76.9	41.4	50.1	49.9
46738	GARRETT	97.6	96.9	0.3	0.3	0.7	0.9	1.7	2.5	7.6	7.2	7.0	7.4	6.0	28.5	24.9	9.8	1.8	73.8	35.6	49.5	50.5
46740	GENEVA	98.4	97.8	0.2	0.2	0.4	0.5	0.9	1.5	9.0	8.6	8.5	8.2	5.9	24.4	21.9	10.4	3.2	68.6	32.3	50.0	50.0
46741	GRABILL	98.4	97.6	0.1	0.2	0.4	0.6	0.7	1.3	9.6	9.5	9.3	8.4	6.2	25.7	22.3	7.9	1.0	66.3	30.9	49.6	50.4
46742	HAMILTON	98.7	98.2	0.1	0.1	0.1	0.1	1.1	1.7	6.7	7.1	7.4	7.1	4.7	24.4	29.1	12.1	1.4	74.3	39.8	50.2	49.8
46743	HARLAN	98.7	98.1	0.3	0.4	0.1	0.1	0.7	1.1	8.9	9.0	9.0	7.6	4.8	26.0	24.8	8.6	1.2	68.1	33.9	51.3	48.7
46745	HOAGLAND	98.9	98.3	0.2	0.4	0.3	0.4	1.0	1.9	6.0	6.6	7.0	7.2	4.8	23.5	32.4	11.2	1.3	76.0	40.6	49.7	50.3
46746	HOWE	92.5	89.2	0.3	0.3	0.5	0.8	8.1	12.2	8.3	8.3	8.2	6.8	5.1	26.2	26.1	9.9	1.1	71.0	35.1	51.3	48.7
46747	HUDSON	98.4	97.9	0.1	0.1	0.1	0.1	0.9	1.4	7.3	7.2	7.4	6.7	4.9	26.6	26.8	11.9	1.2	74.0	38.6	51.4	48.6
46748	HUNTERTOWN	97.8	96.5	0.5	0.8	0.6	0.9	0.9	1.7	6.3	6.7	7.4	7.8	5.2	24.8	32.0	9.0	0.9	74.8	39.3	49.7	50.3
46750	HUNTINGTON	98.1	98.0	0.2	0.2	0.4	0.4	0.9	1.0	6.9	6.8	6.6	7.5	7.4	25.6	25.9	11.2	2.1	75.6	36.5	48.8	51.2
46755	KENDALLVILLE	96.6	95.1	0.4	0.5	0.6	0.9	2.7	4.5	8.0	7.2	6.9	6.6	6.2	27.7	25.3	9.9	2.1	74.0	35.9	48.6	51.4
46759	KEYSTONE	98.2	97.8	0.1	0.1	0.1	0.1	1.4	2.2	5.3	5.9	6.4	7.3	5.0	24.7	30.9	13.1	1.4	77.8	42.2	51.5	48.5
46760	KIMMELL	98.3	97.8	0.2	0.2	0.2	0.4	1.7	2.9	6.0	6.3	6.7	7.5	5.5	25.1	30.7	10.9	1.3	76.5	40.2	52.0	48.0
46761	LAGRANGE	95.4	93.3	0.3	0.3	0.3	0.5	4.6	7.0	9.2	8.4	8.4	7.7	5.8	25.4	22.8	10.5	1.8	69.3	33.1	50.2	49.8
46763	LAOTTO	97.7	96.2	0.7	0.4	0.2	1.9	0.9	1.2	6.5	7.1	7.6	6.7	4.2	25.8	30.5	10.7	0.9	74.6	39.7	51.2	48.8
46764	LARWILL	98.1	97.5	0.2	0.2	0.2	0.3	1.1	1.5	6.7	7.2	8.0	7.5	5.1	25.4	29.1	9.6	1.3	73.3	38.0	51.6	48.4
46765	LEO	97.9	96.8	0.4	0.6	0.5	0.8	0.7	1.3	7.0	7.6	8.4	8.4	4.8	23.6	29.9	9.1	1.2	71.5	38.3	49.1	50.9
46766	LIBERTY CENTER	97.2	96.3	0.2	0.1	0.3	0.6	1.2	1.9	5.8	6.4	7.0	7.3	5.4	23.0	32.4	11.0	1.6	76.1	41.0	49.9	50.1
46767	LIGONIER	80.8	73.8	0.3	0.4	0.5	0.6	25.2	34.6	10.3	10.0	8.8	7.5	6.5	28.5	20.1	7.3	1.1	66.4	29.5	51.9	48.1
46770	MARKLE	99.1	98.8	0.1	0.1	0.2	0.3	0.8	1.2	6.6	6.8	7.0	7.5	5.3	25.3	29.2	10.6	1.6	74.8	38.7	50.3	49.7
46772	MONROE	99.0	98.6	0.0	0.0	0.0	0.0	1.1	1.6	12.2	10.9	10.1	9.0	6.2	25.3	18.0	7.3	1.1	61.1	26.1	51.2	48.8
46773	MONROEVILLE	97.9	96.9	0.2	0.3	0.1	0.2	1.4	2.6	7.2	7.5	7.8	7.3	4.9	26.1	26.7	10.9	1.6	72.9	37.9	49.8	50.2
46774	NEW HAVEN	97.8	96.7	0.6	1.0	0.3	0.4	1.3	2.3	6.7	6.8	6.9	6.9	5.6	25.8	27.4	12.2	1.8	75.4	38.4	49.0	51.0
46776	ORLAND	98.0	97.3	0.1	0.1	0.2	0.3	1.1	1.7	5.9	6.2	6.4	7.0	4.4	27.0	28.9	12.7	1.4	77.2	40.7	52.3	47.7
46777	OSSIAN	98.5	98.0	0.1	0.2	0.2	0.2	1.0	1.5	6.9	7.8	7.9	7.6	5.0	26.4	26.2	10.2	2.0	72.7	36.9	49.8	50.2
46779	PLEASANT LAKE	97.6	96.7	0.1	0.2	0.3	0.5	2.5	3.7	6.7	6.9	7.0	6.4	4.9	25.8	29.0	12.1	1.2	75.5	39.9	50.5	49.5
46781	PONETO	98.3	98.0	0.0	0.0	0.1	0.1	0.7	1.0	6.4	6.8	7.0	7.1	5.1	25.4	29.7	10.9	1.6	75.6	39.6	50.3	49.7
46783	ROANOKE	98.1	97.6	0.4	0.5	0.3	0.5	1.0	1.3	5.8	6.4	6.9	6.6	4.9	23.7	33.3	10.9	1.4	76.6	41.9	49.6	50.4
46784	ROME CITY	98.3	97.8	0.2	0.2	0.2	0.4	1.0	1.7	7.7	7.6	7.8	6.9	5.3	26.5	26.3	10.8	1.0	72.5	37.2	49.9	50.1
46785	SAINT JOE	98.2	97.5	0.2	0.3	0.0	0.0	1.8	2.7	7.4	7.8	7.9	7.5	5.0	25.9	27.3	9.9	1.3	72.2	37.0	52.6	47.4
46787	SOUTH WHITLEY	98.6	98.2	0.1	0.2	0.2	0.3	0.8	1.3	7.7	7.8	7.7	7.0	6.0	26.1	26.1	9.9	1.6	72.4	35.8	49.7	50.3
46788	SPENCERVILLE	98.5	97.9	0.3	0.4	0.1	0.1	0.7	1.2	7.6	7.9	8.4	8.3	4.9	24.2	28.1	9.3	1.2	70.7	36.3	51.0	49.0
46791	UNIONDALE	99.7	99.5	0.0	0.0	0.1	0.2	0.2	0.3	6.2	6.6	7.2	7.7	5.3	24.8	29.9	10.8	1.6	75.3	40.0	52.4	47.6
46792	WARREN	98.9	98.9	0.1	0.1	0.1	0.1	1.0	1.1	5.3	5.7	6.0	6.3	4.7	22.4	27.2	14.6	7.8	79.1	44.7	47.4	52.6
46793	WATERLOO	97.0	95.9	0.2	0.2	0.2	0.3	2.3	3.5	7.4	7.5	7.4	6.9	6.0	26.0	28.4	9.5	1.0	73.5	37.0	51.4	48.6
46794	WAWAKA	97.5	96.4	0.2	0.2	0.2	0.3	2.3	3.8	7.9	7.9	7.9	7.0	5.4	26.1	26.6	10.4	1.0	72.0	36.7	51.0	49.0
46795	WOLCOTTVILLE	98.5	98.1	0.1	0.2	0.2	0.3	0.9	1.3	7.4	7.6	7.6	6.5	4.7	24.9	26.7	13.3	1.3	73.4	38.7	50.7	49.3
46797	WOODBURN	98.7	97.8	0.3	0.5	0.1	0.1	1.3	2.4	7.9	7.9	7.8	7.3	6.2	25.4	26.3	10.1	1.1	71.9	34.7	49.8	50.2
46798	YODER	96.7	95.0	0.7	1.1	0.4	0.7	1.7	3.0	5.5	5.9	6.7	7.2	4.9	24.5	33.0	11.1	1.2	77.5	41.4	49.7	50.3
46802	FORT WAYNE	72.6	64.0	15.4	19.7	1.8	2.2	12.3	18.2	6.5	5.9	5.2	7.1	9.3	32.3	24.1	8.2	1.4	78.6	33.9	55.2	44.8
46803	FORT WAYNE	40.3	34.2	51.0	55.5	1.3	1.3	9.1	11.9	9.9	9.3	8.0	9.4	8.6	25.3	20.6	7.8	1.1	67.9	28.3	50.0	50.0
	INDIANA	87.5	85.6	8.4	8.9	1.0	1.5	3.5	5.0	6.9	6.8	6.8	7.2	6.9	26.5	26.2	10.8	1.9	75.4	36.8	49.3	50.7
	UNITED STATES	75.1	72.0	12.3	12.7	3.8	4.6	12.5	15.7	6.8	6.7	6.6	7.1	6.9	27.0	26.0	10.9	1.9	75.7	36.9	49.2	50.8

ZIP CODE #	POST OFFICE NAME	2009 Per Capita Income	2009 HH Income Base	2009 HOUSEHOLD INCOME DISTRIBUTION (%) Less than $25,000	$25,000 to $49,999	$50,000 to $99,999	$100,000 to $149,999	$150,000 or More	MEDIAN HOUSEHOLD INCOME 2009	2014	2009 National Centile	2009 State Centile	2009 Home Value Base	2009 HOME VALUE DISTRIBUTION (%) Less than $50,000	$50,000 to $89,999	$90,000 to $174,999	$175,000 to $399,999	$400,000 or More	2009 Median Home Value
46532	HAMLET	19776	798	22.7	30.8	40.5	4.8	1.3	47058	49205	54	32	657	16.7	29.4	44.6	8.5	0.8	93269
46534	KNOX	20351	4342	25.6	30.0	36.4	5.4	2.6	45245	46770	49	24	3458	12.1	25.6	51.7	9.3	1.3	101147
46536	LAKEVILLE	24036	1187	16.2	26.1	46.8	7.7	3.3	55623	57050	72	71	992	6.7	22.7	49.9	18.4	2.3	111592
46538	LEESBURG	27992	1818	13.9	28.3	43.9	10.1	3.9	56427	57022	73	74	1534	15.3	16.4	38.9	22.6	6.8	116784
46539	MENTONE	22310	902	18.1	29.3	42.9	6.9	2.9	52392	54277	67	60	721	22.9	30.4	38.8	6.9	1.0	85727
46540	MIDDLEBURY	22843	3710	11.7	24.9	48.3	10.1	5.0	61304	62301	79	85	3123	9.6	8.4	47.1	31.8	3.1	151088
46542	MILFORD	23116	1569	15.4	30.0	42.4	9.0	3.3	53470	54585	69	65	1211	14.0	22.5	45.4	17.3	0.7	106904
46543	MILLERSBURG	20401	939	9.6	26.7	51.2	8.5	3.9	59154	59964	76	80	796	5.7	19.3	46.0	24.7	4.3	128935
46544	MISHAWAKA	24392	13103	20.9	27.8	40.9	7.5	2.9	51092	53453	64	52	9144	9.9	35.7	46.5	7.2	0.6	92998
46545	MISHAWAKA	25754	11849	20.7	32.4	38.0	5.9	3.0	46973	50851	54	31	6018	9.7	33.9	42.3	13.3	0.7	96514
46550	NAPPANEE	23688	4417	13.2	24.0	47.8	10.9	4.1	62221	63313	80	86	3303	13.2	17.7	47.7	19.3	2.0	113140
46552	NEW CARLISLE	23233	2418	18.2	25.0	46.3	8.1	2.4	55800	57608	72	72	1968	3.6	27.1	50.8	16.5	2.0	113993
46553	NEW PARIS	23225	1153	10.9	25.9	49.2	9.5	4.4	61218	62341	79	84	966	6.1	18.3	60.8	12.6	2.2	120128
46554	NORTH LIBERTY	24821	1617	16.2	25.5	44.5	10.7	3.1	56422	57500	73	74	1344	3.9	25.4	49.9	18.8	1.9	109273
46555	NORTH WEBSTER	24621	1138	18.0	30.3	40.9	8.7	2.1	51224	53025	64	53	908	9.4	22.2	49.6	17.1	1.8	110465
46556	NOTRE DAME	12825	15	20.0	33.3	26.7	6.7	13.3	47351	47351	55	33	12	0.0	16.7	75.0	8.3	0.0	116667
46561	OSCEOLA	24853	4102	8.6	22.8	54.8	10.5	3.3	63406	64136	82	89	3649	2.1	20.7	66.1	11.0	0.2	114823
46562	PIERCETON	21370	1627	19.9	30.7	41.8	5.3	2.3	49551	51991	60	44	1355	25.1	23.5	35.1	15.7	0.6	91779
46563	PLYMOUTH	23666	9212	19.1	26.4	42.2	8.5	3.9	53790	55173	69	66	6818	11.2	23.3	49.5	14.2	1.7	107855
46565	SHIPSHEWANA	18414	2295	14.2	29.7	44.1	8.2	3.8	55695	56058	72	72	1875	8.7	11.9	44.1	31.2	4.1	141620
46567	SYRACUSE	28574	4033	14.5	27.0	43.7	9.6	5.2	57426	57753	75	76	3177	9.2	20.0	40.9	22.9	7.1	129462
46570	TIPPECANOE	20287	415	17.1	33.5	42.9	4.8	1.7	49574	52127	60	44	355	20.8	20.3	49.6	7.3	2.0	98750
46571	TOPEKA	16175	1734	15.7	32.1	43.3	6.1	2.8	51342	52007	64	54	1373	11.7	16.1	34.7	31.4	6.0	139208
46573	WAKARUSA	24176	1331	15.1	26.8	45.8	7.4	4.8	57080	59362	74	76	1108	9.6	12.9	54.1	19.9	3.5	125994
46574	WALKERTON	22874	3259	18.8	28.3	42.6	7.4	2.9	51967	53685	66	58	2675	6.9	29.0	49.5	13.3	1.3	103790
46580	WARSAW	24044	8358	19.9	27.1	41.2	7.7	4.2	52504	54238	67	61	6167	15.2	26.4	45.1	12.1	1.2	99531
46582	WARSAW	23784	4531	14.6	26.9	46.3	9.3	3.0	57377	57916	74	76	3766	24.2	13.5	44.2	17.4	0.6	107635
46590	WINONA LAKE	24595	1460	14.0	27.0	45.6	8.1	5.3	58862	60486	76	79	1029	10.2	23.7	44.9	17.6	3.6	108610
46601	SOUTH BEND	15861	2368	55.5	22.4	18.0	3.0	1.1	21069	21613	2	1	536	23.7	44.2	30.2	1.5	0.4	74808
46613	SOUTH BEND	16167	4061	31.3	34.8	29.9	3.1	0.9	38096	40331	27	7	2656	34.9	57.1	7.3	0.6	0.0	57737
46614	SOUTH BEND	28633	12744	17.8	25.3	42.1	10.1	4.7	57466	58926	75	77	10104	4.7	28.5	52.4	12.7	1.7	105796
46615	SOUTH BEND	23619	6662	22.8	33.6	34.7	5.7	3.2	44197	47778	46	20	4122	6.7	53.8	34.4	4.8	0.3	83741
46616	SOUTH BEND	20663	2599	26.4	30.0	33.2	7.2	3.2	42933	46608	42	14	1483	19.6	46.7	32.4	1.3	0.1	76943
46617	SOUTH BEND	24681	4162	25.0	26.2	35.2	9.5	4.2	48257	51737	57	37	2783	10.2	29.9	50.7	8.2	1.0	97296
46619	SOUTH BEND	18641	7566	24.5	30.6	37.5	6.0	1.3	44224	49149	46	20	5976	22.9	43.0	29.6	4.3	0.3	73311
46628	SOUTH BEND	22185	10506	22.2	28.8	40.8	6.0	2.1	48979	52120	59	41	7353	13.8	39.2	39.0	7.1	1.0	86354
46635	SOUTH BEND	32903	2583	12.4	18.1	43.4	17.6	8.4	71380	73534	88	94	2187	3.3	15.5	59.1	21.0	1.1	119966
46637	SOUTH BEND	27816	6370	20.0	23.3	42.7	9.7	4.2	57479	59646	75	77	4373	5.1	25.3	60.3	8.6	0.7	106375
46701	ALBION	23052	2938	14.7	29.1	45.2	8.6	2.4	55875	56808	72	73	2465	12.9	20.1	48.3	16.8	2.0	108967
46702	ANDREWS	22827	864	16.0	35.3	38.4	8.1	2.2	48847	51817	59	40	683	12.6	25.5	44.9	15.2	1.8	106342
46703	ANGOLA	24906	7132	16.6	28.0	43.5	8.0	3.9	54244	54952	70	68	5069	16.1	17.9	45.2	16.7	4.1	111928
46705	ASHLEY	22922	716	21.9	27.4	42.5	5.3	2.9	50558	52646	62	50	558	15.8	33.2	39.1	10.0	2.0	91250
46706	AUBURN	27314	7263	15.6	23.7	45.4	11.1	4.2	60508	60584	78	83	5784	14.8	13.8	51.2	18.1	2.1	118302
46710	AVILLA	23308	1753	17.7	26.8	43.6	9.9	2.1	54391	55506	70	68	1326	9.0	11.6	58.5	19.0	1.8	120695
46711	BERNE	18497	2557	22.7	33.0	34.9	7.6	1.8	44461	47843	47	21	1879	8.9	26.4	52.2	11.4	1.0	104548
46714	BLUFFTON	23886	5921	18.7	30.5	39.5	8.1	3.2	50766	54300	63	51	4508	15.6	29.2	43.9	10.7	0.5	95309
46721	BUTLER	21158	1871	17.9	29.9	43.7	6.6	1.9	51728	53557	65	56	1487	16.7	29.4	44.0	9.5	0.3	94675
46723	CHURUBUSCO	24383	2834	16.2	26.0	44.3	10.8	2.7	57681	59486	75	77	2453	17.5	18.8	47.5	15.2	0.9	103363
46725	COLUMBIA CITY	25183	9094	16.1	27.5	44.2	8.9	3.2	56164	58289	73	73	7450	12.0	19.0	50.0	17.3	1.6	113577
46730	CORUNNA	21475	539	17.6	31.0	38.6	9.3	3.5	51302	53429	64	54	474	7.8	15.2	52.7	18.8	5.5	121065
46731	CRAIGVILLE	24973	239	10.0	24.7	46.9	14.2	4.2	63037	63661	81	88	214	5.6	21.5	42.5	29.4	0.9	128846
46732	CROMWELL	20364	1241	16.0	29.2	44.7	8.1	1.9	53819	55122	69	66	971	26.9	16.8	44.4	10.9	1.0	97410
46733	DECATUR	24172	7490	16.5	29.3	41.1	10.2	2.9	53223	54210	68	65	5765	12.0	21.8	50.8	14.1	1.1	108679
46737	FREMONT	25107	2683	17.3	28.5	43.4	7.6	3.2	53038	53918	68	64	2275	13.7	19.2	40.8	20.9	5.4	116707
46738	GARRETT	24013	3063	16.2	27.3	47.5	6.7	2.4	56343	57185	73	73	2464	18.1	30.0	45.5	6.2	0.2	91661
46740	GENEVA	17863	1298	24.2	29.9	37.3	6.9	1.8	45847	49054	51	26	972	16.3	29.9	43.6	9.6	0.6	93814
46741	GRABILL	17811	1347	13.1	32.8	44.0	7.8	2.2	52702	55108	67	63	1171	11.4	13.8	60.1	13.3	1.4	111627
46742	HAMILTON	24099	1421	17.0	30.5	39.8	8.6	4.1	52499	53987	67	61	1200	12.0	22.1	44.0	19.3	2.7	113393
46743	HARLAN	21847	795	11.1	28.3	49.2	9.3	2.1	57429	59025	75	77	678	10.2	14.5	62.1	11.8	1.5	116556
46745	HOAGLAND	24007	603	14.6	22.9	49.3	10.8	2.5	62323	62792	80	87	542	10.1	21.0	54.2	14.4	0.2	109737
46746	HOWE	19677	1721	15.7	35.4	41.0	6.3	1.6	49074	50750	59	42	1443	12.0	24.4	49.8	13.0	0.9	107743
46747	HUDSON	23456	1140	13.7	32.5	46.3	5.8	1.7	52191	52985	66	59	993	12.4	33.3	42.2	10.8	1.3	94521
46748	HUNTERTOWN	29227	1538	7.6	19.8	48.0	16.6	8.0	71415	72020	88	94	1348	2.6	17.4	55.4	21.6	3.0	127665
46750	HUNTINGTON	24000	10611	18.5	29.1	41.2	7.8	3.3	52286	54322	66	59	7993	11.0	28.8	47.4	12.0	0.7	98089
46755	KENDALLVILLE	23021	6176	19.2	31.0	39.2	8.3	2.3	49834	52278	61	45	4438	13.6	21.6	49.8	14.2	0.9	104843
46759	KEYSTONE	20931	288	15.6	32.6	45.5	5.6	0.7	51723	56661	65	56	253	9.1	20.2	65.2	5.5	0.0	110129
46760	KIMMELL	21460	619	15.0	33.8	40.9	8.6	1.8	51113	53210	64	52	539	10.2	28.8	45.3	14.8	0.9	100833
46761	LAGRANGE	19088	3944	19.2	32.7	39.3	6.9	1.9	48484	50263	58	37	3080	11.9	22.9	45.7	17.7	1.8	112548
46763	LAOTTO	24692	692	16.0	24.1	45.4	11.6	2.9	58483	58248	76	79	613	4.7	9.0	54.3	27.6	4.4	143169
46764	LARWILL	22956	630	13.3	29.7	45.2	9.2	2.5	56699	58972	74	75	549	13.8	19.5	44.4	21.1	1.1	110767
46765	LEO	27586	1590	7.6	19.3	47.5	20.1	5.5	76211	76271	90	96	1448	0.8	13.1	53.5	31.3	1.4	141422
46766	LIBERTY CENTER	21704	238	17.6	24.4	46.2	6.7	5.0	58887	60473	76	80	211	10.4	24.2	45.5	18.5	1.4	107500
46767	LIGONIER	18397	2839	14.2	33.7	41.2	8.7	2.1	51948	54070	66	58	2130	14.1	24.9	47.8	11.8	1.4	98298
46770	MARKLE	24716	906	14.0	22.6	48.7	12.1	2.5	61854	62412	80	86	760	10.0	25.7	53.6	9.9	0.9	103313
46772	MONROE	16228	792	13.0	32.1	43.9	7.4	3.5	53348	54626	69	65	696	2.3	24.4	57.2	14.8	1.3	115263
46773	MONROEVILLE	21120	1380	18.7	25.4	46.3	7.6	2.0	53754	55614	69	66	1170	13.2	27.9	47.6	9.9	1.4	99369
46774	NEW HAVEN	25291	6185	12.3	23.8	52.0	9.3	2.6	60387	62024	78	82	4947	7.2	37.3	47.8	7.2	0.5	94345
46776	ORLAND	25590	594	12.8	30.8	46.6	7.1	2.7	54524	54998	70	69	509	17.7	24.0	43.2	12.4	2.8	99659
46777	OSSIAN	24746	2468	11.7	23.7	52.0	10.3	2.4	62499	63386	81	87	2069	10.5	23.8	49.1	15.4	1.3	107378
46779	PLEASANT LAKE	25485	737	15.3	33.1	41.5	6.2	3.8	51418	53516	65	55	633	20.9	20.5	45.0	11.8	1.7	99561
46781	PONETO	18523	248	14.5	38.7	42.7	3.2	0.8	47932	51813	56	36	216	11.1	23.1	55.1	10.6	0.0	106364
46783	ROANOKE	27144	2168	10.4	26.3	45.0	13.9	4.5	62022	62181	80	86	1893	9.2	12.8	52.1	22.6	3.2	125720
46784	ROME CITY	21779	954	16.2	33.4	40.6	7.5	2.2	50257	52647	62	47	755	13.4	22.5	43.3	18.8	2.0	106944
46785	SAINT JOE	21618	526	16.5	30.4	41.8	7.0	4.2	53079	54618	68	64	462	19.5	21.0	43.3	15.6	0.6	105183
46787	SOUTH WHITLEY	23507	1509	19.8	30.1	38.4	9.1	2.7	50104	53639	61	47	1227	13.4	29.2	45.9	10.3	1.3	98243
46788	SPENCERVILLE	21531	1048	13.2	22.3	50.5	11.0	3.1	62275	62124	80	86	952	6.7	13.8	55.6	22.1	1.9	129503
46791	UNIONDALE	22841	381	13.6	27.0	47.8	8.9	2.6	58420	60522	76	78	340	12.4	30.6	48.8	7.9	0.3	96857
46792	WARREN	22613	1519	16.4	31.4	42.1	7.6	2.5	51870	53957	66	57	1211	14.7	26.8	47.2	8.5	2.7	96926
46793	WATERLOO	24066	1710	15.0	25.2	47.0	10.5	2.3	57959	57901	75	78	1429	16.0	25.9	39.5	17.6	1.0	101689
46794	WAWAKA	22881	569	12.7	29.3	47.6	7.2	3.2	55195	55741	72	70	508	11.6	12.4	55.7	18.7	1.6	124702
46795	WOLCOTTVILLE	23277	2384	14.9	32.0	43.0	6.9	3.2	52570	53017	67	61	2029	5.7	21.2	48.3	20.4	4.4	123962
46797	WOODBURN	24069	1439	12.9	21.3	53.9	9.0	2.9	61263	61448	79	85	1199	12.7	30.4	46.3	9.8	0.8	97455
46798	YODER	25663	832	8.8	28.5	47.8	12.6	2.3	58763	60000	76	79	763	18.0	26.2	41.4	13.2	1.2	96642
46802	FORT WAYNE	19598	4648	38.5	30.7	25.5	3.0	2.2	32288	33514	12	3	1610	42.6	35.8	19.4	2.0	0.1	55980
46803	FORT WAYNE	15641	3886	41.8	28.9	24.5	3.5	1.3	31317	32265	10	2	1990	64.0	28.4	6.9	0.6	0.0	38926
	INDIANA	26003		19.5	26.3	38.6	10.5	5.1	54105	56493				12.2	24.1	44.1	17.2	2.4	108938
	UNITED STATES	27277		20.9	24.4	35.3	11.7	7.6	54719	56938				9.3	13.1	31.6	32.6	13.5	162279

SPENDING POTENTIAL INDICES

ZIP CODE #	POST OFFICE NAME	FINANCIAL SERVICES: Auto Loan	Home Loan	Investments	Retirement Plans	THE HOME: Home Improvements: Home Repair	Lawn & Garden	Furnishings: Computers & Hardware-Personal	Major Appliances	TV, Radio, Sound Equipment	Furniture	ENTERTAINMENT: Dine out/ Carry out	Sports Equipment	Fees & Tickets	Toys & Games	Travel	Cable TV	PERSONAL: Apparel & Services	Auto Repairs	Health Insurance	Pets & Supplies
46532	HAMLET	85	69	73	70	70	86	70	80	75	66	73	61	61	77	67	80	50	75	83	95
46534	KNOX	85	70	74	71	71	85	74	81	78	68	76	61	65	79	70	83	52	78	85	96
46536	LAKEVILLE	94	89	93	90	89	103	85	96	89	81	88	72	83	90	88	94	60	91	101	112
46538	LEESBURG	106	95	103	96	98	113	93	106	97	89	95	79	86	97	94	103	65	100	111	124
46539	MENTONE	91	84	76	85	81	95	84	88	87	79	86	69	79	89	81	91	59	86	95	106
46540	MIDDLEBURY	107	107	97	109	105	112	99	106	101	99	101	81	100	104	101	103	69	101	106	125
46542	MILFORD	93	87	81	90	86	97	87	92	89	82	88	71	83	91	85	93	60	89	96	109
46543	MILLERSBURG	97	105	87	107	100	105	98	99	97	95	97	78	101	100	100	98	68	97	102	118
46544	MISHAWAKA	84	81	72	82	78	86	84	82	85	80	85	64	82	86	81	88	59	84	89	99
46545	MISHAWAKA	82	72	66	75	69	73	82	75	82	79	83	60	77	83	76	83	57	80	79	91
46550	NAPPANEE	105	99	90	100	97	107	99	102	101	95	100	79	95	103	96	104	69	100	107	122
46552	NEW CARLISLE	84	89	81	90	87	95	82	88	84	79	84	66	85	85	86	87	58	84	93	103
46553	NEW PARIS	99	99	87	102	96	107	96	100	97	91	96	78	95	99	96	100	66	97	105	119
46554	NORTH LIBERTY	93	93	82	96	91	100	90	94	91	85	90	73	89	93	90	93	62	91	98	111
46555	NORTH WEBSTER	90	80	82	83	81	96	80	90	83	73	82	68	73	84	79	88	56	84	94	105
46556	NOTRE DAME	96	83	81	87	81	83	104	88	103	99	104	72	97	101	95	102	73	100	97	110
46561	OSCEOLA	102	103	95	104	102	108	97	103	98	94	98	79	97	100	99	101	68	99	105	120
46562	PIERCETON	91	77	78	77	76	91	77	85	82	74	81	65	69	84	74	86	55	81	89	102
46563	PLYMOUTH	92	87	81	89	86	96	88	92	90	82	89	70	84	91	86	94	61	89	97	108
46565	SHIPSHEWANA	99	92	85	89	91	94	90	95	90	91	91	72	84	93	88	91	63	92	92	110
46567	SYRACUSE	105	98	100	100	99	110	97	105	99	92	98	80	92	100	98	103	67	101	109	124
46570	TIPPECANOE	85	77	76	80	78	91	76	86	78	69	77	65	70	80	76	83	52	79	88	100
46571	TOPEKA	93	81	82	82	81	95	79	89	83	76	82	68	72	86	78	88	56	84	92	106
46573	WAKARUSA	102	97	92	98	97	106	92	101	94	90	94	76	89	97	92	98	64	95	102	118
46574	WALKERTON	87	86	81	87	85	96	82	89	85	78	84	67	81	86	84	89	58	85	95	104
46580	WARSAW	94	85	80	86	83	95	87	90	90	84	89	69	82	92	83	94	61	89	96	108
46582	WARSAW	99	92	85	90	90	97	88	94	91	89	91	70	84	94	85	94	62	91	95	111
46590	WINONA LAKE	101	98	82	97	92	91	98	94	97	99	97	72	95	100	92	96	67	95	92	112
46601	SOUTH BEND	43	33	32	36	32	36	46	38	49	43	49	31	42	47	40	51	34	45	46	49
46613	SOUTH BEND	67	55	48	56	52	62	64	60	67	59	65	47	57	68	56	70	45	64	68	74
46614	SOUTH BEND	94	99	89	100	96	101	96	96	97	94	97	73	99	97	97	99	67	96	103	113
46615	SOUTH BEND	75	71	63	73	68	74	78	72	79	73	78	57	75	79	73	80	54	76	80	88
46616	SOUTH BEND	74	67	56	69	62	69	78	69	79	71	78	56	73	79	70	80	55	75	76	85
46617	SOUTH BEND	84	82	75	83	79	85	87	82	88	84	88	63	86	88	84	90	61	86	90	99
46619	SOUTH BEND	76	70	64	69	68	77	71	73	75	70	74	54	68	75	69	79	51	74	80	87
46628	SOUTH BEND	79	77	69	79	74	80	78	77	81	77	81	59	78	81	77	83	56	79	83	93
46635	SOUTH BEND	115	125	126	127	128	129	116	122	117	118	116	90	123	115	123	119	82	119	126	141
46637	SOUTH BEND	91	87	84	89	87	93	93	90	93	88	93	69	90	93	89	95	64	92	97	107
46701	ALBION	95	87	83	89	86	99	85	92	88	81	87	71	81	90	84	92	60	88	96	110
46702	ANDREWS	94	86	81	86	86	95	83	91	86	80	85	68	77	89	81	90	58	86	93	107
46703	ANGOLA	93	87	81	88	84	92	89	90	90	86	90	70	84	92	86	92	62	90	93	107
46705	ASHLEY	100	76	84	76	76	97	78	90	85	75	83	69	65	88	73	92	56	85	94	108
46706	AUBURN	99	98	87	99	95	102	97	98	97	94	97	76	95	99	95	99	67	97	101	116
46710	AVILLA	94	89	82	90	88	95	85	91	87	84	86	68	82	89	84	89	59	87	92	107
46711	BERNE	84	70	80	70	70	87	73	81	77	67	76	63	65	77	72	83	52	79	88	97
46714	BLUFFTON	89	81	78	82	80	91	83	87	86	78	85	67	78	87	80	90	58	85	92	103
46721	BUTLER	93	78	79	79	78	94	79	88	83	74	82	67	70	86	76	89	56	83	92	105
46723	CHURUBUSCO	97	95	84	96	93	100	90	95	92	88	91	72	88	94	89	94	63	92	97	113
46725	COLUMBIA CITY	92	89	82	91	87	96	88	92	90	84	89	70	85	91	87	93	61	90	96	109
46730	CORUNNA	95	86	86	89	88	102	85	96	88	77	86	73	78	90	85	93	59	89	99	112
46731	CRAIGVILLE	105	105	98	109	105	115	99	108	100	94	99	83	97	103	101	104	69	102	110	126
46732	CROMWELL	101	82	84	81	81	97	82	92	87	80	86	69	71	91	77	93	58	87	95	110
46733	DECATUR	93	86	82	88	85	98	86	92	89	80	87	71	81	90	84	93	60	89	98	109
46737	FREMONT	103	85	106	84	88	105	84	100	89	81	88	74	74	89	85	95	59	93	101	117
46738	GARRETT	93	88	77	88	84	95	87	90	89	83	88	70	83	92	84	92	61	88	95	108
46740	GENEVA	90	69	82	69	70	91	75	85	80	67	78	66	62	81	71	87	53	81	92	102
46741	GRABILL	91	91	82	91	89	94	84	90	85	84	85	68	83	88	85	87	59	86	90	106
46742	HAMILTON	96	88	87	91	90	103	87	98	89	79	88	74	80	91	86	94	60	90	100	113
46743	HARLAN	93	93	87	97	93	102	88	96	89	83	88	74	87	91	90	92	61	90	97	112
46745	HOAGLAND	99	99	92	102	98	107	93	101	94	88	93	78	92	96	95	97	64	95	103	118
46746	HOWE	90	76	78	77	76	92	76	86	80	71	79	65	67	82	73	86	53	80	89	102
46747	HUDSON	98	79	84	80	80	98	80	91	85	75	84	70	69	88	76	92	57	86	95	109
46748	HUNTERTOWN	114	129	110	132	124	124	117	118	114	117	115	93	125	118	121	114	81	115	118	139
46750	HUNTINGTON	90	85	78	86	83	93	86	88	89	82	88	68	83	90	84	92	60	88	94	105
46755	KENDALLVILLE	84	79	68	81	76	85	83	81	84	77	83	64	78	86	78	86	57	82	87	98
46759	KEYSTONE	83	76	75	79	77	89	75	84	77	68	76	64	69	79	75	82	52	78	87	98
46760	KIMMELL	95	79	83	80	79	97	79	90	84	74	83	69	69	87	76	90	56	84	94	107
46761	LAGRANGE	92	77	78	77	76	91	77	86	82	74	80	65	68	84	73	87	55	81	89	102
46763	LAOTTO	100	96	92	99	96	108	92	102	94	86	93	78	88	96	93	98	64	95	104	119
46764	LARWILL	98	94	90	98	95	106	90	100	92	84	91	76	87	94	92	96	62	93	102	116
46765	LEO	110	134	118	135	130	123	115	118	111	118	112	92	128	114	124	109	80	113	112	137
46766	LIBERTY CENTER	95	86	85	90	88	102	85	96	88	77	86	73	78	89	85	93	59	89	99	111
46767	LIGONIER	95	86	81	82	85	87	86	90	86	87	86	68	79	89	83	87	60	88	88	104
46770	MARKLE	95	96	85	99	93	103	92	96	93	87	92	75	91	95	92	95	63	93	100	114
46772	MONROE	97	85	85	86	82	100	86	92	89	80	88	73	78	91	83	93	60	90	98	112
46773	MONROEVILLE	94	80	82	82	81	97	80	91	84	74	83	69	71	86	78	90	56	85	94	107
46774	NEW HAVEN	92	100	86	100	95	101	92	94	93	91	93	72	97	95	95	95	65	93	99	111
46776	ORLAND	98	89	88	92	90	105	88	99	90	79	89	75	81	92	87	96	61	91	102	115
46777	OSSIAN	97	99	84	99	95	98	92	95	92	93	93	73	93	96	92	93	64	92	95	112
46779	PLEASANT LAKE	100	91	88	93	92	104	90	99	93	84	91	75	83	95	89	97	62	93	101	116
46781	PONETO	80	72	72	76	74	85	71	81	74	65	72	61	66	75	71	78	49	75	83	94
46783	ROANOKE	107	107	98	109	106	113	100	107	101	97	100	82	99	103	101	103	69	102	108	126
46784	ROME CITY	96	78	81	77	78	94	78	88	84	76	82	66	68	87	74	89	56	83	91	105
46785	SAINT JOE	95	87	86	90	89	102	86	97	88	77	87	73	79	90	86	93	59	89	100	112
46787	SOUTH WHITLEY	91	82	75	85	81	94	86	89	89	79	87	69	79	90	82	93	60	87	95	106
46788	SPENCERVILLE	98	101	92	104	100	107	93	101	94	90	94	78	94	96	97	97	65	95	102	118
46791	UNIONDALE	94	88	86	92	90	102	86	96	88	79	87	73	81	90	86	93	59	89	99	112
46792	WARREN	90	84	79	87	84	96	83	91	85	76	84	69	78	87	83	90	58	86	95	106
46793	WATERLOO	94	92	81	93	90	96	89	93	90	87	90	71	87	93	88	92	62	90	95	110
46794	WAWAKA	97	89	88	92	90	104	87	99	90	79	88	75	81	92	87	95	60	91	102	115
46795	WOLCOTTVILLE	93	85	84	88	86	99	84	94	86	76	85	71	77	88	83	91	58	87	97	109
46797	WOODBURN	95	98	83	100	93	102	94	96	94	90	94	75	94	96	94	97	65	94	101	114
46798	YODER	98	99	89	101	98	103	92	98	93	92	93	74	92	96	93	95	64	94	98	115
46802	FORT WAYNE	58	47	44	49	45	52	63	54	64	56	64	43	55	63	54	67	45	60	62	67
46803	FORT WAYNE	58	47	42	48	45	52	57	52	60	54	59	40	51	60	50	63	41	57	59	65
	INDIANA	97	91	86	93	89	96	93	94	95	91	94	73	90	96	90	97	65	94	97	112
	UNITED STATES	100	100	100	100	100	100	100	100	100	100	100	100	100	100	100	100	100	100	100	100

ZIP CODE #	POST OFFICE NAME	COUNTY FIPS CODE	POPULATION 2000	POPULATION 2009	POPULATION 2014	2000-2009 ANNUAL RATE % Rate	2000-2009 ANNUAL RATE State Centile	HOUSEHOLDS 2000	HOUSEHOLDS 2009	HOUSEHOLDS 2014	HOUSEHOLDS % Annual Rate 2000-2009	HOUSEHOLDS 2009 Average HH Size	FAMILIES 2000	FAMILIES 2009	FAMILIES % Annual Rate 2000-2009
46804	FORT WAYNE	003	26143	28674	29907	1.0	81	10505	11743	12323	1.2	2.42	7290	7757	0.7
46805	FORT WAYNE	003	22204	21425	21245	-0.4	18	9639	9427	9407	-0.2	2.16	5051	4508	-1.2
46806	FORT WAYNE	003	26596	25266	24886	-0.6	8	9423	9096	9019	-0.4	2.77	6679	6078	-1.0
46807	FORT WAYNE	003	17253	16442	16215	-0.5	13	6605	6378	6322	-0.4	2.52	4133	3713	-1.2
46808	FORT WAYNE	003	18989	19023	19190	0.0	37	8141	8334	8470	0.3	2.24	4655	4436	-0.5
46809	FORT WAYNE	003	8677	8811	8921	0.2	49	3776	3944	4029	0.5	2.22	2324	2249	-0.4
46814	FORT WAYNE	003	7437	10771	12231	4.1	98	2371	3533	4041	4.4	3.05	2164	3165	4.2
46815	FORT WAYNE	003	26287	26681	26955	0.2	49	10293	10757	10974	0.5	2.44	7238	7128	-0.2
46816	FORT WAYNE	003	17517	17411	17477	-0.1	31	7252	7417	7524	0.2	2.31	4422	4170	-0.6
46818	FORT WAYNE	003	14262	17546	18995	2.3	95	5479	6796	7370	2.4	2.54	3871	4698	2.1
46819	FORT WAYNE	003	9278	9274	9318	0.0	37	3816	3935	3993	0.3	2.34	2530	2441	-0.4
46825	FORT WAYNE	003	25174	28534	30132	1.4	89	10088	11695	12445	1.6	2.40	6649	7256	0.9
46835	FORT WAYNE	003	30988	34649	36389	1.2	86	12205	13968	14787	1.5	2.44	8298	9098	1.0
46845	FORT WAYNE	003	15557	21331	23814	3.5	97	5186	7235	8121	3.7	2.94	4505	6127	3.4
46901	KOKOMO	067	39881	38137	37403	-0.5	13	16199	15629	15384	-0.4	2.40	10691	9848	-0.9
46902	KOKOMO	067	35356	36070	36005	0.2	49	15079	15508	15549	0.3	2.31	10073	9918	-0.2
46910	AKRON	049	3259	3364	3365	0.3	56	1178	1223	1226	0.4	2.75	896	900	0.0
46911	AMBOY	103	1514	1464	1429	-0.4	18	560	563	556	0.1	2.60	448	438	-0.2
46913	BRINGHURST	015	1345	1371	1361	0.2	49	476	496	495	0.4	2.76	388	395	0.2
46914	BUNKER HILL	103	2552	2386	2296	-0.7	5	992	958	932	-0.4	2.49	745	694	-0.8
46917	CAMDEN	015	1816	1844	1824	0.2	49	698	721	716	0.4	2.56	521	520	0.0
46919	CONVERSE	053	2313	2205	2138	-0.5	13	913	905	886	-0.1	2.44	697	666	-0.5
46920	CUTLER	015	1466	1540	1574	0.5	66	567	610	627	0.8	2.52	428	446	0.4
46923	DELPHI	015	8532	8896	9005	0.5	66	3190	3373	3427	0.6	2.60	2304	2350	0.2
46926	DENVER	103	1919	1914	1887	0.0	37	699	721	719	0.3	2.65	562	563	0.0
46928	FAIRMOUNT	053	4983	4639	4447	-0.8	4	1991	1906	1843	-0.5	2.43	1462	1347	-0.9
46929	FLORA	015	3300	3306	3242	0.0	37	1287	1309	1287	0.2	2.46	939	921	-0.2
46932	GALVESTON	017	3680	3694	3645	0.0	37	1413	1449	1436	0.3	2.55	1098	1090	-0.1
46933	GAS CITY	053	6153	5796	5573	-0.6	8	2478	2400	2330	-0.3	2.38	1761	1635	-0.8
46936	GREENTOWN	067	6427	6417	6388	0.0	37	2368	2381	2376	0.1	2.67	1857	1807	-0.3
46938	JONESBORO	053	3557	3261	3107	-0.9	3	1429	1349	1298	-0.6	2.42	1054	959	-1.0
46939	KEWANNA	049	2236	2191	2170	-0.2	27	913	911	905	0.0	2.41	638	613	-0.4
46940	LA FONTAINE	169	3115	3008	2919	-0.4	18	1223	1218	1193	0.0	2.37	910	874	-0.4
46941	LAGRO	169	1466	1489	1478	0.2	49	530	551	551	0.4	2.70	419	423	0.1
46947	LOGANSPORT	017	30442	29399	28560	-0.4	18	11759	11456	11135	-0.3	2.48	7893	7365	-0.7
46950	LUCERNE	017	654	633	616	-0.4	18	254	252	246	-0.1	2.51	204	197	-0.4
46951	MACY	103	2641	2637	2605	0.0	37	974	998	995	0.3	2.64	751	746	-0.1
46952	MARION	053	22243	21004	20254	-0.6	8	9326	8979	8719	-0.4	2.27	6285	5810	-0.8
46953	MARION	053	26110	24139	23091	-0.8	4	9825	9091	8719	-0.8	2.36	6510	5759	-1.3
46960	MONTEREY	131	1351	1429	1448	0.6	70	494	534	544	0.8	2.67	367	384	0.5
46962	NORTH MANCHESTER	169	10222	9736	9432	-0.5	13	3629	3531	3436	-0.3	2.39	2539	2376	-0.7
46970	PERU	103	25763	26669	26045	0.4	60	9874	9834	9667	0.0	2.38	6806	6514	-0.5
46974	ROANN	169	1406	1351	1305	-0.4	18	513	506	493	-0.1	2.66	408	391	-0.5
46975	ROCHESTER	049	14403	14574	14540	0.1	43	5713	5861	5862	0.3	2.46	4011	3960	-0.1
46978	ROYAL CENTER	017	2232	2137	2067	-0.5	13	855	838	814	-0.2	2.55	642	607	-0.6
46979	RUSSIAVILLE	067	4394	4767	4844	0.9	79	1596	1750	1786	1.0	2.72	1290	1372	0.7
46982	SILVER LAKE	085	2732	2748	2720	0.1	43	1014	1054	1052	0.4	2.61	791	797	0.1
46985	STAR CITY	131	1561	1557	1541	0.0	37	566	576	574	0.2	2.70	447	443	-0.1
46986	SWAYZEE	053	1971	1867	1792	-0.6	8	771	748	724	-0.3	2.50	602	565	-0.7
46988	TWELVE MILE	017	1169	1147	1129	-0.2	27	387	387	382	0.0	2.66	292	283	-0.3
46989	UPLAND	053	5986	6174	6061	0.3	56	1584	1552	1517	-0.2	2.67	1207	1142	-0.6
46990	URBANA	169	768	771	762	0.0	37	268	276	275	0.3	2.76	215	215	0.0
46991	VAN BUREN	053	1702	1624	1575	-0.5	13	650	638	624	-0.2	2.52	495	470	-0.6
46992	WABASH	169	18132	17085	16479	-0.6	8	7112	6874	6678	-0.4	2.40	4947	4593	-0.8
46994	WALTON	017	2900	2809	2736	-0.3	22	1088	1075	1051	-0.1	2.61	828	791	-0.5
46996	WINAMAC	131	7215	7268	7210	0.1	43	2803	2870	2858	0.3	2.47	1997	1971	-0.1
47001	AURORA	029	10259	10579	10704	0.3	56	3871	4102	4186	0.6	2.57	2844	2904	0.2
47003	WEST COLLEGE CORNER	161	1010	1012	992	0.0	37	376	380	374	0.1	2.65	272	264	-0.3
47006	BATESVILLE	137	10535	11622	11979	1.1	84	3777	4260	4417	1.3	2.66	2840	3117	1.0
47010	BATH	047	143	151	154	0.6	70	53	58	60	1.0	2.34	42	44	0.5
47011	BENNINGTON	155	1157	1320	1383	1.4	89	399	463	488	1.6	2.85	318	358	1.3
47012	BROOKVILLE	047	9679	10223	10424	0.6	70	3583	3879	3988	0.9	2.59	2662	2796	0.5
47016	CEDAR GROVE	047	847	921	958	0.9	79	304	344	362	1.3	2.68	243	267	1.0
47017	CROSS PLAINS	137	645	717	745	1.2	86	259	297	311	1.5	2.41	187	206	1.1
47018	DILLSBORO	029	3989	4458	4696	1.2	86	1481	1713	1824	1.6	2.53	1095	1215	1.1
47020	FLORENCE	155	987	1014	997	0.3	56	369	389	385	0.6	2.61	286	292	0.2
47022	GUILFORD	029	2791	3150	3352	1.3	87	942	1091	1170	1.6	2.89	774	871	1.3
47023	HOLTON	137	1646	1808	1873	1.0	81	577	654	685	1.4	2.76	446	490	1.0
47024	LAUREL	047	3358	3500	3549	0.4	60	1186	1277	1309	0.8	2.74	952	993	0.5
47025	LAWRENCEBURG	029	20562	22701	23736	1.1	84	7607	8604	9062	1.3	2.60	5648	6184	1.0
47030	METAMORA	047	1347	1390	1405	0.3	56	480	511	521	0.7	2.72	382	394	0.3
47031	MILAN	137	4726	5160	5289	1.0	81	1737	1955	2023	1.3	2.60	1300	1412	0.9
47032	MOORES HILL	029	3231	3658	3883	1.4	89	1077	1254	1344	1.7	2.91	886	1001	1.3
47036	OLDENBURG	047	1090	1178	1218	0.8	76	327	368	385	1.3	3.07	264	287	0.9
47037	OSGOOD	137	4495	4662	4581	0.4	60	1678	1779	1761	0.6	2.58	1240	1267	0.2
47038	PATRIOT	155	1265	1359	1395	0.8	76	447	497	516	1.2	2.73	353	380	0.8
47040	RISING SUN	115	5031	5287	5309	0.5	66	1993	2156	2183	0.9	2.43	1420	1478	0.4
47041	SUNMAN	029	5186	5854	6152	1.3	87	1828	2124	2252	1.6	2.76	1458	1643	1.3
47042	VERSAILLES	137	4131	4529	4666	1.0	81	1612	1808	1874	1.2	2.48	1169	1264	0.8
47043	VEVAY	155	4815	5195	5286	0.8	76	1923	2118	2165	1.0	2.41	1348	1429	0.6
47060	WEST HARRISON	029	6128	7250	7743	1.8	93	2175	2635	2833	2.1	2.75	1752	2059	1.8
47102	AUSTIN	143	7740	8003	8122	0.4	60	2894	3103	3181	0.8	2.58	2207	2291	0.4
47106	BORDEN	019	4631	5019	5393	0.9	79	1740	1949	2120	1.2	2.56	1376	1482	0.8
47108	CAMPBELLSBURG	175	2392	2456	2479	0.3	56	900	954	972	0.6	2.57	655	667	0.2
47110	CENTRAL	061	180	193	198	0.8	76	64	71	74	1.1	2.72	46	50	0.9
47111	CHARLESTOWN	019	11899	13612	14530	1.5	91	4434	5249	5670	1.8	2.57	3368	3824	1.4
47112	CORYDON	061	13844	15611	16344	1.3	87	5315	6191	6549	1.7	2.47	3819	4291	1.3
47114	CRANDALL	061	374	399	408	0.7	73	143	158	163	1.1	2.53	115	124	0.8
47115	DEPAUW	061	2450	2544	2569	0.4	60	923	990	1009	0.8	2.57	700	728	0.4
47116	ECKERTY	025	1014	1012	992	0.0	37	393	407	403	0.4	2.49	286	286	0.0
47117	ELIZABETH	061	4167	4469	4570	0.8	76	1523	1685	1740	1.1	2.65	1203	1296	0.8
47118	ENGLISH	025	3539	3643	3650	0.3	56	1379	1470	1488	0.7	2.45	992	1020	0.3
47119	FLOYDS KNOBS	043	9489	10636	11196	1.2	86	3307	3816	4053	1.6	2.78	2791	3125	1.2
47120	FREDERICKSBURG	175	953	1081	1134	1.4	89	350	407	430	1.6	2.66	273	308	1.3
47122	GEORGETOWN	043	8509	9475	9928	1.2	86	3018	3451	3646	1.5	2.74	2515	2795	1.1
	INDIANA					0.7					0.8	2.49			0.4
	UNITED STATES					1.0					1.1	2.59			0.9

ZIP CODE #	POST OFFICE NAME	RACE (%) White 2000	White 2009	Black 2000	Black 2009	Asian/Pacific 2000	Asian/Pacific 2009	% Hispanic Origin 2000	% Hispanic Origin 2009	2009 AGE DISTRIBUTION (%) 0-4	5-9	10-14	15-19	20-24	25-44	45-64	65-84	85+	18+	MEDIAN AGE 2009	% 2009 Males	% 2009 Females
46804	FORT WAYNE	92.7	89.0	2.6	4.0	2.1	3.1	2.4	4.3	6.8	6.7	6.8	6.6	6.0	26.8	28.4	10.2	1.7	75.7	38.0	48.7	51.3
46805	FORT WAYNE	89.3	84.7	4.4	6.4	1.7	2.4	5.0	7.9	7.4	6.9	6.6	6.1	6.5	29.8	22.3	10.5	3.9	75.4	35.8	48.1	51.9
46806	FORT WAYNE	30.8	24.9	58.9	63.3	0.9	0.9	10.5	13.1	9.8	9.4	8.7	8.9	7.9	25.5	21.6	7.2	0.9	66.5	28.4	47.4	52.6
46807	FORT WAYNE	79.7	72.1	10.4	14.0	1.5	2.0	9.1	14.1	9.0	7.9	7.0	7.8	7.6	29.1	22.8	7.2	1.6	71.7	31.9	48.2	51.8
46808	FORT WAYNE	92.3	88.7	2.2	3.3	1.2	1.7	4.2	7.3	6.8	6.6	6.3	7.3	7.1	29.7	25.2	9.4	1.6	76.3	35.2	50.1	49.9
46809	FORT WAYNE	91.3	87.3	3.9	5.6	0.4	0.6	4.6	7.7	6.9	6.6	6.3	6.1	6.1	26.6	27.0	12.0	2.4	76.3	38.5	49.0	51.0
46814	FORT WAYNE	94.1	90.3	1.5	2.5	2.8	4.7	1.6	2.9	6.5	7.6	9.0	9.0	4.9	20.6	34.7	7.4	0.4	71.2	39.3	49.4	50.6
46815	FORT WAYNE	91.0	86.7	4.9	7.3	1.3	1.9	2.2	3.9	6.8	6.8	6.9	6.8	5.7	25.3	26.5	12.5	2.7	75.3	38.4	47.5	52.5
46816	FORT WAYNE	58.0	49.2	33.7	40.5	1.4	1.7	6.0	8.4	8.1	7.4	6.9	7.0	7.4	27.9	23.3	9.6	2.3	73.6	33.2	47.8	52.2
46818	FORT WAYNE	94.7	91.6	1.6	2.9	1.3	2.4	1.9	3.1	7.7	7.6	7.4	6.7	5.2	28.5	26.1	9.6	1.1	72.9	36.7	49.7	50.3
46819	FORT WAYNE	91.0	86.8	5.2	7.6	0.4	0.6	3.4	5.9	6.7	6.4	6.4	6.3	6.7	25.5	27.0	12.7	2.3	76.8	38.4	49.5	50.5
46825	FORT WAYNE	89.0	83.9	4.4	6.5	3.3	4.8	2.6	4.4	8.0	7.5	7.2	6.6	6.6	28.9	23.8	9.7	1.8	73.3	34.8	48.1	51.9
46835	FORT WAYNE	92.2	88.6	3.6	5.4	1.8	2.7	2.0	3.4	7.2	6.8	6.8	6.5	6.9	28.6	25.6	9.9	1.7	75.2	35.9	49.5	50.5
46845	FORT WAYNE	96.4	94.3	1.0	1.7	1.3	2.0	0.9	1.8	7.3	8.2	8.8	8.3	4.2	24.3	30.4	7.8	0.7	70.1	38.1	49.8	50.2
46901	KOKOMO	87.7	85.9	8.8	9.7	0.4	0.6	2.3	3.4	6.9	6.9	7.0	6.9	5.8	25.4	26.9	12.2	2.0	74.9	38.1	48.5	51.5
46902	KOKOMO	89.8	87.1	5.7	6.9	1.9	2.8	2.0	2.9	7.0	6.3	6.2	6.1	6.0	25.7	27.0	13.7	1.9	76.8	39.3	48.2	51.8
46910	AKRON	95.0	92.9	0.1	0.1	0.0	0.0	7.8	11.3	6.6	6.9	7.1	7.4	5.6	26.5	26.8	11.4	1.7	74.9	37.9	50.8	49.2
46911	AMBOY	98.3	98.0	0.5	0.5	0.1	0.2	2.3	3.3	5.5	5.9	6.7	7.3	5.1	24.5	30.5	12.7	1.6	77.3	41.4	51.0	49.0
46913	BRINGHURST	98.4	97.9	0.1	0.1	0.1	0.1	1.3	2.0	6.1	6.6	7.1	6.9	4.9	23.8	30.1	13.1	1.4	76.0	41.3	51.3	48.7
46914	BUNKER HILL	96.6	96.4	0.9	0.7	0.3	0.5	1.0	1.5	6.8	7.0	7.2	7.0	5.4	25.1	29.0	10.9	1.5	74.6	38.5	49.5	50.5
46917	CAMDEN	99.1	99.0	0.2	0.3	0.0	0.0	0.6	0.9	7.4	7.7	7.8	6.8	4.6	24.6	27.8	11.3	2.1	72.8	38.8	49.1	50.9
46919	CONVERSE	97.7	97.0	0.1	0.2	0.3	0.4	2.5	3.7	5.8	6.1	6.2	6.8	5.5	24.4	30.0	13.5	1.7	77.8	41.3	49.1	50.9
46920	CUTLER	99.0	98.8	0.1	0.1	0.0	0.0	1.0	1.6	6.8	7.2	7.3	6.8	4.5	24.7	28.7	12.3	1.7	74.4	40.0	51.0	49.0
46923	DELPHI	96.4	95.0	0.2	0.2	0.1	0.2	4.9	7.2	7.0	7.1	7.1	6.8	5.5	25.7	27.6	11.4	1.9	74.6	38.5	50.5	49.5
46926	DENVER	97.1	96.9	0.1	0.1	0.1	0.1	0.7	1.0	6.2	6.6	6.9	7.4	5.7	25.3	29.4	11.2	1.3	75.8	39.5	51.1	48.9
46928	FAIRMOUNT	98.4	97.9	0.4	0.5	0.1	0.2	0.6	0.9	5.9	6.1	6.5	7.2	5.0	24.9	28.9	13.7	1.8	77.1	41.2	49.0	51.0
46929	FLORA	98.4	97.8	0.4	0.5	0.1	0.1	1.8	2.9	6.5	6.6	6.7	6.6	5.7	25.0	26.3	13.2	3.6	76.2	39.6	47.9	52.1
46932	GALVESTON	98.3	97.7	0.3	0.3	0.2	0.4	1.3	2.2	6.2	6.6	7.0	6.7	4.8	25.9	30.2	11.2	1.2	76.0	39.7	49.4	50.6
46933	GAS CITY	97.2	96.2	0.4	0.6	0.2	0.3	1.7	2.6	6.6	6.4	6.4	6.4	6.1	27.0	26.9	12.3	1.8	76.5	38.1	48.4	51.6
46936	GREENTOWN	97.7	96.9	0.5	0.7	0.3	0.5	1.0	1.6	6.0	6.4	6.7	7.0	5.4	23.5	30.6	12.2	2.1	76.5	41.2	49.1	50.9
46938	JONESBORO	97.8	97.1	0.3	0.3	0.2	0.2	1.4	2.1	5.8	5.9	6.3	7.1	5.2	25.1	29.2	13.9	1.5	77.7	41.2	48.8	51.2
46939	KEWANNA	97.6	97.1	1.0	1.1	0.1	0.1	0.4	0.7	6.4	6.7	6.9	7.1	4.7	22.5	28.3	15.0	2.4	75.6	41.6	49.5	50.5
46940	LA FONTAINE	97.8	97.3	0.2	0.3	0.1	0.2	1.1	1.6	5.4	5.8	6.4	6.9	5.1	24.0	30.0	13.8	2.7	77.9	42.4	50.1	49.9
46941	LAGRO	98.6	97.9	0.1	0.1	0.2	0.4	0.3	0.7	6.4	6.4	6.9	7.5	6.0	23.6	29.8	12.1	1.3	75.7	39.8	50.8	49.2
46947	LOGANSPORT	92.4	89.8	1.5	1.7	0.7	1.0	8.8	12.8	7.1	6.5	6.3	6.9	6.1	25.9	26.2	12.5	2.5	75.6	38.1	50.5	49.5
46950	LUCERNE	99.5	99.4	0.0	0.0	0.2	0.3	0.2	0.2	6.8	7.3	7.7	6.6	4.1	24.6	27.8	13.4	1.6	74.1	40.5	50.4	49.6
46951	MACY	97.9	97.5	0.1	0.1	0.0	0.1	0.8	1.1	6.1	6.5	6.8	7.6	5.2	24.3	30.0	12.2	1.3	75.7	40.3	51.8	48.2
46952	MARION	91.3	88.9	4.4	5.5	1.2	1.7	2.5	3.8	5.7	5.8	6.1	6.2	5.1	23.3	29.4	15.6	2.9	78.6	43.3	48.4	51.6
46953	MARION	79.8	76.8	16.0	17.9	0.3	0.5	3.4	4.7	6.1	5.9	5.9	9.2	9.0	23.1	24.8	13.5	2.5	78.1	37.1	47.9	52.1
46960	MONTEREY	93.6	92.2	3.4	3.8	0.6	1.0	1.3	2.0	6.4	6.7	7.1	6.5	4.8	25.4	28.7	12.7	1.7	75.4	39.3	50.9	49.1
46962	NORTH MANCHESTER	97.0	96.1	0.6	0.7	0.6	0.9	1.5	2.2	5.5	5.6	5.7	9.4	9.9	21.9	23.9	13.6	4.6	79.6	37.3	47.2	52.8
46970	PERU	92.2	90.8	4.0	4.6	0.4	0.6	1.3	2.0	6.0	5.8	5.8	6.4	7.3	29.3	26.3	11.1	2.0	78.6	38.0	54.1	45.9
46974	ROANN	97.6	97.0	0.1	0.1	0.2	0.4	0.8	1.2	5.8	5.9	6.4	6.8	6.2	25.5	29.3	12.3	1.8	77.7	40.0	49.1	50.9
46975	ROCHESTER	96.4	95.5	0.7	0.9	0.5	0.8	1.4	2.2	6.7	6.7	6.8	6.6	5.3	24.8	27.8	13.1	2.2	75.7	39.8	49.6	50.4
46978	ROYAL CENTER	98.6	98.1	0.3	0.4	0.1	0.1	0.5	0.8	7.0	7.2	7.0	6.7	6.0	25.1	27.2	12.1	1.8	74.8	37.9	50.7	49.3
46979	RUSSIAVILLE	97.6	96.9	0.7	0.9	0.5	0.7	0.9	1.4	6.3	6.7	7.2	7.3	5.3	24.4	30.7	10.8	1.2	74.9	39.8	49.5	50.5
46982	SILVER LAKE	97.2	96.2	0.1	0.1	0.1	0.1	2.4	3.6	6.8	6.7	6.8	6.7	5.8	27.1	27.5	11.3	1.2	75.6	38.0	49.6	50.4
46985	STAR CITY	98.9	98.6	0.1	0.2	0.1	0.1	0.7	1.2	6.2	6.5	7.1	7.6	5.0	24.3	30.2	11.6	1.5	75.6	40.3	51.5	48.5
46986	SWAYZEE	96.9	95.7	0.4	0.6	0.2	0.2	1.7	2.6	5.2	5.7	6.3	6.8	4.6	24.2	32.0	13.3	1.8	78.6	43.1	48.4	51.6
46988	TWELVE MILE	96.2	95.5	2.5	3.0	0.2	0.3	0.9	1.4	6.4	6.8	7.1	5.8	4.8	24.6	29.8	12.8	1.9	75.9	41.4	53.8	46.2
46989	UPLAND	95.9	94.5	1.0	1.4	1.0	1.6	1.7	2.7	3.7	4.0	4.6	18.2	24.1	15.8	20.1	8.3	1.2	84.3	24.1	49.5	50.5
46990	URBANA	98.4	97.8	0.0	0.1	0.1	0.3	0.5	1.0	6.2	6.4	6.7	7.5	6.1	24.0	28.9	12.5	1.7	76.1	39.9	50.7	49.3
46991	VAN BUREN	98.1	97.5	0.2	0.3	0.1	0.2	1.1	1.7	6.2	6.3	6.7	7.1	5.5	23.9	28.4	13.5	2.5	76.5	40.8	49.0	51.0
46992	WABASH	97.4	96.8	0.4	0.4	0.5	0.7	1.1	1.7	6.3	6.2	6.4	6.9	5.8	25.2	27.4	13.6	2.2	76.7	39.7	49.2	50.8
46994	WALTON	95.6	93.6	0.3	0.4	0.2	0.3	5.2	8.2	6.3	6.6	6.8	7.2	5.2	23.9	29.8	12.5	1.7	75.9	40.6	49.2	50.8
46996	WINAMAC	97.9	97.4	0.6	0.7	0.2	0.4	1.2	1.7	5.9	6.2	6.6	7.1	5.3	24.0	28.7	13.7	2.5	77.1	41.1	50.0	50.0
47001	AURORA	98.7	98.4	0.1	0.1	0.3	0.5	0.5	0.7	6.8	6.7	6.7	6.6	6.0	26.7	27.9	11.4	1.2	75.8	38.4	49.7	50.3
47003	WEST COLLEGE CORNER	98.6	98.6	0.1	0.1	0.1	0.1	0.2	0.2	8.6	9.1	8.7	7.2	5.5	26.4	24.8	8.4	1.3	69.0	34.2	51.1	48.9
47006	BATESVILLE	97.8	97.0	0.0	0.1	0.8	1.2	1.0	1.5	7.2	7.5	7.8	7.5	4.8	24.7	27.4	10.8	2.4	72.7	38.6	49.2	50.8
47010	BATH	99.3	99.3	0.0	0.0	0.0	0.0	0.7	0.7	6.0	6.6	6.6	6.0	4.0	23.8	27.8	12.6	6.6	76.8	43.0	48.3	51.7
47011	BENNINGTON	98.9	98.6	0.0	0.1	0.1	0.1	0.8	1.3	7.0	7.1	7.5	7.1	5.5	27.1	26.4	11.2	1.1	73.9	37.1	51.5	48.5
47012	BROOKVILLE	99.1	98.8	0.0	0.1	0.2	0.3	0.5	0.7	6.7	7.0	7.2	7.1	5.1	25.6	27.2	12.1	2.1	74.7	39.0	50.0	50.0
47016	CEDAR GROVE	99.5	99.3	0.0	0.0	0.1	0.1	0.2	0.4	6.5	6.6	6.8	6.7	5.4	27.1	29.3	10.2	1.2	75.8	38.4	50.2	49.8
47017	CROSS PLAINS	99.5	99.3	0.0	0.0	0.0	0.0	0.5	0.7	5.6	6.0	6.3	6.6	4.5	26.5	28.9	13.7	2.1	78.1	42.0	54.5	45.5
47018	DILLSBORO	99.0	98.7	0.1	0.1	0.2	0.2	0.6	0.9	6.1	6.2	6.4	6.4	5.6	23.5	29.1	13.9	2.8	77.3	41.9	48.6	51.4
47020	FLORENCE	99.1	98.9	0.4	0.5	0.2	0.2	1.1	1.7	7.3	7.6	7.7	6.5	4.5	26.6	27.8	11.2	0.7	73.3	37.0	51.2	48.8
47022	GUILFORD	99.3	98.6	0.0	0.4	0.1	0.2	0.2	0.3	6.1	6.7	7.4	7.2	4.9	25.4	30.8	10.3	1.1	75.1	40.0	50.9	49.1
47023	HOLTON	99.4	99.2	0.0	0.0	0.1	0.1	0.6	0.9	6.5	6.9	7.2	7.0	5.0	26.2	28.5	11.3	1.3	75.0	38.9	50.2	49.8
47024	LAUREL	98.7	98.5	0.1	0.1	0.1	0.1	0.5	0.8	7.8	7.8	7.9	7.1	5.4	27.7	25.3	10.1	0.8	71.9	35.8	50.7	49.3
47025	LAWRENCEBURG	97.2	96.5	1.3	1.5	0.4	0.6	0.7	1.0	7.0	7.0	7.1	6.6	5.2	26.5	28.8	10.2	1.6	74.8	38.4	49.1	50.9
47030	METAMORA	99.0	98.8	0.1	0.1	0.1	0.2	0.5	0.8	7.1	7.3	7.8	7.8	5.2	27.8	26.3	10.0	0.7	72.8	36.3	51.1	48.9
47031	MILAN	98.2	97.8	0.1	0.1	0.3	0.4	0.6	0.9	7.0	7.1	7.4	7.0	5.5	26.2	26.9	11.1	1.8	74.0	37.8	50.3	49.7
47032	MOORES HILL	97.8	97.3	0.1	0.1	0.3	0.5	0.8	1.2	7.2	7.3	7.5	7.3	5.9	26.5	27.7	9.5	1.1	73.5	36.9	50.6	49.4
47036	OLDENBURG	98.9	98.6	0.1	0.2	0.4	0.5	0.3	0.5	5.3	6.8	8.1	7.0	4.4	24.9	28.0	12.9	2.6	75.1	40.5	50.1	49.9
47037	OSGOOD	98.9	98.7	0.1	0.1	0.1	0.2	0.6	0.9	7.9	7.8	7.7	7.3	5.6	25.2	25.1	11.2	2.2	71.8	36.9	49.5	50.5
47038	PATRIOT	97.7	97.2	0.7	0.9	0.0	0.0	1.2	1.8	6.0	6.0	6.3	8.0	6.8	26.8	29.7	9.5	0.9	76.8	38.3	53.3	46.7
47040	RISING SUN	98.6	98.5	0.5	0.6	0.2	0.2	0.5	0.7	6.1	5.9	6.5	6.6	6.0	25.2	27.9	13.7	2.1	77.3	40.7	49.6	50.4
47041	SUNMAN	98.3	97.7	0.0	0.1	0.1	0.1	1.4	2.2	7.8	8.1	8.1	7.1	4.7	25.5	27.1	10.4	1.2	71.4	37.5	50.8	49.2
47042	VERSAILLES	99.1	99.0	0.0	0.0	0.1	0.2	0.4	0.6	6.9	6.9	6.8	6.4	5.7	25.3	26.9	13.4	1.7	75.5	38.8	48.1	51.9
47043	VEVAY	98.9	98.8	0.2	0.2	0.1	0.1	0.8	1.1	5.9	6.0	6.7	6.7	5.6	24.4	28.1	14.4	2.2	77.2	40.7	49.9	50.1
47060	WEST HARRISON	99.1	98.9	0.1	0.2	0.3	0.4	0.5	0.7	6.4	7.0	7.4	7.2	4.6	26.8	31.0	8.7	0.9	74.7	39.0	50.7	49.3
47102	AUSTIN	98.7	98.2	0.1	0.1	0.2	0.3	1.3	1.9	7.9	7.4	7.3	6.5	6.1	27.3	26.3	10.1	1.0	73.4	36.2	49.8	50.2
47106	BORDEN	97.8	96.9	0.2	0.3	0.2	0.4	1.2	2.0	6.1	6.7	7.0	6.4	4.7	26.1	31.1	10.9	1.0	76.3	40.1	50.8	49.2
47108	CAMPBELLSBURG	98.6	98.3	0.3	0.3	0.1	0.2	0.5	0.7	7.4	7.5	7.2	6.3	5.6	26.5	26.9	11.3	1.2	74.0	37.0	51.1	48.9
47110	CENTRAL	98.9	97.9	0.0	0.0	0.0	0.5	1.1	1.6	7.8	7.8	7.3	5.7	5.2	27.5	29.0	9.3	0.5	73.6	37.5	49.7	50.3
47111	CHARLESTOWN	94.6	93.0	1.9	2.4	0.3	0.5	3.1	4.5	7.5	7.3	7.3	6.6	5.2	27.8	27.3	9.8	1.2	73.8	37.2	49.3	50.7
47112	CORYDON	98.1	97.7	0.6	0.7	0.2	0.3	1.1	1.6	6.3	6.4	6.7	6.4	5.5	26.4	28.6	11.9	1.9	76.7	39.6	49.6	50.4
47114	CRANDALL	98.4	98.2	0.5	0.8	0.0	0.0	0.8	1.3	6.0	6.5	6.5	6.3	5.0	25.8	32.3	10.8	0.8	76.7	40.9	49.4	50.6
47115	DEPAUW	98.8	98.5	0.2	0.2	0.2	0.3	0.1	0.2	6.1	6.5	6.6	6.3	5.0	25.3	31.4	11.5	1.3	76.8	40.8	49.6	50.4
47116	ECKERTY	98.8	98.4	0.1	0.1	0.3	0.4	0.6	1.0	5.9	6.1	6.6	7.2	5.9	24.4	29.7	12.7	1.3	76.9	40.5	51.5	48.5
47117	ELIZABETH	98.4	98.1	0.2	0.2	0.1	0.2	0.5	0.8	5.9	6.2	6.6	6.6	4.7	25.6	32.1	11.1	1.2	77.2	41.2	49.3	50.7
47118	ENGLISH	98.2	97.8	0.2	0.2	0.3	0.3	1.0	1.4	6.1	6.2	6.5	6.4	5.5	25.6	30.2	11.9	1.5	77.5	40.2	49.5	50.5
47119	FLOYDS KNOBS	98.6	98.2	0.3	0.3	0.4	0.6	0.6	1.0	5.4	6.6	7.5	7.9	4.6	24.2	33.1	9.8	0.8	75.2	41.1	49.5	50.5
47120	FREDERICKSBURG	98.2	97.8	0.5	0.6	0.2	0.3	0.5	0.8	6.3	6.5	6.6	6.6	5.9	27.9	29.2	10.0	1.0	76.6	38.1	52.9	47.1
47122	GEORGETOWN	98.5	98.1	0.4	0.5	0.2	0.3	0.6	0.9	5.8	6.5	7.1	7.3	4.6	25.9	32.9	9.2	0.8	76.0	40.3	50.5	49.5
	INDIANA	87.5	85.6	8.4	8.9	1.0	1.5	3.5	5.0	6.9	6.8	6.8	7.2	6.9	26.5	26.2	10.8	1.9	75.4	36.8	49.3	50.7
	UNITED STATES	75.1	72.0	12.3	12.7	3.8	4.6	12.5	15.7	6.8	6.7	6.6	7.1	6.9	27.0	26.0	10.9	1.9	75.7	36.9	49.2	50.8

ZIP CODE #	POST OFFICE NAME	2009 Per Capita Income	2009 HH Income Base	2009 HOUSEHOLD INCOME DISTRIBUTION (%) Less than $25,000	$25,000 to $49,999	$50,000 to $99,999	$100,000 to $149,999	$150,000 or More	MEDIAN HOUSEHOLD INCOME 2009	2014	2009 National Centile	2009 State Centile	2009 Home Value Base	2009 HOME VALUE DISTRIBUTION (%) Less than $50,000	$50,000 to $89,999	$90,000 to $174,999	$175,000 to $399,999	$400,000 or More	2009 Median Home Value
46804	FORT WAYNE	36011	11743	10.2	15.8	45.8	17.9	10.3	73818	75572	89	95	8872	0.9	8.4	70.7	18.9	1.2	132288
46805	FORT WAYNE	23986	9427	22.1	33.8	36.7	5.2	2.2	43461	47273	44	16	5397	11.0	62.8	24.8	1.1	0.2	74581
46806	FORT WAYNE	15227	9096	33.4	35.1	26.2	4.2	1.1	34510	35794	17	4	5401	43.1	47.0	9.5	0.3	0.1	53931
46807	FORT WAYNE	22639	6378	21.5	28.3	41.0	5.6	3.5	50092	52898	61	47	4171	20.4	52.1	24.0	3.2	0.3	69393
46808	FORT WAYNE	22455	8334	24.6	30.3	39.4	4.7	1.0	44295	49618	46	20	5278	20.9	56.4	20.8	1.8	0.0	68792
46809	FORT WAYNE	24691	3944	21.1	29.2	42.2	5.2	2.2	49566	52202	60	44	2719	15.2	53.5	29.6	1.6	0.1	76460
46814	FORT WAYNE	57096	3533	4.7	6.5	25.5	13.3	49.9	149820	151365	100	100	3417	2.7	3.0	19.5	50.9	24.0	247952
46815	FORT WAYNE	28989	10757	13.1	21.2	49.4	11.3	5.0	64160	65174	82	89	7972	0.7	21.6	72.3	5.3	0.1	107730
46816	FORT WAYNE	22767	7417	25.9	27.2	38.5	6.3	2.1	45443	50491	50	24	3918	17.8	44.3	34.2	3.2	0.6	81088
46818	FORT WAYNE	25744	6796	12.9	25.4	48.2	10.4	3.2	59588	61803	77	81	5974	27.3	16.7	42.9	12.4	0.7	98517
46819	FORT WAYNE	25760	3935	17.1	25.9	47.3	7.1	2.6	55103	57038	71	70	2786	13.3	35.7	45.7	5.1	0.2	90637
46825	FORT WAYNE	27133	11695	14.9	26.0	45.2	9.5	4.5	56460	57773	73	74	7529	9.7	27.1	53.9	8.6	0.7	101878
46835	FORT WAYNE	29924	13968	11.6	19.6	51.2	12.6	5.1	66348	67041	84	92	10271	1.8	22.9	65.9	8.5	0.9	106083
46845	FORT WAYNE	36531	7235	3.8	11.9	40.8	27.5	16.0	90294	90049	95	99	6851	1.7	7.2	53.9	34.1	3.1	154363
46901	KOKOMO	25497	15629	22.4	27.1	35.5	10.7	4.2	50482	54109	62	49	11064	18.6	38.4	35.8	6.7	0.5	83469
46902	KOKOMO	30181	15508	17.1	23.8	41.9	11.2	6.0	60272	62048	78	82	10629	8.2	38.7	42.1	10.3	0.8	93060
46910	AKRON	18420	1223	21.8	35.7	36.5	5.2	0.8	44662	46536	47	21	990	14.4	30.5	47.3	7.2	0.6	93676
46911	AMBOY	23954	563	16.9	26.6	43.9	9.4	3.2	55720	56134	72	72	483	12.2	37.5	39.3	10.4	0.6	90556
46913	BRINGHURST	24445	496	12.9	26.6	45.2	10.7	4.6	60507	61168	78	83	446	11.2	17.7	53.6	14.8	2.7	110682
46914	BUNKER HILL	21955	958	22.0	29.2	38.8	8.4	1.6	49039	51364	59	41	758	22.6	27.0	42.6	7.7	0.1	90492
46917	CAMDEN	20797	721	18.7	32.6	40.5	7.2	1.0	48935	51082	59	41	593	18.5	37.8	36.8	6.1	0.8	83421
46919	CONVERSE	24710	905	20.0	27.7	39.0	9.4	3.9	52395	54340	67	60	738	10.3	43.5	37.4	8.0	0.8	87255
46920	CUTLER	24017	610	17.0	26.6	44.1	10.7	1.6	55424	57610	72	71	502	16.3	21.5	49.6	12.2	0.4	103814
46923	DELPHI	22277	3373	20.3	26.7	43.0	7.3	2.7	52518	54869	67	61	2572	10.5	32.0	45.4	11.0	1.0	96784
46926	DENVER	20474	721	16.8	36.2	39.7	5.8	1.5	47302	50937	55	33	629	15.6	34.2	42.0	7.8	0.5	90326
46928	FAIRMOUNT	22631	1906	20.2	29.1	43.4	5.6	1.7	50688	53161	63	50	1503	19.3	37.1	38.5	4.7	0.4	82689
46929	FLORA	24161	1309	18.8	26.5	44.3	7.0	3.4	53225	55057	68	65	1004	12.9	31.5	48.8	6.3	0.5	94667
46932	GALVESTON	26928	1449	12.6	28.3	41.3	13.3	4.6	60077	59931	77	82	1223	9.2	20.6	60.5	9.2	0.5	105711
46933	GAS CITY	24949	2400	21.9	27.5	38.0	10.0	2.6	50548	52824	62	50	1850	12.4	49.0	36.0	2.6	0.1	84150
46936	GREENTOWN	27272	2381	12.9	23.4	43.0	14.0	6.7	64580	65540	83	90	1994	9.1	24.1	52.6	13.3	1.0	108058
46938	JONESBORO	22986	1349	20.2	28.8	42.8	7.1	1.1	50870	53050	63	51	1111	21.2	42.4	32.8	3.5	0.2	79788
46939	KEWANNA	20886	911	24.8	30.1	38.5	5.6	1.0	44357	47507	46	21	745	16.1	35.6	37.6	8.6	2.1	87727
46940	LA FONTAINE	25740	1218	16.1	24.6	47.0	10.1	2.2	58016	58871	75	78	997	16.1	25.7	43.8	13.1	1.2	97342
46941	LAGRO	21078	551	16.3	31.6	44.1	5.8	2.2	51307	52855	64	54	491	15.5	27.3	46.0	9.8	1.4	98256
46947	LOGANSPORT	22753	11456	21.1	31.0	36.6	8.1	3.2	47959	51035	56	36	8025	14.5	40.1	37.2	7.6	0.6	86614
46950	LUCERNE	21315	252	15.1	44.0	31.3	8.3	1.2	44729	46840	47	22	220	11.4	36.4	44.1	7.3	0.9	92273
46951	MACY	20102	998	17.4	36.8	38.8	5.0	2.0	46489	50066	53	30	846	16.7	29.1	42.9	9.5	1.9	95625
46952	MARION	26776	8979	22.7	29.1	33.7	9.8	4.7	48489	51285	58	37	6270	10.3	33.5	44.2	11.1	0.8	96494
46953	MARION	19968	9091	31.3	30.2	30.4	6.3	1.8	40389	42586	34	9	6363	26.6	39.3	30.3	3.3	0.5	73596
46960	MONTEREY	18466	534	28.8	33.7	29.0	5.1	3.4	39639	41440	32	8	448	23.7	36.6	26.1	12.5	1.1	80213
46962	NORTH MANCHESTER	23012	3531	18.1	30.0	41.4	8.6	1.9	52034	54197	66	58	2594	11.9	30.2	47.7	9.4	0.8	97295
46970	PERU	22264	9834	23.0	27.5	40.0	7.1	2.4	49464	52055	60	43	7133	20.7	35.9	35.9	7.0	0.6	83955
46974	ROANN	20463	506	17.6	31.8	43.5	5.7	1.4	50396	52675	62	48	424	20.3	31.4	39.2	8.7	0.5	88511
46975	ROCHESTER	22445	5861	20.1	32.0	39.1	6.5	2.3	47900	49394	56	35	4504	15.0	32.6	41.1	10.1	1.2	92314
46978	ROYAL CENTER	23866	838	15.6	29.2	43.2	10.4	1.6	55919	57175	73	73	692	15.5	37.7	39.6	6.1	1.2	87556
46979	RUSSIAVILLE	28512	1750	11.1	20.2	45.9	16.4	6.4	68156	68115	86	93	1565	5.7	25.9	52.1	14.8	1.5	107328
46982	SILVER LAKE	19449	1054	19.9	34.5	40.2	3.9	1.4	46165	49809	52	28	888	21.4	32.0	40.5	5.7	0.3	85946
46985	STAR CITY	18896	576	18.8	41.0	34.0	5.4	0.9	43527	44822	44	17	484	30.4	20.7	41.5	6.2	1.2	88684
46986	SWAYZEE	22574	748	19.8	28.3	42.4	8.6	0.9	51829	54132	66	57	641	13.1	34.0	45.4	7.0	0.5	93627
46988	TWELVE MILE	21867	387	13.7	36.7	38.2	8.3	3.1	49545	52790	60	43	323	9.0	35.6	44.3	9.9	1.2	93302
46989	UPLAND	19254	1552	18.7	29.2	41.0	8.5	2.6	51791	53747	65	57	1224	9.9	30.5	49.6	9.7	0.3	99008
46990	URBANA	20288	276	14.1	30.8	48.2	6.2	0.7	54171	55141	70	67	242	19.4	29.3	39.7	10.7	0.8	91500
46991	VAN BUREN	22858	638	19.6	29.6	39.8	8.8	2.2	50738	53024	63	51	514	18.1	35.0	39.3	6.6	1.0	87333
46992	WABASH	23909	6874	20.7	28.8	39.9	7.7	2.9	50406	52643	62	48	5070	13.4	35.6	41.9	8.5	0.6	90864
46994	WALTON	24221	1075	16.2	27.4	43.6	9.5	3.3	56760	57732	74	75	862	14.8	25.1	51.4	8.2	0.5	99255
46996	WINAMAC	21990	2870	22.1	36.7	31.9	5.9	3.4	43460	45000	44	16	2235	17.5	31.8	39.6	9.6	1.6	90699
47001	AURORA	23183	4102	18.2	28.6	43.1	7.4	2.7	52974	56096	68	63	3059	11.0	26.4	43.8	17.3	1.5	107252
47003	WEST COLLEGE CORNER	18783	380	18.9	46.6	26.8	5.8	1.8	41536	42508	38	12	266	19.9	37.2	32.7	4.5	5.6	81739
47006	BATESVILLE	26373	4260	13.4	23.2	47.1	10.5	5.9	62111	61773	80	86	3282	3.5	11.2	54.1	26.6	4.5	139273
47010	BATH	22596	58	20.7	27.6	43.1	3.4	5.2	51177	53230	64	53	43	11.6	34.9	37.2	14.0	2.3	97500
47011	BENNINGTON	17446	463	25.3	31.3	37.8	4.3	1.3	43281	44448	43	15	393	10.2	22.1	49.1	16.0	2.5	109861
47012	BROOKVILLE	21655	3879	21.1	30.1	38.6	7.8	2.4	48888	52483	59	40	3011	13.3	27.8	41.5	15.8	1.6	101729
47016	CEDAR GROVE	22946	344	16.3	28.2	45.9	7.0	2.6	54789	57149	71	69	289	15.9	20.1	41.2	19.0	3.8	113720
47017	CROSS PLAINS	21216	297	22.2	29.6	40.4	7.7	0.0	48735	50491	58	39	251	12.7	17.1	41.4	26.7	2.0	119837
47018	DILLSBORO	22683	1713	18.4	30.1	41.4	8.2	1.8	51376	54419	65	55	1343	12.7	18.6	42.8	23.4	2.5	117779
47020	FLORENCE	26518	389	20.8	31.6	38.0	5.9	3.6	47883	47668	56	35	313	16.6	25.9	43.5	12.8	1.3	99792
47022	GUILFORD	22953	1091	10.6	31.1	45.1	10.0	3.2	60631	64204	78	84	988	6.4	14.1	41.2	36.3	2.0	153053
47023	HOLTON	19196	654	21.6	32.1	37.3	7.2	1.8	46934	48865	54	31	547	17.2	24.9	40.4	16.5	1.1	100710
47024	LAUREL	18532	1277	23.6	33.1	37.5	4.5	1.3	45219	48153	49	24	1043	28.1	30.4	30.3	9.1	2.1	77056
47025	LAWRENCEBURG	27812	8604	14.7	21.0	44.7	13.6	6.0	65098	69490	83	90	6535	4.7	13.6	48.9	30.3	2.4	144367
47030	METAMORA	19604	511	18.8	32.3	41.7	6.1	1.2	49196	52635	59	43	426	13.1	23.7	45.3	17.1	0.7	106071
47031	MILAN	21148	1955	21.5	27.7	42.6	6.5	1.6	50535	51840	62	50	1550	15.6	25.0	41.9	15.5	1.9	101389
47032	MOORES HILL	21159	1254	18.2	27.0	44.7	7.6	2.6	53991	56265	70	67	1040	15.3	26.6	35.3	20.2	2.6	97925
47036	OLDENBURG	20562	368	19.6	25.0	43.5	7.3	4.6	55625	58143	72	72	312	12.2	17.6	40.4	26.9	2.9	131522
47037	OSGOOD	19880	1779	24.1	30.0	39.0	5.7	1.2	46429	48956	53	29	1373	16.0	23.4	44.3	14.8	1.6	103858
47038	PATRIOT	19923	497	19.9	30.0	42.5	5.6	2.0	50051	49023	61	46	405	21.5	24.9	41.5	10.1	2.0	95800
47040	RISING SUN	24574	2156	20.3	26.8	41.7	8.9	2.4	52872	55311	68	63	1630	14.8	15.6	47.5	18.5	3.6	115248
47041	SUNMAN	21629	2124	16.8	26.2	47.6	7.6	1.9	56493	57517	73	74	1775	7.8	17.9	39.7	32.8	1.9	137597
47042	VERSAILLES	21076	1808	23.1	30.9	38.2	5.9	1.9	46600	48882	53	30	1365	12.6	27.8	44.7	13.3	1.6	100376
47043	VEVAY	19886	2118	30.5	29.2	34.3	4.4	1.7	42092	44228	40	13	1555	11.3	30.6	43.2	12.9	2.1	100644
47060	WEST HARRISON	26439	2635	12.7	22.3	47.4	12.5	5.2	64954	67818	83	90	2238	7.6	16.0	40.6	31.0	4.7	146500
47102	AUSTIN	18266	3103	31.4	31.6	30.2	5.3	1.5	40308	42191	34	9	2282	19.1	37.9	35.8	7.0	0.2	83484
47106	BORDEN	25124	1949	14.2	30.1	43.7	8.7	3.4	54440	55933	70	68	1694	11.0	18.5	41.4	24.3	4.7	124810
47108	CAMPBELLSBURG	18120	954	30.6	28.1	36.7	3.6	1.0	40856	44522	36	10	769	20.2	34.9	35.2	9.6	0.1	85523
47110	CENTRAL	19609	71	14.1	38.0	46.5	1.4	0.0	47996	50000	57	36	62	12.9	43.5	27.4	16.1	0.0	80000
47111	CHARLESTOWN	21636	5249	24.4	26.8	38.2	7.8	2.7	48731	51915	58	39	3802	10.5	25.2	42.8	18.7	2.7	111423
47112	CORYDON	23933	6191	20.2	27.3	40.8	8.6	3.2	51721	54289	65	56	4883	13.1	21.4	44.8	19.5	1.1	114917
47114	CRANDALL	25508	158	11.4	28.5	46.8	12.0	1.3	59297	61247	77	80	143	16.8	18.9	42.0	21.0	1.4	111413
47115	DEPAUW	23460	990	22.4	31.2	35.2	7.9	3.3	47910	50931	56	36	842	17.2	25.2	41.6	12.9	3.1	102000
47116	ECKERTY	20577	407	27.5	31.4	34.9	4.7	1.5	43272	43037	43	15	360	22.5	33.3	35.3	6.1	2.8	85227
47117	ELIZABETH	23702	1685	14.0	31.5	43.8	8.0	2.7	52857	55388	68	63	1507	12.8	26.5	36.8	21.4	2.4	108018
47118	ENGLISH	17336	1470	35.7	28.6	30.3	4.4	1.0	37203	37592	24	6	1202	27.1	34.0	30.6	7.3	0.9	77381
47119	FLOYDS KNOBS	33641	3816	9.2	17.7	42.7	18.3	12.0	74931	73271	89	96	3506	2.9	5.9	51.1	33.6	6.5	160264
47120	FREDERICKSBURG	16146	407	30.7	30.7	35.1	2.9	0.5	42550	45720	41	13	348	22.1	23.3	39.7	12.9	2.0	96667
47122	GEORGETOWN	26164	3451	10.5	23.8	48.1	13.3	4.3	63351	64232	82	88	3145	6.8	14.9	48.0	28.6	1.6	137347
	INDIANA	26003		19.5	26.3	38.6	10.5	5.1	54105	56493				12.2	24.1	44.1	17.2	2.4	108938
	UNITED STATES	27277		20.9	24.4	35.3	11.7	7.6	54719	56938				9.3	13.1	31.6	32.6	13.5	162279

ZIP CODE #	POST OFFICE NAME	FINANCIAL SERVICES: Auto Loan	FINANCIAL SERVICES: Home Loan	FINANCIAL SERVICES: Invest-ments	FINANCIAL SERVICES: Retire-ment Plans	THE HOME: Home Improvements: Home Repair	THE HOME: Home Improvements: Lawn & Garden	THE HOME: Furnishings: Comput-ers & Hard-ware-Personal	THE HOME: Furnishings: Major Appli-ances	THE HOME: Furnishings: TV, Radio, Sound Equip-ment	THE HOME: Furnishings: Furni-ture	ENTERTAINMENT: Dine out/ Carry out	ENTERTAINMENT: Sports Equip-ment	ENTERTAINMENT: Fees & Tickets	ENTERTAINMENT: Toys & Games	ENTERTAINMENT: Travel	ENTERTAINMENT: Cable TV	PERSONAL: Apparel & Services	PERSONAL: Auto Repairs	PERSONAL: Health Insur-ance	PERSONAL: Pets & Supplies
46804	FORT WAYNE	126	132	120	133	129	122	126	124	122	130	124	97	129	126	126	120	87	123	119	144
46805	FORT WAYNE	75	67	59	70	64	71	77	70	78	72	78	56	73	78	71	80	54	75	78	86
46806	FORT WAYNE	62	54	45	55	49	58	60	56	63	58	63	44	57	64	54	65	43	60	62	70
46807	FORT WAYNE	82	77	64	78	72	78	84	77	85	80	85	61	80	86	77	86	59	82	83	94
46808	FORT WAYNE	71	66	59	68	63	71	73	69	75	68	74	54	70	75	68	77	52	72	76	83
46809	FORT WAYNE	77	73	65	74	70	78	78	75	81	73	80	58	76	81	74	84	55	78	84	91
46814	FORT WAYNE	237	298	278	309	298	254	246	252	228	272	231	205	286	241	267	212	172	231	211	282
46815	FORT WAYNE	99	107	96	107	104	106	100	101	101	100	101	76	105	102	102	102	70	100	105	119
46816	FORT WAYNE	79	68	58	70	64	73	77	72	79	72	78	58	70	80	69	81	54	76	79	88
46818	FORT WAYNE	101	98	86	97	95	96	94	97	94	95	94	75	91	98	92	94	65	94	94	113
46819	FORT WAYNE	87	80	76	83	80	85	86	84	87	83	88	65	83	88	83	89	61	87	89	100
46825	FORT WAYNE	96	92	79	94	88	89	95	90	94	95	95	71	93	97	91	94	66	93	91	108
46835	FORT WAYNE	105	106	91	108	100	100	107	100	105	107	106	81	107	108	104	103	74	103	101	120
46845	FORT WAYNE	147	181	165	184	178	158	152	156	143	164	145	124	172	149	164	136	105	146	137	177
46901	KOKOMO	91	83	80	84	81	93	87	89	90	82	89	68	82	91	83	94	61	89	96	106
46902	KOKOMO	99	97	90	99	95	102	99	98	101	96	100	75	99	101	97	103	70	100	105	117
46910	AKRON	83	70	72	71	70	85	70	80	74	65	72	61	62	76	68	79	49	74	83	94
46911	AMBOY	96	88	87	92	90	104	87	98	89	78	88	74	80	91	87	95	60	90	101	114
46913	BRINGHURST	109	93	103	95	95	115	93	108	97	84	96	82	82	99	92	104	65	100	112	126
46914	BUNKER HILL	92	74	79	74	74	92	75	86	80	70	79	65	64	83	71	86	53	80	90	102
46917	CAMDEN	82	75	74	78	77	88	74	84	76	67	75	63	68	78	74	81	51	77	86	97
46919	CONVERSE	90	86	79	89	85	97	84	91	87	78	85	70	80	88	84	90	58	86	96	107
46920	CUTLER	94	86	85	89	87	101	84	95	87	76	85	72	78	89	84	92	58	88	98	111
46923	DELPHI	89	79	77	82	80	92	82	88	85	75	83	68	75	86	79	89	57	85	93	104
46926	DENVER	91	73	78	74	74	92	74	85	79	70	78	65	64	82	71	85	53	80	89	101
46928	FAIRMOUNT	82	78	76	80	78	90	76	83	79	70	78	64	73	80	77	83	53	80	89	98
46929	FLORA	92	84	81	85	81	96	84	89	87	78	86	69	79	88	82	91	59	87	96	107
46932	GALVESTON	107	97	96	101	99	114	95	108	99	87	97	82	88	101	95	104	66	100	111	125
46933	GAS CITY	85	86	69	88	80	90	85	83	86	80	86	66	85	88	83	89	59	85	92	101
46936	GREENTOWN	103	110	97	112	107	114	102	107	103	99	103	82	105	105	105	106	71	103	112	126
46938	JONESBORO	85	78	73	80	76	89	78	83	80	72	79	64	73	82	76	84	54	80	89	99
46939	KEWANNA	84	65	84	65	67	89	68	82	73	60	71	63	56	73	67	79	47	76	87	97
46940	LA FONTAINE	94	88	82	92	88	101	87	95	90	80	88	73	83	91	87	94	60	90	99	111
46941	LAGRO	98	76	83	76	76	97	78	89	84	74	82	68	65	87	73	91	56	84	93	107
46947	LOGANSPORT	86	76	73	77	75	87	81	83	84	75	83	64	75	85	77	88	57	83	90	99
46950	LUCERNE	92	68	97	69	71	98	73	89	76	61	75	72	57	76	73	83	49	83	94	108
46951	MACY	89	70	89	71	73	94	72	87	76	64	75	67	61	76	72	82	50	80	90	103
46952	MARION	89	86	83	87	86	96	86	90	89	83	88	67	85	89	86	93	61	89	97	106
46953	MARION	78	63	65	63	62	77	69	73	73	64	71	56	60	74	64	78	49	72	80	88
46960	MONTEREY	88	64	84	62	65	87	66	80	72	62	71	61	53	73	63	79	47	75	84	96
46962	NORTH MANCHESTER	92	79	82	80	79	95	81	89	86	76	84	68	74	87	79	91	57	86	96	106
46970	PERU	87	75	75	76	74	88	79	84	82	73	81	64	71	83	75	87	55	82	89	100
46974	ROANN	95	72	80	71	72	93	74	86	81	71	79	66	62	84	69	88	53	81	90	103
46975	ROCHESTER	88	75	79	75	75	90	77	84	81	72	80	64	69	82	74	86	54	81	90	100
46978	ROYAL CENTER	92	85	81	88	83	98	86	91	88	78	86	71	81	89	84	91	59	88	97	109
46979	RUSSIAVILLE	108	118	99	121	113	119	109	111	109	107	109	87	114	111	112	110	76	109	115	132
46982	SILVER LAKE	89	67	75	66	67	86	69	80	75	66	74	61	57	78	64	81	50	75	84	96
46985	STAR CITY	83	69	79	72	71	88	71	82	73	62	72	64	61	74	71	78	48	76	85	97
46986	SWAYZEE	88	79	81	82	81	94	78	89	81	70	79	68	71	82	78	86	54	82	92	104
46988	TWELVE MILE	94	86	85	89	88	101	85	96	87	76	86	72	78	89	84	92	58	88	98	111
46989	UPLAND	86	86	78	89	85	92	84	87	85	80	84	67	83	86	84	87	58	85	91	103
46990	URBANA	98	75	82	74	75	96	77	88	83	73	82	68	64	86	72	90	55	83	93	106
46991	VAN BUREN	85	82	72	85	80	91	82	85	83	76	82	66	79	85	80	87	56	83	91	101
46992	WABASH	89	78	78	79	77	92	81	87	86	75	84	66	74	86	78	91	57	85	94	103
46994	WALTON	99	89	90	92	91	106	88	100	91	79	89	75	81	93	88	96	61	92	103	116
46996	WINAMAC	92	71	88	71	73	95	74	89	80	67	78	68	62	80	73	87	52	82	94	105
47001	AURORA	89	86	76	86	83	90	84	87	86	82	85	66	82	88	82	88	59	85	90	103
47003	WEST COLLEGE CORNER	82	71	72	69	70	79	69	76	72	68	71	57	62	74	67	75	48	73	77	91
47006	BATESVILLE	102	106	95	109	104	110	100	104	100	98	100	80	102	102	102	102	69	101	106	123
47010	BATH	86	78	77	81	80	92	77	87	79	70	78	66	71	81	77	84	53	80	90	101
47011	BENNINGTON	85	68	73	67	68	83	68	77	73	66	72	58	58	75	64	78	48	73	80	93
47012	BROOKVILLE	88	79	78	80	79	91	79	87	82	74	80	65	72	83	77	86	55	82	90	102
47016	CEDAR GROVE	96	90	82	90	89	96	86	92	88	85	88	69	82	91	84	91	60	88	93	109
47017	CROSS PLAINS	80	72	72	75	74	85	71	80	74	64	72	61	66	75	71	78	49	74	83	94
47018	DILLSBORO	89	80	81	82	82	93	81	89	84	75	82	67	75	85	80	88	56	85	93	104
47020	FLORENCE	125	90	103	87	89	118	93	108	103	91	101	83	75	108	85	113	68	103	114	132
47022	GUILFORD	94	103	90	106	100	103	93	98	92	92	92	76	97	94	97	93	64	93	97	115
47023	HOLTON	84	74	75	76	75	89	73	83	77	67	75	63	66	78	72	81	51	77	86	97
47024	LAUREL	89	67	75	66	67	87	69	80	75	66	74	61	57	78	64	82	50	75	84	96
47025	LAWRENCEBURG	104	109	95	109	104	106	103	104	103	103	103	80	105	106	103	104	72	102	105	122
47030	METAMORA	90	74	75	72	73	86	73	81	78	73	77	61	64	81	69	83	52	78	84	98
47031	MILAN	90	75	80	75	74	92	76	85	81	72	80	65	67	82	73	86	54	81	90	102
47032	MOORES HILL	97	89	83	89	89	97	86	93	89	84	88	69	81	91	84	92	60	89	95	110
47036	OLDENBURG	95	95	88	98	95	103	89	97	90	85	90	75	88	92	92	93	62	91	99	114
47037	OSGOOD	83	69	70	70	69	84	72	79	76	67	74	60	63	78	68	81	51	75	83	94
47038	PATRIOT	97	72	80	70	71	92	74	84	81	72	79	64	61	84	67	87	54	80	89	103
47040	RISING SUN	89	84	77	84	82	90	85	87	87	82	86	65	81	88	82	90	59	86	92	103
47041	SUNMAN	94	85	87	86	85	99	82	92	85	78	84	71	76	87	82	90	58	87	95	109
47042	VERSAILLES	84	69	77	70	71	86	73	81	77	68	75	61	64	77	70	82	51	78	86	96
47043	VEVAY	80	61	77	60	63	80	65	76	71	61	70	57	55	70	63	77	47	72	81	90
47060	WEST HARRISON	105	112	98	115	109	112	102	107	101	102	102	82	106	104	105	102	71	102	106	126
47102	AUSTIN	76	60	59	60	59	73	67	69	71	63	69	53	57	73	59	75	47	69	75	84
47106	BORDEN	101	93	90	94	92	105	89	98	92	87	92	75	84	95	88	97	63	93	100	116
47108	CAMPBELLSBURG	84	60	70	59	60	80	63	73	70	61	68	56	50	73	57	76	46	69	77	89
47110	CENTRAL	96	69	79	67	69	91	72	84	80	70	78	64	58	83	65	87	53	79	88	102
47111	CHARLESTOWN	81	82	71	81	79	83	79	80	80	78	80	61	78	82	78	81	55	79	82	95
47112	CORYDON	93	82	83	82	82	94	83	90	87	79	85	67	76	88	80	91	58	87	94	106
47114	CRANDALL	103	95	84	92	93	97	90	95	93	93	93	69	85	97	85	96	63	92	95	113
47115	DEPAUW	102	80	100	80	82	106	81	98	87	75	86	74	69	88	80	95	57	90	102	116
47116	ECKERTY	92	66	76	64	66	88	69	80	76	67	75	62	55	80	63	83	50	76	85	98
47117	ELIZABETH	97	89	88	93	91	104	87	99	90	79	89	75	81	92	88	95	60	91	101	114
47118	ENGLISH	77	55	67	53	55	74	57	68	64	55	62	52	45	66	52	70	42	64	71	82
47119	FLOYDS KNOBS	128	148	136	152	147	145	131	137	128	134	129	105	142	130	141	128	91	131	134	159
47120	FREDERICKSBURG	77	56	64	54	55	74	58	67	64	56	63	52	46	67	53	70	42	64	71	82
47122	GEORGETOWN	105	110	98	112	108	111	101	107	100	100	100	82	103	103	104	101	70	101	105	125
	INDIANA	97	91	86	93	89	96	93	94	95	91	94	73	90	96	90	97	65	94	97	112
	UNITED STATES	100	100	100	100	100	100	100	100	100	100	100	100	100	100	100	100	100	100	100	100

ZIP CODE			POPULATION			2000-2009 ANNUAL RATE		HOUSEHOLDS					FAMILIES		
#	POST OFFICE NAME	COUNTY FIPS CODE	2000	2009	2014	% Rate	State Centile	2000	2009	2014	% Annual Rate 2000-2009	2009 Average HH Size	2000	2009	% Annual Rate 2000-2009
47123	GRANTSBURG	025	93	96	96	0.3	56	44	47	47	0.7	2.02	33	33	0.0
47124	GREENVILLE	043	3767	4067	4211	0.8	76	1301	1446	1514	1.1	2.81	1088	1173	0.8
47125	HARDINSBURG	117	1831	1880	1899	0.3	56	680	717	729	0.6	2.62	517	528	0.2
47126	HENRYVILLE	019	3515	3900	4115	1.1	84	1277	1483	1585	1.6	2.57	1003	1124	1.2
47129	CLARKSVILLE	019	20554	21050	21466	0.3	56	8705	9210	9512	0.6	2.22	5288	5232	-0.1
47130	JEFFERSONVILLE	019	38783	44279	47238	1.4	89	16080	19168	20697	1.9	2.27	10551	12095	1.5
47135	LACONIA	061	1154	1204	1222	0.5	66	445	477	487	0.8	2.52	338	352	0.4
47136	LANESVILLE	061	4041	4557	4791	1.3	87	1465	1702	1806	1.6	2.68	1176	1326	1.3
47137	LEAVENWORTH	025	1519	1496	1475	-0.2	27	575	582	580	0.1	2.50	434	426	-0.2
47138	LEXINGTON	077	4253	4511	4626	0.6	70	1583	1734	1797	1.0	2.60	1251	1326	0.6
47140	MARENGO	117	2485	2527	2511	0.2	49	976	1020	1022	0.5	2.48	690	693	0.0
47141	MARYSVILLE	019	1486	1677	1779	1.3	87	533	621	667	1.7	2.69	433	487	1.3
47142	MAUCKPORT	061	835	894	916	0.7	73	331	367	381	1.1	2.44	240	257	0.7
47143	MEMPHIS	019	2412	3511	3913	4.1	98	899	1374	1550	4.7	2.56	734	1082	4.3
47145	MILLTOWN	025	2103	2229	2273	0.6	70	800	873	899	0.9	2.53	617	652	0.6
47147	NABB	019	969	1062	1111	1.0	81	377	428	453	1.4	2.47	292	319	1.0
47150	NEW ALBANY	043	47019	47405	47824	0.1	43	19227	19762	20066	0.3	2.35	12737	12442	-0.3
47160	NEW MIDDLETOWN	061	134	147	154	1.0	81	51	58	61	1.4	2.53	41	45	1.0
47161	NEW SALISBURY	061	3318	3463	3528	0.5	66	1198	1298	1336	0.9	2.67	931	980	0.6
47162	NEW WASHINGTON	019	769	854	898	1.1	84	259	298	318	1.5	2.81	196	216	1.1
47163	OTISCO	019	1684	1875	1982	1.2	86	613	711	761	1.6	2.63	510	571	1.2
47164	PALMYRA	061	3324	3537	3631	0.7	73	1223	1341	1392	1.0	2.62	944	1004	0.7
47165	PEKIN	175	5918	6369	6560	0.8	76	2180	2398	2486	1.0	2.66	1661	1765	0.7
47166	RAMSEY	061	1228	1250	1257	0.2	49	456	483	491	0.6	2.59	354	364	0.3
47167	SALEM	175	14663	15139	15305	0.3	56	5608	5912	6011	0.6	2.50	4039	4112	0.2
47170	SCOTTSBURG	143	13319	13899	14119	0.5	66	5226	5626	5773	0.8	2.43	3727	3867	0.4
47172	SELLERSBURG	019	11489	13849	15044	2.0	93	4411	5553	6104	2.5	2.46	3268	3932	2.0
47174	SULPHUR	025	58	58	56	0.0	37	21	22	21	0.5	2.64	16	16	0.0
47175	TASWELL	025	733	733	720	0.0	37	292	303	300	0.4	2.42	217	218	0.0
47177	UNDERWOOD	143	1184	1296	1354	1.0	81	442	505	534	1.5	2.54	359	397	1.1
47201	COLUMBUS	005	37490	39311	40314	0.5	66	14946	15701	16132	0.5	2.47	10422	10558	0.1
47203	COLUMBUS	005	25218	27312	28343	0.9	79	9809	10627	11053	0.9	2.53	7158	7463	0.5
47220	BROWNSTOWN	071	5373	5589	5691	0.4	60	2048	2201	2259	0.8	2.48	1519	1573	0.4
47223	BUTLERVILLE	079	1753	1806	1822	0.3	56	533	563	573	0.6	2.92	410	419	0.2
47224	CANAAN	077	640	717	749	1.2	86	219	252	265	1.5	2.85	176	196	1.2
47227	COMMISKEY	079	1232	1289	1311	0.5	66	462	497	509	0.8	2.59	364	380	0.5
47229	CROTHERSVILLE	071	3257	3229	3225	-0.1	31	1276	1305	1315	0.2	2.47	970	958	-0.1
47230	DEPUTY	077	2046	2145	2180	0.5	66	770	826	846	0.8	2.60	605	629	0.4
47231	DUPONT	077	1149	1217	1251	0.6	70	401	436	452	0.9	2.78	309	325	0.5
47232	ELIZABETHTOWN	005	2442	2579	2657	0.6	70	938	1004	1038	0.7	2.57	756	787	0.4
47234	FLAT ROCK	145	1281	1302	1317	0.2	49	483	506	516	0.5	2.57	381	388	0.2
47235	FREETOWN	071	1571	1575	1573	0.0	37	609	634	639	0.4	2.46	454	455	0.0
47236	GRAMMER	005	111	112	113	0.1	43	44	45	45	0.2	2.49	37	37	0.0
47240	GREENSBURG	031	20068	20688	20877	0.3	56	7719	8249	8421	0.7	2.47	5611	5784	0.3
47243	HANOVER	077	6142	6506	6640	0.6	70	1927	2105	2175	1.0	2.55	1428	1501	0.5
47244	HARTSVILLE	005	807	816	823	0.1	43	285	289	293	0.2	2.82	228	224	-0.2
47246	HOPE	005	4506	4474	4486	-0.1	31	1579	1574	1584	0.0	2.79	1237	1195	-0.4
47250	MADISON	077	20796	21331	21494	0.3	56	8465	8925	9069	0.6	2.31	5630	5687	0.1
47260	MEDORA	071	1846	1848	1831	0.0	37	699	720	721	0.3	2.57	538	534	-0.1
47264	NORMAN	071	1575	1523	1498	-0.4	18	623	623	618	0.0	2.44	480	464	-0.4
47265	NORTH VERNON	079	19688	20606	20935	0.5	66	7378	7880	8049	0.7	2.57	5436	5612	0.3
47270	PARIS CROSSING	079	952	1011	1038	0.7	73	347	379	392	1.0	2.67	279	296	0.6
47272	SAINT PAUL	031	1986	2142	2209	0.8	76	704	780	811	1.1	2.75	555	597	0.8
47273	SCIPIO	079	2047	2140	2182	0.5	66	722	772	792	0.7	2.77	573	595	0.4
47274	SEYMOUR	071	28143	29094	29491	0.4	60	10959	11626	11883	0.6	2.47	7723	7900	0.2
47281	VALLONIA	071	1456	1682	1769	1.6	91	555	651	689	1.7	2.58	441	503	1.4
47282	VERNON	079	317	322	323	0.2	49	113	117	118	0.4	2.66	80	79	-0.1
47283	WESTPORT	031	3521	3574	3569	0.2	49	1316	1387	1402	0.6	2.57	995	1015	0.2
47302	MUNCIE	035	30276	27819	26657	-0.9	3	12678	11929	11515	-0.7	2.31	8408	7589	-1.1
47303	MUNCIE	035	31297	30583	29865	-0.2	27	11042	10875	10645	-0.2	2.27	5837	5372	-0.9
47304	MUNCIE	035	28438	29090	28756	0.2	49	11908	12450	12390	0.5	2.28	7620	7524	-0.1
47305	MUNCIE	035	4912	4207	3954	-1.7	0	2239	1930	1817	-1.6	2.04	922	734	-2.4
47306	MUNCIE	035	256	257	249	0.0	37	153	143	138	-0.7	1.72	41	35	-1.7
47320	ALBANY	035	4275	3984	3831	-0.8	4	1689	1607	1555	-0.5	2.44	1227	1126	-0.9
47325	BROWNSVILLE	161	755	757	747	0.0	37	272	280	279	0.3	2.69	221	221	0.0
47326	BRYANT	075	2027	2046	2031	0.1	43	612	616	610	0.1	3.32	487	477	-0.2
47327	CAMBRIDGE CITY	177	5516	5352	5218	-0.3	22	2180	2140	2096	-0.2	2.48	1598	1512	-0.6
47330	CENTERVILLE	177	5433	5394	5300	-0.1	31	2050	2070	2046	0.1	2.55	1599	1562	-0.3
47331	CONNERSVILLE	041	24981	23771	23043	-0.5	13	9964	9740	9514	-0.2	2.39	6967	6550	-0.7
47334	DALEVILLE	035	3284	3384	3363	0.3	56	1292	1361	1363	0.6	2.48	962	977	0.2
47336	DUNKIRK	075	4006	3893	3808	-0.3	22	1629	1611	1584	-0.1	2.39	1168	1112	-0.5
47338	EATON	035	2972	2747	2637	-0.8	4	1151	1098	1063	-0.5	2.49	878	810	-0.9
47339	ECONOMY	177	617	624	619	0.1	43	223	227	226	0.2	2.75	178	176	-0.1
47340	FARMLAND	135	3155	3050	2977	-0.4	18	1214	1198	1177	-0.1	2.54	911	868	-0.5
47341	FOUNTAIN CITY	177	2069	1992	1947	-0.4	18	776	759	746	-0.2	2.62	617	585	-0.6
47342	GASTON	035	2967	2853	2769	-0.4	18	1098	1071	1045	-0.3	2.59	852	805	-0.6
47345	GREENS FORK	177	1398	1410	1403	0.1	43	506	515	514	0.2	2.74	400	395	-0.1
47346	HAGERSTOWN	177	3950	3846	3751	-0.3	22	1611	1583	1549	-0.2	2.43	1161	1096	-0.6
47348	HARTFORD CITY	009	10845	10351	10021	-0.5	13	4372	4308	4207	-0.2	2.37	3094	2937	-0.6
47352	LEWISVILLE	065	890	893	886	0.0	37	340	352	351	0.4	2.54	268	269	0.0
47353	LIBERTY	161	5811	5875	5877	0.1	43	2225	2296	2308	0.3	2.53	1643	1639	0.0
47354	LOSANTVILLE	135	1161	1107	1072	-0.5	13	458	448	437	-0.2	2.47	356	338	-0.6
47355	LYNN	135	3037	2886	2793	-0.5	13	1206	1176	1145	-0.3	2.45	887	833	-0.7
47356	MIDDLETOWN	065	6521	6628	6553	0.2	49	2529	2566	2549	0.2	2.49	1887	1847	-0.2
47357	MILTON	177	1182	1135	1102	-0.4	18	454	444	435	-0.2	2.56	357	339	-0.6
47358	MODOC	135	1094	1040	1006	-0.5	13	408	399	389	-0.2	2.61	311	295	-0.6
47359	MONTPELIER	009	3270	3113	3002	-0.5	13	1302	1272	1236	-0.3	2.45	928	871	-0.7
47360	MOORELAND	065	1521	1503	1479	-0.1	31	561	568	563	0.1	2.65	444	436	-0.2
47362	NEW CASTLE	065	29568	29060	28298	-0.2	27	12128	11861	11616	-0.2	2.33	8401	7897	-0.7
47368	PARKER CITY	135	2826	2785	2746	-0.2	27	1100	1114	1106	0.1	2.44	805	784	-0.3
47369	PENNVILLE	075	1359	1381	1371	0.2	49	526	540	537	0.3	2.56	376	372	-0.1
47371	PORTLAND	075	12407	12260	12065	-0.1	31	4873	4877	4817	0.0	2.47	3447	3323	-0.4
47373	REDKEY	075	2411	2408	2380	0.0	37	969	992	986	0.3	2.43	695	684	-0.2
47374	RICHMOND	177	49948	47741	46373	-0.5	13	20386	19680	19192	-0.4	2.31	13151	12111	-0.9
47380	RIDGEVILLE	135	2228	2131	2069	-0.5	13	852	833	814	-0.2	2.56	641	606	-0.6
	INDIANA					0.7					0.8	2.49			0.4
	UNITED STATES					1.0					1.1	2.59			0.9

ZIP CODE		RACE (%)								2009 AGE DISTRIBUTION (%)										MEDIAN AGE		
#	POST OFFICE NAME	White		Black		Asian/Pacific		% Hispanic Origin														
		2000	2009	2000	2009	2000	2009	2000	2009	0-4	5-9	10-14	15-19	20-24	25-44	45-64	65-84	85+	18+	2009	% 2009 Males	% 2009 Females
47123	GRANTSBURG	97.8	97.9	0.0	0.0	0.0	0.0	1.1	1.0	6.3	6.3	6.3	6.3	6.3	25.0	31.3	11.5	1.0	78.1	40.0	50.0	50.0
47124	GREENVILLE	98.0	97.3	0.5	0.6	0.3	0.5	0.7	1.1	6.4	7.4	7.9	7.5	4.6	28.9	29.1	7.4	0.9	73.6	37.6	50.2	49.8
47125	HARDINSBURG	98.9	98.7	0.2	0.3	0.2	0.3	0.8	1.2	5.9	5.8	6.2	7.9	6.6	26.6	29.8	10.3	0.9	77.3	38.9	50.5	49.5
47126	HENRYVILLE	98.2	97.7	0.8	1.1	0.1	0.2	0.5	0.8	6.1	6.3	6.7	6.3	5.0	28.9	29.8	9.9	0.9	77.0	39.0	51.8	48.2
47129	CLARKSVILLE	90.1	87.6	6.0	7.1	0.9	1.3	2.9	4.5	6.4	5.9	5.4	5.8	6.9	27.2	25.3	13.7	3.4	79.0	39.1	47.7	52.3
47130	JEFFERSONVILLE	84.0	81.5	12.5	14.0	0.8	1.2	1.6	2.4	6.5	6.3	6.4	6.3	6.1	27.9	27.5	11.3	1.6	77.0	38.2	48.5	51.5
47135	LACONIA	99.1	98.8	0.0	0.1	0.5	0.7	0.7	1.1	6.1	6.4	7.0	7.1	5.0	24.8	31.1	11.2	1.4	76.2	40.7	51.7	48.3
47136	LANESVILLE	98.3	97.8	0.5	0.6	0.4	0.6	0.5	0.8	6.0	6.6	7.2	6.8	4.3	25.0	32.0	11.0	1.1	76.0	41.2	50.0	50.0
47137	LEAVENWORTH	98.0	97.5	0.2	0.3	0.3	0.3	1.3	1.8	6.4	6.5	6.9	6.4	4.9	24.3	29.3	13.1	2.3	76.4	40.5	51.9	48.1
47138	LEXINGTON	98.4	97.8	0.2	0.2	0.1	0.2	0.8	1.2	6.1	6.3	6.7	6.9	5.4	26.9	29.7	11.0	1.0	76.7	40.0	50.6	49.4
47140	MARENGO	98.7	98.2	0.2	0.2	0.2	0.4	0.8	1.1	6.3	6.4	6.7	7.3	5.6	26.9	28.2	11.4	1.3	76.0	38.4	51.3	48.7
47141	MARYSVILLE	98.5	98.0	0.2	0.2	0.1	0.2	0.6	1.0	6.7	7.2	7.2	6.3	4.4	26.9	29.0	11.2	1.2	75.1	39.3	49.9	50.1
47142	MAUCKPORT	98.3	97.8	0.1	0.1	0.2	0.4	0.8	1.3	7.3	7.5	7.3	5.9	5.4	27.2	28.6	10.2	0.7	74.3	37.8	50.6	49.4
47143	MEMPHIS	98.3	98.0	0.1	0.2	0.2	0.3	0.2	0.4	4.8	5.3	5.9	6.5	4.9	24.1	35.3	12.3	1.0	80.0	43.9	49.8	50.2
47145	MILLTOWN	98.2	97.8	0.0	0.0	0.2	0.3	0.9	1.2	6.4	6.4	6.6	6.7	6.3	25.6	29.3	11.5	1.3	76.1	39.1	49.8	50.2
47147	NABB	99.0	98.8	0.2	0.2	0.1	0.2	0.5	0.8	6.1	6.3	6.6	6.2	4.6	26.6	30.2	11.9	1.5	77.3	40.7	49.2	50.8
47150	NEW ALBANY	90.7	88.7	6.4	7.5	0.5	0.8	1.3	1.9	6.8	6.3	6.0	6.2	6.3	27.1	26.6	12.3	2.3	77.0	38.3	47.5	52.5
47160	NEW MIDDLETOWN	97.0	97.3	0.7	0.7	0.0	0.0	0.7	1.4	6.8	6.8	6.8	6.8	4.8	25.9	29.9	10.9	1.4	75.5	40.2	49.7	50.3
47161	NEW SALISBURY	98.5	98.2	0.4	0.4	0.2	0.2	2.2	3.2	6.8	6.8	6.8	6.3	5.4	28.5	29.2	9.2	0.9	75.6	37.7	51.0	49.0
47162	NEW WASHINGTON	97.7	96.8	0.8	0.9	0.0	0.1	0.8	1.2	6.7	6.8	7.1	6.2	4.2	28.0	28.7	11.0	1.3	76.1	39.0	50.2	49.8
47163	OTISCO	98.1	97.5	0.3	0.4	0.3	0.4	0.8	1.4	6.5	7.0	7.0	5.8	4.2	26.8	30.1	11.7	1.0	75.9	40.2	51.2	48.8
47164	PALMYRA	98.7	98.4	0.2	0.1	0.2	0.3	0.9	1.4	6.7	6.8	6.7	6.5	5.9	28.6	28.5	9.4	0.9	75.7	37.5	49.4	50.6
47165	PEKIN	98.6	98.3	0.1	0.1	0.2	0.3	1.2	1.8	6.7	6.7	7.0	7.3	5.8	28.7	28.2	8.7	0.9	75.1	37.2	50.4	49.6
47166	RAMSEY	98.8	98.5	0.2	0.3	0.2	0.2	1.7	2.6	6.5	6.6	6.7	6.2	5.1	27.9	30.1	9.8	1.0	76.2	38.8	50.6	49.4
47167	SALEM	98.9	98.6	0.1	0.1	0.2	0.3	0.6	0.9	6.6	6.6	6.7	6.4	5.4	26.1	27.8	12.2	2.2	76.2	39.4	49.5	50.5
47170	SCOTTSBURG	98.6	98.2	0.1	0.1	0.2	0.3	0.8	1.2	7.3	7.1	7.0	6.4	5.7	27.9	26.1	10.9	1.5	74.7	37.1	49.6	50.4
47172	SELLERSBURG	97.7	96.8	0.7	0.9	0.6	1.0	1.0	1.5	7.0	7.0	6.9	6.1	5.0	27.1	27.8	11.4	1.8	75.3	38.9	48.5	51.5
47174	SULPHUR	98.2	98.3	0.0	0.0	0.0	0.0	1.8	1.7	6.9	6.9	6.9	6.9	8.6	24.1	29.3	10.3	0.0	72.4	36.3	50.0	50.0
47175	TASWELL	98.6	98.5	0.1	0.1	0.4	0.5	0.4	0.7	6.0	6.4	6.7	6.5	5.7	23.6	29.7	14.1	1.2	76.8	41.5	52.7	47.3
47177	UNDERWOOD	98.5	98.2	0.3	0.4	0.1	0.2	0.5	0.9	6.2	6.6	6.9	6.3	4.8	26.8	30.3	11.3	0.8	76.3	40.1	51.5	48.5
47201	COLUMBUS	93.4	91.5	2.1	2.3	2.1	3.1	2.7	4.0	7.1	7.0	7.0	6.7	5.8	26.8	26.8	11.4	1.6	74.8	37.8	49.9	50.1
47203	COLUMBUS	93.9	91.9	1.9	2.2	2.3	3.5	1.9	2.7	7.0	7.1	7.1	6.6	5.2	24.3	27.9	12.7	2.1	74.4	39.5	48.3	51.7
47220	BROWNSTOWN	98.8	98.4	0.1	0.1	0.3	0.5	0.5	0.8	6.6	7.0	6.9	7.1	5.1	25.4	26.4	13.1	2.5	75.0	39.8	48.6	51.4
47223	BUTLERVILLE	97.2	96.5	0.9	1.0	0.3	0.6	0.7	1.0	6.5	6.5	7.1	7.2	5.1	28.6	29.3	8.7	0.9	75.1	38.6	51.2	48.8
47224	CANAAN	98.4	97.9	0.3	0.4	0.3	0.4	1.1	1.7	7.8	7.8	7.8	7.3	6.1	26.1	25.8	10.3	1.0	72.1	35.6	50.6	49.4
47227	COMMISKEY	98.8	98.4	0.3	0.4	0.2	0.2	0.4	0.6	6.3	6.7	7.0	7.0	5.2	26.9	28.5	11.3	1.2	75.7	38.8	50.3	49.7
47229	CROTHERSVILLE	98.7	98.4	0.1	0.1	0.4	0.5	1.1	1.6	6.7	6.8	6.9	6.6	5.0	26.4	28.0	12.3	1.3	75.5	39.3	50.6	49.4
47230	DEPUTY	98.2	97.9	0.1	0.1	0.1	0.2	0.9	1.4	6.2	6.4	6.8	7.0	5.5	26.2	29.4	11.4	1.1	76.3	39.6	49.9	50.1
47231	DUPONT	97.2	96.7	0.8	0.9	0.5	0.7	0.8	1.2	7.1	7.1	7.4	7.6	6.5	26.6	27.2	9.4	1.0	73.5	36.2	51.7	48.3
47232	ELIZABETHTOWN	97.6	96.9	0.7	0.8	0.1	0.1	2.5	3.8	6.3	6.7	7.0	6.4	4.6	26.6	30.0	11.4	1.0	76.0	40.2	50.3	49.7
47234	FLAT ROCK	99.4	99.3	0.1	0.1	0.1	0.1	0.4	0.5	5.7	6.2	6.5	6.3	4.7	25.6	32.6	10.8	1.8	77.6	41.7	51.2	48.8
47235	FREETOWN	98.3	98.0	0.1	0.1	0.1	0.1	0.9	1.4	5.5	5.9	6.1	5.5	4.9	26.0	30.9	13.3	2.0	79.0	42.1	51.0	49.0
47236	GRAMMER	96.4	95.5	1.8	2.7	0.0	0.0	0.0	0.0	5.4	5.4	6.3	6.3	3.6	27.7	30.4	13.4	1.8	79.5	42.7	51.8	48.2
47240	GREENSBURG	98.3	97.7	0.1	0.1	0.9	1.3	0.6	0.9	7.1	7.0	7.0	6.4	5.3	26.7	26.5	11.7	2.2	74.9	38.1	49.7	50.3
47243	HANOVER	96.3	95.3	1.4	1.7	0.8	1.2	1.2	1.7	5.8	5.6	5.8	13.0	13.5	22.1	22.6	10.1	1.4	78.6	30.6	48.1	51.9
47244	HARTSVILLE	98.5	97.9	0.5	0.6	0.5	0.7	0.5	0.7	6.5	6.9	7.4	7.1	5.1	24.6	29.4	11.9	1.1	74.9	39.9	51.3	48.7
47246	HOPE	98.6	98.2	0.4	0.5	0.2	0.2	1.0	1.5	7.2	7.3	7.5	7.4	6.0	25.5	26.8	10.2	2.1	73.5	37.3	50.2	49.8
47250	MADISON	95.8	94.8	1.7	1.9	0.6	0.9	1.1	1.6	6.2	6.2	6.1	6.3	5.6	25.6	28.5	13.2	2.2	77.5	40.6	49.5	50.5
47260	MEDORA	99.1	98.9	0.0	0.0	0.3	0.3	1.0	1.5	6.8	6.9	7.3	6.7	6.2	24.4	28.1	12.3	1.5	74.9	38.7	50.1	49.9
47264	NORMAN	98.7	98.6	0.0	0.0	0.2	0.3	0.7	1.1	6.6	6.9	7.2	6.8	5.4	25.4	29.2	11.5	1.1	75.1	39.7	51.4	48.6
47265	NORTH VERNON	97.1	96.5	0.9	1.0	0.3	0.5	0.8	1.2	7.9	7.6	7.3	7.1	5.8	26.9	25.4	10.5	1.5	72.7	36.2	49.3	50.7
47270	PARIS CROSSING	99.3	99.1	0.0	0.1	0.0	0.0	0.2	0.3	5.4	6.0	6.6	7.2	4.8	25.7	31.1	12.0	1.1	77.5	40.9	51.8	48.2
47272	SAINT PAUL	98.8	98.6	0.1	0.0	0.2	0.2	0.8	1.1	8.3	8.3	8.0	7.5	6.3	24.8	27.0	8.8	0.9	70.8	35.2	49.3	50.7
47273	SCIPIO	98.1	97.7	0.2	0.2	0.1	0.2	0.6	0.9	7.1	6.9	7.0	7.1	5.7	26.7	28.6	10.2	0.8	74.7	38.1	49.7	50.3
47274	SEYMOUR	94.8	93.1	0.8	0.9	1.1	1.5	3.6	5.3	7.2	7.2	6.9	6.3	5.2	28.5	25.9	10.8	2.0	74.7	37.3	49.7	50.3
47281	VALLONIA	99.2	99.2	0.1	0.1	0.1	0.1	0.3	0.5	5.9	6.2	6.7	7.3	5.2	25.7	29.5	12.0	1.6	76.7	40.5	52.3	47.7
47282	VERNON	98.4	97.8	1.3	1.6	0.0	0.0	0.0	0.3	6.5	6.8	7.1	6.8	4.3	28.0	28.0	10.6	1.9	74.8	38.8	52.8	47.2
47283	WESTPORT	99.1	98.9	0.1	0.1	0.1	0.2	0.2	0.3	7.8	7.8	7.6	6.5	5.3	27.0	25.2	11.4	1.4	72.8	36.8	50.1	49.9
47302	MUNCIE	87.9	86.7	9.9	10.7	0.2	0.3	1.1	1.5	7.1	6.9	6.8	6.9	5.8	25.4	26.2	13.1	1.8	74.7	38.3	48.2	51.8
47303	MUNCIE	87.9	85.7	9.5	11.0	0.6	0.9	1.3	2.0	4.4	4.0	4.1	16.3	23.6	18.8	17.4	9.4	2.0	84.8	24.5	47.3	52.7
47304	MUNCIE	92.7	90.5	3.9	5.1	1.6	2.2	1.2	1.8	5.6	5.4	5.6	5.9	9.7	25.4	25.1	14.3	3.1	80.1	38.4	47.8	52.2
47305	MUNCIE	79.3	74.1	16.0	20.2	0.7	0.8	1.5	2.2	6.4	5.3	5.4	7.2	13.6	30.3	22.4	7.5	1.8	78.8	31.8	51.9	48.1
47306	MUNCIE	62.5	53.7	5.9	6.6	26.2	33.9	2.0	2.3	3.1	1.2	1.2	3.9	47.1	35.4	6.2	1.9	0.0	94.2	24.3	48.2	51.8
47320	ALBANY	98.2	97.8	0.5	0.7	0.1	0.1	0.4	0.5	5.3	5.6	5.8	6.4	5.4	25.3	29.0	14.7	2.5	79.3	42.1	48.7	51.3
47325	BROWNSVILLE	98.9	98.8	0.3	0.3	0.3	0.4	0.4	0.5	6.1	6.6	6.7	6.9	4.6	26.0	30.1	11.8	1.2	76.2	40.6	51.4	48.6
47326	BRYANT	97.3	96.4	0.2	0.2	0.5	0.7	1.3	1.9	11.3	10.2	8.7	8.0	5.2	23.4	22.6	9.7	1.1	64.4	31.0	51.4	48.6
47327	CAMBRIDGE CITY	99.3	99.1	0.2	0.3	0.1	0.2	0.7	1.0	6.5	6.7	6.5	6.5	6.3	24.0	27.4	13.9	2.1	76.2	40.2	48.6	51.4
47330	CENTERVILLE	98.7	98.2	0.3	0.4	0.2	0.3	0.8	1.2	5.8	6.3	6.7	7.3	5.9	24.9	29.0	11.6	2.4	76.6	39.9	48.8	51.2
47331	CONNERSVILLE	97.1	96.5	1.7	2.0	0.3	0.5	0.5	0.8	6.4	6.4	6.4	6.4	5.4	25.7	27.5	13.5	2.4	76.9	39.8	48.8	51.2
47334	DALEVILLE	98.4	97.8	0.3	0.5	0.4	0.7	0.7	1.1	6.0	6.3	6.7	6.6	4.9	23.6	30.6	13.5	1.7	76.9	41.9	48.0	52.0
47336	DUNKIRK	98.1	97.5	0.3	0.3	0.4	0.7	0.6	1.0	6.3	6.3	6.4	6.4	5.4	23.6	28.3	15.2	2.2	77.1	41.7	49.0	51.0
47338	EATON	98.8	98.5	0.1	0.2	0.1	0.1	0.6	0.8	6.4	6.2	6.5	7.5	6.2	25.0	27.2	13.4	1.6	76.4	39.7	50.4	49.6
47339	ECONOMY	98.2	97.8	0.0	0.0	0.5	0.6	0.5	1.0	5.3	5.8	6.1	6.6	5.4	25.0	31.3	13.1	1.4	79.0	42.3	51.3	48.7
47340	FARMLAND	98.8	98.6	0.1	0.1	0.1	0.1	0.3	0.4	6.8	7.1	7.2	7.0	5.4	25.0	27.6	11.9	2.0	74.5	38.7	49.5	50.5
47341	FOUNTAIN CITY	98.1	97.6	0.6	0.8	0.1	0.2	0.2	0.3	5.2	5.3	6.1	7.0	6.2	24.3	31.0	13.3	1.6	79.2	41.9	50.5	49.5
47342	GASTON	98.7	98.2	0.2	0.3	0.0	0.1	0.6	0.9	5.9	6.1	6.4	6.5	5.4	25.3	30.7	12.1	1.7	77.2	41.3	50.0	50.0
47345	GREENS FORK	98.0	97.5	0.4	0.6	0.1	0.2	0.4	0.6	6.4	6.7	7.0	6.7	5.2	23.5	30.2	12.8	1.4	75.7	40.9	50.9	49.1
47346	HAGERSTOWN	99.0	98.7	0.1	0.2	0.1	0.2	0.3	0.4	5.8	5.9	6.1	6.6	5.5	25.1	29.0	14.2	1.9	78.2	41.6	49.3	50.7
47348	HARTFORD CITY	98.5	98.2	0.1	0.1	0.2	0.3	0.5	0.8	6.1	6.2	6.3	6.5	5.7	24.4	28.3	14.2	2.3	77.5	41.1	49.6	50.4
47352	LEWISVILLE	98.5	98.1	0.1	0.1	0.0	0.0	0.8	1.1	5.7	6.0	6.6	6.4	4.7	23.3	31.5	13.9	1.9	77.6	42.9	50.4	49.6
47353	LIBERTY	98.7	98.7	0.3	0.3	0.2	0.2	0.3	0.3	6.9	7.3	7.2	6.7	4.9	25.4	27.1	12.4	2.1	74.2	39.3	49.5	50.5
47354	LOSANTVILLE	98.5	98.1	0.2	0.2	0.1	0.2	0.9	1.4	6.1	6.5	6.9	6.7	4.6	24.6	29.8	13.2	1.6	76.3	41.1	50.4	49.6
47355	LYNN	98.3	97.9	0.2	0.3	0.3	0.4	0.2	0.3	6.9	6.8	6.9	6.8	5.2	25.7	26.1	13.6	1.9	75.1	39.0	49.4	50.6
47356	MIDDLETOWN	98.6	98.2	0.4	0.5	0.3	0.4	0.5	0.7	6.1	6.8	7.0	6.7	5.1	24.2	28.0	13.4	2.7	76.0	40.8	48.4	51.6
47357	MILTON	99.1	98.9	0.3	0.3	0.1	0.1	0.1	0.1	5.4	5.8	6.5	7.8	5.3	24.8	30.5	12.6	1.4	77.4	41.4	50.8	49.2
47358	MODOC	98.6	98.2	0.2	0.3	0.0	0.1	0.4	0.6	6.4	6.7	7.2	6.5	4.6	24.6	29.1	13.0	1.7	75.6	40.7	51.0	49.0
47359	MONTPELIER	98.2	97.9	0.1	0.1	0.0	0.1	0.9	1.3	7.5	7.7	7.5	6.3	5.1	25.0	26.8	12.6	1.6	73.4	38.5	49.7	50.3
47360	MOORELAND	99.0	98.7	0.1	0.1	0.3	0.4	1.0	1.4	7.1	7.3	7.5	6.9	4.4	24.9	28.9	11.7	1.5	73.9	39.8	50.3	49.7
47362	NEW CASTLE	97.4	96.8	1.2	1.4	0.2	0.4	0.9	1.3	5.9	5.9	6.0	6.5	5.7	25.5	27.4	14.4	2.8	78.2	41.0	49.3	50.7
47368	PARKER CITY	99.0	98.8	0.1	0.1	0.1	0.2	0.3	0.5	5.6	6.1	6.5	6.9	5.0	23.9	29.3	13.7	3.0	77.5	42.1	49.1	50.9
47369	PENNVILLE	98.6	98.0	0.3	0.4	0.0	0.0	1.5	2.2	7.1	7.2	7.5	7.9	5.4	24.2	26.0	12.9	1.7	73.2	37.9	50.3	49.7
47371	PORTLAND	97.3	96.2	0.3	0.3	0.4	0.5	2.4	3.6	6.8	6.7	6.9	6.9	5.3	24.9	26.9	13.3	2.5	75.4	39.5	49.0	51.0
47373	REDKEY	98.9	98.6	0.1	0.1	0.1	0.1	0.8	1.2	6.9	7.0	7.3	7.2	5.1	25.0	26.4	13.3	1.8	74.4	39.0	49.7	50.3
47374	RICHMOND	89.2	87.1	7.1	8.2	0.7	1.1	1.7	2.5	6.3	6.0	6.1	6.8	7.0	24.9	26.2	13.9	2.8	77.8	39.3	47.9	52.1
47380	RIDGEVILLE	99.2	99.0	0.0	0.0	0.1	0.1	0.6	1.0	6.6	6.8	7.2	7.1	4.9	25.6	28.1	12.4	1.3	74.9	39.3	50.6	49.4
	INDIANA	87.5	85.6	8.4	8.9	1.0	1.5	3.5	5.0	6.9	6.8	6.8	7.2	6.9	26.5	26.2	10.8	1.9	75.4	36.8	49.3	50.7
	UNITED STATES	75.1	72.0	12.3	12.7	3.8	4.6	12.5	15.7	6.8	6.7	6.6	7.1	6.9	27.0	26.0	10.9	1.9	75.7	36.9	49.2	50.8

#	POST OFFICE NAME	2009 Per Capita Income	2009 HH Income Base	2009 HOUSEHOLD INCOME DISTRIBUTION (%) Less than $25,000	$25,000 to $49,999	$50,000 to $99,999	$100,000 to $149,999	$150,000 or More	MEDIAN HOUSEHOLD INCOME 2009	2014	2009 National Centile	2009 State Centile	2009 Home Value Base	2009 HOME VALUE DISTRIBUTION (%) Less than $50,000	$50,000 to $89,999	$90,000 to $174,999	$175,000 to $399,999	$400,000 or More	2009 Median Home Value
47123	GRANTSBURG	20825	47	38.3	29.8	27.7	4.3	0.0	35544	35544	19	5	39	28.2	38.5	25.6	7.7	0.0	71667
47124	GREENVILLE	27261	1446	9.3	25.0	42.9	16.0	6.8	65357	66909	84	91	1305	5.5	12.0	44.6	34.9	3.0	147950
47125	HARDINSBURG	19981	717	25.2	36.3	30.7	5.2	2.6	40148	42752	33	9	625	25.1	27.5	35.5	10.2	1.6	87295
47126	HENRYVILLE	22428	1483	15.8	29.7	46.7	6.6	1.2	54973	57256	71	70	1210	17.7	19.0	40.4	19.8	3.1	110427
47129	CLARKSVILLE	24622	9210	23.5	31.8	35.6	5.9	3.1	44711	48469	47	22	5243	15.6	20.4	57.3	6.3	0.4	107141
47130	JEFFERSONVILLE	27835	19168	18.4	26.5	40.7	10.4	4.0	55093	57542	71	70	12791	8.6	18.4	57.4	14.5	1.1	117799
47135	LACONIA	21805	477	26.6	23.5	41.1	5.9	2.9	49893	53130	61	45	423	18.4	25.1	41.6	12.3	2.6	101645
47136	LANESVILLE	25653	1702	14.4	20.0	49.5	12.7	3.4	63132	63638	81	88	1523	6.1	17.9	47.1	27.5	1.4	131220
47137	LEAVENWORTH	18919	582	34.2	27.5	30.4	5.2	2.7	37854	38092	26	6	478	21.1	39.5	27.8	10.3	1.3	79250
47138	LEXINGTON	19582	1734	17.6	36.4	40.2	5.2	0.6	46657	49341	53	30	1488	17.9	25.5	43.1	12.2	1.3	100000
47140	MARENGO	16077	1020	33.4	39.3	23.7	2.8	0.7	33987	34717	15	4	794	25.1	36.0	34.5	2.9	1.5	74576
47141	MARYSVILLE	20888	621	18.5	35.3	37.2	5.3	3.7	47690	50702	56	34	548	18.1	23.4	38.5	17.9	2.2	107971
47142	MAUCKPORT	21859	367	16.3	38.4	41.1	2.5	1.6	45932	50417	51	26	321	15.3	39.3	27.7	17.1	0.6	83095
47143	MEMPHIS	27346	1374	14.8	27.4	41.6	11.1	5.1	59193	60200	76	80	1225	13.1	13.0	40.8	29.0	4.2	140427
47145	MILLTOWN	18768	873	28.4	28.6	36.3	6.0	0.7	45363	45551	49	24	755	17.9	31.8	44.0	5.6	0.8	90294
47147	NABB	20877	428	21.0	37.6	32.7	7.2	1.4	45114	46691	49	23	364	18.1	29.7	36.8	12.9	2.5	93333
47150	NEW ALBANY	25724	19762	22.6	26.2	38.2	8.5	4.5	51020	54126	64	52	12513	5.9	26.2	52.0	14.9	1.0	111718
47160	NEW MIDDLETOWN	24639	58	15.5	25.9	48.3	8.6	1.7	55708	57013	72	72	52	11.5	28.8	50.0	9.6	0.0	100000
47161	NEW SALISBURY	22516	1298	16.6	29.2	43.7	7.4	3.2	53638	57128	69	66	1104	18.2	22.8	39.4	17.2	2.4	104688
47162	NEW WASHINGTON	19098	298	21.5	32.2	37.2	7.0	2.0	47447	50153	55	34	247	15.8	32.0	36.0	13.4	2.8	94231
47163	OTISCO	22166	711	18.3	31.1	39.2	8.6	2.8	50509	53140	62	49	640	13.9	18.1	42.2	23.4	2.3	120604
47164	PALMYRA	21156	1341	19.8	30.8	40.4	6.9	2.1	49553	52953	60	44	1112	13.0	25.2	49.4	11.2	1.2	105375
47165	PEKIN	20275	2398	23.5	29.6	38.6	6.3	2.1	46796	49073	54	30	1966	15.4	29.9	42.9	10.6	1.2	94973
47166	RAMSEY	22926	483	20.5	27.5	40.8	7.9	3.3	51609	55124	65	56	415	17.1	22.9	45.1	13.0	1.9	103598
47167	SALEM	19836	5912	26.4	31.3	35.3	5.1	1.8	43443	45955	44	16	4646	15.7	30.3	41.6	11.0	1.3	95000
47170	SCOTTSBURG	20920	5626	24.7	33.5	33.9	5.5	2.3	44176	46544	46	20	4219	17.9	25.4	44.0	11.9	0.8	98003
47172	SELLERSBURG	28353	5553	12.0	28.9	41.2	12.7	5.2	59409	60513	77	81	4526	14.4	10.0	49.4	23.8	2.5	131621
47174	SULPHUR	18039	22	36.4	22.7	36.4	4.5	0.0	37303	32344	24	6	19	15.8	42.1	31.6	10.5	0.0	87000
47175	TASWELL	23153	303	25.7	29.4	36.6	6.3	2.0	45836	45858	51	26	271	21.8	31.0	36.5	7.7	3.0	87321
47177	UNDERWOOD	22985	505	14.5	34.5	41.8	6.7	2.6	50963	53593	63	51	447	18.8	19.7	38.9	20.8	1.8	108789
47201	COLUMBUS	25733	15701	19.8	26.9	38.6	10.4	4.4	53130	56399	68	65	10917	17.1	18.6	43.7	17.7	2.9	109572
47203	COLUMBUS	28636	10627	14.7	24.2	41.2	13.3	6.6	62640	64300	81	87	8224	14.0	6.6	57.1	21.0	1.3	131494
47220	BROWNSTOWN	21936	2201	20.9	32.2	38.0	6.2	2.7	47737	49704	56	34	1708	20.4	22.9	41.3	13.0	2.3	101100
47223	BUTLERVILLE	18216	563	17.6	37.5	37.8	5.3	1.8	47265	50027	55	33	462	22.3	26.2	43.1	7.1	1.3	91556
47224	CANAAN	17527	252	19.8	38.1	36.9	4.4	0.8	45732	46399	50	25	212	11.8	18.4	47.2	21.2	1.4	113953
47227	COMMISKEY	20572	497	18.3	35.2	38.8	6.2	1.4	47797	50039	56	35	421	15.7	27.3	43.7	11.4	1.9	98939
47229	CROTHERSVILLE	21424	1305	20.4	37.5	33.5	7.1	1.5	43212	45953	43	15	1057	22.4	31.2	37.7	7.8	0.9	86652
47230	DEPUTY	19822	826	18.6	37.2	37.7	5.9	0.6	45571	47764	50	25	723	19.1	26.1	45.6	8.0	1.1	95074
47231	DUPONT	18020	436	19.3	38.5	36.9	4.1	1.1	46224	47800	52	28	373	26.8	32.2	35.4	4.6	1.1	76304
47232	ELIZABETHTOWN	23530	1004	15.7	32.9	39.6	9.4	2.4	51191	54460	64	53	881	27.4	14.5	44.7	12.0	1.4	103865
47234	FLAT ROCK	22784	506	13.8	37.5	38.3	8.5	1.8	49128	52482	59	42	421	3.8	32.3	46.8	13.1	4.0	105993
47235	FREETOWN	23247	634	18.6	36.4	35.2	6.8	3.0	47108	48749	54	32	538	19.5	21.9	40.3	16.0	2.2	106471
47236	GRAMMER	24181	45	6.7	46.7	35.6	6.7	4.4	48574	51472	58	39	41	12.2	17.1	48.8	19.5	2.4	113750
47240	GREENSBURG	24014	8249	18.0	30.3	40.8	8.2	2.7	51396	53439	65	55	5953	9.8	18.5	54.0	15.9	1.7	114652
47243	HANOVER	20139	2105	18.7	29.8	43.3	6.5	1.7	51263	52101	64	54	1548	12.1	34.4	42.7	9.3	1.4	93464
47244	HARTSVILLE	23951	289	10.7	29.1	45.7	10.0	4.5	61185	62293	79	84	241	7.9	22.0	49.8	17.4	2.9	114250
47246	HOPE	21223	1574	17.3	28.0	44.2	8.5	2.0	54434	57862	70	68	1271	16.1	30.4	43.4	9.8	0.3	94588
47250	MADISON	23956	8925	23.5	27.7	38.4	7.6	2.8	48956	50502	59	41	6398	13.9	24.1	45.9	14.4	1.6	105674
47260	MEDORA	17436	720	30.0	36.1	28.9	4.0	1.0	38441	40126	28	7	615	35.9	28.6	27.0	7.6	0.8	68111
47264	NORMAN	21804	623	19.6	36.8	35.8	6.7	1.1	45941	47590	51	27	533	23.1	20.6	38.1	15.8	2.4	100164
47265	NORTH VERNON	21254	7880	20.4	31.1	39.9	6.4	2.1	48816	51218	58	40	6011	21.4	29.3	40.0	8.2	1.1	89133
47270	PARIS CROSSING	20532	379	14.8	37.5	40.4	5.5	1.8	47936	50989	56	36	334	12.9	24.3	48.5	12.9	1.5	111275
47272	SAINT PAUL	20223	780	17.9	33.1	42.4	4.7	1.8	49268	52277	59	43	620	22.1	24.8	43.1	9.2	0.8	92879
47273	SCIPIO	20556	772	19.4	29.7	38.9	10.8	1.3	50686	52575	63	50	669	20.5	20.5	48.0	9.6	1.5	107091
47274	SEYMOUR	23895	11626	19.3	29.1	41.6	6.8	3.2	51403	52598	65	55	8283	17.2	22.9	46.3	12.8	0.9	103216
47281	VALLONIA	19933	651	19.4	33.5	41.3	4.5	1.4	47796	50188	56	34	570	13.2	24.4	48.8	10.2	3.5	106422
47282	VERNON	20786	117	23.1	35.0	30.8	9.4	1.7	43728	45763	45	18	93	16.1	25.8	48.4	9.7	0.0	101974
47283	WESTPORT	22414	1387	16.4	32.4	41.9	7.1	2.3	50968	53141	63	52	1112	13.8	23.9	46.3	14.4	1.6	103846
47302	MUNCIE	20844	11929	32.4	31.7	28.1	5.1	2.6	37822	40265	26	6	8248	32.4	46.5	18.5	2.5	0.2	62100
47303	MUNCIE	19137	10875	34.8	28.9	29.4	5.0	1.9	36237	38485	21	5	6017	23.8	41.5	31.7	2.7	0.2	74894
47304	MUNCIE	30955	12450	18.7	24.6	38.0	12.3	6.4	58529	59053	76	79	8701	3.9	30.9	54.6	9.8	0.9	102912
47305	MUNCIE	15683	1930	52.8	27.6	17.2	1.3	1.1	23070	23835	2	1	549	58.3	31.3	8.7	1.1	0.5	44167
47306	MUNCIE	8466	143	96.5	0.0	0.0	3.5	0.0	8938	9324	0	0	5	0.0	0.0	100.0	0.0	0.0	145833
47320	ALBANY	23202	1607	18.0	37.2	35.1	6.3	3.4	46053	48483	51	27	1279	12.5	44.6	35.8	6.6	0.5	85628
47325	BROWNSVILLE	25716	280	16.8	25.0	46.4	9.3	2.5	56521	55980	73	74	238	16.0	23.9	47.1	13.0	0.0	102717
47326	BRYANT	15338	616	19.5	36.0	40.1	3.7	0.6	46108	48753	52	28	529	16.6	28.7	45.4	7.4	1.9	94455
47327	CAMBRIDGE CITY	21406	2140	21.8	33.6	35.9	6.5	2.1	45287	48462	49	24	1608	12.3	35.5	41.7	9.9	0.6	92400
47330	CENTERVILLE	22440	2070	18.0	32.1	39.8	7.9	2.3	49955	52474	61	45	1602	9.5	27.2	47.8	14.4	1.2	104297
47331	CONNERSVILLE	23727	9740	22.7	28.6	37.8	7.5	3.3	48490	51126	58	38	6920	11.8	32.8	46.6	7.9	0.8	94675
47334	DALEVILLE	28758	1361	12.6	25.9	44.9	10.2	6.5	63089	64436	81	88	1125	4.8	33.1	53.2	8.6	0.3	100321
47336	DUNKIRK	20935	1611	20.4	35.9	36.7	6.3	0.7	45752	47931	51	25	1259	23.3	47.4	25.2	3.2	1.0	73276
47338	EATON	23225	1098	18.8	32.2	38.8	7.7	2.5	49060	51747	59	42	918	23.1	37.9	32.9	5.7	0.4	77952
47339	ECONOMY	18891	227	24.7	34.8	30.8	8.8	0.9	44362	46185	46	21	197	11.7	22.3	46.7	17.8	1.5	114732
47340	FARMLAND	24086	1198	16.8	29.8	42.2	8.4	2.8	52856	53851	68	63	991	13.0	38.8	39.8	7.4	1.0	88669
47341	FOUNTAIN CITY	22869	759	18.8	28.3	41.0	8.8	3.0	52412	54237	67	60	640	9.1	25.5	50.9	14.4	0.2	104832
47342	GASTON	24207	1071	12.5	35.8	37.7	11.4	2.6	52632	55785	67	62	894	10.5	42.3	38.4	7.2	1.7	87706
47345	GREENS FORK	20304	515	16.9	33.2	42.3	6.2	1.4	49949	52077	61	45	430	19.3	21.6	44.0	12.6	2.6	98864
47346	HAGERSTOWN	23619	1583	20.0	30.4	39.9	8.0	1.8	49727	52395	60	44	1289	11.1	26.4	49.0	13.0	0.5	104275
47348	HARTFORD CITY	21143	4308	22.5	34.3	36.8	5.0	1.4	44194	46395	46	20	3402	15.8	43.6	34.7	5.3	0.6	81878
47352	LEWISVILLE	26603	352	16.2	27.3	38.9	9.9	7.7	59517	58758	77	81	284	10.2	28.2	45.8	13.7	2.1	99706
47353	LIBERTY	22309	2296	19.4	35.4	35.4	7.4	2.4	46412	48338	53	29	1736	12.2	28.2	44.8	12.5	2.4	99076
47354	LOSANTVILLE	20571	448	22.3	36.4	34.4	6.0	0.9	43626	45358	44	17	389	22.9	31.9	33.4	11.8	0.0	85595
47355	LYNN	21494	1176	23.2	31.3	37.4	6.9	1.2	45784	47797	51	26	915	16.1	36.0	43.6	3.8	0.5	88659
47356	MIDDLETOWN	24288	2566	17.9	28.7	40.2	10.3	2.9	52963	54791	68	63	2087	10.8	21.4	49.4	17.4	1.0	113386
47357	MILTON	21782	444	18.2	34.9	37.2	7.9	1.8	47170	50511	55	32	352	17.0	26.7	35.5	19.6	1.1	97857
47358	MODOC	19204	399	26.3	31.3	35.6	5.3	1.5	43794	45781	45	18	331	20.5	31.4	37.8	10.0	0.3	88289
47359	MONTPELIER	20255	1272	25.1	30.7	37.2	6.3	0.8	44353	46650	46	20	963	21.6	38.9	34.9	4.5	0.1	81398
47360	MOORELAND	20855	568	16.7	37.0	37.1	7.4	1.8	47398	50148	55	33	495	17.0	25.9	41.2	15.8	0.2	98068
47362	NEW CASTLE	23830	11861	24.2	29.4	34.9	8.2	3.3	46689	50016	53	30	8731	14.4	31.7	44.9	8.2	0.8	94008
47368	PARKER CITY	22238	1114	19.3	37.7	32.9	7.6	2.4	45110	46674	49	23	898	15.7	36.2	42.3	5.5	0.3	88426
47369	PENNVILLE	17931	540	23.5	38.3	33.9	3.1	1.1	39755	42746	32	8	409	31.8	30.3	29.3	6.1	2.4	73167
47371	PORTLAND	21436	4877	21.8	33.4	37.0	6.2	1.7	45709	48168	50	25	3738	14.5	35.1	41.6	8.0	0.8	90360
47373	REDKEY	19999	992	25.0	34.4	34.1	5.6	0.9	43362	45705	43	16	770	21.4	46.2	28.8	3.1	0.4	74286
47374	RICHMOND	22791	19680	27.0	29.2	34.4	6.5	2.9	43876	47182	45	18	12619	15.6	32.6	43.0	8.1	0.7	91905
47380	RIDGEVILLE	19292	833	23.8	35.7	35.3	4.2	1.1	42864	44820	42	14	675	23.7	39.1	29.8	6.2	1.2	75290
	INDIANA	26003		19.5	26.3	38.6	10.5	5.1	54105	56493				12.2	24.1	44.1	17.2	2.4	108938
	UNITED STATES	27277		20.9	24.4	35.3	11.7	7.6	54719	56938				9.3	13.1	31.6	32.6	13.5	162279

ZIP CODE #	POST OFFICE NAME	FINANCIAL SERVICES: Auto Loan	Home Loan	Invest-ments	Retire-ment Plans	THE HOME: Home Improvements: Home Repair	Lawn & Garden	Furnishings: Comput-ers & Hard-ware-Personal	Major Appli-ances	TV, Radio, Sound Equip-ment	Furni-ture	ENTERTAINMENT: Dine out/ Carry out	Sports Equip-ment	Fees & Tickets	Toys & Games	Travel	Cable TV	PERSONAL: Apparel & Services	Auto Repairs	Health Insur-ance	Pets & Supplies
47123	GRANTSBURG	77	55	63	53	55	73	57	66	63	56	62	51	46	66	52	69	42	63	70	81
47124	GREENVILLE	111	122	103	122	117	114	109	112	106	112	107	87	113	111	111	105	75	107	107	130
47125	HARDINSBURG	95	68	78	66	67	90	71	82	78	69	77	63	57	82	64	85	52	78	87	100
47126	HENRYVILLE	93	85	77	84	84	90	81	87	84	82	84	64	76	87	78	87	57	83	88	103
47129	CLARKSVILLE	79	72	68	73	70	79	79	77	82	74	81	59	75	81	75	85	56	80	85	92
47130	JEFFERSONVILLE	91	89	81	89	85	90	91	89	92	89	92	69	89	93	88	93	64	91	93	106
47135	LACONIA	85	78	77	81	79	92	77	86	79	69	78	65	70	81	76	84	53	80	89	100
47136	LANESVILLE	100	103	94	107	102	109	96	103	96	92	96	80	97	98	99	99	66	98	104	121
47137	LEAVENWORTH	86	62	77	60	62	84	64	77	71	61	69	58	51	72	60	77	46	72	80	92
47138	LEXINGTON	87	69	73	68	69	85	70	79	75	67	74	60	60	78	66	80	50	75	83	95
47140	MARENGO	73	49	67	47	49	71	52	64	60	50	58	50	40	61	48	66	39	60	68	78
47141	MARYSVILLE	87	80	78	82	81	93	78	88	81	72	79	66	72	83	78	85	54	81	90	102
47142	MAUCKPORT	96	69	79	67	69	91	72	83	80	70	78	64	58	83	65	87	52	79	88	102
47143	MEMPHIS	105	102	97	106	102	113	97	107	99	91	98	82	95	101	99	103	67	100	109	125
47145	MILLTOWN	86	62	72	60	61	82	64	75	71	62	70	58	51	74	59	78	47	71	79	91
47147	NABB	84	71	73	72	72	86	71	81	75	66	74	61	63	77	69	80	50	75	84	95
47150	NEW ALBANY	89	84	75	84	81	87	88	86	89	85	88	66	84	90	83	91	61	87	91	102
47160	NEW MIDDLETOWN	97	88	87	92	90	104	87	98	90	79	88	74	80	91	87	95	60	91	101	114
47161	NEW SALISBURY	96	89	78	86	87	91	84	89	87	87	87	64	79	90	80	89	59	86	89	105
47162	NEW WASHINGTON	85	78	73	78	78	86	75	83	78	72	77	61	70	80	74	81	52	78	84	97
47163	OTISCO	88	86	80	88	86	93	81	89	83	78	82	67	79	85	82	86	56	83	90	104
47164	PALMYRA	96	76	80	73	75	91	76	85	82	75	81	64	65	85	70	88	55	82	89	103
47165	PEKIN	90	76	74	74	75	85	74	81	79	75	78	60	66	82	70	83	53	78	83	97
47166	RAMSEY	94	86	79	85	85	92	83	89	85	82	85	66	77	88	80	89	58	85	90	105
47167	SALEM	85	65	75	64	65	84	68	78	74	64	73	59	57	76	64	80	49	74	83	94
47170	SCOTTSBURG	83	69	67	69	68	79	72	76	76	70	74	57	64	78	66	80	51	75	80	91
47172	SELLERSBURG	101	105	93	105	102	105	99	101	99	99	99	77	101	102	100	101	69	99	104	119
47174	SULPHUR	86	62	71	60	61	82	64	75	71	62	70	57	51	74	58	78	47	71	79	91
47175	TASWELL	101	73	83	71	72	96	75	88	84	74	82	67	61	87	69	91	55	83	93	107
47177	UNDERWOOD	92	84	80	85	84	93	82	90	84	79	84	67	76	87	80	88	57	85	91	105
47201	COLUMBUS	94	89	82	90	87	95	91	92	93	88	92	71	87	94	88	95	64	92	96	109
47203	COLUMBUS	106	106	100	107	105	108	103	105	104	103	104	81	103	106	103	105	72	104	106	124
47220	BROWNSTOWN	89	74	84	74	74	93	75	86	80	70	78	66	67	80	74	85	53	81	91	102
47223	BUTLERVILLE	99	71	81	69	70	94	74	86	82	72	80	66	59	85	67	89	54	81	90	104
47224	CANAAN	84	70	69	68	69	79	69	75	73	70	72	56	61	76	64	77	49	72	77	90
47227	COMMISKEY	85	74	76	76	75	89	74	84	77	68	76	64	66	79	72	82	52	78	87	98
47229	CROTHERSVILLE	93	70	78	69	70	90	72	83	79	69	77	64	59	82	67	85	52	78	87	100
47230	DEPUTY	90	68	76	67	68	88	70	81	76	67	75	62	58	79	65	83	50	76	85	97
47231	DUPONT	87	67	72	65	66	82	69	77	74	68	73	59	58	78	63	79	50	74	80	93
47232	ELIZABETHTOWN	94	87	82	89	88	97	84	92	87	81	86	69	79	89	83	90	59	87	94	108
47234	FLAT ROCK	91	83	82	86	85	97	82	92	84	74	83	70	76	86	82	89	56	85	95	107
47235	FREETOWN	97	78	83	78	78	97	79	90	84	74	83	69	68	87	75	91	56	84	94	107
47236	GRAMMER	93	85	84	88	87	100	84	95	86	76	85	72	77	88	84	91	58	87	97	110
47240	GREENSBURG	89	84	79	86	83	93	84	89	86	79	85	68	80	87	83	89	58	86	93	105
47243	HANOVER	88	73	73	73	73	86	77	82	81	74	80	62	68	83	72	86	54	81	88	98
47244	HARTSVILLE	104	96	94	100	98	112	94	106	97	86	95	80	88	99	94	102	65	98	108	123
47246	HOPE	93	84	80	85	82	96	83	89	86	79	85	69	77	89	81	91	58	86	94	107
47250	MADISON	86	76	77	76	77	87	78	83	82	75	81	62	73	82	76	86	55	82	89	98
47260	MEDORA	82	56	73	54	56	79	59	71	67	57	65	55	46	69	55	74	44	68	75	87
47264	NORMAN	94	71	78	69	70	89	72	83	79	71	78	63	60	82	67	85	52	79	86	100
47265	NORTH VERNON	86	76	71	76	74	85	78	82	81	74	79	62	71	83	73	84	54	80	85	97
47270	PARIS CROSSING	86	77	77	80	78	91	76	86	79	69	77	65	70	80	76	84	53	80	89	100
47272	SAINT PAUL	98	73	82	72	73	95	75	87	83	72	81	67	62	86	69	90	55	82	92	105
47273	SCIPIO	91	84	74	81	81	85	80	84	82	82	82	62	75	86	76	84	56	82	84	99
47274	SEYMOUR	88	85	74	85	82	90	84	86	86	81	85	66	81	88	81	88	58	85	90	102
47281	VALLONIA	84	71	73	72	71	86	71	81	75	66	73	61	62	77	69	80	50	75	84	95
47282	VERNON	87	79	78	82	81	93	78	88	80	70	79	67	72	82	78	85	54	81	91	102
47283	WESTPORT	88	81	73	82	78	91	81	85	84	76	83	66	77	86	78	88	57	83	91	102
47302	MUNCIE	73	62	60	63	60	72	68	69	72	64	70	53	62	73	63	76	48	70	76	83
47303	MUNCIE	69	54	51	56	52	60	75	62	72	64	71	51	61	71	60	72	49	68	66	76
47304	MUNCIE	101	97	94	100	96	101	105	99	103	100	104	77	102	103	100	104	72	102	104	118
47305	MUNCIE	45	35	32	37	33	38	48	40	50	43	50	32	42	49	40	52	35	46	46	50
47306	MUNCIE	22	9	9	11	8	11	31	15	24	21	25	16	18	24	16	22	18	22	15	21
47320	ALBANY	85	81	74	84	79	91	80	85	82	74	81	66	76	84	79	86	55	82	90	101
47325	BROWNSVILLE	107	98	97	102	100	115	96	109	99	87	98	82	89	101	96	105	67	100	112	126
47326	BRYANT	85	69	73	70	70	86	70	80	74	65	73	61	61	77	67	80	50	75	83	95
47327	CAMBRIDGE CITY	82	74	72	76	73	87	74	81	77	68	76	62	69	78	73	81	52	77	86	96
47330	CENTERVILLE	83	84	71	86	80	89	82	83	83	77	82	65	81	84	81	85	57	82	89	99
47331	CONNERSVILLE	87	77	76	78	76	89	80	84	84	75	82	64	74	84	77	88	56	83	91	100
47334	DALEVILLE	94	109	101	107	107	115	95	103	100	95	100	74	106	99	104	105	70	100	115	119
47336	DUNKIRK	81	64	74	64	65	83	69	78	74	62	72	59	59	74	66	80	49	75	85	93
47338	EATON	90	81	77	81	79	93	80	86	84	77	83	66	75	86	78	89	57	84	93	103
47339	ECONOMY	80	73	73	76	75	86	72	82	75	65	73	62	67	76	72	79	50	75	84	95
47340	FARMLAND	90	87	77	90	84	96	86	90	88	80	87	70	84	90	85	92	60	88	96	107
47341	FOUNTAIN CITY	89	85	76	88	83	95	85	89	86	78	85	69	81	88	83	90	58	86	95	106
47342	GASTON	93	92	82	95	90	100	89	94	91	84	90	73	87	93	89	94	62	91	99	111
47345	GREENS FORK	86	78	78	82	80	92	77	87	80	70	78	66	71	81	77	84	53	81	90	101
47346	HAGERSTOWN	86	81	75	84	80	92	81	86	83	74	81	67	77	84	80	86	56	82	91	102
47348	HARTFORD CITY	79	66	68	67	66	81	70	76	74	64	72	58	62	75	66	79	49	74	82	90
47352	LEWISVILLE	103	96	94	99	97	112	94	105	97	85	95	79	88	98	94	102	65	98	110	122
47353	LIBERTY	88	78	85	79	77	94	78	87	81	72	80	68	71	82	78	85	54	84	92	104
47354	LOSANTVILLE	86	68	74	69	69	86	69	80	75	65	73	61	60	77	66	80	50	75	83	95
47355	LYNN	84	71	75	71	70	87	73	81	77	67	76	62	65	78	70	82	51	77	87	96
47356	MIDDLETOWN	92	89	85	90	88	100	85	93	88	80	87	70	82	90	86	93	60	88	98	109
47357	MILTON	94	75	85	75	75	95	76	88	81	71	80	68	65	83	73	87	54	83	92	106
47358	MODOC	83	68	72	69	69	84	69	79	73	64	72	60	60	75	66	79	49	73	82	93
47359	MONTPELIER	84	64	76	64	65	85	67	79	73	62	71	60	56	74	64	80	48	74	84	94
47360	MOORELAND	85	78	77	81	79	92	77	87	79	69	78	66	71	81	77	84	53	80	89	101
47362	NEW CASTLE	85	76	74	77	75	88	80	83	83	74	82	63	74	84	76	88	56	82	91	99
47368	PARKER CITY	88	73	83	74	75	93	75	88	80	67	78	66	66	80	74	86	53	81	92	102
47369	PENNVILLE	78	61	67	61	62	78	63	72	68	59	66	55	53	70	59	73	45	68	75	86
47371	PORTLAND	85	71	75	72	71	87	74	82	78	68	76	62	65	79	71	84	52	78	88	97
47373	REDKEY	77	63	68	63	63	79	68	75	72	61	70	57	58	72	64	77	47	72	81	88
47374	RICHMOND	79	70	67	71	69	79	77	77	80	71	78	59	71	79	72	83	54	78	84	92
47380	RIDGEVILLE	83	67	71	67	67	83	68	77	72	64	71	59	58	75	64	78	48	73	81	92
	INDIANA	97	91	86	93	89	96	93	94	95	91	94	73	90	96	90	97	65	94	97	112
	UNITED STATES	100	100	100	100	100	100	100	100	100	100	100	100	100	100	100	100	100	100	100	100

ZIP CODE			POPULATION			2000-2009 ANNUAL RATE		HOUSEHOLDS					FAMILIES		
#	POST OFFICE NAME	COUNTY FIPS CODE	2000	2009	2014	% Rate	State Centile	2000	2009	2014	% Annual Rate 2000-2009	2009 Average HH Size	2000	2009	% Annual Rate 2000-2009
47381	SALAMONIA	075	190	195	195	0.3	56	69	72	72	0.5	2.71	56	57	0.2
47382	SARATOGA	135	261	254	246	-0.3	22	106	105	102	-0.1	2.42	82	78	-0.5
47383	SELMA	035	2764	2719	2662	-0.2	27	1055	1069	1056	0.1	2.52	817	801	-0.2
47384	SHIRLEY	065	2418	2670	2795	1.1	84	892	1007	1063	1.3	2.65	682	742	0.9
47385	SPICELAND	065	1801	1724	1672	-0.5	13	721	713	698	-0.1	2.42	540	516	-0.5
47386	SPRINGPORT	065	1293	1247	1212	-0.4	18	491	488	478	-0.1	2.56	407	394	-0.4
47387	STRAUGHN	065	803	810	801	0.1	43	303	316	315	0.5	2.56	236	238	0.1
47390	UNION CITY	135	5558	5251	5073	-0.6	8	2301	2229	2170	-0.3	2.34	1544	1435	-0.8
47392	WEBSTER	177	175	168	163	-0.4	18	65	63	61	-0.3	2.67	53	50	-0.6
47393	WILLIAMSBURG	177	1294	1279	1254	-0.1	31	423	421	414	-0.1	3.04	352	342	-0.3
47394	WINCHESTER	135	8696	8236	7971	-0.6	8	3542	3434	3345	-0.3	2.34	2448	2282	-0.8
47396	YORKTOWN	035	6543	6540	6432	0.0	37	2493	2549	2523	0.2	2.54	1869	1849	-0.1
47401	BLOOMINGTON	105	33121	36983	39022	1.2	86	14457	16046	16943	1.1	2.24	7474	7864	0.6
47403	BLOOMINGTON	105	25499	28946	30722	1.4	89	10731	12250	13055	1.4	2.31	6475	6907	0.7
47404	BLOOMINGTON	105	18077	19300	19992	0.7	73	7484	8072	8411	0.8	2.33	4250	4265	0.0
47405	BLOOMINGTON	105	833	844	849	0.1	43	1	1	1	0.0	3.00	0	0	0.0
47406	BLOOMINGTON	105	7755	7777	7797	0.0	37	453	488	510	0.8	1.62	138	130	-0.6
47408	BLOOMINGTON	105	25512	26534	27222	0.4	60	10069	10567	10928	0.5	2.10	3693	3606	-0.3
47421	BEDFORD	093	28315	27795	27478	-0.2	27	11603	11752	11730	0.1	2.32	8012	7802	-0.3
47424	BLOOMFIELD	055	9829	9499	9270	-0.4	18	4021	3975	3900	-0.1	2.36	2841	2706	-0.5
47427	COAL CITY	119	1748	1958	2028	1.2	86	637	729	759	1.5	2.69	499	553	1.1
47429	ELLETTSVILLE	105	7094	7271	7467	0.3	56	2670	2742	2822	0.3	2.65	1959	1928	-0.2
47431	FREEDOM	119	1155	1168	1141	0.1	43	450	469	464	0.4	2.49	357	362	0.2
47432	FRENCH LICK	117	4233	4303	4322	0.2	49	1727	1804	1826	0.5	2.32	1174	1182	0.1
47433	GOSPORT	119	4412	4480	4498	0.2	49	1639	1699	1717	0.4	2.60	1243	1241	0.0
47436	HELTONVILLE	093	1773	1685	1654	-0.5	13	707	697	690	-0.2	2.42	532	507	-0.5
47438	JASONVILLE	021	4553	4320	4189	-0.6	8	1766	1688	1640	-0.5	2.50	1236	1140	-0.9
47441	LINTON	055	10102	11163	11300	1.1	84	4184	4743	4834	1.4	2.30	2820	3067	0.9
47443	LYONS	055	1746	1634	1578	-0.7	5	653	617	597	-0.6	2.56	478	438	-0.9
47446	MITCHELL	093	9790	9877	9867	0.1	43	3902	4104	4155	0.5	2.38	2821	2848	0.1
47448	NASHVILLE	013	7217	7438	7472	0.3	56	2981	3160	3200	0.6	2.32	2151	2193	0.2
47449	NEWBERRY	055	392	369	356	-0.7	5	159	153	149	-0.4	2.41	118	110	-0.8
47451	OOLITIC	093	1203	1243	1255	0.4	60	525	564	576	0.8	2.20	355	364	0.3
47452	ORLEANS	117	4554	4528	4486	-0.1	31	1741	1765	1760	0.1	2.57	1234	1205	-0.3
47453	OWENSBURG	055	1327	1155	1097	-1.5	1	526	468	447	-1.3	2.47	393	339	-1.6
47454	PAOLI	117	7326	7368	7353	0.1	43	2890	2992	3013	0.4	2.40	2010	1997	-0.1
47456	QUINCY	119	2380	2564	2622	0.8	76	901	989	1019	1.0	2.59	695	738	0.7
47459	SOLSBERRY	055	2365	2403	2374	0.2	49	907	944	940	0.4	2.54	682	689	0.1
47460	SPENCER	119	10242	10943	11094	0.7	73	3946	4307	4389	1.0	2.49	2904	3076	0.6
47462	SPRINGVILLE	093	3649	3491	3444	-0.5	13	1334	1309	1302	-0.2	2.67	1036	987	-0.5
47465	SWITZ CITY	055	913	851	826	-0.8	4	348	329	321	-0.6	2.53	257	238	-0.8
47468	UNIONVILLE	105	1146	1143	1141	0.0	37	481	484	486	0.1	2.36	357	346	-0.3
47469	WEST BADEN SPRINGS	117	1797	1906	1953	0.6	70	723	796	822	1.0	2.39	514	544	0.6
47470	WILLIAMS	093	2588	2597	2582	0.0	37	963	996	1001	0.4	2.61	734	736	0.0
47471	WORTHINGTON	055	2447	2301	2219	-0.7	5	1020	973	942	-0.5	2.36	707	652	-0.9
47501	WASHINGTON	027	16459	16607	16686	0.1	43	6545	6672	6713	0.2	2.42	4386	4287	-0.2
47512	BICKNELL	083	4648	4304	4175	-0.8	4	1899	1787	1743	-0.7	2.38	1295	1166	-1.1
47513	BIRDSEYE	037	1658	1682	1665	0.2	49	643	676	676	0.5	2.49	460	464	0.1
47514	BRANCHVILLE	123	1213	1561	1624	2.8	96	106	119	130	1.3	6.84	88	96	0.9
47515	BRISTOW	123	1027	1096	1127	0.7	73	367	415	434	1.3	2.53	289	316	1.0
47516	BRUCEVILLE	083	1160	1247	1262	0.8	76	466	515	524	1.1	2.42	353	376	0.7
47519	CANNELBURG	027	1568	1593	1602	0.2	49	446	459	463	0.3	3.39	377	378	0.0
47520	CANNELTON	123	2554	2618	2640	0.3	56	1022	1086	1113	0.7	2.37	695	702	0.1
47521	CELESTINE	037	824	851	858	0.3	56	281	300	306	0.7	2.84	225	233	0.4
47522	CRANE	101	223	205	196	-0.9	3	99	94	91	-0.6	2.18	74	68	-0.9
47523	DALE	173	3223	3252	3256	0.1	43	1196	1239	1250	0.4	2.57	876	871	-0.1
47524	DECKER	083	562	552	549	-0.2	27	217	219	219	0.1	2.52	158	153	-0.3
47525	DERBY	123	615	641	655	0.4	60	247	273	284	1.1	2.35	191	203	0.7
47527	DUBOIS	037	2063	2167	2211	0.5	66	771	838	863	0.9	2.59	570	598	0.5
47528	EDWARDSPORT	083	534	507	493	-0.6	8	214	207	204	-0.4	2.45	155	143	-0.9
47529	ELNORA	027	2424	2433	2431	0.0	37	792	801	800	0.1	3.04	616	604	-0.2
47531	EVANSTON	147	596	612	605	0.3	56	216	228	227	0.6	2.68	169	173	0.3
47532	FERDINAND	037	4641	4720	4712	0.2	49	1566	1641	1651	0.5	2.72	1205	1224	0.2
47537	GENTRYVILLE	173	783	808	823	0.3	56	280	296	303	0.6	2.73	229	236	0.3
47541	HOLLAND	037	1336	1402	1432	0.5	66	499	540	558	0.9	2.60	374	390	0.5
47542	HUNTINGBURG	037	8737	9065	9190	0.4	60	3247	3448	3522	0.7	2.57	2338	2393	0.3
47546	JASPER	037	19333	20887	21466	0.8	76	7427	8243	8538	1.1	2.49	5266	5641	0.7
47550	LAMAR	147	269	281	282	0.5	66	99	106	108	0.7	2.65	78	82	0.5
47551	LEOPOLD	123	519	556	573	0.7	73	196	221	233	1.3	2.43	152	166	1.0
47552	LINCOLN CITY	147	248	289	306	1.7	92	86	102	109	1.9	2.83	70	81	1.6
47553	LOOGOOTEE	101	6163	6030	5897	-0.2	27	2473	2501	2470	0.1	2.39	1680	1631	-0.3
47556	MARIAH HILL	147	195	214	220	1.0	81	70	78	81	1.2	2.65	56	60	0.7
47557	MONROE CITY	083	1326	1275	1250	-0.4	18	528	522	516	-0.1	2.44	387	368	-0.5
47558	MONTGOMERY	027	2990	3040	3056	0.2	49	911	938	945	0.3	3.22	744	747	0.0
47561	OAKTOWN	083	2242	2206	2183	-0.2	27	876	884	880	0.1	2.43	635	615	-0.3
47562	ODON	027	4753	4905	4955	0.3	56	1581	1652	1672	0.5	2.94	1229	1240	0.1
47564	OTWELL	125	1427	1473	1467	0.3	56	575	607	608	0.6	2.43	409	415	0.2
47567	PETERSBURG	125	6161	6127	6033	-0.1	31	2482	2506	2476	0.1	2.38	1752	1704	-0.3
47568	PLAINVILLE	027	930	935	938	0.1	43	372	378	379	0.2	2.45	281	276	-0.2
47574	ROME	123	223	212	211	-0.5	13	88	88	89	0.0	2.41	69	67	-0.3
47575	SAINT ANTHONY	037	1283	1319	1319	0.3	56	456	485	490	0.7	2.66	358	370	0.4
47576	SAINT CROIX	123	416	434	442	0.5	66	150	165	171	1.0	2.63	118	126	0.7
47577	SAINT MEINRAD	147	1031	1041	1028	0.1	43	340	354	353	0.4	2.66	264	265	0.0
47578	SANDBORN	083	886	853	836	-0.4	18	375	368	363	-0.2	2.30	253	236	-0.7
47579	SANTA CLAUS	147	2384	2757	2912	1.6	91	857	1011	1074	1.8	2.73	697	798	1.5
47580	SCHNELLVILLE	037	272	280	282	0.3	56	97	103	105	0.7	2.72	77	79	0.3
47581	SHOALS	101	4439	4269	4142	-0.4	18	1776	1773	1740	0.0	2.38	1255	1205	-0.4
47585	STENDAL	125	444	466	466	0.5	66	181	193	193	0.7	2.41	136	140	0.3
47586	TELL CITY	123	11396	10882	10676	-0.5	13	4714	4659	4644	-0.1	2.20	3180	3011	-0.6
47588	TROY	123	412	361	347	-1.4	1	180	166	162	-0.9	2.16	132	117	-1.3
47590	VELPEN	125	671	708	710	0.6	70	243	261	262	0.8	2.71	183	190	0.4
47591	VINCENNES	083	26809	25622	25177	-0.5	13	10546	10379	10254	-0.2	2.26	6581	6171	-0.7
47597	WHEATLAND	083	1089	1137	1139	0.5	66	431	463	467	0.8	2.45	319	329	0.3
47598	WINSLOW	125	3439	3599	3591	0.5	66	1349	1434	1436	0.7	2.51	981	1005	0.3
47601	BOONVILLE	173	14113	14572	14876	0.3	56	5442	5787	5969	0.7	2.47	4015	4104	0.2
	INDIANA					0.7					0.8	2.49			0.4
	UNITED STATES					1.0					1.1	2.59			0.9

ZIP CODE #	POST OFFICE NAME	RACE (%) White 2000	White 2009	Black 2000	Black 2009	Asian/Pacific 2000	Asian/Pacific 2009	% Hispanic Origin 2000	% Hispanic Origin 2009	2009 AGE DISTRIBUTION (%) 0-4	5-9	10-14	15-19	20-24	25-44	45-64	65-84	85+	18+	MEDIAN AGE 2009	% 2009 Males	% 2009 Females
47381	SALAMONIA	96.8	95.9	0.0	0.0	1.6	2.6	1.1	2.1	7.2	7.2	7.2	7.7	6.7	26.2	26.7	10.3	1.0	73.8	36.6	50.8	49.2
47382	SARATOGA	99.2	98.8	0.0	0.0	0.0	0.4	1.5	2.4	7.5	7.9	7.9	6.3	5.1	24.0	29.1	11.0	1.2	72.8	38.7	52.0	48.0
47383	SELMA	98.3	97.8	0.4	0.5	0.1	0.2	0.4	0.6	6.3	6.3	6.5	6.5	5.6	24.0	29.5	13.5	1.9	76.8	41.4	49.1	50.9
47384	SHIRLEY	99.0	98.7	0.1	0.1	0.2	0.4	0.5	0.6	7.0	7.1	7.3	6.8	5.4	26.5	26.7	11.6	1.6	74.5	37.9	49.5	50.5
47385	SPICELAND	98.9	98.6	0.1	0.1	0.1	0.1	1.3	1.9	6.0	6.3	6.4	5.5	4.4	27.0	28.8	13.7	1.9	77.8	41.1	48.4	51.6
47386	SPRINGPORT	98.9	98.8	0.5	0.5	0.2	0.2	0.5	0.7	5.4	6.2	6.9	6.3	4.0	22.7	33.8	13.6	1.3	77.6	44.0	52.0	48.0
47387	STRAUGHN	99.1	98.9	0.2	0.2	0.1	0.1	0.7	1.1	4.0	4.2	4.8	7.0	4.8	26.5	32.1	14.6	2.0	82.7	44.0	49.1	50.9
47390	UNION CITY	95.7	94.1	0.7	0.9	0.3	0.4	3.3	5.0	7.1	6.7	6.5	6.8	5.9	24.2	26.4	14.2	2.3	75.7	39.2	48.9	51.1
47392	WEBSTER	98.3	97.6	0.6	0.6	0.0	0.0	0.6	0.6	4.2	4.8	8.3	9.5	3.6	25.0	32.7	10.7	1.2	75.0	41.8	51.2	48.8
47393	WILLIAMSBURG	97.9	97.3	0.2	0.2	0.0	0.0	1.2	2.0	6.2	6.7	7.5	8.3	5.6	24.9	29.1	10.6	1.2	74.4	38.7	52.5	47.5
47394	WINCHESTER	98.6	98.2	0.1	0.2	0.3	0.4	1.1	1.6	6.4	6.5	6.4	5.8	5.3	24.1	27.9	14.7	2.9	77.1	41.3	48.6	51.4
47396	YORKTOWN	98.0	97.4	0.7	0.9	0.2	0.4	0.7	1.1	6.1	6.4	7.0	6.7	5.0	23.1	30.0	13.7	2.0	76.4	41.9	47.8	52.2
47401	BLOOMINGTON	91.3	88.3	2.1	2.3	3.9	6.0	1.9	2.8	5.1	4.7	4.8	6.4	16.8	26.4	23.9	10.3	1.7	82.4	33.0	48.7	51.3
47403	BLOOMINGTON	93.1	91.3	3.3	3.9	1.2	1.9	1.4	2.2	7.1	6.4	6.1	6.0	9.2	30.2	23.7	9.7	1.6	76.8	34.7	49.0	51.0
47404	BLOOMINGTON	91.9	89.9	3.7	4.3	1.2	1.9	1.7	2.5	6.6	5.8	5.6	7.0	14.8	26.6	23.7	8.5	1.3	78.3	32.0	50.3	49.7
47405	BLOOMINGTON	81.2	75.7	8.2	8.8	8.0	12.2	2.9	4.0	0.1	0.1	0.0	58.6	33.6	6.3	0.9	0.0	0.2	99.5	19.2	44.7	55.3
47406	BLOOMINGTON	82.0	77.2	5.6	6.0	9.5	13.5	2.4	3.2	0.9	0.5	0.2	54.4	34.4	8.4	1.0	0.2	0.1	98.2	19.4	45.6	54.4
47408	BLOOMINGTON	87.9	84.2	3.2	3.6	5.8	8.4	2.6	3.7	2.4	2.5	2.7	14.4	33.0	20.4	15.4	7.4	1.9	90.5	24.2	50.4	49.6
47421	BEDFORD	97.7	97.0	0.5	0.6	0.4	0.6	1.1	1.5	6.1	6.2	6.4	6.1	4.9	24.9	28.3	14.4	2.5	77.4	41.5	48.9	51.1
47424	BLOOMFIELD	98.5	98.1	0.1	0.1	0.2	0.3	0.7	1.1	6.1	6.3	6.5	6.3	5.0	26.1	29.4	12.3	1.9	77.0	40.6	50.6	49.4
47427	COAL CITY	98.5	98.2	0.0	0.0	0.1	0.2	1.1	1.5	6.3	6.6	7.0	7.7	6.3	23.9	27.9	12.9	1.4	75.3	39.3	49.4	50.6
47429	ELLETTSVILLE	96.6	95.7	1.1	1.3	0.6	0.9	0.8	1.3	6.7	6.8	7.2	7.4	5.6	27.4	29.0	9.0	1.1	74.7	37.8	49.6	50.4
47431	FREEDOM	98.2	97.9	0.3	0.3	0.3	0.3	1.6	2.3	5.3	5.9	6.6	6.4	4.4	23.9	32.4	13.9	1.3	78.0	43.4	51.2	48.8
47432	FRENCH LICK	96.5	96.0	1.9	2.2	0.2	0.3	0.3	0.4	5.8	5.9	6.0	6.1	5.4	23.4	29.1	15.8	2.5	78.5	43.1	49.8	50.2
47433	GOSPORT	98.4	98.1	0.3	0.4	0.2	0.4	0.6	0.9	6.0	6.2	6.7	7.0	5.0	24.6	30.2	12.5	1.8	76.5	41.4	50.2	49.8
47436	HELTONVILLE	98.9	98.6	0.0	0.0	0.3	0.4	0.6	0.8	6.2	6.8	7.1	5.8	3.9	26.9	29.6	12.6	1.1	76.3	40.7	50.9	49.1
47438	JASONVILLE	98.7	98.3	0.1	0.1	0.2	0.3	0.8	1.3	6.5	6.5	6.5	6.8	6.2	25.2	26.4	13.1	2.8	76.3	39.0	48.5	51.5
47441	LINTON	98.5	98.1	0.1	0.1	0.3	0.5	1.0	1.4	5.9	6.1	6.3	5.9	5.0	23.7	28.0	15.8	3.3	78.0	42.8	47.9	52.1
47443	LYONS	99.1	98.9	0.0	0.0	0.2	0.2	0.5	0.9	6.8	6.7	6.7	6.4	5.1	24.1	27.7	13.3	3.2	75.4	40.6	49.4	50.6
47446	MITCHELL	98.4	98.0	0.3	0.4	0.1	0.1	0.6	0.8	6.6	6.5	6.8	7.0	5.5	24.7	27.8	13.0	2.1	75.8	40.3	48.9	51.1
47448	NASHVILLE	98.1	97.7	0.3	0.3	0.3	0.4	0.8	1.1	4.8	5.3	5.9	5.6	4.1	23.1	35.3	14.1	1.8	80.2	45.7	49.6	50.4
47449	NEWBERRY	99.2	98.9	0.0	0.0	0.0	0.0	0.8	1.1	6.8	6.8	6.8	6.0	4.6	24.1	29.3	14.1	1.6	75.9	41.7	52.3	47.7
47451	OOLITIC	98.8	98.5	0.0	0.0	0.1	0.1	0.2	0.3	6.3	6.5	6.5	5.7	4.5	25.0	28.7	14.8	1.9	77.1	41.3	47.0	53.0
47452	ORLEANS	98.4	98.0	0.2	0.3	0.1	0.1	0.6	0.9	7.9	7.6	7.8	7.5	5.4	24.7	25.3	11.8	2.1	72.1	36.7	49.1	50.9
47453	OWENSBURG	98.9	98.7	0.0	0.0	0.0	0.0	1.1	1.7	5.9	6.3	7.1	5.5	5.5	28.8	30.5	9.2	1.2	77.2	38.5	52.2	47.8
47454	PAOLI	98.5	98.2	0.2	0.2	0.2	0.3	0.5	0.8	6.6	6.7	6.6	6.5	5.5	24.7	28.3	12.7	2.3	76.1	40.1	49.0	51.0
47456	QUINCY	98.4	98.0	0.3	0.3	0.1	0.2	0.6	0.8	5.9	6.2	6.6	6.8	5.1	24.9	30.3	13.1	1.1	77.0	41.4	50.7	49.3
47459	SOLSBERRY	98.9	98.5	0.1	0.1	0.1	0.2	0.5	0.7	6.7	6.7	6.8	6.8	5.2	28.5	29.3	9.0	0.9	75.4	38.2	50.5	49.5
47460	SPENCER	98.2	97.9	0.2	0.2	0.2	0.3	0.7	0.9	6.7	6.7	6.9	6.5	5.7	25.5	28.7	11.5	1.8	75.6	39.4	48.9	51.1
47462	SPRINGVILLE	97.6	97.0	0.1	0.1	0.3	0.5	1.2	1.6	6.4	6.6	6.8	6.7	5.1	28.0	29.0	10.4	1.0	76.1	38.8	51.1	48.9
47465	SWITZ CITY	98.0	97.4	0.1	0.1	0.3	0.5	0.9	1.5	6.5	6.7	7.1	6.5	4.6	23.7	29.4	13.9	1.8	75.8	41.2	49.6	50.4
47468	UNIONVILLE	98.3	97.7	0.0	0.0	0.3	0.5	0.8	1.2	4.9	5.9	6.6	6.5	4.5	24.9	35.5	10.1	1.0	78.1	43.0	51.1	48.9
47469	WEST BADEN SPRINGS	97.0	96.3	1.0	1.2	0.4	0.5	1.5	2.2	6.4	6.7	6.5	5.8	5.5	24.3	30.4	12.7	1.7	76.9	40.6	48.4	51.6
47470	WILLIAMS	98.1	97.8	0.1	0.1	0.2	0.3	0.6	0.8	6.0	6.4	6.9	6.9	5.1	24.7	31.0	11.9	1.1	76.4	40.8	49.3	50.7
47471	WORTHINGTON	98.7	98.5	0.0	0.0	0.2	0.2	0.4	0.6	5.6	5.6	5.9	6.3	5.5	23.6	29.2	15.9	2.5	79.1	43.1	48.5	51.5
47501	WASHINGTON	96.3	95.0	0.8	0.9	0.4	0.5	3.2	4.8	6.6	6.4	6.6	6.4	5.9	24.0	27.1	14.0	3.0	76.4	40.2	48.7	51.3
47512	BICKNELL	98.4	98.0	0.4	0.4	0.2	0.2	0.5	0.7	7.0	6.8	6.5	6.4	5.9	23.6	26.8	14.5	2.5	75.8	40.2	48.0	52.0
47513	BIRDSEYE	99.0	98.9	0.0	0.0	0.1	0.2	1.5	2.2	7.5	7.7	7.7	6.7	5.5	26.6	27.0	9.9	1.3	72.9	37.3	50.8	49.2
47514	BRANCHVILLE	85.3	87.6	12.7	10.5	0.1	0.1	1.2	1.1	3.8	3.6	3.8	6.5	15.4	42.2	19.2	4.9	0.6	85.8	33.0	74.1	25.9
47515	BRISTOW	98.4	98.6	1.1	0.9	0.0	0.0	0.7	0.6	5.6	5.7	5.9	6.4	6.1	27.9	29.6	11.3	1.5	78.8	39.8	53.7	46.3
47516	BRUCEVILLE	98.9	98.6	0.2	0.2	0.1	0.1	0.5	0.8	6.1	6.3	6.2	6.6	5.5	23.3	30.6	13.9	1.5	77.5	42.3	49.1	50.9
47519	CANNELBURG	99.2	98.9	0.0	0.0	0.1	0.2	0.6	1.0	11.0	10.6	10.1	9.2	5.4	24.8	19.6	7.5	1.8	62.5	27.8	49.7	50.3
47520	CANNELTON	98.8	98.9	0.1	0.1	0.0	0.0	0.5	0.5	6.3	6.4	6.7	6.6	5.2	27.1	29.2	10.9	1.5	76.4	38.8	51.0	49.0
47521	CELESTINE	99.9	99.9	0.0	0.0	0.1	0.1	0.4	0.5	8.1	8.5	8.3	6.6	4.6	25.6	28.4	8.5	1.4	70.9	37.1	52.3	47.7
47522	CRANE	98.2	98.0	0.0	0.0	0.4	0.5	0.4	0.5	6.3	6.8	7.3	6.3	3.9	21.5	31.7	14.6	1.5	75.1	43.1	49.3	50.7
47523	DALE	95.7	93.8	0.5	0.6	0.1	0.2	4.9	7.3	6.5	6.9	7.2	6.9	5.4	25.9	27.9	11.2	2.2	75.0	38.3	49.1	50.9
47524	DECKER	99.3	99.1	0.5	0.7	0.0	0.0	0.4	0.5	5.4	7.2	8.5	8.9	4.3	23.9	29.5	10.0	2.2	73.6	39.0	51.8	48.2
47525	DERBY	99.3	99.4	0.0	0.0	0.0	0.0	0.2	0.3	4.7	5.1	6.4	7.8	4.8	24.6	34.2	10.8	1.6	78.3	42.5	51.5	48.5
47527	DUBOIS	99.3	99.1	0.0	0.0	0.1	0.2	0.5	0.8	7.1	7.0	7.1	6.7	6.0	27.4	27.5	9.8	1.4	74.7	36.8	50.9	49.1
47528	EDWARDSPORT	97.2	96.6	0.4	0.4	0.2	0.2	1.5	2.2	4.5	4.5	7.5	8.9	5.7	26.2	29.2	11.6	1.8	77.9	40.8	50.3	49.7
47529	ELNORA	98.9	98.5	0.0	0.0	0.1	0.2	0.7	1.0	8.7	8.5	8.2	7.8	5.2	24.0	24.8	11.0	1.7	69.5	34.4	50.9	49.1
47531	EVANSTON	98.5	98.2	0.3	0.5	0.2	0.2	1.7	2.6	5.9	6.5	7.0	7.5	4.4	24.5	31.0	12.1	1.0	75.8	41.2	52.3	47.7
47532	FERDINAND	99.2	98.9	0.1	0.1	0.2	0.3	0.6	0.9	6.9	7.3	7.6	7.2	4.9	25.4	27.1	11.2	2.4	73.6	39.2	49.4	50.6
47537	GENTRYVILLE	98.5	98.3	0.0	0.0	0.1	0.1	0.9	1.2	5.6	5.8	6.4	6.8	5.3	23.9	33.5	11.4	1.2	78.1	42.0	50.6	49.4
47541	HOLLAND	98.7	98.1	0.0	0.0	0.2	0.4	1.2	2.0	6.6	6.9	7.1	7.1	5.0	25.7	28.8	11.3	1.4	74.9	38.9	51.5	48.5
47542	HUNTINGBURG	94.8	92.6	0.1	0.1	0.2	0.3	6.5	9.5	6.9	6.9	6.9	6.9	5.6	25.5	27.2	11.8	2.1	74.8	38.5	49.1	50.9
47546	JASPER	97.8	96.8	0.2	0.3	0.3	0.4	2.3	3.6	7.0	7.0	7.1	6.8	5.6	25.5	28.0	10.9	2.0	74.6	38.5	49.8	50.2
47550	LAMAR	98.9	98.6	0.4	0.4	0.0	0.4	1.1	1.8	6.0	6.4	7.1	7.1	4.6	24.6	31.7	11.4	1.1	76.2	41.3	52.0	48.0
47551	LEOPOLD	98.5	98.7	1.0	0.7	0.0	0.0	0.2	0.4	4.5	4.9	6.1	7.9	5.9	25.7	33.3	10.1	1.6	79.3	41.4	53.2	46.8
47552	LINCOLN CITY	98.8	98.3	0.0	0.0	0.4	0.7	0.8	1.0	7.3	8.0	8.0	6.6	4.2	27.3	26.6	11.1	1.0	72.7	38.3	51.9	48.1
47553	LOOGOOTEE	98.9	98.7	0.1	0.1	0.2	0.3	0.4	0.5	6.3	6.5	6.8	6.7	5.2	23.7	29.5	13.1	2.3	76.2	41.3	50.5	49.5
47556	MARIAH HILL	99.0	98.1	0.0	0.0	0.5	0.5	1.0	1.9	6.5	7.5	7.9	7.5	4.7	27.1	25.7	11.7	1.4	72.9	37.9	51.4	48.6
47557	MONROE CITY	99.4	99.2	0.1	0.1	0.1	0.2	0.4	0.6	5.9	6.3	6.3	5.9	5.2	23.9	31.4	13.1	2.1	78.0	42.7	50.9	49.1
47558	MONTGOMERY	99.2	98.9	0.0	0.0	0.1	0.2	0.5	0.8	9.4	9.2	9.0	7.8	5.6	25.1	24.2	8.4	1.2	67.7	32.0	50.5	49.5
47561	OAKTOWN	99.0	98.7	0.1	0.1	0.2	0.3	0.9	1.3	6.1	6.2	6.1	6.2	4.9	23.7	28.9	14.2	3.7	77.9	42.6	49.4	50.6
47562	ODON	98.9	98.5	0.1	0.1	0.2	0.3	0.8	1.2	9.0	8.7	8.5	7.9	5.3	24.1	23.2	11.3	2.0	68.7	33.4	50.2	49.8
47564	OTWELL	99.2	99.0	0.1	0.1	0.1	0.2	0.6	0.9	6.5	6.9	7.1	6.7	5.2	25.0	28.4	12.4	1.8	75.4	39.4	50.8	49.2
47567	PETERSBURG	99.3	99.1	0.1	0.1	0.1	0.2	0.4	0.5	5.6	6.0	6.1	5.8	4.8	23.7	29.3	15.6	3.0	78.7	43.5	50.2	49.8
47568	PLAINVILLE	98.8	98.5	0.1	0.1	0.1	0.2	1.4	2.2	7.2	7.3	7.5	6.4	4.2	25.3	25.8	14.0	2.4	73.8	39.3	51.0	49.0
47574	ROME	99.6	99.5	0.0	0.0	0.0	0.0	0.4	0.5	6.1	6.6	6.6	6.6	5.2	25.9	31.1	10.8	0.9	76.9	40.0	50.9	49.1
47575	SAINT ANTHONY	99.4	99.1	0.0	0.0	0.2	0.2	0.5	0.8	7.2	7.7	8.0	6.9	4.5	25.7	28.5	9.9	1.5	72.5	38.5	49.3	50.7
47576	SAINT CROIX	99.8	99.8	0.0	0.0	0.0	0.0	0.2	0.2	6.5	6.5	6.5	7.1	6.9	26.5	29.0	10.1	0.9	76.0	37.5	49.8	50.2
47577	SAINT MEINRAD	98.7	98.4	0.3	0.4	0.5	0.7	1.2	1.6	5.6	6.0	6.2	6.4	4.9	25.9	30.5	12.6	1.9	78.0	41.4	54.9	45.1
47578	SANDBORN	98.3	98.1	0.2	0.2	0.1	0.1	0.5	0.6	4.7	4.7	5.0	6.3	6.0	21.8	31.5	16.6	3.3	81.8	45.9	48.5	51.5
47579	SANTA CLAUS	98.8	98.2	0.0	0.0	0.4	0.6	1.0	1.5	7.4	7.9	7.9	7.0	4.5	27.1	26.7	10.6	0.9	72.4	37.9	51.2	48.8
47580	SCHNELLVILLE	100.0	100.0	0.0	0.0	0.0	0.0	0.4	0.4	7.9	8.6	8.6	6.4	4.3	26.8	27.9	8.2	1.4	70.7	36.8	50.7	49.3
47581	SHOALS	98.9	98.6	0.2	0.3	0.1	0.1	0.5	0.9	6.0	6.2	6.4	6.3	5.7	25.6	29.0	13.3	1.6	77.7	40.4	51.4	48.6
47585	STENDAL	99.1	99.1	0.2	0.2	0.0	0.0	0.5	0.6	6.2	6.2	6.9	7.3	5.6	27.7	27.3	11.8	1.1	76.2	38.7	50.2	49.8
47586	TELL CITY	98.2	98.0	0.9	1.0	0.2	0.2	0.8	0.8	5.2	5.5	5.8	6.0	5.8	26.0	28.0	14.4	3.2	80.0	41.7	50.7	49.3
47588	TROY	99.8	99.7	0.0	0.0	0.0	0.0	0.5	0.6	5.5	5.5	5.8	6.4	6.1	27.4	31.3	10.8	1.1	79.2	40.3	51.5	48.5
47590	VELPEN	99.3	99.2	0.1	0.1	0.0	0.0	0.6	1.0	6.4	6.5	7.1	7.3	5.4	26.4	28.8	11.0	1.1	75.7	38.8	51.1	48.9
47591	VINCENNES	95.3	94.2	2.6	3.0	0.8	1.1	0.9	1.4	5.7	5.5	5.4	10.0	9.5	22.7	25.6	12.9	2.7	79.5	37.3	50.1	49.9
47597	WHEATLAND	99.0	98.7	0.2	0.3	0.2	0.3	0.4	0.5	5.7	6.1	6.3	6.5	4.5	24.4	31.0	13.5	2.0	77.8	42.8	50.1	49.9
47598	WINSLOW	98.8	98.5	0.1	0.1	0.3	0.4	1.0	1.5	6.4	6.5	6.8	6.6	5.2	25.0	28.6	13.5	1.4	76.2	40.1	50.8	49.2
47601	BOONVILLE	98.7	98.5	0.5	0.5	0.2	0.2	0.4	0.6	6.1	6.5	6.4	6.4	5.5	25.9	29.3	12.0	2.0	76.9	40.2	49.7	50.3
	INDIANA	87.5	85.6	8.4	8.9	1.0	1.5	3.5	5.0	6.9	6.8	6.8	7.2	6.9	26.5	26.2	10.8	1.9	75.4	36.8	49.3	50.7
	UNITED STATES	75.1	72.0	12.3	12.7	3.8	4.6	12.5	15.7	6.8	6.7	6.6	7.1	6.9	27.0	26.0	10.9	1.9	75.7	36.9	49.2	50.8

ZIP CODE		2009 Per Capita Income	2009 HH Income Base	2009 HOUSEHOLD INCOME DISTRIBUTION (%)					MEDIAN HOUSEHOLD INCOME				2009 Home Value Base	2009 HOME VALUE DISTRIBUTION (%)					2009 Median Home Value
#	POST OFFICE NAME			Less than $25,000	$25,000 to $49,999	$50,000 to $99,999	$100,000 to $149,999	$150,000 or More	2009	2014	2009 National Centile	2009 State Centile		Less than $50,000	$50,000 to $89,999	$90,000 to $174,999	$175,000 to $399,999	$400,000 or More	
47381	SALAMONIA	17944	72	20.8	36.1	38.9	4.2	0.0	45000	45904	48	22	60	25.0	41.7	20.0	10.0	3.3	80000
47382	SARATOGA	23461	105	22.9	24.8	43.8	6.7	1.9	51753	51767	65	57	83	10.8	37.3	39.8	9.6	2.4	91667
47383	SELMA	27212	1069	15.9	24.7	43.1	8.9	7.4	60160	60660	78	82	884	10.2	35.6	48.0	6.0	0.2	92701
47384	SHIRLEY	21870	1007	18.6	30.0	41.2	8.2	2.0	51208	53730	64	53	846	13.4	23.2	51.7	10.4	1.4	103655
47385	SPICELAND	24931	713	21.6	25.7	38.0	12.2	2.5	53300	55189	69	65	572	6.1	34.3	47.4	10.8	1.4	100815
47386	SPRINGPORT	26728	488	13.1	25.4	47.7	8.0	5.7	60584	60000	78	83	441	6.6	19.0	61.9	12.5	0.0	120742
47387	STRAUGHN	23878	316	24.4	23.1	38.9	9.5	4.1	52968	54650	68	63	269	13.0	34.6	37.2	13.8	1.5	92826
47390	UNION CITY	19740	2229	33.1	29.0	33.0	3.8	1.0	40373	41942	34	9	1575	24.8	40.6	30.0	4.0	0.5	78766
47392	WEBSTER	19906	63	20.6	38.1	33.3	7.9	0.0	43353	50583	43	16	56	3.6	19.6	64.3	12.5	0.0	115625
47393	WILLIAMSBURG	19859	421	15.2	33.5	42.0	6.7	2.6	51130	52911	64	52	359	12.0	24.0	49.9	13.1	1.1	105754
47394	WINCHESTER	22360	3434	25.1	32.2	34.7	5.6	2.3	43690	45904	44	17	2437	16.6	38.7	36.9	6.9	0.9	85844
47396	YORKTOWN	30099	2549	12.1	24.9	41.9	12.7	8.5	64524	65270	83	90	2090	5.2	34.1	49.0	9.9	1.9	101361
47401	BLOOMINGTON	30351	16046	27.1	21.9	30.7	11.6	8.7	51256	54289	64	54	9071	4.8	8.2	42.5	38.3	6.2	164408
47403	BLOOMINGTON	22686	12250	24.8	32.3	35.8	5.0	2.1	43788	46185	45	18	7262	22.5	16.4	48.0	11.9	1.3	106821
47404	BLOOMINGTON	21242	8072	31.0	30.2	29.9	6.8	2.1	41196	42669	37	11	4626	22.8	14.5	44.4	17.2	1.1	110684
47405	BLOOMINGTON	11881	1	100.0	0.0	0.0	0.0	0.0	5000	5000	0	0	0	0.0	0.0	0.0	0.0	0.0	0
47406	BLOOMINGTON	12862	488	80.3	13.5	5.5	0.6	0.0	12357	12423	1	1	5	0.0	0.0	100.0	0.0	0.0	112500
47408	BLOOMINGTON	20193	10567	44.3	24.2	22.3	6.5	2.9	29911	30600	8	2	3684	9.5	8.4	47.6	30.0	4.5	147669
47421	BEDFORD	23052	11752	25.6	28.4	36.2	7.7	2.0	46232	49128	52	28	8989	16.3	33.5	40.0	9.8	0.5	90359
47424	BLOOMFIELD	21947	3975	25.8	29.8	35.3	7.6	1.5	45783	46683	51	26	3187	18.6	30.9	39.6	10.4	0.6	90594
47427	COAL CITY	17083	729	28.1	34.0	33.7	3.0	1.1	40561	42670	35	10	618	24.3	33.3	27.3	9.1	6.0	77885
47429	ELLETTSVILLE	22822	2742	16.4	29.6	43.1	8.5	2.4	53244	54742	68	65	2115	11.7	19.1	56.5	12.3	0.5	112222
47431	FREEDOM	21253	469	23.7	34.8	36.0	2.3	3.2	44111	46837	46	19	404	12.1	30.9	48.5	6.9	1.5	99655
47432	FRENCH LICK	20298	1699	29.3	32.2	32.4	3.5	2.5	41812	43107	39	12	1388	26.8	28.0	33.4	10.7	1.1	84174
47433	GOSPORT	21525	1699	19.5	32.9	37.3	8.1	2.2	47840	49642	56	35	1358	15.7	25.0	42.8	16.0	0.5	106343
47436	HELTONVILLE	24941	697	15.9	31.7	40.0	8.9	3.4	52597	54236	67	62	606	17.7	25.4	42.1	14.2	0.7	97368
47438	JASONVILLE	16647	1688	36.5	28.7	30.6	3.6	0.6	35000	36897	18	4	1296	35.8	34.3	25.3	4.5	0.2	65177
47441	LINTON	21837	4743	28.2	30.0	33.0	7.5	1.4	41909	44014	39	13	3632	25.1	34.5	31.5	8.5	0.4	78448
47443	LYONS	17817	617	28.0	35.8	30.1	4.4	1.6	41789	43951	39	12	492	36.2	39.8	22.4	1.6	0.0	61587
47446	MITCHELL	20350	4104	25.8	32.5	35.7	5.0	1.0	43260	45872	43	15	3259	24.0	32.1	33.7	9.5	0.6	82405
47448	NASHVILLE	26534	3160	17.9	28.3	40.9	9.5	3.4	53006	55286	68	64	2564	8.8	16.0	47.2	25.0	3.0	132449
47449	NEWBERRY	20159	153	34.6	30.7	24.8	5.9	3.9	37112	39233	24	6	135	23.0	31.1	34.1	11.9	0.0	85000
47451	OOLITIC	22347	564	31.9	31.0	26.6	8.2	2.3	40477	42384	34	10	383	17.5	36.0	40.2	5.7	0.5	85781
47452	ORLEANS	18625	1765	29.5	35.5	28.0	4.5	2.5	38985	40737	30	7	1368	17.6	42.0	33.6	6.3	0.5	81902
47453	OWENSBURG	19849	468	26.1	36.5	30.6	4.9	1.9	39004	41245	30	8	424	20.5	23.3	46.5	9.7	0.0	96047
47454	PAOLI	19495	2992	31.1	33.8	28.9	4.4	1.8	36279	38161	21	5	2344	24.7	35.8	31.2	7.7	0.5	77706
47456	QUINCY	21187	989	18.5	34.8	37.5	7.6	1.6	47424	48806	55	33	854	14.8	22.6	41.5	20.1	1.1	111983
47459	SOLSBERRY	20082	944	22.4	35.0	34.5	7.8	0.3	45124	46047	49	23	826	25.5	23.6	37.4	12.2	1.2	90972
47460	SPENCER	20886	4307	22.0	34.5	35.3	6.1	2.1	44728	46672	47	22	3387	15.2	26.4	44.0	13.3	1.1	99845
47462	SPRINGVILLE	21416	1309	19.5	29.7	40.9	7.5	2.4	50468	51874	62	49	1161	20.7	27.0	41.6	8.4	2.4	92412
47465	SWITZ CITY	20292	329	25.5	24.6	42.6	6.1	1.2	49817	50309	61	45	274	22.6	35.0	33.6	8.4	0.4	84000
47468	UNIONVILLE	26420	484	16.9	28.7	42.4	8.1	3.9	54816	56962	71	69	412	15.8	19.9	39.1	23.5	1.7	114035
47469	WEST BADEN SPRINGS	22243	796	31.8	28.6	32.9	4.0	2.6	41908	43423	39	12	632	32.6	30.4	29.4	7.4	0.2	74600
47470	WILLIAMS	20202	996	22.0	32.2	38.9	5.5	1.4	47329	49491	55	33	877	22.1	25.2	42.8	8.8	1.1	93790
47471	WORTHINGTON	22154	973	29.1	29.8	33.4	5.3	2.4	43708	45526	44	17	799	24.0	40.1	29.7	5.5	0.8	72536
47501	WASHINGTON	20840	6672	29.4	30.5	32.6	4.9	2.5	40896	43446	36	11	4910	17.2	38.2	36.3	7.5	0.7	85507
47512	BICKNELL	18431	1787	37.5	28.0	27.9	5.1	1.5	34481	37075	16	4	1284	37.7	43.2	16.5	2.5	0.1	57315
47513	BIRDSEYE	20296	676	24.9	28.0	40.8	5.5	0.9	47364	50478	55	33	568	27.3	26.2	35.2	9.7	1.6	85652
47514	BRANCHVILLE	10682	119	15.1	33.6	43.7	5.9	1.7	50956	52488	63	51	114	7.0	30.7	53.5	8.8	0.0	105645
47515	BRISTOW	20547	415	18.1	32.8	41.0	6.0	2.2	49168	50663	59	42	371	18.6	22.4	45.8	10.0	3.2	104119
47516	BRUCEVILLE	20903	515	29.3	29.1	34.2	5.0	2.3	43548	46444	44	17	440	21.1	45.0	25.9	5.2	2.7	76364
47519	CANNELBURG	13927	459	27.5	30.3	38.1	2.6	1.5	42575	45519	41	14	395	10.9	29.1	42.8	16.2	1.0	103178
47520	CANNELTON	19761	1086	27.9	30.6	37.0	3.9	0.6	42524	45092	41	13	826	22.3	39.7	32.8	4.7	0.5	78778
47521	CELESTINE	20930	300	11.0	24.3	58.7	6.0	0.0	59460	58785	77	81	267	11.6	17.2	48.7	18.0	4.5	113611
47522	CRANE	25372	94	13.8	37.2	40.4	8.5	0.0	48914	49537	59	40	77	22.1	36.4	32.5	9.1	0.0	79167
47523	DALE	20494	1239	19.9	32.0	41.9	4.8	1.5	48527	50857	58	38	964	16.6	37.0	35.1	8.6	2.7	87009
47524	DECKER	19568	219	31.1	35.2	27.4	2.3	4.1	38405	40950	28	7	177	51.4	26.0	12.4	6.2	4.0	48750
47525	DERBY	21543	273	19.8	35.2	40.7	4.4	0.0	46488	48267	53	29	247	19.4	23.9	47.4	9.3	0.0	96111
47527	DUBOIS	21601	838	12.2	35.9	46.3	4.5	1.1	51686	53719	65	56	718	20.5	24.0	46.8	8.1	0.7	95556
47528	EDWARDSPORT	20075	207	30.0	24.6	37.2	8.2	0.0	45227	47373	49	24	169	45.0	20.7	29.6	4.1	0.6	59444
47529	ELNORA	16982	801	28.1	34.2	29.2	5.1	3.4	40478	42128	34	10	678	27.3	27.9	35.0	9.0	0.9	84444
47531	EVANSTON	21746	228	14.9	29.8	45.6	9.6	0.0	54108	54674	70	67	202	11.4	22.3	49.0	13.9	3.5	110811
47532	FERDINAND	22154	1641	14.7	28.3	45.2	9.6	2.3	55873	56561	72	73	1383	10.7	20.7	49.9	17.1	1.6	111675
47537	GENTRYVILLE	19111	296	19.3	28.4	45.6	5.4	1.4	50927	51850	63	51	262	21.4	31.7	34.0	10.7	2.3	87419
47541	HOLLAND	22323	540	19.6	32.2	38.7	5.6	3.9	48690	51320	58	39	458	17.0	34.7	40.4	7.4	0.4	87895
47542	HUNTINGBURG	21851	3448	20.8	30.6	39.2	7.1	2.3	48613	51424	58	39	2590	15.6	28.9	42.1	12.2	1.3	96000
47546	JASPER	27147	8243	15.7	24.9	44.4	10.7	4.3	58465	58753	76	79	6143	7.3	18.8	51.0	20.7	2.2	119614
47550	LAMAR	22620	106	15.1	30.2	45.3	9.4	0.0	53065	53810	68	64	92	10.9	22.8	45.7	17.4	3.3	110938
47551	LEOPOLD	20734	221	19.9	34.4	39.8	5.4	0.5	47047	48486	54	32	203	14.8	29.1	45.8	10.3	0.0	96579
47552	LINCOLN CITY	25026	102	10.8	22.5	50.0	10.8	5.9	60000	58081	77	81	92	5.4	12.0	54.3	23.9	4.3	137500
47553	LOOGOOTEE	22195	2501	25.5	29.0	38.1	4.9	2.5	46018	47348	51	27	1988	19.8	39.4	32.6	7.6	0.6	81719
47556	MARIAH HILL	25382	78	14.1	24.4	46.2	10.3	5.1	57828	57941	75	77	68	11.8	17.6	47.1	19.1	4.4	122727
47557	MONROE CITY	21441	522	23.6	30.7	37.4	7.3	1.1	45983	48957	51	27	401	17.0	45.4	28.7	7.0	2.0	79681
47558	MONTGOMERY	16309	938	21.4	30.0	40.3	6.3	2.0	48570	50658	58	38	815	9.2	26.6	50.3	11.9	2.0	105806
47561	OAKTOWN	20495	884	31.7	27.7	31.4	6.4	2.7	41411	44268	37	11	698	22.2	46.7	26.2	3.6	1.3	71034
47562	ODON	18159	1652	22.6	34.1	34.8	6.2	2.3	44227	46509	46	20	1379	17.9	33.8	37.6	10.3	0.4	88657
47564	OTWELL	21203	607	21.3	31.3	40.9	5.9	0.7	46790	49000	54	30	515	25.2	29.1	37.1	8.2	0.4	85909
47567	PETERSBURG	19814	2506	27.3	32.5	35.1	4.3	0.9	41432	43425	37	12	1991	30.8	33.5	31.1	4.4	0.2	72207
47568	PLAINVILLE	21603	378	22.5	28.8	42.1	5.6	1.1	48650	50527	58	39	313	17.9	39.9	36.1	4.5	1.6	84432
47574	ROME	22034	88	20.5	29.5	44.3	5.7	0.0	50000	51429	61	46	76	23.7	22.4	47.4	6.6	0.0	93000
47575	SAINT ANTHONY	23310	485	14.2	30.3	42.9	10.1	2.5	54601	55834	71	69	429	12.1	21.2	44.3	21.0	1.4	115625
47576	SAINT CROIX	19834	165	22.4	29.1	38.8	9.1	0.6	49005	50393	59	41	147	10.2	38.8	41.5	8.8	0.7	91364
47577	SAINT MEINRAD	23032	354	16.4	29.1	38.7	11.6	4.2	53731	54411	69	66	302	21.5	24.2	39.4	12.9	2.0	100000
47578	SANDBORN	24582	368	29.9	23.1	37.8	5.7	3.5	45713	49791	50	25	305	43.3	38.0	12.5	2.6	3.6	55857
47579	SANTA CLAUS	25770	1011	11.9	22.6	49.1	10.9	5.6	59727	58366	77	81	901	5.5	12.1	54.4	23.8	4.2	136355
47580	SCHNELLVILLE	21503	103	13.6	26.2	52.4	6.8	1.0	56495	56681	73	74	91	12.1	20.9	46.2	18.7	2.2	109167
47581	SHOALS	20673	1773	26.3	30.2	36.5	5.4	1.6	44792	46196	48	22	1461	33.4	33.4	27.7	4.4	1.1	69083
47585	STENDAL	22576	193	24.4	31.6	33.7	7.8	2.6	44171	46153	46	19	165	31.5	34.5	26.7	5.5	1.8	78500
47586	TELL CITY	23250	4659	27.5	29.0	34.8	6.1	2.6	43719	45976	44	18	3521	13.0	36.7	41.7	8.0	0.5	90292
47588	TROY	22855	166	24.1	33.7	34.9	6.0	1.2	44566	45747	47	21	141	19.1	38.3	31.9	9.9	0.7	81250
47590	VELPEN	19989	261	20.3	35.2	34.5	8.4	1.5	45149	47207	49	23	226	25.7	31.4	31.0	10.6	1.3	84839
47591	VINCENNES	21468	10379	32.5	27.8	30.8	6.0	2.9	40145	42479	33	9	6716	17.2	38.3	34.8	8.7	1.0	84244
47597	WHEATLAND	23334	463	20.1	28.7	40.8	7.1	3.2	51140	53032	64	52	350	22.3	43.1	26.6	5.7	2.3	75641
47598	WINSLOW	19522	1434	25.0	34.8	33.9	5.3	1.0	42350	44620	40	13	1185	29.0	32.0	33.8	5.0	0.2	80114
47601	BOONVILLE	22518	5787	22.7	29.2	37.7	8.6	1.9	48441	51012	58	37	4594	19.4	38.5	30.7	10.3	1.2	82713
	INDIANA	26003		19.5	26.3	38.6	10.5	5.1	54105	56493				12.2	24.1	44.1	17.2	2.4	108938
	UNITED STATES	27277		20.9	24.4	35.3	11.7	7.6	54719	56938				9.3	13.1	31.6	32.6	13.5	162279

#	POST OFFICE NAME	FINANCIAL SERVICES: Auto Loan	FINANCIAL SERVICES: Home Loan	FINANCIAL SERVICES: Invest-ments	FINANCIAL SERVICES: Retire-ment Plans	THE HOME: Home Improvements: Home Repair	THE HOME: Home Improvements: Lawn & Garden	THE HOME: Furnishings: Comput-ers & Hard-ware-Personal	THE HOME: Furnishings: Major Appli-ances	THE HOME: Furnishings: TV, Radio, Sound Equip-ment	THE HOME: Furnishings: Furni-ture	ENTERTAINMENT: Dine out/ Carry out	ENTERTAINMENT: Sports Equip-ment	ENTERTAINMENT: Fees & Tickets	ENTERTAINMENT: Toys & Games	ENTERTAINMENT: Travel	ENTERTAINMENT: Cable TV	PERSONAL: Apparel & Services	PERSONAL: Auto Repairs	PERSONAL: Health Insur-ance	PERSONAL: Pets & Supplies
47381	SALAMONIA	88	63	72	61	63	83	65	76	73	64	71	59	53	76	60	79	48	72	80	93
47382	SARATOGA	88	80	79	83	82	94	79	89	81	71	80	67	73	83	79	86	55	82	92	104
47383	SELMA	102	98	88	101	96	109	97	102	99	90	98	79	94	101	96	103	67	99	109	121
47384	SHIRLEY	85	83	74	86	81	92	82	86	83	76	82	67	79	85	81	86	56	83	91	102
47385	SPICELAND	90	86	84	88	88	100	83	93	86	77	85	69	80	87	85	91	58	87	98	107
47386	SPRINGPORT	106	96	95	100	98	114	95	107	98	86	96	81	88	100	95	104	66	99	111	125
47387	STRAUGHN	95	86	85	90	88	102	85	96	88	77	86	73	79	90	85	93	59	89	99	112
47390	UNION CITY	75	59	66	59	59	76	64	71	69	58	67	54	55	69	60	74	45	69	77	85
47392	WEBSTER	82	75	74	78	76	88	74	83	76	67	75	63	68	78	74	81	51	77	86	97
47393	WILLIAMSBURG	93	85	84	89	87	100	84	95	87	76	85	72	77	88	84	92	58	87	98	110
47394	WINCHESTER	84	69	77	70	70	88	73	82	78	66	76	62	64	78	70	83	51	78	89	97
47396	YORKTOWN	109	114	110	116	113	121	107	113	108	104	108	86	110	109	111	111	75	109	117	132
47401	BLOOMINGTON	100	88	84	92	86	88	108	92	102	99	103	76	97	103	94	100	72	99	93	112
47403	BLOOMINGTON	79	69	65	70	67	71	79	73	78	75	78	58	71	79	71	78	54	76	75	88
47404	BLOOMINGTON	74	61	56	63	59	64	80	66	75	70	75	55	68	76	66	75	53	72	68	81
47405	BLOOMINGTON	8	3	3	4	3	4	11	6	8	7	9	6	6	8	6	8	6	8	5	7
47406	BLOOMINGTON	27	11	11	14	10	13	38	19	30	25	30	20	22	29	20	27	22	26	19	25
47408	BLOOMINGTON	67	46	46	51	45	50	82	56	71	65	72	51	61	71	58	68	51	67	57	71
47421	BEDFORD	86	72	79	71	72	88	73	83	79	69	77	62	65	79	71	85	52	79	89	98
47424	BLOOMFIELD	85	71	79	70	71	87	71	82	76	67	74	61	63	76	69	81	50	77	85	96
47427	COAL CITY	83	59	69	58	59	79	62	72	69	60	67	55	50	71	56	75	45	68	76	88
47429	ELLETTSVILLE	85	92	78	93	88	92	85	86	85	85	85	66	88	87	86	86	59	85	89	102
47431	FREEDOM	82	75	74	78	76	88	74	83	76	67	75	63	68	77	73	80	51	77	86	97
47432	FRENCH LICK	81	60	73	59	60	79	65	74	71	61	69	56	53	71	60	77	47	71	79	89
47433	GOSPORT	88	80	79	82	80	92	78	87	81	74	80	66	72	83	77	85	55	81	89	102
47436	HELTONVILLE	94	87	83	88	87	96	84	92	87	81	86	69	79	89	83	90	59	87	93	108
47438	JASONVILLE	65	54	53	56	54	65	60	62	62	54	60	48	52	63	55	66	41	61	67	74
47441	LINTON	81	67	80	66	68	87	68	80	74	63	72	59	60	73	68	80	49	75	87	94
47443	LYONS	80	58	82	56	60	83	61	76	68	56	66	57	49	67	60	75	44	71	81	90
47446	MITCHELL	83	63	72	62	62	82	66	75	72	62	71	58	55	74	61	78	48	72	81	91
47448	NASHVILLE	98	86	107	87	90	104	85	99	88	80	87	74	78	87	88	92	59	93	100	115
47449	NEWBERRY	87	62	89	60	65	88	64	81	71	59	70	61	51	70	63	78	46	74	84	96
47451	OOLITIC	83	62	80	60	64	85	66	79	73	61	71	59	55	72	64	79	47	74	86	93
47452	ORLEANS	83	62	70	61	62	80	66	74	71	62	70	58	54	73	60	77	47	71	79	90
47453	OWENSBURG	84	66	80	64	67	83	66	78	71	64	70	58	56	72	64	76	47	73	80	93
47454	PAOLI	81	60	74	59	60	80	64	75	70	59	68	57	52	70	60	76	46	71	80	90
47456	QUINCY	86	78	75	80	79	89	76	85	79	72	78	63	71	81	75	83	53	79	87	99
47459	SOLSBERRY	85	72	75	70	72	82	70	78	74	70	73	58	63	76	67	78	50	75	80	93
47460	SPENCER	84	74	70	73	73	82	73	78	76	72	76	59	67	79	69	80	51	76	81	94
47462	SPRINGVILLE	95	79	81	78	79	93	78	88	83	77	82	66	69	86	75	89	56	83	90	105
47465	SWITZ CITY	87	69	87	68	71	91	69	84	75	64	74	63	59	75	69	81	49	78	88	99
47468	UNIONVILLE	97	89	106	91	92	104	86	99	88	81	87	75	81	87	90	91	59	93	99	115
47469	WEST BADEN SPRINGS	96	68	85	66	68	93	71	85	79	68	78	66	57	82	66	87	52	80	89	103
47470	WILLIAMS	87	72	76	73	72	89	72	83	77	67	75	63	63	79	69	82	51	77	86	98
47471	WORTHINGTON	86	67	83	67	69	90	71	85	77	63	74	63	60	76	69	83	50	79	90	99
47501	WASHINGTON	79	67	70	67	67	80	71	76	75	66	74	57	64	75	67	80	50	75	82	90
47512	BICKNELL	72	53	67	53	54	72	61	68	66	54	64	52	50	65	57	71	43	67	75	82
47513	BIRDSEYE	87	67	74	67	67	86	69	79	75	65	73	61	58	77	65	81	49	74	83	95
47514	BRANCHVILLE	105	75	87	73	75	99	78	91	87	76	85	70	63	90	71	94	57	86	96	111
47515	BRISTOW	85	73	75	75	74	88	73	83	77	67	75	63	65	79	71	82	51	77	86	97
47516	BRUCEVILLE	87	62	92	61	65	92	68	84	74	58	72	66	53	72	67	81	47	79	91	101
47519	CANNELBURG	78	65	68	66	65	79	65	74	69	60	68	56	57	71	63	74	46	69	77	88
47520	CANNELTON	84	61	70	60	61	81	64	74	70	62	69	57	51	73	58	76	46	70	78	90
47521	CELESTINE	92	84	83	87	85	99	83	93	85	75	84	71	76	87	82	90	57	86	96	108
47522	CRANE	99	71	101	69	73	100	73	92	81	68	79	69	58	80	72	89	52	85	96	110
47523	DALE	93	70	81	69	70	91	72	84	78	69	77	64	60	81	68	85	52	79	88	101
47524	DECKER	88	61	97	61	63	93	67	84	70	55	69	69	49	69	67	76	45	78	88	103
47525	DERBY	91	65	87	63	67	90	67	83	74	63	73	63	54	75	65	82	48	77	87	99
47527	DUBOIS	90	76	75	77	74	91	77	84	82	74	81	65	70	84	73	87	55	81	90	101
47528	EDWARDSPORT	88	63	90	61	65	89	65	82	72	60	70	62	52	71	64	79	46	75	85	98
47529	ELNORA	90	64	91	64	67	93	70	85	75	60	73	67	54	74	68	82	48	80	91	103
47531	EVANSTON	90	82	82	86	84	97	81	92	84	73	82	69	75	85	81	89	56	85	95	107
47532	FERDINAND	91	91	83	94	90	98	86	93	87	82	87	71	85	89	88	90	60	88	95	109
47537	GENTRYVILLE	85	71	76	73	73	88	72	82	76	66	74	62	63	78	70	81	50	76	85	97
47541	HOLLAND	88	83	81	86	84	95	81	90	83	74	81	68	76	84	81	87	56	84	92	105
47542	HUNTINGBURG	86	78	76	78	77	87	80	84	82	76	81	64	74	83	77	86	56	82	87	99
47546	JASPER	98	97	88	99	95	103	97	98	98	92	97	76	95	99	96	100	67	97	103	117
47550	LAMAR	92	85	84	89	87	99	83	94	86	76	84	71	78	88	84	91	58	87	96	109
47551	LEOPOLD	91	66	87	64	67	91	68	83	75	64	74	63	54	76	65	82	49	77	87	100
47552	LINCOLN CITY	99	111	96	115	108	109	99	103	98	100	98	81	106	100	105	98	69	99	102	122
47553	LOOGOOTEE	90	68	85	68	70	92	72	86	78	66	76	65	60	79	69	85	51	80	91	101
47556	MARIAH HILL	101	102	94	106	102	110	96	104	96	92	96	80	96	99	99	99	66	98	105	121
47557	MONROE CITY	88	70	87	70	72	92	70	85	76	65	74	64	60	76	70	82	50	78	88	101
47558	MONTGOMERY	84	73	74	76	74	88	73	83	76	67	75	63	66	78	72	81	51	77	85	97
47561	OAKTOWN	88	62	92	61	65	91	67	84	73	59	71	65	52	72	66	80	47	78	89	100
47562	ODON	92	69	88	69	70	94	73	87	78	65	77	67	59	79	70	85	51	81	92	104
47564	OTWELL	91	67	76	66	67	88	70	81	77	67	75	62	57	80	64	83	51	76	85	98
47567	PETERSBURG	83	60	80	58	61	84	63	78	70	58	68	59	50	70	61	77	46	72	83	93
47568	PLAINVILLE	83	75	75	78	76	89	74	84	76	67	75	63	68	78	74	81	51	77	86	97
47574	ROME	96	69	79	67	69	91	72	83	79	70	78	64	58	83	65	86	52	79	88	101
47575	SAINT ANTHONY	93	93	86	96	92	101	87	95	88	83	88	73	86	90	89	91	60	89	97	111
47576	SAINT CROIX	94	68	78	66	67	89	70	82	78	68	76	63	56	81	64	85	51	77	86	100
47577	SAINT MEINRAD	98	92	89	95	93	106	89	100	92	82	90	76	84	93	90	96	62	93	103	116
47578	SANDBORN	97	70	98	68	72	101	75	94	84	68	81	70	60	83	73	93	54	87	101	110
47579	SANTA CLAUS	99	109	95	113	106	109	98	103	97	98	98	80	104	100	103	98	68	99	102	121
47580	SCHNELLVILLE	91	82	82	86	84	97	81	92	84	74	82	69	75	86	81	89	56	85	95	107
47581	SHOALS	86	64	76	62	64	85	67	79	73	62	71	60	54	75	63	80	48	74	84	94
47585	STENDAL	98	71	81	69	70	93	73	85	81	72	80	66	59	85	67	89	54	81	90	104
47586	TELL CITY	86	67	78	67	68	87	72	82	78	66	76	62	61	78	68	84	51	78	88	97
47588	TROY	89	64	74	62	64	85	67	78	74	65	73	60	54	77	61	81	49	74	82	95
47590	VELPEN	97	71	80	69	71	92	73	85	81	71	79	65	60	84	67	88	53	80	89	103
47591	VINCENNES	75	65	66	66	65	75	72	72	74	67	73	56	65	74	67	77	50	73	78	87
47597	WHEATLAND	97	74	100	75	77	103	78	94	82	67	81	75	63	82	78	88	53	88	99	113
47598	WINSLOW	87	62	76	61	63	85	66	78	73	62	71	59	53	75	61	80	48	73	83	94
47601	BOONVILLE	85	79	74	80	77	89	79	83	81	74	80	64	74	83	77	85	55	81	88	99
	INDIANA	97	91	86	93	89	96	93	94	95	91	94	73	90	96	90	97	65	94	97	112
	UNITED STATES	100	100	100	100	100	100	100	100	100	100	100	100	100	100	100	100	100	100	100	100

POPULATION CHANGE

47610-47954

ZIP CODE #	POST OFFICE NAME	COUNTY FIPS CODE	POPULATION 2000	POPULATION 2009	POPULATION 2014	2000-2009 ANNUAL RATE % Rate	2000-2009 ANNUAL RATE State Centile	HOUSEHOLDS 2000	HOUSEHOLDS 2009	HOUSEHOLDS 2014	HOUSEHOLDS % Annual Rate 2000-2009	HOUSEHOLDS 2009 Average HH Size	FAMILIES 2000	FAMILIES 2009	FAMILIES % Annual Rate 2000-2009
47610	CHANDLER	173	5261	5603	5808	0.7	73	1954	2160	2265	1.1	2.57	1509	1615	0.7
47611	CHRISNEY	147	1857	1963	2001	0.6	70	699	753	772	0.8	2.61	528	552	0.5
47612	CYNTHIANA	129	997	1006	997	0.1	43	364	371	369	0.2	2.71	280	277	-0.1
47613	ELBERFELD	051	3548	3977	4146	1.2	86	1356	1566	1647	1.6	2.54	1041	1165	1.2
47615	GRANDVIEW	147	1747	1928	1996	1.1	84	652	740	772	1.4	2.61	497	545	1.0
47616	GRIFFIN	129	327	321	315	-0.2	27	134	135	133	0.1	2.38	99	96	-0.3
47619	LYNNVILLE	173	1421	1617	1729	1.4	89	589	698	755	1.9	2.32	428	485	1.4
47620	MOUNT VERNON	129	14682	14306	13991	-0.3	22	5652	5623	5530	-0.1	2.52	4156	4001	-0.4
47630	NEWBURGH	173	27497	32878	35665	2.0	93	9927	12264	13441	2.3	2.65	8021	9650	2.0
47631	NEW HARMONY	129	1963	2026	2016	0.3	56	796	845	846	0.6	2.28	552	562	0.2
47633	POSEYVILLE	129	2533	2603	2585	0.3	56	942	986	984	0.5	2.61	695	701	0.1
47634	RICHLAND	147	2437	2519	2517	0.4	60	955	1014	1018	0.7	2.48	744	766	0.3
47635	ROCKPORT	147	5622	5588	5533	-0.1	31	2151	2175	2163	0.1	2.51	1575	1540	-0.2
47637	TENNYSON	173	1613	1726	1800	0.7	73	598	664	699	1.1	2.60	481	519	0.8
47638	WADESVILLE	129	3308	3357	3321	0.2	49	1180	1223	1218	0.4	2.74	935	941	0.1
47639	HAUBSTADT	051	3766	4966	5329	3.0	97	1349	1830	1979	3.4	2.71	1053	1381	3.0
47640	HAZLETON	051	1297	1290	1283	-0.1	31	496	504	505	0.2	2.56	384	378	-0.2
47647	BUCKSKIN	051	233	229	221	-0.2	27	100	101	98	0.1	2.27	75	73	-0.3
47648	FORT BRANCH	051	3954	3854	3846	-0.3	22	1567	1567	1574	0.0	2.46	1127	1079	-0.5
47649	FRANCISCO	051	1478	1494	1487	0.1	43	590	615	618	0.4	2.43	437	440	0.1
47660	OAKLAND CITY	125	4800	4922	4963	0.3	56	1873	1970	2002	0.5	2.35	1291	1301	0.1
47665	OWENSVILLE	051	3749	3916	3973	0.5	66	1408	1492	1519	0.6	2.59	1052	1076	0.2
47666	PATOKA	051	1334	1350	1355	0.1	43	547	571	578	0.5	2.36	409	414	0.1
47670	PRINCETON	051	11495	11224	11104	-0.3	22	4753	4753	4733	0.0	2.29	3148	3009	-0.5
47708	EVANSVILLE	163	946	952	955	0.1	43	231	240	244	0.4	1.37	60	55	-0.9
47710	EVANSVILLE	163	21522	20301	19945	-0.6	8	9045	8727	8630	-0.4	2.21	5397	4908	-1.0
47711	EVANSVILLE	163	28458	29669	30181	0.5	66	11998	12724	13004	0.6	2.32	8015	8183	0.2
47712	EVANSVILLE	163	25042	24970	24956	0.0	37	9482	9694	9760	0.2	2.35	5969	5758	-0.4
47713	EVANSVILLE	163	12306	11184	10818	-1.0	2	5151	4748	4610	-0.9	2.27	2739	2343	-1.7
47714	EVANSVILLE	163	34924	33449	32963	-0.5	13	14835	14516	14398	-0.2	2.20	8951	8186	-1.0
47715	EVANSVILLE	163	24418	25789	26412	0.6	70	11127	12193	12636	1.0	2.10	6361	6356	0.0
47720	EVANSVILLE	163	16857	17246	17514	0.2	49	6396	6719	6876	0.5	2.53	4872	4908	0.1
47722	EVANSVILLE	163	1008	994	987	-0.2	27	15	14	14	-0.7	2.57	5	4	-2.4
47725	EVANSVILLE	163	9388	13471	15114	4.0	98	3380	4959	5599	4.2	2.72	2890	4138	4.0
47802	TERRE HAUTE	167	31252	33756	34076	0.8	76	12002	12651	12867	0.6	2.35	7859	7897	0.1
47803	TERRE HAUTE	167	19895	20013	20108	0.1	43	8168	8393	8472	0.3	2.28	5158	5041	-0.2
47804	TERRE HAUTE	167	11054	10599	10437	-0.5	13	4574	4466	4416	-0.3	2.27	2750	2536	-0.9
47805	TERRE HAUTE	167	12541	12493	12478	0.0	37	4928	5038	5068	0.2	2.48	3555	3490	-0.2
47807	TERRE HAUTE	167	17337	16338	16008	-0.6	8	6141	5820	5704	-0.6	2.21	2913	2555	-1.4
47809	TERRE HAUTE	167	151	133	127	-1.4	1	72	64	62	-1.3	2.08	31	26	-1.9
47832	BLOOMINGDALE	121	808	775	752	-0.4	18	316	301	292	-0.5	2.51	236	219	-0.8
47833	BOWLING GREEN	021	1156	1163	1158	0.1	43	427	437	438	0.3	2.66	329	326	-0.1
47834	BRAZIL	021	19838	20281	20210	0.2	49	7663	7932	7924	0.4	2.52	5517	5513	0.0
47836	BRIDGETON	121	489	462	446	-0.6	8	189	181	176	-0.5	2.55	152	143	-0.7
47837	CARBON	121	949	918	901	-0.4	18	347	342	337	-0.2	2.68	270	258	-0.5
47838	CARLISLE	153	4227	4314	4311	0.2	49	850	893	895	0.5	2.66	642	651	0.2
47840	CENTERPOINT	021	1640	1716	1722	0.5	66	593	627	630	0.6	2.70	456	466	0.2
47841	CLAY CITY	021	2351	2323	2294	-0.1	31	961	969	961	0.1	2.40	685	665	-0.3
47842	CLINTON	165	10628	10518	10351	-0.1	31	4325	4339	4281	0.0	2.36	2924	2816	-0.4
47846	CORY	021	735	756	755	0.3	56	297	310	311	0.5	2.44	209	209	0.0
47847	DANA	165	1182	1152	1128	-0.3	22	452	446	437	-0.1	2.56	341	325	-0.5
47848	DUGGER	153	1340	1353	1343	0.1	43	560	580	579	0.4	2.33	410	409	0.0
47849	FAIRBANKS	153	321	329	327	0.3	56	117	122	122	0.5	2.70	93	94	0.1
47850	FARMERSBURG	153	2773	2732	2702	-0.2	27	1069	1077	1070	0.1	2.53	797	775	-0.3
47854	HILLSDALE	165	987	957	936	-0.3	22	377	373	368	-0.1	2.53	292	280	-0.5
47858	LEWIS	021	634	616	606	-0.3	22	234	233	231	0.0	2.64	184	178	-0.4
47859	MARSHALL	121	793	772	753	-0.3	22	295	287	280	-0.3	2.67	228	216	-0.6
47861	MEROM	153	684	693	688	0.1	43	254	263	263	0.4	2.63	200	201	0.1
47862	MONTEZUMA	121	1414	1340	1300	-0.6	8	565	541	525	-0.5	2.45	414	385	-0.8
47866	PIMENTO	167	447	431	424	-0.4	18	184	183	181	-0.1	2.36	144	139	-0.4
47868	POLAND	119	3429	3627	3680	0.6	70	1280	1376	1403	0.8	2.64	938	966	0.3
47872	ROCKVILLE	121	9429	10160	10146	0.8	76	3373	3585	3596	0.7	2.42	2343	2388	0.2
47874	ROSEDALE	121	3994	3837	3752	-0.4	18	1544	1508	1479	-0.3	2.53	1175	1115	-0.6
47879	SHELBURN	153	3937	3838	3774	-0.3	22	1534	1522	1503	-0.1	2.51	1129	1081	-0.5
47882	SULLIVAN	153	8756	8639	8517	-0.1	31	3530	3535	3499	0.0	2.35	2380	2287	-0.4
47885	WEST TERRE HAUTE	167	10608	10264	10162	-0.4	18	3968	3937	3921	-0.1	2.50	2900	2766	-0.5
47901	LAFAYETTE	157	3345	3476	3590	0.4	60	1746	1891	1977	0.9	1.80	601	563	-0.7
47904	LAFAYETTE	157	16104	15986	16125	-0.1	31	6773	6932	7062	0.3	2.20	3606	3373	-0.7
47905	LAFAYETTE	157	36429	39404	41331	0.9	79	14926	16592	17525	1.2	2.35	9593	10128	0.6
47906	WEST LAFAYETTE	157	57485	64539	68300	1.3	87	18174	21754	23600	2.0	2.31	8974	10082	1.3
47907	WEST LAFAYETTE	157	1	1	1	0.0	37	1	1	1	0.0	1.00	0	0	0.0
47909	LAFAYETTE	157	30147	36828	40122	2.2	94	11642	14504	15867	2.4	2.54	8103	9755	2.0
47917	AMBIA	171	465	446	431	-0.4	18	184	181	176	-0.2	2.46	143	136	-0.5
47918	ATTICA	045	6652	6480	6311	-0.3	22	2579	2538	2480	-0.2	2.53	1837	1745	-0.6
47920	BATTLE GROUND	157	1818	1955	2041	0.8	76	676	757	798	1.2	2.58	515	551	0.7
47921	BOSWELL	007	1129	1068	1032	-0.6	8	444	426	412	-0.4	2.51	314	291	-0.8
47922	BROOK	111	1742	1714	1683	-0.2	27	627	626	616	0.0	2.65	461	443	-0.4
47923	BROOKSTON	181	3566	3609	3616	0.1	43	1368	1412	1420	0.3	2.55	1069	1068	0.0
47926	BURNETTSVILLE	181	1074	1050	1033	-0.2	27	398	397	392	0.0	2.64	307	296	-0.4
47928	CAYUGA	165	2448	2397	2348	-0.2	27	987	991	978	0.0	2.40	700	676	-0.4
47929	CHALMERS	181	839	906	917	0.8	76	300	326	330	0.9	2.78	233	245	0.5
47930	CLARKS HILL	157	1309	1432	1507	1.0	81	462	516	547	1.2	2.78	357	382	0.7
47932	COVINGTON	045	5623	5570	5460	-0.1	31	2231	2258	2223	0.1	2.41	1611	1574	-0.3
47933	CRAWFORDSVILLE	107	26778	27116	26964	0.1	43	10458	10699	10652	0.2	2.43	7129	7001	-0.2
47940	DARLINGTON	107	1935	1980	1972	0.2	49	719	744	743	0.4	2.66	555	556	0.0
47942	EARL PARK	007	907	831	796	-0.9	3	321	299	287	-0.8	2.62	232	208	-1.2
47943	FAIR OAKS	073	814	912	956	1.2	86	284	325	342	1.5	2.81	235	263	1.2
47944	FOWLER	007	3833	3625	3506	-0.6	8	1460	1401	1358	-0.4	2.51	1023	944	-0.9
47946	FRANCESVILLE	131	2032	2153	2164	0.6	70	743	801	810	0.8	2.62	555	579	0.5
47948	GOODLAND	111	1496	1567	1561	0.5	66	570	603	603	0.6	2.60	418	427	0.2
47949	HILLSBORO	045	1295	1208	1167	-0.7	5	493	468	453	-0.6	2.58	372	342	-0.9
47950	IDAVILLE	181	813	778	762	-0.5	13	321	313	308	-0.3	2.49	236	222	-0.7
47951	KENTLAND	111	2325	2159	2084	-0.8	4	935	887	858	-0.6	2.38	637	577	-1.1
47952	KINGMAN	045	3111	3034	2959	-0.3	22	1210	1193	1168	-0.2	2.54	876	834	-0.5
47954	LADOGA	107	2509	2468	2437	-0.2	27	919	916	907	0.0	2.63	709	685	-0.4
	INDIANA					0.7					0.8	2.49			0.4
	UNITED STATES					1.0					1.1	2.59			0.9

#	POST OFFICE NAME	RACE (%) White 2000	White 2009	Black 2000	Black 2009	Asian/Pacific 2000	Asian/Pacific 2009	% Hispanic Origin 2000	% Hispanic Origin 2009	2009 AGE DISTRIBUTION (%) 0-4	5-9	10-14	15-19	20-24	25-44	45-64	65-84	85+	18+	MEDIAN AGE 2009	% 2009 Males	% 2009 Females
47610	CHANDLER	98.7	98.4	0.4	0.4	0.2	0.2	0.6	0.8	6.6	6.6	7.1	6.7	5.6	26.8	28.8	10.6	1.3	75.3	38.5	49.7	50.3
47611	CHRISNEY	98.5	98.1	0.2	0.3	0.1	0.2	0.8	1.2	6.7	6.8	7.3	7.1	4.6	25.1	29.3	11.7	1.4	74.8	39.8	50.3	49.7
47612	CYNTHIANA	98.9	98.6	0.0	0.0	0.2	0.3	0.3	0.5	7.3	7.3	7.5	7.5	6.3	23.7	28.8	10.3	1.5	73.5	37.8	48.7	51.3
47613	ELBERFELD	99.3	99.1	0.1	0.1	0.1	0.2	0.3	0.4	5.7	6.0	6.4	6.8	5.0	25.1	30.4	13.1	1.6	77.7	41.8	50.5	49.5
47615	GRANDVIEW	98.1	97.7	0.9	1.1	0.2	0.4	0.4	0.6	6.0	6.2	6.7	7.5	5.3	25.6	29.6	12.0	1.1	76.5	40.4	50.9	49.1
47616	GRIFFIN	99.4	99.4	0.0	0.0	0.3	0.3	0.0	0.0	5.0	5.6	6.5	5.9	4.7	21.2	34.6	15.0	1.6	79.4	45.6	50.5	49.5
47619	LYNNVILLE	99.2	99.1	0.0	0.0	0.1	0.2	0.0	0.0	5.6	6.0	6.1	5.2	4.2	25.2	32.9	13.2	1.5	79.1	43.3	50.8	49.2
47620	MOUNT VERNON	97.2	96.6	1.5	1.7	0.2	0.3	0.6	0.9	6.6	6.8	7.0	6.8	5.8	25.1	29.0	11.2	1.6	75.5	39.2	49.7	50.3
47630	NEWBURGH	96.2	95.3	1.6	1.8	1.1	1.7	0.9	1.3	6.8	7.0	7.5	7.2	5.2	25.4	29.6	9.7	1.5	74.1	38.6	48.9	51.1
47631	NEW HARMONY	98.8	98.7	0.1	0.1	0.2	0.2	0.3	0.4	5.0	5.3	5.8	6.1	4.9	21.5	31.0	16.3	4.0	79.6	45.9	48.0	52.0
47633	POSEYVILLE	99.1	98.9	0.1	0.2	0.0	0.1	0.1	0.1	6.1	6.4	6.9	7.4	5.6	21.9	30.7	12.8	2.3	75.5	41.6	50.4	49.6
47634	RICHLAND	98.4	97.9	0.2	0.2	0.1	0.2	0.7	1.1	6.0	6.2	6.6	6.6	4.7	25.8	29.9	13.0	1.3	77.2	40.9	49.8	50.2
47635	ROCKPORT	97.3	96.8	1.3	1.5	0.2	0.2	0.7	1.1	6.0	6.4	6.7	6.7	4.8	24.2	29.8	13.0	2.4	76.5	41.6	49.4	50.6
47637	TENNYSON	99.2	99.1	0.1	0.1	0.1	0.1	0.4	0.7	6.1	6.3	6.5	6.7	5.4	25.7	31.7	10.6	0.9	76.9	40.3	49.8	50.2
47638	WADESVILLE	98.8	98.4	0.2	0.3	0.2	0.3	0.3	0.5	6.3	7.1	7.8	7.4	4.9	24.9	31.5	9.1	0.9	74.0	39.2	49.8	50.2
47639	HAUBSTADT	99.5	99.4	0.1	0.1	0.2	0.3	0.3	0.5	7.0	7.3	7.5	7.0	5.0	25.0	29.2	10.5	1.4	73.3	39.0	50.6	49.4
47640	HAZLETON	98.1	97.8	0.6	0.7	0.2	0.2	0.2	0.3	5.3	5.9	6.4	6.9	4.7	24.6	32.6	11.9	1.7	78.2	42.0	50.9	49.1
47647	BUCKSKIN	98.7	98.3	0.4	0.4	0.0	0.0	0.9	1.3	7.4	7.4	7.4	6.1	3.5	25.8	27.1	13.1	2.2	73.4	39.9	50.7	49.3
47648	FORT BRANCH	98.9	98.5	0.3	0.3	0.2	0.4	0.5	0.7	6.1	6.5	6.9	6.8	4.6	26.0	29.1	12.1	1.8	76.3	40.3	49.4	50.6
47649	FRANCISCO	98.3	97.9	0.8	1.0	0.1	0.2	0.3	0.5	5.0	5.4	5.9	5.8	4.2	26.8	32.2	13.0	1.8	80.1	42.7	50.3	49.7
47660	OAKLAND CITY	98.3	97.7	0.4	0.5	0.3	0.5	1.1	1.6	5.5	5.5	5.9	8.1	8.0	22.3	26.6	14.9	3.1	78.9	40.7	48.4	51.6
47665	OWENSVILLE	98.5	98.1	0.5	0.6	0.1	0.2	0.9	1.3	6.3	6.5	6.8	6.7	5.9	25.1	28.3	12.1	2.3	76.2	40.1	49.2	50.8
47666	PATOKA	96.0	95.3	2.9	3.5	0.3	0.4	0.2	0.4	6.1	6.7	6.9	5.8	4.4	24.1	31.3	13.1	1.6	76.6	42.1	51.3	48.7
47670	PRINCETON	92.7	90.8	4.4	5.3	1.1	1.8	0.9	1.4	6.6	6.1	6.0	6.0	5.6	25.2	26.8	14.5	3.3	77.6	40.8	48.4	51.6
47708	EVANSVILLE	73.2	66.5	24.0	30.0	0.7	0.9	1.6	2.2	0.7	1.4	0.6	2.8	5.4	36.8	23.0	20.4	8.9	96.7	46.6	60.8	39.2
47710	EVANSVILLE	93.4	91.6	4.4	5.6	0.5	0.7	0.9	1.4	6.0	5.9	6.0	6.1	6.0	24.4	26.0	15.6	3.8	78.2	41.5	47.2	52.8
47711	EVANSVILLE	95.3	93.9	2.5	3.2	0.7	1.1	0.9	1.3	6.3	6.1	6.3	6.3	5.5	25.8	28.9	12.5	2.2	77.5	40.5	48.4	51.6
47712	EVANSVILLE	97.0	95.9	1.4	1.9	0.6	1.0	0.7	1.0	5.2	5.1	5.2	9.8	9.9	26.9	25.3	10.5	2.1	81.2	34.5	47.7	52.3
47713	EVANSVILLE	47.0	40.2	49.7	56.2	0.3	0.4	1.2	1.6	7.5	6.9	6.3	7.1	6.9	25.7	25.2	11.7	2.8	74.9	36.7	47.3	52.7
47714	EVANSVILLE	85.7	82.3	11.3	14.1	0.6	0.9	1.2	1.7	6.8	6.4	5.8	6.7	8.1	27.3	24.3	12.0	2.8	77.5	36.6	46.7	53.3
47715	EVANSVILLE	89.6	86.1	6.4	8.4	1.8	2.7	1.4	2.2	6.2	5.8	5.7	5.7	7.8	27.1	25.5	13.3	2.9	79.1	37.6	47.5	52.5
47720	EVANSVILLE	98.3	97.8	0.5	0.7	0.3	0.4	0.4	0.7	6.1	6.5	6.9	6.5	5.0	24.0	30.1	12.9	2.1	76.3	41.5	49.1	50.9
47722	EVANSVILLE	91.3	88.2	3.0	3.9	3.9	5.4	1.7	2.6	0.4	0.4	0.2	38.3	51.2	4.7	2.5	1.6	0.6	98.3	21.0	33.0	67.0
47725	EVANSVILLE	97.2	96.0	1.0	1.4	1.1	1.7	0.6	0.9	5.9	6.5	7.3	6.9	4.2	23.6	32.3	12.1	1.2	75.9	42.1	50.0	50.0
47802	TERRE HAUTE	89.0	85.4	6.6	8.9	2.0	2.9	1.7	2.7	6.1	5.6	5.5	5.7	7.3	30.0	26.1	11.5	2.2	79.3	38.0	53.4	46.6
47803	TERRE HAUTE	93.5	92.6	4.1	4.3	0.9	1.4	1.1	1.4	5.7	5.7	5.9	7.4	7.7	24.0	27.6	13.4	2.7	79.1	39.9	49.2	50.8
47804	TERRE HAUTE	92.8	92.1	5.1	5.4	0.3	0.4	0.9	1.2	6.1	5.9	5.9	6.3	6.2	24.9	25.2	15.0	4.3	78.2	40.5	46.2	53.8
47805	TERRE HAUTE	96.8	96.2	1.7	1.9	0.4	0.6	0.8	1.0	6.0	6.1	6.7	8.3	6.6	25.1	27.4	12.4	1.6	76.9	38.2	50.1	49.9
47807	TERRE HAUTE	78.6	76.4	15.3	15.9	2.3	3.4	1.5	1.9	6.0	5.3	4.8	14.9	22.8	22.8	15.2	6.8	1.5	80.9	24.2	49.4	50.6
47809	TERRE HAUTE	74.0	71.4	19.3	20.3	2.0	3.0	2.0	2.3	9.0	6.8	5.3	6.8	22.6	24.8	18.0	5.3	1.5	76.7	24.9	51.9	48.1
47832	BLOOMINGDALE	98.0	97.5	0.9	1.2	0.1	0.1	0.5	0.5	6.8	6.8	7.2	7.2	6.5	26.1	26.7	11.0	1.7	74.7	36.6	49.9	50.1
47833	BOWLING GREEN	98.1	97.9	0.1	0.1	0.2	0.2	1.0	1.6	6.4	6.8	7.2	7.4	5.8	24.9	30.0	10.1	1.2	74.9	38.7	50.4	49.6
47834	BRAZIL	98.3	97.9	0.4	0.5	0.1	0.2	0.6	0.9	6.4	6.5	6.6	6.8	5.4	25.4	27.8	12.7	2.4	76.3	39.8	48.8	51.2
47836	BRIDGETON	98.6	98.5	0.0	0.0	0.6	0.6	0.4	0.6	4.8	5.4	5.8	6.7	5.0	24.0	34.4	12.3	1.5	79.9	43.8	49.8	50.2
47837	CARBON	98.8	98.5	0.3	0.3	0.0	0.0	0.7	1.2	6.3	6.6	7.0	7.4	5.1	25.1	29.5	11.9	1.1	75.4	39.7	49.0	51.0
47838	CARLISLE	77.2	74.1	19.9	22.3	0.1	0.2	1.6	2.2	3.4	3.5	3.6	4.6	11.2	41.8	23.0	8.0	0.9	87.1	35.8	72.4	27.6
47840	CENTERPOINT	98.2	97.9	0.1	0.1	0.1	0.2	0.5	0.8	7.4	7.7	7.8	6.1	4.9	24.2	28.1	11.7	2.0	73.0	38.6	48.8	51.2
47841	CLAY CITY	98.9	98.8	0.0	0.0	0.0	0.0	0.6	1.0	6.1	6.1	6.2	6.1	5.0	24.5	28.2	15.2	2.6	77.9	41.9	48.8	51.2
47842	CLINTON	98.3	97.9	0.3	0.4	0.1	0.1	0.7	1.0	6.3	6.3	6.3	5.9	5.2	25.2	28.2	13.5	3.0	77.6	41.1	48.4	51.6
47846	CORY	99.5	99.2	0.0	0.0	0.4	0.7	0.3	0.3	5.7	6.0	6.2	6.5	5.0	27.0	29.6	12.0	2.0	78.2	40.7	50.4	49.6
47847	DANA	98.1	97.3	0.4	0.5	0.3	0.5	1.2	1.7	6.8	6.9	7.2	6.9	5.7	24.1	29.1	11.5	1.6	74.7	39.2	50.1	49.9
47848	DUGGER	98.8	98.5	0.0	0.0	0.2	0.4	0.8	1.3	5.2	5.4	5.8	5.9	5.0	25.6	31.0	14.5	1.8	80.1	43.2	49.9	50.1
47849	FAIRBANKS	99.4	99.1	0.0	0.0	0.0	0.0	0.6	0.9	5.5	6.1	6.7	7.6	4.6	24.6	30.1	13.4	1.5	76.6	41.8	52.0	48.0
47850	FARMERSBURG	98.2	97.8	0.1	0.1	0.2	0.3	0.7	1.0	6.3	6.5	6.8	6.7	4.8	24.7	28.9	13.5	1.9	76.1	40.7	50.7	49.3
47854	HILLSDALE	98.6	98.3	0.1	0.2	0.4	0.4	0.4	0.6	5.3	5.7	6.2	6.6	5.1	23.3	33.6	12.3	1.8	78.6	43.2	50.7	49.3
47858	LEWIS	98.9	98.5	0.2	0.2	0.3	0.6	0.8	1.0	5.7	6.3	6.3	6.0	4.4	25.5	30.8	13.0	1.9	78.1	42.0	49.0	51.0
47859	MARSHALL	98.6	98.4	0.4	0.4	0.1	0.1	0.3	0.3	6.0	6.3	6.6	6.6	5.3	24.7	30.6	11.8	2.1	76.7	41.4	51.9	48.1
47861	MEROM	99.3	99.1	0.1	0.1	0.0	0.0	0.1	0.3	5.8	6.3	6.3	6.3	4.8	25.8	30.4	12.6	1.6	77.6	41.1	51.1	48.9
47862	MONTEZUMA	96.6	96.2	1.6	1.8	0.1	0.2	0.8	1.0	7.0	6.9	6.9	6.2	5.6	25.1	27.5	13.1	1.6	75.2	38.4	50.4	49.6
47866	PIMENTO	98.2	97.9	0.2	0.2	0.9	1.2	0.9	1.2	5.1	6.0	6.0	5.3	3.9	24.8	32.9	13.7	2.1	79.6	44.1	48.3	51.7
47868	POLAND	97.5	97.0	0.5	0.6	0.1	0.2	0.7	1.0	6.2	6.3	6.7	6.8	6.3	24.9	30.7	11.1	1.1	76.7	39.8	50.9	49.1
47872	ROCKVILLE	94.7	94.0	3.5	3.8	0.2	0.4	0.8	1.1	5.0	5.0	5.3	5.8	6.0	27.1	28.9	14.7	2.3	81.2	42.1	45.1	54.9
47874	ROSEDALE	98.9	98.6	0.3	0.4	0.3	0.4	0.3	0.5	5.7	5.9	6.5	7.5	5.3	25.6	30.0	12.0	1.4	77.0	40.4	49.3	50.7
47879	SHELBURN	98.5	98.2	0.2	0.2	0.1	0.2	0.4	0.6	7.0	7.4	7.2	6.3	4.5	26.2	28.1	11.7	1.6	74.4	38.5	51.1	48.9
47882	SULLIVAN	97.8	97.4	0.8	1.0	0.2	0.3	0.7	1.1	5.8	5.8	5.9	6.3	5.5	24.7	28.0	14.8	3.3	78.7	42.1	48.2	51.8
47885	WEST TERRE HAUTE	98.7	98.4	0.1	0.1	0.3	0.5	0.5	0.6	5.8	6.1	6.3	7.2	6.2	24.7	28.1	13.1	2.5	77.8	40.7	47.3	52.7
47901	LAFAYETTE	86.8	82.9	4.6	5.2	1.6	2.6	9.4	13.9	5.4	4.1	4.1	5.5	22.1	32.2	18.8	6.6	1.2	83.9	28.3	53.9	46.1
47904	LAFAYETTE	89.6	85.2	3.2	4.2	1.0	1.8	8.0	12.3	6.4	5.9	5.5	6.1	9.5	32.2	21.5	10.2	2.7	79.2	34.1	50.4	49.6
47905	LAFAYETTE	91.2	88.0	2.3	2.8	1.6	2.6	6.7	9.7	6.7	6.6	6.5	6.5	6.7	29.1	26.1	10.1	1.7	76.2	36.2	49.8	50.2
47906	WEST LAFAYETTE	84.8	78.1	2.5	4.4	9.8	13.9	3.0	4.5	3.8	3.5	3.6	17.0	30.7	19.9	14.1	6.1	1.5	87.3	23.6	54.1	45.9
47907	WEST LAFAYETTE	100.0	100.0	0.0	0.0	0.0	0.0	0.0	0.0	0.0	0.0	0.0	0.0	100.0	0.0	0.0	0.0	0.0	100.0	22.5	100.0	0.0
47909	LAFAYETTE	91.9	90.0	2.6	2.8	0.8	1.1	6.5	8.8	8.3	7.8	7.3	6.8	6.6	31.9	22.8	7.6	0.9	72.5	32.8	49.6	50.4
47917	AMBIA	94.8	93.0	0.2	0.4	0.0	0.0	6.9	9.9	5.6	6.5	6.7	6.7	4.0	23.8	30.7	13.7	2.2	77.1	42.6	51.8	48.2
47918	ATTICA	98.3	97.9	0.1	0.1	0.2	0.3	1.1	1.5	6.9	7.2	7.2	7.1	5.5	24.5	26.7	12.6	2.3	74.2	39.0	50.4	49.6
47920	BATTLE GROUND	97.3	96.5	0.4	0.3	0.2	0.3	1.7	2.8	5.8	7.1	7.6	7.2	4.0	25.6	31.6	10.2	1.0	75.1	40.3	49.7	50.3
47921	BOSWELL	93.6	91.2	0.2	0.2	0.2	0.3	7.6	11.3	7.6	7.3	6.7	6.0	6.0	25.3	24.7	13.6	2.8	74.7	38.3	47.8	52.2
47922	BROOK	96.4	96.2	0.2	0.2	0.3	0.4	5.4	5.5	6.5	6.6	6.8	6.6	5.1	24.0	26.3	14.2	4.0	75.8	41.3	47.8	52.2
47923	BROOKSTON	98.6	98.0	0.1	0.1	0.3	0.5	1.1	1.8	6.7	7.1	7.5	7.3	4.7	25.4	29.8	10.3	1.3	74.1	39.2	49.2	50.8
47926	BURNETTSVILLE	98.9	98.6	0.0	0.0	0.0	0.0	1.1	1.7	5.4	6.1	6.7	7.0	4.6	25.2	32.1	11.7	1.1	77.3	41.2	52.3	47.7
47928	CAYUGA	98.5	98.3	0.1	0.2	0.2	0.3	0.7	0.9	5.9	6.1	6.2	6.0	5.5	25.0	28.6	14.8	1.8	78.2	41.5	51.0	49.0
47929	CHALMERS	98.6	98.1	0.0	0.0	0.0	0.1	1.2	1.9	6.8	7.3	7.7	7.2	3.9	25.6	29.6	10.6	1.3	73.5	39.6	48.9	51.1
47930	CLARKS HILL	97.7	96.9	0.3	0.3	0.5	0.8	1.5	2.3	8.0	8.2	8.6	8.4	5.2	24.6	27.4	8.7	0.9	70.0	35.2	48.4	51.6
47932	COVINGTON	98.7	98.3	0.3	0.3	0.3	0.5	0.5	0.8	5.7	6.0	6.2	6.0	5.2	24.2	29.0	15.0	2.7	78.3	42.6	49.9	50.1
47933	CRAWFORDSVILLE	95.9	94.6	1.0	1.1	0.6	0.9	2.1	3.1	6.4	6.4	6.6	7.8	6.9	24.1	26.5	12.9	2.3	76.4	38.6	49.9	50.1
47940	DARLINGTON	99.2	98.9	0.1	0.2	0.1	0.2	0.5	0.7	7.3	7.7	8.2	8.2	4.1	24.1	27.7	11.2	1.5	71.5	38.9	49.9	50.1
47942	EARL PARK	98.0	97.4	0.1	0.1	0.1	0.1	2.2	3.2	6.6	6.7	7.0	6.7	4.3	25.0	26.0	12.8	4.8	75.5	40.5	49.7	50.3
47943	FAIR OAKS	97.7	97.4	0.6	0.7	0.2	0.2	3.4	4.9	7.8	8.2	8.1	6.8	4.7	25.2	27.9	10.3	1.0	71.6	37.1	50.8	49.2
47944	FOWLER	97.3	96.4	0.3	0.4	0.1	0.1	2.1	3.1	6.6	7.2	7.2	7.6	6.0	24.1	25.6	12.9	2.7	73.8	38.3	50.6	49.4
47946	FRANCESVILLE	98.6	98.2	0.0	0.1	0.2	0.2	1.3	1.9	6.6	7.1	7.7	7.5	4.4	22.5	27.1	13.8	3.3	73.3	40.8	50.3	49.7
47948	GOODLAND	97.6	97.5	0.1	0.1	0.1	0.2	3.3	3.4	6.9	7.1	7.3	7.2	5.5	25.7	26.6	11.7	1.9	74.2	38.3	48.8	51.2
47949	HILLSBORO	99.4	99.3	0.0	0.0	0.2	0.2	0.4	0.4	6.8	6.9	7.4	7.8	5.3	25.2	27.2	11.6	1.8	74.3	39.4	50.1	49.9
47950	IDAVILLE	98.4	97.8	0.1	0.1	0.2	0.4	1.0	1.5	6.3	6.6	7.2	6.8	5.0	25.2	28.9	12.5	1.5	75.7	39.9	50.8	49.2
47951	KENTLAND	98.2	98.0	0.2	0.2	0.3	0.3	2.9	3.0	5.2	5.7	7.3	6.9	5.7	23.7	28.9	14.1	2.5	77.8	41.6	49.6	50.4
47952	KINGMAN	99.1	98.9	0.0	0.0	0.1	0.1	0.5	0.8	6.4	6.4	6.8	7.1	6.0	24.4	27.6	13.8	1.6	76.2	39.9	52.1	47.9
47954	LADOGA	99.2	98.9	0.1	0.1	0.2	0.3	0.4	0.7	6.8	7.2	7.5	7.0	5.0	23.7	28.0	12.1	2.7	74.1	40.0	50.6	49.4
	INDIANA	87.5	85.6	8.4	8.9	1.0	1.5	3.5	5.0	6.9	6.8	6.8	7.2	6.9	26.5	26.2	10.8	1.9	75.4	36.8	49.3	50.7
	UNITED STATES	75.1	72.0	12.3	12.7	3.8	4.6	12.5	15.7	6.8	6.7	6.6	7.1	6.9	27.0	26.0	10.9	1.9	75.7	36.9	49.2	50.8

C 47610-47954

ZIP CODE #	POST OFFICE NAME	2009 Per Capita Income	2009 HH Income Base	2009 HOUSEHOLD INCOME DISTRIBUTION (%) Less than $25,000	$25,000 to $49,999	$50,000 to $99,999	$100,000 to $149,999	$150,000 or More	MEDIAN HOUSEHOLD INCOME 2009	2014	2009 National Centile	2009 State Centile	2009 Home Value Base	2009 HOME VALUE DISTRIBUTION (%) Less than $50,000	$50,000 to $89,999	$90,000 to $174,999	$175,000 to $399,999	$400,000 or More	2009 Median Home Value
47610	CHANDLER	22096	2160	17.7	30.2	44.5	6.3	1.3	51590	53985	65	56	1821	19.5	41.2	31.4	6.7	1.3	81239
47611	CHRISNEY	21223	753	19.3	30.1	41.8	6.6	2.1	50309	51591	62	48	630	16.0	29.8	37.6	13.8	2.7	94483
47612	CYNTHIANA	18952	371	22.1	32.6	40.7	3.5	1.1	46240	50096	52	29	300	33.0	32.0	31.7	3.3	0.0	69630
47613	ELBERFELD	21577	1566	17.0	35.2	40.4	5.7	1.6	48559	50166	58	38	1319	14.7	36.3	36.5	11.9	0.5	88893
47615	GRANDVIEW	20206	740	21.5	32.0	38.1	7.2	1.2	46845	49743	54	31	606	20.8	32.2	36.3	9.2	1.5	87429
47616	GRIFFIN	20960	135	20.0	32.6	41.5	5.9	0.0	47674	51070	56	34	115	33.0	41.7	22.6	2.6	0.0	66765
47619	LYNNVILLE	23099	698	18.6	34.5	40.4	5.7	0.7	47876	49847	56	35	576	25.0	37.0	29.3	8.3	0.3	77692
47620	MOUNT VERNON	24064	5623	22.1	24.3	39.8	10.7	3.1	54120	57023	70	67	4447	15.7	28.6	43.7	11.4	0.6	96222
47630	NEWBURGH	32299	12264	9.9	17.1	46.0	18.0	9.0	75023	77594	89	96	10289	4.9	10.4	54.2	27.3	3.4	137071
47631	NEW HARMONY	23475	845	27.6	27.7	34.0	7.2	3.6	44721	48227	47	22	664	23.0	29.5	37.0	8.1	2.3	86531
47633	POSEYVILLE	21935	986	20.1	27.9	40.4	8.6	3.0	51393	53894	65	55	815	22.6	40.1	30.8	6.3	0.2	78952
47634	RICHLAND	20630	1014	19.8	33.7	39.3	6.5	0.7	47531	50129	55	34	881	18.6	31.3	40.7	8.7	0.6	90083
47635	ROCKPORT	20488	2175	25.6	29.6	35.2	8.0	1.6	45172	48283	49	24	1727	15.0	35.2	40.5	9.1	0.2	89829
47637	TENNYSON	20480	664	19.0	30.6	44.9	4.8	0.8	50357	52594	62	48	569	24.6	34.8	33.6	5.8	1.2	79878
47638	WADESVILLE	23922	1223	13.7	24.9	46.8	11.5	3.1	60649	61393	78	84	1054	4.6	19.5	59.2	15.4	1.2	116224
47639	HAUBSTADT	25414	1830	13.4	23.1	49.2	10.4	3.9	62691	60928	81	87	1585	6.1	16.9	52.6	23.4	0.9	122898
47640	HAZLETON	19262	504	26.0	33.3	34.1	5.4	1.2	41904	44171	39	12	452	39.8	26.3	28.8	5.1	0.0	69355
47647	BUCKSKIN	21555	101	22.8	33.7	38.6	5.0	0.0	44599	47332	47	21	79	30.4	26.6	27.8	12.7	2.5	76429
47648	FORT BRANCH	24540	1567	15.6	29.5	42.6	9.8	2.4	52526	53806	70	68	1240	10.7	33.6	44.6	11.0	0.1	95426
47649	FRANCISCO	23346	615	17.2	30.1	44.4	6.3	2.0	52253	51706	66	59	545	21.8	39.1	32.3	6.8	0.0	83161
47660	OAKLAND CITY	20649	1970	27.4	30.3	34.0	7.0	1.4	43581	46567	44	17	1501	27.4	39.2	28.6	4.8	0.0	72138
47665	OWENSVILLE	21203	1492	20.4	28.6	41.6	7.8	1.5	50738	51469	63	51	1236	25.4	35.6	32.8	5.3	1.0	78571
47666	PATOKA	23115	571	26.4	29.9	35.7	5.1	2.8	44109	47043	46	19	491	36.0	23.8	32.6	6.5	1.0	68243
47670	PRINCETON	20980	4753	30.3	29.1	32.2	6.9	1.5	40474	43868	34	10	3306	24.1	40.4	30.4	4.7	0.4	75031
47708	EVANSVILLE	18730	240	54.2	19.2	15.4	6.3	5.0	20725	22299	2	1	32	0.0	0.0	100.0	0.0	0.0	157609
47710	EVANSVILLE	21580	8727	33.4	30.3	28.7	5.1	2.4	37580	40617	25	6	5025	22.1	41.0	31.0	5.5	0.4	79696
47711	EVANSVILLE	26669	12724	19.9	29.2	38.3	9.0	3.6	50801	53235	63	51	9764	12.6	35.5	42.0	9.4	0.6	91748
47712	EVANSVILLE	24735	9694	22.5	27.6	38.4	7.5	4.1	49958	52343	61	46	6681	12.8	33.2	44.0	9.0	1.0	93882
47713	EVANSVILLE	16809	4748	45.1	30.8	19.7	2.9	1.5	27914	28306	6	2	2106	45.3	35.8	15.4	3.0	0.5	53793
47714	EVANSVILLE	23196	14516	26.2	32.4	33.8	5.2	2.4	42974	45999	42	14	9083	10.0	53.2	34.1	2.5	0.2	81986
47715	EVANSVILLE	30049	12193	20.6	29.1	37.9	7.0	5.4	50271	52225	62	48	6379	3.7	17.5	64.7	12.7	1.4	112157
47720	EVANSVILLE	26910	6719	14.9	25.8	44.2	10.6	4.5	60554	60243	78	83	6012	17.5	20.2	46.6	14.2	1.4	103749
47722	EVANSVILLE	10745	14	57.1	21.4	14.3	7.1	0.0	17928	25000	1	1	5	0.0	100.0	0.0	0.0	0.0	71667
47725	EVANSVILLE	37932	4959	6.0	13.2	47.1	20.1	13.6	81304	81669	93	98	4638	0.9	9.4	54.3	28.6	6.7	143384
47802	TERRE HAUTE	23029	12651	23.1	31.0	35.3	6.7	3.9	46089	49635	52	27	8394	12.5	33.8	41.6	10.7	1.4	93667
47803	TERRE HAUTE	28569	8393	19.2	28.2	37.4	9.2	6.1	52986	55071	68	64	6262	12.3	36.4	39.2	11.0	1.0	91205
47804	TERRE HAUTE	19687	4466	34.0	30.4	29.4	4.1	2.1	35815	38355	20	5	2934	30.5	49.4	19.3	0.7	0.1	62860
47805	TERRE HAUTE	25051	5038	20.6	26.7	40.5	8.8	3.5	52239	54088	66	59	4028	12.1	36.7	45.0	5.5	0.6	90877
47807	TERRE HAUTE	14695	5820	50.4	29.3	17.5	2.2	0.7	24690	24914	3	2	2094	54.0	34.7	10.0	1.1	0.2	47804
47809	TERRE HAUTE	12077	64	65.6	21.9	10.9	1.6	0.0	16410	15828	1	1	15	66.7	33.3	0.0	0.0	0.0	28750
47832	BLOOMINGDALE	21178	301	24.3	31.2	33.9	6.6	4.0	43385	44441	44	16	251	31.9	40.2	20.3	5.2	2.4	71731
47833	BOWLING GREEN	18742	437	22.9	34.6	35.2	6.2	1.1	44081	46634	46	19	374	24.6	18.7	35.3	16.8	4.5	103000
47834	BRAZIL	21003	7932	24.9	29.2	36.9	6.7	2.2	46195	49569	52	28	6134	17.5	37.2	37.3	7.7	0.3	85820
47836	BRIDGETON	20031	181	24.9	32.0	34.3	8.3	0.6	44176	43727	46	20	162	23.5	26.5	36.4	11.7	1.9	90000
47837	CARBON	18578	342	26.0	30.7	36.0	6.7	0.6	43904	46684	45	18	299	24.4	30.8	39.1	5.7	0.0	85694
47838	CARLISLE	16336	893	26.5	34.2	31.6	4.6	3.1	42975	44878	42	15	731	25.2	39.4	30.6	4.2	0.5	70088
47840	CENTERPOINT	21860	627	16.9	30.5	42.9	5.9	3.8	51936	53587	66	57	525	20.2	20.4	48.2	10.3	1.0	99340
47841	CLAY CITY	21445	969	22.7	36.2	33.1	6.1	1.9	43075	46082	43	15	778	22.1	36.8	37.7	2.6	0.9	82418
47842	CLINTON	22632	4339	28.3	29.0	33.8	5.9	3.1	42882	45179	42	14	3317	24.0	41.0	29.5	5.3	0.2	74461
47846	CORY	19467	310	19.7	42.9	32.9	3.9	0.6	42281	43390	40	13	261	25.7	22.2	42.1	10.0	0.0	92750
47847	DANA	21167	446	21.5	35.0	35.7	6.1	1.8	45148	46367	49	23	375	22.4	42.4	29.6	5.6	0.0	72568
47848	DUGGER	18887	580	30.0	32.2	33.8	3.4	0.5	40000	42436	33	8	490	29.0	41.8	25.9	3.3	0.0	68116
47849	FAIRBANKS	21297	122	22.1	27.0	39.3	7.4	4.1	50499	53013	62	49	106	17.0	27.4	42.5	13.2	0.0	95455
47850	FARMERSBURG	19852	1077	26.8	30.9	34.0	5.8	2.5	42770	46329	42	14	899	22.4	42.9	29.6	4.9	0.2	76193
47854	HILLSDALE	25799	373	17.7	29.8	38.1	10.2	4.3	52435	52074	67	60	324	17.0	31.8	39.8	11.4	0.0	91111
47858	LEWIS	22616	233	21.5	32.6	35.6	5.2	5.2	42624	50408	41	14	202	21.3	32.2	36.6	9.4	0.5	85625
47859	MARSHALL	20276	287	19.5	28.2	42.9	9.4	0.0	51145	50725	64	52	224	19.6	35.3	28.1	15.2	1.8	85417
47861	MEROM	19680	263	22.1	31.6	38.8	6.1	1.5	46895	50446	54	31	226	18.6	47.3	28.8	5.3	0.0	77500
47862	MONTEZUMA	19019	541	26.8	37.7	28.1	6.1	1.3	40987	42585	36	11	422	37.4	40.5	17.5	4.3	0.2	60000
47866	PIMENTO	29572	183	20.8	26.2	37.7	7.1	8.2	51735	53102	65	57	156	8.3	33.3	47.4	9.6	1.3	105172
47868	POLAND	19132	1376	21.8	35.6	35.8	5.5	1.4	44070	46010	46	19	1188	26.3	23.1	33.7	14.8	2.0	90779
47872	ROCKVILLE	20775	3585	24.7	32.4	34.1	6.4	2.5	43496	44548	44	16	2757	20.4	35.5	34.2	8.6	1.3	84347
47874	ROSEDALE	22102	1508	19.4	30.0	42.0	7.2	1.5	50583	51357	63	50	1287	21.0	38.2	34.9	5.4	0.6	82114
47879	SHELBURN	18509	1522	29.5	34.5	28.7	5.0	2.3	38712	41143	29	7	1262	28.7	38.3	28.8	3.6	0.6	70000
47882	SULLIVAN	20932	3535	28.0	32.7	31.5	5.9	1.9	41018	43486	36	11	2640	20.6	40.6	33.3	5.1	0.5	77526
47885	WEST TERRE HAUTE	19863	3937	27.2	32.7	32.1	6.0	2.0	40850	43193	35	10	3135	25.6	31.5	34.8	7.8	0.3	80915
47901	LAFAYETTE	21126	1891	44.2	31.3	19.9	3.2	1.4	27194	27424	5	2	370	14.1	29.5	40.5	13.8	2.2	102113
47904	LAFAYETTE	22397	6932	26.1	33.6	34.3	4.2	1.8	41324	43820	37	11	3517	14.6	41.8	38.9	4.5	0.2	85882
47905	LAFAYETTE	28727	16592	17.3	24.6	42.3	10.2	5.5	57235	57646	74	76	10516	7.6	12.3	58.0	19.6	2.5	126613
47906	WEST LAFAYETTE	23157	21754	33.7	23.9	26.3	8.9	7.1	39152	42234	30	8	9583	12.3	4.6	49.2	30.1	3.9	145758
47907	WEST LAFAYETTE	0	0	0.0	0.0	0.0	0.0	0.0	0	0	0	0	0	0.0	0.0	0.0	0.0	0.0	0
47909	LAFAYETTE	27238	14504	11.7	25.2	47.2	11.6	4.2	61545	62262	79	85	9983	3.9	12.9	65.1	17.0	1.1	120371
47917	AMBIA	20448	146	20.4	35.9	37.0	6.1	0.6	46047	49203	51	27	146	26.0	34.2	35.6	4.1	0.0	73333
47918	ATTICA	21351	2538	21.6	32.7	36.5	7.7	1.5	46279	48769	52	29	1941	15.2	29.6	45.5	8.9	0.8	94786
47920	BATTLE GROUND	23791	757	15.2	31.8	40.4	9.2	3.3	52115	53619	66	58	627	11.8	14.2	47.8	24.4	1.8	121798
47921	BOSWELL	20630	426	23.0	32.9	35.9	7.0	1.2	46196	48626	52	28	339	20.4	44.0	33.6	2.1	0.0	76848
47922	BROOK	18697	626	23.6	31.9	37.7	5.6	1.1	45840	49296	51	26	474	7.4	42.0	41.8	7.6	1.3	90600
47923	BROOKSTON	23667	1412	13.2	29.2	48.3	7.2	2.0	57094	58010	74	76	1149	5.9	16.8	60.3	15.8	1.1	115369
47926	BURNETTSVILLE	22364	397	18.9	28.2	43.1	7.6	2.3	52292	53977	66	59	332	12.7	34.6	47.3	5.1	0.3	92727
47928	CAYUGA	21236	991	27.1	30.2	34.2	5.9	2.6	42107	45224	40	13	845	21.7	47.8	27.3	3.1	0.1	72525
47929	CHALMERS	21266	326	17.8	25.8	47.5	7.1	1.8	54210	55101	70	67	269	8.9	23.8	53.2	11.2	3.0	108269
47930	CLARKS HILL	18841	516	20.2	32.4	40.7	5.2	1.6	47890	51217	56	35	398	27.4	25.4	34.4	11.3	1.5	86667
47932	COVINGTON	25138	2258	19.2	28.3	41.0	9.1	2.5	52225	53220	66	59	1782	14.8	31.3	46.2	7.1	0.7	93977
47933	CRAWFORDSVILLE	24236	10699	21.3	26.0	41.2	8.2	3.3	52302	54045	66	60	7530	10.1	22.8	51.5	14.4	1.2	111278
47940	DARLINGTON	21772	744	18.7	29.7	42.7	7.5	1.3	51272	53201	64	54	624	10.6	22.8	47.6	17.3	1.8	110560
47942	EARL PARK	18184	299	19.4	40.8	35.8	2.0	2.0	37993	41644	27	7	218	19.7	33.9	41.7	4.6	0.0	87241
47943	FAIR OAKS	21838	325	11.4	30.2	49.2	8.3	0.9	60494	61025	78	82	266	4.9	7.1	47.0	38.0	3.0	162500
47944	FOWLER	24304	1401	17.0	28.6	42.0	9.9	2.6	54634	56069	71	69	1059	13.5	32.1	49.8	4.5	0.1	94009
47946	FRANCESVILLE	19810	801	20.1	34.2	40.0	3.6	2.1	47180	48278	55	32	656	12.7	34.5	43.0	9.1	0.8	92533
47948	GOODLAND	19158	603	22.4	32.8	38.6	5.5	0.7	46860	49800	54	31	441	12.5	51.2	31.5	3.9	0.9	78984
47949	HILLSBORO	21058	468	20.1	27.6	46.6	3.6	2.1	51198	51972	64	53	393	19.6	39.2	36.9	4.3	0.0	85400
47950	IDAVILLE	22330	313	15.3	36.7	40.9	5.4	1.6	48161	50896	57	36	261	34.1	20.3	36.0	7.7	1.9	82333
47951	KENTLAND	22834	887	20.2	33.5	38.1	5.7	2.5	46855	50556	54	31	625	9.9	43.4	37.3	9.4	0.0	86694
47952	KINGMAN	17523	1193	29.6	36.5	29.6	3.0	1.3	36804	40263	23	6	959	35.1	39.6	21.3	3.4	0.5	70407
47954	LADOGA	21716	916	16.5	27.6	48.6	6.3	1.0	55204	56277	72	70	729	8.8	24.8	57.3	9.1	0.0	110244
	INDIANA	26003		19.5	26.3	38.6	10.5	5.1	54105	56493				12.2	24.1	44.1	17.2	2.4	108938
	UNITED STATES	27277		20.9	24.4	35.3	11.7	7.6	54719	56938				9.3	13.1	31.6	32.6	13.5	162279

ZIP CODE #	POST OFFICE NAME	FINANCIAL SERVICES: Auto Loan	Home Loan	Invest-ments	Retire-ment Plans	THE HOME: Home Improvements: Home Repair	Lawn & Garden	Furnishings: Computers & Hardware-Personal	Major Appli-ances	TV, Radio, Sound Equip-ment	Furni-ture	ENTERTAINMENT: Dine out/Carry out	Sports Equip-ment	Fees & Tickets	Toys & Games	Travel	Cable TV	PERSONAL: Apparel & Services	Auto Repairs	Health Insur-ance	Pets & Supplies
47610	CHANDLER	87	83	75	83	80	88	80	84	82	79	81	65	77	84	79	84	56	82	86	100
47611	CHRISNEY	86	78	78	81	79	92	77	86	79	71	78	66	71	81	76	84	53	80	89	101
47612	CYNTHIANA	92	67	76	65	66	88	69	81	77	67	75	62	56	80	63	84	51	76	85	98
47613	ELBERFELD	87	76	77	78	77	91	76	86	79	70	78	65	68	81	74	84	53	80	89	101
47615	GRANDVIEW	89	71	76	71	71	89	72	83	77	68	76	63	61	80	68	83	51	77	86	99
47616	GRIFFIN	89	64	91	62	66	90	65	83	73	61	71	62	52	72	65	80	47	76	87	99
47619	LYNNVILLE	95	69	97	67	71	97	70	89	78	65	77	67	56	78	70	86	51	82	93	106
47620	MOUNT VERNON	90	87	78	89	85	93	86	89	88	83	87	68	83	89	84	90	60	87	93	106
47630	NEWBURGH	123	136	121	136	132	124	123	124	118	129	120	97	130	123	126	115	85	120	116	143
47631	NEW HARMONY	88	73	85	74	75	93	74	87	79	68	78	66	65	80	74	86	52	81	92	102
47633	POSEYVILLE	91	80	85	83	82	97	79	91	83	73	81	69	72	84	79	88	55	84	94	106
47634	RICHLAND	83	71	73	72	72	86	71	80	74	65	73	61	63	76	69	79	50	75	83	95
47635	ROCKPORT	81	72	74	74	73	87	72	82	75	65	73	62	65	76	71	80	50	76	85	95
47637	TENNYSON	94	70	82	68	70	92	72	84	79	69	77	65	59	81	67	86	52	79	89	102
47638	WADESVILLE	94	100	89	103	98	103	92	98	91	90	91	76	94	94	96	93	63	93	98	114
47639	HAUBSTADT	98	105	91	108	101	107	97	101	97	95	96	78	100	99	100	98	67	97	103	119
47640	HAZLETON	84	65	76	66	66	85	67	78	72	62	71	61	56	74	64	78	48	73	82	94
47647	BUCKSKIN	76	69	68	72	70	81	68	77	70	61	69	58	63	71	68	74	47	71	79	89
47648	FORT BRANCH	91	86	85	87	85	98	84	92	86	79	85	70	80	87	84	90	58	87	96	108
47649	FRANCISCO	88	80	79	83	82	94	79	89	81	71	80	67	73	83	79	86	55	82	92	103
47660	OAKLAND CITY	85	61	82	60	63	87	66	81	74	60	71	60	53	73	63	81	48	75	87	95
47665	OWENSVILLE	94	74	81	72	74	91	75	85	81	74	80	64	64	84	70	87	54	81	89	102
47666	PATOKA	92	74	79	74	74	92	75	86	80	70	79	65	64	83	71	86	53	80	90	102
47670	PRINCETON	75	63	65	64	63	75	69	72	72	63	70	55	61	72	64	76	48	71	78	86
47708	EVANSVILLE	47	35	43	40	37	43	57	46	62	51	61	36	51	53	51	66	43	57	65	60
47710	EVANSVILLE	69	63	62	63	63	71	68	68	72	65	71	51	65	71	65	76	49	70	77	81
47711	EVANSVILLE	88	88	78	89	85	93	87	88	89	84	89	67	87	90	86	92	61	88	94	105
47712	EVANSVILLE	87	84	76	86	81	89	87	86	88	83	87	67	84	89	84	90	60	87	91	103
47713	EVANSVILLE	56	46	43	47	44	52	54	51	58	52	57	39	50	58	49	61	40	55	58	63
47714	EVANSVILLE	75	68	60	70	65	72	76	70	77	71	76	56	72	77	70	78	53	75	77	86
47715	EVANSVILLE	91	81	77	84	79	80	92	84	92	91	93	67	88	92	87	91	65	90	87	101
47720	EVANSVILLE	99	103	93	104	101	105	96	101	97	95	96	77	98	98	98	98	67	97	102	118
47722	EVANSVILLE	52	22	22	27	20	26	74	36	58	50	59	39	43	57	39	53	42	51	36	49
47725	EVANSVILLE	139	166	159	169	166	159	143	151	139	148	140	115	159	141	156	138	100	143	145	174
47802	TERRE HAUTE	83	76	74	78	75	83	82	81	84	78	83	62	77	84	78	86	57	82	86	97
47803	TERRE HAUTE	96	94	88	95	93	99	94	95	96	93	95	72	93	97	93	98	66	95	101	113
47804	TERRE HAUTE	68	56	58	57	55	67	64	64	68	59	66	50	57	67	59	71	45	66	73	78
47805	TERRE HAUTE	88	87	81	87	84	95	84	88	87	81	86	67	84	88	84	90	59	87	95	105
47807	TERRE HAUTE	48	36	34	38	35	40	52	42	52	45	51	35	43	51	42	53	36	48	48	53
47809	TERRE HAUTE	38	24	23	27	24	26	45	30	40	35	40	28	33	40	31	39	28	37	32	39
47832	BLOOMINGDALE	96	70	80	69	70	92	73	84	80	70	78	65	59	83	67	87	53	80	89	102
47833	BOWLING GREEN	85	67	72	67	67	84	68	78	73	64	72	60	58	76	65	79	49	73	82	93
47834	BRAZIL	83	72	74	73	72	86	74	81	78	68	76	62	67	78	72	83	52	78	87	96
47836	BRIDGETON	88	67	88	66	69	91	68	84	74	63	73	63	57	74	68	81	49	77	87	99
47837	CARBON	86	66	75	66	67	85	68	79	74	64	72	60	57	76	64	80	49	74	82	94
47838	CARLISLE	89	65	91	63	67	91	67	84	73	62	72	63	54	73	66	81	48	77	87	100
47840	CENTERPOINT	92	84	83	87	85	99	83	93	85	75	84	71	76	87	82	90	57	86	96	108
47841	CLAY CITY	89	64	90	62	67	92	68	85	76	62	73	64	55	75	66	83	49	79	91	100
47842	CLINTON	87	70	77	71	70	89	75	83	80	68	78	63	65	80	71	86	53	80	90	99
47846	CORY	84	61	86	59	63	86	62	79	69	58	68	59	50	69	62	76	45	73	82	94
47847	DANA	96	71	85	70	72	94	73	87	80	70	79	66	60	82	69	87	53	81	91	104
47848	DUGGER	79	56	81	55	58	80	58	74	64	54	63	55	46	64	57	71	42	68	77	87
47849	FAIRBANKS	89	81	80	84	83	96	80	90	82	72	81	68	74	84	80	87	55	83	93	105
47850	FARMERSBURG	85	64	83	63	66	88	67	82	74	61	72	61	56	73	66	80	48	76	87	96
47854	HILLSDALE	108	89	103	91	92	113	90	106	95	82	93	80	78	96	89	102	63	98	110	124
47858	LEWIS	96	82	90	85	84	102	82	95	86	75	85	72	73	87	82	92	57	88	99	111
47859	MARSHALL	85	76	77	79	78	91	75	86	78	68	76	65	69	79	75	83	52	79	88	100
47861	MEROM	80	73	72	76	75	86	72	81	74	65	73	62	67	76	72	79	50	75	84	95
47862	MONTEZUMA	82	59	74	57	60	81	63	75	70	59	68	57	50	71	59	76	45	70	80	90
47866	PIMENTO	108	98	97	102	100	116	97	109	100	88	98	83	90	102	97	106	67	101	113	127
47868	POLAND	85	70	70	69	70	81	69	77	74	69	73	57	62	77	65	78	50	73	79	92
47872	ROCKVILLE	87	68	88	67	71	90	72	85	78	66	76	63	62	77	71	85	51	80	91	100
47874	ROSEDALE	89	78	83	78	77	93	77	86	81	73	80	66	71	82	76	86	54	82	91	103
47879	SHELBURN	82	60	77	58	61	82	62	75	69	58	67	57	50	69	59	75	45	70	79	90
47882	SULLIVAN	79	65	76	65	67	83	68	77	73	63	71	57	60	73	66	79	48	74	84	91
47885	WEST TERRE HAUTE	81	67	71	68	68	82	70	78	74	64	72	59	62	75	67	79	49	74	82	92
47901	LAFAYETTE	56	40	38	43	39	42	64	47	60	54	60	41	51	60	49	59	42	56	50	59
47904	LAFAYETTE	73	63	56	66	60	67	76	67	75	69	75	55	68	76	67	76	52	72	73	83
47905	LAFAYETTE	98	95	86	96	92	93	98	95	97	97	98	74	96	99	95	97	68	97	96	112
47906	WEST LAFAYETTE	89	69	66	73	67	70	101	77	92	87	92	66	83	92	79	88	65	87	77	95
47907	WEST LAFAYETTE	0	0	0	0	0	0	0	0	0	0	0	0	0	0	0	0	0	0	0	0
47909	LAFAYETTE	102	99	83	100	93	93	101	95	99	101	100	76	98	103	96	97	69	97	94	114
47917	AMBIA	90	62	99	62	65	95	69	86	72	56	71	71	50	70	68	78	46	80	90	105
47918	ATTICA	85	71	76	72	72	89	75	84	80	68	78	64	66	80	72	85	53	80	90	99
47920	BATTLE GROUND	92	89	93	91	89	98	85	93	87	83	86	71	84	87	88	89	59	89	95	110
47921	BOSWELL	87	64	88	62	66	91	69	85	76	61	74	64	56	75	67	84	49	79	92	100
47922	BROOK	80	67	75	69	69	85	68	80	73	62	71	60	60	73	68	78	48	74	84	93
47923	BROOKSTON	89	88	82	91	87	96	85	91	86	80	85	70	83	87	86	89	59	87	94	107
47926	BURNETTSVILLE	92	83	83	87	85	98	82	93	85	74	83	70	76	87	82	90	57	86	96	108
47928	CAYUGA	89	65	83	64	67	89	68	83	75	64	74	62	56	76	65	83	49	77	88	98
47929	CHALMERS	91	84	87	87	85	98	82	92	84	75	83	71	76	85	83	88	56	86	95	109
47930	CLARKS HILL	89	70	76	71	71	88	71	82	77	67	75	63	61	79	68	83	51	77	86	98
47932	COVINGTON	97	83	90	85	84	103	84	96	89	77	87	73	76	90	83	95	59	90	101	113
47933	CRAWFORDSVILLE	88	82	77	84	81	92	85	87	88	79	86	66	81	88	82	91	59	86	94	103
47940	DARLINGTON	88	84	80	87	84	95	81	90	82	75	81	68	77	84	82	86	56	83	91	104
47942	EARL PARK	86	60	93	60	62	90	66	81	69	54	68	67	49	68	66	75	44	76	86	100
47943	FAIR OAKS	95	87	86	90	88	102	85	96	88	77	86	73	79	90	85	93	59	89	99	112
47944	FOWLER	92	86	83	88	82	98	87	90	89	80	88	73	83	90	86	92	60	90	98	110
47946	FRANCESVILLE	86	70	85	72	72	92	72	85	75	63	74	67	61	75	72	80	49	79	88	101
47948	GOODLAND	86	63	79	62	64	86	67	80	74	62	72	61	54	75	63	81	48	75	85	95
47949	HILLSBORO	91	74	78	74	74	92	75	85	80	70	78	65	65	82	71	85	53	80	89	101
47950	IDAVILLE	96	74	81	74	74	94	76	87	82	72	80	67	64	85	71	88	54	82	91	104
47951	KENTLAND	82	78	72	80	77	88	77	83	79	71	78	64	73	81	76	83	53	79	87	98
47952	KINGMAN	80	58	66	56	58	76	60	70	67	58	65	54	49	69	55	72	44	66	74	85
47954	LADOGA	89	81	81	85	83	96	80	91	83	73	81	69	74	84	80	88	55	84	93	105
	INDIANA	97	91	86	93	89	96	93	94	95	91	94	73	90	96	90	97	65	94	97	112
	UNITED STATES	100	100	100	100	100	100	100	100	100	100	100	100	100	100	100	100	100	100	100	100

47955-47995

ZIP CODE			POPULATION			2000-2009 ANNUAL RATE		HOUSEHOLDS					FAMILIES		
#	POST OFFICE NAME	COUNTY FIPS CODE	2000	2009	2014	% Rate	State Centile	2000	2009	2014	% Annual Rate 2000-2009	2009 Average HH Size	2000	2009	% Annual Rate 2000-2009
47955	LINDEN	107	1044	1015	1000	-0.3	22	424	420	414	-0.1	2.42	299	284	-0.6
47957	MEDARYVILLE	131	1979	2018	2007	0.2	49	693	727	727	0.5	2.61	513	520	0.1
47959	MONON	181	2778	2681	2637	-0.4	18	1037	1004	988	-0.3	2.65	733	682	-0.8
47960	MONTICELLO	181	15815	15270	15017	-0.4	18	6316	6178	6091	-0.2	2.42	4473	4209	-0.7
47963	MOROCCO	111	2287	2224	2176	-0.3	22	904	894	879	-0.1	2.49	628	594	-0.6
47967	NEW RICHMOND	107	1073	1056	1044	-0.2	27	408	409	406	0.0	2.58	313	304	-0.3
47968	NEW ROSS	107	1314	1334	1330	0.2	49	505	521	521	0.3	2.56	381	381	0.0
47970	OTTERBEIN	171	2003	1969	1940	-0.2	27	759	761	755	0.0	2.59	567	550	-0.3
47971	OXFORD	007	1873	1896	1879	0.1	43	710	733	731	0.3	2.53	515	513	0.0
47974	PERRYSVILLE	165	1175	1152	1131	-0.2	27	464	467	462	0.1	2.46	335	324	-0.4
47975	PINE VILLAGE	171	685	715	719	0.5	66	278	297	301	0.7	2.40	204	209	0.3
47977	REMINGTON	073	2364	2423	2428	0.3	56	890	924	930	0.4	2.62	649	647	0.0
47978	RENSSELAER	073	11023	11735	12023	0.7	73	3963	4323	4464	0.9	2.52	2884	3032	0.5
47980	REYNOLDS	181	1226	1293	1301	0.6	70	436	461	465	0.6	2.80	339	348	0.3
47981	ROMNEY	157	822	792	782	-0.4	18	293	289	288	-0.1	2.74	233	221	-0.6
47987	VEEDERSBURG	045	4437	4244	4120	-0.5	13	1714	1669	1627	-0.3	2.54	1268	1194	-0.6
47989	WAVELAND	107	980	1036	1040	0.6	70	377	405	408	0.8	2.56	277	287	0.4
47990	WAYNETOWN	107	1485	1446	1421	-0.3	22	584	574	566	-0.2	2.49	433	411	-0.6
47991	WEST LEBANON	171	1012	1104	1136	0.9	79	392	441	457	1.3	2.50	309	337	0.9
47992	WESTPOINT	157	1395	1433	1472	0.3	56	503	536	556	0.7	2.67	399	408	0.2
47993	WILLIAMSPORT	171	3883	3968	3914	0.2	49	1485	1555	1542	0.5	2.49	1083	1096	0.1
47994	WINGATE	107	572	565	560	-0.1	31	218	219	217	0.0	2.58	163	158	-0.3
47995	WOLCOTT	181	1701	1636	1606	-0.4	18	643	625	616	-0.3	2.60	482	452	-0.7
	INDIANA					0.7					0.8	2.49			0.4
	UNITED STATES					1.0					1.1	2.59			0.9

ZIP CODE #	POST OFFICE NAME	RACE (%) White 2000	White 2009	Black 2000	Black 2009	Asian/Pacific 2000	Asian/Pacific 2009	% Hispanic Origin 2000	% Hispanic Origin 2009	2009 AGE DISTRIBUTION (%) 0-4	5-9	10-14	15-19	20-24	25-44	45-64	65-84	85+	18+	MEDIAN AGE 2009	% 2009 Males	% 2009 Females
47955	LINDEN	98.2	97.8	0.5	0.6	0.0	0.1	0.7	1.0	6.2	6.2	6.3	6.5	6.5	24.6	30.3	11.6	1.7	77.5	40.0	51.2	48.8
47957	MEDARYVILLE	95.7	94.9	2.4	2.7	0.1	0.1	2.7	3.9	6.4	6.2	6.3	7.2	7.1	27.3	26.6	11.5	1.4	76.6	37.7	53.0	47.0
47959	MONON	88.7	83.8	0.1	0.1	0.2	0.3	12.5	18.4	6.2	6.0	6.3	7.6	6.3	28.9	25.6	11.4	1.7	77.1	37.1	51.0	49.0
47960	MONTICELLO	95.1	93.0	0.2	0.2	0.3	0.5	5.7	8.5	5.9	6.1	6.2	6.1	5.1	24.9	28.6	14.8	2.4	78.0	41.7	49.9	50.1
47963	MOROCCO	98.4	98.4	0.2	0.2	0.3	0.4	1.6	1.7	5.9	6.1	6.6	6.6	5.0	25.4	28.8	13.6	2.0	77.2	40.7	50.6	49.4
47967	NEW RICHMOND	98.8	98.7	0.6	0.7	0.1	0.1	0.3	0.4	6.8	7.5	7.7	7.1	4.6	25.9	28.3	10.6	1.5	73.5	38.3	50.3	49.7
47968	NEW ROSS	98.9	98.6	0.1	0.1	0.0	0.1	0.7	1.1	6.4	6.7	7.0	7.0	4.9	26.5	29.8	10.0	1.6	75.5	39.5	52.2	47.8
47970	OTTERBEIN	98.5	98.1	0.0	0.1	0.1	0.2	0.6	1.0	7.0	7.4	7.3	7.4	6.1	27.8	26.1	9.6	1.4	73.6	36.0	50.8	49.2
47971	OXFORD	97.3	96.5	0.1	0.2	0.1	0.1	0.9	1.5	6.4	6.9	7.1	6.9	4.7	25.1	27.5	12.5	2.9	74.9	40.3	51.2	48.8
47974	PERRYSVILLE	99.1	98.8	0.1	0.1	0.2	0.3	0.2	0.2	5.6	5.9	6.9	6.6	4.1	23.9	30.8	14.1	2.3	77.6	42.8	51.1	48.9
47975	PINE VILLAGE	99.1	99.2	0.0	0.0	0.0	0.0	0.3	0.4	6.0	6.4	7.1	6.9	4.1	25.2	29.9	12.6	1.8	76.1	41.6	49.9	50.1
47977	REMINGTON	98.8	98.3	0.3	0.3	0.5	0.8	1.1	1.6	7.6	7.5	7.4	7.3	5.8	25.7	26.3	10.7	1.7	73.0	36.3	49.9	50.1
47978	RENSSELAER	97.5	96.7	0.6	0.6	0.2	0.3	2.7	4.1	6.4	6.3	6.4	8.8	8.6	24.3	25.4	11.5	2.2	76.7	36.3	49.9	50.1
47980	REYNOLDS	94.9	92.8	0.2	0.2	0.2	0.2	4.6	7.2	7.8	7.9	8.0	7.3	5.4	24.5	27.7	10.2	1.2	72.0	36.7	49.7	50.3
47981	ROMNEY	98.9	98.7	0.0	0.0	0.1	0.1	0.1	0.4	6.9	7.7	8.1	8.2	5.4	24.2	28.9	9.2	1.3	72.1	38.0	50.5	49.5
47987	VEEDERSBURG	99.0	98.7	0.1	0.1	0.1	0.1	1.8	2.8	6.9	6.8	7.0	6.9	5.6	25.0	26.6	13.4	1.8	75.1	38.8	49.7	50.3
47989	WAVELAND	97.9	97.2	0.1	0.1	0.2	0.3	0.7	1.1	6.6	6.8	7.3	7.9	5.0	25.6	28.5	10.8	1.5	74.4	39.1	50.4	49.6
47990	WAYNETOWN	99.0	98.8	0.2	0.2	0.1	0.1	0.3	0.6	7.3	7.3	7.5	7.1	5.1	26.2	24.8	12.2	2.5	73.2	37.7	48.6	51.4
47991	WEST LEBANON	98.8	98.6	0.0	0.0	0.2	0.2	0.7	1.1	6.4	6.8	7.1	6.6	5.2	23.2	28.9	14.3	1.5	75.7	41.3	50.5	49.5
47992	WESTPOINT	99.2	98.9	0.1	0.1	0.3	0.4	0.9	1.5	5.7	6.4	6.8	7.4	5.9	25.0	29.9	11.4	1.7	76.6	39.9	50.5	49.5
47993	WILLIAMSPORT	99.3	99.0	0.1	0.1	0.2	0.4	0.3	0.5	6.2	6.3	6.6	7.0	5.4	23.9	27.5	14.7	2.6	76.6	41.3	50.3	49.7
47994	WINGATE	99.7	99.6	0.0	0.0	0.2	0.2	0.7	0.9	6.4	6.7	7.4	8.3	4.4	23.7	29.2	12.4	1.4	74.3	40.3	48.3	51.7
47995	WOLCOTT	98.0	97.5	0.7	0.9	0.0	0.0	1.3	2.0	8.1	7.1	7.3	7.2	5.0	24.9	26.8	11.8	1.9	73.0	37.4	48.7	51.3
	INDIANA	87.5	85.6	8.4	8.9	1.0	1.5	3.5	5.0	6.9	6.8	6.8	7.2	6.9	26.5	26.2	10.8	1.9	75.4	36.8	49.3	50.7
	UNITED STATES	75.1	72.0	12.3	12.7	3.8	4.6	12.5	15.7	6.8	6.7	6.6	7.1	6.9	27.0	26.0	10.9	1.9	75.7	36.9	49.2	50.8

INCOME

ZIP CODE #	POST OFFICE NAME	2009 Per Capita Income	2009 HH Income Base	2009 HOUSEHOLD INCOME DISTRIBUTION (%) Less than $25,000	$25,000 to $49,999	$50,000 to $99,999	$100,000 to $149,999	$150,000 or More	MEDIAN HOUSEHOLD INCOME 2009	2014	2009 National Centile	2009 State Centile	2009 Home Value Base	2009 HOME VALUE DISTRIBUTION (%) Less than $50,000	$50,000 to $89,999	$90,000 to $174,999	$175,000 to $399,999	$400,000 or More	2009 Median Home Value
47955	LINDEN	24620	420	18.8	25.5	45.5	8.6	1.7	55244	56723	72	70	331	15.4	29.0	47.1	7.3	1.2	95286
47957	MEDARYVILLE	16914	727	28.5	35.1	31.4	4.1	1.0	38616	40382	28	7	613	24.0	26.6	40.9	8.3	0.2	89314
47959	MONON	17622	1004	24.3	37.7	32.2	4.6	1.2	39754	42585	32	8	716	26.5	35.5	32.0	5.0	1.0	76349
47960	MONTICELLO	23064	6178	19.0	30.8	40.6	7.3	2.3	50160	52309	62	47	4726	11.3	24.5	49.0	13.6	1.5	105408
47963	MOROCCO	21494	894	24.8	31.0	35.3	5.5	3.4	46113	49105	52	28	667	9.7	37.6	37.8	14.7	0.1	92823
47967	NEW RICHMOND	22679	409	15.2	28.6	46.9	7.3	2.0	55605	56864	72	71	332	10.8	27.7	53.0	7.8	0.6	103302
47968	NEW ROSS	22797	521	15.7	32.8	40.3	10.6	0.6	51214	53472	64	53	440	11.4	32.5	45.9	9.3	0.9	95400
47970	OTTERBEIN	23592	761	14.8	29.7	43.8	9.9	1.8	55308	56005	72	70	570	9.5	28.6	48.4	11.6	1.9	102757
47971	OXFORD	21530	733	16.5	35.6	39.7	6.7	1.5	48510	50958	58	38	573	7.7	43.8	45.5	3.0	0.0	88768
47974	PERRYSVILLE	22288	467	25.3	29.8	36.2	6.2	2.6	44931	46762	48	22	361	21.3	39.6	32.1	6.9	0.0	79146
47975	PINE VILLAGE	23576	297	17.5	32.7	38.7	10.1	1.0	49860	51630	61	45	238	13.0	31.5	43.7	6.3	5.5	96500
47977	REMINGTON	24268	924	17.5	28.8	39.9	9.8	3.9	53930	56424	70	66	645	9.9	27.3	53.2	9.5	0.2	102790
47978	RENSSELAER	22694	4323	22.3	30.4	35.5	8.4	3.4	48232	51029	57	36	3104	5.8	23.6	48.7	19.5	2.4	116091
47980	REYNOLDS	19765	461	25.2	24.5	42.5	5.6	2.2	50202	52177	62	47	343	12.2	34.1	42.6	9.6	1.5	93676
47981	ROMNEY	23889	289	11.8	36.0	36.3	12.5	3.5	52487	54808	67	61	236	7.6	8.9	53.4	27.5	2.5	135000
47987	VEEDERSBURG	21281	1669	20.7	30.3	42.6	4.8	1.7	49309	51048	60	43	1326	19.2	41.4	33.9	4.8	0.6	83843
47989	WAVELAND	21558	405	19.0	25.4	48.6	6.4	0.5	52692	53835	67	62	315	13.0	38.7	38.7	9.2	0.3	88472
47990	WAYNETOWN	23785	574	16.9	27.2	46.5	7.8	1.6	55618	56888	72	71	450	10.4	30.7	49.6	8.2	1.1	97143
47991	WEST LEBANON	24415	441	20.0	27.2	40.1	7.5	5.2	52666	53531	67	62	350	15.1	37.4	40.9	6.6	0.0	88125
47992	WESTPOINT	29352	536	5.2	26.3	47.0	15.9	5.6	69237	68938	86	94	444	3.6	16.0	59.0	18.5	2.9	118692
47993	WILLIAMSPORT	23075	1555	19.5	27.3	42.9	7.7	2.6	52439	53509	67	61	1204	16.4	34.5	39.5	8.2	1.4	89320
47994	WINGATE	19482	219	23.7	32.4	37.0	5.9	0.9	45159	48429	49	23	181	19.9	22.1	47.0	8.8	2.2	101838
47995	WOLCOTT	22013	625	18.4	30.1	43.4	5.6	2.6	51644	54427	65	56	471	14.6	33.3	42.3	8.1	1.7	93167
	INDIANA	26003		19.5	26.3	38.6	10.5	5.1	54105	56493				12.2	24.1	44.1	17.2	2.4	108938
	UNITED STATES	27277		20.9	24.4	35.3	11.7	7.6	54719	56938				9.3	13.1	31.6	32.6	13.5	162279

ZIP CODE	FINANCIAL SERVICES				THE HOME						ENTERTAINMENT						PERSONAL			
					Home Improvements		Furnishings													
# POST OFFICE NAME	Auto Loan	Home Loan	Invest-ments	Retire-ment Plans	Home Repair	Lawn & Garden	Comput-ers & Hard-ware-Personal	Major Appli-ances	TV, Radio, Sound Equip-ment	Furni-ture	Dine out/ Carry out	Sports Equip-ment	Fees & Tickets	Toys & Games	Travel	Cable TV	Apparel & Services	Auto Repairs	Health Insur-ance	Pets & Supplies
47955 LINDEN	84	85	69	87	80	90	85	83	86	80	85	66	85	88	83	88	59	84	92	101
47957 MEDARYVILLE	80	58	67	57	58	77	60	70	67	58	65	54	49	69	55	73	44	67	74	86
47959 MONON	83	60	71	59	60	80	63	74	70	60	68	56	51	72	58	76	46	70	78	89
47960 MONTICELLO	88	77	84	78	77	91	78	86	81	73	80	66	72	82	77	86	55	83	91	102
47963 MOROCCO	91	69	82	69	70	92	72	85	79	67	77	65	60	80	69	86	52	80	91	101
47967 NEW RICHMOND	92	82	84	85	84	98	81	92	84	73	82	70	74	85	81	89	56	85	95	108
47968 NEW ROSS	89	84	81	87	85	96	81	91	83	75	82	69	77	85	82	87	56	84	93	105
47970 OTTERBEIN	88	89	76	91	85	95	86	88	87	82	87	69	86	89	86	90	60	87	94	106
47971 OXFORD	85	78	77	81	79	91	76	86	79	69	77	65	71	80	77	83	53	80	89	100
47974 PERRYSVILLE	90	71	86	71	73	95	74	89	80	67	78	66	63	80	73	87	53	82	94	103
47975 PINE VILLAGE	88	80	79	83	82	94	79	89	81	71	80	67	73	83	79	86	54	82	92	103
47977 REMINGTON	95	91	83	94	89	102	89	95	91	83	90	74	86	93	89	95	62	91	100	113
47978 RENSSELAER	89	80	78	82	80	92	84	87	86	77	85	67	77	87	81	90	58	86	93	104
47980 REYNOLDS	94	74	83	75	75	95	76	88	81	70	79	68	64	83	73	87	54	82	92	105
47981 ROMNEY	96	98	96	101	97	105	91	99	91	88	91	78	91	92	95	93	63	94	99	117
47987 VEEDERSBURG	90	73	75	73	71	90	74	82	80	71	78	64	65	82	70	85	53	79	88	100
47989 WAVELAND	85	78	77	81	79	92	77	87	79	69	78	66	71	81	77	84	53	80	89	101
47990 WAYNETOWN	86	85	71	87	80	92	84	85	86	79	85	67	83	88	82	89	58	85	93	102
47991 WEST LEBANON	99	80	95	81	82	105	83	98	89	75	87	74	71	89	82	97	59	91	104	115
47992 WESTPOINT	107	121	119	120	118	127	106	115	108	105	109	88	116	109	116	111	76	111	120	135
47993 WILLIAMSPORT	92	77	87	78	78	98	80	91	84	72	82	70	70	85	78	90	56	86	97	108
47994 WINGATE	78	71	70	74	72	84	70	79	72	63	71	60	64	74	70	76	48	73	81	92
47995 WOLCOTT	87	81	77	83	79	93	81	86	83	74	82	67	76	84	80	86	56	83	92	103
INDIANA	97	91	86	93	89	96	93	94	95	91	94	73	90	96	90	97	65	94	97	112
UNITED STATES	100	100	100	100	100	100	100	100	100	100	100	100	100	100	100	100	100	100	100	100

POPULATION CHANGE

ZIP CODE #	POST OFFICE NAME	COUNTY FIPS CODE	POPULATION 2000	POPULATION 2009	POPULATION 2014	2000-2009 ANNUAL RATE % Rate	2000-2009 ANNUAL RATE State Centile	HOUSEHOLDS 2000	HOUSEHOLDS 2009	HOUSEHOLDS 2014	HOUSEHOLDS % Annual Rate 2000-2009	HOUSEHOLDS 2009 Average HH Size	FAMILIES 2000	FAMILIES 2009	FAMILIES % Annual Rate 2000-2009
50001	ACKWORTH	181	567	819	897	4.1	99	203	304	336	4.5	2.69	166	245	4.3
50002	ADAIR	077	1365	1286	1243	-0.6	20	580	565	549	-0.3	2.26	375	355	-0.6
50003	ADEL	049	6045	7228	8406	2.0	96	2279	2823	3303	2.3	2.52	1638	2009	2.2
50005	ALBION	127	826	818	814	-0.1	51	311	318	318	0.2	2.57	245	246	0.0
50006	ALDEN	083	1940	1908	1867	-0.2	46	749	754	744	0.1	2.53	551	544	-0.1
50007	ALLEMAN	153	484	557	601	1.5	94	154	185	202	2.0	3.01	135	158	1.7
50008	ALLERTON	185	888	837	807	-0.6	20	356	341	330	-0.5	2.45	249	234	-0.7
50009	ALTOONA	153	12004	16002	18062	3.2	98	4435	6062	6857	3.4	2.62	3358	4427	3.0
50010	AMES	169	25113	27585	28425	1.0	90	10843	12167	12590	1.3	2.23	6273	7081	1.3
50011	AMES	169	1347	1405	1407	0.5	79	0	0	0	0.0	0.00	0	0	0.0
50013	AMES	169	1118	1415	1416	2.6	98	0	0	0	0.0	0.00	0	0	0.0
50014	AMES	169	26695	30123	31874	1.3	93	8563	10326	11124	2.0	2.31	3767	4356	1.6
50020	ANITA	029	1386	1371	1350	-0.1	51	584	595	589	0.2	2.28	389	387	-0.1
50021	ANKENY	153	15017	22127	25048	4.3	99	5776	8460	9586	4.2	2.59	4169	6078	4.2
50022	ATLANTIC	029	8736	8341	8093	-0.5	27	3670	3598	3509	-0.2	2.22	2376	2270	-0.5
50023	ANKENY	153	16614	24476	28055	4.3	99	6210	9661	11168	4.9	2.49	4439	7003	5.1
50025	AUDUBON	009	3886	3652	3550	-0.7	15	1581	1518	1479	-0.4	2.33	1091	1025	-0.7
50026	BAGLEY	077	698	707	698	0.1	63	281	290	287	0.3	2.42	207	210	0.2
50027	BARNES CITY	123	340	334	332	-0.2	46	150	152	152	0.1	2.20	109	108	-0.1
50028	BAXTER	099	1597	1691	1698	0.6	83	656	715	724	0.9	2.33	458	486	0.6
50029	BAYARD	077	780	730	703	-0.7	15	308	296	287	-0.4	2.43	217	204	-0.7
50033	BEVINGTON	121	57	60	62	0.6	83	20	22	22	1.0	2.68	15	17	1.4
50034	BLAIRSBURG	079	474	449	433	-0.6	20	179	174	169	-0.3	2.57	137	131	-0.5
50035	BONDURANT	153	2995	4400	5105	4.2	99	1048	1585	1855	4.6	2.78	833	1226	4.3
50036	BOONE	015	16484	16820	16984	0.2	68	6746	7038	7131	0.5	2.34	4452	4532	0.2
50038	BOONEVILLE	049	6	7	8	1.7	95	3	4	4	3.2	1.75	2	3	4.5
50039	BOUTON	049	420	449	498	0.7	85	168	185	207	1.0	2.43	120	129	0.8
50040	BOXHOLM	015	237	242	242	0.2	68	111	115	116	0.4	2.10	76	77	0.1
50041	BRADFORD	069	32	30	30	-0.7	15	12	12	12	0.0	2.50	9	8	-1.3
50042	BRAYTON	009	425	415	408	-0.3	40	167	165	162	-0.1	2.52	127	123	-0.3
50044	BUSSEY	125	863	861	854	0.0	58	340	349	348	0.3	2.47	251	251	0.0
50046	CAMBRIDGE	169	1415	1415	1436	0.0	58	531	556	570	0.5	2.54	382	389	0.2
50047	CARLISLE	181	5337	5759	6062	0.8	87	2029	2261	2406	1.2	2.50	1526	1662	0.9
50048	CASEY	077	974	925	899	-0.6	20	395	388	379	-0.2	2.34	290	279	-0.4
50049	CHARITON	117	7174	7021	6930	-0.2	46	2885	2848	2806	-0.1	2.42	1910	1839	-0.4
50050	CHURDAN	073	751	764	759	0.2	68	320	330	328	0.3	2.32	222	224	0.1
50051	CLEMONS	127	331	321	318	-0.3	40	138	138	137	0.0	2.33	105	103	-0.2
50052	CLIO	185	153	148	144	-0.4	32	69	68	66	-0.2	2.18	48	46	-0.5
50054	COLFAX	099	3573	3571	3545	0.0	58	1343	1376	1375	0.3	2.54	983	984	0.0
50055	COLLINS	169	943	918	902	-0.3	40	379	382	379	0.1	2.38	282	277	-0.2
50056	COLO	169	1342	1294	1275	-0.4	32	511	514	512	0.1	2.52	376	369	-0.2
50057	COLUMBIA	125	257	258	257	0.0	58	98	102	102	0.4	2.53	81	83	0.3
50058	COON RAPIDS	027	1969	1895	1854	-0.4	32	804	795	786	-0.1	2.30	535	515	-0.4
50059	COOPER	073	44	42	40	-0.5	27	15	14	14	-0.7	3.00	11	11	0.0
50060	CORYDON	185	2747	2609	2523	-0.6	20	1149	1116	1081	-0.3	2.28	751	712	-0.6
50061	CUMMING	121	1199	1380	1601	1.5	94	427	502	584	1.8	2.73	365	420	1.5
50062	DALLAS	125	408	420	425	0.3	72	153	164	167	0.8	2.56	122	129	0.6
50063	DALLAS CENTER	049	2322	2753	3176	1.9	96	851	1036	1208	2.1	2.57	643	769	2.0
50064	DANA	073	138	131	126	-0.6	20	49	46	44	-0.7	2.85	34	31	-1.0
50065	DAVIS CITY	053	800	773	756	-0.4	32	312	305	298	-0.2	2.47	228	219	-0.4
50066	DAWSON	049	339	446	546	3.0	98	135	183	225	3.3	2.44	109	145	3.1
50067	DECATUR	053	425	414	405	-0.3	40	175	173	170	-0.1	2.39	119	115	-0.4
50068	DERBY	117	359	368	366	0.3	72	138	140	139	0.2	2.62	104	104	0.0
50069	DE SOTO	049	1023	1361	1681	3.1	98	379	523	649	3.5	2.60	292	397	3.4
50070	DEXTER	049	1497	1774	2025	1.9	96	587	708	807	2.0	2.48	441	521	1.8
50071	DOWS	197	1270	1196	1155	-0.6	20	546	526	510	-0.4	2.23	361	339	-0.7
50072	EARLHAM	121	2378	2863	3204	2.0	96	884	1085	1214	2.2	2.62	679	818	2.0
50073	ELKHART	153	890	986	1058	1.1	91	361	413	447	1.5	2.39	266	291	1.0
50074	ELLSTON	159	624	599	582	-0.4	32	268	263	256	-0.2	2.28	192	184	-0.5
50075	ELLSWORTH	079	934	908	885	-0.3	40	355	352	345	-0.1	2.58	261	254	-0.3
50076	EXIRA	009	1588	1573	1555	-0.1	51	665	670	664	0.1	2.26	441	433	-0.2
50101	GALT	197	52	50	49	-0.4	32	24	24	23	0.0	2.08	17	17	0.0
50102	GARDEN CITY	083	43	40	39	-0.8	11	16	15	15	-0.7	2.67	11	11	0.0
50103	GARDEN GROVE	053	689	612	585	-1.3	2	263	237	226	-1.1	2.58	204	181	-1.3
50104	GIBSON	107	167	161	157	-0.4	32	63	63	62	0.0	2.56	45	44	-0.2
50105	GILBERT	169	1037	1033	1031	0.0	58	356	367	370	0.3	2.81	273	269	-0.2
50106	GILMAN	127	1103	1145	1154	0.4	76	456	486	491	0.7	2.36	321	334	0.4
50107	GRAND JUNCTION	073	1223	1187	1148	-0.3	40	471	448	431	-0.5	2.65	330	308	-0.7
50108	GRAND RIVER	053	545	535	525	-0.2	46	235	234	230	0.0	2.29	161	155	-0.4
50109	GRANGER	049	1747	2592	3042	4.4	99	644	989	1175	4.7	2.57	493	736	4.4
50111	GRIMES	153	5799	8971	10394	4.8	99	2163	3471	4043	5.2	2.58	1663	2530	4.6
50112	GRINNELL	157	11410	11495	11362	0.1	63	4362	4506	4491	0.4	2.24	2754	2771	0.1
50115	GUTHRIE CENTER	077	2769	2596	2507	-0.7	15	1129	1082	1047	-0.5	2.34	749	700	-0.7
50116	HAMILTON	125	363	365	364	0.1	63	131	135	135	0.3	2.70	97	98	0.1
50117	HAMLIN	009	233	239	239	0.3	72	92	96	96	0.5	2.49	65	66	0.2
50118	HARTFORD	181	906	1118	1220	2.3	97	330	424	467	2.7	2.64	261	329	2.5
50119	HARVEY	125	486	513	526	0.6	83	190	207	213	0.9	2.48	143	152	0.7
50120	HAVERHILL	127	395	399	399	0.1	63	136	140	141	0.3	2.85	102	103	0.1
50122	HUBBARD	083	1524	1471	1426	-0.4	32	610	598	580	-0.2	2.36	429	410	-0.5
50123	HUMESTON	185	793	749	724	-0.6	20	374	357	345	-0.5	2.09	262	245	-0.7
50124	HUXLEY	169	2775	3188	3355	1.5	94	1083	1302	1385	2.0	2.43	785	920	1.7
50125	INDIANOLA	181	17283	19473	20588	1.3	93	6223	7179	7658	1.6	2.50	4493	5097	1.4
50126	IOWA FALLS	083	7015	6668	6453	-0.5	27	2952	2866	2784	-0.3	2.20	1863	1760	-0.6
50127	IRA	099	33	34	34	0.3	72	14	15	15	0.7	2.27	12	12	0.0
50128	JAMAICA	077	398	413	415	0.4	76	163	172	173	0.6	2.40	121	125	0.4
50129	JEFFERSON	073	5698	5391	5196	-0.6	20	2334	2214	2128	-0.6	2.32	1536	1420	-0.8
50130	JEWELL	079	1697	1761	1749	0.4	76	657	688	684	0.5	2.54	481	494	0.3
50131	JOHNSTON	153	8955	15728	18902	6.3	99	3332	6007	7269	6.6	2.58	2449	4248	6.1
50132	KAMRAR	079	402	382	369	-0.6	20	155	151	147	-0.3	2.53	120	115	-0.5
50133	KELLERTON	159	570	554	538	-0.3	40	222	218	211	-0.2	2.54	152	145	-0.5
50134	KELLEY	169	646	655	663	0.1	63	236	252	258	0.7	2.59	163	168	0.3
50135	KELLOGG	099	1583	1664	1671	0.5	79	637	692	700	0.9	2.40	475	504	0.6
50136	KESWICK	107	610	587	572	-0.4	32	240	237	232	-0.1	2.48	180	174	-0.4
50138	KNOXVILLE	125	11675	11794	11785	0.1	63	4626	4765	4792	0.3	2.36	3135	3145	0.0
50139	LACONA	181	1118	1352	1467	2.1	97	419	529	582	2.6	2.56	317	389	2.2
	IOWA					0.4					0.7	2.40			0.4
	UNITED STATES					1.0					1.1	2.59			0.9

ZIP CODE #	POST OFFICE NAME	RACE (%) White 2000	White 2009	Black 2000	Black 2009	Asian/Pacific 2000	Asian/Pacific 2009	% Hispanic Origin 2000	% Hispanic Origin 2009	2009 AGE DISTRIBUTION (%) 0-4	5-9	10-14	15-19	20-24	25-44	45-64	65-84	85+	18+	MEDIAN AGE 2009	% 2009 Males	% 2009 Females
50001	ACKWORTH	98.4	98.2	0.4	0.5	0.2	0.2	0.9	1.3	6.1	6.8	7.3	7.3	4.8	22.8	32.6	11.1	1.1	75.1	41.4	49.6	50.4
50002	ADAIR	98.8	98.4	0.1	0.1	0.3	0.5	1.2	1.6	5.3	5.6	5.8	5.9	5.2	23.3	29.3	16.2	3.5	79.5	44.3	49.5	50.5
50003	ADEL	98.1	97.2	0.1	0.2	0.4	0.6	1.0	2.3	6.0	6.7	7.3	7.4	5.4	23.4	30.5	10.8	2.5	75.2	41.0	49.5	50.5
50005	ALBION	98.7	98.0	0.0	0.0	0.5	0.6	1.2	2.1	6.6	7.2	7.5	7.0	4.5	23.0	28.5	14.4	1.3	74.4	40.8	50.7	49.3
50006	ALDEN	98.4	97.7	0.0	0.0	0.2	0.2	3.1	4.6	6.1	7.3	7.9	7.1	3.9	24.0	29.4	12.6	1.7	74.2	40.2	49.8	50.2
50007	ALLEMAN	99.6	99.5	0.0	0.0	0.0	0.2	0.4	0.9	7.7	8.3	8.8	7.0	4.1	22.4	32.1	8.6	0.9	70.7	39.0	52.6	47.4
50008	ALLERTON	99.4	99.3	0.0	0.0	0.1	0.2	0.7	1.0	5.7	5.9	6.2	7.2	5.9	22.6	27.6	15.9	3.1	77.9	42.4	48.3	51.7
50009	ALTOONA	96.2	94.1	0.8	1.5	0.8	1.3	1.6	2.8	8.5	7.9	7.6	7.6	6.2	28.5	25.1	7.6	0.9	71.1	33.5	48.2	51.8
50010	AMES	88.0	84.5	2.5	2.6	7.5	10.6	1.7	2.3	5.8	5.0	5.1	5.8	13.4	28.2	24.4	10.2	2.1	80.7	34.0	49.3	50.7
50011	AMES	90.7	86.9	3.9	4.8	3.3	5.3	1.7	2.6	0.1	0.0	0.0	54.9	44.1	1.0	0.0	0.0	0.0	97.2	19.5	56.1	43.9
50013	AMES	90.7	87.0	3.8	4.7	3.2	5.3	1.7	2.5	0.1	0.0	0.0	54.9	44.0	1.0	0.0	0.0	0.0	97.2	19.5	56.2	43.8
50014	AMES	87.7	81.8	2.4	3.0	7.5	12.3	2.2	3.0	3.6	3.0	3.0	14.9	36.1	19.9	14.3	4.4	0.9	88.0	23.5	54.4	45.6
50020	ANITA	99.4	99.1	0.0	0.0	0.1	0.2	0.4	0.5	5.0	5.3	5.5	6.1	5.3	21.6	29.9	17.9	3.5	80.5	45.8	50.3	49.7
50021	ANKENY	96.9	94.9	0.8	1.5	0.8	1.5	1.2	2.0	8.6	8.1	7.7	6.3	6.0	29.9	24.0	7.9	1.5	71.7	34.9	48.4	51.6
50022	ATLANTIC	98.6	98.1	0.2	0.3	0.3	0.4	0.8	1.2	5.4	5.8	5.8	6.3	5.2	21.9	27.8	17.0	4.8	79.0	44.7	48.0	52.0
50023	ANKENY	97.0	95.1	0.9	1.6	1.0	1.6	0.9	1.7	8.1	7.9	7.4	6.9	6.2	30.8	24.9	7.0	0.8	72.5	34.1	49.2	50.8
50025	AUDUBON	99.3	99.2	0.2	0.2	0.1	0.1	0.4	0.7	6.3	5.9	6.4	6.6	4.8	19.4	26.5	18.6	5.5	77.4	45.4	47.5	52.5
50026	BAGLEY	98.0	98.0	0.3	0.3	0.0	0.0	2.2	2.4	6.1	6.8	6.9	6.2	3.3	21.5	30.8	16.5	1.8	76.4	44.4	50.5	49.5
50027	BARNES CITY	99.4	99.4	0.3	0.3	0.0	0.0	0.3	0.3	5.7	6.3	6.9	6.6	4.8	21.0	34.4	12.3	2.1	76.9	44.1	55.1	44.9
50028	BAXTER	98.9	98.6	0.6	0.8	0.3	0.5	0.0	0.0	6.3	6.6	6.7	6.6	5.1	25.5	28.2	12.4	2.6	76.4	40.1	49.4	50.6
50029	BAYARD	98.3	98.2	0.0	0.0	0.4	0.4	1.3	1.4	4.9	5.5	6.2	7.0	4.2	22.1	31.2	15.3	3.6	78.5	45.1	51.2	48.8
50033	BEVINGTON	100.0	100.0	0.0	0.0	0.0	0.0	0.0	0.0	6.7	6.7	6.7	6.7	3.3	28.3	31.7	10.0	0.0	73.3	41.4	48.3	51.7
50034	BLAIRSBURG	97.9	97.1	0.0	0.0	0.4	0.7	1.7	2.7	5.3	6.0	6.5	6.5	4.5	21.8	32.1	15.1	2.2	78.2	44.5	51.7	48.3
50035	BONDURANT	98.5	97.7	0.1	0.1	0.2	0.4	0.8	1.4	7.4	7.7	8.0	8.4	5.8	27.0	27.5	7.5	0.7	71.7	35.8	49.7	50.3
50036	BOONE	98.4	97.9	0.3	0.4	0.2	0.4	0.9	1.3	6.4	6.1	6.1	6.2	6.1	25.7	27.3	12.8	3.3	77.6	39.6	48.4	51.6
50038	BOONEVILLE	100.0	100.0	0.0	0.0	0.0	0.0	0.0	0.0	0.0	0.0	0.0	0.0	0.0	14.3	85.7	0.0	0.0	100.0	49.2	28.6	71.4
50039	BOUTON	98.6	98.2	0.2	0.2	0.2	0.2	1.4	3.3	5.6	6.2	6.7	6.5	4.7	21.6	35.2	12.0	1.6	77.5	44.1	52.1	47.9
50040	BOXHOLM	100.0	100.0	0.0	0.0	0.0	0.0	0.4	0.4	5.0	5.8	6.6	7.9	4.1	20.2	33.1	14.9	2.5	77.3	45.2	52.5	47.5
50041	BRADFORD	100.0	100.0	0.0	0.0	0.0	0.0	0.0	0.0	3.3	6.7	6.7	6.7	6.7	26.7	26.7	16.7	0.0	76.7	40.0	50.0	50.0
50042	BRAYTON	99.3	99.3	0.0	0.0	0.2	0.2	0.5	0.7	6.5	7.2	7.7	8.0	4.6	19.8	28.4	14.9	2.9	73.7	42.2	49.6	50.4
50044	BUSSEY	98.5	98.3	0.2	0.2	0.2	0.3	0.5	0.6	6.9	6.9	6.7	6.9	5.6	24.2	27.6	13.6	1.7	75.5	39.7	53.7	46.3
50046	CAMBRIDGE	96.5	95.4	0.7	0.9	0.5	0.8	1.8	2.7	7.3	7.5	7.5	6.6	5.0	28.1	27.4	9.1	1.4	73.7	37.4	48.8	51.2
50047	CARLISLE	97.8	96.9	0.3	0.5	0.4	0.7	1.4	2.1	7.0	7.2	7.5	6.7	4.7	25.8	27.6	11.5	1.9	74.1	38.7	48.7	51.3
50048	CASEY	98.6	98.5	0.1	0.1	0.2	0.2	1.1	1.3	5.6	6.1	6.7	6.6	4.0	20.6	30.4	16.8	3.2	77.3	45.2	49.4	50.6
50049	CHARITON	98.5	98.0	0.2	0.2	0.3	0.5	0.9	1.3	6.1	6.1	6.4	6.9	5.7	22.3	27.2	15.6	3.8	77.1	42.2	48.8	51.2
50050	CHURDAN	99.2	98.8	0.1	0.3	0.0	0.0	0.8	1.3	6.2	5.6	5.1	7.1	4.1	19.2	29.3	20.5	2.9	78.0	47.1	51.2	48.8
50051	CLEMONS	97.6	96.6	0.3	0.3	0.0	0.0	1.5	2.5	5.6	6.2	6.9	6.2	4.0	23.4	33.0	12.8	1.9	77.3	43.6	52.6	47.4
50052	CLIO	100.0	100.0	0.0	0.0	0.0	0.0	0.7	1.4	5.4	6.1	6.1	5.4	5.4	20.9	27.0	19.6	4.1	79.1	45.6	49.3	50.7
50054	COLFAX	98.4	98.0	0.3	0.4	0.1	0.2	0.9	1.3	6.4	6.8	7.2	7.4	5.2	25.0	28.6	12.0	1.4	74.8	39.5	50.8	49.2
50055	COLLINS	98.6	98.1	0.1	0.1	0.4	0.8	0.3	0.5	6.1	6.8	7.1	6.6	4.2	23.3	31.2	12.3	2.4	75.9	41.8	50.9	49.1
50056	COLO	97.9	97.2	0.7	0.9	0.5	0.9	0.3	0.4	6.5	6.3	6.6	7.0	6.6	26.0	27.7	11.1	1.9	76.1	37.7	50.9	49.1
50057	COLUMBIA	98.1	97.3	0.0	0.4	0.4	0.8	0.0	0.0	5.0	5.8	7.0	7.8	5.4	24.8	31.0	12.0	1.2	77.5	41.1	52.3	47.7
50058	COON RAPIDS	98.9	98.7	0.5	0.6	0.1	0.1	1.5	2.2	5.8	6.0	6.1	6.0	5.0	21.3	27.4	17.3	5.0	78.3	44.8	49.6	50.4
50059	COOPER	100.0	97.6	0.0	0.0	0.0	0.0	2.4	2.4	4.8	4.8	4.8	4.8	4.8	19.0	38.1	19.0	0.0	81.0	48.0	50.0	50.0
50060	CORYDON	99.1	98.9	0.1	0.1	0.2	0.3	0.4	0.5	5.3	5.5	5.8	6.6	4.8	20.1	27.8	18.9	5.3	79.1	46.4	47.0	53.0
50061	CUMMING	98.1	97.5	0.3	0.3	0.6	0.9	0.9	1.5	6.2	7.2	8.0	7.4	4.6	22.5	33.8	9.6	0.8	74.0	41.5	50.3	49.7
50062	DALLAS	98.8	98.6	0.0	0.0	0.2	0.2	0.2	0.2	4.8	4.8	5.7	7.6	5.5	23.8	30.5	15.7	1.7	80.0	43.3	52.1	47.9
50063	DALLAS CENTER	98.8	97.9	0.3	0.3	0.1	0.1	0.5	1.3	6.0	6.6	7.2	6.9	4.7	22.4	31.7	11.6	2.9	75.6	42.5	50.5	49.5
50064	DANA	98.5	96.9	0.0	0.0	0.0	0.8	2.9	3.1	6.9	6.9	7.6	6.9	3.8	23.7	29.8	12.2	2.3	74.0	40.8	52.7	47.3
50065	DAVIS CITY	97.2	96.6	0.6	0.6	0.3	0.5	1.3	1.7	6.9	7.4	7.6	8.2	4.5	20.4	27.0	15.5	2.5	73.5	40.8	49.4	50.6
50066	DAWSON	99.1	98.7	0.0	0.0	0.0	0.0	0.3	1.1	5.2	5.6	6.3	6.7	4.5	21.3	34.3	14.6	1.6	78.9	45.2	49.3	50.7
50067	DECATUR	97.4	96.9	0.2	0.2	0.2	0.2	1.9	2.7	7.2	7.7	7.5	6.5	3.9	22.5	26.8	15.7	2.2	73.2	40.8	50.7	49.3
50068	DERBY	96.6	95.1	0.0	0.0	1.1	1.9	1.4	2.2	7.3	7.3	7.6	7.3	5.4	20.9	28.0	14.1	1.9	72.8	40.0	50.0	50.0
50069	DE SOTO	98.5	97.8	0.1	0.1	0.6	1.0	0.6	1.3	7.8	7.9	7.9	6.5	5.1	27.0	28.2	8.8	0.7	72.3	36.6	50.8	49.2
50070	DEXTER	98.3	97.5	0.1	0.1	0.7	1.1	0.8	1.7	6.8	7.0	7.4	6.8	5.1	24.7	29.0	11.2	1.9	74.4	39.8	50.7	49.3
50071	DOWS	95.3	93.0	0.1	0.1	0.4	0.7	7.2	10.4	5.0	5.4	5.8	5.9	3.8	23.4	30.8	16.0	3.9	80.2	45.4	50.6	49.4
50072	EARLHAM	98.8	98.4	0.1	0.1	0.2	0.3	0.8	1.3	7.7	7.9	8.1	7.1	5.0	25.7	27.4	9.3	1.7	71.6	37.8	50.4	49.6
50073	ELKHART	98.9	98.2	0.4	0.8	0.3	0.6	0.4	0.6	6.6	7.4	7.6	6.1	4.0	26.1	30.1	10.2	1.9	74.6	39.6	51.2	48.8
50074	ELLSTON	98.9	98.7	0.2	0.2	0.2	0.3	0.2	0.2	4.8	5.2	5.5	5.2	3.8	17.7	31.9	23.5	2.3	81.1	50.3	50.3	49.7
50075	ELLSWORTH	95.2	92.7	0.3	0.3	0.4	0.8	5.8	8.6	6.1	6.8	7.0	6.6	4.5	24.6	29.7	12.6	2.1	76.0	40.6	50.2	49.8
50076	EXIRA	98.7	98.3	0.1	0.1	0.5	0.8	0.5	0.7	5.1	5.3	5.7	6.4	5.3	20.0	27.5	18.5	6.1	79.4	46.5	47.7	52.3
50101	GALT	96.1	94.0	0.0	0.0	0.0	0.0	5.9	6.0	6.0	6.0	8.0	6.0	4.0	20.0	34.0	14.0	2.0	76.0	45.0	52.0	48.0
50102	GARDEN CITY	97.7	97.5	0.0	0.0	0.0	0.0	2.3	5.0	5.0	5.0	5.0	5.0	5.0	20.0	35.0	15.0	5.0	80.0	47.5	45.0	55.0
50103	GARDEN GROVE	99.0	98.7	0.0	0.0	0.1	0.3	0.3	0.5	4.9	5.9	8.0	9.2	3.6	22.5	30.9	14.5	0.5	75.3	42.5	52.9	47.1
50104	GIBSON	99.4	98.8	0.0	0.0	0.0	0.0	0.6	1.2	4.3	5.0	5.6	6.2	5.0	23.6	32.9	14.9	2.5	81.4	45.2	48.4	51.6
50105	GILBERT	96.8	95.2	0.5	0.7	1.7	3.0	1.0	1.4	6.8	7.1	7.2	7.5	5.9	28.8	28.2	7.6	1.0	74.4	36.1	49.8	50.2
50106	GILMAN	94.8	92.9	0.1	0.2	0.1	0.2	3.8	5.9	6.1	6.3	6.6	7.4	6.6	24.3	29.6	11.0	2.0	76.5	39.4	50.8	49.2
50107	GRAND JUNCTION	98.3	97.6	0.1	0.1	0.1	0.3	1.1	1.7	7.3	7.1	7.0	7.7	6.7	24.5	24.4	12.9	2.4	74.1	37.3	52.6	47.4
50108	GRAND RIVER	97.4	96.8	0.2	0.2	0.2	0.4	1.8	2.6	7.1	7.7	7.5	6.5	3.9	22.6	26.7	15.9	2.1	73.5	40.8	50.7	49.3
50109	GRANGER	98.9	98.3	0.2	0.3	0.4	0.6	0.5	0.9	6.6	7.2	7.7	7.1	4.6	24.4	30.5	10.0	2.0	73.7	40.3	50.3	49.7
50111	GRIMES	97.2	95.6	0.4	0.6	0.9	1.7	1.1	2.0	9.7	9.0	8.0	6.7	4.9	32.6	23.1	5.4	0.7	69.1	32.5	48.7	51.3
50112	GRINNELL	95.6	94.3	0.9	1.1	1.8	2.6	1.3	1.9	5.4	5.2	5.3	10.0	11.9	19.7	24.7	13.9	3.9	80.2	37.9	47.2	52.8
50115	GUTHRIE CENTER	98.5	98.4	0.1	0.1	0.1	0.1	1.2	1.3	5.6	6.0	5.7	6.6	4.5	20.9	28.3	17.6	4.7	78.1	45.4	48.3	51.7
50116	HAMILTON	97.8	97.5	0.5	0.8	0.3	0.3	0.5	0.8	6.8	6.8	6.8	7.1	5.8	23.8	27.7	13.4	1.6	75.3	39.4	53.7	46.3
50117	HAMLIN	100.0	99.2	0.0	0.0	0.0	0.4	0.4	0.4	6.7	6.7	7.9	7.5	4.2	22.2	28.5	14.2	2.1	73.6	41.5	51.5	48.5
50118	HARTFORD	96.4	95.3	0.0	0.0	0.0	0.0	2.9	4.3	6.0	6.6	7.0	7.2	4.6	26.1	29.2	12.3	1.2	75.8	40.3	50.7	49.3
50119	HARVEY	99.8	99.8	0.2	0.2	0.0	0.0	0.0	0.0	7.2	7.6	7.4	5.8	5.1	26.3	27.7	11.3	1.6	73.9	38.9	51.9	48.1
50120	HAVERHILL	98.0	97.2	0.0	0.0	0.8	1.3	1.3	2.0	6.3	6.8	7.0	7.0	5.0	21.8	31.3	12.8	2.0	75.9	42.1	48.9	51.1
50122	HUBBARD	99.1	98.6	0.0	0.0	0.1	0.3	0.8	1.2	5.7	6.3	7.2	7.0	4.1	20.5	26.5	17.3	5.4	76.3	44.3	49.2	50.8
50123	HUMESTON	98.9	98.5	0.1	0.3	0.3	0.4	0.6	0.8	6.4	7.2	7.2	6.5	3.6	20.6	29.9	15.9	2.7	74.8	43.8	48.6	51.4
50124	HUXLEY	97.8	97.1	0.2	0.2	0.4	0.6	1.0	1.5	7.3	7.5	7.4	6.8	4.9	29.9	26.9	7.9	1.5	73.9	35.2	48.8	51.2
50125	INDIANOLA	98.1	97.5	0.4	0.4	0.5	0.9	0.8	1.2	6.2	6.3	6.6	8.4	8.3	23.6	26.5	11.4	2.6	76.8	37.5	48.0	52.0
50126	IOWA FALLS	97.6	96.8	1.0	1.2	0.3	0.5	1.1	1.7	5.5	5.2	5.4	8.1	7.0	21.7	26.2	16.2	4.5	80.2	42.4	48.7	51.3
50127	IRA	100.0	100.0	0.0	0.0	0.0	0.0	0.0	0.0	5.9	5.9	5.9	5.9	5.9	23.5	32.4	14.7	0.0	76.5	42.5	47.1	52.9
50128	JAMAICA	98.0	97.8	0.3	0.2	0.0	0.0	2.0	1.9	6.1	6.5	6.8	6.1	3.4	21.1	32.0	16.2	1.9	77.2	45.1	50.4	49.6
50129	JEFFERSON	98.1	97.5	0.1	0.2	0.3	0.5	1.6	2.4	5.5	5.6	5.7	6.5	5.4	20.1	28.0	16.5	6.6	78.9	45.7	46.9	53.1
50130	JEWELL	96.8	94.9	0.2	0.2	1.5	2.6	1.6	2.4	7.0	7.2	7.3	7.7	6.0	24.1	27.8	11.0	2.0	72.9	38.6	52.7	47.3
50131	JOHNSTON	96.3	93.6	0.6	0.9	1.9	3.8	1.5	2.6	7.5	7.8	8.6	7.4	3.6	29.6	27.0	7.0	1.5	70.7	37.0	48.7	51.3
50132	KAMRAR	98.5	97.9	0.0	0.0	0.2	0.5	1.2	1.6	5.5	6.3	6.5	6.8	4.5	21.7	31.9	14.9	1.8	77.2	43.9	51.8	48.2
50133	KELLERTON	98.9	98.7	0.0	0.0	0.0	0.0	0.4	0.5	8.1	7.9	7.0	5.8	6.9	22.0	24.5	15.0	2.7	73.1	36.3	46.9	53.1
50134	KELLEY	97.1	96.3	0.5	0.5	1.1	1.7	1.1	1.5	7.0	6.9	6.7	6.9	6.1	28.9	25.8	9.3	2.4	75.3	35.9	50.2	49.8
50135	KELLOGG	98.3	97.8	0.3	0.4	0.5	0.9	0.7	1.0	5.1	5.7	6.1	6.8	4.9	21.5	33.3	14.9	1.7	78.8	45.0	50.7	49.3
50136	KESWICK	99.0	99.0	0.0	0.0	0.2	0.2	0.5	0.7	6.1	6.8	6.8	7.2	4.6	21.8	30.3	13.6	2.7	75.6	42.3	49.9	50.1
50138	KNOXVILLE	97.4	96.7	0.9	1.1	0.4	0.6	0.8	1.2	6.3	6.2	6.3	6.7	5.6	23.2	28.2	14.6	3.0	77.1	41.9	50.6	49.4
50139	LACONA	98.6	98.1	0.0	0.0	0.3	0.4	0.4	0.5	5.7	6.3	6.8	6.9	4.9	24.1	30.6	12.7	2.0	76.9	42.0	50.8	49.2
	IOWA	93.9	91.9	2.1	2.5	1.3	2.1	2.8	4.1	6.5	6.4	6.5	7.3	7.1	25.2	26.5	11.9	2.6	76.5	38.1	49.3	50.7
	UNITED STATES	75.1	72.0	12.3	12.7	3.8	4.6	12.5	15.7	6.8	6.7	6.6	7.1	6.9	27.0	26.0	10.9	1.9	75.7	36.9	49.2	50.8

#	POST OFFICE NAME	2009 Per Capita Income	2009 HH Income Base	2009 HOUSEHOLD INCOME DISTRIBUTION (%) Less than $25,000	$25,000 to $49,999	$50,000 to $99,999	$100,000 to $149,999	$150,000 or More	MEDIAN HOUSEHOLD INCOME 2009	2014	2009 National Centile	2009 State Centile	2009 Home Value Base	2009 HOME VALUE DISTRIBUTION (%) Less than $50,000	$50,000 to $89,999	$90,000 to $174,999	$175,000 to $399,999	$400,000 or More	2009 Median Home Value
50001	ACKWORTH	22582	304	12.2	34.2	43.8	8.6	1.3	54163	59580	70	84	269	11.5	8.6	29.4	46.5	4.1	176250
50002	ADAIR	21839	565	25.7	34.3	33.8	4.6	1.6	41360	42844	37	22	447	27.5	37.6	30.0	4.0	0.9	73977
50003	ADEL	26134	2823	14.1	27.9	44.0	9.5	4.5	57197	59492	74	89	2159	14.6	13.0	31.0	31.0	10.4	144555
50005	ALBION	20702	318	17.0	34.0	42.5	6.0	0.6	49175	51700	59	66	267	23.2	27.3	33.7	13.1	2.6	89444
50006	ALDEN	20806	754	22.0	33.4	36.6	6.1	1.9	45400	45895	49	46	579	25.6	30.4	33.3	8.3	2.4	81375
50007	ALLEMAN	21909	185	12.4	23.2	54.1	8.6	1.6	62285	64936	80	94	155	5.8	18.7	32.3	43.2	0.0	156250
50008	ALLERTON	18262	341	29.9	36.1	28.2	4.1	1.8	37403	38923	25	7	278	60.4	19.1	16.2	3.6	0.7	43556
50009	ALTOONA	27680	6062	11.4	23.7	45.3	15.1	4.5	67343	73553	85	97	4567	3.9	7.9	55.8	31.6	0.8	145200
50010	AMES	29796	12167	23.1	24.5	35.6	10.4	6.4	52637	55528	67	79	7074	9.3	5.7	44.4	36.8	3.9	154146
50011	AMES	13327	0	0.0	0.0	0.0	0.0	0.0	0	0	0	0	0	0.0	0.0	0.0	0.0	0.0	0
50013	AMES	13321	0	0.0	0.0	0.0	0.0	0.0	0	0	0	0	0	0.0	0.0	0.0	0.0	0.0	0
50014	AMES	24066	10326	28.6	25.6	30.3	9.5	5.9	45274	48883	49	46	4304	7.0	3.3	36.8	48.1	4.9	182442
50020	ANITA	19790	595	33.4	30.3	30.9	4.2	1.2	38275	40437	28	9	470	30.2	35.5	27.0	6.2	1.1	71333
50021	ANKENY	33197	8460	10.8	19.9	40.2	19.6	9.5	74131	77538	89	98	6682	8.5	5.7	38.4	43.9	3.5	170214
50022	ATLANTIC	22442	3598	24.4	34.7	32.9	5.6	2.4	42984	45471	42	31	2590	15.5	32.6	42.2	9.1	0.6	92356
50023	ANKENY	36900	9661	9.4	19.8	38.6	19.1	13.2	76244	80097	90	99	7423	2.5	4.0	39.1	49.7	4.7	185561
50025	AUDUBON	23577	1518	26.9	32.4	31.9	5.1	3.7	43635	45939	44	35	1196	21.1	36.7	33.6	6.5	2.1	79394
50026	BAGLEY	24320	290	23.1	28.6	36.6	8.3	3.4	48495	50559	58	63	241	18.3	24.9	31.5	19.5	5.8	102574
50027	BARNES CITY	23526	152	23.0	30.9	37.5	5.9	2.6	47118	50398	54	57	106	24.5	24.5	33.0	10.4	7.5	93333
50028	BAXTER	24864	715	18.6	27.7	44.3	7.7	1.7	52912	54157	68	80	517	10.3	18.8	56.7	12.0	2.3	114489
50029	BAYARD	24031	296	30.7	32.1	26.7	6.1	4.4	40000	42544	33	15	227	30.0	27.8	32.2	8.8	1.3	72647
50033	BEVINGTON	23709	22	18.2	27.3	40.9	9.1	4.5	52835	60000	68	80	19	5.3	15.8	21.1	42.1	15.8	206250
50034	BLAIRSBURG	20577	174	21.3	31.0	42.5	4.0	1.1	48613	49544	58	64	131	25.2	26.7	32.8	11.5	3.8	87727
50035	BONDURANT	26875	1585	13.5	19.3	48.6	13.1	5.4	67266	70701	85	97	1353	4.9	7.7	61.7	25.2	0.5	124019
50036	BOONE	25578	7038	21.2	27.2	40.8	7.2	3.6	51438	53544	65	75	5132	15.7	29.5	37.9	15.4	1.5	96806
50038	BOONEVILLE	44286	4	0.0	0.0	100.0	0.0	0.0	75000	75000	89	98	0	0.0	0.0	0.0	0.0	0.0	0
50039	BOUTON	21865	185	18.4	41.6	30.3	7.6	2.2	42563	43612	41	29	145	20.0	29.7	26.9	21.4	2.1	90625
50040	BOXHOLM	22825	115	26.1	36.5	31.3	6.1	0.0	42933	45439	42	31	93	26.9	24.7	31.2	14.0	3.2	87500
50041	BRADFORD	24660	12	16.7	25.0	41.7	16.7	0.0	60000	54356	77	92	9	0.0	44.4	55.6	0.0	0.0	92500
50042	BRAYTON	19742	165	23.6	40.6	30.3	3.0	2.4	37318	38303	25	7	132	26.5	28.8	28.0	11.4	5.3	80000
50044	BUSSEY	19768	349	26.6	32.7	34.4	5.7	0.6	42337	45505	40	27	292	38.4	28.8	24.3	8.6	0.0	65000
50046	CAMBRIDGE	22578	556	18.5	30.6	41.2	7.9	1.8	50649	52513	63	72	454	21.4	22.2	33.9	18.9	3.5	102532
50047	CARLISLE	25758	2261	17.4	24.1	45.7	9.7	3.1	58677	61528	76	90	1840	18.9	13.0	44.3	21.4	2.4	127827
50048	CASEY	24417	388	23.7	32.0	36.3	4.6	3.4	44380	46894	46	41	305	30.5	29.8	30.2	6.9	2.6	78810
50049	CHARITON	18838	2848	33.0	30.8	30.9	3.9	1.5	38424	39723	28	10	2166	28.5	30.9	31.0	8.2	1.4	77632
50050	CHURDAN	19564	330	34.2	35.2	25.8	1.8	3.0	33145	34542	14	2	253	53.0	23.3	17.4	3.2	3.2	47973
50051	CLEMONS	22741	138	17.4	31.2	46.4	4.3	0.7	50748	52925	63	73	108	33.3	18.5	36.1	10.2	1.9	87143
50052	CLIO	23670	68	30.9	26.5	32.4	8.8	1.5	43892	46559	45	37	54	50.0	25.9	11.1	9.3	3.7	50000
50054	COLFAX	21756	1376	23.1	27.3	37.6	10.3	1.6	49503	51817	60	67	1116	13.6	22.6	47.3	16.0	0.4	107977
50055	COLLINS	23759	382	16.8	31.7	44.5	5.5	1.6	50950	52682	63	73	305	29.5	15.1	33.4	18.0	3.9	105060
50056	COLO	24162	514	14.4	29.0	47.7	7.0	1.9	54218	54674	70	84	413	24.9	32.7	34.4	7.3	0.7	80735
50057	COLUMBIA	20211	102	18.6	35.3	40.2	5.9	0.0	47336	50000	55	58	90	23.3	23.3	40.0	11.1	2.2	96000
50058	COON RAPIDS	22052	795	25.3	36.1	32.2	4.7	1.8	42249	44204	40	26	601	28.0	34.1	33.3	4.3	0.3	76023
50059	COOPER	15893	14	28.6	28.6	35.7	7.1	0.0	42500	42500	41	28	11	9.1	27.3	63.6	0.0	0.0	102500
50060	CORYDON	20699	1116	32.6	31.9	28.1	4.7	2.7	38205	40125	27	9	861	30.7	33.9	30.0	4.6	0.8	70948
50061	CUMMING	39197	502	5.4	13.3	45.6	21.3	14.3	81505	85172	93	99	449	2.0	4.5	33.9	44.5	15.1	205903
50062	DALLAS	21278	164	20.1	28.0	45.7	4.9	1.2	51106	52587	64	75	143	17.5	28.0	38.5	13.3	2.8	97222
50063	DALLAS CENTER	24272	1036	15.8	24.5	47.9	9.3	2.5	60062	61657	77	92	849	7.9	14.0	38.2	34.5	5.4	145147
50064	DANA	19534	46	17.4	39.1	34.8	6.5	2.2	45000	46534	48	44	36	50.0	30.6	11.1	5.6	2.8	50000
50065	DAVIS CITY	16712	305	32.8	43.3	20.0	2.3	1.6	33141	33312	14	2	243	43.6	26.3	21.8	7.8	0.4	61071
50066	DAWSON	26534	183	18.0	27.3	42.6	8.7	3.3	56167	58313	73	88	154	26.6	19.5	26.6	22.1	5.2	98571
50067	DECATUR	16752	173	36.4	40.5	19.7	2.3	1.2	32413	32601	12	1	139	40.3	27.3	16.5	15.1	0.7	63125
50068	DERBY	16583	140	28.6	34.3	32.9	4.3	0.0	41006	42045	36	20	120	20.8	23.3	34.2	17.5	4.2	101563
50069	DE SOTO	23531	523	12.6	27.5	53.2	5.5	1.1	60164	61799	78	92	450	40.0	20.2	24.2	12.4	3.1	69286
50070	DEXTER	23257	708	19.1	25.7	46.6	6.6	2.0	54120	55367	70	84	594	14.8	30.6	38.9	13.1	2.5	96750
50071	DOWS	20456	526	27.4	34.0	34.6	3.0	1.0	40561	42821	35	17	392	38.3	31.6	19.4	9.2	1.5	62647
50072	EARLHAM	23954	1085	19.1	24.8	44.1	8.7	3.3	56025	58332	73	88	885	9.5	14.9	42.7	27.5	5.4	137596
50073	ELKHART	26471	413	17.9	24.0	47.5	9.2	1.5	61099	63753	79	93	330	18.5	11.8	33.6	32.7	3.3	131897
50074	ELLSTON	19208	263	31.6	33.8	27.8	6.1	0.8	36058	38446	21	4	214	32.2	25.7	26.2	14.0	1.9	75263
50075	ELLSWORTH	20234	352	23.3	34.7	33.8	6.0	2.3	43574	46181	44	35	254	16.9	22.8	41.3	18.1	0.8	104245
50076	EXIRA	18796	670	35.2	33.4	27.2	3.1	1.0	35539	37172	19	4	539	34.7	28.9	28.2	6.9	1.3	66184
50101	GALT	21980	24	20.8	33.3	45.8	0.0	0.0	47330	45707	55	58	18	38.9	22.2	22.2	16.7	0.0	70000
50102	GARDEN CITY	18563	15	20.0	40.0	33.3	6.7	0.0	42343	47351	40	27	11	9.1	36.4	54.5	0.0	0.0	95000
50103	GARDEN GROVE	21168	237	34.6	29.5	28.3	3.4	4.2	36595	37584	22	5	194	32.0	25.8	27.8	11.3	3.1	76429
50104	GIBSON	20548	63	23.8	33.3	38.1	4.8	0.0	44307	46142	46	40	51	21.6	37.3	31.4	5.9	3.9	75000
50105	GILBERT	19958	367	23.4	26.2	38.4	10.6	1.4	50281	52158	62	71	296	36.8	8.1	35.1	18.6	1.4	106875
50106	GILMAN	22184	486	25.5	27.2	40.7	5.6	1.0	47541	51020	56	60	380	23.9	31.1	36.1	7.6	1.3	84063
50107	GRAND JUNCTION	17213	448	33.0	29.7	33.0	2.9	1.3	38577	40257	28	11	330	46.4	36.4	12.4	4.5	0.3	52857
50108	GRAND RIVER	17415	234	36.3	40.2	20.1	2.6	0.9	32833	32895	13	2	189	36.0	28.0	18.0	15.9	2.1	70333
50109	GRANGER	28864	989	13.7	21.8	43.7	15.7	5.2	62051	64003	80	94	826	7.1	11.5	42.5	32.3	6.5	150000
50111	GRIMES	33843	3471	7.8	21.4	39.8	21.6	9.4	72419	76158	88	98	2832	6.5	12.1	45.9	30.6	4.9	151163
50112	GRINNELL	24347	4506	22.5	30.0	36.4	7.3	3.9	47808	49850	56	61	3100	11.4	21.4	46.2	19.5	1.5	116623
50115	GUTHRIE CENTER	21781	1082	29.1	28.8	34.2	5.7	2.1	41435	44505	37	22	836	27.3	36.2	29.7	5.0	1.8	74412
50116	HAMILTON	17526	135	26.7	32.6	35.6	5.2	0.0	42585	45323	41	29	115	39.1	29.6	24.3	7.0	0.0	64375
50117	HAMLIN	17898	96	29.2	35.4	30.2	5.2	0.0	39363	40913	31	13	75	30.7	30.7	33.3	5.3	0.0	78333
50118	HARTFORD	22958	424	14.9	29.5	47.6	5.7	2.4	54280	57433	70	84	397	22.2	18.6	40.6	18.6	0.0	107008
50119	HARVEY	19418	207	23.2	35.7	35.7	5.3	0.0	43181	45622	43	32	170	33.5	32.9	21.2	9.4	2.9	65385
50120	HAVERHILL	19491	140	15.0	33.6	46.4	5.0	0.0	51032	53109	64	74	116	13.8	25.0	44.0	16.4	0.9	104545
50122	HUBBARD	24260	598	20.6	36.3	34.4	5.5	3.2	44868	46326	48	44	480	19.6	33.3	41.0	5.6	0.4	86889
50123	HUMESTON	20595	357	35.6	33.3	25.2	4.8	1.1	35241	36737	18	3	283	34.3	34.3	22.3	7.8	1.4	62885
50124	HUXLEY	26461	1302	16.0	26.0	43.5	11.2	3.3	60065	59286	77	92	997	32.1	7.6	38.1	21.6	0.6	111894
50125	INDIANOLA	25168	7179	17.0	25.4	43.1	10.9	3.5	58808	62266	76	91	5234	10.7	7.4	44.5	34.9	2.6	149196
50126	IOWA FALLS	24318	2866	24.6	31.8	33.3	7.5	2.9	44651	46006	47	43	2050	19.7	32.9	36.3	9.3	1.9	86709
50127	IRA	24944	15	26.7	26.7	33.3	13.3	0.0	47351	52087	55	59	14	0.0	7.1	35.7	57.1	0.0	200000
50128	JAMAICA	24948	172	23.3	27.9	36.6	8.7	3.5	48910	50191	59	65	144	18.1	25.0	31.3	20.1	5.6	102500
50129	JEFFERSON	22450	2214	25.8	28.3	37.3	6.9	1.8	45834	48091	51	49	1679	20.0	35.9	38.4	4.7	1.1	84730
50130	JEWELL	25165	688	16.0	28.5	43.2	9.6	2.8	55207	57385	72	87	527	11.4	23.9	52.2	12.1	0.4	108169
50131	JOHNSTON	45694	6007	9.7	15.5	30.6	19.1	25.2	87422	89373	94	100	4396	0.6	2.0	17.1	68.4	11.9	240835
50132	KAMRAR	21309	151	19.9	31.8	42.4	4.6	1.3	48999	50175	59	66	113	22.1	26.5	35.4	11.5	4.4	93000
50133	KELLERTON	14970	218	33.5	42.2	22.9	0.5	0.9	35430	36368	19	4	162	49.4	27.8	9.9	8.6	4.3	50588
50134	KELLEY	27623	252	12.7	24.6	45.2	12.7	4.8	64480	64364	83	96	181	7.2	13.3	54.1	21.5	3.9	127016
50135	KELLOGG	24432	692	19.7	30.1	39.5	9.5	1.3	50250	52547	62	71	589	13.8	15.4	45.3	23.8	1.7	117935
50136	KESWICK	22129	237	23.6	31.6	39.2	3.0	2.5	44813	45646	48	43	197	22.8	29.9	38.6	5.6	3.0	82143
50138	KNOXVILLE	22999	4765	23.4	27.8	38.8	7.2	2.9	48775	51524	58	65	3511	16.2	30.2	42.7	10.5	0.4	94922
50139	LACONA	19956	529	21.2	34.2	38.9	5.5	0.2	45615	48686	50	48	437	18.5	27.7	33.9	17.4	2.5	95500
	IOWA	25379		21.1	28.2	37.9	8.6	4.3	50616	52941				14.7	22.5	41.6	18.6	2.6	110128
	UNITED STATES	27277		20.9	24.4	35.3	11.7	7.6	54719	56938				9.3	13.1	31.6	32.6	13.5	162279

ZIP CODE #	POST OFFICE NAME	FINANCIAL SERVICES: Auto Loan	Home Loan	Invest-ments	Retire-ment Plans	THE HOME: Home Improvements: Home Repair	Lawn & Garden	Furnishings: Comput-ers & Hard-ware-Personal	Major Appli-ances	TV, Radio, Sound Equip-ment	Furni-ture	ENTERTAINMENT: Dine out/ Carry out	Sports Equip-ment	Fees & Tickets	Toys & Games	Travel	Cable TV	PERSONAL: Apparel & Services	Auto Repairs	Health Insur-ance	Pets & Supplies
50001	ACKWORTH	85	95	82	98	93	94	85	89	84	86	84	69	91	86	90	84	59	85	88	104
50002	ADAIR	85	60	89	59	63	90	66	82	72	57	70	64	52	71	65	79	46	77	89	98
50003	ADEL	95	98	93	99	97	100	93	95	93	93	94	73	95	95	95	94	65	94	97	113
50005	ALBION	83	74	77	77	76	90	74	84	76	66	75	64	67	77	74	81	51	78	87	98
50006	ALDEN	94	65	103	65	68	99	72	89	75	58	74	74	53	73	72	82	48	83	94	110
50007	ALLEMAN	92	103	89	107	100	102	92	96	91	93	91	75	99	93	98	91	64	92	95	113
50008	ALLERTON	77	55	79	54	57	80	60	74	66	52	64	57	47	65	58	72	42	69	80	88
50009	ALTOONA	110	109	91	107	102	96	106	102	103	111	105	80	104	108	101	100	73	102	95	120
50010	AMES	95	86	84	90	85	86	105	89	98	97	99	73	96	98	93	96	70	96	90	108
50011	AMES	0	0	0	0	0	0	0	0	0	0	0	0	0	0	0	0	0	0	0	0
50013	AMES	0	0	0	0	0	0	0	0	0	0	0	0	0	0	0	0	0	0	0	0
50014	AMES	91	67	64	73	65	69	107	77	96	90	97	69	85	96	81	92	68	90	78	97
50020	ANITA	78	55	80	54	57	81	60	75	66	53	64	57	47	65	59	73	43	70	81	89
50021	ANKENY	124	131	117	134	126	118	125	121	120	130	122	97	129	126	125	116	87	120	113	141
50022	ATLANTIC	79	67	77	67	68	84	70	78	74	64	72	59	62	73	68	79	49	75	85	93
50023	ANKENY	135	141	126	143	137	128	134	131	129	140	131	105	138	135	133	125	93	129	122	153
50025	AUDUBON	96	68	99	67	71	100	75	92	81	65	79	71	58	80	73	90	52	86	100	110
50026	BAGLEY	106	73	116	72	76	111	81	100	84	65	83	83	59	82	80	91	54	94	106	123
50027	BARNES CITY	92	64	102	63	67	98	71	88	73	57	73	73	52	72	70	80	47	82	93	108
50028	BAXTER	85	83	71	86	80	91	83	84	84	77	83	66	81	86	81	87	57	83	91	101
50029	BAYARD	105	72	115	72	76	111	80	100	83	65	82	82	59	82	80	91	53	93	105	123
50033	BEVINGTON	89	100	86	103	97	98	90	93	88	90	89	73	96	90	95	88	62	90	92	110
50034	BLAIRSBURG	95	65	104	65	68	100	72	90	75	59	74	74	53	74	72	82	48	84	95	111
50035	BONDURANT	111	118	98	116	111	106	106	108	104	112	105	82	108	108	106	102	73	104	101	126
50036	BOONE	89	83	80	84	82	92	86	88	87	81	86	68	81	88	83	90	59	88	94	105
50038	BOONEVILLE	124	114	101	111	112	117	108	114	112	112	112	83	102	116	103	115	76	111	115	136
50039	BOUTON	95	65	104	65	68	100	72	90	75	59	75	74	53	74	72	82	48	84	95	111
50040	BOXHOLM	86	59	94	59	62	91	66	82	68	53	67	67	48	67	65	74	44	76	86	100
50041	BRADFORD	110	76	121	76	79	116	84	105	88	68	87	86	62	86	84	96	56	98	111	129
50042	BRAYTON	89	61	98	61	64	94	68	84	71	55	70	70	50	69	67	77	45	79	89	104
50044	BUSSEY	86	64	72	63	64	83	66	76	72	63	71	59	55	75	61	78	48	72	80	92
50046	CAMBRIDGE	91	85	76	83	83	87	80	85	82	83	82	62	77	86	77	85	56	82	85	100
50047	CARLISLE	93	100	89	100	97	100	90	94	91	91	92	71	94	94	93	93	64	91	96	111
50048	CASEY	103	71	112	70	74	108	78	97	82	64	81	80	58	81	78	90	53	91	103	119
50049	CHARITON	77	56	77	55	58	79	62	74	68	55	66	56	50	66	59	74	44	70	80	88
50050	CHURDAN	81	56	89	56	58	85	62	77	64	50	64	64	45	63	62	70	41	72	81	95
50051	CLEMONS	95	65	104	65	68	100	72	90	75	59	74	74	53	74	72	82	48	84	95	110
50052	CLIO	88	63	89	61	65	91	69	85	76	61	74	64	55	75	66	84	49	79	92	100
50054	COLFAX	87	78	82	79	78	93	77	87	80	71	78	66	71	81	77	84	53	81	91	102
50055	COLLINS	99	72	106	72	75	105	78	95	81	65	80	77	60	80	78	88	52	89	100	116
50056	COLO	92	84	84	85	80	98	86	90	88	78	87	73	79	88	84	91	59	89	98	110
50057	COLUMBIA	79	72	71	75	74	85	71	80	73	64	72	61	66	75	71	78	49	74	83	93
50058	COON RAPIDS	81	68	86	67	70	90	69	82	74	62	73	62	62	73	70	80	49	77	90	96
50059	COOPER	85	59	94	59	61	90	65	81	68	53	67	67	48	66	65	74	43	76	85	100
50060	CORYDON	82	58	85	57	60	86	64	79	70	55	68	61	50	68	62	76	45	74	85	94
50061	CUMMING	144	178	165	182	176	162	151	156	143	158	145	122	171	147	165	139	105	148	143	179
50062	DALLAS	86	75	79	78	77	91	75	86	79	68	77	65	68	80	75	84	52	80	90	100
50063	DALLAS CENTER	93	95	87	98	94	101	88	95	89	85	88	74	89	91	91	91	61	90	96	112
50064	DANA	99	68	109	68	72	105	76	94	79	62	78	78	56	77	76	86	51	88	100	116
50065	DAVIS CITY	74	50	79	51	53	76	58	69	59	47	59	58	42	58	56	64	38	65	73	85
50066	DAWSON	116	80	127	79	83	122	88	110	92	72	91	91	65	90	88	100	59	102	116	135
50067	DECATUR	72	49	79	49	52	76	55	68	57	44	56	56	40	56	54	62	37	63	72	84
50068	DERBY	78	54	85	54	56	82	59	74	62	48	61	61	44	61	59	68	40	69	78	91
50069	DE SOTO	98	90	80	87	88	92	85	90	88	89	88	66	81	92	81	91	60	87	90	107
50070	DEXTER	90	80	83	80	77	94	80	87	84	75	83	68	74	84	79	88	56	85	93	105
50071	DOWS	82	56	90	56	59	87	63	78	65	51	64	64	46	64	62	71	42	73	82	96
50072	EARLHAM	98	93	86	92	91	97	88	94	90	89	90	70	85	93	86	92	61	90	94	111
50073	ELKHART	88	99	85	102	96	97	89	92	87	89	88	72	94	89	94	87	61	89	91	108
50074	ELLSTON	73	58	92	57	63	77	58	74	62	54	61	54	50	59	63	66	40	68	74	86
50075	ELLSWORTH	93	64	102	64	67	98	71	89	74	58	73	73	52	73	71	81	48	83	94	109
50076	EXIRA	75	53	80	52	55	79	58	72	62	49	61	57	44	61	57	68	40	67	77	87
50101	GALT	82	56	90	56	59	86	63	78	65	51	64	64	46	64	62	71	42	73	82	96
50102	GARDEN CITY	89	61	97	61	64	93	68	84	70	55	70	69	49	69	67	77	45	78	89	103
50103	GARDEN GROVE	98	67	107	67	70	103	75	93	78	60	77	77	55	76	74	85	50	87	98	114
50104	GIBSON	94	65	103	64	68	99	72	89	75	58	74	74	53	73	71	81	48	83	94	110
50105	GILBERT	90	83	73	80	81	85	78	83	81	81	81	60	74	84	74	83	55	80	83	98
50106	GILMAN	77	74	65	76	71	82	74	76	76	69	75	60	71	77	72	78	51	75	82	91
50107	GRAND JUNCTION	78	56	79	55	58	81	61	75	67	54	65	57	48	66	59	74	43	70	81	89
50108	GRAND RIVER	71	49	78	49	51	75	54	68	57	44	56	56	40	55	54	62	36	63	71	83
50109	GRANGER	108	116	107	119	115	117	105	113	104	103	104	87	108	107	109	105	73	106	109	130
50111	GRIMES	130	143	119	139	135	121	127	127	120	136	122	100	131	128	126	115	86	121	112	145
50112	GRINNELL	86	76	80	77	77	88	82	85	85	77	83	64	75	84	79	88	57	85	91	101
50115	GUTHRIE CENTER	89	63	91	62	65	92	69	85	75	60	73	65	54	74	67	83	48	79	92	101
50116	HAMILTON	83	62	70	61	62	81	64	74	70	62	69	57	53	73	59	76	46	70	78	90
50117	HAMLIN	80	55	87	55	57	84	61	76	63	49	63	63	45	62	61	69	41	71	80	93
50118	HARTFORD	94	85	85	89	87	101	84	95	87	76	85	72	78	89	84	92	58	88	98	110
50119	HARVEY	86	63	71	61	62	82	65	75	72	63	70	58	53	75	59	78	47	71	80	92
50120	HAVERHILL	88	77	83	79	79	94	77	88	80	68	78	68	69	81	77	85	53	82	92	104
50122	HUBBARD	101	71	105	70	74	106	78	97	85	67	83	75	61	84	76	94	55	90	104	116
50123	HUMESTON	77	53	85	53	55	81	59	73	61	48	60	60	43	60	59	67	39	68	77	90
50124	HUXLEY	102	98	84	94	94	94	91	94	92	95	93	70	88	96	87	93	63	91	92	111
50125	INDIANOLA	92	95	88	97	94	98	92	94	93	90	92	71	94	93	93	95	64	93	98	111
50126	IOWA FALLS	82	74	80	73	74	88	75	82	80	70	79	61	71	79	75	85	54	80	90	97
50127	IRA	79	89	76	91	86	87	79	82	78	79	78	64	85	80	84	78	55	79	82	97
50128	JAMAICA	107	74	118	73	77	113	82	102	85	66	84	84	60	83	81	93	55	95	107	125
50129	JEFFERSON	88	66	88	66	69	91	72	85	78	65	76	65	60	77	70	84	51	81	92	101
50130	JEWELL	96	89	86	90	84	102	91	94	92	83	92	76	85	93	89	96	62	93	103	115
50131	JOHNSTON	166	201	178	207	198	173	169	172	158	186	160	141	191	168	180	148	117	159	148	194
50132	KAMRAR	96	66	106	66	69	102	74	91	77	60	76	76	54	75	73	84	49	85	97	113
50133	KELLERTON	64	46	64	45	48	67	51	62	56	45	54	47	41	55	49	62	36	58	68	73
50134	KELLEY	107	111	93	109	105	99	103	102	100	108	102	78	103	105	101	98	71	100	96	120
50135	KELLOGG	91	83	82	86	85	98	82	92	84	74	83	70	75	86	82	89	56	85	95	107
50136	KESWICK	98	67	108	67	71	103	75	93	78	61	77	77	55	76	74	85	50	87	98	114
50138	KNOXVILLE	84	75	76	76	75	88	77	84	81	71	79	63	71	81	75	85	54	81	90	99
50139	LACONA	87	66	91	67	68	92	70	84	72	59	72	68	56	72	70	78	47	78	88	102
	IOWA	93	84	87	85	83	95	87	91	89	82	88	71	81	90	85	92	61	90	96	108
	UNITED STATES	100	100	100	100	100	100	100	100	100	100	100	100	100	100	100	100	100	100	100	100

ZIP CODE			POPULATION			2000-2009 ANNUAL RATE		HOUSEHOLDS					FAMILIES		
#	POST OFFICE NAME	COUNTY FIPS CODE	2000	2009	2014	% Rate	State Centile	2000	2009	2014	% Annual Rate 2000-2009	2009 Average HH Size	2000	2009	% Annual Rate 2000-2009
50140	LAMONI	053	2828	2978	2992	0.6	83	953	1037	1045	0.9	2.23	523	560	0.7
50141	LAUREL	127	595	591	589	-0.1	51	231	234	234	0.1	2.53	171	170	-0.1
50142	LE GRAND	127	860	887	891	0.3	72	329	349	352	0.6	2.54	252	262	0.4
50143	LEIGHTON	123	664	692	703	0.4	76	229	244	248	0.7	2.79	193	203	0.5
50144	LEON	053	2579	2344	2251	-1.0	6	1069	978	939	-1.0	2.33	677	606	-1.2
50146	LINDEN	049	489	545	618	1.2	93	195	223	253	1.5	2.44	152	171	1.3
50147	LINEVILLE	185	403	390	378	-0.4	32	174	171	166	-0.2	2.28	121	116	-0.5
50148	LISCOMB	127	412	417	418	0.1	63	170	176	176	0.4	2.37	123	124	0.1
50149	LORIMOR	121	937	930	928	-0.1	51	377	385	387	0.2	2.42	267	268	0.0
50150	LOVILIA	135	1073	1028	991	-0.5	27	414	406	394	-0.2	2.53	311	300	-0.4
50151	LUCAS	117	754	797	805	0.6	83	310	330	334	0.7	2.42	228	239	0.5
50152	LUTHER	015	21	22	23	0.5	79	9	10	10	1.1	2.20	8	8	0.0
50153	LYNNVILLE	099	757	786	788	0.4	76	276	296	299	0.8	2.66	217	228	0.5
50154	MC CALLSBURG	169	527	504	498	-0.5	27	202	203	203	0.1	2.48	157	155	-0.1
50155	MACKSBURG	121	267	287	295	0.8	87	100	110	113	1.0	2.61	81	88	0.9
50156	MADRID	015	4235	4473	4625	0.6	83	1588	1718	1784	0.9	2.52	1179	1250	0.6
50157	MALCOM	157	796	815	818	0.3	72	320	341	346	0.7	2.34	248	259	0.5
50158	MARSHALLTOWN	127	30496	30618	30521	0.0	58	11871	12003	11968	0.1	2.44	7937	7839	-0.1
50161	MAXWELL	153	1940	2121	2238	1.0	90	719	781	828	0.9	2.72	562	596	0.6
50162	MELBOURNE	127	1243	1319	1332	0.6	83	491	530	536	0.8	2.49	349	367	0.5
50163	MELCHER	125	1187	1226	1231	0.4	76	474	508	515	0.8	2.41	330	344	0.5
50164	MENLO	077	652	652	641	0.0	58	274	280	277	0.2	2.33	200	200	0.0
50165	MILLERTON	185	57	55	53	-0.4	32	24	24	23	0.0	2.29	18	17	-0.6
50166	MILO	181	1574	1792	1934	1.4	94	568	667	727	1.8	2.69	449	518	1.6
50167	MINBURN	049	761	868	991	1.4	94	293	343	395	1.7	2.53	213	245	1.5
50168	MINGO	099	721	804	818	1.2	93	287	328	336	1.5	2.42	223	250	1.2
50169	MITCHELLVILLE	153	2734	2923	3038	0.7	85	909	1007	1059	1.1	2.53	671	718	0.7
50170	MONROE	099	2747	2803	2805	0.2	68	1085	1137	1147	0.5	2.47	804	822	0.2
50171	MONTEZUMA	157	2909	3006	3022	0.4	76	1202	1291	1314	0.8	2.27	845	886	0.5
50173	MONTOUR	171	783	842	853	0.8	87	290	319	324	1.0	2.62	216	233	0.8
50174	MURRAY	039	1364	1428	1428	0.5	79	529	561	562	0.6	2.55	396	412	0.4
50201	NEVADA	169	8304	7872	7699	-0.6	20	3301	3247	3206	-0.2	2.36	2251	2147	-0.5
50206	NEW PROVIDENCE	083	504	480	465	-0.5	27	203	199	193	-0.2	2.40	147	141	-0.4
50207	NEW SHARON	123	2650	2720	2743	0.3	72	1018	1066	1080	0.5	2.51	768	786	0.3
50208	NEWTON	099	20901	20254	19928	-0.3	40	8344	8267	8174	-0.1	2.28	5522	5337	-0.4
50210	NEW VIRGINIA	181	1666	2004	2148	2.0	96	641	799	864	2.4	2.47	502	614	2.2
50211	NORWALK	181	9122	9823	10250	0.8	87	3134	3485	3671	1.2	2.76	2545	2790	1.0
50212	OGDEN	015	3338	3448	3488	0.4	76	1319	1377	1394	0.5	2.46	970	993	0.3
50213	OSCEOLA	039	6365	6326	6229	-0.1	51	2538	2520	2478	-0.1	2.46	1696	1644	-0.3
50214	OTLEY	125	872	955	1019	1.0	90	307	347	372	1.3	2.75	263	291	1.1
50216	PANORA	077	2677	2864	2873	0.7	85	1111	1223	1230	1.0	2.29	767	825	0.8
50217	PATON	073	627	597	577	-0.5	27	258	244	235	-0.6	2.45	183	170	-0.8
50218	PATTERSON	121	101	107	109	0.6	83	42	46	47	1.0	2.28	32	35	1.0
50219	PELLA	125	12823	14035	14393	1.0	90	4476	4953	5113	1.1	2.50	3203	3492	0.9
50220	PERRY	049	8954	9491	10350	0.6	83	3314	3534	3866	0.7	2.61	2318	2433	0.5
50222	PERU	121	573	635	666	1.1	91	202	229	241	1.4	2.77	164	184	1.3
50223	PILOT MOUND	015	433	443	443	0.2	68	182	189	190	0.4	2.34	125	126	0.1
50225	PLEASANTVILLE	125	2602	2793	2876	0.8	87	1016	1111	1151	1.0	2.47	725	765	0.6
50226	POLK CITY	153	3478	5021	5801	4.0	99	1225	1864	2175	4.6	2.67	1002	1496	4.4
50227	POPEJOY	069	30	29	28	-0.4	32	13	13	13	0.0	2.23	9	9	0.0
50228	PRAIRIE CITY	099	2169	2239	2247	0.3	72	847	904	914	0.7	2.42	625	652	0.5
50229	PROLE	181	1498	1730	1872	1.6	95	559	672	734	2.0	2.57	439	519	1.8
50230	RADCLIFFE	083	1229	1158	1116	-0.6	20	488	471	455	-0.4	2.46	357	337	-0.6
50231	RANDALL	079	148	144	139	-0.3	40	68	67	65	-0.2	2.15	54	52	-0.4
50232	REASNOR	099	554	569	568	0.3	72	206	222	225	0.8	1.92	172	183	0.7
50233	REDFIELD	049	1358	1710	2048	2.5	97	551	718	867	2.9	2.38	384	487	2.6
50234	RHODES	127	494	505	507	0.2	68	201	209	210	0.4	2.41	147	149	0.1
50235	RIPPEY	073	537	531	518	-0.1	51	209	206	200	-0.2	2.58	155	150	-0.4
50236	ROLAND	169	1587	1574	1570	-0.1	51	576	594	598	0.3	2.65	440	442	0.0
50237	RUNNELLS	153	2293	2505	2699	1.0	90	805	898	973	1.2	2.79	686	749	1.0
50238	RUSSELL	117	874	876	865	0.0	58	372	377	374	0.1	2.32	238	235	-0.1
50239	SAINT ANTHONY	127	232	223	220	-0.4	32	87	86	85	-0.1	2.59	66	64	-0.3
50240	SAINT CHARLES	121	1949	2260	2435	1.6	95	747	891	967	1.9	2.54	572	670	1.7
50242	SEARSBORO	157	465	460	447	-0.1	51	191	194	190	0.2	2.37	146	145	-0.1
50244	SLATER	153	1714	1684	1684	-0.2	46	684	707	716	0.4	2.38	487	490	0.1
50246	STANHOPE	079	893	876	858	-0.2	46	344	342	336	-0.1	2.56	249	243	-0.3
50247	STATE CENTER	127	2114	2140	2138	0.1	63	841	875	878	0.4	2.40	579	588	0.2
50248	STORY CITY	169	4351	4411	4426	0.1	63	1715	1803	1827	0.5	2.32	1129	1151	0.2
50249	STRATFORD	079	1397	1356	1327	-0.3	40	540	535	524	-0.1	2.42	362	349	-0.4
50250	STUART	001	2422	2542	2544	0.5	79	975	1048	1053	0.8	2.37	678	713	0.5
50251	SULLY	099	1483	1465	1448	-0.1	51	555	565	564	0.2	2.59	450	450	0.0
50252	SWAN	125	461	505	532	1.0	90	154	171	182	1.1	2.95	126	137	0.9
50254	THAYER	175	387	396	398	0.2	68	156	165	167	0.6	2.40	117	121	0.4
50256	TRACY	125	512	533	543	0.4	76	205	220	226	0.8	2.40	155	162	0.5
50257	TRURO	121	922	1094	1179	1.9	96	340	412	446	2.1	2.66	263	312	1.9
50258	UNION	083	1044	1010	982	-0.4	32	422	416	405	-0.2	2.42	311	301	-0.4
50261	VAN METER	121	1966	2293	2609	1.7	95	740	890	1020	2.0	2.58	560	661	1.8
50262	VAN WERT	053	414	401	392	-0.3	40	170	168	165	-0.1	2.39	121	118	-0.3
50263	WAUKEE	049	6718	15091	19992	9.1	100	2484	5648	7481	9.3	2.67	1920	4297	9.1
50264	WELDON	053	526	518	509	-0.2	46	210	211	208	0.1	2.45	155	154	-0.1
50265	WEST DES MOINES	153	30144	32833	34718	0.9	89	12662	14272	15192	1.3	2.28	7905	8472	0.8
50266	WEST DES MOINES	049	16868	23791	27986	3.8	98	7378	10748	12733	4.2	2.21	4198	5893	3.7
50268	WHAT CHEER	107	1023	992	974	-0.3	40	447	447	443	0.0	2.22	283	276	-0.3
50271	WILLIAMS	079	780	741	714	-0.6	20	315	308	298	-0.2	2.40	243	234	-0.4
50272	WILLIAMSON	117	435	433	431	0.0	58	175	176	175	0.1	2.45	133	131	-0.2
50273	WINTERSET	121	7468	8314	8737	1.2	93	2869	3279	3455	1.5	2.48	2016	2255	1.2
50274	WIOTA	029	528	502	486	-0.5	27	210	203	197	-0.4	2.35	155	147	-0.6
50275	WOODBURN	039	728	747	742	0.3	72	266	275	274	0.4	2.68	207	211	0.2
50276	WOODWARD	015	2610	2680	2905	0.3	72	903	973	1075	0.8	2.52	624	648	0.4
50277	YALE	077	501	548	560	1.0	90	212	237	243	1.2	2.31	159	175	1.0
50278	ZEARING	169	916	786	741	-1.6	0	336	297	282	-1.3	2.53	246	212	-1.6
50309	DES MOINES	153	5011	5529	5831	1.1	91	2272	2695	2924	1.9	1.51	575	612	0.7
50310	DES MOINES	153	31425	31505	32174	0.0	58	13413	13863	14251	0.4	2.23	8212	8066	-0.2
50311	DES MOINES	153	18765	18926	19321	0.1	63	7564	7869	8109	0.4	2.15	3877	3793	-0.2
50312	DES MOINES	153	16310	16383	16739	0.0	58	7618	7875	8088	0.4	2.03	3791	3701	-0.3
	IOWA					0.4					0.7	2.40			0.4
	UNITED STATES					1.0					1.1	2.59			0.9

ZIP CODE # POST OFFICE NAME	RACE (%) White 2000	White 2009	Black 2000	Black 2009	Asian/Pacific 2000	Asian/Pacific 2009	% Hispanic Origin 2000	% Hispanic Origin 2009	2009 AGE DISTRIBUTION (%) 0-4	5-9	10-14	15-19	20-24	25-44	45-64	65-84	85+	18+	MEDIAN AGE 2009	% 2009 Males	% 2009 Females
50140 LAMONI	92.6	91.0	2.5	2.9	1.7	2.6	2.6	3.6	4.3	3.5	4.2	14.9	19.2	17.6	19.7	13.1	3.6	84.8	28.6	48.3	51.7
50141 LAUREL	98.3	97.6	0.0	0.0	0.5	0.7	1.2	2.0	6.6	6.9	7.3	6.8	5.1	22.0	31.5	12.0	1.9	74.8	41.7	49.9	50.1
50142 LE GRAND	97.8	97.0	0.3	0.5	0.3	0.6	1.9	3.0	7.0	7.1	7.4	7.7	5.7	25.3	26.5	11.7	1.6	74.1	37.5	47.5	52.5
50143 LEIGHTON	99.2	99.3	0.0	0.0	0.3	0.3	0.2	0.1	7.7	8.1	7.9	7.5	4.5	24.6	27.9	10.5	1.3	71.2	37.7	50.7	49.3
50144 LEON	98.6	98.1	0.2	0.2	0.4	0.7	1.4	1.9	6.5	6.5	6.8	7.0	5.2	22.4	26.3	14.6	4.7	75.4	41.2	47.7	52.3
50146 LINDEN	98.8	98.5	0.0	0.0	0.2	0.2	0.8	2.0	5.9	6.2	7.0	7.3	3.9	21.7	33.8	12.3	2.0	76.3	43.7	52.3	47.7
50147 LINEVILLE	99.3	99.2	0.0	0.0	0.5	0.5	0.7	1.0	5.4	5.6	5.4	5.4	5.6	20.3	29.5	18.5	4.4	80.5	47.0	47.2	52.8
50148 LISCOMB	98.5	98.1	0.0	0.0	0.2	0.2	0.2	0.5	5.3	5.8	6.5	7.0	4.1	24.0	31.7	13.7	2.2	77.9	43.4	49.9	50.1
50149 LORIMOR	97.8	97.0	0.0	0.0	0.2	0.6	0.9	1.2	6.7	6.3	6.7	6.6	5.2	24.6	28.3	14.2	1.5	76.2	40.5	50.8	49.2
50150 LOVILIA	99.0	98.9	0.1	0.1	0.1	0.1	0.2	0.2	8.0	8.0	8.2	7.6	5.6	24.3	24.5	12.2	1.7	71.1	36.5	50.1	49.9
50151 LUCAS	98.9	98.4	0.0	0.0	0.3	0.4	1.2	1.8	6.0	6.5	6.5	6.4	4.8	22.0	29.7	16.2	1.9	77.2	43.3	49.3	50.7
50152 LUTHER	100.0	100.0	0.0	0.0	0.0	0.0	0.0	0.0	4.5	9.1	9.1	9.1	9.1	27.3	31.8	0.0	0.0	68.2	35.0	40.9	59.1
50153 LYNNVILLE	99.9	99.7	0.0	0.0	0.1	0.3	0.8	1.0	6.4	7.0	7.4	8.9	5.0	22.3	29.0	12.6	1.5	73.7	40.0	51.8	48.2
50154 MC CALLSBURG	99.2	98.8	0.4	0.6	0.2	0.2	0.4	0.6	4.8	6.2	8.3	8.5	3.8	23.6	30.0	13.9	1.0	74.6	41.8	53.6	46.4
50155 MACKSBURG	97.0	96.2	0.0	0.0	0.4	0.3	1.5	2.4	6.6	6.6	7.3	6.6	3.8	23.7	29.3	14.3	1.7	75.3	41.4	49.1	50.9
50156 MADRID	99.0	98.6	0.2	0.2	0.3	0.4	0.9	1.2	6.7	6.7	6.9	6.7	5.1	24.7	27.4	12.2	3.6	75.5	40.1	48.9	51.1
50157 MALCOM	98.7	98.3	0.1	0.1	0.3	0.5	0.5	0.7	5.6	6.4	6.7	7.1	4.5	22.3	30.8	14.4	2.1	76.8	43.2	52.0	48.0
50158 MARSHALLTOWN	88.2	83.7	1.2	1.4	1.0	1.4	11.1	16.0	6.6	6.1	6.3	6.6	6.2	24.1	26.9	14.3	3.0	77.0	40.2	50.1	49.9
50161 MAXWELL	98.8	98.3	0.0	0.0	0.4	0.8	0.4	0.5	7.2	7.4	7.8	7.1	4.9	24.5	29.1	10.3	1.6	73.1	39.1	50.8	49.2
50162 MELBOURNE	99.1	98.8	0.1	0.1	0.2	0.4	0.5	1.0	6.7	6.7	6.7	6.7	5.5	28.3	27.3	10.5	1.6	75.7	37.4	50.0	50.0
50163 MELCHER	98.5	98.0	0.2	0.2	0.5	0.7	0.3	0.4	5.6	5.5	5.8	6.8	6.5	24.1	27.9	14.9	2.8	78.2	41.0	48.3	51.7
50164 MENLO	98.9	98.8	0.0	0.0	0.0	0.0	0.9	1.1	5.4	4.6	7.7	7.1	4.6	23.6	29.8	15.2	2.1	77.0	43.0	50.5	49.5
50165 MILLERTON	98.2	98.2	0.0	0.0	0.0	0.0	1.8	0.0	3.6	5.5	5.5	7.3	5.5	21.8	29.1	18.2	3.6	78.2	45.5	47.3	52.7
50166 MILO	98.9	98.6	0.1	0.1	0.2	0.3	0.4	0.5	6.9	7.3	7.5	7.4	5.1	25.2	28.1	10.9	1.6	73.6	38.9	50.9	49.1
50167 MINBURN	99.1	98.5	0.1	0.1	0.0	0.1	0.9	2.3	6.1	6.7	7.1	6.9	4.5	22.0	32.7	12.2	1.7	75.7	42.9	50.3	49.7
50168 MINGO	98.5	98.3	0.1	0.1	0.1	0.2	1.1	1.4	5.7	6.2	7.0	7.1	4.4	23.8	31.8	12.2	1.9	76.7	42.3	49.8	50.2
50169 MITCHELLVILLE	94.0	91.5	2.9	4.2	0.6	1.1	1.5	2.6	6.3	6.4	6.4	6.5	6.5	31.1	25.1	9.6	2.2	77.1	36.3	44.3	55.7
50170 MONROE	98.0	97.4	0.1	0.1	0.4	0.7	1.0	1.4	6.7	7.2	7.2	7.2	5.1	25.8	27.6	11.7	1.6	74.3	38.8	49.8	50.2
50171 MONTEZUMA	98.9	98.5	0.1	0.2	0.3	0.5	0.3	0.6	5.0	5.2	5.5	5.6	5.1	21.8	31.7	16.8	3.3	82.1	46.3	50.2	49.8
50173 MONTOUR	77.9	77.2	0.1	0.1	0.0	0.0	2.6	2.6	6.8	7.1	7.4	7.4	5.3	24.3	27.4	12.8	1.4	74.1	38.9	52.0	48.0
50174 MURRAY	98.7	98.7	0.4	0.4	0.1	0.1	0.8	0.9	5.7	5.9	6.4	7.3	6.1	24.2	29.2	13.4	1.8	77.7	40.7	51.1	48.9
50201 NEVADA	97.2	96.1	0.5	0.7	0.7	1.2	0.9	1.3	6.6	6.2	6.2	6.5	7.1	26.6	26.7	11.2	2.9	76.9	37.9	48.7	51.3
50206 NEW PROVIDENCE	98.8	98.1	0.0	0.0	0.2	0.4	1.0	1.5	6.0	6.9	8.1	6.9	3.5	22.9	30.2	13.1	2.3	74.4	41.7	52.9	47.1
50207 NEW SHARON	99.0	99.0	0.1	0.1	0.3	0.3	0.5	0.5	6.5	6.8	7.2	7.3	4.9	23.5	28.3	12.1	3.4	74.7	40.7	49.6	50.4
50208 NEWTON	96.9	95.9	1.2	1.4	0.6	1.1	1.2	1.8	6.2	6.0	6.0	6.1	6.3	26.0	26.5	13.9	3.1	77.9	40.1	50.8	49.2
50210 NEW VIRGINIA	98.8	98.5	0.1	0.2	0.2	0.3	0.7	0.8	5.7	6.3	6.7	5.9	4.4	23.0	32.5	13.3	2.2	77.4	43.5	51.2	48.8
50211 NORWALK	97.8	96.9	0.2	0.3	0.6	0.9	1.4	2.1	7.6	7.9	8.0	7.6	5.7	25.5	27.9	8.3	1.5	71.4	36.4	48.2	51.8
50212 OGDEN	99.1	98.8	0.1	0.1	0.1	0.2	0.6	0.9	6.0	6.2	7.0	7.3	4.7	23.1	29.7	13.4	2.7	76.2	42.0	49.1	50.9
50213 OSCEOLA	96.2	96.1	0.1	0.1	0.5	0.5	5.0	5.1	6.7	6.5	6.6	6.4	6.1	23.7	27.2	13.4	3.5	76.2	40.3	48.8	51.2
50214 OTLEY	97.8	97.3	0.2	0.2	1.0	1.5	0.5	0.6	8.0	8.5	9.1	8.1	4.2	25.0	27.7	8.7	0.7	69.3	37.6	51.2	48.8
50216 PANORA	98.6	98.7	0.3	0.3	0.3	0.3	0.9	0.8	5.7	5.9	6.1	5.9	4.3	21.3	30.0	17.3	3.5	78.2	45.5	50.1	49.9
50217 PATON	97.9	97.3	0.2	0.2	0.3	0.5	2.2	3.2	6.4	6.9	7.0	7.2	4.4	22.6	29.5	13.4	2.7	75.2	41.7	51.9	48.1
50218 PATTERSON	99.0	98.1	0.0	0.0	0.0	0.0	1.0	0.0	6.5	6.5	7.5	6.5	3.7	26.2	29.9	11.2	1.9	74.8	40.8	50.5	49.5
50219 PELLA	96.8	95.5	0.1	0.2	2.0	2.9	0.9	1.4	5.8	6.0	6.1	10.6	11.1	21.8	23.5	11.7	3.6	80.0	35.2	48.9	51.1
50220 PERRY	85.1	74.5	1.0	1.1	0.8	1.0	21.0	36.3	7.5	6.9	6.7	6.9	5.8	25.6	24.5	12.8	3.4	74.7	37.9	49.8	50.2
50222 PERU	97.7	97.0	0.0	0.0	0.2	0.3	1.2	1.9	6.3	6.6	7.1	7.1	4.3	23.3	29.4	14.2	1.7	75.6	41.5	49.6	50.4
50223 PILOT MOUND	100.0	99.8	0.0	0.0	0.0	0.2	0.2	0.2	4.7	5.4	6.3	7.4	4.3	20.3	34.1	15.1	2.3	78.8	45.8	52.8	47.2
50225 PLEASANTVILLE	98.8	98.4	0.1	0.1	0.4	0.6	1.3	1.9	6.9	6.8	6.9	7.6	6.3	23.2	27.0	12.3	3.0	76.3	39.7	49.3	50.7
50226 POLK CITY	98.4	97.3	0.3	0.6	0.3	0.6	0.7	1.3	7.7	8.3	8.7	6.8	3.9	26.8	28.9	7.9	1.0	70.6	38.0	50.8	49.2
50227 POPEJOY	96.7	96.6	0.0	0.0	0.0	0.0	3.3	3.4	6.9	6.9	6.9	6.9	3.4	27.6	27.6	13.8	0.0	72.4	38.8	51.7	48.3
50228 PRAIRIE CITY	98.4	97.9	0.3	0.4	0.3	0.5	0.9	1.2	6.3	6.8	7.3	6.5	4.1	24.8	28.4	12.7	3.0	75.4	41.0	49.9	50.1
50229 PROLE	98.5	97.9	0.0	0.0	0.3	0.6	1.0	1.5	6.0	6.6	7.5	7.3	4.6	23.5	32.9	10.6	1.0	75.4	41.0	49.9	50.1
50230 RADCLIFFE	97.8	96.8	0.0	0.1	0.1	0.1	2.9	4.4	5.6	6.6	7.0	6.5	4.2	23.6	31.1	12.3	3.2	76.8	42.5	50.9	49.1
50231 RANDALL	98.0	97.9	0.7	0.7	0.0	0.0	1.4	1.4	4.9	6.3	6.9	6.9	4.2	19.4	37.5	12.5	1.4	77.1	45.6	53.5	46.5
50232 REASNOR	94.0	92.4	4.5	5.4	0.4	0.7	1.4	2.3	4.9	5.3	5.8	5.6	7.7	31.5	26.2	11.1	1.9	80.7	38.3	62.6	37.4
50233 REDFIELD	98.7	98.1	0.0	0.0	0.1	0.1	0.8	1.9	5.8	5.7	6.4	6.7	5.3	23.1	29.8	14.7	2.5	78.0	42.8	51.0	49.0
50234 RHODES	98.2	97.2	0.0	0.0	0.4	0.6	0.8	1.4	5.7	6.5	6.9	6.9	5.0	22.4	31.5	13.5	1.6	76.6	42.5	50.1	49.9
50235 RIPPEY	97.4	96.6	0.4	0.4	0.2	0.4	2.0	3.0	6.6	7.0	7.2	7.2	4.7	23.4	29.0	12.8	2.3	74.8	40.4	53.7	46.3
50236 ROLAND	99.1	98.6	0.1	0.1	0.3	0.5	0.7	1.1	7.4	7.8	8.3	8.1	5.1	25.1	28.0	8.5	1.7	71.4	37.7	49.7	50.3
50237 RUNNELLS	98.3	97.6	0.1	0.2	0.2	0.4	0.9	1.6	6.2	6.9	7.6	7.5	4.5	23.3	32.5	10.4	1.0	74.6	41.2	48.9	51.1
50238 RUSSELL	98.4	97.9	0.0	0.0	0.3	0.5	0.7	0.9	6.8	6.6	6.7	6.7	4.8	21.9	27.2	15.5	3.7	75.7	41.4	49.0	51.0
50239 SAINT ANTHONY	97.4	96.4	0.4	0.4	0.0	0.0	1.7	2.7	5.4	6.3	6.7	6.3	3.6	24.2	33.6	12.1	1.8	77.1	43.5	53.4	46.6
50240 SAINT CHARLES	98.6	98.2	0.0	0.0	0.1	0.2	0.9	1.4	6.2	7.0	7.7	6.8	4.4	24.6	31.5	10.4	1.3	74.7	40.6	51.1	48.9
50242 SEARSBORO	98.9	98.5	0.0	0.0	0.2	0.4	0.2	0.2	5.9	6.5	7.0	5.9	3.9	21.1	34.3	13.9	1.5	76.5	44.8	52.0	48.0
50244 SLATER	99.4	99.2	0.2	0.3	0.2	0.2	0.1	0.2	6.8	7.3	7.5	6.5	5.0	24.7	28.9	11.0	2.2	74.2	39.3	49.9	50.1
50246 STANHOPE	99.1	98.9	0.0	0.0	0.0	0.0	0.8	1.1	5.5	6.2	6.7	7.2	4.3	21.6	32.5	13.5	2.5	77.1	43.9	51.3	48.7
50247 STATE CENTER	98.1	96.9	0.0	0.0	0.2	0.3	1.7	2.9	5.7	6.2	6.7	7.4	4.4	24.2	29.1	12.7	3.7	76.6	42.0	49.7	50.3
50248 STORY CITY	98.4	97.7	0.5	0.6	0.4	0.7	0.6	0.9	5.9	6.3	6.6	6.5	5.2	22.7	28.2	12.5	6.2	77.1	42.6	48.1	51.9
50249 STRATFORD	99.2	98.9	0.0	0.0	0.1	0.1	0.5	0.7	5.7	5.9	6.0	6.3	4.7	21.0	29.1	16.7	4.6	77.9	45.2	51.8	48.2
50250 STUART	98.6	98.4	0.0	0.0	0.1	0.1	0.9	1.1	6.6	6.8	6.9	6.0	5.1	23.8	28.2	12.9	3.8	76.1	40.8	50.0	50.0
50251 SULLY	99.8	99.7	0.0	0.0	0.2	0.3	0.3	0.4	6.8	7.2	7.2	6.8	5.2	22.5	28.5	13.7	2.0	74.5	40.4	51.6	48.4
50252 SWAN	99.3	99.0	0.0	0.2	0.2	0.2	0.9	1.2	6.7	7.1	7.3	7.3	5.0	24.4	29.5	11.3	1.4	74.1	40.5	49.7	50.3
50254 THAYER	99.2	96.5	0.0	0.0	0.3	2.8	0.5	0.5	4.8	5.3	5.8	6.1	4.0	21.7	34.1	15.4	2.8	80.1	46.3	51.5	48.5
50256 TRACY	99.2	99.1	0.4	0.6	0.2	0.2	0.2	0.2	6.9	7.3	7.1	6.4	4.9	25.3	28.1	12.2	1.7	74.5	39.5	51.2	48.8
50257 TRURO	97.8	97.3	0.1	0.1	0.2	0.4	0.9	1.2	6.8	7.1	7.8	7.9	4.9	22.6	29.3	12.1	1.6	73.5	39.8	50.1	49.9
50258 UNION	98.8	98.3	0.1	0.1	0.2	0.4	0.8	1.1	5.6	6.6	7.4	7.2	3.7	22.6	29.4	15.3	2.1	75.5	42.5	50.2	49.8
50261 VAN METER	98.0	97.1	0.3	0.3	0.6	0.8	1.2	2.4	6.3	6.8	7.3	7.1	5.5	24.8	31.4	9.9	0.8	75.2	39.9	49.4	50.6
50262 VAN WERT	98.8	98.5	0.0	0.0	0.0	0.0	1.2	1.5	6.0	6.5	6.7	7.0	3.7	23.4	29.4	15.0	2.2	76.3	42.4	50.9	49.1
50263 WAUKEE	98.1	96.5	0.4	0.7	0.7	1.3	0.8	2.5	9.1	8.9	8.5	6.5	4.5	30.2	25.3	6.4	0.6	69.3	34.6	50.0	50.0
50264 WELDON	98.1	97.9	0.0	0.0	0.0	0.0	1.9	2.1	5.6	6.6	6.9	6.9	3.5	23.6	30.9	14.3	1.7	76.4	42.6	51.4	48.6
50265 WEST DES MOINES	93.1	88.9	1.5	2.3	2.7	4.9	3.1	5.0	7.0	6.6	6.4	5.7	6.9	31.6	25.0	9.0	1.8	76.4	35.7	48.4	51.6
50266 WEST DES MOINES	92.0	88.6	2.4	2.9	2.9	4.5	2.8	5.0	8.8	7.7	7.0	5.9	6.4	36.6	20.6	6.2	0.8	72.9	32.3	48.4	51.6
50268 WHAT CHEER	98.6	98.4	0.0	0.0	0.0	0.0	0.5	0.8	5.4	5.8	6.3	6.8	4.9	22.5	28.6	16.1	3.5	78.2	43.3	48.3	51.7
50271 WILLIAMS	98.2	97.7	0.1	0.1	0.4	0.5	1.2	1.6	5.4	6.1	6.6	6.6	4.3	21.7	32.0	15.1	2.2	77.7	44.4	51.8	48.2
50272 WILLIAMSON	98.4	98.4	0.2	0.2	0.2	0.2	0.7	0.9	4.8	5.3	6.0	7.4	5.1	21.5	33.0	15.2	1.6	79.2	44.9	50.1	49.9
50273 WINTERSET	98.8	98.3	0.1	0.1	0.2	0.4	0.7	1.0	6.9	6.8	6.9	6.6	5.7	23.8	27.4	12.5	3.5	75.1	39.7	48.8	51.2
50274 WIOTA	99.4	99.4	0.0	0.0	0.0	0.0	0.2	0.2	5.8	6.6	6.8	6.0	3.2	19.9	28.3	18.7	4.8	76.9	46.1	50.0	50.0
50275 WOODBURN	95.6	95.6	0.0	0.0	0.1	0.1	3.8	3.9	6.7	7.6	7.4	6.3	3.9	22.6	30.5	13.1	1.9	74.2	41.4	51.9	48.1
50276 WOODWARD	97.7	96.4	0.8	0.9	0.6	0.9	0.8	1.8	5.3	5.3	6.0	8.5	6.5	24.2	30.9	10.9	2.3	77.2	40.7	50.6	49.4
50277 YALE	99.0	99.1	0.2	0.2	0.2	0.2	0.6	0.7	4.9	5.3	5.8	5.1	3.6	20.1	35.2	17.7	2.2	80.7	48.1	50.9	49.1
50278 ZEARING	98.0	97.5	0.1	0.1	0.5	0.9	0.4	0.6	7.3	7.0	6.6	5.9	6.6	24.3	25.8	12.5	4.1	75.2	38.9	47.3	52.7
50309 DES MOINES	72.2	63.2	15.3	20.0	3.4	5.1	9.1	13.1	5.3	3.9	3.4	4.9	6.5	29.4	24.7	16.0	6.0	85.0	42.6	55.6	44.4
50310 DES MOINES	86.9	81.3	5.9	8.2	2.8	4.7	3.1	4.8	6.9	6.3	6.1	5.7	6.6	29.9	25.1	10.6	2.7	77.0	37.6	47.8	52.2
50311 DES MOINES	81.4	75.8	9.1	11.3	3.3	5.2	5.6	7.9	6.6	5.4	4.8	9.7	15.0	28.0	21.5	7.3	1.5	80.2	29.8	48.1	51.9
50312 DES MOINES	89.4	85.3	5.9	7.8	1.5	2.6	2.7	4.5	5.3	5.1	5.3	5.4	6.9	26.8	27.8	12.7	4.7	80.9	41.4	47.8	52.2
IOWA	93.9	91.9	2.1	2.5	1.3	2.1	2.8	4.1	6.5	6.4	6.5	7.3	7.1	25.2	26.5	11.9	2.6	76.5	38.1	49.3	50.7
UNITED STATES	75.1	72.0	12.3	12.7	3.8	4.6	12.5	15.7	6.8	6.7	6.6	7.1	6.9	27.0	26.0	10.9	1.9	75.7	36.9	49.2	50.8

INCOME

ZIP CODE				2009 HOUSEHOLD INCOME DISTRIBUTION (%)					MEDIAN HOUSEHOLD INCOME					2009 HOME VALUE DISTRIBUTION (%)					
#	POST OFFICE NAME	2009 Per Capita Income	2009 HH Income Base	Less than $25,000	$25,000 to $49,999	$50,000 to $99,999	$100,000 to $149,999	$150,000 or More	2009	2014	2009 National Centile	2009 State Centile	2009 Home Value Base	Less than $50,000	$50,000 to $89,999	$90,000 to $174,999	$175,000 to $399,999	$400,000 or More	2009 Median Home Value
50140	LAMONI	18945	1037	39.4	25.5	26.8	5.2	3.1	33186	34331	14	2	622	24.6	25.6	40.2	9.5	0.2	89722
50141	LAUREL	22420	234	15.8	31.2	47.0	5.1	0.9	52303	53716	66	79	193	13.5	26.4	43.0	15.5	1.6	104435
50142	LE GRAND	22666	349	19.8	24.1	47.0	8.0	1.1	54465	54919	70	85	283	17.3	34.3	42.8	5.7	0.0	88875
50143	LEIGHTON	21080	244	15.2	34.4	41.8	7.0	1.6	50248	52082	62	71	193	10.4	13.5	49.2	18.1	8.8	120663
50144	LEON	16492	978	36.4	36.8	25.1	0.9	0.8	33531	33682	14	2	687	40.2	30.0	25.8	3.5	0.6	59926
50146	LINDEN	23793	223	16.1	30.0	46.2	5.8	1.8	54582	56371	71	85	173	10.4	24.3	33.5	28.9	2.9	116532
50147	LINEVILLE	22682	171	32.2	26.9	29.8	8.2	2.9	42331	44445	40	26	136	52.9	25.0	10.3	8.1	3.7	46000
50148	LISCOMB	21234	176	22.7	31.8	40.3	5.1	0.0	47461	50000	55	59	132	15.2	16.7	45.5	19.7	3.0	123529
50149	LORIMOR	17410	385	31.9	36.9	27.5	3.1	0.5	37029	38121	24	6	312	39.4	25.6	26.0	8.7	0.3	63684
50150	LOVILIA	16496	406	31.3	32.5	33.3	3.0	0.0	39276	40315	31	13	351	36.2	37.9	21.4	2.6	2.0	63293
50151	LUCAS	21977	330	26.1	30.6	37.3	3.6	2.4	45192	47240	49	45	286	36.7	13.6	34.6	14.7	0.3	89167
50152	LUTHER	31757	10	0.0	30.0	60.0	10.0	0.0	63627	60000	82	96	8	0.0	0.0	50.0	50.0	0.0	175000
50153	LYNNVILLE	22765	296	13.2	31.4	43.9	9.1	2.4	53922	54599	70	84	234	8.5	21.4	51.3	14.5	4.3	112891
50154	MC CALLSBURG	20088	203	27.1	28.6	39.4	4.9	0.0	46800	48968	54	56	157	25.5	26.1	35.0	10.8	2.5	87917
50155	MACKSBURG	18867	110	24.5	33.6	35.5	5.5	0.9	43206	46955	43	32	93	36.6	19.4	29.0	15.1	0.0	78333
50156	MADRID	27457	1718	10.9	28.2	45.8	10.8	4.2	60258	60379	78	93	1379	9.1	23.4	46.0	17.3	4.3	116716
50157	MALCOM	23279	341	18.2	30.2	44.0	6.2	1.5	51699	51699	65	76	262	16.0	21.0	37.0	22.1	3.8	111111
50158	MARSHALLTOWN	23427	12003	22.5	29.3	36.6	8.0	3.6	48497	51457	58	64	8651	15.8	29.7	41.8	12.1	0.6	97170
50161	MAXWELL	23296	781	18.2	25.2	46.7	6.7	3.2	54831	55648	71	86	638	18.5	21.0	33.7	24.8	2.0	108500
50162	MELBOURNE	25719	530	13.4	25.5	49.8	9.1	2.3	61474	61083	79	94	426	16.4	29.3	44.6	8.7	0.9	96429
50163	MELCHER	20820	508	29.5	26.8	36.8	4.9	2.0	45262	48724	49	46	434	33.9	40.1	23.5	2.5	0.0	65263
50164	MENLO	22544	280	27.5	35.4	30.4	5.0	1.8	41311	42813	37	22	225	27.6	34.2	34.2	3.6	0.4	81452
50165	MILLERTON	16761	24	37.5	37.5	25.0	0.0	0.0	32300	33593	12	1	21	28.6	23.8	42.9	0.0	4.8	85000
50166	MILO	21379	667	15.6	32.2	45.3	6.0	0.9	51879	55187	66	77	563	10.8	18.1	41.4	28.4	1.2	122294
50167	MINBURN	22260	343	20.4	27.4	43.1	7.3	1.7	51952	53097	66	77	273	12.1	19.4	37.4	29.3	1.8	120750
50168	MINGO	25412	328	16.2	30.2	41.2	10.7	1.8	52637	54088	67	79	277	9.0	14.8	46.9	27.4	1.8	128716
50169	MITCHELLVILLE	24469	1007	16.4	23.3	47.0	10.3	3.0	61348	63542	79	93	761	8.5	15.0	53.9	21.7	0.9	123348
50170	MONROE	23895	1137	18.9	27.7	41.9	9.7	1.8	53282	54564	68	82	910	11.0	22.6	51.0	13.5	1.9	109132
50171	MONTEZUMA	24917	1291	20.7	30.1	40.4	6.1	2.6	49181	50865	59	66	986	14.1	26.6	39.1	18.6	1.6	104011
50173	MONTOUR	17213	319	27.9	32.9	35.4	2.5	1.3	39024	42081	30	12	256	21.9	27.3	38.7	9.8	2.3	91250
50174	MURRAY	17860	561	25.3	37.1	33.0	4.3	0.4	40840	42542	35	19	448	25.4	38.2	24.3	9.2	2.9	77556
50201	NEVADA	26332	3247	17.1	26.5	44.5	9.1	2.9	54618	55319	71	85	2369	21.8	21.1	42.4	13.0	1.6	100664
50206	NEW PROVIDENCE	23872	199	18.1	37.2	38.2	2.0	4.5	46136	47457	52	51	150	23.3	27.3	35.3	12.7	1.3	89375
50207	NEW SHARON	20290	1066	22.3	30.9	39.9	6.2	0.8	48028	50637	57	62	801	13.0	27.3	39.6	16.4	3.7	105248
50208	NEWTON	25756	8267	20.4	26.6	41.1	8.2	3.6	52616	54703	67	79	5968	9.1	23.4	47.6	18.4	1.4	110975
50210	NEW VIRGINIA	22734	799	19.1	28.9	43.6	5.8	2.6	51027	52346	64	74	699	10.6	21.3	33.8	30.9	3.4	123946
50211	NORWALK	31203	3485	8.8	13.8	49.2	20.1	8.1	77387	79416	91	99	2954	3.5	5.1	50.5	36.9	4.0	157975
50212	OGDEN	23880	1377	19.2	29.2	42.9	5.7	3.0	50962	52747	63	74	1139	15.9	22.1	42.1	18.6	1.3	107405
50213	OSCEOLA	20820	2520	25.4	31.2	35.2	6.3	2.0	43706	45806	44	36	1744	16.1	33.1	38.4	11.6	0.9	91648
50214	OTLEY	23853	347	15.6	19.3	51.0	11.5	2.6	63847	62811	82	96	314	1.0	12.7	44.3	36.9	5.1	154167
50216	PANORA	24598	1223	25.7	29.6	33.8	6.4	4.6	45035	47570	48	44	979	14.8	28.1	34.8	17.2	5.1	99521
50217	PATON	22570	244	20.1	36.9	33.6	6.6	2.9	44408	46699	47	41	190	40.5	29.5	20.0	8.4	1.6	59000
50218	PATTERSON	27871	46	10.9	23.9	54.3	8.7	2.2	61540	61280	79	94	40	12.5	12.5	22.5	37.5	15.0	187500
50219	PELLA	25422	4953	16.5	23.4	44.7	12.0	3.5	59709	59869	77	92	3575	4.7	7.5	46.4	36.5	4.9	158539
50220	PERRY	20549	3534	21.9	31.7	38.3	6.1	2.0	45929	47978	51	49	2381	17.6	26.6	40.7	14.1	1.0	98343
50222	PERU	18897	229	23.6	30.1	37.6	7.0	1.7	46608	50989	53	55	195	26.2	22.1	31.3	16.4	4.1	94375
50223	PILOT MOUND	20445	189	25.4	36.5	32.8	5.3	0.0	43387	45835	44	33	153	26.1	24.2	34.6	13.1	2.0	89500
50225	PLEASANTVILLE	23319	1111	20.5	27.5	41.3	9.0	1.6	51772	54053	65	77	881	17.6	19.3	45.5	15.1	2.5	108538
50226	POLK CITY	35133	1864	6.6	15.4	45.9	20.1	12.0	76541	79291	90	99	1609	1.6	6.5	43.6	42.4	5.9	171904
50227	POPEJOY	22523	13	23.1	38.5	30.8	7.7	0.0	42330	42330	40	26	10	30.0	20.0	50.0	0.0	0.0	95000
50228	PRAIRIE CITY	24895	904	19.7	25.7	40.8	11.2	2.7	53846	55187	69	83	713	6.6	14.6	59.2	17.5	2.1	126225
50229	PROLE	26752	672	12.5	26.5	44.6	12.4	4.0	61318	63972	79	93	581	7.1	12.0	39.1	37.3	4.5	155847
50230	RADCLIFFE	23047	471	18.3	31.4	41.2	6.8	2.3	50195	49927	62	70	357	18.2	30.8	41.2	8.7	1.1	91346
50231	RANDALL	30907	67	20.9	28.4	37.3	7.5	6.0	50700	50504	63	72	54	7.4	22.2	40.7	25.9	3.7	120833
50232	REASNOR	29716	222	10.8	31.5	41.4	13.1	3.2	57385	58304	74	89	196	5.6	14.3	46.9	30.6	2.6	134783
50233	REDFIELD	21788	718	20.8	34.8	37.9	5.7	0.8	45500	46892	50	47	579	26.3	33.3	28.7	9.5	2.2	77222
50234	RHODES	24451	209	20.1	24.9	43.5	7.2	4.3	53228	54406	68	81	173	13.3	24.3	39.3	19.1	4.0	107849
50235	RIPPEY	22746	206	20.4	35.0	33.0	6.3	5.3	45695	47162	50	48	159	35.2	32.1	24.5	5.0	3.1	60455
50236	ROLAND	22968	594	12.0	27.1	51.9	7.4	1.7	55760	55318	72	87	498	6.4	19.3	56.2	18.1	0.0	120872
50237	RUNNELLS	27116	898	13.3	16.0	50.9	14.4	5.5	70618	74594	87	98	800	0.9	9.4	32.6	50.8	6.4	194257
50238	RUSSELL	19307	377	27.1	41.1	24.9	5.8	1.1	38651	39631	29	11	300	44.3	25.7	26.7	3.0	0.3	58095
50239	SAINT ANTHONY	20088	86	18.6	30.2	45.3	4.7	1.2	50602	52536	63	72	68	36.8	20.6	32.4	10.3	0.0	80000
50240	SAINT CHARLES	27023	891	13.7	24.2	46.8	11.8	3.5	60400	61314	78	93	768	9.1	13.9	40.2	33.3	3.4	148131
50242	SEARSBORO	23252	194	20.6	33.0	37.1	6.2	3.1	46027	49499	51	50	156	22.4	17.3	32.1	23.1	5.1	106944
50244	SLATER	26748	707	13.4	28.1	45.5	10.6	2.3	59007	59049	76	91	561	20.0	15.9	52.4	11.8	0.0	107686
50246	STANHOPE	23266	342	17.5	31.3	39.2	10.2	1.8	51055	51935	64	74	260	20.8	27.3	39.6	11.2	1.2	92174
50247	STATE CENTER	24008	875	23.0	28.9	37.5	8.2	2.4	48260	51318	57	62	647	12.2	21.3	50.1	15.0	1.4	110052
50248	STORY CITY	25804	1803	19.0	27.1	43.9	7.3	2.7	53777	55130	69	83	1292	8.9	17.3	51.0	20.7	2.1	117470
50249	STRATFORD	20882	535	24.5	34.0	33.1	6.4	2.1	41782	45311	39	24	404	19.3	31.9	38.9	6.4	3.5	88837
50250	STUART	22466	1048	21.5	31.7	39.6	5.4	1.8	47200	49563	55	58	765	18.8	22.9	48.2	6.3	3.8	103109
50251	SULLY	23745	565	11.2	31.3	45.7	9.7	2.1	55198	55396	72	86	463	6.3	19.7	55.9	16.6	1.5	117479
50252	SWAN	21100	171	19.9	23.4	43.9	11.7	1.2	59516	60442	77	91	152	13.8	13.8	43.4	25.7	3.3	135000
50254	THAYER	20962	165	24.2	31.5	37.0	6.7	0.6	44655	46678	47	43	139	23.7	24.5	31.7	17.3	2.9	96250
50256	TRACY	20113	220	24.1	35.9	35.0	5.0	0.0	42848	45761	42	30	182	33.5	30.8	24.7	8.8	2.2	69167
50257	TRURO	21560	412	25.0	21.8	43.2	5.8	4.1	52306	54472	67	79	333	14.7	33.0	32.1	9.3	10.8	94688
50258	UNION	20099	416	19.7	39.2	36.3	4.1	0.7	42466	45071	41	28	332	33.4	35.2	23.2	7.2	0.9	66471
50261	VAN METER	26144	890	14.9	26.4	46.3	8.2	4.2	59020	60620	76	91	738	29.0	12.1	26.8	26.7	5.4	121538
50262	VAN WERT	21900	168	30.4	33.3	30.4	3.0	3.0	38178	40381	27	9	136	42.6	27.2	19.1	8.8	2.2	60000
50263	WAUKEE	36797	5648	7.3	19.2	41.1	19.0	13.4	80666	82258	92	99	4730	6.1	9.3	19.8	46.8	17.9	214487
50264	WELDON	22764	211	27.5	32.2	32.2	3.8	4.3	40204	43657	33	16	170	38.8	24.1	25.3	10.0	1.8	70000
50265	WEST DES MOINES	37553	14272	8.6	22.9	42.5	16.7	9.3	68382	72676	86	97	9262	3.5	5.8	41.1	43.8	5.7	174135
50266	WEST DES MOINES	40373	10748	13.5	22.1	37.4	13.5	13.5	65886	68111	84	96	6109	1.0	1.6	25.1	62.2	10.2	229082
50268	WHAT CHEER	21438	447	33.8	31.8	30.0	2.7	1.8	38695	40501	29	11	375	49.9	30.7	15.5	2.1	1.9	50135
50271	WILLIAMS	22205	308	20.5	31.5	42.9	4.2	1.0	48844	49829	59	65	233	24.0	26.6	34.3	11.2	3.9	89211
50272	WILLIAMSON	18439	176	27.8	30.7	38.6	2.8	0.0	42355	45615	40	27	149	16.8	26.8	36.9	15.4	4.0	101442
50273	WINTERSET	23077	3279	22.5	29.4	36.8	7.6	3.7	47984	51568	57	61	2424	10.9	19.8	42.8	22.2	4.4	119880
50274	WIOTA	19527	203	32.5	34.5	26.6	4.9	1.5	41048	41678	36	20	161	28.0	20.5	29.2	18.0	4.3	94167
50275	WOODBURN	20018	275	25.1	33.5	33.5	4.7	3.3	41051	44016	36	20	222	24.8	17.1	39.6	18.5	0.0	108784
50276	WOODWARD	22020	973	20.9	28.9	39.4	8.8	2.1	50198	51734	62	70	758	17.4	23.4	38.9	19.4	0.9	103740
50277	YALE	26707	237	24.1	29.5	32.9	6.3	7.2	46610	49802	53	55	195	12.8	26.7	25.6	27.7	7.2	122794
50278	ZEARING	21888	297	15.5	33.0	42.4	8.4	0.7	51133	53277	64	75	235	31.1	30.2	29.8	8.1	0.9	74412
50309	DES MOINES	20185	2695	55.6	26.0	14.8	1.7	1.9	21510	21653	2	1	407	28.7	16.2	39.6	12.0	3.4	96833
50310	DES MOINES	29480	13863	13.7	26.9	45.4	10.7	3.4	60138	62665	77	92	9366	2.4	15.4	70.5	11.1	0.6	121466
50311	DES MOINES	25904	7869	20.3	28.9	40.6	7.8	2.3	50820	54389	63	73	4489	4.8	15.5	65.9	13.6	0.3	121007
50312	DES MOINES	37947	7875	17.7	26.6	35.0	11.6	9.1	56952	60335	74	89	4661	4.8	13.9	43.0	30.5	7.8	145309
	IOWA	25379		21.1	28.2	37.9	8.6	4.3	50616	52941				14.7	22.5	41.6	18.6	2.6	110128
	UNITED STATES	27277		20.9	24.4	35.3	11.7	7.6	54719	56938				9.3	13.1	31.6	32.6	13.5	162279

ZIP CODE		FINANCIAL SERVICES				THE HOME						ENTERTAINMENT						PERSONAL			
						Home Improvements		Furnishings													
#	POST OFFICE NAME	Auto Loan	Home Loan	Invest-ments	Retire-ment Plans	Home Repair	Lawn & Garden	Comput-ers & Hard-ware-Personal	Major Appli-ances	TV, Radio, Sound Equip-ment	Furni-ture	Dine out/ Carry out	Sports Equip-ment	Fees & Tickets	Toys & Games	Travel	Cable TV	Apparel & Services	Auto Repairs	Health Insur-ance	Pets & Supplies
50140	LAMONI	70	52	57	55	53	61	72	63	69	62	69	52	58	69	60	70	48	68	67	77
50141	LAUREL	88	80	79	83	81	94	79	89	81	71	80	67	73	83	79	86	54	82	92	103
50142	LE GRAND	80	83	64	84	76	86	82	79	83	78	83	63	83	85	80	85	57	81	88	97
50143	LEIGHTON	106	73	116	73	76	112	81	100	84	65	83	83	59	82	80	92	54	94	106	123
50144	LEON	66	47	67	46	49	69	51	64	57	45	55	48	41	56	50	63	37	59	69	75
50146	LINDEN	104	72	114	72	75	110	79	99	83	65	82	81	58	81	79	90	53	92	104	121
50147	LINEVILLE	88	63	89	61	65	92	69	85	77	61	74	64	55	75	67	84	49	79	93	100
50148	LISCOMB	90	62	99	62	65	95	69	85	71	56	71	71	50	70	68	78	46	80	90	105
50149	LORIMOR	76	54	69	53	54	74	57	68	62	52	61	53	44	63	53	67	40	64	71	83
50150	LOVILIA	75	54	62	53	54	72	56	65	62	55	61	50	45	65	51	68	41	62	69	80
50151	LUCAS	93	69	95	68	71	95	70	88	77	66	76	66	58	77	70	84	50	81	91	104
50152	LUTHER	97	110	94	113	106	108	98	102	96	98	97	79	104	99	103	96	68	98	101	120
50153	LYNNVILLE	94	85	86	88	87	101	84	95	87	76	85	72	77	88	84	92	58	88	98	111
50154	MC CALLSBURG	89	61	98	61	64	94	68	85	71	55	70	70	50	69	68	77	45	79	89	104
50155	MACKSBURG	88	61	97	60	63	93	67	84	70	54	69	69	49	69	67	76	45	78	88	103
50156	MADRID	100	102	91	105	100	106	100	101	100	97	99	78	100	101	100	102	69	100	106	120
50157	MALCOM	90	74	88	76	76	96	76	89	79	66	77	69	65	79	75	84	52	82	93	105
50158	MARSHALLTOWN	84	79	76	80	78	87	82	83	85	78	84	63	79	85	80	88	58	84	90	99
50161	MAXWELL	95	92	88	96	93	103	88	97	90	82	89	74	85	92	89	94	61	91	99	113
50162	MELBOURNE	94	90	81	92	86	100	91	93	92	84	91	74	87	94	89	96	62	92	101	112
50163	MELCHER	85	61	85	60	63	89	67	82	74	60	72	61	54	73	65	82	48	77	90	97
50164	MENLO	90	64	91	63	67	94	70	87	77	62	75	66	55	76	68	85	50	81	94	103
50165	MILLERTON	69	47	75	47	49	72	52	65	55	43	54	54	38	54	52	60	35	61	69	80
50166	MILO	86	84	80	87	84	93	80	88	81	75	80	67	78	83	82	84	55	82	89	103
50167	MINBURN	93	75	92	77	77	99	78	91	80	67	79	72	66	81	78	86	53	85	95	109
50168	MINGO	89	94	85	97	92	98	87	93	86	84	86	72	88	89	90	88	60	88	93	108
50169	MITCHELLVILLE	94	96	78	98	90	95	95	92	94	93	94	73	95	97	93	95	65	93	96	110
50170	MONROE	89	83	81	85	81	95	83	89	84	76	83	70	78	85	82	88	57	86	94	106
50171	MONTEZUMA	93	76	99	76	80	97	78	92	82	73	81	69	68	81	79	88	54	87	95	108
50173	MONTOUR	81	58	72	56	58	79	61	72	67	57	66	56	48	69	57	73	44	68	76	88
50174	MURRAY	82	58	72	57	59	79	61	72	67	58	66	56	48	70	57	73	44	68	76	88
50201	NEVADA	94	85	83	86	84	93	90	91	91	86	91	70	84	92	86	93	62	91	96	108
50206	NEW PROVIDENCE	102	71	112	71	74	108	78	97	82	64	81	80	58	80	78	89	52	91	103	120
50207	NEW SHARON	86	67	87	69	70	91	70	84	73	60	72	67	58	73	70	79	48	78	88	101
50208	NEWTON	88	84	80	85	82	92	86	88	88	81	87	67	83	88	84	91	60	87	95	104
50210	NEW VIRGINIA	86	82	79	85	82	93	79	87	80	73	79	67	75	82	80	84	54	81	89	102
50211	NORWALK	126	141	119	139	134	125	124	126	120	131	122	97	130	125	126	117	85	121	116	146
50212	OGDEN	86	86	86	87	86	98	81	90	84	76	83	67	81	84	84	88	57	85	96	105
50213	OSCEOLA	83	66	82	66	68	86	71	81	75	65	74	62	60	74	69	81	49	78	87	96
50214	OTLEY	91	103	89	106	100	101	92	96	90	92	91	75	98	93	97	91	64	92	95	113
50216	PANORA	97	71	107	70	75	102	76	95	82	68	80	72	61	80	76	90	53	88	100	112
50217	PATON	99	68	108	68	71	104	75	94	78	61	78	77	55	77	75	86	50	88	99	115
50218	PATTERSON	89	101	87	104	98	99	90	94	89	90	89	73	96	91	95	89	62	90	93	110
50219	PELLA	97	98	93	99	97	103	95	98	96	93	95	75	95	97	96	98	66	97	102	116
50220	PERRY	83	73	73	74	71	85	76	80	79	71	78	63	70	80	73	83	53	79	86	96
50222	PERU	93	65	101	65	68	98	72	88	74	59	74	73	53	73	71	81	48	83	93	109
50223	PILOT MOUND	86	59	94	59	62	90	65	81	68	53	67	67	48	67	65	74	44	76	86	100
50225	PLEASANTVILLE	90	80	81	81	81	92	81	87	84	78	83	66	75	85	79	88	57	84	91	104
50226	POLK CITY	130	156	137	159	152	140	133	137	127	140	129	109	148	132	142	123	92	129	125	157
50227	POPEJOY	90	62	99	62	65	95	69	85	71	56	71	71	50	70	68	78	46	80	90	105
50228	PRAIRIE CITY	92	88	86	91	89	100	85	94	86	79	85	72	81	88	86	90	59	88	96	110
50229	PROLE	96	108	93	111	105	106	96	100	95	97	95	78	103	97	102	95	67	96	99	118
50230	RADCLIFFE	101	70	111	70	73	107	77	96	80	63	80	80	57	79	77	88	52	90	102	118
50231	RANDALL	119	82	130	82	86	125	91	113	94	74	93	93	66	93	90	103	61	105	119	139
50232	REASNOR	111	91	109	93	93	118	93	109	97	81	95	86	79	97	93	103	64	102	114	130
50233	REDFIELD	87	65	88	63	67	91	69	85	76	62	74	64	57	75	68	83	49	79	91	100
50234	RHODES	91	83	82	87	85	98	82	93	85	74	83	70	76	86	82	90	57	86	96	108
50235	RIPPEY	105	72	115	72	76	111	80	99	83	65	82	82	59	82	80	91	53	93	105	122
50236	ROLAND	85	95	83	98	92	94	85	89	84	85	84	70	90	86	90	84	59	86	88	105
50237	RUNNELLS	105	121	104	123	117	115	106	110	104	108	104	86	115	107	113	103	73	106	107	129
50238	RUSSELL	76	55	77	53	57	80	60	74	66	53	64	56	48	65	58	73	43	69	80	87
50239	SAINT ANTHONY	92	64	101	64	67	98	71	88	74	58	73	73	53	73	71	81	48	82	93	108
50240	SAINT CHARLES	96	107	93	110	104	106	96	100	95	96	95	78	102	97	101	95	66	96	99	118
50242	SEARSBORO	98	68	109	68	72	103	75	94	78	62	77	76	56	76	75	85	50	87	98	114
50244	SLATER	83	101	90	101	97	99	87	90	88	88	89	68	99	89	95	89	62	88	94	105
50246	STANHOPE	107	73	117	73	77	112	81	101	85	66	84	84	60	83	81	92	54	94	107	124
50247	STATE CENTER	92	81	85	84	83	98	81	92	83	72	82	71	73	85	81	89	56	85	95	108
50248	STORY CITY	92	87	87	89	88	97	86	92	87	82	87	70	82	88	86	90	59	89	96	109
50249	STRATFORD	89	63	93	62	65	93	69	86	75	59	73	67	53	73	68	82	48	80	92	103
50250	STUART	85	73	80	73	71	89	74	82	78	69	77	64	67	78	72	82	52	79	88	99
50251	SULLY	98	85	93	88	87	105	85	98	88	76	87	76	76	89	85	94	59	91	102	115
50252	SWAN	87	98	84	101	95	96	87	91	86	88	86	71	93	88	92	86	60	87	90	107
50254	THAYER	90	62	98	62	65	95	69	85	72	56	71	70	51	70	68	78	46	79	90	105
50256	TRACY	86	63	74	62	63	84	66	77	72	62	70	59	53	74	61	78	47	72	81	93
50257	TRURO	90	80	83	83	82	96	80	91	82	71	81	69	72	83	79	87	55	84	94	106
50258	UNION	87	60	96	60	63	92	67	83	69	54	68	68	49	68	66	75	44	77	87	102
50261	VAN METER	104	101	89	100	99	102	94	99	96	97	96	73	92	99	92	98	66	96	99	117
50262	VAN WERT	93	64	103	64	67	99	71	89	74	58	73	73	52	73	71	81	48	83	94	109
50263	WAUKEE	143	164	141	162	157	137	142	142	133	154	136	114	152	142	145	125	97	134	123	161
50264	WELDON	100	69	110	69	72	105	76	95	79	62	78	78	56	78	76	87	51	89	100	117
50265	WEST DES MOINES	124	116	108	121	112	110	126	115	124	126	125	92	123	126	119	121	88	121	115	138
50266	WEST DES MOINES	131	126	113	132	121	112	131	119	126	136	129	100	131	132	125	121	92	123	112	142
50268	WHAT CHEER	82	58	84	57	60	85	64	79	70	55	68	60	50	68	62	77	45	73	85	94
50271	WILLIAMS	96	66	105	66	69	101	73	91	76	59	75	75	53	74	73	83	49	85	96	112
50272	WILLIAMSON	81	57	85	56	59	83	60	76	65	54	64	59	47	65	60	72	42	70	79	91
50273	WINTERSET	90	77	86	78	78	94	81	88	83	75	82	68	73	83	79	88	56	86	94	105
50274	WIOTA	83	57	92	57	60	88	64	79	66	52	66	66	47	65	63	72	43	74	84	98
50275	WOODBURN	94	68	100	69	71	100	74	90	77	61	76	74	57	76	74	83	50	84	95	110
50276	WOODWARD	84	82	75	84	81	89	81	84	82	78	81	65	80	83	81	84	56	82	88	100
50277	YALE	105	81	130	80	88	111	83	105	87	75	86	79	69	83	88	93	57	97	105	123
50278	ZEARING	81	80	68	81	74	86	80	79	81	75	81	64	79	83	78	84	55	80	88	97
50309	DES MOINES	42	31	36	35	32	37	48	40	52	44	52	31	43	46	43	56	36	49	54	51
50310	DES MOINES	93	92	82	93	88	93	95	91	96	92	96	71	95	96	92	97	67	94	98	109
50311	DES MOINES	85	74	69	77	71	74	90	78	87	84	88	63	81	88	79	86	61	84	80	95
50312	DES MOINES	108	106	106	109	107	106	113	107	112	113	112	83	113	111	111	111	79	111	110	126
	IOWA	93	84	87	85	83	95	87	91	89	82	88	71	81	90	85	92	61	90	96	108
	UNITED STATES	100	100	100	100	100	100	100	100	100	100	100	100	100	100	100	100	100	100	100	100

ZIP CODE #	POST OFFICE NAME	COUNTY FIPS CODE	POPULATION 2000	POPULATION 2009	POPULATION 2014	2000-2009 ANNUAL RATE % Rate	2000-2009 ANNUAL RATE State Centile	HOUSEHOLDS 2000	HOUSEHOLDS 2009	HOUSEHOLDS 2014	HOUSEHOLDS % Annual Rate 2000-2009	HOUSEHOLDS 2009 Average HH Size	FAMILIES 2000	FAMILIES 2009	FAMILIES % Annual Rate 2000-2009
50313	DES MOINES	153	16414	16705	17126	0.2	68	6687	6983	7202	0.5	2.38	4357	4358	0.0
50314	DES MOINES	153	12127	12425	12736	0.3	72	4390	4518	4638	0.3	2.64	2543	2490	-0.2
50315	DES MOINES	153	37457	37586	38491	0.0	58	15137	15768	16278	0.4	2.35	9822	9762	-0.1
50316	DES MOINES	153	16667	16742	17018	0.0	58	6051	6143	6268	0.2	2.63	3867	3741	-0.4
50317	DES MOINES	153	34584	36661	38297	0.6	83	13501	14774	15526	1.0	2.46	9329	9799	0.5
50320	DES MOINES	153	13947	17249	18960	2.3	97	5271	6705	7430	2.6	2.57	3798	4654	2.2
50321	DES MOINES	153	7227	7841	8278	0.9	89	2839	3209	3427	1.3	2.33	1741	1861	0.7
50322	URBANDALE	153	33022	35131	36954	0.7	85	13360	14764	15649	1.1	2.36	9053	9583	0.6
50323	URBANDALE	153	974	6202	8391	22.2	100	325	2166	2949	22.8	2.86	288	1844	22.2
50325	CLIVE	153	12540	14704	16531	1.7	95	4611	5348	5947	1.6	2.75	3538	4018	1.4
50327	DES MOINES	153	6328	9316	10656	4.3	99	2320	3520	4055	4.6	2.63	1807	2679	4.3
50401	MASON CITY	033	31242	29836	28958	-0.5	27	13168	12931	12609	-0.2	2.24	8124	7762	-0.5
50420	ALEXANDER	069	431	420	412	-0.3	40	181	180	178	-0.1	2.33	131	128	-0.3
50421	BELMOND	197	3267	2959	2809	-1.1	5	1380	1275	1212	-0.9	2.27	881	793	-1.1
50423	BRITT	081	3113	2946	2847	-0.6	20	1255	1223	1189	-0.3	2.36	826	785	-0.5
50424	BUFFALO CENTER	189	1574	1500	1454	-0.5	27	665	651	634	-0.2	2.23	443	423	-0.5
50428	CLEAR LAKE	033	10038	9431	9108	-0.7	15	4190	4044	3917	-0.4	2.27	2800	2638	-0.6
50430	CORWITH	081	669	640	619	-0.5	27	262	258	251	-0.2	2.48	184	178	-0.4
50432	CRYSTAL LAKE	081	292	272	262	-0.8	11	127	122	119	-0.4	2.23	90	85	-0.6
50433	DOUGHERTY	033	246	245	241	0.0	58	99	101	100	0.2	2.43	75	74	-0.1
50434	FERTILE	195	541	560	561	0.4	76	217	229	231	0.6	2.45	167	173	0.4
50435	FLOYD	067	851	878	874	0.3	72	315	332	332	0.6	2.64	255	264	0.4
50436	FOREST CITY	189	6208	5847	5664	-0.6	20	2360	2305	2245	-0.3	2.39	1608	1535	-0.5
50438	GARNER	081	4113	4023	3943	-0.2	46	1619	1634	1611	0.1	2.43	1161	1148	-0.1
50439	GOODELL	081	387	361	346	-0.7	15	157	150	145	-0.5	2.41	117	110	-0.7
50440	GRAFTON	195	525	502	492	-0.5	27	206	201	198	-0.3	2.50	151	145	-0.4
50441	HAMPTON	069	5684	5537	5461	-0.3	40	2357	2322	2294	-0.2	2.31	1545	1484	-0.4
50444	HANLONTOWN	195	358	369	370	0.3	72	140	148	149	0.6	2.49	107	111	0.4
50446	JOICE	195	600	591	583	-0.2	46	239	242	239	0.1	2.44	179	177	-0.1
50447	KANAWHA	081	1282	1210	1169	-0.6	20	508	490	475	-0.4	2.40	349	329	-0.6
50448	KENSETT	195	749	706	687	-0.6	20	310	299	293	-0.4	2.36	222	210	-0.6
50449	KLEMME	081	851	849	841	0.0	58	338	340	337	0.1	2.50	248	244	-0.2
50450	LAKE MILLS	189	2954	2810	2728	-0.5	27	1266	1249	1220	-0.1	2.19	825	793	-0.4
50451	LAKOTA	109	698	622	586	-1.2	4	286	262	249	-0.9	2.37	202	181	-1.2
50452	LATIMER	069	1144	1138	1129	-0.1	51	440	442	439	0.0	2.57	319	314	-0.2
50453	LELAND	189	577	549	532	-0.5	27	230	226	220	-0.2	2.43	179	173	-0.4
50454	LITTLE CEDAR	131	154	155	155	0.1	63	63	64	64	0.2	2.38	46	46	0.0
50455	MC INTIRE	131	466	464	462	0.0	58	155	156	156	0.1	2.96	119	117	-0.2
50456	MANLY	195	1770	1732	1704	-0.2	46	725	723	714	0.0	2.36	488	475	-0.3
50457	MESERVEY	033	351	348	344	-0.1	51	161	163	162	0.1	2.13	110	109	-0.1
50458	NORA SPRINGS	067	2045	2091	2081	0.2	68	787	831	832	0.6	2.43	561	578	0.3
50459	NORTHWOOD	195	3098	2956	2892	-0.5	27	1341	1317	1295	-0.2	2.19	879	843	-0.5
50460	ORCHARD	131	372	369	367	-0.1	51	132	134	133	0.2	2.71	102	101	-0.1
50461	OSAGE	131	5690	5484	5406	-0.4	32	2331	2288	2260	-0.2	2.35	1586	1522	-0.4
50464	PLYMOUTH	195	673	631	607	-0.7	15	263	253	245	-0.4	2.49	199	188	-0.6
50465	RAKE	189	259	240	231	-0.8	11	124	118	114	-0.5	2.03	76	70	-0.9
50466	RICEVILLE	089	1797	1783	1768	-0.1	51	676	685	682	0.1	2.56	478	474	-0.1
50467	ROCK FALLS	033	92	85	82	-0.9	8	37	35	34	-0.6	2.43	28	26	-0.8
50468	ROCKFORD	067	1711	1667	1635	-0.3	40	650	653	645	0.0	2.55	449	440	-0.2
50469	ROCKWELL	033	1676	1636	1607	-0.3	40	617	619	611	0.0	2.58	456	449	-0.2
50470	ROWAN	197	325	315	305	-0.3	40	138	136	132	-0.2	2.32	100	97	-0.3
50471	RUDD	067	782	811	808	0.4	76	309	331	332	0.7	2.39	226	237	0.5
50472	SAINT ANSGAR	131	2384	2487	2496	0.5	79	921	982	990	0.7	2.46	652	681	0.5
50473	SCARVILLE	189	335	318	309	-0.6	20	130	128	125	-0.2	2.48	100	96	-0.4
50475	SHEFFIELD	069	1647	1698	1697	0.3	72	640	675	678	0.6	2.42	462	477	0.3
50476	STACYVILLE	131	771	786	788	0.2	68	307	322	324	0.5	2.35	206	211	0.3
50477	SWALEDALE	033	378	377	371	0.0	58	143	146	144	0.2	2.58	108	108	0.0
50478	THOMPSON	189	1028	999	972	-0.3	40	428	421	411	-0.2	2.37	306	295	-0.4
50479	THORNTON	033	748	741	732	-0.1	51	314	318	315	0.1	2.33	215	212	-0.2
50480	TITONKA	109	1120	1002	950	-1.2	4	452	415	396	-0.9	2.35	321	289	-1.1
50482	VENTURA	033	864	851	829	-0.2	46	354	352	344	-0.1	2.42	255	249	-0.3
50483	WESLEY	109	918	881	850	-0.4	32	341	335	326	-0.2	2.63	248	238	-0.4
50484	WODEN	081	538	503	483	-0.7	15	213	204	197	-0.5	2.47	153	143	-0.7
50501	FORT DODGE	187	30416	29271	28395	-0.4	32	12010	11692	11372	-0.3	2.28	7530	7136	-0.6
50510	ALBERT CITY	021	1250	1214	1201	-0.3	40	494	493	489	0.0	2.40	349	340	-0.3
50511	ALGONA	109	7488	7000	6746	-0.7	15	3070	2972	2887	-0.4	2.30	2057	1945	-0.6
50514	ARMSTRONG	063	1555	1440	1385	-0.8	11	648	624	606	-0.4	2.23	431	405	-0.7
50515	AYRSHIRE	147	376	354	340	-0.6	20	155	151	146	-0.3	2.34	115	110	-0.5
50516	BADGER	187	757	761	754	0.1	63	285	298	297	0.5	2.55	220	225	0.2
50517	BANCROFT	109	1149	1016	962	-1.3	2	460	423	404	-0.9	2.32	303	272	-1.2
50518	BARNUM	187	388	379	368	-0.3	40	142	142	138	0.0	2.67	111	109	-0.2
50519	BODE	109	724	695	679	-0.4	32	296	292	287	-0.1	2.36	226	219	-0.3
50520	BRADGATE	091	267	233	221	-1.5	1	112	101	97	-1.1	2.31	85	76	-1.2
50521	BURNSIDE	187	16	15	14	-0.7	15	5	5	5	0.0	3.00	4	4	0.0
50522	BURT	109	896	804	762	-1.2	4	350	323	308	-0.9	2.34	242	218	-1.1
50523	CALLENDER	187	785	762	738	-0.3	40	303	301	294	-0.1	2.53	225	218	-0.3
50524	CLARE	187	699	683	664	-0.3	40	250	249	244	0.0	2.74	195	191	-0.2
50525	CLARION	197	3926	3696	3550	-0.7	15	1636	1557	1495	-0.5	2.32	1073	996	-0.8
50527	CURLEW	147	283	261	250	-0.9	8	115	110	106	-0.5	2.37	82	77	-0.7
50528	CYLINDER	147	484	448	429	-0.8	11	182	173	166	-0.5	2.59	143	134	-0.7
50529	DAKOTA CITY	091	895	831	800	-0.8	11	348	334	324	-0.4	2.49	249	234	-0.7
50530	DAYTON	187	1303	1244	1207	-0.5	27	507	493	479	-0.3	2.43	351	332	-0.6
50531	DOLLIVER	063	278	265	256	-0.5	27	116	114	111	-0.2	2.10	88	85	-0.4
50532	DUNCOMBE	187	1023	1020	1010	0.0	58	402	417	415	0.4	2.45	282	284	0.1
50533	EAGLE GROVE	197	4299	3915	3723	-1.0	6	1729	1596	1518	-0.9	2.40	1160	1044	-1.1
50535	EARLY	161	985	894	847	-1.0	6	397	372	356	-0.7	2.40	283	260	-0.9
50536	EMMETSBURG	147	4689	4472	4345	-0.5	27	1889	1867	1825	-0.1	2.23	1148	1104	-0.4
50538	FARNHAMVILLE	025	568	509	480	-1.2	4	247	226	215	-1.0	2.25	174	156	-1.2
50539	FENTON	109	676	606	574	-1.2	4	292	272	260	-0.8	2.23	197	179	-1.0
50540	FONDA	151	1221	1075	1011	-1.4	1	500	450	426	-1.1	2.31	326	287	-1.4
50541	GILMORE CITY	151	968	918	887	-0.6	20	401	392	381	-0.2	2.33	282	269	-0.5
50542	GOLDFIELD	197	972	972	962	0.0	58	407	418	415	0.3	2.33	278	280	0.1
50543	GOWRIE	187	1527	1453	1407	-0.5	27	608	589	572	-0.3	2.39	411	388	-0.6
50544	HARCOURT	187	568	540	522	-0.5	27	228	221	215	-0.3	2.44	160	152	-0.6
50545	HARDY	091	287	273	265	-0.5	27	104	99	96	-0.5	2.76	74	69	-0.8
	IOWA					0.4					0.7	2.40			0.4
	UNITED STATES					1.0					1.1	2.59			0.9

ZIP CODE #	POST OFFICE NAME	RACE (%) White 2000	White 2009	Black 2000	Black 2009	Asian/Pacific 2000	Asian/Pacific 2009	% Hispanic Origin 2000	% Hispanic Origin 2009	2009 AGE DISTRIBUTION (%) 0-4	5-9	10-14	15-19	20-24	25-44	45-64	65-84	85+	18+	MEDIAN AGE 2009	% 2009 Males	% 2009 Females
50313	DES MOINES	87.9	82.4	4.2	5.7	3.0	4.9	5.1	7.9	7.0	6.8	6.7	6.5	6.0	26.9	26.8	11.5	1.7	75.4	38.2	49.7	50.3
50314	DES MOINES	37.2	28.9	37.3	40.1	11.1	14.2	15.6	19.5	9.5	8.8	7.7	7.3	7.7	27.6	20.9	9.1	1.5	69.7	30.0	48.9	51.1
50315	DES MOINES	89.2	83.6	3.0	4.4	2.4	4.0	6.8	10.8	7.5	6.9	6.6	6.5	7.1	29.4	24.0	10.3	1.6	75.0	35.1	48.8	51.2
50316	DES MOINES	67.3	58.1	15.7	18.3	6.4	9.4	12.6	18.0	8.4	7.4	7.1	8.2	8.0	27.1	22.8	8.7	2.2	72.4	32.7	48.9	51.1
50317	DES MOINES	91.9	87.5	2.3	3.3	2.1	3.8	4.2	6.8	7.0	6.8	6.6	6.5	5.8	27.2	25.9	12.3	2.0	75.6	37.8	48.6	51.4
50320	DES MOINES	83.9	77.4	5.6	6.8	4.1	6.6	9.2	13.9	9.6	8.7	7.9	6.8	6.1	29.9	22.1	8.2	0.8	69.6	32.4	49.7	50.3
50321	DES MOINES	90.7	85.4	4.0	6.0	1.7	2.9	3.5	6.0	6.0	5.4	5.3	8.4	8.8	28.1	25.4	11.2	1.4	80.1	34.7	47.4	52.6
50322	URBANDALE	95.0	91.9	1.6	2.5	1.8	3.3	1.8	3.0	6.2	6.4	6.7	6.5	5.5	26.6	28.9	11.5	1.8	76.6	39.7	48.2	51.8
50323	URBANDALE	94.3	92.4	1.2	1.8	3.4	4.2	1.4	2.8	10.6	10.3	9.4	6.5	3.0	32.4	23.5	4.0	0.3	65.3	33.4	49.8	50.2
50325	CLIVE	93.1	89.8	1.2	1.6	2.9	4.9	2.6	4.0	8.5	9.1	9.2	7.0	4.6	25.6	28.3	7.4	0.4	68.6	36.5	49.5	50.5
50327	DES MOINES	95.6	92.6	0.6	1.1	1.6	3.1	2.2	3.7	7.0	7.4	7.7	6.7	4.4	26.7	28.8	9.8	1.4	73.7	38.7	48.7	51.3
50401	MASON CITY	95.6	94.1	1.1	1.4	0.8	1.2	3.3	4.8	6.2	6.1	6.0	7.1	6.5	25.0	26.4	13.5	3.1	77.8	39.5	47.9	52.1
50420	ALEXANDER	97.0	95.5	0.0	0.0	0.0	0.0	2.8	4.5	5.0	5.5	5.7	6.2	5.0	21.4	33.8	15.0	2.4	80.0	45.6	52.4	47.6
50421	BELMOND	94.9	92.8	0.2	0.3	0.2	0.4	5.2	7.8	5.4	5.8	6.2	6.2	5.2	20.9	29.9	15.4	5.1	78.7	45.3	48.4	51.6
50423	BRITT	95.8	93.6	0.0	0.1	0.2	0.4	4.6	7.0	6.0	6.6	6.7	6.6	4.9	21.6	28.2	15.4	4.1	76.3	43.0	49.0	51.0
50424	BUFFALO CENTER	98.2	97.3	0.0	0.0	0.3	0.5	2.4	3.5	6.3	6.5	6.6	5.8	4.6	19.0	27.2	17.8	6.2	77.1	45.9	49.7	50.3
50428	CLEAR LAKE	97.2	96.0	0.2	0.3	0.9	1.4	1.8	2.7	5.5	5.7	6.0	5.9	5.2	22.9	31.2	14.8	2.8	79.0	44.0	48.8	51.2
50430	CORWITH	98.1	97.0	0.0	0.0	0.3	0.6	2.7	3.9	5.2	6.9	8.6	7.5	3.6	22.7	28.0	15.2	2.5	73.6	41.7	50.2	49.8
50432	CRYSTAL LAKE	98.0	97.1	0.0	0.0	0.3	0.4	2.0	3.3	5.1	5.9	6.3	6.3	4.0	23.9	32.0	14.3	2.2	78.3	43.8	50.0	50.0
50433	DOUGHERTY	99.6	98.4	0.0	0.4	0.0	0.4	0.4	0.8	4.9	7.3	9.0	8.2	4.1	23.3	29.4	12.7	1.2	73.1	40.1	50.6	49.4
50434	FERTILE	97.6	96.8	0.2	0.4	0.2	0.4	1.8	2.7	5.9	6.6	7.3	6.8	3.6	22.5	31.4	13.6	2.3	75.9	43.1	49.1	50.9
50435	FLOYD	99.1	98.6	0.0	0.0	0.5	0.8	0.1	0.2	6.3	6.6	6.9	6.5	5.1	22.0	30.6	14.5	1.5	76.1	42.3	50.7	49.3
50436	FOREST CITY	96.7	95.3	0.4	0.5	1.0	1.6	2.4	3.5	6.0	6.0	6.4	8.9	7.3	23.6	27.4	12.0	2.4	77.4	37.9	49.8	50.2
50438	GARNER	98.8	98.2	0.1	0.1	0.4	0.7	1.1	1.6	6.1	6.4	6.9	7.0	5.5	23.0	29.5	12.6	3.1	76.1	41.3	48.9	51.1
50439	GOODELL	97.4	96.4	0.5	0.6	0.5	0.8	2.6	3.9	4.7	6.4	7.8	9.4	5.0	24.7	31.3	9.7	1.1	74.2	41.0	52.6	47.4
50440	GRAFTON	99.4	99.4	0.0	0.0	0.2	0.2	0.2	0.4	5.6	5.4	8.6	7.6	4.2	24.3	28.9	12.7	2.8	75.1	41.6	52.2	47.8
50441	HAMPTON	92.7	89.3	0.1	0.1	0.2	0.3	8.8	12.9	6.0	6.1	5.8	6.4	5.2	22.3	27.1	16.8	4.2	78.3	43.3	48.6	51.4
50444	HANLONTOWN	97.5	97.0	0.3	0.3	0.3	0.3	1.9	2.4	6.0	6.5	7.3	6.8	3.8	22.8	31.2	13.6	2.2	75.6	42.8	49.3	50.7
50446	JOICE	98.5	98.0	0.2	0.2	0.2	0.2	1.2	1.5	5.9	6.6	6.9	7.1	3.9	24.9	27.6	15.2	1.9	75.3	41.6	50.8	49.2
50447	KANAWHA	97.7	96.9	0.1	0.1	0.3	0.4	1.9	2.7	6.7	6.8	6.9	6.3	5.2	19.8	27.1	16.0	5.1	75.6	43.6	50.1	49.9
50448	KENSETT	99.3	98.9	0.0	0.0	0.1	0.4	1.3	1.8	4.8	5.4	6.4	6.4	4.1	22.8	32.6	15.2	2.4	79.5	45.1	52.7	47.3
50449	KLEMME	98.9	98.5	0.0	0.0	0.1	0.2	2.2	3.2	7.9	7.9	8.2	7.7	5.1	26.0	24.5	10.2	2.5	71.0	36.2	49.6	50.4
50450	LAKE MILLS	98.3	97.7	0.0	0.0	0.5	0.9	1.7	2.5	5.1	5.1	5.4	6.3	6.0	22.5	29.6	15.1	4.9	80.4	44.6	48.0	52.0
50451	LAKOTA	99.0	98.6	0.1	0.2	0.0	0.2	1.6	2.3	5.9	6.9	6.9	6.1	4.0	19.1	32.0	16.4	2.6	76.4	45.5	52.6	47.4
50452	LATIMER	94.5	91.5	0.0	0.0	0.1	0.2	7.3	11.2	6.2	6.6	6.9	6.6	4.2	22.5	29.3	14.9	3.0	76.3	42.4	50.9	49.1
50453	LELAND	98.1	97.4	0.0	0.0	0.3	0.5	1.2	1.6	5.3	6.4	7.5	7.3	4.9	22.0	31.7	13.5	1.5	75.8	42.7	51.0	49.0
50454	LITTLE CEDAR	99.3	99.4	0.7	0.6	0.0	0.0	0.7	0.6	7.1	8.4	7.7	7.7	4.5	20.0	27.7	13.5	3.2	71.6	40.8	52.9	47.1
50455	MC INTIRE	98.3	98.1	1.3	1.5	0.2	0.2	0.6	1.1	9.3	9.5	9.1	9.3	5.6	21.3	23.1	11.4	1.5	66.6	32.7	53.2	46.8
50456	MANLY	97.7	97.2	0.8	1.0	0.2	0.3	1.5	2.1	6.9	6.9	7.2	7.4	5.3	23.6	26.2	13.3	3.4	74.2	39.0	49.2	50.8
50457	MESERVEY	98.9	98.3	0.0	0.0	0.0	0.0	1.7	2.6	4.6	4.9	5.5	5.5	4.3	22.1	33.9	16.1	3.2	81.6	46.5	49.1	50.9
50458	NORA SPRINGS	99.6	99.3	0.0	0.0	0.0	0.0	0.9	1.3	6.2	7.0	7.3	6.4	3.9	24.4	29.8	12.1	3.0	75.4	41.2	50.8	49.2
50459	NORTHWOOD	98.3	97.9	0.1	0.1	0.2	0.3	2.0	2.9	5.1	5.5	5.9	6.3	4.1	23.5	28.9	16.0	4.8	79.2	44.7	49.8	50.2
50460	ORCHARD	100.0	100.0	0.0	0.0	0.0	0.0	0.5	0.8	7.3	7.6	7.9	8.1	4.6	20.9	29.5	12.2	1.9	71.3	40.6	50.7	49.3
50461	OSAGE	99.2	99.0	0.1	0.1	0.2	0.3	0.6	0.9	5.9	6.7	6.9	7.0	4.6	21.7	27.5	15.4	4.4	75.9	42.7	48.7	51.3
50464	PLYMOUTH	99.0	98.6	0.0	0.0	0.3	0.5	0.9	1.4	4.8	5.2	6.2	6.3	5.1	23.6	32.8	13.8	2.2	79.9	44.1	50.7	49.3
50465	RAKE	96.9	95.8	0.0	0.0	0.0	0.0	4.2	6.3	5.0	5.4	5.8	5.8	4.2	26.3	30.8	13.8	2.9	79.6	42.9	52.9	47.1
50466	RICEVILLE	99.3	99.2	0.3	0.3	0.1	0.1	0.2	0.2	7.3	6.6	6.6	8.5	4.9	20.3	27.4	14.9	3.6	74.1	41.6	50.8	49.2
50467	ROCK FALLS	100.0	98.8	0.0	0.0	0.0	0.0	1.1	2.4	4.7	4.7	4.7	5.9	5.9	22.4	36.5	12.9	2.4	83.5	45.8	50.6	49.4
50468	ROCKFORD	98.8	98.5	0.2	0.2	0.1	0.2	0.8	1.1	6.5	6.8	7.2	7.6	5.3	23.5	27.7	12.9	2.6	74.9	40.1	50.4	49.6
50469	ROCKWELL	98.2	97.7	0.1	0.2	0.2	0.4	1.4	2.1	6.3	6.8	7.2	6.8	5.9	22.2	26.9	14.4	3.5	75.1	40.8	49.6	50.4
50470	ROWAN	95.1	93.0	0.6	1.0	0.3	0.6	4.9	7.6	5.4	6.3	7.0	6.0	3.5	19.7	34.9	14.3	2.9	77.1	46.3	52.4	47.6
50471	RUDD	99.0	98.6	0.0	0.0	0.0	0.0	1.4	2.1	6.5	7.2	7.5	7.0	4.2	21.8	30.7	12.5	2.6	74.4	41.6	50.3	49.7
50472	SAINT ANSGAR	99.4	99.0	0.0	0.0	0.3	0.6	0.8	1.1	5.4	6.1	6.6	7.1	4.6	20.5	29.0	15.8	4.9	77.5	44.7	48.0	52.0
50473	SCARVILLE	97.6	97.2	0.0	0.0	0.3	0.3	1.5	1.9	5.0	5.3	6.0	6.0	5.3	22.6	32.7	14.8	2.2	80.2	44.8	51.3	48.7
50475	SHEFFIELD	98.5	97.7	0.1	0.1	0.3	0.5	1.5	2.3	5.9	6.4	6.7	6.1	4.3	20.6	28.2	16.8	5.0	77.0	44.9	49.4	50.6
50476	STACYVILLE	99.2	99.0	0.1	0.1	0.1	0.3	0.3	0.5	5.9	6.5	6.5	6.5	4.1	20.4	27.6	17.3	5.3	76.6	45.1	51.0	49.0
50477	SWALEDALE	98.7	98.7	0.3	0.3	0.3	0.3	0.8	1.1	4.8	7.4	9.0	7.7	4.0	22.8	30.5	12.7	1.1	73.5	40.9	50.7	49.3
50478	THOMPSON	97.8	96.9	0.0	0.0	0.3	0.5	1.5	2.1	6.3	6.9	7.0	6.5	4.3	23.8	28.9	13.7	2.5	75.7	41.1	52.9	47.1
50479	THORNTON	98.8	98.5	0.0	0.0	0.0	0.0	1.6	2.3	4.5	5.1	5.7	5.8	4.3	22.4	32.9	16.1	3.2	81.1	46.2	50.5	49.5
50480	TITONKA	99.1	99.0	0.1	0.1	0.1	0.1	0.6	0.9	5.9	6.6	6.8	6.5	4.1	20.0	28.6	16.9	4.7	76.1	45.1	50.0	50.0
50482	VENTURA	99.0	98.5	0.1	0.1	0.3	0.7	0.8	1.3	4.2	5.1	6.1	6.3	3.6	19.4	37.3	15.7	2.2	80.4	47.9	50.9	49.1
50483	WESLEY	98.9	98.5	0.0	0.0	0.1	0.2	0.5	0.8	6.7	7.3	7.7	7.7	4.3	21.0	28.1	14.8	2.4	73.4	41.1	51.0	49.0
50484	WODEN	98.5	98.2	0.0	0.0	0.0	0.0	0.9	1.4	7.0	7.4	7.6	7.8	4.6	21.3	28.8	13.7	2.0	73.4	40.7	50.5	49.5
50501	FORT DODGE	91.8	89.3	4.4	5.3	0.8	1.5	2.8	4.1	6.3	6.1	6.1	8.5	8.4	22.9	24.6	13.3	3.8	77.8	37.5	48.9	51.1
50510	ALBERT CITY	98.7	98.2	0.1	0.1	0.2	0.2	1.0	1.6	5.1	6.3	6.8	6.9	3.9	21.3	31.4	14.3	4.0	77.1	44.7	50.5	49.5
50511	ALGONA	98.6	98.0	0.1	0.1	0.7	1.1	0.7	1.0	5.3	5.4	5.7	6.7	6.0	21.9	29.4	15.6	4.0	79.2	44.1	48.0	52.0
50514	ARMSTRONG	99.1	98.8	0.1	0.1	0.1	0.3	0.4	0.6	5.4	5.7	5.8	5.5	4.8	20.1	29.9	17.9	4.8	79.5	46.9	48.6	51.4
50515	AYRSHIRE	98.9	98.6	0.0	0.0	0.3	0.3	0.8	0.8	5.9	6.5	7.3	7.3	4.0	20.1	30.5	16.7	1.7	75.4	44.0	51.1	48.9
50516	BADGER	98.5	98.0	0.7	0.9	0.1	0.1	0.8	1.2	7.6	8.0	8.3	6.7	4.9	23.3	28.8	11.0	1.4	72.0	38.5	51.4	48.6
50517	BANCROFT	99.3	99.1	0.1	0.1	0.0	0.0	1.0	1.6	6.5	6.7	6.9	7.4	4.9	21.4	24.9	15.9	5.4	74.6	42.0	46.9	53.1
50518	BARNUM	98.7	98.2	0.0	0.0	0.0	0.3	0.8	1.6	6.1	6.9	7.7	8.2	4.7	21.1	32.7	11.3	1.3	74.4	41.4	52.8	47.2
50519	BODE	98.2	97.1	0.0	0.0	1.1	1.7	0.8	1.3	5.9	6.5	7.1	7.3	3.7	23.6	29.5	13.5	2.9	75.7	42.0	51.2	48.8
50520	BRADGATE	98.9	98.7	0.0	0.0	0.4	0.4	0.0	0.0	5.2	6.4	6.0	5.6	4.3	21.0	33.9	15.5	2.1	78.5	46.0	51.5	48.5
50521	BURNSIDE	100.0	100.0	0.0	0.0	0.0	0.0	0.0	0.0	0.0	6.7	6.7	0.0	0.0	20.0	66.7	0.0	0.0	86.7	49.2	60.0	40.0
50522	BURT	99.2	99.0	0.2	0.2	0.2	0.4	0.4	0.6	5.1	5.6	5.8	7.7	5.3	23.4	28.2	15.2	3.6	78.5	42.6	48.3	51.7
50523	CALLENDER	99.1	98.8	0.1	0.3	0.0	0.0	0.9	1.4	5.9	6.4	6.7	7.0	4.5	21.7	31.9	13.5	2.5	76.8	43.4	50.5	49.5
50524	CLARE	98.6	98.1	0.0	0.0	0.1	0.1	0.9	1.5	6.1	6.9	7.5	8.2	4.7	20.9	32.8	11.6	1.3	74.2	41.6	52.6	47.4
50525	CLARION	94.5	92.0	0.2	0.2	0.2	0.3	8.1	11.9	6.0	5.8	6.2	7.0	4.9	22.2	27.7	16.0	4.2	77.4	43.4	49.1	50.9
50527	CURLEW	98.9	98.9	0.0	0.0	0.4	0.4	0.4	0.4	5.4	5.7	6.5	7.3	4.6	20.3	30.7	16.9	2.7	77.8	45.1	51.0	49.0
50528	CYLINDER	98.6	98.2	0.2	0.2	0.2	0.2	0.8	1.1	5.8	7.4	8.5	8.3	3.6	21.4	30.4	13.2	1.6	72.5	41.7	51.8	48.2
50529	DAKOTA CITY	98.7	98.1	0.1	0.1	0.1	0.2	1.5	2.2	6.5	6.3	6.1	6.9	7.8	28.3	27.3	9.5	1.3	77.1	35.7	51.4	48.6
50530	DAYTON	98.6	98.2	0.1	0.1	0.3	0.5	0.5	0.6	6.0	6.1	5.9	6.4	5.7	22.4	26.9	16.0	4.4	78.2	42.9	49.8	50.2
50531	DOLLIVER	97.8	97.4	0.7	0.8	0.4	0.4	2.5	3.8	4.9	5.7	8.3	13.2	3.4	21.1	27.9	13.6	1.9	70.6	38.9	49.4	50.6
50532	DUNCOMBE	97.7	96.9	0.0	0.0	0.2	0.3	1.6	2.3	6.7	6.7	6.8	6.4	5.6	24.9	28.3	12.8	1.9	76.0	40.2	49.3	50.7
50533	EAGLE GROVE	97.5	96.5	0.2	0.2	0.1	0.2	1.9	2.9	6.3	6.4	6.4	6.9	5.4	21.9	27.9	14.9	3.9	76.6	42.3	49.2	50.8
50535	EARLY	96.8	95.5	0.5	0.6	0.0	0.0	2.9	4.6	6.2	6.5	7.6	7.7	3.8	23.2	29.5	13.0	2.6	74.7	41.6	50.8	49.2
50536	EMMETSBURG	98.6	97.2	0.1	1.0	0.5	0.8	0.8	1.1	5.1	5.1	5.6	9.1	7.0	19.9	26.8	16.4	5.0	80.6	43.3	48.5	51.5
50538	FARNHAMVILLE	98.6	98.2	0.0	0.0	0.0	0.0	0.9	1.4	5.7	5.9	6.7	5.9	4.7	21.6	28.9	17.1	3.5	78.2	44.6	48.9	51.1
50539	FENTON	98.8	98.5	0.0	0.0	0.0	0.0	0.3	0.3	5.6	6.6	7.1	8.4	3.3	20.1	29.5	15.5	3.8	75.2	44.1	49.0	51.0
50540	FONDA	98.9	98.6	0.2	0.2	0.0	0.0	1.3	2.0	5.2	5.4	5.7	6.0	6.2	18.0	31.7	16.7	5.0	79.6	46.9	51.9	48.1
50541	GILMORE CITY	98.9	98.6	0.1	0.1	0.1	0.2	0.5	0.7	5.2	6.4	7.0	7.5	4.5	21.9	31.4	13.7	2.4	76.3	42.9	51.1	48.9
50542	GOLDFIELD	98.9	98.6	0.0	0.0	0.1	0.1	1.7	2.7	5.1	5.5	6.3	7.2	5.2	22.3	28.8	16.8	2.8	78.8	43.8	51.6	48.4
50543	GOWRIE	98.6	98.1	0.2	0.2	0.3	0.5	0.9	1.4	5.2	5.4	5.7	6.8	6.0	21.7	27.9	16.6	4.7	78.9	44.3	48.9	51.1
50544	HARCOURT	98.8	98.0	0.2	0.2	0.5	0.9	0.9	1.5	5.2	6.1	6.3	5.2	3.9	24.4	32.8	14.1	2.0	79.1	44.0	52.0	48.0
50545	HARDY	98.6	98.2	0.0	0.0	0.3	0.4	0.7	1.1	5.5	7.3	8.8	8.1	2.6	24.2	26.4	14.7	2.6	74.0	41.0	52.4	47.6
	IOWA	93.9	91.9	2.1	2.5	1.3	2.1	2.8	4.1	6.5	6.4	6.5	7.3	7.1	25.2	26.5	11.9	2.6	76.5	38.1	49.3	50.7
	UNITED STATES	75.1	72.0	12.3	12.7	3.8	4.6	12.5	15.7	6.8	6.7	6.6	7.1	6.9	27.0	26.0	10.9	1.9	75.7	36.9	49.2	50.8

ZIP CODE #	POST OFFICE NAME	2009 Per Capita Income	2009 HH Income Base	2009 HOUSEHOLD INCOME DISTRIBUTION (%) Less than $25,000	$25,000 to $49,999	$50,000 to $99,999	$100,000 to $149,999	$150,000 or More	MEDIAN HOUSEHOLD INCOME 2009	2014	2009 National Centile	2009 State Centile	2009 Home Value Base	2009 HOME VALUE DISTRIBUTION (%) Less than $50,000	$50,000 to $89,999	$90,000 to $174,999	$175,000 to $399,999	$400,000 or More	2009 Median Home Value
50313	DES MOINES	23290	6983	19.8	31.3	40.9	6.2	1.7	48822	52025	58	65	5279	9.5	41.7	41.4	7.4	0.0	89070
50314	DES MOINES	14676	4518	38.2	36.2	21.7	3.1	0.9	31814	32023	11	1	1631	36.4	41.1	19.9	2.4	0.2	59933
50315	DES MOINES	24018	15768	21.0	27.1	43.2	7.1	1.6	51606	54140	65	76	10428	10.4	33.0	52.6	3.9	0.1	97143
50316	DES MOINES	18595	6143	27.6	31.7	33.9	5.4	1.5	41987	43643	39	25	3958	21.7	46.8	30.3	1.2	0.0	77500
50317	DES MOINES	22552	14774	21.2	30.6	39.6	6.7	1.9	48097	51482	57	62	11341	13.3	37.4	44.7	3.9	0.7	89468
50320	DES MOINES	24076	6705	18.4	27.4	43.0	8.5	2.8	54463	58456	70	85	4870	29.5	13.9	37.9	17.4	1.3	107061
50321	DES MOINES	35622	3209	12.2	25.7	34.3	16.5	11.3	63049	64872	81	95	1988	13.2	2.4	24.3	53.4	6.7	194179
50322	URBANDALE	34782	14764	9.7	21.5	43.8	16.7	8.3	69184	73373	86	98	10981	2.5	4.1	50.9	41.1	1.4	164337
50323	URBANDALE	44325	2166	5.1	7.5	48.4	16.3	22.6	87956	89342	95	100	1981	1.0	4.4	28.5	46.1	19.9	232701
50325	CLIVE	46397	5348	5.9	15.2	34.9	18.2	25.9	91079	97756	95	100	4149	1.3	3.3	14.8	59.1	21.5	254378
50327	DES MOINES	29858	3520	8.2	20.9	44.3	21.0	5.6	72333	76001	88	98	2860	5.0	10.2	49.1	33.0	2.7	153337
50401	MASON CITY	25783	12931	24.1	29.2	35.3	7.6	3.9	46825	48599	54	56	8874	10.7	31.8	43.8	12.8	0.9	100416
50420	ALEXANDER	21688	180	22.2	36.7	34.4	5.6	1.1	43907	45589	45	38	140	30.7	38.6	23.6	5.7	1.4	70000
50421	BELMOND	22076	1275	25.6	32.0	35.7	5.9	0.9	42961	44616	42	31	960	14.3	38.8	39.9	6.4	0.7	87157
50423	BRITT	19880	1223	23.2	35.4	36.7	3.7	1.0	43738	46172	45	36	960	25.2	37.9	31.6	4.5	0.8	77419
50424	BUFFALO CENTER	21701	651	25.7	34.3	33.6	4.3	2.2	40581	44194	35	18	533	43.7	33.8	18.6	2.4	1.5	56837
50428	CLEAR LAKE	25778	4044	24.2	27.1	37.8	7.4	3.6	48600	49576	58	64	3063	10.3	20.3	48.1	15.6	5.7	113009
50430	CORWITH	18777	258	29.5	35.3	27.9	7.0	0.4	40598	41956	35	18	201	39.8	29.9	22.4	5.5	2.5	59762
50432	CRYSTAL LAKE	23013	122	21.3	34.4	36.9	7.4	0.0	46360	48382	52	53	98	24.5	30.6	33.7	11.2	0.0	80000
50433	DOUGHERTY	21528	101	17.8	35.6	41.6	4.0	1.0	47650	47525	56	60	78	37.2	19.2	32.1	10.3	1.3	76667
50434	FERTILE	20438	229	24.5	35.4	35.4	3.5	1.3	42496	45657	41	28	193	21.2	43.0	28.5	7.3	0.0	77000
50435	FLOYD	21851	332	21.7	32.8	35.2	6.9	3.3	46463	47425	53	54	283	15.2	23.0	47.7	13.8	0.4	106703
50436	FOREST CITY	24774	2305	17.0	30.1	44.1	6.1	2.7	52426	52982	67	79	1734	16.3	34.7	40.9	8.0	0.2	89220
50438	GARNER	24907	1634	18.7	28.9	42.7	6.1	3.7	51451	52430	65	75	1290	11.8	30.3	45.8	11.5	0.6	100750
50439	GOODELL	20510	150	13.3	46.0	36.7	3.3	0.7	45287	46536	49	46	120	25.0	28.3	32.5	10.0	4.2	85556
50440	GRAFTON	19113	201	20.9	36.8	38.8	3.5	0.0	43531	45000	44	34	162	19.1	33.3	34.6	8.0	4.9	86000
50441	HAMPTON	24204	2322	25.8	28.9	35.7	6.8	2.8	45512	47836	50	47	1671	21.6	36.4	33.5	7.7	0.8	82006
50444	HANLONTOWN	19901	148	25.0	34.5	35.8	3.4	1.4	42847	46027	42	30	125	22.4	43.2	27.2	7.2	0.0	75938
50446	JOICE	21996	242	19.8	37.2	35.1	6.6	1.2	46012	47413	51	50	201	20.9	37.8	31.8	9.0	0.5	81250
50447	KANAWHA	21741	490	18.4	38.6	37.6	4.1	1.4	45245	46610	49	46	385	41.3	26.0	23.9	6.2	2.6	59853
50448	KENSETT	20149	299	25.4	29.8	40.8	3.3	0.7	46192	48629	52	52	248	23.4	32.7	31.5	9.7	2.8	79565
50449	KLEMME	18919	340	22.9	35.0	36.5	5.0	0.6	42435	44634	41	28	251	43.0	36.7	14.7	3.6	2.0	56250
50450	LAKE MILLS	26252	1249	20.1	30.4	36.3	10.7	2.4	49322	51470	60	67	914	10.8	31.2	43.5	13.1	1.3	102249
50451	LAKOTA	19549	262	33.6	29.4	28.6	6.1	2.3	36543	39311	22	5	213	50.7	21.6	17.4	7.5	2.8	49571
50452	LATIMER	19851	442	23.5	36.0	32.8	5.4	2.3	43541	46061	44	34	342	29.2	29.2	32.2	7.6	1.8	81471
50453	LELAND	23855	226	11.5	34.1	45.1	8.4	0.9	52208	52649	66	78	190	17.4	24.7	44.7	11.6	1.6	102703
50454	LITTLE CEDAR	19654	64	26.6	40.6	26.6	6.3	0.0	40729	43162	35	18	53	30.2	30.2	24.5	9.4	5.7	76250
50455	MC INTIRE	15883	156	25.6	39.1	28.8	5.1	1.3	42144	43138	40	25	132	36.4	24.2	23.5	9.8	6.1	70000
50456	MANLY	20877	723	23.0	32.4	39.8	4.4	0.4	45564	47835	50	47	558	26.3	38.2	30.3	4.5	0.7	76087
50457	MESERVEY	20482	163	23.3	44.2	28.8	3.7	0.0	39459	42349	31	13	130	33.1	34.6	25.4	6.2	0.8	65714
50458	NORA SPRINGS	20624	831	24.8	32.3	36.1	5.4	1.4	44064	45984	46	39	667	19.3	25.6	42.6	9.9	2.5	99054
50459	NORTHWOOD	22944	1317	25.2	33.0	33.9	5.8	2.0	44113	46233	46	39	1010	15.7	34.6	37.7	10.8	1.2	89663
50460	ORCHARD	21012	134	18.7	35.1	34.3	9.0	3.0	47743	47847	56	61	112	14.3	29.5	28.6	18.8	8.9	104545
50461	OSAGE	21147	2288	26.0	33.1	33.9	5.4	1.5	42450	44485	41	28	1823	11.1	33.4	43.0	11.2	1.3	98816
50464	PLYMOUTH	19180	253	20.2	39.5	36.8	3.2	0.4	42830	45637	42	30	213	19.7	31.9	36.2	10.8	1.4	88056
50465	RAKE	24460	118	28.0	33.1	32.2	5.9	0.8	38339	39371	28	10	95	56.8	13.7	16.8	12.6	0.0	44583
50466	RICEVILLE	19942	685	28.5	29.1	35.8	5.0	1.8	44017	45625	45	39	549	25.7	33.0	27.5	11.7	2.2	80104
50467	ROCK FALLS	19805	35	20.0	37.1	40.0	2.9	0.0	45739	46091	50	48	30	20.0	30.0	40.0	10.0	0.0	90000
50468	ROCKFORD	20464	653	25.4	30.5	37.2	4.3	2.6	45167	46317	49	45	492	26.0	27.8	34.8	10.2	1.2	86545
50469	ROCKWELL	22185	619	17.8	28.1	45.1	7.4	1.6	53124	53225	68	81	515	19.6	28.9	42.7	7.0	1.7	92206
50470	ROWAN	19894	136	25.0	34.6	37.5	2.2	0.7	44526	45000	47	42	104	40.4	25.0	25.0	9.6	0.0	62857
50471	RUDD	20909	331	26.3	32.6	33.2	4.8	3.0	44080	45661	46	39	259	26.6	31.3	34.4	6.6	1.2	80682
50472	SAINT ANSGAR	20108	982	26.1	30.7	36.8	5.9	0.6	43636	45000	44	35	818	17.6	24.7	44.6	12.5	0.6	101210
50473	SCARVILLE	22047	128	12.5	37.5	43.0	7.0	0.0	50000	51244	61	70	109	30.3	25.7	33.0	6.4	4.6	84091
50475	SHEFFIELD	21912	675	23.6	30.1	36.1	7.9	2.4	47293	49041	55	58	554	22.7	33.8	35.4	6.7	1.4	84286
50476	STACYVILLE	19353	322	24.5	43.5	26.4	4.7	0.9	40000	41575	33	15	264	29.5	35.6	26.9	6.8	1.1	73750
50477	SWALEDALE	20002	146	17.1	36.3	42.5	4.1	0.0	47568	47471	56	60	113	37.2	19.5	31.9	9.7	1.8	73750
50478	THOMPSON	21941	421	20.7	39.0	34.2	4.0	2.1	43682	46202	44	36	323	40.9	28.8	24.5	5.0	0.9	59516
50479	THORNTON	19042	318	23.3	44.3	28.0	4.4	0.0	39443	42615	31	13	254	33.5	33.5	26.0	5.5	1.6	66154
50480	TITONKA	21565	415	24.8	33.7	34.9	4.1	2.4	44689	46357	47	43	347	35.4	35.4	19.9	6.1	3.2	62500
50482	VENTURA	26699	352	18.8	29.0	40.1	8.5	3.7	52167	52241	66	78	296	7.1	15.5	41.9	27.7	7.8	132143
50483	WESLEY	21593	335	21.5	30.7	38.8	7.2	1.8	48235	50414	57	62	267	26.2	37.5	24.7	11.2	0.4	75000
50484	WODEN	19490	204	23.0	39.7	32.4	4.4	0.5	42643	45486	41	29	151	39.1	35.8	17.2	7.3	0.7	59706
50501	FORT DODGE	24092	11692	24.6	31.0	33.3	7.7	3.3	45490	48253	50	47	8076	17.3	32.0	39.5	10.1	1.1	90914
50510	ALBERT CITY	18513	493	28.2	39.6	27.0	4.3	1.0	38332	40061	28	10	389	40.9	33.2	21.1	2.6	2.3	57553
50511	ALGONA	22443	2972	26.2	31.8	33.5	6.0	2.5	43855	45809	45	37	2264	17.5	32.1	38.1	12.2	0.1	90602
50514	ARMSTRONG	22110	624	25.6	32.5	35.1	5.4	1.3	43794	45547	45	36	514	37.7	29.6	26.5	4.7	1.6	68788
50515	AYRSHIRE	19288	151	30.5	33.8	32.5	2.0	1.3	38501	40000	28	10	117	29.9	30.8	24.8	12.8	1.7	76250
50516	BADGER	23228	298	14.1	32.9	44.6	6.7	1.7	54352	54529	70	84	241	9.1	14.1	63.5	13.3	0.0	118134
50517	BANCROFT	19660	423	30.7	33.3	29.3	5.0	1.7	40060	41205	33	15	330	34.8	34.5	26.7	3.0	0.9	67200
50518	BARNUM	21667	142	24.6	31.7	33.1	4.2	6.3	46613	48036	53	55	117	13.7	26.5	35.9	18.8	5.1	102679
50519	BODE	22463	292	20.9	38.4	33.6	4.8	2.4	45000	45744	48	44	224	34.8	27.2	25.0	9.8	3.1	66667
50520	BRADGATE	21749	101	25.7	33.7	33.7	5.0	2.0	44599	46845	47	42	81	44.4	23.5	22.2	6.2	3.7	56429
50521	BURNSIDE	23500	5	0.0	0.0	100.0	0.0	0.0	66333	66333	84	97	4	0.0	0.0	100.0	0.0	0.0	112500
50522	BURT	19340	323	30.0	32.5	32.8	3.4	1.2	39859	41075	32	14	262	48.1	32.8	14.1	3.4	1.5	52083
50523	CALLENDER	20955	301	25.6	30.6	34.6	6.6	2.7	45117	47358	49	45	240	16.3	29.2	42.9	8.3	3.3	95500
50524	CLARE	20849	249	24.9	31.7	33.3	4.4	5.6	46529	47608	53	54	204	15.7	27.0	33.8	18.1	5.4	98824
50525	CLARION	24347	1557	21.8	28.4	40.6	5.8	3.3	49772	50333	60	68	1123	21.2	38.0	34.8	4.2	1.8	78218
50527	CURLEW	21238	110	31.8	32.7	29.1	3.6	2.7	37960	38756	27	8	88	46.6	26.1	20.5	6.8	0.0	55000
50528	CYLINDER	26634	173	19.1	26.6	42.2	4.6	7.5	53271	53125	68	82	119	18.5	26.9	40.3	9.2	5.0	94583
50529	DAKOTA CITY	22869	334	18.9	32.9	39.5	7.2	1.5	48577	49291	58	64	273	14.7	47.3	35.9	2.2	0.0	81216
50530	DAYTON	19973	493	26.6	31.6	36.9	3.2	1.6	44729	47203	47	43	367	25.9	34.9	31.1	6.8	1.4	76282
50531	DOLLIVER	24948	114	19.3	40.4	29.8	7.0	3.5	43447	44539	44	33	90	21.1	26.7	40.0	8.9	3.3	94000
50532	DUNCOMBE	21749	417	19.9	40.0	35.5	3.4	1.2	42409	45089	41	27	333	26.7	24.0	40.8	7.2	1.2	88438
50533	EAGLE GROVE	24727	1596	24.6	29.3	36.3	6.0	3.8	46544	47865	53	55	1193	36.5	36.0	23.5	3.8	0.3	60446
50535	EARLY	20286	372	29.3	31.2	34.1	4.6	0.8	42511	45000	41	28	290	30.7	33.4	28.6	4.1	3.1	74706
50536	EMMETSBURG	23224	1867	26.0	33.0	33.8	5.2	2.0	42336	44143	40	26	1310	16.1	37.4	38.2	7.6	0.7	86134
50538	FARNHAMVILLE	25977	226	21.2	38.1	31.4	4.0	5.3	43898	44785	45	37	179	36.3	42.5	17.9	2.2	1.1	63235
50539	FENTON	20880	272	30.1	36.8	28.3	2.6	2.2	40398	40945	34	17	213	47.9	33.3	13.6	3.8	1.4	52143
50540	FONDA	20779	450	29.8	34.9	30.4	3.1	1.8	40121	40968	33	16	357	46.2	32.5	18.5	2.0	0.8	53649
50541	GILMORE CITY	21580	392	26.8	32.1	32.4	5.9	2.8	42900	45396	42	31	301	35.9	36.9	18.6	8.3	0.3	59239
50542	GOLDFIELD	21203	418	26.8	31.1	35.9	5.0	1.2	43958	45294	45	38	323	39.0	33.1	22.0	5.0	0.9	63958
50543	GOWRIE	21537	589	27.2	29.5	34.5	6.8	2.0	44342	47955	46	40	430	19.3	31.2	40.5	8.1	0.9	89459
50544	HARCOURT	26715	221	20.4	32.1	38.0	6.3	3.2	47897	50859	56	61	168	29.8	22.6	36.9	8.3	2.4	85000
50545	HARDY	18293	99	22.2	32.3	38.4	7.1	0.0	46145	47597	52	51	81	38.3	27.2	18.5	12.3	3.7	65000
	IOWA	25379		21.1	28.2	37.9	8.6	4.3	50616	52941				14.7	22.5	41.6	18.6	2.6	110128
	UNITED STATES	27277		20.9	24.4	35.3	11.7	7.6	54719	56938				9.3	13.1	31.6	32.6	13.5	162279

ZIP CODE		FINANCIAL SERVICES				THE HOME						ENTERTAINMENT						PERSONAL			
						Home Improvements		Furnishings													
#	POST OFFICE NAME	Auto Loan	Home Loan	Investments	Retirement Plans	Home Repair	Lawn & Garden	Computers & Hardware-Personal	Major Appliances	TV, Radio, Sound Equipment	Furniture	Dine out/ Carry out	Sports Equipment	Fees & Tickets	Toys & Games	Travel	Cable TV	Apparel & Services	Auto Repairs	Health Insurance	Pets & Supplies
50313	DES MOINES	77	79	66	80	74	83	79	77	80	75	80	60	80	82	77	83	55	79	85	93
50314	DES MOINES	57	43	38	46	40	45	57	48	59	54	59	40	51	59	48	60	41	56	53	61
50315	DES MOINES	82	77	64	78	72	79	82	77	83	79	83	61	79	85	77	84	57	81	83	94
50316	DES MOINES	68	63	52	65	58	66	72	64	74	66	73	52	69	74	65	76	51	70	72	80
50317	DES MOINES	80	78	69	79	74	83	79	79	81	76	80	61	77	82	77	83	55	79	86	94
50320	DES MOINES	94	88	76	86	84	83	90	86	89	92	90	67	86	92	85	88	62	88	85	103
50321	DES MOINES	118	118	115	121	117	114	123	116	121	124	122	91	124	121	122	120	86	121	118	139
50322	URBANDALE	114	124	114	126	121	119	117	116	115	119	116	90	123	117	120	114	82	115	115	136
50323	URBANDALE	180	219	189	225	213	179	182	184	167	204	170	153	206	181	191	153	125	168	150	205
50325	CLIVE	177	200	188	207	199	177	183	179	173	194	176	144	199	180	189	165	127	174	161	206
50327	DES MOINES	108	126	113	127	122	115	112	112	107	115	109	88	121	111	117	105	77	109	106	131
50401	MASON CITY	83	79	75	80	77	86	83	83	85	78	84	63	80	85	80	88	58	84	91	99
50420	ALEXANDER	91	62	99	62	65	95	69	86	72	56	71	71	51	70	69	78	46	80	91	106
50421	BELMOND	86	62	88	60	64	90	67	83	74	59	72	64	53	73	66	82	48	78	90	99
50423	BRITT	81	58	84	57	60	85	63	78	69	55	67	60	49	68	62	76	44	73	85	93
50424	BUFFALO CENTER	84	60	86	58	62	88	65	81	72	57	70	62	52	71	64	79	46	76	88	96
50428	CLEAR LAKE	90	80	90	81	82	94	83	90	85	79	84	67	77	84	83	89	57	88	95	106
50430	CORWITH	83	57	91	57	60	88	64	79	66	52	65	65	47	65	63	72	42	74	84	97
50432	CRYSTAL LAKE	92	63	101	63	66	97	70	87	73	57	72	72	51	71	70	79	47	81	92	107
50433	DOUGHERTY	93	64	103	64	67	99	71	89	74	58	73	73	52	73	71	81	48	83	94	109
50434	FERTILE	89	62	98	62	64	94	68	85	71	55	70	70	50	70	68	77	46	79	89	104
50435	FLOYD	92	79	87	82	81	99	80	92	83	71	81	71	71	84	80	88	55	85	96	108
50436	FOREST CITY	93	82	86	83	81	97	86	91	88	79	87	71	78	88	84	92	59	90	98	109
50438	GARNER	95	84	95	82	85	102	82	94	87	78	86	70	76	87	83	93	58	90	101	111
50439	GOODELL	88	61	97	61	64	93	67	84	70	55	69	69	49	69	67	76	45	78	88	103
50440	GRAFTON	85	59	94	59	61	90	65	81	68	53	67	67	48	66	65	74	43	76	86	100
50441	HAMPTON	87	75	76	76	73	89	81	83	83	74	82	66	72	84	76	87	56	83	91	101
50444	HANLONTOWN	88	62	96	62	64	93	68	84	71	55	70	69	50	69	68	77	45	78	88	103
50446	JOICE	95	67	102	67	70	100	74	90	76	60	75	74	55	75	73	83	49	84	95	111
50447	KANAWHA	90	64	92	63	67	94	70	87	77	62	75	67	55	76	69	85	50	81	94	103
50448	KENSETT	83	60	88	61	63	87	65	79	68	54	67	65	50	67	65	73	44	74	83	97
50449	KLEMME	85	61	72	59	61	82	64	74	70	61	69	58	51	73	58	77	46	71	79	91
50450	LAKE MILLS	88	79	86	79	81	93	81	88	84	76	83	65	75	83	81	89	56	86	95	103
50451	LAKOTA	83	57	91	57	60	88	63	79	66	51	65	65	46	65	63	72	42	74	83	97
50452	LATIMER	91	63	100	63	66	96	70	87	73	57	72	72	51	71	69	79	47	81	92	107
50453	LELAND	95	77	94	79	80	102	80	94	83	69	82	74	68	83	80	89	55	87	98	112
50454	LITTLE CEDAR	84	58	92	58	60	89	64	80	67	52	66	66	47	65	64	73	43	74	84	98
50455	MC INTIRE	84	58	93	58	61	89	64	80	67	52	66	66	47	66	64	73	43	75	84	98
50456	MANLY	78	65	72	65	64	82	68	76	72	62	71	59	61	72	66	77	48	73	83	91
50457	MESERVEY	78	54	86	54	56	83	60	74	62	48	61	61	44	61	59	68	40	69	78	91
50458	NORA SPRINGS	84	68	83	69	70	89	70	83	73	61	71	65	59	73	70	78	48	77	86	98
50459	NORTHWOOD	85	66	85	66	68	90	69	83	73	60	72	65	57	73	68	79	48	77	88	99
50460	ORCHARD	102	70	111	70	74	107	78	97	82	64	81	79	58	80	77	89	52	90	103	119
50461	OSAGE	85	63	86	63	65	89	68	82	73	59	71	64	54	72	66	79	47	77	88	98
50464	PLYMOUTH	77	65	74	67	67	82	66	77	68	58	67	60	58	69	66	73	45	71	80	91
50465	RAKE	89	61	98	61	64	94	68	84	71	55	70	70	50	69	68	77	45	79	89	104
50466	RICEVILLE	90	63	95	62	66	94	69	86	74	58	73	68	53	73	68	81	48	80	92	104
50467	ROCK FALLS	74	68	67	71	69	80	67	76	69	60	68	57	62	70	67	73	46	70	78	88
50468	ROCKFORD	90	64	94	63	66	95	70	87	76	60	74	68	54	75	69	84	49	81	93	104
50469	ROCKWELL	88	79	85	80	77	94	81	87	83	74	82	69	75	83	80	86	55	85	93	105
50470	ROWAN	82	57	90	57	59	87	63	78	65	51	65	65	46	64	63	71	42	73	83	96
50471	RUDD	90	62	99	62	65	95	69	86	72	56	71	71	50	70	68	78	46	80	90	105
50472	SAINT ANSGAR	87	61	91	60	64	91	67	83	72	57	71	65	52	71	66	80	47	78	89	100
50473	SCARVILLE	98	67	108	67	71	103	75	93	78	61	77	77	55	76	74	85	50	87	98	114
50475	SHEFFIELD	93	66	97	65	69	98	72	90	79	62	77	70	56	77	71	86	50	84	96	107
50476	STACYVILLE	82	57	90	56	59	87	63	78	65	51	65	65	46	64	62	71	42	73	82	96
50477	SWALEDALE	92	64	102	64	67	97	70	88	73	58	72	72	52	72	70	80	47	82	92	107
50478	THOMPSON	93	64	102	64	67	98	71	88	74	58	73	73	52	73	71	81	47	83	93	109
50479	THORNTON	79	55	87	55	57	84	61	75	63	49	62	62	45	62	60	69	40	70	79	92
50480	TITONKA	92	63	101	63	66	97	70	87	73	57	72	72	51	71	70	79	47	81	92	107
50482	VENTURA	109	85	137	84	93	115	87	110	90	80	89	81	73	86	93	97	59	101	109	128
50483	WESLEY	101	70	111	70	73	107	78	96	81	63	80	80	57	79	77	88	52	90	102	119
50484	WODEN	86	59	94	59	62	91	66	82	68	53	67	67	48	67	65	74	44	76	86	100
50501	FORT DODGE	85	75	77	76	75	88	81	83	84	75	83	63	75	84	77	88	57	83	91	99
50510	ALBERT CITY	80	55	88	55	58	84	61	76	64	50	63	63	45	62	61	69	41	71	80	94
50511	ALGONA	81	69	79	69	70	85	72	80	76	66	74	60	64	75	71	81	50	77	87	95
50514	ARMSTRONG	86	61	89	60	63	90	67	83	73	58	71	64	52	72	65	80	47	77	89	99
50515	AYRSHIRE	81	56	89	55	58	85	62	77	64	50	64	63	45	63	61	70	41	72	81	94
50516	BADGER	92	83	84	87	85	99	82	94	85	74	84	71	75	87	82	90	57	86	97	109
50517	BANCROFT	79	56	81	55	59	83	62	76	68	54	66	58	48	67	60	75	44	71	83	91
50518	BARNUM	103	71	113	71	75	109	79	98	82	64	81	81	58	81	79	90	53	91	103	120
50519	BODE	95	65	105	65	69	100	73	90	76	59	75	75	53	74	72	82	49	84	95	111
50520	BRADGATE	90	62	99	62	65	95	69	85	71	56	70	70	50	70	68	78	46	80	90	105
50521	BURNSIDE	126	87	138	87	91	133	96	120	100	78	99	99	71	98	96	109	64	112	126	147
50522	BURT	80	56	82	55	59	83	62	77	68	54	66	59	48	66	60	74	43	72	83	91
50523	CALLENDER	95	65	104	65	68	100	72	90	75	59	74	74	53	74	72	82	48	84	95	111
50524	CLARE	102	70	112	70	74	108	78	97	81	63	80	80	57	80	78	89	52	91	103	119
50525	CLARION	92	74	89	75	74	97	79	89	83	70	81	70	68	82	77	88	54	86	96	107
50527	CURLEW	90	62	99	62	65	95	69	86	72	56	71	71	50	70	68	78	46	80	90	105
50528	CYLINDER	123	85	135	85	89	130	94	117	98	76	97	97	69	96	94	107	63	109	124	144
50529	DAKOTA CITY	79	82	65	83	76	85	81	79	82	77	82	62	82	84	79	84	56	80	88	95
50530	DAYTON	84	60	86	59	62	88	66	81	72	57	70	62	52	71	64	79	46	76	88	96
50531	DOLLIVER	98	68	108	67	71	104	75	93	78	61	77	77	55	77	75	85	50	87	99	115
50532	DUNCOMBE	96	68	83	67	69	92	72	84	79	68	78	66	57	82	66	86	52	80	89	103
50533	EAGLE GROVE	95	79	86	79	78	98	83	92	88	75	86	71	73	88	80	94	58	89	99	110
50535	EARLY	87	60	96	60	63	92	67	83	69	54	68	68	49	68	66	76	44	77	87	102
50536	EMMETSBURG	89	66	90	66	69	93	73	86	78	64	76	66	59	77	71	85	51	82	93	103
50538	FARNHAMVILLE	99	71	100	69	74	104	78	96	87	69	84	72	62	85	75	95	56	90	105	113
50539	FENTON	83	57	91	57	60	88	64	79	66	51	65	65	47	65	63	72	42	74	83	97
50540	FONDA	84	59	88	58	62	88	65	81	71	56	69	63	50	69	64	78	45	76	87	97
50541	GILMORE CITY	89	62	97	62	65	94	69	85	72	56	71	69	51	71	68	79	46	80	90	104
50542	GOLDFIELD	84	60	85	59	62	88	66	81	73	58	70	62	52	71	64	80	47	76	88	96
50543	GOWRIE	89	63	91	62	66	93	69	86	77	61	74	65	55	75	68	84	49	80	93	102
50544	HARCOURT	117	80	128	80	84	123	89	111	93	72	92	92	65	91	89	101	59	103	117	136
50545	HARDY	90	62	99	62	65	95	69	86	72	56	71	71	50	70	69	78	46	80	90	105
	IOWA	93	84	87	85	83	95	87	91	89	82	88	71	81	90	85	92	61	90	96	108
	UNITED STATES	100	100	100	100	100	100	100	100	100	100	100	100	100	100	100	100	100	100	100	100

POPULATION CHANGE

A 50546-50671

ZIP CODE #	POST OFFICE NAME	COUNTY FIPS CODE	POPULATION 2000	POPULATION 2009	POPULATION 2014	2000-2009 ANNUAL RATE % Rate	2000-2009 ANNUAL RATE State Centile	HOUSEHOLDS 2000	HOUSEHOLDS 2009	HOUSEHOLDS 2014	HOUSEHOLDS % Annual Rate 2000-2009	HOUSEHOLDS 2009 Average HH Size	FAMILIES 2000	FAMILIES 2009	FAMILIES % Annual Rate 2000-2009
50546	HAVELOCK	151	507	450	425	-1.3	2	203	186	177	-0.9	2.42	149	134	-1.1
50548	HUMBOLDT	091	5727	5458	5305	-0.5	27	2428	2369	2315	-0.3	2.23	1546	1469	-0.6
50551	JOLLEY	025	206	186	176	-1.1	5	88	82	78	-0.8	2.27	67	62	-0.8
50552	KNIERIM	025	109	117	117	0.8	87	53	57	57	0.8	1.74	40	42	0.5
50554	LAURENS	151	1876	1671	1575	-1.2	4	817	750	711	-0.9	2.17	520	465	-1.2
50556	LEDYARD	109	368	330	313	-1.2	4	164	151	145	-0.9	2.19	115	104	-1.1
50557	LEHIGH	187	900	884	867	-0.2	46	390	395	391	0.1	2.24	257	252	-0.2
50558	LIVERMORE	091	735	710	692	-0.4	32	287	280	274	-0.3	2.53	197	189	-0.4
50559	LONE ROCK	109	393	351	333	-1.2	4	161	149	143	-0.8	2.36	111	100	-1.1
50560	LU VERNE	109	639	607	586	-0.6	20	267	262	255	-0.2	2.31	194	187	-0.4
50561	LYTTON	025	561	508	482	-1.1	5	239	222	212	-0.8	2.16	163	148	-1.0
50562	MALLARD	147	610	564	540	-0.8	11	239	228	220	-0.5	2.47	172	162	-0.6
50563	MANSON	025	2758	2603	2505	-0.6	20	1157	1109	1072	-0.5	2.29	798	748	-0.7
50565	MARATHON	021	561	544	539	-0.3	40	242	240	238	-0.1	2.27	177	172	-0.3
50566	MOORLAND	187	447	429	415	-0.4	32	182	178	174	-0.2	2.41	144	139	-0.4
50567	NEMAHA	161	292	268	255	-0.9	8	114	108	103	-0.6	2.48	85	79	-0.8
50568	NEWELL	021	1434	1503	1520	0.5	79	552	596	604	0.8	2.45	388	410	0.6
50569	OTHO	187	876	997	1012	1.4	94	358	422	432	1.8	2.36	252	290	1.5
50570	OTTOSEN	091	308	294	286	-0.5	27	100	98	96	-0.2	2.98	76	73	-0.4
50571	PALMER	151	547	492	468	-1.1	5	220	204	195	-0.8	2.41	159	143	-1.1
50573	PLOVER	151	46	41	38	-1.2	4	16	15	14	-0.7	2.73	12	11	-0.9
50574	POCAHONTAS	151	2528	2277	2154	-1.1	5	1089	1011	963	-0.8	2.20	722	655	-1.0
50575	POMEROY	025	1002	984	966	-0.2	46	437	442	437	0.1	2.12	279	273	-0.2
50576	REMBRANDT	021	462	449	445	-0.3	40	180	179	178	-0.1	2.47	130	126	-0.3
50577	RENWICK	091	547	519	502	-0.6	20	226	215	208	-0.5	2.41	163	152	-0.8
50578	RINGSTED	063	718	671	648	-0.7	15	316	310	302	-0.2	2.16	218	209	-0.5
50579	ROCKWELL CITY	025	2908	2643	2520	-1.0	6	1062	965	915	-1.0	2.35	687	610	-1.3
50581	ROLFE	151	1186	1051	990	-1.3	2	481	437	414	-1.0	2.36	331	293	-1.3
50582	RUTLAND	091	328	289	276	-1.4	1	129	118	113	-1.0	2.45	98	88	-1.2
50583	SAC CITY	161	3177	2854	2699	-1.2	4	1382	1278	1217	-0.8	2.18	876	790	-1.1
50585	SIOUX RAPIDS	041	1208	1147	1128	-0.6	20	506	493	486	-0.3	2.29	334	318	-0.5
50586	SOMERS	025	372	378	375	0.2	68	137	140	140	0.2	2.21	98	98	0.0
50588	STORM LAKE	021	12477	12283	12240	-0.2	46	4376	4333	4301	-0.1	2.59	2910	2814	-0.4
50590	SWEA CITY	109	1133	1029	978	-1.0	6	475	444	426	-0.7	2.32	314	286	-1.0
50591	THOR	091	370	350	340	-0.6	20	153	147	143	-0.4	2.38	110	103	-0.7
50594	VINCENT	187	310	279	266	-1.1	5	130	122	117	-0.7	2.29	98	90	-0.9
50595	WEBSTER CITY	079	9320	8947	8678	-0.4	32	3941	3899	3806	-0.1	2.26	2577	2484	-0.4
50597	WEST BEND	147	1427	1352	1306	-0.6	20	556	539	524	-0.3	2.38	377	359	-0.5
50598	WHITTEMORE	109	1013	953	920	-0.7	15	409	400	389	-0.2	2.38	289	276	-0.5
50599	WOOLSTOCK	197	442	399	378	-1.1	5	187	173	165	-0.8	2.31	143	130	-1.0
50601	ACKLEY	069	2808	2656	2569	-0.6	20	1101	1046	1011	-0.6	2.44	781	728	-0.8
50602	ALLISON	023	1578	1491	1446	-0.6	20	631	622	608	-0.2	2.30	442	426	-0.4
50603	ALTA VISTA	037	611	581	564	-0.5	27	239	233	228	-0.3	2.49	178	171	-0.4
50604	APLINGTON	023	1756	1655	1602	-0.6	20	708	693	676	-0.2	2.32	519	500	-0.4
50605	AREDALE	023	229	245	244	0.7	85	84	91	91	0.9	2.69	63	67	0.7
50606	ARLINGTON	065	1025	979	944	-0.5	27	412	405	394	-0.2	2.42	294	282	-0.4
50607	AURORA	019	520	510	504	-0.2	46	203	204	203	0.1	2.50	152	150	-0.1
50608	AUSTINVILLE	023	12	13	13	0.9	89	5	5	5	0.0	2.60	4	4	0.0
50609	BEAMAN	075	501	489	480	-0.3	40	196	196	194	0.0	2.49	149	146	-0.2
50611	BRISTOW	023	459	484	478	0.6	83	171	185	184	0.9	2.62	135	142	0.5
50612	BUCKINGHAM	171	285	284	282	0.0	58	109	112	112	0.3	2.54	82	82	0.0
50613	CEDAR FALLS	013	38557	39101	39676	0.2	68	13737	14755	15074	0.8	2.40	8310	8667	0.5
50614	CEDAR FALLS	013	48	689	697	33.4	100	25	31	32	2.4	5.19	16	19	1.9
50616	CHARLES CITY	067	10616	10166	9930	-0.5	27	4393	4320	4240	-0.2	2.28	2937	2815	-0.5
50619	CLARKSVILLE	023	2652	2533	2457	-0.5	27	1027	1021	1002	-0.1	2.43	765	746	-0.3
50621	CONRAD	075	1506	1541	1535	0.2	68	614	644	643	0.5	2.35	428	439	0.3
50622	DENVER	017	2954	3294	3418	1.2	93	1118	1283	1344	1.5	2.54	888	1002	1.3
50624	DIKE	075	1607	1745	1762	0.9	89	623	691	700	1.1	2.53	472	513	0.9
50625	DUMONT	023	1152	1152	1130	0.0	58	460	467	460	0.2	2.40	315	312	-0.1
50626	DUNKERTON	013	1740	1772	1772	0.2	68	605	635	638	0.5	2.79	484	499	0.3
50627	ELDORA	083	3765	3560	3439	-0.6	20	1480	1411	1360	-0.5	2.27	954	886	-0.8
50628	ELMA	089	1587	1528	1494	-0.4	32	614	609	599	-0.1	2.39	427	414	-0.3
50629	FAIRBANK	019	2456	2434	2406	-0.1	51	862	885	883	0.3	2.75	661	667	0.1
50630	FREDERICKSBURG	037	1793	1750	1720	-0.3	40	704	716	710	0.2	2.41	512	509	-0.1
50632	GARWIN	171	1071	1108	1113	0.4	76	419	441	445	0.6	2.51	311	320	0.3
50633	GENEVA	069	443	427	419	-0.4	32	172	170	168	-0.1	2.51	120	117	-0.3
50634	GILBERTVILLE	013	766	745	734	-0.3	40	296	300	299	0.1	2.48	224	223	0.0
50635	GLADBROOK	171	1917	1881	1868	-0.2	46	774	767	760	-0.1	2.38	538	521	-0.3
50636	GREENE	023	2001	1876	1808	-0.7	15	870	845	822	-0.3	2.20	601	571	-0.6
50638	GRUNDY CENTER	075	3391	3319	3264	-0.2	46	1403	1407	1389	0.0	2.30	961	941	-0.2
50641	HAZLETON	019	1809	1876	1888	0.4	76	625	671	683	0.8	2.79	437	458	0.5
50642	HOLLAND	075	491	482	474	-0.2	46	194	195	193	0.1	2.47	154	152	-0.1
50643	HUDSON	013	2624	2786	2859	0.6	83	973	1068	1104	1.0	2.61	769	830	0.8
50644	INDEPENDENCE	019	8828	8636	8551	-0.2	46	3410	3423	3412	0.0	2.40	2331	2287	-0.2
50645	IONIA	037	1205	1159	1129	-0.4	32	453	450	442	-0.1	2.55	339	331	-0.3
50647	JANESVILLE	017	1733	1837	1882	0.6	83	697	765	790	1.0	2.40	533	573	0.8
50648	JESUP	013	3603	3813	3885	0.6	83	1331	1455	1494	1.0	2.62	996	1068	0.8
50649	KESLEY	023	46	43	41	-0.7	15	18	17	17	-0.6	2.53	15	14	-0.7
50650	LAMONT	019	845	836	827	-0.1	51	340	347	346	0.2	2.41	240	239	0.0
50651	LA PORTE CITY	013	3991	4001	3983	0.0	58	1537	1578	1578	0.3	2.51	1131	1140	0.1
50652	LINCOLN	171	29	27	27	-0.8	11	10	9	9	-1.1	3.00	8	7	-1.4
50653	MARBLE ROCK	067	717	681	665	-0.6	20	300	296	291	-0.1	2.30	220	213	-0.3
50654	MASONVILLE	019	578	575	567	-0.1	51	209	215	214	0.3	2.67	164	166	0.1
50655	MAYNARD	065	791	763	736	-0.4	32	330	330	321	0.0	2.31	229	223	-0.3
50658	NASHUA	037	2469	2509	2484	0.2	68	1010	1052	1049	0.4	2.38	717	731	0.2
50659	NEW HAMPTON	037	5779	5342	5141	-0.8	11	2310	2214	2147	-0.5	2.35	1554	1455	-0.7
50660	NEW HARTFORD	023	1380	1368	1340	-0.1	51	544	562	557	0.4	2.43	422	429	0.2
50662	OELWEIN	065	7558	6995	6680	-0.8	11	3138	2982	2865	-0.5	2.28	2072	1919	-0.8
50665	PARKERSBURG	023	3217	3143	3072	-0.3	40	1295	1307	1288	0.1	2.40	951	942	-0.1
50666	PLAINFIELD	017	1033	1115	1149	0.8	87	423	475	493	1.3	2.35	305	335	1.0
50667	RAYMOND	013	59	59	59	0.0	58	24	25	25	0.4	2.36	19	19	0.0
50668	READLYN	017	1402	1394	1364	-0.1	51	551	568	561	0.3	2.45	410	413	0.1
50669	REINBECK	075	2613	2535	2486	-0.3	40	1057	1042	1022	-0.2	2.40	759	732	-0.4
50670	SHELL ROCK	023	1859	1806	1767	-0.3	40	746	760	750	0.2	2.33	543	541	0.0
50671	STANLEY	065	333	327	322	-0.2	46	116	117	116	0.1	2.79	87	86	-0.1
	IOWA					0.4					0.7	2.40			0.4
	UNITED STATES					1.0					1.1	2.59			0.9

ZIP CODE #	POST OFFICE NAME	RACE (%) White 2000	White 2009	Black 2000	Black 2009	Asian/Pacific 2000	Asian/Pacific 2009	% Hispanic Origin 2000	% Hispanic Origin 2009	2009 AGE DISTRIBUTION (%) 0-4	5-9	10-14	15-19	20-24	25-44	45-64	65-84	85+	18+	MEDIAN AGE 2009	% 2009 Males	% 2009 Females
50546	HAVELOCK	97.6	97.3	0.2	0.2	0.4	0.4	0.8	1.1	4.4	5.1	5.3	6.9	5.1	20.0	34.2	16.0	2.9	80.9	46.6	51.3	48.7
50548	HUMBOLDT	98.6	98.0	0.2	0.2	0.2	0.4	1.3	2.0	5.9	5.7	5.7	6.1	5.5	20.6	27.1	18.1	5.3	78.9	45.4	48.0	52.0
50551	JOLLEY	99.5	99.5	0.0	0.0	0.0	0.0	1.0	1.1	4.8	5.4	5.9	6.5	4.8	18.8	36.0	15.6	2.2	79.6	47.5	54.8	45.2
50552	KNIERIM	88.1	85.5	7.3	7.7	0.0	0.9	3.7	5.1	2.6	2.6	3.4	4.3	7.7	47.0	23.1	7.7	1.7	88.9	37.3	74.4	25.6
50554	LAURENS	98.8	98.4	0.0	0.0	0.4	0.7	0.9	1.3	4.8	5.0	6.6	7.4	5.0	20.8	28.7	16.9	4.9	78.3	45.3	48.7	51.3
50556	LEDYARD	98.6	98.5	0.0	0.0	0.3	0.3	1.4	2.1	5.8	6.7	7.0	6.4	4.5	19.7	31.2	16.1	2.7	76.7	45.0	50.9	49.1
50557	LEHIGH	98.4	98.0	0.2	0.3	0.2	0.2	0.3	0.6	4.9	5.4	5.5	6.1	6.1	18.8	33.6	17.1	2.5	80.8	46.8	51.8	48.2
50558	LIVERMORE	99.6	99.4	0.0	0.0	0.1	0.1	0.3	0.6	3.9	4.6	5.2	6.9	5.2	22.1	34.1	14.9	3.0	81.4	46.1	50.4	49.6
50559	LONE ROCK	98.7	98.6	0.3	0.3	0.0	0.0	0.3	0.0	5.4	6.6	7.1	8.5	3.1	20.2	30.8	14.5	3.7	75.2	44.2	49.3	50.7
50560	LU VERNE	98.9	98.4	0.0	0.0	0.2	0.3	0.6	1.0	5.8	6.3	6.6	6.6	3.8	21.7	30.0	17.0	2.3	77.4	44.3	52.9	47.1
50561	LYTTON	98.8	98.6	0.4	0.4	0.2	0.2	1.1	1.6	5.1	5.5	5.9	6.5	4.7	20.7	28.3	16.7	6.5	78.9	46.2	50.2	49.8
50562	MALLARD	98.7	98.2	0.2	0.2	0.2	0.5	0.3	0.4	5.7	6.4	6.6	6.9	4.6	20.9	30.9	15.4	2.7	77.0	44.1	51.8	48.2
50563	MANSON	98.8	98.3	0.3	0.3	0.2	0.4	0.5	0.7	5.4	5.8	5.9	6.0	5.3	20.1	29.8	16.9	4.8	79.0	46.0	48.5	51.5
50565	MARATHON	98.0	97.1	0.2	0.2	0.0	0.0	2.0	3.5	4.4	5.0	5.9	7.4	4.8	20.6	33.8	16.0	2.2	80.3	46.3	53.1	46.9
50566	MOORLAND	98.7	98.4	0.4	0.7	0.2	0.2	0.9	1.2	5.6	6.1	6.8	6.8	4.2	20.7	32.2	15.2	2.6	77.4	44.9	49.9	50.1
50567	NEMAHA	97.6	96.6	0.0	0.0	0.7	1.1	1.0	1.5	6.3	7.1	7.5	6.3	4.1	21.6	31.0	13.8	2.2	75.0	42.9	52.2	47.8
50568	NEWELL	97.6	96.0	0.2	0.3	0.6	1.1	2.1	3.5	5.9	7.1	7.3	6.7	5.1	21.2	28.1	14.2	4.4	75.4	42.6	48.7	51.3
50569	OTHO	98.1	97.4	0.7	1.0	0.1	0.2	0.6	0.9	6.1	6.5	6.7	6.4	5.8	24.4	29.6	12.9	1.5	76.6	39.8	49.1	50.9
50570	OTTOSEN	97.7	96.6	0.0	0.0	1.6	2.4	0.6	1.0	5.8	6.5	7.1	6.8	4.1	24.1	28.9	13.6	3.1	75.9	41.6	51.0	49.0
50571	PALMER	98.4	98.0	1.1	1.4	0.2	0.2	0.5	0.8	4.7	5.9	6.5	7.5	4.5	19.9	34.1	14.6	2.2	78.0	45.5	52.8	47.2
50573	PLOVER	97.8	97.6	0.0	0.0	0.0	0.0	0.0	0.0	4.9	4.9	4.9	7.3	4.9	19.5	29.3	19.5	4.9	78.0	46.9	48.8	51.2
50574	POCAHONTAS	98.3	97.9	0.3	0.4	0.1	0.1	0.8	1.2	5.3	5.7	5.9	6.7	5.1	18.6	30.1	18.1	4.5	78.8	46.8	47.7	52.3
50575	POMEROY	99.5	99.5	0.1	0.1	0.0	0.0	0.4	0.6	5.5	5.7	5.7	5.5	5.9	20.1	27.4	17.9	6.3	79.3	46.4	48.2	51.8
50576	REMBRANDT	97.4	96.0	0.0	0.0	0.2	0.2	2.6	4.2	5.3	6.0	6.7	5.6	4.7	20.9	36.1	12.7	2.0	78.4	45.5	52.8	47.2
50577	RENWICK	98.7	98.3	0.0	0.0	0.2	0.4	0.9	1.2	5.2	6.7	7.5	7.3	3.5	22.9	29.3	15.0	2.5	76.1	42.8	52.0	48.0
50578	RINGSTED	99.7	99.7	0.0	0.0	0.1	0.1	0.0	0.0	4.5	4.9	5.5	6.4	4.6	22.4	33.7	14.6	3.4	80.9	46.0	50.5	49.5
50579	ROCKWELL CITY	96.3	95.2	1.7	2.1	0.3	0.4	1.3	2.0	4.4	4.8	5.1	5.7	5.6	26.8	27.8	15.6	4.3	83.4	43.4	53.7	46.3
50581	ROLFE	98.3	97.8	0.3	0.3	0.2	0.4	0.7	1.0	5.6	6.0	6.1	6.9	6.0	19.5	28.3	17.1	4.5	77.9	44.9	49.0	51.0
50582	RUTLAND	98.8	98.3	0.0	0.0	0.6	1.0	0.3	0.0	5.5	6.6	6.2	5.5	4.5	21.8	32.2	15.2	2.4	77.9	44.8	50.9	49.1
50583	SAC CITY	98.8	98.4	0.2	0.2	0.1	0.2	0.7	1.1	4.9	5.1	5.4	6.0	5.3	21.5	29.5	17.2	5.0	80.5	46.2	47.9	52.1
50585	SIOUX RAPIDS	98.8	98.2	0.2	0.2	0.1	0.2	1.3	2.2	5.3	5.7	6.5	6.5	5.2	19.7	32.0	14.6	4.4	78.5	45.7	49.3	50.7
50586	SOMERS	94.9	94.2	2.7	2.9	0.3	0.3	1.6	2.6	4.2	5.8	6.9	6.6	4.8	31.5	26.2	11.6	2.4	78.8	38.9	59.0	41.0
50588	STORM LAKE	82.5	75.4	0.4	0.5	6.8	10.2	18.0	24.3	6.3	6.4	6.5	8.9	9.3	24.5	23.8	11.3	3.0	76.7	35.5	50.2	49.8
50590	SWEA CITY	98.1	97.2	0.0	0.0	0.2	0.3	1.9	2.9	6.3	6.7	6.2	5.9	5.2	20.3	29.6	16.3	3.3	77.3	44.4	49.9	50.1
50591	THOR	98.9	98.3	0.0	0.0	0.5	0.9	0.5	0.9	6.0	6.6	7.1	7.1	4.3	21.7	30.3	14.3	2.6	75.4	42.8	54.6	45.4
50594	VINCENT	97.4	96.1	0.0	0.0	0.3	0.7	1.9	3.6	5.0	5.7	5.4	5.4	4.7	22.6	32.3	16.5	2.5	81.0	45.8	52.0	48.0
50595	WEBSTER CITY	95.9	94.1	0.3	0.4	2.2	3.6	1.2	1.8	6.8	6.3	6.5	6.5	5.6	23.9	26.2	14.6	3.5	76.3	40.5	48.5	51.5
50597	WEST BEND	99.2	98.8	0.1	0.1	0.1	0.3	0.7	1.1	5.0	5.3	5.8	7.4	5.7	19.6	29.4	16.4	5.3	79.1	45.7	48.7	51.3
50598	WHITTEMORE	98.8	98.6	0.6	0.6	0.1	0.2	0.5	0.6	6.3	6.9	7.3	7.6	4.5	21.8	29.8	13.1	2.6	74.7	41.5	51.9	48.1
50599	WOOLSTOCK	98.9	98.2	0.0	0.0	0.2	0.5	1.1	1.5	4.8	5.8	6.3	6.8	3.8	17.3	36.6	16.3	2.5	78.9	47.4	50.1	49.9
50601	ACKLEY	95.5	93.6	0.2	0.2	0.4	0.6	5.5	7.8	6.0	6.3	6.2	5.8	4.9	20.0	28.2	17.4	5.1	77.7	45.4	48.3	51.7
50602	ALLISON	99.2	99.0	0.0	0.0	0.3	0.3	0.5	0.7	5.1	5.7	6.1	6.8	4.6	22.9	26.7	17.0	5.2	78.8	44.1	49.6	50.4
50603	ALTA VISTA	99.3	99.1	0.0	0.0	0.2	0.2	0.3	0.7	7.1	7.6	7.4	6.7	4.1	24.1	28.7	12.4	1.9	73.7	40.1	52.8	47.2
50604	APLINGTON	99.0	98.6	0.0	0.0	0.2	0.4	0.5	0.7	5.8	6.0	6.3	6.8	4.9	20.2	27.7	17.6	4.7	77.2	45.0	48.2	51.8
50605	AREDALE	98.7	98.0	0.0	0.0	0.0	0.0	0.9	1.6	6.1	8.2	6.9	7.8	4.9	22.9	26.1	15.1	2.0	73.9	39.8	50.6	49.4
50606	ARLINGTON	98.9	98.6	0.1	0.2	0.1	0.2	0.3	0.3	5.8	6.4	7.0	7.3	4.0	21.2	31.5	13.6	3.2	76.1	43.4	49.1	50.9
50607	AURORA	97.1	97.1	0.8	0.8	0.0	0.0	0.4	0.2	7.3	7.5	7.6	6.7	4.7	21.8	30.2	12.2	2.2	73.3	40.9	51.4	48.6
50608	AUSTINVILLE	100.0	100.0	0.0	0.0	0.0	0.0	0.0	0.0	7.7	7.7	7.7	0.0	7.7	23.1	46.2	0.0	0.0	76.9	43.8	69.2	30.8
50609	BEAMAN	98.6	98.6	0.0	0.0	0.6	0.6	0.2	0.2	5.7	6.5	7.0	7.0	4.5	20.2	33.7	13.5	1.8	76.3	44.2	50.7	49.3
50611	BRISTOW	98.5	97.9	0.0	0.0	0.0	0.0	1.1	1.7	5.8	7.4	6.6	7.6	5.4	23.6	26.7	15.1	1.9	75.4	40.3	51.2	48.8
50612	BUCKINGHAM	98.6	98.6	0.3	0.4	0.3	0.4	0.7	0.7	5.6	5.6	6.3	6.3	5.3	21.8	31.0	15.5	2.5	78.5	44.2	50.7	49.3
50613	CEDAR FALLS	95.3	94.8	1.5	1.7	1.6	1.8	1.0	1.1	4.7	4.4	4.4	9.6	17.0	24.2	22.9	10.1	2.6	83.6	31.5	47.3	52.7
50614	CEDAR FALLS	95.7	94.6	2.1	2.3	2.1	1.9	0.0	1.0	0.6	1.0	1.2	42.8	38.9	4.4	5.5	2.2	3.5	94.9	20.6	40.1	59.9
50616	CHARLES CITY	97.4	96.4	0.3	0.4	0.7	1.2	1.7	2.5	6.2	6.0	6.1	6.7	5.2	21.8	26.8	16.9	4.2	77.4	43.3	47.4	52.6
50619	CLARKSVILLE	99.1	98.9	0.0	0.0	0.3	0.3	0.3	0.4	6.3	6.7	6.8	6.3	4.5	22.9	28.8	13.9	3.9	76.2	42.3	49.5	50.5
50621	CONRAD	98.6	98.6	0.0	0.0	0.3	0.3	0.5	0.4	6.7	6.7	6.7	6.6	5.5	20.2	28.7	14.8	4.1	75.5	42.8	48.4	51.6
50622	DENVER	98.8	98.4	0.1	0.1	0.1	0.2	0.7	1.0	6.0	6.6	7.0	6.5	4.5	22.7	31.9	12.6	2.3	75.9	42.7	50.0	50.0
50624	DIKE	98.8	98.9	0.1	0.1	0.2	0.2	0.7	0.7	5.5	6.2	6.9	7.2	4.6	25.8	29.1	13.1	1.5	76.9	40.5	50.5	49.5
50625	DUMONT	98.9	98.3	0.2	0.2	0.3	0.7	1.0	1.6	5.3	5.7	5.8	7.0	5.5	22.0	27.3	16.6	4.9	78.6	44.0	49.5	50.5
50626	DUNKERTON	98.0	97.9	0.0	0.0	1.1	1.2	0.8	0.7	6.8	6.9	6.9	7.2	5.9	27.0	27.9	10.3	1.0	75.0	37.4	50.9	49.1
50627	ELDORA	96.0	94.5	1.1	1.3	0.8	1.3	2.5	3.8	5.4	5.5	5.8	11.5	5.7	19.0	27.8	14.8	4.5	74.2	42.0	49.8	50.2
50628	ELMA	99.5	99.4	0.1	0.1	0.1	0.1	0.1	0.2	5.6	6.1	6.2	6.5	3.9	22.3	28.3	16.4	4.7	78.1	44.6	50.0	50.0
50629	FAIRBANK	98.4	98.3	0.3	0.4	0.7	0.7	0.9	1.1	9.0	9.0	8.8	8.2	6.0	23.6	24.4	9.7	1.3	68.1	31.9	51.2	48.8
50630	FREDERICKSBURG	97.4	96.3	0.2	0.2	0.4	0.7	1.7	2.5	7.2	7.1	7.3	6.5	5.3	21.9	28.1	13.5	3.1	74.3	40.8	50.1	49.9
50632	GARWIN	97.2	97.1	0.1	0.1	0.0	0.0	1.9	2.0	6.8	6.2	6.4	6.8	6.2	23.6	29.6	12.6	1.8	76.4	40.4	50.8	49.2
50633	GENEVA	98.6	98.1	0.0	0.0	0.2	0.2	1.1	1.6	4.0	5.6	6.6	9.4	4.7	22.7	31.1	13.6	2.3	77.3	43.0	51.1	48.9
50634	GILBERTVILLE	99.1	99.1	0.3	0.3	0.3	0.3	0.8	0.8	5.4	6.0	6.4	7.7	5.2	21.6	31.8	14.1	1.7	77.3	43.3	50.3	49.7
50635	GLADBROOK	99.0	98.9	0.1	0.1	0.0	0.0	0.9	0.9	5.4	5.4	6.0	7.2	5.4	20.9	28.0	17.2	4.5	78.3	44.7	47.4	52.6
50636	GREENE	99.3	99.0	0.2	0.2	0.3	0.5	0.9	1.2	4.6	5.0	5.2	5.8	5.2	21.3	30.3	18.6	4.1	81.2	47.0	50.4	49.6
50638	GRUNDY CENTER	99.1	99.1	0.1	0.1	0.2	0.2	0.7	0.7	5.3	5.6	6.0	6.6	4.9	21.9	28.2	16.8	4.6	78.8	44.7	47.8	52.2
50641	HAZLETON	98.2	98.1	0.1	0.1	0.2	0.2	1.5	1.5	9.3	8.9	8.6	7.2	6.4	26.1	23.5	8.9	1.1	68.8	32.5	52.0	48.0
50642	HOLLAND	98.8	98.8	0.2	0.2	0.4	0.4	0.4	0.6	5.4	6.2	7.1	7.3	4.1	24.3	29.3	14.1	2.3	76.8	42.2	51.7	48.3
50643	HUDSON	98.6	98.5	0.1	0.1	0.6	0.6	0.5	0.5	5.6	6.2	7.1	7.7	5.0	22.4	32.4	12.3	1.4	76.3	42.1	48.7	51.3
50644	INDEPENDENCE	98.1	98.1	0.3	0.3	0.6	0.6	0.6	0.6	6.1	6.2	6.9	6.7	5.5	23.9	27.7	13.4	3.5	76.2	40.9	49.0	51.0
50645	IONIA	99.0	98.7	0.0	0.0	0.2	0.3	0.5	0.8	5.8	7.2	7.8	7.6	4.2	21.9	30.7	13.3	1.5	74.4	41.6	51.6	48.4
50647	JANESVILLE	98.7	98.1	0.2	0.3	0.5	0.7	0.3	0.5	5.1	5.4	5.9	5.7	4.2	23.6	33.7	14.9	1.5	80.0	45.1	49.9	50.1
50648	JESUP	99.2	99.2	0.1	0.1	0.1	0.1	0.6	0.5	6.5	6.7	6.8	7.1	5.4	24.7	28.4	12.3	2.0	75.3	39.3	49.8	50.2
50649	KESLEY	100.0	100.0	0.0	0.0	0.0	0.0	0.0	0.0	4.7	7.0	7.0	9.3	2.3	23.3	30.2	16.3	0.0	76.7	42.5	58.1	41.9
50650	LAMONT	99.1	99.0	0.2	0.2	0.2	0.2	0.4	0.4	6.7	7.3	8.0	7.2	3.9	23.2	29.7	11.8	2.2	73.2	39.9	53.1	46.9
50651	LA PORTE CITY	99.1	99.0	0.1	0.1	0.2	0.1	0.3	0.3	6.7	6.9	6.9	6.6	5.4	24.1	27.4	13.0	2.9	75.3	39.7	49.0	51.0
50652	LINCOLN	100.0	100.0	0.0	0.0	0.0	0.0	0.0	0.0	7.4	7.4	7.4	7.4	7.4	29.6	29.6	3.7	0.0	70.4	33.8	51.9	48.1
50653	MARBLE ROCK	99.2	98.8	0.0	0.0	0.6	0.9	0.4	0.7	5.6	5.9	6.6	7.5	4.6	22.8	31.3	13.7	2.2	77.2	42.9	52.1	47.9
50654	MASONVILLE	99.1	99.0	0.2	0.2	0.2	0.2	0.5	0.9	7.0	7.5	7.8	7.7	4.5	23.7	28.2	12.0	1.7	72.9	39.3	50.8	49.2
50655	MAYNARD	99.7	99.7	0.0	0.0	0.0	0.0	0.3	0.4	6.6	7.3	7.5	5.9	4.1	23.2	30.7	12.5	2.4	74.7	42.1	53.7	46.3
50658	NASHUA	99.3	99.1	0.1	0.1	0.2	0.2	0.2	0.4	5.5	5.7	6.2	7.0	5.5	22.4	27.9	16.9	2.8	78.4	43.1	49.7	50.3
50659	NEW HAMPTON	98.8	98.5	0.0	0.0	0.3	0.6	0.4	0.5	5.7	6.2	6.5	6.4	5.0	23.7	27.7	15.0	3.9	77.3	42.4	49.6	50.4
50660	NEW HARTFORD	98.8	98.6	0.1	0.1	0.1	0.2	1.2	1.5	5.5	6.0	6.7	6.4	4.2	25.1	31.6	12.9	1.6	77.8	41.7	50.2	49.8
50662	OELWEIN	97.4	96.6	0.4	0.5	0.4	0.7	2.2	3.2	6.4	6.4	6.2	6.2	5.7	22.9	25.8	15.8	4.5	77.0	41.6	47.5	52.5
50665	PARKERSBURG	99.1	99.0	0.1	0.1	0.1	0.1	0.5	0.6	5.7	6.3	6.8	6.8	5.2	22.9	29.1	14.6	2.6	77.0	42.2	48.8	51.2
50666	PLAINFIELD	99.6	99.5	0.0	0.0	0.1	0.2	0.5	0.7	5.7	6.0	6.5	6.6	4.2	25.4	30.1	13.4	2.0	77.5	41.4	51.8	48.2
50667	RAYMOND	100.0	100.0	0.0	0.0	0.0	0.0	1.7	0.0	6.8	6.8	6.8	6.8	3.4	27.1	28.8	13.6	0.0	72.9	39.4	50.8	49.2
50668	READLYN	98.6	98.2	0.3	0.4	0.6	0.9	0.4	0.7	5.9	5.9	6.5	7.6	5.2	21.9	29.6	14.9	2.6	77.0	42.7	50.2	49.8
50669	REINBECK	99.3	99.3	0.1	0.1	0.3	0.4	0.5	0.5	5.1	5.4	6.0	6.9	5.0	22.1	29.5	16.1	3.9	79.0	44.6	49.5	50.5
50670	SHELL ROCK	98.6	98.2	0.2	0.2	0.3	0.6	0.3	0.4	5.4	5.8	6.2	6.1	4.8	24.5	31.8	12.3	3.2	78.6	42.6	50.7	49.3
50671	STANLEY	97.9	97.9	0.6	0.6	0.0	0.0	0.3	0.3	7.0	7.6	7.6	6.7	4.6	21.7	29.4	13.1	2.1	73.4	41.0	50.8	49.2
	IOWA	93.9	91.9	2.1	2.5	1.3	2.1	2.8	4.1	6.5	6.4	6.5	7.3	7.1	25.2	26.5	11.9	2.6	76.5	38.1	49.3	50.7
	UNITED STATES	75.1	72.0	12.3	12.7	3.8	4.6	12.5	15.7	6.8	6.7	6.6	7.1	6.9	27.0	26.0	10.9	1.9	75.7	36.9	49.2	50.8

#	POST OFFICE NAME	2009 Per Capita Income	2009 HH Income Base	2009 HOUSEHOLD INCOME DISTRIBUTION (%) Less than $25,000	$25,000 to $49,999	$50,000 to $99,999	$100,000 to $149,999	$150,000 or More	MEDIAN HOUSEHOLD INCOME 2009	2014	2009 National Centile	2009 State Centile	2009 Home Value Base	2009 HOME VALUE DISTRIBUTION (%) Less than $50,000	$50,000 to $89,999	$90,000 to $174,999	$175,000 to $399,999	$400,000 or More	2009 Median Home Value
50546	HAVELOCK	19786	186	25.8	39.2	30.1	2.7	2.2	40000	40939	33	15	149	45.6	23.5	29.5	0.7	0.7	55909
50548	HUMBOLDT	26324	2369	22.8	24.9	41.0	7.2	4.1	51979	52512	66	78	1755	12.6	24.4	49.5	12.6	0.9	106966
50551	JOLLEY	26933	82	17.1	40.2	34.1	4.9	3.7	46487	48146	53	54	61	24.6	24.6	32.8	18.0	0.0	91667
50552	KNIERIM	24874	57	35.1	29.8	35.1	0.0	0.0	35752	36716	20	4	45	22.2	35.6	35.6	2.2	4.4	72500
50554	LAURENS	23606	750	28.5	32.4	32.3	3.6	3.2	42140	44478	40	25	582	28.7	39.5	26.8	4.5	0.5	70968
50556	LEDYARD	22250	151	30.5	31.8	28.5	7.9	1.3	39688	42366	32	14	117	49.6	23.1	15.4	7.7	4.3	50625
50557	LEHIGH	21354	395	28.9	31.9	33.2	4.6	1.5	41952	44867	39	24	317	33.4	26.5	33.4	5.0	1.6	73400
50558	LIVERMORE	18474	280	27.9	37.1	29.6	3.6	1.8	40180	41441	33	16	227	38.8	34.4	19.4	4.4	3.1	62600
50559	LONE ROCK	18680	149	32.2	35.6	27.5	2.7	2.0	38738	41131	29	11	116	44.8	31.9	17.2	4.3	1.7	55455
50560	LU VERNE	19349	262	28.2	38.9	27.5	4.6	0.8	37195	38746	24	6	195	46.7	27.7	19.5	3.6	2.6	54063
50561	LYTTON	23259	222	22.1	40.5	31.1	4.1	2.3	44017	45535	45	39	161	34.2	26.7	29.8	8.1	1.2	72500
50562	MALLARD	21886	228	31.6	32.5	27.6	3.1	5.3	37929	40000	26	8	176	51.7	22.7	21.6	3.4	0.6	49189
50563	MANSON	24391	1109	27.5	28.2	34.3	6.8	3.2	46062	47368	52	51	851	13.3	39.2	37.8	8.0	1.6	87584
50565	MARATHON	17835	240	32.9	41.3	22.1	2.5	1.3	35459	37322	19	4	172	44.8	19.2	22.1	8.1	5.8	56000
50566	MOORLAND	25849	178	19.7	26.4	42.1	5.6	6.2	53230	53672	68	82	145	16.6	26.2	44.1	9.0	4.1	98750
50567	NEMAHA	22612	108	24.1	25.0	42.6	7.4	0.9	50684	52322	63	72	76	21.1	25.0	42.1	6.6	5.3	94286
50568	NEWELL	18530	596	24.8	38.4	30.9	5.9	0.0	41164	43068	37	21	467	30.8	32.3	31.0	4.3	1.5	73676
50569	OTHO	22966	422	19.0	33.4	39.1	7.6	0.9	48138	50262	57	62	328	24.7	42.7	31.1	0.6	0.9	73273
50570	OTTOSEN	17505	98	21.4	38.8	33.7	4.1	2.0	44369	46199	46	40	74	37.8	28.4	23.0	8.1	2.7	61667
50571	PALMER	19563	204	30.4	27.5	36.3	4.9	1.0	42773	45204	42	30	155	41.9	33.5	15.5	7.1	1.9	55682
50573	PLOVER	14329	15	26.7	46.7	26.7	0.0	0.0	33972	35000	15	3	12	41.7	33.3	25.0	0.0	0.0	60000
50574	POCAHONTAS	24079	1011	27.9	32.9	30.8	5.1	3.3	42199	43568	40	25	813	28.0	39.4	27.1	4.8	0.7	69384
50575	POMEROY	21922	442	29.2	38.7	25.6	4.3	2.3	35551	36394	19	4	344	40.1	29.1	27.3	3.2	0.3	66875
50576	REMBRANDT	19448	179	24.0	40.8	31.3	3.4	0.6	40156	41528	33	16	130	42.3	19.2	30.0	8.5	0.0	59091
50577	RENWICK	20956	215	22.8	31.6	38.6	6.0	0.9	46236	46675	52	52	175	32.6	28.0	21.7	13.1	4.6	72917
50578	RINGSTED	23722	310	31.6	31.6	27.7	5.8	3.2	38712	39704	29	11	232	38.8	22.8	25.4	10.8	2.2	71250
50579	ROCKWELL CITY	19987	965	27.2	32.4	33.8	4.5	2.2	40895	41658	36	19	731	22.6	40.9	31.5	4.4	0.7	75379
50581	ROLFE	18895	437	31.1	34.8	27.5	4.8	1.8	38649	39350	29	11	347	54.2	24.8	19.3	1.2	0.6	47157
50582	RUTLAND	20396	118	25.4	33.9	33.9	5.1	1.7	44376	46542	46	40	93	41.9	25.8	21.5	6.5	4.3	58333
50583	SAC CITY	21820	1278	30.4	35.8	27.2	4.6	2.0	39251	40522	30	13	959	31.7	36.1	28.3	2.7	1.3	66818
50585	SIOUX RAPIDS	20487	493	27.0	35.7	31.6	4.3	1.4	39108	41060	30	13	374	43.3	32.9	19.3	2.9	1.6	55682
50586	SOMERS	18203	140	35.7	28.6	32.1	3.6	0.0	35920	38451	20	4	115	35.7	31.3	30.4	0.9	1.7	62917
50588	STORM LAKE	20733	4333	24.1	29.9	36.2	6.3	3.6	46354	49049	52	53	2932	10.8	30.5	43.7	12.3	2.7	101316
50590	SWEA CITY	19398	444	30.6	33.1	30.4	4.7	1.1	38759	40195	29	12	346	51.4	29.5	13.0	3.8	2.3	49254
50591	THOR	21639	147	21.8	29.3	41.5	7.5	0.0	48408	50185	58	63	118	33.9	26.3	24.6	14.4	0.8	64000
50594	VINCENT	24737	122	19.7	22.1	52.5	5.7	0.0	58935	56719	76	91	105	12.4	21.0	39.0	21.0	6.7	116477
50595	WEBSTER CITY	25663	3899	22.2	28.6	39.1	7.2	2.8	49178	50857	59	66	2783	14.9	33.2	43.3	7.3	1.3	92229
50597	WEST BEND	23601	539	23.6	35.1	33.0	3.7	4.6	43983	45783	45	38	446	27.6	32.1	31.4	8.3	0.7	75758
50598	WHITTEMORE	20495	400	25.3	34.8	34.5	4.0	1.5	43534	45082	44	34	309	33.3	26.9	32.4	5.5	1.9	67857
50599	WOOLSTOCK	25959	173	13.9	30.1	45.1	9.2	1.7	54734	53967	71	85	135	23.0	36.3	28.1	11.1	1.5	74231
50601	ACKLEY	21203	1046	24.7	31.5	36.2	5.4	2.1	45647	47158	50	48	823	25.2	41.1	28.9	3.5	1.3	74837
50602	ALLISON	22062	622	23.2	33.6	35.5	6.3	1.4	46056	47526	51	51	498	15.7	46.0	29.1	6.8	2.4	80333
50603	ALTA VISTA	21140	233	18.5	37.8	36.1	5.6	2.1	45658	47189	50	48	194	28.4	25.3	35.6	9.3	1.5	83636
50604	APLINGTON	22260	693	24.0	32.6	36.5	5.2	1.7	44583	47407	47	42	571	18.2	32.7	39.1	8.9	1.1	88962
50605	AREDALE	18601	91	24.2	34.1	35.2	4.4	2.2	43631	45315	44	35	72	36.1	26.4	25.0	9.7	2.8	68000
50606	ARLINGTON	19694	405	33.3	31.6	27.2	3.5	4.4	37315	37967	25	7	312	33.7	30.8	21.5	10.9	3.2	66452
50607	AURORA	22583	204	31.4	30.4	27.0	4.9	6.4	41141	43418	36	20	165	29.7	26.7	28.5	10.3	4.8	78214
50608	AUSTINVILLE	19613	5	0.0	60.0	40.0	0.0	0.0	47183	47183	55	57	4	50.0	25.0	25.0	0.0	0.0	60000
50609	BEAMAN	22024	196	16.3	36.7	40.3	5.1	1.5	47967	50000	57	61	143	16.1	22.4	39.2	21.7	0.7	110326
50611	BRISTOW	18622	185	21.1	39.5	34.6	3.8	1.1	43528	46120	44	34	147	31.3	25.9	29.3	10.9	2.7	80455
50612	BUCKINGHAM	23746	112	19.6	25.9	42.0	9.8	2.7	53361	53083	69	82	88	6.8	21.6	45.5	20.5	5.7	118056
50613	CEDAR FALLS	26164	14755	22.7	24.2	37.4	9.3	6.4	53069	54725	68	81	9708	9.8	11.6	49.1	26.6	2.8	134629
50614	CEDAR FALLS	14254	31	16.1	19.4	32.3	12.9	19.4	66720	60000	85	97	21	0.0	4.8	47.6	47.6	0.0	170833
50616	CHARLES CITY	22432	4320	27.0	29.1	37.1	5.0	1.8	43916	45860	45	38	3105	12.2	33.2	43.3	10.9	0.4	96233
50619	CLARKSVILLE	20947	1021	26.8	30.2	35.4	6.3	1.4	43884	45972	45	37	799	21.3	30.8	38.4	7.9	1.6	87574
50621	CONRAD	26276	644	18.2	26.6	42.4	10.6	2.3	56144	58975	73	88	495	9.5	25.9	46.7	18.0	0.0	108513
50622	DENVER	26398	1283	15.1	28.7	40.1	11.4	4.7	55705	56581	72	87	1075	5.9	7.3	48.2	34.2	4.4	149709
50624	DIKE	23338	691	18.2	29.8	41.5	7.8	2.6	51366	53034	65	75	559	8.6	16.8	49.2	22.9	2.5	124629
50625	DUMONT	18921	467	30.8	33.0	30.6	4.3	1.3	38367	40142	28	10	366	43.2	33.6	18.3	4.1	0.8	56410
50626	DUNKERTON	19957	635	15.3	33.4	45.8	3.8	1.7	50741	52522	63	72	507	13.0	24.5	46.0	15.0	1.6	110901
50627	ELDORA	21009	1411	26.5	31.3	36.2	4.7	1.3	44657	45389	47	43	1032	27.1	36.9	29.1	6.2	0.7	76455
50628	ELMA	18691	609	28.2	32.0	34.5	4.8	0.5	42642	45321	41	29	485	34.0	29.7	23.3	10.3	2.7	73438
50629	FAIRBANK	17716	885	28.6	30.4	34.6	5.4	1.0	42819	44136	42	30	703	16.1	23.3	43.1	14.4	3.1	107480
50630	FREDERICKSBURG	20716	716	22.9	32.1	38.3	4.7	2.0	44087	46237	46	39	582	12.4	32.1	45.0	9.6	0.9	98205
50632	GARWIN	23366	441	17.0	27.4	46.5	7.7	1.4	53762	54527	69	83	349	16.6	39.5	31.5	12.0	0.3	84189
50633	GENEVA	23496	170	19.4	29.4	40.0	7.1	4.1	50818	51794	63	73	134	32.1	35.8	17.9	11.2	3.0	68182
50634	GILBERTVILLE	23972	300	15.0	33.0	41.0	9.0	2.0	51222	53206	64	75	258	3.1	22.9	49.6	22.9	1.6	127703
50635	GLADBROOK	23157	767	19.4	34.3	36.5	6.4	3.4	46951	48149	54	57	614	15.6	35.3	40.2	6.5	2.3	88929
50636	GREENE	23364	845	24.7	30.4	36.8	6.4	1.7	46463	47861	53	54	693	22.9	32.6	34.8	8.7	1.0	83889
50638	GRUNDY CENTER	23772	1407	19.7	32.0	39.1	7.6	1.6	48724	51430	58	65	1124	11.1	28.4	49.0	10.5	1.0	104883
50641	HAZLETON	16139	671	29.1	32.5	35.3	1.9	1.2	40831	41917	35	18	537	38.5	23.3	28.7	9.1	0.4	67167
50642	HOLLAND	22625	195	18.5	39.0	34.9	5.1	2.6	45413	47179	49	46	156	12.8	35.9	38.5	9.6	3.2	92500
50643	HUDSON	27275	1068	11.3	27.3	44.1	11.3	5.9	61522	60845	79	94	889	4.2	11.5	47.8	31.5	5.1	143695
50644	INDEPENDENCE	25282	3423	21.0	31.9	36.1	7.0	4.0	47558	48728	56	60	2623	10.9	26.2	48.4	11.7	2.8	107160
50645	IONIA	19428	450	22.7	31.6	40.7	4.0	1.1	46365	47633	52	53	380	18.9	25.3	36.8	14.2	4.7	101190
50647	JANESVILLE	27419	765	16.2	28.0	44.3	7.7	3.8	55230	56101	72	87	628	7.2	13.7	41.1	33.0	5.1	147603
50648	JESUP	21678	1455	19.1	27.8	45.2	6.2	1.7	52302	52667	66	78	1195	13.6	26.0	44.4	14.6	1.3	105969
50649	KESLEY	19942	17	17.6	41.2	35.3	5.9	0.0	43583	46091	44	35	13	0.0	30.8	46.2	23.1	0.0	118750
50650	LAMONT	20039	347	33.1	28.8	30.5	5.5	2.0	37032	39218	24	6	256	29.7	28.9	26.6	12.5	2.3	78571
50651	LA PORTE CITY	24149	1578	19.6	25.3	44.4	7.9	2.7	53268	54415	68	82	1260	12.9	29.9	44.0	12.0	1.2	101872
50652	LINCOLN	14074	9	22.2	44.4	33.3	0.0	0.0	42288	42288	40	26	7	0.0	42.9	57.1	0.0	0.0	106250
50653	MARBLE ROCK	24801	296	23.0	29.7	37.8	5.7	3.7	48367	48552	57	63	234	19.7	20.9	39.7	14.5	5.1	103804
50654	MASONVILLE	20479	215	20.9	33.5	35.8	7.9	1.9	46236	46615	52	52	170	17.6	17.1	37.1	22.9	5.3	116667
50655	MAYNARD	20671	330	28.5	30.6	35.2	5.2	0.6	43636	45491	44	35	262	16.8	34.7	34.7	11.5	2.3	88571
50658	NASHUA	20055	1052	25.1	36.2	31.9	5.8	1.0	41385	43476	37	22	849	22.7	30.3	35.8	10.1	1.1	86136
50659	NEW HAMPTON	24529	2214	19.8	27.5	42.8	7.5	2.4	52212	51951	66	78	1712	12.5	25.3	48.6	13.0	0.6	105714
50660	NEW HARTFORD	22340	562	22.6	30.1	37.9	8.4	1.1	47589	49614	56	60	458	18.8	27.3	33.4	17.7	2.8	96207
50662	OELWEIN	21707	2982	31.0	30.8	32.7	3.9	1.7	38204	39124	27	9	2215	24.7	37.7	32.9	4.0	0.8	76206
50665	PARKERSBURG	22915	1307	24.3	30.1	35.2	8.0	2.4	46070	48788	52	51	1049	11.2	28.0	49.5	10.1	1.1	104550
50666	PLAINFIELD	22522	475	21.5	30.3	42.1	4.4	1.7	48702	51141	58	65	393	12.5	24.4	50.6	10.9	1.5	105168
50667	RAYMOND	25055	25	20.0	24.0	48.0	8.0	0.0	54473	53167	70	85	22	9.1	18.2	59.1	13.6	0.0	114286
50668	READLYN	23889	568	19.4	24.6	44.5	10.2	1.2	54804	55724	71	86	480	5.4	19.8	56.9	14.4	3.5	117828
50669	REINBECK	22566	1042	19.4	34.8	36.6	7.0	2.2	47185	49137	55	58	840	13.8	28.7	42.5	12.3	2.7	101442
50670	SHELL ROCK	23729	760	20.5	27.2	42.4	8.6	1.3	51618	52217	65	76	604	7.9	28.5	45.5	15.7	2.3	108582
50671	STANLEY	20289	117	31.6	29.9	26.5	5.1	6.8	40973	45000	36	20	94	26.6	27.7	29.8	11.7	4.3	82000
	IOWA	25379		21.1	28.2	37.9	8.6	4.3	50616	52941				14.7	22.5	41.6	18.6	2.6	110128
	UNITED STATES	27277		20.9	24.4	35.3	11.7	7.6	54719	56938				9.3	13.1	31.6	32.6	13.5	162279

#	POST OFFICE NAME	FINANCIAL SERVICES: Auto Loan	FINANCIAL SERVICES: Home Loan	FINANCIAL SERVICES: Invest-ments	FINANCIAL SERVICES: Retire-ment Plans	THE HOME: Home Improvements: Home Repair	THE HOME: Home Improvements: Lawn & Garden	THE HOME: Furnishings: Comput-ers & Hard-ware-Personal	THE HOME: Furnishings: Major Appli-ances	THE HOME: Furnishings: TV, Radio, Sound Equip-ment	THE HOME: Furnishings: Furni-ture	ENTERTAINMENT: Dine out/ Carry out	ENTERTAINMENT: Sports Equip-ment	ENTERTAINMENT: Fees & Tickets	ENTERTAINMENT: Toys & Games	ENTERTAINMENT: Travel	ENTERTAINMENT: Cable TV	PERSONAL: Apparel & Services	PERSONAL: Auto Repairs	PERSONAL: Health Insur-ance	PERSONAL: Pets & Supplies
50546	HAVELOCK	86	59	94	59	62	90	65	81	68	53	67	67	48	67	65	74	44	76	86	100
50548	HUMBOLDT	89	81	90	81	83	98	81	91	86	77	85	67	77	85	83	91	58	88	99	106
50551	JOLLEY	109	76	121	75	79	115	83	104	87	68	86	85	62	85	83	94	56	97	109	127
50552	KNIERIM	67	46	74	46	48	71	51	64	53	42	53	53	38	52	51	58	34	60	67	79
50554	LAURENS	90	63	95	63	66	95	70	87	75	59	74	68	54	74	69	83	48	81	93	104
50556	LEDYARD	87	60	95	60	63	92	66	83	69	54	68	68	49	68	66	75	44	77	87	102
50557	LEHIGH	82	58	83	57	61	85	64	79	70	56	68	60	50	69	62	77	45	74	85	94
50558	LIVERMORE	84	58	92	57	60	88	64	79	66	52	66	66	47	65	64	72	43	74	84	98
50559	LONE ROCK	79	54	86	54	57	83	60	75	63	49	62	62	44	61	60	68	40	70	79	92
50560	LU VERNE	80	55	88	55	58	84	61	76	64	50	63	63	45	62	61	69	41	71	80	94
50561	LYTTON	89	63	93	62	66	94	69	86	75	59	73	67	53	74	68	82	48	80	92	103
50562	MALLARD	97	67	106	66	70	102	74	92	77	60	76	76	54	75	74	84	49	86	97	113
50563	MANSON	89	75	98	73	78	98	75	90	81	69	80	67	67	79	77	88	53	85	97	106
50565	MARATHON	72	50	79	50	52	76	55	69	57	45	57	57	40	56	55	63	37	64	72	84
50566	MOORLAND	111	77	122	76	80	118	85	106	88	69	87	87	62	87	85	97	57	99	112	130
50567	NEMAHA	100	69	110	69	72	106	77	95	80	62	79	79	56	78	76	87	51	89	101	117
50568	NEWELL	78	56	80	55	58	82	61	76	67	53	65	58	48	66	60	74	43	71	82	90
50569	OTHO	77	77	64	79	72	82	77	76	78	73	78	61	77	80	75	80	53	77	84	93
50570	OTTOSEN	94	64	103	64	67	99	71	89	74	58	73	73	52	73	71	81	48	83	94	109
50571	PALMER	84	58	93	58	61	89	64	80	67	52	66	66	47	66	64	73	43	75	85	99
50573	PLOVER	70	48	77	48	50	74	54	66	56	43	55	55	39	55	53	61	36	62	70	82
50574	POCAHONTAS	93	66	99	65	68	98	72	90	77	61	76	71	55	76	71	85	50	84	96	108
50575	POMEROY	81	58	84	57	60	85	63	78	69	56	67	60	50	68	62	76	45	73	85	93
50576	REMBRANDT	86	59	95	59	62	91	66	82	69	53	68	68	48	67	66	75	44	77	87	101
50577	RENWICK	90	62	99	62	65	95	69	86	72	56	71	71	51	70	69	78	46	80	91	106
50578	RINGSTED	92	63	101	63	66	97	70	87	73	57	72	72	51	71	70	79	47	81	92	107
50579	ROCKWELL CITY	85	61	87	59	63	89	66	82	73	58	71	63	52	71	65	80	47	76	89	97
50581	ROLFE	77	55	79	54	57	80	60	74	66	52	64	57	47	65	58	72	42	69	80	88
50582	RUTLAND	89	61	98	61	64	94	68	85	71	55	70	70	50	70	68	77	46	79	90	104
50583	SAC CITY	82	58	83	57	61	86	64	79	71	56	68	60	51	69	62	78	45	74	86	94
50585	SIOUX RAPIDS	81	58	84	56	60	85	63	78	69	55	67	60	49	68	62	76	44	73	84	93
50586	SOMERS	76	52	84	52	55	81	58	72	61	47	60	60	43	59	58	66	39	68	76	89
50588	STORM LAKE	90	73	79	73	73	89	77	84	82	73	80	64	67	83	72	87	55	82	89	101
50590	SWEA CITY	78	55	81	54	57	81	60	75	66	52	64	58	47	64	59	72	42	70	81	89
50591	THOR	92	63	101	63	66	97	70	87	73	57	72	72	52	72	70	80	47	82	92	108
50594	VINCENT	101	70	111	69	73	107	77	96	80	63	79	79	57	79	77	88	52	90	101	118
50595	WEBSTER CITY	90	79	78	80	77	91	83	86	85	77	84	67	76	86	79	89	57	85	93	103
50597	WEST BEND	99	70	103	69	73	104	77	96	84	66	82	74	60	82	75	92	54	89	103	114
50598	WHITTEMORE	87	60	96	60	63	92	67	83	69	54	68	68	49	68	66	76	44	77	87	102
50599	WOOLSTOCK	107	74	118	73	77	113	82	102	85	66	84	84	60	83	81	93	55	95	107	125
50601	ACKLEY	91	64	96	63	67	96	71	88	76	60	74	69	54	75	69	83	49	82	94	106
50602	ALLISON	89	63	91	62	65	93	69	85	75	60	73	66	54	74	67	83	49	80	92	102
50603	ALTA VISTA	94	65	103	65	68	99	72	89	75	58	74	74	53	73	72	82	48	83	94	110
50604	APLINGTON	90	64	93	63	66	94	70	87	76	61	74	67	55	75	68	84	49	81	94	103
50605	AREDALE	90	62	98	61	64	95	68	85	71	55	70	70	50	70	68	78	46	79	90	105
50606	ARLINGTON	85	59	93	58	61	90	65	81	68	53	67	67	48	66	65	74	43	75	85	99
50607	AURORA	101	69	111	69	73	107	77	96	80	62	79	79	56	79	77	87	51	89	101	118
50608	AUSTINVILLE	91	63	100	63	66	96	70	86	72	56	72	72	51	71	69	79	46	81	91	107
50609	BEAMAN	98	68	108	67	71	104	75	93	78	61	77	77	55	77	75	85	50	87	99	115
50611	BRISTOW	87	60	96	60	63	92	67	83	69	54	68	68	49	68	66	75	44	77	87	102
50612	BUCKINGHAM	95	79	95	80	82	99	84	93	86	77	85	72	74	86	83	91	58	90	99	111
50613	CEDAR FALLS	93	88	85	90	87	90	98	90	96	93	96	71	93	95	92	96	67	94	94	108
50614	CEDAR FALLS	122	124	118	127	121	120	127	120	125	128	127	95	129	125	125	124	89	124	122	144
50616	CHARLES CITY	81	68	79	68	69	86	71	80	75	65	74	61	63	75	70	80	50	77	87	95
50619	CLARKSVILLE	89	63	92	62	65	93	69	85	75	59	73	66	54	73	68	82	48	80	92	102
50621	CONRAD	98	81	95	82	84	100	87	95	90	81	89	73	77	89	85	95	60	93	102	113
50622	DENVER	101	99	94	103	99	109	94	103	95	89	94	79	92	97	96	98	65	97	104	121
50624	DIKE	93	82	86	85	84	99	82	93	84	73	83	71	74	86	82	90	56	86	97	109
50625	DUMONT	79	56	82	55	58	83	61	76	67	53	65	59	48	66	60	73	43	71	82	91
50626	DUNKERTON	86	83	74	83	81	85	78	82	79	79	79	61	76	82	77	81	54	79	83	97
50627	ELDORA	82	62	81	61	64	84	68	79	73	61	71	60	56	72	65	79	47	75	86	94
50628	ELMA	81	56	89	56	58	85	62	77	64	50	64	63	45	63	62	70	41	72	81	95
50629	FAIRBANK	87	63	80	62	63	86	66	78	71	61	70	62	53	73	63	77	47	74	82	95
50630	FREDERICKSBURG	87	61	92	60	64	91	68	84	73	58	71	66	52	72	66	80	47	78	90	101
50632	GARWIN	89	81	80	83	78	94	83	87	85	75	84	69	77	85	81	88	57	86	94	105
50633	GENEVA	106	73	116	72	76	111	81	100	84	65	83	83	59	82	80	91	54	94	106	123
50634	GILBERTVILLE	92	84	83	87	86	99	83	94	85	75	84	71	76	87	83	90	57	86	96	109
50635	GLADBROOK	95	69	97	67	71	100	75	92	82	65	80	70	59	81	73	90	53	86	100	109
50636	GREENE	83	68	88	66	69	91	69	83	74	62	73	63	60	73	70	81	49	78	90	98
50638	GRUNDY CENTER	86	75	87	75	76	95	75	87	80	68	78	65	68	79	76	86	53	82	94	102
50641	HAZLETON	81	59	67	57	58	77	61	71	67	59	66	54	49	70	55	73	44	67	75	86
50642	HOLLAND	100	69	110	69	72	106	76	95	79	62	79	78	56	78	76	87	51	89	100	117
50643	HUDSON	99	112	96	115	108	110	100	104	98	100	99	81	106	101	105	98	69	100	103	122
50644	INDEPENDENCE	94	86	91	86	87	102	85	95	90	79	88	71	80	89	86	95	60	91	103	111
50645	IONIA	85	64	88	65	66	90	68	82	71	57	70	66	54	70	68	76	46	76	86	99
50647	JANESVILLE	100	95	94	98	97	108	91	102	94	85	92	77	87	95	93	98	63	95	105	119
50648	JESUP	84	81	83	82	82	95	77	87	81	72	80	65	75	81	80	86	55	82	94	102
50649	KESLEY	90	62	99	62	65	95	69	86	72	56	71	71	50	70	69	78	46	80	90	105
50650	LAMONT	86	59	95	59	62	91	66	82	69	53	68	68	48	67	66	75	44	77	87	101
50651	LA PORTE CITY	88	87	82	88	85	97	84	90	87	79	86	69	83	88	85	91	59	87	98	106
50652	LINCOLN	76	52	83	52	54	80	58	72	60	47	59	59	42	59	57	65	38	67	76	88
50653	MARBLE ROCK	102	70	112	70	73	108	78	97	81	63	80	80	57	79	78	88	52	90	102	119
50654	MASONVILLE	96	69	105	69	72	102	75	92	78	62	77	76	57	76	75	84	50	86	97	113
50655	MAYNARD	85	59	94	59	61	90	65	81	68	53	67	67	48	66	65	74	43	76	86	100
50658	NASHUA	82	58	84	57	61	86	64	79	70	56	68	60	50	69	62	77	45	74	86	94
50659	NEW HAMPTON	88	80	89	80	80	98	79	89	84	73	82	68	75	83	81	89	56	86	98	105
50660	NEW HARTFORD	90	76	79	76	75	90	74	83	79	73	78	64	67	82	72	84	53	79	86	100
50662	OELWEIN	80	64	71	63	63	81	70	76	74	63	72	59	60	74	65	79	49	74	83	91
50665	PARKERSBURG	88	72	93	71	74	97	74	88	79	66	78	67	65	78	75	86	52	83	96	104
50666	PLAINFIELD	83	74	78	76	75	89	73	84	76	66	74	64	66	77	73	80	50	78	87	98
50667	RAYMOND	92	83	83	87	85	98	82	93	85	74	83	70	76	86	82	90	57	86	96	108
50668	READLYN	88	81	96	80	83	102	79	91	83	72	82	69	74	81	82	89	55	87	101	108
50669	REINBECK	81	77	80	78	79	91	74	84	78	69	77	62	72	78	77	83	52	79	90	97
50670	SHELL ROCK	81	81	71	83	78	87	79	81	79	74	79	64	78	81	78	82	54	79	86	97
50671	STANLEY	101	70	111	70	73	107	77	96	81	63	80	79	57	79	77	88	52	90	102	118
	IOWA	93	84	87	85	83	95	87	91	89	82	88	71	81	90	85	92	61	90	96	108
	UNITED STATES	100	100	100	100	100	100	100	100	100	100	100	100	100	100	100	100	100	100	100	100

ZIP CODE			POPULATION			2000-2009 ANNUAL RATE		HOUSEHOLDS					FAMILIES		
#	POST OFFICE NAME	COUNTY FIPS CODE	2000	2009	2014	% Rate	State Centile	2000	2009	2014	% Annual Rate 2000-2009	2009 Average HH Size	2000	2009	% Annual Rate 2000-2009
50672	STEAMBOAT ROCK	083	664	634	612	-0.5	27	274	266	257	-0.3	2.38	185	175	-0.6
50674	SUMNER	017	3978	3878	3802	-0.3	40	1578	1586	1568	0.1	2.39	1123	1104	-0.2
50675	TRAER	171	2366	2316	2294	-0.2	46	969	970	964	0.0	2.31	668	653	-0.2
50676	TRIPOLI	017	2026	2183	2237	0.8	87	800	875	902	1.0	2.46	562	600	0.7
50677	WAVERLY	017	11248	11688	11783	0.4	76	4088	4344	4410	0.7	2.37	2822	2930	0.4
50680	WELLSBURG	075	1219	1232	1219	0.1	63	520	536	533	0.3	2.30	348	349	0.0
50681	WESTGATE	065	524	537	531	0.3	72	191	203	202	0.7	2.65	147	153	0.4
50682	WINTHROP	019	1619	1627	1634	0.1	63	621	643	650	0.4	2.53	442	447	0.1
50701	WATERLOO	013	29452	29582	29651	0.0	58	12331	12823	12938	0.4	2.28	7862	7958	0.1
50702	WATERLOO	013	20802	20416	20272	-0.2	46	8683	8707	8681	0.0	2.26	5382	5273	-0.2
50703	WATERLOO	013	21286	20256	19854	-0.5	27	8115	7877	7756	-0.3	2.53	5347	5071	-0.6
50707	EVANSDALE	013	8087	8027	8022	-0.1	51	3166	3260	3282	0.3	2.46	2252	2266	0.1
50801	CRESTON	175	9416	9129	9021	-0.3	40	4034	4036	4027	0.0	2.20	2512	2444	-0.3
50830	AFTON	175	1667	1695	1706	0.2	68	671	699	710	0.4	2.32	470	477	0.2
50833	BEDFORD	173	2633	2448	2341	-0.8	11	1067	1004	961	-0.7	2.39	701	644	-0.9
50835	BENTON	159	175	166	160	-0.6	20	72	70	68	-0.3	2.37	53	51	-0.4
50836	BLOCKTON	173	452	417	397	-0.9	8	197	185	178	-0.7	2.25	142	131	-0.9
50837	BRIDGEWATER	001	420	397	384	-0.6	20	188	182	177	-0.4	2.18	137	130	-0.6
50840	CLEARFIELD	173	491	476	469	-0.3	40	210	211	209	0.1	2.14	141	138	-0.2
50841	CORNING	003	3068	2775	2637	-1.1	5	1295	1193	1136	-0.9	2.25	810	724	-1.2
50843	CUMBERLAND	029	626	595	575	-0.5	27	264	256	249	-0.3	2.32	189	179	-0.6
50845	DIAGONAL	159	766	739	718	-0.4	32	322	317	309	-0.2	2.33	221	213	-0.4
50846	FONTANELLE	001	1327	1241	1198	-0.7	15	543	519	502	-0.5	2.32	377	352	-0.7
50847	GRANT	137	44	41	40	-0.8	11	20	19	19	-0.6	2.16	15	14	-0.7
50848	GRAVITY	173	578	522	494	-1.1	5	225	207	197	-0.9	2.52	176	160	-1.0
50849	GREENFIELD	001	2955	2746	2643	-0.8	11	1234	1159	1115	-0.7	2.30	811	744	-0.9
50851	LENOX	173	2141	1971	1889	-0.9	8	849	799	767	-0.7	2.36	564	519	-0.9
50853	MASSENA	029	776	754	739	-0.3	40	328	328	324	0.0	2.30	229	224	-0.2
50854	MOUNT AYR	159	2499	2398	2327	-0.4	32	1028	1005	976	-0.2	2.29	678	647	-0.5
50857	NODAWAY	003	449	422	405	-0.7	15	172	166	159	-0.4	2.43	118	111	-0.7
50858	ORIENT	001	962	877	838	-1.0	6	371	345	331	-0.8	2.52	284	261	-0.9
50859	PRESCOTT	003	602	563	538	-0.7	15	252	242	233	-0.4	2.33	186	175	-0.7
50860	REDDING	159	453	431	419	-0.5	27	168	163	159	-0.3	2.51	122	117	-0.5
50861	SHANNON CITY	175	260	256	255	-0.2	46	119	123	123	0.4	2.08	87	88	0.1
50862	SHARPSBURG	173	169	151	144	-1.2	4	65	60	57	-0.9	2.52	52	47	-1.1
50863	TINGLEY	159	308	295	287	-0.5	27	141	138	135	-0.2	2.14	101	97	-0.4
50864	VILLISCA	137	2151	2002	1925	-0.8	11	892	845	814	-0.6	2.30	592	547	-0.9
51001	AKRON	149	2256	2253	2234	0.0	58	929	955	953	0.3	2.36	639	640	0.0
51002	ALTA	021	2735	2703	2694	-0.1	51	1040	1048	1046	0.1	2.56	757	746	-0.2
51003	ALTON	167	1616	1732	1781	0.8	87	597	659	683	1.1	2.63	420	454	0.8
51004	ANTHON	193	1178	1175	1171	0.0	58	488	502	503	0.3	2.34	334	335	0.0
51005	AURELIA	035	1643	1476	1397	-1.2	4	638	588	560	-0.9	2.42	460	416	-1.1
51006	BATTLE CREEK	093	1216	1066	999	-1.4	1	487	446	421	-0.9	2.31	316	282	-1.2
51007	BRONSON	193	655	711	722	0.9	89	247	275	281	1.2	2.59	191	209	1.0
51009	CALUMET	141	198	185	177	-0.7	15	84	80	78	-0.5	2.31	65	61	-0.7
51010	CASTANA	133	529	533	528	0.1	63	223	230	228	0.3	2.31	150	150	0.0
51011	CHATSWORTH	167	89	97	101	0.9	89	36	41	43	1.4	2.37	26	29	1.2
51012	CHEROKEE	035	6898	6233	5905	-1.1	5	2952	2772	2646	-0.7	2.17	1854	1695	-1.0
51014	CLEGHORN	035	588	526	496	-1.2	4	233	216	206	-0.8	2.44	174	159	-1.0
51016	CORRECTIONVILLE	193	1505	1475	1463	-0.2	46	588	592	590	0.1	2.43	406	399	-0.2
51018	CUSHING	193	403	399	395	-0.1	51	165	169	168	0.3	2.36	119	119	0.0
51019	DANBURY	193	830	786	770	-0.6	20	337	329	325	-0.3	2.39	238	227	-0.5
51020	GALVA	093	601	510	470	-1.8	0	254	223	207	-1.4	2.29	191	164	-1.6
51022	GRANVILLE	141	869	860	853	-0.1	51	312	316	316	0.1	2.72	235	235	0.0
51023	HAWARDEN	167	3046	2997	2987	-0.2	46	1234	1244	1247	0.1	2.35	824	806	-0.2
51024	HINTON	149	2075	2300	2335	1.1	91	734	841	861	1.5	2.73	586	660	1.3
51025	HOLSTEIN	093	2220	2121	2057	-0.5	27	904	897	879	-0.1	2.31	623	604	-0.3
51026	HORNICK	193	940	906	894	-0.4	32	354	351	349	-0.1	2.58	261	254	-0.3
51027	IRETON	167	1228	1243	1252	0.1	63	449	473	481	0.6	2.63	363	376	0.4
51028	KINGSLEY	149	2012	2115	2121	0.5	79	787	857	867	0.9	2.42	558	594	0.7
51029	LARRABEE	035	299	275	261	-0.9	8	132	126	121	-0.5	2.18	100	94	-0.7
51030	LAWTON	193	1459	1522	1535	0.5	79	515	548	554	0.7	2.75	414	433	0.5
51031	LE MARS	149	12206	11989	11822	-0.2	46	4643	4676	4635	0.1	2.51	3262	3212	-0.2
51033	LINN GROVE	021	569	551	545	-0.3	40	227	225	223	-0.1	2.41	163	158	-0.3
51034	MAPLETON	133	2136	1827	1735	-1.7	0	849	778	743	-0.9	2.26	548	490	-1.2
51035	MARCUS	035	1852	1648	1553	-1.3	2	717	661	627	-0.9	2.43	484	436	-1.1
51036	MAURICE	167	693	676	672	-0.3	40	237	239	239	0.1	2.83	196	196	0.0
51037	MERIDEN	035	411	369	349	-1.2	4	174	162	155	-0.8	2.28	132	121	-0.9
51038	MERRILL	149	1469	1467	1453	0.0	58	546	563	562	0.3	2.61	426	431	0.1
51039	MOVILLE	193	2435	2502	2514	0.3	72	922	962	970	0.5	2.59	692	707	0.2
51040	ONAWA	133	3983	3738	3595	-0.7	15	1682	1605	1550	-0.5	2.26	1042	969	-0.8
51041	ORANGE CITY	167	6657	6965	7024	0.5	79	2030	2143	2184	0.6	2.63	1559	1617	0.4
51044	OTO	193	295	286	284	-0.3	40	119	119	118	0.0	2.40	88	87	-0.1
51046	PAULLINA	141	1846	1720	1650	-0.8	11	772	734	708	-0.5	2.29	532	496	-0.8
51047	PETERSON	041	809	772	752	-0.5	27	346	342	336	-0.1	2.25	246	238	-0.4
51048	PIERSON	193	668	622	605	-0.8	11	261	248	243	-0.6	2.44	194	181	-0.7
51049	QUIMBY	035	619	549	515	-1.3	2	250	229	217	-0.9	2.40	183	164	-1.2
51050	REMSEN	149	2799	2841	2828	0.2	68	1012	1064	1068	0.5	2.61	754	777	0.3
51051	RODNEY	133	114	117	116	0.3	72	52	54	54	0.4	2.17	35	36	0.3
51052	SALIX	193	1026	1023	1023	0.0	58	397	407	408	0.3	2.51	288	289	0.0
51053	SCHALLER	161	1323	1213	1156	-0.9	8	512	484	464	-0.6	2.51	372	344	-0.8
51054	SERGEANT BLUFF	193	4085	4197	4241	0.3	72	1413	1496	1521	0.6	2.79	1120	1164	0.4
51055	SLOAN	193	1409	1406	1404	0.0	58	581	598	600	0.3	2.35	396	398	0.1
51056	SMITHLAND	193	477	464	461	-0.3	40	198	198	198	0.0	2.34	148	146	-0.1
51058	SUTHERLAND	141	1104	1028	989	-0.8	11	474	450	435	-0.6	2.21	324	301	-0.8
51060	UTE	133	610	576	557	-0.6	20	276	269	261	-0.3	2.14	189	180	-0.5
51061	WASHTA	035	559	510	483	-1.0	6	221	209	200	-0.6	2.44	165	154	-0.7
51062	WESTFIELD	149	758	758	754	0.0	58	282	291	291	0.3	2.60	218	221	0.1
51063	WHITING	133	1073	1072	1026	0.0	58	430	404	388	-0.7	2.45	286	262	-0.9
51101	SIOUX CITY	193	803	903	928	1.3	93	364	384	389	0.6	2.00	146	148	0.1
51103	SIOUX CITY	193	17525	17276	17144	-0.2	46	6135	6103	6060	-0.1	2.72	4218	4100	-0.3
51104	SIOUX CITY	193	21262	20803	20612	-0.2	46	8249	8169	8107	-0.1	2.50	5403	5210	-0.4
51105	SIOUX CITY	193	11859	11399	11179	-0.4	32	4222	3984	3892	-0.6	2.78	2569	2351	-1.0
51106	SIOUX CITY	193	27105	27197	27176	0.0	58	10352	10563	10575	0.2	2.47	7086	7067	0.0
51108	SIOUX CITY	193	6577	6632	6628	0.1	63	2587	2683	2694	0.4	2.40	1782	1807	0.2
	IOWA					0.4					0.7	2.40			0.4
	UNITED STATES					1.0					1.1	2.59			0.9

ZIP CODE		RACE (%)						% Hispanic Origin		2009 AGE DISTRIBUTION (%)										MEDIAN AGE	% 2009 Males	% 2009 Females
#	POST OFFICE NAME	White		Black		Asian/Pacific																
		2000	2009	2000	2009	2000	2009	2000	2009	0-4	5-9	10-14	15-19	20-24	25-44	45-64	65-84	85+	18+	2009		
50672	STEAMBOAT ROCK	96.8	95.6	0.3	0.3	0.3	0.5	3.0	4.6	6.3	6.3	6.3	5.8	6.0	21.5	28.5	16.1	3.2	77.8	43.2	51.7	48.3
50674	SUMNER	98.9	98.4	0.1	0.2	0.5	0.8	0.7	1.0	6.0	6.5	6.7	6.8	5.2	23.3	27.1	14.4	4.0	76.3	41.5	49.6	50.4
50675	TRAER	98.9	98.8	0.3	0.3	0.1	0.1	0.4	0.4	6.4	6.8	6.7	5.8	4.2	21.4	27.0	16.6	5.1	76.3	44.1	48.7	51.3
50676	TRIPOLI	99.0	98.7	0.1	0.2	0.1	0.2	0.3	0.5	6.8	7.0	7.1	7.5	4.9	22.9	26.5	13.8	3.5	74.3	40.2	49.4	50.6
50677	WAVERLY	97.5	96.7	0.9	1.0	0.8	1.3	0.6	0.8	5.1	4.9	5.9	10.6	11.3	20.1	25.0	14.0	3.2	80.1	37.8	47.7	52.3
50680	WELLSBURG	98.9	98.9	0.1	0.1	0.4	0.4	0.2	0.2	5.5	5.9	6.1	6.5	5.4	20.0	29.6	16.8	4.1	78.3	45.3	49.3	50.7
50681	WESTGATE	99.4	98.9	0.2	0.2	0.0	0.2	1.3	2.0	6.5	7.4	7.4	6.7	4.1	22.0	31.5	12.7	1.7	74.1	42.0	52.5	47.5
50682	WINTHROP	98.9	98.8	0.2	0.2	0.1	0.2	0.4	0.4	6.9	7.2	7.3	6.8	4.7	24.2	28.6	12.5	1.9	74.4	39.5	51.0	49.0
50701	WATERLOO	92.4	91.8	4.2	4.5	1.0	1.1	1.8	1.9	6.5	6.4	6.3	5.9	5.7	27.6	27.2	12.2	2.1	77.3	38.4	48.6	51.4
50702	WATERLOO	91.8	91.2	4.2	4.5	1.0	1.0	1.7	1.8	6.6	6.1	6.0	5.6	6.6	26.1	23.9	14.5	4.4	78.0	39.1	47.9	52.1
50703	WATERLOO	62.5	61.4	32.2	33.1	0.4	0.4	3.9	3.9	7.2	7.1	6.9	7.8	7.2	25.8	25.6	10.8	1.7	74.1	35.0	48.4	51.6
50707	EVANSDALE	87.9	87.6	7.8	7.8	0.9	1.0	2.4	2.4	6.8	6.9	7.1	6.7	5.8	26.1	27.4	11.8	1.5	74.9	37.5	49.4	50.6
50801	CRESTON	98.3	97.8	0.3	0.4	0.3	0.5	1.1	1.6	6.1	6.1	6.1	7.0	6.0	23.4	27.4	14.4	3.6	78.0	41.1	47.7	52.3
50830	AFTON	99.0	97.5	0.0	0.1	0.1	1.1	1.3	1.9	5.7	5.9	6.3	7.0	5.4	22.4	29.7	14.6	3.0	80.4	43.0	49.1	50.9
50833	BEDFORD	98.4	97.8	0.0	0.0	0.2	0.2	1.4	2.2	6.0	6.4	6.5	6.3	5.3	21.9	26.4	16.6	4.7	77.2	43.0	48.3	51.7
50835	BENTON	99.4	99.4	0.0	0.0	0.6	0.6	0.0	0.0	4.2	5.4	5.4	7.2	3.6	22.9	32.5	15.7	3.0	80.1	45.7	51.2	48.8
50836	BLOCKTON	99.3	99.0	0.0	0.0	0.4	0.7	0.2	0.2	5.8	6.2	6.0	5.0	4.8	23.0	30.0	16.3	2.9	78.9	44.3	49.6	50.4
50837	BRIDGEWATER	99.5	99.2	0.0	0.0	0.2	0.5	0.2	0.3	5.5	5.8	6.5	6.5	4.0	21.7	31.7	15.6	2.5	78.1	44.9	53.1	46.9
50840	CLEARFIELD	97.8	97.3	0.0	0.0	0.0	0.0	1.6	2.5	4.8	4.8	4.6	5.5	5.5	21.8	27.3	20.2	5.5	82.6	47.8	45.4	54.6
50841	CORNING	99.0	98.7	0.1	0.1	0.2	0.3	0.6	0.8	5.7	5.9	6.1	6.5	5.2	21.2	28.1	17.3	4.3	77.9	44.6	49.1	50.9
50843	CUMBERLAND	98.2	97.8	0.5	0.7	0.2	0.2	1.6	2.4	4.4	5.0	5.7	7.6	5.0	23.0	32.3	14.8	2.2	80.0	44.5	52.1	47.9
50845	DIAGONAL	99.7	99.6	0.0	0.0	0.0	0.1	0.1	0.1	6.8	7.3	6.9	5.0	3.8	24.9	28.7	13.9	2.7	75.9	41.3	50.9	49.1
50846	FONTANELLE	99.2	99.0	0.1	0.1	0.1	0.1	0.5	0.6	5.9	6.1	6.0	5.8	5.0	19.9	28.3	17.4	5.6	77.9	45.9	48.6	51.4
50847	GRANT	100.0	100.0	0.0	0.0	0.0	0.0	0.0	0.0	4.9	4.9	4.9	7.3	4.9	22.0	29.3	19.5	2.4	78.0	45.6	51.2	48.8
50848	GRAVITY	98.6	98.3	0.2	0.2	0.3	0.6	1.2	1.5	4.6	7.1	7.7	7.9	4.4	20.7	28.5	17.4	1.7	75.3	42.7	53.6	46.4
50849	GREENFIELD	99.1	98.8	0.1	0.1	0.3	0.5	0.4	0.6	5.3	5.3	5.8	7.0	5.6	21.8	27.3	16.5	5.4	79.2	44.4	47.9	52.1
50851	LENOX	96.1	94.4	0.0	0.1	0.6	1.1	9.5	13.6	6.1	6.6	6.5	6.0	4.3	22.8	27.2	15.8	4.6	77.2	42.9	49.7	50.3
50853	MASSENA	99.9	99.9	0.0	0.0	0.0	0.0	0.1	0.1	5.0	5.6	6.0	5.8	3.4	22.9	32.9	15.5	2.8	79.8	45.8	52.5	47.5
50854	MOUNT AYR	99.0	98.7	0.1	0.1	0.2	0.4	0.3	0.5	5.9	6.0	6.1	6.0	4.9	20.3	26.3	18.6	6.0	78.0	45.7	47.3	52.7
50857	NODAWAY	98.4	97.9	0.0	0.0	0.2	0.5	0.4	0.9	4.5	4.7	5.5	7.6	5.0	20.6	30.1	19.2	2.8	80.1	46.4	50.0	50.0
50858	ORIENT	99.0	98.7	0.0	0.0	0.1	0.1	0.8	1.3	5.4	6.0	7.0	7.5	4.3	23.0	31.0	13.8	1.9	77.0	42.6	52.9	47.1
50859	PRESCOTT	98.7	98.6	0.0	0.0	0.2	0.2	0.7	0.9	5.9	6.4	6.7	6.4	3.9	21.7	31.4	15.1	2.5	76.9	44.1	52.4	47.6
50860	REDDING	98.9	98.8	0.4	0.5	0.0	0.0	0.0	0.0	7.4	7.7	7.9	6.7	3.7	20.6	26.9	14.4	4.6	72.9	42.2	50.8	49.2
50861	SHANNON CITY	100.0	99.6	0.0	0.0	0.0	0.4	0.0	0.0	4.7	5.5	5.5	5.1	3.5	21.5	34.0	17.6	2.7	80.9	47.4	52.3	47.7
50862	SHARPSBURG	98.2	97.4	0.0	0.0	1.2	2.0	0.0	0.0	6.0	6.6	6.6	6.6	4.6	20.5	31.1	14.6	3.3	76.8	44.1	50.3	49.7
50863	TINGLEY	98.7	98.6	0.3	0.3	0.3	0.3	0.0	0.0	4.4	4.7	5.4	5.1	3.4	17.6	32.9	24.1	2.4	82.4	51.3	50.8	49.2
50864	VILLISCA	99.1	98.8	0.1	0.1	0.0	0.1	0.5	0.7	5.1	5.2	5.6	6.7	5.4	20.6	29.4	17.0	4.8	79.5	45.8	47.6	52.4
51001	AKRON	98.8	98.4	0.2	0.3	0.1	0.2	0.7	1.1	5.8	6.0	6.5	7.4	5.1	23.9	27.3	15.0	3.1	77.2	41.5	49.6	50.4
51002	ALTA	93.9	90.5	0.5	0.6	1.1	1.8	8.0	12.7	6.0	6.4	7.4	7.6	5.6	24.6	26.7	13.1	2.6	75.2	39.6	49.9	50.1
51003	ALTON	98.9	98.6	0.1	0.1	0.2	0.3	1.2	1.7	6.2	6.8	6.9	7.4	5.5	24.1	30.6	10.4	2.1	75.5	38.8	49.6	50.4
51004	ANTHON	99.2	98.7	0.0	0.0	0.1	0.1	1.0	1.9	5.9	6.2	6.5	7.1	5.2	20.8	29.3	15.9	3.2	77.2	43.7	48.7	51.3
51005	AURELIA	98.9	98.3	0.1	0.1	0.2	0.3	1.0	1.5	5.4	6.0	6.1	5.6	5.5	20.3	28.5	17.5	5.2	78.7	45.7	49.0	51.0
51006	BATTLE CREEK	99.3	99.0	0.0	0.0	0.1	0.2	0.7	1.0	4.7	4.7	5.5	6.8	5.2	21.1	27.9	18.9	5.3	80.5	46.6	49.4	50.6
51007	BRONSON	98.9	98.3	0.0	0.0	0.5	0.7	0.8	1.3	5.1	6.5	8.2	8.2	4.5	26.2	30.7	9.7	1.1	74.8	40.0	52.7	47.3
51009	CALUMET	99.0	98.4	0.0	0.0	0.0	0.5	0.0	0.0	5.4	5.9	7.0	7.6	4.3	21.6	31.9	14.6	1.6	75.7	43.7	53.0	47.0
51010	CASTANA	98.7	97.7	0.0	0.4	0.2	0.6	0.6	0.9	5.4	5.8	6.9	7.9	3.9	22.1	30.0	15.2	2.6	76.9	43.1	50.7	49.3
51011	CHATSWORTH	98.9	97.9	0.0	0.0	1.1	1.0	1.1	1.0	5.2	6.2	7.2	6.2	5.2	22.7	30.9	14.4	2.1	78.4	43.2	52.6	47.4
51012	CHEROKEE	97.8	97.0	0.5	0.6	0.6	0.9	1.3	2.0	5.3	5.6	6.3	7.3	5.3	21.3	29.3	15.9	3.6	78.1	44.0	49.1	50.9
51014	CLEGHORN	99.5	99.4	0.2	0.2	0.2	0.2	0.2	0.2	5.7	6.7	6.8	5.3	4.0	22.2	31.6	15.6	2.1	77.4	44.5	50.4	49.6
51016	CORRECTIONVILLE	98.3	97.2	0.0	0.0	0.2	0.3	2.6	4.5	6.6	6.5	6.6	6.6	5.0	21.6	27.9	14.8	4.3	76.3	42.4	50.3	49.7
51018	CUSHING	99.0	98.5	0.0	0.0	0.0	0.0	2.0	3.5	6.3	6.8	7.0	7.0	3.8	23.8	29.8	13.3	2.3	75.4	41.0	50.9	49.1
51019	DANBURY	99.5	99.4	0.0	0.0	0.1	0.1	0.2	0.3	5.9	6.5	7.0	7.8	3.9	23.5	29.1	14.0	2.3	75.8	41.9	51.5	48.5
51020	GALVA	99.3	99.0	0.0	0.0	0.3	0.6	0.2	0.2	5.3	6.1	7.1	6.3	3.5	22.4	31.2	15.1	3.1	77.3	44.6	49.8	50.2
51022	GRANVILLE	97.8	97.1	0.5	0.5	0.2	0.3	1.4	2.1	6.7	7.1	7.7	8.7	5.0	21.9	28.6	11.9	2.4	72.9	39.5	51.7	48.3
51023	HAWARDEN	94.6	92.2	0.3	0.5	0.4	0.5	5.5	8.3	6.0	5.7	6.0	7.0	6.2	23.2	27.3	14.9	3.6	78.0	41.3	48.6	51.4
51024	HINTON	98.5	97.9	0.3	0.4	0.4	0.6	0.7	1.1	5.9	6.4	7.1	7.0	5.0	24.4	32.4	10.3	1.4	76.3	40.8	51.3	48.7
51025	HOLSTEIN	99.2	98.9	0.0	0.0	0.3	0.5	0.3	0.5	6.6	6.6	6.6	5.7	5.2	21.9	26.9	15.9	4.7	76.4	42.7	47.4	52.6
51026	HORNICK	97.6	96.6	0.2	0.2	0.2	0.3	0.4	1.0	6.3	7.2	7.5	6.7	3.6	22.6	31.9	12.4	1.8	74.6	42.2	51.5	48.5
51027	IRETON	98.9	98.2	0.0	0.0	0.5	0.9	0.8	1.3	6.3	6.8	7.2	7.8	4.7	24.1	29.4	12.1	1.4	74.8	39.8	50.8	49.2
51028	KINGSLEY	98.6	97.9	0.2	0.3	0.4	0.8	0.5	0.9	6.6	7.0	7.0	6.6	5.1	22.7	25.8	15.3	4.0	74.9	41.0	49.6	50.4
51029	LARRABEE	99.7	99.6	0.0	0.0	0.0	0.0	0.0	0.0	4.7	5.8	6.9	7.6	4.0	19.3	35.6	14.2	1.8	77.5	45.9	52.4	47.6
51030	LAWTON	98.6	98.1	0.1	0.1	0.6	1.0	0.2	0.3	7.2	7.8	8.3	7.9	4.5	24.9	28.4	9.4	1.6	71.6	37.7	49.4	50.6
51031	LE MARS	97.6	96.8	0.4	0.5	0.4	0.6	2.0	3.0	7.3	7.2	7.4	7.2	6.0	24.7	26.2	11.3	2.7	73.4	37.2	49.6	50.4
51033	LINN GROVE	97.7	96.4	0.0	0.0	0.2	0.4	2.1	3.6	5.1	6.2	6.7	5.4	4.5	21.4	35.4	13.1	2.2	78.6	45.4	51.7	48.3
51034	MAPLETON	98.8	95.2	0.1	1.7	0.1	1.9	0.4	0.5	5.0	5.2	5.6	6.2	5.3	18.0	27.3	19.4	8.0	80.3	48.3	47.5	52.5
51035	MARCUS	98.6	98.1	0.1	0.1	0.5	0.8	0.4	0.5	5.2	5.5	6.0	6.7	5.2	21.1	28.0	17.8	4.6	78.5	45.2	49.6	50.4
51036	MAURICE	98.4	97.5	0.0	0.0	0.7	1.2	1.6	2.2	6.5	7.4	7.5	7.2	4.9	24.7	29.4	10.8	1.5	74.1	37.8	50.6	49.4
51037	MERIDEN	99.5	99.2	0.2	0.3	0.0	0.3	0.2	0.3	6.0	6.8	7.3	5.7	3.8	22.8	30.9	14.9	1.9	76.2	43.5	49.9	50.1
51038	MERRILL	98.8	98.2	0.2	0.3	0.2	0.3	1.0	1.6	6.1	6.8	7.6	8.3	5.0	23.9	28.8	11.8	1.8	74.2	39.6	51.9	48.1
51039	MOVILLE	98.4	97.6	0.2	0.3	0.4	0.6	0.9	1.5	7.6	8.0	8.0	7.8	5.2	24.0	26.8	10.6	2.0	71.3	36.7	50.3	49.7
51040	ONAWA	98.0	97.4	0.1	0.1	0.2	0.3	1.0	1.4	5.8	5.9	6.1	6.3	4.9	21.6	27.0	17.5	4.9	78.1	44.5	48.4	51.6
51041	ORANGE CITY	97.7	96.6	0.4	0.5	0.9	1.5	1.1	1.7	6.5	6.2	6.0	12.5	14.4	20.0	20.6	10.4	3.5	77.2	28.8	46.9	53.1
51044	OTO	98.6	97.9	0.0	0.0	0.3	0.3	0.3	1.0	5.6	5.6	6.3	7.0	4.2	22.0	32.2	15.0	2.1	78.0	44.5	52.8	47.2
51046	PAULLINA	99.2	99.0	0.1	0.1	0.2	0.3	0.7	1.0	5.1	5.5	5.9	6.2	4.7	20.0	29.0	18.8	4.8	79.6	46.9	49.5	50.5
51047	PETERSON	99.1	98.8	0.0	0.0	0.1	0.3	0.7	1.3	4.8	5.7	6.1	5.6	3.9	21.1	35.1	15.2	2.6	80.1	46.8	53.1	46.9
51048	PIERSON	98.1	97.1	0.1	0.3	0.4	0.8	1.0	1.9	7.4	7.4	7.4	6.1	4.5	22.2	28.3	13.7	3.1	73.8	41.1	49.7	50.3
51049	QUIMBY	98.7	98.2	0.3	0.4	0.2	0.2	1.0	1.5	6.6	6.9	7.3	7.1	4.6	23.0	29.7	13.1	1.8	74.9	40.7	50.8	49.2
51050	REMSEN	99.3	99.0	0.1	0.1	0.1	0.2	0.5	0.7	7.1	7.7	8.3	8.1	4.6	23.3	26.0	11.4	3.4	71.6	38.4	50.7	49.3
51051	RODNEY	99.1	98.3	0.0	0.0	0.0	0.0	0.9	0.9	5.1	6.0	6.8	8.5	3.4	22.2	32.5	13.7	1.7	76.9	43.2	51.3	48.7
51052	SALIX	98.5	97.7	0.0	0.0	0.3	0.7	0.8	1.4	5.1	8.1	8.6	8.4	3.3	25.8	28.0	10.9	1.9	72.0	38.6	50.8	49.2
51053	SCHALLER	97.5	96.6	0.2	0.2	0.2	0.4	2.4	3.5	6.5	6.7	8.3	7.7	4.8	22.6	27.9	13.2	2.3	73.5	40.0	51.6	48.4
51054	SERGEANT BLUFF	95.2	92.5	0.8	1.0	1.6	3.0	1.6	2.7	7.6	7.9	8.1	8.1	5.7	26.2	27.7	8.0	0.7	71.4	34.9	50.5	49.5
51055	SLOAN	97.7	96.9	0.1	0.1	0.2	0.4	0.8	1.4	6.8	5.8	7.2	8.7	4.1	22.6	28.2	14.6	2.1	74.8	40.9	47.8	52.2
51056	SMITHLAND	98.3	97.8	0.2	0.2	0.2	0.4	0.4	0.9	5.2	5.6	6.0	6.9	4.5	22.0	32.5	14.9	2.4	78.7	44.8	52.8	47.2
51058	SUTHERLAND	98.5	98.2	0.2	0.2	0.1	0.1	0.4	0.5	5.1	5.3	5.9	6.5	4.7	19.7	30.3	16.5	6.0	79.5	46.9	50.4	49.6
51060	UTE	99.3	99.1	0.2	0.2	0.0	0.0	0.2	0.3	4.7	5.2	5.4	6.1	4.5	17.9	29.0	24.0	3.3	80.9	49.4	48.3	51.7
51061	WASHTA	99.1	98.4	0.2	0.2	0.4	0.8	0.5	0.6	5.9	6.5	6.9	6.5	4.9	20.6	31.4	15.5	2.0	76.7	44.0	51.6	48.4
51062	WESTFIELD	97.2	96.7	0.1	0.1	0.4	0.5	0.9	1.3	4.9	5.5	6.3	6.6	5.1	23.1	33.9	13.2	1.3	79.0	43.9	50.0	50.0
51063	WHITING	97.9	96.7	0.0	0.0	0.0	0.4	1.1	1.8	4.9	5.6	5.9	8.0	7.7	21.3	29.2	13.8	3.5	81.9	41.6	50.0	50.0
51101	SIOUX CITY	59.0	51.2	6.9	7.4	7.2	9.0	30.8	37.5	7.8	7.0	6.3	8.1	8.5	32.4	20.6	8.0	1.3	75.3	32.3	58.9	41.1
51103	SIOUX CITY	77.5	71.0	4.8	5.5	3.6	5.5	15.3	21.4	8.5	7.5	7.0	7.7	8.0	26.3	23.1	9.8	2.1	72.8	32.9	48.9	51.1
51104	SIOUX CITY	89.5	85.2	1.8	2.2	2.9	4.6	7.2	10.7	7.2	7.0	7.1	6.9	6.1	26.3	25.4	11.0	2.7	74.3	37.0	48.4	51.6
51105	SIOUX CITY	67.1	58.6	3.9	4.2	6.5	9.2	26.6	35.0	9.9	8.7	7.7	7.6	8.0	28.6	20.2	8.0	1.3	69.4	30.0	51.3	48.7
51106	SIOUX CITY	93.6	90.3	0.9	1.2	1.1	2.0	4.9	7.8	7.3	7.1	6.8	7.3	7.0	26.6	24.4	11.0	2.4	74.9	35.6	48.1	51.9
51108	SIOUX CITY	95.5	93.1	0.6	0.9	0.8	1.5	3.4	5.6	6.5	6.6	6.7	6.9	6.1	24.9	27.8	12.0	2.5	75.9	39.0	48.8	51.2
	IOWA	93.9	91.9	2.1	2.5	1.3	2.1	2.8	4.1	6.5	6.4	6.5	7.3	7.1	25.2	26.5	11.9	2.6	76.5	38.1	49.3	50.7
	UNITED STATES	75.1	72.0	12.3	12.7	3.8	4.6	12.5	15.7	6.8	6.7	6.6	7.1	6.9	27.0	26.0	10.9	1.9	75.7	36.9	49.2	50.8

ZIP CODE #	POST OFFICE NAME	2009 Per Capita Income	2009 HH Income Base	2009 HOUSEHOLD INCOME DISTRIBUTION (%) Less than $25,000	$25,000 to $49,999	$50,000 to $99,999	$100,000 to $149,999	$150,000 or More	MEDIAN HOUSEHOLD INCOME 2009	2014	2009 National Centile	2009 State Centile	2009 Home Value Base	2009 HOME VALUE DISTRIBUTION (%) Less than $50,000	$50,000 to $89,999	$90,000 to $174,999	$175,000 to $399,999	$400,000 or More	2009 Median Home Value
50672	STEAMBOAT ROCK	19941	266	28.2	37.2	28.2	4.9	1.5	39090	41312	30	12	205	31.2	32.7	27.8	4.4	3.9	72391
50674	SUMNER	21878	1586	23.2	32.3	37.2	5.4	1.9	45244	48075	49	46	1280	10.0	34.0	42.3	10.9	2.8	99872
50675	TRAER	21886	970	22.8	31.1	38.8	6.7	0.6	46889	48283	54	56	774	16.4	24.5	44.1	12.5	2.5	102795
50676	TRIPOLI	22265	875	22.2	32.1	36.0	6.9	2.9	45926	49642	51	49	707	12.9	32.0	42.7	10.5	2.0	100084
50677	WAVERLY	25436	4344	16.9	29.4	40.6	8.8	4.4	53869	55662	69	83	3209	5.0	13.4	53.5	25.1	3.0	135017
50680	WELLSBURG	20972	536	24.4	39.0	31.2	3.7	1.7	41158	43853	37	21	437	35.7	40.5	17.6	4.8	1.4	60283
50681	WESTGATE	20456	203	21.7	34.0	35.0	8.4	1.0	45187	46527	49	45	168	19.0	26.8	37.5	14.3	2.4	95833
50682	WINTHROP	21791	643	24.9	30.5	36.5	5.1	3.0	46279	47236	52	52	509	13.2	27.5	39.9	15.5	3.9	104905
50701	WATERLOO	29394	12823	20.5	26.4	37.9	9.0	6.2	52621	54464	67	79	8995	12.9	22.4	45.2	17.2	2.4	110944
50702	WATERLOO	23739	8707	22.8	30.0	39.1	6.1	2.0	46776	50872	53	56	5760	8.3	44.3	42.7	4.1	0.6	88011
50703	WATERLOO	18424	7877	32.0	31.8	29.8	4.6	1.8	37148	39306	24	6	5351	38.6	38.0	17.7	4.9	0.8	59350
50707	EVANSDALE	20710	3260	24.5	33.0	35.7	5.5	1.3	43381	46704	43	33	2407	19.5	43.7	33.2	3.7	0.0	79576
50801	CRESTON	23018	4036	27.2	31.0	34.1	5.4	2.4	42232	44731	40	25	2827	21.8	30.8	38.2	8.1	1.1	86748
50830	AFTON	19060	699	30.2	34.2	30.8	4.1	0.7	40126	40949	33	16	536	30.2	32.8	26.7	9.0	1.3	73415
50833	BEDFORD	18789	1004	32.4	33.2	30.1	3.3	1.1	38626	39816	29	11	773	36.0	36.2	22.3	4.9	0.6	64077
50835	BENTON	23151	70	32.9	28.6	30.0	5.7	2.9	37310	40000	24	7	55	36.4	20.0	21.8	12.7	9.1	68333
50836	BLOCKTON	23583	185	28.6	36.2	29.2	2.2	3.8	39830	40910	32	14	147	34.0	34.0	21.8	9.5	0.7	75000
50837	BRIDGEWATER	20624	182	27.5	38.5	29.1	4.4	0.5	38949	40557	30	12	140	47.9	24.3	20.0	7.9	0.0	52308
50840	CLEARFIELD	19875	211	36.5	34.1	22.7	4.3	2.4	32714	33747	13	2	161	58.4	21.7	16.1	3.1	0.6	42500
50841	CORNING	19579	1193	30.2	33.9	31.0	4.1	0.8	37806	38551	26	8	885	33.1	33.6	27.0	5.6	0.7	67958
50843	CUMBERLAND	19705	256	32.8	34.8	27.7	2.7	2.0	37196	37965	24	7	199	31.2	26.6	28.6	12.1	1.5	81842
50845	DIAGONAL	19233	317	32.2	37.5	24.9	3.8	1.6	36189	36654	21	5	248	45.2	22.2	15.7	15.7	1.2	56000
50846	FONTANELLE	20704	519	22.7	36.6	36.6	3.1	1.0	42746	44839	42	30	418	30.9	31.6	29.2	7.4	1.0	75862
50847	GRANT	25878	19	21.1	26.3	47.4	5.3	0.0	52140	50924	66	78	15	26.7	26.7	40.0	6.7	0.0	85000
50848	GRAVITY	17423	207	40.6	21.7	34.3	2.4	1.0	38118	41285	27	9	164	42.1	36.6	18.3	3.0	0.0	55200
50849	GREENFIELD	23752	1159	25.7	28.3	37.8	5.0	3.2	46314	48118	52	53	860	16.2	41.3	34.4	7.7	0.5	83469
50851	LENOX	19326	799	28.0	36.4	29.7	4.0	1.9	39306	40563	31	13	576	31.8	31.1	29.5	5.4	2.3	70811
50853	MASSENA	19552	328	34.5	32.6	28.4	3.0	1.5	35000	36983	18	3	254	36.6	27.2	19.3	10.6	6.3	64118
50854	MOUNT AYR	18763	1005	35.4	32.3	27.3	3.8	1.2	35847	37340	20	4	734	27.0	39.4	27.8	5.3	0.5	73333
50857	NODAWAY	18523	166	31.3	28.9	34.9	4.8	0.0	38197	38971	27	9	134	38.1	29.9	28.4	2.2	1.5	66667
50858	ORIENT	20805	345	19.4	32.2	40.6	7.2	0.6	48639	50087	58	64	256	28.9	30.9	30.1	9.4	0.8	79000
50859	PRESCOTT	19371	242	28.1	36.4	30.2	4.1	1.2	37603	38714	26	8	193	32.6	23.8	27.5	14.0	2.1	71667
50860	REDDING	16315	163	35.6	33.7	28.2	2.5	0.0	36242	37486	21	5	125	30.4	32.0	30.4	6.4	0.8	73000
50861	SHANNON CITY	20706	123	35.8	31.7	28.5	2.4	1.6	32553	34060	12	2	103	28.2	37.9	20.4	13.6	0.0	75938
50862	SHARPSBURG	15874	60	31.7	41.7	25.0	1.7	0.0	37292	38586	24	7	49	38.8	24.5	34.7	2.0	0.0	67000
50863	TINGLEY	20797	138	31.9	34.1	26.1	7.2	0.7	35559	38827	19	4	113	31.0	24.8	28.3	14.2	1.8	77500
50864	VILLISCA	21415	845	28.3	34.3	29.3	6.4	1.7	39606	40849	32	14	665	40.9	27.5	23.3	6.3	2.0	60098
51001	AKRON	22933	955	26.2	33.6	32.0	5.7	2.5	41896	44568	39	24	718	11.7	27.6	47.1	10.6	3.1	103962
51002	ALTA	22766	1048	19.5	32.2	39.3	5.9	3.1	48312	50698	57	63	787	19.3	24.0	41.3	13.0	2.4	98750
51003	ALTON	18855	659	19.6	35.5	40.4	3.5	1.1	46311	48690	52	53	535	14.0	27.7	42.8	14.8	0.7	99674
51004	ANTHON	21788	502	30.3	31.1	31.7	3.8	3.2	39587	43084	31	14	408	33.3	29.2	26.2	9.6	1.7	71071
51005	AURELIA	22465	588	21.8	28.9	42.3	4.4	2.6	49335	50080	60	67	474	19.4	34.0	41.6	3.8	1.3	85789
51006	BATTLE CREEK	21670	446	26.2	35.0	32.3	4.3	2.2	41057	42589	36	20	350	38.0	34.6	21.4	4.6	1.4	60000
51007	BRONSON	23239	275	17.1	26.9	46.2	8.7	1.1	54034	54384	70	84	239	5.0	15.5	52.3	23.8	3.3	122461
51009	CALUMET	24174	80	21.3	35.0	33.8	6.3	3.8	46697	48146	53	55	62	24.2	37.1	25.8	8.1	4.8	81250
51010	CASTANA	18106	230	35.2	32.6	28.3	2.6	1.3	33812	35638	15	3	181	44.2	23.8	22.7	7.2	2.2	56563
51011	CHATSWORTH	22356	41	22.0	39.0	26.8	7.3	4.9	41151	45546	37	21	31	25.8	19.4	32.3	12.9	9.7	95000
51012	CHEROKEE	23833	2772	25.4	33.3	32.0	6.7	2.5	42964	44439	42	31	1957	21.9	41.1	28.3	7.9	0.9	77179
51014	CLEGHORN	20546	216	24.1	34.7	37.5	2.3	1.4	44667	46147	47	43	162	24.7	29.0	38.9	6.2	1.2	84545
51016	CORRECTIONVILLE	20596	592	29.7	32.1	29.9	5.7	2.5	40221	43478	33	16	466	37.1	29.6	27.3	4.5	1.5	64878
51018	CUSHING	21575	169	26.6	33.1	34.9	4.1	1.2	42131	44445	40	25	128	43.8	28.1	21.9	4.7	1.6	58889
51019	DANBURY	19885	329	30.4	35.6	28.6	4.0	1.5	39881	41834	32	14	243	24.3	26.3	37.0	11.9	0.4	89118
51020	GALVA	23353	223	26.5	41.3	23.3	4.9	4.0	38886	41188	29	12	178	39.9	27.5	21.9	10.1	0.6	57826
51022	GRANVILLE	18492	316	26.9	32.9	30.4	7.3	2.5	45133	46389	49	45	252	21.4	30.6	28.6	16.7	2.8	86875
51023	HAWARDEN	21891	1244	24.7	30.5	36.6	6.0	2.3	44516	47260	47	42	948	24.1	30.5	35.8	7.6	2.1	84819
51024	HINTON	25548	841	14.6	23.3	45.9	10.6	5.6	61708	60218	80	94	706	4.5	13.5	43.5	31.7	6.8	149048
51025	HOLSTEIN	22011	897	26.5	29.7	36.3	5.7	1.8	44454	45092	47	41	668	21.0	36.2	34.3	6.6	1.9	80588
51026	HORNICK	22444	351	19.4	32.8	37.6	5.4	4.8	47669	50353	56	60	280	24.6	20.0	39.6	12.9	2.9	100847
51027	IRETON	19427	473	19.7	35.9	39.1	3.6	1.7	46535	48160	53	54	379	16.9	20.8	44.9	11.9	5.5	103799
51028	KINGSLEY	23384	857	17.9	35.5	37.9	5.3	3.5	46901	48709	54	57	673	12.3	24.1	47.5	12.8	3.3	108613
51029	LARRABEE	24682	126	17.5	31.7	44.4	4.8	1.6	50585	50919	63	72	103	26.2	17.5	39.8	9.7	6.8	97222
51030	LAWTON	23011	548	15.9	26.3	46.2	10.6	1.1	56140	56171	73	88	463	9.3	15.6	50.8	23.5	0.9	120184
51031	LE MARS	24341	4676	21.8	27.7	38.6	8.1	3.9	50461	51830	62	71	3453	8.6	18.2	50.5	20.8	1.9	119126
51033	LINN GROVE	19936	225	22.7	40.4	32.9	3.1	0.9	41194	42493	37	21	166	42.8	20.5	27.7	8.4	0.6	58000
51034	MAPLETON	21685	778	29.8	33.2	31.1	3.3	2.6	39911	40635	32	14	610	26.9	35.1	32.1	5.6	0.3	75593
51035	MARCUS	22798	661	23.4	31.5	37.7	3.9	3.5	46479	47097	53	54	535	23.6	33.1	33.1	8.4	1.9	82900
51036	MAURICE	20496	239	11.3	33.9	46.0	8.4	0.4	52971	52803	68	80	194	12.9	24.2	45.4	15.5	2.1	106667
51037	MERIDEN	22725	162	22.8	32.7	40.1	2.5	1.9	46398	47150	53	53	122	21.3	28.7	42.6	5.7	1.6	90000
51038	MERRILL	23387	563	17.6	29.3	41.9	6.7	4.4	52254	52286	66	78	482	9.5	21.0	49.6	17.6	2.3	115733
51039	MOVILLE	21886	962	21.0	28.9	42.2	5.3	2.6	50086	52188	61	70	744	13.2	23.8	48.1	14.0	0.9	107632
51040	ONAWA	22851	1605	28.1	30.3	34.7	4.6	2.2	44467	45725	47	41	1191	24.0	36.9	34.2	4.2	0.8	80263
51041	ORANGE CITY	21845	2143	16.1	30.1	43.2	7.3	3.4	52986	53581	68	81	1717	4.5	17.2	52.5	23.1	2.7	129907
51044	OTO	20221	119	26.9	31.9	33.6	7.6	0.0	44541	47063	47	42	92	30.4	25.0	32.6	9.8	2.2	80000
51046	PAULLINA	21932	734	22.8	35.4	34.7	5.0	2.0	43159	45847	43	32	601	27.6	39.9	27.1	3.8	1.5	73526
51047	PETERSON	21151	342	21.1	40.6	34.5	2.9	0.9	42719	45114	42	30	267	36.7	25.1	25.5	10.1	2.6	63947
51048	PIERSON	21564	248	16.5	39.5	38.3	3.6	2.0	45526	48556	50	47	198	29.3	33.3	24.2	12.1	1.0	71538
51049	QUIMBY	18823	229	30.6	32.3	32.3	3.9	0.9	38281	41042	28	9	169	34.3	27.2	29.0	8.9	0.6	70455
51050	REMSEN	20057	1064	20.6	32.6	39.9	5.0	1.9	46940	49454	54	57	860	7.0	23.1	56.5	11.2	2.2	112281
51051	RODNEY	19485	54	37.0	33.3	25.9	1.9	1.9	32311	33606	12	1	43	44.2	23.3	25.6	4.7	2.3	56250
51052	SALIX	24767	407	16.7	33.9	34.6	12.8	2.0	49426	52352	60	67	329	18.5	25.2	38.3	17.6	0.3	104481
51053	SCHALLER	19621	484	20.9	38.4	36.2	4.1	0.4	43804	46165	45	36	378	26.5	34.1	30.4	7.9	1.1	78378
51054	SERGEANT BLUFF	24085	1496	14.1	27.6	43.2	11.6	3.5	59044	57680	76	91	1109	19.3	15.5	39.0	25.5	0.6	118826
51055	SLOAN	25194	598	20.2	25.8	41.6	11.0	1.3	53351	54281	69	82	452	13.3	27.0	51.3	8.4	0.0	103000
51056	SMITHLAND	21114	198	26.3	30.8	34.3	8.6	0.0	45294	48072	49	46	155	32.3	24.5	31.6	9.0	2.6	77500
51058	SUTHERLAND	21841	450	25.8	33.3	35.8	3.8	1.3	43719	45536	44	36	367	43.3	36.0	16.6	2.7	1.4	56447
51060	UTE	22464	269	25.7	35.3	34.2	2.2	2.6	40958	41659	36	19	214	38.3	37.4	20.1	2.3	1.9	60909
51061	WASHTA	19523	209	25.4	37.3	31.6	4.3	1.4	42183	43062	40	25	146	24.7	27.4	32.9	12.3	2.7	87500
51062	WESTFIELD	28791	291	19.2	21.6	40.2	10.3	8.6	59780	57141	77	92	241	12.0	14.1	32.0	26.1	15.8	149519
51063	WHITING	20695	404	25.7	31.9	33.4	7.9	1.0	43522	45000	44	34	305	29.5	30.5	31.5	7.2	1.3	75179
51101	SIOUX CITY	17037	384	47.9	29.9	21.1	0.3	0.8	26433	27018	4	1	40	50.0	40.0	7.5	2.5	0.0	50000
51103	SIOUX CITY	19166	6103	25.3	32.3	34.5	5.4	2.4	43820	46961	45	37	3986	18.5	43.3	34.1	3.7	0.4	80728
51104	SIOUX CITY	30627	8169	15.7	24.7	40.0	11.4	8.3	60551	61359	78	93	5553	4.7	23.2	52.0	17.9	2.3	113497
51105	SIOUX CITY	15787	3984	32.8	35.9	26.4	3.0	1.8	35000	36978	18	3	1922	47.5	38.7	12.2	1.7	0.0	52438
51106	SIOUX CITY	26410	10563	15.5	27.2	40.6	12.6	4.1	56486	57532	73	89	7766	7.4	24.8	53.3	13.9	0.6	109067
51108	SIOUX CITY	25934	2683	17.7	30.9	39.5	7.7	4.2	51047	52915	64	74	2099	28.0	21.3	31.5	16.5	2.6	91368
	IOWA	25379		21.1	28.2	37.9	8.6	4.3	50616	52941				14.7	22.5	41.6	18.6	2.6	110128
	UNITED STATES	27277		20.9	24.4	35.3	11.7	7.6	54719	56938				9.3	13.1	31.6	32.6	13.5	162279

ZIP CODE #	POST OFFICE NAME	FINANCIAL SERVICES: Auto Loan	Home Loan	Invest-ments	Retire-ment Plans	THE HOME: Home Improvements: Home Repair	Lawn & Garden	Furnishings: Comput-ers & Hard-ware-Personal	Major Appli-ances	TV, Radio, Sound Equip-ment	Furni-ture	ENTERTAINMENT: Dine out/ Carry out	Sports Equip-ment	Fees & Tickets	Toys & Games	Travel	Cable TV	PERSONAL: Apparel & Services	Auto Repairs	Health Insur-ance	Pets & Supplies
50672	STEAMBOAT ROCK	81	58	82	56	60	84	63	78	70	56	68	59	50	69	61	77	45	73	85	92
50674	SUMNER	82	72	82	72	71	89	73	81	75	65	75	64	66	75	73	80	50	78	88	98
50675	TRAER	80	68	85	67	70	89	69	81	74	62	72	61	62	72	70	80	49	77	89	96
50676	TRIPOLI	90	72	87	73	74	95	75	89	80	67	78	67	64	80	74	87	52	82	94	104
50677	WAVERLY	92	89	91	90	91	99	89	94	92	87	91	70	87	91	90	95	62	93	102	110
50680	WELLSBURG	83	59	85	58	61	87	65	80	71	56	69	61	50	69	63	78	45	74	86	95
50681	WESTGATE	97	67	106	66	70	102	74	92	77	60	76	76	54	75	74	84	49	86	97	113
50682	WINTHROP	97	69	104	69	72	102	75	93	78	62	77	76	57	77	75	85	51	86	98	113
50701	WATERLOO	96	94	87	95	92	99	95	95	97	93	97	73	94	98	93	99	67	96	101	113
50702	WATERLOO	77	74	68	75	72	80	77	76	79	73	79	58	75	79	75	82	54	78	84	91
50703	WATERLOO	68	60	55	61	58	67	66	64	70	62	68	49	62	69	61	73	47	67	72	78
50707	EVANSDALE	75	70	69	70	68	82	70	75	74	66	73	57	67	74	69	78	50	74	83	89
50801	CRESTON	77	69	70	69	67	81	71	75	75	66	73	58	66	75	69	79	50	75	83	90
50830	AFTON	77	55	80	54	57	81	60	74	65	52	64	58	47	64	59	72	42	69	80	89
50833	BEDFORD	77	55	79	54	57	81	60	75	66	53	64	57	48	65	59	73	43	70	81	88
50835	BENTON	98	68	108	67	71	104	75	93	78	61	77	77	55	76	75	85	50	87	98	115
50836	BLOCKTON	95	68	99	66	70	97	70	89	77	64	76	68	55	76	70	85	50	82	93	107
50837	BRIDGEWATER	80	55	88	55	58	85	61	76	64	50	63	63	45	63	61	70	41	71	81	94
50840	CLEARFIELD	73	53	74	51	55	76	58	71	64	51	62	53	46	63	56	71	41	66	77	84
50841	CORNING	73	57	77	56	59	79	60	72	64	53	63	55	50	63	60	70	42	68	78	86
50843	CUMBERLAND	82	56	90	56	59	86	63	78	65	51	64	64	46	64	62	71	42	73	82	96
50845	DIAGONAL	80	55	88	55	58	85	61	76	64	50	63	63	45	62	61	69	41	71	80	94
50846	FONTANELLE	84	59	86	58	62	88	65	81	71	56	69	62	51	70	63	78	46	75	87	96
50847	GRANT	100	69	110	69	72	105	76	95	79	62	78	78	56	78	76	87	51	89	100	117
50848	GRAVITY	79	54	86	54	57	83	60	75	62	49	62	62	44	61	60	68	40	70	79	92
50849	GREENFIELD	92	69	93	68	71	96	75	89	81	67	79	68	61	80	73	88	53	84	97	106
50851	LENOX	80	57	83	55	59	84	62	77	68	54	66	59	48	66	61	74	43	72	83	92
50853	MASSENA	80	55	88	55	58	85	61	76	64	50	63	63	45	63	61	70	41	71	81	94
50854	MOUNT AYR	74	53	77	52	55	78	58	72	64	51	62	55	46	62	57	70	41	67	78	85
50857	NODAWAY	80	56	86	55	58	84	62	77	66	52	64	61	47	64	61	72	42	72	82	93
50858	ORIENT	94	65	103	65	68	99	72	89	75	58	74	74	53	73	71	82	48	83	94	110
50859	PRESCOTT	81	55	88	55	58	85	62	76	64	50	63	63	45	63	61	70	41	71	81	94
50860	REDDING	74	51	81	51	53	78	57	70	59	46	58	58	41	58	56	64	38	66	74	86
50861	SHANNON CITY	77	53	85	53	55	81	59	73	61	48	61	60	43	60	59	67	39	68	77	90
50862	SHARPSBURG	71	49	78	49	51	75	55	68	57	44	56	56	40	56	54	62	36	63	72	83
50863	TINGLEY	74	59	95	58	65	79	59	75	62	55	61	55	51	59	64	66	41	70	75	88
50864	VILLISCA	85	61	88	60	63	89	67	82	73	58	71	63	52	72	65	80	47	77	89	98
51001	AKRON	88	71	85	72	73	93	74	87	79	66	77	66	63	79	73	85	52	81	92	102
51002	ALTA	84	83	76	85	79	91	83	84	84	78	83	67	81	85	82	86	57	84	91	102
51003	ALTON	79	68	75	70	70	85	69	79	71	61	70	61	61	72	69	76	47	73	82	93
51004	ANTHON	88	62	90	61	65	92	68	85	75	59	73	65	53	73	67	82	48	79	91	101
51005	AURELIA	95	67	98	66	70	99	74	91	81	64	79	70	58	79	72	89	52	85	99	109
51006	BATTLE CREEK	87	62	90	61	64	91	68	84	74	59	72	65	53	73	66	82	48	78	91	100
51007	BRONSON	94	84	86	87	86	101	83	95	86	75	85	72	76	88	83	91	58	88	98	111
51009	CALUMET	100	69	110	69	72	105	76	95	79	62	79	78	56	78	76	87	51	89	100	117
51010	CASTANA	75	52	81	51	54	79	57	71	60	47	59	58	42	59	57	65	38	66	75	87
51011	CHATSWORTH	95	65	104	65	68	100	72	90	75	59	74	74	53	74	72	82	48	84	95	110
51012	CHEROKEE	84	67	83	66	69	89	71	82	77	65	75	62	61	76	70	83	50	79	90	97
51014	CLEGHORN	89	62	98	61	64	94	68	85	71	55	70	70	50	70	68	78	46	79	90	105
51016	CORRECTIONVILLE	87	62	91	61	64	91	68	84	74	58	72	65	52	72	66	81	47	78	90	100
51018	CUSHING	91	63	100	63	66	96	70	86	72	56	72	71	51	71	69	79	46	81	91	106
51019	DANBURY	85	58	93	58	61	90	65	81	68	53	67	67	48	66	65	74	43	75	85	99
51020	GALVA	95	66	105	66	69	101	73	91	76	59	75	75	54	74	73	83	49	85	96	111
51022	GRANVILLE	90	62	99	62	65	95	69	85	71	56	71	71	50	70	68	78	46	80	90	105
51023	HAWARDEN	86	64	78	63	64	86	72	81	77	64	75	62	58	77	67	84	50	79	88	97
51024	HINTON	101	106	100	109	104	111	98	104	97	95	97	82	100	99	102	98	67	100	104	123
51025	HOLSTEIN	88	63	91	61	65	92	69	85	75	60	73	66	54	74	67	83	48	79	92	101
51026	HORNICK	104	71	114	71	75	109	79	98	82	64	81	81	58	81	79	90	53	92	104	121
51027	IRETON	91	63	100	63	66	96	70	87	73	56	72	72	51	71	69	79	47	81	92	107
51028	KINGSLEY	83	81	90	79	82	97	76	87	81	71	80	65	75	79	81	87	54	83	97	102
51029	LARRABEE	96	66	106	66	69	102	74	91	77	60	76	76	54	75	73	83	49	85	97	113
51030	LAWTON	90	98	86	101	96	99	89	94	88	87	88	73	92	90	93	89	61	90	94	110
51031	LE MARS	94	83	86	84	83	95	87	92	89	81	88	71	80	90	84	93	60	90	96	109
51033	LINN GROVE	86	60	95	59	62	91	66	82	69	54	68	68	48	67	66	75	44	77	87	101
51034	MAPLETON	84	61	85	59	63	88	66	82	74	59	71	61	53	72	64	81	47	76	89	96
51035	MARCUS	96	68	100	67	71	101	75	93	82	65	80	72	58	80	73	90	53	87	100	111
51036	MAURICE	104	71	114	71	75	109	79	98	82	64	81	81	58	81	79	90	53	92	104	121
51037	MERIDEN	93	64	102	64	67	98	71	88	74	57	73	73	52	72	70	80	47	82	93	108
51038	MERRILL	94	87	87	90	88	101	85	95	87	78	86	73	79	88	86	91	58	88	98	111
51039	MOVILLE	94	80	85	78	79	92	79	87	82	77	81	66	70	84	76	85	55	84	89	105
51040	ONAWA	85	67	88	65	69	92	70	84	76	62	74	64	59	75	70	83	50	79	92	99
51041	ORANGE CITY	97	83	92	85	86	100	88	96	91	82	89	72	79	90	86	95	61	93	101	113
51044	OTO	87	60	95	60	63	92	66	82	69	54	68	68	49	68	66	75	44	77	87	102
51046	PAULLINA	87	62	90	61	64	91	68	84	74	59	72	65	53	73	66	81	48	78	91	100
51047	PETERSON	85	59	94	59	61	90	65	81	68	53	67	67	48	66	65	74	43	76	85	100
51048	PIERSON	95	65	104	65	68	100	73	90	76	59	75	74	54	74	72	83	49	84	95	111
51049	QUIMBY	81	56	89	55	58	85	62	77	64	50	63	63	45	63	61	70	41	72	81	94
51050	REMSEN	85	72	82	74	74	91	73	85	76	64	74	66	64	76	73	81	50	79	88	100
51051	RODNEY	75	52	82	52	54	79	58	71	60	47	59	59	42	59	57	66	39	67	76	88
51052	SALIX	98	86	91	90	88	105	86	99	89	77	88	76	78	91	86	95	60	91	102	115
51053	SCHALLER	85	60	88	59	62	89	66	82	72	57	70	63	51	71	64	79	46	76	88	97
51054	SERGEANT BLUFF	106	100	91	98	99	102	94	100	97	97	97	73	91	100	91	99	66	96	99	118
51055	SLOAN	86	83	73	85	78	92	84	84	85	78	85	68	82	87	82	88	58	85	93	103
51056	SMITHLAND	88	61	97	61	64	93	68	84	70	55	69	69	49	69	67	77	45	78	89	103
51058	SUTHERLAND	84	60	87	59	62	88	66	81	71	57	70	63	51	70	64	79	46	76	88	97
51060	UTE	82	59	83	57	61	86	64	79	71	57	69	60	51	70	62	78	46	74	86	94
51061	WASHTA	85	59	94	58	61	90	65	81	68	53	67	67	48	66	65	74	43	76	85	100
51062	WESTFIELD	105	117	102	120	114	116	105	110	104	105	104	86	111	106	111	104	73	105	109	129
51063	WHITING	90	64	93	62	66	94	70	87	76	61	74	67	55	75	68	84	49	81	93	103
51101	SIOUX CITY	49	40	41	41	40	45	51	47	54	46	53	36	46	52	45	56	37	51	53	56
51103	SIOUX CITY	76	69	61	70	66	76	76	73	78	70	77	57	71	79	70	81	53	76	81	88
51104	SIOUX CITY	108	108	99	110	106	112	110	108	111	107	110	83	110	111	109	113	77	110	115	128
51105	SIOUX CITY	64	54	49	54	51	56	64	59	66	60	66	46	58	66	57	67	46	63	63	71
51106	SIOUX CITY	93	96	83	97	91	98	95	93	95	92	95	72	96	97	93	97	66	94	99	111
51108	SIOUX CITY	90	90	78	91	86	90	91	88	90	89	91	69	90	92	89	91	63	90	92	105
	IOWA	93	84	87	85	83	95	87	91	89	82	88	71	81	90	85	92	61	90	96	108
	UNITED STATES	100	100	100	100	100	100	100	100	100	100	100	100	100	100	100	100	100	100	100	100

51109-51544

ZIP CODE #	POST OFFICE NAME	COUNTY FIPS CODE	POPULATION 2000	POPULATION 2009	POPULATION 2014	2000-2009 ANNUAL RATE % Rate	2000-2009 ANNUAL RATE State Centile	HOUSEHOLDS 2000	HOUSEHOLDS 2009	HOUSEHOLDS 2014	HOUSEHOLDS % Annual Rate 2000-2009	HOUSEHOLDS 2009 Average HH Size	FAMILIES 2000	FAMILIES 2009	FAMILIES % Annual Rate 2000-2009
51109	SIOUX CITY	149	2844	2797	2784	-0.2	46	1184	1199	1197	0.1	2.33	762	750	-0.2
51111	SIOUX CITY	193	143	140	140	-0.2	46	49	49	49	0.0	2.61	37	36	-0.3
51201	SHELDON	141	6217	6015	5877	-0.4	32	2406	2387	2345	-0.1	2.38	1637	1589	-0.3
51230	ALVORD	119	500	486	475	-0.3	40	159	161	159	0.1	3.02	131	130	-0.1
51231	ARCHER	141	263	255	251	-0.3	40	103	103	102	0.0	2.48	87	86	-0.1
51232	ASHTON	143	1029	979	941	-0.5	27	385	374	361	-0.3	2.60	286	273	-0.5
51234	BOYDEN	167	1235	1270	1290	0.3	72	456	484	496	0.6	2.59	361	377	0.5
51235	DOON	119	1043	1001	975	-0.4	32	350	351	345	0.0	2.85	284	280	-0.2
51237	GEORGE	119	1802	1743	1690	-0.4	32	750	749	731	0.0	2.26	514	501	-0.3
51238	HOSPERS	167	1233	1205	1197	-0.2	46	442	446	446	0.1	2.70	344	341	-0.1
51239	HULL	167	2954	3116	3182	0.6	83	971	1049	1080	0.8	2.91	779	830	0.7
51240	INWOOD	119	1854	1835	1804	-0.1	51	634	651	646	0.3	2.75	488	493	0.1
51241	LARCHWOOD	119	1888	1868	1838	-0.1	51	701	725	720	0.4	2.58	540	548	0.2
51243	LITTLE ROCK	119	814	780	753	-0.5	27	313	308	299	-0.2	2.53	230	222	-0.4
51245	PRIMGHAR	141	1425	1338	1293	-0.7	15	576	550	534	-0.5	2.32	383	358	-0.7
51246	ROCK RAPIDS	119	3788	3553	3406	-0.7	15	1494	1444	1397	-0.4	2.39	1059	1001	-0.6
51247	ROCK VALLEY	167	4453	4635	4722	0.4	76	1617	1739	1789	0.8	2.58	1188	1255	0.6
51248	SANBORN	141	1908	1876	1837	-0.2	46	739	748	737	0.1	2.39	527	519	-0.2
51249	SIBLEY	143	3770	3434	3247	-1.0	6	1523	1421	1351	-0.7	2.34	1034	943	-1.0
51250	SIOUX CENTER	167	7220	7754	7905	0.8	87	2196	2362	2428	0.8	2.69	1679	1775	0.6
51301	SPENCER	041	12872	12565	12326	-0.3	40	5438	5477	5411	0.1	2.25	3464	3404	-0.2
51331	ARNOLDS PARK	059	1041	1159	1213	1.2	93	510	580	612	1.4	2.00	322	355	1.1
51333	DICKENS	041	622	583	563	-0.7	15	227	220	214	-0.3	2.65	173	164	-0.6
51334	ESTHERVILLE	063	8377	7984	7748	-0.5	27	3319	3254	3184	-0.2	2.31	2137	2041	-0.5
51338	EVERLY	041	1039	989	964	-0.5	27	415	409	401	-0.2	2.42	297	286	-0.4
51342	GRAETTINGER	147	1275	1211	1169	-0.6	20	535	521	506	-0.3	2.30	343	327	-0.5
51343	GREENVILLE	041	332	309	298	-0.8	11	142	137	134	-0.4	2.26	101	96	-0.5
51345	HARRIS	143	443	430	413	-0.3	40	171	170	165	-0.1	2.53	129	126	-0.3
51346	HARTLEY	141	2724	2530	2425	-0.8	11	1070	1003	964	-0.7	2.43	732	670	-1.0
51347	LAKE PARK	059	1378	1417	1448	0.3	72	569	609	629	0.7	2.25	396	415	0.5
51350	MELVIN	143	473	453	434	-0.5	27	196	192	185	-0.2	2.35	137	131	-0.5
51351	MILFORD	059	4330	4669	4824	0.8	87	1867	2077	2160	1.2	2.22	1232	1331	0.8
51354	OCHEYEDAN	143	1267	1180	1122	-0.8	11	492	468	447	-0.5	2.52	355	331	-0.8
51355	OKOBOJI	059	844	735	692	-1.5	1	442	377	357	-1.7	1.87	264	217	-2.1
51357	ROYAL	041	810	766	743	-0.6	20	322	314	307	-0.3	2.44	221	211	-0.5
51358	RUTHVEN	147	1361	1342	1294	-0.2	46	582	568	553	-0.3	2.26	396	378	-0.5
51360	SPIRIT LAKE	059	7830	8170	8328	0.5	79	3328	3568	3662	0.8	2.25	2256	2365	0.5
51363	SUPERIOR	059	179	207	220	1.6	95	73	88	94	2.0	2.35	54	64	1.9
51364	TERRIL	059	837	920	975	1.0	90	322	384	410	1.9	2.40	242	281	1.6
51365	WALLINGFORD	063	226	212	205	-0.7	15	99	97	94	-0.2	2.08	73	70	-0.5
51366	WEBB	041	445	410	393	-0.9	8	179	170	165	-0.6	2.41	134	125	-0.7
51401	CARROLL	027	12649	12414	12260	-0.2	46	5020	5122	5117	0.2	2.36	3310	3297	0.0
51430	ARCADIA	027	908	919	914	0.1	63	324	343	346	0.6	2.68	245	254	0.4
51431	ARTHUR	093	460	411	386	-1.2	4	187	175	166	-0.7	2.35	139	127	-1.0
51433	AUBURN	161	764	705	671	-0.9	8	301	287	275	-0.5	2.46	212	197	-0.8
51436	BREDA	027	870	829	813	-0.5	27	350	348	346	-0.1	2.38	243	236	-0.3
51439	CHARTER OAK	047	1138	1119	1106	-0.2	46	486	488	484	0.0	2.29	332	326	-0.2
51440	DEDHAM	027	453	444	438	-0.2	46	172	176	176	0.2	2.52	121	121	0.0
51441	DELOIT	047	362	346	340	-0.5	27	141	139	137	-0.2	2.49	101	97	-0.4
51442	DENISON	047	8931	8917	8852	0.0	58	3254	3264	3235	0.0	2.56	2201	2157	-0.2
51443	GLIDDEN	027	2097	2084	2063	-0.1	51	811	833	834	0.3	2.33	560	561	0.0
51444	HALBUR	027	11	10	10	-1.0	6	3	3	3	0.0	3.33	2	2	0.0
51445	IDA GROVE	093	3189	2779	2587	-1.5	1	1322	1196	1124	-1.1	2.28	871	769	-1.3
51446	IRWIN	165	669	713	713	0.7	85	279	310	313	1.1	2.30	203	221	0.9
51447	KIRKMAN	165	292	306	305	0.5	79	113	123	124	0.9	2.49	86	92	0.7
51448	KIRON	047	660	628	616	-0.5	27	282	277	273	-0.2	2.27	200	193	-0.4
51449	LAKE CITY	025	2421	2271	2168	-0.7	15	1023	954	912	-0.8	2.24	656	597	-1.0
51450	LAKE VIEW	161	1777	1672	1617	-0.7	15	767	743	724	-0.3	2.20	512	483	-0.6
51451	LANESBORO	027	44	42	42	-0.5	27	17	17	17	0.0	2.47	13	13	0.0
51452	LIDDERDALE	027	65	63	62	-0.3	40	17	17	17	0.0	3.71	13	13	0.0
51453	LOHRVILLE	025	817	793	778	-0.3	40	332	328	323	-0.1	2.42	232	224	-0.4
51454	MANILLA	047	1517	1507	1496	-0.1	51	565	581	580	0.3	2.50	399	402	0.1
51455	MANNING	027	2324	2201	2143	-0.6	20	935	904	888	-0.4	2.35	611	577	-0.6
51458	ODEBOLT	161	1730	1598	1528	-0.9	8	674	639	614	-0.6	2.38	455	421	-0.8
51460	RICKETTS	047	54	52	51	-0.4	32	20	20	19	0.0	2.60	14	14	0.0
51461	SCHLESWIG	047	1134	1127	1119	-0.1	51	480	488	486	0.2	2.31	331	329	-0.1
51462	SCRANTON	073	1150	1113	1077	-0.4	32	471	461	447	-0.2	2.41	330	316	-0.5
51463	TEMPLETON	027	609	582	572	-0.5	27	240	239	237	0.0	2.44	172	167	-0.3
51465	VAIL	047	916	894	881	-0.3	40	346	348	346	0.1	2.57	254	251	-0.1
51466	WALL LAKE	161	1216	1143	1104	-0.7	15	470	450	435	-0.5	2.40	326	306	-0.7
51467	WESTSIDE	047	550	538	530	-0.2	46	225	227	225	0.1	2.37	165	164	-0.1
51501	COUNCIL BLUFFS	155	33992	34725	34922	0.2	68	13129	13757	13926	0.5	2.51	8780	8933	0.2
51503	COUNCIL BLUFFS	155	33704	35305	35860	0.5	79	13093	14041	14333	0.8	2.42	9130	9637	0.6
51510	CARTER LAKE	155	3248	3487	3595	0.8	87	1221	1367	1422	1.2	2.55	914	999	1.0
51520	ARION	047	279	294	296	0.6	83	101	109	111	0.8	2.70	82	87	0.6
51521	AVOCA	155	2152	2256	2281	0.5	79	858	917	933	0.7	2.35	618	643	0.4
51523	BLENCOE	133	338	325	314	-0.4	32	158	157	154	-0.1	2.06	113	110	-0.3
51525	CARSON	155	1127	1156	1157	0.3	72	454	479	483	0.6	2.41	332	342	0.3
51526	CRESCENT	155	1394	1685	1798	2.1	97	515	633	679	2.3	2.52	409	493	2.0
51527	DEFIANCE	165	639	658	654	0.3	72	224	240	240	0.7	2.72	172	182	0.6
51528	DOW CITY	047	1125	1141	1137	0.2	68	446	465	466	0.5	2.45	328	335	0.2
51529	DUNLAP	085	1787	1708	1669	-0.5	27	720	709	696	-0.2	2.33	478	459	-0.4
51530	EARLING	165	1084	927	897	-1.7	0	397	357	348	-1.1	2.47	274	242	-1.3
51531	ELK HORN	165	1003	936	903	-0.7	15	380	363	351	-0.5	2.34	280	263	-0.7
51532	ELLIOTT	137	795	741	713	-0.8	11	312	297	287	-0.5	2.49	236	220	-0.8
51533	EMERSON	137	1074	1074	1073	0.0	58	404	414	416	0.3	2.59	297	297	0.0
51534	GLENWOOD	129	8674	9268	9601	0.7	85	3033	3334	3472	1.0	2.61	2232	2410	0.8
51535	GRISWOLD	029	2054	2078	2056	0.1	63	812	833	826	0.3	2.43	572	574	0.0
51536	HANCOCK	155	554	549	548	-0.1	51	217	221	222	0.2	2.48	161	160	-0.1
51537	HARLAN	165	7063	6690	6459	-0.6	20	2842	2786	2706	-0.2	2.36	2007	1924	-0.5
51540	HASTINGS	129	438	471	490	0.8	87	175	195	204	1.2	2.42	130	142	1.0
51541	HENDERSON	129	389	377	373	-0.3	40	164	165	164	0.1	2.28	121	119	-0.2
51542	HONEY CREEK	155	1154	1315	1374	1.4	94	428	506	532	1.8	2.60	336	390	1.6
51543	KIMBALLTON	009	443	444	440	0.0	58	178	182	180	0.2	2.43	131	131	0.0
51544	LEWIS	029	787	745	721	-0.6	20	324	313	305	-0.4	2.38	240	228	-0.6
	IOWA					0.4					0.7	2.40			0.4
	UNITED STATES					1.0					1.1	2.59			0.9

ZIP CODE #	POST OFFICE NAME	RACE (%) White 2000	White 2009	Black 2000	Black 2009	Asian/Pacific 2000	Asian/Pacific 2009	% Hispanic Origin 2000	% Hispanic Origin 2009	2009 AGE DISTRIBUTION (%) 0-4	5-9	10-14	15-19	20-24	25-44	45-64	65-84	85+	18+	MEDIAN AGE 2009	% 2009 Males	% 2009 Females
51109	SIOUX CITY	94.1	91.8	1.4	1.9	0.6	1.0	4.0	6.5	6.1	6.0	6.1	6.7	6.5	27.6	27.2	12.0	1.8	77.8	38.2	50.8	49.2
51111	SIOUX CITY	86.7	81.4	0.0	0.0	2.8	5.7	7.0	10.7	9.3	9.3	7.1	5.7	10.0	30.0	25.0	3.6	0.0	71.4	30.5	47.9	52.1
51201	SHELDON	97.7	96.8	0.4	0.4	0.7	1.1	2.2	3.1	6.7	6.8	6.8	6.7	5.6	26.0	24.6	13.1	3.8	75.9	38.5	50.1	49.9
51230	ALVORD	99.6	99.6	0.0	0.0	0.0	0.0	0.2	0.2	9.5	9.7	9.5	7.8	4.5	25.5	23.3	9.5	0.8	66.5	33.2	52.9	47.1
51231	ARCHER	98.9	98.4	0.0	0.0	0.8	1.2	1.5	2.0	7.1	7.5	8.6	7.8	4.7	23.5	27.5	11.8	1.6	71.8	37.7	51.0	49.0
51232	ASHTON	99.3	99.1	0.1	0.1	0.1	0.2	0.6	0.8	6.9	7.3	7.3	6.7	4.9	23.7	28.2	13.1	1.9	74.1	40.0	50.2	49.8
51234	BOYDEN	98.7	98.0	0.2	0.2	0.3	0.6	1.9	2.9	7.9	8.5	8.3	7.0	4.6	23.6	26.6	11.7	1.8	71.0	37.1	53.9	46.1
51235	DOON	99.8	99.7	0.0	0.0	0.0	0.1	0.2	0.2	8.2	8.5	8.7	8.1	4.6	25.2	25.4	10.3	1.1	69.4	35.3	53.1	46.9
51237	GEORGE	99.1	99.0	0.2	0.2	0.1	0.1	0.3	0.5	5.1	5.3	5.8	6.4	4.8	21.0	27.9	18.8	4.9	79.3	46.1	49.0	51.0
51238	HOSPERS	97.2	96.3	0.0	0.0	0.4	0.7	1.1	1.7	7.6	8.0	8.0	7.0	4.6	23.2	26.7	13.1	2.0	72.1	38.5	50.6	49.4
51239	HULL	95.7	93.5	0.1	0.2	0.8	1.4	4.6	7.0	8.4	8.6	8.6	7.9	4.8	24.8	23.8	10.0	2.9	69.2	34.6	50.5	49.5
51240	INWOOD	98.2	97.7	0.2	0.3	0.1	0.2	1.2	1.7	7.8	8.1	8.3	7.6	4.7	24.1	24.9	11.2	3.2	70.8	36.8	49.9	50.1
51241	LARCHWOOD	99.0	98.8	0.0	0.0	0.2	0.4	0.2	0.3	7.4	8.1	7.9	7.0	4.6	25.3	27.2	10.3	2.2	72.2	36.9	51.3	48.7
51243	LITTLE ROCK	99.5	99.5	0.0	0.0	0.2	0.3	0.2	0.3	6.2	6.5	7.3	7.6	4.5	22.9	27.2	15.0	2.8	75.3	41.5	49.2	50.8
51245	PRIMGHAR	98.0	97.1	0.4	0.5	1.0	1.5	0.9	1.4	5.0	5.3	5.7	6.1	5.6	20.7	29.4	17.6	4.6	80.0	46.1	49.4	50.6
51246	ROCK RAPIDS	99.3	99.1	0.1	0.1	0.3	0.4	0.2	0.3	6.2	6.3	6.6	7.1	5.4	22.4	27.0	14.8	4.2	76.4	41.5	48.5	51.5
51247	ROCK VALLEY	98.7	98.1	0.1	0.1	0.2	0.4	1.2	1.8	7.3	7.1	7.5	8.8	5.3	23.1	24.4	13.8	2.8	72.7	37.5	49.3	50.7
51248	SANBORN	99.0	98.6	0.2	0.2	0.2	0.2	0.6	1.1	5.1	5.3	6.2	6.9	5.1	21.7	25.8	18.3	5.6	78.7	44.7	48.0	52.0
51249	SIBLEY	97.7	96.8	0.2	0.2	0.3	0.4	2.1	3.1	6.2	6.2	6.1	6.2	5.9	22.5	26.8	15.4	4.7	77.7	42.4	47.7	52.3
51250	SIOUX CENTER	96.9	95.6	0.1	0.1	0.8	1.3	4.0	5.7	6.2	6.3	6.5	13.4	14.1	21.2	21.0	8.9	2.3	76.9	28.3	48.7	51.3
51301	SPENCER	97.7	96.7	0.2	0.2	1.1	1.8	1.3	1.9	6.3	6.2	6.3	6.4	5.8	25.0	27.2	13.4	3.4	77.3	40.2	47.4	52.6
51331	ARNOLDS PARK	97.3	96.9	0.6	0.6	0.3	0.3	0.3	0.4	5.6	6.5	6.9	5.2	2.8	24.8	30.1	15.8	2.3	78.3	43.7	49.8	50.2
51333	DICKENS	99.4	99.1	0.0	0.0	0.5	0.7	0.2	0.2	5.5	6.3	6.7	7.9	4.3	21.8	32.4	13.0	2.1	76.5	43.1	49.9	50.1
51334	ESTHERVILLE	96.9	95.6	0.3	0.3	0.4	0.6	5.4	7.9	5.5	5.5	6.5	9.3	6.7	22.4	25.6	14.2	4.2	77.2	40.1	49.0	51.0
51338	EVERLY	99.2	99.0	0.1	0.1	0.1	0.2	0.2	0.3	6.2	6.2	7.2	7.1	4.1	25.5	29.5	12.1	2.1	76.1	41.3	51.8	48.2
51342	GRAETTINGER	98.7	98.5	0.1	0.1	0.2	0.2	0.9	1.3	6.6	6.5	7.2	7.2	5.0	23.3	26.6	14.7	2.9	74.4	40.0	48.6	51.4
51343	GREENVILLE	97.9	97.7	1.2	1.3	0.0	0.0	1.5	1.9	4.9	6.1	8.7	7.1	3.2	23.6	32.7	12.0	1.6	75.4	42.9	51.5	48.5
51345	HARRIS	98.0	97.2	0.0	0.0	0.5	0.7	1.6	2.3	4.7	8.8	8.4	7.7	4.7	24.7	27.0	12.3	1.9	72.6	40.0	51.6	48.4
51346	HARTLEY	97.4	96.6	0.8	0.9	0.3	0.6	3.2	4.7	6.3	6.3	6.9	6.8	5.1	22.1	27.8	13.9	4.8	75.8	42.1	50.2	49.8
51347	LAKE PARK	99.1	98.8	0.1	0.1	0.1	0.1	0.8	1.2	5.1	5.2	5.8	6.2	4.9	23.3	28.0	16.9	4.7	79.7	44.7	49.5	50.5
51350	MELVIN	97.0	96.0	0.0	0.0	0.0	0.0	2.5	3.8	4.6	5.5	6.2	5.7	4.2	21.0	35.1	15.2	2.4	79.9	46.6	50.1	49.9
51351	MILFORD	98.8	98.5	0.2	0.2	0.3	0.5	0.9	1.2	5.3	5.2	5.9	6.2	4.9	22.2	29.6	17.5	3.3	79.6	45.3	49.5	50.5
51354	OCHEYEDAN	98.8	98.4	0.0	0.0	0.2	0.3	1.3	1.9	6.0	8.0	8.2	7.1	3.9	23.5	28.3	13.0	2.0	73.1	40.1	51.4	48.6
51355	OKOBOJI	99.1	98.4	0.1	0.3	0.0	0.1	0.5	0.8	3.5	3.8	4.1	4.5	4.2	20.7	34.7	21.6	2.9	88.6	51.7	50.7	49.3
51357	ROYAL	99.6	99.6	0.0	0.0	0.0	0.0	1.1	1.7	6.1	6.4	7.0	6.9	4.3	26.1	29.0	11.7	2.3	76.1	40.3	51.6	48.4
51358	RUTHVEN	97.9	97.0	0.0	0.1	0.3	0.7	1.0	1.3	5.7	6.0	6.0	6.9	5.7	23.4	27.1	16.1	3.1	80.4	41.7	48.5	51.5
51360	SPIRIT LAKE	99.1	98.9	0.1	0.2	0.1	0.2	0.6	0.9	5.2	5.4	5.8	5.4	4.7	20.9	32.1	16.8	3.6	80.4	46.7	48.0	52.0
51363	SUPERIOR	99.4	99.5	0.0	0.0	0.6	0.5	0.6	1.0	3.4	4.3	4.8	4.8	2.9	17.9	36.7	22.7	2.4	84.5	52.8	49.8	50.2
51364	TERRIL	98.7	98.5	0.4	0.3	0.4	0.5	0.5	0.8	5.4	6.3	7.0	6.5	3.9	23.5	32.3	13.3	1.8	77.5	43.3	51.5	48.5
51365	WALLINGFORD	97.8	97.6	0.4	0.5	0.0	0.0	2.7	3.3	4.2	6.1	8.5	9.9	3.8	22.2	28.8	14.2	2.4	74.1	41.9	50.5	49.5
51366	WEBB	98.9	98.3	0.2	0.2	0.7	1.0	0.4	0.5	5.9	6.8	7.6	7.6	4.4	21.2	32.0	12.7	2.0	74.6	42.7	49.8	50.2
51401	CARROLL	98.7	98.1	0.2	0.2	0.5	0.7	0.5	0.8	6.1	6.3	7.0	7.3	5.8	23.4	26.1	14.2	3.7	76.0	40.5	48.6	51.4
51430	ARCADIA	99.8	99.7	0.0	0.0	0.2	0.3	0.1	0.2	7.8	8.3	7.6	7.1	4.8	23.1	26.3	12.7	2.3	71.9	38.1	52.8	47.2
51431	ARTHUR	98.7	98.5	0.0	0.0	0.2	0.2	0.9	1.0	6.1	6.3	7.1	7.3	4.9	22.6	31.4	12.4	1.9	75.7	41.6	52.3	47.7
51433	AUBURN	99.3	99.1	0.0	0.0	0.1	0.3	0.4	0.6	6.4	7.4	7.4	6.4	4.1	23.7	30.2	12.2	2.3	75.0	40.4	53.0	47.0
51436	BREDA	99.1	98.8	0.2	0.2	0.3	0.6	0.5	0.6	6.2	6.6	7.2	7.4	5.1	22.9	28.1	13.6	2.9	75.2	40.7	52.8	47.2
51439	CHARTER OAK	99.3	98.9	0.0	0.0	0.2	0.3	0.6	1.1	6.3	7.0	7.3	7.0	4.1	21.6	29.4	14.7	2.6	75.0	42.1	52.3	47.7
51440	DEDHAM	98.2	97.5	0.9	1.1	0.0	0.0	1.1	1.8	7.7	8.1	7.9	6.8	4.1	24.5	26.4	12.6	2.0	72.3	38.1	52.7	47.3
51441	DELOIT	96.1	94.5	0.3	0.3	0.3	0.3	3.0	4.6	4.3	7.2	9.5	7.5	3.2	22.5	30.9	13.3	1.4	74.0	42.0	51.4	48.6
51442	DENISON	88.5	83.9	1.3	1.6	0.8	1.2	15.4	22.0	6.9	6.7	6.5	8.2	6.4	24.8	25.3	11.8	3.4	74.8	37.3	50.3	49.7
51443	GLIDDEN	99.3	99.1	0.0	0.0	0.1	0.2	0.2	0.4	4.7	5.1	6.0	7.3	5.9	25.1	31.1	12.4	2.4	79.3	42.2	50.1	49.9
51444	HALBUR	100.0	100.0	0.0	0.0	0.0	0.0	0.0	0.0	0.0	0.0	0.0	0.0	0.0	30.0	70.0	0.0	0.0	100.0	48.3	50.0	50.0
51445	IDA GROVE	98.7	98.3	0.2	0.3	0.3	0.4	0.6	1.0	5.6	5.7	6.3	6.9	5.5	20.7	29.8	15.9	3.7	78.1	44.4	48.7	51.3
51446	IRWIN	99.0	98.6	0.1	0.1	0.0	0.0	1.0	1.5	6.5	7.2	7.3	6.5	3.8	21.7	29.3	15.3	2.5	75.0	42.6	48.2	51.8
51447	KIRKMAN	99.0	98.0	0.0	0.0	0.0	0.0	1.4	2.3	6.5	7.2	7.2	6.9	4.6	21.6	30.7	13.4	2.0	75.2	41.8	51.3	48.7
51448	KIRON	97.6	96.5	0.2	0.2	0.2	0.3	1.7	2.7	5.7	6.8	7.8	6.7	3.7	22.5	31.2	13.5	2.1	75.2	42.6	51.4	48.6
51449	LAKE CITY	98.9	98.6	0.0	0.1	0.2	0.4	0.9	1.3	5.6	6.0	6.3	6.9	5.6	19.0	27.4	17.4	5.7	79.4	45.4	47.2	52.8
51450	LAKE VIEW	99.2	99.1	0.3	0.3	0.1	0.1	0.3	0.4	5.5	5.6	5.5	5.1	4.7	17.5	30.6	21.2	4.3	80.1	49.4	48.9	51.1
51451	LANESBORO	100.0	100.0	0.0	0.0	0.0	0.0	0.0	0.0	4.8	9.5	9.5	9.5	4.8	26.2	21.4	14.3	0.0	66.7	36.7	52.4	47.6
51452	LIDDERDALE	100.0	100.0	0.0	0.0	0.0	0.0	0.0	0.0	6.3	7.9	7.9	9.5	6.3	23.8	25.4	12.7	0.0	69.8	35.6	50.8	49.2
51453	LOHRVILLE	99.1	99.0	0.1	0.1	0.1	0.1	0.7	1.1	5.2	7.1	8.7	7.7	3.7	23.2	27.6	14.0	2.9	74.0	40.7	50.1	49.9
51454	MANILLA	98.4	97.8	0.1	0.3	0.1	0.1	0.5	0.9	6.9	6.6	6.7	6.1	5.2	20.3	27.4	16.1	4.6	76.0	43.4	49.7	50.3
51455	MANNING	98.9	98.5	0.0	0.0	0.4	0.7	0.4	0.5	6.0	6.0	6.7	7.1	5.2	19.7	27.8	16.4	5.0	76.3	44.3	47.8	52.2
51458	ODEBOLT	99.0	98.6	0.4	0.4	0.2	0.4	0.5	0.7	5.8	6.0	6.5	6.6	4.7	21.5	27.2	15.7	6.1	77.0	44.2	47.9	52.1
51460	RICKETTS	100.0	100.0	0.0	0.0	0.0	0.0	0.0	0.0	7.7	7.7	7.7	5.8	3.8	23.1	28.8	15.4	0.0	71.2	38.8	51.9	48.1
51461	SCHLESWIG	99.6	99.4	0.0	0.0	0.1	0.2	1.0	1.5	5.9	6.1	6.5	6.6	5.1	20.2	27.4	18.1	4.1	77.5	44.7	49.0	51.0
51462	SCRANTON	97.9	97.2	0.2	0.2	0.2	0.2	2.3	3.3	5.8	6.4	6.7	6.6	4.1	21.1	30.0	16.6	2.6	76.9	44.3	50.5	49.5
51463	TEMPLETON	99.0	99.0	0.2	0.2	0.0	0.0	0.2	0.2	7.2	7.6	7.2	7.4	5.0	20.8	31.3	11.7	1.9	73.2	40.7	51.9	48.1
51465	VAIL	98.5	97.7	0.3	0.3	0.1	0.2	1.3	2.1	5.6	6.5	7.3	7.2	4.3	21.7	30.6	14.8	2.1	76.2	43.3	51.2	48.8
51466	WALL LAKE	98.6	98.4	0.1	0.1	0.2	0.3	0.3	0.5	6.4	6.6	6.5	5.9	5.3	22.9	24.3	16.0	6.0	76.6	41.5	49.2	50.8
51467	WESTSIDE	98.5	98.0	0.4	0.4	0.2	0.2	1.3	1.9	5.8	6.3	6.9	7.1	4.3	21.9	30.9	14.9	2.0	76.6	43.5	51.5	48.5
51501	COUNCIL BLUFFS	93.8	91.6	1.2	1.5	0.6	1.0	5.5	8.1	7.7	7.2	6.8	6.9	6.9	28.4	24.7	10.3	1.3	74.2	35.0	49.1	50.9
51503	COUNCIL BLUFFS	96.7	95.6	0.6	0.8	0.6	0.9	2.4	3.5	6.0	5.8	6.3	7.4	6.5	24.1	28.2	12.9	2.7	77.6	40.1	48.3	51.7
51510	CARTER LAKE	96.7	95.7	0.2	0.3	0.2	0.4	2.9	4.4	6.3	6.6	6.9	6.8	5.7	25.8	28.6	12.2	1.2	75.9	39.0	50.4	49.6
51520	ARION	95.7	93.9	0.4	0.3	0.4	0.3	4.3	6.8	6.8	6.8	7.1	6.8	4.8	22.1	34.4	10.9	0.3	74.5	42.0	53.4	46.6
51521	AVOCA	99.1	98.8	0.1	0.1	0.0	0.1	1.2	1.9	5.6	5.9	6.2	6.3	5.0	23.8	27.7	15.7	3.8	77.9	42.7	49.5	50.5
51523	BLENCOE	98.2	97.8	0.0	0.0	0.0	0.0	0.6	0.9	4.6	5.2	5.8	6.2	4.3	20.6	33.2	17.2	2.8	80.3	46.9	52.0	48.0
51525	CARSON	98.8	98.5	0.1	0.1	0.4	0.5	0.1	0.2	5.5	6.4	7.3	6.8	3.8	24.0	31.5	12.5	2.1	76.4	42.1	48.3	51.7
51526	CRESCENT	98.4	97.9	0.6	0.7	0.2	0.4	2.2	2.8	4.3	4.9	5.9	6.7	5.3	25.7	34.1	12.1	1.1	80.8	42.9	52.9	47.1
51527	DEFIANCE	98.4	97.7	0.0	0.0	0.2	0.2	1.4	2.4	6.5	7.3	7.4	7.0	4.3	20.4	31.6	13.4	2.1	74.8	42.8	52.7	47.3
51528	DOW CITY	97.1	95.4	0.1	0.1	0.7	1.3	1.7	2.7	5.2	6.2	7.4	7.5	4.6	22.1	32.3	13.7	1.1	76.2	42.9	51.6	48.4
51529	DUNLAP	98.2	97.9	0.1	0.2	0.2	0.2	0.8	1.1	4.9	5.2	5.6	6.7	5.9	21.6	29.9	16.5	3.7	79.8	45.1	50.1	49.9
51530	EARLING	99.1	99.2	0.0	0.0	0.0	0.0	0.7	0.9	6.5	7.8	8.1	7.3	3.6	18.2	27.7	16.7	4.1	76.5	43.9	49.6	50.4
51531	ELK HORN	99.3	98.8	0.0	0.1	0.5	0.9	0.2	0.2	4.1	4.2	4.6	7.2	5.3	17.5	27.5	20.1	9.6	81.6	49.5	47.4	52.6
51532	ELLIOTT	98.9	98.5	0.0	0.1	0.3	0.4	0.0	0.0	6.6	7.2	7.2	5.7	4.3	23.3	29.7	14.0	2.0	75.4	41.4	52.4	47.6
51533	EMERSON	99.2	99.1	0.1	0.1	0.1	0.1	0.5	0.7	4.9	5.2	6.1	7.4	5.9	21.2	32.9	14.1	2.2	79.2	44.4	50.5	49.5
51534	GLENWOOD	97.6	96.9	0.4	0.5	0.3	0.6	1.4	2.1	6.7	6.6	6.8	7.3	6.0	25.7	28.2	10.9	1.7	75.5	38.5	49.9	50.1
51535	GRISWOLD	98.9	98.6	0.3	0.4	0.0	0.1	0.8	1.2	5.7	6.7	7.3	6.6	4.1	21.1	27.4	17.3	3.8	76.0	43.8	49.2	50.8
51536	HANCOCK	98.4	97.4	0.7	1.1	0.2	0.4	0.4	0.7	4.9	6.0	6.7	6.9	4.7	22.4	31.5	14.4	2.4	78.0	43.8	50.5	49.5
51537	HARLAN	98.5	98.1	0.1	0.1	0.4	0.6	0.6	0.9	5.7	6.0	6.6	7.0	5.2	21.1	28.4	16.1	3.9	77.2	43.7	48.3	51.7
51540	HASTINGS	99.3	99.2	0.0	0.0	0.0	0.0	0.9	1.3	5.7	6.6	7.4	6.6	3.4	21.2	34.0	13.0	2.1	76.4	44.1	50.1	49.9
51541	HENDERSON	99.2	99.2	0.0	0.0	0.3	0.3	1.0	1.6	4.2	4.8	5.8	6.4	5.0	21.2	35.8	14.6	2.1	81.2	46.4	53.3	46.7
51542	HONEY CREEK	98.1	97.6	0.3	0.3	0.3	0.4	0.8	1.2	5.0	5.7	6.5	6.7	4.3	21.7	35.8	13.1	1.1	78.6	45.0	52.2	47.8
51543	KIMBALLTON	99.1	98.6	0.2	0.2	0.2	0.5	0.5	0.7	6.3	6.8	7.4	7.7	4.3	22.1	29.7	14.0	1.8	74.5	41.9	51.1	48.9
51544	LEWIS	99.4	99.2	0.1	0.3	0.0	0.0	0.3	0.3	5.2	5.9	6.7	7.2	4.3	19.6	35.3	13.6	2.1	77.6	45.5	50.1	49.9
	IOWA	93.9	91.9	2.1	2.5	1.3	2.1	2.8	4.1	6.5	6.4	6.5	7.3	7.1	25.2	26.5	11.9	2.6	76.5	38.1	49.3	50.7
	UNITED STATES	75.1	72.0	12.3	12.7	3.8	4.6	12.5	15.7	6.8	6.7	6.6	7.1	6.9	27.0	26.0	10.9	1.9	75.7	36.9	49.2	50.8

ZIP CODE #	POST OFFICE NAME	2009 Per Capita Income	2009 HH Income Base	2009 Household Income Distribution (%): Less than $25,000	$25,000 to $49,999	$50,000 to $99,999	$100,000 to $149,999	$150,000 or More	Median Household Income: 2009	2014	2009 National Centile	2009 State Centile	2009 Home Value Base	2009 Home Value Distribution (%): Less than $50,000	$50,000 to $89,999	$90,000 to $174,999	$175,000 to $399,999	$400,000 or More	2009 Median Home Value
51109	SIOUX CITY	24549	1199	27.6	25.1	33.4	10.3	3.5	47164	50672	55	57	879	11.9	45.1	36.5	4.8	1.7	82013
51111	SIOUX CITY	24028	49	0.0	40.8	53.1	4.1	2.0	62881	62376	81	95	5	0.0	0.0	0.0	100.0	0.0	275000
51201	SHELDON	21756	2387	23.4	33.3	35.2	6.8	1.3	45147	46517	49	45	1734	10.0	30.9	44.5	14.1	0.5	101833
51230	ALVORD	17146	161	15.5	37.3	41.0	6.2	0.0	47975	48344	57	61	135	14.1	32.6	41.5	11.9	0.0	97500
51231	ARCHER	21064	103	15.5	36.9	41.7	4.9	1.0	48469	50000	58	63	80	20.0	40.0	32.5	5.0	2.5	76000
51232	ASHTON	19908	374	25.4	30.5	36.4	4.5	3.2	45194	47041	49	45	310	26.5	38.1	30.3	4.5	0.6	73704
51234	BOYDEN	19804	484	19.2	33.5	41.1	5.6	0.6	48302	49600	57	63	402	11.7	32.1	45.5	8.5	2.2	98333
51235	DOON	18118	351	16.0	36.8	41.9	5.4	0.0	48092	48529	57	62	299	18.1	32.4	40.5	7.7	1.3	89444
51237	GEORGE	20287	749	30.2	32.7	31.2	4.4	1.5	41129	43343	36	20	598	29.8	39.3	25.9	2.8	2.2	68769
51238	HOSPERS	19311	446	20.0	35.2	38.1	5.4	1.3	45939	48410	51	50	372	16.9	33.3	36.0	10.5	3.2	89412
51239	HULL	18179	1049	19.1	33.1	41.3	4.6	2.0	48672	50183	58	64	893	8.2	26.5	51.2	13.0	1.1	108393
51240	INWOOD	18002	651	23.2	33.8	35.9	7.1	0.0	44434	45917	47	41	529	12.1	26.7	45.6	14.6	1.1	106829
51241	LARCHWOOD	22843	725	17.5	32.7	40.3	7.2	2.3	49810	50567	61	69	613	9.3	24.5	46.3	17.9	2.0	111405
51243	LITTLE ROCK	18545	308	26.9	33.1	35.1	3.2	1.6	42964	45767	42	31	254	41.3	31.9	23.6	2.8	0.4	57333
51245	PRIMGHAR	22449	550	25.5	33.1	34.5	3.1	3.8	43929	46045	45	38	440	40.2	33.4	20.9	4.5	0.9	63103
51246	ROCK RAPIDS	22294	1444	22.4	29.8	38.0	7.8	2.1	47766	50241	56	61	1153	16.4	33.7	39.5	9.5	1.0	89960
51247	ROCK VALLEY	20504	1739	23.4	30.3	38.6	4.9	2.8	47284	49127	55	58	1403	8.8	21.0	52.5	17.3	0.4	115267
51248	SANBORN	21393	748	20.5	35.2	38.1	4.3	2.0	45938	47626	51	50	597	19.9	33.7	37.5	7.7	1.2	85612
51249	SIBLEY	21998	1421	28.8	27.0	35.5	6.1	2.6	44065	46494	46	39	1071	21.2	32.1	40.4	5.2	1.0	85203
51250	SIOUX CENTER	20894	2362	20.4	25.6	44.3	6.5	3.2	53030	53220	68	81	1867	5.8	10.1	49.7	32.7	1.6	145694
51301	SPENCER	24690	5477	25.7	30.0	34.4	6.3	3.6	44567	46297	47	42	3677	10.7	25.7	47.7	13.8	2.0	108234
51331	ARNOLDS PARK	27175	580	24.1	35.9	31.6	5.2	3.3	41651	44831	38	24	430	15.3	22.1	32.6	22.3	7.7	111250
51333	DICKENS	19832	220	23.2	31.4	39.1	4.1	2.3	46056	47031	51	51	170	28.8	28.8	29.4	9.4	3.5	74286
51334	ESTHERVILLE	22015	3254	23.6	35.1	32.8	6.0	2.5	42038	43421	39	25	2391	21.2	38.1	33.8	6.3	0.7	80328
51338	EVERLY	20938	409	18.1	38.6	39.6	3.4	0.2	45625	46290	50	48	321	22.1	32.1	34.9	7.5	3.4	85909
51342	GRAETTINGER	21016	521	30.3	32.8	29.4	5.8	1.7	39555	40297	31	14	403	29.5	38.2	29.0	2.7	0.5	71098
51343	GREENVILLE	25480	137	28.5	32.8	32.8	2.9	2.9	41441	41904	37	22	104	36.5	23.1	28.8	4.8	6.7	68333
51345	HARRIS	19716	170	21.2	35.9	37.1	5.3	0.6	43512	45760	44	34	126	31.0	30.2	34.1	4.8	0.0	73333
51346	HARTLEY	20391	1003	25.2	34.5	34.2	4.0	2.1	42890	44725	42	30	779	30.3	40.4	25.4	3.2	0.6	69345
51347	LAKE PARK	22372	609	22.3	34.2	36.5	4.8	2.3	44941	48386	48	44	495	18.2	36.6	33.5	9.9	1.8	85300
51350	MELVIN	22788	192	29.2	31.3	29.2	5.2	5.2	41533	43120	38	23	158	51.9	24.1	17.7	6.3	0.0	49063
51351	MILFORD	26450	2077	20.6	29.8	39.5	6.5	3.6	49662	51828	60	68	1569	11.2	21.9	43.9	14.7	8.3	113444
51354	OCHEYEDAN	17508	468	28.4	39.5	26.7	4.3	1.1	38228	39149	27	9	368	36.7	36.1	25.0	2.2	0.0	61875
51355	OKOBOJI	34376	377	21.5	32.6	32.6	7.7	5.6	45845	49280	51	49	306	18.6	5.6	27.1	36.6	12.1	169444
51357	ROYAL	22599	314	31.5	22.9	33.4	7.3	4.8	46677	48019	53	55	231	19.5	48.1	21.2	8.7	2.6	74038
51358	RUTHVEN	20982	568	27.8	34.3	32.6	3.5	1.8	40104	41417	33	15	447	32.4	34.5	26.6	5.4	1.1	70122
51360	SPIRIT LAKE	27411	3568	20.2	30.5	37.0	7.1	5.3	49334	51650	60	67	2818	9.3	14.2	40.5	28.4	7.7	137130
51363	SUPERIOR	26101	88	22.7	31.8	34.1	5.7	5.7	45914	50000	51	49	77	10.4	13.0	35.1	35.1	6.5	148438
51364	TERRIL	22946	384	15.6	34.4	43.2	4.7	2.1	50000	51574	61	70	301	23.9	23.9	33.9	14.6	3.7	94333
51365	WALLINGFORD	24271	97	21.6	35.1	36.1	6.2	1.0	45317	46988	49	46	76	19.7	27.6	39.5	10.5	2.6	94000
51366	WEBB	20767	170	26.5	34.7	32.9	4.1	1.8	40908	44172	36	19	131	38.2	30.5	20.6	7.6	3.1	61154
51401	CARROLL	25348	5122	22.5	26.5	39.5	7.7	3.8	50952	50530	63	73	3697	8.7	19.2	53.2	16.7	2.2	115354
51430	ARCADIA	18983	343	24.5	34.1	34.1	3.8	3.5	41583	42974	38	23	278	17.3	30.9	37.4	6.5	7.9	93333
51431	ARTHUR	23424	175	28.6	30.3	34.3	4.6	2.3	42348	43723	40	27	132	20.5	40.2	27.3	8.3	3.8	73333
51433	AUBURN	23439	287	23.7	30.7	33.4	6.3	5.9	47118	49866	54	57	219	29.7	28.8	32.9	6.4	2.3	76538
51436	BREDA	21675	348	27.9	37.4	26.1	3.2	5.5	39808	42672	32	14	283	17.3	29.0	38.9	7.8	7.1	97500
51439	CHARTER OAK	20208	488	28.5	33.8	33.0	3.3	1.4	41383	43542	37	22	378	38.6	33.1	22.0	4.8	1.6	62174
51440	DEDHAM	16995	176	26.7	38.1	33.0	2.3	0.0	42487	44330	41	28	141	29.8	29.8	30.5	9.2	0.7	75500
51441	DELOIT	21059	139	25.9	38.8	28.1	4.3	2.9	40501	41878	34	17	112	37.5	18.8	38.4	4.5	0.9	80000
51442	DENISON	19617	3264	25.2	33.5	33.5	5.8	2.0	43451	46111	44	33	2232	12.5	28.5	46.9	11.4	0.6	102244
51443	GLIDDEN	22818	833	23.5	30.9	36.3	7.1	2.3	45864	46864	51	49	644	20.2	30.3	40.8	7.3	1.4	89388
51444	HALBUR	19000	3	0.0	0.0	100.0	0.0	0.0	63750	52500	82	96	0	0.0	0.0	0.0	0.0	0.0	0
51445	IDA GROVE	24700	1196	26.9	27.3	36.7	5.4	3.8	45826	46819	51	49	844	22.0	35.9	33.1	7.8	1.2	81067
51446	IRWIN	19868	310	28.1	31.6	35.2	4.5	0.6	40000	44371	33	15	224	27.7	33.5	22.8	13.4	2.7	80000
51447	KIRKMAN	19105	123	24.4	31.7	39.0	4.9	0.0	44603	46529	47	42	97	23.7	28.9	34.0	12.4	1.0	87222
51448	KIRON	21344	277	28.5	35.0	31.4	3.6	1.4	41534	43229	38	23	220	25.5	36.4	27.3	9.1	1.8	76000
51449	LAKE CITY	20890	954	29.4	32.2	32.1	5.5	0.9	40522	41540	34	17	743	29.9	30.1	31.0	7.0	2.0	79868
51450	LAKE VIEW	21421	743	31.2	32.2	29.9	4.4	2.3	37070	39225	24	6	576	23.6	29.2	35.9	10.6	0.7	86981
51451	LANESBORO	18155	17	29.4	35.3	29.4	5.9	0.0	38575	45673	28	10	14	7.1	28.6	42.9	21.4	0.0	108333
51452	LIDDERDALE	12103	17	29.4	35.3	29.4	5.9	0.0	38575	45673	28	10	14	7.1	28.6	42.9	21.4	0.0	108333
51453	LOHRVILLE	19619	328	32.0	29.3	32.3	5.5	0.9	40404	41834	34	17	273	42.1	30.4	26.0	1.1	0.4	57167
51454	MANILLA	17767	581	26.9	35.1	34.4	2.8	0.9	40863	42769	36	19	466	38.8	34.8	20.6	5.2	0.6	64722
51455	MANNING	21188	904	29.0	32.0	31.3	5.1	2.7	41322	43003	37	22	694	22.0	40.6	28.1	7.2	2.0	76400
51458	ODEBOLT	19572	639	30.7	32.4	29.7	6.3	0.9	40278	42769	34	17	496	31.3	37.3	26.8	3.8	0.8	67750
51460	RICKETTS	18160	20	20.0	35.0	40.0	5.0	0.0	47309	47368	55	58	15	33.3	26.7	26.7	13.3	0.0	75000
51461	SCHLESWIG	19935	488	28.5	34.0	33.2	3.3	1.0	40844	43141	35	19	395	27.8	40.8	27.6	3.0	0.8	69872
51462	SCRANTON	17680	461	28.4	40.3	27.8	3.0	0.4	37098	39188	24	6	347	32.3	28.8	30.0	6.6	2.3	73824
51463	TEMPLETON	24622	239	29.3	29.7	30.1	6.7	4.2	40953	42683	36	19	193	14.5	28.0	43.0	9.3	5.2	98529
51465	VAIL	20674	348	23.0	40.5	32.2	3.2	1.1	41699	42638	38	24	277	31.8	27.1	37.2	3.2	0.7	80200
51466	WALL LAKE	20134	450	24.7	36.4	32.2	5.8	0.9	42466	44700	41	28	363	27.3	33.6	32.8	4.4	1.9	76029
51467	WESTSIDE	22456	227	22.5	41.4	31.7	3.1	1.3	41613	42929	38	24	181	30.4	27.6	39.8	2.2	0.0	81471
51501	COUNCIL BLUFFS	21510	13757	22.7	32.1	36.6	6.8	1.8	45985	49846	51	50	9170	16.2	36.9	44.5	1.9	0.5	87105
51503	COUNCIL BLUFFS	29357	14041	16.4	26.1	37.5	13.0	7.1	58128	59961	75	90	9935	3.8	12.3	51.7	29.4	2.8	137032
51510	CARTER LAKE	23636	1367	19.8	31.4	39.4	5.4	4.0	49197	52150	59	66	1180	24.0	31.8	38.6	5.2	0.4	83761
51520	ARION	17033	109	30.3	32.1	33.9	2.8	0.9	40242	41647	33	16	82	32.9	12.2	31.7	19.5	3.7	100000
51521	AVOCA	24160	917	14.8	36.1	39.9	7.3	1.9	49427	51895	60	67	695	16.1	26.0	46.8	9.8	1.3	102348
51523	BLENCOE	28054	157	24.8	22.9	40.1	10.2	1.9	51866	52531	66	77	120	23.3	24.2	37.5	12.5	2.5	94286
51525	CARSON	22588	479	21.5	28.8	42.4	6.3	1.0	49753	52406	60	68	368	11.1	23.4	49.5	14.7	1.4	110448
51526	CRESCENT	30376	633	7.3	24.5	45.7	16.7	5.8	67578	67371	85	97	566	2.5	8.8	47.7	38.0	3.0	154098
51527	DEFIANCE	17559	240	24.2	33.8	36.7	5.0	0.4	43901	46189	45	38	194	22.2	27.8	36.6	11.9	1.5	90000
51528	DOW CITY	18633	465	27.3	37.4	31.2	3.2	0.9	40918	42262	36	19	349	35.0	29.5	23.2	10.3	2.0	71607
51529	DUNLAP	22566	709	26.0	33.6	32.4	4.8	3.2	42450	45513	41	28	557	29.8	30.7	27.1	10.6	1.8	74853
51530	EARLING	19309	357	21.3	37.5	37.0	3.6	0.6	43437	45688	44	33	284	14.4	28.9	41.9	11.6	3.2	98261
51531	ELK HORN	22526	363	17.1	34.7	40.8	4.4	3.0	48256	50076	57	62	294	15.3	34.0	40.5	5.8	4.4	90556
51532	ELLIOTT	20173	297	29.6	27.6	35.0	6.1	1.7	44580	47369	47	42	240	39.6	23.8	26.3	7.9	2.5	72941
51533	EMERSON	21323	414	21.0	37.4	31.2	8.2	2.2	43820	46045	45	37	335	23.9	37.0	30.4	7.5	1.2	74565
51534	GLENWOOD	23886	3334	17.2	26.5	42.5	10.1	3.7	56308	59363	73	88	2568	7.1	15.1	50.3	25.0	2.4	124699
51535	GRISWOLD	20248	833	23.2	35.7	35.3	4.9	1.0	43196	45000	43	32	659	18.7	36.1	36.3	8.3	0.6	81923
51536	HANCOCK	21710	221	26.2	30.3	32.6	7.2	3.6	43634	47662	44	35	158	19.0	15.8	44.3	13.9	7.0	107353
51537	HARLAN	23922	2786	21.0	29.4	39.5	7.3	2.8	49627	51337	60	68	2119	10.8	27.3	45.1	15.1	1.7	105674
51540	HASTINGS	20619	195	27.2	31.3	35.4	4.6	1.5	43529	46259	44	34	142	32.4	24.6	24.6	12.0	6.3	78571
51541	HENDERSON	25831	165	19.4	33.9	36.4	6.7	3.6	47351	50427	55	59	127	17.3	26.8	33.1	19.7	3.1	98333
51542	HONEY CREEK	26788	506	10.1	26.5	47.4	12.3	3.8	61260	61534	79	93	450	10.7	6.2	41.8	36.2	5.1	150625
51543	KIMBALLTON	19516	182	28.6	36.8	28.6	4.4	1.6	39391	41246	31	13	142	26.8	29.6	33.1	7.7	2.8	83571
51544	LEWIS	21832	313	23.0	34.2	36.1	5.4	1.3	43481	45889	44	33	248	27.4	38.7	26.2	6.9	0.8	73333
	IOWA	25379		21.1	28.2	37.9	8.6	4.3	50616	52941				14.7	22.5	41.6	18.6	2.6	110128
	UNITED STATES	27277		20.9	24.4	35.3	11.7	7.6	54719	56938				9.3	13.1	31.6	32.6	13.5	162279

ZIP CODE #	POST OFFICE NAME	FINANCIAL SERVICES: Auto Loan	Home Loan	Invest-ments	Retire-ment Plans	THE HOME: Home Improvements: Home Repair	Lawn & Garden	Furnishings: Comput-ers & Hard-ware-Personal	Major Appli-ances	TV, Radio, Sound Equip-ment	Furni-ture	ENTERTAINMENT: Dine out/ Carry out	Sports Equip-ment	Fees & Tickets	Toys & Games	Travel	Cable TV	PERSONAL: Apparel & Services	Auto Repairs	Health Insur-ance	Pets & Supplies
51109	SIOUX CITY	88	74	72	75	72	88	81	83	85	75	83	64	73	86	75	90	57	84	91	100
51111	SIOUX CITY	99	88	76	90	83	79	98	87	94	99	96	72	91	99	89	91	67	93	83	105
51201	SHELDON	84	70	76	71	69	87	74	81	77	66	76	63	65	78	71	82	51	78	87	97
51230	ALVORD	93	64	102	64	67	98	71	88	74	57	73	73	52	72	70	80	47	82	93	108
51231	ARCHER	93	64	102	64	67	98	71	88	74	58	73	73	52	73	71	81	48	83	93	109
51232	ASHTON	93	64	102	64	67	98	71	88	74	57	73	73	52	72	70	80	47	82	93	108
51234	BOYDEN	92	63	101	63	66	97	70	87	73	57	72	72	52	72	70	80	47	82	92	108
51235	DOON	92	64	101	63	66	97	71	88	73	57	73	72	52	72	70	80	47	82	93	108
51237	GEORGE	80	57	83	56	59	84	62	77	68	54	66	60	48	66	61	74	44	72	83	92
51238	HOSPERS	93	64	102	64	67	98	71	88	74	58	73	73	52	73	71	81	47	83	93	109
51239	HULL	90	69	93	70	72	96	73	88	76	62	75	70	59	76	73	82	49	82	92	106
51240	INWOOD	89	61	98	61	64	94	68	85	71	55	70	70	50	69	68	77	45	79	89	104
51241	LARCHWOOD	98	78	99	79	80	105	81	96	84	69	83	76	67	84	81	90	55	89	100	115
51243	LITTLE ROCK	84	58	92	58	60	89	64	80	67	52	66	66	47	65	64	73	43	74	84	98
51245	PRIMGHAR	91	65	94	64	67	96	71	88	78	62	75	68	55	76	69	85	50	82	95	105
51246	ROCK RAPIDS	89	68	88	68	69	93	73	86	79	65	77	67	61	78	72	85	51	82	93	103
51247	ROCK VALLEY	88	70	87	71	72	94	73	87	77	64	76	67	61	77	72	83	51	81	91	103
51248	SANBORN	89	64	91	62	66	93	70	86	76	61	74	66	55	75	68	84	49	80	93	102
51249	SIBLEY	82	68	81	67	69	88	71	81	76	64	74	61	62	75	70	82	50	78	89	96
51250	SIOUX CENTER	96	84	90	85	85	100	84	93	87	79	86	72	77	88	84	91	58	89	97	111
51301	SPENCER	85	74	77	75	73	87	79	83	82	73	80	64	72	82	76	86	55	82	89	99
51331	ARNOLDS PARK	96	70	103	68	74	98	72	91	78	67	77	68	58	77	72	86	51	84	94	108
51333	DICKENS	94	65	103	65	68	99	72	89	75	58	74	74	53	73	71	81	48	83	94	110
51334	ESTHERVILLE	84	67	77	67	67	86	73	80	77	65	75	62	62	77	69	82	51	78	87	96
51338	EVERLY	91	62	99	62	65	96	69	86	72	56	71	71	51	71	69	78	46	80	91	106
51342	GRAETTINGER	83	59	85	58	61	87	65	80	71	57	69	61	51	70	63	78	46	75	87	95
51343	GREENVILLE	103	71	113	71	74	108	78	98	82	64	81	81	57	80	78	89	52	91	103	120
51345	HARRIS	89	61	98	61	64	94	68	85	71	55	70	70	50	69	68	77	45	79	89	104
51346	HARTLEY	86	61	89	60	64	90	67	83	74	58	71	64	52	72	66	81	47	78	90	99
51347	LAKE PARK	87	62	89	61	65	91	68	84	75	60	73	64	54	74	66	83	48	79	91	100
51350	MELVIN	96	66	105	66	69	101	73	91	76	59	75	75	54	75	73	83	49	85	96	112
51351	MILFORD	91	80	94	80	82	97	81	90	85	78	84	68	75	83	82	89	57	88	98	107
51354	OCHEYEDAN	79	54	87	54	57	83	60	75	63	49	62	62	44	61	60	68	40	70	79	92
51355	OKOBOJI	109	88	142	87	97	116	88	112	92	83	91	81	77	87	96	98	61	103	111	129
51357	ROYAL	99	68	108	68	71	104	75	94	78	61	77	77	55	77	75	85	50	87	99	115
51358	RUTHVEN	83	59	87	58	61	87	65	80	70	56	68	62	50	69	63	77	45	75	86	96
51360	SPIRIT LAKE	96	85	103	84	89	100	85	96	89	83	88	69	79	87	87	93	60	92	100	112
51363	SUPERIOR	102	82	132	81	90	108	82	104	86	77	85	76	71	82	89	92	56	96	103	121
51364	TERRIL	98	68	109	68	72	103	75	93	78	62	77	76	56	76	75	85	50	87	98	114
51365	WALLINGFORD	92	64	101	63	67	97	71	88	73	57	73	72	52	72	70	80	47	82	93	108
51366	WEBB	90	62	98	61	64	95	68	85	71	55	70	70	50	70	68	78	46	79	90	105
51401	CARROLL	92	81	91	82	83	98	84	92	87	78	86	70	77	86	83	92	59	89	99	109
51430	ARCADIA	91	63	100	62	65	96	69	86	72	56	71	71	51	71	69	79	46	81	91	106
51431	ARTHUR	98	68	108	68	71	104	75	93	78	61	77	77	55	77	75	85	50	87	99	115
51433	AUBURN	103	71	113	71	74	109	79	98	82	64	81	81	58	80	78	89	52	91	103	120
51436	BREDA	92	64	101	63	66	97	71	88	73	57	73	72	52	72	70	80	47	82	93	108
51439	CHARTER OAK	83	57	91	57	60	87	63	79	66	51	65	65	46	65	63	72	42	73	83	97
51440	DEDHAM	77	53	84	53	55	81	59	73	61	47	60	60	43	60	58	66	39	68	77	90
51441	DELOIT	94	64	103	64	67	99	72	89	74	58	74	74	52	73	71	81	48	83	94	109
51442	DENISON	83	67	75	67	67	84	71	79	75	65	74	61	61	76	68	80	50	76	85	94
51443	GLIDDEN	95	67	99	66	70	99	74	91	80	63	78	71	57	78	72	88	51	85	98	109
51444	HALBUR	113	78	124	78	82	119	86	107	90	70	89	89	63	88	86	98	58	100	114	132
51445	IDA GROVE	91	73	95	72	75	99	76	91	83	68	81	68	66	81	76	90	54	86	100	107
51446	IRWIN	82	56	90	56	59	86	62	78	65	51	64	64	46	64	62	71	42	72	82	95
51447	KIRKMAN	84	59	91	59	61	89	65	80	68	53	67	66	49	66	65	73	44	75	85	98
51448	KIRON	87	60	95	59	62	91	66	82	69	54	68	68	48	67	66	75	44	77	87	101
51449	LAKE CITY	82	58	84	57	61	86	64	79	70	56	68	60	50	69	62	77	45	74	86	94
51450	LAKE VIEW	77	62	85	59	66	83	64	77	68	61	67	56	55	65	65	74	44	73	84	91
51451	LANESBORO	80	55	88	55	58	85	61	76	64	50	63	63	45	62	61	69	41	71	80	94
51452	LIDDERDALE	80	55	88	55	58	85	61	76	64	50	63	63	45	62	61	69	41	71	80	94
51453	LOHRVILLE	84	58	92	58	61	89	65	80	68	53	67	66	48	66	64	74	43	75	85	98
51454	MANILLA	77	55	80	54	57	81	60	74	65	52	64	58	47	64	59	72	42	69	80	89
51455	MANNING	87	62	90	60	64	91	68	84	74	59	72	64	53	72	66	81	47	78	90	100
51458	ODEBOLT	82	58	87	57	60	87	64	79	69	54	67	62	49	67	63	75	44	74	85	95
51460	RICKETTS	84	58	93	58	61	89	64	80	67	52	66	66	47	66	64	73	43	75	85	99
51461	SCHLESWIG	79	56	81	55	58	82	61	76	68	54	66	58	48	66	60	74	44	71	82	90
51462	SCRANTON	76	52	84	52	55	80	58	72	61	47	60	60	43	59	58	66	39	68	76	89
51463	TEMPLETON	107	74	118	74	77	113	82	102	85	66	84	84	60	84	81	93	55	95	107	125
51465	VAIL	95	65	104	65	68	100	73	90	75	59	75	75	53	74	72	82	48	84	95	111
51466	WALL LAKE	84	60	87	59	62	88	66	81	72	57	70	63	52	71	64	79	46	76	88	97
51467	WESTSIDE	95	65	105	65	69	100	73	90	76	59	75	75	53	74	72	82	48	84	95	111
51501	COUNCIL BLUFFS	78	73	63	74	70	78	77	75	79	74	79	58	74	80	73	82	54	77	82	91
51503	COUNCIL BLUFFS	101	103	96	105	101	106	103	102	103	101	103	78	104	104	103	105	72	103	107	121
51510	CARTER LAKE	87	88	79	87	85	93	84	88	86	82	86	66	84	87	84	90	59	86	94	103
51520	ARION	82	57	90	56	59	87	63	78	65	51	65	64	46	64	62	71	42	73	82	96
51521	AVOCA	90	77	93	75	78	100	77	91	84	71	82	67	70	82	78	91	55	86	101	106
51523	BLENCOE	104	71	114	71	75	110	79	99	82	64	82	81	58	81	79	90	53	92	104	121
51525	CARSON	86	76	82	78	77	93	76	87	78	68	77	67	68	79	76	82	52	80	89	102
51526	CRESCENT	108	124	108	127	120	122	110	114	109	110	109	88	119	111	117	109	77	110	115	134
51527	DEFIANCE	86	59	94	59	62	90	65	81	68	53	67	67	48	67	65	74	44	76	86	100
51528	DOW CITY	82	58	86	56	60	84	61	77	66	54	65	60	47	65	60	72	43	71	80	92
51529	DUNLAP	92	65	96	64	68	97	72	89	78	62	76	69	55	76	70	85	50	83	95	106
51530	EARLING	87	60	95	59	62	91	66	82	69	54	68	68	48	67	66	75	44	77	87	101
51531	ELK HORN	74	80	81	79	81	90	73	81	78	71	77	58	77	76	79	83	53	78	92	93
51532	ELLIOTT	90	64	94	62	66	92	67	84	73	60	72	65	52	72	66	80	47	78	88	101
51533	EMERSON	93	70	92	70	72	97	75	90	81	66	79	69	61	80	73	88	52	84	97	107
51534	GLENWOOD	94	92	83	92	89	93	92	92	92	90	92	70	89	93	89	93	63	92	94	109
51535	GRISWOLD	87	61	92	60	63	91	67	83	72	56	70	66	51	70	66	79	46	78	89	101
51536	HANCOCK	92	70	96	71	72	98	74	89	77	63	76	72	59	76	74	83	50	83	93	108
51537	HARLAN	85	78	85	77	78	93	78	86	82	73	81	64	73	81	78	87	55	83	94	101
51540	HASTINGS	89	61	98	61	64	94	68	85	71	55	70	70	50	69	68	77	45	79	89	104
51541	HENDERSON	105	73	114	73	77	111	81	100	84	66	83	82	60	82	80	91	54	93	105	122
51542	HONEY CREEK	97	109	94	112	106	107	98	101	96	98	97	79	104	98	103	96	67	98	100	119
51543	KIMBALLTON	85	58	93	58	61	90	65	81	68	53	67	67	48	66	65	74	43	75	85	99
51544	LEWIS	93	64	102	64	67	98	71	88	74	58	73	73	52	72	71	81	47	82	93	109
	IOWA	93	84	87	85	83	95	87	91	89	82	88	71	81	90	85	92	61	90	96	108
	UNITED STATES	100	100	100	100	100	100	100	100	100	100	100	100	100	100	100	100	100	100	100	100

ZIP CODE #	POST OFFICE NAME	COUNTY FIPS CODE	POPULATION 2000	POPULATION 2009	POPULATION 2014	2000-2009 ANNUAL RATE % Rate	2000-2009 ANNUAL RATE State Centile	HOUSEHOLDS 2000	HOUSEHOLDS 2009	HOUSEHOLDS 2014	HOUSEHOLDS % Annual Rate 2000-2009	HOUSEHOLDS 2009 Average HH Size	FAMILIES 2000	FAMILIES 2009	FAMILIES % Annual Rate 2000-2009
51545	LITTLE SIOUX	085	473	484	481	0.2	68	190	197	197	0.4	2.46	129	130	0.1
51546	LOGAN	085	3002	3067	3047	0.2	68	1128	1164	1159	0.3	2.58	799	808	0.1
51548	MC CLELLAND	155	481	512	525	0.7	85	175	192	199	1.0	2.67	134	144	0.8
51549	MACEDONIA	155	513	528	529	0.3	72	199	210	211	0.6	2.51	150	155	0.4
51550	MAGNOLIA	085	156	161	161	0.3	72	66	70	70	0.6	2.30	51	52	0.2
51551	MALVERN	129	1880	1957	2016	0.4	76	725	785	815	0.9	2.41	512	542	0.6
51552	MARNE	029	283	271	262	-0.5	27	107	106	103	-0.1	2.55	83	81	-0.3
51553	MINDEN	155	927	973	996	0.5	79	357	391	403	1.0	2.49	270	289	0.7
51555	MISSOURI VALLEY	085	5335	5265	5190	-0.1	51	2079	2104	2083	0.1	2.45	1455	1442	-0.1
51556	MODALE	085	488	513	513	0.5	79	211	225	225	0.7	2.28	161	167	0.4
51557	MONDAMIN	085	826	835	828	0.1	63	328	339	337	0.4	2.46	241	243	0.1
51558	MOORHEAD	133	520	454	429	-1.5	1	225	204	194	-1.1	2.23	161	143	-1.3
51559	NEOLA	155	1799	1932	1994	0.8	87	682	763	793	1.2	2.53	517	565	1.0
51560	OAKLAND	155	2140	2192	2198	0.3	72	851	897	906	0.6	2.37	599	615	0.3
51561	PACIFIC JUNCTION	129	1286	1421	1485	1.1	91	494	562	592	1.4	2.53	387	432	1.2
51562	PANAMA	165	476	445	427	-0.7	15	186	180	175	-0.4	2.46	135	128	-0.6
51563	PERSIA	085	855	896	894	0.5	79	309	331	333	0.7	2.71	250	265	0.6
51564	PISGAH	085	684	690	683	0.1	63	281	289	287	0.3	2.39	196	196	0.0
51565	PORTSMOUTH	165	622	593	573	-0.5	27	235	231	224	-0.2	2.57	178	171	-0.4
51566	RED OAK	137	7480	7016	6747	-0.7	15	3168	3008	2897	-0.6	2.28	2051	1900	-0.8
51570	SHELBY	165	1201	1206	1194	0.0	58	459	475	474	0.4	2.52	327	331	0.1
51571	SILVER CITY	129	665	710	734	0.7	85	263	287	298	0.9	2.47	206	221	0.8
51572	SOLDIER	133	546	500	478	-0.9	8	241	229	221	-0.6	2.18	158	147	-0.8
51573	STANTON	137	1158	1074	1034	-0.8	11	448	424	409	-0.6	2.42	326	302	-0.8
51575	TREYNOR	155	1376	1443	1475	0.5	79	511	555	572	0.9	2.60	398	423	0.7
51576	UNDERWOOD	155	1547	1644	1687	0.7	85	550	598	617	0.9	2.75	422	449	0.7
51577	WALNUT	155	1209	1342	1356	1.1	91	475	538	548	1.4	2.49	351	387	1.1
51578	WESTPHALIA	165	46	43	41	-0.7	15	13	13	12	0.0	3.31	9	9	0.0
51579	WOODBINE	085	2370	2385	2359	0.1	63	923	952	947	0.3	2.43	639	642	0.1
51601	SHENANDOAH	145	6432	5958	5687	-0.8	11	2768	2625	2522	-0.6	2.20	1750	1616	-0.9
51630	BLANCHARD	145	186	168	159	-1.1	5	78	73	70	-0.7	2.30	57	53	-0.8
51631	BRADDYVILLE	145	348	313	297	-1.1	5	140	130	124	-0.8	2.41	108	99	-0.9
51632	CLARINDA	145	7632	7441	7211	-0.3	40	2775	2682	2597	-0.4	2.25	1829	1725	-0.6
51636	COIN	145	497	473	462	-0.5	27	205	203	201	-0.1	2.33	149	144	-0.4
51637	COLLEGE SPRINGS	145	233	210	199	-1.1	5	87	81	77	-0.8	2.59	67	61	-1.0
51638	ESSEX	145	1499	1381	1317	-0.9	8	599	572	550	-0.5	2.41	453	425	-0.7
51639	FARRAGUT	071	911	930	927	0.2	68	378	396	397	0.5	2.35	272	279	0.3
51640	HAMBURG	071	1804	1749	1719	-0.3	40	757	749	738	-0.1	2.33	514	498	-0.3
51645	IMOGENE	071	255	256	255	0.0	58	106	110	111	0.4	2.33	76	77	0.1
51646	NEW MARKET	173	820	791	759	-0.4	32	353	348	337	-0.2	2.27	251	243	-0.3
51647	NORTHBORO	145	240	222	213	-0.8	11	96	92	89	-0.5	2.41	70	66	-0.6
51648	PERCIVAL	071	278	266	259	-0.5	27	114	112	110	-0.2	2.38	82	79	-0.4
51649	RANDOLPH	071	430	423	417	-0.2	46	162	164	163	0.1	2.56	115	114	-0.1
51650	RIVERTON	071	398	373	361	-0.7	15	167	160	156	-0.5	2.33	114	106	-0.8
51651	SHAMBAUGH	145	21	21	20	0.0	58	8	8	8	0.0	2.63	6	6	0.0
51652	SIDNEY	071	1972	1882	1837	-0.5	27	756	737	721	-0.3	2.44	535	511	-0.5
51653	TABOR	071	1366	1316	1301	-0.4	32	528	524	521	-0.1	2.40	376	366	-0.3
51654	THURMAN	071	536	511	497	-0.5	27	210	206	201	-0.2	2.48	152	146	-0.4
51656	YORKTOWN	145	58	54	52	-0.8	11	20	19	19	-0.6	2.84	16	15	-0.7
52001	DUBUQUE	061	43992	43969	44096	0.0	58	17340	17855	18124	0.3	2.24	10653	10599	-0.1
52002	DUBUQUE	061	11680	13562	14428	1.6	95	4283	5195	5597	2.1	2.59	3246	3857	1.9
52003	DUBUQUE	061	13593	14333	14724	0.6	83	5013	5516	5748	1.0	2.51	3761	4032	0.8
52030	ANDREW	097	435	445	443	0.2	68	157	166	167	0.6	2.63	123	127	0.3
52031	BELLEVUE	097	4922	5009	5006	0.2	68	1840	1939	1954	0.6	2.54	1360	1408	0.4
52032	BERNARD	097	1337	1453	1504	0.9	89	499	568	593	1.4	2.56	364	403	1.1
52033	CASCADE	105	3033	3248	3358	0.7	85	1123	1256	1316	1.2	2.53	812	877	0.8
52035	COLESBURG	043	1054	1009	978	-0.5	27	408	407	399	0.0	2.48	316	310	-0.2
52036	DELAWARE	055	51	48	46	-0.7	15	19	18	18	-0.6	2.67	15	14	-0.7
52037	DELMAR	045	1382	1468	1477	0.7	85	508	551	558	0.9	2.65	396	421	0.7
52038	DUNDEE	055	525	529	520	0.1	63	195	204	202	0.5	2.59	157	162	0.3
52039	DURANGO	061	947	999	1042	0.6	83	320	357	379	1.2	2.80	265	289	0.9
52040	DYERSVILLE	055	5352	5517	5588	0.3	72	2007	2139	2197	0.7	2.55	1487	1534	0.3
52041	EARLVILLE	055	1674	1587	1531	-0.6	20	580	568	553	-0.2	2.79	438	421	-0.4
52042	EDGEWOOD	043	1687	1746	1729	0.4	76	594	633	632	0.7	2.66	454	474	0.5
52043	ELKADER	043	2416	2386	2341	-0.1	51	995	1018	1008	0.2	2.25	672	671	0.0
52044	ELKPORT	043	238	225	217	-0.6	20	95	94	92	-0.1	2.39	64	61	-0.5
52045	EPWORTH	061	2105	2487	2634	1.8	96	691	854	919	2.3	2.77	544	654	2.0
52046	FARLEY	061	2107	2274	2368	0.8	87	722	820	868	1.4	2.76	550	604	1.0
52047	FARMERSBURG	043	706	721	712	0.2	68	274	291	290	0.7	2.48	208	217	0.5
52048	GARBER	043	401	389	379	-0.3	40	166	168	165	0.1	2.30	119	118	-0.1
52049	GARNAVILLO	043	1323	1292	1266	-0.3	40	552	563	557	0.2	2.22	368	365	-0.1
52050	GREELEY	055	621	585	565	-0.6	20	230	226	220	-0.2	2.58	180	174	-0.4
52052	GUTTENBERG	043	3341	3156	3058	-0.6	20	1334	1299	1268	-0.3	2.33	914	872	-0.5
52053	HOLY CROSS	061	1216	1249	1271	0.3	72	429	463	477	0.8	2.70	347	367	0.6
52054	LA MOTTE	097	1008	1099	1125	0.9	89	354	404	418	1.4	2.72	286	321	1.3
52057	MANCHESTER	055	8409	8144	7906	-0.3	40	3234	3214	3142	-0.1	2.48	2257	2198	-0.3
52060	MAQUOKETA	097	8744	8642	8533	-0.1	51	3594	3677	3669	0.2	2.30	2346	2333	-0.1
52064	MILES	097	820	758	734	-0.8	11	314	303	297	-0.4	2.50	229	217	-0.6
52065	NEW VIENNA	061	1225	1267	1295	0.4	76	443	483	502	0.9	2.62	351	374	0.7
52068	PEOSTA	061	2341	2981	3302	2.6	98	789	1065	1200	3.3	2.78	671	885	3.0
52069	PRESTON	097	1561	1521	1501	-0.3	40	637	654	653	0.3	2.31	426	426	0.0
52070	SABULA	097	1172	1128	1093	-0.4	32	525	531	520	0.1	2.12	350	344	-0.2
52071	SAINT DONATUS	097	105	111	118	0.6	83	42	43	46	0.3	2.58	33	33	0.0
52072	SAINT OLAF	043	366	374	370	0.2	68	140	149	148	0.7	2.48	110	115	0.5
52073	SHERRILL	061	1426	1598	1684	1.2	93	489	575	614	1.8	2.78	411	474	1.6
52074	SPRAGUEVILLE	097	355	343	337	-0.4	32	131	132	131	0.1	2.59	106	106	0.0
52076	STRAWBERRY POINT	043	2316	2258	2205	-0.3	40	844	848	835	0.1	2.53	593	583	-0.2
52077	VOLGA	043	462	456	448	-0.1	51	177	180	178	0.2	2.53	128	127	-0.1
52078	WORTHINGTON	061	934	990	1018	0.6	83	306	342	358	1.2	2.86	241	262	0.9
52079	ZWINGLE	097	826	867	884	0.5	79	309	341	352	1.1	2.54	235	253	0.8
52101	DECORAH	191	13811	14040	14058	0.2	68	4861	5099	5147	0.5	2.32	3163	3243	0.3
52132	CALMAR	191	2362	2298	2254	-0.3	40	941	953	945	0.1	2.41	629	620	-0.2
52133	CASTALIA	191	664	636	625	-0.5	27	245	244	242	0.0	2.60	182	177	-0.3
52134	CHESTER	089	513	493	481	-0.4	32	194	190	186	-0.2	2.59	142	137	-0.4
52135	CLERMONT	065	908	909	900	0.0	58	374	382	380	0.2	2.38	253	252	0.0
	IOWA					0.4					0.7	2.40			0.4
	UNITED STATES					1.0					1.1	2.59			0.9

ZIP CODE #	POST OFFICE NAME	RACE (%) White 2000	White 2009	Black 2000	Black 2009	Asian/Pacific 2000	Asian/Pacific 2009	% Hispanic Origin 2000	% Hispanic Origin 2009	2009 AGE DISTRIBUTION (%) 0-4	5-9	10-14	15-19	20-24	25-44	45-64	65-84	85+	18+	MEDIAN AGE 2009	% 2009 Males	% 2009 Females
51545	LITTLE SIOUX	98.7	98.8	0.2	0.2	0.2	0.2	0.6	0.6	6.2	5.8	5.8	7.0	6.8	20.0	28.5	16.9	2.9	78.1	43.5	49.0	51.0
51546	LOGAN	98.7	98.6	0.1	0.1	0.2	0.2	0.8	0.7	6.4	7.1	7.2	7.3	4.7	23.2	27.8	13.2	3.1	74.2	40.8	50.8	49.2
51548	MC CLELLAND	98.3	97.5	0.2	0.2	0.2	0.4	0.8	1.4	7.2	7.8	8.0	6.8	4.5	23.2	30.7	10.9	0.8	72.9	39.8	52.9	47.1
51549	MACEDONIA	98.2	97.9	0.0	0.0	0.2	0.4	0.4	0.6	4.9	5.7	6.3	7.2	4.5	23.1	33.7	12.3	2.3	78.6	43.7	51.5	48.5
51550	MAGNOLIA	99.4	99.4	0.0	0.0	0.0	0.0	1.3	0.6	5.6	6.8	6.8	8.1	5.0	21.1	32.9	12.4	1.2	75.2	42.5	52.8	47.2
51551	MALVERN	98.7	98.5	0.1	0.1	0.1	0.2	0.6	1.0	6.0	6.0	6.4	6.7	5.5	21.6	29.7	14.7	3.3	77.0	43.0	49.5	50.5
51552	MARNE	98.9	98.5	0.0	0.0	0.4	0.7	0.4	0.4	4.4	5.2	5.9	7.0	4.1	20.7	35.8	15.1	1.8	80.1	46.4	50.6	49.4
51553	MINDEN	99.2	99.0	0.0	0.0	0.1	0.1	0.4	0.8	6.3	6.5	7.0	7.0	5.2	25.4	29.8	11.3	1.5	76.0	40.2	50.2	49.8
51555	MISSOURI VALLEY	98.8	98.8	0.0	0.0	0.1	0.1	0.8	0.9	6.2	6.0	6.2	6.7	5.9	25.0	27.6	13.6	2.9	77.5	40.4	48.6	51.4
51556	MODALE	98.4	97.9	0.0	0.0	0.2	0.2	0.2	0.2	6.2	6.8	7.2	6.4	3.9	22.4	32.0	13.5	1.6	75.4	42.7	53.4	46.6
51557	MONDAMIN	98.3	98.3	0.0	0.0	0.2	0.2	1.3	1.2	4.9	5.7	6.3	7.1	5.3	21.9	33.7	13.4	1.7	78.7	44.0	50.7	49.3
51558	MOORHEAD	99.2	98.7	0.0	0.0	0.6	1.1	0.0	0.0	5.1	5.7	6.4	7.0	4.0	21.1	30.4	17.6	2.6	78.4	45.4	50.7	49.3
51559	NEOLA	98.7	98.1	0.2	0.2	0.4	0.7	0.7	1.0	6.9	7.2	7.5	6.8	4.8	25.1	28.7	11.2	1.8	74.0	39.1	48.9	51.1
51560	OAKLAND	98.5	98.0	0.3	0.5	0.2	0.3	0.4	0.6	5.7	6.2	6.6	6.7	5.7	24.0	27.0	13.7	4.4	77.0	41.1	48.7	51.3
51561	PACIFIC JUNCTION	98.0	97.3	0.1	0.1	0.5	0.8	1.2	1.8	5.3	6.0	6.7	7.1	4.7	23.2	34.8	11.0	1.3	77.7	42.8	51.9	48.1
51562	PANAMA	99.2	99.3	0.0	0.0	0.2	0.2	0.2	0.2	6.5	8.1	8.8	7.0	2.9	23.8	24.9	15.5	2.5	71.9	40.1	49.7	50.3
51563	PERSIA	99.4	99.4	0.4	0.3	0.1	0.1	0.7	0.8	6.7	7.3	7.6	7.5	5.1	21.9	29.5	12.9	1.6	73.7	40.4	50.9	49.1
51564	PISGAH	98.7	98.7	0.3	0.3	0.1	0.1	0.9	0.9	5.9	5.8	5.9	7.1	6.2	21.4	28.4	16.2	2.9	78.1	43.0	49.0	51.0
51565	PORTSMOUTH	99.2	99.0	0.0	0.0	0.2	0.3	0.3	0.3	7.4	8.1	7.9	6.7	3.5	22.3	28.3	14.0	1.7	72.2	40.6	51.1	48.9
51566	RED OAK	97.7	96.8	0.1	0.1	0.3	0.6	1.8	2.7	6.7	6.2	6.1	6.7	5.9	22.5	27.4	14.4	4.0	76.8	41.5	47.0	53.0
51570	SHELBY	98.7	98.4	0.0	0.0	0.2	0.2	0.7	1.0	6.0	6.7	7.0	7.0	4.3	23.0	30.0	13.8	2.2	75.7	42.2	50.8	49.2
51571	SILVER CITY	98.3	97.9	0.3	0.3	0.5	0.7	1.1	1.7	6.6	7.3	7.9	7.5	4.5	23.1	30.8	10.8	1.4	73.4	40.5	50.6	49.4
51572	SOLDIER	98.2	97.6	0.5	0.6	0.0	0.2	0.4	0.6	5.2	6.0	6.2	6.2	3.6	21.0	32.6	16.6	2.6	78.4	46.0	51.2	48.8
51573	STANTON	99.1	98.8	0.0	0.0	0.1	0.2	0.4	0.7	4.5	6.7	7.4	7.7	3.0	22.6	26.6	15.8	5.7	76.1	43.7	48.6	51.4
51575	TREYNOR	99.6	99.4	0.1	0.1	0.2	0.4	0.2	0.3	5.4	5.9	6.7	8.0	5.9	23.2	30.6	12.3	2.1	77.1	41.4	49.8	50.2
51576	UNDERWOOD	98.4	97.9	0.1	0.1	0.3	0.6	0.9	1.4	7.0	7.4	7.7	7.2	4.6	24.4	30.0	10.4	1.2	73.4	39.2	49.3	50.7
51577	WALNUT	98.2	96.9	0.4	0.9	0.2	0.8	0.8	1.4	6.2	6.6	6.9	6.6	4.4	23.9	29.4	13.6	2.5	76.2	41.2	49.9	50.1
51578	WESTPHALIA	100.0	100.0	0.0	0.0	0.0	0.0	0.0	0.0	4.7	9.3	9.3	7.0	2.3	25.6	20.9	18.6	2.3	72.1	39.4	51.2	48.8
51579	WOODBINE	98.4	98.4	0.1	0.1	0.3	0.3	0.6	0.6	6.5	7.1	6.9	6.9	4.9	22.9	25.9	14.4	4.5	75.0	41.0	49.2	50.8
51601	SHENANDOAH	97.9	97.3	0.1	0.1	0.2	0.4	2.5	3.5	6.2	6.1	6.1	5.9	5.5	22.4	26.5	16.2	5.1	78.1	43.0	47.4	52.6
51630	BLANCHARD	98.4	97.6	0.0	0.0	0.5	0.6	1.6	1.8	5.4	6.0	6.0	6.5	4.8	23.2	31.0	14.3	3.0	78.6	43.3	53.0	47.0
51631	BRADDYVILLE	99.4	99.4	0.0	0.0	0.0	0.0	0.0	0.0	6.7	7.3	7.3	7.0	4.8	20.1	30.4	14.7	1.6	74.1	41.9	50.5	49.5
51632	CLARINDA	93.6	92.0	3.6	4.2	0.9	1.4	1.2	1.8	4.7	4.6	5.6	8.3	6.6	27.1	25.1	14.4	3.6	79.0	39.8	55.2	44.8
51636	COIN	99.6	99.6	0.0	0.0	0.0	0.0	0.6	0.6	4.0	4.4	5.1	6.3	4.9	23.9	33.4	15.0	3.0	82.7	45.8	49.0	51.0
51637	COLLEGE SPRINGS	99.6	99.5	0.0	0.0	0.0	0.0	0.0	0.0	6.7	7.1	7.1	7.1	4.8	20.0	31.4	13.8	1.9	74.8	42.3	51.4	48.6
51638	ESSEX	98.1	97.8	0.1	0.1	0.0	0.0	0.5	0.7	6.4	7.0	7.2	5.9	4.1	22.1	31.6	13.5	2.2	75.7	43.0	50.0	50.0
51639	FARRAGUT	98.0	97.5	0.0	0.0	0.3	0.4	1.2	1.8	4.4	4.8	5.7	7.6	4.8	21.3	32.0	16.2	3.0	80.3	45.7	50.2	49.8
51640	HAMBURG	97.1	96.0	0.1	0.1	0.4	0.6	4.0	5.7	6.1	6.2	6.5	6.5	4.7	23.1	27.8	16.1	3.0	77.3	42.5	49.9	50.1
51645	IMOGENE	98.8	98.0	0.0	0.0	0.0	0.4	0.8	1.2	6.6	6.6	7.0	6.6	4.3	21.5	31.6	13.7	2.0	75.0	42.8	52.0	48.0
51646	NEW MARKET	98.5	97.7	0.0	0.0	0.2	0.4	1.3	2.1	5.4	5.9	6.6	8.0	5.2	23.6	26.5	15.9	2.8	76.9	41.9	49.2	50.8
51647	NORTHBORO	97.5	96.8	0.0	0.0	0.4	0.5	1.7	2.3	4.5	5.4	5.4	6.3	5.0	24.3	31.1	14.9	3.2	80.2	44.2	52.3	47.7
51648	PERCIVAL	97.1	95.5	0.0	0.0	0.4	0.4	3.2	4.9	5.3	7.1	7.9	6.4	2.6	24.1	32.7	12.8	1.1	75.2	42.9	50.4	49.6
51649	RANDOLPH	98.4	98.1	0.0	0.0	0.2	0.2	0.7	0.9	6.6	6.6	6.9	6.6	4.7	21.7	30.3	13.9	2.6	75.7	42.6	52.2	47.8
51650	RIVERTON	99.0	98.7	0.0	0.0	0.3	0.3	2.0	2.7	4.3	4.8	5.6	7.5	4.8	23.9	30.8	15.8	2.4	80.7	44.2	53.9	46.1
51651	SHAMBAUGH	100.0	100.0	0.0	0.0	0.0	0.0	0.0	0.0	4.8	9.5	9.5	9.5	0.0	23.8	38.1	4.8	0.0	66.7	41.3	52.4	47.6
51652	SIDNEY	98.3	97.6	0.1	0.2	0.2	0.3	2.0	3.1	6.5	6.5	6.6	6.6	5.3	20.9	28.9	14.6	4.0	75.9	43.0	49.5	50.5
51653	TABOR	99.0	98.6	0.0	0.0	0.1	0.2	1.1	1.7	5.2	5.5	6.1	6.0	5.8	21.3	29.3	16.2	4.8	79.0	45.2	47.4	52.6
51654	THURMAN	97.0	95.7	0.0	0.0	0.2	0.4	3.2	4.7	5.3	6.8	8.0	6.5	2.5	24.5	32.9	12.3	1.2	75.3	42.7	50.5	49.5
51656	YORKTOWN	98.3	98.1	0.0	0.0	0.0	0.0	0.0	0.0	5.6	5.6	7.4	5.6	3.7	24.1	31.5	14.8	1.9	79.6	43.8	46.3	53.7
52001	DUBUQUE	95.9	94.5	1.4	1.7	0.6	1.0	1.9	2.8	6.0	5.8	5.8	8.0	8.8	23.9	24.7	13.3	3.7	78.7	38.0	47.5	52.5
52002	DUBUQUE	97.2	96.1	0.5	0.7	1.3	1.9	0.8	1.1	6.9	7.3	7.8	7.3	5.3	24.7	28.5	10.6	1.5	73.3	38.2	49.2	50.8
52003	DUBUQUE	98.3	97.6	0.4	0.5	0.5	0.8	0.5	0.9	6.3	6.6	7.1	6.9	5.0	23.3	29.0	13.3	2.6	75.4	41.3	48.2	51.8
52030	ANDREW	99.3	98.9	0.0	0.0	0.0	0.0	1.1	1.6	6.1	6.5	7.0	7.4	5.4	24.3	29.4	12.6	1.3	75.1	40.5	49.4	50.6
52031	BELLEVUE	99.6	99.5	0.0	0.0	0.1	0.1	0.3	0.5	5.8	6.5	6.9	7.5	4.9	23.0	28.8	13.8	2.8	75.7	41.7	50.5	49.5
52032	BERNARD	99.7	99.6	0.1	0.1	0.0	0.1	0.1	0.2	5.4	5.9	6.7	7.8	5.0	22.0	32.3	13.4	1.5	77.2	43.0	53.2	46.8
52033	CASCADE	99.4	99.1	0.0	0.0	0.1	0.1	0.5	0.7	7.3	7.5	7.5	6.9	5.0	25.0	26.5	11.3	2.8	73.1	37.9	51.6	48.4
52035	COLESBURG	99.5	99.4	0.0	0.0	0.1	0.1	0.6	0.8	6.6	7.4	8.0	7.6	4.3	23.3	28.5	12.6	1.6	73.1	39.9	50.7	49.3
52036	DELAWARE	100.0	100.0	0.0	0.0	0.0	0.0	0.0	0.0	8.3	8.3	8.3	8.3	4.2	25.0	22.9	14.6	0.0	68.8	36.3	50.0	50.0
52037	DELMAR	99.1	98.7	0.1	0.1	0.1	0.1	0.4	0.8	5.7	7.4	8.5	7.9	3.6	24.3	28.2	12.9	1.6	73.2	39.9	50.3	49.7
52038	DUNDEE	99.0	98.7	0.0	0.0	0.0	0.2	0.8	1.3	6.2	6.8	7.4	8.1	4.7	23.3	29.7	12.1	1.7	74.7	40.7	49.9	50.1
52039	DURANGO	98.9	98.6	0.4	0.5	0.1	0.2	0.5	0.8	7.3	7.7	8.0	7.3	4.7	24.1	28.5	11.3	1.0	72.3	38.8	52.9	47.1
52040	DYERSVILLE	99.0	98.5	0.4	0.5	0.2	0.4	0.4	0.6	7.9	8.0	7.6	6.9	5.4	24.1	25.4	12.4	2.4	72.0	37.3	49.7	50.3
52041	EARLVILLE	99.2	98.9	0.1	0.1	0.1	0.2	0.8	1.1	6.6	7.0	7.1	7.8	5.5	24.9	28.5	11.0	1.6	74.4	38.3	51.0	49.0
52042	EDGEWOOD	99.3	99.1	0.0	0.0	0.2	0.3	0.4	0.6	6.1	6.6	7.0	7.5	4.5	22.7	28.3	13.6	3.8	75.3	41.7	48.4	51.6
52043	ELKADER	99.1	99.0	0.2	0.2	0.0	0.0	0.1	0.1	4.7	5.1	5.6	6.4	5.0	20.4	31.4	16.8	4.7	80.4	46.8	47.9	52.1
52044	ELKPORT	98.7	98.2	0.0	0.0	0.4	0.9	0.4	0.4	7.1	7.1	8.0	6.7	3.6	25.3	29.3	10.7	2.2	73.3	40.1	52.4	47.6
52045	EPWORTH	95.2	92.8	0.4	0.6	3.6	5.5	0.5	0.8	7.0	7.6	7.8	6.9	5.5	27.3	27.4	9.4	1.0	75.7	36.2	52.2	47.8
52046	FARLEY	99.0	98.6	0.1	0.2	0.3	0.5	0.7	1.0	8.0	8.5	8.4	6.8	4.7	27.1	25.4	9.6	1.5	70.5	36.2	50.5	49.5
52047	FARMERSBURG	99.3	98.9	0.0	0.0	0.1	0.1	0.7	1.2	6.1	6.9	8.6	7.5	4.0	24.7	26.4	13.6	2.2	73.2	39.9	52.3	47.7
52048	GARBER	99.0	98.7	0.0	0.0	0.3	0.5	0.3	0.3	6.9	7.5	8.0	7.5	3.9	24.9	29.6	10.0	1.8	72.8	39.4	52.2	47.8
52049	GARNAVILLO	99.7	99.5	0.3	0.4	0.0	0.0	0.5	0.8	4.6	4.6	4.7	5.4	5.7	21.3	30.7	18.7	4.5	82.6	47.5	50.9	49.1
52050	GREELEY	99.4	99.1	0.3	0.5	0.0	0.0	0.5	0.9	6.7	7.0	7.2	7.0	4.4	25.0	30.8	10.4	1.5	74.7	39.4	50.3	49.7
52052	GUTTENBERG	99.0	98.8	0.3	0.3	0.1	0.2	0.5	0.7	5.2	5.5	6.2	6.2	4.5	21.1	30.0	16.9	4.4	78.9	45.8	49.2	50.8
52053	HOLY CROSS	99.2	98.8	0.2	0.3	0.1	0.1	0.7	1.1	6.7	7.2	8.3	7.8	4.4	23.5	29.7	11.3	1.0	72.7	39.4	53.2	46.8
52054	LA MOTTE	98.8	98.5	0.0	0.0	0.0	0.1	0.1	0.1	6.6	7.5	7.6	7.0	4.5	23.6	29.6	12.2	1.4	73.7	40.7	51.2	48.8
52057	MANCHESTER	99.2	98.9	0.1	0.1	0.2	0.3	0.8	1.2	6.3	6.8	7.1	7.2	5.7	23.8	26.5	13.5	3.1	75.2	39.6	48.5	51.5
52060	MAQUOKETA	98.4	98.0	0.1	0.2	0.4	0.5	1.0	1.4	6.1	6.4	6.4	7.1	5.7	23.2	26.8	14.6	3.8	76.7	41.2	48.2	51.8
52064	MILES	99.0	98.9	0.1	0.1	0.0	0.0	0.0	0.0	6.5	7.0	7.4	6.5	3.7	22.4	31.8	12.8	2.0	75.1	42.5	50.4	49.6
52065	NEW VIENNA	99.8	99.8	0.0	0.0	0.1	0.1	0.2	0.3	6.8	7.2	7.7	7.6	3.8	23.6	28.3	13.5	1.6	73.6	40.0	53.6	46.4
52068	PEOSTA	99.3	99.0	0.1	0.2	0.2	0.3	0.4	0.7	8.1	8.7	9.4	7.4	4.2	24.4	28.1	9.0	0.7	68.9	37.1	49.9	50.1
52069	PRESTON	99.5	99.5	0.2	0.2	0.2	0.2	0.2	0.3	5.9	6.0	6.8	6.8	4.2	27.1	28.5	12.5	2.2	76.7	40.3	50.4	49.6
52070	SABULA	99.3	99.3	0.0	0.0	0.0	0.0	0.7	1.0	5.8	6.3	6.4	5.9	3.6	22.7	29.6	17.2	2.6	77.9	44.6	49.7	50.3
52071	SAINT DONATUS	100.0	100.0	0.0	0.0	0.0	0.0	0.0	0.0	5.4	6.3	7.2	8.1	4.5	21.6	30.6	14.4	1.8	75.7	42.5	51.4	48.6
52072	SAINT OLAF	100.0	99.7	0.0	0.0	0.0	0.0	0.3	0.3	6.1	7.0	7.5	7.2	4.5	22.2	30.2	13.6	1.6	74.9	41.5	51.9	48.1
52073	SHERRILL	99.2	98.6	0.3	0.4	0.0	0.1	0.6	1.0	7.1	7.3	7.6	6.8	4.8	24.3	28.4	12.6	1.1	73.8	40.2	52.9	47.1
52074	SPRAGUEVILLE	99.4	99.1	0.3	0.3	0.0	0.3	0.3	0.3	5.8	6.4	8.5	8.5	3.8	23.9	29.2	13.1	0.9	73.5	40.3	52.5	47.5
52076	STRAWBERRY POINT	98.9	98.8	0.0	0.0	0.0	0.1	0.6	0.8	6.5	6.7	7.3	7.4	4.7	22.5	27.0	13.4	4.6	74.5	41.1	48.2	51.8
52077	VOLGA	97.2	96.5	0.0	0.0	0.0	0.2	0.9	1.1	7.2	7.7	7.9	7.2	4.6	21.3	29.6	12.5	2.0	71.9	40.8	50.2	49.8
52078	WORTHINGTON	99.8	99.7	0.0	0.0	0.0	0.1	0.2	0.3	7.0	7.7	7.7	6.9	4.5	24.7	28.2	11.2	2.1	72.8	38.4	52.4	47.6
52079	ZWINGLE	99.3	98.8	0.1	0.2	0.2	0.3	0.5	0.7	6.0	6.8	7.6	7.8	4.8	22.5	32.2	11.0	1.3	74.6	40.8	52.0	48.0
52101	DECORAH	97.2	95.1	0.7	1.6	1.1	1.8	0.9	1.5	4.4	4.8	5.3	10.7	13.5	20.3	24.5	12.5	3.9	82.3	36.4	47.9	52.1
52132	CALMAR	98.9	98.5	0.1	0.1	0.3	0.6	0.5	0.7	6.6	7.1	7.1	8.7	6.0	24.0	26.0	12.1	2.3	74.4	38.5	52.0	48.0
52133	CASTALIA	98.6	98.0	0.0	0.0	0.5	0.6	1.4	2.0	5.7	6.1	6.8	7.1	4.1	23.1	32.1	13.4	1.7	76.9	43.1	53.0	47.0
52134	CHESTER	99.2	99.2	0.0	0.0	0.2	0.2	0.2	0.4	5.7	6.1	6.5	7.9	4.7	23.3	29.4	14.0	2.4	76.7	42.0	49.9	50.1
52135	CLERMONT	98.0	97.0	0.0	0.0	0.0	0.1	2.5	3.7	6.2	6.6	6.9	7.3	4.2	23.5	27.0	16.4	2.0	75.7	42.3	52.4	47.6
	IOWA	93.9	91.9	2.1	2.5	1.3	2.1	2.8	4.1	6.5	6.4	6.5	7.3	7.1	25.2	26.5	11.9	2.6	76.5	38.1	49.3	50.7
	UNITED STATES	75.1	72.0	12.3	12.7	3.8	4.6	12.5	15.7	6.8	6.7	6.6	7.1	6.9	27.0	26.0	10.9	1.9	75.7	36.9	49.2	50.8

ZIP CODE #	POST OFFICE NAME	2009 Per Capita Income	2009 HH Income Base	2009 HOUSEHOLD INCOME DISTRIBUTION (%) Less than $25,000	$25,000 to $49,999	$50,000 to $99,999	$100,000 to $149,999	$150,000 or More	MEDIAN HOUSEHOLD INCOME 2009	2014	2009 National Centile	2009 State Centile	2009 Home Value Base	2009 HOME VALUE DISTRIBUTION (%) Less than $50,000	$50,000 to $89,999	$90,000 to $174,999	$175,000 to $399,999	$400,000 or More	2009 Median Home Value
51545	LITTLE SIOUX	16921	197	34.5	34.5	26.4	3.0	1.5	35407	37657	19	4	148	45.9	32.4	14.9	6.1	0.7	53333
51546	LOGAN	21298	1164	22.9	30.2	38.7	5.9	2.4	47393	50132	55	59	925	14.7	24.8	45.5	13.6	1.4	105549
51548	MC CLELLAND	24972	192	17.7	24.0	42.2	12.0	4.2	56503	57335	73	89	144	4.2	4.2	41.7	42.4	7.6	175000
51549	MACEDONIA	19719	210	26.2	32.4	33.3	7.1	1.0	43074	46637	43	32	159	12.6	25.2	40.9	20.1	1.3	112500
51550	MAGNOLIA	24434	70	21.4	30.0	41.4	5.7	1.4	48899	51309	59	65	57	17.5	24.6	40.4	14.0	3.5	103750
51551	MALVERN	22623	785	25.6	28.7	34.9	7.6	3.2	45928	50228	51	49	624	18.4	33.2	36.1	10.4	1.9	88214
51552	MARNE	20035	106	18.9	39.6	34.0	7.5	0.0	45794	47652	51	49	85	11.8	20.0	50.6	15.3	2.4	108523
51553	MINDEN	23694	391	20.7	26.1	43.2	8.2	1.8	52969	55453	68	80	302	5.0	11.9	55.0	26.2	2.0	126163
51555	MISSOURI VALLEY	23969	2104	20.2	26.4	42.3	8.2	3.0	52941	54130	68	80	1571	14.5	23.7	43.1	17.5	1.1	105180
51556	MODALE	24846	225	18.2	34.2	35.1	10.7	1.8	47898	50575	56	61	187	18.2	24.1	34.2	22.5	1.1	105603
51557	MONDAMIN	23278	339	21.5	28.3	42.2	5.3	2.7	50090	51261	61	70	278	20.1	28.1	35.3	13.7	2.9	92778
51558	MOORHEAD	22786	204	28.9	33.3	25.5	7.8	4.4	40966	41534	36	20	156	39.7	30.1	16.0	11.5	2.6	61111
51559	NEOLA	23339	763	18.0	25.4	47.8	6.4	2.4	54900	56454	71	86	594	4.9	14.8	58.8	20.5	1.0	119604
51560	OAKLAND	25047	897	19.1	30.9	38.7	8.4	3.0	50048	53399	61	70	695	8.8	24.3	54.2	11.7	1.0	107500
51561	PACIFIC JUNCTION	24642	562	16.7	29.7	39.7	10.7	3.2	52552	55477	67	79	487	18.1	18.3	31.2	28.1	4.3	122406
51562	PANAMA	19882	180	21.7	38.3	34.4	5.0	0.6	43174	45739	43	32	148	12.2	33.1	36.5	13.5	4.7	97000
51563	PERSIA	20691	331	19.6	25.4	46.2	8.5	0.3	53230	53198	68	82	265	11.7	17.0	49.4	17.4	4.5	116604
51564	PISGAH	18656	289	32.9	32.5	29.4	3.8	1.4	37317	39067	25	7	217	40.6	28.1	19.4	10.1	1.8	58913
51565	PORTSMOUTH	20789	231	20.3	32.5	36.8	10.0	0.4	46642	49542	53	55	191	9.4	32.5	39.3	18.8	0.0	100368
51566	RED OAK	20688	3008	27.7	34.7	30.8	5.5	1.3	41247	43311	37	21	2120	25.8	32.5	34.7	6.3	0.7	78281
51570	SHELBY	19524	475	21.7	36.4	37.1	4.4	0.4	44300	46609	46	40	367	13.4	27.0	46.3	12.5	0.8	101993
51571	SILVER CITY	26745	287	17.1	30.3	40.1	8.7	3.8	51989	54900	66	78	245	8.2	13.9	37.1	30.6	10.2	150543
51572	SOLDIER	17964	229	32.3	44.5	19.7	3.1	0.4	34872	36096	17	3	169	39.1	27.2	17.8	13.6	2.4	64375
51573	STANTON	20552	424	22.9	30.0	40.3	6.4	0.5	47550	50849	56	60	333	21.6	35.1	34.8	7.2	1.2	81964
51575	TREYNOR	27209	555	14.2	20.5	46.8	14.4	4.0	66504	67302	85	97	444	1.8	6.3	62.8	24.3	4.7	142800
51576	UNDERWOOD	23788	598	15.1	26.1	45.2	9.5	4.2	57434	58240	75	89	478	5.6	6.3	54.4	30.3	3.3	135156
51577	WALNUT	20036	538	20.3	38.7	35.9	4.6	0.6	43764	46689	45	36	426	16.4	28.4	46.0	8.2	0.9	94681
51578	WESTPHALIA	13870	13	23.1	38.5	38.5	0.0	0.0	42330	40000	40	26	11	9.1	36.4	54.5	0.0	0.0	95000
51579	WOODBINE	19581	952	31.2	26.7	35.3	5.6	1.3	41543	45316	38	23	694	12.8	29.8	43.5	12.5	1.3	100194
51601	SHENANDOAH	21824	2625	31.9	29.6	30.7	5.3	2.4	40239	42251	33	16	1773	28.9	31.8	33.1	5.8	0.6	75397
51630	BLANCHARD	21746	73	23.3	37.0	31.5	4.1	4.1	43932	45739	45	38	58	29.3	27.6	32.8	6.9	3.4	83333
51631	BRADDYVILLE	20793	130	19.2	36.2	40.8	3.8	0.0	46365	47839	52	53	110	32.7	31.8	30.0	5.5	0.0	67000
51632	CLARINDA	22941	2682	24.1	28.2	37.3	7.6	2.8	48151	50037	57	62	1952	19.0	31.1	41.0	8.5	0.4	89844
51636	COIN	21667	203	25.6	32.5	35.5	4.9	1.5	43676	45518	44	35	162	38.9	28.4	24.7	6.8	1.2	64615
51637	COLLEGE SPRINGS	19259	81	19.8	35.8	40.7	3.7	0.0	46133	48626	52	51	68	30.9	32.4	30.9	5.9	0.0	68333
51638	ESSEX	23433	572	19.1	30.1	43.9	5.2	1.7	50689	52199	63	72	438	24.0	35.6	32.6	7.8	0.0	76316
51639	FARRAGUT	23419	396	28.0	27.5	38.1	3.3	3.0	45000	46501	48	44	302	26.2	32.1	31.5	9.9	0.3	81935
51640	HAMBURG	21250	749	29.9	28.8	33.9	4.9	2.4	41191	44197	37	21	555	22.7	30.5	36.4	8.8	1.6	85732
51645	IMOGENE	26336	110	20.0	33.6	35.5	6.4	4.5	46549	50645	53	55	79	25.3	27.8	35.4	10.1	1.3	85000
51646	NEW MARKET	21980	348	26.4	28.7	39.9	4.3	0.6	45237	48649	49	45	279	30.8	33.0	28.0	6.1	2.2	70263
51647	NORTHBORO	20963	92	23.9	35.9	33.7	3.3	3.3	43956	45962	45	38	72	25.0	29.2	34.7	8.3	2.8	86250
51648	PERCIVAL	24866	112	23.2	29.5	36.6	8.0	2.7	48184	49481	57	62	90	22.2	20.0	43.3	12.2	2.2	98750
51649	RANDOLPH	24748	164	18.9	31.7	36.6	6.7	6.1	49318	50146	60	67	117	19.7	26.5	39.3	13.7	0.9	97500
51650	RIVERTON	19229	160	31.9	26.3	38.1	3.8	0.0	43901	45337	45	38	121	48.8	24.8	17.4	9.1	0.0	51500
51651	SHAMBAUGH	21170	8	12.5	25.0	62.5	0.0	0.0	60000	63351	77	92	7	28.6	28.6	42.9	0.0	0.0	75000
51652	SIDNEY	20300	737	24.7	25.4	44.9	3.5	1.5	49903	50101	61	69	546	18.5	31.7	39.7	7.0	3.1	89756
51653	TABOR	23519	524	24.4	23.1	41.8	8.0	2.7	53699	54118	69	83	401	12.2	21.7	50.1	15.5	0.5	108912
51654	THURMAN	23924	206	22.3	30.1	36.9	8.3	2.4	48388	48795	58	63	165	23.0	20.0	41.8	12.7	2.4	97667
51656	YORKTOWN	19540	19	26.3	26.3	42.1	5.3	0.0	47368	54641	55	59	15	20.0	26.7	40.0	13.3	0.0	95000
52001	DUBUQUE	23986	17855	24.0	32.7	33.7	6.3	3.2	44917	47700	48	44	11640	7.3	21.7	56.1	13.5	1.5	113034
52002	DUBUQUE	26327	5195	14.3	26.2	43.3	12.6	3.7	59461	59169	77	91	3976	4.6	4.3	54.5	34.3	2.3	152605
52003	DUBUQUE	30485	5516	13.1	27.7	40.4	10.4	8.4	57927	58089	75	90	4746	19.9	7.4	38.1	28.2	6.5	136690
52030	ANDREW	20902	166	19.3	37.3	36.7	4.2	2.4	45958	50307	51	50	139	8.6	13.7	51.8	22.3	3.6	121591
52031	BELLEVUE	20594	1939	25.5	30.0	36.7	5.7	2.1	46295	49362	52	52	1570	11.5	15.7	48.3	21.5	3.0	121012
52032	BERNARD	23190	568	28.0	21.5	40.0	7.2	3.3	50418	52409	62	71	471	15.1	14.4	32.5	30.1	7.9	128618
52033	CASCADE	22346	1256	22.3	27.1	43.8	4.5	2.3	50593	52839	63	72	943	6.7	20.4	55.4	13.7	3.9	116685
52035	COLESBURG	21841	407	23.1	34.9	34.2	4.9	2.9	45533	46794	50	47	331	21.5	23.9	37.2	11.5	6.0	98158
52036	DELAWARE	16042	18	22.2	38.9	38.9	0.0	0.0	40000	45000	33	15	14	21.4	28.6	42.9	0.0	7.1	90000
52037	DELMAR	19506	551	23.8	29.0	39.2	6.7	1.3	46528	50210	53	54	449	15.4	25.2	45.7	11.1	2.7	105186
52038	DUNDEE	20695	204	19.1	38.7	32.4	7.8	2.0	44148	45000	46	40	166	18.1	16.9	36.7	24.7	3.6	115517
52039	DURANGO	26089	357	11.8	31.4	40.3	9.2	7.3	56180	57099	73	88	303	7.6	8.9	40.9	36.3	6.3	156250
52040	DYERSVILLE	22906	2139	17.9	31.7	42.2	5.9	2.3	50346	52542	62	71	1748	6.9	13.7	48.4	28.3	2.7	132692
52041	EARLVILLE	17849	568	21.3	32.9	41.5	3.5	0.7	46449	47444	53	54	453	17.4	26.9	42.6	8.2	4.9	100140
52042	EDGEWOOD	20395	633	23.7	37.1	29.7	6.0	3.5	43855	45250	45	37	507	17.4	23.3	42.8	11.8	4.7	102388
52043	ELKADER	21851	1018	23.5	35.5	35.6	3.5	2.0	44087	46055	46	39	786	14.1	29.6	43.4	11.1	1.8	96712
52044	ELKPORT	21760	94	37.2	30.9	22.3	6.4	3.2	32778	32931	13	2	77	24.7	24.7	33.8	15.6	1.3	91000
52045	EPWORTH	21047	854	17.9	33.5	36.9	8.8	2.9	48883	51618	59	65	700	7.1	12.3	51.6	24.9	4.1	125575
52046	FARLEY	20054	820	19.0	33.7	38.3	6.8	2.2	47660	50774	56	60	665	2.1	15.3	58.0	20.2	4.4	122688
52047	FARMERSBURG	18525	291	21.6	42.3	30.9	4.1	1.0	41480	43285	38	23	224	15.6	33.0	37.5	11.2	2.7	91579
52048	GARBER	22911	168	35.1	32.1	24.4	5.4	3.0	36320	40324	21	5	138	23.9	23.9	33.3	17.4	1.4	93333
52049	GARNAVILLO	23694	563	22.2	35.5	34.6	5.9	1.8	43453	46145	44	33	434	15.2	33.9	41.7	5.5	3.7	90833
52050	GREELEY	18102	226	20.8	41.2	35.0	2.2	0.9	41613	44017	38	24	173	26.0	25.4	30.6	8.7	9.2	88214
52052	GUTTENBERG	21089	1299	29.3	33.9	29.1	5.5	2.2	38977	40286	30	12	1014	11.3	22.0	51.8	12.4	2.5	112000
52053	HOLY CROSS	22490	463	16.2	31.3	43.2	5.6	3.7	51752	53361	65	76	383	8.9	15.4	45.4	24.5	5.7	128125
52054	LA MOTTE	19972	404	23.3	26.7	41.6	7.2	1.2	50000	51878	61	70	334	12.3	15.3	43.1	24.0	5.4	133182
52057	MANCHESTER	22505	3214	26.4	30.0	34.0	6.3	3.4	44164	45256	46	40	2439	10.0	24.4	49.8	13.6	2.1	107634
52060	MAQUOKETA	20795	3677	28.1	34.1	31.6	4.5	1.7	40167	40976	33	16	2625	16.4	27.2	42.1	13.0	1.3	99158
52064	MILES	18966	303	29.7	28.7	36.3	4.6	0.7	41213	43152	37	21	240	21.3	25.8	42.1	7.5	3.3	94118
52065	NEW VIENNA	20760	483	23.2	29.6	38.3	7.5	1.4	47532	50647	55	59	395	10.4	18.2	41.8	21.5	8.1	124423
52068	PEOSTA	26686	1065	11.4	20.6	50.8	12.7	4.6	64452	63444	83	96	949	6.4	2.1	34.7	51.5	5.3	186944
52069	PRESTON	21154	654	26.0	31.2	38.2	3.5	1.1	44119	46939	46	40	493	11.8	26.4	42.8	15.6	3.4	105778
52070	SABULA	22104	531	29.6	35.6	28.8	4.0	2.1	36887	38012	23	6	413	23.5	24.2	34.9	13.8	3.6	94318
52071	SAINT DONATUS	19369	43	20.9	30.2	44.2	4.7	0.0	49423	51046	60	67	38	5.3	15.8	50.0	28.9	0.0	130000
52072	SAINT OLAF	19430	149	24.2	39.6	30.2	4.0	2.0	40605	42075	35	18	114	17.5	21.9	40.4	16.7	3.5	107292
52073	SHERRILL	23673	575	17.2	27.0	41.4	9.6	4.9	54817	55891	71	86	501	12.4	6.8	46.1	32.7	2.0	142620
52074	SPRAGUEVILLE	20648	132	22.7	33.3	37.9	4.5	1.5	45497	48656	50	47	106	15.1	12.3	42.5	24.5	5.7	128571
52076	STRAWBERRY POINT	19359	848	25.6	33.1	35.6	3.5	2.1	42866	44736	42	30	662	14.7	30.5	43.8	9.4	1.7	95517
52077	VOLGA	17545	180	30.0	33.3	32.2	2.8	1.7	38370	41018	28	10	143	23.8	23.8	28.7	21.0	2.8	100735
52078	WORTHINGTON	17022	342	24.3	32.5	40.1	2.6	0.6	42368	46887	41	27	278	3.2	20.9	43.2	18.3	14.4	125806
52079	ZWINGLE	22417	341	22.0	32.8	34.6	7.0	3.5	45597	50111	50	48	277	14.4	13.7	29.6	39.4	2.9	149479
52101	DECORAH	22818	5099	21.0	29.1	40.1	6.9	2.9	49881	50539	61	69	3648	6.5	18.6	46.4	24.9	3.6	126144
52132	CALMAR	21992	953	27.2	29.0	37.6	4.4	1.9	43503	46208	44	34	716	12.7	30.7	41.8	13.3	1.5	98246
52133	CASTALIA	18785	244	23.8	32.0	39.3	4.9	0.0	45000	46359	48	44	193	21.2	29.5	24.4	19.7	5.2	89063
52134	CHESTER	19090	190	26.8	31.1	34.7	6.8	0.5	44080	46142	46	39	150	28.0	28.0	32.0	8.7	3.3	81000
52135	CLERMONT	19768	382	24.9	39.8	31.2	3.1	1.0	40729	41461	35	18	310	14.5	31.3	42.3	11.0	1.0	98125
	IOWA	25379		21.1	28.2	37.9	8.6	4.3	50616	52941				14.7	22.5	41.6	18.6	2.6	110128
	UNITED STATES	27277		20.9	24.4	35.3	11.7	7.6	54719	56938				9.3	13.1	31.6	32.6	13.5	162279

ZIP CODE #	POST OFFICE NAME	FINANCIAL SERVICES: Auto Loan	Home Loan	Invest-ments	Retire-ment Plans	THE HOME: Home Improvements: Home Repair	Lawn & Garden	Furnishings: Comput-ers & Hard-ware-Personal	Major Appli-ances	TV, Radio, Sound Equip-ment	Furni-ture	ENTERTAINMENT: Dine out/ Carry out	Sports Equip-ment	Fees & Tickets	Toys & Games	Travel	Cable TV	PERSONAL: Apparel & Services	Auto Repairs	Health Insur-ance	Pets & Supplies
51545	LITTLE SIOUX	70	51	71	49	52	73	55	68	62	49	59	51	44	60	53	68	40	64	74	80
51546	LOGAN	91	72	90	73	75	97	76	90	80	66	78	69	63	80	75	86	52	84	95	106
51548	MC CLELLAND	93	104	90	108	101	103	93	97	92	94	92	76	100	94	99	92	65	93	96	114
51549	MACEDONIA	87	63	95	63	65	92	68	83	70	56	70	68	52	69	68	76	45	78	87	102
51550	MAGNOLIA	92	76	90	78	78	98	78	91	80	68	79	71	66	81	77	86	53	84	94	108
51551	MALVERN	92	70	93	69	72	97	74	90	81	67	78	68	62	80	73	88	52	84	96	106
51552	MARNE	91	63	100	63	66	96	70	86	73	57	72	71	52	71	70	79	47	81	91	106
51553	MINDEN	90	84	82	87	85	97	82	92	84	75	83	70	77	86	82	89	57	85	94	107
51555	MISSOURI VALLEY	86	83	75	85	81	88	85	85	85	81	85	66	82	86	83	87	58	85	90	101
51556	MODALE	101	70	111	70	73	107	77	96	80	63	80	79	57	79	77	88	52	90	102	118
51557	MONDAMIN	90	80	84	83	81	97	80	91	82	71	81	70	72	83	79	87	55	84	94	106
51558	MOORHEAD	91	62	100	62	65	96	69	86	72	56	71	71	51	71	69	79	46	80	91	106
51559	NEOLA	91	84	82	87	85	98	82	92	85	75	83	70	77	86	82	89	57	85	95	107
51560	OAKLAND	89	85	78	87	82	95	85	88	86	79	86	70	82	88	84	90	59	87	95	106
51561	PACIFIC JUNCTION	100	88	100	88	88	105	84	98	88	82	88	75	78	89	86	93	60	92	100	116
51562	PANAMA	88	60	96	60	63	93	67	83	70	54	69	69	49	68	67	76	45	78	88	102
51563	PERSIA	87	79	78	82	81	93	78	88	80	70	79	67	72	82	78	85	54	81	91	102
51564	PISGAH	76	54	78	53	57	80	60	74	65	52	63	57	47	64	58	72	42	69	80	88
51565	PORTSMOUTH	95	66	105	65	69	101	73	91	76	59	75	75	53	74	73	83	49	85	96	111
51566	RED OAK	74	62	67	62	62	77	66	72	70	61	69	54	58	70	63	75	47	70	79	85
51570	SHELBY	87	62	93	62	64	92	67	83	70	56	69	68	51	69	67	77	45	77	88	101
51571	SILVER CITY	95	102	94	104	99	104	92	98	91	91	92	77	96	93	97	93	64	94	98	116
51572	SOLDIER	70	48	77	48	50	74	54	67	56	43	55	55	39	55	53	61	36	62	70	82
51573	STANTON	82	69	79	71	70	87	70	81	73	62	71	63	61	73	70	78	48	75	85	96
51575	TREYNOR	92	112	100	113	108	110	96	101	97	98	98	76	110	99	106	99	69	98	105	117
51576	UNDERWOOD	97	97	90	100	97	105	91	99	92	87	91	76	90	94	94	95	63	93	101	116
51577	WALNUT	89	61	98	61	64	94	68	85	71	55	70	70	50	69	68	77	45	79	89	104
51578	WESTPHALIA	82	56	90	56	59	87	63	78	65	51	64	64	46	64	62	71	42	73	82	96
51579	WOODBINE	83	59	85	57	61	86	64	80	70	56	68	61	50	69	63	77	45	74	86	95
51601	SHENANDOAH	74	62	71	62	63	78	67	73	72	61	70	55	59	70	65	77	48	72	81	87
51630	BLANCHARD	87	63	93	64	66	92	69	84	71	57	70	68	53	70	68	77	46	78	88	102
51631	BRADDYVILLE	78	71	70	74	72	83	70	79	72	63	71	60	64	73	70	76	48	73	81	91
51632	CLARINDA	90	73	85	73	73	93	79	87	82	71	81	67	68	82	76	87	54	84	94	104
51636	COIN	90	62	99	62	65	95	69	86	72	56	71	71	51	70	69	78	46	80	90	105
51637	COLLEGE SPRINGS	77	70	70	73	72	83	69	78	72	63	70	59	64	73	69	76	48	72	81	91
51638	ESSEX	93	76	92	77	78	99	78	92	81	68	80	72	66	81	78	87	53	85	96	109
51639	FARRAGUT	98	68	108	68	71	104	75	93	78	61	77	77	55	77	75	85	50	87	99	115
51640	HAMBURG	80	66	77	67	68	85	68	80	72	60	70	60	59	72	67	77	47	74	84	93
51645	IMOGENE	109	75	119	75	79	115	84	104	87	68	86	85	62	86	83	95	56	97	110	127
51646	NEW MARKET	85	61	87	60	63	89	67	82	74	59	71	63	53	72	65	81	47	77	89	98
51647	NORTHBORO	90	62	99	62	65	95	69	86	72	56	71	71	51	70	69	78	46	80	91	106
51648	PERCIVAL	105	73	114	73	76	111	81	100	84	66	83	82	60	82	80	91	54	93	105	123
51649	RANDOLPH	112	79	121	79	82	118	87	107	91	72	90	87	65	89	86	99	58	100	113	131
51650	RIVERTON	80	55	88	55	58	85	61	76	64	50	63	63	45	62	61	69	41	71	80	94
51651	SHAMBAUGH	99	68	109	68	72	105	76	94	79	61	78	78	56	77	76	86	51	88	100	116
51652	SIDNEY	87	63	88	61	65	90	67	83	74	60	72	63	54	73	65	81	48	77	89	98
51653	TABOR	87	78	82	79	79	89	81	86	83	77	82	65	75	83	80	86	56	84	91	101
51654	THURMAN	106	73	117	73	76	112	81	101	84	66	83	83	59	83	81	92	54	94	106	124
51656	YORKTOWN	99	68	109	68	72	105	76	94	79	61	78	78	56	77	75	86	51	88	100	116
52001	DUBUQUE	78	76	70	77	74	82	79	78	82	75	81	59	78	81	77	85	56	80	87	93
52002	DUBUQUE	97	102	93	104	100	103	96	99	96	95	96	77	99	98	99	97	67	96	100	116
52003	DUBUQUE	111	118	110	118	116	120	108	114	109	109	109	85	113	110	112	111	76	110	117	133
52030	ANDREW	86	78	77	81	80	92	77	87	80	70	78	66	71	81	77	84	53	80	90	101
52031	BELLEVUE	85	71	81	73	73	90	72	84	76	64	74	65	63	76	72	81	50	78	88	99
52032	BERNARD	101	77	104	78	80	107	82	98	85	69	83	78	66	84	81	91	55	91	102	118
52033	CASCADE	89	78	82	80	78	95	80	88	82	71	81	69	72	83	79	86	55	84	93	105
52035	COLESBURG	97	67	106	66	70	102	74	92	77	60	76	76	54	75	74	84	49	86	97	113
52036	DELAWARE	73	55	76	56	57	78	59	71	61	50	60	57	47	61	59	66	40	66	74	86
52037	DELMAR	92	64	101	64	67	97	71	88	74	58	73	72	52	72	70	80	47	82	93	108
52038	DUNDEE	96	66	105	66	69	101	73	91	76	59	75	75	54	75	73	83	49	85	96	112
52039	DURANGO	117	101	116	104	103	125	101	116	103	91	102	92	90	104	102	109	69	109	119	138
52040	DYERSVILLE	85	85	79	85	82	93	82	85	84	77	83	67	81	84	83	87	57	84	93	102
52041	EARLVILLE	81	67	79	69	69	86	69	80	71	60	70	63	59	72	69	76	47	74	83	95
52042	EDGEWOOD	98	68	108	67	71	104	75	93	78	61	77	77	55	77	75	85	50	87	99	115
52043	ELKADER	78	67	83	65	68	87	67	79	72	60	71	60	60	70	68	78	47	75	87	93
52044	ELKPORT	93	64	102	64	67	98	71	88	74	58	73	73	52	73	71	81	47	83	93	109
52045	EPWORTH	91	85	85	88	86	98	83	93	84	76	83	71	77	86	84	89	57	86	95	108
52046	FARLEY	88	77	84	79	78	94	77	88	79	69	78	68	69	80	77	84	53	82	91	104
52047	FARMERSBURG	82	56	90	56	59	87	63	78	65	51	64	64	46	64	62	71	42	73	82	96
52048	GARBER	95	65	104	65	68	100	72	90	75	59	74	74	53	74	72	82	48	84	95	111
52049	GARNAVILLO	90	65	91	63	68	94	71	88	79	63	76	66	57	78	69	87	51	82	96	103
52050	GREELEY	84	57	92	57	60	88	64	79	66	52	66	66	47	65	63	72	43	74	84	98
52052	GUTTENBERG	86	62	95	61	66	91	67	84	72	58	70	65	53	70	67	79	46	78	88	100
52053	HOLY CROSS	106	77	115	77	80	112	83	101	86	69	85	83	64	85	83	93	56	95	106	124
52054	LA MOTTE	84	77	78	79	78	91	76	85	78	68	76	65	70	79	76	82	52	79	88	100
52057	MANCHESTER	85	78	77	80	77	91	78	84	81	73	80	65	74	82	78	85	55	82	90	100
52060	MAQUOKETA	73	64	65	65	64	76	67	72	71	61	69	55	61	71	65	75	47	70	78	85
52064	MILES	85	58	93	58	61	89	65	80	67	53	67	66	48	66	64	73	43	75	85	99
52065	NEW VIENNA	97	67	107	67	70	103	74	92	77	60	76	76	54	76	74	84	50	86	98	114
52068	PEOSTA	107	114	105	117	112	117	104	110	103	102	103	87	108	105	109	104	72	106	110	130
52069	PRESTON	79	67	77	69	68	85	68	79	70	59	69	61	59	71	68	75	46	73	82	93
52070	SABULA	84	60	87	58	62	86	62	79	68	56	67	60	49	67	62	75	44	72	82	94
52071	SAINT DONATUS	77	71	70	73	72	83	70	79	72	63	70	59	64	73	69	76	48	73	81	91
52072	SAINT OLAF	86	59	94	59	62	91	66	82	69	54	68	67	48	67	65	75	44	76	87	100
52073	SHERRILL	105	91	98	94	93	112	91	105	94	81	93	81	81	95	91	100	63	97	109	123
52074	SPRAGUEVILLE	94	67	101	68	70	100	73	90	76	60	75	74	56	75	73	83	49	84	95	110
52076	STRAWBERRY POINT	89	63	94	61	65	92	67	84	72	58	71	66	51	71	66	79	46	77	88	101
52077	VOLGA	79	55	87	54	57	84	61	75	63	49	62	62	44	62	60	69	40	70	80	93
52078	WORTHINGTON	85	61	90	61	63	90	67	81	69	56	69	67	52	69	66	75	45	76	86	99
52079	ZWINGLE	101	71	109	71	74	106	78	96	81	64	80	79	58	80	78	88	52	90	101	118
52101	DECORAH	85	78	84	79	78	90	80	85	81	75	81	66	75	81	80	84	55	83	90	101
52132	CALMAR	95	65	104	65	68	100	72	90	75	59	74	74	53	74	72	82	48	84	95	111
52133	CASTALIA	87	60	96	60	63	92	67	83	69	54	69	69	49	68	66	76	45	77	88	102
52134	CHESTER	89	61	97	61	64	93	68	84	70	55	70	70	50	69	67	77	45	79	89	103
52135	CLERMONT	84	58	92	58	61	89	64	80	67	52	66	66	47	66	64	73	43	75	84	98
	IOWA	93	84	87	85	83	95	87	91	89	82	88	71	81	90	85	92	61	90	96	108
	UNITED STATES	100	100	100	100	100	100	100	100	100	100	100	100	100	100	100	100	100	100	100	100

ZIP CODE #	POST OFFICE NAME	COUNTY FIPS CODE	POPULATION 2000	POPULATION 2009	POPULATION 2014	2000-2009 ANNUAL RATE % Rate	2000-2009 ANNUAL RATE State Centile	HOUSEHOLDS 2000	HOUSEHOLDS 2009	HOUSEHOLDS 2014	HOUSEHOLDS % Annual Rate 2000-2009	HOUSEHOLDS 2009 Average HH Size	FAMILIES 2000	FAMILIES 2009	FAMILIES % Annual Rate 2000-2009
52136	CRESCO	089	5978	5792	5661	-0.3	40	2403	2375	2331	-0.1	2.36	1543	1488	-0.4
52140	DORCHESTER	005	687	723	744	0.6	83	266	289	301	0.9	2.50	197	209	0.6
52141	ELGIN	065	1526	1545	1524	0.1	63	619	645	642	0.4	2.38	407	413	0.2
52142	FAYETTE	065	1967	1809	1737	-0.9	8	603	552	526	-1.0	2.42	399	357	-1.2
52144	FORT ATKINSON	191	1405	1318	1282	-0.7	15	512	502	494	-0.2	2.62	357	342	-0.5
52146	HARPERS FERRY	005	1002	1043	1057	0.4	76	405	437	447	0.8	2.26	292	308	0.6
52147	HAWKEYE	065	1151	1105	1064	-0.4	32	462	455	441	-0.2	2.43	331	319	-0.4
52151	LANSING	005	2267	2348	2379	0.4	76	903	973	995	0.8	2.35	619	650	0.5
52154	LAWLER	037	1155	1073	1032	-0.8	11	446	430	418	-0.4	2.49	325	307	-0.6
52155	LIME SPRINGS	089	1223	1159	1122	-0.6	20	487	470	457	-0.4	2.44	348	329	-0.6
52156	LUANA	043	665	659	648	-0.1	51	255	262	260	0.3	2.52	194	195	0.1
52157	MC GREGOR	043	2180	2175	2138	0.0	58	918	957	949	0.5	2.22	579	587	0.1
52158	MARQUETTE	043	18	18	17	0.0	58	6	6	6	0.0	2.83	4	4	0.0
52159	MONONA	005	2345	2320	2275	-0.1	51	945	964	955	0.2	2.40	654	652	0.0
52160	NEW ALBIN	005	895	878	858	-0.2	46	368	374	368	0.2	2.35	249	246	-0.1
52161	OSSIAN	191	1397	1438	1448	0.3	72	518	558	568	0.8	2.52	383	403	0.6
52162	POSTVILLE	005	3395	3594	3641	0.6	83	1220	1293	1311	0.6	2.72	875	906	0.4
52163	PROTIVIN	089	295	287	283	-0.3	40	147	148	146	0.1	1.94	103	102	-0.1
52164	RANDALIA	065	297	282	270	-0.6	20	106	104	100	-0.2	2.70	85	82	-0.4
52165	RIDGEWAY	191	1095	1104	1104	0.1	63	420	445	450	0.6	2.48	299	310	0.4
52169	WADENA	065	433	421	413	-0.3	40	180	181	179	0.1	2.33	132	129	-0.2
52170	WATERVILLE	005	561	569	573	0.2	68	201	211	215	0.5	2.68	157	163	0.4
52171	WAUCOMA	065	1254	1163	1115	-0.8	11	482	463	448	-0.4	2.51	343	322	-0.7
52172	WAUKON	005	6249	6161	6090	-0.2	46	2507	2544	2529	0.2	2.34	1647	1633	-0.1
52175	WEST UNION	065	3688	3457	3324	-0.7	15	1531	1472	1420	-0.4	2.24	985	924	-0.7
52201	AINSWORTH	183	1249	1334	1373	0.7	85	467	512	529	1.0	2.61	363	390	0.8
52202	ALBURNETT	113	1023	1137	1201	1.1	91	367	423	452	1.5	2.69	300	339	1.3
52203	AMANA	095	1927	2073	2119	0.8	87	772	851	875	1.1	2.35	543	587	0.8
52205	ANAMOSA	105	8377	8723	8784	0.4	76	2854	3039	3095	0.7	2.37	1996	2081	0.5
52206	ATKINS	011	1728	1739	1736	0.1	63	610	621	622	0.2	2.80	487	486	0.0
52207	BALDWIN	097	444	432	425	-0.3	40	180	183	182	0.2	2.36	125	124	-0.1
52208	BELLE PLAINE	011	3266	3190	3144	-0.3	40	1360	1347	1335	-0.1	2.31	867	833	-0.4
52209	BLAIRSTOWN	011	974	1027	1050	0.6	83	392	426	439	0.9	2.41	284	302	0.7
52210	BRANDON	019	725	755	765	0.4	76	282	304	310	0.8	2.48	218	230	0.6
52211	BROOKLYN	157	2635	2672	2668	0.2	68	1068	1119	1128	0.5	2.34	721	737	0.2
52212	CENTER JUNCTION	105	348	357	360	0.3	72	145	155	157	0.7	2.30	102	106	0.4
52213	CENTER POINT	113	3617	3551	3558	-0.2	46	1352	1375	1392	0.2	2.58	1033	1023	-0.1
52214	CENTRAL CITY	113	2982	3268	3434	1.0	90	1197	1362	1448	1.4	2.40	864	953	1.1
52215	CHELSEA	171	931	979	986	0.5	79	340	359	362	0.6	2.73	265	275	0.4
52216	CLARENCE	031	1424	1467	1484	0.3	72	579	608	619	0.5	2.34	393	404	0.3
52217	CLUTIER	171	643	649	649	0.1	63	269	278	279	0.4	2.33	193	195	0.1
52218	COGGON	113	1946	2053	2119	0.6	83	700	763	795	0.9	2.69	543	577	0.7
52219	PRAIRIEBURG	113	175	203	217	1.6	95	69	84	91	2.1	2.42	54	64	1.9
52220	CONROY	095	178	180	177	0.1	63	63	65	64	0.3	2.77	50	51	0.2
52221	GUERNSEY	157	139	139	135	0.0	58	60	62	61	0.4	2.24	43	44	0.2
52222	DEEP RIVER	157	807	811	795	0.1	63	313	327	324	0.5	2.48	225	230	0.2
52223	DELHI	055	1367	1341	1311	-0.2	46	525	529	523	0.1	2.44	413	409	-0.1
52224	DYSART	171	2017	2049	2055	0.2	68	795	821	826	0.3	2.44	575	581	0.1
52225	ELBERON	171	464	466	467	0.0	58	174	179	180	0.3	2.59	131	132	0.1
52227	ELY	113	1869	2437	2695	2.9	98	691	936	1044	3.3	2.60	513	680	3.1
52228	FAIRFAX	113	2156	2779	3081	2.8	98	808	1106	1241	3.5	2.51	656	875	3.2
52229	GARRISON	011	782	850	882	0.9	89	303	335	348	1.1	2.54	225	243	0.8
52231	HARPER	107	390	385	378	-0.1	51	148	151	150	0.2	2.55	114	114	0.0
52232	HARTWICK	157	231	234	234	0.1	63	98	103	103	0.5	2.27	71	73	0.3
52233	HIAWATHA	113	6441	7032	7239	1.0	90	2852	3172	3279	1.2	2.19	1691	1860	1.0
52236	HOMESTEAD	095	502	507	500	0.1	63	190	196	194	0.3	2.58	152	154	0.1
52237	HOPKINTON	055	1663	1634	1596	-0.2	46	603	611	602	0.1	2.65	451	446	-0.1
52240	IOWA CITY	103	31706	33648	35541	0.6	83	12967	14518	15546	1.2	2.17	6097	6458	0.6
52241	CORALVILLE	103	13689	16366	17599	1.9	96	6172	7439	8016	2.0	2.18	3112	3635	1.7
52242	IOWA CITY	103	802	1646	1646	8.1	100	1	2	2	7.8	5.00	0	1	0.0
52245	IOWA CITY	103	20584	22720	23684	1.1	91	7266	8377	8852	1.6	2.32	3735	4156	1.2
52246	IOWA CITY	103	19927	21232	22082	0.7	85	8889	9952	10465	1.2	2.04	4136	4347	0.5
52247	KALONA	183	5266	5717	5936	0.9	89	1781	1999	2090	1.3	2.82	1292	1418	1.0
52248	KEOTA	183	1827	1895	1904	0.4	76	727	783	791	0.8	2.38	487	511	0.5
52249	KEYSTONE	011	1075	1218	1275	1.4	94	418	484	509	1.6	2.43	289	327	1.3
52251	LADORA	095	578	625	638	0.8	87	223	248	254	1.2	2.52	163	177	0.9
52253	LISBON	031	2823	3081	3216	0.9	89	1051	1191	1259	1.4	2.59	772	847	1.0
52254	LOST NATION	045	1033	1065	1063	0.3	72	423	443	445	0.5	2.40	301	308	0.2
52255	LOWDEN	031	1285	1301	1308	0.1	63	527	547	553	0.4	2.38	377	383	0.2
52257	LUZERNE	011	337	339	333	0.1	63	118	122	121	0.4	2.78	96	98	0.2
52301	MARENGO	095	4303	4265	4221	-0.1	51	1741	1754	1740	0.1	2.38	1163	1144	-0.2
52302	MARION	113	28873	34983	37873	2.1	97	11202	14136	15447	2.5	2.43	7833	9623	2.2
52305	MARTELLE	105	624	622	624	0.0	58	245	255	259	0.4	2.44	188	191	0.2
52306	MECHANICSVILLE	031	1849	1890	1908	0.2	68	703	739	751	0.5	2.48	512	525	0.3
52307	MIDDLE AMANA	095	3	3	3	0.0	58	1	1	1	0.0	3.00	1	1	0.0
52308	MILLERSBURG	095	20	21	22	0.5	79	8	9	9	1.3	2.33	6	6	0.0
52309	MONMOUTH	097	471	458	451	-0.3	40	179	182	181	0.2	2.51	125	124	-0.1
52310	MONTICELLO	105	6225	6093	6021	-0.2	46	2468	2487	2480	0.1	2.38	1728	1703	-0.2
52313	MOUNT AUBURN	011	427	469	487	1.0	90	158	175	182	1.1	2.68	131	143	1.0
52314	MOUNT VERNON	113	4736	5594	5818	1.8	96	1611	1831	1939	1.4	2.54	1187	1311	1.1
52315	NEWHALL	011	1127	1256	1308	1.2	93	448	509	533	1.4	2.47	325	360	1.1
52316	NORTH ENGLISH	095	1794	1852	1845	0.3	72	714	746	745	0.5	2.40	490	501	0.2
52317	NORTH LIBERTY	103	6768	12759	15320	7.1	100	2780	5557	6736	7.8	2.30	1852	3522	7.2
52318	NORWAY	011	1840	2256	2416	2.2	97	621	767	822	2.3	2.94	511	620	2.1
52320	OLIN	105	1184	1194	1195	0.1	63	472	492	497	0.4	2.43	328	333	0.2
52321	ONSLOW	105	438	448	451	0.2	68	180	192	195	0.7	2.32	129	135	0.5
52322	OXFORD	103	2294	2555	2720	1.2	93	891	1040	1121	1.7	2.45	651	734	1.3
52323	OXFORD JUNCTION	105	970	957	946	-0.1	51	391	398	396	0.2	2.40	257	254	-0.1
52324	PALO	113	1686	2043	2224	2.1	97	646	825	906	2.7	2.47	516	649	2.5
52325	PARNELL	095	765	851	880	1.2	93	284	321	332	1.3	2.61	226	251	1.1
52326	QUASQUETON	019	486	538	554	1.1	91	192	218	227	1.4	2.47	151	169	1.2
52327	RIVERSIDE	183	2890	3089	3257	0.7	85	1073	1187	1263	1.1	2.59	742	799	0.8
52328	ROBINS	113	1529	2190	2468	4.0	99	497	734	836	4.3	2.96	400	559	3.7
52329	ROWLEY	019	893	896	898	0.0	58	333	344	348	0.4	2.60	270	275	0.2
52330	RYAN	055	964	928	895	-0.4	32	341	339	330	-0.1	2.74	259	252	-0.3
	IOWA					0.4					0.7	2.40			0.4
	UNITED STATES					1.0					1.1	2.59			0.9

POPULATION COMPOSITION

ZIP CODE #	POST OFFICE NAME	RACE (%) White 2000	White 2009	Black 2000	Black 2009	Asian/Pacific 2000	Asian/Pacific 2009	% Hispanic Origin 2000	% Hispanic Origin 2009	2009 AGE DISTRIBUTION (%) 0-4	5-9	10-14	15-19	20-24	25-44	45-64	65-84	85+	18+	MEDIAN AGE 2009	% 2009 Males	% 2009 Females
52136	CRESCO	98.9	98.6	0.2	0.2	0.2	0.3	0.7	1.0	6.4	6.7	7.0	6.6	4.9	23.1	25.9	15.0	4.3	75.6	41.6	48.9	51.1
52140	DORCHESTER	98.7	98.5	0.0	0.0	0.1	0.1	0.6	0.8	5.8	6.1	6.6	7.1	4.6	21.3	32.8	14.4	1.4	76.6	43.8	53.1	46.9
52141	ELGIN	99.2	98.8	0.1	0.1	0.1	0.2	0.8	1.3	6.0	6.3	6.7	6.9	4.9	21.7	28.9	15.5	3.3	76.6	43.0	50.4	49.6
52142	FAYETTE	92.4	89.6	3.5	4.4	1.7	2.8	2.1	3.2	5.2	5.3	5.0	10.4	16.7	19.9	21.4	12.7	3.4	83.1	31.4	52.7	47.3
52144	FORT ATKINSON	99.2	98.9	0.0	0.0	0.4	0.5	0.4	0.7	6.1	6.7	6.8	8.0	4.5	23.4	28.1	14.2	2.3	75.2	41.4	51.8	48.2
52146	HARPERS FERRY	98.1	97.7	0.8	1.0	0.0	0.0	0.8	1.2	5.3	5.8	6.1	5.7	4.8	20.8	29.1	20.2	2.1	78.8	46.0	52.9	47.1
52147	HAWKEYE	99.2	99.0	0.0	0.0	0.2	0.3	0.5	0.8	5.7	6.3	7.0	8.1	3.9	22.3	30.2	13.9	2.6	76.1	42.8	52.4	47.6
52151	LANSING	99.2	98.8	0.1	0.1	0.2	0.4	0.6	0.9	5.9	6.3	6.5	6.0	4.7	20.7	29.0	17.6	3.3	77.1	44.9	49.9	50.1
52154	LAWLER	99.2	99.0	0.0	0.0	0.1	0.2	1.0	1.4	4.7	6.4	6.8	7.0	4.8	23.9	29.5	14.9	2.0	77.1	42.4	51.6	48.4
52155	LIME SPRINGS	98.9	98.5	0.0	0.0	0.2	0.4	1.3	2.0	6.7	7.3	7.2	6.6	4.6	22.5	28.6	13.5	2.8	74.5	41.7	51.1	48.9
52156	LUANA	97.7	97.1	0.2	0.3	0.0	0.0	3.9	5.5	6.1	7.1	7.6	7.1	4.7	26.1	28.7	11.7	0.9	74.7	38.9	51.6	48.4
52157	MC GREGOR	99.3	99.1	0.1	0.1	0.0	0.1	0.9	1.4	6.3	6.5	6.6	5.4	4.2	23.9	28.4	15.7	3.0	77.1	42.9	50.7	49.3
52158	MARQUETTE	100.0	100.0	0.0	0.0	0.0	0.0	0.0	0.0	11.1	11.1	11.1	0.0	0.0	44.4	22.2	0.0	0.0	66.7	32.5	50.0	50.0
52159	MONONA	98.7	98.3	0.1	0.1	0.3	0.4	0.6	0.9	5.7	6.3	6.8	6.9	5.6	23.2	27.9	14.7	2.8	76.6	41.6	49.1	50.9
52160	NEW ALBIN	97.2	96.2	0.0	0.0	0.2	0.3	1.5	2.2	7.1	6.9	6.9	6.2	5.1	23.1	28.8	13.4	2.4	75.2	40.9	50.6	49.4
52161	OSSIAN	99.6	99.4	0.1	0.1	0.1	0.2	0.6	1.0	6.7	7.1	7.2	7.6	4.5	23.6	27.9	12.4	3.0	73.6	40.4	51.4	48.6
52162	POSTVILLE	86.2	80.5	0.1	0.1	0.6	0.9	13.6	19.6	6.3	6.7	7.1	6.6	4.3	26.9	27.5	11.6	2.9	75.4	39.1	51.9	48.1
52163	PROTIVIN	99.0	99.0	0.0	0.0	0.3	0.3	0.0	0.0	5.2	5.9	6.6	7.0	4.2	22.3	30.7	15.7	2.4	77.7	44.2	51.9	48.1
52164	RANDALIA	99.7	99.6	0.0	0.0	0.0	0.0	0.7	0.7	6.0	6.7	6.7	6.7	4.6	23.8	30.5	13.1	1.8	77.0	41.8	52.1	47.9
52165	RIDGEWAY	99.2	98.8	0.2	0.3	0.4	0.5	0.7	1.2	5.5	6.3	6.5	6.6	4.5	22.6	32.4	13.8	1.8	77.7	43.6	52.6	47.4
52169	WADENA	98.8	98.3	0.2	0.5	0.2	0.2	0.2	0.2	6.4	7.4	8.1	8.1	4.3	19.2	31.1	13.5	1.9	73.2	42.0	49.4	50.6
52170	WATERVILLE	99.3	98.8	0.2	0.2	0.0	0.2	0.7	1.2	4.9	7.7	9.3	8.3	4.9	23.9	28.5	11.6	0.9	72.4	39.3	52.9	47.1
52171	WAUCOMA	99.4	99.2	0.0	0.0	0.1	0.1	0.5	0.9	5.8	6.6	7.0	7.1	4.1	23.7	28.9	14.5	2.2	76.1	41.5	51.0	49.0
52172	WAUKON	98.8	98.3	0.1	0.2	0.2	0.4	0.6	1.0	6.0	6.2	6.4	6.9	5.4	22.2	27.6	15.2	4.1	77.7	42.4	48.6	51.4
52175	WEST UNION	97.6	96.7	0.3	0.4	0.6	1.1	1.4	2.0	5.6	5.7	5.8	6.7	6.2	23.8	26.8	15.0	4.2	78.7	42.1	50.7	49.3
52201	AINSWORTH	96.2	94.3	0.0	0.0	0.1	0.1	5.6	8.4	8.6	8.9	8.8	6.2	3.8	24.3	26.8	11.1	1.4	69.7	38.6	53.2	46.8
52202	ALBURNETT	99.3	99.1	0.0	0.0	0.2	0.4	0.2	0.4	6.8	7.2	7.9	7.7	4.5	26.3	28.0	10.5	1.1	73.2	37.9	51.1	48.9
52203	AMANA	99.0	98.6	0.2	0.2	0.3	0.5	0.5	0.6	5.1	5.7	6.6	6.8	3.9	21.3	30.9	14.9	4.8	78.2	45.4	47.9	52.1
52205	ANAMOSA	93.5	92.2	4.0	4.8	0.4	0.6	1.6	2.3	5.1	5.3	5.2	6.1	7.7	30.2	26.5	11.6	2.4	80.9	38.7	57.1	42.9
52206	ATKINS	98.9	98.6	0.5	0.6	0.1	0.2	0.8	1.2	8.8	9.2	9.2	7.0	4.4	25.2	26.7	8.5	0.9	68.2	36.4	51.5	48.5
52207	BALDWIN	99.5	99.3	0.0	0.0	0.0	0.2	0.2	0.5	4.4	6.3	8.1	7.2	4.4	23.6	29.6	14.6	1.9	76.4	42.2	51.2	48.8
52208	BELLE PLAINE	98.9	98.7	0.1	0.1	0.3	0.5	0.7	1.1	5.7	5.8	5.9	7.1	6.1	24.2	27.3	13.3	4.5	78.0	41.3	49.8	50.2
52209	BLAIRSTOWN	99.3	99.0	0.0	0.0	0.0	0.0	0.3	0.6	5.7	6.1	6.8	7.4	4.8	24.6	30.4	11.7	2.4	76.7	41.4	50.5	49.5
52210	BRANDON	99.4	99.5	0.0	0.0	0.0	0.0	0.0	0.0	6.2	6.4	6.6	6.8	4.6	26.9	28.5	12.2	1.9	76.6	39.4	50.9	49.1
52211	BROOKLYN	98.1	97.3	0.1	0.1	0.1	0.2	1.4	2.2	5.6	5.9	6.3	6.8	5.2	22.8	30.2	13.8	3.4	77.9	43.0	49.4	50.6
52212	CENTER JUNCTION	99.1	98.6	0.0	0.0	0.0	0.3	0.0	0.0	5.9	6.4	7.0	6.7	3.9	22.4	30.3	15.4	2.0	76.2	43.2	51.5	48.5
52213	CENTER POINT	98.5	98.1	0.4	0.5	0.1	0.2	0.5	0.8	7.5	8.0	8.3	7.4	4.6	26.6	27.3	8.7	1.6	71.4	37.7	50.6	49.4
52214	CENTRAL CITY	98.9	98.7	0.0	0.1	0.2	0.3	0.5	0.7	6.5	6.6	6.8	6.8	4.9	24.2	29.2	13.0	2.1	75.9	40.7	49.7	50.3
52215	CHELSEA	91.2	90.9	0.0	0.1	0.2	0.3	10.2	10.5	8.1	7.8	7.5	6.0	4.3	23.4	27.7	12.9	2.5	73.0	39.8	51.8	48.2
52216	CLARENCE	98.9	98.7	0.1	0.1	0.1	0.2	0.5	0.7	6.2	6.3	6.5	6.7	4.5	21.1	27.3	16.4	5.0	76.6	44.1	47.6	52.4
52217	CLUTIER	98.3	98.3	0.2	0.2	0.2	0.2	0.5	0.5	6.6	7.1	7.4	6.5	4.0	20.6	29.9	15.4	2.5	75.0	43.3	52.4	47.6
52218	COGGON	99.4	99.3	0.1	0.1	0.2	0.2	0.4	0.5	7.5	8.3	7.4	6.5	4.1	24.8	26.3	13.8	1.4	72.5	38.7	49.7	50.3
52219	PRAIRIEBURG	100.0	99.5	0.0	0.0	0.0	0.0	0.0	0.5	5.4	6.4	6.4	6.4	4.4	25.6	31.0	13.3	1.0	77.3	41.6	52.7	47.3
52220	CONROY	98.9	98.9	0.0	0.0	0.6	0.6	0.0	0.0	6.1	6.7	6.7	7.8	5.6	22.8	32.2	11.1	1.1	75.6	40.8	50.6	49.4
52221	GUERNSEY	98.6	97.8	0.0	0.0	0.0	0.0	2.2	2.9	6.5	6.5	7.2	6.5	4.3	23.0	28.8	15.1	2.2	75.5	42.7	51.8	48.2
52222	DEEP RIVER	98.3	97.5	0.0	0.0	0.0	0.0	2.0	3.0	6.5	6.8	7.2	6.9	3.9	22.3	30.0	14.5	1.8	75.1	42.6	50.8	49.2
52223	DELHI	99.6	99.4	0.1	0.1	0.1	0.1	0.1	0.1	5.5	6.2	6.5	6.8	4.3	22.3	33.1	13.7	1.6	77.0	43.9	50.0	50.0
52224	DYSART	98.7	98.5	0.2	0.2	0.4	0.4	0.5	0.6	6.2	6.6	7.1	7.2	5.2	20.8	27.3	15.8	3.9	75.9	42.7	50.3	49.7
52225	ELBERON	97.8	97.6	0.2	0.2	0.2	0.2	1.5	1.7	6.9	7.3	7.5	6.0	4.1	24.0	29.0	12.9	2.4	74.7	40.0	52.1	47.9
52227	ELY	98.0	97.3	0.4	0.6	0.2	0.4	1.0	1.5	7.4	7.8	7.9	6.9	4.5	28.5	28.1	7.9	1.1	72.6	36.9	50.8	49.2
52228	FAIRFAX	97.9	97.0	0.5	0.7	0.4	0.7	0.8	1.3	7.1	7.6	7.9	6.7	4.2	25.6	27.9	12.1	1.1	73.2	39.2	49.9	50.1
52229	GARRISON	98.6	98.2	0.1	0.1	0.4	0.7	0.8	1.2	5.8	6.2	6.6	6.7	4.2	22.1	32.7	14.0	1.6	77.4	43.9	51.1	48.9
52231	HARPER	99.0	99.0	0.0	0.0	0.5	0.5	0.3	0.5	6.0	7.0	8.1	8.1	4.2	21.3	31.7	11.9	1.8	74.0	41.6	50.6	49.4
52232	HARTWICK	98.7	97.9	0.0	0.4	0.0	0.4	0.9	1.3	4.7	6.0	6.4	6.8	4.3	22.2	31.6	16.2	1.7	78.2	44.7	52.6	47.4
52233	HIAWATHA	94.2	92.3	2.2	2.7	1.7	2.8	1.3	1.8	7.4	6.9	6.6	6.5	7.2	31.6	24.4	8.0	1.4	75.4	34.1	49.0	51.0
52236	HOMESTEAD	99.2	98.8	0.0	0.0	0.4	0.6	0.0	0.0	6.3	6.7	7.1	7.3	5.5	23.3	30.8	11.4	1.6	75.7	40.5	50.1	49.9
52237	HOPKINTON	99.0	98.8	0.1	0.1	0.1	0.2	0.4	0.5	6.5	7.3	7.8	9.0	4.8	23.7	28.0	11.3	1.5	72.2	38.5	51.3	48.7
52240	IOWA CITY	90.1	85.9	3.4	4.3	3.0	5.1	3.4	5.1	5.2	4.8	4.7	8.8	22.2	26.7	20.4	6.3	1.0	82.6	27.6	50.5	49.5
52241	CORALVILLE	86.5	82.4	4.5	5.0	5.5	8.8	3.0	4.0	7.5	6.0	5.3	5.7	12.4	35.4	20.8	5.8	1.1	78.0	30.8	49.0	51.0
52242	IOWA CITY	93.0	88.9	2.5	3.9	2.7	4.9	1.5	2.3	0.9	0.8	0.9	55.8	29.5	6.1	3.2	1.9	1.2	94.8	19.3	47.9	52.1
52245	IOWA CITY	92.7	89.3	2.3	2.9	2.7	4.8	2.2	3.3	3.8	3.8	4.0	13.7	20.9	22.0	22.1	8.2	1.5	85.7	27.8	49.1	50.9
52246	IOWA CITY	81.2	73.6	4.5	5.3	11.0	17.3	2.6	3.7	5.8	4.8	4.2	6.2	16.2	37.9	17.6	5.6	1.5	82.8	29.6	49.9	50.1
52247	KALONA	98.1	97.4	0.2	0.3	0.3	0.6	1.1	1.7	7.7	8.0	8.1	7.6	4.8	23.0	26.9	11.0	2.9	71.4	37.2	48.0	52.0
52248	KEOTA	98.8	98.3	0.0	0.0	0.4	0.6	0.6	0.9	5.8	6.1	6.7	7.4	4.6	23.0	29.1	13.2	4.1	76.8	42.4	48.9	51.1
52249	KEYSTONE	99.3	99.3	0.2	0.2	0.1	0.1	0.3	0.3	5.3	5.4	5.7	7.1	5.6	22.2	27.3	15.6	5.7	79.0	44.1	48.7	51.3
52251	LADORA	99.5	99.2	0.2	0.3	0.0	0.0	1.4	1.9	5.6	5.9	6.7	8.3	4.5	23.4	30.1	13.1	2.4	76.2	42.3	52.6	47.4
52253	LISBON	98.1	97.6	0.3	0.4	0.1	0.2	0.8	1.2	7.4	7.7	8.0	7.1	5.3	25.0	29.1	9.1	1.3	72.5	37.5	51.4	48.6
52254	LOST NATION	98.8	98.5	0.0	0.0	0.5	0.7	0.7	0.9	6.8	7.3	7.4	6.3	5.1	23.4	27.4	13.9	2.4	74.6	39.9	49.0	51.0
52255	LOWDEN	98.9	98.5	0.2	0.2	0.1	0.2	1.2	1.7	6.1	6.4	6.5	6.5	5.1	19.9	31.1	15.1	3.4	77.0	44.7	50.1	49.9
52257	LUZERNE	99.4	99.4	0.3	0.3	0.0	0.0	0.0	0.0	4.4	5.3	5.9	6.8	5.0	22.7	35.7	12.4	1.8	79.9	44.9	54.0	46.0
52301	MARENGO	98.5	97.9	0.2	0.3	0.4	0.8	0.9	1.3	6.2	6.5	6.6	7.2	5.5	24.4	27.5	12.7	3.4	76.1	40.7	49.3	50.7
52302	MARION	97.0	95.6	0.6	0.8	1.0	1.9	1.0	1.5	7.3	7.0	6.9	6.6	5.8	29.1	25.3	10.3	1.7	74.6	36.1	48.8	51.2
52305	MARTELLE	99.0	98.9	0.2	0.2	0.2	0.2	0.2	0.2	5.8	6.3	7.2	6.9	3.2	25.6	30.9	12.5	1.6	76.0	41.6	51.3	48.7
52306	MECHANICSVILLE	98.6	98.2	0.1	0.1	0.1	0.2	1.0	1.5	6.2	6.5	6.6	6.7	5.6	24.7	28.3	11.9	3.7	76.6	40.5	49.2	50.8
52307	MIDDLE AMANA	100.0	100.0	0.0	0.0	0.0	0.0	0.0	0.0	0.0	0.0	0.0	0.0	0.0	0.0	100.0	0.0	0.0	100.0	48.8	33.3	66.7
52308	MILLERSBURG	100.0	100.0	0.0	0.0	0.0	0.0	0.0	0.0	9.5	9.5	9.5	9.5	0.0	23.8	38.1	0.0	0.0	61.9	38.8	47.6	52.4
52309	MONMOUTH	99.6	99.3	0.0	0.0	0.0	0.0	0.2	0.4	4.4	6.1	7.9	7.6	4.6	23.4	29.7	14.4	2.0	76.6	42.1	51.7	48.3
52310	MONTICELLO	99.1	98.8	0.1	0.1	0.1	0.1	0.9	1.3	6.1	6.5	6.9	7.1	4.7	23.4	27.8	14.4	3.2	75.7	41.6	48.5	51.5
52313	MOUNT AUBURN	98.1	97.4	0.0	0.0	0.2	0.4	0.5	0.9	6.6	7.2	7.7	7.7	4.1	21.7	31.6	11.9	1.5	73.6	41.2	51.4	48.6
52314	MOUNT VERNON	97.4	95.1	0.5	1.4	0.6	1.6	0.8	1.4	5.5	5.4	5.9	11.2	14.3	21.8	25.3	8.8	2.0	80.8	31.4	48.7	51.3
52315	NEWHALL	99.6	99.4	0.0	0.0	0.1	0.2	0.5	0.7	6.3	6.6	7.0	7.9	5.4	23.8	28.4	12.1	2.5	75.2	40.2	49.0	51.0
52316	NORTH ENGLISH	98.9	98.6	0.2	0.3	0.1	0.2	1.0	1.4	6.8	7.1	7.2	6.6	4.8	22.0	26.5	13.5	5.6	74.8	41.7	48.4	51.6
52317	NORTH LIBERTY	95.7	93.7	1.2	1.6	1.4	2.3	2.0	3.1	8.3	7.5	6.9	6.8	8.6	32.0	23.2	5.9	0.7	73.3	31.9	49.2	50.8
52318	NORWAY	98.9	98.7	0.3	0.4	0.1	0.1	0.3	0.4	8.6	9.4	8.9	7.1	3.8	30.8	21.9	8.3	1.2	68.2	33.9	51.1	48.9
52320	OLIN	98.2	97.7	0.7	0.8	0.2	0.3	0.8	1.2	6.8	6.8	6.4	6.9	6.4	25.0	26.9	12.6	2.3	75.9	39.0	50.8	49.2
52321	ONSLOW	99.1	99.1	0.0	0.0	0.0	0.0	0.2	0.2	5.8	6.3	6.7	6.7	4.0	22.3	31.5	15.0	1.8	76.8	43.6	51.6	48.4
52322	OXFORD	97.9	97.1	0.3	0.4	0.5	0.8	0.8	1.3	5.5	5.8	6.5	7.3	5.0	25.7	32.1	10.8	1.3	77.8	41.3	51.6	48.4
52323	OXFORD JUNCTION	98.0	97.6	0.1	0.1	0.1	0.2	0.4	0.5	5.5	5.6	5.9	6.6	5.9	22.6	29.7	15.0	3.2	79.1	43.2	49.2	50.8
52324	PALO	97.7	96.7	0.7	0.8	0.8	1.3	0.6	0.8	5.6	6.2	7.0	8.1	5.4	24.6	33.7	8.5	0.9	76.1	40.5	51.0	49.0
52325	PARNELL	98.8	98.1	0.1	0.2	0.5	0.8	1.2	1.6	7.3	7.6	8.0	8.0	4.8	22.1	28.3	12.2	1.6	72.2	39.6	50.2	49.8
52326	QUASQUETON	97.3	97.6	0.6	0.6	0.8	0.7	0.6	0.6	6.1	6.1	6.9	7.2	5.4	24.5	29.2	12.8	1.7	76.2	40.4	51.9	48.1
52327	RIVERSIDE	96.7	95.7	0.7	0.9	0.4	0.7	1.5	2.2	7.7	7.8	7.8	6.9	5.0	27.1	28.1	8.3	1.4	72.4	36.5	49.8	50.2
52328	ROBINS	95.8	93.5	1.2	1.9	1.2	2.3	1.5	2.2	8.7	8.1	8.1	7.8	6.7	26.8	25.9	6.8	1.0	70.1	32.8	50.0	50.0
52329	ROWLEY	99.3	99.3	0.1	0.1	0.3	0.3	0.1	0.1	6.3	6.5	6.8	7.5	5.4	23.7	30.5	11.9	1.6	75.8	40.7	51.9	48.1
52330	RYAN	99.6	99.5	0.0	0.0	0.0	0.0	0.5	0.8	8.0	8.2	7.9	7.0	4.4	25.3	26.5	11.2	1.5	71.4	37.9	51.3	48.7
	IOWA	93.9	91.9	2.1	2.5	1.3	2.1	2.8	4.1	6.5	6.4	6.5	7.3	7.1	25.2	26.5	11.9	2.6	76.5	38.1	49.3	50.7
	UNITED STATES	75.1	72.0	12.3	12.7	3.8	4.6	12.5	15.7	6.8	6.7	6.6	7.1	6.9	27.0	26.0	10.9	1.9	75.7	36.9	49.2	50.8

#	POST OFFICE NAME	2009 Per Capita Income	2009 HH Income Base	2009 HOUSEHOLD INCOME DISTRIBUTION (%) Less than $25,000	$25,000 to $49,999	$50,000 to $99,999	$100,000 to $149,999	$150,000 or More	MEDIAN HOUSEHOLD INCOME 2009	2014	2009 National Centile	2009 State Centile	2009 Home Value Base	2009 HOME VALUE DISTRIBUTION (%) Less than $50,000	$50,000 to $89,999	$90,000 to $174,999	$175,000 to $399,999	$400,000 or More	2009 Median Home Value
52136	CRESCO	22110	2375	25.3	32.8	34.3	4.7	2.9	42657	44906	41	29	1861	16.0	33.9	38.1	10.4	1.7	90236
52140	DORCHESTER	18522	289	17.0	47.4	33.9	1.4	0.3	43260	45266	43	32	241	20.7	26.6	32.8	16.6	3.3	95417
52141	ELGIN	19279	645	29.8	31.9	34.4	3.3	0.6	41404	42726	37	22	485	16.5	31.8	40.2	10.3	1.2	92931
52142	FAYETTE	19588	552	27.5	31.9	30.3	7.4	2.9	42571	43999	41	29	400	18.5	30.5	37.0	11.0	3.0	92000
52144	FORT ATKINSON	19821	502	28.3	31.1	33.3	5.4	2.0	43822	46451	45	37	404	19.6	25.5	44.3	8.9	1.7	97407
52146	HARPERS FERRY	19617	437	27.2	37.8	29.5	5.3	0.2	38621	39913	29	11	376	14.6	29.3	44.7	10.4	1.1	99200
52147	HAWKEYE	20535	455	25.7	41.3	27.0	3.3	2.6	39005	39829	30	12	366	23.2	30.9	32.5	11.5	1.9	85313
52151	LANSING	21011	973	22.6	39.0	32.2	4.9	1.3	41563	43779	38	23	781	23.6	21.4	39.8	12.8	2.4	100599
52154	LAWLER	21549	430	23.5	34.4	37.0	3.0	2.1	44066	46240	46	39	358	19.0	24.0	39.7	16.8	0.6	100309
52155	LIME SPRINGS	19707	470	24.9	34.7	34.3	5.1	1.1	43760	45641	45	36	398	22.1	32.4	31.9	11.6	2.0	86087
52156	LUANA	17740	262	26.7	39.3	30.2	2.3	1.5	40599	42204	35	18	184	16.3	17.9	42.4	16.8	6.5	110811
52157	MC GREGOR	21240	957	26.6	37.7	29.8	4.7	1.1	40653	42154	35	18	695	21.4	28.5	35.1	12.1	2.9	90135
52158	MARQUETTE	13946	6	33.3	33.3	33.3	0.0	0.0	40000	45000	33	15	4	0.0	0.0	100.0	0.0	0.0	112500
52159	MONONA	21805	964	22.2	35.9	34.2	5.3	2.4	44506	46427	47	41	741	15.2	32.1	43.0	7.8	1.8	92910
52160	NEW ALBIN	23227	374	27.0	32.9	33.4	3.7	2.9	42616	44495	41	29	312	31.4	27.6	29.8	10.6	0.6	75000
52161	OSSIAN	19694	558	24.2	33.3	36.0	5.2	1.3	44637	46192	47	43	437	12.6	22.9	45.5	13.7	5.3	108059
52162	POSTVILLE	17535	1293	27.5	33.4	32.9	3.9	2.2	41445	43242	38	23	922	13.8	33.3	39.4	9.8	3.8	93699
52163	PROTIVIN	29724	148	20.3	42.6	27.7	6.8	2.7	42554	43255	41	29	122	16.4	24.6	35.2	18.9	4.9	105208
52164	RANDALIA	19008	104	24.0	31.7	38.5	4.8	1.0	43441	44082	44	33	78	16.7	32.1	34.6	11.5	5.1	93333
52165	RIDGEWAY	21412	445	22.5	32.4	37.8	4.5	2.9	46504	48163	53	54	353	16.7	20.1	38.2	18.4	6.5	110142
52169	WADENA	21957	181	28.7	34.3	27.6	5.5	3.9	38110	39764	27	8	136	26.5	21.3	37.5	11.0	3.7	95000
52170	WATERVILLE	19595	211	18.0	46.0	28.0	4.7	3.3	42314	44129	40	26	171	22.2	19.9	36.8	17.5	3.5	103750
52171	WAUCOMA	21076	463	25.7	38.2	30.7	3.0	2.4	40826	43483	35	18	375	28.3	23.2	33.9	12.5	2.1	87381
52172	WAUKON	20646	2544	28.5	32.6	31.8	5.6	1.6	41719	43686	38	24	1877	17.2	25.1	41.8	14.0	2.0	101473
52175	WEST UNION	23141	1472	24.9	30.6	36.2	5.6	2.6	46256	47186	52	52	1075	18.4	29.3	39.9	11.5	0.8	93403
52201	AINSWORTH	20913	512	16.6	33.8	42.4	5.9	1.4	49689	52463	60	68	398	14.3	23.6	38.7	22.6	0.8	112736
52202	ALBURNETT	24755	423	16.5	18.2	53.0	9.7	2.6	64124	67221	82	96	344	3.8	8.1	54.4	32.3	1.5	147917
52203	AMANA	26359	851	19.4	26.4	39.5	10.6	4.1	53350	53768	69	82	688	9.4	3.6	29.9	50.3	6.7	187903
52205	ANAMOSA	23544	3039	21.6	27.4	38.2	9.5	3.3	50996	53519	64	74	2308	13.8	24.7	42.5	17.5	1.5	107126
52206	ATKINS	24298	621	10.8	22.1	53.6	11.8	1.8	66199	66079	84	96	528	4.2	8.9	46.6	37.1	3.2	147845
52207	BALDWIN	19720	183	27.3	34.4	31.1	6.0	1.1	38375	39707	28	10	144	39.6	18.8	25.7	9.7	6.3	70000
52208	BELLE PLAINE	22113	1347	24.6	25.7	42.7	6.5	0.5	49631	52249	60	68	1015	26.6	36.0	31.3	5.6	0.5	77102
52209	BLAIRSTOWN	22893	426	20.0	29.3	43.0	7.7	0.0	50775	53861	63	73	334	7.8	29.6	45.2	13.5	3.9	109091
52210	BRANDON	26696	304	20.7	30.9	37.5	4.9	5.9	48498	50000	58	64	241	16.2	19.9	37.8	19.5	6.6	108750
52211	BROOKLYN	22520	1119	23.1	33.4	35.1	6.2	2.2	45313	47553	49	46	858	15.7	28.6	38.1	14.8	2.8	96364
52212	CENTER JUNCTION	19894	155	25.2	37.4	32.9	4.5	0.0	41136	43318	36	20	121	25.6	29.8	33.1	7.4	4.1	82778
52213	CENTER POINT	24145	1375	15.2	26.2	48.8	8.1	1.7	59126	61263	76	91	1139	6.0	15.3	51.4	23.5	3.8	132919
52214	CENTRAL CITY	23852	1362	19.5	31.4	41.7	5.4	2.0	49186	52291	59	66	1065	11.8	19.0	43.4	21.6	4.2	118199
52215	CHELSEA	19553	359	18.7	33.7	41.2	5.3	1.1	48646	49230	58	64	311	31.8	19.6	37.9	9.6	1.0	87500
52216	CLARENCE	22055	608	24.3	30.6	35.0	8.7	1.3	46781	49356	53	56	454	13.4	29.1	45.2	10.6	1.8	99444
52217	CLUTIER	21964	278	27.3	28.1	35.6	6.8	2.2	42193	42359	40	25	217	16.1	28.6	21.7	27.6	6.0	103125
52218	COGGON	23706	763	14.2	27.8	46.0	9.7	2.4	58039	59931	75	90	613	14.8	18.4	44.2	18.9	3.6	116557
52219	PRAIRIEBURG	23441	84	17.9	32.1	41.7	7.1	1.2	50000	55449	61	70	66	15.2	15.2	40.9	25.8	3.0	119231
52220	CONROY	22449	65	9.2	30.8	53.8	6.2	0.0	57790	55750	75	90	53	5.7	11.3	49.1	32.1	1.9	144643
52221	GUERNSEY	21477	62	25.8	29.0	41.9	3.2	0.0	46142	47332	52	51	50	26.0	26.0	24.0	16.0	8.0	87500
52222	DEEP RIVER	19439	327	24.5	30.9	40.1	3.7	0.9	45754	48319	51	48	264	22.3	26.1	29.2	15.5	6.8	94000
52223	DELHI	23018	529	19.7	29.1	40.5	8.9	1.9	50965	51010	63	74	448	10.7	13.6	47.1	25.0	3.6	123958
52224	DYSART	25276	821	17.3	24.8	45.4	9.1	3.3	56029	56621	73	88	652	8.9	18.3	49.4	19.5	4.0	118838
52225	ELBERON	19862	179	17.3	39.7	35.8	5.6	1.7	45974	46479	51	50	145	30.3	20.7	38.6	7.6	2.8	88750
52227	ELY	26201	936	16.0	22.4	45.6	11.3	4.6	64235	67576	83	96	702	5.7	6.3	44.4	37.0	6.6	162069
52228	FAIRFAX	29961	1106	11.2	21.8	45.9	15.8	5.2	67682	71174	85	97	975	4.1	8.4	41.3	43.3	2.9	165335
52229	GARRISON	20949	335	20.6	32.5	37.9	8.4	0.6	46790	50208	54	56	257	19.5	19.5	37.4	21.4	2.3	113487
52231	HARPER	19460	151	23.2	32.5	39.1	4.0	1.3	46575	47301	53	55	115	12.2	30.4	44.3	10.4	2.6	100568
52232	HARTWICK	24475	103	20.4	28.2	43.7	6.8	1.0	51030	52498	64	74	86	15.1	26.7	34.9	22.1	1.2	102273
52233	HIAWATHA	32500	3172	9.3	33.1	40.4	10.9	6.3	58026	61425	75	90	1976	31.8	4.5	32.8	27.6	3.2	130525
52236	HOMESTEAD	24106	196	9.7	31.6	51.5	6.6	0.5	56981	56318	74	89	158	3.8	11.4	51.3	32.3	1.3	144318
52237	HOPKINTON	17597	611	26.7	32.1	35.8	4.9	0.5	43087	45359	43	32	493	15.6	18.9	40.8	18.9	5.9	112219
52240	IOWA CITY	25744	14518	30.4	25.3	32.0	7.3	5.0	42999	47212	42	31	7519	23.4	9.0	36.1	26.5	5.0	133808
52241	CORALVILLE	30918	7439	19.1	28.5	34.5	11.2	6.7	52060	55236	66	78	3638	4.3	5.0	45.0	40.4	5.2	167147
52242	IOWA CITY	13459	2	0.0	0.0	0.0	100.0	0.0	112500	112500	98	100	0	0.0	0.0	0.0	0.0	0.0	0
52245	IOWA CITY	29416	8377	22.2	21.8	35.4	11.2	9.4	56270	57811	73	88	5026	9.7	5.2	36.7	41.9	6.5	172159
52246	IOWA CITY	30663	9952	31.2	23.7	28.1	9.5	7.5	43546	48281	44	34	4126	9.5	6.3	27.2	51.0	6.1	193830
52247	KALONA	19192	1999	25.1	30.3	36.4	4.9	3.4	44101	49308	46	39	1505	10.8	14.0	45.3	25.8	4.2	135445
52248	KEOTA	21151	783	22.2	33.5	37.0	6.4	0.9	45573	47050	50	47	624	14.9	33.2	43.3	6.6	2.1	92000
52249	KEYSTONE	23447	484	15.3	30.8	44.0	8.7	1.2	52876	54972	68	80	385	8.1	41.3	41.0	8.1	1.6	91136
52251	LADORA	21524	248	19.8	27.0	46.0	6.9	0.4	52449	53210	67	79	207	23.7	28.5	25.1	20.3	2.4	87000
52253	LISBON	23740	1191	20.3	26.7	41.8	8.1	3.0	52748	55070	67	80	910	8.4	14.9	47.8	26.0	2.9	127559
52254	LOST NATION	19260	443	23.5	36.8	35.7	3.2	0.9	41862	45892	39	24	323	19.2	32.2	38.7	8.4	1.5	88269
52255	LOWDEN	22815	547	25.4	28.9	34.4	9.3	2.0	46840	49316	54	56	435	14.9	24.6	46.2	12.6	1.6	104332
52257	LUZERNE	20628	122	18.0	26.2	45.1	9.8	0.8	55939	57903	73	88	95	13.7	17.9	45.3	17.9	5.3	113587
52301	MARENGO	22845	1754	21.6	26.7	44.6	6.0	1.1	51583	52475	65	76	1329	15.0	25.3	44.2	14.7	0.7	103524
52302	MARION	32852	14136	11.9	22.9	42.3	13.8	9.1	66831	71320	85	97	11193	13.0	9.2	49.9	25.3	2.6	135805
52305	MARTELLE	25187	255	18.4	27.5	42.0	9.0	3.1	53743	55011	69	83	202	6.9	25.2	47.0	17.8	3.0	119531
52306	MECHANICSVILLE	22865	739	20.3	30.2	39.0	8.3	2.3	49617	51307	60	68	587	12.9	22.3	43.8	19.1	1.9	109300
52307	MIDDLE AMANA	0	0	0.0	0.0	0.0	0.0	0.0	0	0	0	0	0	0.0	0.0	0.0	0.0	0.0	0
52308	MILLERSBURG	20322	9	11.1	55.6	33.3	0.0	0.0	42288	47295	40	26	7	0.0	57.1	28.6	14.3	0.0	85000
52309	MONMOUTH	18880	182	26.9	34.1	31.9	6.0	1.1	38743	40462	29	11	144	39.6	20.1	26.4	9.0	4.9	70000
52310	MONTICELLO	21643	2487	21.4	32.0	40.0	5.3	1.4	47512	50579	55	59	1861	9.8	26.7	46.0	14.9	2.5	108100
52313	MOUNT AUBURN	22410	175	12.6	36.0	41.7	5.7	4.0	50878	53721	63	73	144	9.7	24.3	40.3	23.6	2.1	127885
52314	MOUNT VERNON	25182	1831	15.2	21.0	47.3	12.1	4.4	63610	66203	82	95	1432	9.5	7.7	45.5	34.4	2.9	152363
52315	NEWHALL	24310	509	15.1	29.7	45.8	7.9	1.6	54828	56561	71	86	407	3.4	14.0	64.1	16.2	2.2	120717
52316	NORTH ENGLISH	21272	746	20.6	33.8	38.5	5.6	1.5	46147	48661	52	52	596	17.4	35.6	35.4	9.2	2.3	85714
52317	NORTH LIBERTY	37218	5557	11.8	24.4	43.2	10.3	10.3	62733	62877	81	95	3999	21.8	11.3	28.1	29.5	9.4	143114
52318	NORWAY	28074	767	6.1	16.8	49.2	23.1	4.8	77966	78897	91	99	648	5.9	10.8	40.1	42.3	0.9	156967
52320	OLIN	23655	492	24.0	27.0	39.2	5.9	3.9	49114	51737	59	66	379	22.2	32.2	36.1	7.9	1.6	85541
52321	ONSLOW	20900	192	23.4	35.9	33.9	5.7	1.0	43732	45745	45	36	151	19.9	29.1	39.1	7.9	4.0	91500
52322	OXFORD	24153	1040	18.8	29.1	40.1	8.9	3.0	51974	54668	66	77	830	24.1	16.4	25.4	24.1	10.0	123661
52323	OXFORD JUNCTION	18061	398	30.7	37.4	27.1	4.0	0.8	37310	38778	24	7	304	35.2	39.8	16.4	6.9	1.6	69545
52324	PALO	33005	825	9.0	18.5	48.5	16.7	7.3	72741	75909	88	98	726	11.4	7.6	33.2	44.5	3.3	169521
52325	PARNELL	23065	321	11.8	29.3	48.9	6.5	3.4	55353	54915	72	87	261	10.3	16.5	40.2	26.1	6.9	142151
52326	QUASQUETON	23505	218	20.2	33.0	39.9	4.6	2.3	47782	48366	56	61	184	12.5	25.5	40.8	20.7	0.5	107759
52327	RIVERSIDE	21412	1187	21.1	29.1	41.1	6.7	2.0	49774	52629	60	68	906	18.2	13.5	46.8	20.6	0.9	119771
52328	ROBINS	32224	734	6.1	15.9	44.3	20.8	12.8	80917	82307	92	99	613	0.0	3.3	36.4	55.5	4.9	197679
52329	ROWLEY	21279	344	18.0	32.0	42.4	6.7	0.9	50000	50421	61	70	284	12.3	19.7	46.5	15.1	6.3	122143
52330	RYAN	19433	339	17.7	31.9	44.2	5.0	1.2	50294	49363	62	71	263	11.4	7.2	64.6	11.0	5.7	117031
	IOWA	25379		21.1	28.2	37.9	8.6	4.3	50616	52941				14.7	22.5	41.6	18.6	2.6	110128
	UNITED STATES	27277		20.9	24.4	35.3	11.7	7.6	54719	56938				9.3	13.1	31.6	32.6	13.5	162279

#	POST OFFICE NAME	FINANCIAL SERVICES				THE HOME						ENTERTAINMENT						PERSONAL			
						Home Improvements		Furnishings													
ZIP CODE		Auto Loan	Home Loan	Investments	Retirement Plans	Home Repair	Lawn & Garden	Computers & Hardware-Personal	Major Appliances	TV, Radio, Sound Equipment	Furniture	Dine out/Carry out	Sports Equipment	Fees & Tickets	Toys & Games	Travel	Cable TV	Apparel & Services	Auto Repairs	Health Insurance	Pets & Supplies
52136	CRESCO	88	67	86	67	68	92	72	85	77	63	75	66	59	77	70	84	50	80	91	102
52140	DORCHESTER	83	57	90	57	60	87	63	78	66	52	65	64	47	65	63	72	42	73	83	96
52141	ELGIN	80	56	83	55	59	84	62	77	67	53	65	60	48	66	61	74	43	71	82	92
52142	FAYETTE	87	66	88	66	68	91	72	85	77	64	75	65	59	76	70	83	50	80	91	101
52144	FORT ATKINSON	93	64	102	64	67	98	71	88	74	57	73	73	52	72	71	80	47	82	93	109
52146	HARPERS FERRY	81	58	83	56	60	82	59	75	66	55	64	57	47	65	59	72	43	69	78	90
52147	HAWKEYE	89	61	98	61	64	94	68	85	71	55	70	70	50	69	68	77	45	79	89	104
52151	LANSING	86	65	88	65	67	90	67	83	72	59	71	64	54	71	67	78	47	76	86	99
52154	LAWLER	96	68	101	66	70	99	72	90	78	63	76	71	55	77	71	85	50	83	95	109
52155	LIME SPRINGS	86	59	95	59	62	91	66	82	68	53	68	68	48	67	65	75	44	76	86	101
52156	LUANA	80	55	88	55	57	84	61	76	63	49	63	63	45	62	61	69	41	71	80	93
52157	MC GREGOR	83	60	86	58	62	86	63	79	69	57	68	60	50	69	62	76	45	73	84	94
52158	MARQUETTE	72	52	74	50	54	73	53	67	59	49	58	51	42	58	53	65	38	62	70	80
52159	MONONA	90	64	92	63	67	94	70	87	77	61	75	66	55	76	68	85	49	81	94	103
52160	NEW ALBIN	96	70	98	69	73	98	72	91	79	67	78	68	58	79	71	87	52	83	94	108
52161	OSSIAN	89	61	98	61	64	94	68	85	71	55	70	70	50	70	68	77	46	79	90	104
52162	POSTVILLE	86	60	87	59	62	88	65	80	69	56	68	64	49	69	63	76	45	75	84	98
52163	PROTIVIN	103	71	113	71	74	109	79	98	82	64	81	81	58	80	78	89	53	91	103	120
52164	RANDALIA	92	63	101	63	66	97	70	87	73	57	72	72	52	72	70	80	47	81	92	107
52165	RIDGEWAY	95	65	104	65	68	100	73	90	75	59	75	75	53	74	72	82	48	84	95	111
52169	WADENA	91	63	100	63	66	96	70	87	73	57	72	72	51	71	69	79	47	81	92	107
52170	WATERVILLE	94	65	103	65	68	99	72	89	75	59	74	73	53	73	71	82	48	83	94	110
52171	WAUCOMA	95	65	104	65	68	100	72	90	75	59	74	74	53	74	72	82	48	84	95	110
52172	WAUKON	84	60	86	59	62	88	65	81	72	57	70	62	51	70	64	79	46	75	87	96
52175	WEST UNION	84	68	82	67	69	89	72	82	77	65	76	63	62	77	70	83	51	79	90	98
52201	AINSWORTH	97	67	107	67	70	103	74	92	77	60	77	76	55	76	74	84	50	86	98	114
52202	ALBURNETT	93	104	90	107	101	103	93	97	92	93	92	76	99	94	98	92	64	93	96	114
52203	AMANA	90	96	88	100	95	99	88	94	88	86	87	72	91	89	92	89	61	89	94	110
52205	ANAMOSA	87	89	78	90	85	93	86	87	87	83	86	68	86	88	86	89	60	87	92	104
52206	ATKINS	95	107	92	110	104	104	96	99	94	96	94	78	102	97	101	94	66	95	97	116
52207	BALDWIN	83	59	86	57	61	85	62	78	67	55	66	60	48	67	61	74	44	72	82	94
52208	BELLE PLAINE	81	69	75	70	69	85	71	80	75	65	73	61	64	75	70	80	50	76	86	94
52209	BLAIRSTOWN	86	78	77	81	79	92	77	87	79	69	78	66	71	81	77	84	53	80	89	101
52210	BRANDON	102	94	92	98	96	110	92	104	95	84	93	79	85	97	92	100	64	96	107	121
52211	BROOKLYN	85	72	80	73	73	90	73	85	77	66	75	64	64	78	72	83	51	79	89	99
52212	CENTER JUNCTION	81	57	88	57	59	85	63	77	65	52	64	64	47	64	62	71	42	72	81	95
52213	CENTER POINT	92	93	85	96	92	99	87	94	88	84	87	72	87	90	89	90	60	89	95	110
52214	CENTRAL CITY	88	79	81	81	78	94	80	87	82	73	81	69	74	83	79	86	55	84	92	104
52215	CHELSEA	92	68	96	69	71	97	73	88	76	61	75	71	58	75	73	82	49	82	93	107
52216	CLARENCE	90	64	92	63	66	94	70	87	77	61	74	66	55	75	68	84	49	81	94	103
52217	CLUTIER	92	63	101	63	66	97	70	87	73	57	72	72	51	71	70	79	47	81	92	107
52218	COGGON	98	88	89	91	87	104	89	96	92	81	91	76	83	93	88	96	61	93	103	116
52219	PRAIRIEBURG	88	80	79	83	82	94	79	89	81	71	80	67	73	83	79	86	54	82	92	103
52220	CONROY	96	88	87	91	89	103	86	98	89	78	88	74	80	91	86	94	60	90	101	113
52221	GUERNSEY	86	59	95	59	62	91	66	82	68	53	68	68	48	67	65	75	44	76	86	101
52222	DEEP RIVER	86	59	94	59	62	91	66	82	68	53	68	68	48	67	66	75	44	76	86	101
52223	DELHI	96	76	102	77	77	102	79	93	80	68	80	76	65	80	80	86	53	87	97	113
52224	DYSART	94	85	98	85	87	104	85	96	89	79	88	72	80	87	87	95	60	92	105	113
52225	ELBERON	89	65	98	65	68	96	70	86	73	58	72	70	54	72	71	80	47	81	92	105
52227	ELY	96	106	92	109	103	104	96	99	94	96	95	77	101	97	100	94	66	96	98	117
52228	FAIRFAX	108	117	102	119	114	115	106	111	104	107	105	86	110	108	110	104	73	106	108	129
52229	GARRISON	95	65	104	65	68	100	73	90	76	59	75	75	53	74	72	82	48	84	95	111
52231	HARPER	89	61	97	61	64	94	68	84	70	55	70	70	50	69	67	77	45	79	89	104
52232	HARTWICK	88	77	83	79	79	95	77	89	80	69	78	68	69	81	77	85	53	82	92	104
52233	HIAWATHA	105	97	88	100	93	93	105	96	103	105	104	77	102	106	99	102	73	102	97	116
52236	HOMESTEAD	96	88	87	92	90	103	87	98	89	79	88	74	80	91	87	94	60	90	101	114
52237	HOPKINTON	84	59	79	58	60	84	63	76	68	57	67	60	49	69	60	74	44	71	80	93
52240	IOWA CITY	86	69	66	72	67	69	95	75	87	85	88	64	79	87	77	84	62	84	74	92
52241	CORALVILLE	104	78	73	85	75	76	102	85	101	101	102	72	91	104	88	98	72	97	86	105
52242	IOWA CITY	172	73	72	90	67	85	243	119	193	164	196	130	143	188	130	176	139	170	120	162
52245	IOWA CITY	104	101	100	104	101	98	115	101	107	110	108	82	109	107	107	104	77	106	99	121
52246	IOWA CITY	97	79	71	83	75	75	101	83	96	95	97	71	88	99	85	93	68	91	81	101
52247	KALONA	94	70	96	70	73	98	74	90	78	65	77	70	59	78	73	85	51	83	94	108
52248	KEOTA	87	62	91	61	64	92	68	84	74	58	72	65	53	72	66	81	47	79	91	101
52249	KEYSTONE	81	84	87	82	84	97	77	87	82	74	81	63	80	80	83	88	56	83	97	101
52251	LADORA	97	67	107	67	70	102	74	92	77	60	76	76	54	76	74	84	49	86	97	113
52253	LISBON	97	91	84	89	89	94	85	91	88	87	88	68	82	91	83	90	60	88	92	108
52254	LOST NATION	80	57	83	56	59	84	62	77	68	54	66	60	48	66	61	74	43	72	83	92
52255	LOWDEN	93	66	97	65	69	98	73	90	79	63	77	70	57	78	71	87	51	84	97	107
52257	LUZERNE	89	81	80	84	82	95	80	90	82	72	81	68	74	84	80	87	55	83	93	105
52301	MARENGO	83	76	74	78	73	88	77	81	79	71	78	65	73	80	76	82	53	80	88	98
52302	MARION	118	123	105	121	117	115	115	115	114	119	115	89	117	118	114	112	80	113	113	134
52305	MARTELLE	108	78	117	78	80	114	84	103	87	70	86	85	64	86	84	94	56	96	108	126
52306	MECHANICSVILLE	84	83	75	84	79	90	81	83	82	76	82	66	80	83	81	84	56	82	89	101
52307	MIDDLE AMANA	0	0	0	0	0	0	0	0	0	0	0	0	0	0	0	0	0	0	0	0
52308	MILLERSBURG	85	58	93	58	61	89	65	80	67	52	67	67	47	66	64	73	43	75	85	99
52309	MONMOUTH	84	60	88	58	62	87	63	80	69	56	68	61	49	68	62	76	44	73	83	95
52310	MONTICELLO	83	70	79	71	70	88	72	82	75	65	74	63	63	75	71	80	50	77	87	97
52313	MOUNT AUBURN	107	74	118	74	77	113	82	102	85	66	84	84	60	84	82	93	55	95	108	125
52314	MOUNT VERNON	98	107	97	107	104	106	97	100	98	99	99	75	103	100	101	99	69	98	102	118
52315	NEWHALL	92	85	84	89	87	99	83	94	86	76	84	71	78	88	84	91	58	87	97	109
52316	NORTH ENGLISH	89	64	91	63	66	93	70	86	76	60	74	66	55	74	68	83	49	80	92	102
52317	NORTH LIBERTY	128	115	103	117	110	104	128	114	123	130	125	93	120	128	117	119	87	122	109	137
52318	NORWAY	126	137	110	131	127	111	121	120	113	131	116	96	123	123	119	107	81	114	104	136
52320	OLIN	84	81	72	82	76	89	82	82	83	76	82	66	78	84	79	85	56	83	90	100
52321	ONSLOW	87	60	94	59	62	91	66	82	69	54	68	67	49	68	66	76	44	77	87	101
52322	OXFORD	91	87	81	88	87	93	83	89	84	81	84	67	80	87	82	87	58	85	90	105
52323	OXFORD JUNCTION	74	53	75	52	55	77	58	71	64	51	62	54	46	63	56	71	41	67	78	84
52324	PALO	113	132	119	133	129	124	115	120	111	116	112	94	124	115	122	110	79	114	113	138
52325	PARNELL	99	81	98	84	84	106	84	98	87	73	85	77	71	87	84	93	57	91	102	117
52326	QUASQUETON	90	82	81	85	83	96	81	91	83	73	82	69	74	85	81	88	56	84	94	106
52327	RIVERSIDE	91	78	82	76	77	89	78	85	80	76	80	65	69	82	75	83	54	82	86	102
52328	ROBINS	136	147	130	150	141	129	139	132	132	144	135	108	146	138	140	127	96	132	121	155
52329	ROWLEY	88	77	83	79	78	94	77	88	79	68	78	68	69	80	77	84	53	82	91	104
52330	RYAN	94	66	103	66	69	99	73	90	75	60	75	74	55	74	73	82	49	84	94	110
	IOWA	93	84	87	85	83	95	87	91	89	82	88	71	81	90	85	92	61	90	96	108
	UNITED STATES	100	100	100	100	100	100	100	100	100	100	100	100	100	100	100	100	100	100	100	100

POPULATION CHANGE

52332-52640

#	POST OFFICE NAME	COUNTY FIPS CODE	POPULATION 2000	POPULATION 2009	POPULATION 2014	2000-2009 ANNUAL RATE % Rate	2000-2009 ANNUAL RATE State Centile	HOUSEHOLDS 2000	HOUSEHOLDS 2009	HOUSEHOLDS 2014	HOUSEHOLDS % Annual Rate 2000-2009	HOUSEHOLDS 2009 Average HH Size	FAMILIES 2000	FAMILIES 2009	FAMILIES % Annual Rate 2000-2009
52332	SHELLSBURG	011	1700	1999	2140	1.8	96	628	756	815	2.0	2.62	469	553	1.8
52333	SOLON	103	6076	5808	6127	-0.5	27	1889	2170	2316	1.5	2.64	1529	1700	1.2
52334	SOUTH AMANA	095	224	229	227	0.2	68	85	89	88	0.5	2.56	65	67	0.3
52335	SOUTH ENGLISH	107	647	652	646	0.1	63	260	270	271	0.4	2.41	189	193	0.2
52336	SPRINGVILLE	113	2189	2261	2324	0.4	76	824	890	925	0.8	2.53	609	639	0.5
52337	STANWOOD	031	912	881	867	-0.4	32	369	364	361	-0.1	2.42	267	258	-0.4
52338	SWISHER	103	2713	3057	3261	1.3	93	966	1141	1231	1.8	2.68	793	909	1.5
52339	TAMA	171	4086	4107	4095	0.1	63	1510	1535	1532	0.2	2.62	1062	1057	-0.1
52340	TIFFIN	103	1024	1202	1423	1.7	95	426	523	627	2.2	2.30	283	332	1.7
52341	TODDVILLE	113	1281	1433	1518	1.2	93	456	534	572	1.7	2.68	371	426	1.5
52342	TOLEDO	171	3556	3468	3431	-0.3	40	1371	1362	1350	-0.1	2.40	932	902	-0.4
52345	URBANA	011	956	927	917	-0.3	40	340	336	334	-0.1	2.76	259	251	-0.3
52346	VAN HORNE	011	1174	1222	1226	0.4	76	436	461	464	0.6	2.64	317	327	0.3
52347	VICTOR	095	1485	1509	1490	0.2	68	588	610	606	0.4	2.45	419	425	0.2
52348	VINING	171	72	71	70	-0.2	46	32	32	32	0.0	2.22	25	24	-0.4
52349	VINTON	011	7569	7894	7950	0.5	79	3040	3240	3279	0.7	2.37	2118	2208	0.5
52352	WALKER	113	1851	2011	2106	0.9	89	675	764	808	1.3	2.63	523	578	1.1
52353	WASHINGTON	183	9172	9170	9167	0.0	58	3663	3754	3768	0.3	2.37	2482	2485	0.0
52354	WATKINS	011	449	483	500	0.8	87	164	181	188	1.1	2.67	117	126	0.8
52355	WEBSTER	107	362	363	360	0.0	58	128	132	132	0.3	2.75	93	94	0.1
52356	WELLMAN	183	2600	2787	2870	0.8	87	978	1078	1117	1.1	2.53	704	760	0.8
52358	WEST BRANCH	031	3606	3830	3926	0.7	85	1377	1512	1559	1.0	2.49	981	1052	0.8
52359	WEST CHESTER	183	264	283	292	0.8	87	113	125	130	1.1	2.25	84	91	0.9
52361	WILLIAMSBURG	095	3980	4214	4265	0.6	83	1545	1660	1682	0.8	2.51	1056	1107	0.5
52362	WYOMING	105	1131	1117	1107	-0.1	51	480	492	491	0.3	2.27	321	321	0.0
52401	CEDAR RAPIDS	113	2135	2232	2285	0.5	79	1103	1175	1214	0.7	1.73	382	385	0.1
52402	CEDAR RAPIDS	113	38892	41479	43161	0.7	85	15834	17439	18299	1.0	2.28	9874	10574	0.7
52403	CEDAR RAPIDS	113	25737	25277	25508	-0.2	46	10502	10812	11013	0.3	2.30	6712	6696	0.0
52404	CEDAR RAPIDS	113	32951	36164	37988	1.0	90	13887	15843	16813	1.4	2.23	8248	9090	1.1
52405	CEDAR RAPIDS	113	24273	24883	25418	0.3	72	9664	10297	10608	0.7	2.37	6595	6845	0.4
52411	CEDAR RAPIDS	113	5236	6360	6934	2.1	97	1735	2176	2392	2.5	2.92	1431	1761	2.3
52501	OTTUMWA	179	30730	30376	30138	-0.1	51	12617	12716	12656	0.1	2.31	8241	8098	-0.2
52530	AGENCY	179	960	1104	1155	1.5	94	404	479	504	1.9	2.30	299	345	1.6
52531	ALBIA	135	6119	5862	5706	-0.5	27	2484	2431	2374	-0.2	2.34	1648	1574	-0.5
52533	BATAVIA	101	1200	1204	1205	0.0	58	469	488	491	0.4	2.45	333	338	0.2
52534	BEACON	123	460	458	458	0.0	58	187	193	194	0.3	2.36	148	149	0.1
52535	BIRMINGHAM	177	939	1057	1103	1.3	93	395	456	477	1.6	2.31	278	313	1.3
52536	BLAKESBURG	179	915	977	996	0.7	85	375	413	425	1.0	2.37	279	301	0.8
52537	BLOOMFIELD	051	6688	6760	6783	0.1	63	2545	2618	2634	0.3	2.53	1787	1798	0.1
52540	BRIGHTON	101	1538	1556	1564	0.1	63	619	647	654	0.5	2.40	436	445	0.2
52542	CANTRIL	177	486	493	497	0.2	68	206	215	218	0.5	2.29	145	147	0.1
52543	CEDAR	123	257	268	273	0.5	79	90	97	100	0.8	2.76	71	75	0.6
52544	CENTERVILLE	007	8255	7643	7331	-0.8	11	3511	3333	3215	-0.6	2.23	2221	2054	-0.8
52548	CHILLICOTHE	179	90	95	96	0.6	83	38	41	42	0.8	2.32	30	32	0.7
52549	CINCINNATI	007	760	759	747	0.0	58	306	315	312	0.3	2.41	212	213	0.1
52550	DELTA	107	679	654	639	-0.4	32	283	277	271	-0.2	2.36	187	178	-0.5
52551	DOUDS	177	382	390	392	0.2	68	155	162	164	0.5	2.40	113	116	0.3
52552	DRAKESVILLE	051	1085	1118	1132	0.3	72	392	412	419	0.5	2.62	287	296	0.3
52553	EDDYVILLE	123	1638	1663	1674	0.2	68	641	668	676	0.4	2.49	454	459	0.1
52554	ELDON	179	1429	1514	1541	0.6	83	607	660	677	0.9	2.29	405	427	0.6
52555	EXLINE	007	355	384	385	0.9	89	138	153	154	1.1	2.51	104	112	0.8
52556	FAIRFIELD	101	11857	11628	11513	-0.2	46	5026	5034	5013	0.0	2.21	3127	3046	-0.3
52557	FAIRFIELD	101	606	575	564	-0.6	20	158	152	150	-0.4	3.07	96	89	-0.8
52560	FLORIS	051	485	497	503	0.3	72	188	197	199	0.5	2.52	146	150	0.3
52561	FREMONT	123	1007	1167	1221	1.6	95	394	464	488	1.8	2.52	286	329	1.5
52563	HEDRICK	107	1719	1694	1674	-0.2	46	672	677	672	0.1	2.49	493	487	-0.1
52565	KEOSAUQUA	177	2102	2117	2122	0.1	63	858	884	891	0.3	2.25	558	560	0.0
52566	KIRKVILLE	179	218	229	233	0.5	79	73	79	81	0.9	2.90	58	62	0.7
52567	LIBERTYVILLE	101	559	551	547	-0.2	46	223	227	227	0.2	2.35	166	165	-0.1
52569	MELROSE	135	658	642	631	-0.3	40	276	278	275	0.1	2.31	208	205	-0.2
52570	MILTON	177	910	878	867	-0.4	32	327	319	315	-0.3	2.75	243	232	-0.5
52571	MORAVIA	007	1319	1309	1293	-0.1	51	566	583	580	0.3	2.25	397	396	0.0
52572	MOULTON	007	1177	1166	1142	-0.1	51	503	511	503	0.2	2.28	332	326	-0.2
52573	MOUNT STERLING	177	240	243	246	0.1	63	95	99	101	0.4	2.45	67	68	0.2
52574	MYSTIC	007	1058	1067	1056	0.1	63	421	440	439	0.5	2.43	287	292	0.2
52576	OLLIE	107	569	572	567	0.1	63	234	240	239	0.3	2.38	167	167	0.0
52577	OSKALOOSA	123	15058	14772	14688	-0.2	46	6128	6173	6172	0.1	2.32	4048	3973	-0.2
52580	PACKWOOD	101	530	522	518	-0.2	46	218	222	222	0.2	2.35	156	156	0.0
52581	PLANO	007	405	412	408	0.2	68	180	189	188	0.5	2.18	132	135	0.2
52583	PROMISE CITY	185	401	386	373	-0.4	32	161	158	154	-0.2	2.44	117	113	-0.4
52584	PULASKI	051	460	469	473	0.2	68	156	162	164	0.4	2.82	123	126	0.3
52585	RICHLAND	107	996	1009	1004	0.1	63	410	424	424	0.4	2.38	292	295	0.1
52586	ROSE HILL	123	590	611	620	0.4	76	233	249	255	0.7	2.45	181	190	0.5
52588	SELMA	177	462	466	465	0.1	63	199	206	207	0.4	2.26	142	144	0.2
52590	SEYMOUR	185	1195	1065	1012	-1.2	4	475	429	408	-1.1	2.41	327	289	-1.3
52591	SIGOURNEY	107	3237	2943	2835	-1.0	6	1285	1196	1154	-0.8	2.38	864	787	-1.0
52593	UDELL	007	129	138	139	0.7	85	49	55	55	1.3	2.51	38	42	1.1
52594	UNIONVILLE	007	399	420	420	0.6	83	152	166	167	1.0	2.53	116	124	0.7
52601	BURLINGTON	057	31005	29494	28876	-0.5	27	12756	12442	12253	-0.3	2.31	8321	7909	-0.5
52619	ARGYLE	111	828	809	789	-0.3	40	287	288	283	0.0	2.68	222	219	-0.1
52620	BONAPARTE	177	853	864	859	0.1	63	334	344	344	0.3	2.51	228	229	0.0
52621	CRAWFORDSVILLE	183	663	691	695	0.4	76	248	263	266	0.6	2.63	188	196	0.5
52623	DANVILLE	057	1910	1911	1896	0.0	58	721	741	742	0.3	2.52	558	563	0.1
52624	DENMARK	111	459	426	407	-0.8	11	170	163	157	-0.5	2.61	132	124	-0.7
52625	DONNELLSON	111	2585	2522	2459	-0.3	40	1003	1005	986	0.0	2.41	757	743	-0.2
52626	FARMINGTON	111	1389	1326	1302	-0.5	27	577	566	559	-0.2	2.34	377	360	-0.5
52627	FORT MADISON	111	13697	12943	12499	-0.6	20	5486	5266	5100	-0.4	2.25	3540	3304	-0.7
52630	HILLSBORO	111	551	561	558	0.2	68	218	229	229	0.5	2.45	157	162	0.3
52631	HOUGHTON	111	18	18	18	0.0	58	7	7	7	0.0	2.57	5	5	0.0
52632	KEOKUK	111	13803	12742	12198	-0.9	8	5659	5351	5155	-0.6	2.33	3706	3414	-0.9
52635	LOCKRIDGE	101	758	732	723	-0.4	32	285	285	283	0.0	2.57	209	204	-0.3
52637	MEDIAPOLIS	057	2542	2487	2446	-0.2	46	982	984	973	0.0	2.40	696	680	-0.3
52638	MIDDLETOWN	057	692	686	676	-0.1	51	248	252	251	0.2	2.69	194	193	-0.1
52639	MONTROSE	111	2173	2155	2120	-0.1	51	797	818	812	0.3	2.50	573	576	0.1
52640	MORNING SUN	115	1413	1396	1382	-0.1	51	541	538	532	-0.1	2.52	403	394	-0.2
	IOWA					0.4					0.7	2.40			0.4
	UNITED STATES					1.0					1.1	2.59			0.9

POPULATION COMPOSITION

ZIP CODE #	POST OFFICE NAME	RACE (%) White 2000	White 2009	Black 2000	Black 2009	Asian/Pacific 2000	Asian/Pacific 2009	% Hispanic Origin 2000	% Hispanic Origin 2009	2009 AGE DISTRIBUTION (%) 0-4	5-9	10-14	15-19	20-24	25-44	45-64	65-84	85+	18+	MEDIAN AGE 2009	% 2009 Males	% 2009 Females
52332	SHELLSBURG	99.3	99.1	0.1	0.2	0.1	0.2	0.6	1.0	6.1	6.6	7.1	7.2	4.9	23.4	32.1	11.3	1.5	75.1	41.9	52.3	47.7
52333	SOLON	98.5	95.5	0.3	1.6	0.2	1.8	0.8	1.1	5.5	6.1	6.4	11.2	10.8	19.5	29.6	8.6	2.2	78.3	36.8	51.1	48.9
52334	SOUTH AMANA	99.1	99.1	0.0	0.0	0.4	0.4	0.0	0.0	5.7	6.6	7.0	7.0	5.7	22.7	31.0	12.7	1.7	76.0	41.7	50.2	49.8
52335	SOUTH ENGLISH	99.2	99.2	0.0	0.0	0.3	0.3	0.3	0.5	6.6	7.8	7.7	7.1	4.4	21.0	31.7	11.5	2.1	73.3	41.3	50.3	49.7
52336	SPRINGVILLE	98.7	98.2	0.1	0.2	0.4	0.7	0.5	0.7	6.8	6.8	6.9	6.9	5.8	25.4	28.9	10.9	1.5	75.4	38.2	50.6	49.4
52337	STANWOOD	98.1	98.0	0.2	0.2	0.3	0.5	0.2	0.3	5.8	6.4	6.8	6.5	3.7	25.0	30.4	13.2	2.3	77.1	42.4	51.5	48.5
52338	SWISHER	98.1	97.2	0.2	0.3	0.7	1.3	0.4	0.7	6.1	7.1	7.5	7.0	3.8	24.8	33.2	9.5	0.9	74.7	41.1	50.6	49.4
52339	TAMA	78.8	78.5	0.3	0.3	0.3	0.3	8.3	8.3	8.4	7.4	7.0	7.4	6.1	22.6	24.2	13.5	3.4	72.4	37.3	48.6	51.4
52340	TIFFIN	96.3	94.6	1.0	1.3	1.0	1.7	2.0	3.0	7.9	7.2	6.7	6.9	8.5	31.8	24.0	6.2	0.7	74.1	32.5	49.7	50.3
52341	TODDVILLE	97.6	96.5	0.5	0.7	0.9	1.5	0.6	1.0	5.1	5.8	6.7	7.0	4.4	23.7	35.4	10.8	1.1	78.0	43.1	51.9	48.1
52342	TOLEDO	87.0	86.7	0.4	0.4	0.3	0.3	4.2	4.3	6.3	6.2	6.4	7.7	5.2	22.9	26.7	14.9	3.7	75.7	41.1	48.5	51.5
52345	URBANA	99.2	99.1	0.4	0.4	0.1	0.1	0.8	1.2	8.1	7.8	7.8	7.6	5.4	31.0	23.4	7.9	1.2	71.8	35.5	50.8	49.2
52346	VAN HORNE	98.2	97.7	0.5	0.7	0.3	0.4	0.4	0.7	6.6	7.3	7.4	7.5	4.2	23.8	29.1	11.8	2.2	73.2	40.4	51.6	48.4
52347	VICTOR	98.7	98.1	0.1	0.1	0.3	0.5	0.9	1.5	5.4	6.3	6.8	7.2	4.6	21.3	31.9	13.5	3.2	76.9	43.8	49.6	50.4
52348	VINING	97.2	97.2	0.0	0.0	0.0	0.0	1.4	1.4	7.0	8.5	8.5	5.6	4.2	23.9	25.4	14.1	2.8	70.4	38.1	50.7	49.3
52349	VINTON	98.5	98.1	0.2	0.3	0.3	0.4	0.8	1.1	6.2	6.3	6.3	6.8	5.5	23.5	28.1	14.0	3.3	77.1	41.8	50.0	50.0
52352	WALKER	99.0	98.7	0.2	0.2	0.1	0.1	0.2	0.2	6.8	7.2	7.3	7.2	4.7	25.0	28.7	11.4	1.7	74.3	39.4	50.5	49.5
52353	WASHINGTON	95.6	93.8	0.5	0.6	0.4	0.6	4.3	6.4	6.2	6.3	6.5	6.5	5.3	22.7	27.3	14.8	4.3	76.9	42.1	47.9	52.1
52354	WATKINS	99.3	99.0	0.0	0.0	0.0	0.0	0.4	0.6	6.2	6.6	7.0	7.7	4.8	25.5	28.2	11.6	2.5	75.2	40.1	49.3	50.7
52355	WEBSTER	99.4	99.4	0.0	0.0	0.0	0.0	0.6	0.8	6.6	7.7	7.7	7.2	4.4	21.5	30.6	12.1	2.2	73.3	41.1	51.0	49.0
52356	WELLMAN	98.6	98.1	0.1	0.1	0.1	0.2	1.0	1.5	6.7	6.9	7.2	7.1	5.0	22.2	27.6	13.7	3.6	74.6	41.2	50.0	50.0
52358	WEST BRANCH	97.3	96.3	0.4	0.4	0.7	1.2	1.6	2.3	6.3	6.5	6.7	6.3	5.2	24.8	31.0	10.7	2.6	76.4	40.7	48.0	52.0
52359	WEST CHESTER	98.1	97.2	0.0	0.0	0.0	0.4	0.8	1.4	6.4	7.1	7.8	7.1	3.9	21.9	31.8	12.7	1.4	74.2	41.8	51.2	48.8
52361	WILLIAMSBURG	98.2	97.5	0.1	0.1	0.4	0.5	1.5	2.2	6.7	6.5	6.8	8.0	6.5	22.9	27.6	12.3	2.6	74.6	39.3	48.4	51.6
52362	WYOMING	98.9	98.7	0.4	0.4	0.0	0.1	0.4	0.5	5.6	5.5	5.6	6.7	5.6	21.8	29.1	17.5	2.6	79.3	44.3	49.3	50.7
52401	CEDAR RAPIDS	70.4	62.9	17.9	21.7	6.4	9.5	3.4	4.9	6.3	5.9	5.4	6.4	7.5	25.9	23.3	14.0	5.3	79.2	39.3	48.5	51.5
52402	CEDAR RAPIDS	92.9	90.4	2.8	3.6	2.0	3.3	1.7	2.5	7.3	6.9	6.6	7.6	7.7	28.8	24.1	9.3	1.7	75.3	34.5	49.0	51.0
52403	CEDAR RAPIDS	89.5	86.3	6.2	7.9	1.3	2.2	1.8	2.7	6.4	6.5	7.0	7.0	5.5	24.5	28.1	12.0	2.9	75.9	40.1	48.7	51.3
52404	CEDAR RAPIDS	92.6	90.4	2.9	3.6	1.6	2.6	1.8	2.6	7.3	6.7	6.4	6.9	7.5	29.7	23.2	10.2	2.0	75.9	34.3	49.4	50.6
52405	CEDAR RAPIDS	94.9	93.1	1.7	2.2	1.5	2.5	1.3	2.0	6.5	6.7	6.8	6.6	5.2	27.2	27.0	11.4	2.5	75.9	39.0	49.0	51.0
52411	CEDAR RAPIDS	96.9	95.6	0.5	0.6	1.3	2.0	1.1	1.6	6.3	7.3	8.3	7.7	3.8	21.8	34.3	9.5	0.9	73.0	41.9	50.0	50.0
52501	OTTUMWA	95.9	95.8	1.1	1.1	0.7	0.7	2.5	2.5	5.9	6.0	6.1	6.9	6.1	24.6	27.1	14.2	3.2	78.4	40.4	49.0	51.0
52530	AGENCY	99.0	98.7	0.1	0.2	0.3	0.5	0.4	0.6	5.1	5.7	6.3	6.3	4.5	21.0	33.2	15.6	2.3	79.0	45.6	49.7	50.3
52531	ALBIA	98.2	98.0	0.2	0.3	0.5	0.5	0.6	0.9	6.5	6.5	6.4	6.4	5.4	23.2	26.7	14.8	4.2	76.6	41.6	48.6	51.4
52533	BATAVIA	97.9	97.2	0.1	0.1	1.1	1.7	1.1	1.5	5.6	6.3	6.6	6.1	4.2	22.0	35.0	12.1	1.9	77.7	44.3	50.8	49.2
52534	BEACON	98.5	98.5	0.2	0.2	0.0	0.0	0.2	0.2	6.1	6.6	6.8	6.3	4.6	24.7	30.6	12.9	1.5	76.4	41.0	51.1	48.9
52535	BIRMINGHAM	99.3	99.1	0.0	0.0	0.2	0.3	1.0	1.3	5.2	5.6	6.0	6.0	4.6	23.2	31.3	15.8	2.4	79.6	44.6	52.0	48.0
52536	BLAKESBURG	98.5	98.5	0.1	0.1	0.3	0.3	1.1	1.1	6.3	6.8	6.9	5.2	4.0	25.9	30.5	12.7	1.7	76.8	41.5	50.5	49.5
52537	BLOOMFIELD	98.3	97.8	0.1	0.2	0.3	0.4	0.7	1.0	6.8	6.7	7.0	6.6	4.8	22.7	27.9	14.2	3.3	75.3	41.3	50.0	50.0
52540	BRIGHTON	99.0	98.6	0.4	0.5	0.4	0.6	0.3	0.5	6.0	6.3	6.9	6.9	4.6	24.4	30.2	13.0	1.6	76.4	41.3	50.5	49.5
52542	CANTRIL	98.4	98.0	0.2	0.2	0.4	0.4	0.4	0.4	5.7	6.1	6.7	7.1	4.3	22.3	29.2	16.6	2.0	77.3	43.6	54.4	45.6
52543	CEDAR	98.1	97.8	0.4	0.4	0.4	0.4	0.8	0.7	6.0	6.3	7.5	7.8	4.9	25.0	29.9	11.2	1.5	75.4	40.5	53.4	46.6
52544	CENTERVILLE	97.7	97.0	0.6	0.8	0.4	0.6	1.3	1.9	6.1	5.9	5.9	6.4	6.0	23.3	26.6	15.5	4.2	78.0	41.8	47.2	52.8
52548	CHILLICOTHE	100.0	100.0	0.0	0.0	0.0	0.0	0.0	0.0	4.2	4.2	5.3	7.4	6.3	22.1	34.7	13.7	2.1	83.2	45.4	52.6	47.4
52549	CINCINNATI	98.6	98.3	0.0	0.0	0.0	0.0	0.7	1.1	6.6	7.0	6.9	6.7	4.5	22.5	29.6	13.8	2.4	75.5	42.1	51.8	48.2
52550	DELTA	98.2	97.6	0.3	0.5	0.4	0.6	1.0	1.5	5.8	6.0	6.1	7.3	5.0	24.6	26.8	15.7	2.6	77.5	41.0	47.9	52.1
52551	DOUDS	98.4	98.2	0.0	0.0	0.5	0.5	0.5	0.8	5.9	6.4	6.2	5.9	4.9	23.1	29.5	16.2	2.1	77.9	43.2	48.7	51.3
52552	DRAKESVILLE	98.9	98.5	0.0	0.1	0.2	0.3	0.6	0.8	7.2	7.6	7.8	6.9	4.3	22.8	26.2	13.1	4.1	73.1	39.5	49.8	50.2
52553	EDDYVILLE	99.0	99.0	0.1	0.1	0.2	0.2	0.6	0.6	6.6	6.9	7.0	6.3	5.5	25.3	29.6	11.4	1.4	75.6	38.8	49.7	50.3
52554	ELDON	98.3	98.3	0.1	0.1	0.1	0.1	1.1	1.1	6.2	6.3	6.5	6.9	5.2	22.8	28.5	15.1	2.6	76.7	42.3	48.8	51.2
52555	EXLINE	99.2	98.7	0.3	0.5	0.3	0.5	0.8	1.3	4.4	4.9	6.0	7.8	4.4	22.1	33.3	15.1	1.8	79.9	45.2	50.5	49.5
52556	FAIRFIELD	95.4	93.9	0.7	0.9	2.0	3.0	2.1	3.0	5.1	5.3	6.1	6.6	6.2	21.7	34.8	11.2	3.0	79.2	44.1	48.6	51.4
52557	FAIRFIELD	92.2	89.9	1.8	2.1	3.3	4.9	3.5	5.0	3.8	4.2	5.2	8.9	8.0	16.2	46.8	6.1	0.9	82.1	45.9	49.2	50.8
52560	FLORIS	99.0	98.8	0.0	0.0	0.2	0.4	0.8	1.0	6.2	6.6	6.6	5.6	4.6	22.9	30.0	15.7	1.6	76.9	43.1	51.3	48.7
52561	FREMONT	99.2	99.1	0.1	0.1	0.1	0.1	0.3	0.3	7.4	7.8	8.4	6.9	4.3	26.2	26.0	10.7	2.2	71.8	37.6	50.3	49.7
52563	HEDRICK	98.8	98.6	0.1	0.1	0.2	0.2	0.6	0.7	5.6	6.8	6.8	6.9	4.8	23.5	28.0	14.3	2.4	75.3	40.9	49.1	50.9
52565	KEOSAUQUA	98.6	98.4	0.1	0.1	0.4	0.4	0.3	0.4	5.0	5.2	5.4	6.3	5.1	21.5	28.5	17.6	5.4	80.3	46.1	47.4	52.6
52566	KIRKVILLE	99.1	99.1	0.0	0.0	0.5	0.4	0.5	0.4	3.9	4.4	5.7	7.9	6.6	22.3	34.1	13.5	1.7	81.7	44.6	52.0	48.0
52567	LIBERTYVILLE	98.7	98.4	0.2	0.2	0.2	0.4	0.4	0.5	5.1	5.6	6.2	7.1	4.9	24.3	33.8	11.3	1.8	78.8	42.8	50.6	49.4
52569	MELROSE	99.2	99.2	0.2	0.2	0.3	0.3	0.2	0.2	5.5	5.8	5.9	5.3	4.2	21.0	31.0	19.5	1.9	79.6	46.6	52.5	47.5
52570	MILTON	98.2	98.1	0.1	0.1	0.2	0.2	1.4	1.9	8.0	8.5	7.6	7.7	7.1	19.9	21.1	15.1	4.9	70.4	37.4	53.0	47.0
52571	MORAVIA	99.1	98.9	0.1	0.2	0.1	0.1	0.4	0.5	5.7	5.9	5.7	5.4	5.2	21.8	29.6	17.6	3.0	79.4	45.1	48.4	51.6
52572	MOULTON	98.3	97.9	0.3	0.3	0.2	0.3	0.4	0.6	5.2	5.5	5.6	6.3	5.1	24.2	28.4	16.6	3.2	79.7	43.4	49.6	50.4
52573	MOUNT STERLING	98.3	97.5	0.0	0.4	0.4	0.4	0.4	0.8	5.3	6.2	7.0	7.0	4.1	22.6	29.2	16.5	2.1	77.0	43.6	53.9	46.1
52574	MYSTIC	99.1	99.1	0.1	0.2	0.1	0.1	0.3	0.5	5.3	5.4	6.0	6.7	5.0	25.1	29.8	14.2	2.3	79.0	42.3	49.7	50.3
52576	OLLIE	99.5	99.0	0.0	0.0	0.0	0.2	0.5	0.7	5.9	6.5	7.3	7.3	3.3	23.1	29.9	14.3	2.3	75.5	42.9	51.2	48.8
52577	OSKALOOSA	96.3	96.3	0.9	0.9	1.2	1.2	1.1	1.1	6.8	6.3	6.3	7.0	7.3	25.0	25.5	12.8	3.1	76.6	38.1	49.6	50.4
52580	PACKWOOD	98.7	98.1	0.0	0.0	0.2	0.2	1.3	2.1	6.3	6.9	7.3	6.9	3.4	24.1	31.6	11.3	2.1	74.9	41.3	50.8	49.2
52581	PLANO	98.5	98.3	0.2	0.5	0.2	0.2	1.0	1.2	5.1	5.6	5.8	5.6	3.6	22.3	32.8	16.7	2.4	79.9	46.3	49.5	50.5
52583	PROMISE CITY	97.8	96.9	0.0	0.0	0.3	0.8	1.0	1.0	4.1	4.9	5.2	7.3	4.9	21.5	31.1	18.7	2.3	81.3	46.1	48.7	51.3
52584	PULASKI	97.4	96.4	0.9	1.3	0.0	0.0	1.1	1.9	7.2	7.7	8.1	8.5	4.5	20.7	27.9	13.0	2.3	70.8	39.9	50.3	49.7
52585	RICHLAND	99.2	98.8	0.1	0.1	0.1	0.2	0.5	0.8	6.0	6.4	7.2	7.2	3.5	23.1	29.7	14.4	2.4	75.6	42.9	50.6	49.4
52586	ROSE HILL	98.3	98.4	0.3	0.3	0.2	0.2	0.7	0.7	5.9	6.4	7.4	7.7	4.6	24.2	31.1	11.5	1.3	75.5	41.1	54.3	45.7
52588	SELMA	98.1	97.9	0.0	0.0	0.6	0.6	0.6	1.1	5.8	6.0	5.8	5.8	4.7	22.5	31.1	16.1	2.1	79.2	44.5	49.4	50.6
52590	SEYMOUR	98.1	97.5	0.0	0.0	0.0	0.0	1.5	2.3	5.6	5.4	5.7	6.4	5.8	21.3	28.5	16.8	4.5	79.1	44.8	47.8	52.2
52591	SIGOURNEY	99.0	98.6	0.1	0.2	0.4	0.7	0.6	0.8	5.9	6.1	6.7	7.1	5.0	22.0	26.4	15.4	5.4	76.7	42.5	47.5	52.5
52593	UDELL	99.2	99.3	0.0	0.0	0.0	0.0	0.8	1.4	4.3	5.1	5.8	7.2	4.3	21.7	33.3	15.2	2.9	80.4	45.7	51.4	48.6
52594	UNIONVILLE	98.7	98.6	0.0	0.0	0.3	0.2	0.8	1.2	5.0	5.5	6.2	6.9	4.5	21.9	31.9	15.7	2.4	79.0	45.0	51.0	49.0
52601	BURLINGTON	92.4	90.5	4.5	5.4	0.7	1.1	1.9	2.8	6.5	6.2	6.1	6.4	6.2	24.6	27.3	13.6	3.1	77.4	40.0	48.4	51.6
52619	ARGYLE	98.4	97.8	0.4	0.5	0.1	0.2	1.0	1.5	5.4	5.8	6.3	7.3	5.7	22.6	31.9	13.3	1.6	79.9	42.6	51.4	48.6
52620	BONAPARTE	99.2	99.0	0.0	0.0	0.5	0.6	1.8	2.3	6.6	6.5	6.6	7.2	6.5	24.8	28.5	11.3	2.1	75.9	38.2	49.0	51.0
52621	CRAWFORDSVILLE	98.5	98.3	0.2	0.1	0.0	0.0	1.5	2.5	6.4	7.2	7.2	7.5	4.1	21.9	33.3	10.9	1.6	74.4	42.0	50.4	49.6
52623	DANVILLE	98.1	97.6	0.5	0.6	0.3	0.4	0.6	1.0	5.7	6.2	6.6	7.3	4.3	24.2	29.9	12.4	3.4	76.7	41.9	49.7	50.3
52624	DENMARK	99.3	98.8	0.0	0.0	0.0	0.2	0.7	0.9	6.1	6.6	6.8	6.8	4.9	22.5	30.0	14.1	2.1	76.3	42.0	48.4	51.6
52625	DONNELLSON	98.8	98.2	0.2	0.4	0.2	0.3	1.0	1.5	5.4	5.5	5.9	7.1	5.7	22.9	30.0	14.2	3.3	79.7	42.9	48.4	51.6
52626	FARMINGTON	99.1	99.1	0.1	0.1	0.1	0.1	0.4	0.5	5.6	5.7	6.1	6.6	5.4	21.5	30.8	15.2	3.0	78.5	44.3	48.0	52.0
52627	FORT MADISON	91.6	89.0	4.1	5.0	0.7	1.1	4.7	6.9	5.5	5.5	5.7	6.0	6.2	25.3	28.8	13.9	3.1	80.2	41.7	51.4	48.6
52630	HILLSBORO	98.9	98.6	0.2	0.2	0.2	0.5	0.4	0.4	7.3	7.5	7.3	6.1	4.8	23.4	30.1	11.6	2.0	73.8	40.8	49.9	50.1
52631	HOUGHTON	100.0	100.0	0.0	0.0	0.0	0.0	0.0	0.0	11.1	11.1	11.1	5.6	0.0	22.2	38.9	0.0	0.0	61.1	40.0	50.0	50.0
52632	KEOKUK	93.7	92.3	3.4	4.0	0.5	0.8	1.0	1.5	6.7	6.3	6.4	6.6	6.3	23.5	27.0	14.2	3.1	76.6	40.3	48.2	51.8
52635	LOCKRIDGE	99.6	99.6	0.0	0.0	0.3	0.3	0.4	0.5	6.3	6.7	7.0	6.3	4.2	24.7	31.4	11.9	1.5	76.0	41.5	50.5	49.5
52637	MEDIAPOLIS	99.0	98.6	0.2	0.3	0.3	0.5	0.6	0.8	6.9	6.6	6.4	7.0	4.5	23.0	25.6	15.6	4.4	75.8	41.8	48.3	51.7
52638	MIDDLETOWN	95.9	94.0	1.3	1.7	0.7	1.3	1.7	2.8	5.0	7.3	7.4	8.0	5.1	24.5	31.0	10.2	1.5	74.9	40.7	50.9	49.1
52639	MONTROSE	96.2	92.9	1.5	1.7	0.1	2.8	2.2	2.9	5.0	5.3	5.8	6.6	5.1	22.3	32.6	14.4	2.9	82.5	44.9	52.0	48.0
52640	MORNING SUN	97.5	96.1	0.1	0.2	0.4	0.6	4.6	7.2	7.7	7.7	7.7	6.4	4.7	24.2	25.8	13.1	2.7	72.4	38.7	49.1	50.9
	IOWA	93.9	91.9	2.1	2.5	1.3	2.1	2.8	4.1	6.5	6.4	6.5	7.3	7.1	25.2	26.5	11.9	2.6	76.5	38.1	49.3	50.7
	UNITED STATES	75.1	72.0	12.3	12.7	3.8	4.6	12.5	15.7	6.8	6.7	6.6	7.1	6.9	27.0	26.0	10.9	1.9	75.7	36.9	49.2	50.8

ZIP CODE #	POST OFFICE NAME	2009 Per Capita Income	2009 HH Income Base	2009 HOUSEHOLD INCOME DISTRIBUTION (%) Less than $25,000	$25,000 to $49,999	$50,000 to $99,999	$100,000 to $149,999	$150,000 or More	MEDIAN HOUSEHOLD INCOME 2009	2014	2009 National Centile	2009 State Centile	2009 Home Value Base	2009 HOME VALUE DISTRIBUTION (%) Less than $50,000	$50,000 to $89,999	$90,000 to $174,999	$175,000 to $399,999	$400,000 or More	2009 Median Home Value
52332	SHELLSBURG	20999	756	18.4	32.1	41.4	7.4	0.7	49579	52400	60	67	655	21.2	11.3	42.9	22.4	2.1	120406
52333	SOLON	37125	2170	6.9	15.2	42.3	23.8	11.8	81929	82255	93	99	1873	2.0	4.0	28.2	50.9	14.9	219195
52334	SOUTH AMANA	22623	89	13.5	30.3	49.4	6.7	0.0	54995	53676	71	86	70	2.9	11.4	50.0	34.3	1.4	144444
52335	SOUTH ENGLISH	21070	270	21.1	32.2	40.7	5.6	0.4	47593	48285	56	60	214	23.4	33.6	33.6	5.6	3.7	82105
52336	SPRINGVILLE	25098	890	14.2	24.8	49.2	9.2	2.6	61224	62831	79	93	711	11.8	12.1	50.6	21.9	3.5	127744
52337	STANWOOD	22961	364	21.2	27.2	43.7	4.9	3.0	51065	52208	64	74	278	11.5	26.3	46.0	15.1	1.1	105743
52338	SWISHER	33860	1141	7.7	11.7	51.9	19.8	8.9	78445	78559	91	99	995	0.5	3.2	28.1	55.6	12.6	218152
52339	TAMA	19882	1535	26.6	28.6	37.5	5.0	2.4	45436	47210	50	47	1126	19.4	31.8	43.3	4.6	0.8	88667
52340	TIFFIN	33748	523	13.0	26.4	43.2	9.9	7.5	59102	60201	76	91	373	24.7	12.1	27.3	27.6	8.3	133468
52341	TODDVILLE	27707	534	14.8	23.4	42.7	13.9	5.2	62475	65005	81	94	477	0.8	11.3	35.8	43.0	9.0	182422
52342	TOLEDO	22218	1362	22.4	32.6	35.4	6.7	2.9	45680	47537	50	48	1013	17.2	30.7	42.3	9.2	0.7	92986
52345	URBANA	22593	336	16.1	29.5	44.3	6.8	3.3	52997	55078	68	81	291	7.9	19.9	50.9	19.6	1.7	120905
52346	VAN HORNE	20960	461	16.9	26.5	49.7	6.3	0.7	53516	55065	69	83	366	6.8	20.8	53.8	14.5	4.1	114720
52347	VICTOR	20967	610	23.9	28.7	41.1	5.2	1.0	47442	50297	55	59	485	12.8	36.5	42.5	7.0	1.2	90854
52348	VINING	22871	32	18.8	43.8	31.3	3.1	3.1	42348	45000	40	27	26	34.6	15.4	42.3	7.7	0.0	90000
52349	VINTON	23652	3240	23.1	29.2	38.0	7.7	2.1	48340	51420	57	63	2464	13.4	28.7	42.7	14.2	1.0	100951
52352	WALKER	21713	764	15.8	34.6	40.3	7.6	1.7	49709	51716	60	68	615	10.1	17.7	44.9	25.2	2.1	124662
52353	WASHINGTON	23350	3754	21.8	27.1	42.5	6.3	2.3	50833	52999	63	73	2744	11.3	27.2	47.5	13.0	1.1	106355
52354	WATKINS	21252	181	19.3	29.8	42.0	8.3	0.6	50916	54014	63	73	143	5.6	28.7	48.3	14.0	3.5	112109
52355	WEBSTER	19402	132	23.5	30.3	38.6	6.8	0.8	46322	48198	52	53	108	28.7	32.4	27.8	7.4	3.7	76667
52356	WELLMAN	21566	1078	18.8	35.0	38.7	5.5	2.0	47216	50511	55	58	859	14.4	26.7	40.9	15.7	2.3	106161
52358	WEST BRANCH	24660	1512	15.1	27.9	45.8	9.5	1.7	56542	56494	73	89	1183	14.1	15.0	43.5	22.8	4.6	126078
52359	WEST CHESTER	25026	125	16.0	33.6	44.0	4.8	1.6	50232	52951	62	70	99	13.1	21.2	43.4	21.2	1.0	116406
52361	WILLIAMSBURG	23371	1660	15.6	32.2	42.4	6.7	3.1	51807	52859	66	77	1259	8.3	14.5	52.9	21.6	2.8	132459
52362	WYOMING	21861	492	26.6	31.7	32.3	8.1	1.2	44160	46901	46	40	376	27.4	42.3	22.6	6.4	1.3	68929
52401	CEDAR RAPIDS	18028	1175	59.1	20.9	17.4	1.5	1.2	20460	20000	2	1	300	44.7	39.7	14.7	0.0	1.0	53902
52402	CEDAR RAPIDS	31661	17439	13.8	24.3	42.5	12.3	7.0	63380	66905	82	95	12065	3.8	9.7	55.5	29.0	1.9	140971
52403	CEDAR RAPIDS	32819	10812	16.2	27.7	36.4	10.8	9.0	59761	62860	77	92	7779	4.5	13.9	50.6	24.0	7.1	131663
52404	CEDAR RAPIDS	25617	15843	20.5	29.1	41.3	6.6	2.5	50428	53574	62	71	10372	20.1	20.1	50.1	9.2	0.5	104252
52405	CEDAR RAPIDS	28678	10297	13.3	23.8	47.9	11.4	3.6	63538	67077	82	95	7855	3.2	14.4	64.9	17.1	0.5	126443
52411	CEDAR RAPIDS	37956	2176	5.1	13.5	40.9	22.5	18.1	85484	87293	94	100	2093	11.1	3.0	20.1	54.9	10.9	223633
52501	OTTUMWA	21554	12716	28.0	33.9	30.5	5.0	2.6	40960	43248	36	19	9468	26.8	34.2	29.6	8.2	1.2	74639
52530	AGENCY	22381	479	22.5	32.8	36.7	6.9	1.0	46500	48981	53	54	399	13.3	30.6	41.6	13.5	1.0	96806
52531	ALBIA	21804	2431	29.1	29.4	33.3	6.1	2.2	43222	44341	43	32	1845	25.3	30.6	36.3	7.5	0.4	83364
52533	BATAVIA	24885	488	19.9	36.3	32.2	7.8	3.9	45000	46068	48	44	383	32.1	22.7	30.0	12.0	3.1	77069
52534	BEACON	24013	193	13.5	38.9	38.3	6.7	2.6	48612	50993	58	64	173	21.4	29.5	33.5	15.6	0.0	89118
52535	BIRMINGHAM	18178	456	30.0	34.4	32.7	2.4	0.4	38734	41051	29	11	377	31.0	32.1	30.5	5.8	0.5	70962
52536	BLAKESBURG	21337	413	21.3	38.3	34.4	5.1	1.0	43045	45698	43	31	342	25.7	30.7	32.7	9.9	0.9	80435
52537	BLOOMFIELD	18548	2618	29.5	30.2	35.0	4.5	0.9	40395	41498	34	17	2075	25.3	27.1	35.5	10.6	1.6	86906
52540	BRIGHTON	19065	647	26.4	39.1	30.6	2.9	0.9	39524	41420	31	13	498	30.3	30.3	29.1	7.6	2.6	75714
52542	CANTRIL	22627	215	27.4	32.1	32.6	5.1	2.8	41473	45296	38	23	180	27.8	28.3	25.0	16.7	2.2	76000
52543	CEDAR	21592	97	19.6	26.8	42.3	8.2	3.1	53064	54068	68	81	79	24.1	16.5	36.7	21.5	1.3	106731
52544	CENTERVILLE	19395	3333	35.0	30.8	29.0	3.8	1.4	36332	37453	22	5	2278	30.2	35.1	27.4	6.6	0.7	69255
52548	CHILLICOTHE	23677	41	17.1	36.6	36.6	4.9	4.9	47343	50000	55	58	35	28.6	25.7	34.3	11.4	0.0	82500
52549	CINCINNATI	17979	315	29.5	38.1	27.0	5.4	0.0	36629	37122	22	5	278	45.3	23.4	23.4	7.6	0.4	65000
52550	DELTA	21331	277	30.3	32.5	30.3	4.0	2.9	37505	38761	25	8	213	53.5	22.1	16.9	5.6	1.9	46053
52551	DOUDS	16883	162	28.4	45.7	22.8	3.1	0.0	38303	39240	28	9	137	33.6	25.5	29.9	10.2	0.7	76111
52552	DRAKESVILLE	17405	412	30.1	35.9	28.9	3.9	1.2	36848	38037	23	6	343	21.6	29.2	33.5	13.7	2.0	89242
52553	EDDYVILLE	21335	668	26.9	31.0	34.4	5.4	2.2	44387	46752	46	41	500	25.8	31.6	32.4	9.4	0.8	81778
52554	ELDON	18827	660	31.5	36.5	27.4	3.8	0.8	36385	37919	22	5	540	43.9	34.8	16.3	3.3	1.7	56735
52555	EXLINE	15520	153	35.9	39.9	20.3	2.0	2.0	31486	31655	11	1	126	30.2	25.4	30.2	13.5	0.8	83000
52556	FAIRFIELD	25676	5034	26.5	30.9	30.1	7.8	4.7	42578	44766	41	29	3320	18.3	26.2	39.2	13.9	2.3	98867
52557	FAIRFIELD	16768	152	33.6	23.7	32.2	7.2	3.3	41147	43643	36	21	55	5.5	50.9	30.9	7.3	5.5	86818
52560	FLORIS	17774	197	32.0	28.9	36.5	1.5	1.0	38851	39467	29	12	163	32.5	16.0	39.3	8.6	3.7	96250
52561	FREMONT	21179	464	25.9	26.9	38.1	7.5	1.5	47538	50481	56	59	379	23.5	36.9	32.7	6.6	0.3	81023
52563	HEDRICK	21069	677	27.2	31.5	33.1	5.8	2.5	42987	45094	42	31	529	34.2	27.2	28.2	5.7	4.7	73594
52565	KEOSAUQUA	19628	884	28.7	40.2	25.3	4.1	1.7	38958	40345	30	12	675	28.3	31.6	30.1	9.5	0.6	76250
52566	KIRKVILLE	18869	79	20.3	38.0	32.9	3.8	5.1	44444	46930	47	41	68	26.5	25.0	36.8	10.3	1.5	87500
52567	LIBERTYVILLE	23541	227	18.5	41.4	33.9	2.2	4.0	44592	45697	47	42	184	24.5	17.9	35.3	17.4	4.9	103472
52569	MELROSE	20037	278	21.9	46.0	27.3	3.6	1.1	42127	43000	40	25	241	29.5	30.7	29.0	7.5	3.3	73824
52570	MILTON	13578	319	39.5	38.9	19.7	0.9	0.9	31402	32976	10	1	261	48.7	24.9	19.9	6.5	0.0	51522
52571	MORAVIA	20151	583	32.4	37.7	25.0	3.3	1.5	36421	37045	22	5	472	31.4	31.6	28.8	7.6	0.6	70000
52572	MOULTON	19155	511	37.2	35.4	24.3	1.8	1.4	33254	34029	14	2	386	42.2	25.1	24.4	7.5	0.8	63500
52573	MOUNT STERLING	21238	99	26.3	32.3	34.3	5.1	2.0	42363	45970	41	27	83	26.5	27.7	27.7	16.9	1.2	79000
52574	MYSTIC	16666	440	36.8	35.9	23.6	2.5	1.1	33863	34652	15	3	361	41.8	31.0	22.2	4.7	0.3	58194
52576	OLLIE	19644	240	31.3	27.9	35.4	4.6	0.8	41396	43654	37	22	188	20.7	30.9	43.1	4.3	1.1	88421
52577	OSKALOOSA	23929	6173	25.2	28.6	37.0	5.9	3.3	47162	50165	55	57	4209	17.6	30.5	39.0	11.8	1.0	92710
52580	PACKWOOD	22250	222	19.8	40.5	30.6	7.7	1.4	43305	43819	43	33	170	31.2	22.9	38.2	7.6	0.0	78333
52581	PLANO	20501	189	28.0	39.2	27.0	3.2	2.6	37761	39097	26	8	159	24.5	25.2	39.6	9.4	1.3	90714
52583	PROMISE CITY	16097	158	34.8	39.2	23.4	0.6	1.9	35000	37352	18	3	134	30.6	26.1	34.3	5.2	3.7	80000
52584	PULASKI	16913	162	30.2	32.1	30.2	6.2	1.2	40000	41542	33	15	136	28.7	22.1	37.5	10.3	1.5	88750
52585	RICHLAND	19548	424	30.2	29.5	35.6	4.2	0.5	41217	44393	37	21	332	21.4	29.5	44.0	3.6	1.5	89063
52586	ROSE HILL	23434	249	20.9	27.7	40.6	7.2	3.6	51078	53058	64	75	197	23.9	17.3	36.5	19.8	2.5	107917
52588	SELMA	17934	206	31.6	40.8	24.3	3.4	0.0	37167	38958	24	6	174	32.2	25.3	29.9	11.5	1.1	76000
52590	SEYMOUR	18401	429	35.2	33.3	24.5	4.4	2.6	34919	35529	17	3	337	53.1	24.6	16.6	4.5	1.2	46250
52591	SIGOURNEY	21343	1196	29.2	28.7	34.0	5.4	2.8	40827	43373	35	18	902	22.0	36.3	32.8	8.0	1.0	81868
52593	UDELL	17953	55	27.3	32.7	38.2	1.8	0.0	42358	45760	40	27	47	21.3	19.1	42.6	14.9	2.1	105682
52594	UNIONVILLE	19387	166	28.3	33.7	33.7	3.0	1.2	40448	41449	34	17	139	23.7	23.7	37.4	13.7	1.4	95000
52601	BURLINGTON	24733	12442	25.1	29.4	35.7	6.3	3.4	46072	48948	52	51	9008	16.7	33.9	37.7	10.5	1.2	89357
52619	ARGYLE	19808	288	22.6	32.3	37.5	5.2	2.4	46799	48509	54	56	247	19.4	20.6	43.3	14.6	2.0	107813
52620	BONAPARTE	18195	344	27.9	33.4	34.9	2.6	1.2	41458	44174	38	23	266	35.0	29.3	24.1	11.7	0.0	65833
52621	CRAWFORDSVILLE	22167	263	15.2	30.0	43.0	9.9	1.9	53405	55226	69	82	209	12.0	29.2	33.5	18.2	7.2	105515
52623	DANVILLE	23484	741	18.5	24.4	48.0	6.6	2.4	54368	54642	70	85	624	12.0	23.9	48.4	13.9	1.8	107167
52624	DENMARK	23202	163	11.7	36.2	46.0	3.1	3.1	51637	52990	65	76	143	9.1	28.0	52.4	10.5	0.0	106389
52625	DONNELLSON	22760	1005	18.7	31.5	41.8	6.3	1.7	49810	51079	61	69	814	15.0	28.1	42.4	12.4	2.1	98889
52626	FARMINGTON	22442	566	27.4	32.5	34.8	3.5	1.8	40271	42633	34	17	442	25.1	35.7	28.3	10.4	0.5	73077
52627	FORT MADISON	24024	5266	25.0	29.4	35.6	6.6	3.4	46066	48907	52	51	3836	24.3	37.4	30.7	6.6	0.9	77849
52630	HILLSBORO	22948	229	20.5	27.9	44.1	3.9	3.5	51222	52240	64	75	181	20.4	22.1	41.4	15.5	0.6	103516
52631	HOUGHTON	23999	7	0.0	14.3	85.7	0.0	0.0	62635	62635	81	95	5	0.0	40.0	60.0	0.0	0.0	112500
52632	KEOKUK	22665	5351	28.2	30.9	31.4	6.0	3.5	42332	45102	40	26	3871	32.4	30.9	28.8	7.1	0.9	72228
52635	LOCKRIDGE	17907	285	21.8	37.9	36.5	3.9	0.0	44859	46192	48	43	231	31.6	19.9	25.5	16.0	6.9	88409
52637	MEDIAPOLIS	23754	984	23.0	28.5	37.8	7.4	3.4	48955	51178	59	66	810	17.3	21.5	49.9	10.2	1.1	102000
52638	MIDDLETOWN	20245	252	20.6	28.6	43.7	5.2	2.0	50636	52286	63	72	216	26.4	17.6	44.0	11.1	0.9	100000
52639	MONTROSE	20406	818	26.3	31.5	34.4	6.2	1.6	43606	45923	44	35	664	24.4	31.3	34.5	9.0	0.8	83214
52640	MORNING SUN	21452	538	21.2	33.1	37.7	5.4	2.6	46750	48815	53	56	427	33.7	32.8	25.3	6.8	1.4	68429
	IOWA	25379		21.1	28.2	37.9	8.6	4.3	50616	52941				14.7	22.5	41.6	18.6	2.6	110128
	UNITED STATES	27277		20.9	24.4	35.3	11.7	7.6	54719	56938				9.3	13.1	31.6	32.6	13.5	162279

ZIP CODE #	POST OFFICE NAME	FINANCIAL SERVICES				THE HOME						ENTERTAINMENT						PERSONAL			
						Home Improvements		Furnishings													
		Auto Loan	Home Loan	Invest-ments	Retire-ment Plans	Home Repair	Lawn & Garden	Comput-ers & Hard-ware-Personal	Major Appli-ances	TV, Radio, Sound Equip-ment	Furni-ture	Dine out/ Carry out	Sports Equip-ment	Fees & Tickets	Toys & Games	Travel	Cable TV	Apparel & Services	Auto Repairs	Health Insur-ance	Pets & Supplies
52332	SHELLSBURG	86	78	77	81	79	92	77	87	79	69	78	66	71	81	77	84	53	80	89	101
52333	SOLON	130	159	154	160	159	146	139	142	133	144	135	109	155	134	152	131	97	137	135	164
52334	SOUTH AMANA	90	82	81	85	84	97	81	91	83	73	82	69	75	85	81	88	56	84	94	106
52335	SOUTH ENGLISH	91	63	100	62	66	96	69	86	72	56	71	71	51	71	69	79	46	81	91	106
52336	SPRINGVILLE	90	95	78	97	90	96	90	90	90	88	90	71	92	92	90	92	62	90	95	108
52337	STANWOOD	88	77	82	80	79	94	77	88	80	69	78	68	69	81	77	85	53	82	91	103
52338	SWISHER	123	147	135	150	145	138	127	132	123	132	124	102	140	125	138	121	88	126	126	153
52339	TAMA	84	69	72	68	69	82	73	79	77	70	76	60	64	78	69	81	52	77	83	94
52340	TIFFIN	118	104	89	105	98	96	116	104	112	117	114	85	107	117	105	109	79	111	101	125
52341	TODDVILLE	104	117	100	120	113	115	104	108	102	104	103	85	111	105	110	103	72	104	107	127
52342	TOLEDO	86	73	87	71	74	93	74	86	79	68	78	64	66	78	74	85	52	81	93	101
52345	URBANA	100	92	81	89	90	94	87	92	90	90	90	67	82	94	83	92	61	89	92	109
52346	VAN HORNE	98	70	105	70	73	103	76	93	79	62	78	76	57	78	76	86	51	87	98	114
52347	VICTOR	82	71	78	73	73	88	72	82	74	63	73	64	63	75	71	79	49	76	85	97
52348	VINING	91	62	100	62	65	96	69	86	72	56	71	71	51	71	69	79	46	80	91	106
52349	VINTON	84	78	78	78	77	89	79	84	82	74	81	63	75	82	78	87	56	82	91	99
52352	WALKER	89	81	83	83	82	95	79	90	82	72	80	69	73	83	80	86	55	83	92	105
52353	WASHINGTON	84	77	80	77	76	91	77	84	81	72	80	64	73	81	77	85	54	82	92	100
52354	WATKINS	88	81	79	84	82	93	79	89	81	72	80	67	73	83	79	85	55	82	91	103
52355	WEBSTER	95	66	105	65	69	101	73	91	76	59	75	75	53	74	72	83	49	85	96	111
52356	WELLMAN	95	67	99	66	70	100	74	91	80	63	78	71	57	79	72	88	51	85	98	110
52358	WEST BRANCH	95	88	86	89	88	96	87	93	89	85	88	69	82	90	85	92	60	89	95	109
52359	WEST CHESTER	101	69	111	69	73	106	77	96	80	62	79	79	56	79	77	87	51	89	101	118
52361	WILLIAMSBURG	92	77	88	79	80	94	83	90	85	77	84	68	74	85	81	90	57	88	96	106
52362	WYOMING	85	61	87	59	63	89	66	82	73	58	71	63	52	72	64	80	47	76	89	97
52401	CEDAR RAPIDS	43	33	35	36	32	38	45	39	49	43	49	30	41	46	40	51	34	45	49	50
52402	CEDAR RAPIDS	105	103	94	106	100	100	107	101	106	107	107	80	107	108	104	105	75	104	102	120
52403	CEDAR RAPIDS	104	109	107	110	109	111	106	107	108	107	108	80	111	107	109	110	76	108	113	125
52404	CEDAR RAPIDS	84	77	69	78	74	78	84	79	84	81	84	62	80	86	78	85	59	83	83	95
52405	CEDAR RAPIDS	94	103	91	103	99	103	95	97	97	95	97	73	102	98	99	98	68	96	102	113
52411	CEDAR RAPIDS	147	181	180	186	184	170	154	162	148	164	150	122	175	148	172	145	107	154	153	186
52501	OTTUMWA	76	67	70	67	67	80	70	75	74	65	72	57	65	74	68	78	49	74	82	89
52530	AGENCY	82	72	76	74	73	87	71	82	74	65	73	62	64	75	71	79	49	76	85	96
52531	ALBIA	85	66	83	66	67	89	70	83	76	63	74	62	59	75	68	82	49	78	89	98
52533	BATAVIA	107	77	114	78	80	113	84	102	87	70	86	83	64	86	83	95	56	95	108	125
52534	BEACON	88	80	79	84	82	95	79	89	82	72	80	68	73	83	79	86	55	83	92	104
52535	BIRMINGHAM	75	54	77	53	56	76	56	70	61	51	60	54	44	61	55	67	40	65	73	84
52536	BLAKESBURG	78	71	70	74	73	84	70	79	72	63	71	60	65	74	70	77	49	73	82	92
52537	BLOOMFIELD	81	60	81	60	62	84	64	77	69	56	67	61	51	69	62	75	45	72	82	93
52540	BRIGHTON	82	58	78	57	59	82	62	75	67	56	66	59	48	68	59	73	44	70	79	91
52542	CANTRIL	93	64	102	64	67	98	71	88	74	58	73	73	52	72	70	80	47	82	93	108
52543	CEDAR	104	75	111	76	78	110	82	100	85	68	84	81	63	84	81	92	55	93	105	122
52544	CENTERVILLE	71	52	68	52	54	72	60	68	65	53	63	52	49	63	57	70	42	66	75	81
52548	CHILLICOTHE	85	77	77	81	79	91	76	86	79	69	77	65	70	80	76	83	53	80	89	100
52549	CINCINNATI	77	55	80	54	57	79	57	73	63	52	62	55	45	62	57	69	41	67	76	87
52550	DELTA	86	61	88	60	64	90	67	83	74	59	72	63	53	73	65	82	48	78	90	99
52551	DOUDS	72	51	77	50	53	75	54	68	58	47	58	54	42	58	54	64	38	63	72	83
52552	DRAKESVILLE	82	56	90	56	59	87	63	78	65	51	65	64	46	64	62	71	42	73	82	96
52553	EDDYVILLE	91	71	79	71	72	90	72	84	78	68	77	64	61	80	69	84	52	78	88	100
52554	ELDON	74	54	74	52	56	76	57	71	64	52	62	53	46	63	56	70	41	66	76	84
52555	EXLINE	70	48	76	48	50	74	53	66	55	43	55	55	39	54	53	60	35	62	70	81
52556	FAIRFIELD	86	79	82	80	79	90	82	85	83	77	82	66	77	83	80	87	57	84	91	101
52557	FAIRFIELD	75	76	72	77	74	73	78	73	76	78	77	58	79	76	76	76	54	75	74	88
52560	FLORIS	76	60	75	59	61	79	60	73	65	55	64	55	51	65	60	70	43	67	76	86
52561	FREMONT	85	73	80	76	75	91	74	85	76	66	75	65	66	77	74	81	51	78	88	100
52563	HEDRICK	91	64	96	63	67	96	71	88	76	60	74	69	54	75	69	84	49	82	94	106
52565	KEOSAUQUA	78	56	80	54	58	81	60	75	66	53	64	57	47	65	59	73	43	69	80	89
52566	KIRKVILLE	85	77	76	80	79	91	76	86	78	69	77	65	70	80	76	83	53	79	89	100
52567	LIBERTYVILLE	88	78	82	81	80	95	78	89	81	70	79	68	70	82	78	85	54	82	92	104
52569	MELROSE	83	59	85	57	61	84	61	77	67	56	66	59	48	67	60	74	44	71	81	93
52570	MILTON	67	46	73	46	48	71	51	63	53	41	52	52	37	52	51	58	34	59	67	78
52571	MORAVIA	78	56	80	55	58	81	61	75	66	53	64	58	48	65	59	73	43	70	81	89
52572	MOULTON	75	53	78	52	56	79	59	73	64	51	62	56	46	63	57	70	41	68	78	87
52573	MOUNT STERLING	93	64	102	64	67	98	71	88	74	58	73	73	52	73	71	81	47	83	93	109
52574	MYSTIC	73	51	66	50	52	72	55	65	59	50	58	51	43	61	51	65	39	61	69	80
52576	OLLIE	84	58	92	57	60	88	64	79	67	52	66	66	47	65	64	73	43	74	84	98
52577	OSKALOOSA	86	73	78	74	73	87	79	84	82	73	81	64	71	82	75	87	55	83	90	100
52580	PACKWOOD	94	64	103	64	67	99	71	89	74	58	73	73	52	73	71	81	48	83	94	109
52581	PLANO	80	55	88	55	58	84	61	76	63	49	63	63	45	62	61	69	41	71	80	93
52583	PROMISE CITY	70	48	77	48	51	74	54	67	56	44	55	55	39	55	53	61	36	62	70	82
52584	PULASKI	86	59	94	59	62	91	66	81	68	53	67	67	48	67	65	74	44	76	86	100
52585	RICHLAND	83	57	91	57	60	88	64	79	66	51	65	65	47	65	63	72	42	74	83	97
52586	ROSE HILL	103	71	113	71	74	108	79	98	82	64	81	81	58	80	78	89	52	91	103	120
52588	SELMA	72	51	78	50	53	76	55	68	58	46	57	55	41	57	55	63	37	64	72	83
52590	SEYMOUR	77	55	79	54	57	80	60	74	66	52	64	57	47	64	58	72	42	69	80	88
52591	SIGOURNEY	88	63	91	61	65	92	69	85	75	60	73	65	54	74	67	83	48	79	92	101
52593	UDELL	81	55	88	55	58	85	62	76	64	50	63	63	45	63	61	70	41	71	81	94
52594	UNIONVILLE	87	60	94	60	63	92	67	83	70	55	69	67	50	69	66	77	45	77	88	101
52601	BURLINGTON	83	78	73	79	77	87	82	82	85	77	83	62	79	85	79	88	58	83	90	98
52619	ARGYLE	84	75	77	78	77	90	75	85	77	67	76	65	68	79	75	82	52	79	88	99
52620	BONAPARTE	82	59	71	57	59	79	62	72	68	59	67	56	49	70	57	74	45	68	77	88
52621	CRAWFORDSVILLE	104	72	114	71	75	110	80	99	83	64	82	82	58	81	79	90	53	92	104	122
52623	DANVILLE	93	84	84	88	86	100	83	94	86	75	84	71	77	88	83	91	58	87	97	109
52624	DENMARK	94	86	85	89	87	101	84	95	87	76	85	72	78	89	84	92	58	88	98	111
52625	DONNELLSON	88	76	84	77	75	94	78	86	80	69	79	69	69	80	77	84	53	83	92	104
52626	FARMINGTON	90	64	92	63	67	94	70	87	77	61	75	66	55	76	68	85	50	81	94	103
52627	FORT MADISON	85	75	80	74	75	90	77	84	82	72	81	63	71	82	76	88	55	82	93	100
52630	HILLSBORO	101	71	97	70	72	101	76	92	82	68	81	73	59	83	73	89	53	86	97	112
52631	HOUGHTON	110	76	121	76	79	116	84	105	88	68	87	87	62	86	84	96	56	98	111	129
52632	KEOKUK	80	69	69	70	68	81	75	77	79	70	77	59	68	78	71	83	53	77	85	92
52635	LOCKRIDGE	82	57	89	57	59	86	63	78	66	51	65	64	46	65	62	71	42	73	82	96
52637	MEDIAPOLIS	89	82	80	85	81	95	82	88	84	75	83	69	77	85	81	88	56	84	93	105
52638	MIDDLETOWN	92	74	79	74	74	92	75	86	80	70	79	65	64	83	71	86	53	80	89	102
52639	MONTROSE	88	68	87	68	70	91	69	85	75	64	74	64	58	75	69	82	49	78	88	100
52640	MORNING SUN	98	70	87	68	70	96	74	87	81	69	79	68	58	83	69	88	53	82	92	107
	IOWA	93	84	87	85	83	95	87	91	89	82	88	71	81	90	85	92	61	90	96	108
	UNITED STATES	100	100	100	100	100	100	100	100	100	100	100	100	100	100	100	100	100	100	100	100

POPULATION CHANGE

ZIP CODE #	POST OFFICE NAME	COUNTY FIPS CODE	POPULATION 2000	POPULATION 2009	POPULATION 2014	2000-2009 ANNUAL RATE % Rate	2000-2009 ANNUAL RATE State Centile	HOUSEHOLDS 2000	HOUSEHOLDS 2009	HOUSEHOLDS 2014	HOUSEHOLDS % Annual Rate 2000-2009	HOUSEHOLDS 2009 Average HH Size	FAMILIES 2000	FAMILIES 2009	FAMILIES % Annual Rate 2000-2009
52641	MOUNT PLEASANT	087	12327	12357	12206	0.0	58	4494	4543	4498	0.1	2.37	2998	2961	-0.1
52644	MOUNT UNION	087	454	454	449	0.0	58	175	181	180	0.4	2.51	139	141	0.2
52645	NEW LONDON	087	3225	3081	3006	-0.5	27	1272	1248	1224	-0.2	2.43	925	889	-0.4
52646	OAKVILLE	115	836	790	772	-0.6	20	319	308	301	-0.4	2.56	230	216	-0.7
52647	OLDS	087	224	218	215	-0.3	40	93	93	92	0.0	2.34	72	71	-0.2
52649	SALEM	087	1005	1036	1033	0.3	72	411	437	438	0.7	2.37	299	311	0.4
52650	SPERRY	057	840	871	871	0.4	76	304	325	328	0.7	2.68	237	248	0.5
52651	STOCKPORT	177	519	527	531	0.2	68	214	223	227	0.4	2.36	152	155	0.2
52653	WAPELLO	115	3897	3788	3729	-0.3	40	1485	1458	1435	-0.2	2.55	1073	1034	-0.4
52654	WAYLAND	087	1707	1661	1635	-0.3	40	640	637	630	-0.1	2.54	488	478	-0.2
52655	WEST BURLINGTON	057	4616	4503	4432	-0.3	40	1983	1987	1973	0.0	2.22	1317	1284	-0.3
52656	WEST POINT	111	2459	2436	2407	-0.1	51	966	994	991	0.3	2.40	692	695	0.0
52657	SAINT PAUL	111	69	69	69	0.0	58	34	36	36	0.6	1.92	26	26	0.0
52658	WEVER	111	1272	1198	1152	-0.6	20	484	467	453	-0.4	2.55	390	371	-0.5
52659	WINFIELD	087	1679	1736	1732	0.4	76	646	681	683	0.6	2.48	444	458	0.3
52660	YARMOUTH	057	306	330	334	0.8	87	114	125	128	1.0	2.64	88	95	0.8
52701	ANDOVER	045	32	31	31	-0.3	40	11	11	11	0.0	2.82	9	9	0.0
52720	ATALISSA	139	1003	1041	1060	0.4	76	383	413	424	0.8	2.47	277	291	0.5
52721	BENNETT	031	869	853	840	-0.2	46	342	346	342	0.1	2.47	269	268	0.0
52722	BETTENDORF	163	33247	35091	35931	0.6	83	13228	14194	14590	0.8	2.45	9278	9753	0.5
52726	BLUE GRASS	163	4052	4181	4249	0.3	72	1447	1545	1586	0.7	2.70	1177	1236	0.5
52727	BRYANT	045	439	460	462	0.5	79	155	167	169	0.8	2.75	117	123	0.5
52728	BUFFALO	163	1208	1273	1307	0.6	83	450	491	510	0.9	2.59	376	404	0.8
52729	CALAMUS	045	802	885	899	1.1	91	324	368	378	1.4	2.40	242	270	1.2
52730	CAMANCHE	045	4748	4725	4696	-0.1	51	2004	2079	2085	0.4	2.27	1396	1411	0.1
52731	CHARLOTTE	045	1067	1032	1020	-0.4	32	345	346	345	0.0	2.70	265	261	-0.2
52732	CLINTON	045	29663	28535	28029	-0.4	32	12114	11996	11870	-0.1	2.31	7908	7626	-0.4
52738	COLUMBUS JUNCTION	115	4195	4154	4108	-0.1	51	1516	1512	1496	0.0	2.71	1117	1093	-0.2
52739	CONESVILLE	139	653	666	677	0.2	68	224	237	243	0.6	2.67	170	177	0.4
52742	DE WITT	045	7457	7550	7522	0.1	63	2901	3012	3020	0.4	2.48	2043	2070	0.1
52745	DIXON	163	701	708	708	0.1	63	267	278	281	0.4	2.55	210	215	0.3
52746	DONAHUE	163	1007	1058	1082	0.5	79	354	384	396	0.9	2.74	289	309	0.7
52747	DURANT	031	2077	2187	2225	0.6	83	812	875	896	0.8	2.49	595	630	0.6
52748	ELDRIDGE	163	7116	8502	9082	1.9	96	2526	3123	3369	2.3	2.72	1982	2406	2.1
52749	FRUITLAND	139	598	674	706	1.3	93	205	238	251	1.6	2.83	164	187	1.4
52750	GOOSE LAKE	045	628	647	648	0.3	72	233	249	251	0.7	2.60	181	189	0.5
52751	GRAND MOUND	045	1028	1076	1079	0.5	79	380	409	413	0.8	2.63	305	323	0.6
52753	LE CLAIRE	163	4232	4584	4731	0.9	89	1641	1833	1910	1.2	2.50	1252	1339	0.7
52754	LETTS	139	1729	1713	1710	-0.1	51	633	647	650	0.2	2.60	481	482	0.0
52755	LONE TREE	103	1834	1908	1974	0.4	76	702	758	794	0.8	2.47	512	533	0.4
52756	LONG GROVE	163	2116	2252	2320	0.7	85	758	833	866	1.0	2.68	626	677	0.9
52760	MOSCOW	139	656	730	760	1.2	93	246	282	296	1.5	2.59	187	210	1.3
52761	MUSCATINE	139	30263	31124	31452	0.3	72	11635	12317	12517	0.6	2.49	8191	8495	0.4
52765	NEW LIBERTY	163	467	463	460	-0.1	51	165	169	169	0.3	2.74	130	131	0.1
52766	NICHOLS	139	875	905	906	0.4	76	343	362	365	0.6	2.50	255	263	0.3
52768	PRINCETON	163	1458	1451	1442	-0.1	51	544	557	559	0.3	2.61	412	412	0.0
52769	STOCKTON	139	757	785	798	0.4	76	282	304	312	0.8	2.58	225	238	0.6
52772	TIPTON	031	4936	4906	4880	-0.1	51	1997	2029	2030	0.2	2.38	1391	1386	0.0
52773	WALCOTT	163	2280	2315	2319	0.2	68	897	941	953	0.5	2.46	656	672	0.3
52774	WELTON	045	59	61	62	0.4	76	19	20	21	0.6	3.05	16	16	0.0
52776	WEST LIBERTY	139	4261	4580	4714	0.8	87	1486	1630	1684	1.0	2.78	1076	1153	0.8
52777	WHEATLAND	045	1434	1468	1465	0.3	72	551	577	579	0.5	2.47	398	407	0.2
52778	WILTON	031	3763	4041	4162	0.8	87	1441	1592	1652	1.1	2.53	1051	1134	0.8
52801	DAVENPORT	163	1048	1067	1070	0.2	68	587	602	606	0.3	1.36	92	86	-0.7
52802	DAVENPORT	163	11897	11627	11524	-0.2	46	4407	4357	4341	-0.1	2.58	2775	2658	-0.5
52803	DAVENPORT	163	24400	23525	23199	-0.4	32	9785	9604	9537	-0.2	2.30	5558	5259	-0.6
52804	DAVENPORT	163	24934	25284	25507	0.2	68	9845	10194	10348	0.4	2.43	6657	6724	0.1
52806	DAVENPORT	163	27142	28729	29493	0.6	83	10400	11325	11732	0.9	2.50	7407	7841	0.6
52807	DAVENPORT	163	11406	12430	12884	0.9	89	5043	5646	5896	1.2	2.19	3025	3257	0.8
	IOWA					0.4					0.7	2.40			0.4
	UNITED STATES					1.0					1.1	2.59			0.9

POPULATION COMPOSITION

ZIP CODE # POST OFFICE NAME	RACE (%) White 2000	White 2009	Black 2000	Black 2009	Asian/Pacific 2000	Asian/Pacific 2009	% Hispanic Origin 2000	% Hispanic Origin 2009	2009 AGE DISTRIBUTION (%) 0-4	5-9	10-14	15-19	20-24	25-44	45-64	65-84	85+	18+	MEDIAN AGE 2009	% 2009 Males	% 2009 Females
52641 MOUNT PLEASANT	92.5	92.0	2.3	2.3	2.9	3.3	1.5	1.5	5.9	5.9	5.9	7.3	7.8	27.6	25.4	11.2	3.0	78.2	37.7	52.2	47.8
52644 MOUNT UNION	98.2	98.2	0.2	0.2	0.4	0.4	0.7	0.7	6.2	6.8	7.5	7.0	4.6	25.6	30.6	10.4	1.3	74.9	40.4	51.3	48.7
52645 NEW LONDON	98.4	98.3	0.2	0.2	0.4	0.5	0.6	0.7	6.0	6.3	6.7	6.5	5.3	26.2	28.3	11.9	2.7	76.9	40.3	49.2	50.8
52646 OAKVILLE	99.0	98.9	0.2	0.3	0.4	0.5	0.6	0.9	7.8	8.1	8.7	7.2	4.8	25.2	24.8	11.5	1.8	70.8	37.1	51.0	49.0
52647 OLDS	97.8	97.7	0.4	0.5	0.4	0.5	1.8	2.3	7.3	7.3	7.3	6.9	3.7	23.4	27.5	13.8	2.8	72.9	40.9	49.1	50.9
52649 SALEM	98.3	98.2	0.1	0.1	0.5	0.7	0.4	0.4	6.2	6.8	6.8	6.0	4.9	22.4	31.9	13.1	2.0	76.5	42.7	49.9	50.1
52650 SPERRY	99.2	98.7	0.0	0.0	0.1	0.2	0.4	0.6	6.0	6.5	7.2	7.1	4.5	23.2	32.3	11.8	1.4	75.8	41.4	51.4	48.6
52651 STOCKPORT	97.7	97.0	0.0	0.0	0.4	0.4	1.3	2.1	5.3	5.7	6.5	6.5	4.0	24.9	30.9	14.0	2.3	78.4	42.8	51.6	48.4
52653 WAPELLO	96.6	95.0	0.2	0.2	0.2	0.3	7.0	10.8	7.4	7.1	7.0	6.5	6.0	26.6	25.2	11.6	2.6	74.5	36.9	49.3	50.7
52654 WAYLAND	98.3	98.1	0.0	0.0	0.4	0.5	0.9	1.0	5.5	6.1	6.3	6.9	4.7	23.8	28.9	14.2	3.6	77.2	42.2	48.7	51.3
52655 WEST BURLINGTON	95.4	93.9	2.2	2.8	0.8	1.2	2.4	3.5	5.2	5.4	6.1	6.4	5.4	23.9	30.5	14.6	2.6	79.6	43.2	49.5	50.5
52656 WEST POINT	99.5	99.3	0.0	0.0	0.0	0.1	0.6	0.9	5.5	6.0	6.3	6.6	4.6	22.7	31.4	13.4	3.5	77.7	43.8	48.0	52.0
52657 SAINT PAUL	100.0	100.0	0.0	0.0	0.0	0.0	0.0	0.0	8.7	8.7	8.7	5.8	2.9	24.6	24.6	13.0	2.9	68.1	38.1	49.3	50.7
52658 WEVER	98.4	97.8	0.2	0.3	0.2	0.3	1.2	1.8	5.4	6.0	6.6	7.0	4.6	21.7	33.3	13.4	1.9	77.7	44.0	49.0	51.0
52659 WINFIELD	98.0	97.8	0.4	0.3	0.3	0.3	1.7	1.9	6.6	6.6	6.6	7.1	5.8	22.7	27.4	13.0	4.1	75.0	40.9	49.4	50.6
52660 YARMOUTH	98.4	97.9	0.3	0.3	0.7	1.2	0.3	0.6	6.1	6.7	7.3	7.3	3.9	21.5	30.6	14.5	2.1	75.2	42.9	50.6	49.4
52701 ANDOVER	100.0	100.0	0.0	0.0	0.0	0.0	0.0	0.0	6.5	6.5	6.5	6.5	6.5	25.8	29.0	12.9	0.0	74.2	38.8	48.4	51.6
52720 ATALISSA	97.9	97.0	0.6	0.9	0.2	0.4	2.6	3.9	6.3	6.7	6.7	6.1	4.6	24.8	31.6	11.5	1.5	76.4	41.7	51.9	48.1
52721 BENNETT	98.8	98.6	0.0	0.0	0.1	0.2	1.0	1.5	6.0	6.3	6.7	6.7	4.1	24.6	29.0	14.3	2.3	76.8	42.2	51.5	48.5
52722 BETTENDORF	95.2	93.2	1.5	1.9	1.4	2.4	2.4	3.6	5.9	6.3	7.1	7.2	5.5	23.8	31.2	11.1	1.9	76.7	41.0	48.9	51.1
52726 BLUE GRASS	97.7	96.9	0.5	0.6	0.2	0.4	1.9	3.0	5.5	6.1	6.5	6.8	4.8	24.8	32.6	12.1	1.0	77.7	42.3	50.4	49.6
52727 BRYANT	99.1	99.1	0.0	0.0	0.0	0.0	0.9	1.3	7.2	7.6	8.0	7.6	5.4	23.9	28.0	10.9	1.3	72.6	38.0	51.7	48.3
52728 BUFFALO	97.5	96.6	0.7	0.9	0.2	0.3	2.3	3.6	5.3	5.7	6.5	6.9	4.9	24.0	34.5	11.2	0.9	78.2	42.8	50.6	49.4
52729 CALAMUS	99.0	98.6	0.0	0.0	0.0	0.0	0.9	1.4	5.9	6.2	6.6	7.0	5.1	25.6	29.7	12.0	1.9	77.2	41.1	49.3	50.7
52730 CAMANCHE	98.0	97.5	0.5	0.6	0.2	0.3	0.6	1.0	5.6	5.5	5.7	6.0	5.1	24.2	32.4	13.7	1.7	79.7	43.3	49.5	50.5
52731 CHARLOTTE	98.3	98.0	0.4	0.5	0.4	0.5	1.1	1.6	5.9	6.7	6.6	6.7	5.1	25.2	29.2	13.5	1.2	76.8	41.1	51.3	48.7
52732 CLINTON	94.1	92.5	3.0	3.8	0.8	1.1	1.6	2.3	6.5	6.4	6.3	6.7	6.2	23.7	27.5	13.7	3.1	76.8	40.2	48.2	51.8
52738 COLUMBUS JUNCTION	88.4	84.3	0.4	0.4	0.1	0.2	25.4	33.7	7.3	7.6	8.1	7.6	5.8	25.8	24.7	10.9	2.2	71.9	36.0	50.2	49.8
52739 CONESVILLE	93.3	89.9	0.2	0.3	0.3	0.3	15.3	22.8	5.4	6.3	7.1	7.1	4.4	23.0	29.3	13.1	4.5	76.4	42.7	50.0	50.0
52742 DE WITT	98.4	97.9	0.2	0.2	0.5	0.7	0.9	1.3	6.8	6.7	6.9	7.1	6.9	23.8	27.2	12.0	2.7	75.0	38.9	48.8	51.2
52745 DIXON	98.4	98.0	0.4	0.6	0.1	0.1	0.4	0.8	5.9	6.5	7.2	6.6	4.4	22.7	33.6	11.7	1.3	76.1	42.6	51.4	48.6
52746 DONAHUE	98.9	98.5	0.3	0.4	0.0	0.1	0.4	0.6	5.5	6.9	8.4	7.3	3.7	24.1	33.1	9.9	1.1	74.4	41.2	51.8	48.2
52747 DURANT	98.8	98.3	0.1	0.2	0.2	0.3	0.9	1.4	6.5	6.8	6.8	6.9	5.4	25.5	27.7	12.3	2.1	75.4	38.9	49.2	50.8
52748 ELDRIDGE	98.0	97.4	0.4	0.5	0.3	0.5	1.3	2.1	7.2	7.5	7.8	6.1	27.1	28.0	8.3	0.8	73.3	35.8	49.6	50.4	
52749 FRUITLAND	95.8	93.3	0.0	0.0	0.5	0.9	4.9	7.6	5.9	6.4	6.8	7.0	5.0	26.9	31.8	9.6	0.6	76.4	40.1	50.0	50.0
52750 GOOSE LAKE	98.9	98.6	0.0	0.0	0.0	0.0	1.1	1.7	6.3	7.4	8.0	8.3	5.4	23.0	29.7	10.4	1.4	72.5	39.1	51.9	48.1
52751 GRAND MOUND	98.2	97.5	0.2	0.2	0.2	0.5	0.7	1.0	7.2	7.6	7.6	6.5	5.0	23.7	29.1	11.7	1.5	73.4	39.9	50.0	50.0
52753 LE CLAIRE	97.6	96.5	0.2	0.3	0.5	0.9	2.0	3.2	5.8	6.4	6.7	6.2	4.8	24.8	32.1	12.1	1.2	77.3	41.9	49.4	50.6
52754 LETTS	94.3	91.6	0.3	0.4	0.4	0.6	10.7	16.1	6.3	6.7	7.0	6.9	5.3	23.7	29.4	11.9	2.7	75.6	40.3	49.5	50.5
52755 LONE TREE	98.5	98.0	0.5	0.7	0.1	0.2	0.9	1.3	7.2	7.3	7.5	6.8	4.9	25.2	27.1	11.4	2.6	73.5	39.4	50.7	49.3
52756 LONG GROVE	99.0	98.6	0.2	0.3	0.1	0.3	0.5	0.8	6.0	7.1	8.1	7.0	4.2	24.0	32.8	9.9	0.9	74.2	40.7	51.5	48.5
52760 MOSCOW	97.4	96.4	0.2	0.3	0.5	0.7	1.4	2.2	5.1	5.8	6.3	6.6	4.7	22.9	33.8	13.6	1.4	78.8	44.0	50.7	49.3
52761 MUSCATINE	91.9	88.7	0.9	1.0	0.6	0.9	10.5	15.2	7.0	6.9	6.8	6.9	5.8	26.1	27.7	11.0	1.9	75.1	37.7	49.4	50.6
52765 NEW LIBERTY	98.5	98.5	0.4	0.4	0.2	0.2	0.4	0.9	6.3	6.9	6.9	6.7	4.5	22.2	32.0	13.0	1.5	76.0	42.3	50.5	49.5
52766 NICHOLS	89.2	84.4	0.7	0.7	1.9	2.8	13.6	20.1	5.7	6.3	7.0	7.1	4.5	26.7	30.7	10.5	1.4	76.6	40.0	52.2	47.8
52768 PRINCETON	98.4	97.7	0.1	0.2	0.1	0.3	1.0	1.5	6.0	6.3	6.8	7.1	5.2	22.9	32.9	11.7	1.2	76.7	42.3	51.9	48.1
52769 STOCKTON	99.2	99.1	0.3	0.3	0.1	0.3	0.8	1.1	5.2	8.2	7.4	6.5	4.8	23.9	32.2	10.7	1.0	74.6	40.8	50.7	49.3
52772 TIPTON	98.7	98.4	0.3	0.3	0.3	0.5	0.8	1.2	5.9	6.2	6.4	6.3	4.7	24.6	29.4	13.5	3.0	77.6	42.1	50.8	49.2
52773 WALCOTT	97.7	96.7	0.4	0.5	0.4	0.7	1.0	1.6	6.7	6.8	7.3	7.0	4.8	26.6	28.6	10.7	1.6	74.9	39.6	49.2	50.8
52774 WELTON	98.3	98.4	0.0	0.0	0.0	0.0	0.0	0.0	8.2	8.2	6.6	6.6	6.6	24.6	26.2	11.5	1.6	70.5	36.9	47.5	52.5
52776 WEST LIBERTY	73.9	65.5	0.3	0.3	3.0	3.6	31.9	42.2	7.4	7.4	7.1	7.2	6.5	28.7	24.4	9.2	2.2	73.5	34.7	49.8	50.2
52777 WHEATLAND	98.4	98.0	0.2	0.3	0.1	0.1	0.6	0.9	6.3	6.5	6.8	7.4	5.2	21.4	28.6	13.4	4.5	75.5	42.0	49.2	50.8
52778 WILTON	97.7	96.7	0.2	0.2	0.4	0.6	2.1	3.3	7.0	6.7	6.6	7.1	6.6	26.9	26.7	10.5	2.0	75.4	36.8	48.9	51.1
52801 DAVENPORT	73.5	67.5	20.7	25.2	0.6	0.7	5.3	7.8	2.2	2.2	1.7	5.2	6.8	30.7	30.0	17.6	3.4	92.4	45.6	61.3	38.7
52802 DAVENPORT	82.3	76.9	6.8	8.1	1.7	2.5	10.5	15.3	7.6	6.9	6.5	7.5	8.2	27.9	23.6	9.7	2.0	74.5	34.3	50.6	49.4
52803 DAVENPORT	79.2	74.7	13.9	16.2	1.7	2.5	5.3	7.7	7.4	7.0	6.5	7.9	9.6	28.3	22.8	8.6	1.8	75.0	33.0	49.0	51.0
52804 DAVENPORT	87.1	82.9	6.0	7.4	2.3	3.6	5.2	7.7	6.8	6.6	6.5	6.5	6.1	26.6	25.8	12.5	2.6	76.1	38.1	48.5	51.5
52806 DAVENPORT	85.0	80.6	9.0	11.2	2.0	3.3	3.9	5.9	8.1	7.3	6.9	6.6	6.3	28.4	24.6	9.8	2.0	73.8	35.1	47.9	52.1
52807 DAVENPORT	88.0	83.9	6.5	8.3	2.1	3.6	2.9	4.3	6.9	6.1	6.2	6.7	9.5	25.7	28.0	9.6	1.3	76.6	35.3	49.1	50.9
IOWA	93.9	91.9	2.1	2.5	1.3	2.1	2.8	4.1	6.5	6.4	6.5	7.3	7.1	25.2	26.5	11.9	2.6	76.5	38.1	49.3	50.7
UNITED STATES	75.1	72.0	12.3	12.7	3.8	4.6	12.5	15.7	6.8	6.7	6.6	7.1	6.9	27.0	26.0	10.9	1.9	75.7	36.9	49.2	50.8

ZIP CODE #	POST OFFICE NAME	2009 Per Capita Income	2009 HH Income Base	2009 HOUSEHOLD INCOME DISTRIBUTION (%)					MEDIAN HOUSEHOLD INCOME				2009 Home Value Base	2009 HOME VALUE DISTRIBUTION (%)					2009 Median Home Value
				Less than $25,000	$25,000 to $49,999	$50,000 to $99,999	$100,000 to $149,999	$150,000 or More	2009	2014	2009 National Centile	2009 State Centile		Less than $50,000	$50,000 to $89,999	$90,000 to $174,999	$175,000 to $399,999	$400,000 or More	
52641	MOUNT PLEASANT	22440	4543	24.6	26.3	37.5	8.2	3.3	49021	51251	59	66	3202	16.4	18.9	47.2	16.1	1.5	109542
52644	MOUNT UNION	23976	181	16.0	23.8	51.4	6.6	2.2	58116	56636	75	90	148	12.2	25.0	43.2	19.6	0.0	108871
52645	NEW LONDON	23786	1248	18.4	28.7	43.3	7.1	2.6	52771	53630	68	80	987	18.3	31.0	39.9	10.4	0.3	91083
52646	OAKVILLE	20937	308	22.1	32.8	38.3	3.9	2.9	45959	46987	51	50	238	41.2	26.5	26.1	5.5	0.8	65714
52647	OLDS	24436	93	17.2	31.2	44.1	6.5	1.1	51254	52177	64	75	71	18.3	11.3	50.7	16.9	2.8	116406
52649	SALEM	21147	437	25.9	31.4	37.5	3.4	1.8	46190	47934	52	52	354	24.3	24.9	33.6	15.5	1.7	91429
52650	SPERRY	24748	325	12.3	31.4	42.2	10.2	4.0	57592	58093	75	89	278	11.2	17.3	44.6	23.4	3.6	123000
52651	STOCKPORT	17790	223	26.0	40.8	29.6	3.6	0.0	37844	39054	26	8	185	31.4	26.5	29.7	9.2	3.2	72778
52653	WAPELLO	21369	1458	21.3	30.2	40.1	6.6	1.8	48469	49159	58	63	1139	22.2	28.4	39.2	9.1	1.1	89369
52654	WAYLAND	19128	637	24.3	32.2	38.3	3.8	1.4	44513	49447	47	41	485	14.8	31.3	40.4	10.3	3.1	95441
52655	WEST BURLINGTON	26367	1987	21.0	26.9	41.2	8.0	2.9	51291	52602	64	75	1466	20.7	25.2	43.2	9.3	1.4	96277
52656	WEST POINT	27718	994	16.8	26.5	43.9	9.2	3.7	55921	55704	73	87	818	10.4	19.3	52.1	17.5	0.7	114033
52657	SAINT PAUL	30409	36	19.4	25.0	47.2	5.6	2.8	54495	51316	70	85	28	7.1	25.0	60.7	7.1	0.0	108333
52658	WEVER	26886	467	16.9	28.1	43.9	6.9	4.3	54412	54636	70	85	409	12.2	20.5	46.0	20.5	0.7	111821
52659	WINFIELD	21571	681	26.1	26.7	38.6	6.9	1.6	46297	50369	52	52	508	20.1	31.1	41.1	6.7	1.0	88696
52660	YARMOUTH	21889	125	15.2	35.2	38.4	8.8	2.4	49778	51625	61	69	99	9.1	35.4	40.4	12.1	3.0	97857
52701	ANDOVER	14516	11	27.3	45.5	27.3	0.0	0.0	37303	37303	24	7	9	0.0	11.1	66.7	22.2	0.0	145833
52720	ATALISSA	25001	413	18.4	29.1	41.2	6.8	4.6	51506	51963	65	76	328	12.8	23.8	42.4	19.2	1.8	113636
52721	BENNETT	23318	346	16.5	27.2	48.3	6.6	1.4	54118	54374	70	84	270	7.8	21.9	44.4	18.5	7.4	118750
52722	BETTENDORF	34615	14194	13.4	17.9	41.9	15.7	11.0	69006	69694	86	98	11132	3.6	8.8	48.3	33.3	5.9	144797
52726	BLUE GRASS	26644	1545	13.8	20.1	50.4	10.4	5.4	63422	63574	82	95	1335	5.8	13.5	47.5	30.0	3.2	133811
52727	BRYANT	19594	167	15.6	30.5	47.3	6.0	0.6	51788	52556	65	77	134	5.2	23.1	52.2	12.7	6.7	126042
52728	BUFFALO	30666	491	12.8	16.9	49.1	13.4	7.7	69239	68538	86	98	437	5.5	13.3	37.1	39.8	4.3	157770
52729	CALAMUS	22407	368	16.8	29.6	46.7	6.3	0.5	51520	52477	65	76	300	15.7	26.3	46.7	7.7	3.7	103438
52730	CAMANCHE	25613	2079	21.2	25.3	42.2	9.0	2.3	53173	54851	68	81	1627	19.4	20.0	50.1	10.1	0.5	103624
52731	CHARLOTTE	18544	346	22.5	32.4	37.3	6.6	1.2	46334	49664	52	53	262	13.0	21.8	40.5	19.1	5.7	115476
52732	CLINTON	22651	11996	26.2	29.5	36.1	6.0	2.3	45116	47833	49	45	8431	19.4	35.0	35.6	8.7	1.2	85129
52738	COLUMBUS JUNCTION	21529	1512	19.0	30.7	39.0	8.5	2.7	50239	51121	62	70	1128	18.3	28.2	43.7	8.7	1.2	95263
52739	CONESVILLE	22670	237	23.6	21.5	40.5	10.1	4.2	53079	53197	68	81	197	12.2	18.8	38.1	24.9	6.1	122845
52742	DE WITT	25718	3012	19.5	21.9	44.6	10.5	3.6	60550	60543	78	93	2224	3.1	15.1	58.3	22.4	1.2	127590
52745	DIXON	23891	278	20.9	20.9	47.1	9.0	2.2	55334	57760	72	87	219	13.2	13.7	39.7	27.4	5.9	136250
52746	DONAHUE	25639	384	15.1	19.8	49.2	11.7	4.2	61686	62657	80	94	339	8.0	11.2	42.2	36.0	2.7	149734
52747	DURANT	24541	875	17.4	26.1	43.9	10.2	2.5	55124	54947	71	86	666	4.2	14.0	56.2	24.0	1.7	125952
52748	ELDRIDGE	26375	3123	10.6	23.7	47.6	13.6	4.5	64206	64369	83	96	2353	5.7	4.5	54.3	34.7	0.7	148260
52749	FRUITLAND	22466	238	16.4	19.3	54.2	8.4	1.7	62697	60889	81	95	212	11.8	11.3	55.7	19.3	1.9	130682
52750	GOOSE LAKE	21089	249	16.9	29.7	45.8	6.4	1.2	51712	52866	65	76	199	6.0	19.6	52.3	14.1	8.0	127016
52751	GRAND MOUND	21172	409	18.6	28.6	45.0	6.8	1.0	51803	52774	66	77	338	11.8	18.6	50.0	17.2	2.4	115064
52753	LE CLAIRE	27823	1833	12.9	26.6	43.4	12.4	4.6	58654	60608	76	90	1516	2.6	14.8	53.4	24.8	4.4	126941
52754	LETTS	20976	647	21.2	32.3	36.9	7.4	2.2	47047	48619	54	57	527	16.3	25.0	38.1	17.6	2.8	105417
52755	LONE TREE	25120	758	19.3	19.7	52.0	6.7	2.4	57624	58331	75	89	553	9.4	22.1	41.6	24.4	2.5	124500
52756	LONG GROVE	27372	833	15.2	18.6	51.1	9.6	5.4	62225	62889	80	94	746	11.5	13.8	40.1	31.8	2.8	138529
52760	MOSCOW	20192	282	20.9	23.8	51.1	3.9	0.4	52709	52454	67	80	226	7.5	18.6	56.6	16.4	0.9	116667
52761	MUSCATINE	25861	12317	20.7	26.0	38.1	10.6	4.7	53642	54410	69	83	9266	15.6	21.1	40.7	20.6	2.1	109660
52765	NEW LIBERTY	20449	169	24.3	21.3	45.0	7.1	2.4	54227	56679	70	84	122	4.1	15.6	36.9	32.8	10.7	155000
52766	NICHOLS	21767	362	20.2	29.3	42.5	6.4	1.7	50281	51402	62	71	295	14.6	25.1	43.1	13.9	3.4	104009
52768	PRINCETON	22919	557	17.1	29.1	42.7	9.3	1.8	53462	56392	69	82	470	16.2	15.1	41.1	25.5	2.1	122152
52769	STOCKTON	21694	304	21.1	29.3	41.4	5.6	2.6	49734	50862	60	68	226	8.8	16.8	35.0	31.4	8.0	139583
52772	TIPTON	22479	2029	21.0	31.8	39.6	6.1	1.4	47873	49967	56	61	1534	12.3	13.8	51.8	18.7	3.4	120872
52773	WALCOTT	23679	941	17.9	25.6	47.6	7.2	1.7	53586	55834	69	83	743	21.5	12.4	49.1	15.3	1.6	113845
52774	WELTON	16475	20	20.0	30.0	45.0	5.0	0.0	50000	50947	61	70	17	5.9	11.8	58.8	23.5	0.0	122500
52776	WEST LIBERTY	21507	1630	15.8	28.3	46.3	7.3	2.3	55399	56485	72	87	1154	6.8	15.9	57.8	17.2	2.3	119218
52777	WHEATLAND	19080	577	24.6	35.9	33.3	6.1	0.2	43285	45936	43	32	448	16.1	32.1	38.2	12.9	0.7	92581
52778	WILTON	24185	1592	15.1	26.1	48.2	8.6	1.9	58662	59038	76	90	1222	13.8	16.5	56.4	12.7	0.6	112253
52801	DAVENPORT	15620	602	74.6	15.3	7.0	3.0	0.2	13596	13838	1	0	17	29.4	58.8	11.8	0.0	0.0	58750
52802	DAVENPORT	16983	4357	29.5	35.6	31.0	2.7	1.1	37838	39321	26	8	2776	31.2	54.2	12.8	1.5	0.4	60605
52803	DAVENPORT	24380	9604	26.2	24.5	38.2	7.7	3.5	48724	52302	58	65	5785	8.0	29.8	50.5	10.8	0.9	104290
52804	DAVENPORT	24209	10194	20.6	26.7	42.4	7.3	3.0	51976	54719	66	77	7653	11.5	29.5	52.9	5.7	0.4	99291
52806	DAVENPORT	24803	11325	18.8	25.7	42.0	10.4	3.1	55074	58556	71	86	7974	10.3	19.8	56.4	13.0	0.5	112010
52807	DAVENPORT	33922	5646	21.5	23.6	32.4	12.5	10.0	55472	57999	72	87	3122	0.6	6.3	36.5	47.8	8.7	195020
	IOWA	25379		21.1	28.2	37.9	8.6	4.3	50616	52941				14.7	22.5	41.6	18.6	2.6	110128
	UNITED STATES	27277		20.9	24.4	35.3	11.7	7.6	54719	56938				9.3	13.1	31.6	32.6	13.5	162279

ZIP CODE #	POST OFFICE NAME	FINANCIAL SERVICES: Auto Loan	Home Loan	Invest-ments	Retire-ment Plans	THE HOME: Home Improvements: Home Repair	Lawn & Garden	Furnishings: Comput-ers & Hard-ware-Personal	Major Appli-ances	TV, Radio, Sound Equip-ment	Furni-ture	ENTERTAINMENT: Dine out/ Carry out	Sports Equip-ment	Fees & Tickets	Toys & Games	Travel	Cable TV	PERSONAL: Apparel & Services	Auto Repairs	Health Insur-ance	Pets & Supplies
52641	MOUNT PLEASANT	84	78	75	78	76	86	80	82	82	76	81	64	75	83	77	84	56	82	87	98
52644	MOUNT UNION	97	82	93	84	84	104	83	97	86	73	85	75	72	87	83	92	57	89	100	114
52645	NEW LONDON	88	82	77	85	82	94	82	89	84	75	82	68	77	85	81	88	56	84	93	104
52646	OAKVILLE	94	71	79	70	71	91	73	84	80	70	78	65	60	83	68	86	53	79	88	102
52647	OLDS	102	70	112	70	74	108	78	97	81	63	80	80	57	80	78	89	52	91	103	120
52649	SALEM	80	69	73	72	71	85	69	79	72	62	71	61	62	73	69	77	48	74	82	93
52650	SPERRY	96	100	91	104	99	105	93	99	93	90	92	77	94	95	96	95	64	94	100	116
52651	STOCKPORT	75	52	83	52	54	79	57	71	60	47	59	59	42	59	57	65	38	67	75	88
52653	WAPELLO	85	76	70	77	73	87	77	80	80	73	79	63	72	82	73	84	54	79	87	97
52654	WAYLAND	86	61	93	62	64	91	67	82	70	55	69	67	51	69	67	76	45	77	87	101
52655	WEST BURLINGTON	86	85	78	86	83	94	82	87	85	78	84	66	81	86	82	89	58	84	94	103
52656	WEST POINT	95	99	99	99	99	110	91	101	95	88	94	75	94	94	97	99	65	96	108	118
52657	SAINT PAUL	104	72	114	72	75	110	80	99	83	64	82	82	58	81	79	90	53	92	104	122
52658	WEVER	107	97	96	101	99	114	96	108	99	87	97	82	88	101	96	104	66	100	111	126
52659	WINFIELD	93	66	96	65	69	97	72	90	79	63	77	69	57	78	71	87	51	84	97	107
52660	YARMOUTH	101	73	107	74	76	107	79	97	82	66	81	79	61	81	79	89	53	90	102	118
52701	ANDOVER	73	50	80	50	53	77	56	69	58	45	57	57	41	57	56	63	37	65	73	85
52720	ATALISSA	94	90	86	93	91	102	87	96	89	81	88	73	83	91	88	93	60	90	98	112
52721	BENNETT	103	71	113	71	74	108	79	98	82	64	81	81	58	80	78	89	52	91	103	120
52722	BETTENDORF	115	128	122	131	128	123	121	120	118	123	119	93	129	119	125	117	85	119	118	140
52726	BLUE GRASS	107	107	101	110	106	116	101	110	101	96	101	85	99	103	103	104	69	103	111	128
52727	BRYANT	87	74	83	76	76	93	75	86	77	66	76	67	65	78	75	82	51	80	90	102
52728	BUFFALO	111	124	108	128	121	123	111	116	110	111	110	91	118	113	117	110	77	112	115	137
52729	CALAMUS	84	76	76	79	77	90	75	85	77	67	76	65	69	79	75	82	52	78	88	99
52730	CAMANCHE	85	84	79	84	82	92	80	86	83	77	83	64	79	84	81	87	57	83	93	101
52731	CHARLOTTE	92	64	100	63	66	97	70	87	73	57	72	72	52	72	70	80	47	81	92	107
52732	CLINTON	78	70	70	71	69	81	74	76	78	70	76	58	69	77	71	82	52	77	85	91
52738	COLUMBUS JUNCTION	93	80	85	79	78	93	83	89	84	78	84	70	74	85	80	87	57	87	92	106
52739	CONESVILLE	98	86	91	89	88	105	86	98	89	77	87	75	77	90	86	94	59	91	102	115
52742	DE WITT	94	88	85	90	88	98	91	93	93	86	92	71	87	93	89	96	63	93	100	111
52745	DIXON	94	88	96	90	87	101	84	94	85	79	85	75	80	86	87	88	58	89	95	113
52746	DONAHUE	98	110	95	114	107	108	99	103	97	99	98	80	105	100	104	97	68	99	102	121
52747	DURANT	93	86	82	88	85	99	86	92	88	79	87	72	81	90	85	92	59	88	98	110
52748	ELDRIDGE	101	111	97	111	107	104	102	103	100	103	101	80	106	102	105	99	71	100	100	120
52749	FRUITLAND	96	96	84	96	94	97	89	93	90	91	90	70	89	93	89	92	62	90	93	110
52750	GOOSE LAKE	90	73	89	75	76	96	76	89	78	66	77	70	64	79	75	84	52	82	93	106
52751	GRAND MOUND	88	77	83	80	79	95	77	89	80	69	78	68	69	81	77	85	53	82	92	104
52753	LE CLAIRE	98	108	95	110	105	104	98	100	96	100	97	77	104	99	102	96	68	97	99	118
52754	LETTS	86	77	77	79	78	91	76	86	79	69	78	65	69	81	75	84	53	80	89	101
52755	LONE TREE	88	93	78	96	88	95	89	89	89	86	88	70	91	91	89	90	61	88	94	107
52756	LONG GROVE	105	113	100	117	111	115	103	109	102	101	103	85	107	105	108	104	71	104	109	128
52760	MOSCOW	81	74	73	77	75	87	73	82	75	66	74	62	67	76	73	79	50	76	85	95
52761	MUSCATINE	93	92	82	93	89	97	92	92	94	89	93	71	91	95	90	96	64	92	98	110
52765	NEW LIBERTY	100	69	110	69	72	106	77	95	80	62	79	79	56	78	76	87	51	89	100	117
52766	NICHOLS	83	78	76	81	79	89	76	84	78	70	76	64	72	79	77	81	52	78	86	98
52768	PRINCETON	90	87	83	90	87	97	83	92	85	78	84	70	80	86	85	88	58	86	94	107
52769	STOCKTON	100	69	110	69	72	106	77	95	80	62	79	79	56	78	76	87	51	89	100	117
52772	TIPTON	83	76	80	76	76	89	74	83	77	70	76	62	69	77	74	81	52	78	87	97
52773	WALCOTT	91	86	79	85	84	90	81	87	83	82	83	65	78	86	80	85	57	83	87	103
52774	WELTON	78	71	70	74	72	84	70	79	72	63	71	60	64	73	70	76	48	73	81	92
52776	WEST LIBERTY	87	87	73	86	83	89	86	86	86	83	86	67	84	88	84	87	59	86	90	102
52777	WHEATLAND	82	58	86	57	61	86	64	79	69	55	67	62	49	68	63	76	44	74	85	95
52778	WILTON	88	88	73	89	82	93	87	87	88	82	88	69	86	90	85	91	60	87	95	105
52801	DAVENPORT	26	19	23	22	20	24	32	25	34	28	34	20	28	29	28	36	23	31	35	33
52802	DAVENPORT	66	55	49	56	52	62	64	60	67	59	65	48	57	67	57	70	45	64	67	74
52803	DAVENPORT	81	75	67	78	72	77	84	77	85	80	85	61	81	85	78	86	59	82	83	94
52804	DAVENPORT	82	85	76	85	82	90	83	84	85	79	85	64	85	86	83	88	59	84	92	99
52806	DAVENPORT	91	91	83	89	89	90	88	89	89	89	89	67	88	90	87	90	62	89	91	105
52807	DAVENPORT	107	99	94	103	96	94	109	99	107	109	109	80	106	109	104	105	76	105	99	119
	IOWA	93	84	87	85	83	95	87	91	89	82	88	71	81	90	85	92	61	90	96	108
	UNITED STATES	100	100	100	100	100	100	100	100	100	100	100	100	100	100	100	100	100	100	100	100

POPULATION CHANGE

 66002-66218

ZIP CODE #	POST OFFICE NAME	COUNTY FIPS CODE	POPULATION 2000	POPULATION 2009	POPULATION 2014	2000-2009 ANNUAL RATE % Rate	2000-2009 ANNUAL RATE State Centile	HOUSEHOLDS 2000	HOUSEHOLDS 2009	HOUSEHOLDS 2014	HOUSEHOLDS % Annual Rate 2000-2009	HOUSEHOLDS 2009 Average HH Size	FAMILIES 2000	FAMILIES 2009	FAMILIES % Annual Rate 2000-2009
66002	ATCHISON	005	13366	13086	12902	-0.2	56	4990	4953	4897	-0.1	2.43	3313	3254	-0.2
66006	BALDWIN CITY	045	6157	7723	8509	2.5	96	2076	2698	3007	2.9	2.63	1582	2020	2.7
66007	BASEHOR	103	4073	5268	5793	2.8	97	1481	1944	2155	3.0	2.71	1210	1571	2.9
66008	BENDENA	043	329	350	352	0.7	84	119	128	129	0.8	2.73	93	99	0.7
66010	BLUE MOUND	107	622	737	783	1.9	95	258	309	328	2.0	2.39	181	215	1.9
66012	BONNER SPRINGS	103	9448	10141	10472	0.8	86	3474	3745	3872	0.8	2.70	2622	2810	0.8
66013	BUCYRUS	121	1731	1856	1984	0.8	86	588	633	683	0.8	2.93	505	533	0.6
66014	CENTERVILLE	107	356	386	391	0.9	87	150	165	167	1.0	2.34	112	122	0.9
66015	COLONY	003	712	682	663	-0.5	41	277	268	262	-0.4	2.54	213	205	-0.4
66016	CUMMINGS	005	593	624	628	0.6	82	204	219	221	0.8	2.85	164	174	0.6
66017	DENTON	043	333	302	289	-1.1	17	132	123	118	-0.8	2.46	90	83	-0.9
66018	DE SOTO	091	4924	6320	7067	2.7	97	1756	2285	2575	2.9	2.77	1382	1744	2.5
66020	EASTON	103	1802	1981	2068	1.0	88	636	713	751	1.2	2.72	519	574	1.1
66021	EDGERTON	091	2260	2760	3051	2.2	96	787	983	1097	2.4	2.80	642	782	2.2
66023	EFFINGHAM	005	1310	1327	1321	0.1	68	518	534	534	0.3	2.49	378	384	0.2
66025	EUDORA	045	5782	7341	8168	2.6	97	2142	2792	3129	2.9	2.60	1565	2000	2.7
66026	FONTANA	121	658	631	625	-0.5	41	256	250	249	-0.3	2.52	201	193	-0.4
66027	FORT LEAVENWORTH	103	8940	9448	9629	0.6	82	1545	1638	1695	0.6	3.82	1504	1584	0.6
66030	GARDNER	091	11089	18024	21334	5.4	99	3944	6411	7636	5.4	2.77	2980	4671	5.0
66031	NEW CENTURY	091	161	160	199	-0.1	59	5	5	6	0.0	2.60	4	4	0.0
66032	GARNETT	003	5025	4950	4870	-0.2	56	2034	2020	1989	-0.1	2.39	1351	1326	-0.2
66033	GREELEY	003	844	905	916	0.8	86	322	350	355	0.9	2.58	254	273	0.8
66035	HIGHLAND	043	1294	1245	1215	-0.4	48	444	434	424	-0.2	2.12	262	253	-0.4
66039	KINCAID	003	698	689	675	-0.1	59	268	268	264	0.0	2.57	202	200	-0.1
66040	LACYGNE	107	3171	3274	3328	0.3	74	1256	1316	1345	0.5	2.47	923	956	0.4
66041	LANCASTER	005	810	835	835	0.3	74	304	319	321	0.5	2.62	232	241	0.4
66042	LANE	059	684	748	781	1.0	88	257	286	301	1.2	2.62	203	224	1.1
66043	LANSING	103	8938	10365	11008	1.6	94	2445	2963	3194	2.1	2.79	1905	2291	2.0
66044	LAWRENCE	045	26566	27601	28432	0.4	76	11180	11832	12277	0.6	2.10	4644	4789	0.3
66045	LAWRENCE	045	5855	6250	6474	0.7	84	787	976	1078	2.4	2.35	227	267	1.8
66046	LAWRENCE	045	17642	19060	20029	0.8	86	7120	7828	8285	1.0	2.32	4035	4331	0.8
66047	LAWRENCE	045	16241	19588	21312	2.0	95	6527	8051	8820	2.3	2.41	3726	4446	1.9
66048	LEAVENWORTH	103	31938	34617	36034	0.9	87	12333	13561	14194	1.0	2.45	8292	9008	0.9
66049	LAWRENCE	045	20135	24574	26998	2.2	96	8127	10110	11192	2.4	2.42	4985	6031	2.1
66050	LECOMPTON	045	1793	2084	2257	1.6	94	644	763	829	1.8	2.73	496	578	1.7
66052	LINWOOD	103	1719	1906	2001	1.1	89	636	718	757	1.3	2.65	506	562	1.1
66053	LOUISBURG	121	5520	6636	7249	2.0	95	1942	2373	2608	2.2	2.75	1524	1833	2.0
66054	MC LOUTH	087	2566	2822	2908	1.0	88	949	1053	1087	1.1	2.68	749	825	1.1
66056	MOUND CITY	107	1758	1813	1786	0.3	74	708	740	731	0.5	2.38	509	528	0.4
66058	MUSCOTAH	005	381	386	385	0.1	68	150	155	155	0.4	2.49	110	111	0.1
66060	NORTONVILLE	087	1146	1224	1243	0.7	84	415	448	456	0.8	2.65	311	331	0.7
66061	OLATHE	091	42055	51850	56833	2.3	96	15181	18886	20802	2.4	2.71	11002	13653	2.4
66062	OLATHE	091	54565	71573	79621	3.0	97	18339	24746	27836	3.3	2.85	14642	19468	3.1
66064	OSAWATOMIE	121	6216	6116	6125	-0.2	56	2369	2363	2377	0.0	2.46	1594	1557	-0.3
66066	OSKALOOSA	087	2688	2924	2972	0.9	87	992	1094	1115	1.1	2.58	727	794	1.0
66067	OTTAWA	059	15421	16415	16876	0.7	84	5976	6435	6634	0.8	2.47	4062	4328	0.7
66070	OZAWKIE	087	2272	2436	2450	0.8	86	854	925	933	0.9	2.63	660	709	0.8
66071	PAOLA	121	11687	12963	13665	1.1	89	4321	4863	5145	1.3	2.60	3216	3553	1.1
66072	PARKER	107	999	1142	1197	1.5	92	371	425	445	1.5	2.69	285	324	1.4
66073	PERRY	087	2331	2451	2454	0.5	79	859	913	919	0.7	2.68	655	691	0.6
66075	PLEASANTON	107	2375	2576	2638	0.9	87	953	1047	1076	1.0	2.44	674	734	0.9
66076	POMONA	059	2281	2539	2675	1.2	91	845	950	1002	1.3	2.67	634	707	1.2
66078	PRINCETON	059	924	1038	1093	1.3	91	339	382	403	1.3	2.70	270	301	1.2
66079	RANTOUL	059	800	881	916	1.0	88	278	308	320	1.1	2.86	219	240	1.0
66080	RICHMOND	059	1080	1236	1309	1.5	92	375	434	460	1.6	2.77	295	339	1.5
66083	SPRING HILL	121	6324	8522	9563	3.3	98	2189	3041	3433	3.6	2.79	1812	2486	3.5
66085	STILWELL	091	5377	7341	8195	3.4	98	1800	2520	2833	3.7	2.91	1593	2215	3.6
66086	TONGANOXIE	103	6892	8228	8847	1.9	95	2468	2997	3241	2.1	2.72	1958	2364	2.1
66087	TROY	043	2195	2176	2137	-0.1	59	865	871	860	0.1	2.49	620	619	0.0
66088	VALLEY FALLS	087	2473	2469	2439	0.0	64	911	913	901	0.0	2.62	648	643	-0.1
66090	WATHENA	043	3474	3295	3185	-0.6	36	1362	1317	1280	-0.4	2.47	951	909	-0.5
66091	WELDA	003	347	343	337	-0.1	59	138	138	136	0.0	2.49	105	104	-0.1
66092	WELLSVILLE	059	3580	3958	4171	1.1	89	1342	1506	1596	1.3	2.59	1016	1126	1.1
66093	WESTPHALIA	003	593	579	568	-0.3	52	221	217	213	-0.2	2.67	170	166	-0.3
66094	WHITE CLOUD	043	517	486	467	-0.7	32	211	204	198	-0.4	2.38	143	137	-0.5
66095	WILLIAMSBURG	059	859	912	934	0.6	82	336	361	371	0.8	2.53	258	274	0.7
66097	WINCHESTER	087	1134	1139	1107	0.0	64	403	409	398	0.2	2.68	311	313	0.1
66101	KANSAS CITY	209	14791	13683	13431	-0.8	28	5443	4901	4792	-1.1	2.69	3071	2687	-1.4
66102	KANSAS CITY	209	28471	27828	27659	-0.2	56	10307	9878	9785	-0.5	2.80	6729	6309	-0.7
66103	KANSAS CITY	209	14497	13455	13220	-0.8	28	6636	6171	6061	-0.8	2.18	3104	2796	-1.1
66104	KANSAS CITY	209	27410	25466	25028	-0.8	28	10266	9587	9430	-0.7	2.61	6921	6326	-1.0
66105	KANSAS CITY	209	3212	2910	2831	-1.1	17	985	872	845	-1.3	3.34	703	611	-1.5
66106	KANSAS CITY	209	24220	23141	22924	-0.5	41	8751	8385	8305	-0.5	2.76	6355	5984	-0.6
66109	KANSAS CITY	209	15885	19490	20510	2.2	96	5717	6962	7312	2.2	2.79	4548	5555	2.2
66111	KANSAS CITY	209	9525	9633	9675	0.1	68	3621	3693	3715	0.2	2.55	2532	2532	0.0
66112	KANSAS CITY	209	12085	11885	11850	-0.2	56	4984	4915	4905	-0.2	2.37	3119	3006	-0.4
66113	EDWARDSVILLE	209	1472	1379	1357	-0.7	32	578	544	536	-0.7	2.53	404	373	-0.9
66118	KANSAS CITY	209	1	1	1	0.0	64	1	1	1	0.0	1.00	0	0	0.0
66202	MISSION	091	17219	17021	17254	-0.1	59	8495	8641	8844	0.2	1.95	4298	4104	-0.5
66203	SHAWNEE	091	20007	20162	20589	0.1	68	8569	8901	9183	0.4	2.24	5377	5311	-0.1
66204	OVERLAND PARK	091	18794	19466	20135	0.4	76	8519	9124	9546	0.7	2.10	4722	4757	0.1
66205	MISSION	091	13548	13825	14019	0.2	70	6060	6364	6522	0.5	2.17	3644	3609	-0.1
66206	LEAWOOD	091	9971	9829	9958	-0.2	56	4107	4171	4264	0.2	2.31	2942	2872	-0.3
66207	OVERLAND PARK	091	13230	13290	13696	0.0	64	5358	5535	5754	0.4	2.37	3888	3900	0.0
66208	PRAIRIE VILLAGE	091	21220	21256	21664	0.0	64	9139	9415	9686	0.3	2.24	5996	5887	-0.2
66209	LEAWOOD	091	18873	22391	24440	1.9	95	6616	8230	9119	2.4	2.67	5192	6186	1.9
66210	OVERLAND PARK	091	18255	19021	19702	0.4	76	7820	8398	8782	0.8	2.25	4801	4894	0.2
66211	LEAWOOD	091	3424	4804	5359	3.7	98	1426	2109	2392	4.3	2.20	1014	1412	3.6
66212	OVERLAND PARK	091	33790	34179	34951	0.1	68	14824	15359	15830	0.4	2.21	8894	8730	-0.2
66213	OVERLAND PARK	091	26069	29064	30731	1.2	91	9509	10653	11306	1.2	2.72	6886	7444	0.8
66214	OVERLAND PARK	091	12054	12176	12431	0.1	68	5334	5535	5706	0.4	2.20	3072	2998	-0.3
66215	LENEXA	091	25690	27388	28653	0.7	84	10027	10925	11502	0.9	2.44	6718	7043	0.5
66216	SHAWNEE	091	23728	25499	26925	0.8	86	8437	9264	9846	1.0	2.73	6650	7150	0.8
66217	SHAWNEE	091	3532	5393	6101	4.7	98	1412	2168	2469	4.7	2.49	1050	1563	4.4
66218	SHAWNEE	091	3387	6530	8038	7.4	99	1159	2287	2840	7.6	2.85	1010	1982	7.6
	KANSAS					0.6					0.6	2.49			0.5
	UNITED STATES					1.0					1.1	2.59			0.9

ZIP CODE #	POST OFFICE NAME	RACE (%) White 2000	White 2009	Black 2000	Black 2009	Asian/Pacific 2000	Asian/Pacific 2009	% Hispanic Origin 2000	% Hispanic Origin 2009	2009 AGE DISTRIBUTION (%) 0-4	5-9	10-14	15-19	20-24	25-44	45-64	65-84	85+	18+	MEDIAN AGE 2009	% 2009 Males	% 2009 Females
66002	ATCHISON	90.2	88.8	6.5	7.1	0.5	0.7	2.3	3.3	6.7	6.5	6.7	9.0	7.9	23.3	23.9	13.0	3.2	75.5	35.8	48.3	51.7
66006	BALDWIN CITY	95.5	94.5	0.8	0.9	0.5	0.7	1.5	2.2	5.7	6.0	6.6	9.7	9.6	21.1	28.6	10.6	2.0	76.7	37.8	50.0	50.0
66007	BASEHOR	97.1	96.2	0.4	0.5	0.5	0.8	1.8	2.8	5.5	6.0	6.7	7.0	5.1	24.1	32.3	11.9	1.3	77.5	41.9	48.8	51.2
66008	BENDENA	98.2	98.0	0.0	0.0	0.3	0.6	0.3	0.6	6.9	7.7	7.7	6.9	4.0	21.7	31.1	11.7	2.3	73.1	41.3	47.4	52.6
66010	BLUE MOUND	99.2	98.9	0.0	0.0	0.2	0.3	1.0	1.4	5.3	5.7	6.2	6.5	6.0	21.6	30.7	15.9	2.2	79.0	43.9	50.9	49.1
66012	BONNER SPRINGS	92.0	89.7	3.1	3.6	0.4	0.7	5.1	8.1	6.8	6.8	7.3	7.2	6.0	25.8	27.6	10.6	1.8	74.7	37.5	48.6	51.4
66013	BUCYRUS	97.1	96.1	0.3	0.4	0.4	0.6	1.7	2.7	6.2	7.2	8.4	7.5	4.3	23.1	32.8	9.8	0.8	73.4	41.1	50.1	49.9
66014	CENTERVILLE	97.5	97.4	0.3	0.3	0.0	0.0	0.6	1.0	5.2	5.4	6.0	6.0	5.2	18.7	35.0	16.3	2.3	79.5	46.9	51.8	48.2
66015	COLONY	97.5	97.4	0.6	0.6	0.1	0.1	0.8	1.0	5.1	5.6	6.2	7.2	5.3	21.0	30.2	16.4	3.1	78.9	44.8	50.6	49.4
66016	CUMMINGS	97.0	96.5	1.5	1.8	0.2	0.2	1.0	1.4	6.7	7.4	7.4	6.7	5.4	22.3	29.6	12.7	1.8	74.7	40.9	49.8	50.2
66017	DENTON	99.4	99.3	0.0	0.0	0.0	0.0	0.3	0.0	6.6	7.3	7.9	7.3	4.3	23.5	29.1	11.3	2.6	73.5	39.1	52.3	47.7
66018	DE SOTO	95.1	93.4	0.2	0.2	0.6	0.9	6.3	9.8	7.8	8.1	8.3	7.8	5.2	27.6	26.1	8.1	0.9	70.8	34.6	50.0	50.0
66020	EASTON	96.2	95.0	0.8	1.0	0.9	1.4	1.2	1.9	5.8	5.8	6.3	7.2	6.0	23.8	30.6	12.6	2.0	77.6	41.5	50.7	49.3
66021	EDGERTON	96.3	95.5	0.4	0.4	0.2	0.3	1.9	3.2	8.5	8.5	8.3	7.3	5.1	29.4	25.1	7.0	0.6	70.4	33.8	52.0	48.0
66023	EFFINGHAM	97.9	97.4	0.2	0.2	0.2	0.4	0.5	1.0	6.1	6.5	6.7	7.0	4.6	23.0	29.8	14.2	2.1	76.4	41.8	49.9	50.1
66025	EUDORA	95.4	94.2	0.5	0.6	0.4	0.7	2.3	3.4	7.9	7.4	7.2	7.6	7.3	28.5	23.8	8.5	1.9	72.8	33.8	47.8	52.2
66026	FONTANA	98.3	97.9	0.3	0.3	0.0	0.0	0.9	1.6	4.4	6.3	8.1	6.8	4.1	23.8	32.5	12.0	1.9	76.4	42.8	50.6	49.4
66027	FORT LEAVENWORTH	68.8	64.2	23.0	25.5	1.8	2.6	7.7	11.0	11.3	11.9	7.1	4.2	6.7	49.2	9.3	0.4	0.0	66.9	29.1	66.1	33.9
66030	GARDNER	94.4	92.2	1.4	1.7	0.9	1.5	2.7	4.6	9.8	9.0	8.3	7.0	6.2	31.6	21.3	5.9	0.9	68.5	31.9	49.6	50.4
66031	NEW CENTURY	91.3	88.8	3.1	3.1	0.6	1.3	3.7	6.3	7.5	8.1	8.1	6.9	4.4	29.4	26.9	8.1	0.6	72.5	36.9	51.9	48.1
66032	GARNETT	97.3	97.2	0.3	0.3	0.3	0.3	1.2	1.3	6.8	6.8	6.8	6.6	5.1	22.2	25.8	15.4	4.4	75.4	41.3	49.0	51.0
66033	GREELEY	98.1	97.9	0.1	0.2	0.2	0.3	0.8	1.0	6.1	6.5	6.6	6.9	4.3	22.3	30.1	15.2	2.0	76.2	43.0	51.5	48.5
66035	HIGHLAND	90.2	88.8	4.6	5.0	0.5	0.6	1.5	2.1	3.5	3.5	3.6	19.5	11.6	18.4	22.2	13.2	4.4	86.3	33.3	48.4	51.6
66039	KINCAID	96.3	96.2	0.4	0.4	0.3	0.3	1.0	1.2	4.5	4.8	5.4	7.1	5.4	21.2	32.9	16.0	2.8	81.1	45.9	51.2	48.8
66040	LACYGNE	96.8	96.3	0.5	0.5	0.3	0.3	1.1	1.7	6.7	7.2	7.8	6.2	4.1	22.7	29.3	14.3	1.8	74.2	41.7	50.2	49.8
66041	LANCASTER	98.1	97.6	0.4	0.4	0.0	0.1	0.4	0.6	6.0	6.6	6.7	6.8	5.0	24.4	29.6	12.9	1.9	76.4	40.9	51.6	48.4
66042	LANE	96.8	96.1	0.4	0.5	0.1	0.3	0.7	1.1	5.9	6.8	6.8	6.3	5.6	23.8	31.3	12.3	1.2	76.5	41.0	51.1	48.9
66043	LANSING	82.6	80.7	11.2	11.6	1.4	2.2	3.8	5.4	5.1	5.4	5.7	6.3	7.6	31.6	28.8	8.0	1.5	80.0	37.8	58.6	41.4
66044	LAWRENCE	85.4	82.5	5.2	5.8	1.7	2.5	3.8	5.7	4.8	4.1	4.0	10.2	27.7	25.8	16.7	5.7	0.9	84.5	24.9	49.8	50.2
66045	LAWRENCE	74.3	67.6	7.8	8.0	13.2	18.8	4.7	6.5	1.5	0.8	0.5	44.6	38.5	12.4	1.4	0.3	0.0	96.6	20.3	48.8	51.2
66046	LAWRENCE	79.5	76.1	5.1	5.4	4.3	6.2	4.1	5.8	6.7	5.7	5.3	6.9	16.8	32.0	18.5	7.2	0.9	79.2	29.1	50.4	49.6
66047	LAWRENCE	88.5	85.3	3.3	3.6	3.3	5.0	2.6	3.9	5.6	5.3	5.7	7.0	18.7	26.4	21.6	7.8	2.0	79.6	29.4	49.5	50.5
66048	LEAVENWORTH	81.8	79.0	12.3	13.5	1.4	2.1	3.8	5.5	6.9	6.5	6.4	6.6	6.7	25.5	28.2	11.3	1.8	76.2	38.4	49.5	50.5
66049	LAWRENCE	88.0	85.3	4.3	4.8	3.0	4.4	2.8	4.2	6.0	5.9	6.0	6.6	11.3	29.1	25.7	8.2	1.2	78.5	33.7	49.8	50.2
66050	LECOMPTON	93.9	92.5	1.0	1.2	0.8	1.2	1.8	2.6	6.8	7.2	7.7	8.0	5.7	24.0	29.8	9.7	1.0	73.4	38.2	49.3	50.7
66052	LINWOOD	95.8	94.3	0.6	0.8	0.2	0.3	3.6	5.5	6.7	7.3	7.5	6.2	4.7	23.1	31.5	12.7	0.9	74.6	41.0	49.8	50.2
66053	LOUISBURG	97.6	97.1	0.3	0.4	0.2	0.3	1.1	1.6	7.1	7.4	7.7	6.8	4.9	25.4	28.8	9.7	2.3	73.4	39.0	49.1	50.9
66054	MC LOUTH	96.2	95.6	0.7	0.8	0.2	0.2	1.1	1.7	6.3	7.0	7.2	6.9	4.8	24.8	30.3	11.4	1.3	75.2	40.5	50.4	49.6
66056	MOUND CITY	97.8	97.5	0.9	0.9	0.1	0.2	0.7	0.9	5.6	5.8	6.1	6.4	5.5	20.5	29.8	17.7	3.3	78.3	45.1	48.9	51.1
66058	MUSCOTAH	96.1	94.8	1.1	1.0	0.0	0.3	1.1	1.8	6.5	7.0	6.7	6.7	4.1	25.1	28.5	13.5	1.8	75.1	41.0	50.8	49.2
66060	NORTONVILLE	97.7	97.1	0.4	0.5	0.0	0.1	1.1	1.7	6.4	6.9	7.4	7.4	4.3	22.1	27.3	14.0	4.2	74.5	41.8	50.4	49.6
66061	OLATHE	86.7	84.2	4.0	4.0	2.4	3.4	7.7	10.1	8.5	8.4	7.9	6.9	5.7	31.6	23.7	6.5	1.0	70.9	33.3	50.0	50.0
66062	OLATHE	90.6	88.3	3.2	3.5	2.9	4.2	3.5	5.2	9.6	8.9	8.3	7.1	5.7	33.1	22.5	4.7	0.6	68.7	31.9	49.6	50.4
66064	OSAWATOMIE	93.6	92.3	3.1	3.5	0.2	0.3	2.3	3.4	7.6	7.2	6.7	6.7	6.6	26.6	25.0	11.5	2.2	74.5	36.7	48.5	51.5
66066	OSKALOOSA	96.4	95.7	0.5	0.5	0.1	0.2	2.0	2.8	5.7	6.1	6.6	6.7	5.4	23.6	32.1	11.6	2.2	77.4	42.1	51.6	48.4
66067	OTTAWA	93.8	92.7	1.9	2.0	0.4	0.6	3.5	5.0	7.0	6.7	6.5	7.6	7.3	25.1	24.9	11.8	3.1	75.6	36.7	49.6	50.4
66070	OZAWKIE	96.9	96.4	0.5	0.6	0.1	0.1	0.8	1.3	5.9	5.9	7.3	7.3	4.1	23.9	33.9	10.6	1.1	76.1	42.5	51.2	48.8
66071	PAOLA	95.7	94.8	1.8	2.1	0.2	0.3	1.7	2.5	6.5	6.7	7.1	7.2	5.9	24.2	29.2	11.3	1.8	75.2	39.5	49.5	50.5
66072	PARKER	97.5	96.9	0.9	1.0	0.0	0.0	0.7	1.1	7.4	7.8	7.6	6.0	4.7	22.2	29.2	13.2	1.9	73.5	40.9	50.6	49.4
66073	PERRY	94.6	93.8	0.4	0.4	0.4	0.6	1.2	1.7	5.8	6.2	6.6	6.7	5.6	25.1	31.5	11.0	1.6	77.4	40.6	50.1	49.9
66075	PLEASANTON	97.9	97.6	0.5	0.6	0.0	0.0	0.8	1.1	6.4	6.6	6.7	6.2	4.8	22.4	29.2	14.7	2.9	76.3	41.9	49.4	50.6
66076	POMONA	96.4	95.7	0.0	0.0	0.0	0.1	1.5	2.1	6.3	6.5	6.9	7.2	5.6	23.4	30.1	12.6	1.4	75.9	40.6	50.8	49.2
66078	PRINCETON	95.8	95.0	0.2	0.3	0.2	0.4	1.0	1.4	6.2	6.7	7.0	7.2	5.4	22.9	31.2	11.8	1.5	75.5	40.7	51.0	49.0
66079	RANTOUL	97.1	96.6	0.1	0.1	0.1	0.2	2.0	3.0	6.2	7.0	7.0	7.2	4.2	24.5	30.5	11.7	1.6	74.9	41.1	51.1	48.9
66080	RICHMOND	97.2	96.7	0.1	0.1	0.4	0.6	1.0	1.5	7.4	7.4	7.1	7.0	5.9	24.3	25.7	12.6	2.5	73.3	38.0	49.4	50.6
66083	SPRING HILL	96.9	96.2	0.6	0.8	0.2	0.4	2.1	3.1	7.6	7.9	8.0	7.2	5.0	27.4	28.2	7.9	0.9	71.9	36.8	50.5	49.5
66085	STILWELL	96.7	94.8	0.6	1.0	1.1	2.1	1.7	2.6	7.6	8.6	9.3	8.4	4.1	23.1	31.3	7.1	0.4	68.9	37.8	49.9	50.1
66086	TONGANOXIE	96.2	95.5	1.0	1.2	0.3	0.5	1.8	2.8	6.7	7.2	7.4	6.8	5.0	25.9	29.2	10.1	1.7	74.4	38.6	49.9	50.1
66087	TROY	98.6	98.1	0.1	0.2	0.3	0.4	1.1	1.7	6.9	7.2	7.5	6.6	5.2	23.4	28.3	12.3	2.5	74.2	39.6	50.5	49.5
66088	VALLEY FALLS	97.7	97.2	0.5	0.5	0.2	0.3	0.8	1.3	7.2	7.7	7.7	7.1	4.2	23.5	27.9	12.0	2.6	73.0	39.7	51.1	48.9
66090	WATHENA	94.4	93.6	2.6	2.9	0.2	0.2	1.2	1.7	7.1	7.0	6.9	6.9	5.6	25.0	27.5	11.4	2.5	74.7	37.6	49.4	50.6
66091	WELDA	97.1	97.1	0.3	0.3	0.3	0.3	0.9	0.9	6.4	6.4	7.0	7.0	5.0	22.2	29.2	14.6	2.3	75.8	41.9	51.6	48.4
66092	WELLSVILLE	97.9	97.5	0.2	0.3	0.1	0.1	1.0	1.6	6.8	7.3	7.4	7.2	5.5	25.6	27.6	10.7	1.9	73.9	38.4	49.8	50.2
66093	WESTPHALIA	98.5	98.4	0.2	0.2	0.0	0.0	0.7	0.5	9.5	9.5	8.8	6.7	3.8	22.1	24.9	12.6	2.1	67.9	36.6	52.8	47.2
66094	WHITE CLOUD	83.2	80.7	1.9	2.1	0.4	0.6	1.7	2.9	6.2	6.6	6.4	5.6	4.1	25.9	30.2	13.6	1.4	77.6	41.6	51.2	48.8
66095	WILLIAMSBURG	97.6	97.1	0.1	0.1	0.0	0.0	0.6	1.0	6.9	7.1	7.1	6.3	5.0	23.6	28.8	13.7	1.4	75.0	40.6	50.9	49.1
66097	WINCHESTER	97.6	97.2	0.3	0.3	0.1	0.2	1.3	2.0	7.1	7.6	7.3	6.1	5.2	22.5	27.4	13.4	3.5	73.7	40.5	49.2	50.8
66101	KANSAS CITY	35.7	33.0	40.4	37.3	2.8	3.5	30.1	38.9	10.0	8.6	7.2	7.6	8.2	26.6	20.6	9.2	2.0	69.9	30.6	50.6	49.4
66102	KANSAS CITY	48.8	43.5	32.0	31.7	2.3	3.0	24.3	32.7	9.6	8.6	7.7	7.5	7.4	28.5	21.4	7.9	1.4	69.7	30.7	49.9	50.1
66103	KANSAS CITY	67.1	60.2	12.6	12.4	4.1	5.7	24.9	34.8	8.0	5.9	5.3	5.9	12.3	35.6	19.4	6.5	1.0	77.7	29.5	50.9	49.1
66104	KANSAS CITY	32.4	30.0	61.2	61.7	1.1	1.6	5.4	7.8	7.2	7.4	7.2	7.8	6.9	24.4	25.2	11.5	2.4	73.4	35.6	46.9	53.1
66105	KANSAS CITY	59.5	50.9	1.3	1.2	1.3	1.6	50.5	63.8	10.9	10.3	9.3	8.6	5.9	27.6	19.0	7.5	0.9	64.1	28.7	50.2	49.8
66106	KANSAS CITY	77.5	72.4	7.7	7.7	1.4	2.0	19.3	27.3	8.7	8.0	7.2	7.1	6.9	27.0	24.0	9.7	1.3	71.9	33.0	48.9	51.1
66109	KANSAS CITY	76.3	75.0	19.1	18.9	0.6	0.8	3.7	6.0	6.0	6.4	6.9	7.2	5.5	25.0	30.6	11.1	1.4	76.3	40.0	49.5	50.5
66111	KANSAS CITY	80.0	76.1	14.1	15.9	0.4	0.6	5.4	8.6	7.3	6.6	6.4	6.5	6.4	26.3	26.6	12.1	1.8	75.8	37.7	48.7	51.3
66112	KANSAS CITY	54.7	49.1	37.0	39.7	1.0	1.4	7.2	11.1	7.3	6.4	6.2	6.3	7.5	26.9	23.5	12.7	3.3	76.5	36.4	46.0	54.0
66113	EDWARDSVILLE	92.5	89.4	1.2	1.4	0.5	0.8	6.3	10.5	9.6	8.8	7.9	7.2	7.0	30.2	20.6	8.0	0.8	69.4	31.3	48.2	51.8
66118	KANSAS CITY	50.0	100.0	50.0	0.0	0.0	0.0	0.0	0.0	0.0	0.0	0.0	0.0	0.0	0.0	100.0	0.0	0.0	100.0	62.5	100.0	0.0
66202	MISSION	88.7	85.4	3.7	4.0	2.5	3.7	5.8	8.9	5.6	5.2	5.1	5.2	9.5	31.0	25.0	11.0	2.3	81.1	37.0	48.1	51.9
66203	SHAWNEE	89.1	85.8	3.7	4.0	1.7	2.6	6.0	9.4	6.4	6.1	6.0	5.7	6.1	28.8	26.2	12.3	2.3	77.9	38.8	48.1	51.9
66204	OVERLAND PARK	90.3	87.2	2.9	3.2	2.3	3.5	5.7	8.8	6.3	5.9	5.7	5.6	7.2	32.0	24.2	10.7	2.5	78.7	37.1	48.2	51.8
66205	MISSION	94.0	91.4	1.4	1.7	1.4	2.6	4.8	7.4	6.1	5.9	5.9	5.2	5.9	28.3	28.4	11.6	2.6	78.8	40.5	47.7	52.3
66206	LEAWOOD	97.3	96.3	0.3	0.4	1.1	1.8	1.2	1.9	4.7	5.7	6.8	6.0	3.8	15.6	33.6	18.2	5.6	78.6	49.2	47.1	52.9
66207	OVERLAND PARK	95.6	94.1	1.0	1.1	1.9	3.0	1.8	2.8	4.4	5.2	6.3	6.4	3.8	15.6	33.6	20.8	4.0	80.0	50.2	46.7	53.3
66208	PRAIRIE VILLAGE	96.6	95.5	0.7	0.8	0.8	1.3	2.2	3.6	5.6	5.8	6.6	6.3	5.0	23.4	29.8	14.1	3.4	77.8	43.2	47.0	53.0
66209	LEAWOOD	94.6	92.5	1.6	1.8	2.8	4.4	1.3	2.0	5.1	6.4	7.9	8.1	4.5	18.4	34.8	11.9	3.0	75.2	44.8	48.1	51.9
66210	OVERLAND PARK	89.6	86.1	2.7	2.9	4.8	7.3	3.2	5.0	5.6	5.6	5.9	5.8	7.7	29.8	30.1	8.4	1.0	79.3	37.6	49.1	50.9
66211	LEAWOOD	94.0	91.9	1.5	1.7	3.1	4.6	1.3	2.2	3.7	4.5	5.7	6.6	3.9	17.6	36.4	17.8	3.8	81.8	50.1	48.0	52.0
66212	OVERLAND PARK	88.3	85.0	3.2	3.5	4.6	6.5	5.7	8.3	5.4	5.2	5.4	5.6	7.0	26.7	26.9	14.9	2.8	80.5	40.7	48.1	51.9
66213	OVERLAND PARK	90.1	86.8	2.5	2.7	5.5	8.1	2.3	3.6	8.8	9.1	8.8	6.9	4.0	32.3	25.3	4.3	0.6	68.6	34.5	49.1	50.9
66214	OVERLAND PARK	86.6	82.5	3.9	4.1	4.9	7.2	5.4	8.1	5.8	5.1	5.3	5.7	8.9	31.1	27.0	9.9	1.2	80.7	36.2	50.4	49.6
66215	LENEXA	90.3	87.6	3.1	3.3	3.1	4.5	4.1	6.1	5.7	5.9	6.5	6.5	6.7	26.3	28.7	10.2	3.5	77.9	39.7	48.2	51.8
66216	SHAWNEE	89.3	86.2	3.2	3.4	4.1	6.0	3.7	5.6	6.4	7.1	7.4	7.1	5.1	25.4	31.3	9.2	1.0	74.6	39.3	48.9	51.1
66217	SHAWNEE	92.6	86.4	2.4	4.4	2.0	4.2	3.3	5.8	6.0	6.7	7.1	6.9	7.3	27.2	29.7	8.5	0.7	76.0	36.9	50.4	49.6
66218	SHAWNEE	94.1	92.1	1.4	1.5	1.0	1.7	3.8	5.7	10.3	10.3	9.5	6.0	2.9	33.2	23.2	4.3	0.3	65.9	35.6	50.8	49.2
	KANSAS	86.1	83.7	5.7	5.9	1.8	2.6	7.0	9.4	7.1	6.9	6.9	7.3	7.3	25.9	25.7	10.7	2.2	75.0	36.3	49.6	50.4
	UNITED STATES	75.1	72.0	12.3	12.7	3.8	4.6	12.5	15.7	6.8	6.7	6.6	7.1	6.9	27.0	26.0	10.9	1.9	75.7	36.9	49.2	50.8

INCOME

#	POST OFFICE NAME	2009 Per Capita Income	2009 HH Income Base	2009 Household Income Distribution (%) Less than $25,000	$25,000 to $49,999	$50,000 to $99,999	$100,000 to $149,999	$150,000 or More	Median Household Income 2009	2014	2009 National Centile	2009 State Centile	2009 Home Value Base	2009 Home Value Distribution (%) Less than $50,000	$50,000 to $89,999	$90,000 to $174,999	$175,000 to $399,999	$400,000 or More	2009 Median Home Value
66002	ATCHISON	19109	4953	28.4	33.1	32.6	4.4	1.4	41610	44216	38	43	3467	20.9	33.4	34.3	10.5	0.8	83266
66006	BALDWIN CITY	26174	2698	12.4	24.6	48.5	9.8	4.7	63686	63078	82	91	2069	13.8	9.4	34.8	35.0	7.0	154438
66007	BASEHOR	28026	1944	10.2	21.9	46.1	17.2	4.6	70939	74690	87	94	1681	2.1	8.6	56.6	30.9	1.7	150949
66008	BENDENA	19950	128	14.8	29.7	50.8	3.9	0.8	53343	53897	69	81	102	29.4	21.6	35.3	11.8	2.0	88571
66010	BLUE MOUND	24584	309	29.1	21.0	42.4	4.9	2.6	49753	50558	60	73	273	35.9	18.7	30.8	13.2	1.5	79667
66012	BONNER SPRINGS	25459	3745	17.1	20.7	44.2	13.0	5.0	60994	61620	79	89	2824	13.0	15.2	44.2	25.7	1.9	121172
66013	BUCYRUS	31549	633	8.8	16.0	40.0	25.3	10.0	80197	81140	92	96	562	3.7	10.0	25.4	45.4	15.5	201744
66014	CENTERVILLE	21748	165	26.1	29.1	37.6	4.8	2.4	44608	47137	47	56	145	42.1	15.2	29.0	12.4	1.4	68750
66015	COLONY	17192	268	30.6	32.1	34.3	1.9	1.1	38183	41702	27	25	219	28.8	32.0	30.1	6.8	2.3	76053
66016	CUMMINGS	19022	219	16.9	31.5	44.3	6.4	0.9	51216	53541	64	77	192	18.2	18.8	37.5	24.5	1.0	112963
66017	DENTON	17241	123	37.4	30.9	27.6	2.4	1.6	35194	37529	18	10	93	54.8	23.7	11.8	7.5	2.2	45500
66018	DE SOTO	29497	2285	9.4	22.3	41.9	20.1	6.3	67180	67817	85	93	1664	9.9	8.8	39.7	37.6	4.0	153788
66020	EASTON	22377	713	15.1	29.9	46.7	5.9	2.4	55822	59451	72	84	584	24.3	9.6	40.2	24.3	1.5	115506
66021	EDGERTON	25955	983	8.3	23.3	51.1	14.1	3.2	64769	66184	83	92	831	10.3	12.0	56.4	17.8	3.4	115787
66023	EFFINGHAM	19781	534	22.7	31.8	41.6	3.4	0.6	46445	50177	53	62	439	23.7	29.4	34.9	11.6	0.5	86860
66025	EUDORA	24264	2792	14.5	25.1	49.7	8.3	2.4	58621	59507	76	87	1795	15.9	5.3	50.0	25.9	2.9	133861
66026	FONTANA	24809	250	14.4	25.6	54.0	4.4	1.6	59117	60302	76	87	219	23.7	13.2	33.8	21.9	7.3	115625
66027	FORT LEAVENWORTH	17577	1638	3.8	23.7	61.5	9.3	1.6	70652	74558	87	94	27	0.0	0.0	66.7	33.3	0.0	146875
66030	GARDNER	26968	6411	9.3	21.5	49.2	15.8	4.2	68144	66702	86	93	4863	17.1	7.7	48.9	24.8	1.5	138345
66031	NEW CENTURY	2841	5	0.0	0.0	100.0	0.0	0.0	66333	75000	84	92	4	0.0	0.0	75.0	25.0	0.0	150000
66032	GARNETT	19720	2020	26.8	35.4	32.5	4.1	1.3	40562	42372	35	36	1534	24.6	25.5	37.5	11.7	0.7	89765
66033	GREELEY	21445	350	17.4	29.7	46.6	4.9	1.4	52123	54197	66	78	310	19.0	25.5	34.8	18.1	2.6	100000
66035	HIGHLAND	18674	434	37.6	29.7	28.1	3.0	1.6	36043	38412	21	14	286	38.1	31.8	26.2	3.8	0.0	62400
66039	KINCAID	16559	268	31.7	35.4	28.7	2.6	1.5	36735	38485	23	18	229	38.9	21.4	23.1	15.3	1.3	73235
66040	LACYGNE	22127	1316	19.6	27.7	47.0	4.7	1.0	52050	51866	66	78	1091	25.7	23.5	34.3	14.1	2.5	91056
66041	LANCASTER	19533	319	20.1	32.0	44.8	1.9	1.3	47962	50842	57	66	264	25.0	31.1	25.0	15.5	3.4	80000
66042	LANE	22600	286	13.6	32.2	46.5	5.9	1.7	53280	55214	68	81	254	26.8	20.9	38.2	11.8	2.4	92857
66043	LANSING	27260	2963	6.5	13.1	59.1	14.4	7.0	77651	79225	91	96	2281	10.2	12.6	46.7	29.3	1.1	134474
66044	LAWRENCE	20512	11832	36.6	31.9	26.3	3.1	2.1	33769	36071	15	7	4734	19.0	20.2	38.7	19.5	2.6	105667
66045	LAWRENCE	13445	976	68.9	20.6	10.2	0.3	0.0	18363	18776	1	1	25	0.0	0.0	52.0	48.0	0.0	148214
66046	LAWRENCE	23489	7828	21.6	31.5	39.1	5.9	2.0	47418	50694	55	65	3946	13.1	4.4	59.3	21.5	1.7	130282
66047	LAWRENCE	30157	8051	19.2	24.3	38.9	9.7	8.0	57653	57869	75	86	4166	8.8	3.1	34.3	44.3	9.5	182047
66048	LEAVENWORTH	24982	13561	19.0	28.2	40.2	9.2	3.4	52603	56065	67	79	8458	14.2	27.5	40.2	17.3	0.9	98201
66049	LAWRENCE	31823	10110	18.9	23.2	34.7	13.2	10.0	60582	60122	78	89	6020	1.0	4.2	35.8	53.9	5.1	189082
66050	LECOMPTON	22727	763	13.4	29.2	49.0	6.3	2.1	57063	57934	74	85	629	18.9	8.1	43.7	26.2	3.0	127373
66052	LINWOOD	24836	718	12.7	28.3	49.2	7.0	2.9	59002	63018	76	87	606	6.9	17.2	43.1	26.7	6.1	135317
66053	LOUISBURG	25687	2373	12.3	23.6	48.0	11.7	4.4	63238	65491	81	91	1917	8.5	16.0	40.9	28.5	6.2	137871
66054	MC LOUTH	22143	1053	18.3	26.6	45.5	7.4	2.2	54286	57773	70	82	897	15.2	16.2	41.6	24.2	2.9	118912
66056	MOUND CITY	20090	740	30.1	30.1	33.5	3.9	2.3	40328	44308	34	34	615	44.6	25.9	23.7	5.5	0.3	57976
66058	MUSCOTAH	19471	155	28.4	27.1	40.6	2.6	1.3	44170	49610	46	54	128	43.0	24.2	19.5	12.5	0.8	56429
66060	NORTONVILLE	20977	448	19.4	31.5	41.5	5.6	2.0	49092	52231	59	71	373	26.8	33.2	29.5	10.5	0.0	77667
66061	OLATHE	31487	18886	9.7	20.9	40.4	20.7	8.3	72436	75942	88	94	12971	4.5	6.6	45.5	37.4	6.0	163504
66062	OLATHE	35070	24746	5.6	11.0	41.0	30.1	12.3	89766	97985	95	98	18391	0.9	0.6	32.2	64.1	2.3	191355
66064	OSAWATOMIE	20994	2363	25.0	34.2	32.6	6.0	2.2	41916	44191	39	44	1624	43.1	26.8	21.6	7.6	1.0	57778
66066	OSKALOOSA	21730	1094	20.0	28.6	42.0	7.2	2.1	51181	54700	64	77	893	19.4	23.5	36.8	18.6	1.7	101321
66067	OTTAWA	21882	6435	22.5	28.7	40.9	5.8	2.1	48517	51958	58	68	4346	20.7	27.3	40.2	11.4	0.5	92304
66070	OZAWKIE	24641	925	10.5	25.4	53.7	7.7	2.7	61166	62145	79	90	854	14.9	20.1	46.3	18.1	0.6	112736
66071	PAOLA	25834	4863	17.2	25.5	43.1	9.2	4.9	57509	61156	75	86	3753	12.3	20.7	37.4	26.8	2.9	120218
66072	PARKER	18584	425	20.2	33.2	43.1	3.5	0.0	47349	48146	55	64	381	29.1	22.8	31.0	16.8	0.3	86739
66073	PERRY	22307	913	20.3	24.4	47.0	5.5	2.8	53654	56478	69	81	744	16.5	18.1	39.4	23.0	3.0	114348
66075	PLEASANTON	17671	1047	33.8	32.2	29.0	4.2	0.8	36296	37917	21	16	786	40.5	25.1	25.7	7.3	1.5	63279
66076	POMONA	18940	950	20.0	34.5	40.5	4.2	0.7	45931	50000	51	60	755	25.0	21.7	42.9	10.3	0.0	94153
66078	PRINCETON	21143	382	13.4	31.7	47.9	6.5	0.5	53815	55368	69	82	338	28.7	17.8	27.8	24.6	1.2	97059
66079	RANTOUL	20045	308	21.1	24.7	44.5	8.8	1.0	53874	55209	69	82	275	19.6	13.8	45.1	20.0	1.5	111824
66080	RICHMOND	19696	434	18.7	32.0	45.2	2.3	1.8	49476	52593	60	72	371	35.3	33.2	23.7	7.0	0.8	67750
66083	SPRING HILL	28924	3041	9.3	19.3	47.6	17.6	6.2	72438	75796	88	94	2529	1.5	7.3	54.8	30.0	6.3	150250
66085	STILWELL	50265	2520	2.2	7.6	33.5	30.3	26.4	109924	113720	98	99	2315	0.4	1.8	19.3	58.1	20.4	245409
66086	TONGANOXIE	23840	2997	13.8	25.6	47.8	10.3	2.4	60928	64325	79	89	2416	6.2	13.6	48.7	28.6	3.0	140175
66087	TROY	18855	871	27.7	33.3	34.9	2.8	1.4	41053	43233	36	40	686	32.5	33.5	27.4	6.1	0.4	72361
66088	VALLEY FALLS	20463	913	22.1	28.5	42.3	4.9	2.2	49319	52169	60	72	700	22.9	24.9	38.7	10.4	3.1	92963
66090	WATHENA	18495	1317	29.3	33.3	32.5	3.9	1.1	40734	42650	35	37	987	37.5	29.6	27.2	5.2	0.6	65725
66091	WELDA	16801	138	31.9	35.5	28.3	2.9	1.4	37326	38886	25	20	118	37.3	22.0	23.7	16.1	0.8	73750
66092	WELLSVILLE	23532	1506	17.9	24.0	49.2	6.7	2.2	57153	57903	74	85	1232	12.3	17.0	48.1	20.3	2.4	114216
66093	WESTPHALIA	15876	217	31.3	33.6	32.7	1.8	0.5	39767	41272	32	30	185	28.6	22.7	29.7	18.4	0.5	87222
66094	WHITE CLOUD	20060	204	27.0	31.9	34.8	4.4	2.0	41253	43911	37	40	133	39.1	24.1	28.6	8.3	0.0	69167
66095	WILLIAMSBURG	20608	361	26.0	28.3	37.4	5.5	2.8	45142	50091	49	58	279	25.1	21.9	26.2	23.7	3.2	94048
66097	WINCHESTER	19266	409	20.8	28.6	45.2	3.9	1.5	50422	54068	62	75	329	31.6	21.0	31.0	13.1	3.3	83929
66101	KANSAS CITY	13218	4901	48.0	28.9	19.5	2.0	1.5	26205	26959	4	1	2244	80.1	15.5	4.2	0.2	0.0	33757
66102	KANSAS CITY	16137	9878	32.4	33.8	27.5	4.8	1.5	36614	39253	22	17	5623	50.5	37.6	11.3	0.5	0.0	49669
66103	KANSAS CITY	20093	6171	32.2	34.8	28.5	3.2	1.3	37157	40106	24	19	2242	34.6	52.9	11.2	1.1	0.3	60599
66104	KANSAS CITY	19047	9587	28.9	30.5	32.7	5.8	2.1	41582	44270	38	42	6686	41.0	42.9	15.6	0.5	0.0	58149
66105	KANSAS CITY	14063	872	34.5	31.2	27.3	5.4	1.6	33387	35182	14	6	533	80.9	15.8	2.1	0.6	0.8	26853
66106	KANSAS CITY	20024	8385	20.7	30.9	40.0	6.6	1.8	48596	51645	58	69	5651	20.7	45.4	32.8	0.8	0.3	74190
66109	KANSAS CITY	27985	6962	9.8	20.0	46.0	18.2	6.1	70001	71090	87	93	6008	4.0	21.3	55.9	17.2	1.6	114028
66111	KANSAS CITY	22584	3693	16.1	30.8	44.2	7.3	1.5	52769	54644	68	80	2687	30.1	31.3	32.3	5.8	0.6	76561
66112	KANSAS CITY	24130	4915	20.3	30.7	39.3	7.0	2.7	49203	51829	59	71	2555	6.9	43.6	45.9	3.4	0.2	89451
66113	EDWARDSVILLE	20528	544	23.2	33.6	39.0	2.8	1.5	42706	46167	42	48	496	88.1	9.3	2.2	0.0	0.4	24324
66118	KANSAS CITY	112500	1	0.0	0.0	0.0	100.0	0.0	112500	112500	98	99	1	0.0	0.0	0.0	100.0	0.0	225000
66202	MISSION	33839	8641	16.0	28.0	41.3	11.1	3.7	55900	54505	73	84	4736	2.1	3.1	70.7	23.5	0.6	137885
66203	SHAWNEE	30558	8901	13.4	24.6	44.6	14.0	3.4	61067	59241	79	89	5862	3.2	6.0	69.8	20.6	0.3	140451
66204	OVERLAND PARK	30606	9124	11.7	28.3	46.6	10.9	2.5	57763	56854	75	86	4929	1.7	4.9	77.9	15.0	0.5	127828
66205	MISSION	41520	6364	9.1	21.6	39.0	20.3	10.0	73644	75232	89	95	5332	1.6	4.8	51.4	35.4	6.8	160512
66206	LEAWOOD	48420	4171	5.5	13.8	32.0	32.2	16.5	96855	102008	96	98	3720	1.2	0.7	8.9	69.5	19.6	280842
66207	OVERLAND PARK	43074	5535	6.6	15.7	39.0	24.4	14.4	83957	87033	93	97	4709	0.5	0.1	23.0	63.7	12.7	214461
66208	PRAIRIE VILLAGE	48665	9415	6.7	16.5	40.6	18.3	17.8	80026	83785	92	96	8296	0.6	2.1	42.7	36.5	18.1	181619
66209	LEAWOOD	60879	8230	5.5	10.0	25.5	22.9	36.1	124439	121590	99	100	6695	1.3	0.3	1.2	65.5	31.8	350386
66210	OVERLAND PARK	40942	8398	5.9	14.9	44.1	26.3	8.9	80076	82975	92	96	5216	0.7	1.3	24.2	73.3	0.6	216975
66211	LEAWOOD	68256	2109	5.5	15.7	19.8	24.5	34.4	113647	117169	98	99	1634	0.0	0.4	13.5	35.7	50.4	407692
66212	OVERLAND PARK	33040	15359	13.0	24.6	41.7	16.0	4.8	63049	60342	81	91	9035	2.1	4.7	50.9	40.9	1.4	164510
66213	OVERLAND PARK	50690	10653	5.5	10.5	26.7	26.0	31.3	111947	114914	98	99	7540	1.8	0.4	4.2	81.6	11.9	301068
66214	OVERLAND PARK	33833	5535	12.5	26.5	37.6	18.3	5.1	61241	57854	79	90	2867	0.8	2.8	37.3	59.1	0.0	184030
66215	LENEXA	36274	10925	8.0	20.4	38.5	22.1	11.0	76236	78144	90	95	7330	1.1	1.1	35.1	61.5	1.2	186718
66216	SHAWNEE	37198	9264	7.3	14.9	39.2	22.7	15.9	83221	88178	93	97	7759	1.0	3.4	34.3	54.1	7.3	189206
66217	SHAWNEE	46851	2168	6.1	11.9	35.3	25.3	21.4	93675	99648	96	98	1427	2.5	0.9	18.1	63.3	15.3	250151
66218	SHAWNEE	40300	2287	3.0	4.5	33.2	46.3	13.0	107492	109402	98	99	2065	2.7	0.0	15.5	78.8	3.1	212101
	KANSAS	26028		20.3	26.8	37.6	9.9	5.4	52748	54940				18.1	21.6	35.7	21.6	3.0	107692
	UNITED STATES	27277		20.9	24.4	35.3	11.7	7.6	54719	56938				9.3	13.1	31.6	32.6	13.5	162279

ZIP CODE	FINANCIAL SERVICES				THE HOME						ENTERTAINMENT						PERSONAL			
					Home Improvements		Furnishings													
# POST OFFICE NAME	Auto Loan	Home Loan	Invest-ments	Retire-ment Plans	Home Repair	Lawn & Garden	Comput-ers & Hard-ware-Personal	Major Appli-ances	TV, Radio, Sound Equip-ment	Furni-ture	Dine out/ Carry out	Sports Equip-ment	Fees & Tickets	Toys & Games	Travel	Cable TV	Apparel & Services	Auto Repairs	Health Insur-ance	Pets & Supplies
66002 ATCHISON	73	62	64	63	62	74	66	71	69	61	68	54	59	70	63	74	46	69	77	84
66006 BALDWIN CITY	102	105	99	107	105	109	100	105	101	99	100	80	101	101	103	102	69	102	107	123
66007 BASEHOR	101	121	107	122	117	117	105	109	104	106	105	83	117	106	114	105	74	105	110	127
66008 BENDENA	98	67	107	67	70	103	75	93	77	60	77	77	55	76	74	85	50	86	98	114
66010 BLUE MOUND	105	75	108	73	78	106	77	98	85	72	84	74	62	85	76	94	55	90	102	116
66012 BONNER SPRINGS	97	103	87	103	98	97	99	96	97	99	98	75	101	100	97	97	68	96	96	114
66013 BUCYRUS	124	151	143	155	151	141	129	134	124	135	125	104	146	126	142	121	90	128	126	155
66014 CENTERVILLE	90	65	92	64	68	92	67	85	74	62	73	64	54	74	66	81	48	78	88	101
66015 COLONY	78	54	86	54	56	82	60	74	62	49	61	61	44	61	59	68	40	69	78	91
66016 CUMMINGS	84	76	76	80	78	90	75	85	78	68	76	64	70	79	75	82	52	79	88	99
66017 DENTON	76	52	83	52	54	80	58	72	60	47	59	59	42	59	58	66	39	67	76	88
66018 DE SOTO	122	129	106	126	121	115	117	118	114	123	116	89	118	119	115	111	80	114	110	137
66020 EASTON	94	92	81	91	90	93	85	90	87	88	87	67	84	90	84	89	60	87	90	106
66021 EDGERTON	107	115	96	113	109	104	104	105	101	108	103	80	106	106	104	99	71	102	99	123
66023 EFFINGHAM	85	63	89	64	65	90	67	82	70	56	69	66	53	69	67	76	45	76	86	99
66025 EUDORA	94	93	79	94	89	86	92	89	90	94	91	70	91	93	89	88	63	89	85	105
66026 FONTANA	105	82	113	83	86	111	86	103	89	75	88	81	71	88	87	96	58	96	107	123
66027 FORT LEAVENWORTH	124	65	49	75	58	55	117	81	110	108	115	80	89	132	84	101	81	103	73	98
66030 GARDNER	112	115	96	113	109	105	109	107	106	113	107	84	109	111	106	103	74	106	102	125
66031 NEW CENTURY	104	117	101	121	114	115	105	109	103	105	103	85	112	105	110	103	72	105	108	128
66032 GARNETT	79	60	82	59	62	84	63	77	69	56	67	59	52	68	63	75	45	72	84	92
66033 GREELEY	97	70	104	70	73	103	76	93	79	63	78	76	58	78	76	86	51	87	98	113
66035 HIGHLAND	71	51	73	50	53	75	56	69	62	49	60	52	44	61	54	68	40	64	75	82
66039 KINCAID	76	54	80	53	56	78	56	71	62	51	61	55	44	61	56	68	40	66	75	86
66040 LACYGNE	94	73	97	71	75	96	73	89	79	69	78	67	62	79	73	85	52	83	92	106
66041 LANCASTER	83	70	79	72	71	88	71	82	73	62	72	64	62	74	71	78	48	76	85	97
66042 LANE	92	84	81	86	85	96	82	92	85	77	84	69	76	87	81	89	57	85	94	107
66043 LANSING	122	133	113	131	127	121	120	121	117	125	118	93	124	122	121	115	83	118	115	141
66044 LAWRENCE	65	48	43	51	45	50	75	55	69	62	69	49	59	69	56	67	48	65	58	70
66045 LAWRENCE	35	15	15	18	14	17	50	24	39	34	40	27	29	39	27	36	28	35	24	33
66046 LAWRENCE	83	71	63	73	68	68	86	73	82	81	83	61	76	84	74	80	58	79	73	89
66047 LAWRENCE	104	93	88	97	91	91	113	96	107	105	108	79	103	108	100	105	76	104	97	117
66048 LEAVENWORTH	87	86	79	88	84	90	88	86	90	85	89	67	88	90	87	92	62	88	93	103
66049 LAWRENCE	110	105	97	109	103	99	118	103	111	113	112	86	112	114	108	108	80	109	100	124
66050 LECOMPTON	95	94	82	93	91	94	87	91	88	89	88	68	86	91	86	90	61	88	91	108
66052 LINWOOD	98	97	91	101	97	106	92	101	93	87	92	77	90	95	94	96	64	94	102	117
66053 LOUISBURG	100	110	96	111	107	108	100	103	99	101	99	79	105	101	103	99	69	100	103	121
66054 MC LOUTH	87	89	82	92	88	95	83	89	83	80	83	69	83	85	85	85	57	84	90	105
66056 MOUND CITY	86	62	88	60	64	87	63	81	70	59	69	60	51	70	63	77	46	74	84	96
66058 MUSCOTAH	87	60	95	60	62	92	66	82	69	54	68	68	49	68	66	75	44	77	87	101
66060 NORTONVILLE	98	71	104	71	74	103	77	94	80	63	79	76	59	79	76	86	51	87	99	114
66061 OLATHE	124	132	115	131	127	116	125	121	119	131	121	96	128	125	123	115	86	119	111	140
66062 OLATHE	147	160	138	161	153	136	146	142	138	157	141	115	153	147	146	131	100	138	126	164
66064 OSAWATOMIE	80	72	65	72	69	79	74	76	77	71	76	58	69	78	70	80	52	76	81	91
66066 OSKALOOSA	95	77	100	76	79	99	76	92	81	72	80	69	66	81	77	87	54	85	94	109
66067 OTTAWA	80	74	69	76	72	82	78	78	80	73	79	61	74	80	75	82	54	79	85	94
66070 OZAWKIE	100	94	114	95	97	107	89	103	90	86	90	77	86	89	95	93	61	96	101	120
66071 PAOLA	98	99	90	101	97	104	96	99	96	93	96	76	95	98	96	98	66	97	102	117
66072 PARKER	78	70	73	72	72	84	69	79	72	63	70	60	63	73	69	76	48	73	81	92
66073 PERRY	93	89	82	88	88	92	83	89	85	85	85	66	81	88	82	87	58	86	89	105
66075 PLEASANTON	76	54	77	53	56	78	57	72	63	52	62	54	46	63	56	70	41	66	76	85
66076 POMONA	86	67	85	67	69	89	68	83	73	62	72	62	57	74	67	80	48	76	86	98
66078 PRINCETON	90	80	81	83	81	96	79	90	83	72	81	68	72	84	78	88	55	83	93	105
66079 RANTOUL	89	81	80	84	83	95	80	90	82	72	81	68	74	84	80	87	55	83	93	105
66080 RICHMOND	96	72	84	72	73	95	75	87	81	70	79	68	61	83	70	87	53	82	91	105
66083 SPRING HILL	116	130	111	130	125	118	115	117	111	119	112	91	122	116	119	108	79	112	110	136
66085 STILWELL	199	250	230	257	247	214	207	211	192	226	196	171	239	203	225	180	144	196	180	238
66086 TONGANOXIE	93	100	88	101	97	98	91	94	91	92	91	73	95	93	94	91	64	92	94	111
66087 TROY	79	60	79	60	62	83	64	77	68	56	67	59	52	68	63	74	44	71	82	91
66088 VALLEY FALLS	93	70	98	70	72	98	73	89	77	64	76	71	59	77	73	84	50	83	93	108
66090 WATHENA	76	60	71	59	60	75	63	71	67	59	66	55	53	67	60	71	44	69	74	86
66091 WELDA	75	52	79	52	55	77	56	70	60	49	59	55	43	59	55	66	39	65	74	85
66092 WELLSVILLE	91	91	79	92	88	94	86	90	87	85	87	68	85	90	85	89	60	87	92	106
66093 WESTPHALIA	76	52	83	52	55	80	58	72	60	47	59	59	42	59	58	66	39	67	76	88
66094 WHITE CLOUD	85	59	94	59	62	90	65	81	68	53	67	67	48	67	65	74	44	76	86	100
66095 WILLIAMSBURG	92	67	93	66	70	94	69	86	76	64	74	65	56	75	68	83	49	79	90	103
66097 WINCHESTER	81	73	75	76	75	87	72	82	75	65	73	62	66	76	72	79	50	76	85	96
66101 KANSAS CITY	52	40	37	41	39	46	49	46	54	48	53	34	44	53	43	57	37	51	54	57
66102 KANSAS CITY	67	56	48	57	53	61	65	61	68	62	67	47	59	68	58	70	47	65	67	74
66103 KANSAS CITY	67	46	41	50	43	49	67	54	68	62	68	46	56	68	54	68	47	63	59	68
66104 KANSAS CITY	72	65	58	66	62	72	69	68	74	68	73	51	67	73	65	78	50	71	78	83
66105 KANSAS CITY	77	62	48	54	59	61	64	67	69	69	69	44	56	70	57	72	48	68	67	75
66106 KANSAS CITY	80	75	62	76	70	79	79	76	81	75	80	60	76	83	74	84	56	79	83	92
66109 KANSAS CITY	107	122	106	122	117	117	110	111	109	111	109	85	118	111	114	109	77	109	113	130
66111 KANSAS CITY	84	84	73	84	80	85	83	82	83	81	83	63	82	85	81	85	58	82	85	98
66112 KANSAS CITY	83	75	68	76	72	78	83	78	85	80	84	61	78	85	78	86	58	83	84	94
66113 EDWARDSVILLE	81	76	64	72	72	73	75	74	75	78	75	56	71	78	70	75	52	75	73	88
66118 KANSAS CITY	0	0	0	0	0	0	0	0	0	0	0	0	0	0	0	0	0	0	0	0
66202 MISSION	94	86	79	89	83	84	97	87	96	95	98	70	94	97	91	96	68	94	91	105
66203 SHAWNEE	99	97	88	97	94	95	99	96	99	99	99	75	98	100	96	99	69	98	97	113
66204 OVERLAND PARK	92	86	79	88	83	85	94	87	94	93	94	68	91	94	89	93	66	92	90	104
66205 MISSION	120	134	133	136	135	130	127	126	125	131	126	96	137	124	134	124	89	126	127	147
66206 LEAWOOD	140	179	202	182	193	176	156	166	151	168	150	120	182	145	180	150	109	158	165	186
66207 OVERLAND PARK	133	161	173	162	170	165	139	152	139	148	139	107	159	135	158	142	98	145	158	172
66208 PRAIRIE VILLAGE	143	169	172	171	172	166	151	157	150	157	150	116	170	148	165	150	107	153	159	180
66209 LEAWOOD	210	266	280	276	277	248	229	237	218	245	219	181	267	217	257	212	161	225	221	268
66210 OVERLAND PARK	132	130	122	136	127	120	135	124	130	137	133	101	136	134	131	127	94	129	120	148
66211 LEAWOOD	191	252	287	258	274	242	213	229	202	233	201	167	254	196	250	197	148	214	216	254
66212 OVERLAND PARK	102	100	97	103	99	100	105	99	105	105	106	77	106	105	104	105	74	104	104	118
66213 OVERLAND PARK	199	218	193	227	211	185	200	193	188	216	192	161	214	201	202	176	139	186	167	221
66214 OVERLAND PARK	107	98	94	102	96	95	108	98	107	109	109	78	106	108	103	106	76	105	100	118
66215 LENEXA	124	129	125	134	128	123	128	123	126	132	127	97	134	127	130	124	90	125	122	144
66216 SHAWNEE	140	164	150	165	160	148	144	145	139	152	141	113	159	143	152	135	100	141	136	168
66217 SHAWNEE	167	170	162	179	168	153	169	158	162	177	164	128	176	168	167	155	119	161	145	186
66218 SHAWNEE	160	196	175	202	193	165	164	167	152	181	154	136	186	162	175	141	113	154	140	187
KANSAS	98	90	91	91	89	97	94	95	94	90	94	74	88	96	90	96	65	95	98	113
UNITED STATES	100	100	100	100	100	100	100	100	100	100	100	100	100	100	100	100	100	100	100	100

ZIP CODE #	POST OFFICE NAME	COUNTY FIPS CODE	POPULATION 2000	POPULATION 2009	POPULATION 2014	2000-2009 ANNUAL RATE % Rate	2000-2009 ANNUAL RATE State Centile	HOUSEHOLDS 2000	HOUSEHOLDS 2009	HOUSEHOLDS 2014	HOUSEHOLDS % Annual Rate 2000-2009	HOUSEHOLDS 2009 Average HH Size	FAMILIES 2000	FAMILIES 2009	FAMILIES % Annual Rate 2000-2009
66219	LENEXA	091	8022	9720	10548	2.1	96	3101	3991	4413	2.8	2.44	2006	2325	1.6
66220	LENEXA	091	1623	4702	5998	12.2	100	579	1693	2182	12.3	2.78	503	1422	11.9
66221	OVERLAND PARK	091	6249	15207	19360	10.1	100	1805	4351	5562	10.0	3.50	1708	4095	9.9
66223	OVERLAND PARK	091	12862	23457	28007	6.7	99	4111	7590	9105	6.9	3.09	3566	6486	6.7
66224	OVERLAND PARK	091	6358	11337	13978	6.5	99	2046	3573	4408	6.2	3.17	1753	3053	6.2
66226	SHAWNEE	091	6662	11903	14306	6.5	99	2174	3949	4794	6.7	3.01	1930	3429	6.4
66227	LENEXA	091	1519	3303	4088	8.8	100	549	1288	1613	9.7	2.56	465	1065	9.4
66401	ALMA	197	2152	2144	2133	0.0	64	840	847	845	0.1	2.47	610	609	0.0
66402	AUBURN	177	2665	2851	2932	0.7	84	927	1019	1056	1.0	2.80	766	831	0.9
66403	AXTELL	117	751	727	708	-0.4	48	281	274	267	-0.3	2.59	213	206	-0.4
66404	BAILEYVILLE	131	594	535	508	-1.1	17	195	177	169	-1.0	3.02	155	141	-1.0
66406	BEATTIE	117	583	569	555	-0.3	52	230	226	221	-0.2	2.49	160	156	-0.3
66407	BELVUE	149	381	439	469	1.5	92	127	144	154	1.4	3.05	97	109	1.3
66408	BERN	131	465	423	404	-1.0	19	171	156	149	-1.0	2.71	139	127	-1.0
66409	BERRYTON	177	3010	3360	3514	1.2	91	1075	1231	1297	1.5	2.73	908	1027	1.3
66411	BLUE RAPIDS	117	1328	1242	1195	-0.7	32	530	500	482	-0.6	2.41	364	339	-0.8
66412	BREMEN	117	417	400	389	-0.4	48	153	149	145	-0.3	2.68	118	114	-0.4
66413	BURLINGAME	139	1889	1807	1754	-0.5	41	774	755	736	-0.3	2.35	532	512	-0.4
66414	CARBONDALE	139	3064	2952	2872	-0.4	48	1164	1142	1117	-0.2	2.58	870	846	-0.3
66415	CENTRALIA	131	736	771	771	0.5	79	296	315	316	0.7	2.35	194	205	0.6
66416	CIRCLEVILLE	085	462	485	488	0.5	79	181	193	195	0.7	2.51	139	146	0.5
66417	CORNING	131	680	637	616	-0.7	32	235	219	211	-0.8	2.88	177	164	-0.8
66418	DELIA	085	658	725	754	1.1	89	216	239	249	1.1	3.03	174	191	1.0
66419	DENISON	085	511	565	587	1.1	89	180	203	212	1.3	2.77	142	158	1.2
66422	EMMETT	149	537	615	654	1.5	92	195	221	234	1.4	2.78	151	169	1.2
66423	ESKRIDGE	197	772	827	844	0.7	84	290	315	322	0.9	2.45	204	219	0.8
66424	EVEREST	013	624	608	592	-0.3	52	249	245	239	-0.2	2.48	181	177	-0.2
66425	FAIRVIEW	013	575	550	537	-0.5	41	238	234	231	-0.2	2.35	176	172	-0.2
66427	FRANKFORT	117	1477	1381	1330	-0.7	32	588	553	533	-0.7	2.41	405	376	-0.8
66428	GOFF	131	552	510	488	-0.9	23	189	172	163	-1.0	2.97	141	127	-1.1
66429	GRANTVILLE	087	535	552	545	0.3	74	198	206	204	0.4	2.68	155	161	0.4
66431	HARVEYVILLE	197	919	944	942	0.3	74	345	357	358	0.4	2.64	267	274	0.3
66432	HAVENSVILLE	149	478	474	474	-0.1	59	185	187	187	0.1	2.53	142	143	0.1
66434	HIAWATHA	013	5205	5071	4943	-0.3	52	2151	2127	2081	-0.1	2.32	1430	1401	-0.2
66436	HOLTON	085	5344	5424	5435	0.2	70	2133	2196	2211	0.3	2.37	1444	1465	0.2
66438	HOME	117	321	313	305	-0.3	52	116	114	111	-0.2	2.72	81	78	-0.4
66439	HORTON	013	2923	2765	2666	-0.6	36	1148	1095	1057	-0.5	2.47	762	719	-0.6
66440	HOYT	085	2029	2391	2538	1.8	95	714	859	916	2.0	2.78	585	697	1.9
66441	JUNCTION CITY	061	22244	20455	19529	-0.9	23	8852	8285	7947	-0.7	2.44	6091	5661	-0.8
66442	FORT RILEY	061	11180	11522	11541	0.3	74	2059	2147	2167	0.5	3.64	2020	2104	0.4
66449	LEONARDVILLE	161	943	991	1028	0.5	79	352	382	401	0.9	2.49	261	276	0.6
66451	LYNDON	139	2367	2647	2673	1.2	91	916	1031	1042	1.3	2.55	696	776	1.2
66502	MANHATTAN	161	39830	42151	43494	0.6	82	15874	17354	18120	1.0	2.22	7612	8084	0.7
66503	MANHATTAN	161	10802	11861	12375	1.0	88	4156	4765	5038	1.5	2.42	2882	3237	1.3
66506	MANHATTAN	161	2256	2364	2367	0.5	79	10	14	15	3.7	1.57	3	4	3.2
66507	MAPLE HILL	197	1180	1252	1278	0.6	82	447	481	492	0.8	2.60	355	379	0.7
66508	MARYSVILLE	117	4240	3994	3861	-0.6	36	1805	1725	1671	-0.5	2.24	1149	1086	-0.6
66509	MAYETTA	085	2130	2417	2535	1.4	92	723	835	880	1.6	2.89	576	658	1.4
66510	MELVERN	139	909	901	883	-0.1	59	352	355	350	0.1	2.53	261	261	0.0
66512	MERIDEN	087	3109	3308	3349	0.7	84	1151	1239	1256	0.8	2.67	918	982	0.7
66514	MILFORD	061	1577	1491	1421	-0.6	36	573	555	533	-0.3	2.69	465	447	-0.4
66515	MORRILL	013	479	469	461	-0.2	56	176	176	175	0.0	2.66	130	129	-0.1
66516	NETAWAKA	085	382	378	371	-0.1	59	142	143	142	0.1	2.64	112	112	0.0
66517	OGDEN	161	1763	1817	1887	0.3	74	691	747	786	0.8	2.43	480	506	0.6
66518	OKETO	117	238	229	223	-0.4	48	99	97	94	-0.2	2.35	75	72	-0.4
66520	OLSBURG	149	582	651	693	1.2	91	235	267	285	1.4	2.44	181	205	1.4
66521	ONAGA	149	1478	1553	1601	0.5	79	588	632	656	0.8	2.36	385	406	0.6
66522	ONEIDA	131	223	200	190	-1.2	14	78	71	67	-1.0	2.82	62	56	-1.1
66523	OSAGE CITY	139	4059	3991	3910	-0.2	56	1608	1589	1558	-0.1	2.45	1102	1077	-0.2
66524	OVERBROOK	045	2318	2380	2397	0.3	74	856	896	905	0.5	2.57	651	674	0.4
66526	PAXICO	197	1306	1300	1296	0.0	64	474	481	481	0.2	2.70	357	359	0.1
66527	POWHATTAN	013	367	300	276	-2.2	2	135	113	105	-1.9	2.65	102	85	-2.0
66528	QUENEMO	139	588	696	713	1.8	95	211	248	253	1.8	2.81	167	194	1.6
66531	RILEY	161	1464	1609	1657	1.0	88	498	562	587	1.3	2.71	381	421	1.1
66532	ROBINSON	013	741	692	664	-0.7	32	283	269	259	-0.5	2.53	205	193	-0.6
66533	ROSSVILLE	177	1561	1619	1647	0.4	76	576	614	630	0.7	2.61	440	460	0.5
66534	SABETHA	131	3561	3427	3335	-0.4	48	1285	1236	1199	-0.4	2.49	883	842	-0.5
66535	SAINT GEORGE	149	2319	2597	2742	1.2	91	894	1012	1071	1.3	2.57	639	714	1.2
66536	SAINT MARYS	149	2994	3114	3193	0.4	76	972	1010	1035	0.4	2.97	679	697	0.3
66537	SCRANTON	139	1163	1252	1252	0.8	86	429	468	471	0.9	2.68	313	337	0.8
66538	SENECA	131	3362	3311	3248	-0.2	56	1308	1307	1285	0.0	2.45	865	858	-0.1
66539	SILVER LAKE	177	2690	2829	2903	0.5	79	984	1071	1109	0.9	2.61	772	826	0.7
66540	SOLDIER	085	525	554	559	0.6	82	187	200	203	0.7	2.77	144	152	0.6
66541	SUMMERFIELD	117	276	268	261	-0.3	52	97	95	92	-0.2	2.75	73	71	-0.3
66542	TECUMSEH	177	2981	3161	3248	0.6	82	1064	1167	1211	1.0	2.71	910	988	0.9
66543	VASSAR	139	766	853	857	1.2	91	308	345	348	1.2	2.47	244	272	1.2
66544	VERMILLION	117	404	385	372	-0.5	41	170	164	159	-0.4	2.33	127	122	-0.4
66546	WAKARUSA	177	1052	1078	1091	0.3	74	403	426	436	0.6	2.53	319	331	0.4
66547	WAMEGO	149	6441	7201	7626	1.2	91	2391	2703	2868	1.3	2.64	1781	1994	1.2
66548	WATERVILLE	117	988	901	860	-1.0	19	410	373	357	-1.0	2.42	278	250	-1.1
66549	WESTMORELAND	149	1479	1579	1645	0.7	84	577	622	649	0.8	2.47	426	456	0.7
66550	WETMORE	131	625	581	556	-0.8	28	233	212	201	-1.0	2.74	172	155	-1.1
66552	WHITING	085	438	481	499	1.0	88	188	211	220	1.3	2.28	139	153	1.0
66554	RANDOLPH	161	616	669	696	0.9	87	253	285	301	1.3	2.29	186	204	1.0
66603	TOPEKA	177	2038	2014	2011	-0.1	59	917	915	918	0.0	2.09	397	377	-0.6
66604	TOPEKA	177	23014	22538	22382	-0.2	56	10206	10264	10273	0.1	2.14	5783	5644	-0.3
66605	TOPEKA	177	19067	19280	19419	0.1	68	7311	7630	7755	0.5	2.50	5246	5389	0.3
66606	TOPEKA	177	12217	11783	11644	-0.4	48	5664	5615	5591	-0.1	2.00	2882	2753	-0.5
66607	TOPEKA	177	9977	9982	10010	0.0	64	3312	3349	3370	0.1	2.69	2183	2149	-0.2
66608	TOPEKA	177	5729	5585	5547	-0.3	52	2400	2412	2419	0.1	2.16	1413	1381	-0.2
66609	TOPEKA	177	6396	6998	7282	1.0	88	2723	3024	3153	1.1	2.30	1735	1924	1.1
66610	TOPEKA	177	6496	7903	8410	2.1	96	2275	2848	3062	2.5	2.68	1870	2322	2.4
66611	TOPEKA	177	9580	9294	9198	-0.3	52	4520	4512	4503	0.0	2.03	2479	2395	-0.4
66612	TOPEKA	177	2943	2969	2984	0.1	68	1610	1636	1650	0.2	1.75	599	582	-0.3
66614	TOPEKA	177	31210	32710	33526	0.5	79	13156	14056	14466	0.7	2.25	8378	8803	0.5
	KANSAS					0.6					0.6	2.49			0.5
	UNITED STATES					1.0					1.1	2.59			0.9

POPULATION COMPOSITION

ZIP CODE #	POST OFFICE NAME	RACE (%) White 2000	White 2009	Black 2000	Black 2009	Asian/Pacific 2000	Asian/Pacific 2009	% Hispanic Origin 2000	% Hispanic Origin 2009	2009 AGE DISTRIBUTION (%) 0-4	5-9	10-14	15-19	20-24	25-44	45-64	65-84	85+	18+	MEDIAN AGE 2009	% 2009 Males	% 2009 Females
66219	LENEXA	90.9	87.4	2.8	3.3	3.5	5.3	2.6	4.4	6.9	6.6	6.9	6.9	7.6	34.0	26.8	4.1	0.3	75.6	33.2	50.3	49.7
66220	LENEXA	95.4	93.9	2.0	2.2	1.4	2.3	2.1	3.4	6.0	7.3	8.5	7.3	3.2	21.5	36.3	9.1	0.6	73.5	42.7	49.1	50.9
66221	OVERLAND PARK	94.5	92.5	1.9	2.1	2.4	3.8	1.3	2.1	8.9	9.9	10.5	9.4	4.8	22.6	29.8	3.8	0.3	64.7	31.1	49.5	50.5
66223	OVERLAND PARK	92.6	89.7	1.9	2.4	3.3	4.9	2.4	4.1	11.0	10.7	9.7	7.1	3.2	31.6	23.3	3.2	0.2	63.7	32.5	49.7	50.3
66224	OVERLAND PARK	92.2	90.4	2.9	3.0	3.0	4.3	1.8	2.7	10.3	10.5	10.4	7.7	4.8	24.2	26.5	5.2	0.4	63.6	31.6	48.5	51.5
66226	SHAWNEE	94.4	92.7	1.8	1.9	1.6	2.0	2.9	4.8	10.5	11.0	10.2	6.6	3.0	30.9	23.4	4.0	0.3	63.9	35.2	50.0	50.0
66227	LENEXA	97.2	96.3	0.4	0.5	0.4	0.6	1.7	3.0	5.8	6.6	7.5	7.3	3.9	23.6	34.8	9.5	1.0	75.5	42.1	50.2	49.8
66401	ALMA	97.2	96.5	0.3	0.3	0.1	0.1	2.3	3.3	6.0	6.3	7.2	6.7	4.6	22.9	29.2	14.2	3.0	76.1	42.4	50.8	49.2
66402	AUBURN	96.1	94.9	0.5	0.6	0.5	0.6	2.7	4.3	6.1	6.6	7.1	8.0	6.2	24.2	31.0	9.8	1.0	75.3	38.4	48.1	51.9
66403	AXTELL	98.1	97.8	0.1	0.1	0.1	0.1	0.8	1.1	5.9	6.6	7.0	7.2	4.3	20.9	30.1	15.0	3.0	75.1	43.7	50.2	49.8
66404	BAILEYVILLE	99.0	98.5	0.2	0.2	0.0	0.2	0.8	1.3	8.2	8.6	8.4	8.2	4.9	20.7	26.7	12.5	1.7	69.7	37.6	52.5	47.5
66406	BEATTIE	97.6	97.2	0.2	0.2	0.2	0.2	1.4	2.1	5.4	6.2	6.7	6.7	4.7	21.4	32.7	13.7	2.5	77.0	44.0	51.7	48.3
66407	BELVUE	97.9	97.5	0.0	0.0	0.0	0.0	1.6	2.1	9.3	9.8	8.2	7.1	5.7	23.9	23.2	10.7	2.1	68.3	34.5	51.0	49.0
66408	BERN	98.9	98.6	0.0	0.0	0.2	0.5	0.9	1.4	7.8	8.5	8.5	8.3	4.7	18.2	29.3	12.8	1.9	70.2	39.3	52.0	48.0
66409	BERRYTON	96.2	95.0	1.5	1.8	0.4	0.5	2.7	4.3	5.2	5.9	6.8	7.0	4.7	20.7	36.8	12.0	0.9	77.7	44.8	51.1	48.9
66411	BLUE RAPIDS	98.2	97.9	0.2	0.2	0.1	0.1	0.6	0.8	6.0	6.0	5.9	6.3	5.9	21.2	27.1	17.3	4.3	77.8	43.8	49.8	50.2
66412	BREMEN	97.1	96.8	0.2	0.3	0.0	0.0	0.5	0.5	4.0	4.5	4.8	6.0	4.8	22.5	32.8	18.3	2.5	83.0	47.1	52.5	47.5
66413	BURLINGAME	98.1	97.6	0.3	0.3	0.0	0.0	0.7	1.1	5.4	6.2	6.6	6.7	4.3	21.9	30.5	14.9	3.4	77.0	44.1	48.3	51.7
66414	CARBONDALE	97.5	97.0	0.3	0.3	0.2	0.3	2.3	3.4	6.6	7.0	7.0	7.7	5.9	24.2	29.8	10.7	1.2	74.8	39.4	48.8	51.2
66415	CENTRALIA	98.0	97.5	0.1	0.1	0.3	0.3	2.0	3.0	6.5	6.5	6.5	7.3	5.8	19.3	27.1	14.8	6.2	75.9	43.2	50.7	49.3
66416	CIRCLEVILLE	92.0	91.3	0.4	0.4	0.2	0.4	1.5	2.1	7.2	7.6	8.0	6.4	4.1	22.5	30.7	12.0	1.4	73.0	40.7	52.8	47.2
66417	CORNING	97.8	97.6	0.6	0.6	0.4	0.5	0.4	0.9	7.8	8.3	7.8	6.9	4.6	20.3	27.9	13.0	3.3	71.6	39.7	51.5	48.5
66418	DELIA	71.0	69.8	0.5	0.4	0.2	0.1	1.5	1.8	8.4	8.6	8.6	8.3	5.7	22.2	26.5	10.9	1.0	69.4	35.9	50.1	49.9
66419	DENISON	96.5	95.8	0.4	0.5	0.0	0.0	1.0	1.2	6.9	7.6	7.8	6.5	3.7	24.2	28.5	13.3	1.4	73.3	40.1	51.5	48.5
66422	EMMETT	92.8	92.7	0.2	0.2	0.2	0.2	1.5	2.1	9.3	9.9	8.5	7.2	5.7	23.6	23.3	10.9	1.8	67.8	34.3	50.9	49.1
66423	ESKRIDGE	97.9	97.6	0.8	0.8	0.3	0.4	1.0	1.7	5.7	5.9	6.2	6.0	4.5	22.0	32.0	15.4	2.3	79.1	44.8	49.2	50.8
66424	EVEREST	94.1	92.6	1.8	2.0	0.2	0.3	2.1	3.1	5.9	6.6	6.9	6.7	3.9	25.2	30.4	11.8	2.5	76.3	41.3	51.0	49.0
66425	FAIRVIEW	90.8	91.1	1.4	1.5	0.0	0.0	1.4	1.8	5.6	6.0	6.4	6.7	4.4	22.0	32.4	14.4	2.2	78.0	44.2	48.2	51.8
66427	FRANKFORT	98.5	98.4	0.5	0.6	0.1	0.1	0.6	0.7	4.3	5.1	6.4	7.1	5.4	19.6	28.0	18.0	6.1	79.5	46.4	49.6	50.4
66428	GOFF	97.6	97.5	0.7	0.8	0.2	0.2	0.5	0.6	8.4	8.8	8.8	8.2	4.3	21.8	25.7	11.8	2.4	68.8	36.8	52.0	48.0
66429	GRANTVILLE	95.9	94.7	0.2	0.2	0.4	0.5	1.9	2.9	5.3	5.6	6.0	6.3	5.3	23.6	33.9	12.9	1.3	79.3	43.5	52.5	47.5
66431	HARVEYVILLE	97.7	97.1	0.2	0.2	0.3	0.4	1.0	1.3	6.1	6.8	7.2	6.9	3.9	21.4	32.7	13.2	1.7	75.5	43.2	51.2	48.8
66432	HAVENSVILLE	96.7	96.2	0.2	0.2	0.2	0.2	1.3	1.7	6.5	7.2	7.6	6.3	4.2	21.5	30.4	14.1	2.1	74.5	42.6	54.0	46.0
66434	HIAWATHA	90.4	88.8	2.2	2.4	0.1	0.2	2.4	3.5	6.2	6.1	6.2	6.4	5.5	21.9	27.6	15.3	4.7	77.5	43.0	48.3	51.7
66436	HOLTON	93.8	93.0	0.8	0.9	0.2	0.3	1.6	2.2	6.6	6.6	6.5	6.1	5.7	22.9	26.2	14.6	4.8	76.2	41.5	47.6	52.4
66438	HOME	98.1	97.4	0.3	0.3	0.0	0.0	1.6	2.2	5.1	6.1	7.0	7.0	4.5	21.4	32.6	13.7	2.6	76.7	44.1	51.8	48.2
66439	HORTON	81.2	79.3	0.9	1.0	0.5	0.7	2.5	3.4	7.3	7.3	7.3	7.2	5.2	22.5	24.5	14.5	4.2	73.5	39.3	48.4	51.6
66440	HOYT	91.1	90.5	0.1	0.1	0.1	0.3	2.0	2.7	7.0	7.2	8.1	7.6	4.9	25.4	28.7	10.2	0.9	72.9	38.6	50.5	49.5
66441	JUNCTION CITY	62.8	58.7	23.3	23.9	3.9	5.3	7.6	10.6	8.3	7.5	6.7	6.6	7.5	28.1	23.6	10.0	1.6	73.6	33.2	48.8	51.2
66442	FORT RILEY	61.8	57.7	22.9	23.3	2.6	3.3	13.3	18.0	13.7	9.3	5.8	9.1	27.3	33.2	1.4	0.1	0.0	68.7	22.2	63.2	36.8
66449	LEONARDVILLE	97.9	97.5	0.0	0.0	0.1	0.2	1.7	2.5	4.8	5.7	6.1	6.8	4.4	20.3	30.5	16.0	5.4	78.7	46.2	49.8	50.2
66451	LYNDON	97.7	96.9	0.0	0.0	0.3	0.5	0.9	1.4	5.6	6.1	6.6	6.8	5.4	23.2	31.0	13.2	2.2	77.3	42.2	51.1	48.9
66502	MANHATTAN	87.4	84.8	4.8	5.1	3.6	5.1	3.7	5.4	4.9	4.0	3.9	9.9	29.2	23.6	15.8	6.9	1.8	84.3	24.7	52.4	47.6
66503	MANHATTAN	89.8	87.3	3.5	3.7	3.6	5.2	2.5	3.5	5.7	5.9	6.2	7.3	9.0	26.5	27.5	9.8	2.2	78.0	37.3	50.0	50.0
66506	MANHATTAN	89.7	87.6	5.6	6.0	1.7	2.5	3.5	5.1	0.0	0.0	0.0	71.4	26.9	1.6	0.2	0.0	0.0	99.9	18.5	38.2	61.8
66507	MAPLE HILL	96.4	95.6	0.8	0.9	0.3	0.4	2.0	2.7	7.3	7.7	7.7	6.5	4.6	22.8	28.7	13.4	1.4	73.4	40.3	51.0	49.0
66508	MARYSVILLE	98.2	97.8	0.2	0.2	0.4	0.5	0.7	1.0	5.1	5.4	5.7	5.9	5.8	21.4	29.7	15.9	5.1	79.7	45.4	48.3	51.7
66509	MAYETTA	83.2	82.4	0.3	0.4	0.1	0.2	1.2	1.5	7.4	7.6	9.0	8.2	4.6	23.6	27.9	10.7	0.9	70.9	37.5	50.6	49.4
66510	MELVERN	97.8	97.6	0.0	0.0	0.1	0.1	1.1	1.7	6.9	7.0	6.9	5.8	5.2	24.3	29.3	12.3	2.3	75.2	40.0	51.1	48.9
66512	MERIDEN	97.2	96.6	0.4	0.4	0.1	0.2	1.4	2.1	6.8	7.0	7.5	6.9	5.1	25.6	29.8	10.4	0.9	74.4	39.8	51.3	48.7
66514	MILFORD	84.3	80.9	5.5	5.7	2.5	3.2	5.6	8.3	6.2	6.3	6.5	6.8	6.0	25.4	30.9	11.3	0.7	76.7	39.0	50.7	49.3
66515	MORRILL	97.7	97.0	1.5	1.7	0.0	0.0	0.8	1.3	5.1	5.8	6.0	6.8	4.3	21.3	33.5	15.1	2.1	78.9	45.4	48.4	51.6
66516	NETAWAKA	92.4	92.3	0.0	0.0	0.5	0.8	0.8	1.1	7.4	7.7	7.9	7.1	4.2	21.4	31.7	10.6	1.9	72.5	40.0	52.6	47.4
66517	OGDEN	77.5	74.1	11.4	12.1	2.7	3.7	7.0	9.7	10.5	8.8	7.3	7.0	9.6	33.9	17.2	5.2	0.6	69.3	28.0	50.5	49.5
66518	OKETO	97.1	96.9	0.0	0.0	0.0	0.0	0.8	0.9	4.4	5.2	5.2	6.1	4.8	22.7	32.3	17.0	2.2	80.8	45.9	52.4	47.6
66520	OLSBURG	97.6	97.4	0.7	0.6	0.0	0.0	1.5	2.2	5.4	6.3	6.9	6.8	3.5	21.4	33.6	14.1	2.0	77.1	44.8	52.5	47.5
66521	ONAGA	97.2	96.6	0.3	0.3	0.3	0.5	1.8	2.6	6.4	6.6	7.0	6.6	4.4	21.4	26.5	16.4	4.8	75.7	43.1	51.1	48.9
66522	ONEIDA	99.1	99.0	0.0	0.0	0.0	0.0	0.9	1.5	8.0	8.5	8.0	8.0	4.5	21.0	27.0	13.0	2.0	70.0	38.6	52.5	47.5
66523	OSAGE CITY	96.9	96.4	0.3	0.3	0.3	0.4	2.0	3.0	7.1	7.0	7.0	6.8	5.3	21.1	26.7	14.8	4.0	74.2	41.1	48.7	51.3
66524	OVERBROOK	97.6	97.1	0.2	0.2	0.1	0.2	1.2	1.8	5.9	6.2	7.1	6.3	4.8	22.6	29.6	13.9	3.6	76.5	42.9	49.2	50.8
66526	PAXICO	97.2	96.7	0.4	0.4	0.2	0.2	1.8	2.8	7.5	7.5	8.1	7.5	6.0	23.5	28.1	10.5	1.4	72.2	37.8	50.8	49.2
66527	POWHATTAN	47.8	43.7	0.3	0.3	0.0	0.0	5.2	6.7	8.3	8.3	8.3	6.7	5.0	23.7	27.7	10.0	2.0	71.0	34.8	47.7	52.3
66528	QUENEMO	94.9	93.7	0.2	0.3	1.0	1.4	1.2	1.9	7.6	7.6	7.9	7.5	6.5	22.7	28.6	10.5	1.1	72.3	37.0	50.0	50.0
66531	RILEY	91.1	89.6	3.7	3.9	0.8	1.1	3.1	4.4	6.3	6.8	8.4	10.4	7.7	26.3	23.1	8.8	2.2	71.6	33.4	52.0	48.0
66532	ROBINSON	95.3	94.1	0.3	0.3	0.1	0.1	1.2	1.7	5.1	5.9	7.7	9.5	4.0	21.0	30.9	14.6	1.3	75.9	42.5	53.3	46.7
66533	ROSSVILLE	96.1	94.7	0.1	0.1	0.4	0.6	2.7	4.3	6.9	7.5	7.9	7.6	4.6	24.3	28.0	11.2	2.0	72.8	39.0	50.7	49.3
66534	SABETHA	98.0	97.6	0.8	0.8	0.2	0.2	0.5	0.8	7.2	7.2	6.9	5.9	5.0	20.3	24.0	16.3	7.2	74.8	42.9	47.8	52.2
66535	SAINT GEORGE	95.3	94.4	1.1	1.2	0.5	0.7	1.9	2.8	7.0	6.9	6.9	6.5	5.6	29.5	27.7	8.8	1.0	75.2	36.4	48.6	51.4
66536	SAINT MARYS	95.6	94.8	0.7	0.7	0.6	0.8	4.1	5.8	9.9	10.2	8.9	8.5	5.7	21.4	21.6	10.9	3.0	65.7	31.3	49.3	50.7
66537	SCRANTON	95.3	94.4	0.5	0.6	0.5	0.7	1.5	2.2	7.5	7.7	7.9	7.4	4.8	23.6	27.8	12.0	1.2	72.2	38.4	49.7	50.3
66538	SENECA	98.9	98.7	0.3	0.4	0.1	0.1	0.7	0.9	7.1	6.9	6.9	6.9	5.7	20.5	25.7	15.7	4.7	74.5	41.5	48.9	51.1
66539	SILVER LAKE	96.7	95.6	0.3	0.3	0.3	0.4	1.7	2.7	6.0	7.0	7.8	7.6	4.2	25.0	30.4	10.6	1.4	73.8	40.2	51.4	48.6
66540	SOLDIER	90.1	89.4	0.4	0.4	0.2	0.4	1.5	2.0	7.4	7.8	8.1	6.5	4.3	22.4	30.5	11.6	1.4	72.6	40.1	52.2	47.8
66541	SUMMERFIELD	98.5	98.1	0.0	0.0	0.0	0.0	0.7	0.7	6.0	6.7	6.7	6.7	4.5	21.3	30.2	14.9	3.0	75.4	43.7	49.6	50.4
66542	TECUMSEH	94.9	93.5	1.6	2.0	0.2	0.3	3.0	4.7	4.6	5.5	6.5	6.5	4.7	18.5	36.1	16.0	1.5	79.3	47.1	48.8	51.2
66543	VASSAR	97.8	97.1	0.0	0.0	0.3	0.5	1.0	1.6	5.3	6.0	6.3	6.2	4.9	21.3	33.3	15.4	1.3	78.5	45.0	49.8	50.2
66544	VERMILLION	98.8	98.7	0.7	0.8	0.0	0.0	1.0	1.3	3.9	6.0	9.1	9.1	3.9	18.7	29.4	16.4	3.6	74.8	44.6	52.2	47.8
66546	WAKARUSA	93.5	92.1	2.4	2.6	0.4	0.6	2.2	3.4	6.2	6.5	6.9	6.8	6.1	23.8	32.7	10.3	0.6	76.2	40.6	50.3	49.7
66547	WAMEGO	96.8	96.3	0.6	0.7	0.2	0.3	1.8	2.6	7.4	7.4	7.4	7.0	5.9	26.2	27.3	9.5	1.9	73.4	36.8	49.0	51.0
66548	WATERVILLE	98.0	97.6	0.1	0.1	0.2	0.3	1.0	1.3	6.8	6.7	6.4	6.8	6.2	19.3	26.7	17.1	4.0	75.9	43.1	49.7	50.3
66549	WESTMORELAND	97.8	97.4	0.1	0.1	0.1	0.1	1.8	2.7	6.3	7.1	7.3	6.3	3.8	21.4	30.1	14.0	3.5	75.0	43.3	50.7	49.3
66550	WETMORE	97.4	96.9	0.8	0.9	0.2	0.3	0.6	0.9	8.3	8.3	9.0	8.8	4.5	21.9	25.6	11.5	2.2	68.8	36.8	52.2	47.8
66552	WHITING	95.9	95.4	0.9	1.0	0.2	0.2	0.5	0.6	5.0	5.6	6.2	7.3	4.2	22.0	32.0	15.4	2.3	78.4	44.8	50.7	49.3
66554	RANDOLPH	97.2	96.7	0.3	0.3	0.3	0.4	1.8	2.5	5.2	6.0	6.3	5.8	4.2	22.0	31.8	14.8	3.9	78.6	45.3	50.4	49.6
66603	TOPEKA	64.1	58.0	17.1	18.2	0.5	0.7	16.9	24.2	8.5	7.0	5.9	8.1	9.4	29.2	23.2	7.3	1.3	74.5	31.8	54.8	45.2
66604	TOPEKA	83.2	80.1	9.6	10.5	0.9	1.3	5.9	9.0	6.6	6.1	5.9	6.4	7.0	26.9	25.4	12.5	3.0	77.9	38.2	46.7	53.3
66605	TOPEKA	69.1	64.8	20.3	21.6	0.7	0.9	9.9	14.4	7.5	7.3	7.3	7.3	6.4	23.7	27.3	11.6	1.6	73.4	37.0	47.4	52.6
66606	TOPEKA	85.5	82.4	7.5	8.4	0.8	1.1	5.8	8.8	6.1	5.8	5.6	5.5	5.8	26.7	26.2	13.6	4.6	79.2	40.6	46.9	53.1
66607	TOPEKA	51.7	46.7	26.8	26.6	0.3	0.4	24.9	32.8	8.3	7.4	6.7	7.7	8.3	28.3	22.1	9.8	1.5	73.0	32.6	50.9	49.1
66608	TOPEKA	87.3	84.5	5.0	5.8	0.4	0.6	5.4	8.3	7.1	6.9	6.4	9.5	6.4	25.2	25.9	10.9	1.7	73.7	35.8	51.5	48.5
66609	TOPEKA	84.3	81.1	9.0	9.8	1.2	1.5	6.6	10.2	6.4	6.5	6.4	6.3	6.1	29.2	27.0	10.8	1.4	77.1	36.6	48.4	51.6
66610	TOPEKA	91.4	89.2	3.8	4.3	1.5	2.2	3.1	5.0	5.4	5.7	6.7	7.2	4.8	21.1	34.0	12.8	2.3	77.3	44.3	48.6	51.4
66611	TOPEKA	84.2	80.6	8.6	9.9	1.6	2.2	4.6	7.1	6.2	5.4	5.4	5.5	6.1	26.0	25.3	15.7	4.6	79.7	41.2	47.0	53.0
66612	TOPEKA	56.0	50.8	30.6	32.3	1.1	1.4	10.8	15.6	7.6	6.6	5.5	6.5	8.7	28.5	25.1	9.7	1.7	77.1	34.7	51.0	49.0
66614	TOPEKA	88.2	85.2	5.5	6.2	2.1	3.0	4.1	6.3	6.1	5.8	6.0	6.1	5.5	26.5	27.8	13.4	2.6	78.1	40.0	47.8	52.2
	KANSAS	86.1	83.7	5.7	5.9	1.8	2.6	7.0	9.4	7.1	6.9	6.9	7.3	7.3	25.9	25.7	10.7	2.2	75.0	36.3	49.6	50.4
	UNITED STATES	75.1	72.0	12.3	12.7	3.8	4.6	12.5	15.7	6.8	6.7	6.6	7.1	6.9	27.0	26.0	10.9	1.9	75.7	36.9	49.2	50.8

INCOME

#	POST OFFICE NAME	2009 Per Capita Income	2009 HH Income Base	2009 Household Income Distribution (%): Less than $25,000	$25,000 to $49,999	$50,000 to $99,999	$100,000 to $149,999	$150,000 or More	Median Household Income: 2009	2014	2009 National Centile	2009 State Centile	2009 Home Value Base	2009 Home Value Distribution (%): Less than $50,000	$50,000 to $89,999	$90,000 to $174,999	$175,000 to $399,999	$400,000 or More	2009 Median Home Value
66219	LENEXA	38901	3991	5.1	16.4	38.2	28.4	11.9	83756	86195	93	97	2102	0.0	0.0	10.3	87.0	2.7	226015
66220	LENEXA	58641	1693	0.2	7.4	19.8	35.2	37.3	130264	131310	99	100	1507	0.0	0.0	14.2	57.9	27.9	312005
66221	OVERLAND PARK	62808	4351	0.7	4.9	13.5	19.0	61.8	173619	178055	100	100	3807	0.5	0.0	1.8	60.3	37.4	364820
66223	OVERLAND PARK	45991	7590	2.1	5.6	25.8	36.9	29.6	124274	125646	99	99	5688	1.1	0.0	10.6	80.2	8.2	243229
66224	OVERLAND PARK	55614	3573	4.2	9.4	22.2	21.1	43.1	133638	132422	99	100	2915	0.6	1.0	17.9	50.3	30.2	300772
66226	SHAWNEE	37961	3949	2.5	6.6	38.5	37.3	15.1	102296	105682	97	98	3619	0.6	1.0	19.4	74.9	4.0	205539
66227	LENEXA	37840	1288	7.5	12.1	46.3	25.6	8.5	80723	85490	92	96	1160	0.8	0.9	34.1	57.7	6.5	194249
66401	ALMA	21361	847	16.5	33.3	44.3	4.7	1.2	50083	52129	61	74	690	23.0	28.4	36.7	11.7	0.1	88387
66402	AUBURN	25043	1019	9.4	28.0	48.1	9.9	4.6	59412	58730	77	88	912	3.6	24.6	46.1	23.8	2.0	111222
66403	AXTELL	17271	274	29.9	34.3	32.1	2.2	1.5	37831	39610	26	23	233	43.8	25.8	20.2	9.4	0.9	59667
66404	BAILEYVILLE	15797	177	26.6	32.2	37.9	2.3	1.1	41280	43098	37	41	148	25.0	31.1	20.9	16.2	6.8	81000
66406	BEATTIE	18830	226	31.4	30.5	33.2	3.1	1.8	40520	41819	34	36	182	45.1	27.5	18.7	8.8	0.0	54737
66407	BELVUE	17283	144	22.9	36.1	34.0	4.9	2.1	45000	46579	48	57	113	21.2	21.2	40.7	12.4	4.4	100893
66408	BERN	18024	156	23.1	34.6	37.2	3.2	1.9	45000	46210	48	57	132	34.8	24.2	17.4	18.2	5.3	74000
66409	BERRYTON	26242	1231	10.9	22.0	48.7	14.8	3.7	66737	64649	85	93	1124	13.8	9.0	43.2	31.5	2.5	143646
66411	BLUE RAPIDS	19420	500	27.4	37.2	28.8	4.0	2.6	38718	40905	29	27	393	54.5	23.9	19.1	2.0	0.5	46818
66412	BREMEN	16481	149	25.5	38.9	30.9	3.4	1.3	38255	39761	27	25	123	28.5	29.3	30.9	9.8	1.6	80500
66413	BURLINGAME	20811	755	25.4	31.5	37.1	5.3	0.7	43075	45894	43	50	596	29.2	29.7	32.9	7.0	1.2	78936
66414	CARBONDALE	19676	1142	22.8	30.5	41.2	5.3	0.2	46977	48823	54	63	908	16.7	29.4	41.1	12.0	0.8	93571
66415	CENTRALIA	17160	315	40.3	34.0	21.3	1.9	2.5	29390	30396	7	2	245	35.1	34.3	26.1	3.7	0.8	70806
66416	CIRCLEVILLE	21702	193	23.8	28.0	38.9	6.2	3.1	48422	50851	58	68	167	18.6	26.3	30.5	23.4	1.2	100543
66417	CORNING	14585	219	26.9	37.9	34.2	0.9	0.0	39832	40128	32	31	187	32.6	17.1	35.8	12.3	2.1	90417
66418	DELIA	20150	239	16.7	33.9	40.2	5.9	3.3	49410	51373	60	72	199	22.6	25.1	35.2	14.6	2.5	91667
66419	DENISON	19914	203	14.8	34.0	46.3	3.0	2.0	51049	52823	64	77	173	22.0	16.2	36.4	23.7	1.7	104435
66422	EMMETT	19307	221	22.2	36.7	33.5	4.5	3.2	44874	46694	48	56	176	21.6	21.6	40.9	12.5	3.4	98000
66423	ESKRIDGE	18946	315	24.1	27.9	43.8	4.1	0.0	48324	50753	57	68	254	29.1	46.9	16.9	7.1	0.0	67419
66424	EVEREST	17886	245	29.8	30.2	36.7	2.4	0.8	38534	42698	28	26	199	33.7	26.1	26.1	9.5	4.5	72083
66425	FAIRVIEW	21925	234	23.5	30.8	41.0	4.3	0.4	45762	49661	51	59	193	34.2	21.8	33.2	9.8	1.0	78125
66427	FRANKFORT	17929	553	28.6	39.6	27.7	1.8	2.4	36416	38604	22	16	469	45.6	20.0	26.4	5.8	2.1	56406
66428	GOFF	16185	172	24.4	31.4	40.1	2.9	1.2	43998	46817	45	53	147	40.8	25.2	20.4	12.9	0.7	66500
66429	GRANTVILLE	25936	206	10.7	18.4	57.8	7.8	5.3	59152	60154	76	87	176	9.7	33.5	44.9	11.9	0.0	101042
66431	HARVEYVILLE	20787	357	19.9	30.5	42.9	4.2	2.5	49665	51692	60	72	296	21.6	26.7	33.1	18.6	0.0	92941
66432	HAVENSVILLE	20209	187	22.5	29.4	42.8	3.7	1.6	48420	50101	58	68	157	28.7	21.0	28.7	19.7	1.9	91000
66434	HIAWATHA	20424	2127	29.1	27.7	37.1	5.2	0.8	43495	46900	44	51	1439	21.5	30.6	39.0	8.5	0.3	87393
66436	HOLTON	21800	2196	22.9	31.7	37.2	6.5	1.7	44718	48711	47	56	1589	20.5	24.9	37.9	15.3	1.4	96250
66438	HOME	17396	114	29.8	32.5	34.2	2.6	0.9	40489	42348	34	35	92	44.6	25.0	20.7	9.8	0.0	55556
66439	HORTON	15351	1095	40.5	32.7	24.1	2.2	0.5	31699	32891	11	4	786	45.3	28.2	22.6	3.6	0.3	56271
66440	HOYT	20556	859	16.5	26.8	49.9	5.7	1.0	54014	54294	70	82	747	11.8	24.0	47.8	16.2	0.3	104827
66441	JUNCTION CITY	21566	8285	24.3	35.1	32.7	5.2	2.6	41883	44922	39	44	4559	18.9	37.0	35.0	8.6	0.5	84245
66442	FORT RILEY	13773	2147	19.5	46.7	29.3	3.3	1.2	40882	42305	36	38	32	0.0	15.6	65.6	18.8	0.0	115278
66449	LEONARDVILLE	21943	382	19.9	38.5	33.5	3.7	4.5	43668	45854	44	52	296	20.6	26.7	35.1	12.8	4.7	93636
66451	LYNDON	20612	1031	20.5	30.5	43.0	4.8	1.3	49075	50896	59	71	849	23.2	31.3	31.9	12.5	1.1	84867
66502	MANHATTAN	21072	17354	36.8	25.8	29.0	5.6	2.8	35563	37964	19	12	7632	12.6	12.6	52.1	20.9	1.8	122563
66503	MANHATTAN	32019	4765	11.7	23.5	43.2	13.0	8.6	65075	64718	83	92	3188	3.1	4.6	35.8	48.6	7.8	187623
66506	MANHATTAN	15511	14	64.3	35.7	0.0	0.0	0.0	17143	16000	1	0	0	0.0	0.0	0.0	0.0	0.0	0
66507	MAPLE HILL	21849	481	18.7	26.8	45.5	7.5	1.5	52666	53989	67	79	416	13.5	13.2	47.8	25.2	0.2	118243
66508	MARYSVILLE	21557	1725	29.3	33.0	29.7	5.6	2.4	40192	42137	33	33	1264	24.2	27.1	35.4	11.7	1.6	88072
66509	MAYETTA	20130	835	15.6	31.6	45.9	4.6	2.4	52026	53361	66	78	712	22.2	20.4	39.5	17.1	0.8	99138
66510	MELVERN	21741	355	22.3	28.2	42.3	3.9	3.4	49665	50856	60	72	279	24.0	21.1	39.8	13.6	1.4	94655
66512	MERIDEN	22829	1239	15.7	20.7	55.2	7.3	1.2	60341	61160	78	88	1114	17.3	15.7	43.8	22.3	0.9	114480
66514	MILFORD	22751	555	13.2	36.0	40.0	7.7	3.1	50811	53503	63	77	416	14.4	8.9	59.6	17.1	0.0	131176
66515	MORRILL	19758	176	22.7	29.5	42.6	4.5	0.6	47649	51074	56	65	146	32.9	21.9	33.6	10.3	1.4	80000
66516	NETAWAKA	20301	143	19.6	28.7	44.8	5.6	1.4	51648	53666	65	78	119	24.4	23.5	26.9	25.2	0.0	93571
66517	OGDEN	19374	747	29.7	32.3	31.5	5.6	0.9	41261	42734	37	41	400	21.5	20.3	54.3	4.0	0.0	101316
66518	OKETO	18964	97	26.8	36.1	33.0	3.1	1.0	38809	40912	29	27	79	32.9	27.8	27.8	10.1	1.3	77222
66520	OLSBURG	22064	267	17.2	32.6	43.4	5.6	1.1	50125	50844	61	74	229	14.4	29.3	30.1	19.7	6.6	99667
66521	ONAGA	18632	632	30.2	35.0	30.9	3.3	0.6	39508	41659	31	29	481	30.6	30.8	26.2	10.2	2.3	75833
66522	ONEIDA	16798	71	26.8	31.0	39.4	2.8	0.0	40765	43666	35	38	59	25.4	32.2	18.6	15.3	8.5	79000
66523	OSAGE CITY	19545	1589	28.8	34.0	31.1	4.4	1.8	40996	43163	36	39	1146	17.5	29.4	42.9	10.2	0.0	93789
66524	OVERBROOK	23998	896	17.5	24.0	49.0	7.7	1.8	59697	59055	77	88	767	15.0	18.8	42.8	19.8	3.7	112764
66526	PAXICO	20063	481	20.4	29.3	44.1	4.6	1.7	50161	52243	62	74	408	22.5	26.2	36.8	12.3	2.2	91667
66527	POWHATTAN	15195	113	28.3	42.5	26.5	2.7	0.0	36415	37286	22	16	86	39.5	24.4	24.4	11.6	0.0	70000
66528	QUENEMO	15952	248	26.6	34.3	36.7	2.4	0.0	40744	42758	35	37	200	51.5	14.0	20.0	9.5	5.0	48000
66531	RILEY	18854	562	23.1	31.0	39.9	3.7	2.3	45678	47919	50	59	419	6.7	38.4	39.9	11.0	4.1	95125
66532	ROBINSON	16648	269	33.5	34.2	27.5	3.7	1.1	35085	36273	18	10	209	32.5	27.8	33.0	6.2	0.5	77813
66533	ROSSVILLE	23855	614	12.5	33.1	45.3	6.7	2.4	53164	55118	68	81	471	11.7	27.0	47.3	14.0	0.0	102885
66534	SABETHA	21197	1236	26.5	30.8	35.3	4.0	3.4	44298	46039	46	55	970	19.4	34.8	30.8	13.9	1.0	84143
66535	SAINT GEORGE	20019	1012	22.4	37.9	33.2	4.6	1.8	43488	45666	44	51	810	25.8	10.9	39.0	20.2	4.1	119207
66536	SAINT MARYS	18073	1010	21.4	29.9	40.3	6.5	1.9	48873	50484	59	70	774	8.4	16.3	57.6	15.2	2.5	122310
66537	SCRANTON	19157	468	20.1	35.3	38.7	4.9	1.1	46100	48590	52	61	381	35.4	29.1	27.3	7.6	0.5	69815
66538	SENECA	19152	1307	28.2	35.7	31.9	2.8	1.5	40074	41723	33	33	1024	16.4	27.2	39.9	14.7	1.7	99420
66539	SILVER LAKE	24764	1071	12.1	28.4	49.3	7.4	2.8	58525	59021	76	87	843	5.7	15.4	55.6	23.0	0.2	123550
66540	SOLDIER	19920	200	23.0	28.5	40.0	6.0	2.5	48740	51322	58	70	172	18.6	25.6	31.4	23.3	1.2	100000
66541	SUMMERFIELD	16118	95	32.6	33.7	29.5	2.1	2.1	35955	37944	20	14	81	44.4	28.4	18.5	8.6	0.0	57500
66542	TECUMSEH	29729	1167	8.1	15.2	53.5	18.6	4.7	72516	73374	88	95	1074	8.4	12.6	54.5	24.4	0.2	131753
66543	VASSAR	23287	345	14.5	28.7	50.1	5.5	1.2	55533	55580	72	84	310	11.6	26.1	41.6	19.0	1.6	101563
66544	VERMILLION	20318	164	22.6	39.0	34.1	1.8	2.4	40681	41892	35	37	143	35.7	9.8	34.3	14.7	5.6	97222
66546	WAKARUSA	27310	426	12.0	31.5	41.8	11.0	3.8	57232	58267	74	85	335	22.7	16.4	36.7	22.7	1.5	110174
66547	WAMEGO	21591	2703	19.8	27.0	43.9	7.5	1.9	52967	52774	68	80	2038	9.0	10.1	53.9	25.2	1.8	128954
66548	WATERVILLE	20932	373	30.0	32.2	31.4	3.5	2.9	38685	41139	29	27	311	33.1	37.6	23.8	4.2	1.3	70946
66549	WESTMORELAND	20407	622	24.1	33.4	35.9	5.0	1.6	44591	46756	47	55	495	16.8	26.1	36.6	17.8	2.8	99342
66550	WETMORE	18148	212	24.1	29.7	41.0	3.8	1.4	45921	48653	51	60	181	43.6	28.7	15.5	12.2	0.0	61000
66552	WHITING	20861	211	28.9	34.6	29.9	3.8	2.8	42290	44223	40	46	185	28.1	17.8	32.4	19.5	2.2	101563
66554	RANDOLPH	26350	285	18.6	28.1	43.2	5.6	4.6	52858	54063	68	80	226	14.2	20.8	37.2	22.6	5.3	115323
66603	TOPEKA	14486	915	53.7	30.8	13.3	1.1	1.1	22688	23118	2	1	222	63.5	26.6	7.2	2.7	0.0	40909
66604	TOPEKA	27423	10264	23.1	29.3	37.0	7.0	3.6	47364	51200	55	64	6190	14.8	44.5	34.0	5.6	1.1	81876
66605	TOPEKA	22404	7630	23.1	27.9	38.1	8.4	2.6	48857	52055	59	70	5318	27.8	28.5	37.0	6.7	0.0	77788
66606	TOPEKA	26258	5615	24.7	32.6	33.8	6.0	2.9	42670	46632	41	48	2988	18.1	49.5	23.4	8.1	1.0	74039
66607	TOPEKA	15379	3349	37.6	36.6	21.3	2.9	1.5	32726	33843	13	5	1799	68.4	22.7	7.6	1.3	0.0	38729
66608	TOPEKA	19344	2412	31.8	33.1	32.5	2.3	0.4	36093	39423	21	14	1613	65.9	27.5	6.0	0.6	0.0	37188
66609	TOPEKA	26042	3024	16.5	30.4	41.2	9.1	2.8	52670	55906	67	79	2150	43.4	17.0	31.6	8.0	0.0	66364
66610	TOPEKA	36234	2848	5.4	12.3	51.6	18.0	12.7	81564	82703	93	97	2486	2.3	6.6	40.4	44.4	6.2	176194
66611	TOPEKA	29228	4512	18.6	30.0	39.3	8.6	3.5	51092	53716	64	77	2612	11.3	45.3	32.4	10.6	0.5	82366
66612	TOPEKA	16764	1636	56.3	27.6	14.5	0.7	0.9	20749	21636	2	1	342	71.3	17.0	8.2	3.5	0.0	37130
66614	TOPEKA	31304	14056	13.5	25.7	42.4	12.8	5.6	61651	62488	80	90	9390	2.7	20.5	51.1	23.6	2.1	124079
	KANSAS	26028		20.3	26.8	37.6	9.9	5.4	52748	54940				18.1	21.6	35.7	21.6	3.0	107692
	UNITED STATES	27277		20.9	24.4	35.3	11.7	7.6	54719	56938				9.3	13.1	31.6	32.6	13.5	162279

ZIP CODE #	POST OFFICE NAME	FINANCIAL SERVICES: Auto Loan	FINANCIAL SERVICES: Home Loan	FINANCIAL SERVICES: Investments	FINANCIAL SERVICES: Retirement Plans	THE HOME: Home Improvements: Home Repair	THE HOME: Home Improvements: Lawn & Garden	THE HOME: Furnishings: Computers & Hardware Personal	THE HOME: Furnishings: Major Appliances	THE HOME: Furnishings: TV, Radio, Sound Equipment	THE HOME: Furnishings: Furniture	ENTERTAINMENT: Dine out/ Carry out	ENTERTAINMENT: Sports Equipment	ENTERTAINMENT: Fees & Tickets	ENTERTAINMENT: Toys & Games	ENTERTAINMENT: Travel	ENTERTAINMENT: Cable TV	PERSONAL: Apparel & Services	PERSONAL: Auto Repairs	PERSONAL: Health Insurance	PERSONAL: Pets & Supplies
66219	LENEXA	138	135	124	143	131	120	139	127	133	145	135	106	141	139	134	126	97	130	116	150
66220	LENEXA	209	274	282	287	283	248	226	236	212	245	215	184	270	215	256	203	159	220	209	267
66221	OVERLAND PARK	308	377	334	389	370	313	313	318	289	350	294	263	357	311	333	265	217	291	261	355
66223	OVERLAND PARK	202	245	211	252	238	201	203	206	187	228	191	171	230	203	214	171	140	188	168	229
66224	OVERLAND PARK	250	304	262	313	296	249	253	255	233	284	237	213	286	252	266	213	174	233	209	285
66226	SHAWNEE	159	195	172	199	190	164	163	165	151	178	154	135	184	161	174	141	112	153	141	187
66227	LENEXA	129	161	155	163	161	147	136	141	129	144	131	108	154	131	150	126	94	134	131	162
66401	ALMA	89	68	89	68	70	93	72	87	77	63	75	67	59	76	71	83	50	81	92	103
66402	AUBURN	103	110	92	110	105	102	99	101	97	103	99	78	102	101	100	96	68	98	97	119
66403	AXTELL	80	55	88	55	58	85	61	76	64	50	63	63	45	63	61	70	41	71	80	94
66404	BAILEYVILLE	85	59	94	59	61	90	65	81	68	53	67	67	48	67	65	74	44	76	86	100
66406	BEATTIE	84	58	92	58	61	89	64	80	67	52	66	66	47	65	64	73	43	74	84	98
66407	BELVUE	84	78	69	76	76	79	73	78	76	76	76	57	70	79	70	78	52	75	78	92
66408	BERN	87	60	96	60	63	92	67	83	69	54	69	69	49	68	66	76	45	77	88	102
66409	BERRYTON	101	112	97	115	109	110	100	104	99	101	99	81	106	102	105	99	69	100	103	123
66411	BLUE RAPIDS	80	57	82	56	60	84	63	78	69	55	67	59	50	68	61	76	45	72	84	92
66412	BREMEN	79	54	87	54	57	83	60	75	63	49	62	62	44	62	60	69	40	70	79	92
66413	BURLINGAME	84	61	85	60	63	88	66	81	72	58	70	62	53	71	65	79	46	75	87	96
66414	CARBONDALE	76	75	68	75	72	79	71	74	72	70	72	58	70	74	71	74	49	73	77	89
66415	CENTRALIA	69	49	70	48	51	72	54	67	60	47	58	50	43	59	52	66	38	62	72	79
66416	CIRCLEVILLE	98	67	107	67	70	103	74	93	77	60	77	77	55	76	74	84	50	86	98	114
66417	CORNING	74	52	81	51	54	78	57	71	60	47	59	58	42	59	57	66	39	66	75	87
66418	DELIA	95	86	85	90	88	102	85	96	88	77	86	73	78	89	85	93	59	89	99	112
66419	DENISON	97	69	104	70	72	102	76	93	79	62	78	76	57	77	75	85	51	86	98	113
66422	EMMETT	86	79	71	77	77	82	75	80	77	76	77	59	70	80	72	80	53	77	81	95
66423	ESKRIDGE	84	60	87	58	62	85	62	79	68	57	67	59	49	68	61	75	44	72	82	94
66424	EVEREST	79	55	87	54	57	84	61	75	63	49	62	62	44	62	60	69	40	70	80	93
66425	FAIRVIEW	92	63	101	63	66	97	70	87	73	57	72	72	52	72	70	80	47	82	92	108
66427	FRANKFORT	75	53	77	52	55	78	58	72	63	50	62	55	45	62	57	70	41	67	78	86
66428	GOFF	86	59	94	59	62	91	66	81	68	53	67	67	48	67	65	74	44	76	86	100
66429	GRANTVILLE	109	99	96	101	100	113	97	108	100	90	98	81	90	102	96	105	67	100	110	126
66431	HARVEYVILLE	93	72	100	72	74	99	75	90	77	65	77	73	61	77	76	83	51	84	94	110
66432	HAVENSVILLE	92	63	101	63	66	97	70	87	73	57	72	72	51	71	70	79	47	81	92	107
66434	HIAWATHA	76	62	76	62	63	81	65	75	69	59	68	57	57	68	64	74	46	72	82	89
66436	HOLTON	86	66	84	66	68	87	72	82	76	65	75	63	60	75	70	81	50	79	87	98
66438	HOME	85	58	93	58	61	90	65	81	67	53	67	67	47	66	64	74	43	75	85	99
66439	HORTON	65	46	67	45	48	68	51	63	56	44	54	48	40	55	49	61	36	58	68	74
66440	HOYT	83	87	78	90	85	91	80	86	80	78	80	66	81	82	83	82	55	81	86	100
66441	JUNCTION CITY	78	69	65	70	67	74	76	74	77	72	77	58	70	78	71	79	53	76	79	89
66442	FORT RILEY	83	43	32	50	38	37	78	54	73	72	77	54	59	88	56	67	54	69	49	66
66449	LEONARDVILLE	98	68	108	68	71	104	75	94	78	61	78	77	56	77	75	85	50	87	99	115
66451	LYNDON	83	73	74	76	75	88	73	83	76	66	74	63	66	78	72	81	51	76	85	96
66502	MANHATTAN	72	51	48	54	49	54	82	60	75	69	75	53	63	75	61	73	53	70	62	76
66503	MANHATTAN	110	117	108	120	114	109	112	109	109	115	111	86	117	112	114	107	78	110	106	129
66506	MANHATTAN	29	12	12	15	11	14	41	20	33	28	33	22	24	32	22	30	24	29	20	28
66507	MAPLE HILL	84	84	78	87	84	92	79	87	80	75	80	66	78	82	81	83	55	81	88	101
66508	MARYSVILLE	81	62	81	61	64	86	66	80	71	58	69	60	54	71	64	78	46	74	85	94
66509	MAYETTA	91	82	83	85	83	98	81	92	84	73	82	70	74	85	81	89	56	85	95	107
66510	MELVERN	86	78	77	81	79	92	77	87	79	69	78	66	70	81	76	84	53	80	89	101
66512	MERIDEN	92	92	86	92	90	95	85	91	86	86	86	68	84	88	86	88	59	87	90	107
66514	MILFORD	98	90	80	87	88	92	85	90	88	89	88	66	80	92	81	91	60	87	90	107
66515	MORRILL	94	65	103	65	68	99	72	89	75	58	74	74	53	73	72	82	48	83	94	110
66516	NETAWAKA	96	66	105	66	69	101	73	91	76	59	75	75	54	75	73	83	49	85	96	112
66517	OGDEN	72	62	53	63	58	56	71	62	69	71	70	51	65	71	63	66	48	67	60	75
66518	OKETO	80	55	88	55	58	84	61	76	63	49	63	63	45	62	61	69	41	71	80	93
66520	OLSBURG	96	66	106	66	69	102	73	91	76	60	76	75	54	75	73	83	49	85	96	112
66521	ONAGA	77	54	80	54	57	80	60	74	65	51	63	57	46	63	58	71	42	69	79	88
66522	ONEIDA	85	58	93	58	61	89	65	80	67	52	66	66	47	66	64	73	43	75	85	99
66523	OSAGE CITY	80	61	79	60	63	84	65	78	71	58	69	59	53	70	63	77	46	73	84	92
66524	OVERBROOK	90	90	85	93	90	96	88	92	88	86	88	70	87	89	89	90	61	89	94	108
66526	PAXICO	85	79	72	79	78	84	75	81	78	76	78	60	72	81	73	81	53	78	82	96
66527	POWHATTAN	72	50	79	50	52	76	55	68	57	45	57	57	40	56	55	63	37	64	72	84
66528	QUENEMO	81	58	67	56	58	77	60	70	67	59	66	54	49	70	55	73	44	66	74	85
66531	RILEY	92	63	99	63	66	95	71	87	74	58	73	72	52	73	70	80	48	82	91	107
66532	ROBINSON	75	52	82	52	54	79	58	72	60	47	59	59	42	59	57	66	39	67	76	88
66533	ROSSVILLE	98	88	102	90	89	106	87	98	87	79	87	79	79	88	89	91	59	93	100	118
66534	SABETHA	93	66	95	65	69	97	73	90	80	64	77	68	57	78	71	88	51	84	97	106
66535	SAINT GEORGE	82	76	67	73	74	77	71	76	74	74	74	55	68	77	68	76	50	73	76	90
66536	SAINT MARYS	81	77	70	79	75	86	76	80	78	70	77	62	72	79	74	81	52	78	85	96
66537	SCRANTON	90	66	92	65	69	92	68	85	74	63	73	64	55	74	67	81	48	78	88	101
66538	SENECA	81	58	83	56	60	85	63	78	69	55	67	60	50	68	61	76	45	73	85	93
66539	SILVER LAKE	90	102	88	105	99	100	91	95	89	91	90	74	97	92	96	90	63	91	94	111
66540	SOLDIER	97	69	105	69	72	103	75	93	78	62	78	76	57	77	75	85	51	87	98	114
66541	SUMMERFIELD	79	55	87	54	57	84	61	75	63	49	62	62	44	62	60	69	40	70	79	93
66542	TECUMSEH	106	130	126	133	130	125	111	117	108	116	110	87	126	109	124	108	78	112	115	135
66543	VASSAR	90	81	81	84	82	96	80	90	83	73	81	69	73	85	79	88	55	84	93	105
66544	VERMILLION	85	58	92	58	61	89	65	80	68	53	67	66	48	66	64	74	43	75	85	98
66546	WAKARUSA	98	106	91	109	102	103	98	99	96	98	97	78	102	99	101	96	68	97	98	117
66547	WAMEGO	82	87	74	88	83	86	81	82	80	81	81	64	83	83	82	81	56	81	83	98
66548	WATERVILLE	86	62	88	60	64	90	67	84	74	59	72	64	53	73	66	82	48	78	91	99
66549	WESTMORELAND	90	63	99	63	66	95	69	86	72	56	71	71	51	71	69	78	46	80	91	106
66550	WETMORE	89	61	98	61	64	94	68	84	71	55	70	70	50	69	68	77	45	79	89	104
66552	WHITING	85	58	93	58	61	90	65	81	68	53	67	67	48	66	65	74	43	75	85	99
66554	RANDOLPH	98	84	103	85	85	105	84	97	85	76	85	78	74	85	86	90	57	92	100	117
66603	TOPEKA	42	33	30	35	31	35	45	37	46	41	46	31	40	46	38	47	33	43	41	47
66604	TOPEKA	83	79	73	80	77	83	85	81	87	82	86	63	83	86	82	88	60	85	89	98
66605	TOPEKA	82	78	72	79	76	84	79	80	82	77	81	61	77	82	77	84	56	81	86	95
66606	TOPEKA	72	71	66	72	70	76	75	72	78	72	78	55	76	76	74	81	54	76	83	87
66607	TOPEKA	62	52	47	51	49	55	59	57	62	56	61	43	53	62	53	64	43	60	61	68
66608	TOPEKA	67	55	53	54	53	63	61	61	63	58	62	47	53	65	55	66	42	62	66	74
66609	TOPEKA	91	84	72	85	80	80	87	82	87	89	88	65	84	90	81	85	61	85	81	99
66610	TOPEKA	135	161	152	163	160	147	140	144	133	148	135	110	154	136	150	130	96	137	134	165
66611	TOPEKA	82	81	77	82	80	85	85	82	86	82	86	63	84	85	83	88	60	85	90	98
66612	TOPEKA	41	31	32	33	31	36	42	38	45	39	44	29	37	43	37	47	31	42	45	47
66614	TOPEKA	100	103	97	105	102	101	102	100	101	103	102	77	104	102	102	101	71	101	102	118
	KANSAS	98	90	91	91	89	97	94	95	94	90	94	74	88	96	90	96	65	95	98	113
	UNITED STATES	100	100	100	100	100	100	100	100	100	100	100	100	100	100	100	100	100	100	100	100

ZIP CODE #	POST OFFICE NAME	COUNTY FIPS CODE	POPULATION 2000	POPULATION 2009	POPULATION 2014	2000-2009 ANNUAL RATE % Rate	2000-2009 ANNUAL RATE State Centile	HOUSEHOLDS 2000	HOUSEHOLDS 2009	HOUSEHOLDS 2014	HOUSEHOLDS % Annual Rate 2000-2009	HOUSEHOLDS 2009 Average HH Size	FAMILIES 2000	FAMILIES 2009	FAMILIES % Annual Rate 2000-2009
66615	TOPEKA	177	1967	3005	3271	4.7	98	534	955	1065	6.5	2.83	421	755	6.5
66616	TOPEKA	177	6307	6144	6091	-0.3	52	2576	2576	2575	0.0	2.38	1651	1610	-0.3
66617	TOPEKA	177	8176	8662	8885	0.6	82	3006	3276	3388	0.9	2.64	2483	2678	0.8
66618	TOPEKA	177	7783	9170	9754	1.8	95	2706	3316	3565	2.2	2.74	2274	2759	2.1
66619	TOPEKA	177	3345	3317	3302	-0.1	59	1120	1151	1160	0.3	2.88	886	884	0.0
66701	FORT SCOTT	011	12563	12065	11785	-0.4	48	5064	4896	4784	-0.4	2.40	3344	3202	-0.5
66710	ALTOONA	205	854	806	779	-0.6	36	348	333	323	-0.5	2.42	246	233	-0.6
66711	ARCADIA	037	690	735	750	0.7	84	279	295	301	0.6	2.48	195	204	0.5
66712	ARMA	037	2098	2163	2192	0.3	74	893	926	940	0.4	2.28	558	569	0.2
66713	BAXTER SPRINGS	021	6073	5659	5428	-0.8	28	2370	2208	2117	-0.8	2.52	1642	1513	-0.9
66714	BENEDICT	205	858	855	845	0.0	64	350	354	351	0.1	2.42	259	259	0.0
66716	BRONSON	011	747	705	682	-0.6	36	303	291	283	-0.4	2.42	204	192	-0.7
66717	BUFFALO	205	414	447	454	0.8	86	162	177	180	1.0	2.53	113	123	0.9
66720	CHANUTE	133	10947	10523	10255	-0.4	48	4463	4307	4195	-0.4	2.36	2970	2838	-0.5
66724	CHEROKEE	037	1078	1081	1084	0.0	64	436	441	442	0.1	2.45	293	292	0.0
66725	COLUMBUS	021	5995	5623	5429	-0.7	32	2412	2273	2192	-0.6	2.41	1641	1530	-0.8
66728	CRESTLINE	021	50	53	54	0.6	82	20	22	22	1.0	2.41	15	16	0.7
66732	ELSMORE	001	284	268	259	-0.6	36	112	108	104	-0.4	2.44	79	75	-0.6
66733	ERIE	133	2409	2271	2197	-0.6	36	952	906	878	-0.5	2.44	688	649	-0.6
66734	FARLINGTON	037	365	372	375	0.2	70	153	157	159	0.3	2.37	109	111	0.2
66735	FRANKLIN	037	458	522	545	1.4	92	191	219	230	1.5	2.37	130	147	1.3
66736	FREDONIA	205	4116	3880	3747	-0.6	36	1723	1630	1575	-0.6	2.31	1141	1068	-0.7
66738	FULTON	011	412	394	383	-0.5	41	151	146	143	-0.4	2.68	109	104	-0.5
66739	GALENA	021	5845	5654	5497	-0.4	48	2261	2209	2151	-0.3	2.52	1608	1557	-0.3
66740	GALESBURG	133	886	843	820	-0.5	41	334	320	311	-0.5	2.63	268	255	-0.5
66743	GIRARD	037	4335	4255	4230	-0.2	56	1656	1632	1623	-0.2	2.48	1184	1153	-0.3
66746	HEPLER	037	272	276	278	0.2	70	101	104	105	0.3	2.65	72	73	0.1
66748	HUMBOLDT	001	2792	2658	2560	-0.5	41	1138	1102	1067	-0.3	2.37	788	754	-0.5
66749	IOLA	001	8662	8163	7867	-0.6	36	3495	3347	3238	-0.5	2.36	2286	2167	-0.6
66751	LA HARPE	001	1032	975	936	-0.6	36	386	367	354	-0.5	2.65	285	269	-0.6
66753	MC CUNE	037	1187	1264	1291	0.7	84	451	486	498	0.8	2.60	340	362	0.7
66754	MAPLETON	011	382	360	348	-0.6	36	154	147	143	-0.5	2.45	109	102	-0.7
66755	MORAN	001	1205	1137	1099	-0.6	36	482	464	449	-0.4	2.41	341	325	-0.5
66756	MULBERRY	037	1066	1232	1293	1.6	94	429	500	526	1.7	2.46	292	335	1.5
66757	NEODESHA	205	3657	3438	3322	-0.7	32	1453	1369	1323	-0.6	2.43	964	899	-0.8
66758	NEOSHO FALLS	207	239	232	228	-0.3	52	106	106	105	0.0	2.19	75	74	-0.1
66759	NEW ALBANY	205	398	372	359	-0.7	32	154	146	141	-0.6	2.52	116	109	-0.7
66761	PIQUA	207	315	296	290	-0.7	32	123	119	118	-0.4	2.49	90	86	-0.5
66762	PITTSBURG	037	23963	23856	23861	0.0	64	9770	9745	9739	0.0	2.30	5556	5467	-0.2
66763	FRONTENAC	037	3035	3212	3286	0.6	82	1244	1327	1358	0.7	2.32	792	832	0.5
66767	PRESCOTT	107	534	547	537	0.3	74	210	219	215	0.5	2.31	145	150	0.4
66769	REDFIELD	011	591	590	583	0.0	64	221	225	224	0.2	2.60	160	161	0.1
66770	RIVERTON	021	1021	1068	1073	0.5	79	399	424	426	0.7	2.52	309	325	0.5
66771	SAINT PAUL	133	1110	1095	1080	-0.1	59	389	388	383	0.0	2.69	276	271	-0.2
66772	SAVONBURG	001	287	273	264	-0.5	41	112	108	105	-0.4	2.48	80	76	-0.6
66773	SCAMMON	021	1163	1046	997	-1.1	17	454	410	392	-1.1	2.55	326	291	-1.2
66775	STARK	133	232	219	213	-0.6	36	91	87	85	-0.5	2.52	72	69	-0.5
66776	THAYER	133	1406	1396	1384	-0.1	59	515	515	511	0.0	2.71	411	408	-0.1
66777	TORONTO	207	698	675	666	-0.4	48	319	317	316	-0.1	1.96	187	184	-0.2
66778	TREECE	021	149	148	146	-0.1	59	59	59	59	0.0	2.51	45	45	0.0
66779	UNIONTOWN	011	683	710	710	0.4	76	267	283	285	0.6	2.48	198	207	0.5
66780	WALNUT	037	568	572	573	0.1	68	228	233	234	0.2	2.45	168	170	0.1
66781	WEIR	021	1415	1283	1225	-1.1	17	559	509	486	-1.0	2.52	392	353	-1.1
66783	YATES CENTER	207	2526	2393	2350	-0.6	36	1090	1051	1037	-0.4	2.22	698	666	-0.5
66801	EMPORIA	111	30236	30452	30485	0.1	68	11533	11662	11677	0.1	2.48	7017	7008	0.0
66830	ADMIRE	111	381	393	398	0.3	74	140	147	150	0.5	2.67	104	108	0.4
66833	ALLEN	111	539	557	564	0.4	76	216	228	232	0.6	2.44	158	165	0.5
66834	ALTA VISTA	197	687	690	686	0.0	64	286	293	293	0.3	2.35	206	209	0.2
66835	AMERICUS	111	1351	1315	1301	-0.3	52	512	508	505	-0.1	2.59	394	388	-0.2
66838	BURDICK	127	190	176	171	-0.8	28	80	75	73	-0.7	2.33	60	56	-0.7
66839	BURLINGTON	031	4175	4038	3918	-0.4	48	1638	1594	1546	-0.3	2.45	1109	1068	-0.4
66840	BURNS	017	899	865	848	-0.4	48	333	322	317	-0.4	2.69	264	254	-0.4
66842	CASSODAY	015	303	309	312	0.2	70	123	126	127	0.3	2.45	100	101	0.1
66843	CEDAR POINT	017	184	175	170	-0.5	41	81	79	78	-0.3	2.22	55	53	-0.4
66845	COTTONWOOD FALLS	017	1246	1312	1316	0.6	82	501	538	543	0.8	2.23	310	329	0.6
66846	COUNCIL GROVE	127	3644	3517	3444	-0.4	48	1525	1488	1460	-0.3	2.31	1039	1003	-0.4
66849	DWIGHT	127	471	457	446	-0.3	52	203	201	197	-0.1	2.27	144	141	-0.2
66850	ELMDALE	017	126	122	120	-0.3	52	57	56	56	-0.2	2.18	40	39	-0.3
66851	FLORENCE	115	850	796	765	-0.7	32	326	304	291	-0.8	2.44	238	221	-0.8
66852	GRIDLEY	031	668	698	693	0.5	79	275	288	286	0.5	2.42	199	207	0.4
66853	HAMILTON	073	548	466	432	-1.7	7	232	199	185	-1.6	2.33	172	147	-1.7
66854	HARTFORD	111	967	928	912	-0.4	48	374	364	360	-0.3	2.47	264	255	-0.4
66856	LEBO	031	1676	1722	1706	0.3	74	653	671	666	0.3	2.56	497	507	0.2
66857	LE ROY	031	946	879	842	-0.8	28	391	367	352	-0.7	2.40	296	276	-0.8
66858	LINCOLNVILLE	115	533	513	498	-0.4	48	198	191	185	-0.4	2.69	138	132	-0.5
66859	LOST SPRINGS	115	195	183	177	-0.7	32	79	75	72	-0.6	2.44	60	57	-0.6
66860	MADISON	073	1432	1243	1168	-1.5	9	575	502	471	-1.5	2.37	385	334	-1.5
66861	MARION	115	3437	3316	3217	-0.4	48	1399	1350	1308	-0.4	2.37	973	931	-0.5
66862	MATFIELD GREEN	017	155	146	142	-0.6	36	73	70	69	-0.5	2.09	49	47	-0.4
66864	NEOSHO RAPIDS	111	596	602	604	0.1	68	231	238	240	0.3	2.52	181	185	0.2
66865	OLPE	111	1089	1067	1061	-0.2	56	399	398	397	0.0	2.68	307	304	-0.1
66866	PEABODY	115	1946	1880	1825	-0.4	48	737	714	692	-0.3	2.48	532	511	-0.4
66868	READING	111	755	776	784	0.3	74	284	298	302	0.5	2.60	217	226	0.4
66869	STRONG CITY	017	1151	1101	1079	-0.5	41	464	455	449	-0.2	2.42	316	308	-0.3
66870	VIRGIL	073	382	346	331	-1.1	17	156	144	138	-0.9	2.40	113	103	-1.0
66871	WAVERLY	031	1374	1344	1305	-0.2	56	533	524	508	-0.2	2.48	376	367	-0.3
66872	WHITE CITY	127	994	1007	1000	0.1	68	412	423	422	0.3	2.38	296	301	0.2
66873	WILSEY	127	337	313	304	-0.8	28	134	126	122	-0.7	2.48	100	93	-0.8
66901	CONCORDIA	029	7163	6634	6325	-0.8	28	2875	2687	2564	-0.7	2.26	1831	1693	-0.8
66930	AGENDA	157	175	147	134	-1.9	4	76	65	59	-1.7	2.26	54	46	-1.7
66932	ATHOL	183	134	112	103	-1.9	4	60	51	47	-1.7	2.16	42	36	-1.7
66933	BARNES	201	354	321	305	-1.1	17	156	144	138	-0.9	2.22	116	107	-0.9
66935	BELLEVILLE	157	3216	2926	2747	-1.0	19	1431	1317	1238	-0.9	2.12	885	808	-1.0
66936	BURR OAK	089	516	429	392	-2.0	4	235	201	185	-1.7	2.13	145	122	-1.8
66937	CLIFTON	201	957	880	843	-0.9	23	400	375	361	-0.7	2.35	286	266	-0.8
	KANSAS					0.6					0.6	2.49			0.5
	UNITED STATES					1.0					1.1	2.59			0.9

# ZIP CODE	POST OFFICE NAME	RACE (%) White 2000	White 2009	Black 2000	Black 2009	Asian/Pacific 2000	Asian/Pacific 2009	% Hispanic Origin 2000	% Hispanic Origin 2009	2009 AGE DISTRIBUTION (%) 0-4	5-9	10-14	15-19	20-24	25-44	45-64	65-84	85+	18+	MEDIAN AGE 2009	% 2009 Males	% 2009 Females
66615	TOPEKA	88.3	86.1	7.2	7.3	1.0	1.9	2.8	4.9	6.6	5.9	6.2	6.2	4.3	31.3	28.0	10.1	1.4	77.2	38.4	45.6	54.4
66616	TOPEKA	79.4	73.5	1.9	2.2	0.3	0.3	24.9	33.8	7.5	7.3	6.9	6.5	5.8	27.1	24.4	12.3	2.1	74.4	36.8	50.0	50.0
66617	TOPEKA	96.3	95.0	0.6	0.7	0.3	0.4	3.0	4.7	5.9	6.6	7.2	6.8	4.9	22.2	32.3	13.0	1.1	76.1	42.5	50.1	49.9
66618	TOPEKA	95.8	94.7	1.0	1.2	0.4	0.6	2.5	3.9	5.7	6.5	7.3	7.7	4.5	23.3	32.4	11.7	0.9	75.6	41.7	50.4	49.6
66619	TOPEKA	85.8	82.8	7.1	8.0	0.8	1.1	5.2	7.9	9.8	7.9	7.2	7.9	10.9	29.9	21.2	4.9	0.4	69.9	27.9	49.2	50.8
66701	FORT SCOTT	93.5	92.5	3.7	4.0	0.4	0.6	1.4	2.0	6.7	6.2	6.2	7.4	6.4	23.6	25.7	14.1	3.7	76.6	39.3	48.1	51.9
66710	ALTOONA	97.9	97.6	0.1	0.1	0.0	0.1	0.6	0.7	6.5	6.2	6.6	6.7	6.1	21.5	27.5	16.6	2.4	77.0	41.9	49.9	50.1
66711	ARCADIA	96.5	96.1	0.6	0.5	0.1	0.1	0.9	1.2	6.3	6.3	6.1	6.4	5.9	24.4	29.0	12.9	2.9	77.1	40.9	49.9	50.1
66712	ARMA	97.5	97.1	0.4	0.5	0.1	0.2	0.9	1.3	6.7	6.7	6.4	5.5	4.9	23.0	27.5	14.8	4.5	76.7	42.5	47.4	52.6
66713	BAXTER SPRINGS	88.8	87.5	0.9	1.0	0.4	0.5	1.3	1.8	7.1	7.1	6.8	7.0	5.8	24.8	25.5	13.0	2.9	74.6	38.6	48.8	51.2
66714	BENEDICT	97.7	97.7	0.1	0.1	0.0	0.0	0.8	1.1	5.0	5.6	6.1	6.2	4.8	21.6	32.2	16.4	2.1	79.6	45.4	49.7	50.3
66716	BRONSON	96.5	96.0	0.9	1.1	0.3	0.3	0.8	1.1	4.1	4.3	4.7	8.1	5.4	23.3	30.5	17.2	2.6	82.3	45.1	50.1	49.9
66717	BUFFALO	97.8	97.5	0.0	0.0	0.0	0.0	0.2	0.7	5.6	6.0	6.5	6.9	5.8	20.6	31.1	15.4	2.0	77.9	43.7	48.3	51.7
66720	CHANUTE	93.7	92.4	1.3	1.4	0.4	0.6	3.5	4.8	6.6	6.2	6.1	7.6	6.7	23.4	25.9	14.2	3.3	77.1	39.4	47.5	52.5
66724	CHEROKEE	95.7	95.1	0.2	0.2	0.2	0.3	0.6	0.9	5.9	6.0	6.3	6.6	6.1	23.6	29.1	14.0	2.4	77.8	42.0	49.1	50.9
66725	COLUMBUS	94.6	93.7	0.4	0.4	0.4	0.6	1.4	2.1	6.7	6.8	6.9	6.7	5.5	23.3	26.6	14.1	3.3	75.4	40.2	47.6	52.4
66728	CRESTLINE	93.9	90.6	2.0	1.9	0.0	0.0	2.0	1.9	5.7	5.7	7.5	7.5	3.8	26.4	30.2	11.3	1.9	73.6	40.6	47.2	52.8
66732	ELSMORE	97.2	96.3	0.4	0.7	0.4	0.7	0.4	0.7	4.5	5.2	5.2	7.1	4.9	20.5	31.7	17.2	3.7	80.6	46.5	50.0	50.0
66733	ERIE	97.4	96.8	0.2	0.2	0.1	0.1	1.7	2.4	4.7	5.9	6.8	7.4	5.1	21.5	30.4	15.1	3.1	77.9	43.9	49.6	50.4
66734	FARLINGTON	98.4	97.3	0.0	0.3	0.3	0.5	0.5	0.5	7.0	7.3	7.5	6.2	4.0	22.6	27.4	15.6	2.4	74.2	41.5	50.8	49.2
66735	FRANKLIN	95.9	95.6	1.3	1.3	0.0	0.0	0.9	1.3	5.7	5.9	6.1	5.7	5.0	24.9	30.8	13.0	2.7	78.5	42.6	50.8	49.2
66736	FREDONIA	96.5	95.6	0.5	0.6	0.5	0.8	2.0	2.9	5.7	5.8	6.0	6.5	5.7	21.3	27.1	17.4	4.5	78.5	44.2	48.0	52.0
66738	FULTON	97.1	96.2	0.0	0.3	0.5	0.8	0.5	0.8	4.8	7.6	7.6	7.6	4.8	22.1	29.7	12.9	2.8	75.1	41.9	50.5	49.5
66739	GALENA	91.1	90.0	0.7	0.7	0.1	0.2	1.6	2.2	6.9	6.7	7.0	6.8	5.6	25.2	26.6	13.1	2.1	75.1	38.9	48.7	51.3
66740	GALESBURG	96.5	96.1	0.2	0.2	0.1	0.1	2.0	2.8	6.5	7.0	7.1	6.0	4.6	23.7	31.6	11.9	1.5	75.6	41.1	52.3	47.7
66743	GIRARD	97.3	96.8	0.7	0.8	0.2	0.3	0.7	1.1	6.0	5.9	6.3	6.9	5.8	23.8	26.8	14.2	4.3	77.4	41.4	48.9	51.1
66746	HEPLER	98.2	97.8	0.0	0.0	0.4	0.4	0.4	0.7	7.2	7.6	7.2	6.2	4.0	22.1	26.8	16.3	2.5	73.6	41.5	50.7	49.3
66748	HUMBOLDT	94.0	92.5	1.3	1.4	0.1	0.2	4.3	6.4	5.2	5.4	5.6	5.8	5.6	22.8	30.2	16.0	3.5	80.4	44.7	50.0	50.0
66749	IOLA	94.4	93.4	2.1	2.3	0.3	0.4	1.6	2.4	6.8	6.2	6.1	7.6	6.9	23.5	26.4	13.3	3.2	76.9	38.4	48.4	51.6
66751	LA HARPE	95.7	94.9	0.5	0.6	0.4	0.6	0.8	1.0	5.6	5.8	6.1	7.5	7.1	24.7	29.2	12.3	1.6	78.2	39.5	50.2	49.8
66753	MC CUNE	97.6	97.2	0.0	0.0	0.1	0.2	1.0	1.6	5.8	6.2	6.4	6.3	4.3	24.6	30.8	13.6	2.1	77.7	42.4	51.3	48.7
66754	MAPLETON	96.9	96.1	0.3	0.3	0.5	0.8	0.5	0.6	4.4	6.7	6.9	7.8	5.0	22.5	30.3	13.9	2.5	76.9	42.7	50.8	49.2
66755	MORAN	96.9	96.2	0.5	0.6	0.4	0.6	0.5	0.7	4.7	5.1	5.6	7.0	4.9	20.8	31.4	16.7	3.8	80.1	46.1	50.2	49.8
66756	MULBERRY	95.9	95.5	1.3	1.5	0.0	0.0	0.9	1.4	5.5	5.8	6.1	5.8	5.1	25.1	31.5	12.7	2.4	79.1	42.6	51.0	49.0
66757	NEODESHA	96.6	95.8	0.3	0.3	0.2	0.3	2.0	2.9	6.2	6.3	7.2	7.5	5.9	22.9	26.6	13.3	4.2	75.6	40.1	48.3	51.7
66758	NEOSHO FALLS	96.2	95.7	0.8	0.9	0.0	0.0	0.8	1.3	8.6	8.6	8.6	5.2	3.9	20.3	28.0	15.1	1.7	70.7	41.3	52.6	47.4
66759	NEW ALBANY	96.5	95.7	1.0	1.1	0.3	0.5	1.3	1.9	4.3	4.8	5.6	6.5	5.1	20.4	33.3	17.7	2.2	80.9	46.9	50.0	50.0
66761	PIQUA	98.4	98.3	0.3	0.3	0.0	0.0	0.3	0.3	4.7	4.7	5.4	4.7	5.1	22.6	34.8	15.2	2.7	81.8	46.5	52.4	47.6
66762	PITTSBURG	91.0	88.7	2.6	2.9	1.8	2.7	3.3	4.9	6.7	5.9	5.5	8.7	13.4	25.3	21.3	10.5	2.7	78.6	31.4	49.2	50.8
66763	FRONTENAC	97.5	96.9	0.2	0.2	0.1	0.1	0.9	1.5	6.6	6.4	6.5	6.0	4.8	24.2	25.8	14.4	5.2	76.7	41.2	46.6	53.4
66767	PRESCOTT	98.3	98.0	0.9	1.1	0.2	0.2	1.5	2.0	4.6	5.1	5.1	5.5	4.4	19.2	30.5	16.8	8.8	81.7	49.2	51.4	48.6
66769	REDFIELD	97.1	96.3	0.5	0.5	0.2	0.5	1.0	1.5	5.6	6.1	6.6	7.1	4.6	23.1	29.8	14.2	2.9	77.1	42.5	51.2	48.8
66770	RIVERTON	93.0	92.0	1.1	1.2	0.3	0.5	1.2	1.7	6.1	6.5	7.0	6.4	4.7	26.0	29.7	12.3	1.4	76.5	40.0	50.6	49.4
66771	SAINT PAUL	97.5	96.7	0.2	0.2	0.5	0.6	1.9	2.6	5.9	6.3	6.3	7.1	4.7	23.8	27.2	14.2	4.5	76.4	41.8	49.0	51.0
66772	SAVONBURG	97.2	96.0	0.3	0.7	0.3	0.7	0.7	0.7	4.4	5.1	5.9	7.0	4.8	20.5	31.9	16.8	3.7	80.6	46.4	50.2	49.8
66773	SCAMMON	95.2	94.5	0.3	0.4	0.2	0.3	0.6	0.9	6.2	6.8	7.3	7.5	5.0	24.0	27.7	13.0	2.6	75.1	40.2	49.3	50.7
66775	STARK	98.3	97.7	0.0	0.0	0.0	0.0	1.3	1.8	5.5	6.4	7.3	6.4	3.7	19.6	33.3	15.5	2.3	76.3	45.8	52.5	47.5
66776	THAYER	96.2	95.5	0.0	0.0	0.1	0.1	2.4	3.4	7.1	6.9	6.9	7.2	6.4	24.9	27.1	12.1	1.4	74.7	37.9	51.8	48.2
66777	TORONTO	94.3	93.3	2.6	2.8	0.1	0.1	2.0	3.0	3.3	3.3	3.3	4.0	7.0	17.2	32.7	25.9	3.4	87.4	54.0	54.5	45.5
66778	TREECE	91.3	89.9	1.3	1.4	0.0	0.0	0.0	0.0	6.1	6.1	6.1	6.1	6.1	25.7	29.7	12.8	1.4	78.4	40.9	52.7	47.3
66779	UNIONTOWN	97.2	96.3	0.4	0.4	0.1	0.4	1.2	1.7	5.6	6.2	6.6	7.2	4.4	23.7	29.9	13.8	2.7	76.8	42.0	51.7	48.3
66780	WALNUT	98.1	97.7	0.2	0.2	0.2	0.3	0.4	0.7	6.5	7.2	7.3	6.8	4.0	22.7	28.0	15.4	2.1	74.7	41.6	51.0	49.0
66781	WEIR	97.0	96.5	0.2	0.3	0.1	0.2	0.8	1.1	8.2	8.2	8.0	6.8	5.3	24.8	26.3	11.1	1.4	71.4	36.8	51.7	48.3
66783	YATES CENTER	97.6	97.4	0.4	0.5	0.0	0.0	1.3	1.8	5.4	5.4	5.4	5.0	5.8	22.0	29.1	16.6	5.2	80.5	45.7	47.4	52.6
66801	EMPORIA	80.6	75.1	2.6	2.7	2.4	3.2	19.5	26.6	7.1	6.5	6.0	8.9	12.5	25.9	21.9	8.8	2.4	76.6	30.6	49.3	50.7
66830	ADMIRE	97.4	96.2	0.3	0.5	0.3	0.5	1.8	3.1	6.1	6.6	7.4	7.6	3.8	23.9	31.0	12.0	1.5	74.8	41.4	52.2	47.8
66833	ALLEN	97.2	96.2	0.6	0.5	0.4	0.7	1.7	2.7	6.3	6.8	7.2	7.4	3.9	23.5	31.1	12.4	1.4	75.0	41.5	52.1	47.9
66834	ALTA VISTA	97.5	97.1	0.3	0.3	0.3	0.4	2.8	4.1	4.3	4.9	5.2	5.5	4.6	22.6	34.2	16.4	2.2	82.0	46.7	53.3	46.7
66835	AMERICUS	96.7	95.3	0.3	0.3	0.2	0.3	1.8	3.1	6.5	7.0	7.2	7.2	4.9	23.2	30.8	11.6	1.4	74.7	40.4	47.6	52.4
66838	BURDICK	97.9	97.2	0.0	0.0	0.0	0.0	1.1	1.1	6.3	6.3	6.8	7.4	4.0	19.3	29.0	17.6	3.4	75.0	45.0	49.4	50.6
66839	BURLINGTON	96.2	95.4	0.3	0.3	0.6	0.8	1.7	2.5	6.3	6.6	6.4	6.9	5.2	24.6	28.9	11.4	3.5	75.7	40.5	48.5	51.5
66840	BURNS	97.9	97.6	0.3	0.3	0.1	0.2	1.4	2.2	7.2	7.7	8.1	6.8	3.9	19.7	29.5	15.0	2.1	72.7	42.5	52.4	47.6
66842	CASSODAY	97.0	96.4	0.3	0.3	0.3	0.3	2.3	3.6	7.8	8.4	8.4	8.1	4.2	19.7	27.2	14.6	1.6	70.2	40.1	52.1	47.9
66843	CEDAR POINT	97.8	97.7	0.0	0.0	0.0	0.0	1.6	1.1	5.7	6.9	7.4	5.7	4.0	20.6	32.6	14.9	2.3	76.6	44.7	52.0	48.0
66845	COTTONWOOD FALLS	95.7	95.7	1.8	1.8	0.2	0.2	2.1	2.1	5.8	5.9	5.9	6.5	5.7	23.6	25.8	15.9	4.9	78.3	42.5	48.8	51.2
66846	COUNCIL GROVE	98.1	97.7	0.3	0.3	0.2	0.3	2.2	3.2	5.7	5.8	6.1	6.6	5.8	20.0	29.5	16.2	4.4	78.0	45.0	49.2	50.8
66849	DWIGHT	95.6	94.5	0.2	0.2	0.4	0.4	4.0	5.9	5.3	6.1	6.6	5.9	5.0	20.4	33.7	14.7	2.4	78.1	45.4	51.0	49.0
66850	ELMDALE	97.6	97.5	0.0	0.0	0.0	0.0	2.4	1.6	4.9	5.7	6.6	5.7	4.1	22.1	34.4	13.9	2.5	78.7	45.6	54.1	45.9
66851	FLORENCE	95.6	94.5	0.6	0.6	0.2	0.3	3.2	4.6	5.2	5.2	5.5	6.9	5.0	20.2	28.5	20.2	3.3	79.0	46.5	47.0	53.0
66852	GRIDLEY	97.2	96.6	0.6	0.6	0.1	0.3	1.2	1.7	4.7	5.3	6.3	8.2	4.3	22.3	31.9	13.9	3.0	78.7	44.1	51.1	48.9
66853	HAMILTON	96.9	95.7	0.5	0.6	0.2	0.4	1.3	2.1	5.8	6.0	6.7	7.1	4.5	22.5	28.3	16.3	2.8	77.0	42.7	51.7	48.3
66854	HARTFORD	98.2	97.8	0.2	0.2	0.2	0.3	1.6	2.6	5.7	6.0	6.4	7.4	5.2	21.4	32.3	13.7	1.8	77.3	43.2	51.1	48.9
66856	LEBO	97.6	96.6	0.0	0.0	0.2	0.3	2.3	3.3	6.0	6.2	6.7	7.4	5.3	24.0	30.0	12.4	2.0	76.4	41.0	51.2	48.8
66857	LE ROY	98.1	97.7	0.1	0.1	0.0	0.0	0.7	0.9	5.9	6.5	6.6	6.7	3.8	21.0	31.3	15.9	2.3	76.7	44.6	51.9	48.1
66858	LINCOLNVILLE	95.9	94.9	0.9	1.0	0.2	0.2	2.6	3.5	8.4	8.2	8.6	5.8	3.9	20.7	27.7	14.2	2.5	71.3	39.9	50.7	49.3
66859	LOST SPRINGS	96.4	95.6	0.0	0.0	0.0	0.0	3.6	4.9	7.1	7.1	7.1	6.0	4.4	20.2	30.1	14.8	3.3	74.9	43.3	49.7	50.3
66860	MADISON	97.0	96.4	0.1	0.2	0.1	0.2	1.3	1.9	5.2	5.5	6.5	7.1	5.0	20.7	29.9	15.6	4.5	77.6	45.0	50.4	49.6
66861	MARION	97.4	97.0	0.1	0.2	0.1	0.1	1.3	1.9	6.1	6.3	6.4	6.3	4.8	19.2	29.0	17.0	4.9	76.7	45.6	49.1	50.9
66862	MATFIELD GREEN	97.4	97.3	0.0	0.0	0.0	0.0	1.3	1.4	6.2	6.8	6.8	5.5	3.4	17.8	34.9	15.8	2.7	77.4	46.5	53.4	46.6
66864	NEOSHO RAPIDS	97.3	95.8	0.3	0.5	0.0	0.2	3.7	6.1	5.0	5.5	6.1	7.1	5.6	21.4	32.9	15.0	1.3	78.1	44.4	51.5	48.5
66865	OLPE	98.4	97.9	0.2	0.2	0.3	0.5	1.8	3.1	6.7	7.2	7.2	7.6	5.7	22.9	30.0	10.9	1.8	74.0	39.6	53.1	46.9
66866	PEABODY	96.5	95.9	1.2	1.3	0.1	0.2	2.5	3.7	5.1	5.4	6.0	7.4	5.4	21.9	29.7	15.3	3.8	79.0	44.1	49.1	50.9
66868	READING	97.4	96.3	0.3	0.3	0.1	0.4	2.1	3.5	5.3	6.1	7.7	8.6	3.9	24.0	31.3	11.5	1.7	75.0	41.7	51.8	48.2
66869	STRONG CITY	97.8	97.7	0.6	0.6	0.2	0.2	1.6	1.7	6.2	6.6	6.7	5.7	4.5	22.6	32.0	13.5	2.1	76.9	42.9	53.4	46.6
66870	VIRGIL	97.1	96.5	0.3	0.3	0.3	0.3	1.0	1.7	5.2	5.5	5.5	6.1	4.6	20.5	29.8	20.2	2.6	80.1	46.9	50.9	49.1
66871	WAVERLY	97.7	97.3	0.4	0.4	0.1	0.2	1.0	1.4	6.2	6.5	6.9	6.6	4.4	21.9	29.9	13.5	3.9	75.6	42.8	48.4	51.6
66872	WHITE CITY	96.3	95.1	0.6	0.7	0.3	0.4	2.3	3.5	6.0	6.1	6.3	6.5	5.6	22.1	28.7	16.1	2.8	77.7	43.1	48.7	51.3
66873	WILSEY	97.3	96.8	0.3	0.3	0.3	0.3	0.9	1.3	6.1	6.4	7.0	7.0	3.8	18.8	29.4	17.9	3.5	75.1	45.5	50.8	49.2
66901	CONCORDIA	98.0	97.6	0.5	0.5	0.3	0.5	0.7	0.9	5.5	5.4	5.5	9.1	6.2	21.5	24.9	16.2	5.7	79.7	42.2	46.5	53.5
66930	AGENDA	99.4	99.3	0.0	0.0	0.0	0.0	1.1	2.0	4.8	4.8	4.8	4.8	4.8	17.7	36.7	18.4	3.4	83.0	48.9	51.7	48.3
66932	ATHOL	99.2	99.1	0.0	0.0	0.0	0.0	0.8	0.9	4.5	5.4	5.4	5.4	3.6	18.8	33.9	18.8	4.5	81.3	48.3	51.8	48.2
66933	BARNES	99.2	99.1	0.0	0.0	0.3	0.3	0.3	0.3	6.9	7.2	7.5	6.5	3.7	17.8	28.3	18.1	4.0	74.1	45.3	52.0	48.0
66935	BELLEVILLE	98.2	97.8	0.3	0.3	0.3	0.4	1.0	1.4	4.1	4.7	5.0	5.4	4.2	18.5	29.3	21.6	7.2	82.4	50.8	46.8	53.2
66936	BURR OAK	97.5	97.0	0.0	0.0	0.0	0.0	0.6	0.7	5.8	6.5	6.3	5.1	3.5	20.0	31.0	18.2	3.5	78.1	46.7	48.7	51.3
66937	CLIFTON	98.3	98.2	0.1	0.1	0.1	0.1	0.8	1.0	6.0	6.7	6.9	6.6	4.1	22.3	30.2	14.5	2.6	76.0	42.7	51.1	48.9
	KANSAS	86.1	83.7	5.7	5.9	1.8	2.6	7.0	9.4	7.1	6.9	6.9	7.3	7.3	25.9	25.7	10.7	2.2	75.0	36.3	49.6	50.4
	UNITED STATES	75.1	72.0	12.3	12.7	3.8	4.6	12.5	15.7	6.8	6.7	6.6	7.1	6.9	27.0	26.0	10.9	1.9	75.7	36.9	49.2	50.8

ZIP CODE #	POST OFFICE NAME	2009 Per Capita Income	2009 HH Income Base	2009 Household Income Distribution (%): Less than $25,000	$25,000 to $49,999	$50,000 to $99,999	$100,000 to $149,999	$150,000 or More	Median Household Income: 2009	2014	2009 National Centile	2009 State Centile	2009 Home Value Base	2009 Home Value Distribution (%): Less than $50,000	$50,000 to $89,999	$90,000 to $174,999	$175,000 to $399,999	$400,000 or More	2009 Median Home Value
66615	TOPEKA	27277	955	7.2	20.4	45.1	20.4	6.8	73659	75239	89	95	828	3.6	7.0	55.9	30.8	2.7	140714
66616	TOPEKA	19984	2576	26.2	34.0	35.9	3.5	0.5	41858	44909	39	44	1881	39.9	53.5	5.7	0.3	0.5	55640
66617	TOPEKA	29021	3276	6.9	18.3	60.5	10.0	4.3	71088	70836	87	94	2980	6.7	15.7	60.0	16.9	0.6	118175
66618	TOPEKA	27430	3316	7.2	15.4	64.4	9.4	3.5	70184	68099	87	93	3057	3.9	11.5	60.7	22.7	1.2	131196
66619	TOPEKA	21175	1151	11.5	39.7	40.6	6.6	1.7	49300	52546	60	72	551	26.3	35.8	26.1	11.3	0.5	75923
66701	FORT SCOTT	19239	4896	29.8	33.3	31.6	3.1	2.1	38484	40367	28	26	3463	31.0	31.6	28.2	8.4	0.8	73914
66710	ALTOONA	17972	333	33.9	36.3	24.6	2.4	2.7	33166	34365	14	6	275	52.4	18.2	22.9	5.1	1.5	47045
66711	ARCADIA	19296	295	37.3	26.8	28.5	4.4	3.1	34018	37626	16	7	238	42.9	16.4	22.7	18.1	0.0	70000
66712	ARMA	17747	926	36.2	34.1	25.7	3.2	0.8	32967	34535	13	6	657	30.3	32.9	28.3	8.5	0.0	73431
66713	BAXTER SPRINGS	16813	2208	33.1	32.6	31.0	2.2	1.1	34779	37135	17	9	1571	34.1	25.0	32.3	7.8	0.7	76515
66714	BENEDICT	19459	354	30.5	29.7	34.2	3.1	2.5	40223	43656	33	33	309	37.5	25.9	28.8	7.1	0.6	71087
66716	BRONSON	15770	291	35.4	41.2	19.6	2.4	1.4	32906	33120	13	6	252	42.5	27.4	20.2	4.4	5.6	61923
66717	BUFFALO	17212	177	34.5	28.8	32.8	2.8	1.1	36665	40771	23	18	158	50.0	24.7	20.9	3.8	0.6	50000
66720	CHANUTE	20995	4307	28.6	33.1	31.5	4.1	2.7	40876	42825	36	38	3048	34.2	31.8	25.2	8.0	0.9	67576
66724	CHEROKEE	17298	441	27.0	44.2	25.4	2.5	0.9	36583	38577	22	17	355	48.7	24.5	20.0	6.5	0.3	51731
66725	COLUMBUS	18027	2273	35.0	30.0	29.7	3.7	1.6	35743	37608	20	13	1712	35.0	28.9	27.7	7.8	0.6	69067
66728	CRESTLINE	20754	22	22.7	27.3	45.5	4.5	0.0	50000	50000	61	74	19	15.8	26.3	47.4	10.5	0.0	102500
66732	ELSMORE	18180	108	30.6	32.4	33.3	2.8	0.9	37808	40000	26	23	87	33.3	26.4	24.1	10.3	5.7	74167
66733	ERIE	19460	906	26.4	35.8	32.7	4.3	0.9	40756	42394	35	37	708	32.3	29.0	30.6	8.1	0.0	71667
66734	FARLINGTON	20816	157	28.0	25.5	42.0	3.2	1.3	46815	50487	54	62	132	37.1	22.0	26.5	14.4	0.0	80000
66735	FRANKLIN	17804	219	32.9	33.8	30.1	3.2	0.0	35136	37021	18	10	174	44.3	25.3	22.4	5.2	2.9	58333
66736	FREDONIA	17954	1630	33.3	37.9	24.2	3.6	1.1	34558	34762	17	8	1267	36.2	30.2	26.0	6.8	0.8	63313
66738	FULTON	18000	146	39.0	21.2	34.9	2.7	2.1	34301	45461	16	8	127	40.9	22.8	27.6	3.1	5.5	64167
66739	GALENA	16708	2209	33.5	32.4	30.0	2.9	1.3	37019	38164	24	19	1652	34.3	32.3	27.7	5.5	0.2	64362
66740	GALESBURG	19535	320	21.3	36.6	34.7	5.6	1.9	43338	46502	43	50	273	30.4	29.7	31.1	7.7	1.1	75313
66743	GIRARD	20863	1632	26.1	31.3	35.5	4.3	2.9	44109	47253	46	54	1243	24.8	26.7	33.6	14.5	0.4	87016
66746	HEPLER	18553	104	26.0	26.0	43.3	2.9	1.9	48210	51249	57	67	88	36.4	23.9	26.1	13.6	0.0	81000
66748	HUMBOLDT	19837	1102	30.5	32.6	33.5	2.0	1.5	40052	41694	33	33	868	40.0	33.1	23.4	3.1	0.5	57250
66749	IOLA	19185	3347	31.2	32.7	31.1	3.3	1.8	39345	41233	31	29	2380	34.0	32.3	25.8	6.9	1.0	65438
66751	LA HARPE	17344	367	29.4	31.9	33.2	4.4	1.1	38454	40609	28	26	286	34.6	28.0	27.6	9.4	0.3	69091
66753	MC CUNE	19057	486	26.7	35.0	34.4	2.7	1.2	40244	42572	33	34	400	35.3	27.0	23.5	12.8	1.5	68214
66754	MAPLETON	18693	147	40.1	25.9	29.9	2.7	1.4	31782	33636	11	4	129	43.4	23.3	23.3	3.1	7.0	59444
66755	MORAN	18470	464	30.6	32.1	33.6	2.6	1.1	38073	39559	27	24	375	34.1	25.9	25.1	10.9	4.0	73125
66756	MULBERRY	17225	500	32.0	34.4	30.0	3.2	0.4	35562	37807	19	12	398	46.0	23.6	21.9	5.3	3.3	56154
66757	NEODESHA	17231	1369	34.5	28.0	34.0	2.8	0.8	38445	42014	28	25	964	37.8	36.0	22.9	2.8	0.5	59219
66758	NEOSHO FALLS	15759	106	45.3	34.0	17.9	2.8	0.0	28408	30171	6	1	86	43.0	19.8	27.9	4.7	4.7	58571
66759	NEW ALBANY	19909	146	27.4	32.2	32.2	4.8	3.4	42629	45856	41	48	128	33.6	23.4	25.8	14.1	3.1	78750
66761	PIQUA	17020	119	31.9	32.8	32.8	1.7	0.8	33722	37353	15	7	102	25.5	35.3	27.5	9.8	2.0	84500
66762	PITTSBURG	19938	9745	37.3	25.8	29.5	4.8	2.6	35278	38056	19	11	5489	22.2	29.1	30.4	16.0	2.4	88021
66763	FRONTENAC	19908	1327	29.5	32.2	34.4	2.3	1.7	40490	43017	34	35	1000	22.0	26.8	41.4	9.8	0.0	91481
66767	PRESCOTT	18486	219	39.3	17.4	39.7	3.7	0.0	39656	42397	32	30	183	41.5	27.3	25.1	6.0	0.0	66786
66769	REDFIELD	17318	225	30.2	32.4	32.0	4.4	0.9	39811	40411	32	30	189	35.4	28.6	28.6	5.3	2.1	66563
66770	RIVERTON	19826	424	23.6	32.1	38.7	4.2	1.4	46236	50087	52	61	354	20.1	29.7	39.3	10.7	0.3	90500
66771	SAINT PAUL	19401	388	25.5	30.4	38.1	3.9	2.1	43383	47779	44	51	313	32.9	27.2	30.7	8.6	0.6	71842
66772	SAVONBURG	18058	108	30.6	32.4	32.4	3.7	0.9	37808	40453	26	23	87	32.2	26.4	25.3	10.3	5.7	75833
66773	SCAMMON	16595	410	33.7	32.4	28.3	4.4	1.2	37809	40000	26	23	343	44.6	22.4	26.2	6.7	0.0	56607
66775	STARK	18631	87	24.1	37.9	31.0	6.9	0.0	40369	42353	34	35	75	28.0	26.7	40.0	5.3	0.0	84167
66776	THAYER	18268	515	21.6	34.2	38.4	5.4	0.4	43788	48287	45	52	431	30.6	21.3	38.1	9.0	0.9	86458
66777	TORONTO	20140	317	32.8	40.4	21.8	4.1	0.9	32364	33291	12	4	271	48.0	19.6	22.9	9.6	0.0	54583
66778	TREECE	15216	59	39.0	30.5	28.8	1.7	0.0	30429	31333	9	2	51	37.3	21.6	31.4	9.8	0.0	75000
66779	UNIONTOWN	19187	283	27.9	31.8	33.6	4.9	1.8	41484	43476	38	42	236	31.8	27.5	30.9	7.6	2.1	72500
66780	WALNUT	20037	233	25.8	27.5	43.8	2.1	0.9	46984	50847	54	64	196	33.2	25.5	27.6	13.8	0.0	79167
66781	WEIR	17996	509	28.7	36.0	30.8	4.1	0.4	39129	40417	30	28	425	39.3	25.2	26.6	8.9	0.0	65000
66783	YATES CENTER	17465	1051	39.9	34.4	21.0	3.7	1.0	30546	31051	9	2	828	41.2	28.4	23.2	5.4	1.8	62951
66801	EMPORIA	20338	11662	28.3	29.9	33.3	6.3	2.3	42250	45187	40	46	6641	20.2	25.4	41.1	12.3	1.0	96339
66830	ADMIRE	20305	147	19.0	34.7	37.4	6.8	2.0	46449	50586	53	62	120	23.3	32.5	30.8	11.7	1.7	81250
66833	ALLEN	21945	228	17.5	34.6	40.4	6.1	1.3	47602	51316	56	65	185	25.9	35.1	27.6	9.2	2.2	72917
66834	ALTA VISTA	20516	293	24.6	35.5	34.5	3.1	2.4	42101	45627	40	45	228	38.6	25.4	33.3	2.2	0.4	66923
66835	AMERICUS	19742	508	19.3	32.5	43.1	3.9	1.2	48597	51132	58	69	391	18.7	29.4	37.1	14.1	0.8	91786
66838	BURDICK	21333	75	25.3	42.7	25.3	4.0	2.7	36906	38026	23	19	65	46.2	20.0	24.6	9.2	0.0	58333
66839	BURLINGTON	21150	1594	25.1	30.3	35.6	7.0	1.9	45102	46549	49	57	1193	18.2	31.3	36.1	13.6	0.8	90663
66840	BURNS	19352	322	21.7	33.2	40.4	3.7	0.9	44707	47558	47	56	257	31.5	24.9	29.2	11.3	3.1	81316
66842	CASSODAY	25346	126	16.7	27.8	50.0	4.8	0.8	56636	60250	74	85	103	27.2	26.2	31.1	11.7	3.9	85625
66843	CEDAR POINT	23502	79	25.3	29.1	39.2	5.1	1.3	45570	48231	50	59	60	23.3	16.7	35.0	23.3	1.7	112500
66845	COTTONWOOD FALLS	18788	538	31.8	36.2	28.1	2.8	1.1	36578	38713	22	17	382	28.8	34.8	28.3	7.6	0.5	73030
66846	COUNCIL GROVE	21923	1488	29.8	32.5	30.2	4.7	2.7	39134	40630	30	28	1108	26.7	27.9	30.8	13.1	1.5	81500
66849	DWIGHT	18993	201	31.3	33.3	31.3	2.5	1.5	37551	39354	25	21	160	41.9	25.6	17.5	15.0	0.0	61875
66850	ELMDALE	26846	56	21.4	30.4	35.7	8.9	3.6	48214	48214	57	67	46	23.9	10.9	28.3	34.8	2.2	141667
66851	FLORENCE	18935	304	32.6	36.8	25.3	3.0	2.3	35467	37206	19	12	236	54.2	29.7	7.6	5.9	2.5	47297
66852	GRIDLEY	22661	288	26.4	30.9	34.7	4.9	3.1	43488	45383	44	51	228	43.4	27.2	19.7	8.8	0.9	56818
66853	HAMILTON	18710	199	28.6	36.2	30.7	3.5	1.0	38638	42686	29	27	153	57.5	19.0	17.0	4.6	2.0	43611
66854	HARTFORD	19925	364	24.2	33.8	37.4	3.0	1.6	44201	47132	46	54	298	31.9	21.1	34.2	11.1	1.7	84706
66856	LEBO	20263	671	22.2	29.8	40.8	6.3	0.9	48143	48549	57	67	529	15.7	23.8	47.6	11.2	1.7	102867
66857	LE ROY	21585	367	22.9	32.4	37.6	4.6	2.5	45849	47165	51	59	313	25.2	29.4	31.0	14.1	0.3	84821
66858	LINCOLNVILLE	16440	191	33.0	33.0	30.4	3.7	0.0	40604	41996	35	37	163	46.0	23.9	23.3	6.7	0.0	53824
66859	LOST SPRINGS	18183	75	36.0	29.3	29.3	4.0	1.3	37367	41144	25	21	65	46.2	21.5	21.5	9.2	1.5	53571
66860	MADISON	19454	502	30.7	33.3	30.7	3.4	2.0	39541	41369	31	29	385	41.3	24.7	24.4	7.5	2.1	62885
66861	MARION	20125	1350	28.1	31.6	34.9	4.2	1.2	40732	42356	35	37	1075	22.8	32.3	34.6	9.9	0.5	83736
66862	MATFIELD GREEN	23417	70	27.1	30.0	37.1	4.3	1.4	42355	44094	40	47	51	27.5	21.6	33.3	13.7	3.9	92500
66864	NEOSHO RAPIDS	21938	238	18.5	32.8	40.8	5.9	2.1	48906	51730	59	70	205	20.0	18.0	40.5	19.5	2.0	111513
66865	OLPE	18657	398	17.6	36.2	43.7	2.5	0.0	47490	50522	55	65	327	17.7	20.8	42.5	18.3	0.6	108631
66866	PEABODY	19380	714	23.0	37.4	33.3	4.8	1.5	42197	43446	40	45	551	25.4	37.9	27.0	8.5	1.1	71923
66868	READING	21125	298	19.5	34.6	37.2	7.0	1.7	46152	50637	52	61	250	22.0	22.4	38.4	16.4	0.8	97368
66869	STRONG CITY	20471	455	27.7	30.1	34.7	5.9	1.5	42914	45636	42	49	341	40.8	17.6	24.9	15.8	0.9	69545
66870	VIRGIL	18154	144	29.2	34.0	32.6	3.5	0.7	40400	45000	34	35	113	54.0	20.4	15.9	8.8	0.9	45500
66871	WAVERLY	19620	524	27.1	32.1	34.2	4.4	2.3	42336	43760	40	46	431	27.8	26.2	30.6	12.5	2.8	84531
66872	WHITE CITY	19701	423	23.9	34.8	39.0	1.9	0.5	44435	45578	47	55	334	36.8	29.3	26.0	6.6	1.2	67500
66873	WILSEY	20339	126	26.2	41.3	27.0	4.0	1.6	36826	38148	23	18	109	45.0	19.3	25.7	10.1	0.0	61000
66901	CONCORDIA	21431	2687	29.4	32.4	32.6	3.2	2.5	40221	42194	33	33	1892	33.6	33.7	29.2	3.3	0.1	70357
66930	AGENDA	19785	65	23.1	41.5	30.8	3.1	1.5	41900	41728	39	44	54	75.9	9.3	11.1	1.9	1.9	30000
66932	ATHOL	19181	51	27.5	33.3	37.3	2.0	0.0	39077	47408	30	28	42	45.2	28.6	21.4	4.8	0.0	52857
66933	BARNES	19682	144	30.6	41.0	23.6	2.1	2.8	35330	35000	19	11	116	49.1	12.1	28.4	3.4	6.9	52000
66935	BELLEVILLE	20754	1317	33.2	35.9	25.5	3.4	2.0	35281	36497	19	11	1017	42.5	26.8	25.6	4.2	0.9	60284
66936	BURR OAK	18080	201	37.8	39.3	19.4	1.5	2.0	32461	33604	12	5	160	66.3	15.0	14.4	4.4	0.0	29286
66937	CLIFTON	19070	375	36.5	31.7	26.1	2.9	2.7	35091	36132	18	10	295	49.8	26.4	16.3	6.4	1.0	50185
	KANSAS	26028		20.3	26.8	37.6	9.9	5.4	52748	54940				18.1	21.6	35.7	21.6	3.0	107692
	UNITED STATES	27277		20.9	24.4	35.3	11.7	7.6	54719	56938				9.3	13.1	31.6	32.6	13.5	162279

ZIP CODE #	POST OFFICE NAME	FINANCIAL SERVICES				THE HOME						ENTERTAINMENT						PERSONAL			
						Home Improvements		Furnishings													
		Auto Loan	Home Loan	Invest-ments	Retire-ment Plans	Home Repair	Lawn & Garden	Comput-ers & Hard-ware-Personal	Major Appli-ances	TV, Radio, Sound Equip-ment	Furni-ture	Dine out/ Carry out	Sports Equip-ment	Fees & Tickets	Toys & Games	Travel	Cable TV	Apparel & Services	Auto Repairs	Health Insur-ance	Pets & Supplies
66615	TOPEKA	119	131	109	128	124	114	116	117	112	123	113	92	121	118	117	108	79	112	108	135
66616	TOPEKA	71	63	58	64	60	73	68	68	70	63	69	53	62	71	63	74	47	69	76	83
66617	TOPEKA	105	120	105	121	116	118	106	111	106	107	107	85	115	109	113	107	75	107	112	130
66618	TOPEKA	104	119	103	121	115	116	105	109	104	106	105	85	114	107	112	105	73	106	110	128
66619	TOPEKA	92	83	72	85	79	78	90	83	88	91	89	67	85	91	83	86	62	87	81	100
66701	FORT SCOTT	73	59	65	60	60	74	65	70	69	58	67	54	56	68	61	73	45	69	77	84
66710	ALTOONA	75	53	77	52	55	78	58	72	64	51	62	55	46	63	57	70	41	67	78	85
66711	ARCADIA	81	58	82	57	61	85	64	79	71	57	69	59	51	70	62	78	46	74	86	93
66712	ARMA	69	49	69	48	51	72	54	67	60	48	58	50	43	59	52	66	39	62	72	78
66713	BAXTER SPRINGS	70	56	66	55	56	72	57	67	62	53	61	51	49	63	55	67	41	63	71	80
66714	BENEDICT	84	59	89	58	62	87	63	79	68	55	67	62	48	67	62	74	44	73	83	96
66716	BRONSON	68	49	71	47	50	69	50	64	55	46	54	49	40	55	50	61	36	59	67	76
66717	BUFFALO	78	56	80	54	58	79	57	73	63	53	62	54	46	63	56	70	41	67	76	86
66720	CHANUTE	76	66	68	66	65	79	70	74	73	65	72	57	64	73	67	78	49	73	82	88
66724	CHEROKEE	72	52	73	51	54	75	56	70	63	50	61	53	45	61	55	69	40	65	76	83
66725	COLUMBUS	73	54	70	53	55	75	59	70	64	53	63	53	48	64	56	70	42	66	75	83
66728	CRESTLINE	77	71	70	73	72	83	70	79	72	63	70	59	64	73	69	76	48	73	81	91
66732	ELSMORE	79	55	87	54	57	84	61	75	63	49	62	62	44	62	60	69	40	70	80	93
66733	ERIE	82	59	84	59	62	86	64	79	70	56	68	61	51	69	63	76	45	74	85	94
66734	FARLINGTON	88	61	96	60	63	92	67	83	70	55	69	68	50	69	67	77	45	78	88	102
66735	FRANKLIN	75	54	77	52	56	76	55	70	62	51	60	53	44	61	55	68	40	65	74	83
66736	FREDONIA	70	51	67	50	52	71	56	67	62	50	60	51	46	61	54	67	40	63	72	79
66738	FULTON	86	62	87	61	65	87	64	81	70	59	69	60	52	70	63	77	46	74	84	96
66739	GALENA	70	54	59	54	54	69	58	65	63	54	61	49	49	64	54	67	41	62	69	77
66740	GALESBURG	92	64	96	63	67	95	70	86	74	60	73	69	53	73	68	81	48	80	91	105
66743	GIRARD	81	71	77	72	71	86	73	80	76	67	75	61	66	76	72	81	51	77	86	95
66746	HEPLER	88	61	97	60	63	93	67	84	70	54	69	69	49	69	67	76	45	78	88	103
66748	HUMBOLDT	81	58	83	57	60	84	63	78	69	55	67	60	50	68	61	76	45	73	84	92
66749	IOLA	71	58	64	58	58	72	63	69	67	58	66	52	55	67	60	72	45	67	75	82
66751	LA HARPE	83	59	71	58	59	80	62	73	68	59	67	57	49	71	57	74	45	69	77	89
66753	MC CUNE	88	62	95	62	64	93	68	84	70	55	70	69	51	69	67	77	45	78	88	102
66754	MAPLETON	82	59	84	57	61	83	60	76	67	56	66	57	48	66	59	73	43	70	80	91
66755	MORAN	80	55	87	55	57	84	61	76	63	49	63	63	45	62	61	69	41	71	80	93
66756	MULBERRY	76	54	78	52	56	77	56	71	62	52	61	53	45	61	55	68	40	65	74	84
66757	NEODESHA	68	54	62	53	54	68	58	64	62	54	61	49	50	62	55	66	41	62	69	77
66758	NEOSHO FALLS	62	42	68	42	44	65	47	59	49	38	48	48	35	48	47	53	31	55	62	72
66759	NEW ALBANY	90	64	94	62	66	92	67	85	73	59	72	66	52	72	66	80	47	78	88	102
66761	PIQUA	76	52	83	52	55	80	58	72	60	47	59	59	42	59	58	66	39	67	76	88
66762	PITTSBURG	69	58	56	60	57	64	70	64	70	64	69	51	61	70	61	71	48	68	68	78
66763	FRONTENAC	79	57	80	56	59	83	62	77	69	56	67	57	50	68	60	76	44	71	83	90
66767	PRESCOTT	77	55	79	54	57	78	57	72	63	53	62	54	45	63	56	69	41	66	75	86
66769	REDFIELD	80	56	87	55	58	84	61	76	64	51	63	62	46	63	61	70	41	71	80	93
66770	RIVERTON	81	69	71	71	70	84	69	78	72	64	71	60	61	74	67	77	48	73	81	92
66771	SAINT PAUL	94	65	102	65	68	99	72	89	75	59	74	73	53	74	71	82	48	83	94	109
66772	SAVONBURG	80	55	88	55	58	85	61	76	64	50	63	63	45	63	61	70	41	71	81	94
66773	SCAMMON	75	54	78	53	56	77	56	71	61	51	60	55	44	61	56	67	40	65	74	85
66775	STARK	84	58	92	58	60	89	64	80	67	52	66	66	47	65	64	73	43	74	84	98
66776	THAYER	87	65	76	64	65	85	67	78	73	63	72	61	55	76	63	79	48	74	82	95
66777	TORONTO	59	56	72	52	62	68	54	63	57	58	55	42	53	52	58	60	37	61	70	73
66778	TREECE	68	49	70	47	51	69	50	64	56	47	55	48	40	55	50	61	36	58	66	76
66779	UNIONTOWN	85	59	93	59	62	90	65	81	68	53	67	67	48	67	65	74	44	76	85	99
66780	WALNUT	88	61	97	60	63	93	67	83	70	54	69	69	49	69	67	76	45	78	88	103
66781	WEIR	79	60	67	59	60	77	62	71	67	59	66	55	51	69	58	73	44	67	75	86
66783	YATES CENTER	66	48	68	47	50	69	52	64	57	46	55	48	42	56	51	62	37	60	69	76
66801	EMPORIA	75	65	61	66	63	69	76	70	76	71	75	56	68	76	68	76	52	74	74	84
66830	ADMIRE	97	67	107	67	70	102	74	92	77	60	76	76	54	76	74	84	49	86	97	113
66833	ALLEN	96	66	105	66	69	101	73	91	76	59	75	75	54	75	73	83	49	85	96	112
66834	ALTA VISTA	86	59	95	59	62	91	66	82	69	53	68	68	48	67	66	75	44	77	87	101
66835	AMERICUS	79	72	72	75	73	85	71	80	73	64	72	61	65	75	71	78	49	74	83	94
66838	BURDICK	89	61	98	61	64	94	68	85	71	55	70	70	50	70	68	77	45	79	89	104
66839	BURLINGTON	85	70	82	69	71	88	71	82	76	67	75	62	62	76	70	81	50	78	87	97
66840	BURNS	93	64	102	64	67	98	71	88	74	58	73	73	52	72	71	81	47	82	93	109
66842	CASSODAY	111	76	122	76	80	117	85	105	88	69	87	87	62	87	84	96	57	99	111	130
66843	CEDAR POINT	93	64	102	64	67	98	71	88	74	58	73	73	52	73	71	81	47	83	93	109
66845	COTTONWOOD FALLS	73	52	74	51	54	76	57	70	63	50	61	54	45	61	55	69	40	66	76	83
66846	COUNCIL GROVE	85	64	86	63	66	89	69	82	75	62	73	63	57	73	68	81	48	78	89	98
66849	DWIGHT	77	53	85	53	56	81	59	73	61	48	61	61	43	60	59	67	39	68	77	90
66850	ELMDALE	105	72	115	72	75	110	80	99	83	65	82	82	59	81	79	91	53	93	105	122
66851	FLORENCE	79	57	80	56	59	83	62	77	69	55	67	58	50	68	60	76	44	72	84	91
66852	GRIDLEY	96	69	104	70	72	102	75	92	78	62	77	76	58	77	75	84	50	86	96	113
66853	HAMILTON	78	56	81	54	58	80	58	73	63	53	62	56	46	63	57	70	41	67	76	88
66854	HARTFORD	86	65	87	64	67	88	66	82	72	61	71	61	55	72	65	78	47	75	84	97
66856	LEBO	80	74	73	77	75	86	72	81	74	66	73	62	67	76	72	79	50	75	84	95
66857	LE ROY	92	64	102	63	67	98	71	88	73	57	73	73	52	72	70	80	47	82	93	108
66858	LINCOLNVILLE	79	54	87	54	57	83	60	75	63	49	62	62	44	62	60	68	40	70	79	92
66859	LOST SPRINGS	79	55	87	54	57	84	61	75	63	49	62	62	44	62	60	69	40	70	80	93
66860	MADISON	79	57	81	56	59	83	62	77	68	54	66	59	49	67	61	75	44	71	83	91
66861	MARION	83	61	93	60	65	86	64	81	69	58	68	61	52	67	65	75	45	75	84	95
66862	MATFIELD GREEN	87	60	96	60	63	92	67	83	69	54	69	69	49	68	66	76	45	77	88	102
66864	NEOSHO RAPIDS	86	78	77	81	80	92	77	87	79	69	78	66	71	81	77	84	53	80	89	101
66865	OLPE	78	70	71	73	72	83	69	79	72	63	70	60	64	73	69	76	48	73	81	91
66866	PEABODY	80	64	80	64	63	85	68	77	70	58	69	63	57	69	67	74	46	74	83	94
66868	READING	97	69	105	69	72	103	75	93	78	62	77	76	56	77	75	85	50	86	98	114
66869	STRONG CITY	89	62	94	61	65	91	66	83	71	58	70	65	51	71	66	78	46	77	87	101
66870	VIRGIL	72	58	79	55	62	77	58	71	63	57	61	51	50	60	59	68	41	67	76	83
66871	WAVERLY	88	62	91	61	65	90	65	82	71	59	70	63	51	70	64	78	46	76	86	98
66872	WHITE CITY	81	57	84	56	60	85	63	78	69	54	67	60	49	67	61	75	44	73	84	93
66873	WILSEY	90	62	99	62	65	95	69	85	72	56	71	71	50	70	68	78	46	80	90	105
66901	CONCORDIA	78	64	79	63	65	83	68	77	72	62	71	58	59	71	67	78	48	74	84	91
66930	AGENDA	80	55	88	55	58	84	61	76	64	50	63	63	45	62	61	69	41	71	80	93
66932	ATHOL	74	51	82	51	53	78	57	70	59	46	58	58	42	58	56	64	38	66	74	87
66933	BARNES	78	54	86	54	56	83	60	74	62	48	61	61	44	61	59	68	40	69	79	91
66935	BELLEVILLE	72	57	75	56	59	78	59	72	65	53	63	54	51	63	59	71	42	67	78	84
66936	BURR OAK	69	47	76	47	50	73	53	65	55	43	54	54	39	54	52	60	35	61	69	81
66937	CLIFTON	80	55	88	55	58	84	61	76	64	50	63	63	45	62	61	69	41	71	80	93
	KANSAS	98	90	91	91	89	97	94	95	94	90	94	74	88	96	90	96	65	95	98	113
	UNITED STATES	100	100	100	100	100	100	100	100	100	100	100	100	100	100	100	100	100	100	100	100

ZIP CODE #	POST OFFICE NAME	COUNTY FIPS CODE	POPULATION 2000	POPULATION 2009	POPULATION 2014	2000-2009 ANNUAL RATE % Rate	2000-2009 ANNUAL RATE State Centile	HOUSEHOLDS 2000	HOUSEHOLDS 2009	HOUSEHOLDS 2014	HOUSEHOLDS % Annual Rate 2000-2009	HOUSEHOLDS 2009 Average HH Size	FAMILIES 2000	FAMILIES 2009	FAMILIES % Annual Rate 2000-2009
66938	CLYDE	029	1107	1010	957	-1.0	19	469	435	413	-0.8	2.26	315	290	-0.9
66939	COURTLAND	157	450	385	353	-1.7	7	195	166	152	-1.7	2.32	142	120	-1.8
66940	CUBA	157	378	320	293	-1.8	6	172	147	135	-1.7	2.18	123	105	-1.7
66941	ESBON	089	316	260	237	-2.1	3	143	121	111	-1.8	2.15	94	79	-1.9
66942	FORMOSO	089	220	180	164	-2.1	3	104	88	80	-1.8	2.05	76	63	-2.0
66943	GREENLEAF	201	552	508	482	-0.9	23	245	230	220	-0.7	2.14	153	142	-0.8
66944	HADDAM	201	277	246	231	-1.3	12	121	109	102	-1.1	2.19	82	73	-1.2
66945	HANOVER	201	1116	1080	1059	-0.4	48	444	439	434	-0.1	2.40	295	288	-0.3
66946	HOLLENBERG	201	155	139	132	-1.2	14	65	59	56	-1.0	2.34	48	43	-1.2
66948	JAMESTOWN	029	479	456	435	-0.5	41	176	167	159	-0.6	2.59	126	119	-0.6
66949	JEWELL	089	645	601	567	-0.8	28	294	282	268	-0.4	2.13	181	172	-0.5
66951	KENSINGTON	183	619	521	480	-1.8	6	264	223	205	-1.8	2.28	185	156	-1.8
66952	LEBANON	183	448	370	339	-2.0	4	206	172	158	-1.9	2.15	150	125	-2.0
66953	LINN	201	735	666	629	-1.1	17	278	254	240	-1.0	2.39	191	174	-1.0
66955	MAHASKA	201	161	143	134	-1.3	12	53	48	45	-1.1	2.88	36	32	-1.3
66956	MANKATO	089	1732	1542	1436	-1.2	14	759	694	652	-1.0	2.16	487	441	-1.1
66958	MORROWVILLE	201	403	359	337	-1.2	14	165	148	139	-1.2	2.35	112	100	-1.2
66959	MUNDEN	157	242	218	202	-1.1	17	97	89	83	-0.9	2.45	69	62	-1.1
66960	NARKA	157	174	157	145	-1.1	17	82	75	70	-1.0	2.09	58	53	-1.0
66961	NORWAY	157	158	135	124	-1.7	7	56	48	44	-1.7	2.81	41	34	-2.0
66962	PALMER	201	330	300	285	-1.0	19	126	116	110	-0.9	2.36	88	80	-1.0
66963	RANDALL	089	172	140	128	-2.2	2	74	61	56	-2.1	2.30	53	44	-2.0
66964	REPUBLIC	157	262	203	186	-2.7	0	127	99	91	-2.7	2.05	88	68	-2.7
66966	SCANDIA	157	780	629	577	-2.3	1	321	259	237	-2.3	2.43	226	182	-2.3
66967	SMITH CENTER	183	2531	2334	2203	-0.9	23	1097	1015	957	-0.8	2.22	717	656	-1.0
66968	WASHINGTON	201	1824	1628	1535	-1.2	14	781	706	668	-1.1	2.23	492	440	-1.2
66970	WEBBER	089	190	155	141	-2.2	2	86	72	66	-1.9	2.15	62	52	-1.9
67001	ANDALE	173	1321	1354	1387	0.3	74	407	428	441	0.5	3.16	332	344	0.4
67002	ANDOVER	015	9220	12468	13885	3.3	98	3163	4353	4875	3.5	2.82	2499	3408	3.4
67003	ANTHONY	077	2834	2554	2402	-1.1	17	1227	1109	1043	-1.1	2.25	783	700	-1.2
67004	ARGONIA	191	940	886	856	-0.6	36	360	341	330	-0.6	2.60	250	234	-0.7
67005	ARKANSAS CITY	035	16238	15273	14752	-0.7	32	6510	6210	6014	-0.5	2.38	4406	4163	-0.6
67008	ATLANTA	035	606	582	569	-0.4	48	237	230	225	-0.3	2.53	180	173	-0.4
67009	ATTICA	077	949	879	840	-0.8	28	388	363	346	-0.7	2.17	251	232	-0.8
67010	AUGUSTA	015	13023	13660	14033	0.5	79	4926	5233	5390	0.7	2.58	3648	3845	0.6
67013	BELLE PLAINE	191	3134	2985	2907	-0.5	41	1167	1133	1109	-0.3	2.63	886	853	-0.4
67016	BENTLEY	173	392	385	387	-0.2	56	148	148	150	0.0	2.60	119	118	-0.1
67017	BENTON	015	2120	2457	2623	1.6	94	754	879	938	1.7	2.79	610	703	1.5
67018	BLUFF CITY	077	180	150	138	-2.0	4	79	67	62	-1.8	2.24	56	47	-1.9
67019	BURDEN	035	1052	999	969	-0.6	36	389	373	362	-0.5	2.68	293	278	-0.6
67020	BURRTON	079	1867	1868	1849	0.0	64	712	722	717	0.2	2.58	535	536	0.0
67021	BYERS	151	131	122	119	-0.8	28	54	51	50	-0.6	2.39	40	37	-0.8
67022	CALDWELL	191	1849	1619	1537	-1.4	11	797	706	671	-1.3	2.21	504	440	-1.5
67023	CAMBRIDGE	035	264	250	242	-0.6	36	105	100	97	-0.5	2.49	78	74	-0.6
67024	CEDAR VALE	019	1229	1136	1090	-0.8	28	486	447	428	-0.9	2.37	341	310	-1.0
67025	CHENEY	173	3065	3233	3335	0.6	82	1094	1171	1214	0.7	2.71	832	872	0.5
67026	CLEARWATER	173	4347	4814	5139	1.1	89	1528	1761	1890	1.5	2.70	1245	1411	1.4
67028	COATS	151	184	172	167	-0.7	32	75	71	70	-0.6	2.42	55	52	-0.6
67029	COLDWATER	033	1131	1083	1075	-0.5	41	510	505	508	-0.1	2.09	302	296	-0.2
67030	COLWICH	173	2305	2430	2548	0.6	82	677	733	774	0.9	3.25	584	626	0.8
67031	CONWAY SPRINGS	191	2283	2181	2121	-0.5	41	761	735	717	-0.4	2.89	560	535	-0.5
67035	CUNNINGHAM	095	1020	891	843	-1.5	9	381	336	318	-1.3	2.45	277	243	-1.4
67036	DANVILLE	077	175	155	145	-1.3	12	78	70	66	-1.2	2.21	58	51	-1.4
67037	DERBY	173	22553	26166	27928	1.6	94	7867	9290	9959	1.8	2.80	6345	7408	1.7
67038	DEXTER	035	651	669	669	0.3	74	220	227	227	0.3	2.80	164	168	0.3
67039	DOUGLASS	015	3500	3902	4102	1.2	91	1255	1419	1499	1.3	2.71	978	1092	1.2
67042	EL DORADO	015	16975	17266	17482	0.2	70	6437	6644	6755	0.3	2.38	4265	4325	0.2
67045	EUREKA	073	3911	3739	3594	-0.5	41	1660	1587	1523	-0.5	2.27	1043	986	-0.6
67047	FALL RIVER	073	580	578	574	0.0	64	270	273	272	0.1	2.12	187	188	0.1
67049	FREEPORT	077	52	46	43	-1.3	12	20	18	17	-1.1	2.56	15	13	-1.5
67050	GARDEN PLAIN	173	1804	1880	1944	0.4	76	582	621	647	0.7	3.01	455	476	0.5
67051	GEUDA SPRINGS	191	496	471	459	-0.6	36	198	192	188	-0.3	2.45	159	153	-0.4
67052	GODDARD	173	5842	6880	7574	1.8	95	1881	2278	2526	2.1	2.97	1567	1870	1.9
67053	GOESSEL	115	461	439	426	-0.5	41	174	166	160	-0.5	2.49	138	131	-0.6
67054	GREENSBURG	097	1842	1513	1380	-2.1	3	822	688	631	-1.9	2.18	526	433	-2.1
67055	GREENWICH	173	23	30	36	2.9	97	11	15	18	3.4	1.93	9	12	3.2
67056	HALSTEAD	079	2694	2713	2694	0.1	68	1048	1071	1070	0.2	2.51	769	779	0.1
67057	HARDTNER	007	275	259	248	-0.6	36	125	120	116	-0.4	2.16	77	74	-0.4
67058	HARPER	077	2202	1947	1824	-1.3	12	920	821	771	-1.2	2.35	601	531	-1.3
67059	HAVILAND	097	1145	1076	1020	-0.7	32	422	401	380	-0.6	2.45	309	290	-0.7
67060	HAYSVILLE	173	11451	13099	13795	1.5	92	4087	4744	5024	1.6	2.74	3189	3639	1.4
67061	HAZELTON	007	199	181	172	-1.0	19	75	69	66	-0.9	2.54	54	50	-0.8
67062	HESSTON	079	3998	4206	4274	0.5	79	1383	1492	1525	0.8	2.54	1038	1109	0.7
67063	HILLSBORO	115	3856	3760	3669	-0.3	52	1427	1375	1333	-0.4	2.42	1000	954	-0.5
67065	ISABEL	151	249	240	233	-0.4	48	95	94	92	-0.1	2.55	72	71	-0.2
67066	IUKA	151	374	365	359	-0.3	52	147	146	144	-0.1	2.50	113	111	-0.2
67067	KECHI	173	1232	1435	1727	1.7	94	418	487	590	1.7	2.94	348	400	1.5
67068	KINGMAN	095	5609	5254	5050	-0.7	32	2200	2078	2001	-0.6	2.48	1539	1441	-0.7
67070	KIOWA	007	1164	1075	1028	-0.9	23	505	477	458	-0.6	2.21	337	315	-0.7
67071	LAKE CITY	007	97	93	89	-0.5	41	41	40	39	-0.3	2.33	30	29	-0.4
67072	LATHAM	015	301	319	328	0.6	82	122	131	136	0.8	2.44	91	97	0.7
67073	LEHIGH	115	335	356	358	0.7	84	117	124	125	0.6	2.87	103	108	0.5
67074	LEON	015	1897	1984	2027	0.5	79	677	724	746	0.7	2.64	516	543	0.6
67101	MAIZE	173	2585	3329	3709	2.8	97	882	1146	1282	2.9	2.90	727	935	2.8
67102	MAPLE CITY	035	52	53	53	0.2	70	21	22	22	0.5	2.41	17	18	0.6
67103	MAYFIELD	191	271	273	272	0.1	68	103	106	106	0.3	2.58	83	84	0.1
67104	MEDICINE LODGE	007	2786	2562	2442	-0.9	23	1169	1097	1052	-0.7	2.30	785	728	-0.8
67105	MILAN	191	237	229	224	-0.4	48	86	84	83	-0.3	2.73	70	68	-0.3
67106	MILTON	191	483	482	479	0.0	64	164	165	164	0.1	2.92	134	134	0.0
67107	MOUNDRIDGE	113	2777	2809	2811	0.1	68	1039	1062	1066	0.2	2.49	755	763	0.1
67108	MOUNT HOPE	173	1663	1704	1731	0.3	74	575	603	617	0.5	2.75	436	449	0.3
67109	MULLINVILLE	097	400	379	355	-0.8	28	167	159	150	-0.5	2.38	124	116	-0.7
67110	MULVANE	191	7683	8269	8541	0.8	86	2799	3063	3178	1.0	2.68	2181	2361	0.9
67111	MURDOCK	095	269	260	253	-0.4	48	100	98	96	-0.2	2.65	81	79	-0.3
67112	NASHVILLE	095	259	227	214	-1.4	11	107	96	91	-1.2	2.36	83	74	-1.2
	KANSAS					0.6					0.6	2.49			0.5
	UNITED STATES					1.0					1.1	2.59			0.9

POPULATION COMPOSITION

ZIP CODE #	POST OFFICE NAME	RACE (%) White 2000	White 2009	Black 2000	Black 2009	Asian/Pacific 2000	Asian/Pacific 2009	% Hispanic Origin 2000	% Hispanic Origin 2009	2009 AGE DISTRIBUTION (%) 0-4	5-9	10-14	15-19	20-24	25-44	45-64	65-84	85+	18+	MEDIAN AGE 2009	% 2009 Males	% 2009 Females
66938	CLYDE	99.4	99.3	0.0	0.0	0.0	0.0	0.4	0.6	5.0	5.1	5.3	5.6	5.4	22.4	26.5	18.3	6.2	80.4	45.8	48.2	51.8
66939	COURTLAND	98.7	98.4	0.7	0.8	0.0	0.0	1.3	1.8	5.7	6.5	7.3	7.0	4.9	17.7	33.0	14.8	3.1	75.8	45.5	50.1	49.9
66940	CUBA	98.9	98.8	0.0	0.0	0.0	0.0	1.3	1.6	5.0	5.0	5.6	5.0	4.7	17.5	34.1	19.4	3.8	81.3	49.0	52.5	47.5
66941	ESBON	98.4	98.1	0.0	0.0	0.0	0.0	0.6	0.8	5.4	5.8	6.2	6.2	3.8	18.8	33.1	17.7	3.1	78.8	47.4	50.0	50.0
66942	FORMOSO	99.5	99.4	0.0	0.0	0.0	0.0	0.5	0.6	3.9	5.0	5.6	5.0	3.3	16.7	32.8	24.4	3.3	82.2	51.4	51.1	48.9
66943	GREENLEAF	99.5	99.4	0.0	0.0	0.0	0.0	0.9	1.6	4.3	4.3	4.7	6.9	6.3	19.7	31.7	17.7	4.3	82.3	46.9	52.0	48.0
66944	HADDAM	98.2	98.0	0.0	0.0	0.0	0.0	0.4	0.0	6.5	7.3	7.3	6.1	4.1	19.9	26.0	17.5	5.3	74.4	44.1	53.3	46.7
66945	HANOVER	98.9	98.8	0.4	0.4	0.0	0.0	0.4	0.5	6.0	6.7	6.8	6.2	4.4	20.9	28.1	16.8	4.2	76.8	44.0	52.4	47.6
66946	HOLLENBERG	99.4	99.3	0.0	0.0	0.0	0.0	1.3	1.4	7.2	8.6	7.2	5.8	4.3	19.4	28.1	17.3	2.2	72.7	43.1	54.0	46.0
66948	JAMESTOWN	98.1	98.0	0.0	0.0	0.2	0.2	0.2	0.2	6.1	6.1	6.1	6.6	4.4	21.9	27.2	16.4	5.0	77.2	44.0	50.9	49.1
66949	JEWELL	99.8	99.8	0.0	0.0	0.0	0.0	1.1	1.2	6.0	5.8	6.2	6.0	5.7	19.8	28.3	17.8	4.5	78.2	45.5	47.4	52.6
66951	KENSINGTON	98.4	97.9	0.3	0.4	0.0	0.2	0.8	1.3	4.4	5.2	5.6	5.8	4.2	17.9	33.2	18.8	5.0	80.8	48.7	50.7	49.3
66952	LEBANON	98.4	97.8	0.2	0.3	0.0	0.0	1.1	1.6	4.6	5.4	5.9	5.9	3.8	18.4	32.4	20.0	3.5	80.0	48.5	50.8	49.2
66953	LINN	99.2	99.1	0.1	0.2	0.0	0.0	0.7	1.1	4.8	5.4	5.7	6.3	4.1	18.9	27.3	18.8	8.7	79.3	47.8	49.7	50.3
66955	MAHASKA	98.1	97.9	0.0	0.0	0.0	0.0	0.0	0.0	6.3	7.7	7.7	7.0	4.2	18.2	26.6	17.5	4.9	74.1	44.2	53.1	46.9
66956	MANKATO	98.8	98.6	0.0	0.0	0.1	0.1	0.7	0.8	3.9	4.3	4.9	6.0	5.3	17.4	32.2	20.4	5.5	82.7	50.2	50.3	49.7
66958	MORROWVILLE	98.3	98.1	0.0	0.0	0.0	0.0	0.2	0.6	6.7	7.0	7.0	6.7	4.2	19.8	26.2	17.3	5.3	74.9	44.1	52.6	47.4
66959	MUNDEN	99.2	98.6	0.0	0.0	0.0	0.0	0.4	0.5	6.4	6.9	6.9	6.0	4.1	20.6	29.8	16.5	2.8	75.7	44.3	54.6	45.4
66960	NARKA	98.9	98.7	0.0	0.0	0.0	0.0	0.0	0.6	6.4	7.6	7.0	5.7	3.8	19.7	29.9	17.2	2.5	75.8	44.8	55.4	44.6
66961	NORWAY	99.4	99.3	0.6	0.7	0.0	0.0	1.3	1.5	5.9	6.7	7.4	7.4	5.2	17.0	32.6	14.1	3.7	75.6	45.2	50.4	49.6
66962	PALMER	99.1	99.0	0.0	0.0	0.0	0.0	0.6	1.0	5.0	5.7	5.7	6.3	3.7	18.7	28.0	18.3	8.7	79.0	47.8	49.7	50.3
66963	RANDALL	99.4	99.3	0.0	0.0	0.0	0.0	0.6	0.7	4.3	5.0	5.7	7.1	3.6	17.1	37.1	17.1	2.9	80.7	49.2	52.9	47.1
66964	REPUBLIC	99.6	99.5	0.0	0.0	0.0	0.0	0.4	0.5	3.4	4.4	4.9	5.9	4.9	18.2	38.4	16.3	3.4	83.3	49.9	52.2	47.8
66966	SCANDIA	99.2	99.0	0.3	0.3	0.0	0.0	0.8	1.1	4.8	5.2	6.2	6.5	4.9	18.3	34.5	16.2	3.3	79.8	47.4	50.4	49.6
66967	SMITH CENTER	99.1	98.9	0.0	0.0	0.2	0.3	0.6	0.8	4.2	4.9	5.1	5.8	4.7	18.6	28.1	20.8	7.7	81.6	49.6	47.4	52.6
66968	WASHINGTON	99.1	98.8	0.1	0.1	0.0	0.0	0.8	1.3	6.0	6.1	6.0	5.4	4.9	20.1	27.8	18.0	5.8	78.2	46.2	49.6	50.4
66970	WEBBER	99.5	99.4	0.0	0.0	0.0	0.0	0.5	0.6	3.9	4.5	5.8	5.2	3.2	16.1	33.5	24.5	3.2	82.6	51.9	51.6	48.4
67001	ANDALE	98.8	98.2	0.2	0.2	0.0	0.0	1.7	3.0	10.2	9.7	9.6	9.1	5.9	22.7	22.7	8.9	1.1	64.8	30.1	52.1	47.9
67002	ANDOVER	95.0	93.9	0.6	0.7	1.0	1.4	2.1	3.1	7.5	7.8	8.2	8.3	4.8	25.7	27.1	8.4	2.1	70.8	36.6	49.1	50.9
67003	ANTHONY	96.3	95.6	0.2	0.3	0.2	0.2	1.3	1.9	6.7	6.8	6.5	6.3	5.7	21.0	24.8	17.5	4.6	76.0	42.2	49.2	50.8
67004	ARGONIA	96.8	96.2	0.2	0.2	0.1	0.1	1.5	2.3	6.0	6.1	6.8	7.9	7.2	20.9	27.3	14.9	2.9	76.2	41.0	49.8	50.2
67005	ARKANSAS CITY	89.1	87.3	3.4	3.6	0.5	0.8	3.9	5.7	6.7	6.4	6.4	7.8	6.2	23.4	26.7	13.6	2.9	76.4	39.1	48.1	51.9
67008	ATLANTA	95.2	94.7	0.2	0.2	0.2	0.2	1.2	1.9	6.4	6.7	6.9	7.4	5.5	22.7	29.7	13.1	1.7	75.4	40.6	49.8	50.2
67009	ATTICA	98.1	97.8	0.3	0.3	0.2	0.3	0.6	0.8	4.3	4.4	5.0	5.2	4.9	20.5	27.4	19.0	9.2	82.8	49.8	46.8	53.2
67010	AUGUSTA	96.0	95.1	0.3	0.3	0.4	0.5	2.4	3.5	6.7	6.9	7.3	7.5	6.0	25.4	27.3	10.7	2.3	74.3	37.9	49.3	50.7
67013	BELLE PLAINE	94.0	92.8	0.1	0.1	0.2	0.3	2.1	3.0	6.0	6.8	7.7	8.1	5.4	24.2	28.9	11.6	1.3	74.4	39.1	50.6	49.4
67016	BENTLEY	94.1	90.4	0.0	0.0	0.0	0.3	5.1	8.6	6.8	6.8	7.3	8.6	6.8	26.5	28.1	8.6	0.8	74.0	37.4	51.7	48.3
67017	BENTON	96.5	95.0	1.0	1.4	0.5	1.1	1.3	2.2	6.8	7.3	7.8	7.4	4.8	23.9	30.6	9.9	1.4	73.4	39.5	51.4	48.6
67018	BLUFF CITY	98.3	98.0	0.0	0.0	0.0	0.0	1.1	0.7	4.7	6.0	6.0	6.7	3.3	18.7	31.3	20.7	2.7	79.3	48.2	50.7	49.3
67019	BURDEN	94.8	93.9	0.2	0.2	0.1	0.1	1.1	1.8	6.3	6.7	6.6	7.3	5.2	22.9	28.8	14.1	2.0	75.8	40.8	48.9	51.1
67020	BURRTON	95.0	93.6	0.7	0.8	0.1	0.2	3.7	5.7	7.2	7.4	7.5	7.3	5.6	26.1	27.2	10.4	1.3	73.3	36.1	49.0	51.0
67021	BYERS	95.4	93.4	0.0	0.0	0.8	0.8	3.1	4.9	6.6	6.6	7.4	5.7	4.1	24.6	29.5	13.1	2.5	74.6	41.3	50.0	50.0
67022	CALDWELL	96.6	96.0	0.1	0.1	0.3	0.5	1.1	1.7	5.3	5.6	6.3	6.5	5.1	20.5	28.3	17.0	5.4	78.4	45.5	48.2	51.8
67023	CAMBRIDGE	94.3	93.6	0.4	0.4	0.0	0.0	1.1	2.0	6.4	6.8	6.4	7.6	5.2	22.8	28.8	14.0	2.0	76.0	40.7	48.4	51.6
67024	CEDAR VALE	93.7	92.7	0.2	0.3	0.0	0.0	1.5	2.2	5.5	5.5	5.5	6.7	6.0	18.2	26.7	20.4	5.5	79.0	46.9	50.0	50.0
67025	CHENEY	97.4	96.4	0.1	0.2	0.0	0.1	1.5	2.6	6.8	7.3	7.8	8.7	5.8	22.4	29.3	9.5	2.4	72.3	38.6	50.8	49.2
67026	CLEARWATER	96.7	95.6	0.2	0.3	0.4	0.7	1.2	2.2	6.9	7.5	8.0	8.1	5.4	22.4	29.5	10.4	1.7	72.5	38.3	49.7	50.3
67028	COATS	95.6	93.6	0.0	0.0	0.5	1.2	3.3	4.7	6.4	7.0	7.6	5.8	4.1	23.8	29.7	13.4	2.3	75.0	41.4	48.8	51.2
67029	COLDWATER	98.1	98.1	0.1	0.1	0.4	0.4	1.7	1.8	5.6	5.8	6.1	6.2	4.8	18.7	27.9	19.4	5.5	78.3	47.1	47.3	52.7
67030	COLWICH	98.1	97.2	0.0	0.0	0.4	0.7	1.0	1.7	9.1	9.3	10.1	9.9	4.8	23.3	24.4	7.2	1.9	65.3	32.4	51.1	48.9
67031	CONWAY SPRINGS	97.2	96.4	0.2	0.2	0.1	0.2	1.5	2.3	9.1	8.7	8.4	8.3	5.0	21.7	23.8	11.6	3.3	68.0	35.0	48.0	52.0
67035	CUNNINGHAM	98.5	98.1	0.4	0.4	0.1	0.1	1.0	1.7	4.5	5.3	5.7	7.0	4.4	18.0	30.4	19.3	5.5	79.3	48.8	49.0	51.0
67036	DANVILLE	97.7	97.4	0.6	0.6	0.6	0.6	0.6	0.6	5.2	6.5	6.5	5.2	4.5	19.4	36.1	14.2	2.6	79.4	46.6	52.3	47.7
67037	DERBY	94.2	92.0	1.3	1.8	1.1	1.8	2.8	4.7	6.8	7.4	8.3	8.4	5.2	25.9	28.2	8.8	1.0	71.9	36.9	48.8	51.2
67038	DEXTER	92.3	91.5	0.3	0.3	0.0	0.0	0.8	1.2	6.0	6.1	7.0	8.4	4.0	21.4	28.1	14.3	4.6	75.8	43.0	49.5	50.5
67039	DOUGLASS	96.9	96.3	0.2	0.2	0.3	0.4	1.3	2.1	6.9	7.1	7.4	7.3	6.5	24.6	28.3	10.3	1.7	74.0	37.1	49.8	50.2
67042	EL DORADO	92.4	91.1	3.6	4.1	0.3	0.4	3.0	4.4	6.8	6.6	6.4	6.7	6.8	27.2	24.8	12.1	2.6	76.8	36.9	51.6	48.4
67045	EUREKA	96.3	95.5	0.1	0.1	0.1	0.2	2.2	3.3	6.2	6.2	6.0	5.9	5.4	20.6	27.0	17.3	5.3	78.0	44.7	47.9	52.1
67047	FALL RIVER	97.2	96.7	0.0	0.0	0.0	0.0	0.9	1.0	4.0	4.3	4.2	4.2	4.7	16.6	33.7	26.0	2.4	85.3	52.6	50.7	49.3
67049	FREEPORT	100.0	100.0	0.0	0.0	0.0	0.0	0.0	0.0	4.3	4.3	4.3	4.3	4.3	17.4	41.3	17.4	2.2	82.6	50.6	50.0	50.0
67050	GARDEN PLAIN	97.2	96.1	0.3	0.5	0.2	0.4	1.6	2.9	8.5	8.9	9.3	9.8	5.0	22.3	26.2	8.9	1.1	66.9	34.0	51.0	49.0
67051	GEUDA SPRINGS	95.0	94.1	0.8	0.8	0.4	0.4	2.0	3.0	5.9	6.8	7.2	7.0	4.0	22.5	31.6	13.2	1.7	75.6	42.3	51.2	48.8
67052	GODDARD	95.4	93.6	0.8	1.1	0.4	0.6	1.7	3.0	7.0	7.2	7.8	9.2	6.0	24.5	28.2	8.8	1.3	71.6	35.6	50.0	50.0
67053	GOESSEL	97.2	96.6	0.0	0.0	0.7	0.9	1.3	1.8	4.3	4.8	5.7	7.5	5.5	18.5	32.8	15.3	5.7	80.2	46.9	48.3	51.7
67054	GREENSBURG	97.1	96.3	0.0	0.0	0.1	0.1	1.6	2.4	5.4	5.6	5.9	6.4	5.0	19.8	30.0	17.8	4.0	78.8	46.4	49.0	51.0
67055	GREENWICH	91.3	86.7	4.3	3.3	4.3	6.7	4.3	3.3	6.7	6.7	6.7	6.7	10.0	26.7	36.7	0.0	0.0	73.3	35.0	43.3	56.7
67056	HALSTEAD	96.8	95.9	0.2	0.3	0.4	0.6	2.1	3.2	6.5	6.5	6.4	6.6	6.3	24.0	28.0	13.5	2.4	76.3	39.9	48.5	51.5
67057	HARDTNER	97.1	96.5	0.4	0.4	0.0	0.0	2.5	3.5	5.0	5.8	6.2	5.0	4.2	17.8	32.0	19.3	4.6	79.5	48.9	48.6	51.4
67058	HARPER	97.9	97.3	0.2	0.2	0.1	0.1	1.0	1.5	5.4	5.4	6.0	6.6	6.1	20.5	29.7	16.2	4.1	78.7	45.0	48.5	51.5
67059	HAVILAND	96.0	94.9	0.6	0.7	0.4	0.5	4.3	5.9	6.3	6.9	6.6	8.1	6.2	23.0	27.4	13.2	2.2	75.6	38.7	49.2	50.8
67060	HAYSVILLE	94.1	91.9	0.5	0.6	0.6	0.9	3.1	5.3	7.0	7.2	7.6	7.6	5.9	25.3	27.4	10.9	1.2	73.5	37.6	49.8	50.2
67061	HAZELTON	94.5	93.4	0.5	0.6	0.0	0.0	4.0	5.5	5.5	6.1	6.6	7.2	5.0	18.2	29.8	17.1	4.4	75.7	45.9	48.1	51.9
67062	HESSTON	95.1	93.7	1.3	1.5	0.7	1.1	2.7	4.1	5.6	5.7	6.5	11.2	6.9	21.0	24.2	13.9	5.0	78.0	39.2	49.1	50.9
67063	HILLSBORO	97.4	96.7	0.5	0.5	0.3	0.5	1.6	2.4	4.9	5.3	5.7	8.7	9.0	20.1	24.7	15.6	6.0	80.1	41.7	48.6	51.4
67065	ISABEL	97.2	96.7	0.4	0.4	0.0	0.0	0.8	1.7	5.0	5.8	5.8	6.3	4.6	18.8	32.5	18.8	2.5	79.2	47.5	49.2	50.8
67066	IUKA	98.7	98.4	0.0	0.0	0.0	0.3	1.3	1.6	6.0	6.8	7.4	6.8	4.1	19.5	32.3	15.1	1.9	75.1	44.4	52.6	47.4
67067	KECHI	87.9	83.7	6.3	8.0	2.3	3.6	2.6	4.5	7.9	8.8	9.1	7.5	4.3	25.9	29.2	6.6	0.8	69.3	36.6	49.8	50.2
67068	KINGMAN	97.5	97.0	0.2	0.2	0.3	0.4	1.6	2.4	6.9	6.9	7.0	6.8	5.7	21.1	26.9	15.1	3.7	75.0	41.3	49.1	50.9
67070	KIOWA	95.8	94.7	0.3	0.4	0.1	0.1	3.3	4.8	5.4	6.0	6.3	6.1	4.6	18.3	31.1	17.7	4.6	78.0	47.2	48.8	51.2
67071	LAKE CITY	97.9	97.8	0.0	0.0	0.0	0.0	1.0	1.1	4.3	5.4	5.4	6.5	4.3	19.4	31.2	20.4	3.2	79.6	48.8	47.3	52.7
67072	LATHAM	96.0	95.0	0.7	0.6	0.0	0.0	2.3	3.8	6.9	6.9	7.2	7.2	6.6	24.5	28.8	10.7	1.3	74.3	37.5	49.2	50.8
67073	LEHIGH	97.6	96.3	0.9	1.1	0.0	0.3	2.1	3.4	5.9	6.7	7.3	8.4	4.2	18.5	32.3	14.9	1.7	74.7	44.0	50.3	49.7
67074	LEON	94.1	93.2	2.0	2.2	0.2	0.2	2.6	3.9	6.1	6.3	6.7	7.1	6.7	25.1	30.3	10.5	1.2	76.5	39.0	51.9	48.1
67101	MAIZE	94.7	92.9	0.7	1.0	0.7	1.3	2.2	3.9	7.0	7.3	7.5	7.7	5.4	25.1	29.5	9.5	0.9	73.4	37.4	50.0	50.0
67102	MAPLE CITY	96.2	96.2	0.0	0.0	0.0	0.0	1.9	0.0	7.5	7.5	7.5	7.5	3.8	22.6	26.4	15.1	1.9	69.8	40.6	49.1	50.9
67103	MAYFIELD	96.7	96.0	0.4	0.4	0.4	0.4	1.8	2.6	6.6	7.7	8.4	9.2	4.4	19.4	32.2	11.4	0.7	71.1	40.9	49.8	50.2
67104	MEDICINE LODGE	97.8	97.3	0.4	0.4	0.1	0.1	1.6	2.3	5.2	5.6	5.8	6.6	4.8	21.3	31.0	16.0	3.6	79.1	45.4	49.1	50.9
67105	MILAN	96.6	96.1	0.0	0.0	0.4	0.4	2.1	3.5	7.4	8.3	7.9	7.9	6.1	21.4	29.3	10.5	1.3	71.2	37.0	50.2	49.8
67106	MILTON	96.7	95.9	0.0	0.0	0.2	0.2	2.3	3.3	7.7	7.7	8.3	8.1	6.4	21.8	28.2	10.6	1.2	71.2	36.0	49.4	50.6
67107	MOUNDRIDGE	97.7	97.1	0.4	0.4	0.1	0.2	1.5	2.2	6.3	6.8	7.1	6.5	4.9	21.1	26.5	15.6	5.3	75.3	42.8	48.1	51.9
67108	MOUNT HOPE	97.1	95.7	0.3	0.5	0.2	0.4	2.4	4.1	7.0	6.7	6.9	8.0	7.9	22.4	26.5	12.0	2.8	74.5	38.2	48.6	51.4
67109	MULLINVILLE	98.0	97.6	0.0	0.0	0.5	0.5	2.0	2.6	5.8	6.3	6.9	7.1	4.5	21.6	31.1	14.2	2.4	76.8	43.0	53.6	46.4
67110	MULVANE	96.0	94.9	0.2	0.3	0.3	0.5	2.5	4.2	7.0	7.1	7.2	7.6	6.3	26.0	27.3	10.0	1.4	73.9	35.8	48.6	51.4
67111	MURDOCK	97.8	97.7	0.0	0.0	0.0	0.0	0.4	0.4	6.2	6.9	7.7	8.1	5.8	20.4	30.0	13.1	1.9	73.8	41.6	53.5	46.5
67112	NASHVILLE	98.5	97.8	0.0	0.0	0.0	0.0	1.5	2.2	5.3	6.2	6.6	6.6	5.3	20.7	31.7	14.5	3.1	77.5	44.4	51.5	48.5
	KANSAS	86.1	83.7	5.7	5.9	1.8	2.6	7.0	9.4	7.1	6.9	6.9	7.3	7.3	25.9	25.7	10.7	2.2	75.0	36.3	49.6	50.4
	UNITED STATES	75.1	72.0	12.3	12.7	3.8	4.6	12.5	15.7	6.8	6.7	6.6	7.1	6.9	27.0	26.0	10.9	1.9	75.7	36.9	49.2	50.8

ZIP CODE #	POST OFFICE NAME	2009 Per Capita Income	2009 HH Income Base	2009 Household Income Distribution (%): Less than $25,000	$25,000 to $49,999	$50,000 to $99,999	$100,000 to $149,999	$150,000 or More	Median Household Income: 2009	2014	2009 National Centile	2009 State Centile	2009 Home Value Base	2009 Home Value Distribution (%): Less than $50,000	$50,000 to $89,999	$90,000 to $174,999	$175,000 to $399,999	$400,000 or More	2009 Median Home Value
66938	CLYDE	21206	435	27.1	39.8	28.0	3.0	2.1	38466	40076	28	26	355	43.7	29.6	22.3	4.5	0.0	59000
66939	COURTLAND	18470	166	30.7	33.7	31.3	3.0	1.2	39094	41745	30	28	128	46.1	25.8	18.0	8.6	1.6	56250
66940	CUBA	21043	147	23.8	42.9	29.3	2.0	2.0	41024	42905	36	39	123	69.1	12.2	12.2	4.9	1.6	32750
66941	ESBON	19580	121	31.4	39.7	24.8	2.5	1.7	37324	38955	25	20	99	55.6	18.2	19.2	6.1	1.0	39375
66942	FORMOSO	21781	88	36.4	38.6	19.3	3.4	2.3	35627	36511	20	12	74	60.8	13.5	10.8	8.1	6.8	36250
66943	GREENLEAF	18636	230	33.0	41.3	21.7	2.2	1.7	32863	33168	13	5	189	52.4	23.8	21.2	1.1	1.6	47857
66944	HADDAM	17500	109	39.4	33.9	22.9	3.7	0.0	31832	32498	11	4	87	59.8	18.4	17.2	4.6	0.0	34500
66945	HANOVER	18065	439	30.1	31.9	34.4	3.2	0.5	39878	42936	32	31	349	42.1	25.8	23.5	7.4	1.1	62273
66946	HOLLENBERG	19561	59	25.4	33.9	39.0	1.7	0.0	39430	45000	31	29	48	33.3	22.9	33.3	10.4	0.0	75000
66948	JAMESTOWN	23754	167	18.0	42.5	30.5	3.6	5.4	38691	39388	29	27	142	48.6	32.4	18.3	0.7	0.0	52000
66949	JEWELL	19689	282	36.9	36.2	23.8	1.4	1.8	36260	38085	21	16	216	61.1	16.2	19.9	1.9	0.9	39000
66951	KENSINGTON	18570	223	30.0	31.8	35.0	2.7	0.4	37143	40384	24	19	182	43.4	29.1	20.9	4.4	2.2	55000
66952	LEBANON	18457	172	29.1	37.2	32.0	1.7	0.0	34589	37721	17	8	138	52.9	15.2	23.9	7.2	0.7	46923
66953	LINN	18677	254	26.4	42.9	26.0	2.8	2.0	35740	36644	20	13	200	44.0	32.0	21.0	3.0	0.0	54444
66955	MAHASKA	13131	48	37.5	33.3	25.0	4.2	0.0	32781	32265	13	5	38	52.6	21.1	18.4	7.9	0.0	45000
66956	MANKATO	20784	694	32.0	34.1	28.5	3.7	1.6	37750	40102	26	22	537	49.2	27.9	17.9	3.5	1.5	51023
66958	MORROWVILLE	16428	148	39.9	34.5	20.3	4.1	1.4	31471	32269	10	3	118	57.6	19.5	17.8	5.1	0.0	37500
66959	MUNDEN	20993	89	30.3	36.0	28.1	1.1	4.5	38622	39529	29	27	76	51.3	23.7	10.5	14.5	0.0	48000
66960	NARKA	24642	75	29.3	36.0	28.0	1.3	5.3	39438	40000	31	29	64	53.1	21.9	9.4	15.6	0.0	45000
66961	NORWAY	15127	48	31.3	31.3	35.4	2.1	0.0	40000	45000	33	32	37	51.4	24.3	16.2	8.1	0.0	48333
66962	PALMER	19012	116	25.9	41.4	28.4	2.6	1.7	36125	36297	21	14	92	42.4	35.9	19.6	2.2	0.0	55000
66963	RANDALL	20779	61	23.0	39.3	32.8	3.3	1.6	42578	45000	41	48	51	37.3	23.5	27.5	7.8	3.9	67000
66964	REPUBLIC	22762	99	28.3	33.3	33.3	5.1	0.0	40964	45573	36	39	79	43.0	24.1	21.5	10.1	1.3	65000
66966	SCANDIA	18583	259	28.6	32.8	33.6	4.6	0.4	41131	43866	36	40	204	46.1	24.5	19.6	8.8	1.0	58000
66967	SMITH CENTER	17743	1015	35.0	34.9	26.1	3.8	0.2	31991	32511	11	4	786	40.2	30.7	24.4	3.7	1.0	60000
66968	WASHINGTON	18557	706	29.7	39.5	28.2	1.8	0.7	36702	37577	23	18	549	37.7	34.4	24.2	3.3	0.4	59783
66970	WEBBER	20916	72	36.1	38.9	19.4	2.8	2.8	35731	36830	20	13	60	58.3	13.3	11.7	8.3	8.3	38333
67001	ANDALE	20675	428	9.6	29.0	50.9	8.2	2.3	61456	61971	79	90	363	8.0	17.9	55.1	18.7	0.3	119038
67002	ANDOVER	28584	4353	11.2	23.1	41.5	15.3	8.9	68462	69610	86	93	3491	12.4	13.7	40.3	30.7	2.9	136321
67003	ANTHONY	17347	1109	41.5	29.0	25.1	3.4	1.0	30746	32249	9	3	786	33.8	39.7	22.3	3.8	0.4	62136
67004	ARGONIA	18836	341	27.0	36.1	30.8	4.1	2.1	40894	42752	36	38	271	48.3	20.7	23.2	6.6	1.1	53000
67005	ARKANSAS CITY	19735	6210	31.9	28.9	33.3	4.0	2.0	39177	42182	30	28	4369	31.1	34.7	27.4	6.5	0.3	68038
67008	ATLANTA	20512	230	25.7	28.7	38.3	4.8	2.6	45414	47362	49	58	183	35.5	20.2	29.5	12.0	2.7	78125
67009	ATTICA	20489	363	32.2	35.0	28.4	2.8	1.7	38164	39306	27	24	281	49.1	28.1	17.4	4.6	0.7	50926
67010	AUGUSTA	23995	5233	18.3	24.5	45.7	8.7	2.8	57157	59561	74	85	4064	17.2	24.7	43.7	13.0	1.4	97847
67013	BELLE PLAINE	23801	1133	16.9	23.8	46.9	9.4	3.0	60134	60057	77	88	942	21.9	30.8	40.3	6.9	0.1	86154
67016	BENTLEY	20598	148	16.9	34.5	43.9	4.7	0.0	48995	56000	59	70	125	23.2	49.6	23.2	4.0	0.0	74318
67017	BENTON	25504	879	13.0	25.7	48.0	6.8	6.5	62595	63712	81	91	741	11.5	19.6	43.3	20.4	5.3	111123
67018	BLUFF CITY	21085	67	32.8	29.9	32.8	3.0	1.5	37976	45000	27	23	52	26.9	23.1	32.7	13.5	3.8	90000
67019	BURDEN	17713	373	29.8	30.3	34.3	4.3	1.3	40885	43524	36	38	285	39.6	22.1	26.0	9.5	2.8	65938
67020	BURRTON	21480	722	18.4	31.3	42.9	5.8	1.5	50218	53475	62	74	551	27.6	32.8	30.1	9.3	0.2	76765
67021	BYERS	22021	51	25.5	37.3	29.4	3.9	3.9	40551	43618	35	36	40	50.0	17.5	25.0	7.5	0.0	50000
67022	CALDWELL	20090	706	35.1	30.0	29.6	3.5	1.7	36983	40151	24	19	559	53.3	25.9	17.7	2.9	0.2	47063
67023	CAMBRIDGE	18620	100	31.0	31.0	32.0	4.0	2.0	39200	42336	30	28	75	44.0	22.7	22.7	8.0	2.7	57500
67024	CEDAR VALE	19118	447	33.6	36.2	26.0	2.7	1.6	37180	38221	24	20	365	49.0	26.3	14.8	7.7	2.2	51167
67025	CHENEY	21696	1171	15.4	29.8	46.6	6.6	1.6	53888	56343	69	82	956	18.9	31.5	34.8	13.9	0.8	89579
67026	CLEARWATER	24384	1761	12.3	24.4	50.1	10.6	2.7	61387	61658	79	90	1466	9.3	22.2	52.4	15.3	0.8	107780
67028	COATS	21694	71	25.4	35.2	31.0	4.2	4.2	41366	43894	37	41	56	50.0	19.6	23.2	5.4	1.8	50000
67029	COLDWATER	20133	505	31.9	36.0	27.7	2.6	1.8	34767	36183	17	9	370	46.2	28.1	20.5	5.1	0.0	53415
67030	COLWICH	21702	733	10.6	28.1	45.4	11.5	4.4	61164	62051	79	90	630	4.6	21.7	45.1	24.9	3.7	121212
67031	CONWAY SPRINGS	18807	735	20.4	28.7	43.5	5.4	1.9	50688	52898	63	76	579	31.4	31.4	27.8	8.3	1.0	74206
67035	CUNNINGHAM	19293	336	19.9	42.9	32.7	3.9	0.6	42447	44306	41	47	270	39.6	29.6	23.3	5.6	1.9	62174
67036	DANVILLE	24828	70	25.7	30.0	37.1	5.7	1.4	43640	50000	44	52	56	14.3	25.0	44.6	16.1	0.0	105000
67037	DERBY	28850	9290	8.5	16.3	51.0	17.0	7.2	74366	75806	89	95	7280	4.7	18.8	52.4	23.5	0.6	129203
67038	DEXTER	18100	227	30.4	29.5	34.8	1.8	3.5	43021	45951	42	50	164	36.0	29.9	23.8	7.3	3.0	67692
67039	DOUGLASS	23875	1419	14.2	26.9	46.3	8.7	3.9	59503	61041	77	88	1150	18.8	28.2	37.3	15.0	0.8	93241
67042	EL DORADO	21795	6644	26.4	29.7	36.0	4.9	2.9	44154	48169	46	54	4498	24.7	36.8	28.2	9.6	0.7	78245
67045	EUREKA	18116	1587	35.5	34.1	26.3	2.5	1.6	33294	33973	14	6	1132	43.3	28.2	19.9	7.6	1.1	55507
67047	FALL RIVER	21646	273	30.4	29.7	34.4	4.0	1.5	41893	45461	39	44	224	38.4	20.5	22.3	16.5	2.2	60000
67049	FREEPORT	18261	18	27.8	33.3	33.3	5.6	0.0	40000	47361	33	32	14	7.1	35.7	35.7	21.4	0.0	100000
67050	GARDEN PLAIN	22113	621	18.4	23.2	46.7	7.9	3.9	60553	61364	78	88	523	8.4	23.7	45.7	21.0	1.1	111851
67051	GEUDA SPRINGS	23261	192	16.1	27.6	47.4	7.3	1.6	53875	54415	69	82	161	31.1	25.5	36.0	7.5	0.0	83000
67052	GODDARD	23422	2278	13.3	25.4	45.3	11.8	4.2	61684	62186	80	90	1939	13.4	14.9	44.2	24.6	2.9	123745
67053	GOESSEL	19780	166	21.1	33.1	42.8	2.4	0.6	46932	48052	54	63	141	7.1	25.5	50.4	17.0	0.0	112083
67054	GREENSBURG	20116	688	33.1	31.8	30.1	3.6	1.3	34891	38237	17	9	491	39.7	35.2	22.2	2.4	0.4	63125
67055	GREENWICH	55907	15	0.0	0.0	53.3	20.0	26.7	96845	100000	96	98	13	0.0	0.0	46.2	53.8	0.0	181250
67056	HALSTEAD	25626	1071	15.8	27.9	44.9	7.7	3.7	56568	60120	73	84	817	15.8	28.4	45.9	9.8	0.1	94847
67057	HARDTNER	22741	120	30.8	33.3	29.2	4.2	2.5	37819	39477	26	23	93	45.2	24.7	25.8	2.2	2.2	59000
67058	HARPER	20587	821	26.7	36.9	31.3	3.2	1.9	40040	42239	33	33	618	35.8	27.3	29.4	7.3	0.2	66735
67059	HAVILAND	18793	401	23.7	39.7	31.9	3.7	1.0	40562	41635	35	36	292	49.0	31.5	14.4	4.1	1.0	51034
67060	HAYSVILLE	22987	4744	13.2	26.8	50.5	7.5	2.1	59033	60461	76	87	3936	13.8	40.6	39.9	5.5	0.2	86140
67061	HAZELTON	17513	69	27.5	36.2	34.8	1.4	0.0	37729	40000	26	22	57	64.9	15.8	15.8	3.5	0.0	32500
67062	HESSTON	23302	1492	15.9	28.6	43.0	10.7	1.9	55109	58261	71	83	1036	11.0	15.5	57.7	15.4	0.3	117143
67063	HILLSBORO	19390	1375	23.5	35.3	36.5	3.3	1.4	43747	45805	45	52	1042	17.4	30.7	40.6	10.3	1.1	93390
67065	ISABEL	20604	94	23.4	34.0	35.1	3.2	4.3	44080	46986	46	53	74	37.8	17.6	28.4	9.5	6.8	84286
67066	IUKA	20974	146	15.1	38.4	41.8	4.1	0.7	47082	48371	54	64	124	31.5	18.5	44.4	4.0	1.6	90000
67067	KECHI	29616	487	6.2	12.7	53.6	17.7	9.9	77048	77545	91	96	444	3.8	8.3	54.7	31.8	1.4	150962
67068	KINGMAN	22344	2078	24.8	27.3	39.0	6.1	2.7	48055	49978	57	67	1580	21.2	30.6	33.3	13.4	1.5	86744
67070	KIOWA	21119	477	29.1	34.4	31.7	2.5	2.3	38056	39589	27	24	381	53.0	21.0	21.5	3.1	1.3	44524
67071	LAKE CITY	22545	40	27.5	35.0	27.5	2.5	7.5	40000	41148	33	32	31	45.2	19.4	22.6	6.5	6.5	65000
67072	LATHAM	21793	131	24.4	28.2	40.5	5.3	1.5	47672	52281	56	66	104	35.6	25.0	22.1	15.4	1.9	72500
67073	LEHIGH	18270	124	13.7	39.5	41.1	4.8	0.8	48293	48985	57	68	112	22.3	18.8	44.6	9.8	4.5	111364
67074	LEON	20886	724	23.1	26.7	42.7	5.8	1.8	50280	54571	62	75	594	28.8	22.4	28.8	17.8	2.2	87879
67101	MAIZE	26823	1146	7.9	23.3	51.0	12.0	5.8	69625	69274	87	93	1001	14.3	22.0	37.9	25.3	0.6	105258
67102	MAPLE CITY	23017	22	18.2	31.8	45.5	4.5	0.0	50000	53237	61	74	18	16.7	22.2	38.9	22.2	0.0	100000
67103	MAYFIELD	21965	106	17.0	32.1	40.6	6.6	3.8	50526	52695	62	76	90	24.4	21.1	40.0	14.4	0.0	94000
67104	MEDICINE LODGE	20016	1097	25.2	37.7	31.9	4.2	1.0	41873	43555	39	44	795	46.5	26.2	22.6	3.5	1.1	54365
67105	MILAN	22846	84	16.7	23.8	48.8	6.0	4.8	56824	57172	74	85	71	28.2	16.9	36.6	16.9	1.4	97000
67106	MILTON	21463	165	15.2	24.8	50.9	6.1	3.0	57071	58342	74	85	140	27.1	17.1	36.4	16.4	2.9	98000
67107	MOUNDRIDGE	23330	1062	15.2	28.9	45.1	8.6	2.3	53638	54780	69	81	779	12.3	20.3	51.2	15.4	0.8	113113
67108	MOUNT HOPE	21478	603	15.9	30.5	43.8	7.1	2.7	53341	56560	69	81	488	20.3	30.3	41.4	7.6	0.4	89400
67109	MULLINVILLE	22355	159	16.4	35.8	39.6	5.7	2.5	46974	50375	54	63	117	37.6	29.9	20.5	10.3	1.7	65909
67110	MULVANE	24910	3063	13.9	22.5	49.3	10.8	3.5	61933	63217	80	91	2465	8.9	26.9	54.4	9.2	0.6	99548
67111	MURDOCK	21904	98	19.4	24.5	44.9	10.2	1.0	54949	55613	71	83	82	17.1	18.3	50.0	12.2	2.4	106944
67112	NASHVILLE	18889	96	28.1	42.7	25.0	3.1	1.0	40000	40980	33	32	77	54.5	18.2	18.2	5.2	3.9	41250
	KANSAS	26028		20.3	26.8	37.6	9.9	5.4	52748	54940				18.1	21.6	35.7	21.6	3.0	107692
	UNITED STATES	27277		20.9	24.4	35.3	11.7	7.6	54719	56938				9.3	13.1	31.6	32.6	13.5	162279

ZIP CODE #	POST OFFICE NAME	FINANCIAL SERVICES: Auto Loan	Home Loan	Invest-ments	Retire-ment Plans	THE HOME: Home Improvements: Home Repair	Lawn & Garden	Furnishings: Comput-ers & Hard-ware-Personal	Major Appli-ances	TV, Radio, Sound Equip-ment	Furni-ture	ENTERTAINMENT: Dine out/ Carry out	Sports Equip-ment	Fees & Tickets	Toys & Games	Travel	Cable TV	PERSONAL: Apparel & Services	Auto Repairs	Health Insur-ance	Pets & Supplies
66938	CLYDE	83	59	85	58	61	87	64	80	71	56	69	61	51	69	63	78	45	74	86	95
66939	COURTLAND	77	53	84	53	55	81	59	73	61	47	60	60	43	60	58	66	39	68	77	89
66940	CUBA	82	56	90	56	59	86	63	78	65	51	64	64	46	64	62	71	42	73	82	96
66941	ESBON	75	52	83	52	54	79	57	71	60	47	59	59	42	59	57	65	38	67	75	88
66942	FORMOSO	80	55	87	55	57	84	61	76	63	49	63	63	45	62	61	69	41	71	80	93
66943	GREENLEAF	69	49	70	48	51	72	54	66	59	47	57	50	42	58	52	65	38	62	72	79
66944	HADDAM	69	47	75	47	49	72	52	65	55	43	54	54	38	54	52	60	35	61	69	80
66945	HANOVER	78	53	85	53	56	82	59	74	62	48	61	61	43	61	59	67	40	69	78	91
66946	HOLLENBERG	82	56	90	56	59	87	63	78	65	51	64	64	46	64	62	71	42	73	82	96
66948	JAMESTOWN	112	77	123	77	81	118	86	106	89	69	88	88	63	87	85	97	57	99	112	131
66949	JEWELL	71	51	73	50	53	75	56	69	62	49	60	52	44	61	54	68	40	64	75	82
66951	KENSINGTON	76	52	84	52	55	80	58	72	60	47	60	60	43	59	58	66	39	67	76	89
66952	LEBANON	71	49	78	49	51	75	54	67	56	44	56	56	40	55	54	61	36	63	71	83
66953	LINN	81	56	88	56	58	85	62	77	65	51	64	63	46	63	61	71	42	72	81	94
66955	MAHASKA	67	46	74	46	48	71	51	64	53	42	53	53	38	52	51	58	34	60	67	78
66956	MANKATO	78	55	80	54	57	81	61	75	66	52	64	58	47	65	59	73	42	70	81	89
66958	MORROWVILLE	69	48	76	47	50	73	53	66	55	43	54	54	39	54	53	60	35	61	69	81
66959	MUNDEN	92	63	101	63	66	97	70	87	73	57	72	72	51	72	70	80	47	81	92	107
66960	NARKA	92	63	101	63	66	97	70	88	73	57	72	72	52	72	70	80	47	82	92	108
66961	NORWAY	76	52	84	52	55	80	58	72	60	47	60	60	43	59	58	66	39	67	76	89
66962	PALMER	82	56	90	56	59	86	62	78	65	51	64	64	46	64	62	71	42	72	82	95
66963	RANDALL	85	59	93	58	61	90	65	81	68	53	67	67	48	66	65	74	43	76	85	99
66964	REPUBLIC	83	57	92	57	60	88	64	79	66	52	66	66	47	65	63	72	43	74	84	97
66966	SCANDIA	81	56	89	55	58	85	62	77	64	50	63	63	45	63	61	70	41	72	81	94
66967	SMITH CENTER	68	48	69	47	50	71	53	65	58	46	56	50	42	57	51	64	37	61	71	77
66968	WASHINGTON	71	51	73	50	53	75	56	69	61	49	59	53	44	60	54	67	39	64	75	82
66970	WEBBER	81	55	88	55	58	85	61	76	64	50	63	63	45	63	61	70	41	71	81	94
67001	ANDALE	100	94	91	97	95	108	91	102	93	84	92	77	86	95	92	98	63	94	104	118
67002	ANDOVER	119	131	109	130	124	116	117	118	112	122	113	93	121	118	118	108	79	113	109	136
67003	ANTHONY	66	48	67	46	49	69	52	64	58	46	56	48	41	57	50	64	37	60	70	76
67004	ARGONIA	82	61	81	61	63	86	66	80	72	58	70	60	54	71	64	79	47	74	86	94
67005	ARKANSAS CITY	76	60	67	61	61	77	66	72	70	60	68	55	56	70	62	75	46	70	78	86
67008	ATLANTA	88	70	85	69	71	90	70	84	75	66	74	63	60	76	69	81	50	78	87	99
67009	ATTICA	78	56	81	55	58	82	61	76	67	53	65	58	48	66	60	74	43	71	82	90
67010	AUGUSTA	90	89	79	92	87	93	89	89	89	85	88	69	88	90	87	91	61	89	93	106
67013	BELLE PLAINE	88	93	77	95	88	95	89	89	89	86	89	70	91	91	89	90	61	88	94	107
67016	BENTLEY	86	79	70	76	77	81	75	79	77	78	77	57	71	81	71	79	53	76	79	94
67017	BENTON	100	112	97	115	109	109	100	104	98	101	99	81	106	101	105	98	69	99	101	122
67018	BLUFF CITY	84	58	93	58	61	89	64	80	67	52	66	66	47	66	64	73	43	75	85	99
67019	BURDEN	84	61	86	60	63	86	63	79	69	57	68	60	50	68	62	75	45	73	82	94
67020	BURRTON	85	77	75	78	74	89	78	82	80	72	79	65	73	81	76	83	54	81	88	99
67021	BYERS	94	65	103	65	68	99	72	89	75	58	74	74	53	73	72	82	48	83	94	110
67022	CALDWELL	77	55	79	54	57	80	60	74	66	52	64	57	47	65	58	72	42	69	80	88
67023	CAMBRIDGE	83	59	85	57	61	84	61	78	67	56	66	59	49	67	60	74	44	71	81	92
67024	CEDAR VALE	79	56	82	55	59	83	61	76	67	54	65	59	48	66	60	74	43	71	82	91
67025	CHENEY	89	86	82	89	86	97	82	91	84	76	83	70	79	86	83	88	57	85	93	106
67026	CLEARWATER	90	104	92	106	101	103	92	96	91	92	92	74	100	93	98	92	64	93	97	112
67028	COATS	94	65	103	64	68	99	72	89	75	58	74	74	53	73	71	81	48	83	94	110
67029	COLDWATER	72	52	74	50	54	76	56	70	62	49	60	53	44	61	55	68	40	65	76	83
67030	COLWICH	98	113	97	115	109	108	100	103	97	101	98	81	107	100	105	97	69	99	101	121
67031	CONWAY SPRINGS	83	76	74	79	75	89	77	83	79	70	78	65	71	80	76	82	53	79	88	98
67035	CUNNINGHAM	86	59	94	59	62	91	66	81	68	53	67	67	48	67	65	74	44	76	86	100
67036	DANVILLE	98	68	108	67	71	104	75	93	78	61	77	77	55	77	75	85	50	87	99	115
67037	DERBY	115	129	113	128	124	118	115	117	112	120	113	91	122	116	118	109	79	113	111	135
67038	DEXTER	91	63	100	63	66	96	70	87	72	56	72	72	51	71	69	79	46	81	91	106
67039	DOUGLASS	94	96	80	97	91	98	92	93	93	90	93	72	92	95	91	95	64	92	98	111
67042	EL DORADO	79	72	70	73	71	82	75	78	78	71	77	59	70	78	72	81	53	77	84	92
67045	EUREKA	70	51	72	49	53	74	55	68	61	49	59	52	44	60	54	67	39	64	74	81
67047	FALL RIVER	70	63	83	59	69	78	61	73	65	63	63	50	58	60	66	69	42	70	81	85
67049	FREEPORT	83	57	92	57	60	88	64	79	66	52	66	65	47	65	63	72	43	74	84	97
67050	GARDEN PLAIN	93	105	90	108	102	103	94	97	92	94	93	76	100	94	99	92	65	94	96	114
67051	GEUDA SPRINGS	100	71	108	72	75	106	78	96	81	64	80	79	59	80	78	88	52	89	101	117
67052	GODDARD	105	109	93	107	104	103	99	102	98	103	99	77	99	102	98	98	68	98	98	119
67053	GOESSEL	77	70	70	73	72	83	69	78	71	63	70	59	64	73	69	76	48	72	81	91
67054	GREENSBURG	75	53	75	52	55	78	58	72	65	52	63	54	47	64	57	71	42	67	79	85
67055	GREENWICH	158	191	165	197	186	157	159	161	146	179	149	134	180	159	167	134	110	147	131	179
67056	HALSTEAD	99	87	91	88	86	103	91	96	93	84	92	76	83	93	89	97	63	95	104	116
67057	HARDTNER	88	60	96	60	63	93	67	83	70	54	69	69	49	68	67	76	45	78	88	103
67058	HARPER	83	59	85	58	61	87	65	80	71	57	69	61	51	70	63	78	46	75	87	95
67059	HAVILAND	84	58	92	57	60	88	64	79	67	52	66	66	47	65	64	73	43	74	84	98
67060	HAYSVILLE	96	91	85	91	89	100	88	95	91	85	90	72	84	93	87	94	61	91	98	112
67061	HAZELTON	80	55	87	55	57	84	61	76	63	49	63	63	45	62	61	69	41	71	80	93
67062	HESSTON	96	86	84	85	86	94	86	91	89	86	88	67	80	90	83	92	60	89	94	108
67063	HILLSBORO	76	63	77	62	65	82	65	76	70	59	68	57	58	69	65	75	46	72	82	89
67065	ISABEL	94	65	103	65	68	99	72	89	75	58	74	74	53	73	71	82	48	83	94	110
67066	IUKA	94	64	103	64	68	99	72	89	74	58	74	74	52	73	71	81	48	83	94	110
67067	KECHI	118	148	129	148	142	127	124	126	116	131	118	100	139	121	133	111	85	119	111	144
67068	KINGMAN	91	72	90	72	74	96	76	89	81	68	79	69	64	80	75	87	53	84	95	106
67070	KIOWA	84	58	92	58	60	89	64	80	67	52	66	66	47	65	64	73	43	74	84	98
67071	LAKE CITY	94	64	103	64	67	99	72	89	74	58	74	74	52	73	71	81	48	83	94	109
67072	LATHAM	85	78	70	75	76	81	74	79	77	76	77	57	69	80	70	79	52	76	79	93
67073	LEHIGH	94	65	103	64	68	99	72	89	75	58	74	74	52	73	71	81	48	83	94	110
67074	LEON	88	81	74	80	80	87	77	84	80	77	80	62	73	83	75	83	54	80	85	99
67101	MAIZE	113	123	103	123	117	115	110	113	108	114	109	87	114	112	113	107	76	109	109	132
67102	MAPLE CITY	99	68	109	68	71	105	76	94	79	61	78	78	55	77	75	86	51	88	99	116
67103	MAYFIELD	101	70	111	69	73	107	77	96	80	63	79	79	57	79	77	88	52	90	101	118
67104	MEDICINE LODGE	81	57	87	56	59	86	63	78	66	52	65	62	47	65	62	73	43	73	83	94
67105	MILAN	99	86	92	89	88	106	86	99	89	77	88	76	77	90	86	95	59	92	102	116
67106	MILTON	95	90	87	93	91	103	87	97	89	80	88	74	82	91	88	94	60	90	100	113
67107	MOUNDRIDGE	90	81	85	82	80	94	83	89	85	78	84	69	77	85	82	89	57	87	95	106
67108	MOUNT HOPE	87	85	73	87	81	92	84	86	86	79	85	68	82	88	83	89	58	85	93	103
67109	MULLINVILLE	95	66	105	65	69	101	73	90	76	59	75	75	53	74	72	83	49	84	96	111
67110	MULVANE	101	100	90	99	96	100	94	98	95	95	95	75	92	98	93	96	65	95	97	116
67111	MURDOCK	90	82	81	85	84	97	81	91	83	73	82	69	75	85	81	88	56	84	94	106
67112	NASHVILLE	80	55	88	55	58	84	61	76	63	49	63	63	45	62	61	69	41	71	80	93
	KANSAS	98	90	91	91	89	97	94	95	94	90	94	74	88	96	90	96	65	95	98	113
	UNITED STATES	100	100	100	100	100	100	100	100	100	100	100	100	100	100	100	100	100	100	100	100

POPULATION CHANGE

ZIP CODE #	POST OFFICE NAME	COUNTY FIPS CODE	POPULATION 2000	POPULATION 2009	POPULATION 2014	2000-2009 ANNUAL RATE % Rate	2000-2009 ANNUAL RATE State Centile	HOUSEHOLDS 2000	HOUSEHOLDS 2009	HOUSEHOLDS 2014	HOUSEHOLDS % Annual Rate 2000-2009	HOUSEHOLDS 2009 Average HH Size	FAMILIES 2000	FAMILIES 2009	FAMILIES % Annual Rate 2000-2009
67114	NEWTON	079	20960	21451	21530	0.3	74	8172	8454	8507	0.4	2.46	5695	5840	0.3
67117	NORTH NEWTON	079	1511	1575	1600	0.4	76	601	647	662	0.8	1.88	342	363	0.6
67118	NORWICH	095	790	788	783	0.0	64	292	294	294	0.1	2.59	216	216	0.0
67119	OXFORD	191	1670	1570	1522	-0.7	32	650	622	605	-0.5	2.45	476	451	-0.6
67120	PECK	191	1394	1444	1479	0.4	76	482	514	529	0.7	2.80	388	409	0.6
67122	PIEDMONT	073	294	259	244	-1.4	11	122	109	103	-1.2	2.38	88	78	-1.3
67123	POTWIN	015	701	745	768	0.7	84	274	295	304	0.8	2.53	194	205	0.6
67124	PRATT	151	7979	7909	7837	-0.1	59	3309	3320	3300	0.0	2.28	2148	2133	-0.1
67127	PROTECTION	033	734	707	704	-0.4	48	312	309	310	-0.1	2.16	204	200	-0.2
67131	ROCK	035	353	338	328	-0.5	41	134	130	126	-0.3	2.60	105	101	-0.4
67132	ROSALIA	015	437	466	479	0.7	84	163	176	183	0.8	2.65	122	130	0.7
67133	ROSE HILL	015	6058	6516	6761	0.8	86	1930	2112	2203	1.0	3.06	1636	1773	0.9
67134	SAWYER	151	432	404	394	-0.7	32	153	146	143	-0.5	2.77	113	106	-0.7
67135	SEDGWICK	079	3075	3227	3279	0.5	79	1085	1164	1190	0.8	2.70	876	928	0.6
67137	SEVERY	073	830	733	692	-1.3	12	348	311	294	-1.2	2.36	257	228	-1.3
67138	SHARON	007	437	396	377	-1.1	17	181	166	159	-0.9	2.37	123	112	-1.0
67140	SOUTH HAVEN	191	870	819	790	-0.7	32	321	307	297	-0.5	2.67	237	224	-0.6
67142	SPIVEY	095	411	376	360	-1.0	19	165	154	149	-0.7	2.42	124	115	-0.8
67143	SUN CITY	007	166	159	153	-0.5	41	68	67	65	-0.2	2.37	51	50	-0.2
67144	TOWANDA	015	2948	3160	3267	0.8	86	1034	1125	1166	0.9	2.81	860	926	0.8
67146	UDALL	035	1860	2011	2011	0.8	86	687	755	762	1.0	2.66	537	584	0.9
67147	VALLEY CENTER	173	8012	8799	9286	1.0	88	2843	3180	3370	1.2	2.75	2245	2465	1.0
67149	VIOLA	173	992	1132	1200	1.4	92	321	370	394	1.5	3.04	267	303	1.4
67150	WALDRON	077	144	120	111	-2.0	4	61	52	48	-1.7	2.31	43	36	-1.9
67151	WALTON	079	579	576	573	-0.1	59	215	215	214	0.0	2.67	174	174	0.0
67152	WELLINGTON	191	10246	9757	9477	-0.5	41	3991	3828	3723	-0.4	2.50	2772	2632	-0.6
67154	WHITEWATER	015	1501	1584	1619	0.6	82	492	522	535	0.6	2.91	389	407	0.5
67155	WILMORE	033	102	98	97	-0.4	48	50	50	50	0.0	1.96	35	35	0.0
67156	WINFIELD	035	15141	14635	14282	-0.4	48	5708	5569	5440	-0.3	2.40	3812	3673	-0.4
67159	ZENDA	095	210	184	174	-1.4	11	88	79	75	-1.2	2.33	68	61	-1.2
67202	WICHITA	173	824	958	1022	1.6	94	399	524	579	3.0	1.27	86	95	1.1
67203	WICHITA	173	30247	29564	29519	-0.2	56	13238	13162	13217	-0.1	2.14	7111	6834	-0.4
67204	WICHITA	173	20326	20397	20758	0.0	64	7944	8122	8313	0.2	2.50	5488	5472	0.0
67205	WICHITA	173	8303	14142	16347	5.9	99	2703	4781	5561	6.4	2.96	2309	4006	6.1
67206	WICHITA	173	13570	15039	15780	1.1	89	5709	6401	6729	1.2	2.32	3743	4124	1.1
67207	WICHITA	173	23362	24688	25456	0.6	82	10369	11078	11449	0.7	2.22	5958	6147	0.3
67208	WICHITA	173	18790	18347	18290	-0.3	52	7832	7748	7757	-0.1	2.33	4555	4360	-0.5
67209	WICHITA	173	12387	13707	14378	1.1	89	4574	5108	5370	1.2	2.66	3429	3803	1.1
67210	WICHITA	173	11710	11743	11899	0.0	64	3822	3851	3905	0.1	2.93	2909	2898	0.0
67211	WICHITA	173	21084	20194	20057	-0.5	41	9290	8968	8939	-0.4	2.24	5014	4649	-0.8
67212	WICHITA	173	46246	46542	47151	0.1	68	17932	18432	18768	0.3	2.51	12602	12690	0.1
67213	WICHITA	173	21485	20852	20793	-0.3	52	9045	8982	9019	-0.1	2.26	5074	4849	-0.5
67214	WICHITA	173	18004	16987	16741	-0.6	36	6846	6485	6406	-0.6	2.54	4041	3717	-0.9
67215	WICHITA	173	4772	5545	5918	1.6	94	1599	1891	2030	1.8	2.93	1325	1552	1.7
67216	WICHITA	173	24363	23857	23949	-0.2	56	9303	9283	9361	0.0	2.57	6394	6219	-0.3
67217	WICHITA	173	29472	30049	30572	0.2	70	11537	11910	12153	0.3	2.52	8006	8057	0.1
67218	WICHITA	173	22785	22479	22561	-0.1	59	10301	10280	10346	0.0	2.16	5520	5298	-0.4
67219	WICHITA	173	10520	11803	12240	1.3	91	3712	4201	4373	1.3	2.80	2777	3114	1.2
67220	WICHITA	173	11532	13577	14505	1.8	95	4302	5152	5539	2.0	2.63	3043	3569	1.7
67221	MCCONNELL AFB	173	540	528	530	-0.2	56	11	11	11	0.0	2.55	11	11	0.0
67223	WICHITA	173	494	580	646	1.8	95	145	177	199	2.2	3.26	132	160	2.1
67226	WICHITA	173	15677	18210	19680	1.6	94	6184	7216	7775	1.7	2.48	4149	4783	1.5
67227	WICHITA	173	273	305	321	1.2	91	90	103	109	1.5	2.96	76	85	1.2
67228	WICHITA	173	377	1312	1586	14.4	100	120	452	550	15.4	2.83	96	356	15.2
67230	WICHITA	173	5890	8569	9594	4.1	98	2007	2924	3284	4.2	2.92	1755	2501	3.9
67232	WICHITA	173	266	271	276	0.2	70	98	102	104	0.4	2.66	76	76	0.0
67235	WICHITA	173	5889	9882	11327	5.8	99	1859	3207	3705	6.1	3.08	1654	2786	5.8
67301	INDEPENDENCE	125	13583	12936	12646	-0.5	41	5561	5376	5273	-0.4	2.34	3721	3559	-0.5
67330	ALTAMONT	099	1443	1431	1413	-0.1	59	554	559	554	0.1	2.52	408	409	0.0
67332	BARTLETT	099	435	451	452	0.4	76	155	164	165	0.6	2.75	121	128	0.6
67333	CANEY	125	3346	3188	3113	-0.5	41	1330	1281	1257	-0.4	2.47	952	907	-0.5
67335	CHERRYVALE	125	3346	3236	3174	-0.4	48	1352	1321	1298	-0.3	2.42	920	898	-0.3
67336	CHETOPA	021	1819	1753	1713	-0.4	48	779	765	752	-0.2	2.24	509	494	-0.3
67337	COFFEYVILLE	125	15210	14044	13644	-0.9	23	6329	5920	5771	-0.7	2.29	4128	3809	-0.9
67341	DENNIS	099	474	473	469	0.0	64	190	194	194	0.2	2.44	144	146	0.1
67342	EDNA	099	755	815	824	0.8	86	323	354	359	1.0	2.30	226	247	1.0
67344	ELK CITY	125	901	982	996	0.9	87	363	404	412	1.2	2.43	262	288	1.0
67345	ELK FALLS	049	196	175	167	-1.2	14	90	81	77	-1.1	2.16	63	56	-1.3
67346	GRENOLA	049	380	340	324	-1.2	14	166	150	144	-1.1	2.27	114	101	-1.3
67347	HAVANA	125	269	260	258	-0.4	48	115	114	113	-0.1	2.28	88	87	-0.1
67349	HOWARD	049	1122	1170	1169	0.5	79	487	511	511	0.5	2.19	315	327	0.4
67351	LIBERTY	125	430	411	401	-0.5	41	175	171	168	-0.2	2.40	135	131	-0.3
67352	LONGTON	049	598	549	526	-0.9	23	243	223	214	-0.9	2.46	165	150	-1.0
67353	MOLINE	049	654	586	559	-1.2	14	295	265	252	-1.2	2.08	180	159	-1.3
67354	MOUND VALLEY	099	819	850	852	0.4	76	322	341	344	0.6	2.49	240	251	0.5
67355	NIOTAZE	019	277	248	234	-1.2	14	109	98	92	-1.1	2.53	76	68	-1.2
67356	OSWEGO	099	3003	2961	2929	-0.2	56	1155	1150	1139	0.0	2.34	783	772	-0.2
67357	PARSONS	099	13661	13162	12873	-0.4	48	5552	5414	5311	-0.3	2.33	3551	3423	-0.4
67360	PERU	019	550	518	501	-0.6	36	238	225	217	-0.6	2.27	164	154	-0.7
67361	SEDAN	019	2250	2169	2102	-0.4	48	938	903	874	-0.4	2.32	634	605	-0.5
67401	SALINA	169	49495	50571	51038	0.2	70	19918	20528	20753	0.3	2.40	13020	13275	0.2
67410	ABILENE	041	9954	9976	9856	0.0	64	4120	4196	4162	0.2	2.34	2782	2806	0.1
67416	ASSARIA	169	1214	1266	1288	0.5	79	427	446	453	0.5	2.77	347	358	0.3
67417	AURORA	029	185	160	149	-1.6	8	69	61	57	-1.3	2.62	54	48	-1.3
67418	BARNARD	105	270	222	206	-2.1	3	123	103	96	-1.9	2.16	90	75	-2.0
67420	BELOIT	123	5082	4623	4382	-1.0	19	2028	1869	1775	-0.9	2.29	1309	1193	-1.0
67422	BENNINGTON	143	1101	1327	1359	2.0	95	414	503	516	2.1	2.64	313	376	2.0
67423	BEVERLY	105	436	365	339	-1.9	4	168	141	132	-1.9	2.59	126	106	-1.9
67425	BROOKVILLE	169	544	589	606	0.9	87	220	243	251	1.1	2.41	161	176	1.0
67427	BUSHTON	159	494	476	459	-0.4	48	198	193	186	-0.3	2.47	141	136	-0.4
67428	CANTON	113	1557	1611	1631	0.4	76	577	605	614	0.5	2.59	455	474	0.4
67430	CAWKER CITY	123	578	539	513	-0.8	28	283	271	261	-0.5	1.99	188	179	-0.5
67431	CHAPMAN	041	2177	2150	2117	-0.1	59	853	860	851	0.1	2.44	632	631	0.0
67432	CLAY CENTER	027	6166	6050	6037	-0.2	56	2593	2574	2577	-0.1	2.30	1744	1714	-0.2
67436	DELPHOS	143	722	674	647	-0.7	32	296	278	267	-0.7	2.42	214	199	-0.8
	KANSAS					0.6					0.6	2.49			0.5
	UNITED STATES					1.0					1.1	2.59			0.9

ZIP CODE #	POST OFFICE NAME	RACE (%) White 2000	White 2009	Black 2000	Black 2009	Asian/Pacific 2000	Asian/Pacific 2009	% Hispanic Origin 2000	% Hispanic Origin 2009	2009 AGE DISTRIBUTION (%) 0-4	5-9	10-14	15-19	20-24	25-44	45-64	65-84	85+	18+	MEDIAN AGE 2009	% 2009 Males	% 2009 Females
67114	NEWTON	88.5	85.0	2.0	2.1	0.6	0.9	11.0	15.6	7.0	6.7	7.0	7.0	6.1	24.3	26.8	12.1	3.0	74.7	38.6	49.0	51.0
67117	NORTH NEWTON	94.2	92.6	1.9	2.1	0.7	0.8	2.7	4.2	3.0	2.6	2.5	8.1	13.1	17.5	18.1	24.3	10.9	89.9	50.0	44.4	55.6
67118	NORWICH	95.3	94.7	0.1	0.1	0.1	0.1	1.4	1.9	6.0	6.6	6.9	7.4	5.1	20.1	30.7	13.7	3.7	75.5	43.6	48.5	51.5
67119	OXFORD	95.7	94.9	0.3	0.3	0.4	0.6	1.8	2.6	4.5	4.9	5.2	6.7	6.2	23.2	30.7	14.6	4.0	80.6	44.5	47.8	52.2
67120	PECK	95.3	94.1	0.2	0.3	0.2	0.4	1.8	2.8	5.5	6.2	7.3	7.9	5.1	23.5	33.3	10.3	0.9	76.0	41.2	51.1	48.9
67122	PIEDMONT	95.9	94.2	0.0	0.0	0.0	0.0	1.7	3.1	5.0	5.4	6.2	5.8	4.2	21.6	32.0	17.4	2.3	79.2	46.1	49.8	50.2
67123	POTWIN	95.6	95.0	0.0	0.0	0.1	0.1	1.4	2.0	7.9	7.7	7.1	6.0	6.7	24.2	27.5	11.3	1.6	73.7	36.9	51.4	48.6
67124	PRATT	94.9	93.4	1.2	1.3	0.6	0.9	3.3	4.8	5.9	6.0	6.0	7.4	6.5	21.8	27.8	14.8	3.9	78.2	41.6	48.6	51.4
67127	PROTECTION	97.4	97.3	0.0	0.0	0.1	0.1	2.0	2.1	5.5	5.9	6.2	5.7	4.5	16.8	28.3	21.2	5.8	78.5	48.8	52.2	47.8
67131	ROCK	95.5	94.7	0.3	0.3	0.3	0.9	1.4	2.1	5.3	5.9	6.2	7.7	5.0	21.9	31.7	14.8	1.5	77.8	43.4	50.0	50.0
67132	ROSALIA	96.1	95.3	0.7	0.6	0.0	0.0	2.5	3.6	7.1	6.9	7.1	7.1	6.7	24.5	29.2	10.5	1.1	74.7	37.5	49.4	50.6
67133	ROSE HILL	96.3	95.5	0.6	0.7	0.5	0.7	1.7	2.6	7.2	7.4	7.9	8.7	6.6	25.1	29.0	7.4	0.9	71.8	35.0	49.9	50.1
67134	SAWYER	95.4	94.1	0.2	0.2	0.7	1.0	3.0	4.5	6.4	6.9	7.2	6.4	4.0	23.5	30.0	13.1	2.5	75.5	41.5	50.0	50.0
67135	SEDGWICK	95.6	94.0	0.2	0.3	0.2	0.3	2.9	4.7	6.7	6.8	7.0	7.5	6.2	24.0	29.0	10.9	1.8	74.3	39.0	49.4	50.6
67137	SEVERY	96.0	95.1	0.0	0.0	0.0	0.0	1.3	1.9	5.3	5.7	6.1	5.7	4.4	21.7	32.7	16.4	1.9	79.5	45.6	49.9	50.1
67138	SHARON	97.0	96.5	0.5	0.5	0.2	0.3	1.1	1.5	6.8	7.3	7.1	7.3	5.1	20.7	27.8	14.6	3.3	73.7	41.7	50.0	50.0
67140	SOUTH HAVEN	95.4	94.5	0.1	0.1	0.1	0.1	1.7	2.7	6.3	7.0	7.7	8.5	4.4	22.5	30.0	11.6	2.0	73.5	40.5	49.8	50.2
67142	SPIVEY	98.3	97.9	0.2	0.3	0.0	0.0	1.5	2.1	5.1	5.9	6.4	6.6	4.8	19.9	33.2	15.4	2.7	78.5	45.9	53.2	46.8
67143	SUN CITY	96.4	96.2	0.6	0.6	0.0	0.0	1.2	1.3	5.0	5.7	5.7	6.3	4.4	19.5	31.4	19.5	2.5	79.9	47.5	48.4	51.6
67144	TOWANDA	96.9	96.3	0.3	0.3	0.3	0.5	0.9	1.5	7.1	7.3	7.5	7.3	6.3	24.1	30.2	9.3	0.8	73.6	36.8	50.3	49.7
67146	UDALL	96.2	95.5	0.4	0.4	0.1	0.2	2.0	3.0	7.1	7.6	8.0	7.5	4.9	24.6	28.9	10.3	1.1	72.6	37.3	49.4	50.6
67147	VALLEY CENTER	96.2	94.9	0.6	0.8	0.3	0.5	1.8	3.1	7.3	7.5	7.6	7.5	6.0	24.9	28.5	9.7	1.1	73.0	36.7	49.8	50.2
67149	VIOLA	96.5	95.1	0.3	0.4	0.1	0.2	1.7	2.9	7.0	7.8	8.4	8.4	5.5	22.2	30.7	9.1	1.0	71.3	37.5	49.5	50.5
67150	WALDRON	98.6	98.3	0.0	0.0	0.0	0.0	0.7	0.8	5.8	5.8	5.8	6.7	4.2	20.0	29.2	20.0	2.5	79.2	46.1	49.2	50.8
67151	WALTON	97.4	96.7	0.5	0.5	0.0	0.2	1.9	3.0	7.5	7.3	9.4	7.6	4.2	26.4	26.9	9.5	1.2	71.0	37.4	53.3	46.7
67152	WELLINGTON	93.0	91.2	1.5	1.7	0.4	0.5	6.4	9.2	7.3	6.9	7.0	6.9	6.2	23.7	26.5	12.8	2.7	74.5	38.3	48.9	51.1
67154	WHITEWATER	97.4	96.8	0.1	0.1	0.2	0.3	1.3	1.9	5.8	8.3	8.0	8.5	3.7	21.2	26.1	13.4	5.1	72.2	40.8	50.1	49.9
67155	WILMORE	99.0	99.0	0.0	0.0	0.0	0.0	0.0	0.0	6.1	7.1	7.1	6.1	4.1	18.4	36.7	12.2	2.0	77.6	45.6	53.1	46.9
67156	WINFIELD	89.6	86.9	2.7	3.0	3.1	4.4	4.0	5.7	6.4	6.2	6.2	7.8	7.8	24.6	25.2	12.6	3.2	76.8	38.0	50.0	50.0
67159	ZENDA	98.6	97.8	0.0	0.0	0.0	0.0	1.4	2.7	5.4	6.0	6.0	6.5	5.4	20.1	33.7	14.1	2.7	78.3	45.4	53.3	46.7
67202	WICHITA	65.0	57.1	22.9	27.0	1.8	2.8	9.5	13.0	2.1	1.6	1.5	2.7	12.7	47.4	26.7	4.7	0.6	93.7	36.8	72.5	27.5
67203	WICHITA	78.7	72.4	5.6	6.2	1.2	1.7	17.2	24.4	7.1	6.7	6.3	6.3	6.6	29.6	24.0	10.7	2.7	76.3	36.0	50.4	49.6
67204	WICHITA	78.7	73.3	3.6	3.8	2.0	2.6	21.8	28.6	7.0	6.9	6.8	6.6	5.8	24.5	26.9	13.1	2.4	75.2	38.7	50.0	50.0
67205	WICHITA	93.6	90.8	0.8	1.0	2.6	3.7	2.6	4.5	8.4	9.1	9.3	7.6	3.9	28.2	26.7	6.2	0.5	67.9	36.0	50.6	49.4
67206	WICHITA	88.4	84.1	4.1	5.0	4.3	6.6	2.6	4.5	5.9	5.9	6.4	6.6	6.4	23.5	28.0	14.4	2.9	77.6	41.2	48.4	51.6
67207	WICHITA	74.0	67.0	11.5	13.2	8.1	11.8	5.2	7.9	7.8	6.9	6.4	6.1	7.6	31.6	23.3	8.9	1.4	75.4	33.6	49.1	50.9
67208	WICHITA	58.1	53.1	30.7	33.0	5.3	6.9	4.0	6.2	7.4	7.2	7.0	7.3	10.7	26.9	22.8	8.9	1.9	74.3	31.7	48.9	51.1
67209	WICHITA	89.0	84.6	2.4	2.9	2.9	4.5	5.2	8.6	9.3	8.6	7.9	6.6	5.5	30.0	22.8	8.1	1.2	70.0	34.1	49.6	50.4
67210	WICHITA	61.3	54.1	10.7	11.8	11.6	14.4	18.0	23.3	12.0	10.0	8.2	8.0	10.0	31.7	15.8	3.9	0.5	65.3	25.9	51.9	48.1
67211	WICHITA	75.3	67.9	8.4	9.6	3.5	5.1	13.3	20.3	8.1	7.2	6.3	6.8	7.4	28.8	24.3	8.9	2.1	74.4	34.3	50.1	49.9
67212	WICHITA	89.8	85.8	2.4	3.1	2.4	3.7	4.9	8.2	7.3	7.3	7.3	7.0	6.1	26.8	26.4	10.0	1.6	73.6	36.2	48.9	51.1
67213	WICHITA	81.3	75.0	5.4	6.4	1.7	2.4	11.8	18.7	8.1	7.4	6.6	6.6	7.1	28.5	23.0	9.5	3.1	74.3	34.2	49.5	50.5
67214	WICHITA	25.2	21.8	53.9	53.6	4.5	5.1	19.2	24.0	9.1	8.6	7.9	8.2	8.0	26.3	21.3	9.0	1.5	69.5	30.6	49.6	50.4
67215	WICHITA	91.9	89.3	1.2	1.4	3.2	4.8	4.0	6.3	8.1	8.5	8.6	8.3	5.3	26.5	27.4	6.9	0.5	69.4	34.4	49.4	50.6
67216	WICHITA	75.6	68.9	7.7	8.8	6.5	8.9	7.9	12.3	9.0	8.3	7.8	7.4	6.8	27.9	22.8	8.9	1.1	70.5	32.4	49.4	50.6
67217	WICHITA	84.0	78.5	4.3	5.2	3.5	5.3	6.3	10.2	8.4	8.0	7.5	7.0	6.2	27.5	23.8	10.6	1.1	71.9	34.1	49.1	50.9
67218	WICHITA	74.5	68.1	11.1	12.4	3.8	5.4	11.1	16.4	8.1	7.2	6.3	5.9	6.8	29.1	22.7	10.9	3.1	75.0	35.4	48.6	51.4
67219	WICHITA	58.2	59.2	32.6	29.4	0.9	1.3	8.2	10.8	8.7	8.9	8.4	8.6	6.5	26.1	23.7	8.3	0.7	68.7	31.8	48.9	51.1
67220	WICHITA	60.3	55.0	28.7	30.3	6.1	8.6	3.5	5.4	8.0	7.4	7.2	6.8	7.5	29.6	24.3	8.3	1.0	73.4	33.9	49.2	50.8
67221	MCCONNELL AFB	73.8	66.9	15.4	18.2	2.4	3.6	7.4	11.6	14.4	11.2	8.1	7.6	18.9	35.8	3.6	0.4	0.0	63.6	22.3	56.1	43.9
67223	WICHITA	96.6	95.2	0.6	0.7	0.8	1.4	1.8	3.3	7.8	8.1	9.1	9.3	5.0	23.8	29.3	6.9	0.7	69.1	35.7	51.0	49.0
67226	WICHITA	83.3	77.7	6.8	8.2	6.2	9.3	3.1	5.1	7.7	7.4	7.3	6.5	6.1	29.0	25.3	7.8	2.8	73.5	35.3	48.3	51.7
67227	WICHITA	97.8	97.4	0.0	0.0	0.0	0.0	1.5	2.6	4.9	5.9	6.9	7.2	5.6	22.6	34.8	11.1	1.0	77.7	42.4	50.2	49.8
67228	WICHITA	89.4	85.4	3.4	4.4	4.2	6.9	2.4	4.0	9.5	9.6	9.8	7.5	3.9	27.9	24.8	5.2	1.8	65.9	32.8	48.9	51.1
67230	WICHITA	92.6	88.9	1.7	2.5	3.2	5.4	1.3	2.4	6.3	7.9	8.7	7.6	3.2	22.1	32.1	10.6	1.4	71.6	41.4	49.7	50.3
67232	WICHITA	92.1	88.6	1.1	1.5	2.6	4.1	3.0	5.5	6.6	6.6	7.0	6.6	6.3	26.2	30.6	9.2	0.7	76.0	36.4	51.7	48.3
67235	WICHITA	93.9	91.3	1.0	1.4	1.7	2.2	3.1	5.1	7.7	8.1	8.5	8.3	5.3	25.2	29.3	7.0	0.5	70.3	35.5	49.4	50.6
67301	INDEPENDENCE	88.8	86.7	5.9	6.7	0.5	0.8	3.3	4.9	6.6	6.3	6.5	7.3	6.5	23.8	26.5	13.8	3.0	76.6	39.8	49.0	51.0
67330	ALTAMONT	95.7	95.0	0.1	0.1	0.2	0.3	0.7	0.8	6.4	6.1	6.9	8.0	5.7	23.1	26.3	13.8	3.6	75.0	40.7	48.4	51.6
67332	BARTLETT	93.5	92.5	0.0	0.0	0.5	0.9	1.2	1.3	4.2	5.8	8.6	10.0	3.1	23.1	30.4	12.2	2.7	74.5	42.0	51.4	48.6
67333	CANEY	90.6	89.2	0.2	0.3	0.1	0.1	2.1	3.1	6.3	6.2	6.6	7.3	5.8	22.7	28.4	13.8	2.8	76.3	40.8	47.9	52.1
67335	CHERRYVALE	94.6	93.5	0.2	0.3	0.1	0.1	2.4	3.5	6.6	6.6	6.6	6.6	5.7	23.6	27.6	13.9	2.8	76.3	40.6	48.5	51.5
67336	CHETOPA	90.5	89.8	1.6	1.8	0.0	0.0	0.9	1.3	5.2	5.4	6.0	6.6	4.7	21.1	28.8	18.3	3.9	79.4	45.6	48.9	51.1
67337	COFFEYVILLE	79.4	77.2	9.1	9.6	0.6	0.9	3.3	4.8	6.0	6.1	6.3	7.0	6.0	22.7	26.1	15.9	3.9	77.8	41.4	48.0	52.0
67341	DENNIS	99.2	98.9	0.0	0.0	0.0	0.0	1.5	1.9	5.5	5.9	6.3	6.1	5.1	22.0	33.0	14.2	1.9	79.1	44.5	52.6	47.4
67342	EDNA	89.6	88.6	0.1	0.1	0.1	0.2	0.5	0.7	5.2	5.4	6.1	8.0	5.8	21.3	30.9	13.7	3.6	78.5	43.8	48.3	51.7
67344	ELK CITY	94.9	93.7	0.0	0.0	0.1	0.2	1.8	2.9	5.2	5.7	6.1	6.4	5.2	19.8	32.8	16.2	2.6	79.0	46.1	50.2	49.8
67345	ELK FALLS	96.9	94.9	0.0	0.0	0.0	0.0	2.1	3.4	4.6	4.6	5.1	5.1	4.6	16.0	38.3	18.3	3.4	82.9	50.8	51.4	48.6
67346	GRENOLA	95.0	93.2	0.0	0.0	0.3	0.3	2.4	3.8	4.7	4.7	5.3	5.0	3.5	19.7	31.8	22.4	2.9	81.8	50.0	48.5	51.5
67347	HAVANA	91.4	90.4	0.7	0.8	0.0	0.0	0.4	0.4	3.5	3.8	4.2	6.2	5.8	18.8	38.1	17.3	2.3	84.6	49.3	53.1	46.9
67349	HOWARD	95.0	94.5	0.4	0.4	0.4	0.4	1.8	2.6	4.8	4.4	4.9	6.6	5.9	19.1	27.9	19.8	6.5	81.3	48.2	47.0	53.0
67351	LIBERTY	94.2	92.9	1.2	1.5	0.0	0.0	2.3	3.4	4.1	5.1	6.1	7.5	4.4	20.4	33.6	16.5	2.2	80.3	46.4	51.8	48.2
67352	LONGTON	94.8	93.8	0.0	0.0	0.2	0.2	2.0	2.7	5.6	5.5	5.5	7.3	7.7	20.8	28.2	16.6	2.9	79.6	42.6	48.5	51.5
67353	MOLINE	94.8	93.3	0.3	0.3	0.0	0.0	2.9	4.1	5.3	4.6	4.6	4.6	5.3	20.0	24.1	24.7	6.8	82.3	50.3	48.0	52.0
67354	MOUND VALLEY	93.5	92.8	0.0	0.0	0.1	0.1	1.8	2.4	7.6	7.6	7.3	5.9	5.2	25.6	27.3	11.9	1.5	74.0	37.7	48.2	51.8
67355	NIOTAZE	92.0	91.5	0.4	0.4	0.0	0.0	1.4	2.4	4.0	4.0	4.0	6.9	5.6	22.6	33.1	17.3	2.4	84.3	46.6	47.6	52.4
67356	OSWEGO	92.7	91.7	2.4	2.6	0.2	0.2	1.8	2.5	6.0	6.2	6.3	8.1	8.7	22.4	25.5	13.6	3.1	76.9	38.0	52.2	47.8
67357	PARSONS	87.0	85.2	7.0	7.6	0.5	0.7	4.2	5.6	6.7	6.2	6.1	6.8	7.2	24.0	26.3	13.0	3.7	77.2	39.1	48.8	51.2
67360	PERU	93.1	92.7	0.2	0.2	0.0	0.0	1.1	1.4	4.4	4.4	4.6	6.9	5.6	20.3	29.9	19.9	3.9	82.6	47.4	47.3	52.7
67361	SEDAN	94.2	93.4	0.3	0.3	0.2	0.4	1.3	2.0	5.3	5.4	5.5	6.4	5.9	19.5	26.9	19.7	5.5	80.1	46.5	47.2	52.8
67401	SALINA	88.6	85.6	3.3	3.5	1.9	2.7	6.3	9.1	7.0	6.6	6.6	7.3	7.0	25.6	26.0	11.7	2.3	75.5	37.2	49.3	50.7
67410	ABILENE	96.3	96.2	0.7	0.8	0.3	0.3	2.3	2.4	6.1	6.3	6.4	6.5	5.3	22.6	28.6	15.1	3.1	76.9	42.4	49.0	51.0
67416	ASSARIA	96.5	95.2	0.2	0.3	0.2	0.3	2.1	3.2	7.5	7.4	8.7	7.0	5.6	23.8	29.4	9.6	1.0	71.9	37.7	51.6	48.4
67417	AURORA	99.5	99.4	0.0	0.0	0.0	0.0	0.5	0.6	5.0	6.3	6.3	6.3	4.4	20.6	33.1	16.3	1.9	78.8	45.7	55.0	45.0
67418	BARNARD	99.6	99.5	0.0	0.0	0.0	0.0	0.4	0.9	4.5	4.5	5.0	5.4	4.5	19.4	35.1	18.9	2.7	82.4	49.2	49.5	50.5
67420	BELOIT	97.4	96.9	0.6	0.7	0.3	0.5	1.0	1.4	5.2	5.4	5.9	9.5	4.6	21.1	28.3	14.8	5.1	78.5	43.3	49.6	50.4
67422	BENNINGTON	98.2	98.2	0.2	0.2	0.4	0.3	0.8	1.0	6.0	6.3	7.3	8.0	4.7	22.6	31.7	12.1	1.4	75.4	42.0	51.3	48.7
67423	BEVERLY	97.7	96.4	0.0	0.0	0.2	0.5	1.6	2.7	5.5	6.6	7.7	8.2	3.3	21.4	32.6	12.6	2.2	75.3	43.2	50.1	49.9
67425	BROOKVILLE	98.3	98.0	0.0	0.0	0.0	0.0	2.2	3.2	5.6	6.1	7.5	8.1	3.7	24.1	31.6	12.1	1.2	75.0	41.8	54.2	45.8
67427	BUSHTON	98.0	97.3	0.2	0.2	0.2	0.4	1.6	2.5	3.6	4.2	4.6	5.5	4.8	20.6	35.9	17.6	3.2	84.0	49.0	49.8	50.2
67428	CANTON	98.1	97.6	0.1	0.1	0.4	0.6	1.0	1.4	6.1	6.3	7.1	7.2	5.3	24.2	27.6	12.9	3.3	75.8	40.3	48.5	51.5
67430	CAWKER CITY	97.6	97.2	0.3	0.4	0.3	0.6	0.7	1.1	5.0	5.0	5.4	5.6	5.8	18.7	30.8	20.2	3.5	81.3	47.9	49.9	50.1
67431	CHAPMAN	95.6	95.4	0.4	0.4	0.4	0.4	2.2	2.3	5.3	5.6	5.9	6.5	5.6	22.7	30.6	13.4	4.4	79.0	43.7	49.2	50.8
67432	CLAY CENTER	97.8	97.4	0.6	0.6	0.2	0.3	0.8	1.2	5.4	5.4	5.9	6.4	5.6	21.8	28.5	16.3	4.9	79.4	44.7	49.5	50.5
67436	DELPHOS	98.8	98.7	0.0	0.0	0.0	0.0	1.2	1.3	5.5	5.9	6.4	7.3	4.5	20.6	33.1	14.4	2.4	77.6	44.9	52.1	47.9
	KANSAS	86.1	83.7	5.7	5.9	1.8	2.6	7.0	9.4	7.1	6.9	6.9	7.3	7.3	25.9	25.7	10.7	2.2	75.0	36.3	49.6	50.4
	UNITED STATES	75.1	72.0	12.3	12.7	3.8	4.6	12.5	15.7	6.8	6.7	6.6	7.1	6.9	27.0	26.0	10.9	1.9	75.7	36.9	49.2	50.8

ZIP CODE #	POST OFFICE NAME	2009 Per Capita Income	2009 HH Income Base	2009 HOUSEHOLD INCOME DISTRIBUTION (%) Less than $25,000	$25,000 to $49,999	$50,000 to $99,999	$100,000 to $149,999	$150,000 or More	MEDIAN HOUSEHOLD INCOME 2009	2014	2009 National Centile	2009 State Centile	2009 Home Value Base	2009 HOME VALUE DISTRIBUTION (%) Less than $50,000	$50,000 to $89,999	$90,000 to $174,999	$175,000 to $399,999	$400,000 or More	2009 Median Home Value
67114	NEWTON	23169	8454	19.8	29.4	41.6	7.1	2.0	50647	54324	63	76	5956	19.0	30.2	39.9	10.5	0.4	90622
67117	NORTH NEWTON	28393	647	28.1	19.3	41.7	6.5	4.3	53001	57800	68	80	442	4.3	18.8	60.9	14.9	1.1	114623
67118	NORWICH	19973	294	21.4	34.4	35.4	7.5	1.4	43667	46436	44	52	231	27.3	19.5	39.4	13.9	0.0	95000
67119	OXFORD	21426	622	24.0	30.1	38.9	5.6	1.4	46006	50140	51	61	485	32.8	28.7	32.2	5.6	0.8	78023
67120	PECK	22749	514	12.1	24.3	53.3	9.1	1.2	61145	60886	79	89	453	14.3	23.0	47.0	15.0	0.7	101935
67122	PIEDMONT	21122	109	25.7	30.3	39.4	2.8	1.8	41391	45455	37	41	90	42.2	12.2	23.3	15.6	6.7	75000
67123	POTWIN	26760	295	16.6	25.8	45.8	7.5	4.4	55942	57653	73	84	236	39.4	30.9	16.9	10.6	2.1	65556
67124	PRATT	22309	3320	25.4	30.4	36.7	5.0	2.4	44249	46280	46	55	2374	22.6	32.2	29.6	14.8	0.9	83989
67127	PROTECTION	21894	309	31.4	42.1	23.0	1.3	2.3	34085	34346	16	7	231	53.7	21.2	16.0	9.1	0.0	44688
67131	ROCK	19676	130	22.3	27.7	43.8	5.4	0.8	50000	50000	61	74	110	21.8	19.1	37.3	15.5	6.4	99091
67132	ROSALIA	19974	176	23.9	27.8	41.5	5.7	1.1	48521	52358	58	69	139	36.0	25.9	20.9	15.1	2.2	71364
67133	ROSE HILL	25895	2112	9.2	16.2	52.2	17.3	5.1	76337	76059	90	95	1844	5.4	12.4	62.6	18.5	1.1	121367
67134	SAWYER	18892	146	25.3	35.6	31.5	4.1	3.4	40900	43743	36	39	117	48.7	20.5	22.2	6.8	1.7	52500
67135	SEDGWICK	23223	1164	13.1	29.6	45.8	8.8	2.7	58267	60770	75	86	974	19.4	29.6	36.4	12.9	1.6	90935
67137	SEVERY	22004	311	24.4	30.5	38.6	2.6	3.9	43257	46926	43	50	255	43.9	11.8	23.9	18.0	2.4	72143
67138	SHARON	19074	166	31.3	30.7	33.1	3.6	1.2	40000	42054	33	32	127	55.1	22.0	19.7	3.1	0.0	45667
67140	SOUTH HAVEN	18096	307	25.7	30.0	40.1	3.3	1.0	45124	48485	49	57	248	47.6	28.2	20.2	3.6	0.4	52727
67142	SPIVEY	19751	154	24.0	40.3	28.6	6.5	0.6	40308	42132	34	34	124	36.3	29.0	22.6	10.5	1.6	64545
67143	SUN CITY	22225	67	26.9	34.3	29.9	3.0	6.0	41737	47338	38	43	51	39.2	19.6	21.6	11.8	7.8	82500
67144	TOWANDA	22312	1125	14.1	28.0	47.1	8.5	2.2	58364	60470	76	86	993	19.9	32.9	24.7	19.3	3.1	85746
67146	UDALL	21215	755	17.6	31.4	41.3	8.2	1.5	50847	50437	63	77	636	14.9	24.5	41.8	17.0	1.7	102647
67147	VALLEY CENTER	25066	3180	9.2	26.4	50.4	10.3	3.6	62595	63672	81	91	2594	11.1	24.1	43.1	19.0	2.8	110188
67149	VIOLA	21202	370	12.2	24.1	52.7	8.9	2.2	60000	60476	77	88	317	12.3	24.0	42.0	21.1	0.6	107986
67150	WALDRON	20351	52	30.8	30.8	32.7	3.8	1.9	40000	40000	33	32	41	31.7	22.0	29.3	12.2	4.9	77500
67151	WALTON	21969	215	11.2	30.2	50.2	7.9	0.5	54200	55892	70	82	175	16.6	30.3	36.0	17.1	0.0	92500
67152	WELLINGTON	21160	3828	24.8	28.2	38.9	6.2	1.8	46711	50759	53	62	2669	31.9	36.5	26.6	4.6	0.4	71923
67154	WHITEWATER	22190	522	15.5	31.0	42.7	7.1	3.6	54748	59866	71	83	425	13.6	21.4	54.4	8.9	1.6	100457
67155	WILMORE	22418	50	22.0	40.0	38.0	0.0	0.0	40000	42376	33	32	35	40.0	31.4	14.3	14.3	0.0	57000
67156	WINFIELD	21856	5569	25.8	29.0	37.5	5.2	2.5	44892	46803	48	56	3803	21.8	29.5	35.3	12.3	1.1	88238
67159	ZENDA	19165	79	26.6	43.0	25.3	3.8	1.3	40233	41071	33	34	64	51.6	20.3	20.3	3.1	4.7	46667
67202	WICHITA	22502	524	47.9	34.0	13.9	3.6	0.6	25988	25897	4	1	21	81.0	14.3	0.0	4.8	0.0	41875
67203	WICHITA	23566	13162	23.2	33.8	36.8	4.5	1.7	44101	47786	46	54	7058	16.3	46.2	35.0	2.3	0.2	79157
67204	WICHITA	22517	8122	22.8	27.4	40.9	6.5	2.5	49886	53585	61	73	5688	18.1	37.8	34.0	9.6	0.5	83876
67205	WICHITA	37239	4781	5.5	11.5	41.8	22.7	18.5	87899	86391	95	97	4235	5.2	6.2	37.9	45.6	5.2	176293
67206	WICHITA	41020	6401	14.7	18.9	37.4	13.4	15.6	73234	71251	88	95	4338	3.1	5.0	39.3	40.4	12.2	180973
67207	WICHITA	28716	11078	15.5	29.1	43.2	8.3	3.9	55011	57728	71	83	5590	8.3	23.9	57.3	9.1	1.3	106535
67208	WICHITA	23404	7748	29.4	26.8	34.0	6.2	3.6	43018	46758	42	49	4409	16.5	32.6	38.3	10.5	2.2	90928
67209	WICHITA	28427	5108	8.2	19.3	55.8	11.9	4.8	71265	72331	87	94	4062	4.6	15.7	71.8	7.8	0.2	112987
67210	WICHITA	19538	3851	21.2	29.6	39.3	7.4	2.5	49258	53477	59	71	1694	39.4	15.6	40.9	4.0	0.1	72459
67211	WICHITA	19982	8968	29.2	38.2	27.9	3.6	1.2	36651	38580	23	18	4430	33.8	54.4	10.6	1.1	0.1	59010
67212	WICHITA	27816	18432	11.7	23.1	49.9	11.5	3.8	64112	65134	82	92	12912	3.8	18.5	65.7	11.6	0.4	115121
67213	WICHITA	19055	8982	30.2	35.8	30.5	2.4	1.0	36528	39343	22	17	4440	45.5	49.3	4.5	0.7	0.0	52721
67214	WICHITA	14103	6485	46.3	30.2	20.3	2.5	0.7	27147	27697	5	1	2629	67.6	25.9	5.7	0.8	0.0	38931
67215	WICHITA	27115	1891	4.3	11.6	64.5	15.5	4.1	71690	72019	88	94	1764	8.2	12.2	70.4	8.4	0.7	109929
67216	WICHITA	20672	9283	21.3	30.9	42.1	4.4	1.3	47986	51691	57	66	6371	44.5	39.2	15.0	1.1	0.2	54670
67217	WICHITA	22278	11910	17.2	31.4	44.4	5.5	1.5	50980	54154	64	77	8640	23.7	53.8	21.6	0.8	0.1	69517
67218	WICHITA	22649	10280	26.9	33.7	33.4	4.2	1.8	40917	43588	36	39	5347	18.2	54.5	22.0	5.1	0.2	72060
67219	WICHITA	19558	4201	24.4	27.3	39.9	6.3	2.2	48278	52534	57	67	3057	38.3	36.0	21.7	3.9	0.0	60138
67220	WICHITA	26374	5152	15.5	19.2	48.6	12.7	3.9	65336	66597	84	92	3660	4.5	16.0	67.9	11.1	0.5	114408
67221	MCCONNELL AFB	4120	11	0.0	45.5	54.5	0.0	0.0	54545	51995	70	83	0	0.0	0.0	0.0	0.0	0.0	0
67223	WICHITA	33997	177	4.5	13.0	44.1	22.6	15.8	86768	88037	94	97	166	3.0	6.0	38.6	47.0	5.4	179762
67226	WICHITA	36657	7216	9.6	18.4	42.4	17.0	12.6	76740	76647	90	96	4592	1.9	7.5	44.9	41.2	4.4	163007
67227	WICHITA	22396	103	11.7	23.3	49.5	13.6	1.9	60934	60994	79	89	96	8.3	17.7	51.0	20.8	2.1	115278
67228	WICHITA	38634	452	4.4	13.3	42.0	21.0	19.2	88132	90865	95	98	379	3.7	6.9	42.7	39.8	6.9	167378
67230	WICHITA	44961	2924	4.7	10.2	28.6	25.9	30.7	111792	108199	98	99	2734	2.0	1.3	23.0	58.5	15.3	222253
67232	WICHITA	25711	102	9.8	25.5	53.9	5.9	4.9	55480	56198	72	84	78	12.8	6.4	46.2	33.3	1.3	140000
67235	WICHITA	37376	3207	5.3	13.0	37.9	23.6	20.2	91740	92833	95	98	2972	3.9	2.8	36.1	52.6	4.6	187022
67301	INDEPENDENCE	21006	5376	29.6	29.8	34.1	4.5	2.0	41648	45060	38	43	3736	25.5	30.8	32.0	10.9	0.8	79696
67330	ALTAMONT	18180	559	27.9	32.0	36.0	3.8	0.4	41374	45336	37	41	448	23.2	36.6	30.8	7.6	1.8	80000
67332	BARTLETT	16513	164	26.8	35.4	36.0	1.8	0.0	39190	42358	30	28	137	24.1	25.5	32.1	10.9	7.3	90833
67333	CANEY	19264	1281	29.7	32.2	32.6	4.4	1.2	40578	42604	35	37	956	32.6	31.0	28.6	7.0	0.8	70000
67335	CHERRYVALE	17481	1321	36.4	31.6	28.7	2.4	0.9	36407	38485	22	16	1011	41.5	29.9	20.7	6.4	1.5	59096
67336	CHETOPA	16400	765	40.9	36.9	20.3	1.6	0.4	30605	31315	9	2	559	51.3	32.4	13.4	2.7	0.2	48864
67337	COFFEYVILLE	19232	5920	35.2	31.7	27.7	4.1	1.3	36215	38519	21	15	4153	36.9	30.1	25.0	7.2	0.7	62677
67341	DENNIS	20591	194	29.9	25.3	38.7	5.2	1.0	43816	48240	45	52	168	20.8	16.7	39.3	19.6	3.6	108621
67342	EDNA	21548	354	29.9	26.3	41.2	1.1	1.4	43852	47083	45	53	268	37.7	29.9	25.0	7.1	0.4	70476
67344	ELK CITY	19243	404	37.6	27.2	30.0	2.7	2.5	34563	40721	17	8	339	50.1	25.4	12.4	8.3	3.8	49737
67345	ELK FALLS	20159	81	34.6	30.9	30.9	3.7	0.0	35763	40767	20	13	66	31.8	13.6	36.4	6.1	12.1	95000
67346	GRENOLA	20689	150	30.0	28.0	37.3	4.0	0.7	35761	38917	20	13	125	37.6	16.8	25.6	9.6	10.4	75000
67347	HAVANA	19446	114	30.7	27.2	39.5	2.6	0.0	42339	43825	40	46	97	39.2	22.7	25.8	12.4	0.0	68750
67349	HOWARD	19156	511	33.9	36.0	26.4	2.2	1.6	33863	36301	15	7	400	57.0	16.8	21.3	3.0	2.0	45882
67351	LIBERTY	23993	171	18.7	28.7	45.6	5.3	1.8	52284	54648	66	79	141	17.0	22.7	42.6	12.8	5.0	109559
67352	LONGTON	14174	223	42.6	35.9	18.4	2.7	0.4	28769	28898	6	2	174	46.6	23.0	19.0	6.9	4.6	54615
67353	MOLINE	21240	265	39.6	33.6	20.0	4.5	2.3	30442	31379	9	2	221	58.8	15.4	20.8	3.6	1.4	33750
67354	MOUND VALLEY	15440	341	41.6	32.6	23.2	2.1	0.6	30951	35511	10	3	270	46.7	20.0	21.1	11.1	1.1	56000
67355	NIOTAZE	15621	98	30.6	36.7	29.6	3.1	0.0	37973	40000	27	23	84	54.8	20.2	20.2	1.2	3.6	37500
67356	OSWEGO	17432	1150	33.0	31.4	33.3	2.2	0.1	38418	41752	28	25	877	39.8	28.7	24.7	5.9	0.8	62188
67357	PARSONS	20300	5414	28.8	33.4	31.3	5.0	1.6	39800	42214	32	30	3740	37.5	27.1	25.4	8.9	1.1	65685
67360	PERU	17609	225	34.7	36.0	25.3	3.1	0.9	34839	35976	17	9	189	50.8	22.2	18.0	4.8	4.2	48636
67361	SEDAN	18552	903	36.2	36.4	22.0	3.1	2.2	32501	33249	12	5	716	47.2	25.1	19.8	6.0	1.8	53279
67401	SALINA	23888	20528	20.8	30.6	39.2	6.2	3.1	48609	51743	58	69	13868	8.7	22.6	45.3	21.5	1.9	116855
67410	ABILENE	22250	4196	24.2	28.2	41.0	4.8	1.8	47634	49269	56	65	3095	13.2	26.5	42.3	16.5	1.4	102740
67416	ASSARIA	20882	446	15.0	33.0	45.3	4.5	2.2	51351	53077	65	78	380	16.1	18.2	39.2	23.9	2.6	124324
67417	AURORA	17517	61	26.2	36.1	31.1	4.9	1.6	40760	44088	35	38	51	29.4	37.3	27.5	5.9	0.0	78333
67418	BARNARD	19696	103	29.1	44.7	24.3	1.9	0.0	39644	40000	32	29	77	51.9	20.8	19.5	5.2	2.6	47000
67420	BELOIT	22211	1869	25.0	34.5	33.4	4.9	2.2	42992	45258	42	49	1374	27.2	28.7	29.8	13.1	1.2	81980
67422	BENNINGTON	20213	503	19.1	30.4	44.3	4.2	2.0	50276	50181	62	75	423	11.6	23.9	38.8	22.7	3.1	113705
67423	BEVERLY	16887	141	27.0	39.0	29.1	2.8	2.1	37319	38977	25	20	115	36.5	30.4	24.3	6.1	2.6	69000
67425	BROOKVILLE	24149	243	18.5	35.4	36.6	6.2	3.3	45959	50180	51	60	204	19.1	25.5	31.9	22.1	1.5	100758
67427	BUSHTON	21298	193	25.9	29.0	39.9	4.1	1.0	45226	45691	49	58	164	53.7	17.7	22.6	6.1	0.0	47000
67428	CANTON	20502	605	19.2	33.7	41.2	3.6	2.3	47493	51314	55	65	492	19.7	20.9	44.5	12.8	2.0	103750
67430	CAWKER CITY	23274	271	35.8	31.7	25.8	4.1	2.6	34832	36002	17	9	211	41.7	32.7	20.4	3.3	1.9	59722
67431	CHAPMAN	22555	860	18.5	28.6	43.7	8.4	0.8	52393	53136	67	79	646	14.1	30.2	43.0	11.5	1.2	96981
67432	CLAY CENTER	20577	2574	27.6	32.0	35.0	4.3	1.0	40895	42839	36	39	1939	27.4	29.3	30.6	12.4	0.2	79325
67436	DELPHOS	20800	278	21.2	41.4	29.5	5.8	2.2	42480	44699	41	47	238	39.5	26.9	21.4	11.8	0.4	62941
	KANSAS	26028		20.3	26.8	37.6	9.9	5.4	52748	54940				18.1	21.6	35.7	21.6	3.0	107692
	UNITED STATES	27277		20.9	24.4	35.3	11.7	7.6	54719	56938				9.3	13.1	31.6	32.6	13.5	162279

ZIP CODE #	POST OFFICE NAME	FINANCIAL SERVICES				THE HOME						ENTERTAINMENT						PERSONAL			
						Home Improvements		Furnishings													
		Auto Loan	Home Loan	Invest-ments	Retire-ment Plans	Home Repair	Lawn & Garden	Comput-ers & Hard-ware-Personal	Major Appli-ances	TV, Radio, Sound Equip-ment	Furni-ture	Dine out/ Carry out	Sports Equip-ment	Fees & Tickets	Toys & Games	Travel	Cable TV	Apparel & Services	Auto Repairs	Health Insur-ance	Pets & Supplies
67114	NEWTON	88	79	76	79	78	89	81	84	84	78	83	64	76	85	78	87	57	83	90	101
67117	NORTH NEWTON	74	80	86	80	84	89	81	82	86	80	85	57	87	79	86	92	59	85	102	95
67118	NORWICH	81	73	73	76	75	87	72	82	75	65	73	62	67	76	72	79	50	75	84	95
67119	OXFORD	89	66	90	65	68	94	71	87	78	63	75	66	57	76	69	85	50	81	94	103
67120	PECK	92	98	86	100	96	99	89	94	89	89	89	72	92	91	92	90	62	90	93	110
67122	PIEDMONT	90	63	96	62	65	93	68	85	72	57	71	68	51	71	67	79	46	79	89	103
67123	POTWIN	96	96	79	98	89	102	96	94	98	91	97	75	96	99	94	100	67	96	104	115
67124	PRATT	80	69	82	68	70	86	70	80	75	66	73	60	64	73	70	80	50	77	86	94
67127	PROTECTION	82	59	84	57	61	86	64	79	71	56	69	60	51	70	62	78	46	74	86	94
67131	ROCK	79	72	71	75	74	85	71	80	73	64	72	61	66	75	71	78	49	74	83	93
67132	ROSALIA	85	78	70	75	76	80	74	78	76	76	76	57	69	79	70	79	52	76	79	93
67133	ROSE HILL	117	127	105	125	120	115	113	115	110	119	112	89	117	115	115	108	78	111	108	134
67134	SAWYER	93	64	103	64	67	99	71	89	74	58	73	73	52	73	71	81	48	83	94	109
67135	SEDGWICK	96	90	84	90	87	99	89	92	91	86	90	72	85	93	87	94	62	91	98	112
67137	SEVERY	91	65	101	64	68	97	71	87	74	59	73	71	53	72	71	80	47	82	93	107
67138	SHARON	81	56	89	56	58	85	62	77	64	50	64	63	45	63	61	70	41	72	81	95
67140	SOUTH HAVEN	86	59	95	59	62	91	66	82	69	53	68	68	48	67	66	75	44	77	87	101
67142	SPIVEY	84	60	90	61	63	89	66	80	68	54	67	66	50	67	65	74	44	75	85	98
67143	SUN CITY	94	65	104	65	68	100	72	90	75	58	74	74	53	73	72	82	48	84	95	110
67144	TOWANDA	101	92	82	89	90	94	87	92	90	91	90	67	83	94	83	93	62	89	93	110
67146	UDALL	87	80	79	84	82	93	79	88	81	72	80	67	73	82	79	85	54	82	91	103
67147	VALLEY CENTER	103	106	90	105	101	103	97	100	97	100	98	76	98	101	97	98	68	97	99	118
67149	VIOLA	90	101	87	104	98	99	90	94	89	91	89	73	96	91	95	89	62	90	93	111
67150	WALDRON	84	58	92	58	60	89	64	80	67	52	66	66	47	65	64	73	43	74	84	98
67151	WALTON	101	76	108	76	78	107	81	97	83	68	82	79	64	82	81	89	54	91	102	118
67152	WELLINGTON	83	70	76	70	69	86	74	81	78	68	76	62	66	78	71	83	52	79	88	96
67154	WHITEWATER	101	93	94	96	94	109	91	102	93	83	92	78	84	95	91	98	63	95	105	120
67155	WILMORE	79	54	86	54	57	83	60	75	62	49	62	62	44	61	60	68	40	70	79	92
67156	WINFIELD	82	73	78	73	73	86	75	81	78	70	77	62	69	78	74	82	52	79	87	96
67159	ZENDA	80	55	88	55	57	84	61	76	63	49	63	63	45	62	61	69	41	71	80	93
67202	WICHITA	39	30	34	33	30	35	47	38	50	42	50	29	42	44	41	53	35	46	51	49
67203	WICHITA	74	67	59	67	64	70	74	70	76	71	75	54	70	76	68	78	52	73	76	84
67204	WICHITA	81	79	71	79	77	83	79	81	81	76	81	60	78	82	78	84	56	80	86	95
67205	WICHITA	162	180	161	184	176	163	156	161	149	168	151	131	168	159	161	143	108	150	143	184
67206	WICHITA	134	142	138	145	142	136	136	134	133	142	135	103	143	135	139	131	95	134	133	156
67207	WICHITA	95	84	73	86	80	81	94	85	93	94	94	69	88	96	86	92	65	91	86	103
67208	WICHITA	78	69	62	72	66	72	83	72	82	76	81	58	76	81	73	82	57	78	78	89
67209	WICHITA	111	116	103	115	111	106	109	108	106	114	107	85	111	111	108	103	75	106	102	126
67210	WICHITA	87	71	60	72	66	64	87	74	85	86	87	62	78	90	76	82	62	83	71	89
67211	WICHITA	65	54	48	55	52	59	66	60	68	60	67	47	59	68	57	70	47	65	66	73
67212	WICHITA	100	103	91	104	99	99	100	98	99	101	100	77	102	102	99	98	70	98	98	115
67213	WICHITA	65	53	47	54	51	60	63	59	66	58	64	46	55	66	55	69	44	63	66	72
67214	WICHITA	52	42	38	42	40	47	50	47	54	49	53	35	46	53	44	57	37	51	54	57
67215	WICHITA	116	128	108	125	122	112	114	114	109	120	111	88	119	114	115	106	78	110	105	132
67216	WICHITA	83	72	66	71	69	77	76	76	78	75	77	58	69	80	70	80	53	77	79	91
67217	WICHITA	82	79	66	79	75	82	80	79	82	78	81	61	78	83	76	83	56	80	84	95
67218	WICHITA	68	64	56	65	61	66	71	65	73	67	72	52	68	72	66	74	50	70	72	80
67219	WICHITA	83	76	66	75	72	77	77	76	80	79	80	58	74	82	72	82	55	78	80	92
67220	WICHITA	100	104	91	104	99	94	100	97	97	104	99	76	102	100	99	95	69	97	94	113
67221	MCCONNELL AFB	97	50	38	58	45	43	91	63	86	85	90	63	69	103	66	79	63	81	57	77
67223	WICHITA	151	185	162	186	179	164	157	160	149	163	152	127	175	155	169	145	108	153	147	185
67226	WICHITA	131	137	124	142	133	121	134	126	127	140	129	103	138	133	132	121	93	126	116	147
67227	WICHITA	92	104	90	107	101	102	93	97	91	93	92	76	99	94	98	92	64	93	96	114
67228	WICHITA	158	191	165	197	186	157	159	161	146	179	149	134	180	159	167	134	110	147	131	179
67230	WICHITA	170	221	230	229	230	199	184	192	171	201	173	149	218	174	209	163	128	178	169	215
67232	WICHITA	110	101	89	97	98	103	95	101	99	99	99	73	90	103	91	101	67	98	101	120
67235	WICHITA	165	191	167	193	186	167	163	167	155	177	157	133	179	164	170	148	113	156	147	191
67301	INDEPENDENCE	77	64	66	65	64	77	70	74	73	64	71	56	62	74	66	77	49	73	80	88
67330	ALTAMONT	77	58	78	57	59	81	62	75	67	55	65	57	50	66	60	73	44	70	81	89
67332	BARTLETT	81	56	88	56	59	85	62	77	65	51	64	63	46	63	62	70	42	72	81	94
67333	CANEY	80	60	79	59	62	83	64	78	70	57	68	58	53	69	62	77	45	72	84	91
67335	CHERRYVALE	72	54	66	54	55	73	57	68	62	52	61	51	47	63	55	68	41	63	72	80
67336	CHETOPA	63	45	64	44	46	65	49	61	54	43	52	46	39	53	48	60	35	56	66	72
67337	COFFEYVILLE	70	57	66	57	57	72	61	68	65	56	64	51	53	64	59	70	43	66	74	81
67341	DENNIS	78	71	70	74	72	83	70	79	72	63	71	60	64	73	70	76	48	73	81	92
67342	EDNA	77	69	71	72	71	83	69	78	71	62	70	60	63	72	69	75	48	72	81	91
67344	ELK CITY	82	60	83	59	62	84	62	77	68	57	67	58	50	68	61	75	44	71	81	92
67345	ELK FALLS	78	54	85	53	56	82	59	74	62	48	61	60	44	61	59	68	40	69	78	90
67346	GRENOLA	84	60	86	58	62	85	62	78	68	57	67	59	49	68	61	75	44	72	82	93
67347	HAVANA	79	57	81	55	59	80	58	74	65	54	63	56	47	64	58	71	42	68	77	88
67349	HOWARD	72	52	73	50	54	75	56	70	62	50	60	53	45	61	55	69	40	65	76	82
67351	LIBERTY	89	81	81	85	83	96	80	91	83	73	81	69	74	84	80	88	55	84	93	105
67352	LONGTON	60	43	61	42	44	62	47	58	51	41	50	44	37	50	45	57	33	54	62	68
67353	MOLINE	76	55	77	53	57	80	60	74	67	53	64	55	48	65	58	73	43	69	80	87
67354	MOUND VALLEY	68	50	59	49	50	66	52	61	57	49	56	47	42	59	48	62	38	57	64	74
67355	NIOTAZE	71	51	72	49	52	72	52	66	58	48	57	50	42	57	51	63	37	61	69	78
67356	OSWEGO	69	52	69	51	53	72	55	67	61	49	59	51	45	60	54	66	39	63	73	79
67357	PARSONS	72	61	60	62	61	72	68	69	71	63	69	53	61	71	63	75	48	70	76	83
67360	PERU	71	51	73	49	53	72	53	67	58	49	57	50	42	58	52	64	38	61	70	79
67361	SEDAN	74	53	75	52	55	77	57	71	64	51	62	54	46	63	56	70	41	66	77	84
67401	SALINA	83	80	73	81	77	83	83	81	84	80	83	63	81	85	80	85	58	82	86	97
67410	ABILENE	83	69	80	69	69	87	72	81	76	65	75	62	63	76	71	81	50	78	88	97
67416	ASSARIA	93	85	81	83	84	91	81	87	83	81	83	65	76	86	79	86	57	84	88	104
67417	AURORA	82	57	90	56	59	87	63	78	65	51	65	64	46	64	62	71	42	73	82	96
67418	BARNARD	76	52	83	52	55	80	58	72	60	47	60	60	42	59	58	66	39	67	76	89
67420	BELOIT	88	66	95	66	69	95	70	86	74	60	73	68	56	73	71	81	48	81	92	104
67422	BENNINGTON	83	75	75	78	77	89	74	84	77	67	75	64	68	78	74	81	51	77	86	98
67423	BEVERLY	78	54	86	54	56	82	60	74	62	48	61	61	44	61	59	68	40	69	78	91
67425	BROOKVILLE	103	72	113	72	75	109	80	98	83	65	82	81	59	81	79	90	53	92	104	121
67427	BUSHTON	94	65	103	64	68	99	72	89	75	58	74	74	53	73	71	81	48	83	94	110
67428	CANTON	95	69	86	68	70	94	72	86	78	67	77	67	58	80	68	85	51	81	90	104
67430	CAWKER CITY	78	56	78	55	58	82	61	76	69	55	66	57	49	67	59	76	44	71	83	89
67431	CHAPMAN	83	77	83	77	76	92	76	83	79	70	78	65	72	78	77	84	53	81	92	100
67432	CLAY CENTER	77	60	80	59	62	81	64	76	69	58	68	57	55	68	63	75	45	72	82	89
67436	DELPHOS	90	62	99	62	65	95	69	86	72	56	71	71	50	70	69	78	46	80	90	105
	KANSAS	98	90	91	91	89	97	94	95	94	90	94	74	88	96	90	96	65	95	98	113
	UNITED STATES	100	100	100	100	100	100	100	100	100	100	100	100	100	100	100	100	100	100	100	100

POPULATION CHANGE

ZIP CODE #	POST OFFICE NAME	COUNTY FIPS CODE	POPULATION 2000	POPULATION 2009	POPULATION 2014	2000-2009 ANNUAL RATE % Rate	2000-2009 ANNUAL RATE State Centile	HOUSEHOLDS 2000	HOUSEHOLDS 2009	HOUSEHOLDS 2014	HOUSEHOLDS % Annual Rate 2000-2009	HOUSEHOLDS 2009 Average HH Size	FAMILIES 2000	FAMILIES 2009	FAMILIES % Annual Rate 2000-2009
67437	DOWNS	141	1248	1111	1038	-1.2	14	560	506	475	-1.1	2.09	336	300	-1.2
67438	DURHAM	115	309	287	275	-0.8	28	126	117	112	-0.8	2.45	89	83	-0.8
67439	ELLSWORTH	053	3581	3545	3507	-0.1	59	1230	1231	1220	0.0	2.26	806	798	-0.1
67441	ENTERPRISE	041	1123	1098	1076	-0.2	56	413	412	406	0.0	2.57	302	299	-0.1
67442	FALUN	169	260	279	288	0.8	86	107	116	120	0.9	2.40	82	88	0.8
67443	GALVA	113	1539	1589	1588	0.3	74	548	571	572	0.4	2.78	455	472	0.4
67444	GENESEO	159	536	522	506	-0.3	52	242	239	232	-0.1	2.18	171	167	-0.3
67445	GLASCO	029	686	591	550	-1.6	8	295	254	236	-1.6	2.20	196	167	-1.7
67446	GLEN ELDER	123	626	574	545	-0.9	23	262	248	238	-0.6	2.31	175	164	-0.7
67447	GREEN	027	360	362	364	0.1	68	136	140	142	0.3	2.57	107	110	0.3
67448	GYPSUM	169	1319	1379	1402	0.5	79	492	516	524	0.5	2.67	384	399	0.4
67449	HERINGTON	127	3289	3207	3147	-0.3	52	1410	1392	1369	-0.1	2.25	879	856	-0.3
67450	HOLYROOD	053	598	583	574	-0.3	52	267	262	258	-0.2	2.22	190	185	-0.3
67451	HOPE	041	1068	1064	1049	0.0	64	443	449	445	0.1	2.37	327	328	0.0
67452	HUNTER	123	132	107	98	-2.2	2	65	54	50	-2.0	1.98	45	38	-1.8
67454	KANOPOLIS	053	665	654	645	-0.2	56	296	299	297	0.1	2.19	190	190	0.0
67455	LINCOLN	105	1906	1901	1863	0.0	64	834	839	823	0.1	2.18	532	531	0.0
67456	LINDSBORG	113	4444	4496	4484	0.1	68	1660	1692	1690	0.2	2.32	1105	1114	0.1
67457	LITTLE RIVER	159	879	811	772	-0.9	23	321	295	280	-0.9	2.58	233	212	-1.0
67458	LONGFORD	027	280	273	271	-0.3	52	116	116	116	0.0	2.35	89	89	0.0
67459	LORRAINE	053	273	267	263	-0.2	56	97	96	94	-0.1	2.78	69	67	-0.3
67460	MCPHERSON	113	16015	16373	16417	0.2	70	6159	6362	6392	0.4	2.46	4291	4391	0.2
67464	MARQUETTE	113	1015	1023	1012	0.1	68	410	421	417	0.3	2.33	282	287	0.2
67466	MILTONVALE	029	740	661	624	-1.2	14	317	285	269	-1.1	2.26	202	181	-1.2
67467	MINNEAPOLIS	143	3132	3005	2919	-0.4	48	1246	1200	1164	-0.4	2.35	836	794	-0.6
67468	MORGANVILLE	027	370	371	372	0.0	64	132	135	137	0.2	2.75	105	107	0.2
67470	NEW CAMBRIA	169	542	554	559	0.2	70	210	218	221	0.4	2.53	164	169	0.3
67473	OSBORNE	141	2075	1863	1754	-1.2	14	879	802	756	-1.0	2.25	544	490	-1.1
67474	PORTIS	141	216	196	186	-1.0	19	94	86	82	-1.0	2.14	60	54	-1.1
67475	RAMONA	115	189	179	173	-0.6	36	76	72	70	-0.6	2.49	58	55	-0.6
67476	ROXBURY	113	25	27	27	0.8	86	11	12	12	0.9	2.25	9	10	1.1
67478	SIMPSON	123	168	155	147	-0.9	23	67	63	60	-0.7	2.44	44	41	-0.8
67480	SOLOMON	143	1732	1837	1842	0.6	82	674	717	721	0.7	2.54	511	539	0.6
67481	SYLVAN GROVE	105	966	913	888	-0.6	36	404	389	381	-0.4	2.35	291	279	-0.5
67482	TALMAGE	041	108	111	110	0.3	74	44	46	46	0.5	2.39	36	37	0.3
67483	TAMPA	115	364	339	325	-0.8	28	136	127	122	-0.7	2.67	98	91	-0.8
67484	TESCOTT	143	1015	1019	1007	0.0	64	382	383	378	0.0	2.66	284	282	-0.1
67485	TIPTON	123	384	313	288	-2.2	2	162	136	126	-1.9	2.30	113	93	-2.1
67487	WAKEFIELD	027	1263	1219	1209	-0.4	48	480	473	471	-0.2	2.52	353	345	-0.2
67490	WILSON	053	1027	999	982	-0.3	52	429	424	418	-0.1	2.21	276	269	-0.3
67491	WINDOM	113	395	391	384	-0.1	59	155	155	153	0.0	2.52	122	121	-0.1
67492	WOODBINE	041	328	316	309	-0.4	48	127	125	123	-0.2	2.53	92	90	-0.2
67501	HUTCHINSON	155	27621	26350	25855	-0.5	41	10534	10093	9906	-0.5	2.37	6577	6217	-0.6
67502	HUTCHINSON	155	23337	23565	23489	0.1	68	9530	9801	9815	0.3	2.35	6789	6899	0.2
67505	SOUTH HUTCHINSON	155	2514	2418	2375	-0.4	48	1129	1106	1093	-0.2	2.06	674	648	-0.4
67510	ABBYVILLE	155	426	396	386	-0.8	28	160	151	148	-0.6	2.62	122	114	-0.7
67511	ALBERT	009	283	271	266	-0.5	41	119	117	115	-0.2	2.32	87	84	-0.4
67512	ALDEN	159	260	251	242	-0.4	48	107	104	100	-0.3	2.41	82	79	-0.4
67513	ALEXANDER	165	139	117	108	-1.8	6	60	51	48	-1.7	2.29	40	34	-1.7
67514	ARLINGTON	155	754	725	712	-0.4	48	313	302	297	-0.4	2.40	220	209	-0.6
67516	BAZINE	135	441	373	344	-1.8	6	212	185	172	-1.5	2.02	140	121	-1.6
67518	BEELER	135	70	60	56	-1.7	7	29	25	24	-1.6	2.32	19	16	-1.8
67519	BELPRE	047	223	198	186	-1.3	12	94	82	77	-1.5	2.41	69	61	-1.3
67520	BISON	165	319	310	298	-0.3	52	129	127	123	-0.2	2.44	85	83	-0.3
67521	BROWNELL	135	142	120	111	-1.8	6	60	52	49	-1.5	2.31	40	34	-1.7
67522	BUHLER	155	1980	1915	1881	-0.4	48	700	688	679	-0.2	2.67	563	549	-0.3
67523	BURDETT	145	338	272	249	-2.3	1	142	115	106	-2.3	2.37	104	84	-2.3
67524	CHASE	159	707	626	589	-1.3	12	275	244	231	-1.3	2.57	197	174	-1.3
67525	CLAFLIN	009	1281	1229	1205	-0.4	48	491	478	470	-0.3	2.57	354	342	-0.4
67526	ELLINWOOD	009	2753	2682	2641	-0.3	52	1125	1113	1101	-0.1	2.35	763	747	-0.2
67529	GARFIELD	145	332	267	244	-2.3	1	132	107	98	-2.2	2.50	98	79	-2.3
67530	GREAT BEND	009	19351	18929	18677	-0.2	56	7814	7741	7672	-0.1	2.36	5094	4994	-0.2
67543	HAVEN	155	2027	2154	2173	0.7	84	774	833	843	0.8	2.59	581	618	0.7
67544	HOISINGTON	009	3711	3605	3543	-0.3	52	1546	1525	1508	-0.1	2.30	1011	987	-0.3
67545	HUDSON	185	311	283	271	-1.0	19	135	124	120	-0.9	2.28	94	86	-1.0
67546	INMAN	113	2601	2654	2667	0.2	70	951	984	993	0.4	2.61	730	747	0.2
67547	KINSLEY	047	2012	1868	1787	-0.8	28	899	842	806	-0.7	2.15	540	502	-0.8
67548	LA CROSSE	165	1475	1476	1448	0.0	64	629	641	631	0.2	2.17	408	411	0.1
67550	LARNED	145	6301	5799	5516	-0.9	23	2357	2162	2042	-0.9	2.26	1506	1369	-1.0
67552	LEWIS	047	770	685	646	-1.3	12	287	253	238	-1.4	2.71	213	187	-1.4
67553	LIEBENTHAL	165	211	178	165	-1.8	6	89	76	70	-1.7	2.34	59	50	-1.8
67554	LYONS	159	4622	4388	4218	-0.6	36	1851	1754	1683	-0.6	2.44	1274	1195	-0.7
67556	MC CRACKEN	165	304	256	237	-1.8	6	145	124	115	-1.7	2.06	96	81	-1.8
67557	MACKSVILLE	185	770	708	683	-0.9	23	288	266	256	-0.9	2.66	209	191	-1.0
67559	NEKOMA	165	65	55	51	-1.8	6	31	27	25	-1.5	2.04	20	17	-1.7
67560	NESS CITY	135	1977	1789	1682	-1.1	17	873	817	775	-0.7	2.13	556	515	-0.8
67561	NICKERSON	155	1664	1606	1582	-0.4	48	630	620	614	-0.2	2.58	487	475	-0.3
67563	OFFERLE	047	404	372	356	-0.9	23	163	150	143	-0.9	2.48	126	115	-1.0
67564	OLMITZ	009	315	298	292	-0.6	36	124	118	116	-0.5	2.53	93	88	-0.6
67565	OTIS	165	590	551	525	-0.7	32	256	243	233	-0.6	2.27	169	159	-0.7
67566	PARTRIDGE	155	689	731	739	0.6	82	234	250	253	0.7	2.92	187	199	0.7
67567	PAWNEE ROCK	009	544	521	512	-0.5	41	189	185	183	-0.2	2.82	138	134	-0.3
67568	PLEVNA	155	287	265	257	-0.9	23	129	121	118	-0.7	2.19	98	90	-0.9
67570	PRETTY PRAIRIE	155	1175	1243	1253	0.6	82	471	505	510	0.8	2.46	357	378	0.6
67572	RANSOM	135	479	411	379	-1.6	8	199	174	162	-1.4	2.28	130	113	-1.5
67573	RAYMOND	159	211	203	196	-0.4	48	91	88	85	-0.4	2.31	70	67	-0.5
67574	ROZEL	145	262	211	193	-2.3	1	108	88	80	-2.2	2.40	79	64	-2.3
67575	RUSH CENTER	165	447	377	349	-1.8	6	208	178	166	-1.7	2.12	137	116	-1.8
67576	SAINT JOHN	185	2197	2027	1955	-0.9	23	920	854	825	-0.8	2.34	590	543	-0.9
67578	STAFFORD	185	1496	1408	1366	-0.7	32	661	628	611	-0.6	2.16	398	374	-0.7
67579	STERLING	159	3284	3142	3053	-0.5	41	1056	1009	973	-0.5	2.39	728	689	-0.6
67581	SYLVIA	155	513	466	449	-1.0	19	205	188	182	-0.9	2.48	144	130	-1.1
67583	TURON	155	1186	1134	1109	-0.5	41	491	474	466	-0.4	2.39	353	337	-0.5
67584	UTICA	135	345	296	274	-1.6	8	143	125	116	-1.4	2.28	93	81	-1.5
67601	HAYS	051	23329	23125	23082	-0.1	59	9474	9622	9678	0.2	2.29	5592	5611	0.0
	KANSAS					0.6					0.6	2.49			0.5
	UNITED STATES					1.0					1.1	2.59			0.9

ZIP CODE #	POST OFFICE NAME	RACE (%) White 2000	White 2009	Black 2000	Black 2009	Asian/Pacific 2000	Asian/Pacific 2009	% Hispanic Origin 2000	% Hispanic Origin 2009	2009 AGE DISTRIBUTION (%) 0-4	5-9	10-14	15-19	20-24	25-44	45-64	65-84	85+	18+	MEDIAN AGE 2009	% 2009 Males	% 2009 Females
67437	DOWNS	99.0	98.6	0.0	0.0	0.2	0.4	0.4	0.5	4.9	5.0	5.0	5.2	6.6	19.4	28.6	18.5	6.9	81.8	47.9	48.8	51.2
67438	DURHAM	96.4	95.1	0.0	0.0	0.0	0.0	3.9	5.2	8.7	8.4	8.4	8.0	3.8	23.0	25.1	12.2	2.4	69.3	36.9	54.7	45.3
67439	ELLSWORTH	90.1	89.8	6.3	6.5	0.4	0.5	3.6	3.8	4.2	4.4	5.2	6.1	7.5	27.2	26.1	14.7	4.5	82.6	41.4	56.5	43.5
67441	ENTERPRISE	96.9	96.8	0.2	0.2	0.1	0.1	1.5	1.5	5.6	5.9	6.6	6.8	4.6	22.8	28.9	14.6	4.2	77.1	43.3	48.4	51.6
67442	FALUN	97.3	97.1	0.0	0.0	0.4	0.4	5.0	7.5	7.2	6.1	7.5	9.3	3.2	26.9	28.0	11.5	0.4	72.4	39.6	51.3	48.7
67443	GALVA	97.8	97.3	0.1	0.1	0.5	0.6	0.8	1.3	6.9	7.4	7.9	7.0	4.5	24.4	29.8	10.9	1.2	73.3	39.1	50.7	49.3
67444	GENESEO	98.3	97.9	0.0	0.0	0.2	0.2	1.7	2.3	3.6	4.4	4.8	5.6	4.4	20.3	35.8	18.0	3.1	83.9	49.0	50.2	49.8
67445	GLASCO	98.8	98.5	0.0	0.0	0.1	0.3	0.1	0.2	4.2	4.6	5.1	5.8	4.2	18.1	30.6	20.1	7.3	82.1	50.3	50.6	49.4
67446	GLEN ELDER	97.8	97.2	0.3	0.3	0.3	0.5	0.6	1.2	4.9	4.9	5.4	5.6	5.7	18.8	31.0	20.2	3.5	81.7	47.9	49.8	50.2
67447	GREEN	98.1	96.7	0.6	0.6	0.0	0.3	1.1	1.7	5.0	5.5	6.1	6.9	4.4	21.8	33.7	14.1	2.5	78.7	45.2	50.6	49.4
67448	GYPSUM	97.5	96.9	0.4	0.4	0.4	0.4	1.0	1.5	5.4	6.0	7.3	7.1	4.3	21.7	32.6	13.6	2.1	76.9	43.8	51.5	48.5
67449	HERINGTON	95.8	95.6	0.9	0.9	0.5	0.5	3.7	4.1	5.6	5.3	5.7	6.5	5.5	21.2	27.3	17.8	5.1	79.3	45.1	48.2	51.8
67450	HOLYROOD	98.0	97.9	0.5	0.5	0.0	0.0	2.0	2.1	4.6	5.1	5.7	6.9	5.1	20.1	34.0	15.3	3.3	80.1	46.3	50.6	49.4
67451	HOPE	98.1	98.1	0.3	0.3	0.3	0.3	0.6	0.6	4.4	5.0	5.6	7.4	4.6	20.5	34.6	14.9	2.9	80.4	46.3	52.3	47.7
67452	HUNTER	99.2	99.1	0.0	0.0	0.0	0.0	0.0	0.0	3.7	4.7	5.6	7.5	5.6	17.8	34.6	17.8	2.8	82.2	47.8	49.5	50.5
67454	KANOPOLIS	96.1	95.9	0.3	0.3	0.2	0.2	10.4	11.0	3.2	3.5	4.1	6.1	6.1	21.7	33.6	18.2	3.4	85.5	48.1	50.3	49.7
67455	LINCOLN	98.0	97.7	0.2	0.2	0.2	0.3	1.0	1.5	5.7	5.9	5.9	5.4	4.8	20.1	27.6	18.4	6.2	79.1	46.6	47.2	52.8
67456	LINDSBORG	97.1	96.6	0.9	1.0	0.3	0.4	1.8	2.8	5.2	5.0	5.4	10.1	11.1	20.7	25.1	13.2	4.4	79.9	38.4	49.5	50.5
67457	LITTLE RIVER	97.4	96.7	0.0	0.0	0.0	0.0	1.7	2.6	6.7	7.2	7.3	7.2	3.5	22.6	26.0	14.2	5.5	74.6	41.6	47.6	52.4
67458	LONGFORD	98.2	98.2	0.4	0.4	0.0	0.0	0.7	1.1	6.6	7.0	7.3	6.6	3.7	22.0	30.0	14.3	2.6	74.7	42.6	53.5	46.5
67459	LORRAINE	98.2	98.1	0.4	0.4	0.0	0.0	1.8	1.9	4.9	5.2	5.6	6.7	4.9	20.2	33.7	15.4	3.4	79.8	46.3	50.6	49.4
67460	MCPHERSON	95.4	94.3	1.2	1.3	0.5	0.8	2.6	3.9	6.4	6.3	6.4	7.5	7.9	23.8	26.4	12.4	2.9	76.8	37.6	48.7	51.3
67464	MARQUETTE	98.7	98.6	0.0	0.0	0.1	0.1	0.7	1.0	4.8	5.5	6.0	6.1	4.0	22.2	31.7	15.2	4.7	79.8	45.9	50.4	49.6
67466	MILTONVALE	98.5	98.3	0.1	0.2	0.1	0.2	1.1	1.5	4.2	4.1	4.7	6.7	6.8	21.0	29.2	17.1	6.2	82.5	46.6	49.9	50.1
67467	MINNEAPOLIS	97.3	97.2	0.9	0.9	0.1	0.1	1.4	1.5	5.3	5.5	6.0	6.7	4.9	22.0	28.2	15.9	5.6	78.9	44.7	48.7	51.3
67468	MORGANVILLE	97.8	96.8	0.5	0.5	0.0	0.3	1.1	1.3	4.9	5.4	5.9	7.0	4.6	22.1	34.5	13.5	2.2	79.0	45.1	51.2	48.8
67470	NEW CAMBRIA	93.7	92.6	2.4	2.3	0.6	0.7	2.8	4.0	5.4	6.1	6.7	7.6	4.9	21.3	34.3	12.5	1.3	76.9	43.6	51.6	48.4
67473	OSBORNE	98.2	97.8	0.1	0.1	0.2	0.4	0.2	0.4	5.0	5.2	5.7	7.1	5.4	18.5	29.9	17.2	6.0	79.3	46.8	48.1	51.9
67474	PORTIS	98.1	97.4	0.5	0.5	0.0	0.5	0.5	0.0	4.6	5.1	5.6	6.1	4.1	18.4	30.6	17.9	7.7	80.6	48.8	46.9	53.1
67475	RAMONA	96.8	96.1	0.0	0.0	0.0	0.0	3.2	4.5	6.7	6.7	6.7	6.1	4.5	20.1	31.3	15.1	2.8	76.0	44.3	50.3	49.7
67476	ROXBURY	100.0	100.0	0.0	0.0	0.0	0.0	0.0	0.0	7.4	7.4	7.4	7.4	7.4	25.9	29.6	7.4	0.0	70.4	36.3	48.1	51.9
67478	SIMPSON	98.2	98.1	0.0	0.0	0.6	0.6	1.2	1.3	4.5	5.8	5.8	7.1	3.9	24.5	30.3	14.8	3.2	80.0	43.9	54.2	45.8
67480	SOLOMON	98.2	98.0	0.1	0.1	0.2	0.2	1.7	1.9	6.4	7.0	7.6	8.1	4.7	22.5	29.5	12.5	1.7	73.0	41.2	51.1	48.9
67481	SYLVAN GROVE	98.9	98.8	0.0	0.0	0.0	0.0	0.8	1.3	4.2	4.7	5.1	6.1	5.0	19.3	35.3	17.2	3.1	82.3	48.1	51.6	48.4
67482	TALMAGE	96.3	96.4	0.0	0.0	0.9	0.9	0.9	1.8	5.4	7.2	7.2	7.2	4.5	23.4	30.6	12.6	1.8	75.7	41.6	49.5	50.5
67483	TAMPA	96.4	95.3	0.0	0.0	0.0	0.0	3.6	5.3	8.3	8.3	8.0	7.4	3.8	22.7	25.7	13.3	2.7	70.8	38.3	54.0	46.0
67484	TESCOTT	96.5	96.3	0.4	0.4	0.2	0.2	1.7	2.1	6.2	6.8	7.0	6.7	4.7	22.9	31.2	12.9	1.8	75.8	42.0	52.5	47.5
67485	TIPTON	99.2	99.0	0.0	0.0	0.0	0.0	0.3	0.6	4.5	4.5	5.8	7.3	5.1	18.5	34.5	16.9	2.9	80.5	47.2	51.1	48.9
67487	WAKEFIELD	97.0	96.6	0.7	0.7	0.1	0.1	1.0	1.6	6.7	6.6	6.6	6.8	5.9	24.2	27.9	12.2	3.0	75.4	40.3	52.4	47.6
67490	WILSON	99.0	99.0	0.0	0.0	0.0	0.0	1.2	1.2	5.1	5.2	6.9	7.4	4.8	18.4	27.9	18.4	5.8	77.7	46.4	47.5	52.5
67491	WINDOM	98.0	97.4	0.3	0.3	0.3	0.5	0.5	0.5	5.6	5.9	6.9	6.6	4.1	22.3	33.8	13.0	1.8	77.5	44.0	50.1	49.9
67492	WOODBINE	97.9	97.8	0.0	0.0	0.3	0.3	0.6	0.6	5.7	6.6	6.6	7.0	5.1	21.2	32.3	13.9	1.6	76.6	43.6	51.9	48.1
67501	HUTCHINSON	85.7	82.5	5.5	5.9	0.5	0.7	9.7	13.9	7.0	6.5	6.4	7.3	8.5	28.7	24.0	10.0	1.7	76.3	34.7	53.4	46.6
67502	HUTCHINSON	95.5	94.1	1.3	1.5	0.7	1.0	2.8	4.4	5.5	5.6	6.1	6.2	5.0	21.5	29.5	16.3	4.3	78.9	45.1	47.7	52.3
67505	SOUTH HUTCHINSON	94.0	91.7	0.8	0.9	0.2	0.3	5.0	7.6	6.3	5.8	5.5	5.2	4.3	21.8	24.9	18.0	8.3	79.2	46.0	46.2	53.8
67510	ABBYVILLE	98.6	98.5	0.0	0.0	0.0	0.0	0.2	0.3	6.8	7.6	7.3	5.6	3.0	19.7	31.8	16.7	1.5	74.7	45.0	52.5	47.5
67511	ALBERT	98.6	98.2	0.0	0.0	0.0	0.0	1.1	2.2	5.2	5.9	8.9	9.2	3.3	22.1	30.6	13.7	1.1	73.1	42.0	50.2	49.8
67512	ALDEN	97.3	96.8	0.0	0.0	0.4	0.4	2.7	4.0	6.4	7.2	7.2	6.4	3.6	21.9	29.9	14.7	2.8	74.5	42.5	51.0	49.0
67513	ALEXANDER	99.3	99.1	0.0	0.0	0.0	0.0	0.7	0.9	3.4	4.3	5.1	6.8	4.3	17.1	34.2	20.5	4.3	83.8	49.4	52.1	47.9
67514	ARLINGTON	97.3	96.6	0.7	0.7	0.0	0.0	1.5	2.1	6.1	6.8	7.4	7.6	4.1	19.9	29.4	15.7	3.0	75.0	43.3	50.1	49.9
67516	BAZINE	97.7	97.1	0.0	0.0	0.0	0.0	1.6	2.4	3.8	4.3	4.8	6.2	3.8	18.5	36.5	19.3	2.9	83.4	49.5	52.8	47.2
67518	BEELER	100.0	100.0	0.0	0.0	0.0	0.0	0.0	0.0	5.0	6.7	6.7	6.7	3.3	18.3	31.7	15.0	6.7	75.0	46.7	50.0	50.0
67519	BELPRE	85.7	80.3	0.4	0.5	0.0	0.0	18.8	26.3	7.1	7.1	7.6	6.1	4.0	24.7	26.8	14.6	2.0	74.2	40.4	51.0	49.0
67520	BISON	98.1	97.7	0.9	1.0	0.0	0.0	1.3	1.6	6.5	6.5	6.5	5.8	5.8	20.3	29.4	16.5	2.9	77.4	43.9	49.0	51.0
67521	BROWNELL	98.6	97.5	0.0	0.0	0.0	0.0	1.4	2.5	4.2	4.2	4.2	6.7	3.3	19.2	35.8	19.2	3.3	84.2	49.5	53.3	46.7
67522	BUHLER	98.2	97.8	0.2	0.2	0.1	0.1	1.5	2.3	6.4	6.8	7.5	7.7	5.2	21.7	28.8	11.4	4.5	74.0	41.1	47.8	52.2
67523	BURDETT	97.6	97.1	0.3	0.4	0.0	0.0	1.8	2.6	6.6	7.4	7.4	5.9	4.0	20.6	30.1	15.4	2.6	74.3	43.4	49.6	50.4
67524	CHASE	96.0	94.6	0.0	0.0	0.0	0.0	5.0	7.3	8.0	8.1	7.7	7.3	5.0	21.2	26.7	13.9	2.1	71.4	39.4	48.4	51.6
67525	CLAFLIN	98.8	98.4	0.2	0.2	0.4	0.6	1.1	2.0	5.9	6.5	7.1	8.3	5.0	20.5	29.9	14.2	2.5	74.6	42.4	50.1	49.9
67526	ELLINWOOD	97.2	96.3	0.2	0.2	0.0	0.0	1.7	2.9	6.2	6.5	6.7	6.3	5.4	20.4	29.3	15.0	4.1	76.5	43.6	47.6	52.4
67529	GARFIELD	97.9	97.0	0.3	0.4	0.0	0.0	1.8	2.6	6.4	7.1	7.9	6.4	3.7	21.3	30.0	14.6	2.6	74.2	42.8	50.2	49.8
67530	GREAT BEND	91.1	88.4	1.4	1.5	0.3	0.5	11.2	15.7	6.6	6.4	6.6	7.8	6.6	22.9	26.3	13.8	3.1	76.2	39.1	48.6	51.4
67543	HAVEN	97.7	97.0	0.2	0.2	0.1	0.3	1.1	1.7	6.7	7.3	7.3	6.9	5.2	23.9	28.8	12.0	1.8	74.3	39.1	50.4	49.6
67544	HOISINGTON	95.9	94.6	1.0	1.2	0.1	0.1	3.0	5.0	5.8	6.0	6.4	6.9	5.1	22.2	28.2	15.5	4.0	77.6	43.0	48.2	51.8
67545	HUDSON	98.1	97.9	0.0	0.0	0.0	0.0	1.6	2.1	5.7	6.0	6.7	6.4	4.9	19.1	33.6	15.9	1.8	77.4	45.6	52.3	47.7
67546	INMAN	98.4	98.0	0.2	0.2	0.0	0.0	0.9	1.5	5.8	6.2	7.0	7.6	4.9	22.3	27.4	13.3	5.6	75.9	42.3	49.4	50.6
67547	KINSLEY	95.0	93.1	0.4	0.4	0.4	0.5	6.8	10.0	5.5	5.9	5.8	5.7	5.4	21.4	28.2	17.8	4.4	79.6	45.3	48.8	51.2
67548	LA CROSSE	98.3	98.0	0.3	0.3	0.1	0.2	1.3	1.9	5.4	5.4	5.5	5.6	5.0	20.8	27.1	18.0	7.2	80.3	46.9	47.5	52.5
67550	LARNED	90.0	88.0	5.7	6.6	0.6	0.7	4.5	6.4	5.4	5.5	6.2	7.9	5.9	23.6	27.0	14.7	3.7	77.5	41.4	53.9	46.1
67552	LEWIS	87.5	82.6	0.3	0.3	0.1	0.1	16.0	22.6	6.9	7.3	7.4	6.6	4.4	24.2	27.3	13.6	2.3	74.2	40.2	50.8	49.2
67553	LIEBENTHAL	99.1	98.9	0.0	0.0	0.0	0.0	0.5	0.6	3.9	3.9	5.1	6.7	3.9	16.9	36.0	19.7	3.9	82.6	49.7	53.9	46.1
67554	LYONS	92.2	90.1	1.7	1.8	0.4	0.5	10.2	14.6	6.7	6.9	6.7	6.4	5.5	21.9	26.3	15.9	3.8	75.6	41.4	48.5	51.5
67556	MC CRACKEN	99.0	98.8	0.0	0.0	0.0	0.0	0.3	0.4	3.5	4.3	4.7	6.6	4.3	16.4	36.7	19.5	3.9	83.2	50.0	53.5	46.5
67557	MACKSVILLE	89.4	85.3	0.1	0.1	0.1	0.3	13.0	18.6	6.6	7.2	7.2	6.8	4.8	22.3	29.4	13.4	2.3	74.7	41.4	51.3	48.7
67559	NEKOMA	100.0	100.0	0.0	0.0	0.0	0.0	0.0	0.0	3.6	3.6	3.6	5.5	3.6	18.2	38.2	20.0	3.6	83.6	49.6	52.7	47.3
67560	NESS CITY	98.0	97.4	0.1	0.1	0.1	0.1	2.0	2.9	5.6	6.3	6.4	5.5	4.2	19.1	30.6	16.7	5.6	77.6	46.6	50.0	50.0
67561	NICKERSON	96.8	96.0	0.4	0.4	0.1	0.1	2.4	3.8	7.0	7.4	7.5	6.2	5.4	23.4	30.2	11.2	1.7	74.0	39.9	50.4	49.6
67563	OFFERLE	96.0	93.8	0.0	0.0	0.5	0.5	4.5	7.0	5.6	6.5	6.7	7.0	4.6	21.5	32.5	13.4	2.2	76.9	43.5	54.3	45.7
67564	OLMITZ	96.8	96.0	1.0	1.3	0.0	0.0	1.0	1.7	5.4	5.0	7.7	9.4	3.4	22.8	29.9	14.8	1.7	75.8	42.8	52.7	47.3
67565	OTIS	98.0	97.6	0.7	0.7	0.2	0.2	1.2	1.5	6.0	6.0	6.0	6.0	5.3	20.5	29.6	17.6	3.1	78.4	45.2	49.2	50.8
67566	PARTRIDGE	95.6	94.4	0.7	0.8	0.1	0.3	1.2	1.9	7.9	8.5	8.5	7.5	4.5	22.8	26.0	12.6	1.6	70.2	37.2	49.4	50.6
67567	PAWNEE ROCK	98.7	98.3	0.0	0.0	0.0	0.0	1.3	2.1	5.4	6.0	9.0	9.2	3.6	21.9	30.5	13.2	1.2	72.7	41.6	50.3	49.7
67568	PLEVNA	99.0	98.5	0.0	0.0	0.0	0.0	0.0	0.0	6.8	7.5	7.5	5.7	3.0	18.9	31.7	17.4	1.5	74.0	45.4	52.5	47.5
67570	PRETTY PRAIRIE	97.8	97.0	0.1	0.2	0.3	0.4	1.4	2.3	5.1	5.6	6.4	7.9	5.3	21.6	32.2	13.6	2.4	78.0	43.7	52.9	47.1
67572	RANSOM	99.0	98.8	0.0	0.0	0.0	0.0	0.4	0.5	4.9	5.6	6.1	6.6	3.9	18.5	30.9	18.0	5.6	78.6	47.5	49.6	50.4
67573	RAYMOND	97.2	96.1	0.0	0.0	0.5	0.5	2.4	3.9	5.9	6.9	7.4	6.9	3.4	21.7	29.1	15.8	3.0	74.9	42.8	50.2	49.8
67574	ROZEL	97.3	96.2	0.4	0.5	0.0	0.0	1.9	2.8	6.6	7.6	7.1	5.7	3.8	21.3	29.9	15.6	2.4	74.9	43.1	49.3	50.7
67575	RUSH CENTER	98.7	98.1	0.0	0.0	0.2	0.3	1.1	1.6	3.7	4.2	5.0	6.1	3.7	20.4	30.8	22.0	4.0	83.0	48.5	49.9	50.1
67576	SAINT JOHN	95.4	93.8	0.2	0.2	0.2	0.2	4.9	7.2	6.2	6.2	6.5	6.8	5.7	20.9	28.7	15.3	3.7	76.4	43.1	49.9	50.1
67578	STAFFORD	96.5	95.5	0.1	0.1	0.0	0.0	3.1	4.5	5.2	5.5	5.7	6.4	5.9	18.0	29.0	18.1	6.3	79.3	47.2	47.8	52.2
67579	STERLING	95.9	94.8	1.3	1.4	0.6	0.8	1.8	2.7	4.9	5.1	5.3	14.1	18.2	18.5	20.8	11.1	1.9	81.2	27.3	47.7	52.3
67581	SYLVIA	97.9	97.2	0.0	0.0	0.4	0.6	1.2	1.7	5.2	5.4	6.2	7.7	4.7	20.4	32.2	15.2	3.0	78.1	45.2	51.9	48.1
67583	TURON	96.2	94.9	0.2	0.2	0.1	0.2	3.3	5.0	6.1	6.7	6.8	6.7	4.4	21.1	30.3	15.3	2.6	76.2	43.6	51.0	49.0
67584	UTICA	99.4	99.3	0.0	0.0	0.0	0.0	0.3	0.0	5.1	5.7	6.4	6.8	4.1	18.9	29.4	17.6	6.1	77.4	46.7	48.3	51.7
67601	HAYS	95.6	94.2	0.8	0.8	1.0	1.4	2.6	3.8	5.8	5.2	5.4	9.4	14.5	23.7	22.6	11.0	2.4	79.7	32.1	49.1	50.9
	KANSAS	86.1	83.7	5.7	5.9	1.8	2.6	7.0	9.4	7.1	6.9	6.9	7.3	7.3	25.9	25.7	10.7	2.2	75.0	36.3	49.6	50.4
	UNITED STATES	75.1	72.0	12.3	12.7	3.8	4.6	12.5	15.7	6.8	6.7	6.6	7.1	6.9	27.0	26.0	10.9	1.9	75.7	36.9	49.2	50.8

INCOME

ZIP CODE #	POST OFFICE NAME	2009 Per Capita Income	2009 HH Income Base	2009 Household Income Distribution (%): Less than $25,000	$25,000 to $49,999	$50,000 to $99,999	$100,000 to $149,999	$150,000 or More	Median Household Income: 2009	2014	2009 National Centile	2009 State Centile	2009 Home Value Base	2009 Home Value Distribution (%): Less than $50,000	$50,000 to $89,999	$90,000 to $174,999	$175,000 to $399,999	$400,000 or More	2009 Median Home Value
67437	DOWNS	18627	506	38.1	35.0	22.9	2.6	1.4	31465	33518	10	3	409	52.3	25.7	18.6	2.7	0.7	47889
67438	DURHAM	22530	117	29.1	26.5	35.9	0.9	7.7	43827	45000	45	53	99	37.4	17.2	27.3	18.2	0.0	81000
67439	ELLSWORTH	20949	1231	26.4	26.7	40.5	5.6	0.8	46955	48502	54	63	920	26.4	33.4	31.5	8.5	0.2	75588
67441	ENTERPRISE	20717	412	21.6	33.7	37.9	4.4	2.4	46212	47388	52	61	324	22.8	34.6	29.6	11.7	1.2	77917
67442	FALUN	21078	116	21.6	35.3	37.1	5.2	0.9	41164	47393	37	40	95	14.7	26.3	42.1	16.8	0.0	99444
67443	GALVA	19690	571	17.2	33.8	41.7	5.8	1.6	49317	51936	60	72	472	11.2	18.4	47.9	19.7	2.8	119706
67444	GENESEO	24532	239	25.5	28.5	38.9	5.0	2.1	45958	46860	51	60	204	50.0	18.1	22.5	8.8	0.5	50000
67445	GLASCO	18756	254	31.9	36.2	29.1	2.8	0.0	36516	37966	22	17	207	58.0	23.2	11.6	7.2	0.0	42500
67446	GLEN ELDER	20084	248	35.5	31.5	27.0	4.0	2.0	35228	36777	18	11	194	42.3	32.0	20.6	3.6	1.5	59375
67447	GREEN	18503	140	20.7	37.9	37.9	2.9	0.7	44064	46123	46	53	111	33.3	21.6	33.3	11.7	0.0	77000
67448	GYPSUM	20663	516	19.0	32.6	41.3	5.0	2.1	48557	51557	58	69	431	15.1	25.1	37.8	18.6	3.5	108272
67449	HERINGTON	19597	1392	34.6	34.3	25.9	3.8	1.4	36005	38156	21	14	1008	35.6	33.3	24.2	5.8	1.1	64737
67450	HOLYROOD	21547	262	26.7	30.9	37.4	3.8	1.1	44199	45949	46	54	216	45.8	29.2	20.8	2.8	1.4	56000
67451	HOPE	20588	449	23.4	36.1	36.3	3.6	0.7	42259	44297	40	46	372	22.8	26.6	36.8	12.9	0.8	90909
67452	HUNTER	24764	54	25.9	27.8	42.6	3.7	0.0	46547	45000	53	62	43	37.2	23.3	30.2	7.0	2.3	71667
67454	KANOPOLIS	20864	299	27.8	38.5	28.8	3.7	1.3	38553	40385	28	26	255	49.4	22.7	22.4	5.1	0.4	51154
67455	LINCOLN	20068	839	32.3	33.5	29.1	3.9	1.2	37190	38969	24	20	642	39.9	32.4	22.4	4.5	0.8	61455
67456	LINDSBORG	24142	1692	19.7	28.1	42.0	7.0	3.1	51647	53457	65	78	1270	10.2	23.5	46.2	18.4	1.7	112209
67457	LITTLE RIVER	18568	295	26.8	30.5	36.3	5.8	0.7	43312	44742	43	50	242	44.2	16.5	29.3	9.9	0.0	64444
67458	LONGFORD	20106	116	31.0	42.2	18.1	7.8	0.9	35322	36239	19	11	94	28.7	36.2	19.1	14.9	1.1	69000
67459	LORRAINE	17221	96	27.1	31.3	36.5	4.2	1.0	43615	46300	44	51	79	45.6	29.1	20.3	3.8	1.3	55833
67460	MCPHERSON	24367	6362	18.8	25.7	45.9	6.9	2.8	54952	56222	71	83	4442	9.1	19.3	52.5	17.7	1.3	118271
67464	MARQUETTE	24526	421	23.8	28.0	38.0	5.2	5.0	48493	51410	58	68	350	26.6	29.1	28.9	12.3	3.1	82000
67466	MILTONVALE	18230	285	32.3	41.1	21.8	3.9	1.1	32195	33027	12	4	229	55.5	20.5	18.3	5.7	0.0	44565
67467	MINNEAPOLIS	20990	1200	23.9	34.1	36.2	3.8	2.1	43562	45277	44	51	936	21.0	29.9	36.1	12.0	1.0	88636
67468	MORGANVILLE	17060	135	20.0	38.5	38.5	3.0	0.0	44234	46315	46	55	108	32.4	21.3	34.3	12.0	0.0	80000
67470	NEW CAMBRIA	29457	218	17.0	22.5	41.3	11.9	7.3	63732	63515	82	92	183	10.9	11.5	25.1	47.0	5.5	183654
67473	OSBORNE	19992	802	30.4	37.7	25.9	4.5	1.5	36188	37569	21	15	620	46.5	27.1	19.5	5.8	1.1	54681
67474	PORTIS	22093	86	25.6	46.5	20.9	4.7	2.3	36478	38594	22	16	67	49.3	25.4	16.4	7.5	1.5	51250
67475	RAMONA	18226	72	33.3	29.2	33.3	2.8	1.4	40000	42355	33	32	62	46.8	19.4	24.2	8.1	1.6	54000
67476	ROXBURY	28038	12	8.3	25.0	58.3	8.3	0.0	62486	64058	81	91	10	10.0	10.0	50.0	30.0	0.0	125000
67478	SIMPSON	19153	63	28.6	31.7	34.9	1.6	3.2	43353	46140	43	51	43	46.5	23.3	20.9	9.3	0.0	55000
67480	SOLOMON	21361	717	19.8	25.7	48.4	5.4	0.7	53117	53755	68	80	559	14.5	22.9	42.6	17.4	2.7	108868
67481	SYLVAN GROVE	21410	389	29.3	37.5	30.6	2.1	0.5	36136	39393	21	15	312	40.7	28.2	23.4	7.1	0.6	58788
67482	TALMAGE	23945	46	17.4	23.9	52.2	6.5	0.0	57672	56168	75	86	37	0.0	13.5	43.2	37.8	5.4	159375
67483	TAMPA	20247	127	30.7	27.6	34.6	1.6	5.5	42038	44090	39	45	108	41.7	16.7	25.9	15.7	0.0	64000
67484	TESCOTT	19451	383	25.3	24.5	44.1	3.9	2.1	50048	50492	61	74	324	22.2	38.6	25.6	13.0	0.6	73077
67485	TIPTON	20816	136	27.9	28.7	39.0	4.4	0.0	43638	47889	44	52	109	37.6	23.9	27.5	7.3	3.7	70625
67487	WAKEFIELD	20838	473	20.9	33.6	38.5	5.3	1.7	45638	47945	50	59	361	13.3	26.9	48.5	11.1	0.3	102471
67490	WILSON	21644	424	27.4	29.5	36.8	5.9	0.5	44257	46097	46	55	343	37.0	34.7	24.2	4.1	0.0	62321
67491	WINDOM	25642	155	11.6	27.7	51.0	7.1	2.6	58432	59252	76	87	133	11.3	20.3	42.9	22.6	3.0	116447
67492	WOODBINE	20050	125	19.2	36.0	39.2	2.4	3.2	45322	46796	49	58	104	24.0	21.2	37.5	16.3	1.0	98333
67501	HUTCHINSON	18406	10093	30.8	35.0	29.4	3.7	1.2	37447	40170	25	21	6323	34.3	41.0	21.8	2.5	0.3	64730
67502	HUTCHINSON	28232	9801	16.0	27.9	43.4	7.9	4.7	56022	55875	73	84	7418	4.4	17.4	52.9	22.3	2.9	130126
67505	SOUTH HUTCHINSON	21426	1106	36.0	29.4	29.6	3.4	1.6	36531	38819	22	17	692	21.8	28.8	43.5	5.2	0.7	89403
67510	ABBYVILLE	21048	151	21.2	29.8	44.4	4.6	0.0	48844	51257	59	70	124	35.5	31.5	27.4	5.6	0.0	64737
67511	ALBERT	21522	117	17.1	35.9	44.4	2.6	0.0	47901	50912	56	66	96	37.5	29.2	30.2	3.1	0.0	65714
67512	ALDEN	21668	104	25.0	33.7	38.5	1.9	1.0	45434	45789	50	59	87	44.8	32.2	16.1	6.9	0.0	54091
67513	ALEXANDER	19242	51	33.3	27.5	33.3	5.9	0.0	38649	42374	29	27	43	62.8	16.3	14.0	4.7	2.3	38750
67514	ARLINGTON	18054	302	27.5	38.1	31.8	2.0	0.7	37615	40557	26	22	236	39.8	34.3	17.4	5.5	3.0	63750
67516	BAZINE	24143	185	28.6	32.4	30.8	5.9	2.2	40941	42859	36	39	144	48.6	28.5	17.4	4.9	0.7	52000
67518	BEELER	17809	25	32.0	32.0	32.0	4.0	0.0	38610	35000	28	26	20	60.0	20.0	20.0	0.0	0.0	40000
67519	BELPRE	19143	82	34.1	35.4	26.8	1.2	2.4	36144	39092	21	15	63	47.6	31.7	15.9	1.6	3.2	53000
67520	BISON	18207	127	33.1	33.9	29.1	3.9	0.0	35276	35317	19	11	102	49.0	27.5	18.6	4.9	0.0	50769
67521	BROWNELL	21239	52	28.8	32.7	30.8	5.8	1.9	40000	40752	33	32	40	50.0	30.0	17.5	2.5	0.0	50000
67522	BUHLER	22660	688	15.4	31.1	43.5	7.0	3.1	53050	53619	68	80	561	13.5	30.8	42.4	13.0	0.2	96848
67523	BURDETT	22483	115	18.3	36.5	37.4	6.1	1.7	45977	46515	51	60	91	49.5	27.5	16.5	5.5	1.1	50625
67524	CHASE	17460	244	26.2	36.1	34.4	2.9	0.4	41433	43971	37	42	198	66.7	22.7	8.6	1.0	1.0	37750
67525	CLAFLIN	18777	478	25.1	34.5	35.1	3.6	1.7	39859	43396	32	31	392	24.7	30.1	36.5	8.2	0.5	80952
67526	ELLINWOOD	19537	1113	30.5	33.3	30.4	4.2	1.6	37478	40177	25	21	866	27.9	35.6	27.9	8.1	0.5	69263
67529	GARFIELD	21218	107	17.8	39.3	33.6	6.5	2.8	44647	45485	47	56	85	44.7	29.4	20.0	5.9	0.0	56429
67530	GREAT BEND	21097	7741	29.4	30.7	33.1	4.9	2.0	41966	44867	39	45	5316	24.0	29.0	37.3	8.7	1.0	85106
67543	HAVEN	20406	833	19.3	33.1	40.5	5.9	1.2	47590	50324	56	65	628	13.1	30.3	43.0	13.4	0.3	99333
67544	HOISINGTON	18367	1525	32.7	35.6	27.1	4.1	0.5	34527	35682	17	8	1185	37.0	32.2	27.0	3.8	0.0	60372
67545	HUDSON	18377	124	29.0	38.7	29.8	2.4	0.0	38177	40000	27	25	99	35.4	27.3	30.3	5.1	2.0	75000
67546	INMAN	20628	984	19.9	31.6	40.5	6.4	1.5	48739	51707	58	70	820	7.9	19.9	56.3	14.9	1.0	118314
67547	KINSLEY	20570	842	34.4	34.6	26.0	3.1	1.9	33669	34297	15	7	642	45.6	33.0	17.3	3.0	1.1	54308
67548	LA CROSSE	20386	641	31.4	34.8	29.3	2.8	1.7	36650	37754	23	18	512	42.2	30.9	19.9	7.0	0.0	56557
67550	LARNED	21964	2162	24.5	34.0	33.7	4.6	3.2	42087	43205	40	45	1586	30.5	36.4	25.9	6.6	0.6	69157
67552	LEWIS	17661	253	29.6	34.8	32.0	2.0	1.6	40522	41546	34	36	197	46.2	29.9	17.8	1.5	4.6	55769
67553	LIEBENTHAL	18136	76	35.5	27.6	31.6	5.3	0.0	35000	40000	18	10	63	66.7	14.3	11.1	6.3	1.6	35833
67554	LYONS	19966	1754	27.1	31.2	34.5	5.5	1.5	42914	44721	42	49	1271	32.2	38.0	22.4	6.5	0.9	66702
67556	MC CRACKEN	20545	124	35.5	26.6	32.3	5.6	0.0	35000	40575	18	10	104	69.2	15.4	10.6	3.8	1.0	31250
67557	MACKSVILLE	18059	266	27.1	28.6	39.1	5.3	0.0	44411	46891	47	55	198	39.9	27.3	23.7	7.1	2.0	64444
67559	NEKOMA	22488	27	33.3	29.6	33.3	3.7	0.0	38616	42376	28	26	23	65.2	17.4	13.0	4.3	0.0	41250
67560	NESS CITY	22469	817	28.6	33.7	31.9	4.4	1.3	40120	41988	33	33	606	38.8	31.0	23.8	6.1	0.3	63396
67561	NICKERSON	19022	620	20.8	36.8	37.3	4.0	1.1	42750	45920	42	49	474	27.4	38.6	26.2	7.2	0.6	73404
67563	OFFERLE	22796	150	14.0	38.0	40.0	6.0	2.0	48624	51249	58	69	122	31.1	31.1	24.6	5.7	7.4	77500
67564	OLMITZ	18164	118	23.7	39.8	28.8	7.6	0.0	40000	41516	33	32	98	33.7	35.7	29.6	1.0	0.0	61429
67565	OTIS	20112	243	31.7	33.7	29.2	3.7	1.6	36571	37672	22	17	197	47.7	25.9	19.3	6.1	1.0	52143
67566	PARTRIDGE	15635	250	27.2	36.8	32.4	2.8	0.8	41220	43369	37	40	199	29.6	24.1	37.7	7.0	1.5	85000
67567	PAWNEE ROCK	17796	185	16.8	35.7	44.3	3.2	0.0	48252	51002	57	67	151	39.7	29.8	26.5	4.0	0.0	62083
67568	PLEVNA	25660	121	20.7	28.9	45.5	5.0	0.0	50289	52460	62	75	100	36.0	31.0	28.0	5.0	0.0	64118
67570	PRETTY PRAIRIE	21446	505	23.6	29.9	40.2	4.6	1.8	45946	49526	51	60	412	24.0	30.6	32.8	11.7	1.0	85000
67572	RANSOM	20163	174	30.5	30.5	33.3	4.0	1.7	41132	42854	36	40	137	48.9	27.0	20.4	3.6	0.0	51875
67573	RAYMOND	22665	88	25.0	33.0	38.6	2.3	1.1	45548	46231	50	59	73	45.2	31.5	16.4	6.8	0.0	54375
67574	ROZEL	22043	88	17.0	35.2	38.6	6.8	2.3	47868	46972	56	66	69	50.7	27.5	15.9	5.8	0.0	49286
67575	RUSH CENTER	24106	178	27.5	34.3	32.6	3.4	2.2	40313	42856	34	34	148	45.9	20.3	21.6	10.1	2.0	58571
67576	SAINT JOHN	19804	854	27.5	35.8	32.6	2.7	1.4	40327	41733	34	34	650	38.5	28.5	26.3	6.0	0.8	62759
67578	STAFFORD	18666	628	33.4	40.0	22.6	2.7	1.3	33453	34362	14	6	499	57.1	22.8	16.0	3.2	0.8	41125
67579	STERLING	19658	1009	25.5	31.2	37.8	3.8	1.8	45032	46529	48	57	756	31.6	22.6	32.9	11.6	1.2	83333
67581	SYLVIA	17203	188	33.5	34.6	27.7	2.7	1.6	36287	40000	21	16	148	49.3	25.0	23.0	2.0	0.7	50909
67583	TURON	17494	474	30.0	37.6	29.5	2.5	0.4	37316	40258	25	20	389	45.2	20.6	29.3	4.4	0.5	57400
67584	UTICA	20046	125	31.2	29.6	33.6	4.0	1.6	40846	41998	35	38	99	49.5	26.3	21.2	3.0	0.0	50833
67601	HAYS	24284	9622	27.8	27.7	34.6	6.1	3.9	44113	47032	46	54	5792	10.0	14.8	53.0	20.3	2.0	122015
	KANSAS	26028		20.3	26.8	37.6	9.9	5.4	52748	54940				18.1	21.6	35.7	21.6	3.0	107692
	UNITED STATES	27277		20.9	24.4	35.3	11.7	7.6	54719	56938				9.3	13.1	31.6	32.6	13.5	162279

ZIP CODE		FINANCIAL SERVICES				THE HOME						ENTERTAINMENT						PERSONAL			
						Home Improvements		Furnishings													
#	POST OFFICE NAME	Auto Loan	Home Loan	Invest-ments	Retire-ment Plans	Home Repair	Lawn & Garden	Comput-ers & Hard-ware-Personal	Major Appli-ances	TV, Radio, Sound Equip-ment	Furni-ture	Dine out/ Carry out	Sports Equip-ment	Fees & Tickets	Toys & Games	Travel	Cable TV	Apparel & Services	Auto Repairs	Health Insur-ance	Pets & Supplies
67437	DOWNS	67	48	67	47	50	70	52	65	58	46	56	49	42	57	51	64	37	60	70	76
67438	DURHAM	99	68	109	68	71	104	75	94	79	61	78	78	55	77	75	86	50	88	99	115
67439	ELLSWORTH	78	67	80	67	69	85	69	79	73	64	72	59	62	72	69	78	49	75	86	92
67441	ENTERPRISE	96	66	105	66	69	101	73	91	76	59	75	75	54	75	73	83	49	85	96	112
67442	FALUN	89	64	94	64	66	92	69	84	72	59	71	68	53	71	68	78	47	79	88	103
67443	GALVA	89	74	86	77	76	95	76	88	78	67	77	69	66	79	76	84	52	82	91	104
67444	GENESEO	96	66	105	66	69	101	73	91	76	59	75	75	54	75	73	83	49	85	96	112
67445	GLASCO	75	51	82	51	54	79	57	71	59	46	59	59	42	58	57	65	38	66	75	87
67446	GLEN ELDER	79	57	80	55	59	82	62	77	69	55	66	58	49	67	60	76	44	71	83	90
67447	GREEN	85	59	94	58	61	90	65	81	68	53	67	67	48	66	65	74	43	76	85	100
67448	GYPSUM	93	73	97	74	75	99	76	90	78	65	77	73	63	78	76	84	51	84	94	109
67449	HERINGTON	74	54	72	53	55	76	60	71	66	53	64	54	48	65	57	71	42	68	77	85
67450	HOLYROOD	86	59	94	59	62	90	65	81	68	53	67	67	48	67	65	74	44	76	86	100
67451	HOPE	87	60	96	60	63	92	67	83	69	54	69	68	49	68	66	76	44	77	87	102
67452	HUNTER	88	60	96	60	63	93	67	83	70	54	69	69	49	68	67	76	45	78	88	102
67454	KANOPOLIS	78	56	79	54	58	81	61	75	67	54	65	57	48	66	59	74	43	70	82	89
67455	LINCOLN	75	54	77	52	56	79	59	73	65	52	63	55	46	64	57	71	42	68	79	86
67456	LINDSBORG	89	80	84	80	80	93	83	88	85	78	84	67	76	85	81	89	57	86	95	105
67457	LITTLE RIVER	87	60	95	59	62	91	66	82	69	54	68	68	48	67	66	75	44	77	87	101
67458	LONGFORD	85	58	93	58	61	89	65	80	67	52	66	66	47	66	64	73	43	75	85	99
67459	LORRAINE	86	59	94	59	62	90	65	81	68	53	67	67	48	67	65	74	44	76	86	100
67460	MCPHERSON	90	84	79	85	82	92	86	88	88	83	87	68	82	89	84	91	60	88	94	105
67464	MARQUETTE	104	71	114	71	75	109	79	98	82	64	81	81	58	81	79	90	53	92	104	121
67466	MILTONVALE	71	50	72	49	52	74	55	68	61	49	59	52	44	60	54	67	39	64	74	81
67467	MINNEAPOLIS	86	61	89	60	64	90	67	83	73	58	71	64	52	72	66	81	47	77	90	99
67468	MORGANVILLE	84	58	92	58	60	88	64	80	67	52	66	66	47	65	64	73	43	74	84	98
67470	NEW CAMBRIA	106	113	99	116	110	114	105	108	105	104	105	84	109	107	108	106	73	105	109	128
67473	OSBORNE	79	56	84	55	58	83	61	76	66	52	64	60	47	64	60	72	42	71	81	91
67474	PORTIS	86	59	94	59	62	91	66	82	69	53	68	67	48	67	65	75	44	76	86	100
67475	RAMONA	81	56	89	56	58	86	62	77	64	50	64	64	45	63	62	70	41	72	81	95
67476	ROXBURY	98	89	88	93	91	105	88	99	91	79	89	75	81	92	88	96	61	91	102	115
67478	SIMPSON	84	58	92	58	60	89	64	80	67	52	66	66	47	65	64	73	43	74	84	98
67480	SOLOMON	86	76	83	78	78	92	75	86	77	68	76	67	68	78	76	82	52	80	89	102
67481	SYLVAN GROVE	73	50	80	50	53	77	56	69	58	45	57	57	41	57	56	63	37	65	73	85
67482	TALMAGE	103	71	113	71	74	108	78	98	82	64	81	81	57	80	78	89	52	91	103	120
67483	TAMPA	97	66	106	66	70	102	74	92	77	60	76	76	54	75	73	84	49	86	97	113
67484	TESCOTT	92	64	102	63	67	98	71	88	73	57	73	73	52	72	70	80	47	82	93	108
67485	TIPTON	86	59	94	59	62	90	65	81	68	53	67	67	48	67	65	74	44	76	86	100
67487	WAKEFIELD	86	76	75	73	75	83	73	80	76	73	76	60	67	78	70	79	51	77	81	96
67490	WILSON	83	59	85	58	62	87	65	81	72	57	69	61	51	70	63	79	46	75	87	95
67491	WINDOM	116	79	127	79	83	122	88	110	92	71	91	91	65	90	88	100	59	102	116	135
67492	WOODBINE	91	62	100	62	65	96	69	86	72	56	71	71	51	71	69	79	46	80	91	106
67501	HUTCHINSON	67	57	54	58	55	66	64	63	66	58	65	50	57	67	58	69	44	65	69	77
67502	HUTCHINSON	92	98	94	99	98	102	93	96	94	93	94	72	97	94	97	97	66	95	102	113
67505	SOUTH HUTCHINSON	73	57	63	56	57	71	61	67	67	58	65	50	53	67	57	72	45	66	73	80
67510	ABBYVILLE	99	68	108	68	71	104	75	94	78	61	78	77	55	77	75	86	50	87	99	115
67511	ALBERT	89	61	98	61	64	94	68	85	71	55	70	70	50	69	68	77	45	79	89	104
67512	ALDEN	94	64	103	64	67	99	71	89	74	58	73	73	52	73	71	81	48	83	94	109
67513	ALEXANDER	79	54	87	54	57	83	60	75	63	49	62	62	44	61	60	68	40	70	79	92
67514	ARLINGTON	78	53	85	53	56	82	59	74	62	48	61	61	43	60	59	67	39	69	78	91
67516	BAZINE	87	60	96	60	63	92	66	83	69	54	68	68	49	68	66	75	44	77	87	102
67518	BEELER	74	51	81	51	53	78	56	70	59	46	58	58	41	58	56	64	38	65	74	86
67519	BELPRE	83	57	91	57	60	87	63	78	66	51	65	65	46	64	63	72	42	73	83	97
67520	BISON	75	54	76	53	56	79	59	73	66	52	63	55	47	65	57	72	42	68	80	86
67521	BROWNELL	88	60	96	60	63	92	67	83	70	54	69	69	49	68	67	76	45	78	88	102
67522	BUHLER	96	86	87	90	88	103	85	97	88	77	86	74	78	90	85	93	59	89	100	113
67523	BURDETT	95	65	104	65	68	100	73	90	76	59	75	75	53	74	72	82	48	84	95	111
67524	CHASE	80	57	83	55	59	82	59	75	65	54	64	57	47	65	58	72	42	69	78	89
67525	CLAFLIN	86	59	95	59	62	91	66	82	69	53	68	68	48	67	66	75	44	76	86	101
67526	ELLINWOOD	82	57	86	56	60	85	62	77	67	54	66	61	48	66	61	73	43	72	82	93
67529	GARFIELD	95	65	104	65	68	100	72	90	75	59	74	74	53	74	72	82	48	84	95	111
67530	GREAT BEND	76	67	69	67	67	78	70	75	73	66	72	55	64	73	68	77	49	73	80	87
67543	HAVEN	85	72	81	74	74	91	73	85	76	64	74	66	64	76	73	81	50	78	88	100
67544	HOISINGTON	73	52	74	51	54	76	56	70	62	50	60	53	45	61	55	69	40	65	76	83
67545	HUDSON	75	52	82	51	54	79	57	71	60	46	59	59	42	58	57	65	38	66	75	88
67546	INMAN	91	69	94	68	71	96	73	89	79	65	77	69	60	78	72	86	51	83	95	106
67547	KINSLEY	76	54	77	53	56	79	59	73	66	52	64	55	47	64	58	72	42	68	80	87
67548	LA CROSSE	76	55	76	53	57	79	60	74	66	53	64	55	48	65	58	73	43	69	80	86
67550	LARNED	89	65	90	64	68	92	70	85	77	63	75	65	57	76	69	84	50	80	92	101
67552	LEWIS	86	59	94	59	62	90	65	81	68	53	67	67	48	67	65	74	44	76	86	100
67553	LIEBENTHAL	76	52	83	52	55	80	58	72	60	47	60	60	42	59	58	66	39	67	76	89
67554	LYONS	79	63	81	62	65	86	65	79	72	59	70	59	56	70	65	78	47	74	86	92
67556	MC CRACKEN	76	52	83	52	55	80	58	72	60	47	60	60	42	59	58	66	39	67	76	89
67557	MACKSVILLE	86	59	94	59	62	91	66	82	68	53	68	67	48	67	65	74	44	76	86	100
67559	NEKOMA	82	56	90	56	59	86	63	78	65	51	64	64	46	64	62	71	42	73	82	96
67560	NESS CITY	84	59	89	58	62	88	65	81	70	55	68	64	50	69	64	77	45	75	86	97
67561	NICKERSON	88	63	83	62	64	88	67	80	72	60	71	63	52	73	63	78	47	75	84	97
67563	OFFERLE	101	70	111	69	73	107	77	96	80	63	79	79	57	79	77	88	52	90	101	118
67564	OLMITZ	82	56	90	56	59	87	63	78	65	51	64	64	46	64	62	71	42	73	82	96
67565	OTIS	78	56	81	55	58	82	61	76	67	53	65	58	48	66	60	73	43	70	82	90
67566	PARTRIDGE	82	56	90	56	59	86	62	78	65	51	64	64	46	64	62	71	42	72	82	95
67567	PAWNEE ROCK	90	62	98	62	65	95	68	85	71	55	70	70	50	70	68	78	46	79	90	105
67568	PLEVNA	101	69	110	69	72	106	77	95	80	62	79	79	56	78	76	87	51	89	101	117
67570	PRETTY PRAIRIE	92	67	98	67	70	97	72	88	75	60	74	72	56	74	72	81	49	82	93	107
67572	RANSOM	83	57	91	57	60	88	63	79	66	51	65	65	46	65	63	72	42	74	83	97
67573	RAYMOND	94	64	103	64	67	99	71	89	74	58	73	73	52	73	71	81	48	83	94	109
67574	ROZEL	95	65	104	65	68	100	72	90	75	58	74	74	53	74	72	82	48	84	95	110
67575	RUSH CENTER	91	63	100	63	66	96	70	87	73	57	72	72	51	71	69	79	47	81	92	107
67576	SAINT JOHN	80	57	83	56	59	84	62	77	68	54	66	60	48	67	61	75	44	72	83	92
67578	STAFFORD	69	50	70	48	51	72	54	67	60	48	58	51	43	59	53	66	38	62	73	79
67579	STERLING	82	63	81	63	65	84	69	79	73	62	71	60	58	72	67	79	48	76	85	94
67581	SYLVIA	76	52	84	52	55	80	58	72	61	47	60	60	43	59	58	66	39	68	76	89
67583	TURON	75	51	82	51	54	79	57	71	59	46	59	59	42	58	57	65	38	66	75	87
67584	UTICA	82	57	90	57	59	87	63	78	65	51	65	65	46	64	63	71	42	73	83	96
67601	HAYS	82	73	71	75	72	76	85	77	83	79	83	62	78	83	77	83	58	81	80	93
	KANSAS	98	90	91	91	89	97	94	95	94	90	94	74	88	96	90	96	65	95	98	113
	UNITED STATES	100	100	100	100	100	100	100	100	100	100	100	100	100	100	100	100	100	100	100	100

POPULATION CHANGE

ZIP CODE #	POST OFFICE NAME	COUNTY FIPS CODE	POPULATION 2000	POPULATION 2009	POPULATION 2014	2000-2009 ANNUAL RATE % Rate	2000-2009 ANNUAL RATE State Centile	HOUSEHOLDS 2000	HOUSEHOLDS 2009	HOUSEHOLDS 2014	HOUSEHOLDS % Annual Rate 2000-2009	HOUSEHOLDS 2009 Average HH Size	FAMILIES 2000	FAMILIES 2009	FAMILIES % Annual Rate 2000-2009
67621	AGRA	147	599	518	484	-1.6	8	241	208	194	-1.6	2.49	180	154	-1.7
67622	ALMENA	137	614	589	574	-0.4	48	254	239	228	-0.7	1.68	174	162	-0.8
67623	ALTON	141	303	263	245	-1.5	9	139	123	115	-1.3	2.14	91	80	-1.4
67625	BOGUE	065	361	314	296	-1.5	9	153	136	129	-1.3	2.31	108	95	-1.4
67626	BUNKER HILL	167	221	195	185	-1.3	12	101	91	87	-1.1	2.14	67	59	-1.4
67627	CATHARINE	051	8	8	7	0.0	64	3	3	3	0.0	2.67	2	2	0.0
67628	CEDAR	183	66	56	51	-1.8	6	23	19	18	-2.0	2.84	16	14	-1.4
67629	CLAYTON	137	66	54	50	-2.1	3	27	23	21	-1.7	2.35	19	16	-1.8
67631	COLLYER	195	428	365	340	-1.7	7	182	161	152	-1.3	2.27	133	117	-1.4
67632	DAMAR	163	219	203	195	-0.8	28	90	85	82	-0.6	2.39	61	58	-0.5
67634	DORRANCE	167	346	305	290	-1.4	11	154	139	133	-1.1	2.19	102	91	-1.2
67635	DRESDEN	039	122	98	89	-2.3	1	50	41	38	-2.1	2.39	35	29	-2.0
67637	ELLIS	051	2326	2292	2280	-0.2	56	969	988	994	0.2	2.26	666	670	0.1
67638	GAYLORD	183	738	621	574	-1.8	6	303	256	236	-1.8	2.37	212	178	-1.9
67639	GLADE	147	298	259	241	-1.5	9	121	104	98	-1.6	2.47	90	77	-1.7
67640	GORHAM	167	512	462	441	-1.1	17	214	197	190	-0.9	2.35	151	138	-1.0
67642	HILL CITY	065	2112	1966	1889	-0.8	28	907	871	845	-0.4	2.18	596	567	-0.5
67643	JENNINGS	039	258	208	189	-2.3	1	124	103	94	-2.0	2.02	86	71	-2.1
67644	KIRWIN	147	342	297	277	-1.5	9	135	117	109	-1.5	2.54	101	86	-1.7
67645	LENORA	137	716	593	546	-2.0	4	306	257	237	-1.9	2.27	215	179	-2.0
67646	LOGAN	147	711	599	561	-1.8	6	286	241	225	-1.8	2.31	198	165	-2.0
67647	LONG ISLAND	147	256	258	257	0.1	68	107	110	110	0.3	2.35	79	81	0.3
67648	LUCAS	167	526	533	532	0.1	68	219	226	227	0.3	2.20	146	149	0.2
67649	LURAY	167	281	271	264	-0.4	48	136	134	131	-0.2	2.01	86	84	-0.3
67650	MORLAND	065	458	388	363	-1.8	6	195	170	160	-1.5	2.28	138	120	-1.5
67651	NATOMA	141	607	529	494	-1.5	9	265	235	220	-1.3	2.25	175	154	-1.4
67653	NORCATUR	039	275	221	201	-2.3	1	124	103	94	-2.0	2.15	86	71	-2.1
67654	NORTON	137	4557	4237	4059	-0.8	28	1679	1562	1492	-0.8	2.39	1064	979	-0.9
67656	OGALLAH	195	401	341	318	-1.7	7	159	141	133	-1.3	2.42	117	103	-1.4
67657	PALCO	163	344	320	306	-0.8	28	156	148	142	-0.6	2.16	107	100	-0.7
67658	PARADISE	167	151	144	139	-0.5	41	67	65	63	-0.3	2.22	43	42	-0.3
67659	PENOKEE	065	15	13	12	-1.5	9	8	7	7	-1.4	1.86	6	5	-2.0
67660	PFEIFER	051	25	24	24	-0.4	48	9	9	9	0.0	2.67	6	6	0.0
67661	PHILLIPSBURG	147	3500	3266	3129	-0.7	32	1482	1400	1343	-0.6	2.26	983	920	-0.7
67663	PLAINVILLE	163	2843	2590	2465	-1.0	19	1180	1098	1052	-0.8	2.32	782	719	-0.9
67664	PRAIRIE VIEW	147	295	296	294	0.0	64	124	127	126	0.3	2.32	92	93	0.1
67665	RUSSELL	167	5278	4900	4714	-0.8	28	2288	2142	2063	-0.7	2.21	1410	1305	-0.8
67669	STOCKTON	163	2014	1868	1794	-0.8	28	820	767	738	-0.7	2.23	529	489	-0.8
67671	VICTORIA	051	1732	1623	1588	-0.7	32	701	679	670	-0.3	2.26	479	458	-0.5
67672	WAKEENEY	195	2490	2308	2202	-0.8	28	1071	1026	987	-0.5	2.14	686	651	-0.6
67673	WALDO	167	90	86	84	-0.5	41	44	43	42	-0.2	2.00	28	27	-0.4
67675	WOODSTON	163	275	253	243	-0.9	23	120	113	109	-0.6	2.24	80	75	-0.7
67701	COLBY	193	7060	6433	6106	-1.0	19	2776	2581	2461	-0.8	2.38	1790	1646	-0.9
67730	ATWOOD	153	1976	1811	1707	-0.9	23	840	795	756	-0.6	2.21	539	504	-0.7
67731	BIRD CITY	023	771	718	694	-0.8	28	352	330	320	-0.7	2.18	223	207	-0.8
67732	BREWSTER	193	401	353	331	-1.4	11	160	145	137	-1.1	2.43	122	110	-1.1
67733	EDSON	181	257	236	223	-0.9	23	95	89	84	-0.7	2.65	76	71	-0.7
67734	GEM	193	132	116	109	-1.4	11	52	47	44	-1.1	2.47	38	34	-1.2
67735	GOODLAND	181	6013	5456	5167	-1.0	19	2468	2273	2161	-0.9	2.34	1567	1427	-1.0
67736	GOVE	063	321	289	274	-1.1	17	126	115	110	-1.0	2.51	88	80	-1.0
67737	GRAINFIELD	063	430	381	359	-1.3	12	183	165	156	-1.1	2.31	123	110	-1.2
67738	GRINNELL	063	565	498	469	-1.4	11	244	219	207	-1.2	2.27	163	145	-1.3
67739	HERNDON	153	363	297	271	-2.1	3	164	139	128	-1.8	2.14	117	98	-1.9
67740	HOXIE	179	2197	2054	1979	-0.7	32	872	833	808	-0.5	2.41	624	591	-0.6
67741	KANORADO	181	464	401	376	-1.6	8	184	163	154	-1.3	2.46	131	115	-1.4
67743	LEVANT	193	150	132	123	-1.4	11	58	52	49	-1.2	2.54	44	39	-1.3
67744	LUDELL	153	136	111	102	-2.2	2	54	46	42	-1.7	2.41	38	32	-1.8
67745	MC DONALD	153	491	399	365	-2.2	2	211	177	164	-1.9	2.25	154	128	-2.0
67748	OAKLEY	109	2509	2246	2112	-1.2	14	1027	933	880	-1.0	2.35	698	629	-1.1
67749	OBERLIN	039	2680	2449	2318	-1.0	19	1143	1064	1011	-0.8	2.19	738	680	-0.9
67751	PARK	063	315	295	283	-0.7	32	135	129	124	-0.5	2.29	103	97	-0.6
67752	QUINTER	063	1437	1358	1302	-0.6	36	557	533	513	-0.5	2.45	385	364	-0.6
67753	REXFORD	193	325	287	269	-1.3	12	145	130	123	-1.2	2.21	107	95	-1.3
67756	SAINT FRANCIS	023	2394	2321	2280	-0.3	52	1008	985	968	-0.2	2.30	697	675	-0.3
67757	SELDEN	179	753	677	642	-1.1	17	305	281	269	-0.9	2.41	209	191	-1.0
67758	SHARON SPRINGS	199	1096	1011	966	-0.9	23	439	413	397	-0.7	2.39	294	274	-0.8
67761	WALLACE	199	290	267	255	-0.9	23	111	104	100	-0.7	2.57	86	80	-0.8
67762	WESKAN	199	393	363	348	-0.9	23	133	125	121	-0.7	2.90	104	97	-0.8
67764	WINONA	109	645	572	536	-1.3	12	253	229	216	-1.1	2.49	186	167	-1.2
67801	DODGE CITY	057	29150	30880	31572	0.6	82	9607	9868	10023	0.3	3.06	6930	7054	0.2
67831	ASHLAND	025	1183	1158	1154	-0.2	56	504	491	489	-0.3	2.32	341	328	-0.4
67834	BUCKLIN	057	926	959	972	0.4	76	360	365	367	0.1	2.51	249	251	0.1
67835	CIMARRON	055	2797	2835	2811	0.1	68	1017	1030	1020	0.1	2.73	769	772	0.0
67837	COPELAND	069	544	547	541	0.1	68	189	190	187	0.1	2.88	146	146	0.0
67838	DEERFIELD	093	1274	1309	1319	0.3	74	408	422	425	0.4	3.10	337	346	0.3
67839	DIGHTON	101	1731	1588	1521	-0.9	23	746	695	669	-0.8	2.25	490	452	-0.9
67840	ENGLEWOOD	025	171	168	167	-0.2	56	73	71	71	-0.3	2.32	49	47	-0.4
67841	ENSIGN	069	330	318	310	-0.4	48	122	117	113	-0.5	2.72	100	95	-0.6
67842	FORD	057	513	516	518	0.1	68	188	185	184	-0.2	2.78	149	146	-0.2
67844	FOWLER	119	884	875	857	-0.1	59	356	347	338	-0.3	2.43	250	241	-0.4
67846	GARDEN CITY	055	37386	35966	34860	-0.4	48	11975	11453	11070	-0.5	3.09	8925	8467	-0.6
67849	HANSTON	083	576	535	520	-0.8	28	209	195	190	-0.7	2.74	161	151	-0.7
67850	HEALY	101	424	386	370	-1.0	19	164	152	146	-0.8	2.53	123	113	-0.9
67851	HOLCOMB	055	2661	2601	2530	-0.2	56	797	780	759	-0.2	3.33	683	666	-0.3
67853	INGALLS	069	927	938	929	0.1	68	310	314	311	0.1	2.98	246	247	0.0
67854	JETMORE	083	1509	1558	1563	0.3	74	587	610	612	0.4	2.50	420	432	0.3
67855	JOHNSON	187	2094	1925	1840	-0.9	23	739	685	655	-0.8	2.73	544	500	-0.9
67857	KENDALL	075	101	102	102	0.1	68	38	38	38	0.0	2.61	25	25	0.0
67859	KISMET	175	1684	1682	1689	0.0	64	533	516	512	-0.3	3.26	432	415	-0.4
67860	LAKIN	093	3296	3320	3325	0.1	68	1147	1158	1159	0.1	2.83	874	875	0.0
67861	LEOTI	203	2389	2215	2129	-0.8	28	916	871	845	-0.5	2.51	681	643	-0.6
67862	MANTER	187	312	290	277	-0.8	28	119	112	108	-0.7	2.59	94	88	-0.7
67863	MARIENTHAL	171	267	242	230	-1.1	17	100	93	90	-0.8	2.60	82	76	-0.8
67864	MEADE	119	2191	2156	2111	-0.2	56	844	821	799	-0.3	2.53	600	578	-0.4
67865	MINNEOLA	025	1169	1139	1135	-0.3	52	453	439	435	-0.3	2.54	327	314	-0.4
	KANSAS					0.6					0.6	2.49			0.5
	UNITED STATES					1.0					1.1	2.59			0.9

ZIP CODE #	POST OFFICE NAME	RACE (%) White 2000	White 2009	Black 2000	Black 2009	Asian/Pacific 2000	Asian/Pacific 2009	% Hispanic Origin 2000	% Hispanic Origin 2009	2009 AGE DISTRIBUTION (%) 0-4	5-9	10-14	15-19	20-24	25-44	45-64	65-84	85+	18+	MEDIAN AGE 2009	% 2009 Males	% 2009 Females
67621	AGRA	99.0	98.8	0.0	0.0	0.0	0.0	0.3	0.6	6.4	6.9	7.3	6.4	4.2	21.4	32.4	12.7	2.1	75.3	42.9	51.2	48.8
67622	ALMENA	79.6	77.2	15.5	16.1	0.7	1.0	4.9	6.8	3.6	3.7	3.7	4.6	12.1	40.4	20.7	8.8	2.4	86.2	36.1	73.5	26.5
67623	ALTON	99.7	99.2	0.0	0.0	0.0	0.0	0.7	1.1	5.3	5.7	5.7	6.8	4.2	20.2	31.2	16.7	4.2	78.7	46.2	51.0	49.0
67625	BOGUE	91.7	91.1	6.6	7.0	0.0	0.0	0.8	1.3	4.1	5.1	5.1	5.7	4.8	20.4	34.1	17.8	2.9	82.2	47.0	53.8	46.2
67626	BUNKER HILL	99.1	99.0	0.0	0.0	0.5	0.5	1.4	2.1	4.1	4.6	5.6	4.6	4.1	16.9	38.5	18.5	3.1	83.1	49.4	51.3	48.7
67627	CATHARINE	100.0	100.0	0.0	0.0	0.0	0.0	0.0	0.0	0.0	0.0	0.0	0.0	0.0	37.5	62.5	0.0	0.0	100.0	46.7	50.0	50.0
67628	CEDAR	98.5	98.2	0.0	0.0	0.0	0.0	1.5	0.0	3.6	5.4	5.4	5.4	3.6	17.9	35.7	17.9	5.4	80.4	49.2	51.8	48.2
67629	CLAYTON	100.0	100.0	0.0	0.0	0.0	0.0	0.0	0.0	5.6	5.6	7.4	5.6	3.7	22.2	31.5	14.8	3.7	75.9	45.0	50.0	50.0
67631	COLLYER	98.4	97.8	0.2	0.3	0.0	0.0	1.4	1.6	5.2	6.3	6.8	6.6	3.6	19.7	33.7	15.9	2.2	77.8	46.0	52.9	47.1
67632	DAMAR	98.2	98.0	0.9	1.0	0.0	0.0	0.9	1.5	6.9	7.9	7.9	6.9	3.9	20.7	27.6	15.3	3.0	72.4	41.7	49.8	50.2
67634	DORRANCE	99.1	99.0	0.0	0.0	0.3	0.3	1.2	1.6	4.3	4.9	5.2	4.6	4.3	17.0	38.4	18.4	3.0	82.3	49.1	52.1	47.9
67635	DRESDEN	98.4	98.0	0.8	1.0	0.0	0.0	0.8	1.0	4.1	5.1	5.1	6.1	4.1	19.4	36.7	16.3	3.1	82.7	48.3	54.1	45.9
67637	ELLIS	98.6	98.2	0.0	0.0	0.0	0.0	1.6	2.5	5.6	5.6	6.1	6.4	5.1	24.8	27.6	14.5	4.3	78.4	42.3	48.1	51.9
67638	GAYLORD	98.2	97.7	0.3	0.3	0.0	0.2	0.8	1.0	4.5	5.2	5.5	5.8	4.5	17.9	32.7	19.0	5.0	80.8	48.7	50.7	49.3
67639	GLADE	98.0	97.7	0.3	0.4	0.0	0.0	0.7	0.8	6.6	6.6	6.9	6.9	4.2	18.5	29.7	17.8	2.7	75.3	45.1	52.5	47.5
67640	GORHAM	98.8	98.5	0.0	0.0	0.2	0.2	0.6	0.9	5.6	6.7	6.7	5.4	4.1	22.5	31.0	15.6	2.4	77.7	44.2	49.1	50.9
67642	HILL CITY	94.9	93.9	3.1	3.4	0.4	0.6	0.9	1.4	4.3	4.7	5.0	5.6	5.2	18.9	30.3	21.4	4.6	82.2	48.8	47.0	53.0
67643	JENNINGS	98.1	97.6	0.4	0.5	0.4	0.5	0.8	1.0	4.3	5.3	5.3	5.8	4.8	20.2	33.7	17.3	3.4	81.7	47.5	53.8	46.2
67644	KIRWIN	98.0	97.6	0.3	0.3	0.0	0.0	0.6	1.0	6.4	6.7	7.1	7.4	4.4	18.2	30.3	17.2	2.4	75.1	44.9	53.9	46.1
67645	LENORA	98.3	98.0	0.7	0.8	0.1	0.2	0.7	1.2	5.7	6.4	6.4	6.4	3.9	22.4	31.4	14.8	2.5	77.2	43.9	50.6	49.4
67646	LOGAN	99.3	99.2	0.1	0.2	0.1	0.2	0.1	0.2	5.2	5.7	6.2	5.7	4.3	19.4	30.4	16.5	6.7	78.8	47.8	46.9	53.1
67647	LONG ISLAND	98.8	98.4	0.4	0.4	0.0	0.4	0.8	0.8	6.2	6.6	6.6	5.4	3.9	20.5	29.1	18.2	3.5	76.7	45.6	50.8	49.2
67648	LUCAS	98.1	97.7	1.1	1.1	0.0	0.0	0.4	0.6	3.9	4.7	5.3	6.6	3.9	17.1	31.3	20.1	7.1	81.2	51.1	48.2	51.8
67649	LURAY	96.4	95.9	0.0	0.0	0.0	0.0	1.1	1.5	5.2	5.5	5.5	6.3	3.3	19.2	28.0	22.5	4.4	79.3	48.2	48.3	51.7
67650	MORLAND	97.4	96.9	1.1	1.3	0.2	0.3	0.2	0.5	5.9	6.7	7.0	6.2	3.6	20.1	29.9	18.0	2.6	76.5	45.3	51.5	48.5
67651	NATOMA	99.2	99.1	0.0	0.0	0.2	0.2	0.7	0.9	5.3	5.7	6.0	6.6	4.3	20.4	31.0	16.6	4.0	78.8	45.9	50.9	49.1
67653	NORCATUR	98.2	97.7	0.4	0.5	0.4	0.5	0.7	0.9	4.1	5.0	5.4	6.3	4.5	19.0	35.3	17.2	3.2	81.4	48.1	54.3	45.7
67654	NORTON	94.3	93.4	3.1	3.3	0.5	0.6	2.3	3.4	5.0	5.1	5.5	6.1	7.1	23.9	27.2	15.3	4.9	80.2	42.9	53.7	46.3
67656	OGALLAH	99.0	98.8	0.0	0.0	0.0	0.0	1.0	1.2	5.3	6.2	7.0	6.7	4.1	19.1	33.7	15.8	2.1	77.4	45.9	52.5	47.5
67657	PALCO	98.0	97.8	0.9	0.9	0.0	0.0	1.2	1.6	6.9	7.5	7.5	6.9	4.1	20.3	28.1	15.9	2.8	73.8	42.4	50.0	50.0
67658	PARADISE	96.7	96.5	0.0	0.0	0.0	0.0	1.3	1.4	4.9	6.3	5.6	6.3	3.5	20.1	27.8	21.5	4.2	79.2	47.1	49.3	50.7
67659	PENOKEE	93.3	92.3	6.7	7.7	0.0	0.0	0.0	0.0	0.0	0.0	0.0	0.0	0.0	23.1	76.9	0.0	0.0	100.0	49.4	69.2	30.8
67660	PFEIFER	100.0	100.0	0.0	0.0	0.0	0.0	0.0	0.0	4.2	4.2	8.3	8.3	8.3	29.2	33.3	4.2	0.0	75.0	37.5	50.0	50.0
67661	PHILLIPSBURG	97.9	97.4	0.3	0.3	0.7	1.1	0.9	1.2	5.5	5.5	5.8	6.1	5.4	21.6	28.0	17.0	5.1	79.0	45.1	48.5	51.5
67663	PLAINVILLE	98.3	98.1	0.5	0.5	0.2	0.2	0.5	0.6	6.4	6.7	6.5	6.4	5.4	22.2	26.3	15.8	4.2	76.1	41.7	48.7	51.3
67664	PRAIRIE VIEW	99.0	98.6	0.3	0.3	0.0	0.3	0.7	0.7	6.1	6.4	6.8	5.4	4.1	20.6	29.1	17.9	3.7	77.0	45.5	50.7	49.3
67665	RUSSELL	97.3	96.9	0.6	0.6	0.4	0.6	0.9	1.4	5.6	5.7	5.7	6.1	5.2	21.1	28.5	17.6	4.5	79.1	45.4	48.6	51.4
67669	STOCKTON	95.0	94.1	2.2	2.4	0.2	0.4	1.8	2.7	5.2	5.8	6.0	6.2	6.3	23.3	27.4	15.1	4.8	78.8	43.0	51.4	48.6
67671	VICTORIA	99.4	99.3	0.0	0.0	0.1	0.1	0.7	1.0	5.7	6.0	5.9	5.4	4.4	23.2	26.7	17.7	4.9	78.9	44.5	49.5	50.5
67672	WAKEENEY	97.5	97.0	0.2	0.2	0.7	1.0	0.7	0.8	4.9	5.4	5.8	6.5	4.5	20.1	29.0	18.0	5.8	79.3	46.8	46.9	53.1
67673	WALDO	96.7	95.3	0.0	0.0	0.0	0.0	1.1	1.2	5.8	5.8	5.8	7.0	2.3	18.6	26.7	23.3	4.7	79.1	47.9	51.2	48.8
67675	WOODSTON	98.5	98.0	0.4	0.4	0.4	0.8	1.5	2.0	4.7	7.1	9.1	7.1	2.4	22.5	34.4	11.1	1.6	74.3	43.1	54.2	45.8
67701	COLBY	97.0	96.1	0.5	0.5	0.3	0.5	1.9	2.8	6.7	6.5	6.3	8.2	6.5	25.4	25.4	12.0	2.8	76.7	35.7	47.7	52.3
67730	ATWOOD	98.6	98.4	0.3	0.3	0.1	0.1	0.5	0.7	4.9	5.1	5.6	5.9	5.1	17.8	29.8	20.0	5.9	80.0	48.7	49.0	51.0
67731	BIRD CITY	97.9	97.1	0.1	0.1	0.0	0.0	3.4	5.0	5.0	5.4	6.4	7.5	3.9	19.8	29.5	18.2	4.2	78.4	46.4	50.8	49.2
67732	BREWSTER	97.5	95.8	0.0	0.0	0.0	0.3	2.5	4.0	6.2	6.8	7.9	7.6	4.5	20.4	32.0	12.7	1.7	73.9	42.0	50.1	49.9
67733	EDSON	96.1	94.9	0.4	0.4	0.0	0.0	4.3	5.9	5.9	6.8	7.2	7.6	5.1	20.8	30.1	14.8	1.7	75.0	42.1	51.3	48.7
67734	GEM	98.5	98.3	0.0	0.0	0.0	0.0	0.8	1.7	6.9	7.8	7.8	6.9	5.2	24.1	26.7	12.9	1.7	72.4	37.5	51.7	48.3
67735	GOODLAND	93.8	91.6	0.4	0.4	0.3	0.4	8.3	12.0	6.3	6.1	6.4	7.6	6.6	24.0	25.3	14.7	3.0	77.5	38.6	51.2	48.8
67736	GOVE	98.1	97.9	0.0	0.0	0.0	0.0	1.2	1.4	5.9	6.6	6.9	6.9	4.2	19.4	31.5	16.3	2.4	76.1	45.1	51.9	48.1
67737	GRAINFIELD	98.8	98.7	0.0	0.0	0.0	0.0	1.4	1.8	5.2	6.0	6.8	7.3	4.2	18.9	32.0	16.8	2.6	77.2	45.9	51.2	48.8
67738	GRINNELL	98.9	98.8	0.0	0.0	0.0	0.0	1.6	1.6	5.2	5.8	6.8	7.6	4.2	18.9	31.1	17.5	2.8	77.1	45.9	50.0	50.0
67739	HERNDON	98.4	98.0	0.3	0.3	0.3	0.3	1.6	2.4	3.7	4.4	5.1	7.7	5.1	15.8	36.0	18.9	3.4	81.8	49.5	53.9	46.1
67740	HOXIE	98.7	98.4	0.2	0.2	0.1	0.1	1.3	1.7	4.8	6.0	7.0	7.4	3.6	20.7	30.0	16.7	3.8	77.3	45.3	49.8	50.2
67741	KANORADO	92.9	90.0	0.0	0.0	0.9	1.2	12.7	18.2	4.0	4.2	5.5	8.7	4.7	22.7	32.4	16.0	1.7	81.3	45.1	51.4	48.6
67743	LEVANT	97.3	95.5	0.0	0.0	0.0	0.0	2.7	4.5	6.1	6.8	8.3	7.6	4.5	21.2	31.1	12.9	1.5	74.2	41.3	50.8	49.2
67744	LUDELL	99.3	98.2	0.0	0.0	0.0	0.9	2.2	2.7	3.6	4.5	4.5	8.1	5.4	14.4	36.0	19.8	3.6	82.0	50.2	54.1	45.9
67745	MC DONALD	98.2	98.0	0.6	0.8	0.2	0.3	1.0	1.3	4.0	4.8	5.5	6.8	5.0	18.5	34.8	17.8	2.8	81.5	48.4	52.6	47.4
67748	OAKLEY	96.7	95.8	0.5	0.6	0.2	0.2	1.6	2.3	6.1	5.8	5.9	6.3	6.0	20.9	28.5	16.1	4.4	78.1	44.0	48.3	51.7
67749	OBERLIN	97.8	97.3	0.5	0.6	0.2	0.2	1.0	1.5	4.7	5.1	5.5	6.9	4.9	18.7	29.0	19.2	6.1	80.2	48.0	48.8	51.2
67751	PARK	97.8	97.6	0.0	0.0	0.0	0.0	1.0	0.7	6.8	7.8	7.5	5.8	4.7	21.0	30.2	14.6	1.7	73.9	41.7	50.8	49.2
67752	QUINTER	97.5	97.3	0.1	0.1	0.2	0.2	1.1	1.2	6.1	6.7	7.1	6.8	4.1	18.2	28.4	16.4	6.1	75.5	45.6	48.2	51.8
67753	REXFORD	98.8	98.3	0.0	0.0	0.0	0.0	0.9	1.4	7.3	8.0	8.0	7.3	4.5	23.0	28.6	11.8	1.4	72.1	37.6	52.6	47.4
67756	SAINT FRANCIS	97.9	97.3	0.1	0.1	0.5	0.6	2.3	3.4	4.8	5.6	6.6	6.4	4.2	21.6	28.5	16.9	5.3	78.8	45.5	50.1	49.9
67757	SELDEN	98.5	98.1	0.1	0.1	0.5	0.7	2.0	2.8	5.8	6.8	6.8	6.2	4.4	22.3	29.8	15.1	2.8	76.8	43.2	52.3	47.7
67758	SHARON SPRINGS	95.5	94.2	0.4	0.4	0.3	0.4	4.3	6.3	5.8	6.2	6.4	7.2	4.1	21.2	29.2	16.0	3.9	76.9	44.1	48.4	51.6
67761	WALLACE	93.8	92.1	1.0	1.1	0.0	0.0	5.2	7.5	7.1	7.1	7.5	8.6	5.2	19.5	31.8	11.2	1.9	72.7	40.5	52.4	47.6
67762	WESKAN	93.1	91.2	1.0	1.1	0.0	0.0	5.6	8.3	6.6	7.2	7.7	8.8	5.2	19.8	31.4	11.6	1.7	73.0	40.4	51.5	48.5
67764	WINONA	97.2	96.3	0.8	0.9	0.3	0.5	1.9	2.8	9.3	5.9	6.3	7.9	5.8	22.9	25.2	14.9	1.9	73.4	38.8	50.7	49.3
67801	DODGE CITY	72.4	66.6	1.8	1.7	2.4	3.0	41.3	51.3	9.8	8.6	7.7	8.1	8.0	27.7	20.0	8.2	1.9	69.2	29.8	51.6	48.4
67831	ASHLAND	94.6	94.3	0.2	0.2	0.1	0.1	4.3	4.6	6.6	7.3	7.5	6.6	3.9	19.7	28.6	15.6	4.1	74.0	43.7	50.3	49.7
67834	BUCKLIN	95.7	93.8	0.3	0.4	0.3	0.5	3.3	6.0	6.4	6.8	6.7	5.8	4.4	22.4	29.6	13.3	4.6	76.0	42.9	49.8	50.2
67835	CIMARRON	92.5	91.9	0.3	0.3	0.3	0.2	9.9	10.9	7.7	7.8	7.7	8.0	5.9	26.5	26.4	8.3	1.7	71.3	34.5	49.1	50.9
67837	COPELAND	91.5	91.2	0.0	0.0	0.0	0.0	9.0	9.5	7.9	8.0	8.8	10.8	5.5	25.4	23.4	9.0	1.3	68.2	32.0	54.1	45.9
67838	DEERFIELD	76.7	75.4	0.2	0.3	0.5	0.5	30.7	32.4	9.9	10.0	9.9	8.5	4.5	25.0	23.5	7.9	0.8	64.9	32.0	52.7	47.3
67839	DIGHTON	97.6	96.9	0.0	0.0	0.2	0.3	1.5	2.3	5.3	5.7	6.0	6.6	4.7	21.8	30.1	15.9	3.9	78.1	44.9	50.4	49.6
67840	ENGLEWOOD	94.2	94.0	0.0	0.0	0.0	0.0	4.7	4.8	6.5	7.7	7.7	6.5	3.6	19.6	29.2	14.9	4.2	73.2	43.6	50.6	49.4
67841	ENSIGN	91.5	90.9	0.0	0.0	0.3	0.3	11.9	12.9	8.8	8.8	8.2	8.2	5.0	26.4	26.4	6.9	1.3	68.9	32.6	52.2	47.8
67842	FORD	95.9	93.6	0.4	0.4	0.0	0.0	6.4	11.0	6.6	7.4	7.4	6.6	4.1	25.2	29.7	11.6	1.6	74.4	40.0	50.6	49.4
67844	FOWLER	94.9	94.5	0.2	0.2	0.0	0.0	7.0	7.7	6.2	6.6	7.1	6.9	4.1	22.9	26.2	15.3	4.8	75.0	42.2	48.6	51.4
67846	GARDEN CITY	67.8	61.5	1.3	1.5	3.2	3.9	45.3	54.8	10.6	9.3	8.4	8.5	7.5	28.2	20.0	6.4	1.1	66.7	28.6	51.0	49.0
67849	HANSTON	97.2	97.0	1.2	1.3	0.0	0.0	2.1	2.2	4.3	5.6	6.7	6.9	4.7	21.3	32.9	14.8	2.8	79.1	45.3	52.1	47.9
67850	HEALY	98.1	97.7	0.0	0.0	0.0	0.0	1.2	1.8	6.2	6.5	6.7	7.0	4.7	21.2	30.1	14.5	3.1	75.9	43.3	49.0	51.0
67851	HOLCOMB	83.5	76.8	0.9	1.1	0.3	0.4	21.3	30.9	9.4	9.3	8.8	9.3	7.8	27.4	23.2	4.5	0.3	66.8	28.2	49.8	50.2
67853	INGALLS	91.4	90.7	0.1	0.1	0.0	0.0	10.1	11.0	7.8	7.9	9.6	10.0	5.3	26.2	24.1	8.4	0.6	67.4	32.3	51.9	48.1
67854	JETMORE	97.3	97.3	0.8	0.8	0.0	0.0	2.9	3.0	5.8	6.9	7.8	7.3	4.8	21.9	26.1	15.5	4.0	74.2	41.8	48.5	51.5
67855	JOHNSON	83.6	78.6	0.7	0.8	0.2	0.3	25.1	33.6	8.3	8.5	8.2	6.9	4.3	26.6	24.5	10.8	1.9	70.3	35.8	51.8	48.2
67857	KENDALL	88.2	87.3	1.0	1.0	1.0	1.0	12.7	13.7	6.9	7.8	7.8	6.9	3.9	21.6	25.5	14.7	4.9	72.5	40.8	49.0	51.0
67859	KISMET	77.7	70.5	0.5	0.5	0.1	0.1	37.6	51.5	9.3	8.7	8.1	7.6	7.8	27.8	23.4	6.7	0.6	69.4	29.8	51.7	48.3
67860	LAKIN	81.9	81.0	0.7	0.7	0.4	0.4	24.7	26.1	8.8	8.7	8.4	7.9	6.2	24.8	24.4	9.0	1.7	68.7	32.6	51.3	48.7
67861	LEOTI	85.8	80.9	0.1	0.1	0.1	0.1	19.2	26.3	8.2	8.7	8.4	6.5	3.9	24.1	25.5	11.7	3.0	70.3	37.7	51.2	48.8
67862	MANTER	90.0	85.9	0.0	0.0	0.0	0.0	14.5	20.3	6.6	7.2	7.2	7.6	5.2	25.2	27.6	12.1	1.4	74.1	37.9	52.1	47.9
67863	MARIENTHAL	95.5	93.4	0.0	0.0	0.0	0.0	4.9	7.4	6.6	7.9	7.9	7.0	4.5	23.1	30.6	11.2	1.2	72.3	40.0	53.3	46.7
67864	MEADE	94.2	93.9	0.6	0.6	0.4	0.4	5.4	5.8	6.7	6.7	6.8	7.5	5.6	21.8	25.8	15.0	4.1	75.0	41.0	49.2	50.8
67865	MINNEOLA	97.3	96.8	0.3	0.4	0.1	0.1	3.9	4.7	5.7	6.2	6.8	7.4	4.3	21.3	29.3	15.1	3.8	75.9	43.5	49.4	50.6
	KANSAS	86.1	83.7	5.7	5.9	1.8	2.6	7.0	9.4	7.1	6.9	6.9	7.3	7.3	25.9	25.7	10.7	2.2	75.0	36.3	49.6	50.4
	UNITED STATES	75.1	72.0	12.3	12.7	3.8	4.6	12.5	15.7	6.8	6.7	6.6	7.1	6.9	27.0	26.0	10.9	1.9	75.7	36.9	49.2	50.8

ZIP CODE #	POST OFFICE NAME	2009 Per Capita Income	2009 HH Income Base	2009 HOUSEHOLD INCOME DISTRIBUTION (%) Less than $25,000	$25,000 to $49,999	$50,000 to $99,999	$100,000 to $149,999	$150,000 or More	MEDIAN HOUSEHOLD INCOME 2009	2014	2009 National Centile	2009 State Centile	2009 Home Value Base	2009 HOME VALUE DISTRIBUTION (%) Less than $50,000	$50,000 to $89,999	$90,000 to $174,999	$175,000 to $399,999	$400,000 or More	2009 Median Home Value
67621	AGRA	19926	208	29.8	32.7	31.7	2.4	3.4	36135	39445	21	15	161	46.6	17.4	30.4	3.1	2.5	56875
67622	ALMENA	24820	239	30.5	41.4	23.4	1.3	3.3	35812	36340	20	13	192	45.8	31.3	20.3	2.6	0.0	53478
67623	ALTON	18788	123	34.1	34.1	27.6	3.3	0.8	34644	37644	17	8	95	44.2	25.3	16.8	7.4	6.3	57857
67625	BOGUE	21372	136	36.0	33.1	25.0	1.5	4.4	35000	36947	18	10	111	42.3	29.7	23.4	2.7	1.8	60625
67626	BUNKER HILL	27414	91	26.4	30.8	31.9	4.4	6.6	40450	42412	34	35	72	62.5	22.2	12.5	2.8	0.0	41000
67627	CATHARINE	0	0	0.0	0.0	0.0	0.0	0.0	0	52500	0	0	0	0.0	0.0	0.0	0.0	0.0	0
67628	CEDAR	13534	19	31.6	31.6	36.8	0.0	0.0	37351	47500	25	21	15	46.7	33.3	20.0	0.0	0.0	52500
67629	CLAYTON	18183	23	21.7	39.1	39.1	0.0	0.0	41115	42367	36	40	18	50.0	27.8	22.2	0.0	0.0	50000
67631	COLLYER	18503	161	33.5	27.3	35.4	3.7	0.0	34826	37880	17	9	130	42.3	21.5	30.0	3.1	3.1	65000
67632	DAMAR	18687	85	28.2	37.6	31.8	2.4	0.0	38042	41151	27	24	66	57.6	24.2	12.1	6.1	0.0	43750
67634	DORRANCE	26724	139	26.6	30.2	32.4	5.0	5.8	40322	41182	34	34	110	58.2	23.6	14.5	3.6	0.0	41000
67635	DRESDEN	18385	41	29.3	34.1	34.1	2.4	0.0	36144	37351	21	15	32	46.9	28.1	15.6	6.3	3.1	53333
67637	ELLIS	20593	988	28.1	33.5	32.9	4.6	0.9	40546	42782	34	36	752	28.9	32.4	32.8	5.5	0.4	75672
67638	GAYLORD	17989	256	30.1	30.9	35.9	2.7	0.4	37708	40661	26	22	209	42.1	32.1	20.1	3.8	1.9	54853
67639	GLADE	19271	104	28.8	34.6	31.7	3.8	1.0	41815	42983	39	43	87	55.2	16.1	24.1	4.6	0.0	45000
67640	GORHAM	21209	197	21.3	36.5	33.0	6.6	2.5	43283	46162	43	50	157	31.2	23.6	34.4	8.9	1.9	80625
67642	HILL CITY	20266	871	31.8	35.6	27.4	3.6	1.6	36750	37569	23	18	672	37.8	34.8	24.9	2.4	0.1	63846
67643	JENNINGS	21482	103	29.1	35.9	31.1	2.9	1.0	35450	37363	19	12	80	47.5	28.8	13.8	8.8	1.3	52857
67644	KIRWIN	18721	117	29.1	34.2	32.5	3.4	0.9	41862	43366	39	44	98	58.2	14.3	22.4	5.1	0.0	43846
67645	LENORA	19073	257	22.6	38.1	37.4	1.6	0.4	42206	45206	40	45	202	47.0	26.7	20.3	5.0	1.0	54000
67646	LOGAN	18470	241	29.5	34.4	32.0	4.1	0.0	38230	41194	27	25	192	49.0	29.7	18.8	1.6	1.0	50952
67647	LONG ISLAND	20083	110	24.5	33.6	38.2	2.7	0.9	42707	42970	42	48	90	37.8	27.8	28.9	5.6	0.0	72857
67648	LUCAS	19561	226	33.6	34.5	25.7	5.3	0.9	37557	38025	25	21	186	56.5	20.4	17.2	5.9	0.0	42000
67649	LURAY	18596	134	36.6	40.3	18.7	3.7	0.7	31356	31409	10	3	107	65.4	13.1	12.1	5.6	3.7	32500
67650	MORLAND	21848	170	34.1	27.1	31.2	4.7	2.9	40448	43465	34	35	144	47.2	26.4	22.2	4.2	0.0	55714
67651	NATOMA	17963	235	33.2	34.5	29.4	2.6	0.4	35611	37498	20	12	181	44.8	24.9	17.7	7.2	5.5	57308
67653	NORCATUR	20219	103	29.1	35.9	31.1	2.9	1.0	35450	37363	19	12	80	47.5	28.8	13.8	8.8	1.3	52857
67654	NORTON	18143	1562	31.1	36.6	27.5	2.8	2.0	36027	37370	21	14	1195	32.0	31.4	32.7	3.4	0.5	73281
67656	OGALLAH	17446	141	34.8	26.2	34.8	4.3	0.0	33975	34774	15	7	114	44.7	21.1	28.1	3.5	2.6	61429
67657	PALCO	20773	148	28.4	37.2	30.4	2.7	1.4	38167	40000	27	24	116	60.3	23.3	10.3	6.0	0.0	40769
67658	PARADISE	17808	65	36.9	38.5	21.5	3.1	0.0	31094	31572	10	3	52	63.5	13.5	15.4	5.8	1.9	33750
67659	PENOKEE	15000	7	57.1	14.3	28.6	0.0	0.0	17143	17143	1	0	6	66.7	0.0	33.3	0.0	0.0	45000
67660	PFEIFER	13229	9	33.3	44.4	22.2	0.0	0.0	32265	37278	12	4	7	0.0	14.3	85.7	0.0	0.0	112500
67661	PHILLIPSBURG	22323	1400	26.1	30.1	39.1	2.7	2.0	45242	46625	49	58	1061	30.3	28.0	36.9	3.6	1.2	79226
67663	PLAINVILLE	17905	1098	28.4	41.9	26.8	2.0	0.9	35515	36934	19	12	836	36.6	37.1	19.9	5.5	1.0	61900
67664	PRAIRIE VIEW	20112	127	24.4	33.9	37.8	3.1	0.8	42662	43187	41	48	103	38.8	27.2	29.1	4.9	0.0	70714
67665	RUSSELL	19421	2142	36.9	30.5	26.0	4.9	1.7	33390	34744	14	6	1557	33.7	33.3	26.1	6.5	0.4	68929
67669	STOCKTON	19417	767	30.2	36.2	30.0	2.5	1.0	36905	39136	23	19	586	43.7	27.3	22.0	5.3	1.7	58409
67671	VICTORIA	20797	679	28.0	34.5	32.5	3.8	1.2	39739	42341	32	30	544	21.3	25.9	44.5	8.3	0.0	93125
67672	WAKEENEY	21192	1026	32.4	30.3	32.2	3.6	1.6	37211	38917	24	20	826	34.9	27.8	31.6	5.1	0.6	70755
67673	WALDO	18897	43	39.5	41.9	16.3	2.3	0.0	29403	30000	7	2	34	67.6	11.8	11.8	5.9	2.9	30000
67675	WOODSTON	17749	113	32.7	31.0	34.5	1.8	0.0	36244	38285	21	15	89	37.1	24.7	27.0	4.5	6.7	74167
67701	COLBY	23707	2581	23.3	29.7	35.8	7.9	3.3	46851	49349	54	63	1743	13.2	26.7	46.1	12.9	1.1	99643
67730	ATWOOD	19638	795	32.2	32.6	29.9	4.0	1.3	37681	40000	26	22	599	40.7	25.7	28.9	4.7	0.0	63367
67731	BIRD CITY	20743	330	37.6	31.2	24.2	3.6	3.3	32797	33546	13	5	254	37.4	26.4	22.8	8.7	4.7	70556
67732	BREWSTER	23084	145	24.1	33.8	34.5	6.2	1.4	42349	45752	40	47	116	37.1	22.4	30.2	8.6	1.7	71667
67733	EDSON	23554	89	14.6	30.3	47.2	5.6	2.2	54520	56140	70	83	69	17.4	29.0	33.3	17.4	2.9	96250
67734	GEM	23424	47	19.1	27.7	44.7	6.4	2.1	52593	52354	67	79	36	36.1	19.4	30.6	11.1	2.8	75000
67735	GOODLAND	21028	2273	26.8	33.3	33.3	5.0	1.5	41484	43490	38	42	1552	20.6	33.9	34.1	10.6	0.8	84052
67736	GOVE	20360	115	27.8	32.2	33.0	4.3	2.6	41426	44209	37	42	93	43.0	28.0	22.6	6.5	0.0	58125
67737	GRAINFIELD	22466	165	27.3	31.5	33.9	4.8	2.4	42343	45569	40	47	137	43.8	30.7	19.7	5.8	0.0	57083
67738	GRINNELL	22928	219	27.9	30.6	35.2	4.6	1.8	42676	44785	41	48	183	45.4	31.1	18.0	5.5	0.0	55000
67739	HERNDON	22088	139	31.7	31.7	28.8	5.8	2.2	38091	38882	27	24	111	53.2	18.9	18.0	9.9	0.0	47083
67740	HOXIE	20445	833	27.1	35.1	31.2	4.1	2.5	41584	43628	38	42	678	31.3	24.9	36.6	5.6	1.6	81765
67741	KANORADO	13989	163	33.7	47.2	18.4	0.6	0.0	32521	33769	12	5	116	39.7	46.6	13.8	0.0	0.0	64000
67743	LEVANT	22132	52	23.1	32.7	36.5	5.8	1.9	45000	44082	48	57	42	38.1	21.4	28.6	9.5	2.4	70000
67744	LUDELL	19375	46	34.8	32.6	23.9	6.5	2.2	35000	38178	18	10	37	54.1	18.9	16.2	10.8	0.0	46250
67745	MC DONALD	21687	177	28.2	28.8	36.2	6.2	0.6	42976	45772	42	49	138	49.3	21.0	23.9	5.8	0.0	51429
67748	OAKLEY	20026	933	27.3	36.3	29.2	5.5	1.7	37918	39798	26	23	710	31.8	32.7	28.6	6.8	0.1	73390
67749	OBERLIN	18373	1064	31.1	39.2	26.2	3.2	0.3	35914	36508	20	13	802	37.8	28.2	30.9	2.2	0.9	66364
67751	PARK	21269	129	27.9	33.3	32.6	3.9	2.3	39739	41312	32	30	97	40.2	20.6	32.0	7.2	0.0	76250
67752	QUINTER	18981	533	26.6	35.3	32.8	3.8	1.5	40511	42270	34	35	415	24.6	32.0	35.4	7.7	0.2	82763
67753	REXFORD	26400	130	18.5	28.5	43.1	7.7	2.3	52459	52875	67	79	100	35.0	21.0	31.0	10.0	3.0	76000
67756	SAINT FRANCIS	20073	985	27.5	42.2	24.7	4.3	1.3	37738	39680	26	22	758	29.6	28.1	31.3	9.6	1.5	76531
67757	SELDEN	17362	281	29.5	38.8	28.8	1.8	1.1	39813	42209	32	30	232	39.7	26.3	24.1	9.5	0.4	63846
67758	SHARON SPRINGS	20441	413	29.1	29.8	34.1	4.4	2.7	41840	42741	39	43	332	38.3	30.1	28.3	3.0	0.3	62647
67761	WALLACE	21478	104	29.8	32.7	26.9	5.8	4.8	37345	40000	25	21	74	40.5	32.4	20.3	4.1	2.7	62857
67762	WESKAN	18935	125	31.2	30.4	27.2	6.4	4.8	38072	37648	27	24	89	38.2	32.6	21.3	5.6	2.2	65000
67764	WINONA	22170	229	19.2	39.7	32.3	4.4	4.4	42015	44539	39	45	170	44.7	21.8	27.6	5.9	0.0	57500
67801	DODGE CITY	19109	9868	20.7	29.5	39.8	6.2	3.7	49782	52548	61	73	6228	20.2	25.9	41.4	11.5	0.9	95137
67831	ASHLAND	21958	491	26.9	34.0	32.0	4.1	3.1	41365	42738	37	41	379	40.9	34.0	18.5	5.8	0.8	60714
67834	BUCKLIN	21770	365	21.6	29.6	41.4	4.1	3.3	49187	51560	59	71	295	23.4	40.7	28.1	7.8	0.0	76711
67835	CIMARRON	21026	1030	19.4	31.7	40.4	5.4	3.1	49084	49685	59	71	753	20.2	18.7	46.7	13.3	1.1	104344
67837	COPELAND	20769	190	17.9	35.8	37.4	5.3	3.7	46943	48532	54	63	143	23.1	23.1	42.7	11.2	0.0	97857
67838	DEERFIELD	17194	422	21.3	31.3	39.6	4.7	3.1	47253	48879	55	64	306	38.6	19.0	29.4	12.1	1.0	74286
67839	DIGHTON	22959	695	25.8	33.2	34.1	4.3	2.6	42830	43873	42	49	538	36.6	35.1	23.4	4.5	0.4	64894
67840	ENGLEWOOD	21939	71	26.8	32.4	33.8	4.2	2.8	42338	42338	40	46	55	41.8	36.4	16.4	5.5	0.0	59000
67841	ENSIGN	21270	117	20.5	33.3	39.3	3.4	3.4	47039	48616	54	64	92	34.8	17.4	39.1	8.7	0.0	86000
67842	FORD	19925	185	17.8	33.5	41.1	5.4	2.2	49012	51676	59	71	147	36.7	15.0	25.9	19.0	3.4	83750
67844	FOWLER	21234	347	21.6	38.6	33.7	4.0	2.0	44003	45922	45	53	261	32.6	24.9	33.3	8.8	0.4	77917
67846	GARDEN CITY	19508	11453	19.1	30.2	39.7	7.5	3.5	50575	52921	63	76	7307	20.3	21.8	43.1	13.8	1.0	100857
67849	HANSTON	18393	195	22.1	33.8	39.0	3.1	2.1	46795	47810	54	62	161	37.3	23.0	31.1	6.8	1.9	76500
67850	HEALY	21074	152	20.4	34.2	37.5	4.6	3.3	46377	47331	52	61	115	19.1	40.9	33.9	6.1	0.0	78750
67851	HOLCOMB	19284	780	12.4	26.8	51.2	6.7	2.9	61014	60799	79	89	612	9.6	22.9	55.1	11.1	1.3	105189
67853	INGALLS	19517	314	17.5	37.6	33.8	7.6	3.5	45908	48297	51	60	218	19.3	27.5	37.6	15.1	0.5	93333
67854	JETMORE	19294	610	28.0	33.8	32.1	4.3	1.8	41343	42963	37	41	467	27.4	33.4	31.0	6.2	1.9	75921
67855	JOHNSON	21235	685	22.8	29.2	39.3	5.3	3.5	48144	50280	57	67	467	27.6	27.2	36.0	9.2	0.0	84512
67857	KENDALL	19269	38	23.7	34.2	34.2	5.3	2.6	43179	43179	43	50	28	14.3	28.6	50.0	7.1	0.0	100000
67859	KISMET	18040	516	18.8	31.0	39.9	6.6	3.7	50116	52011	61	74	375	37.9	31.2	22.9	8.0	0.0	65313
67860	LAKIN	18533	1158	22.5	31.4	37.9	6.0	2.2	46897	47731	54	63	859	20.0	23.5	42.4	12.8	1.3	99407
67861	LEOTI	19934	871	27.9	31.9	32.7	5.1	2.4	41677	43353	38	43	650	35.5	25.7	32.8	4.9	1.1	72391
67862	MANTER	24764	112	18.8	26.8	42.0	6.3	6.3	52840	53340	68	80	73	20.5	26.0	35.6	17.8	0.0	98333
67863	MARIENTHAL	24974	93	20.4	29.0	36.6	7.5	6.5	50461	52583	62	75	64	26.6	25.0	39.1	7.8	1.6	87500
67864	MEADE	19410	821	25.8	35.2	31.2	6.6	1.2	42328	43957	40	46	627	29.2	32.2	30.8	5.3	2.6	73936
67865	MINNEOLA	20192	439	26.9	30.1	36.4	3.9	2.7	42361	44606	41	47	334	28.4	24.0	33.2	12.0	2.4	84286
	KANSAS	26028		20.3	26.8	37.6	9.9	5.4	52748	54940				18.1	21.6	35.7	21.6	3.0	107692
	UNITED STATES	27277		20.9	24.4	35.3	11.7	7.6	54719	56938				9.3	13.1	31.6	32.6	13.5	162279

ZIP CODE #	POST OFFICE NAME	FINANCIAL SERVICES: Auto Loan	Home Loan	Invest-ments	Retire-ment Plans	THE HOME: Home Improvements: Home Repair	Lawn & Garden	Furnishings: Comput-ers & Hard-ware-Personal	Major Appli-ances	TV, Radio, Sound Equip-ment	Furni-ture	ENTERTAINMENT: Dine out/ Carry out	Sports Equip-ment	Fees & Tickets	Toys & Games	Travel	Cable TV	PERSONAL: Apparel & Services	Auto Repairs	Health Insur-ance	Pets & Supplies
67621	AGRA	89	61	97	61	64	94	68	84	70	55	70	70	50	69	67	77	45	79	89	104
67622	ALMENA	77	53	85	53	56	82	59	73	61	48	61	61	43	60	59	67	39	69	78	90
67623	ALTON	72	49	79	49	52	76	55	68	57	44	56	56	40	56	55	62	37	64	72	84
67625	BOGUE	88	61	97	61	64	93	67	84	70	55	69	69	49	69	67	76	45	78	88	103
67626	BUNKER HILL	105	72	115	72	76	111	80	100	83	65	82	82	59	82	80	91	54	93	105	123
67627	CATHARINE	0	0	0	0	0	0	0	0	0	0	0	0	0	0	0	0	0	0	0	0
67628	CEDAR	69	48	76	48	50	73	53	66	55	43	55	54	39	54	53	60	35	62	70	81
67629	CLAYTON	76	53	84	52	55	81	58	72	61	47	60	60	43	59	58	66	39	68	77	89
67631	COLLYER	75	52	82	51	54	79	57	71	60	46	59	59	42	58	57	65	38	66	75	88
67632	DAMAR	80	55	88	55	57	84	61	76	63	49	63	63	45	62	61	69	41	71	80	93
67634	DORRANCE	105	72	115	72	75	111	80	100	83	65	82	82	59	82	80	91	53	93	105	122
67635	DRESDEN	79	54	86	54	57	83	60	75	62	49	62	62	44	61	60	68	40	70	79	92
67637	ELLIS	74	61	70	61	60	78	64	72	68	58	67	56	57	68	63	73	45	70	79	86
67638	GAYLORD	76	53	84	52	55	81	58	73	61	47	60	60	43	60	58	66	39	68	77	89
67639	GLADE	85	59	93	59	62	90	65	81	68	53	67	67	48	67	65	74	44	76	86	99
67640	GORHAM	89	61	98	61	64	94	68	84	71	55	70	70	50	69	68	77	45	79	89	104
67642	HILL CITY	76	54	77	53	56	79	59	73	66	52	63	56	47	64	58	72	42	68	80	87
67643	JENNINGS	78	53	85	53	56	82	59	74	62	48	61	61	43	60	59	67	40	69	78	91
67644	KIRWIN	85	58	93	58	61	90	65	81	68	53	67	67	48	66	65	74	43	75	85	99
67645	LENORA	78	53	85	53	56	82	59	74	62	48	61	61	43	60	59	67	40	69	78	91
67646	LOGAN	77	53	85	53	56	82	59	73	61	48	61	61	43	60	59	67	39	68	77	90
67647	LONG ISLAND	84	58	92	58	61	89	64	80	67	52	66	66	47	66	64	73	43	75	84	98
67648	LUCAS	78	54	86	54	56	82	60	74	62	48	61	61	44	61	59	68	40	69	78	91
67649	LURAY	67	46	74	46	48	71	51	64	53	41	53	53	38	52	51	58	34	59	67	78
67650	MORLAND	89	61	98	61	64	94	68	85	71	55	70	70	50	69	68	77	45	79	89	104
67651	NATOMA	72	50	79	50	52	76	55	69	57	45	57	57	40	56	55	63	37	64	72	84
67653	NORCATUR	78	53	85	53	56	82	59	74	62	48	61	61	43	60	59	67	40	69	78	91
67654	NORTON	75	54	76	53	56	79	59	73	65	52	63	55	47	64	57	72	42	68	79	86
67656	OGALLAH	75	52	83	52	54	80	58	72	60	47	59	59	42	59	57	65	38	67	76	88
67657	PALCO	80	55	88	55	58	85	61	76	64	50	63	63	45	63	61	70	41	71	81	94
67658	PARADISE	71	49	77	48	51	74	54	67	56	44	55	55	39	55	54	61	36	63	71	82
67659	PENOKEE	49	34	53	34	36	52	38	47	40	31	39	38	28	39	37	44	26	44	50	57
67660	PFEIFER	63	43	69	43	45	67	48	60	50	39	50	50	35	49	48	55	32	56	63	74
67661	PHILLIPSBURG	81	66	84	65	68	89	68	81	74	62	72	61	60	73	68	81	49	77	89	96
67663	PLAINVILLE	71	51	73	50	53	75	56	69	61	49	59	53	44	60	54	67	39	64	75	82
67664	PRAIRIE VIEW	84	58	92	57	60	88	64	79	66	52	66	66	47	65	64	73	43	74	84	98
67665	RUSSELL	73	53	74	51	55	77	57	71	64	51	62	53	46	63	56	70	41	66	77	84
67669	STOCKTON	76	54	77	53	56	79	59	73	65	52	63	56	46	64	57	71	42	68	79	87
67671	VICTORIA	74	64	79	62	65	83	64	75	69	58	67	57	58	67	65	74	45	71	83	89
67672	WAKEENEY	75	59	80	59	61	82	62	75	66	54	65	58	52	65	62	72	43	70	81	89
67673	WALDO	68	46	74	46	49	71	52	64	54	42	53	53	38	53	51	59	34	60	68	79
67675	WOODSTON	71	49	78	49	51	75	54	67	56	44	56	56	40	55	54	62	36	63	71	83
67701	COLBY	92	75	86	75	76	91	81	87	83	74	82	68	70	83	77	87	56	86	92	105
67730	ATWOOD	75	53	77	52	55	78	58	72	64	51	62	55	46	63	57	71	41	67	78	86
67731	BIRD CITY	81	56	89	55	58	85	62	77	64	50	63	63	45	63	61	70	41	72	81	94
67732	BREWSTER	101	69	110	69	72	106	77	95	80	62	79	79	56	78	76	87	51	89	101	117
67733	EDSON	112	77	123	77	80	118	85	106	89	69	88	88	62	87	85	97	57	99	112	130
67734	GEM	103	71	114	71	74	109	79	98	82	64	81	81	58	81	79	90	53	92	104	121
67735	GOODLAND	81	63	78	62	64	82	69	77	73	62	71	60	58	72	66	78	48	75	83	92
67736	GOVE	92	63	100	63	66	97	70	87	73	57	72	72	51	71	70	79	47	81	92	107
67737	GRAINFIELD	93	64	102	64	67	98	71	88	74	57	73	73	52	72	70	80	47	82	93	108
67738	GRINNELL	93	64	102	64	67	98	71	88	74	58	73	73	52	73	71	81	48	83	93	109
67739	HERNDON	84	58	93	58	61	89	64	80	67	52	66	66	47	66	64	73	43	75	85	99
67740	HOXIE	89	61	97	61	64	94	68	84	70	55	70	70	50	69	67	77	45	79	89	104
67741	KANORADO	62	42	68	42	44	65	47	58	49	38	48	48	34	48	47	53	31	55	62	72
67743	LEVANT	100	69	110	69	72	106	77	95	80	62	79	79	56	78	76	87	51	89	101	117
67744	LUDELL	84	58	92	57	60	88	64	79	66	52	66	66	47	65	64	72	43	74	84	98
67745	MC DONALD	87	60	96	60	63	92	67	83	69	54	69	69	49	68	66	76	45	77	88	102
67748	OAKLEY	80	58	81	56	60	84	63	78	70	56	68	59	50	69	61	77	45	73	85	92
67749	OBERLIN	70	50	73	49	52	74	54	67	59	47	57	53	42	58	53	65	38	63	73	81
67751	PARK	87	60	96	60	63	92	66	83	69	54	68	68	49	68	66	75	44	77	87	102
67752	QUINTER	84	58	92	57	60	88	64	79	67	52	66	66	47	65	64	73	43	74	84	98
67753	REXFORD	104	72	114	72	75	110	80	99	83	64	82	82	58	81	79	90	53	92	104	122
67756	SAINT FRANCIS	81	57	86	56	59	85	63	78	67	53	66	62	48	66	62	74	43	73	83	94
67757	SELDEN	75	51	82	51	54	79	57	71	59	46	59	59	42	58	57	65	38	66	75	87
67758	SHARON SPRINGS	88	60	96	60	63	93	67	83	70	54	69	69	49	68	67	76	45	78	88	103
67761	WALLACE	99	68	108	68	71	104	75	94	78	61	77	77	55	77	75	85	50	87	99	115
67762	WESKAN	98	68	108	67	71	104	75	93	78	61	77	77	55	77	75	85	50	87	99	115
67764	WINONA	98	68	106	67	71	103	75	93	79	62	78	76	56	77	74	86	51	87	99	114
67801	DODGE CITY	86	83	75	79	81	79	84	83	83	86	84	63	81	85	81	83	59	84	82	96
67831	ASHLAND	91	63	100	63	66	97	70	87	73	57	72	72	51	71	69	79	47	81	92	107
67834	BUCKLIN	99	68	109	68	71	105	76	94	79	61	78	78	55	77	75	86	51	88	99	116
67835	CIMARRON	95	81	84	79	81	92	80	88	83	78	82	66	71	85	77	86	55	84	89	105
67837	COPELAND	107	74	117	73	77	113	82	101	85	66	84	84	60	83	81	93	54	95	107	125
67838	DEERFIELD	95	66	105	65	69	101	73	90	76	59	75	75	53	74	72	83	49	85	96	111
67839	DIGHTON	91	64	98	63	67	96	70	87	75	59	73	70	53	73	69	82	48	81	93	106
67840	ENGLEWOOD	92	63	101	63	66	97	70	87	73	57	72	72	51	71	70	79	47	81	92	107
67841	ENSIGN	103	71	114	71	74	109	79	98	82	64	81	81	58	81	79	90	53	92	104	121
67842	FORD	99	68	109	68	71	105	76	94	79	61	78	78	56	77	75	86	51	88	100	116
67844	FOWLER	93	64	102	64	67	98	71	89	74	58	73	73	52	73	71	81	48	83	94	109
67846	GARDEN CITY	91	85	77	82	82	81	88	85	86	89	87	66	83	89	83	86	61	87	84	100
67849	HANSTON	90	62	99	62	65	95	69	86	72	56	71	71	50	70	69	78	46	80	90	105
67850	HEALY	94	65	102	65	68	99	72	90	76	60	75	73	54	75	72	83	49	84	95	110
67851	HOLCOMB	100	99	88	95	94	92	92	94	90	95	91	72	89	94	89	89	63	91	89	111
67853	INGALLS	104	72	114	72	75	110	80	99	83	64	82	82	58	81	79	90	53	92	104	122
67854	JETMORE	83	59	86	58	61	87	65	80	71	56	69	62	50	69	63	78	45	75	87	96
67855	JOHNSON	105	72	115	72	75	110	80	99	83	65	82	82	58	81	79	91	53	93	105	122
67857	KENDALL	91	62	99	62	65	96	69	86	72	56	71	71	51	71	69	78	46	80	91	106
67859	KISMET	98	82	79	78	79	90	82	87	86	84	86	67	73	90	76	89	58	86	88	105
67860	LAKIN	87	74	77	72	74	84	73	80	76	72	75	61	65	78	70	79	51	77	82	96
67861	LEOTI	90	63	96	62	65	94	68	85	72	58	71	68	51	71	67	79	46	79	89	103
67862	MANTER	115	79	126	79	83	121	88	109	91	71	90	90	64	89	87	99	58	102	115	134
67863	MARIENTHAL	116	80	128	80	84	123	89	110	92	72	91	91	65	91	88	101	59	103	117	136
67864	MEADE	84	60	86	59	63	88	66	82	73	58	70	62	52	71	64	80	47	76	88	96
67865	MINNEOLA	92	63	101	63	66	97	70	88	73	57	72	72	52	72	70	80	47	82	92	108
	KANSAS	98	90	91	91	89	97	94	95	94	90	94	74	88	96	90	96	65	95	98	113
	UNITED STATES	100	100	100	100	100	100	100	100	100	100	100	100	100	100	100	100	100	100	100	100

67867-67954

ZIP CODE #	POST OFFICE NAME	COUNTY FIPS CODE	POPULATION 2000	POPULATION 2009	POPULATION 2014	2000-2009 ANNUAL RATE % Rate	2000-2009 ANNUAL RATE State Centile	HOUSEHOLDS 2000	HOUSEHOLDS 2009	HOUSEHOLDS 2014	HOUSEHOLDS % Annual Rate 2000-2009	HOUSEHOLDS 2009 Average HH Size	FAMILIES 2000	FAMILIES 2009	FAMILIES % Annual Rate 2000-2009
67867	MONTEZUMA	069	1547	1571	1558	0.2	70	503	510	506	0.1	2.86	373	376	0.1
67868	PIERCEVILLE	055	175	177	176	0.1	68	59	60	59	0.2	2.95	48	48	0.0
67869	PLAINS	119	1603	1598	1570	0.0	64	547	533	519	-0.3	3.00	417	403	-0.4
67870	SATANTA	175	2171	2164	2122	0.0	64	722	711	694	-0.2	3.00	562	549	-0.3
67871	SCOTT CITY	171	5039	4582	4346	-1.0	19	2013	1871	1786	-0.8	2.40	1408	1296	-0.9
67876	SPEARVILLE	057	1177	1222	1250	0.4	76	430	437	443	0.2	2.77	322	324	0.1
67877	SUBLETTE	081	2493	2406	2341	-0.4	48	874	841	817	-0.4	2.86	688	657	-0.5
67878	SYRACUSE	075	2569	2589	2600	0.1	68	1016	1005	1002	-0.1	2.54	691	676	-0.2
67879	TRIBUNE	071	1534	1349	1256	-1.4	11	602	544	510	-1.1	2.43	414	370	-1.2
67880	ULYSSES	067	7909	7598	7401	-0.4	48	2742	2688	2634	-0.2	2.80	2099	2043	-0.3
67882	WRIGHT	057	423	438	446	0.4	76	158	160	162	0.1	2.72	120	120	0.0
67901	LIBERAL	175	20469	21413	21799	0.5	79	6771	6927	7005	0.2	3.03	4976	5050	0.2
67950	ELKHART	129	2561	2353	2249	-0.9	23	959	888	850	-0.8	2.59	698	641	-0.9
67951	HUGOTON	189	4609	4461	4377	-0.4	48	1692	1625	1590	-0.4	2.71	1221	1163	-0.5
67952	MOSCOW	189	854	806	787	-0.6	36	296	280	273	-0.6	2.88	236	222	-0.7
67953	RICHFIELD	129	218	204	196	-0.7	32	93	87	84	-0.7	2.34	71	66	-0.8
67954	ROLLA	129	717	671	645	-0.7	32	254	239	230	-0.7	2.81	193	180	-0.8
	KANSAS					0.6					0.6	2.49			0.5
	UNITED STATES					1.0					1.1	2.59			0.9

ZIP CODE		RACE (%)						% Hispanic Origin		2009 AGE DISTRIBUTION (%)										MEDIAN AGE		
#	POST OFFICE NAME	White		Black		Asian/Pacific																
		2000	2009	2000	2009	2000	2009	2000	2009	0-4	5-9	10-14	15-19	20-24	25-44	45-64	65-84	85+	18+	2009	% 2009 Males	% 2009 Females
67867	MONTEZUMA	93.2	92.9	0.1	0.1	0.1	0.1	8.9	9.5	8.3	8.3	8.4	7.6	4.6	23.7	21.1	11.8	6.0	70.0	35.8	47.1	52.9
67868	PIERCEVILLE	83.0	75.1	0.6	0.6	0.6	0.6	19.9	29.9	10.2	10.7	9.0	7.9	6.2	27.7	21.5	6.2	0.6	65.5	29.4	51.4	48.6
67869	PLAINS	85.0	84.1	0.2	0.2	0.1	0.1	20.5	21.7	10.5	10.8	10.1	7.4	3.9	25.9	21.1	9.0	1.2	63.7	31.9	51.5	48.5
67870	SATANTA	83.0	78.0	0.4	0.4	0.6	0.7	28.7	37.8	9.1	8.6	8.9	8.1	5.2	25.3	23.6	9.1	2.2	68.1	33.2	50.5	49.5
67871	SCOTT CITY	95.4	93.7	0.1	0.1	0.1	0.2	6.4	9.2	6.0	6.3	6.6	6.7	5.5	22.1	29.7	13.6	3.5	76.8	42.4	48.8	51.2
67876	SPEARVILLE	97.9	97.0	0.1	0.2	0.0	0.0	5.3	9.2	5.6	6.1	6.5	7.7	4.8	23.3	30.3	13.4	2.3	76.4	42.2	51.8	48.2
67877	SUBLETTE	86.9	83.0	0.1	0.1	0.6	0.8	18.9	25.6	9.3	8.4	8.4	8.1	6.2	25.3	24.2	8.9	1.2	68.6	32.3	51.9	48.1
67878	SYRACUSE	81.4	80.4	0.5	0.5	0.5	0.5	20.9	22.2	7.1	7.4	7.5	6.7	4.5	23.9	26.7	13.2	3.1	73.6	39.2	50.3	49.7
67879	TRIBUNE	93.1	90.5	0.2	0.2	0.2	0.2	11.5	16.4	6.8	7.0	8.0	8.0	4.3	22.3	26.6	13.9	3.0	72.8	40.2	50.2	49.8
67880	ULYSSES	77.0	70.9	0.2	0.3	0.4	0.4	34.7	44.3	8.9	8.7	8.1	7.4	6.6	26.3	24.4	8.3	1.3	69.8	32.4	50.5	49.5
67882	WRIGHT	94.8	92.2	0.5	0.5	0.2	0.5	9.2	15.1	5.9	5.9	6.4	7.3	5.3	24.4	29.7	13.2	1.8	77.4	41.2	51.6	48.4
67901	LIBERAL	64.1	58.2	4.1	3.7	3.2	3.9	42.9	51.8	9.8	8.8	7.9	7.9	8.0	28.9	19.9	7.2	1.6	69.0	29.2	51.1	48.9
67950	ELKHART	89.0	85.2	0.1	0.1	1.1	1.6	13.7	19.0	8.4	8.1	7.4	6.3	6.2	24.2	25.0	12.0	2.3	72.2	35.8	48.3	51.7
67951	HUGOTON	82.4	77.0	1.0	1.1	0.3	0.4	22.1	29.9	8.5	8.4	7.9	7.3	5.6	25.3	24.3	10.4	2.3	70.6	34.5	49.7	50.3
67952	MOSCOW	86.1	81.9	0.7	0.7	0.2	0.2	19.5	26.8	8.7	9.2	8.9	7.1	4.0	24.8	26.4	9.8	1.1	68.6	35.8	50.7	49.3
67953	RICHFIELD	86.3	82.8	0.5	0.5	0.9	1.0	15.1	21.6	8.3	9.3	8.8	7.8	3.4	21.1	26.5	13.2	1.5	67.6	37.7	48.5	51.5
67954	ROLLA	86.8	82.6	0.4	0.4	0.8	1.0	15.3	21.3	8.3	8.6	8.8	8.3	3.7	21.9	26.1	12.8	1.3	68.9	37.3	49.0	51.0
	KANSAS	86.1	83.7	5.7	5.9	1.8	2.6	7.0	9.4	7.1	6.9	6.9	7.3	7.3	25.9	25.7	10.7	2.2	75.0	36.3	49.6	50.4
	UNITED STATES	75.1	72.0	12.3	12.7	3.8	4.6	12.5	15.7	6.8	6.7	6.6	7.1	6.9	27.0	26.0	10.9	1.9	75.7	36.9	49.2	50.8

INCOME

ZIP CODE #	POST OFFICE NAME	2009 Per Capita Income	2009 HH Income Base	2009 Household Income Distribution (%): Less than $25,000	$25,000 to $49,999	$50,000 to $99,999	$100,000 to $149,999	$150,000 or More	Median Household Income: 2009	2014	2009 National Centile	2009 State Centile	2009 Home Value Base	2009 Home Value Distribution (%): Less than $50,000	$50,000 to $89,999	$90,000 to $174,999	$175,000 to $399,999	$400,000 or More	2009 Median Home Value
67867	MONTEZUMA	21312	510	17.8	36.1	36.9	4.7	4.5	46436	49079	53	61	374	15.5	29.4	42.2	12.8	0.0	100368
67868	PIERCEVILLE	19368	60	5.0	41.7	45.0	5.0	3.3	51595	52864	65	78	43	25.6	30.2	18.6	25.6	0.0	83750
67869	PLAINS	18566	533	23.8	28.7	38.3	6.4	2.8	47930	49133	56	66	378	18.8	32.5	36.0	11.4	1.3	88148
67870	SATANTA	18427	711	22.8	33.6	35.9	5.3	2.4	45048	47351	48	57	500	27.2	30.8	29.6	11.6	0.8	76176
67871	SCOTT CITY	25636	1871	24.5	25.1	38.2	7.8	4.5	50364	50521	62	75	1395	20.1	29.7	39.8	7.4	3.0	90266
67876	SPEARVILLE	21107	437	19.2	30.0	41.6	6.6	2.5	50778	53261	63	76	348	15.2	23.6	42.8	14.4	4.0	102459
67877	SUBLETTE	21506	841	16.6	35.3	37.6	6.3	4.2	48428	50465	58	68	627	22.8	22.3	38.0	15.8	1.1	98243
67878	SYRACUSE	18927	1005	27.8	35.5	30.3	3.9	2.5	39503	40641	31	29	705	22.6	34.6	33.0	9.2	0.6	81984
67879	TRIBUNE	23260	544	24.8	35.5	30.3	5.7	3.7	41793	41848	39	43	407	32.4	29.2	28.3	9.6	0.5	75500
67880	ULYSSES	21265	2688	17.8	32.3	39.6	7.8	2.5	49941	52050	61	73	2011	23.4	22.3	35.1	18.9	0.3	95149
67882	WRIGHT	21138	160	18.1	31.9	41.9	5.6	2.5	50000	52205	61	74	111	17.1	22.5	44.1	15.3	0.9	111719
67901	LIBERAL	18828	6927	22.0	30.0	37.3	7.3	3.4	47886	50908	56	66	4372	20.5	25.8	37.4	14.3	1.9	95016
67950	ELKHART	21619	888	19.7	34.7	36.7	6.4	2.5	46563	48137	53	62	644	22.2	32.5	37.9	7.1	0.3	85522
67951	HUGOTON	21336	1625	18.2	31.1	41.7	6.6	2.3	50680	50958	63	76	1232	20.5	25.4	36.3	16.2	1.6	95204
67952	MOSCOW	23377	280	15.4	33.9	38.9	5.4	6.4	50569	51693	63	76	207	21.7	24.6	27.1	22.2	4.3	97500
67953	RICHFIELD	22460	87	25.3	31.0	40.2	3.4	0.0	44596	46530	47	56	60	26.7	33.3	31.7	8.3	0.0	78333
67954	ROLLA	18650	239	25.9	29.7	38.9	3.8	1.7	45160	47187	49	58	164	27.4	32.9	30.5	9.1	0.0	77500
	KANSAS	26028		20.3	26.8	37.6	9.9	5.4	52748	54940				18.1	21.6	35.7	21.6	3.0	107692
	UNITED STATES	27277		20.9	24.4	35.3	11.7	7.6	54719	56938				9.3	13.1	31.6	32.6	13.5	162279

ZIP CODE	FINANCIAL SERVICES				THE HOME						ENTERTAINMENT						PERSONAL			
					Home Improvements		Furnishings													
# POST OFFICE NAME	Auto Loan	Home Loan	Invest-ments	Retire-ment Plans	Home Repair	Lawn & Garden	Comput-ers & Hard-ware-Personal	Major Appli-ances	TV, Radio, Sound Equip-ment	Furni-ture	Dine out/ Carry out	Sports Equip-ment	Fees & Tickets	Toys & Games	Travel	Cable TV	Apparel & Services	Auto Repairs	Health Insur-ance	Pets & Supplies
67867 MONTEZUMA	111	77	122	76	80	117	85	106	88	69	87	87	62	87	85	96	57	99	112	130
67868 PIERCEVILLE	102	70	112	70	74	108	78	97	81	63	80	80	57	80	78	89	52	91	102	119
67869 PLAINS	99	68	109	68	72	105	76	94	79	62	78	78	56	78	76	86	51	88	100	116
67870 SATANTA	99	68	108	68	71	104	76	94	79	62	78	77	56	77	75	86	51	88	99	115
67871 SCOTT CITY	101	81	108	82	84	107	85	99	88	77	87	78	73	87	86	94	58	94	104	119
67876 SPEARVILLE	105	72	115	72	75	111	80	99	83	65	82	82	59	82	80	91	53	93	105	122
67877 SUBLETTE	106	82	105	80	83	107	85	99	88	76	87	78	69	88	83	94	58	94	103	120
67878 SYRACUSE	86	59	95	59	62	91	66	82	68	53	68	68	48	67	65	75	44	76	86	101
67879 TRIBUNE	102	70	112	70	73	107	78	97	81	63	80	80	57	79	77	88	52	90	102	119
67880 ULYSSES	91	87	79	86	84	92	84	88	85	82	85	67	81	88	82	88	58	86	90	105
67882 WRIGHT	100	72	104	72	74	100	80	94	82	69	82	77	62	81	78	87	54	89	97	114
67901 LIBERAL	86	79	70	76	77	75	83	80	82	84	83	61	78	83	78	81	58	83	78	93
67950 ELKHART	88	78	77	78	79	86	79	84	82	78	81	62	73	83	76	85	55	82	87	99
67951 HUGOTON	95	77	91	76	77	98	80	91	84	73	83	71	68	84	78	89	55	87	96	110
67952 MOSCOW	120	83	132	83	87	127	92	114	96	74	95	94	67	94	91	104	61	107	121	141
67953 RICHFIELD	94	65	103	65	68	99	72	89	75	58	74	74	53	73	72	82	48	83	94	110
67954 ROLLA	94	64	103	64	67	99	72	89	74	58	74	73	52	73	71	81	48	83	94	109
KANSAS	98	90	91	91	89	97	94	95	94	90	94	74	88	96	90	96	65	95	98	113
UNITED STATES	100	100	100	100	100	100	100	100	100	100	100	100	100	100	100	100	100	100	100	100

ZIP CODE #	POST OFFICE NAME	COUNTY FIPS CODE	POPULATION 2000	POPULATION 2009	POPULATION 2014	2000-2009 ANNUAL RATE % Rate	2000-2009 ANNUAL RATE State Centile	HOUSEHOLDS 2000	HOUSEHOLDS 2009	HOUSEHOLDS 2014	HOUSEHOLDS % Annual Rate 2000-2009	HOUSEHOLDS 2009 Average HH Size	FAMILIES 2000	FAMILIES 2009	FAMILIES % Annual Rate 2000-2009
40003	BAGDAD	211	1733	2059	2240	1.9	94	641	774	845	2.1	2.66	518	607	1.7
40004	BARDSTOWN	179	23249	27603	30133	1.9	94	8760	10744	11846	2.2	2.53	6276	7409	1.8
40006	BEDFORD	223	4325	4973	5234	1.5	90	1649	1939	2054	1.8	2.54	1211	1375	1.4
40007	BETHLEHEM	103	312	311	306	0.0	39	119	120	119	0.1	2.59	89	86	-0.4
40008	BLOOMFIELD	179	3411	4248	4685	2.4	96	1304	1644	1822	2.5	2.58	986	1201	2.2
40009	BRADFORDSVILLE	155	1100	1122	1136	0.2	48	440	459	469	0.5	2.44	317	318	0.0
40010	BUCKNER	185	291	619	723	8.5	100	91	197	231	8.7	3.14	78	165	8.4
40011	CAMPBELLSBURG	103	2500	2793	2916	1.2	86	958	1083	1134	1.3	2.58	729	799	1.0
40012	CHAPLIN	179	528	620	673	1.8	93	216	259	282	2.0	2.39	165	191	1.6
40013	COXS CREEK	179	5225	6682	7405	2.7	97	1807	2399	2693	3.1	2.69	1471	1897	2.8
40014	CRESTWOOD	185	14835	19674	22128	3.1	97	5083	6788	7679	3.2	2.89	4314	5636	2.9
40019	EMINENCE	103	3547	3658	3664	0.3	54	1432	1496	1504	0.5	2.44	996	993	0.0
40022	FINCHVILLE	211	685	832	903	2.1	95	262	327	364	2.4	2.00	214	259	2.1
40023	FISHERVILLE	111	2204	3625	4228	5.5	99	773	1282	1505	5.6	2.78	650	1047	5.3
40025	GLENVIEW	111	204	221	228	0.9	80	79	88	91	1.2	2.51	58	61	0.5
40026	GOSHEN	185	4595	5490	5972	1.9	94	1495	1793	1961	2.0	3.06	1299	1523	1.7
40031	LA GRANGE	185	18247	22352	24334	2.2	95	5323	6888	7654	2.8	2.70	4132	5188	2.5
40033	LEBANON	155	12161	12427	12593	0.2	48	4382	4620	4733	0.6	2.48	3107	3154	0.2
40036	LOCKPORT	103	364	377	377	0.4	60	146	153	154	0.5	2.46	111	113	0.2
40037	LORETTO	155	2627	2786	2869	0.6	69	921	1021	1065	1.1	2.61	684	729	0.7
40040	MACKVILLE	229	696	775	812	1.2	86	279	321	340	1.5	2.41	211	234	1.1
40045	MILTON	223	2871	3267	3412	1.4	89	1148	1341	1414	1.7	2.44	831	933	1.3
40046	MOUNT EDEN	215	1470	1989	2348	3.3	98	553	764	904	3.6	2.60	429	576	3.2
40047	MOUNT WASHINGTON	029	13048	18229	20960	3.7	99	4717	6696	7763	3.9	2.70	3793	5263	3.6
40050	NEW CASTLE	103	1791	1990	2093	1.1	85	710	812	861	1.5	2.38	496	545	1.0
40051	NEW HAVEN	179	4397	4842	5099	1.0	83	1611	1839	1960	1.4	2.61	1202	1320	1.0
40052	NEW HOPE	155	731	834	884	1.4	89	274	325	349	1.9	2.51	206	235	1.4
40055	PENDLETON	223	1724	2085	2227	2.1	95	624	765	820	2.2	2.73	493	587	1.9
40056	PEWEE VALLEY	185	3146	3675	3940	1.7	93	1101	1302	1404	1.8	2.75	876	1000	1.4
40057	PLEASUREVILLE	103	3137	3334	3398	0.7	74	1200	1292	1322	0.8	2.58	898	937	0.5
40059	PROSPECT	185	11312	15666	17673	3.6	98	4129	5660	6372	3.5	2.75	3428	4585	3.2
40060	RAYWICK	155	912	990	1029	0.9	80	344	389	409	1.3	2.47	253	275	0.9
40061	SAINT CATHARINE	229	275	294	304	0.7	74	21	24	25	1.5	2.54	17	18	0.6
40062	SAINT FRANCIS	155	102	119	127	1.7	93	40	49	52	2.2	2.43	29	34	1.7
40065	SHELBYVILLE	211	21698	27759	31160	2.7	97	8199	10619	11954	2.8	2.57	5968	7452	2.4
40067	SIMPSONVILLE	211	4575	5775	6510	2.6	97	1317	1791	2064	3.4	2.81	1049	1380	3.0
40068	SMITHFIELD	103	1747	2038	2143	1.7	93	633	746	786	1.8	2.73	502	575	1.5
40069	SPRINGFIELD	229	7106	7523	7734	0.6	69	2744	2988	3104	0.9	2.44	1966	2062	0.5
40070	SULPHUR	103	591	631	665	0.7	74	229	250	265	1.0	2.52	183	194	0.6
40071	TAYLORSVILLE	215	10633	15918	19074	4.5	99	3815	5823	7007	4.7	2.72	3056	4517	4.3
40075	TURNERS STATION	103	1067	1142	1163	0.7	74	405	438	446	0.9	2.61	312	327	0.5
40076	WADDY	211	2320	2793	3058	2.0	95	870	1058	1160	2.1	2.63	699	825	1.8
40077	WESTPORT	185	718	840	900	1.7	93	283	334	359	1.8	2.51	213	242	1.4
40078	WILLISBURG	229	2269	2459	2556	0.9	80	853	954	1003	1.2	2.52	653	706	0.8
40104	BATTLETOWN	163	1090	1067	1045	-0.2	26	424	433	428	0.2	2.46	321	316	-0.2
40107	BOSTON	179	2335	2588	2744	1.1	85	870	999	1073	1.5	2.58	656	726	1.1
40108	BRANDENBURG	163	9259	10184	10566	1.0	83	3491	3967	4159	1.4	2.54	2655	2922	1.0
40109	BROOKS	029	2981	3464	3766	1.6	91	1125	1352	1490	2.0	2.56	840	967	1.5
40111	CLOVERPORT	027	2908	2921	2932	0.0	39	1134	1171	1186	0.3	2.47	826	822	-0.1
40115	CUSTER	027	1016	1079	1106	0.7	74	381	411	424	0.8	2.63	298	312	0.5
40117	EKRON	163	2802	2979	3030	0.7	74	1009	1099	1128	0.9	2.71	792	835	0.6
40118	FAIRDALE	111	9285	9509	9640	0.3	54	3599	3799	3889	0.6	2.50	2643	2654	0.0
40119	FALLS OF ROUGH	027	2388	2627	2710	1.0	83	993	1129	1176	1.4	2.33	748	822	1.0
40121	FORT KNOX	093	12353	11921	11716	-0.4	18	2742	2723	2693	-0.1	3.38	2585	2546	-0.2
40140	GARFIELD	027	204	214	219	0.5	64	79	84	86	0.7	2.55	62	64	0.3
40142	GUSTON	163	1841	1968	2019	0.7	74	661	729	756	1.1	2.70	535	574	0.8
40143	HARDINSBURG	027	3983	4261	4385	0.7	74	1572	1733	1801	1.1	2.33	1087	1151	0.6
40144	HARNED	027	1847	1951	1998	0.6	69	721	782	807	0.9	2.47	513	535	0.5
40145	HUDSON	027	136	144	147	0.6	69	45	48	49	0.7	3.00	35	37	0.6
40146	IRVINGTON	027	3286	3363	3411	0.3	54	1303	1361	1390	0.5	2.47	952	960	0.1
40150	LEBANON JUNCTION	029	4460	4793	5045	0.8	77	1656	1823	1934	1.0	2.63	1255	1330	0.6
40152	MC DANIELS	027	61	64	66	0.5	64	28	30	31	0.7	2.13	20	21	0.5
40155	MULDRAUGH	163	1303	1254	1237	-0.4	18	520	504	499	-0.3	2.49	320	294	-0.9
40157	PAYNEVILLE	163	1437	1548	1592	0.8	77	532	597	619	1.3	2.59	405	439	0.9
40160	RADCLIFF	093	23932	24851	25436	0.4	60	9188	9950	10291	0.9	2.48	6383	6637	0.4
40161	RHODELIA	163	111	128	136	1.6	91	39	46	49	1.8	2.78	30	34	1.4
40162	RINEYVILLE	093	3098	3463	3719	1.2	86	1083	1257	1367	1.6	2.75	876	986	1.3
40165	SHEPHERDSVILLE	029	26831	33945	38085	2.6	97	9771	12719	14404	2.9	2.66	7801	9880	2.6
40170	STEPHENSPORT	027	220	222	223	0.1	45	96	99	101	0.3	2.18	68	68	0.0
40171	UNION STAR	027	626	645	658	0.3	54	220	233	239	0.6	2.77	164	168	0.3
40175	VINE GROVE	163	11436	12609	13125	1.1	85	4148	4762	5025	1.5	2.64	3187	3532	1.1
40176	WEBSTER	027	610	684	719	1.2	86	214	247	262	1.6	2.77	163	182	1.2
40177	WEST POINT	093	1853	1859	1884	0.0	39	716	750	768	0.5	2.46	503	506	0.1
40178	WESTVIEW	027	255	270	276	0.6	69	114	123	127	0.8	2.20	81	84	0.4
40202	LOUISVILLE	111	4875	4681	4629	-0.4	18	2475	2458	2462	-0.1	1.62	780	674	-1.6
40203	LOUISVILLE	111	20238	19742	19584	-0.3	22	9038	8921	8898	-0.1	1.99	3869	3497	-1.1
40204	LOUISVILLE	111	15606	14839	14595	-0.5	13	7857	7637	7567	-0.3	1.88	3259	2859	-1.4
40205	LOUISVILLE	111	23798	22979	22716	-0.4	18	10814	10708	10681	-0.1	2.05	5928	5413	-1.0
40206	LOUISVILLE	111	19682	19468	19426	-0.1	32	9465	9605	9676	0.2	1.89	4383	4043	-0.9
40207	LOUISVILLE	111	30165	29541	29385	-0.2	26	13968	14020	14065	0.0	2.08	7960	7415	-0.8
40208	LOUISVILLE	111	12935	12483	12309	-0.4	18	5977	5819	5770	-0.3	2.02	2559	2263	-1.3
40209	LOUISVILLE	111	487	443	432	-1.0	1	213	198	195	-0.8	2.17	124	106	-1.7
40210	LOUISVILLE	111	16378	15414	15109	-0.7	5	6436	6202	6132	-0.4	2.47	4185	3790	-1.1
40211	LOUISVILLE	111	23729	23780	23897	0.0	39	9137	9338	9453	0.2	2.55	6068	5851	-0.4
40212	LOUISVILLE	111	19916	18581	18148	-0.7	5	7245	6926	6821	-0.5	2.68	5036	4543	-1.1
40213	LOUISVILLE	111	18157	17316	17085	-0.5	13	7716	7552	7519	-0.2	2.24	4833	4404	-1.0
40214	LOUISVILLE	111	44803	44075	43895	-0.2	26	18711	18756	18816	0.0	2.34	12013	11317	-0.6
40215	LOUISVILLE	111	25075	23819	23395	-0.6	9	10378	9996	9871	-0.4	2.35	6377	5714	-1.2
40216	LOUISVILLE	111	40088	39024	38774	-0.3	22	16791	16801	16843	0.0	2.31	11102	10458	-0.6
40217	LOUISVILLE	111	12844	12370	12218	-0.4	18	5841	5756	5731	-0.2	2.12	3170	2874	-1.1
40218	LOUISVILLE	111	29988	29879	29858	0.0	39	13187	13418	13522	0.2	2.20	7716	7306	-0.6
40219	LOUISVILLE	111	35539	35253	35471	-0.1	32	14125	14435	14663	0.2	2.41	9801	9453	-0.4
40220	LOUISVILLE	111	32964	32850	32996	0.0	39	14252	14537	14713	0.2	2.21	8701	8272	-0.5
40222	LOUISVILLE	111	20425	20264	20240	-0.1	32	9246	9369	9436	0.1	2.09	5524	5226	-0.6
40223	LOUISVILLE	111	22885	23240	23471	0.2	48	9237	9567	9729	0.4	2.37	6176	6038	-0.2
	KENTUCKY					0.7					1.0	2.41			0.6
	UNITED STATES					1.0					1.1	2.59			0.9

ZIP CODE #	POST OFFICE NAME	RACE (%) White 2000	White 2009	Black 2000	Black 2009	Asian/Pacific 2000	Asian/Pacific 2009	% Hispanic Origin 2000	% Hispanic Origin 2009	2009 AGE DISTRIBUTION (%) 0-4	5-9	10-14	15-19	20-24	25-44	45-64	65-84	85+	18+	MEDIAN AGE 2009	% 2009 Males	% 2009 Females
40003	BAGDAD	96.7	95.5	1.6	1.8	0.1	0.1	1.8	3.3	5.8	6.6	7.5	7.6	4.6	25.6	29.6	11.1	1.7	75.2	40.0	51.4	48.6
40004	BARDSTOWN	90.1	88.9	7.9	8.4	0.7	1.1	1.1	1.7	7.8	7.2	7.0	6.9	7.1	27.6	25.7	9.4	1.3	73.7	35.0	48.7	51.3
40006	BEDFORD	97.9	97.1	0.3	0.3	0.1	0.1	1.3	2.1	6.6	6.6	6.9	7.1	5.8	27.0	28.3	9.8	1.8	75.5	38.4	49.4	50.6
40007	BETHLEHEM	98.1	97.1	0.3	0.3	0.3	0.6	1.3	1.9	6.1	6.1	6.4	6.4	6.1	27.0	31.2	9.6	1.0	77.5	38.9	50.2	49.8
40008	BLOOMFIELD	94.9	94.0	3.7	4.0	0.1	0.2	1.6	2.6	6.7	6.9	7.1	6.5	5.3	26.1	28.7	11.2	1.6	75.3	38.8	50.2	49.8
40009	BRADFORDSVILLE	97.8	97.1	0.4	0.4	0.0	0.0	1.1	1.9	6.4	6.3	6.2	6.4	5.8	28.0	28.4	11.1	1.3	77.1	38.6	50.2	49.8
40010	BUCKNER	96.9	96.3	1.7	1.9	0.3	0.6	0.7	1.3	6.1	6.9	7.8	8.1	4.7	23.4	33.3	9.0	0.6	74.0	40.6	49.1	50.9
40011	CAMPBELLSBURG	95.9	94.6	1.6	1.7	0.9	1.3	1.7	2.7	6.7	7.2	7.6	6.8	4.7	25.4	28.6	11.5	1.5	74.2	39.1	50.3	49.7
40012	CHAPLIN	98.7	98.2	0.6	0.5	0.0	0.2	1.3	2.4	6.3	6.3	6.6	6.0	5.3	25.3	29.0	13.2	1.9	77.3	41.0	50.8	49.2
40013	COXS CREEK	97.2	96.8	1.6	1.6	0.2	0.4	0.9	1.4	6.4	6.9	7.1	7.0	4.8	25.5	29.9	10.9	1.5	75.1	40.0	49.7	50.3
40014	CRESTWOOD	96.6	95.2	1.6	2.2	0.4	0.6	1.1	2.0	6.6	7.4	8.1	7.8	4.6	25.3	31.6	7.9	0.8	72.8	38.7	49.2	50.8
40019	EMINENCE	87.5	85.2	8.1	8.6	0.3	0.4	3.7	6.2	7.3	7.2	7.0	6.3	5.9	26.0	27.6	11.3	1.5	74.7	37.7	49.8	50.2
40022	FINCHVILLE	85.4	83.1	13.0	14.5	0.4	0.6	1.3	2.3	4.3	5.0	6.0	8.1	5.2	30.4	31.3	9.0	0.7	79.6	40.1	41.3	58.7
40023	FISHERVILLE	95.9	94.7	2.2	2.6	0.6	0.9	1.3	2.2	6.0	6.6	7.3	6.8	3.9	24.4	33.8	10.0	1.2	75.8	41.8	50.1	49.9
40025	GLENVIEW	93.1	90.5	3.9	5.0	2.0	3.6	0.5	0.9	3.2	4.1	5.0	5.0	2.7	15.8	38.0	23.5	2.7	84.6	54.1	48.0	52.0
40026	GOSHEN	97.1	96.3	0.7	0.8	0.5	0.7	0.8	1.4	6.8	7.9	8.9	8.6	4.8	23.0	33.6	6.0	0.4	70.7	38.8	49.4	50.6
40031	LA GRANGE	89.4	88.0	8.1	8.5	0.3	0.5	1.6	2.6	5.8	6.1	6.5	6.3	6.1	31.5	28.5	8.3	1.0	77.8	38.2	57.0	43.0
40033	LEBANON	84.9	83.3	13.3	14.1	0.6	0.9	0.7	1.2	6.6	6.5	6.4	6.3	6.8	28.7	25.6	11.1	2.0	76.7	37.2	51.3	48.7
40036	LOCKPORT	98.1	97.3	0.3	0.3	0.3	0.5	1.9	2.7	7.2	7.2	7.7	6.6	5.0	24.9	28.9	11.1	1.3	73.5	38.5	50.9	49.1
40037	LORETTO	98.2	97.5	0.4	0.4	0.2	0.3	0.9	1.6	7.7	7.5	7.5	6.5	5.6	26.4	25.7	10.1	3.0	73.4	37.0	48.0	52.0
40040	MACKVILLE	98.1	97.8	0.7	0.8	0.0	0.0	1.0	1.7	5.9	6.3	6.5	6.2	4.6	26.5	29.7	12.9	1.4	77.4	41.1	48.9	51.1
40045	MILTON	98.2	97.7	0.2	0.2	0.1	0.1	1.3	2.1	6.5	6.7	6.9	6.3	4.8	27.7	28.4	11.3	1.4	75.9	39.7	49.3	50.7
40046	MOUNT EDEN	98.6	98.2	0.3	0.3	0.1	0.1	1.0	1.6	6.6	6.9	7.2	7.2	5.1	28.9	28.4	8.8	0.9	74.8	38.2	51.2	48.8
40047	MOUNT WASHINGTON	98.4	98.1	0.3	0.3	0.2	0.4	0.6	0.9	7.2	7.5	7.6	6.9	4.5	28.2	28.0	9.1	1.1	73.4	37.9	49.0	51.0
40050	NEW CASTLE	93.2	91.6	4.5	4.9	0.1	0.1	2.1	3.5	6.1	6.3	6.2	6.1	4.8	24.6	27.9	15.2	2.8	77.7	42.1	46.9	53.1
40051	NEW HAVEN	98.2	97.7	0.5	0.6	0.2	0.3	0.8	1.4	6.9	7.1	7.2	6.8	5.8	26.4	28.6	10.2	1.0	74.8	37.9	51.6	48.4
40052	NEW HOPE	98.1	97.2	0.3	0.2	0.3	0.4	1.4	2.4	6.7	6.7	7.0	6.8	6.1	27.2	28.9	9.5	1.1	75.3	37.5	52.8	47.2
40055	PENDLETON	96.5	95.5	1.2	1.4	0.2	0.2	1.5	2.4	6.6	6.8	7.1	6.7	4.9	26.7	30.8	9.5	0.9	75.3	39.5	50.6	49.4
40056	PEWEE VALLEY	95.1	93.9	3.1	3.6	0.5	0.8	1.3	2.1	6.3	7.0	7.3	6.8	4.7	23.3	30.3	11.8	2.4	75.0	41.3	47.9	52.1
40057	PLEASUREVILLE	96.4	94.9	1.0	1.0	0.2	0.2	2.9	4.7	6.6	6.9	7.3	6.7	5.1	25.7	28.8	11.2	1.6	75.0	39.1	51.0	49.0
40059	PROSPECT	91.9	89.6	4.6	5.4	1.9	3.1	1.0	1.7	5.9	7.4	8.8	7.6	3.4	18.4	35.9	11.4	1.2	72.9	44.0	49.4	50.6
40060	RAYWICK	96.9	96.5	2.2	2.3	0.3	0.4	0.8	1.0	6.9	7.0	6.6	5.7	5.8	30.8	27.3	9.1	1.0	76.3	36.5	52.3	47.7
40061	SAINT CATHARINE	87.3	85.4	9.8	10.9	0.7	1.0	1.8	3.1	6.5	6.5	6.8	10.2	6.8	22.4	24.1	13.6	3.1	75.5	37.8	48.6	51.4
40062	SAINT FRANCIS	98.0	97.5	0.0	0.0	0.0	0.0	2.0	2.5	7.6	7.6	7.6	6.7	5.0	29.4	26.9	8.4	0.8	73.1	35.3	50.4	49.6
40065	SHELBYVILLE	85.0	82.6	9.6	9.7	0.6	0.9	5.7	9.0	7.1	7.1	6.9	6.4	5.6	28.0	26.7	10.4	1.7	74.9	37.5	49.7	50.3
40067	SIMPSONVILLE	81.6	78.5	14.5	15.5	0.5	0.7	3.3	5.5	6.2	6.3	6.4	9.4	6.4	27.0	28.0	9.1	0.8	75.4	37.4	46.5	53.5
40068	SMITHFIELD	96.1	95.4	2.2	2.3	0.2	0.3	1.1	1.9	6.4	6.8	7.1	6.4	5.2	25.8	31.8	9.5	1.0	75.7	40.0	51.1	48.9
40069	SPRINGFIELD	86.9	85.6	10.8	11.4	0.4	0.5	1.8	3.0	5.9	6.0	6.4	7.3	5.6	24.6	27.8	13.8	2.6	77.5	40.9	48.3	51.7
40070	SULPHUR	95.3	92.9	1.2	1.4	0.3	0.5	2.7	4.6	6.3	6.7	6.5	6.0	5.1	28.2	29.6	10.8	0.8	76.7	39.5	50.4	49.6
40071	TAYLORSVILLE	97.5	96.9	1.2	1.3	0.1	0.2	1.1	1.8	7.1	7.1	7.1	6.7	4.9	29.0	28.2	8.8	1.1	74.5	37.7	50.3	49.7
40075	TURNERS STATION	97.6	96.8	0.8	1.0	0.6	0.7	0.9	1.5	5.6	6.5	7.3	6.1	4.6	26.4	29.6	12.3	1.6	76.6	40.7	51.5	48.5
40076	WADDY	97.1	96.1	1.0	1.1	0.0	0.1	1.5	2.6	6.3	6.7	7.1	6.5	4.4	27.5	30.0	10.3	1.0	75.6	40.1	50.7	49.3
40077	WESTPORT	96.9	96.3	0.8	1.1	0.4	0.6	0.4	0.6	4.9	5.6	6.7	7.0	4.3	23.1	37.9	9.4	1.2	78.3	44.1	50.1	49.9
40078	WILLISBURG	98.0	97.4	0.9	1.0	0.2	0.3	1.1	2.0	5.8	6.1	6.5	8.6	5.3	26.6	28.9	10.6	1.5	75.6	39.0	53.3	46.7
40104	BATTLETOWN	97.6	96.9	0.4	0.4	0.3	0.6	0.5	0.7	5.9	6.3	7.4	7.6	4.5	26.7	29.0	11.2	1.4	75.6	39.6	50.2	49.8
40107	BOSTON	98.8	98.5	0.2	0.2	0.1	0.2	0.6	0.9	6.4	6.2	6.6	7.1	6.1	27.7	29.1	9.8	1.0	76.4	38.2	50.7	49.3
40108	BRANDENBURG	96.5	95.7	1.7	1.8	0.2	0.4	0.7	1.2	6.7	6.8	6.8	6.7	5.9	26.4	28.3	11.3	1.1	75.5	38.4	48.8	51.2
40109	BROOKS	97.5	96.9	0.6	0.8	0.2	0.3	0.8	1.5	6.7	6.9	6.9	6.6	5.5	27.2	29.9	9.9	0.5	75.3	38.2	50.2	49.8
40111	CLOVERPORT	97.7	97.3	1.1	1.2	0.0	0.1	0.8	1.4	6.8	7.0	7.3	6.0	4.6	24.4	29.3	13.3	1.4	75.2	40.3	50.6	49.4
40115	CUSTER	97.2	96.8	0.3	0.4	0.2	0.2	0.7	1.3	6.3	6.1	6.4	6.2	6.1	26.0	29.7	11.9	1.2	77.4	39.7	51.3	48.7
40117	EKRON	94.3	93.0	3.2	3.6	0.4	0.5	1.0	1.7	7.1	7.2	7.4	7.1	5.8	27.0	28.9	8.9	0.6	74.0	36.9	50.7	49.3
40118	FAIRDALE	97.1	95.9	0.9	1.1	0.3	0.5	1.2	2.1	7.3	7.2	6.9	6.9	6.1	28.5	25.4	10.6	1.0	74.3	35.8	48.9	51.1
40119	FALLS OF ROUGH	99.0	98.8	0.3	0.3	0.1	0.1	0.2	0.3	5.1	5.3	5.8	6.3	5.4	23.6	31.1	15.9	1.6	80.1	43.9	53.0	47.0
40121	FORT KNOX	66.3	61.6	23.0	23.7	2.1	2.8	10.3	16.0	13.1	10.4	7.8	11.2	18.9	35.6	2.8	0.1	0.0	65.0	22.0	61.0	39.0
40140	GARFIELD	99.0	98.6	0.0	0.0	0.0	0.0	1.0	1.4	6.5	5.6	6.5	6.1	6.1	24.3	30.4	13.1	1.4	77.1	41.1	50.5	49.5
40142	GUSTON	95.9	95.0	2.2	2.5	0.4	0.7	0.4	0.8	7.3	7.4	7.4	7.0	5.6	27.7	26.9	9.9	0.9	73.7	36.4	50.4	49.6
40143	HARDINSBURG	93.6	93.0	5.2	5.5	0.2	0.2	1.0	1.5	6.0	6.0	6.1	6.1	5.9	24.9	28.7	13.6	2.6	78.3	41.0	47.8	52.2
40144	HARNED	96.5	96.1	2.3	2.4	0.1	0.1	0.8	1.2	5.8	5.9	6.3	5.8	5.1	23.9	30.8	14.1	2.2	78.3	42.7	47.6	52.4
40145	HUDSON	98.5	98.6	0.0	0.0	0.0	0.0	0.7	1.4	6.9	5.6	6.9	6.3	6.3	23.6	29.2	13.9	1.4	77.1	40.6	50.0	50.0
40146	IRVINGTON	91.6	90.9	7.0	7.4	0.2	0.3	0.7	1.0	6.5	7.3	7.4	6.6	5.1	24.3	27.2	14.0	1.6	74.5	39.9	48.1	51.9
40150	LEBANON JUNCT ON	98.2	97.8	0.3	0.4	0.2	0.4	0.6	0.9	5.2	7.2	7.2	7.9	5.3	26.8	29.8	9.9	0.8	75.7	38.5	50.6	49.4
40152	MC DANIELS	100.0	100.0	0.0	0.0	0.0	0.0	0.0	1.6	6.3	6.3	6.3	6.3	3.1	20.3	31.3	18.8	1.6	75.0	46.3	50.0	50.0
40155	MULDRAUGH	82.3	78.8	10.0	10.8	1.1	1.7	7.0	10.7	9.0	8.1	7.0	6.9	7.6	31.3	24.4	5.0	0.7	71.9	31.5	50.3	49.7
40157	PAYNEVILLE	97.5	96.9	0.6	0.6	0.1	0.2	0.7	1.2	7.6	7.6	7.6	6.5	5.6	26.2	27.8	9.8	1.2	73.2	36.9	51.9	48.1
40160	RADCLIFF	66.1	61.6	23.0	24.0	3.7	5.2	5.2	8.2	7.7	7.1	7.3	7.2	7.2	28.6	25.0	8.9	0.9	73.3	34.1	49.1	50.9
40161	RHODELIA	97.3	96.9	0.9	0.8	0.0	0.0	0.9	1.6	7.8	7.8	7.0	6.3	6.3	25.8	28.1	9.4	1.6	72.7	36.9	52.3	47.7
40162	RINEYVILLE	93.3	91.4	2.6	3.0	1.1	1.6	1.6	2.8	6.2	6.6	6.9	6.8	5.5	26.4	31.3	9.4	0.8	76.1	39.3	49.6	50.4
40165	SHEPHERDSVILLE	97.9	97.4	0.5	0.5	0.3	0.5	0.6	1.0	7.4	7.0	7.0	6.6	5.9	28.3	28.1	9.0	0.7	74.6	36.7	49.9	50.1
40170	STEPHENSPORT	98.2	98.2	0.9	0.9	0.0	0.0	0.5	0.0	5.9	6.8	6.8	6.3	5.0	23.0	31.1	14.0	1.4	76.1	42.3	51.4	48.6
40171	UNION STAR	98.1	97.8	0.2	0.2	0.0	0.0	1.3	2.0	5.6	6.0	6.2	5.9	4.5	24.5	32.7	13.2	1.4	78.4	42.9	50.4	49.6
40175	VINE GROVE	89.2	86.8	6.1	6.7	1.6	2.3	2.0	3.3	6.5	6.7	6.7	6.8	6.2	26.7	29.5	9.9	1.0	76.0	38.1	50.0	50.0
40176	WEBSTER	97.7	97.1	0.5	0.6	0.0	0.0	1.0	1.6	7.5	7.5	7.2	6.0	5.6	25.7	28.9	10.4	1.3	74.1	38.0	52.3	47.7
40177	WEST POINT	97.2	96.5	1.3	1.4	0.2	0.3	1.1	1.8	6.5	6.3	6.3	7.0	6.7	28.7	26.9	10.9	0.6	76.7	36.7	51.0	49.0
40178	WESTVIEW	98.4	98.1	0.4	0.4	0.0	0.0	0.8	1.1	5.9	6.3	6.3	5.6	4.1	21.5	31.5	17.4	1.5	77.4	45.3	48.9	51.1
40202	LOUISVILLE	27.2	24.1	67.7	69.5	2.5	3.5	1.9	2.6	7.7	6.9	5.3	5.5	7.8	27.9	22.6	14.1	2.3	77.3	36.4	51.4	48.6
40203	LOUISVILLE	35.3	30.9	61.3	65.1	0.4	0.5	1.5	2.2	8.6	7.6	6.3	6.9	8.8	26.0	21.2	10.6	4.1	73.7	33.8	46.7	53.3
40204	LOUISVILLE	85.6	83.5	11.5	12.5	0.8	1.2	1.2	2.0	5.2	4.4	3.7	4.4	7.7	34.5	26.6	10.8	2.5	84.2	38.2	48.5	51.5
40205	LOUISVILLE	96.0	94.6	1.8	2.2	0.9	1.5	0.9	1.5	4.4	4.3	4.7	5.7	6.8	26.6	30.4	13.5	3.6	83.8	43.3	47.1	52.9
40206	LOUISVILLE	86.5	83.2	9.6	11.2	1.8	2.8	1.9	3.1	4.7	4.5	4.4	4.6	8.3	31.4	27.8	11.3	3.1	83.9	39.7	47.8	52.2
40207	LOUISVILLE	94.6	92.5	2.3	2.9	1.8	3.0	1.1	1.9	5.4	5.2	5.5	5.0	5.7	25.6	28.5	15.1	4.0	80.8	43.2	47.0	53.0
40208	LOUISVILLE	60.8	55.0	32.8	36.7	2.2	3.3	2.4	3.7	6.3	5.3	5.2	8.2	14.4	29.8	23.1	6.6	1.1	79.7	30.7	50.9	49.1
40209	LOUISVILLE	88.5	84.7	7.0	8.8	2.3	3.4	2.3	3.4	6.1	6.1	5.6	7.7	6.5	25.5	28.4	12.0	2.0	79.0	39.6	50.3	49.7
40210	LOUISVILLE	9.5	8.0	88.7	90.1	0.1	0.1	0.8	1.0	7.5	7.6	7.5	8.4	7.1	22.4	26.3	11.6	1.7	72.5	35.9	46.0	54.0
40211	LOUISVILLE	3.1	2.6	95.1	95.6	0.1	0.1	0.7	0.9	7.3	7.9	8.2	8.6	6.5	22.5	24.9	11.9	2.3	71.3	35.9	45.0	55.0
40212	LOUISVILLE	43.5	40.5	54.4	57.1	0.1	0.1	0.7	1.1	7.6	7.9	7.8	8.6	6.9	23.8	26.2	9.9	1.2	71.5	34.3	46.9	53.1
40213	LOUISVILLE	80.6	77.6	16.2	18.0	0.9	1.3	1.9	3.0	6.1	6.2	6.2	6.1	6.1	26.7	26.8	13.1	2.7	77.7	39.0	48.3	51.7
40214	LOUISVILLE	84.8	81.3	7.8	8.9	4.1	5.7	3.6	5.3	6.9	6.6	6.2	6.1	6.4	28.2	26.3	11.5	1.9	76.7	37.3	48.9	51.1
40215	LOUISVILLE	69.8	66.0	25.9	28.4	0.9	1.4	2.2	3.4	8.6	8.3	7.3	7.2	6.9	26.8	24.4	8.6	1.8	71.4	33.3	47.2	52.8
40216	LOUISVILLE	75.8	72.4	21.9	24.4	0.5	0.8	1.2	2.0	6.0	5.9	5.9	6.1	5.6	24.9	28.7	14.3	2.4	78.4	41.5	47.6	52.4
40217	LOUISVILLE	90.0	87.6	6.7	7.9	1.3	2.0	1.3	2.1	5.6	5.4	5.2	5.4	7.4	28.6	27.7	12.0	2.8	80.8	39.5	48.6	51.4
40218	LOUISVILLE	58.1	54.1	36.6	38.6	1.7	2.5	3.3	5.1	6.8	6.5	6.3	6.7	7.6	26.8	24.9	11.8	2.6	76.4	36.8	46.9	53.1
40219	LOUISVILLE	80.1	77.1	15.9	17.4	1.1	1.7	2.7	4.3	6.8	6.5	6.2	6.3	6.6	27.0	25.8	12.9	2.0	76.7	38.0	48.2	51.8
40220	LOUISVILLE	86.0	82.2	9.7	11.7	1.7	2.7	2.0	3.3	5.7	5.7	5.8	5.6	5.3	27.0	27.6	14.0	3.3	79.4	41.3	47.3	52.7
40222	LOUISVILLE	89.2	85.8	5.9	7.0	2.8	4.4	1.8	3.0	5.2	5.1	5.3	5.0	5.5	25.1	28.4	16.3	4.3	81.4	44.1	47.2	52.8
40223	LOUISVILLE	88.0	84.6	7.3	8.7	2.5	3.9	2.1	3.4	5.4	5.9	6.9	7.0	5.0	23.3	31.2	12.7	2.6	77.1	42.6	47.7	52.3
	KENTUCKY	90.1	88.9	7.3	7.5	0.8	1.2	1.5	2.4	6.5	6.5	6.5	6.8	6.5	27.0	27.1	11.3	1.8	76.6	37.9	49.1	50.9
	UNITED STATES	75.1	72.0	12.3	12.7	3.8	4.6	12.5	15.7	6.8	6.7	6.6	7.1	6.9	27.0	26.0	10.9	1.9	75.7	36.9	49.2	50.8

ZIP CODE #	POST OFFICE NAME	2009 Per Capita Income	2009 HH Income Base	2009 HOUSEHOLD INCOME DISTRIBUTION (%) Less than $25,000	$25,000 to $49,999	$50,000 to $99,999	$100,000 to $149,999	$150,000 or More	MEDIAN HOUSEHOLD INCOME 2009	2014	2009 National Centile	2009 State Centile	2009 Home Value Base	2009 HOME VALUE DISTRIBUTION (%) Less than $50,000	$50,000 to $89,999	$90,000 to $174,999	$175,000 to $399,999	$400,000 or More	2009 Median Home Value
40003	BAGDAD	22166	774	15.6	35.8	39.4	7.5	1.7	48701	49261	58	84	639	7.0	16.4	37.4	33.3	5.8	132237
40004	BARDSTOWN	23362	10744	23.7	26.1	38.8	7.3	4.1	50148	52682	62	86	7899	8.4	17.4	48.0	23.8	2.5	121280
40006	BEDFORD	19564	1939	26.4	33.0	32.9	6.3	1.5	42866	46008	42	72	1551	23.7	22.1	35.7	17.1	1.5	97198
40007	BETHLEHEM	24514	120	28.3	21.7	35.8	8.3	5.8	50000	51685	61	86	91	30.8	11.0	41.8	16.5	0.0	104464
40008	BLOOMFIELD	19268	1644	28.6	27.4	36.5	5.6	1.9	44014	46460	45	75	1336	15.6	18.8	41.2	21.8	2.7	112560
40009	BRADFORDSVILLE	19092	459	44.4	24.8	24.0	3.9	2.8	28717	31350	6	34	354	42.4	20.1	31.9	4.5	1.1	64000
40010	BUCKNER	44388	197	4.1	11.2	31.5	26.4	26.9	105140	108548	97	99	174	1.1	4.0	14.9	56.3	23.6	273077
40011	CAMPBELLSBURG	20017	1083	27.6	27.3	37.0	5.8	2.2	46556	48484	53	82	879	16.7	23.3	42.8	13.5	3.6	99511
40012	CHAPLIN	22114	259	22.4	30.9	39.8	5.0	1.9	45693	50000	50	80	216	18.1	22.2	39.8	18.1	1.9	100000
40013	COXS CREEK	23431	2399	18.5	22.0	46.1	9.0	4.3	56337	58780	73	92	2133	10.9	15.3	37.6	31.2	4.9	142375
40014	CRESTWOOD	37603	6788	6.0	13.5	35.5	28.1	16.9	91699	98453	95	99	5909	1.5	2.3	26.0	58.5	11.6	235311
40019	EMINENCE	20282	1496	32.5	27.5	31.6	5.5	2.9	41441	45268	37	69	1006	10.5	25.0	47.4	15.7	1.4	102871
40022	FINCHVILLE	33674	327	19.0	18.0	36.1	17.4	9.5	73591	77770	89	97	283	3.5	2.8	21.9	50.9	20.8	247222
40023	FISHERVILLE	32793	1282	10.5	18.4	40.4	17.1	13.6	75665	78035	90	98	1176	5.9	6.1	23.3	51.4	13.4	228571
40025	GLENVIEW	64740	88	9.1	10.2	25.0	17.0	38.6	111095	112027	98	100	82	0.0	3.7	15.9	35.4	45.1	355556
40026	GOSHEN	42317	1793	3.2	11.4	30.8	29.0	25.6	107024	110151	98	100	1690	1.9	0.8	19.6	66.3	11.4	208943
40031	LA GRANGE	27397	6888	14.2	22.2	35.3	17.9	10.3	68449	67884	86	96	5644	6.2	6.3	36.4	44.3	6.7	177662
40033	LEBANON	18945	4620	33.7	32.0	27.6	4.1	2.6	36430	39030	22	55	3452	15.1	27.9	44.0	11.6	1.4	95776
40036	LOCKPORT	25578	153	23.5	22.9	43.1	7.8	2.6	53498	53732	69	89	123	25.2	17.9	35.8	18.7	2.4	101875
40037	LORETTO	18402	1021	25.4	33.7	34.6	5.6	0.8	42702	43132	41	72	883	21.1	25.1	39.6	13.4	0.8	93564
40040	MACKVILLE	20428	321	24.6	36.4	31.8	4.7	2.5	42776	43643	42	72	257	22.2	28.4	37.4	9.7	2.3	88846
40045	MILTON	21331	1341	26.0	26.3	40.6	4.6	2.5	47711	50389	56	83	1092	20.8	28.5	34.6	14.0	2.1	91067
40046	MOUNT EDEN	23466	764	17.5	22.9	47.1	10.9	1.6	58106	60216	75	93	668	16.2	8.7	35.2	34.1	5.8	156389
40047	MOUNT WASHINGTON	23970	6696	15.1	25.5	46.6	9.5	3.3	58495	60963	76	93	5574	2.5	3.6	46.2	44.7	3.0	171355
40050	NEW CASTLE	20101	812	35.6	20.4	35.0	6.2	2.8	40773	45592	35	66	572	14.2	23.8	42.5	16.8	2.8	103879
40051	NEW HAVEN	19433	1839	28.0	27.1	38.3	4.1	2.4	44392	46761	47	76	1495	16.2	21.1	44.2	17.1	1.3	106788
40052	NEW HOPE	18924	325	30.8	28.3	33.2	6.2	1.5	39086	41499	30	62	278	23.7	22.7	35.3	16.9	1.4	95556
40055	PENDLETON	23293	765	16.7	34.8	33.5	11.4	3.7	49192	50579	59	85	674	16.9	13.2	39.6	25.4	4.9	129787
40056	PEWEE VALLEY	34698	1302	11.2	17.1	36.2	22.0	13.6	80470	82785	92	98	1184	4.0	1.8	40.9	39.9	13.5	182407
40057	PLEASUREVILLE	21874	1292	24.2	27.9	39.0	6.2	2.6	47978	50000	57	83	1005	19.0	20.1	39.6	18.0	3.3	103882
40059	PROSPECT	60107	5660	4.2	9.8	23.5	21.0	41.5	128807	130358	99	100	5276	1.1	2.7	8.4	47.8	39.9	350047
40060	RAYWICK	20728	389	22.6	31.4	39.3	5.4	1.3	46509	46625	53	82	331	22.4	20.5	45.6	11.2	0.3	97833
40061	SAINT CATHARINE	5659	24	20.8	29.2	45.8	4.2	0.0	50000	48624	61	86	21	0.0	19.0	57.1	19.0	4.8	122917
40062	SAINT FRANCIS	20008	49	28.6	32.7	32.7	6.1	0.0	41711	43621	38	69	42	26.2	26.2	35.7	11.9	0.0	85000
40065	SHELBYVILLE	24869	10619	19.7	25.0	40.8	10.3	4.2	57416	60515	75	92	7177	2.4	10.7	42.6	38.2	6.1	161341
40067	SIMPSONVILLE	29363	1791	11.4	21.2	39.9	16.4	11.1	76930	79426	91	98	1467	1.5	4.8	35.3	35.1	23.2	208648
40068	SMITHFIELD	25362	746	17.0	29.2	36.7	11.4	5.6	54777	55327	71	90	653	15.5	16.1	36.1	27.4	4.9	124290
40069	SPRINGFIELD	20621	2988	30.6	31.0	30.3	4.9	3.2	40970	42961	36	67	2303	14.9	27.1	41.3	13.6	3.0	98946
40070	SULPHUR	24947	250	19.2	23.2	43.6	10.4	3.6	55838	55644	72	91	222	11.3	23.4	32.4	28.4	4.5	126087
40071	TAYLORSVILLE	24301	5823	17.8	23.1	44.7	10.7	3.7	60909	63375	79	94	4817	9.9	10.4	29.2	43.7	6.9	176508
40075	TURNERS STATION	20694	438	23.7	24.2	44.5	5.7	1.8	52183	52976	66	88	375	24.3	18.9	34.4	14.7	7.7	97286
40076	WADDY	22407	1058	15.9	27.9	47.5	6.7	2.0	54669	55202	71	90	914	6.9	11.7	43.9	34.1	3.4	134155
40077	WESTPORT	29244	334	12.3	25.7	40.4	15.6	6.0	65994	63308	84	96	290	7.6	3.4	32.4	47.9	8.6	192593
40078	WILLISBURG	18430	954	30.2	33.3	32.7	2.3	1.5	39665	42096	32	64	835	23.4	28.3	32.2	14.7	1.4	86351
40104	BATTLETOWN	19938	433	26.1	35.3	29.8	7.4	1.4	40776	43276	35	67	377	25.7	26.5	31.8	13.8	2.1	87424
40107	BOSTON	19192	999	24.6	34.0	34.3	4.8	2.2	44500	45545	47	77	870	19.8	19.5	40.5	17.9	2.3	108962
40108	BRANDENBURG	22785	3967	22.0	27.3	39.7	7.7	3.4	50610	52360	63	87	3198	14.2	22.3	40.7	21.6	1.2	107648
40109	BROOKS	23318	1352	12.5	33.8	43.3	8.7	1.6	53378	55673	69	89	1226	42.4	9.0	27.7	19.7	1.3	83462
40111	CLOVERPORT	18589	1171	35.7	29.1	28.5	4.3	2.4	34834	37068	17	50	915	34.8	28.2	31.7	5.4	0.0	70288
40115	CUSTER	19125	411	27.7	30.7	36.7	3.6	1.2	44918	44629	48	77	368	25.3	31.3	30.7	11.4	1.4	82258
40117	EKRON	18726	1099	23.8	33.2	36.9	4.3	1.7	46290	48141	52	81	959	17.6	29.7	39.7	12.6	0.3	93446
40118	FAIRDALE	22001	3799	22.5	27.3	41.8	6.7	1.7	50162	52262	62	86	3018	29.3	26.2	39.3	5.2	0.0	84377
40119	FALLS OF ROUGH	19273	1129	29.0	36.3	30.2	3.5	1.1	37828	38321	26	59	994	25.4	28.8	33.7	11.4	0.8	80000
40121	FORT KNOX	15072	2723	11.4	47.2	35.4	4.1	1.8	44536	46554	47	77	61	32.8	9.8	29.5	26.2	1.6	110227
40140	GARFIELD	16775	84	33.3	34.5	28.6	3.6	0.0	35000	35902	18	50	75	41.3	21.3	30.7	6.7	0.0	67500
40142	GUSTON	21658	729	22.6	24.8	41.8	7.7	3.0	52363	54238	67	88	628	18.5	23.7	39.5	17.5	0.8	101546
40143	HARDINSBURG	19950	1733	37.2	29.3	26.5	4.0	3.1	36610	38003	22	56	1303	23.1	32.8	34.3	8.2	1.6	83831
40144	HARNED	19278	782	34.5	30.4	29.0	3.5	2.6	39036	39831	30	62	638	24.5	30.4	33.2	9.9	2.0	84918
40145	HUDSON	13972	48	33.3	33.3	29.2	4.2	0.0	37365	39076	25	58	43	39.5	25.6	32.6	2.3	0.0	75000
40146	IRVINGTON	18181	1361	31.5	33.9	29.6	3.5	1.5	38793	39243	29	62	1090	23.5	29.6	35.1	9.4	2.4	86264
40150	LEBANON JUNCTION	20529	1823	24.1	28.3	39.8	5.8	2.0	46842	49419	54	82	1500	11.0	20.3	43.5	23.9	1.3	120610
40152	MC DANIELS	21214	30	30.0	33.3	33.3	3.3	0.0	33134	31635	14	45	26	30.8	23.1	42.3	3.8	0.0	86667
40155	MULDRAUGH	18940	504	24.4	37.1	32.9	4.8	0.8	42071	45962	39	70	188	51.1	31.9	10.1	6.9	0.0	48947
40157	PAYNEVILLE	18972	597	25.8	34.3	33.2	4.7	2.0	37802	41157	26	59	526	27.8	31.6	25.5	14.6	0.6	77292
40160	RADCLIFF	22951	9950	21.5	29.8	38.8	6.9	3.0	48724	50889	58	84	5841	18.2	14.0	56.8	10.4	0.7	111339
40161	RHODELIA	17404	46	28.3	34.8	32.6	2.2	2.2	34020	34568	16	48	41	31.7	29.3	24.4	14.6	0.0	73750
40162	RINEYVILLE	23174	1257	17.9	27.4	43.2	8.4	3.1	55352	56643	72	91	1088	18.6	11.5	46.5	21.3	2.1	130846
40165	SHEPHERDSVILLE	23336	12719	18.5	24.2	44.8	8.9	3.6	56088	58747	73	91	10370	13.0	11.5	37.7	35.7	2.1	151641
40170	STEPHENSPORT	20997	99	39.4	28.3	27.3	2.0	3.0	32290	34135	12	44	78	29.5	21.8	39.7	9.0	0.0	86667
40171	UNION STAR	15384	233	35.6	33.5	27.9	1.7	1.3	35136	36443	18	51	204	37.3	20.1	30.9	7.4	4.4	76000
40175	VINE GROVE	21920	4762	17.6	32.4	41.0	6.7	2.4	50032	51348	61	86	3942	12.7	20.6	50.0	15.7	1.1	110764
40176	WEBSTER	16940	247	30.0	33.6	31.6	2.8	2.0	34350	36830	16	48	218	33.5	28.9	22.5	13.3	1.8	72105
40177	WEST POINT	18772	750	28.0	33.1	34.1	3.9	0.9	39877	43219	32	65	521	28.6	30.5	29.0	11.5	0.4	77625
40178	WESTVIEW	20473	123	31.7	35.8	29.3	1.6	1.6	32272	34028	12	44	106	30.2	24.5	39.6	5.7	0.0	85455
40202	LOUISVILLE	14642	2458	71.2	13.8	12.3	1.7	0.9	12162	12460	1	1	98	30.6	24.5	33.7	11.2	0.0	82857
40203	LOUISVILLE	13768	8921	60.0	24.4	13.3	1.7	0.6	18016	18678	1	3	1587	38.4	31.2	25.8	4.5	0.0	63319
40204	LOUISVILLE	29615	7637	26.3	30.2	31.3	7.4	4.7	42626	44362	41	71	3441	8.2	26.3	37.2	22.4	5.9	115027
40205	LOUISVILLE	39437	10708	13.0	21.4	39.4	16.5	9.6	65328	66622	84	96	7812	1.2	5.9	40.0	48.2	4.7	179558
40206	LOUISVILLE	34190	9605	22.4	33.2	29.0	7.6	7.8	44345	46046	46	76	4737	2.7	14.5	47.6	25.3	9.9	134786
40207	LOUISVILLE	44695	14020	12.9	20.9	38.8	14.8	12.7	68592	69504	86	96	9794	0.5	2.8	33.9	50.4	12.3	193454
40208	LOUISVILLE	20103	5819	40.5	31.3	22.4	3.8	2.0	30747	32976	9	39	1829	13.8	47.7	29.0	8.4	1.1	79400
40209	LOUISVILLE	17481	198	36.4	39.9	20.2	2.0	1.5	30609	31350	9	38	98	14.3	43.9	40.8	1.0	0.0	82727
40210	LOUISVILLE	15548	6202	46.4	26.1	22.9	3.1	1.6	27196	29139	5	29	3339	33.6	45.9	19.9	0.4	0.2	63871
40211	LOUISVILLE	15024	9338	46.5	26.5	21.9	3.6	1.6	26988	28406	5	28	5085	24.7	49.7	24.2	1.1	0.3	70199
40212	LOUISVILLE	14784	6926	42.5	28.8	24.2	3.1	1.4	29702	31733	8	36	3943	31.8	46.9	20.9	0.3	0.0	63779
40213	LOUISVILLE	25064	7552	23.1	32.8	34.0	6.8	3.3	42743	44867	42	72	4770	9.0	27.3	50.1	12.1	1.4	100660
40214	LOUISVILLE	23899	18756	24.4	28.8	35.7	8.4	2.7	45765	49617	51	80	10446	6.7	20.8	55.5	16.1	0.8	113298
40215	LOUISVILLE	16793	9996	40.0	28.9	27.5	2.8	0.8	31301	34157	10	41	5007	9.0	57.2	32.7	1.1	0.0	79874
40216	LOUISVILLE	23122	16801	23.9	29.5	37.9	6.8	1.9	45680	49304	50	80	12003	5.9	21.5	68.4	4.1	0.1	107411
40217	LOUISVILLE	25012	5756	25.9	28.8	35.6	7.6	2.1	44209	47057	46	75	3827	5.5	24.1	63.7	5.8	0.9	106611
40218	LOUISVILLE	24472	13418	25.4	28.3	36.9	6.9	2.4	44919	48324	48	77	6944	5.0	22.6	59.7	12.3	0.4	113686
40219	LOUISVILLE	23403	14435	21.9	27.9	40.2	8.1	2.0	50186	52598	62	86	9301	4.4	13.7	75.4	6.4	0.1	114974
40220	LOUISVILLE	32022	14537	14.3	22.9	42.6	14.8	5.3	61308	63477	79	94	9465	1.1	3.9	62.3	32.1	0.6	153930
40222	LOUISVILLE	42197	9369	14.5	20.4	36.7	14.8	13.7	64870	66076	83	95	5770	1.6	3.8	26.7	55.3	12.7	208896
40223	LOUISVILLE	42270	9567	8.9	18.8	38.7	18.0	15.6	76040	75582	90	98	6891	0.5	2.5	34.8	54.2	8.0	203184
	KENTUCKY	23409		28.5	27.2	32.3	7.7	4.3	44205	46476				19.8	20.7	38.3	18.6	2.6	103937
	UNITED STATES	27277		20.9	24.4	35.3	11.7	7.6	54719	56938				9.3	13.1	31.6	32.6	13.5	162279

#	POST OFFICE NAME	FINANCIAL SERVICES: Auto Loan	Home Loan	Investments	Retirement Plans	THE HOME: Home Improvements: Home Repair	Lawn & Garden	Furnishings: Computers & Hardware-Personal	Major Appliances	TV, Radio, Sound Equipment	Furniture	ENTERTAINMENT: Dine out/Carry out	Sports Equipment	Fees & Tickets	Toys & Games	Travel	Cable TV	PERSONAL: Apparel & Services	Auto Repairs	Health Insurance	Pets & Supplies
40003	BAGDAD	92	83	83	86	84	98	82	93	85	74	83	70	75	86	81	90	57	86	96	108
40004	BARDSTOWN	92	81	75	81	79	86	86	85	87	83	87	66	78	89	80	89	60	86	88	102
40006	BEDFORD	87	67	72	65	66	83	68	77	74	67	73	58	57	77	62	79	49	73	80	93
40007	BETHLEHEM	115	82	95	80	82	109	86	100	95	83	93	77	69	99	78	104	63	94	105	121
40008	BLOOMFIELD	88	66	72	64	65	83	67	77	74	66	73	59	56	77	62	80	49	73	81	94
40009	BRADFORDSVILLE	84	60	69	59	60	80	63	73	70	61	68	56	50	73	57	76	46	69	77	89
40010	BUCKNER	188	236	207	235	227	204	198	201	185	208	189	160	223	194	213	178	136	191	179	231
40011	CAMPBELLSBURG	84	71	75	72	72	87	71	81	75	66	74	62	63	77	69	80	50	76	84	96
40012	CHAPLIN	96	69	79	67	68	91	71	83	79	69	78	64	57	83	65	86	52	79	88	101
40013	COXS CREEK	98	95	87	96	94	101	89	96	91	87	91	73	87	94	89	94	62	92	97	113
40014	CRESTWOOD	150	177	163	178	174	160	153	157	147	162	149	121	169	151	163	143	107	150	144	181
40019	EMINENCE	83	64	67	64	63	79	69	74	74	66	72	57	58	76	62	79	49	73	79	90
40022	FINCHVILLE	110	124	107	128	120	122	111	115	109	111	110	90	118	112	117	109	77	111	114	136
40023	FISHERVILLE	124	148	141	153	148	142	128	134	124	134	125	103	143	126	140	123	89	128	129	156
40025	GLENVIEW	194	271	328	278	303	252	228	244	208	254	206	180	279	200	274	198	155	225	218	266
40026	GOSHEN	172	219	201	222	215	192	182	187	171	193	174	148	209	178	200	164	127	176	166	214
40031	LA GRANGE	120	126	113	127	123	124	116	120	115	118	116	91	119	119	118	116	81	116	119	141
40033	LEBANON	80	62	68	62	62	79	67	74	72	62	70	57	56	73	62	78	48	72	80	89
40036	LOCKPORT	114	82	94	79	81	108	85	99	94	83	92	76	68	98	77	103	62	94	104	120
40037	LORETTO	87	64	72	62	63	83	66	76	73	65	71	58	54	76	60	79	48	72	80	93
40040	MACKVILLE	80	68	70	69	69	83	68	77	72	63	70	59	60	74	66	77	48	72	80	91
40045	MILTON	89	69	76	69	70	88	71	82	77	67	75	62	60	79	67	83	51	77	85	98
40046	MOUNT EDEN	97	89	81	88	88	94	85	91	88	87	88	67	80	91	82	91	60	87	92	108
40047	MOUNT WASHINGTON	98	98	87	98	96	100	91	96	92	92	92	72	90	95	91	94	63	92	96	113
40050	NEW CASTLE	81	62	77	60	63	82	65	77	71	61	70	57	55	71	62	77	47	73	83	91
40051	NEW HAVEN	90	67	74	65	67	86	69	79	76	68	74	60	57	79	63	82	50	75	83	96
40052	NEW HOPE	86	62	71	60	62	82	65	75	72	63	70	58	52	75	59	78	47	71	79	91
40055	PENDLETON	99	95	83	93	92	96	88	93	91	91	91	69	86	94	86	93	62	90	93	111
40056	PEWEE VALLEY	139	154	140	151	151	143	136	141	134	145	135	104	144	136	141	132	94	135	136	163
40057	PLEASUREVILLE	99	74	83	74	75	96	77	88	84	73	82	68	63	87	71	91	55	83	93	107
40059	PROSPECT	206	280	311	292	300	255	230	243	214	254	214	187	282	214	269	204	162	225	213	270
40060	RAYWICK	92	68	77	66	68	89	70	81	77	68	76	62	57	80	64	84	51	77	86	98
40061	SAINT CATHARINE	76	70	69	73	71	82	69	78	71	62	70	59	63	72	69	75	47	72	80	90
40062	SAINT FRANCIS	88	63	72	61	63	83	65	76	73	64	71	59	53	76	60	79	48	72	80	93
40065	SHELBYVILLE	90	91	82	92	88	91	92	90	92	89	93	70	92	94	90	94	65	91	93	107
40067	SIMPSONVILLE	118	140	133	141	139	132	126	128	123	128	124	99	138	123	136	122	88	125	125	149
40068	SMITHFIELD	109	104	92	101	101	104	97	102	99	100	99	75	93	103	94	101	68	98	101	121
40069	SPRINGFIELD	85	67	80	66	68	88	69	82	75	63	73	62	58	76	67	81	49	76	86	97
40070	SULPHUR	101	93	82	90	91	95	88	93	91	91	91	67	83	95	83	93	62	90	93	110
40071	TAYLORSVILLE	97	98	86	100	96	100	93	96	94	93	94	74	93	97	93	96	65	94	97	114
40075	TURNERS STATION	90	73	85	73	75	93	73	87	78	67	77	66	63	79	72	84	52	80	90	102
40076	WADDY	87	88	81	91	87	94	82	89	83	79	82	68	82	85	85	85	57	84	90	104
40077	WESTPORT	103	115	99	119	112	113	103	107	101	103	102	84	110	104	109	102	71	103	106	126
40078	WILLISBURG	84	61	70	59	60	80	63	73	70	61	69	56	51	73	57	76	46	69	77	89
40104	BATTLETOWN	88	63	82	61	64	87	65	80	72	62	71	60	52	74	62	79	47	74	84	96
40107	BOSTON	85	68	70	66	67	81	68	76	73	68	72	57	59	76	63	78	49	72	78	91
40108	BRANDENBURG	93	82	76	80	80	88	81	86	85	82	84	63	75	88	76	88	57	84	88	102
40109	BROOKS	89	89	78	89	86	89	85	87	85	85	85	67	83	88	84	86	59	85	87	103
40111	CLOVERPORT	84	58	79	56	59	82	61	75	68	58	67	57	48	69	57	75	44	70	79	91
40115	CUSTER	91	65	75	63	65	86	68	79	75	66	74	60	54	78	62	82	49	75	83	96
40117	EKRON	85	72	70	69	70	80	70	77	74	71	74	57	62	77	65	78	50	74	78	92
40118	FAIRDALE	81	80	69	79	77	82	78	79	79	77	79	60	77	81	76	81	54	78	83	93
40119	FALLS OF ROUGH	81	58	70	56	58	78	60	71	67	58	65	54	48	69	56	73	44	67	75	86
40121	FORT KNOX	95	49	37	57	44	42	89	62	84	83	88	62	68	101	64	77	62	79	56	75
40140	GARFIELD	77	55	64	54	55	73	58	67	64	56	63	51	46	67	52	70	42	63	71	82
40142	GUSTON	97	84	79	81	82	91	81	87	85	83	85	65	74	89	76	89	57	84	89	105
40143	HARDINSBURG	83	59	80	58	61	84	63	78	70	58	68	58	51	70	61	77	46	72	83	92
40144	HARNED	84	61	82	59	62	85	63	78	70	59	69	59	51	71	61	77	46	73	83	93
40145	HUDSON	76	54	62	53	54	72	56	66	63	55	61	51	45	65	51	68	41	62	69	80
40146	IRVINGTON	75	59	73	59	61	78	60	73	65	55	64	55	51	65	60	71	43	67	77	86
40150	LEBANON JUNCTION	83	75	76	77	75	88	75	83	78	69	76	63	70	79	74	82	52	78	87	97
40152	MC DANIELS	81	58	83	56	60	82	59	76	66	55	65	57	48	66	59	73	43	69	79	90
40155	MULDRAUGH	71	65	55	63	61	64	69	65	69	68	69	51	64	71	63	70	48	68	66	79
40157	PAYNEVILLE	89	64	75	62	64	85	66	78	73	64	72	60	53	76	61	80	48	73	82	94
40160	RADCLIFF	86	79	70	79	76	77	83	80	83	84	83	62	78	85	77	82	57	82	79	95
40161	RHODELIA	87	63	75	61	63	84	65	77	72	63	71	59	52	75	60	79	47	72	81	93
40162	RINEYVILLE	100	94	86	93	92	99	89	95	91	90	91	71	85	95	87	94	62	91	95	112
40165	SHEPHERDSVILLE	94	92	82	91	89	93	88	91	88	88	89	69	86	91	86	90	61	89	91	107
40170	STEPHENSPORT	83	59	85	57	62	84	61	77	68	57	66	58	49	67	60	74	44	71	81	92
40171	UNION STAR	76	54	78	53	57	77	56	71	62	52	61	53	45	62	55	68	40	65	74	85
40175	VINE GROVE	88	85	77	84	83	88	81	85	83	82	83	63	79	85	80	85	57	83	87	100
40176	WEBSTER	84	60	76	59	61	82	63	75	69	60	68	57	50	71	59	76	46	70	79	91
40177	WEST POINT	72	61	54	61	59	67	67	66	69	64	68	50	59	71	59	72	47	67	71	79
40178	WESTVIEW	80	57	82	56	60	81	59	75	65	55	64	56	47	65	58	72	42	69	78	89
40202	LOUISVILLE	32	24	24	26	23	27	35	29	38	33	37	23	31	35	30	40	26	35	36	37
40203	LOUISVILLE	38	27	27	30	26	31	40	33	43	37	43	26	35	41	33	46	30	39	41	43
40204	LOUISVILLE	80	71	68	74	69	72	84	74	84	80	84	60	79	83	77	84	59	81	79	91
40205	LOUISVILLE	111	123	122	125	124	122	117	117	116	119	117	88	125	114	123	117	82	117	122	137
40206	LOUISVILLE	95	86	84	90	85	86	100	89	99	97	99	72	96	99	93	98	70	96	92	108
40207	LOUISVILLE	127	135	137	138	137	131	134	130	131	137	132	100	141	130	137	130	94	132	131	152
40208	LOUISVILLE	61	46	42	49	44	50	65	52	64	58	64	44	55	64	53	65	45	60	57	66
40209	LOUISVILLE	59	45	41	46	43	54	56	52	59	52	57	41	48	59	47	62	39	56	59	64
40210	LOUISVILLE	56	48	44	49	46	55	52	51	58	53	57	37	50	56	48	61	39	54	60	64
40211	LOUISVILLE	56	48	45	49	46	55	51	51	57	53	56	37	50	56	48	61	38	54	60	64
40212	LOUISVILLE	57	50	45	51	47	56	55	53	60	54	59	39	52	58	50	63	40	56	61	66
40213	LOUISVILLE	79	77	70	78	74	81	81	78	83	78	82	60	80	82	78	85	57	81	85	93
40214	LOUISVILLE	80	76	69	77	74	79	80	77	82	77	81	60	78	82	77	83	56	80	82	93
40215	LOUISVILLE	58	47	41	49	44	52	57	52	61	53	59	41	52	61	50	63	41	57	59	65
40216	LOUISVILLE	75	73	67	74	71	80	75	75	78	72	77	57	74	78	73	81	53	76	83	89
40217	LOUISVILLE	74	71	63	72	68	76	78	73	79	72	78	57	74	78	72	81	54	76	81	88
40218	LOUISVILLE	77	69	64	71	67	72	78	72	80	75	80	56	74	79	73	81	55	77	79	88
40219	LOUISVILLE	79	79	69	79	75	81	81	78	82	78	82	60	80	83	78	84	57	81	85	93
40220	LOUISVILLE	97	103	98	104	102	104	101	100	101	101	102	75	105	101	103	103	71	101	106	117
40222	LOUISVILLE	120	130	136	134	134	125	130	126	125	133	126	97	137	123	135	123	90	127	125	147
40223	LOUISVILLE	138	153	152	156	154	147	143	144	141	148	142	109	154	140	150	140	101	142	143	167
	KENTUCKY	90	77	81	77	76	88	80	85	83	78	83	65	73	85	76	87	57	83	88	101
	UNITED STATES	100	100	100	100	100	100	100	100	100	100	100	100	100	100	100	100	100	100	100	100

POPULATION CHANGE

ZIP CODE #	POST OFFICE NAME	COUNTY FIPS CODE	POPULATION 2000	POPULATION 2009	POPULATION 2014	2000-2009 ANNUAL RATE % Rate	2000-2009 ANNUAL RATE State Centile	HOUSEHOLDS 2000	HOUSEHOLDS 2009	HOUSEHOLDS 2014	HOUSEHOLDS % Annual Rate 2000-2009	HOUSEHOLDS 2009 Average HH Size	FAMILIES 2000	FAMILIES 2009	FAMILIES % Annual Rate 2000-2009
40228	LOUISVILLE	111	12874	15791	16914	2.2	95	4965	6259	6748	2.5	2.52	3658	4388	2.0
40229	LOUISVILLE	111	29164	33796	36119	1.6	91	10307	12325	13315	2.0	2.71	8167	9437	1.6
40241	LOUISVILLE	111	22314	26396	28079	1.8	93	8704	10591	11381	2.1	2.49	6307	7284	1.6
40242	LOUISVILLE	111	11281	11103	11059	-0.2	26	4674	4731	4759	0.1	2.31	3085	2937	-0.5
40243	LOUISVILLE	111	9008	10025	10417	1.2	86	3648	4192	4404	1.5	2.39	2688	2944	1.0
40245	LOUISVILLE	111	16151	27544	32346	5.9	100	5659	9777	11551	6.1	2.82	4690	7905	5.8
40258	LOUISVILLE	111	23985	25402	26062	0.6	69	9458	10314	10682	0.9	2.46	6863	7124	0.4
40272	LOUISVILLE	111	34330	34664	34966	0.1	45	12766	13260	13503	0.4	2.60	9713	9638	-0.1
40291	LOUISVILLE	111	27372	32457	34671	1.9	94	10560	12888	13914	2.2	2.52	7949	9320	1.7
40292	LOUISVILLE	111	794	799	799	0.1	45	0	0	0	0.0	0.00	0	0	0.0
40299	LOUISVILLE	111	30365	34766	36642	1.5	90	11738	13573	14369	1.6	2.54	8641	9624	1.2
40311	CARLISLE	181	6931	7012	7056	0.1	45	2763	2846	2880	0.3	2.43	1986	1971	-0.1
40312	CLAY CITY	197	5996	6443	6656	0.8	77	2237	2502	2620	1.2	2.57	1710	1850	0.9
40313	CLEARFIELD	205	2421	2573	2645	0.7	74	1028	1126	1167	1.0	2.26	676	698	0.3
40316	DENNISTON	165	213	234	243	1.0	83	77	88	92	1.5	2.58	57	63	1.1
40322	FRENCHBURG	165	3795	3924	3963	0.4	60	1441	1540	1574	0.7	2.43	1068	1103	0.3
40324	GEORGETOWN	209	28136	39323	46434	3.7	99	10304	14854	17730	4.0	2.55	7547	10517	3.7
40328	GRAVEL SWITCH	155	1539	1597	1631	0.4	60	594	635	655	0.7	2.50	447	460	0.3
40330	HARRODSBURG	167	19226	20414	21032	0.7	74	7809	8487	8810	0.9	2.39	5567	5822	0.5
40336	IRVINE	065	13648	13549	13479	-0.1	32	5410	5570	5609	0.3	2.41	3946	3917	-0.1
40337	JEFFERSONVILLE	173	4736	5349	5724	1.3	88	1752	2050	2218	1.7	2.60	1363	1544	1.4
40342	LAWRENCEBURG	005	18754	21730	23322	1.6	91	7183	8487	9158	1.8	2.54	5416	6189	1.5
40346	MEANS	165	979	1039	1060	0.6	69	375	412	425	1.0	2.51	293	312	0.7
40347	MIDWAY	239	2343	2592	2715	1.1	85	903	1039	1100	1.5	2.36	601	659	1.0
40350	MOOREFIELD	181	382	391	395	0.3	54	141	147	149	0.5	2.66	109	109	0.0
40351	MOREHEAD	205	20100	20444	20643	0.2	48	7059	7346	7478	0.4	2.36	4660	4638	-0.1
40353	MOUNT STERLING	173	17751	20439	21931	1.5	90	7126	8439	9142	1.8	2.38	5055	5761	1.4
40355	NEW LIBERTY	187	918	1074	1169	1.7	93	352	418	457	1.9	2.57	263	302	1.5
40356	NICHOLASVILLE	113	32077	40542	45035	2.6	97	11752	15180	16990	2.8	2.65	9077	11358	2.5
40358	OLYMPIA	011	565	650	690	1.5	90	219	253	271	1.6	2.57	170	190	1.2
40359	OWENTON	187	7666	8013	8232	0.5	64	3000	3189	3289	0.7	2.48	2172	2222	0.2
40360	OWINGSVILLE	011	6573	6927	7040	0.6	69	2596	2803	2871	0.8	2.43	1874	1949	0.4
40361	PARIS	017	18159	18803	19134	0.4	60	7231	7687	7888	0.7	2.42	5106	5217	0.2
40370	SADIEVILLE	209	3337	3967	4383	1.9	94	1224	1497	1670	2.2	2.65	981	1163	1.9
40371	SALT LICK	011	2445	2677	2786	1.0	83	1002	1143	1203	1.4	2.34	712	781	1.0
40372	SALVISA	167	1986	2162	2240	0.9	80	766	855	893	1.2	2.53	589	635	0.8
40374	SHARPSBURG	011	1633	1674	1694	0.3	54	684	722	738	0.6	2.32	485	492	0.2
40376	SLADE	197	316	331	339	0.5	64	131	143	149	1.0	2.31	96	101	0.6
40379	STAMPING GROUND	209	2991	3711	4286	2.4	96	1115	1432	1668	2.7	2.59	873	1083	2.4
40380	STANTON	197	6945	7055	7131	0.2	48	2684	2834	2902	0.6	2.45	1984	2021	0.2
40383	VERSAILLES	239	20633	22503	23465	0.9	80	7879	8819	9275	1.2	2.53	5994	6501	0.9
40385	WACO	151	2650	3154	3451	1.9	94	1016	1222	1345	2.0	2.58	796	922	1.6
40387	WELLINGTON	165	1678	1829	1884	0.9	80	687	774	805	1.3	2.31	515	560	0.9
40390	WILMORE	113	7399	8122	8655	1.0	83	2186	2505	2712	1.5	2.66	1660	1836	1.1
40391	WINCHESTER	049	32653	36224	38081	1.1	85	12821	14634	15527	1.4	2.45	9389	10336	1.0
40402	ANNVILLE	109	2911	3216	3340	1.1	85	1106	1263	1328	1.4	2.51	841	930	1.1
40403	BEREA	151	20775	24804	27035	1.9	94	7780	9472	10428	2.2	2.49	5644	6556	1.6
40409	BRODHEAD	203	3610	3857	3940	0.7	74	1435	1581	1631	1.1	2.40	1058	1121	0.6
40419	CRAB ORCHARD	137	4570	5083	5335	1.2	86	1724	1965	2079	1.4	2.57	1262	1385	1.0
40422	DANVILLE	021	23120	24083	24602	0.4	60	8766	9386	9680	0.7	2.30	5992	6154	0.3
40437	HUSTONVILLE	137	3798	4335	4546	1.4	89	1508	1763	1868	1.7	2.46	1111	1254	1.3
40440	JUNCTION CITY	021	2400	2576	2667	0.8	77	916	1014	1060	1.1	2.54	679	721	0.7
40442	KINGS MOUNTAIN	045	1305	1390	1426	0.7	74	542	597	619	1.1	2.32	394	418	0.6
40444	LANCASTER	079	12187	14011	15048	1.5	90	4742	5508	5928	1.6	2.53	3578	4027	1.3
40445	LIVINGSTON	203	534	537	534	0.1	45	217	226	227	0.4	2.37	155	155	0.0
40447	MC KEE	109	8193	8425	8552	0.3	54	3270	3476	3566	0.7	2.41	2400	2461	0.3
40456	MOUNT VERNON	203	10858	10849	10811	0.0	39	4333	4474	4507	0.3	2.38	3125	3111	0.0
40460	ORLANDO	203	232	235	237	0.1	45	93	98	100	0.6	2.40	69	70	0.2
40461	PAINT LICK	079	2431	2745	2937	1.3	88	940	1078	1161	1.5	2.55	748	829	1.1
40464	PARKSVILLE	021	896	959	993	0.7	74	349	385	403	1.1	2.49	270	287	0.7
40468	PERRYVILLE	021	1652	1776	1844	0.8	77	679	751	787	1.1	2.36	507	539	0.7
40472	RAVENNA	065	1736	1637	1602	-0.6	9	723	707	700	-0.2	2.30	505	472	-0.7
40475	RICHMOND	151	47851	55086	59301	1.5	90	18491	21578	23417	1.7	2.36	11852	13217	1.2
40481	SANDGAP	109	304	292	287	-0.4	18	121	121	120	0.0	2.39	86	82	-0.5
40484	STANFORD	137	11344	12574	13150	1.1	85	4465	5106	5391	1.5	2.42	3236	3567	1.1
40486	TYNER	109	2083	2101	2118	0.1	45	814	849	865	0.5	2.47	630	637	0.1
40489	WAYNESBURG	137	4144	4399	4500	0.6	69	1634	1797	1858	1.0	2.44	1213	1288	0.7
40502	LEXINGTON	067	27072	25559	25169	-0.6	9	13066	12830	12795	-0.2	1.98	6631	5887	-1.3
40503	LEXINGTON	067	27685	27907	28336	0.1	45	11615	12178	12494	0.5	2.22	7269	7162	-0.2
40504	LEXINGTON	067	24189	24073	24215	-0.1	32	10882	11172	11359	0.3	2.09	5728	5318	-0.8
40505	LEXINGTON	067	26433	25565	25505	-0.4	18	11113	11242	11358	0.1	2.26	7129	6694	-0.7
40507	LEXINGTON	067	2256	2412	2481	0.7	74	1175	1336	1407	1.4	1.51	268	257	-0.5
40508	LEXINGTON	067	25931	25722	25818	-0.1	32	9099	9341	9514	0.3	2.03	3535	3188	-1.1
40509	LEXINGTON	067	20360	28596	31996	3.7	99	8896	12685	14304	3.9	2.24	5345	7458	3.7
40510	LEXINGTON	067	1126	1118	1376	-0.1	32	305	289	363	-0.6	3.44	225	202	-1.2
40511	LEXINGTON	067	18372	27992	31480	4.7	99	6618	10627	12113	5.3	2.39	4254	6605	4.9
40513	LEXINGTON	067	8403	9745	10417	1.6	91	3179	3870	4192	2.1	2.51	2368	2728	1.5
40514	LEXINGTON	067	11303	13617	14766	2.0	95	3905	4971	5468	2.6	2.74	3282	4002	2.2
40515	LEXINGTON	067	28325	32333	34296	1.4	89	11095	13032	13947	1.8	2.46	7481	8400	1.3
40516	LEXINGTON	067	2628	3084	3363	1.7	93	979	1185	1311	2.1	2.58	737	829	1.3
40517	LEXINGTON	067	36337	36145	36336	-0.1	32	16412	17044	17343	0.4	2.11	8705	8244	-0.6
40601	FRANKFORT	073	48684	49950	50652	0.3	54	20278	21387	21883	0.6	2.25	13116	13196	0.1
40701	CORBIN	235	29491	31607	32734	0.8	77	11647	12841	13427	1.1	2.42	8340	8864	0.7
40729	EAST BERNSTADT	125	5390	5929	6253	1.0	83	2077	2374	2533	1.5	2.50	1587	1750	1.1
40734	GRAY	121	2894	2860	2833	-0.1	32	1053	1071	1073	0.2	2.67	824	814	-0.1
40737	KEAVY	125	1616	1815	1918	1.3	88	601	697	746	1.6	2.60	484	544	1.3
40740	LILY	125	2475	2780	2941	1.3	88	930	1081	1157	1.6	2.55	693	775	1.2
40741	LONDON	125	19012	20949	21963	1.1	85	7405	8419	8921	1.4	2.42	5451	6011	1.1
40744	LONDON	125	16500	18200	19185	1.1	85	6308	7203	7681	1.4	2.53	4911	5425	1.1
40759	ROCKHOLDS	235	2378	2541	2634	0.7	74	870	959	1005	1.1	2.63	680	725	0.7
40763	SILER	235	605	686	724	1.4	89	248	291	311	1.7	2.35	182	205	1.3
40769	WILLIAMSBURG	235	17956	18921	19517	0.6	69	6817	7407	7721	0.9	2.43	4780	4975	0.4
40771	WOODBINE	121	371	381	390	0.3	54	146	155	161	0.6	2.26	107	109	0.2
40801	AGES BROOKSIDE	095	176	166	161	-0.6	9	68	67	66	-0.2	2.48	49	47	-0.4
40806	BAXTER	095	3290	3157	3079	-0.4	18	1308	1301	1286	-0.1	2.41	922	883	-0.5
	KENTUCKY					0.7					1.0	2.41			0.6
	UNITED STATES					1.0					1.1	2.59			0.9

ZIP CODE #	POST OFFICE NAME	RACE (%) White 2000	White 2009	Black 2000	Black 2009	Asian/Pacific 2000	Asian/Pacific 2009	% Hispanic Origin 2000	% Hispanic Origin 2009	2009 AGE DISTRIBUTION (%) 0-4	5-9	10-14	15-19	20-24	25-44	45-64	65-84	85+	18+	MEDIAN AGE 2009	% 2009 Males	% 2009 Females
40228	LOUISVILLE	88.2	85.8	8.7	9.8	0.9	1.4	2.0	3.4	6.8	6.7	6.7	6.6	6.1	27.8	27.3	11.1	1.2	75.9	37.5	49.0	51.0
40229	LOUISVILLE	94.1	92.5	3.2	3.7	0.6	1.0	1.2	2.1	7.8	7.4	7.2	7.0	6.0	31.2	24.9	7.9	0.6	73.4	34.8	50.0	50.0
40241	LOUISVILLE	85.3	81.2	9.1	10.7	3.4	5.3	1.6	2.7	7.4	7.5	7.6	6.7	5.1	26.2	28.4	9.5	1.6	73.3	38.1	48.4	51.6
40242	LOUISVILLE	89.7	86.6	6.1	7.3	1.8	2.9	2.1	3.4	5.8	5.9	6.3	6.1	5.1	26.1	28.9	14.0	1.9	78.3	41.1	48.0	52.0
40243	LOUISVILLE	91.4	89.3	5.8	6.8	1.1	1.7	1.8	2.8	5.3	5.9	6.8	6.8	4.6	22.0	32.4	14.4	1.9	77.8	44.0	47.9	52.1
40245	LOUISVILLE	86.4	84.6	9.2	9.3	2.1	3.3	2.8	4.3	8.2	8.7	9.0	6.9	3.7	27.6	29.2	6.2	0.5	69.6	36.6	48.8	51.2
40258	LOUISVILLE	94.1	92.2	4.1	5.4	0.4	0.7	0.8	1.3	6.5	6.4	6.4	6.3	5.9	27.3	27.1	12.7	1.4	76.9	38.5	48.7	51.3
40272	LOUISVILLE	95.4	93.9	2.2	2.8	0.4	0.7	0.9	1.7	6.8	6.8	6.8	6.5	5.7	26.6	27.0	12.2	1.5	75.5	38.0	48.3	51.7
40291	LOUISVILLE	89.8	88.3	6.5	6.9	1.4	1.9	1.7	2.6	6.5	6.7	6.8	6.5	5.2	27.9	28.9	10.6	1.0	76.0	38.4	48.9	51.1
40292	LOUISVILLE	56.0	49.7	36.5	40.8	2.9	4.3	2.8	4.3	0.3	0.5	0.3	69.0	24.9	4.4	0.5	0.3	0.0	98.6	18.6	47.6	52.4
40299	LOUISVILLE	90.5	88.3	6.1	7.0	1.1	1.8	1.8	2.7	7.1	7.3	7.5	6.3	4.3	27.2	28.5	10.3	1.5	74.1	39.0	48.7	51.3
40311	CARLISLE	98.0	97.8	1.0	1.1	0.1	0.1	0.7	0.8	6.0	6.3	6.7	6.1	4.9	26.1	27.9	13.3	2.6	77.3	40.9	48.9	51.1
40312	CLAY CITY	97.9	97.6	1.0	1.1	0.1	0.1	0.7	1.1	6.8	7.3	7.5	7.3	5.7	28.1	26.8	9.6	0.9	73.8	36.2	50.1	49.9
40313	CLEARFIELD	96.9	96.0	0.9	0.9	0.5	0.8	1.5	2.4	6.6	6.8	6.6	5.9	5.6	30.2	25.8	11.3	1.2	77.3	36.8	49.3	50.7
40316	DENNISTON	96.2	95.7	2.3	2.6	0.0	0.0	1.4	2.1	5.6	5.6	5.6	7.3	6.4	26.5	29.9	12.4	0.9	79.5	39.7	52.1	47.9
40322	FRENCHBURG	97.7	97.5	1.4	1.5	0.0	0.1	1.1	1.6	5.8	6.1	6.3	8.5	5.5	24.8	28.1	12.9	2.0	76.9	39.6	49.3	50.7
40324	GEORGETOWN	91.0	89.7	6.1	6.3	0.6	0.9	1.8	2.9	7.9	7.4	6.9	7.4	7.4	30.9	23.3	7.7	1.2	74.0	33.4	48.9	51.1
40328	GRAVEL SWITCH	98.1	97.7	0.6	0.8	0.1	0.2	0.6	1.0	6.2	6.2	6.4	6.4	5.2	26.1	29.8	11.6	1.9	77.0	40.5	50.8	49.2
40330	HARRODSBURG	93.6	92.5	4.0	4.2	0.5	0.8	1.4	2.2	6.3	6.4	6.6	6.6	4.7	25.6	28.3	13.5	2.1	76.6	40.7	48.8	51.2
40336	IRVINE	99.1	98.9	0.1	0.1	0.0	0.1	0.5	0.8	6.3	6.3	6.5	6.6	5.2	27.3	27.7	12.4	1.7	76.8	39.6	48.6	51.4
40337	JEFFERSONVILLE	98.2	97.8	0.3	0.4	0.1	0.1	0.9	1.6	7.7	7.6	8.0	6.7	5.4	28.2	26.6	9.0	0.8	72.5	36.1	51.7	48.3
40342	LAWRENCEBURG	96.5	96.0	2.4	2.5	0.1	0.2	0.8	1.3	7.2	7.5	7.6	6.5	4.7	28.2	27.1	9.6	1.5	73.5	37.7	49.2	50.8
40346	MEANS	99.4	99.3	0.2	0.2	0.0	0.0	0.6	1.0	6.6	6.7	6.9	7.2	5.9	27.3	29.2	9.3	0.8	74.9	37.0	52.1	47.9
40347	MIDWAY	90.3	88.2	5.9	6.3	0.3	0.5	4.9	7.9	5.9	6.2	6.4	7.4	5.9	27.4	29.0	10.3	1.5	78.0	39.2	48.1	51.9
40350	MOOREFIELD	99.5	99.2	0.3	0.5	0.0	0.0	0.8	0.5	6.6	6.6	7.2	6.6	5.4	28.9	28.1	9.7	0.8	75.4	37.5	51.7	48.3
40351	MOREHEAD	95.9	93.1	1.6	3.5	0.9	1.4	1.0	1.8	5.6	5.2	5.0	11.0	14.1	24.6	22.5	10.5	1.5	79.4	31.9	48.9	51.1
40353	MOUNT STERLING	94.2	93.5	4.3	4.6	0.2	0.2	1.2	1.9	6.5	6.6	6.7	6.3	5.1	27.2	27.6	11.8	2.1	76.2	39.0	48.6	51.4
40355	NEW LIBERTY	94.0	93.5	4.0	3.8	0.1	0.2	1.2	2.0	6.6	6.8	7.1	6.3	4.8	26.4	28.9	11.7	1.3	75.5	39.1	50.6	49.4
40356	NICHOLASVILLE	94.2	93.1	3.4	3.6	0.5	0.8	1.3	2.1	7.5	7.2	7.1	6.9	6.8	28.3	26.2	8.8	1.1	73.8	35.2	49.2	50.8
40358	OLYMPIA	98.6	98.2	0.4	0.3	0.0	0.2	0.5	0.9	6.3	6.3	6.9	6.2	5.2	28.3	28.6	10.9	1.2	76.8	38.8	51.4	48.6
40359	OWENTON	97.4	96.8	0.8	0.8	0.3	0.5	0.9	1.5	5.8	6.6	7.0	6.9	5.1	24.6	28.4	13.3	2.3	76.4	40.4	49.5	50.5
40360	OWINGSVILLE	97.4	96.9	1.5	1.6	0.0	0.0	0.9	1.4	6.7	6.9	6.9	6.1	4.6	26.1	27.8	12.1	2.7	75.7	39.9	48.9	51.1
40361	PARIS	90.0	88.6	7.3	7.7	0.1	0.2	2.6	4.1	6.4	6.3	6.4	6.6	6.3	25.3	28.2	12.5	2.0	76.8	39.7	48.9	51.1
40370	SADIEVILLE	97.3	96.9	1.2	1.2	0.2	0.3	0.6	1.0	5.8	6.3	7.0	7.3	4.9	26.6	32.4	8.8	0.8	76.4	40.1	51.2	48.8
40371	SALT LICK	98.8	98.5	0.2	0.1	0.0	0.0	0.2	0.4	6.1	6.3	6.5	6.3	4.9	26.0	30.4	12.4	1.2	77.2	40.9	49.2	50.8
40372	SALVISA	98.5	98.1	0.4	0.5	0.3	0.4	0.2	0.4	6.4	7.0	7.1	5.9	4.2	23.9	32.2	12.0	1.3	75.8	42.0	49.6	50.4
40374	SHARPSBURG	91.7	90.2	5.9	6.4	0.0	0.0	1.6	2.6	6.0	6.2	6.6	6.7	4.6	24.3	29.3	14.5	1.9	77.1	42.1	50.8	49.2
40376	SLADE	99.4	99.4	0.0	0.0	0.0	0.0	0.6	1.2	5.7	5.7	6.6	6.3	5.4	26.9	29.6	12.4	1.2	78.2	39.9	51.1	48.9
40379	STAMPING GROUND	97.2	96.6	1.3	1.3	0.2	0.2	0.9	1.5	6.9	7.0	7.4	7.0	5.0	27.2	28.9	9.4	1.2	74.4	38.1	51.0	49.0
40380	STANTON	99.1	98.9	0.3	0.3	0.0	0.1	0.7	1.1	6.6	6.7	6.9	6.4	5.4	27.8	27.3	11.4	1.4	75.9	38.0	49.7	50.3
40383	VERSAILLES	92.2	91.1	5.5	5.7	0.3	0.5	2.7	4.5	5.9	6.3	6.8	6.9	5.2	25.7	31.1	10.8	1.4	76.7	40.4	48.5	51.5
40385	WACO	98.5	98.2	0.6	0.7	0.0	0.0	0.8	1.3	5.8	5.8	6.5	7.1	5.5	27.4	30.1	10.9	1.0	77.5	39.7	48.9	51.1
40387	WELLINGTON	96.8	96.5	1.7	1.8	0.1	0.1	1.3	1.7	6.0	5.9	6.1	7.4	6.2	26.8	28.5	12.3	0.8	77.7	38.5	51.6	48.4
40390	WILMORE	95.0	93.6	1.9	1.9	1.6	2.6	1.5	2.4	6.5	6.2	5.4	10.3	13.2	26.9	20.0	9.8	1.8	78.5	30.1	50.2	49.8
40391	WINCHESTER	93.5	92.6	4.8	5.1	0.2	0.3	1.2	1.9	6.4	6.4	6.5	6.5	5.6	27.1	28.2	11.5	1.6	76.4	39.2	48.6	51.4
40402	ANNVILLE	98.8	98.7	0.1	0.1	0.0	0.0	0.7	1.2	6.6	6.7	7.2	7.2	5.5	27.7	26.4	10.9	1.7	75.1	37.8	50.2	49.8
40403	BEREA	95.0	94.1	2.6	2.8	0.6	0.9	0.9	1.4	6.6	6.3	6.3	8.2	7.7	27.9	25.5	9.9	1.5	77.0	35.7	48.4	51.6
40409	BRODHEAD	99.1	98.9	0.1	0.1	0.2	0.3	0.6	0.9	6.4	6.4	6.7	6.6	5.3	26.7	27.2	12.6	2.0	76.4	39.9	49.1	50.9
40419	CRAB ORCHARD	98.4	98.0	0.6	0.7	0.0	0.0	0.8	1.4	6.8	6.7	6.9	7.1	5.8	26.5	26.4	12.0	1.8	75.1	38.3	49.8	50.2
40422	DANVILLE	85.9	84.4	11.4	12.0	0.7	1.1	1.4	2.3	5.1	5.2	5.7	7.4	8.3	25.2	27.5	13.3	2.3	80.2	39.7	49.7	50.3
40437	HUSTONVILLE	97.7	97.2	0.7	0.7	0.1	0.2	0.9	1.5	6.3	6.4	6.6	6.4	5.2	27.8	28.0	11.7	1.5	76.6	39.1	50.1	49.9
40440	JUNCTION CITY	97.4	96.7	1.0	1.0	0.2	0.3	2.4	3.9	7.1	7.0	7.2	7.5	5.4	27.8	26.5	10.3	1.2	73.8	37.0	49.2	50.8
40442	KINGS MOUNTAIN	98.4	97.8	0.2	0.1	0.0	0.1	1.1	1.8	5.9	6.0	6.4	6.8	5.3	25.7	29.1	13.2	1.7	77.6	40.9	51.2	48.8
40444	LANCASTER	95.2	94.5	3.6	3.8	0.0	0.1	1.5	2.4	6.1	6.5	6.8	6.6	5.1	27.1	28.1	11.9	1.9	76.6	39.8	49.5	50.5
40445	LIVINGSTON	97.9	97.8	0.2	0.2	0.0	0.0	1.3	1.9	4.8	5.8	5.6	5.8	4.7	28.9	30.0	12.8	1.7	79.7	41.7	50.7	49.3
40447	MC KEE	99.3	99.2	0.1	0.1	0.0	0.0	0.6	0.9	6.6	6.4	6.7	7.3	6.4	26.4	28.1	10.4	1.6	75.9	37.8	48.7	51.3
40456	MOUNT VERNON	98.8	98.6	0.2	0.2	0.1	0.2	0.6	0.9	5.9	6.4	6.8	6.4	5.8	27.4	27.5	12.0	1.8	76.7	39.0	49.7	50.3
40460	ORLANDO	97.0	96.6	0.0	0.0	0.0	0.0	0.4	0.4	5.5	6.8	6.4	8.5	5.1	27.2	28.9	10.6	0.9	74.9	39.6	52.8	47.2
40461	PAINT LICK	97.7	96.9	0.7	0.8	0.4	0.6	1.0	1.6	6.1	6.3	6.6	6.3	5.3	28.1	29.6	10.5	1.3	77.2	39.4	49.9	50.1
40464	PARKSVILLE	97.2	96.6	0.8	0.8	0.1	0.2	0.6	0.9	5.8	6.0	6.8	7.6	4.1	26.6	30.6	11.2	1.4	76.6	40.8	51.4	48.6
40468	PERRYVILLE	95.7	94.8	2.5	2.8	0.1	0.2	0.5	1.0	6.3	6.8	7.1	6.1	4.5	23.6	31.1	12.8	1.7	76.1	42.0	48.5	51.5
40472	RAVENNA	99.0	98.8	0.3	0.3	0.0	0.1	0.6	1.0	4.6	5.3	5.8	6.2	5.6	26.2	29.4	14.5	2.4	80.9	42.6	48.0	52.0
40475	RICHMOND	91.9	90.7	5.4	5.7	0.8	1.3	1.0	1.7	6.2	5.6	5.5	8.6	13.7	27.8	22.4	9.0	1.3	79.5	31.7	48.8	51.2
40481	SANDGAP	99.3	99.0	0.0	0.0	0.0	0.0	0.3	0.3	8.2	5.5	6.5	7.9	9.2	24.7	26.4	9.9	1.7	75.3	34.4	49.7	50.3
40484	STANFORD	94.2	93.5	4.3	4.5	0.1	0.2	0.9	1.4	6.9	6.7	6.7	6.5	6.1	27.0	26.5	11.8	1.8	75.6	38.2	48.7	51.3
40486	TYNER	99.3	99.1	0.0	0.0	0.0	0.0	0.2	0.2	6.0	6.0	6.3	6.8	5.3	28.0	27.8	12.1	1.6	77.2	39.4	49.6	50.4
40489	WAYNESBURG	98.6	98.0	0.2	0.2	0.1	0.2	1.0	1.8	6.4	6.5	6.7	6.6	5.6	26.1	27.3	13.3	1.5	76.4	39.4	49.8	50.2
40502	LEXINGTON	93.1	90.8	2.7	3.0	2.3	3.5	1.8	3.0	4.2	3.9	4.0	4.8	9.6	30.6	27.8	12.5	2.5	85.2	39.2	48.5	51.5
40503	LEXINGTON	92.2	89.6	2.6	2.9	3.1	4.7	2.1	3.6	5.0	5.0	5.4	6.4	8.9	26.7	27.7	12.8	2.2	81.3	39.8	48.2	51.8
40504	LEXINGTON	82.8	79.8	11.4	12.0	0.9	1.3	8.8	13.6	6.2	5.4	4.8	5.8	10.8	28.4	23.3	12.1	3.0	80.6	35.9	49.4	50.6
40505	LEXINGTON	78.7	75.6	17.4	18.9	0.6	1.0	3.2	5.3	6.0	5.9	5.9	6.0	6.0	27.2	28.0	13.3	1.6	78.6	40.0	48.4	51.6
40507	LEXINGTON	63.0	61.0	32.1	32.1	1.6	2.3	4.3	6.5	2.9	2.3	2.0	4.8	16.4	34.5	23.1	11.6	2.4	90.9	36.3	56.8	43.2
40508	LEXINGTON	60.1	56.8	31.5	31.5	5.2	7.7	3.2	5.1	3.9	3.6	3.3	17.9	25.5	22.8	16.0	6.0	1.1	86.9	24.2	51.2	48.8
40509	LEXINGTON	81.2	80.2	12.7	11.4	3.1	4.6	2.5	3.8	7.9	7.3	6.6	5.2	5.4	36.5	22.6	7.3	1.3	75.2	35.2	48.9	51.1
40510	LEXINGTON	85.0	84.2	11.8	11.9	1.3	1.9	17.1	26.2	3.8	4.2	4.8	5.2	4.9	24.0	32.8	18.2	2.1	84.3	46.8	52.8	47.2
40511	LEXINGTON	53.5	59.8	40.5	32.9	0.8	1.4	8.1	11.1	6.3	6.3	6.1	5.8	5.7	32.2	26.1	10.4	1.2	77.9	37.6	51.7	48.3
40513	LEXINGTON	91.3	87.8	2.5	2.8	4.8	7.6	1.0	1.7	5.0	5.2	5.9	7.3	6.6	24.7	34.5	9.8	1.1	79.5	41.6	48.4	51.6
40514	LEXINGTON	93.1	90.8	3.1	3.5	2.1	3.4	1.2	2.2	8.4	8.5	8.6	7.2	4.6	30.0	28.1	4.4	0.3	69.9	34.9	48.8	51.2
40515	LEXINGTON	88.7	85.8	5.8	6.1	3.3	5.3	1.6	2.7	7.4	7.6	7.7	6.5	5.8	33.6	25.7	4.8	0.8	73.1	34.3	49.1	50.9
40516	LEXINGTON	87.2	84.2	9.5	11.2	0.6	0.9	2.4	4.0	7.0	6.8	6.6	5.8	3.9	30.4	26.8	11.3	1.4	75.3	38.3	47.7	52.3
40517	LEXINGTON	81.6	78.3	13.1	14.4	2.2	3.4	1.7	3.0	7.3	5.9	5.1	6.0	11.7	37.2	19.1	6.6	1.1	78.6	30.4	48.0	52.0
40601	FRANKFORT	88.2	86.8	9.2	9.7	0.7	1.1	1.1	1.9	5.9	5.9	5.9	6.6	6.5	27.2	28.7	11.6	1.7	78.6	39.5	48.8	51.2
40701	CORBIN	98.3	97.9	0.1	0.1	0.3	0.5	0.7	1.1	6.9	6.9	6.9	6.4	5.4	25.6	26.9	12.9	2.1	75.3	39.1	47.9	52.1
40729	EAST BERNSTADT	96.5	96.0	1.8	2.0	0.1	0.2	0.7	1.1	6.5	6.9	7.1	6.8	5.2	26.7	28.5	11.0	1.4	75.5	38.6	49.5	50.5
40734	GRAY	98.2	97.9	0.4	0.5	0.0	0.0	0.3	0.6	7.1	7.3	7.3	6.7	5.7	26.7	27.6	10.3	1.2	74.1	37.0	50.9	49.1
40737	KEAVY	98.1	97.8	0.1	0.1	0.1	0.1	0.6	1.0	7.4	7.3	7.5	6.9	5.2	27.8	26.3	10.6	1.0	73.6	37.1	49.0	51.0
40740	LILY	98.3	98.2	0.1	0.1	0.1	0.1	0.4	0.7	8.5	8.1	7.6	6.5	5.9	28.2	24.8	9.3	1.1	71.9	34.8	49.2	50.8
40741	LONDON	97.5	97.1	0.8	0.8	0.4	0.6	0.5	0.8	6.3	6.4	6.6	6.1	5.3	27.2	28.4	11.9	1.9	76.9	39.3	49.2	50.8
40744	LONDON	97.9	97.4	0.4	0.4	0.5	0.8	0.7	1.1	6.9	7.0	7.1	6.3	5.2	28.3	27.7	10.5	1.0	75.0	37.9	49.5	50.5
40759	ROCKHOLDS	98.8	98.5	0.2	0.2	0.1	0.2	1.0	1.4	6.5	7.6	6.7	6.8	5.6	26.5	27.9	10.7	1.7	75.0	37.7	50.4	49.6
40763	SILER	99.0	98.8	0.0	0.0	0.2	0.1	0.2	0.3	6.1	6.3	6.7	7.3	5.8	24.6	29.0	12.4	1.7	75.5	40.8	51.3	48.7
40769	WILLIAMSBURG	98.1	97.7	0.6	0.7	0.2	0.2	0.6	1.0	6.2	6.6	6.5	8.4	8.0	25.3	25.8	11.3	1.8	76.4	36.2	48.5	51.5
40771	WOODBINE	98.4	97.9	0.0	0.0	0.0	0.3	0.3	0.3	5.8	6.0	6.0	6.3	4.7	22.3	28.3	15.2	5.2	78.0	44.1	46.2	53.8
40801	AGES BROOKSIDE	94.3	93.4	5.1	6.0	0.0	0.0	1.1	1.8	7.2	7.2	7.8	7.2	5.4	22.9	28.3	12.7	1.2	72.9	39.4	46.4	53.6
40806	BAXTER	94.8	93.8	2.1	2.2	0.9	1.3	0.6	1.0	6.1	6.2	6.7	6.5	5.8	25.9	29.3	12.1	1.3	76.9	39.8	48.2	51.8
	KENTUCKY	90.1	88.9	7.3	7.5	0.8	1.2	1.5	2.4	6.5	6.5	6.5	6.8	6.5	27.0	27.1	11.3	1.8	76.6	37.9	49.1	50.9
	UNITED STATES	75.1	72.0	12.3	12.7	3.8	4.6	12.5	15.7	6.8	6.7	6.6	7.1	6.9	27.0	26.0	10.9	1.9	75.7	36.9	49.2	50.8

ZIP CODE #	POST OFFICE NAME	2009 Per Capita Income	2009 HH Income Base	2009 Household Income Distribution (%) Less than $25,000	$25,000 to $49,999	$50,000 to $99,999	$100,000 to $149,999	$150,000 or More	Median Household Income 2009	2014	2009 National Centile	2009 State Centile	2009 Home Value Base	2009 Home Value Distribution (%) Less than $50,000	$50,000 to $89,999	$90,000 to $174,999	$175,000 to $399,999	$400,000 or More	2009 Median Home Value
40228	LOUISVILLE	27954	6259	13.1	23.3	44.8	15.2	3.6	61292	63971	79	94	4893	1.3	6.8	67.4	23.6	0.7	140951
40229	LOUISVILLE	24439	12325	13.0	24.1	49.5	10.6	2.9	60200	62007	78	93	9899	4.3	9.1	71.3	14.4	0.8	120391
40241	LOUISVILLE	45506	10591	7.2	14.7	36.8	21.2	20.1	86105	86058	94	99	8058	0.2	1.2	30.6	60.7	7.3	207053
40242	LOUISVILLE	34750	4731	10.5	22.0	41.5	18.0	7.9	69103	70308	86	97	3426	1.1	3.8	46.0	48.4	0.6	173253
40243	LOUISVILLE	39240	4192	8.8	17.5	39.9	21.9	12.0	75956	77475	90	98	3503	0.4	3.2	38.2	56.9	1.3	187182
40245	LOUISVILLE	53709	9777	5.8	8.1	30.3	21.5	34.4	109703	111391	98	100	8640	1.2	4.4	23.3	51.8	19.3	263736
40258	LOUISVILLE	24539	10314	16.6	26.3	45.9	9.5	1.7	54961	58080	71	91	8397	8.1	15.2	70.5	6.1	0.1	110517
40272	LOUISVILLE	23742	13260	16.2	27.4	44.8	9.1	2.5	54496	57389	70	90	10958	11.6	18.4	56.4	13.3	0.3	108112
40291	LOUISVILLE	31680	12888	9.0	19.9	46.7	18.6	5.9	70267	71650	87	97	10298	3.4	6.1	56.6	32.1	1.9	149241
40292	LOUISVILLE	11141	0	0.0	0.0	0.0	0.0	0.0	0	0	0	0	0	0.0	0.0	0.0	0.0	0.0	0
40299	LOUISVILLE	32544	13573	9.9	17.8	43.7	20.5	8.2	73945	74730	89	97	11060	0.6	3.4	53.8	40.2	2.1	163173
40311	CARLISLE	18981	2846	35.3	32.1	25.5	4.9	2.1	36579	37682	22	55	2115	28.3	31.1	33.3	6.1	1.1	76849
40312	CLAY CITY	14056	2502	42.6	32.4	22.8	1.7	0.5	28811	29123	6	34	1967	39.0	29.5	27.8	3.7	0.0	63872
40313	CLEARFIELD	17977	1126	43.1	26.8	25.7	2.6	1.9	30585	32601	9	38	774	39.5	25.1	26.7	8.0	0.6	65192
40316	DENNISTON	13677	88	45.5	34.1	19.3	1.1	0.0	28878	29055	7	35	76	28.9	40.8	30.3	0.0	0.0	71667
40322	FRENCHBURG	15090	1540	47.6	29.0	20.4	2.3	0.8	27165	28517	5	29	1200	40.5	27.7	26.5	4.9	0.4	63238
40324	GEORGETOWN	30120	14854	16.0	21.9	38.4	15.2	8.4	65417	68617	84	96	10126	9.3	7.2	38.0	38.2	7.4	167582
40328	GRAVEL SWITCH	17823	635	36.7	28.7	28.3	4.6	1.7	36374	39157	22	55	523	33.8	21.6	34.4	9.4	0.8	79783
40330	HARRODSBURG	21592	8487	26.7	31.2	33.8	6.2	2.1	43023	44879	42	73	6279	9.8	24.3	45.7	17.8	2.4	109986
40336	IRVINE	15376	5570	44.5	31.9	19.4	2.9	1.3	28639	29836	6	34	4142	42.4	31.4	20.8	5.4	0.0	57960
40337	JEFFERSONVILLE	15852	2050	33.6	36.0	26.6	2.9	0.8	35769	38826	20	53	1705	37.7	23.7	30.7	6.6	1.3	70701
40342	LAWRENCEBURG	23933	8487	16.9	24.4	48.5	8.2	2.0	56068	55947	73	91	6756	6.9	14.7	49.9	26.9	1.6	131743
40346	MEANS	14464	412	48.1	28.2	19.9	2.9	1.0	26653	28276	4	26	340	42.4	26.8	27.6	3.2	0.0	64167
40347	MIDWAY	29225	1039	23.4	21.1	39.6	10.6	5.4	60614	62869	78	94	693	12.3	15.0	34.9	30.2	7.6	142960
40350	MOOREFIELD	18843	147	33.3	36.1	25.2	4.1	1.4	39741	40102	32	64	120	30.0	27.5	37.5	5.0	0.0	79091
40351	MOREHEAD	18415	7346	36.2	29.6	26.9	4.7	2.6	35874	37827	20	54	5190	29.0	26.1	31.6	11.9	1.4	83450
40353	MOUNT STERLING	22383	8439	28.5	29.2	32.9	5.8	3.6	43133	45298	43	73	5850	14.5	20.2	44.2	18.7	2.3	109916
40355	NEW LIBERTY	19071	418	26.6	28.7	38.5	6.2	0.0	46522	47289	53	82	337	24.6	15.4	33.5	22.0	4.5	109122
40356	NICHOLASVILLE	26528	15180	16.8	27.0	38.6	10.1	7.4	55068	57852	71	91	10512	8.6	10.3	44.3	29.7	7.1	145018
40358	OLYMPIA	18097	253	29.2	39.5	26.9	3.6	0.8	36917	37068	23	56	225	39.6	24.4	27.6	8.4	0.0	65000
40359	OWENTON	19263	3189	31.4	29.6	31.5	5.1	2.4	39810	41697	32	64	2471	22.1	27.0	37.0	11.8	2.1	91211
40360	OWINGSVILLE	18044	2803	39.0	28.5	26.3	4.2	2.0	34458	36558	16	49	2191	31.2	28.3	30.5	9.3	0.7	78273
40361	PARIS	23301	7687	27.7	28.6	32.3	7.4	4.0	45173	47177	49	78	5068	10.2	18.4	49.3	17.3	4.9	114304
40370	SADIEVILLE	23897	1497	20.3	24.4	41.3	10.0	3.9	56750	57301	74	92	1275	17.6	17.4	32.2	29.6	3.2	128064
40371	SALT LICK	18036	1143	40.4	32.4	22.4	2.6	2.2	30112	31018	8	37	958	41.5	26.1	21.5	10.6	0.2	62258
40372	SALVISA	24462	855	15.4	30.3	43.6	8.2	2.5	53730	52300	69	89	741	7.8	15.1	49.5	26.3	1.2	119536
40374	SHARPSBURG	18118	722	45.0	30.5	19.0	3.0	2.5	27191	28096	5	29	552	40.9	23.2	25.7	8.2	2.0	71429
40376	SLADE	18935	143	37.1	25.2	32.2	4.2	1.4	39453	44111	31	63	118	50.0	20.3	17.8	11.0	0.8	50000
40379	STAMPING GROUND	22713	1432	24.7	29.1	32.0	10.3	3.9	45949	46866	51	81	1148	22.4	16.3	29.3	30.1	2.0	117982
40380	STANTON	18588	2834	36.8	30.7	25.6	3.9	3.0	34224	35846	16	48	2003	30.6	25.6	35.1	7.8	0.9	82665
40383	VERSAILLES	29778	8819	14.3	24.0	41.4	13.3	6.9	64299	68017	83	95	6577	2.8	6.1	45.2	38.9	6.9	166652
40385	WACO	17029	1222	31.3	30.7	32.7	5.0	0.3	38252	41698	27	60	1022	25.0	25.6	32.3	16.6	0.5	89268
40387	WELLINGTON	14885	774	44.4	34.9	18.9	1.4	0.4	30133	30442	8	37	668	33.8	34.6	30.4	1.2	0.0	69455
40390	WILMORE	20523	2505	25.4	26.8	36.2	7.7	3.9	45860	49736	51	80	1421	5.2	8.2	38.6	43.2	4.8	169911
40391	WINCHESTER	24171	14634	23.8	24.1	40.8	7.8	3.5	51683	53757	65	88	10098	14.8	15.9	41.0	25.5	2.7	122952
40402	ANNVILLE	14313	1263	45.6	33.8	17.7	1.9	1.0	28124	30180	6	31	1080	37.1	25.8	25.8	11.0	0.2	71591
40403	BEREA	19229	9472	28.1	32.8	32.1	4.9	2.2	42004	43925	39	70	6551	22.1	19.8	42.5	15.0	0.6	99441
40409	BRODHEAD	16368	1581	45.2	24.0	26.9	3.0	0.9	30693	32348	9	39	1233	37.6	28.8	26.5	6.8	0.3	67346
40419	CRAB ORCHARD	15272	1965	41.3	30.2	24.1	2.7	1.7	32048	33367	12	43	1568	28.6	29.8	34.5	6.8	0.3	78155
40422	DANVILLE	24024	9386	28.5	27.9	32.3	6.9	4.3	44538	46438	47	77	6399	11.2	18.4	47.3	20.2	2.8	112686
40437	HUSTONVILLE	16801	1763	41.5	26.8	26.8	3.5	1.4	31753	34058	11	42	1440	33.1	24.0	34.8	7.2	0.8	78382
40440	JUNCTION CITY	18317	1014	35.2	29.3	30.0	4.1	1.4	37583	40653	25	59	734	26.2	36.2	33.0	4.6	0.0	76308
40442	KINGS MOUNTAIN	16514	597	45.9	35.2	16.6	0.8	1.5	27232	28914	5	29	499	41.9	31.1	20.6	5.6	0.8	55956
40444	LANCASTER	21876	5508	26.5	27.8	37.7	5.2	2.8	45289	45773	49	79	4219	9.8	21.0	47.3	20.9	1.0	115130
40445	LIVINGSTON	13302	226	50.9	29.2	19.5	0.4	0.0	24432	26443	3	20	190	61.6	25.8	12.1	0.5	0.0	39615
40447	MC KEE	12742	3476	51.1	31.6	15.6	1.3	0.5	24234	25362	3	20	2706	44.0	28.6	24.1	3.4	0.0	57212
40456	MOUNT VERNON	15333	4474	45.9	28.9	21.5	2.7	1.1	28435	29394	6	32	3543	40.3	29.9	24.0	5.2	0.6	60057
40460	ORLANDO	12128	98	52.0	33.7	14.3	0.0	0.0	23919	25469	3	19	87	51.7	31.0	17.2	0.0	0.0	48333
40461	PAINT LICK	19504	1078	30.5	26.3	35.9	4.8	2.5	44457	45751	47	76	864	19.7	16.8	40.9	21.9	0.8	106818
40464	PARKSVILLE	19456	385	32.5	27.0	33.0	5.5	2.1	42469	44905	41	71	330	26.7	22.4	37.9	12.1	0.9	90938
40468	PERRYVILLE	23475	751	25.4	27.2	38.6	5.1	3.7	47430	47802	55	83	592	7.4	18.4	51.0	21.5	1.7	109549
40472	RAVENNA	16657	707	41.7	28.7	26.0	2.7	0.8	30524	33203	9	38	534	39.3	41.8	15.9	3.0	0.0	57215
40475	RICHMOND	21731	21578	30.1	28.0	32.5	6.1	3.2	42010	44725	39	70	11921	15.3	16.8	39.1	27.2	1.5	125681
40481	SANDGAP	10491	121	62.0	26.4	11.6	0.0	0.0	15721	20263	1	1	77	42.9	23.4	31.2	2.6	0.0	57857
40484	STANFORD	18451	5106	34.8	29.3	30.2	3.9	1.7	36832	37271	23	56	3860	20.6	25.7	42.7	10.0	0.9	93669
40486	TYNER	12630	849	51.6	32.3	15.2	0.5	0.5	24088	25254	3	19	711	36.7	34.5	27.1	1.7	0.0	65548
40489	WAYNESBURG	16094	1797	38.0	39.3	19.2	2.4	1.1	32051	33012	12	43	1509	38.1	26.2	27.3	7.3	1.1	65060
40502	LEXINGTON	40853	12830	20.8	24.9	32.6	10.1	11.6	53850	55697	69	90	6899	1.2	4.0	26.0	50.8	18.0	230270
40503	LEXINGTON	32369	12178	15.5	21.8	43.6	12.9	6.2	60170	62253	78	93	8573	1.3	5.0	58.3	34.6	0.9	151245
40504	LEXINGTON	23178	11172	29.1	29.7	34.3	5.1	1.8	39688	42047	32	64	4769	3.1	10.1	70.2	15.6	0.8	121802
40505	LEXINGTON	24214	11242	24.5	28.2	40.0	5.0	2.3	44483	49303	47	76	6552	5.8	20.8	65.3	7.6	0.5	104962
40507	LEXINGTON	22141	1336	52.8	23.0	19.6	2.2	2.5	22813	23334	2	16	244	16.0	16.8	22.5	34.0	10.7	153333
40508	LEXINGTON	15253	9341	53.5	25.7	17.2	2.0	1.6	22442	23407	2	14	2230	31.5	30.6	18.3	16.2	3.4	73574
40509	LEXINGTON	38986	12685	14.0	20.0	40.1	14.9	11.0	66984	68349	85	96	7809	3.4	6.0	45.3	35.0	10.3	165906
40510	LEXINGTON	21660	289	15.2	17.0	49.1	10.7	8.0	70166	70971	87	97	221	1.4	6.3	32.1	48.4	11.8	193750
40511	LEXINGTON	27751	10627	20.6	20.0	41.5	12.0	5.8	57645	61249	75	93	6599	11.6	16.0	38.8	28.0	5.5	138150
40513	LEXINGTON	44948	3870	9.2	10.4	38.7	18.8	22.8	87376	85970	94	99	3039	2.0	1.8	13.7	68.6	13.8	267368
40514	LEXINGTON	39753	4971	3.6	6.5	49.0	22.8	18.1	89654	90235	95	99	4666	0.5	0.2	46.1	52.7	0.4	178586
40515	LEXINGTON	38103	13032	8.5	18.4	45.1	13.4	14.6	74404	75566	89	97	8942	1.4	3.2	46.5	42.6	6.3	172112
40516	LEXINGTON	30037	1185	13.6	24.1	44.9	12.1	5.4	65129	66256	83	95	814	1.8	2.7	41.3	38.7	15.5	182870
40517	LEXINGTON	24714	17044	24.4	28.8	39.7	5.4	1.7	44321	47618	46	76	6811	1.9	9.9	77.4	10.7	0.2	121235
40601	FRANKFORT	27618	21387	21.6	25.5	38.1	9.8	4.9	52450	52855	67	89	14020	12.6	15.3	50.1	20.3	1.8	116749
40701	CORBIN	17595	12841	41.2	30.8	21.9	3.8	2.3	30956	33496	10	40	9407	29.9	25.9	34.6	7.8	1.8	82019
40729	EAST BERNSTADT	14358	2374	48.3	31.0	17.4	2.4	1.0	26289	30059	4	25	1980	42.2	28.0	24.0	5.7	0.2	61145
40734	GRAY	13027	1071	46.2	31.8	18.3	2.7	0.9	26670	28270	4	27	869	37.1	21.9	32.7	7.8	0.6	69167
40737	KEAVY	16376	697	35.6	41.2	17.6	3.2	2.4	33014	34335	13	45	582	31.1	24.1	37.8	5.3	1.7	80000
40740	LILY	16894	1081	39.4	32.6	23.8	2.2	2.0	32819	34962	13	45	802	38.4	29.1	25.9	6.4	0.2	68913
40741	LONDON	17745	8419	37.4	30.5	26.4	3.9	1.8	35421	37006	19	52	6305	26.1	26.4	32.9	13.1	1.6	85597
40744	LONDON	19083	7203	34.3	31.4	27.2	4.2	2.9	37691	38919	26	59	5692	23.5	22.5	39.2	13.6	1.1	95271
40759	ROCKHOLDS	13848	959	45.3	34.3	18.0	1.0	1.4	27132	28021	5	28	769	47.3	26.1	20.2	6.0	0.4	53417
40763	SILER	10056	291	67.4	22.3	8.9	1.4	0.0	17340	17363	1	2	226	64.6	31.9	3.5	0.0	0.0	37250
40769	WILLIAMSBURG	14064	7407	49.5	30.6	16.3	2.2	1.4	25248	25526	3	23	5166	47.9	27.2	21.5	3.2	0.2	52831
40771	WOODBINE	14542	155	44.5	38.7	16.1	0.6	0.0	27602	28367	5	30	116	45.7	25.9	22.4	5.2	0.9	53846
40801	AGES BROOKSIDE	11755	67	58.2	28.4	11.9	0.0	1.5	17924	17207	1	3	44	45.5	40.9	13.6	0.0	0.0	53333
40806	BAXTER	16213	1301	44.3	28.9	22.0	2.8	2.0	28970	31116	7	35	904	33.6	35.8	26.0	4.3	0.2	67045
	KENTUCKY	23409		28.5	27.2	32.3	7.7	4.3	44205	46476				19.8	20.7	38.3	18.6	2.6	103937
	UNITED STATES	27277		20.9	24.4	35.3	11.7	7.6	54719	56938				9.3	13.1	31.6	32.6	13.5	162279

ZIP CODE #	POST OFFICE NAME	FINANCIAL SERVICES: Auto Loan	Home Loan	Invest-ments	Retire-ment Plans	THE HOME: Home Improvements: Home Repair	Lawn & Garden	Furnishings: Comput-ers & Hard-ware-Personal	Major Appli-ances	TV, Radio, Sound Equip-ment	Furni-ture	ENTERTAINMENT: Dine out/ Carry out	Sports Equip-ment	Fees & Tickets	Toys & Games	Travel	Cable TV	PERSONAL: Apparel & Services	Auto Repairs	Health Insur-ance	Pets & Supplies
40228	LOUISVILLE	100	106	91	104	100	98	101	98	99	103	101	76	103	103	100	98	70	98	97	115
40229	LOUISVILLE	98	99	84	99	94	97	95	95	95	95	95	73	94	98	93	95	66	94	96	113
40241	LOUISVILLE	160	175	161	178	172	157	163	160	156	172	158	127	172	161	166	150	113	156	148	184
40242	LOUISVILLE	111	120	115	122	119	119	114	114	113	116	114	87	121	114	118	114	80	114	117	133
40243	LOUISVILLE	125	145	142	147	146	142	130	135	128	134	129	101	143	128	141	129	91	131	136	156
40245	LOUISVILLE	211	256	233	261	252	217	215	219	200	237	204	177	243	213	229	187	149	203	186	247
40258	LOUISVILLE	84	89	75	89	84	91	85	85	86	83	86	65	87	88	85	88	60	85	92	101
40272	LOUISVILLE	88	90	78	90	86	95	87	88	89	84	88	68	87	90	86	91	61	88	95	105
40291	LOUISVILLE	110	123	111	122	119	116	112	113	111	115	112	86	119	113	116	110	79	111	112	132
40292	LOUISVILLE	0	0	0	0	0	0	0	0	0	0	0	0	0	0	0	0	0	0	0	0
40299	LOUISVILLE	116	130	118	131	127	122	117	119	114	121	116	92	125	118	122	113	81	116	116	138
40311	CARLISLE	83	59	77	57	59	82	62	75	69	58	67	57	49	70	58	75	45	70	79	90
40312	CLAY CITY	66	46	58	44	45	64	48	58	54	46	53	45	37	56	44	60	35	54	61	71
40313	CLEARFIELD	69	54	62	52	53	65	56	63	60	55	59	48	48	61	53	63	40	61	64	75
40316	DENNISTON	64	46	53	45	46	61	48	55	53	46	52	43	38	55	43	58	35	53	58	67
40322	FRENCHBURG	68	46	63	44	46	66	49	60	55	47	54	46	37	57	45	61	36	56	63	73
40324	GEORGETOWN	116	118	100	117	112	108	114	111	111	117	112	88	113	116	110	108	78	110	106	130
40328	GRAVEL SWITCH	78	59	67	58	59	76	60	70	66	58	65	54	50	68	56	72	44	66	74	85
40330	HARRODSBURG	80	71	75	71	72	83	72	79	75	68	74	59	66	75	71	79	50	76	83	93
40336	IRVINE	67	47	59	45	46	64	50	59	56	47	54	45	39	57	46	61	36	56	62	72
40337	JEFFERSONVILLE	74	53	61	52	53	71	56	65	62	54	60	50	45	64	50	67	41	61	68	79
40342	LAWRENCEBURG	94	87	84	88	86	96	86	92	88	82	87	71	81	90	84	91	60	88	94	108
40346	MEANS	67	44	63	42	44	66	47	59	54	45	53	46	36	55	44	60	35	56	62	72
40347	MIDWAY	119	99	113	97	99	118	98	111	102	94	102	86	86	103	96	107	68	106	114	134
40350	MOOREFIELD	90	65	75	63	65	86	68	79	75	66	73	60	54	78	61	82	49	74	83	96
40351	MOREHEAD	76	60	63	59	60	70	66	68	68	63	68	52	56	70	59	72	46	68	71	82
40353	MOUNT STERLING	82	74	72	74	73	84	75	80	78	71	77	61	70	79	72	82	53	78	84	95
40355	NEW LIBERTY	80	68	69	68	68	81	68	76	71	64	70	57	60	74	65	76	48	71	78	90
40356	NICHOLASVILLE	104	100	92	102	97	98	102	99	101	102	101	78	100	103	98	100	71	100	98	118
40358	OLYMPIA	84	60	69	59	60	80	63	73	70	61	68	56	50	72	57	76	46	69	77	89
40359	OWENTON	82	62	79	61	63	84	64	78	70	59	69	58	53	71	62	77	46	72	82	92
40360	OWINGSVILLE	79	56	72	54	56	78	59	71	66	56	64	54	47	67	55	72	43	67	75	86
40361	PARIS	85	76	76	77	75	87	80	83	83	74	81	64	74	83	77	86	56	82	89	99
40370	SADIEVILLE	98	94	87	94	92	99	88	94	90	89	90	72	86	93	87	93	62	90	95	112
40371	SALT LICK	77	53	74	51	54	76	56	69	63	53	61	53	43	63	53	69	41	64	72	84
40372	SALVISA	94	89	86	92	90	102	86	96	88	79	87	73	81	90	87	93	60	89	99	112
40374	SHARPSBURG	76	52	76	50	54	76	55	69	62	51	61	53	43	62	53	68	40	65	73	84
40376	SLADE	79	57	65	55	56	75	59	69	66	58	64	53	47	68	54	71	43	65	73	84
40379	STAMPING GROUND	102	80	86	78	79	98	80	91	87	80	85	70	69	90	75	92	58	86	94	110
40380	STANTON	80	60	68	58	59	77	62	71	68	61	67	54	51	71	57	74	45	68	75	86
40383	VERSAILLES	111	115	105	115	112	114	106	111	106	109	106	84	108	109	108	107	74	107	109	130
40385	WACO	76	60	63	58	59	72	60	68	65	60	64	51	51	67	56	69	43	64	70	81
40387	WELLINGTON	62	45	51	43	44	59	47	54	52	45	51	42	37	54	42	56	34	51	57	66
40390	WILMORE	86	81	76	83	80	82	86	83	86	86	86	64	84	87	83	86	60	85	85	98
40391	WINCHESTER	90	82	78	82	81	89	84	86	86	82	86	65	79	88	80	89	59	86	90	102
40402	ANNVILLE	65	47	56	45	47	62	48	57	54	47	53	44	39	55	45	59	35	54	60	69
40403	BEREA	76	67	63	67	65	74	69	71	72	67	71	55	63	73	64	74	48	70	75	86
40409	BRODHEAD	72	50	64	48	50	69	52	63	59	51	58	49	41	61	48	65	39	59	66	77
40419	CRAB ORCHARD	72	50	63	48	50	69	52	62	59	50	57	48	41	61	48	64	38	59	66	76
40422	DANVILLE	89	79	85	79	80	91	81	87	85	78	83	65	76	84	80	89	57	85	93	103
40437	HUSTONVILLE	75	53	62	52	53	71	56	65	62	54	61	50	44	64	51	67	41	62	69	79
40440	JUNCTION CITY	80	59	63	58	58	75	64	70	70	61	68	54	53	72	57	75	46	69	76	86
40442	KINGS MOUNTAIN	70	48	63	46	48	68	51	62	57	49	56	48	39	59	47	63	37	58	65	75
40444	LANCASTER	83	79	78	79	78	88	76	83	80	74	79	62	74	80	76	83	54	80	88	98
40445	LIVINGSTON	59	38	56	36	38	57	41	51	47	39	46	40	31	48	38	53	31	48	54	63
40447	MC KEE	57	38	54	36	38	56	40	50	46	38	45	39	30	47	37	51	30	47	53	61
40456	MOUNT VERNON	67	45	62	43	45	65	48	59	55	46	54	46	37	56	45	61	36	56	62	72
40460	ORLANDO	54	35	52	33	35	53	38	48	44	36	42	37	28	44	35	49	28	45	50	58
40461	PAINT LICK	83	68	77	67	68	85	67	78	72	64	71	60	59	73	66	77	48	73	81	93
40464	PARKSVILLE	84	64	71	64	65	82	66	76	72	63	70	58	55	74	62	77	47	71	80	91
40468	PERRYVILLE	92	75	89	75	77	96	75	90	80	69	79	68	65	81	75	87	53	83	93	105
40472	RAVENNA	67	47	66	45	48	68	51	63	57	46	55	48	40	57	48	63	37	59	68	75
40475	RICHMOND	81	67	66	69	66	72	78	74	79	74	79	59	69	80	70	80	54	77	76	89
40481	SANDGAP	47	30	45	29	30	46	33	41	38	31	37	32	24	38	30	42	24	39	43	50
40484	STANFORD	75	57	63	57	57	72	62	68	67	59	66	52	53	68	57	72	45	66	72	82
40486	TYNER	57	39	52	37	39	55	41	50	47	39	46	39	32	48	38	52	30	47	53	61
40489	WAYNESBURG	71	50	62	48	50	69	52	62	59	51	58	48	41	61	48	64	38	59	66	76
40502	LEXINGTON	113	110	109	114	109	108	118	110	116	118	117	87	118	116	115	115	82	115	112	131
40503	LEXINGTON	101	103	99	105	102	105	106	102	105	103	105	79	106	105	104	105	74	104	106	120
40504	LEXINGTON	70	58	56	61	57	61	74	64	73	69	74	52	66	73	65	74	51	71	69	78
40505	LEXINGTON	79	74	66	75	71	80	78	77	81	74	79	59	75	81	74	83	55	79	85	92
40507	LEXINGTON	50	39	39	42	38	41	57	45	55	51	56	38	49	53	48	56	39	53	51	56
40508	LEXINGTON	49	33	32	35	32	37	56	41	53	46	53	35	43	52	41	53	37	49	45	52
40509	LEXINGTON	131	125	117	128	121	113	129	121	123	133	125	99	126	129	123	118	89	123	111	142
40510	LEXINGTON	103	122	125	122	126	126	106	116	108	111	108	81	119	105	118	111	75	110	123	131
40511	LEXINGTON	103	100	92	99	96	100	99	99	101	100	101	76	97	103	96	102	70	99	102	117
40513	LEXINGTON	151	175	171	179	175	162	160	159	154	166	156	124	175	156	170	151	112	156	151	185
40514	LEXINGTON	160	184	153	181	174	150	158	158	147	173	150	128	169	159	160	137	107	148	134	178
40515	LEXINGTON	137	146	128	149	141	127	136	132	130	145	132	106	142	137	136	124	94	130	119	153
40516	LEXINGTON	113	127	111	124	123	112	111	114	107	120	108	88	118	112	115	103	76	108	105	129
40517	LEXINGTON	81	60	53	64	56	57	80	65	78	79	80	55	69	81	67	76	55	75	66	81
40601	FRANKFORT	93	87	85	88	86	92	90	91	92	87	91	69	87	92	88	94	63	91	95	107
40701	CORBIN	73	55	66	54	55	71	58	67	63	56	62	50	48	64	54	68	42	64	70	80
40729	EAST BERNSTADT	66	44	62	42	44	65	47	58	54	45	52	45	36	55	43	60	35	55	61	71
40734	GRAY	64	44	56	42	44	61	46	55	52	45	51	43	36	54	42	57	34	52	59	68
40737	KEAVY	77	55	64	54	55	73	57	67	64	56	62	51	46	66	52	70	42	63	71	81
40740	LILY	74	58	62	56	57	69	59	66	64	59	63	50	51	66	55	67	43	64	67	79
40741	LONDON	73	57	67	55	57	72	59	68	64	56	63	51	50	65	56	69	42	64	71	81
40744	LONDON	82	65	69	64	65	79	66	74	71	65	70	56	57	73	62	76	47	71	77	89
40759	ROCKHOLDS	67	45	63	43	45	66	48	59	54	45	53	46	37	55	45	60	35	56	62	72
40763	SILER	44	29	42	27	29	43	31	39	35	29	35	30	23	36	29	40	23	36	41	48
40769	WILLIAMSBURG	60	42	57	40	42	59	46	54	52	43	50	42	36	52	43	57	34	52	58	66
40771	WOODBINE	62	40	60	38	40	61	43	54	50	41	49	42	32	51	40	56	32	51	58	67
40801	AGES BROOKSIDE	54	35	52	33	35	53	38	48	44	36	43	37	28	44	35	49	28	45	50	59
40806	BAXTER	70	48	67	46	48	69	52	63	58	49	57	48	40	59	49	65	38	60	67	76
	KENTUCKY	90	77	81	77	76	88	80	85	83	78	83	65	73	85	76	87	57	83	88	101
	UNITED STATES	100	100	100	100	100	100	100	100	100	100	100	100	100	100	100	100	100	100	100	100

POPULATION CHANGE

ZIP CODE #	POST OFFICE NAME	COUNTY FIPS CODE	POPULATION 2000	POPULATION 2009	POPULATION 2014	2000-2009 ANNUAL RATE % Rate	2000-2009 ANNUAL RATE State Centile	HOUSEHOLDS 2000	HOUSEHOLDS 2009	HOUSEHOLDS 2014	HOUSEHOLDS % Annual Rate 2000-2009	HOUSEHOLDS 2009 Average HH Size	FAMILIES 2000	FAMILIES 2009	FAMILIES % Annual Rate 2000-2009
40807	BENHAM	095	137	127	122	-0.8	3	58	56	55	-0.4	2.27	36	33	-0.9
40808	BIG LAUREL	095	332	307	296	-0.8	3	131	127	124	-0.3	2.40	100	93	-0.8
40810	BLEDSOE	095	1412	1321	1278	-0.7	5	545	534	524	-0.2	2.47	419	398	-0.6
40813	CALVIN	013	1161	1264	1297	0.9	80	339	394	411	1.6	2.62	259	293	1.3
40815	CAWOOD	095	1345	1286	1254	-0.5	13	518	518	513	0.0	2.48	374	360	-0.4
40816	CHAPPELL	131	72	68	66	-0.6	9	30	30	29	0.0	2.27	22	21	-0.5
40818	COALGOOD	095	380	365	357	-0.4	18	156	157	156	0.1	2.32	115	111	-0.4
40819	COLDIRON	095	740	714	696	-0.4	18	299	298	294	0.0	2.40	223	215	-0.4
40820	CRANKS	095	559	536	524	-0.5	13	218	219	217	0.0	2.45	159	154	-0.3
40823	CUMBERLAND	095	5516	4889	4681	-1.3	0	2304	2126	2060	-0.9	2.26	1578	1393	-1.3
40824	DAYHOIT	095	22	21	21	-0.5	13	6	6	6	0.0	3.50	4	4	0.0
40826	EOLIA	133	620	582	566	-0.7	5	236	232	229	-0.2	2.51	186	178	-0.5
40828	EVARTS	095	5311	5051	4917	-0.5	13	2046	2033	2008	-0.1	2.48	1488	1425	-0.5
40829	GRAYS KNOB	095	68	65	64	-0.5	13	22	22	22	0.0	2.95	17	17	0.0
40831	HARLAN	095	7919	7592	7416	-0.5	13	3231	3226	3191	0.0	2.27	2223	2128	-0.5
40840	HELTON	131	278	261	254	-0.7	5	113	112	110	-0.1	2.33	86	83	-0.4
40843	HOLMES MILL	095	165	159	157	-0.4	18	57	58	57	0.2	2.74	42	41	-0.3
40845	HULEN	013	1817	1729	1696	-0.5	13	677	672	668	-0.1	2.57	519	498	-0.4
40847	KENVIR	095	91	88	86	-0.4	18	30	30	30	0.0	2.93	22	22	0.0
40855	LYNCH	095	74	70	68	-0.6	9	26	26	25	0.0	2.69	20	19	-0.6
40858	MOZELLE	131	2047	1941	1884	-0.6	9	800	801	788	0.0	2.42	605	586	-0.3
40862	PARTRIDGE	133	946	944	932	0.0	39	370	387	387	0.5	2.44	290	294	0.1
40863	PATHFORK	095	583	642	646	1.0	83	227	260	265	1.5	2.47	170	187	1.0
40865	PUTNEY	095	529	510	501	-0.4	18	210	212	211	0.1	2.41	155	151	-0.3
40868	STINNETT	131	1213	1145	1107	-0.6	9	463	459	450	-0.1	2.49	358	344	-0.4
40870	TOTZ	095	593	560	542	-0.6	9	242	239	234	-0.1	2.34	183	176	-0.4
40873	WALLINS CREEK	095	3461	3342	3266	-0.4	18	1397	1407	1394	0.1	2.38	1004	973	-0.3
40902	ARJAY	013	1248	1161	1130	-0.8	3	491	478	471	-0.3	2.42	358	335	-0.7
40903	ARTEMUS	121	463	507	527	1.0	83	180	206	217	1.5	2.46	130	143	1.0
40906	BARBOURVILLE	121	9480	10100	10347	0.7	74	3767	4156	4310	1.1	2.33	2622	2780	0.6
40913	BEVERLY	121	209	212	215	0.2	48	77	81	83	0.5	2.60	56	57	0.2
40914	BIG CREEK	051	2392	2199	2110	-0.9	2	887	858	834	-0.4	2.56	688	645	-0.7
40915	BIMBLE	121	1077	1151	1186	0.7	74	406	450	469	1.1	2.55	321	346	0.8
40921	BRYANTS STORE	121	264	276	283	0.5	64	102	111	115	0.9	2.49	74	77	0.4
40923	CANNON	121	2370	2516	2587	0.6	69	879	970	1009	1.1	2.59	700	751	0.8
40927	CLOSPLINT	095	589	569	559	-0.4	18	226	229	228	0.1	2.48	166	162	-0.3
40930	DEWITT	013	245	257	258	0.5	64	95	104	106	1.0	2.47	64	67	0.5
40935	FLAT LICK	121	2173	2029	1995	-0.7	5	843	816	810	-0.4	2.48	636	597	-0.7
40940	FRAKES	013	1265	1249	1250	-0.1	32	520	535	542	0.3	2.32	384	380	-0.1
40943	GIRDLER	121	239	254	261	0.7	74	95	105	109	1.1	2.42	76	82	0.8
40946	GREEN ROAD	121	774	821	844	0.6	69	275	303	316	1.1	2.71	220	237	0.8
40949	HEIDRICK	121	1525	1644	1697	0.8	77	600	671	702	1.2	2.45	430	464	0.8
40953	HINKLE	121	202	171	162	-1.8	0	78	69	66	-1.3	2.48	58	49	-1.8
40958	KETTLE ISLAND	013	553	525	515	-0.6	9	209	207	206	-0.1	2.54	158	152	-0.4
40962	MANCHESTER	051	17579	17446	17085	-0.1	32	6113	6335	6271	0.4	2.46	4549	4556	0.0
40964	MARY ALICE	095	114	109	108	-0.5	13	41	41	41	0.0	2.66	32	31	-0.3
40965	MIDDLESBORO	013	14056	13536	13301	-0.4	18	5857	5861	5835	0.0	2.28	3986	3817	-0.5
40972	ONEIDA	051	2722	2439	2310	-1.2	1	920	845	805	-0.9	2.55	702	624	-1.3
40977	PINEVILLE	013	9320	9333	9248	0.0	39	3660	3819	3840	0.5	2.35	2673	2691	0.1
40979	ROARK	131	372	352	342	-0.6	9	142	142	140	0.0	2.48	111	108	-0.3
40982	SCALF	121	1278	1347	1382	0.6	69	495	542	563	1.0	2.49	359	379	0.6
40983	SEXTONS CREEK	051	1804	1774	1731	-0.2	26	611	628	620	0.3	2.75	484	485	0.0
40988	STONEY FORK	013	565	533	522	-0.6	9	225	222	221	-0.1	2.40	169	161	-0.5
40995	TROSPER	121	1123	1147	1153	0.2	48	450	478	486	0.7	2.40	325	332	0.2
40997	WALKER	121	242	252	257	0.4	60	93	101	104	0.9	2.49	67	70	0.5
41001	ALEXANDRIA	037	16488	17241	17435	0.5	64	5786	6329	6487	1.0	2.72	4618	4881	0.6
41002	AUGUSTA	023	2507	2630	2681	0.5	64	985	1053	1078	0.7	2.46	701	721	0.3
41003	BERRY	097	2306	2617	2725	1.4	89	829	952	997	1.5	2.75	652	724	1.1
41004	BROOKSVILLE	023	3848	4096	4187	0.7	74	1511	1649	1699	0.9	2.48	1103	1160	0.5
41005	BURLINGTON	015	15184	21667	25387	3.9	99	5250	7760	9185	4.3	2.76	4119	5793	3.8
41006	BUTLER	191	4492	4772	4873	0.7	74	1560	1687	1729	0.8	2.79	1245	1309	0.5
41007	CALIFORNIA	037	3135	3230	3249	0.3	54	1055	1121	1139	0.7	2.86	855	883	0.3
41008	CARROLLTON	041	7449	7755	7925	0.4	60	2974	3159	3250	0.7	2.39	2012	2045	0.2
41010	CORINTH	081	3042	3501	3748	1.5	90	1131	1321	1422	1.7	2.65	873	987	1.3
41011	COVINGTON	117	27783	26502	26232	-0.5	13	12474	12349	12368	-0.1	2.07	6301	5716	-1.0
41014	COVINGTON	117	7853	7431	7318	-0.6	9	3277	3229	3222	-0.2	2.29	1886	1710	-1.1
41015	LATONIA	117	20829	21655	22046	0.4	60	8008	8556	8807	0.7	2.50	5536	5619	0.2
41016	COVINGTON	117	6281	6560	6697	0.5	64	2598	2815	2910	0.9	2.32	1584	1573	-0.1
41017	FT MITCHELL	117	39256	40518	41312	0.3	54	14969	16027	16532	0.7	2.50	10616	10815	0.2
41018	ERLANGER	117	26463	27336	27977	0.4	60	10236	10962	11339	0.7	2.48	7078	7164	0.1
41030	CRITTENDEN	081	5381	6232	6712	1.6	91	1901	2259	2449	1.9	2.75	1482	1704	1.5
41031	CYNTHIANA	097	14764	15529	15911	0.5	64	5840	6265	6458	0.8	2.44	4143	4277	0.3
41033	DE MOSSVILLE	191	1644	1766	1816	0.8	77	564	618	639	1.0	2.82	459	489	0.7
41034	DOVER	161	1080	1184	1227	1.0	83	414	470	491	1.4	2.52	314	344	1.0
41035	DRY RIDGE	081	9416	11101	11784	1.8	93	3374	4046	4315	2.0	2.73	2621	3049	1.6
41039	EWING	069	2489	2461	2457	-0.1	32	921	930	933	0.1	2.63	706	689	-0.3
41040	FALMOUTH	191	7204	7541	7656	0.5	64	2673	2810	2854	0.5	2.66	1966	1993	0.1
41041	FLEMINGSBURG	069	6655	6713	6760	0.1	45	2664	2730	2761	0.3	2.42	1907	1880	-0.2
41042	FLORENCE	015	41848	53470	60011	2.7	97	16281	21210	23961	2.9	2.51	11254	14033	2.4
41043	FOSTER	023	1953	1995	2008	0.2	48	748	788	801	0.6	2.53	563	574	0.2
41044	GERMANTOWN	023	618	679	703	1.0	83	239	269	281	1.3	2.52	181	197	0.9
41045	GHENT	041	1338	1432	1473	0.7	74	453	497	515	1.0	2.86	340	360	0.6
41046	GLENCOE	187	1423	1408	1401	-0.1	32	510	513	513	0.1	2.74	393	383	-0.3
41048	HEBRON	015	8191	13926	16952	5.9	100	2657	4628	5681	6.2	3.01	2288	3885	5.9
41049	HILLSBORO	069	2046	2074	2102	0.1	45	777	802	817	0.3	2.58	583	580	-0.1
41051	INDEPENDENCE	117	16433	22626	25065	3.5	98	5582	7934	8889	3.9	2.85	4581	6284	3.5
41052	JONESVILLE	081	287	310	320	0.8	77	91	100	104	1.0	3.08	72	77	0.7
41055	MAYSLICK	161	1616	1759	1812	0.9	80	617	681	706	1.1	2.58	462	490	0.6
41056	MAYSVILLE	161	13916	14091	14223	0.1	45	5742	5966	6072	0.4	2.31	3866	3844	-0.1
41059	MELBOURNE	037	2644	2675	2670	0.1	45	970	1016	1026	0.5	2.60	746	755	0.1
41063	MORNING VIEW	117	3610	3645	3690	0.1	45	1254	1317	1351	0.5	2.75	992	999	0.1
41064	MOUNT OLIVET	201	2261	2314	2323	0.3	54	866	898	905	0.4	2.50	622	621	0.0
41071	NEWPORT	037	22202	20872	20329	-0.7	5	9359	9116	8974	-0.3	2.20	5588	5133	-0.9
41073	BELLEVUE	037	6524	6275	6169	-0.4	18	2779	2779	2759	0.0	2.26	1675	1580	-0.6
41074	DAYTON	037	5922	5654	5538	-0.5	13	2179	2158	2137	-0.1	2.59	1505	1426	-0.6
	KENTUCKY					0.7					1.0	2.41			0.6
	UNITED STATES					1.0					1.1	2.59			0.9

ZIP CODE		RACE (%)								2009 AGE DISTRIBUTION (%)										MEDIAN AGE		
#	POST OFFICE NAME	White		Black		Asian/Pacific		% Hispanic Origin														
		2000	2009	2000	2009	2000	2009	2000	2009	0-4	5-9	10-14	15-19	20-24	25-44	45-64	65-84	85+	18+	2009	% 2009 Males	% 2009 Females
40807	BENHAM	75.7	74.0	22.8	24.4	0.0	0.0	0.0	0.0	5.5	5.5	5.5	7.1	5.5	20.5	30.7	16.5	3.1	78.7	45.3	48.0	52.0
40808	BIG LAUREL	99.1	99.0	0.0	0.0	0.0	0.0	0.3	0.7	6.8	6.8	7.2	6.5	5.9	23.1	30.3	11.7	1.6	75.2	39.6	48.9	51.1
40810	BLEDSOE	99.4	99.2	0.0	0.0	0.0	0.0	0.4	0.7	6.1	7.3	7.0	7.2	6.1	25.1	29.7	10.2	1.2	74.6	37.6	49.4	50.6
40813	CALVIN	94.6	94.1	4.6	4.8	0.1	0.2	0.2	0.3	6.3	6.0	6.0	5.9	8.1	27.8	26.3	10.7	2.9	78.4	37.8	53.7	46.3
40815	CAWOOD	99.0	98.9	0.1	0.2	0.0	0.0	0.5	0.9	6.5	7.2	6.8	6.7	6.0	26.5	28.5	10.6	1.2	75.6	37.1	49.5	50.5
40816	CHAPPELL	100.0	100.0	0.0	0.0	0.0	0.0	1.4	2.9	5.9	7.4	7.4	5.9	5.9	25.0	30.9	10.3	1.5	73.5	40.0	45.6	54.4
40818	COALGOOD	100.0	100.0	0.0	0.0	0.0	0.0	0.8	1.4	7.1	6.8	6.6	5.8	6.0	26.6	29.6	10.4	1.1	75.9	37.4	48.2	51.8
40819	COLDIRON	98.4	98.3	0.0	0.0	0.0	0.0	0.4	0.7	7.0	7.3	7.6	6.9	4.6	25.1	29.0	10.9	1.7	73.8	39.3	47.2	52.8
40820	CRANKS	97.5	97.2	0.4	0.4	0.2	0.2	0.2	0.4	5.2	7.3	7.8	8.8	4.9	27.2	28.2	9.9	0.7	74.4	37.0	49.1	50.9
40823	CUMBERLAND	91.7	90.9	7.0	7.7	0.0	0.0	0.7	1.0	6.1	5.8	5.8	7.0	5.8	22.0	29.4	15.1	3.0	78.2	43.0	47.1	52.9
40824	DAYHOIT	100.0	100.0	0.0	0.0	0.0	0.0	0.0	0.0	9.5	9.5	9.5	9.5	0.0	38.1	23.8	0.0	0.0	61.9	31.3	47.6	52.4
40826	EOLIA	99.8	99.8	0.0	0.0	0.0	0.0	0.3	0.5	5.7	6.5	6.4	9.6	6.4	29.4	27.5	7.2	1.4	75.9	36.6	53.4	46.6
40828	EVARTS	96.6	96.3	2.2	2.3	0.1	0.1	0.8	1.3	6.4	6.7	6.9	7.8	6.4	24.9	29.4	10.1	1.4	75.3	38.5	48.8	51.2
40829	GRAYS KNOB	97.0	96.9	0.0	0.0	0.0	0.0	0.0	0.0	6.2	6.2	6.2	6.2	4.6	24.6	32.3	12.3	1.5	75.4	41.9	49.2	50.8
40831	HARLAN	94.2	93.2	3.0	3.3	0.8	1.2	0.5	0.9	5.5	5.6	5.7	5.9	5.4	23.2	29.8	15.8	3.1	79.7	44.0	46.7	53.3
40840	HELTON	99.3	99.2	0.4	0.4	0.0	0.0	0.7	0.8	6.1	6.5	6.9	6.9	5.4	26.4	31.0	10.0	0.8	75.9	39.0	50.2	49.8
40843	HOLMES MILL	98.2	97.5	0.6	1.3	0.0	0.0	0.6	0.6	5.0	7.5	7.5	8.2	7.5	26.4	25.2	11.9	0.6	75.5	35.3	49.1	50.9
40845	HULEN	99.1	98.9	0.1	0.1	0.1	0.1	0.7	1.2	5.5	6.1	6.1	7.6	5.1	27.3	29.0	11.9	1.4	77.9	40.0	50.7	49.3
40847	KENVIR	97.8	97.7	0.0	0.0	0.0	0.0	0.0	0.0	4.5	6.8	8.0	9.1	4.5	28.4	29.5	9.1	0.0	75.0	37.5	48.9	51.1
40855	LYNCH	95.9	95.7	2.7	2.9	0.0	0.0	0.0	0.0	7.1	7.1	5.7	11.4	7.1	25.7	24.3	10.0	1.4	75.7	34.0	47.1	52.9
40858	MOZELLE	99.3	99.2	0.1	0.1	0.0	0.1	0.6	1.0	6.1	6.0	6.9	7.6	6.6	27.7	28.9	9.3	1.0	76.1	37.8	50.1	49.9
40862	PARTRIDGE	99.0	98.8	0.0	0.0	0.0	0.0	0.6	1.2	5.5	5.8	6.3	7.1	4.8	25.5	30.3	13.6	1.2	78.2	41.6	50.1	49.9
40863	PATHFORK	98.3	98.0	0.3	0.3	0.7	0.9	1.4	2.2	5.8	5.8	6.2	6.5	5.1	26.3	30.1	12.9	1.2	78.2	41.1	50.3	49.7
40865	PUTNEY	99.1	99.0	0.0	0.0	0.0	0.0	0.8	1.4	4.7	5.5	6.1	6.3	5.3	25.5	34.7	10.2	1.8	80.0	42.3	49.4	50.6
40868	STINNETT	99.4	99.2	0.1	0.1	0.0	0.0	0.7	1.3	5.9	6.4	6.5	6.8	6.1	27.4	29.1	10.4	1.4	76.9	39.0	48.6	51.4
40870	TOTZ	98.7	98.2	0.0	0.0	0.2	0.2	1.5	2.7	4.6	4.3	7.7	7.3	4.5	22.9	37.7	8.9	2.1	79.8	44.1	47.7	52.3
40873	WALLINS CREEK	98.2	97.9	0.1	0.1	0.0	0.0	0.8	1.2	6.0	7.1	7.5	6.5	4.7	26.3	29.1	11.6	1.2	75.1	39.4	48.3	51.7
40902	ARJAY	99.4	99.3	0.2	0.2	0.0	0.0	0.5	0.8	6.6	7.3	5.9	6.5	6.5	26.5	28.7	10.8	1.1	76.1	37.5	49.4	50.6
40903	ARTEMUS	96.1	95.7	2.8	3.0	0.2	0.2	0.2	0.4	6.9	7.5	6.7	6.1	5.3	26.4	27.6	11.6	1.8	75.1	38.0	48.9	51.1
40906	BARBOURVILLE	96.5	96.0	1.9	2.0	0.1	0.2	0.6	1.0	6.9	6.9	6.5	7.2	7.0	25.4	25.6	12.3	2.2	75.7	37.1	48.5	51.5
40913	BEVERLY	99.5	99.1	0.0	0.0	0.0	0.0	0.5	0.9	8.0	8.0	8.0	6.1	4.7	27.8	26.9	9.4	0.9	70.8	37.3	47.6	52.4
40914	BIG CREEK	99.3	99.2	0.0	0.0	0.0	0.0	0.7	1.0	5.9	7.2	8.4	8.4	7.2	28.1	24.8	8.6	1.4	73.0	34.8	50.0	50.0
40915	BIMBLE	98.6	98.3	0.1	0.0	0.2	0.3	0.7	1.1	7.4	7.3	7.4	7.0	5.1	28.9	27.0	9.0	0.9	73.8	36.3	49.3	50.7
40921	BRYANTS STORE	99.2	99.3	0.4	0.4	0.0	0.0	0.0	0.0	5.8	6.9	6.9	6.2	5.1	25.7	29.3	12.7	1.4	76.8	39.8	51.1	48.9
40923	CANNON	99.5	99.4	0.1	0.1	0.0	0.0	0.4	0.7	7.4	7.6	7.1	7.4	6.3	25.7	28.9	8.8	0.8	72.9	35.6	49.4	50.6
40927	CLOSPLINT	97.8	97.5	0.8	1.1	0.2	0.2	0.3	0.7	5.1	7.6	7.0	8.4	7.2	25.7	27.1	10.9	1.1	75.4	35.9	49.6	50.4
40930	DEWITT	97.2	97.3	1.6	1.6	0.0	0.0	1.2	1.9	5.4	7.4	7.0	8.6	5.4	25.7	30.0	8.9	1.6	75.9	38.1	47.1	52.9
40935	FLAT LICK	98.3	98.2	0.8	0.7	0.0	0.0	0.7	1.2	7.3	7.4	7.3	6.4	5.7	25.0	28.5	11.0	1.3	73.8	38.2	48.5	51.5
40940	FRAKES	99.5	99.4	0.0	0.0	0.1	0.2	0.8	1.3	4.2	5.3	6.2	7.0	6.6	25.3	32.1	11.8	1.4	79.3	41.3	50.9	49.1
40943	GIRDLER	99.2	99.2	0.0	0.0	0.0	0.0	0.0	0.4	6.7	7.1	7.1	7.9	6.3	25.6	29.5	9.1	0.8	73.6	36.7	48.8	51.2
40946	GREEN ROAD	99.2	99.0	0.1	0.2	0.0	0.0	0.1	0.2	6.9	6.9	7.1	8.0	6.0	25.5	29.4	9.4	0.9	73.6	36.7	48.5	51.5
40949	HEIDRICK	96.9	96.4	1.6	1.7	0.2	0.4	0.5	0.8	6.9	7.0	7.1	6.6	5.6	26.6	28.3	10.5	1.3	75.1	38.0	48.9	51.1
40953	HINKLE	97.5	97.7	1.5	1.2	0.0	0.0	1.0	1.8	6.4	7.0	7.0	7.0	5.3	23.4	31.0	11.1	1.8	74.9	40.2	46.8	53.2
40958	KETTLE ISLAND	99.3	99.0	0.0	0.0	0.2	0.2	0.4	0.8	6.5	6.5	6.1	5.7	5.7	25.7	30.3	11.6	1.9	77.7	39.8	48.4	51.6
40962	MANCHESTER	92.2	91.6	6.3	6.6	0.1	0.2	1.6	2.3	5.5	6.2	6.4	6.4	6.1	30.7	27.2	10.1	1.4	78.0	37.6	54.2	45.8
40964	MARY ALICE	96.5	95.4	0.9	0.9	0.0	0.0	0.9	0.9	6.4	6.4	6.4	7.3	4.6	25.7	31.2	10.1	1.8	76.1	40.3	49.5	50.5
40965	MIDDLESBORO	94.1	93.2	3.8	4.0	0.7	1.0	0.7	1.2	6.5	6.4	6.1	6.3	6.1	25.1	27.6	13.6	2.2	77.1	40.0	46.9	53.1
40972	ONEIDA	96.7	96.1	2.1	2.3	0.2	0.3	0.9	1.4	4.9	6.0	8.2	15.0	5.7	23.4	25.3	9.8	1.6	70.4	33.4	50.6	49.4
40977	PINEVILLE	97.1	96.7	1.4	1.5	0.2	0.2	0.5	0.9	5.9	6.0	6.1	6.4	6.0	26.1	29.3	12.5	1.8	78.2	40.5	48.8	51.2
40979	ROARK	99.5	99.4	0.3	0.3	0.0	0.0	0.5	0.9	6.3	6.0	7.1	7.1	5.4	27.6	31.3	9.4	0.0	75.9	38.9	50.9	49.1
40982	SCALF	99.4	99.3	0.0	0.0	0.0	0.0	0.5	0.8	7.5	8.6	7.3	7.8	5.9	26.7	25.8	9.2	1.1	72.2	33.2	49.6	50.4
40983	SEXTONS CREEK	98.9	98.6	0.4	0.5	0.1	0.1	0.4	0.7	6.5	6.8	7.0	6.8	4.9	26.8	28.6	10.5	2.0	75.4	38.9	49.5	50.5
40988	STONEY FORK	99.6	99.4	0.0	0.0	0.0	0.0	0.5	0.9	6.4	6.4	6.2	5.6	5.4	25.7	30.6	12.0	1.7	77.5	40.2	48.4	51.6
40995	TROSPER	99.2	99.0	0.1	0.1	0.1	0.2	0.9	1.5	4.8	7.1	7.1	7.1	6.3	24.7	31.6	10.6	0.9	77.3	39.4	51.4	48.6
40997	WALKER	99.2	99.2	0.0	0.0	0.0	0.0	0.4	1.2	8.7	8.3	7.9	6.3	4.8	27.8	26.2	8.7	1.2	70.2	36.7	47.6	52.4
41001	ALEXANDRIA	98.9	98.4	0.1	0.1	0.3	0.5	0.5	1.0	7.5	7.6	7.5	6.8	5.3	28.0	27.1	9.3	1.0	73.2	36.3	49.5	50.5
41002	AUGUSTA	98.1	98.0	0.8	0.8	0.1	0.2	0.6	1.1	6.7	6.7	6.8	6.2	5.4	25.5	27.1	13.7	2.0	76.1	39.9	49.6	50.4
41003	BERRY	97.6	96.9	0.3	0.4	0.1	0.2	1.4	2.3	6.9	7.1	7.1	6.6	5.6	27.8	28.1	9.8	1.0	74.7	37.6	50.7	49.3
41004	BROOKSVILLE	98.5	98.2	0.5	0.6	0.1	0.1	0.5	0.8	6.7	6.8	6.9	6.5	5.3	26.7	28.2	11.5	1.5	75.6	38.8	50.2	49.8
41005	BURLINGTON	95.6	94.1	1.5	1.6	1.0	1.5	1.5	2.7	8.7	8.3	7.8	6.9	5.7	32.0	23.8	6.3	0.5	71.0	32.9	50.7	49.3
41006	BUTLER	98.9	98.5	0.1	0.1	0.2	0.3	0.4	0.6	7.2	7.1	7.3	7.8	5.8	27.3	27.0	9.1	1.3	73.5	36.7	49.4	50.6
41007	CALIFORNIA	98.9	98.5	0.2	0.2	0.3	0.4	0.6	1.1	7.1	7.5	8.5	8.2	4.4	25.5	27.7	10.2	0.8	71.3	37.7	48.6	51.4
41008	CARROLLTON	94.8	93.4	1.9	2.0	0.3	0.4	3.5	5.7	6.5	6.3	6.4	6.4	5.6	27.9	26.8	12.2	1.8	76.8	38.5	50.1	49.9
41010	CORINTH	98.1	97.7	0.6	0.6	0.2	0.3	0.7	1.0	7.0	7.1	7.1	6.9	5.8	26.7	28.3	9.9	1.2	74.5	37.4	51.1	48.9
41011	COVINGTON	83.8	81.7	13.3	14.5	0.5	0.8	1.5	2.4	6.8	6.3	5.8	5.7	6.7	29.7	25.2	11.3	2.4	77.7	37.3	50.0	50.0
41014	COVINGTON	89.8	87.8	7.2	8.5	0.3	0.4	1.0	1.6	7.1	6.8	6.2	6.2	8.1	30.1	24.8	9.4	1.3	76.2	34.7	48.9	51.1
41015	LATONIA	97.0	96.2	1.2	1.4	0.5	0.7	0.9	1.5	7.4	6.9	6.7	6.7	5.7	27.3	26.8	10.4	2.2	75.0	37.6	48.6	51.4
41016	COVINGTON	98.2	97.6	0.5	0.7	0.2	0.3	0.7	1.2	7.1	6.5	6.4	6.8	7.2	28.0	25.1	11.0	1.9	75.9	36.1	49.4	50.6
41017	FT MITCHELL	97.0	95.7	0.9	1.2	1.1	1.7	0.9	1.6	6.7	6.7	6.9	6.7	6.2	27.4	27.9	10.1	1.5	75.8	37.2	48.5	51.5
41018	ERLANGER	94.7	93.4	3.0	3.4	0.6	1.0	1.7	2.8	8.0	7.5	7.0	6.4	6.4	30.4	23.9	9.0	1.5	73.7	34.7	49.1	50.9
41030	CRITTENDEN	98.3	97.8	0.4	0.4	0.1	0.2	1.0	1.7	8.1	8.2	7.2	7.7	6.8	30.4	24.4	6.6	0.6	71.7	32.1	49.5	50.5
41031	CYNTHIANA	95.2	94.3	3.0	3.2	0.2	0.3	1.1	1.8	6.2	6.4	6.6	6.4	4.9	26.5	28.4	12.5	2.2	77.0	40.4	48.8	51.2
41033	DE MOSSVILLE	98.4	98.0	0.9	1.0	0.2	0.3	0.5	0.8	6.7	6.7	7.0	7.4	5.7	29.0	26.7	9.6	1.1	74.7	37.1	53.1	46.9
41034	DOVER	96.4	95.4	1.8	1.9	0.4	0.5	0.9	1.5	5.9	6.3	6.9	6.8	4.2	24.9	31.0	12.3	1.5	76.5	41.5	50.4	49.6
41035	DRY RIDGE	98.3	97.8	0.2	0.3	0.4	0.6	1.0	1.7	8.4	8.1	7.4	7.1	6.6	29.6	24.2	7.7	0.8	71.7	33.3	49.4	50.6
41039	EWING	98.1	97.5	0.8	0.9	0.1	0.2	0.6	1.0	6.3	6.1	6.6	7.6	6.1	28.4	26.9	10.7	1.3	76.1	38.5	50.7	49.3
41040	FALMOUTH	98.0	97.6	0.7	0.8	0.0	0.1	0.9	1.5	6.8	6.7	6.7	7.1	6.1	27.2	27.3	10.7	1.4	75.4	37.5	50.5	49.5
41041	FLEMINGSBURG	96.0	95.2	2.4	2.7	0.2	0.4	0.9	1.4	6.7	6.6	6.8	6.1	5.0	25.4	27.9	13.2	2.4	76.2	40.0	48.2	51.8
41042	FLORENCE	93.8	92.0	2.0	2.1	1.6	2.6	2.8	4.5	8.0	7.3	7.0	6.7	6.6	31.0	23.8	8.3	1.3	73.6	34.1	48.4	51.6
41043	FOSTER	99.4	99.3	0.1	0.1	0.1	0.1	0.3	0.4	6.1	6.2	6.5	6.9	6.0	26.6	29.7	10.6	1.4	77.0	39.1	50.1	49.9
41044	GERMANTOWN	97.4	96.6	1.5	1.8	0.2	0.3	0.5	0.9	6.5	6.5	6.8	7.1	5.6	27.5	28.6	10.3	1.2	75.8	38.9	49.8	50.2
41045	GHENT	94.0	92.8	3.4	3.5	0.0	0.1	2.6	4.3	7.8	7.9	7.5	6.8	5.6	28.1	26.5	8.8	1.0	72.5	36.2	50.8	49.2
41046	GLENCOE	97.9	97.2	0.7	0.7	0.1	0.3	1.2	2.1	7.6	7.6	7.7	7.2	5.5	28.0	26.3	8.9	1.1	72.6	35.7	51.1	48.9
41048	HEBRON	96.3	95.2	1.5	1.7	0.9	1.3	1.2	1.9	9.6	9.2	8.7	7.1	4.7	31.2	23.8	5.3	0.5	68.0	32.4	49.4	50.6
41049	HILLSBORO	98.6	98.2	0.2	0.2	0.1	0.3	0.8	1.3	7.1	7.1	7.1	6.3	5.2	28.1	26.9	11.0	1.3	74.9	37.5	49.7	50.3
41051	INDEPENDENCE	97.7	96.7	0.6	0.8	0.4	0.7	1.0	1.7	8.5	7.9	7.4	6.8	5.9	30.8	24.1	7.8	0.9	72.0	34.0	50.5	49.5
41052	JONESVILLE	97.6	96.8	0.0	0.0	0.3	0.3	1.7	2.6	7.1	7.1	7.1	6.5	5.2	27.1	28.4	10.6	1.0	74.8	38.4	51.0	49.0
41055	MAYSLICK	94.5	93.1	3.6	4.0	0.1	0.1	1.8	3.1	6.6	7.3	7.3	6.0	3.9	25.9	30.2	11.1	1.8	75.0	40.6	51.1	48.9
41056	MAYSVILLE	89.9	88.8	8.1	8.6	0.4	0.7	0.8	1.4	6.0	6.1	6.2	6.1	5.7	25.5	28.5	13.4	2.5	77.9	41.0	48.3	51.7
41059	MELBOURNE	99.1	98.8	0.1	0.1	0.3	0.4	0.7	1.1	6.2	6.8	7.4	7.3	5.9	26.0	27.8	11.1	1.4	75.2	38.5	50.4	49.6
41063	MORNING VIEW	98.7	98.4	0.5	0.5	0.0	0.0	0.3	0.5	6.0	6.4	6.8	8.3	5.2	26.8	30.0	9.5	0.9	75.5	39.0	51.4	48.6
41064	MOUNT OLIVET	98.6	98.7	0.0	0.0	0.0	0.0	0.9	0.9	5.5	5.7	6.2	6.6	4.5	23.6	29.5	15.7	2.7	78.6	43.7	49.0	51.0
41071	NEWPORT	92.4	91.1	4.7	5.1	0.6	1.0	1.5	2.4	7.8	6.7	5.8	6.8	8.6	29.1	23.1	10.1	1.9	76.1	34.2	48.4	51.6
41073	BELLEVUE	98.4	97.9	0.2	0.2	0.4	0.6	0.9	1.5	7.1	6.6	6.3	6.3	7.2	29.3	25.0	10.3	1.8	76.3	36.1	48.4	51.6
41074	DAYTON	98.4	98.1	0.5	0.5	0.2	0.3	0.6	1.0	8.3	7.9	7.0	6.6	7.3	28.9	23.7	9.3	1.2	73.0	32.9	49.2	50.8
	KENTUCKY	90.1	88.9	7.3	7.5	0.8	1.2	1.5	2.4	6.5	6.5	6.5	6.8	6.5	27.0	27.1	11.3	1.8	76.6	37.9	49.1	50.9
	UNITED STATES	75.1	72.0	12.3	12.7	3.8	4.6	12.5	15.7	6.8	6.7	6.6	7.1	6.9	27.0	26.0	10.9	1.9	75.7	36.9	49.2	50.8

ZIP CODE #	POST OFFICE NAME	2009 Per Capita Income	2009 HH Income Base	2009 Household Income Distribution (%): Less than $25,000	$25,000 to $49,999	$50,000 to $99,999	$100,000 to $149,999	$150,000 or More	Median Household Income: 2009	2014	2009 National Centile	2009 State Centile	2009 Home Value Base	2009 Home Value Distribution (%): Less than $50,000	$50,000 to $89,999	$90,000 to $174,999	$175,000 to $399,999	$400,000 or More	2009 Median Home Value
40807	BENHAM	12185	56	57.1	25.0	16.1	1.8	0.0	18048	19388	1	3	43	65.1	27.9	7.0	0.0	0.0	39583
40808	BIG LAUREL	11961	127	59.8	21.3	18.9	0.0	0.0	18460	18842	1	4	101	59.4	34.7	4.0	2.0	0.0	44063
40810	BLEDSOE	11578	534	56.0	26.6	17.4	0.0	0.0	20000	20331	1	7	431	56.6	29.5	13.7	0.2	0.0	43372
40813	CALVIN	9207	394	65.7	24.4	9.9	0.0	0.0	16718	16899	1	2	250	53.2	23.6	22.4	0.4	0.4	47500
40815	CAWOOD	10076	518	60.8	29.5	7.9	1.7	0.0	18109	18071	1	4	387	55.3	28.2	14.0	2.6	0.0	46204
40816	CHAPPELL	9118	30	80.0	16.7	3.3	0.0	0.0	15000	17790	1	1	26	65.4	26.9	7.7	0.0	0.0	44286
40818	COALGOOD	11864	157	56.7	29.9	11.5	1.9	0.0	19634	19728	1	7	121	57.0	30.6	9.1	3.3	0.0	46852
40819	COLDIRON	11772	298	58.4	25.5	13.4	1.7	1.0	19170	20180	1	6	236	51.7	26.3	18.6	3.4	0.0	46667
40820	CRANKS	8420	219	68.0	26.5	4.1	1.4	0.0	14855	14616	1	1	166	63.3	18.7	17.5	0.6	0.0	37353
40823	CUMBERLAND	14703	2126	52.0	28.8	16.3	1.8	1.1	22831	24100	2	16	1550	49.4	36.1	13.4	1.0	0.1	50592
40824	DAYHOIT	4762	6	66.7	33.3	0.0	0.0	0.0	15000	17500	1	1	4	50.0	25.0	25.0	0.0	0.0	50000
40826	EOLIA	10222	232	64.7	21.6	12.5	0.0	1.3	18394	19518	1	4	202	52.0	35.6	12.4	0.0	0.0	48095
40828	EVARTS	12872	2033	57.9	26.6	13.2	0.7	1.6	18615	18639	1	4	1601	57.0	28.2	14.2	0.5	0.0	44668
40829	GRAYS KNOB	9923	22	50.0	36.4	13.6	0.0	0.0	25000	25000	3	22	16	50.0	37.5	12.5	0.0	0.0	50000
40831	HARLAN	16922	3226	47.2	29.2	18.1	3.5	2.0	27208	29108	5	29	2110	39.0	31.8	22.3	6.6	0.3	61932
40840	HELTON	12100	112	58.0	25.9	15.2	0.9	0.0	19164	20529	1	5	92	60.9	25.0	14.1	0.0	0.0	40000
40843	HOLMES MILL	11940	58	53.4	34.5	10.3	0.0	1.7	22275	23286	2	14	48	54.2	27.1	18.8	0.0	0.0	47143
40845	HULEN	14594	672	57.1	26.0	12.2	1.9	2.7	20085	21636	1	7	561	48.7	29.9	20.3	1.1	0.0	51389
40847	KENVIR	6637	30	70.0	26.7	3.3	0.0	0.0	11343	10000	1	0	23	73.9	13.0	13.0	0.0	0.0	23750
40855	LYNCH	11271	26	57.7	23.1	19.2	0.0	0.0	18039	27336	1	3	17	35.3	41.2	23.5	0.0	0.0	67500
40858	MOZELLE	12382	801	56.7	23.2	18.0	2.1	0.0	19109	19652	1	5	663	60.6	27.3	11.8	0.3	0.0	39309
40862	PARTRIDGE	13131	387	50.6	27.9	19.9	1.6	0.0	24672	26734	3	21	346	52.3	31.8	12.1	3.8	0.0	47778
40863	PATHFORK	10749	260	58.5	26.9	11.9	2.7	0.0	18669	18361	1	5	218	60.6	32.6	6.9	0.0	0.0	45306
40865	PUTNEY	16024	212	44.3	29.7	20.3	2.8	2.8	31285	35156	10	41	167	43.7	33.5	22.8	0.0	0.0	68750
40868	STINNETT	12775	459	55.3	25.3	15.5	3.3	0.7	20535	21422	2	9	387	56.6	26.4	16.0	1.0	0.0	43625
40870	TOTZ	18952	239	39.3	36.0	21.3	1.7	1.7	28527	29063	6	32	214	43.9	34.6	18.7	2.8	0.0	53611
40873	WALLINS CREEK	13082	1407	54.7	29.2	13.7	1.7	0.7	20874	21817	2	10	1108	47.8	31.6	18.0	2.5	0.1	52202
40902	ARJAY	9712	478	69.0	20.1	10.0	0.8	0.0	16770	17078	1	2	382	70.9	20.2	8.1	0.8	0.0	28214
40903	ARTEMUS	12972	206	53.9	27.7	13.1	5.3	0.0	22531	23062	2	14	141	44.7	18.4	27.0	9.2	0.7	56818
40906	BARBOURVILLE	13757	4156	54.5	26.8	14.4	3.3	1.0	20749	21769	2	9	2702	40.7	25.6	23.8	9.4	0.5	60813
40913	BEVERLY	9257	81	59.3	33.3	7.4	0.0	0.0	19763	19709	1	7	63	73.0	15.9	11.1	0.0	0.0	29500
40914	BIG CREEK	10555	858	64.3	20.2	13.9	1.4	0.2	17544	17327	1	2	700	61.3	28.0	9.6	1.0	0.1	40920
40915	BIMBLE	14513	450	38.2	41.3	15.3	4.4	0.7	33882	38373	15	47	368	29.3	20.4	35.1	14.4	0.8	90385
40921	BRYANTS STORE	11422	111	51.4	36.0	9.9	0.9	1.8	23332	22828	2	17	90	51.1	30.0	15.6	3.3	0.0	48750
40923	CANNON	12036	970	54.9	26.9	16.4	1.5	0.2	21140	21298	2	11	788	45.3	32.4	20.6	1.8	0.0	54205
40927	CLOSPLINT	13229	229	52.8	34.5	10.5	0.0	2.2	22972	23425	2	16	191	57.6	26.7	15.7	0.0	0.0	45469
40930	DEWITT	12203	104	59.6	16.3	21.2	1.9	1.0	17153	17419	1	2	63	68.3	20.6	7.9	3.2	0.0	32917
40935	FLAT LICK	10979	816	57.6	31.4	8.9	2.1	0.0	20818	21231	2	10	614	63.7	15.0	17.8	3.6	0.0	35439
40940	FRAKES	13412	535	56.3	28.2	13.5	0.9	1.1	19895	21423	1	7	455	59.3	26.2	13.6	0.9	0.0	41327
40943	GIRDLER	13778	105	54.3	26.7	16.2	2.9	0.0	21959	21368	2	12	87	41.4	32.2	25.3	1.1	0.0	57500
40946	GREEN ROAD	12612	303	53.1	26.7	16.8	2.6	0.7	22706	22163	2	15	254	38.2	33.5	27.2	1.2	0.0	59375
40949	HEIDRICK	12507	671	56.0	28.5	11.3	3.1	1.0	21136	22016	2	11	460	29.3	33.7	28.7	8.3	0.0	73542
40953	HINKLE	12236	69	50.7	34.8	11.6	2.9	0.0	24504	25000	3	21	50	48.0	16.0	28.0	8.0	0.0	65000
40958	KETTLE ISLAND	13626	207	46.4	30.4	19.8	2.4	1.0	27296	27094	5	30	180	59.4	31.1	7.8	1.7	0.0	43462
40962	MANCHESTER	12990	6335	57.3	22.9	16.3	2.6	1.0	20092	20412	1	7	4652	52.3	24.1	19.6	3.7	0.2	47657
40964	MARY ALICE	10390	41	51.2	36.6	12.2	0.0	0.0	23596	26122	3	18	30	50.0	33.3	16.7	0.0	0.0	50000
40965	MIDDLESBORO	15699	5861	48.4	30.1	17.7	2.5	1.3	25941	27240	4	24	3632	35.6	32.9	24.8	6.3	0.5	67993
40972	ONEIDA	10715	845	57.6	28.3	12.7	1.4	0.0	20380	20352	1	8	642	58.3	29.3	11.5	0.9	0.0	41846
40977	PINEVILLE	14404	3819	50.5	28.9	17.2	1.9	1.5	24363	24814	3	20	2688	48.0	29.6	18.6	3.4	0.3	52488
40979	ROARK	12386	142	51.4	29.6	16.9	2.1	0.0	23404	23588	2	17	116	62.1	22.4	15.5	0.0	0.0	42632
40982	SCALF	8426	542	72.9	20.8	5.4	0.9	0.0	14539	14497	1	1	444	74.5	11.9	12.2	1.4	0.0	31136
40983	SEXTONS CREEK	10131	628	58.0	26.6	13.2	2.2	0.0	19207	19940	1	6	509	52.7	33.2	12.0	1.8	0.4	47545
40988	STONEY FORK	13486	222	50.5	28.8	18.0	1.8	0.9	24517	23744	3	21	192	59.4	30.7	7.8	2.1	0.0	42174
40995	TROSPER	12849	478	50.4	32.4	15.1	2.1	0.0	24454	27350	3	21	375	65.6	26.9	7.5	0.0	0.0	39470
40997	WALKER	9739	101	58.4	35.6	5.9	0.0	0.0	20228	21292	1	8	77	74.0	13.0	13.0	0.0	0.0	30417
41001	ALEXANDRIA	27653	6329	11.2	18.7	50.8	14.1	5.2	67622	68924	85	96	5417	7.9	7.4	56.3	26.2	2.2	135830
41002	AUGUSTA	18782	1053	27.7	33.2	35.1	3.0	0.9	42202	44932	40	70	767	24.4	28.7	35.3	11.3	0.3	86544
41003	BERRY	17728	952	23.4	36.6	32.9	6.6	0.5	43621	44682	44	74	771	25.3	26.2	36.2	10.9	1.4	88506
41004	BROOKSVILLE	19801	1649	27.2	31.8	33.8	5.8	1.3	43635	45813	44	74	1281	27.0	28.6	34.9	8.6	0.9	80203
41005	BURLINGTON	30480	7760	8.3	17.6	44.2	22.9	6.9	76435	80254	90	98	5801	3.4	5.5	39.2	48.2	3.7	178243
41006	BUTLER	20256	1687	19.3	26.4	44.8	7.3	2.2	52801	54230	68	89	1350	15.3	18.7	41.0	25.0	0.1	113348
41007	CALIFORNIA	24805	1121	14.6	22.8	46.1	10.2	6.2	60998	63191	79	94	995	12.7	14.2	42.2	28.6	2.3	122434
41008	CARROLLTON	21314	3159	32.5	22.0	37.2	6.2	2.1	45673	46295	50	80	2033	17.9	19.7	44.7	16.6	1.2	104591
41010	CORINTH	18855	1321	25.0	35.0	33.2	4.4	2.3	41431	43255	37	69	1099	23.7	26.0	33.1	15.6	1.5	90329
41011	COVINGTON	28065	12349	29.0	28.2	28.4	9.2	5.2	43315	44373	43	73	5159	11.3	19.0	41.2	26.1	2.3	126615
41014	COVINGTON	21502	3229	29.2	33.9	29.3	6.1	1.5	39612	41478	32	63	1664	23.5	48.4	24.8	3.2	0.1	73715
41015	LATONIA	25673	8556	20.7	26.3	36.2	11.9	4.9	53434	54454	69	89	6172	6.3	31.1	42.2	19.3	1.1	99962
41016	COVINGTON	23564	2815	25.3	29.2	35.5	7.7	2.3	45156	47107	49	78	1699	10.7	38.2	48.9	2.0	0.2	90573
41017	FT MITCHELL	39355	16027	8.9	18.7	39.3	18.7	14.3	76657	81135	90	98	11904	2.0	3.8	45.5	41.4	7.2	172464
41018	ERLANGER	27633	10962	13.5	27.4	44.9	9.7	4.5	60409	62723	78	94	7495	9.2	12.2	65.0	13.3	0.3	113638
41030	CRITTENDEN	24161	2259	12.6	29.0	44.3	10.6	3.5	57067	59977	74	92	1621	24.2	14.5	39.3	19.4	2.5	109565
41031	CYNTHIANA	21829	6265	24.1	32.1	34.7	6.6	2.5	45520	46527	50	79	4345	11.0	23.0	45.7	18.1	2.2	108448
41033	DE MOSSVILLE	18447	618	17.3	31.2	46.3	5.0	0.2	50782	52049	63	87	520	21.3	34.2	33.7	10.4	0.4	82750
41034	DOVER	21803	470	24.5	36.4	31.1	4.3	3.8	43216	43184	43	73	398	26.9	20.6	42.0	8.3	2.3	92273
41035	DRY RIDGE	21872	4046	18.0	27.6	43.7	8.1	2.6	53256	56279	68	89	3064	25.4	13.1	39.5	20.2	1.9	112703
41039	EWING	16955	930	34.7	27.6	32.6	4.1	1.0	39137	40756	30	63	761	26.8	28.1	31.5	11.0	2.5	85787
41040	FALMOUTH	18760	2810	31.2	25.5	36.6	4.8	1.9	43910	46360	45	75	2091	14.1	27.6	46.2	11.2	0.9	98032
41041	FLEMINGSBURG	19197	2730	35.2	30.3	27.4	4.4	2.6	37114	38718	24	57	2037	19.7	34.8	30.9	13.4	1.2	84618
41042	FLORENCE	30658	21210	13.7	22.2	39.2	17.6	7.3	65289	67281	84	95	14069	9.9	5.2	43.3	39.6	2.0	157191
41043	FOSTER	20563	788	23.0	33.8	33.8	8.0	1.5	43777	47054	45	74	659	22.2	24.3	33.2	18.5	1.8	95875
41044	GERMANTOWN	22893	269	24.5	31.6	34.2	5.6	4.1	45963	46845	51	81	219	32.9	21.5	29.7	11.0	5.0	82083
41045	GHENT	20333	497	22.5	27.2	40.4	7.2	2.6	50402	50704	62	86	376	19.9	23.9	36.7	14.4	5.1	96389
41046	GLENCOE	18248	513	26.9	31.4	32.9	7.0	1.8	42991	45981	42	73	418	17.0	22.7	40.2	17.9	2.2	104231
41048	HEBRON	40352	4628	4.8	11.0	35.8	27.6	20.9	97293	104132	96	99	4009	0.2	8.8	28.7	48.7	13.5	193914
41049	HILLSBORO	15199	802	33.5	41.9	19.8	3.5	1.2	31700	34507	11	42	659	34.1	34.6	25.9	4.4	0.9	67174
41051	INDEPENDENCE	27155	7934	10.2	18.7	50.6	15.5	5.0	70585	76442	87	97	6577	5.5	10.0	54.4	29.2	0.8	142986
41052	JONESVILLE	16881	100	20.0	30.0	44.0	6.0	0.0	50000	51388	61	86	83	20.5	14.5	37.3	26.5	1.2	119318
41055	MAYSLICK	19465	681	33.8	33.0	25.7	4.1	3.4	35175	37480	18	51	515	18.8	22.1	37.1	19.6	2.3	97750
41056	MAYSVILLE	20867	5966	33.0	32.2	26.6	5.5	2.7	36979	38912	24	57	3928	21.7	26.8	37.7	12.3	1.4	91418
41059	MELBOURNE	27097	1016	15.3	21.7	43.4	13.3	6.4	59908	62487	77	93	802	13.2	13.0	45.1	25.7	3.0	119006
41063	MORNING VIEW	22859	1317	19.5	24.0	44.3	9.6	2.6	56144	57297	73	92	1122	10.0	17.2	47.3	23.3	2.2	132143
41064	MOUNT OLIVET	16668	898	34.5	30.8	30.3	3.8	0.6	37295	38139	24	57	706	34.8	24.2	33.0	7.8	0.1	75349
41071	NEWPORT	24767	9116	27.8	27.9	33.1	7.0	4.1	42843	44536	42	72	4679	14.1	32.3	41.9	11.2	0.5	93671
41073	BELLEVUE	25754	2779	22.2	25.5	42.9	7.2	2.3	51956	54976	66	88	1853	6.7	46.5	43.7	3.1	0.1	87763
41074	DAYTON	20650	2158	29.0	28.6	33.5	5.7	3.2	42482	44260	41	71	1308	17.2	49.5	26.7	4.9	1.7	74510
	KENTUCKY	23409		28.5	27.2	32.3	7.7	4.3	44205	46476				19.8	20.7	38.3	18.6	2.6	103937
	UNITED STATES	27277		20.9	24.4	35.3	11.7	7.6	54719	56938				9.3	13.1	31.6	32.6	13.5	162279

ZIP CODE #	POST OFFICE NAME	FINANCIAL SERVICES: Auto Loan	FINANCIAL SERVICES: Home Loan	FINANCIAL SERVICES: Invest-ments	FINANCIAL SERVICES: Retire-ment Plans	THE HOME: Home Improvements: Home Repair	THE HOME: Home Improvements: Lawn & Garden	THE HOME: Furnishings: Comput-ers & Hard-ware-Personal	THE HOME: Furnishings: Major Appli-ances	THE HOME: Furnishings: TV, Radio, Sound Equip-ment	THE HOME: Furnishings: Furni-ture	ENTERTAINMENT: Dine out/ Carry out	ENTERTAINMENT: Sports Equip-ment	ENTERTAINMENT: Fees & Tickets	ENTERTAINMENT: Toys & Games	ENTERTAINMENT: Travel	ENTERTAINMENT: Cable TV	PERSONAL: Apparel & Services	PERSONAL: Auto Repairs	PERSONAL: Health Insur-ance	PERSONAL: Pets & Supplies
40807	BENHAM	47	34	47	33	35	49	37	45	41	33	40	34	29	40	35	45	26	42	49	53
40808	BIG LAUREL	54	35	52	33	35	53	37	47	43	35	42	37	28	44	35	48	28	44	50	58
40810	BLEDSOE	53	35	51	33	35	52	37	47	43	35	42	36	28	44	35	48	28	44	49	58
40813	CALVIN	41	27	38	26	27	40	30	36	34	28	33	28	23	34	27	37	22	34	38	44
40815	CAWOOD	47	30	45	29	30	46	32	41	37	31	37	32	24	38	30	42	24	38	43	50
40816	CHAPPELL	38	25	37	24	25	38	27	34	31	25	30	26	20	31	25	35	20	32	36	42
40818	COALGOOD	51	33	49	31	33	50	36	45	41	34	40	35	27	42	33	46	27	42	48	55
40819	COLDIRON	52	34	51	32	34	51	37	46	42	35	41	36	27	43	34	47	27	43	49	57
40820	CRANKS	38	25	37	24	25	38	27	34	31	25	30	26	20	31	25	34	20	32	36	41
40823	CUMBERLAND	58	40	56	39	41	58	44	54	50	41	48	41	35	50	42	55	32	51	58	64
40824	DAYHOIT	31	20	30	19	20	30	22	27	25	21	24	21	16	25	20	28	16	26	29	34
40826	EOLIA	48	31	46	29	31	47	33	42	38	32	37	33	25	39	31	43	25	39	44	52
40828	EVARTS	59	39	57	37	39	58	41	52	48	39	47	41	31	49	39	53	31	49	55	64
40829	GRAYS KNOB	55	36	53	33	35	53	38	48	44	36	43	37	28	45	35	49	28	45	51	59
40831	HARLAN	64	48	63	47	49	65	51	60	58	49	56	45	44	57	49	63	38	58	66	72
40840	HELTON	52	34	51	32	34	51	37	46	42	35	41	36	27	43	34	47	27	43	49	57
40843	HOLMES MILL	61	40	59	37	40	60	42	53	49	40	48	42	32	50	40	55	32	50	57	66
40845	HULEN	70	46	67	43	45	68	49	61	56	46	55	48	36	57	45	63	36	58	65	75
40847	KENVIR	36	24	35	22	24	35	25	32	29	24	28	25	19	30	24	33	19	30	34	39
40855	LYNCH	56	37	54	35	37	55	39	50	45	37	44	39	29	46	37	51	29	47	52	61
40858	MOZELLE	56	36	54	34	36	55	39	49	45	37	44	38	29	46	36	50	29	46	52	60
40862	PARTRIDGE	60	39	57	37	39	58	42	52	48	39	47	41	31	49	39	53	31	49	55	64
40863	PATHFORK	49	32	48	30	32	48	34	43	40	33	39	34	26	40	32	44	26	41	46	53
40865	PUTNEY	72	47	69	44	47	70	50	63	58	48	56	49	37	59	47	64	37	59	67	77
40868	STINNETT	59	39	57	36	39	58	41	52	48	39	47	41	31	48	39	53	31	49	55	64
40870	TOTZ	83	54	80	51	54	81	58	73	66	55	65	57	43	68	54	74	43	68	77	89
40873	WALLINS CREEK	58	38	56	35	38	57	40	51	47	38	45	40	30	47	38	52	30	48	54	62
40902	ARJAY	44	29	42	27	28	43	31	38	35	29	34	30	23	36	28	39	23	36	41	47
40903	ARTEMUS	59	39	57	36	39	58	41	52	48	39	47	41	31	49	39	53	31	49	55	64
40906	BARBOURVILLE	56	39	53	38	39	55	43	51	48	40	47	39	34	48	40	53	31	49	54	62
40913	BEVERLY	45	29	43	27	29	44	31	39	36	30	35	31	23	37	29	40	23	37	42	48
40914	BIG CREEK	50	33	49	31	33	49	35	44	40	33	40	34	26	41	33	45	26	42	47	54
40915	BIMBLE	62	52	51	50	51	59	51	56	54	52	54	42	45	56	48	57	36	54	57	67
40921	BRYANTS STORE	53	34	51	32	34	52	37	46	43	35	41	36	28	43	34	47	27	44	49	57
40923	CANNON	58	38	56	36	38	57	40	51	47	38	46	40	30	48	38	52	30	48	54	63
40927	CLOSPLINT	61	40	59	38	40	60	43	54	49	41	48	42	32	50	40	55	32	51	57	66
40930	DEWITT	56	37	54	34	36	55	39	49	45	37	44	38	29	46	36	50	29	46	52	61
40935	FLAT LICK	51	33	49	31	33	50	35	45	41	34	40	35	26	42	33	46	26	42	47	55
40940	FRAKES	58	38	56	36	38	57	40	51	47	38	46	40	30	47	38	52	30	48	54	63
40943	GIRDLER	62	40	60	38	40	61	43	54	50	41	49	42	32	51	40	56	32	51	58	67
40946	GREEN ROAD	64	41	61	39	41	62	44	56	51	42	50	44	33	52	41	57	33	53	59	69
40949	HEIDRICK	56	38	51	37	38	54	40	49	46	39	45	38	31	47	37	51	30	46	52	60
40953	HINKLE	56	37	54	35	37	55	39	50	45	37	44	39	29	46	37	51	29	47	52	61
40958	KETTLE ISLAND	64	42	62	39	42	63	45	56	52	43	50	44	34	53	42	58	33	53	60	69
40962	MANCHESTER	59	39	57	37	40	58	42	52	48	40	47	41	32	49	40	53	31	49	56	64
40964	MARY ALICE	51	33	50	32	33	50	36	45	41	34	40	35	27	42	33	46	27	42	48	56
40965	MIDDLESBORO	61	44	56	43	44	60	48	56	54	45	52	43	39	54	45	59	35	54	60	67
40972	ONEIDA	50	33	48	31	32	49	35	44	40	33	39	34	26	41	33	45	26	41	46	54
40977	PINEVILLE	62	42	60	40	42	61	45	56	51	42	50	43	34	51	42	56	33	52	59	68
40979	ROARK	57	37	55	35	37	56	40	50	46	38	45	39	30	47	37	51	30	47	53	62
40982	SCALF	39	25	38	24	25	38	27	34	31	26	31	27	20	32	25	35	20	32	36	42
40983	SEXTONS CREEK	52	34	50	32	33	51	36	45	41	34	40	35	27	42	34	46	27	43	48	56
40988	STONEY FORK	60	39	58	37	39	59	42	53	48	40	47	41	31	49	39	54	31	50	56	65
40995	TROSPER	57	37	55	35	37	56	40	50	46	38	45	39	30	47	37	51	30	47	53	62
40997	WALKER	45	29	43	28	29	44	31	39	36	30	35	31	23	37	29	40	23	37	42	49
41001	ALEXANDRIA	107	118	103	118	114	112	106	109	104	108	105	85	112	108	110	104	74	105	106	127
41002	AUGUSTA	82	59	73	57	59	80	62	74	69	59	67	56	50	70	58	76	45	70	79	89
41003	BERRY	86	64	72	63	64	83	66	76	72	64	71	58	54	75	61	79	48	72	80	92
41004	BROOKSVILLE	88	63	77	62	64	85	66	78	73	63	72	60	53	75	61	80	48	74	82	95
41005	BURLINGTON	125	135	113	134	128	117	123	121	117	130	119	97	126	124	122	112	84	117	109	140
41006	BUTLER	95	80	79	78	79	91	78	86	83	79	82	64	70	86	73	88	56	82	88	103
41007	CALIFORNIA	104	106	99	108	105	114	98	107	101	94	100	81	99	103	101	105	69	101	110	125
41008	CARROLLTON	82	70	70	69	69	81	72	77	76	70	74	58	65	77	68	79	51	75	82	92
41010	CORINTH	88	66	74	64	65	85	68	78	74	66	73	60	56	77	62	81	49	74	82	95
41011	COVINGTON	81	72	69	75	70	76	85	77	88	81	88	60	81	86	79	91	62	84	86	94
41014	COVINGTON	71	61	54	63	58	66	73	66	74	67	73	53	66	75	64	76	51	71	73	81
41015	LATONIA	93	94	83	94	89	96	91	92	93	89	92	71	91	95	90	94	64	91	96	109
41016	COVINGTON	78	73	63	75	70	80	78	76	81	73	79	59	75	81	74	84	55	78	85	92
41017	FT MITCHELL	138	147	138	149	145	139	141	139	138	144	140	108	148	141	144	137	99	139	137	162
41018	ERLANGER	98	100	85	99	95	97	99	96	98	98	99	74	98	101	96	99	69	97	98	113
41030	CRITTENDEN	104	98	85	95	95	97	94	97	96	98	96	72	90	100	90	97	66	95	96	115
41031	CYNTHIANA	85	72	75	73	73	88	74	83	78	69	77	62	66	80	72	84	52	78	87	97
41033	DE MOSSVILLE	92	69	77	67	68	89	71	82	78	69	76	63	58	81	65	84	51	77	86	99
41034	DOVER	98	69	102	68	71	101	75	92	79	63	78	75	56	78	73	86	51	86	97	112
41035	DRY RIDGE	95	88	77	84	85	88	84	87	86	88	86	65	80	90	80	88	59	86	87	104
41039	EWING	81	58	67	56	58	77	60	70	67	59	66	54	48	70	55	73	44	66	74	85
41040	FALMOUTH	84	66	73	64	66	82	68	77	74	66	72	58	58	75	64	79	49	74	82	92
41041	FLEMINGSBURG	82	60	71	59	60	79	64	73	70	60	68	56	52	72	58	76	46	70	78	89
41042	FLORENCE	114	113	99	113	108	101	113	107	109	117	110	86	111	114	108	105	77	108	101	126
41043	FOSTER	91	70	75	68	69	87	71	80	77	70	76	61	59	80	65	83	51	77	84	97
41044	GERMANTOWN	100	79	82	76	78	94	79	89	85	79	84	67	68	89	73	91	57	85	92	107
41045	GHENT	96	84	78	81	82	90	81	87	85	83	84	64	74	88	76	88	57	84	88	104
41046	GLENCOE	87	68	71	66	67	82	68	77	74	68	73	58	58	77	63	79	49	73	80	93
41048	HEBRON	176	204	171	203	194	170	175	176	164	191	167	142	189	176	179	154	120	164	151	198
41049	HILLSBORO	71	51	58	49	50	67	53	61	59	51	57	47	42	61	48	64	39	58	65	75
41051	INDEPENDENCE	113	120	103	118	115	109	111	112	108	114	109	88	113	113	111	106	76	108	105	129
41052	JONESVILLE	82	75	70	75	75	82	72	79	75	71	74	58	68	77	70	78	51	75	80	93
41055	MAYSLICK	90	62	98	62	65	95	69	85	71	56	71	70	50	70	68	78	46	79	90	105
41056	MAYSVILLE	78	63	70	63	64	78	67	74	72	63	70	56	58	72	64	76	48	72	79	88
41059	MELBOURNE	102	103	95	104	101	107	101	103	101	96	100	80	99	103	100	104	70	101	105	121
41063	MORNING VIEW	96	93	86	94	92	100	88	95	90	85	89	72	85	92	88	93	61	90	97	112
41064	MOUNT OLIVET	75	54	77	52	56	76	55	70	61	51	60	53	44	61	55	67	40	64	73	83
41071	NEWPORT	80	69	61	71	65	72	81	73	83	77	82	58	75	83	73	85	57	79	80	90
41073	BELLEVUE	82	79	68	80	75	84	83	80	85	78	84	62	81	86	79	88	58	83	89	97
41074	DAYTON	78	68	62	70	66	77	77	74	81	72	79	57	71	81	70	84	55	78	83	90
	KENTUCKY	90	77	81	77	76	88	80	85	83	78	83	65	73	85	76	87	57	83	88	101
	UNITED STATES	100	100	100	100	100	100	100	100	100	100	100	100	100	100	100	100	100	100	100	100

ZIP CODE #	POST OFFICE NAME	COUNTY FIPS CODE	POPULATION 2000	POPULATION 2009	POPULATION 2014	2000-2009 ANNUAL RATE % Rate	2000-2009 ANNUAL RATE State Centile	HOUSEHOLDS 2000	HOUSEHOLDS 2009	HOUSEHOLDS 2014	HOUSEHOLDS % Annual Rate 2000-2009	HOUSEHOLDS 2009 Average HH Size	FAMILIES 2000	FAMILIES 2009	FAMILIES % Annual Rate 2000-2009
41075	FORT THOMAS	037	16489	16158	15929	-0.2	26	6732	6801	6774	0.1	2.33	4292	4125	-0.4
41076	NEWPORT	037	14538	14989	15085	0.3	54	5626	6106	6238	0.9	2.33	3650	3737	0.3
41080	PETERSBURG	015	1895	2540	2898	3.2	97	641	885	1021	3.5	2.87	525	695	3.1
41083	SANDERS	041	1135	1328	1398	1.7	93	425	513	544	2.1	2.53	308	358	1.6
41085	SILVER GROVE	037	780	795	796	0.2	48	287	303	307	0.6	2.62	191	192	0.1
41086	SPARTA	077	1551	1767	1809	1.4	89	553	645	666	1.7	2.71	403	453	1.3
41091	UNION	015	10726	16679	19832	4.9	99	3529	5643	6773	5.2	2.96	3013	4643	4.8
41092	VERONA	015	2886	3360	3613	1.7	93	1005	1199	1300	1.9	2.80	812	935	1.5
41093	WALLINGFORD	069	2370	3193	3523	3.3	98	913	1262	1406	3.6	2.52	700	932	3.1
41094	WALTON	015	7906	10347	11865	3.0	97	2802	3791	4390	3.3	2.73	2206	2855	2.8
41095	WARSAW	077	4079	4417	4515	0.9	80	1572	1735	1783	1.1	2.50	1130	1203	0.7
41097	WILLIAMSTOWN	081	6437	6926	7164	0.8	77	2442	2677	2785	1.0	2.54	1776	1873	0.6
41098	WORTHVILLE	041	983	1025	1051	0.5	64	366	390	403	0.7	2.63	267	274	0.3
41101	ASHLAND	019	19501	18696	18499	-0.5	13	8398	8201	8169	-0.3	2.23	5398	5040	-0.7
41102	ASHLAND	019	20924	20903	20850	0.0	39	8029	8181	8228	0.2	2.35	5989	5866	-0.2
41121	ARGILLITE	089	1141	1140	1142	0.0	39	427	440	446	0.3	2.59	336	336	0.0
41124	BLAINE	127	1019	1031	1042	0.1	45	385	404	413	0.5	2.55	300	306	0.2
41129	CATLETTSBURG	019	9780	9998	10038	0.2	48	3797	3989	4038	0.5	2.47	2904	2954	0.2
41132	DENTON	043	328	336	339	0.3	54	126	133	136	0.6	2.52	98	100	0.2
41135	EMERSON	135	514	508	502	-0.1	32	195	198	198	0.2	2.57	152	150	-0.1
41139	FLATWOODS	089	8239	8106	8079	-0.2	26	3354	3425	3455	0.2	2.34	2495	2459	-0.2
41141	GARRISON	135	3616	3540	3490	-0.2	26	1360	1371	1366	0.1	2.58	1050	1028	-0.2
41143	GRAYSON	043	13400	13507	13547	0.1	45	5037	5254	5329	0.5	2.45	3812	3852	0.1
41144	GREENUP	089	11313	11768	12000	0.4	60	4323	4655	4798	0.8	2.49	3327	3473	0.5
41146	HITCHINS	043	611	634	642	0.4	60	228	245	251	0.8	2.59	179	186	0.4
41149	ISONVILLE	063	1210	1285	1327	0.7	74	446	490	512	1.0	2.62	341	363	0.7
41159	MARTHA	127	700	702	707	0.0	39	242	251	255	0.4	2.80	191	192	0.1
41164	OLIVE HILL	043	11522	12074	12273	0.5	64	4560	4943	5084	0.9	2.44	3347	3501	0.5
41166	QUINCY	135	1116	1079	1065	-0.4	18	410	407	405	-0.1	2.65	330	319	-0.4
41168	RUSH	019	3113	3124	3132	0.0	39	1152	1191	1204	0.4	2.58	913	914	0.0
41169	RUSSELL	089	5562	5494	5478	-0.1	32	2244	2294	2315	0.2	2.36	1660	1635	-0.2
41171	SANDY HOOK	063	5129	5460	5641	0.7	74	2043	2262	2368	1.1	2.39	1474	1572	0.7
41174	SOUTH PORTSMOUTH	089	757	711	693	-0.7	5	303	292	288	-0.4	2.30	224	209	-0.7
41175	SOUTH SHORE	089	6102	6216	6273	0.2	48	2418	2548	2603	0.6	2.43	1817	1848	0.2
41179	VANCEBURG	135	5557	5793	5868	0.5	64	2148	2317	2370	0.8	2.41	1538	1598	0.4
41180	WEBBVILLE	127	783	758	751	-0.4	18	318	319	319	0.0	2.38	235	228	-0.3
41183	WORTHINGTON	089	1682	1747	1775	0.4	60	670	719	738	0.8	2.41	519	540	0.4
41189	TOLLESBORO	135	3279	3172	3122	-0.4	18	1305	1296	1287	-0.1	2.45	975	938	-0.4
41201	ADAMS	127	801	871	908	0.9	80	311	350	368	1.3	2.49	236	258	1.0
41204	BOONS CAMP	115	447	561	605	2.5	96	169	220	241	2.9	2.55	129	162	2.5
41214	DEBORD	159	1156	2045	2002	6.4	100	431	427	416	-0.1	2.57	334	320	-0.5
41216	EAST POINT	071	2043	2074	2096	0.2	48	777	821	839	0.6	2.52	625	642	0.3
41219	FLATGAP	115	2065	2229	2305	0.8	77	794	888	929	1.2	2.51	615	666	0.9
41222	HAGERHILL	115	2628	2491	2456	-0.6	9	1000	981	977	-0.2	2.50	760	721	-0.6
41224	INEZ	159	5327	5644	5446	0.6	69	2019	1993	1940	-0.1	2.49	1517	1448	-0.5
41226	KEATON	115	401	430	443	0.8	77	147	163	170	1.1	2.64	118	127	0.8
41230	LOUISA	127	9830	10331	10606	0.5	64	3774	4091	4244	0.9	2.49	2783	2911	0.5
41231	LOVELY	159	890	834	797	-0.7	5	336	330	319	-0.2	2.53	256	244	-0.5
41232	LOWMANSVILLE	127	1984	2176	2270	1.0	83	745	839	882	1.3	2.59	591	647	1.0
41234	MEALLY	115	194	200	204	0.3	54	75	81	83	0.8	2.43	57	60	0.6
41238	OIL SPRINGS	115	1216	1424	1512	1.7	93	486	591	635	2.1	2.41	381	450	1.8
41240	PAINTSVILLE	115	7075	7044	7055	0.0	39	2802	2862	2893	0.2	2.33	1995	1963	-0.2
41250	PILGRIM	159	985	917	875	-0.8	3	377	367	355	-0.3	2.50	292	276	-0.6
41254	RIVER	159	367	382	377	0.4	60	135	146	146	0.9	2.62	111	117	0.6
41255	SITKA	115	285	299	306	0.5	64	113	123	128	0.9	2.43	84	88	0.5
41256	STAFFORDSVILLE	115	1653	1724	1753	0.5	64	641	691	710	0.8	2.49	499	519	0.4
41257	STAMBAUGH	115	801	801	804	0.0	39	298	309	314	0.4	2.59	229	229	0.0
41260	THELMA	115	2055	2175	2233	0.6	69	801	882	917	1.0	2.37	614	654	0.7
41262	TOMAHAWK	159	1725	1711	1675	-0.1	32	638	657	652	0.3	2.60	498	498	0.0
41263	TUTOR KEY	115	418	431	438	0.3	54	158	169	174	0.7	2.55	129	134	0.4
41265	VAN LEAR	115	2053	2107	2141	0.3	54	784	833	854	0.7	2.52	608	626	0.3
41267	WARFIELD	159	2128	1966	1870	-0.9	2	840	812	783	-0.4	2.41	613	571	-0.8
41271	WILLIAMSPORT	115	233	294	317	2.5	96	94	123	135	2.9	2.39	72	91	2.6
41274	WITTENSVILLE	115	1040	1002	989	-0.4	18	411	408	407	-0.1	2.46	311	298	-0.5
41301	CAMPTON	237	6339	6348	6293	0.0	39	2546	2628	2631	0.3	2.36	1790	1776	-0.1
41311	BEATTYVILLE	129	7626	7388	7213	-0.3	22	2862	2872	2833	0.0	2.32	2034	1962	-0.4
41314	BOONEVILLE	189	4316	4360	4329	0.1	45	1688	1752	1754	0.4	2.43	1234	1236	0.0
41317	CLAYHOLE	025	710	676	658	-0.5	13	273	268	264	-0.2	2.52	206	195	-0.6
41332	HAZEL GREEN	175	1313	1333	1325	0.2	48	541	568	571	0.5	2.35	410	417	0.2
41338	ISLAND CITY	189	431	407	394	-0.6	9	164	159	156	-0.3	2.56	125	118	-0.6
41339	JACKSON	025	12237	12156	12065	-0.1	32	4689	4838	4861	0.3	2.44	3412	3394	-0.1
41348	LOST CREEK	025	1278	1275	1268	0.0	39	477	492	495	0.3	2.59	359	358	0.0
41351	MISTLETOE	189	92	90	89	-0.2	26	29	29	29	0.0	3.10	22	22	0.0
41360	PINE RIDGE	237	455	462	462	0.2	48	158	167	169	0.6	2.71	113	115	0.2
41364	RICETOWN	189	405	396	389	-0.2	26	160	162	160	0.1	2.44	121	119	-0.2
41365	ROGERS	237	560	597	606	0.7	74	221	243	249	1.0	2.44	159	167	0.5
41366	ROUSSEAU	025	204	210	211	0.3	54	84	90	92	0.7	2.33	62	64	0.3
41367	ROWDY	193	601	579	567	-0.4	18	233	235	233	0.1	2.46	171	166	-0.3
41385	VANCLEVE	025	891	851	832	-0.5	13	348	346	342	-0.1	2.33	269	259	-0.4
41386	VINCENT	189	330	313	306	-0.6	9	131	129	127	-0.2	2.43	96	90	-0.7
41397	ZOE	129	124	117	113	-0.6	9	50	49	48	-0.2	2.39	37	35	-0.6
41425	EZEL	175	1332	1297	1273	-0.3	22	496	494	489	0.0	2.57	377	364	-0.4
41464	ROYALTON	153	353	363	365	0.3	54	125	133	136	0.7	2.73	97	100	0.3
41465	SALYERSVILLE	153	12295	12425	12410	0.1	45	4644	4896	4956	0.6	2.50	3559	3634	0.2
41472	WEST LIBERTY	175	11441	11953	12088	0.5	64	3771	4108	4210	0.9	2.47	2825	2975	0.6
41501	PIKEVILLE	195	25219	24974	24501	-0.1	32	10329	10666	10599	0.3	2.28	7262	7215	-0.1
41503	SOUTH WILLIAMSON	195	743	705	683	-0.6	9	308	301	295	-0.2	2.17	207	192	-0.8
41512	ASHCAMP	195	507	485	472	-0.5	13	177	177	175	0.0	2.69	137	133	-0.3
41513	BELCHER	195	567	531	515	-0.7	5	230	226	222	-0.2	2.35	177	168	-0.6
41514	BELFRY	195	3745	3579	3470	-0.5	13	1538	1530	1503	-0.1	2.34	1139	1093	-0.4
41519	CANADA	195	451	456	451	0.1	45	181	192	192	0.6	2.38	145	149	0.3
41522	ELKHORN CITY	195	6328	6026	5852	-0.5	13	2550	2540	2499	0.0	2.32	1904	1834	-0.4
41524	FEDSCREEK	195	235	216	208	-0.9	2	96	92	90	-0.5	2.35	66	61	-0.8
41527	FOREST HILLS	195	855	844	829	-0.1	32	340	349	347	0.3	2.42	272	271	0.0
41528	FREEBURN	195	1374	1278	1231	-0.8	3	558	545	533	-0.3	2.34	417	393	-0.6
	KENTUCKY					0.7					1.0	2.41			0.6
	UNITED STATES					1.0					1.1	2.59			0.9

ZIP CODE #	POST OFFICE NAME	RACE (%) White 2000	White 2009	Black 2000	Black 2009	Asian/Pacific 2000	Asian/Pacific 2009	% Hispanic Origin 2000	% Hispanic Origin 2009	2009 AGE DISTRIBUTION (%) 0-4	5-9	10-14	15-19	20-24	25-44	45-64	65-84	85+	18+	MEDIAN AGE 2009	% 2009 Males	% 2009 Females
41075	FORT THOMAS	97.5	96.8	0.7	0.8	0.6	1.0	0.7	1.2	5.9	5.9	6.0	6.3	6.5	26.2	27.7	12.8	2.8	78.5	40.1	47.9	52.1
41076	NEWPORT	96.9	95.9	1.2	1.3	1.0	1.5	0.6	0.9	5.7	5.5	5.6	7.1	7.0	26.3	26.1	14.1	2.6	79.8	39.6	47.1	52.9
41080	PETERSBURG	98.4	97.9	0.3	0.3	0.0	0.0	0.7	1.4	6.1	6.6	7.2	7.3	5.5	26.5	31.4	8.6	0.7	75.5	38.8	51.3	48.7
41083	SANDERS	96.9	95.8	1.7	2.0	0.2	0.3	1.9	3.2	7.8	7.8	7.6	6.4	5.2	26.3	28.3	9.6	1.1	72.7	37.9	51.3	48.7
41085	SILVER GROVE	98.3	97.9	0.3	0.3	0.1	0.1	2.3	4.0	8.3	7.8	7.2	6.8	6.8	28.4	23.0	10.6	1.1	72.8	34.6	54.0	46.0
41086	SPARTA	96.1	94.9	2.3	2.9	0.2	0.3	1.1	1.8	7.1	7.2	7.5	7.1	5.4	26.1	27.5	10.6	1.5	73.8	37.9	50.0	50.0
41091	UNION	96.7	95.2	0.4	0.5	1.7	2.7	1.0	1.7	7.7	8.0	8.1	7.4	4.6	26.4	31.1	6.2	0.5	71.4	37.5	50.1	49.9
41092	VERONA	98.2	97.7	0.2	0.3	0.3	0.4	1.0	1.7	6.1	6.8	7.4	8.1	5.1	26.5	30.2	9.1	0.7	74.8	38.6	50.3	49.7
41093	WALLINGFORD	98.9	98.8	0.4	0.3	0.0	0.0	0.6	1.0	6.7	6.7	7.0	6.5	5.0	27.5	28.2	11.1	1.2	75.2	38.7	50.1	49.9
41094	WALTON	97.6	96.8	0.6	0.8	0.5	0.8	0.9	1.6	7.2	7.6	7.6	7.4	5.4	27.2	28.3	8.5	0.9	72.9	36.7	49.9	50.1
41095	WARSAW	96.2	95.6	2.0	2.0	0.2	0.4	1.0	1.6	7.2	7.3	7.6	7.2	5.2	26.6	26.9	10.3	1.8	73.5	37.7	49.8	50.2
41097	WILLIAMSTOWN	98.3	97.6	0.1	0.1	0.5	0.7	1.1	1.8	7.5	7.4	7.1	6.4	5.5	27.0	25.6	11.6	2.0	73.9	37.6	49.3	50.7
41098	WORTHVILLE	98.4	97.6	0.2	0.2	0.1	0.2	2.4	3.9	6.5	6.7	6.9	6.8	5.4	27.2	28.1	11.3	1.0	75.5	38.4	50.6	49.4
41101	ASHLAND	95.6	94.8	2.2	2.3	0.6	1.0	0.7	1.1	5.7	5.4	5.6	6.2	5.5	23.9	28.2	16.4	3.1	79.5	43.2	46.2	53.8
41102	ASHLAND	95.0	94.4	3.6	3.8	0.3	0.5	2.0	3.2	4.8	5.1	5.5	5.4	4.9	27.4	30.4	14.7	1.8	81.3	42.9	51.9	48.1
41121	ARGILLITE	98.8	98.6	0.4	0.4	0.0	0.0	0.6	1.1	6.4	6.5	6.8	6.9	4.8	26.4	28.9	12.1	1.1	76.1	39.8	50.1	49.9
41124	BLAINE	98.6	98.3	0.0	0.0	0.0	0.0	0.2	0.4	5.5	6.2	8.6	7.1	7.0	24.5	28.2	11.2	1.6	75.0	36.2	50.4	49.6
41129	CATLETTSBURG	98.7	98.4	0.6	0.6	0.1	0.2	0.2	0.4	5.2	5.5	5.9	5.9	4.9	26.4	30.9	13.8	1.4	79.7	42.3	49.7	50.3
41132	DENTON	99.1	98.8	0.0	0.0	0.0	0.3	0.6	0.9	7.4	7.1	7.4	6.8	5.4	26.5	27.4	10.4	1.5	73.5	37.7	50.6	49.4
41135	EMERSON	99.4	99.4	0.0	0.0	0.0	0.0	0.4	0.4	5.1	7.3	6.3	7.9	4.9	28.3	26.2	11.8	2.2	77.0	37.5	50.0	50.0
41139	FLATWOODS	98.5	98.1	0.3	0.3	0.3	0.4	0.5	0.8	5.2	5.5	5.7	5.8	5.2	24.7	29.2	16.2	2.5	80.0	43.3	47.0	53.0
41141	GARRISON	98.9	98.9	0.3	0.3	0.0	0.0	0.2	0.2	7.2	7.1	7.3	7.5	5.8	27.3	26.1	10.2	1.4	74.0	36.2	48.3	51.7
41143	GRAYSON	98.9	98.6	0.2	0.2	0.2	0.3	0.6	1.0	6.3	6.4	6.6	7.7	6.6	26.6	26.6	11.6	1.8	76.7	37.8	49.0	51.0
41144	GREENUP	97.7	97.3	1.2	1.2	0.2	0.3	0.7	1.1	6.1	6.2	6.5	6.3	5.0	25.3	29.3	13.7	1.6	77.3	41.2	49.1	50.9
41146	HITCHINS	99.5	99.2	0.0	0.0	0.2	0.2	0.5	0.9	7.6	7.9	7.7	7.1	5.2	26.5	26.7	10.3	1.1	72.6	37.0	50.8	49.2
41149	ISONVILLE	99.2	99.1	0.1	0.1	0.0	0.0	0.6	0.9	7.2	7.2	7.2	6.9	5.8	25.1	27.2	12.2	1.2	74.2	37.9	50.3	49.7
41159	MARTHA	99.0	98.6	0.0	0.0	0.0	0.0	0.1	0.3	5.6	6.3	8.3	7.1	6.8	24.9	27.9	11.4	1.7	75.1	36.4	50.7	49.3
41164	OLIVE HILL	99.1	98.9	0.1	0.1	0.0	0.0	0.7	1.1	6.3	6.4	6.6	6.5	4.9	26.4	28.6	12.8	1.4	76.6	39.8	49.4	50.6
41166	QUINCY	99.4	99.4	0.0	0.0	0.1	0.1	0.3	0.3	6.4	6.4	7.0	7.7	5.6	27.9	26.8	11.2	1.1	75.4	37.4	50.6	49.4
41168	RUSH	98.3	98.0	0.7	0.8	0.2	0.3	0.4	0.6	6.0	6.1	6.8	7.5	5.1	27.8	29.1	10.6	0.9	76.0	39.1	50.3	49.7
41169	RUSSELL	97.7	96.9	0.7	0.7	0.9	1.3	0.6	1.0	5.2	5.5	5.8	5.8	4.9	23.8	30.9	16.0	2.2	79.9	44.3	47.5	52.5
41171	SANDY HOOK	99.0	98.9	0.0	0.0	0.0	0.0	0.6	0.8	6.3	6.4	6.5	6.4	5.0	24.9	29.3	13.1	2.1	76.8	40.7	48.7	51.3
41174	SOUTH PORTSMOUTH	98.0	97.7	0.1	0.1	0.0	0.0	0.0	0.0	5.8	6.3	6.5	5.9	4.1	25.5	28.3	14.3	3.4	77.5	42.0	47.1	52.9
41175	SOUTH SHORE	98.5	98.2	0.1	0.1	0.1	0.2	0.2	0.4	6.1	6.3	6.6	6.4	5.0	26.0	27.2	14.8	1.6	77.0	40.4	48.4	51.6
41179	VANCEBURG	99.0	99.1	0.3	0.3	0.0	0.0	0.4	0.4	6.2	6.6	6.5	6.3	4.9	26.4	28.6	12.6	2.0	76.9	39.9	50.4	49.6
41180	WEBBVILLE	98.1	97.8	0.0	0.0	0.0	0.0	0.5	0.9	6.3	6.6	6.7	6.5	4.7	26.3	30.3	11.1	1.5	76.3	40.6	52.5	47.5
41183	WORTHINGTON	98.7	98.3	0.1	0.1	0.0	0.0	0.8	1.3	4.4	4.5	5.2	6.6	5.1	23.4	32.0	16.5	2.3	81.9	45.5	47.2	52.8
41189	TOLLESBORO	98.5	98.4	0.2	0.2	0.0	0.0	0.8	0.8	5.9	6.1	6.4	6.1	4.8	28.0	29.4	11.9	1.5	77.9	40.1	51.0	49.0
41201	ADAMS	99.0	98.9	0.0	0.0	0.0	0.0	0.0	0.0	6.2	6.8	6.9	6.8	4.7	25.1	30.9	11.5	1.1	76.0	39.4	51.7	48.3
41204	BOONS CAMP	98.9	98.6	0.2	0.2	0.0	0.0	0.9	1.2	6.2	6.6	6.8	7.3	5.9	24.2	30.1	11.4	1.4	75.9	39.7	48.5	51.5
41214	DEBORD	99.5	99.5	0.0	0.0	0.1	0.0	0.5	0.8	3.1	3.6	3.8	6.9	11.1	43.3	22.0	5.6	0.6	85.4	34.4	71.6	28.4
41216	EAST POINT	98.7	98.6	0.2	0.2	0.4	0.4	0.6	0.8	6.3	6.5	6.6	5.8	5.4	26.5	31.8	10.1	1.1	77.1	40.8	48.0	52.0
41219	FLATGAP	99.1	98.7	0.1	0.2	0.1	0.3	0.5	0.8	5.8	6.1	6.5	6.4	5.3	26.1	29.5	12.6	1.7	77.7	40.5	51.0	49.0
41222	HAGERHILL	98.2	97.9	0.3	0.3	0.2	0.2	0.8	1.4	6.0	6.1	7.0	6.9	5.4	26.3	31.4	9.8	1.2	76.5	39.5	48.5	51.5
41224	INEZ	99.3	99.3	0.0	0.0	0.1	0.1	0.6	0.9	5.9	6.2	6.3	7.5	7.4	30.1	26.7	8.8	1.1	76.6	36.1	54.2	45.8
41226	KEATON	99.5	99.3	0.0	0.0	0.0	0.2	0.7	1.2	7.2	7.2	7.0	7.4	5.6	27.7	24.9	11.4	1.6	74.4	36.9	50.9	49.1
41230	LOUISA	98.9	98.7	0.1	0.1	0.1	0.2	0.5	0.8	5.8	5.9	6.2	6.5	5.6	26.3	29.1	12.8	1.9	78.0	40.6	48.7	51.3
41231	LOVELY	99.2	99.2	0.1	0.1	0.1	0.1	0.7	1.1	6.2	7.2	7.4	8.9	7.1	27.1	26.4	9.1	0.6	73.4	35.1	51.0	49.0
41232	LOWMANSVILLE	99.6	99.6	0.1	0.0	0.1	0.1	0.2	0.4	6.4	6.7	7.1	7.5	6.4	26.2	29.7	9.1	0.7	74.6	36.9	50.9	49.1
41234	MEALLY	98.5	98.0	0.5	0.5	0.5	0.5	0.5	0.5	6.0	6.0	6.0	7.0	6.0	24.5	33.5	10.0	1.0	78.0	41.1	50.0	50.0
41238	OIL SPRINGS	99.3	99.2	0.2	0.1	0.0	0.1	0.9	1.4	6.5	5.6	6.0	5.9	5.4	27.3	30.8	10.7	1.7	78.1	39.7	49.1	50.9
41240	PAINTSVILLE	98.4	98.1	0.3	0.4	0.4	0.6	0.6	0.8	5.4	5.6	5.6	6.1	5.4	25.5	29.2	14.9	2.4	79.6	42.3	46.9	53.1
41250	PILGRIM	99.4	99.2	0.0	0.0	0.1	0.1	0.7	1.1	5.9	7.2	7.6	8.5	6.9	27.0	27.6	8.7	0.5	73.7	35.9	51.3	48.7
41254	RIVER	99.5	99.2	0.0	0.0	0.0	0.0	1.4	2.4	6.8	8.4	9.7	7.3	6.8	28.5	25.4	6.3	0.8	70.2	32.0	50.0	50.0
41255	SITKA	98.6	98.3	0.3	0.3	0.7	1.0	0.7	1.3	5.7	6.0	8.0	8.0	5.7	26.1	29.1	9.7	1.7	75.3	37.8	48.8	51.2
41256	STAFFORDSVILLE	98.8	98.4	0.0	0.0	0.7	1.0	0.4	0.6	6.1	5.9	6.3	6.3	5.0	25.9	32.7	10.6	1.2	77.6	40.7	48.3	51.7
41257	STAMBAUGH	99.0	98.8	0.1	0.1	0.5	0.7	0.5	0.7	5.9	6.5	6.7	8.4	5.6	26.3	29.7	9.7	1.1	75.4	38.1	49.1	50.9
41260	THELMA	98.1	97.8	0.8	0.9	0.1	0.1	0.6	0.9	6.0	6.3	6.4	6.3	5.7	25.6	29.9	12.0	1.8	77.8	40.4	48.4	51.6
41262	TOMAHAWK	99.1	98.9	0.0	0.0	0.2	0.2	1.0	1.9	7.0	8.5	8.5	7.2	6.0	26.9	26.7	8.4	0.7	70.8	34.4	50.5	49.5
41263	TUTOR KEY	100.0	99.8	0.0	0.0	0.0	0.2	0.7	0.9	5.6	5.8	6.0	6.0	4.6	25.3	32.5	12.8	1.4	78.7	42.6	49.4	50.6
41265	VAN LEAR	98.8	98.4	0.0	0.0	0.4	0.6	0.6	1.0	6.5	6.8	6.8	6.3	5.4	24.9	31.6	10.7	1.1	76.3	40.5	48.1	51.9
41267	WARFIELD	99.0	98.8	0.0	0.1	0.2	0.3	0.3	0.6	8.5	8.5	8.1	7.4	5.5	26.2	25.3	9.4	1.0	70.3	33.9	48.1	51.9
41271	WILLIAMSPORT	98.7	98.6	0.0	0.0	0.0	0.0	0.9	1.4	6.5	6.5	6.8	7.5	6.1	24.8	29.3	11.2	1.4	75.9	39.0	49.0	51.0
41274	WITTENSVILLE	98.6	97.9	0.1	0.1	0.7	1.1	0.5	0.7	5.8	6.1	6.1	6.9	5.2	26.8	30.6	11.3	1.2	77.6	40.2	47.7	52.3
41301	CAMPTON	99.2	99.1	0.3	0.3	0.1	0.1	0.5	0.6	6.3	6.9	7.5	6.4	5.1	25.6	27.7	12.2	2.1	75.2	39.3	49.4	50.6
41311	BEATTYVILLE	95.0	94.5	3.9	4.1	0.1	0.1	0.4	0.6	5.2	5.3	5.6	6.5	7.2	27.5	27.7	12.8	2.2	80.0	40.1	52.2	47.8
41314	BOONEVILLE	99.2	99.2	0.1	0.1	0.0	0.0	0.8	0.9	5.4	6.2	6.1	7.0	6.3	24.1	28.9	13.5	2.5	77.8	41.2	49.6	50.4
41317	CLAYHOLE	99.3	99.3	0.0	0.0	0.0	0.0	2.5	4.1	5.5	6.8	6.4	8.6	7.4	27.1	26.9	10.2	1.2	75.7	37.6	51.5	48.5
41332	HAZEL GREEN	99.5	99.4	0.1	0.2	0.0	0.0	0.5	0.5	5.9	6.1	6.3	6.2	5.3	26.1	30.1	12.5	1.6	77.9	40.6	49.8	50.2
41338	ISLAND CITY	99.1	99.0	0.2	0.2	0.2	0.2	0.9	1.0	5.7	6.1	6.1	6.1	4.4	24.8	29.5	15.5	1.7	78.1	42.8	47.7	52.3
41339	JACKSON	98.7	98.3	0.4	0.4	0.4	0.6	0.6	0.9	5.6	6.5	6.6	7.5	6.3	25.6	28.9	11.2	1.7	76.7	38.7	49.3	50.7
41348	LOST CREEK	99.0	98.8	0.3	0.3	0.0	0.1	0.7	1.2	7.0	7.1	7.3	7.5	5.5	25.7	27.8	11.1	1.0	73.9	38.0	49.2	50.8
41351	MISTLETOE	100.0	100.0	0.0	0.0	0.0	0.0	0.0	0.0	5.6	5.6	5.6	6.7	5.6	26.7	27.8	14.4	2.2	81.1	41.9	53.3	46.7
41360	PINE RIDGE	98.9	98.9	0.7	0.6	0.0	0.0	0.4	0.4	7.1	7.1	7.8	6.7	5.4	25.3	29.0	10.4	1.1	73.6	37.7	50.2	49.8
41364	RICETOWN	99.5	99.5	0.0	0.0	0.0	0.0	0.2	0.3	5.6	5.8	6.6	7.3	5.6	24.2	28.8	14.4	1.8	77.5	41.4	53.0	47.0
41365	ROGERS	98.9	98.8	0.2	0.2	0.2	0.2	0.4	0.3	7.4	7.4	7.5	7.0	5.0	25.6	28.6	10.2	1.2	73.5	37.9	50.9	49.1
41366	ROUSSEAU	99.5	99.5	0.0	0.0	0.0	0.0	0.5	0.5	4.3	7.1	7.1	5.2	6.7	25.2	33.8	9.5	1.0	77.6	40.4	49.0	51.0
41367	ROWDY	99.7	99.5	0.0	0.0	0.0	0.0	0.2	0.3	6.6	6.2	6.0	7.6	6.2	27.3	29.2	9.2	1.7	78.1	37.3	50.4	49.6
41385	VANCLEVE	97.6	97.1	1.1	1.2	0.6	0.9	0.3	0.7	5.3	5.6	5.8	7.5	8.3	24.4	29.8	12.0	1.2	78.5	39.5	50.2	49.8
41386	VINCENT	98.8	98.7	0.0	0.0	0.0	0.0	0.9	1.0	4.8	5.1	5.4	5.4	4.5	24.6	31.3	16.9	1.9	81.2	45.1	52.7	47.3
41397	ZOE	97.6	97.4	1.6	1.7	0.0	0.0	0.0	0.0	5.1	5.1	6.8	7.7	6.0	25.6	29.9	12.0	1.7	78.6	39.8	51.3	48.7
41425	EZEL	98.5	98.1	0.3	0.3	0.5	0.7	0.5	0.7	5.7	5.9	6.6	8.2	4.8	26.8	29.1	11.5	1.3	75.7	38.9	51.4	48.6
41464	ROYALTON	99.2	98.9	0.0	0.0	0.0	0.0	0.6	0.8	7.4	7.4	7.4	7.2	5.5	25.6	28.4	10.2	0.8	73.0	36.8	51.2	48.8
41465	SALYERSVILLE	99.3	99.2	0.2	0.2	0.1	0.1	0.4	0.7	6.9	6.8	7.1	7.2	6.0	27.1	27.5	9.9	1.6	74.9	37.1	49.2	50.8
41472	WEST LIBERTY	93.7	93.1	5.3	5.6	0.2	0.2	0.7	1.0	5.2	5.5	5.8	6.2	7.6	31.3	26.2	10.4	1.7	79.8	37.5	56.2	43.8
41501	PIKEVILLE	97.7	97.1	0.7	0.8	0.7	1.0	0.8	1.2	6.0	6.1	6.2	6.6	6.4	26.9	28.7	11.7	1.6	77.9	39.4	48.6	51.4
41503	SOUTH WILLIAMSON	93.5	91.3	0.5	0.6	4.4	6.2	0.3	0.4	4.3	5.0	5.1	4.5	4.3	19.4	32.8	21.3	3.4	82.8	50.2	45.4	54.6
41512	ASHCAMP	98.2	97.7	0.6	0.6	0.2	0.2	0.6	0.8	5.2	5.8	7.2	7.8	5.6	26.8	31.3	9.3	1.0	76.5	39.2	51.8	48.2
41513	BELCHER	99.1	99.1	0.0	0.0	0.0	0.0	0.2	0.4	4.7	4.9	5.8	6.2	3.8	25.6	33.5	14.1	1.3	80.4	44.3	49.3	50.7
41514	BELFRY	97.5	96.9	0.8	0.9	0.6	0.9	0.3	0.4	6.1	6.6	6.6	6.1	5.6	25.6	30.6	11.6	1.1	76.7	40.3	47.5	52.5
41519	CANADA	99.8	99.8	0.0	0.0	0.0	0.0	0.7	0.9	6.1	6.6	7.0	6.8	5.7	27.2	28.1	11.0	1.5	75.2	38.2	48.7	51.3
41522	ELKHORN CITY	99.1	99.0	0.3	0.3	0.0	0.0	0.6	0.8	4.9	5.7	6.6	6.5	5.4	25.0	31.1	13.1	1.8	78.5	41.7	49.2	50.8
41524	FEDSCREEK	97.9	97.2	0.0	0.0	0.4	0.5	1.7	2.8	6.9	6.0	4.2	8.8	4.6	27.3	31.5	9.7	0.9	78.2	39.7	49.5	50.5
41527	FOREST HILLS	94.7	93.2	1.4	1.4	2.5	3.6	0.7	1.1	5.9	6.6	6.6	5.2	4.0	28.9	29.1	11.8	1.7	77.5	40.0	47.6	52.4
41528	FREEBURN	99.1	98.9	0.1	0.2	0.1	0.2	1.1	1.6	6.7	7.1	5.7	7.4	6.8	27.8	28.7	9.2	0.6	75.9	35.9	49.8	50.2
	KENTUCKY	90.1	88.9	7.3	7.5	0.8	1.2	1.5	2.4	6.5	6.5	6.5	6.8	6.5	27.0	27.1	11.3	1.8	76.6	37.9	49.1	50.9
	UNITED STATES	75.1	72.0	12.3	12.7	3.8	4.6	12.5	15.7	6.8	6.7	6.6	7.1	6.9	27.0	26.0	10.9	1.9	75.7	36.9	49.2	50.8

INCOME

#	POST OFFICE NAME	2009 Per Capita Income	2009 HH Income Base	2009 Household Income Distribution (%) Less than $25,000	$25,000 to $49,999	$50,000 to $99,999	$100,000 to $149,999	$150,000 or More	Median Household Income 2009	2014	2009 National Centile	2009 State Centile	2009 Home Value Base	2009 Home Value Distribution (%) Less than $50,000	$50,000 to $89,999	$90,000 to $174,999	$175,000 to $399,999	$400,000 or More	2009 Median Home Value
41075	FORT THOMAS	33831	6801	16.1	20.8	40.8	12.8	9.6	63648	65790	82	95	4700	2.7	6.9	55.4	30.9	4.1	150856
41076	NEWPORT	30056	6106	13.9	22.4	44.4	13.4	6.0	62600	64140	81	95	4663	1.6	22.7	50.5	23.1	2.1	118922
41080	PETERSBURG	25639	885	14.7	22.6	39.9	17.6	5.2	60791	60309	79	94	743	13.5	20.1	31.4	31.2	3.9	134201
41083	SANDERS	19745	513	26.3	31.8	34.5	5.5	1.9	43521	44901	44	74	410	35.6	28.8	23.4	8.8	3.4	70588
41085	SILVER GROVE	19127	303	23.1	33.3	36.6	5.6	1.3	41670	44632	38	69	213	33.8	22.5	38.0	5.2	0.5	82500
41086	SPARTA	18602	645	28.5	29.1	33.6	6.4	2.3	43861	46876	45	75	496	17.5	20.0	38.5	21.6	2.4	110145
41091	UNION	39809	5643	6.1	15.6	30.1	28.1	20.1	96597	103983	96	99	5195	8.4	2.7	18.6	55.9	14.5	236792
41092	VERONA	24437	1199	15.3	28.5	38.5	12.7	4.9	57169	55254	74	92	1047	10.4	20.0	30.5	29.9	9.3	138194
41093	WALLINGFORD	16430	1262	37.4	31.3	26.5	3.9	1.0	33749	35184	15	47	1060	33.0	32.0	27.8	5.5	1.7	72170
41094	WALTON	28539	3791	14.3	22.6	39.2	16.8	7.2	64030	63663	82	95	3073	17.2	8.3	34.1	33.4	7.1	146937
41095	WARSAW	20420	1735	28.4	27.9	35.3	6.1	2.4	44859	47361	48	77	1282	17.7	20.3	42.7	17.2	2.1	102854
41097	WILLIAMSTOWN	20348	2677	25.3	30.6	35.9	6.3	1.9	44466	47362	47	76	1993	19.8	21.6	39.9	16.9	1.8	104716
41098	WORTHVILLE	17664	390	27.9	34.1	33.1	3.6	1.3	40000	41502	33	65	307	45.0	25.7	21.8	5.5	2.0	55536
41101	ASHLAND	23476	8201	33.4	27.4	28.1	6.5	4.7	39864	42838	32	64	5243	15.4	33.9	34.8	13.4	2.5	90979
41102	ASHLAND	23442	8181	26.2	29.5	33.5	7.0	3.9	45072	46730	48	78	6482	17.2	25.5	44.1	11.9	1.3	98058
41121	ARGILLITE	16204	440	27.5	37.5	30.9	4.1	0.0	37248	40120	24	57	378	46.6	16.4	30.2	6.9	0.0	58125
41124	BLAINE	11159	404	61.6	23.8	11.6	2.0	1.0	18684	20363	1	5	322	51.2	26.4	21.7	0.3	0.3	48788
41129	CATLETTSBURG	20849	3989	29.8	27.8	34.1	6.3	2.0	42628	44783	41	72	3272	27.4	24.9	35.1	10.9	1.7	86324
41132	DENTON	15020	133	39.8	32.3	25.6	1.5	0.8	34535	35000	17	49	114	44.7	30.7	18.4	6.1	0.0	55455
41135	EMERSON	11747	198	52.5	29.3	15.7	2.5	0.0	23227	23824	2	17	175	66.3	17.7	14.3	0.6	1.1	38152
41139	FLATWOODS	21514	3425	29.2	31.6	31.1	5.1	3.1	40465	42558	34	66	2651	14.9	40.4	36.7	7.8	0.3	85613
41141	GARRISON	14244	1371	43.7	27.9	25.1	3.2	0.1	28558	30156	6	33	1175	42.8	37.0	17.5	2.6	0.0	55523
41143	GRAYSON	17609	5254	36.8	29.9	27.7	4.2	1.4	35701	35928	20	53	4117	32.4	30.1	30.2	6.6	0.7	72140
41144	GREENUP	17291	4655	35.5	30.0	29.5	4.3	0.8	36625	39982	22	56	3900	33.9	25.0	32.7	7.9	0.3	76360
41146	HITCHINS	14534	245	38.0	31.8	29.4	0.8	0.0	36530	36000	22	55	213	47.9	28.6	19.2	4.2	0.0	52143
41149	ISONVILLE	11576	490	58.4	23.3	14.5	3.9	0.0	20816	21224	2	9	412	40.3	38.3	17.2	4.1	0.0	62400
41159	MARTHA	10155	251	61.8	24.3	11.2	2.4	0.4	18756	20587	1	5	199	50.3	24.6	25.1	0.0	0.0	49773
41164	OLIVE HILL	15248	4943	44.2	28.4	23.8	2.8	0.9	29447	30070	7	36	4099	44.4	29.8	19.6	5.9	0.3	56322
41166	QUINCY	16950	407	35.4	31.4	29.7	2.0	1.5	33221	34459	14	45	357	51.3	21.3	22.7	3.9	0.8	48929
41168	RUSH	19033	1191	32.5	23.0	38.6	4.7	1.2	45034	46625	48	78	1003	32.4	25.3	27.0	14.8	0.5	77500
41169	RUSSELL	27140	2294	20.4	28.0	37.5	9.0	5.1	52137	51755	66	88	1808	15.4	24.8	43.0	15.1	1.7	103081
41171	SANDY HOOK	15572	2262	48.3	27.6	18.9	3.4	1.8	26417	27989	4	25	1836	42.3	27.3	24.2	5.9	0.3	61532
41174	SOUTH PORTSMOUTH	17988	292	42.8	24.3	26.4	3.8	2.7	30937	34625	10	40	234	32.9	34.6	27.4	5.1	0.0	67097
41175	SOUTH SHORE	17195	2548	38.6	28.0	28.9	3.1	1.4	33291	37507	14	45	2008	30.6	30.1	32.1	7.0	0.3	77933
41179	VANCEBURG	13029	2317	52.4	29.5	15.5	1.9	0.8	23477	24384	2	18	1742	49.9	30.3	14.9	4.2	0.6	50055
41180	WEBBVILLE	14265	319	43.9	34.5	19.4	1.6	0.6	28751	30416	6	34	267	50.9	27.0	18.7	2.2	1.1	48958
41183	WORTHINGTON	22213	719	30.2	28.9	32.1	6.1	2.6	41909	44300	39	70	618	21.2	43.2	32.4	3.2	0.0	80532
41189	TOLLESBORO	16884	1296	37.0	34.2	23.9	3.3	1.5	34180	38699	16	48	1084	40.8	27.2	28.3	3.2	0.5	60870
41201	ADAMS	13922	350	53.7	22.0	21.4	0.6	2.3	22070	22996	2	13	298	56.4	13.1	16.4	12.4	1.7	39167
41204	BOONS CAMP	13363	220	43.6	34.5	20.9	0.9	0.0	28508	28772	6	32	191	45.5	34.6	15.7	4.2	0.0	54474
41214	DEBORD	14100	427	47.8	23.0	22.2	3.3	3.7	26314	28445	4	25	366	43.4	23.0	17.2	14.2	2.2	61250
41216	EAST POINT	21099	821	30.1	29.5	32.2	5.1	3.2	40232	42666	33	66	677	27.3	18.5	40.8	12.0	1.5	95182
41219	FLATGAP	14647	888	44.8	34.7	17.6	1.9	1.0	27946	29090	6	31	760	39.7	33.6	20.8	5.9	0.0	58667
41222	HAGERHILL	15433	981	46.4	26.0	22.2	3.9	1.5	28827	30680	6	34	772	35.1	29.7	27.1	7.4	0.8	67843
41224	INEZ	13592	1993	51.5	25.2	20.2	2.1	1.1	23935	24576	3	19	1610	47.0	23.9	23.2	5.7	0.3	54153
41226	KEATON	14283	163	36.8	47.9	13.5	0.6	1.2	30693	31012	9	39	139	33.1	35.3	23.0	8.6	0.0	63462
41230	LOUISA	15457	4091	45.3	28.9	20.4	3.7	1.6	27949	29461	6	31	3072	40.0	28.1	26.0	5.3	0.6	63761
41231	LOVELY	11146	330	57.3	25.8	16.1	0.9	0.0	20725	21645	2	9	275	45.5	28.4	23.3	2.9	0.0	55435
41232	LOWMANSVILLE	12815	839	48.6	28.5	20.9	1.9	0.1	25705	25445	4	24	715	43.4	26.7	21.8	6.0	2.1	62386
41234	MEALLY	15875	81	42.0	32.1	21.0	3.7	1.2	29582	29698	7	36	63	38.1	30.2	28.6	3.2	0.0	66250
41238	OIL SPRINGS	16925	591	39.9	33.0	22.0	3.9	1.2	31289	33470	10	41	518	36.5	31.5	27.4	4.1	0.6	68750
41240	PAINTSVILLE	19035	2862	41.8	27.6	23.4	4.1	3.1	31578	32899	11	42	1934	32.3	24.3	34.5	8.2	0.7	79189
41250	PILGRIM	12353	367	56.1	25.6	16.9	1.1	0.3	20960	22339	2	10	312	43.3	28.2	25.6	2.9	0.0	58400
41254	RIVER	9270	146	63.0	27.4	6.8	2.7	0.0	16101	17029	1	1	125	66.4	25.6	6.4	1.6	0.0	29405
41255	SITKA	14669	123	56.9	19.5	19.5	1.6	2.4	19788	21775	1	7	97	45.4	21.6	25.8	7.2	0.0	54500
41256	STAFFORDSVILLE	20108	691	35.7	35.0	22.0	3.5	3.8	34005	36635	16	47	542	36.2	26.4	27.9	6.6	3.0	70196
41257	STAMBAUGH	14142	309	49.8	23.9	21.0	3.6	1.6	25183	27323	3	23	245	46.1	18.4	30.2	5.3	0.0	55000
41260	THELMA	17471	882	35.3	32.4	26.9	4.1	1.4	32421	33275	12	44	643	34.5	31.1	30.3	3.9	0.2	66132
41262	TOMAHAWK	12097	657	52.4	31.1	12.2	2.9	1.5	22700	23049	2	15	549	51.9	28.1	10.9	7.3	1.8	47083
41263	TUTOR KEY	14904	169	44.4	27.2	24.9	2.4	1.2	29223	29584	7	35	147	43.5	15.0	35.4	6.1	0.0	74375
41265	VAN LEAR	16513	833	38.3	32.9	23.5	4.1	1.2	31169	31454	10	41	680	41.3	29.3	24.6	3.5	1.3	62889
41267	WARFIELD	11175	812	61.8	22.9	13.3	1.7	0.2	17631	18281	1	3	513	47.8	20.3	29.4	2.5	0.0	55750
41271	WILLIAMSPORT	14244	123	43.9	34.1	21.1	0.8	0.0	28585	28648	6	33	107	46.7	33.6	15.0	4.7	0.0	53500
41274	WITTENSVILLE	16055	408	47.5	26.7	21.1	2.2	2.5	26605	28159	4	26	297	38.0	27.3	26.9	6.4	1.3	64250
41301	CAMPTON	13550	2628	50.8	31.4	15.7	1.3	0.9	24227	24565	3	20	1943	51.8	26.7	17.4	3.4	0.7	47633
41311	BEATTYVILLE	15220	2872	51.8	27.9	15.5	2.8	2.0	23113	23728	2	16	2185	48.3	26.0	22.5	2.9	0.3	52060
41314	BOONEVILLE	12428	1752	60.1	21.7	15.6	1.6	1.0	18803	19327	1	5	1354	53.0	30.8	14.4	1.6	0.3	47143
41317	CLAYHOLE	13096	268	53.4	19.4	23.5	3.7	0.0	21372	24430	2	12	219	57.5	22.4	16.9	3.2	0.0	41750
41332	HAZEL GREEN	15303	568	43.5	33.6	20.1	1.8	1.1	28154	29777	6	32	449	39.9	34.7	21.4	3.1	0.9	59891
41338	ISLAND CITY	9787	159	59.7	26.4	13.8	0.0	0.0	20357	20479	1	8	131	68.7	21.4	9.9	0.0	0.0	40577
41339	JACKSON	13590	4838	51.1	27.9	17.5	2.6	0.9	23881	24761	3	18	3677	56.1	19.9	19.5	3.9	0.6	41783
41348	LOST CREEK	14049	492	53.3	19.9	24.4	1.2	1.2	22487	24261	2	14	402	57.7	22.1	17.4	2.7	0.0	39348
41351	MISTLETOE	8333	29	62.1	27.6	3.4	3.4	3.4	19213	17192	1	6	25	36.0	48.0	12.0	4.0	0.0	57000
41360	PINE RIDGE	10602	167	59.9	21.6	16.8	1.2	0.6	17964	18484	1	3	138	46.4	24.6	26.8	2.2	0.0	53846
41364	RICETOWN	10403	162	66.7	24.7	3.7	3.1	1.9	17045	17370	1	2	138	38.4	41.3	14.5	5.8	0.0	60000
41365	ROGERS	11063	243	62.1	21.0	16.5	0.4	0.0	17654	18166	1	3	206	37.4	28.6	32.0	1.9	0.0	62000
41366	ROUSSEAU	13388	90	50.0	32.2	12.2	3.3	2.2	25000	22279	3	22	74	68.9	14.9	14.9	1.4	0.0	40667
41367	ROWDY	13938	235	47.2	31.5	16.6	3.4	1.3	26520	25961	4	26	192	45.8	32.3	15.1	6.8	0.0	54000
41385	VANCLEVE	13720	346	52.0	30.9	15.3	0.9	0.9	23215	25748	2	17	249	51.0	27.7	21.3	0.0	0.0	49000
41386	VINCENT	9983	129	59.7	30.2	10.1	0.0	0.0	20435	21370	2	8	106	65.1	28.3	6.6	0.0	0.0	26429
41397	ZOE	13738	49	55.1	30.6	12.2	0.0	2.0	20718	21073	2	9	42	54.8	23.8	11.9	9.5	0.0	43333
41425	EZEL	16608	494	44.3	27.3	23.5	4.3	0.6	29802	30599	8	36	411	36.0	34.1	20.0	8.8	1.2	73356
41464	ROYALTON	10949	133	57.1	21.8	18.8	2.3	0.0	19412	20857	1	6	115	66.1	20.9	9.6	2.6	0.9	38393
41465	SALYERSVILLE	13409	4896	51.5	26.8	18.0	2.3	1.3	23511	24556	2	18	3988	49.5	25.7	20.2	4.3	0.3	50601
41472	WEST LIBERTY	15198	4108	47.4	29.8	18.1	2.9	1.9	27154	28176	5	29	3240	41.3	28.0	23.5	6.7	0.5	62676
41501	PIKEVILLE	19994	10666	41.7	26.6	24.5	4.3	2.8	30887	31950	10	39	7607	37.1	22.1	29.6	9.5	1.7	72406
41503	SOUTH WILLIAMSON	30315	301	28.9	25.2	32.6	6.6	6.6	46219	47826	52	81	227	3.5	48.9	35.7	11.9	0.0	88382
41512	ASHCAMP	11663	177	51.4	30.5	15.8	2.3	0.0	24212	25547	3	19	154	48.7	27.3	22.7	0.6	0.6	51538
41513	BELCHER	16559	226	36.3	33.6	24.8	5.3	0.0	33524	35372	14	46	201	38.8	36.3	19.9	2.5	2.5	63864
41514	BELFRY	17412	1530	41.4	28.4	24.8	3.4	2.0	32247	34387	12	43	1167	31.0	27.9	36.3	4.3	0.4	77372
41519	CANADA	14196	192	45.8	30.2	21.4	2.6	0.0	26583	27217	4	26	168	39.9	28.0	30.4	1.8	0.0	62500
41522	ELKHORN CITY	16722	2540	45.8	30.2	20.1	2.5	1.4	27269	28043	5	29	2109	41.1	35.6	19.5	3.3	0.5	57034
41524	FEDSCREEK	10809	92	57.6	35.9	6.5	0.0	0.0	20936	22515	2	10	78	47.4	32.1	20.5	0.0	0.0	51538
41527	FOREST HILLS	24336	349	27.5	27.5	36.1	3.7	5.2	46496	48408	53	82	262	14.9	14.9	51.5	16.0	2.7	116071
41528	FREEBURN	13274	545	53.2	27.9	15.6	2.0	1.3	22822	24555	2	16	437	57.2	28.6	14.2	0.0	0.0	40455
	KENTUCKY	23409		28.5	27.2	32.3	7.7	4.3	44205	46476				19.8	20.7	38.3	18.6	2.6	103937
	UNITED STATES	27277		20.9	24.4	35.3	11.7	7.6	54719	56938				9.3	13.1	31.6	32.6	13.5	162279

ZIP CODE #	POST OFFICE NAME	FINANCIAL SERVICES: Auto Loan	Home Loan	Invest-ments	Retire-ment Plans	THE HOME: Home Improvements: Home Repair	Lawn & Garden	Furnishings: Comput-ers & Hard-ware-Personal	Major Appli-ances	TV, Radio, Sound Equip-ment	Furni-ture	ENTERTAINMENT: Dine out/ Carry out	Sports Equip-ment	Fees & Tickets	Toys & Games	Travel	Cable TV	PERSONAL: Apparel & Services	Auto Repairs	Health Insur-ance	Pets & Supplies
41075	FORT THOMAS	108	116	111	117	115	115	113	112	112	112	113	86	117	112	116	113	79	113	116	131
41076	NEWPORT	102	100	96	102	100	106	102	102	103	99	103	78	101	103	102	106	72	103	109	121
41080	PETERSBURG	109	113	98	113	110	112	103	108	103	105	104	82	104	107	104	105	72	104	107	127
41083	SANDERS	90	66	75	65	66	86	68	79	75	66	74	61	56	78	63	82	50	75	83	96
41085	SILVER GROVE	77	62	55	63	59	72	73	70	77	67	74	55	63	78	63	81	51	73	78	86
41086	SPARTA	86	69	72	68	69	83	69	78	74	68	73	59	60	77	65	79	50	74	81	94
41091	UNION	168	196	169	201	190	170	168	171	158	182	160	139	184	169	175	149	116	159	149	194
41092	VERONA	106	103	91	101	100	104	95	101	98	99	98	75	94	101	94	99	67	97	100	119
41093	WALLINGFORD	75	54	62	52	53	71	56	65	62	54	61	50	45	65	51	68	41	62	69	79
41094	WALTON	114	120	104	119	116	115	110	112	109	113	110	86	112	113	110	109	76	109	110	133
41095	WARSAW	87	72	71	69	70	82	70	78	75	71	75	58	62	79	66	80	51	75	80	94
41097	WILLIAMSTOWN	86	71	74	70	70	84	72	79	76	69	75	60	63	78	68	81	51	76	82	95
41098	WORTHVILLE	84	60	69	58	60	80	63	73	69	61	68	56	50	72	57	76	46	69	77	89
41101	ASHLAND	78	67	76	68	69	82	73	78	78	68	76	58	67	75	71	83	52	77	87	92
41102	ASHLAND	90	78	91	77	80	96	77	90	83	73	82	66	71	82	78	89	55	85	95	105
41121	ARGILLITE	76	54	63	53	54	72	57	66	63	55	62	51	45	65	51	68	41	62	69	80
41124	BLAINE	53	35	51	33	34	52	37	47	43	35	42	36	28	43	34	48	28	44	49	57
41129	CATLETTSBURG	86	70	80	68	71	86	70	82	76	68	74	60	61	76	68	81	50	77	85	97
41132	DENTON	70	47	68	44	47	69	49	62	56	47	55	48	38	57	47	63	37	58	65	76
41135	EMERSON	56	37	54	34	36	55	39	49	45	37	44	38	29	46	36	50	29	46	52	61
41139	FLATWOODS	79	67	77	67	68	85	68	78	74	63	72	59	62	73	68	79	49	75	86	92
41141	GARRISON	67	46	60	44	46	65	49	59	55	47	54	45	38	57	45	61	36	55	62	72
41143	GRAYSON	77	58	69	55	57	75	59	69	65	57	64	52	49	67	55	70	43	65	72	84
41144	GREENUP	77	54	74	52	55	77	57	70	64	54	63	54	45	65	54	70	42	66	74	85
41146	HITCHINS	70	46	67	43	45	69	49	61	56	46	55	48	37	57	46	63	36	58	65	76
41149	ISONVILLE	56	37	54	35	37	55	39	50	45	37	44	39	29	46	37	51	29	47	52	61
41159	MARTHA	53	34	51	32	34	52	37	46	43	35	41	36	28	43	34	47	27	44	49	57
41164	OLIVE HILL	68	47	63	45	47	66	49	60	55	47	54	46	38	57	46	61	36	57	63	73
41166	QUINCY	81	58	67	57	58	77	61	70	67	59	66	54	49	70	55	73	44	67	74	86
41168	RUSH	83	69	70	67	68	79	68	75	72	68	71	56	60	75	64	76	48	72	77	90
41169	RUSSELL	92	92	92	93	92	104	88	95	92	86	91	71	89	91	91	96	63	93	104	112
41171	SANDY HOOK	69	46	67	43	46	68	48	61	56	46	54	47	37	56	46	62	36	57	64	75
41174	SOUTH PORTSMOUTH	75	54	77	52	56	77	55	71	62	52	60	53	44	61	55	68	40	65	73	84
41175	SOUTH SHORE	73	53	69	51	54	74	56	68	62	52	60	51	45	62	53	68	40	63	72	81
41179	VANCEBURG	58	39	55	37	39	57	41	51	47	39	46	40	32	47	39	52	30	48	54	63
41180	WEBBVILLE	62	42	61	40	42	62	44	56	50	42	49	43	34	51	42	56	33	52	59	68
41183	WORTHINGTON	79	74	83	72	75	90	71	83	78	67	76	60	69	76	74	84	52	78	92	96
41189	TOLLESBORO	74	53	68	52	54	73	55	67	61	52	60	51	44	62	52	67	40	62	70	80
41201	ADAMS	64	42	62	40	42	63	45	57	52	43	51	44	34	53	42	58	34	53	60	70
41204	BOONS CAMP	63	41	61	39	41	62	44	56	51	42	50	43	33	52	41	57	33	52	59	69
41214	DEBORD	76	50	73	47	49	75	53	67	61	50	60	52	40	62	50	68	40	63	71	82
41216	EAST POINT	90	74	82	72	74	87	72	83	77	72	77	61	64	79	70	82	51	78	85	99
41219	FLATGAP	68	46	62	43	45	66	48	59	55	46	54	46	37	56	45	61	36	56	63	73
41222	HAGERHILL	71	48	70	46	48	70	50	64	57	48	56	49	39	58	48	64	37	59	67	77
41224	INEZ	64	42	62	39	42	63	45	56	52	42	50	44	33	52	42	58	33	53	59	69
41226	KEATON	68	49	56	47	49	65	51	59	56	49	55	45	41	59	46	61	37	56	62	72
41230	LOUISA	67	49	64	47	49	67	51	62	57	49	56	47	42	57	49	62	37	58	66	74
41231	LOVELY	52	34	51	32	34	51	37	46	42	35	41	36	27	43	34	47	27	43	49	57
41232	LOWMANSVILLE	61	40	60	38	40	60	43	54	50	41	48	42	32	50	40	55	32	51	57	67
41234	MEALLY	71	48	67	45	48	69	51	62	58	48	56	48	39	59	47	64	38	59	66	76
41238	OIL SPRINGS	74	51	74	49	53	74	53	68	60	50	59	51	42	60	52	66	39	63	71	81
41240	PAINTSVILLE	78	57	74	55	58	77	61	71	67	58	66	54	50	67	58	73	44	68	76	86
41250	PILGRIM	57	37	55	35	37	56	40	50	46	38	45	39	30	47	37	52	30	47	53	62
41254	RIVER	45	29	44	28	29	44	31	40	36	30	35	31	24	37	29	40	23	37	42	49
41255	SITKA	66	43	64	41	43	65	46	58	53	44	52	45	35	54	43	60	34	55	62	72
41256	STAFFORDSVILLE	92	62	91	59	62	91	65	82	75	62	73	64	50	75	62	83	48	77	87	100
41257	STAMBAUGH	68	44	66	42	44	67	48	60	55	45	54	47	36	56	44	61	35	56	63	74
41260	THELMA	76	52	73	50	53	75	55	68	62	52	61	52	43	63	52	69	41	64	72	83
41262	TOMAHAWK	59	38	56	36	38	57	41	51	47	39	46	40	31	48	38	53	30	48	54	63
41263	TUTOR KEY	70	47	69	44	47	69	49	62	56	47	55	48	38	57	47	63	37	58	66	76
41265	VAN LEAR	76	53	72	51	53	75	55	68	62	52	60	52	43	63	52	68	40	63	71	82
41267	WARFIELD	50	33	48	31	32	49	35	44	40	33	39	34	26	41	33	45	26	41	46	54
41271	WILLIAMSPORT	63	41	61	39	41	62	44	56	51	42	50	43	33	52	41	57	33	52	59	68
41274	WITTENSVILLE	73	48	71	45	48	72	51	64	59	49	58	50	38	60	48	66	38	61	68	79
41301	CAMPTON	59	39	56	37	39	58	42	52	48	40	47	40	32	49	39	53	31	49	55	64
41311	BEATTYVILLE	65	43	62	41	44	63	48	58	54	45	53	45	37	55	44	60	35	55	62	71
41314	BOONEVILLE	53	36	49	35	36	52	39	47	46	38	44	36	31	46	36	51	30	46	51	58
41317	CLAYHOLE	61	40	59	38	40	60	43	54	49	41	48	42	32	50	40	55	32	51	57	66
41332	HAZEL GREEN	66	45	62	43	45	64	47	58	54	45	52	45	36	55	44	59	35	55	61	71
41338	ISLAND CITY	47	30	45	29	30	46	32	41	37	31	37	32	24	38	30	42	24	39	43	50
41339	JACKSON	61	41	60	39	41	61	43	55	50	41	48	42	33	50	41	55	32	51	58	67
41348	LOST CREEK	68	44	65	42	44	66	47	59	54	45	53	46	35	55	44	61	35	56	63	73
41351	MISTLETOE	48	31	46	30	31	47	34	42	39	32	38	33	25	39	31	43	25	40	45	52
41360	PINE RIDGE	53	35	51	33	35	52	37	47	43	35	42	36	28	44	35	48	28	44	49	57
41364	RICETOWN	47	31	46	29	31	46	33	42	38	31	37	32	25	39	31	42	25	39	44	51
41365	ROGERS	50	33	49	31	33	49	35	44	40	33	40	34	26	41	33	45	26	42	47	54
41366	ROUSSEAU	58	38	56	36	38	57	41	51	47	39	46	40	30	48	38	52	30	48	54	63
41367	ROWDY	64	42	62	39	41	63	45	56	51	42	50	44	33	52	42	57	33	53	59	69
41385	VANCLEVE	60	39	58	37	39	59	42	53	48	40	47	41	31	49	39	54	31	49	56	65
41386	VINCENT	45	29	43	28	29	44	31	40	36	30	35	31	24	37	29	40	23	37	42	49
41397	ZOE	61	40	59	37	40	60	43	54	49	40	48	42	32	50	40	55	32	50	57	66
41425	EZEL	77	55	69	54	56	75	57	69	64	55	62	52	46	65	54	70	42	64	72	83
41464	ROYALTON	56	36	54	34	36	54	39	49	45	37	44	38	29	45	36	50	29	46	52	60
41465	SALYERSVILLE	62	41	60	39	41	61	44	55	50	42	49	43	33	51	41	56	33	52	58	67
41472	WEST LIBERTY	70	49	66	47	49	69	52	62	58	49	57	48	41	59	48	64	38	59	66	76
41501	PIKEVILLE	79	58	71	56	58	76	62	71	69	60	67	54	51	69	58	74	45	69	76	86
41503	SOUTH WILLIAMSON	91	103	98	100	103	112	91	100	98	90	97	70	100	96	99	104	67	97	114	115
41512	ASHCAMP	58	38	56	36	38	57	41	51	47	39	46	40	31	48	38	52	30	48	54	63
41513	BELCHER	70	50	71	48	52	71	51	65	57	48	56	49	41	56	50	62	37	60	68	77
41514	BELFRY	74	51	71	48	51	73	53	66	60	51	59	51	41	61	50	67	39	62	69	81
41519	CANADA	63	41	60	38	41	61	44	55	50	42	49	43	33	51	41	56	33	52	58	68
41522	ELKHORN CITY	72	47	70	45	47	71	51	64	58	48	57	49	38	59	48	65	38	60	68	78
41524	FEDSCREEK	47	31	46	29	31	46	33	41	38	31	37	32	25	39	31	42	25	39	44	51
41527	FOREST HILLS	94	87	77	84	85	89	82	87	85	85	85	63	78	88	78	87	58	84	87	103
41528	FREEBURN	58	38	56	36	38	57	40	51	47	38	45	40	30	47	38	52	30	48	54	63
	KENTUCKY	90	77	81	77	76	88	80	85	83	78	83	65	73	85	76	87	57	83	88	101
	UNITED STATES	100	100	100	100	100	100	100	100	100	100	100	100	100	100	100	100	100	100	100	100

POPULATION CHANGE

ZIP CODE #	POST OFFICE NAME	COUNTY FIPS CODE	POPULATION 2000	POPULATION 2009	POPULATION 2014	2000-2009 ANNUAL RATE % Rate	2000-2009 ANNUAL RATE State Centile	HOUSEHOLDS 2000	HOUSEHOLDS 2009	HOUSEHOLDS 2014	HOUSEHOLDS % Annual Rate 2000-2009	HOUSEHOLDS 2009 Average HH Size	FAMILIES 2000	FAMILIES 2009	FAMILIES % Annual Rate 2000-2009
41531	HARDY	195	715	707	691	-0.1	32	274	279	277	0.2	2.53	199	195	-0.2
41535	HUDDY	195	485	463	447	-0.5	13	193	191	187	-0.1	2.42	142	135	-0.5
41537	JENKINS	195	5875	5640	5495	-0.4	18	2374	2376	2347	0.0	2.36	1758	1699	-0.4
41539	KIMPER	195	2272	2159	2094	-0.5	13	866	863	849	0.0	2.50	671	648	-0.4
41540	LICK CREEK	195	447	452	445	0.1	45	174	185	185	0.7	2.44	137	141	0.3
41543	MC ANDREWS	195	397	413	409	0.4	60	169	182	182	0.8	2.27	121	125	0.4
41544	MC CARR	195	780	751	732	-0.4	18	309	312	307	0.1	2.41	237	231	-0.3
41548	MOUTHCARD	195	673	673	660	0.0	39	281	294	293	0.5	2.29	220	224	0.2
41553	PHELPS	195	2761	2765	2724	0.0	39	1077	1133	1131	0.5	2.35	813	826	0.2
41554	PHYLLIS	195	1206	1197	1174	-0.1	32	485	505	502	0.4	2.37	369	371	0.1
41555	PINSONFORK	195	690	650	625	-0.6	9	265	259	253	-0.2	2.51	194	182	-0.7
41557	RACCOON	195	2219	2204	2165	-0.1	32	889	927	922	0.5	2.38	678	684	0.1
41558	RANSOM	195	1169	1211	1201	0.4	60	452	490	493	0.9	2.47	361	381	0.6
41559	REGINA	195	657	639	625	-0.3	22	254	258	255	0.2	2.48	201	199	-0.1
41560	ROBINSON CREEK	195	289	285	279	-0.2	26	115	118	117	0.3	2.42	92	92	0.0
41562	SHELBIANA	195	2301	2226	2172	-0.4	18	881	893	883	0.1	2.49	666	653	-0.2
41563	SHELBY GAP	195	570	543	526	-0.5	13	236	235	232	0.0	2.31	182	176	-0.4
41564	SIDNEY	195	1646	1641	1614	0.0	39	635	663	661	0.5	2.48	502	510	0.2
41566	STEELE	195	1092	1002	960	-0.9	2	424	408	397	-0.4	2.46	314	292	-0.8
41567	STONE	195	1220	1225	1202	0.0	39	478	497	494	0.4	2.46	346	346	0.0
41568	STOPOVER	195	1172	1146	1122	-0.2	26	480	492	489	0.3	2.33	351	347	-0.1
41571	VARNEY	195	474	452	439	-0.5	13	204	204	201	0.0	2.22	153	147	-0.4
41572	VIRGIE	195	2973	3004	2962	0.1	45	1161	1225	1225	0.6	2.45	905	927	0.3
41601	ALLEN	071	891	886	885	-0.1	32	388	403	408	0.4	2.20	282	282	0.0
41602	AUXIER	071	1271	1273	1274	0.0	39	522	549	557	0.5	2.32	384	388	0.1
41603	BANNER	071	1910	2025	2068	0.6	69	719	798	827	1.1	2.54	550	591	0.8
41604	BEAVER	071	772	773	774	0.0	39	298	311	316	0.5	2.49	221	223	0.1
41605	BETSY LAYNE	071	1048	1050	1048	0.0	39	425	445	451	0.5	2.36	303	305	0.1
41606	BEVINSVILLE	071	2870	2830	2805	-0.2	26	920	940	943	0.2	2.49	681	671	-0.2
41607	BLUE RIVER	071	560	556	555	-0.1	32	213	222	226	0.4	2.50	164	165	0.1
41615	DANA	071	57	64	66	1.3	88	22	26	27	1.8	2.46	17	20	1.8
41616	DAVID	071	93	105	110	1.3	88	35	42	44	2.0	2.50	28	32	1.5
41621	DWALE	071	230	222	217	-0.4	18	89	90	89	0.1	2.30	63	61	-0.3
41622	EASTERN	071	65	63	62	-0.3	22	26	26	26	0.0	2.42	20	19	-0.6
41630	GARRETT	071	1400	1353	1337	-0.4	18	576	585	587	0.2	2.31	420	411	-0.2
41631	GRETHEL	071	2003	2005	2014	0.0	39	792	833	848	0.5	2.40	581	589	0.1
41632	GUNLOCK	153	678	694	701	0.3	54	253	269	275	0.7	2.58	200	206	0.3
41635	HAROLD	071	2961	3005	3034	0.2	48	1212	1293	1323	0.7	2.32	890	914	0.3
41636	HI HAT	071	714	673	660	-0.6	9	304	301	299	-0.1	2.21	224	213	-0.5
41640	HUEYSVILLE	071	1148	1103	1084	-0.4	18	464	468	467	0.1	2.35	345	337	-0.3
41642	IVEL	071	1572	1591	1601	0.1	45	622	661	675	0.7	2.41	449	459	0.2
41643	LACKEY	071	55	54	54	-0.2	26	25	26	26	0.4	2.08	18	18	0.0
41645	LANGLEY	071	1374	1338	1320	-0.3	22	548	558	558	0.2	2.39	412	405	-0.2
41647	MC DOWELL	071	1647	1708	1735	0.4	60	645	701	721	0.9	2.43	482	505	0.5
41649	MARTIN	071	2180	2166	2167	-0.1	32	909	948	961	0.5	2.26	619	618	0.0
41650	MELVIN	071	513	509	506	-0.1	32	205	211	213	0.3	2.23	152	151	-0.1
41653	PRESTONSBURG	071	12249	12175	12147	-0.1	32	5022	5223	5282	0.4	2.25	3542	3545	0.0
41655	PRINTER	071	992	991	996	0.0	39	395	415	422	0.5	2.38	271	273	0.1
41660	TEABERRY	071	1786	1807	1821	0.1	45	691	733	750	0.6	2.46	527	541	0.3
41666	WAYLAND	071	982	963	959	-0.2	26	398	411	415	0.3	2.34	284	282	-0.1
41701	HAZARD	193	15013	15201	15304	0.1	45	5928	6252	6374	0.6	2.38	4243	4306	0.2
41712	ARY	193	665	622	606	-0.7	5	253	249	246	-0.2	2.50	183	172	-0.7
41714	BEAR BRANCH	131	476	449	435	-0.6	9	192	190	186	-0.1	2.36	147	141	-0.4
41719	BONNYMAN	193	761	811	831	0.7	74	301	338	352	1.3	2.33	223	241	0.8
41721	BUCKHORN	193	751	853	894	1.4	89	274	328	350	2.0	2.50	215	249	1.6
41722	BULAN	119	2370	2331	2307	-0.2	26	924	950	954	0.3	2.45	686	682	-0.1
41723	BUSY	193	1772	1733	1715	-0.2	26	643	659	661	0.3	2.63	511	510	0.0
41725	CARRIE	119	858	852	853	-0.1	32	338	353	359	0.5	2.41	253	255	0.1
41727	CHAVIES	193	595	562	553	-0.6	9	238	236	235	-0.1	2.38	191	184	-0.4
41729	COMBS	193	285	332	352	1.7	93	112	139	149	2.4	2.25	82	97	1.8
41731	CORNETTSVILLE	193	1430	1433	1440	0.0	39	569	598	609	0.5	2.40	436	443	0.2
41735	DELPHIA	193	292	279	276	-0.5	13	115	115	116	0.0	2.43	89	87	-0.2
41736	DICE	193	127	122	119	-0.4	18	54	54	54	0.0	2.26	39	38	-0.3
41740	EMMALENA	119	1224	1216	1217	-0.1	32	486	508	516	0.5	2.39	363	367	0.1
41745	GAYS CREEK	193	348	392	410	1.3	88	129	153	162	1.9	2.48	101	115	1.4
41746	HAPPY	193	902	883	869	-0.2	26	333	340	339	0.2	2.60	253	249	-0.2
41749	HYDEN	131	3545	3357	3253	-0.6	9	1397	1387	1361	-0.1	2.35	1019	975	-0.5
41754	KRYPTON	193	710	754	776	0.7	74	254	283	295	1.2	2.66	203	220	0.9
41759	SASSAFRAS	119	714	729	734	0.2	48	285	304	311	0.7	2.40	217	224	0.3
41760	SCUDDY	193	551	536	527	-0.3	22	198	202	201	0.2	2.65	148	146	-0.1
41763	SLEMP	193	309	294	290	-0.5	13	124	124	124	0.0	2.37	96	93	-0.3
41764	SMILAX	131	738	716	700	-0.3	22	300	308	304	0.3	2.32	227	226	0.0
41766	THOUSANDSTICKS	131	679	642	622	-0.6	9	260	257	253	-0.1	2.50	203	195	-0.4
41772	VEST	119	96	95	95	-0.1	32	38	40	40	0.6	2.38	28	28	0.0
41773	VICCO	193	1173	1157	1146	-0.1	32	471	486	489	0.3	2.38	353	351	-0.1
41774	VIPER	193	3008	3111	3173	0.4	60	1183	1281	1325	0.9	2.43	928	975	0.5
41775	WENDOVER	131	38	37	36	-0.3	22	18	18	18	0.0	1.89	13	13	0.0
41776	WOOTON	131	2265	2205	2155	-0.3	22	903	927	918	0.3	2.37	675	670	-0.1
41777	YEADDISS	131	455	458	451	0.1	45	180	191	191	0.6	2.40	136	139	0.2
41804	BLACKEY	133	623	624	618	0.0	39	241	253	254	0.5	2.47	175	177	0.1
41812	DEANE	133	606	554	534	-1.0	1	244	234	228	-0.5	2.37	189	176	-0.8
41815	ERMINE	133	690	732	732	0.6	69	248	274	278	1.1	2.67	196	209	0.7
41817	GARNER	119	1221	1198	1182	-0.2	26	364	372	371	0.2	2.59	269	265	-0.2
41819	GORDON	133	498	517	517	0.4	60	198	215	218	0.9	2.40	157	166	0.6
41821	HALLIE	133	1184	1204	1196	0.2	48	469	499	503	0.7	2.41	342	351	0.3
41822	HINDMAN	119	1700	1709	1707	0.1	45	702	739	748	0.6	2.19	499	505	0.1
41824	ISOM	133	699	691	681	-0.1	32	318	330	330	0.4	2.09	229	228	0.0
41825	JACKHORN	133	161	147	141	-1.0	1	61	58	57	-0.5	2.53	44	40	-1.0
41826	JEREMIAH	133	845	897	901	0.6	69	359	399	406	1.1	2.25	263	282	0.8
41828	KITE	119	780	811	821	0.4	60	290	315	324	0.9	2.57	232	246	0.6
41831	LEBURN	119	2105	2069	2032	-0.2	26	791	812	809	0.3	2.53	561	554	-0.1
41832	LETCHER	133	209	229	232	1.0	83	88	101	104	1.5	2.27	68	75	1.1
41833	LINEFORK	133	312	316	314	0.1	45	118	125	125	0.6	2.53	92	95	0.3
41834	LITTCARR	119	676	671	669	-0.1	32	274	287	290	0.5	2.34	196	196	0.0
41835	MC ROBERTS	133	692	624	599	-1.1	1	266	251	244	-0.6	2.49	202	184	-1.0
	KENTUCKY					0.7					1.0	2.41			0.6
	UNITED STATES					1.0					1.1	2.59			0.9

ZIP CODE #	POST OFFICE NAME	RACE (%) White 2000	White 2009	Black 2000	Black 2009	Asian/Pacific 2000	Asian/Pacific 2009	% Hispanic Origin 2000	% Hispanic Origin 2009	2009 AGE DISTRIBUTION (%) 0-4	5-9	10-14	15-19	20-24	25-44	45-64	65-84	85+	18+	MEDIAN AGE 2009	% 2009 Males	% 2009 Females
41531	HARDY	97.6	97.6	1.3	1.3	0.3	0.3	0.3	0.3	5.8	6.2	5.7	6.2	4.8	26.0	31.5	12.6	1.1	78.2	41.5	47.0	53.0
41535	HUDDY	99.2	99.1	0.4	0.4	0.0	0.0	0.2	0.4	5.8	6.3	6.7	6.9	4.8	25.5	29.8	12.5	1.7	76.9	40.7	50.1	49.9
41537	JENKINS	98.7	98.4	0.5	0.6	0.2	0.4	0.5	0.7	5.7	6.1	6.2	5.7	4.8	25.4	31.1	13.3	1.8	78.4	42.0	49.2	50.8
41539	KIMPER	99.1	98.9	0.0	0.0	0.3	0.4	0.6	0.9	6.2	6.3	6.5	6.6	5.6	29.2	28.9	9.6	1.2	77.0	38.4	49.7	50.3
41540	LICK CREEK	99.8	99.6	0.0	0.0	0.0	0.0	0.7	0.9	6.0	5.8	5.8	7.1	5.5	27.4	32.1	9.5	0.9	78.3	39.5	51.3	48.7
41543	MC ANDREWS	98.7	98.3	0.5	0.5	0.0	0.0	0.0	0.2	7.0	7.5	8.0	6.3	4.6	23.7	29.8	11.4	1.7	73.1	39.9	48.7	51.3
41544	MC CARR	98.3	97.9	0.0	0.0	0.4	0.4	1.3	2.0	5.3	6.8	5.9	6.3	6.1	26.1	32.0	10.4	1.2	77.9	40.7	47.0	53.0
41548	MOUTHCARD	99.6	99.6	0.0	0.0	0.0	0.0	0.6	0.9	5.8	6.1	5.8	7.3	5.5	27.3	32.1	9.4	0.7	78.2	39.4	51.1	48.9
41553	PHELPS	99.0	98.8	0.2	0.2	0.1	0.1	0.7	1.0	5.6	6.0	6.0	5.9	5.1	25.5	29.8	14.5	1.6	79.0	42.1	49.6	50.4
41554	PHYLLIS	98.4	98.1	0.2	0.3	0.5	0.5	0.7	1.2	5.7	5.8	6.1	6.1	5.1	25.8	32.1	11.9	1.4	78.7	41.4	50.5	49.5
41555	PINSONFORK	96.5	96.2	2.3	2.5	0.0	0.0	0.0	0.0	6.2	6.6	6.9	6.6	4.5	25.7	30.6	11.5	1.4	76.3	40.5	50.0	50.0
41557	RACCOON	99.1	98.8	0.1	0.1	0.2	0.3	0.5	0.9	6.0	5.4	5.5	6.3	5.5	27.0	33.0	10.1	1.0	79.3	40.2	48.1	51.9
41558	RANSOM	98.2	97.7	0.1	0.1	0.4	0.7	1.4	2.0	5.9	7.0	6.4	7.4	7.3	27.3	28.5	8.7	1.4	75.8	37.1	49.3	50.7
41559	REGINA	99.1	98.9	0.0	0.0	0.0	0.0	0.6	0.9	5.8	6.1	5.9	6.4	5.8	27.2	30.7	11.0	1.1	78.1	40.4	49.1	50.9
41560	ROBINSON CREEK	99.0	98.9	0.0	0.0	0.7	0.7	0.7	1.4	6.0	6.7	7.0	5.6	4.2	28.8	29.8	10.9	1.1	76.5	39.4	49.8	50.2
41562	SHELBIANA	99.4	99.2	0.0	0.0	0.1	0.2	0.3	0.6	6.2	6.2	6.4	6.0	5.3	27.2	30.1	11.3	1.1	77.4	39.7	49.8	50.2
41563	SHELBY GAP	98.2	97.8	0.0	0.0	0.4	0.4	0.9	1.3	5.0	5.7	6.4	6.8	5.0	27.1	33.0	9.9	1.1	78.8	41.1	50.5	49.5
41564	SIDNEY	99.7	99.6	0.1	0.1	0.0	0.0	0.5	0.7	5.9	6.5	6.9	6.9	5.9	26.8	28.5	10.9	1.5	75.8	38.5	48.9	51.1
41566	STEELE	98.7	98.5	0.0	0.0	0.3	0.3	1.0	1.5	6.4	6.1	5.9	9.0	5.3	29.0	28.5	8.8	1.0	76.1	37.5	51.1	48.9
41567	STONE	98.9	98.8	0.4	0.4	0.0	0.0	0.2	0.2	6.7	6.9	7.4	6.5	4.7	24.5	29.4	12.2	1.7	74.8	40.1	49.5	50.5
41568	STOPOVER	98.9	98.7	0.1	0.1	0.1	0.1	0.5	0.8	6.5	7.1	6.9	7.0	7.5	27.4	28.0	9.1	0.6	75.3	35.0	51.6	48.4
41571	VARNEY	99.6	99.3	0.0	0.0	0.0	0.0	0.2	0.2	4.6	5.3	5.1	8.6	7.5	25.2	31.6	10.0	2.0	80.3	40.6	49.6	50.4
41572	VIRGIE	99.8	99.7	0.0	0.0	0.1	0.2	0.7	1.1	5.6	6.1	5.8	7.6	6.0	27.9	28.9	11.3	0.9	77.7	39.2	49.6	50.4
41601	ALLEN	99.0	99.0	0.4	0.5	0.0	0.0	0.2	0.2	5.6	5.9	6.2	5.9	4.3	27.8	30.1	12.4	1.8	78.6	41.2	45.6	54.4
41602	AUXIER	98.5	98.5	0.2	0.2	0.3	0.3	0.6	0.6	6.4	6.8	6.8	5.7	4.3	26.6	29.3	12.4	1.6	76.2	40.3	46.6	53.4
41603	BANNER	98.4	98.3	0.7	0.8	0.3	0.3	0.6	0.6	6.6	7.0	7.7	7.1	6.6	28.5	27.2	8.1	1.2	73.8	35.8	50.5	49.5
41604	BEAVER	99.0	99.0	0.1	0.1	0.0	0.0	0.9	0.8	6.1	6.1	6.5	7.4	6.1	24.7	29.2	12.7	1.3	77.0	39.9	48.1	51.9
41605	BETSY LAYNE	97.7	97.7	0.5	0.5	0.5	0.5	0.3	0.3	5.3	5.5	6.0	6.1	4.9	26.3	31.0	13.6	1.3	79.2	42.3	49.3	50.7
41606	BEVINSVILLE	86.6	86.2	12.5	12.9	0.0	0.0	0.8	0.8	5.2	5.1	5.2	5.7	11.2	31.2	25.4	9.8	1.3	80.8	35.5	57.2	42.8
41607	BLUE RIVER	98.6	98.6	0.5	0.5	0.2	0.2	0.9	0.7	5.9	5.9	5.9	6.1	5.2	29.1	29.5	11.0	1.3	78.4	39.6	50.9	49.1
41615	DANA	100.0	100.0	0.0	0.0	0.0	0.0	0.0	0.0	6.3	6.3	7.8	7.8	6.3	31.3	26.6	7.8	0.0	71.9	35.0	48.4	51.6
41616	DAVID	100.0	99.0	0.0	0.0	0.0	1.0	1.1	1.0	4.8	5.7	5.7	6.7	5.7	31.4	29.5	9.5	1.0	80.0	38.4	52.4	47.6
41621	DWALE	94.8	94.6	3.5	3.6	0.0	0.0	1.3	0.9	7.7	7.2	7.2	9.5	6.3	25.7	25.2	10.4	0.9	73.0	36.1	49.5	50.5
41622	EASTERN	100.0	100.0	0.0	0.0	0.0	0.0	0.0	0.0	4.8	6.3	6.3	6.3	6.3	31.7	25.4	11.1	1.6	76.2	37.5	49.2	50.8
41630	GARRETT	98.9	98.8	0.0	0.0	0.6	0.6	0.4	0.4	4.8	5.5	5.6	6.5	5.2	24.9	33.0	12.7	1.8	80.0	43.0	50.6	49.4
41631	GRETHEL	98.4	98.4	0.1	0.1	0.9	0.9	0.4	0.3	6.3	6.2	6.8	6.2	4.9	25.5	31.5	11.0	1.5	76.8	40.5	49.7	50.3
41632	GUNLOCK	99.1	98.8	0.0	0.0	0.0	0.0	0.1	0.3	7.6	7.6	7.2	6.9	5.8	26.7	27.7	9.4	1.2	73.2	36.4	49.3	50.7
41635	HAROLD	99.3	99.3	0.3	0.3	0.1	0.1	0.4	0.4	6.7	6.5	6.3	7.5	6.8	27.1	29.0	9.1	1.1	76.0	37.4	50.2	49.8
41636	HI HAT	99.3	99.3	0.0	0.0	0.1	0.1	0.1	0.1	5.3	5.8	5.8	5.1	4.6	26.3	31.9	13.2	1.9	79.6	43.0	47.3	52.7
41640	HUEYSVILLE	99.3	99.3	0.1	0.1	0.2	0.2	0.4	0.5	4.1	5.5	5.8	6.7	6.1	28.9	30.4	11.2	1.4	80.3	40.6	50.0	50.0
41642	IVEL	97.8	97.8	1.3	1.3	0.2	0.2	0.5	0.5	7.0	7.0	6.6	6.2	5.8	29.0	27.0	10.1	1.2	75.4	37.1	49.5	50.5
41643	LACKEY	100.0	100.0	0.0	0.0	0.0	0.0	0.0	0.0	3.7	5.6	9.3	7.4	3.7	25.9	29.6	13.0	1.9	74.1	41.3	50.0	50.0
41645	LANGLEY	99.5	99.5	0.0	0.0	0.3	0.3	0.6	0.6	6.4	7.0	6.9	6.1	5.7	28.6	27.7	9.9	1.8	76.1	37.7	47.8	52.2
41647	MC DOWELL	99.1	99.1	0.0	0.0	0.1	0.1	0.4	0.5	6.6	7.4	6.4	5.9	6.1	25.5	30.6	10.1	1.4	75.6	38.3	48.7	51.3
41649	MARTIN	98.7	98.7	0.2	0.2	0.6	0.6	0.4	0.4	5.8	6.1	6.2	6.0	4.9	26.7	29.0	13.3	2.1	78.3	41.0	46.1	53.9
41650	MELVIN	93.4	93.3	5.8	5.9	0.0	0.0	0.8	0.8	5.7	5.7	5.9	6.5	7.9	27.9	27.5	11.6	1.4	78.6	37.9	51.9	48.1
41653	PRESTONSBURG	98.2	98.2	0.6	0.7	0.4	0.4	0.8	0.8	5.4	5.6	5.8	6.4	5.4	27.2	28.7	13.2	2.2	79.2	41.0	48.7	51.3
41655	PRINTER	98.9	98.9	0.0	0.0	0.8	0.8	0.4	0.4	4.9	5.5	6.3	7.5	7.2	25.6	29.4	11.8	1.8	78.2	39.6	50.2	49.8
41660	TEABERRY	99.5	99.4	0.1	0.1	0.0	0.0	1.1	1.0	6.9	5.9	6.7	7.6	7.6	26.4	30.4	7.5	1.0	75.4	36.8	49.2	50.8
41666	WAYLAND	99.2	99.2	0.0	0.0	0.3	0.3	0.5	0.5	4.7	6.9	8.1	7.2	3.9	26.6	28.8	11.7	2.2	76.0	40.0	50.2	49.8
41701	HAZARD	95.5	94.9	3.1	3.3	0.7	1.1	0.7	1.0	5.9	6.2	6.1	6.7	5.9	27.0	29.1	11.4	1.7	78.4	39.4	48.4	51.6
41712	ARY	99.7	99.8	0.2	0.0	0.0	0.0	0.0	0.0	5.6	5.9	5.9	8.7	6.6	25.7	30.7	9.0	1.8	79.9	38.9	50.0	50.0
41714	BEAR BRANCH	98.7	98.2	0.0	0.0	0.0	0.0	0.2	0.4	7.6	6.2	6.7	7.1	8.5	28.1	25.4	9.4	1.1	74.2	35.4	48.1	51.9
41719	BONNYMAN	97.8	96.4	0.3	0.4	1.8	3.1	0.1	0.2	5.9	5.8	6.4	6.0	5.7	29.0	30.3	9.9	1.0	78.3	39.8	49.7	50.3
41721	BUCKHORN	98.9	98.7	0.4	0.5	0.4	0.6	0.1	0.4	4.5	5.4	8.2	11.3	5.5	25.7	27.7	10.9	0.9	73.2	37.8	50.4	49.6
41722	BULAN	98.5	98.2	0.6	0.8	0.2	0.3	0.5	0.8	6.2	6.3	6.3	6.7	5.3	26.9	29.9	10.9	1.5	77.1	39.7	50.3	49.7
41723	BUSY	99.4	99.2	0.0	0.0	0.2	0.3	0.4	0.7	6.8	5.9	6.7	8.7	7.4	26.3	28.7	8.5	1.1	75.3	36.7	49.8	50.2
41725	CARRIE	98.7	98.7	0.3	0.4	0.0	0.0	0.5	0.4	6.7	6.5	6.1	7.7	6.2	27.2	28.4	9.3	1.9	76.2	37.7	50.7	49.3
41727	CHAVIES	99.8	99.8	0.0	0.0	0.0	0.0	0.0	0.0	6.0	6.4	6.2	4.3	4.8	29.9	29.9	11.6	0.9	78.8	39.9	51.2	48.8
41729	COMBS	95.4	93.4	0.7	0.6	3.9	6.0	0.0	0.3	5.1	5.4	5.7	6.3	5.1	27.4	31.9	11.7	1.2	79.8	42.0	48.8	51.2
41731	CORNETTSVILLE	99.2	99.0	0.1	0.1	0.1	0.1	0.8	1.2	5.4	5.3	6.5	6.5	6.5	26.3	31.6	10.3	1.7	78.6	40.3	48.8	51.2
41735	DELPHIA	99.0	98.9	0.7	0.7	0.0	0.0	0.3	0.4	5.7	5.7	6.8	7.2	6.1	29.4	28.7	9.0	1.4	76.3	38.0	50.9	49.1
41736	DICE	100.0	100.0	0.0	0.0	0.0	0.0	0.0	0.0	5.7	6.6	5.7	9.0	7.4	26.2	28.7	8.2	2.5	80.3	37.1	50.8	49.2
41740	EMMALENA	98.8	98.8	0.3	0.3	0.0	0.0	0.4	0.4	6.6	6.5	6.1	7.6	6.2	27.0	28.7	9.5	1.9	76.3	38.0	50.6	49.4
41745	GAYS CREEK	99.4	99.2	0.3	0.3	0.3	0.5	0.3	0.3	4.6	5.6	7.9	10.5	6.1	26.0	27.8	10.5	1.0	74.0	37.5	50.5	49.5
41746	HAPPY	99.3	99.2	0.1	0.1	0.1	0.1	0.2	0.3	6.2	6.0	6.0	8.3	6.5	26.6	30.4	8.7	1.4	76.4	38.3	48.9	51.1
41749	HYDEN	99.0	98.7	0.1	0.1	0.3	0.4	0.6	0.9	5.5	5.7	6.0	6.2	5.2	25.5	30.4	13.1	2.4	78.8	42.2	47.6	52.4
41754	KRYPTON	99.0	98.9	0.0	0.0	0.1	0.1	0.4	0.7	5.3	6.8	8.0	8.0	6.4	31.3	25.6	8.2	0.5	75.1	35.7	50.3	49.7
41759	SASSAFRAS	95.8	95.7	3.4	3.4	0.0	0.0	0.8	0.7	5.1	5.9	6.4	8.4	6.0	25.5	31.0	10.2	1.5	77.5	39.4	50.5	49.5
41760	SCUDDY	99.6	99.6	0.2	0.2	0.0	0.0	0.5	0.9	7.1	6.2	7.5	8.8	6.9	25.9	28.2	8.6	0.9	73.5	34.5	48.7	51.3
41763	SLEMP	99.0	99.0	0.6	0.7	0.0	0.0	0.3	0.3	5.8	5.4	7.1	7.1	5.8	31.0	27.6	8.8	1.4	76.5	37.4	50.3	49.7
41764	SMILAX	99.2	99.0	0.0	0.0	0.1	0.1	0.8	1.4	5.3	5.4	6.8	6.7	8.0	27.0	30.3	9.1	1.4	78.5	38.8	49.6	50.4
41766	THOUSANDSTICKS	99.1	98.8	0.0	0.0	0.0	0.0	0.4	0.8	7.0	6.5	6.5	7.5	8.3	28.8	24.8	9.3	1.2	74.8	35.3	49.1	50.9
41772	VEST	99.0	98.9	0.0	0.0	0.0	0.0	0.0	0.0	6.3	6.3	6.3	7.4	6.3	25.3	30.5	10.5	1.1	76.8	38.8	52.6	47.4
41773	VICCO	99.2	99.1	0.3	0.3	0.0	0.1	0.3	0.6	6.1	6.1	6.5	7.9	6.2	26.1	29.8	10.1	1.2	76.3	38.4	49.1	50.9
41774	VIPER	99.5	99.4	0.0	0.0	0.1	0.2	0.6	1.0	4.4	6.1	6.1	7.3	5.9	27.7	32.6	8.9	1.2	78.8	40.2	48.8	51.2
41775	WENDOVER	100.0	100.0	0.0	0.0	0.0	0.0	0.0	0.0	5.4	5.4	5.4	5.4	5.4	21.6	32.4	16.2	2.7	78.4	45.6	48.6	51.4
41776	WOOTON	99.2	98.9	0.0	0.0	0.1	0.3	0.7	1.2	6.2	5.6	6.3	6.7	7.4	27.6	29.0	10.0	1.2	77.7	38.1	49.3	50.7
41777	YEADDISS	99.3	99.1	0.0	0.0	0.2	0.4	0.9	1.5	5.2	5.9	7.0	8.1	7.0	28.2	28.6	9.2	0.9	76.6	37.6	49.1	50.9
41804	BLACKEY	99.5	99.4	0.0	0.0	0.0	0.0	0.3	0.5	4.2	5.4	5.6	8.0	6.4	24.2	32.2	12.0	1.9	79.6	42.4	49.4	50.6
41812	DEANE	99.3	99.3	0.2	0.2	0.0	0.0	0.3	0.5	5.2	6.3	6.3	7.0	7.0	26.2	30.7	9.6	1.6	77.8	39.4	50.0	50.0
41815	ERMINE	99.6	99.6	0.0	0.0	0.0	0.0	0.4	0.5	6.8	7.1	7.1	6.4	4.5	26.5	30.6	10.0	1.0	74.9	38.9	51.1	48.9
41817	GARNER	98.4	98.3	0.4	0.4	0.6	0.6	0.6	0.5	5.6	5.7	5.3	12.9	12.6	22.4	25.4	9.1	1.1	79.0	32.7	48.1	51.9
41819	GORDON	100.0	100.0	0.0	0.0	0.0	0.0	0.0	0.0	5.2	6.2	7.2	8.1	9.1	27.3	26.9	8.1	1.9	76.6	36.4	50.7	49.3
41821	HALLIE	99.7	99.7	0.0	0.0	0.0	0.0	0.1	0.1	4.9	5.6	7.0	7.9	7.1	26.7	29.1	9.7	2.2	77.4	39.0	48.9	51.1
41822	HINDMAN	98.9	98.9	0.1	0.1	0.1	0.1	1.3	1.3	5.9	6.0	6.1	7.0	5.9	24.6	28.9	12.8	2.8	77.6	41.3	47.1	52.9
41824	ISOM	99.6	99.3	0.1	0.1	0.0	0.1	0.3	0.4	4.9	5.6	5.6	7.2	6.7	26.2	32.3	10.0	1.4	79.5	40.5	48.9	51.1
41825	JACKHORN	98.8	98.6	0.6	0.7	0.0	0.0	0.0	0.0	6.8	6.8	6.8	6.8	4.8	25.2	29.3	11.6	2.0	75.5	39.2	49.0	51.0
41826	JEREMIAH	99.2	99.0	0.1	0.2	0.0	0.0	0.1	0.2	3.8	4.5	5.6	8.1	6.8	24.3	32.9	12.0	2.0	81.0	43.2	48.6	51.4
41828	KITE	99.5	99.5	0.0	0.0	0.0	0.0	0.3	0.2	6.4	7.3	6.5	7.5	6.8	26.5	27.9	9.7	1.4	74.8	36.9	50.6	49.4
41831	LEBURN	97.9	97.9	0.0	0.0	0.3	0.3	1.0	0.9	5.7	6.1	6.1	6.5	4.7	26.3	30.9	12.1	1.5	78.1	41.3	49.2	50.8
41832	LETCHER	99.0	98.7	0.0	0.0	0.0	0.0	0.0	0.4	3.9	3.9	6.1	8.7	7.0	23.6	32.3	12.2	2.2	80.3	43.2	48.5	51.5
41833	LINEFORK	100.0	100.0	0.0	0.0	0.0	0.0	0.0	0.0	5.7	6.3	7.0	7.6	7.9	27.8	27.2	8.9	1.6	76.3	36.6	51.6	48.4
41834	LITTCARR	99.3	99.3	0.1	0.1	0.0	0.0	0.4	0.4	5.7	6.0	6.0	5.1	4.3	26.5	30.3	14.9	1.3	79.3	42.7	49.8	50.2
41835	MC ROBERTS	93.5	92.8	5.8	6.4	0.0	0.0	0.9	1.4	6.1	6.1	6.3	6.6	5.4	22.8	32.1	12.8	1.9	77.4	42.6	51.1	48.9
	KENTUCKY	90.1	88.9	7.3	7.5	0.8	1.2	1.5	2.4	6.5	6.5	6.5	6.8	6.5	27.0	27.1	11.3	1.8	76.6	37.9	49.1	50.9
	UNITED STATES	75.1	72.0	12.3	12.7	3.8	4.6	12.5	15.7	6.8	6.7	6.6	7.1	6.9	27.0	26.0	10.9	1.9	75.7	36.9	49.2	50.8

KENTUCKY

INCOME

C 41531-41835

#	POST OFFICE NAME	2009 Per Capita Income	2009 HH Income Base	2009 Household Income Distribution (%): Less than $25,000	$25,000 to $49,999	$50,000 to $99,999	$100,000 to $149,999	$150,000 or More	Median Household Income: 2009	2014	2009 National Centile	2009 State Centile	2009 Home Value Base	2009 Home Value Distribution (%): Less than $50,000	$50,000 to $89,999	$90,000 to $174,999	$175,000 to $399,999	$400,000 or More	2009 Median Home Value
41531	HARDY	17318	279	37.3	28.3	28.0	3.2	3.2	34501	37155	17	49	215	38.6	21.9	36.3	2.8	0.5	68333
41535	HUDDY	17732	191	41.4	25.1	27.7	4.7	1.0	38656	42156	29	62	161	31.7	20.5	42.9	5.0	0.0	87083
41537	JENKINS	15644	2376	45.6	28.5	22.1	2.8	0.9	28687	29690	6	34	1895	40.4	31.2	25.9	2.5	0.0	58139
41539	KIMPER	16687	863	34.9	34.1	25.6	4.5	0.9	35107	36609	18	50	698	42.1	31.1	19.3	7.4	0.0	61778
41540	LICK CREEK	15707	185	36.2	35.7	23.8	4.3	0.0	35134	36213	18	51	159	35.8	35.2	25.2	3.8	0.0	61000
41543	MC ANDREWS	14861	182	50.0	24.7	23.1	1.1	1.1	25000	26939	3	22	149	35.6	40.9	16.8	4.0	2.7	60882
41544	MC CARR	16505	312	50.3	16.3	27.2	5.4	0.6	24752	26866	3	21	263	40.3	27.0	23.6	9.1	0.0	67667
41548	MOUTHCARD	16604	294	37.1	35.4	23.5	4.1	0.0	33767	35585	15	47	253	37.2	34.4	24.5	4.0	0.0	60652
41553	PHELPS	14587	1133	50.8	28.5	18.7	0.4	1.6	24430	25792	3	20	955	45.1	31.9	21.6	0.5	0.8	55671
41554	PHYLLIS	12121	505	58.2	23.2	16.6	1.8	0.2	20561	22328	2	9	423	48.0	25.1	26.7	0.2	0.0	52024
41555	PINSONFORK	13743	259	44.8	35.1	17.4	2.7	0.0	28596	29583	6	33	213	50.7	23.5	25.8	0.0	0.0	49167
41557	RACCOON	17445	927	33.9	34.3	27.8	3.2	0.8	35289	37252	19	52	757	23.1	35.9	34.3	6.1	0.5	81104
41558	RANSOM	13963	490	49.6	23.9	24.9	1.4	0.2	25244	26381	3	23	430	46.5	34.4	17.0	2.1	0.0	53488
41559	REGINA	14571	258	41.5	31.8	23.3	3.5	0.0	29102	29515	7	35	223	41.3	34.5	20.2	2.7	1.3	61136
41560	ROBINSON CREEK	17679	118	34.7	33.1	27.1	4.2	0.8	35000	37363	18	50	99	36.4	25.3	30.3	8.1	0.0	71875
41562	SHELBIANA	15743	893	46.5	28.0	20.2	3.0	2.4	26617	27338	4	26	748	48.4	24.6	23.5	3.2	0.3	52069
41563	SHELBY GAP	13491	235	52.8	29.4	15.3	2.6	0.0	23430	24764	2	17	206	51.0	27.7	21.4	0.0	0.0	48571
41564	SIDNEY	13931	663	44.2	31.8	21.1	2.7	0.2	27506	28192	5	30	575	39.5	27.1	32.2	1.2	0.0	62875
41566	STEELE	12902	408	48.3	34.3	15.7	0.7	1.0	25742	26520	4	24	354	46.9	30.5	20.3	2.3	0.0	52619
41567	STONE	15166	497	46.5	25.2	24.9	2.4	1.0	28349	31323	6	32	410	34.9	32.4	26.8	4.1	1.7	66765
41568	STOPOVER	11523	492	56.3	31.3	12.2	0.2	0.0	21862	23058	2	12	419	57.5	20.8	21.7	0.0	0.0	44919
41571	VARNEY	17518	204	36.3	37.3	23.5	2.9	0.0	36401	39245	22	55	171	43.9	18.7	37.4	0.0	0.0	57000
41572	VIRGIE	18656	1225	38.8	27.8	27.3	4.1	2.0	33694	36057	15	46	1035	42.6	30.7	24.9	1.4	0.4	59107
41601	ALLEN	18834	403	29.5	41.4	24.8	4.0	0.2	36148	40342	21	54	338	40.2	31.1	24.9	3.8	0.0	63448
41602	AUXIER	15828	549	47.9	24.6	22.6	3.8	1.1	26959	27859	5	28	389	33.9	39.1	21.1	5.9	0.0	69559
41603	BANNER	12490	798	51.9	29.2	17.4	1.3	0.3	23755	24519	3	18	628	34.2	36.8	25.0	3.7	0.3	62615
41604	BEAVER	11639	311	51.4	33.4	13.5	1.6	0.0	22571	24676	2	15	241	57.3	26.6	10.4	5.8	0.0	44697
41605	BETSY LAYNE	22999	445	30.6	36.0	25.2	4.0	4.3	40901	43597	36	67	350	34.0	28.9	26.0	11.1	0.0	71613
41606	BEVINSVILLE	12858	940	58.9	26.5	10.9	1.6	2.1	18676	20072	1	5	774	61.9	27.5	9.2	1.4	0.0	41154
41607	BLUE RIVER	16956	222	38.7	31.5	24.3	2.3	3.2	31704	32827	11	42	181	33.7	26.0	32.6	7.2	0.6	73667
41615	DANA	11846	26	57.7	26.9	15.4	0.0	0.0	21420	22817	2	12	21	28.6	47.6	23.8	0.0	0.0	61667
41616	DAVID	14289	42	50.0	23.8	23.8	2.4	0.0	25000	35000	3	22	35	48.6	34.3	14.3	2.9	0.0	51000
41621	DWALE	11969	90	54.4	28.9	13.3	2.2	1.1	21473	20691	2	12	55	40.0	27.3	25.5	7.3	0.0	63750
41622	EASTERN	14722	26	50.0	26.9	19.2	3.8	0.0	25000	27290	3	22	22	36.4	40.9	22.7	0.0	0.0	60000
41630	GARRETT	14149	585	55.0	23.8	16.2	4.8	0.2	21641	22421	2	12	464	52.2	26.7	18.8	2.4	0.0	47059
41631	GRETHEL	14570	833	54.6	24.7	15.5	3.5	1.7	21972	22544	2	13	631	53.9	29.8	15.1	1.3	0.0	45625
41632	GUNLOCK	12736	269	52.4	31.6	14.1	0.7	1.1	22761	24577	2	15	222	62.6	21.6	10.8	5.0	0.0	38958
41635	HAROLD	15160	1293	53.2	24.7	19.2	2.6	0.4	22060	23332	2	13	988	43.3	30.7	16.6	9.3	0.1	58684
41636	HI HAT	13423	301	63.5	18.9	14.3	2.7	0.7	18488	20633	1	4	235	53.2	23.8	18.7	4.3	0.0	45588
41640	HUEYSVILLE	14682	468	49.6	28.0	16.9	5.3	0.2	25194	25295	3	23	385	44.2	36.6	16.9	2.3	0.0	55769
41642	IVEL	16852	661	44.3	29.5	22.1	2.1	2.0	30985	33957	10	40	495	33.7	24.8	30.3	10.3	0.8	76875
41643	LACKEY	15762	26	53.8	30.8	11.5	3.8	0.0	22265	22265	2	13	20	55.0	35.0	10.0	0.0	0.0	46667
41645	LANGLEY	14013	558	48.2	28.9	19.4	3.4	0.2	26016	26817	4	25	434	43.1	37.1	18.9	0.9	0.0	56250
41647	MC DOWELL	14403	701	54.1	25.7	17.4	1.6	1.3	22735	23890	2	15	557	56.2	24.1	16.7	3.1	0.0	42813
41649	MARTIN	15658	948	44.0	34.2	18.5	2.4	0.9	30051	30975	8	37	658	41.9	34.0	21.3	2.6	0.2	61455
41650	MELVIN	13806	211	55.9	28.9	12.3	1.9	0.9	19575	20939	1	6	170	60.0	27.6	9.4	2.9	0.0	42917
41653	PRESTONSBURG	17865	5223	44.4	28.4	20.9	4.2	2.0	28734	29861	6	34	3804	34.9	29.9	25.2	9.7	0.4	68791
41655	PRINTER	11578	415	64.1	21.2	13.3	1.2	0.2	18841	20432	1	5	319	43.6	36.4	17.2	2.8	0.0	57885
41660	TEABERRY	12522	733	60.8	22.8	12.7	1.8	1.9	18167	19092	1	4	620	65.3	22.4	11.0	0.2	1.1	40306
41666	WAYLAND	13689	411	53.3	26.5	15.6	4.1	0.5	22445	23169	2	14	317	53.6	32.8	13.2	0.3	0.0	47386
41701	HAZARD	16180	6252	46.5	26.0	22.6	2.9	1.9	27967	28966	6	31	4518	40.1	28.0	25.6	5.6	0.6	65795
41712	ARY	13871	249	47.4	32.9	14.9	3.2	1.6	26620	27477	4	26	203	51.7	25.6	13.8	8.9	0.0	47813
41714	BEAR BRANCH	11128	190	59.5	25.8	14.2	0.5	0.0	19567	20000	1	6	155	68.4	27.7	3.9	0.0	0.0	35313
41719	BONNYMAN	17988	338	41.7	28.1	23.1	5.6	1.5	32557	35000	13	44	278	49.6	24.8	17.6	6.8	1.1	50476
41721	BUCKHORN	12829	328	55.8	26.2	12.2	4.6	1.2	21164	21840	2	11	270	55.6	28.9	14.8	0.7	0.0	46512
41722	BULAN	14230	950	45.9	27.1	24.1	2.8	0.1	28610	29360	6	33	793	52.7	25.5	18.2	3.0	0.6	47346
41723	BUSY	12302	659	54.0	24.4	19.7	1.5	0.3	22505	23061	2	14	542	57.9	29.9	8.9	3.3	0.0	44557
41725	CARRIE	14082	353	49.9	26.6	20.7	2.3	0.6	25097	25578	3	23	300	51.3	29.0	17.0	2.7	0.0	48667
41727	CHAVIES	18650	236	30.9	33.9	30.9	4.2	0.0	40000	42955	33	65	198	45.5	23.2	26.3	3.5	1.5	56429
41729	COMBS	20453	139	33.8	28.8	27.3	8.6	1.4	39073	41532	30	62	116	37.1	33.6	14.7	13.8	0.9	63750
41731	CORNETTSVILLE	14557	598	49.8	30.9	15.6	2.2	1.5	25071	25302	3	23	504	52.8	26.0	20.6	0.6	0.0	46500
41735	DELPHIA	12647	115	51.3	33.0	13.9	1.7	0.0	23920	23932	3	19	88	52.3	26.1	21.6	0.0	0.0	48000
41736	DICE	15395	54	46.3	33.3	14.8	3.7	1.9	27294	28168	5	30	44	54.5	25.0	13.6	6.8	0.0	45000
41740	EMMALENA	14232	508	50.0	26.6	20.5	2.4	0.6	25000	25507	3	22	430	51.4	29.1	17.0	2.6	0.0	48571
41745	GAYS CREEK	12901	153	55.6	26.1	13.1	3.9	1.3	20980	21800	2	11	126	57.9	27.8	13.5	0.8	0.0	44118
41746	HAPPY	10476	340	64.1	19.4	13.2	2.6	0.6	17052	18290	1	2	273	54.9	21.2	21.2	2.6	0.0	45500
41749	HYDEN	13720	1387	52.9	27.4	16.1	2.9	0.7	22555	22732	2	14	1109	52.5	25.3	19.7	1.8	0.6	48179
41754	KRYPTON	14437	283	43.1	36.4	17.3	0.7	2.5	30846	32492	9	39	237	46.4	32.5	16.9	4.2	0.0	57083
41759	SASSAFRAS	16504	304	42.4	30.3	22.0	4.6	0.7	30196	31921	8	37	258	46.1	26.0	26.0	1.9	0.0	56667
41760	SCUDDY	10092	202	60.4	23.8	14.4	1.5	0.0	18577	20086	1	4	158	51.3	22.2	22.8	3.8	0.0	48571
41763	SLEMP	12654	124	51.6	33.1	13.7	1.6	0.0	23580	23433	3	18	93	52.7	25.8	21.5	0.0	0.0	47500
41764	SMILAX	13943	308	46.1	34.1	17.9	1.9	0.0	26487	28587	4	25	256	62.9	26.2	9.8	1.2	0.0	36500
41766	THOUSANDSTICKS	12149	257	55.3	28.8	13.2	1.9	0.8	20889	22756	2	10	214	68.7	20.6	10.7	0.0	0.0	35263
41772	VEST	14387	40	52.5	25.0	20.0	2.5	0.0	23546	25000	2	18	34	52.9	29.4	17.6	0.0	0.0	46667
41773	VICCO	12938	486	57.8	22.2	16.7	2.9	0.4	20206	21326	1	8	394	48.2	24.4	23.4	3.8	0.3	52692
41774	VIPER	17479	1281	41.8	29.4	24.5	2.3	2.0	30545	32596	9	38	1102	37.8	36.2	20.2	5.4	0.3	61667
41775	WENDOVER	14735	18	50.0	38.9	11.1	0.0	0.0	25000	25000	3	22	15	60.0	26.7	13.3	0.0	0.0	45000
41776	WOOTON	13459	927	52.9	27.8	16.6	2.4	0.3	22937	23723	2	16	749	61.4	27.0	10.0	1.5	0.1	40284
41777	YEADDISS	15145	191	43.5	31.9	20.9	2.6	1.0	29045	31655	7	35	165	72.1	21.8	6.1	0.0	0.0	31731
41804	BLACKEY	13581	253	45.8	32.0	20.9	0.8	0.4	27557	29288	5	30	217	52.5	30.4	14.3	2.8	0.0	47800
41812	DEANE	11988	234	63.7	16.7	17.9	1.7	0.0	19564	20699	1	6	184	47.8	33.2	19.0	0.0	0.0	52500
41815	ERMINE	12361	274	46.4	33.2	18.2	0.4	1.8	26705	26198	4	27	219	53.0	29.7	15.1	2.3	0.0	43500
41817	GARNER	13679	372	51.1	25.3	18.3	3.2	2.2	24397	24324	3	20	278	42.8	28.1	19.8	9.0	0.4	59524
41819	GORDON	10559	215	60.9	29.3	9.3	0.5	0.0	21346	21777	2	11	173	64.7	19.7	15.6	0.0	0.0	30341
41821	HALLIE	14880	499	46.7	27.3	23.6	2.2	0.2	28139	29858	6	32	437	58.6	22.7	17.2	1.6	0.0	38304
41822	HINDMAN	17128	739	48.3	25.2	20.4	4.5	1.6	27074	30000	5	28	512	39.6	28.9	24.8	6.3	0.4	62727
41824	ISOM	15414	330	53.6	24.2	18.8	3.0	0.3	23212	23448	2	17	271	54.2	22.1	22.9	0.7	0.0	45208
41825	JACKHORN	12775	58	41.4	36.2	22.4	0.0	0.0	29028	27277	7	35	45	60.0	35.6	4.4	0.0	0.0	41000
41826	JEREMIAH	16644	399	39.3	34.1	23.6	2.0	1.0	30830	34605	9	39	341	39.0	29.3	27.3	4.4	0.0	72386
41828	KITE	12323	315	53.7	27.3	16.8	2.2	0.0	23313	23897	2	17	266	52.6	32.7	14.7	0.0	0.0	47308
41831	LEBURN	14633	812	49.1	25.7	19.5	3.2	2.5	25586	26567	4	24	610	45.4	26.4	20.7	7.2	0.3	55957
41832	LETCHER	18684	101	27.7	39.6	28.7	2.0	2.0	37544	40320	25	59	88	22.7	36.4	34.1	6.8	0.0	81111
41833	LINEFORK	11261	125	59.2	22.4	17.6	0.8	0.0	21352	22151	2	12	102	66.7	17.6	14.7	1.0	0.0	32308
41834	LITTCARR	15043	287	57.8	18.5	17.8	4.9	1.0	21053	22197	2	11	236	40.7	27.1	26.7	4.7	0.8	61579
41835	MC ROBERTS	12084	251	60.2	28.3	7.6	3.2	0.8	22698	22756	2	15	225	54.2	36.9	7.1	1.8	0.0	46481
	KENTUCKY	23409		28.5	27.2	32.3	7.7	4.3	44205	46476				19.8	20.7	38.3	18.6	2.6	103937
	UNITED STATES	27277		20.9	24.4	35.3	11.7	7.6	54719	56938				9.3	13.1	31.6	32.6	13.5	162279

ZIP CODE #	POST OFFICE NAME	FINANCIAL SERVICES: Auto Loan	Home Loan	Invest-ments	Retire-ment Plans	THE HOME: Home Improvements: Home Repair	Lawn & Garden	Furnishings: Comput-ers & Hard-ware-Personal	Major Appli-ances	TV, Radio, Sound Equip-ment	Furni-ture	ENTERTAINMENT: Dine out/ Carry out	Sports Equip-ment	Fees & Tickets	Toys & Games	Travel	Cable TV	PERSONAL: Apparel & Services	Auto Repairs	Health Insur-ance	Pets & Supplies
41531	HARDY	79	55	80	53	57	80	57	73	64	54	63	55	45	64	56	71	42	67	76	87
41535	HUDDY	77	55	79	53	57	78	56	72	63	53	62	54	45	63	55	69	41	66	75	85
41537	JENKINS	66	46	66	44	46	67	48	61	55	45	53	46	38	55	46	61	35	57	64	73
41539	KIMPER	75	54	65	52	54	72	56	66	62	54	61	51	45	64	52	68	41	62	70	80
41540	LICK CREEK	71	47	69	44	46	70	50	63	57	47	56	49	37	58	46	64	37	59	66	77
41543	MC ANDREWS	63	41	60	39	41	61	44	55	50	42	49	43	33	51	41	56	33	52	58	68
41544	MC CARR	74	48	71	45	48	72	52	65	59	49	58	51	39	60	48	66	38	61	69	80
41548	MOUTHCARD	71	46	68	43	46	69	49	62	57	47	56	48	37	58	46	63	37	58	66	76
41553	PHELPS	64	42	62	39	42	63	45	56	52	43	50	44	33	53	42	58	33	53	60	69
41554	PHYLLIS	53	35	51	33	35	52	37	47	43	35	42	37	28	44	35	48	28	44	50	58
41555	PINSONFORK	64	42	62	39	42	63	45	56	52	43	50	44	33	52	42	58	33	53	60	69
41557	RACCOON	75	53	68	51	54	73	55	67	62	53	60	51	44	63	52	67	40	62	70	81
41558	RANSOM	64	42	62	39	42	63	45	56	52	43	50	44	34	53	42	58	33	53	60	69
41559	REGINA	66	45	65	43	46	66	47	60	53	44	52	46	37	53	45	59	34	55	63	72
41560	ROBINSON CREEK	77	55	64	54	55	73	58	67	64	56	63	51	46	67	52	70	42	63	71	81
41562	SHELBIANA	73	48	68	46	48	71	51	64	59	49	57	49	39	60	48	65	38	60	67	78
41563	SHELBY GAP	58	38	56	36	38	57	40	51	47	38	46	40	30	47	38	52	30	48	54	63
41564	SIDNEY	64	42	62	39	42	63	45	56	52	42	50	44	33	52	42	58	33	53	60	69
41566	STEELE	59	38	57	36	38	58	41	52	47	39	46	40	31	48	38	53	31	49	55	64
41567	STONE	69	46	68	44	47	68	49	62	55	46	54	47	37	56	46	62	36	57	65	75
41568	STOPOVER	50	33	48	31	32	49	35	44	40	33	39	34	26	41	32	45	26	41	46	54
41571	VARNEY	72	47	70	44	47	71	50	63	58	48	57	49	38	59	47	65	38	60	67	78
41572	VIRGIE	85	55	82	52	55	83	59	75	68	56	67	58	44	70	55	76	44	70	79	92
41601	ALLEN	73	54	72	53	56	73	55	68	60	52	59	51	45	60	54	66	39	63	70	80
41602	AUXIER	67	45	66	43	46	67	48	60	54	45	53	46	37	55	45	60	35	56	63	73
41603	BANNER	58	39	55	37	39	57	41	51	47	40	46	40	32	48	39	52	31	48	54	63
41604	BEAVER	54	35	52	33	35	53	38	47	43	36	42	37	28	44	35	48	28	44	50	58
41605	BETSY LAYNE	97	69	95	67	71	97	72	89	80	67	78	67	57	80	69	87	52	83	93	107
41606	BEVINSVILLE	60	39	58	37	39	59	42	53	49	40	47	41	32	49	39	54	31	50	56	65
41607	BLUE RIVER	73	58	64	56	57	70	57	65	62	58	62	49	50	64	54	66	41	63	67	79
41615	DANA	54	35	52	33	35	53	38	48	44	36	43	37	28	44	35	49	28	45	50	59
41616	DAVID	66	44	64	41	43	65	46	58	53	44	52	45	35	54	43	59	35	55	61	72
41621	DWALE	51	33	49	31	33	50	36	45	41	34	40	35	27	42	33	46	27	42	48	55
41622	EASTERN	66	43	64	41	43	65	46	58	53	44	52	45	35	54	43	60	35	55	62	72
41630	GARRETT	61	40	59	37	40	60	42	53	49	40	48	42	32	50	40	55	32	50	56	66
41631	GRETHEL	64	44	63	42	44	64	46	58	52	43	51	44	35	52	44	57	34	54	61	70
41632	GUNLOCK	61	40	59	38	40	60	43	54	49	40	48	42	32	50	40	55	32	51	57	66
41635	HAROLD	65	43	64	41	44	64	46	58	52	43	51	45	35	53	43	58	34	54	61	71
41636	HI HAT	55	36	53	34	36	54	39	49	45	37	43	38	29	45	36	50	29	46	51	60
41640	HUEYSVILLE	64	42	62	39	42	63	45	56	52	43	51	44	34	53	42	58	33	53	60	70
41642	IVEL	74	51	67	49	51	72	54	65	61	51	59	50	42	62	50	67	39	61	69	80
41643	LACKEY	61	40	59	37	40	60	42	53	49	40	48	42	32	50	40	55	32	50	57	66
41645	LANGLEY	60	41	55	39	40	58	45	53	50	42	49	41	35	51	41	56	33	51	57	65
41647	MC DOWELL	65	42	63	40	42	64	45	57	52	43	51	45	34	53	42	58	34	54	60	70
41649	MARTIN	60	44	57	43	45	61	48	57	53	44	51	43	39	53	45	58	34	54	61	68
41650	MELVIN	58	38	56	36	38	57	40	51	47	38	45	40	30	47	38	52	30	48	54	63
41653	PRESTONSBURG	69	52	67	50	52	69	54	63	60	52	59	48	46	60	52	65	39	61	68	77
41655	PRINTER	50	33	49	32	34	50	36	45	41	34	40	35	27	42	34	46	27	42	48	55
41660	TEABERRY	57	37	55	35	37	56	40	50	46	38	45	39	30	47	37	51	30	47	53	62
41666	WAYLAND	60	39	58	37	39	58	42	52	48	40	47	41	31	49	39	54	31	49	55	64
41701	HAZARD	68	47	65	45	47	67	51	62	58	48	57	48	41	58	48	64	38	59	66	75
41712	ARY	64	42	62	40	42	63	45	57	52	43	51	44	34	53	42	58	34	53	60	70
41714	BEAR BRANCH	49	32	47	30	32	48	34	43	39	32	38	34	26	40	32	44	25	40	45	53
41719	BONNYMAN	77	53	77	50	54	77	55	70	63	52	61	54	43	63	53	69	41	65	73	85
41721	BUCKHORN	60	39	58	37	39	59	42	52	48	40	47	41	31	49	39	54	31	49	56	65
41722	BULAN	65	42	63	40	42	64	45	57	52	43	51	45	34	53	42	58	34	54	60	70
41723	BUSY	60	39	58	37	39	59	42	53	48	40	47	41	31	49	39	54	31	50	56	65
41725	CARRIE	63	41	61	39	41	62	44	56	51	42	50	43	33	52	41	57	33	52	59	68
41727	CHAVIES	80	57	68	55	57	77	60	70	66	58	65	54	48	69	54	73	44	66	74	85
41729	COMBS	84	60	86	58	63	85	62	79	69	58	68	59	50	68	61	76	45	72	82	94
41731	CORNETTSVILLE	65	42	63	40	42	64	45	57	52	43	51	44	34	53	42	58	34	54	60	70
41735	DELPHIA	57	37	55	35	37	56	40	50	46	38	45	39	30	47	37	51	30	47	53	62
41736	DICE	65	42	62	40	42	63	45	57	52	43	51	44	34	53	42	58	34	53	60	70
41740	EMMALENA	63	41	61	39	41	62	44	56	51	42	50	43	33	52	41	57	33	52	59	68
41745	GAYS CREEK	60	39	58	37	39	59	42	52	48	40	47	41	31	49	39	54	31	49	55	65
41746	HAPPY	51	33	49	31	33	50	35	44	41	34	40	35	26	41	33	45	26	42	47	55
41749	HYDEN	60	39	58	37	39	59	42	53	48	40	47	41	31	49	39	54	31	50	56	65
41754	KRYPTON	72	47	69	44	46	70	50	63	58	47	56	49	37	59	47	64	37	59	66	77
41759	SASSAFRAS	74	48	71	45	48	72	51	65	59	49	58	50	38	60	48	66	38	61	68	80
41760	SCUDDY	50	32	48	31	32	49	35	44	40	33	39	34	26	41	32	45	26	41	46	54
41763	SLEMP	56	36	54	34	36	55	39	49	45	37	44	38	29	46	36	50	29	46	52	60
41764	SMILAX	60	39	58	37	39	59	42	53	49	40	47	41	31	49	39	54	31	50	56	65
41766	THOUSANDSTICKS	56	37	54	35	37	55	39	50	45	37	44	39	29	46	37	51	29	47	52	61
41772	VEST	64	41	61	39	41	62	44	56	51	42	50	44	33	52	41	57	33	53	59	69
41773	VICCO	57	37	55	35	37	56	40	50	46	38	45	39	30	47	37	51	30	47	53	62
41774	VIPER	79	51	76	48	51	77	55	69	64	52	62	54	41	65	51	71	41	65	73	85
41775	WENDOVER	53	34	51	32	34	52	37	46	42	35	41	36	28	43	34	47	27	44	49	57
41776	WOOTON	59	39	57	36	39	58	41	52	48	39	47	41	31	49	39	53	31	49	55	64
41777	YEADDISS	68	44	65	41	44	66	47	59	54	45	53	46	35	55	44	61	35	56	63	73
41804	BLACKEY	62	41	60	39	41	61	44	55	50	41	49	43	33	51	41	56	32	51	58	67
41812	DEANE	53	34	51	32	34	52	37	46	42	35	41	36	28	43	34	47	27	44	49	57
41815	ERMINE	61	40	59	38	40	60	43	54	49	41	48	42	32	50	40	55	32	51	57	66
41817	GARNER	68	44	65	42	44	67	47	60	55	45	53	47	35	56	44	61	35	56	63	73
41819	GORDON	47	31	46	29	31	46	33	41	38	31	37	32	25	39	31	42	25	39	44	51
41821	HALLIE	67	44	64	41	43	65	47	59	54	44	52	46	35	55	43	60	35	55	62	72
41822	HINDMAN	71	46	68	44	46	70	50	62	57	47	56	49	37	58	46	64	37	59	66	77
41824	ISOM	60	39	58	37	39	59	42	53	48	40	47	41	31	49	39	54	31	50	56	65
41825	JACKHORN	60	39	58	37	39	59	42	53	48	40	47	41	31	49	39	54	31	50	56	65
41826	JEREMIAH	68	47	68	45	48	68	49	62	55	46	54	47	38	55	47	61	36	57	65	75
41828	KITE	59	38	57	36	38	58	41	52	47	39	46	40	31	48	38	53	31	49	55	64
41831	LEBURN	69	45	66	42	45	68	48	61	55	46	54	47	36	56	45	62	36	57	64	74
41832	LETCHER	76	54	78	52	56	77	56	71	62	52	61	53	44	61	55	68	40	65	74	84
41833	LINEFORK	53	35	51	32	34	52	37	47	43	35	42	36	28	43	34	48	28	44	49	57
41834	LITTCARR	65	43	63	40	42	64	46	57	53	43	51	45	34	54	43	59	34	54	61	71
41835	MC ROBERTS	56	36	54	34	36	55	39	49	45	37	44	38	29	46	36	50	29	46	52	60
	KENTUCKY	90	77	81	77	76	88	80	85	83	78	83	65	73	85	76	87	57	83	88	101
	UNITED STATES	100	100	100	100	100	100	100	100	100	100	100	100	100	100	100	100	100	100	100	100

POPULATION CHANGE

ZIP CODE #	POST OFFICE NAME	COUNTY FIPS CODE	POPULATION 2000	POPULATION 2009	POPULATION 2014	2000-2009 ANNUAL RATE % Rate	2000-2009 ANNUAL RATE State Centile	HOUSEHOLDS 2000	HOUSEHOLDS 2009	HOUSEHOLDS 2014	HOUSEHOLDS % Annual Rate 2000-2009	HOUSEHOLDS 2009 Average HH Size	FAMILIES 2000	FAMILIES 2009	FAMILIES % Annual Rate 2000-2009
41836	MALLIE	119	637	622	614	-0.3	22	234	240	239	0.3	2.34	176	174	-0.1
41837	MAYKING	133	735	721	707	-0.2	26	257	260	259	0.1	2.77	208	205	-0.2
41838	MILLSTONE	133	428	388	371	-1.1	1	169	159	155	-0.7	2.43	125	114	-1.0
41839	MOUSIE	119	1280	1222	1200	-0.5	13	501	501	498	0.0	2.39	359	346	-0.4
41840	NEON	133	2425	2198	2110	-1.1	1	987	933	907	-0.6	2.35	727	664	-1.0
41843	PINE TOP	119	1043	1018	1003	-0.3	22	420	431	431	0.3	2.36	319	316	-0.1
41844	PIPPA PASSES	119	658	657	655	0.0	39	231	242	243	0.5	2.19	176	179	0.2
41845	PREMIUM	133	354	349	345	-0.2	26	156	161	162	0.3	2.17	107	106	-0.1
41847	REDFOX	119	862	845	835	-0.2	26	340	351	351	0.3	2.41	256	255	0.0
41848	ROXANA	133	64	62	62	-0.3	22	28	29	29	0.4	2.14	19	19	0.0
41855	THORNTON	133	673	618	596	-0.9	2	262	251	245	-0.5	2.46	200	186	-0.8
41858	WHITESBURG	133	8789	8526	8363	-0.3	22	3504	3543	3520	0.1	2.36	2566	2500	-0.3
41859	DEMA	119	319	330	334	0.4	60	119	129	132	0.9	2.56	96	101	0.6
41861	RAVEN	119	309	304	299	-0.2	26	117	120	120	0.3	2.41	87	87	0.0
41862	TOPMOST	119	1268	1333	1353	0.5	64	455	498	513	1.0	2.68	360	383	0.7
42001	PADUCAH	145	28222	28097	28248	0.0	39	12249	12449	12596	0.2	2.22	7912	7680	-0.3
42003	PADUCAH	145	29995	29727	29820	-0.1	32	12629	12819	12961	0.2	2.25	8335	8080	-0.3
42020	ALMO	035	1972	2277	2416	1.6	91	775	911	972	1.8	2.49	566	639	1.3
42021	ARLINGTON	039	1487	1419	1374	-0.5	13	631	616	600	-0.3	2.30	437	409	-0.7
42023	BARDWELL	039	2615	2592	2540	-0.1	32	1112	1121	1104	0.1	2.30	778	752	-0.4
42024	BARLOW	007	1417	1397	1386	-0.2	26	608	608	605	0.0	2.30	410	393	-0.5
42025	BENTON	157	18939	19947	20485	0.6	69	7731	8315	8595	0.8	2.36	5606	5813	0.4
42027	BOAZ	083	2072	2120	2145	0.2	48	829	868	884	0.5	2.41	620	624	0.1
42028	BURNA	139	652	625	612	-0.5	13	263	255	251	-0.3	2.45	185	172	-0.8
42029	CALVERT CITY	157	5366	5348	5367	0.0	39	2168	2219	2247	0.3	2.32	1540	1514	-0.2
42031	CLINTON	105	3950	3711	3571	-0.7	5	1644	1584	1535	-0.4	2.25	1132	1045	-0.9
42032	COLUMBUS	105	274	277	274	0.1	45	115	118	117	0.3	2.35	80	79	-0.1
42035	CUNNINGHAM	039	1267	1214	1181	-0.5	13	462	452	443	-0.2	2.59	355	337	-0.6
42036	DEXTER	035	1247	1320	1363	0.6	69	469	506	526	0.8	2.61	352	368	0.5
42038	EDDYVILLE	143	5303	5430	5405	0.3	54	1770	1853	1851	0.5	2.22	1243	1250	0.1
42039	FANCY FARM	083	1589	1652	1673	0.4	60	622	658	669	0.6	2.50	473	484	0.2
42040	FARMINGTON	083	1134	1162	1179	0.3	54	458	478	487	0.5	2.40	343	346	0.1
42041	FULTON	075	5428	4974	4734	-0.9	2	2319	2163	2068	-0.8	2.27	1548	1386	-1.2
42044	GILBERTSVILLE	157	3168	3412	3534	0.8	77	1378	1518	1584	1.1	2.22	1003	1064	0.6
42045	GRAND RIVERS	139	2402	2455	2453	0.2	48	1014	1060	1066	0.5	2.31	738	742	0.1
42047	HAMPTON	139	339	322	315	-0.6	9	140	135	132	-0.4	2.39	97	90	-0.8
42048	HARDIN	157	2441	2599	2681	0.7	74	1040	1133	1178	0.9	2.29	767	806	0.5
42049	HAZEL	035	1763	1881	1955	0.7	74	727	793	829	0.9	2.37	511	537	0.5
42050	HICKMAN	075	3580	3134	2937	-1.4	0	1428	1272	1196	-1.2	2.31	961	820	-1.7
42051	HICKORY	083	2748	2858	2904	0.4	60	1054	1116	1139	0.6	2.52	790	807	0.2
42053	KEVIL	007	4518	4758	4868	0.6	69	1806	1937	1991	0.8	2.45	1388	1433	0.3
42054	KIRKSEY	035	1222	1325	1375	0.9	80	418	469	493	1.3	2.61	320	348	0.9
42055	KUTTAWA	143	2556	2630	2656	0.3	54	1040	1094	1110	0.5	2.25	735	744	0.1
42056	LA CENTER	007	2289	2319	2327	0.1	45	911	941	950	0.4	2.37	642	638	-0.1
42058	LEDBETTER	139	2321	2266	2230	-0.3	22	920	919	911	0.0	2.46	680	656	-0.4
42064	MARION	055	8761	8465	8353	-0.4	18	3580	3513	3483	-0.2	2.37	2522	2379	-0.6
42066	MAYFIELD	083	23091	23203	23289	0.1	45	9336	9466	9520	0.1	2.38	6431	6252	-0.3
42069	MELBER	083	969	992	1004	0.3	54	370	386	393	0.5	2.49	276	278	0.1
42071	MURRAY	035	26630	27908	28663	0.5	64	10893	11752	12196	0.8	2.13	6425	6537	0.2
42076	NEW CONCORD	035	1037	1219	1300	1.8	93	460	553	594	2.0	2.20	329	381	1.6
42078	SALEM	139	1988	1929	1897	-0.3	22	820	807	797	-0.2	2.29	566	534	-0.6
42079	SEDALIA	083	1241	1259	1273	0.2	48	475	489	496	0.3	2.57	359	357	-0.1
42081	SMITHLAND	139	2030	2055	2044	0.1	45	805	827	825	0.3	2.43	596	592	-0.1
42082	SYMSONIA	083	1930	1951	1965	0.1	45	818	845	857	0.4	2.31	598	595	-0.1
42083	TILINE	139	270	271	270	0.0	39	109	111	111	0.2	2.44	84	82	-0.3
42085	WATER VALLEY	083	923	888	872	-0.4	18	387	380	375	-0.2	2.34	291	276	-0.6
42086	WEST PADUCAH	145	3889	3892	3922	0.0	39	1543	1583	1608	0.3	2.45	1173	1155	-0.2
42087	WICKLIFFE	007	2552	2526	2517	-0.1	32	1031	1039	1040	0.1	2.38	735	712	-0.3
42088	WINGO	083	2530	2628	2672	0.4	60	983	1038	1058	0.6	2.53	765	782	0.2
42101	BOWLING GREEN	227	47841	51423	53792	0.8	77	17482	19270	20336	1.1	2.41	10896	11451	0.5
42103	BOWLING GREEN	227	15939	17992	19280	1.3	88	6579	7641	8243	1.6	2.32	4414	4870	1.1
42104	BOWLING GREEN	227	20749	28422	32333	3.5	98	8344	11766	13484	3.8	2.38	5765	7698	3.2
42120	ADOLPHUS	003	2208	2435	2543	1.1	85	820	914	959	1.2	2.66	618	666	0.8
42122	ALVATON	227	3162	3809	4164	2.0	95	1177	1467	1613	2.4	2.60	963	1163	2.1
42123	AUSTIN	009	704	743	770	0.6	69	284	305	318	0.8	2.44	212	219	0.4
42124	BEAUMONT	169	6	6	6	0.0	39	2	2	2	0.0	3.00	2	2	0.0
42127	CAVE CITY	009	5262	5892	6198	1.2	86	2149	2467	2615	1.5	2.39	1533	1686	1.0
42129	EDMONTON	169	6488	6710	6824	0.4	60	2612	2769	2837	0.6	2.38	1852	1887	0.2
42130	EIGHTY EIGHT	009	110	122	128	1.1	85	49	56	59	1.5	2.18	39	43	1.1
42131	ETOILE	009	94	99	102	0.6	69	41	44	46	0.8	2.25	31	32	0.3
42133	FOUNTAIN RUN	171	1400	1436	1456	0.3	54	597	620	630	0.4	2.32	429	429	0.0
42134	FRANKLIN	213	15841	16795	17322	0.6	69	6224	6721	6971	0.8	2.46	4484	4662	0.4
42140	GAMALIEL	171	1262	1310	1312	0.4	60	505	533	535	0.6	2.46	365	370	0.1
42141	GLASGOW	009	27539	29728	30984	0.8	77	11144	12322	12940	1.1	2.36	7864	8371	0.7
42151	HESTAND	171	305	297	293	-0.3	22	111	109	107	-0.2	2.54	78	73	-0.7
42153	HOLLAND	003	372	384	398	0.3	54	146	155	161	0.6	2.48	110	112	0.2
42154	KNOB LICK	169	782	806	818	0.3	54	314	330	337	0.5	2.44	232	235	0.1
42156	LUCAS	009	316	337	350	0.7	74	125	136	142	0.9	2.48	94	99	0.6
42157	MOUNT HERMON	171	485	484	481	0.0	39	188	192	193	0.2	2.52	142	140	-0.2
42159	OAKLAND	227	1494	1588	1662	0.7	74	577	625	658	0.9	2.54	449	468	0.4
42160	PARK CITY	009	2383	2686	2848	1.3	88	947	1084	1157	1.5	2.48	698	768	1.0
42163	ROCKY HILL	061	188	194	198	0.3	54	81	86	88	0.6	2.26	62	63	0.2
42164	SCOTTSVILLE	003	14548	15502	16045	0.7	74	5678	6148	6388	0.9	2.49	4179	4365	0.5
42166	SUMMER SHADE	169	2274	2438	2515	0.8	77	921	1011	1050	1.0	2.41	678	718	0.6
42167	TOMPKINSVILLE	171	8806	8638	8528	-0.2	26	3550	3536	3505	0.0	2.41	2522	2415	-0.5
42170	WOODBURN	213	1408	1559	1652	1.1	85	512	584	624	1.4	2.64	399	439	1.0
42171	SMITHS GROVE	227	5589	6129	6448	1.0	83	2104	2362	2502	1.3	2.59	1627	1765	0.9
42202	ADAIRVILLE	141	2352	2416	2448	0.3	54	949	1006	1030	0.6	2.40	681	695	0.2
42204	ALLENSVILLE	219	598	583	579	-0.3	22	224	222	221	-0.1	2.60	169	162	-0.5
42206	AUBURN	141	4866	5486	5784	1.3	88	1785	2056	2181	1.5	2.63	1368	1524	1.2
42207	BEE SPRING	061	1347	1304	1291	-0.4	18	556	556	556	0.0	2.35	415	401	-0.4
42210	BROWNSVILLE	061	4134	4280	4361	0.4	60	1649	1760	1812	0.7	2.38	1201	1235	0.3
42211	CADIZ	221	11753	12617	12956	0.8	77	4887	5358	5539	1.0	2.33	3510	3706	0.6
42214	CENTER	169	806	805	803	0.0	39	294	297	297	0.1	2.71	223	218	-0.2
42215	CERULEAN	047	1293	1323	1349	0.2	48	498	525	540	0.6	2.50	396	405	0.2
	KENTUCKY					0.7					1.0	2.41			0.6
	UNITED STATES					1.0					1.1	2.59			0.9

POPULATION COMPOSITION

ZIP CODE #	POST OFFICE NAME	RACE (%) White 2000	White 2009	Black 2000	Black 2009	Asian/Pacific 2000	Asian/Pacific 2009	% Hispanic Origin 2000	% Hispanic Origin 2009	2009 AGE DISTRIBUTION (%) 0-4	5-9	10-14	15-19	20-24	25-44	45-64	65-84	85+	18+	MEDIAN AGE 2009	% 2009 Males	% 2009 Females
41836	MALLIE	98.4	98.4	1.1	1.1	0.2	0.2	0.6	0.5	5.6	5.8	5.8	11.4	10.5	24.0	28.0	7.7	1.3	77.7	34.4	48.4	51.6
41837	MAYKING	99.9	99.9	0.0	0.0	0.0	0.0	0.4	0.7	7.5	6.9	5.7	7.5	7.8	25.9	30.2	7.5	1.0	75.2	36.6	49.7	50.3
41838	MILLSTONE	99.1	99.0	0.2	0.3	0.0	0.0	0.7	1.0	6.4	6.4	6.4	6.2	5.9	25.3	28.9	12.9	1.5	76.8	39.8	51.8	48.2
41839	MOUSIE	98.6	98.5	0.2	0.2	0.3	0.3	0.5	0.6	5.6	6.8	5.6	6.8	5.0	27.4	30.2	11.2	1.4	77.7	40.7	50.0	50.0
41840	NEON	97.7	97.5	1.4	1.6	0.1	0.1	0.7	1.1	5.6	6.6	6.4	6.2	5.3	24.8	31.0	12.3	1.8	77.7	40.7	49.5	50.5
41843	PINE TOP	99.4	99.4	0.2	0.2	0.1	0.1	0.5	0.5	6.0	6.3	6.4	8.8	6.6	26.1	30.7	7.5	1.6	75.7	37.3	48.6	51.4
41844	PIPPA PASSES	98.9	98.9	0.3	0.3	0.3	0.3	0.6	0.6	5.9	6.1	5.5	14.2	14.3	22.4	23.4	7.2	1.1	77.6	29.0	48.4	51.6
41845	PREMIUM	99.7	99.7	0.0	0.0	0.0	0.0	0.3	0.6	4.3	5.2	5.2	7.7	6.3	24.4	33.2	11.5	2.3	81.1	42.9	48.4	51.6
41847	REDFOX	92.8	92.7	6.4	6.5	0.0	0.0	0.9	0.9	5.2	5.6	5.7	6.3	6.0	24.1	32.7	12.4	2.0	79.6	42.9	49.7	50.3
41848	ROXANA	100.0	100.0	0.0	0.0	0.0	0.0	0.0	0.0	3.2	4.8	4.8	8.1	6.5	22.6	33.9	14.5	1.6	80.6	45.0	51.6	48.4
41855	THORNTON	99.3	99.0	0.1	0.2	0.4	0.6	0.3	0.5	6.0	6.1	6.1	7.0	6.1	25.1	31.7	10.4	1.5	77.7	39.9	49.0	51.0
41858	WHITESBURG	98.8	98.3	0.2	0.2	0.6	1.0	0.5	0.8	5.6	5.7	5.9	6.5	6.0	25.4	31.2	12.0	1.8	78.9	41.2	48.6	51.4
41859	DEMA	99.7	99.7	0.0	0.0	0.0	0.0	0.3	0.3	6.7	7.6	6.7	7.9	7.0	27.0	26.7	9.4	1.2	73.9	35.7	50.3	49.7
41861	RAVEN	98.1	98.0	0.3	0.3	0.6	0.7	0.3	0.3	5.9	6.3	6.6	6.9	4.6	25.7	29.9	12.8	1.3	76.0	41.1	49.0	51.0
41862	TOPMOST	99.2	99.2	0.0	0.0	0.1	0.1	0.3	0.3	6.0	6.5	6.2	6.2	6.0	26.5	30.4	10.7	1.5	77.4	39.7	51.4	48.6
42001	PADUCAH	83.3	82.2	14.3	14.7	0.7	1.0	1.2	1.7	5.6	5.8	6.3	6.5	5.0	23.7	29.6	14.5	3.1	78.3	42.9	47.3	52.7
42003	PADUCAH	87.6	86.2	9.9	10.7	0.5	0.7	1.1	1.6	6.0	5.9	6.0	6.2	5.4	25.0	28.8	14.0	2.7	78.4	41.6	47.6	52.4
42020	ALMO	97.3	96.4	0.9	1.0	0.4	0.6	1.9	3.1	6.5	6.5	6.8	6.6	7.4	26.0	26.9	11.6	1.6	76.2	38.0	49.1	50.9
42021	ARLINGTON	97.4	97.0	2.1	2.3	0.1	0.1	0.9	1.3	6.7	7.0	6.8	5.7	4.7	24.6	27.1	15.0	2.4	76.0	40.9	49.0	51.0
42023	BARDWELL	97.5	97.0	1.0	1.1	0.1	0.2	1.1	1.8	5.8	5.8	6.0	5.9	5.3	25.3	27.8	15.3	2.7	78.9	42.1	48.4	51.6
42024	BARLOW	94.5	93.8	3.6	4.0	0.0	0.0	0.6	1.1	6.3	6.8	7.2	6.3	4.1	25.3	29.0	13.0	2.1	75.9	41.0	51.2	48.8
42025	BENTON	98.5	98.1	0.2	0.2	0.2	0.3	0.8	1.3	5.1	5.3	5.7	6.0	4.7	25.1	29.7	15.9	2.6	80.3	43.6	49.1	50.9
42027	BOAZ	97.3	96.6	1.1	1.3	0.0	0.0	1.0	1.7	6.3	6.5	6.7	5.9	5.0	27.8	29.7	10.9	1.3	77.2	39.8	50.0	50.0
42028	BURNA	98.8	98.7	0.2	0.2	0.0	0.0	0.3	0.3	5.1	5.4	5.9	6.2	4.8	23.7	29.9	16.5	2.4	79.5	44.2	49.9	50.1
42029	CALVERT CITY	98.7	98.3	0.0	0.0	0.2	0.3	0.8	1.3	5.2	5.4	5.8	5.9	4.8	23.7	29.5	15.9	3.7	79.8	44.3	48.2	51.8
42031	CLINTON	87.1	86.1	11.0	11.6	0.1	0.1	1.1	1.8	5.6	5.6	5.8	5.9	5.0	23.6	28.9	15.7	3.7	79.1	43.8	47.2	52.8
42032	COLUMBUS	84.2	82.3	12.8	13.7	0.0	0.0	2.2	4.0	7.2	7.6	7.2	6.5	4.3	25.3	27.1	13.4	1.4	73.6	39.8	51.3	48.7
42035	CUNNINGHAM	97.9	97.4	0.2	0.2	0.0	0.0	0.6	0.9	5.7	5.8	6.1	6.5	5.7	26.6	27.6	12.4	3.5	78.2	40.7	47.0	53.0
42036	DEXTER	98.4	97.7	0.2	0.3	0.2	0.4	1.3	2.2	6.1	6.1	6.5	6.9	5.9	27.0	28.3	11.8	1.4	77.1	39.5	49.2	50.8
42038	EDDYVILLE	89.7	88.6	8.9	9.5	0.2	0.3	0.9	1.5	3.4	3.9	3.8	3.7	6.6	32.9	28.8	15.2	1.6	86.6	42.4	61.4	38.6
42039	FANCY FARM	96.7	96.2	2.0	2.0	0.0	0.1	0.8	1.4	7.6	7.6	7.4	6.6	5.8	26.2	26.4	10.8	1.6	73.2	36.8	49.5	50.5
42040	FARMINGTON	97.7	97.1	1.1	1.2	0.2	0.3	1.0	1.6	5.9	6.1	6.5	6.4	4.8	26.3	29.3	12.8	1.9	77.6	41.1	50.4	49.6
42041	FULTON	81.9	80.8	16.1	16.4	0.4	0.7	0.9	1.4	6.4	6.4	6.3	6.1	5.4	22.5	27.8	15.6	3.4	77.1	42.4	46.5	53.5
42044	GILBERTSVILLE	98.4	97.9	0.0	0.0	0.1	0.1	0.7	1.2	4.0	4.4	4.9	5.3	3.7	20.5	34.5	20.2	2.4	83.4	49.2	50.1	49.9
42045	GRAND RIVERS	98.0	98.0	0.0	0.0	0.0	0.0	0.5	0.5	5.0	5.9	6.1	5.3	4.0	25.5	31.9	14.9	1.4	79.9	43.6	50.3	49.7
42047	HAMPTON	98.2	98.1	0.3	0.3	0.0	0.0	0.6	0.6	5.0	5.3	5.6	6.2	4.7	24.2	30.4	16.5	2.2	80.4	44.4	50.3	49.7
42048	HARDIN	99.0	98.6	0.0	0.0	0.1	0.2	0.8	1.3	5.4	5.7	5.9	5.6	4.3	22.6	32.1	16.3	1.9	79.5	45.2	50.1	49.9
42049	HAZEL	97.7	97.1	1.6	1.8	0.1	0.3	0.6	1.0	5.7	6.0	6.1	6.1	4.6	24.7	31.5	13.2	2.1	78.3	42.6	48.6	51.4
42050	HICKMAN	72.8	71.0	26.3	27.9	0.0	0.0	0.4	0.6	6.2	6.2	6.1	7.0	7.7	25.5	26.0	13.3	2.0	77.2	38.2	49.7	50.3
42051	HICKORY	97.1	95.9	0.8	0.9	0.1	0.2	1.4	2.5	6.5	6.6	6.9	6.8	5.3	25.9	27.8	12.4	1.7	75.9	39.4	49.8	50.2
42053	KEVIL	97.6	97.1	1.2	1.3	0.2	0.3	0.7	1.1	6.4	6.7	6.9	6.1	4.8	26.6	29.2	11.8	1.5	76.2	40.2	50.3	49.7
42054	KIRKSEY	96.6	95.9	2.4	2.6	0.2	0.2	2.1	3.5	5.3	5.4	5.7	6.1	5.7	28.5	29.8	11.8	1.5	80.2	41.0	53.1	46.9
42055	KUTTAWA	96.4	95.9	2.1	2.2	0.2	0.3	0.4	0.6	3.9	4.6	5.1	5.1	3.7	20.0	33.9	18.9	4.8	83.1	49.5	48.2	51.8
42056	LA CENTER	92.8	92.0	5.6	5.9	0.2	0.3	0.6	1.0	5.8	6.0	6.1	5.8	4.9	23.2	27.9	16.1	4.1	78.4	43.6	47.3	52.7
42058	LEDBETTER	99.0	99.0	0.3	0.3	0.1	0.1	0.8	0.9	6.0	5.8	6.1	7.2	6.8	27.2	31.4	8.4	1.1	77.4	38.6	50.6	49.4
42064	MARION	98.2	97.8	0.7	0.7	0.1	0.1	0.5	0.7	5.7	5.7	6.0	6.1	5.1	23.9	28.9	15.9	2.6	78.9	43.0	48.6	51.4
42066	MAYFIELD	89.8	88.0	6.5	6.9	0.3	0.4	3.2	5.2	6.7	6.4	6.3	6.2	5.7	24.8	26.5	14.3	3.2	76.8	40.2	48.7	51.3
42069	MELBER	96.6	95.4	1.4	1.6	0.1	0.2	2.0	3.3	6.3	6.6	7.0	7.3	4.9	24.4	29.5	12.0	2.1	75.4	40.9	49.6	50.4
42071	MURRAY	92.3	90.6	4.3	4.5	1.7	2.6	1.4	2.2	4.6	4.4	4.5	9.0	15.9	22.0	23.3	13.6	2.8	83.8	34.8	47.9	52.1
42076	NEW CONCORD	98.5	97.9	0.2	0.2	0.3	0.5	0.5	0.8	4.3	5.4	5.3	5.1	2.5	21.3	36.4	17.1	2.5	81.5	48.9	48.5	51.5
42078	SALEM	98.7	98.7	0.2	0.2	0.1	0.1	0.6	0.6	4.9	5.1	5.5	5.8	4.4	22.7	30.0	18.1	3.7	80.8	46.2	47.7	52.3
42079	SEDALIA	98.0	97.1	0.7	0.8	0.2	0.2	1.3	2.2	5.8	6.8	7.7	7.0	5.1	25.5	27.7	12.6	1.8	75.5	39.4	50.0	50.0
42081	SMITHLAND	98.4	98.3	0.1	0.1	0.0	0.0	1.3	1.3	5.1	5.6	6.2	6.5	4.2	25.3	30.6	14.3	2.3	79.3	43.1	48.4	51.6
42082	SYMSONIA	99.0	98.7	0.2	0.2	0.1	0.1	0.4	0.8	5.1	5.3	5.8	6.1	4.5	23.7	31.8	15.5	2.2	79.9	44.6	50.0	50.0
42083	TILINE	97.4	97.4	0.0	0.0	0.0	0.0	0.7	0.7	4.8	7.0	7.7	6.6	3.7	26.9	31.7	10.0	1.5	76.4	40.1	49.4	50.6
42085	WATER VALLEY	97.1	96.3	1.6	1.8	0.1	0.2	0.9	1.5	5.9	6.4	6.4	5.5	4.3	24.1	30.2	15.2	2.0	77.9	43.2	49.9	50.1
42086	WEST PADUCAH	96.0	95.0	2.4	2.9	0.4	0.5	0.5	0.8	5.9	6.2	6.4	5.9	4.8	25.9	31.2	12.3	1.5	77.9	41.6	49.5	50.5
42087	WICKLIFFE	96.2	95.4	1.3	1.3	0.4	0.6	0.8	1.3	4.9	5.4	5.7	5.7	4.8	25.4	32.1	14.4	1.7	80.6	43.7	51.5	48.5
42088	WINGO	97.2	96.3	1.6	1.8	0.1	0.2	1.0	1.8	6.8	7.0	7.3	6.8	5.3	24.6	28.5	11.9	1.8	74.3	39.5	49.7	50.3
42101	BOWLING GREEN	82.0	79.0	12.2	12.9	1.5	2.2	3.8	6.2	6.3	5.9	5.6	10.4	13.5	27.2	21.5	8.3	1.3	78.6	30.1	49.5	50.5
42103	BOWLING GREEN	92.9	90.8	3.8	4.2	1.3	2.1	1.9	3.5	5.8	6.0	6.3	6.2	5.4	26.7	29.4	12.1	2.0	78.1	40.2	49.8	50.2
42104	BOWLING GREEN	91.7	89.5	4.9	5.5	1.7	2.8	1.3	2.3	7.2	6.8	6.6	5.9	6.2	30.0	25.1	10.6	1.7	75.8	36.0	48.2	51.8
42120	ADOLPHUS	97.8	96.9	0.1	0.2	0.1	0.1	1.2	2.1	7.3	7.0	7.1	7.2	6.1	28.1	25.4	10.7	1.2	74.3	36.2	49.8	50.2
42122	ALVATON	96.4	95.2	2.0	2.3	0.4	0.7	1.0	1.8	5.8	6.9	7.1	7.5	4.4	28.8	31.0	7.7	0.8	75.3	39.5	50.1	49.9
42123	AUSTIN	98.7	98.3	0.1	0.1	0.0	0.1	0.6	0.9	5.7	5.8	6.3	7.0	5.0	25.2	29.6	13.9	1.6	77.9	41.8	50.6	49.4
42124	BEAUMONT	100.0	100.0	0.0	0.0	0.0	0.0	0.0	0.0	0.0	0.0	0.0	0.0	0.0	50.0	50.0	0.0	0.0	100.0	42.5	33.3	66.7
42127	CAVE CITY	93.6	92.6	5.1	5.6	0.5	0.8	0.7	1.2	5.7	6.2	6.5	6.2	4.8	24.6	30.3	13.8	1.8	77.6	42.2	49.6	50.4
42129	EDMONTON	97.7	97.3	1.3	1.3	0.1	0.1	0.4	0.7	6.4	6.5	6.7	6.5	5.3	25.9	26.8	13.8	2.2	76.4	40.0	48.2	51.8
42130	EIGHTY EIGHT	99.1	99.2	0.9	0.8	0.0	0.0	0.0	0.8	6.6	6.6	6.6	5.7	4.1	28.7	27.9	12.3	1.6	76.2	39.5	52.5	47.5
42131	ETOILE	98.9	99.0	0.0	0.0	0.0	0.0	1.1	1.0	6.1	6.1	7.1	8.1	4.0	25.3	28.3	14.1	1.0	74.7	40.9	50.5	49.5
42133	FOUNTAIN RUN	97.0	96.0	1.0	1.0	0.1	0.1	2.1	3.3	5.9	5.8	6.4	6.8	5.1	25.9	27.5	14.4	2.1	77.6	40.6	49.6	50.4
42134	FRANKLIN	87.6	86.4	10.4	10.9	0.6	0.9	0.9	1.5	7.3	7.2	7.3	6.5	5.3	26.6	26.4	11.5	1.9	74.1	37.9	48.7	51.3
42140	GAMALIEL	97.1	96.0	0.4	0.4	0.0	0.0	1.9	3.0	6.4	6.4	6.9	6.9	5.1	26.0	27.4	13.2	1.7	75.9	39.8	50.1	49.9
42141	GLASGOW	93.7	92.8	4.5	4.7	0.5	0.7	1.0	1.7	6.4	6.4	6.5	6.2	5.3	25.6	27.5	13.5	2.5	76.9	40.3	48.2	51.8
42151	HESTAND	93.1	91.6	3.6	3.7	0.0	0.0	2.6	3.7	6.7	6.7	7.1	6.7	4.4	24.2	23.9	14.8	5.4	75.1	39.9	47.1	52.9
42153	HOLLAND	97.6	96.9	0.3	0.5	0.3	0.5	0.8	1.3	6.0	6.0	6.3	6.3	5.7	25.5	28.9	13.8	1.6	77.9	40.0	51.8	48.2
42154	KNOB LICK	95.3	94.8	3.8	4.1	0.1	0.1	0.4	0.7	6.9	7.1	7.3	6.8	5.1	26.6	26.7	11.9	1.6	74.3	38.4	50.1	49.9
42156	LUCAS	99.1	98.8	0.0	0.0	0.0	0.0	0.3	0.6	5.6	5.6	6.2	7.1	5.0	25.5	29.4	13.9	1.5	77.7	41.6	51.3	48.7
42157	MOUNT HERMON	98.8	98.6	1.0	1.0	0.0	0.2	0.2	0.4	6.8	7.0	7.4	6.0	3.1	26.7	27.7	13.8	1.4	74.8	40.3	51.4	48.6
42159	OAKLAND	88.5	86.2	10.1	11.6	0.1	0.1	1.1	2.1	6.4	6.7	7.1	7.0	4.4	27.0	28.4	11.6	1.4	75.2	39.7	49.9	50.1
42160	PARK CITY	96.3	95.7	2.7	3.0	0.1	0.2	0.5	1.0	6.8	7.0	7.0	6.3	5.2	26.3	27.8	12.1	1.5	75.3	38.7	50.3	49.7
42163	ROCKY HILL	98.4	98.5	0.5	0.5	0.0	0.0	0.5	0.5	6.7	6.7	6.7	5.7	4.1	25.3	29.9	13.4	1.5	76.3	40.5	50.0	50.0
42164	SCOTTSVILLE	97.6	97.2	1.3	1.3	0.1	0.2	0.7	1.2	6.7	6.7	6.8	6.6	5.2	26.6	27.0	12.5	1.8	75.7	38.9	49.4	50.6
42166	SUMMER SHADE	98.2	97.9	1.0	1.1	0.0	0.0	0.9	1.5	5.5	5.7	6.3	6.5	4.6	26.0	30.3	13.5	1.6	78.4	41.9	50.0	50.0
42167	TOMPKINSVILLE	95.2	94.4	3.3	3.5	0.0	0.0	1.3	2.1	6.2	6.4	6.4	6.1	4.7	25.8	27.8	14.2	2.3	77.1	40.7	48.9	51.1
42170	WOODBURN	94.1	92.9	4.5	5.1	0.5	0.8	0.8	1.3	6.5	7.0	7.2	6.1	4.2	25.4	29.3	12.3	1.9	75.1	40.6	50.7	49.3
42171	SMITHS GROVE	94.7	93.6	3.8	4.4	0.1	0.1	0.8	1.5	6.7	6.9	7.1	6.7	4.7	27.4	28.1	11.2	1.2	75.1	38.4	49.2	50.8
42202	ADAIRVILLE	87.9	86.2	10.2	11.2	0.0	0.0	2.4	4.0	6.3	6.5	6.7	6.7	5.0	26.9	27.5	12.6	1.7	76.4	38.9	49.8	50.2
42204	ALLENSVILLE	81.1	79.1	16.4	17.5	0.2	0.2	1.8	3.1	8.7	8.2	8.6	7.5	5.0	24.9	24.9	10.5	1.7	69.6	35.3	49.7	50.3
42206	AUBURN	95.7	95.2	3.1	3.4	0.1	0.2	0.5	0.9	7.5	7.4	7.7	7.2	5.2	27.0	25.8	10.2	2.0	72.5	36.9	48.5	51.5
42207	BEE SPRING	99.3	99.2	0.0	0.0	0.1	0.2	0.7	1.2	5.7	5.8	6.1	5.6	3.9	25.7	29.1	16.4	1.8	79.0	43.1	51.3	48.7
42210	BROWNSVILLE	98.6	98.5	0.1	0.1	0.0	0.1	0.5	0.9	6.4	6.5	6.6	6.1	5.0	25.7	26.9	14.1	2.7	76.7	40.0	48.0	52.0
42211	CADIZ	88.9	87.9	9.2	9.7	0.3	0.4	0.9	1.5	5.7	5.8	6.2	6.0	4.5	23.5	29.7	16.7	2.0	78.5	43.8	49.4	50.6
42214	CENTER	97.1	97.0	1.6	1.7	0.0	0.0	0.9	1.4	7.0	7.2	7.5	6.3	4.6	26.3	27.6	12.2	1.4	74.4	38.4	49.9	50.1
42215	CERULEAN	87.8	86.8	10.9	11.5	0.3	0.5	0.7	1.1	6.4	6.7	7.0	6.8	4.8	25.1	29.3	12.5	1.3	76.3	40.7	49.2	50.8
	KENTUCKY	90.1	88.9	7.3	7.5	0.8	1.2	1.5	2.4	6.5	6.5	6.5	6.8	6.5	27.0	27.1	11.3	1.8	76.6	37.9	49.1	50.9
	UNITED STATES	75.1	72.0	12.3	12.7	3.8	4.6	12.5	15.7	6.8	6.7	6.6	7.1	6.9	27.0	26.0	10.9	1.9	75.7	36.9	49.2	50.8

INCOME

#	POST OFFICE NAME	2009 Per Capita Income	2009 HH Income Base	2009 Household Income Distribution (%): Less than $25,000	$25,000 to $49,999	$50,000 to $99,999	$100,000 to $149,999	$150,000 or More	Median Household Income: 2009	2014	2009 National Centile	2009 State Centile	2009 Home Value Base	2009 Home Value Distribution (%): Less than $50,000	$50,000 to $89,999	$90,000 to $174,999	$175,000 to $399,999	$400,000 or More	2009 Median Home Value
41836	MALLIE	14206	240	52.5	27.5	15.4	3.3	1.3	23211	22983	2	16	180	47.2	26.7	21.7	4.4	0.0	52500
41837	MAYKING	15805	260	45.4	20.8	27.3	3.5	3.1	28878	28842	7	35	213	52.1	28.6	13.1	5.2	0.9	48125
41838	MILLSTONE	13207	159	59.1	22.0	17.6	0.6	0.6	21967	22544	2	13	126	57.9	27.0	11.9	1.6	1.6	44444
41839	MOUSIE	12798	501	54.7	24.6	18.2	2.6	0.0	21964	23406	2	13	393	54.2	28.2	13.5	4.1	0.0	43125
41840	NEON	14110	933	52.5	25.4	20.4	1.1	0.6	24062	24181	3	19	767	59.1	31.2	8.6	0.7	0.5	42908
41843	PINE TOP	12136	431	57.1	26.0	14.2	2.8	0.0	20643	21587	2	9	341	46.6	31.4	19.9	1.8	0.3	52212
41844	PIPPA PASSES	16313	242	50.0	26.9	16.5	3.7	2.9	25000	25852	3	22	178	46.1	28.7	19.1	5.6	0.6	53182
41845	PREMIUM	13871	161	50.9	29.8	18.0	1.2	0.0	24404	25881	3	20	135	65.2	25.2	9.6	0.0	0.0	40682
41847	REDFOX	13246	351	49.9	32.8	14.0	3.4	0.0	25146	24928	3	23	284	60.2	15.5	21.1	3.2	0.0	41944
41848	ROXANA	14041	29	44.8	34.5	20.7	0.0	0.0	28596	32361	6	33	25	68.0	28.0	4.0	0.0	0.0	43571
41855	THORNTON	12545	251	61.4	25.1	10.0	1.6	2.0	22187	22504	2	13	208	54.3	25.5	17.3	2.4	0.5	47500
41858	WHITESBURG	16674	3543	48.5	24.7	21.6	3.4	1.7	25849	25857	4	24	2748	45.1	25.8	24.0	4.3	0.9	56904
41859	DEMA	12035	129	55.8	27.9	13.2	3.1	0.0	22493	23290	2	14	110	51.8	34.5	13.6	0.0	0.0	48000
41861	RAVEN	12832	120	55.8	24.2	17.5	2.5	0.0	22742	23543	2	15	99	44.4	31.3	17.2	7.1	0.0	56875
41862	TOPMOST	12579	498	49.2	26.1	23.9	0.8	0.0	25438	25326	4	24	414	55.1	27.3	17.6	0.0	0.0	45435
42001	PADUCAH	28304	12449	27.0	25.0	34.1	8.0	6.0	47881	47565	56	83	8399	15.9	25.0	36.5	19.9	2.8	106504
42003	PADUCAH	20993	12819	34.6	28.2	29.2	5.6	2.3	37563	40489	25	59	8560	30.3	25.3	31.7	12.3	0.5	80105
42020	ALMO	19741	911	27.6	34.7	31.9	3.8	2.0	40716	42701	35	66	751	27.8	29.3	34.4	7.7	0.8	77881
42021	ARLINGTON	19318	616	34.4	34.6	25.6	4.1	1.3	35849	37123	20	53	497	41.9	33.0	20.5	4.0	0.6	56532
42023	BARDWELL	19194	1121	31.6	40.9	21.9	3.9	1.8	35371	36501	19	52	922	37.3	36.1	22.0	4.1	0.4	62169
42024	BARLOW	18533	608	30.3	38.2	26.6	3.6	1.3	35561	38848	19	52	485	39.0	28.0	25.6	6.4	1.0	60897
42025	BENTON	21812	8315	27.1	29.6	34.5	6.5	2.3	44025	43982	45	75	6856	18.6	24.8	38.4	16.7	1.5	98404
42027	BOAZ	22236	868	26.3	28.1	36.5	6.0	3.1	46742	47724	53	82	747	24.1	27.4	33.7	14.1	0.7	86034
42028	BURNA	17959	255	32.2	35.3	27.8	3.5	1.2	37042	39324	24	57	216	41.2	26.9	27.3	3.2	1.4	61875
42029	CALVERT CITY	24433	2219	22.8	30.9	34.7	8.2	3.3	47033	47083	54	83	1761	24.9	29.0	33.1	12.9	0.0	85516
42031	CLINTON	20181	1584	36.9	29.7	27.0	4.0	2.5	36732	40523	23	56	1262	42.0	33.4	19.5	4.3	0.9	60808
42032	COLUMBUS	18595	118	33.9	37.3	22.0	6.8	0.0	35487	38816	19	52	104	59.6	19.2	17.3	1.0	2.9	40000
42035	CUNNINGHAM	18651	452	21.7	39.8	30.3	6.2	2.0	42332	43422	40	70	404	27.2	31.2	34.2	7.4	0.0	76786
42036	DEXTER	18286	506	33.2	32.6	28.7	3.0	2.6	38495	41212	28	61	435	34.0	31.7	21.1	10.1	3.0	66806
42038	EDDYVILLE	18687	1853	31.8	31.0	30.2	5.7	1.4	38398	40710	28	61	1449	20.0	25.3	35.7	16.9	2.1	95437
42039	FANCY FARM	18633	658	31.0	31.0	32.5	3.8	1.7	41109	43543	36	67	540	29.1	25.9	36.7	7.8	0.6	82895
42040	FARMINGTON	20882	478	26.2	30.5	34.9	6.5	1.9	43263	45374	43	73	406	24.6	27.8	38.2	8.4	1.0	87143
42041	FULTON	21140	2163	35.9	28.3	28.1	5.1	2.6	35870	39219	20	54	1499	39.4	31.8	23.9	4.5	0.3	59382
42044	GILBERTSVILLE	26382	1518	25.0	27.0	35.4	8.0	4.7	48110	47316	57	83	1291	12.9	17.5	38.9	29.2	1.5	120228
42045	GRAND RIVERS	20910	1060	25.5	35.6	32.5	4.9	1.5	39390	41339	31	63	883	34.5	26.7	29.3	7.7	1.7	73269
42047	HAMPTON	17974	135	36.3	34.8	24.4	3.0	1.5	35196	37487	18	51	115	42.6	26.1	27.8	1.7	1.7	59444
42048	HARDIN	17442	1133	39.6	30.6	25.3	3.4	1.0	30619	32846	9	38	935	25.5	23.3	33.5	16.9	0.9	92018
42049	HAZEL	20117	793	27.2	37.1	29.8	4.0	1.9	38424	42517	28	61	654	24.3	26.5	32.1	15.3	1.8	88913
42050	HICKMAN	15430	1272	45.1	31.6	20.4	2.3	0.6	28634	30769	6	33	835	47.1	36.4	13.7	2.4	0.5	52207
42051	HICKORY	19935	1116	30.4	31.2	29.4	7.0	2.1	41677	43871	38	69	960	27.1	30.9	32.3	9.5	0.2	80128
42053	KEVIL	21672	1937	23.1	30.9	37.9	5.7	2.3	45500	45172	50	79	1638	24.2	32.8	31.0	9.8	2.2	81739
42054	KIRKSEY	20789	469	18.3	37.7	35.4	5.5	3.0	45223	45952	49	79	418	26.8	18.9	37.8	14.8	1.7	97826
42055	KUTTAWA	22327	1094	28.1	31.6	31.1	6.7	2.6	42725	43662	42	72	957	25.8	28.4	30.1	14.6	1.0	83955
42056	LA CENTER	19731	941	31.7	29.2	31.0	6.9	1.2	39829	41045	32	64	750	36.5	25.9	30.3	7.3	0.0	71458
42058	LEDBETTER	20722	919	23.2	33.3	36.2	5.0	2.3	44378	44880	46	76	791	16.8	43.9	33.5	5.3	0.5	82028
42064	MARION	18227	3513	35.6	31.3	27.6	4.0	1.6	35831	36689	20	53	2808	35.0	36.1	23.5	5.2	0.2	62910
42066	MAYFIELD	19682	9466	36.3	28.6	27.5	5.2	2.4	36468	40747	22	55	6908	26.0	30.3	35.3	7.8	0.5	82521
42069	MELBER	20608	386	27.5	34.2	26.7	10.4	1.3	43062	45045	43	73	338	19.8	32.0	30.2	17.2	0.9	88667
42071	MURRAY	22489	11752	31.9	30.9	27.7	6.1	3.4	39100	41819	30	62	7453	16.7	20.7	44.7	16.1	1.8	105788
42076	NEW CONCORD	19576	553	31.6	38.2	23.7	4.7	1.8	33968	40000	15	47	480	41.7	20.8	22.5	12.9	2.1	57407
42078	SALEM	19619	807	32.3	33.5	28.7	3.8	1.6	36880	39138	23	56	684	42.8	30.4	22.8	3.7	0.3	58033
42079	SEDALIA	19574	489	30.5	29.2	32.7	4.5	3.1	41356	43132	37	68	426	34.5	26.1	29.1	7.0	3.3	75135
42081	SMITHLAND	20317	827	31.7	31.9	29.9	4.8	1.7	37557	40953	25	59	707	32.8	35.9	21.8	6.5	3.0	75149
42082	SYMSONIA	22013	845	31.4	31.2	27.2	7.2	3.0	41772	43880	39	70	719	25.2	27.3	35.3	12.2	0.0	86569
42083	TILINE	19160	111	29.7	27.9	33.3	9.0	0.0	37360	40574	25	58	101	24.8	32.7	25.7	13.9	3.0	80625
42085	WATER VALLEY	18666	380	35.0	31.6	27.9	4.5	1.1	40140	42169	33	65	317	33.8	32.2	28.7	5.4	0.0	65270
42086	WEST PADUCAH	20795	1583	23.8	31.9	36.6	6.8	0.9	45627	45458	50	79	1363	28.4	25.5	28.9	15.5	1.7	82132
42087	WICKLIFFE	22451	1039	31.6	28.2	32.1	5.0	3.1	40129	41338	33	65	866	35.1	29.2	24.2	9.4	2.1	67143
42088	WINGO	21670	1038	27.9	27.8	35.5	5.8	2.9	45586	46794	50	79	887	29.5	33.3	31.3	5.2	0.7	77911
42101	BOWLING GREEN	18755	19270	34.0	30.3	29.8	3.6	2.4	35855	40954	20	53	10887	23.3	20.0	45.4	9.9	1.4	97223
42103	BOWLING GREEN	31143	7641	19.0	24.8	37.8	10.6	7.9	56888	55720	74	92	5532	10.4	4.4	35.8	42.8	6.5	173035
42104	BOWLING GREEN	29618	11766	18.9	24.7	36.9	12.6	6.9	56121	55939	73	91	7701	3.9	4.9	45.9	41.7	3.6	165474
42120	ADOLPHUS	15819	914	29.6	36.7	31.4	1.8	0.5	38308	40148	28	61	755	36.3	27.3	29.8	6.2	0.4	67603
42122	ALVATON	26253	1467	14.0	27.5	43.8	10.8	3.8	58071	56476	75	93	1334	12.4	9.4	50.5	24.2	3.5	133137
42123	AUSTIN	22249	305	28.2	34.8	28.9	4.6	3.6	41360	43769	37	68	253	17.8	24.5	46.2	10.3	1.2	95909
42124	BEAUMONT	0	0	0.0	0.0	0.0	0.0	0.0	0	0	0	0	0	0.0	0.0	0.0	0.0	0.0	0
42127	CAVE CITY	19617	2467	38.3	28.5	26.2	3.9	3.1	34440	38169	16	49	1792	23.9	29.7	36.2	8.3	2.0	85963
42129	EDMONTON	16134	2769	42.3	31.6	22.6	2.0	1.5	29315	30233	7	36	2154	40.9	29.9	22.3	6.7	0.2	61484
42130	EIGHTY EIGHT	20830	56	25.0	33.9	39.3	1.8	0.0	42337	44521	40	71	49	20.4	34.7	30.6	14.3	0.0	85833
42131	ETOILE	23448	44	36.4	34.1	25.0	2.3	2.3	36518	41800	22	55	37	21.6	21.6	45.9	10.8	0.0	95000
42133	FOUNTAIN RUN	18843	620	37.6	33.4	24.2	2.6	2.3	33900	38085	15	47	499	33.7	27.5	27.9	10.4	0.6	70517
42134	FRANKLIN	21020	6721	24.9	30.4	37.0	5.7	2.0	45806	46914	51	80	4854	13.5	21.3	47.6	15.9	1.7	104918
42140	GAMALIEL	14794	533	41.8	36.0	19.7	1.7	0.8	28559	30073	6	33	430	32.8	42.6	19.8	4.9	0.0	66786
42141	GLASGOW	21423	12322	30.9	29.4	32.2	4.8	2.6	41424	43757	37	69	8750	15.1	26.4	42.9	13.8	1.9	100492
42151	HESTAND	13346	109	45.0	28.4	23.9	2.8	0.0	26861	27845	5	27	72	29.2	27.8	31.9	6.9	4.2	81667
42153	HOLLAND	16810	155	36.1	35.5	23.9	3.9	0.6	34016	36649	16	48	130	29.2	26.9	27.7	14.6	1.5	82000
42154	KNOB LICK	17894	330	36.4	29.1	28.5	3.6	2.4	33607	37630	15	46	259	27.8	28.2	37.8	5.8	0.4	79444
42156	LUCAS	21158	136	27.9	35.3	28.7	5.9	2.2	41114	42724	36	67	112	14.3	29.5	46.4	8.9	0.9	95000
42157	MOUNT HERMON	13976	192	40.1	35.4	21.4	2.1	1.0	35000	38022	18	50	156	34.6	25.0	25.6	12.2	2.6	68333
42159	OAKLAND	24115	625	23.2	25.9	40.5	6.1	4.3	51053	52309	64	88	540	9.3	22.6	48.1	16.1	3.9	108947
42160	PARK CITY	17324	1084	34.6	32.4	27.7	4.4	0.9	34417	37552	16	48	850	21.8	31.8	33.8	11.4	1.5	86216
42163	ROCKY HILL	19629	86	33.7	32.6	26.7	4.7	2.3	33294	33297	14	45	73	21.9	24.7	42.5	11.0	0.0	94167
42164	SCOTTSVILLE	18336	6148	32.8	30.6	31.4	3.1	2.0	39124	41008	30	63	4813	24.6	28.2	33.7	12.5	1.0	85163
42166	SUMMER SHADE	16645	1011	37.6	33.2	25.2	3.4	0.6	30658	32890	9	38	866	27.7	33.8	31.4	6.6	0.5	75190
42167	TOMPKINSVILLE	15946	3536	46.0	29.8	20.3	1.9	1.9	27466	28061	5	30	2634	38.9	23.5	30.6	6.2	0.9	70061
42170	WOODBURN	22751	584	18.8	29.8	40.9	6.7	3.8	51002	51497	64	87	500	17.2	11.0	43.8	25.8	2.2	124013
42171	SMITHS GROVE	18981	2362	27.8	32.4	33.5	4.4	1.8	41349	43915	37	68	2029	17.7	24.4	42.7	13.6	1.6	98867
42202	ADAIRVILLE	20750	1006	26.3	32.3	35.7	3.7	2.0	43782	45261	45	74	752	26.7	26.5	32.8	9.8	4.1	84286
42204	ALLENSVILLE	19363	222	28.4	30.2	36.0	3.2	2.3	45000	44404	48	78	172	29.7	23.3	36.6	6.4	4.1	85455
42206	AUBURN	18139	2056	29.6	28.3	37.3	3.6	1.2	43966	45112	45	75	1658	22.6	27.2	37.9	11.9	0.4	90182
42207	BEE SPRING	16302	556	41.4	32.2	24.1	1.8	0.5	32623	35332	13	44	494	30.4	33.8	29.4	6.5	0.0	75246
42210	BROWNSVILLE	17967	1760	46.3	28.5	21.1	2.2	2.0	27030	28199	5	28	1402	29.3	34.7	27.6	7.7	0.6	72000
42211	CADIZ	20949	5358	30.7	31.1	31.5	4.6	2.1	41021	43031	36	67	4369	17.9	24.9	37.7	17.3	2.2	99121
42214	CENTER	17059	297	46.8	24.6	21.2	2.7	4.7	27063	28746	5	28	240	37.9	27.9	31.7	2.5	0.0	69333
42215	CERULEAN	19908	525	27.0	27.2	40.0	4.4	1.3	46367	47277	52	82	432	24.8	21.3	35.9	15.5	2.5	100000
	KENTUCKY	23409		28.5	27.2	32.3	7.7	4.3	44205	46476				19.8	20.7	38.3	18.6	2.6	103937
	UNITED STATES	27277		20.9	24.4	35.3	11.7	7.6	54719	56938				9.3	13.1	31.6	32.6	13.5	162279

#	POST OFFICE NAME	FINANCIAL SERVICES: Auto Loan	Home Loan	Investments	Retirement Plans	THE HOME: Home Improvements: Home Repair	Lawn & Garden	Furnishings: Computers & Hardware-Personal	Major Appliances	TV, Radio, Sound Equipment	Furniture	ENTERTAINMENT: Dine out/Carry out	Sports Equipment	Fees & Tickets	Toys & Games	Travel	Cable TV	PERSONAL: Apparel & Services	Auto Repairs	Health Insurance	Pets & Supplies
41836	MALLIE	63	41	61	39	41	62	44	55	50	42	49	43	33	51	41	56	33	52	58	68
41837	MAYKING	82	53	79	50	53	80	57	72	66	54	64	56	43	67	53	73	42	67	76	88
41838	MILLSTONE	60	39	58	37	39	59	42	53	48	40	47	41	31	49	39	54	31	50	56	65
41839	MOUSIE	57	37	55	35	37	56	40	50	46	38	45	39	30	47	37	51	30	47	53	62
41840	NEON	62	40	60	38	40	61	43	54	50	41	49	42	32	51	40	55	32	51	57	67
41843	PINE TOP	53	35	51	33	35	52	37	47	43	35	42	37	28	44	35	48	28	44	50	58
41844	PIPPA PASSES	71	46	68	43	46	69	49	62	57	47	55	48	37	58	46	63	37	58	66	76
41845	PREMIUM	56	36	54	34	36	55	39	49	45	37	44	38	29	46	36	50	29	46	52	60
41847	REDFOX	59	39	57	36	39	58	41	52	48	39	47	41	31	49	39	53	31	49	55	64
41848	ROXANA	56	36	54	34	36	55	39	49	45	37	44	38	29	46	36	50	29	46	52	60
41855	THORNTON	57	37	55	35	37	56	40	50	46	38	45	39	30	47	37	52	30	48	53	62
41858	WHITESBURG	73	48	71	46	48	72	51	65	59	48	57	50	39	60	49	66	38	61	69	79
41859	DEMA	57	37	55	35	37	56	40	50	46	38	45	39	30	47	37	51	30	47	53	62
41861	RAVEN	58	38	56	35	37	57	40	51	46	38	45	40	30	47	38	52	30	48	54	62
41862	TOPMOST	63	41	60	38	41	61	44	55	50	41	49	43	33	51	41	56	33	52	58	68
42001	PADUCAH	90	88	89	89	89	96	88	92	91	87	90	68	87	90	88	94	62	91	97	108
42003	PADUCAH	73	62	64	63	62	73	67	70	71	64	69	53	61	70	63	74	48	70	76	83
42020	ALMO	84	63	69	63	63	80	70	75	74	65	72	59	57	76	62	79	49	73	79	91
42021	ARLINGTON	78	56	70	55	57	77	60	71	66	56	64	54	48	67	56	73	43	67	76	85
42023	BARDWELL	78	56	69	54	57	77	59	71	66	56	64	54	48	67	55	72	43	66	75	85
42024	BARLOW	76	54	78	53	56	77	56	71	62	52	61	53	45	62	55	68	40	65	74	84
42025	BENTON	83	70	81	70	72	87	71	82	75	66	74	61	63	75	70	80	50	77	86	96
42027	BOAZ	88	78	72	75	76	83	75	80	78	77	78	59	69	82	70	81	53	78	81	96
42028	BURNA	78	56	81	54	58	80	58	73	64	54	63	55	46	64	57	70	42	67	76	87
42029	CALVERT CITY	92	77	88	78	79	96	80	91	84	74	82	68	70	84	78	90	56	86	96	106
42031	CLINTON	83	58	79	56	59	82	61	75	68	57	67	57	48	69	58	75	44	70	79	90
42032	COLUMBUS	79	57	65	55	56	75	59	68	65	57	64	53	47	68	53	71	43	65	72	83
42035	CUNNINGHAM	88	63	75	61	63	84	66	77	73	64	71	59	53	76	60	80	48	73	81	94
42036	DEXTER	86	62	71	60	61	82	64	75	71	63	70	57	52	74	58	78	47	71	79	91
42038	EDDYVILLE	78	59	90	58	64	82	62	77	66	57	65	57	52	64	64	72	43	72	80	90
42039	FANCY FARM	84	60	70	59	60	80	63	73	70	61	68	56	50	73	57	76	46	69	77	89
42040	FARMINGTON	86	67	84	67	69	89	68	82	73	62	72	62	57	73	67	79	48	76	85	97
42041	FULTON	79	62	69	61	62	78	67	73	72	62	70	56	57	73	62	77	48	71	79	88
42044	GILBERTSVILLE	98	79	118	78	85	103	79	99	83	74	82	73	69	80	84	89	55	91	99	115
42045	GRAND RIVERS	84	64	82	62	66	84	64	78	70	62	69	58	54	71	63	76	46	73	81	93
42047	HAMPTON	77	55	79	53	57	78	56	72	62	52	61	54	45	62	56	69	41	66	74	85
42048	HARDIN	70	51	78	50	54	72	53	67	58	49	57	50	43	57	54	63	38	62	69	79
42049	HAZEL	84	62	85	60	64	86	63	79	69	58	68	60	51	69	62	76	45	73	82	94
42050	HICKMAN	59	43	51	43	43	58	48	54	54	46	53	40	41	54	44	59	36	53	60	65
42051	HICKORY	90	66	80	64	66	88	68	81	75	65	73	61	55	77	64	81	49	76	84	97
42053	KEVIL	91	72	84	70	73	90	72	84	78	70	77	63	62	79	69	83	51	79	87	100
42054	KIRKSEY	97	74	97	73	76	100	75	92	81	69	80	69	62	81	74	89	53	85	96	109
42055	KUTTAWA	91	67	100	65	71	93	68	87	75	64	73	65	56	73	70	81	48	80	89	103
42056	LA CENTER	80	60	80	60	62	83	63	78	70	57	68	58	52	69	62	76	45	72	83	91
42058	LEDBETTER	91	65	94	63	68	93	67	85	74	62	73	64	54	74	66	82	48	78	89	101
42064	MARION	76	56	71	54	57	76	58	70	64	54	63	53	47	65	56	70	42	66	74	84
42066	MAYFIELD	77	60	68	60	61	76	66	72	70	61	69	54	56	71	61	76	47	70	78	86
42069	MELBER	91	68	91	66	70	92	69	85	76	65	74	64	57	76	68	82	49	79	88	102
42071	MURRAY	79	60	68	62	61	73	76	72	76	67	75	58	63	76	66	79	52	75	76	88
42076	NEW CONCORD	66	60	77	55	65	73	57	69	61	61	60	46	55	57	62	65	40	65	75	79
42078	SALEM	82	59	84	57	61	83	60	76	67	56	65	57	48	66	59	73	43	70	79	91
42079	SEDALIA	90	64	92	62	67	91	66	84	73	62	72	63	53	73	65	81	48	77	88	100
42081	SMITHLAND	89	64	91	62	66	90	65	83	73	61	71	62	53	72	65	80	47	76	86	99
42082	SYMSONIA	88	67	88	66	69	90	68	84	74	63	72	63	56	74	67	80	48	77	87	99
42083	TILINE	84	60	86	58	62	85	61	78	68	57	67	59	49	68	61	75	44	72	81	93
42085	WATER VALLEY	78	56	79	54	58	79	57	73	64	54	63	55	46	63	56	70	41	67	76	86
42086	WEST PADUCAH	86	71	79	69	71	84	69	80	74	69	73	59	61	75	67	78	49	75	81	95
42087	WICKLIFFE	96	69	98	67	72	98	71	90	79	66	77	67	57	78	70	86	51	82	94	107
42088	WINGO	99	71	84	69	71	95	74	86	82	71	80	66	59	85	68	89	54	82	91	105
42101	BOWLING GREEN	71	60	55	61	58	64	69	65	70	65	70	51	62	71	61	71	48	68	68	79
42103	BOWLING GREEN	104	105	99	108	104	105	104	103	103	104	103	80	105	104	104	103	72	103	103	122
42104	BOWLING GREEN	103	104	95	105	102	99	102	100	100	104	101	79	103	103	101	99	71	100	98	117
42120	ADOLPHUS	76	55	63	53	54	72	57	66	63	55	62	51	46	66	52	69	42	63	70	80
42122	ALVATON	97	107	92	109	103	104	96	100	94	97	95	78	101	97	100	94	66	96	98	117
42123	AUSTIN	98	70	85	68	70	94	73	86	80	69	79	67	58	83	67	88	53	81	91	105
42124	BEAUMONT	0	0	0	0	0	0	0	0	0	0	0	0	0	0	0	0	0	0	0	0
42127	CAVE CITY	82	59	81	58	61	83	62	77	69	57	67	58	50	69	61	75	45	71	81	91
42129	EDMONTON	69	49	59	48	49	66	52	61	58	50	56	47	42	59	48	63	38	58	65	74
42130	EIGHTY EIGHT	82	59	68	57	58	78	61	71	68	60	67	55	49	71	56	74	45	67	75	87
42131	ETOILE	95	67	88	66	68	94	71	85	77	65	76	68	55	79	67	84	50	80	90	104
42133	FOUNTAIN RUN	79	57	65	55	56	75	59	68	65	57	64	53	47	68	53	71	43	65	72	83
42134	FRANKLIN	82	72	71	72	71	83	73	78	76	69	75	60	67	78	70	80	51	76	83	93
42140	GAMALIEL	66	47	54	46	47	62	49	57	54	48	53	44	39	57	45	59	36	54	60	69
42141	GLASGOW	80	68	72	68	68	81	71	76	75	67	74	58	64	75	68	80	50	75	82	91
42151	HESTAND	62	44	51	43	44	59	46	54	51	45	50	41	37	53	42	56	34	51	56	65
42153	HOLLAND	75	54	62	52	54	71	56	65	62	55	61	50	45	65	51	68	41	62	69	79
42154	KNOB LICK	79	56	72	55	56	78	59	71	64	54	63	55	46	66	56	70	42	66	74	86
42156	LUCAS	94	68	83	66	68	91	70	84	78	68	76	64	56	80	65	85	51	79	88	101
42157	MOUNT HERMON	63	43	69	43	45	66	48	60	50	39	50	49	35	49	48	55	32	56	63	73
42159	OAKLAND	96	88	83	89	88	97	85	93	88	83	87	69	80	91	83	92	60	88	95	110
42160	PARK CITY	76	55	70	53	55	75	57	69	64	54	62	52	46	65	54	70	42	65	73	83
42163	ROCKY HILL	79	57	79	55	58	80	58	73	65	55	64	55	47	65	57	71	42	67	76	87
42164	SCOTTSVILLE	81	59	71	58	60	79	62	73	68	59	67	56	50	70	58	74	45	69	77	88
42166	SUMMER SHADE	72	52	68	50	53	71	53	65	59	50	58	50	43	60	51	65	39	61	68	79
42167	TOMPKINSVILLE	69	48	63	47	49	68	51	62	57	48	56	48	40	58	48	63	37	58	66	75
42170	WOODBURN	94	86	83	89	87	98	84	93	87	79	85	70	79	89	83	91	58	87	95	109
42171	SMITHS GROVE	84	66	72	66	67	83	67	77	72	64	71	59	58	75	64	78	48	72	81	92
42202	ADAIRVILLE	88	66	72	64	66	83	68	77	74	67	73	59	56	77	62	80	49	73	81	93
42204	ALLENSVILLE	90	64	88	63	66	91	69	83	73	61	72	66	53	74	66	80	48	78	87	101
42206	AUBURN	86	63	71	61	63	82	65	75	71	63	70	57	53	74	59	78	47	71	79	91
42207	BEE SPRING	68	49	68	48	50	69	50	63	56	47	55	48	40	56	49	61	36	58	66	75
42210	BROWNSVILLE	79	54	71	52	54	76	57	69	64	55	63	53	44	66	52	71	42	65	73	84
42211	CADIZ	84	64	85	63	66	85	66	80	71	62	70	59	55	71	65	77	47	74	82	94
42214	CENTER	83	59	75	58	60	81	62	74	68	59	67	58	49	70	58	75	45	70	78	90
42215	CERULEAN	87	66	80	65	67	87	67	80	73	63	72	61	56	75	64	80	48	75	84	96
	KENTUCKY	90	77	81	77	76	88	80	85	83	78	83	65	73	85	76	87	57	83	88	101
	UNITED STATES	100	100	100	100	100	100	100	100	100	100	100	100	100	100	100	100	100	100	100	100

ZIP CODE	POST OFFICE NAME	COUNTY FIPS CODE	POPULATION 2000	POPULATION 2009	POPULATION 2014	2000-2009 ANNUAL RATE % Rate	2000-2009 ANNUAL RATE State Centile	HOUSEHOLDS 2000	HOUSEHOLDS 2009	HOUSEHOLDS 2014	HOUSEHOLDS % Annual Rate 2000-2009	HOUSEHOLDS 2009 Average HH Size	FAMILIES 2000	FAMILIES 2009	FAMILIES % Annual Rate 2000-2009
42217	CROFTON	047	3760	3852	3986	0.3	54	1449	1541	1611	0.7	2.47	1109	1141	0.3
42220	ELKTON	219	6199	6482	6618	0.5	64	2414	2558	2620	0.6	2.50	1810	1853	0.3
42232	GRACEY	047	653	747	780	1.5	90	249	293	308	1.8	2.55	197	225	1.4
42234	GUTHRIE	219	2457	2423	2418	-0.2	26	891	894	897	0.0	2.69	618	595	-0.4
42236	HERNDON	047	814	839	871	0.3	54	304	318	332	0.5	2.64	230	232	0.1
42240	HOPKINSVILLE	047	40352	42955	44152	0.7	74	15955	17572	18237	1.0	2.37	11056	11710	0.6
42252	JETSON	031	243	250	251	0.3	54	88	93	94	0.6	2.69	68	69	0.2
42254	LA FAYETTE	047	279	285	293	0.2	48	112	117	121	0.5	2.44	84	85	0.1
42256	LEWISBURG	141	4782	4841	4864	0.1	45	1967	2037	2062	0.4	2.38	1410	1405	0.0
42259	MAMMOTH CAVE	061	1010	1093	1130	0.9	80	386	431	451	1.2	2.43	288	311	0.8
42261	MORGANTOWN	031	10253	10530	10436	0.3	54	3979	4185	4177	0.5	2.46	2897	2940	0.2
42262	OAK GROVE	047	7827	9810	10623	2.5	96	2808	3495	3786	2.4	2.80	2026	2434	2.0
42265	OLMSTEAD	141	1116	1082	1074	-0.3	22	423	422	422	0.0	2.54	316	304	-0.4
42266	PEMBROKE	047	2290	2497	2640	0.9	80	807	892	944	1.1	2.73	604	640	0.6
42273	ROCHESTER	031	557	522	506	-0.7	5	224	213	208	-0.5	2.45	166	153	-0.9
42274	ROCKFIELD	227	1902	2370	2605	2.4	96	697	892	988	2.7	2.64	535	657	2.2
42275	ROUNDHILL	031	929	960	970	0.4	60	355	377	385	0.7	2.55	265	272	0.3
42276	RUSSELLVILLE	141	14782	14600	14582	-0.1	32	5911	5978	6014	0.1	2.40	4197	4076	-0.3
42280	SHARON GROVE	219	662	718	740	0.9	80	259	286	297	1.1	2.51	196	209	0.7
42285	SWEEDEN	061	192	187	186	-0.3	22	87	88	88	0.1	2.13	67	65	-0.3
42286	TRENTON	219	1535	1531	1539	0.0	39	585	588	592	0.1	2.60	429	416	-0.3
42287	WELCHS CREEK	031	469	473	472	0.1	45	192	199	200	0.4	2.38	148	149	0.1
42301	OWENSBORO	059	40420	42257	43256	0.5	64	16316	17705	18296	0.9	2.32	10845	11232	0.4
42303	OWENSBORO	059	35929	37987	39071	0.6	69	14332	15718	16325	1.0	2.33	9613	10124	0.6
42320	BEAVER DAM	183	7596	8058	8248	0.6	69	2975	3230	3330	0.9	2.46	2193	2298	0.5
42321	BEECH CREEK	177	613	577	564	-0.7	5	243	237	234	-0.3	2.43	187	178	-0.5
42323	BEECHMONT	177	855	797	775	-0.8	3	352	340	334	-0.4	2.34	271	253	-0.7
42324	BELTON	177	1274	1327	1330	0.4	60	496	537	544	0.9	2.47	377	394	0.5
42325	BREMEN	177	2303	2423	2439	0.6	69	915	990	1006	0.9	2.45	707	741	0.5
42326	BROWDER	177	285	301	302	0.6	69	122	134	136	1.0	2.25	87	91	0.5
42327	CALHOUN	149	4271	4277	4234	0.0	39	1678	1719	1712	0.3	2.43	1244	1231	-0.1
42328	CENTERTOWN	183	1603	1624	1630	0.1	45	607	633	641	0.5	2.56	480	486	0.1
42330	CENTRAL CITY	177	9812	9777	9687	0.0	39	3587	3656	3653	0.2	2.41	2566	2515	-0.2
42333	CROMWELL	183	959	1025	1054	0.7	74	361	397	412	1.0	2.56	277	295	0.7
42337	DRAKESBORO	177	2078	2060	2041	-0.1	32	819	843	845	0.3	2.44	606	602	-0.1
42338	DUNDEE	183	196	210	216	0.7	74	75	82	85	1.0	2.56	56	59	0.6
42339	DUNMOR	177	817	852	854	0.5	64	319	345	350	0.9	2.47	243	255	0.5
42343	FORDSVILLE	183	2225	2339	2384	0.5	64	882	956	983	0.9	2.38	616	640	0.4
42344	GRAHAM	177	987	937	917	-0.6	9	390	384	380	-0.2	2.44	293	278	-0.6
42345	GREENVILLE	177	11213	10788	10585	-0.4	18	4475	4441	4397	-0.1	2.30	3263	3120	-0.5
42347	HARTFORD	183	5474	5464	5449	0.0	39	2171	2216	2227	0.2	2.39	1548	1520	-0.2
42348	HAWESVILLE	091	4444	4725	4851	0.7	74	1665	1830	1901	1.0	2.57	1275	1358	0.7
42349	HORSE BRANCH	183	1665	1735	1766	0.4	60	626	672	690	0.8	2.58	468	485	0.4
42350	ISLAND	149	1386	1305	1267	-0.6	9	584	567	555	-0.3	2.30	418	391	-0.7
42351	LEWISPORT	091	4022	3964	3947	-0.2	26	1542	1575	1585	0.2	2.48	1171	1156	-0.1
42352	LIVERMORE	149	2214	2247	2225	0.2	48	887	921	921	0.4	2.44	624	623	0.0
42354	MC HENRY	183	342	386	405	1.3	88	129	148	156	1.5	2.61	102	114	1.2
42355	MACEO	059	2031	1994	1987	-0.2	26	756	775	782	0.3	2.57	598	592	-0.1
42361	OLATON	183	555	579	590	0.5	64	215	230	236	0.7	2.52	159	164	0.3
42366	PHILPOT	059	5979	6223	6387	0.4	60	2049	2240	2325	1.0	2.75	1706	1815	0.7
42367	POWDERLY	177	935	936	929	0.0	39	378	392	393	0.4	2.39	257	255	-0.1
42368	REYNOLDS STATION	091	1036	1133	1176	1.0	83	379	428	449	1.3	2.65	290	317	1.0
42369	ROCKPORT	183	386	409	421	0.6	69	152	165	171	0.9	2.48	120	127	0.6
42371	RUMSEY	149	634	619	609	-0.3	22	262	263	260	0.0	2.35	180	173	-0.4
42372	SACRAMENTO	149	2008	2047	2035	0.2	48	804	843	846	0.5	2.43	593	600	0.1
42376	UTICA	059	5425	5475	5518	0.1	45	1982	2081	2120	0.5	2.63	1592	1621	0.2
42378	WHITESVILLE	183	2899	3147	3272	0.9	80	1040	1180	1241	1.4	2.66	819	899	1.0
42404	CLAY	233	2744	2683	2639	-0.2	26	1109	1111	1100	0.0	2.41	807	779	-0.4
42406	CORYDON	101	3146	3137	3121	0.0	39	1166	1195	1201	0.3	2.63	921	911	-0.1
42408	DAWSON SPRINGS	107	7018	6936	6914	-0.1	32	2772	2801	2813	0.1	2.41	2019	1963	-0.3
42409	DIXON	233	2418	2478	2493	0.3	54	951	997	1008	0.5	2.41	715	724	0.1
42410	EARLINGTON	107	1948	1835	1795	-0.6	9	814	791	781	-0.3	2.32	546	504	-0.9
42411	FREDONIA	033	1463	1432	1431	-0.2	26	600	604	608	0.1	2.36	459	448	-0.3
42413	HANSON	107	2355	2579	2667	1.0	83	868	981	1024	1.3	2.62	709	779	1.0
42420	HENDERSON	101	36941	38013	38522	0.3	54	15191	16042	16389	0.6	2.32	10248	10367	0.1
42431	MADISONVILLE	107	27522	27189	27074	-0.1	32	11416	11575	11620	0.1	2.30	7811	7576	-0.3
42436	MANITOU	107	1122	1255	1305	1.2	86	425	489	513	1.5	2.56	356	399	1.2
42437	MORGANFIELD	225	8416	8140	7953	-0.4	18	2796	2769	2718	-0.1	2.47	1966	1870	-0.5
42441	NEBO	107	1585	1588	1590	0.0	39	619	639	646	0.3	2.48	478	476	0.0
42442	NORTONVILLE	107	3233	3359	3397	0.4	60	1262	1349	1377	0.7	2.49	951	979	0.3
42445	PRINCETON	033	11368	11216	11177	-0.1	32	4717	4750	4765	0.1	2.30	3262	3151	-0.4
42450	PROVIDENCE	233	4448	4101	3972	-0.9	2	1809	1699	1655	-0.7	2.37	1291	1166	-1.1
42451	REED	101	1013	1063	1084	0.5	64	376	405	417	0.8	2.62	303	315	0.4
42452	ROBARDS	101	2274	2437	2512	0.8	77	827	914	953	1.1	2.67	659	704	0.7
42453	SAINT CHARLES	107	503	506	507	0.1	45	199	206	209	0.4	2.46	160	161	0.1
42455	SEBREE	233	3430	3681	3751	0.8	77	1281	1394	1428	0.9	2.56	926	969	0.5
42456	SLAUGHTERS	233	1614	1739	1782	0.8	77	625	689	710	1.1	2.51	492	526	0.7
42458	SPOTTSVILLE	101	944	1003	1032	0.7	74	354	387	402	1.0	2.59	289	306	0.6
42459	STURGIS	225	4902	4677	4538	-0.5	13	1993	1944	1901	-0.3	2.39	1436	1348	-0.7
42461	UNIONTOWN	225	1646	1603	1576	-0.3	22	676	682	679	0.1	2.35	487	472	-0.3
42462	WAVERLY	225	1621	1650	1645	0.2	48	592	624	628	0.6	2.58	470	479	0.2
42464	WHITE PLAINS	107	1760	1816	1835	0.3	54	661	701	714	0.6	2.59	522	536	0.3
42501	SOMERSET	199	16619	16464	16557	-0.1	32	6818	6922	7010	0.2	2.30	4578	4462	-0.3
42503	SOMERSET	199	18649	20647	21618	1.1	85	7476	8518	9018	1.4	2.36	5524	6048	1.0
42516	BETHELRIDGE	045	355	342	338	-0.4	18	146	145	144	-0.1	2.36	106	102	-0.4
42518	BRONSTON	231	2979	3416	3618	1.5	90	1201	1433	1535	1.9	2.35	892	1022	1.5
42519	BURNSIDE	199	3383	3623	3758	0.7	74	1403	1557	1634	1.1	2.32	989	1048	0.6
42528	DUNNVILLE	045	1470	1651	1729	1.3	88	572	658	695	1.5	2.51	403	444	1.1
42533	FERGUSON	199	911	902	908	-0.1	32	377	387	394	0.3	2.33	266	259	-0.3
42539	LIBERTY	045	9916	10372	10609	0.5	64	4050	4367	4510	0.8	2.33	2834	2936	0.4
42541	MIDDLEBURG	045	517	558	577	0.8	77	199	221	231	1.1	2.52	142	151	0.7
42544	NANCY	199	4718	4890	5035	0.4	60	1948	2085	2168	0.7	2.34	1442	1484	0.3
42553	SCIENCE HILL	199	4623	5311	5630	1.5	90	1795	2121	2269	1.8	2.49	1362	1552	1.4
42565	WINDSOR	045	556	581	594	0.5	64	226	243	250	0.8	2.31	161	166	0.3
42566	YOSEMITE	045	437	443	448	0.1	45	171	179	183	0.5	2.47	125	127	0.2
	KENTUCKY					0.7					1.0	2.41			0.6
	UNITED STATES					1.0					1.1	2.59			0.9

ZIP CODE #	POST OFFICE NAME	RACE (%) White 2000	White 2009	Black 2000	Black 2009	Asian/Pacific 2000	Asian/Pacific 2009	% Hispanic Origin 2000	% Hispanic Origin 2009	2009 AGE DISTRIBUTION (%) 0-4	5-9	10-14	15-19	20-24	25-44	45-64	65-84	85+	18+	MEDIAN AGE 2009	% 2009 Males	% 2009 Females
42217	CROFTON	94.3	93.1	4.2	5.0	0.2	0.3	0.5	0.8	6.5	6.7	7.0	6.3	4.9	26.5	28.2	12.5	1.4	76.1	40.0	49.6	50.4
42220	ELKTON	93.3	92.2	5.1	5.5	0.1	0.2	1.6	2.7	6.9	6.8	7.0	6.4	5.3	26.5	27.1	12.2	1.9	75.3	38.6	49.4	50.6
42232	GRACEY	91.7	90.4	6.3	7.1	0.5	0.7	1.1	1.6	5.9	6.4	6.7	6.3	3.7	25.2	30.5	13.9	1.3	77.1	42.3	50.5	49.5
42234	GUTHRIE	76.2	73.9	21.0	22.3	0.3	0.5	2.1	3.4	8.5	8.5	8.6	7.6	5.0	25.5	24.1	10.4	1.7	69.5	34.7	49.8	50.2
42236	HERNDON	92.4	90.6	5.2	6.0	0.5	0.6	1.7	3.0	8.0	8.2	8.0	6.7	4.3	26.9	26.7	10.1	1.1	71.5	37.1	50.5	49.5
42240	HOPKINSVILLE	70.7	69.7	26.5	26.6	0.7	1.1	1.5	2.4	7.2	7.0	7.0	6.9	5.8	25.9	25.4	12.5	2.3	75.5	37.6	47.7	52.3
42252	JETSON	98.8	98.0	0.4	0.4	0.0	0.0	0.4	1.2	7.2	6.8	6.8	5.6	6.4	29.6	26.4	10.4	0.8	75.6	37.0	51.6	48.4
42254	LA FAYETTE	92.1	90.2	5.4	6.0	0.4	0.7	1.8	3.2	8.1	8.4	8.1	6.7	4.2	28.1	25.6	9.8	1.1	71.2	36.5	50.2	49.8
42256	LEWISBURG	98.5	98.0	0.3	0.3	0.2	0.3	0.5	0.9	6.3	6.4	6.5	6.1	5.1	25.6	29.1	13.3	1.7	77.1	40.8	49.9	50.1
42259	MAMMOTH CAVE	95.6	95.4	3.4	3.4	0.1	0.1	0.9	1.5	3.9	4.1	4.4	8.1	6.2	22.3	32.0	17.4	1.6	82.8	45.6	51.4	48.6
42261	MORGANTOWN	97.8	97.1	0.6	0.7	0.1	0.2	1.2	1.9	6.5	6.4	6.3	6.5	5.9	27.2	27.3	12.0	1.9	76.7	38.5	49.4	50.6
42262	OAK GROVE	64.6	60.6	23.9	24.6	1.9	2.4	8.7	13.3	15.6	8.5	5.2	5.8	19.4	35.4	7.7	2.0	0.3	68.7	23.8	52.4	47.6
42265	OLMSTEAD	92.6	91.6	5.7	6.2	0.2	0.3	1.3	2.2	7.2	7.5	7.4	5.9	4.5	25.8	27.1	12.5	2.1	74.2	38.7	49.6	50.4
42266	PEMBROKE	82.0	79.2	14.4	15.4	0.7	0.9	1.8	3.6	8.8	8.2	7.6	6.1	5.7	25.1	24.4	11.9	2.3	72.4	35.2	50.3	49.7
42273	ROCHESTER	97.8	97.3	0.0	0.0	0.2	0.4	0.0	0.0	4.8	4.8	5.2	6.3	5.0	26.1	28.4	16.7	2.9	82.0	43.6	49.8	50.2
42274	ROCKFIELD	96.6	95.9	1.6	1.8	0.3	0.3	0.6	1.1	5.9	6.2	6.5	6.3	5.3	28.7	31.5	8.4	1.1	77.3	38.7	49.9	50.1
42275	ROUNDHILL	99.2	99.0	0.1	0.1	0.0	0.0	0.3	0.5	6.7	6.8	6.6	6.0	6.0	27.4	26.9	12.5	1.1	76.4	38.4	51.3	48.7
42276	RUSSELLVILLE	87.4	86.0	10.6	11.4	0.3	0.4	1.2	2.0	6.8	6.8	6.8	6.5	5.3	25.9	27.6	12.2	2.0	75.5	39.0	48.1	51.9
42280	SHARON GROVE	97.6	96.5	0.0	0.0	0.2	0.1	2.0	3.3	8.2	7.8	7.8	6.5	5.2	29.5	23.5	10.2	1.3	72.1	36.0	50.6	49.4
42285	SWEEDEN	99.5	99.5	0.0	0.0	0.0	0.0	0.5	0.5	6.4	6.4	5.9	5.9	5.3	27.8	26.2	14.4	1.6	77.5	40.2	49.2	50.8
42286	TRENTON	91.5	90.0	6.2	6.8	0.4	0.7	1.2	2.0	8.1	8.1	8.0	6.2	3.9	26.1	25.5	12.2	1.9	71.9	37.8	50.0	50.0
42287	WELCHS CREEK	98.9	98.5	0.2	0.2	0.0	0.0	0.4	0.6	7.2	7.0	7.0	6.1	5.9	28.3	27.3	10.1	1.1	75.1	36.9	51.0	49.0
42301	OWENSBORO	91.3	90.2	6.6	7.0	0.4	0.6	1.0	1.6	6.6	6.6	6.5	6.8	6.3	25.3	26.5	13.1	2.4	76.5	38.5	47.7	52.3
42303	OWENSBORO	94.2	93.3	3.5	3.6	0.6	1.0	1.1	1.8	6.9	6.9	6.7	6.6	5.7	26.2	26.5	12.0	2.5	75.4	38.2	48.2	51.8
42320	BEAVER DAM	96.2	95.1	1.5	1.6	0.3	0.5	1.6	2.6	6.2	5.9	5.9	6.2	5.6	25.5	28.5	13.8	2.4	78.3	41.1	48.4	51.6
42321	BEECH CREEK	98.0	97.2	1.1	1.4	0.0	0.0	0.3	0.5	7.6	7.6	7.3	5.9	5.4	25.5	27.2	12.1	1.4	73.7	37.8	48.7	51.3
42323	BEECHMONT	99.1	98.9	0.2	0.3	0.0	0.0	0.2	0.4	7.7	7.7	7.2	5.8	5.5	25.6	27.4	11.9	1.4	74.0	37.7	49.6	50.4
42324	BELTON	98.3	97.6	0.3	0.4	0.2	0.2	1.4	2.2	6.7	6.7	6.7	5.4	5.0	25.5	28.5	13.6	1.8	76.6	40.4	50.6	49.4
42325	BREMEN	99.4	99.1	0.0	0.0	0.0	0.1	0.6	0.9	5.9	5.9	6.2	6.6	5.0	26.6	29.6	12.8	1.4	77.9	41.0	50.0	50.0
42326	BROWDER	98.2	97.7	0.7	0.7	0.7	1.0	0.7	1.0	7.3	7.3	7.0	5.6	4.7	23.9	28.6	14.3	1.3	74.4	40.1	49.5	50.5
42327	CALHOUN	99.0	99.0	0.2	0.2	0.0	0.0	0.7	0.7	5.8	5.9	6.1	5.8	5.2	25.5	29.9	13.5	2.3	78.8	41.8	48.7	51.3
42328	CENTERTOWN	99.1	98.8	0.1	0.1	0.0	0.0	0.9	1.5	6.8	6.7	7.2	6.9	5.4	28.0	25.1	12.4	1.5	75.1	37.5	51.2	48.8
42330	CENTRAL CITY	91.6	90.8	7.2	7.6	0.2	0.3	0.6	0.9	5.3	5.5	5.7	5.8	6.3	28.0	27.4	13.6	2.3	80.2	40.3	52.4	47.6
42333	CROMWELL	97.9	97.3	0.4	0.4	0.2	0.3	1.4	2.2	6.2	6.1	6.3	6.5	5.6	27.3	28.0	12.4	1.5	77.3	39.1	49.6	50.4
42337	DRAKESBORO	91.2	90.4	7.0	7.5	0.1	0.1	1.2	1.7	7.8	7.8	7.8	6.7	5.1	24.7	26.4	12.1	1.6	72.3	37.7	48.1	51.9
42338	DUNDEE	97.0	96.7	0.5	0.5	0.5	0.5	1.5	1.9	6.7	6.7	6.7	6.2	5.7	24.3	28.6	13.8	1.4	75.7	39.6	50.0	50.0
42339	DUNMOR	98.2	97.5	0.4	0.5	0.0	0.1	1.3	2.2	6.2	6.3	6.3	5.2	4.8	25.7	29.3	14.0	2.1	78.1	41.6	51.1	48.9
42343	FORDSVILLE	99.5	99.4	0.1	0.1	0.1	0.1	0.5	0.9	6.3	6.4	6.6	6.7	5.3	24.7	27.5	14.0	2.5	76.3	40.5	50.0	50.0
42344	GRAHAM	99.4	99.4	0.4	0.4	0.0	0.0	0.2	0.2	7.3	7.5	7.0	5.8	4.5	25.1	27.5	13.1	2.2	74.6	39.8	48.2	51.8
42345	GREENVILLE	93.6	92.8	5.1	5.5	0.1	0.2	0.8	1.2	5.5	5.7	5.9	6.8	5.4	23.2	29.1	15.2	3.3	78.8	43.1	48.2	51.8
42347	HARTFORD	97.6	97.1	0.8	0.8	0.2	0.4	0.9	1.4	6.4	6.5	6.4	6.0	5.4	25.2	27.4	13.5	3.2	77.0	40.4	48.9	51.1
42348	HAWESVILLE	98.4	98.1	0.6	0.6	0.1	0.1	0.5	0.9	7.3	7.3	7.5	7.2	5.6	25.9	27.6	10.5	1.1	73.5	37.8	50.0	50.0
42349	HORSE BRANCH	98.7	98.2	0.2	0.3	0.4	0.6	0.4	0.7	5.8	5.9	6.1	6.1	4.5	27.1	29.7	13.6	1.2	78.5	41.0	50.0	50.0
42350	ISLAND	99.4	99.3	0.1	0.2	0.0	0.0	0.5	0.5	6.9	7.0	7.1	5.4	4.1	24.8	29.8	13.1	1.6	75.4	41.2	49.2	50.8
42351	LEWISPORT	97.5	96.9	1.1	1.3	0.3	0.5	1.1	1.8	7.1	7.1	6.9	6.4	5.3	27.5	27.7	10.1	1.8	75.0	37.4	48.9	51.1
42352	LIVERMORE	98.6	98.5	0.0	0.0	0.0	0.0	1.4	1.4	7.1	7.3	7.2	6.3	5.0	24.5	28.3	12.7	1.6	74.9	39.4	48.7	51.3
42354	MC HENRY	98.5	98.2	0.0	0.0	0.3	0.5	0.3	0.8	6.7	6.7	6.7	7.0	6.2	30.1	26.9	8.3	1.3	75.4	37.1	50.3	49.7
42355	MACEO	98.8	98.5	0.3	0.4	0.3	0.5	0.6	0.9	6.2	6.6	6.8	6.8	5.6	26.4	30.6	10.0	1.0	76.2	39.2	51.6	48.4
42361	OLATON	98.6	98.1	0.2	0.2	0.4	0.7	0.7	1.2	5.9	5.9	6.2	6.7	4.7	25.4	29.7	14.0	1.6	77.9	41.4	50.3	49.7
42366	PHILPOT	99.1	98.8	0.1	0.1	0.2	0.3	0.6	1.0	6.7	7.0	7.2	7.0	5.3	26.5	29.2	9.9	1.1	74.5	38.3	50.4	49.6
42367	POWDERLY	96.5	96.0	2.8	3.0	0.0	0.0	0.6	1.0	6.5	6.9	6.7	5.8	4.4	25.7	28.7	13.7	1.5	76.2	40.2	49.7	50.3
42368	REYNOLDS STATION	98.9	98.8	0.3	0.4	0.0	0.0	0.4	0.6	7.2	7.2	7.1	6.8	5.6	26.0	26.8	12.1	1.0	74.1	37.6	50.8	49.2
42369	ROCKPORT	99.2	99.3	0.0	0.0	0.0	0.0	0.0	0.0	6.8	6.8	6.8	5.1	4.2	24.9	29.6	14.2	1.5	76.3	40.9	49.4	50.6
42371	RUMSEY	98.9	98.9	0.3	0.3	0.0	0.0	0.3	0.3	5.8	6.1	6.3	5.5	4.7	24.1	28.4	16.2	2.9	78.2	43.4	49.3	50.7
42372	SACRAMENTO	97.2	97.1	1.2	1.3	0.1	0.1	0.6	0.6	6.5	6.7	7.0	6.1	3.8	27.1	27.2	13.7	1.8	75.9	40.2	51.6	48.4
42376	UTICA	98.4	98.0	0.7	0.7	0.1	0.3	0.3	0.4	6.4	6.4	6.9	6.8	5.5	26.6	29.7	10.7	1.0	76.1	39.4	49.6	50.4
42378	WHITESVILLE	99.2	99.0	0.2	0.2	0.1	0.1	0.3	0.5	7.8	7.6	7.6	7.1	6.0	26.9	25.4	10.2	1.3	72.6	35.9	49.0	51.0
42404	CLAY	97.8	97.7	1.2	1.4	0.3	0.3	0.3	0.3	5.5	5.6	6.1	6.3	4.7	26.9	29.9	13.4	1.7	78.9	41.7	51.4	48.6
42406	CORYDON	94.6	93.9	4.2	4.6	0.1	0.2	0.6	1.0	6.2	7.1	7.0	6.8	4.9	27.0	29.2	10.7	1.0	75.4	39.1	49.3	50.7
42408	DAWSON SPRINGS	98.2	98.1	0.7	0.8	0.1	0.1	0.3	0.3	5.7	5.8	6.2	6.2	5.3	25.0	28.3	15.0	2.5	78.4	41.9	48.6	51.4
42409	DIXON	96.2	96.1	2.6	2.6	0.0	0.0	0.5	0.5	4.8	5.2	5.6	6.9	5.4	27.8	31.3	11.5	1.6	79.9	41.2	50.8	49.2
42410	EARLINGTON	84.4	83.4	14.5	15.4	0.2	0.2	0.8	0.7	6.5	5.9	6.0	6.7	6.2	22.3	29.0	15.0	2.3	77.8	41.6	46.2	53.8
42411	FREDONIA	97.8	97.5	1.2	1.3	0.1	0.1	0.7	1.1	5.5	5.7	6.0	5.9	4.2	25.1	29.9	15.9	1.7	79.0	43.2	49.7	50.3
42413	HANSON	98.2	98.2	0.6	0.6	0.4	0.4	0.6	0.7	5.7	6.1	7.1	6.6	4.9	26.5	32.0	10.2	0.9	76.7	40.5	49.5	50.5
42420	HENDERSON	90.0	88.9	8.2	8.6	0.4	0.6	1.0	1.7	6.3	6.3	6.4	6.2	5.9	26.9	27.9	12.1	2.0	77.1	39.2	48.4	51.6
42431	MADISONVILLE	88.8	88.5	9.0	9.3	0.5	0.5	1.2	1.2	5.9	6.0	6.2	6.2	5.5	25.1	28.5	13.9	2.8	78.1	41.4	47.2	52.8
42436	MANITOU	98.1	98.1	0.5	0.6	0.5	0.5	0.5	0.6	5.7	6.0	6.6	6.7	4.6	27.3	32.5	10.0	0.7	77.7	40.6	50.0	50.0
42437	MORGANFIELD	78.1	76.2	19.0	19.9	0.2	0.3	2.3	3.5	6.0	5.9	6.0	14.5	10.0	22.2	23.6	9.9	1.8	74.8	31.5	52.3	47.7
42441	NEBO	98.3	98.2	0.6	0.7	0.3	0.3	0.3	0.4	5.4	5.5	6.2	6.8	5.7	24.9	32.9	11.5	1.1	78.8	41.7	50.7	49.3
42442	NORTONVILLE	97.4	97.3	1.5	1.5	0.1	0.1	0.6	0.7	6.4	6.9	7.2	6.8	5.1	26.2	28.6	11.3	1.6	75.1	39.1	49.6	50.4
42445	PRINCETON	93.0	92.3	5.6	6.0	0.2	0.2	0.6	1.0	5.4	5.6	5.9	6.0	4.8	23.6	29.6	16.1	3.0	79.3	44.0	48.4	51.6
42450	PROVIDENCE	86.1	84.8	12.4	13.7	0.1	0.1	0.7	0.7	6.2	6.3	6.3	6.4	5.8	25.3	27.2	14.1	2.4	77.4	40.2	47.9	52.1
42451	REED	98.3	97.6	0.6	0.8	0.6	0.9	1.1	1.9	5.8	6.2	6.6	6.5	5.6	25.7	32.3	10.3	0.9	77.4	41.0	50.2	49.8
42452	ROBARDS	98.3	98.0	0.4	0.5	0.1	0.2	0.5	0.7	5.8	6.6	6.9	6.9	4.3	26.6	31.2	10.7	1.0	76.3	40.6	50.7	49.3
42453	SAINT CHARLES	98.8	98.8	0.4	0.4	0.2	0.2	0.2	0.2	6.3	6.7	6.7	5.9	4.5	24.9	29.4	14.0	1.4	76.7	41.5	49.4	50.6
42455	SEBREE	96.6	96.7	0.3	0.4	0.1	0.1	5.7	5.5	6.9	6.9	7.0	6.3	4.8	27.0	26.2	12.2	2.7	75.3	38.1	49.6	50.4
42456	SLAUGHTERS	98.8	98.7	0.3	0.3	0.2	0.2	0.8	0.7	6.2	6.6	6.8	6.0	4.7	26.3	29.6	12.4	1.5	76.5	40.3	49.4	50.6
42458	SPOTTSVILLE	98.3	97.7	0.7	0.9	0.3	0.6	1.0	1.7	5.9	6.3	6.8	6.5	5.1	25.4	32.9	10.3	0.9	77.0	41.2	50.6	49.4
42459	STURGIS	93.1	92.3	5.5	6.0	0.1	0.2	0.9	1.4	5.8	6.0	6.2	5.9	5.1	25.1	29.7	13.9	2.2	78.6	41.8	48.1	51.9
42461	UNIONTOWN	94.7	94.1	4.7	5.1	0.1	0.1	0.2	0.4	7.0	6.9	6.9	6.2	5.9	27.4	26.9	11.3	1.4	75.8	37.9	49.7	50.3
42462	WAVERLY	94.9	94.4	4.5	4.9	0.1	0.1	0.7	1.3	6.5	6.7	6.6	5.9	5.4	28.0	29.5	10.2	1.2	76.7	38.7	49.3	50.7
42464	WHITE PLAINS	98.1	97.9	1.0	1.2	0.1	0.1	1.0	1.0	5.8	6.9	6.4	7.0	5.9	26.9	28.8	10.7	1.4	76.4	38.6	49.1	50.9
42501	SOMERSET	96.2	95.6	2.1	2.2	0.4	0.6	0.8	1.4	5.9	5.8	6.1	5.8	5.5	24.8	26.8	15.9	3.4	78.6	42.0	46.5	53.5
42503	SOMERSET	97.4	96.7	1.1	1.2	0.6	1.0	0.8	1.3	5.9	6.0	6.4	6.3	5.2	26.6	28.7	13.4	1.6	77.7	40.8	49.5	50.5
42516	BETHELRIDGE	98.0	97.7	0.6	0.6	0.0	0.3	1.7	2.9	6.1	6.1	6.1	5.8	5.3	25.4	30.1	13.2	1.8	78.1	41.5	49.1	50.9
42518	BRONSTON	98.4	98.0	0.5	0.5	0.2	0.3	0.5	0.9	5.8	6.0	7.0	6.8	5.2	24.9	29.9	13.2	1.3	76.4	41.1	50.3	49.7
42519	BURNSIDE	98.1	97.7	0.2	0.2	0.0	0.0	0.7	1.2	5.3	5.5	6.0	6.7	5.2	24.5	30.0	15.4	1.3	78.9	42.9	50.7	49.3
42528	DUNNVILLE	99.3	99.1	0.1	0.1	0.1	0.1	0.8	1.3	7.1	7.2	7.3	6.7	5.1	26.4	26.3	12.4	1.5	74.3	38.2	50.0	50.0
42533	FERGUSON	95.8	94.9	2.2	2.3	0.4	0.7	1.0	1.8	5.5	5.5	6.8	7.1	5.3	27.7	28.0	12.6	1.3	77.6	39.4	49.0	51.0
42539	LIBERTY	98.3	97.8	0.4	0.4	0.1	0.2	1.3	2.1	6.3	6.5	6.5	6.5	5.2	24.6	27.8	14.3	2.2	76.8	40.8	48.8	51.2
42541	MIDDLEBURG	98.5	98.0	0.0	0.0	0.0	0.0	1.2	2.2	7.0	7.0	7.3	6.5	4.7	25.6	26.9	13.8	1.3	74.4	39.4	49.8	50.2
42544	NANCY	99.0	98.7	0.1	0.1	0.2	0.2	0.7	1.2	5.5	5.8	6.0	5.8	4.5	24.1	32.2	14.3	1.7	79.1	43.8	49.7	50.3
42553	SCIENCE HILL	98.9	98.6	0.3	0.4	0.1	0.1	0.6	1.0	5.6	5.8	6.2	6.2	5.3	26.1	30.6	12.8	1.4	78.5	41.4	50.4	49.6
42565	WINDSOR	97.7	97.1	1.1	1.2	0.2	0.2	1.3	2.1	7.4	7.6	7.6	7.4	6.0	24.3	25.8	12.6	1.4	73.1	37.3	49.9	50.1
42566	YOSEMITE	98.2	97.3	0.2	0.2	0.0	0.2	1.6	2.5	5.9	6.1	6.3	6.5	5.6	26.6	29.1	12.2	1.6	77.7	40.5	50.8	49.2
	KENTUCKY	90.1	88.9	7.3	7.5	0.8	1.2	1.5	2.4	6.5	6.5	6.5	6.8	6.5	27.0	27.1	11.3	1.8	76.6	37.9	49.1	50.9
	UNITED STATES	75.1	72.0	12.3	12.7	3.8	4.6	12.5	15.7	6.8	6.7	6.6	7.1	6.9	27.0	26.0	10.9	1.9	75.7	36.9	49.2	50.8

#	POST OFFICE NAME	2009 Per Capita Income	2009 HH Income Base	2009 Household Income Distribution (%): Less than $25,000	$25,000 to $49,999	$50,000 to $99,999	$100,000 to $149,999	$150,000 or More	Median Household Income: 2009	2014	2009 National Centile	2009 State Centile	2009 Home Value Base	2009 Home Value Distribution (%): Less than $50,000	$50,000 to $89,999	$90,000 to $174,999	$175,000 to $399,999	$400,000 or More	2009 Median Home Value
42217	CROFTON	18080	1541	29.7	35.2	30.1	4.1	0.8	38596	41872	28	61	1243	32.5	26.6	31.2	7.7	1.9	74888
42220	ELKTON	17389	2558	35.1	31.7	28.8	2.7	1.6	36021	37064	21	54	2022	29.3	35.8	28.1	6.3	0.4	72282
42232	GRACEY	23202	293	19.8	31.4	38.2	7.5	3.1	49186	50278	59	84	247	7.7	15.0	43.3	28.7	5.3	142500
42234	GUTHRIE	15969	894	35.9	32.6	27.3	3.5	0.8	36685	36032	23	56	606	36.8	31.5	25.1	5.1	1.5	66136
42236	HERNDON	20966	318	21.1	34.9	34.3	6.3	3.5	45937	47005	51	81	237	15.6	19.4	45.1	16.9	3.0	107372
42240	HOPKINSVILLE	21138	17572	30.9	28.9	31.7	5.7	2.7	41403	44768	37	68	11012	14.9	22.1	45.3	15.6	2.2	108194
42252	JETSON	16360	93	33.3	33.3	28.0	2.2	3.2	37349	37577	25	58	78	33.3	28.2	34.6	3.8	0.0	73333
42254	LA FAYETTE	21867	117	20.5	35.0	36.8	5.1	2.6	45847	47321	51	80	85	15.3	21.2	48.2	15.3	0.0	102500
42256	LEWISBURG	18764	2037	35.1	32.7	27.0	3.0	2.2	35646	38517	20	52	1677	33.0	29.8	27.0	9.4	0.8	72007
42259	MAMMOTH CAVE	14237	431	41.8	37.4	18.3	2.6	0.0	31266	31717	10	41	379	31.1	32.2	31.4	5.3	0.0	72738
42261	MORGANTOWN	17838	4185	33.9	31.4	30.6	3.0	1.1	37522	38803	25	58	3247	35.6	29.4	29.6	5.1	0.3	71313
42262	OAK GROVE	18165	3495	17.4	45.8	31.0	3.9	1.9	43478	45560	44	74	1564	15.1	20.0	60.5	3.4	1.0	96754
42265	OLMSTEAD	21963	422	19.9	29.4	41.7	5.0	4.0	50497	49708	62	87	330	17.9	29.4	29.1	19.1	4.5	93750
42266	PEMBROKE	17656	892	30.7	36.4	24.9	4.1	3.8	40000	42587	33	65	634	13.4	24.9	38.6	16.6	6.5	103022
42273	ROCHESTER	22055	213	28.6	30.5	30.5	8.5	1.9	45107	45000	49	78	189	36.0	29.1	22.8	12.2	0.0	66333
42274	ROCKFIELD	19113	892	26.5	24.2	45.9	2.1	1.3	49398	50620	60	85	756	25.5	15.3	38.5	15.9	4.8	98415
42275	ROUNDHILL	14606	377	41.1	31.8	24.7	0.8	1.6	31324	32923	10	41	319	33.5	32.9	27.9	4.7	0.9	67857
42276	RUSSELLVILLE	20102	5978	31.0	30.9	31.5	4.2	2.4	39709	41600	32	64	4338	20.6	31.5	35.4	11.6	1.0	87554
42280	SHARON GROVE	15606	286	29.7	37.4	30.8	2.1	0.0	33295	34259	14	46	242	24.8	40.1	21.9	12.4	0.8	70000
42285	SWEEDEN	19733	88	30.7	37.5	28.4	2.3	1.1	38600	41111	28	61	78	26.9	35.9	29.5	7.7	0.0	76923
42286	TRENTON	21393	588	34.5	25.3	30.1	6.3	3.7	38218	37790	27	60	458	19.2	27.1	33.4	17.2	3.1	94595
42287	WELCHS CREEK	18339	199	33.7	33.2	29.6	1.5	2.0	38116	38685	27	60	171	36.3	27.5	33.3	2.9	0.0	70385
42301	OWENSBORO	23434	17705	26.5	29.1	35.6	5.7	3.1	46323	48534	52	81	11453	10.1	30.6	47.4	11.0	0.9	97456
42303	OWENSBORO	25521	15718	25.5	27.2	34.1	8.7	4.6	48159	50363	57	83	10971	11.8	27.5	42.3	16.9	1.6	99190
42320	BEAVER DAM	18148	3230	35.7	31.6	26.4	4.8	1.5	35684	37631	20	53	2432	33.3	31.4	30.8	4.3	0.3	73161
42321	BEECH CREEK	17320	237	34.6	31.2	30.0	3.4	0.8	38130	39600	27	60	203	33.5	30.0	30.5	5.9	0.0	70278
42323	BEECHMONT	18464	340	30.6	33.8	31.8	2.9	0.9	40532	41805	34	66	288	29.9	30.2	34.4	5.6	0.0	74444
42324	BELTON	16433	537	33.5	35.9	26.3	4.1	0.2	34892	37094	17	50	484	30.2	33.1	32.0	4.8	0.0	73617
42325	BREMEN	17555	990	33.2	36.3	26.5	3.4	0.6	38032	38868	27	59	872	31.8	32.8	27.4	7.2	0.8	72386
42326	BROWDER	19024	134	25.4	35.8	36.6	2.2	0.0	40000	40000	33	65	123	42.3	28.5	25.2	4.1	0.0	59500
42327	CALHOUN	20202	1719	30.1	33.5	31.2	2.4	2.7	41231	41492	37	68	1421	33.6	29.8	27.2	8.1	1.4	73319
42328	CENTERTOWN	17558	633	26.7	32.9	37.4	2.1	0.9	44808	45259	48	77	541	37.0	37.7	21.4	3.9	0.0	59156
42330	CENTRAL CITY	17158	3656	38.2	30.4	25.8	4.0	1.6	34852	36521	17	50	2925	37.9	29.0	26.6	6.1	0.5	67672
42333	CROMWELL	16001	397	33.5	35.5	26.4	4.0	0.5	37351	39273	25	58	332	42.2	31.3	22.0	4.5	0.0	62381
42337	DRAKESBORO	14983	843	45.2	29.4	21.9	2.4	1.1	27916	30381	6	31	735	52.1	28.7	17.6	1.6	0.0	47652
42338	DUNDEE	17274	82	31.7	26.8	39.0	2.4	0.0	37356	38619	25	58	74	33.8	23.0	33.8	9.5	0.0	75000
42339	DUNMOR	16548	345	35.1	35.1	24.6	4.9	0.3	34444	37503	16	49	312	28.8	32.1	34.3	4.8	0.0	76333
42343	FORDSVILLE	18008	956	39.7	27.3	29.3	2.2	1.5	32863	35098	13	45	797	42.3	29.2	23.6	4.9	0.0	58425
42344	GRAHAM	14687	384	37.2	44.5	16.7	1.0	0.5	31861	32944	11	43	325	61.8	27.7	8.3	1.8	0.3	43790
42345	GREENVILLE	20850	4441	36.0	28.0	28.0	4.9	3.1	38091	39361	27	60	3551	25.8	33.8	30.6	8.5	1.3	77922
42347	HARTFORD	19155	2216	33.4	31.7	29.4	3.4	2.1	36372	37994	22	54	1696	27.9	32.7	30.7	8.3	0.3	77462
42348	HAWESVILLE	20309	1830	25.4	29.9	36.9	6.2	1.5	46072	47698	52	81	1567	29.6	26.2	31.5	12.2	0.5	83092
42349	HORSE BRANCH	14409	672	41.8	32.7	21.3	4.0	0.1	31985	34292	11	43	581	41.8	30.5	20.8	6.7	0.2	62159
42350	ISLAND	17573	567	33.9	34.9	27.5	3.2	0.5	34355	36632	16	48	496	48.2	26.2	21.4	3.4	0.8	52903
42351	LEWISPORT	21382	1575	24.3	27.9	38.9	7.0	1.8	48206	49934	57	84	1241	25.1	30.5	32.1	12.1	0.2	80070
42352	LIVERMORE	17856	921	39.5	29.4	24.9	4.9	1.3	31922	34343	11	43	675	36.1	30.2	29.6	3.6	0.4	67766
42354	MC HENRY	15714	148	36.5	34.5	25.7	2.0	1.4	33767	36118	15	47	129	48.8	37.2	14.0	0.0	0.0	50938
42355	MACEO	21805	775	20.4	32.3	37.3	7.0	3.1	48298	50063	57	84	703	31.9	23.3	34.6	9.5	0.7	82234
42361	OLATON	16581	230	35.7	32.6	27.8	3.0	0.9	35274	36272	19	51	199	33.2	25.1	31.2	9.5	1.0	76071
42366	PHILPOT	24168	2240	14.4	25.3	47.5	9.9	2.9	61941	61356	80	95	2072	9.5	19.8	45.9	22.3	2.4	119164
42367	POWDERLY	13532	392	46.2	34.4	17.3	1.8	0.3	26806	29165	4	27	311	55.0	29.6	13.5	1.9	0.0	45921
42368	REYNOLDS STATION	20206	428	27.1	29.7	35.7	4.7	2.8	44613	46615	47	77	375	41.6	21.3	32.0	5.1	0.0	72200
42369	ROCKPORT	19986	165	33.3	34.5	26.1	4.2	1.8	38744	39461	29	62	146	39.0	30.1	22.6	8.2	0.0	67000
42371	RUMSEY	17896	263	38.8	33.5	23.6	1.9	2.3	32543	35375	12	44	207	38.6	28.0	25.1	8.2	0.0	65769
42372	SACRAMENTO	18327	843	32.7	32.7	30.2	2.8	1.4	38054	40000	27	60	691	36.9	33.4	23.6	6.1	0.0	65702
42376	UTICA	23070	2081	18.7	32.0	38.4	8.4	2.5	49549	50750	60	85	1845	17.3	26.8	39.7	14.1	2.1	94415
42378	WHITESVILLE	19744	1180	24.2	33.1	36.3	4.9	1.4	44227	45960	46	75	1039	24.1	25.8	39.8	10.2	0.1	90127
42404	CLAY	18857	1111	30.8	32.0	32.3	3.9	1.1	38420	41037	28	61	908	44.2	30.5	19.5	5.0	0.9	54818
42406	CORYDON	20954	1195	20.8	29.5	40.0	8.6	1.1	49723	50814	60	85	991	26.1	31.9	32.2	9.8	0.0	80422
42408	DAWSON SPRINGS	16342	2801	38.7	34.8	22.6	3.1	0.9	30921	34155	10	39	2193	47.7	31.1	18.9	2.0	0.4	52682
42409	DIXON	20571	997	29.8	28.0	35.1	5.2	1.9	42355	43571	40	71	812	33.7	28.1	32.6	4.7	0.9	69194
42410	EARLINGTON	15599	791	45.1	29.5	22.9	2.3	0.3	27958	30893	6	31	575	51.1	34.3	13.7	0.9	0.0	48917
42411	FREDONIA	19700	604	28.5	36.4	28.3	4.1	2.6	40878	43212	36	67	519	34.7	32.0	25.6	7.5	0.2	66196
42413	HANSON	23071	981	20.3	28.3	41.1	6.7	3.6	51005	50931	64	88	876	19.9	31.4	33.6	14.2	1.0	88226
42420	HENDERSON	23672	16042	28.7	27.4	33.8	6.5	3.7	44961	46994	48	78	10305	21.7	25.3	39.0	12.9	1.1	93037
42431	MADISONVILLE	22941	11575	30.2	30.7	30.6	5.0	3.5	41619	43768	38	69	8096	26.9	32.9	32.3	7.4	0.6	76462
42436	MANITOU	24292	489	17.2	33.5	36.0	8.0	5.3	49457	50174	60	85	439	18.5	32.3	29.6	16.9	2.7	88833
42437	MORGANFIELD	22565	2769	25.0	26.3	38.3	6.6	3.7	48568	48395	58	84	2086	29.9	29.3	34.3	5.9	0.5	77820
42441	NEBO	19807	639	26.9	36.8	31.1	2.0	3.1	41231	44045	37	68	554	36.1	30.0	26.5	6.3	1.1	70159
42442	NORTONVILLE	15817	1349	36.6	34.6	25.6	2.7	0.4	34712	38816	17	49	1125	43.0	34.3	20.4	2.0	0.3	57269
42445	PRINCETON	19267	4750	35.6	31.6	27.1	3.6	2.0	34934	36519	17	50	3614	34.1	31.2	27.7	6.6	0.5	68868
42450	PROVIDENCE	18488	1699	38.6	29.5	24.0	5.5	2.4	35280	37325	19	51	1257	56.9	22.8	19.5	0.4	0.4	45399
42451	REED	21449	405	18.3	33.6	40.5	6.4	1.2	48810	49272	58	84	353	36.3	30.3	28.0	4.8	0.6	66304
42452	ROBARDS	23110	914	16.1	29.0	44.7	8.5	1.6	54469	53412	70	90	786	15.8	27.1	40.5	16.0	0.6	95895
42453	SAINT CHARLES	15869	206	40.3	35.4	20.4	2.9	1.0	30508	33999	9	37	185	52.4	24.3	21.6	0.5	1.1	47857
42455	SEBREE	18674	1394	28.0	32.2	34.5	4.3	1.0	41212	42847	37	68	1066	31.1	35.2	29.2	4.0	0.5	69167
42456	SLAUGHTERS	21604	689	23.1	26.1	43.5	4.9	2.3	50482	49592	62	87	602	29.2	28.6	31.2	9.1	1.8	79091
42458	SPOTTSVILLE	23029	387	23.3	26.1	40.6	7.5	2.6	50736	51483	63	87	345	32.8	28.4	31.9	6.1	0.9	73000
42459	STURGIS	20755	1944	30.9	30.1	31.4	4.6	3.0	41304	42650	37	68	1527	35.5	34.4	25.1	4.6	0.3	64735
42461	UNIONTOWN	19733	682	30.4	34.5	29.6	4.1	1.5	39500	42452	31	63	571	50.4	28.0	15.1	6.5	0.0	49648
42462	WAVERLY	20341	624	19.7	29.6	45.2	5.1	0.3	50611	51269	63	87	534	30.0	35.8	25.5	8.6	0.2	72813
42464	WHITE PLAINS	16281	701	33.4	36.1	25.5	2.9	2.1	34437	38239	16	49	601	42.6	29.3	21.8	4.8	1.5	57946
42501	SOMERSET	17476	6922	39.1	33.9	22.1	3.1	1.8	31367	34042	10	41	4652	24.8	34.1	33.9	6.3	0.9	81996
42503	SOMERSET	20802	8518	30.5	31.3	30.4	4.9	2.8	40222	41599	33	66	6551	19.6	18.3	44.3	16.0	1.7	105470
42516	BETHELRIDGE	19732	145	46.2	32.4	15.2	2.1	4.1	27077	28160	5	28	126	40.5	38.1	19.0	2.4	0.0	59231
42518	BRONSTON	21419	1433	31.7	34.5	25.5	5.0	3.3	37468	39304	25	58	1168	28.4	30.1	33.3	8.2	0.0	80748
42519	BURNSIDE	14978	1557	45.3	36.7	14.9	1.3	1.7	26791	28365	4	27	1272	48.0	32.5	16.2	3.0	0.2	51908
42528	DUNNVILLE	14115	658	42.7	35.7	18.4	2.1	1.1	30000	31146	8	36	549	45.4	21.9	21.9	10.9	0.0	55000
42533	FERGUSON	20768	387	31.5	33.9	26.4	3.1	5.2	38204	39632	27	60	243	29.6	33.3	29.2	5.8	2.1	71944
42539	LIBERTY	15440	4367	48.2	29.7	18.4	1.9	1.7	26028	26256	4	25	3469	39.1	29.2	26.2	5.1	0.3	63723
42541	MIDDLEBURG	14547	221	43.4	28.1	26.2	0.9	1.4	31027	34171	10	40	181	40.3	28.2	30.4	1.1	0.0	57609
42544	NANCY	16864	2085	40.9	38.2	17.5	2.3	1.1	30158	32422	8	37	1729	34.0	24.7	32.8	7.9	0.6	77457
42553	SCIENCE HILL	16899	2121	37.6	30.8	26.6	3.9	1.1	33545	36427	14	46	1730	29.9	29.9	30.2	8.6	1.4	77652
42565	WINDSOR	13126	243	58.8	23.5	14.4	2.9	0.4	20427	21624	2	8	197	50.8	18.3	17.8	13.2	0.0	49375
42566	YOSEMITE	17824	179	40.2	40.8	14.5	1.7	2.8	31440	34688	10	41	150	44.0	37.3	15.3	2.7	0.7	55625
	KENTUCKY	23409		28.5	27.2	32.3	7.7	4.3	44205	46476				19.8	20.7	38.3	18.6	2.6	103937
	UNITED STATES	27277		20.9	24.4	35.3	11.7	7.6	54719	56938				9.3	13.1	31.6	32.6	13.5	162279

ZIP CODE #	POST OFFICE NAME	FINANCIAL SERVICES: Auto Loan	FINANCIAL SERVICES: Home Loan	FINANCIAL SERVICES: Investments	FINANCIAL SERVICES: Retirement Plans	THE HOME – Home Improvements: Home Repair	THE HOME – Home Improvements: Lawn & Garden	THE HOME – Furnishings: Computers & Hardware-Personal	THE HOME – Furnishings: Major Appliances	THE HOME – Furnishings: TV, Radio, Sound Equipment	THE HOME – Furnishings: Furniture	ENTERTAINMENT: Dine out/Carry out	ENTERTAINMENT: Sports Equipment	ENTERTAINMENT: Fees & Tickets	ENTERTAINMENT: Toys & Games	ENTERTAINMENT: Travel	ENTERTAINMENT: Cable TV	PERSONAL: Apparel & Services	PERSONAL: Auto Repairs	PERSONAL: Health Insurance	PERSONAL: Pets & Supplies
42217	CROFTON	81	58	71	56	58	78	60	72	67	58	65	55	48	68	56	73	44	67	75	87
42220	ELKTON	79	56	66	55	56	75	59	69	65	57	64	53	47	68	54	71	43	65	72	84
42232	GRACEY	92	84	82	87	85	97	82	92	85	76	84	69	76	87	82	90	57	86	95	107
42234	GUTHRIE	78	55	68	54	55	75	58	68	64	55	63	53	46	66	54	70	42	65	72	84
42236	HERNDON	88	81	73	79	80	85	77	82	80	79	80	60	73	83	74	82	54	79	83	97
42240	HOPKINSVILLE	77	68	69	68	67	78	70	74	74	68	73	55	66	74	68	78	50	73	80	88
42252	JETSON	79	57	66	55	57	75	59	69	66	58	64	53	48	69	54	72	43	65	73	84
42254	LA FAYETTE	85	79	70	76	77	80	74	78	77	77	77	57	70	80	71	79	52	76	79	93
42256	LEWISBURG	80	57	72	56	58	78	59	72	66	57	65	55	48	68	56	72	43	67	75	86
42259	MAMMOTH CAVE	62	45	64	43	46	63	46	58	51	43	50	44	37	50	45	56	33	53	61	69
42261	MORGANTOWN	77	56	64	55	56	74	60	68	66	57	65	52	49	68	55	72	44	66	73	83
42262	OAK GROVE	89	49	40	55	44	45	83	61	78	77	82	59	63	93	62	73	57	75	56	74
42265	OLMSTEAD	89	79	77	80	80	91	78	86	81	74	80	65	71	83	76	85	54	81	88	101
42266	PEMBROKE	87	62	91	60	64	89	64	82	70	58	69	63	50	70	64	77	46	75	85	98
42273	ROCHESTER	97	69	99	67	72	98	71	90	79	66	77	68	57	78	70	87	51	83	94	107
42274	ROCKFIELD	82	74	67	72	72	77	70	75	73	73	73	55	66	76	67	76	50	72	75	89
42275	ROUNDHILL	68	47	61	45	46	66	49	60	56	47	54	46	38	57	45	61	36	56	63	73
42276	RUSSELLVILLE	81	64	69	64	64	80	67	75	72	63	70	57	57	74	63	77	48	72	80	90
42280	SHARON GROVE	71	51	58	49	50	67	53	61	59	51	57	47	42	61	48	64	39	58	65	75
42285	SWEEDEN	76	54	62	53	54	72	57	66	63	55	61	51	45	65	51	68	41	62	69	80
42286	TRENTON	100	69	108	68	72	104	76	94	79	63	78	77	56	78	75	87	51	88	99	115
42287	WELCHS CREEK	79	56	65	55	56	75	59	68	65	57	64	53	47	68	53	71	43	65	72	83
42301	OWENSBORO	79	75	70	76	74	82	77	78	80	75	79	59	75	80	75	83	55	79	85	93
42303	OWENSBORO	85	85	77	86	83	88	86	85	87	83	87	66	85	88	84	89	61	86	91	101
42320	BEAVER DAM	78	58	71	56	58	78	60	71	66	57	65	54	50	68	57	73	44	67	76	85
42321	BEECH CREEK	76	54	65	52	54	73	57	67	63	55	62	51	45	65	52	69	41	63	70	81
42323	BEECHMONT	78	56	64	55	56	74	58	68	65	57	63	52	47	67	53	71	43	64	72	83
42324	BELTON	73	52	65	51	53	71	54	65	60	52	59	50	44	62	51	66	39	61	68	78
42325	BREMEN	77	55	72	54	56	76	57	70	63	54	62	53	46	64	54	69	41	65	73	84
42326	BROWDER	77	55	64	54	55	73	58	67	64	56	63	51	46	67	52	70	42	63	71	82
42327	CALHOUN	88	63	84	61	64	88	66	81	73	61	71	61	53	73	63	80	47	75	85	97
42328	CENTERTOWN	81	58	68	57	58	77	61	71	67	59	66	54	49	70	55	73	44	67	75	86
42330	CENTRAL CITY	74	55	69	53	56	74	57	68	63	54	62	51	47	64	54	69	41	64	73	81
42333	CROMWELL	74	53	64	51	53	71	55	65	61	53	60	50	44	63	51	67	40	61	69	79
42337	DRAKESBORO	67	45	62	43	45	65	48	59	55	46	54	46	37	56	44	61	36	56	62	72
42338	DUNDEE	80	57	66	56	57	76	60	69	66	58	65	53	48	69	54	72	44	66	73	84
42339	DUNMOR	73	53	68	51	53	72	54	66	60	52	59	50	44	62	52	66	39	62	69	80
42343	FORDSVILLE	78	56	64	54	56	74	58	68	65	57	63	52	47	67	53	71	43	64	72	83
42344	GRAHAM	67	43	64	41	43	65	46	59	54	44	52	46	35	55	43	60	35	55	62	72
42345	GREENVILLE	83	63	82	62	65	86	65	79	72	61	70	59	55	72	64	78	47	74	84	94
42347	HARTFORD	80	59	74	58	60	80	62	74	69	58	67	56	51	69	59	75	45	70	80	89
42348	HAWESVILLE	93	68	77	67	68	89	71	82	78	69	76	63	57	81	65	85	51	78	86	99
42349	HORSE BRANCH	67	48	67	46	49	67	49	62	54	46	53	46	39	54	48	60	35	57	64	74
42350	ISLAND	72	52	74	50	54	73	53	68	59	49	58	51	42	59	53	65	38	62	70	80
42351	LEWISPORT	84	75	68	74	73	82	75	79	78	73	77	59	69	80	71	81	53	77	82	94
42352	LIVERMORE	80	53	77	51	53	79	57	71	65	54	63	55	43	66	53	72	42	67	75	87
42354	MC HENRY	74	53	61	52	53	70	55	64	61	54	60	49	44	64	50	67	40	61	68	78
42355	MACEO	87	80	76	81	80	90	78	86	81	74	80	65	73	83	77	84	54	81	88	101
42361	OLATON	75	54	71	52	55	74	55	68	61	52	60	52	44	62	53	67	40	63	71	82
42366	PHILPOT	99	100	90	102	98	105	93	99	94	92	94	76	93	97	94	97	65	95	100	117
42367	POWDERLY	60	39	58	37	39	59	42	53	48	40	47	41	31	49	39	54	31	50	56	65
42368	REYNOLDS STATION	97	69	80	67	69	92	72	84	80	70	78	64	58	83	66	87	53	79	88	102
42369	ROCKPORT	88	63	91	61	66	90	65	83	72	61	71	62	52	72	64	79	47	76	86	98
42371	RUMSEY	73	53	74	51	55	75	56	70	62	51	60	52	45	61	54	68	40	64	74	82
42372	SACRAMENTO	80	57	77	55	59	79	59	73	65	56	64	55	47	66	57	72	43	68	76	87
42376	UTICA	99	86	84	85	85	97	84	93	88	82	87	69	76	91	80	93	59	88	95	110
42378	WHITESVILLE	93	69	77	67	69	89	71	82	78	70	77	63	58	82	65	85	52	78	86	99
42404	CLAY	82	59	73	57	59	80	61	73	67	58	66	56	49	69	57	74	44	68	77	88
42406	CORYDON	90	76	78	77	77	91	76	86	80	72	79	65	68	82	73	85	53	80	88	101
42408	DAWSON SPRINGS	69	49	65	48	50	69	53	64	59	49	57	48	42	59	50	65	38	60	68	76
42409	DIXON	86	68	81	66	69	85	68	80	73	66	72	59	58	74	66	78	48	75	82	95
42410	EARLINGTON	61	44	52	44	44	59	50	55	55	46	53	43	41	55	45	59	36	54	59	67
42411	FREDONIA	83	60	85	58	62	84	61	78	68	57	67	58	49	67	61	75	44	71	81	92
42413	HANSON	95	87	82	88	87	96	84	92	87	82	86	69	79	90	82	91	59	87	94	109
42420	HENDERSON	82	74	70	75	73	81	79	79	81	75	80	61	74	82	75	84	55	80	85	95
42431	MADISONVILLE	83	71	76	71	70	84	74	80	78	70	77	60	67	78	71	83	52	78	85	95
42436	MANITOU	100	91	83	89	90	95	87	93	90	88	90	68	82	93	83	93	61	89	94	110
42437	MORGANFIELD	91	85	80	85	83	95	84	89	88	81	87	68	81	89	83	92	59	87	96	106
42441	NEBO	87	65	77	63	65	84	66	78	73	64	71	59	55	75	62	79	48	73	81	94
42442	NORTONVILLE	72	49	66	47	49	70	52	63	59	50	58	49	40	60	48	65	38	60	67	78
42445	PRINCETON	75	58	76	57	60	79	60	73	65	55	64	54	51	65	59	71	43	68	77	85
42450	PROVIDENCE	76	55	64	54	54	73	61	67	67	57	65	52	49	68	55	72	44	66	73	82
42451	REED	95	76	81	77	77	95	77	88	83	72	81	67	66	85	73	89	55	83	92	105
42452	ROBARDS	93	90	85	93	90	100	86	94	87	81	87	72	83	89	87	91	59	88	96	110
42453	SAINT CHARLES	72	48	68	45	48	70	51	63	58	49	57	49	38	60	47	65	38	60	67	78
42455	SEBREE	86	63	71	62	63	83	66	76	72	63	71	58	54	75	60	78	48	72	80	92
42456	SLAUGHTERS	85	77	75	79	78	89	76	84	78	71	77	63	70	80	74	82	53	79	86	98
42458	SPOTTSVILLE	95	83	84	85	84	100	83	94	86	76	85	71	75	88	81	92	58	87	97	110
42459	STURGIS	84	64	80	63	66	86	67	80	73	61	71	60	56	73	65	80	48	75	85	95
42461	UNIONTOWN	83	60	69	59	60	79	62	73	69	61	68	56	50	72	57	75	46	69	77	88
42462	WAVERLY	89	74	73	72	73	84	73	80	78	74	77	60	65	81	68	82	52	77	82	96
42464	WHITE PLAINS	77	53	69	51	53	74	56	68	63	54	62	52	44	65	52	69	41	64	71	82
42501	SOMERSET	66	50	61	50	52	66	55	63	60	51	59	47	47	60	52	66	40	60	68	74
42503	SOMERSET	81	67	73	65	67	81	67	76	73	65	72	57	60	74	65	78	48	73	81	90
42516	BETHELRIDGE	87	56	83	53	56	85	60	76	70	57	68	59	45	71	56	78	45	72	80	94
42518	BRONSTON	86	67	82	64	69	87	68	80	74	68	73	59	58	74	66	81	49	76	86	95
42519	BURNSIDE	63	43	57	42	44	61	46	56	52	44	51	43	36	53	43	57	34	53	60	68
42528	DUNNVILLE	64	46	54	44	45	61	48	56	53	46	52	43	38	55	43	58	35	53	59	68
42533	FERGUSON	82	59	82	57	61	85	64	79	72	57	69	59	52	70	62	79	46	74	87	93
42539	LIBERTY	65	45	62	43	46	65	48	59	54	45	53	45	37	55	45	59	35	55	62	71
42541	MIDDLEBURG	66	48	55	46	47	63	49	58	55	48	54	44	40	57	45	60	36	55	61	70
42544	NANCY	71	50	72	48	52	71	52	65	58	49	57	49	41	58	51	64	38	61	69	78
42553	SCIENCE HILL	75	54	69	53	55	74	56	68	62	53	61	52	45	63	53	68	41	63	71	82
42565	WINDSOR	56	38	51	36	38	54	40	49	45	38	44	38	31	47	37	50	30	46	52	60
42566	YOSEMITE	81	56	71	53	55	78	59	70	66	56	65	54	46	68	54	73	43	66	74	86
	KENTUCKY	90	77	81	77	76	88	80	85	83	78	83	65	73	85	76	87	57	83	88	101
	UNITED STATES	100	100	100	100	100	100	100	100	100	100	100	100	100	100	100	100	100	100	100	100

KENTUCKY

POPULATION CHANGE

42567-45275

#	POST OFFICE NAME	COUNTY FIPS CODE	POPULATION 2000	POPULATION 2009	POPULATION 2014	2000-2009 ANNUAL RATE % Rate	2000-2009 ANNUAL RATE State Centile	HOUSEHOLDS 2000	HOUSEHOLDS 2009	HOUSEHOLDS 2014	HOUSEHOLDS % Annual Rate 2000-2009	HOUSEHOLDS 2009 Average HH Size	FAMILIES 2000	FAMILIES 2009	FAMILIES % Annual Rate 2000-2009
42567	EUBANK	199	5295	5743	5981	0.9	80	2072	2328	2449	1.3	2.46	1573	1705	0.9
42602	ALBANY	053	8700	8792	8840	0.1	45	3692	3853	3916	0.5	2.27	2527	2527	0.0
42603	ALPHA	231	3494	3587	3640	0.3	54	1334	1413	1448	0.6	2.51	1023	1050	0.3
42629	JAMESTOWN	207	4678	4861	4969	0.4	60	1973	2113	2182	0.7	2.24	1364	1403	0.3
42633	MONTICELLO	231	16171	16708	16964	0.4	60	6482	6898	7071	0.7	2.40	4705	4828	0.3
42634	PARKERS LAKE	147	1592	1587	1592	0.0	39	582	607	617	0.5	2.51	433	436	0.1
42635	PINE KNOT	147	4298	5906	5894	3.5	98	1613	1623	1639	0.1	2.41	1145	1106	-0.4
42638	REVELO	147	211	219	223	0.4	60	81	87	89	0.8	2.52	57	58	0.2
42642	RUSSELL SPRINGS	207	12318	12966	13313	0.6	69	5267	5704	5912	0.9	2.27	3653	3794	0.4
42647	STEARNS	147	4441	4613	4695	0.4	60	1738	1879	1938	0.8	2.44	1297	1355	0.5
42649	STRUNK	147	1974	2139	2199	0.9	80	738	822	854	1.2	2.60	560	602	0.8
42653	WHITLEY CITY	147	4564	4748	4832	0.4	60	1768	1922	1983	0.9	2.43	1265	1323	0.5
42701	ELIZABETHTOWN	093	38960	43663	45856	1.2	86	15342	17796	18884	1.6	2.40	10977	12314	1.3
42712	BIG CLIFTY	085	1763	1852	1900	0.5	64	690	747	774	0.9	2.48	522	546	0.5
42713	BONNIEVILLE	099	1622	1781	1838	1.0	83	640	714	740	1.2	2.49	469	504	0.8
42715	BREEDING	001	341	354	359	0.4	60	136	146	150	0.8	2.42	100	104	0.4
42716	BUFFALO	123	1404	1494	1534	0.7	74	537	584	604	0.9	2.56	418	440	0.6
42717	BURKESVILLE	057	7338	7194	7032	-0.2	26	3061	3070	3022	0.0	2.31	2094	2011	-0.4
42718	CAMPBELLSVILLE	217	22754	23386	23730	0.3	54	9205	9696	9915	0.6	2.34	6530	6616	0.1
42721	CANEYVILLE	085	3731	3845	3898	0.3	54	1498	1588	1624	0.6	2.42	1087	1109	0.2
42722	CANMER	099	588	675	709	1.5	90	226	263	277	1.7	2.57	169	191	1.3
42724	CECILIA	093	4425	4872	5089	1.0	83	1667	1914	2025	1.5	2.55	1311	1456	1.1
42726	CLARKSON	085	4252	4449	4553	0.5	64	1746	1880	1941	0.8	2.36	1302	1353	0.4
42728	COLUMBIA	001	14354	14531	14643	0.1	45	5622	5867	5968	0.5	2.35	3963	3975	0.0
42729	CUB RUN	099	1342	1480	1535	1.1	85	517	578	603	1.2	2.52	378	407	0.8
42731	DUBRE	169	322	324	323	0.1	45	129	133	133	0.3	2.44	94	94	0.0
42732	EASTVIEW	093	1906	1980	2025	0.4	60	717	773	800	0.8	2.56	545	567	0.4
42733	ELK HORN	217	1404	1469	1499	0.5	64	505	539	554	0.7	2.73	385	396	0.3
42740	GLENDALE	093	1687	1781	1819	0.6	69	619	674	696	0.9	2.64	496	524	0.6
42741	GLENS FORK	001	674	681	687	0.1	45	273	287	293	0.5	2.37	190	191	0.1
42742	GRADYVILLE	001	227	227	228	0.0	39	85	88	89	0.4	2.58	67	68	0.2
42743	GREENSBURG	087	9339	9243	9172	-0.1	32	3861	3896	3887	0.1	2.33	2747	2668	-0.3
42746	HARDYVILLE	099	1710	1895	1970	1.1	85	631	708	739	1.3	2.68	471	512	0.9
42748	HODGENVILLE	123	7784	8060	8168	0.4	60	3114	3285	3347	0.6	2.39	2220	2255	0.2
42749	HORSE CAVE	099	5681	5744	5759	0.1	45	2282	2361	2380	0.4	2.36	1590	1579	-0.1
42753	KNIFLEY	001	691	759	784	1.0	83	268	299	311	1.2	2.54	206	222	0.8
42754	LEITCHFIELD	085	15362	16033	16369	0.5	64	6096	6508	6693	0.7	2.42	4356	4479	0.3
42757	MAGNOLIA	099	3208	3399	3462	0.6	69	1246	1337	1367	0.8	2.54	943	978	0.4
42762	MILLWOOD	085	378	386	388	0.2	48	133	139	140	0.5	2.78	99	99	0.0
42764	MOUNT SHERMAN	087	846	893	907	0.6	69	338	365	373	0.8	2.45	254	264	0.4
42765	MUNFORDVILLE	099	5172	5819	6063	1.3	88	1975	2248	2352	1.4	2.56	1361	1484	0.9
42776	SONORA	093	2477	2689	2782	0.9	80	865	965	1008	1.2	2.71	668	720	0.8
42782	SUMMERSVILLE	087	892	918	920	0.3	54	329	346	349	0.5	2.65	255	260	0.2
42784	UPTON	099	2643	2907	3025	1.0	83	1015	1145	1201	1.3	2.53	755	820	0.9
42788	WHITE MILLS	093	337	338	336	0.0	39	117	120	121	0.3	2.82	93	92	-0.1
45275	CINCINNATI	015	360	385	402	0.7	74	157	175	186	1.2	1.97	100	103	0.3
	KENTUCKY					0.7					1.0	2.41			0.6
	UNITED STATES					1.0					1.1	2.59			0.9

ZIP CODE #	POST OFFICE NAME	RACE (%) White 2000	White 2009	Black 2000	Black 2009	Asian/Pacific 2000	Asian/Pacific 2009	% Hispanic Origin 2000	% Hispanic Origin 2009	2009 AGE DISTRIBUTION (%) 0-4	5-9	10-14	15-19	20-24	25-44	45-64	65-84	85+	18+	MEDIAN AGE 2009	% 2009 Males	% 2009 Females
42567	EUBANK	98.8	98.4	0.2	0.2	0.1	0.2	1.3	2.1	6.0	6.1	6.3	6.2	5.5	26.9	28.6	13.1	1.5	77.7	40.3	50.6	49.4
42602	ALBANY	99.1	98.9	0.1	0.1	0.2	0.2	1.2	2.1	6.2	6.5	6.4	5.7	4.3	25.2	28.8	14.8	2.0	77.3	41.9	48.6	51.4
42603	ALPHA	99.0	98.9	0.5	0.5	0.0	0.0	1.3	2.1	6.8	6.8	7.1	7.6	5.5	27.0	26.5	11.3	1.4	74.2	37.8	50.7	49.3
42629	JAMESTOWN	97.5	97.1	1.5	1.6	0.2	0.3	0.8	1.3	5.6	5.9	6.3	5.8	4.3	23.7	29.9	15.7	2.8	78.5	43.8	49.1	50.9
42633	MONTICELLO	96.5	95.8	1.7	1.8	0.1	0.1	1.5	2.5	6.6	6.7	6.9	6.4	5.6	26.2	27.5	12.4	1.7	75.8	39.0	49.5	50.5
42634	PARKERS LAKE	98.4	97.9	0.1	0.1	0.0	0.0	0.4	0.8	7.1	8.0	7.2	6.6	6.6	25.3	28.5	9.8	0.8	73.3	36.1	51.5	48.5
42635	PINE KNOT	96.0	96.1	2.1	1.8	0.0	0.1	1.0	1.4	4.9	5.1	4.8	8.5	9.7	36.2	21.8	7.8	1.1	79.7	34.3	63.2	36.8
42638	REVELO	98.6	98.2	0.0	0.0	0.0	0.0	0.5	0.9	5.5	5.5	5.9	8.2	6.4	23.7	29.2	13.7	1.8	78.5	41.6	48.9	51.1
42642	RUSSELL SPRINGS	98.7	98.3	0.2	0.2	0.1	0.2	0.8	1.4	5.4	5.8	5.9	6.0	4.8	25.0	30.0	15.1	1.9	79.1	42.9	48.5	51.5
42647	STEARNS	98.5	98.1	0.2	0.2	0.0	0.0	0.5	0.9	6.2	6.2	7.1	7.3	5.8	25.4	28.6	12.0	1.3	75.9	38.9	49.0	51.0
42649	STRUNK	98.9	98.7	0.1	0.0	0.1	0.1	0.6	1.0	7.4	8.2	7.6	7.4	6.0	26.7	25.7	9.6	1.3	71.9	35.5	48.6	51.4
42653	WHITLEY CITY	98.8	98.4	0.1	0.2	0.0	0.0	0.5	0.8	6.3	6.5	7.5	7.7	6.5	25.9	28.8	9.6	1.2	75.0	36.9	48.8	51.2
42701	ELIZABETHTOWN	89.5	87.3	6.7	7.4	1.6	2.4	1.6	2.7	6.6	6.7	6.8	6.8	5.7	27.4	27.7	10.6	1.7	75.5	38.0	48.9	51.1
42712	BIG CLIFTY	98.9	98.5	0.1	0.1	0.1	0.2	0.7	1.2	6.5	6.6	6.9	6.3	4.9	28.0	28.8	10.9	1.2	76.2	38.9	51.5	48.5
42713	BONNIEVILLE	96.8	96.2	2.0	2.3	0.1	0.1	0.4	0.7	6.6	6.6	6.9	7.1	5.4	25.6	27.9	12.4	1.6	75.6	39.5	49.2	50.8
42715	BREEDING	96.8	96.3	1.2	1.1	0.3	0.3	0.3	0.6	6.2	6.5	6.8	6.5	5.1	24.9	29.1	13.6	1.4	76.3	40.0	48.9	51.1
42716	BUFFALO	97.4	96.8	1.4	1.5	0.6	0.9	0.6	1.0	5.5	6.2	6.6	6.4	4.8	25.2	31.3	12.6	1.5	77.8	41.7	49.5	50.5
42717	BURKESVILLE	95.4	94.8	3.3	3.5	0.1	0.1	0.6	1.0	5.8	6.0	6.3	6.3	4.9	23.6	28.6	15.9	2.6	77.9	42.9	48.6	51.4
42718	CAMPBELLSVILLE	93.5	92.8	5.1	5.5	0.2	0.3	0.8	1.4	5.9	5.9	6.1	7.1	6.2	23.9	28.6	14.2	2.1	78.3	41.2	48.6	51.4
42721	CANEYVILLE	99.1	98.9	0.1	0.1	0.0	0.0	0.4	0.7	6.0	6.1	6.4	7.0	5.3	26.0	28.2	13.5	1.6	77.2	40.0	49.4	50.6
42722	CANMER	91.3	90.2	6.6	7.4	0.0	0.0	1.0	1.3	6.5	7.1	7.0	6.1	4.1	24.6	29.5	13.5	1.6	75.7	41.3	50.7	49.3
42724	CECILIA	98.2	97.6	0.6	0.7	0.2	0.4	0.7	1.3	5.7	6.1	6.5	6.5	5.0	25.3	31.8	11.9	1.2	77.7	41.7	50.2	49.8
42726	CLARKSON	98.7	98.2	0.1	0.1	0.3	0.4	1.0	1.6	6.1	6.1	6.4	5.8	5.1	24.6	31.0	13.7	1.3	77.8	42.0	50.6	49.4
42728	COLUMBIA	95.6	95.0	2.9	3.1	0.3	0.5	0.8	1.2	6.0	6.0	6.2	7.4	6.9	25.1	26.9	13.5	2.1	78.1	39.4	48.6	51.4
42729	CUB RUN	97.8	97.6	1.3	1.3	0.1	0.1	0.9	1.5	6.8	6.6	6.6	7.8	6.5	23.6	27.6	13.3	1.3	75.3	38.4	51.4	48.6
42731	DUBRE	96.9	96.9	0.9	0.9	0.3	0.3	0.6	0.6	6.5	6.5	6.5	6.8	4.9	25.9	26.9	14.5	1.5	76.2	40.2	49.7	50.3
42732	EASTVIEW	98.6	98.0	0.3	0.3	0.5	0.8	0.6	1.2	6.1	6.3	6.3	6.0	5.3	25.9	30.3	12.5	1.4	77.6	40.7	50.6	49.4
42733	ELK HORN	98.8	98.5	0.3	0.3	0.0	0.0	0.7	1.2	7.1	7.0	7.1	6.9	6.2	25.5	27.2	12.0	1.0	74.5	37.4	51.3	48.7
42740	GLENDALE	96.4	95.3	1.4	1.6	0.7	1.2	1.1	1.9	6.4	6.7	6.9	6.6	4.9	25.0	30.5	11.6	1.3	75.9	40.2	49.2	50.8
42741	GLENS FORK	97.6	97.1	1.0	1.2	0.1	0.1	1.0	1.9	5.4	5.9	6.0	4.8	4.3	24.4	33.0	14.2	1.9	79.6	44.5	51.1	48.9
42742	GRADYVILLE	98.2	98.2	0.9	0.9	0.0	0.0	1.3	2.2	7.5	7.5	7.5	5.7	5.3	28.6	24.7	12.3	0.9	73.6	36.3	49.3	50.7
42743	GREENSBURG	96.0	95.9	2.8	2.8	0.1	0.1	1.0	1.0	5.3	5.4	5.7	6.0	5.2	24.3	29.9	15.6	2.7	79.8	43.7	49.5	50.5
42746	HARDYVILLE	94.0	93.2	4.4	5.0	0.4	0.4	1.6	2.4	6.5	6.5	6.6	6.8	5.5	27.2	28.3	11.0	1.5	76.1	39.0	49.9	50.1
42748	HODGENVILLE	92.9	92.1	5.1	5.4	0.1	0.2	1.2	1.9	6.3	6.3	6.3	6.6	4.9	25.0	28.5	13.5	2.6	77.1	41.1	48.3	51.7
42749	HORSE CAVE	87.9	86.8	10.8	11.6	0.1	0.2	0.7	1.1	6.2	6.5	6.6	6.2	4.8	26.6	27.3	13.6	2.2	76.7	40.0	49.5	50.5
42753	KNIFLEY	98.3	97.6	0.7	0.8	0.0	0.1	0.9	1.6	7.5	7.2	7.4	7.6	7.4	26.1	26.2	9.6	0.9	73.3	35.2	51.4	48.6
42754	LEITCHFIELD	97.9	97.5	0.7	0.8	0.1	0.2	0.8	1.3	6.5	6.4	6.5	6.6	5.6	26.4	27.0	13.0	1.9	76.6	39.0	49.4	50.6
42757	MAGNOLIA	97.8	97.4	0.6	0.7	0.2	0.3	1.2	1.9	6.5	6.7	7.3	6.9	5.0	25.8	28.1	12.0	1.6	75.1	39.3	49.7	50.3
42762	MILLWOOD	97.9	97.2	0.3	0.3	0.3	0.3	0.8	1.0	5.7	5.7	6.2	6.7	5.7	26.9	29.8	11.9	1.3	78.2	39.8	49.7	50.3
42764	MOUNT SHERMAN	97.3	96.8	1.4	1.6	0.4	0.6	0.6	1.0	5.7	6.2	6.4	5.7	4.9	25.6	30.7	13.1	1.7	78.4	41.8	49.5	50.5
42765	MUNFORDVILLE	93.3	92.5	5.6	6.1	0.1	0.1	0.8	1.3	7.0	7.0	7.1	6.6	5.5	24.9	27.0	13.1	1.7	74.8	38.8	49.3	50.7
42776	SONORA	96.4	95.5	1.6	1.9	0.4	0.6	0.7	1.3	7.5	6.8	7.5	9.2	5.1	23.7	27.4	11.0	1.7	71.4	37.1	49.5	50.5
42782	SUMMERSVILLE	97.0	96.8	1.9	2.1	0.0	0.0	0.9	0.9	6.2	6.3	7.0	7.3	4.9	26.3	28.0	12.1	2.0	75.9	39.7	50.9	49.1
42784	UPTON	96.6	95.9	1.4	1.7	0.2	0.2	0.6	1.0	6.3	7.4	6.9	7.2	5.5	25.1	28.1	11.5	2.0	74.9	38.6	50.4	49.6
42788	WHITE MILLS	98.5	97.9	0.0	0.0	0.0	0.3	1.8	3.3	5.9	6.2	6.8	7.1	5.3	23.1	32.2	12.1	1.2	76.6	41.6	50.9	49.1
45275	CINCINNATI	98.3	97.7	0.6	0.8	0.6	0.8	0.3	0.8	7.3	6.8	6.5	5.5	4.7	24.4	23.4	17.1	4.4	76.6	40.9	43.9	56.1
	KENTUCKY	90.1	88.9	7.3	7.5	0.8	1.2	1.5	2.4	6.5	6.5	6.5	6.8	6.5	27.0	27.1	11.3	1.8	76.6	37.9	49.1	50.9
	UNITED STATES	75.1	72.0	12.3	12.7	3.8	4.6	12.5	15.7	6.8	6.7	6.6	7.1	6.9	27.0	26.0	10.9	1.9	75.7	36.9	49.2	50.8

INCOME

#	ZIP CODE / POST OFFICE NAME	2009 Per Capita Income	2009 HH Income Base	2009 HOUSEHOLD INCOME DISTRIBUTION (%) Less than $25,000	$25,000 to $49,999	$50,000 to $99,999	$100,000 to $149,999	$150,000 or More	MEDIAN HOUSEHOLD INCOME 2009	2014	2009 National Centile	2009 State Centile	2009 Home Value Base	2009 HOME VALUE DISTRIBUTION (%) Less than $50,000	$50,000 to $89,999	$90,000 to $174,999	$175,000 to $399,999	$400,000 or More	2009 Median Home Value
42567	EUBANK	16066	2328	41.6	29.2	24.8	3.6	0.8	30931	33161	10	40	1986	37.1	26.0	27.6	8.0	1.4	69667
42602	ALBANY	15788	3853	51.5	28.0	17.2	2.2	1.2	23950	25094	3	19	2956	45.1	30.4	18.8	5.2	0.5	56293
42603	ALPHA	15223	1413	44.8	32.8	18.6	2.1	1.8	28474	30622	6	32	1203	49.6	26.0	18.4	5.5	0.5	50429
42629	JAMESTOWN	15653	2113	48.0	30.7	17.3	3.2	0.9	26634	27944	4	26	1668	32.4	26.9	29.0	10.4	1.4	75912
42633	MONTICELLO	15666	6898	49.2	29.5	17.3	1.7	2.3	25479	26259	4	24	5152	42.0	27.7	23.3	6.4	0.6	59448
42634	PARKERS LAKE	13912	607	55.2	32.9	8.9	0.8	2.1	20830	21525	2	10	506	64.4	25.5	7.9	1.6	0.6	36500
42635	PINE KNOT	11942	1623	54.5	29.7	13.9	1.7	0.3	20962	22577	2	10	1177	45.1	27.7	26.0	0.8	0.3	56765
42638	REVELO	11086	87	57.5	25.3	17.2	0.0	0.0	20297	23393	1	8	70	54.3	27.1	18.6	0.0	0.0	32500
42642	RUSSELL SPRINGS	16226	5704	46.4	32.5	16.8	2.7	1.6	27511	28552	5	30	4571	32.7	31.0	29.0	6.1	1.2	71870
42647	STEARNS	12462	1879	49.8	34.5	13.8	1.2	0.6	25068	25586	3	22	1468	48.2	29.4	20.4	1.7	0.3	52596
42649	STRUNK	11645	822	54.5	30.8	13.0	0.7	1.0	21204	22259	2	11	643	53.5	27.4	16.2	3.0	0.0	47384
42653	WHITLEY CITY	13270	1922	49.6	35.2	12.6	1.9	0.7	25182	25755	3	23	1408	40.8	29.6	24.3	5.1	0.1	60492
42701	ELIZABETHTOWN	25433	17796	20.5	29.2	38.0	8.1	4.2	50285	51961	62	86	12460	10.3	14.8	44.7	26.0	4.1	133810
42712	BIG CLIFTY	16700	747	30.9	40.3	24.5	3.7	0.5	35653	37039	20	53	644	26.2	26.9	35.9	9.5	1.6	82857
42713	BONNIEVILLE	16257	714	38.5	32.9	23.2	4.2	1.1	31069	31027	10	40	597	33.5	28.0	29.3	8.7	0.5	73289
42715	BREEDING	17503	146	40.4	33.6	19.2	2.7	4.1	28257	28510	6	32	116	51.7	19.8	23.3	3.4	1.7	48333
42716	BUFFALO	18721	584	28.1	35.1	31.2	3.9	1.7	39478	42579	31	63	499	15.0	30.5	39.1	14.4	1.0	95233
42717	BURKESVILLE	15544	3070	47.8	31.5	17.0	2.5	1.2	26908	28006	5	27	2381	37.6	31.7	25.4	4.7	0.6	64677
42718	CAMPBELLSVILLE	19181	9696	36.0	31.8	26.1	4.0	2.1	36050	37390	21	54	7070	16.2	28.5	44.5	9.9	0.9	94857
42721	CANEYVILLE	16733	1588	39.1	32.9	22.8	3.5	1.6	31444	32748	10	42	1279	31.0	28.1	30.4	8.8	1.6	76205
42722	CANMER	14552	263	43.0	25.9	27.8	3.4	0.0	31467	34746	10	42	220	27.7	26.4	35.9	10.0	0.0	84706
42724	CECILIA	20522	1914	19.4	36.3	37.4	5.9	1.0	45668	47499	50	79	1716	20.3	14.9	41.7	18.9	4.2	114831
42726	CLARKSON	18720	1880	28.6	37.5	28.4	4.2	1.3	36920	37741	23	57	1607	28.1	28.6	35.0	8.1	0.3	77359
42728	COLUMBIA	18371	5867	42.6	27.9	24.1	2.6	2.9	30116	30883	8	37	4628	29.9	30.7	31.3	7.2	0.9	77584
42729	CUB RUN	13814	578	39.1	40.1	19.2	1.4	0.2	32106	32551	12	43	507	27.8	29.6	35.3	7.3	0.0	81071
42731	DUBRE	14988	133	46.6	30.8	19.5	1.5	1.5	26665	27264	4	27	114	44.7	32.5	18.4	4.4	0.0	53750
42732	EASTVIEW	18618	773	26.3	35.7	32.6	4.4	1.0	42362	43773	41	71	681	29.2	20.9	31.4	17.2	1.3	89868
42733	ELK HORN	12855	539	47.5	31.9	19.3	0.6	0.7	26228	28271	4	25	449	33.6	31.0	29.6	2.7	3.1	67375
42740	GLENDALE	21584	674	18.5	26.7	46.1	7.4	1.2	53959	55071	70	90	577	8.8	14.7	46.4	28.9	1.0	135954
42741	GLENS FORK	17892	287	42.9	30.7	18.8	4.2	3.5	27762	28495	5	31	246	37.4	35.0	23.6	3.7	0.4	68889
42742	GRADYVILLE	16516	88	38.6	29.5	28.4	1.1	2.3	35903	37993	20	54	77	33.8	23.4	29.9	13.0	0.0	83125
42743	GREENSBURG	17803	3896	42.5	29.5	22.9	3.4	1.7	30579	30139	9	38	3004	28.5	37.9	28.0	5.3	0.3	72230
42746	HARDYVILLE	13977	708	38.1	31.8	27.0	3.1	0.0	33645	36409	15	46	586	29.5	28.2	34.3	8.0	0.0	79231
42748	HODGENVILLE	20454	3285	31.0	29.4	31.4	6.1	2.0	42429	44094	41	71	2496	16.7	25.1	39.9	16.2	2.1	102850
42749	HORSE CAVE	18498	2361	41.6	28.8	24.4	3.7	1.5	30984	31559	10	40	1656	21.3	34.4	38.4	5.4	0.5	83380
42753	KNIFLEY	14309	299	42.5	26.1	29.8	1.7	0.0	29635	30518	8	36	262	44.3	30.2	22.1	2.3	1.1	60476
42754	LEITCHFIELD	18603	6508	34.2	33.4	26.6	4.1	1.8	35129	35891	18	51	4832	23.9	30.0	37.3	8.5	0.3	84566
42757	MAGNOLIA	18707	1337	30.8	33.7	29.8	3.7	2.1	37318	40027	25	57	1151	23.9	27.7	33.4	13.0	1.9	87716
42762	MILLWOOD	21247	139	30.2	25.9	36.7	4.3	2.9	43835	45653	45	74	107	38.3	19.6	29.9	12.1	0.0	68750
42764	MOUNT SHERMAN	23655	365	29.9	31.8	30.1	4.4	3.8	40596	44085	35	66	308	26.3	29.9	31.8	11.4	0.6	80500
42765	MUNFORDVILLE	16118	2248	40.6	31.5	22.7	2.9	2.3	31598	32435	11	42	1709	23.1	31.9	36.5	7.1	1.4	84419
42776	SONORA	16157	965	33.9	30.6	30.2	4.7	0.7	35577	38725	19	52	787	21.7	27.7	32.4	14.7	3.4	90542
42782	SUMMERSVILLE	14684	346	33.5	40.2	22.5	3.8	0.0	32317	32632	12	44	292	46.2	26.0	25.3	2.4	0.0	53929
42784	UPTON	16144	1145	34.1	37.5	23.8	3.7	1.0	33570	36084	15	46	966	27.5	30.6	30.3	9.3	2.2	78400
42788	WHITE MILLS	21285	120	21.7	22.5	41.7	11.7	2.5	54481	55395	70	90	106	28.3	25.5	24.5	21.7	0.0	84286
45275	CINCINNATI	29113	175	12.6	38.9	34.3	12.6	1.7	49467	50493	60	85	154	76.6	11.7	9.7	1.9	0.0	36053
	KENTUCKY	23409		28.5	27.2	32.3	7.7	4.3	44205	46476				19.8	20.7	38.3	18.6	2.6	103937
	UNITED STATES	27277		20.9	24.4	35.3	11.7	7.6	54719	56938				9.3	13.1	31.6	32.6	13.5	162279

ZIP CODE	FINANCIAL SERVICES				THE HOME						ENTERTAINMENT						PERSONAL			
					Home Improvements		Furnishings													
# POST OFFICE NAME	Auto Loan	Home Loan	Invest-ments	Retire-ment Plans	Home Repair	Lawn & Garden	Comput-ers & Hard-ware-Personal	Major Appli-ances	TV, Radio, Sound Equip-ment	Furni-ture	Dine out/ Carry out	Sports Equip-ment	Fees & Tickets	Toys & Games	Travel	Cable TV	Apparel & Services	Auto Repairs	Health Insur-ance	Pets & Supplies
42567 EUBANK	71	51	62	49	51	69	53	63	59	51	58	48	42	61	49	64	39	59	66	76
42602 ALBANY	65	45	62	43	45	64	47	58	53	45	52	45	36	54	44	59	35	55	62	71
42603 ALPHA	69	49	58	48	49	66	51	60	57	50	56	46	41	59	47	63	38	57	64	73
42629 JAMESTOWN	63	45	64	44	47	64	46	59	51	43	51	44	37	51	46	57	33	54	61	70
42633 MONTICELLO	67	47	62	45	47	66	50	60	56	48	55	46	40	57	47	62	37	57	64	73
42634 PARKERS LAKE	65	43	63	40	42	64	46	57	53	43	51	45	34	54	43	59	34	54	61	71
42635 PINE KNOT	54	35	52	33	35	52	37	47	43	35	42	37	28	44	35	48	28	44	50	58
42638 REVELO	52	34	50	32	34	51	36	46	42	34	41	36	27	42	34	47	27	43	48	56
42642 RUSSELL SPRINGS	64	47	62	45	48	64	49	60	54	46	53	45	40	54	47	59	35	56	63	71
42647 STEARNS	57	37	55	35	37	55	39	50	46	37	44	39	30	46	37	51	29	47	53	61
42649 STRUNK	56	37	54	35	37	55	39	50	45	37	44	39	29	46	37	51	29	47	52	61
42653 WHITLEY CITY	60	39	58	37	39	59	42	53	48	40	47	41	31	49	39	54	31	50	56	65
42701 ELIZABETHTOWN	93	89	80	89	86	90	88	89	89	87	89	68	85	91	85	90	61	88	90	105
42712 BIG CLIFTY	75	54	62	52	53	71	56	65	62	54	61	50	45	64	51	67	41	62	69	79
42713 BONNIEVILLE	73	52	67	51	53	71	54	65	60	52	59	50	43	61	51	65	39	61	68	79
42715 BREEDING	77	55	63	53	55	73	57	67	63	56	62	51	46	66	52	69	42	63	70	81
42716 BUFFALO	76	66	71	68	68	81	66	76	69	60	68	57	59	70	66	73	46	70	79	89
42717 BURKESVILLE	63	45	61	44	46	63	48	58	53	45	52	44	38	53	46	58	35	55	62	70
42718 CAMPBELLSVILLE	73	59	68	59	60	75	62	71	67	57	65	53	54	67	60	72	44	67	76	84
42721 CANEYVILLE	74	51	66	49	52	71	54	65	60	52	59	50	42	62	50	66	39	61	68	79
42722 CANMER	67	46	73	46	48	70	51	63	53	41	52	52	37	52	51	58	34	59	67	78
42724 CECILIA	87	71	76	72	72	88	72	82	76	67	75	63	62	79	69	82	51	77	86	97
42726 CLARKSON	76	58	68	56	59	75	60	69	65	59	64	51	50	66	56	71	43	66	74	83
42728 COLUMBIA	77	55	71	54	56	76	59	70	65	55	64	53	47	66	55	71	43	66	75	84
42729 CUB RUN	63	45	57	44	46	61	47	56	52	45	51	43	37	53	44	57	34	53	59	68
42731 DUBRE	66	47	55	46	47	63	49	58	54	48	53	44	39	57	45	59	36	54	61	70
42732 EASTVIEW	85	62	76	61	63	83	64	76	70	61	69	58	52	72	60	77	46	71	80	92
42733 ELK HORN	63	45	53	44	45	60	47	55	52	46	51	42	38	54	43	57	34	52	58	67
42740 GLENDALE	90	81	79	83	81	93	79	88	82	74	81	67	73	84	78	86	55	82	91	103
42741 GLENS FORK	76	54	78	53	56	77	56	71	62	52	61	53	45	61	55	68	40	65	74	84
42742 GRADYVILLE	77	55	63	54	55	73	57	67	64	56	62	51	46	66	52	69	42	63	70	81
42743 GREENSBURG	73	53	69	52	54	73	56	67	62	52	60	51	45	62	53	67	40	63	71	81
42746 HARDYVILLE	67	47	63	47	48	67	51	61	55	46	54	48	39	56	48	60	36	57	64	74
42748 HODGENVILLE	82	66	72	65	66	81	68	76	73	64	71	58	59	74	64	78	48	73	81	91
42749 HORSE CAVE	78	55	76	53	56	79	59	72	65	54	64	56	46	65	56	71	42	67	77	87
42753 KNIFLEY	66	47	54	46	47	62	49	57	54	48	53	44	39	57	45	59	36	54	60	69
42754 LEITCHFIELD	78	58	66	57	58	75	62	70	68	59	66	53	51	69	57	73	45	67	74	84
42757 MAGNOLIA	86	61	74	60	61	83	64	75	71	61	69	59	51	73	59	77	46	71	80	92
42762 MILLWOOD	107	76	88	74	76	101	80	92	88	77	86	71	64	92	72	96	58	88	98	113
42764 MOUNT SHERMAN	99	77	93	77	79	101	78	94	84	72	83	71	66	85	76	91	55	86	97	111
42765 MUNFORDVILLE	73	54	64	52	54	71	56	65	61	54	60	50	45	63	52	67	40	62	69	79
42776 SONORA	79	57	71	55	57	77	59	71	65	56	64	54	47	67	55	71	43	66	74	85
42782 SUMMERSVILLE	70	50	62	49	51	68	52	62	58	50	57	47	42	59	49	63	38	58	65	75
42784 UPTON	73	53	69	51	54	73	54	67	60	51	59	50	43	61	52	66	39	62	70	80
42788 WHITE MILLS	93	85	84	88	86	100	83	94	86	75	84	71	77	88	83	91	58	87	97	109
45275 CINCINNATI	95	89	76	85	85	86	88	87	88	92	89	67	83	92	83	88	61	88	86	104
KENTUCKY	90	77	81	77	76	88	80	85	83	78	83	65	73	85	76	87	57	83	88	101
UNITED STATES	100	100	100	100	100	100	100	100	100	100	100	100	100	100	100	100	100	100	100	100

POPULATION CHANGE

ZIP CODE #	POST OFFICE NAME	COUNTY FIPS CODE	POPULATION 2000	POPULATION 2009	POPULATION 2014	2000-2009 ANNUAL RATE % Rate	2000-2009 ANNUAL RATE State Centile	HOUSEHOLDS 2000	HOUSEHOLDS 2009	HOUSEHOLDS 2014	HOUSEHOLDS % Annual Rate 2000-2009	HOUSEHOLDS 2009 Average HH Size	FAMILIES 2000	FAMILIES 2009	FAMILIES % Annual Rate 2000-2009
70001	METAIRIE	051	39365	37535	36799	-0.5	21	18388	17492	17177	-0.5	2.14	10024	9305	-0.8
70002	METAIRIE	051	19423	18528	18134	-0.5	21	8865	8435	8270	-0.5	2.19	5047	4682	-0.8
70003	METAIRIE	051	43344	41573	40759	-0.4	24	16711	16074	15799	-0.4	2.57	12091	11405	-0.6
70005	METAIRIE	051	25465	24027	23456	-0.6	17	12114	11442	11191	-0.6	2.10	6770	6219	-0.9
70006	METAIRIE	051	16656	15284	14891	-0.9	10	7027	6397	6237	-1.0	2.37	4641	4182	-1.1
70030	DES ALLEMANDS	089	4133	3752	3736	-1.0	9	1498	1367	1364	-1.0	2.74	1190	1077	-1.1
70031	AMA	089	1385	1067	1005	-2.8	5	477	370	349	-2.7	2.88	376	290	-2.8
70032	ARABI	087	8093	2726	5221	-11.1	0	3474	1233	2404	-10.6	2.15	2246	772	-10.9
70036	BARATARIA	051	1328	1248	1216	-0.7	14	498	469	458	-0.6	2.66	367	338	-0.9
70037	BELLE CHASSE	075	12130	15564	16419	2.7	96	4130	5389	5712	2.9	2.85	3300	4233	2.7
70039	BOUTTE	089	2389	2815	2948	1.8	91	820	975	1024	1.9	2.88	624	732	1.7
70040	BRAITHWAITE	075	3246	3058	3041	-0.6	17	999	1009	1015	0.1	2.79	775	771	-0.1
70041	BURAS	075	7206	4944	4533	-4.0	4	2461	1736	1607	-3.7	2.84	1859	1282	-3.9
70043	CHALMETTE	087	32084	12863	27013	-9.4	0	12327	5137	10792	-9.0	2.50	8827	3557	-9.4
70047	DESTREHAN	089	12674	15131	15936	1.9	91	4114	4931	5200	2.0	3.03	3431	4069	1.9
70049	EDGARD	095	2737	3304	3565	2.1	93	885	1093	1188	2.3	3.02	717	874	2.2
70051	GARYVILLE	095	2095	2243	2318	0.7	74	687	753	784	1.0	2.97	540	584	0.9
70052	GRAMERCY	093	3216	3340	3381	0.4	61	1138	1211	1237	0.7	2.75	876	920	0.5
70053	GRETNA	051	17414	16747	16555	-0.4	24	6956	6755	6695	-0.3	2.39	4281	4046	-0.6
70056	GRETNA	051	40353	38411	37944	-0.5	21	14592	13806	13658	-0.6	2.77	10802	10071	-0.8
70057	HAHNVILLE	089	3528	3134	3117	-1.3	7	1219	1074	1068	-1.4	2.83	928	806	-1.5
70058	HARVEY	051	41973	39983	39512	-0.5	21	13690	12921	12773	-0.6	3.06	10851	10205	-0.7
70062	KENNER	051	18945	18210	17895	-0.4	24	6737	6481	6379	-0.4	2.78	4808	4534	-0.6
70065	KENNER	051	53584	51130	50344	-0.5	21	19607	18739	18482	-0.5	2.71	14199	13316	-0.7
70067	LAFITTE	051	4196	4117	4075	-0.2	29	1437	1411	1400	-0.2	2.92	1137	1096	-0.4
70068	LA PLACE	095	30446	35521	37624	1.7	90	10058	11934	12714	1.9	2.94	8047	9450	1.8
70070	LULING	089	11457	12437	12866	0.9	80	3883	4247	4404	1.0	2.90	3206	3493	0.9
70071	LUTCHER	093	3807	3984	4010	0.5	66	1275	1349	1370	0.6	2.83	1007	1053	0.5
70072	MARRERO	051	56998	57364	57153	0.1	44	19065	19199	19155	0.1	2.96	15109	15063	0.0
70075	MERAUX	087	8066	3799	7460	-7.8	1	2958	1403	2788	-7.7	2.71	2195	1042	-7.7
70076	MOUNT AIRY	095	683	731	748	0.7	74	226	248	255	1.0	2.95	180	195	0.9
70079	NORCO	089	3706	4092	4237	1.1	82	1364	1530	1590	1.2	2.67	1013	1118	1.1
70080	PARADIS	089	1408	1664	1768	1.8	91	494	588	626	1.9	2.83	378	440	1.7
70081	PILOTTOWN	075	4	3	3	-3.1	5	1	1	1	0.0	1.00	1	0	-100.0
70083	PORT SULPHUR	075	4155	3476	3338	-1.9	5	1424	1231	1196	-1.6	2.81	1058	894	-1.8
70084	RESERVE	095	7450	8053	8308	0.8	77	2553	2813	2925	1.1	2.86	1917	2076	0.9
70085	SAINT BERNARD	087	7460	4387	6445	-5.6	3	2565	1567	2307	-5.2	2.78	1963	1185	-5.3
70086	SAINT JAMES	093	2243	2379	2388	0.6	71	675	722	731	0.7	3.13	551	583	0.6
70087	SAINT ROSE	089	6597	8424	9062	2.7	96	2310	2976	3208	2.8	2.83	1766	2239	2.6
70090	VACHERIE	093	7317	7686	7819	0.5	66	2429	2622	2692	0.8	2.93	1940	2070	0.7
70091	VENICE	075	241	166	153	-4.0	4	91	65	60	-3.6	2.54	67	46	-4.0
70092	VIOLET	087	11301	5417	9783	-7.6	2	3714	1812	3281	-7.5	2.98	3009	1454	-7.6
70094	WESTWEGO	051	34150	34598	34484	0.1	44	11843	11983	11958	0.1	2.87	8954	8935	0.0
70112	NEW ORLEANS	071	6342	4246	5470	-4.2	4	2439	1748	2274	-3.5	2.42	1295	882	-4.1
70113	NEW ORLEANS	071	10421	7765	9894	-3.1	5	4162	3014	3861	-3.4	2.56	2096	1537	-3.3
70114	NEW ORLEANS	071	28469	25275	28095	-1.3	7	10381	8821	9860	-1.7	2.84	6706	5817	-1.5
70115	NEW ORLEANS	071	40371	36707	41543	-1.0	9	18230	16115	18269	-1.3	2.24	8710	7781	-1.2
70116	NEW ORLEANS	071	16895	13727	16749	-2.2	5	8014	6457	7769	-2.3	2.12	3326	2617	-2.6
70117	NEW ORLEANS	071	51258	24001	32728	-7.9	1	18804	8909	12054	-7.8	2.69	12073	5371	-8.4
70118	NEW ORLEANS	071	37235	35142	41017	-0.6	17	15210	12900	15314	-1.8	2.39	7907	6703	-1.8
70119	NEW ORLEANS	071	49794	33814	44864	-4.1	4	18440	13168	17661	-3.6	2.41	9832	7096	-3.5
70121	NEW ORLEANS	051	12998	12471	12260	-0.4	24	5930	5728	5640	-0.4	2.11	3188	2978	-0.7
70122	NEW ORLEANS	071	46533	24384	34814	-6.7	2	17819	8820	12847	-7.3	2.65	11946	5976	-7.2
70123	NEW ORLEANS	051	27721	26686	26222	-0.4	24	12149	11806	11651	-0.3	2.24	7477	7043	-0.6
70124	NEW ORLEANS	071	23000	11756	18094	-7.0	2	10753	5166	8105	-7.6	2.28	6152	3106	-7.1
70125	NEW ORLEANS	071	23442	14106	18853	-5.3	3	8790	5095	7042	-5.7	2.52	5205	2998	-5.8
70126	NEW ORLEANS	071	40834	17411	24969	-8.8	1	14561	5937	8582	-9.2	2.92	10584	4437	-9.0
70127	NEW ORLEANS	071	30570	13911	19612	-8.2	1	11396	4913	6934	-8.7	2.82	7944	3531	-8.4
70128	NEW ORLEANS	071	21448	13384	17775	-5.0	3	6974	4141	5564	-5.5	3.22	5478	3308	-5.3
70129	NEW ORLEANS	071	14979	8389	10443	-6.1	2	4662	2374	3023	-7.0	3.52	3651	1942	-6.6
70130	NEW ORLEANS	071	14770	13610	14722	-0.9	10	7312	6534	7121	-1.2	2.04	2676	2466	-0.9
70131	NEW ORLEANS	071	28325	29354	31061	0.4	61	10307	10184	10915	-0.1	2.87	7396	7476	0.1
70301	THIBODAUX	057	39652	41042	41422	0.4	61	14312	15031	15238	0.5	2.65	10368	10740	0.4
70339	PIERRE PART	007	5647	5815	5755	0.3	53	2157	2285	2284	0.6	2.54	1627	1702	0.5
70341	BELLE ROSE	007	4276	4193	4098	-0.2	29	1451	1463	1445	0.1	2.87	1122	1118	0.0
70342	BERWICK	101	4183	3921	3771	-0.7	14	1565	1489	1442	-0.5	2.63	1120	1047	-0.7
70343	BOURG	109	4493	4893	5003	0.9	80	1459	1630	1681	1.2	3.00	1249	1382	1.1
70344	CHAUVIN	109	6962	7150	7193	0.3	53	2338	2451	2487	0.5	2.92	1908	1976	0.4
70345	CUT OFF	057	13256	13772	13781	0.4	61	4624	4862	4891	0.5	2.80	3668	3807	0.4
70346	DONALDSONVILLE	005	11384	12290	13141	0.8	77	3897	4343	4688	1.2	2.77	2909	3189	1.0
70353	DULAC	109	2160	2010	1954	-0.8	12	672	638	623	-0.6	3.15	541	503	-0.8
70354	GALLIANO	057	4652	4928	4975	0.6	71	1690	1810	1837	0.7	2.72	1300	1372	0.6
70355	GHEENS	057	579	603	600	0.4	61	178	187	187	0.5	3.22	142	148	0.4
70356	GIBSON	109	1913	1982	2002	0.4	61	666	704	716	0.6	2.82	521	543	0.4
70357	GOLDEN MEADOW	057	3337	3245	3193	-0.3	27	1212	1182	1168	-0.3	2.74	880	844	-0.5
70358	GRAND ISLE	051	1541	1336	1274	-1.5	6	622	541	517	-1.5	2.45	436	371	-1.7
70359	GRAY	109	6629	7921	8312	1.9	91	2243	2724	2881	2.1	2.91	1740	2089	2.0
70360	HOUMA	109	21511	24105	25093	1.2	84	7639	8677	9077	1.4	2.71	5738	6461	1.3
70363	HOUMA	109	26957	27916	28119	0.4	61	8659	9102	9218	0.5	2.99	6763	7028	0.4
70364	HOUMA	057	27505	28848	29239	0.5	66	10217	10881	11089	0.7	2.64	7303	7655	0.5
70372	LABADIEVILLE	007	3028	3042	2998	0.0	38	1116	1153	1148	0.4	2.64	854	872	0.2
70374	LOCKPORT	057	10598	10879	10915	0.3	53	3750	3887	3917	0.4	2.80	2926	2994	0.2
70375	MATHEWS	057	549	576	577	0.5	66	199	211	213	0.6	2.73	159	166	0.5
70377	MONTEGUT	109	4086	4206	4235	0.3	53	1332	1394	1412	0.5	3.02	1066	1101	0.3
70380	MORGAN CITY	099	23257	22744	22196	-0.2	29	8769	8797	8660	0.0	2.55	6186	6119	-0.1
70390	NAPOLEONVILLE	007	7807	7709	7553	-0.1	35	2615	2643	2610	0.1	2.84	2019	2019	0.0
70392	PATTERSON	101	7190	7226	7091	0.1	44	2568	2635	2604	0.3	2.73	1922	1957	0.2
70394	RACELAND	057	13353	14081	14296	0.6	71	4773	5085	5188	0.7	2.75	3718	3905	0.5
70395	SCHRIEVER	109	4715	5239	5410	1.1	82	1587	1797	1868	1.4	2.91	1300	1458	1.2
70397	THERIOT	109	1610	1602	1593	-0.1	35	489	497	498	0.2	3.22	403	405	0.1
70401	HAMMOND	105	16828	20650	22546	2.2	93	6529	8093	8897	2.3	2.42	3947	4829	2.2
70402	HAMMOND	105	1032	1188	1225	1.5	88	0	0	0	0.0	0.00	0	0	0.0
70403	HAMMOND	105	20785	25334	27743	2.2	93	7766	9563	10531	2.3	2.58	5362	6510	2.1
70420	ABITA SPRINGS	103	4932	6745	7677	3.4	99	1825	2479	2829	3.4	2.72	1357	1809	3.2
70422	AMITE	091	14843	16276	17022	1.0	80	5233	5798	6101	1.1	2.70	3818	4171	1.0
	LOUISIANA					0.0					0.1	2.60			0.1
	UNITED STATES					1.0					1.1	2.59			0.9

#	POST OFFICE NAME	RACE (%) White 2000	White 2009	Black 2000	Black 2009	Asian/Pacific 2000	Asian/Pacific 2009	% Hispanic Origin 2000	% Hispanic Origin 2009	2009 AGE DISTRIBUTION (%) 0-4	5-9	10-14	15-19	20-24	25-44	45-64	65-84	85+	18+	MEDIAN AGE 2009	% 2009 Males	% 2009 Females
70001	METAIRIE	86.4	81.4	7.9	10.7	2.1	3.1	6.7	8.2	5.7	5.2	5.1	5.3	7.7	28.9	27.1	12.5	2.5	81.0	39.4	48.1	51.9
70002	METAIRIE	82.8	76.7	6.0	8.0	5.0	7.6	10.9	13.0	5.0	4.4	4.5	5.2	7.1	26.7	28.3	16.1	2.6	83.0	42.7	48.6	51.4
70003	METAIRIE	83.5	78.9	11.0	13.3	1.8	2.9	7.2	9.2	6.0	6.1	6.4	6.2	5.4	24.4	28.8	14.6	2.1	77.6	41.8	47.6	52.4
70005	METAIRIE	94.8	92.4	0.9	1.3	2.3	3.6	4.4	5.7	4.6	4.6	5.0	5.1	5.7	25.0	29.7	16.6	3.8	82.7	45.0	47.6	52.4
70006	METAIRIE	86.7	80.9	3.0	4.3	5.3	8.2	9.2	11.5	5.6	5.5	5.7	5.2	5.2	26.0	28.4	15.8	2.6	80.0	42.7	47.3	52.7
70030	DES ALLEMANDS	89.5	88.0	8.2	9.2	0.1	0.1	2.1	2.6	7.1	7.1	7.6	6.8	5.4	27.8	28.0	9.3	0.9	73.9	36.9	49.8	50.2
70031	AMA	67.0	59.7	32.2	39.2	0.2	0.4	1.1	1.4	6.0	7.3	7.0	9.8	6.4	26.0	28.0	9.0	0.5	72.9	36.5	50.5	49.5
70032	ARABI	94.8	89.7	2.0	6.2	0.8	1.1	5.0	6.4	4.9	5.0	4.9	5.1	5.1	24.9	27.6	18.6	3.9	82.0	45.0	48.1	51.9
70036	BARATARIA	87.0	80.4	11.1	17.0	0.0	0.0	1.9	2.5	5.4	5.8	6.1	5.8	4.5	24.7	31.3	15.0	1.4	79.1	43.4	49.3	50.7
70037	BELLE CHASSE	87.5	81.5	9.0	13.5	0.8	1.5	2.2	2.5	8.6	7.9	7.5	6.9	6.5	29.9	23.5	8.4	0.8	71.5	33.3	49.4	50.6
70039	BOUTTE	40.1	30.4	57.4	67.2	0.2	0.1	2.6	2.5	9.0	8.7	7.9	7.9	7.4	26.1	23.8	8.1	1.1	69.6	31.1	47.4	52.6
70040	BRAITHWAITE	43.1	39.2	54.9	58.8	0.4	0.5	1.8	1.9	6.8	6.7	6.9	7.0	6.2	26.7	26.6	11.3	1.8	75.4	37.6	50.3	49.7
70041	BURAS	65.1	59.3	22.8	24.9	7.6	10.6	1.2	1.4	7.8	7.7	7.5	7.5	7.3	26.3	25.7	9.3	0.9	72.4	33.7	50.3	49.7
70043	CHALMETTE	93.0	89.1	2.1	4.7	1.8	2.4	4.8	5.8	6.3	5.9	5.7	5.8	6.2	27.4	27.0	13.7	2.1	78.7	39.3	48.1	51.9
70047	DESTREHAN	80.9	74.8	16.6	22.1	0.9	1.1	3.6	4.2	7.1	7.9	8.6	8.0	5.0	25.8	29.3	7.3	1.1	71.1	37.1	48.8	51.2
70049	EDGARD	4.7	3.8	94.8	95.6	0.0	0.0	0.1	0.1	7.0	7.3	7.5	7.9	6.6	23.3	27.0	11.7	1.6	73.3	37.0	46.0	54.0
70051	GARYVILLE	47.2	44.6	51.6	53.9	0.3	0.4	0.8	0.8	7.8	7.6	9.3	9.2	6.5	24.2	23.6	10.0	1.7	70.0	34.0	46.5	53.5
70052	GRAMERCY	64.3	59.9	34.1	38.3	0.1	0.1	0.7	0.8	7.1	7.7	8.0	7.2	4.9	26.8	25.2	12.0	1.1	73.0	37.8	49.0	51.0
70053	GRETNA	54.6	46.4	37.2	43.6	3.2	4.3	6.3	7.2	7.2	6.4	6.0	6.5	7.8	27.4	24.9	11.8	1.9	76.6	36.4	50.1	49.9
70056	GRETNA	59.1	51.3	30.8	36.2	4.3	6.1	8.1	9.0	7.6	7.0	6.5	6.7	7.3	28.4	25.8	9.8	0.9	74.9	34.9	48.3	51.7
70057	HAHNVILLE	39.5	26.8	59.3	72.0	0.1	0.1	1.0	1.1	7.7	7.8	8.4	7.9	6.7	27.9	23.8	8.5	1.3	71.0	33.9	49.5	50.5
70058	HARVEY	40.0	33.3	50.6	55.4	5.6	7.3	5.3	5.5	8.0	7.9	7.6	8.0	7.5	28.2	25.5	6.6	0.7	71.4	32.4	48.0	52.0
70062	KENNER	49.2	41.8	45.5	51.9	1.0	1.3	7.1	7.9	8.0	8.0	7.6	7.7	6.4	25.9	24.5	10.1	1.8	71.6	35.0	46.8	53.2
70065	KENNER	75.3	68.0	14.2	18.5	3.5	5.1	15.6	17.7	6.6	6.6	6.7	6.7	6.4	28.7	28.0	9.3	1.0	76.0	36.5	48.5	51.5
70067	LAFITTE	92.3	89.6	1.3	2.1	1.1	1.8	2.3	2.9	6.2	6.5	6.6	6.0	5.4	28.1	29.0	11.2	0.9	77.0	38.1	51.2	48.8
70068	LA PLACE	60.5	55.9	36.2	39.9	0.7	0.9	3.7	4.4	8.1	8.1	7.9	7.6	6.3	28.1	26.0	7.2	0.8	71.3	33.5	48.9	51.1
70070	LULING	81.3	79.0	16.3	18.0	0.8	1.0	2.5	3.0	7.0	7.3	7.4	7.5	5.6	27.0	28.6	8.5	1.1	73.6	36.5	47.8	52.2
70071	LUTCHER	51.2	49.5	48.5	50.1	0.0	0.0	0.4	0.5	6.0	6.2	6.9	8.4	5.4	23.3	27.6	12.8	3.3	75.9	40.4	47.4	52.6
70072	MARRERO	57.9	51.1	36.1	41.1	2.9	4.0	4.5	5.3	7.3	7.6	7.7	7.7	6.1	27.0	26.2	9.2	1.1	72.5	35.1	47.3	52.7
70075	MERAUX	92.3	87.0	4.0	7.9	1.7	2.7	3.7	4.3	7.0	7.0	7.1	7.0	5.7	27.7	28.3	9.1	1.2	74.6	37.4	47.5	52.5
70076	MOUNT AIRY	44.1	39.4	55.2	59.8	0.0	0.0	0.4	0.5	7.1	7.4	7.5	7.7	5.6	23.1	28.5	11.6	1.5	73.2	38.2	50.2	49.8
70079	NORCO	75.6	77.9	22.4	19.5	0.3	0.4	2.0	2.4	6.2	6.4	6.5	7.1	5.8	26.2	27.2	12.5	2.0	76.5	38.9	48.1	51.9
70080	PARADIS	84.7	78.7	12.6	18.1	0.4	0.4	2.3	2.9	8.5	8.0	7.2	6.9	8.2	27.8	25.6	7.1	0.8	72.4	32.0	50.8	49.2
70081	PILOTTOWN	25.0	0.0	75.0	100.0	0.0	0.0	0.0	0.0	0.0	0.0	0.0	0.0	100.0	0.0	0.0	0.0	0.0	100.0	22.5	66.7	33.3
70083	PORT SULPHUR	47.2	37.7	42.3	49.9	0.8	0.8	1.0	1.1	7.1	7.2	7.3	7.5	6.1	25.1	27.8	10.6	1.3	73.7	37.0	49.2	50.8
70084	RESERVE	45.6	43.3	52.8	54.8	0.3	0.5	1.0	1.2	8.1	8.4	8.1	7.8	5.9	25.2	24.9	10.3	1.3	70.4	33.8	48.3	51.7
70085	SAINT BERNARD	89.2	77.8	7.4	18.3	0.3	0.4	8.6	9.0	7.3	7.0	6.7	7.1	7.4	27.5	26.8	9.3	1.0	74.8	35.1	49.9	50.1
70086	SAINT JAMES	11.4	9.1	88.0	90.2	0.0	0.0	1.2	1.3	7.5	7.4	8.4	10.5	6.2	24.1	25.1	9.4	1.4	69.4	32.7	47.6	52.4
70087	SAINT ROSE	55.5	48.1	41.2	48.1	0.5	0.5	4.5	5.0	7.2	7.9	8.1	8.1	6.2	29.5	24.4	7.9	0.6	71.6	33.8	48.3	51.7
70090	VACHERIE	45.7	41.3	53.9	58.2	0.0	0.0	0.6	0.6	7.2	7.3	7.2	6.7	5.9	26.3	28.0	10.2	1.1	74.3	36.8	48.5	51.5
70091	VENICE	82.6	75.3	6.2	7.2	5.0	9.0	0.8	1.8	8.4	9.0	8.4	6.0	6.0	25.3	26.5	9.0	1.2	69.9	34.5	52.4	47.6
70092	VIOLET	66.9	50.9	29.9	46.0	0.8	1.0	4.5	4.3	7.3	7.3	7.3	7.7	6.2	28.2	27.0	8.3	0.6	73.4	34.9	48.5	51.5
70094	WESTWEGO	56.8	48.1	36.2	43.2	3.7	4.9	4.2	4.9	7.7	7.3	7.1	7.9	7.4	26.1	25.2	10.4	1.0	73.1	34.3	47.7	52.3
70112	NEW ORLEANS	17.6	15.2	78.0	81.0	2.9	2.3	1.3	1.7	10.7	10.3	8.1	7.8	9.4	25.6	19.0	7.7	1.2	65.8	27.3	45.7	54.3
70113	NEW ORLEANS	8.2	6.5	89.7	91.3	0.7	0.8	1.6	1.9	7.1	7.8	7.9	8.3	6.8	24.2	24.5	11.4	1.9	72.1	34.6	46.1	53.9
70114	NEW ORLEANS	22.0	15.9	73.5	79.9	1.2	1.2	4.3	4.4	9.0	8.9	8.6	8.1	7.9	25.9	21.9	7.9	1.7	68.5	30.0	45.5	54.5
70115	NEW ORLEANS	45.6	40.9	51.0	54.8	0.9	1.4	3.2	4.7	5.9	5.5	5.2	5.7	8.0	32.3	25.1	10.1	2.2	80.0	36.3	47.2	52.8
70116	NEW ORLEANS	28.6	28.3	68.8	68.5	0.5	0.8	2.5	3.3	6.3	6.4	5.4	5.9	6.8	27.2	28.6	11.5	1.9	78.4	39.2	50.6	49.4
70117	NEW ORLEANS	9.4	11.4	88.8	86.4	0.2	0.3	2.0	3.2	7.5	7.5	7.4	7.9	7.5	25.4	25.5	9.9	1.4	72.8	34.3	47.0	53.0
70118	NEW ORLEANS	45.0	45.0	51.1	49.2	1.5	2.7	3.2	5.3	5.2	5.0	4.9	9.4	15.2	26.6	22.0	10.1	1.7	80.9	31.5	48.5	51.5
70119	NEW ORLEANS	23.6	21.2	71.5	73.7	0.9	1.0	5.6	6.7	6.3	6.2	5.8	6.9	8.5	28.9	25.7	9.5	2.0	77.7	36.0	49.2	50.8
70121	NEW ORLEANS	74.1	68.9	21.5	25.4	1.4	2.1	4.9	5.9	5.2	5.2	4.9	5.1	6.4	28.2	29.2	12.5	3.2	81.5	41.6	48.6	51.4
70122	NEW ORLEANS	23.0	18.1	73.2	77.7	1.1	1.5	3.2	3.7	6.0	6.4	6.4	9.0	8.1	23.3	26.4	12.1	2.3	76.9	37.0	44.8	55.2
70123	NEW ORLEANS	89.4	86.2	7.4	9.3	1.2	2.0	3.1	4.0	5.1	5.0	5.4	5.5	6.7	26.9	29.2	13.8	2.5	81.1	41.5	48.1	51.9
70124	NEW ORLEANS	95.6	92.5	1.3	2.6	1.2	2.2	3.9	7.0	5.4	5.3	5.8	5.4	5.7	24.4	31.2	12.9	3.9	80.3	43.7	47.6	52.4
70125	NEW ORLEANS	24.6	24.1	72.4	71.8	1.1	1.8	2.6	3.9	6.5	6.1	5.5	12.4	9.8	25.4	22.3	9.7	2.3	78.3	31.7	43.4	56.6
70126	NEW ORLEANS	10.4	6.8	87.0	90.7	0.8	0.9	1.5	1.6	7.2	7.3	7.2	7.8	7.6	25.4	25.5	10.5	1.5	73.8	34.2	45.8	54.2
70127	NEW ORLEANS	11.2	7.7	85.8	89.1	1.0	1.4	1.6	1.7	7.5	7.7	7.8	8.2	7.2	25.4	26.0	8.8	1.4	72.0	33.9	44.9	55.1
70128	NEW ORLEANS	8.5	5.4	86.5	89.4	3.0	3.4	1.6	1.5	6.8	7.6	7.9	8.6	7.0	27.0	27.7	6.6	0.8	72.3	32.9	46.2	53.8
70129	NEW ORLEANS	14.9	9.5	50.6	51.0	32.4	37.5	2.2	2.6	9.7	8.8	7.7	8.1	8.6	27.6	21.3	7.4	0.7	68.9	29.1	47.5	52.5
70130	NEW ORLEANS	46.7	39.3	48.7	55.2	1.3	1.8	4.7	6.4	5.7	5.7	5.3	6.1	9.3	32.0	24.8	9.1	2.0	79.7	34.4	49.6	50.4
70131	NEW ORLEANS	49.7	40.5	41.9	49.7	5.4	6.6	4.1	5.4	7.3	7.5	7.8	7.5	6.7	25.5	26.1	10.3	1.3	72.8	36.0	47.0	53.0
70301	THIBODAUX	76.3	71.4	21.7	26.1	0.6	0.8	1.0	1.2	7.0	6.8	6.6	7.7	7.3	28.0	25.2	9.9	1.5	75.5	34.9	48.2	51.8
70339	PIERRE PART	98.2	97.6	1.0	1.3	0.0	0.0	1.0	1.3	6.6	6.6	6.8	6.7	5.9	27.3	28.2	10.8	1.0	75.9	37.9	48.7	51.3
70341	BELLE ROSE	47.9	42.1	51.4	57.2	0.1	0.1	1.2	1.3	7.2	7.2	7.1	7.3	5.9	26.9	27.0	10.0	1.4	74.1	36.0	49.3	50.7
70342	BERWICK	86.1	82.9	8.6	9.9	0.8	1.3	1.5	2.0	7.7	7.3	7.2	7.8	6.0	26.8	25.9	10.2	1.1	72.8	35.9	48.2	51.8
70343	BOURG	90.3	87.6	2.9	3.4	0.3	0.4	0.6	0.8	6.8	7.1	7.1	7.4	6.4	27.3	28.5	8.6	0.8	74.4	36.4	50.4	49.6
70344	CHAUVIN	92.4	90.5	4.3	5.0	0.3	0.5	0.7	1.0	7.0	7.1	7.0	6.8	5.7	26.5	27.6	11.2	1.0	74.8	37.8	50.7	49.3
70345	CUT OFF	88.4	85.0	3.5	4.8	1.8	2.7	2.5	3.2	7.1	7.2	7.3	6.8	5.4	27.3	26.6	10.8	1.4	74.0	37.5	49.2	50.8
70346	DONALDSONVILLE	35.1	29.1	63.6	69.4	0.1	0.2	1.4	1.5	8.3	8.0	7.8	7.8	6.9	25.3	24.5	9.8	1.7	71.2	33.2	46.5	53.5
70353	DULAC	57.3	49.7	3.8	4.3	0.6	0.8	1.7	2.0	7.7	8.0	7.9	8.3	6.9	24.1	26.2	10.0	1.0	71.4	34.2	50.9	49.1
70354	GALLIANO	91.1	88.8	0.5	0.7	0.7	1.1	1.0	1.3	6.8	6.9	7.1	7.0	5.5	27.0	25.4	13.1	1.3	74.8	37.8	50.0	50.0
70355	GHEENS	94.6	92.4	2.8	4.1	0.2	0.3	1.9	2.5	7.3	7.3	7.0	7.0	6.8	29.2	25.2	9.5	0.8	74.1	35.5	50.2	49.8
70356	GIBSON	48.4	42.1	48.9	54.5	0.4	0.5	1.3	1.4	6.9	6.7	6.8	7.2	6.3	24.6	29.3	11.3	1.0	75.2	38.5	48.1	51.9
70357	GOLDEN MEADOW	89.2	86.6	0.6	0.8	0.3	0.5	1.3	1.7	7.1	7.0	7.2	7.0	5.3	26.7	25.9	12.0	1.7	74.3	38.0	49.5	50.5
70358	GRAND ISLE	96.0	94.7	0.2	0.3	0.2	0.3	1.5	1.9	5.0	5.5	6.1	7.0	4.7	24.9	30.7	15.0	1.0	79.3	42.5	50.7	49.3
70359	GRAY	68.0	64.7	28.4	30.8	0.3	0.4	1.3	1.7	8.8	8.3	7.7	7.7	7.5	28.6	24.2	6.8	0.5	70.5	31.3	48.9	51.1
70360	HOUMA	79.6	77.8	17.0	17.6	0.7	1.0	1.7	2.1	7.0	7.1	7.0	6.8	5.9	26.1	28.1	10.1	1.8	74.6	37.9	47.8	52.2
70363	HOUMA	58.3	52.7	27.7	29.6	1.7	2.4	1.7	2.0	8.6	7.9	7.2	7.9	7.8	28.2	23.1	8.6	0.9	71.6	31.6	49.4	50.6
70364	HOUMA	85.3	82.1	9.6	11.2	0.5	0.8	2.1	2.7	7.7	7.2	6.7	6.9	7.0	29.7	24.0	9.5	1.3	74.1	34.0	49.1	50.9
70372	LABADIEVILLE	70.4	65.4	28.1	32.8	0.1	0.2	1.2	1.4	7.1	7.4	7.6	7.8	5.4	26.5	27.1	9.9	1.3	73.2	36.9	48.3	51.7
70374	LOCKPORT	90.3	87.6	2.9	3.9	0.5	0.9	1.6	2.1	6.8	6.9	6.9	7.2	5.9	27.8	27.4	9.9	1.2	75.1	37.3	50.0	50.0
70375	MATHEWS	93.8	91.1	3.6	5.4	0.2	0.3	2.0	2.4	7.3	7.1	6.9	6.9	6.4	29.2	25.3	9.9	0.9	74.5	35.8	49.8	50.2
70377	MONTEGUT	79.1	73.3	1.6	2.0	0.0	0.0	1.1	1.3	7.7	7.5	7.3	7.6	7.0	26.6	26.4	8.8	1.0	72.9	34.8	51.2	48.8
70380	MORGAN CITY	76.1	72.7	16.7	18.2	3.2	4.1	3.5	4.3	7.3	7.1	7.1	7.1	6.1	26.4	26.4	11.2	1.3	74.0	36.8	49.4	50.6
70390	NAPOLEONVILLE	51.1	45.2	48.1	53.7	0.1	0.1	0.9	1.0	7.1	7.3	7.3	7.4	5.7	25.9	27.0	10.5	2.0	73.9	37.3	48.1	51.9
70392	PATTERSON	62.6	59.6	33.6	35.2	0.5	0.8	2.0	2.6	7.2	7.9	7.6	8.0	6.1	27.4	26.5	8.4	0.9	72.1	34.8	48.9	51.1
70394	RACELAND	77.9	73.2	19.6	23.9	0.3	0.5	1.3	1.5	7.1	7.2	7.2	6.7	5.3	26.6	27.4	11.0	1.6	74.4	37.9	48.5	51.5
70395	SCHRIEVER	80.3	76.1	16.6	19.7	0.5	0.7	1.2	1.6	7.4	7.4	7.3	6.9	6.0	29.3	26.4	8.5	0.8	73.6	35.2	48.3	51.7
70397	THERIOT	76.6	70.6	1.8	2.2	0.1	0.1	2.1	2.7	6.6	6.9	8.4	10.3	6.9	24.8	25.7	9.8	0.5	71.7	34.3	51.7	48.3
70401	HAMMOND	64.9	58.5	32.4	38.2	0.7	0.8	2.0	2.4	7.0	6.6	6.2	9.3	13.6	27.0	21.5	7.9	0.9	76.4	29.2	47.6	52.4
70402	HAMMOND	67.7	59.4	29.9	37.8	0.3	0.3	1.2	1.3	1.1	1.5	1.3	40.0	33.3	8.4	7.7	6.2	0.4	94.8	20.9	39.3	60.7
70403	HAMMOND	64.8	59.0	33.3	38.8	0.6	0.7	1.4	1.6	7.3	7.1	7.0	6.9	6.4	28.7	24.8	9.8	2.0	74.5	35.0	47.6	52.4
70420	ABITA SPRINGS	92.1	89.4	5.2	6.9	0.4	0.7	2.6	3.3	8.3	8.3	8.0	6.5	5.0	29.5	25.8	7.8	0.9	71.3	34.9	47.4	52.6
70422	AMITE	54.1	48.9	44.3	49.3	0.3	0.4	1.1	1.2	7.3	7.2	7.4	7.5	6.5	25.3	26.6	10.8	1.4	73.6	36.2	50.0	50.0
	LOUISIANA	63.9	61.9	32.5	33.7	1.3	1.6	2.4	2.8	7.2	7.0	6.9	7.3	7.1	26.8	25.7	10.4	1.6	74.6	35.6	48.6	51.4
	UNITED STATES	75.1	72.0	12.3	12.7	3.8	4.6	12.5	15.7	6.8	6.7	6.6	7.1	6.9	27.0	26.0	10.9	1.9	75.7	36.9	49.2	50.8

ZIP CODE #	POST OFFICE NAME	2009 Per Capita Income	2009 HH Income Base	2009 Household Income Distribution (%): Less than $25,000	$25,000 to $49,999	$50,000 to $99,999	$100,000 to $149,999	$150,000 or More	Median Household Income: 2009	2014	2009 National Centile	2009 State Centile	2009 Home Value Base	2009 Home Value Distribution (%): Less than $50,000	$50,000 to $89,999	$90,000 to $174,999	$175,000 to $399,999	$400,000 or More	2009 Median Home Value
70001	METAIRIE	25288	17492	26.3	32.2	32.1	6.3	3.1	42711	45296	42	79	8824	1.6	4.8	37.2	51.0	5.4	186985
70002	METAIRIE	28782	8435	26.4	28.2	29.2	9.6	6.6	44795	47571	48	84	4323	2.7	3.1	17.3	57.6	19.4	261287
70003	METAIRIE	23487	16074	23.2	27.5	36.4	8.7	4.2	49246	51107	59	90	12329	2.3	6.4	49.6	38.4	3.4	162267
70005	METAIRIE	33393	11442	25.2	27.4	30.1	9.1	8.3	47534	49606	55	89	7114	0.6	2.4	21.8	52.3	22.9	238973
70006	METAIRIE	26275	6397	22.5	28.0	34.5	9.9	5.1	49404	51122	60	91	3758	0.5	0.9	23.0	65.4	10.3	221307
70030	DES ALLEMANDS	18897	1367	29.7	25.3	37.6	5.9	1.5	45967	43775	51	86	1185	14.3	19.4	36.4	27.7	2.2	120491
70031	AMA	20731	370	24.3	26.8	35.7	10.3	3.0	49149	51388	59	90	322	6.5	15.8	55.9	20.8	0.9	126000
70032	ARABI	21251	1233	42.2	30.9	21.8	2.8	2.4	31094	32699	10	40	930	10.1	70.6	17.7	1.5	0.0	73627
70036	BARATARIA	14571	469	37.3	40.3	17.5	3.4	1.5	30212	29173	8	34	386	15.8	16.6	35.8	29.0	2.8	129861
70037	BELLE CHASSE	21093	5389	21.3	28.4	36.2	10.9	3.3	50226	51789	62	92	3824	16.2	6.1	25.3	44.7	7.7	182667
70039	BOUTTE	14425	975	41.7	26.1	28.0	3.0	1.2	32424	30905	12	48	650	26.9	25.2	31.1	16.8	0.0	87200
70040	BRAITHWAITE	15389	1009	39.4	32.2	20.4	5.1	2.9	32786	31479	13	49	888	35.2	19.7	11.1	31.1	2.8	69800
70041	BURAS	15729	1736	36.8	27.1	29.8	4.3	2.0	36784	37475	23	64	1487	48.4	24.9	20.8	5.6	0.2	51880
70043	CHALMETTE	18507	5137	37.8	31.1	24.3	4.2	2.6	33730	35581	15	54	3436	9.4	53.2	33.0	4.2	0.2	83328
70047	DESTREHAN	25347	4931	15.3	22.4	37.5	16.3	8.4	61629	64884	80	99	4183	3.2	8.3	29.1	47.8	11.6	198039
70049	EDGARD	11751	1093	46.2	31.4	16.8	5.1	0.5	27173	27023	5	18	885	38.9	18.3	30.7	12.0	0.1	66288
70051	GARYVILLE	12832	753	39.4	28.7	28.7	2.7	0.5	33064	32453	13	50	587	25.9	30.7	38.7	3.6	1.2	82736
70052	GRAMERCY	16920	1211	32.0	29.4	30.6	7.0	0.9	39951	40230	32	72	1011	20.8	20.0	43.4	14.3	1.5	105870
70053	GRETNA	16571	6755	39.8	36.2	19.2	3.2	1.6	31090	30319	10	40	3263	7.0	26.8	50.2	14.4	1.6	110202
70056	GRETNA	20624	13806	22.9	29.2	36.4	8.6	2.9	48128	50306	57	89	8444	0.5	7.4	65.9	21.1	5.2	142308
70057	HAHNVILLE	16304	1074	37.0	28.5	26.3	6.4	1.9	40046	39249	33	73	821	19.1	11.4	44.8	24.6	0.0	126062
70058	HARVEY	18086	12921	28.3	26.3	34.3	7.8	3.3	45426	47958	50	85	8914	2.4	13.2	65.0	16.8	2.6	128586
70062	KENNER	14206	6481	39.9	32.4	22.7	4.4	0.6	31193	30401	10	41	3348	6.3	18.6	57.4	16.6	1.1	119437
70065	KENNER	24473	18739	19.4	29.0	36.5	9.6	5.5	51438	52989	65	94	11950	1.2	6.5	45.3	38.3	8.6	167916
70067	LAFITTE	17124	1411	33.5	26.3	31.0	6.6	2.7	39147	44147	30	71	1203	21.9	19.0	28.9	25.8	4.3	110018
70068	LA PLACE	19078	11934	23.0	27.1	38.7	9.5	1.8	49894	51587	61	91	9644	6.1	8.9	57.2	25.6	2.2	136179
70070	LULING	24001	4247	16.7	20.6	41.7	17.4	3.4	63435	66604	82	99	3563	1.9	3.3	36.9	53.9	4.0	195543
70071	LUTCHER	17426	1349	37.6	25.2	25.6	8.9	2.7	35812	37242	20	60	1125	17.3	15.2	42.3	25.2	0.0	119612
70072	MARRERO	17723	19199	27.9	29.3	34.5	5.8	2.5	43629	46176	44	81	14655	3.1	23.0	59.2	12.6	2.2	115006
70075	MERAUX	20446	1403	28.7	24.4	34.9	8.6	3.4	45614	42727	50	86	1148	12.1	38.6	40.3	9.0	0.0	89497
70076	MOUNT AIRY	14729	248	45.2	16.1	32.7	6.0	0.0	31860	33319	11	46	217	36.4	18.0	29.5	12.9	3.2	84412
70079	NORCO	18557	1530	28.2	28.3	36.5	5.1	1.8	43593	41797	44	81	1267	6.0	12.5	59.0	22.2	0.4	126875
70080	PARADIS	19029	588	26.4	34.0	29.1	8.7	1.9	42373	41575	41	77	436	17.0	26.6	35.3	21.1	0.0	98485
70081	PILOTTOWN	9680	0	0.0	0.0	0.0	0.0	0.0	0	0	0	0	0	0.0	0.0	0.0	0.0	0.0	0
70083	PORT SULPHUR	15775	1231	44.2	25.0	25.9	2.4	2.5	29881	28655	8	33	1085	30.7	32.4	27.1	8.8	0.9	74114
70084	RESERVE	15516	2813	35.7	26.8	31.1	4.7	1.6	37910	39292	26	68	2177	13.5	27.4	38.2	19.6	1.4	104260
70085	SAINT BERNARD	14992	1567	42.7	32.5	17.7	3.7	3.4	30304	31368	9	35	1275	42.0	40.7	9.8	6.0	1.5	54143
70086	SAINT JAMES	12918	722	38.2	29.9	27.8	2.4	1.7	32029	32061	11	46	601	33.8	20.8	31.1	11.3	3.0	83293
70087	SAINT ROSE	16080	2976	27.3	34.6	32.6	4.7	0.7	40058	39340	33	73	2113	7.6	11.6	67.9	11.2	1.7	130630
70090	VACHERIE	16807	2622	35.4	23.1	31.9	8.1	1.5	38492	39012	28	69	2250	19.3	16.5	44.5	18.8	1.0	114818
70091	VENICE	13688	65	43.1	27.7	27.7	1.5	0.0	28574	27261	6	26	61	62.3	19.7	18.0	0.0	0.0	26875
70092	VIOLET	15579	1812	40.8	28.9	23.8	3.3	3.1	31447	32132	10	43	1464	16.3	59.4	20.7	2.9	0.8	68833
70094	WESTWEGO	13913	11983	37.1	34.0	25.1	3.0	0.8	32954	32581	13	49	8311	11.6	43.0	37.9	6.9	0.6	87215
70112	NEW ORLEANS	10107	1748	70.8	16.3	9.8	1.8	1.3	13116	13524	1	1	156	6.4	29.5	34.0	21.2	9.0	123611
70113	NEW ORLEANS	9930	3014	63.7	23.4	11.0	1.3	0.5	16343	17171	1	2	563	11.7	30.9	44.9	10.3	2.1	96484
70114	NEW ORLEANS	13062	8821	43.9	31.1	21.3	2.7	1.1	28904	30492	7	27	3856	8.1	38.5	40.1	12.3	1.0	94486
70115	NEW ORLEANS	22311	16115	39.0	28.2	23.4	4.9	4.5	33786	35449	15	54	6402	4.7	12.1	31.3	31.8	20.1	185702
70116	NEW ORLEANS	17611	6457	48.7	30.8	15.8	2.6	2.1	25635	26696	4	13	1758	9.3	15.5	36.2	16.6	22.4	135736
70117	NEW ORLEANS	11862	8909	51.1	30.2	16.3	1.6	0.8	24220	25887	3	9	3821	12.1	42.0	36.4	8.6	1.0	87218
70118	NEW ORLEANS	21829	12900	39.0	27.3	22.3	5.6	5.7	33115	35047	14	50	5834	2.7	18.2	31.6	29.4	18.1	166216
70119	NEW ORLEANS	14848	13168	46.5	31.2	18.9	2.3	1.0	26834	27618	5	17	4620	6.3	23.7	47.3	20.0	2.7	116507
70121	NEW ORLEANS	22540	5728	33.4	30.3	27.8	6.6	1.9	36820	37999	23	65	3258	2.8	9.2	60.3	27.3	0.4	144733
70122	NEW ORLEANS	18009	8820	32.5	30.3	29.4	5.2	2.6	38360	38486	28	69	5751	2.7	17.5	57.6	18.2	4.0	122332
70123	NEW ORLEANS	29472	11806	20.7	27.5	36.1	9.9	5.8	51557	52997	65	94	7164	1.6	3.8	32.0	50.4	12.2	205115
70124	NEW ORLEANS	34356	5166	17.7	25.8	35.3	11.2	10.1	56290	54329	73	98	3621	0.6	3.8	17.4	53.7	24.5	271154
70125	NEW ORLEANS	17212	5095	44.5	22.8	24.0	5.9	2.8	29375	30028	7	30	2237	4.3	14.8	37.9	36.9	6.1	159596
70126	NEW ORLEANS	15347	5937	32.4	32.2	29.5	4.9	1.1	36860	37599	23	65	3558	5.3	27.3	55.3	11.5	0.6	108477
70127	NEW ORLEANS	16700	4913	31.1	28.5	34.3	5.0	1.1	40680	40748	35	74	2866	1.5	13.8	69.8	13.4	1.5	125102
70128	NEW ORLEANS	17277	4141	23.1	26.5	40.5	7.9	1.9	50211	47698	62	92	2886	1.0	11.5	64.0	20.2	3.3	136834
70129	NEW ORLEANS	11392	2374	39.7	34.2	21.1	3.7	1.3	33287	35391	14	51	1269	7.6	20.0	61.5	9.5	1.3	114614
70130	NEW ORLEANS	23699	6534	41.5	30.1	19.5	4.7	4.2	31505	33172	11	43	1671	4.0	11.4	26.8	32.9	24.8	222744
70131	NEW ORLEANS	23917	10184	20.4	26.9	35.0	10.9	6.8	52299	51150	66	94	6839	2.2	15.4	39.0	37.3	6.1	159089
70301	THIBODAUX	18557	15031	33.0	28.4	29.8	6.2	2.7	38349	40390	28	68	10670	16.7	19.1	36.2	24.6	3.4	124081
70339	PIERRE PART	18399	2285	30.5	27.9	36.1	4.6	1.0	40711	40157	35	75	2019	29.6	17.8	33.2	18.8	0.6	95095
70341	BELLE ROSE	15806	1463	41.0	23.9	25.4	7.9	1.8	35357	35601	19	59	1232	31.4	14.6	33.8	18.6	1.6	96125
70342	BERWICK	16697	1489	35.6	29.7	28.3	5.8	0.7	36499	36549	22	62	1084	28.6	22.0	32.4	13.9	3.0	88600
70343	BOURG	18971	1630	22.4	27.9	40.8	6.6	2.4	49778	48609	61	91	1457	15.3	12.8	40.4	27.7	3.8	130848
70344	CHAUVIN	14801	2451	41.2	29.1	23.9	3.5	2.4	31230	30567	10	41	2123	22.6	25.9	34.4	12.8	4.4	92043
70345	CUT OFF	18344	4862	26.8	30.5	34.9	6.0	1.8	44468	45461	47	83	4067	14.0	17.6	45.9	19.7	2.8	122449
70346	DONALDSONVILLE	15328	4343	44.6	24.4	24.0	5.4	1.6	30315	30854	9	36	2803	22.9	17.3	42.6	16.6	0.6	109178
70353	DULAC	11120	638	48.3	27.9	21.5	1.3	1.1	25980	26426	4	14	518	27.6	26.3	40.5	4.8	0.8	82593
70354	GALLIANO	14558	1810	42.8	32.5	20.3	2.8	1.6	29436	29480	7	30	1518	21.3	27.1	37.4	10.5	3.6	93000
70355	GHEENS	14220	187	27.8	35.3	33.7	1.1	2.1	39326	40126	31	71	155	19.4	28.4	32.9	18.7	0.6	92917
70356	GIBSON	12973	704	50.7	28.1	18.5	1.4	1.3	24497	25735	3	10	597	27.6	19.9	35.8	14.2	2.3	102415
70357	GOLDEN MEADOW	13334	1182	44.4	28.1	24.5	2.5	0.6	28545	28530	6	26	941	26.5	30.7	27.8	12.1	2.9	80878
70358	GRAND ISLE	19922	541	32.5	37.7	22.7	4.4	2.6	35383	35770	19	59	426	24.2	26.3	39.2	7.3	3.1	89556
70359	GRAY	15551	2724	31.8	30.4	30.8	6.2	0.8	38419	40328	28	69	2135	20.3	24.3	41.1	13.4	0.9	102276
70360	HOUMA	25884	8677	25.1	21.4	33.9	12.4	7.2	54279	54205	70	96	6698	6.9	10.5	33.4	40.3	8.9	172846
70363	HOUMA	13977	9102	37.1	31.2	26.7	3.6	1.5	33684	33692	15	53	6594	20.2	23.9	45.4	9.0	1.5	100611
70364	HOUMA	18567	10881	29.2	29.7	34.1	5.9	1.1	42259	43758	40	77	7337	14.0	14.8	51.9	18.1	1.2	126096
70372	LABADIEVILLE	16694	1153	37.6	26.0	30.4	5.6	0.3	36721	36510	23	64	934	22.3	25.7	38.7	12.6	0.7	92676
70374	LOCKPORT	17681	3887	28.4	27.8	36.7	6.3	0.9	44289	45274	46	83	3125	19.8	18.2	41.5	17.4	3.1	112028
70375	MATHEWS	17171	211	27.5	34.1	34.6	1.9	1.9	40413	40342	34	74	174	19.0	27.0	33.9	19.5	0.6	95833
70377	MONTEGUT	13267	1394	36.2	34.0	26.0	2.9	0.9	36704	37317	23	63	1199	21.4	25.0	43.6	9.0	1.0	95058
70380	MORGAN CITY	16726	8797	36.7	30.3	27.2	4.6	1.2	34095	35151	16	55	6301	26.1	18.7	42.0	11.5	1.7	97849
70390	NAPOLEONVILLE	15392	2643	42.6	26.1	23.7	5.0	2.6	29897	29954	8	33	2070	27.6	20.7	32.3	17.4	2.0	94675
70392	PATTERSON	15391	2635	37.6	27.4	29.0	5.6	0.4	34595	35227	17	56	1957	21.2	24.7	42.5	10.4	1.2	96681
70394	RACELAND	18274	5085	32.9	31.3	27.2	5.4	3.2	37255	40023	24	66	4038	15.9	20.5	43.6	17.9	2.1	115306
70395	SCHRIEVER	19469	1797	24.5	30.3	35.3	7.0	2.9	46423	46863	53	87	1507	13.3	14.6	45.9	20.6	5.6	128679
70397	THERIOT	14486	497	46.3	21.3	24.7	3.8	3.8	28136	28052	6	23	439	14.1	21.9	36.4	22.1	5.5	111623
70401	HAMMOND	16656	8093	41.9	29.9	21.5	5.2	1.5	30896	30902	10	39	4506	11.1	16.2	36.9	29.7	6.2	137262
70402	HAMMOND	8988	0	0.0	0.0	0.0	0.0	0.0	0	0	0	0	0	0.0	0.0	0.0	0.0	0.0	0
70403	HAMMOND	16962	9563	39.8	26.3	26.4	5.9	1.6	32573	33129	13	48	6615	15.2	16.7	35.8	27.2	5.0	129201
70420	ABITA SPRINGS	22042	2479	17.3	30.6	40.8	6.8	4.5	51156	51006	64	93	2003	3.8	7.1	34.6	47.6	6.9	185475
70422	AMITE	14751	5798	42.0	30.7	22.1	3.8	1.4	30588	30763	9	37	4540	26.1	17.6	34.3	18.2	3.8	103317
	LOUISIANA	19176		34.0	28.2	28.2	6.6	3.0	37868	38644				16.9	18.7	37.2	22.8	4.3	118738
	UNITED STATES	27277		20.9	24.4	35.3	11.7	7.6	54719	56938				9.3	13.1	31.6	32.6	13.5	162279

ZIP CODE		FINANCIAL SERVICES				THE HOME						ENTERTAINMENT						PERSONAL			
						Home Improvements		Furnishings													
#	POST OFFICE NAME	Auto Loan	Home Loan	Invest-ments	Retire-ment Plans	Home Repair	Lawn & Garden	Comput-ers & Hard-ware-Personal	Major Appli-ances	TV, Radio, Sound Equip-ment	Furni-ture	Dine out/ Carry out	Sports Equip-ment	Fees & Tickets	Toys & Games	Travel	Cable TV	Apparel & Services	Auto Repairs	Health Insur-ance	Pets & Supplies
70001	METAIRIE	77	70	68	73	69	72	78	73	79	77	79	56	76	79	75	79	55	77	77	87
70002	METAIRIE	85	84	86	87	85	84	90	85	90	91	91	66	92	88	90	90	64	89	89	101
70003	METAIRIE	82	88	83	90	87	89	84	85	85	85	86	64	89	85	87	87	60	85	89	100
70005	METAIRIE	93	97	101	100	100	99	99	97	99	100	99	73	103	96	102	99	70	99	102	113
70006	METAIRIE	84	88	88	90	89	89	88	87	88	89	89	66	92	87	91	89	62	88	91	102
70030	DES ALLEMANDS	83	74	75	73	72	85	71	79	75	70	74	61	66	77	70	78	51	75	80	94
70031	AMA	91	86	84	89	87	98	83	93	85	77	84	71	79	87	84	89	58	86	95	108
70032	ARABI	66	64	65	63	64	74	63	68	67	59	66	50	62	66	64	71	45	66	76	79
70036	BARATARIA	69	50	71	48	51	70	51	65	56	47	55	49	41	56	50	62	37	59	67	77
70037	BELLE CHASSE	89	87	77	87	85	83	87	85	86	87	87	67	86	90	85	85	61	85	83	100
70039	BOUTTE	64	56	50	54	53	59	58	58	62	60	61	43	54	62	54	64	42	60	62	70
70040	BRAITHWAITE	75	59	66	56	58	71	59	67	64	59	63	51	51	66	55	68	42	64	69	81
70041	BURAS	77	59	69	56	58	73	61	69	66	61	65	53	51	68	57	70	44	67	70	83
70043	CHALMETTE	68	63	62	63	62	69	65	66	67	63	66	50	62	67	63	69	46	67	71	78
70047	DESTREHAN	111	123	114	122	120	114	108	112	106	114	107	86	115	109	113	104	75	107	105	130
70049	EDGARD	55	45	49	44	44	56	47	51	53	47	52	37	43	52	44	58	35	52	58	63
70051	GARYVILLE	66	45	59	44	45	64	50	58	58	49	56	44	41	57	46	64	38	57	64	72
70052	GRAMERCY	83	60	72	58	60	80	62	73	69	61	68	56	51	71	58	76	46	69	78	89
70053	GRETNA	58	50	47	51	48	55	57	54	60	54	59	42	53	59	52	62	41	57	61	66
70056	GRETNA	80	80	71	81	76	77	82	77	82	82	82	61	82	83	80	81	58	81	79	93
70057	HAHNVILLE	72	63	60	64	63	72	64	68	68	63	67	50	59	69	61	72	46	67	73	82
70058	HARVEY	82	78	69	79	74	77	79	77	80	80	80	60	78	82	75	80	56	78	78	92
70062	KENNER	57	50	46	51	47	55	55	53	59	53	58	41	53	59	51	62	40	56	60	65
70065	KENNER	94	97	89	97	95	91	96	93	93	98	94	72	97	95	95	92	67	94	90	109
70067	LAFITTE	90	64	81	62	64	88	68	80	74	63	72	63	53	75	63	80	48	76	85	98
70068	LA PLACE	86	83	77	81	79	83	79	82	80	80	80	63	77	83	77	81	55	80	81	97
70070	LULING	97	111	94	110	105	103	98	99	97	101	98	77	106	100	102	96	69	97	98	116
70071	LUTCHER	77	68	75	66	67	82	66	75	72	65	71	56	63	72	66	78	49	73	81	89
70072	MARRERO	77	74	68	74	71	76	73	74	76	74	76	56	72	76	72	77	52	75	77	88
70075	MERAUX	78	85	77	83	83	81	78	80	77	80	78	60	81	78	79	77	54	78	79	92
70076	MOUNT AIRY	81	53	78	50	52	79	56	71	65	54	63	55	42	66	53	72	42	67	75	87
70079	NORCO	68	74	64	74	70	76	68	69	70	68	70	53	73	71	71	72	49	70	76	83
70080	PARADIS	84	78	67	74	74	76	77	77	78	80	78	59	72	81	72	78	54	78	76	92
70081	PILOTTOWN	0	0	0	0	0	0	0	0	0	0	0	0	0	0	0	0	0	0	0	0
70083	PORT SULPHUR	82	54	77	52	54	80	58	72	66	55	65	56	44	68	54	74	43	68	76	89
70084	RESERVE	68	61	61	61	60	70	61	66	64	59	64	49	57	65	59	68	43	64	71	79
70085	SAINT BERNARD	68	59	56	56	57	63	59	62	61	60	60	47	53	63	55	62	41	61	62	74
70086	SAINT JAMES	75	49	72	46	49	74	52	66	60	50	59	52	39	62	49	67	39	62	70	81
70087	SAINT ROSE	68	63	55	63	60	62	65	62	66	67	66	48	63	67	61	66	46	65	64	75
70090	VACHERIE	86	64	78	63	65	85	66	78	73	63	71	60	55	74	63	79	48	74	82	94
70091	VENICE	65	42	62	40	42	63	45	57	52	43	51	44	34	53	42	58	34	53	60	70
70092	VIOLET	77	65	69	63	63	73	64	70	67	64	67	53	57	69	61	70	45	68	71	84
70094	WESTWEGO	60	52	50	52	50	58	56	56	59	55	58	43	52	59	52	61	40	58	61	68
70112	NEW ORLEANS	36	22	21	25	21	24	38	28	39	34	39	24	31	38	29	39	27	35	32	37
70113	NEW ORLEANS	35	26	26	28	25	30	36	31	39	34	39	24	32	38	31	42	27	36	37	39
70114	NEW ORLEANS	53	43	39	45	40	45	53	46	56	52	56	37	49	56	47	57	39	52	52	59
70115	NEW ORLEANS	68	62	63	66	62	62	73	64	74	70	74	52	71	73	69	74	53	70	68	79
70116	NEW ORLEANS	50	44	46	47	44	45	54	47	55	51	56	37	52	54	50	57	40	52	51	58
70117	NEW ORLEANS	45	38	36	39	37	43	44	42	49	43	48	31	42	48	40	51	33	45	48	52
70118	NEW ORLEANS	76	68	68	71	67	70	82	71	82	77	82	57	77	80	74	82	58	78	76	87
70119	NEW ORLEANS	49	44	42	45	43	46	51	46	54	49	53	35	49	53	47	56	38	51	52	57
70121	NEW ORLEANS	67	65	62	66	64	67	69	66	70	67	70	50	68	69	67	71	49	68	71	79
70122	NEW ORLEANS	67	65	61	66	63	69	67	66	70	67	70	49	68	69	66	73	48	68	73	79
70123	NEW ORLEANS	89	92	91	94	92	92	94	90	94	93	95	70	97	93	96	95	67	93	95	107
70124	NEW ORLEANS	103	117	123	120	121	111	112	110	107	116	107	85	121	106	118	105	77	109	107	127
70125	NEW ORLEANS	62	56	53	58	55	60	62	59	66	62	65	45	61	64	58	68	45	63	65	72
70126	NEW ORLEANS	64	59	53	60	56	62	62	60	66	63	66	45	61	66	59	68	45	63	66	73
70127	NEW ORLEANS	65	62	57	63	59	65	65	63	69	65	69	47	65	68	63	72	48	66	70	77
70128	NEW ORLEANS	82	80	70	81	76	76	79	77	79	82	80	59	79	81	76	79	56	78	77	92
70129	NEW ORLEANS	60	49	47	49	48	49	58	54	59	58	59	42	52	60	52	60	42	58	55	65
70130	NEW ORLEANS	65	54	56	59	53	54	73	59	73	67	74	50	67	71	64	73	53	68	64	74
70131	NEW ORLEANS	95	96	92	99	94	95	97	93	98	99	98	72	101	98	97	98	69	96	96	111
70301	THIBODAUX	78	67	67	66	66	75	69	72	73	68	72	54	63	74	65	76	49	72	76	87
70339	PIERRE PART	85	61	70	59	60	80	63	73	70	61	69	56	51	73	57	76	46	70	77	89
70341	BELLE ROSE	81	59	72	56	58	78	60	71	67	59	66	55	49	69	56	73	44	68	74	87
70342	BERWICK	73	58	64	57	56	69	61	66	65	59	64	51	52	66	56	68	43	65	68	80
70343	BOURG	91	82	82	81	80	91	78	86	82	79	81	65	74	84	77	85	56	82	87	103
70344	CHAUVIN	78	55	76	53	56	77	57	71	64	54	62	54	45	64	55	70	41	66	74	85
70345	CUT OFF	87	70	75	70	70	86	70	80	76	68	74	61	61	78	67	81	50	76	83	96
70346	DONALDSONVILLE	67	52	55	53	50	64	58	60	64	56	63	46	52	64	53	68	43	62	67	75
70353	DULAC	65	42	63	40	42	64	45	57	52	43	51	45	34	53	42	58	34	54	61	70
70354	GALLIANO	72	50	72	48	51	72	52	66	58	49	57	50	40	59	50	65	38	61	69	79
70355	GHEENS	83	59	68	58	59	79	62	72	69	60	67	55	50	71	56	75	45	68	76	88
70356	GIBSON	68	44	66	42	44	67	47	60	55	45	53	47	35	56	44	61	35	56	63	73
70357	GOLDEN MEADOW	67	45	66	43	46	67	48	60	54	45	53	46	37	54	46	60	35	56	63	73
70358	GRAND ISLE	84	65	82	64	67	84	66	79	71	63	70	60	55	71	65	76	47	74	81	94
70359	GRAY	76	63	63	60	61	71	63	68	66	63	66	51	55	69	59	69	45	66	69	82
70360	HOUMA	105	104	99	104	101	106	100	103	101	101	101	79	99	103	99	102	70	101	103	121
70363	HOUMA	67	55	56	54	53	63	59	61	62	57	61	47	52	63	54	65	42	61	64	74
70364	HOUMA	75	68	63	67	65	71	70	70	71	70	71	54	65	73	66	73	49	70	72	84
70372	LABADIEVILLE	76	58	68	58	58	76	59	70	65	56	63	54	50	66	57	70	43	66	73	84
70374	LOCKPORT	86	65	74	64	65	85	67	78	73	64	72	60	56	75	63	79	48	73	82	94
70375	MATHEWS	84	62	69	60	61	79	63	73	70	62	69	56	52	73	58	76	46	69	77	89
70377	MONTEGUT	73	51	64	49	50	70	53	64	60	51	59	49	42	62	49	66	39	60	67	78
70380	MORGAN CITY	69	57	58	57	56	67	59	63	63	58	62	48	53	64	56	67	42	62	67	76
70390	NAPOLEONVILLE	74	56	69	55	56	74	58	68	65	56	64	52	49	65	56	71	43	65	73	83
70392	PATTERSON	68	57	55	56	55	64	58	61	62	58	61	46	52	64	54	65	42	61	64	75
70394	RACELAND	84	68	74	67	67	83	68	77	74	67	73	58	60	75	65	79	49	74	81	93
70395	SCHRIEVER	92	82	79	80	81	88	78	85	82	81	82	63	73	85	75	85	56	82	85	101
70397	THERIOT	80	60	82	61	63	84	64	77	67	55	66	61	51	66	64	72	43	72	81	93
70401	HAMMOND	63	48	46	49	46	52	63	54	62	57	62	44	52	63	52	63	43	59	57	67
70402	HAMMOND	0	0	0	0	0	0	0	0	0	0	0	0	0	0	0	0	0	0	0	0
70403	HAMMOND	68	60	55	59	59	64	62	63	65	62	64	47	58	66	58	67	44	63	66	75
70420	ABITA SPRINGS	93	94	79	91	89	85	86	87	84	91	85	66	85	89	83	83	59	84	82	102
70422	AMITE	70	50	65	48	50	69	53	63	59	51	58	48	43	60	50	65	39	60	67	76
	LOUISIANA	78	67	68	67	66	75	70	72	73	70	73	55	65	74	67	76	50	73	76	87
	UNITED STATES	100	100	100	100	100	100	100	100	100	100	100	100	100	100	100	100	100	100	100	100

POPULATION CHANGE

ZIP CODE #	POST OFFICE NAME	COUNTY FIPS CODE	POPULATION 2000	POPULATION 2009	POPULATION 2014	2000-2009 ANNUAL RATE % Rate	2000-2009 ANNUAL RATE State Centile	HOUSEHOLDS 2000	HOUSEHOLDS 2009	HOUSEHOLDS 2014	HOUSEHOLDS % Annual Rate 2000-2009	HOUSEHOLDS 2009 Average HH Size	FAMILIES 2000	FAMILIES 2009	FAMILIES % Annual Rate 2000-2009
70426	ANGIE	117	6450	6701	6787	0.4	61	1893	2063	2111	0.9	2.71	1425	1526	0.7
70427	BOGALUSA	117	20618	20114	19780	-0.3	27	8250	8186	8098	-0.1	2.43	5610	5463	-0.3
70431	BUSH	103	4746	5240	5721	1.1	82	1749	1956	2146	1.2	2.67	1392	1533	1.0
70433	COVINGTON	103	25025	33764	38785	3.3	98	9212	12585	14505	3.4	2.63	6775	9139	3.3
70435	COVINGTON	103	11649	15736	18129	3.3	98	4067	5578	6465	3.5	2.80	3229	4360	3.3
70436	FLUKER	105	203	246	270	2.1	93	60	73	81	2.1	3.37	43	51	1.9
70437	FOLSOM	103	5825	7287	8215	2.5	95	2129	2702	3066	2.6	2.69	1647	2058	2.4
70438	FRANKLINTON	117	15981	17793	18381	1.2	84	5992	6837	7118	1.4	2.56	4378	4909	1.2
70441	GREENSBURG	091	3738	3668	3645	-0.2	29	1403	1416	1422	0.1	2.55	984	977	-0.1
70442	HUSSER	105	500	558	589	1.2	84	180	203	215	1.3	2.74	134	148	1.1
70443	INDEPENDENCE	105	8130	9549	10448	1.8	91	2893	3430	3773	1.9	2.76	2162	2526	1.7
70444	KENTWOOD	105	10066	11647	12466	1.6	89	3681	4303	4629	1.7	2.68	2668	3076	1.6
70445	LACOMBE	103	8832	11540	13194	2.9	97	3233	4302	4947	3.1	2.65	2425	3175	3.0
70446	LORANGER	105	4885	5310	5558	0.9	80	1703	1865	1960	1.0	2.83	1328	1435	0.8
70447	MADISONVILLE	103	4643	9060	11232	7.5	100	1716	3413	4262	7.7	2.65	1306	2529	7.4
70448	MANDEVILLE	103	20339	26864	30500	3.1	97	7174	9499	10796	3.1	2.79	5629	7410	3.0
70449	MAUREPAS	063	2922	3605	4022	2.3	94	1172	1464	1646	2.4	2.46	843	1037	2.3
70450	MOUNT HERMON	117	2223	2477	2556	1.2	84	836	954	993	1.4	2.60	626	702	1.2
70452	PEARL RIVER	103	11294	14635	16725	2.8	96	4124	5403	6202	3.0	2.71	3137	4044	2.8
70453	PINE GROVE	091	673	685	690	0.2	49	219	229	232	0.5	2.99	168	173	0.3
70454	PONCHATOULA	105	19500	24202	26551	2.4	95	7154	8922	9830	2.4	2.70	5313	6531	2.3
70455	ROBERT	105	1396	1508	1577	0.8	77	515	561	588	0.9	2.69	395	426	0.8
70456	ROSELAND	105	2937	3402	3666	1.6	89	1049	1223	1323	1.7	2.71	755	864	1.5
70458	SLIDELL	103	32841	34658	36466	0.6	71	12511	13249	13969	0.6	2.59	9214	9675	0.5
70460	SLIDELL	103	20440	24884	27529	2.1	93	7296	8958	9961	2.2	2.77	5579	6737	2.1
70461	SLIDELL	103	22726	28707	32251	2.6	96	7867	9997	11272	2.6	2.86	6238	7824	2.5
70462	SPRINGFIELD	063	4844	5683	6217	1.7	90	1852	2199	2419	1.9	2.58	1401	1635	1.7
70466	TICKFAW	105	7399	8775	9577	1.9	91	2671	3191	3494	1.9	2.73	1966	2326	1.8
70467	VARNADO	117	12	12	12	0.0	38	7	8	8	1.5	1.50	5	4	-2.4
70471	MANDEVILLE	103	17027	20654	22673	2.1	93	5993	7292	8021	2.1	2.80	4519	5426	2.0
70501	LAFAYETTE	055	30723	31039	31331	0.1	44	11280	11694	11925	0.4	2.51	7132	7167	0.1
70503	LAFAYETTE	055	26424	27358	27937	0.4	61	9758	10288	10570	0.6	2.48	6666	6910	0.4
70504	LAFAYETTE	055	287	311	325	0.9	80	111	125	131	1.3	2.42	75	82	1.0
70506	LAFAYETTE	055	35708	37090	37918	0.4	61	15226	16178	16644	0.7	2.26	8825	9143	0.4
70507	LAFAYETTE	055	14663	15546	16047	0.6	71	5399	5863	6092	0.9	2.62	3915	4176	0.7
70508	LAFAYETTE	055	26965	31434	33521	1.7	90	10694	12799	13766	2.0	2.43	7072	8245	1.7
70510	ABBEVILLE	113	24044	25487	25996	0.6	71	8871	9559	9810	0.8	2.62	6362	6759	0.7
70512	ARNAUDVILLE	097	8961	10017	10506	1.2	84	3217	3664	3871	1.4	2.71	2472	2775	1.3
70514	BALDWIN	101	4242	3901	3728	-0.9	10	1389	1309	1261	-0.6	2.85	1051	975	-0.8
70515	BASILE	001	4071	4237	4280	0.4	61	1220	1304	1329	0.7	2.60	852	895	0.5
70516	BRANCH	001	1294	1481	1557	1.5	88	441	514	544	1.7	2.88	354	407	1.5
70517	BREAUX BRIDGE	099	23854	26370	27331	1.1	82	8424	9528	9962	1.3	2.72	6370	7120	1.2
70518	BROUSSARD	055	10547	11869	12478	1.3	85	3782	4382	4649	1.6	2.69	2837	3230	1.4
70520	CARENCRO	055	15039	17152	18205	1.4	87	5245	6161	6599	1.8	2.76	4064	4704	1.6
70525	CHURCH POINT	001	11737	12190	12408	0.4	61	4208	4444	4553	0.6	2.71	3130	3262	0.4
70526	CROWLEY	001	20960	21147	21204	0.1	44	7554	7724	7785	0.2	2.65	5502	5542	0.1
70528	DELCAMBRE	113	2304	2396	2418	0.4	61	875	923	936	0.6	2.60	667	694	0.4
70529	DUSON	055	9673	11033	11714	1.4	87	3491	4083	4370	1.7	2.70	2643	3039	1.5
70531	EGAN	001	990	1005	1005	0.2	49	351	361	364	0.3	2.78	269	272	0.1
70532	ELTON	053	2829	2751	2704	-0.3	27	1045	1038	1030	-0.1	2.29	776	757	-0.3
70533	ERATH	113	7832	8147	8258	0.4	61	2739	2900	2957	0.6	2.77	2088	2179	0.5
70535	EUNICE	001	18825	19540	19852	0.4	61	6889	7210	7365	0.5	2.67	4979	5136	0.3
70537	EVANGELINE	001	708	732	740	0.4	61	264	278	283	0.6	2.63	212	220	0.4
70538	FRANKLIN	101	15406	14683	14216	-0.5	21	5399	5264	5141	-0.3	2.76	4082	3930	-0.4
70542	GUEYDAN	113	3662	3482	3482	-0.5	21	1425	1378	1383	-0.4	2.48	999	948	-0.6
70543	IOTA	001	3316	3559	3661	0.8	77	1209	1315	1359	0.9	2.70	912	977	0.7
70544	JEANERETTE	045	11902	11834	11756	-0.1	35	3935	3965	3961	0.1	2.96	3023	2998	-0.1
70546	JENNINGS	053	16393	16281	16037	-0.1	35	5899	5942	5883	0.1	2.69	4365	4344	-0.1
70548	KAPLAN	113	10925	11604	11886	0.7	74	4117	4430	4558	0.8	2.58	2934	3108	0.6
70549	LAKE ARTHUR	053	4160	4167	4121	0.0	38	1606	1645	1637	0.3	2.53	1134	1139	0.0
70552	LOREAUVILLE	045	1354	1496	1547	1.1	82	470	525	545	1.2	2.85	371	408	1.0
70554	MAMOU	039	6535	6836	6867	0.5	66	2449	2597	2619	0.6	2.57	1727	1798	0.4
70555	MAURICE	113	4966	5590	5854	1.3	85	1770	2017	2123	1.4	2.76	1364	1533	1.3
70559	MORSE	001	3085	3118	3130	0.1	44	1111	1144	1155	0.3	2.72	848	860	0.2
70560	NEW IBERIA	045	43040	44360	44770	0.3	53	14891	15468	15670	0.4	2.78	11031	11304	0.3
70563	NEW IBERIA	045	17307	18480	18897	0.7	74	6186	6648	6822	0.8	2.75	4829	5134	0.7
70570	OPELOUSAS	097	44697	46990	48094	0.5	66	16392	17413	17923	0.7	2.64	11592	12139	0.5
70577	PORT BARRE	097	4227	4418	4507	0.5	66	1547	1638	1681	0.6	2.68	1163	1211	0.4
70578	RAYNE	001	14993	16013	16430	0.7	74	5414	5873	6059	0.9	2.70	3978	4252	0.7
70581	ROANOKE	053	865	981	998	1.4	87	296	342	350	1.6	2.87	241	275	1.4
70582	SAINT MARTINVILLE	099	19158	20292	20748	0.6	71	6680	7247	7469	0.9	2.75	5009	5359	0.7
70583	SCOTT	055	10960	11897	12409	0.9	80	3967	4419	4647	1.2	2.69	2948	3217	0.9
70584	SUNSET	097	6026	6753	7058	1.2	84	2288	2603	2742	1.4	2.59	1696	1897	1.2
70586	VILLE PLATTE	039	22840	23582	23572	0.3	53	8325	8556	8605	0.3	2.61	6021	6113	0.2
70589	WASHINGTON	097	3835	4039	4142	0.6	71	1435	1528	1576	0.7	2.61	1022	1069	0.5
70591	WELSH	053	5238	5353	5319	0.2	49	1904	1985	1985	0.5	2.64	1423	1460	0.3
70592	YOUNGSVILLE	055	11996	15850	17551	3.1	97	4227	5727	6400	3.3	2.77	3297	4390	3.1
70601	LAKE CHARLES	019	35114	33882	33447	-0.4	24	14221	13959	13869	-0.2	2.36	8754	8385	-0.5
70605	LAKE CHARLES	019	28495	29660	30160	0.4	61	10969	11700	11993	0.7	2.50	7893	8268	0.5
70607	LAKE CHARLES	019	23043	24006	24374	0.4	61	8810	9435	9662	0.7	2.53	6206	6528	0.5
70609	LAKE CHARLES	019	816	802	802	-0.2	29	1	1	1	0.0	1.00	0	0	0.0
70611	LAKE CHARLES	019	16910	17795	18208	0.6	71	5874	6367	6573	0.9	2.79	4826	5171	0.7
70615	LAKE CHARLES	019	12844	14217	14816	1.1	82	4226	4917	5207	1.7	2.60	3046	3465	1.4
70630	BELL CITY	019	1337	1410	1435	0.6	71	490	530	544	0.9	2.66	381	404	0.6
70631	CAMERON	023	3644	2269	2190	-5.0	3	1314	843	820	-4.7	2.65	963	608	-4.9
70632	CREOLE	023	674	400	368	-5.5	3	242	147	136	-5.2	2.71	187	111	-5.5
70633	DEQUINCY	019	8210	8541	8732	0.4	61	2803	2985	3071	0.7	2.74	2068	2167	0.5
70634	DERIDDER	011	23540	23922	24237	0.2	49	8945	9283	9482	0.4	2.53	6574	6714	0.2
70637	DRY CREEK	011	732	793	824	0.9	80	268	296	310	1.1	2.68	198	215	0.9
70639	EVANS	115	509	471	448	-0.8	12	192	180	173	-0.7	2.62	143	132	-0.9
70643	GRAND CHENIER	023	910	432	398	-7.7	1	352	171	158	-7.5	2.51	263	125	-7.7
70645	HACKBERRY	023	1699	1693	1673	0.0	38	626	639	635	0.2	2.65	458	462	0.1
70647	IOWA	019	8017	8411	8553	0.5	66	2846	3079	3159	0.9	2.73	2223	2372	0.7
70648	KINDER	003	8352	8471	8519	0.2	49	2562	2669	2710	0.4	2.74	1906	1956	0.3
70650	LACASSINE	053	11	12	12	0.9	80	6	7	7	1.7	1.71	5	5	0.0
	LOUISIANA					0.0					0.1	2.60			0.1
	UNITED STATES					1.0					1.1	2.59			0.9

#	POST OFFICE NAME	White 2000	White 2009	Black 2000	Black 2009	Asian/Pacific 2000	Asian/Pacific 2009	% Hispanic Origin 2000	% Hispanic Origin 2009	0-4	5-9	10-14	15-19	20-24	25-44	45-64	65-84	85+	18+	MEDIAN AGE 2009	% 2009 Males	% 2009 Females
70426	ANGIE	53.8	48.1	45.7	51.2	0.0	0.0	0.7	0.8	6.2	6.3	6.3	7.1	9.5	31.2	23.0	9.3	1.1	77.3	33.9	56.4	43.6
70427	BOGALUSA	69.2	66.4	29.4	31.7	0.3	0.4	0.7	0.9	7.0	7.3	7.3	6.8	5.2	23.0	27.0	14.0	2.4	74.2	39.2	47.1	52.9
70431	BUSH	97.7	96.9	1.1	1.5	0.1	0.2	1.3	1.7	5.8	6.2	6.8	6.9	5.1	25.8	30.7	11.9	1.0	77.1	40.3	50.1	49.9
70433	COVINGTON	86.3	84.5	11.3	12.4	0.6	0.9	2.3	3.0	7.8	7.9	7.8	6.7	4.8	27.1	26.8	9.7	1.5	72.1	36.6	48.4	51.6
70435	COVINGTON	89.6	87.7	8.9	10.2	0.3	0.4	1.5	1.9	6.4	6.9	7.3	7.4	5.3	24.8	30.4	10.6	1.0	74.8	39.2	49.4	50.6
70436	FLUKER	31.5	24.4	67.0	74.4	0.5	0.4	1.5	1.6	7.7	7.3	7.3	7.7	6.1	24.4	26.8	11.0	1.6	73.2	36.1	48.4	51.6
70437	FOLSOM	85.2	81.7	12.8	16.0	0.2	0.3	2.6	3.1	6.4	7.1	7.0	6.9	5.0	24.7	30.9	11.0	1.0	74.9	40.1	48.5	51.5
70438	FRANKLINTON	71.4	68.4	27.8	30.6	0.1	0.1	0.9	1.1	7.2	7.2	7.0	6.7	5.7	24.2	27.5	12.5	1.9	74.4	38.5	48.5	51.5
70441	GREENSBURG	42.9	40.7	56.0	58.2	0.1	0.1	1.2	1.3	7.0	6.9	7.0	7.4	5.7	23.6	27.0	13.3	2.2	74.7	39.2	48.2	51.8
70442	HUSSER	82.8	76.5	15.6	21.1	0.2	0.4	1.4	1.6	7.3	7.5	7.5	7.3	5.4	25.3	28.0	10.6	1.1	73.1	36.6	49.6	50.4
70443	INDEPENDENCE	71.5	65.8	26.4	31.7	0.2	0.3	2.2	2.6	7.4	7.4	7.2	7.1	6.3	26.7	26.3	10.3	1.3	73.7	35.8	49.3	50.7
70444	KENTWOOD	60.5	54.6	38.5	44.3	0.1	0.2	0.9	1.0	7.6	7.6	7.7	7.6	6.4	24.1	25.6	11.4	2.0	72.3	35.9	48.8	51.2
70445	LACOMBE	70.6	64.4	24.1	29.2	0.5	0.6	2.5	2.9	6.1	6.4	6.8	6.7	5.2	25.0	30.9	11.6	1.4	76.5	40.3	48.4	51.6
70446	LORANGER	90.6	87.1	7.8	10.8	0.1	0.1	1.5	2.0	7.8	7.8	7.9	7.5	5.5	27.2	26.1	9.5	0.8	71.8	35.1	49.8	50.2
70447	MADISONVILLE	92.1	88.7	5.3	7.7	0.6	0.8	2.6	3.4	6.4	7.0	7.6	7.3	4.5	25.7	31.5	9.1	1.0	74.4	39.7	49.9	50.1
70448	MANDEVILLE	93.3	90.7	4.2	6.0	0.7	1.0	2.4	3.2	8.9	8.5	8.5	6.8	3.5	31.0	24.9	7.1	0.8	69.3	35.5	48.9	51.1
70449	MAUREPAS	93.2	90.2	5.4	8.0	0.2	0.3	1.7	2.2	6.3	6.6	6.8	5.9	4.8	25.5	30.9	12.3	1.1	76.7	40.7	50.1	49.9
70450	MOUNT HERMON	75.9	68.9	23.1	29.9	0.1	0.1	0.6	0.7	6.7	6.8	6.7	6.7	5.5	23.3	29.1	13.7	1.5	75.7	40.4	48.4	51.6
70452	PEARL RIVER	91.2	87.8	6.5	9.3	0.3	0.4	1.6	2.0	6.9	6.9	7.0	6.8	6.0	26.1	28.7	10.7	1.0	75.1	37.9	50.0	50.0
70453	PINE GROVE	43.5	42.9	55.7	56.1	0.0	0.0	0.7	0.7	8.2	8.3	8.0	7.4	6.3	23.6	28.0	9.1	1.0	71.1	35.3	48.9	51.1
70454	PONCHATOULA	84.2	80.2	14.4	18.0	0.3	0.4	1.1	1.4	7.2	7.2	7.2	7.0	6.0	26.9	27.2	10.0	1.3	74.0	36.3	49.0	51.0
70455	ROBERT	96.6	95.2	1.6	2.4	0.0	0.0	1.4	1.9	7.6	7.6	7.8	6.9	5.4	27.5	26.9	9.5	0.7	72.7	35.8	49.4	50.6
70456	ROSELAND	44.7	35.9	53.9	62.6	0.3	0.4	1.1	1.1	7.0	7.0	7.0	7.7	6.4	24.9	27.2	11.3	1.5	74.3	36.9	49.5	50.5
70458	SLIDELL	87.7	84.6	8.9	10.7	1.0	1.6	2.7	3.3	6.1	6.2	6.5	6.6	5.6	25.5	28.8	12.8	2.0	77.1	40.3	48.4	51.6
70460	SLIDELL	74.2	68.8	21.6	26.3	0.5	0.7	2.7	3.2	7.8	7.7	7.5	7.0	5.9	28.1	26.4	8.8	0.9	72.7	35.0	48.8	51.2
70461	SLIDELL	86.0	81.4	9.6	12.8	1.8	2.6	3.4	4.1	6.8	7.4	7.9	7.9	5.4	25.4	30.6	7.7	0.9	72.8	37.4	49.5	50.5
70462	SPRINGFIELD	88.2	83.3	11.0	15.6	0.2	0.2	0.7	0.9	5.9	6.1	6.6	6.7	4.9	25.0	31.0	12.8	1.1	77.2	41.4	50.1	49.9
70466	TICKFAW	79.0	73.2	18.3	23.6	0.2	0.3	2.6	3.0	7.6	7.3	7.1	7.2	6.9	29.1	25.3	8.6	0.9	73.7	34.0	48.5	51.5
70467	VARNADO	33.3	25.0	66.7	75.0	0.0	0.0	0.0	0.0	0.0	0.0	0.0	8.3	25.0	66.7	0.0	0.0	0.0	100.0	30.0	100.0	0.0
70471	MANDEVILLE	94.8	92.7	2.6	3.6	1.0	1.5	2.5	3.2	7.0	7.3	7.8	7.8	5.3	24.8	29.7	8.7	1.6	72.6	38.1	48.2	51.8
70501	LAFAYETTE	29.4	25.0	68.7	72.7	0.4	0.5	1.2	1.3	7.2	7.2	6.9	7.1	8.3	26.4	24.0	11.2	1.7	74.5	34.3	48.5	51.5
70503	LAFAYETTE	89.8	86.9	6.2	7.7	2.3	3.3	2.1	2.6	5.6	6.0	6.5	9.8	9.5	24.0	25.9	11.1	1.6	77.6	35.6	48.0	52.0
70504	LAFAYETTE	97.2	96.5	2.1	2.6	0.7	1.0	0.7	0.6	4.5	4.8	5.8	5.8	3.9	15.8	30.2	23.5	5.8	81.7	51.3	49.2	50.8
70506	LAFAYETTE	80.3	75.4	15.7	19.3	1.8	2.5	2.2	2.8	6.7	6.1	5.7	6.6	9.6	31.2	23.1	9.3	1.6	78.0	33.0	47.9	52.1
70507	LAFAYETTE	65.0	58.6	32.5	38.3	0.7	0.9	1.5	1.8	8.2	7.6	7.1	7.3	7.3	28.8	23.9	8.5	1.2	72.6	32.6	47.7	52.3
70508	LAFAYETTE	89.2	86.1	7.7	9.6	1.3	1.9	2.1	2.6	7.4	6.9	6.5	6.3	7.0	30.5	26.4	7.8	1.1	75.4	34.4	48.5	51.5
70510	ABBEVILLE	72.8	67.7	22.4	25.6	3.4	5.0	1.6	1.9	7.5	7.2	7.2	7.1	5.9	25.5	25.8	11.7	2.0	73.7	37.0	48.4	51.6
70512	ARNAUDVILLE	79.5	76.0	19.5	22.7	0.1	0.1	0.8	1.0	7.0	7.2	7.2	7.3	5.9	25.3	27.7	10.7	1.5	74.0	37.5	48.8	51.2
70514	BALDWIN	38.0	32.9	51.7	55.0	0.7	1.1	1.4	1.6	7.8	7.4	8.3	8.0	6.7	26.7	24.9	9.3	0.8	71.3	34.1	51.3	48.7
70515	BASILE	73.4	69.3	25.6	29.5	0.2	0.3	0.9	1.0	6.1	6.2	6.3	7.1	9.8	30.3	22.5	9.6	2.1	77.4	34.4	57.2	42.8
70516	BRANCH	91.8	88.9	7.3	10.0	0.1	0.1	0.5	0.6	7.0	7.2	7.2	7.5	5.5	28.1	27.1	9.3	1.1	73.8	36.1	50.5	49.5
70517	BREAUX BRIDGE	69.5	65.2	28.2	31.6	1.3	1.8	0.7	0.9	7.7	8.0	7.7	7.4	6.4	26.8	25.7	9.0	1.3	72.1	34.5	49.6	50.4
70518	BROUSSARD	80.4	77.1	16.5	18.9	1.5	1.9	1.6	2.0	8.7	8.7	8.0	6.7	5.9	30.6	24.5	6.3	0.6	70.3	32.9	49.5	50.5
70520	CARENCRO	71.2	66.4	27.1	31.3	0.4	0.6	1.2	1.4	7.8	7.6	7.5	7.9	7.0	27.1	26.2	7.8	1.1	72.2	33.7	49.2	50.8
70525	CHURCH POINT	76.6	72.0	22.2	26.5	0.1	0.2	1.3	1.6	7.8	7.9	7.7	7.6	6.5	25.1	25.3	10.6	1.7	71.8	35.2	49.1	50.9
70526	CROWLEY	75.2	73.2	23.7	25.3	0.2	0.3	0.9	1.1	8.1	7.8	7.6	7.3	6.2	24.7	24.6	11.7	2.1	72.3	35.3	48.4	51.6
70528	DELCAMBRE	88.4	84.3	8.8	11.9	0.3	0.5	1.6	2.0	8.2	8.0	8.1	7.1	5.6	28.2	24.3	9.5	1.0	71.2	34.7	49.8	50.2
70529	DUSON	83.0	78.8	14.6	18.0	0.4	0.6	1.8	2.2	8.2	7.9	7.4	7.0	6.8	29.5	25.4	7.3	0.7	72.3	33.3	48.9	51.1
70531	EGAN	97.8	97.3	0.4	0.6	0.2	0.2	0.7	0.9	8.2	7.8	7.6	6.4	6.5	26.4	24.7	11.4	1.2	72.0	35.0	49.8	50.2
70532	ELTON	57.1	53.5	37.1	40.7	0.3	0.3	0.9	1.0	6.6	6.8	6.9	6.9	6.9	31.0	23.7	10.2	1.1	75.5	35.4	55.5	44.5
70533	ERATH	91.2	87.4	6.2	8.7	1.2	2.0	1.1	1.4	7.5	7.7	8.0	7.0	5.8	27.0	25.5	9.8	1.7	72.4	35.7	48.9	51.1
70535	EUNICE	74.9	72.0	23.8	26.3	0.2	0.3	1.1	1.3	7.9	7.6	7.3	7.4	6.6	24.4	25.2	11.8	1.7	72.6	35.0	48.7	51.3
70537	EVANGELINE	98.6	98.1	0.4	0.5	0.1	0.3	0.7	1.0	7.1	7.1	7.2	7.0	6.4	25.5	28.1	10.4	1.1	74.3	36.8	51.2	48.8
70538	FRANKLIN	51.9	47.4	45.5	49.3	0.6	1.0	0.7	0.8	7.7	7.9	8.2	8.0	5.8	23.1	26.9	10.7	1.8	71.0	36.5	47.6	52.4
70542	GUEYDAN	92.8	90.6	6.4	8.5	0.1	0.1	0.9	1.1	6.1	6.6	6.5	6.1	4.6	24.2	28.8	14.1	2.9	77.1	41.7	47.5	52.5
70543	IOTA	93.6	91.5	5.6	7.5	0.1	0.1	0.7	0.9	8.3	8.1	7.8	6.9	6.0	25.5	25.7	10.3	1.4	71.5	35.5	50.4	49.6
70544	JEANERETTE	45.8	40.6	51.4	56.0	0.3	0.4	1.7	1.9	7.9	7.8	8.5	8.3	6.7	23.4	25.6	10.2	1.7	70.6	34.6	47.6	52.4
70546	JENNINGS	78.5	77.7	20.0	20.7	0.3	0.3	1.0	1.1	7.8	7.5	7.3	7.3	6.3	24.7	25.2	12.0	1.8	72.8	36.2	48.1	51.9
70548	KAPLAN	91.2	88.3	7.3	9.7	0.3	0.6	1.1	1.4	6.8	6.7	6.7	6.6	5.8	26.0	26.8	12.2	2.4	75.6	38.4	48.4	51.6
70549	LAKE ARTHUR	90.9	89.6	8.1	9.3	0.1	0.1	0.6	0.6	7.5	7.6	7.5	6.7	5.1	25.0	27.0	11.9	1.7	73.2	37.4	48.5	51.5
70552	LOREAUVILLE	76.3	71.4	23.4	28.2	0.1	0.1	0.7	0.8	8.6	8.4	8.1	6.8	5.9	27.6	24.1	9.4	1.2	70.8	34.3	50.3	49.7
70554	MAMOU	72.0	67.0	26.8	31.5	0.1	0.2	0.9	1.0	8.2	8.1	7.9	7.6	6.0	23.9	24.4	11.8	2.0	70.9	35.6	48.3	51.7
70555	MAURICE	87.3	82.4	10.7	14.8	0.7	1.1	1.4	1.8	6.8	6.9	7.0	7.5	6.1	28.6	26.8	9.1	1.3	74.6	36.6	50.3	49.7
70559	MORSE	94.8	92.8	4.2	5.7	0.0	0.0	0.8	1.1	7.4	8.6	7.4	7.5	6.4	24.5	26.6	10.3	1.3	72.1	35.3	49.7	50.3
70560	NEW IBERIA	60.7	56.6	34.1	36.6	2.7	3.7	1.5	1.9	8.4	8.0	7.6	7.3	6.7	26.4	24.3	9.8	1.5	71.6	34.1	48.4	51.6
70563	NEW IBERIA	84.0	80.1	14.1	17.3	0.7	1.1	1.4	1.7	7.1	7.2	7.4	7.4	5.7	25.5	27.4	10.4	1.8	73.7	37.4	48.2	51.8
70570	OPELOUSAS	43.5	39.7	55.0	58.5	0.3	0.4	0.8	0.9	8.0	7.8	7.4	7.5	6.4	24.2	25.2	11.6	2.0	72.1	35.6	47.2	52.8
70577	PORT BARRE	79.1	74.7	20.2	24.3	0.1	0.2	0.6	0.7	7.4	7.4	7.4	7.6	6.0	25.0	26.8	11.2	1.3	73.2	36.9	49.2	50.8
70578	RAYNE	77.1	73.8	21.9	25.0	0.2	0.2	0.9	1.1	7.9	7.8	7.5	7.3	6.3	26.2	25.4	10.2	1.6	72.3	35.1	48.1	51.9
70581	ROANOKE	87.2	85.2	11.4	13.4	0.1	0.1	0.5	0.6	7.4	7.4	8.0	8.2	6.5	24.1	27.4	9.8	1.2	72.1	35.0	50.1	49.9
70582	SAINT MARTINVILLE	59.3	56.5	39.1	41.5	0.5	0.6	1.0	1.1	7.7	7.6	7.5	7.4	6.3	26.4	26.0	10.0	1.4	72.7	35.3	48.7	51.3
70583	SCOTT	75.9	71.8	22.0	25.4	0.6	0.9	1.4	1.7	8.7	8.5	7.9	7.1	7.1	29.2	24.5	6.4	0.7	70.6	31.9	48.7	51.3
70584	SUNSET	61.2	57.5	37.7	41.1	0.1	0.1	1.1	1.2	7.7	7.5	7.3	7.2	5.9	25.7	27.6	9.9	1.2	73.1	36.4	48.7	51.3
70586	VILLE PLATTE	67.7	65.0	31.4	33.8	0.1	0.2	1.1	1.3	8.1	7.7	7.4	7.3	6.5	25.5	24.4	11.3	1.8	72.4	35.2	49.9	50.1
70589	WASHINGTON	54.8	50.3	44.1	48.4	0.1	0.1	0.9	1.0	7.9	8.0	7.7	7.0	5.2	23.6	24.8	13.5	2.3	71.8	38.0	48.8	51.2
70591	WELSH	81.2	79.2	17.6	19.6	0.1	0.1	1.0	1.0	7.4	7.4	7.5	7.2	5.6	25.1	25.9	11.8	2.1	73.2	36.7	49.0	51.0
70592	YOUNGSVILLE	88.7	84.7	8.7	11.7	1.1	1.5	1.6	2.1	8.7	8.3	8.0	7.0	5.6	31.7	24.3	5.9	0.6	70.6	33.3	49.5	50.5
70601	LAKE CHARLES	36.4	28.4	60.9	68.7	0.7	0.9	1.2	1.2	7.3	7.1	6.7	7.0	6.6	24.4	25.1	13.2	2.8	74.6	37.5	46.7	53.3
70605	LAKE CHARLES	91.5	86.3	5.6	9.5	1.4	2.2	1.6	2.0	6.2	6.1	6.4	6.7	6.2	25.9	28.1	12.4	2.0	77.2	39.4	47.9	52.1
70607	LAKE CHARLES	67.4	58.3	29.6	38.1	0.9	1.3	1.4	1.5	8.6	7.8	7.1	6.9	8.1	30.2	22.6	8.0	0.8	72.5	31.3	49.1	50.9
70609	LAKE CHARLES	61.2	46.5	31.0	43.9	4.5	5.9	2.7	3.0	0.0	0.0	0.0	51.9	42.6	5.2	0.2	0.0	0.0	99.9	19.8	45.3	54.7
70611	LAKE CHARLES	93.2	89.0	4.7	8.1	0.4	0.6	1.4	1.8	7.5	7.4	7.4	7.4	6.1	29.1	27.1	7.5	0.6	73.2	34.7	49.4	50.6
70615	LAKE CHARLES	41.5	35.2	55.9	61.8	0.5	0.7	1.4	1.5	7.0	6.3	6.5	7.8	8.1	28.0	25.5	9.8	1.0	75.6	34.9	51.7	48.3
70630	BELL CITY	98.1	96.9	0.7	1.5	0.1	0.1	1.3	1.8	7.4	7.3	7.2	7.0	6.0	26.9	26.2	11.1	0.9	73.8	37.0	50.5	49.5
70631	CAMERON	86.6	82.8	9.3	11.2	0.6	1.3	4.0	5.4	7.4	7.3	7.3	6.9	5.7	25.6	27.4	11.1	1.3	73.5	37.4	52.1	47.9
70632	CREOLE	94.9	91.8	3.4	5.5	0.1	0.3	1.6	3.0	4.5	5.8	8.3	8.5	7.3	26.5	25.8	11.0	2.5	75.8	39.2	50.5	49.5
70633	DEQUINCY	83.4	78.2	14.8	19.6	0.3	0.5	0.8	1.0	7.3	7.2	7.1	6.9	6.2	26.9	24.7	11.9	1.6	74.1	36.4	50.7	49.3
70634	DERIDDER	80.3	76.7	16.0	18.3	0.8	1.2	1.9	2.5	7.1	7.0	7.1	7.1	6.0	25.3	26.6	12.1	1.7	74.3	37.7	48.9	51.1
70637	DRY CREEK	97.1	96.2	0.5	0.8	0.1	0.1	0.5	0.8	6.4	6.7	6.9	7.1	5.5	24.1	29.6	12.2	1.4	75.7	40.1	51.7	48.3
70639	EVANS	94.9	93.4	0.8	1.1	0.2	0.4	1.6	2.3	8.3	8.3	7.6	6.6	4.9	26.3	23.8	13.0	1.3	71.3	36.9	50.3	49.7
70643	GRAND CHENIER	97.5	95.6	0.8	1.4	1.0	1.4	0.9	1.9	4.2	6.7	8.3	7.9	5.8	26.4	27.5	11.3	1.9	75.7	39.4	49.5	50.5
70645	HACKBERRY	97.5	95.6	0.5	0.9	0.7	1.1	1.1	2.2	6.0	6.3	6.5	6.1	5.3	24.3	31.7	12.8	1.1	77.5	40.9	49.3	50.7
70647	IOWA	85.3	78.6	12.5	18.7	0.3	0.4	1.2	1.4	7.4	7.3	7.3	7.7	6.2	27.8	26.1	9.2	0.9	73.1	35.1	49.4	50.6
70648	KINDER	71.0	68.7	24.1	26.3	0.4	0.5	1.1	1.3	6.3	6.4	6.6	6.8	6.7	30.5	24.3	10.7	1.6	76.4	36.4	55.2	44.8
70650	LACASSINE	100.0	100.0	0.0	0.0	0.0	0.0	0.0	0.0	0.0	8.3	0.0	0.0	0.0	41.7	50.0	0.0	0.0	91.7	45.0	75.0	25.0
	LOUISIANA	63.9	61.9	32.5	33.7	1.3	1.6	2.4	2.8	7.2	7.0	6.9	7.3	7.1	26.8	25.7	10.4	1.6	74.6	35.6	48.6	51.4
	UNITED STATES	75.1	72.0	12.3	12.7	3.8	4.6	12.5	15.7	6.8	6.7	6.6	7.1	6.9	27.0	26.0	10.9	1.9	75.7	36.9	49.2	50.8

ZIP CODE #	POST OFFICE NAME	2009 Per Capita Income	2009 HH Income Base	2009 Household Income Distribution (%): Less than $25,000	$25,000 to $49,999	$50,000 to $99,999	$100,000 to $149,999	$150,000 or More	Median Household Income: 2009	2014	2009 National Centile	2009 State Centile	2009 Home Value Base	2009 Home Value Distribution (%): Less than $50,000	$50,000 to $89,999	$90,000 to $174,999	$175,000 to $399,999	$400,000 or More	2009 Median Home Value
70426	ANGIE	13588	2063	42.1	33.2	21.4	2.6	0.7	28920	28985	7	27	1644	38.1	21.5	26.9	12.3	1.2	70423
70427	BOGALUSA	14851	8186	46.9	29.2	19.2	3.7	0.9	26820	27558	4	17	5728	26.8	30.9	29.5	11.3	1.6	78934
70431	BUSH	20889	1956	27.0	26.6	36.7	5.9	3.8	45517	43614	50	86	1703	11.9	10.4	28.0	37.8	11.9	173007
70433	COVINGTON	29472	12585	19.0	22.9	35.1	12.7	10.3	58458	61931	76	98	9429	3.4	4.3	26.9	50.3	15.0	221348
70435	COVINGTON	22198	5578	24.3	28.1	34.0	8.1	5.5	47490	44494	55	88	4906	8.6	7.5	29.6	39.5	14.7	195392
70436	FLUKER	9062	73	58.9	24.7	13.7	2.7	0.0	18335	19612	1	3	56	48.2	14.3	25.0	10.7	1.8	55000
70437	FOLSOM	20695	2702	27.5	27.0	34.9	6.9	3.7	44943	42270	48	84	2348	9.5	7.1	27.9	42.7	12.9	202362
70438	FRANKLINTON	15226	6837	45.1	29.2	20.2	3.8	1.6	27598	28044	5	20	5519	27.5	20.0	32.3	17.1	3.1	97036
70441	GREENSBURG	13408	1416	50.2	24.5	21.2	3.5	0.6	24842	26566	3	10	1169	30.5	22.3	29.3	12.1	5.7	83796
70442	HUSSER	15383	203	36.5	29.1	28.1	4.9	1.5	33327	33101	14	51	166	24.7	13.3	37.3	20.5	4.2	111458
70443	INDEPENDENCE	15903	3430	39.0	29.1	25.5	3.5	2.8	32511	32788	12	48	2767	24.1	19.0	35.7	18.6	2.5	106191
70444	KENTWOOD	13994	4303	45.8	27.4	22.6	3.3	1.0	28048	28551	6	22	3466	28.0	17.1	28.4	21.3	5.3	103399
70445	LACOMBE	20878	4302	29.8	25.2	33.6	8.7	2.7	44330	41969	46	83	3662	8.9	12.1	37.1	36.6	5.2	151045
70446	LORANGER	16249	1865	32.1	31.4	29.4	5.4	1.7	39142	38712	30	71	1580	16.9	12.4	37.4	28.3	5.0	129360
70447	MADISONVILLE	28382	3413	21.7	23.9	33.5	12.9	8.1	54995	57129	71	97	2799	6.8	5.5	29.2	41.2	17.3	209099
70448	MANDEVILLE	33359	9499	12.3	16.3	37.4	21.6	12.3	77690	78821	91	100	8013	2.2	2.6	18.3	64.7	12.2	250943
70449	MAUREPAS	17878	1464	31.9	32.7	30.2	4.3	0.9	34953	34423	17	57	1220	15.5	20.6	35.3	24.8	3.8	120000
70450	MOUNT HERMON	14392	954	40.1	38.3	17.9	2.1	1.6	28384	28170	6	25	801	23.1	22.1	27.7	21.6	5.5	98556
70452	PEARL RIVER	17981	5403	34.8	26.4	29.5	6.9	2.4	37540	37794	25	67	4309	16.9	14.1	40.0	26.2	2.8	125778
70453	PINE GROVE	13219	229	43.7	27.9	24.0	2.6	1.7	29460	30784	7	30	199	32.2	15.1	34.2	15.1	3.5	95500
70454	PONCHATOULA	17411	8922	35.4	27.9	28.2	6.3	2.2	35220	35897	18	59	7007	14.9	13.5	35.7	30.5	5.3	137863
70455	ROBERT	17393	561	31.4	29.6	31.6	6.1	1.4	40224	39463	33	74	492	17.1	15.0	31.5	33.3	3.0	132927
70456	ROSELAND	12707	1223	49.7	27.7	18.4	3.4	0.8	25204	26456	3	11	960	38.2	17.7	27.4	13.6	3.0	71935
70458	SLIDELL	24726	13249	20.0	26.1	39.4	10.0	4.4	53020	54623	68	95	10077	2.8	6.0	51.2	35.0	5.0	155342
70460	SLIDELL	21467	8958	25.5	25.0	36.7	9.5	3.3	49323	48094	60	90	7093	6.4	9.7	54.2	26.1	3.6	138673
70461	SLIDELL	25592	9997	18.9	18.7	41.5	14.2	6.6	62000	64335	80	99	8105	6.6	4.7	32.0	47.4	9.3	193672
70462	SPRINGFIELD	17559	2199	34.7	31.0	27.0	5.3	2.0	35286	35522	19	59	1890	18.2	17.1	38.0	22.0	4.6	127697
70466	TICKFAW	16408	3191	36.6	27.7	29.7	4.5	1.4	34965	35941	18	57	2464	24.2	17.7	34.5	21.8	1.8	107625
70467	VARNADO	21666	8	75.0	0.0	25.0	0.0	0.0	15000	25000	1	1	6	0.0	66.7	33.3	0.0	0.0	57500
70471	MANDEVILLE	34443	7292	14.6	18.0	32.7	19.2	15.5	73278	74164	88	100	5533	0.9	3.2	16.9	54.3	24.7	273025
70501	LAFAYETTE	13717	11694	52.2	27.0	17.0	2.3	1.4	23272	24536	2	8	6237	21.5	29.6	38.1	8.6	2.2	88715
70503	LAFAYETTE	30199	10288	23.6	22.3	32.3	12.0	9.9	54853	54236	71	97	7262	1.2	1.5	34.8	47.3	15.1	207053
70504	LAFAYETTE	33960	125	14.4	15.2	42.4	16.8	11.2	69319	71494	86	99	113	1.8	0.0	30.1	63.7	4.4	221250
70506	LAFAYETTE	21546	16178	32.2	28.4	31.1	5.9	2.5	40499	41929	34	74	8564	7.3	11.7	51.4	27.8	1.9	137048
70507	LAFAYETTE	19229	5863	28.5	30.3	32.4	6.8	2.0	42587	44561	41	78	3909	17.8	16.7	43.6	20.6	1.3	123289
70508	LAFAYETTE	29275	12799	19.5	25.0	35.6	12.8	7.1	55431	55132	72	97	8123	7.8	4.1	30.4	45.9	11.9	198112
70510	ABBEVILLE	15420	9559	42.9	28.4	22.9	4.2	1.6	30016	29760	8	34	6967	23.6	22.6	33.9	17.0	2.8	97673
70512	ARNAUDVILLE	15485	3664	38.9	27.5	28.2	4.6	0.8	33714	34845	15	53	3097	22.7	21.7	36.8	17.7	1.0	99122
70514	BALDWIN	13111	1309	44.6	28.2	22.8	3.7	0.7	28594	28285	6	26	1109	41.2	20.4	28.9	9.0	0.5	66132
70515	BASILE	13907	1304	48.8	27.9	17.9	3.7	1.7	25722	26606	4	13	981	39.4	22.0	28.5	9.9	0.1	66091
70516	BRANCH	16184	514	34.2	28.8	29.8	5.8	1.4	37849	37820	26	67	426	25.6	19.0	36.4	18.1	0.9	99583
70517	BREAUX BRIDGE	15726	9528	37.9	29.0	26.8	4.9	1.4	34644	36271	17	56	7758	23.0	23.0	33.6	18.5	1.8	98253
70518	BROUSSARD	22107	4382	25.5	26.4	34.9	9.2	4.0	48120	47736	57	89	3403	16.9	14.2	35.9	28.6	4.5	136212
70520	CARENCRO	17809	6161	31.8	29.8	30.3	5.8	2.3	39906	41377	32	72	4763	16.9	19.5	37.5	22.1	4.0	116298
70525	CHURCH POINT	13738	4444	42.9	30.0	23.5	2.9	0.8	29787	29831	8	32	3313	26.7	28.5	30.9	11.4	2.5	83417
70526	CROWLEY	15775	7724	41.6	29.5	22.4	4.5	2.0	29815	29712	8	33	5041	22.6	26.4	34.1	14.3	2.6	91452
70528	DELCAMBRE	17606	923	33.9	29.9	28.3	7.0	0.9	36719	36406	23	63	715	28.3	23.5	33.4	14.4	0.4	86711
70529	DUSON	17548	4083	32.7	29.7	30.3	5.8	1.5	40950	42054	36	76	3117	24.1	18.9	37.2	17.9	1.9	105444
70531	EGAN	15080	361	42.1	24.9	28.5	3.3	1.1	31113	30809	10	40	307	32.2	27.0	25.7	9.1	5.9	82297
70532	ELTON	17151	1038	46.2	26.1	20.8	5.2	1.6	28394	29433	6	25	819	35.7	28.0	25.0	10.4	1.0	63545
70533	ERATH	16379	2900	34.6	29.6	28.7	5.4	1.6	35750	36203	20	60	2336	22.9	21.2	36.3	17.6	1.9	102708
70535	EUNICE	14512	7210	45.0	27.7	22.6	3.1	1.7	28342	28586	6	24	4978	26.2	26.2	34.5	12.4	0.7	85890
70537	EVANGELINE	14356	278	46.0	25.5	24.1	3.6	0.7	27547	28161	5	20	244	33.2	25.4	31.6	7.0	2.9	80870
70538	FRANKLIN	14647	5264	44.0	28.7	21.2	4.4	1.7	29342	29615	7	29	3907	26.5	25.6	33.7	12.9	1.3	86873
70542	GUEYDAN	16635	1378	40.8	28.9	24.2	4.5	1.7	32372	32780	12	47	1140	28.0	29.4	28.6	11.8	2.3	80968
70543	IOTA	14720	1315	43.0	27.5	23.2	5.2	1.2	29565	29712	7	31	1044	33.3	24.5	31.9	9.8	0.5	76866
70544	JEANERETTE	13678	3965	43.2	27.6	23.4	4.0	1.8	29743	29878	8	32	3067	27.6	31.1	29.1	10.1	2.1	76597
70546	JENNINGS	14612	5942	42.2	28.8	24.1	3.8	1.2	30229	30380	8	35	4250	23.0	27.4	38.2	10.0	1.3	89420
70548	KAPLAN	15725	4430	40.5	27.8	26.0	4.7	1.1	32546	33217	12	48	3387	27.5	26.3	32.8	12.3	1.0	83128
70549	LAKE ARTHUR	16093	1645	42.6	28.8	22.2	4.9	1.5	31188	32741	10	40	1217	32.4	29.9	29.2	6.9	1.6	74053
70552	LOREAUVILLE	16259	525	37.0	28.8	27.8	4.8	1.7	35082	35265	18	58	439	26.7	23.5	38.7	10.9	0.2	89783
70554	MAMOU	12356	2597	56.1	24.6	15.8	2.3	1.1	20039	21677	1	4	1643	38.0	22.5	29.7	8.9	0.9	66649
70555	MAURICE	17389	2017	31.1	30.7	31.3	4.8	2.0	37986	37805	27	68	1672	24.2	21.5	27.8	23.1	3.3	102516
70559	MORSE	14220	1144	43.1	30.0	22.0	2.9	2.0	29591	29919	7	31	916	40.2	28.1	26.9	4.8	0.1	60779
70560	NEW IBERIA	14919	15468	40.6	29.2	24.1	4.5	1.6	31346	31500	10	42	10467	25.4	22.7	37.7	12.8	1.5	92924
70563	NEW IBERIA	20834	6648	27.5	26.2	33.7	8.8	3.8	46915	44197	54	87	5444	11.7	14.9	44.4	25.2	3.9	126078
70570	OPELOUSAS	13185	17413	51.3	25.9	18.3	3.2	1.3	23832	25552	3	9	11590	24.9	28.3	31.1	14.1	1.6	85175
70577	PORT BARRE	14313	1638	43.0	31.3	20.7	3.7	1.3	29757	29804	8	32	1284	32.9	22.7	31.3	11.8	1.2	77833
70578	RAYNE	15518	5873	42.0	29.5	22.6	3.8	2.1	30419	30492	9	36	4133	27.8	23.2	32.8	14.5	1.7	88521
70581	ROANOKE	15435	342	31.6	34.8	26.6	6.1	0.9	36292	36490	21	62	296	22.6	24.7	45.6	6.1	1.0	93478
70582	SAINT MARTINVILLE	15015	7247	39.8	27.6	28.0	3.5	1.2	33031	34833	13	50	5646	25.2	26.3	32.3	14.4	1.8	88061
70583	SCOTT	17072	4419	31.9	32.2	29.4	4.9	1.5	39762	41016	32	71	3434	32.5	21.1	28.9	15.3	2.2	83107
70584	SUNSET	15769	2603	44.3	25.7	23.7	4.6	1.7	29367	29206	7	29	1942	25.1	22.5	29.5	20.1	2.8	96301
70586	VILLE PLATTE	13261	8556	52.2	23.8	19.6	3.3	1.1	23009	24066	2	7	5886	27.1	30.4	30.5	11.0	1.0	78649
70589	WASHINGTON	13550	1528	53.1	25.4	16.7	3.4	1.4	22905	24492	2	7	1110	25.2	29.3	33.9	10.1	1.5	84186
70591	WELSH	15590	1985	39.5	30.6	24.4	3.8	1.6	31459	31563	10	43	1503	27.3	28.9	35.5	8.0	0.3	82094
70592	YOUNGSVILLE	23759	5727	19.2	28.3	35.1	12.7	4.7	53135	51267	68	95	4695	17.1	10.6	33.4	34.1	4.9	143282
70601	LAKE CHARLES	16134	13959	46.4	29.7	18.6	3.7	1.6	27123	27321	5	18	7349	12.5	38.3	39.2	8.4	1.6	89185
70605	LAKE CHARLES	28749	11700	22.3	25.1	32.0	13.4	7.2	52842	51893	68	95	8936	9.8	9.5	38.0	33.3	9.4	155817
70607	LAKE CHARLES	19109	9435	30.2	31.9	29.6	6.7	1.6	39316	41284	31	71	6157	19.0	30.6	36.9	12.9	0.6	90817
70609	LAKE CHARLES	13183	0	0.0	0.0	0.0	0.0	0.0	0	0	0	0	0	0.0	0.0	0.0	0.0	0.0	0
70611	LAKE CHARLES	22716	6367	21.8	24.9	38.2	11.0	4.1	52562	51455	67	95	5279	16.7	13.5	36.1	31.5	2.2	139648
70615	LAKE CHARLES	16001	4917	39.7	29.2	25.1	4.9	1.1	33017	33021	13	50	3329	31.7	31.8	27.2	8.1	1.3	71481
70630	BELL CITY	18782	530	26.8	33.2	30.4	8.5	1.1	43057	43917	43	79	451	26.8	30.2	29.9	10.6	2.4	84273
70631	CAMERON	17000	843	40.0	27.2	24.2	5.9	2.7	31514	32069	11	44	699	43.8	30.0	22.0	2.1	2.0	57373
70632	CREOLE	14712	147	36.1	29.9	31.3	2.7	0.0	33821	35000	15	54	126	39.7	28.6	29.4	0.8	1.6	66667
70633	DEQUINCY	15562	2985	37.0	30.8	26.2	4.7	1.3	33116	32358	14	51	2315	29.8	30.7	26.0	12.5	0.9	76944
70634	DERIDDER	18628	9283	33.4	29.7	28.1	6.8	1.9	37666	37593	26	67	6929	23.4	21.2	37.4	16.4	1.7	100112
70637	DRY CREEK	15281	296	38.5	30.7	25.3	5.1	0.3	31645	30997	11	45	269	33.8	21.9	36.4	5.9	1.9	79667
70639	EVANS	14788	180	39.4	34.4	20.6	3.9	1.7	30761	30180	9	38	153	34.0	20.3	25.5	17.0	3.3	79286
70643	GRAND CHENIER	17503	171	38.0	28.1	28.7	2.9	2.3	30245	28836	8	35	145	41.4	22.8	34.5	0.7	0.7	65500
70645	HACKBERRY	17596	639	31.6	27.4	35.1	5.6	0.3	40465	41224	34	74	551	44.8	27.4	18.7	8.0	1.1	58636
70647	IOWA	17122	3079	31.9	32.0	29.2	5.6	1.4	39936	40819	32	72	2477	30.3	23.7	34.8	10.2	1.0	83299
70648	KINDER	17044	2669	35.0	25.4	32.5	5.2	1.9	38478	37977	28	69	2030	22.2	24.9	38.7	13.4	0.8	94797
70650	LACASSINE	21167	7	57.1	0.0	42.9	0.0	0.0	17143	27208	1	2	6	0.0	33.3	66.7	0.0	0.0	95000
	LOUISIANA	19176		34.0	28.2	28.2	6.6	3.0	37868	38644				16.9	18.7	37.2	22.8	4.3	118738
	UNITED STATES	27277		20.9	24.4	35.3	11.7	7.6	54719	56938				9.3	13.1	31.6	32.6	13.5	162279

ZIP CODE #	POST OFFICE NAME	FINANCIAL SERVICES: Auto Loan	FINANCIAL SERVICES: Home Loan	FINANCIAL SERVICES: Investments	FINANCIAL SERVICES: Retirement Plans	THE HOME – Home Improvements: Home Repair	THE HOME – Home Improvements: Lawn & Garden	THE HOME – Furnishings: Computers & Hardware-Personal	THE HOME – Furnishings: Major Appliances	THE HOME – Furnishings: TV, Radio, Sound Equipment	THE HOME – Furnishings: Furniture	ENTERTAINMENT: Dine out/Carry out	ENTERTAINMENT: Sports Equipment	ENTERTAINMENT: Fees & Tickets	ENTERTAINMENT: Toys & Games	ENTERTAINMENT: Travel	ENTERTAINMENT: Cable TV	PERSONAL: Apparel & Services	PERSONAL: Auto Repairs	PERSONAL: Health Insurance	PERSONAL: Pets & Supplies
70426	ANGIE	68	46	64	43	46	67	49	60	55	46	54	47	37	57	45	62	36	57	63	74
70427	BOGALUSA	58	45	53	44	45	59	48	54	54	47	52	40	42	53	46	59	35	53	61	65
70431	BUSH	86	84	75	83	82	86	78	82	80	79	80	62	76	82	77	81	55	80	83	98
70433	COVINGTON	115	123	109	122	119	112	111	113	109	118	110	87	116	113	112	106	77	109	106	131
70435	COVINGTON	93	93	87	93	91	95	87	92	88	88	88	69	87	90	88	90	61	89	92	109
70436	FLUKER	56	37	54	35	37	55	40	50	46	38	45	39	30	46	37	51	30	47	53	61
70437	FOLSOM	91	79	91	77	81	90	76	87	80	76	79	63	70	80	76	83	53	83	87	102
70438	FRANKLINTON	68	49	65	48	50	68	52	62	58	49	57	47	42	58	49	63	38	59	66	75
70441	GREENSBURG	63	42	61	39	41	62	44	56	51	42	50	44	33	52	41	57	33	53	59	69
70442	HUSSER	72	58	68	56	58	71	57	67	61	56	61	50	49	62	55	65	41	63	68	79
70443	INDEPENDENCE	77	58	70	55	57	74	59	69	65	58	64	53	49	66	56	69	43	66	71	83
70444	KENTWOOD	66	47	59	45	46	64	49	58	56	48	55	44	40	57	46	62	37	56	63	71
70445	LACOMBE	89	81	84	79	81	88	76	84	79	78	79	63	73	81	76	82	54	80	84	100
70446	LORANGER	76	66	65	64	65	72	63	70	67	65	67	51	58	69	61	70	45	67	71	83
70447	MADISONVILLE	105	120	105	122	116	114	106	110	103	108	104	86	114	106	112	102	73	105	106	128
70448	MANDEVILLE	134	155	136	155	150	132	135	136	127	146	129	108	146	134	139	120	92	128	119	154
70449	MAUREPAS	78	57	73	55	58	77	59	71	65	56	64	54	48	66	56	71	42	66	74	85
70450	MOUNT HERMON	69	46	68	44	47	68	49	62	55	46	54	47	37	56	46	62	36	57	65	75
70452	PEARL RIVER	81	67	75	65	67	79	67	75	71	66	70	57	59	72	64	74	47	72	76	90
70453	PINE GROVE	72	49	69	46	49	71	52	64	59	50	58	49	40	60	48	65	38	60	67	78
70454	PONCHATOULA	76	65	65	64	64	73	65	70	68	65	68	53	60	70	62	71	46	68	72	84
70455	ROBERT	75	69	61	67	67	70	65	69	68	68	68	50	62	70	62	69	46	67	69	82
70456	ROSELAND	63	42	61	40	42	62	45	56	51	42	50	44	34	52	42	57	33	53	59	69
70458	SLIDELL	91	96	88	96	93	94	90	92	90	92	91	69	93	92	92	91	63	90	93	107
70460	SLIDELL	90	90	80	87	86	86	84	86	84	88	85	66	83	87	82	84	59	84	84	101
70461	SLIDELL	104	118	110	117	115	108	104	107	100	108	101	83	111	103	109	98	72	102	99	124
70462	SPRINGFIELD	80	59	78	58	60	80	60	74	66	57	65	56	49	67	59	72	43	69	77	88
70466	TICKFAW	74	63	62	60	61	69	62	67	66	64	65	51	56	68	59	68	44	65	68	80
70467	VARNADO	60	39	58	37	39	59	42	53	49	40	47	41	32	49	39	54	31	50	56	65
70471	MANDEVILLE	138	152	143	154	151	136	139	138	133	148	135	109	148	138	143	128	96	134	126	159
70501	LAFAYETTE	51	41	38	42	39	47	48	46	52	47	51	34	44	52	43	55	35	49	53	57
70503	LAFAYETTE	106	114	112	117	114	111	114	109	109	113	110	85	117	109	114	108	78	110	108	128
70504	LAFAYETTE	109	129	133	129	134	136	112	123	115	117	115	85	126	111	126	119	80	118	133	140
70506	LAFAYETTE	72	63	58	65	61	62	72	65	72	71	72	52	67	73	66	71	50	70	67	79
70507	LAFAYETTE	76	71	63	69	67	69	73	70	73	74	74	54	69	75	68	73	51	72	71	84
70508	LAFAYETTE	104	105	95	106	101	94	104	99	100	108	102	79	105	104	102	97	72	100	93	116
70510	ABBEVILLE	67	53	60	51	52	66	54	62	60	53	59	46	47	60	52	65	40	60	66	75
70512	ARNAUDVILLE	76	54	68	51	53	73	56	67	62	54	61	51	45	64	52	68	41	63	70	81
70514	BALDWIN	63	47	55	46	46	60	50	56	56	49	55	43	43	56	47	60	37	55	61	69
70515	BASILE	67	46	65	44	46	66	48	60	54	45	53	46	37	55	46	60	35	56	63	73
70516	BRANCH	80	63	75	61	63	79	64	74	67	60	67	57	53	68	61	72	44	70	76	89
70517	BREAUX BRIDGE	75	55	66	53	54	72	57	66	64	56	63	51	48	65	53	69	42	64	70	81
70518	BROUSSARD	92	90	75	87	85	84	85	85	85	89	86	65	83	89	81	85	59	84	82	101
70520	CARENCRO	75	70	62	68	68	70	70	70	71	72	71	53	67	73	67	72	49	70	71	83
70525	CHURCH POINT	65	46	57	45	46	63	50	58	56	48	55	44	40	57	46	61	37	56	62	71
70526	CROWLEY	67	55	55	55	54	65	58	62	63	56	61	47	52	63	54	67	42	61	67	75
70528	DELCAMBRE	82	59	68	58	59	78	62	72	68	60	67	55	49	71	56	75	45	68	76	87
70529	DUSON	79	64	66	63	63	73	66	71	70	66	69	54	58	72	61	73	47	69	72	85
70531	EGAN	76	54	62	53	54	72	57	66	63	55	61	51	45	65	51	68	41	62	69	80
70532	ELTON	74	51	73	48	51	74	53	67	60	50	59	51	41	61	51	67	39	62	70	81
70533	ERATH	80	61	69	59	61	77	62	71	67	60	66	54	52	69	58	73	44	67	75	86
70535	EUNICE	65	48	56	47	48	63	53	59	58	50	57	45	44	59	48	63	38	58	64	71
70537	EVANGELINE	69	47	63	45	47	67	50	61	56	48	55	47	38	58	46	62	37	57	64	74
70538	FRANKLIN	69	50	62	49	49	67	54	62	61	52	59	47	45	61	50	66	40	60	67	76
70542	GUEYDAN	76	51	78	49	52	77	55	69	60	49	59	55	41	60	53	67	39	65	73	85
70543	IOTA	73	50	68	48	50	71	53	64	59	50	58	50	40	60	49	65	38	61	68	79
70544	JEANERETTE	69	51	63	50	50	69	53	62	60	52	59	47	45	61	50	66	40	60	68	76
70546	JENNINGS	65	50	57	50	50	64	53	60	58	51	57	45	46	59	50	63	39	58	65	72
70548	KAPLAN	71	52	67	50	52	70	54	65	60	51	59	49	44	61	52	66	39	61	69	78
70549	LAKE ARTHUR	73	50	73	48	51	74	54	67	60	49	59	52	41	60	51	66	39	63	71	81
70552	LOREAUVILLE	84	60	69	58	60	79	62	73	69	61	68	56	50	72	57	75	46	69	77	88
70554	MAMOU	55	39	48	38	39	53	42	49	48	41	46	37	34	48	39	52	31	47	53	60
70555	MAURICE	77	71	63	69	69	73	67	71	69	70	69	52	63	72	64	71	47	69	71	84
70559	MORSE	72	47	69	44	47	71	50	63	58	48	57	49	38	59	47	65	37	60	67	78
70560	NEW IBERIA	67	54	55	53	53	64	57	61	62	57	61	45	51	63	53	66	42	61	66	74
70563	NEW IBERIA	87	84	81	84	83	90	80	85	82	80	82	65	78	84	80	85	56	82	87	101
70570	OPELOUSAS	56	44	48	43	43	54	47	51	52	47	51	38	41	52	43	56	35	51	56	62
70577	PORT BARRE	70	48	67	45	48	69	50	63	57	48	56	48	39	58	47	63	37	59	66	76
70578	RAYNE	70	54	59	52	53	68	57	63	63	55	61	48	48	64	52	68	41	62	68	77
70581	ROANOKE	80	57	66	56	57	76	60	69	66	58	65	53	48	69	54	72	44	66	73	85
70582	SAINT MARTINVILLE	71	54	60	52	53	67	56	63	61	56	60	48	48	63	52	66	41	61	66	76
70583	SCOTT	73	63	58	61	60	66	65	66	68	65	67	50	59	70	60	70	46	66	67	79
70584	SUNSET	69	52	59	51	51	66	56	61	61	54	60	47	47	62	51	65	40	60	65	75
70586	VILLE PLATTE	58	43	51	42	43	55	47	52	52	45	51	39	39	52	43	56	34	51	57	63
70589	WASHINGTON	60	43	56	42	44	60	47	55	53	45	51	41	39	52	44	58	34	53	60	67
70591	WELSH	73	52	69	50	53	73	55	67	61	51	60	51	43	62	52	67	40	63	71	81
70592	YOUNGSVILLE	103	103	86	99	98	93	94	96	93	100	94	73	92	98	91	91	65	92	90	112
70601	LAKE CHARLES	56	46	44	47	45	53	53	52	58	52	57	39	49	57	49	61	39	55	59	63
70605	LAKE CHARLES	101	108	104	109	108	107	101	104	101	104	102	78	106	102	105	102	71	102	105	121
70607	LAKE CHARLES	74	64	56	64	61	64	70	66	71	70	72	52	65	73	64	72	49	69	68	80
70609	LAKE CHARLES	0	0	0	0	0	0	0	0	0	0	0	0	0	0	0	0	0	0	0	0
70611	LAKE CHARLES	101	95	85	92	92	95	89	93	91	93	91	70	85	95	85	92	62	90	92	110
70615	LAKE CHARLES	64	57	51	57	55	61	59	59	63	60	62	44	56	63	56	65	43	61	64	72
70630	BELL CITY	89	65	77	63	65	85	67	78	74	66	73	60	55	77	62	81	49	74	82	95
70631	CAMERON	83	57	74	54	56	80	60	72	68	57	66	56	46	69	55	74	44	68	76	89
70632	CREOLE	72	50	73	49	52	72	52	66	58	49	57	50	41	58	51	64	38	61	69	79
70633	DEQUINCY	72	54	63	53	54	71	58	66	64	56	62	50	49	65	54	69	42	64	71	79
70634	DERIDDER	78	64	68	62	63	76	65	72	70	64	69	54	57	71	61	74	46	69	76	86
70637	DRY CREEK	74	51	74	49	53	74	54	68	60	50	59	52	42	60	52	67	39	63	71	82
70639	EVANS	69	50	71	48	51	70	51	65	56	47	55	49	41	56	50	62	37	59	67	77
70643	GRAND CHENIER	79	56	81	54	58	80	58	73	64	54	63	55	46	64	57	71	42	67	76	87
70645	HACKBERRY	83	60	85	58	62	85	61	78	68	57	67	58	49	67	61	75	44	71	81	93
70647	IOWA	79	65	66	62	63	74	64	71	68	65	68	53	56	71	60	72	46	68	72	85
70648	KINDER	80	63	71	63	63	80	66	75	71	62	70	57	57	72	63	77	47	72	79	89
70650	LACASSINE	65	47	54	46	47	62	49	57	54	48	53	44	39	57	44	59	36	54	60	69
	LOUISIANA	78	67	68	67	66	75	70	72	73	70	73	55	65	74	67	76	50	73	76	87
	UNITED STATES	100	100	100	100	100	100	100	100	100	100	100	100	100	100	100	100	100	100	100	100

POPULATION CHANGE

ZIP CODE #	POST OFFICE NAME	COUNTY FIPS CODE	POPULATION 2000	POPULATION 2009	POPULATION 2014	2000-2009 ANNUAL RATE % Rate	2000-2009 ANNUAL RATE State Centile	HOUSEHOLDS 2000	HOUSEHOLDS 2009	HOUSEHOLDS 2014	HOUSEHOLDS % Annual Rate 2000-2009	HOUSEHOLDS 2009 Average HH Size	FAMILIES 2000	FAMILIES 2009	FAMILIES % Annual Rate 2000-2009
70652	LONGVILLE	011	2059	2512	2730	2.2	93	747	929	1019	2.4	2.65	596	730	2.2
70653	MERRYVILLE	011	3311	3484	3593	0.6	71	1287	1391	1450	0.8	2.46	951	1008	0.6
70654	MITTIE	003	523	535	539	0.2	49	197	206	209	0.5	2.60	148	152	0.3
70655	OBERLIN	003	3259	3343	3382	0.3	53	1219	1283	1310	0.6	2.45	856	886	0.4
70656	PITKIN	115	4286	4258	4206	-0.1	35	1560	1569	1558	0.1	2.71	1207	1197	-0.1
70657	RAGLEY	011	3497	4383	4741	2.5	95	1202	1542	1682	2.7	2.84	993	1260	2.6
70658	REEVES	003	984	1086	1130	1.1	82	366	412	431	1.3	2.64	287	320	1.2
70660	SINGER	011	1544	1665	1735	0.8	77	552	625	664	1.4	2.06	437	487	1.2
70661	STARKS	019	2442	2604	2671	0.7	74	973	1064	1100	1.0	2.45	721	775	0.8
70662	SUGARTOWN	011	424	463	487	1.0	80	157	175	186	1.2	2.65	123	135	1.0
70663	SULPHUR	019	27328	27547	27649	0.1	44	10134	10479	10607	0.4	2.58	7394	7537	0.2
70665	SULPHUR	019	9142	9972	10332	0.9	80	3239	3619	3775	1.2	2.75	2564	2830	1.1
70668	VINTON	019	6443	6584	6660	0.2	49	2356	2458	2504	0.5	2.64	1781	1826	0.3
70669	WESTLAKE	019	10309	10160	10152	-0.2	29	3846	3886	3912	0.1	2.61	2914	2897	-0.1
70706	DENHAM SPRINGS	063	13072	19932	23889	4.7	99	4394	6777	8167	4.8	2.94	3676	5598	4.7
70710	ADDIS	121	2757	3400	3679	2.3	94	982	1232	1344	2.5	2.76	739	916	2.3
70711	ALBANY	063	3491	4706	5317	3.3	98	1282	1737	1975	3.3	2.70	1003	1340	3.2
70712	ANGOLA	125	5496	5489	5475	0.0	38	169	171	168	0.1	2.85	136	136	0.0
70714	BAKER	033	20244	21162	21213	0.5	66	7004	7532	7594	0.8	2.74	5445	5761	0.6
70715	BATCHELOR	077	1683	1680	1678	0.0	38	614	628	632	0.2	2.68	458	462	0.1
70719	BRUSLY	121	3919	4240	4421	0.9	80	1395	1547	1627	1.1	2.74	1117	1222	1.0
70721	CARVILLE	047	508	476	460	-0.7	14	181	173	168	-0.5	2.67	126	117	-0.8
70722	CLINTON	037	6302	6401	6269	0.2	49	2162	2270	2247	0.5	2.68	1633	1691	0.4
70723	CONVENT	093	1999	2038	2012	0.2	49	613	616	611	0.1	3.10	467	465	0.0
70725	DARROW	005	1038	1694	2203	5.4	99	318	543	714	6.0	3.12	250	419	5.7
70726	DENHAM SPRINGS	063	36696	48748	55848	3.1	97	13136	17620	20286	3.2	2.75	10113	13427	3.1
70729	ERWINVILLE	121	572	590	606	0.3	53	211	223	230	0.6	2.65	163	169	0.4
70730	ETHEL	037	4193	4163	4060	-0.1	35	1394	1431	1410	0.3	2.74	1074	1089	0.2
70732	FORDOCHE	077	1450	1453	1443	0.0	38	533	547	549	0.3	2.65	423	429	0.2
70733	FRENCH SETTLEMENT	063	1368	1709	1902	2.4	95	508	640	716	2.5	2.67	397	491	2.3
70734	GEISMAR	005	3480	6882	8772	7.7	100	1193	2394	3068	7.8	2.87	910	1798	7.6
70736	GLYNN	077	512	541	554	0.6	71	179	194	200	0.9	2.79	134	143	0.7
70737	GONZALES	005	28391	36835	42346	2.9	97	10007	13266	15362	3.1	2.76	7646	10006	3.0
70739	GREENWELL SPRINGS	033	10237	10949	11204	0.7	74	3565	3914	4040	1.0	2.80	2954	3205	0.9
70740	GROSSE TETE	047	1301	1346	1341	0.4	61	488	518	519	0.6	2.60	369	386	0.5
70744	HOLDEN	063	4766	5896	6571	2.3	94	1654	2067	2317	2.4	2.84	1282	1576	2.3
70748	JACKSON	037	6707	6532	6405	-0.3	27	1638	1644	1611	0.0	2.64	1199	1188	-0.1
70749	JARREAU	077	1587	1703	1753	0.8	77	667	734	762	1.0	2.32	459	497	0.9
70750	KROTZ SPRINGS	097	1936	1951	1955	0.1	44	738	752	758	0.2	2.59	536	536	0.0
70752	LAKELAND	077	747	787	807	0.6	71	283	306	316	0.8	2.57	218	232	0.7
70753	LETTSWORTH	077	1316	1326	1320	0.1	44	451	464	466	0.3	2.86	342	348	0.2
70754	LIVINGSTON	063	7299	8824	9959	2.1	93	2597	3184	3611	2.2	2.74	2047	2474	2.1
70755	LIVONIA	077	2233	2271	2282	0.2	49	812	844	854	0.4	2.69	630	648	0.3
70756	LOTTIE	077	452	452	449	0.0	38	164	166	165	0.1	2.72	123	123	0.0
70757	MARINGOUIN	047	3325	3208	3137	-0.4	24	1107	1086	1069	-0.2	2.95	849	823	-0.3
70759	MORGANZA	077	1111	1079	1067	-0.3	27	423	421	420	-0.1	2.56	304	297	-0.3
70760	NEW ROADS	077	7031	6951	6901	-0.1	35	2521	2557	2560	0.2	2.62	1787	1786	0.0
70761	NORWOOD	037	929	880	859	-0.6	17	356	346	340	-0.3	2.54	249	237	-0.5
70762	OSCAR	077	783	846	873	0.8	77	306	338	352	1.1	2.50	238	259	0.9
70763	PAULINA	093	3270	3463	3527	0.6	71	1074	1164	1196	0.9	2.97	880	945	0.8
70764	PLAQUEMINE	047	17786	17467	17139	-0.2	29	6286	6295	6215	0.0	2.72	4694	4643	-0.1
70767	PORT ALLEN	121	14353	14877	15209	0.4	61	5075	5373	5535	0.6	2.66	3717	3880	0.5
70769	PRAIRIEVILLE	005	23596	35834	43063	4.6	99	8178	12680	15341	4.9	2.83	6628	10133	4.7
70770	PRIDE	033	3633	3787	3847	0.4	61	1254	1346	1379	0.8	2.81	1022	1083	0.6
70772	ROSEDALE	047	753	711	689	-0.6	17	264	254	248	-0.4	2.80	197	187	-0.6
70773	ROUGON	077	392	415	425	0.6	71	153	166	172	0.9	2.50	112	120	0.7
70774	SAINT AMANT	005	7576	9417	10720	2.4	95	2677	3406	3907	2.6	2.76	2121	2662	2.5
70775	SAINT FRANCISVILLE	125	9569	9963	9973	0.4	61	3460	3657	3680	0.6	2.68	2556	2665	0.5
70776	SAINT GABRIEL	047	5334	5515	5550	0.4	61	843	917	931	0.9	2.81	618	662	0.7
70777	SLAUGHTER	037	4014	4094	4036	0.2	49	1423	1498	1494	0.6	2.73	1144	1193	0.5
70778	SORRENTO	005	1616	2044	2370	2.6	96	585	757	885	2.8	2.70	448	572	2.7
70780	SUNSHINE	047	884	962	966	0.9	80	308	341	345	1.1	2.82	227	246	0.9
70783	VENTRESS	077	2441	2604	2676	0.7	74	938	1028	1066	1.0	2.45	676	730	0.8
70785	WALKER	063	15267	20511	23745	3.2	98	5302	7237	8432	3.4	2.83	4211	5656	3.2
70788	WHITE CASTLE	047	4454	4263	4148	-0.5	21	1550	1522	1495	-0.2	2.80	1201	1165	-0.3
70789	WILSON	037	772	723	692	-0.7	14	269	261	252	-0.3	2.75	184	174	-0.6
70791	ZACHARY	033	20133	22920	23969	1.4	87	6890	8060	8495	1.7	2.82	5447	6309	1.6
70792	UNCLE SAM	093	142	147	148	0.4	61	48	51	51	0.7	2.88	36	38	0.6
70801	BATON ROUGE	033	66	62	62	-0.7	14	53	51	51	-0.4	1.22	8	7	-1.4
70802	BATON ROUGE	033	30828	28655	27856	-0.8	12	11924	11404	11188	-0.5	2.36	6578	6093	-0.8
70803	BATON ROUGE	033	3876	3459	3509	-1.2	7	16	16	18	0.0	2.56	3	3	0.0
70805	BATON ROUGE	033	31143	31292	31117	0.1	44	10898	11003	10978	0.1	2.83	7475	7390	-0.1
70806	BATON ROUGE	033	27355	26451	26025	-0.4	24	12280	12099	11963	-0.2	2.10	6326	6042	-0.5
70807	BATON ROUGE	033	19087	18830	18922	-0.1	35	5875	6010	6099	0.2	2.77	4299	4313	0.0
70808	BATON ROUGE	033	30259	30094	29814	-0.1	35	13593	13904	13900	0.2	2.10	7355	7247	-0.2
70809	BATON ROUGE	033	19881	22860	23915	1.5	88	9090	10459	10919	1.5	2.14	4883	5634	1.6
70810	BATON ROUGE	033	30137	35528	37503	1.8	91	11242	13450	14269	2.0	2.64	8062	9410	1.7
70811	BATON ROUGE	033	13423	13067	12920	-0.3	27	4666	4671	4662	0.0	2.77	3570	3515	-0.2
70812	BATON ROUGE	033	12178	12017	11834	-0.1	35	3830	3866	3837	0.1	3.08	3112	3096	-0.1
70813	BATON ROUGE	033	2095	1904	1899	-1.0	9	63	64	63	0.2	4.89	55	55	0.0
70814	BATON ROUGE	033	13994	14066	13999	0.1	44	5047	5122	5122	0.2	2.73	3800	3798	0.0
70815	BATON ROUGE	033	28971	28924	28681	0.0	38	11294	11465	11438	0.2	2.49	7826	7780	-0.1
70816	BATON ROUGE	033	35357	37561	38234	0.7	74	15173	16369	16728	0.8	2.28	9202	9732	0.6
70817	BATON ROUGE	033	28644	32143	33432	1.3	85	10309	11909	12505	1.6	2.70	8222	9339	1.4
70818	BATON ROUGE	033	10092	10108	10041	0.0	38	3613	3722	3731	0.3	2.71	2986	3038	0.2
70819	BATON ROUGE	033	4879	4896	4862	0.0	38	1766	1836	1842	0.4	2.54	1276	1300	0.2
70820	BATON ROUGE	033	14829	16858	17524	1.4	87	6393	7215	7498	1.3	2.33	2237	2355	0.6
71001	ARCADIA	013	4814	4616	4506	-0.5	21	1763	1720	1689	-0.3	2.51	1233	1182	-0.5
71002	ASHLAND	069	225	214	211	-0.5	21	99	96	95	-0.3	2.23	71	68	-0.5
71003	ATHENS	027	1060	1052	1033	-0.1	35	423	426	421	0.1	2.47	298	295	-0.1
71004	BELCHER	017	625	638	638	0.2	49	226	231	232	0.2	2.74	160	161	0.1
71006	BENTON	015	9586	11854	13020	2.3	94	3507	4446	4926	2.6	2.64	2805	3498	2.4
71007	BETHANY	017	882	942	958	0.7	74	341	370	379	0.9	2.55	264	282	0.7
71008	BIENVILLE	013	790	785	773	-0.1	35	331	337	335	0.2	2.33	224	224	0.0
71016	CASTOR	013	2057	2149	2146	0.5	66	748	785	786	0.5	2.74	555	574	0.4
	LOUISIANA					0.0					0.1	2.60			0.1
	UNITED STATES					1.0					1.1	2.59			0.9

ZIP CODE #	POST OFFICE NAME	RACE (%) White 2000	White 2009	Black 2000	Black 2009	Asian/Pacific 2000	Asian/Pacific 2009	% Hispanic Origin 2000	% Hispanic Origin 2009	2009 AGE DISTRIBUTION (%) 0-4	5-9	10-14	15-19	20-24	25-44	45-64	65-84	85+	18+	MEDIAN AGE 2009	% 2009 Males	% 2009 Females
70652	LONGVILLE	95.9	94.5	2.5	3.2	0.3	0.4	0.7	1.0	8.2	7.9	7.7	7.2	6.7	27.0	24.4	10.0	1.0	71.8	34.0	50.9	49.1
70653	MERRYVILLE	90.3	87.7	7.5	9.3	0.0	0.1	1.8	2.2	6.7	6.6	6.8	6.3	5.3	24.9	28.3	13.4	1.7	76.0	40.0	49.1	50.9
70654	MITTIE	97.9	97.6	0.4	0.6	0.0	0.0	1.1	1.3	7.1	7.1	7.3	7.9	6.4	23.4	27.5	12.0	1.5	73.5	37.8	49.3	50.7
70655	OBERLIN	66.8	63.4	31.0	34.4	0.2	0.2	0.8	1.0	7.3	7.1	7.1	7.2	6.3	25.1	25.0	12.7	2.2	74.1	37.3	49.4	50.6
70656	PITKIN	94.5	92.8	1.0	1.3	0.1	0.2	1.0	1.5	7.5	7.5	7.5	7.2	5.5	25.6	26.1	11.9	1.1	73.0	36.7	49.2	50.8
70657	RAGLEY	97.2	96.3	1.4	1.9	0.2	0.3	0.4	0.6	8.0	7.9	7.8	7.2	5.6	27.7	25.5	9.6	0.8	71.8	35.2	50.9	49.1
70658	REEVES	95.7	94.9	2.4	2.9	0.2	0.4	0.3	0.4	7.4	7.5	7.5	7.0	5.1	26.2	26.2	12.2	1.0	73.4	37.3	50.6	49.4
70660	SINGER	84.5	79.4	12.4	16.2	1.5	2.3	1.1	1.4	5.3	5.2	5.6	7.2	9.1	34.8	23.8	8.2	0.7	79.9	35.5	60.5	39.5
70661	STARKS	95.7	93.2	2.9	5.1	0.0	0.1	0.3	0.4	6.9	7.2	7.3	5.7	4.7	24.5	29.5	12.9	1.2	75.0	39.6	50.1	49.9
70662	SUGARTOWN	95.0	93.1	2.6	3.5	0.2	0.4	0.7	0.9	8.0	7.3	7.6	7.8	6.9	27.2	24.2	10.2	0.9	71.9	34.9	50.5	49.5
70663	SULPHUR	92.5	89.0	5.5	8.3	0.4	0.5	1.4	1.8	7.4	7.1	6.8	6.4	6.1	27.1	26.3	11.1	1.7	74.7	36.6	49.1	50.9
70665	SULPHUR	97.6	96.2	0.8	1.5	0.3	0.4	1.2	1.6	7.8	7.7	7.4	6.9	6.4	27.8	26.3	8.9	0.8	72.7	34.8	49.8	50.2
70668	VINTON	83.9	77.8	14.2	20.0	0.2	0.3	1.0	1.1	7.1	7.0	7.2	6.9	6.5	25.3	26.6	12.2	1.2	74.4	37.5	49.2	50.8
70669	WESTLAKE	84.0	78.1	14.2	19.6	0.2	0.3	1.5	1.9	7.0	6.9	6.7	7.1	6.1	26.3	27.6	11.2	1.2	75.0	37.0	49.4	50.6
70706	DENHAM SPRINGS	95.4	95.2	3.5	3.4	0.1	0.2	1.1	1.4	8.4	8.1	7.8	7.5	5.8	30.6	24.5	6.8	0.6	71.0	33.4	49.9	50.1
70710	ADDIS	70.9	65.9	27.6	32.2	0.1	0.1	1.7	2.1	7.5	7.1	6.8	7.6	7.9	30.2	25.2	6.9	0.7	74.0	32.8	49.3	50.7
70711	ALBANY	91.1	87.3	7.1	10.6	0.1	0.1	1.2	1.5	7.9	7.4	7.1	7.2	6.9	29.1	24.8	8.7	0.9	73.0	33.9	49.1	50.9
70712	ANGOLA	29.6	26.1	70.2	73.6	0.1	0.1	1.8	2.0	0.7	0.6	0.5	1.4	9.9	61.7	24.0	1.2	0.0	97.5	37.3	95.8	4.2
70714	BAKER	53.4	44.1	44.9	54.0	0.3	0.4	0.8	0.9	7.2	7.4	7.5	8.8	5.9	26.7	25.0	10.4	1.1	72.2	34.4	47.7	52.3
70715	BATCHELOR	52.1	45.8	46.5	52.4	0.1	0.2	1.9	2.1	8.5	8.0	7.5	6.9	5.8	22.6	25.4	13.3	2.1	71.8	36.4	47.1	52.9
70719	BRUSLY	71.2	66.7	27.1	31.1	0.2	0.2	1.6	2.1	7.2	7.3	7.2	7.2	6.3	28.4	27.5	8.1	0.8	73.8	35.5	49.2	50.8
70721	CARVILLE	16.5	14.1	81.5	83.6	0.8	1.1	3.1	3.2	8.2	8.4	8.0	8.2	6.9	26.7	22.3	9.9	1.5	70.8	31.8	46.2	53.8
70722	CLINTON	51.9	47.8	47.1	51.0	0.1	0.2	1.1	1.3	6.8	7.4	7.7	7.3	5.9	24.1	27.4	11.4	1.9	73.3	37.8	49.1	50.9
70723	CONVENT	23.2	18.5	76.2	80.7	0.0	0.0	0.2	0.2	6.6	7.8	8.9	7.3	7.4	25.2	26.3	9.2	1.3	72.1	34.2	49.5	50.5
70725	DARROW	35.0	28.0	63.2	70.0	0.4	0.4	1.0	1.1	7.5	7.4	7.4	7.5	5.9	27.9	26.7	8.7	0.9	73.0	35.8	50.0	50.0
70726	DENHAM SPRINGS	94.6	94.2	3.8	3.8	0.3	0.4	1.3	1.6	7.6	7.4	7.2	6.9	6.2	29.0	26.1	8.6	1.1	73.6	35.3	49.3	50.7
70729	ERWINVILLE	68.3	63.7	30.6	34.9	0.0	0.0	0.7	0.7	7.1	6.8	6.3	6.1	8.6	26.8	28.0	9.7	0.7	76.1	35.2	49.7	50.3
70730	ETHEL	55.2	51.5	43.5	46.7	0.3	0.4	0.8	0.9	6.6	6.7	6.8	6.7	5.3	26.5	27.7	12.2	1.5	75.7	38.9	50.8	49.2
70732	FORDOCHE	85.4	81.8	13.7	16.9	0.2	0.3	0.7	0.8	6.8	6.9	7.1	6.6	5.4	28.0	26.9	11.1	1.2	74.7	38.2	48.9	51.1
70733	FRENCH SETTLEMENT	99.3	99.1	0.2	0.4	0.0	0.0	1.3	1.6	6.9	6.9	6.9	6.4	6.1	26.2	28.9	10.5	1.1	75.3	37.8	49.7	50.3
70734	GEISMAR	63.9	61.9	34.3	35.9	0.2	0.2	1.8	2.2	8.8	8.3	7.7	7.3	7.2	28.2	24.4	7.3	0.8	70.8	32.1	49.0	51.0
70736	GLYNN	72.1	67.3	25.0	29.2	0.4	0.4	1.8	2.0	6.1	6.5	6.5	5.9	5.0	25.3	30.9	12.2	1.7	77.3	41.7	49.9	50.1
70737	GONZALES	79.6	73.5	17.1	22.2	0.4	0.5	4.0	5.1	7.9	7.8	7.7	7.2	6.0	29.4	25.1	8.0	1.0	72.1	34.4	49.3	50.7
70739	GREENWELL SPRINGS	94.0	91.7	4.5	6.2	0.3	0.4	0.9	1.2	6.6	7.0	7.4	7.4	5.1	28.2	28.6	8.8	0.8	74.3	37.3	48.8	51.2
70740	GROSSE TETE	73.8	69.6	25.3	29.2	0.3	0.5	0.6	0.8	6.8	7.2	7.3	6.7	4.9	24.4	30.8	10.7	1.1	74.9	39.3	48.1	51.9
70744	HOLDEN	93.4	89.9	5.1	8.2	0.1	0.1	1.2	1.5	7.3	6.9	7.0	7.5	6.9	27.7	26.5	9.3	0.9	73.9	35.4	49.3	50.7
70748	JACKSON	46.8	42.4	52.0	56.0	0.4	0.5	0.5	0.6	5.1	5.2	5.3	5.3	7.4	36.1	25.5	9.0	1.1	81.4	37.3	63.2	36.8
70749	JARREAU	89.5	86.8	9.0	11.3	0.3	0.4	0.9	1.2	5.7	5.8	5.5	5.5	4.9	24.1	33.1	13.6	1.9	79.7	44.0	50.6	49.4
70750	KROTZ SPRINGS	99.2	99.0	0.2	0.2	0.1	0.1	0.7	0.8	7.3	7.5	7.2	6.6	5.1	27.4	26.7	10.8	1.4	73.8	37.0	50.8	49.2
70752	LAKELAND	66.1	60.4	30.7	35.8	0.3	0.3	2.1	2.5	6.2	6.4	6.4	6.6	5.5	25.5	30.7	11.3	1.4	77.0	41.1	49.2	50.8
70753	LETTSWORTH	39.6	34.1	58.8	64.0	0.0	0.0	0.6	0.7	7.8	8.0	8.1	7.4	6.0	22.2	28.1	10.9	1.4	71.7	36.4	48.3	51.7
70754	LIVINGSTON	96.7	95.4	2.1	3.0	0.1	0.2	0.7	0.9	7.5	7.3	7.2	7.0	6.4	29.0	25.9	9.0	0.8	73.8	35.0	50.7	49.3
70755	LIVONIA	85.3	82.3	14.1	16.9	0.0	0.0	0.5	0.7	7.2	7.2	7.2	6.7	5.7	26.9	27.4	10.5	1.2	74.3	37.5	50.4	49.6
70756	LOTTIE	60.8	54.9	38.6	44.2	0.0	0.0	0.7	0.7	7.5	7.5	7.3	7.7	6.2	26.1	26.8	9.7	1.1	73.0	35.4	48.0	52.0
70757	MARINGOUIN	38.9	35.2	60.2	63.7	0.4	0.6	0.2	0.3	7.8	7.9	7.9	7.8	6.1	24.7	26.5	10.0	1.4	71.7	34.8	47.3	52.7
70759	MORGANZA	61.4	55.8	38.0	43.4	0.1	0.1	0.5	0.6	6.3	6.2	6.5	6.9	5.7	24.5	27.8	14.1	2.0	76.9	40.1	49.4	50.6
70760	NEW ROADS	36.1	32.4	62.6	65.9	0.5	0.7	0.9	0.9	6.9	7.2	7.2	7.5	5.9	22.3	26.2	13.4	3.4	74.1	38.9	46.7	53.3
70761	NORWOOD	41.6	37.2	57.7	61.8	0.1	0.1	0.5	0.5	7.4	7.6	7.4	6.9	6.1	24.2	28.3	10.8	1.3	73.4	36.9	48.5	51.5
70762	OSCAR	90.8	88.8	8.5	10.6	0.0	0.0	1.1	1.3	6.4	6.5	6.5	7.2	6.3	25.5	31.1	9.5	1.1	76.5	39.9	49.4	50.6
70763	PAULINA	83.5	79.7	15.9	19.4	0.2	0.2	0.8	1.0	7.0	7.9	7.9	8.0	6.0	26.6	27.9	7.8	0.9	72.3	34.7	48.7	51.3
70764	PLAQUEMINE	56.3	52.1	42.6	46.5	0.2	0.3	1.1	1.2	6.8	7.1	7.0	7.4	6.3	25.9	26.7	11.1	1.6	74.5	36.8	48.5	51.5
70767	PORT ALLEN	58.7	55.2	39.5	42.5	0.3	0.3	1.4	1.7	7.0	7.2	7.0	6.7	6.2	27.7	26.7	10.1	1.3	74.7	36.3	49.4	50.6
70769	PRAIRIEVILLE	91.0	88.5	6.8	8.6	0.5	0.7	1.8	2.5	8.7	8.2	7.7	6.8	5.7	32.1	24.6	5.7	0.5	71.1	33.2	49.8	50.2
70770	PRIDE	92.9	90.7	5.9	7.7	0.2	0.3	0.8	1.1	6.4	6.6	6.9	6.6	5.2	26.9	30.7	9.9	0.8	76.0	39.1	49.7	50.3
70772	ROSEDALE	55.2	49.6	43.7	48.8	0.7	1.0	0.1	0.1	7.6	7.7	7.7	7.6	5.9	24.6	27.8	9.6	1.4	72.2	36.6	48.7	51.3
70773	ROUGON	77.6	73.0	19.9	23.6	0.3	0.5	1.5	1.9	6.0	6.5	6.5	5.5	5.1	25.5	30.6	12.5	1.7	77.6	41.5	50.6	49.4
70774	SAINT AMANT	98.3	97.6	0.5	0.7	0.3	0.4	0.8	1.1	7.8	7.8	7.7	7.0	5.6	28.8	26.5	8.0	0.6	72.2	35.5	50.0	50.0
70775	SAINT FRANCISVILLE	59.4	55.1	39.4	43.5	0.3	0.3	0.6	0.7	6.7	6.8	7.3	7.7	6.2	24.5	29.0	10.2	1.5	73.9	37.4	48.8	51.2
70776	SAINT GABRIEL	37.3	35.0	61.8	63.8	0.2	0.3	1.0	1.2	3.4	3.5	3.5	5.2	11.8	46.3	21.1	4.8	0.5	87.3	34.5	59.9	40.1
70777	SLAUGHTER	68.4	64.3	30.5	34.2	0.2	0.3	0.6	0.7	7.0	7.2	7.2	7.3	5.9	26.7	28.2	9.6	0.9	74.1	36.5	50.2	49.8
70778	SORRENTO	80.4	74.8	18.1	23.1	0.2	0.3	2.0	2.6	8.7	8.3	8.0	6.8	6.0	27.9	25.2	8.3	0.7	71.1	33.5	52.9	47.1
70780	SUNSHINE	52.2	46.6	46.9	52.4	0.3	0.4	0.9	1.0	7.9	8.3	8.0	7.9	5.0	26.4	25.1	10.5	0.9	70.7	35.5	48.5	51.5
70783	VENTRESS	75.8	71.5	22.9	26.8	0.1	0.2	2.2	2.6	5.9	5.8	5.7	6.6	6.0	26.0	31.3	11.4	1.4	78.5	41.1	51.0	49.0
70785	WALKER	94.7	92.9	3.8	5.3	0.2	0.2	0.9	1.2	8.4	8.0	7.6	7.1	6.1	30.5	24.2	7.3	0.7	71.4	33.3	50.2	49.8
70788	WHITE CASTLE	42.2	38.2	56.8	60.6	0.2	0.2	1.5	1.6	7.3	7.5	7.5	7.8	6.1	24.1	27.1	10.9	1.8	72.9	36.6	47.0	53.0
70789	WILSON	40.5	36.2	58.7	62.9	0.0	0.0	0.4	0.4	7.1	7.3	7.6	7.5	5.9	25.2	27.2	10.9	1.2	73.4	36.4	48.0	52.0
70791	ZACHARY	66.6	58.4	32.0	39.8	0.4	0.5	0.8	1.0	6.8	7.1	7.3	7.4	6.0	26.3	28.2	9.5	1.4	74.2	36.5	48.4	51.6
70792	UNCLE SAM	62.0	55.1	38.0	44.9	0.0	0.0	0.7	0.0	6.8	6.8	6.8	8.8	5.4	24.5	30.6	8.8	1.4	73.5	38.4	51.7	48.3
70801	BATON ROUGE	49.3	40.3	44.8	53.2	1.5	1.6	1.5	1.6	3.2	0.0	0.0	3.2	8.1	46.8	30.6	6.5	1.6	96.8	37.0	67.7	32.3
70802	BATON ROUGE	17.0	14.3	78.4	80.1	3.0	3.8	1.3	1.4	7.0	7.1	6.5	10.7	11.0	25.5	21.0	9.5	1.7	75.4	29.7	47.9	52.1
70803	BATON ROUGE	81.2	74.2	14.6	19.8	1.7	2.6	3.1	4.0	0.2	0.3	0.1	53.0	38.3	5.5	1.9	0.5	0.1	98.9	19.7	35.0	65.0
70805	BATON ROUGE	10.4	7.5	87.5	90.3	0.9	1.0	1.0	0.9	9.1	9.2	8.5	9.0	7.8	25.7	22.9	6.9	0.8	67.8	29.2	46.0	54.0
70806	BATON ROUGE	51.9	47.8	45.9	49.4	0.9	1.2	1.4	1.5	7.3	6.6	5.8	6.0	8.2	28.5	22.9	11.4	3.4	77.1	35.4	46.2	53.8
70807	BATON ROUGE	3.8	2.6	95.4	96.6	0.1	0.1	0.7	0.7	8.0	8.1	8.0	11.7	8.7	23.6	21.3	9.4	1.3	70.2	29.4	49.1	50.9
70808	BATON ROUGE	80.9	76.1	13.6	16.1	3.7	5.4	2.0	2.5	4.8	4.7	5.0	7.5	12.2	26.1	25.2	11.6	2.9	82.5	36.0	48.8	51.2
70809	BATON ROUGE	85.5	78.4	11.0	16.6	1.9	2.9	2.1	2.7	5.8	5.0	5.0	5.6	9.7	28.6	25.8	11.9	2.7	81.2	36.9	47.2	52.8
70810	BATON ROUGE	63.9	55.4	30.9	37.9	2.8	3.8	3.4	3.8	7.5	7.3	7.5	7.0	7.4	29.0	26.4	7.3	0.6	73.7	34.1	48.4	51.6
70811	BATON ROUGE	29.6	23.8	68.6	74.2	0.8	1.0	0.7	0.7	7.1	7.2	7.4	8.0	6.9	24.8	26.9	10.5	1.3	73.3	35.1	46.8	53.2
70812	BATON ROUGE	8.3	6.2	90.6	92.6	0.2	0.2	0.9	0.9	8.6	9.2	8.9	9.1	8.0	24.2	25.0	6.2	0.7	67.6	29.2	46.0	54.0
70813	BATON ROUGE	0.4	0.4	98.5	98.5	0.1	0.1	0.6	0.6	1.9	2.2	1.3	38.6	45.9	5.5	3.6	1.0	0.1	93.5	20.7	53.9	46.1
70814	BATON ROUGE	34.6	26.9	61.0	68.0	3.0	3.6	1.6	1.6	8.2	7.9	7.6	7.5	6.8	28.3	24.1	8.5	1.2	71.8	33.6	47.6	52.4
70815	BATON ROUGE	67.2	60.9	24.9	29.1	6.1	7.7	1.9	2.2	6.9	6.2	6.1	6.7	7.2	24.7	24.8	14.9	2.6	76.9	38.3	47.4	52.6
70816	BATON ROUGE	77.8	72.1	17.4	21.3	2.7	3.8	3.0	3.6	7.2	6.3	5.9	6.3	8.7	32.5	23.8	8.3	1.1	77.0	33.4	48.6	51.4
70817	BATON ROUGE	90.7	86.6	5.9	8.3	1.9	3.0	1.7	2.2	7.3	7.9	8.0	7.2	4.9	29.1	28.9	6.1	0.5	72.1	36.5	49.3	50.7
70818	BATON ROUGE	94.6	92.5	3.9	5.4	0.3	0.5	0.8	1.1	6.6	6.9	6.9	6.6	5.0	27.1	29.1	10.9	0.9	75.3	38.3	48.2	51.8
70819	BATON ROUGE	81.2	74.9	13.5	17.9	2.1	3.0	3.7	4.6	7.2	7.0	6.7	5.9	5.0	29.2	24.1	12.0	2.8	75.5	37.5	46.0	54.0
70820	BATON ROUGE	67.2	62.7	24.0	25.3	4.9	7.1	4.9	5.8	5.6	3.9	3.6	14.1	37.4	21.9	11.4	1.9	0.2	84.3	23.0	52.0	48.0
71001	ARCADIA	43.8	39.6	54.7	58.6	0.2	0.3	1.3	1.5	7.0	7.1	6.5	7.1	6.3	22.6	24.7	14.0	4.8	75.1	39.7	46.2	53.8
71002	ASHLAND	82.2	78.0	16.0	19.6	0.4	0.5	0.4	0.5	5.6	5.6	6.1	5.6	5.1	23.4	29.4	16.4	2.8	79.0	43.9	50.5	49.5
71003	ATHENS	59.4	55.2	39.2	43.2	0.2	0.2	0.8	0.8	5.8	5.8	6.2	7.3	5.9	24.1	28.8	14.1	2.0	77.7	41.4	46.6	53.4
71004	BELCHER	53.1	43.9	42.7	50.6	0.0	0.0	3.7	4.9	6.3	6.3	6.4	7.1	5.8	23.7	29.9	12.7	1.9	76.5	41.0	52.0	48.0
71006	BENTON	80.1	77.2	17.7	19.9	0.4	0.5	1.9	2.5	5.9	6.8	7.2	6.6	4.9	23.6	32.1	12.0	1.0	76.1	41.6	48.9	51.1
71007	BETHANY	73.6	64.8	23.5	31.2	0.3	0.5	1.2	1.7	5.2	5.3	5.8	6.5	6.1	25.3	32.4	12.4	1.1	79.8	41.9	49.3	50.7
71008	BIENVILLE	56.7	51.2	42.8	47.9	0.0	0.1	0.3	0.3	5.6	5.7	5.7	6.4	5.9	21.4	31.5	15.5	2.3	79.1	44.3	49.4	50.6
71016	CASTOR	82.5	79.6	16.1	18.4	0.2	0.3	1.0	1.3	7.6	7.5	7.3	7.2	6.7	24.8	25.6	11.6	1.6	73.2	36.7	50.1	49.9
	LOUISIANA	63.9	61.9	32.5	33.7	1.3	1.6	2.4	2.8	7.2	7.0	6.9	7.3	7.1	26.8	25.7	10.4	1.6	74.6	35.6	48.6	51.4
	UNITED STATES	75.1	72.0	12.3	12.7	3.8	4.6	12.5	15.7	6.8	6.7	6.6	7.1	6.9	27.0	26.0	10.9	1.9	75.7	36.9	49.2	50.8

70652-71016

#	POST OFFICE NAME	2009 Per Capita Income	2009 HH Income Base	2009 Household Income Distribution (%) Less than $25,000	$25,000 to $49,999	$50,000 to $99,999	$100,000 to $149,999	$150,000 or More	Median Household Income 2009	2014	2009 National Centile	2009 State Centile	2009 Home Value Base	2009 Home Value Distribution (%) Less than $50,000	$50,000 to $89,999	$90,000 to $174,999	$175,000 to $399,999	$400,000 or More	2009 Median Home Value
70652	LONGVILLE	16974	929	31.5	31.6	31.1	4.7	1.0	36685	37265	23	63	810	35.8	24.4	25.9	10.5	3.3	70244
70653	MERRYVILLE	16580	1391	41.8	29.2	23.3	4.9	0.9	31082	31085	10	39	1141	31.9	26.3	30.2	11.3	0.3	76186
70654	MITTIE	15032	206	49.5	20.9	25.7	2.9	1.0	25397	26332	3	12	184	40.8	23.9	23.9	10.3	1.1	63000
70655	OBERLIN	15566	1283	41.0	31.2	23.6	3.6	0.6	30737	30221	9	38	999	34.2	24.3	29.6	9.9	1.9	74926
70656	PITKIN	15118	1569	40.9	28.9	24.2	4.5	1.6	31585	31657	11	44	1347	35.6	22.7	31.8	8.8	1.0	74275
70657	RAGLEY	18869	1542	25.7	31.1	34.0	5.9	3.2	43052	41863	43	79	1356	29.5	23.0	30.3	14.5	2.7	85000
70658	REEVES	15721	412	40.3	32.8	22.8	1.7	2.4	33565	35690	14	52	350	28.0	34.3	28.9	8.9	0.0	73824
70660	SINGER	17915	625	33.3	38.1	25.1	3.0	0.5	34573	35093	17	56	539	47.1	14.5	22.1	13.9	2.4	54189
70661	STARKS	17379	1064	36.6	32.1	25.8	4.5	1.0	34741	34791	17	57	911	33.2	26.9	30.4	8.3	1.2	77549
70662	SUGARTOWN	16820	175	26.9	37.1	29.1	6.9	0.0	36805	35682	23	64	156	35.9	22.4	30.1	11.5	0.0	70000
70663	SULPHUR	19920	10479	27.7	28.2	34.9	7.1	2.2	44335	45918	46	83	7953	17.4	22.0	44.8	14.8	1.0	108426
70665	SULPHUR	22717	3619	19.4	28.6	37.0	11.1	3.9	51470	49866	65	94	3074	20.5	19.3	36.1	21.0	3.1	111914
70668	VINTON	15981	2458	34.7	31.9	29.0	3.5	0.8	35425	35745	19	59	1918	30.7	26.1	32.3	8.7	2.3	78333
70669	WESTLAKE	19857	3886	28.6	28.7	34.5	6.1	2.2	43897	45451	45	82	2967	14.5	23.9	45.9	14.5	1.2	107643
70706	DENHAM SPRINGS	20227	6777	20.4	27.2	39.8	10.4	2.2	52210	53986	66	94	6003	10.2	14.0	33.2	40.1	2.5	156282
70710	ADDIS	18094	1232	24.6	32.9	34.5	7.0	1.1	44136	45832	46	82	1015	33.3	12.1	34.1	20.1	0.4	103590
70711	ALBANY	17610	1737	33.3	28.6	29.7	6.3	2.1	38359	38083	28	69	1372	21.9	18.2	37.7	19.4	2.8	112338
70712	ANGOLA	13811	171	0.6	40.9	58.5	0.0	0.0	53843	54427	69	96	70	37.1	28.6	15.7	18.6	0.0	60000
70714	BAKER	18203	7532	26.6	30.8	34.3	7.0	1.3	44474	45777	47	83	5772	8.9	26.2	48.0	14.4	2.5	107926
70715	BATCHELOR	13355	628	44.9	35.4	15.4	3.3	1.0	28301	28144	6	24	469	27.3	30.3	16.0	22.0	4.5	79306
70719	BRUSLY	21223	1547	24.6	24.9	35.9	12.3	2.3	50447	49542	62	92	1294	17.8	9.4	36.5	33.2	3.2	141588
70721	CARVILLE	14577	173	43.4	29.5	22.0	2.9	2.3	28977	30000	7	28	117	38.5	17.9	35.9	7.7	0.0	77000
70722	CLINTON	17318	2270	37.4	27.3	26.7	6.4	2.2	33715	36720	15	53	1874	24.8	15.1	30.4	25.1	4.6	116327
70723	CONVENT	12391	616	41.1	27.8	28.6	1.5	1.1	29894	29167	8	33	495	45.5	28.7	16.0	9.9	0.0	54592
70725	DARROW	16547	543	32.4	30.4	25.2	8.5	3.5	41624	40667	38	76	504	4.0	10.5	34.7	30.4	20.4	178448
70726	DENHAM SPRINGS	19381	17620	23.5	30.0	37.0	7.8	1.6	46886	49746	54	87	14246	13.8	12.1	40.3	31.2	2.5	139732
70729	ERWINVILLE	18690	223	26.9	30.9	34.1	6.7	1.3	44749	46071	47	84	179	30.7	14.0	28.5	23.5	3.4	126875
70730	ETHEL	17865	1431	35.6	25.9	29.4	7.4	1.7	38658	40410	29	70	1250	23.3	19.8	31.9	20.0	5.0	107847
70732	FORDOCHE	19373	547	26.7	31.8	33.1	6.9	1.5	43190	42428	43	80	466	22.7	18.9	42.7	14.8	0.9	106908
70733	FRENCH SETTLEMENT	18347	640	23.6	35.5	35.3	5.2	0.5	45465	46908	50	85	554	11.6	17.0	36.8	30.0	4.7	132456
70734	GEISMAR	19430	2394	22.3	32.0	34.4	9.0	2.4	47010	46088	54	88	2092	18.9	19.2	28.9	25.6	7.4	123571
70736	GLYNN	17906	194	35.1	27.8	27.3	6.7	3.1	38524	38525	28	70	155	22.6	18.7	31.0	25.2	2.6	111719
70737	GONZALES	19678	13266	24.1	25.7	41.1	7.6	1.5	50154	50620	62	91	10338	10.9	13.4	37.9	33.8	4.0	150059
70739	GREENWELL SPRINGS	23234	3914	15.0	24.9	44.7	12.7	2.6	58261	57955	75	98	3267	4.1	5.5	48.9	39.4	2.1	157437
70740	GROSSE TETE	16174	518	31.1	37.8	26.6	4.4	0.0	35000	36165	18	58	440	32.0	24.8	29.8	12.3	1.1	81667
70744	HOLDEN	16566	2067	34.6	27.9	30.1	5.0	2.4	38123	38001	27	68	1665	21.9	17.1	33.3	23.6	4.1	119177
70748	JACKSON	16361	1644	39.1	26.6	25.7	6.0	2.6	33969	36701	15	54	1242	30.6	22.4	26.5	15.5	5.0	85595
70749	JARREAU	22791	734	27.0	30.7	32.2	7.6	2.6	43502	42390	44	80	587	17.9	16.9	26.1	30.5	8.7	135577
70750	KROTZ SPRINGS	15427	752	39.5	30.3	26.7	3.2	0.3	32122	32149	12	47	608	34.4	27.5	28.8	9.4	0.0	69750
70752	LAKELAND	19359	306	37.9	25.2	27.5	6.2	3.3	35467	35886	19	60	249	23.7	17.7	32.9	24.1	1.6	114904
70753	LETTSWORTH	10143	464	58.8	27.6	11.0	2.6	0.0	19820	22809	1	4	357	40.6	31.4	19.9	8.1	0.0	59571
70754	LIVINGSTON	17778	3184	28.3	28.9	36.5	4.9	1.4	43693	45743	44	81	2727	16.1	20.4	38.3	23.6	1.5	119483
70755	LIVONIA	18025	844	31.5	28.8	32.3	6.0	1.3	40738	40767	35	75	685	21.0	20.3	40.1	18.0	0.6	105062
70756	LOTTIE	17819	166	39.2	25.3	27.7	6.0	1.8	35000	38088	18	58	134	33.6	14.2	28.4	23.9	0.0	97500
70757	MARINGOUIN	13619	1086	43.6	28.0	22.3	5.0	1.1	29683	31257	8	31	818	29.8	23.6	31.7	13.1	1.8	85333
70759	MORGANZA	17571	421	39.7	25.9	27.1	5.5	1.9	35764	37492	20	60	301	17.6	20.3	36.2	24.3	1.7	114236
70760	NEW ROADS	15071	2557	47.1	25.8	21.0	4.2	1.9	27348	28116	5	19	1789	18.8	25.2	34.3	17.9	3.7	98333
70761	NORWOOD	15048	346	44.5	29.5	20.5	4.0	1.4	27395	28354	5	20	273	30.0	15.8	27.5	23.8	2.9	102717
70762	OSCAR	22319	338	23.7	26.0	40.8	7.7	1.8	50312	46903	62	92	277	14.8	12.6	31.8	37.5	3.2	150481
70763	PAULINA	20030	1164	19.6	24.9	39.3	15.5	0.7	54154	53306	70	96	1014	17.8	19.8	30.6	30.7	1.2	121698
70764	PLAQUEMINE	16978	6295	38.0	27.6	25.4	6.5	2.6	33697	35708	15	53	4797	24.6	21.4	33.6	18.6	1.8	99159
70767	PORT ALLEN	18108	5373	31.5	30.1	29.2	7.2	2.0	40768	42596	35	75	4053	17.2	19.4	42.4	19.2	1.8	111273
70769	PRAIRIEVILLE	25588	12680	15.2	17.5	46.9	16.6	3.9	66755	68596	85	99	11164	9.3	9.2	28.7	45.1	7.8	183665
70770	PRIDE	21185	1346	16.3	30.0	42.6	9.7	1.5	53697	51509	69	96	1184	11.3	13.5	41.6	28.9	4.6	141346
70772	ROSEDALE	16152	254	35.4	28.0	28.0	8.7	0.0	35000	37190	18	58	206	26.7	18.4	30.1	22.3	2.4	102679
70773	ROUGON	20220	166	33.1	29.5	27.7	7.2	2.4	40000	40476	33	73	132	22.7	19.7	28.8	25.8	3.0	108333
70774	SAINT AMANT	18275	3406	25.0	32.5	34.4	7.3	0.9	43180	42270	43	80	2889	14.6	17.4	34.2	29.0	4.9	138610
70775	SAINT FRANCISVILLE	20791	3657	31.5	25.0	30.5	9.2	3.8	43981	46422	45	82	2773	19.3	12.8	29.6	26.9	11.5	134138
70776	SAINT GABRIEL	15893	917	31.7	26.7	32.3	5.5	3.8	38556	38392	28	70	746	18.2	16.0	34.0	22.7	9.1	117672
70777	SLAUGHTER	19920	1498	28.0	26.8	35.2	7.7	2.1	45120	44089	49	84	1269	19.3	21.1	33.6	23.1	2.8	111683
70778	SORRENTO	17672	757	33.4	25.1	34.9	5.4	1.2	43243	41518	43	80	621	18.7	23.3	42.2	14.7	1.1	107885
70780	SUNSHINE	15233	341	41.6	20.5	30.5	4.7	2.6	32104	32965	12	46	293	24.6	23.5	30.4	11.6	9.9	93235
70783	VENTRESS	20953	1028	28.0	26.6	36.5	6.4	2.5	42957	41860	42	79	846	15.1	15.7	30.6	31.2	7.3	139607
70785	WALKER	18229	7237	22.6	33.6	35.7	6.6	1.5	45438	47946	50	85	5911	13.1	16.1	38.8	28.5	3.5	139799
70788	WHITE CASTLE	14130	1522	47.4	24.9	21.7	4.5	1.5	26621	28044	4	16	1077	25.6	26.0	31.4	16.4	0.6	87697
70789	WILSON	14787	261	44.8	27.6	21.8	3.8	1.9	27716	28457	5	21	196	31.6	16.3	32.7	18.9	0.5	94444
70791	ZACHARY	20980	8060	24.1	24.6	36.7	11.9	2.6	51250	50106	64	93	6453	13.6	15.3	37.4	29.9	3.8	132997
70792	UNCLE SAM	19108	51	33.3	13.7	33.3	17.6	2.0	54626	54626	71	97	46	30.4	21.7	37.0	6.5	4.3	85000
70801	BATON ROUGE	11898	51	100.0	0.0	0.0	0.0	0.0	15490	15490	1	2	2	0.0	0.0	0.0	100.0	0.0	350000
70802	BATON ROUGE	11460	11404	61.7	25.2	10.9	1.5	0.6	18153	19451	1	3	4549	33.3	41.0	21.1	3.2	1.5	64269
70803	BATON ROUGE	11384	16	75.0	12.5	6.3	6.3	0.0	12093	12110	1	1	3	0.0	0.0	66.7	0.0	33.3	118750
70805	BATON ROUGE	11291	11003	51.8	29.0	16.3	2.1	0.8	23681	25129	3	8	5518	22.4	51.5	24.8	0.9	0.3	71098
70806	BATON ROUGE	22615	12099	40.4	28.1	22.3	5.7	3.5	31788	31640	11	46	5446	4.3	12.9	41.0	35.7	6.1	153930
70807	BATON ROUGE	12396	6010	54.6	23.6	17.9	3.0	0.9	21635	23290	2	6	3460	25.2	32.9	34.9	6.4	0.7	80939
70808	BATON ROUGE	34116	13904	27.3	23.0	28.6	11.4	9.6	49589	48862	60	91	8125	1.5	4.0	26.2	52.0	16.3	221964
70809	BATON ROUGE	32510	10459	21.7	29.0	31.4	10.3	7.6	49224	48486	59	90	5613	4.4	5.1	41.8	33.5	15.2	171247
70810	BATON ROUGE	31746	13450	17.5	24.0	33.5	13.6	11.4	60734	60926	78	98	9238	0.8	6.7	40.0	33.2	19.3	185156
70811	BATON ROUGE	16295	4671	34.4	29.7	29.3	5.5	1.1	36807	37669	23	64	3631	10.3	26.8	54.5	7.7	0.7	104134
70812	BATON ROUGE	12428	3866	40.4	31.8	23.2	4.2	0.4	31221	30158	10	41	2778	8.2	38.9	49.0	3.5	0.4	92277
70813	BATON ROUGE	12427	64	62.5	10.9	21.9	0.0	4.7	17425	18847	1	3	33	27.3	48.5	24.2	0.0	0.0	80556
70814	BATON ROUGE	19586	5122	22.1	33.8	36.1	6.1	1.9	45987	46603	51	86	3851	1.4	7.1	83.7	7.8	0.1	129543
70815	BATON ROUGE	23037	11465	23.9	31.2	33.0	8.7	3.2	45512	46326	50	86	7582	2.0	8.2	49.7	39.5	0.6	157675
70816	BATON ROUGE	26533	16369	18.8	32.9	34.5	9.9	4.0	48531	48274	58	89	8374	3.2	3.7	50.6	39.3	3.3	164325
70817	BATON ROUGE	31016	11909	10.0	19.7	41.9	20.4	8.0	71238	71833	87	100	9697	0.6	1.9	37.3	54.7	5.5	193956
70818	BATON ROUGE	23844	3722	17.1	27.1	41.0	11.3	3.4	55261	53908	72	97	3165	7.3	6.7	48.2	36.2	1.6	145833
70819	BATON ROUGE	21952	1836	15.8	33.1	40.8	9.0	1.2	50595	48965	63	93	1385	2.6	20.5	74.0	2.9	0.0	111257
70820	BATON ROUGE	15547	7215	54.9	24.2	13.6	5.3	2.0	21403	23198	2	6	1670	1.0	3.5	35.3	50.8	9.5	252273
71001	ARCADIA	14607	1720	46.6	26.2	22.1	4.2	0.9	26978	27438	5	17	1191	35.0	28.4	28.0	7.8	0.8	68641
71002	ASHLAND	17261	96	47.9	24.0	21.9	3.1	3.1	28195	29433	6	23	79	51.9	22.8	20.3	5.1	0.0	48846
71003	ATHENS	17454	426	43.0	25.1	24.9	4.9	2.1	29812	29508	8	33	355	37.2	21.1	33.0	8.5	0.3	70357
71004	BELCHER	17118	231	35.9	34.2	23.8	3.5	2.6	35868	39083	20	61	171	42.7	20.5	18.1	12.9	5.8	57353
71006	BENTON	24314	4446	24.2	23.1	37.2	10.8	4.7	53283	54498	68	96	3819	11.7	15.5	34.4	27.6	10.8	141420
71007	BETHANY	21420	370	28.6	25.4	34.9	8.4	2.7	47250	44445	55	88	320	20.6	16.6	36.6	25.0	1.3	117262
71008	BIENVILLE	15395	337	46.6	28.5	21.7	2.4	0.9	27005	27114	5	18	280	43.9	26.1	22.1	7.1	0.7	60000
71016	CASTOR	12982	785	42.9	31.0	23.4	1.9	0.8	29157	29195	7	28	658	48.8	18.4	26.0	6.1	0.8	52353
	LOUISIANA	19176		34.0	28.2	28.2	6.6	3.0	37868	38644				16.9	18.7	37.2	22.8	4.3	118738
	UNITED STATES	27277		20.9	24.4	35.3	11.7	7.6	54719	56938				9.3	13.1	31.6	32.6	13.5	162279

ZIP CODE		FINANCIAL SERVICES				THE HOME						ENTERTAINMENT						PERSONAL			
						Home Improvements		Furnishings													
#	POST OFFICE NAME	Auto Loan	Home Loan	Invest-ments	Retire-ment Plans	Home Repair	Lawn & Garden	Comput-ers & Hard-ware-Personal	Major Appli-ances	TV, Radio, Sound Equip-ment	Furni-ture	Dine out/ Carry out	Sports Equip-ment	Fees & Tickets	Toys & Games	Travel	Cable TV	Apparel & Services	Auto Repairs	Health Insur-ance	Pets & Supplies
70652	LONGVILLE	78	61	63	59	60	72	62	69	67	62	66	53	53	70	57	71	45	66	71	83
70653	MERRYVILLE	74	52	70	50	52	73	54	66	61	51	59	51	42	62	51	67	40	62	70	81
70654	MITTIE	73	47	70	45	47	71	51	64	58	48	57	50	38	59	47	65	38	60	67	78
70655	OBERLIN	65	50	55	48	49	62	53	58	58	51	56	45	45	59	48	62	38	57	62	71
70656	PITKIN	74	52	67	51	53	72	55	66	61	52	60	50	43	62	51	67	40	62	69	80
70657	RAGLEY	90	75	77	73	74	86	73	82	78	74	78	61	65	81	70	82	52	78	84	98
70658	REEVES	74	53	76	51	55	75	54	69	60	51	59	52	44	60	54	66	39	63	72	82
70660	SINGER	72	51	59	50	51	68	54	62	59	52	58	48	43	62	49	65	39	59	66	76
70661	STARKS	76	55	71	53	56	75	57	69	63	54	62	52	45	64	54	69	41	64	72	83
70662	SUGARTOWN	80	58	66	56	57	76	60	70	67	58	65	54	48	69	55	73	44	66	74	85
70663	SULPHUR	77	73	68	72	71	78	72	75	75	71	74	56	70	76	70	78	51	74	79	89
70665	SULPHUR	94	93	80	92	89	92	89	90	89	91	89	69	87	92	87	90	62	89	90	107
70668	VINTON	71	55	65	54	54	71	57	66	63	54	61	50	48	63	54	68	41	63	70	79
70669	WESTLAKE	81	72	67	72	71	79	73	76	76	71	75	57	67	78	69	79	51	75	80	91
70706	DENHAM SPRINGS	94	90	79	87	87	87	84	88	85	88	85	65	81	89	81	85	58	84	85	103
70710	ADDIS	79	73	63	70	70	72	71	72	72	74	72	54	67	75	67	73	49	71	72	86
70711	ALBANY	75	70	61	67	67	69	67	69	69	70	69	51	63	72	64	70	47	68	69	82
70712	ANGOLA	89	84	71	79	79	80	82	82	83	86	83	62	78	86	77	83	57	82	80	97
70714	BAKER	72	73	61	73	68	74	70	69	72	70	72	53	71	73	69	74	50	70	75	84
70715	BATCHELOR	65	43	63	41	44	65	47	58	53	44	52	45	36	54	44	59	34	55	62	71
70719	BRUSLY	88	88	76	86	85	87	82	85	83	84	83	64	81	86	81	84	57	83	84	101
70721	CARVILLE	58	49	40	51	44	53	54	50	59	54	58	40	52	59	49	61	40	55	57	65
70722	CLINTON	80	62	77	60	62	81	62	74	69	60	68	56	53	69	61	75	45	70	79	90
70723	CONVENT	71	46	69	44	46	70	50	62	57	47	56	49	37	58	46	64	37	59	66	77
70725	DARROW	83	76	67	74	74	78	72	76	75	75	75	55	68	78	68	77	51	74	76	90
70726	DENHAM SPRINGS	84	78	69	76	76	79	75	78	77	78	77	57	71	80	72	78	53	76	78	92
70729	ERWINVILLE	77	72	61	69	69	69	71	71	71	74	72	54	67	74	67	71	49	71	69	84
70730	ETHEL	85	68	75	65	67	81	67	76	73	68	72	57	59	75	64	77	49	73	78	92
70732	FORDOCHE	93	66	77	65	66	88	69	81	77	67	75	62	56	80	63	84	51	76	85	98
70733	FRENCH SETTLEMENT	88	63	73	62	63	84	66	77	73	64	72	59	53	76	60	80	48	73	81	94
70734	GEISMAR	88	82	71	78	79	80	79	81	81	83	81	60	75	84	75	81	55	80	80	96
70736	GLYNN	92	62	84	59	62	89	66	80	75	63	73	62	50	77	61	83	49	76	85	99
70737	GONZALES	87	78	70	76	75	81	76	79	79	78	79	58	71	82	71	82	54	78	81	95
70739	GREENWELL SPRINGS	94	102	90	102	99	97	91	94	90	95	91	71	95	93	94	90	63	91	92	110
70740	GROSSE TETE	78	51	75	48	51	77	54	69	63	52	61	54	41	64	51	70	41	65	73	84
70744	HOLDEN	79	65	65	63	64	74	65	71	69	66	69	54	57	72	61	73	47	69	73	85
70748	JACKSON	83	62	77	59	61	82	63	75	70	62	69	57	52	72	60	76	46	71	78	91
70749	JARREAU	91	70	98	68	73	92	71	87	76	68	75	65	59	76	71	82	50	81	88	103
70750	KROTZ SPRINGS	74	50	68	47	49	72	53	64	60	50	59	50	40	61	49	66	39	61	68	79
70752	LAKELAND	91	62	87	58	61	89	65	81	74	62	73	62	50	76	61	82	48	76	85	99
70753	LETTSWORTH	54	35	52	33	35	53	38	47	43	36	42	37	28	44	35	48	28	45	50	58
70754	LIVINGSTON	81	69	66	67	67	76	68	73	71	69	71	55	61	74	63	74	48	71	74	87
70755	LIVONIA	85	63	73	62	63	82	65	76	72	64	71	58	54	74	61	78	47	72	80	92
70756	LOTTIE	90	59	85	56	59	88	63	79	73	60	71	61	48	74	59	81	47	74	83	97
70757	MARINGOUIN	75	49	71	46	49	73	52	65	60	50	59	51	40	61	49	67	39	62	69	80
70759	MORGANZA	75	55	73	53	56	78	60	72	67	54	65	54	49	66	57	74	43	68	80	85
70760	NEW ROADS	62	49	55	49	49	63	53	58	59	52	58	42	48	58	50	64	39	58	66	70
70761	NORWOOD	71	46	69	44	46	70	50	62	57	47	56	49	37	58	46	64	37	59	66	77
70762	OSCAR	91	81	83	78	81	87	77	85	80	79	80	62	72	82	75	83	54	81	85	100
70763	PAULINA	101	83	85	80	82	95	81	90	87	82	86	67	72	90	77	92	58	87	93	109
70764	PLAQUEMINE	76	60	66	58	59	74	63	70	69	62	68	52	55	69	59	74	46	68	75	84
70767	PORT ALLEN	73	69	62	69	67	72	68	70	71	69	70	51	66	72	66	73	48	69	73	83
70769	PRAIRIEVILLE	112	114	95	109	108	101	104	105	101	111	103	81	103	108	101	99	71	101	97	122
70770	PRIDE	93	89	80	87	87	91	83	88	85	85	85	66	80	88	81	87	58	85	88	105
70772	ROSEDALE	84	55	81	52	55	82	59	74	68	56	66	58	44	69	55	75	44	70	78	91
70773	ROUGON	93	64	82	61	63	89	67	81	76	65	74	63	52	78	62	83	49	76	85	99
70774	SAINT AMANT	85	71	69	69	70	80	69	76	74	71	73	57	62	77	65	78	50	73	78	91
70775	SAINT FRANCISVILLE	93	77	84	74	77	90	77	86	82	76	81	64	68	83	73	87	55	83	89	103
70776	SAINT GABRIEL	86	73	69	72	70	81	73	77	78	74	78	58	67	80	68	82	53	77	80	94
70777	SLAUGHTER	91	77	78	74	75	87	74	83	79	76	79	61	67	82	71	83	53	79	84	99
70778	SORRENTO	75	70	61	67	68	69	67	69	69	70	69	51	64	72	64	70	47	68	69	82
70780	SUNSHINE	80	52	77	49	52	78	56	70	64	53	63	55	42	65	52	72	42	66	74	86
70783	VENTRESS	85	73	91	71	75	86	71	83	74	70	73	60	64	74	72	78	49	78	83	97
70785	WALKER	82	77	67	74	74	75	73	75	74	76	74	56	69	77	69	75	51	73	74	89
70788	WHITE CASTLE	70	48	64	46	47	68	52	62	60	50	58	47	41	60	48	66	39	60	67	76
70789	WILSON	75	50	72	47	50	73	53	66	61	51	59	51	40	62	50	68	39	62	70	81
70791	ZACHARY	92	88	84	86	84	91	82	88	84	84	84	67	80	87	81	86	58	85	87	104
70792	UNCLE SAM	102	67	99	63	67	100	71	90	82	68	80	70	53	84	67	92	53	85	95	111
70801	BATON ROUGE	20	15	16	17	15	15	22	17	22	21	22	15	20	22	19	21	16	20	18	22
70802	BATON ROUGE	40	29	28	31	28	34	39	34	41	37	41	26	34	40	32	43	28	38	40	43
70803	BATON ROUGE	43	18	18	22	17	21	60	30	48	41	49	32	36	47	32	44	35	42	30	40
70805	BATON ROUGE	47	39	33	41	35	43	44	41	48	44	48	32	42	48	39	50	33	45	47	52
70806	BATON ROUGE	68	57	57	60	57	62	70	63	72	67	72	49	65	71	63	74	50	69	70	77
70807	BATON ROUGE	49	41	39	42	39	48	46	45	52	46	51	32	43	50	42	55	35	48	53	56
70808	BATON ROUGE	102	96	97	100	96	96	111	98	106	106	106	78	106	105	103	104	75	104	100	117
70809	BATON ROUGE	102	88	86	94	87	86	106	92	103	103	104	76	99	104	96	100	74	100	92	111
70810	BATON ROUGE	117	125	119	128	123	115	122	116	116	125	118	92	127	119	121	113	84	116	109	136
70811	BATON ROUGE	64	63	57	64	60	68	62	63	66	61	65	47	63	66	61	68	45	64	70	76
70812	BATON ROUGE	55	51	43	52	47	54	52	51	57	53	56	38	52	56	49	59	38	54	58	64
70813	BATON ROUGE	61	38	33	43	35	44	60	47	67	56	65	38	51	65	47	70	46	58	57	63
70814	BATON ROUGE	77	77	65	76	72	75	77	74	77	76	78	57	76	79	73	78	54	76	78	89
70815	BATON ROUGE	80	79	76	80	79	82	82	80	83	81	83	60	82	82	81	84	58	82	85	94
70816	BATON ROUGE	91	79	72	82	76	75	89	80	88	90	90	64	84	91	82	87	62	86	80	97
70817	BATON ROUGE	118	133	119	134	129	118	120	119	114	126	116	94	128	119	123	110	83	116	109	138
70818	BATON ROUGE	97	99	89	99	97	98	91	96	91	93	91	72	91	94	92	91	63	91	93	112
70819	BATON ROUGE	77	84	74	83	81	83	80	80	80	79	81	61	84	81	81	82	56	80	84	94
70820	BATON ROUGE	55	34	31	38	32	34	66	42	58	53	59	40	48	58	45	54	41	53	42	54
71001	ARCADIA	62	46	58	45	46	62	48	57	55	47	54	42	42	55	46	61	36	55	63	69
71002	ASHLAND	72	47	69	44	46	70	50	63	58	47	56	49	37	59	47	64	37	59	66	77
71003	ATHENS	80	52	77	49	52	79	56	70	65	53	63	55	42	66	52	72	42	66	74	87
71004	BELCHER	86	58	85	56	59	86	61	78	70	58	68	60	47	70	59	77	45	72	81	94
71006	BENTON	95	95	101	97	96	102	88	96	90	90	90	73	90	90	92	92	62	92	96	113
71007	BETHANY	88	80	71	78	79	82	76	80	79	79	79	58	72	82	72	81	54	78	81	96
71008	BIENVILLE	66	44	65	42	44	65	47	59	53	44	52	46	35	54	44	59	34	55	62	72
71016	CASTOR	65	44	59	42	44	63	47	57	53	45	52	44	36	55	43	59	35	54	60	70
	LOUISIANA	78	67	68	67	66	75	70	72	73	70	73	55	65	74	67	76	50	73	76	87
	UNITED STATES	100	100	100	100	100	100	100	100	100	100	100	100	100	100	100	100	100	100	100	100

ZIP CODE #	POST OFFICE NAME	COUNTY FIPS CODE	POPULATION 2000	POPULATION 2009	POPULATION 2014	2000-2009 ANNUAL RATE % Rate	2000-2009 ANNUAL RATE State Centile	HOUSEHOLDS 2000	HOUSEHOLDS 2009	HOUSEHOLDS 2014	HOUSEHOLDS % Annual Rate 2000-2009	HOUSEHOLDS 2009 Average HH Size	FAMILIES 2000	FAMILIES 2009	FAMILIES % Annual Rate 2000-2009
71018	COTTON VALLEY	119	1937	1910	1893	-0.2	29	796	801	800	0.1	2.37	555	547	-0.2
71019	COUSHATTA	081	9770	9632	9436	-0.2	29	3461	3429	3364	-0.1	2.73	2556	2497	-0.3
71023	DOYLINE	119	3549	3598	3594	0.1	44	1412	1453	1459	0.3	2.48	1030	1042	0.1
71024	DUBBERLY	119	1299	1353	1354	0.4	61	516	548	553	0.7	2.43	383	400	0.5
71027	FRIERSON	031	1496	1637	1701	1.0	80	576	644	674	1.2	2.54	430	474	1.1
71028	GIBSLAND	013	2023	1904	1849	-0.7	14	847	817	801	-0.4	2.33	557	527	-0.6
71029	GILLIAM	017	238	222	216	-0.7	14	90	85	83	-0.6	2.60	63	58	-0.9
71030	GLOSTER	031	1237	1267	1273	0.3	53	448	469	475	0.5	2.70	347	359	0.4
71031	GOLDONNA	069	1036	1059	1059	0.2	49	400	417	420	0.5	2.54	296	304	0.3
71032	GRAND CANE	031	1547	1734	1816	1.2	84	627	718	758	1.5	2.42	461	519	1.3
71033	GREENWOOD	017	3028	3182	3200	0.5	66	1180	1257	1269	0.7	2.53	860	899	0.5
71034	HALL SUMMIT	081	264	249	239	-0.6	17	101	96	92	-0.5	2.59	75	70	-0.7
71037	HAUGHTON	015	17202	19963	21359	1.6	89	6153	7337	7927	1.9	2.72	4825	5628	1.7
71038	HAYNESVILLE	027	5836	5791	5616	-0.1	35	1964	1883	1822	-0.5	2.62	1339	1261	-0.6
71039	HEFLIN	119	2083	2146	2143	0.3	53	792	831	835	0.5	2.58	566	584	0.3
71040	HOMER	027	8047	7894	7668	-0.2	29	3140	3064	2991	-0.3	2.34	2180	2093	-0.4
71043	HOSSTON	017	608	573	558	-0.6	17	233	223	219	-0.5	2.57	165	155	-0.7
71044	IDA	017	937	893	872	-0.5	21	390	378	371	-0.3	2.36	278	264	-0.6
71045	JAMESTOWN	013	880	873	862	-0.1	35	349	351	348	0.1	2.49	237	234	-0.1
71046	KEATCHIE	031	1394	1571	1644	1.3	85	548	636	672	1.6	2.39	408	465	1.4
71047	KEITHVILLE	017	11143	12594	13044	1.3	85	3853	4418	4600	1.5	2.73	2993	3373	1.3
71048	LISBON	027	81	82	81	0.1	44	40	41	41	0.3	2.00	29	29	0.0
71049	LOGANSPORT	031	3739	3901	3953	0.5	66	1457	1545	1576	0.6	2.51	1037	1081	0.5
71051	ELM GROVE	015	2017	2253	2385	1.2	84	773	887	949	1.5	2.54	572	632	1.1
71052	MANSFIELD	031	11127	11319	11348	0.2	49	4186	4329	4368	0.4	2.55	2906	2958	0.2
71055	MINDEN	119	19961	19528	19252	-0.2	29	7851	7803	7733	-0.1	2.43	5428	5314	-0.2
71060	MOORINGSPORT	017	2676	2971	3069	1.1	82	1038	1164	1209	1.2	2.55	778	860	1.1
71061	OIL CITY	017	1966	1882	1845	-0.5	21	803	781	770	-0.3	2.41	533	505	-0.6
71063	PELICAN	031	873	882	877	0.1	44	331	340	340	0.3	2.59	229	232	0.1
71064	PLAIN DEALING	015	4242	4564	4757	0.8	77	1573	1752	1846	1.2	2.46	1079	1165	0.8
71065	PLEASANT HILL	085	1272	1366	1391	0.8	77	484	528	540	0.9	2.50	349	375	0.8
71067	PRINCETON	015	2571	3042	3305	1.8	91	942	1147	1259	2.2	2.65	704	836	1.9
71068	RINGGOLD	013	3555	3462	3401	-0.3	27	1453	1440	1421	-0.1	2.35	968	941	-0.3
71069	RODESSA	017	752	725	712	-0.4	24	305	299	295	-0.2	2.42	210	202	-0.4
71070	SALINE	069	1707	1694	1675	-0.1	35	691	701	699	0.2	2.42	494	494	0.0
71071	SAREPTA	119	3250	3335	3328	0.3	53	1247	1303	1310	0.5	2.55	907	932	0.3
71072	SHONGALOO	119	1566	1594	1593	0.2	49	614	635	638	0.4	2.49	463	471	0.2
71073	SIBLEY	119	2484	2666	2692	0.8	77	880	964	981	1.0	2.60	643	692	0.8
71075	SPRINGHILL	119	7011	6820	6720	-0.3	27	2919	2888	2864	-0.1	2.31	1941	1882	-0.3
71078	STONEWALL	031	4057	4281	4388	0.6	71	1506	1624	1675	0.8	2.64	1145	1218	0.7
71079	SUMMERFIELD	027	311	314	310	0.1	44	110	113	113	0.3	2.78	81	82	0.1
71082	VIVIAN	017	5469	5404	5329	-0.1	35	2142	2141	2120	0.0	2.48	1436	1404	-0.2
71101	SHREVEPORT	017	9892	9249	9013	-0.7	14	3974	3711	3618	-0.7	2.24	1907	1712	-1.2
71103	SHREVEPORT	017	10618	9729	9429	-0.9	10	3784	3463	3358	-1.0	2.54	2288	2040	-1.2
71104	SHREVEPORT	017	15199	14575	14270	-0.5	21	6730	6464	6341	-0.4	2.16	3418	3172	-0.8
71105	SHREVEPORT	017	20084	20536	20564	0.2	49	9380	9728	9802	0.4	2.10	5382	5382	0.0
71106	SHREVEPORT	017	33265	34879	35311	0.5	66	12044	12656	12832	0.5	2.69	8689	9068	0.5
71107	SHREVEPORT	017	30768	32306	32686	0.5	66	10810	11543	11750	0.7	2.71	8084	8482	0.5
71108	SHREVEPORT	017	20909	20763	20500	-0.1	35	7522	7414	7325	-0.2	2.80	5330	5153	-0.4
71109	SHREVEPORT	017	25965	24623	24021	-0.6	17	9377	8975	8789	-0.5	2.71	6423	6012	-0.7
71110	BARKSDALE AFB	015	3459	3503	3524	0.1	44	718	742	754	0.4	3.62	708	731	0.3
71111	BOSSIER CITY	015	31054	36154	38614	1.7	90	11952	14128	15157	1.8	2.51	8208	9620	1.7
71112	BOSSIER CITY	015	27336	30330	31920	1.1	82	10574	12010	12730	1.4	2.50	7518	8429	1.2
71115	SHREVEPORT	017	10404	10967	11103	0.6	71	4989	5300	5384	0.7	1.98	2606	2701	0.4
71118	SHREVEPORT	017	23867	23684	23476	-0.1	35	9608	9665	9623	0.1	2.41	6728	6631	-0.2
71119	SHREVEPORT	017	11139	11248	11183	0.1	44	4386	4468	4455	0.2	2.50	3182	3186	0.0
71129	SHREVEPORT	017	12040	12546	12641	0.4	61	4987	5263	5327	0.6	2.38	3255	3352	0.3
71201	MONROE	073	21859	21147	20817	-0.4	24	9706	9453	9335	-0.3	2.19	5486	5202	-0.6
71202	MONROE	073	30628	29514	29139	-0.4	24	9629	9367	9273	-0.3	3.02	7245	6919	-0.5
71203	MONROE	073	33185	35377	36192	0.7	74	12521	13568	13946	0.9	2.50	8508	9063	0.7
71209	MONROE	073	845	767	765	-1.0	9	7	7	7	0.0	2.57	2	2	0.0
71219	BASKIN	041	1179	1217	1219	0.3	53	433	456	459	0.6	2.66	330	342	0.4
71220	BASTROP	067	25931	24732	23917	-0.5	21	9543	9315	9080	-0.3	2.57	6996	6731	-0.4
71222	BERNICE	111	3821	3930	3920	0.3	53	1486	1562	1570	0.5	2.45	1038	1073	0.4
71223	BONITA	067	697	636	605	-1.0	9	265	249	239	-0.7	2.55	178	163	-0.9
71225	CALHOUN	073	5086	5782	6046	1.4	87	1860	2131	2238	1.5	2.71	1497	1689	1.3
71226	CHATHAM	049	1712	1736	1721	0.2	49	694	721	720	0.4	2.41	493	504	0.2
71227	CHOUDRANT	061	3287	3456	3492	0.5	66	1269	1364	1390	0.8	2.53	968	1025	0.6
71229	COLLINSTON	067	1424	1441	1430	0.1	44	443	461	461	0.4	2.84	328	337	0.3
71232	DELHI	083	6421	6166	6033	-0.4	24	2383	2336	2300	-0.2	2.54	1734	1674	-0.4
71234	DOWNSVILLE	111	3817	4137	4247	0.9	80	1500	1663	1722	1.1	2.49	1121	1225	1.0
71235	DUBACH	061	4015	4064	4060	0.1	44	1570	1623	1633	0.4	2.50	1185	1208	0.2
71237	EPPS	123	1453	1318	1249	-1.0	9	336	298	277	-1.3	3.02	254	222	-1.4
71238	EROS	049	2397	2526	2542	0.6	71	890	954	965	0.8	2.65	701	738	0.6
71241	FARMERVILLE	111	9498	9520	9456	0.0	38	3673	3767	3771	0.3	2.43	2686	2718	0.1
71243	FORT NECESSITY	041	243	231	224	-0.5	21	96	93	91	-0.3	2.48	73	70	-0.5
71245	GRAMBLING	061	2645	4390	4360	5.6	100	1146	1156	1152	0.1	2.18	637	624	-0.2
71250	JONES	067	328	303	289	-0.9	10	122	116	112	-0.5	2.61	84	78	-0.8
71251	JONESBORO	049	9588	9360	9186	-0.3	27	3807	3791	3748	0.0	2.40	2656	2603	-0.2
71254	LAKE PROVIDENCE	035	7753	7115	6756	-0.9	10	2432	2263	2152	-0.8	2.82	1731	1588	-0.9
71256	LILLIE	111	595	591	579	-0.1	35	219	223	219	0.2	2.65	156	156	0.0
71259	MANGHAM	083	1736	1862	1876	0.8	77	674	739	751	1.0	2.52	504	545	0.8
71260	MARION	111	3400	3492	3520	0.3	53	1324	1393	1416	0.6	2.51	953	989	0.4
71261	MER ROUGE	067	1729	1610	1547	-0.8	12	652	623	604	-0.5	2.55	482	454	-0.6
71263	OAK GROVE	123	8778	8352	8022	-0.5	21	3347	3233	3120	-0.4	2.51	2428	2312	-0.5
71264	OAK RIDGE	067	1020	906	860	-1.3	7	391	357	342	-1.0	2.53	277	248	-1.2
71266	PIONEER	123	2153	1938	1810	-1.1	7	802	726	678	-1.1	2.49	589	526	-1.2
71268	QUITMAN	049	2877	2879	2846	0.0	38	1070	1094	1090	0.2	2.60	785	789	0.1
71269	RAYVILLE	083	12846	12729	12568	-0.1	35	4435	4494	4469	0.1	2.62	3245	3241	0.0
71270	RUSTON	061	31083	29363	29365	-0.6	17	10759	11147	11210	0.4	2.37	6530	6624	0.2
71275	SIMSBORO	061	2399	2456	2463	0.3	53	863	904	912	0.5	2.70	638	657	0.3
71276	SONDHEIMER	035	675	579	542	-1.6	6	242	207	193	-1.7	2.35	185	156	-1.8
71277	SPEARSVILLE	111	2034	1999	1975	-0.2	29	759	759	756	0.0	2.63	552	544	-0.2
71280	STERLINGTON	111	2717	2855	2898	0.5	66	1016	1088	1112	0.7	2.59	774	819	0.6
71282	TALLULAH	065	13522	12146	11685	-1.2	7	4383	4112	3964	-0.7	2.72	3077	2841	-0.9
	LOUISIANA					0.0					0.1	2.60			0.1
	UNITED STATES					1.0					1.1	2.59			0.9

ZIP CODE #	POST OFFICE NAME	RACE (%) White 2000	White 2009	Black 2000	Black 2009	Asian/Pacific 2000	Asian/Pacific 2009	% Hispanic Origin 2000	% Hispanic Origin 2009	2009 AGE DISTRIBUTION (%) 0-4	5-9	10-14	15-19	20-24	25-44	45-64	65-84	85+	18+	MEDIAN AGE 2009	% 2009 Males	% 2009 Females
71018	COTTON VALLEY	67.7	61.5	30.5	36.2	0.0	0.1	1.3	1.5	6.9	7.4	6.9	5.3	5.4	23.9	28.6	13.5	2.1	75.4	39.5	48.4	51.6
71019	COUSHATTA	57.9	54.1	40.8	44.3	0.1	0.1	1.0	1.2	7.7	7.2	7.9	8.4	6.2	23.1	25.3	11.9	2.2	71.9	36.1	47.7	52.3
71023	DOYLINE	84.8	80.8	13.0	16.5	0.5	0.8	1.1	1.3	5.6	5.9	5.9	5.5	5.1	23.5	31.8	15.3	1.4	79.3	43.8	49.5	50.5
71024	DUBBERLY	68.9	62.3	28.9	35.1	0.1	0.1	1.5	1.8	6.2	6.5	6.7	5.9	4.2	25.1	29.8	13.7	1.8	76.9	41.7	48.0	52.0
71027	FRIERSON	71.7	67.4	26.2	30.1	0.2	0.2	1.5	2.1	6.8	7.0	7.1	6.4	6.2	25.5	29.4	10.7	1.0	75.3	38.5	50.5	49.5
71028	GIBSLAND	35.7	31.7	63.1	66.8	0.1	0.2	0.5	0.6	6.0	6.2	6.3	7.3	5.8	24.3	27.5	14.0	2.7	76.9	40.8	47.6	52.4
71029	GILLIAM	63.3	54.1	35.9	44.6	0.0	0.0	0.4	0.5	5.0	6.3	8.1	8.1	5.0	23.0	28.4	14.0	2.3	75.2	41.0	50.5	49.5
71030	GLOSTER	61.6	56.3	35.9	40.7	0.1	0.1	2.0	2.3	6.9	6.9	7.0	6.4	6.0	27.2	28.7	9.6	1.2	75.1	37.1	50.0	50.0
71031	GOLDONNA	95.4	94.1	3.4	4.2	0.1	0.1	1.0	1.5	6.7	7.3	7.1	6.0	4.3	24.3	28.5	14.2	1.6	75.2	40.6	50.4	49.6
71032	GRAND CANE	63.2	58.3	35.4	39.9	0.0	0.0	1.0	1.3	6.0	6.4	6.7	6.3	4.8	22.8	31.1	13.9	2.0	77.0	42.8	49.6	50.4
71033	GREENWOOD	73.2	64.6	24.2	32.1	0.5	0.6	1.6	1.9	5.4	5.6	6.1	6.7	5.7	25.5	31.8	12.0	1.2	78.7	41.1	49.0	51.0
71034	HALL SUMMIT	83.4	80.7	15.5	18.1	0.0	0.0	0.8	1.2	6.4	6.8	6.4	6.0	4.8	24.9	26.9	15.3	2.4	76.3	40.8	47.8	52.2
71037	HAUGHTON	83.0	78.6	13.7	17.1	0.6	0.8	2.2	2.9	7.6	7.4	7.5	7.2	6.3	27.1	27.1	9.0	0.8	72.9	35.5	49.2	50.8
71038	HAYNESVILLE	53.1	48.7	46.2	50.5	0.1	0.1	0.7	0.9	5.7	6.0	6.3	6.4	6.2	27.7	25.2	13.1	3.5	78.0	39.2	53.5	46.5
71039	HEFLIN	65.2	58.7	33.4	39.6	0.1	0.1	1.4	1.7	6.5	6.5	6.7	6.8	5.8	23.3	29.2	13.4	1.7	76.2	40.6	49.3	50.7
71040	HOMER	49.9	46.7	49.3	52.2	0.2	0.2	0.8	0.9	5.8	6.0	6.2	6.8	6.2	24.3	26.6	14.9	3.2	77.8	41.0	50.9	49.1
71043	HOSSTON	67.4	58.1	31.8	40.8	0.2	0.2	0.3	0.3	4.5	5.6	7.9	8.0	5.1	21.8	28.6	16.2	2.3	76.6	42.8	50.1	49.9
71044	IDA	65.5	56.2	33.1	42.1	0.0	0.0	0.7	0.9	5.5	5.6	5.9	6.8	6.2	20.5	28.9	18.1	2.5	78.8	44.6	49.0	51.0
71045	JAMESTOWN	73.7	69.3	24.7	28.6	0.2	0.3	1.4	1.8	7.0	7.1	6.9	6.4	5.4	22.6	27.9	14.4	2.3	75.1	40.8	49.0	51.0
71046	KEATCHIE	71.7	67.0	25.9	29.9	0.1	0.1	1.9	2.4	6.1	6.4	6.8	6.9	5.3	24.8	30.2	11.8	1.5	76.0	40.2	50.9	49.1
71047	KEITHVILLE	79.8	73.2	17.6	23.4	0.3	0.4	1.7	2.2	6.5	6.4	6.4	6.6	6.5	28.7	27.2	10.8	0.9	76.7	37.1	52.3	47.7
71048	LISBON	46.3	41.5	53.8	57.3	0.0	0.0	1.3	0.0	7.3	7.3	7.3	7.3	6.1	24.4	23.2	14.6	2.4	73.2	37.5	50.0	50.0
71049	LOGANSPORT	71.0	67.0	27.9	31.6	0.2	0.2	1.3	1.6	7.4	7.7	7.8	7.5	5.0	23.0	26.1	13.6	1.8	72.2	38.0	47.8	52.2
71051	ELM GROVE	75.4	69.8	22.4	27.2	0.7	1.0	1.1	1.4	5.6	5.8	6.5	7.1	5.4	24.5	31.6	12.0	1.4	77.6	41.1	50.7	49.3
71052	MANSFIELD	39.1	35.2	59.4	62.9	0.2	0.2	1.5	1.7	7.5	7.4	7.1	7.4	6.5	23.4	25.8	12.0	2.7	73.4	36.8	46.5	53.5
71055	MINDEN	56.9	53.4	41.4	44.6	0.3	0.3	0.7	0.8	6.9	6.9	6.8	6.6	6.0	24.1	26.5	13.6	2.6	75.3	39.0	48.1	51.9
71060	MOORINGSPORT	85.7	81.0	12.2	16.1	0.1	0.1	1.3	1.7	6.6	6.8	6.9	6.9	5.7	26.0	28.0	11.8	1.3	75.5	38.2	48.5	51.5
71061	OIL CITY	70.1	61.5	28.8	37.1	0.1	0.1	1.2	1.4	7.4	7.4	7.1	6.4	5.5	23.5	26.8	14.1	1.8	74.1	38.5	48.5	51.5
71063	PELICAN	47.3	42.3	51.2	56.0	0.1	0.1	1.6	1.6	5.7	5.8	6.0	7.8	6.6	23.2	28.6	13.8	2.5	77.9	40.9	48.9	51.1
71064	PLAIN DEALING	50.8	44.3	47.8	54.0	0.1	0.1	1.2	1.4	6.4	6.4	6.6	6.7	6.2	24.7	26.9	13.7	2.4	76.3	39.7	49.9	50.1
71065	PLEASANT HILL	71.4	65.7	23.3	27.5	0.1	0.1	2.4	3.0	6.4	6.4	6.3	7.2	5.7	24.9	26.4	14.1	2.6	75.9	40.3	46.5	53.5
71067	PRINCETON	75.9	70.8	21.9	26.2	0.3	0.4	1.6	2.1	7.1	6.9	6.9	7.2	6.8	26.6	26.8	10.6	1.1	74.7	36.9	49.3	50.7
71068	RINGGOLD	59.8	55.2	39.0	43.4	0.1	0.1	0.8	1.0	6.7	6.9	6.8	6.6	5.5	21.6	26.8	15.6	3.4	75.4	41.5	48.2	51.8
71069	RODESSA	69.4	61.5	28.4	35.6	0.0	0.1	0.8	1.1	6.3	6.3	6.9	6.9	5.2	22.2	28.1	15.4	2.5	76.3	41.8	50.1	49.9
71070	SALINE	74.2	70.0	24.6	28.4	0.1	0.2	0.7	0.8	6.1	6.3	6.3	6.6	5.4	23.7	29.0	14.5	2.2	77.3	41.6	49.9	50.1
71071	SAREPTA	79.1	77.0	19.1	20.4	0.1	0.1	1.9	2.5	6.4	6.5	6.3	5.7	5.7	25.2	28.3	13.7	2.2	77.3	40.1	47.9	52.1
71072	SHONGALOO	89.7	86.6	9.7	12.5	0.1	0.2	0.4	0.6	6.0	6.3	7.2	6.0	3.6	25.4	29.8	13.4	2.3	76.6	42.1	52.1	47.9
71073	SIBLEY	63.2	57.2	34.8	40.2	0.1	0.1	0.9	1.2	6.3	6.5	6.6	6.5	6.1	26.2	28.2	12.3	1.3	76.9	38.9	52.1	47.9
71075	SPRINGHILL	68.5	66.3	30.1	31.9	0.3	0.4	0.7	0.9	6.4	6.0	6.1	6.7	5.7	22.6	25.8	17.2	3.5	77.5	42.0	46.5	53.5
71078	STONEWALL	74.6	70.5	22.3	25.6	0.2	0.2	1.9	2.4	6.5	6.6	6.8	6.4	6.2	25.8	29.5	11.1	1.1	76.2	39.2	50.1	49.9
71079	SUMMERFIELD	43.5	39.2	55.8	59.9	0.0	0.0	0.6	1.0	7.3	7.3	7.0	7.6	6.1	23.2	26.1	13.4	1.9	73.6	37.9	45.9	54.1
71082	VIVIAN	71.7	65.6	26.6	32.1	0.3	0.4	0.8	0.9	7.4	7.3	7.0	6.7	6.0	22.1	26.1	14.1	3.3	73.9	39.4	46.8	53.2
71101	SHREVEPORT	24.3	20.6	73.1	76.3	0.4	0.5	2.4	2.6	8.2	7.7	6.4	7.0	6.7	23.3	24.3	12.9	3.5	73.7	36.4	48.4	51.6
71103	SHREVEPORT	8.4	6.2	90.3	92.3	0.3	0.3	0.8	0.8	7.0	6.8	6.8	7.3	6.2	21.1	24.5	15.6	4.6	74.8	40.4	45.9	54.1
71104	SHREVEPORT	68.9	62.5	26.6	31.7	1.3	1.7	2.6	3.2	6.9	5.7	5.3	7.3	10.2	29.9	22.8	9.4	2.4	78.9	33.4	47.5	52.5
71105	SHREVEPORT	88.9	84.5	7.4	10.3	2.0	2.8	2.1	2.7	5.6	5.3	5.2	5.9	7.7	28.3	25.1	13.6	3.3	80.6	38.8	47.4	52.6
71106	SHREVEPORT	51.0	49.6	47.0	47.7	0.9	1.3	1.0	1.2	7.2	7.4	7.4	7.3	6.1	23.0	27.4	11.6	2.6	73.3	38.3	47.0	53.0
71107	SHREVEPORT	46.1	43.4	52.0	54.2	0.2	0.3	1.2	1.4	7.4	7.4	7.1	7.5	6.9	25.8	26.1	10.5	1.3	73.7	35.1	48.9	51.1
71108	SHREVEPORT	29.7	23.2	68.3	74.7	0.4	0.5	1.1	1.1	8.4	8.6	8.2	8.5	7.6	26.5	22.2	8.6	1.4	69.5	31.0	46.4	53.6
71109	SHREVEPORT	9.6	7.2	89.2	91.4	0.2	0.2	0.8	0.8	7.2	7.7	7.9	8.8	7.2	23.5	25.5	10.4	1.8	71.9	34.0	46.0	54.0
71110	BARKSDALE AFB	68.6	62.2	22.7	26.5	2.3	2.8	7.6	9.6	13.1	10.7	8.5	11.1	22.2	31.2	3.1	0.1	0.0	64.1	21.5	57.3	42.7
71111	BOSSIER CITY	70.8	69.2	24.1	24.4	1.7	2.4	3.2	3.9	8.3	7.7	7.6	7.3	6.5	28.1	23.9	9.1	1.6	71.9	34.1	48.1	51.9
71112	BOSSIER CITY	76.0	71.5	18.1	20.5	2.0	2.8	4.0	5.1	7.4	7.0	6.6	6.4	6.5	29.1	24.7	11.0	1.4	75.3	35.5	48.9	51.1
71115	SHREVEPORT	82.6	76.5	13.2	18.0	1.9	2.6	2.1	2.7	5.6	5.0	4.9	6.8	10.0	27.7	23.6	12.5	3.8	81.3	36.5	45.3	54.7
71118	SHREVEPORT	80.3	74.7	16.3	20.9	1.1	1.5	2.0	2.5	6.5	6.1	6.2	6.1	6.1	26.1	26.1	14.0	2.8	77.5	39.3	46.6	53.4
71119	SHREVEPORT	51.0	42.6	47.1	55.2	0.5	0.6	1.1	1.3	5.7	5.8	6.3	6.2	5.4	26.0	29.2	13.8	1.6	78.1	40.9	48.5	51.5
71129	SHREVEPORT	61.9	54.0	35.0	42.2	0.5	0.7	2.3	2.6	7.7	6.9	6.4	6.6	8.9	29.0	25.0	8.4	0.9	74.8	33.2	48.3	51.7
71201	MONROE	67.7	62.9	29.8	33.7	1.4	2.0	1.2	1.4	6.5	6.0	5.8	5.7	7.3	27.0	24.4	14.1	3.2	78.4	38.1	46.3	53.7
71202	MONROE	15.1	11.2	83.8	87.6	0.2	0.3	0.9	0.9	9.0	9.4	9.5	10.2	7.7	24.2	21.0	7.8	1.2	65.7	28.0	46.7	53.3
71203	MONROE	62.4	56.2	35.2	40.7	1.1	1.4	1.1	1.3	7.2	7.0	6.8	8.1	9.4	28.0	22.4	9.8	1.4	75.1	32.6	47.0	53.0
71209	MONROE	49.8	36.9	43.7	55.3	4.4	5.5	1.8	2.0	2.2	1.4	1.6	36.0	36.0	12.0	5.7	4.4	0.7	93.6	21.2	36.0	64.0
71219	BASKIN	84.7	80.9	14.2	17.7	0.2	0.2	0.7	0.8	6.9	7.1	6.9	6.4	5.8	24.2	28.3	12.5	1.9	75.3	39.4	49.8	50.2
71220	BASTROP	56.0	52.7	43.1	46.2	0.2	0.3	0.7	0.7	7.2	7.2	7.1	7.2	6.1	25.1	25.2	12.5	2.3	74.0	37.0	47.6	52.4
71222	BERNICE	57.5	52.5	38.7	42.5	0.3	0.4	4.2	5.3	7.0	7.2	6.9	6.2	5.2	24.5	26.1	14.3	2.7	75.1	39.4	47.4	52.6
71223	BONITA	48.9	42.1	49.3	55.5	0.1	0.2	1.3	1.4	5.8	6.1	6.1	6.1	6.1	22.2	29.2	15.7	2.5	78.5	42.5	50.6	49.4
71225	CALHOUN	91.8	87.8	6.5	9.9	0.2	0.4	1.0	1.4	6.8	6.8	6.9	6.8	5.6	28.1	27.5	10.5	1.0	75.3	37.5	49.7	50.3
71226	CHATHAM	74.1	70.0	24.8	28.7	0.1	0.2	0.6	0.7	6.9	7.2	7.1	6.3	4.9	24.9	28.6	12.3	1.7	74.8	39.6	49.4	50.6
71227	CHOUDRANT	86.9	83.9	12.1	14.7	0.1	0.1	0.9	1.2	6.2	6.3	6.6	6.5	5.5	27.8	29.0	10.7	1.4	76.9	38.8	49.8	50.2
71229	COLLINSTON	58.2	52.4	41.1	46.6	0.2	0.3	1.5	1.7	5.8	6.0	6.0	6.5	7.2	29.1	26.9	11.2	1.4	78.3	37.3	54.1	45.9
71232	DELHI	53.0	47.9	45.7	50.3	0.3	0.4	1.3	1.5	7.5	7.8	7.3	6.7	5.5	23.7	25.4	13.4	2.7	73.4	37.8	46.7	53.3
71234	DOWNSVILLE	93.0	90.9	5.8	7.5	0.1	0.1	0.7	1.0	6.2	6.2	6.4	6.0	5.2	26.8	29.3	12.5	1.3	77.5	40.4	50.2	49.8
71235	DUBACH	81.1	77.6	17.5	20.5	0.2	0.3	0.9	1.2	6.8	7.0	7.0	6.4	5.0	25.3	28.8	12.2	1.6	75.2	39.4	49.1	50.9
71237	EPPS	51.9	46.4	47.2	52.5	0.1	0.1	1.2	1.4	4.3	4.2	4.5	7.1	13.9	33.9	21.8	9.0	1.3	83.6	33.2	64.8	35.2
71238	EROS	85.5	80.2	13.0	17.7	0.2	0.3	1.2	1.4	6.7	6.9	7.0	6.7	5.6	26.3	28.9	10.8	1.1	75.3	38.5	49.1	50.9
71241	FARMERVILLE	67.9	64.9	30.2	32.5	0.4	0.6	1.6	2.1	7.0	6.5	6.6	6.5	5.6	24.6	26.7	13.9	2.5	75.8	39.7	48.6	51.4
71243	FORT NECESSITY	90.6	87.9	8.2	10.4	0.0	0.0	0.8	1.3	6.5	7.4	6.9	5.6	5.2	26.8	29.0	10.8	1.7	74.9	38.8	50.2	49.8
71245	GRAMBLING	5.7	21.3	92.2	76.1	0.3	0.5	1.1	1.3	6.2	5.5	5.5	10.6	18.5	23.5	19.7	8.9	1.5	79.5	27.6	49.8	50.2
71250	JONES	54.1	47.5	44.3	50.2	0.0	0.0	1.2	1.3	5.9	6.3	6.3	6.3	6.3	23.4	28.4	14.9	2.3	77.9	40.8	50.2	49.8
71251	JONESBORO	67.1	64.3	31.7	34.1	0.3	0.4	0.5	0.6	6.5	6.6	6.6	6.2	5.4	24.4	26.3	15.0	3.0	76.6	40.5	47.6	52.4
71254	LAKE PROVIDENCE	25.8	23.7	73.1	74.9	0.4	0.5	1.1	1.3	7.9	8.3	7.7	8.8	8.1	24.9	21.4	10.8	2.1	70.8	31.5	49.8	50.2
71256	LILLIE	51.7	46.2	46.8	51.9	0.0	0.0	1.0	1.5	8.1	8.1	7.8	7.1	5.1	25.2	24.2	12.7	1.7	71.6	36.3	48.7	51.3
71259	MANGHAM	76.9	73.7	22.6	25.6	0.1	0.1	1.0	1.3	6.7	6.8	7.0	6.7	5.3	23.6	28.2	13.9	1.8	75.2	40.4	47.8	52.2
71260	MARION	69.5	65.1	28.2	31.9	0.4	0.6	2.3	2.8	6.7	6.8	6.7	6.2	5.3	24.6	29.1	12.9	1.7	76.0	40.4	49.8	50.2
71261	MER ROUGE	54.6	48.1	44.5	50.9	0.1	0.2	1.0	1.1	7.1	7.3	7.0	6.4	5.7	23.3	27.9	13.1	2.2	74.7	38.8	48.0	52.0
71263	OAK GROVE	86.3	84.2	12.3	14.0	0.2	0.2	1.4	1.9	6.4	6.6	6.7	6.6	5.2	23.3	28.1	14.2	2.9	76.1	41.0	48.4	51.6
71264	OAK RIDGE	61.9	57.8	37.6	41.6	0.1	0.1	0.8	0.9	6.5	7.2	6.8	5.4	4.4	23.6	29.8	14.1	2.1	76.2	41.6	48.8	51.2
71266	PIONEER	71.9	67.5	26.9	31.1	0.1	0.1	1.1	1.2	6.1	6.1	6.2	7.1	6.9	26.8	25.1	13.5	2.0	77.4	37.9	52.2	47.8
71268	QUITMAN	73.9	69.9	25.1	28.9	0.1	0.1	0.6	0.7	6.6	6.7	6.5	6.1	5.1	25.8	27.2	13.4	2.4	76.5	39.8	48.5	51.5
71269	RAYVILLE	61.4	57.7	37.6	41.0	0.1	0.2	0.9	1.1	7.3	7.4	7.1	6.8	6.4	26.0	25.0	11.8	2.2	74.1	36.3	47.7	52.3
71270	RUSTON	56.3	55.8	40.6	39.9	1.7	2.5	1.2	1.5	6.2	5.6	5.4	12.3	16.7	23.0	19.5	9.3	2.0	79.2	27.5	48.7	51.3
71275	SIMSBORO	53.7	47.5	44.9	50.7	0.0	0.0	1.4	1.7	7.3	7.0	6.3	6.2	7.4	28.5	26.2	9.7	1.4	75.7	34.5	49.6	50.4
71276	SONDHEIMER	61.6	55.4	37.4	43.2	0.0	0.0	1.8	1.9	6.9	6.9	6.2	5.9	8.5	29.7	23.0	11.6	1.4	76.5	35.2	59.1	40.9
71277	SPEARSVILLE	67.4	61.8	30.7	35.7	0.0	0.1	2.0	2.6	7.9	6.9	7.0	6.0	5.9	24.4	27.2	12.9	2.0	74.5	38.7	49.1	50.9
71280	STERLINGTON	83.5	77.5	14.2	19.4	0.4	0.6	2.1	2.7	6.5	6.4	6.3	6.1	6.7	26.2	28.0	12.3	1.6	77.2	38.4	47.8	52.2
71282	TALLULAH	37.6	34.2	60.6	63.5	0.2	0.2	2.1	2.5	8.7	8.3	7.7	9.9	7.3	24.0	22.2	10.1	1.8	68.8	30.9	49.9	50.1
	LOUISIANA	63.9	61.9	32.5	33.7	1.3	1.6	2.4	2.8	7.2	7.0	6.9	7.3	7.1	26.8	25.7	10.4	1.6	74.6	35.6	48.6	51.4
	UNITED STATES	75.1	72.0	12.3	12.7	3.8	4.6	12.5	15.7	6.8	6.7	6.6	7.1	6.9	27.0	26.0	10.9	1.9	75.7	36.9	49.2	50.8

#	POST OFFICE NAME	2009 Per Capita Income	2009 HH Income Base	2009 Household Income Distribution (%): Less than $25,000	$25,000 to $49,999	$50,000 to $99,999	$100,000 to $149,999	$150,000 or More	Median Household Income: 2009	2014	2009 National Centile	2009 State Centile	2009 Home Value Base	2009 Home Value Distribution (%): Less than $50,000	$50,000 to $89,999	$90,000 to $174,999	$175,000 to $399,999	$400,000 or More	2009 Median Home Value
71018	COTTON VALLEY	17008	801	42.8	28.2	23.3	4.5	1.1	29255	29719	7	29	608	42.9	25.2	23.4	7.6	1.0	60250
71019	COUSHATTA	13620	3429	46.8	29.1	20.0	2.8	1.3	26755	27340	4	16	2585	37.1	26.0	29.4	6.2	1.4	67139
71023	DOYLINE	19061	1453	30.5	36.1	27.9	4.1	1.3	36235	36322	21	61	1211	29.6	22.0	29.7	14.8	3.9	87622
71024	DUBBERLY	17406	548	33.8	36.1	24.1	4.7	1.3	33428	33946	14	51	462	31.6	22.1	32.3	9.7	4.3	82917
71027	FRIERSON	17946	644	27.8	32.8	34.5	3.4	1.6	41298	39705	37	76	545	24.6	24.2	30.5	19.1	1.7	92600
71028	GIBSLAND	16037	817	47.5	29.0	18.8	3.2	1.5	26226	26881	4	14	625	49.0	23.7	19.8	5.3	2.2	51548
71029	GILLIAM	16014	85	41.2	34.1	17.6	3.5	3.5	29026	29743	7	28	69	47.8	23.2	20.3	8.7	0.0	53000
71030	GLOSTER	19991	469	27.7	29.4	32.8	7.7	2.3	42706	41512	42	78	387	24.5	16.0	37.0	17.3	5.2	110750
71031	GOLDONNA	15651	417	38.4	35.7	20.1	5.0	0.7	30243	29417	8	35	348	46.6	23.3	23.0	7.2	0.0	56000
71032	GRAND CANE	16934	718	41.1	25.2	28.4	4.5	0.8	31379	32221	10	42	600	29.3	20.8	30.7	15.2	4.0	89773
71033	GREENWOOD	20595	1257	31.5	27.8	29.4	8.0	3.2	43079	42031	43	80	963	22.2	18.9	29.5	26.4	3.0	114698
71034	HALL SUMMIT	14357	96	39.6	36.5	21.9	2.1	0.0	30000	29585	8	34	77	31.2	22.1	42.9	3.9	0.0	81667
71037	HAUGHTON	20195	7337	21.4	29.5	40.7	6.3	2.1	49011	50697	59	90	6058	23.6	15.2	42.9	17.4	0.9	120078
71038	HAYNESVILLE	14613	1883	45.4	29.7	20.2	2.9	1.8	28079	28657	6	22	1374	41.5	21.8	23.4	12.2	1.1	62051
71039	HEFLIN	15573	831	37.2	32.6	27.4	1.9	0.8	31464	31175	10	43	668	33.2	23.5	27.8	10.0	5.4	81818
71040	HOMER	16817	3064	43.2	30.8	20.0	4.2	1.7	29564	29769	7	31	2263	32.0	22.7	30.1	13.3	1.9	80139
71043	HOSSTON	15286	223	44.8	29.6	19.3	3.6	2.7	27508	27866	5	20	187	46.5	24.1	20.3	8.0	1.1	53421
71044	IDA	14266	378	50.5	28.3	18.8	1.6	0.8	24604	25876	3	10	323	48.6	27.6	18.3	3.4	2.2	50714
71045	JAMESTOWN	14004	351	45.0	31.3	20.8	1.7	1.1	27808	28242	5	21	294	44.2	22.4	19.4	11.2	2.7	58947
71046	KEATCHIE	18532	636	38.1	24.7	30.7	5.0	1.6	34483	35349	16	56	547	25.4	19.9	29.6	20.8	4.2	103831
71047	KEITHVILLE	20041	4418	27.8	25.4	35.4	9.0	2.4	46662	44181	53	87	3713	27.1	21.8	29.4	20.3	1.5	92249
71048	LISBON	18018	41	48.8	22.0	26.8	2.4	0.0	25723	26657	4	13	34	44.1	26.5	20.6	8.8	0.0	60000
71049	LOGANSPORT	14532	1545	45.2	27.7	23.6	2.9	0.5	28366	29899	6	24	1194	29.5	28.7	26.3	13.7	1.8	78235
71051	ELM GROVE	19252	887	32.4	24.6	36.8	4.4	1.9	40787	40074	35	76	741	29.8	20.1	25.9	17.0	7.2	90238
71052	MANSFIELD	13933	4329	49.0	26.1	20.9	3.0	0.9	25655	27094	4	13	2901	31.8	31.6	27.7	8.7	0.2	72045
71055	MINDEN	17285	7803	41.2	29.7	22.0	5.0	2.1	30650	30927	9	37	5443	27.5	26.9	30.1	14.1	1.5	82373
71060	MOORINGSPORT	18597	1164	29.3	29.3	34.8	5.8	0.9	41830	41874	39	77	949	28.1	27.8	30.9	11.6	1.6	79694
71061	OIL CITY	15097	781	47.9	31.0	17.5	1.5	2.0	26307	27298	4	15	525	39.6	28.0	19.6	8.0	4.8	60469
71063	PELICAN	11318	340	54.1	28.5	16.5	0.9	0.0	22941	24118	2	7	267	25.8	32.2	37.1	4.9	0.0	82037
71064	PLAIN DEALING	14427	1752	46.9	28.2	21.6	2.5	0.9	27355	27047	5	19	1379	32.7	28.1	29.6	7.7	1.9	74455
71065	PLEASANT HILL	15911	528	45.6	27.1	21.0	4.4	1.9	29349	30283	7	29	387	37.7	30.7	26.6	3.9	1.0	63036
71067	PRINCETON	17889	1147	28.5	27.8	39.4	3.3	1.0	43809	44926	45	81	921	30.7	23.0	36.9	9.2	0.1	83727
71068	RINGGOLD	13980	1440	50.0	28.3	18.7	2.4	0.6	25000	26213	3	11	1102	38.7	27.3	22.6	9.9	1.5	65568
71069	RODESSA	13993	299	47.5	33.4	16.4	2.3	0.3	26603	28226	4	15	256	49.6	25.0	21.9	2.7	0.8	50256
71070	SALINE	15776	701	45.6	28.2	21.4	3.0	1.7	28217	28826	6	23	591	47.5	20.8	24.2	6.6	0.8	54028
71071	SAREPTA	15473	1303	38.4	33.1	23.9	3.2	1.3	31977	32649	11	46	1033	29.8	27.0	33.4	9.2	0.6	75635
71072	SHONGALOO	17601	635	26.8	40.8	27.2	4.9	0.3	37101	36970	24	65	553	40.3	25.7	28.8	4.5	0.7	64630
71073	SIBLEY	16819	964	35.7	32.8	26.7	3.4	1.5	33882	33903	15	54	758	35.4	17.4	32.3	8.3	6.6	82222
71075	SPRINGHILL	17346	2888	44.4	32.4	18.8	2.3	2.1	28106	28617	6	22	2018	30.4	34.3	26.5	8.3	0.4	71548
71078	STONEWALL	18449	1624	28.3	30.2	34.1	6.0	1.5	42477	40531	41	78	1369	21.5	18.3	36.6	21.6	2.0	113432
71079	SUMMERFIELD	13078	113	46.9	22.1	26.5	3.5	0.9	26990	26549	5	17	94	39.4	27.7	20.2	11.7	1.1	67500
71082	VIVIAN	15939	2141	41.9	30.0	24.0	2.4	1.7	29106	28819	7	28	1579	36.5	34.3	22.7	5.1	1.5	58340
71101	SHREVEPORT	11638	3711	63.1	25.3	10.3	0.6	0.7	16713	17744	1	2	1100	38.7	44.9	10.8	4.1	1.5	58435
71103	SHREVEPORT	12130	3463	61.3	23.7	12.4	1.2	1.4	17993	19278	1	3	1633	48.1	38.6	9.6	2.6	1.0	51292
71104	SHREVEPORT	20497	6464	36.1	34.1	22.8	4.8	2.2	33571	35380	15	52	3247	9.5	30.9	45.7	11.5	2.4	103047
71105	SHREVEPORT	27915	9728	20.7	32.5	34.9	8.3	3.6	47124	44022	54	88	5762	1.3	7.0	65.4	25.7	0.6	139976
71106	SHREVEPORT	28214	12656	34.6	21.6	22.0	10.1	11.7	40682	41573	35	75	8654	15.3	19.5	20.5	29.8	14.9	144534
71107	SHREVEPORT	16264	11543	39.5	26.8	26.1	5.9	1.7	34485	36373	16	56	8161	23.9	23.7	35.5	14.4	2.5	95407
71108	SHREVEPORT	12466	7414	44.7	34.0	18.9	1.5	0.9	27704	28225	5	21	4665	28.9	47.1	22.5	1.5	0.1	64245
71109	SHREVEPORT	12286	8975	51.6	29.3	15.9	2.3	0.9	23821	25568	3	9	4878	39.5	36.3	20.7	2.9	0.6	58156
71110	BARKSDALE AFB	14537	742	11.9	36.7	43.1	8.4	0.0	50765	51352	63	93	7	0.0	0.0	100.0	0.0	0.0	137500
71111	BOSSIER CITY	22600	14128	29.7	26.7	29.9	8.9	4.8	42634	44839	41	78	8190	8.6	16.7	32.1	35.7	6.9	151289
71112	BOSSIER CITY	21025	12010	22.9	29.6	39.5	6.3	1.7	47607	49766	56	89	8290	9.3	18.2	55.9	15.9	0.7	119849
71115	SHREVEPORT	30345	5300	23.2	32.0	29.4	9.4	5.9	45415	43147	49	85	2839	1.3	7.0	51.8	35.4	4.5	154937
71118	SHREVEPORT	21254	9665	24.2	32.8	34.6	7.1	1.3	44573	42965	47	84	6345	2.2	14.6	67.9	14.8	0.5	124046
71119	SHREVEPORT	24169	4468	19.1	29.8	39.2	8.5	3.4	50816	48264	63	93	3520	13.0	16.6	44.5	22.6	3.3	123002
71129	SHREVEPORT	20558	5263	30.7	30.0	29.4	8.3	1.6	40055	40506	33	73	3145	23.9	16.8	40.7	17.2	1.4	111012
71201	MONROE	27413	9453	34.4	25.8	25.4	7.8	6.6	38902	39957	29	70	4993	6.4	10.3	39.2	32.3	11.8	155706
71202	MONROE	11195	9367	50.9	28.3	17.6	2.4	0.8	24313	25683	3	9	5151	33.7	39.4	22.6	4.0	0.3	63223
71203	MONROE	19079	13568	33.8	28.6	28.9	6.3	2.4	37828	39148	26	67	8196	15.7	17.9	46.9	16.6	2.9	113354
71209	MONROE	9110	7	57.1	42.9	0.0	0.0	0.0	22183	22183	2	6	0	0.0	0.0	0.0	0.0	0.0	0
71219	BASKIN	15059	456	46.3	26.1	22.4	3.5	1.8	27293	27689	5	19	389	35.5	31.1	24.4	8.2	0.8	66705
71220	BASTROP	15360	9315	44.2	27.3	23.4	3.7	1.5	28949	29041	7	27	6516	34.3	27.9	26.9	9.9	0.9	69558
71222	BERNICE	15079	1562	43.0	32.7	19.7	3.5	1.3	28936	30125	7	27	1214	31.6	26.6	30.6	9.3	1.8	80741
71223	BONITA	13707	249	59.8	29.3	7.6	0.8	2.4	19425	21816	1	4	183	57.4	20.8	16.4	4.9	0.5	39375
71225	CALHOUN	20048	2131	26.3	32.4	29.8	8.6	2.9	42974	42071	42	79	1804	23.7	11.5	35.4	23.7	5.8	125781
71226	CHATHAM	16721	721	41.6	30.2	20.8	6.0	1.4	29678	29649	8	31	589	38.5	22.6	28.0	7.8	3.1	65833
71227	CHOUDRANT	19099	1364	27.0	32.8	33.4	5.2	1.5	41949	40824	39	77	1136	30.1	18.7	31.1	17.1	3.1	92800
71229	COLLINSTON	14671	461	39.3	29.7	24.5	4.3	2.2	31119	30100	10	40	372	44.9	23.7	24.5	6.2	0.8	58261
71232	DELHI	14708	2336	45.9	29.0	20.2	3.7	1.2	27609	28128	5	21	1675	35.5	27.6	25.1	11.8	0.0	68197
71234	DOWNSVILLE	17254	1663	30.7	37.0	27.1	4.7	0.5	35156	36276	18	58	1444	30.5	20.8	31.7	14.0	2.9	88113
71235	DUBACH	18961	1623	34.7	27.9	29.4	6.1	1.9	36153	36980	21	61	1338	25.3	20.7	31.1	19.7	3.3	99643
71237	EPPS	12250	298	46.6	31.9	18.5	2.3	0.7	26714	27478	4	16	228	43.4	31.1	20.6	4.8	0.0	57895
71238	EROS	18193	954	33.3	31.6	26.1	7.1	1.9	36799	38115	23	64	835	28.1	22.0	30.4	16.3	3.1	89717
71241	FARMERVILLE	17400	3767	37.0	31.2	25.9	4.6	1.2	32775	34656	13	49	2942	26.8	24.1	33.2	13.0	2.9	88531
71243	FORT NECESSITY	15126	93	46.2	34.4	14.0	3.2	2.2	26235	26539	4	15	76	43.4	23.7	18.4	13.2	1.3	55000
71245	GRAMBLING	14875	1156	52.9	27.1	15.2	3.4	1.5	22902	25181	2	7	504	7.3	26.2	45.4	19.2	1.8	112000
71250	JONES	13873	116	56.9	30.2	9.5	0.9	2.6	20847	22757	2	5	86	53.5	23.3	18.6	4.7	0.0	44000
71251	JONESBORO	16765	3791	40.5	27.8	26.1	4.4	1.3	31547	31574	11	44	2773	28.7	30.4	30.0	9.3	1.6	75076
71254	LAKE PROVIDENCE	11040	2263	56.3	29.4	11.6	1.6	1.1	20582	22095	2	4	1335	49.0	27.0	20.4	2.8	0.7	51205
71256	LILLIE	15134	223	43.9	21.5	30.5	3.6	0.4	29426	30322	7	30	183	39.9	27.9	22.4	7.7	2.2	61250
71259	MANGHAM	17486	739	39.5	30.7	23.0	4.3	2.4	31587	31544	11	45	596	30.9	34.6	24.5	10.1	0.0	70208
71260	MARION	15855	1393	42.3	31.3	20.8	4.6	1.0	30023	30928	8	34	1130	37.7	23.3	26.3	9.7	3.0	68889
71261	MER ROUGE	15371	623	49.8	24.1	21.2	3.0	1.9	25149	26245	3	11	444	46.4	25.9	19.8	6.5	1.4	55333
71263	OAK GROVE	15154	3233	45.4	29.1	21.0	3.2	1.3	27765	28113	5	21	2535	39.5	25.5	25.4	7.4	2.2	63785
71264	OAK RIDGE	16283	357	52.7	23.0	16.2	4.8	3.4	23146	25156	2	7	275	29.5	19.3	32.4	17.5	1.5	91522
71266	PIONEER	13311	726	50.0	31.0	16.1	2.1	0.8	25000	25831	3	11	583	46.5	28.1	22.0	3.4	0.0	54271
71268	QUITMAN	17099	1094	34.9	33.1	24.5	5.8	1.7	35000	35558	18	58	891	33.1	21.1	31.5	12.0	2.2	79884
71269	RAYVILLE	14114	4494	49.3	25.6	20.2	3.2	1.7	25416	26363	4	12	3151	29.0	27.9	28.2	14.1	0.7	78630
71270	RUSTON	17342	11147	45.9	23.7	23.4	4.5	2.5	28218	28976	6	23	5982	17.9	16.9	39.8	21.4	4.1	115525
71275	SIMSBORO	15701	904	32.9	34.2	27.2	5.3	0.4	36491	37079	22	62	702	29.2	28.2	30.8	10.7	1.1	77568
71276	SONDHEIMER	16719	207	31.4	40.1	22.7	5.8	0.0	34277	34780	16	55	155	46.5	32.3	18.1	0.6	2.6	61250
71277	SPEARSVILLE	16354	759	35.7	32.0	26.6	3.7	2.0	33717	35080	15	53	650	32.8	24.6	30.8	9.7	2.2	78400
71280	STERLINGTON	22321	1088	29.5	26.5	30.4	8.7	4.9	43576	42551	44	81	870	21.4	25.1	35.7	13.7	4.1	97045
71282	TALLULAH	11914	4112	52.4	30.1	14.5	2.2	0.8	23330	24967	2	8	2505	40.1	30.3	22.8	5.9	1.0	61698
	LOUISIANA	19176		34.0	28.2	28.2	6.6	3.0	37868	38644				16.9	18.7	37.2	22.8	4.3	118738
	UNITED STATES	27277		20.9	24.4	35.3	11.7	7.6	54719	56938				9.3	13.1	31.6	32.6	13.5	162279

ZIP CODE		FINANCIAL SERVICES				THE HOME						ENTERTAINMENT						PERSONAL			
						Home Improvements		Furnishings													
#	POST OFFICE NAME	Auto Loan	Home Loan	Invest-ments	Retire-ment Plans	Home Repair	Lawn & Garden	Comput-ers & Hard-ware-Personal	Major Appli-ances	TV, Radio, Sound Equip-ment	Furni-ture	Dine out/ Carry out	Sports Equip-ment	Fees & Tickets	Toys & Games	Travel	Cable TV	Apparel & Services	Auto Repairs	Health Insur-ance	Pets & Supplies
71018	COTTON VALLEY	74	50	71	47	50	73	53	66	60	50	59	51	40	61	49	67	39	62	69	80
71019	COUSHATTA	66	45	60	44	45	63	49	58	56	47	55	45	39	57	45	61	37	56	62	71
71023	DOYLINE	85	60	86	57	61	86	62	78	69	58	68	59	49	69	60	77	45	72	82	94
71024	DUBBERLY	76	54	78	52	56	77	56	71	62	52	61	53	44	62	55	68	40	65	74	85
71027	FRIERSON	82	59	69	57	59	78	61	72	68	60	67	55	49	71	56	74	45	68	76	87
71028	GIBSLAND	69	45	67	43	45	68	48	61	56	46	54	48	36	57	45	62	36	57	64	75
71029	GILLIAM	78	51	75	48	50	76	54	68	62	51	61	53	41	63	50	70	40	64	72	84
71030	GLOSTER	88	78	75	76	77	84	75	81	78	77	78	59	69	81	71	81	53	78	82	96
71031	GOLDONNA	73	49	72	47	50	72	52	65	59	49	58	50	40	59	49	65	38	61	69	80
71032	GRAND CANE	73	52	75	50	54	74	54	68	60	50	59	51	43	60	53	66	39	63	71	81
71033	GREENWOOD	84	76	69	74	75	79	72	77	75	75	75	56	68	78	69	78	51	75	78	92
71034	HALL SUMMIT	67	48	68	46	49	68	49	62	54	45	53	47	39	54	48	60	35	57	65	74
71037	HAUGHTON	85	82	72	79	79	80	77	80	78	81	79	60	75	81	75	79	54	78	78	94
71038	HAYNESVILLE	69	49	68	47	49	70	51	63	58	48	56	48	41	58	49	64	38	59	67	76
71039	HEFLIN	74	49	73	47	50	73	52	66	60	49	58	51	40	60	50	66	39	62	70	81
71040	HOMER	66	51	65	49	52	68	53	62	60	53	58	45	46	58	52	65	39	60	69	75
71043	HOSSTON	73	48	70	45	47	72	51	64	59	48	57	50	38	60	48	66	38	60	68	79
71044	IDA	63	41	60	39	41	61	44	55	50	42	49	43	33	51	41	56	33	52	58	68
71045	JAMESTOWN	64	43	63	41	44	63	45	57	52	43	50	44	35	52	44	57	33	53	60	70
71046	KEATCHIE	77	60	75	58	61	77	60	72	65	58	64	54	51	65	58	70	43	67	74	86
71047	KEITHVILLE	90	80	75	77	78	85	77	82	80	79	80	61	71	84	73	83	55	80	83	99
71048	LISBON	67	44	65	41	44	66	47	59	54	44	53	46	35	55	44	60	35	55	62	72
71049	LOGANSPORT	66	46	66	44	47	66	48	61	54	45	53	46	37	54	46	60	35	56	63	73
71051	ELM GROVE	82	67	76	65	67	80	66	76	71	66	70	57	58	72	64	75	47	72	78	91
71052	MANSFIELD	58	42	50	42	41	56	48	53	54	45	52	39	40	53	44	59	35	53	59	64
71055	MINDEN	65	55	56	55	54	64	58	61	63	57	61	45	54	62	55	66	42	61	67	73
71060	MOORINGSPORT	78	66	69	64	65	76	65	73	69	64	68	54	58	71	62	73	46	70	75	86
71061	OIL CITY	68	44	65	42	44	66	47	59	54	45	53	46	35	55	44	61	35	56	63	73
71063	PELICAN	55	36	53	34	35	54	38	48	44	36	43	37	29	45	36	49	28	45	51	59
71064	PLAIN DEALING	66	44	64	41	44	65	46	58	53	44	52	45	35	54	44	59	34	55	62	71
71065	PLEASANT HILL	74	49	72	46	49	73	52	66	60	49	58	51	39	61	49	67	39	62	69	80
71067	PRINCETON	80	65	70	62	63	76	65	72	69	65	69	55	57	72	61	73	47	70	74	87
71068	RINGGOLD	58	40	54	39	40	57	43	52	49	42	48	39	35	49	40	54	32	50	56	63
71069	RODESSA	63	42	61	39	42	62	44	56	51	42	49	43	33	51	42	56	33	52	59	68
71070	SALINE	70	47	69	44	47	69	50	63	57	47	55	48	38	57	47	63	37	59	66	76
71071	SAREPTA	69	50	60	49	50	67	53	62	59	51	58	46	43	60	49	64	39	59	66	75
71072	SHONGALOO	78	56	80	54	58	80	58	73	64	54	63	55	46	64	57	70	41	67	76	87
71073	SIBLEY	80	56	81	53	57	80	58	73	65	54	64	56	45	65	56	72	42	68	77	88
71075	SPRINGHILL	64	50	58	49	50	65	54	61	60	51	58	45	47	59	51	65	39	60	68	73
71078	STONEWALL	81	69	67	67	67	77	67	73	71	68	71	54	60	74	63	75	48	70	75	88
71079	SUMMERFIELD	68	44	65	41	44	66	47	59	54	45	53	46	35	55	44	61	35	56	63	73
71082	VIVIAN	67	48	65	47	49	67	53	63	59	49	58	47	43	59	50	65	39	60	68	75
71101	SHREVEPORT	36	27	26	29	26	31	36	32	40	34	39	24	33	38	31	42	27	36	38	40
71103	SHREVEPORT	45	36	34	36	34	43	41	40	47	42	45	29	38	45	37	50	31	44	49	50
71104	SHREVEPORT	64	57	52	59	55	59	66	59	67	63	66	47	62	66	60	68	46	64	64	73
71105	SHREVEPORT	84	76	74	78	76	81	84	80	86	82	86	61	81	85	80	87	59	84	87	96
71106	SHREVEPORT	106	107	105	111	107	111	106	106	110	110	109	79	111	108	107	112	77	107	112	126
71107	SHREVEPORT	67	58	55	58	57	64	61	62	66	61	65	46	58	66	57	69	44	63	68	75
71108	SHREVEPORT	52	44	37	45	41	48	49	46	53	48	52	35	46	53	44	55	36	49	53	58
71109	SHREVEPORT	49	40	37	41	38	46	45	44	51	45	49	32	42	49	41	54	34	47	52	55
71110	BARKSDALE AFB	95	49	37	57	44	42	89	62	84	83	89	62	68	101	65	77	62	79	56	75
71111	BOSSIER CITY	82	79	73	81	77	77	82	78	82	83	82	61	81	83	79	82	58	80	79	93
71112	BOSSIER CITY	79	74	66	73	70	76	75	75	77	74	76	57	72	78	71	78	53	75	78	89
71115	SHREVEPORT	89	79	77	83	78	80	92	82	90	88	91	66	86	91	84	90	63	88	85	99
71118	SHREVEPORT	73	72	66	73	70	72	73	71	74	73	74	54	73	75	72	75	52	73	75	84
71119	SHREVEPORT	86	91	83	90	88	93	84	87	85	84	86	66	87	87	86	88	59	86	91	103
71129	SHREVEPORT	75	63	57	63	60	63	71	66	72	71	73	52	65	74	65	72	50	71	67	80
71201	MONROE	85	77	77	80	77	81	88	81	89	85	89	63	84	87	83	90	62	86	88	98
71202	MONROE	51	41	37	42	38	46	46	44	51	46	50	33	43	51	41	54	34	48	51	56
71203	MONROE	73	63	58	64	61	65	70	66	71	69	71	51	64	72	64	72	49	69	69	80
71209	MONROE	33	21	21	23	21	23	39	27	35	31	35	24	29	35	28	34	25	33	28	34
71219	BASKIN	74	48	72	46	48	73	52	65	60	49	58	51	39	61	48	67	39	62	69	80
71220	BASTROP	65	49	57	49	49	64	53	60	59	51	58	45	45	59	50	64	39	59	65	72
71222	BERNICE	68	46	67	44	47	67	48	61	55	46	54	47	37	56	46	61	36	57	64	74
71223	BONITA	65	43	62	40	42	64	45	57	52	43	51	45	34	53	42	58	34	54	60	70
71225	CALHOUN	87	80	71	78	78	82	76	80	78	79	78	58	72	82	72	81	53	78	80	95
71226	CHATHAM	71	51	67	50	51	71	53	65	60	50	58	50	43	61	51	65	39	61	68	79
71227	CHOUDRANT	82	67	70	65	66	79	66	74	71	66	70	56	58	73	62	75	47	71	76	89
71229	COLLINSTON	75	54	70	52	54	74	56	68	62	53	61	52	45	64	53	68	41	64	71	82
71232	DELHI	66	46	63	45	46	66	49	60	56	46	54	46	39	56	47	61	36	57	64	73
71234	DOWNSVILLE	76	57	68	55	57	74	58	68	63	56	62	51	48	65	54	68	42	64	71	82
71235	DUBACH	81	64	76	62	64	80	64	75	69	62	68	57	55	70	62	74	46	71	77	90
71237	EPPS	66	44	64	42	44	65	46	59	53	44	52	45	35	54	44	59	34	55	62	71
71238	EROS	82	66	72	63	65	79	65	74	71	66	70	56	57	73	62	75	47	71	76	89
71241	FARMERVILLE	76	54	69	52	54	74	57	68	64	54	62	52	46	64	54	69	42	65	72	82
71243	FORT NECESSITY	67	48	69	47	50	68	49	63	55	46	54	47	39	54	49	60	35	58	65	75
71245	GRAMBLING	50	39	41	40	39	45	53	47	54	47	53	37	45	52	45	56	37	51	53	57
71250	JONES	67	44	63	42	44	65	47	59	54	45	53	46	36	55	44	60	35	55	62	72
71251	JONESBORO	67	51	63	51	52	69	54	63	60	51	58	47	46	59	52	65	39	60	69	76
71254	LAKE PROVIDENCE	49	35	41	35	35	47	40	44	46	40	45	32	35	45	37	51	30	45	51	54
71256	LILLIE	75	49	72	46	48	73	52	66	60	49	59	51	39	61	49	67	39	62	69	81
71259	MANGHAM	80	55	80	52	56	80	57	73	65	54	64	56	45	65	55	72	42	68	76	88
71260	MARION	73	49	71	47	50	72	52	65	59	49	58	50	40	60	49	65	38	61	69	79
71261	MER ROUGE	73	48	70	45	48	72	51	64	59	49	57	50	38	60	48	66	38	60	68	79
71263	OAK GROVE	68	48	69	47	50	69	50	64	56	47	55	48	40	56	49	62	36	58	67	76
71264	OAK RIDGE	75	51	75	49	52	75	54	68	61	51	60	52	41	62	51	68	40	63	71	82
71266	PIONEER	60	41	60	39	42	60	43	55	49	41	48	42	33	49	42	54	32	51	57	66
71268	QUITMAN	80	57	77	55	58	79	59	72	66	57	65	55	47	67	56	72	43	68	75	87
71269	RAYVILLE	64	45	58	44	45	62	49	58	56	47	54	43	40	55	46	61	36	56	63	70
71270	RUSTON	62	50	47	52	48	53	65	55	64	59	64	45	56	64	54	65	44	61	59	68
71275	SIMSBORO	70	59	61	56	58	65	59	64	62	60	61	48	53	63	56	64	42	62	64	76
71276	SONDHEIMER	75	50	76	48	51	76	54	68	60	48	59	54	40	60	52	66	39	64	72	83
71277	SPEARSVILLE	78	55	67	54	55	75	58	68	64	56	63	52	46	66	53	70	42	64	72	83
71280	STERLINGTON	90	82	83	82	80	94	80	87	84	78	83	67	76	85	79	88	57	84	92	104
71282	TALLULAH	52	37	45	37	37	50	43	47	49	41	47	35	36	48	39	53	32	48	53	58
	LOUISIANA	78	67	68	67	66	75	70	72	73	70	73	55	65	74	67	76	50	73	76	87
	UNITED STATES	100	100	100	100	100	100	100	100	100	100	100	100	100	100	100	100	100	100	100	100

ZIP CODE #	POST OFFICE NAME	COUNTY FIPS CODE	POPULATION 2000	POPULATION 2009	POPULATION 2014	2000-2009 ANNUAL RATE % Rate	2000-2009 ANNUAL RATE State Centile	HOUSEHOLDS 2000	HOUSEHOLDS 2009	HOUSEHOLDS 2014	HOUSEHOLDS % Annual Rate 2000-2009	HOUSEHOLDS 2009 Average HH Size	FAMILIES 2000	FAMILIES 2009	FAMILIES % Annual Rate 2000-2009
71286	TRANSYLVANIA	035	989	846	796	-1.7	6	293	241	223	-2.1	2.52	223	181	-2.2
71291	WEST MONROE	073	31205	32602	33101	0.5	66	12388	13010	13247	0.5	2.47	8636	8922	0.4
71292	WEST MONROE	073	20133	20825	21072	0.4	61	7549	7860	7983	0.4	2.65	5703	5860	0.3
71295	WINNSBORO	041	14532	13894	13564	-0.5	21	5248	5113	5024	-0.3	2.59	3849	3703	-0.4
71301	ALEXANDRIA	079	24047	23803	23656	-0.1	35	9243	9198	9173	-0.1	2.49	5841	5665	-0.3
71302	ALEXANDRIA	079	14702	14566	14509	-0.1	35	5579	5668	5693	0.2	2.54	3889	3872	0.0
71303	ALEXANDRIA	079	19053	20037	20374	0.5	66	7076	7648	7852	0.8	2.46	4954	5241	0.6
71316	ACME	029	49	51	51	0.4	61	21	22	22	0.5	2.32	16	17	0.7
71322	BUNKIE	009	7603	7892	7888	0.4	61	2691	2831	2848	0.5	2.72	1970	2040	0.4
71323	CENTER POINT	009	903	1007	1040	1.2	84	309	356	372	1.5	2.65	244	278	1.4
71325	CHENEYVILLE	079	1405	1460	1481	0.4	61	467	505	518	0.8	2.54	337	356	0.6
71326	CLAYTON	107	1907	1830	1779	-0.4	24	709	696	681	-0.2	2.63	484	468	-0.4
71327	COTTONPORT	009	5486	5636	5644	0.3	53	1409	1510	1525	0.8	2.55	1012	1068	0.6
71328	DEVILLE	079	6904	8060	8546	1.7	90	2470	2947	3150	1.9	2.73	2029	2390	1.8
71331	EFFIE	009	825	858	866	0.4	61	326	347	353	0.7	2.47	252	265	0.5
71333	EVERGREEN	009	852	866	854	0.2	49	365	382	379	0.5	2.03	247	254	0.3
71334	FERRIDAY	029	8981	8655	8422	-0.4	24	3420	3384	3323	-0.1	2.48	2372	2307	-0.3
71336	GILBERT	041	1983	1888	1836	-0.5	21	756	737	723	-0.3	2.52	561	538	-0.5
71340	HARRISONBURG	025	1906	1845	1816	-0.4	24	595	587	582	-0.1	2.48	439	427	-0.3
71341	HESSMER	009	3046	3221	3256	0.6	71	1142	1236	1260	0.9	2.55	838	894	0.7
71342	JENA	059	6718	6820	6862	0.2	49	2585	2664	2694	0.3	2.47	1805	1829	0.1
71343	JONESVILLE	025	7909	7794	7695	-0.2	29	3019	3063	3055	0.2	2.43	2250	2256	0.0
71346	LECOMPTE	079	2848	3058	3140	0.8	77	1040	1141	1180	1.0	2.66	726	781	0.8
71350	MANSURA	009	4305	4261	4181	-0.1	35	1619	1641	1621	0.1	2.49	1157	1153	0.0
71351	MARKSVILLE	009	11174	11287	11159	0.1	44	4173	4311	4293	0.4	2.55	2957	3008	0.2
71353	MELVILLE	097	1860	1848	1845	-0.1	35	724	729	733	0.1	2.53	507	501	-0.1
71354	MONTEREY	029	1766	1797	1774	0.2	49	687	716	712	0.4	2.41	524	539	0.3
71355	MOREAUVILLE	009	2779	2794	2746	0.1	44	1118	1148	1137	0.3	2.42	780	788	0.1
71356	MORROW	097	246	258	263	0.5	66	103	110	113	0.7	2.35	70	73	0.5
71357	NEWELLTON	107	3316	3084	2967	-0.8	12	1121	1060	1022	-0.6	2.47	795	740	-0.8
71358	PALMETTO	097	1027	1058	1072	0.3	53	392	409	418	0.5	2.48	288	295	0.3
71360	PINEVILLE	079	33253	35203	36012	0.6	71	12144	13140	13540	0.9	2.51	8564	9143	0.7
71362	PLAUCHEVILLE	009	1960	2108	2154	0.8	77	730	806	831	1.1	2.54	522	567	0.9
71366	SAINT JOSEPH	107	1831	1703	1637	-0.8	12	683	654	634	-0.5	2.57	466	438	-0.7
71367	SAINT LANDRY	039	1280	1379	1415	0.8	77	475	522	539	1.0	2.64	349	376	0.8
71368	SICILY ISLAND	025	1445	1469	1466	0.2	49	582	606	609	0.4	2.42	417	427	0.3
71369	SIMMESPORT	009	3142	3159	3091	0.1	44	1073	1106	1087	0.3	2.59	765	775	0.1
71371	TROUT	059	2791	2791	2792	0.0	38	1023	1037	1043	0.1	2.46	754	754	0.0
71373	VIDALIA	029	7566	7165	6930	-0.6	17	2710	2602	2530	-0.4	2.70	2008	1900	-0.6
71375	WATERPROOF	107	950	873	833	-0.9	10	399	378	365	-0.6	2.31	236	218	-0.9
71378	WISNER	041	2586	2455	2395	-0.6	17	950	923	906	-0.3	2.54	682	651	-0.5
71401	AIMWELL	025	130	121	118	-0.8	12	49	47	46	-0.4	2.57	38	36	-0.6
71403	ANACOCO	115	4243	4319	4275	0.2	49	1660	1726	1720	0.4	2.50	1248	1281	0.3
71404	ATLANTA	127	2242	2108	2060	-0.7	14	300	292	283	-0.3	3.61	221	212	-0.4
71405	BALL	079	5194	5591	5771	0.8	77	2024	2250	2350	1.2	2.35	1477	1610	0.9
71406	BELMONT	085	292	284	279	-0.3	27	112	111	110	-0.1	2.54	82	80	-0.3
71407	BENTLEY	043	1139	1294	1351	1.4	87	411	477	503	1.6	2.71	329	377	1.5
71409	BOYCE	079	6174	6698	6919	0.9	80	2373	2645	2759	1.2	2.49	1752	1918	1.0
71411	CAMPTI	069	3137	3250	3294	0.4	61	1195	1259	1285	0.6	2.58	849	880	0.4
71416	CLOUTIERVILLE	069	1042	1105	1133	0.6	71	412	446	460	0.9	2.48	283	300	0.6
71417	COLFAX	043	4969	5138	5267	0.4	61	1848	1948	2012	0.6	2.57	1336	1387	0.4
71418	COLUMBIA	021	6700	6771	6694	0.1	44	2617	2704	2693	0.4	2.44	1831	1866	0.2
71419	CONVERSE	085	2066	2166	2190	0.5	66	827	878	892	0.6	2.46	606	633	0.5
71422	DODSON	127	1869	1792	1724	-0.5	21	707	688	665	-0.3	2.57	526	505	-0.4
71423	DRY PRONG	043	4280	4606	4791	0.8	77	1587	1739	1821	1.0	2.64	1230	1331	0.9
71424	ELMER	079	1380	1570	1672	1.4	87	503	590	635	1.7	2.62	391	451	1.6
71425	ENTERPRISE	025	110	103	101	-0.7	14	51	49	49	-0.4	2.10	39	38	-0.3
71426	FISHER	085	182	174	170	-0.5	21	70	68	67	-0.3	2.56	52	50	-0.4
71427	FLATWOODS	079	346	358	362	0.4	61	129	137	139	0.7	2.61	94	98	0.5
71429	FLORIEN	085	3341	3431	3439	0.3	53	1317	1384	1398	0.5	2.48	977	1010	0.4
71430	FOREST HILL	079	2360	2488	2541	0.6	71	851	910	933	0.7	2.73	645	677	0.5
71432	GEORGETOWN	043	1073	1244	1314	1.6	89	431	508	538	1.8	2.45	315	366	1.6
71433	GLENMORA	079	4259	4442	4525	0.5	66	1619	1728	1774	0.7	2.56	1193	1250	0.5
71435	GRAYSON	021	3661	3650	3602	0.0	38	1254	1281	1273	0.2	2.44	928	935	0.1
71438	HINESTON	115	1417	1508	1539	0.7	74	509	555	572	0.9	2.68	400	429	0.8
71439	HORNBECK	115	1738	1787	1780	0.3	53	671	701	703	0.5	2.55	496	512	0.3
71441	KELLY	021	649	656	648	0.1	44	246	255	254	0.4	2.56	192	196	0.2
71446	LEESVILLE	115	23508	21958	21149	-0.7	14	9250	8803	8532	-0.5	2.45	6349	5958	-0.7
71447	LENA	079	1280	1322	1340	0.3	53	496	524	535	0.6	2.52	356	369	0.4
71449	MANY	085	9138	9244	9227	0.1	44	3619	3735	3753	0.3	2.39	2543	2591	0.2
71450	MARTHAVILLE	069	1048	1047	1059	0.0	38	419	427	435	0.2	2.45	302	303	0.0
71454	MONTGOMERY	043	2495	2577	2637	0.4	61	1016	1073	1107	0.6	2.40	713	740	0.4
71455	MORA	069	279	287	291	0.3	53	102	107	109	0.5	2.68	74	76	0.3
71456	NATCHEZ	069	844	1025	1092	2.1	93	341	427	457	2.5	2.40	237	292	2.3
71457	NATCHITOCHES	069	27707	28150	28589	0.2	49	9773	10321	10568	0.6	2.52	6319	6553	0.4
71459	FORT POLK	115	14504	13208	12640	-1.0	9	3468	3128	2976	-1.1	3.26	3220	2896	-1.1
71461	NEWLLANO	115	2119	1897	1812	-1.2	7	829	751	721	-1.1	2.53	577	520	-1.1
71462	NOBLE	085	1527	1611	1631	0.6	71	591	637	649	0.8	2.48	421	446	0.6
71463	OAKDALE	003	11684	11314	11371	-0.3	27	3581	3696	3744	0.3	2.54	2577	2621	0.2
71465	OLLA	059	3135	3182	3197	0.2	49	1215	1253	1268	0.3	2.53	897	912	0.2
71466	OTIS	079	640	681	702	0.7	74	236	257	267	0.9	2.65	180	193	0.8
71467	POLLOCK	043	4536	6445	6660	3.9	99	1690	1883	1978	1.2	2.60	1289	1417	1.0
71468	PROVENCAL	069	499	519	531	0.4	61	209	221	228	0.6	2.35	146	152	0.4
71469	ROBELINE	069	3519	3674	3764	0.5	66	1386	1473	1516	0.7	2.49	1015	1064	0.5
71472	SIEPER	079	153	163	168	0.7	74	63	69	71	1.0	2.36	48	52	0.9
71473	SIKES	127	566	560	551	-0.1	35	233	233	230	0.0	2.40	170	168	-0.1
71479	TULLOS	127	2058	2072	2072	0.1	44	635	650	653	0.3	2.51	462	468	0.1
71483	WINNFIELD	127	10754	10049	9603	-0.7	14	4144	3936	3774	-0.6	2.41	2912	2723	-0.7
71485	WOODWORTH	079	1753	2232	2373	2.6	96	636	820	876	2.8	2.72	497	632	2.6
71486	ZWOLLE	085	4714	4834	4834	0.3	53	1836	1919	1932	0.5	2.51	1282	1316	0.3
	LOUISIANA					0.0					0.1	2.60			0.1
	UNITED STATES					1.0					1.1	2.59			0.9

ZIP CODE #	POST OFFICE NAME	RACE (%) White 2000	White 2009	Black 2000	Black 2009	Asian/Pacific 2000	Asian/Pacific 2009	% Hispanic Origin 2000	% Hispanic Origin 2009	2009 AGE DISTRIBUTION (%) 0-4	5-9	10-14	15-19	20-24	25-44	45-64	65-84	85+	18+	MEDIAN AGE 2009	% 2009 Males	% 2009 Females
71286	TRANSYLVANIA	57.1	50.5	42.0	48.3	0.1	0.1	1.6	1.8	6.0	6.0	5.6	6.0	10.2	34.3	20.8	9.9	1.2	79.3	33.8	64.4	35.6
71291	WEST MONROE	90.0	86.6	8.2	10.9	0.4	0.6	1.2	1.6	7.2	6.9	6.7	6.5	5.9	28.4	24.7	11.6	2.0	75.2	36.6	47.4	52.6
71292	WEST MONROE	88.3	84.6	10.1	13.3	0.3	0.5	1.5	1.9	7.0	7.1	6.9	6.6	5.8	27.7	26.6	11.2	1.1	75.0	36.9	49.0	51.0
71295	WINNSBORO	64.9	61.8	33.9	36.7	0.3	0.3	0.6	0.7	7.2	7.3	7.0	6.9	6.2	24.6	25.2	13.0	2.6	74.2	37.6	48.6	51.4
71301	ALEXANDRIA	45.7	39.0	51.2	57.1	1.4	1.9	1.2	1.4	7.3	7.6	7.2	7.5	6.5	25.0	24.6	11.5	2.8	73.3	36.0	46.1	53.9
71302	ALEXANDRIA	20.9	18.6	77.8	79.8	0.4	0.4	0.5	0.6	7.2	7.4	7.2	7.4	6.2	23.5	26.4	12.9	1.8	73.5	37.4	46.3	53.7
71303	ALEXANDRIA	69.5	63.0	27.4	32.9	1.4	2.1	1.3	1.6	7.4	6.8	6.9	7.3	6.5	25.1	24.7	13.0	2.4	74.2	37.4	47.0	53.0
71316	ACME	93.9	92.2	4.1	5.9	0.0	0.0	0.0	0.0	5.9	5.9	5.9	7.8	3.9	27.5	29.4	11.8	2.0	74.5	40.6	52.9	47.1
71322	BUNKIE	57.7	52.1	41.0	46.2	0.2	0.3	1.5	1.8	7.8	7.7	7.4	7.4	6.0	23.7	24.8	12.6	2.5	72.5	36.8	48.1	51.9
71323	CENTER POINT	96.5	95.4	2.2	2.8	0.0	0.0	0.4	0.6	5.9	5.9	6.2	5.8	3.8	26.6	28.7	14.3	3.0	78.3	42.3	48.4	51.6
71325	CHENEYVILLE	51.6	45.0	46.7	52.9	0.0	0.0	2.3	2.5	6.0	6.2	6.7	6.8	6.6	26.0	26.6	12.6	2.5	76.5	38.7	48.2	51.8
71326	CLAYTON	43.4	38.8	55.7	60.2	0.0	0.0	0.7	0.8	8.0	8.0	8.1	7.8	5.8	21.7	26.3	12.1	2.1	71.0	36.3	47.5	52.5
71327	COTTONPORT	50.9	47.4	47.9	51.0	0.1	0.1	0.6	0.8	5.7	5.5	5.3	5.9	9.1	37.0	22.1	8.1	1.3	80.1	34.2	60.7	39.3
71328	DEVILLE	97.3	96.2	0.5	0.7	0.2	0.3	0.7	0.9	7.3	7.3	7.3	6.9	5.9	28.0	27.0	9.5	0.9	73.7	36.4	49.4	50.6
71331	EFFIE	97.8	97.1	0.7	1.0	0.2	0.2	1.0	1.2	7.6	7.6	7.8	6.8	4.9	26.7	25.8	11.9	1.0	72.8	37.7	50.7	49.3
71333	EVERGREEN	71.7	67.1	26.6	30.8	0.5	0.7	1.4	1.6	4.6	4.7	5.0	6.5	6.6	29.8	28.5	12.6	1.7	81.6	40.0	55.8	44.2
71334	FERRIDAY	47.3	43.6	51.6	55.0	0.2	0.3	0.8	0.9	7.8	7.3	7.0	6.7	5.8	20.6	27.7	14.5	2.6	73.6	40.1	47.5	52.5
71336	GILBERT	77.9	73.6	20.7	24.5	0.0	0.0	1.2	1.5	6.5	6.3	6.4	6.8	6.5	23.9	27.4	14.4	1.9	76.5	40.6	48.9	51.1
71340	HARRISONBURG	75.1	70.8	23.5	27.2	0.6	0.8	0.5	0.7	4.8	5.1	5.0	6.7	9.8	30.7	25.9	10.7	1.3	81.6	36.3	60.2	39.8
71341	HESSMER	94.0	92.4	4.4	5.4	0.0	0.0	1.3	1.7	7.5	7.5	7.3	6.2	5.2	26.4	25.3	12.2	2.4	73.8	37.9	48.8	51.2
71342	JENA	84.1	82.1	14.1	15.6	0.3	0.4	0.9	1.0	6.4	6.6	6.8	7.5	5.2	23.0	27.3	14.7	2.5	75.3	40.7	47.3	52.7
71343	JONESVILLE	71.3	68.5	27.2	29.6	0.1	0.2	1.8	2.2	6.6	6.7	6.8	6.5	5.4	25.5	28.0	12.5	2.1	75.8	39.2	50.5	49.5
71346	LECOMPTE	54.3	49.0	43.7	48.4	0.2	0.3	2.0	2.4	7.3	7.5	7.3	7.1	5.3	24.2	27.1	12.1	2.0	73.3	38.0	47.4	52.6
71350	MANSURA	61.3	56.5	36.6	40.9	0.1	0.1	0.8	0.8	6.6	7.3	7.3	6.8	5.4	24.9	24.6	13.4	3.7	74.3	39.1	48.5	51.5
71351	MARKSVILLE	68.0	64.5	28.3	31.1	0.2	0.3	0.8	0.9	6.8	7.0	6.8	6.9	6.3	25.6	26.7	11.9	1.9	75.0	37.4	47.2	52.8
71353	MELVILLE	58.9	53.5	39.4	44.5	0.6	0.8	1.4	1.5	8.8	8.8	8.4	7.4	5.5	22.2	24.1	13.0	1.7	69.5	35.5	47.0	53.0
71354	MONTEREY	90.1	87.4	7.6	9.7	0.1	0.2	1.9	2.4	6.7	6.8	6.7	6.0	5.5	25.1	28.3	13.4	1.5	76.0	40.3	51.8	48.2
71355	MOREAUVILLE	79.8	76.3	18.5	21.5	0.1	0.2	1.1	1.3	6.8	7.0	7.2	6.9	5.3	23.6	28.1	13.2	2.1	75.0	39.4	48.9	51.1
71356	MORROW	72.2	66.3	26.1	31.4	0.4	0.4	1.2	1.2	7.0	7.0	7.0	7.0	5.4	22.5	26.7	14.7	2.7	74.4	40.6	47.3	52.7
71357	NEWELLTON	53.2	49.8	45.6	48.8	0.2	0.2	1.8	2.1	5.0	5.4	6.0	7.5	8.1	25.3	27.1	13.0	2.5	79.4	39.0	54.5	45.5
71358	PALMETTO	44.2	40.2	54.3	58.0	0.2	0.3	0.7	0.8	6.9	6.9	7.1	6.7	5.5	23.3	25.1	15.3	3.2	74.6	39.8	49.7	50.3
71360	PINEVILLE	82.5	78.0	14.1	17.6	1.1	1.4	1.2	1.6	6.7	6.6	6.6	7.1	6.4	26.6	26.8	11.7	1.6	76.1	37.7	48.8	51.2
71362	PLAUCHEVILLE	93.3	91.8	5.6	6.7	0.4	0.6	1.1	1.3	7.1	7.1	6.8	6.0	4.9	24.9	26.7	14.0	2.5	75.0	39.9	49.7	50.3
71366	SAINT JOSEPH	35.4	31.2	63.0	66.8	0.2	0.2	0.7	0.9	8.3	9.0	8.3	7.4	6.5	20.4	27.4	10.5	2.1	70.2	35.0	46.2	53.8
71367	SAINT LANDRY	91.4	89.0	6.7	8.6	0.1	0.1	1.3	1.7	7.6	7.6	7.3	6.1	5.2	26.6	26.9	11.1	1.5	73.7	37.3	51.6	48.4
71368	SICILY ISLAND	64.8	59.5	33.6	38.6	0.0	0.0	1.7	2.0	7.1	7.3	7.4	7.4	5.7	22.1	27.9	13.1	1.9	73.7	39.1	48.1	51.9
71369	SIMMESPORT	58.2	53.4	40.7	45.3	0.2	0.2	0.8	0.9	7.8	7.9	7.5	6.8	6.4	26.4	24.2	11.3	1.8	72.4	35.0	43.2	56.8
71371	TROUT	86.8	84.6	11.5	13.3	0.0	0.0	0.6	0.7	5.9	5.9	6.9	12.1	5.1	23.6	26.7	11.3	2.4	72.2	37.7	51.9	48.1
71373	VIDALIA	72.8	68.8	25.8	29.3	0.3	0.4	1.4	1.8	6.7	6.6	6.9	7.6	7.0	24.4	27.6	11.7	1.5	75.4	37.4	49.4	50.6
71375	WATERPROOF	23.2	19.9	76.1	79.2	0.0	0.0	0.7	0.8	6.8	4.9	8.0	8.8	6.4	16.5	29.7	14.4	4.5	74.2	43.8	43.3	56.7
71378	WISNER	60.6	55.5	38.1	42.8	0.0	0.0	1.3	1.6	8.0	8.0	7.5	6.7	5.8	20.9	25.0	15.2	3.0	72.4	39.1	46.7	53.3
71401	AIMWELL	96.9	96.7	2.3	2.5	0.0	0.0	0.8	0.8	5.8	5.8	5.8	5.8	5.0	24.0	31.4	14.9	1.7	79.3	42.9	50.4	49.6
71403	ANACOCO	94.9	93.0	0.5	0.6	0.4	0.7	1.5	2.1	6.3	6.5	6.8	6.8	4.9	24.6	29.2	13.5	1.3	76.1	40.9	49.6	50.4
71404	ATLANTA	49.7	44.4	49.0	54.1	0.2	0.2	0.4	0.4	2.9	3.0	3.3	4.2	10.9	45.6	21.1	7.6	1.2	88.5	35.6	74.4	25.6
71405	BALL	92.6	89.6	5.7	8.0	0.3	0.5	1.4	1.8	7.0	6.9	6.6	6.4	6.7	29.5	25.6	10.2	1.0	75.6	35.4	51.1	48.9
71406	BELMONT	83.6	79.6	10.3	12.7	0.0	0.0	1.7	2.1	7.4	7.7	7.4	6.7	4.9	24.3	27.1	12.7	1.8	73.2	37.9	51.1	48.9
71407	BENTLEY	96.5	95.1	0.4	0.7	0.2	0.3	1.4	1.7	7.3	7.2	7.7	8.3	6.2	26.1	26.2	9.6	1.4	72.7	36.1	51.2	48.8
71409	BOYCE	74.4	70.9	22.2	24.7	0.2	0.3	1.3	1.7	7.1	7.6	7.7	7.2	5.3	25.7	27.2	11.1	1.0	73.1	37.0	48.6	51.4
71411	CAMPTI	64.9	60.7	34.2	38.2	0.0	0.0	1.2	1.5	8.3	8.4	8.6	8.2	5.5	24.2	25.2	10.3	1.4	69.5	34.6	47.8	52.2
71416	CLOUTIERVILLE	57.4	51.0	28.8	33.1	0.1	0.2	2.8	3.3	6.6	6.6	6.5	6.6	5.7	23.2	27.8	14.6	2.4	76.1	41.1	49.3	50.7
71417	COLFAX	59.4	52.2	38.6	45.4	0.2	0.2	0.7	0.9	7.3	7.3	7.2	7.2	5.7	23.3	26.9	12.7	2.4	73.7	38.5	47.7	52.3
71418	COLUMBIA	81.2	80.0	17.2	18.3	0.1	0.1	1.6	1.7	6.4	6.8	6.9	6.5	5.2	23.9	28.4	13.9	2.1	75.9	40.6	48.2	51.8
71419	CONVERSE	84.7	81.0	6.9	8.2	0.0	0.0	2.7	3.3	5.2	6.3	7.0	6.9	4.7	22.2	29.6	16.0	2.1	77.2	43.1	49.8	50.2
71422	DODSON	86.1	83.2	12.4	14.8	0.4	0.5	1.4	1.8	6.5	6.5	6.7	6.5	5.4	25.8	28.7	12.3	1.6	75.6	39.3	49.5	50.5
71423	DRY PRONG	95.1	93.1	0.9	1.5	0.4	0.6	1.4	1.8	7.7	7.8	7.8	7.0	5.1	26.2	26.5	10.9	1.0	72.3	37.0	50.0	50.0
71424	ELMER	96.3	94.8	1.7	2.4	0.1	0.1	1.2	1.6	7.3	7.3	7.4	6.6	4.7	25.6	27.9	11.3	1.9	73.7	39.0	48.7	51.3
71425	ENTERPRISE	96.3	94.2	2.8	3.9	0.0	0.0	0.9	1.0	5.8	5.8	5.8	5.8	4.9	23.3	29.1	17.5	1.9	79.6	43.5	51.5	48.5
71426	FISHER	75.8	70.1	21.4	26.4	0.0	0.0	0.5	1.1	5.7	6.3	6.3	5.7	5.7	23.0	31.6	13.8	1.7	78.2	42.9	48.3	51.7
71427	FLATWOODS	74.1	67.0	14.7	20.1	0.3	0.3	0.6	0.8	6.4	6.4	6.1	6.7	6.4	24.0	28.5	14.0	1.4	76.8	40.6	50.0	50.0
71429	FLORIEN	84.4	81.4	13.5	15.9	0.0	0.1	0.8	1.1	5.9	5.9	5.9	5.9	5.5	22.2	30.0	16.9	1.8	78.7	43.9	49.2	50.8
71430	FOREST HILL	86.0	80.7	4.2	5.8	1.8	2.8	10.2	13.0	6.8	7.0	7.1	6.5	5.1	26.2	28.1	11.9	1.3	75.0	38.8	49.9	50.1
71432	GEORGETOWN	99.4	99.0	0.2	0.3	0.0	0.0	0.9	1.2	7.2	7.2	7.2	6.5	5.1	26.3	26.0	12.8	1.5	74.1	38.0	48.2	51.8
71433	GLENMORA	82.5	78.7	13.5	16.1	0.4	0.6	2.3	3.0	7.1	7.2	7.1	6.9	5.8	24.8	26.9	12.5	1.8	74.4	37.9	48.6	51.4
71435	GRAYSON	77.6	76.2	20.6	22.0	0.1	0.1	1.3	1.3	5.4	5.7	5.9	6.9	8.4	29.7	25.2	10.9	1.8	79.1	36.6	54.9	45.1
71438	HINESTON	96.0	94.8	0.4	0.6	0.1	0.1	0.9	1.3	7.7	7.8	7.5	6.1	4.8	26.2	26.7	11.3	1.9	73.1	37.8	49.3	50.7
71439	HORNBECK	93.6	91.3	2.2	2.9	0.5	0.8	1.1	1.6	6.4	6.5	6.9	6.7	4.7	25.7	28.3	13.2	1.7	76.1	40.1	49.2	50.8
71441	KELLY	94.1	93.6	4.5	4.9	0.2	0.2	0.9	0.9	6.7	7.6	7.5	7.0	4.9	27.7	27.4	9.9	1.2	73.5	36.9	51.4	48.6
71446	LEESVILLE	74.7	70.8	17.1	18.6	1.9	2.7	4.4	5.4	7.8	7.0	6.4	6.6	8.1	26.7	25.0	11.0	1.5	74.8	34.7	50.0	50.0
71447	LENA	75.3	68.6	14.2	18.7	0.2	0.3	1.2	1.4	6.5	6.5	6.4	6.6	5.9	24.1	28.1	14.3	1.6	76.7	40.8	49.7	50.3
71449	MANY	72.6	69.3	22.5	24.4	0.3	0.4	1.8	2.3	6.5	6.4	6.2	6.1	5.7	22.6	26.8	17.2	2.6	77.3	42.0	48.8	51.2
71450	MARTHAVILLE	79.2	74.9	15.1	18.0	0.2	0.3	1.9	2.3	7.1	7.1	7.2	6.4	5.1	23.7	28.7	13.1	1.7	74.7	39.3	49.4	50.6
71454	MONTGOMERY	84.0	76.5	13.3	20.3	0.0	0.0	1.2	1.4	6.5	6.9	7.2	7.1	5.0	23.7	28.4	13.3	1.8	74.9	40.0	49.9	50.1
71455	MORA	76.8	70.0	12.9	17.4	0.4	0.3	0.7	1.0	6.3	6.3	6.3	6.3	5.9	24.0	28.9	14.3	1.7	77.4	41.5	50.2	49.8
71456	NATCHEZ	48.6	41.7	41.9	47.8	0.1	0.2	1.9	2.0	6.1	7.0	7.3	8.7	6.0	24.8	27.5	11.1	1.4	74.1	37.1	50.2	49.8
71457	NATCHITOCHES	51.1	47.3	45.4	48.4	0.6	0.8	1.4	1.7	7.2	6.6	6.4	11.1	11.9	24.2	21.4	9.4	1.8	75.9	29.5	47.5	52.5
71459	FORT POLK	59.6	52.5	26.5	29.7	2.6	3.5	11.6	14.7	14.7	9.6	5.8	7.9	24.3	35.8	1.8	0.1	0.0	67.6	22.5	59.4	40.6
71461	NEWLLANO	48.6	41.7	38.2	41.6	4.1	5.4	8.3	10.2	7.4	6.4	6.0	7.4	10.8	30.5	24.2	6.9	0.5	76.0	31.0	50.6	49.4
71462	NOBLE	64.6	58.4	2.9	3.2	0.1	0.1	5.3	6.3	7.4	7.5	7.1	5.9	5.4	24.0	25.6	14.5	2.5	74.0	39.3	49.7	50.3
71463	OAKDALE	71.8	71.2	25.5	26.0	0.9	0.9	8.8	9.2	6.4	6.4	6.4	6.3	6.7	31.3	23.7	11.1	1.6	76.9	36.3	55.8	44.2
71465	OLLA	94.2	93.1	4.4	5.2	0.2	0.4	0.8	1.1	6.8	6.9	7.0	7.4	5.7	26.3	26.5	11.9	1.5	74.7	37.7	48.3	51.7
71466	OTIS	97.0	95.2	1.1	1.8	0.0	0.1	0.9	1.2	7.5	7.2	7.5	6.8	5.6	26.6	27.3	10.6	1.0	73.7	37.4	49.3	50.7
71467	POLLOCK	97.0	95.8	0.5	0.9	0.2	0.2	1.2	1.6	5.8	5.9	5.9	6.6	7.9	33.8	23.7	9.2	1.2	77.8	35.6	60.0	40.0
71468	PROVENCAL	89.2	85.7	6.6	8.7	0.0	0.2	1.0	1.2	5.8	6.0	6.6	6.2	4.6	23.7	29.5	15.6	2.1	77.8	43.0	48.7	51.3
71469	ROBELINE	84.5	81.2	11.8	14.2	0.1	0.1	1.5	1.8	7.2	7.3	7.3	6.2	5.0	25.5	27.1	12.8	1.7	74.3	38.5	48.6	51.4
71472	SIEPER	96.7	95.1	1.3	1.8	0.0	0.0	0.7	1.2	7.4	7.4	7.4	6.7	5.5	26.4	27.6	10.4	1.2	73.6	37.3	49.1	50.9
71473	SIKES	94.5	93.2	3.5	4.5	0.0	0.0	1.2	1.6	6.3	6.6	6.8	5.7	5.0	25.9	29.8	12.1	1.8	76.6	40.1	50.4	49.6
71479	TULLOS	80.8	77.7	17.5	20.1	0.0	0.0	1.1	1.3	4.6	4.7	4.9	5.9	9.8	33.2	24.4	11.1	1.4	82.5	36.8	60.9	39.1
71483	WINNFIELD	63.1	59.5	35.2	38.4	0.2	0.3	0.8	1.0	7.2	6.6	6.9	7.2	6.3	24.6	26.0	12.6	2.5	74.9	38.1	49.0	51.0
71485	WOODWORTH	88.0	85.3	9.7	11.9	0.1	0.2	2.1	2.3	7.7	8.2	7.8	6.3	4.8	27.3	27.9	9.2	0.9	72.3	36.0	50.7	49.3
71486	ZWOLLE	56.6	51.2	19.3	20.3	0.3	0.4	5.6	6.6	7.6	7.7	7.2	6.8	5.6	22.4	27.3	13.7	1.6	72.8	39.0	48.9	51.1
	LOUISIANA	63.9	61.9	32.5	33.7	1.3	1.6	2.4	2.8	7.2	7.0	6.9	7.3	7.1	26.8	25.7	10.4	1.6	74.6	35.6	48.6	51.4
	UNITED STATES	75.1	72.0	12.3	12.7	3.8	4.6	12.5	15.7	6.8	6.7	6.6	7.1	6.9	27.0	26.0	10.9	1.9	75.7	36.9	49.2	50.8

ZIP CODE #	POST OFFICE NAME	2009 Per Capita Income	2009 HH Income Base	2009 HOUSEHOLD INCOME DISTRIBUTION (%) Less than $25,000	$25,000 to $49,999	$50,000 to $99,999	$100,000 to $149,999	$150,000 or More	MEDIAN HOUSEHOLD INCOME 2009	2014	2009 National Centile	2009 State Centile	2009 Home Value Base	2009 HOME VALUE DISTRIBUTION (%) Less than $50,000	$50,000 to $89,999	$90,000 to $174,999	$175,000 to $399,999	$400,000 or More	2009 Median Home Value
71286	TRANSYLVANIA	14369	241	35.3	43.2	16.6	3.7	1.2	30800	30112	9	39	178	47.8	36.5	14.0	0.6	1.1	52353
71291	WEST MONROE	22300	13010	28.7	26.7	32.9	8.7	3.0	44286	42901	46	82	8769	13.4	13.8	43.1	27.1	2.7	129408
71292	WEST MONROE	17548	7860	33.4	32.4	26.9	5.4	2.0	35767	37420	20	60	5976	29.8	25.0	29.0	14.5	1.6	83720
71295	WINNSBORO	13406	5113	48.6	32.9	15.0	2.2	1.3	25687	26609	4	13	3805	40.1	27.3	23.6	8.7	0.3	62586
71301	ALEXANDRIA	16454	9198	47.5	27.2	19.2	3.6	2.5	27458	28246	5	20	4794	17.6	27.3	39.1	11.2	4.7	97675
71302	ALEXANDRIA	14071	5668	48.4	29.0	17.8	3.6	1.1	26498	27328	4	15	3515	24.6	34.5	32.9	6.4	1.7	81294
71303	ALEXANDRIA	22805	7648	30.5	29.4	27.7	7.1	5.2	40135	39887	33	73	4777	8.5	13.8	39.5	33.0	5.3	144338
71316	ACME	16565	22	36.4	36.4	27.3	0.0	0.0	32290	35000	12	47	19	26.3	26.3	42.1	5.3	0.0	85000
71322	BUNKIE	13115	2831	50.4	25.3	20.0	3.1	1.1	24556	25872	3	10	1875	32.9	25.2	30.6	9.2	2.2	76116
71323	CENTER POINT	15898	356	29.2	41.9	24.2	3.1	1.7	36392	37029	22	62	323	35.9	23.2	29.7	11.1	0.0	78500
71325	CHENEYVILLE	13380	505	53.9	24.0	18.8	2.2	1.2	22488	23580	2	6	370	37.3	24.9	25.1	11.9	0.8	70000
71326	CLAYTON	11092	696	62.4	22.6	11.9	2.2	1.0	17884	19794	1	3	500	50.8	25.4	17.4	4.0	2.4	49231
71327	COTTONPORT	13900	1510	48.6	28.2	17.9	4.1	1.2	25626	26471	4	12	1067	24.8	27.8	35.6	10.9	0.8	86868
71328	DEVILLE	18215	2947	28.1	30.2	33.6	6.3	1.8	42334	40600	40	77	2605	21.4	17.8	38.4	20.9	1.5	108991
71331	EFFIE	15449	347	39.8	35.2	21.3	2.3	1.4	30861	30672	9	39	299	38.5	18.1	34.1	8.0	1.3	80250
71333	EVERGREEN	19057	382	42.9	32.5	19.1	4.2	1.3	30505	31823	9	36	278	32.4	29.9	25.5	10.8	1.4	74737
71334	FERRIDAY	12691	3384	55.9	26.1	14.4	2.5	1.2	21018	23181	2	5	2392	41.9	27.1	18.9	10.5	1.5	58694
71336	GILBERT	14787	737	45.0	31.9	19.4	2.3	1.4	27834	28318	5	22	574	41.8	32.2	20.0	5.9	0.0	58868
71340	HARRISONBURG	14711	587	43.8	27.9	23.9	3.9	0.5	28318	28274	6	24	493	36.9	20.5	32.9	9.1	0.6	78409
71341	HESSMER	13450	1236	46.4	32.8	17.2	3.2	0.6	26849	27334	5	17	993	26.1	26.4	38.6	8.7	0.3	84896
71342	JENA	15865	2664	41.0	28.9	25.3	4.0	0.9	31374	31619	10	42	2178	31.7	24.8	31.7	10.3	1.5	78468
71343	JONESVILLE	14990	3063	46.6	32.4	16.1	3.8	1.2	26740	27308	4	16	2554	42.9	22.6	25.3	7.7	1.4	58873
71346	LECOMPTE	14881	1141	47.0	26.3	21.6	3.2	1.8	29920	30415	8	34	808	26.9	24.9	28.7	16.2	3.3	88313
71350	MANSURA	14600	1641	46.3	28.0	22.5	2.4	0.8	27293	27817	5	19	1173	24.0	24.4	41.0	10.3	0.3	92407
71351	MARKSVILLE	14486	4311	47.8	28.7	18.7	2.8	2.0	26114	26769	4	14	3155	25.6	28.2	34.0	10.6	1.5	83875
71353	MELVILLE	11412	729	55.4	26.7	17.0	0.5	0.3	21495	23298	2	6	518	41.7	30.3	21.8	6.2	0.0	60000
71354	MONTEREY	15553	716	37.3	33.9	25.8	2.9	0.0	31507	31227	11	44	612	35.9	19.4	33.5	9.8	1.3	78095
71355	MOREAUVILLE	16538	1148	41.9	28.4	25.7	2.7	1.3	30673	30299	9	37	911	26.0	23.4	41.6	8.6	0.4	90809
71356	MORROW	14830	110	50.0	31.8	15.5	1.8	0.9	25000	26086	3	11	86	30.2	38.4	26.7	4.7	0.0	73846
71357	NEWELLTON	15982	1060	46.2	32.3	14.1	4.7	2.7	27260	27083	5	19	741	28.5	22.3	22.5	19.8	6.9	88625
71358	PALMETTO	13019	409	52.3	23.7	21.0	2.7	0.2	23359	24650	2	8	313	31.3	35.8	24.3	8.6	0.0	71207
71360	PINEVILLE	19645	13140	32.9	29.5	28.5	6.3	2.7	36720	37894	23	63	9235	17.6	20.1	41.2	18.3	2.8	111698
71362	PLAUCHEVILLE	15327	806	44.4	26.4	24.3	3.1	1.7	28809	28951	6	27	640	29.1	29.1	33.6	8.3	0.0	75789
71366	SAINT JOSEPH	11451	654	57.6	27.7	12.5	1.2	0.9	20377	20768	1	4	436	50.7	25.9	15.8	4.8	2.8	49348
71367	SAINT LANDRY	15274	522	38.1	33.0	22.4	5.6	1.0	32131	31762	12	47	435	26.0	25.5	33.6	13.8	1.1	87593
71368	SICILY ISLAND	14290	606	55.1	21.9	18.0	3.1	1.8	20596	22341	2	5	481	48.2	20.6	21.2	9.4	0.6	53542
71369	SIMMESPORT	12270	1106	57.1	24.1	14.6	3.0	1.2	20593	22247	2	5	816	39.0	24.8	26.0	10.2	0.1	65088
71371	TROUT	16375	1037	39.9	28.5	24.9	5.2	1.4	31212	30905	10	41	898	40.1	19.8	30.8	8.2	1.0	68913
71373	VIDALIA	14818	2602	41.1	29.7	24.8	2.9	1.6	30856	30628	9	39	1990	24.3	35.8	33.8	5.5	0.7	80099
71375	WATERPROOF	16394	378	68.5	16.4	6.3	5.6	3.2	14360	15324	1	1	251	65.3	21.1	10.8	1.2	1.6	37500
71378	WISNER	13488	923	51.9	28.7	15.9	2.0	1.5	23702	25569	3	9	679	37.1	29.0	27.4	6.5	0.0	66371
71401	AIMWELL	12128	47	48.9	29.8	19.1	2.1	0.0	25414	25683	3	12	42	42.9	23.8	26.2	7.1	0.0	60000
71403	ANACOCO	17026	1726	32.4	35.9	27.2	3.6	0.9	36679	36849	23	63	1463	32.3	23.9	34.1	9.2	0.5	80376
71404	ATLANTA	12283	292	38.4	35.3	21.6	2.4	2.4	30711	30661	9	38	247	46.6	17.0	30.8	5.7	0.0	57727
71405	BALL	18372	2250	31.3	35.9	27.2	4.9	0.8	37260	38158	24	66	1586	17.0	25.0	46.7	10.4	0.9	100189
71406	BELMONT	16025	111	27.0	41.4	27.0	4.5	0.0	37338	36503	25	66	99	50.5	21.2	16.2	8.1	4.0	49583
71407	BENTLEY	17033	477	35.2	24.9	32.9	5.7	1.3	37240	36984	24	66	394	23.4	22.3	28.4	25.9	0.0	98095
71409	BOYCE	18041	2645	34.9	29.7	30.3	3.6	1.5	36279	37867	21	61	2110	22.9	23.8	33.7	16.3	3.2	98293
71411	CAMPTI	12928	1259	48.2	28.0	21.0	2.4	0.3	25864	26641	4	14	902	39.7	22.6	27.3	9.0	1.4	68511
71416	CLOUTIERVILLE	15636	446	46.4	31.8	15.7	4.3	1.8	28681	28690	6	26	326	32.5	24.2	32.2	8.6	2.5	78667
71417	COLFAX	13968	1948	46.5	29.8	19.3	3.5	0.9	27091	28308	5	18	1515	35.7	25.4	24.7	12.1	2.0	72120
71418	COLUMBIA	15953	2704	44.1	27.7	23.0	3.9	1.3	28587	28947	6	26	2046	33.4	25.4	29.6	10.5	1.1	77231
71419	CONVERSE	15315	878	44.6	30.2	20.3	4.1	0.8	29766	30404	8	32	742	37.2	27.4	29.1	4.4	1.9	70769
71422	DODSON	15468	688	38.7	34.6	20.6	4.8	1.3	30750	30253	9	38	569	48.5	20.0	25.1	5.6	0.7	52297
71423	DRY PRONG	17745	1739	33.2	33.2	25.9	5.8	1.9	35967	36848	20	61	1484	25.6	19.0	34.0	19.7	1.8	100815
71424	ELMER	19050	590	35.4	29.3	26.3	5.9	3.1	37731	38739	26	67	512	21.7	19.9	35.0	17.6	5.9	105137
71425	ENTERPRISE	14246	49	51.0	30.6	16.3	2.0	0.0	24400	24490	3	10	44	34.1	13.6	45.5	6.8	0.0	93333
71426	FISHER	15974	68	42.6	32.4	19.1	5.9	0.0	28370	29623	6	24	59	42.4	20.3	25.4	11.9	0.0	61667
71427	FLATWOODS	14031	137	35.8	43.8	16.8	2.9	0.7	31619	32215	11	45	114	36.0	22.8	30.7	10.5	0.0	76667
71429	FLORIEN	17195	1384	39.1	34.8	20.2	3.6	2.2	30522	30829	9	37	1184	31.7	24.1	31.1	12.8	0.3	81605
71430	FOREST HILL	16827	910	35.2	29.0	28.2	5.7	1.9	37362	37904	25	66	724	23.9	25.8	29.6	15.6	5.1	90400
71432	GEORGETOWN	18699	508	38.6	29.5	22.6	7.7	1.6	32941	35141	13	49	405	42.0	24.2	22.2	10.4	1.2	60625
71433	GLENMORA	15217	1728	46.2	27.7	20.7	4.2	1.3	29200	29711	7	29	1372	36.2	27.1	24.7	9.0	2.9	69877
71435	GRAYSON	16266	1281	40.3	29.7	25.3	3.2	1.6	32131	32772	12	47	1067	41.7	25.0	23.5	9.6	0.2	61197
71438	HINESTON	14916	555	39.1	32.6	23.6	3.4	1.3	31753	31753	11	45	491	32.0	23.8	35.0	5.3	3.9	82500
71439	HORNBECK	14754	701	35.8	36.7	25.4	1.9	0.3	33047	33457	13	50	590	36.6	22.4	31.7	8.1	1.2	72581
71441	KELLY	18238	255	38.0	29.0	27.8	2.4	2.7	34010	35000	16	55	222	36.5	26.6	22.5	14.4	0.0	65882
71446	LEESVILLE	17236	8803	34.6	34.8	24.7	4.4	1.4	33556	33980	14	52	5485	30.1	24.3	35.1	8.9	1.6	82885
71447	LENA	14719	524	37.4	43.1	16.0	2.7	0.8	31570	32062	11	44	429	35.9	23.1	30.8	10.0	0.2	75313
71449	MANY	16743	3735	43.6	29.0	21.5	3.9	2.0	28375	28925	6	25	2826	30.6	21.3	28.4	17.5	2.2	86788
71450	MARTHAVILLE	18047	427	38.4	29.0	27.2	3.0	2.3	32969	33453	13	49	358	34.6	20.4	27.4	12.6	5.0	82500
71454	MONTGOMERY	16685	1073	40.8	32.1	22.4	2.8	2.0	30666	31811	9	37	901	36.6	27.6	30.2	5.4	0.1	65804
71455	MORA	13810	107	36.4	45.8	15.9	1.9	0.0	31473	31763	10	43	89	33.7	23.6	32.6	10.1	0.0	80714
71456	NATCHEZ	17109	427	45.9	29.0	19.0	3.0	3.0	28196	28871	6	23	304	28.0	19.4	29.6	18.1	4.9	94444
71457	NATCHITOCHES	16163	10321	45.0	27.0	21.0	4.5	2.4	28441	28892	6	25	5980	19.6	18.0	38.7	20.7	3.1	111215
71459	FORT POLK	13762	3128	18.6	48.4	29.9	2.4	0.7	39889	38584	32	72	85	42.4	32.9	15.3	9.4	0.0	54333
71461	NEWLLANO	18528	751	29.7	33.4	30.0	6.1	0.8	40771	39613	35	76	345	13.9	43.8	40.3	2.0	0.0	78043
71462	NOBLE	15766	637	37.8	34.4	23.1	3.1	1.6	31331	31213	10	42	560	43.4	22.9	24.3	7.5	2.0	58222
71463	OAKDALE	13829	3696	48.4	29.7	16.6	4.1	1.1	25911	26856	4	14	2617	31.8	26.4	32.9	7.6	1.2	76462
71465	OLLA	16923	1253	38.5	33.0	22.3	4.1	2.1	33498	35088	14	51	994	41.0	24.7	22.9	10.8	0.5	60758
71466	OTIS	16460	257	31.5	35.0	28.4	5.1	0.0	36974	38767	24	65	214	29.4	24.3	34.6	9.3	2.3	83333
71467	POLLOCK	15858	1883	35.2	33.2	25.2	5.5	1.0	34333	35462	16	55	1495	27.9	22.4	33.0	14.8	1.9	89521
71468	PROVENCAL	15439	221	41.2	38.5	17.2	2.3	0.9	30437	30746	9	36	184	39.7	22.8	28.8	8.7	0.0	68750
71469	ROBELINE	17160	1473	39.9	31.2	23.6	3.6	1.8	31192	30996	10	41	1196	36.4	18.6	31.6	11.3	2.2	78413
71472	SIEPER	18345	69	31.9	33.3	29.0	5.8	0.0	38659	39089	29	70	58	27.6	24.1	37.9	8.6	1.7	86667
71473	SIKES	16913	233	34.8	36.9	23.2	3.9	1.3	33670	34596	15	52	198	50.5	23.2	14.1	9.1	3.0	49500
71479	TULLOS	14599	650	40.6	34.3	21.7	2.9	0.5	30347	30323	9	36	552	56.3	24.8	14.5	3.1	1.3	43000
71483	WINNFIELD	14622	3936	47.2	30.7	17.5	3.5	1.1	26718	27624	4	16	2723	44.5	25.9	20.5	8.1	1.1	58592
71485	WOODWORTH	21259	820	25.0	29.3	33.7	8.0	4.0	46976	45670	54	87	679	11.3	19.3	36.1	27.4	5.9	123777
71486	ZWOLLE	16086	1919	42.3	29.1	23.2	3.7	1.7	29383	29561	7	30	1553	42.0	21.2	25.4	10.1	1.2	64104
	LOUISIANA	19176		34.0	28.2	28.2	6.6	3.0	37868	38644				16.9	18.7	37.2	22.8	4.3	118738
	UNITED STATES	27277		20.9	24.4	35.3	11.7	7.6	54719	56938				9.3	13.1	31.6	32.6	13.5	162279

ZIP CODE		FINANCIAL SERVICES				THE HOME						ENTERTAINMENT						PERSONAL			
						Home Improvements		Furnishings													
#	POST OFFICE NAME	Auto Loan	Home Loan	Invest-ments	Retire-ment Plans	Home Repair	Lawn & Garden	Comput-ers & Hard-ware-Personal	Major Appli-ances	TV, Radio, Sound Equip-ment	Furni-ture	Dine out/ Carry out	Sports Equip-ment	Fees & Tickets	Toys & Games	Travel	Cable TV	Apparel & Services	Auto Repairs	Health Insur-ance	Pets & Supplies
71286	TRANSYLVANIA	69	45	68	43	46	69	49	62	56	45	54	49	37	56	46	62	36	58	65	76
71291	WEST MONROE	81	78	73	78	77	80	78	79	80	78	79	60	76	81	76	81	55	79	82	93
71292	WEST MONROE	77	63	66	62	62	74	64	70	68	63	67	53	57	70	60	72	46	68	73	84
71295	WINNSBORO	59	43	54	42	43	59	46	54	52	44	51	40	38	52	43	57	34	52	59	65
71301	ALEXANDRIA	60	53	49	54	51	58	57	56	61	57	61	42	55	61	54	64	42	59	63	68
71302	ALEXANDRIA	53	46	44	46	44	54	48	50	53	48	52	36	46	52	45	57	36	51	57	61
71303	ALEXANDRIA	81	80	77	82	79	83	80	80	83	81	82	60	81	82	80	84	57	81	85	95
71316	ACME	69	49	70	48	51	70	50	64	56	47	55	48	40	56	50	62	36	59	67	76
71322	BUNKIE	58	44	50	44	44	57	48	53	53	46	52	40	41	53	45	58	35	53	59	65
71323	CENTER POINT	76	55	76	53	56	77	56	71	62	53	61	53	45	62	55	68	40	65	74	84
71325	CHENEYVILLE	56	41	47	40	40	54	45	50	52	45	50	37	38	51	41	57	34	50	57	62
71326	CLAYTON	53	35	51	33	35	52	38	47	44	36	43	36	29	44	35	49	28	45	50	58
71327	COTTONPORT	63	44	57	42	44	61	47	56	55	46	53	42	39	54	44	60	36	55	62	69
71328	DEVILLE	82	72	67	69	70	77	69	74	72	71	72	55	63	75	65	75	49	72	75	89
71331	EFFIE	69	49	57	48	49	65	51	60	57	50	56	46	41	60	47	62	38	57	63	73
71333	EVERGREEN	74	49	72	46	48	73	52	65	60	49	58	51	39	61	48	67	39	62	69	80
71334	FERRIDAY	52	38	48	37	38	51	41	47	47	41	46	35	35	46	39	52	31	47	53	58
71336	GILBERT	69	46	63	44	46	67	49	60	56	47	55	47	38	57	45	62	36	57	64	74
71340	HARRISONBURG	69	46	68	44	47	68	49	62	55	46	54	47	37	56	47	62	36	58	65	75
71341	HESSMER	63	43	60	41	43	62	45	56	51	43	50	43	35	52	42	57	33	52	59	68
71342	JENA	67	49	65	49	51	68	52	63	58	49	57	47	43	58	50	64	38	60	68	75
71343	JONESVILLE	67	46	65	44	46	66	48	60	54	45	53	46	37	55	46	60	35	56	63	73
71346	LECOMPTE	65	48	58	48	48	64	52	59	59	51	58	43	45	58	49	65	39	59	66	72
71350	MANSURA	63	45	59	44	45	63	48	57	54	46	53	43	39	54	45	60	35	55	62	70
71351	MARKSVILLE	64	46	58	44	46	62	49	57	55	48	54	43	40	55	46	61	36	55	62	70
71353	MELVILLE	49	35	43	34	34	48	38	44	44	37	42	32	32	43	35	48	29	43	49	53
71354	MONTEREY	68	48	69	46	49	68	49	63	55	46	54	47	39	55	48	61	36	58	66	75
71355	MOREAUVILLE	69	50	69	48	51	71	53	66	59	48	57	49	43	58	52	65	38	61	71	78
71356	MORROW	60	42	60	41	44	62	46	57	52	42	50	43	36	51	44	57	33	53	62	68
71357	NEWELLTON	73	51	76	49	52	73	53	67	59	50	58	51	42	59	52	65	38	62	69	81
71358	PALMETTO	58	39	57	37	40	58	42	53	48	39	47	41	33	48	40	53	31	50	56	64
71360	PINEVILLE	78	70	70	69	69	76	70	74	73	70	72	56	66	74	68	75	50	73	76	88
71362	PLAUCHEVILLE	71	49	71	47	50	71	51	65	58	48	56	49	40	58	50	64	37	60	68	78
71366	SAINT JOSEPH	46	35	37	35	34	44	39	41	45	39	44	29	35	44	35	49	30	43	49	51
71367	SAINT LANDRY	72	52	68	50	53	71	54	66	59	51	58	50	43	60	51	65	39	61	69	79
71368	SICILY ISLAND	64	43	63	41	43	63	45	57	51	43	50	44	35	52	43	57	33	53	60	69
71369	SIMMESPORT	55	38	50	36	37	53	41	48	48	40	46	37	33	48	38	53	31	47	53	60
71371	TROUT	74	52	71	50	52	73	54	67	61	51	59	51	42	62	51	67	39	62	70	81
71373	VIDALIA	64	52	56	51	50	65	54	59	60	52	58	45	49	60	51	64	39	59	66	72
71375	WATERPROOF	56	44	43	45	43	54	50	51	58	52	56	36	46	56	45	63	38	54	62	63
71378	WISNER	61	42	60	40	42	62	45	56	51	42	50	43	35	51	43	57	33	53	60	68
71401	AIMWELL	57	39	57	37	40	57	41	52	46	38	45	39	32	46	39	51	30	48	54	62
71403	ANACOCO	74	56	75	54	58	75	56	70	62	53	61	52	47	62	56	67	40	65	72	83
71404	ATLANTA	76	51	74	48	51	75	53	67	61	50	60	52	41	62	51	68	39	63	71	82
71405	BALL	72	61	64	59	60	69	61	67	64	61	63	50	54	65	58	66	43	64	68	79
71406	BELMONT	76	50	72	47	50	74	53	67	61	51	60	52	40	62	49	68	40	63	70	82
71407	BENTLEY	84	60	70	58	59	80	62	73	69	60	68	56	50	72	57	75	45	69	77	88
71409	BOYCE	71	63	58	62	62	68	62	65	66	64	65	48	59	68	59	69	45	65	68	79
71411	CAMPTI	62	40	60	38	40	61	43	55	50	41	49	43	32	51	40	56	32	51	58	67
71416	CLOUTIERVILLE	72	47	70	45	47	71	50	63	58	48	56	49	38	59	47	64	37	60	67	78
71417	COLFAX	61	44	56	43	44	60	47	56	54	46	52	41	39	53	45	59	35	54	61	67
71418	COLUMBIA	68	49	65	47	49	68	51	62	58	49	57	46	42	57	49	64	38	59	67	75
71419	CONVERSE	68	47	68	45	49	69	49	63	56	46	54	48	39	56	48	61	36	58	65	75
71422	DODSON	73	50	68	48	50	71	52	64	59	50	58	50	41	60	49	65	39	60	68	78
71423	DRY PRONG	79	65	75	63	65	79	63	74	68	62	67	55	56	69	62	72	45	69	75	88
71424	ELMER	84	69	78	68	69	84	68	79	72	66	72	60	60	74	67	77	48	74	81	94
71425	ENTERPRISE	53	38	55	37	40	54	39	50	44	37	43	38	31	43	39	48	28	46	52	59
71426	FISHER	73	52	75	51	54	74	54	68	60	50	58	51	43	59	53	66	39	63	71	81
71427	FLATWOODS	68	44	66	42	44	67	48	60	55	45	54	47	36	56	44	61	35	56	63	74
71429	FLORIEN	73	55	77	52	58	76	56	70	62	55	61	51	47	61	56	68	40	65	74	83
71430	FOREST HILL	83	58	84	56	60	83	60	76	67	56	66	58	48	67	59	74	44	70	80	91
71432	GEORGETOWN	83	59	70	58	59	79	61	72	68	60	67	55	49	71	57	74	45	68	76	88
71433	GLENMORA	70	49	68	47	50	70	51	64	58	48	56	49	41	58	49	64	37	59	67	77
71435	GRAYSON	75	51	71	49	51	74	54	67	61	51	60	51	41	62	50	68	40	62	70	81
71438	HINESTON	72	52	67	50	52	71	53	65	59	51	58	49	43	60	51	65	39	60	68	78
71439	HORNBECK	67	48	69	47	50	68	49	63	55	46	54	47	40	54	49	60	36	58	65	75
71441	KELLY	84	60	81	58	62	83	62	77	69	59	68	58	50	70	60	76	45	71	80	92
71446	LEESVILLE	69	53	57	54	53	62	60	62	63	57	62	48	52	64	55	65	43	62	64	74
71447	LENA	68	46	67	43	46	68	48	61	55	46	54	47	37	56	46	61	36	57	64	74
71449	MANY	63	52	61	51	54	64	54	61	59	54	58	44	49	58	53	63	39	60	66	72
71450	MARTHAVILLE	81	55	80	53	56	80	58	73	65	54	64	56	45	66	55	72	42	68	77	88
71454	MONTGOMERY	74	49	72	47	49	73	52	66	60	49	58	51	40	60	49	66	39	62	69	80
71455	MORA	68	45	67	43	46	67	48	61	55	46	54	47	37	56	46	61	36	57	64	74
71456	NATCHEZ	76	50	74	47	50	75	53	67	61	51	60	52	40	62	50	69	40	63	71	83
71457	NATCHITOCHES	65	50	54	50	49	59	59	58	62	56	61	46	51	62	53	65	42	61	63	71
71459	FORT POLK	80	41	31	48	37	35	75	52	70	70	74	52	57	85	54	65	52	66	47	63
71461	NEWLLANO	69	59	50	61	56	58	71	61	70	66	70	50	64	71	62	69	48	67	64	75
71462	NOBLE	71	50	67	48	51	70	52	64	58	49	57	49	41	58	50	63	38	60	67	77
71463	OAKDALE	60	43	56	42	44	60	47	55	53	45	52	41	39	52	44	58	34	53	60	67
71465	OLLA	77	55	65	54	55	74	58	67	64	56	63	52	46	67	53	70	42	64	71	82
71466	OTIS	79	56	65	55	56	75	59	68	65	57	64	53	47	68	53	71	43	65	72	83
71467	POLLOCK	74	59	70	57	60	73	58	69	63	57	62	51	50	64	57	67	42	65	71	82
71468	PROVENCAL	65	46	66	45	48	66	48	61	53	44	52	45	38	52	47	58	34	56	63	72
71469	ROBELINE	77	55	74	52	55	76	56	70	63	54	62	53	45	64	54	69	41	65	73	84
71472	SIEPER	78	56	65	55	56	74	58	68	65	57	63	52	47	67	53	71	43	64	72	83
71473	SIKES	73	52	66	51	53	71	54	65	60	52	59	50	43	62	51	66	39	61	68	79
71479	TULLOS	69	47	68	45	48	68	49	62	56	46	54	47	38	56	47	62	36	58	65	75
71483	WINNFIELD	59	42	52	42	42	57	47	54	54	45	52	40	39	53	44	58	35	53	59	65
71485	WOODWORTH	89	87	77	86	85	88	81	85	82	83	82	64	79	85	80	84	57	82	85	101
71486	ZWOLLE	69	52	72	49	54	71	53	65	59	52	58	48	44	58	53	64	38	62	70	78
	LOUISIANA	78	67	68	67	66	75	70	72	73	70	73	55	65	74	67	76	50	73	76	87
	UNITED STATES	100	100	100	100	100	100	100	100	100	100	100	100	100	100	100	100	100	100	100	100

ZIP CODE #	POST OFFICE NAME	COUNTY FIPS CODE	POPULATION 2000	POPULATION 2009	POPULATION 2014	2000-2009 ANNUAL RATE % Rate	2000-2009 ANNUAL RATE State Centile	HOUSEHOLDS 2000	HOUSEHOLDS 2009	HOUSEHOLDS 2014	HOUSEHOLDS % Annual Rate 2000-2009	HOUSEHOLDS 2009 Average HH Size	FAMILIES 2000	FAMILIES 2009	FAMILIES % Annual Rate 2000-2009
03901	BERWICK	031	6376	7584	8094	1.9	96	2329	2817	3032	2.1	2.67	1731	2055	1.9
03902	CAPE NEDDICK	031	1968	2290	2438	1.7	94	843	1002	1075	1.9	2.29	556	646	1.6
03903	ELIOT	031	5957	5933	5875	0.0	33	2308	2348	2340	0.2	2.53	1706	1703	0.0
03904	KITTERY	031	7248	7620	7700	0.5	57	3083	3285	3349	0.7	2.25	1873	1939	0.4
03905	KITTERY POINT	031	2295	2357	2354	0.3	50	995	1040	1047	0.5	2.24	656	668	0.2
03906	NORTH BERWICK	031	4362	5199	5545	1.9	96	1609	1951	2098	2.1	2.63	1193	1419	1.9
03907	OGUNQUIT	031	1219	1377	1459	1.3	88	664	764	813	1.5	1.80	344	383	1.2
03908	SOUTH BERWICK	031	6697	7292	7485	0.9	77	2412	2652	2738	1.0	2.73	1854	2004	0.8
03909	YORK	031	10862	11858	12221	1.0	80	4384	4865	5057	1.1	2.38	3128	3405	0.9
04001	ACTON	031	2158	2677	2909	2.4	98	863	1100	1204	2.7	2.43	622	778	2.4
04002	ALFRED	031	6512	7467	7890	1.5	91	2445	2851	3040	1.7	2.56	1823	2089	1.5
04003	BAILEY ISLAND	005	512	537	574	0.5	57	257	286	309	1.2	1.87	151	162	0.8
04005	BIDDEFORD	031	22491	24025	24401	0.7	66	9185	9885	10123	0.8	2.31	5723	6025	0.6
04006	BIDDEFORD POOL	031	162	174	176	0.8	71	69	74	75	0.8	2.24	33	33	0.0
04008	BOWDOINHAM	023	2931	3108	3154	0.6	62	1148	1258	1290	1.0	2.46	843	908	0.8
04009	BRIDGTON	005	4525	5210	5475	1.5	91	1793	2101	2224	1.7	2.44	1209	1374	1.4
04010	BROWNFIELD	017	1388	1419	1429	0.2	46	573	612	624	0.7	2.32	394	412	0.5
04011	BRUNSWICK	005	21218	22304	22605	0.5	57	8170	8758	8977	0.8	2.28	5159	5395	0.5
04015	CASCO	005	3354	3774	3943	1.3	88	1277	1488	1571	1.7	2.51	924	1051	1.4
04017	CHEBEAGUE ISLAND	005	356	382	395	0.8	71	170	188	196	1.1	2.02	127	136	0.7
04019	CLIFF ISLAND	005	87	88	88	0.1	39	39	40	40	0.3	2.20	31	31	0.0
04020	CORNISH	031	1272	1416	1488	1.2	87	522	593	627	1.4	2.38	341	376	1.1
04021	CUMBERLAND CENTER	005	5516	5753	5856	0.5	57	1898	2025	2079	0.7	2.84	1558	1636	0.5
04022	DENMARK	017	854	869	874	0.2	46	352	376	382	0.7	2.31	241	252	0.5
04024	EAST BALDWIN	005	424	385	372	-1.0	1	168	158	154	-0.7	2.44	130	120	-0.9
04027	LEBANON	031	5058	5902	6258	1.7	94	1809	2154	2303	1.9	2.74	1395	1633	1.7
04029	SEBAGO	005	1504	1545	1550	0.3	50	620	655	665	0.6	2.36	442	457	0.4
04030	EAST WATERBORO	031	1867	2088	2193	1.2	87	698	795	842	1.4	2.62	542	605	1.2
04032	FREEPORT	005	7876	8309	8488	0.6	62	3096	3351	3452	0.9	2.42	2178	2294	0.6
04037	FRYEBURG	017	3384	3960	4189	1.7	94	1364	1663	1781	2.2	2.32	924	1102	1.9
04038	GORHAM	005	14145	15570	16101	1.0	80	4877	5462	5700	1.2	2.62	3531	3867	1.0
04039	GRAY	005	6612	7095	7282	0.8	71	2539	2822	2929	1.1	2.50	1825	1976	0.9
04040	HARRISON	005	2606	3064	3246	1.8	95	1022	1239	1326	2.1	2.47	729	859	1.8
04041	HIRAM	017	1413	1731	1854	2.2	97	530	669	725	2.5	2.59	385	477	2.3
04042	HOLLIS CENTER	031	4192	4752	4987	1.4	90	1526	1774	1878	1.6	2.67	1155	1319	1.4
04043	KENNEBUNK	031	10501	11956	12560	1.4	90	4241	4869	5142	1.5	2.42	2907	3273	1.3
04046	KENNEBUNKPORT	031	7253	8075	8383	1.2	87	2961	3350	3505	1.3	2.41	2078	2298	1.1
04047	PARSONSFIELD	031	1584	1943	2101	2.2	97	634	793	865	2.4	2.43	439	537	2.2
04048	LIMERICK	031	2249	2981	3282	3.1	100	855	1155	1284	3.3	2.57	612	810	3.1
04049	LIMINGTON	031	3400	4084	4360	2.0	97	1140	1386	1497	2.1	2.78	892	1067	2.0
04050	LONG ISLAND	005	202	209	211	0.4	53	93	99	101	0.7	2.11	61	63	0.3
04051	LOVELL	017	927	946	943	0.2	46	372	393	397	0.6	2.41	271	281	0.4
04055	NAPLES	005	3431	3641	3707	0.6	62	1359	1492	1538	1.0	2.43	973	1039	0.7
04061	NORTH WATERBORO	031	2583	2953	3118	1.5	91	857	981	1039	1.5	3.01	693	782	1.3
04062	WINDHAM	005	14787	16048	16563	0.9	77	5480	6136	6408	1.2	2.49	3989	4355	1.0
04064	OLD ORCHARD BEACH	031	8829	9437	9685	0.7	66	4284	4657	4806	0.9	2.02	2251	2363	0.5
04066	ORRS ISLAND	005	660	817	888	2.3	98	302	387	424	2.7	2.11	193	240	2.4
04068	PORTER	017	1448	1472	1478	0.2	46	566	596	605	0.6	2.47	413	427	0.4
04069	POWNAL	005	1506	1629	1687	0.9	77	568	636	666	1.2	2.56	445	489	1.0
04071	RAYMOND	005	4706	6133	6702	2.9	100	1782	2408	2660	3.3	2.55	1374	1820	3.1
04072	SACO	031	16849	18407	18947	1.0	80	6811	7509	7771	1.1	2.41	4599	4982	0.9
04073	SANFORD	031	16356	17348	17706	0.6	62	6498	6995	7196	0.8	2.43	4259	4481	0.6
04074	SCARBOROUGH	005	16606	18257	18911	1.0	80	6282	7042	7355	1.2	2.55	4559	4979	1.0
04076	SHAPLEIGH	031	2329	2893	3136	2.4	98	915	1160	1267	2.6	2.49	676	840	2.4
04079	HARPSWELL	005	4017	4370	4492	0.9	77	1760	1986	2063	1.3	2.20	1175	1285	1.0
04083	SPRINGVALE	031	4334	4975	5221	1.5	91	1731	2019	2136	1.7	2.43	1158	1320	1.4
04084	STANDISH	005	7557	8867	9322	1.7	94	2604	3174	3391	2.2	2.59	1991	2374	1.9
04085	STEEP FALLS	005	1732	1997	2133	1.6	93	601	713	770	1.9	2.80	473	550	1.6
04086	TOPSHAM	023	9100	9895	10171	0.9	77	3424	3851	3999	1.3	2.52	2463	2715	1.1
04087	WATERBORO	031	1519	1537	1545	0.1	39	562	579	586	0.3	2.65	407	409	0.1
04088	WATERFORD	017	1852	1871	1864	0.1	39	750	791	797	0.6	2.37	544	563	0.4
04090	WELLS	031	9423	10887	11528	1.6	93	4014	4730	5046	1.8	2.30	2698	3105	1.5
04091	WEST BALDWIN	005	802	720	693	-1.2	0	297	277	269	-0.8	2.60	232	212	-1.0
04092	WESTBROOK	005	16248	16852	17070	0.4	53	6910	7397	7563	0.7	2.25	4295	4464	0.4
04093	BUXTON	031	7486	8428	8783	1.3	88	2811	3230	3397	1.5	2.60	2100	2368	1.3
04095	WEST NEWFIELD	031	1338	1687	1830	2.5	99	500	643	703	2.8	2.61	373	471	2.6
04096	YARMOUTH	005	8407	8523	8554	0.1	39	3444	3588	3636	0.4	2.34	2315	2339	0.1
04097	NORTH YARMOUTH	005	3212	3567	3719	1.1	83	1117	1277	1345	1.5	2.79	923	1038	1.3
04101	PORTLAND	005	17053	17152	17124	0.1	39	8726	8905	8956	0.2	1.76	2598	2507	-0.4
04102	PORTLAND	005	17018	16831	16716	-0.1	25	8076	8234	8259	0.2	1.99	3549	3446	-0.3
04103	PORTLAND	005	29177	29935	30160	0.3	50	12444	13073	13290	0.5	2.23	7122	7224	0.2
04105	FALMOUTH	005	10295	11440	11852	1.1	83	3942	4383	4557	1.2	2.55	2833	3088	0.9
04106	SOUTH PORTLAND	005	23568	24804	25224	0.6	62	10174	11005	11298	0.9	2.20	6125	6398	0.5
04107	CAPE ELIZABETH	005	9082	9261	9282	0.2	46	3494	3664	3708	0.5	2.50	2609	2671	0.3
04108	PEAKS ISLAND	005	920	925	921	0.1	39	431	445	447	0.3	2.07	249	247	-0.1
04109	PORTLAND	005	5	6	6	2.0	97	3	4	4	3.2	1.50	2	0	-100.0
04110	CUMBERLAND FORESIDE	005	1206	1295	1337	0.8	71	464	513	534	1.1	2.51	345	373	0.8
04210	AUBURN	001	23276	23630	23736	0.2	46	9784	10277	10436	0.5	2.22	5924	6057	0.2
04216	ANDOVER	017	762	752	746	-0.1	25	337	348	350	0.3	2.16	233	236	0.1
04217	BETHEL	017	2874	2924	2924	0.2	46	1224	1292	1309	0.6	2.26	812	840	0.4
04219	BRYANT POND	017	1627	1701	1724	0.5	57	657	719	740	1.0	2.35	464	498	0.8
04220	BUCKFIELD	017	2229	2717	2910	2.2	97	858	1096	1189	2.7	2.48	618	775	2.5
04221	CANTON	017	1587	1583	1575	0.0	33	579	595	598	0.3	2.47	406	410	0.1
04222	DURHAM	001	3322	3925	4172	1.8	95	1202	1462	1568	2.1	2.68	961	1152	2.0
04224	DIXFIELD	017	3034	3036	3016	0.0	33	1209	1254	1260	0.4	2.41	869	884	0.2
04226	EAST ANDOVER	017	262	258	256	-0.2	21	102	105	106	0.3	2.46	71	71	0.0
04228	EAST LIVERMORE	001	41	39	38	-0.5	7	16	16	15	0.0	2.31	12	11	-0.9
04231	STONEHAM	017	331	356	367	0.8	71	147	165	173	1.3	2.16	103	114	1.1
04236	GREENE	001	4074	4504	4685	1.1	83	1493	1706	1794	1.5	2.63	1185	1334	1.3
04237	HANOVER	017	251	244	240	-0.3	16	106	108	107	0.2	2.26	73	72	-0.1
04238	HEBRON	017	988	1141	1205	1.6	93	366	443	474	2.1	2.58	279	333	1.9
04239	JAY	007	5052	5146	5200	0.2	46	2043	2175	2226	0.7	2.36	1465	1533	0.5
04240	LEWISTON	001	35881	36534	36771	0.2	46	15351	16261	16549	0.6	2.10	8704	8916	0.3
04250	LISBON	001	3662	3772	3812	0.3	50	1524	1624	1659	0.7	2.31	1010	1051	0.4
04252	LISBON FALLS	001	5314	5534	5596	0.4	53	2060	2206	2253	0.7	2.51	1460	1529	0.5
	MAINE					0.6					0.9	2.32			0.7
	UNITED STATES					1.0					1.1	2.59			0.9

ZIP CODE #	POST OFFICE NAME	RACE (%) White 2000	White 2009	Black 2000	Black 2009	Asian/Pacific 2000	Asian/Pacific 2009	% Hispanic Origin 2000	% Hispanic Origin 2009	2009 AGE DISTRIBUTION (%) 0-4	5-9	10-14	15-19	20-24	25-44	45-64	65-84	85+	18+	MEDIAN AGE 2009	% 2009 Males	% 2009 Females
03901	BERWICK	97.3	96.5	0.4	0.5	1.2	1.8	0.5	0.8	6.4	6.6	6.8	7.3	6.3	26.4	30.1	9.0	1.1	75.8	38.4	48.9	51.1
03902	CAPE NEDDICK	98.9	98.6	0.2	0.2	0.3	0.3	0.8	1.4	4.6	5.2	5.2	5.4	2.9	22.8	38.3	14.1	1.5	81.3	46.9	49.7	50.3
03903	ELIOT	98.4	98.0	0.2	0.3	0.4	0.6	0.5	0.8	5.5	6.2	6.7	6.3	4.7	21.9	34.7	12.2	1.8	77.7	44.0	48.0	52.0
03904	KITTERY	95.3	93.8	2.2	2.8	0.7	1.1	1.8	2.7	6.2	5.8	5.8	6.0	8.0	27.3	27.3	11.4	2.3	78.5	38.6	48.9	51.1
03905	KITTERY POINT	98.3	97.8	0.6	0.8	0.4	0.6	0.6	1.0	4.5	4.8	5.5	5.9	3.7	18.3	34.9	19.1	3.3	81.4	49.0	47.4	52.6
03906	NORTH BERWICK	97.1	96.4	0.6	0.8	0.8	1.2	0.6	1.0	5.8	6.2	6.6	6.8	5.3	25.2	31.6	10.5	1.9	77.0	41.1	49.6	50.4
03907	OGUNQUIT	98.5	97.9	0.5	0.7	0.5	0.8	0.7	1.0	1.7	2.9	2.5	1.8	2.0	13.9	42.8	28.7	3.6	91.5	58.4	52.2	47.8
03908	SOUTH BERWICK	97.6	97.0	0.3	0.4	0.7	1.0	0.7	1.1	6.6	7.1	7.5	7.7	5.8	24.1	31.2	8.6	1.3	73.9	39.2	48.9	51.1
03909	YORK	98.3	97.8	0.3	0.3	0.6	0.8	0.7	1.1	4.5	5.3	6.5	6.2	3.6	19.1	35.4	16.4	3.1	79.6	47.6	48.1	51.9
04001	ACTON	98.4	98.2	0.1	0.1	0.2	0.3	0.9	1.4	5.1	5.6	6.2	6.3	4.5	21.2	34.9	14.5	1.6	79.2	45.6	50.1	49.9
04002	ALFRED	98.5	98.2	0.3	0.4	0.3	0.5	0.2	0.4	4.9	5.7	6.4	6.3	4.6	24.5	33.6	12.8	1.2	78.7	43.4	50.9	49.1
04003	BAILEY ISLAND	98.4	97.8	0.4	0.4	0.4	0.6	1.2	2.0	4.3	4.7	5.0	4.7	3.0	19.6	36.1	20.3	2.4	82.3	50.2	49.9	50.1
04005	BIDDEFORD	96.8	96.0	0.6	0.8	1.0	1.4	0.6	1.0	6.1	5.8	5.8	7.6	7.1	26.6	25.5	12.5	2.9	78.4	38.5	47.7	52.3
04006	BIDDEFORD POOL	98.2	97.7	0.0	0.0	1.2	1.7	0.0	0.6	1.1	2.3	2.9	1.1	19.0	15.5	32.8	23.0	2.3	93.1	50.8	40.2	59.8
04008	BOWDOINHAM	97.7	97.2	0.4	0.5	0.5	0.8	0.5	0.7	5.2	5.7	6.4	6.6	5.2	24.2	35.0	10.3	1.3	78.1	42.7	49.8	50.2
04009	BRIDGTON	97.4	96.9	0.4	0.6	0.3	0.4	0.8	1.4	5.2	5.5	5.5	7.5	5.1	22.2	31.8	14.9	2.3	80.3	44.2	50.2	49.8
04010	BROWNFIELD	98.8	98.7	0.1	0.1	0.1	0.1	0.4	0.7	4.4	6.2	6.5	7.3	3.8	23.6	33.6	12.5	2.0	77.9	43.9	49.3	50.7
04011	BRUNSWICK	94.4	92.6	1.7	2.3	1.7	2.6	1.6	2.5	5.9	5.3	5.4	9.6	10.8	21.9	25.4	12.6	3.0	79.2	37.1	48.3	51.7
04015	CASCO	97.9	97.4	0.3	0.4	0.5	0.8	0.5	0.8	5.8	6.2	7.1	6.9	4.8	26.7	30.1	11.1	1.4	76.3	40.7	49.8	50.2
04017	CHEBEAGUE ISLAND	99.2	98.4	0.0	0.3	0.6	0.8	0.8	1.6	5.2	6.3	7.9	7.3	3.7	16.0	34.0	16.8	2.9	74.9	47.2	47.4	52.6
04019	CLIFF ISLAND	96.6	95.5	0.0	0.0	1.1	2.3	0.0	0.0	5.7	5.7	5.7	8.0	2.3	17.0	39.8	14.8	1.1	78.4	49.2	46.6	53.4
04020	CORNISH	98.3	97.9	0.2	0.4	0.4	0.6	0.6	0.9	5.3	5.9	6.9	7.3	4.0	22.7	31.8	14.3	1.7	76.3	43.6	49.2	50.8
04021	CUMBERLAND CENTER	98.7	98.3	0.1	0.2	0.4	0.6	0.6	1.0	6.5	7.8	8.5	8.2	3.9	21.2	33.0	9.6	1.3	71.8	41.2	48.4	51.6
04022	DENMARK	97.9	97.5	0.4	0.5	0.5	0.7	1.1	1.7	4.1	6.3	6.4	7.0	3.3	24.4	33.0	13.1	2.2	77.7	44.1	48.4	51.6
04024	EAST BALDWIN	99.1	98.4	0.2	0.5	0.2	0.5	0.5	0.8	5.5	6.2	7.0	6.2	4.2	24.2	30.9	14.0	1.8	77.1	42.9	49.4	50.6
04027	LEBANON	98.5	98.2	0.3	0.4	0.3	0.4	0.6	1.1	5.8	6.3	7.4	8.0	5.7	26.2	30.7	8.9	1.1	75.5	39.3	49.6	50.4
04029	SEBAGO	98.4	98.0	0.3	0.5	0.1	0.3	0.3	0.6	4.1	6.0	7.8	5.0	3.1	23.9	34.8	13.9	1.4	78.7	45.1	49.6	50.4
04030	EAST WATERBORO	98.2	97.7	0.2	0.3	0.5	0.7	0.7	1.1	5.7	6.5	7.2	7.3	3.9	26.3	32.6	9.2	1.1	75.5	40.8	50.3	49.7
04032	FREEPORT	97.2	96.5	0.4	0.5	1.1	1.5	0.7	1.2	5.5	6.1	6.9	6.9	5.1	22.0	33.0	12.3	2.2	77.1	43.4	48.6	51.4
04037	FRYEBURG	98.2	97.8	0.3	0.5	0.4	0.6	1.1	1.4	3.5	5.5	6.6	7.7	4.3	22.9	33.5	13.4	2.7	78.9	44.7	48.1	51.9
04038	GORHAM	97.6	96.9	0.4	0.6	0.6	1.0	0.6	1.0	5.9	6.0	6.3	10.6	9.5	23.6	27.5	8.9	1.7	77.6	35.8	48.4	51.6
04039	GRAY	97.9	97.2	0.4	0.6	0.5	0.7	0.6	1.0	5.6	6.2	6.5	6.3	5.1	28.9	31.1	9.1	1.2	77.4	39.9	51.0	49.0
04040	HARRISON	98.6	98.2	0.6	0.8	0.0	0.0	0.5	0.8	5.7	6.5	6.5	8.1	4.0	23.9	30.8	13.4	1.1	77.2	41.9	50.8	49.2
04041	HIRAM	97.6	97.2	0.1	0.1	0.3	0.4	0.4	0.7	6.6	7.0	7.5	7.1	4.9	22.9	31.1	11.9	1.1	74.5	40.9	48.9	51.1
04042	HOLLIS CENTER	98.8	98.7	0.1	0.2	0.2	0.3	0.5	0.7	6.1	7.0	8.0	7.0	5.3	27.5	29.8	8.3	0.9	74.5	38.2	49.8	50.2
04043	KENNEBUNK	98.0	97.5	0.2	0.3	0.9	1.3	0.5	0.8	5.1	5.6	6.4	7.2	5.7	20.7	32.2	13.9	3.2	78.0	44.5	47.0	53.0
04046	KENNEBUNKPORT	98.4	97.9	0.2	0.2	0.5	0.8	0.6	0.9	4.9	5.7	6.5	6.2	3.7	21.4	35.6	14.3	1.8	78.8	45.9	47.8	52.2
04047	PARSONSFIELD	98.2	97.9	0.1	0.2	0.2	0.3	0.8	1.3	5.8	5.9	7.5	6.0	4.4	24.6	29.6	13.5	2.6	76.4	41.7	50.1	49.9
04048	LIMERICK	98.2	98.0	0.3	0.3	0.4	0.0	0.1	0.4	0.6	6.5	6.9	7.6	7.5	4.9	25.8	29.7	9.8	1.3	74.5	39.2	50.1	49.9
04049	LIMINGTON	98.3	97.9	0.4	0.6	0.2	0.3	0.3	0.5	5.8	6.2	6.5	7.8	5.6	26.6	29.2	9.1	3.3	76.6	39.4	48.7	51.3
04050	LONG ISLAND	97.0	96.7	0.0	0.0	1.0	1.4	0.5	1.0	4.3	5.3	8.6	6.7	1.4	19.6	35.9	17.7	0.5	77.0	46.7	49.3	50.7
04051	LOVELL	99.1	99.0	0.0	0.0	0.1	0.2	0.3	0.5	4.3	6.0	7.3	6.9	3.4	22.9	33.4	14.3	1.5	77.7	44.5	51.8	48.2
04055	NAPLES	98.2	97.9	0.1	0.2	0.3	0.5	0.2	0.4	4.9	6.9	6.7	6.3	3.6	26.0	30.0	13.7	1.8	77.2	42.2	50.5	49.5
04061	NORTH WATERBORO	98.5	98.3	0.1	0.1	0.1	0.2	0.9	1.4	10.3	9.5	8.9	7.4	5.2	32.4	21.8	4.1	0.3	66.7	31.4	50.1	49.9
04062	WINDHAM	97.6	97.0	0.5	0.7	0.4	0.6	0.4	0.7	6.0	6.3	6.5	6.4	6.1	28.2	29.3	9.7	1.4	77.1	39.3	50.6	49.4
04064	OLD ORCHARD BEACH	97.5	96.9	0.6	0.8	0.5	0.7	1.0	1.6	4.8	4.6	4.6	5.2	6.9	26.2	31.4	14.1	2.2	82.7	43.4	48.9	51.1
04066	ORRS ISLAND	98.3	97.3	0.0	0.1	1.1	1.6	1.5	2.3	4.3	4.9	5.0	4.0	3.4	17.6	38.1	20.8	1.8	83.1	50.6	49.0	51.0
04068	PORTER	97.0	96.7	0.3	0.4	0.3	0.5	0.7	1.0	5.2	5.8	6.2	7.0	4.7	25.3	30.8	13.2	1.7	78.3	42.2	49.0	51.0
04069	POWNAL	97.9	97.4	0.5	0.6	0.4	0.5	0.7	1.0	5.1	6.0	6.9	6.1	4.2	21.7	37.9	11.1	1.0	78.3	45.0	50.2	49.8
04071	RAYMOND	98.4	98.0	0.4	0.5	0.3	0.4	0.6	0.8	5.4	6.1	6.7	6.5	4.8	25.4	33.5	10.4	1.2	77.6	42.1	49.6	50.4
04072	SACO	97.9	97.5	0.3	0.4	0.6	0.8	0.6	0.9	6.3	6.2	6.6	6.7	6.0	27.2	27.7	11.1	2.3	76.3	39.3	48.1	51.9
04073	SANFORD	95.7	94.3	0.5	0.6	2.1	3.1	1.1	1.7	6.7	6.6	6.4	7.1	6.6	26.4	26.0	11.7	2.6	75.8	37.6	48.6	51.4
04074	SCARBOROUGH	97.4	96.5	0.4	0.5	1.2	1.7	0.5	0.8	6.2	6.8	7.4	7.0	4.7	22.3	31.3	12.5	2.0	75.0	42.3	48.8	51.2
04076	SHAPLEIGH	98.4	98.0	0.2	0.3	0.4	0.7	0.9	1.4	5.1	5.8	6.6	6.5	4.1	24.8	32.8	12.3	1.8	78.0	43.3	50.1	49.9
04079	HARPSWELL	97.9	97.3	0.3	0.4	0.5	0.7	1.3	2.0	4.1	5.0	5.6	4.7	3.3	21.6	37.3	16.3	2.2	81.9	48.4	49.3	50.7
04083	SPRINGVALE	95.7	94.4	0.4	0.5	2.1	3.2	0.5	0.8	6.7	6.2	6.1	6.7	7.3	26.8	26.3	11.2	2.8	76.7	37.2	47.6	52.4
04084	STANDISH	98.1	97.6	0.4	0.6	0.3	0.4	0.5	0.8	6.1	6.5	6.6	9.6	8.2	26.5	27.3	8.4	0.9	76.9	36.3	48.8	51.2
04085	STEEP FALLS	98.2	97.5	0.2	0.3	0.5	0.9	0.3	0.6	6.0	6.7	7.1	6.7	4.3	29.0	31.7	7.7	0.8	76.1	39.2	48.5	51.5
04086	TOPSHAM	95.2	93.8	1.3	1.8	1.4	2.0	1.2	2.0	6.6	6.8	6.5	6.7	5.6	26.5	27.1	11.0	3.0	75.5	38.7	48.4	51.6
04087	WATERBORO	99.1	99.0	0.1	0.1	0.1	0.2	0.4	0.7	7.0	7.3	7.7	7.6	5.1	27.3	29.3	7.8	0.9	73.1	37.9	50.4	49.6
04088	WATERFORD	98.7	98.4	0.1	0.1	0.2	0.3	0.4	0.7	5.0	5.8	7.0	6.0	3.8	23.5	33.8	13.4	1.7	78.2	44.3	49.3	50.7
04090	WELLS	98.2	97.8	0.2	0.3	0.5	0.7	0.6	1.0	4.4	5.0	5.5	5.5	3.9	21.6	36.4	15.8	1.9	81.7	47.3	48.9	51.1
04091	WEST BALDWIN	99.0	98.5	0.2	0.4	0.4	0.7	0.5	0.8	5.8	6.4	6.7	6.5	4.2	24.4	30.4	13.8	1.8	76.9	42.4	49.3	50.7
04092	WESTBROOK	96.7	95.8	0.9	1.2	0.8	1.3	0.9	1.4	6.0	5.8	5.9	6.2	6.4	26.0	28.1	12.8	2.8	78.4	40.7	48.0	52.0
04093	BUXTON	97.8	97.3	0.4	0.6	0.7	1.0	0.6	0.9	5.6	6.5	7.0	6.8	4.2	27.7	31.9	9.2	1.1	76.3	40.7	50.4	49.6
04095	WEST NEWFIELD	97.9	97.7	0.1	0.1	0.1	0.1	0.7	1.1	5.7	6.3	7.2	8.1	3.7	25.3	31.6	10.2	1.8	75.3	41.2	51.5	48.5
04096	YARMOUTH	98.5	98.1	0.4	0.5	0.4	0.6	0.6	1.0	4.7	5.2	6.2	6.6	5.8	21.4	34.0	13.4	2.7	79.8	45.1	47.8	52.2
04097	NORTH YARMOUTH	98.7	98.2	0.1	0.1	0.6	0.9	0.5	0.8	6.1	7.3	8.6	8.2	4.1	21.6	34.8	8.1	1.1	72.8	41.7	48.5	51.5
04101	PORTLAND	87.0	83.1	4.6	6.1	3.6	5.2	2.8	4.3	4.5	3.3	2.9	5.8	13.1	38.0	21.2	8.7	2.7	86.9	33.9	50.9	49.1
04102	PORTLAND	91.6	88.7	2.2	2.9	3.4	5.1	1.4	2.1	4.7	4.0	3.9	4.9	10.5	33.0	25.8	10.8	2.4	84.4	37.0	48.4	51.6
04103	PORTLAND	93.4	91.2	1.8	2.4	2.8	4.2	0.9	1.3	5.6	5.3	5.4	5.5	7.1	28.7	27.0	11.9	3.4	80.2	39.8	46.3	53.7
04105	FALMOUTH	97.7	97.0	0.2	0.3	1.2	1.8	0.5	0.8	6.0	7.1	8.4	7.7	3.8	18.1	33.0	12.2	3.7	73.3	44.3	47.6	52.4
04106	SOUTH PORTLAND	95.8	94.3	0.6	0.9	1.6	2.5	1.1	1.8	5.6	5.5	5.7	7.1	6.9	26.6	28.3	11.9	2.5	78.8	40.2	47.8	52.2
04107	CAPE ELIZABETH	98.0	97.3	0.3	0.4	1.0	1.6	0.5	0.8	4.4	5.3	6.8	7.7	4.7	16.5	37.0	14.6	3.1	78.5	47.6	47.8	52.2
04108	PEAKS ISLAND	97.8	97.3	0.0	0.0	1.0	1.5	0.9	1.5	5.5	4.3	7.6	4.9	1.3	22.8	37.8	13.8	1.9	78.6	46.6	47.7	52.3
04109	PORTLAND	100.0	100.0	0.0	0.0	0.0	0.0	0.0	0.0	0.0	0.0	0.0	0.0	0.0	0.0	100.0	0.0	0.0	100.0	52.5	33.3	66.7
04110	CUMBERLAND FORESIDE	98.8	98.5	0.1	0.2	0.6	0.8	0.9	1.5	5.2	6.2	7.6	7.2	3.6	15.9	34.8	16.7	2.9	75.6	47.6	47.6	52.4
04210	AUBURN	97.0	96.4	0.6	0.8	0.6	0.9	0.7	1.2	5.7	5.5	5.5	6.3	6.4	25.3	28.5	13.3	3.6	79.4	41.7	47.8	52.2
04216	ANDOVER	98.8	98.7	0.3	0.3	0.1	0.1	0.1	0.3	4.1	5.2	6.3	5.9	3.6	21.4	38.6	13.2	1.9	80.2	46.6	52.0	48.0
04217	BETHEL	98.2	97.8	0.2	0.2	0.5	0.7	0.6	1.0	5.2	5.3	6.2	6.1	4.9	24.4	31.4	14.8	1.8	79.3	43.6	49.1	50.9
04219	BRYANT POND	98.7	98.5	0.1	0.1	0.1	0.2	0.6	0.9	5.2	5.1	7.8	6.9	3.9	24.4	31.3	13.8	1.6	77.0	42.7	51.2	48.8
04220	BUCKFIELD	98.3	98.1	0.0	0.0	0.3	0.4	0.5	0.7	5.9	6.4	6.9	6.9	4.9	24.5	32.4	10.8	1.3	76.6	41.4	49.4	50.6
04221	CANTON	98.7	98.4	0.1	0.1	0.4	0.5	0.8	1.3	5.5	6.2	7.4	6.4	3.9	25.0	28.1	14.3	3.2	76.8	42.2	48.6	51.4
04222	DURHAM	98.9	98.7	0.1	0.2	0.3	0.4	0.7	1.0	5.7	6.4	7.2	6.7	4.2	26.3	35.1	7.8	0.7	76.3	41.6	50.0	50.0
04224	DIXFIELD	98.2	97.7	0.0	0.1	0.5	0.7	0.8	1.2	5.5	6.0	6.8	6.8	4.7	22.6	31.7	14.0	2.0	76.7	43.4	48.9	51.1
04226	EAST ANDOVER	98.9	98.4	0.4	0.4	0.0	0.4	0.4	0.4	4.3	5.0	6.2	6.2	3.9	21.3	37.6	13.6	1.9	79.8	46.5	51.2	48.8
04228	EAST LIVERMORE	100.0	97.4	0.0	0.0	0.0	0.0	0.0	0.0	5.1	5.1	7.7	7.7	5.1	20.5	30.8	12.8	5.1	74.4	43.8	51.3	48.7
04231	STONEHAM	98.5	97.8	0.0	0.0	0.3	0.6	0.3	0.3	4.5	6.2	7.0	6.5	3.7	24.2	32.9	14.0	1.1	77.8	43.6	50.3	49.7
04236	GREENE	98.5	98.1	0.5	0.6	0.3	0.4	0.7	1.2	5.7	6.2	6.8	6.7	4.4	27.1	32.7	9.6	1.0	76.8	41.3	49.7	50.3
04237	HANOVER	99.2	99.2	0.0	0.0	0.0	0.0	0.8	1.2	4.9	4.1	7.0	6.1	3.3	23.0	34.0	16.8	0.8	80.3	45.7	52.9	47.1
04238	HEBRON	97.8	97.3	0.1	0.2	0.6	0.8	0.8	1.2	5.3	5.6	6.3	6.1	5.3	26.2	36.3	8.0	1.0	78.9	41.9	51.4	48.6
04239	JAY	97.9	97.7	0.3	0.3	0.3	0.4	0.5	0.8	5.7	5.8	6.1	6.8	5.9	23.9	29.6	14.5	1.7	78.1	42.1	48.7	51.3
04240	LEWISTON	95.8	94.8	1.1	1.4	0.9	1.3	1.2	2.0	5.7	5.3	5.2	7.3	8.3	24.8	25.6	14.3	3.5	80.3	39.8	47.8	52.2
04250	LISBON	97.5	97.0	0.7	0.9	0.6	0.7	0.5	0.8	7.0	6.8	6.8	6.5	5.9	25.9	27.2	12.2	1.7	75.4	38.9	49.0	51.0
04252	LISBON FALLS	97.3	96.7	0.6	0.8	0.4	0.6	0.9	1.4	6.9	6.7	6.6	6.6	6.3	27.9	27.4	10.2	1.3	75.7	37.2	49.3	50.7
	MAINE	96.9	96.3	0.5	0.7	0.7	1.1	0.7	1.1	5.4	5.6	6.1	6.9	6.2	24.7	30.2	12.7	2.3	78.8	41.6	48.8	51.2
	UNITED STATES	75.1	72.0	12.3	12.7	3.8	4.6	12.5	15.7	6.8	6.7	6.6	7.1	6.9	27.0	26.0	10.9	1.9	75.7	36.9	49.2	50.8

#	POST OFFICE NAME	2009 Per Capita Income	2009 HH Income Base	2009 Household Income Distribution (%): Less than $25,000	$25,000 to $49,999	$50,000 to $99,999	$100,000 to $149,999	$150,000 or More	Median Household Income: 2009	2014	2009 National Centile	2009 State Centile	2009 Home Value Base	2009 Home Value Distribution (%): Less than $50,000	$50,000 to $89,999	$90,000 to $174,999	$175,000 to $399,999	$400,000 or More	2009 Median Home Value
03901	BERWICK	23018	2817	20.3	22.7	45.9	7.9	3.3	56487	59487	73	87	2138	2.5	7.7	34.9	53.8	1.0	183667
03902	CAPE NEDDICK	42496	1002	11.7	13.1	43.9	17.2	14.2	78740	78868	91	99	860	0.0	1.4	6.4	56.6	35.6	347234
03903	ELIOT	30974	2348	14.3	20.1	39.9	19.3	6.5	69941	71309	87	98	1913	1.4	2.7	12.9	64.1	19.0	261941
03904	KITTERY	26791	3285	18.3	28.4	41.8	8.8	2.7	53455	56768	69	84	1908	5.0	3.1	22.3	59.4	10.2	223108
03905	KITTERY POINT	34308	1040	13.1	21.9	44.4	12.3	8.3	62747	64918	81	94	831	5.8	2.0	7.9	44.3	40.0	338603
03906	NORTH BERWICK	25131	1951	13.4	23.5	50.9	9.8	2.5	61114	62515	79	92	1603	0.6	2.4	38.9	51.8	6.4	191037
03907	OGUNQUIT	46602	764	13.9	23.7	39.0	11.8	11.6	65376	67427	84	96	587	0.0	0.2	2.4	53.3	44.1	374632
03908	SOUTH BERWICK	26959	2652	10.2	20.3	51.1	14.1	4.4	69629	71199	87	97	2066	0.0	2.7	22.6	67.2	7.5	226482
03909	YORK	37869	4865	11.3	23.2	36.0	16.8	12.7	70672	72663	87	98	3930	1.4	0.3	6.0	54.6	37.8	347489
04001	ACTON	23243	1100	19.3	34.1	38.0	5.5	3.1	47382	49940	55	67	982	1.7	4.4	28.2	53.2	12.5	217081
04002	ALFRED	23874	2851	17.6	26.4	45.7	6.9	3.3	54370	56453	70	85	2469	2.4	6.0	34.0	53.5	4.2	187634
04003	BAILEY ISLAND	32292	286	21.3	25.2	40.6	7.3	5.6	52075	54658	66	81	217	1.4	0.0	25.3	43.3	30.0	269792
04005	BIDDEFORD	22535	9885	28.4	28.0	33.3	7.7	2.6	43596	46784	44	52	5039	1.1	1.6	29.7	60.2	7.3	202910
04006	BIDDEFORD POOL	36151	74	18.9	25.7	31.1	12.2	12.2	60000	76186	77	91	48	0.0	0.0	4.2	16.7	79.2	692308
04008	BOWDOINHAM	26817	1258	21.2	22.7	40.3	9.5	6.3	55261	58351	72	86	1058	2.5	6.4	31.7	51.1	8.3	193657
04009	BRIDGTON	21629	2101	23.8	31.0	37.8	3.9	3.4	43827	48419	45	53	1570	1.7	6.6	52.3	32.2	7.2	153158
04010	BROWNFIELD	21130	612	25.0	34.8	32.7	5.1	2.5	41917	42539	39	46	542	3.0	12.2	38.6	39.9	6.5	169949
04011	BRUNSWICK	26036	8758	21.7	26.3	37.5	9.9	4.7	51393	53799	65	80	5576	12.5	5.1	22.2	47.8	12.4	208532
04015	CASCO	24714	1488	19.5	27.5	40.7	8.0	4.3	52225	54985	66	82	1231	3.7	4.5	39.1	44.9	7.8	181492
04017	CHEBEAGUE ISLAND	61711	188	9.0	12.8	37.2	9.0	31.9	87182	90138	94	100	171	0.0	0.6	11.1	38.0	50.3	401852
04019	CLIFF ISLAND	23900	40	27.5	42.5	22.5	5.0	2.5	39014	39014	30	36	24	0.0	0.0	16.7	50.0	33.3	250000
04020	CORNISH	21215	593	26.8	27.7	38.6	5.7	1.2	45531	49014	50	59	467	1.9	4.7	44.5	45.8	3.0	173036
04021	CUMBERLAND CENTER	41352	2025	8.4	14.8	35.7	19.5	21.7	86688	87840	94	99	1846	0.3	0.4	8.3	60.9	30.1	315826
04022	DENMARK	25720	376	22.3	29.3	35.6	8.8	4.0	46182	46447	52	61	325	1.2	4.9	31.4	46.2	16.3	219118
04024	EAST BALDWIN	20532	158	22.8	32.3	39.9	3.8	1.3	45000	48791	48	57	138	3.6	8.7	51.4	32.6	3.6	158036
04027	LEBANON	18858	2154	24.8	27.7	39.0	7.4	1.1	47437	50626	55	68	1890	6.8	7.3	38.7	44.1	3.1	169058
04029	SEBAGO	24482	655	16.3	32.5	42.4	6.4	2.3	50647	52938	63	78	556	0.7	6.1	44.4	40.3	8.5	173250
04030	EAST WATERBORO	23611	795	10.8	31.2	49.4	5.8	2.8	57615	60368	75	88	682	2.9	0.3	44.6	48.7	3.5	179032
04032	FREEPORT	34278	3351	16.1	19.4	40.6	12.8	11.0	66305	68347	84	96	2609	3.7	4.0	17.9	49.3	25.2	267120
04037	FRYEBURG	22222	1663	28.0	33.6	30.6	6.0	1.9	42124	44368	40	47	1300	4.0	6.2	38.0	43.1	8.8	184677
04038	GORHAM	27008	5462	15.4	20.4	46.0	11.5	6.7	64084	66250	82	95	4377	5.7	2.0	22.0	62.6	7.7	215394
04039	GRAY	29433	2822	9.6	23.3	50.9	10.9	5.2	63154	64729	81	94	2190	3.2	2.8	28.4	61.5	4.2	204626
04040	HARRISON	22409	1239	22.8	31.6	37.0	5.4	3.1	44068	49084	46	54	1056	4.1	7.3	45.4	34.7	8.6	164857
04041	HIRAM	19149	669	29.3	32.3	31.8	4.5	2.1	41168	42822	37	42	554	4.9	9.4	45.1	37.5	3.1	157667
04042	HOLLIS CENTER	24907	1774	13.1	21.1	54.8	7.7	3.2	63675	64557	82	94	1492	5.2	5.7	27.4	57.3	4.4	192090
04043	KENNEBUNK	33107	4869	12.3	23.9	39.9	13.5	10.3	65624	67324	84	96	3857	0.0	1.6	15.1	59.5	23.8	268163
04046	KENNEBUNKPORT	35129	3350	11.8	22.0	42.7	13.3	10.1	66816	68263	85	96	2805	1.4	4.4	13.4	48.3	32.5	293136
04047	PARSONSFIELD	20095	793	24.7	39.2	29.1	4.9	2.0	39631	41715	32	37	643	5.6	6.1	49.8	29.7	8.9	155242
04048	LIMERICK	22573	1155	22.3	27.8	40.3	6.5	3.0	49885	52304	61	75	948	3.3	5.5	47.0	39.1	5.1	166717
04049	LIMINGTON	20140	1386	21.0	26.8	43.6	6.3	2.3	51353	53244	65	80	1179	5.5	5.7	43.0	43.4	2.4	169107
04050	LONG ISLAND	22452	99	29.3	24.2	45.5	1.0	0.0	46393	46394	53	63	73	0.0	5.5	9.6	31.5	53.4	417857
04051	LOVELL	20568	393	26.2	33.8	33.1	5.6	1.3	40278	41636	34	40	334	3.3	6.3	32.9	41.3	16.2	197321
04055	NAPLES	22581	1492	21.1	30.2	40.6	6.2	1.9	48503	50967	58	71	1235	3.0	4.5	46.6	37.0	8.9	167530
04061	NORTH WATERBORO	20914	981	8.8	27.7	56.2	6.3	1.0	59021	60690	76	90	888	1.7	1.4	63.2	32.7	1.1	162879
04062	WINDHAM	26367	6136	12.7	25.3	48.9	9.0	4.0	59661	62240	77	90	4901	1.7	2.1	34.0	55.4	6.9	197967
04064	OLD ORCHARD BEACH	25784	4657	25.8	29.0	38.7	4.5	2.1	44732	48676	47	56	2555	7.0	7.7	43.9	38.3	3.1	158321
04066	ORRS ISLAND	30280	387	15.5	25.6	43.9	9.8	5.2	55722	58390	72	86	290	0.0	1.4	32.8	49.0	16.9	214179
04068	PORTER	19150	596	25.8	34.9	34.1	3.5	1.7	41362	42897	37	43	482	3.5	12.4	46.3	34.4	3.3	156563
04069	POWNAL	32385	636	11.9	19.3	46.9	14.2	7.7	68992	70278	86	97	566	1.9	0.7	15.4	61.5	20.5	246715
04071	RAYMOND	31851	2408	9.3	21.6	51.8	8.2	9.1	64857	66123	83	95	2077	0.0	0.0	28.2	56.5	15.3	229986
04072	SACO	25930	7509	20.9	23.6	42.3	9.1	4.1	56782	60377	74	88	5000	4.3	3.2	25.6	59.0	7.9	205681
04073	SANFORD	20425	6995	29.0	29.9	34.0	5.5	1.6	40341	43873	34	41	4405	4.5	5.8	55.3	32.6	1.7	158897
04074	SCARBOROUGH	34523	7042	10.1	19.6	38.4	22.9	8.9	73679	74134	89	98	5705	1.7	1.2	11.4	65.5	20.2	272225
04076	SHAPLEIGH	24073	1160	12.5	31.8	46.2	7.2	2.3	53208	55090	68	83	1028	0.7	4.2	36.9	51.2	7.1	192418
04079	HARPSWELL	34236	1986	21.2	30.0	31.6	8.5	8.7	48964	51467	59	73	1559	4.0	2.2	20.7	39.4	33.7	291274
04083	SPRINGVALE	23600	2019	24.8	26.2	37.8	6.1	5.1	49000	52172	59	73	1260	0.0	8.7	54.4	35.2	1.7	154680
04084	STANDISH	25869	3174	11.2	25.2	51.1	7.6	4.9	61748	63434	80	93	2753	5.8	3.1	26.8	57.8	6.6	202205
04085	STEEP FALLS	21808	713	12.2	24.5	56.1	6.2	1.0	58883	61154	76	89	650	0.8	4.2	37.8	54.6	2.6	184631
04086	TOPSHAM	26265	3851	13.9	26.6	44.9	10.6	3.9	60276	62423	78	91	2703	3.6	3.0	26.7	62.2	4.5	205251
04087	WATERBORO	22817	579	16.1	35.6	37.3	5.7	5.4	48880	51054	59	72	476	5.0	2.3	42.4	45.2	5.0	175397
04088	WATERFORD	20702	791	27.6	34.0	31.6	4.9	1.9	39957	40633	32	38	668	3.6	9.3	34.6	39.7	12.9	183854
04090	WELLS	29858	4730	15.5	26.6	42.1	9.9	5.9	58976	61243	76	89	3854	1.6	2.8	16.7	55.9	23.0	263402
04091	WEST BALDWIN	19012	277	22.7	31.4	40.8	3.6	1.4	45818	49144	51	60	243	5.3	9.1	49.8	32.1	3.7	155398
04092	WESTBROOK	24821	7397	23.4	28.0	39.0	7.1	2.4	48084	51702	57	70	4419	5.0	2.3	33.7	56.5	2.5	186887
04093	BUXTON	25692	3230	15.3	21.9	50.2	8.6	4.0	61431	62868	79	92	2732	0.3	4.7	32.7	59.8	2.5	195968
04095	WEST NEWFIELD	20772	643	20.5	31.4	41.5	5.1	1.4	47284	51229	55	67	557	2.0	5.0	50.1	40.8	2.2	166906
04096	YARMOUTH	43981	3588	12.1	15.4	40.1	15.5	16.9	77842	78533	91	98	2520	0.5	1.1	6.4	53.5	38.6	329412
04097	NORTH YARMOUTH	33824	1277	6.0	14.8	46.4	21.5	11.3	78632	79725	91	99	1162	0.4	0.7	12.7	66.9	19.3	264773
04101	PORTLAND	24349	8905	36.6	31.0	26.3	4.0	2.1	34148	35674	16	16	1354	0.9	2.4	38.5	48.9	9.3	197561
04102	PORTLAND	31973	8234	23.5	26.5	36.6	8.0	5.4	50048	52613	61	76	3480	0.4	1.0	24.8	61.8	12.0	218898
04103	PORTLAND	29104	13073	18.7	24.4	43.4	9.0	4.5	55979	59330	73	86	7552	0.5	0.6	29.4	64.8	4.7	210610
04105	FALMOUTH	50683	4383	8.5	12.5	33.8	17.4	27.7	91169	92234	95	100	3651	0.0	0.2	7.8	45.1	46.9	384037
04106	SOUTH PORTLAND	28797	11005	18.4	25.0	44.2	8.6	3.8	54752	57485	71	85	6897	0.4	0.9	36.7	57.6	4.5	193117
04107	CAPE ELIZABETH	50658	3664	8.5	12.2	31.3	20.7	27.3	95250	96741	96	100	3210	0.3	0.2	9.2	52.4	37.9	328545
04108	PEAKS ISLAND	36009	445	19.8	21.8	42.7	11.9	3.8	56633	59205	74	87	339	2.9	1.8	25.1	41.3	28.9	265351
04109	PORTLAND	41667	4	0.0	50.0	50.0	0.0	0.0	57500	57500	75	88	4	0.0	0.0	0.0	0.0	100.0	500000
04110	CUMBERLAND FORESIDE	49700	513	9.0	12.7	38.0	9.0	31.4	86708	90458	94	99	468	0.0	0.6	11.3	37.4	50.6	404000
04210	AUBURN	23399	10277	28.5	29.5	32.6	6.7	2.8	42580	45833	41	49	5878	3.4	6.5	60.3	26.0	3.8	144075
04216	ANDOVER	25445	348	27.9	28.4	33.6	5.7	4.3	44038	45567	45	54	295	9.8	11.2	34.6	35.6	8.8	164423
04217	BETHEL	22677	1292	26.5	33.0	32.5	5.3	2.6	41614	42951	38	45	961	5.3	5.5	34.4	39.0	15.7	197750
04219	BRYANT POND	22137	719	21.7	38.4	32.7	4.5	2.8	44151	45353	46	54	605	9.6	14.2	36.5	32.7	6.9	150962
04220	BUCKFIELD	21738	1096	18.2	37.4	36.4	6.3	1.6	45678	46002	50	59	927	6.8	10.4	46.0	33.2	3.7	155529
04221	CANTON	18073	595	31.9	26.7	36.1	3.9	1.3	41926	43838	39	46	479	13.6	22.1	35.7	25.5	3.1	126453
04222	DURHAM	26869	1462	11.4	24.5	48.1	11.4	4.7	65083	64905	83	95	1303	0.3	6.1	28.5	60.2	4.9	213838
04224	DIXFIELD	19511	1254	26.1	32.2	35.8	5.3	0.6	43481	45424	44	51	1013	9.0	17.6	54.0	17.3	2.2	127153
04226	EAST ANDOVER	22448	105	27.6	28.6	33.3	5.7	4.8	44451	45489	47	55	89	10.1	12.4	34.8	32.6	10.1	161458
04228	EAST LIVERMORE	19938	16	18.8	50.0	25.0	6.3	0.0	42270	42343	40	47	14	7.1	28.6	50.0	14.3	0.0	116667
04231	STONEHAM	26205	165	24.8	30.3	35.2	6.7	3.0	44692	45796	47	56	144	6.9	10.4	37.5	35.4	9.7	166250
04236	GREENE	24697	1706	11.0	26.7	51.6	8.3	2.5	60232	60885	78	91	1507	2.2	6.0	47.4	40.2	4.1	166056
04237	HANOVER	26139	108	24.1	28.7	38.9	4.6	3.7	46882	46427	54	65	89	4.5	2.2	33.7	47.2	12.4	198611
04238	HEBRON	24676	443	10.8	26.2	51.7	9.5	1.8	57982	58746	75	89	357	2.2	9.0	34.2	47.9	6.7	185313
04239	JAY	21893	2175	27.2	29.1	35.8	6.5	1.4	44623	46003	47	55	1756	8.2	11.8	51.0	25.7	3.2	149728
04240	LEWISTON	21119	16261	35.9	29.9	27.5	4.7	2.0	35707	38050	20	23	7614	5.2	7.8	59.8	25.7	1.4	142670
04250	LISBON	21533	1624	22.6	36.8	34.5	3.7	2.3	43294	46296	43	50	1168	19.6	11.0	47.3	20.3	1.9	128059
04252	LISBON FALLS	23037	2206	16.6	31.5	42.7	6.6	2.6	51165	51850	64	79	1612	12.3	4.4	58.4	24.1	0.8	143266
	MAINE	24559		25.0	28.4	35.2	7.5	3.8	46650	48581				6.4	9.4	36.7	38.7	8.8	170226
	UNITED STATES	27277		20.9	24.4	35.3	11.7	7.6	54719	56938				9.3	13.1	31.6	32.6	13.5	162279

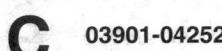

ZIP CODE #	POST OFFICE NAME	FINANCIAL SERVICES: Auto Loan	Home Loan	Invest-ments	Retire-ment Plans	THE HOME: Home Improvements: Home Repair	Lawn & Garden	Furnishings: Comput-ers & Hard-ware-Personal	Major Appli-ances	TV, Radio, Sound Equip-ment	Furni-ture	ENTERTAINMENT: Dine out/ Carry out	Sports Equip-ment	Fees & Tickets	Toys & Games	Travel	Cable TV	PERSONAL: Apparel & Services	Auto Repairs	Health Insur-ance	Pets & Supplies
03901	BERWICK	88	94	83	93	91	92	87	89	87	87	87	68	89	89	88	87	61	87	89	105
03902	CAPE NEDDICK	134	145	169	146	157	159	130	146	133	141	132	100	142	126	145	137	92	140	155	167
03903	ELIOT	106	123	115	126	122	117	110	113	107	113	108	87	119	108	117	106	76	109	110	131
03904	KITTERY	87	87	80	88	85	86	88	85	87	88	88	66	88	89	86	87	61	87	87	101
03905	KITTERY POINT	104	118	118	117	121	123	105	113	107	110	107	80	115	105	115	110	75	109	121	130
03906	NORTH BERWICK	91	103	91	104	100	100	94	96	92	93	93	75	100	94	98	92	65	93	95	112
03907	OGUNQUIT	115	122	165	120	140	143	109	129	115	124	113	81	120	104	126	121	78	123	144	146
03908	SOUTH BERWICK	100	117	105	117	114	108	105	105	101	106	102	83	114	103	111	100	73	103	101	123
03909	YORK	131	141	165	142	147	147	126	140	124	130	125	104	133	122	139	125	87	132	136	161
04001	ACTON	91	78	101	79	82	97	77	92	80	71	79	69	69	79	80	85	53	85	93	107
04002	ALFRED	91	91	91	92	93	100	85	94	87	85	86	70	85	87	89	90	59	89	97	110
04003	BAILEY ISLAND	101	81	131	80	89	107	81	103	85	76	84	75	70	80	88	90	56	95	102	119
04005	BIDDEFORD	73	72	67	73	70	73	76	73	77	73	77	56	76	77	74	78	54	76	77	87
04006	BIDDEFORD POOL	115	121	165	120	140	143	109	129	115	123	113	80	120	103	126	120	78	123	143	146
04008	BOWDOINHAM	100	100	88	100	98	101	92	97	94	95	94	73	92	97	92	95	65	94	97	115
04009	BRIDGTON	84	72	89	73	76	88	73	85	76	68	75	63	66	75	75	80	51	80	87	98
04010	BROWNFIELD	82	65	106	64	72	86	65	83	69	61	68	61	57	65	71	73	45	77	82	96
04011	BRUNSWICK	89	85	88	87	86	89	90	88	90	89	91	68	88	90	89	92	63	90	93	104
04015	CASCO	98	90	101	89	92	100	86	97	88	85	88	71	81	89	88	91	60	92	96	113
04017	CHEBEAGUE ISLAND	165	204	209	210	210	193	174	184	167	186	168	137	198	166	195	163	121	174	174	210
04019	CLIFF ISLAND	88	70	113	69	77	93	70	89	74	66	73	65	61	70	76	78	48	82	88	103
04020	CORNISH	78	71	71	74	73	84	70	79	73	64	71	60	65	74	70	77	49	73	82	92
04021	CUMBERLAND CENTER	157	196	182	197	193	175	165	170	156	174	159	132	187	160	181	152	114	162	156	195
04022	DENMARK	99	79	128	78	87	105	79	101	83	74	82	74	69	79	86	89	55	93	100	117
04024	EAST BALDWIN	78	70	73	73	72	84	69	79	72	63	70	60	64	73	70	76	48	73	81	92
04027	LEBANON	82	75	69	74	74	80	72	78	74	72	74	57	67	77	70	77	50	74	79	92
04029	SEBAGO	96	77	122	76	85	102	77	98	81	72	80	71	67	77	83	86	53	90	97	113
04030	EAST WATERBORO	86	97	84	100	94	95	87	90	85	87	86	71	93	88	92	85	60	87	89	106
04032	FREEPORT	118	128	124	130	129	122	120	120	116	124	117	93	126	118	124	114	83	118	116	140
04037	FRYEBURG	86	70	106	69	76	90	70	87	73	66	72	63	62	70	75	78	48	81	87	101
04038	GORHAM	100	114	105	114	112	108	104	105	102	106	103	81	112	103	110	102	73	103	104	122
04039	GRAY	99	113	101	114	111	108	104	105	102	103	103	82	111	104	110	102	73	103	104	123
04040	HARRISON	89	75	100	76	80	94	76	90	79	70	77	67	67	77	79	83	52	84	91	105
04041	HIRAM	77	70	69	73	71	82	69	78	71	62	70	59	64	72	69	75	48	72	80	90
04042	HOLLIS CENTER	90	103	91	104	100	99	94	95	92	93	93	75	101	94	99	92	66	93	95	112
04043	KENNEBUNK	111	122	122	123	123	121	113	117	112	116	112	88	120	111	119	112	79	114	117	136
04046	KENNEBUNKPORT	120	129	136	129	134	134	115	126	117	123	117	89	123	115	124	119	81	120	128	146
04047	PARSONSFIELD	82	65	106	64	72	86	65	83	69	61	68	61	57	65	71	73	45	77	82	96
04048	LIMERICK	92	84	79	84	84	93	81	89	84	78	83	66	76	86	79	87	56	84	91	104
04049	LIMINGTON	91	83	77	83	83	90	80	87	83	79	82	64	75	85	78	86	56	82	88	102
04050	LONG ISLAND	79	63	102	62	70	84	63	80	66	59	65	59	55	63	69	71	44	74	79	93
04051	LOVELL	83	66	107	65	73	87	66	84	69	62	68	61	57	66	72	74	45	78	83	97
04055	NAPLES	91	74	117	73	81	97	74	93	77	69	76	68	64	73	79	82	51	86	92	108
04061	NORTH WATERBORO	95	102	84	99	96	88	91	92	87	97	89	72	92	93	90	84	62	87	83	105
04062	WINDHAM	92	102	94	101	100	98	95	96	94	95	95	73	101	96	99	94	67	95	95	112
04064	OLD ORCHARD BEACH	77	69	65	69	67	71	76	72	76	74	76	56	71	77	71	77	53	75	76	86
04066	ORRS ISLAND	107	85	138	84	94	113	85	109	89	80	88	79	74	85	93	95	59	100	107	126
04068	PORTER	73	67	66	69	68	79	66	74	68	59	67	56	61	69	66	72	45	69	77	86
04069	POWNAL	115	130	112	134	127	128	116	121	114	117	115	94	124	117	123	114	80	116	119	142
04071	RAYMOND	120	121	131	123	122	131	112	125	112	110	112	95	112	112	119	115	77	118	123	146
04072	SACO	88	92	87	92	90	88	90	88	89	90	89	69	92	90	91	89	63	89	88	104
04073	SANFORD	73	68	63	68	66	72	72	70	73	68	73	55	68	74	68	75	51	72	74	84
04074	SCARBOROUGH	120	140	135	142	139	129	126	127	121	131	122	99	138	122	135	118	87	124	120	147
04076	SHAPLEIGH	91	88	102	89	90	98	82	94	83	80	83	71	81	83	88	86	57	88	93	109
04079	HARPSWELL	126	101	162	99	110	133	101	128	105	94	104	93	87	100	109	112	69	118	126	148
04083	SPRINGVALE	77	83	80	82	83	81	82	81	82	80	82	63	85	82	84	82	58	82	83	94
04084	STANDISH	106	106	100	105	104	106	97	104	98	100	99	78	97	101	98	99	68	99	101	122
04085	STEEP FALLS	85	96	83	99	93	94	86	89	84	86	85	70	91	86	90	84	59	86	88	105
04086	TOPSHAM	93	99	87	100	95	93	96	93	94	96	95	74	99	96	97	93	67	94	92	110
04087	WATERBORO	94	91	80	89	88	92	84	89	86	87	87	66	82	90	83	88	59	86	89	106
04088	WATERFORD	82	65	106	64	72	86	65	83	68	61	68	61	57	65	71	73	45	77	82	96
04090	WELLS	101	101	119	102	106	113	93	106	95	95	94	77	95	92	102	98	65	101	108	123
04091	WEST BALDWIN	77	70	69	73	71	82	69	78	71	62	70	59	63	72	69	75	48	72	80	90
04092	WESTBROOK	78	79	76	79	77	83	79	79	81	76	80	60	80	80	79	83	56	80	85	93
04093	BUXTON	93	105	90	108	102	103	94	98	92	94	93	76	100	95	99	92	65	94	97	115
04095	WEST NEWFIELD	91	73	117	72	80	96	73	92	76	68	75	67	63	72	79	81	50	85	91	107
04096	YARMOUTH	136	159	166	163	165	152	147	149	141	154	142	113	162	140	159	139	102	146	144	171
04097	NORTH YARMOUTH	126	157	150	159	156	142	132	138	126	140	128	105	150	128	146	122	92	130	127	158
04101	PORTLAND	62	48	48	52	46	49	69	54	68	63	69	46	60	66	59	68	48	64	60	69
04102	PORTLAND	87	82	83	87	82	78	97	83	93	93	95	70	94	93	91	91	68	91	84	101
04103	PORTLAND	90	92	87	93	90	89	95	89	94	94	95	70	97	94	94	93	67	93	92	106
04105	FALMOUTH	164	214	228	217	224	202	181	190	174	190	175	142	214	173	206	172	129	180	182	213
04106	SOUTH PORTLAND	86	89	85	90	88	87	92	87	91	90	92	68	94	91	92	92	65	91	91	103
04107	CAPE ELIZABETH	163	205	223	209	217	195	178	188	169	192	170	139	204	165	203	165	123	178	178	212
04108	PEAKS ISLAND	104	106	105	108	105	104	107	103	106	108	107	80	109	105	107	105	75	105	106	122
04109	PORTLAND	86	90	123	90	104	107	81	96	86	92	84	60	89	77	94	90	58	92	107	109
04110	CUMBERLAND FORESIDE	165	204	209	210	210	193	174	184	167	186	168	137	198	166	195	163	121	174	174	210
04210	AUBURN	75	70	69	72	70	77	75	74	77	71	76	56	72	76	72	80	53	76	82	89
04216	ANDOVER	92	73	119	72	81	97	73	93	77	69	76	68	64	73	80	82	50	86	92	108
04217	BETHEL	80	69	83	70	73	84	71	81	73	67	72	60	64	72	72	77	49	77	83	94
04219	BRYANT POND	86	70	109	69	76	91	70	88	73	65	72	64	61	70	75	78	48	81	87	102
04220	BUCKFIELD	83	76	75	79	78	90	75	85	77	68	76	64	69	79	75	82	52	78	87	98
04221	CANTON	78	61	77	60	63	81	61	75	66	57	65	56	52	67	61	72	44	69	78	88
04222	DURHAM	100	113	97	116	110	111	101	105	99	101	100	82	108	102	107	100	70	101	104	124
04224	DIXFIELD	74	65	69	66	66	79	65	75	68	59	67	56	58	69	64	73	45	69	78	87
04226	EAST ANDOVER	92	74	119	72	81	97	74	94	77	69	76	68	64	73	80	82	51	86	92	109
04228	EAST LIVERMORE	85	61	87	59	63	86	62	79	69	58	68	59	50	69	61	76	45	73	82	94
04231	STONEHAM	94	75	122	74	83	100	76	96	79	71	78	70	65	75	82	84	52	89	95	111
04236	GREENE	91	102	88	105	99	100	91	95	90	91	90	74	97	92	96	90	63	91	94	112
04237	HANOVER	98	79	127	78	87	104	79	100	83	74	82	73	68	78	86	88	54	93	99	116
04238	HEBRON	89	100	86	103	97	98	89	93	88	89	88	72	95	90	94	88	62	89	92	109
04239	JAY	79	74	71	74	74	81	72	78	75	70	74	57	68	76	71	78	50	75	81	91
04240	LEWISTON	65	58	56	60	57	64	66	63	67	61	67	48	61	66	62	70	46	66	70	76
04250	LISBON	81	65	71	65	66	80	69	76	73	67	72	57	61	74	65	78	49	73	80	90
04252	LISBON FALLS	83	83	70	84	78	88	81	81	83	78	83	64	82	85	80	86	57	82	89	98
	MAINE	87	79	87	80	81	89	81	86	83	78	82	65	76	83	81	86	57	84	89	102
	UNITED STATES	100	100	100	100	100	100	100	100	100	100	100	100	100	100	100	100	100	100	100	100

ZIP CODE #	POST OFFICE NAME	COUNTY FIPS CODE	POPULATION 2000	POPULATION 2009	POPULATION 2014	2000-2009 ANNUAL RATE % Rate	2000-2009 ANNUAL RATE State Centile	HOUSEHOLDS 2000	HOUSEHOLDS 2009	HOUSEHOLDS 2014	HOUSEHOLDS % Annual Rate 2000-2009	HOUSEHOLDS 2009 Average HH Size	FAMILIES 2000	FAMILIES 2009	FAMILIES % Annual Rate 2000-2009
04253	LIVERMORE	001	2092	2370	2483	1.4	90	837	978	1036	1.7	2.42	598	685	1.5
04254	LIVERMORE FALLS	001	3165	3136	3126	-0.1	25	1297	1323	1334	0.2	2.33	819	813	-0.1
04255	GREENWOOD	017	641	694	719	0.9	77	255	289	304	1.4	2.40	178	198	1.2
04256	MECHANIC FALLS	001	3084	3203	3227	0.4	53	1149	1217	1236	0.6	2.61	832	865	0.4
04257	MEXICO	017	2959	2980	2977	0.1	39	1298	1360	1376	0.5	2.18	832	852	0.3
04258	MINOT	001	2204	2253	2258	0.2	46	786	825	835	0.5	2.72	635	657	0.4
04259	MONMOUTH	011	2857	3346	3546	1.7	94	1069	1295	1388	2.1	2.58	808	961	1.9
04260	NEW GLOUCESTER	005	4769	5191	5365	0.9	77	1747	1973	2063	1.3	2.62	1303	1437	1.1
04261	NEWRY	017	348	343	340	-0.2	21	145	150	151	0.4	2.29	100	102	0.2
04263	LEEDS	001	2001	1900	1863	-0.6	3	736	722	716	-0.2	2.63	548	528	-0.4
04265	NORTH MONMOUTH	011	921	977	1000	0.6	62	362	398	413	1.0	2.45	266	287	0.8
04266	NORTH TURNER	001	3	3	3	0.0	33	1	1	1	0.0	3.00	1	1	0.0
04268	NORWAY	017	4643	4855	4948	0.5	57	1985	2150	2214	0.9	2.21	1267	1338	0.6
04270	OXFORD	017	5364	6072	6356	1.3	88	2013	2364	2508	1.8	2.56	1496	1727	1.6
04274	POLAND	001	4912	5672	5983	1.6	93	1854	2213	2363	1.9	2.56	1442	1694	1.8
04275	ROXBURY	017	505	512	512	0.1	39	215	228	231	0.6	2.25	146	150	0.3
04276	RUMFORD	017	6472	6274	6181	-0.3	16	2876	2900	2896	0.1	2.12	1755	1725	-0.2
04280	SABATTUS	001	5738	6216	6391	0.9	77	2154	2388	2476	1.1	2.59	1646	1795	0.9
04281	SOUTH PARIS	017	4966	5368	5525	0.8	71	2051	2299	2400	1.2	2.23	1295	1417	1.0
04282	TURNER	001	4937	5363	5539	0.9	77	1752	1946	2026	1.1	2.75	1381	1511	1.0
04284	WAYNE	011	1088	1182	1224	0.9	77	454	513	537	1.3	2.30	322	356	1.1
04285	WELD	007	402	403	401	0.0	33	176	185	186	0.5	2.18	130	135	0.4
04287	BOWDOIN	023	2666	2770	2786	0.4	53	958	1031	1051	0.8	2.68	743	786	0.6
04289	WEST PARIS	017	1817	1871	1869	0.3	50	680	719	726	0.6	2.44	484	502	0.4
04290	PERU	017	1515	1623	1673	0.7	66	585	652	680	1.2	2.49	437	478	1.0
04292	SUMNER	017	813	881	910	0.9	77	313	355	372	1.4	2.48	235	262	1.2
04294	WILTON	007	4214	4172	4125	-0.1	25	1700	1754	1759	0.3	2.38	1173	1187	0.1
04330	AUGUSTA	011	24731	25194	25389	0.2	46	10876	11517	11742	0.6	2.13	6329	6498	0.3
04341	COOPERS MILLS	015	7	7	7	0.0	33	4	4	4	0.0	1.75	3	3	0.0
04342	DRESDEN	015	1625	1914	2011	1.8	95	642	783	835	2.2	2.44	455	543	1.9
04344	FARMINGDALE	011	2834	2944	2979	0.4	53	1208	1302	1334	0.8	2.23	779	815	0.5
04345	GARDINER	011	11442	12475	12906	0.9	77	4553	5146	5386	1.3	2.39	3106	3437	1.1
04346	RANDOLPH	011	2104	2171	2183	0.3	50	910	974	991	0.7	2.23	593	618	0.4
04347	HALLOWELL	011	2330	2296	2279	-0.2	21	1093	1112	1114	0.2	1.98	571	561	-0.2
04348	JEFFERSON	015	2891	3016	3021	0.5	57	1144	1252	1273	1.0	2.40	822	883	0.8
04349	KENTS HILL	011	1031	1149	1199	1.2	87	414	479	506	1.6	2.40	295	335	1.4
04350	LITCHFIELD	011	3110	3462	3599	1.2	87	1190	1380	1455	1.6	2.51	897	1022	1.4
04351	MANCHESTER	011	2463	2741	2856	1.2	87	979	1117	1176	1.4	2.45	735	824	1.2
04352	MOUNT VERNON	011	1425	1562	1625	1.0	80	566	644	677	1.4	2.42	421	470	1.2
04353	WHITEFIELD	015	2351	2586	2680	1.0	80	869	1006	1057	1.6	2.51	638	725	1.4
04354	PALERMO	027	1215	1405	1479	1.6	93	488	591	631	2.1	2.38	362	431	1.9
04355	READFIELD	011	2473	2837	2986	1.5	91	908	1069	1136	1.8	2.65	704	817	1.6
04357	RICHMOND	023	3022	3025	2990	0.0	33	1184	1224	1222	0.4	2.45	822	831	0.1
04358	SOUTH CHINA	011	4106	4622	4830	1.3	88	1549	1805	1907	1.7	2.56	1176	1347	1.5
04360	VIENNA	011	517	581	608	1.3	88	210	245	259	1.7	2.37	155	178	1.5
04363	WINDSOR	011	2164	2284	2334	0.6	62	835	913	943	1.0	2.50	612	656	0.8
04364	WINTHROP	011	6254	6560	6693	0.5	57	2506	2727	2817	0.9	2.33	1748	1862	0.7
04401	BANGOR	019	41873	43517	44116	0.4	53	17663	18751	19185	0.6	2.18	10168	10595	0.4
04406	ABBOT	021	769	762	751	-0.1	25	338	354	354	0.5	2.15	242	249	0.3
04408	AURORA	009	173	190	197	1.0	80	72	83	87	1.5	2.29	46	52	1.3
04410	BRADFORD	019	1112	1019	983	-0.9	1	406	384	376	-0.6	2.65	302	280	-0.8
04411	BRADLEY	019	1140	1164	1177	0.2	46	473	501	513	0.6	2.32	335	347	0.4
04412	BREWER	019	8987	9093	9136	0.1	39	3842	4008	4073	0.5	2.23	2401	2438	0.2
04413	BROOKTON	029	186	177	173	-0.5	7	77	77	77	0.0	2.30	51	50	-0.2
04414	BROWNVILLE	021	1233	1177	1149	-0.5	7	552	557	551	0.1	2.11	355	350	-0.2
04416	BUCKSPORT	009	5441	5539	5540	0.2	46	2272	2426	2458	0.7	2.27	1523	1592	0.5
04417	BURLINGTON	019	558	570	575	0.2	46	223	237	241	0.7	2.41	159	165	0.4
04418	GREENBUSH	019	1847	1881	1902	0.2	46	684	724	741	0.6	2.60	503	522	0.4
04419	CARMEL	019	2312	2235	2218	-0.4	11	895	900	905	0.1	2.48	680	671	-0.1
04421	CASTINE	009	1337	1411	1431	0.6	62	370	412	427	1.2	2.09	221	240	0.9
04422	CHARLESTON	019	1471	1604	1651	0.9	77	459	520	545	1.4	2.55	356	396	1.2
04424	DANFORTH	029	962	918	898	-0.5	7	411	412	408	0.0	2.20	282	278	-0.2
04426	DOVER FOXCROFT	021	4654	4920	4901	0.6	62	1845	2013	2032	0.9	2.34	1288	1379	0.7
04427	CORINTH	019	2511	2873	3016	1.5	91	959	1132	1200	1.8	2.53	715	828	1.6
04428	EDDINGTON	019	2786	2935	2997	0.6	62	1125	1226	1266	0.9	2.37	808	860	0.7
04429	HOLDEN	009	4258	4375	4424	0.3	50	1720	1834	1875	0.7	2.39	1241	1300	0.5
04430	EAST MILLINOCKET	019	1828	1762	1738	-0.4	11	780	781	780	0.0	2.26	555	543	-0.2
04434	ETNA	019	1012	1026	1026	0.1	39	392	413	419	0.6	2.48	295	305	0.4
04435	EXETER	019	881	939	964	0.7	66	343	378	393	1.1	2.48	260	282	0.9
04438	FRANKFORT	027	1116	1332	1419	1.9	96	426	535	576	2.5	2.49	320	394	2.3
04441	GREENVILLE	021	1746	1683	1646	-0.4	11	795	796	788	0.0	2.08	479	468	-0.3
04442	GREENVILLE JUNCTION	021	97	95	91	-0.2	21	44	45	44	0.2	2.11	27	27	0.0
04443	GUILFORD	021	2335	2215	2150	-0.6	3	950	943	929	-0.1	2.35	647	631	-0.3
04444	HAMPDEN	019	7593	8250	8518	0.9	77	2952	3313	3462	1.3	2.49	2171	2387	1.0
04448	HOWLAND	019	1547	1555	1560	0.1	39	635	661	671	0.4	2.28	424	430	0.2
04449	HUDSON	019	1343	1490	1547	1.1	83	488	559	589	1.5	2.67	371	417	1.3
04450	KENDUSKEAG	019	1171	1285	1338	1.0	80	470	536	564	1.4	2.40	330	368	1.2
04451	KINGMAN	003	320	310	306	-0.3	16	136	137	137	0.1	2.26	103	102	-0.1
04453	LAGRANGE	019	930	958	970	0.3	50	355	381	391	0.8	2.51	239	251	0.5
04454	LAMBERT LAKE	029	55	52	51	-0.6	3	23	23	23	0.0	2.26	15	15	0.0
04455	LEE	019	914	922	915	0.1	39	321	333	335	0.4	2.74	265	270	0.2
04456	LEVANT	019	2171	2769	3008	2.7	99	784	1035	1136	3.0	2.68	610	792	2.9
04457	LINCOLN	019	6146	6532	6693	0.7	66	2466	2719	2824	1.1	2.37	1742	1876	0.8
04459	MATTAWAMKEAG	019	670	672	673	0.0	33	271	282	286	0.4	2.38	188	192	0.2
04460	MEDWAY	003	1628	1498	1456	-0.9	1	647	620	610	-0.5	2.42	481	452	-0.7
04461	MILFORD	019	2532	2547	2567	0.1	39	995	1040	1060	0.5	2.45	675	688	0.2
04462	MILLINOCKET	019	5204	5063	5021	-0.3	16	2296	2319	2326	0.1	2.16	1557	1534	-0.2
04463	MILO	021	2883	2925	2889	0.2	46	1226	1299	1302	0.6	2.25	818	848	0.4
04464	MONSON	021	668	637	623	-0.5	7	302	304	301	0.1	2.09	188	185	-0.2
04468	OLD TOWN	019	10068	10748	11031	0.7	66	4192	4619	4797	1.1	2.27	2556	2750	0.8
04469	ORONO	019	1633	1786	1786	1.0	80	1	1	1	0.0	1.00	0	0	0.0
04471	ORIENT	003	546	528	520	-0.4	11	220	222	222	0.1	2.37	165	164	-0.1
04472	ORLAND	009	2127	2365	2456	1.2	87	879	1024	1077	1.7	2.31	629	720	1.5
04473	ORONO	019	7557	8073	8238	0.7	66	2722	2996	3108	1.0	2.15	1314	1410	0.8
04474	ORRINGTON	019	3526	3785	3894	0.8	71	1396	1549	1613	1.1	2.44	1043	1135	0.9
	MAINE					0.6					0.9	2.32			0.7
	UNITED STATES					1.0					1.1	2.59			0.9

ZIP CODE #	POST OFFICE NAME	RACE (%) White 2000	White 2009	Black 2000	Black 2009	Asian/Pacific 2000	Asian/Pacific 2009	% Hispanic Origin 2000	% Hispanic Origin 2009	2009 AGE DISTRIBUTION (%) 0-4	5-9	10-14	15-19	20-24	25-44	45-64	65-84	85+	18+	MEDIAN AGE 2009	% 2009 Males	% 2009 Females
04253	LIVERMORE	99.0	98.9	0.2	0.3	0.0	0.0	0.3	0.5	5.5	5.9	6.2	6.0	4.8	24.7	31.8	13.7	1.4	78.8	43.1	53.8	46.2
04254	LIVERMORE FALLS	97.3	96.7	0.5	0.7	0.2	0.3	1.0	1.7	6.6	6.6	6.9	7.7	6.4	24.3	25.3	13.4	2.7	74.4	37.9	48.8	51.2
04255	GREENWOOD	97.8	97.6	0.2	0.1	0.3	0.4	0.3	0.4	4.9	5.9	7.1	6.5	3.6	24.9	32.3	13.7	1.2	77.4	42.9	50.3	49.7
04256	MECHANIC FALLS	97.3	96.7	0.5	0.7	0.6	1.0	0.5	0.8	6.4	6.5	6.9	7.0	5.3	27.4	29.3	9.6	1.5	75.8	39.2	49.3	50.7
04257	MEXICO	97.9	97.3	0.2	0.3	0.9	1.4	0.3	0.4	5.3	5.4	5.6	6.3	5.9	21.5	30.6	16.5	2.8	79.5	44.9	48.6	51.4
04258	MINOT	98.2	97.9	0.2	0.3	0.4	0.5	0.4	0.5	6.0	6.5	7.0	6.9	4.6	25.9	32.8	9.4	1.0	75.6	41.1	49.5	50.5
04259	MONMOUTH	98.8	98.5	0.1	0.2	0.1	0.2	0.8	1.2	6.4	6.9	7.1	7.0	5.7	24.2	32.3	9.4	1.0	75.2	40.1	47.8	52.2
04260	NEW GLOUCESTER	98.2	97.7	0.2	0.3	0.5	0.8	0.6	0.9	6.8	7.5	8.1	6.9	4.8	30.0	27.7	7.6	0.6	73.0	36.9	50.7	49.3
04261	NEWRY	99.1	98.5	0.3	0.3	0.0	0.3	0.3	0.3	4.1	5.2	6.4	5.8	3.8	22.2	37.3	13.4	1.7	80.5	46.2	51.6	48.4
04263	LEEDS	99.1	98.9	0.2	0.3	0.1	0.2	0.5	0.8	5.3	6.7	8.2	8.3	4.8	27.6	29.4	8.8	1.0	74.0	37.7	50.5	49.5
04265	NORTH MONMOUTH	97.6	97.2	0.9	1.1	0.2	0.3	0.4	0.6	6.2	6.9	7.3	6.6	4.1	23.3	32.9	11.6	1.2	75.4	42.2	48.4	51.6
04266	NORTH TURNER	100.0	100.0	0.0	0.0	0.0	0.0	0.0	0.0	0.0	0.0	0.0	0.0	0.0	33.3	66.7	0.0	0.0	100.0	47.5	33.3	66.7
04268	NORWAY	97.8	97.4	0.3	0.4	0.4	0.6	0.5	0.8	5.3	5.4	5.2	5.7	5.6	23.3	30.6	15.0	3.6	80.2	44.5	47.4	52.6
04270	OXFORD	97.9	97.7	0.3	0.3	0.3	0.4	0.4	0.7	5.7	6.2	7.0	6.3	4.7	24.8	32.5	11.7	1.3	77.0	42.1	49.7	50.3
04274	POLAND	98.5	98.3	0.3	0.4	0.2	0.3	0.3	0.5	5.6	6.1	6.6	6.4	4.7	24.6	33.8	11.1	1.1	77.5	42.7	50.1	49.9
04275	ROXBURY	98.2	97.9	0.2	0.2	0.8	1.2	0.0	0.2	3.9	4.3	4.7	5.9	5.7	20.9	34.2	17.8	2.7	82.6	47.4	50.8	49.2
04276	RUMFORD	98.7	98.4	0.1	0.1	0.3	0.4	0.6	1.0	5.6	5.4	5.4	6.2	6.2	22.3	28.3	16.8	3.8	79.6	44.1	47.6	52.4
04280	SABATTUS	98.0	97.5	0.2	0.3	0.4	0.6	0.5	0.7	6.4	6.5	6.8	6.6	5.4	27.9	29.7	9.7	1.0	76.2	39.5	50.5	49.5
04281	SOUTH PARIS	97.9	97.4	0.3	0.4	0.9	1.3	0.4	0.6	5.3	5.2	5.4	6.0	5.9	24.3	28.2	16.4	3.5	80.5	43.6	48.0	52.0
04282	TURNER	96.8	95.6	0.1	0.1	0.3	0.5	2.8	4.2	6.4	7.0	7.4	7.2	5.3	25.6	31.3	8.9	1.0	74.6	39.3	49.6	50.4
04284	WAYNE	98.5	98.4	0.3	0.3	0.1	0.2	0.2	0.3	2.7	5.8	8.0	7.2	2.5	21.6	35.0	14.9	2.5	78.5	46.1	51.3	48.7
04285	WELD	98.0	97.5	0.2	0.2	0.0	0.0	0.5	1.0	5.2	6.0	7.7	6.2	1.7	27.0	32.5	12.4	1.2	76.9	42.7	53.6	46.4
04287	BOWDOIN	97.8	97.4	0.3	0.3	0.3	0.5	0.7	1.2	6.1	6.5	6.8	7.2	6.0	25.5	33.2	7.9	0.8	76.4	40.0	49.3	50.7
04289	WEST PARIS	98.8	98.7	0.1	0.2	0.1	0.1	0.3	0.5	6.0	6.4	6.5	5.7	4.2	22.2	29.0	14.7	5.2	77.4	44.2	47.4	52.6
04290	PERU	99.3	99.2	0.0	0.0	0.1	0.2	0.4	0.7	4.6	6.3	7.0	8.1	4.9	23.7	30.1	13.4	2.0	76.6	42.3	50.3	49.7
04292	SUMNER	98.5	98.4	0.1	0.1	0.0	0.0	0.5	0.8	5.3	5.9	6.1	5.3	4.5	23.8	35.4	11.9	1.6	79.3	44.1	49.1	50.9
04294	WILTON	97.5	96.9	0.4	0.6	0.8	1.2	0.4	0.7	5.6	5.7	5.9	6.6	6.4	23.9	30.6	13.5	1.8	78.9	41.8	48.0	52.0
04330	AUGUSTA	96.7	95.7	0.4	0.6	1.1	1.7	0.8	1.2	5.2	5.2	5.4	5.9	5.9	25.6	29.8	14.3	2.7	80.7	42.6	48.3	51.7
04341	COOPERS MILLS	100.0	100.0	0.0	0.0	0.0	0.0	0.0	0.0	0.0	0.0	0.0	0.0	0.0	42.9	57.1	0.0	0.0	100.0	47.5	42.9	57.1
04342	DRESDEN	97.4	97.1	0.2	0.3	0.5	0.7	0.1	0.1	6.4	6.7	7.4	7.2	4.8	25.2	30.6	10.6	1.2	75.0	40.2	51.4	48.6
04344	FARMINGDALE	97.5	96.9	0.7	0.9	0.5	0.8	0.5	0.8	6.2	6.1	6.2	6.0	5.4	24.5	29.0	14.4	2.2	77.7	41.7	45.9	54.1
04345	GARDINER	97.3	96.7	0.4	0.5	0.3	0.4	0.7	1.1	5.6	5.8	6.0	6.5	5.6	25.1	31.8	11.9	1.8	78.5	42.1	49.0	51.0
04346	RANDOLPH	97.3	96.8	0.4	0.6	0.2	0.4	0.8	1.3	6.1	5.9	6.0	6.4	6.1	24.0	28.2	15.1	2.1	77.8	42.0	48.8	51.2
04347	HALLOWELL	97.2	96.5	0.4	0.5	0.9	1.4	1.1	1.9	4.0	3.7	4.0	5.7	9.1	23.3	33.7	13.4	3.1	84.5	45.1	47.6	52.4
04348	JEFFERSON	98.6	98.4	0.1	0.1	0.2	0.3	0.4	0.7	5.2	5.8	6.5	6.8	3.5	23.9	34.7	12.1	1.3	77.7	43.9	49.4	50.6
04349	KENTS HILL	98.4	98.0	0.0	0.0	0.6	0.9	0.4	0.7	5.6	6.2	5.4	7.4	3.6	25.8	34.7	10.0	1.4	76.8	42.8	50.6	49.4
04350	LITCHFIELD	98.4	97.9	0.1	0.1	0.4	0.6	0.8	1.3	5.5	6.1	6.8	6.5	4.9	25.4	33.3	10.3	1.1	77.2	41.8	49.8	50.2
04351	MANCHESTER	97.8	97.5	0.0	0.1	0.4	0.5	0.4	0.6	5.1	5.9	6.5	6.3	4.2	20.4	36.6	13.0	2.0	78.6	45.8	48.9	51.1
04352	MOUNT VERNON	97.6	97.3	0.3	0.4	0.4	0.4	0.4	0.6	4.4	6.1	7.1	8.0	4.0	24.2	36.0	9.0	1.0	76.3	42.5	50.8	49.2
04353	WHITEFIELD	97.3	96.8	0.2	0.2	0.5	0.7	0.9	1.3	4.8	5.1	5.8	7.5	5.7	26.0	32.3	10.8	2.0	78.8	42.1	48.8	51.2
04354	PALERMO	97.7	97.4	0.3	0.4	0.3	0.4	0.2	0.4	5.6	6.1	7.2	5.5	3.1	26.5	32.9	11.4	1.9	77.1	42.6	50.6	49.4
04355	READFIELD	97.7	97.4	0.1	0.1	0.5	0.7	1.0	1.7	6.1	6.6	7.4	6.9	4.5	24.1	31.9	11.2	1.3	75.5	41.3	51.1	48.9
04357	RICHMOND	98.2	97.7	0.4	0.6	0.3	0.5	0.8	1.3	6.1	6.2	6.5	6.9	6.2	25.1	30.5	11.2	1.2	76.4	40.4	48.7	51.3
04358	SOUTH CHINA	98.0	97.5	0.1	0.2	0.4	0.6	0.6	1.0	5.4	5.9	6.9	7.6	5.3	25.9	33.3	8.6	1.2	77.0	40.6	49.7	50.3
04360	VIENNA	98.5	98.1	0.2	0.2	0.0	0.2	0.4	0.5	4.3	5.5	8.6	5.9	4.3	24.1	36.0	10.3	1.0	77.5	43.4	49.6	50.4
04363	WINDSOR	98.4	98.1	0.3	0.4	0.1	0.2	0.6	0.9	6.4	6.7	6.8	6.6	5.5	26.9	29.2	10.8	1.2	76.1	39.6	48.1	51.9
04364	WINTHROP	98.4	98.0	0.3	0.4	0.4	0.6	0.5	0.9	4.6	5.3	6.2	5.9	5.3	22.9	33.4	13.8	2.6	80.0	44.9	49.7	50.3
04401	BANGOR	95.7	94.7	0.8	1.0	1.0	1.5	0.9	1.4	5.6	5.3	5.4	7.2	8.0	27.2	27.5	11.5	2.2	79.7	38.6	48.0	52.0
04406	ABBOT	97.9	97.9	0.1	0.1	0.1	0.1	0.1	0.1	3.9	4.1	5.4	6.3	3.1	23.2	37.9	15.0	1.0	81.9	46.9	50.4	49.6
04408	AURORA	98.8	98.4	0.0	0.0	0.0	0.0	0.6	1.1	5.8	5.3	7.4	5.8	3.7	26.3	35.8	9.5	0.5	76.8	42.3	51.1	48.9
04410	BRADFORD	97.4	96.9	0.4	0.5	0.0	0.0	0.9	1.5	7.0	7.1	7.0	6.8	5.8	27.8	28.1	9.4	1.2	74.7	38.1	52.8	47.2
04411	BRADLEY	98.3	98.0	0.2	0.3	0.2	0.3	0.6	1.0	5.2	5.4	5.8	5.8	4.5	28.6	30.8	12.5	1.5	80.0	41.4	49.7	50.3
04412	BREWER	97.6	97.0	0.3	0.4	0.6	0.9	0.6	1.0	5.5	5.4	5.6	6.2	7.1	25.0	28.3	14.2	2.8	79.5	41.6	48.1	51.9
04413	BROOKTON	95.2	93.2	0.5	0.6	0.0	0.0	1.1	1.7	4.0	4.0	4.5	4.0	4.5	23.2	36.2	18.1	1.7	85.9	48.8	52.5	47.5
04414	BROWNVILLE	98.1	98.0	0.0	0.0	0.1	0.1	0.8	0.8	4.3	4.8	5.3	5.7	4.8	20.2	34.7	16.9	3.2	81.9	47.9	50.3	49.7
04416	BUCKSPORT	98.1	97.9	0.1	0.1	0.2	0.3	0.8	1.3	5.2	5.5	6.2	6.6	6.0	24.8	31.0	12.6	2.1	79.0	42.0	48.4	51.6
04417	BURLINGTON	99.3	99.1	0.0	0.0	0.2	0.4	0.4	0.7	5.3	4.7	6.3	8.2	5.4	26.7	31.4	10.7	1.2	78.4	41.6	52.3	47.7
04418	GREENBUSH	96.9	96.3	0.5	0.7	0.1	0.2	0.3	0.5	5.6	5.8	7.7	9.5	5.4	30.1	27.9	7.2	0.6	74.4	37.2	51.0	49.0
04419	CARMEL	98.1	97.7	0.2	0.2	0.4	0.6	0.3	0.5	5.4	5.9	6.2	6.9	5.2	26.1	33.2	10.3	0.9	78.3	41.6	50.8	49.2
04421	CASTINE	97.1	96.3	0.7	0.9	0.7	1.1	0.6	0.9	2.8	2.5	3.0	13.3	28.6	13.6	22.0	12.4	1.8	90.5	25.0	64.3	35.7
04422	CHARLESTON	98.2	97.8	0.7	0.9	0.2	0.3	0.3	0.4	4.8	6.1	6.5	8.9	6.7	31.1	28.2	7.2	0.5	77.2	37.0	52.4	47.6
04424	DANFORTH	99.4	99.1	0.1	0.1	0.2	0.2	0.1	0.1	4.7	4.8	5.9	6.0	5.6	21.1	31.2	18.5	2.3	80.3	46.4	50.4	49.6
04426	DOVER FOXCROFT	97.0	97.1	0.2	0.2	0.5	0.5	0.9	0.9	4.5	4.8	5.9	6.7	5.1	23.2	31.1	15.2	3.5	80.1	44.8	48.7	51.3
04427	CORINTH	98.2	97.6	0.1	0.1	0.1	0.1	0.8	1.3	6.5	6.6	6.9	6.5	4.7	27.5	29.7	10.5	1.3	75.8	39.2	49.7	50.3
04428	EDDINGTON	97.9	97.6	0.2	0.2	0.3	0.4	0.4	0.5	4.7	5.2	5.4	6.1	5.6	25.3	32.1	14.3	1.3	80.7	43.6	49.4	50.6
04429	HOLDEN	98.1	97.7	0.2	0.3	0.5	0.7	0.3	0.5	5.0	5.4	6.7	7.0	3.9	25.6	35.2	10.3	1.0	77.9	43.0	50.8	49.2
04430	EAST MILLINOCKET	98.3	98.0	0.0	0.0	0.4	0.6	0.3	0.5	4.7	5.6	6.9	6.5	4.4	20.3	29.5	19.7	2.4	78.5	45.9	48.2	51.8
04434	ETNA	99.1	98.8	0.2	0.3	0.3	0.5	0.1	0.2	7.0	7.2	7.2	5.6	4.2	27.6	29.9	10.4	0.9	75.0	39.0	48.2	51.8
04435	EXETER	99.0	98.9	0.0	0.0	0.0	0.0	0.1	0.2	5.6	5.4	6.9	5.2	4.6	27.4	31.4	12.7	0.7	78.5	41.3	51.0	49.0
04438	FRANKFORT	97.7	97.3	0.1	0.2	0.3	0.4	0.4	0.5	7.0	7.1	6.8	5.7	5.2	29.7	29.0	8.8	0.8	75.5	37.6	48.4	51.6
04441	GREENVILLE	98.8	98.8	0.1	0.1	0.2	0.2	0.2	0.2	5.1	4.8	5.0	5.2	7.5	18.2	33.8	16.2	4.2	81.2	47.7	48.4	51.6
04442	GREENVILLE JUNCTION	97.9	97.9	0.0	0.0	0.0	0.0	0.0	0.0	4.2	10.5	2.1	6.3	1.1	23.2	41.1	11.6	0.0	80.0	45.9	54.7	45.3
04443	GUILFORD	97.0	97.0	0.3	0.3	0.4	0.4	0.4	0.4	5.0	5.6	6.5	6.3	4.2	23.7	32.3	14.5	1.9	78.8	44.0	49.9	50.1
04444	HAMPDEN	97.9	97.4	0.4	0.5	0.6	0.8	0.5	0.8	5.0	5.5	6.1	6.8	5.7	24.0	34.3	11.4	1.3	79.1	42.9	49.2	50.8
04448	HOWLAND	98.3	97.9	0.2	0.3	0.1	0.2	0.1	0.3	5.7	5.9	6.2	6.1	4.7	22.9	29.5	15.9	3.0	78.1	44.0	46.5	53.5
04449	HUDSON	97.8	97.5	0.5	0.7	0.1	0.1	0.2	0.3	6.8	6.8	6.6	6.2	5.8	28.9	29.9	8.3	0.5	75.8	38.2	50.1	49.9
04450	KENDUSKEAG	97.0	96.7	0.3	0.5	0.0	0.0	0.3	0.6	5.5	5.2	5.8	7.4	6.0	28.5	31.4	10.0	0.3	79.4	40.6	49.3	50.7
04451	KINGMAN	98.1	98.1	0.6	0.6	0.3	0.3	0.3	0.6	4.2	5.8	7.7	6.8	4.8	24.8	30.0	14.8	1.0	77.1	42.5	50.3	49.7
04453	LAGRANGE	97.5	97.0	0.4	0.6	0.5	0.7	0.2	0.3	5.8	5.9	6.2	7.0	6.1	26.2	30.8	10.6	1.4	77.8	40.3	48.7	51.3
04454	LAMBERT LAKE	96.3	94.2	0.0	0.0	0.0	0.0	1.9	1.9	3.8	3.8	5.8	3.8	3.8	25.0	34.6	17.3	1.9	82.7	47.5	48.1	51.9
04455	LEE	98.8	98.6	0.0	0.0	0.1	0.3	0.1	0.2	5.4	6.2	8.2	8.0	3.6	27.7	24.8	14.3	1.7	74.1	40.0	51.0	49.0
04456	LEVANT	97.5	97.1	0.1	0.2	0.2	0.3	0.7	1.2	6.4	6.5	7.0	8.2	5.9	27.1	29.9	8.5	0.7	75.2	38.7	49.4	50.6
04457	LINCOLN	98.4	98.0	0.1	0.2	0.4	0.5	0.3	0.5	5.4	5.5	5.9	6.9	5.7	23.2	30.0	14.8	2.6	78.9	43.1	48.4	51.6
04459	MATTAWAMKEAG	98.1	97.9	0.0	0.0	0.0	0.0	0.1	0.3	6.4	6.5	6.7	6.1	4.9	21.3	31.0	15.5	1.6	76.6	43.7	48.4	51.6
04460	MEDWAY	99.2	99.1	0.1	0.1	0.1	0.2	0.2	0.4	4.3	5.4	6.5	7.9	4.2	24.4	35.4	11.1	0.8	78.9	43.4	53.5	46.5
04461	MILFORD	96.6	95.8	0.1	0.1	0.5	0.7	0.5	0.8	5.4	5.6	5.5	5.4	5.2	32.4	29.1	10.4	0.9	80.1	38.9	49.7	50.3
04462	MILLINOCKET	98.5	98.2	0.1	0.1	0.4	0.5	0.2	0.4	3.5	4.1	4.7	6.4	4.9	20.6	34.6	18.1	3.2	83.6	48.4	48.3	51.7
04463	MILO	98.5	98.5	0.3	0.3	0.2	0.2	0.2	0.2	5.6	5.6	5.8	6.1	5.8	22.3	30.3	16.1	2.4	79.4	44.0	48.0	52.0
04464	MONSON	97.9	97.8	0.0	0.0	0.0	0.0	0.4	0.5	5.7	5.8	6.4	6.3	4.4	19.6	33.4	16.3	2.0	77.7	46.1	49.1	50.9
04468	OLD TOWN	90.6	89.8	0.5	0.7	1.5	2.1	0.5	0.8	5.3	5.4	5.6	7.5	9.4	28.2	25.1	11.7	1.9	80.0	36.2	48.5	51.5
04469	ORONO	94.3	92.5	2.3	3.2	1.1	1.6	1.3	2.0	0.0	0.0	0.0	55.5	43.1	1.2	0.1	0.0	0.1	99.8	19.5	51.8	48.2
04471	ORIENT	98.4	97.9	0.4	0.6	0.0	0.0	0.5	0.8	4.9	5.5	8.0	6.3	4.0	24.1	34.7	11.9	0.8	77.3	43.2	51.3	48.7
04472	ORLAND	98.3	98.0	0.0	0.0	0.2	0.4	0.4	0.6	5.2	5.6	6.1	6.6	3.9	24.5	34.6	12.1	1.4	78.8	43.8	50.1	49.9
04473	ORONO	93.4	91.4	1.2	1.5	2.7	4.0	1.2	1.8	3.5	3.4	3.6	13.4	26.6	18.2	19.7	9.6	1.9	86.4	24.9	50.3	49.7
04474	ORRINGTON	99.1	98.9	0.2	0.2	0.2	0.3	0.1	0.2	5.0	5.8	6.6	6.3	4.1	24.0	34.6	12.1	1.4	78.5	43.9	49.8	50.2
	MAINE	96.9	96.3	0.5	0.7	0.7	1.1	0.7	1.1	5.4	5.6	6.1	6.9	6.2	24.7	30.2	12.7	2.3	78.8	41.6	48.8	51.2
	UNITED STATES	75.1	72.0	12.3	12.7	3.8	4.6	12.5	15.7	6.8	6.7	6.6	7.1	6.9	27.0	26.0	10.9	1.9	75.7	36.9	49.2	50.8

ZIP CODE				2009 HOUSEHOLD INCOME DISTRIBUTION (%)					MEDIAN HOUSEHOLD INCOME					2009 HOME VALUE DISTRIBUTION (%)					
#	POST OFFICE NAME	2009 Per Capita Income	2009 HH Income Base	Less than $25,000	$25,000 to $49,999	$50,000 to $99,999	$100,000 to $149,999	$150,000 or More	2009	2014	2009 National Centile	2009 State Centile	2009 Home Value Base	Less than $50,000	$50,000 to $89,999	$90,000 to $174,999	$175,000 to $399,999	$400,000 or More	2009 Median Home Value
04253	LIVERMORE	21907	978	20.9	33.5	37.5	6.5	1.5	47238	47615	55	66	874	6.4	17.2	53.1	23.2	0.1	126103
04254	LIVERMORE FALLS	17946	1323	33.7	39.5	21.7	3.6	1.4	34871	36578	17	20	912	17.2	24.9	45.9	11.7	0.2	99863
04255	GREENWOOD	23977	289	25.3	30.4	34.3	6.6	3.5	44836	46162	48	56	252	7.5	12.3	37.7	34.1	8.3	160606
04256	MECHANIC FALLS	18927	1217	25.4	33.1	35.8	4.3	1.4	43475	46188	44	51	906	10.8	14.5	58.2	14.5	2.1	122765
04257	MEXICO	20080	1360	38.5	27.2	28.5	4.5	1.4	35000	36320	18	21	975	14.7	25.9	47.6	10.6	1.2	104142
04258	MINOT	24468	825	11.2	26.8	49.8	9.1	3.2	59586	60033	77	90	750	2.4	7.2	44.9	40.8	4.7	167975
04259	MONMOUTH	21793	1295	20.9	25.7	44.6	6.8	2.0	51890	51891	66	81	1065	5.0	10.2	40.2	37.8	6.8	166235
04260	NEW GLOUCESTER	24979	1973	13.8	24.4	49.8	9.2	2.8	61966	64228	80	93	1689	4.4	2.7	34.2	53.3	5.4	196315
04261	NEWRY	24033	150	27.3	28.0	35.3	5.3	4.0	45000	45855	48	57	127	9.4	11.0	34.6	36.2	8.7	165441
04263	LEEDS	19871	722	20.8	35.9	35.6	5.8	1.9	46009	47078	51	60	615	4.2	15.3	45.4	32.7	2.4	149531
04265	NORTH MONMOUTH	21817	398	25.4	21.6	44.5	6.8	1.8	52218	51773	66	82	356	8.1	16.0	48.9	23.0	3.9	140530
04266	NORTH TURNER	0	0	0.0	0.0	0.0	0.0	0.0	0	0	0	0	0	0.0	0.0	0.0	0.0	0.0	0
04268	NORWAY	20240	2150	34.3	33.2	25.0	5.7	1.8	33845	35833	15	14	1502	11.4	10.3	43.4	29.0	5.9	149646
04270	OXFORD	21015	2364	19.7	34.0	37.4	6.8	2.2	47424	47345	55	67	2045	9.7	10.4	37.5	38.1	4.4	159733
04274	POLAND	26977	2213	15.2	26.9	41.3	11.3	5.3	56879	56240	74	88	1966	11.0	10.6	35.4	35.4	7.6	158534
04275	ROXBURY	20761	228	30.3	32.9	28.9	7.5	0.4	36719	38102	23	28	177	13.0	20.3	49.2	15.8	1.7	112500
04276	RUMFORD	19960	2900	36.0	31.9	25.9	4.5	1.7	32338	33847	12	10	1735	6.1	20.5	50.1	22.0	1.3	129927
04280	SABATTUS	21268	2388	16.8	31.6	43.4	6.7	1.4	50995	50092	64	79	2042	5.9	14.8	50.8	26.8	1.7	136111
04281	SOUTH PARIS	20989	2299	30.5	28.4	34.4	4.8	1.8	41640	43077	38	45	1550	8.1	10.1	48.2	29.5	4.0	157955
04282	TURNER	26661	1946	14.7	26.8	43.1	9.2	6.2	56072	55971	73	87	1599	4.5	8.6	39.3	42.6	5.0	171284
04284	WAYNE	31829	513	15.6	29.4	37.0	9.0	9.0	54629	53569	71	85	448	0.7	3.8	27.5	46.7	21.4	244355
04285	WELD	19898	185	29.7	34.1	31.9	4.3	0.0	38111	41549	27	33	163	12.9	18.4	43.6	20.2	4.9	128125
04287	BOWDOIN	21573	1031	15.0	31.2	46.3	5.6	1.8	52325	54823	67	83	923	7.7	9.0	38.6	42.3	2.5	165601
04289	WEST PARIS	17202	719	33.4	32.5	29.5	4.2	0.4	36886	38657	23	29	540	7.2	14.3	46.9	27.0	4.6	140493
04290	PERU	20028	652	21.8	33.9	38.7	5.5	0.2	46429	46726	53	63	592	6.6	18.8	46.6	25.3	2.7	141319
04292	SUMNER	21621	355	20.0	33.2	35.8	9.6	1.4	46848	46865	54	65	318	5.0	14.5	53.8	23.9	2.8	139773
04294	WILTON	22218	1754	29.2	27.5	32.7	7.6	2.9	42499	45149	41	48	1359	8.9	16.0	50.8	19.9	4.4	122816
04330	AUGUSTA	22297	11517	32.0	29.4	31.3	5.5	1.8	38999	42899	30	36	6973	5.8	9.2	53.2	28.1	3.8	150128
04341	COOPERS MILLS	40714	4	0.0	0.0	100.0	0.0	0.0	67500	50000	85	97	4	0.0	0.0	100.0	0.0	0.0	125000
04342	DRESDEN	23258	783	21.7	28.0	41.8	6.4	2.2	50155	49906	62	77	667	3.9	10.5	36.4	40.0	9.1	173363
04344	FARMINGDALE	22647	1302	24.3	29.2	39.6	5.0	1.9	46790	48364	54	65	920	7.1	9.8	47.9	33.2	2.1	160654
04345	GARDINER	23459	5146	23.8	28.9	37.1	6.9	3.3	47462	48402	55	68	3776	5.5	9.5	50.1	32.5	2.4	150347
04346	RANDOLPH	20292	974	28.5	32.5	34.7	3.7	0.5	40249	45140	34	40	670	9.1	15.2	56.0	18.2	1.5	137992
04347	HALLOWELL	26164	1112	24.4	30.3	34.4	7.8	3.1	44217	47374	46	54	623	1.4	4.3	42.2	48.6	3.4	181127
04348	JEFFERSON	25351	1252	19.2	28.9	39.8	8.3	3.8	51483	51470	65	80	1090	3.0	6.3	33.7	47.6	9.4	192925
04349	KENTS HILL	22377	479	21.1	29.9	39.2	7.7	2.1	49090	49559	59	73	440	2.3	10.2	41.6	42.0	3.9	168478
04350	LITCHFIELD	22720	1380	16.3	32.0	42.8	6.1	2.8	51149	52203	64	79	1225	6.5	10.2	37.2	45.0	1.1	169308
04351	MANCHESTER	33972	1117	7.6	27.0	43.4	12.5	9.4	63708	63267	82	95	967	1.1	4.1	28.1	48.2	18.4	230280
04352	MOUNT VERNON	24394	644	19.1	31.2	38.8	7.6	3.3	49740	49544	60	74	554	6.0	9.2	41.5	37.2	6.1	164489
04353	WHITEFIELD	20852	1006	25.4	29.9	35.7	6.9	2.1	46520	46696	53	64	880	5.9	9.9	48.2	32.4	3.6	153646
04354	PALERMO	21270	591	27.6	34.3	31.1	4.9	2.0	42544	44563	41	49	540	2.6	7.8	46.9	38.0	4.8	163529
04355	READFIELD	26299	1069	15.1	25.4	43.3	10.3	5.9	58890	56792	76	89	941	1.4	6.4	35.5	49.4	7.3	197359
04357	RICHMOND	22175	1224	25.6	29.4	36.3	7.2	1.6	44746	48832	47	56	916	4.8	8.3	49.1	35.6	2.2	153626
04358	SOUTH CHINA	23648	1805	14.5	35.4	39.0	7.9	3.2	50079	49753	61	76	1505	4.3	8.9	32.8	46.6	7.4	186372
04360	VIENNA	25012	245	25.3	26.5	36.7	6.9	4.5	48556	48807	58	72	216	6.5	14.4	33.8	33.3	12.0	166071
04363	WINDSOR	21188	913	20.8	31.9	40.3	4.9	2.1	47672	48634	56	69	780	8.6	9.2	43.3	36.4	2.4	157460
04364	WINTHROP	23446	2727	21.8	28.2	38.5	9.5	1.9	49979	50400	61	75	2076	8.3	4.4	36.7	44.9	5.7	176570
04401	BANGOR	23881	18751	29.7	29.1	30.6	6.9	3.7	41575	45659	38	45	10457	9.4	10.6	43.6	32.8	3.5	149056
04406	ABBOT	21349	354	31.1	32.5	30.5	4.5	1.4	40000	41218	33	38	314	6.1	26.8	41.1	22.6	3.5	121622
04408	AURORA	17965	83	33.7	33.7	31.3	1.2	0.0	36614	38802	22	27	73	6.8	19.2	46.6	21.9	5.5	139063
04410	BRADFORD	17487	384	23.4	40.4	29.4	6.3	0.5	42316	45903	40	48	317	11.7	19.6	47.9	20.2	0.6	117955
04411	BRADLEY	22310	501	24.4	32.5	36.9	4.6	1.6	45511	47153	50	58	403	6.5	25.8	44.7	22.6	0.5	119792
04412	BREWER	24150	4008	25.9	29.7	34.5	7.4	2.6	45683	47788	50	59	2466	3.3	5.9	55.8	32.0	3.1	152724
04413	BROOKTON	17133	77	40.3	31.2	24.7	3.9	0.0	34084	36737	16	15	66	31.8	25.8	28.8	12.1	1.5	77500
04414	BROWNVILLE	18830	557	39.9	32.1	24.2	2.9	0.9	33090	35819	13	12	462	15.2	33.8	33.1	16.5	1.5	91316
04416	BUCKSPORT	22487	2426	25.3	32.2	33.4	7.9	1.2	43723	45880	45	53	1829	5.1	7.8	45.9	38.2	3.0	161762
04417	BURLINGTON	19374	237	30.4	35.0	28.7	3.4	2.5	40102	42338	33	39	211	19.9	35.1	28.4	16.1	0.5	82500
04418	GREENBUSH	17705	724	27.5	37.8	28.2	5.5	1.0	38608	42233	28	34	636	20.0	28.3	39.2	11.6	0.9	92619
04419	CARMEL	19603	900	23.8	34.0	35.9	5.6	0.8	45689	47329	50	60	793	8.2	15.4	44.9	29.4	2.1	136862
04421	CASTINE	28563	412	15.5	22.6	35.4	15.5	10.9	62597	62615	81	94	290	0.0	3.4	6.9	26.6	63.1	448718
04422	CHARLESTON	18003	520	26.3	34.2	34.2	3.8	1.3	43710	46130	44	52	421	9.7	19.2	52.5	17.3	1.2	118472
04424	DANFORTH	15780	412	48.3	29.6	19.7	1.2	1.2	25891	26471	4	2	339	25.1	30.4	29.5	13.0	2.1	82600
04426	DOVER FOXCROFT	18558	2013	34.2	30.6	29.2	4.7	1.2	35828	37025	20	24	1570	10.4	18.9	42.4	25.2	3.1	126355
04427	CORINTH	21286	1132	21.3	38.6	32.5	5.4	2.2	45147	46648	49	57	950	16.4	16.1	43.2	21.4	2.9	125370
04428	EDDINGTON	22952	1226	20.5	33.3	38.0	6.4	1.9	47081	48205	54	66	999	4.6	14.9	49.8	29.4	1.2	140329
04429	HOLDEN	30682	1834	16.7	24.9	39.1	12.4	6.9	60202	58440	78	91	1594	12.5	6.6	27.9	44.4	8.7	183167
04430	EAST MILLINOCKET	22647	781	30.3	28.0	33.5	6.8	1.3	41450	43997	38	44	588	5.8	43.5	45.4	4.1	1.2	90500
04434	ETNA	18957	413	29.8	31.2	34.4	3.4	1.2	41545	45134	38	45	361	18.3	16.3	43.2	21.6	0.6	117659
04435	EXETER	18379	378	27.2	38.6	29.6	3.4	1.1	41248	44187	37	43	341	17.3	21.7	41.6	18.8	0.6	107115
04438	FRANKFORT	18835	535	27.1	36.3	31.6	3.9	1.1	40610	41967	35	41	467	7.5	16.7	48.6	27.0	0.2	132321
04441	GREENVILLE	22467	796	34.8	31.4	27.1	4.0	2.6	37402	39562	25	30	556	5.8	12.6	45.5	29.5	6.7	147785
04442	GREENVILLE JUNCTION	40610	45	26.7	24.4	22.2	15.6	11.1	49425	48866	60	74	31	0.0	9.7	51.6	22.6	16.1	132500
04443	GUILFORD	16662	943	37.4	33.6	25.5	3.0	0.5	32583	33657	13	11	753	10.9	22.4	42.4	19.1	5.2	118193
04444	HAMPDEN	29642	3313	13.9	23.2	45.3	11.2	6.3	60660	59652	78	92	2615	1.6	6.1	42.8	44.4	5.1	174057
04448	HOWLAND	18349	661	36.0	31.2	28.4	3.8	0.6	35864	38126	20	24	484	18.6	24.4	47.5	8.5	1.0	100253
04449	HUDSON	19612	559	23.6	29.7	40.1	5.2	1.4	46887	48086	54	66	495	14.3	15.2	49.7	20.2	0.6	124306
04450	KENDUSKEAG	20181	536	27.8	35.4	31.0	4.1	1.7	42268	45509	40	47	469	23.2	16.4	46.9	13.2	0.2	108507
04451	KINGMAN	14614	137	51.8	29.2	16.8	0.7	1.5	23945	25213	3	1	123	34.1	28.5	28.5	7.3	1.6	66875
04453	LAGRANGE	17468	381	32.5	31.8	30.4	4.2	1.0	38276	41747	28	33	297	22.2	26.3	40.4	10.8	0.3	92250
04454	LAMBERT LAKE	16538	23	43.5	30.4	21.7	4.3	0.0	32349	27332	12	10	20	40.0	20.0	30.0	10.0	0.0	70000
04455	LEE	18156	333	22.8	42.6	30.3	3.6	0.6	41512	44894	38	44	305	16.4	25.9	43.6	13.4	0.7	103676
04456	LEVANT	21244	1035	21.4	28.9	42.5	4.7	2.5	49779	49071	61	75	917	8.4	15.9	44.5	29.9	1.3	143211
04457	LINCOLN	18372	2719	34.8	31.7	28.8	3.5	1.2	38268	41919	27	33	2155	12.5	23.1	47.1	16.3	1.0	107830
04459	MATTAWAMKEAG	16062	282	42.9	28.7	25.5	2.1	0.7	28374	29773	6	4	223	20.2	43.0	31.8	4.0	0.9	78333
04460	MEDWAY	18723	620	32.1	26.3	38.1	2.7	0.8	40000	44190	33	38	529	24.0	29.5	35.7	10.0	0.8	83148
04461	MILFORD	22133	1040	23.7	27.6	40.3	6.7	1.7	48575	49106	58	72	830	12.4	17.8	50.8	18.4	0.5	121920
04462	MILLINOCKET	21257	2319	37.9	26.1	28.0	7.0	1.0	35396	39062	19	22	1707	15.5	43.5	38.0	3.0	0.0	83604
04463	MILO	16584	1299	39.8	33.3	24.5	2.2	0.3	30875	32097	9	7	1039	21.7	32.1	36.5	9.0	0.7	85183
04464	MONSON	19475	304	38.8	35.9	19.7	3.3	2.3	32468	33274	12	10	241	5.4	29.0	40.2	22.4	2.9	115726
04468	OLD TOWN	20206	4619	35.9	28.8	27.5	5.7	2.1	37669	41490	26	31	2981	14.3	13.4	50.2	21.2	1.0	121938
04469	ORONO	11842	0	0.0	0.0	0.0	0.0	0.0	0	0	0	0	0	0.0	0.0	0.0	0.0	0.0	0
04471	ORIENT	16979	222	41.9	27.9	26.6	2.3	1.4	31493	33243	11	8	191	11.0	25.1	35.6	24.6	3.7	117935
04472	ORLAND	24383	1024	22.9	28.8	36.1	10.4	1.8	48245	48088	57	71	865	6.4	8.8	39.3	36.0	9.6	167300
04473	ORONO	22174	2996	36.2	23.2	27.1	9.3	4.1	40068	44558	33	39	1420	6.1	4.6	31.7	53.9	3.7	188557
04474	ORRINGTON	25329	1549	15.4	28.0	42.1	13.3	1.3	55975	55260	73	86	1337	3.1	8.3	42.7	44.1	1.9	166841
	MAINE	24559		25.0	28.4	35.2	7.5	3.8	46650	48581				6.4	9.4	36.7	38.7	8.8	170226
	UNITED STATES	27277		20.9	24.4	35.3	11.7	7.6	54719	56938				9.3	13.1	31.6	32.6	13.5	162279

ZIP CODE #	POST OFFICE NAME	FINANCIAL SERVICES: Auto Loan	Home Loan	Invest-ments	Retire-ment Plans	THE HOME: Home Improvements: Home Repair	Lawn & Garden	Furnishings: Comput-ers & Hard-ware-Personal	Major Appli-ances	TV, Radio, Sound Equip-ment	Furni-ture	ENTERTAINMENT: Dine out/ Carry out	Sports Equip-ment	Fees & Tickets	Toys & Games	Travel	Cable TV	PERSONAL: Apparel & Services	Auto Repairs	Health Insur-ance	Pets & Supplies
04253	LIVERMORE	82	75	74	78	76	88	74	83	76	67	75	63	68	78	74	81	51	77	86	97
04254	LIVERMORE FALLS	65	51	57	52	51	62	60	61	63	54	62	47	52	62	55	66	42	62	66	73
04255	GREENWOOD	96	77	124	76	84	102	77	98	81	72	80	71	67	76	83	86	53	90	97	113
04256	MECHANIC FALLS	78	72	67	72	71	78	69	75	71	67	71	56	64	73	67	74	48	71	76	88
04257	MEXICO	68	56	68	55	57	73	59	68	65	54	63	50	53	63	58	70	43	65	76	79
04258	MINOT	93	104	91	107	102	103	93	97	92	94	92	76	100	94	99	92	65	93	96	114
04259	MONMOUTH	90	82	74	81	81	86	78	84	81	80	81	61	74	84	75	84	55	80	84	99
04260	NEW GLOUCESTER	96	101	88	102	98	100	92	96	92	93	92	73	94	95	94	93	64	92	95	113
04261	NEWRY	92	73	118	72	81	97	73	93	77	69	76	68	64	73	80	82	50	86	92	108
04263	LEEDS	81	74	73	77	75	87	73	82	75	66	74	62	67	76	73	79	50	76	85	95
04265	NORTH MONMOUTH	83	76	75	79	77	89	74	84	77	68	75	64	69	78	74	81	52	78	87	98
04266	NORTH TURNER	0	0	0	0	0	0	0	0	0	0	0	0	0	0	0	0	0	0	0	0
04268	NORWAY	70	56	77	55	59	72	62	70	66	57	64	52	53	63	61	71	44	68	75	82
04270	OXFORD	90	73	94	73	76	93	73	88	77	68	76	65	64	77	74	83	51	81	89	103
04274	POLAND	104	103	93	105	102	108	96	103	98	95	97	78	95	101	97	100	67	98	104	121
04275	ROXBURY	61	70	66	68	70	76	62	68	66	61	66	47	68	65	67	70	45	66	77	77
04276	RUMFORD	60	56	57	56	57	65	59	62	63	55	61	45	57	61	58	66	42	61	69	72
04280	SABATTUS	89	81	72	79	80	83	77	81	80	80	80	59	73	83	73	82	54	79	82	97
04281	SOUTH PARIS	72	64	66	65	66	74	67	71	69	64	68	53	62	69	65	72	47	70	76	83
04282	TURNER	109	112	98	113	109	112	103	108	103	105	104	81	104	107	104	105	72	104	107	127
04284	WAYNE	122	98	158	96	108	129	98	125	103	92	101	91	85	97	106	109	67	115	123	144
04285	WELD	67	61	61	64	62	72	60	68	62	55	61	52	56	63	60	66	42	63	70	79
04287	BOWDOIN	93	85	76	83	83	87	81	85	84	84	84	62	76	87	77	86	57	83	86	101
04289	WEST PARIS	76	55	78	53	57	77	56	71	62	52	61	53	45	62	56	68	40	66	74	85
04290	PERU	77	70	70	73	72	83	69	78	72	63	70	59	64	73	69	76	48	72	81	91
04292	SUMNER	83	76	75	79	77	89	75	84	77	67	76	64	69	78	75	81	52	78	87	98
04294	WILTON	82	73	72	74	74	83	74	80	76	71	75	59	69	77	72	80	52	77	83	93
04330	AUGUSTA	70	63	66	64	64	72	67	70	70	64	69	52	63	69	66	73	48	70	76	82
04341	COOPERS MILLS	119	95	154	94	104	126	95	121	100	89	98	88	83	95	103	106	65	112	119	140
04342	DRESDEN	91	84	74	81	82	86	79	84	82	82	82	61	75	85	75	84	56	81	84	100
04344	FARMINGDALE	77	68	70	70	70	78	72	76	74	68	73	56	66	74	70	77	50	74	81	89
04345	GARDINER	86	78	77	79	79	88	79	85	82	75	81	63	74	83	77	86	55	82	89	99
04346	RANDOLPH	68	60	62	61	62	69	64	67	66	61	65	50	59	65	62	69	44	66	72	79
04347	HALLOWELL	75	68	68	71	69	73	76	73	77	73	77	56	73	76	73	78	53	76	78	87
04348	JEFFERSON	92	89	104	91	91	100	84	95	85	82	84	72	82	84	89	87	58	90	94	111
04349	KENTS HILL	89	72	116	71	79	95	72	91	75	67	74	67	62	71	78	80	49	84	90	106
04350	LITCHFIELD	93	80	102	78	83	94	77	91	81	76	80	66	70	80	79	85	54	86	91	107
04351	MANCHESTER	125	123	139	125	125	136	115	129	116	112	115	98	113	115	122	119	79	122	128	151
04352	MOUNT VERNON	99	79	127	78	87	104	79	100	83	74	82	73	68	78	86	88	54	93	99	116
04353	WHITEFIELD	85	78	69	76	76	80	74	78	76	76	76	57	70	79	70	79	52	76	78	93
04354	PALERMO	84	68	109	66	74	89	68	86	71	63	70	63	59	67	73	75	46	79	85	100
04355	READFIELD	107	101	122	102	104	115	96	110	97	93	97	83	93	96	102	100	66	103	109	128
04357	RICHMOND	86	78	73	76	77	82	76	80	79	77	79	59	72	81	73	82	54	79	82	95
04358	SOUTH CHINA	98	87	96	84	88	96	83	94	87	84	86	68	77	87	83	90	58	89	93	110
04360	VIENNA	99	79	128	78	87	105	79	101	83	74	82	74	69	79	86	88	54	93	99	117
04363	WINDSOR	85	78	69	76	76	80	74	78	77	77	77	57	70	80	70	79	52	76	78	93
04364	WINTHROP	88	75	94	74	78	91	76	87	80	73	79	64	69	78	77	84	53	83	90	102
04401	BANGOR	77	70	68	72	69	73	78	74	78	75	78	57	74	78	73	80	54	77	78	89
04406	ABBOT	77	61	99	60	67	81	61	78	64	58	64	57	53	61	66	69	42	72	77	90
04408	AURORA	73	53	76	51	55	75	54	69	60	50	59	52	43	59	53	66	39	63	71	82
04410	BRADFORD	74	68	61	66	67	70	65	68	67	67	67	50	61	70	62	69	46	66	69	81
04411	BRADLEY	83	76	68	74	75	78	72	76	75	75	75	56	68	78	69	77	51	74	77	91
04412	BREWER	75	75	71	76	74	78	77	75	79	74	78	57	77	78	76	81	54	77	81	89
04413	BROOKTON	70	50	72	49	52	71	52	66	57	48	56	49	41	57	51	63	37	60	68	78
04414	BROWNVILLE	67	49	68	47	51	70	53	65	59	47	57	49	43	58	51	65	38	61	71	77
04416	BUCKSPORT	78	70	70	71	71	79	72	77	74	69	73	57	67	74	70	77	50	74	81	90
04417	BURLINGTON	84	60	69	59	60	80	63	73	70	61	68	56	50	73	57	76	46	69	77	89
04418	GREENBUSH	82	60	68	59	60	78	62	72	69	61	67	55	51	71	57	74	45	68	75	87
04419	CARMEL	78	72	64	69	70	73	68	72	70	71	70	52	64	73	65	72	48	69	72	85
04421	CASTINE	113	119	161	118	137	140	107	126	113	121	111	79	117	101	123	118	76	120	140	143
04422	CHARLESTON	87	63	89	61	66	88	65	82	72	61	70	61	52	71	64	79	47	75	85	97
04424	DANFORTH	60	43	62	42	45	62	46	58	51	42	50	43	37	50	45	56	33	53	61	68
04426	DOVER FOXCROFT	72	58	72	58	60	76	60	71	64	54	63	53	51	64	59	69	42	66	75	83
04427	CORINTH	90	75	82	73	75	88	73	84	78	73	78	62	65	80	71	82	52	79	85	99
04428	EDDINGTON	84	76	74	77	77	85	77	82	79	74	78	61	71	80	74	82	53	79	86	96
04429	HOLDEN	113	105	132	106	109	122	100	116	102	97	101	87	96	100	107	106	69	109	115	136
04430	EAST MILLINOCKET	81	66	83	64	68	88	68	81	75	62	73	60	60	73	68	82	49	76	90	95
04434	ETNA	76	69	62	67	68	71	66	69	68	68	68	50	62	71	62	70	46	67	70	83
04435	EXETER	82	58	84	57	61	83	60	76	67	56	65	57	48	66	59	73	43	70	79	91
04438	FRANKFORT	75	69	61	67	68	71	65	69	68	68	68	50	62	70	62	70	46	67	69	82
04441	GREENVILLE	71	62	68	63	64	72	66	70	68	63	67	52	61	67	65	71	46	69	75	82
04442	GREENVILLE JUNCTION	143	114	185	113	126	151	115	146	120	107	118	106	99	114	124	128	79	134	144	169
04443	GUILFORD	68	49	71	48	52	70	52	65	57	47	56	49	42	56	51	63	37	60	69	77
04444	HAMPDEN	108	107	101	110	107	115	104	110	105	100	104	83	102	106	105	107	72	106	113	128
04448	HOWLAND	71	53	69	52	55	74	57	69	62	51	60	52	46	62	55	68	41	64	74	81
04449	HUDSON	84	77	68	75	75	79	73	77	75	76	75	56	69	79	69	78	51	75	77	92
04450	KENDUSKEAG	86	62	89	60	64	88	63	81	70	59	69	61	51	70	63	78	46	74	84	96
04451	KINGMAN	59	42	61	41	44	60	43	55	48	40	47	41	35	48	43	53	31	51	57	66
04453	LAGRANGE	78	56	67	55	56	76	59	69	66	57	64	53	47	68	54	72	43	66	74	84
04454	LAMBERT LAKE	67	48	69	46	50	68	49	62	54	46	54	47	39	54	49	60	35	57	65	74
04455	LEE	89	64	91	62	66	90	66	83	73	61	71	62	52	72	65	80	47	76	87	99
04456	LEVANT	91	84	74	81	82	86	79	84	82	82	82	61	75	85	75	84	56	81	84	100
04457	LINCOLN	75	55	71	54	57	76	59	71	65	54	63	53	48	65	56	71	42	66	75	84
04459	MATTAWAMKEAG	68	49	70	47	51	69	50	64	56	47	55	48	40	55	50	61	36	59	67	76
04460	MEDWAY	82	59	69	57	58	78	61	71	67	59	66	55	49	70	56	74	44	67	75	87
04461	MILFORD	87	80	71	77	78	82	75	80	78	78	78	58	71	81	72	80	53	77	80	95
04462	MILLINOCKET	74	59	74	57	60	79	61	73	68	57	66	54	54	67	61	74	45	69	80	85
04463	MILO	63	46	64	45	48	66	50	61	55	44	53	46	40	54	48	61	36	57	67	72
04464	MONSON	69	50	72	49	53	72	54	67	60	49	58	50	44	59	53	66	39	62	72	79
04468	OLD TOWN	67	62	58	63	61	66	67	65	68	63	67	50	63	68	63	70	46	67	70	78
04469	ORONO	0	0	0	0	0	0	0	0	0	0	0	0	0	0	0	0	0	0	0	0
04471	ORIENT	72	52	74	50	54	73	53	67	59	49	58	51	42	58	52	65	38	62	70	80
04472	ORLAND	89	78	92	80	81	95	77	91	80	71	79	68	70	80	79	85	53	84	92	105
04473	ORONO	79	61	64	64	60	65	87	70	81	75	81	59	71	81	70	80	57	78	72	87
04474	ORRINGTON	83	98	85	99	94	96	85	89	85	86	86	68	94	87	92	86	60	86	90	104
	MAINE	87	79	87	80	81	89	81	86	83	78	82	65	76	83	81	86	57	84	89	102
	UNITED STATES	100	100	100	100	100	100	100	100	100	100	100	100	100	100	100	100	100	100	100	100

ZIP CODE #	POST OFFICE NAME	COUNTY FIPS CODE	POPULATION 2000	POPULATION 2009	POPULATION 2014	2000-2009 ANNUAL RATE % Rate	2000-2009 ANNUAL RATE State Centile	HOUSEHOLDS 2000	HOUSEHOLDS 2009	HOUSEHOLDS 2014	HOUSEHOLDS % Annual Rate 2000-2009	HOUSEHOLDS 2009 Average HH Size	FAMILIES 2000	FAMILIES 2009	FAMILIES % Annual Rate 2000-2009
04475	PASSADUMKEAG	019	441	486	508	1.1	83	172	197	208	1.5	2.47	129	145	1.3
04476	PENOBSCOT	009	1346	1447	1483	0.8	71	533	599	623	1.3	2.26	371	409	1.1
04478	ROCKWOOD	025	271	275	277	0.2	46	126	134	138	0.7	2.05	78	81	0.4
04479	SANGERVILLE	021	1503	1479	1456	-0.2	21	657	681	680	0.4	2.17	429	435	0.2
04481	SEBEC	021	668	658	646	-0.2	21	275	286	285	0.4	2.30	196	200	0.2
04487	SPRINGFIELD	019	882	881	880	0.0	33	351	365	369	0.4	2.41	252	256	0.2
04488	STETSON	019	858	895	916	0.5	57	334	362	374	0.9	2.47	238	252	0.6
04490	TOPSFIELD	029	244	235	231	-0.4	11	101	103	102	0.2	2.28	65	64	-0.2
04491	VANCEBORO	029	147	140	137	-0.5	7	68	68	68	0.0	2.06	45	45	0.0
04492	WAITE	029	195	186	182	-0.5	7	86	87	86	0.1	2.14	57	56	-0.2
04493	WEST ENFIELD	019	1760	1801	1816	0.2	46	671	710	725	0.6	2.54	506	525	0.4
04495	WINN	019	390	373	368	-0.5	7	159	158	158	-0.1	2.36	121	118	-0.3
04496	WINTERPORT	027	3704	4033	4145	0.9	77	1428	1621	1689	1.4	2.47	1067	1194	1.2
04497	WYTOPITLOCK	003	398	368	355	-0.8	1	141	135	132	-0.5	2.73	109	103	-0.6
04530	BATH	023	11558	11886	11964	0.3	50	4998	5300	5392	0.6	2.21	3018	3126	0.4
04535	ALNA	015	701	713	703	0.2	46	273	286	286	0.5	2.49	202	208	0.3
04537	BOOTHBAY	015	1895	1920	1898	0.1	39	777	820	820	0.6	2.34	559	579	0.4
04538	BOOTHBAY HARBOR	015	2695	2530	2460	-0.7	2	1270	1247	1227	-0.2	1.97	740	707	-0.5
04539	BRISTOL	015	1286	1353	1362	0.6	62	540	592	604	1.0	2.27	373	401	0.8
04541	CHAMBERLAIN	015	194	210	216	0.9	77	84	95	99	1.3	2.19	55	61	1.1
04543	DAMARISCOTTA	015	1890	1781	1727	-0.6	3	872	854	837	-0.2	1.98	510	483	-0.6
04544	EAST BOOTHBAY	015	379	361	353	-0.5	7	184	183	182	-0.1	1.97	118	115	-0.3
04547	FRIENDSHIP	013	1273	1272	1263	0.0	33	528	547	549	0.4	2.32	368	372	0.1
04548	GEORGETOWN	023	985	1037	1047	0.6	62	423	460	470	0.9	2.25	282	299	0.6
04549	ISLE OF SPRINGS	015	6	6	6	0.0	33	2	2	2	0.0	3.00	1	1	0.0
04551	BREMEN	015	677	726	742	0.8	71	287	318	329	1.1	2.28	207	226	1.0
04553	NEWCASTLE	015	1855	1853	1825	0.0	33	779	810	808	0.4	2.25	521	530	0.2
04554	NEW HARBOR	015	643	698	718	0.9	77	328	372	388	1.4	1.87	208	230	1.1
04555	NOBLEBORO	015	1616	1810	1885	1.2	87	672	790	833	1.8	2.29	461	526	1.4
04556	EDGECOMB	015	1090	1204	1246	1.1	83	466	533	558	1.5	2.26	328	368	1.3
04558	PEMAQUID	015	227	246	253	0.9	77	110	124	130	1.3	1.97	71	79	1.2
04562	PHIPPSBURG	023	2106	2284	2339	0.9	77	859	967	1003	1.3	2.36	623	688	1.1
04563	CUSHING	013	1228	1553	1658	2.6	99	509	663	715	2.9	2.32	360	459	2.7
04564	ROUND POND	015	294	319	327	0.9	77	141	159	166	1.3	1.98	93	103	1.1
04568	SOUTH BRISTOL	015	477	487	484	0.2	46	229	244	245	0.7	2.00	155	161	0.4
04570	SQUIRREL ISLAND	015	3	3	3	0.0	33	2	2	2	0.0	1.50	1	1	0.0
04571	TREVETT	015	321	321	315	0.0	33	126	132	131	0.5	2.43	91	93	0.2
04572	WALDOBORO	015	5046	5425	5535	0.8	71	2035	2274	2345	1.2	2.36	1385	1516	1.0
04573	WALPOLE	015	420	429	426	0.2	46	181	192	194	0.6	2.23	123	128	0.4
04574	WASHINGTON	013	1280	1424	1471	1.2	87	493	573	601	1.6	2.42	344	390	1.4
04576	SOUTHPORT	015	679	677	670	0.0	33	328	343	344	0.5	1.97	216	221	0.2
04578	WISCASSET	015	4376	4854	5013	1.1	83	1804	2082	2178	1.6	2.32	1212	1370	1.3
04579	WOOLWICH	023	2810	3264	3434	1.6	93	1101	1330	1416	2.1	2.45	825	976	1.8
04605	ELLSWORTH	009	11876	12463	12529	0.5	57	4992	5424	5514	0.9	2.25	3312	3529	0.7
04606	ADDISON	029	1072	1055	1039	-0.2	21	432	442	440	0.2	2.36	302	303	0.0
04607	GOULDSBORO	009	1359	1467	1509	0.8	71	571	646	672	1.3	2.23	386	428	1.1
04609	BAR HARBOR	009	5874	6215	6298	0.6	62	2646	2903	2979	1.0	2.07	1447	1544	0.7
04611	BEALS	029	618	589	573	-0.5	7	237	234	230	-0.1	2.47	189	184	-0.3
04612	BERNARD	009	9	9	9	0.0	33	4	4	4	0.0	2.25	3	3	0.0
04613	BIRCH HARBOR	009	244	263	271	0.8	71	98	111	115	1.4	2.37	67	74	1.1
04614	BLUE HILL	009	2191	2414	2492	1.1	83	987	1134	1187	1.5	2.13	628	705	1.3
04616	BROOKLIN	009	1040	1127	1155	0.9	77	458	512	531	1.2	2.20	298	325	0.9
04617	BROOKSVILLE	009	818	1024	1096	2.5	99	366	473	512	2.8	2.16	247	312	2.6
04619	CALAIS	029	3447	3301	3220	-0.5	7	1486	1485	1469	0.0	2.14	905	881	-0.3
04622	CHERRYFIELD	029	1288	1247	1222	-0.3	16	551	560	556	0.2	2.18	356	354	-0.1
04623	COLUMBIA FALLS	029	1273	1312	1299	0.3	50	527	563	564	0.7	2.33	352	369	0.5
04624	COREA	009	331	355	364	0.8	71	119	135	141	1.4	2.29	78	86	1.1
04625	CRANBERRY ISLES	009	54	53	50	-0.2	21	27	27	27	0.0	1.96	14	14	0.0
04626	CUTLER	029	623	598	584	-0.4	11	238	238	236	0.0	2.46	179	176	-0.2
04627	DEER ISLE	009	1526	1623	1638	0.7	66	626	692	705	1.1	2.25	417	451	0.9
04628	DENNYSVILLE	029	678	663	652	-0.2	21	277	284	283	0.3	2.33	191	192	0.1
04630	EAST MACHIAS	029	1689	1639	1613	-0.3	16	712	725	722	0.2	2.15	493	493	0.0
04631	EASTPORT	029	1640	1471	1412	-1.2	0	750	709	688	-0.6	2.03	445	410	-0.9
04634	FRANKLIN	009	2944	3019	3024	0.3	50	1230	1318	1337	0.7	2.28	820	860	0.5
04635	FRENCHBORO	009	38	40	39	0.6	62	18	20	20	1.1	2.00	11	12	0.9
04640	HANCOCK	009	882	964	994	1.0	80	389	443	462	1.4	2.16	251	279	1.1
04642	HARBORSIDE	009	139	181	197	2.9	100	68	91	100	3.2	1.99	46	60	2.9
04643	HARRINGTON	029	865	837	821	-0.4	11	361	365	362	0.1	2.28	254	252	-0.1
04645	ISLE AU HAUT	013	79	88	92	1.2	87	32	36	38	1.3	2.44	21	23	1.0
04646	ISLESFORD	009	74	72	69	-0.3	16	33	34	32	0.3	2.12	17	17	0.0
04648	JONESBORO	029	594	595	620	0.0	33	257	271	286	0.6	2.20	175	181	0.4
04649	JONESPORT	029	1408	1342	1311	-0.5	7	597	599	594	0.0	2.18	397	391	-0.2
04650	LITTLE DEER ISLE	009	227	239	238	0.6	62	100	109	110	0.9	2.19	66	71	0.8
04652	LUBEC	029	2026	1991	1960	-0.2	21	909	932	929	0.3	2.10	536	535	0.0
04653	BASS HARBOR	009	453	476	469	0.5	57	199	216	215	0.9	2.20	127	135	0.7
04654	MACHIAS	029	3619	3638	3586	0.1	39	1471	1561	1558	0.6	2.10	861	899	0.5
04655	MACHIASPORT	029	995	963	947	-0.4	11	342	347	346	0.2	2.62	237	236	0.0
04657	MEDDYBEMPS	029	266	264	260	-0.1	25	109	113	113	0.4	2.32	76	77	0.1
04658	MILBRIDGE	029	1363	1320	1295	-0.3	16	585	596	593	0.2	2.13	384	383	0.0
04660	MOUNT DESERT	009	1058	1182	1219	1.2	87	460	526	548	1.5	2.25	301	336	1.2
04666	PEMBROKE	029	1232	1202	1180	-0.3	16	524	535	533	0.2	2.25	368	370	0.1
04667	PERRY	029	1485	1475	1454	-0.1	25	563	583	583	0.4	2.52	407	414	0.2
04668	PRINCETON	029	1755	1699	1667	-0.3	16	692	703	698	0.2	2.42	476	474	0.0
04669	PROSPECT HARBOR	009	424	456	469	0.8	71	175	198	206	1.3	2.23	118	131	1.1
04671	ROBBINSTON	029	525	518	508	-0.1	25	201	206	205	0.3	2.51	149	150	0.1
04673	SARGENTVILLE	009	66	73	75	1.1	83	27	31	32	1.5	2.35	18	20	1.1
04674	SEAL COVE	009	1067	1171	1198	1.0	80	459	521	539	1.4	2.24	307	341	1.1
04676	SEDGWICK	009	994	1096	1127	1.1	83	423	479	499	1.4	2.29	277	307	1.1
04677	SORRENTO	009	290	323	335	1.2	87	128	149	156	1.7	2.17	93	106	1.4
04679	SOUTHWEST HARBOR	009	1963	2101	2144	0.7	66	897	993	1024	1.1	2.08	534	577	0.8
04680	STEUBEN	029	984	980	964	0.0	33	401	415	414	0.4	2.36	275	279	0.2
04681	STONINGTON	009	1152	1206	1201	0.5	57	502	544	548	0.9	2.21	327	347	0.6
04683	SUNSET	009	123	132	136	0.8	71	55	61	63	1.1	2.16	39	43	1.1
04684	SURRY	009	1361	1521	1573	1.2	87	551	635	665	1.5	2.40	405	459	1.4
04685	SWANS ISLAND	009	327	344	339	0.5	57	142	155	155	1.0	2.22	91	97	0.7
	MAINE					0.6					0.9	2.32			0.7
	UNITED STATES					1.0					1.1	2.59			0.9

ZIP CODE #	POST OFFICE NAME	RACE (%) White 2000	White 2009	Black 2000	Black 2009	Asian/Pacific 2000	Asian/Pacific 2009	% Hispanic Origin 2000	% Hispanic Origin 2009	2009 AGE DISTRIBUTION (%) 0-4	5-9	10-14	15-19	20-24	25-44	45-64	65-84	85+	18+	MEDIAN AGE 2009	% 2009 Males	% 2009 Females
04475	PASSADUMKEAG	98.4	98.4	0.0	0.0	0.2	0.2	0.5	0.8	5.3	5.3	6.2	7.8	6.6	22.2	33.1	11.1	2.3	78.6	42.3	48.6	51.4
04476	PENOBSCOT	98.1	97.7	0.1	0.2	0.3	0.4	0.4	0.7	3.5	3.9	4.6	6.8	3.3	19.6	36.8	17.0	4.4	83.5	49.9	50.1	49.9
04478	ROCKWOOD	97.4	97.1	0.0	0.0	0.0	0.0	0.0	0.4	3.3	4.7	5.8	5.5	1.8	22.5	40.7	14.2	1.5	81.5	48.4	54.5	45.5
04479	SANGERVILLE	98.2	98.2	0.5	0.5	0.3	0.3	0.4	0.3	4.2	4.5	5.0	5.7	5.7	21.8	33.7	16.6	2.8	83.1	46.9	50.1	49.9
04481	SEBEC	98.4	98.3	0.0	0.0	0.3	0.3	0.9	0.9	4.6	5.6	5.9	7.6	3.6	18.5	40.7	11.2	2.1	77.8	46.8	50.5	49.5
04487	SPRINGFIELD	96.1	95.5	0.6	0.8	0.1	0.2	0.7	1.0	4.1	4.5	5.6	6.1	4.8	22.5	32.0	18.8	1.6	82.0	46.4	51.4	48.6
04488	STETSON	98.7	98.5	0.2	0.3	0.0	0.0	0.0	0.0	6.4	5.4	7.7	6.8	5.8	25.9	32.3	8.4	1.3	75.5	39.4	50.9	49.1
04490	TOPSFIELD	97.5	96.6	0.0	0.0	0.0	0.0	0.4	0.4	3.8	3.8	4.3	4.3	3.4	20.0	42.1	17.0	1.3	85.5	51.6	50.2	49.8
04491	VANCEBORO	94.6	93.6	0.7	0.7	0.0	0.0	0.7	1.4	4.3	4.3	4.3	5.0	5.0	22.9	34.3	18.6	1.4	85.0	48.0	53.6	46.4
04492	WAITE	96.4	94.6	0.0	0.0	0.0	0.0	0.5	1.1	3.8	3.8	4.3	4.3	4.3	21.5	38.2	18.3	1.6	85.5	50.3	51.6	48.4
04493	WEST ENFIELD	98.9	98.8	0.1	0.1	0.1	0.1	0.4	0.6	6.4	6.6	7.1	6.9	5.6	23.6	30.5	12.2	1.2	75.7	40.9	50.9	49.1
04495	WINN	98.7	98.4	0.0	0.0	0.0	0.0	0.5	1.1	4.8	5.9	5.9	5.6	5.1	19.6	33.5	17.4	2.1	79.9	46.8	50.7	49.3
04496	WINTERPORT	98.1	97.8	0.2	0.2	0.3	0.3	0.4	0.6	5.4	5.7	6.4	6.5	5.8	26.7	32.6	9.8	1.1	78.4	40.5	50.0	50.0
04497	WYTOPITLOCK	98.5	97.6	0.0	0.3	0.8	1.4	0.0	0.0	3.0	6.0	8.7	6.8	3.8	23.6	33.4	13.6	1.1	76.6	43.9	50.8	49.2
04530	BATH	95.6	94.7	1.3	1.7	0.6	0.8	1.5	2.2	6.5	5.7	6.0	6.2	6.5	25.8	29.2	11.6	2.5	77.9	40.1	48.3	51.7
04535	ALNA	99.6	99.4	0.0	0.0	0.1	0.3	0.1	0.3	4.1	4.6	5.5	6.7	5.3	21.3	35.9	14.6	2.0	81.6	46.3	49.4	50.6
04537	BOOTHBAY	98.7	98.4	0.1	0.1	0.2	0.3	0.6	1.1	4.7	5.6	7.0	6.5	3.8	23.8	32.8	14.2	1.7	78.3	44.1	49.3	50.7
04538	BOOTHBAY HARBOR	98.1	97.7	0.2	0.2	0.6	0.9	0.8	1.3	3.9	4.4	4.2	3.8	3.3	19.1	36.2	21.0	4.1	85.0	52.0	46.7	53.3
04539	BRISTOL	99.1	98.9	0.2	0.1	0.4	0.6	0.2	0.3	4.0	4.1	4.9	5.7	3.5	21.4	36.7	17.7	2.0	83.3	48.8	50.4	49.6
04541	CHAMBERLAIN	99.0	98.6	0.0	0.0	0.5	1.0	0.0	0.5	3.3	3.3	4.8	6.2	3.8	20.0	37.6	18.6	2.4	84.3	49.5	51.0	49.0
04543	DAMARISCOTTA	98.9	98.7	0.2	0.3	0.2	0.3	0.5	0.8	3.8	3.9	4.5	5.3	3.4	17.5	33.2	21.3	7.1	84.0	52.7	45.8	54.2
04544	EAST BOOTHBAY	99.7	99.7	0.0	0.0	0.0	0.0	0.3	0.6	3.3	4.2	3.3	2.8	1.7	15.0	45.7	19.9	4.2	87.3	55.0	47.4	52.6
04547	FRIENDSHIP	99.4	99.2	0.0	0.0	0.0	0.0	0.5	0.9	5.0	5.3	5.3	6.2	3.7	23.9	29.9	17.9	2.9	80.3	45.5	49.5	50.5
04548	GEORGETOWN	98.8	98.6	0.1	0.1	0.3	0.5	0.7	1.1	4.8	4.2	6.2	7.0	3.6	22.4	36.6	13.4	1.7	79.8	45.8	48.9	51.1
04549	ISLE OF SPRINGS	100.0	100.0	0.0	0.0	0.0	0.0	0.0	0.0	0.0	0.0	0.0	0.0	0.0	0.0	83.3	16.7	0.0	100.0	60.0	16.7	83.3
04551	BREMEN	98.4	98.1	0.7	1.0	0.3	0.4	0.6	1.1	5.1	5.6	5.8	4.0	3.2	20.0	36.2	17.5	2.6	81.0	49.0	49.3	50.7
04553	NEWCASTLE	98.8	98.5	0.1	0.2	0.3	0.5	0.7	1.1	3.8	4.4	4.8	5.0	4.5	19.2	38.9	16.2	3.3	83.3	50.4	47.0	53.0
04554	NEW HARBOR	99.4	99.1	0.0	0.0	0.5	0.7	0.5	0.7	2.6	2.9	3.4	3.2	2.4	14.5	38.4	27.4	5.3	89.0	58.3	48.9	51.1
04555	NOBLEBORO	98.6	98.2	0.1	0.2	0.4	0.7	0.5	0.8	4.6	7.0	7.0	6.2	3.5	20.5	34.6	14.7	1.9	77.7	45.7	48.5	51.5
04556	EDGECOMB	98.7	98.6	0.0	0.0	0.2	0.2	0.1	0.2	4.8	5.5	6.6	5.6	2.1	21.7	36.8	13.8	3.2	79.1	47.0	48.3	51.7
04558	PEMAQUID	99.1	98.8	0.0	0.0	0.4	0.8	0.4	0.4	3.3	3.7	4.1	4.9	3.3	17.5	38.2	22.0	3.3	85.4	53.0	50.8	49.2
04562	PHIPPSBURG	98.5	98.3	0.3	0.4	0.2	0.4	0.6	0.9	4.3	4.9	5.6	5.4	3.9	21.3	36.9	16.0	1.6	81.7	47.8	51.7	48.3
04563	CUSHING	99.4	99.4	0.0	0.0	0.1	0.1	0.5	0.7	5.3	5.7	6.1	5.7	3.4	24.1	32.8	14.2	2.6	79.4	44.8	50.6	49.4
04564	ROUND POND	99.0	98.1	0.0	0.3	0.7	1.3	0.0	0.3	3.4	3.8	4.4	6.0	3.8	19.7	37.9	18.5	2.5	84.3	49.9	51.4	48.6
04568	SOUTH BRISTOL	99.0	98.8	0.0	0.0	0.2	0.4	0.4	0.8	3.3	3.7	4.1	4.3	3.1	17.5	37.4	23.6	3.1	86.2	54.5	48.0	52.0
04570	SQUIRREL ISLAND	100.0	100.0	0.0	0.0	0.0	0.0	0.0	0.0	0.0	0.0	0.0	0.0	0.0	0.0	100.0	0.0	0.0	100.0	57.5	33.3	66.7
04571	TREVETT	100.0	99.4	0.0	0.0	0.0	0.3	0.3	0.6	3.7	4.4	5.0	4.4	3.1	19.0	38.6	19.9	1.9	83.8	51.5	51.4	48.6
04572	WALDOBORO	98.6	98.3	0.2	0.3	0.5	0.6	0.3	0.4	5.9	6.2	6.5	5.9	5.0	23.5	30.5	14.1	2.4	77.4	42.8	49.2	50.8
04573	WALPOLE	99.0	99.1	0.0	0.0	0.2	0.2	0.5	0.7	3.0	3.7	4.0	4.4	3.3	16.8	37.1	24.5	3.3	86.2	54.8	48.3	51.7
04574	WASHINGTON	98.8	98.7	0.0	0.0	0.0	0.0	0.4	0.6	4.8	5.4	7.0	7.0	4.4	25.6	34.4	10.3	1.0	78.0	42.2	51.3	48.7
04576	SOUTHPORT	98.8	98.5	0.0	0.0	0.6	0.9	0.0	0.0	2.1	2.5	3.2	3.4	2.7	11.4	42.1	28.2	4.4	90.1	59.1	48.6	51.4
04578	WISCASSET	98.1	97.6	0.3	0.4	0.4	0.6	0.5	0.9	4.8	5.6	6.2	6.2	5.3	23.5	33.5	13.3	1.6	78.8	43.9	49.7	50.3
04579	WOOLWICH	97.6	97.1	0.4	0.5	0.5	0.7	0.8	1.3	4.9	6.2	6.8	6.2	4.4	25.0	33.4	11.9	1.2	78.2	42.8	51.1	48.9
04605	ELLSWORTH	97.5	97.0	0.2	0.3	0.4	0.6	0.5	0.9	5.0	5.7	6.8	6.5	4.1	25.8	30.9	12.8	2.3	78.0	42.6	48.5	51.5
04606	ADDISON	98.0	97.3	0.6	0.8	0.4	0.5	0.2	0.3	4.1	6.5	5.4	8.1	3.9	23.0	34.5	12.6	1.9	78.2	44.2	49.4	50.6
04607	GOULDSBORO	97.3	96.7	0.4	0.6	0.4	0.6	1.3	2.0	5.0	5.1	5.6	6.0	5.0	23.9	33.5	13.6	2.2	80.4	44.5	50.9	49.1
04609	BAR HARBOR	98.1	97.6	0.2	0.2	0.8	1.1	0.6	1.0	4.2	4.5	5.2	6.2	6.1	25.1	32.7	13.0	3.0	82.7	44.1	46.8	53.2
04611	BEALS	97.6	96.8	1.3	1.7	0.2	0.2	2.1	3.1	4.8	5.3	5.9	7.6	4.4	24.4	30.2	14.9	2.4	78.6	43.6	52.5	47.5
04612	BERNARD	100.0	100.0	0.0	0.0	0.0	0.0	0.0	0.0	0.0	0.0	0.0	0.0	0.0	0.0	100.0	0.0	0.0	100.0	58.1	33.3	66.7
04613	BIRCH HARBOR	96.7	96.6	0.4	0.4	0.4	0.8	1.6	2.7	5.3	5.3	5.7	6.1	4.2	24.3	35.0	11.8	2.3	79.1	44.1	52.1	47.9
04614	BLUE HILL	97.9	97.6	0.4	0.5	0.1	0.2	0.1	0.2	3.6	4.3	5.4	7.0	3.9	20.6	37.4	14.7	3.1	82.4	47.8	48.1	51.9
04616	BROOKLIN	98.4	98.0	0.2	0.2	0.5	0.7	0.8	1.2	3.1	3.5	4.2	5.4	4.3	18.5	39.9	18.7	2.4	85.9	51.5	49.1	50.9
04617	BROOKSVILLE	98.7	98.5	0.0	0.0	0.6	0.8	0.4	0.4	4.2	4.6	5.0	4.7	3.5	18.4	39.2	17.9	2.6	83.3	51.1	50.7	49.3
04619	CALAIS	96.8	95.5	0.3	0.5	0.7	1.1	0.7	1.2	5.0	4.9	5.1	6.8	6.4	22.8	29.1	16.0	4.0	81.0	44.2	47.1	52.9
04622	CHERRYFIELD	97.9	97.2	0.1	0.1	0.4	0.6	0.2	0.2	4.5	4.9	5.5	6.2	4.7	21.8	33.4	16.0	3.2	80.8	46.8	47.8	52.2
04623	COLUMBIA FALLS	98.3	97.6	0.1	0.1	0.2	0.2	0.4	0.5	5.0	5.7	5.9	6.4	4.6	24.9	32.0	13.8	1.6	79.3	43.4	50.5	49.5
04624	COREA	94.3	93.0	1.5	2.3	0.6	0.8	2.1	3.7	2.5	3.1	3.4	5.4	7.6	21.1	33.5	20.6	2.8	87.9	49.9	51.3	48.7
04625	CRANBERRY ISLES	98.1	98.1	0.0	0.0	0.0	0.0	0.0	0.0	3.8	1.9	5.7	5.7	3.8	22.6	32.1	20.8	3.8	83.0	48.5	49.1	50.9
04626	CUTLER	96.5	95.3	1.6	2.2	0.5	0.7	2.1	3.3	10.2	10.4	10.4	5.9	2.7	26.1	23.7	9.2	1.5	64.4	35.2	53.0	47.0
04627	DEER ISLE	98.7	98.5	0.1	0.2	0.2	0.3	0.3	0.6	4.5	4.6	5.2	5.9	3.9	19.9	34.3	17.4	4.4	81.6	49.0	48.6	51.4
04628	DENNYSVILLE	98.5	97.7	0.1	0.3	0.0	0.2	0.3	0.3	4.8	5.4	6.2	6.0	3.9	22.9	34.1	14.5	2.1	79.9	45.4	48.9	51.1
04630	EAST MACHIAS	98.2	97.6	0.1	0.1	0.2	0.3	0.1	0.2	4.6	4.8	5.4	6.0	5.4	25.6	32.2	14.2	1.7	81.3	43.6	51.7	48.3
04631	EASTPORT	93.6	91.7	0.4	0.5	0.2	0.2	0.9	1.3	5.3	5.2	5.3	5.0	4.4	20.5	32.0	18.8	3.5	81.6	48.0	47.6	52.4
04634	FRANKLIN	96.9	96.5	0.2	0.2	0.5	0.8	0.3	0.6	5.6	6.0	6.6	6.0	4.2	24.9	33.0	12.1	1.6	77.8	42.9	50.1	49.9
04635	FRENCHBORO	97.4	97.5	0.0	0.0	0.0	0.0	0.0	0.0	5.0	5.0	5.0	5.0	5.0	20.0	35.0	20.0	0.0	80.0	46.7	52.5	47.5
04640	HANCOCK	99.2	99.1	0.2	0.3	0.1	0.2	0.9	1.5	4.3	4.9	4.9	4.3	3.8	22.6	35.3	16.8	3.2	82.7	49.0	47.9	52.1
04642	HARBORSIDE	97.9	98.3	0.0	0.0	1.4	1.1	0.7	0.6	3.9	5.0	5.0	4.4	3.3	16.6	39.8	19.3	2.8	84.0	53.0	51.9	48.1
04643	HARRINGTON	98.0	97.5	0.0	0.0	0.0	0.0	1.6	2.7	4.5	5.1	5.6	6.0	3.9	23.9	32.6	16.1	2.2	80.4	45.6	48.0	52.0
04645	ISLE AU HAUT	100.0	100.0	0.0	0.0	0.0	0.0	3.8	5.7	5.7	8.0	6.8	6.8	3.4	20.5	35.2	12.5	1.1	75.0	44.3	52.3	47.7
04646	ISLESFORD	98.6	98.6	0.0	0.0	0.0	0.0	0.0	0.0	5.6	2.8	6.9	5.6	4.2	22.2	29.2	19.4	4.2	81.9	47.0	45.8	54.2
04648	JONESBORO	99.3	99.0	0.2	0.3	0.0	0.0	0.3	0.5	5.0	5.7	6.1	5.4	3.4	21.2	35.1	15.8	2.4	79.8	46.9	51.6	48.4
04649	JONESPORT	97.8	96.9	0.3	0.5	0.1	0.1	0.4	0.5	5.8	6.1	6.1	5.8	3.5	23.5	29.2	15.9	4.1	78.5	44.3	48.4	51.6
04650	LITTLE DEER ISLE	97.8	97.5	0.4	0.4	0.4	0.8	0.9	1.3	4.6	4.6	5.4	5.9	3.8	18.8	38.9	15.5	2.5	82.0	49.1	54.0	46.0
04652	LUBEC	97.7	96.7	0.3	0.4	0.2	0.4	0.7	1.2	4.6	4.9	5.4	6.0	4.8	21.7	31.8	17.4	3.5	81.3	46.7	47.9	52.1
04653	BASS HARBOR	97.8	97.7	0.0	0.0	0.4	0.6	0.7	0.8	5.3	5.7	6.1	5.3	3.8	19.5	37.2	15.3	1.9	79.4	48.2	47.3	52.7
04654	MACHIAS	96.7	95.7	0.5	0.6	1.0	1.3	0.5	0.8	4.6	4.6	4.8	8.9	10.1	21.4	28.3	14.0	3.3	82.0	40.9	47.9	52.1
04655	MACHIASPORT	98.2	97.5	0.0	0.1	0.2	0.3	0.1	0.1	4.5	4.7	5.2	6.0	5.6	26.1	32.2	14.1	1.7	81.6	43.5	52.2	47.8
04657	MEDDYBEMPS	98.1	97.7	0.4	0.4	0.4	0.4	0.0	0.4	5.7	5.7	6.1	6.1	4.2	21.6	34.5	14.8	1.5	79.5	45.5	50.4	49.6
04658	MILBRIDGE	92.5	88.7	0.0	0.0	0.1	0.3	6.2	9.5	3.9	4.2	4.9	5.5	4.2	23.8	31.7	17.8	4.1	83.9	47.6	49.3	50.7
04660	MOUNT DESERT	98.3	98.0	0.1	0.3	0.3	0.3	0.7	1.0	3.7	4.1	7.2	6.0	2.2	22.9	36.5	15.1	2.1	80.0	46.9	48.5	51.5
04666	PEMBROKE	97.5	96.6	0.1	0.1	0.3	0.5	0.4	0.6	5.2	5.6	6.2	5.9	4.2	21.5	33.6	15.9	2.1	79.5	45.9	48.6	51.4
04667	PERRY	54.5	51.1	0.1	0.1	0.1	0.1	0.7	0.8	7.1	7.3	7.1	7.4	7.2	25.4	27.3	10.2	1.1	73.9	36.1	47.9	52.1
04668	PRINCETON	63.6	61.2	0.1	0.1	0.1	0.1	0.7	1.1	6.7	6.6	6.7	8.8	7.5	26.0	26.4	10.0	1.4	74.9	36.4	50.1	49.9
04669	PROSPECT HARBOR	96.9	96.1	0.5	0.9	0.5	0.4	1.9	2.9	4.6	4.6	5.3	5.9	5.3	23.2	34.2	14.5	2.4	81.6	45.8	51.5	48.5
04671	ROBBINSTON	91.8	89.4	0.0	0.0	0.0	0.0	0.2	0.4	5.6	6.2	6.2	5.8	5.2	23.7	33.0	12.5	1.7	78.8	43.1	49.8	50.2
04673	SARGENTVILLE	98.5	97.3	0.0	0.0	0.0	0.0	1.5	1.4	5.5	5.5	6.8	8.2	2.7	20.5	34.2	15.1	1.4	76.7	45.5	49.3	50.7
04674	SEAL COVE	98.1	97.7	0.5	0.6	0.2	0.3	0.2	0.4	4.6	6.2	6.4	5.6	3.7	26.5	33.4	13.0	0.7	79.1	43.3	48.2	51.8
04676	SEDGWICK	96.6	96.2	0.2	0.3	0.4	0.5	1.1	1.6	5.5	6.2	6.8	7.6	3.6	21.7	32.9	13.7	2.1	76.8	43.8	50.1	49.9
04677	SORRENTO	96.2	96.0	0.0	0.0	0.3	0.3	0.7	0.9	2.8	3.4	3.7	3.4	3.7	19.2	43.3	18.3	2.2	87.6	52.7	49.8	50.2
04679	SOUTHWEST HARBOR	98.4	98.0	0.3	0.4	0.2	0.2	0.6	1.0	4.4	5.6	5.3	5.3	4.1	24.3	31.7	15.9	3.4	81.2	45.7	47.5	52.5
04680	STEUBEN	97.0	95.9	0.3	0.3	0.4	0.6	0.5	0.8	5.5	6.4	6.6	6.2	5.2	26.3	29.7	12.4	1.5	77.6	40.4	49.4	50.6
04681	STONINGTON	96.8	96.3	0.1	0.1	0.4	0.7	0.9	1.3	4.5	4.9	5.4	6.1	4.4	23.9	31.8	16.6	2.5	80.8	45.5	47.4	52.6
04683	SUNSET	99.2	99.2	0.0	0.0	0.0	0.0	0.0	0.0	6.1	6.1	6.1	6.1	4.5	23.5	31.8	13.6	2.3	78.0	43.3	50.0	50.0
04684	SURRY	96.8	96.4	0.1	0.2	0.4	0.6	0.4	0.6	4.7	6.0	8.2	5.9	3.2	22.6	34.7	13.1	1.7	77.3	44.6	49.8	50.2
04685	SWANS ISLAND	98.5	98.5	0.3	0.3	0.0	0.0	0.0	0.0	6.1	6.1	6.4	5.5	3.8	22.7	30.8	16.6	2.0	78.2	44.5	51.5	48.5
	MAINE	96.9	96.3	0.5	0.7	0.7	1.1	0.7	1.1	5.4	5.6	6.1	6.9	6.2	24.7	30.2	12.7	2.3	78.8	41.6	48.8	51.2
	UNITED STATES	75.1	72.0	12.3	12.7	3.8	4.6	12.5	15.7	6.8	6.7	6.6	7.1	6.9	27.0	26.0	10.9	1.9	75.7	36.9	49.2	50.8

ZIP CODE #	POST OFFICE NAME	2009 Per Capita Income	2009 HH Income Base	2009 Household Income Distribution (%): Less than $25,000	$25,000 to $49,999	$50,000 to $99,999	$100,000 to $149,999	$150,000 or More	Median Household Income: 2009	2014	2009 National Centile	2009 State Centile	2009 Home Value Base	2009 Home Value Distribution (%): Less than $50,000	$50,000 to $89,999	$90,000 to $174,999	$175,000 to $399,999	$400,000 or More	2009 Median Home Value
04475	PASSADUMKEAG	20041	197	33.0	31.5	29.9	2.5	3.0	41467	45330	38	44	167	6.6	26.3	61.7	5.4	0.0	109670
04476	PENOBSCOT	23844	599	18.0	35.2	39.2	4.8	2.7	47353	47410	55	67	521	7.1	6.3	34.5	40.1	11.9	183468
04478	ROCKWOOD	20744	134	40.3	29.1	24.6	6.0	0.0	32963	36310	13	12	104	6.7	13.5	37.5	29.8	12.5	156818
04479	SANGERVILLE	17983	681	37.0	35.2	24.5	3.1	0.1	33718	34458	15	14	515	8.2	20.2	47.6	22.5	1.6	125181
04481	SEBEC	18670	286	27.6	35.7	33.6	3.1	0.0	41366	44481	37	43	256	5.9	18.0	36.3	35.2	4.7	157895
04487	SPRINGFIELD	15087	365	44.9	27.9	23.6	2.7	0.8	28113	29888	6	4	326	31.9	26.7	33.1	6.4	1.8	77778
04488	STETSON	17171	362	31.5	43.1	21.5	1.9	1.9	37390	40961	25	30	318	11.6	23.6	38.7	25.2	0.9	116477
04490	TOPSFIELD	18144	103	33.0	39.8	21.4	5.8	0.0	33584	35000	15	14	87	14.9	28.7	33.3	17.2	5.7	106944
04491	VANCEBORO	18268	68	44.1	29.4	22.1	4.4	0.0	30000	40000	8	6	58	31.0	24.1	32.8	10.3	1.7	82500
04492	WAITE	20350	87	39.1	33.3	23.0	4.6	0.0	33357	36851	14	13	74	27.0	27.0	29.7	14.9	1.4	84000
04493	WEST ENFIELD	19773	710	27.6	29.7	35.4	5.4	2.0	43232	46356	43	50	599	15.9	19.0	44.1	20.2	0.8	110842
04495	WINN	17812	158	36.7	34.2	22.8	5.1	1.3	32545	34376	12	11	134	23.1	33.6	31.3	11.2	0.7	81000
04496	WINTERPORT	23013	1621	24.8	26.7	34.6	11.5	2.3	48433	48398	58	71	1341	10.6	10.1	30.4	45.9	3.0	172500
04497	WYTOPITLOCK	12018	135	47.4	33.3	17.8	1.5	0.0	25919	26231	4	2	121	32.2	31.4	24.8	11.6	0.0	67083
04530	BATH	25013	5300	24.3	28.8	36.5	8.2	2.2	46716	50069	53	64	3131	1.4	4.7	40.1	44.7	9.1	185127
04535	ALNA	22720	286	20.6	24.5	45.8	8.4	0.7	53613	53416	69	84	257	2.3	4.7	27.6	52.9	12.5	217500
04537	BOOTHBAY	25462	820	20.6	31.7	33.8	9.8	4.1	48505	48876	58	71	711	0.0	4.4	28.8	48.4	18.4	226010
04538	BOOTHBAY HARBOR	29631	1247	24.1	28.1	32.6	11.1	4.1	47773	48001	56	69	906	3.1	4.1	20.1	52.5	20.2	247037
04539	BRISTOL	24961	592	17.6	34.5	37.0	7.6	3.4	47875	48047	56	69	516	2.3	5.8	26.2	49.4	16.3	205670
04541	CHAMBERLAIN	27606	95	17.9	31.6	40.0	7.4	3.2	50368	51068	62	77	81	6.2	1.2	21.0	51.9	19.8	230357
04543	DAMARISCOTTA	31209	854	25.3	23.4	38.4	6.8	6.1	50826	51982	63	78	613	8.5	3.1	16.3	48.5	23.7	265234
04544	EAST BOOTHBAY	45104	183	15.3	16.4	38.3	15.3	14.8	69425	71600	86	97	160	2.5	1.3	11.3	41.3	43.8	356522
04547	FRIENDSHIP	28136	547	18.3	31.6	32.9	10.8	6.4	50057	50948	61	76	460	4.8	6.1	34.6	38.3	16.3	186413
04548	GEORGETOWN	33504	460	15.4	23.5	42.0	11.7	7.4	61540	63241	79	93	378	1.9	5.6	22.2	48.9	21.4	255208
04549	ISLE OF SPRINGS	0	0	0.0	0.0	0.0	0.0	0.0	0	0	0	0	0	0.0	0.0	0.0	0.0	0.0	0
04551	BREMEN	30058	318	22.6	30.8	31.1	7.5	7.9	45991	46625	51	60	286	2.4	3.8	19.6	45.1	29.0	262903
04553	NEWCASTLE	29363	810	17.4	29.6	37.4	11.4	4.2	52195	52157	66	82	659	2.4	3.0	19.0	49.2	26.4	263889
04554	NEW HARBOR	35059	372	19.1	33.6	31.2	8.3	7.8	47483	47395	55	68	332	0.3	2.7	18.7	48.5	29.8	315190
04555	NOBLEBORO	27740	790	19.9	30.8	37.1	8.2	4.1	49573	49877	60	74	678	3.8	2.8	24.6	54.9	13.9	227350
04556	EDGECOMB	31082	533	16.1	32.5	34.0	10.3	7.1	51504	51719	65	80	462	3.7	3.2	23.8	44.6	24.7	245714
04558	PEMAQUID	31865	124	18.5	32.3	37.1	7.3	4.8	49095	49527	59	73	108	4.6	1.9	21.3	48.1	24.1	250000
04562	PHIPPSBURG	28309	967	19.3	23.7	41.1	10.3	5.6	56317	59945	73	87	831	4.0	9.0	26.5	44.2	16.4	211975
04563	CUSHING	26082	663	17.8	31.5	37.1	9.8	3.8	50575	50141	63	78	566	3.5	9.7	33.7	33.9	19.1	187879
04564	ROUND POND	30275	159	17.6	31.4	39.6	7.5	3.8	50683	51168	63	78	136	5.9	2.2	22.1	50.7	19.1	229545
04568	SOUTH BRISTOL	33485	244	26.2	27.9	31.1	9.8	4.9	47550	47989	56	68	212	1.9	1.4	15.1	46.2	35.4	282609
04570	SQUIRREL ISLAND	0	0	0.0	0.0	0.0	0.0	0.0	0	0	0	0	0	0.0	0.0	0.0	0.0	0.0	0
04571	TREVETT	25895	132	16.7	31.1	37.9	9.1	5.3	51681	50834	65	81	122	0.0	3.3	12.3	51.6	32.8	327586
04572	WALDOBORO	22047	2274	27.7	29.6	34.8	6.2	1.7	43774	46049	45	53	1865	8.6	5.1	38.9	38.4	9.0	170700
04573	WALPOLE	30044	192	25.5	27.6	31.8	9.9	5.2	48170	48318	57	70	166	0.6	1.8	15.1	47.0	35.5	286111
04574	WASHINGTON	19894	573	21.8	37.2	36.0	3.7	1.4	44448	46480	47	55	507	4.7	6.5	43.2	41.4	4.1	166477
04576	SOUTHPORT	43957	343	13.4	32.4	30.6	9.3	14.3	54389	55012	70	85	300	1.3	0.0	13.7	34.3	50.7	405000
04578	WISCASSET	23930	2082	20.9	34.1	32.9	8.9	3.3	46380	47257	52	62	1636	8.4	6.5	19.4	51.2	14.5	220290
04579	WOOLWICH	26597	1330	16.0	30.2	39.0	10.1	4.7	53019	55878	68	83	1141	1.8	8.0	31.1	47.4	11.7	198326
04605	ELLSWORTH	23656	5424	25.8	32.0	32.2	7.0	3.0	43959	46298	45	53	4056	5.1	8.3	31.9	45.0	9.8	188960
04606	ADDISON	18678	442	38.7	31.4	24.9	2.0	2.9	31648	33289	11	8	379	14.5	17.9	35.9	25.1	6.6	128629
04607	GOULDSBORO	23235	646	24.0	34.2	34.1	5.3	2.5	42992	45000	42	50	521	7.3	10.7	39.3	31.9	10.7	161632
04609	BAR HARBOR	29747	2903	24.5	27.9	33.4	8.9	5.3	47735	48048	56	69	1792	1.7	1.5	8.1	57.7	31.0	293266
04611	BEALS	18221	234	34.2	33.3	26.1	5.1	1.3	38893	42165	29	35	196	11.7	21.9	31.6	27.6	7.1	139063
04612	BERNARD	25385	4	0.0	0.0	100.0	0.0	0.0	60000	53333	77	91	3	0.0	0.0	0.0	100.0	0.0	287500
04613	BIRCH HARBOR	22621	111	19.8	33.3	38.7	6.3	1.8	46399	46431	53	63	89	5.6	10.1	46.1	32.6	5.6	159559
04614	BLUE HILL	24624	1134	30.1	30.4	29.0	5.8	4.7	39642	41502	32	37	870	4.0	3.1	20.2	45.9	26.8	282463
04616	BROOKLIN	27401	512	24.8	28.9	33.2	7.8	5.3	46373	47081	52	62	431	4.4	3.7	27.1	39.4	25.3	232692
04617	BROOKSVILLE	27773	473	19.9	37.4	31.5	5.7	5.5	45406	46546	49	58	410	7.3	10.0	24.9	29.5	28.3	220370
04619	CALAIS	21460	1485	42.6	23.6	23.4	7.6	2.8	30608	31310	9	6	928	8.6	22.6	51.0	14.0	3.8	120701
04622	CHERRYFIELD	16486	560	44.5	33.0	18.8	2.5	1.3	28526	29494	6	4	427	10.1	19.7	45.4	17.6	7.3	123185
04623	COLUMBIA FALLS	18171	563	37.7	29.5	27.7	3.7	1.4	34490	35899	16	18	457	16.8	16.8	38.5	23.6	4.2	116728
04624	COREA	24014	135	26.7	26.7	35.6	7.4	3.7	47050	46649	54	66	112	1.8	3.6	25.9	38.4	30.4	234211
04625	CRANBERRY ISLES	25519	27	18.5	37.0	37.0	7.4	0.0	46133	47388	52	61	23	0.0	0.0	8.7	47.8	43.5	362500
04626	CUTLER	18323	238	28.6	38.2	26.5	5.9	0.8	41183	45460	37	42	166	10.2	16.9	33.7	34.9	4.2	153571
04627	DEER ISLE	21824	692	30.5	29.8	31.5	4.9	3.3	40588	45025	35	41	591	5.6	8.8	28.6	34.0	23.0	206176
04628	DENNYSVILLE	17032	284	37.0	33.5	25.4	3.9	0.4	33239	35138	14	13	244	14.8	19.3	40.6	20.1	5.3	119697
04630	EAST MACHIAS	19118	725	31.2	38.1	27.0	2.6	1.1	35601	38026	20	23	587	9.5	14.5	45.3	25.0	5.6	138575
04631	EASTPORT	18719	709	44.9	28.9	22.6	3.0	0.7	28063	29119	6	4	491	15.5	35.0	34.6	13.0	1.8	89609
04634	FRANKLIN	20667	1318	30.4	35.1	28.2	3.6	2.7	38839	41828	29	35	1060	11.0	15.4	40.6	26.9	6.1	145565
04635	FRENCHBORO	22324	20	40.0	25.0	30.0	5.0	0.0	35000	45000	18	21	17	5.9	0.0	23.5	47.1	23.5	262500
04640	HANCOCK	23553	443	24.8	33.4	33.0	6.8	2.0	40817	42423	35	42	376	5.6	6.9	26.1	46.0	15.4	198370
04642	HARBORSIDE	34404	91	19.8	33.0	29.7	8.8	8.8	48065	47756	57	70	80	2.5	8.8	22.5	32.5	33.8	281250
04643	HARRINGTON	16723	365	37.5	36.2	24.4	1.4	0.5	31749	32467	11	9	299	19.4	15.7	42.5	16.4	6.0	120313
04645	ISLE AU HAUT	15824	36	38.9	36.1	19.4	5.6	0.0	33153	33158	14	12	29	0.0	0.0	27.6	37.9	34.5	227500
04646	ISLESFORD	26345	34	23.5	29.4	32.4	8.8	5.9	47361	52103	55	67	30	0.0	0.0	13.3	43.3	43.3	350000
04648	JONESBORO	18968	271	39.1	29.5	24.7	4.8	1.8	32189	32989	12	10	234	12.0	20.1	38.9	19.7	9.4	128704
04649	JONESPORT	19672	599	42.9	29.5	19.9	4.2	3.5	30855	32814	9	7	487	11.3	18.5	36.8	29.8	3.7	136184
04650	LITTLE DEER ISLE	25337	109	30.3	27.5	29.4	6.4	6.4	41391	45490	37	44	94	5.3	10.6	26.6	37.2	20.2	205882
04652	LUBEC	16005	932	47.4	32.6	17.2	2.1	0.6	26336	27097	4	3	728	17.4	21.4	38.5	16.3	6.3	109474
04653	BASS HARBOR	23879	216	23.6	30.6	37.0	6.5	2.3	45000	46757	48	57	164	3.7	2.4	17.1	53.7	23.2	272000
04654	MACHIAS	18443	1561	40.2	29.9	24.7	3.7	1.5	31716	32728	11	8	1060	13.1	13.9	45.4	24.3	3.3	136250
04655	MACHIASPORT	15713	347	32.3	38.3	25.9	2.6	0.9	34900	37850	17	20	276	10.9	14.9	43.1	25.7	5.4	137500
04657	MEDDYBEMPS	18415	113	29.2	36.3	31.9	2.7	0.0	36939	43014	23	29	101	7.9	10.9	51.5	23.8	5.9	142361
04658	MILBRIDGE	15615	596	45.3	33.2	18.8	2.0	0.7	27526	27766	5	3	473	14.8	17.1	32.3	30.4	5.3	133807
04660	MOUNT DESERT	32697	526	12.9	30.0	39.2	11.0	6.8	60530	57500	78	92	417	1.9	1.0	6.7	40.3	50.1	400820
04666	PEMBROKE	16663	535	42.4	30.8	22.6	4.1	0.0	29096	29720	7	5	465	15.1	22.2	39.4	21.3	2.2	112500
04667	PERRY	15139	583	44.3	28.6	22.5	3.4	1.2	30803	31832	9	7	471	18.3	21.4	35.9	19.7	4.7	107543
04668	PRINCETON	16305	703	40.3	31.0	24.5	3.6	0.7	30891	31658	10	7	526	17.5	24.0	42.2	14.1	2.3	103125
04669	PROSPECT HARBOR	24438	198	22.2	31.3	37.4	6.6	2.5	46393	46581	53	63	160	5.0	8.8	39.4	34.4	12.5	168750
04671	ROBBINSTON	18159	206	34.5	31.6	27.2	3.9	2.9	38058	41151	27	32	183	13.7	19.1	31.7	27.3	8.2	129605
04673	SARGENTVILLE	19384	31	25.8	32.3	38.7	3.2	0.0	43633	45000	44	52	26	3.8	11.5	19.2	42.3	23.1	225000
04674	SEAL COVE	24984	521	22.5	31.5	33.4	10.4	2.3	46355	46995	52	62	407	2.9	4.9	24.3	51.6	16.2	235909
04676	SEDGWICK	23531	479	25.7	32.2	33.8	6.1	2.3	43591	45616	44	52	397	9.3	11.6	21.7	36.3	21.2	205909
04677	SORRENTO	32407	149	14.8	28.2	38.9	12.8	5.4	53958	54626	70	84	123	0.0	1.6	27.6	47.2	23.6	241250
04679	SOUTHWEST HARBOR	26908	993	29.2	26.3	30.1	11.3	3.1	45412	46778	49	58	647	2.5	2.5	20.4	53.6	21.0	237326
04680	STEUBEN	17066	415	38.8	30.4	26.3	3.4	1.2	33475	35291	14	13	358	18.2	15.4	43.3	18.4	4.7	123333
04681	STONINGTON	20931	544	32.5	32.9	28.1	3.9	2.6	38210	42198	27	33	417	6.7	8.6	36.0	32.6	16.1	171944
04683	SUNSET	23210	61	29.5	32.8	27.9	4.9	4.9	40760	45260	35	42	53	5.7	5.7	30.2	37.7	20.8	209375
04684	SURRY	23766	635	25.7	27.7	37.5	4.9	4.3	46802	47051	54	65	533	2.1	8.4	35.8	34.7	18.9	192411
04685	SWANS ISLAND	20478	155	38.1	27.1	25.8	7.1	1.9	38649	42098	29	34	127	15.0	3.9	17.3	47.2	16.5	222059
	MAINE	24559		25.0	28.4	35.2	7.5	3.8	46650	48581				6.4	9.4	36.7	38.7	8.8	170226
	UNITED STATES	27277		20.9	24.4	35.3	11.7	7.6	54719	56938				9.3	13.1	31.6	32.6	13.5	162279

ZIP CODE #	POST OFFICE NAME	FINANCIAL SERVICES				THE HOME						ENTERTAINMENT						PERSONAL			
						Home Improvements		Furnishings													
		Auto Loan	Home Loan	Invest-ments	Retire-ment Plans	Home Repair	Lawn & Garden	Comput-ers & Hard-ware-Personal	Major Appli-ances	TV, Radio, Sound Equip-ment	Furni-ture	Dine out/ Carry out	Sports Equip-ment	Fees & Tickets	Toys & Games	Travel	Cable TV	Apparel & Services	Auto Repairs	Health Insur-ance	Pets & Supplies
04475	PASSADUMKEAG	89	64	74	62	64	85	67	77	74	65	72	60	53	77	61	81	49	73	82	94
04476	PENOBSCOT	93	75	120	73	82	98	75	95	78	70	77	69	65	74	81	83	51	87	94	110
04478	ROCKWOOD	71	57	92	56	62	75	57	72	60	53	59	53	49	57	62	63	39	67	71	84
04479	SANGERVILLE	68	49	69	47	50	70	52	65	57	47	56	48	41	57	50	63	37	60	69	76
04481	SEBEC	72	57	91	56	62	76	57	73	60	54	60	53	49	58	61	65	40	67	72	85
04487	SPRINGFIELD	65	47	67	45	48	66	48	61	53	44	52	46	38	53	47	58	34	56	63	72
04488	STETSON	76	54	78	53	56	77	56	71	62	52	61	53	45	61	55	68	40	65	74	84
04490	TOPSFIELD	69	55	88	54	60	73	55	70	58	52	57	51	48	55	59	62	38	65	70	82
04491	VANCEBORO	67	48	69	47	50	68	49	63	55	46	54	47	39	54	49	60	36	58	65	75
04492	WAITE	76	56	84	55	60	78	57	73	63	54	62	54	47	61	59	68	41	67	75	86
04493	WEST ENFIELD	86	67	73	67	67	85	68	79	74	65	72	60	58	76	64	80	49	74	82	94
04495	WINN	75	54	77	52	56	76	55	70	61	51	60	53	44	61	55	67	40	64	73	84
04496	WINTERPORT	92	84	76	81	82	87	79	84	82	82	82	62	75	86	76	85	56	82	85	100
04497	WYTOPITLOCK	59	42	60	41	43	59	43	55	48	40	47	41	34	47	43	53	31	50	57	65
04530	BATH	84	71	78	73	72	81	80	81	82	75	81	62	73	81	76	84	55	82	85	96
04535	ALNA	80	88	80	90	86	88	79	84	78	79	78	65	83	80	84	79	55	80	83	98
04537	BOOTHBAY	99	80	128	78	87	105	80	101	83	75	82	74	69	79	86	89	55	93	100	117
04538	BOOTHBAY HARBOR	97	80	126	79	89	104	79	100	83	76	82	71	71	78	86	88	55	92	100	115
04539	BRISTOL	95	76	123	75	83	100	76	97	80	71	79	71	66	76	82	85	52	89	95	112
04541	CHAMBERLAIN	101	81	131	80	89	107	81	103	85	76	84	75	70	81	88	91	56	95	102	119
04543	DAMARISCOTTA	97	89	131	88	100	111	84	103	88	87	87	70	83	82	94	93	59	97	108	118
04544	EAST BOOTHBAY	122	129	175	128	148	152	116	137	122	131	120	85	127	110	134	128	82	130	152	155
04547	FRIENDSHIP	113	84	135	83	91	119	88	111	92	78	91	86	71	89	92	99	60	103	113	132
04548	GEORGETOWN	126	101	163	99	111	133	101	128	106	95	104	94	87	100	109	113	69	118	127	149
04549	ISLE OF SPRINGS	0	0	0	0	0	0	0	0	0	0	0	0	0	0	0	0	0	0	0	0
04551	BREMEN	114	92	148	90	101	121	92	116	96	86	95	85	79	91	99	102	63	107	115	135
04553	NEWCASTLE	111	89	144	88	98	118	89	113	93	84	92	83	77	89	97	99	61	105	112	131
04554	NEW HARBOR	93	94	131	93	108	113	86	102	90	95	89	65	92	82	98	95	61	97	112	116
04555	NOBLEBORO	106	85	137	83	93	112	85	108	89	80	88	79	74	84	92	95	58	100	106	125
04556	EDGECOMB	117	94	151	92	103	124	94	119	98	88	97	87	81	93	102	105	64	110	118	138
04558	PEMAQUID	99	87	132	86	97	110	83	103	88	84	86	72	79	82	93	93	58	97	106	119
04562	PHIPPSBURG	108	91	122	92	97	115	91	110	95	84	93	81	81	93	95	100	63	101	110	127
04563	CUSHING	102	81	131	80	89	107	81	103	85	76	84	75	70	81	88	91	56	95	102	120
04564	ROUND POND	100	80	130	79	88	106	80	102	84	75	83	75	70	80	87	90	55	94	101	118
04568	SOUTH BRISTOL	111	89	144	88	98	118	89	114	93	84	92	83	77	89	97	100	61	105	112	132
04570	SQUIRREL ISLAND	0	0	0	0	0	0	0	0	0	0	0	0	0	0	0	0	0	0	0	0
04571	TREVETT	105	84	136	83	92	111	84	107	88	79	87	78	73	84	91	94	58	99	106	124
04572	WALDOBORO	87	72	90	70	74	87	71	84	75	69	74	61	62	75	71	79	50	79	84	99
04573	WALPOLE	112	90	145	88	98	118	90	114	94	84	93	83	78	89	97	100	62	105	113	132
04574	WASHINGTON	81	65	105	64	71	86	65	83	68	61	67	60	56	65	71	73	45	76	82	96
04576	SOUTHPORT	119	126	170	124	145	148	113	133	119	128	117	83	124	107	130	125	80	127	148	151
04578	WISCASSET	93	76	97	74	79	94	75	89	80	73	79	66	66	79	76	85	53	84	90	105
04579	WOOLWICH	96	97	90	101	97	104	91	99	92	87	91	76	91	94	94	94	63	93	100	115
04605	ELLSWORTH	88	72	102	71	77	91	73	88	76	69	75	64	64	74	76	81	51	82	89	102
04606	ADDISON	79	57	81	55	59	80	58	74	65	54	63	56	47	64	58	71	42	68	77	88
04607	GOULDSBORO	89	69	108	68	75	93	69	88	74	65	73	65	59	71	74	79	48	81	88	103
04609	BAR HARBOR	92	88	102	89	90	97	87	94	88	86	88	71	86	86	91	91	61	92	96	110
04611	BEALS	81	56	89	56	58	85	62	77	64	50	64	64	45	63	61	70	41	72	81	95
04612	BERNARD	95	76	123	75	84	101	76	97	80	72	79	71	66	76	83	85	52	90	96	112
04613	BIRCH HARBOR	89	72	116	70	79	95	72	91	75	67	74	66	62	71	78	80	49	84	90	105
04614	BLUE HILL	87	70	113	69	77	92	70	89	73	66	72	65	61	70	76	78	48	82	88	103
04616	BROOKLIN	101	81	130	79	88	106	81	102	84	76	83	75	70	80	87	90	55	95	101	119
04617	BROOKSVILLE	100	80	130	79	88	106	80	102	84	75	83	75	70	80	87	90	55	94	101	118
04619	CALAIS	69	63	66	63	64	74	64	70	68	61	67	52	61	67	64	72	46	68	77	82
04622	CHERRYFIELD	64	46	68	45	48	66	48	61	52	44	52	46	38	52	48	58	34	56	63	72
04623	COLUMBIA FALLS	75	54	78	53	57	77	56	71	61	52	60	53	45	61	55	68	40	65	73	84
04624	COREA	99	79	127	78	87	104	79	100	83	74	82	73	68	79	86	88	54	93	99	116
04625	CRANBERRY ISLES	84	67	108	66	73	88	67	85	70	63	69	62	58	67	73	75	46	78	84	99
04626	CUTLER	81	56	89	56	59	86	62	77	65	50	64	64	45	63	62	70	41	72	81	95
04627	DEER ISLE	84	67	108	66	73	88	67	85	70	63	69	62	58	67	73	75	46	78	84	99
04628	DENNYSVILLE	71	51	73	49	53	72	52	66	58	49	57	50	42	57	52	64	38	61	69	79
04630	EAST MACHIAS	75	54	77	52	56	76	55	70	61	51	60	53	44	61	54	67	40	64	73	83
04631	EASTPORT	65	47	65	45	48	68	51	63	57	45	55	47	41	56	49	63	37	59	69	74
04634	FRANKLIN	83	62	84	60	63	84	62	78	69	59	68	58	51	69	62	75	45	72	81	93
04635	FRENCHBORO	80	55	88	55	57	84	61	76	63	49	63	63	45	62	61	69	41	71	80	93
04640	HANCOCK	85	68	110	67	75	90	68	87	71	64	71	63	59	68	74	76	47	80	86	100
04642	HARBORSIDE	114	91	148	90	100	121	91	116	96	86	95	85	79	91	99	102	63	107	115	135
04643	HARRINGTON	68	49	70	47	51	69	50	64	56	47	55	48	40	55	50	61	36	58	66	76
04645	ISLE AU HAUT	69	48	76	47	50	73	53	66	55	43	54	54	39	54	53	60	35	61	69	81
04646	ISLESFORD	93	74	120	73	82	98	75	95	78	70	77	69	65	74	81	83	51	87	94	110
04648	JONESBORO	69	56	90	55	61	73	56	71	58	52	58	52	48	55	60	62	38	65	70	82
04649	JONESPORT	78	53	85	53	56	82	59	74	62	48	61	61	43	60	59	67	40	69	78	91
04650	LITTLE DEER ISLE	93	74	120	73	81	98	74	94	78	70	77	69	64	74	80	83	51	87	93	109
04652	LUBEC	59	42	60	41	44	61	44	56	49	41	48	42	36	49	44	54	32	52	59	66
04653	BASS HARBOR	88	70	113	69	77	93	70	89	74	66	73	65	61	70	76	78	48	82	88	104
04654	MACHIAS	63	51	64	50	53	63	56	62	59	52	58	45	49	57	54	63	39	60	66	72
04655	MACHIASPORT	75	53	77	52	55	76	55	70	61	51	60	52	44	60	54	67	39	64	73	83
04657	MEDDYBEMPS	77	55	79	53	57	78	56	72	62	52	61	54	45	62	56	69	40	66	74	85
04658	MILBRIDGE	60	43	62	42	44	61	44	56	49	41	48	42	35	48	44	54	32	51	58	67
04660	MOUNT DESERT	121	100	153	98	108	128	99	123	103	93	102	90	87	98	107	109	68	114	122	143
04666	PEMBROKE	67	48	69	46	50	68	49	63	55	46	54	47	39	54	49	60	35	57	65	74
04667	PERRY	63	49	55	49	47	61	51	57	57	50	56	43	45	57	49	60	38	56	61	70
04668	PRINCETON	66	51	56	51	50	63	54	59	59	52	58	45	46	60	50	63	39	58	63	72
04669	PROSPECT HARBOR	92	74	119	73	81	98	74	94	77	69	76	69	64	74	80	83	51	87	93	109
04671	ROBBINSTON	82	58	84	57	61	83	60	76	67	56	65	57	48	66	59	73	43	70	79	91
04673	SARGENTVILLE	76	61	98	60	67	81	61	78	64	57	63	57	53	61	66	68	42	72	77	90
04674	SEAL COVE	94	75	121	74	82	99	75	95	78	70	78	70	65	74	81	84	52	88	94	110
04676	SEDGWICK	90	72	116	71	79	95	72	91	75	67	74	67	62	71	78	80	49	84	90	106
04677	SORRENTO	117	94	151	92	103	124	94	119	98	88	97	87	81	93	102	105	64	110	118	138
04679	SOUTHWEST HARBOR	94	75	122	74	83	100	76	96	79	71	78	70	65	75	82	84	52	89	95	111
04680	STEUBEN	72	50	79	49	52	76	55	68	57	45	57	57	40	56	55	62	37	64	72	84
04681	STONINGTON	83	57	91	57	60	87	63	79	66	51	65	65	46	65	63	72	42	73	83	97
04683	SUNSET	84	67	108	66	74	89	67	85	70	63	69	62	58	67	73	75	46	79	84	99
04684	SURRY	95	76	123	75	83	100	76	97	80	71	79	71	66	76	82	85	52	89	95	112
04685	SWANS ISLAND	81	56	89	56	59	86	62	77	65	50	64	64	45	63	62	70	41	72	81	95
	MAINE	87	79	87	80	81	89	81	86	83	78	82	65	76	83	81	86	57	84	89	102
	UNITED STATES	100	100	100	100	100	100	100	100	100	100	100	100	100	100	100	100	100	100	100	100

04691-04957

ZIP CODE #	POST OFFICE NAME	COUNTY FIPS CODE	POPULATION 2000	POPULATION 2009	POPULATION 2014	2000-2009 ANNUAL RATE % Rate	2000-2009 ANNUAL RATE State Centile	HOUSEHOLDS 2000	HOUSEHOLDS 2009	HOUSEHOLDS 2014	HOUSEHOLDS % Annual Rate 2000-2009	HOUSEHOLDS 2009 Average HH Size	FAMILIES 2000	FAMILIES 2009	FAMILIES % Annual Rate 2000-2009
04691	WHITING	029	170	164	161	-0.4	11	72	73	72	0.1	2.25	47	47	0.0
04693	WINTER HARBOR	009	988	1044	1066	0.6	62	402	446	461	1.1	2.34	278	303	0.9
04694	BAILEYVILLE	029	2610	2484	2425	-0.5	7	1090	1091	1080	0.0	2.28	757	743	-0.2
04730	HOULTON	003	10045	9385	9134	-0.7	2	4007	3879	3818	-0.4	2.33	2661	2528	-0.6
04732	ASHLAND	003	1870	1813	1779	-0.3	16	792	796	793	0.1	2.27	515	507	-0.2
04733	BENEDICTA	003	188	190	190	0.1	39	67	71	72	0.6	2.66	48	50	0.4
04734	BLAINE	003	461	455	451	-0.1	25	189	193	193	0.2	2.36	141	142	0.1
04735	BRIDGEWATER	003	635	706	729	1.2	87	259	298	312	1.5	2.37	180	204	1.4
04736	CARIBOU	003	10108	10091	10035	0.0	33	4195	4345	4377	0.4	2.29	2836	2883	0.2
04737	CLAYTON LAKE	003	1	1	1	0.0	33	1	1	1	0.0	1.00	0	0	0.0
04740	EASTON	003	1321	1334	1334	0.1	39	545	574	583	0.6	2.32	371	380	0.3
04741	ESTCOURT STATION	003	4	4	4	0.0	33	3	3	3	0.0	1.33	1	1	0.0
04742	FORT FAIRFIELD	003	3669	3864	3925	0.6	62	1560	1704	1751	1.0	2.26	1041	1118	0.8
04743	FORT KENT	003	5999	5849	5790	-0.3	16	2423	2473	2480	0.2	2.27	1578	1577	0.0
04745	FRENCHVILLE	003	1260	1211	1188	-0.4	11	490	493	490	0.1	2.38	366	363	-0.1
04746	GRAND ISLE	003	533	506	493	-0.6	3	224	222	220	-0.1	2.28	167	163	-0.3
04747	ISLAND FALLS	003	1277	1229	1201	-0.4	11	537	540	535	0.1	2.28	376	371	-0.1
04750	LIMESTONE	003	2468	2432	2430	-0.2	21	857	896	907	0.5	2.26	573	586	0.2
04751	LIMESTONE	003	169	168	168	-0.1	25	59	63	64	0.7	1.98	40	42	0.5
04756	MADAWASKA	003	3730	3660	3629	-0.2	21	1687	1725	1731	0.2	2.07	1059	1061	0.0
04757	MAPLETON	003	2851	2939	2960	0.3	50	1129	1209	1234	0.7	2.43	841	887	0.6
04758	MARS HILL	003	1480	1479	1472	0.0	33	614	634	639	0.3	2.28	414	420	0.2
04760	MONTICELLO	003	790	761	744	-0.4	11	325	326	324	0.0	2.33	230	227	-0.1
04761	NEW LIMERICK	003	541	531	525	-0.2	21	228	233	234	0.2	2.28	153	153	0.0
04762	NEW SWEDEN	003	652	753	783	1.6	93	259	310	328	2.0	2.43	183	215	1.8
04763	OAKFIELD	003	1017	971	952	-0.5	7	415	412	410	-0.1	2.36	284	276	-0.3
04764	OXBOW	003	56	54	53	-0.4	11	29	29	29	0.0	1.86	19	19	0.0
04765	PATTEN	019	1450	1446	1452	0.0	33	613	634	644	0.4	2.23	420	424	0.1
04766	PERHAM	003	442	437	434	-0.1	25	166	170	171	0.3	2.57	117	119	0.2
04768	PORTAGE	003	390	382	378	-0.2	21	183	187	188	0.2	2.04	112	112	0.0
04769	PRESQUE ISLE	003	9472	9467	9447	0.0	33	3949	4123	4173	0.5	2.17	2457	2505	0.2
04772	SAINT AGATHA	003	916	956	968	0.5	57	398	435	447	1.0	2.18	275	295	0.8
04773	SAINT DAVID	003	640	624	614	-0.3	16	240	244	244	0.2	2.55	190	190	0.0
04774	SAINT FRANCIS	003	854	823	806	-0.4	11	376	378	376	0.1	2.18	254	251	-0.1
04776	SHERMAN	003	1063	1040	1033	-0.2	21	422	432	434	0.3	2.41	324	326	0.1
04777	STACYVILLE	019	407	397	392	-0.3	16	163	164	164	0.1	2.42	117	115	-0.2
04779	SINCLAIR	003	290	292	293	0.1	39	125	131	134	0.5	2.23	88	90	0.2
04780	SMYRNA MILLS	003	442	429	421	-0.3	16	185	187	186	0.1	2.29	137	136	-0.1
04781	WALLAGRASS	003	399	384	378	-0.4	11	157	157	157	0.0	2.45	120	119	-0.1
04783	STOCKHOLM	003	629	642	645	0.2	46	279	296	302	0.6	2.17	202	211	0.5
04785	VAN BUREN	003	3005	2964	2946	-0.1	25	1240	1289	1300	0.4	2.16	811	827	0.2
04786	WASHBURN	003	1921	1850	1820	-0.4	11	810	814	811	0.1	2.27	583	576	-0.1
04787	WESTFIELD	003	771	754	744	-0.2	21	287	291	291	0.1	2.53	209	209	0.0
04841	ROCKLAND	013	7729	7355	7164	-0.5	7	3485	3436	3383	-0.2	2.07	1977	1889	-0.5
04843	CAMDEN	013	5283	5497	5528	0.4	53	2406	2562	2600	0.7	2.05	1425	1474	0.4
04847	HOPE	013	1254	1432	1496	1.4	90	494	588	621	1.9	2.42	366	427	1.7
04848	ISLESBORO	027	603	609	599	0.1	39	280	288	287	0.3	2.11	177	178	0.1
04849	LINCOLNVILLE	027	3535	3636	3642	0.3	50	1477	1563	1586	0.6	2.33	1019	1056	0.4
04851	MATINICUS	013	51	49	49	-0.4	11	26	26	26	0.0	1.88	14	14	0.0
04852	MONHEGAN	015	75	73	71	-0.3	16	46	47	46	0.2	1.55	21	21	0.0
04853	NORTH HAVEN	013	381	388	385	0.2	46	162	170	171	0.5	2.28	109	112	0.3
04854	OWLS HEAD	013	1621	1767	1815	0.9	77	732	829	862	1.4	2.11	476	526	1.1
04856	ROCKPORT	013	3212	3804	4008	1.8	95	1371	1677	1785	2.2	2.26	919	1097	1.9
04858	SOUTH THOMASTON	013	1456	1546	1565	0.7	66	607	668	685	1.0	2.31	432	465	0.8
04859	SPRUCE HEAD	013	907	942	937	0.4	53	379	405	409	0.7	2.33	276	289	0.5
04860	TENANTS HARBOR	013	1613	1619	1591	0.0	33	718	744	738	0.4	2.18	466	470	0.1
04861	THOMASTON	013	3603	3668	3616	0.2	46	1374	1423	1416	0.4	2.21	849	852	0.0
04862	UNION	013	3596	3746	3757	0.4	53	1383	1496	1521	0.9	2.47	1007	1069	0.6
04863	VINALHAVEN	013	1235	1261	1251	0.2	46	550	576	577	0.5	2.19	341	348	0.2
04864	WARREN	013	3792	4284	4424	1.3	88	1347	1573	1653	1.7	2.50	970	1105	1.4
04901	WATERVILLE	011	25862	25789	25732	0.0	33	10484	10853	10953	0.4	2.17	6321	6360	0.1
04910	ALBION	011	1901	1870	1850	-0.2	21	701	708	708	0.1	2.61	529	524	-0.1
04911	ANSON	025	1979	1987	1995	0.0	33	772	809	824	0.5	2.45	527	541	0.3
04912	ATHENS	025	845	845	856	0.0	33	328	346	356	0.6	2.38	228	235	0.3
04915	BELFAST	027	8437	9012	9163	0.7	66	3564	3937	4060	1.1	2.21	2264	2446	0.8
04917	BELGRADE	011	2978	3205	3297	0.8	71	1178	1299	1347	1.1	2.46	877	949	0.9
04920	BINGHAM	025	1549	1507	1498	-0.3	16	630	642	648	0.2	2.32	418	418	0.0
04921	BROOKS	027	1744	1879	1924	0.8	71	694	776	805	1.2	2.40	472	519	1.0
04922	BURNHAM	027	1142	1202	1226	0.6	62	442	486	503	1.0	2.47	326	353	0.9
04923	CAMBRIDGE	025	560	554	555	-0.1	25	227	237	240	0.5	2.34	175	180	0.3
04924	CANAAN	025	1921	1993	2030	0.4	53	735	801	827	0.9	2.48	538	576	0.7
04925	CARATUNK	025	123	125	126	0.2	46	50	53	55	0.6	2.36	31	32	0.3
04927	CLINTON	011	3335	3592	3714	0.8	71	1276	1428	1493	1.2	2.51	952	1046	1.0
04928	CORINNA	019	2262	2324	2346	0.3	50	884	927	945	0.5	2.51	654	672	0.3
04929	DETROIT	025	816	954	1006	1.7	94	328	401	429	2.2	2.38	227	272	2.0
04930	DEXTER	019	4278	4074	4006	-0.5	7	1764	1742	1732	-0.1	2.29	1221	1179	-0.4
04932	DIXMONT	019	1002	1137	1194	1.4	90	383	452	481	1.8	2.52	293	339	1.6
04936	EUSTIS	007	403	409	406	0.2	46	187	196	198	0.5	2.09	107	110	0.3
04937	FAIRFIELD	025	7194	7258	7283	0.1	39	2855	3005	3058	0.6	2.35	1955	2017	0.3
04938	FARMINGTON	007	9365	9854	9921	0.6	62	3584	3842	3919	0.8	2.21	2075	2178	0.5
04939	GARLAND	019	986	1047	1075	0.7	66	378	417	434	1.1	2.51	270	291	0.8
04941	FREEDOM	027	1930	2097	2160	0.9	77	765	866	904	1.3	2.36	541	601	1.1
04942	HARMONY	021	1307	1393	1421	0.7	66	540	599	620	1.1	2.32	407	445	1.0
04943	HARTLAND	025	1777	1797	1829	0.1	39	697	744	768	0.7	2.34	488	511	0.5
04945	JACKMAN	025	1032	1004	994	-0.3	16	430	436	438	0.1	2.22	270	268	-0.1
04947	KINGFIELD	007	1572	1566	1549	0.0	33	668	688	689	0.3	2.28	438	442	0.1
04949	LIBERTY	027	919	995	1016	0.9	77	358	401	414	1.2	2.47	255	281	1.1
04950	MADISON	025	4399	4384	4410	0.0	33	1845	1926	1963	0.5	2.22	1240	1267	0.2
04951	MONROE	027	824	867	880	0.6	62	325	358	368	1.1	2.42	217	234	0.8
04952	MORRILL	027	1544	1615	1643	0.5	57	613	672	691	1.0	2.40	444	479	0.8
04953	NEWPORT	019	3014	3144	3189	0.5	57	1274	1371	1409	0.8	2.29	850	893	0.5
04954	NEW PORTLAND	025	135	133	132	-0.2	21	54	56	56	0.4	2.38	37	38	0.3
04955	NEW SHARON	007	1305	1420	1468	0.9	77	523	598	628	1.5	2.37	364	408	1.2
04956	NEW VINEYARD	007	726	729	724	0.0	33	280	293	295	0.5	2.49	199	205	0.3
04957	NORRIDGEWOCK	025	4297	4563	4685	0.7	66	1683	1874	1949	1.2	2.43	1238	1355	1.0
	MAINE					0.6					0.9	2.32			0.7
	UNITED STATES					1.0					1.1	2.59			0.9

#	POST OFFICE NAME	RACE (%) White 2000	White 2009	Black 2000	Black 2009	Asian/Pacific 2000	Asian/Pacific 2009	% Hispanic Origin 2000	% Hispanic Origin 2009	2009 AGE DISTRIBUTION (%) 0-4	5-9	10-14	15-19	20-24	25-44	45-64	65-84	85+	18+	MEDIAN AGE 2009	% 2009 Males	% 2009 Females
04691	WHITING	97.1	95.7	0.0	0.6	0.0	0.0	0.6	0.6	3.7	4.3	4.9	6.7	4.3	22.6	35.4	16.5	1.8	82.9	47.0	48.8	51.2
04693	WINTER HARBOR	90.0	88.8	2.0	2.7	0.7	1.1	3.6	5.7	10.2	9.4	8.3	6.4	5.3	27.9	20.4	10.8	1.2	67.9	32.9	47.8	52.2
04694	BAILEYVILLE	98.3	97.5	0.1	0.1	0.1	0.1	0.5	0.8	5.2	5.6	6.0	6.1	4.4	24.1	31.4	15.2	2.0	79.3	44.0	49.6	50.4
04730	HOULTON	95.2	94.3	0.3	0.3	0.4	0.6	0.5	0.9	5.6	5.9	6.4	7.0	5.6	23.6	28.2	14.6	3.1	77.7	42.0	48.0	52.0
04732	ASHLAND	98.9	98.7	0.0	0.0	0.2	0.2	0.2	0.2	4.6	4.9	5.4	5.6	4.9	23.8	33.5	15.5	1.9	81.4	45.5	51.2	48.8
04733	BENEDICTA	100.0	100.0	0.0	0.0	0.0	0.0	0.0	0.0	2.1	5.3	8.9	10.0	3.7	22.6	32.6	12.6	2.1	76.3	43.5	51.1	48.9
04734	BLAINE	97.0	96.9	0.4	0.4	0.0	0.0	0.2	0.4	6.6	6.8	7.9	5.7	3.5	26.2	28.6	13.4	1.3	74.1	39.4	48.6	51.4
04735	BRIDGEWATER	98.1	97.6	0.0	0.0	0.0	0.0	0.6	1.0	4.2	4.7	5.5	5.8	4.8	21.7	34.1	16.6	2.5	82.0	47.1	51.0	49.0
04736	CARIBOU	96.3	95.3	0.4	0.5	0.9	1.4	0.5	0.7	5.3	5.6	6.1	6.2	5.0	23.0	30.6	15.6	2.5	79.0	44.0	48.9	51.1
04737	CLAYTON LAKE	100.0	100.0	0.0	0.0	0.0	0.0	0.0	0.0	0.0	0.0	0.0	0.0	0.0	100.0	0.0	0.0	0.0	100.0	42.5	100.0	0.0
04740	EASTON	97.3	96.7	0.3	0.4	0.4	0.5	0.5	0.8	5.1	5.7	6.0	5.7	4.9	23.7	33.5	13.6	1.8	79.9	44.2	48.4	51.6
04741	ESTCOURT STATION	100.0	100.0	0.0	0.0	0.0	0.0	0.0	0.0	0.0	0.0	0.0	0.0	0.0	50.0	25.0	25.0	0.0	100.0	45.0	100.0	0.0
04742	FORT FAIRFIELD	98.2	97.8	0.3	0.4	0.1	0.1	0.8	1.3	5.6	5.5	5.7	6.1	6.2	22.6	30.7	15.4	2.2	79.6	43.7	47.2	52.8
04743	FORT KENT	97.5	96.9	0.3	0.4	0.7	1.1	0.4	0.6	5.2	4.9	5.2	6.5	7.2	24.1	29.1	14.9	2.9	80.8	42.4	48.9	51.1
04745	FRENCHVILLE	99.3	99.1	0.1	0.1	0.2	0.2	0.4	0.7	5.0	6.7	6.6	5.8	3.6	24.9	31.0	14.0	2.5	77.7	43.3	48.9	51.1
04746	GRAND ISLE	98.9	98.8	0.0	0.0	0.2	0.2	0.4	0.6	4.2	3.8	4.5	5.5	5.1	15.6	34.4	24.7	2.2	84.2	52.9	47.6	52.4
04747	ISLAND FALLS	99.1	98.9	0.0	0.0	0.1	0.1	0.6	1.1	4.8	5.0	6.0	6.0	4.5	22.7	32.4	15.9	2.7	80.5	45.6	48.1	51.9
04750	LIMESTONE	91.1	88.7	4.3	5.5	1.3	1.7	3.7	5.5	4.4	4.4	4.8	16.0	8.9	20.4	25.5	13.7	2.0	77.6	36.4	52.0	48.0
04751	LIMESTONE	87.0	84.5	7.1	8.3	1.8	2.4	5.9	8.3	4.8	4.8	4.8	22.6	11.9	20.2	20.8	8.9	1.2	72.6	26.0	54.8	45.2
04756	MADAWASKA	98.0	97.5	0.1	0.1	0.8	1.1	0.2	0.3	4.2	4.5	4.8	5.3	4.9	19.6	33.1	20.2	3.4	83.3	49.5	46.5	53.5
04757	MAPLETON	97.9	97.5	0.0	0.0	0.1	0.1	0.4	0.6	5.2	5.9	6.1	6.4	4.3	25.9	32.8	11.8	1.6	78.7	42.8	51.2	48.8
04758	MARS HILL	97.5	97.0	0.1	0.2	0.2	0.3	0.4	0.7	5.2	5.1	5.9	7.4	5.5	22.8	25.3	18.1	4.8	79.0	43.6	47.5	52.5
04760	MONTICELLO	93.3	92.4	0.0	0.0	0.5	0.8	0.1	0.1	4.9	5.1	5.7	6.6	4.5	22.6	32.1	16.4	2.2	80.3	45.4	48.5	51.5
04761	NEW LIMERICK	99.8	99.8	0.0	0.0	0.0	0.0	0.0	0.0	3.4	7.2	6.0	5.3	1.9	23.2	36.9	14.5	1.7	79.3	46.7	49.5	50.5
04762	NEW SWEDEN	95.2	93.5	0.2	0.3	0.5	0.7	2.0	3.3	2.8	4.6	8.0	7.7	2.3	22.4	36.7	12.7	2.8	79.7	45.9	50.9	49.1
04763	OAKFIELD	98.3	97.8	0.0	0.0	0.0	0.0	0.7	1.1	4.1	4.6	5.7	6.9	4.1	23.4	31.6	17.4	2.2	81.1	45.6	48.3	51.7
04764	OXBOW	100.0	100.0	0.0	0.0	0.0	0.0	0.0	1.9	3.7	3.7	3.7	1.9	0.0	14.8	53.7	14.8	3.7	87.0	56.4	53.7	46.3
04765	PATTEN	99.1	99.0	0.2	0.3	0.0	0.0	0.0	0.1	3.9	4.6	5.3	6.5	4.2	20.8	34.9	17.2	2.6	81.7	47.7	51.2	48.8
04766	PERHAM	97.1	96.8	0.2	0.2	0.0	0.0	0.0	0.0	3.7	4.1	4.8	6.9	5.5	24.0	33.9	14.6	2.5	83.3	45.6	49.7	50.3
04768	PORTAGE	99.5	99.2	0.0	0.0	0.0	0.0	0.0	0.3	3.7	3.9	4.7	5.2	4.2	23.0	34.6	18.3	2.4	83.8	48.6	51.3	48.7
04769	PRESQUE ISLE	95.1	94.1	0.4	0.5	0.9	1.3	0.7	1.0	5.4	4.9	5.5	7.2	8.7	24.9	26.5	13.9	2.9	80.9	39.8	47.7	52.3
04772	SAINT AGATHA	99.6	99.3	0.0	0.1	0.1	0.3	0.2	0.4	4.5	4.9	5.2	4.6	4.0	21.0	37.6	16.3	1.9	82.4	49.5	50.7	49.3
04773	SAINT DAVID	98.3	97.9	0.3	0.5	0.5	0.6	0.3	0.5	5.6	5.9	6.1	6.1	5.0	22.1	34.0	14.6	0.6	78.7	44.5	51.0	49.0
04774	SAINT FRANCIS	99.6	99.6	0.1	0.1	0.0	0.0	0.0	0.0	2.6	4.5	5.6	6.7	4.7	20.7	33.9	18.6	2.8	82.5	48.3	48.4	51.6
04776	SHERMAN	98.1	97.7	0.3	0.4	0.0	0.0	0.2	0.4	4.0	5.1	6.0	6.3	4.5	20.4	37.1	14.1	2.5	81.1	47.1	50.0	50.0
04777	STACYVILLE	94.3	93.5	0.0	0.0	0.2	0.3	1.7	2.8	7.3	8.1	7.3	5.5	5.0	19.9	30.7	14.4	1.8	73.8	42.8	45.8	54.2
04779	SINCLAIR	99.7	99.7	0.0	0.0	0.0	0.0	0.0	0.0	3.1	3.8	3.8	3.4	3.4	15.8	40.1	25.0	1.7	87.3	56.1	51.4	48.6
04780	SMYRNA MILLS	97.7	97.2	0.0	0.0	0.2	0.2	0.5	0.7	3.7	4.2	7.9	8.2	3.3	23.1	34.3	14.0	1.4	78.8	44.8	50.1	49.9
04781	WALLAGRASS	99.5	99.2	0.0	0.0	0.0	0.0	0.3	0.5	7.3	7.6	7.8	6.5	4.7	25.0	26.8	13.0	1.3	72.9	39.4	50.5	49.5
04783	STOCKHOLM	98.3	97.8	0.0	0.0	0.0	0.2	0.2	0.5	3.7	4.4	5.1	5.6	4.2	18.4	37.9	19.0	1.7	83.2	50.0	50.6	49.4
04785	VAN BUREN	98.4	98.0	0.1	0.2	0.1	0.2	0.7	1.2	4.1	5.0	6.0	5.4	4.1	21.0	32.3	18.5	3.6	81.3	47.8	47.4	52.6
04786	WASHBURN	98.4	98.2	0.2	0.2	0.2	0.2	0.3	0.4	5.2	5.5	5.6	5.1	4.5	23.1	32.3	16.7	2.0	80.5	45.6	49.2	50.8
04787	WESTFIELD	97.5	96.9	0.4	0.5	0.0	0.0	0.1	0.3	5.0	5.6	6.4	5.3	3.7	23.3	33.4	14.6	2.7	79.2	45.5	49.7	50.3
04841	ROCKLAND	97.9	97.5	0.2	0.3	0.6	0.9	0.6	0.9	5.6	5.2	5.1	5.7	7.0	24.9	28.0	14.5	4.1	80.7	42.3	46.8	53.2
04843	CAMDEN	98.3	98.0	0.2	0.3	0.4	0.6	0.9	1.4	4.3	4.1	4.6	4.9	5.4	19.5	33.3	17.8	6.1	83.4	49.2	45.6	54.4
04847	HOPE	98.6	98.4	0.2	0.2	0.2	0.3	0.8	1.3	5.9	7.5	7.9	5.4	2.5	29.1	32.3	8.4	0.9	75.1	40.5	49.1	50.9
04848	ISLESBORO	98.2	97.4	0.2	0.2	0.2	0.3	1.3	2.1	4.1	5.4	5.6	4.6	2.8	17.6	39.9	17.4	2.6	81.9	50.9	49.1	50.9
04849	LINCOLNVILLE	98.5	98.2	0.1	0.1	0.4	0.5	0.7	1.1	5.2	6.0	6.4	5.0	3.1	23.7	35.6	13.3	1.8	79.0	45.4	49.3	50.7
04851	MATINICUS	100.0	100.0	0.0	0.0	0.0	0.0	0.0	0.0	4.1	0.0	6.1	6.1	2.0	14.3	42.9	22.4	2.0	85.7	53.1	59.2	40.8
04852	MONHEGAN	97.3	95.9	0.0	0.0	2.7	4.1	0.0	0.0	4.1	4.1	1.4	2.7	2.7	26.0	43.8	12.3	2.7	90.4	49.1	52.1	47.9
04853	NORTH HAVEN	95.3	93.8	1.0	1.3	0.0	0.0	2.4	3.1	5.7	6.2	6.4	5.9	3.6	25.8	32.7	11.9	1.8	77.8	42.6	51.5	48.5
04854	OWLS HEAD	99.0	98.9	0.1	0.1	0.2	0.3	0.3	0.5	3.9	4.4	5.1	5.4	3.2	19.8	36.7	18.3	3.2	83.4	50.5	48.6	51.4
04856	ROCKPORT	98.7	98.3	0.2	0.2	0.4	0.7	0.7	1.2	4.5	5.3	6.4	6.0	4.1	20.7	35.4	15.1	2.5	79.6	46.9	47.8	52.2
04858	SOUTH THOMASTON	98.1	97.8	0.3	0.4	0.3	0.5	0.3	0.5	5.2	5.6	5.8	5.4	4.0	22.6	34.9	14.5	2.1	80.2	45.8	48.9	51.1
04859	SPRUCE HEAD	97.9	97.5	0.3	0.4	0.4	0.6	0.4	0.7	5.2	5.3	5.4	5.8	4.9	20.5	34.7	16.3	1.8	80.4	46.8	48.1	51.9
04860	TENANTS HARBOR	99.1	98.9	0.1	0.1	0.3	0.5	0.1	0.2	4.4	5.1	5.4	5.1	3.2	18.7	36.6	18.6	2.8	81.8	50.5	51.1	48.9
04861	THOMASTON	97.8	97.2	0.6	0.8	0.5	0.8	0.4	0.7	4.8	4.5	4.8	5.0	7.0	29.9	28.3	13.1	2.6	82.6	40.8	55.2	44.8
04862	UNION	98.6	98.5	0.2	0.2	0.1	0.2	0.4	0.6	5.9	5.8	7.4	6.9	4.7	24.9	31.6	10.9	1.8	76.2	41.5	49.0	51.0
04863	VINALHAVEN	98.1	97.9	0.0	0.0	0.3	0.5	0.0	0.0	6.5	7.1	7.3	5.9	3.3	23.7	30.4	13.4	2.4	75.3	42.5	49.2	50.8
04864	WARREN	97.5	96.9	0.3	0.4	0.4	0.6	0.7	1.1	5.6	6.0	6.3	6.2	6.2	28.6	30.6	9.5	1.0	77.8	39.1	53.7	46.3
04901	WATERVILLE	96.8	96.0	0.5	0.7	0.8	1.1	0.9	1.4	5.4	5.2	5.4	8.6	9.5	22.6	26.2	13.9	3.2	80.4	39.7	47.1	52.9
04910	ALBION	98.5	98.1	0.1	0.1	0.6	0.9	0.4	0.7	6.3	7.5	7.0	7.2	4.7	26.8	26.7	12.4	1.5	74.8	39.0	48.8	51.2
04911	ANSON	97.8	97.4	0.1	0.2	0.3	0.4	0.4	0.6	5.2	5.5	7.3	7.1	5.2	25.6	30.0	12.5	1.6	77.1	41.0	50.6	49.4
04912	ATHENS	98.9	98.8	0.1	0.1	0.1	0.2	0.6	1.1	5.6	6.2	6.7	7.5	4.0	28.0	30.4	10.2	1.4	76.2	39.7	49.7	50.3
04915	BELFAST	97.3	96.9	0.3	0.4	0.3	0.4	0.8	1.2	5.0	5.2	5.7	5.8	5.8	23.3	30.5	15.0	3.7	80.4	44.4	47.8	52.2
04917	BELGRADE	98.7	98.6	0.1	0.2	0.3	0.4	0.5	0.7	4.8	5.9	7.4	6.6	4.1	26.2	32.6	11.5	1.0	77.4	42.0	48.6	51.4
04920	BINGHAM	98.7	98.7	0.0	0.0	0.1	0.1	0.3	0.5	6.4	5.9	7.4	6.0	4.6	24.8	28.6	14.0	2.3	76.2	41.5	50.8	49.2
04921	BROOKS	98.8	98.7	0.1	0.1	0.1	0.2	0.7	1.1	6.0	6.8	7.4	6.4	4.7	25.1	29.6	12.1	1.9	75.4	40.6	49.8	50.2
04922	BURNHAM	96.8	96.5	0.2	0.2	0.1	0.2	0.4	0.5	5.7	5.9	6.4	7.2	5.9	25.6	31.4	10.6	1.2	77.5	40.6	49.8	50.2
04923	CAMBRIDGE	99.1	98.9	0.2	0.4	0.2	0.2	0.2	0.2	4.7	4.9	5.2	5.1	4.3	23.8	35.6	15.2	1.3	81.9	46.2	48.4	51.6
04924	CANAAN	97.6	97.3	0.2	0.2	0.3	0.5	0.3	0.4	5.7	5.9	6.4	7.2	6.2	27.2	30.7	9.7	1.0	77.7	39.9	49.0	51.0
04925	CARATUNK	97.6	96.8	0.0	0.0	0.0	0.0	0.0	0.0	3.2	4.8	5.6	5.6	1.6	21.6	42.4	13.6	1.6	81.6	49.0	54.4	45.6
04927	CLINTON	98.1	97.8	0.1	0.1	0.1	0.1	1.0	1.6	6.6	6.8	6.8	6.5	5.7	27.6	29.2	9.6	1.1	75.9	38.4	50.9	49.1
04928	CORINNA	98.2	97.9	0.4	0.5	0.1	0.2	0.5	0.7	5.6	5.9	6.5	6.2	4.5	24.1	31.6	14.0	1.5	78.0	42.9	50.5	49.5
04929	DETROIT	98.8	98.5	0.2	0.3	0.0	0.0	0.7	1.2	7.2	7.7	7.5	5.9	4.6	26.0	28.5	11.7	0.8	73.8	39.7	49.8	50.2
04930	DEXTER	98.7	98.4	0.3	0.4	0.1	0.2	0.6	1.0	5.8	6.0	6.1	5.5	4.8	22.8	30.2	16.1	2.8	78.7	44.3	48.0	52.0
04932	DIXMONT	98.5	98.2	0.0	0.0	0.5	0.7	0.2	0.4	6.0	6.5	6.7	5.4	4.4	25.9	34.6	9.7	1.0	77.6	41.9	50.1	49.9
04936	EUSTIS	95.3	94.9	0.7	1.0	0.2	0.2	0.0	0.0	4.4	3.9	4.2	5.4	8.3	23.5	32.3	16.6	1.5	84.4	45.2	52.6	47.4
04937	FAIRFIELD	97.8	97.5	0.3	0.5	0.3	0.5	0.3	0.5	5.7	5.8	6.5	7.8	6.2	25.9	29.2	11.2	1.7	76.9	39.8	48.9	51.1
04938	FARMINGTON	97.7	97.1	0.2	0.3	0.7	1.0	0.8	1.2	4.6	4.6	5.0	12.0	12.2	21.8	24.1	12.6	3.1	81.9	35.4	45.9	54.1
04939	GARLAND	97.8	97.3	0.2	0.3	0.5	0.7	0.4	0.7	6.9	6.7	7.1	7.1	6.6	22.6	31.1	11.1	0.9	75.0	40.0	49.5	50.5
04941	FREEDOM	97.7	97.4	0.2	0.2	0.1	0.1	1.3	2.0	5.9	6.6	6.3	7.1	6.0	23.9	32.5	10.3	1.3	77.1	40.7	51.8	48.2
04942	HARMONY	97.9	97.6	0.2	0.1	0.3	0.5	0.2	0.2	5.1	5.9	6.5	5.6	3.9	22.5	33.7	14.9	1.9	78.8	45.3	50.2	49.8
04943	HARTLAND	98.0	97.8	0.2	0.3	0.1	0.2	0.5	0.7	6.3	6.2	6.2	6.1	5.7	24.0	30.0	13.4	2.1	77.8	41.5	49.1	50.9
04945	JACKMAN	98.1	97.8	0.2	0.2	0.1	0.1	1.8	2.9	5.2	5.8	6.2	5.9	4.5	23.0	33.7	13.6	2.2	78.5	44.7	50.7	49.3
04947	KINGFIELD	98.0	97.7	0.1	0.1	0.4	0.5	0.3	0.3	5.9	7.3	5.9	6.1	5.0	26.1	30.6	11.0	1.9	76.8	40.7	50.2	49.8
04949	LIBERTY	98.8	98.6	0.1	0.1	0.1	0.2	0.4	0.7	7.5	8.1	7.7	5.6	3.6	22.2	32.9	10.6	1.7	72.5	41.1	49.2	50.8
04950	MADISON	98.1	97.9	0.1	0.1	0.2	0.3	0.2	0.4	5.7	5.8	5.9	5.3	4.6	21.8	31.4	16.5	3.0	79.0	45.5	47.9	52.1
04951	MONROE	98.2	98.2	0.1	0.1	0.1	0.1	0.5	0.8	5.8	6.3	7.3	6.9	4.0	25.5	33.1	9.9	1.2	75.8	41.1	50.3	49.7
04952	MORRILL	98.3	98.2	0.0	0.0	0.3	0.4	0.2	0.2	5.9	6.2	6.6	7.2	4.4	25.2	30.7	12.3	1.5	76.9	41.3	50.7	49.3
04953	NEWPORT	98.3	98.0	0.2	0.2	0.4	0.6	0.4	0.7	6.4	5.9	5.9	6.1	6.4	23.8	29.3	14.5	1.8	78.3	41.6	48.7	51.3
04954	NEW PORTLAND	98.5	98.5	0.0	0.0	0.0	0.0	0.7	0.8	5.3	4.5	6.0	6.8	3.8	23.3	35.3	13.5	1.5	78.9	45.2	51.1	48.9
04955	NEW SHARON	98.9	98.7	0.2	0.3	0.3	0.4	0.5	0.8	4.7	5.5	5.7	5.9	4.8	23.4	35.4	13.1	1.5	80.5	45.0	51.0	49.0
04956	NEW VINEYARD	98.1	97.9	0.4	0.5	0.1	0.1	0.3	0.4	6.4	5.6	8.4	9.1	4.3	23.5	31.8	9.7	1.2	73.5	40.9	48.8	51.2
04957	NORRIDGEWOCK	98.3	97.9	0.3	0.4	0.2	0.4	0.4	0.6	5.9	6.4	6.8	6.5	4.4	24.6	31.5	12.5	1.4	76.9	42.0	49.8	50.2
	MAINE	96.9	96.3	0.5	0.7	0.7	1.1	0.7	1.1	5.4	5.6	6.1	6.9	6.2	24.7	30.2	12.7	2.3	78.8	41.6	48.8	51.2
	UNITED STATES	75.1	72.0	12.3	12.7	3.8	4.6	12.5	15.7	6.8	6.7	6.6	7.1	6.9	27.0	26.0	10.9	1.9	75.7	36.9	49.2	50.8

ZIP CODE #	POST OFFICE NAME	2009 Per Capita Income	2009 HH Income Base	2009 Household Income Distribution (%): Less than $25,000	$25,000 to $49,999	$50,000 to $99,999	$100,000 to $149,999	$150,000 or More	Median Household Income: 2009	2014	2009 National Centile	2009 State Centile	2009 Home Value Base	2009 Home Value Distribution (%): Less than $50,000	$50,000 to $89,999	$90,000 to $174,999	$175,000 to $399,999	$400,000 or More	2009 Median Home Value
04691	WHITING	16234	73	43.8	31.5	20.5	2.7	1.4	28584	29167	6	5	61	19.7	19.7	31.1	16.4	13.1	114583
04693	WINTER HARBOR	18037	446	31.8	39.2	23.5	3.8	1.6	35781	39908	20	23	220	9.5	10.0	45.0	30.5	5.0	152143
04694	BAILEYVILLE	20321	1091	32.3	32.3	28.1	6.1	1.2	38684	41295	29	34	915	12.6	20.0	50.3	15.0	2.2	113702
04730	HOULTON	16800	3879	39.6	31.1	24.9	3.2	1.1	32471	33769	12	11	2699	13.9	25.6	44.6	14.1	1.9	105968
04732	ASHLAND	20154	796	32.5	30.3	32.4	3.4	1.4	39575	41964	31	37	644	18.3	27.0	39.8	13.4	1.6	97500
04733	BENEDICTA	15475	71	33.8	26.8	38.0	1.4	0.0	36110	36838	21	25	65	20.0	15.4	47.7	16.9	0.0	115625
04734	BLAINE	17199	193	27.5	45.1	23.8	3.1	0.5	33891	36040	15	15	158	20.3	32.9	38.6	7.0	1.3	87222
04735	BRIDGEWATER	19150	298	37.2	34.2	23.2	3.0	2.3	34337	34611	16	17	241	20.3	27.0	41.1	10.4	1.2	95909
04736	CARIBOU	19347	4345	36.1	30.4	27.3	4.6	1.7	35379	36458	19	22	3108	15.0	22.6	43.7	17.9	0.8	109854
04737	CLAYTON LAKE	0	0	0.0	0.0	0.0	0.0	0.0	0	0	0	0	0	0.0	0.0	0.0	0.0	0.0	0
04740	EASTON	19510	574	34.1	33.4	26.5	4.0	1.9	35793	37104	20	24	435	19.8	32.4	35.2	9.9	2.8	87121
04741	ESTCOURT STATION	24375	3	0.0	100.0	0.0	0.0	0.0	31982	31982	11	9	2	0.0	0.0	50.0	50.0	0.0	162500
04742	FORT FAIRFIELD	18617	1704	37.9	31.4	24.0	5.3	1.5	34515	35671	17	18	1197	13.1	26.8	43.1	17.0	0.0	105755
04743	FORT KENT	19262	2473	37.9	29.3	27.5	3.2	2.1	34347	35742	16	17	1741	9.0	22.4	44.5	22.1	2.1	123431
04745	FRENCHVILLE	19961	493	31.0	29.4	34.3	4.5	0.8	40094	42044	33	39	419	6.7	25.5	52.5	14.1	1.2	120265
04746	GRAND ISLE	17489	222	41.9	24.3	30.2	3.6	0.0	35372	36684	19	22	190	22.1	30.5	38.9	7.4	1.1	87727
04747	ISLAND FALLS	18361	540	36.3	32.0	26.9	3.5	1.3	35111	36407	18	21	438	19.4	28.3	35.8	14.8	1.6	94762
04750	LIMESTONE	19342	896	27.9	31.1	35.3	4.0	1.7	42589	45030	41	49	619	18.7	34.2	33.9	12.6	0.5	86146
04751	LIMESTONE	22847	63	20.6	27.0	47.6	3.2	1.6	51189	50625	64	79	42	21.4	33.3	33.3	11.9	0.0	80000
04756	MADAWASKA	22014	1725	34.3	27.9	32.7	4.0	1.2	36950	37783	23	29	1159	4.3	18.9	52.1	22.1	2.6	126551
04757	MAPLETON	21059	1209	23.7	34.3	35.1	5.0	1.9	43461	45314	44	51	1016	10.0	21.8	44.6	21.0	2.7	121361
04758	MARS HILL	16588	634	43.8	28.4	25.4	1.6	0.8	28839	30606	6	5	416	16.8	32.7	37.7	10.8	1.9	90833
04760	MONTICELLO	15562	326	42.9	33.4	21.5	0.9	1.2	27776	28997	5	3	267	23.2	23.2	42.7	9.7	1.1	95000
04761	NEW LIMERICK	18430	233	32.2	30.9	34.3	2.6	0.0	36364	37540	22	26	191	4.7	18.3	37.7	30.9	8.4	144886
04762	NEW SWEDEN	17663	310	34.2	27.4	32.6	5.2	0.6	37495	40282	25	31	270	12.6	23.3	46.3	16.7	1.1	113953
04763	OAKFIELD	16092	412	39.1	33.0	25.0	2.2	0.7	31846	32512	11	9	333	21.9	33.3	36.9	7.8	0.0	83000
04764	OXBOW	16296	29	48.3	37.9	13.8	0.0	0.0	26103	26103	4	2	28	10.7	25.0	39.3	25.0	0.0	118750
04765	PATTEN	18194	634	40.1	28.7	27.3	2.8	1.1	34279	37209	16	16	491	16.9	31.8	38.1	12.0	1.2	91806
04766	PERHAM	15928	170	31.2	33.5	30.6	4.7	0.0	35000	38836	18	21	153	11.1	22.9	45.8	19.0	1.3	113426
04768	PORTAGE	21970	187	35.8	28.9	31.6	2.1	1.6	37970	38510	27	32	146	16.4	26.0	39.0	15.1	3.4	102941
04769	PRESQUE ISLE	19721	4123	36.2	33.7	24.3	3.8	2.0	34838	36273	17	19	2508	14.3	20.6	45.1	17.1	2.9	116429
04772	SAINT AGATHA	20371	435	34.7	32.2	26.2	6.0	0.9	36973	38161	24	30	323	5.0	13.0	56.0	24.8	1.2	134167
04773	SAINT DAVID	21087	244	34.8	25.0	33.2	5.3	1.6	37934	39498	26	31	214	4.2	19.2	37.9	34.1	4.7	156250
04774	SAINT FRANCIS	17026	378	45.5	28.3	21.7	3.4	1.1	27437	29207	5	3	309	15.9	37.9	41.1	5.2	0.0	86406
04776	SHERMAN	18063	432	35.6	31.3	26.4	4.4	2.3	34227	34715	16	16	386	13.7	23.3	46.6	15.8	0.5	110081
04777	STACYVILLE	15590	164	43.9	36.0	14.0	4.3	1.8	30756	35000	9	6	137	30.7	27.0	31.4	10.2	0.7	79444
04779	SINCLAIR	21683	131	35.1	28.2	29.8	5.3	1.5	34683	35000	17	19	114	4.4	13.2	48.2	30.7	3.5	156250
04780	SMYRNA MILLS	18596	187	36.4	27.3	31.6	4.3	0.5	36895	38788	23	29	167	21.6	25.7	36.5	15.0	1.2	95625
04781	WALLAGRASS	18915	157	27.4	35.7	29.9	5.1	1.9	38838	40986	29	35	140	4.3	17.1	50.7	26.4	1.4	126667
04783	STOCKHOLM	20744	296	34.8	30.7	28.0	4.7	1.7	35000	36436	18	21	260	8.8	21.2	45.8	22.3	1.9	128448
04785	VAN BUREN	15505	1289	50.2	29.6	16.4	2.8	1.1	24877	26217	3	2	819	23.3	34.3	34.2	7.8	0.4	83351
04786	WASHBURN	18741	814	33.2	34.2	28.4	3.1	1.2	36556	38011	22	27	651	17.4	28.7	42.9	10.6	0.5	95426
04787	WESTFIELD	15838	291	31.3	41.9	23.0	3.1	0.7	34402	35098	16	18	255	19.6	31.0	40.8	8.2	0.4	89423
04841	ROCKLAND	20351	3436	37.3	33.1	23.9	4.2	1.6	36124	39898	21	25	1837	4.2	11.6	48.1	31.6	4.4	149701
04843	CAMDEN	33926	2562	24.7	23.9	32.1	11.7	7.6	51705	52935	65	81	1765	3.0	2.1	9.8	51.7	33.4	306250
04847	HOPE	27477	588	16.0	31.0	41.8	7.0	4.3	52178	52460	66	82	501	3.4	1.6	32.7	50.3	12.0	211141
04848	ISLESBORO	30300	288	23.6	27.8	33.3	9.7	5.6	47895	47209	56	70	242	6.6	2.9	14.5	41.3	34.7	289130
04849	LINCOLNVILLE	26698	1563	22.3	27.6	35.4	9.9	4.7	50088	49283	61	76	1312	4.7	4.1	23.3	46.4	21.4	243316
04851	MATINICUS	22602	26	23.1	26.9	50.0	0.0	0.0	50000	50000	61	75	23	26.1	4.3	30.4	34.8	4.3	129167
04852	MONHEGAN	31473	47	25.5	36.2	34.0	2.1	2.1	34284	34235	16	17	31	0.0	0.0	3.2	58.1	38.7	365000
04853	NORTH HAVEN	26269	170	22.4	22.4	42.4	9.4	3.5	52346	52563	67	83	116	0.0	0.0	10.3	60.3	29.3	286667
04854	OWLS HEAD	29833	829	17.7	33.1	34.9	9.5	4.8	49335	50152	60	74	680	2.8	2.9	20.4	54.6	19.3	249580
04856	ROCKPORT	33637	1677	13.8	24.3	41.6	12.2	8.1	61672	60147	80	93	1327	0.6	3.4	11.5	48.5	35.9	310766
04858	SOUTH THOMASTON	27502	668	18.3	28.3	41.0	9.3	3.1	53286	52239	68	84	548	1.5	1.8	23.5	52.7	20.4	240865
04859	SPRUCE HEAD	29116	405	24.0	25.7	35.6	10.1	4.7	50476	48853	62	77	354	1.7	6.8	27.7	41.5	22.3	226316
04860	TENANTS HARBOR	28409	744	24.2	25.1	38.6	8.2	3.9	50499	49924	62	77	613	2.1	2.6	25.6	45.7	24.0	242733
04861	THOMASTON	21698	1423	26.2	31.1	34.1	5.2	3.4	42435	46351	41	48	947	1.3	4.4	42.7	44.7	7.0	179306
04862	UNION	21059	1496	19.6	35.4	38.6	4.8	1.6	46152	47339	52	61	1276	3.9	5.6	39.1	43.0	8.4	179245
04863	VINALHAVEN	30095	576	23.6	30.7	28.8	10.1	6.8	46113	48258	52	61	431	1.4	4.2	28.3	47.6	18.6	224695
04864	WARREN	19976	1573	21.0	39.4	33.3	4.1	2.2	44424	46326	47	55	1332	4.7	2.3	48.9	40.5	3.5	167883
04901	WATERVILLE	21080	10853	33.7	29.2	29.0	5.8	2.2	38040	42530	27	32	6512	4.2	9.6	56.3	26.0	3.9	146789
04910	ALBION	18360	708	28.5	32.9	31.6	5.4	1.6	42475	45650	41	48	624	8.5	11.2	52.6	23.4	4.3	145787
04911	ANSON	17226	809	36.8	32.0	25.7	4.4	1.0	34947	35673	17	20	648	13.9	19.9	44.9	18.8	2.5	115094
04912	ATHENS	18511	346	35.8	32.7	26.3	3.8	1.4	31745	32046	11	8	311	27.0	21.5	30.5	16.1	4.8	92647
04915	BELFAST	22390	3937	30.7	29.6	30.8	6.4	2.6	39716	41526	32	37	2798	9.9	9.0	31.3	40.3	9.5	174518
04917	BELGRADE	24329	1299	22.8	29.0	37.0	6.9	4.3	48561	49514	58	72	1110	3.2	5.7	34.2	42.8	14.1	194388
04920	BINGHAM	17991	642	34.1	35.8	25.9	3.4	0.8	33497	34231	14	13	519	10.8	18.7	57.0	11.8	1.7	111979
04921	BROOKS	18669	776	35.6	29.9	27.3	5.5	1.7	36867	40623	23	28	619	8.2	12.6	42.0	32.6	4.5	151618
04922	BURNHAM	17578	486	32.7	37.0	25.9	3.5	0.8	35814	37798	20	24	426	17.8	15.7	36.4	26.1	4.0	128472
04923	CAMBRIDGE	18307	237	28.3	40.9	25.7	4.2	0.8	36569	37506	22	27	215	13.5	26.5	38.1	19.1	2.8	107386
04924	CANAAN	17493	801	32.5	34.0	27.2	6.1	0.2	35407	36643	19	23	645	12.1	17.5	43.6	25.0	1.9	128209
04925	CARATUNK	18110	53	39.6	30.2	24.5	5.7	0.0	34071	34291	16	15	41	7.3	14.6	36.6	29.3	12.2	153125
04927	CLINTON	18752	1428	29.1	36.0	29.6	3.6	1.7	38154	42297	27	33	1173	12.7	15.8	49.1	20.7	1.7	134387
04928	CORINNA	18549	927	31.4	32.1	32.3	3.2	1.0	40725	45418	35	41	770	15.8	23.6	43.9	15.2	1.4	108984
04929	DETROIT	17531	401	34.2	38.9	20.7	5.5	0.7	35154	35459	18	22	327	17.7	24.2	44.0	14.1	0.0	104261
04930	DEXTER	17432	1742	39.1	32.8	24.1	3.3	0.7	32015	35394	11	9	1266	14.1	30.9	37.4	17.1	0.5	97590
04932	DIXMONT	19887	452	26.3	33.0	32.3	7.1	1.3	41755	44903	39	46	408	12.3	17.2	39.2	29.4	2.0	132273
04936	EUSTIS	19249	196	35.7	33.2	28.6	2.6	0.0	34639	37156	17	19	124	4.8	12.9	46.0	30.6	5.6	141667
04937	FAIRFIELD	22077	3005	23.3	29.8	37.9	7.0	2.0	46319	48195	52	62	2241	8.1	12.4	56.6	19.9	3.0	137828
04938	FARMINGTON	18236	3842	36.2	32.2	26.3	3.1	1.5	34316	36771	16	17	2499	9.5	15.2	47.5	23.1	4.7	134126
04939	GARLAND	15754	417	37.2	35.0	24.2	3.1	0.5	34844	37247	17	19	378	28.8	18.5	42.6	10.1	0.0	95882
04941	FREEDOM	19209	866	30.0	33.1	31.6	4.2	1.0	40155	41542	33	40	737	9.0	17.5	41.9	27.1	4.5	139971
04942	HARMONY	15809	599	41.9	34.9	20.2	2.5	0.5	29132	30135	7	5	529	16.1	22.9	41.8	15.3	4.0	106487
04943	HARTLAND	17635	744	33.6	35.8	26.1	3.8	0.8	34475	35484	16	18	563	13.3	21.5	47.4	16.0	1.8	108446
04945	JACKMAN	20075	436	29.4	35.6	27.5	7.6	0.0	37427	37842	25	30	330	9.4	19.1	50.9	17.6	3.0	121250
04947	KINGFIELD	23038	688	23.4	38.2	30.1	4.9	3.3	41385	44085	37	43	524	3.6	7.8	45.2	33.2	10.1	165489
04949	LIBERTY	20524	401	30.7	26.4	34.7	5.0	3.2	42082	43648	40	47	325	8.0	6.8	42.5	40.9	1.8	165208
04950	MADISON	21584	1926	31.5	33.4	27.2	5.1	2.9	36831	38599	23	28	1436	7.9	17.5	47.4	23.5	3.8	130110
04951	MONROE	19048	358	35.5	28.5	27.4	6.7	2.0	36076	39444	21	25	315	8.3	11.4	36.8	37.1	6.3	161149
04952	MORRILL	19591	672	27.7	35.6	30.4	4.8	1.6	39291	40698	31	36	576	6.3	13.0	43.2	34.0	3.5	157000
04953	NEWPORT	18901	1371	34.9	29.9	31.7	2.3	1.2	36206	39307	21	25	981	13.5	17.6	48.2	18.3	2.3	118897
04954	NEW PORTLAND	18441	56	35.7	32.1	28.6	3.6	0.0	36535	41130	22	27	51	9.8	19.6	45.1	21.6	3.9	126389
04955	NEW SHARON	20428	598	30.3	28.8	33.8	5.5	1.7	42076	43907	40	46	531	10.5	17.7	40.5	30.7	0.6	147500
04956	NEW VINEYARD	18624	293	27.3	41.0	25.9	4.8	1.0	36242	39176	21	26	259	5.8	22.0	51.0	21.2	0.0	124716
04957	NORRIDGEWOCK	21339	1874	28.4	27.6	34.9	6.2	2.9	43447	45427	44	51	1567	8.4	16.1	44.0	27.1	4.3	139419
	MAINE	24559		25.0	28.4	35.2	7.5	3.8	46650	48581				6.4	9.4	36.7	38.7	8.8	170226
	UNITED STATES	27277		20.9	24.4	35.3	11.7	7.6	54719	56938				9.3	13.1	31.6	32.6	13.5	162279

ZIP CODE #	POST OFFICE NAME	FINANCIAL SERVICES: Auto Loan	FINANCIAL SERVICES: Home Loan	FINANCIAL SERVICES: Invest-ments	FINANCIAL SERVICES: Retire-ment Plans	THE HOME: Home Improvements: Home Repair	THE HOME: Home Improvements: Lawn & Garden	THE HOME: Furnishings: Comput-ers & Hard-ware-Personal	THE HOME: Furnishings: Major Appli-ances	THE HOME: Furnishings: TV, Radio, Sound Equip-ment	THE HOME: Furnishings: Furni-ture	ENTERTAINMENT: Dine out/ Carry out	ENTERTAINMENT: Sports Equip-ment	ENTERTAINMENT: Fees & Tickets	ENTERTAINMENT: Toys & Games	ENTERTAINMENT: Travel	ENTERTAINMENT: Cable TV	PERSONAL: Apparel & Services	PERSONAL: Auto Repairs	PERSONAL: Health Insur-ance	PERSONAL: Pets & Supplies
04691	WHITING	65	47	67	45	48	66	48	61	53	45	52	46	38	53	47	58	34	56	63	72
04693	WINTER HARBOR	63	56	58	57	57	64	60	62	62	57	60	46	55	61	58	64	41	62	67	73
04694	BAILEYVILLE	81	58	83	56	60	83	61	77	68	56	66	58	49	67	60	75	44	71	81	91
04730	HOULTON	65	49	64	48	51	66	53	62	58	49	57	47	45	58	52	64	38	60	68	74
04732	ASHLAND	82	59	84	57	61	83	60	77	67	56	66	57	48	66	60	74	43	70	80	91
04733	BENEDICTA	74	53	76	51	55	75	54	69	60	51	59	52	43	60	54	66	39	63	72	82
04734	BLAINE	72	52	74	50	54	74	53	68	59	50	58	51	43	59	53	65	38	62	70	81
04735	BRIDGEWATER	81	58	84	56	60	82	60	76	66	55	65	57	48	65	59	73	43	70	79	90
04736	CARIBOU	71	56	71	55	58	73	61	69	65	56	64	51	52	64	59	71	43	67	75	82
04737	CLAYTON LAKE	0	0	0	0	0	0	0	0	0	0	0	0	0	0	0	0	0	0	0	0
04740	EASTON	80	58	82	56	60	81	60	75	66	56	65	56	48	66	59	72	43	69	78	89
04741	ESTCOURT STATION	58	40	64	40	42	61	44	55	46	36	46	46	33	45	44	50	30	52	58	68
04742	FORT FAIRFIELD	67	52	64	52	54	68	58	65	62	53	61	48	49	61	55	67	41	63	71	76
04743	FORT KENT	69	55	66	55	57	70	62	67	66	56	64	51	53	64	59	70	43	66	74	80
04745	FRENCHVILLE	86	62	88	60	64	87	63	80	70	59	69	60	51	70	63	77	46	74	84	95
04746	GRAND ISLE	67	49	67	47	51	70	53	65	59	47	57	49	43	58	51	65	38	61	71	77
04747	ISLAND FALLS	71	51	72	50	53	74	55	69	62	50	60	51	44	61	54	68	40	64	74	81
04750	LIMESTONE	73	63	67	63	61	77	65	71	69	60	68	55	59	69	63	73	46	69	78	85
04751	LIMESTONE	74	76	60	77	70	79	76	73	77	72	76	58	76	78	73	78	52	75	81	89
04756	MADAWASKA	72	58	68	59	60	74	63	71	68	57	66	53	55	67	61	73	45	68	77	83
04757	MAPLETON	84	70	80	71	72	88	70	82	74	64	73	62	61	75	69	79	49	76	85	96
04758	MARS HILL	64	46	65	45	48	67	51	62	56	45	54	47	41	55	49	62	36	58	68	73
04760	MONTICELLO	65	46	67	45	48	66	48	61	53	44	52	46	38	53	47	58	34	56	63	72
04761	NEW LIMERICK	70	56	90	55	61	74	56	71	59	53	58	52	48	56	61	63	39	66	71	83
04762	NEW SWEDEN	72	57	92	56	63	76	57	73	60	54	59	53	49	57	62	64	39	67	72	84
04763	OAKFIELD	65	47	66	45	48	67	50	63	56	45	54	47	40	55	49	62	36	58	67	74
04764	OXBOW	51	41	65	40	45	54	41	52	42	38	42	38	35	40	44	45	28	48	51	60
04765	PATTEN	72	53	77	51	55	74	54	68	59	50	58	51	44	58	54	65	38	63	70	81
04766	PERHAM	73	52	75	51	54	74	54	68	60	50	59	51	43	59	53	66	39	63	71	81
04768	PORTAGE	80	57	82	55	59	81	59	75	65	55	64	56	47	65	58	72	42	69	78	89
04769	PRESQUE ISLE	65	57	60	57	57	66	61	63	64	58	63	48	57	63	59	68	43	64	70	75
04772	SAINT AGATHA	78	58	80	56	60	80	59	74	65	55	64	56	48	65	58	71	42	68	77	88
04773	SAINT DAVID	83	75	75	78	77	89	75	84	78	68	76	64	69	79	75	82	52	78	87	98
04774	SAINT FRANCIS	65	47	66	45	48	67	49	62	54	45	53	46	39	54	48	60	35	57	65	73
04776	SHERMAN	78	56	80	54	58	79	57	73	63	53	62	55	46	63	56	70	41	67	76	86
04777	STACYVILLE	67	48	69	47	50	68	50	63	55	46	54	47	40	55	49	60	36	58	66	75
04779	SINCLAIR	81	65	104	64	71	85	65	82	68	61	67	60	56	64	70	72	44	76	81	95
04780	SMYRNA MILLS	76	55	78	53	57	77	56	71	62	52	61	53	45	62	55	68	40	65	74	85
04781	WALLAGRASS	72	65	65	68	67	77	64	73	66	58	65	55	59	68	64	70	44	67	75	84
04783	STOCKHOLM	77	59	91	58	64	80	60	76	64	56	63	56	50	62	63	69	42	70	76	89
04785	VAN BUREN	59	42	59	41	44	60	45	56	50	41	49	42	36	49	44	55	32	52	60	66
04786	WASHBURN	74	54	74	52	56	76	56	70	62	52	61	52	46	62	55	69	40	65	74	83
04787	WESTFIELD	72	52	74	50	54	73	53	67	59	49	58	50	42	58	53	64	38	62	70	80
04841	ROCKLAND	64	54	56	56	55	63	61	62	63	56	62	47	55	63	57	66	43	62	66	73
04843	CAMDEN	104	98	126	98	105	114	97	108	101	97	100	78	96	95	104	105	68	105	115	126
04847	HOPE	111	89	143	88	98	117	89	113	93	84	92	83	77	89	96	99	61	104	112	131
04848	ISLESBORO	107	86	138	84	94	113	86	109	90	80	89	79	74	85	93	96	59	100	107	126
04849	LINCOLNVILLE	103	83	131	82	91	109	83	105	87	78	86	77	72	83	90	93	57	97	104	122
04851	MATINICUS	76	52	84	52	55	80	58	72	61	47	60	60	43	59	58	66	39	68	76	89
04852	MONHEGAN	87	60	96	60	63	92	67	83	69	54	69	69	49	68	66	76	45	77	88	102
04853	NORTH HAVEN	107	74	118	74	77	113	82	102	85	66	84	84	60	84	81	93	55	95	107	125
04854	OWLS HEAD	106	85	136	83	93	112	85	107	89	79	88	79	73	84	92	94	58	99	106	125
04856	ROCKPORT	115	110	140	110	117	128	103	120	106	103	105	87	102	102	112	110	71	113	122	139
04858	SOUTH THOMASTON	102	87	112	89	92	109	87	104	90	80	89	77	78	89	90	96	60	96	105	121
04859	SPRUCE HEAD	113	90	146	89	99	119	90	115	95	85	94	84	78	90	98	101	62	106	114	133
04860	TENANTS HARBOR	103	83	133	81	91	109	83	105	86	77	85	77	72	82	90	92	57	97	104	122
04861	THOMASTON	77	68	71	69	70	78	73	76	75	70	74	56	67	75	71	78	51	76	82	89
04862	UNION	86	72	98	71	76	88	71	85	74	69	73	62	63	72	74	78	49	80	84	99
04863	VINALHAVEN	118	81	129	81	85	124	90	112	94	73	93	92	66	92	90	102	60	104	118	138
04864	WARREN	82	75	70	75	74	82	72	79	75	70	74	58	67	77	70	78	50	74	80	93
04901	WATERVILLE	67	63	62	64	63	69	67	67	69	64	69	50	65	68	65	72	48	68	74	79
04910	ALBION	82	66	76	64	67	80	65	76	70	64	69	56	57	71	63	74	46	71	78	90
04911	ANSON	76	54	74	52	56	76	56	69	62	52	61	52	45	62	54	68	40	64	73	83
04912	ATHENS	79	57	81	55	59	81	58	74	65	54	64	56	47	64	58	71	42	68	77	88
04915	BELFAST	80	66	79	65	67	81	68	77	73	66	72	57	61	72	67	78	49	74	82	91
04917	BELGRADE	94	85	113	85	89	101	82	97	83	78	83	72	76	81	88	87	56	91	96	113
04920	BINGHAM	73	53	70	51	54	73	56	68	62	52	60	51	45	62	53	68	40	64	72	81
04921	BROOKS	80	58	82	56	60	82	59	75	66	55	64	56	47	65	58	72	42	69	78	89
04922	BURNHAM	78	56	65	55	56	75	59	68	65	57	64	52	47	68	53	71	43	65	72	83
04923	CAMBRIDGE	76	55	78	53	57	78	56	71	62	52	61	54	45	62	56	69	40	66	74	85
04924	CANAAN	70	64	58	62	62	66	60	64	63	62	63	47	57	65	58	65	43	62	65	77
04925	CARATUNK	71	57	92	56	63	75	57	73	60	53	59	53	49	57	62	64	39	67	72	84
04927	CLINTON	79	66	65	64	65	75	65	71	69	66	68	53	58	72	61	73	46	68	73	85
04928	CORINNA	83	60	85	58	62	84	61	78	68	57	67	58	49	67	60	74	44	71	81	92
04929	DETROIT	75	54	62	53	54	71	56	65	62	55	61	50	45	65	51	68	41	62	69	80
04930	DEXTER	69	51	73	49	53	72	53	67	59	49	57	50	43	58	53	65	38	62	71	79
04932	DIXMONT	80	74	65	71	72	75	70	74	72	72	72	54	66	75	66	74	49	71	74	88
04936	EUSTIS	60	53	55	54	55	61	57	59	59	55	58	44	52	58	55	61	39	59	64	69
04937	FAIRFIELD	79	75	64	75	72	78	75	75	76	73	76	57	72	78	71	78	52	75	79	90
04938	FARMINGTON	67	53	60	54	54	64	62	63	63	57	62	48	53	63	57	66	43	63	66	75
04939	GARLAND	71	51	59	50	51	68	53	62	59	52	58	48	43	62	48	64	39	59	65	75
04941	FREEDOM	82	59	84	57	61	83	60	77	67	56	66	57	48	66	60	73	43	70	80	91
04942	HARMONY	65	47	67	45	49	66	48	61	53	45	52	46	38	53	48	59	35	56	64	73
04943	HARTLAND	74	55	61	53	54	71	56	65	62	55	61	50	46	65	51	67	41	62	68	79
04945	JACKMAN	81	58	84	56	60	82	59	76	66	55	65	57	48	65	59	72	43	69	78	90
04947	KINGFIELD	87	70	113	69	77	92	70	89	73	66	72	65	61	70	76	78	48	82	88	103
04949	LIBERTY	85	68	110	67	75	90	68	86	71	64	70	63	59	67	74	76	47	80	85	100
04950	MADISON	81	61	90	60	65	85	65	80	70	59	68	60	53	68	65	77	46	75	85	94
04951	MONROE	82	59	84	57	61	84	60	77	67	56	66	58	48	67	60	74	44	71	80	92
04952	MORRILL	79	65	73	63	65	78	64	74	68	63	68	54	56	70	62	72	45	69	75	88
04953	NEWPORT	65	55	59	56	57	65	61	64	64	57	62	47	55	63	58	67	43	63	70	75
04954	NEW PORTLAND	73	58	94	58	64	77	59	74	61	55	61	54	51	58	63	65	40	69	73	86
04955	NEW SHARON	75	68	68	71	70	81	67	76	70	61	68	58	62	71	67	74	47	70	79	89
04956	NEW VINEYARD	72	65	65	68	67	77	64	73	67	58	65	55	59	68	64	70	45	67	75	85
04957	NORRIDGEWOCK	83	72	78	74	74	88	72	83	75	65	73	62	65	76	72	79	50	76	85	96
	MAINE	87	79	87	80	81	89	81	86	83	78	82	65	76	83	81	86	57	84	89	102
	UNITED STATES	100	100	100	100	100	100	100	100	100	100	100	100	100	100	100	100	100	100	100	100

#	POST OFFICE NAME	COUNTY FIPS CODE	POPULATION 2000	POPULATION 2009	POPULATION 2014	2000-2009 ANNUAL RATE % Rate	2000-2009 ANNUAL RATE State Centile	HOUSEHOLDS 2000	HOUSEHOLDS 2009	HOUSEHOLDS 2014	HOUSEHOLDS % Annual Rate 2000-2009	HOUSEHOLDS 2009 Average HH Size	FAMILIES 2000	FAMILIES 2009	FAMILIES % Annual Rate 2000-2009
04958	NORTH ANSON	025	2108	2106	2105	0.0	33	864	896	910	0.4	2.34	590	600	0.2
04961	NEW PORTLAND	025	861	850	847	-0.1	25	374	387	392	0.4	2.19	256	260	0.2
04963	OAKLAND	011	7045	7626	7861	0.9	77	2774	3103	3239	1.2	2.45	1962	2150	1.0
04965	PALMYRA	025	2028	2180	2245	0.8	71	797	901	941	1.3	2.42	564	626	1.1
04966	PHILLIPS	007	1734	1724	1716	-0.1	25	710	734	740	0.4	2.34	484	490	0.1
04967	PITTSFIELD	025	4337	4516	4596	0.4	53	1676	1807	1861	0.8	2.42	1180	1249	0.6
04969	PLYMOUTH	019	1332	1372	1383	0.3	50	504	539	551	0.7	2.53	373	390	0.5
04970	RANGELEY	007	1539	1531	1527	-0.1	25	683	707	714	0.4	2.16	455	461	0.1
04971	SAINT ALBANS	025	1866	1963	2011	0.5	57	725	801	831	1.1	2.42	534	580	0.9
04973	SEARSMONT	027	912	992	1024	0.9	77	372	424	444	1.4	2.34	249	279	1.2
04974	SEARSPORT	027	2763	3082	3214	1.2	87	1187	1381	1454	1.6	2.23	769	878	1.4
04976	SKOWHEGAN	025	9293	9310	9337	0.0	33	3848	4018	4088	0.5	2.26	2496	2550	0.2
04978	SMITHFIELD	025	802	816	826	0.2	46	322	345	355	0.7	2.37	247	261	0.6
04979	SOLON	025	1129	1132	1144	0.0	33	493	519	533	0.6	2.16	318	328	0.3
04981	STOCKTON SPRINGS	027	2108	2237	2274	0.6	62	873	967	998	1.1	2.31	613	665	0.9
04982	STRATTON	007	437	441	438	0.1	39	182	190	191	0.5	2.32	109	111	0.2
04983	STRONG	007	1718	1781	1792	0.4	53	679	727	741	0.7	2.42	462	486	0.5
04984	TEMPLE	007	554	550	546	-0.1	25	223	230	231	0.3	2.37	160	162	0.1
04985	WEST FORKS	025	101	100	99	-0.1	25	49	51	51	0.4	1.90	31	31	0.0
04986	THORNDIKE	027	1051	1307	1400	2.4	98	401	522	568	2.9	2.50	292	373	2.7
04987	TROY	027	1078	1061	1040	-0.2	21	419	420	418	0.0	2.43	310	306	-0.1
04988	UNITY	027	1686	1889	1928	1.2	87	629	705	733	1.2	2.24	367	400	0.9
04989	VASSALBORO	011	4119	4436	4568	0.8	71	1575	1749	1821	1.1	2.52	1159	1263	0.9
	MAINE					0.6					0.9	2.32			0.7
	UNITED STATES					1.0					1.1	2.59			0.9

ZIP CODE		RACE (%)								2009 AGE DISTRIBUTION (%)										MEDIAN AGE		
#	POST OFFICE NAME	White		Black		Asian/Pacific		% Hispanic Origin														
		2000	2009	2000	2009	2000	2009	2000	2009	0-4	5-9	10-14	15-19	20-24	25-44	45-64	65-84	85+	18+	2009	% 2009 Males	% 2009 Females
04958	NORTH ANSON	99.0	98.9	0.0	0.0	0.0	0.0	0.2	0.4	5.1	5.4	5.8	5.8	4.9	24.9	31.1	15.3	1.9	79.8	43.8	50.0	50.0
04961	NEW PORTLAND	98.5	98.4	0.0	0.0	0.0	0.0	0.3	0.6	5.3	4.8	5.6	6.4	3.8	23.2	34.5	14.9	1.5	79.6	45.5	50.9	49.1
04963	OAKLAND	98.3	97.9	0.2	0.2	0.5	0.7	0.5	0.8	5.7	6.2	7.5	6.7	5.8	25.5	30.7	10.4	1.5	76.3	40.2	48.9	51.1
04965	PALMYRA	98.6	98.2	0.0	0.0	0.3	0.5	0.3	0.4	6.3	6.5	6.6	6.0	4.7	23.9	30.2	14.3	1.5	76.4	42.3	49.5	50.5
04966	PHILLIPS	99.0	98.8	0.1	0.1	0.1	0.2	0.3	0.5	4.6	5.4	6.0	6.1	3.7	22.0	36.0	14.7	1.5	79.5	46.3	50.0	50.0
04967	PITTSFIELD	96.4	95.7	0.8	1.0	1.1	1.6	0.6	1.2	5.5	6.0	6.5	9.0	6.2	24.8	27.5	12.2	2.2	76.1	39.4	48.4	51.6
04969	PLYMOUTH	98.0	97.5	0.0	0.0	0.1	0.2	0.5	0.8	6.6	7.0	7.4	6.7	5.2	27.0	30.1	9.2	0.8	74.4	38.4	49.1	50.9
04970	RANGELEY	99.0	98.9	0.1	0.1	0.1	0.1	0.2	0.4	4.3	4.8	5.4	5.4	3.5	20.3	38.7	15.9	1.8	81.7	48.7	50.0	50.0
04971	SAINT ALBANS	98.4	97.9	0.2	0.2	0.5	0.8	0.4	0.6	5.9	6.0	6.4	6.4	5.3	25.4	30.8	12.5	1.2	77.5	41.4	51.2	48.8
04973	SEARSMONT	98.5	98.3	0.0	0.0	0.1	0.2	0.7	1.1	5.7	6.4	6.8	6.6	4.2	26.8	31.8	10.3	1.5	76.9	41.1	50.6	49.4
04974	SEARSPORT	98.0	97.7	0.3	0.4	0.0	0.0	0.2	0.3	5.4	5.7	6.2	5.6	4.1	24.2	32.8	14.1	1.8	79.2	44.0	48.7	51.3
04976	SKOWHEGAN	97.8	97.3	0.2	0.3	0.5	0.7	0.7	1.1	5.3	5.4	5.7	6.3	5.8	24.8	29.7	14.0	2.9	79.6	42.5	48.2	51.8
04978	SMITHFIELD	98.5	97.9	0.1	0.1	0.4	0.6	1.0	1.6	5.3	5.9	6.6	6.1	4.4	21.6	32.8	16.1	1.2	78.6	45.1	49.5	50.5
04979	SOLON	99.0	98.8	0.4	0.4	0.1	0.2	0.4	0.6	4.5	4.9	5.6	5.6	4.2	24.5	33.2	15.3	2.2	81.0	45.5	52.4	47.6
04981	STOCKTON SPRINGS	97.2	96.9	0.3	0.4	0.3	0.4	0.6	0.9	4.9	6.3	7.2	6.1	3.8	25.5	32.9	11.8	1.3	77.2	42.4	49.5	50.5
04982	STRATTON	96.1	95.9	0.7	0.7	0.2	0.2	0.0	0.0	4.8	4.8	4.5	5.4	7.3	24.3	32.2	15.2	1.6	82.5	44.1	51.9	48.1
04983	STRONG	98.9	98.6	0.1	0.2	0.1	0.2	1.0	1.6	5.6	6.4	6.3	6.3	4.8	24.7	31.4	12.6	1.9	77.0	42.0	50.1	49.9
04984	TEMPLE	98.7	98.5	0.2	0.4	0.4	0.4	0.5	0.9	5.1	6.5	7.5	7.6	3.8	25.8	30.7	12.0	0.9	75.3	41.3	50.2	49.8
04985	WEST FORKS	98.0	98.0	0.0	0.0	0.0	0.0	1.0	1.0	4.0	6.0	6.0	6.0	3.0	22.0	36.0	15.0	2.0	78.0	46.9	52.0	48.0
04986	THORNDIKE	99.2	99.0	0.1	0.2	0.2	0.3	0.3	0.4	5.3	6.1	6.8	6.9	4.8	26.0	30.1	12.3	1.6	77.1	41.0	51.1	48.9
04987	TROY	97.6	97.4	0.0	0.0	0.3	0.4	0.1	0.3	6.2	6.5	6.8	8.1	6.3	21.3	32.3	11.4	1.0	76.1	41.5	51.5	48.5
04988	UNITY	97.6	97.4	0.4	0.4	0.3	0.4	0.8	1.3	4.4	4.2	4.3	13.0	13.4	22.6	24.6	11.5	1.9	83.0	33.5	51.2	48.8
04989	VASSALBORO	98.6	98.4	0.1	0.2	0.0	0.1	0.6	0.9	6.0	6.2	6.7	7.0	5.7	24.7	31.1	11.3	1.3	76.5	40.8	49.2	50.8
	MAINE	96.9	96.3	0.5	0.7	0.7	1.1	0.7	1.1	5.4	5.6	6.1	6.9	6.2	24.7	30.2	12.7	2.3	78.8	41.6	48.8	51.2
	UNITED STATES	75.1	72.0	12.3	12.7	3.8	4.6	12.5	15.7	6.8	6.7	6.6	7.1	6.9	27.0	26.0	10.9	1.9	75.7	36.9	49.2	50.8

C 04958-04989

#	POST OFFICE NAME	2009 Per Capita Income	2009 HH Income Base	2009 Household Income Distribution (%): Less than $25,000	$25,000 to $49,999	$50,000 to $99,999	$100,000 to $149,999	$150,000 or More	Median Household Income: 2009	2014	2009 National Centile	2009 State Centile	2009 Home Value Base	2009 Home Value Distribution (%): Less than $50,000	$50,000 to $89,999	$90,000 to $174,999	$175,000 to $399,999	$400,000 or More	2009 Median Home Value
04958	NORTH ANSON	16518	896	36.7	36.0	23.7	3.3	0.2	32696	33426	13	11	760	13.2	22.9	39.7	21.1	3.2	113384
04961	NEW PORTLAND	19678	387	32.6	35.1	27.9	3.9	0.5	37443	38628	25	31	346	9.8	19.1	42.5	23.1	5.5	128000
04963	OAKLAND	22093	3103	25.6	30.4	34.0	7.2	2.8	43271	46287	43	50	2429	9.9	11.2	45.0	28.0	5.8	154211
04965	PALMYRA	17502	901	31.6	35.5	29.0	3.3	0.6	38288	40219	28	34	763	15.7	22.7	37.5	20.2	3.9	114229
04966	PHILLIPS	20397	734	27.9	35.7	30.0	4.4	2.0	39777	41399	32	38	611	8.7	15.4	37.0	28.3	10.6	150893
04967	PITTSFIELD	20388	1807	25.5	30.8	35.3	6.5	1.8	42626	45675	41	49	1345	7.6	17.3	52.5	19.3	3.3	121528
04969	PLYMOUTH	19184	539	27.5	35.6	29.3	5.6	2.0	40316	42524	34	40	486	8.8	21.8	50.8	17.1	1.4	117523
04970	RANGELEY	21706	707	28.4	34.8	31.1	3.5	2.1	40042	41528	33	39	574	6.8	15.3	33.3	31.0	13.6	161864
04971	SAINT ALBANS	16253	801	37.5	35.3	23.1	3.5	0.6	32917	34162	13	12	654	17.7	19.3	36.2	23.1	3.7	120890
04973	SEARSMONT	22541	424	23.6	33.0	36.1	5.2	2.1	45675	46173	50	59	357	3.9	10.1	33.9	47.3	4.8	182813
04974	SEARSPORT	22376	1381	29.8	29.5	33.7	4.6	2.3	38919	40446	29	35	1047	12.0	12.3	31.5	34.9	9.3	158288
04976	SKOWHEGAN	19091	4018	34.5	31.8	27.7	4.9	1.2	34043	35000	16	15	2749	12.7	17.5	44.2	23.0	2.6	126855
04978	SMITHFIELD	26039	345	27.0	28.1	33.6	6.4	4.9	45356	46712	49	58	306	7.8	10.5	41.2	28.4	12.1	154286
04979	SOLON	18893	519	34.3	37.2	25.4	1.9	1.2	34152	34839	16	16	412	8.7	18.2	49.3	19.4	4.4	121377
04981	STOCKTON SPRINGS	23912	967	22.3	31.4	37.7	6.1	2.4	46561	46711	53	64	835	6.1	10.5	39.2	36.9	7.3	165300
04982	STRATTON	18941	190	31.6	35.3	28.9	3.2	1.1	36524	39002	22	26	128	4.7	10.9	46.9	31.3	6.3	151471
04983	STRONG	18868	727	32.2	31.6	30.0	4.8	1.4	38090	39943	27	32	580	10.5	18.3	43.3	22.9	5.0	127397
04984	TEMPLE	20581	230	27.4	37.8	26.1	6.1	2.6	38957	40446	30	36	204	14.2	16.2	44.1	21.6	3.9	133333
04985	WEST FORKS	22640	51	33.3	33.3	27.5	5.9	0.0	36706	37954	23	28	39	5.1	17.9	46.2	23.1	7.7	137500
04986	THORNDIKE	17165	522	32.4	33.7	28.9	4.4	0.6	33702	35465	15	14	420	9.8	11.7	43.3	27.1	8.1	153169
04987	TROY	17759	420	28.3	40.2	26.7	4.3	0.5	36408	38980	22	26	355	12.4	16.3	41.1	24.8	5.4	136520
04988	UNITY	17435	705	42.7	27.1	23.7	4.7	1.8	30044	31238	8	6	424	11.3	13.4	38.4	29.0	7.8	157716
04989	VASSALBORO	20832	1749	22.3	32.0	37.8	6.1	1.8	46786	48218	53	64	1387	7.0	7.6	45.9	39.1	0.4	160846
	MAINE	24559		25.0	28.4	35.2	7.5	3.8	46650	48581				6.4	9.4	36.7	38.7	8.8	170226
	UNITED STATES	27277		20.9	24.4	35.3	11.7	7.6	54719	56938				9.3	13.1	31.6	32.6	13.5	162279

ZIP CODE	FINANCIAL SERVICES				THE HOME						ENTERTAINMENT						PERSONAL			
					Home Improvements		Furnishings													
# POST OFFICE NAME	Auto Loan	Home Loan	Invest-ments	Retire-ment Plans	Home Repair	Lawn & Garden	Comput-ers & Hard-ware-Personal	Major Appli-ances	TV, Radio, Sound Equip-ment	Furni-ture	Dine out/ Carry out	Sports Equip-ment	Fees & Tickets	Toys & Games	Travel	Cable TV	Apparel & Services	Auto Repairs	Health Insur-ance	Pets & Supplies
04958 NORTH ANSON	69	50	64	48	51	68	52	62	57	49	56	47	41	58	49	63	37	58	65	75
04961 NEW PORTLAND	73	57	90	56	62	77	57	73	61	54	60	54	49	58	61	65	40	67	73	85
04963 OAKLAND	84	73	82	74	75	83	76	81	78	73	77	61	70	78	75	81	53	80	84	96
04965 PALMYRA	75	54	76	53	56	76	56	70	62	52	61	53	45	61	55	68	40	65	73	83
04966 PHILLIPS	81	63	99	62	68	85	64	81	68	59	67	59	54	65	67	73	44	74	81	94
04967 PITTSFIELD	81	66	77	66	67	85	68	79	73	63	71	60	60	73	67	78	48	74	84	93
04969 PLYMOUTH	78	72	64	69	70	73	68	72	70	70	70	52	64	73	65	72	48	69	72	85
04970 RANGELEY	78	63	101	62	69	83	63	80	66	59	65	58	54	62	68	70	43	74	79	92
04971 SAINT ALBANS	71	51	65	49	52	70	53	64	58	50	57	48	42	59	50	64	38	60	67	77
04973 SEARSMONT	82	74	74	77	76	88	73	83	76	66	74	63	68	77	73	80	51	76	85	96
04974 SEARSPORT	82	69	93	67	72	84	67	81	71	66	70	59	60	69	70	74	47	76	80	95
04976 SKOWHEGAN	69	56	65	56	57	70	60	67	64	55	63	50	52	63	58	69	43	65	72	79
04978 SMITHFIELD	95	87	86	90	89	102	86	97	88	77	87	73	79	90	86	94	59	89	100	112
04979 SOLON	72	52	74	50	54	74	54	68	60	50	59	51	43	59	53	66	39	63	72	81
04981 STOCKTON SPRINGS	89	76	95	78	80	94	76	90	79	69	77	67	68	78	78	83	52	83	91	104
04982 STRATTON	68	58	71	59	61	70	61	68	63	58	62	50	55	62	61	66	42	66	71	79
04983 STRONG	81	59	88	58	63	83	60	77	66	56	65	57	49	65	61	72	43	71	79	91
04984 TEMPLE	88	63	90	61	65	89	64	82	71	60	70	61	51	71	64	79	46	75	85	97
04985 WEST FORKS	76	57	86	56	61	79	58	74	63	54	62	55	48	61	60	68	41	68	75	87
04986 THORNDIKE	77	55	79	53	57	78	56	72	63	52	61	54	45	62	56	69	41	66	75	85
04987 TROY	78	56	80	54	58	79	57	73	64	53	63	55	46	63	57	70	41	67	76	87
04988 UNITY	65	50	63	50	52	65	57	63	62	52	60	47	48	60	54	67	41	62	69	74
04989 VASSALBORO	83	76	71	75	75	82	73	79	76	73	75	58	69	78	71	79	51	76	81	93
MAINE	87	79	87	80	81	89	81	86	83	78	82	65	76	83	81	86	57	84	89	102
UNITED STATES	100	100	100	100	100	100	100	100	100	100	100	100	100	100	100	100	100	100	100	100

20601-20772

ZIP CODE #	POST OFFICE NAME	COUNTY FIPS CODE	POPULATION 2000	POPULATION 2009	POPULATION 2014	2000-2009 ANNUAL RATE % Rate	2000-2009 ANNUAL RATE State Centile	HOUSEHOLDS 2000	HOUSEHOLDS 2009	HOUSEHOLDS 2014	HOUSEHOLDS % Annual Rate 2000-2009	HOUSEHOLDS 2009 Average HH Size	FAMILIES 2000	FAMILIES 2009	FAMILIES % Annual Rate 2000-2009
20601	WALDORF	017	22035	24630	25316	1.2	61	7554	8579	8873	1.4	2.86	5970	6571	1.0
20602	WALDORF	017	21524	24474	27253	1.4	67	7490	8731	9791	1.7	2.78	5565	6302	1.4
20603	WALDORF	017	18530	25347	28069	3.4	97	6163	8495	9456	3.5	2.98	4913	6594	3.2
20606	ABELL	037	410	503	554	2.2	87	159	201	224	2.6	2.50	123	152	2.3
20607	ACCOKEEK	033	7111	9295	10432	2.9	95	2341	3047	3418	2.9	3.04	1871	2372	2.6
20608	AQUASCO	033	1015	1078	1102	0.7	41	362	388	397	0.8	2.78	276	285	0.3
20609	AVENUE	037	920	1144	1260	2.4	91	376	482	535	2.7	2.37	277	344	2.4
20611	BEL ALTON	017	924	1102	1196	1.9	79	328	405	444	2.3	2.70	261	312	1.9
20613	BRANDYWINE	033	8400	10945	12359	2.9	95	2949	3867	4398	3.0	2.73	2250	2835	2.5
20615	BROOMES ISLAND	009	401	422	468	0.6	38	161	174	194	0.8	2.43	129	135	0.5
20616	BRYANS ROAD	017	4917	5715	5979	1.6	73	1806	2140	2254	1.9	2.67	1365	1568	1.5
20617	BRYANTOWN	017	885	991	1013	1.2	61	322	370	382	1.5	2.67	263	293	1.2
20618	BUSHWOOD	037	902	1119	1231	2.4	91	357	456	507	2.7	2.45	260	322	2.3
20619	CALIFORNIA	037	7544	9057	10305	2.0	82	2987	3714	4264	2.4	2.42	2018	2409	1.9
20620	CALLAWAY	037	1632	1810	1912	1.1	58	590	664	704	1.3	2.72	448	491	1.0
20621	CHAPTICO	037	1002	1185	1299	1.8	78	381	463	509	2.1	2.56	299	354	1.8
20622	CHARLOTTE HALL	017	3808	4677	5043	2.2	87	1161	1474	1610	2.6	3.01	972	1208	2.4
20623	CHELTENHAM	033	2521	3074	3213	2.2	87	666	837	873	2.5	3.60	578	707	2.2
20624	CLEMENTS	037	718	909	1019	2.6	92	252	330	373	3.0	2.75	200	256	2.7
20625	COBB ISLAND	017	822	1039	1126	2.6	92	346	442	483	2.7	2.34	208	251	2.1
20626	COLTONS POINT	037	520	636	699	2.2	87	228	288	319	2.6	2.20	160	195	2.2
20628	DAMERON	037	331	465	528	3.7	98	135	191	219	3.8	2.43	91	123	3.3
20630	DRAYDEN	037	305	338	356	1.1	58	120	136	144	1.4	2.49	85	93	1.0
20632	FAULKNER	017	364	497	529	3.4	97	131	182	196	3.6	2.68	100	135	3.3
20634	GREAT MILLS	037	4372	6036	6783	3.5	97	1597	2283	2585	3.9	2.63	1107	1516	3.5
20636	HOLLYWOOD	037	7917	10195	11129	2.8	93	2872	3747	4123	2.9	2.70	2161	2730	2.6
20637	HUGHESVILLE	017	4634	6005	6530	2.8	93	1474	1973	2172	3.2	2.92	1215	1582	2.9
20639	HUNTINGTOWN	009	11983	14699	16070	2.2	87	3843	4752	5212	2.3	3.08	3300	4015	2.1
20640	INDIAN HEAD	017	8126	9600	10052	1.8	78	3007	3565	3748	1.9	2.69	2157	2483	1.5
20645	ISSUE	017	413	490	514	1.9	79	179	218	231	2.2	2.25	135	159	1.8
20646	LA PLATA	017	16406	20061	21739	2.2	87	5626	7116	7818	2.6	2.71	4354	5335	2.2
20650	LEONARDTOWN	037	11085	13778	15167	2.4	91	3864	4950	5506	2.7	2.67	2895	3598	2.4
20653	LEXINGTON PARK	037	19980	24626	27085	2.3	89	7154	9051	10086	2.6	2.55	4728	5751	2.1
20657	LUSBY	009	18090	21281	22601	1.8	78	6120	7097	7525	1.6	2.99	4749	5366	1.3
20658	MARBURY	017	913	933	1001	0.2	23	310	323	351	0.4	2.89	234	235	0.0
20659	MECHANICSVILLE	037	20638	23337	24720	1.3	64	6728	7807	8331	1.6	2.97	5533	6289	1.4
20662	NANJEMOY	017	2664	2913	2965	1.0	54	937	1052	1082	1.3	2.77	711	769	0.9
20664	NEWBURG	017	2779	3388	3618	2.2	87	1001	1260	1360	2.5	2.68	756	919	2.1
20667	PARK HALL	037	194	234	256	2.0	82	78	97	107	2.4	2.31	45	54	2.0
20670	PATUXENT RIVER	037	1741	1768	1773	0.2	23	467	474	479	0.2	2.91	269	260	-0.4
20674	PINEY POINT	037	846	1005	1101	1.9	79	334	403	446	2.1	2.40	233	272	1.7
20675	POMFRET	017	1513	1579	1676	0.5	35	516	556	598	0.8	2.84	443	469	0.6
20676	PORT REPUBLIC	009	3156	4104	4677	2.9	95	1089	1429	1636	3.0	2.87	850	1086	2.7
20677	PORT TOBACCO	017	1502	1820	1925	2.1	83	542	673	719	2.4	2.70	437	529	2.1
20678	PRINCE FREDERICK	009	9248	11369	12455	2.3	89	3122	3909	4308	2.5	2.83	2386	2902	2.1
20680	RIDGE	037	1167	1460	1613	2.5	91	504	650	724	2.8	2.23	339	421	2.4
20684	SAINT INIGOES	037	1106	1413	1584	2.7	92	439	573	650	2.9	2.41	298	374	2.5
20685	SAINT LEONARD	009	5597	7084	7761	2.6	92	1920	2445	2684	2.6	2.89	1527	1901	2.4
20687	SCOTLAND	037	339	416	458	2.2	87	150	190	211	2.6	2.19	84	101	2.0
20688	SOLOMONS	009	1796	2436	2731	3.3	96	799	1114	1259	3.7	2.04	502	672	3.2
20689	SUNDERLAND	009	1091	1251	1357	1.5	69	376	438	477	1.7	2.85	316	360	1.4
20690	TALL TIMBERS	037	659	891	989	3.3	96	279	389	438	3.7	2.16	194	261	3.3
20692	VALLEY LEE	037	463	507	534	1.0	54	181	202	214	1.2	2.51	130	141	0.9
20693	WELCOME	017	1206	1507	1609	2.4	91	431	553	596	2.7	2.73	341	425	2.4
20695	WHITE PLAINS	017	6918	9215	10376	3.1	95	2426	3276	3702	3.3	2.80	1919	2520	3.0
20701	ANNAPOLIS JUNCTION	003	797	793	794	-0.1	10	14	15	15	0.7	2.27	10	10	0.0
20705	BELTSVILLE	033	20337	20502	20338	0.1	17	7403	7472	7426	0.1	2.73	5056	4850	-0.4
20706	LANHAM	033	39414	40025	39557	0.2	23	13718	13908	13759	0.1	2.85	10117	9914	-0.2
20707	LAUREL	033	25695	28235	28770	1.0	54	10740	11783	12025	1.0	2.36	6232	6397	0.3
20708	LAUREL	033	25403	25792	25506	0.2	23	10356	10553	10460	0.2	2.42	6303	6068	-0.4
20710	BLADENSBURG	033	7855	7672	7495	-0.3	6	3165	3076	3003	-0.3	2.49	1763	1607	-1.0
20711	LOTHIAN	003	5918	6337	6486	0.7	41	2247	2440	2515	0.9	2.60	1596	1673	0.5
20712	MOUNT RAINIER	033	9063	8928	8723	-0.2	8	3693	3590	3507	-0.3	2.48	1996	1818	-1.0
20714	NORTH BEACH	003	3207	3844	4161	2.0	82	1302	1585	1725	2.1	2.42	867	989	1.4
20715	BOWIE	033	25231	25627	25377	0.2	23	8725	8899	8840	0.2	2.81	6856	6696	-0.3
20716	BOWIE	033	19598	21114	21377	0.8	47	7520	8240	8409	1.0	2.51	5017	5206	0.4
20720	BOWIE	033	14705	20893	22899	3.9	98	4800	6767	7413	3.8	3.04	3970	5468	3.5
20721	BOWIE	033	22589	26240	27465	1.6	73	7660	8896	9313	1.6	2.93	6000	6745	1.3
20722	BRENTWOOD	033	5383	5262	5130	-0.2	8	1798	1748	1708	-0.3	3.01	1194	1105	-0.8
20723	LAUREL	027	24073	28072	29985	1.7	76	8611	9915	10548	1.5	2.82	6235	6977	1.2
20724	LAUREL	003	13013	14967	15726	1.5	69	5077	6032	6403	1.9	2.41	3267	3701	1.4
20732	CHESAPEAKE BEACH	009	7497	10423	11631	3.6	98	2642	3705	4148	3.7	2.81	2028	2774	3.4
20733	CHURCHTON	003	3395	3628	3706	0.7	41	1221	1324	1360	0.9	2.74	944	991	0.5
20735	CLINTON	033	32971	36252	37276	1.0	54	10870	11996	12375	1.1	2.95	8625	9257	0.8
20736	OWINGS	009	7870	9583	10557	2.2	87	2591	3177	3511	2.2	3.01	2161	2592	2.0
20737	RIVERDALE	033	19099	19890	19686	0.4	30	6061	6146	6083	0.2	3.23	4343	4233	-0.3
20740	COLLEGE PARK	033	30464	31895	31667	0.5	35	8743	8872	8771	0.2	2.50	4290	4015	-0.7
20742	COLLEGE PARK	033	175	179	175	0.2	23	63	62	60	-0.2	2.71	15	13	-1.5
20743	CAPITOL HEIGHTS	033	41620	40712	39763	-0.2	8	14786	14526	14233	-0.2	2.79	10544	9956	-0.6
20744	FORT WASHINGTON	033	50175	52651	53251	0.5	35	17823	18747	18977	0.5	2.80	13456	13731	0.2
20745	OXON HILL	033	27690	27341	27155	-0.1	10	10536	10490	10466	0.0	2.61	7077	6695	-0.6
20746	SUITLAND	033	28530	28766	28475	0.1	17	11249	11340	11243	0.1	2.54	7399	7154	-0.4
20747	DISTRICT HEIGHTS	033	38943	39684	39324	0.2	23	14790	15113	15013	0.2	2.61	10051	9807	-0.3
20748	TEMPLE HILLS	033	38060	37523	36786	-0.2	8	14681	14515	14261	-0.1	2.58	9883	9323	-0.6
20751	DEALE	003	2121	2219	2249	0.5	35	801	850	867	0.6	2.61	557	568	0.2
20754	DUNKIRK	009	6215	7049	7437	1.4	67	2034	2340	2480	1.5	3.01	1785	2024	1.4
20755	FORT GEORGE G MEADE	003	9922	10588	10825	0.7	41	2444	2617	2692	0.7	3.51	2315	2472	0.7
20758	FRIENDSHIP	003	876	890	890	0.2	23	351	364	367	0.4	2.45	253	252	0.0
20759	FULTON	027	2115	2907	3195	3.5	97	690	972	1075	3.8	2.98	605	833	3.5
20762	ANDREWS AIR FORCE BA	033	7925	6509	6146	-2.1	0	1932	1478	1377	-2.9	3.36	1865	1419	-2.9
20763	SAVAGE	027	2172	2276	2351	0.5	35	833	881	915	0.6	2.58	566	567	0.0
20764	SHADY SIDE	003	3867	4121	4194	0.7	41	1465	1584	1622	0.8	2.60	1060	1103	0.4
20769	GLENN DALE	033	4946	6399	6954	2.8	93	1613	2110	2305	2.9	3.03	1297	1648	2.6
20770	GREENBELT	033	21177	21424	21145	0.1	17	9278	9307	9190	0.0	2.30	4897	4591	-0.7
20772	UPPER MARLBORO	033	34475	42722	46087	2.3	89	12200	14993	16218	2.3	2.75	8966	10639	1.9
	MARYLAND					0.9					0.9	2.60			0.5
	UNITED STATES					1.0					1.1	2.59			0.9

ZIP CODE #	POST OFFICE NAME	RACE (%) White 2000	White 2009	Black 2000	Black 2009	Asian/Pacific 2000	Asian/Pacific 2009	% Hispanic Origin 2000	% Hispanic Origin 2009	2009 AGE DISTRIBUTION (%) 0-4	5-9	10-14	15-19	20-24	25-44	45-64	65-84	85+	18+	MEDIAN AGE 2009	% 2009 Males	% 2009 Females
20601	WALDORF	62.9	55.1	30.9	36.5	2.2	3.0	2.5	3.9	7.3	7.1	7.2	7.3	6.2	29.9	27.1	7.3	0.7	73.8	35.9	48.8	51.2
20602	WALDORF	63.4	55.4	30.6	36.6	1.9	2.6	2.8	4.1	8.3	7.6	7.6	7.4	6.9	30.3	24.1	6.7	1.0	71.9	32.9	47.7	52.3
20603	WALDORF	67.6	60.0	24.2	29.1	3.5	4.6	3.7	5.6	7.9	8.0	8.2	7.8	5.2	30.7	26.6	5.1	0.4	70.8	34.3	48.0	52.0
20606	ABELL	89.8	86.5	8.0	10.7	0.7	0.8	1.5	2.2	5.2	5.4	5.6	6.0	5.0	26.0	28.2	16.5	2.2	80.3	43.1	51.1	48.9
20607	ACCOKEEK	45.0	33.6	45.9	54.3	5.2	6.7	2.3	3.7	6.2	6.7	7.2	7.2	5.2	24.2	32.4	9.7	1.1	75.5	40.6	49.2	50.8
20608	AQUASCO	59.4	48.2	36.9	46.5	0.1	0.2	1.9	3.3	5.2	6.4	7.1	7.7	4.5	23.9	31.7	12.2	1.2	76.4	41.9	49.1	50.9
20609	AVENUE	83.0	77.9	15.2	19.6	0.5	0.9	1.3	2.1	5.1	5.2	5.5	5.4	4.2	24.2	29.5	18.4	2.4	81.0	45.2	49.7	50.3
20611	BEL ALTON	80.8	74.5	15.6	20.3	0.9	1.2	2.1	3.5	5.5	6.4	7.5	6.8	4.3	25.1	33.2	10.1	1.1	75.5	41.5	49.1	50.9
20613	BRANDYWINE	61.6	51.3	33.4	41.9	1.2	1.9	1.7	3.4	5.5	6.1	7.3	9.3	4.6	23.1	31.1	11.7	1.3	74.4	41.0	51.1	48.9
20615	BROOMES ISLAND	76.3	69.4	19.5	24.2	1.0	1.7	2.7	4.5	6.4	6.6	7.1	7.8	6.4	24.2	30.3	10.0	1.2	74.2	39.4	48.1	51.9
20616	BRYANS ROAD	51.8	44.8	43.2	48.9	1.4	1.9	2.2	3.3	7.3	7.3	7.5	7.3	4.5	30.8	25.0	9.2	1.0	73.2	37.0	47.2	52.8
20617	BRYANTOWN	79.2	73.1	18.2	22.9	0.7	1.1	1.4	2.2	5.5	6.0	6.6	6.3	4.1	24.2	31.2	14.6	1.5	77.9	43.4	49.9	50.1
20618	BUSHWOOD	75.6	70.0	22.6	27.7	0.7	0.9	1.2	2.0	5.1	5.2	5.5	5.2	3.8	24.0	31.5	17.9	1.9	81.1	45.7	50.0	50.0
20619	CALIFORNIA	83.7	78.5	11.4	14.2	2.5	3.8	2.0	3.3	6.9	6.8	6.8	7.4	6.1	27.7	28.4	8.7	1.1	74.5	37.3	49.0	51.0
20620	CALLAWAY	86.5	81.8	9.2	11.8	1.8	2.7	2.1	3.7	7.1	7.3	7.5	7.6	5.5	26.1	29.7	8.3	0.8	73.0	37.9	50.6	49.4
20621	CHAPTICO	84.6	79.6	13.2	17.1	0.5	0.8	1.5	2.4	7.8	7.5	7.5	6.3	5.3	32.3	22.6	9.5	1.0	73.2	34.6	50.7	49.3
20622	CHARLOTTE HALL	86.6	82.2	10.5	13.6	0.8	1.1	0.9	1.5	6.4	6.8	7.4	7.4	4.3	24.8	28.3	13.1	1.5	74.5	40.4	51.7	48.3
20623	CHELTENHAM	32.4	24.0	60.8	67.7	3.3	3.9	2.3	3.3	6.1	6.3	7.4	9.2	4.7	29.0	30.3	6.6	0.5	74.1	36.6	48.9	51.1
20624	CLEMENTS	84.2	79.0	13.8	18.0	0.4	0.7	1.4	2.2	7.2	7.5	8.1	6.9	5.5	29.3	24.9	9.7	1.0	73.3	35.6	51.9	48.1
20625	COBB ISLAND	95.3	92.9	2.6	3.6	1.3	2.1	0.4	0.7	6.9	6.5	6.1	6.4	5.9	28.7	23.4	13.8	2.3	75.8	36.9	47.6	52.4
20626	COLTONS POINT	85.2	80.3	13.1	17.0	0.6	0.9	1.2	2.0	5.0	5.5	5.7	4.7	3.6	22.5	28.0	21.4	3.6	81.3	46.8	48.6	51.4
20628	DAMERON	84.3	79.4	12.7	15.5	0.9	1.7	1.2	2.6	6.2	6.7	6.5	5.6	4.5	24.1	31.0	14.0	1.5	77.6	42.6	50.1	49.9
20630	DRAYDEN	88.5	83.7	7.5	10.1	1.3	2.4	1.3	2.1	5.6	5.9	6.2	5.6	4.1	23.4	30.8	16.0	2.4	79.0	44.4	50.9	49.1
20632	FAULKNER	77.5	70.6	17.5	22.9	1.1	1.6	0.8	1.6	6.6	6.6	6.4	6.6	6.2	27.0	29.4	9.9	1.2	75.9	38.7	50.3	49.7
20634	GREAT MILLS	69.7	60.6	23.4	29.9	3.5	4.9	2.6	4.2	8.7	7.8	7.1	6.8	6.1	34.9	22.5	5.6	0.4	71.8	32.5	49.1	50.9
20636	HOLLYWOOD	92.4	88.4	4.9	7.5	1.0	1.5	1.4	2.4	6.3	6.8	7.3	7.0	4.6	24.8	30.9	10.6	1.7	74.8	40.8	49.1	50.9
20637	HUGHESVILLE	78.5	72.3	17.9	22.5	1.6	2.4	1.2	2.1	6.5	6.5	7.4	6.8	4.1	27.8	29.2	10.6	1.0	75.3	39.9	51.7	48.3
20639	HUNTINGTOWN	86.0	81.4	11.3	14.7	1.3	1.9	1.3	2.1	6.3	7.1	8.2	8.2	4.6	23.1	33.0	8.7	0.9	73.2	40.4	49.4	50.6
20640	INDIAN HEAD	67.0	59.8	28.1	33.8	1.3	1.8	1.6	2.9	7.6	7.4	7.1	6.9	6.3	27.0	25.4	10.6	1.6	73.4	36.3	49.9	50.1
20645	ISSUE	86.4	81.6	10.9	14.7	1.2	1.6	1.0	1.6	4.5	4.9	5.7	5.3	3.3	19.2	31.6	23.5	2.0	81.2	50.0	51.2	48.8
20646	LA PLATA	77.3	70.7	19.3	24.7	1.2	1.7	1.4	2.4	5.7	6.4	7.0	7.0	4.8	25.1	30.4	11.7	1.9	76.3	41.0	49.2	50.8
20650	LEONARDTOWN	86.2	81.0	10.3	13.7	1.9	2.9	1.3	2.3	6.2	6.6	7.1	7.2	5.1	24.5	29.1	11.9	2.2	75.6	40.6	49.2	50.8
20653	LEXINGTON PARK	68.2	61.4	24.3	28.3	3.3	4.5	3.4	5.4	8.7	7.7	6.7	8.7	10.2	31.1	20.8	5.6	0.5	72.8	29.6	49.8	50.2
20657	LUSBY	82.0	76.5	14.4	18.4	0.9	1.2	2.2	3.9	8.6	7.9	7.6	7.9	6.3	30.4	23.5	6.8	1.1	70.8	32.9	48.5	51.5
20658	MARBURY	49.1	40.6	45.4	53.1	0.9	1.2	1.5	2.3	5.8	6.2	6.5	6.1	5.0	24.1	31.2	13.6	1.4	77.7	42.1	50.5	49.5
20659	MECHANICSVILLE	88.8	85.0	8.5	11.1	0.6	0.9	1.0	1.8	7.2	7.5	7.8	7.4	4.9	27.8	27.9	8.8	0.8	72.9	37.4	50.0	50.0
20662	NANJEMOY	62.5	53.8	35.3	43.4	0.3	0.4	0.9	1.4	6.4	6.6	6.7	6.8	5.1	25.6	30.4	11.3	1.1	76.0	39.7	49.5	50.5
20664	NEWBURG	74.9	67.4	21.6	28.0	1.0	1.4	0.9	1.6	5.4	5.6	5.8	6.3	4.8	23.8	31.6	15.1	1.6	79.2	43.9	50.6	49.4
20667	PARK HALL	84.5	79.5	10.8	13.7	0.5	0.9	2.6	4.7	6.8	6.4	6.0	6.8	6.4	27.4	27.4	11.1	1.7	78.2	37.8	51.7	48.3
20670	PATUXENT RIVER	70.5	63.1	19.4	23.0	3.5	4.8	7.0	11.1	11.0	11.0	7.6	7.7	16.3	42.8	3.6	0.1	0.0	68.2	23.9	65.3	34.7
20674	PINEY POINT	87.4	82.7	8.0	10.4	2.0	3.0	2.1	3.7	5.4	5.1	5.6	4.6	4.6	24.7	34.4	13.7	2.0	81.3	45.1	53.0	47.0
20675	POMFRET	75.0	67.9	19.1	24.4	2.4	3.4	1.1	1.8	5.3	5.9	6.8	7.0	4.1	24.3	34.1	11.9	0.7	77.6	42.8	49.5	50.5
20676	PORT REPUBLIC	82.5	77.0	14.6	18.8	0.6	0.9	1.7	2.8	6.3	6.8	7.3	7.3	5.0	25.7	30.7	9.6	1.3	74.6	39.7	49.0	51.0
20677	PORT TOBACCO	83.0	77.4	13.4	17.8	0.8	1.3	1.1	2.0	4.9	5.9	6.8	6.9	4.1	24.6	33.0	12.8	1.1	77.9	43.1	49.1	50.9
20678	PRINCE FREDERICK	77.0	70.7	20.7	26.1	0.8	1.2	1.2	2.0	6.5	6.9	7.2	7.1	5.7	26.9	28.2	9.6	1.8	75.0	38.0	48.3	51.7
20680	RIDGE	82.9	77.4	14.9	19.4	0.9	1.4	0.5	1.0	5.2	5.6	5.8	5.3	3.8	21.6	33.7	16.8	2.1	80.1	46.6	50.7	49.3
20684	SAINT INIGOES	82.6	77.3	14.5	18.3	1.4	2.1	1.3	2.2	4.6	4.9	5.5	6.9	5.3	22.4	31.9	16.3	2.3	80.2	45.3	50.0	50.0
20685	SAINT LEONARD	86.1	81.3	10.7	14.0	0.9	1.3	1.9	3.2	6.6	7.2	8.2	7.4	4.9	26.4	30.3	8.2	0.8	72.9	38.8	48.9	51.1
20687	SCOTLAND	90.3	86.5	7.1	9.4	0.6	1.0	0.9	1.7	3.4	3.6	4.1	4.6	3.1	23.3	39.2	16.8	1.9	86.3	50.3	49.8	50.2
20688	SOLOMONS	85.2	80.6	12.4	15.7	0.6	0.9	0.7	1.2	4.4	4.3	4.6	5.2	5.0	20.9	27.7	20.4	7.7	83.4	48.8	47.0	53.0
20689	SUNDERLAND	74.9	68.7	23.1	28.6	0.5	0.6	1.1	1.9	4.8	5.4	6.6	7.0	4.2	22.9	36.2	11.8	1.4	78.9	44.6	48.9	51.1
20690	TALL TIMBERS	86.2	81.1	8.8	11.3	2.3	3.3	2.9	4.8	5.6	4.9	5.4	4.4	4.9	25.9	35.6	11.4	1.8	81.4	44.1	54.3	45.7
20692	VALLEY LEE	87.3	82.6	8.6	11.0	1.7	2.2	1.5	2.8	6.1	6.3	6.3	5.9	4.9	24.9	30.0	13.8	1.8	77.5	42.1	50.7	49.3
20693	WELCOME	81.8	75.5	14.9	19.8	0.6	0.9	0.6	1.1	5.2	5.5	5.9	6.5	5.6	24.6	31.9	13.6	1.2	79.4	42.7	48.5	51.5
20695	WHITE PLAINS	68.7	59.5	25.5	32.7	2.0	2.7	2.6	4.2	7.7	7.5	7.2	6.5	5.0	32.0	26.5	6.9	0.7	73.5	35.7	48.1	51.9
20701	ANNAPOLIS JUNCTION	25.1	18.9	74.6	80.7	0.1	0.1	0.6	0.8	0.3	0.3	0.3	2.8	14.9	67.7	13.0	0.8	0.1	98.9	33.3	76.7	23.3
20705	BELTSVILLE	48.3	38.9	32.9	36.4	11.2	13.5	8.4	13.5	6.6	6.0	6.0	6.5	8.4	30.4	25.4	9.6	1.2	77.5	35.2	49.4	50.6
20706	LANHAM	22.3	17.1	67.6	70.6	5.5	6.4	3.9	5.9	7.1	7.1	7.0	7.3	6.7	27.3	27.0	9.4	1.0	74.2	36.0	47.3	52.7
20707	LAUREL	57.5	47.3	30.5	36.3	6.6	8.4	5.7	9.3	6.5	6.2	5.7	5.7	6.8	33.2	25.9	8.8	1.3	78.0	36.6	48.2	51.8
20708	LAUREL	37.4	29.4	51.6	56.2	5.4	6.6	4.9	7.7	8.4	7.3	6.4	6.3	8.1	34.2	21.9	6.7	0.8	74.3	32.0	47.4	52.6
20710	BLADENSBURG	17.8	15.7	68.6	66.6	2.5	2.7	14.8	21.1	8.3	7.1	6.6	7.7	10.3	30.1	21.7	7.3	0.9	73.6	30.4	48.8	51.2
20711	LOTHIAN	81.0	74.0	16.1	21.8	0.6	0.9	1.0	1.8	6.1	6.2	6.7	6.8	6.2	23.7	31.1	11.9	1.3	76.9	41.2	49.6	50.4
20712	MOUNT RAINIER	19.9	16.4	62.4	60.3	2.3	2.4	18.4	25.6	7.4	6.7	6.3	6.4	10.1	32.5	23.0	6.6	1.0	76.0	31.7	48.9	51.1
20714	NORTH BEACH	90.6	87.1	5.8	7.7	0.9	1.4	1.5	2.7	7.6	7.3	7.1	6.6	5.1	32.3	25.4	7.8	0.8	73.8	35.2	47.7	52.3
20715	BOWIE	79.4	71.6	14.6	19.0	2.6	3.8	3.0	6.0	6.4	6.7	6.8	7.4	5.9	24.4	27.9	13.1	1.4	75.7	40.4	48.1	51.9
20716	BOWIE	53.1	42.4	39.9	48.0	3.1	4.1	2.9	5.0	7.7	7.4	7.0	6.1	5.2	33.4	24.3	7.6	1.4	74.0	36.2	47.1	52.9
20720	BOWIE	46.0	38.0	42.1	46.9	7.7	9.9	2.9	4.5	6.9	7.7	8.4	8.2	4.7	25.6	31.4	6.5	0.6	72.0	38.2	48.2	51.8
20721	BOWIE	10.9	8.1	84.2	86.2	2.2	2.5	1.5	1.9	6.6	7.2	8.0	7.1	3.8	26.7	32.3	7.1	1.2	73.6	39.4	46.4	53.6
20722	BRENTWOOD	26.9	20.7	52.7	52.3	4.4	4.8	18.0	26.2	6.5	6.0	6.5	7.7	7.7	27.3	26.7	10.3	1.3	76.5	36.4	48.4	51.6
20723	LAUREL	70.9	63.6	17.4	20.3	7.3	10.2	4.0	6.4	7.8	7.8	8.0	7.3	5.7	30.7	27.0	5.2	0.5	71.5	34.9	49.4	50.6
20724	LAUREL	56.4	46.2	32.1	38.7	6.6	8.7	4.2	6.2	7.8	7.1	6.7	8.0	6.8	31.8	25.1	6.2	0.5	73.4	35.0	49.4	50.6
20732	CHESAPEAKE BEACH	84.9	81.1	11.9	14.4	0.7	1.1	1.4	2.4	7.1	7.8	7.8	7.0	5.0	29.0	28.8	6.7	0.8	72.7	36.5	49.6	50.4
20733	CHURCHTON	88.1	83.8	9.8	13.1	0.4	0.5	1.4	2.4	6.4	7.0	7.5	6.8	4.5	24.8	32.3	9.8	1.0	74.8	40.7	48.8	51.2
20735	CLINTON	21.1	15.2	73.1	77.8	2.6	3.0	1.9	2.8	6.0	6.4	7.0	7.3	4.9	26.1	30.5	10.5	1.4	75.9	40.3	47.4	52.6
20736	OWINGS	85.8	80.9	11.6	15.3	0.8	1.3	1.1	1.9	6.1	6.7	7.5	7.2	4.7	24.4	33.4	9.0	1.1	75.1	40.9	48.9	51.1
20737	RIVERDALE	30.0	25.9	50.5	49.5	4.2	4.6	22.7	30.9	8.8	8.2	7.4	7.9	8.1	30.9	22.1	5.9	0.7	70.9	30.4	50.7	49.3
20740	COLLEGE PARK	68.1	57.0	15.9	19.9	10.5	14.4	5.6	10.2	3.2	3.0	3.0	21.9	24.8	20.7	15.3	6.9	1.2	88.9	23.8	52.0	48.0
20742	COLLEGE PARK	88.0	82.1	4.6	6.1	2.3	3.4	2.3	5.0	0.6	1.7	1.7	8.4	63.1	9.5	9.5	4.5	1.1	96.1	23.0	63.1	36.9
20743	CAPITOL HEIGHTS	3.4	2.5	94.1	94.8	0.3	0.4	1.0	1.3	7.2	7.6	7.6	8.4	6.8	26.0	25.3	10.2	0.9	72.4	35.0	45.9	54.1
20744	FORT WASHINGTON	14.5	10.2	75.8	78.5	6.3	7.2	2.1	2.9	5.8	6.0	6.5	6.8	5.5	26.3	30.6	11.5	1.1	77.5	40.2	47.0	53.0
20745	OXON HILL	8.3	5.8	84.6	85.9	4.3	4.8	1.9	2.6	7.4	7.0	6.9	8.1	8.5	27.3	25.8	8.2	0.7	73.9	33.6	46.1	53.9
20746	SUITLAND	9.0	7.2	87.0	87.9	1.1	1.4	2.4	3.3	7.8	7.5	7.2	8.1	8.0	28.0	24.7	7.8	0.9	72.6	33.0	45.1	54.9
20747	DISTRICT HEIGHTS	6.9	4.7	89.7	91.4	0.8	0.9	1.3	1.7	7.6	7.3	7.0	7.7	8.5	28.5	24.9	7.7	0.9	73.4	32.9	45.3	54.7
20748	TEMPLE HILLS	10.8	7.7	85.6	87.9	1.1	1.2	1.9	2.7	6.2	6.2	6.4	7.3	6.8	27.1	27.3	11.4	1.3	76.7	37.8	46.3	53.7
20751	DEALE	92.6	89.1	5.3	7.6	0.7	1.0	0.7	1.3	5.1	5.8	6.5	6.8	4.3	24.7	34.5	11.0	1.4	78.4	43.1	50.5	49.5
20754	DUNKIRK	91.7	88.6	5.9	7.8	1.0	1.6	0.7	1.1	5.0	5.9	7.1	7.5	4.0	20.8	36.0	12.6	1.1	77.2	44.8	49.5	50.5
20755	FORT GEORGE G MEADE	62.5	53.2	25.1	29.9	3.2	4.2	9.5	14.6	15.3	12.6	8.5	7.0	13.6	38.7	4.1	0.3	0.1	60.3	22.5	52.3	47.7
20758	FRIENDSHIP	92.9	90.1	4.8	6.9	0.5	0.6	0.5	0.9	3.7	4.7	6.0	6.4	3.5	19.9	37.8	16.1	2.0	81.6	47.8	49.9	50.1
20759	FULTON	85.0	77.6	4.2	6.0	8.5	12.7	1.9	3.3	6.1	7.6	8.9	8.2	3.8	18.3	34.1	11.6	1.4	71.9	43.1	50.5	49.5
20762	ANDREWS AIR FORCE BA	65.3	54.6	22.8	27.7	3.3	4.5	8.7	15.3	14.3	10.6	5.8	5.8	15.9	43.2	4.2	0.2	0.0	67.1	24.2	55.9	44.1
20763	SAVAGE	67.8	58.0	20.2	25.4	5.9	7.9	5.3	8.7	8.0	7.7	8.0	7.2	8.1	35.2	18.7	6.1	0.8	71.1	31.8	50.6	49.4
20764	SHADY SIDE	87.6	83.5	9.5	12.2	0.5	0.8	1.3	2.4	7.3	8.0	8.3	6.5	3.4	26.5	30.4	8.7	1.0	72.3	39.4	51.1	48.9
20769	GLENN DALE	37.5	28.9	54.0	60.6	5.4	6.2	2.2	3.5	7.0	7.1	7.0	6.6	5.4	25.5	30.9	9.5	1.0	74.7	39.3	48.3	51.7
20770	GREENBELT	40.0	33.7	41.1	42.7	12.0	14.3	6.5	9.9	6.7	5.9	5.3	5.3	9.1	35.5	24.0	7.3	1.0	79.0	33.8	48.0	52.0
20772	UPPER MARLBORO	33.2	25.3	62.1	68.7	1.6	2.2	2.0	3.0	6.7	6.7	6.8	6.8	5.7	30.2	27.9	8.4	0.8	75.5	37.3	49.0	51.0
	MARYLAND	64.0	59.0	27.9	30.1	4.0	5.3	4.3	6.4	6.5	6.6	6.7	7.1	6.4	26.9	27.4	10.7	1.7	76.0	38.1	48.4	51.6
	UNITED STATES	75.1	72.0	12.3	12.7	3.8	4.6	12.5	15.7	6.8	6.7	6.6	7.1	6.9	27.0	26.0	10.9	1.9	75.7	36.9	49.2	50.8

INCOME

ZIP CODE #	POST OFFICE NAME	2009 Per Capita Income	2009 HH Income Base	2009 Household Income Distribution (%): Less than $25,000	$25,000 to $49,999	$50,000 to $99,999	$100,000 to $149,999	$150,000 or More	Median Household Income: 2009	2014	2009 National Centile	2009 State Centile	2009 Home Value Base	2009 Home Value Distribution (%): Less than $50,000	$50,000 to $89,999	$90,000 to $174,999	$175,000 to $399,999	$400,000 or More	2009 Median Home Value
20601	WALDORF	32466	8579	5.1	13.1	44.0	29.0	8.8	83332	90294	93	71	6624	1.4	0.4	4.0	74.5	19.8	309530
20602	WALDORF	26500	8731	15.5	20.5	39.6	19.1	5.4	66469	70276	85	50	5758	0.6	0.1	8.7	84.1	6.5	259589
20603	WALDORF	35162	8495	3.2	11.4	39.2	30.3	15.9	94250	101290	96	82	6541	0.0	0.5	1.4	67.1	31.0	350596
20606	ABELL	35520	201	19.4	11.9	37.3	19.9	11.4	76488	77076	90	64	168	3.6	1.8	10.7	51.8	32.1	284375
20607	ACCOKEEK	35427	3047	6.0	9.3	38.4	28.9	17.4	94896	97026	96	83	2682	0.0	0.7	4.6	58.6	36.2	342923
20608	AQUASCO	30366	388	13.9	14.4	42.0	20.4	9.3	78629	78639	91	66	301	5.6	1.7	13.3	49.8	29.6	274167
20609	AVENUE	32051	482	21.4	17.8	35.9	17.4	7.5	64396	63420	83	49	396	2.5	2.0	14.9	50.8	29.8	277358
20611	BEL ALTON	37026	405	10.4	13.8	36.3	21.2	18.3	82387	88928	93	69	333	0.9	0.3	3.0	62.2	33.6	330128
20613	BRANDYWINE	30831	3867	10.8	16.4	42.0	22.2	8.5	76932	77691	91	64	3368	4.7	1.6	6.4	63.9	23.4	302505
20615	BROOMES ISLAND	35388	174	12.6	22.4	29.3	27.6	8.0	71439	75792	88	58	148	1.4	0.0	7.4	48.0	43.2	375610
20616	BRYANS ROAD	33312	2140	8.0	13.4	46.8	22.8	9.0	78756	83437	91	66	1830	1.5	0.3	3.3	85.2	9.7	258105
20617	BRYANTOWN	37799	370	7.0	13.2	32.4	30.8	16.5	94722	100000	96	82	334	0.0	2.4	6.0	50.6	41.0	367033
20618	BUSHWOOD	29427	456	20.0	17.1	40.8	16.2	5.9	63576	63218	82	47	375	0.5	1.6	16.0	54.1	27.7	269681
20619	CALIFORNIA	34351	3714	9.2	17.2	45.7	19.9	8.1	76545	77098	90	64	2632	2.6	0.5	13.1	67.9	16.0	282866
20620	CALLAWAY	34054	664	9.2	18.8	36.0	22.1	13.9	81554	82220	93	69	510	1.8	0.8	4.3	52.5	40.6	350000
20621	CHAPTICO	28875	463	10.6	15.3	57.7	12.7	3.7	69358	70691	86	56	406	1.5	0.2	6.2	73.4	18.7	276636
20622	CHARLOTTE HALL	34495	1474	8.1	13.0	33.1	27.4	18.5	93293	96243	96	81	1288	0.4	0.2	4.3	57.9	37.1	354017
20623	CHELTENHAM	32017	837	2.2	4.5	36.9	35.6	20.8	106976	108542	98	90	751	0.0	0.0	0.0	69.8	30.2	342442
20624	CLEMENTS	24503	330	15.8	21.8	46.7	13.3	2.4	63992	62662	82	48	280	3.2	0.4	11.4	67.1	17.9	282857
20625	COBB ISLAND	33421	442	10.0	27.8	46.2	10.9	5.2	58972	60236	76	39	380	0.0	0.0	6.6	80.5	12.9	242958
20626	COLTONS POINT	29955	288	25.3	27.8	27.4	14.9	4.5	47356	46941	55	21	229	4.8	3.1	17.5	45.0	29.7	279167
20628	DAMERON	28171	191	20.9	24.1	34.0	15.2	5.8	54263	54099	70	33	142	6.3	2.1	12.0	52.1	27.5	288000
20630	DRAYDEN	34426	136	9.6	16.9	44.1	20.6	8.8	73406	76210	89	60	103	0.0	2.9	8.7	34.0	54.4	419565
20632	FAULKNER	26861	182	14.3	17.0	47.8	14.8	6.0	63931	65150	82	48	130	1.5	0.0	1.5	84.6	12.3	261364
20634	GREAT MILLS	27788	2283	12.3	21.9	45.6	15.2	5.0	67894	69326	86	54	1569	9.8	1.3	10.6	68.3	9.9	243449
20636	HOLLYWOOD	31539	3747	7.6	18.8	43.4	20.8	9.4	77452	77097	91	65	2969	0.2	0.8	8.5	63.4	27.1	295186
20637	HUGHESVILLE	37082	1973	7.9	15.1	25.6	26.4	25.0	102679	106900	97	88	1731	0.0	0.8	8.3	43.2	47.7	388714
20639	HUNTINGTOWN	39919	4752	4.5	9.0	25.8	32.7	27.9	114795	115946	98	93	4404	0.4	0.4	2.1	35.0	62.1	454158
20640	INDIAN HEAD	27530	3565	14.4	25.6	38.2	15.3	6.4	60748	61184	78	43	2713	3.8	6.0	19.3	61.5	9.4	229972
20645	ISSUE	36638	218	11.5	9.6	49.1	24.3	5.5	77645	80927	91	65	185	0.0	0.0	3.2	47.0	49.7	398718
20646	LA PLATA	35759	7116	10.9	15.6	34.7	22.1	16.7	82407	86842	93	70	5611	0.7	0.2	7.2	57.0	34.9	350783
20650	LEONARDTOWN	30631	4950	14.5	18.7	36.8	20.0	10.0	72476	72213	88	59	3794	0.4	0.4	7.9	56.8	34.5	335132
20653	LEXINGTON PARK	26920	9051	15.3	25.9	39.0	14.3	5.5	59948	61361	77	41	4646	6.4	1.7	14.6	63.8	13.5	264811
20657	LUSBY	28199	7097	8.7	18.0	41.2	24.4	7.6	74858	78036	89	62	5909	0.9	0.2	4.9	75.8	18.3	271000
20658	MARBURY	27216	323	11.8	22.6	38.7	20.4	6.5	69948	73467	87	56	255	0.0	2.0	14.5	76.5	7.1	260938
20659	MECHANICSVILLE	27737	7807	8.9	16.2	47.4	20.4	7.1	75791	75966	90	63	6777	0.7	0.2	6.0	75.7	17.5	290769
20662	NANJEMOY	25030	1052	17.9	23.4	38.8	13.8	6.2	58951	58372	76	39	865	5.8	2.9	11.3	58.5	21.5	278297
20664	NEWBURG	25912	1260	17.1	22.7	43.5	12.7	4.0	60154	58128	78	41	967	0.2	1.8	5.8	63.3	29.0	290156
20667	PARK HALL	27711	97	8.2	38.1	42.3	8.2	3.1	56695	60523	74	37	56	17.9	0.0	0.0	80.4	1.8	230556
20670	PATUXENT RIVER	17490	474	25.3	38.0	29.1	4.9	2.7	39096	42768	30	11	8	0.0	0.0	100.0	0.0	0.0	162500
20674	PINEY POINT	33698	403	11.4	16.1	45.7	16.6	10.2	69370	70388	86	56	305	0.0	2.6	10.2	31.5	55.7	426923
20675	POMFRET	43663	556	4.3	7.4	31.7	31.7	25.0	114390	119705	98	92	516	0.0	0.2	1.4	60.3	38.2	372523
20676	PORT REPUBLIC	36444	1429	7.3	15.8	36.7	24.8	15.4	85011	89419	94	73	1233	0.5	0.0	6.0	51.3	42.3	372946
20677	PORT TOBACCO	41479	673	6.5	11.7	33.0	30.9	17.8	97746	102516	96	84	603	0.3	0.2	2.2	55.6	41.8	373947
20678	PRINCE FREDERICK	30168	3909	15.7	18.6	32.9	22.1	10.6	75142	77730	89	62	2878	2.1	0.7	5.0	58.2	33.9	343190
20680	RIDGE	28891	650	27.4	24.6	25.4	16.2	6.5	47712	47243	56	22	477	3.4	0.4	10.1	46.8	39.4	346842
20684	SAINT INIGOES	31216	573	10.8	24.6	36.0	21.1	7.5	65095	64958	83	49	448	2.5	2.5	7.8	50.4	36.8	338542
20685	SAINT LEONARD	34322	2445	7.3	17.0	31.6	31.5	12.6	89101	94300	95	78	2133	0.4	0.4	5.6	53.5	40.1	356837
20687	SCOTLAND	21888	190	33.7	27.4	26.8	11.1	1.1	36559	38659	22	7	125	4.0	0.0	13.6	44.8	37.6	353030
20688	SOLOMONS	41552	1114	9.2	20.2	38.4	19.5	12.7	68847	72111	86	55	760	0.5	1.3	4.2	44.5	49.5	397516
20689	SUNDERLAND	36914	438	8.4	11.4	31.1	32.4	16.7	98159	101994	96	85	395	1.3	0.3	0.8	41.8	55.9	421364
20690	TALL TIMBERS	36187	389	13.4	16.5	44.2	14.9	11.1	66701	66426	85	51	293	0.0	2.0	10.2	31.7	56.0	427778
20692	VALLEY LEE	34400	202	9.4	18.8	42.1	19.8	9.9	73814	76653	89	60	150	0.7	2.0	7.3	38.0	52.0	407895
20693	WELCOME	37301	553	6.7	16.1	38.3	25.1	13.7	85036	89684	94	73	475	1.9	0.0	6.9	53.9	37.3	356786
20695	WHITE PLAINS	35765	3276	4.9	11.3	42.0	26.6	15.2	88860	94272	95	77	2707	1.3	0.4	1.4	73.3	23.7	343587
20701	ANNAPOLIS JUNCTION	18423	15	20.0	13.3	40.0	20.0	6.7	66333	71832	84	50	12	8.3	8.3	41.7	41.7	0.0	150000
20705	BELTSVILLE	29521	7472	11.0	18.8	42.3	20.4	7.5	72096	75007	88	59	4696	0.0	0.8	3.8	80.1	15.3	296476
20706	LANHAM	28039	13908	10.1	20.4	44.1	17.8	7.6	70839	74616	87	58	8813	0.5	1.2	5.3	82.1	10.8	269062
20707	LAUREL	32616	11783	9.9	23.1	44.5	15.9	6.6	67714	70472	85	53	6904	0.9	0.7	11.2	79.8	7.4	244808
20708	LAUREL	30980	10553	10.2	26.4	43.0	13.9	6.5	63957	66399	82	48	3695	0.4	0.1	7.5	76.4	15.7	313295
20710	BLADENSBURG	19184	3076	26.2	34.9	32.7	5.3	0.9	41294	43649	37	13	784	0.0	1.1	9.7	88.3	0.9	218499
20711	LOTHIAN	30624	2440	16.7	21.9	34.3	17.8	9.3	62016	64952	80	46	2108	30.6	7.7	13.4	13.0	35.3	161111
20712	MOUNT RAINIER	20137	3590	24.9	36.3	31.2	6.1	1.5	43008	44726	42	15	949	0.0	0.6	16.0	83.1	0.2	214130
20714	NORTH BEACH	33475	1585	8.5	18.4	43.2	25.1	4.8	74152	78117	89	61	1144	0.0	0.0	8.0	74.3	17.7	279515
20715	BOWIE	35865	8899	3.2	11.5	45.6	25.6	14.2	87461	88767	94	76	7871	0.1	0.2	0.9	87.8	11.0	283711
20716	BOWIE	38572	8240	4.3	12.4	43.4	27.9	12.0	87180	85395	94	76	5717	0.4	0.0	1.2	82.9	15.6	277527
20720	BOWIE	41495	6767	3.6	4.9	37.7	27.6	26.3	105477	108250	97	89	6034	0.0	0.0	0.8	63.1	36.1	352964
20721	BOWIE	48851	8896	2.4	4.1	29.5	27.3	36.7	122533	121530	99	94	7793	0.0	0.2	1.5	42.8	55.5	419838
20722	BRENTWOOD	19764	1748	19.0	25.8	44.2	8.8	2.2	53950	57171	70	32	1205	1.4	0.5	24.8	72.6	0.7	200182
20723	LAUREL	38734	9915	4.7	14.0	35.1	26.6	19.6	92524	96003	96	80	7042	1.9	1.2	3.6	53.2	40.1	357336
20724	LAUREL	37711	6032	4.7	15.1	45.2	23.9	11.1	78605	85885	91	65	4186	4.0	1.8	2.1	72.8	19.4	305800
20732	CHESAPEAKE BEACH	32802	3705	7.0	13.5	41.4	28.5	9.6	83396	87873	93	71	3140	0.6	0.9	5.8	67.2	25.6	336197
20733	CHURCHTON	34422	1324	7.0	10.0	41.9	31.0	10.0	88229	95682	95	77	1181	0.0	0.1	3.2	64.0	32.7	338218
20735	CLINTON	32387	11996	7.0	10.6	42.5	28.1	11.9	87118	87278	94	75	10385	0.7	0.6	1.6	84.1	13.0	288916
20736	OWINGS	36848	3177	4.8	10.1	33.7	30.7	20.8	101668	104532	97	87	2884	1.5	0.3	3.4	39.0	55.8	425419
20737	RIVERDALE	19933	6146	14.8	29.0	42.3	11.0	2.8	56197	60260	73	36	2969	0.4	0.5	14.7	81.5	2.9	221123
20740	COLLEGE PARK	25398	8872	18.1	19.0	43.1	13.4	6.4	62963	65335	81	47	4806	0.6	0.4	9.0	81.8	8.1	249761
20742	COLLEGE PARK	14577	62	61.3	14.5	11.3	11.3	1.6	20896	21381	2	1	19	0.0	0.0	5.3	84.2	10.5	342308
20743	CAPITOL HEIGHTS	21815	14526	18.8	26.9	41.8	9.9	2.6	53784	57034	69	32	8961	2.5	1.5	20.9	74.0	1.1	210142
20744	FORT WASHINGTON	36226	18747	5.8	12.3	41.9	24.2	15.9	86628	86556	94	75	14442	0.2	0.3	3.6	76.3	19.6	301987
20745	OXON HILL	23067	10490	17.3	32.8	36.7	10.3	2.9	49937	51356	61	25	4612	0.2	3.0	13.2	79.1	4.5	226993
20746	SUITLAND	24180	11340	14.9	31.6	41.2	9.3	3.1	52800	55435	68	30	4534	0.6	1.9	11.6	82.0	3.9	236594
20747	DISTRICT HEIGHTS	24529	15113	13.8	28.5	43.3	11.8	2.6	57784	61361	75	38	7518	0.4	1.0	9.3	88.1	1.2	232581
20748	TEMPLE HILLS	28249	14515	10.7	25.8	44.3	13.6	5.5	62994	65645	81	47	8452	0.4	1.3	8.6	85.5	4.2	248503
20751	DEALE	31888	850	9.6	10.8	53.2	20.6	5.8	74061	79385	89	61	711	0.3	0.1	4.5	57.2	37.8	354474
20754	DUNKIRK	42425	2340	4.6	8.1	22.4	33.0	32.0	123450	124284	99	94	2220	3.0	0.5	4.5	25.8	66.1	466791
20755	FORT GEORGE G MEADE	16732	2617	8.3	39.7	42.4	7.9	1.7	51162	51103	64	28	70	0.0	0.0	0.0	71.4	28.6	357143
20758	FRIENDSHIP	45260	364	4.7	10.7	37.6	29.4	17.6	94585	101674	96	82	312	0.0	0.0	3.8	34.6	61.5	500000
20759	FULTON	61872	972	3.1	3.8	14.8	28.7	49.6	149050	149318	100	98	885	0.3	0.3	0.3	10.6	88.4	642708
20762	ANDREWS AIR FORCE BA	18273	1478	5.1	39.3	44.8	8.9	2.0	54461	57587	70	33	16	0.0	0.0	0.0	100.0	0.0	213636
20763	SAVAGE	25720	881	12.5	31.6	38.5	12.9	4.5	55808	54936	72	35	299	0.0	0.0	0.7	80.9	18.4	350000
20764	SHADY SIDE	41728	1584	5.2	14.9	38.7	29.6	11.6	85778	95841	94	74	1354	0.0	0.0	3.8	75.7	20.5	288740
20769	GLENN DALE	36957	2110	5.9	9.6	34.4	31.2	19.0	100187	101595	97	86	1712	0.0	0.0	1.3	58.6	40.1	368284
20770	GREENBELT	30449	9307	12.4	28.3	41.7	11.8	5.8	57470	60670	75	37	4178	1.5	12.3	37.2	42.6	6.4	171884
20772	UPPER MARLBORO	36844	14993	5.1	10.4	43.1	25.1	16.3	88315	88684	95	77	12627	1.4	1.2	3.6	74.3	19.5	287837
	MARYLAND	32538		15.1	20.5	36.5	16.4	11.5	67267	70086				1.9	2.6	14.3	53.1	28.2	289711
	UNITED STATES	27277		20.9	24.4	35.3	11.7	7.6	54719	56938				9.3	13.1	31.6	32.6	13.5	162279

ZIP CODE #	POST OFFICE NAME	FINANCIAL SERVICES: Auto Loan	FINANCIAL SERVICES: Home Loan	FINANCIAL SERVICES: Invest-ments	FINANCIAL SERVICES: Retire-ment Plans	THE HOME: Home Improvements: Home Repair	THE HOME: Home Improvements: Lawn & Garden	THE HOME: Furnishings: Comput-ers & Hard-ware-Personal	THE HOME: Furnishings: Major Appli-ances	THE HOME: Furnishings: TV, Radio, Sound Equip-ment	THE HOME: Furnishings: Furni-ture	ENTERTAINMENT: Dine out/ Carry out	ENTERTAINMENT: Sports Equip-ment	ENTERTAINMENT: Fees & Tickets	ENTERTAINMENT: Toys & Games	ENTERTAINMENT: Travel	ENTERTAINMENT: Cable TV	PERSONAL: Apparel & Services	PERSONAL: Auto Repairs	PERSONAL: Health Insur-ance	PERSONAL: Pets & Supplies
20601	WALDORF	130	149	133	146	145	129	134	132	127	139	129	104	143	133	138	123	92	129	121	152
20602	WALDORF	104	111	99	110	107	99	107	102	103	109	105	81	110	106	106	101	74	103	98	120
20603	WALDORF	149	169	147	170	163	145	151	149	142	160	145	120	162	150	155	136	104	144	133	171
20606	ABELL	114	140	126	139	136	140	120	126	123	121	124	94	137	123	133	126	87	123	135	147
20607	ACCOKEEK	136	181	178	174	183	160	151	156	143	154	145	118	174	146	169	142	106	149	145	174
20608	AQUASCO	105	137	129	133	135	130	115	120	114	116	116	89	134	116	129	116	83	117	122	137
20609	AVENUE	109	112	128	111	114	126	102	116	106	100	106	85	105	104	111	111	73	111	122	134
20611	BEL ALTON	128	165	169	165	170	153	139	147	133	146	135	108	160	133	157	132	97	139	138	166
20613	BRANDYWINE	105	142	143	134	145	129	118	123	114	118	115	91	137	116	133	115	84	118	119	137
20615	BROOMES ISLAND	102	144	149	134	149	127	119	124	114	119	115	91	140	115	136	114	85	119	117	136
20616	BRYANS ROAD	128	147	127	144	141	127	127	129	121	136	123	101	135	127	131	116	87	123	116	148
20617	BRYANTOWN	129	166	171	166	171	154	140	148	134	147	136	109	161	134	158	133	98	140	139	167
20618	BUSHWOOD	115	101	144	99	107	124	97	118	101	93	100	87	90	97	105	106	67	110	118	137
20619	CALIFORNIA	112	131	123	129	129	119	119	118	114	121	116	92	128	117	125	112	83	116	113	136
20620	CALLAWAY	125	147	136	148	144	133	132	131	126	136	128	103	144	129	139	123	92	128	123	152
20621	CHAPTICO	107	120	100	118	114	106	106	107	102	111	103	84	111	107	108	99	72	102	99	123
20622	CHARLOTTE HALL	142	178	159	178	173	158	150	153	142	157	145	120	170	147	163	138	104	146	141	176
20623	CHELTENHAM	154	198	186	195	198	168	164	168	154	176	156	133	189	162	179	147	115	157	147	186
20624	CLEMENTS	93	106	92	109	103	104	94	98	93	94	94	76	102	95	100	93	65	94	98	115
20625	COBB ISLAND	99	116	109	113	115	106	112	108	109	109	111	85	120	110	117	109	79	110	108	125
20626	COLTONS POINT	87	99	94	96	99	107	87	96	94	86	93	67	96	91	95	99	64	93	110	110
20628	DAMERON	104	97	124	98	102	109	95	106	95	93	95	80	91	93	100	98	66	102	104	124
20630	DRAYDEN	113	131	133	132	135	134	116	124	118	121	118	89	129	115	128	120	83	120	131	142
20632	FAULKNER	96	119	113	112	118	104	102	104	98	105	100	77	112	101	109	97	71	101	97	117
20634	GREAT MILLS	109	116	97	113	109	97	107	104	101	114	104	83	109	108	105	97	73	101	93	120
20636	HOLLYWOOD	116	136	125	139	135	129	120	124	116	123	117	96	131	118	129	115	83	119	119	144
20637	HUGHESVILLE	136	185	197	181	193	170	153	161	146	157	147	118	181	147	176	145	108	153	153	179
20639	HUNTINGTOWN	164	207	190	207	203	183	174	178	164	183	167	139	197	169	190	159	120	170	162	204
20640	INDIAN HEAD	98	111	106	108	111	108	103	104	103	102	104	79	111	105	109	105	74	104	107	120
20645	ISSUE	108	127	131	127	132	134	110	121	113	116	113	84	124	109	124	117	79	116	131	138
20646	LA PLATA	130	154	151	156	155	146	139	141	135	143	136	107	153	135	150	133	97	138	138	163
20650	LEONARDTOWN	115	131	120	132	128	124	117	120	114	121	116	92	126	117	123	113	82	116	116	139
20653	LEXINGTON PARK	104	94	84	97	89	84	104	93	101	106	103	77	99	105	96	97	73	99	88	111
20657	LUSBY	122	139	120	133	133	117	122	122	115	130	117	95	129	122	124	111	83	116	109	138
20658	MARBURY	101	126	112	125	121	123	106	111	108	108	109	83	123	109	118	110	77	109	117	129
20659	MECHANICSVILLE	112	136	119	136	131	123	116	119	112	120	113	93	129	116	125	110	81	114	112	138
20662	NANJEMOY	93	109	111	105	112	108	96	104	95	92	95	77	103	97	104	98	68	98	102	116
20664	NEWBURG	107	101	125	99	105	112	95	109	97	95	97	80	92	95	101	100	66	103	108	126
20667	PARK HALL	82	96	91	94	95	88	93	89	90	91	91	70	99	91	97	90	66	91	89	104
20670	PATUXENT RIVER	89	46	35	54	41	39	84	58	79	78	83	58	64	95	60	72	58	74	52	71
20674	PINEY POINT	127	116	161	115	125	141	110	133	114	107	113	96	105	109	121	121	77	124	135	153
20675	POMFRET	164	203	203	208	207	190	173	181	165	184	167	136	196	165	192	161	120	172	170	208
20676	PORT REPUBLIC	139	172	163	173	173	157	147	152	140	153	142	117	165	144	160	137	102	144	141	172
20677	PORT TOBACCO	146	183	184	185	187	172	156	164	150	163	151	122	177	150	174	148	108	156	156	187
20678	PRINCE FREDERICK	113	139	132	135	138	122	123	122	117	125	118	94	135	120	131	114	86	120	114	139
20680	RIDGE	104	89	133	87	96	112	86	107	90	83	89	78	79	86	94	95	60	99	107	124
20684	SAINT INIGOES	102	115	120	116	118	119	104	111	105	107	105	80	113	103	113	107	73	108	116	128
20685	SAINT LEONARD	131	167	155	165	165	147	140	144	132	146	134	112	159	137	153	128	97	136	131	163
20687	SCOTLAND	80	64	103	63	70	85	64	81	67	60	66	59	55	64	69	71	44	75	80	94
20688	SOLOMONS	115	127	127	128	128	126	123	122	123	124	124	91	131	120	129	125	87	123	130	142
20689	SUNDERLAND	136	174	177	176	178	162	146	154	140	154	141	115	169	140	165	137	102	146	145	175
20690	TALL TIMBERS	134	108	174	106	118	142	108	137	113	101	111	100	93	107	117	120	74	126	135	159
20692	VALLEY LEE	115	132	131	133	134	131	119	124	119	124	120	91	131	117	129	120	84	121	127	143
20693	WELCOME	125	169	175	162	175	153	141	147	135	143	136	109	164	136	160	135	100	141	139	164
20695	WHITE PLAINS	142	167	146	163	161	143	144	145	136	153	138	114	155	143	150	130	98	138	130	165
20701	ANNAPOLIS JUNCTION	112	107	93	103	102	102	105	104	105	109	105	79	101	109	100	105	73	105	102	124
20705	BELTSVILLE	112	115	111	115	114	104	117	108	114	117	116	86	120	117	116	112	83	113	105	127
20706	LANHAM	105	120	117	117	120	109	114	110	111	114	113	85	122	113	118	111	81	112	107	127
20707	LAUREL	108	109	104	111	107	101	113	104	110	113	111	83	114	112	111	107	79	109	102	123
20708	LAUREL	114	93	84	98	88	86	113	96	110	113	112	81	104	114	100	107	79	107	94	117
20710	BLADENSBURG	68	54	52	56	53	49	72	59	70	69	72	50	65	71	64	68	52	69	58	72
20711	LOTHIAN	129	112	123	108	111	127	110	122	114	110	114	92	100	116	108	119	77	117	123	145
20712	MOUNT RAINIER	72	57	53	60	54	54	75	61	74	72	76	52	68	76	66	73	54	72	63	76
20714	NORTH BEACH	117	131	112	127	125	111	118	117	111	125	114	92	123	118	119	107	80	112	105	133
20715	BOWIE	125	171	175	163	176	151	142	147	135	144	137	110	166	138	161	134	101	141	137	162
20716	BOWIE	140	147	134	149	142	129	142	134	136	147	139	109	147	142	141	131	99	136	124	157
20720	BOWIE	170	215	207	219	216	188	179	184	168	193	170	145	207	174	196	160	125	172	161	208
20721	BOWIE	192	237	230	244	239	210	203	206	191	218	193	163	232	197	221	182	141	195	183	235
20722	BRENTWOOD	80	87	80	84	85	81	85	82	83	85	85	63	88	84	86	83	60	84	83	96
20723	LAUREL	157	170	156	174	166	148	158	153	150	168	153	123	167	158	159	143	110	150	137	177
20724	LAUREL	135	127	113	130	121	115	136	123	132	137	134	101	133	137	128	128	95	129	119	147
20732	CHESAPEAKE BEACH	130	151	131	150	145	135	131	134	125	137	127	105	141	131	137	122	90	128	123	154
20733	CHURCHTON	123	158	147	156	156	140	132	136	126	138	128	105	151	129	145	123	92	130	125	155
20735	CLINTON	123	160	153	155	160	142	135	139	129	138	131	106	155	132	149	128	95	133	131	156
20736	OWINGS	144	185	184	183	188	167	155	161	147	163	149	122	178	151	173	144	108	153	149	181
20737	RIVERDALE	81	85	82	84	84	77	93	84	91	89	94	67	95	91	92	90	69	90	83	97
20740	COLLEGE PARK	97	95	95	96	95	90	111	94	104	102	105	77	106	104	102	102	75	102	94	112
20742	COLLEGE PARK	57	35	34	39	33	39	74	46	63	55	64	43	52	62	48	60	45	58	48	59
20743	CAPITOL HEIGHTS	81	83	78	83	80	82	84	80	88	83	89	60	87	87	83	91	63	84	87	98
20744	FORT WASHINGTON	134	161	157	158	162	144	144	144	138	148	140	110	159	141	154	135	101	141	135	163
20745	OXON HILL	80	75	73	78	73	74	86	76	88	83	89	60	85	87	82	89	63	84	82	93
20746	SUITLAND	81	80	77	81	78	77	87	79	89	84	90	61	88	89	84	91	64	86	83	96
20747	DISTRICT HEIGHTS	87	87	82	87	85	81	93	85	92	91	93	67	93	93	90	91	66	91	85	101
20748	TEMPLE HILLS	95	106	104	104	106	99	103	100	102	102	103	76	110	103	106	103	74	102	100	116
20751	DEALE	113	132	122	133	131	128	116	121	114	117	114	93	127	116	125	114	81	117	119	141
20754	DUNKIRK	167	211	217	218	217	197	177	187	168	190	170	142	205	169	199	164	124	175	172	213
20755	FORT GEORGE G MEADE	102	53	40	62	48	45	96	67	90	89	95	66	73	109	69	83	67	85	60	81
20758	FRIENDSHIP	145	181	186	187	187	170	153	162	147	164	148	122	176	146	173	143	107	153	151	185
20759	FULTON	236	313	323	329	324	281	256	267	239	279	242	210	309	244	292	228	182	247	232	301
20762	ANDREWS AIR FORCE BA	109	57	42	66	51	48	102	71	96	95	101	71	78	116	74	88	71	90	64	86
20763	SAVAGE	100	89	77	91	84	80	100	88	96	100	98	73	93	100	90	92	68	94	85	106
20764	SHADY SIDE	145	182	161	182	176	160	153	156	145	160	148	123	173	150	166	140	106	149	142	179
20769	GLENN DALE	144	180	180	176	182	161	158	158	151	161	153	122	178	155	172	149	112	155	148	178
20770	GREENBELT	101	87	85	93	86	84	104	90	102	103	103	74	98	103	96	100	73	99	92	110
20772	UPPER MARLBORO	139	163	155	162	161	144	147	145	140	151	143	114	160	145	155	137	103	142	135	166
	MARYLAND	116	125	123	126	125	119	122	119	120	123	121	92	127	121	124	119	86	120	118	139
	UNITED STATES	100	100	100	100	100	100	100	100	100	100	100	100	100	100	100	100	100	100	100	100

MARYLAND

POPULATION CHANGE

20774-21084

#	POST OFFICE NAME	COUNTY FIPS CODE	POPULATION 2000	POPULATION 2009	POPULATION 2014	2000-2009 ANNUAL RATE % Rate	2000-2009 ANNUAL RATE State Centile	HOUSEHOLDS 2000	HOUSEHOLDS 2009	HOUSEHOLDS 2014	HOUSEHOLDS % Annual Rate 2000-2009	HOUSEHOLDS 2009 Average HH Size	FAMILIES 2000	FAMILIES 2009	FAMILIES % Annual Rate 2000-2009
20774	UPPER MARLBORO	033	34011	40833	42973	2.0	82	12381	14780	15555	1.9	2.75	8881	10281	1.6
20776	HARWOOD	003	3528	3680	3797	0.5	35	1264	1342	1393	0.6	2.74	1021	1054	0.3
20777	HIGHLAND	027	3074	3261	3390	0.6	38	1002	1080	1127	0.8	3.01	887	936	0.6
20778	WEST RIVER	003	1396	1532	1590	1.0	54	507	562	586	1.1	2.72	413	446	0.8
20779	TRACYS LANDING	003	1079	1099	1099	0.2	23	433	450	454	0.4	2.44	301	300	0.0
20781	HYATTSVILLE	033	12776	12830	12674	0.0	12	4420	4370	4319	-0.1	2.89	2855	2681	-0.7
20782	HYATTSVILLE	033	29405	29302	28760	0.0	12	11031	10938	10749	-0.1	2.62	6821	6403	-0.7
20783	HYATTSVILLE	033	45716	46465	45761	0.2	23	14795	14618	14354	-0.1	3.14	10044	9484	-0.6
20784	HYATTSVILLE	033	23904	24309	24064	0.2	23	8306	8450	8380	0.2	2.87	5843	5694	-0.3
20785	HYATTSVILLE	033	40139	40040	39539	0.0	12	13505	13520	13372	0.0	2.95	10306	9973	-0.4
20794	JESSUP	027	13991	14447	14761	0.3	27	2813	2961	3078	0.6	2.77	1977	1978	0.0
20812	GLEN ECHO	031	242	245	247	0.1	17	91	90	90	-0.1	2.72	64	61	-0.5
20814	BETHESDA	031	25548	26855	27514	0.5	35	12243	12977	13382	0.6	2.00	5919	5729	-0.4
20815	CHEVY CHASE	031	27369	27751	27802	0.1	17	12243	12403	12425	0.1	2.21	7248	6949	-0.5
20816	BETHESDA	031	15261	15568	15686	0.2	23	6137	6268	6324	0.2	2.47	4340	4250	-0.2
20817	BETHESDA	031	32832	33705	34333	0.3	27	11890	12188	12406	0.3	2.75	9421	9412	0.0
20818	CABIN JOHN	031	1734	1757	1763	0.1	17	668	676	677	0.1	2.60	499	486	-0.3
20832	OLNEY	031	25200	26753	27105	0.6	38	8342	8775	8883	0.5	3.03	6887	7070	0.3
20833	BROOKEVILLE	031	6396	7102	7430	1.1	58	2072	2281	2382	1.0	3.11	1810	1953	0.8
20837	POOLESVILLE	031	5836	6027	6094	0.3	27	1874	1938	1958	0.4	3.11	1579	1596	0.1
20838	BARNESVILLE	031	207	234	246	1.3	64	67	76	80	1.4	3.05	51	56	1.0
20839	BEALLSVILLE	031	388	427	444	1.0	54	144	158	165	1.0	2.70	110	117	0.7
20841	BOYDS	031	3095	8615	10583	11.7	100	1028	2890	3547	11.8	2.98	785	2107	11.3
20842	DICKERSON	031	1733	1959	2074	1.3	64	672	764	812	1.4	2.55	514	569	1.1
20850	ROCKVILLE	031	30891	41192	44843	3.2	96	11281	15182	16592	3.3	2.63	7888	10387	3.0
20851	ROCKVILLE	031	13034	13044	13032	0.0	12	4640	4640	4637	0.0	2.79	3212	3074	-0.5
20852	ROCKVILLE	031	39256	43396	45139	1.1	58	17791	19563	20319	1.0	2.18	9791	10186	0.4
20853	ROCKVILLE	031	26074	26743	26949	0.3	27	9027	9218	9278	0.2	2.89	7206	7154	-0.1
20854	POTOMAC	031	48944	51267	52389	0.5	35	15853	16573	16909	0.5	3.04	14127	14531	0.3
20855	DERWOOD	031	14874	14986	15191	0.1	17	4784	4780	4839	0.0	3.10	4054	4003	-0.1
20860	SANDY SPRING	031	1209	1335	1382	1.1	58	450	498	518	1.1	2.57	350	375	0.7
20861	ASHTON	031	2162	2509	2661	1.6	73	747	863	915	1.6	2.81	552	612	1.1
20862	BRINKLOW	031	374	443	473	1.8	78	121	142	151	1.7	3.10	104	119	1.5
20866	BURTONSVILLE	031	12032	12845	13059	0.7	41	4252	4459	4514	0.5	2.85	3058	3097	0.1
20868	SPENCERVILLE	031	232	238	239	0.3	27	66	68	68	0.3	3.47	57	57	0.0
20871	CLARKSBURG	031	2829	9658	12011	14.2	100	1009	3445	4283	14.2	2.80	820	2694	13.7
20872	DAMASCUS	031	11578	12446	12810	0.8	47	3852	4151	4279	0.8	3.00	3128	3273	0.5
20874	GERMANTOWN	031	48687	56406	59505	1.6	73	18485	21227	22362	1.5	2.66	12593	13719	0.9
20876	GERMANTOWN	031	20039	23117	24592	1.6	73	6937	7922	8406	1.4	2.92	5101	5639	1.1
20877	GAITHERSBURG	031	33224	35919	37173	0.8	47	11662	12250	12626	0.5	2.88	7685	7728	0.1
20878	GAITHERSBURG	031	55614	63418	66587	1.4	67	19321	22101	23280	1.5	2.87	14556	15937	1.0
20879	GAITHERSBURG	031	25122	27250	27964	0.9	49	8399	9009	9219	0.8	3.02	6207	6443	0.4
20882	GAITHERSBURG	031	13944	15932	16896	1.5	69	4325	4937	5237	1.4	3.22	3831	4300	1.3
20886	MONTGOMERY VILLAGE	031	29270	30071	30277	0.3	27	11309	11466	11510	0.1	2.61	7479	7237	-0.4
20895	KENSINGTON	031	20150	20528	20777	0.2	23	7902	8045	8159	0.2	2.49	5221	5042	-0.4
20901	SILVER SPRING	031	36457	37029	37141	0.2	23	13400	13463	13476	0.1	2.74	9084	8707	-0.5
20902	SILVER SPRING	031	42600	43943	44576	0.3	27	14788	15061	15241	0.2	2.90	10255	9972	-0.3
20903	SILVER SPRING	031	17958	19378	19745	0.8	47	5549	5824	5914	0.5	3.32	4186	4252	0.2
20904	SILVER SPRING	031	47837	55159	57703	1.6	73	17716	20002	20820	1.3	2.74	12470	13613	1.0
20905	SILVER SPRING	031	18234	18883	19148	0.4	30	5843	6061	6146	0.4	3.11	4977	5048	0.2
20906	SILVER SPRING	031	59762	62315	63233	0.5	35	23231	24196	24595	0.4	2.55	14752	14447	-0.2
20910	SILVER SPRING	031	37641	39171	39768	0.4	30	17293	18083	18410	0.5	2.13	8449	8147	-0.4
20912	TAKOMA PARK	031	24210	24314	24295	0.0	12	9282	9190	9164	-0.1	2.58	5432	5098	-0.7
21001	ABERDEEN	025	20782	22787	23414	1.0	54	8110	9110	9428	1.3	2.49	5640	6064	0.8
21005	ABERDEEN PROVING GRO	025	3225	2932	2832	-1.0	1	877	788	767	-1.2	3.33	782	707	-1.1
21009	ABINGDON	025	23501	27989	29822	1.9	79	8737	10507	11250	2.0	2.66	6430	7471	1.6
21010	GUNPOWDER	025	864	692	650	-2.4	0	230	182	171	-2.5	3.79	226	178	-2.5
21012	ARNOLD	003	21014	20668	20470	-0.2	8	7492	7481	7449	0.0	2.73	5754	5574	-0.3
21013	BALDWIN	005	5263	5476	5540	0.4	30	1792	1888	1917	0.6	2.90	1563	1618	0.4
21014	BEL AIR	025	33559	37367	38833	1.2	61	12433	13990	14647	1.3	2.63	9274	10136	1.0
21015	BEL AIR	025	23672	29447	31561	2.4	91	8265	10408	11185	2.5	2.83	6530	7936	2.1
21017	BELCAMP	025	5116	6121	6453	2.0	82	1963	2411	2566	2.2	2.48	1330	1567	1.8
21028	CHURCHVILLE	025	2932	3180	3239	0.9	49	1085	1205	1236	1.1	2.64	909	989	0.9
21029	CLARKSVILLE	027	7903	12054	13479	4.7	99	2383	3460	3859	4.1	3.48	2171	3128	4.0
21030	COCKEYSVILLE	005	22802	23547	23973	0.3	27	10196	10504	10681	0.3	2.23	5397	5260	-0.3
21031	HUNT VALLEY	005	62	81	100	2.9	95	1	2	3	7.8	2.50	1	1	0.0
21032	CROWNSVILLE	003	7991	8640	8911	0.8	47	2869	3169	3293	1.1	2.59	2170	2324	0.7
21034	DARLINGTON	025	3208	3366	3382	0.5	35	1215	1308	1324	0.8	2.56	928	968	0.5
21035	DAVIDSONVILLE	003	7201	7545	7674	0.5	35	2406	2565	2623	0.7	2.94	2092	2189	0.5
21036	DAYTON	027	1146	1230	1330	0.8	47	362	395	429	0.9	3.09	325	348	0.7
21037	EDGEWATER	003	16816	19673	20811	1.7	76	6374	7607	8100	1.9	2.57	4563	5256	1.5
21040	EDGEWOOD	025	22350	24969	26057	1.2	61	8008	9087	9534	1.4	2.74	5950	6557	1.1
21042	ELLICOTT CITY	027	35196	38629	40507	1.0	54	11843	13175	13875	1.2	2.92	10033	10898	0.9
21043	ELLICOTT CITY	027	31707	38875	42449	2.2	87	11988	14550	15875	2.1	2.64	8181	9559	1.7
21044	COLUMBIA	027	40285	42525	44386	0.6	38	15990	17011	17770	0.7	2.44	10352	10370	0.0
21045	COLUMBIA	027	37519	39357	40576	0.5	35	14301	15204	15746	0.7	2.57	10019	10117	0.1
21046	COLUMBIA	027	15079	15411	15697	0.2	23	5916	6138	6285	0.4	2.49	4003	3919	-0.2
21047	FALLSTON	025	10766	11777	12085	1.0	54	3728	4175	4315	1.2	2.82	3245	3573	1.0
21048	FINKSBURG	013	10211	11342	11792	1.1	58	3572	4008	4178	1.3	2.83	2966	3253	1.0
21050	FOREST HILL	025	15108	18227	19395	2.0	82	5270	6534	7011	2.4	2.77	4206	5076	2.1
21051	FORK	005	523	551	564	0.6	38	186	197	203	0.6	2.79	157	163	0.4
21053	FREELAND	005	2951	3248	3371	1.0	54	1024	1134	1182	1.1	2.86	848	916	0.8
21054	GAMBRILLS	003	9872	12153	13080	2.3	89	3416	4305	4655	2.5	2.82	2703	3286	2.1
21056	GIBSON ISLAND	003	310	315	315	0.2	23	136	141	142	0.4	2.23	101	101	0.0
21057	GLEN ARM	005	4164	4241	4251	0.2	23	1497	1520	1527	0.2	2.53	1141	1121	-0.2
21060	GLEN BURNIE	003	27198	27924	28435	0.3	27	10656	11128	11393	0.5	2.48	7003	7006	0.0
21061	GLEN BURNIE	003	50096	51068	51336	0.2	23	19844	20501	20704	0.4	2.48	13051	12902	-0.1
21071	GLYNDON	005	365	379	384	0.4	30	130	136	137	0.5	2.79	100	101	0.1
21074	HAMPSTEAD	013	13485	16165	17288	2.0	82	4804	5776	6191	2.0	2.80	3761	4393	1.7
21075	ELKRIDGE	027	20043	24990	27392	2.4	91	7494	9263	10142	2.3	2.67	5263	6239	1.9
21076	HANOVER	003	8629	10563	11487	2.2	87	2970	3775	4145	2.6	2.78	2323	2842	2.2
21077	HARMANS	003	210	233	243	1.1	58	86	97	102	1.3	2.40	70	78	1.2
21078	HAVRE DE GRACE	025	15193	17829	19818	1.7	76	6024	7062	7801	1.7	2.49	4007	4616	1.5
21082	HYDES	005	625	648	661	0.4	30	225	235	240	0.5	2.76	191	195	0.2
21084	JARRETTSVILLE	025	6668	7113	7225	0.7	41	2244	2451	2507	1.0	2.90	1928	2068	0.8
	MARYLAND					0.9					0.9	2.60			0.5
	UNITED STATES					1.0					1.1	2.59			0.9

ZIP CODE #	POST OFFICE NAME	RACE (%) White 2000	White 2009	Black 2000	Black 2009	Asian/Pacific 2000	Asian/Pacific 2009	% Hispanic Origin 2000	% Hispanic Origin 2009	2009 AGE DISTRIBUTION (%) 0-4	5-9	10-14	15-19	20-24	25-44	45-64	65-84	85+	18+	MEDIAN AGE 2009	% 2009 Males	% 2009 Females
20774	UPPER MARLBORO	8.1	5.8	88.1	89.8	1.2	1.3	1.4	1.8	6.3	6.8	7.2	7.0	4.9	28.3	29.9	8.7	0.9	75.2	38.5	46.0	54.0
20776	HARWOOD	85.2	79.6	12.6	17.3	0.5	0.7	1.6	2.8	5.1	6.0	7.3	6.9	4.1	21.3	35.8	11.9	1.7	77.3	44.6	49.4	50.6
20777	HIGHLAND	90.3	85.5	2.9	4.1	5.1	7.9	1.3	2.4	6.1	7.7	9.4	8.5	3.8	16.5	34.0	13.0	1.2	71.1	43.6	49.6	50.4
20778	WEST RIVER	86.9	81.8	11.5	15.9	0.4	0.6	1.6	2.8	5.9	7.2	8.4	6.7	3.6	18.8	36.6	11.3	1.6	73.6	44.6	49.3	50.7
20779	TRACYS LANDING	93.0	90.0	4.9	7.0	0.4	0.5	0.5	0.8	3.6	4.5	5.7	6.1	3.4	19.6	37.7	17.2	2.2	82.3	48.3	50.0	50.0
20781	HYATTSVILLE	36.3	30.1	44.9	44.5	3.1	3.5	21.7	30.9	7.8	7.2	6.6	7.7	8.6	30.0	23.9	6.8	1.2	73.8	32.1	49.4	50.6
20782	HYATTSVILLE	26.1	22.8	54.7	52.6	3.8	4.3	18.2	25.2	7.5	6.6	6.1	6.4	7.9	30.4	23.6	9.3	2.1	75.9	34.4	47.7	52.3
20783	HYATTSVILLE	31.1	29.7	39.3	35.0	5.7	5.8	39.2	48.8	8.0	7.3	6.4	6.6	7.9	33.8	21.4	7.3	1.1	74.4	32.3	51.4	48.6
20784	HYATTSVILLE	21.0	16.1	69.4	71.6	2.8	3.1	8.0	11.6	7.5	7.1	7.3	7.6	7.4	27.5	26.5	7.9	1.0	73.6	34.4	48.1	51.9
20785	HYATTSVILLE	10.9	8.4	84.3	85.5	1.1	1.3	2.9	4.3	9.5	8.6	7.9	8.4	8.3	28.3	21.7	6.7	0.6	68.9	29.5	46.2	53.8
20794	JESSUP	50.8	42.9	45.2	51.5	1.8	2.4	1.8	3.0	3.9	4.1	4.3	5.0	9.5	45.1	22.9	4.8	0.5	85.0	35.5	65.9	34.1
20812	GLEN ECHO	93.8	90.6	1.6	2.4	2.5	3.7	1.2	2.9	7.3	9.0	10.2	5.3	2.0	20.8	36.3	7.8	1.2	69.8	42.9	51.8	48.2
20814	BETHESDA	84.5	77.3	3.5	4.7	7.6	11.0	6.2	11.5	5.1	5.0	5.3	4.3	6.5	30.9	26.8	12.4	3.7	81.8	40.7	48.2	51.8
20815	CHEVY CHASE	88.3	82.8	3.7	4.9	4.6	6.8	5.0	9.3	4.7	5.3	6.8	5.9	4.2	20.6	31.3	16.4	4.8	79.3	46.6	46.0	54.0
20816	BETHESDA	92.4	88.1	1.3	2.0	4.1	6.3	4.9	9.4	5.8	6.8	8.6	7.0	3.3	18.4	32.3	14.5	3.4	74.2	45.1	47.4	52.6
20817	BETHESDA	83.9	76.8	2.8	3.7	10.1	14.6	5.1	9.3	5.5	6.5	8.0	7.0	3.4	18.3	33.4	15.5	2.6	75.5	45.9	47.3	52.7
20818	CABIN JOHN	85.5	78.6	3.2	4.4	8.9	13.3	3.2	6.0	3.9	5.1	6.5	7.5	4.3	17.7	40.2	13.2	1.5	79.8	47.8	48.4	51.6
20832	OLNEY	77.7	68.5	10.0	13.2	8.0	11.4	5.2	9.3	6.8	7.7	8.5	7.8	4.4	24.2	31.3	8.3	1.1	71.8	39.0	47.9	52.1
20833	BROOKEVILLE	84.1	76.4	6.6	9.1	6.1	9.1	3.8	7.2	6.7	7.9	9.0	7.9	4.0	21.4	32.9	9.3	0.8	71.2	40.8	49.3	50.7
20837	POOLESVILLE	91.9	87.5	4.5	6.7	1.0	1.6	2.9	5.7	6.6	7.8	8.9	8.3	4.1	24.3	32.6	6.7	0.7	70.9	39.1	49.5	50.5
20838	BARNESVILLE	95.6	92.3	1.9	3.0	0.5	0.9	2.4	5.1	5.1	6.0	7.3	6.4	3.4	18.4	36.8	14.5	2.1	76.5	46.6	49.1	50.9
20839	BEALLSVILLE	84.7	78.0	12.2	16.9	1.0	1.6	2.3	4.7	5.9	7.3	8.0	5.9	3.0	24.4	31.6	12.2	1.9	74.5	42.6	50.1	49.9
20841	BOYDS	76.9	61.3	9.6	14.8	10.4	17.7	4.8	9.9	7.2	7.3	7.3	6.0	3.7	27.1	29.2	10.9	1.3	74.3	39.9	48.2	51.8
20842	DICKERSON	89.7	85.3	7.4	10.2	0.8	1.1	2.1	3.9	5.7	6.7	7.7	6.0	3.3	21.1	34.5	13.2	1.8	75.5	44.7	49.8	50.2
20850	ROCKVILLE	68.3	57.9	9.8	10.4	16.0	22.7	8.4	13.4	6.6	6.3	6.6	6.1	5.1	27.2	28.8	11.0	2.4	76.3	39.9	47.8	52.2
20851	ROCKVILLE	64.6	53.2	8.3	9.5	12.4	14.9	19.5	30.8	6.5	6.5	6.4	6.0	5.9	30.3	27.7	9.3	1.4	76.8	38.1	50.4	49.6
20852	ROCKVILLE	70.5	62.7	6.7	7.5	16.2	20.5	10.4	16.2	5.3	5.0	4.8	4.7	5.9	28.8	27.2	14.1	4.2	81.9	42.0	46.4	53.6
20853	ROCKVILLE	72.8	63.2	7.7	9.4	10.3	13.4	12.7	19.9	5.2	5.7	6.6	6.7	4.5	22.0	31.0	16.5	1.8	78.0	44.5	48.5	51.5
20854	POTOMAC	77.9	69.0	4.5	5.9	14.6	20.5	4.7	8.3	5.5	6.6	8.3	7.5	3.7	18.4	33.6	15.0	1.4	74.6	45.0	48.7	51.3
20855	DERWOOD	68.3	58.1	9.4	11.3	14.8	19.4	8.3	13.6	5.9	6.6	7.5	7.4	4.5	23.9	32.8	10.6	0.8	74.8	41.2	49.2	50.8
20860	SANDY SPRING	73.8	64.7	15.9	20.3	6.0	8.2	4.9	8.5	6.0	7.3	8.5	7.7	3.7	18.7	31.9	12.2	3.9	72.7	43.5	47.0	53.0
20861	ASHTON	85.3	78.8	8.6	11.8	3.6	5.3	3.2	6.1	5.1	6.2	7.4	7.3	3.5	17.1	32.8	15.6	4.9	76.3	46.8	47.3	52.7
20862	BRINKLOW	80.4	71.6	8.6	11.5	7.5	11.1	4.0	7.2	7.7	9.0	10.2	8.1	3.4	21.9	31.4	7.4	0.9	67.7	39.1	49.0	51.0
20866	BURTONSVILLE	46.0	37.0	32.1	35.4	16.8	20.8	5.3	8.1	7.1	7.4	7.6	6.7	5.3	32.0	27.0	6.0	0.9	73.6	36.0	47.0	53.0
20868	SPENCERVILLE	74.7	66.0	13.3	17.6	7.7	10.5	3.9	6.7	5.0	5.9	6.7	7.1	5.0	19.7	32.8	16.4	1.3	76.9	45.3	48.7	51.3
20871	CLARKSBURG	91.8	86.4	4.5	6.5	1.6	3.1	1.7	4.1	6.1	6.3	6.8	6.4	4.2	22.9	32.9	13.0	1.5	76.7	43.3	48.9	51.1
20872	DAMASCUS	89.6	83.8	4.7	6.7	2.1	3.3	4.2	8.1	8.1	8.6	8.7	7.6	4.9	28.4	26.5	6.3	0.9	69.3	35.4	48.5	51.5
20874	GERMANTOWN	65.3	55.3	17.2	20.2	9.6	12.9	9.1	14.8	8.8	8.0	7.7	6.2	5.6	35.4	23.7	4.1	0.4	71.4	33.1	48.6	51.4
20876	GERMANTOWN	59.7	50.6	17.5	19.4	15.1	19.1	9.8	14.9	8.9	8.6	8.1	6.8	5.4	33.8	23.5	4.5	0.4	70.0	33.7	48.8	51.2
20877	GAITHERSBURG	52.2	43.9	17.5	17.7	12.7	14.2	25.8	35.4	7.7	7.3	6.7	6.2	6.2	29.9	23.2	9.3	3.4	74.4	35.6	48.7	51.3
20878	GAITHERSBURG	65.3	56.5	8.9	9.8	19.1	24.3	8.9	13.5	7.2	7.7	8.2	7.1	4.9	29.2	29.0	6.2	0.5	72.1	36.6	49.1	50.9
20879	GAITHERSBURG	59.2	49.0	16.5	18.9	14.4	17.7	11.7	18.4	7.6	7.7	7.9	7.3	5.0	29.8	28.4	5.9	0.5	72.2	36.0	48.6	51.4
20882	GAITHERSBURG	88.1	82.5	5.4	7.4	3.9	5.8	3.0	5.7	6.6	7.8	9.3	7.8	3.8	22.2	32.7	8.8	0.9	71.0	40.4	49.4	50.6
20886	MONTGOMERY VILLAGE	60.6	50.9	17.8	20.8	12.1	14.5	12.6	19.7	7.3	6.9	6.8	6.3	6.3	30.9	26.5	8.0	1.0	75.0	36.1	47.8	52.2
20895	KENSINGTON	81.3	74.0	6.4	7.7	5.3	7.2	9.5	16.4	6.3	6.8	7.3	6.0	4.2	23.0	29.8	13.3	3.4	75.6	42.9	47.8	52.2
20901	SILVER SPRING	51.6	42.8	25.0	26.4	8.7	10.2	17.7	25.6	7.2	6.9	7.0	6.4	7.0	28.0	26.8	8.9	1.9	74.9	36.9	48.6	51.4
20902	SILVER SPRING	54.2	44.7	18.5	19.6	9.6	11.0	23.8	33.8	7.1	7.1	7.0	6.4	5.8	27.4	26.1	10.8	2.3	74.8	38.0	48.7	51.3
20903	SILVER SPRING	33.0	28.9	29.4	27.7	13.6	13.9	35.6	43.6	8.1	7.5	7.0	7.6	7.8	31.3	21.8	7.6	1.3	72.9	32.1	50.4	49.6
20904	SILVER SPRING	40.1	31.3	36.6	39.1	15.4	19.4	8.8	12.3	6.6	6.2	6.3	6.5	6.7	30.0	26.5	9.8	1.4	76.8	36.4	46.8	53.2
20905	SILVER SPRING	61.0	51.0	18.8	22.5	15.3	19.7	4.4	7.1	5.3	6.0	7.1	7.4	4.7	21.9	33.6	12.8	1.2	76.8	43.3	49.0	51.0
20906	SILVER SPRING	52.1	44.0	23.1	24.7	11.8	13.5	17.4	24.8	6.0	5.8	5.8	5.9	6.0	25.6	25.7	14.5	4.7	78.8	41.3	46.5	53.5
20910	SILVER SPRING	50.9	42.5	32.5	35.6	5.8	7.1	13.5	19.7	5.7	4.9	4.9	4.8	8.4	33.3	26.4	9.0	2.7	81.6	37.1	47.2	52.8
20912	TAKOMA PARK	42.4	35.4	35.2	36.2	4.8	5.2	21.6	29.1	7.1	6.5	6.2	6.8	7.8	31.2	26.2	7.0	1.2	76.4	34.7	48.5	51.5
21001	ABERDEEN	70.9	63.2	22.8	28.0	2.1	2.8	2.9	4.6	6.9	6.7	6.6	6.8	6.0	25.6	28.0	11.9	1.4	75.6	38.7	48.0	52.0
21005	ABERDEEN PROVING GRO	50.9	40.7	34.4	40.1	4.3	4.9	11.0	16.2	11.9	10.7	10.8	6.5	11.7	41.8	5.8	0.6	0.2	62.6	24.3	53.9	46.1
21009	ABINGDON	87.9	82.0	7.2	10.4	2.4	3.5	2.2	3.9	9.2	8.9	8.5	6.5	4.8	31.6	24.1	5.7	0.7	69.3	34.6	49.6	50.4
21010	GUNPOWDER	58.1	47.8	30.9	36.8	3.2	4.0	8.4	13.0	15.6	14.0	13.9	7.4	5.5	39.6	3.9	0.1	0.0	50.9	19.4	50.1	49.9
21012	ARNOLD	92.3	88.7	4.1	5.8	1.5	2.4	1.8	3.3	6.1	7.0	7.6	6.9	4.2	24.6	31.9	10.4	1.2	74.7	41.2	48.3	51.7
21013	BALDWIN	97.5	95.9	0.4	0.6	1.2	1.9	1.0	2.0	4.5	5.9	7.4	7.6	4.0	18.0	36.9	14.1	1.6	77.2	46.4	48.6	51.4
21014	BEL AIR	94.1	90.9	2.9	4.3	1.7	2.7	1.2	2.2	6.3	6.5	6.9	7.2	5.6	25.6	29.2	10.9	1.9	75.7	39.4	48.4	51.6
21015	BEL AIR	93.3	89.9	3.4	5.0	1.8	2.8	1.4	2.6	7.5	7.6	7.8	7.0	4.7	26.8	28.5	9.0	1.0	72.6	37.9	48.8	51.2
21017	BELCAMP	79.6	72.2	15.2	20.5	1.6	2.2	3.3	5.2	9.2	8.7	8.2	6.4	4.0	35.9	21.8	4.7	1.1	69.8	34.3	47.1	52.9
21028	CHURCHVILLE	95.5	93.3	1.9	2.9	1.6	2.5	1.7	3.1	4.7	5.6	6.6	6.8	4.1	19.5	34.9	16.4	1.5	78.9	46.6	49.9	50.1
21029	CLARKSVILLE	81.6	72.2	4.8	6.9	11.3	17.4	1.9	3.0	8.7	10.1	10.7	8.6	3.6	22.0	29.1	6.6	0.7	64.7	36.2	50.3	49.7
21030	COCKEYSVILLE	81.8	73.8	6.7	9.6	8.8	12.5	2.8	4.5	5.0	4.8	5.0	5.6	10.3	30.0	26.3	11.0	1.9	82.0	37.4	48.4	51.6
21031	HUNT VALLEY	90.3	84.0	6.5	9.9	3.2	6.2	0.0	1.2	4.9	4.9	2.5	4.9	9.9	29.6	22.2	13.6	7.4	85.2	39.4	49.4	50.6
21032	CROWNSVILLE	89.5	85.3	7.6	10.4	1.1	1.7	1.4	2.5	4.9	5.4	6.6	6.0	3.2	25.8	35.1	11.7	1.2	79.4	43.9	50.6	49.4
21034	DARLINGTON	93.4	90.2	4.8	7.1	0.3	0.4	0.9	1.7	5.1	5.6	6.4	7.1	4.4	23.4	32.0	14.5	1.7	78.3	43.7	51.2	48.8
21035	DAVIDSONVILLE	94.3	91.5	3.1	4.5	1.2	1.9	1.6	3.0	5.3	6.7	7.8	7.0	3.7	19.8	36.3	12.2	1.2	75.5	44.8	50.6	49.4
21036	DAYTON	90.8	86.2	3.5	5.0	3.8	5.9	2.1	3.8	6.1	7.7	9.5	8.6	3.7	18.4	34.7	9.9	1.3	70.4	42.1	50.0	50.0
21037	EDGEWATER	93.8	91.1	3.6	4.9	0.6	0.9	2.6	4.5	6.0	6.5	6.9	5.9	4.2	25.5	31.5	11.8	1.7	76.9	42.1	49.6	50.4
21040	EDGEWOOD	68.9	60.7	25.1	31.0	1.6	2.2	3.2	5.0	8.6	8.1	7.6	7.5	7.2	28.8	23.9	7.5	0.7	71.1	32.4	48.0	52.0
21042	ELLICOTT CITY	82.5	75.2	4.5	6.3	11.1	15.7	1.6	2.8	5.1	6.3	7.9	8.2	4.5	19.4	35.7	11.4	1.4	75.1	43.9	49.1	50.9
21043	ELLICOTT CITY	76.2	68.3	9.8	12.6	11.0	14.7	2.7	4.4	8.1	8.3	8.3	6.7	4.8	30.2	25.3	6.8	1.5	70.8	35.9	49.1	50.9
21044	COLUMBIA	67.0	58.0	20.8	25.3	7.8	10.5	3.8	6.0	6.2	6.3	6.5	6.3	5.6	28.8	27.9	10.4	2.1	76.7	39.1	47.8	52.2
21045	COLUMBIA	61.7	52.1	26.0	31.3	6.9	9.1	5.1	7.8	7.3	7.0	7.0	6.5	5.1	31.0	27.3	7.9	0.8	74.2	36.7	48.2	51.8
21046	COLUMBIA	73.6	64.6	16.2	21.0	6.3	8.7	2.7	4.6	6.8	6.6	6.7	6.5	6.9	31.8	28.6	5.5	0.6	75.3	35.5	48.7	51.3
21047	FALLSTON	97.2	95.6	0.9	1.3	1.1	1.7	0.9	1.6	4.6	5.5	6.7	7.0	4.1	19.0	35.7	15.7	1.6	78.8	46.7	49.6	50.4
21048	FINKSBURG	97.6	96.5	0.8	1.1	0.6	0.9	0.6	1.2	5.7	6.7	7.7	7.4	4.2	21.1	33.9	12.1	1.3	75.3	43.3	50.7	49.3
21050	FOREST HILL	95.6	93.3	2.4	3.4	1.0	1.6	0.9	1.7	6.7	6.9	7.4	7.3	4.9	24.1	30.3	10.7	1.7	74.3	40.1	48.8	51.2
21051	FORK	97.7	96.0	0.8	1.3	0.6	0.9	1.0	1.8	3.4	4.2	5.6	7.8	3.6	16.3	37.9	18.3	2.7	80.4	49.3	52.3	47.7
21053	FREELAND	97.7	96.1	0.5	0.9	0.8	1.3	0.4	0.8	5.0	6.2	7.1	7.8	4.4	22.4	35.0	10.9	1.2	76.8	42.9	49.5	50.5
21054	GAMBRILLS	87.4	81.6	7.8	11.1	2.3	3.6	2.0	3.6	6.9	6.5	6.8	6.6	6.7	28.1	28.4	9.3	0.7	75.7	37.5	49.2	50.8
21056	GIBSON ISLAND	98.1	97.5	0.3	0.3	1.0	1.3	0.6	1.6	4.1	5.1	6.0	5.4	2.5	17.5	35.2	21.0	3.2	81.3	50.1	49.5	50.5
21057	GLEN ARM	89.8	85.7	6.6	8.6	2.3	3.7	1.1	1.8	4.1	4.6	6.0	13.6	3.8	15.7	30.6	17.5	4.1	75.4	46.6	51.7	48.3
21060	GLEN BURNIE	81.9	76.0	13.1	16.8	2.1	3.1	2.1	3.5	6.2	6.1	6.1	6.2	5.6	28.4	27.3	12.4	1.7	77.9	39.5	48.7	51.3
21061	GLEN BURNIE	76.5	69.4	15.6	19.4	4.2	5.9	3.1	5.0	7.0	6.6	6.3	6.3	6.9	30.5	24.9	10.1	1.4	76.3	36.1	49.0	51.0
21071	GLYNDON	92.9	88.9	2.2	3.7	3.0	4.7	0.5	1.1	6.6	7.7	9.2	8.2	3.4	20.1	32.5	10.8	1.6	71.5	42.3	50.9	49.1
21074	HAMPSTEAD	97.7	96.7	0.7	1.0	0.6	0.9	0.8	1.5	7.2	7.4	7.7	7.4	4.9	25.8	28.5	9.7	1.3	72.9	38.4	48.8	51.2
21075	ELKRIDGE	79.3	71.4	11.0	14.8	6.2	8.7	2.3	4.0	9.1	9.0	8.0	6.4	5.9	33.2	22.5	5.2	0.6	69.7	34.2	49.4	50.6
21076	HANOVER	75.0	67.9	17.1	20.8	3.7	5.1	3.1	5.1	5.8	6.5	7.0	7.0	4.4	26.3	31.1	10.7	1.2	76.0	40.8	50.0	50.0
21077	HARMANS	66.8	57.5	23.7	29.6	4.3	6.0	3.3	5.6	6.4	6.9	7.3	6.9	4.3	28.3	31.3	8.2	0.4	74.7	39.1	50.2	49.8
21078	HAVRE DE GRACE	82.4	76.1	13.4	17.4	1.4	2.1	1.8	3.0	6.9	6.8	6.6	6.4	5.7	25.6	27.9	12.2	1.9	75.7	39.4	48.3	51.7
21082	HYDES	98.2	96.8	0.3	0.6	0.5	0.8	1.8	3.2	5.1	5.7	6.8	7.4	4.6	17.9	34.4	15.9	2.2	77.6	46.4	48.5	51.5
21084	JARRETTSVILLE	96.9	95.3	1.7	2.4	0.4	0.7	0.7	1.3	5.0	6.1	7.8	7.7	4.1	21.7	35.5	11.0	1.1	76.1	43.5	50.4	49.6
	MARYLAND	64.0	59.0	27.9	30.1	4.0	5.3	4.3	6.4	6.5	6.6	6.7	7.1	6.4	26.9	27.4	10.7	1.7	76.0	38.1	48.4	51.6
	UNITED STATES	75.1	72.0	12.3	12.7	3.8	4.6	12.5	15.7	6.8	6.7	6.6	7.1	6.9	27.0	26.0	10.9	1.9	75.7	36.9	49.2	50.8

ZIP CODE #	POST OFFICE NAME	2009 Per Capita Income	2009 HH Income Base	2009 Household Income Distribution (%): Less than $25,000	$25,000 to $49,999	$50,000 to $99,999	$100,000 to $149,999	$150,000 or More	Median Household Income: 2009	2014	2009 National Centile	2009 State Centile	2009 Home Value Base	2009 Home Value Distribution (%): Less than $50,000	$50,000 to $89,999	$90,000 to $174,999	$175,000 to $399,999	$400,000 or More	2009 Median Home Value
20774	UPPER MARLBORO	36832	14780	5.8	12.8	41.1	24.0	16.3	86257	87357	94	75	11649	0.6	0.5	8.6	70.9	19.4	289615
20776	HARWOOD	46565	1342	10.7	12.1	27.0	23.5	26.6	100264	106542	97	87	1172	5.6	3.1	6.1	18.9	66.3	538911
20777	HIGHLAND	70839	1080	1.5	3.8	14.9	24.4	55.5	159865	161043	100	100	1004	0.0	0.0	0.1	6.7	93.2	696951
20778	WEST RIVER	41506	562	12.8	8.7	29.7	24.7	24.0	97453	104060	96	84	493	0.0	0.0	0.2	32.9	66.9	524068
20779	TRACYS LANDING	44756	450	3.8	10.9	39.8	29.3	16.2	92640	100201	96	80	381	0.0	0.0	3.1	37.5	59.3	498611
20781	HYATTSVILLE	20881	4370	17.9	28.3	41.0	10.5	2.2	53574	56301	69	31	2186	0.1	2.2	15.1	79.7	2.7	224566
20782	HYATTSVILLE	24208	10938	17.7	29.2	38.6	9.5	5.0	52532	54507	67	30	4492	0.9	1.0	6.1	81.1	10.9	247317
20783	HYATTSVILLE	19950	14618	16.3	30.0	40.0	9.9	3.9	52954	54993	68	31	6598	1.2	6.2	14.9	70.7	7.0	244664
20784	HYATTSVILLE	24047	8450	11.9	26.6	44.5	13.1	3.8	62102	64574	80	46	5236	0.6	2.6	11.4	83.2	2.3	228520
20785	HYATTSVILLE	20452	13520	18.4	29.2	39.3	10.1	3.0	52456	55939	67	30	6669	0.6	0.8	29.2	64.9	4.5	209778
20794	JESSUP	25306	2961	9.7	15.8	40.0	25.3	9.3	77118	78383	91	64	2139	3.6	2.6	6.8	69.6	17.3	300498
20812	GLEN ECHO	63718	90	0.0	8.9	20.0	18.9	52.2	153424	156712	100	99	73	0.0	0.0	0.0	2.7	97.3	802885
20814	BETHESDA	62985	12977	9.3	12.4	31.7	20.0	26.6	94334	98362	96	82	6844	0.1	0.7	5.2	21.6	72.4	589154
20815	CHEVY CHASE	78987	12403	6.4	10.1	24.0	21.1	38.4	124555	123601	99	95	8169	0.0	0.2	2.9	13.3	83.6	799846
20816	BETHESDA	83816	6268	3.9	5.6	17.9	20.6	52.0	155505	157117	100	99	5182	0.0	0.2	0.6	8.6	90.6	820236
20817	BETHESDA	75016	12188	3.7	4.9	18.5	20.1	52.8	155784	159307	100	99	10521	0.0	0.4	0.9	5.4	93.3	757152
20818	CABIN JOHN	72807	676	4.7	7.8	24.9	14.2	48.4	146010	152016	100	98	589	0.0	0.0	0.0	10.4	89.6	754375
20832	OLNEY	48242	8775	3.4	6.6	26.8	30.8	32.5	125054	125742	99	95	7685	0.3	0.2	1.6	33.4	64.5	464109
20833	BROOKEVILLE	53237	2281	3.3	5.6	23.5	26.8	40.8	133801	135420	99	96	2078	0.0	0.0	0.2	16.6	83.2	580622
20837	POOLESVILLE	42914	1938	4.9	9.1	28.5	29.2	28.4	112697	114054	98	91	1654	0.0	0.2	1.5	47.7	50.6	404975
20838	BARNESVILLE	52973	76	11.8	5.3	14.5	26.3	42.1	135945	137216	99	97	63	0.0	0.0	0.0	17.5	82.5	683824
20839	BEALLSVILLE	51388	158	8.2	15.2	16.5	33.5	26.6	113735	116171	98	92	123	0.0	1.6	3.3	26.8	68.3	571875
20841	BOYDS	42097	2890	6.4	8.4	29.0	35.9	20.4	110703	112442	98	90	2543	0.0	0.2	11.2	38.4	50.2	401864
20842	DICKERSON	55707	764	9.6	12.8	15.6	28.4	33.6	122533	122421	99	94	618	0.6	0.6	1.5	25.4	71.8	599673
20850	ROCKVILLE	49133	15182	9.0	10.5	31.3	19.1	30.1	98485	105408	96	85	10906	0.6	0.3	4.2	31.8	63.1	500162
20851	ROCKVILLE	30171	4640	10.2	16.8	43.3	22.5	7.2	76466	78553	90	63	3057	0.3	0.2	0.4	92.1	7.1	305715
20852	ROCKVILLE	51585	19563	13.3	16.7	30.3	19.0	20.7	82965	87313	93	71	9962	0.1	0.7	11.7	36.9	50.5	405116
20853	ROCKVILLE	44193	9218	4.6	10.3	32.2	27.9	25.1	104385	107081	97	89	8159	0.3	0.0	3.0	46.8	49.9	399709
20854	POTOMAC	73508	16573	3.3	3.7	15.2	17.1	60.6	180157	184334	100	100	15110	0.3	0.3	0.6	4.4	94.4	851405
20855	DERWOOD	43544	4780	5.6	9.6	26.4	25.4	33.0	121292	122289	99	94	3991	0.5	0.0	0.6	32.7	66.2	459622
20860	SANDY SPRING	53759	498	4.0	10.6	24.3	28.7	32.3	119230	122424	98	93	406	0.0	0.0	0.0	33.0	67.0	506466
20861	ASHTON	44695	863	4.6	13.2	32.7	19.7	29.8	99162	104977	97	86	692	0.0	0.0	0.0	26.9	73.1	544843
20862	BRINKLOW	58480	142	3.5	4.9	19.7	25.4	46.5	142642	144558	100	97	127	0.0	0.0	0.0	11.0	89.0	692500
20866	BURTONSVILLE	36808	4459	5.2	10.9	40.9	28.2	14.8	90754	94669	95	79	3235	0.9	0.1	1.2	70.2	27.5	300342
20868	SPENCERVILLE	42676	68	0.0	2.9	41.2	26.5	29.4	109617	111937	98	90	62	0.0	0.0	0.0	30.6	69.4	466667
20871	CLARKSBURG	47587	3445	5.0	6.0	28.0	32.6	28.3	115038	115662	98	93	3123	0.0	0.0	0.5	37.9	61.6	458535
20872	DAMASCUS	33147	4151	7.8	14.7	38.0	25.1	14.4	85941	89257	94	74	3466	0.6	0.5	7.4	56.0	35.5	354946
20874	GERMANTOWN	37510	21227	5.5	16.7	41.9	22.5	13.4	83108	85983	93	71	14707	0.3	0.4	12.5	65.0	21.9	269541
20876	GERMANTOWN	37644	7922	6.0	11.3	35.5	30.5	16.6	95586	100992	96	83	5703	3.4	0.4	6.6	48.1	41.5	355295
20877	GAITHERSBURG	27966	12250	13.3	22.4	37.4	18.4	8.6	66518	67069	85	50	5517	0.5	2.8	9.5	54.1	33.1	320180
20878	GAITHERSBURG	49743	22101	4.4	10.6	29.2	23.0	32.8	112578	115346	98	91	15759	0.5	1.0	3.3	33.0	62.2	487907
20879	GAITHERSBURG	37442	9009	5.2	11.4	38.8	27.5	17.1	92681	98189	96	80	6895	1.1	0.2	8.9	64.0	25.8	298421
20882	GAITHERSBURG	52008	4937	3.2	5.9	26.3	25.4	39.3	128893	128723	99	96	4556	0.1	0.2	2.0	27.3	70.3	541008
20886	MONTGOMERY VILLAGE	37548	11466	7.6	16.7	40.5	21.3	13.8	81275	84117	93	68	7847	0.1	0.5	18.0	64.0	17.4	245011
20895	KENSINGTON	49707	8045	8.2	11.4	31.0	22.8	26.6	98882	103279	97	86	6236	0.2	0.1	4.1	37.0	58.6	446187
20901	SILVER SPRING	34033	13463	9.8	18.9	37.9	20.5	12.9	79221	81388	92	67	8736	0.4	0.9	4.1	68.5	26.1	350812
20902	SILVER SPRING	31599	15061	12.0	17.5	39.1	19.2	12.2	77461	79329	91	65	10260	0.2	0.3	6.4	70.6	22.6	334749
20903	SILVER SPRING	21418	5824	16.3	28.0	35.9	12.6	7.4	56051	55948	73	35	2715	0.7	0.5	3.2	64.5	31.0	337134
20904	SILVER SPRING	35094	20002	9.0	17.9	39.3	19.5	14.2	78924	81365	92	66	11058	0.6	0.7	3.5	49.7	45.5	383311
20905	SILVER SPRING	45578	6061	3.9	8.0	29.6	25.8	32.6	118291	118494	98	93	5378	0.5	0.4	1.0	28.1	70.1	480522
20906	SILVER SPRING	31572	24196	14.3	21.5	38.0	17.1	9.0	67406	69438	85	52	16478	0.6	1.4	9.3	63.1	25.7	317551
20910	SILVER SPRING	37943	18083	14.5	23.9	36.5	14.4	10.7	62021	61820	80	46	6350	0.3	0.8	7.0	44.0	47.9	392739
20912	TAKOMA PARK	28977	9190	17.4	27.0	34.3	13.2	8.2	55323	55619	72	34	3591	0.3	0.3	2.0	59.1	38.3	362002
21001	ABERDEEN	24701	9110	20.6	26.3	38.4	11.3	3.4	53114	52578	68	31	5822	6.5	3.8	18.6	62.6	8.6	223502
21005	ABERDEEN PROVING GRO	16578	788	8.8	46.6	37.9	5.6	1.1	47243	48081	55	21	74	16.2	27.0	31.1	14.9	10.8	104545
21009	ABINGDON	34367	10507	6.8	13.2	43.2	27.8	8.9	82283	88472	93	69	8388	0.9	0.2	6.0	75.3	17.6	280013
21010	GUNPOWDER	17396	182	2.7	34.1	50.5	11.0	1.6	57582	58663	75	38	7	0.0	0.0	42.9	57.1	0.0	208333
21012	ARNOLD	42443	7481	5.3	11.5	32.8	30.2	20.2	100517	106202	97	87	6354	0.3	0.1	3.1	49.7	46.8	385279
21013	BALDWIN	46407	1888	4.2	11.5	27.4	26.2	30.6	111443	112916	98	91	1734	0.0	0.1	0.5	18.8	80.6	571793
21014	BEL AIR	35276	13990	9.2	17.0	36.5	25.5	11.8	80711	87049	92	68	11280	0.5	0.3	7.7	61.6	29.9	338220
21015	BEL AIR	34728	10408	5.8	15.0	42.7	23.3	13.2	80792	87642	92	68	8625	0.7	0.4	4.8	62.1	31.9	329416
21017	BELCAMP	32464	2411	4.1	13.7	59.6	18.2	4.4	76245	79402	90	63	1683	0.9	0.3	18.2	70.8	9.7	228139
21028	CHURCHVILLE	39941	1205	5.1	16.0	37.8	25.5	15.6	86042	92063	94	74	1090	0.3	0.3	3.3	48.1	48.1	393269
21029	CLARKSVILLE	59905	3460	1.6	1.5	11.8	26.3	58.8	164237	166576	100	100	3217	0.1	0.4	0.3	4.7	94.4	699095
21030	COCKEYSVILLE	38308	10504	13.1	28.3	34.4	12.0	12.1	60605	64525	78	42	4621	0.6	0.5	4.7	43.3	51.0	405975
21031	HUNT VALLEY	2578	0	0.0	0.0	0.0	0.0	0.0	0	81250	0	0	0	0.0	0.0	0.0	0.0	0.0	0
21032	CROWNSVILLE	54879	3169	3.8	10.2	28.3	23.0	34.7	114600	116814	98	92	2770	0.4	0.4	2.5	39.7	57.1	453243
21034	DARLINGTON	26977	1308	15.1	29.4	38.8	10.3	6.5	55754	55133	72	34	1028	3.9	0.6	21.2	51.8	22.6	272609
21035	DAVIDSONVILLE	51602	2565	5.4	8.1	23.1	24.0	39.4	129638	128819	99	96	2365	1.3	0.8	1.6	15.6	80.6	677660
21036	DAYTON	57347	395	2.8	5.8	19.2	22.5	49.6	149051	150401	100	98	357	3.1	0.0	0.0	9.0	88.0	701585
21037	EDGEWATER	40170	7607	7.1	13.3	41.3	24.1	14.1	82822	89212	93	70	6451	0.3	0.1	2.7	55.0	42.0	363868
21040	EDGEWOOD	23890	9087	15.5	24.2	45.6	11.4	3.3	59466	59232	77	40	6134	3.9	3.0	31.3	56.3	5.5	199862
21042	ELLICOTT CITY	51017	13175	4.0	8.7	24.1	25.7	37.6	125222	132225	99	95	11391	0.2	0.2	0.7	20.3	78.6	543267
21043	ELLICOTT CITY	41367	14550	8.4	15.1	29.0	27.1	20.4	93730	95864	96	81	9591	0.2	0.3	2.8	45.3	51.5	407762
21044	COLUMBIA	45405	17011	8.9	15.1	30.4	24.4	21.2	89734	90841	95	78	10335	0.1	0.5	9.1	47.3	43.1	368462
21045	COLUMBIA	40895	15204	8.0	13.6	30.6	29.7	18.1	95340	100256	96	83	10560	0.3	0.4	5.8	68.8	24.8	328732
21046	COLUMBIA	45016	6138	4.9	9.3	37.1	30.4	18.3	97654	100648	96	84	4179	0.2	0.3	2.1	59.2	38.2	354382
21047	FALLSTON	42792	4175	5.5	9.3	30.7	30.3	24.2	107739	112671	98	90	3875	0.2	0.0	1.0	41.9	56.8	428425
21048	FINKSBURG	33900	4008	6.9	15.2	39.3	28.0	10.6	84252	90211	94	72	3643	3.2	0.9	4.1	56.9	34.9	350895
21050	FOREST HILL	35560	6534	6.9	13.2	38.9	27.8	13.1	85685	93035	94	74	5588	0.8	0.5	2.1	52.2	44.4	380502
21051	FORK	36261	197	2.0	15.2	37.1	31.5	14.2	93183	95033	96	80	183	0.0	0.0	0.0	29.0	71.0	507813
21053	FREELAND	31450	1134	8.3	17.5	41.7	23.7	8.7	79823	82157	92	68	991	0.0	0.0	2.1	36.8	61.0	453941
21054	GAMBRILLS	41946	4305	3.4	10.2	38.0	27.9	20.4	97421	102585	96	84	3539	0.0	0.2	2.0	59.3	38.5	353859
21056	GIBSON ISLAND	56963	141	6.4	11.3	34.0	26.2	22.0	95452	102974	96	83	126	1.6	0.0	0.0	16.7	81.7	706897
21057	GLEN ARM	43014	1520	8.8	15.1	35.4	17.9	22.8	86052	85477	94	75	1312	0.0	0.5	3.4	18.2	77.9	570473
21060	GLEN BURNIE	25982	11128	16.2	26.0	43.1	11.8	3.0	57800	57787	75	38	7681	0.3	0.3	11.7	81.3	6.4	234520
21061	GLEN BURNIE	26297	20501	15.2	26.7	42.0	12.8	3.2	57737	56868	75	38	11343	0.3	0.2	7.0	86.9	5.7	249365
21071	GLYNDON	41371	136	3.7	6.6	47.8	22.1	19.9	90894	94415	95	79	116	0.0	0.0	3.4	26.7	69.8	520000
21074	HAMPSTEAD	30582	5776	10.5	15.9	42.1	22.5	9.0	76753	81688	90	64	4838	0.4	0.3	3.5	74.3	21.4	308295
21075	ELKRIDGE	36605	9263	8.0	16.8	35.1	23.9	16.2	82440	80004	93	70	7112	8.0	3.0	5.2	60.9	22.9	308971
21076	HANOVER	36835	3775	6.3	15.1	34.3	29.2	15.2	90245	96194	95	78	3285	9.6	3.3	11.3	52.1	23.8	311459
21077	HARMANS	48984	97	1.0	16.5	27.8	34.0	20.6	105664	107217	97	89	88	11.4	4.5	2.3	58.0	23.9	314815
21078	HAVRE DE GRACE	28778	7062	17.1	24.8	36.3	15.9	5.9	60891	62308	79	44	4623	2.2	0.9	11.1	68.1	17.6	291303
21082	HYDES	39629	235	5.1	14.5	36.6	26.4	17.4	91010	92543	95	79	214	0.0	0.0	0.5	20.1	79.4	583333
21084	JARRETTSVILLE	34903	2451	6.4	14.2	35.9	31.7	11.9	89370	98319	95	78	2240	0.1	0.0	3.9	47.6	48.3	395047
	MARYLAND	32538		15.1	20.5	36.5	16.4	11.5	67267	70086				1.9	2.6	14.3	53.1	28.2	289711
	UNITED STATES	27277		20.9	24.4	35.3	11.7	7.6	54719	56938				9.3	13.1	31.6	32.6	13.5	162279

ZIP CODE #	POST OFFICE NAME	FINANCIAL SERVICES: Auto Loan	FINANCIAL SERVICES: Home Loan	FINANCIAL SERVICES: Invest-ments	FINANCIAL SERVICES: Retire-ment Plans	THE HOME: Home Improvements: Home Repair	THE HOME: Home Improvements: Lawn & Garden	THE HOME: Furnishings: Comput-ers & Hard-ware-Personal	THE HOME: Furnishings: Major Appli-ances	THE HOME: Furnishings: TV, Radio, Sound Equip-ment	THE HOME: Furnishings: Furni-ture	ENTERTAINMENT: Dine out/ Carry out	ENTERTAINMENT: Sports Equip-ment	ENTERTAINMENT: Fees & Tickets	ENTERTAINMENT: Toys & Games	ENTERTAINMENT: Travel	ENTERTAINMENT: Cable TV	PERSONAL: Apparel & Services	PERSONAL: Auto Repairs	PERSONAL: Health Insur-ance	PERSONAL: Pets & Supplies
20774	UPPER MARLBORO	141	157	143	159	153	140	145	142	139	151	142	113	155	144	149	135	101	141	132	165
20776	HARWOOD	167	209	214	216	215	197	177	186	169	189	171	140	204	169	199	165	124	176	174	213
20777	HIGHLAND	273	362	374	381	375	325	296	308	277	322	280	243	358	283	337	263	210	286	268	348
20778	WEST RIVER	148	185	190	191	190	174	157	166	150	168	151	124	180	149	176	146	109	156	155	189
20779	TRACYS LANDING	144	178	183	184	183	169	152	160	145	162	147	119	173	145	170	142	105	152	151	183
20781	HYATTSVILLE	81	80	76	80	79	73	88	80	86	87	88	64	87	86	85	84	63	86	79	94
20782	HYATTSVILLE	86	82	82	83	82	77	93	83	92	91	93	66	92	92	89	91	67	90	84	98
20783	HYATTSVILLE	86	82	78	81	82	72	93	83	88	92	92	67	90	90	88	85	66	90	78	96
20784	HYATTSVILLE	91	97	95	95	96	89	99	92	97	98	99	72	103	99	100	97	71	97	92	108
20785	HYATTSVILLE	83	79	73	80	77	75	87	79	88	85	89	62	86	89	82	88	63	85	80	94
20794	JESSUP	121	131	118	131	127	118	124	120	119	127	121	95	129	123	125	117	86	120	114	140
20812	GLEN ECHO	204	292	359	306	328	275	235	253	221	262	219	190	306	220	283	212	171	232	223	275
20814	BETHESDA	166	173	196	184	181	166	188	170	180	188	183	138	197	177	191	176	133	179	169	200
20815	CHEVY CHASE	220	258	304	274	279	244	251	241	238	262	240	191	284	235	272	230	179	241	227	276
20816	BETHESDA	248	346	420	358	386	320	290	308	266	321	264	231	358	260	345	253	202	284	271	336
20817	BETHESDA	246	344	415	354	383	322	286	305	266	316	264	227	356	260	342	256	201	283	275	333
20818	CABIN JOHN	225	315	382	324	353	293	265	284	242	296	239	209	324	233	318	230	180	262	253	310
20832	OLNEY	190	248	246	253	253	219	205	212	192	220	195	166	242	198	229	184	144	198	187	238
20833	BROOKEVILLE	208	280	295	289	292	253	229	239	215	245	217	185	277	219	263	207	163	223	213	268
20837	POOLESVILLE	174	226	220	233	228	200	186	192	175	200	177	152	219	180	208	167	131	180	169	219
20838	BARNESVILLE	194	271	329	279	303	252	228	244	208	255	206	180	279	200	274	198	155	225	218	266
20839	BEALLSVILLE	171	235	251	239	247	213	191	201	180	202	182	153	233	183	221	176	136	188	181	223
20841	BOYDS	153	213	228	209	224	191	173	182	164	181	165	137	210	168	201	161	123	171	168	199
20842	DICKERSON	175	239	265	242	255	220	198	209	185	213	186	157	238	184	231	180	138	196	191	232
20850	ROCKVILLE	169	201	215	204	210	180	190	185	178	198	180	145	209	177	203	171	132	182	170	210
20851	ROCKVILLE	102	133	139	127	137	118	120	118	114	117	116	90	135	115	132	113	85	118	113	132
20852	ROCKVILLE	144	148	165	158	154	138	168	148	159	164	163	122	171	156	168	155	120	158	144	175
20853	ROCKVILLE	154	214	236	209	228	195	177	186	168	185	168	138	213	168	206	165	125	176	173	204
20854	POTOMAC	271	381	457	396	423	354	311	333	289	347	287	250	393	286	372	276	221	306	294	364
20855	DERWOOD	172	226	236	231	235	205	189	196	178	201	180	151	224	181	214	173	133	185	177	220
20860	SANDY SPRING	177	239	264	249	256	218	198	208	183	217	184	160	240	183	230	174	138	193	183	232
20861	ASHTON	154	214	254	221	237	198	179	191	164	200	163	142	219	159	214	156	123	176	170	210
20862	BRINKLOW	233	309	319	324	319	277	252	263	236	274	239	207	305	241	287	224	179	244	228	297
20866	BURTONSVILLE	148	164	152	167	161	143	152	147	144	161	147	119	162	151	156	138	106	145	133	170
20868	SPENCERVILLE	174	252	286	245	271	232	204	217	194	211	194	158	251	194	243	193	145	205	205	236
20871	CLARKSBURG	157	226	251	220	241	207	183	193	174	187	175	142	224	175	216	174	131	183	182	211
20872	DAMASCUS	134	165	153	161	163	144	140	143	133	148	135	110	156	139	150	129	98	136	130	162
20874	GERMANTOWN	146	144	130	148	139	128	146	135	140	151	143	110	146	147	140	134	101	138	125	159
20876	GERMANTOWN	158	172	152	177	166	147	159	153	150	171	153	126	169	159	159	141	110	149	135	176
20877	GAITHERSBURG	108	113	111	114	113	104	117	109	113	117	116	86	120	113	117	111	83	113	107	127
20878	GAITHERSBURG	196	226	216	235	225	198	204	200	192	218	195	162	225	201	213	182	143	194	177	229
20879	GAITHERSBURG	157	176	160	179	171	155	163	157	155	169	158	127	174	161	167	149	113	156	144	183
20882	GAITHERSBURG	214	283	294	291	294	255	233	244	218	253	220	189	279	222	266	209	164	227	216	273
20886	MONTGOMERY VILLAGE	137	145	134	148	141	131	142	134	137	146	139	108	147	140	142	133	99	136	129	158
20895	KENSINGTON	153	201	224	200	214	183	177	181	166	184	167	136	205	165	201	162	124	174	168	201
20901	SILVER SPRING	116	140	147	137	144	128	133	128	128	130	130	99	146	128	142	127	95	130	125	145
20902	SILVER SPRING	110	140	147	134	145	126	130	128	125	128	127	96	144	123	141	124	93	128	124	143
20903	SILVER SPRING	89	97	97	95	99	84	104	95	98	100	102	76	107	99	104	96	76	100	88	106
20904	SILVER SPRING	132	137	137	140	137	125	140	129	135	141	137	103	145	138	140	132	99	135	124	151
20905	SILVER SPRING	173	239	262	240	254	218	196	207	184	208	185	156	238	185	229	179	138	194	188	228
20906	SILVER SPRING	103	117	125	114	123	115	113	114	111	117	112	83	123	109	122	112	80	115	118	128
20910	SILVER SPRING	107	101	108	108	102	94	122	103	117	116	120	87	119	116	116	114	87	114	103	124
20912	TAKOMA PARK	98	99	103	102	100	89	112	99	106	109	109	82	112	106	110	102	80	106	94	116
21001	ABERDEEN	87	88	82	88	86	89	87	86	88	87	88	65	88	89	86	89	61	87	90	102
21005	ABERDEEN PROVING GRO	94	50	38	57	45	44	92	63	86	83	90	62	69	100	66	79	63	80	58	77
21009	ABINGDON	131	146	126	144	139	124	133	130	126	140	128	104	139	132	133	120	91	126	117	149
21010	GUNPOWDER	116	60	45	70	54	51	109	75	102	101	108	75	83	123	79	94	76	96	68	92
21012	ARNOLD	153	190	190	195	193	174	163	168	155	173	157	130	187	157	180	151	114	160	155	192
21013	BALDWIN	170	226	240	233	236	207	186	196	175	201	177	150	223	176	214	169	131	183	177	220
21014	BEL AIR	125	146	140	146	146	136	131	133	128	135	129	102	143	129	139	126	92	130	130	153
21015	BEL AIR	136	159	144	160	155	142	139	141	133	147	135	111	152	138	147	129	96	135	130	162
21017	BELCAMP	122	136	110	130	127	111	119	118	111	129	114	94	123	120	118	105	80	112	102	134
21028	CHURCHVILLE	139	168	166	171	170	165	144	154	143	150	144	114	163	142	160	143	102	147	153	177
21029	CLARKSVILLE	279	356	345	370	361	308	293	302	272	324	276	243	346	285	323	254	206	277	255	337
21030	COCKEYSVILLE	124	108	107	116	107	104	128	111	124	127	126	91	122	126	118	121	89	121	110	134
21031	HUNT VALLEY	0	0	0	0	0	0	0	0	0	0	0	0	0	0	0	0	0	0	0	0
21032	CROWNSVILLE	193	240	245	247	246	225	204	214	195	218	198	162	234	196	229	191	143	203	200	245
21034	DARLINGTON	98	104	98	106	103	112	95	103	97	91	97	78	98	99	100	101	67	98	108	120
21035	DAVIDSONVILLE	194	251	269	260	263	235	209	222	199	227	200	167	248	199	239	193	147	208	204	251
21036	DAYTON	224	302	323	317	317	273	246	258	230	269	232	201	301	234	283	219	175	238	225	289
21037	EDGEWATER	138	166	163	167	167	155	145	149	140	152	142	113	162	141	158	138	101	144	143	171
21040	EDGEWOOD	96	95	82	95	91	86	95	90	93	98	94	72	95	96	92	90	66	92	86	106
21042	ELLICOTT CITY	191	246	257	256	255	224	208	215	196	223	198	167	245	199	234	189	147	203	193	243
21043	ELLICOTT CITY	157	166	154	172	163	146	160	151	152	168	154	124	168	158	160	144	111	151	137	176
21044	COLUMBIA	153	169	167	173	170	155	161	156	155	167	156	123	172	157	167	150	112	156	148	181
21045	COLUMBIA	150	157	145	162	154	141	153	145	146	159	149	117	159	152	153	141	106	146	135	170
21046	COLUMBIA	163	163	152	169	158	145	165	152	158	170	161	125	168	165	161	151	115	156	141	179
21047	FALLSTON	157	198	203	203	203	186	167	177	160	178	162	132	192	160	188	157	117	167	166	201
21048	FINKSBURG	128	155	147	158	155	146	134	140	129	139	131	107	149	131	146	128	93	133	134	161
21050	FOREST HILL	133	157	149	158	155	143	140	141	134	146	136	109	153	136	149	131	97	137	133	163
21051	FORK	133	165	169	170	169	156	140	149	135	150	136	111	160	134	158	132	98	141	140	170
21053	FREELAND	122	148	131	149	144	135	127	130	121	131	123	102	140	125	136	118	87	124	121	151
21054	GAMBRILLS	163	180	175	186	179	163	170	164	162	177	165	131	182	167	175	157	118	163	153	191
21056	GIBSON ISLAND	152	212	257	218	237	197	178	191	163	199	161	141	218	157	214	155	121	176	170	208
21057	GLEN ARM	147	182	190	182	190	182	155	168	155	162	155	119	179	152	176	157	110	160	172	189
21060	GLEN BURNIE	86	95	87	95	92	91	92	89	91	91	92	69	97	92	94	91	65	91	91	105
21061	GLEN BURNIE	91	92	83	93	88	87	94	88	93	94	94	70	95	95	92	92	66	92	89	105
21071	GLYNDON	152	188	192	193	193	178	160	169	153	171	155	126	182	153	179	150	111	160	160	194
21074	HAMPSTEAD	117	141	129	138	138	125	121	124	116	127	117	95	133	120	129	113	84	118	115	141
21075	ELKRIDGE	143	148	130	149	143	130	143	136	137	150	139	110	146	144	140	131	99	136	124	158
21076	HANOVER	135	169	154	168	165	155	143	148	139	148	141	113	162	142	157	137	100	142	142	169
21077	HARMANS	158	199	175	199	192	172	167	169	156	175	160	135	188	163	180	150	115	161	151	195
21078	HAVRE DE GRACE	100	105	96	105	103	100	103	100	102	104	102	77	105	103	103	101	72	101	102	118
21082	HYDES	134	183	198	180	192	170	150	159	144	155	145	117	179	144	174	143	106	151	151	176
21084	JARRETTSVILLE	133	165	167	170	169	156	141	148	135	150	136	111	160	135	157	132	98	140	140	170
	MARYLAND	116	125	123	126	125	119	122	119	120	123	121	92	127	121	124	119	86	120	118	139
	UNITED STATES	100	100	100	100	100	100	100	100	100	100	100	100	100	100	100	100	100	100	100	100

POPULATION CHANGE

ZIP CODE #	POST OFFICE NAME	COUNTY FIPS CODE	POPULATION 2000	POPULATION 2009	POPULATION 2014	2000-2009 ANNUAL RATE % Rate	2000-2009 ANNUAL RATE State Centile	HOUSEHOLDS 2000	HOUSEHOLDS 2009	HOUSEHOLDS 2014	HOUSEHOLDS % Annual Rate 2000-2009	HOUSEHOLDS 2009 Average HH Size	FAMILIES 2000	FAMILIES 2009	FAMILIES % Annual Rate 2000-2009
21085	JOPPA	025	14590	15696	16018	0.8	47	5597	6189	6370	1.1	2.53	4182	4459	0.7
21087	KINGSVILLE	005	5553	5635	5643	0.2	23	1975	2017	2026	0.2	2.79	1621	1614	0.0
21090	LINTHICUM HEIGHTS	003	9650	9449	9350	-0.2	8	3726	3702	3682	-0.1	2.54	2745	2633	-0.4
21093	LUTHERVILLE TIMONIUM	005	35119	37886	38741	0.8	47	14688	15958	16393	0.9	2.34	10045	10511	0.5
21102	MANCHESTER	013	9038	10423	11034	1.6	73	3061	3559	3782	1.6	2.90	2488	2826	1.4
21104	MARRIOTTSVILLE	027	3189	3933	4380	2.3	89	1013	1246	1394	2.3	3.08	852	1033	2.1
21108	MILLERSVILLE	003	17713	18984	19478	0.8	47	5981	6505	6706	0.9	2.90	4744	5041	0.7
21111	MONKTON	005	4881	5034	5070	0.3	27	1786	1858	1877	0.4	2.70	1428	1444	0.1
21113	ODENTON	003	21408	30764	34307	4.0	98	8014	11568	12951	4.0	2.66	5825	8035	3.5
21114	CROFTON	003	21378	21671	21771	0.1	17	7969	8135	8208	0.2	2.64	5855	5785	-0.1
21117	OWINGS MILLS	005	39221	48958	52645	2.4	91	15991	20157	21796	2.5	2.40	10416	12441	1.9
21120	PARKTON	005	6428	6814	6964	0.6	38	2168	2307	2364	0.7	2.95	1834	1909	0.4
21122	PASADENA	003	57237	59179	59799	0.4	30	20222	21176	21491	0.5	2.79	15873	16142	0.2
21128	PERRY HALL	005	7727	12580	14421	5.4	99	3033	4839	5526	5.2	2.60	2217	3554	5.2
21131	PHOENIX	005	6974	7285	7408	0.5	35	2385	2506	2551	0.5	2.90	2022	2080	0.3
21132	PYLESVILLE	025	2639	2952	3077	1.2	61	898	1024	1074	1.4	2.88	744	831	1.2
21133	RANDALLSTOWN	005	27139	29003	29937	0.7	41	9914	10582	10952	0.7	2.67	6855	7026	0.3
21136	REISTERSTOWN	005	31349	34219	35557	1.0	54	11566	12687	13228	1.0	2.66	8503	8981	0.6
21140	RIVA	003	3417	3492	3538	0.2	23	1233	1284	1308	0.4	2.72	1008	1026	0.2
21144	SEVERN	003	28743	31453	32848	1.0	54	9743	10881	11432	1.2	2.89	7744	8413	0.9
21146	SEVERNA PARK	003	25031	25338	25394	0.1	17	8730	9010	9089	0.3	2.77	7157	7211	0.1
21152	SPARKS GLENCOE	005	5349	5533	5587	0.4	30	2244	2306	2329	0.3	2.40	1458	1432	-0.2
21153	STEVENSON	005	406	437	450	0.8	47	159	172	178	0.9	2.50	134	141	0.6
21154	STREET	025	6049	6356	6419	0.5	35	2069	2223	2259	0.8	2.84	1680	1766	0.5
21155	UPPERCO	005	2562	2726	2791	0.7	41	1011	1082	1111	0.7	2.51	776	804	0.4
21156	UPPER FALLS	005	416	425	427	0.2	23	145	149	150	0.3	2.83	110	109	-0.1
21157	WESTMINSTER	013	34691	38273	39553	1.1	58	12602	13999	14524	1.1	2.59	9023	9692	0.8
21158	WESTMINSTER	013	18438	21279	22426	1.6	73	6506	7512	7927	1.6	2.80	5109	5713	1.2
21160	WHITEFORD	025	2255	2523	2614	1.2	61	797	912	951	1.5	2.76	632	704	1.2
21161	WHITE HALL	025	4974	5261	5349	0.6	38	1717	1841	1881	0.8	2.84	1397	1462	0.5
21162	WHITE MARSH	005	2848	3215	3369	1.3	64	1097	1241	1302	1.3	2.59	814	887	0.9
21163	WOODSTOCK	005	5211	7677	8653	4.3	99	1827	2764	3141	4.6	2.72	1410	2095	4.4
21201	BALTIMORE	510	14107	14366	14428	0.2	23	7639	7693	7739	0.1	1.66	2170	2020	-0.8
21202	BALTIMORE	510	23334	23531	23544	0.1	17	7725	7815	7879	0.1	1.98	2829	2537	-1.2
21204	TOWSON	005	20157	21051	21164	0.5	35	7109	7227	7291	0.2	2.12	3505	3363	-0.4
21205	BALTIMORE	510	18739	17091	16754	-1.0	1	6510	5831	5714	-1.2	2.91	4453	3837	-1.6
21206	BALTIMORE	510	49945	50047	49902	0.0	12	19795	19617	19558	-0.1	2.53	12533	11875	-0.6
21207	GWYNN OAK	005	48238	48352	48364	0.0	12	18492	18505	18539	0.0	2.57	12367	11836	-0.5
21208	PIKESVILLE	005	32656	33979	34525	0.4	30	14038	14593	14866	0.4	2.25	8898	8850	-0.1
21209	BALTIMORE	005	23477	24522	24862	0.5	35	10518	10828	10969	0.3	2.25	6011	5921	-0.2
21210	BALTIMORE	510	11662	11373	11253	-0.3	6	5621	5438	5388	-0.4	1.95	2548	2308	-1.1
21211	BALTIMORE	510	17038	16901	16807	-0.1	10	8121	7964	7916	-0.2	2.10	3842	3544	-0.9
21212	BALTIMORE	510	35740	35920	35922	0.1	17	13749	13685	13695	-0.1	2.39	8421	8002	-0.6
21213	BALTIMORE	510	38364	34829	34092	-1.0	1	13456	11933	11665	-1.3	2.90	9358	8023	-1.7
21214	BALTIMORE	510	20880	20416	20197	-0.2	8	8243	7938	7847	-0.4	2.48	5094	4676	-0.9
21215	BALTIMORE	510	65036	62090	61122	-0.5	3	24732	23387	23033	-0.6	2.62	15725	14181	-1.1
21216	BALTIMORE	510	37146	34797	34063	-0.7	2	13986	12976	12702	-0.8	2.65	9081	8075	-1.3
21217	BALTIMORE	510	42521	38952	37986	-0.9	2	17129	15543	15163	-1.0	2.41	8819	7502	-1.7
21218	BALTIMORE	510	53757	51211	50351	-0.5	3	20437	19122	18768	-0.7	2.39	10184	9061	-1.3
21219	SPARROWS POINT	005	9509	10238	10408	0.8	47	3607	3886	3956	0.8	2.60	2581	2673	0.4
21220	MIDDLE RIVER	005	36498	39115	40279	0.8	47	14165	15289	15795	0.8	2.55	9990	10335	0.4
21221	ESSEX	005	42622	43718	44081	0.3	27	17321	17902	18120	0.4	2.44	11367	11202	-0.2
21222	DUNDALK	005	55261	54388	54191	-0.2	8	22007	21742	21710	-0.1	2.49	15012	14205	-0.6
21223	BALTIMORE	510	30614	28034	27326	-0.9	2	10993	9973	9725	-1.0	2.76	6748	5831	-1.6
21224	BALTIMORE	510	48468	47357	46974	-0.3	6	20027	19345	19198	-0.4	2.41	11592	10600	-1.0
21225	BROOKLYN	003	31072	31322	31258	0.1	17	11794	11827	11816	0.0	2.63	7994	7706	-0.4
21226	CURTIS BAY	510	7066	7057	7140	0.0	12	2787	2780	2816	0.0	2.53	1773	1692	-0.5
21227	HALETHORPE	005	33407	33632	33702	0.1	17	12878	13061	13133	0.2	2.55	8813	8531	-0.4
21228	CATONSVILLE	005	46254	46686	46755	0.1	17	18817	18964	19034	0.1	2.36	11849	11387	-0.4
21229	BALTIMORE	510	50054	48800	48390	-0.3	6	19537	18836	18684	-0.4	2.54	12336	11366	-0.9
21230	BALTIMORE	510	32942	32503	32715	-0.1	10	13866	13652	13772	-0.2	2.34	7569	7002	-0.8
21231	BALTIMORE	510	15562	15019	14893	-0.4	4	7196	6878	6819	-0.5	2.13	3000	2645	-1.4
21234	PARKVILLE	005	66472	69774	70669	0.5	35	27678	28945	29334	0.5	2.39	17746	17746	0.0
21236	NOTTINGHAM	005	39732	40045	40277	0.1	17	16608	16762	16886	0.1	2.36	10551	10126	-0.4
21237	ROSEDALE	005	25582	27851	28712	0.9	49	10372	11288	11649	0.9	2.43	6778	7053	0.4
21239	BALTIMORE	510	28393	28880	28926	0.2	23	11652	11692	11706	0.0	2.44	7165	6900	-0.4
21244	WINDSOR MILL	005	31799	34313	35303	0.8	47	12471	13427	13837	0.8	2.52	8239	8450	0.3
21250	BALTIMORE	005	2418	2736	2736	1.3	64	5	5	5	0.0	1.80	3	3	0.0
21286	TOWSON	005	19687	19630	19555	0.0	12	8719	8647	8628	-0.1	2.14	4872	4585	-0.7
21401	ANNAPOLIS	003	33690	36606	37847	0.9	49	14469	15943	16564	1.1	2.21	8711	9146	0.5
21402	ANNAPOLIS	003	5269	5143	5107	-0.3	6	468	442	433	-0.6	3.37	423	396	-0.7
21403	ANNAPOLIS	003	28793	29005	28986	0.1	17	12340	12620	12680	0.2	2.26	7430	7227	-0.3
21409	ANNAPOLIS	003	18317	19634	20112	0.8	47	6597	7176	7391	0.9	2.72	5066	5347	0.6
21502	CUMBERLAND	001	44707	43158	42023	-0.4	4	17682	17247	16848	-0.3	2.24	11246	10490	-0.7
21520	ACCIDENT	023	2032	2172	2212	0.7	41	762	845	872	1.1	2.56	562	601	0.7
21521	BARTON	023	1100	1050	1015	-0.5	3	430	422	411	-0.2	2.49	315	298	-0.6
21522	BITTINGER	023	180	187	188	0.4	30	59	63	64	0.7	2.97	44	46	0.5
21523	BLOOMINGTON	023	474	509	515	0.8	47	191	212	217	1.1	2.32	150	162	0.8
21530	FLINTSTONE	001	1539	1621	1623	0.6	38	562	608	613	0.9	2.50	431	451	0.5
21531	FRIENDSVILLE	023	2313	2280	2185	-0.2	8	931	946	916	0.2	2.41	661	646	-0.2
21532	FROSTBURG	001	15516	15307	14971	-0.1	10	5835	5835	5728	0.0	2.32	3466	3286	-0.6
21536	GRANTSVILLE	023	3917	4080	4087	0.4	30	1481	1588	1605	0.8	2.51	1107	1148	0.4
21538	KITZMILLER	023	743	773	776	0.4	30	290	308	312	0.7	2.51	221	228	0.3
21539	LONACONING	023	3355	3259	3166	-0.3	6	1339	1329	1299	-0.1	2.40	933	890	-0.5
21540	LUKE	001	80	74	71	-0.8	2	39	37	36	-0.6	1.81	24	21	-1.4
21541	MC HENRY	023	1264	1642	1768	2.9	95	529	721	786	3.4	2.24	367	479	2.9
21545	MOUNT SAVAGE	001	2640	2543	2479	-0.4	4	1030	1018	1001	-0.1	2.45	787	753	-0.5
21550	OAKLAND	023	14436	14464	14229	0.0	12	5566	5728	5684	0.3	2.45	3963	3936	-0.1
21555	OLDTOWN	001	2024	2134	2135	0.6	38	748	812	820	0.9	2.55	565	592	0.5
21557	RAWLINGS	001	2230	2196	2160	-0.2	8	859	870	861	0.1	2.52	655	641	-0.2
21561	SWANTON	023	2410	2515	2502	0.5	35	939	1006	1009	0.7	2.47	691	719	0.4
21562	WESTERNPORT	001	3166	2942	2831	-0.8	2	1274	1213	1175	-0.5	2.33	874	795	-1.0
21601	EASTON	041	19308	22324	23613	1.6	73	8197	9572	10155	1.7	2.27	5217	5870	1.3
21607	BARCLAY	035	434	509	556	1.7	76	159	189	208	1.9	2.69	123	143	1.6
21610	BETTERTON	029	477	554	587	1.6	73	202	242	260	2.0	2.24	152	176	1.6
	MARYLAND					0.9					0.9	2.60			0.5
	UNITED STATES					1.0					1.1	2.59			0.9

ZIP CODE #	POST OFFICE NAME	RACE (%) White 2000	White 2009	Black 2000	Black 2009	Asian/Pacific 2000	Asian/Pacific 2009	% Hispanic Origin 2000	% Hispanic Origin 2009	2009 AGE DISTRIBUTION (%) 0-4	5-9	10-14	15-19	20-24	25-44	45-64	65-84	85+	18+	MEDIAN AGE 2009	% 2009 Males	% 2009 Females
21085	JOPPA	87.8	82.4	8.5	11.8	1.2	1.7	1.8	3.2	5.8	6.0	6.2	5.8	5.0	25.7	30.4	13.8	1.3	78.3	42.0	49.4	50.6
21087	KINGSVILLE	97.2	95.3	0.6	1.0	0.9	1.5	0.9	1.7	4.3	5.5	6.8	6.7	4.0	18.8	35.2	16.7	2.1	79.0	47.1	48.7	51.3
21090	LINTHICUM HEIGHTS	93.9	90.9	1.9	2.6	2.6	4.0	1.2	2.3	4.6	4.9	5.6	6.1	4.7	22.4	31.7	17.2	2.7	80.9	45.9	48.5	51.5
21093	LUTHERVILLE TIMONIUM	89.2	83.3	2.8	4.5	6.5	9.9	1.4	2.5	4.9	5.5	6.3	6.0	4.7	20.6	31.8	17.3	3.0	79.5	46.2	47.3	52.7
21102	MANCHESTER	97.4	96.3	1.0	1.4	0.3	0.5	0.6	1.0	5.9	6.5	7.2	7.3	4.6	24.5	32.2	10.2	1.5	75.6	40.9	49.9	50.1
21104	MARRIOTTSVILLE	92.5	89.2	4.0	5.6	2.2	3.4	0.9	1.5	5.8	6.7	8.0	9.6	4.6	22.2	31.8	10.1	1.2	72.5	40.8	50.6	49.4
21108	MILLERSVILLE	85.8	81.0	8.3	10.4	3.6	5.3	1.9	3.3	6.0	6.6	7.4	7.2	5.4	24.5	31.4	10.5	1.0	75.3	40.1	49.6	50.4
21111	MONKTON	95.5	92.6	3.0	4.9	0.8	1.3	0.7	1.4	4.8	5.9	7.3	7.3	3.8	18.9	36.7	13.5	1.7	76.9	46.1	49.0	51.0
21113	ODENTON	69.9	61.8	22.2	27.4	3.6	4.7	3.6	5.7	8.9	8.3	7.8	6.6	5.6	33.6	23.2	5.5	0.6	70.9	33.9	47.9	52.1
21114	CROFTON	89.9	85.4	5.4	7.6	2.4	3.7	2.5	4.4	8.1	8.2	8.3	6.5	4.9	29.3	26.3	7.4	1.0	71.1	36.1	48.7	51.3
21117	OWINGS MILLS	66.5	54.0	26.4	36.6	3.8	5.0	3.0	4.2	7.0	6.5	6.4	6.3	7.0	32.8	26.3	6.9	0.7	76.0	35.0	48.2	51.8
21120	PARKTON	96.8	94.7	1.2	2.1	0.7	1.1	0.7	1.2	5.6	7.6	8.5	7.6	3.1	22.7	34.1	9.7	1.0	72.8	42.2	50.0	50.0
21122	PASADENA	92.1	89.0	4.9	6.5	1.2	1.8	1.2	2.2	6.5	6.7	7.1	6.7	4.7	27.7	29.5	9.8	1.1	75.3	39.3	49.4	50.6
21128	PERRY HALL	91.5	89.1	2.9	4.1	3.8	4.8	1.9	2.9	5.8	5.8	6.2	6.0	5.5	27.0	29.9	12.2	1.6	78.4	41.0	48.3	51.7
21131	PHOENIX	96.0	93.4	0.9	1.6	2.2	3.5	1.0	1.8	5.0	6.3	8.0	7.8	3.8	16.4	36.4	14.2	2.0	75.5	46.4	48.4	51.6
21132	PYLESVILLE	98.0	96.8	0.5	0.7	0.4	0.6	0.5	1.1	5.7	6.3	7.1	7.3	5.1	24.3	32.2	10.6	1.4	76.4	41.3	48.8	51.2
21133	RANDALLSTOWN	26.9	18.0	68.3	76.7	2.3	2.5	1.6	2.0	6.4	6.4	6.5	6.7	5.8	27.1	27.7	11.2	2.1	76.2	38.7	45.7	54.3
21136	REISTERSTOWN	80.9	72.7	12.8	18.1	3.5	5.2	2.8	4.7	6.6	6.9	7.2	7.2	6.1	27.0	28.0	9.5	1.4	74.6	37.8	48.5	51.5
21140	RIVA	94.5	91.9	3.3	4.6	1.1	1.8	2.1	3.9	5.8	6.6	7.8	6.7	3.3	23.5	33.9	11.5	0.9	75.5	43.1	50.2	49.8
21144	SEVERN	60.7	54.0	30.5	34.5	4.4	5.7	3.6	5.3	7.8	7.4	7.4	7.3	6.6	28.6	27.1	7.2	0.6	72.9	35.1	48.8	51.2
21146	SEVERNA PARK	92.3	88.9	3.9	5.5	2.3	3.5	1.2	2.2	5.7	6.9	8.1	7.1	3.7	20.2	32.9	13.3	2.1	74.4	43.9	48.5	51.5
21152	SPARKS GLENCOE	93.6	89.7	2.0	3.3	3.3	5.3	1.0	2.0	5.7	6.3	7.1	6.4	4.1	22.5	33.5	11.8	2.5	76.8	43.7	47.4	52.6
21153	STEVENSON	90.9	85.4	2.2	3.7	5.7	8.7	1.7	3.0	3.2	5.3	9.2	7.8	3.0	16.7	42.8	10.3	1.8	76.2	46.9	48.3	51.7
21154	STREET	95.2	92.9	2.9	4.1	0.4	0.6	1.0	1.8	5.1	5.8	6.7	7.1	4.9	23.1	34.0	11.8	1.4	77.9	43.2	50.2	49.8
21155	UPPERCO	96.3	93.8	1.7	2.9	0.9	1.4	0.9	1.8	4.8	5.6	6.8	6.8	3.7	20.4	34.8	15.1	1.9	78.2	45.9	49.3	50.7
21156	UPPER FALLS	97.4	95.5	1.9	3.3	0.5	0.7	0.7	1.4	4.0	4.9	6.1	7.3	3.5	16.7	36.0	18.4	3.1	79.3	48.6	48.7	51.3
21157	WESTMINSTER	94.5	92.5	3.3	4.2	0.8	1.3	1.1	1.8	5.6	6.0	6.5	8.1	6.8	23.7	29.5	11.8	2.1	77.7	40.4	48.6	51.4
21158	WESTMINSTER	96.2	94.3	1.4	2.0	1.1	1.7	1.0	1.8	7.1	7.2	7.2	6.8	5.0	26.7	28.4	9.4	2.1	74.0	38.2	48.6	51.4
21160	WHITEFORD	98.2	97.3	0.4	0.7	0.2	0.3	0.8	1.3	6.2	6.6	6.9	7.3	4.8	24.4	29.6	12.8	1.4	75.7	40.7	48.1	51.9
21161	WHITE HALL	97.0	95.3	1.4	2.2	0.6	1.0	0.6	1.2	5.3	6.6	7.8	7.8	3.8	22.5	32.9	11.9	1.4	74.9	42.9	49.9	50.1
21162	WHITE MARSH	94.5	90.9	3.5	6.0	0.5	0.8	0.7	1.3	4.9	5.3	5.8	6.0	4.4	22.7	30.7	18.0	2.3	80.3	45.6	49.5	50.5
21163	WOODSTOCK	57.9	57.9	37.0	34.3	3.4	5.7	1.0	1.5	6.2	7.0	7.8	7.8	4.2	23.0	32.0	10.7	1.3	73.8	41.4	49.2	50.8
21201	BALTIMORE	29.0	19.5	63.8	72.6	4.6	5.2	1.8	2.2	5.1	4.4	3.8	5.3	11.2	33.6	22.1	12.3	2.2	84.0	35.3	49.4	50.6
21202	BALTIMORE	19.9	15.5	76.3	79.6	2.3	2.8	1.1	1.6	3.6	3.5	3.2	6.5	13.3	42.9	18.9	7.0	1.1	87.0	33.1	62.8	37.2
21204	TOWSON	88.2	81.8	7.3	11.1	3.0	4.6	1.9	3.4	3.1	3.1	3.7	16.0	17.1	18.0	19.6	14.3	5.1	87.5	32.5	46.9	53.1
21205	BALTIMORE	19.9	17.8	77.2	78.6	0.8	0.8	1.6	2.3	8.0	9.0	8.6	8.7	7.2	24.2	23.9	9.2	1.2	69.0	31.8	45.5	54.5
21206	BALTIMORE	43.1	32.6	53.8	63.8	0.9	1.0	1.3	1.7	7.0	6.7	6.6	7.4	7.9	26.7	26.2	9.6	1.8	75.2	35.6	46.9	53.1
21207	GWYNN OAK	17.1	11.8	79.5	84.4	1.0	1.2	1.5	1.8	6.6	6.6	6.6	7.2	7.0	25.7	26.6	11.9	1.9	75.7	37.8	45.8	54.2
21208	PIKESVILLE	63.0	55.5	33.1	39.3	1.9	2.6	1.6	2.4	4.9	5.0	5.4	5.8	5.6	20.9	28.9	18.8	4.7	80.9	46.7	46.3	53.7
21209	BALTIMORE	83.2	75.3	10.7	15.9	4.2	6.0	1.7	2.9	6.2	5.1	5.4	5.0	6.5	26.7	27.1	15.1	3.0	80.1	41.2	46.6	53.4
21210	BALTIMORE	88.4	80.5	5.2	9.8	4.5	6.8	1.7	2.9	4.2	3.8	4.0	7.0	9.7	23.6	27.9	16.2	3.6	85.4	43.1	46.6	53.4
21211	BALTIMORE	83.8	74.6	10.5	17.1	3.1	4.4	1.8	3.1	5.2	4.7	4.7	5.4	7.2	29.5	27.6	12.8	2.9	82.3	40.7	48.2	51.8
21212	BALTIMORE	56.0	49.9	39.6	44.1	2.3	3.3	1.7	2.7	5.9	5.9	6.2	9.4	9.6	22.8	26.7	11.3	2.2	78.1	37.7	44.7	55.3
21213	BALTIMORE	10.1	6.3	88.0	91.7	0.7	0.7	0.7	0.7	7.0	7.7	7.7	8.2	7.0	23.7	26.6	10.5	1.6	72.7	36.0	44.7	55.3
21214	BALTIMORE	58.4	43.1	37.6	51.9	1.2	1.5	1.7	2.4	6.3	6.0	6.1	6.9	7.0	25.9	28.3	10.9	2.6	77.6	39.5	47.5	52.5
21215	BALTIMORE	16.4	12.3	81.2	85.1	0.5	0.5	1.1	1.3	6.5	6.7	6.7	7.2	6.6	21.8	26.4	15.3	2.7	75.7	40.3	44.2	55.8
21216	BALTIMORE	1.0	0.5	97.4	98.1	0.2	0.2	0.7	0.7	6.4	6.8	6.9	8.3	7.3	22.4	26.2	13.4	2.4	75.2	38.5	44.5	55.5
21217	BALTIMORE	9.0	6.7	88.5	90.5	1.0	1.3	0.9	1.2	7.2	7.1	6.8	8.1	8.9	26.0	23.5	10.5	1.8	74.7	33.2	45.8	54.2
21218	BALTIMORE	24.6	17.8	68.0	73.3	4.8	5.9	1.7	2.2	4.9	4.9	4.9	11.3	13.4	25.4	24.0	9.9	1.3	81.9	32.1	47.8	52.2
21219	SPARROWS POINT	93.6	90.6	5.1	7.3	0.5	0.9	0.7	1.2	4.6	4.8	5.3	6.4	5.4	23.2	32.0	16.0	2.3	81.5	45.2	49.1	50.9
21220	MIDDLE RIVER	83.6	77.4	12.9	17.6	0.9	1.3	1.5	2.7	7.1	6.6	6.3	6.6	6.7	27.1	27.1	11.0	1.5	76.1	37.5	48.7	51.3
21221	ESSEX	76.1	68.7	19.6	25.2	1.2	1.7	2.2	3.4	6.9	6.3	6.1	6.5	7.5	26.0	27.0	11.9	1.9	76.9	37.7	48.5	51.5
21222	DUNDALK	88.8	84.9	8.2	10.6	0.8	1.3	1.4	2.5	5.9	5.8	5.9	6.5	6.2	24.4	27.8	15.0	2.5	78.4	41.6	47.7	52.3
21223	BALTIMORE	25.7	17.8	70.5	77.7	1.5	1.8	1.1	1.4	7.5	7.7	7.3	7.9	7.3	24.8	25.2	10.7	1.5	72.5	35.3	46.5	53.5
21224	BALTIMORE	71.1	62.5	21.6	27.4	1.4	1.9	4.7	7.2	6.1	6.3	6.1	6.5	6.7	27.3	25.8	12.7	2.6	77.5	38.3	47.3	52.7
21225	BROOKLYN	60.0	53.1	36.0	41.4	1.3	1.9	1.8	2.9	7.8	7.9	7.3	7.4	6.8	25.1	25.2	10.9	1.7	72.6	35.5	46.4	53.6
21226	CURTIS BAY	85.3	77.4	10.5	16.5	2.0	2.8	1.6	2.8	8.8	7.6	7.1	6.1	5.4	31.7	23.9	8.3	1.0	72.7	35.2	48.4	51.6
21227	HALETHORPE	82.1	75.5	12.0	15.9	2.9	4.3	2.4	3.8	7.2	6.4	6.0	6.8	7.2	28.3	25.4	10.9	1.7	76.2	36.3	48.0	52.0
21228	CATONSVILLE	74.9	66.7	18.2	23.9	4.5	6.1	2.0	3.2	5.5	5.4	5.8	5.7	5.5	23.8	28.2	15.1	5.0	79.6	43.8	46.8	53.2
21229	BALTIMORE	23.5	18.0	72.8	77.6	1.9	2.4	1.1	1.4	6.8	6.8	6.7	7.0	7.1	25.0	26.0	12.3	2.4	75.4	37.8	44.5	55.5
21230	BALTIMORE	68.5	61.7	27.8	33.1	1.7	2.4	1.5	2.4	6.2	6.1	5.7	5.9	7.4	31.8	24.9	10.5	1.7	78.5	36.2	48.1	51.9
21231	BALTIMORE	50.8	42.5	38.9	43.6	2.2	2.7	9.8	14.4	5.7	5.2	5.0	5.3	9.4	35.9	23.4	8.7	1.4	81.0	34.7	50.4	49.6
21234	PARKVILLE	76.5	70.9	18.0	21.2	3.5	5.3	1.5	2.4	5.7	5.4	5.6	6.4	7.1	26.8	27.9	12.6	2.5	79.4	40.1	47.3	52.7
21236	NOTTINGHAM	88.0	81.4	5.6	8.8	4.5	6.8	1.7	2.9	5.7	5.6	5.8	5.7	5.8	28.4	25.9	13.6	3.5	79.5	40.2	47.3	52.7
21237	ROSEDALE	78.3	70.2	16.0	21.6	3.2	4.5	2.1	3.4	6.0	5.7	5.5	5.7	6.3	29.6	26.0	12.8	2.5	79.4	39.1	48.0	52.0
21239	BALTIMORE	20.6	14.0	75.7	82.1	1.5	1.7	1.2	1.4	6.1	6.4	6.7	7.0	8.1	25.1	27.4	11.2	2.0	76.6	37.7	44.0	56.0
21244	WINDSOR MILL	19.8	13.5	72.6	78.2	3.8	4.1	2.1	2.5	8.0	6.9	6.6	7.2	7.9	31.2	23.6	7.7	1.0	73.9	33.1	46.6	53.4
21250	BALTIMORE	62.1	48.9	19.3	26.4	13.9	18.3	2.3	3.5	0.0	0.0	0.0	52.2	46.7	0.8	0.1	0.1	0.1	99.3	19.8	48.5	51.5
21286	TOWSON	87.1	80.4	6.5	9.8	4.5	6.9	1.6	2.8	4.3	4.4	4.8	6.9	7.6	21.7	26.4	18.5	5.4	83.6	45.3	44.5	55.5
21401	ANNAPOLIS	74.0	68.8	22.0	25.3	1.5	2.2	3.2	5.2	5.2	5.3	5.4	5.5	5.4	25.2	28.4	16.6	3.0	80.9	43.7	47.8	52.2
21402	ANNAPOLIS	83.9	77.8	8.0	10.3	3.2	4.6	7.5	12.6	4.4	3.8	2.5	22.7	48.6	13.1	4.1	0.7	0.1	88.0	21.7	75.9	24.1
21403	ANNAPOLIS	74.6	67.7	20.0	24.5	1.9	2.6	5.1	7.8	6.0	6.0	6.0	5.0	4.5	27.9	29.8	12.9	1.9	78.8	41.7	48.1	51.9
21409	ANNAPOLIS	88.5	83.7	8.1	11.1	1.3	2.0	1.9	3.3	6.4	7.0	7.7	7.1	4.0	25.7	30.7	10.0	1.4	74.1	40.2	49.1	50.9
21502	CUMBERLAND	90.8	87.7	7.5	9.7	0.6	0.9	0.9	1.5	5.1	4.9	5.1	5.6	6.1	27.3	27.1	15.8	3.0	81.4	42.0	52.0	48.0
21520	ACCIDENT	98.9	98.4	0.2	0.3	0.1	0.3	0.4	0.8	6.1	6.3	6.6	6.8	5.2	24.2	30.5	12.6	1.7	77.0	41.4	48.6	51.4
21521	BARTON	99.5	99.1	0.3	0.4	0.1	0.2	0.1	0.1	5.3	5.5	5.7	5.4	5.2	23.8	29.1	17.2	2.6	80.2	44.2	48.2	51.8
21522	BITTINGER	98.9	98.9	0.0	0.0	0.6	0.5	0.6	0.5	7.5	8.0	7.5	7.0	4.8	24.6	27.3	11.8	1.6	72.7	38.5	49.7	50.3
21523	BLOOMINGTON	97.0	96.1	3.0	3.7	0.0	0.0	0.6	1.2	5.7	6.1	6.1	9.4	3.9	24.4	27.9	14.9	1.6	75.4	40.5	52.1	47.9
21530	FLINTSTONE	95.3	93.3	4.1	5.7	0.1	0.1	0.4	0.7	5.6	5.7	6.2	10.8	4.6	22.9	28.7	14.2	1.4	74.5	40.2	54.6	45.4
21531	FRIENDSVILLE	99.1	98.9	0.2	0.3	0.2	0.3	0.8	1.4	5.6	6.3	6.7	6.5	5.5	23.4	29.3	14.8	2.0	77.6	42.0	50.2	49.8
21532	FROSTBURG	94.4	91.9	3.4	4.9	0.7	1.1	0.8	1.4	4.2	4.3	4.4	11.4	16.0	20.6	22.6	13.4	3.0	84.2	34.2	47.1	52.9
21536	GRANTSVILLE	99.2	98.8	0.2	0.2	0.2	0.4	0.3	0.6	6.7	7.1	7.0	6.5	4.4	25.3	27.1	13.0	2.9	75.0	40.3	49.6	50.4
21538	KITZMILLER	99.2	99.0	0.1	0.1	0.1	0.1	0.3	0.4	7.2	7.9	6.5	6.9	5.3	26.3	26.4	11.6	1.9	74.1	37.8	49.4	50.6
21539	LONACONING	98.6	98.0	0.4	0.6	0.1	0.2	0.3	0.6	6.0	6.2	6.3	6.1	5.0	24.5	26.5	15.6	3.8	77.5	42.0	48.5	51.5
21540	LUKE	100.0	100.0	0.0	0.0	0.0	0.0	0.0	1.4	4.1	4.1	5.4	5.4	5.4	21.6	28.4	21.6	4.1	83.8	47.5	43.2	56.8
21541	MC HENRY	97.9	96.9	0.9	1.3	0.2	0.4	0.4	0.7	4.6	4.9	5.6	6.5	4.0	22.2	34.2	16.4	1.7	81.9	46.3	51.8	48.2
21545	MOUNT SAVAGE	99.1	98.5	0.4	0.5	0.1	0.2	0.4	0.8	5.5	5.4	5.6	5.9	6.1	23.3	28.9	16.5	2.8	79.9	43.7	46.7	53.3
21550	OAKLAND	98.9	98.5	0.3	0.5	0.3	0.4	0.5	0.8	6.0	6.2	6.3	6.6	5.1	24.1	29.1	14.2	2.4	77.6	41.8	49.0	51.0
21555	OLDTOWN	97.5	96.6	1.4	2.0	0.2	0.2	0.6	1.1	5.6	5.7	6.4	8.7	4.5	23.9	28.5	15.1	1.5	76.0	41.6	52.2	47.8
21557	RAWLINGS	98.1	97.2	0.6	0.8	0.5	0.8	0.5	0.9	5.8	6.2	6.5	6.7	4.1	24.5	28.6	15.6	1.9	77.2	42.4	49.0	51.0
21561	SWANTON	98.3	97.8	1.2	1.5	0.0	0.0	0.3	0.6	5.1	5.4	5.4	6.9	4.1	22.9	31.5	16.9	1.7	79.4	45.1	50.5	49.5
21562	WESTERNPORT	99.2	98.7	0.3	0.4	0.2	0.3	0.3	0.5	5.6	5.7	5.5	5.5	5.0	22.2	27.1	19.4	4.0	79.7	45.3	47.1	52.9
21601	EASTON	77.9	72.5	18.6	22.5	1.4	1.9	2.5	4.0	5.5	5.4	5.5	5.7	5.4	22.7	30.1	16.3	3.5	79.9	44.9	47.2	52.8
21607	BARCLAY	90.8	87.2	6.7	8.4	0.0	0.2	2.8	4.9	7.1	7.5	7.9	6.3	4.1	24.4	29.1	12.2	1.6	73.7	40.2	48.9	51.1
21610	BETTERTON	82.2	76.7	15.7	19.9	0.0	0.2	3.1	5.4	4.0	4.3	5.1	5.6	4.0	20.2	35.9	19.1	1.8	83.2	49.9	48.6	51.4
	MARYLAND	64.0	59.0	27.9	30.1	4.0	5.3	4.3	6.4	6.5	6.6	6.7	7.1	6.4	26.9	27.4	10.7	1.7	76.0	38.1	48.4	51.6
	UNITED STATES	75.1	72.0	12.3	12.7	3.8	4.6	12.5	15.7	6.8	6.7	6.6	7.1	6.9	27.0	26.0	10.9	1.9	75.7	36.9	49.2	50.8

ZIP CODE #	POST OFFICE NAME	2009 Per Capita Income	2009 HH Income Base	2009 HOUSEHOLD INCOME DISTRIBUTION (%) Less than $25,000	$25,000 to $49,999	$50,000 to $99,999	$100,000 to $149,999	$150,000 or More	MEDIAN HOUSEHOLD INCOME 2009	2014	2009 National Centile	2009 State Centile	2009 Home Value Base	2009 HOME VALUE DISTRIBUTION (%) Less than $50,000	$50,000 to $89,999	$90,000 to $174,999	$175,000 to $399,999	$400,000 or More	2009 Median Home Value
21085	JOPPA	31307	6189	9.6	19.3	48.4	16.3	6.3	71220	75420	87	58	4968	1.3	0.8	10.2	74.5	13.1	279521
21087	KINGSVILLE	40367	2017	10.1	15.6	31.8	22.9	19.7	86557	88020	94	75	1822	0.5	0.1	4.1	30.4	64.9	475910
21090	LINTHICUM HEIGHTS	33586	3702	9.6	20.2	38.4	24.1	7.7	74511	79484	89	61	3110	0.3	0.0	4.6	77.1	18.0	298188
21093	LUTHERVILLE TIMONIUM	48454	15958	8.1	17.4	34.9	18.4	21.2	83858	84448	93	72	12738	0.4	0.1	0.8	44.2	54.5	427160
21102	MANCHESTER	28523	3559	8.3	19.2	44.1	21.3	7.1	74498	78861	89	61	3056	0.5	0.1	2.0	74.2	23.3	317889
21104	MARRIOTTSVILLE	39554	1246	7.9	8.3	29.9	29.9	23.9	105752	109653	97	89	1158	0.9	0.1	1.9	47.9	49.2	397625
21108	MILLERSVILLE	38568	6505	7.2	16.1	32.7	23.0	21.1	88162	97086	95	77	5236	0.4	0.1	3.3	47.5	48.6	392181
21111	MONKTON	47318	1858	3.1	12.0	35.1	20.3	29.4	99483	104912	97	86	1607	0.2	0.5	1.4	17.1	80.7	653446
21113	ODENTON	35660	11568	5.8	12.9	44.0	26.4	10.9	84513	90761	94	72	8642	1.2	0.5	6.1	70.7	21.4	291303
21114	CROFTON	44805	8135	4.0	10.4	36.2	25.8	23.6	98844	104444	97	85	6264	0.1	0.1	3.4	51.4	45.1	371869
21117	OWINGS MILLS	40125	20157	9.4	19.5	42.4	15.2	13.5	75616	77206	90	62	12116	0.2	0.0	5.1	54.0	40.7	342581
21120	PARKTON	37693	2307	7.4	12.1	36.9	23.4	20.2	90931	93146	95	79	2064	0.3	0.6	3.7	22.5	72.9	516289
21122	PASADENA	32464	21176	7.5	15.1	45.3	23.3	8.8	79069	83453	92	67	18177	0.2	0.2	5.2	69.5	25.0	297943
21128	PERRY HALL	34087	4839	6.1	14.7	48.5	22.7	8.1	78861	78827	92	66	4067	0.3	0.3	1.6	64.3	33.4	348633
21131	PHOENIX	50841	2506	4.8	9.9	27.8	19.9	37.6	119249	120403	98	93	2283	0.3	0.2	0.8	10.1	88.5	677480
21132	PYLESVILLE	28891	1024	9.6	20.4	42.3	19.3	8.4	71728	77116	88	59	893	2.4	0.7	10.0	42.1	44.9	381352
21133	RANDALLSTOWN	28503	10582	12.6	20.8	42.6	17.8	6.1	70068	75252	87	57	7316	0.1	0.3	5.2	81.6	12.9	265081
21136	REISTERSTOWN	34263	12687	8.2	22.0	42.7	14.8	12.2	71144	75326	87	58	9590	0.2	0.2	13.9	52.9	32.8	298315
21140	RIVA	53764	1284	4.2	9.3	30.8	21.7	34.0	111642	113587	98	91	1176	0.0	0.3	3.7	37.6	58.3	454144
21144	SEVERN	31886	10881	10.2	13.3	38.9	26.0	11.5	81898	87898	93	69	7822	2.9	0.9	5.9	60.3	30.0	338114
21146	SEVERNA PARK	48000	9010	5.0	8.5	28.7	28.2	29.6	114365	118244	98	92	8018	0.0	0.2	1.5	33.5	64.8	481340
21152	SPARKS GLENCOE	47138	2306	7.6	15.2	38.8	18.9	19.5	82959	83079	93	71	1659	0.4	0.3	1.3	32.6	65.4	524516
21153	STEVENSON	80548	172	3.5	12.2	23.8	8.7	51.7	155927	165158	100	99	157	0.0	0.0	7.0	3.8	89.2	813776
21154	STREET	26894	2223	13.2	20.7	40.8	19.7	5.6	67482	72309	85	52	1901	3.0	1.1	9.5	51.9	34.5	343690
21155	UPPERCO	40348	1082	9.8	15.2	35.4	26.8	12.8	85214	87099	94	73	901	0.8	0.7	3.2	34.4	60.9	476953
21156	UPPER FALLS	32354	149	13.4	18.1	30.9	26.8	10.7	80628	79878	92	68	128	0.0	0.0	10.2	44.5	45.3	385714
21157	WESTMINSTER	30036	13999	15.3	19.9	37.7	18.8	8.3	68185	71887	86	54	10146	0.3	0.1	3.7	70.0	25.9	322521
21158	WESTMINSTER	29167	7512	8.6	20.3	42.7	21.0	7.3	73312	78141	88	60	6119	0.2	0.2	4.2	70.9	24.6	303024
21160	WHITEFORD	30079	912	7.8	25.0	45.4	9.5	12.3	65157	66938	83	49	754	0.9	4.0	12.1	59.0	24.0	287500
21161	WHITE HALL	33454	1841	7.6	13.4	39.5	26.8	12.6	85055	89714	94	73	1589	0.1	0.1	1.6	41.3	56.8	430912
21162	WHITE MARSH	28429	1241	15.3	15.1	48.0	17.0	4.6	70115	73352	87	57	1066	9.7	2.2	7.2	51.5	29.5	320073
21163	WOODSTOCK	44646	2764	8.0	11.4	31.2	23.6	25.8	98880	101767	97	85	2399	1.0	0.3	2.4	37.1	59.3	462325
21201	BALTIMORE	22094	7693	55.3	20.1	18.3	3.5	2.8	21045	21664	2	1	786	8.9	11.2	20.6	37.2	22.1	205405
21202	BALTIMORE	19465	7815	48.8	23.9	20.6	4.5	2.3	25886	27358	4	1	1412	6.4	17.4	43.7	26.6	5.9	132270
21204	TOWSON	38635	7227	19.9	18.9	31.8	12.1	17.4	65894	68854	84	50	3814	0.0	0.1	2.4	35.9	61.6	482342
21205	BALTIMORE	12547	5831	46.8	31.6	16.7	3.4	1.6	26739	27411	4	2	2908	36.8	37.0	22.2	3.4	0.7	64560
21206	BALTIMORE	20418	19617	26.6	28.9	36.1	6.9	1.5	44788	47011	48	17	11713	0.6	4.1	56.5	37.5	1.3	161769
21207	GWYNN OAK	22924	18505	19.6	28.2	40.7	8.9	2.5	51923	54976	66	29	11217	0.6	1.8	32.1	62.0	3.5	194948
21208	PIKESVILLE	41494	14593	13.7	20.6	37.6	13.9	14.2	68826	72059	86	54	10113	0.2	0.3	14.1	56.1	29.3	269199
21209	BALTIMORE	37752	10828	16.8	21.7	35.6	13.7	12.3	62522	64485	81	46	6392	0.3	0.5	10.6	59.3	29.3	303919
21210	BALTIMORE	56526	5438	19.6	17.5	26.6	12.0	24.3	67052	67141	85	51	3219	0.2	1.3	10.3	26.9	61.2	497439
21211	BALTIMORE	24887	7964	27.0	32.1	32.8	5.3	2.7	42298	44922	40	14	4308	5.1	17.2	56.6	16.5	4.6	124126
21212	BALTIMORE	32434	13685	20.1	22.5	33.8	11.6	12.1	58358	60794	76	39	8904	1.1	3.5	27.6	41.4	26.5	257425
21213	BALTIMORE	14693	11933	38.0	30.6	25.8	4.1	1.6	33411	35716	14	4	7395	10.9	21.8	60.4	3.6	3.3	107745
21214	BALTIMORE	24402	7938	18.8	28.1	40.6	9.7	2.9	53169	55422	68	31	5642	0.4	1.1	51.5	46.0	1.1	172129
21215	BALTIMORE	17484	23387	37.3	28.5	26.7	5.2	2.3	34376	37158	16	5	11922	5.4	14.9	56.0	19.8	3.9	133555
21216	BALTIMORE	15768	12976	38.7	29.2	26.8	3.7	1.5	32430	34468	12	4	7018	7.2	25.0	55.4	9.9	2.5	110712
21217	BALTIMORE	15932	15543	50.0	26.1	18.0	3.4	2.5	24993	25681	3	1	4561	20.6	26.4	26.0	17.4	9.6	95723
21218	BALTIMORE	21011	19122	37.5	26.5	26.3	6.1	3.7	35198	38519	18	6	8603	7.5	16.6	48.6	19.0	8.3	132345
21219	SPARROWS POINT	25478	3886	17.4	24.0	44.3	9.8	4.5	60533	64311	78	42	3046	5.8	3.3	16.8	54.0	20.1	245139
21220	MIDDLE RIVER	23407	15289	17.8	30.0	41.6	8.2	2.4	52019	54461	66	29	9543	5.4	2.3	33.9	44.8	13.6	195128
21221	ESSEX	21600	17902	26.6	28.9	35.5	7.1	1.9	43580	46135	44	15	9660	1.2	0.5	36.9	52.4	9.0	198936
21222	DUNDALK	22298	21742	22.5	27.8	40.8	7.0	1.8	49594	51890	60	25	15125	1.3	2.3	56.8	36.9	2.6	165231
21223	BALTIMORE	13412	9973	45.8	29.8	20.6	2.6	1.3	27705	28909	5	2	4216	26.6	38.3	28.3	4.7	2.0	74313
21224	BALTIMORE	19497	19345	34.5	28.5	29.1	5.9	2.0	37294	39988	24	9	12262	6.1	15.6	55.9	19.6	2.8	129604
21225	BROOKLYN	17703	11827	36.9	27.4	28.1	5.5	2.1	36240	37420	21	7	6429	3.0	10.8	40.4	44.8	1.1	167111
21226	CURTIS BAY	24128	2780	23.1	28.9	31.3	12.7	4.0	47747	49860	56	22	1853	2.4	13.2	21.6	57.0	5.8	214809
21227	HALETHORPE	24138	13061	19.0	25.8	43.3	9.4	2.5	55334	60132	72	34	8316	0.7	1.0	22.2	72.2	3.8	216195
21228	CATONSVILLE	32311	18964	13.7	21.3	41.7	15.2	8.1	67115	70925	85	51	13472	0.4	0.3	7.6	69.9	21.8	289672
21229	BALTIMORE	19197	18836	31.1	30.0	31.2	6.0	1.7	40550	42803	34	12	10630	2.5	11.2	63.3	20.3	2.8	134272
21230	BALTIMORE	25948	13652	29.1	24.3	31.9	9.1	5.6	45978	48588	51	19	7936	4.8	12.8	42.0	29.7	10.7	145876
21231	BALTIMORE	24485	6878	37.3	22.2	29.8	6.6	4.2	39441	42392	31	12	2412	7.8	11.0	27.2	40.3	13.6	194048
21234	PARKVILLE	26627	28945	16.5	27.0	42.5	10.5	3.6	56558	60624	73	37	18938	0.2	0.3	21.0	71.9	6.6	224508
21236	NOTTINGHAM	31374	16762	12.2	21.3	47.1	13.6	5.8	65890	70134	84	49	11254	0.3	0.2	11.9	77.3	10.4	250817
21237	ROSEDALE	27110	11288	14.7	24.8	46.9	10.4	3.3	61473	65594	79	44	7295	1.1	0.2	18.4	73.5	6.8	232675
21239	BALTIMORE	23488	11692	21.3	31.0	36.6	8.0	3.0	47808	49584	56	23	6799	1.8	1.7	72.4	19.5	4.6	149107
21244	WINDSOR MILL	25087	13427	14.4	29.5	43.8	9.6	2.8	56508	61042	73	36	6663	0.5	0.2	13.7	81.2	4.4	230091
21250	BALTIMORE	17750	5	100.0	0.0	0.0	0.0	0.0	6250	6250	0	0	5	0.0	0.0	0.0	100.0	0.0	291667
21286	TOWSON	38560	8647	17.0	19.9	36.0	14.8	12.2	66114	69085	84	50	5499	0.2	0.2	8.1	53.5	38.1	339549
21401	ANNAPOLIS	43270	15943	13.5	18.5	33.4	16.8	17.8	75513	79877	90	62	10815	0.5	0.3	4.6	39.3	55.2	433860
21402	ANNAPOLIS	20607	442	1.8	19.0	54.8	14.7	9.7	70714	73400	87	57	102	10.8	2.9	0.0	10.8	75.5	600000
21403	ANNAPOLIS	43021	12620	12.5	17.9	34.6	19.4	15.6	76304	81422	90	63	7844	0.2	0.1	5.4	44.8	49.5	396925
21409	ANNAPOLIS	43519	7176	6.3	9.8	33.7	30.6	19.6	100278	104815	97	87	6071	0.7	0.4	1.5	56.8	40.7	365127
21502	CUMBERLAND	21193	17247	32.9	30.5	29.1	5.1	2.5	38146	40727	27	10	11798	9.3	18.6	41.1	25.8	5.1	132035
21520	ACCIDENT	18882	845	34.7	29.7	27.6	5.7	2.4	37142	38243	24	8	663	8.4	6.2	33.6	42.2	9.5	178159
21521	BARTON	19812	422	32.2	29.4	31.0	5.7	1.7	40649	42397	35	12	328	12.8	25.3	38.1	20.4	3.4	107979
21522	BITTINGER	14292	63	39.7	33.3	20.6	4.8	1.6	31338	31916	10	4	54	5.6	11.1	48.1	31.5	3.7	145833
21523	BLOOMINGTON	21529	212	27.4	27.4	36.8	6.1	2.4	47191	47933	55	20	182	2.7	15.9	50.0	26.4	4.9	152632
21530	FLINTSTONE	18507	608	27.8	43.8	22.9	4.1	1.5	39155	40533	30	11	499	5.8	9.4	36.7	27.3	20.8	170602
21531	FRIENDSVILLE	18036	946	33.9	34.4	25.6	4.1	2.0	34720	34814	17	5	711	15.9	10.3	38.0	30.4	5.5	151071
21532	FROSTBURG	19696	5835	37.8	25.8	28.4	6.0	1.9	35360	37349	19	7	3697	9.0	13.6	40.1	33.9	3.4	142300
21536	GRANTSVILLE	17692	1588	33.6	33.4	27.3	4.0	1.8	35316	35601	19	6	1200	6.2	9.8	42.3	36.5	5.3	160268
21538	KITZMILLER	17804	308	35.1	35.4	25.0	1.6	2.9	31768	32465	11	4	250	18.4	26.4	36.8	17.2	1.2	104630
21539	LONACONING	19428	1329	31.1	32.7	29.6	5.3	1.4	38328	40452	28	10	961	10.8	29.3	39.8	17.5	2.6	102468
21540	LUKE	19256	37	48.6	27.0	21.6	0.0	2.7	26117	25000	4	2	23	8.7	30.4	56.5	4.3	0.0	101786
21541	MC HENRY	31754	721	22.9	31.6	27.3	8.6	9.6	45856	46633	51	19	590	1.5	5.6	25.1	43.2	24.6	228500
21545	MOUNT SAVAGE	21044	1018	25.2	39.7	27.5	4.3	3.2	41004	43517	36	13	837	13.9	23.4	41.6	15.5	5.6	108942
21550	OAKLAND	19533	5728	32.7	33.6	26.2	4.7	2.7	36823	37397	23	8	4290	5.1	12.0	39.7	34.8	8.4	161581
21555	OLDTOWN	18800	812	23.3	40.1	30.5	4.9	1.1	41123	43256	36	13	677	14.0	16.7	43.7	22.6	3.0	127875
21557	RAWLINGS	19458	870	24.9	34.9	32.4	6.7	1.0	42095	45351	40	14	741	12.8	15.7	31.2	36.4	3.9	152932
21561	SWANTON	23315	1006	23.9	29.3	36.8	7.2	2.9	47277	48902	55	21	839	6.4	13.6	32.5	35.5	11.9	168019
21562	WESTERNPORT	17730	1213	37.2	29.8	30.3	1.6	1.1	35079	37199	18	5	884	8.5	33.8	45.5	10.5	1.7	100299
21601	EASTON	31665	9572	23.7	25.2	35.1	7.6	8.4	51083	53475	64	28	6327	2.1	2.2	18.3	50.4	26.9	257390
21607	BARCLAY	21123	189	18.5	28.6	43.9	6.9	2.1	52013	55685	66	29	154	0.0	0.6	16.9	56.5	26.0	286842
21610	BETTERTON	32810	242	13.6	37.2	33.1	8.7	7.4	48247	50475	57	24	194	3.1	0.0	31.4	31.4	34.0	257692
	MARYLAND	32538		15.1	20.5	36.5	16.4	11.5	67267	70086				1.9	2.6	14.3	53.1	28.2	289711
	UNITED STATES	27277		20.9	24.4	35.3	11.7	7.6	54719	56938				9.3	13.1	31.6	32.6	13.5	162279

#	POST OFFICE NAME	FINANCIAL SERVICES				THE HOME						ENTERTAINMENT						PERSONAL			
						Home Improvements		Furnishings													
ZIP CODE		Auto Loan	Home Loan	Invest-ments	Retire-ment Plans	Home Repair	Lawn & Garden	Comput-ers & Hard-ware-Personal	Major Appli-ances	TV, Radio, Sound Equip-ment	Furni-ture	Dine out/ Carry out	Sports Equip-ment	Fees & Tickets	Toys & Games	Travel	Cable TV	Apparel & Services	Auto Repairs	Health Insur-ance	Pets & Supplies
21085	JOPPA	106	125	114	124	122	118	110	113	109	114	110	85	122	111	118	109	78	110	113	131
21087	KINGSVILLE	148	179	184	182	185	178	154	166	152	163	153	119	175	149	173	153	108	157	166	189
21090	LINTHICUM HEIGHTS	110	133	133	131	135	132	117	123	117	120	118	89	131	115	129	119	83	120	128	141
21093	LUTHERVILLE TIMONIUM	147	178	193	182	188	171	160	165	154	170	154	123	181	151	177	151	112	159	159	187
21102	MANCHESTER	112	134	119	135	130	124	117	120	113	120	114	94	128	116	125	111	81	115	114	139
21104	MARRIOTTSVILLE	163	207	196	210	206	185	172	178	163	183	166	139	199	168	191	158	120	168	162	204
21108	MILLERSVILLE	151	178	174	181	179	162	159	160	152	167	153	123	175	155	169	147	111	155	148	183
21111	MONKTON	162	212	230	219	224	198	178	189	167	193	168	141	210	166	205	162	124	176	173	212
21113	ODENTON	139	145	125	146	137	126	138	132	132	144	135	107	141	139	136	126	95	131	121	154
21114	CROFTON	167	190	174	193	186	166	171	168	161	181	164	135	185	169	177	154	118	163	151	193
21117	OWINGS MILLS	142	133	123	139	128	119	143	128	138	146	140	107	141	143	135	132	100	135	121	153
21120	PARKTON	146	183	187	189	188	171	154	163	147	165	149	123	178	147	173	143	108	153	151	185
21122	PASADENA	124	147	133	146	143	134	127	131	123	134	125	100	140	127	136	120	88	125	124	150
21128	PERRY HALL	121	134	131	137	134	127	125	125	122	129	124	95	134	123	131	121	88	124	123	145
21131	PHOENIX	181	246	282	254	267	229	204	218	191	225	190	163	250	188	240	183	143	202	196	241
21132	PYLESVILLE	106	136	134	133	138	126	116	121	112	117	113	91	132	113	129	112	81	116	116	136
21133	RANDALLSTOWN	105	114	106	115	111	106	110	106	107	112	109	83	115	109	112	106	77	107	105	124
21136	REISTERSTOWN	129	136	126	139	133	125	132	127	128	136	130	100	137	131	133	125	92	128	121	149
21140	RIVA	189	243	250	253	251	224	203	213	192	219	194	163	238	193	229	185	142	199	192	242
21144	SEVERN	129	141	131	142	138	128	132	129	127	136	129	101	139	131	135	124	92	128	122	151
21146	SEVERNA PARK	172	222	234	229	232	206	186	196	176	201	177	148	219	176	212	171	130	184	180	221
21152	SPARKS GLENCOE	148	178	183	182	183	166	159	161	152	167	153	124	179	153	173	149	111	156	152	185
21153	STEVENSON	243	340	412	349	380	315	285	305	261	319	258	225	349	251	343	248	194	282	273	334
21154	STREET	107	120	108	121	118	118	107	112	106	108	106	85	114	108	113	107	74	107	111	131
21155	UPPERCO	135	166	165	170	168	156	141	149	135	150	137	112	160	136	157	133	98	141	140	171
21156	UPPER FALLS	120	143	147	143	148	148	123	135	125	130	126	94	139	122	139	129	88	129	143	154
21157	WESTMINSTER	106	121	118	121	121	117	112	114	110	113	110	86	120	110	118	110	79	112	113	131
21158	WESTMINSTER	114	129	118	130	127	119	117	118	112	121	114	91	124	116	122	110	80	114	111	136
21160	WHITEFORD	105	134	124	131	131	129	113	118	113	115	115	88	131	115	126	115	81	115	122	136
21161	WHITE HALL	126	156	155	160	158	146	133	139	127	141	129	105	150	128	147	124	92	132	131	160
21162	WHITE MARSH	95	117	106	117	113	116	100	105	101	102	102	78	114	102	110	103	72	102	110	122
21163	WOODSTOCK	159	202	206	207	207	184	171	177	163	182	165	136	199	165	191	158	121	168	162	201
21201	BALTIMORE	51	38	39	42	37	40	56	44	57	51	58	37	49	55	48	58	41	53	51	56
21202	BALTIMORE	54	44	44	47	43	45	59	48	61	54	62	39	54	60	51	63	44	56	55	61
21204	TOWSON	132	130	143	135	137	135	148	134	141	141	141	104	145	137	141	141	100	140	141	158
21205	BALTIMORE	46	46	46	45	46	48	49	47	55	45	54	33	50	53	47	60	39	50	54	56
21206	BALTIMORE	71	69	64	70	67	69	73	69	75	72	75	53	74	75	71	76	53	73	73	82
21207	GWYNN OAK	78	83	78	83	81	81	83	80	84	82	85	61	87	84	84	86	60	83	84	95
21208	PIKESVILLE	123	140	147	141	145	141	132	134	132	136	132	99	144	128	142	133	93	134	141	155
21209	BALTIMORE	116	116	116	120	116	114	122	115	121	123	122	89	124	120	122	121	86	120	119	136
21210	BALTIMORE	152	159	172	167	165	151	169	156	161	171	163	126	175	159	172	157	118	162	154	184
21211	BALTIMORE	70	66	63	67	65	68	75	68	77	71	77	53	73	75	71	79	54	74	77	83
21212	BALTIMORE	106	115	117	116	116	113	114	110	115	114	115	83	121	113	116	116	82	113	114	130
21213	BALTIMORE	52	59	59	55	59	58	56	55	63	52	63	37	61	61	56	69	46	58	63	65
21214	BALTIMORE	79	89	83	88	87	85	86	84	86	85	87	65	92	86	89	87	62	86	87	99
21215	BALTIMORE	57	59	60	58	59	62	62	59	67	58	67	42	64	64	61	72	48	63	70	72
21216	BALTIMORE	51	56	57	54	56	57	56	54	61	51	62	37	60	59	55	67	44	57	62	65
21217	BALTIMORE	49	44	45	45	43	45	54	46	58	49	58	35	52	56	49	61	42	53	54	58
21218	BALTIMORE	67	62	63	63	61	63	76	65	77	68	77	50	71	75	68	79	55	72	71	79
21219	SPARROWS POINT	87	103	95	101	101	103	90	95	92	91	93	70	101	93	98	95	65	93	101	110
21220	MIDDLE RIVER	84	86	78	85	83	83	85	83	85	86	85	64	86	86	84	85	60	85	85	98
21221	ESSEX	72	69	64	70	67	70	75	70	76	73	77	55	74	76	72	78	54	75	77	84
21222	DUNDALK	75	78	73	78	77	83	77	78	80	74	79	58	79	79	78	84	55	78	87	92
21223	BALTIMORE	46	48	48	46	47	48	49	47	55	45	55	33	52	54	48	60	40	50	54	56
21224	BALTIMORE	63	62	61	61	61	65	65	64	70	61	69	46	65	68	63	74	49	66	71	76
21225	BROOKLYN	64	60	55	61	57	63	66	61	69	62	69	47	64	69	61	72	48	66	68	75
21226	CURTIS BAY	86	87	73	85	82	78	88	82	88	88	89	65	87	91	83	87	63	84	81	97
21227	HALETHORPE	83	88	81	89	86	84	88	84	87	87	88	66	92	88	89	87	62	87	86	99
21228	CATONSVILLE	102	115	117	114	117	114	108	109	108	111	108	81	118	106	116	108	77	109	114	126
21229	BALTIMORE	63	64	63	63	63	65	67	63	72	64	72	46	69	70	65	76	51	68	71	76
21230	BALTIMORE	81	80	78	80	79	81	87	80	90	81	90	61	87	89	83	93	64	85	87	96
21231	BALTIMORE	73	59	58	64	57	59	78	64	79	73	80	54	72	78	69	79	57	74	69	81
21234	PARKVILLE	86	90	85	91	89	89	91	87	90	90	91	67	94	90	92	91	64	90	91	103
21236	NOTTINGHAM	101	108	103	109	107	104	105	103	104	107	105	79	111	105	108	104	74	104	105	120
21237	ROSEDALE	91	95	88	95	93	91	94	91	94	95	94	70	96	95	94	94	66	93	94	107
21239	BALTIMORE	76	78	74	78	76	79	80	76	84	77	84	56	82	81	78	87	59	80	85	92
21244	WINDSOR MILL	89	89	80	89	85	81	93	85	90	92	92	69	92	93	90	89	65	89	84	101
21250	BALTIMORE	10	4	4	5	4	5	14	7	11	9	11	7	8	11	8	10	8	10	7	9
21286	TOWSON	108	116	123	120	120	119	120	116	120	120	120	87	126	115	124	122	85	119	127	136
21401	ANNAPOLIS	128	140	154	141	148	141	136	138	136	143	136	100	147	131	146	136	96	138	144	159
21402	ANNAPOLIS	156	96	80	108	90	83	150	111	140	142	147	105	122	165	117	130	104	134	100	133
21403	ANNAPOLIS	130	141	142	145	143	135	140	134	136	142	138	105	148	135	144	135	99	137	135	158
21409	ANNAPOLIS	158	198	191	199	199	176	168	173	157	180	159	134	191	161	184	151	115	163	156	196
21502	CUMBERLAND	69	65	66	65	65	75	66	70	71	63	70	51	64	69	66	75	48	70	79	82
21520	ACCIDENT	83	64	88	63	66	86	64	80	70	60	69	60	54	69	65	76	46	74	82	94
21521	BARTON	81	62	81	61	64	86	66	80	72	60	70	60	55	71	64	79	47	75	86	94
21522	BITTINGER	66	60	59	62	61	71	59	67	61	53	60	50	54	62	59	64	41	62	69	77
21523	BLOOMINGTON	77	71	70	74	73	83	70	78	72	64	71	59	65	73	70	76	48	73	80	91
21530	FLINTSTONE	83	59	85	58	62	84	61	78	68	57	66	58	49	67	60	74	44	71	81	92
21531	FRIENDSVILLE	75	54	76	52	56	78	57	72	64	52	62	54	46	63	56	71	41	67	77	85
21532	FROSTBURG	69	58	62	59	59	68	68	67	69	61	68	51	59	68	62	72	46	68	73	79
21536	GRANTSVILLE	74	60	72	60	62	77	60	72	64	55	63	54	52	64	60	69	42	66	74	84
21538	KITZMILLER	80	57	82	55	59	81	59	75	65	55	64	56	47	65	58	72	42	68	78	89
21539	LONACONING	77	59	77	58	61	81	63	75	69	57	67	57	53	68	61	75	45	71	81	88
21540	LUKE	59	43	60	42	44	62	47	58	52	42	50	43	37	51	45	58	34	54	63	68
21541	MC HENRY	120	95	152	94	104	127	96	122	101	90	99	89	82	96	103	108	66	112	121	141
21545	MOUNT SAVAGE	80	68	78	67	68	86	70	80	75	65	74	60	64	75	69	81	50	76	88	94
21550	OAKLAND	79	63	82	62	66	81	65	77	69	62	68	57	56	68	65	74	46	72	80	90
21555	OLDTOWN	79	65	71	66	66	81	66	76	70	61	68	58	57	71	64	75	46	70	79	90
21557	RAWLINGS	83	65	82	65	67	86	66	80	71	61	70	60	56	71	66	77	47	74	83	94
21561	SWANTON	95	78	108	78	83	100	78	95	82	72	81	71	68	80	81	87	54	88	96	111
21562	WESTERNPORT	70	51	69	50	53	73	55	68	61	49	59	51	45	60	53	67	39	63	74	79
21601	EASTON	104	101	113	101	104	110	101	106	103	100	103	78	100	100	104	106	71	105	113	124
21607	BARCLAY	88	80	80	84	82	95	79	89	82	72	80	68	73	83	79	86	55	83	92	104
21610	BETTERTON	124	99	160	97	109	131	99	126	104	93	102	92	86	98	107	111	68	116	124	146
	MARYLAND	116	125	123	126	125	119	122	119	120	123	121	92	127	121	124	119	86	120	118	139
	UNITED STATES	100	100	100	100	100	100	100	100	100	100	100	100	100	100	100	100	100	100	100	100

POPULATION CHANGE

ZIP CODE #	POST OFFICE NAME	COUNTY FIPS CODE	POPULATION 2000	POPULATION 2009	POPULATION 2014	2000-2009 ANNUAL RATE % Rate	2000-2009 ANNUAL RATE State Centile	HOUSEHOLDS 2000	HOUSEHOLDS 2009	HOUSEHOLDS 2014	HOUSEHOLDS % Annual Rate 2000-2009	HOUSEHOLDS 2009 Average HH Size	FAMILIES 2000	FAMILIES 2009	FAMILIES % Annual Rate 2000-2009
21612	BOZMAN	041	731	803	823	1.0	54	344	385	399	1.2	2.09	252	270	0.7
21613	CAMBRIDGE	019	16665	17784	18325	0.7	41	7100	7699	7985	0.9	2.23	4486	4649	0.4
21617	CENTREVILLE	035	6484	9425	10716	4.1	99	2390	3559	4075	4.4	2.58	1769	2553	4.0
21619	CHESTER	035	5334	6102	6509	1.5	69	2201	2569	2763	1.7	2.38	1541	1733	1.3
21620	CHESTERTOWN	029	11948	13043	13305	1.0	54	4730	5249	5401	1.1	2.23	3071	3267	0.7
21622	CHURCH CREEK	019	384	406	417	0.6	38	185	199	206	0.8	2.03	129	133	0.3
21623	CHURCH HILL	035	1523	1828	1990	2.0	82	535	667	734	2.4	2.52	377	455	2.1
21625	CORDOVA	041	2567	2813	2879	1.0	54	897	1002	1032	1.2	2.79	714	772	0.8
21626	CRAPO	019	149	156	160	0.5	35	56	60	62	0.7	2.60	38	38	0.0
21628	CRUMPTON	035	426	480	502	1.3	64	182	208	218	1.5	2.30	135	149	1.1
21629	DENTON	011	8125	9397	10140	1.6	73	3091	3609	3912	1.7	2.50	2210	2493	1.3
21631	EAST NEW MARKET	019	2628	2928	3066	1.2	61	1040	1181	1245	1.4	2.46	766	839	1.0
21632	FEDERALSBURG	011	6287	6798	7110	0.8	47	2469	2692	2826	0.9	2.52	1784	1878	0.6
21634	FISHING CREEK	019	525	531	534	0.1	17	233	240	243	0.3	2.15	158	155	-0.2
21635	GALENA	029	1863	2194	2340	1.8	78	754	922	996	2.2	2.36	545	641	1.8
21636	GOLDSBORO	011	1115	1294	1401	1.6	73	400	466	504	1.7	2.75	308	349	1.4
21638	GRASONVILLE	035	4197	4851	5136	1.6	73	1657	1939	2060	1.7	2.49	1232	1391	1.3
21639	GREENSBORO	011	3910	4800	5308	2.2	87	1437	1762	1949	2.2	2.71	1042	1236	1.9
21640	HENDERSON	011	1619	1892	2047	1.7	76	597	696	753	1.7	2.71	450	509	1.3
21643	HURLOCK	019	5192	5694	5943	1.0	54	1952	2178	2287	1.2	2.60	1414	1521	0.8
21644	INGLESIDE	035	118	122	133	0.4	30	47	50	55	0.7	2.44	36	38	0.6
21645	KENNEDYVILLE	029	1169	1251	1281	0.7	41	414	457	475	1.1	2.50	305	324	0.7
21647	MCDANIEL	041	394	434	444	1.1	58	175	196	202	1.2	2.21	118	126	0.7
21648	MADISON	019	329	338	343	0.3	27	125	131	133	0.5	2.52	86	86	0.0
21649	MARYDEL	011	1684	2091	2292	2.4	91	515	635	696	2.3	3.29	392	470	2.0
21650	MASSEY	029	197	232	247	1.8	78	65	80	86	2.3	2.85	46	55	2.0
21651	MILLINGTON	029	2457	2800	2944	1.4	67	931	1087	1151	1.7	2.53	683	771	1.3
21654	OXFORD	041	1400	1568	1623	1.2	61	668	757	786	1.4	2.07	449	484	0.8
21655	PRESTON	011	4879	5463	5823	1.2	61	1830	2066	2207	1.3	2.64	1420	1558	1.0
21657	QUEEN ANNE	035	938	1064	1156	1.4	67	351	390	423	1.1	2.73	269	295	1.0
21658	QUEENSTOWN	035	3501	3856	3989	1.0	54	1318	1460	1513	1.1	2.62	1045	1130	0.8
21659	RHODESDALE	019	1642	1599	1590	-0.3	6	671	666	666	-0.1	2.40	476	455	-0.5
21660	RIDGELY	011	3370	3912	4226	1.6	73	1221	1434	1556	1.8	2.70	902	1021	1.3
21661	ROCK HALL	029	2755	2744	2693	0.0	12	1246	1283	1275	0.3	2.14	820	806	-0.2
21662	ROYAL OAK	041	604	665	682	1.0	54	264	296	306	1.2	2.25	193	207	0.8
21663	SAINT MICHAELS	041	3702	4160	4340	1.3	64	1716	1963	2060	1.5	2.12	1139	1237	0.9
21665	SHERWOOD	041	224	247	253	1.1	58	101	113	117	1.2	2.18	68	73	0.8
21666	STEVENSVILLE	035	11478	12828	13389	1.2	61	4112	4640	4856	1.3	2.76	3258	3589	1.1
21667	STILL POND	029	312	340	354	0.9	49	117	132	139	1.3	2.57	86	93	0.8
21668	SUDLERSVILLE	035	1655	1963	2101	1.9	79	626	757	813	2.1	2.55	465	545	1.7
21669	TAYLORS ISLAND	019	220	223	224	0.1	17	98	101	102	0.3	2.14	66	65	-0.2
21671	TILGHMAN	041	830	920	959	1.1	58	357	404	422	1.3	2.28	254	275	0.9
21672	TODDVILLE	019	434	455	466	0.5	35	200	213	220	0.7	2.14	134	137	0.2
21673	TRAPPE	041	3264	3647	3792	1.2	61	1259	1414	1476	1.3	2.58	979	1060	0.9
21675	WINGATE	019	45	47	48	0.5	35	22	23	24	0.5	2.04	15	15	0.0
21676	WITTMAN	041	247	272	278	1.0	54	121	136	140	1.3	1.99	81	87	0.8
21677	WOOLFORD	019	308	345	362	1.2	61	129	147	155	1.4	2.35	97	106	1.0
21678	WORTON	029	2284	2559	2671	1.2	61	876	1004	1059	1.5	2.53	668	740	1.1
21679	WYE MILLS	041	320	345	351	0.8	47	123	135	138	1.0	2.56	98	104	0.6
21701	FREDERICK	021	32679	37313	39320	1.4	67	13215	15080	15919	1.4	2.36	8159	8925	1.0
21702	FREDERICK	021	31002	37146	40742	2.0	82	11719	14193	15613	2.1	2.57	8111	9410	1.6
21703	FREDERICK	021	25996	32036	34656	2.3	89	9545	11750	12735	2.3	2.69	6720	7936	1.8
21704	FREDERICK	021	4377	9697	11513	9.0	100	1462	3459	4153	9.8	2.78	1203	2732	9.3
21710	ADAMSTOWN	021	2744	3607	4097	3.0	95	981	1336	1530	3.4	2.69	761	1001	3.0
21711	BIG POOL	043	1016	1104	1150	0.9	49	380	425	447	1.2	2.60	292	315	0.8
21713	BOONSBORO	043	8225	9564	10152	1.6	73	3062	3637	3885	1.9	2.55	2262	2581	1.4
21716	BRUNSWICK	021	4892	5029	5080	0.3	27	1865	1953	1984	0.5	2.58	1312	1304	-0.1
21718	BURKITTSVILLE	021	173	186	192	0.8	47	75	82	85	1.0	2.27	61	65	0.7
21719	CASCADE	043	1582	1818	1941	1.5	69	584	690	743	1.8	2.62	443	503	1.4
21722	CLEAR SPRING	043	5170	5697	5948	1.1	58	1865	2111	2223	1.3	2.68	1489	1634	1.0
21723	COOKSVILLE	027	648	760	821	1.7	76	206	245	265	1.9	3.10	181	210	1.6
21727	EMMITSBURG	021	5649	6601	6936	1.7	76	1533	1842	1982	2.0	2.60	1122	1290	1.5
21733	FAIRPLAY	043	4904	4928	4980	0.1	17	340	375	399	1.1	2.63	277	296	0.7
21737	GLENELG	027	1336	1828	2009	3.4	97	415	572	632	3.5	3.17	370	502	3.4
21738	GLENWOOD	027	2111	2724	3009	2.8	93	645	849	943	3.0	3.21	577	746	2.8
21740	HAGERSTOWN	043	56341	62018	65495	1.0	54	22101	24832	26400	1.3	2.33	13937	15043	0.8
21742	HAGERSTOWN	043	23498	27613	29490	1.8	78	9400	11247	12090	2.0	2.41	6575	7534	1.5
21750	HANCOCK	043	3955	4037	4068	0.2	23	1576	1656	1683	0.5	2.41	1130	1135	0.0
21754	IJAMSVILLE	021	5896	6370	6661	0.8	47	1886	2060	2169	1.0	3.09	1663	1791	0.8
21755	JEFFERSON	021	6394	6869	7054	0.8	47	2220	2418	2496	0.9	2.81	1803	1907	0.6
21756	KEEDYSVILLE	043	2609	3266	3608	2.5	91	907	1154	1282	2.6	2.82	737	907	2.3
21757	KEYMAR	013	3140	3385	3485	0.8	47	1086	1186	1228	1.0	2.79	862	916	0.7
21758	KNOXVILLE	021	3984	4803	5184	2.0	82	1419	1748	1898	2.3	2.75	1093	1290	1.8
21765	LISBON	027	70	82	89	1.7	76	29	34	37	1.7	2.41	25	30	2.0
21766	LITTLE ORLEANS	001	663	674	670	0.2	23	259	271	271	0.5	2.49	196	197	0.1
21767	MAUGANSVILLE	043	1057	1276	1390	2.1	83	465	576	634	2.3	2.20	299	350	1.7
21769	MIDDLETOWN	021	9221	11252	12135	2.2	87	3202	3955	4285	2.3	2.84	2608	3126	2.0
21770	MONROVIA	021	5375	6214	6600	1.6	73	1725	2032	2172	1.8	3.05	1530	1769	1.6
21771	MOUNT AIRY	021	25148	30665	33057	2.2	87	8079	9992	10817	2.3	3.07	6869	8285	2.0
21773	MYERSVILLE	021	5020	5617	5855	1.2	61	1730	1941	2027	1.3	2.89	1418	1547	0.9
21774	NEW MARKET	021	8519	11437	12698	3.2	96	2782	3773	4203	3.3	3.03	2320	3068	3.1
21776	NEW WINDSOR	013	5861	6323	6477	0.8	47	2018	2204	2269	1.0	2.86	1630	1735	0.7
21777	POINT OF ROCKS	021	1071	1223	1354	1.4	67	365	425	472	1.7	2.88	283	319	1.3
21778	ROCKY RIDGE	021	937	994	1016	0.6	38	343	371	381	0.9	2.68	277	290	0.5
21779	ROHRERSVILLE	043	913	1029	1090	1.3	64	324	373	399	1.5	2.75	258	286	1.1
21780	SABILLASVILLE	021	1606	1820	1896	1.4	67	510	589	620	1.6	2.76	412	462	1.2
21782	SHARPSBURG	043	3888	4307	4502	1.1	58	1470	1672	1764	1.4	2.57	1137	1247	1.0
21783	SMITHSBURG	043	9682	12057	12997	2.4	91	3660	4681	5083	2.7	2.56	2784	3394	2.2
21784	SYKESVILLE	013	35000	40086	42050	1.5	69	11619	13376	14087	1.5	2.89	9503	10665	1.3
21787	TANEYTOWN	013	8977	11030	11926	2.3	89	3196	3948	4278	2.3	2.79	2515	3016	2.0
21788	THURMONT	021	10753	11685	12032	0.9	49	4014	4405	4558	1.0	2.63	3063	3240	0.6
21790	TUSCARORA	021	88	99	111	1.3	64	37	43	48	1.6	2.30	28	32	1.5
21791	UNION BRIDGE	021	5407	6125	6443	1.4	67	1877	2154	2279	1.5	2.84	1493	1664	1.2
21793	WALKERSVILLE	021	9416	10361	10766	1.0	54	3131	3493	3647	1.2	2.93	2584	2807	0.9
21794	WEST FRIENDSHIP	027	1876	2223	2476	1.9	79	570	675	754	1.8	3.28	502	586	1.7
	MARYLAND					0.9					0.9	2.60			0.5
	UNITED STATES					1.0					1.1	2.59			0.9

ZIP CODE #	POST OFFICE NAME	RACE (%) White 2000	White 2009	Black 2000	Black 2009	Asian/Pacific 2000	Asian/Pacific 2009	% Hispanic Origin 2000	% Hispanic Origin 2009	2009 AGE DISTRIBUTION (%) 0-4	5-9	10-14	15-19	20-24	25-44	45-64	65-84	85+	18+	MEDIAN AGE 2009	% 2009 Males	% 2009 Females
21612	BOZMAN	95.6	93.3	2.7	4.0	0.3	0.2	0.8	1.6	2.2	2.6	2.9	2.7	2.5	10.7	40.5	33.1	2.7	90.5	60.5	47.1	52.9
21613	CAMBRIDGE	62.7	56.3	35.1	40.6	0.7	1.0	1.2	1.9	5.4	5.6	5.9	6.2	5.6	23.2	28.4	16.4	3.2	79.0	43.5	47.3	52.7
21617	CENTREVILLE	84.7	80.6	13.6	17.1	0.4	0.5	0.7	1.1	6.2	6.4	6.7	6.9	5.4	24.4	29.8	11.9	2.2	76.2	40.8	49.1	50.9
21619	CHESTER	90.6	87.5	6.6	8.2	0.9	1.3	1.1	2.0	5.8	6.2	6.5	6.2	4.4	24.6	30.7	13.9	1.6	77.6	42.6	49.7	50.3
21620	CHESTERTOWN	78.2	72.8	19.2	23.6	0.9	1.3	1.5	2.4	4.6	4.5	5.2	8.8	8.7	20.7	27.0	16.7	3.8	81.9	42.8	46.8	53.2
21622	CHURCH CREEK	93.7	90.1	5.0	7.9	0.3	0.2	0.8	1.2	4.2	4.7	5.2	6.2	3.2	20.9	32.5	20.7	2.5	81.8	48.6	50.0	50.0
21623	CHURCH HILL	80.5	75.5	17.2	21.1	0.4	0.6	1.5	2.6	5.1	5.5	6.1	6.1	4.7	30.1	29.5	11.0	1.9	79.0	40.2	51.6	48.4
21625	CORDOVA	87.3	81.4	11.2	16.1	0.2	0.4	1.1	2.1	5.7	6.2	7.2	7.7	4.4	23.4	31.6	12.5	1.4	75.6	42.0	49.2	50.8
21626	CRAPO	94.6	91.0	4.1	6.4	0.0	0.6	0.7	0.6	3.8	5.1	5.8	5.8	2.6	22.4	31.4	19.9	3.2	81.4	47.7	51.9	48.1
21628	CRUMPTON	84.7	80.4	13.6	17.1	0.2	0.4	1.2	2.1	5.8	6.3	6.5	7.1	5.0	26.0	29.8	12.1	1.5	76.9	40.6	49.4	50.6
21629	DENTON	84.5	80.6	13.3	16.1	0.4	0.6	1.1	1.9	5.1	5.3	6.0	6.9	5.4	24.3	30.0	13.8	3.1	79.2	42.9	49.2	50.8
21631	EAST NEW MARKET	88.2	82.7	10.1	14.6	0.6	1.0	1.4	2.6	5.3	5.8	6.4	6.2	4.1	23.0	32.0	15.1	2.2	78.4	44.5	48.8	51.2
21632	FEDERALSBURG	73.3	65.8	23.8	30.1	0.6	0.8	1.4	2.1	6.8	6.6	6.7	7.1	6.4	24.1	28.0	12.5	1.8	75.6	38.8	47.5	52.5
21634	FISHING CREEK	93.5	90.4	5.1	8.1	0.2	0.2	1.5	2.8	4.7	4.9	5.5	7.0	3.4	19.6	31.8	20.7	2.4	80.0	48.2	53.7	46.3
21635	GALENA	90.2	86.8	7.8	10.0	0.3	0.5	2.3	3.8	5.0	5.3	6.8	5.6	3.4	24.0	33.5	14.7	1.7	78.7	44.9	49.7	50.3
21636	GOLDSBORO	90.4	86.2	6.5	8.7	0.6	1.0	2.6	4.6	6.5	6.9	7.3	7.3	4.9	26.7	29.4	9.9	1.2	74.5	38.8	50.0	50.0
21638	GRASONVILLE	80.5	74.6	17.7	22.7	0.3	0.5	1.4	2.3	5.2	5.6	5.9	5.7	4.9	20.3	32.6	17.7	2.2	79.8	46.5	48.9	51.1
21639	GREENSBORO	87.7	82.6	9.1	12.3	0.7	1.0	1.6	2.8	6.4	6.4	6.8	7.8	6.0	27.6	27.5	10.1	1.5	75.2	38.0	48.5	51.5
21640	HENDERSON	86.2	80.4	6.9	8.9	0.4	0.5	8.0	13.3	7.3	7.1	7.4	7.6	6.2	26.8	26.7	9.5	1.3	73.5	36.0	50.7	49.3
21643	HURLOCK	63.5	53.3	33.6	42.9	0.9	1.1	1.7	2.5	6.1	6.4	6.8	7.3	5.8	25.8	29.2	11.3	1.3	75.8	39.4	47.3	52.7
21644	INGLESIDE	90.7	87.7	6.8	8.2	0.0	0.0	2.5	4.9	6.6	7.4	7.4	6.6	4.1	25.4	29.5	11.5	1.6	73.8	40.5	49.2	50.8
21645	KENNEDYVILLE	80.1	73.5	11.5	14.2	0.1	0.1	13.1	19.6	4.9	5.4	5.8	5.5	5.4	24.7	32.9	13.6	1.9	80.8	43.9	55.1	44.9
21647	MCDANIEL	89.3	84.1	10.4	15.2	0.0	0.0	0.8	1.2	3.9	4.4	4.8	4.8	3.2	16.8	37.1	21.4	3.5	82.9	51.4	50.0	50.0
21648	MADISON	93.0	89.9	5.5	8.3	0.3	0.3	1.5	2.7	4.7	4.7	5.3	6.8	3.3	19.5	32.5	21.0	2.1	80.5	48.5	52.4	47.6
21649	MARYDEL	79.5	71.4	5.0	6.0	0.5	0.7	19.3	29.5	7.8	6.7	7.3	9.1	8.0	26.9	24.8	8.0	1.3	72.7	32.8	53.7	46.3
21650	MASSEY	80.0	73.3	16.9	21.1	0.0	0.4	6.2	9.9	4.7	6.5	6.9	7.3	4.7	23.7	30.6	12.9	2.6	77.2	42.0	52.2	47.8
21651	MILLINGTON	83.3	78.4	13.3	16.6	0.4	0.5	4.5	7.2	5.4	6.3	6.5	7.1	5.2	25.3	30.4	12.3	1.7	77.3	41.1	50.4	49.6
21654	OXFORD	91.2	87.1	7.9	11.5	0.2	0.3	0.6	1.1	3.2	3.4	4.1	4.2	2.6	13.8	37.2	27.7	3.7	86.5	57.4	47.9	52.1
21655	PRESTON	82.2	76.4	16.0	21.1	0.6	0.8	0.2	0.5	5.7	6.3	6.7	6.7	4.4	25.7	30.1	12.9	1.5	77.1	41.5	49.9	50.1
21657	QUEEN ANNE	89.4	86.3	9.4	11.9	0.1	0.2	0.7	1.4	6.0	6.4	7.1	8.1	5.0	25.1	30.4	10.5	1.4	75.5	40.5	50.6	49.4
21658	QUEENSTOWN	89.2	85.6	8.2	10.4	0.7	1.0	1.4	2.5	5.5	6.4	7.1	5.9	3.5	21.2	32.7	16.0	1.7	77.2	45.2	50.4	49.6
21659	RHODESDALE	86.3	80.2	11.8	16.9	0.6	0.9	0.8	1.4	5.3	5.9	6.3	6.3	4.8	22.5	32.5	14.6	1.8	78.5	44.2	48.6	51.4
21660	RIDGELY	79.2	72.1	18.1	23.9	0.8	1.1	2.2	3.7	7.2	7.2	7.4	7.5	6.0	26.6	26.5	10.0	1.6	73.5	37.0	48.7	51.3
21661	ROCK HALL	87.7	83.8	11.0	14.3	0.1	0.1	1.1	1.8	4.3	4.5	4.9	5.5	4.0	18.1	34.6	21.1	3.0	82.8	50.6	47.9	52.1
21662	ROYAL OAK	88.4	83.0	11.3	16.2	0.2	0.3	0.7	1.5	3.6	4.2	5.0	5.4	3.3	14.6	38.6	22.7	2.6	84.1	53.3	49.5	50.5
21663	SAINT MICHAELS	85.7	81.6	13.2	16.6	0.2	0.3	0.7	1.3	3.8	4.2	4.5	5.0	3.8	14.8	33.2	27.2	3.5	84.2	54.4	46.9	53.1
21665	SHERWOOD	90.2	85.4	9.4	13.8	0.0	0.0	0.9	1.2	4.0	4.5	4.9	4.9	3.6	17.8	36.0	21.1	3.2	83.0	50.6	50.6	49.4
21666	STEVENSVILLE	94.9	92.8	2.6	3.3	0.9	1.4	0.9	1.5	7.3	7.5	8.1	6.8	4.0	25.8	29.1	10.2	1.0	72.6	39.4	49.8	50.2
21667	STILL POND	80.2	74.4	16.3	20.9	0.3	0.3	3.2	5.0	4.1	4.4	4.7	4.7	4.1	20.3	36.8	18.8	2.1	83.8	50.5	50.3	49.7
21668	SUDLERSVILLE	91.1	88.4	7.4	9.5	0.1	0.2	2.1	3.6	6.4	6.8	7.0	6.2	4.4	25.0	29.9	12.3	2.0	75.8	41.1	50.5	49.5
21669	TAYLORS ISLAND	94.1	90.1	5.0	8.1	0.0	0.4	1.4	2.7	4.5	4.9	5.4	6.7	3.1	18.8	33.6	20.6	2.2	80.7	49.0	53.4	46.6
21671	TILGHMAN	97.7	96.8	0.6	0.9	0.1	0.2	0.2	0.5	3.5	3.8	4.2	5.2	3.2	20.1	36.7	21.1	2.2	85.2	50.3	51.1	48.9
21672	TODDVILLE	94.0	91.2	4.1	6.4	0.2	0.4	0.5	0.7	4.0	4.8	5.3	5.7	2.9	22.9	31.2	20.2	3.1	82.4	47.8	51.0	49.0
21673	TRAPPE	82.5	76.2	14.7	20.0	0.6	0.7	1.4	2.5	5.9	6.6	6.5	6.1	4.3	24.0	30.4	14.5	1.9	77.1	42.9	49.5	50.5
21675	WINGATE	95.5	93.6	4.5	6.4	0.0	0.0	0.0	0.0	4.3	4.3	4.3	6.4	4.3	23.4	31.9	17.0	4.3	80.9	46.9	51.1	48.9
21676	WITTMAN	89.1	83.8	10.5	15.4	0.0	0.0	0.8	1.1	4.0	4.0	5.1	4.8	3.3	16.9	37.5	21.0	3.3	82.7	51.3	50.7	49.3
21677	WOOLFORD	92.8	88.7	6.5	10.1	0.0	0.3	0.7	0.9	4.1	4.6	5.2	6.1	2.9	18.8	34.2	22.3	1.7	82.0	50.1	47.2	52.8
21678	WORTON	80.3	74.5	18.2	23.3	0.1	0.2	1.5	2.4	5.2	5.5	6.2	6.8	4.8	22.4	31.9	15.6	1.7	78.8	44.3	49.7	50.3
21679	WYE MILLS	88.1	82.3	10.3	14.5	0.0	0.6	1.6	3.2	6.4	6.7	7.5	7.5	4.3	24.3	30.1	11.9	1.2	74.5	40.6	49.9	50.1
21701	FREDERICK	84.1	79.5	11.4	13.7	1.7	2.6	2.4	4.1	7.0	6.8	6.6	6.5	6.3	28.4	25.4	10.6	2.4	75.9	37.8	47.1	52.9
21702	FREDERICK	81.2	75.5	10.1	12.1	3.6	5.1	5.0	7.9	7.2	6.9	6.7	6.6	6.7	28.5	26.3	9.6	1.6	75.1	36.5	48.5	51.5
21703	FREDERICK	81.7	75.2	11.1	14.2	3.2	4.6	3.8	6.4	8.6	8.2	7.9	7.4	6.5	30.3	24.8	5.4	1.0	70.6	33.5	49.7	50.3
21704	FREDERICK	88.0	83.0	9.0	13.3	1.1	1.2	1.1	1.5	6.4	6.8	7.1	6.7	4.7	24.9	29.6	12.3	1.5	75.5	40.8	49.9	50.1
21710	ADAMSTOWN	92.6	90.2	4.4	5.4	0.9	1.3	1.5	2.8	6.7	7.0	7.5	7.1	5.2	23.6	30.2	10.7	2.2	74.5	40.5	49.1	50.9
21711	BIG POOL	98.8	98.3	0.0	0.0	0.2	0.3	0.5	0.9	4.8	5.1	5.6	6.9	5.5	25.3	32.2	13.1	1.4	80.3	43.2	51.1	48.9
21713	BOONSBORO	98.5	97.6	0.4	0.7	0.3	0.5	0.6	1.1	5.0	5.5	6.3	6.5	4.6	23.6	31.4	14.0	3.2	78.8	44.1	48.6	51.4
21716	BRUNSWICK	92.1	88.6	5.4	7.5	0.5	0.8	0.9	1.7	6.6	6.3	6.6	7.5	7.2	27.6	27.6	9.2	1.3	75.7	37.2	48.6	51.4
21718	BURKITTSVILLE	97.1	95.7	1.2	1.6	0.6	1.1	0.6	1.1	4.3	5.4	6.5	7.5	4.8	23.7	33.9	12.4	1.6	78.5	43.7	49.5	50.5
21719	CASCADE	92.9	88.4	3.5	6.3	0.6	0.8	1.7	3.0	7.6	7.3	7.0	7.5	6.5	28.4	25.6	8.7	1.3	73.4	35.4	49.8	50.2
21722	CLEAR SPRING	98.5	97.4	0.6	1.2	0.4	0.7	0.3	0.5	5.9	6.4	7.1	6.7	4.4	25.8	30.6	11.8	1.2	76.3	41.1	51.2	48.8
21723	COOKSVILLE	90.1	85.4	5.9	8.4	1.7	2.6	1.5	2.9	6.7	8.4	9.7	8.3	4.2	19.7	34.2	8.0	0.7	69.7	41.0	49.9	50.1
21727	EMMITSBURG	94.1	91.3	3.5	4.8	0.8	1.2	1.3	2.3	4.9	4.7	4.7	13.8	15.0	22.4	20.9	10.7	2.9	82.2	31.2	48.1	51.9
21733	FAIRPLAY	41.4	33.1	58.2	66.4	0.1	0.1	0.5	0.6	1.1	1.2	1.3	2.1	9.4	62.5	18.7	3.4	0.2	95.5	35.8	89.8	10.2
21737	GLENELG	92.7	89.1	3.7	5.3	2.1	3.1	1.9	3.7	6.9	8.5	10.0	9.1	3.5	18.8	32.9	9.1	1.3	68.0	40.7	50.3	49.7
21738	GLENWOOD	93.2	90.0	3.7	5.2	1.3	2.1	1.2	2.3	6.5	8.0	9.4	8.5	3.9	19.6	34.1	9.2	0.8	70.7	41.5	50.4	49.6
21740	HAGERSTOWN	86.2	81.3	10.8	14.4	0.8	1.2	1.5	2.5	7.0	6.5	6.2	6.4	7.4	28.1	24.9	11.5	2.0	76.5	36.9	50.8	49.2
21742	HAGERSTOWN	92.9	88.2	3.5	6.4	1.7	2.5	1.3	2.2	5.8	6.0	6.4	6.2	4.9	23.8	29.1	15.0	2.8	77.7	42.8	48.1	51.9
21750	HANCOCK	97.8	96.6	0.3	0.5	0.2	0.3	0.7	1.3	5.7	5.9	6.2	6.7	5.0	25.4	28.7	14.7	1.7	78.3	41.6	50.0	50.0
21754	IJAMSVILLE	95.5	93.2	1.8	2.6	1.4	2.3	1.1	2.1	7.1	8.6	9.7	7.7	3.8	19.7	34.6	8.2	0.6	69.6	41.1	49.9	50.1
21755	JEFFERSON	95.8	93.8	1.9	2.7	0.7	1.1	1.2	2.2	6.3	6.7	7.6	7.4	4.5	23.8	32.3	10.1	1.3	74.5	41.0	50.0	50.0
21756	KEEDYSVILLE	97.9	96.4	0.7	1.3	0.4	0.6	1.0	1.8	6.1	6.8	7.6	7.1	4.2	25.3	32.0	9.7	1.1	74.8	40.9	50.9	49.1
21757	KEYMAR	96.6	95.2	2.1	2.8	0.3	0.5	1.2	2.3	5.6	5.9	6.5	8.2	4.8	25.1	30.4	11.7	1.8	76.5	41.1	50.8	49.2
21758	KNOXVILLE	94.2	91.4	4.2	6.0	0.4	0.7	0.7	1.4	5.8	6.3	6.8	6.8	5.0	25.6	31.3	11.1	1.5	76.9	41.2	50.4	49.6
21765	LISBON	91.3	85.4	5.8	8.5	1.4	2.4	1.4	2.4	7.3	7.3	9.8	8.5	4.9	18.3	35.4	8.5	0.0	68.3	41.4	51.2	48.8
21766	LITTLE ORLEANS	99.2	99.0	0.3	0.4	0.0	0.0	0.0	0.0	5.6	5.9	6.2	5.8	4.3	26.0	29.1	15.0	2.1	78.5	42.3	50.4	49.6
21767	MAUGANSVILLE	97.5	96.1	0.7	1.2	0.2	0.2	1.2	2.4	5.9	5.4	5.8	6.2	6.3	25.1	27.0	15.5	2.8	79.2	41.4	46.7	53.3
21769	MIDDLETOWN	97.2	95.7	0.9	1.3	0.7	1.1	1.1	2.2	5.4	6.3	7.5	8.1	4.8	22.9	34.7	9.2	1.1	75.5	41.8	49.4	50.6
21770	MONROVIA	96.0	93.6	1.2	1.7	0.8	1.2	2.1	4.0	6.3	7.2	8.7	7.7	4.2	22.7	34.3	8.3	0.6	72.6	40.8	51.4	48.6
21771	MOUNT AIRY	95.6	93.5	2.1	3.0	0.8	1.2	1.3	2.4	7.3	8.1	8.5	7.8	4.2	24.8	30.5	7.9	0.9	70.8	38.6	49.6	50.4
21773	MYERSVILLE	98.0	97.0	0.4	0.6	0.3	0.5	1.2	2.3	6.2	6.9	7.8	8.0	4.4	24.0	32.2	9.4	1.2	74.1	40.6	50.0	50.0
21774	NEW MARKET	94.0	90.9	2.7	3.9	1.3	2.0	2.3	4.2	9.6	9.0	8.9	7.4	3.7	29.8	25.7	5.5	0.4	67.5	35.0	49.8	50.2
21776	NEW WINDSOR	96.2	94.7	2.4	3.3	0.4	0.6	0.9	1.5	6.4	6.6	7.1	7.3	5.6	25.9	30.5	9.2	1.3	75.2	39.1	49.7	50.3
21777	POINT OF ROCKS	92.8	89.3	3.6	5.0	0.9	1.5	0.7	1.2	7.2	8.2	8.7	7.8	3.8	27.0	29.9	6.7	0.7	71.0	38.6	48.8	51.2
21778	ROCKY RIDGE	98.6	97.5	0.1	0.2	0.4	0.8	0.5	1.0	4.8	5.3	5.6	5.8	4.6	25.5	31.7	15.0	1.6	80.7	43.8	49.2	50.8
21779	ROHRERSVILLE	97.7	96.1	0.8	1.5	0.3	0.5	0.7	1.3	5.3	6.0	6.8	6.5	4.2	25.9	33.2	10.8	1.3	77.5	42.3	51.4	48.6
21780	SABILLASVILLE	90.3	86.4	8.5	11.7	0.3	0.5	1.3	2.4	5.9	6.4	6.5	14.9	3.8	22.9	27.6	10.6	1.2	70.1	37.5	55.2	44.8
21782	SHARPSBURG	98.1	96.9	0.4	0.8	0.5	0.8	0.7	1.3	5.1	6.0	6.4	6.4	4.2	25.6	33.9	11.5	1.0	78.5	42.7	50.4	49.6
21783	SMITHSBURG	95.1	91.2	2.1	4.4	0.8	1.3	1.7	3.1	6.8	6.7	6.9	7.0	5.9	25.8	28.0	11.4	1.5	75.0	38.7	49.7	50.3
21784	SYKESVILLE	94.4	92.1	3.2	4.3	1.1	1.7	1.1	2.0	6.9	7.2	7.7	7.6	5.0	24.8	29.8	9.3	1.8	73.4	39.4	49.9	50.1
21787	TANEYTOWN	96.8	95.2	1.3	1.9	0.4	0.6	1.2	2.2	7.3	7.1	7.1	7.7	6.6	25.9	27.1	9.8	1.4	73.5	36.8	49.6	50.4
21788	THURMONT	98.0	96.9	0.5	0.8	0.4	0.6	0.6	1.2	6.9	6.8	6.8	6.7	5.5	26.7	27.5	11.5	1.6	75.4	38.9	49.4	50.6
21790	TUSCARORA	93.2	90.9	3.4	4.0	1.1	1.0	1.1	2.0	7.1	8.1	8.1	7.1	4.0	27.3	29.3	8.1	1.0	72.7	39.1	48.5	51.5
21791	UNION BRIDGE	95.5	93.6	2.8	3.9	0.5	0.8	0.8	1.5	6.3	6.8	7.2	6.9	5.0	25.0	30.1	11.1	1.5	75.2	40.4	50.4	49.6
21793	WALKERSVILLE	93.8	91.0	3.3	4.4	1.0	1.6	1.4	2.7	5.8	6.3	7.0	8.1	5.7	25.1	31.3	9.2	1.6	75.9	39.4	47.7	52.3
21794	WEST FRIENDSHIP	90.9	86.3	4.8	7.2	2.5	3.7	1.6	3.0	7.1	8.5	10.1	9.2	3.5	19.0	32.5	9.0	1.0	67.7	40.7	50.2	49.8
	MARYLAND	64.0	59.0	27.9	30.1	4.0	5.3	4.3	6.4	6.5	6.6	6.7	7.1	6.4	26.9	27.4	10.7	1.7	76.0	38.1	48.4	51.6
	UNITED STATES	75.1	72.0	12.3	12.7	3.8	4.6	12.5	15.7	6.8	6.7	6.6	7.1	6.9	27.0	26.0	10.9	1.9	75.7	36.9	49.2	50.8

ZIP CODE #	POST OFFICE NAME	2009 Per Capita Income	2009 HH Income Base	2009 HOUSEHOLD INCOME DISTRIBUTION (%) Less than $25,000	$25,000 to $49,999	$50,000 to $99,999	$100,000 to $149,999	$150,000 or More	MEDIAN HOUSEHOLD INCOME 2009	2014	2009 National Centile	2009 State Centile	2009 Home Value Base	2009 HOME VALUE DISTRIBUTION (%) Less than $50,000	$50,000 to $89,999	$90,000 to $174,999	$175,000 to $399,999	$400,000 or More	2009 Median Home Value
21612	BOZMAN	50344	385	13.0	23.6	35.8	9.9	17.7	67778	68180	85	53	335	0.0	0.0	15.5	38.2	46.3	373404
21613	CAMBRIDGE	22615	7699	33.2	27.4	30.6	5.7	3.1	38625	40732	29	11	4612	5.7	6.4	36.0	38.5	13.4	181195
21617	CENTREVILLE	30196	3559	17.7	17.1	42.5	14.5	8.1	69129	72142	86	55	2847	1.3	1.2	6.8	48.9	41.8	364307
21619	CHESTER	36142	2569	10.4	21.3	43.0	14.4	10.9	70112	71307	87	57	2053	1.7	0.6	4.1	61.3	32.3	341653
21620	CHESTERTOWN	27941	5249	23.6	25.8	36.9	8.2	5.5	50443	51755	62	27	3454	1.4	2.7	17.7	53.4	24.7	253003
21622	CHURCH CREEK	29150	199	29.6	35.2	24.6	5.5	5.0	37037	38247	24	8	168	7.7	10.1	36.9	29.2	16.1	165476
21623	CHURCH HILL	27707	667	14.8	26.7	42.6	10.9	4.9	61603	64071	80	45	503	2.8	1.0	17.7	52.1	26.4	264732
21625	CORDOVA	22241	1002	17.6	23.3	47.7	9.5	2.0	56674	58259	74	37	810	1.0	4.0	20.4	55.6	19.1	263636
21626	CRAPO	21509	60	31.7	38.3	21.7	3.3	5.0	35925	35930	20	7	50	12.0	18.0	54.0	12.0	4.0	119444
21628	CRUMPTON	23299	208	21.6	26.9	44.2	6.3	1.0	51344	54934	64	28	174	9.8	14.9	16.1	40.8	18.4	203125
21629	DENTON	23205	3609	20.3	28.3	39.5	8.8	3.1	51068	51424	64	28	2703	2.7	1.8	20.4	62.4	12.6	231129
21631	EAST NEW MARKET	24480	1181	21.9	28.2	38.7	7.3	3.9	49888	51839	61	25	1010	7.3	6.1	34.7	41.7	10.2	179703
21632	FEDERALSBURG	18959	2692	32.8	28.7	31.3	4.9	2.3	39399	41011	31	11	1794	6.7	7.9	34.2	42.8	8.4	177253
21634	FISHING CREEK	29731	240	37.1	37.1	15.4	3.3	7.1	30634	32155	9	3	208	11.5	5.3	29.8	33.7	19.7	192500
21635	GALENA	27400	922	19.7	20.8	46.1	9.0	4.3	60800	61473	79	43	753	1.1	2.8	20.2	58.3	17.7	251061
21636	GOLDSBORO	20104	466	17.4	33.5	41.2	4.9	3.0	49241	49606	59	24	380	11.1	2.9	24.7	52.4	8.9	197872
21638	GRASONVILLE	35445	1939	18.8	16.1	33.6	17.8	13.7	68391	69210	86	54	1536	0.7	0.8	11.9	34.9	51.7	415569
21639	GREENSBORO	19650	1762	22.4	28.7	40.1	7.3	1.6	48570	49456	58	24	1270	0.9	2.4	30.2	60.9	5.7	199083
21640	HENDERSON	17914	696	25.7	33.3	35.1	4.0	1.9	42344	44507	40	14	543	15.5	5.9	30.6	42.2	5.9	170395
21643	HURLOCK	19926	2178	26.1	28.1	38.7	5.2	1.9	46596	48282	53	20	1682	5.4	9.9	43.7	36.6	4.4	159615
21644	INGLESIDE	23311	50	18.0	28.0	44.0	8.0	2.0	52871	56611	68	30	41	0.0	0.0	19.5	53.7	26.8	275000
21645	KENNEDYVILLE	24968	457	18.2	31.1	38.5	7.2	5.0	50588	51202	63	27	345	1.2	1.4	20.6	46.7	30.1	290217
21647	MCDANIEL	26638	196	16.3	34.2	36.7	10.7	2.0	49572	51001	60	25	163	0.0	1.8	30.1	46.0	22.1	280357
21648	MADISON	25045	131	35.1	35.1	18.3	4.6	6.9	33063	35596	13	4	113	11.5	5.3	24.8	36.3	22.1	214583
21649	MARYDEL	14283	635	30.9	27.6	36.2	4.1	1.3	41977	44684	39	14	460	6.3	7.4	30.4	48.0	7.8	187500
21650	MASSEY	20095	80	22.5	27.5	40.0	6.3	3.8	50000	50000	61	26	58	0.0	5.2	41.4	46.6	6.9	187500
21651	MILLINGTON	21171	1087	19.5	33.9	40.1	5.2	1.4	44814	48867	48	17	849	5.7	8.2	26.4	46.5	13.2	197917
21654	OXFORD	51511	757	14.8	21.0	31.7	12.9	19.6	69185	70104	86	55	605	0.5	1.8	6.0	26.6	65.1	517979
21655	PRESTON	20344	2066	18.3	33.3	41.4	4.6	2.3	48077	49217	57	23	1706	4.0	5.9	27.7	56.4	5.9	193772
21657	QUEEN ANNE	27056	390	17.9	18.2	43.8	14.1	5.9	61684	63963	80	45	305	0.7	2.3	12.1	54.8	30.2	328824
21658	QUEENSTOWN	39564	1460	11.6	16.4	31.5	23.9	16.6	82772	83394	93	70	1233	0.6	0.2	3.7	33.2	62.3	492945
21659	RHODESDALE	20286	666	23.4	33.2	38.0	5.1	0.3	44721	47095	47	17	561	11.9	14.3	39.0	28.2	6.6	140577
21660	RIDGELY	20997	1434	19.4	32.6	37.0	8.4	2.6	47384	48373	55	21	1025	2.1	0.5	29.7	60.3	7.4	225000
21661	ROCK HALL	22876	1283	29.9	34.2	28.4	5.9	1.5	39965	41372	32	12	1003	2.7	4.6	39.9	38.0	14.9	181477
21662	ROYAL OAK	48683	296	21.3	18.6	35.8	6.1	18.2	60854	62867	79	43	247	2.8	2.8	10.1	38.9	45.3	368056
21663	SAINT MICHAELS	40256	1963	20.8	22.9	34.7	9.5	12.1	56437	59855	73	36	1462	0.8	2.1	9.9	46.0	41.2	343913
21665	SHERWOOD	26015	113	17.7	35.4	35.4	9.7	1.8	47660	48619	56	22	94	0.0	2.1	29.8	45.7	22.3	268750
21666	STEVENSVILLE	35442	4640	7.9	12.9	42.0	24.1	13.2	84776	86113	94	72	4159	0.3	0.7	1.6	56.6	40.9	373406
21667	STILL POND	24301	132	15.9	33.3	38.6	8.3	3.8	50640	50894	63	27	106	0.0	1.9	24.5	42.5	31.1	290000
21668	SUDLERSVILLE	21294	757	26.0	26.2	39.6	6.1	2.1	47994	51240	57	23	577	3.6	1.7	22.9	52.7	19.1	232181
21669	TAYLORS ISLAND	29774	101	37.6	36.6	15.8	4.0	5.9	30366	31518	9	3	88	11.4	4.5	31.8	33.0	19.3	187500
21671	TILGHMAN	16940	404	34.2	34.4	29.5	2.0	0.0	36815	37906	23	8	334	2.7	0.0	25.4	50.0	21.9	222368
21672	TODDVILLE	26338	213	33.3	36.6	22.5	2.8	4.7	35228	35623	18	6	177	9.0	18.1	57.1	11.9	4.0	120608
21673	TRAPPE	29868	1414	17.4	24.7	38.3	11.5	8.2	58955	60657	76	39	1046	1.7	5.2	23.8	33.0	36.3	270290
21675	WINGATE	28047	23	34.8	39.1	21.7	0.0	4.3	33593	35000	15	5	19	5.3	15.8	63.2	10.5	5.3	122500
21676	WITTMAN	29385	136	16.2	33.8	37.5	11.0	1.5	50000	50703	61	26	113	0.0	2.7	30.1	46.0	21.2	277500
21677	WOOLFORD	24812	147	18.4	31.3	36.7	10.2	3.4	50351	49745	62	26	125	0.8	1.6	20.0	47.2	30.4	265909
21678	WORTON	25923	1004	14.5	32.1	41.6	7.7	4.1	54252	55874	70	33	815	3.2	2.5	28.8	44.5	21.0	210567
21679	WYE MILLS	25101	135	17.0	23.0	48.9	8.1	3.0	55857	56120	72	35	108	0.0	4.6	17.6	62.0	15.7	270000
21701	FREDERICK	34472	15080	14.3	20.6	37.1	18.5	9.6	67852	71918	85	53	9737	0.2	0.4	10.3	66.8	22.3	291046
21702	FREDERICK	32100	14193	12.2	19.9	40.0	18.8	9.1	70355	75693	87	57	9253	0.2	0.2	7.0	63.1	29.4	311046
21703	FREDERICK	30915	11750	9.6	16.8	46.0	19.7	7.9	74087	77308	89	61	8079	1.2	0.2	9.4	66.7	22.5	278385
21704	FREDERICK	35930	3459	9.1	11.4	38.4	25.7	15.4	87940	93274	95	76	3090	0.8	0.0	4.1	47.1	48.0	393448
21710	ADAMSTOWN	36063	1336	14.8	12.4	31.4	26.5	14.9	87223	91897	94	76	1037	0.3	0.1	3.7	52.7	43.3	370921
21711	BIG POOL	20845	425	21.4	32.2	37.9	4.7	3.8	47788	50074	56	22	338	2.1	6.2	39.3	39.3	13.0	183000
21713	BOONSBORO	25221	3637	16.8	29.0	40.2	10.0	4.0	53834	57348	69	32	2888	1.6	0.9	14.3	65.3	18.0	266414
21716	BRUNSWICK	25603	1953	18.2	23.0	43.7	11.9	3.1	59195	58293	76	40	1383	0.9	0.2	20.1	76.5	2.3	215870
21718	BURKITTSVILLE	35387	82	11.0	20.7	47.6	12.2	8.5	67510	66774	85	53	67	0.0	0.0	0.0	62.7	37.3	352778
21719	CASCADE	23660	690	20.4	31.9	34.1	5.9	7.7	47214	52210	55	21	455	4.4	2.9	36.7	48.8	7.3	188221
21722	CLEAR SPRING	23773	2111	14.8	25.6	48.6	7.7	3.3	59309	60988	77	40	1708	3.7	3.5	20.8	60.0	12.1	235355
21723	COOKSVILLE	55415	245	4.1	1.2	20.8	29.4	44.5	139462	142002	99	97	221	0.0	0.0	0.0	14.5	85.5	672059
21727	EMMITSBURG	22316	1842	18.9	24.4	43.1	11.5	2.2	56100	55294	73	35	1209	0.3	0.4	17.9	66.7	14.7	240017
21733	FAIRPLAY	18728	375	14.4	30.4	45.9	7.7	1.6	53721	56970	69	32	309	4.5	4.5	13.6	64.1	13.3	239236
21737	GLENELG	49418	572	3.1	7.2	22.4	24.8	42.5	134488	138752	99	96	515	2.9	0.0	0.0	9.7	87.4	690505
21738	GLENWOOD	55167	849	1.4	4.7	22.1	24.1	47.6	144156	145495	100	98	768	1.0	0.0	0.0	10.7	88.3	689394
21740	HAGERSTOWN	21334	24832	29.1	30.7	32.9	4.8	2.4	43456	46535	44	15	13431	3.5	2.9	34.4	52.2	6.9	191970
21742	HAGERSTOWN	29503	11247	15.8	25.1	40.9	11.4	6.8	60969	62110	79	44	8036	2.1	1.8	16.7	62.0	17.3	245682
21750	HANCOCK	20117	1656	26.1	36.5	31.2	4.8	1.4	43849	46029	45	16	1065	5.4	9.9	41.0	34.6	9.1	161029
21754	IJAMSVILLE	46337	2060	5.5	6.3	23.4	28.2	36.6	124285	126477	99	95	1927	0.0	0.0	1.6	36.9	61.5	457642
21755	JEFFERSON	35382	2418	8.3	12.9	33.5	30.6	14.8	92233	100063	95	79	2055	2.0	0.5	7.3	45.9	44.2	377299
21756	KEEDYSVILLE	26255	1154	13.3	16.1	52.8	11.9	5.9	66807	68423	85	51	1007	1.7	1.1	13.1	62.0	22.1	307119
21757	KEYMAR	25584	1186	14.1	23.8	45.5	11.0	5.6	61690	60746	80	45	889	0.3	1.0	9.4	61.9	27.3	318421
21758	KNOXVILLE	28509	1748	9.8	18.4	46.3	19.2	6.4	68933	70823	86	55	1415	1.8	0.5	9.3	59.2	29.3	323568
21765	LISBON	72302	34	2.9	0.0	20.6	29.4	47.1	144025	147976	100	97	31	0.0	0.0	0.0	16.1	83.9	670455
21766	LITTLE ORLEANS	17368	271	32.1	32.5	31.7	3.7	0.0	38269	40625	27	10	225	8.4	8.9	29.3	44.0	9.3	183152
21767	MAUGANSVILLE	23180	576	26.6	21.2	45.1	7.1	0.0	52317	56445	67	29	313	0.3	4.2	16.6	69.0	9.9	216021
21769	MIDDLETOWN	37978	3955	5.5	13.8	34.2	29.3	17.2	93831	100703	96	81	3319	0.3	0.0	2.6	56.9	40.2	372354
21770	MONROVIA	38714	2032	3.3	7.6	33.9	35.2	19.9	105769	108011	97	89	1920	0.0	0.0	0.7	54.5	44.7	387990
21771	MOUNT AIRY	38901	9992	5.0	9.6	34.0	29.6	21.9	102097	107341	97	88	8949	1.2	0.1	1.4	47.5	49.8	399220
21773	MYERSVILLE	31704	1941	8.4	14.0	42.8	24.6	10.1	79490	84721	92	67	1649	1.4	0.4	11.8	50.4	36.1	352680
21774	NEW MARKET	38328	3773	4.7	6.9	36.8	31.3	20.2	101937	105515	97	88	3402	0.0	0.1	2.2	64.6	33.2	351109
21776	NEW WINDSOR	28591	2204	8.4	20.6	45.3	20.1	5.7	72906	76888	88	60	1813	0.2	0.1	5.0	65.8	28.9	339953
21777	POINT OF ROCKS	36943	425	8.5	4.9	36.7	37.9	12.0	99789	104522	97	86	373	0.0	0.5	8.3	75.1	16.1	321429
21778	ROCKY RIDGE	26858	371	15.9	16.2	49.1	15.6	3.2	67497	70429	85	52	295	3.1	0.7	11.9	55.3	29.2	308209
21779	ROHRERSVILLE	25156	373	15.5	19.6	51.2	8.8	4.8	62596	63449	81	47	314	3.5	1.0	7.6	58.0	29.9	312500
21780	SABILLASVILLE	25795	589	12.6	28.0	41.8	11.9	5.8	59487	61155	77	40	480	2.5	0.8	7.1	63.8	25.8	302521
21782	SHARPSBURG	24784	1672	12.7	29.1	46.2	9.0	2.9	60202	61579	78	41	1384	2.2	3.1	22.5	56.9	15.3	243909
21783	SMITHSBURG	26598	4681	16.5	24.4	42.5	11.3	5.3	60849	62180	79	43	3375	0.9	0.7	15.0	64.8	18.7	259845
21784	SYKESVILLE	36218	13376	7.0	11.2	35.0	29.8	17.1	94658	101727	96	82	11468	0.4	0.1	1.6	57.9	40.0	370760
21787	TANEYTOWN	24265	3948	14.2	24.7	46.2	9.6	5.3	60303	59549	78	42	2982	0.1	0.2	13.4	71.4	14.9	266406
21788	THURMONT	27265	4405	12.8	21.8	48.6	12.0	4.8	63770	64957	82	48	3351	0.8	0.4	5.9	79.9	13.0	281815
21790	TUSCARORA	44346	43	14.0	4.7	34.9	34.9	11.6	94004	96360	96	81	36	0.0	0.0	5.6	72.2	22.2	328571
21791	UNION BRIDGE	28832	2154	11.4	20.2	41.4	19.5	7.5	69491	73707	86	56	1632	0.4	0.1	6.7	62.9	30.0	327009
21793	WALKERSVILLE	30158	3493	6.7	17.1	41.1	24.8	10.3	79132	84743	92	67	2889	0.0	0.1	10.8	69.3	19.8	312911
21794	WEST FRIENDSHIP	45591	675	3.6	6.4	22.1	27.6	40.4	131624	135957	99	96	610	0.0	0.0	0.5	13.3	86.2	682266
	MARYLAND	32538		15.1	20.5	36.5	16.4	11.5	67267	70086				1.9	2.6	14.3	53.1	28.2	289711
	UNITED STATES	27277		20.9	24.4	35.3	11.7	7.6	54719	56938				9.3	13.1	31.6	32.6	13.5	162279

ZIP CODE		FINANCIAL SERVICES				THE HOME						ENTERTAINMENT						PERSONAL			
						Home Improvements		Furnishings													
#	POST OFFICE NAME	Auto Loan	Home Loan	Invest-ments	Retire-ment Plans	Home Repair	Lawn & Garden	Comput-ers & Hard-ware-Personal	Major Appli-ances	TV, Radio, Sound Equip-ment	Furni-ture	Dine out/ Carry out	Sports Equip-ment	Fees & Tickets	Toys & Games	Travel	Cable TV	Apparel & Services	Auto Repairs	Health Insur-ance	Pets & Supplies
21612	BOZMAN	144	152	206	151	175	179	136	161	144	155	142	101	150	130	158	151	97	154	180	182
21613	CAMBRIDGE	72	67	69	68	67	75	71	72	74	68	73	54	69	73	69	77	51	73	79	86
21617	CENTREVILLE	108	121	111	124	119	116	111	112	108	113	110	87	118	110	116	108	77	110	110	132
21619	CHESTER	116	134	120	136	130	130	120	123	118	121	119	95	130	120	128	118	84	120	123	144
21620	CHESTERTOWN	93	90	103	90	92	101	90	96	92	87	92	71	88	90	93	95	63	94	102	112
21622	CHURCH CREEK	102	76	123	76	82	107	80	100	83	70	82	77	65	80	83	90	54	93	102	119
21623	CHURCH HILL	101	112	97	116	109	111	101	105	99	101	100	82	107	102	106	100	70	101	104	124
21625	CORDOVA	87	98	84	100	95	96	87	91	86	87	86	71	93	88	92	86	60	87	90	107
21626	CRAPO	100	69	110	69	72	106	76	95	79	62	79	78	56	78	76	87	51	89	100	117
21628	CRUMPTON	86	79	70	77	77	81	75	79	77	78	77	58	71	81	71	80	53	77	79	94
21629	DENTON	84	85	81	87	84	89	82	85	83	80	83	65	83	83	83	84	57	83	87	101
21631	EAST NEW MARKET	91	86	86	89	88	100	83	94	86	77	85	70	79	87	85	91	58	87	98	109
21632	FEDERALSBURG	76	63	65	63	63	76	67	72	71	63	69	55	59	72	63	75	47	70	77	86
21634	FISHING CREEK	108	86	139	85	95	114	86	110	90	81	89	80	75	86	94	96	59	101	108	127
21635	GALENA	105	89	119	89	94	112	88	107	92	81	90	79	78	90	92	97	61	98	107	124
21636	GOLDSBORO	86	81	78	81	79	89	76	83	79	76	78	64	74	81	76	82	54	79	84	99
21638	GRASONVILLE	130	126	163	127	137	143	122	138	123	122	121	102	121	119	132	126	84	131	137	158
21639	GREENSBORO	71	82	73	82	80	78	75	76	74	75	74	59	81	75	79	74	53	75	75	89
21640	HENDERSON	84	65	71	65	65	82	66	75	71	64	70	58	56	74	62	77	48	71	79	91
21643	HURLOCK	80	75	72	75	72	82	72	77	74	70	74	60	69	76	71	77	51	75	80	92
21644	INGLESIDE	88	80	79	84	82	95	79	89	82	72	80	68	73	83	79	86	55	82	92	104
21645	KENNEDYVILLE	110	83	133	82	89	116	87	109	90	77	89	84	70	87	91	97	59	101	111	129
21647	MCDANIEL	98	79	127	77	86	104	79	100	82	74	81	73	68	78	85	88	54	92	99	116
21648	MADISON	106	85	137	83	93	112	85	108	89	79	88	79	74	84	92	95	58	99	106	125
21649	MARYDEL	82	62	70	61	62	80	63	74	69	61	68	56	52	72	59	75	46	69	77	89
21650	MASSEY	89	81	80	84	82	95	80	90	82	72	81	68	73	84	80	87	55	83	93	105
21651	MILLINGTON	85	77	74	77	77	86	75	82	77	72	77	61	69	79	73	81	52	78	84	97
21654	OXFORD	140	163	212	163	185	176	142	162	143	160	141	108	163	131	167	145	100	153	168	182
21655	PRESTON	81	78	75	81	78	88	75	83	77	69	76	63	72	78	76	80	52	77	85	97
21657	QUEEN ANNE	102	115	101	118	112	112	104	107	102	104	102	83	111	104	109	101	72	103	105	125
21658	QUEENSTOWN	138	167	177	171	174	162	145	155	139	153	139	117	163	138	163	137	100	146	147	176
21659	RHODESDALE	85	64	85	63	66	87	65	80	71	60	69	60	53	71	64	77	46	74	83	95
21660	RIDGELY	75	87	78	87	85	82	80	80	79	79	79	63	86	80	84	79	56	79	80	94
21661	ROCK HALL	82	63	98	62	68	86	65	82	70	60	68	60	55	67	68	75	45	76	84	96
21662	ROYAL OAK	182	146	236	144	160	193	146	186	153	137	151	136	127	145	158	163	100	171	183	215
21663	SAINT MICHAELS	121	117	158	116	132	140	113	130	120	120	117	86	116	110	124	126	80	126	144	149
21665	SHERWOOD	95	76	122	75	83	100	76	96	79	71	78	70	66	75	82	85	52	89	95	112
21666	STEVENSVILLE	136	158	146	158	155	141	139	141	133	148	135	109	151	137	147	129	96	136	130	162
21667	STILL POND	104	83	135	82	92	110	83	106	87	78	86	77	72	83	90	93	57	98	105	123
21668	SUDLERSVILLE	92	73	92	73	75	95	73	88	78	69	77	66	63	78	73	84	52	81	91	104
21669	TAYLORS ISLAND	108	86	139	85	95	114	86	110	90	81	89	80	75	86	93	96	59	101	108	127
21671	TILGHMAN	64	52	83	51	57	68	52	66	54	48	53	48	45	51	56	57	35	60	65	76
21672	TODDVILLE	101	69	110	69	72	106	77	95	80	62	79	79	56	78	76	87	51	89	101	118
21673	TRAPPE	106	114	139	113	121	119	107	116	105	107	105	87	112	102	117	107	74	112	114	133
21675	WINGATE	103	70	113	70	74	108	78	97	81	63	80	80	57	80	78	89	52	91	103	120
21676	WITTMAN	98	78	127	77	86	104	78	100	82	74	81	73	68	78	85	88	54	92	98	116
21677	WOOLFORD	97	78	126	77	85	103	78	99	81	73	80	72	67	77	84	87	53	91	98	115
21678	WORTON	101	93	114	94	97	111	89	105	92	84	92	78	85	91	95	97	62	98	106	121
21679	WYE MILLS	89	101	87	104	98	99	90	93	88	90	89	73	96	91	95	89	62	90	93	110
21701	FREDERICK	114	121	113	123	119	112	120	114	117	121	118	91	124	118	120	115	84	116	112	134
21702	FREDERICK	115	121	114	124	119	111	120	114	116	123	118	91	124	119	120	113	84	116	110	134
21703	FREDERICK	121	126	111	126	121	111	122	116	117	127	119	93	123	122	120	113	84	117	108	136
21704	FREDERICK	125	166	167	159	170	150	139	145	134	141	135	108	161	136	157	134	99	139	138	162
21710	ADAMSTOWN	124	162	160	155	164	143	136	141	130	140	131	105	155	133	151	128	96	135	131	157
21711	BIG POOL	84	76	76	80	78	90	75	85	78	68	76	64	69	79	75	82	52	79	88	99
21713	BOONSBORO	91	98	90	100	97	99	91	95	90	89	91	74	94	92	95	92	63	92	95	111
21716	BRUNSWICK	84	100	92	98	98	94	93	92	91	91	93	71	102	92	98	92	66	92	93	106
21718	BURKITTSVILLE	112	126	108	130	122	124	113	117	111	113	111	91	120	114	119	111	78	112	116	138
21719	CASCADE	81	92	87	91	91	87	89	87	87	85	87	68	94	87	92	87	62	87	87	101
21722	CLEAR SPRING	95	94	88	98	94	103	89	97	90	84	89	75	88	92	91	93	62	91	99	113
21723	COOKSVILLE	220	291	301	306	302	261	238	248	223	259	225	196	288	227	271	212	169	230	216	280
21727	EMMITSBURG	85	92	86	92	91	91	88	89	88	86	88	68	92	88	91	89	62	88	91	104
21733	FAIRPLAY	84	91	80	94	89	92	83	87	82	81	82	68	86	84	86	83	57	83	87	103
21737	GLENELG	201	267	276	281	276	240	218	227	204	237	206	179	264	208	248	194	155	211	198	257
21738	GLENWOOD	226	300	310	315	310	269	245	255	229	267	232	201	296	234	279	218	174	237	222	288
21740	HAGERSTOWN	71	66	62	68	65	69	72	69	73	69	73	54	70	73	69	75	51	72	74	83
21742	HAGERSTOWN	99	106	106	107	107	110	99	104	100	99	100	78	104	100	105	102	70	102	108	121
21750	HANCOCK	79	63	76	64	65	84	66	78	71	59	69	59	56	71	65	77	47	73	83	91
21754	IJAMSVILLE	184	241	246	250	248	218	199	208	187	214	189	161	236	190	225	180	140	194	185	235
21755	JEFFERSON	139	164	153	163	162	146	142	146	135	151	137	112	155	140	151	131	97	138	134	166
21756	KEEDYSVILLE	102	120	104	122	116	112	104	107	101	107	102	85	114	104	111	99	72	103	102	125
21757	KEYMAR	96	115	104	115	113	110	100	104	98	101	99	80	110	100	108	99	70	100	103	121
21758	KNOXVILLE	103	126	119	125	126	119	109	114	106	109	107	87	122	108	119	107	77	109	110	130
21765	LISBON	223	295	305	311	306	265	242	252	226	263	229	199	292	231	275	215	171	233	219	284
21766	LITTLE ORLEANS	77	55	79	54	57	78	57	72	63	53	62	54	46	63	56	69	41	66	75	86
21767	MAUGANSVILLE	77	68	70	69	70	77	73	76	75	70	73	56	67	74	70	78	50	75	81	88
21769	MIDDLETOWN	141	180	174	181	181	162	151	156	143	158	145	121	174	146	168	139	105	148	143	178
21770	MONROVIA	156	200	189	204	199	176	166	171	156	177	158	135	193	161	183	149	116	161	151	194
21771	MOUNT AIRY	159	199	192	203	200	178	167	172	158	179	160	135	192	163	184	152	117	162	154	196
21773	MYERSVILLE	124	151	134	151	147	137	129	133	124	133	125	104	143	128	139	121	89	127	124	153
21774	NEW MARKET	165	197	169	196	189	164	167	168	155	181	158	136	183	166	174	146	114	157	144	190
21776	NEW WINDSOR	112	130	114	130	126	119	116	117	112	118	114	92	125	116	122	111	81	114	112	136
21777	POINT OF ROCKS	143	180	158	179	173	155	151	153	141	158	144	122	170	148	163	136	104	146	137	176
21778	ROCKY RIDGE	96	114	100	115	110	112	99	103	99	100	100	79	110	101	107	100	70	100	106	121
21779	ROHRERSVILLE	96	108	93	112	105	107	97	101	95	97	96	79	103	98	102	95	67	97	100	119
21780	SABILLASVILLE	97	119	110	118	118	112	103	107	100	103	101	82	114	103	112	101	72	103	104	123
21782	SHARPSBURG	90	99	87	102	96	99	89	94	88	88	89	73	93	91	94	89	62	90	94	110
21783	SMITHSBURG	91	104	98	104	103	100	96	97	95	95	95	75	103	96	101	95	68	96	97	113
21784	SYKESVILLE	145	172	162	174	171	155	151	153	144	160	146	119	166	147	161	139	104	147	141	176
21787	TANEYTOWN	90	101	95	101	100	98	96	96	94	93	95	75	101	95	100	95	67	95	97	112
21788	THURMONT	95	112	101	110	109	103	102	101	99	102	101	79	110	102	107	99	71	100	100	117
21790	TUSCARORA	134	173	157	170	169	150	144	147	136	150	138	115	164	141	157	132	100	140	133	167
21791	UNION BRIDGE	107	131	122	129	130	121	115	118	111	116	113	91	127	114	124	111	81	114	113	135
21793	WALKERSVILLE	120	145	129	143	141	132	124	128	120	128	122	99	137	124	133	119	87	123	122	147
21794	WEST FRIENDSHIP	192	254	262	267	263	228	208	216	194	226	196	171	251	198	236	185	147	201	188	244
	MARYLAND	116	125	123	126	125	119	122	119	120	123	121	92	127	121	124	119	86	120	118	139
	UNITED STATES	100	100	100	100	100	100	100	100	100	100	100	100	100	100	100	100	100	100	100	100

ZIP CODE			POPULATION			2000-2009 ANNUAL RATE		HOUSEHOLDS					FAMILIES		
#	POST OFFICE NAME	COUNTY FIPS CODE	2000	2009	2014	% Rate	State Centile	2000	2009	2014	% Annual Rate 2000-2009	2009 Average HH Size	2000	2009	% Annual Rate 2000-2009
21795	WILLIAMSPORT	043	8436	9711	10288	1.5	69	3363	3956	4220	1.8	2.37	2309	2593	1.3
21797	WOODBINE	027	7982	9205	9826	1.6	73	2648	3091	3312	1.7	2.97	2257	2577	1.4
21798	WOODSBORO	021	1895	2205	2329	1.7	76	641	749	795	1.7	2.94	529	601	1.4
21801	SALISBURY	045	27063	31152	33122	1.5	69	9592	11125	11874	1.6	2.57	6398	7238	1.3
21804	SALISBURY	045	30875	36227	39066	1.7	76	12310	14730	15983	2.0	2.41	7881	8955	1.4
21811	BERLIN	047	19677	23554	25420	2.0	82	8263	10122	11005	2.2	2.31	5952	7016	1.8
21813	BISHOPVILLE	047	2293	2479	2522	0.8	47	884	973	996	1.0	2.55	678	721	0.7
21814	BIVALVE	045	434	488	510	1.3	64	178	202	212	1.4	2.42	117	127	0.9
21817	CRISFIELD	039	5419	5462	5471	0.1	17	2301	2361	2381	0.3	2.27	1503	1477	-0.2
21821	DEAL ISLAND	039	1143	1130	1116	-0.1	10	485	492	492	0.2	2.30	330	321	-0.3
21822	EDEN	045	2543	2971	3159	1.7	76	986	1161	1242	1.8	2.31	708	802	1.4
21824	EWELL	039	279	272	268	-0.3	6	127	127	127	0.0	2.14	86	83	-0.4
21826	FRUITLAND	045	3746	4294	4666	1.5	69	1452	1698	1852	1.7	2.53	996	1105	1.1
21829	GIRDLETREE	047	444	476	483	0.8	47	169	183	187	0.9	2.60	129	135	0.5
21830	HEBRON	045	2909	3510	3800	2.1	83	1081	1318	1434	2.2	2.66	845	996	1.8
21835	LINKWOOD	019	396	408	415	0.3	27	170	178	182	0.5	2.26	123	125	0.2
21837	MARDELA SPRINGS	045	2566	2847	2994	1.1	58	978	1106	1169	1.3	2.57	705	768	0.9
21838	MARION STATION	039	1962	2194	2302	1.2	61	782	890	939	1.4	2.46	560	614	1.0
21840	NANTICOKE	045	408	444	457	0.9	49	187	206	213	1.1	2.16	133	140	0.6
21841	NEWARK	047	722	755	769	0.5	35	286	307	314	0.8	2.44	209	215	0.3
21842	OCEAN CITY	047	10146	11389	11904	1.3	64	5014	5713	6008	1.4	1.99	2719	2930	0.8
21849	PARSONSBURG	045	3328	3557	3648	0.7	41	1260	1368	1408	0.9	2.60	947	992	0.5
21850	PITTSVILLE	045	2445	2582	2637	0.6	38	973	1044	1072	0.8	2.47	702	724	0.3
21851	POCOMOKE CITY	047	7326	7468	7703	0.2	23	2893	2980	3083	0.3	2.47	1987	1961	-0.1
21853	PRINCESS ANNE	039	12014	12915	13119	0.8	47	3107	3364	3461	0.9	2.61	1890	1952	0.3
21856	QUANTICO	045	835	986	1064	1.8	78	345	413	446	2.0	2.39	253	291	1.5
21861	SHARPTOWN	045	658	751	789	1.4	67	260	299	314	1.5	2.51	180	198	1.0
21863	SNOW HILL	047	5340	5405	5377	0.1	17	1979	2043	2044	0.3	2.46	1430	1424	0.0
21864	STOCKTON	047	562	607	620	0.8	47	206	225	230	1.0	2.70	157	166	0.6
21865	TYASKIN	045	440	506	538	1.5	69	197	230	245	1.7	2.20	137	153	1.2
21866	TYLERTON	039	85	83	82	-0.3	6	40	40	40	0.0	2.08	27	26	-0.4
21869	VIENNA	019	971	945	940	-0.3	6	415	410	410	-0.1	2.30	285	270	-0.6
21871	WESTOVER	039	2177	2377	2439	1.0	54	842	943	989	1.2	1.66	577	620	0.8
21872	WHALEYVILLE	047	517	590	617	1.4	67	222	258	272	1.6	2.28	162	181	1.2
21874	WILLARDS	045	2369	2461	2489	0.4	30	920	967	981	0.5	2.54	673	680	0.1
21875	DELMAR	045	5209	6237	6665	2.0	82	1954	2371	2541	2.1	2.62	1429	1669	1.7
21901	NORTH EAST	015	12557	16014	17431	2.7	92	4542	5807	6336	2.7	2.74	3407	4229	2.4
21903	PERRYVILLE	015	5435	7011	7748	2.8	93	2070	2682	2983	2.8	2.51	1450	1807	2.4
21904	PORT DEPOSIT	015	6760	7461	7740	1.1	58	2435	2680	2780	1.0	2.77	1845	1969	0.7
21911	RISING SUN	015	9024	10938	11904	2.1	83	3187	3887	4250	2.2	2.77	2486	2949	1.9
21912	WARWICK	015	1031	1362	1492	3.1	95	370	491	540	3.1	2.77	266	340	2.7
21913	CECILTON	015	474	554	610	1.7	76	198	237	263	2.0	2.34	142	164	1.6
21914	CHARLESTOWN	015	644	666	739	0.4	30	255	261	290	0.3	2.54	181	177	-0.2
21915	CHESAPEAKE CITY	015	3081	3585	3822	1.7	76	1231	1444	1545	1.7	2.47	932	1061	1.4
21917	COLORA	015	1891	2167	2278	1.5	69	632	723	763	1.5	2.97	513	576	1.3
21918	CONOWINGO	015	3938	4207	4441	0.7	41	1344	1440	1523	0.7	2.91	1074	1118	0.4
21919	EARLEVILLE	015	2719	3354	3661	2.3	89	1123	1395	1528	2.4	2.38	818	981	2.0
21921	ELKTON	015	38397	46075	49847	2.0	82	13836	16762	18217	2.1	2.70	10177	11944	1.7
	MARYLAND					0.9					0.9	2.60			0.5
	UNITED STATES					1.0					1.1	2.59			0.9

ZIP CODE #	POST OFFICE NAME	RACE (%) White 2000	White 2009	Black 2000	Black 2009	Asian/Pacific 2000	Asian/Pacific 2009	% Hispanic Origin 2000	% Hispanic Origin 2009	2009 AGE DISTRIBUTION (%) 0-4	5-9	10-14	15-19	20-24	25-44	45-64	65-84	85+	18+	MEDIAN AGE 2009	% 2009 Males	% 2009 Females
21795	WILLIAMSPORT	97.9	96.5	0.8	1.5	0.6	0.9	0.5	0.9	5.2	5.5	6.0	5.8	4.7	22.4	29.0	16.6	4.7	79.5	45.2	46.9	53.1
21797	WOODBINE	94.6	92.0	3.2	4.5	0.9	1.4	1.4	2.6	6.0	7.1	8.1	7.9	4.4	21.3	33.7	10.5	1.1	73.5	42.0	49.8	50.2
21798	WOODSBORO	98.3	97.4	0.4	0.5	0.4	0.7	1.1	2.0	6.1	6.7	7.4	7.8	5.1	23.1	31.7	10.7	1.3	74.9	40.9	48.9	51.1
21801	SALISBURY	60.1	53.5	35.8	40.7	1.6	2.3	2.7	4.2	6.6	6.7	6.6	10.3	8.8	22.8	25.6	10.7	1.9	76.0	35.1	46.7	53.3
21804	SALISBURY	75.9	69.2	18.8	23.5	2.6	3.6	2.3	3.7	5.7	5.9	5.9	6.4	7.2	27.3	27.1	12.2	2.2	78.5	38.7	47.9	52.1
21811	BERLIN	84.5	80.0	13.1	16.7	0.7	1.0	1.6	2.6	4.6	4.7	5.0	5.0	3.9	20.2	32.1	22.0	2.4	82.5	49.6	48.6	51.4
21813	BISHOPVILLE	89.8	84.3	8.6	13.3	0.7	1.0	0.7	1.2	5.5	5.6	7.2	6.3	3.5	22.7	35.0	12.5	1.7	77.3	44.5	48.6	51.4
21814	BIVALVE	78.6	69.5	21.0	29.9	0.2	0.2	0.0	0.0	3.7	4.1	4.9	7.2	4.7	20.1	33.8	19.1	2.5	82.8	48.2	49.0	51.0
21817	CRISFIELD	73.3	66.8	23.3	28.5	0.8	1.2	1.4	2.2	6.3	6.2	6.0	6.2	5.0	21.5	28.9	17.1	2.9	77.4	44.2	46.7	53.3
21821	DEAL ISLAND	86.0	81.0	12.6	17.2	0.1	0.1	0.5	0.8	4.1	4.6	5.2	5.8	3.6	20.5	33.2	20.7	2.3	82.6	49.0	48.2	51.8
21822	EDEN	68.2	61.2	29.3	35.6	0.5	0.7	1.1	1.8	5.0	5.4	5.8	9.6	8.8	22.4	29.0	12.4	1.6	80.2	39.3	47.5	52.5
21824	EWELL	93.2	90.8	5.4	7.4	0.0	0.0	0.7	0.7	3.7	4.4	5.1	5.5	3.3	21.3	33.1	20.6	2.9	82.7	49.3	50.7	49.3
21826	FRUITLAND	69.2	60.7	27.1	34.1	1.1	1.5	1.9	3.2	6.7	6.5	6.6	7.1	6.2	24.7	27.8	12.5	1.8	75.7	38.5	46.6	53.4
21829	GIRDLETREE	70.7	58.4	27.7	39.5	0.2	0.4	0.5	0.6	5.3	5.7	6.1	6.5	4.8	23.7	31.9	14.1	1.9	79.2	43.6	47.3	52.7
21830	HEBRON	80.8	72.4	17.2	24.6	0.6	0.8	0.5	0.9	6.9	7.3	7.4	7.4	5.2	27.4	28.1	9.5	0.9	73.8	37.2	48.7	51.3
21835	LINKWOOD	83.6	76.0	15.2	22.3	0.0	0.2	0.8	1.2	5.9	6.4	6.6	5.9	3.9	24.5	30.6	14.0	2.2	77.0	42.9	47.1	52.9
21837	MARDELA SPRINGS	75.7	67.0	22.1	29.5	0.5	0.8	1.6	3.1	5.9	6.7	7.1	6.7	5.4	26.0	29.8	11.2	1.3	76.2	40.0	50.1	49.9
21838	MARION STATION	72.1	63.6	23.9	30.3	0.1	0.2	4.2	6.5	4.8	5.2	5.7	5.6	3.7	21.6	34.2	17.1	2.1	80.6	47.0	49.0	51.0
21840	NANTICOKE	68.6	57.7	30.4	41.0	0.2	0.2	0.7	1.4	2.7	3.2	4.1	5.9	2.7	17.8	34.9	25.2	3.6	86.5	53.3	47.7	52.3
21841	NEWARK	80.7	71.1	16.2	24.4	0.7	1.1	1.7	2.6	5.3	5.8	6.5	5.8	4.1	22.4	35.4	12.6	2.1	77.9	45.0	51.1	48.9
21842	OCEAN CITY	95.4	92.7	2.4	4.1	0.7	1.2	1.3	2.3	3.6	3.7	4.0	4.1	4.3	23.5	30.5	23.5	2.8	86.3	49.3	50.3	49.7
21849	PARSONSBURG	93.0	89.3	4.6	7.1	0.8	1.3	1.0	1.9	6.0	6.2	6.4	6.0	5.3	26.7	31.7	10.5	1.1	77.6	40.7	49.7	50.3
21850	PITTSVILLE	92.2	88.0	4.8	7.4	1.9	2.9	0.8	1.5	7.0	7.3	7.6	6.3	4.2	28.1	28.2	10.2	1.1	74.1	38.3	49.1	50.9
21851	POCOMOKE CITY	60.4	49.8	37.3	47.3	0.5	0.7	0.9	1.4	6.2	6.3	6.7	7.4	6.1	22.4	28.5	13.9	2.5	76.2	41.2	46.3	53.7
21853	PRINCESS ANNE	42.2	34.6	55.7	62.8	0.5	0.6	1.1	1.4	4.4	4.1	4.1	9.6	13.5	32.5	21.3	9.1	1.4	84.7	32.9	57.2	42.8
21856	QUANTICO	62.6	51.3	35.5	46.1	0.2	0.4	0.5	0.7	4.2	4.5	5.1	5.1	3.3	19.3	37.4	19.0	2.2	83.3	49.6	49.5	50.5
21861	SHARPTOWN	91.8	87.5	6.4	9.7	0.5	0.5	0.3	0.8	5.2	5.3	5.9	7.5	5.1	25.2	29.4	14.6	1.9	79.0	42.5	47.4	52.6
21863	SNOW HILL	67.3	57.4	31.3	40.8	0.3	0.4	0.8	1.1	4.9	5.1	5.6	6.6	6.1	24.5	29.2	14.9	3.0	80.1	43.0	49.7	50.3
21864	STOCKTON	68.4	55.8	29.8	41.8	0.5	0.7	0.2	0.3	5.6	5.9	6.1	6.4	4.8	24.9	31.1	13.3	1.8	78.3	42.7	46.1	53.9
21865	TYASKIN	69.8	59.5	28.8	39.1	0.2	0.2	0.2	0.4	3.8	4.2	4.9	6.1	4.2	19.4	36.0	19.2	2.4	83.6	49.1	49.2	50.8
21866	TYLERTON	92.9	90.4	4.7	7.2	0.0	0.0	1.2	0.0	4.8	4.8	4.8	4.8	2.4	21.7	34.9	18.1	3.6	80.7	49.6	51.8	48.2
21869	VIENNA	66.5	56.0	31.6	41.6	0.6	0.8	0.5	0.6	4.2	4.9	5.5	6.9	4.2	21.1	32.7	17.8	2.8	80.6	46.8	48.7	51.3
21871	WESTOVER	54.6	46.5	43.4	50.7	0.3	0.4	1.1	1.7	3.7	3.9	4.2	5.5	8.6	38.0	24.7	10.1	1.3	85.6	37.4	66.2	33.8
21872	WHALEYVILLE	82.6	73.9	15.9	23.9	0.2	0.3	1.2	1.7	4.7	5.4	6.3	6.4	4.1	22.7	34.9	13.4	2.0	79.0	45.2	49.0	51.0
21874	WILLARDS	93.5	90.0	3.8	5.6	1.6	2.4	1.6	3.0	6.9	7.2	7.6	7.0	4.6	27.9	28.3	9.1	1.3	73.8	37.7	50.2	49.8
21875	DELMAR	80.0	72.7	15.7	21.0	1.2	1.8	3.0	4.5	6.6	6.8	6.8	6.9	6.2	26.0	28.6	10.9	1.4	75.7	38.5	48.6	51.4
21901	NORTH EAST	95.7	93.9	2.0	2.5	0.6	1.0	1.2	2.1	6.8	6.7	6.9	7.0	6.0	27.0	28.2	10.2	1.3	75.3	38.1	49.6	50.4
21903	PERRYVILLE	91.0	87.8	5.9	7.8	0.7	1.1	1.9	3.2	6.3	6.3	6.6	7.0	5.3	25.9	29.1	12.1	1.3	76.1	40.3	51.1	48.9
21904	PORT DEPOSIT	93.0	91.0	4.6	5.6	0.6	0.8	1.2	1.9	6.6	6.9	7.1	7.1	5.8	26.3	29.7	9.6	1.0	74.7	38.9	49.7	50.3
21911	RISING SUN	97.7	96.8	0.8	1.1	0.3	0.5	0.8	1.5	6.6	7.0	7.1	7.1	5.5	26.4	28.4	9.8	2.0	74.7	38.5	50.2	49.8
21912	WARWICK	85.9	80.9	11.9	15.6	0.4	0.6	2.1	3.4	6.5	6.9	7.0	6.7	4.8	22.3	30.5	13.5	1.7	75.4	42.0	49.1	50.9
21913	CECILTON	83.5	78.5	14.6	18.6	0.4	0.5	1.9	3.2	6.7	7.0	7.2	6.7	4.7	21.1	30.7	14.1	1.8	74.9	42.5	49.5	50.5
21914	CHARLESTOWN	96.1	94.4	1.9	2.4	0.3	0.5	0.5	0.9	5.4	5.7	6.3	6.5	4.5	27.6	30.8	12.2	1.1	78.4	41.8	51.7	48.3
21915	CHESAPEAKE CITY	95.3	93.2	2.7	3.7	0.3	0.4	1.2	2.1	5.6	6.1	7.0	6.6	4.7	23.8	30.8	13.9	1.6	76.7	42.6	48.6	51.4
21917	COLORA	97.7	97.0	0.8	1.1	0.4	0.5	0.5	0.8	6.6	7.2	7.6	6.8	4.5	26.0	30.9	9.3	1.2	73.7	40.0	50.5	49.5
21918	CONOWINGO	97.5	96.6	0.9	1.3	0.2	0.3	0.4	0.7	6.4	7.0	7.5	7.9	4.8	27.8	29.5	8.4	0.8	74.2	38.4	50.4	49.6
21919	EARLEVILLE	96.2	94.6	2.4	3.2	0.4	0.6	0.8	1.4	4.3	4.9	5.3	6.0	3.5	20.3	36.6	17.1	1.9	81.7	47.9	51.2	48.8
21921	ELKTON	91.3	87.8	5.2	6.9	1.0	1.5	2.0	3.6	7.6	7.4	7.2	7.0	6.0	28.7	25.4	9.3	1.2	73.3	35.7	48.6	51.4
	MARYLAND	64.0	59.0	27.9	30.1	4.0	5.3	4.3	6.4	6.5	6.6	6.7	7.1	6.4	26.9	27.4	10.7	1.7	76.0	38.1	48.4	51.6
	UNITED STATES	75.1	72.0	12.3	12.7	3.8	4.6	12.5	15.7	6.8	6.7	6.6	7.1	6.9	27.0	26.0	10.9	1.9	75.7	36.9	49.2	50.8

ZIP CODE #	POST OFFICE NAME	2009 Per Capita Income	2009 HH Income Base	2009 HOUSEHOLD INCOME DISTRIBUTION (%) Less than $25,000	$25,000 to $49,999	$50,000 to $99,999	$100,000 to $149,999	$150,000 or More	MEDIAN HOUSEHOLD INCOME 2009	2014	2009 National Centile	2009 State Centile	2009 Home Value Base	2009 HOME VALUE DISTRIBUTION (%) Less than $50,000	$50,000 to $89,999	$90,000 to $174,999	$175,000 to $399,999	$400,000 or More	2009 Median Home Value
21795	WILLIAMSPORT	24307	3956	22.5	27.1	38.9	7.8	3.6	50349	54297	62	26	2809	3.2	2.7	24.7	59.8	9.6	221190
21797	WOODBINE	42436	3091	6.2	8.4	32.9	24.8	27.6	104071	110505	97	88	2741	0.8	0.1	0.9	32.6	65.6	492717
21798	WOODSBORO	29825	749	14.7	18.3	41.0	14.8	11.2	68356	72662	86	54	594	0.3	0.3	6.2	59.1	34.0	352261
21801	SALISBURY	23612	11125	26.7	25.7	32.5	9.4	5.7	46833	49793	54	20	6702	3.6	6.8	22.9	49.2	17.5	233439
21804	SALISBURY	23465	14730	24.6	28.1	36.4	7.5	3.4	46927	50144	54	20	9093	2.8	4.3	34.8	48.2	9.8	194343
21811	BERLIN	28501	10122	18.2	26.7	40.5	9.3	5.4	53856	55316	69	32	7857	2.6	3.8	20.9	54.6	18.2	237349
21813	BISHOPVILLE	26695	973	20.1	21.1	41.7	11.5	5.5	58504	60559	76	39	832	4.3	8.5	16.9	43.3	26.9	246500
21814	BIVALVE	20886	202	34.7	30.2	28.7	4.0	2.5	38526	41902	28	10	168	9.5	15.5	41.1	28.0	6.0	140909
21817	CRISFIELD	17620	2361	44.9	26.2	22.7	4.6	1.7	27015	27533	5	2	1514	9.3	11.8	48.0	24.4	6.5	139145
21821	DEAL ISLAND	19668	492	31.1	33.3	31.1	3.5	1.0	38129	40954	27	9	430	10.2	14.0	43.0	24.9	7.9	136765
21822	EDEN	24868	1161	22.0	33.6	33.2	7.8	3.4	45100	47623	49	18	952	14.7	13.3	28.4	30.8	12.8	159278
21824	EWELL	21364	127	34.6	30.7	30.7	0.8	3.1	35276	37777	19	6	111	8.1	18.0	55.0	15.3	3.6	127083
21826	FRUITLAND	22105	1698	25.4	30.9	33.8	6.8	3.1	44866	46979	48	18	1133	11.3	11.7	32.2	31.9	12.9	165818
21829	GIRDLETREE	20573	183	24.6	32.2	37.7	1.6	3.8	43845	45765	45	16	142	6.3	7.7	38.0	33.8	14.1	170588
21830	HEBRON	24446	1318	13.6	26.3	48.3	7.7	4.1	60000	61489	77	41	1066	2.9	6.1	27.9	53.2	9.9	205109
21835	LINKWOOD	28148	178	23.6	24.2	38.2	10.1	3.9	52169	52954	66	29	151	11.9	11.9	27.2	41.1	7.9	170833
21837	MARDELA SPRINGS	20546	1106	24.1	31.0	37.1	5.3	2.4	44277	47961	46	17	886	6.8	11.7	38.4	35.8	7.3	160476
21838	MARION STATION	21106	890	20.3	36.9	36.2	5.1	1.6	46099	47755	52	19	743	7.9	17.1	26.4	36.3	12.2	171453
21840	NANTICOKE	26781	206	20.9	28.6	42.7	7.8	0.0	50879	58318	63	27	179	0.0	1.7	21.2	36.9	40.2	327083
21841	NEWARK	21271	307	26.7	30.9	34.2	3.6	4.6	44239	46390	46	16	258	7.0	1.6	41.5	43.8	6.2	175000
21842	OCEAN CITY	30867	5713	22.0	32.5	33.9	6.3	5.3	45532	48250	50	18	4048	0.7	1.2	20.1	56.8	21.1	266186
21849	PARSONSBURG	22418	1368	18.4	26.3	44.8	8.8	1.6	53959	56066	70	33	1084	8.7	7.7	27.6	48.4	7.7	189348
21850	PITTSVILLE	20891	1044	22.5	31.4	39.8	4.0	2.3	45212	49586	49	18	799	8.9	14.4	42.8	26.5	7.4	147533
21851	POCOMOKE CITY	21211	2980	32.3	29.9	29.5	4.1	4.2	37613	39492	26	9	1969	4.9	10.1	47.0	31.6	6.4	154269
21853	PRINCESS ANNE	16937	3364	39.2	29.3	25.2	3.8	2.4	29082	29977	7	3	1957	13.2	13.1	34.3	27.3	12.2	152652
21856	QUANTICO	24594	413	22.8	34.4	30.0	7.7	5.1	43417	45544	44	15	327	6.1	13.8	25.4	35.2	19.6	208333
21861	SHARPTOWN	19674	299	25.8	27.8	42.5	3.3	0.7	47812	49289	56	23	243	1.2	12.8	52.7	28.4	4.9	151453
21863	SNOW HILL	22077	2043	22.5	29.0	39.6	6.6	2.3	48418	51141	58	24	1472	3.8	8.4	37.2	41.9	8.8	176488
21864	STOCKTON	19280	225	27.1	29.8	38.2	1.8	3.1	39438	44323	31	11	169	9.5	7.7	39.1	30.2	13.6	165278
21865	TYASKIN	24582	230	29.1	31.7	30.0	5.7	3.5	41147	43771	36	13	186	7.5	14.5	34.9	31.2	11.8	154688
21866	TYLERTON	17199	40	40.0	30.0	30.0	0.0	0.0	28062	35000	6	3	35	2.9	14.3	60.0	17.1	5.7	135417
21869	VIENNA	19051	410	32.7	30.7	32.0	4.6	0.0	37670	39095	26	9	335	13.7	12.5	38.5	26.9	8.4	153289
21871	WESTOVER	27203	943	31.3	34.0	25.5	4.3	4.9	36698	39692	23	7	778	12.3	17.4	23.7	39.5	7.2	165714
21872	WHALEYVILLE	27074	258	25.2	29.5	32.2	7.0	6.2	45650	47351	50	19	208	6.3	17.8	30.8	27.9	17.3	164130
21874	WILLARDS	19674	967	22.3	34.9	37.1	3.9	1.8	43686	46581	44	16	744	5.9	10.6	44.2	35.2	4.0	157456
21875	DELMAR	22026	2371	20.6	28.7	39.2	8.5	3.0	50432	52214	62	26	1732	5.1	7.9	33.8	42.1	11.1	184272
21901	NORTH EAST	25132	5807	15.1	24.5	44.4	11.3	4.9	60513	63298	78	42	4334	7.4	2.7	16.8	53.8	19.3	256503
21903	PERRYVILLE	23701	2682	18.0	25.6	44.7	8.7	2.9	55220	59884	72	34	1846	3.6	0.5	24.9	62.5	8.5	221347
21904	PORT DEPOSIT	24599	2680	17.3	19.9	47.0	12.0	3.9	61527	64783	79	45	2186	10.1	6.5	11.3	59.6	12.5	237664
21911	RISING SUN	25140	3887	12.9	24.6	45.8	11.7	4.9	60986	63926	79	44	3075	2.5	1.5	10.4	66.0	19.5	264669
21912	WARWICK	22647	491	27.3	25.3	33.2	7.7	6.5	45498	48873	50	18	363	5.2	5.5	17.1	48.5	23.7	260625
21913	CECILTON	25878	237	29.5	25.7	32.1	6.8	5.9	42358	44787	40	14	178	3.4	3.4	20.2	48.9	24.2	263158
21914	CHARLESTOWN	24656	261	14.2	27.6	46.4	8.4	3.4	56241	60422	73	36	209	6.2	2.4	20.1	55.0	16.3	226429
21915	CHESAPEAKE CITY	31778	1444	13.1	18.8	44.5	15.2	8.4	67246	69600	85	52	1171	2.0	2.7	5.0	62.4	27.8	302075
21917	COLORA	25232	723	11.1	19.1	51.3	14.5	4.0	71736	75674	88	59	608	1.8	0.3	4.3	77.8	15.8	260593
21918	CONOWINGO	22658	1440	14.0	24.2	47.4	10.6	3.9	60699	64217	78	43	1233	9.7	1.7	10.7	66.8	11.0	255000
21919	EARLEVILLE	27875	1395	16.9	23.3	46.5	8.7	4.6	56388	59494	73	36	1188	2.9	3.6	18.9	53.2	21.4	241791
21921	ELKTON	26770	16762	15.3	21.4	43.8	12.5	7.0	62403	65897	80	46	11731	2.7	1.8	14.8	64.2	16.6	249206
	MARYLAND	32538		15.1	20.5	36.5	16.4	11.5	67267	70086				1.9	2.6	14.3	53.1	28.2	289711
	UNITED STATES	27277		20.9	24.4	35.3	11.7	7.6	54719	56938				9.3	13.1	31.6	32.6	13.5	162279

ZIP CODE	FINANCIAL SERVICES				THE HOME						ENTERTAINMENT						PERSONAL			
					Home Improvements		Furnishings													
# POST OFFICE NAME	Auto Loan	Home Loan	Invest-ments	Retire-ment Plans	Home Repair	Lawn & Garden	Comput-ers & Hard-ware-Personal	Major Appli-ances	TV, Radio, Sound Equip-ment	Furni-ture	Dine out/ Carry out	Sports Equip-ment	Fees & Tickets	Toys & Games	Travel	Cable TV	Apparel & Services	Auto Repairs	Health Insur-ance	Pets & Supplies
21795 WILLIAMSPORT	84	81	85	82	82	93	79	87	83	76	82	65	78	82	82	88	56	84	94	102
21797 WOODBINE	162	213	214	217	218	190	176	182	165	187	168	142	208	169	198	160	124	171	163	206
21798 WOODSBORO	119	140	126	141	138	134	123	128	120	123	121	98	134	123	132	120	85	123	125	148
21801 SALISBURY	87	84	78	87	82	85	88	84	90	87	90	65	88	90	85	91	63	87	89	101
21804 SALISBURY	81	78	74	79	77	82	81	80	82	79	82	61	79	82	79	84	57	81	85	95
21811 BERLIN	98	91	123	90	100	110	88	103	93	90	91	71	87	87	95	98	62	98	110	119
21813 BISHOPVILLE	106	97	124	98	101	114	93	109	95	90	94	81	88	93	99	98	64	102	108	127
21814 BIVALVE	90	65	93	63	67	91	66	84	73	62	72	63	53	73	66	81	48	77	88	100
21817 CRISFIELD	64	49	64	48	51	64	54	62	59	50	58	46	46	57	52	64	39	60	67	73
21821 DEAL ISLAND	81	57	86	56	59	84	60	76	65	53	64	60	46	64	60	71	42	70	80	92
21822 EDEN	95	82	88	83	83	98	81	93	85	77	84	70	73	87	80	90	57	87	95	109
21824 EWELL	82	56	90	56	59	86	62	78	65	51	64	64	46	64	62	71	42	73	82	96
21826 FRUITLAND	88	74	79	74	73	82	78	81	81	78	81	63	71	83	74	84	56	81	83	97
21829 GIRDLETREE	91	71	90	71	73	94	72	87	78	66	76	66	61	78	71	84	51	80	91	103
21830 HEBRON	89	100	85	100	95	100	91	92	91	90	92	71	97	93	94	93	64	91	97	109
21835 LINKWOOD	99	90	89	94	92	106	89	101	92	80	90	76	82	94	89	97	62	93	104	117
21837 MARDELA SPRINGS	82	75	74	78	76	88	74	83	76	66	74	63	68	77	73	80	51	77	86	96
21838 MARION STATION	90	67	103	66	71	94	69	88	74	63	73	67	56	72	71	80	48	81	90	104
21840 NANTICOKE	96	77	124	76	85	102	77	98	81	72	80	72	67	77	84	86	53	90	97	114
21841 NEWARK	93	67	96	65	70	94	68	87	76	64	74	65	55	75	68	83	49	80	90	103
21842 OCEAN CITY	86	83	93	82	87	92	85	89	87	85	87	65	84	83	88	90	60	89	98	104
21849 PARSONSBURG	85	89	79	89	87	90	81	85	82	82	82	64	83	84	83	84	57	82	86	100
21850 PITTSVILLE	82	75	69	74	74	81	72	78	74	72	74	57	67	77	70	77	50	74	79	92
21851 POCOMOKE CITY	82	69	79	69	70	84	72	79	77	69	76	59	65	76	70	82	51	77	85	95
21853 PRINCESS ANNE	70	53	60	53	53	63	61	63	64	58	64	48	52	64	56	67	43	64	66	76
21856 QUANTICO	97	79	123	78	86	103	79	99	82	74	81	73	69	79	85	88	54	91	98	115
21861 SHARPTOWN	77	70	69	73	71	82	69	78	71	62	70	59	63	72	69	75	48	72	80	90
21863 SNOW HILL	85	75	81	76	76	90	76	85	79	71	78	64	70	80	76	84	53	81	89	100
21864 STOCKTON	93	67	95	64	69	94	68	87	76	64	74	65	55	75	68	83	49	80	90	103
21865 TYASKIN	94	71	107	69	75	97	72	91	77	67	76	67	60	75	74	84	50	84	92	107
21866 TYLERTON	64	44	70	44	46	67	49	61	51	39	50	50	36	50	48	55	33	57	64	75
21869 VIENNA	74	58	73	58	60	77	59	72	63	54	62	54	50	64	58	69	42	66	74	84
21871 WESTOVER	94	67	97	65	69	96	69	88	76	63	75	67	55	76	69	84	49	81	92	105
21872 WHALEYVILLE	104	83	108	82	85	108	83	101	89	78	88	76	72	88	84	96	59	93	103	119
21874 WILLARDS	80	73	66	72	72	77	70	75	72	71	72	55	66	75	67	75	49	72	75	88
21875 DELMAR	83	83	73	84	81	85	81	82	83	80	83	62	81	84	80	85	57	81	85	97
21901 NORTH EAST	96	105	96	105	103	101	97	99	96	99	97	76	102	98	100	96	68	97	97	115
21903 PERRYVILLE	80	92	83	92	90	87	85	85	83	84	84	67	91	85	89	83	60	84	85	100
21904 PORT DEPOSIT	98	106	94	104	103	99	96	98	95	99	96	75	100	98	98	94	67	96	94	115
21911 RISING SUN	97	106	97	107	104	105	99	102	97	97	98	79	102	100	102	98	69	99	101	119
21912 WARWICK	109	83	107	81	85	109	84	102	91	80	90	76	70	92	82	99	60	95	105	121
21913 CECILTON	108	77	111	75	80	110	79	101	88	74	87	76	64	88	79	97	57	93	105	120
21914 CHARLESTOWN	87	99	85	101	96	97	88	92	87	88	87	72	94	89	93	87	61	88	91	108
21915 CHESAPEAKE CITY	109	123	114	123	121	121	108	114	109	112	110	84	117	111	115	110	77	110	115	133
21917 COLORA	104	121	107	123	118	114	106	110	102	107	103	86	114	106	112	101	73	104	104	127
21918 CONOWINGO	99	103	90	101	100	99	92	97	92	96	93	73	94	96	93	93	65	93	93	113
21919 EARLEVILLE	112	89	142	87	97	118	89	113	94	83	92	83	76	89	96	100	61	104	112	131
21921 ELKTON	104	108	96	108	104	101	105	102	102	106	103	80	106	105	104	101	73	102	99	120
MARYLAND	116	125	123	126	125	119	122	119	120	123	121	92	127	121	124	119	86	120	118	139
UNITED STATES	100	100	100	100	100	100	100	100	100	100	100	100	100	100	100	100	100	100	100	100

ZIP CODE #	POST OFFICE NAME	COUNTY FIPS CODE	POPULATION 2000	POPULATION 2009	POPULATION 2014	2000-2009 ANNUAL RATE % Rate	2000-2009 ANNUAL RATE State Centile	HOUSEHOLDS 2000	HOUSEHOLDS 2009	HOUSEHOLDS 2014	HOUSEHOLDS % Annual Rate 2000-2009	HOUSEHOLDS 2009 Average HH Size	FAMILIES 2000	FAMILIES 2009	FAMILIES % Annual Rate 2000-2009
01001	AGAWAM	013	16249	16211	16109	0.0	32	6866	6925	6905	0.1	2.24	4207	4224	0.0
01002	AMHERST	015	32590	32363	32110	-0.1	23	9795	9922	9899	0.1	2.41	5000	4994	0.0
01003	AMHERST	015	3990	3615	3615	-1.1	0	28	27	27	-0.4	1.19	5	5	0.0
01005	BARRE	027	5113	5382	5443	0.6	76	1889	1986	2015	0.5	2.70	1378	1440	0.5
01007	BELCHERTOWN	015	13029	14287	14728	1.0	91	4907	5474	5678	1.2	2.61	3534	3911	1.1
01008	BLANDFORD	013	1176	1252	1265	0.7	81	437	471	478	0.8	2.66	333	358	0.8
01010	BRIMFIELD	013	3467	3769	3829	0.9	88	1298	1426	1452	1.0	2.64	923	1008	1.0
01011	CHESTER	013	1539	1661	1678	0.8	84	593	650	661	1.0	2.55	432	472	1.0
01012	CHESTERFIELD	015	319	329	332	0.3	58	122	129	131	0.6	2.55	89	93	0.5
01013	CHICOPEE	013	23268	22901	22668	-0.2	14	9661	9589	9517	-0.1	2.34	5870	5792	-0.1
01020	CHICOPEE	013	29494	29173	28915	-0.1	23	12690	12719	12662	0.0	2.28	7829	7790	-0.1
01022	CHICOPEE	013	2006	2111	2131	0.6	76	811	873	885	0.8	1.95	468	500	0.7
01026	CUMMINGTON	015	1387	1471	1497	0.6	76	535	587	606	1.0	2.32	351	382	0.9
01027	EASTHAMPTON	015	17535	17985	18081	0.3	58	7425	7777	7873	0.5	2.31	4614	4791	0.4
01028	EAST LONGMEADOW	013	13945	14433	14474	0.4	65	5196	5434	5469	0.5	2.62	3946	4113	0.4
01030	FEEDING HILLS	013	11895	11871	11802	0.0	32	4394	4434	4423	0.1	2.67	3255	3276	0.1
01031	GILBERTVILLE	027	1587	1658	1666	0.5	71	600	627	633	0.5	2.57	420	433	0.3
01032	GOSHEN	015	267	290	297	0.9	88	116	129	134	1.2	2.25	78	86	1.1
01033	GRANBY	015	6132	6230	6218	0.2	48	2247	2334	2346	0.4	2.65	1662	1714	0.3
01034	GRANVILLE	013	1967	1982	1975	0.1	41	730	745	745	0.2	2.66	530	538	0.2
01035	HADLEY	015	4793	4801	4754	0.0	32	1895	1939	1934	0.2	2.40	1249	1266	0.1
01036	HAMPDEN	013	5314	5723	5794	0.8	84	1866	2029	2063	0.9	2.78	1501	1626	0.9
01038	HATFIELD	015	2527	2665	2708	0.6	76	1049	1130	1157	0.8	2.36	662	705	0.7
01039	HAYDENVILLE	015	1702	1816	1849	0.7	81	725	794	816	1.0	2.28	455	493	0.9
01040	HOLYOKE	013	39937	39673	39345	-0.1	23	14980	14923	14828	0.0	2.57	9484	9387	-0.1
01050	HUNTINGTON	015	2387	2479	2497	0.4	65	885	940	955	0.7	2.64	653	690	0.6
01053	LEEDS	015	1338	1366	1374	0.2	48	522	548	557	0.5	2.36	355	368	0.4
01054	LEVERETT	011	1662	1652	1631	-0.1	23	632	638	633	0.1	2.53	449	451	0.0
01056	LUDLOW	013	21209	21569	21574	0.2	48	7659	7897	7921	0.3	2.52	5513	5666	0.3
01057	MONSON	013	8358	8483	8460	0.2	48	3095	3182	3189	0.3	2.61	2210	2260	0.2
01060	NORTHAMPTON	015	15039	14641	14478	-0.3	9	6636	6605	6566	-0.1	1.90	2546	2497	-0.2
01062	FLORENCE	015	12070	12193	12232	0.1	41	4686	4838	4888	0.3	2.33	2953	3033	0.3
01063	NORTHAMPTON	015	458	444	443	-0.3	9	7	7	7	0.0	2.57	2	2	0.0
01068	OAKHAM	027	1673	1877	1963	1.3	95	578	648	679	1.2	2.90	467	518	1.1
01069	PALMER	013	10056	10131	10085	0.1	41	4068	4122	4113	0.1	2.43	2666	2684	0.1
01070	PLAINFIELD	015	547	562	565	0.3	58	228	240	244	0.6	2.34	157	164	0.5
01071	RUSSELL	013	1498	1493	1486	0.0	32	553	558	558	0.1	2.68	436	439	0.1
01072	SHUTESBURY	011	1464	1421	1394	-0.3	9	544	537	531	-0.1	2.63	394	387	-0.2
01073	SOUTHAMPTON	015	5385	5665	5741	0.5	71	1984	2143	2196	0.8	2.64	1555	1669	0.8
01075	SOUTH HADLEY	015	17196	17117	16991	0.0	32	6586	6738	6743	0.2	2.27	4208	4259	0.1
01077	SOUTHWICK	013	8803	9022	9026	0.3	58	3308	3438	3454	0.4	2.62	2411	2492	0.4
01080	THREE RIVERS	013	2640	2652	2646	0.0	32	1088	1107	1108	0.2	2.39	714	721	0.1
01081	WALES	013	1452	1598	1628	1.0	91	552	616	629	1.2	2.59	402	447	1.2
01082	WARE	015	10438	10572	10534	0.1	41	4295	4435	4448	0.3	2.38	2782	2849	0.3
01084	WEST CHESTERFIELD	015	137	141	143	0.3	58	48	51	52	0.7	2.76	35	37	0.6
01085	WESTFIELD	013	40855	42181	42261	0.3	58	15097	15581	15634	0.3	2.55	10250	10534	0.3
01088	WEST HATFIELD	015	643	649	646	0.1	41	304	314	315	0.4	2.07	192	196	0.2
01089	WEST SPRINGFIELD	013	27802	27970	27848	0.1	41	11811	11952	11926	0.1	2.31	7108	7143	0.1
01092	WEST WARREN	027	2621	2735	2749	0.5	71	1045	1089	1096	0.4	2.51	673	695	0.3
01095	WILBRAHAM	013	13314	13952	14038	0.5	71	4839	5135	5190	0.6	2.67	3829	4042	0.6
01096	WILLIAMSBURG	015	2504	2654	2703	0.6	76	980	1064	1093	0.9	2.49	670	721	0.8
01098	WORTHINGTON	015	1202	1186	1162	-0.1	23	483	488	482	0.1	2.43	353	356	0.1
01103	SPRINGFIELD	013	2948	2960	2936	0.0	32	1717	1689	1670	-0.2	1.69	620	602	-0.3
01104	SPRINGFIELD	013	22754	22519	22315	-0.1	23	9185	9124	9062	-0.1	2.42	5615	5535	-0.2
01105	SPRINGFIELD	013	12985	13016	12936	0.0	32	5140	5179	5158	0.1	2.33	2608	2596	0.0
01106	LONGMEADOW	013	15882	15640	15491	-0.2	14	5887	5856	5817	-0.1	2.60	4500	4456	-0.1
01107	SPRINGFIELD	013	10802	10691	10594	-0.1	23	3487	3479	3459	0.0	3.05	2357	2332	-0.1
01108	SPRINGFIELD	013	25693	25804	25655	0.0	32	9854	9859	9810	0.0	2.61	6047	6003	-0.1
01109	SPRINGFIELD	013	30536	30583	30433	0.0	32	9933	10042	10019	0.1	2.81	6861	6897	0.1
01118	SPRINGFIELD	013	14382	14137	14006	-0.2	14	5756	5729	5696	-0.1	2.45	4064	4023	-0.1
01119	SPRINGFIELD	013	13367	13810	13849	0.4	65	4706	4918	4948	0.5	2.55	3279	3407	0.4
01128	SPRINGFIELD	013	2993	2936	2904	-0.2	14	1052	1046	1039	-0.1	2.77	817	809	-0.1
01129	SPRINGFIELD	013	7054	7036	6985	0.0	32	2795	2819	2811	0.1	2.47	1940	1946	0.0
01151	INDIAN ORCHARD	013	8356	8341	8293	0.0	32	3356	3379	3368	0.1	2.46	2133	2133	0.0
01201	PITTSFIELD	003	47697	45906	44731	-0.4	6	20490	20085	19698	-0.2	2.22	12374	12064	-0.3
01220	ADAMS	003	8809	8345	8079	-0.6	2	3992	3856	3760	-0.4	2.16	2433	2336	-0.4
01222	ASHLEY FALLS	003	792	776	759	-0.2	14	291	289	284	-0.1	2.67	212	209	-0.2
01223	BECKET	003	1982	1960	1931	-0.1	23	776	785	779	0.1	2.47	581	586	0.1
01224	BERKSHIRE	003	146	150	149	0.3	58	59	62	62	0.5	2.42	44	46	0.5
01225	CHESHIRE	003	3437	3284	3200	-0.5	4	1380	1347	1322	-0.3	2.44	996	967	-0.3
01226	DALTON	003	6966	6680	6502	-0.5	4	2732	2671	2619	-0.2	2.46	1872	1821	-0.3
01230	GREAT BARRINGTON	003	10002	9736	9517	-0.3	9	4054	4011	3945	-0.1	2.24	2522	2481	-0.2
01235	HINSDALE	003	2698	2704	2664	0.0	32	1046	1064	1053	0.2	2.54	747	760	0.2
01236	HOUSATONIC	003	1057	1048	1029	-0.1	23	427	432	428	0.1	2.37	295	296	0.0
01237	LANESBORO	003	2103	2119	2097	0.1	41	817	841	839	0.3	2.51	589	603	0.3
01238	LEE	003	6358	6421	6361	0.1	41	2575	2650	2643	0.3	2.36	1709	1752	0.3
01240	LENOX	003	5197	5326	5293	0.3	58	2284	2365	2358	0.4	2.13	1339	1376	0.3
01243	MIDDLEFIELD	015	346	341	334	-0.2	14	138	140	138	0.2	2.44	101	102	0.1
01245	MONTEREY	003	536	520	506	-0.3	9	231	227	222	-0.2	2.10	145	141	-0.3
01247	NORTH ADAMS	003	16852	15869	15330	-0.6	2	7155	6844	6654	-0.5	2.21	4284	4069	-0.6
01253	OTIS	003	1309	1282	1259	-0.2	14	543	544	538	0.0	2.35	370	369	0.0
01254	RICHMOND	003	945	908	884	-0.4	6	384	378	371	-0.2	2.39	284	278	-0.2
01255	SANDISFIELD	003	787	758	737	-0.4	6	315	309	303	-0.2	2.29	205	200	-0.3
01256	SAVOY	003	715	726	719	0.2	48	293	304	304	0.4	2.38	206	213	0.4
01257	SHEFFIELD	003	2256	2314	2297	0.3	58	954	993	991	0.4	2.32	614	636	0.4
01258	SOUTH EGREMONT	003	130	142	145	1.0	91	64	71	73	1.1	2.00	37	41	1.1
01259	SOUTHFIELD	003	651	626	611	-0.4	6	266	260	255	-0.2	2.26	188	183	-0.3
01262	STOCKBRIDGE	003	1502	1433	1388	-0.5	4	710	684	666	-0.4	1.90	382	365	-0.5
01266	WEST STOCKBRIDGE	003	1919	1891	1857	-0.2	14	764	767	759	0.0	2.35	509	508	0.0
01267	WILLIAMSTOWN	003	8890	8609	8433	-0.3	9	2945	2852	2790	-0.3	2.18	1830	1762	-0.4
01270	WINDSOR	003	812	774	750	-0.5	4	295	287	281	-0.3	2.70	224	217	-0.3
01301	GREENFIELD	011	18272	17913	17653	-0.2	14	7981	7959	7887	0.0	2.15	4407	4370	-0.1
01330	ASHFIELD	011	1486	1515	1507	0.2	48	608	631	633	0.4	2.40	418	432	0.4
01331	ATHOL	027	13131	14125	14496	0.8	84	5143	5518	5678	0.8	2.51	3465	3693	0.7
01337	BERNARDSTON	011	2672	2792	2798	0.5	71	1026	1092	1100	0.7	2.54	751	793	0.6
	MASSACHUSETTS					0.3					0.3	2.50			0.3
	UNITED STATES					1.0					1.1	2.59			0.9

ZIP CODE #	POST OFFICE NAME	RACE (%) White 2000	White 2009	Black 2000	Black 2009	Asian/Pacific 2000	Asian/Pacific 2009	% Hispanic Origin 2000	% Hispanic Origin 2009	2009 AGE DISTRIBUTION (%) 0-4	5-9	10-14	15-19	20-24	25-44	45-64	65-84	85+	18+	MEDIAN AGE 2009	% 2009 Males	% 2009 Females
01001	AGAWAM	96.4	94.4	1.1	1.7	1.2	1.9	1.8	3.1	5.2	5.2	5.4	5.5	5.0	24.4	28.8	15.5	5.0	80.9	44.5	46.8	53.2
01002	AMHERST	80.2	74.0	5.1	6.0	8.3	12.2	6.2	8.1	3.1	3.3	3.4	16.9	27.2	19.4	17.8	7.1	1.6	87.6	24.3	47.9	52.1
01003	AMHERST	79.0	71.5	3.7	4.3	12.0	17.8	4.3	5.7	0.1	0.0	0.1	51.9	45.7	2.2	0.1	0.0	0.0	99.6	19.8	50.0	50.0
01005	BARRE	97.6	96.8	0.5	0.7	0.3	0.6	0.8	1.3	6.2	6.4	6.9	7.7	6.0	25.3	29.9	9.6	2.0	75.2	39.6	49.1	50.9
01007	BELCHERTOWN	96.1	94.7	0.8	1.0	1.0	1.7	1.6	2.3	6.3	6.6	7.2	7.2	5.0	26.6	31.4	8.5	1.3	75.1	39.5	48.8	51.2
01008	BLANDFORD	98.7	98.2	0.5	0.7	0.3	0.4	0.3	0.6	5.2	5.8	6.4	5.8	4.9	23.6	35.1	11.8	1.4	79.0	43.8	49.6	50.4
01010	BRIMFIELD	97.7	96.5	0.5	0.8	0.1	0.2	1.3	2.3	5.8	6.5	7.2	6.9	4.7	22.7	34.1	10.6	1.4	76.2	42.5	49.9	50.1
01011	CHESTER	98.2	97.4	0.2	0.3	0.1	0.2	1.2	2.0	5.0	6.0	6.6	6.2	4.6	23.5	35.6	11.1	1.5	78.7	43.8	50.9	49.1
01012	CHESTERFIELD	98.7	98.2	0.0	0.0	0.6	0.6	0.0	0.3	5.5	6.4	7.3	6.4	4.0	24.0	35.9	9.7	0.9	76.9	42.7	50.5	49.5
01013	CHICOPEE	85.3	78.9	2.4	3.0	0.7	1.1	14.8	22.0	6.5	6.2	5.9	7.0	7.3	27.0	25.0	12.3	2.9	77.4	37.7	47.5	52.5
01020	CHICOPEE	94.2	90.9	1.6	2.3	1.1	1.7	3.9	6.8	5.1	5.1	5.2	5.9	5.5	25.1	29.5	15.4	3.1	81.0	43.6	48.0	52.0
01022	CHICOPEE	77.2	68.7	12.3	16.2	1.8	2.5	10.2	15.8	4.6	4.7	4.8	17.7	8.9	20.4	24.1	13.2	1.7	76.0	35.2	50.7	49.3
01026	CUMMINGTON	97.1	96.2	0.4	0.5	0.4	0.5	2.4	3.5	4.1	4.9	6.0	12.7	3.1	25.8	31.7	10.4	1.3	75.1	41.2	50.3	49.7
01027	EASTHAMPTON	95.7	93.9	0.6	0.8	1.6	2.5	2.0	2.8	5.3	5.2	5.5	5.7	6.2	28.3	30.9	10.5	2.3	80.5	41.0	48.7	51.3
01028	EAST LONGMEADOW	97.5	96.1	0.7	1.1	0.9	1.5	0.9	1.6	5.3	5.9	6.9	6.8	4.4	20.5	31.8	14.7	3.8	77.6	45.2	47.6	52.4
01030	FEEDING HILLS	97.1	95.6	0.7	1.0	0.7	1.1	1.9	3.4	5.7	6.1	6.6	6.5	5.0	25.2	32.3	11.0	1.7	77.6	41.7	49.2	50.8
01031	GILBERTVILLE	98.1	97.5	0.6	0.8	0.1	0.2	0.8	1.4	5.5	5.6	6.4	9.8	5.2	23.2	31.1	11.3	1.9	75.8	41.1	49.6	50.4
01032	GOSHEN	98.9	99.0	0.0	0.0	0.4	0.3	1.1	1.4	4.5	5.2	5.9	5.9	3.8	24.5	36.9	12.1	1.4	80.7	45.2	46.6	53.4
01033	GRANBY	96.8	95.4	0.5	0.7	1.0	1.6	1.2	1.8	5.4	5.8	6.6	7.6	4.5	25.1	31.8	11.7	1.5	77.2	41.9	48.8	51.2
01034	GRANVILLE	98.4	97.7	0.4	0.6	0.2	0.4	0.8	1.4	5.8	6.7	7.5	7.0	4.4	20.9	35.3	11.5	1.0	75.2	43.3	52.4	47.6
01035	HADLEY	95.9	94.2	0.8	1.0	1.6	2.5	1.7	2.4	4.6	4.7	5.2	5.3	5.0	24.8	31.8	14.7	3.9	81.9	45.3	47.2	52.8
01036	HAMPDEN	98.3	97.5	0.2	0.3	0.5	0.8	0.6	1.1	5.1	6.4	7.5	7.1	3.9	21.1	32.8	14.0	2.1	76.4	44.3	48.0	52.0
01038	HATFIELD	97.9	97.2	0.2	0.3	0.6	0.9	1.0	1.5	4.6	5.1	5.7	6.3	4.6	21.9	34.2	14.7	3.0	80.8	46.2	48.2	51.8
01039	HAYDENVILLE	97.4	96.4	0.4	0.4	0.7	1.1	0.9	1.4	4.4	4.1	4.6	5.7	7.9	23.8	35.8	11.7	2.0	84.7	44.7	47.3	52.7
01040	HOLYOKE	65.8	58.4	3.7	4.1	0.9	1.2	41.3	50.2	8.3	7.3	7.0	7.5	7.8	24.4	22.1	12.1	3.5	72.9	34.7	47.4	52.6
01050	HUNTINGTON	97.6	96.9	0.4	0.5	0.4	0.6	1.8	2.6	5.9	5.9	6.1	6.8	6.2	25.3	31.7	10.7	1.4	78.1	41.0	49.1	50.9
01053	LEEDS	95.1	93.2	0.3	0.4	0.8	1.3	3.2	4.7	4.6	4.6	5.2	6.7	6.4	21.6	32.4	13.5	4.9	81.3	45.5	43.6	56.4
01054	LEVERETT	95.3	93.8	0.2	0.4	1.4	2.1	1.4	2.1	3.7	4.3	5.5	6.2	4.0	23.1	38.1	13.4	1.6	86.1	47.1	50.6	49.4
01056	LUDLOW	95.8	94.1	2.0	2.6	0.6	0.9	6.5	9.8	5.0	5.2	5.5	6.3	6.5	27.7	28.2	13.3	2.3	80.7	40.9	51.1	48.9
01057	MONSON	97.7	96.6	0.7	1.0	0.3	0.5	1.2	2.1	6.0	6.5	6.8	6.4	5.1	25.4	32.1	10.2	1.4	76.6	41.0	49.1	50.9
01060	NORTHAMPTON	87.7	83.5	2.6	3.1	4.5	6.7	5.9	8.0	3.3	2.8	2.9	9.2	14.8	31.5	24.3	8.9	2.4	88.9	34.2	40.8	59.2
01062	FLORENCE	92.7	90.0	1.6	2.0	1.5	2.5	4.6	6.6	4.7	5.0	5.6	5.7	5.4	22.4	34.2	13.6	3.5	81.2	45.7	48.2	51.8
01063	NORTHAMPTON	79.5	72.1	4.1	5.0	10.9	16.4	4.4	5.9	0.5	0.5	0.5	38.7	49.8	5.9	3.6	0.5	0.2	98.2	21.0	5.4	94.6
01068	OAKHAM	98.3	97.5	0.4	0.5	0.6	1.0	1.0	1.7	5.1	5.8	7.0	8.6	5.2	23.2	36.2	7.9	1.1	76.8	41.7	50.5	49.5
01069	PALMER	96.7	95.0	0.9	1.3	0.7	1.1	1.3	2.3	5.6	5.6	5.9	6.9	6.5	25.3	29.6	11.9	2.7	78.7	41.2	48.9	51.1
01070	PLAINFIELD	98.2	97.7	0.0	0.0	0.2	0.4	0.7	1.1	4.6	7.7	6.2	6.0	2.3	22.4	37.2	11.9	1.6	77.2	45.3	48.9	51.1
01071	RUSSELL	97.4	96.1	0.4	0.7	0.3	0.5	1.5	2.7	6.0	6.3	6.8	6.4	5.2	25.5	31.3	11.3	1.2	77.0	41.0	49.6	50.4
01072	SHUTESBURY	93.8	92.0	1.0	1.3	1.2	1.9	2.1	3.0	4.6	5.3	6.3	7.2	5.3	24.0	39.1	7.4	0.8	83.4	42.9	47.4	52.6
01073	SOUTHAMPTON	98.3	97.5	0.2	0.3	0.6	1.1	0.9	1.3	5.0	5.6	6.8	7.1	4.2	23.7	35.2	10.8	1.6	78.2	43.7	48.2	51.8
01075	SOUTH HADLEY	94.0	91.9	1.2	1.4	2.6	3.9	2.4	3.3	4.5	4.5	5.0	9.6	9.9	21.5	27.8	14.0	3.2	82.6	41.1	42.0	58.0
01077	SOUTHWICK	97.4	96.0	0.5	0.7	0.4	0.6	1.7	3.3	6.1	6.7	7.1	6.9	4.8	25.0	31.6	10.1	1.6	75.3	41.0	50.2	49.8
01080	THREE RIVERS	97.4	96.0	0.3	0.5	0.1	0.2	1.1	2.0	6.3	6.0	5.9	6.9	7.2	27.6	26.9	10.8	2.4	77.5	37.8	47.3	52.7
01081	WALES	97.7	96.7	0.6	0.8	0.2	0.3	0.6	1.1	5.4	6.2	6.7	5.8	4.2	26.8	33.9	10.3	0.8	78.0	42.1	50.3	49.7
01082	WARE	96.6	95.4	0.5	0.7	0.6	1.0	2.0	2.9	6.3	5.9	6.0	6.6	6.7	26.0	27.9	12.1	2.5	77.7	39.8	49.1	50.9
01084	WEST CHESTERFIELD	99.3	97.9	0.0	0.0	0.0	1.4	0.0	0.0	5.0	6.4	7.1	6.4	4.3	24.1	35.5	9.9	1.4	77.3	43.0	49.6	50.4
01085	WESTFIELD	94.6	91.6	0.9	1.3	0.9	1.4	4.9	8.3	5.9	5.8	6.0	8.4	8.3	24.5	27.3	11.5	2.3	78.3	38.3	48.5	51.5
01088	WEST HATFIELD	98.3	97.7	0.2	0.3	0.5	0.6	1.1	1.5	4.6	4.8	4.9	4.9	5.4	24.2	34.4	14.0	2.8	82.9	45.8	49.9	50.1
01089	WEST SPRINGFIELD	90.7	86.1	2.0	2.9	2.0	3.0	5.7	9.6	5.8	5.7	6.0	6.2	6.5	25.7	27.7	13.8	2.7	78.6	40.8	48.8	51.2
01092	WEST WARREN	97.6	96.7	0.4	0.5	0.3	0.4	0.6	1.1	6.2	6.0	6.2	7.2	6.9	26.0	27.3	12.2	2.0	77.3	39.1	49.3	50.7
01095	WILBRAHAM	96.4	94.4	1.2	1.8	1.3	2.1	1.4	2.5	5.2	6.3	7.5	7.1	4.1	18.5	33.3	14.8	3.1	76.2	45.7	48.3	51.7
01096	WILLIAMSBURG	98.7	98.3	0.1	0.1	0.3	0.5	0.6	0.8	4.4	4.9	5.8	6.3	5.0	23.6	37.4	11.2	1.5	81.0	45.0	47.4	52.6
01098	WORTHINGTON	98.5	98.0	0.2	0.4	0.2	0.3	0.9	1.3	4.2	5.2	6.1	6.2	4.5	22.0	38.7	11.6	1.5	80.7	45.9	49.4	50.6
01103	SPRINGFIELD	40.6	33.4	22.3	22.7	3.7	3.9	46.9	56.1	8.0	7.7	6.7	6.4	6.2	33.4	22.6	7.5	1.4	74.4	33.6	47.3	52.7
01104	SPRINGFIELD	63.8	54.7	10.0	11.5	1.1	1.3	33.6	43.5	7.3	6.9	6.5	7.3	7.8	25.8	23.5	12.0	2.9	74.8	35.5	47.6	52.4
01105	SPRINGFIELD	35.1	28.4	23.9	23.8	1.0	1.1	50.1	58.9	9.6	8.5	7.6	7.9	8.9	28.5	19.1	8.0	1.9	69.6	29.3	48.6	51.4
01106	LONGMEADOW	95.0	92.2	0.9	1.3	2.9	4.7	1.4	2.4	5.6	6.4	7.7	7.8	4.9	15.6	32.9	15.3	3.7	75.0	46.1	47.3	52.7
01107	SPRINGFIELD	35.6	31.0	8.8	8.4	0.8	0.9	73.5	78.9	10.3	9.1	7.9	9.3	10.1	25.5	18.5	8.0	1.4	67.1	26.9	47.6	52.4
01108	SPRINGFIELD	61.8	52.3	14.4	16.5	5.4	6.6	23.2	31.5	8.5	7.3	6.5	7.3	9.3	29.5	21.7	8.2	1.6	73.3	31.3	48.3	51.7
01109	SPRINGFIELD	32.2	27.1	49.7	51.4	1.3	1.6	22.6	27.5	7.9	7.8	7.6	11.0	11.4	23.2	20.7	8.7	1.7	71.3	28.1	46.5	53.5
01118	SPRINGFIELD	83.5	76.7	8.8	12.0	2.1	3.1	6.4	10.2	6.6	6.8	6.6	6.5	5.1	25.0	27.7	12.8	3.0	75.8	40.6	46.2	53.8
01119	SPRINGFIELD	70.1	60.5	18.7	23.6	1.4	1.9	11.3	17.0	6.1	6.0	6.2	11.0	10.3	24.3	23.7	10.7	1.8	77.4	33.4	47.8	52.2
01128	SPRINGFIELD	82.5	75.3	11.2	15.3	1.1	1.6	7.2	11.4	6.4	6.7	6.8	6.3	4.8	23.9	29.5	12.9	2.7	76.1	41.5	47.6	52.4
01129	SPRINGFIELD	79.0	71.1	13.6	18.0	1.4	1.9	7.7	12.2	5.9	6.1	6.8	6.6	5.3	26.3	29.8	11.3	1.9	76.9	40.3	47.7	52.3
01151	INDIAN ORCHARD	71.6	62.2	11.9	14.8	0.8	1.2	21.1	30.0	8.6	7.8	7.1	8.0	7.9	28.6	21.5	8.6	1.9	71.6	32.0	48.0	52.0
01201	PITTSFIELD	92.8	91.0	3.5	4.2	1.2	1.7	2.0	2.7	5.9	5.6	5.7	6.3	6.3	23.6	28.0	15.1	3.5	79.0	42.5	48.0	52.0
01220	ADAMS	98.0	97.5	0.4	0.5	0.3	0.4	0.8	1.2	5.5	5.3	5.5	6.5	6.0	23.6	28.4	15.6	3.7	79.8	43.3	47.6	52.4
01222	ASHLEY FALLS	97.3	96.4	1.0	1.3	0.0	0.1	1.5	2.1	6.8	7.6	8.1	7.5	4.3	21.5	33.0	9.5	1.7	72.4	41.3	48.7	51.3
01223	BECKET	97.9	97.3	0.6	0.8	0.4	0.6	1.0	1.3	4.8	5.7	6.9	6.3	3.9	24.4	34.9	11.8	1.3	78.7	43.8	50.7	49.3
01224	BERKSHIRE	97.9	97.3	0.7	0.7	0.7	1.3	0.0	0.0	4.7	6.0	7.3	6.7	3.3	22.7	37.3	10.7	1.3	78.0	44.6	46.7	53.3
01225	CHESHIRE	98.2	97.7	0.4	0.5	0.6	0.9	0.4	0.6	4.9	5.2	5.9	6.4	5.0	23.6	32.9	14.0	2.0	80.0	44.2	49.1	50.9
01226	DALTON	97.8	97.0	0.5	0.6	0.7	1.0	1.0	1.4	5.5	6.0	6.6	6.9	6.1	22.0	30.4	13.8	2.7	77.5	42.7	48.1	51.9
01230	GREAT BARRINGTON	95.6	94.3	1.7	2.1	1.0	1.5	1.8	2.5	4.0	4.8	5.3	8.3	5.0	20.5	32.5	16.0	3.6	80.6	46.4	47.6	52.4
01235	HINSDALE	97.9	97.3	0.4	0.5	0.3	0.5	0.3	0.4	5.0	6.8	7.3	6.8	4.7	26.2	32.0	9.6	1.6	76.6	40.7	51.5	48.5
01236	HOUSATONIC	97.4	96.4	0.9	1.1	0.5	0.8	1.4	2.1	4.5	4.9	5.7	7.3	5.0	21.8	34.2	13.8	3.0	80.2	45.6	47.7	52.3
01237	LANESBORO	97.0	95.9	0.7	0.8	1.2	1.8	0.7	1.0	5.1	5.8	6.7	6.6	4.1	23.6	34.3	11.9	2.0	78.2	43.9	49.6	50.4
01238	LEE	96.9	95.7	0.6	0.7	1.0	1.6	2.4	3.3	4.9	5.1	5.5	5.9	5.4	24.3	31.2	15.1	2.5	80.7	44.2	48.1	51.9
01240	LENOX	96.6	95.5	1.3	1.6	1.1	1.7	1.9	2.7	3.3	4.0	5.9	6.4	4.5	18.8	32.0	19.0	6.1	82.2	49.7	46.0	54.0
01243	MIDDLEFIELD	98.6	98.2	0.3	0.3	0.3	0.3	0.9	1.5	4.1	5.3	5.9	6.5	4.7	22.0	38.7	11.4	1.5	80.6	45.8	49.3	50.7
01245	MONTEREY	96.8	96.0	0.6	0.6	0.6	0.8	1.3	2.1	3.5	3.7	4.6	4.2	4.4	20.6	40.4	17.3	1.3	85.8	50.1	48.1	51.9
01247	NORTH ADAMS	95.5	94.3	1.5	1.8	0.7	1.1	1.8	2.5	5.4	5.1	5.1	7.6	8.9	23.2	26.7	14.7	3.3	80.7	40.7	47.0	53.0
01253	OTIS	96.4	95.6	0.6	0.7	0.9	1.4	0.3	0.4	3.9	5.6	6.5	6.0	3.8	23.9	35.6	13.3	1.3	80.2	45.1	53.0	47.0
01254	RICHMOND	97.1	96.4	1.4	1.8	0.5	0.8	0.3	0.4	3.5	4.2	5.5	5.5	4.1	18.4	36.8	19.3	2.8	83.0	50.2	48.0	52.0
01255	SANDISFIELD	96.8	96.0	0.5	0.7	0.1	0.1	1.0	1.5	4.6	3.7	6.9	4.9	2.8	22.7	36.4	16.8	1.3	81.5	47.0	53.7	46.3
01256	SAVOY	97.5	97.1	0.7	0.8	0.0	0.0	0.7	1.0	5.0	5.8	6.6	6.3	4.1	23.6	36.1	11.2	1.4	78.1	44.1	52.8	47.2
01257	SHEFFIELD	97.4	96.7	1.0	1.3	0.3	0.5	1.3	1.8	4.6	6.1	5.6	5.6	4.4	22.0	33.7	16.0	2.1	79.8	46.1	48.6	51.4
01258	SOUTH EGREMONT	100.0	100.0	0.0	0.0	0.0	0.0	0.0	0.0	5.6	4.2	5.6	0.7	1.4	17.6	50.0	12.0	2.8	84.5	53.8	51.4	48.6
01259	SOUTHFIELD	97.5	97.0	1.5	1.9	0.2	0.2	1.2	1.8	5.0	5.9	7.5	9.6	3.7	22.5	31.5	12.8	1.6	74.8	42.5	52.6	47.4
01262	STOCKBRIDGE	96.4	95.4	1.5	1.8	0.5	0.8	3.5	4.8	3.1	3.3	4.0	5.8	3.8	18.5	34.6	22.1	4.8	86.3	52.5	46.2	53.8
01266	WEST STOCKBRIDGE	98.2	97.6	0.4	0.6	0.7	1.0	0.9	1.4	3.3	4.4	5.1	6.5	3.8	18.5	39.2	16.7	2.7	83.6	50.1	49.0	51.0
01267	WILLIAMSTOWN	91.1	88.5	2.6	3.1	3.1	4.5	2.7	3.6	3.2	3.3	3.8	14.0	17.7	15.1	22.7	15.2	5.0	86.5	35.9	47.0	53.0
01270	WINDSOR	98.9	98.7	0.0	0.0	0.0	0.0	0.1	0.1	5.4	6.2	7.8	7.2	4.3	18.2	39.4	9.9	1.6	76.0	45.5	50.3	49.7
01301	GREENFIELD	93.5	91.6	1.3	1.6	1.1	1.7	3.5	4.8	5.4	5.0	5.3	6.1	6.7	25.8	29.0	12.7	4.0	80.6	42.0	47.5	52.5
01330	ASHFIELD	96.8	95.9	0.6	0.8	0.3	0.6	0.6	0.9	4.6	5.1	6.0	6.4	5.7	22.5	36.0	11.7	1.9	80.4	44.8	49.4	50.6
01331	ATHOL	96.5	95.2	0.6	0.8	0.4	0.7	1.8	2.8	6.0	6.3	6.4	6.6	6.3	25.4	27.9	12.1	3.1	77.1	40.0	48.9	51.1
01337	BERNARDSTON	98.8	98.5	0.2	0.2	0.1	0.1	0.4	0.7	4.0	4.8	5.6	6.3	5.2	22.9	36.2	13.0	2.0	81.2	45.7	49.4	50.6
	MASSACHUSETTS	84.5	81.0	5.4	6.0	3.8	5.4	6.8	8.7	6.1	6.2	6.3	7.1	7.1	26.5	27.1	11.3	2.3	77.4	38.6	48.4	51.6
	UNITED STATES	75.1	72.0	12.3	12.7	3.8	4.6	12.5	15.7	6.8	6.7	6.6	7.1	6.9	27.0	26.0	10.9	1.9	75.7	36.9	49.2	50.8

ZIP CODE #	POST OFFICE NAME	2009 Per Capita Income	2009 HH Income Base	2009 Household Income Distribution (%) Less than $25,000	$25,000 to $49,999	$50,000 to $99,999	$100,000 to $149,999	$150,000 or More	Median Household Income 2009	2014	2009 National Centile	2009 State Centile	2009 Home Value Base	2009 Home Value Distribution (%) Less than $50,000	$50,000 to $89,999	$90,000 to $174,999	$175,000 to $399,999	$400,000 or More	2009 Median Home Value
01001	AGAWAM	28902	6925	14.6	25.4	45.3	11.2	3.5	60228	62408	78	28	4928	0.9	3.4	32.3	59.7	3.8	197765
01002	AMHERST	29866	9922	21.2	21.4	27.7	17.4	12.4	59425	63997	77	27	4800	0.3	0.5	10.0	63.1	26.0	292763
01003	AMHERST	15677	27	33.3	25.9	37.0	3.7	0.0	42288	42288	40	7	1	0.0	0.0	0.0	100.0	0.0	350000
01005	BARRE	26260	1986	14.2	22.7	42.0	15.9	5.2	63412	65817	82	35	1517	3.0	3.8	33.2	55.2	4.7	194596
01007	BELCHERTOWN	30513	5474	12.5	18.9	41.0	20.9	6.7	71732	75140	88	51	4340	2.5	5.8	17.4	65.8	8.6	226274
01008	BLANDFORD	28952	471	10.4	18.0	54.8	10.6	6.2	67947	69254	86	45	407	0.5	1.2	21.9	60.2	16.2	231024
01010	BRIMFIELD	26661	1426	15.6	22.8	45.7	10.9	5.0	63660	65761	82	36	1217	5.4	3.1	21.5	60.2	9.7	227517
01011	CHESTER	25269	650	14.3	25.8	49.1	8.0	2.8	60454	62814	78	29	539	3.3	2.4	35.4	48.8	10.0	196205
01012	CHESTERFIELD	26332	129	12.4	19.4	55.0	12.4	0.8	65757	68931	84	40	109	0.0	1.8	26.6	62.4	9.2	219792
01013	CHICOPEE	20448	9589	31.9	28.4	32.8	5.4	1.6	40788	44827	35	6	4865	0.8	3.7	61.2	33.9	0.4	159652
01020	CHICOPEE	24813	12719	21.7	29.9	38.0	7.9	2.4	48468	51386	58	13	8327	3.1	6.3	48.7	40.7	1.3	166101
01022	CHICOPEE	25592	873	14.1	33.7	46.2	5.3	0.8	51563	54289	65	16	680	1.3	9.1	76.9	12.6	0.0	119043
01026	CUMMINGTON	28181	587	15.2	26.9	43.8	9.7	4.4	56497	60274	73	22	455	0.2	1.5	25.1	56.5	16.7	231649
01027	EASTHAMPTON	30571	7777	17.4	22.2	37.8	17.3	5.3	60520	63106	78	30	4929	0.2	1.2	33.1	60.8	4.7	196197
01028	EAST LONGMEADOW	34667	5434	11.0	19.5	37.3	20.0	12.2	78005	79157	91	62	4645	0.7	0.2	14.7	67.6	16.7	245684
01030	FEEDING HILLS	29290	4434	13.4	17.4	42.8	18.5	8.0	70487	72960	87	49	3379	0.5	0.8	20.6	73.8	4.3	225754
01031	GILBERTVILLE	28635	627	16.1	19.5	42.3	15.0	7.2	63953	66592	82	36	465	0.2	0.4	26.5	54.0	18.9	225852
01032	GOSHEN	32164	129	9.3	24.0	48.1	14.0	4.7	65725	68053	84	40	109	0.0	2.8	24.8	67.9	4.6	217969
01033	GRANBY	32260	2334	9.9	17.9	41.4	24.9	6.0	72753	74898	88	52	1932	0.0	0.2	24.1	64.9	10.8	218309
01034	GRANVILLE	29248	745	13.3	18.4	47.8	12.8	7.8	68563	69999	86	46	634	0.2	1.4	15.6	67.0	15.8	249686
01035	HADLEY	35741	1939	15.4	16.2	36.9	20.4	11.1	73081	75513	88	53	1433	0.8	1.0	7.2	72.4	18.6	282182
01036	HAMPDEN	34092	2029	12.5	12.3	38.3	23.7	13.2	81307	81895	93	67	1787	1.1	0.7	9.6	70.2	18.4	270448
01038	HATFIELD	34249	1130	14.5	20.8	34.1	23.0	7.6	68563	71067	86	46	818	1.1	1.3	6.2	67.6	23.7	296818
01039	HAYDENVILLE	39737	794	12.7	17.3	39.2	18.5	12.3	73695	75632	89	54	575	0.2	1.4	18.6	59.1	20.7	250309
01040	HOLYOKE	18986	14923	34.7	26.7	29.3	6.5	2.8	38962	42741	30	6	6274	1.6	6.5	51.3	36.9	3.8	163665
01050	HUNTINGTON	26370	940	12.7	21.9	47.7	14.4	3.4	64058	66290	82	37	731	1.4	2.1	39.3	52.9	4.4	187738
01053	LEEDS	31656	548	14.1	21.5	42.5	13.9	8.0	65312	69957	84	39	420	0.0	0.0	12.9	76.7	10.5	250000
01054	LEVERETT	40529	638	6.6	17.4	37.5	20.8	17.7	82519	83232	93	70	511	1.2	1.0	8.6	54.8	34.4	311667
01056	LUDLOW	25666	7897	16.3	24.1	43.9	11.6	4.1	61486	63834	79	31	6034	2.2	1.1	32.0	59.2	5.6	203114
01057	MONSON	28740	3182	14.2	18.4	45.3	15.5	6.5	66939	68626	85	43	2525	2.3	1.8	23.2	60.1	12.6	223493
01060	NORTHAMPTON	36870	6605	22.7	21.1	32.4	15.3	8.5	56225	60239	73	22	2593	0.1	2.7	17.5	53.3	26.4	260280
01062	FLORENCE	33152	4838	15.3	19.3	40.3	16.7	8.4	63615	66851	82	35	3505	0.0	1.1	22.5	66.8	9.7	220536
01063	NORTHAMPTON	15326	7	28.6	0.0	14.3	28.6	28.6	129468	129468	99	95	0	0.0	0.0	0.0	0.0	0.0	0
01068	OAKHAM	29880	648	6.2	17.0	44.6	24.8	7.4	79012	80184	92	63	579	0.9	0.7	17.1	70.6	10.7	242430
01069	PALMER	24673	4122	21.3	22.8	44.4	8.1	3.4	55748	60127	72	21	2752	0.8	4.9	34.8	53.7	5.8	192150
01070	PLAINFIELD	27727	240	20.8	32.9	29.6	9.2	7.5	47041	49688	54	11	201	2.0	3.5	28.9	42.8	22.9	222115
01071	RUSSELL	25002	558	13.4	23.5	51.3	9.1	2.7	60776	63168	79	30	448	4.2	2.9	33.5	54.2	5.1	194811
01072	SHUTESBURY	34686	537	7.1	19.2	43.0	19.6	11.2	77643	78013	91	60	438	0.7	0.5	14.4	64.8	19.6	270395
01073	SOUTHAMPTON	36401	2143	7.5	14.6	34.8	33.4	9.8	88554	91300	95	77	1803	0.6	0.8	14.9	69.7	14.1	251246
01075	SOUTH HADLEY	32647	6738	15.1	22.4	36.4	18.0	8.0	61640	65354	80	31	4930	0.6	1.5	27.4	59.6	10.9	211783
01077	SOUTHWICK	28035	3438	14.5	18.8	46.2	15.5	5.0	67869	69898	85	45	2741	0.0	2.0	21.3	59.3	17.4	240549
01080	THREE RIVERS	22569	1107	17.4	34.4	42.2	4.1	1.9	48548	50973	58	13	711	6.2	11.3	37.1	45.4	0.0	169155
01081	WALES	26860	616	8.3	26.9	51.0	10.4	3.4	62945	64552	81	34	512	7.4	9.8	37.7	42.2	2.9	167188
01082	WARE	25093	4435	22.8	28.3	34.8	11.1	3.0	48638	52234	58	14	2915	1.1	7.0	43.7	45.4	2.8	172356
01084	WEST CHESTERFIELD	24174	51	13.7	17.6	56.9	11.8	0.0	66569	69037	85	42	43	0.0	0.0	23.3	67.4	9.3	227083
01085	WESTFIELD	25816	15581	19.8	21.8	41.3	11.7	5.4	59482	61925	77	27	10565	2.2	3.3	28.4	59.0	7.0	208990
01088	WEST HATFIELD	39630	314	10.8	22.3	35.4	23.9	7.6	70860	73843	87	49	235	1.3	4.7	8.5	74.0	11.5	268229
01089	WEST SPRINGFIELD	25838	11952	23.9	25.1	37.6	9.4	4.0	50945	54167	63	16	6971	2.2	1.9	36.5	54.0	5.5	191781
01092	WEST WARREN	21232	1089	23.4	32.1	33.5	8.8	2.1	44197	47533	46	9	686	2.3	5.2	42.0	47.1	3.4	175547
01095	WILBRAHAM	37303	5135	12.6	13.8	36.8	18.1	18.7	81950	83268	93	69	4456	0.0	0.1	8.6	69.8	21.5	292120
01096	WILLIAMSBURG	29163	1064	12.3	22.5	48.1	12.7	4.4	62974	65654	81	35	862	0.5	1.7	20.1	64.2	13.6	236765
01098	WORTHINGTON	34343	488	11.7	22.3	40.2	16.0	9.8	66014	69117	84	41	425	0.9	1.6	26.4	59.8	11.3	221944
01103	SPRINGFIELD	17570	1689	57.4	25.6	14.9	1.7	0.4	20587	22551	2	1	99	13.1	27.3	32.3	21.2	6.1	108088
01104	SPRINGFIELD	18286	9124	36.7	27.4	29.5	5.0	1.4	35134	39080	18	4	4643	1.7	7.5	81.5	8.9	0.4	123025
01105	SPRINGFIELD	13096	5179	56.4	26.6	14.6	1.6	0.8	20641	22018	2	1	822	7.8	16.2	64.2	8.8	3.0	112014
01106	LONGMEADOW	45182	5856	10.5	11.0	33.8	17.7	27.1	90996	92259	95	79	5060	0.3	0.3	2.8	56.4	40.3	361333
01107	SPRINGFIELD	12057	3479	51.4	21.7	21.4	4.1	1.4	23650	25633	3	2	983	1.6	7.1	62.9	26.8	1.6	143003
01108	SPRINGFIELD	19199	9859	29.5	31.3	30.8	5.8	2.6	39959	43687	32	6	4463	1.2	4.9	69.8	23.4	0.7	140094
01109	SPRINGFIELD	15632	10042	37.2	28.3	28.8	4.3	1.3	34156	37666	16	4	5003	1.7	12.9	76.0	7.7	1.7	118086
01118	SPRINGFIELD	28075	5729	15.8	23.1	45.1	10.8	5.1	61730	64069	80	31	4567	1.0	1.6	64.7	32.0	0.7	157402
01119	SPRINGFIELD	21790	4918	21.8	28.9	39.7	7.0	2.6	49497	52877	60	14	3591	7.4	7.9	67.7	16.7	0.3	135914
01128	SPRINGFIELD	25868	1046	13.1	22.1	45.4	12.9	6.5	64652	66472	83	38	886	0.0	0.3	57.4	41.3	0.9	167988
01129	SPRINGFIELD	26559	2819	13.2	28.2	44.0	11.0	3.7	60100	61937	77	28	2270	0.6	6.5	65.2	26.7	1.0	149531
01151	INDIAN ORCHARD	17101	3379	36.6	30.5	28.3	3.6	1.0	33893	36930	15	3	1595	4.3	12.2	66.6	16.1	0.8	127700
01201	PITTSFIELD	26137	20085	25.1	28.3	33.8	8.6	4.2	47113	49453	54	11	12418	1.0	3.0	44.1	42.9	8.9	179142
01220	ADAMS	23979	3856	29.9	28.8	31.7	7.2	2.4	43583	46395	44	8	2354	3.6	6.4	48.6	37.8	3.6	159557
01222	ASHLEY FALLS	26186	289	19.7	17.6	48.4	8.7	5.5	64876	67188	83	38	244	4.9	2.5	7.8	60.2	24.6	274138
01223	BECKET	29663	785	15.2	24.3	41.1	11.6	7.8	61896	63907	80	33	693	1.7	6.1	32.2	42.4	17.6	208578
01224	BERKSHIRE	32006	62	12.9	24.2	35.5	21.0	6.5	68519	75000	86	46	54	0.0	0.0	24.1	55.6	20.4	278571
01225	CHESHIRE	26143	1347	17.2	27.4	38.6	13.6	3.2	56197	60375	73	22	1118	8.1	7.6	21.2	54.1	8.9	208654
01226	DALTON	30305	2671	14.8	24.6	41.3	10.9	8.3	63984	66569	82	36	1989	2.5	3.0	28.7	52.0	13.8	210014
01230	GREAT BARRINGTON	33930	4011	15.2	25.4	37.8	11.2	10.4	61986	64371	80	33	2731	0.5	1.9	6.8	47.3	43.5	363701
01235	HINSDALE	26234	1064	14.3	27.9	42.4	11.0	4.4	58031	61049	75	25	878	2.1	10.1	32.3	42.5	13.0	190190
01236	HOUSATONIC	31737	432	16.2	24.3	38.4	12.3	8.8	61386	63467	79	31	315	0.6	2.5	6.0	57.1	33.7	296635
01237	LANESBORO	28019	841	15.0	25.8	39.0	14.4	5.8	62340	63905	80	33	707	0.7	0.7	33.0	50.6	15.0	219643
01238	LEE	27449	2650	18.8	24.4	40.0	11.4	5.4	56113	59621	73	21	1867	3.1	1.8	13.5	63.2	18.4	246883
01240	LENOX	32158	2365	18.1	23.3	41.2	10.5	6.9	61600	64084	79	31	1628	2.0	1.6	6.0	47.5	42.9	362541
01243	MIDDLEFIELD	34127	140	11.4	21.4	41.4	15.7	10.0	67440	68343	85	44	122	0.0	1.6	26.2	60.7	11.5	224074
01245	MONTEREY	36808	227	13.2	27.3	41.9	7.5	10.1	60238	63732	78	29	180	0.0	0.0	5.0	36.1	58.9	461538
01247	NORTH ADAMS	21251	6844	34.2	29.2	28.8	5.7	2.1	36977	40617	24	5	3908	5.3	7.0	53.5	31.7	2.5	149769
01253	OTIS	32673	544	17.5	19.5	41.9	11.6	9.6	65422	67505	84	40	450	2.2	2.4	20.9	48.0	26.4	264655
01254	RICHMOND	43802	378	7.9	19.0	33.9	23.0	16.1	81085	82465	92	67	333	2.4	0.0	3.3	43.5	50.8	403906
01255	SANDISFIELD	32338	309	14.9	25.9	42.4	8.4	8.4	59046	61848	76	26	261	0.0	0.0	11.5	50.6	37.9	328409
01256	SAVOY	24937	304	18.1	27.6	43.4	7.9	3.0	54559	59100	71	20	274	6.6	14.6	33.6	36.9	8.4	164167
01257	SHEFFIELD	32990	993	15.5	30.5	35.4	8.7	9.9	53753	57807	69	18	761	1.2	2.1	8.0	52.3	36.4	334076
01258	SOUTH EGREMONT	52712	71	12.7	15.5	50.7	8.5	12.7	75996	75941	90	58	65	0.0	0.0	1.5	32.3	66.2	585938
01259	SOUTHFIELD	33818	260	13.5	25.8	39.2	12.7	8.8	61767	63381	80	32	203	2.5	0.0	11.3	45.8	40.4	335000
01262	STOCKBRIDGE	41033	684	18.1	22.8	35.2	12.9	11.0	60000	62749	77	27	431	0.0	0.0	2.3	33.6	64.0	488971
01266	WEST STOCKBRIDGE	39183	767	14.1	18.9	36.9	15.1	15.0	69980	71845	87	48	630	2.5	2.9	5.7	36.3	52.5	416327
01267	WILLIAMSTOWN	34192	2852	20.6	19.4	28.6	16.6	14.8	67555	71010	85	44	2093	10.8	2.3	11.2	34.8	40.9	320293
01270	WINDSOR	29091	287	12.5	24.4	42.9	12.9	7.3	67107	70435	85	44	262	1.9	3.4	25.6	45.4	23.7	275000
01301	GREENFIELD	23833	7959	29.4	28.1	32.5	6.7	3.3	42198	45871	40	7	4344	2.1	1.7	48.4	42.4	5.4	171954
01330	ASHFIELD	31235	631	11.9	21.2	49.9	11.3	5.7	67777	69768	85	45	499	0.4	1.8	24.4	55.1	18.2	231881
01331	ATHOL	21689	5518	23.1	31.2	33.0	10.7	1.9	46074	48404	52	10	4022	2.2	7.9	63.1	24.5	2.3	140572
01337	BERNARDSTON	28041	1092	10.5	28.8	44.4	9.7	6.6	60463	62549	78	29	902	1.7	4.3	28.8	51.1	14.1	207018
	MASSACHUSETTS	34904		17.4	19.0	33.1	18.1	12.4	68225	71891				0.7	1.2	13.3	53.8	31.0	297007
	UNITED STATES	27277		20.9	24.4	35.3	11.7	7.6	54719	56938				9.3	13.1	31.6	32.6	13.5	162279

ZIP CODE		FINANCIAL SERVICES				THE HOME						ENTERTAINMENT						PERSONAL			
						Home Improvements		Furnishings													
#	POST OFFICE NAME	Auto Loan	Home Loan	Invest-ments	Retire-ment Plans	Home Repair	Lawn & Garden	Comput-ers & Hard-ware-Personal	Major Appli-ances	TV, Radio, Sound Equip-ment	Furni-ture	Dine out/ Carry out	Sports Equip-ment	Fees & Tickets	Toys & Games	Travel	Cable TV	Apparel & Services	Auto Repairs	Health Insur-ance	Pets & Supplies
01001	AGAWAM	86	96	92	95	95	95	92	92	93	91	93	70	98	92	96	94	66	93	97	107
01002	AMHERST	118	104	104	110	104	103	135	110	125	122	126	93	120	124	116	121	89	120	110	133
01003	AMHERST	74	31	31	38	29	36	104	51	82	70	84	55	61	80	55	75	59	73	51	69
01005	BARRE	93	109	98	109	106	105	99	100	98	99	99	78	108	99	106	99	70	99	101	117
01007	BELCHERTOWN	105	127	115	126	124	116	112	113	108	114	110	88	124	111	120	107	79	110	109	130
01008	BLANDFORD	100	122	112	121	118	121	104	110	106	105	107	82	118	107	115	108	75	107	116	128
01010	BRIMFIELD	98	111	95	114	107	109	99	103	97	99	98	80	105	100	104	97	68	99	102	121
01011	CHESTER	91	99	94	102	98	101	90	96	89	89	89	74	94	90	95	90	62	92	95	112
01012	CHESTERFIELD	94	105	91	108	102	103	94	98	93	94	93	76	100	95	99	93	65	94	97	115
01013	CHICOPEE	64	63	58	63	61	64	68	64	71	64	71	49	68	70	65	73	50	68	70	76
01020	CHICOPEE	75	81	78	80	80	84	78	80	81	76	81	59	82	80	81	84	56	80	88	93
01022	CHICOPEE	75	79	70	79	76	84	76	78	78	73	78	58	78	78	77	82	54	77	87	92
01026	CUMMINGTON	108	94	132	94	100	116	92	111	94	87	94	82	84	91	99	99	63	103	110	129
01027	EASTHAMPTON	94	102	98	103	101	97	101	97	99	100	100	76	105	99	103	98	71	99	98	115
01028	EAST LONGMEADOW	118	145	143	148	146	141	125	132	124	131	125	98	143	123	140	124	89	127	133	152
01030	FEEDING HILLS	103	125	117	125	123	115	110	112	106	113	108	86	123	108	119	105	77	109	108	129
01031	GILBERTVILLE	102	116	101	118	113	112	105	108	103	105	104	84	112	105	111	103	73	105	107	126
01032	GOSHEN	101	113	98	117	110	111	101	105	100	102	100	82	108	102	107	100	70	101	104	124
01033	GRANBY	111	139	123	138	133	132	117	122	117	120	119	92	135	119	129	118	84	118	124	141
01034	GRANVILLE	108	122	105	126	119	120	109	113	107	109	108	89	116	110	115	107	75	109	112	133
01035	HADLEY	114	136	137	135	139	132	121	125	119	124	120	92	134	118	132	120	85	122	127	143
01036	HAMPDEN	125	155	153	158	156	148	131	139	128	139	130	103	150	128	147	127	92	132	135	159
01038	HATFIELD	104	127	129	125	130	123	111	116	110	114	111	85	125	109	123	111	79	113	117	132
01039	HAYDENVILLE	125	132	128	136	131	127	130	126	127	132	128	98	135	127	132	126	91	127	126	149
01040	HOLYOKE	67	62	59	62	62	61	70	66	71	69	72	51	68	70	67	71	51	70	68	77
01050	HUNTINGTON	93	107	95	108	104	102	98	99	96	97	97	78	105	98	103	96	69	97	98	116
01053	LEEDS	101	115	110	115	114	107	110	107	106	110	108	83	117	107	114	105	77	107	105	124
01054	LEVERETT	137	170	174	174	174	161	144	153	138	154	140	114	164	138	162	136	100	145	144	175
01056	LUDLOW	86	104	95	103	101	101	91	94	92	92	93	71	103	93	99	94	66	93	99	109
01057	MONSON	101	118	105	119	115	110	107	108	104	107	105	85	116	106	113	103	75	106	105	126
01060	NORTHAMPTON	105	96	100	103	96	92	115	99	110	112	113	83	111	110	109	107	80	108	99	120
01062	FLORENCE	107	120	115	122	119	117	113	112	112	115	113	86	122	112	119	112	80	113	115	132
01063	NORTHAMPTON	162	120	124	138	115	116	177	133	171	164	178	122	157	173	152	166	126	160	139	171
01068	OAKHAM	117	147	128	146	141	126	123	125	115	129	117	99	138	120	132	111	85	119	111	143
01069	PALMER	78	88	82	88	87	86	85	84	85	83	85	64	90	84	88	86	60	84	88	98
01070	PLAINFIELD	108	87	140	85	95	115	87	110	91	81	90	81	75	86	94	97	60	102	109	128
01071	RUSSELL	86	107	95	106	102	105	90	95	92	92	93	71	104	93	100	94	65	93	100	110
01072	SHUTESBURY	123	155	136	154	149	134	130	132	122	136	124	105	146	127	140	117	89	125	118	151
01073	SOUTHAMPTON	128	154	155	158	157	145	134	139	129	142	131	105	150	129	148	127	93	134	133	160
01075	SOUTH HADLEY	103	119	114	119	118	117	110	111	110	111	110	83	119	109	117	111	78	110	115	129
01077	SOUTHWICK	99	116	102	117	112	110	103	105	101	104	102	82	113	103	110	101	72	102	104	123
01080	THREE RIVERS	68	80	75	78	79	73	77	74	75	75	76	58	83	76	80	75	55	76	74	86
01081	WALES	97	109	94	113	106	107	98	102	96	98	97	79	104	99	103	96	68	98	100	119
01082	WARE	81	84	78	85	83	84	86	83	85	82	85	65	86	86	85	87	60	85	86	98
01084	WEST CHESTERFIELD	93	105	90	108	102	103	94	97	92	94	93	76	100	95	99	92	65	94	96	115
01085	WESTFIELD	91	97	93	98	96	95	96	94	95	95	96	72	99	95	97	95	67	95	96	110
01088	WEST HATFIELD	111	124	119	126	123	115	117	114	113	119	114	89	124	114	121	111	81	114	111	134
01089	WEST SPRINGFIELD	79	82	80	84	82	82	85	81	86	83	86	63	88	84	85	87	61	85	86	96
01092	WEST WARREN	71	79	73	77	78	74	76	74	75	75	76	58	80	76	78	75	54	75	74	87
01095	WILBRAHAM	130	161	165	164	166	154	139	146	135	146	136	108	158	134	155	134	98	140	143	166
01096	WILLIAMSBURG	101	113	99	116	110	110	102	105	101	103	101	82	109	103	107	100	71	102	104	124
01098	WORTHINGTON	116	131	113	135	127	129	117	122	115	117	116	95	125	118	124	115	81	117	120	143
01103	SPRINGFIELD	34	26	25	29	25	26	44	34	48	36	49	25	38	43	35	51	37	39	37	42
01104	SPRINGFIELD	59	55	51	56	54	57	64	58	65	60	65	46	61	64	60	67	46	63	65	70
01105	SPRINGFIELD	40	30	28	32	28	29	45	35	46	41	47	29	39	45	37	47	34	42	38	44
01106	LONGMEADOW	147	197	221	198	211	185	165	176	157	176	157	129	197	154	193	155	116	166	166	195
01107	SPRINGFIELD	47	40	38	41	39	38	53	45	55	50	56	35	49	53	47	56	41	51	47	54
01108	SPRINGFIELD	69	62	57	63	59	62	74	65	74	69	75	52	69	74	67	75	53	71	70	79
01109	SPRINGFIELD	59	55	51	57	53	57	62	57	65	58	66	43	61	64	58	68	46	61	64	70
01118	SPRINGFIELD	91	105	95	104	101	100	96	96	96	97	97	74	105	97	102	96	68	96	99	112
01119	SPRINGFIELD	78	84	74	83	81	84	80	80	81	79	81	61	83	82	81	83	57	81	85	94
01128	SPRINGFIELD	95	111	98	111	106	108	99	101	100	101	101	77	110	102	106	101	71	100	105	118
01129	SPRINGFIELD	85	101	91	100	97	98	91	92	92	91	93	70	101	93	97	93	65	92	96	108
01151	INDIAN ORCHARD	57	52	47	53	50	53	61	55	63	56	63	43	58	62	56	64	45	59	59	66
01201	PITTSFIELD	79	81	77	82	80	84	82	81	84	80	84	61	84	83	83	87	59	83	89	96
01220	ADAMS	69	72	68	72	71	77	72	72	75	69	74	54	74	73	73	78	51	73	81	85
01222	ASHLEY FALLS	100	108	99	111	106	109	98	104	97	98	97	80	103	99	103	98	68	99	103	122
01223	BECKET	118	103	144	102	109	126	100	121	103	95	102	89	92	99	107	108	69	112	119	140
01224	BERKSHIRE	102	126	129	130	130	120	107	114	103	115	104	84	122	102	120	101	75	108	107	130
01225	CHESHIRE	82	102	91	101	98	100	86	90	87	88	88	67	99	89	96	89	62	88	95	105
01226	DALTON	99	114	109	114	113	111	105	107	104	105	105	81	114	105	112	105	74	105	108	124
01230	GREAT BARRINGTON	113	114	131	115	118	121	111	118	111	110	111	89	112	108	117	112	77	115	118	137
01235	HINSDALE	91	104	91	106	101	101	94	96	92	94	93	75	100	94	99	92	65	93	95	113
01236	HOUSATONIC	99	118	118	119	121	115	106	110	104	109	105	81	118	103	116	104	74	107	110	126
01237	LANESBORO	92	113	110	115	113	110	96	102	95	101	96	76	110	95	108	95	68	98	102	117
01238	LEE	91	97	102	96	97	101	91	96	91	89	92	72	95	91	96	94	64	94	99	112
01240	LENOX	92	101	111	101	105	110	94	101	98	96	98	71	102	93	103	103	68	100	114	117
01243	MIDDLEFIELD	116	130	112	134	127	128	117	121	115	117	115	95	124	118	123	115	81	116	120	143
01245	MONTEREY	135	110	174	108	120	143	109	138	114	103	112	100	95	108	118	121	75	127	136	159
01247	NORTH ADAMS	68	59	60	61	60	67	68	66	70	63	69	50	62	69	63	74	48	69	74	79
01253	OTIS	128	103	166	101	113	136	103	131	108	96	106	95	89	102	111	115	71	120	129	151
01254	RICHMOND	138	171	175	176	176	162	146	154	140	156	141	115	166	139	163	137	101	146	146	176
01255	SANDISFIELD	128	103	166	101	113	136	103	131	107	96	106	95	89	102	111	115	71	120	129	151
01256	SAVOY	92	84	83	87	86	99	83	93	85	75	84	71	76	87	83	90	57	86	96	108
01257	SHEFFIELD	123	103	146	103	111	129	104	125	108	99	107	92	93	104	110	114	72	117	126	145
01258	SOUTH EGREMONT	145	153	207	151	176	180	137	162	145	155	142	101	151	130	159	151	98	154	180	183
01259	SOUTHFIELD	114	121	117	124	120	125	110	118	109	109	110	91	114	111	117	111	76	113	117	139
01262	STOCKBRIDGE	105	117	128	116	123	128	110	117	116	114	116	80	121	108	121	122	80	117	138	135
01266	WEST STOCKBRIDGE	126	145	164	146	156	154	127	141	129	137	129	97	142	123	144	132	90	135	149	161
01267	WILLIAMSTOWN	116	134	144	134	139	136	124	130	124	127	124	95	136	120	136	126	88	127	136	149
01270	WINDSOR	109	123	106	127	119	121	110	114	108	110	109	89	117	111	116	108	76	110	113	135
01301	GREENFIELD	72	69	66	71	68	72	74	71	75	72	75	55	73	75	72	77	53	74	77	85
01330	ASHFIELD	103	115	106	117	113	110	106	107	103	107	104	83	113	105	111	103	74	105	105	126
01331	ATHOL	75	79	73	80	78	81	77	78	78	74	78	60	79	78	79	79	54	77	81	91
01337	BERNARDSTON	97	113	98	115	109	111	99	103	98	100	99	79	108	100	106	99	69	100	104	121
	MASSACHUSETTS	113	129	133	129	131	121	127	122	123	125	125	94	135	122	132	123	90	124	121	141
	UNITED STATES	100	100	100	100	100	100	100	100	100	100	100	100	100	100	100	100	100	100	100	100

01338-01609

ZIP CODE # POST OFFICE NAME	COUNTY FIPS CODE	POPULATION 2000	POPULATION 2009	POPULATION 2014	2000-2009 ANNUAL RATE % Rate	2000-2009 ANNUAL RATE State Centile	HOUSEHOLDS 2000	HOUSEHOLDS 2009	HOUSEHOLDS 2014	HOUSEHOLDS % Annual Rate 2000-2009	HOUSEHOLDS 2009 Average HH Size	FAMILIES 2000	FAMILIES 2009	FAMILIES % Annual Rate 2000-2009
01338 BUCKLAND	011	99	103	103	0.4	65	44	47	47	0.7	2.19	32	34	0.7
01339 CHARLEMONT	011	1714	1657	1622	-0.4	6	649	639	630	-0.2	2.56	446	436	-0.2
01340 COLRAIN	011	2095	2053	2023	-0.2	14	794	794	787	0.0	2.58	561	558	-0.1
01341 CONWAY	011	1622	1781	1805	1.0	91	627	702	716	1.2	2.53	464	516	1.2
01342 DEERFIELD	011	1409	1460	1458	0.4	65	548	578	581	0.6	2.52	392	411	0.5
01343 DRURY	003	123	121	119	-0.2	14	50	50	50	0.0	2.42	37	37	0.0
01344 ERVING	011	903	960	965	0.7	81	375	407	412	0.9	2.36	252	272	0.8
01346 HEATH	011	195	186	181	-0.5	4	73	71	70	-0.3	2.62	52	50	-0.4
01349 MILLERS FALLS	011	1727	1738	1722	0.1	41	693	707	704	0.2	2.45	441	448	0.2
01350 MONROE BRIDGE	011	78	75	73	-0.4	6	36	35	35	-0.3	2.14	23	23	0.0
01351 MONTAGUE	011	1920	2071	2097	0.8	84	779	854	869	1.0	2.42	502	546	0.9
01354 GILL	011	1462	1326	1272	-1.0	1	576	530	510	-0.9	2.49	403	368	-1.0
01355 NEW SALEM	011	783	852	859	0.9	88	320	355	361	1.1	2.40	223	246	1.1
01360 NORTHFIELD	011	2951	3120	3131	0.6	76	1158	1228	1237	0.6	2.53	815	860	0.6
01364 ORANGE	011	7573	7785	7772	0.3	58	3050	3195	3208	0.5	2.43	1983	2065	0.4
01366 PETERSHAM	027	1096	1124	1123	0.3	58	407	418	420	0.3	2.48	278	282	0.2
01367 ROWE	011	486	467	456	-0.4	6	205	201	198	-0.2	2.32	137	133	-0.3
01368 ROYALSTON	027	1238	1441	1525	1.7	99	448	521	552	1.6	2.77	329	380	1.6
01370 SHELBURNE FALLS	011	4613	4752	4743	0.3	58	1836	1925	1933	0.5	2.39	1212	1262	0.4
01373 SOUTH DEERFIELD	011	4506	4535	4498	0.1	41	1880	1922	1917	0.2	2.35	1231	1249	0.2
01375 SUNDERLAND	011	3784	3788	3754	0.0	32	1635	1669	1666	0.2	2.24	767	776	0.1
01376 TURNERS FALLS	011	5414	5416	5369	0.0	32	2369	2405	2394	0.2	2.19	1376	1384	0.1
01378 WARWICK	011	761	785	782	0.3	58	294	309	311	0.5	2.54	210	220	0.5
01379 WENDELL	011	919	938	933	0.2	48	374	390	391	0.5	2.17	223	231	0.4
01420 FITCHBURG	027	39027	40638	41095	0.4	65	14894	15462	15687	0.4	2.52	9335	9668	0.4
01430 ASHBURNHAM	027	5529	6124	6372	1.1	93	1921	2128	2220	1.1	2.87	1533	1689	1.1
01431 ASHBY	017	2866	2928	2963	0.2	48	985	1018	1033	0.4	2.86	789	812	0.3
01432 AYER	017	7229	7300	7343	0.1	41	2959	3016	3043	0.2	2.27	1759	1783	0.1
01434 DEVENS	027	751	1177	1180	5.0	100	1	86	88	61.9	2.56	1	58	55.1
01436 BALDWINVILLE	027	3191	3333	3365	0.5	71	1118	1171	1189	0.5	2.68	798	827	0.4
01440 GARDNER	027	21396	21884	21934	0.2	48	8519	8716	8763	0.2	2.36	5267	5348	0.2
01450 GROTON	017	9543	10353	10672	0.9	88	3269	3553	3667	0.9	2.89	2564	2778	0.9
01451 HARVARD	027	5174	5377	5433	0.4	65	1790	1857	1884	0.4	2.86	1477	1525	0.3
01452 HUBBARDSTON	027	3911	4408	4609	1.3	95	1309	1469	1541	1.3	2.99	1072	1198	1.2
01453 LEOMINSTER	027	41391	41932	41977	0.1	41	16543	16739	16805	0.1	2.48	10933	10977	0.0
01460 LITTLETON	017	8183	8681	8876	0.6	76	2963	3155	3233	0.7	2.71	2218	2353	0.6
01462 LUNENBURG	027	9338	10130	10439	0.9	88	3515	3796	3921	0.8	2.67	2652	2853	0.8
01463 PEPPERELL	017	11212	11860	12121	0.6	76	3870	4130	4234	0.7	2.87	3035	3225	0.7
01464 SHIRLEY	017	6468	8003	8128	2.3	99	2098	2234	2289	0.7	2.54	1451	1542	0.7
01468 TEMPLETON	027	3109	3472	3590	1.2	94	1104	1232	1278	1.2	2.77	869	966	1.2
01469 TOWNSEND	017	6434	6566	6624	0.2	48	2179	2248	2278	0.3	2.92	1729	1777	0.3
01473 WESTMINSTER	027	6862	7272	7433	0.6	76	2516	2664	2732	0.6	2.73	1944	2048	0.6
01474 WEST TOWNSEND	017	2676	2788	2836	0.4	65	903	951	971	0.6	2.93	724	759	0.5
01475 WINCHENDON	027	9541	10462	10848	1.0	91	3421	3731	3873	0.9	2.77	2457	2661	0.9
01501 AUBURN	027	15650	16094	16211	0.3	58	6246	6422	6495	0.3	2.48	4331	4419	0.2
01503 BERLIN	027	2380	2520	2566	0.6	76	872	923	944	0.6	2.72	666	701	0.6
01504 BLACKSTONE	027	8820	9251	9416	0.5	71	3241	3384	3454	0.5	2.72	2360	2448	0.4
01505 BOYLSTON	027	3955	4297	4440	0.9	88	1551	1685	1747	0.9	2.55	1128	1217	0.8
01506 BROOKFIELD	027	3051	3504	3677	1.5	97	1204	1365	1433	1.4	2.57	857	965	1.3
01507 CHARLTON	027	11264	12025	12261	0.7	81	3789	4055	4153	0.7	2.92	3046	3241	0.7
01510 CLINTON	027	13447	14251	14480	0.6	76	5604	5936	6048	0.6	2.38	3407	3587	0.6
01515 EAST BROOKFIELD	027	2097	2271	2329	0.9	88	778	841	865	0.8	2.70	600	645	0.8
01516 DOUGLAS	027	7057	7753	8012	1.0	91	2483	2730	2835	1.0	2.84	1943	2127	1.0
01518 FISKDALE	027	2375	2792	2964	1.8	99	948	1114	1187	1.8	2.50	656	766	1.7
01519 GRAFTON	027	5637	6328	6642	1.3	95	2044	2307	2430	1.3	2.72	1493	1671	1.2
01520 HOLDEN	027	12673	13789	14179	0.9	88	4657	5030	5177	0.8	2.71	3584	3864	0.8
01521 HOLLAND	013	2385	2649	2700	1.1	93	887	995	1019	1.2	2.66	658	735	1.2
01522 JEFFERSON	027	2950	3381	3558	1.5	97	1059	1216	1285	1.5	2.78	838	958	1.5
01523 LANCASTER	027	7357	7178	7528	-0.3	9	2039	2325	2455	1.4	2.82	1543	1750	1.4
01524 LEICESTER	027	6583	7117	7317	0.8	84	2333	2519	2597	0.8	2.74	1722	1847	0.8
01527 MILLBURY	027	12827	13851	14195	0.8	84	4963	5360	5516	0.8	2.52	3466	3718	0.8
01529 MILLVILLE	027	2724	2980	3068	1.0	91	923	995	1024	0.8	2.99	720	771	0.7
01531 NEW BRAINTREE	027	1231	1414	1484	1.5	97	447	510	535	1.4	2.77	352	401	1.4
01532 NORTHBOROUGH	027	14107	14499	14574	0.3	58	4940	5069	5115	0.3	2.83	3891	3972	0.2
01534 NORTHBRIDGE	027	4321	4713	4855	0.9	88	1453	1584	1636	0.9	2.82	1121	1220	0.9
01535 NORTH BROOKFIELD	027	4726	4916	5000	0.4	65	1823	1886	1921	0.4	2.57	1246	1279	0.3
01536 NORTH GRAFTON	027	6439	7109	7269	1.1	93	2480	2719	2787	1.0	2.48	1713	1873	1.0
01537 NORTH OXFORD	027	1702	1821	1856	0.7	81	758	809	826	0.7	2.24	496	524	0.6
01540 OXFORD	027	11393	12057	12263	0.6	76	4195	4430	4517	0.6	2.70	3039	3190	0.5
01541 PRINCETON	027	3354	3661	3790	1.0	91	1164	1269	1320	0.9	2.88	958	1040	0.9
01542 ROCHDALE	027	2089	2295	2374	1.0	91	689	760	791	1.1	2.81	489	536	1.0
01543 RUTLAND	027	6335	7422	7855	1.7	99	2248	2614	2772	1.6	2.79	1690	1957	1.6
01545 SHREWSBURY	027	31550	33813	34480	0.8	84	12323	13087	13370	0.7	2.57	8657	9130	0.6
01550 SOUTHBRIDGE	027	17214	17185	17135	0.0	32	7077	7045	7042	0.0	2.41	4520	4468	-0.1
01560 SOUTH GRAFTON	027	2823	3574	3868	2.6	100	1172	1496	1629	2.7	2.38	747	945	2.6
01562 SPENCER	027	11663	12099	12271	0.4	65	4572	4726	4803	0.4	2.54	3086	3182	0.3
01564 STERLING	027	7268	7945	8181	1.0	91	2578	2822	2916	1.0	2.82	2073	2258	0.9
01566 STURBRIDGE	027	5461	6255	6570	1.5	97	2117	2438	2577	1.5	2.56	1556	1780	1.5
01568 UPTON	027	5526	6323	6625	1.5	97	2002	2251	2361	1.3	2.79	1530	1712	1.2
01569 UXBRIDGE	027	11159	12945	13671	1.6	97	3984	4595	4863	1.6	2.81	3032	3492	1.5
01570 WEBSTER	027	16442	17403	17697	0.6	76	6919	7308	7459	0.6	2.35	4280	4494	0.5
01571 DUDLEY	027	9975	10788	11091	0.9	88	3715	4025	4160	0.9	2.57	2653	2856	0.8
01581 WESTBOROUGH	027	17960	19175	19554	0.7	81	6522	6919	7081	0.6	2.65	4513	4744	0.5
01583 WEST BOYLSTON	027	7492	7862	7999	0.5	71	2417	2563	2626	0.6	2.56	1749	1844	0.6
01585 WEST BROOKFIELD	027	5916	6417	6585	0.9	88	2194	2381	2451	0.9	2.54	1569	1691	0.8
01588 WHITINSVILLE	027	8925	9293	9417	0.4	65	3369	3515	3578	0.5	2.61	2398	2483	0.4
01590 SUTTON	027	8187	8857	9103	0.9	88	2793	3017	3113	0.8	2.93	2267	2439	0.8
01602 WORCESTER	027	20901	21415	21550	0.3	58	8265	8469	8555	0.3	2.44	5380	5468	0.2
01603 WORCESTER	027	18995	19606	19783	0.3	58	7333	7548	7642	0.3	2.52	4419	4518	0.2
01604 WORCESTER	027	31805	32885	33072	0.4	65	13222	13652	13785	0.3	2.35	7736	7912	0.2
01605 WORCESTER	027	24721	26408	26935	0.7	81	9841	10507	10760	0.7	2.41	5674	6010	0.6
01606 WORCESTER	027	20056	20894	21161	0.4	65	8315	8649	8787	0.4	2.37	5265	5438	0.4
01607 WORCESTER	027	8479	8726	8747	0.3	58	3682	3777	3800	0.3	2.30	2094	2130	0.2
01608 WORCESTER	027	3545	3639	3657	0.3	58	1412	1444	1454	0.2	2.44	721	727	0.1
01609 WORCESTER	027	21198	21634	21709	0.2	48	7639	7734	7770	0.1	2.36	3782	3784	0.0
MASSACHUSETTS					0.3					0.3	2.50			0.3
UNITED STATES					1.0					1.1	2.59			0.9

ZIP CODE #	POST OFFICE NAME	RACE (%) White 2000	White 2009	Black 2000	Black 2009	Asian/Pacific 2000	Asian/Pacific 2009	% Hispanic Origin 2000	% Hispanic Origin 2009	2009 AGE DISTRIBUTION (%) 0-4	5-9	10-14	15-19	20-24	25-44	45-64	65-84	85+	18+	MEDIAN AGE 2009	% 2009 Males	% 2009 Females
01338	BUCKLAND	97.0	96.1	1.0	1.0	1.0	1.0	1.0	1.0	4.9	5.8	6.8	6.8	4.9	23.3	33.0	12.6	1.9	77.7	43.4	51.5	48.5
01339	CHARLEMONT	96.6	95.7	0.3	0.4	0.6	0.9	1.4	1.9	5.1	5.7	6.7	6.6	5.1	23.8	32.3	12.9	1.8	78.5	42.9	49.6	50.4
01340	COLRAIN	98.2	97.9	0.3	0.3	0.3	0.5	0.9	1.2	5.6	6.3	7.1	7.1	4.8	24.2	32.5	11.0	1.4	76.5	41.7	49.9	50.1
01341	CONWAY	98.6	98.0	0.2	0.2	0.6	0.8	0.9	1.5	4.2	4.9	6.2	6.6	4.0	22.0	39.2	11.3	1.5	79.8	46.0	49.2	50.8
01342	DEERFIELD	97.9	97.0	0.4	0.5	0.9	1.3	1.0	1.4	4.4	5.2	6.2	6.8	4.5	21.8	36.1	12.9	2.0	79.4	45.6	48.4	51.6
01343	DRURY	96.8	96.7	0.8	0.8	0.8	0.8	0.8	0.8	4.1	5.0	9.1	6.6	1.7	28.1	31.4	13.2	0.8	76.9	42.5	52.9	47.1
01344	ERVING	97.2	96.6	0.1	0.1	0.1	0.2	0.7	1.0	5.4	5.6	5.8	6.4	6.0	26.9	30.3	11.6	2.0	79.2	40.5	50.1	49.9
01346	HEATH	97.9	96.8	0.0	0.0	0.5	1.1	1.0	1.6	6.5	7.0	7.5	7.0	4.3	24.7	31.2	10.8	1.1	74.2	40.0	52.2	47.8
01349	MILLERS FALLS	95.5	94.4	0.5	0.6	0.9	1.2	1.5	2.0	5.9	5.8	5.8	6.4	6.9	28.3	28.9	10.0	2.0	78.6	38.8	48.8	51.2
01350	MONROE BRIDGE	98.7	96.0	0.0	0.0	0.0	0.0	2.6	2.7	5.3	5.3	5.3	6.7	5.3	25.3	32.0	13.3	1.3	78.7	41.9	49.3	50.7
01351	MONTAGUE	95.6	94.2	0.7	0.9	1.2	1.8	1.4	2.0	5.7	5.7	5.7	5.4	5.7	24.7	33.4	11.9	1.8	79.5	43.0	46.2	53.8
01354	GILL	97.6	96.9	0.3	0.3	0.8	1.1	0.7	0.9	4.0	4.5	5.8	7.5	5.0	21.3	38.4	11.2	2.3	81.3	46.0	49.7	50.3
01355	NEW SALEM	95.4	94.2	0.8	0.9	0.8	1.2	0.9	1.3	4.2	5.4	6.5	6.9	4.3	19.8	39.7	11.7	1.4	79.5	46.5	49.4	50.6
01360	NORTHFIELD	98.5	98.1	0.1	0.1	0.2	0.3	0.6	0.8	5.4	6.0	6.6	6.7	5.2	23.3	33.0	11.8	1.9	77.6	42.7	48.8	51.2
01364	ORANGE	96.3	95.2	1.1	1.3	0.5	0.8	1.6	2.3	5.6	5.6	6.1	7.1	6.9	23.9	29.7	12.9	2.2	78.4	41.1	48.0	52.0
01366	PETERSHAM	97.3	96.2	0.6	0.9	0.3	0.4	1.1	1.9	5.1	5.5	6.1	5.4	3.2	23.8	33.4	14.8	2.8	79.2	45.4	50.9	49.1
01367	ROWE	96.9	96.1	0.4	0.4	0.4	0.6	1.9	2.6	5.4	5.8	6.9	6.6	4.9	24.0	31.0	13.9	1.5	78.2	42.5	49.7	50.3
01368	ROYALSTON	98.6	97.8	0.1	0.1	0.6	0.9	1.1	1.9	5.3	6.2	7.0	7.8	5.2	23.7	35.2	8.3	1.5	76.8	41.8	50.9	49.1
01370	SHELBURNE FALLS	96.9	96.1	0.4	0.5	0.5	0.8	1.0	1.3	4.2	4.8	5.7	7.0	5.5	22.3	33.6	13.9	3.0	80.9	45.3	48.8	51.2
01373	SOUTH DEERFIELD	97.3	96.3	0.5	0.6	0.8	1.2	1.6	2.3	4.6	4.5	5.6	6.1	4.3	24.3	35.0	13.6	2.0	82.4	45.4	49.8	50.2
01375	SUNDERLAND	88.8	84.8	2.4	2.7	6.5	9.6	2.4	3.2	5.0	5.2	4.2	5.0	20.2	30.5	21.2	7.3	1.3	82.8	29.7	49.1	50.9
01376	TURNERS FALLS	95.1	93.7	0.9	1.1	0.9	1.4	3.1	4.2	6.1	5.6	5.4	5.9	7.1	24.8	27.2	14.6	3.2	79.3	41.0	47.7	52.3
01378	WARWICK	96.2	95.2	0.1	0.1	0.3	0.4	1.4	1.9	5.5	6.5	7.0	6.0	4.1	24.6	34.1	10.8	1.4	77.1	42.4	49.7	50.3
01379	WENDELL	92.6	90.7	3.4	4.2	0.4	0.6	1.4	2.0	4.1	4.7	6.6	9.6	4.2	25.9	35.7	8.6	0.6	78.0	41.8	51.2	48.8
01420	FITCHBURG	81.8	76.4	3.7	4.2	4.3	6.0	15.0	20.3	6.9	6.5	6.2	8.0	8.9	26.3	23.6	11.0	2.7	76.1	34.9	47.9	52.1
01430	ASHBURNHAM	97.6	96.6	0.2	0.3	0.6	1.0	1.7	2.7	5.6	7.1	8.7	7.8	4.8	25.7	31.3	8.1	1.0	73.5	39.2	50.9	49.1
01431	ASHBY	98.0	97.4	0.3	0.4	0.3	0.5	0.8	1.3	5.6	6.3	7.4	7.4	4.7	23.8	34.9	8.8	1.1	76.1	41.4	50.9	49.1
01432	AYER	85.9	82.1	5.7	6.7	3.0	4.5	4.7	6.5	6.9	6.7	6.4	8.3	6.0	28.6	25.3	9.6	2.2	75.3	37.4	49.3	50.7
01434	DEVENS	63.0	61.3	32.0	32.7	1.6	2.0	40.7	48.3	1.3	1.2	1.3	1.8	6.7	61.7	22.3	3.6	0.3	95.8	37.3	90.1	9.9
01436	BALDWINVILLE	98.0	97.1	0.2	0.3	0.3	0.6	1.9	3.0	6.6	6.5	6.5	6.8	6.5	24.2	28.4	11.6	3.0	76.0	39.9	49.6	50.4
01440	GARDNER	93.3	90.7	2.2	2.9	1.4	2.2	4.0	6.2	6.2	5.9	5.7	6.4	6.7	27.9	26.3	12.0	2.8	78.2	38.9	51.3	48.7
01450	GROTON	97.2	96.1	0.4	0.5	1.0	1.6	1.2	1.7	7.4	8.9	10.1	8.5	4.2	20.5	32.1	7.3	1.0	68.0	39.2	49.6	50.4
01451	HARVARD	95.8	93.8	0.6	0.8	2.1	3.4	1.1	1.8	5.4	7.0	9.3	8.4	3.8	15.5	37.8	11.5	1.1	72.6	45.3	49.1	50.9
01452	HUBBARDSTON	98.4	97.5	0.2	0.2	0.5	0.8	1.3	2.2	6.8	7.6	8.5	8.4	4.6	24.4	31.8	7.1	0.8	71.5	39.1	50.3	49.7
01453	LEOMINSTER	87.1	82.9	3.7	4.5	2.5	3.7	11.0	15.5	7.0	6.9	6.7	6.6	6.1	26.9	26.5	11.0	2.2	75.2	38.2	48.4	51.6
01460	LITTLETON	96.5	95.0	0.3	0.4	1.7	2.8	1.0	1.4	7.2	8.2	8.9	7.3	3.7	22.2	30.2	10.2	2.1	70.8	41.0	47.9	52.1
01462	LUNENBURG	97.0	95.8	0.7	0.9	0.8	1.3	1.1	1.9	5.7	6.3	7.1	6.9	4.3	23.9	32.9	11.3	1.6	76.5	42.5	49.2	50.8
01463	PEPPERELL	97.2	96.1	0.5	0.6	0.7	1.1	1.0	1.5	7.4	7.6	7.9	7.6	5.3	25.8	29.8	7.5	1.0	72.2	37.6	49.4	50.6
01464	SHIRLEY	84.1	79.7	6.6	7.7	2.2	3.8	6.8	8.9	5.2	5.3	5.5	9.3	10.0	29.8	25.6	8.2	1.2	81.2	35.4	56.4	43.6
01468	TEMPLETON	98.3	97.5	0.5	0.7	0.2	0.4	1.0	1.6	6.2	6.9	7.5	7.0	4.2	24.7	32.3	10.1	1.0	74.8	41.3	50.9	49.1
01469	TOWNSEND	97.5	96.6	0.8	1.0	0.2	0.4	1.3	2.0	6.6	7.2	7.8	7.7	5.3	26.3	31.5	6.7	0.8	73.6	37.4	49.6	50.4
01473	WESTMINSTER	97.5	96.3	0.5	0.6	1.1	1.9	1.1	1.8	5.7	6.3	7.1	7.1	4.6	23.5	34.2	9.8	1.5	76.3	42.0	49.6	50.4
01474	WEST TOWNSEND	97.8	97.0	0.6	0.8	0.3	0.5	0.9	1.4	6.6	7.4	7.6	7.0	4.9	25.8	30.8	9.2	0.9	74.1	39.3	49.9	50.1
01475	WINCHENDON	96.0	94.2	0.8	1.1	0.7	1.1	2.0	3.3	7.4	7.6	7.9	7.4	5.7	27.3	25.9	9.3	1.5	72.3	35.9	49.5	50.5
01501	AUBURN	97.5	96.4	0.6	0.8	0.9	1.5	1.1	1.7	5.2	5.7	6.1	6.3	4.8	23.5	30.2	14.9	3.2	78.9	43.9	47.4	52.6
01503	BERLIN	97.6	96.5	0.2	0.2	1.0	1.6	0.5	0.9	6.5	7.2	7.9	6.2	4.2	22.8	32.3	11.2	1.7	74.0	42.3	50.4	49.6
01504	BLACKSTONE	97.4	96.2	0.3	0.4	0.8	1.3	1.0	1.7	6.5	6.8	7.2	7.2	6.1	28.8	27.3	8.7	1.4	74.8	37.1	49.6	50.4
01505	BOYLSTON	96.6	95.1	0.7	0.9	1.4	2.3	0.6	1.0	5.3	6.1	6.8	6.9	4.7	23.1	32.5	13.2	1.6	77.4	43.2	49.2	50.8
01506	BROOKFIELD	98.1	97.5	0.2	0.3	0.3	0.5	0.6	1.0	5.9	6.2	6.2	6.4	5.3	22.7	32.5	13.0	1.8	77.9	43.2	49.7	50.3
01507	CHARLTON	98.1	97.2	0.2	0.3	0.5	0.9	1.0	1.6	6.7	7.3	7.8	7.8	4.8	26.3	29.8	7.7	1.7	72.8	38.7	48.5	51.5
01510	CLINTON	88.2	83.3	2.6	3.3	0.9	1.4	11.6	17.1	6.2	5.9	6.2	6.2	6.0	28.4	26.7	11.7	2.7	78.0	39.3	48.5	51.5
01515	EAST BROOKFIELD	98.5	97.9	0.4	0.6	0.1	0.2	0.8	1.2	5.7	6.3	7.0	7.1	4.5	24.0	31.4	12.1	2.0	76.6	41.8	49.8	50.2
01516	DOUGLAS	97.4	96.2	0.5	0.7	0.7	1.2	0.9	1.5	7.6	8.0	8.2	7.2	5.0	27.9	28.2	6.8	1.1	71.6	37.3	49.6	50.4
01518	FISKDALE	96.3	94.6	0.6	0.8	0.5	1.0	2.3	3.8	6.3	6.3	6.7	7.0	6.2	24.4	28.7	12.2	2.1	75.7	40.3	48.1	51.9
01519	GRAFTON	96.2	94.2	0.6	1.0	1.8	3.0	1.2	2.0	7.2	7.6	7.9	6.4	4.1	25.3	30.6	9.5	1.3	72.9	40.4	48.0	52.0
01520	HOLDEN	97.2	95.9	0.6	0.8	1.1	1.7	1.0	1.6	6.0	6.7	7.5	7.1	4.6	20.7	31.6	13.0	2.7	75.2	43.2	48.1	51.9
01521	HOLLAND	96.9	95.7	0.1	0.1	0.3	0.5	1.4	2.5	5.7	7.1	8.3	6.9	3.8	27.4	31.5	8.3	0.9	74.4	39.7	51.6	48.4
01522	JEFFERSON	98.4	97.5	0.2	0.3	0.6	1.0	0.9	1.5	6.5	7.1	7.7	7.8	5.3	23.7	32.4	8.4	1.0	73.7	39.8	49.7	50.3
01523	LANCASTER	84.5	79.6	10.6	12.8	1.2	3.2	7.5	10.6	5.1	5.5	5.9	11.2	6.0	28.0	27.0	9.5	1.8	80.0	37.2	53.7	46.3
01524	LEICESTER	96.3	94.7	1.1	1.6	0.9	1.4	1.7	2.8	5.6	5.9	6.5	8.5	6.1	25.4	29.3	10.8	1.9	77.5	39.4	48.4	51.6
01527	MILLBURY	97.2	96.0	0.5	0.7	1.1	1.7	1.0	1.6	5.9	6.1	6.2	6.4	5.5	25.6	28.1	13.3	2.9	77.8	41.4	48.5	51.5
01529	MILLVILLE	97.7	96.9	0.8	1.0	0.2	0.3	0.6	1.0	7.8	8.0	8.1	8.1	6.1	27.1	26.9	7.0	1.0	70.7	35.9	50.0	50.0
01531	NEW BRAINTREE	98.5	98.1	0.2	0.3	0.1	0.1	0.5	0.8	6.5	6.8	6.8	6.8	6.1	24.5	32.3	8.6	1.6	76.0	40.0	49.1	50.9
01532	NORTHBOROUGH	93.0	89.5	0.7	0.9	5.1	8.1	1.3	2.0	6.7	7.5	8.6	8.0	4.2	22.5	31.3	9.8	1.3	71.6	40.8	49.1	50.9
01534	NORTHBRIDGE	97.7	96.6	0.3	0.4	0.3	0.6	1.6	2.5	6.6	7.0	7.4	7.3	5.1	23.4	28.3	11.3	3.5	74.3	40.8	48.0	52.0
01535	NORTH BROOKFIELD	97.7	96.8	0.3	0.5	0.2	0.4	1.1	1.7	5.9	6.4	7.1	7.1	6.4	26.8	27.9	10.4	2.0	76.1	38.4	48.8	51.2
01536	NORTH GRAFTON	94.9	93.3	2.1	2.3	1.5	2.5	2.9	3.9	6.5	6.7	7.0	9.5	5.3	25.1	28.1	10.1	1.7	73.7	39.2	48.1	51.9
01537	NORTH OXFORD	95.9	94.1	1.1	1.4	1.2	2.0	2.3	3.6	6.3	6.2	5.6	6.5	5.8	29.0	28.1	11.1	1.4	77.6	39.2	49.9	50.1
01540	OXFORD	96.8	95.3	0.8	1.1	0.8	1.3	1.9	3.1	6.4	7.0	6.9	6.5	5.2	27.9	28.7	9.9	1.6	75.6	39.1	48.6	51.4
01541	PRINCETON	96.8	95.1	0.3	0.4	1.0	1.6	1.5	2.4	5.0	6.4	8.1	8.5	3.8	20.2	37.4	9.3	1.1	74.8	43.7	50.5	49.5
01542	ROCHDALE	96.6	95.1	1.2	1.7	0.9	1.4	1.4	2.3	6.1	6.1	6.4	6.7	5.8	27.5	26.1	11.7	3.6	77.4	39.2	47.9	52.1
01543	RUTLAND	96.6	95.4	1.0	1.3	0.5	0.8	1.3	2.1	7.3	8.0	8.8	8.4	4.9	25.1	28.6	7.7	1.1	70.2	37.3	50.6	49.4
01545	SHREWSBURY	89.1	84.1	1.5	1.9	7.6	11.7	1.6	2.4	7.5	7.5	7.4	6.3	4.7	25.5	27.9	10.9	2.4	73.6	39.7	48.8	51.2
01550	SOUTHBRIDGE	85.2	80.0	1.4	1.8	1.6	2.2	20.2	28.0	6.8	6.5	6.0	6.7	7.1	27.7	24.7	11.6	2.8	76.6	37.3	48.7	51.3
01560	SOUTH GRAFTON	97.7	96.6	0.5	0.6	0.5	0.9	1.0	1.6	7.3	7.0	6.9	6.7	6.6	29.6	24.6	9.4	2.0	74.5	36.2	49.3	50.7
01562	SPENCER	97.9	97.1	0.6	0.8	0.3	0.5	1.3	2.1	6.4	6.2	6.3	6.2	6.0	27.1	28.9	11.1	1.8	77.3	39.1	49.3	50.7
01564	STERLING	98.1	97.2	0.6	0.8	0.4	0.7	0.8	1.3	6.0	6.9	8.0	7.6	3.7	22.7	34.5	9.4	1.2	74.0	42.1	49.5	50.5
01566	STURBRIDGE	97.5	96.3	0.3	0.4	1.5	2.4	0.9	1.4	5.5	5.9	6.5	6.7	5.2	23.7	31.4	13.1	2.1	77.9	42.8	49.4	50.6
01568	UPTON	97.3	95.8	0.5	0.8	1.0	1.7	0.7	1.3	8.2	9.5	9.9	7.2	3.5	21.2	30.6	8.3	1.6	70.6	40.2	49.0	51.0
01569	UXBRIDGE	98.0	97.2	0.2	0.2	0.7	1.1	0.9	1.5	7.6	7.9	8.1	7.5	5.0	26.4	28.0	8.1	1.4	71.6	37.6	49.4	50.6
01570	WEBSTER	94.8	92.8	1.1	1.4	0.9	1.5	4.0	6.1	6.5	6.3	6.2	6.1	5.9	26.0	27.2	12.5	3.2	77.2	40.1	48.6	51.4
01571	DUDLEY	96.8	95.4	0.5	0.6	0.7	1.2	2.0	3.3	5.9	6.0	6.3	8.5	7.3	26.0	27.7	10.4	1.8	77.5	38.4	50.0	50.0
01581	WESTBOROUGH	88.2	82.8	1.4	1.8	8.1	12.3	3.3	4.9	6.6	7.2	8.1	8.0	4.6	25.1	28.6	9.0	2.6	72.6	39.0	49.7	50.3
01583	WEST BOYLSTON	91.6	89.0	5.3	6.7	0.9	1.4	4.8	7.1	4.2	4.7	5.4	7.4	7.3	27.0	28.8	12.3	2.8	81.4	41.1	56.0	44.0
01585	WEST BROOKFIELD	97.8	96.9	0.4	0.5	0.3	0.5	1.1	1.9	5.5	5.5	5.9	6.6	6.4	23.0	29.2	13.4	4.5	78.9	42.9	46.5	53.5
01588	WHITINSVILLE	95.6	94.0	0.7	0.9	0.4	0.6	1.9	3.1	7.5	7.1	7.2	7.1	6.5	25.8	26.1	10.2	2.6	73.8	37.6	47.6	52.4
01590	SUTTON	98.2	97.3	0.3	0.4	0.6	1.0	0.7	1.2	7.0	8.2	8.7	7.6	4.3	24.3	30.6	8.2	1.1	71.0	39.1	49.8	50.2
01602	WORCESTER	86.9	82.3	4.1	5.1	3.1	4.7	6.1	9.0	5.6	5.5	5.7	7.6	7.2	25.0	27.4	13.0	3.0	79.2	40.3	46.9	53.1
01603	WORCESTER	75.4	68.7	5.9	6.9	8.2	11.1	14.6	19.3	6.8	6.4	6.1	7.1	8.6	27.9	23.1	11.2	2.8	76.2	35.7	47.9	52.1
01604	WORCESTER	82.9	77.4	4.8	5.9	5.3	7.6	9.0	12.6	6.5	6.1	5.8	6.2	7.0	29.7	24.1	11.8	2.9	77.8	37.7	48.4	51.6
01605	WORCESTER	72.0	67.4	11.3	12.1	3.5	5.0	22.2	26.8	7.6	7.0	6.4	6.8	7.8	27.0	22.7	11.1	3.5	74.7	35.5	47.4	52.6
01606	WORCESTER	87.2	83.9	4.8	5.6	2.2	3.3	8.8	11.1	6.5	6.1	6.2	6.1	6.4	26.6	26.4	12.1	3.6	77.5	39.6	47.6	52.4
01607	WORCESTER	75.9	68.6	8.5	10.2	5.1	7.3	11.4	16.3	7.6	6.9	6.1	6.1	7.8	30.1	23.3	10.0	2.1	75.8	35.2	48.7	51.3
01608	WORCESTER	40.7	35.9	12.7	12.3	6.0	7.0	57.3	63.4	8.6	9.9	8.8	8.4	8.1	28.9	19.8	6.3	1.3	67.6	29.1	48.6	51.4
01609	WORCESTER	76.2	70.9	6.8	7.5	4.5	6.3	15.9	20.2	4.9	4.3	4.4	12.8	16.5	23.6	20.9	10.1	2.5	83.2	29.6	51.0	49.0
	MASSACHUSETTS	84.5	81.0	5.4	6.0	3.8	5.4	6.8	8.7	6.1	6.2	6.3	7.1	7.1	26.5	27.1	11.3	2.3	77.4	38.6	48.4	51.6
	UNITED STATES	75.1	72.0	12.3	12.7	3.8	4.6	12.5	15.7	6.8	6.7	6.6	7.1	6.9	27.0	26.0	10.9	1.9	75.7	36.9	49.2	50.8

#	ZIP CODE POST OFFICE NAME	2009 Per Capita Income	2009 HH Income Base	2009 HOUSEHOLD INCOME DISTRIBUTION (%) Less than $25,000	$25,000 to $49,999	$50,000 to $99,999	$100,000 to $149,999	$150,000 or More	MEDIAN HOUSEHOLD INCOME 2009	2014	2009 National Centile	2009 State Centile	2009 Home Value Base	2009 HOME VALUE DISTRIBUTION (%) Less than $50,000	$50,000 to $89,999	$90,000 to $174,999	$175,000 to $399,999	$400,000 or More	2009 Median Home Value
01338	BUCKLAND	32721	47	12.8	19.1	55.3	8.5	4.3	67393	69904	85	44	40	0.0	2.5	27.5	60.0	10.0	215000
01339	CHARLEMONT	25459	639	17.2	25.2	45.7	7.5	4.4	59010	62089	76	26	502	4.6	3.6	34.5	49.6	7.8	192453
01340	COLRAIN	24674	794	14.4	29.7	47.1	5.5	3.3	55108	58336	71	20	657	4.7	5.5	36.5	44.4	8.8	183958
01341	CONWAY	34864	702	8.1	17.2	44.7	19.4	10.5	77770	78068	91	60	588	0.2	0.9	11.7	60.7	26.5	292045
01342	DEERFIELD	31311	578	15.2	16.3	41.5	18.5	8.5	72988	73699	88	53	447	0.0	3.1	19.7	64.4	12.8	237617
01343	DRURY	24925	50	16.0	30.0	44.0	8.0	2.0	53546	57172	69	18	46	2.2	8.7	52.2	37.0	0.0	150000
01344	ERVING	25750	407	17.7	31.7	38.8	8.8	2.9	50642	54123	63	16	319	2.2	4.1	60.8	32.6	0.3	157753
01346	HEATH	25762	71	15.5	26.8	46.5	7.0	4.2	57530	63310	75	24	59	1.7	5.1	39.0	44.1	10.2	187500
01349	MILLERS FALLS	23214	707	16.8	38.9	33.1	7.8	3.4	47402	48662	55	12	508	3.9	2.2	59.3	32.3	2.4	159146
01350	MONROE BRIDGE	29964	35	20.0	25.7	45.7	5.7	2.9	53274	60937	68	18	27	3.7	0.0	40.7	51.9	3.7	187500
01351	MONTAGUE	29192	854	11.7	23.4	47.2	14.5	3.2	70993	74659	87	50	664	2.3	0.9	21.4	60.8	14.6	221774
01354	GILL	28962	530	15.3	22.6	43.6	12.5	6.0	63666	66468	82	36	428	0.9	0.9	37.9	53.0	7.2	193966
01355	NEW SALEM	28963	355	13.2	19.7	55.8	8.2	3.1	64556	66677	83	38	310	0.0	1.9	32.6	52.9	12.6	209483
01360	NORTHFIELD	26950	1228	12.5	26.1	47.3	10.9	3.3	64470	66521	83	37	946	0.0	0.3	30.9	62.7	6.1	211500
01364	ORANGE	21839	3195	23.3	31.0	38.6	5.4	1.7	46794	49124	54	11	2148	3.6	12.3	58.0	23.7	2.3	136779
01366	PETERSHAM	28849	418	13.9	24.6	36.6	18.9	6.0	61779	64045	80	32	340	0.3	2.6	20.0	53.8	23.2	251515
01367	ROWE	27364	201	17.9	25.9	44.3	7.5	4.5	55799	59377	72	21	158	7.0	4.4	38.0	45.6	5.1	176563
01368	ROYALSTON	23761	521	13.8	25.5	46.1	9.8	4.8	57550	60855	75	24	445	2.0	5.2	42.7	40.4	9.7	175223
01370	SHELBURNE FALLS	26881	1925	16.8	26.6	44.5	8.4	3.6	59266	62241	77	26	1341	0.7	1.9	31.5	54.9	11.0	210128
01373	SOUTH DEERFIELD	35565	1922	12.4	19.8	38.8	17.9	11.1	70149	71776	87	48	1449	0.3	0.2	11.5	75.6	12.4	260727
01375	SUNDERLAND	27431	1669	24.9	21.7	39.9	9.1	4.4	52883	56151	68	18	778	2.3	0.0	6.6	73.5	17.6	276036
01376	TURNERS FALLS	20177	2405	36.7	29.4	27.8	4.1	2.1	33554	37189	14	3	1304	2.5	4.3	50.8	39.2	3.3	166281
01378	WARWICK	25608	309	12.0	33.3	41.1	9.4	4.2	54365	58199	70	19	265	0.4	3.8	41.5	52.5	1.9	183712
01379	WENDELL	28360	390	16.7	27.9	42.8	8.7	3.8	56641	60846	74	23	324	3.7	11.1	42.6	41.7	0.9	164655
01420	FITCHBURG	22026	15462	26.2	26.3	33.6	11.0	2.8	47520	50183	55	13	8217	1.4	3.7	49.5	42.2	3.2	168700
01430	ASHBURNHAM	28128	2128	10.9	15.6	44.3	22.9	6.3	75187	77163	89	56	1846	0.4	1.8	28.8	63.5	5.5	208073
01431	ASHBY	29142	1018	8.3	17.9	42.2	25.9	5.7	80201	82429	92	65	908	0.6	0.2	20.3	70.5	8.5	230189
01432	AYER	34351	3016	16.8	20.7	35.5	17.9	9.1	61875	66951	80	32	1719	2.2	0.8	12.9	73.7	10.4	245450
01434	DEVENS	15394	86	62.8	22.1	7.0	3.5	4.7	16398	15907	1	1	78	0.0	1.3	25.6	53.8	19.2	233333
01436	BALDWINVILLE	24488	1171	16.8	25.6	37.2	15.8	4.5	58979	62606	76	26	889	1.9	0.6	49.2	44.0	4.4	172661
01440	GARDNER	23873	8716	23.4	28.1	34.7	11.1	2.8	48476	51380	58	13	4897	1.4	3.6	54.4	37.9	2.7	162699
01450	GROTON	48342	3553	6.2	8.6	27.4	26.7	31.2	112829	118653	98	90	2918	0.0	0.0	2.5	43.4	54.1	419608
01451	HARVARD	57473	1857	2.2	7.8	16.6	24.1	49.2	148179	153306	100	98	1637	0.0	0.0	0.5	11.1	88.5	631076
01452	HUBBARDSTON	29972	1469	9.7	8.8	45.3	25.9	10.2	81800	82749	93	68	1307	1.1	2.1	23.9	63.8	9.2	230340
01453	LEOMINSTER	27794	16739	19.0	23.0	35.8	16.1	6.0	58447	62102	76	25	9735	1.0	2.3	27.9	60.5	8.3	214401
01460	LITTLETON	44148	3155	10.1	9.5	31.3	26.1	23.0	97996	104162	96	83	2574	3.0	0.4	3.3	51.4	41.9	369001
01462	LUNENBURG	34512	3796	10.5	19.6	34.3	23.7	12.0	77852	80004	91	61	3246	2.7	1.0	18.5	53.6	24.2	262850
01463	PEPPERELL	36271	4130	8.9	13.6	34.2	28.4	15.0	87494	93215	94	75	3239	2.9	1.3	9.6	68.4	17.8	287157
01464	SHIRLEY	27108	2234	12.6	19.5	36.8	23.1	8.1	73943	77204	89	54	1584	3.2	0.6	20.8	66.2	9.2	236127
01468	TEMPLETON	24937	1232	18.8	17.5	46.4	13.3	3.9	64524	67497	83	37	1076	2.6	3.3	37.6	51.3	5.2	184722
01469	TOWNSEND	30795	2248	9.6	14.6	40.1	27.6	8.1	82900	86070	93	71	1839	1.1	0.5	9.6	82.8	6.0	242045
01473	WESTMINSTER	31282	2664	10.0	14.7	41.0	27.1	7.2	75704	77890	90	57	2239	0.0	0.9	22.1	64.4	12.6	231916
01474	WEST TOWNSEND	32075	951	5.8	13.9	43.6	27.2	9.5	84411	87948	94	72	802	1.0	0.6	19.5	72.1	6.9	230043
01475	WINCHENDON	23495	3731	21.4	23.0	37.1	14.3	4.2	56265	60813	73	22	2718	0.6	5.2	46.1	44.6	3.6	172621
01501	AUBURN	30444	6422	15.8	19.7	38.6	18.0	7.8	65800	68442	84	40	5180	1.9	3.2	22.7	66.5	5.7	216089
01503	BERLIN	36467	923	10.9	17.3	26.5	31.1	14.1	89936	91341	95	78	736	0.0	0.0	3.0	40.4	56.7	425926
01504	BLACKSTONE	27809	3384	13.2	21.7	38.9	20.1	6.1	70480	73909	87	49	2371	0.5	0.9	15.9	71.3	11.3	235049
01505	BOYLSTON	39991	1685	9.2	15.5	34.7	23.3	17.3	85106	85721	94	73	1387	0.7	0.0	10.2	52.6	36.5	319872
01506	BROOKFIELD	25825	1365	16.5	24.3	41.5	12.7	4.9	58149	61841	75	25	1095	5.3	12.1	27.5	49.1	5.9	186467
01507	CHARLTON	30656	4055	11.0	10.4	39.0	30.5	9.2	83796	86145	93	71	3296	0.5	0.7	17.4	69.1	12.4	245775
01510	CLINTON	28923	5936	17.5	22.7	40.5	13.8	5.5	59343	62843	77	26	3293	0.4	1.1	17.5	73.7	7.3	228702
01515	EAST BROOKFIELD	28752	841	13.0	19.1	43.9	17.6	6.4	66619	68669	85	43	690	0.3	0.0	30.7	63.5	5.5	202571
01516	DOUGLAS	30206	2730	9.6	13.2	42.7	26.5	8.0	80812	82020	92	66	2184	1.1	1.7	11.3	75.1	10.8	247559
01518	FISKDALE	31464	1114	18.4	16.5	36.3	18.4	10.4	66423	69419	84	42	756	0.5	1.7	31.0	52.8	14.0	221132
01519	GRAFTON	37837	2307	9.8	13.7	32.7	27.4	16.3	88328	91133	95	76	1856	0.0	0.5	6.4	52.2	41.0	361872
01520	HOLDEN	35648	5030	9.4	14.2	38.1	24.0	14.4	83145	84675	93	71	4390	0.1	0.0	10.9	65.7	23.3	270153
01521	HOLLAND	27089	995	13.1	19.0	51.4	11.6	5.0	66424	67750	84	42	846	0.8	2.7	41.4	47.8	7.3	184430
01522	JEFFERSON	35773	1216	9.9	15.9	28.5	26.6	19.1	90122	90750	95	78	1008	0.0	0.5	13.7	62.4	23.4	280479
01523	LANCASTER	32046	2325	13.6	10.6	37.4	25.5	12.8	81249	83368	93	67	1822	0.0	0.4	8.9	59.4	31.2	299492
01524	LEICESTER	27509	2519	14.8	18.6	39.3	23.0	4.2	75014	76278	89	55	1937	0.0	0.0	29.2	66.8	4.0	207177
01527	MILLBURY	30500	5360	15.3	21.1	34.5	20.9	8.2	66687	70342	85	43	3823	0.9	1.2	19.3	68.9	9.7	231015
01529	MILLVILLE	26976	995	11.2	14.8	45.6	21.7	6.7	75265	77950	89	56	788	0.0	2.7	31.7	60.3	5.3	208451
01531	NEW BRAINTREE	25552	510	14.1	21.6	43.9	16.5	3.9	62942	65955	81	34	383	1.6	1.3	23.0	59.5	14.6	234451
01532	NORTHBOROUGH	42974	5069	6.3	10.5	30.0	25.3	27.9	105138	106042	97	88	4171	0.0	0.1	3.5	48.3	48.1	393382
01534	NORTHBRIDGE	29037	1584	11.0	17.4	37.9	24.3	9.4	75406	78676	90	57	1275	0.2	1.2	7.7	75.8	15.2	265088
01535	NORTH BROOKFIELD	25771	1886	18.8	22.1	42.0	11.5	5.6	57663	61184	75	24	1309	0.5	0.8	32.3	57.8	8.6	200890
01536	NORTH GRAFTON	34919	2719	12.0	17.5	33.8	26.2	10.6	77070	79162	91	59	2066	0.0	1.0	7.3	67.5	24.2	291760
01537	NORTH OXFORD	32700	809	11.5	21.1	43.8	17.2	6.4	66616	68187	85	42	587	0.7	9.2	34.6	50.3	5.3	182966
01540	OXFORD	27837	4430	15.9	17.5	40.3	19.8	6.5	68988	71868	86	47	3321	0.1	1.7	29.9	62.6	5.7	200081
01541	PRINCETON	43198	1269	6.5	6.9	29.5	29.9	27.3	110832	113700	98	89	1124	0.0	0.0	4.8	48.8	46.4	383794
01542	ROCHDALE	27761	760	11.1	20.7	36.7	24.7	6.8	70300	73513	87	48	565	0.0	2.1	31.0	62.7	4.2	198639
01543	RUTLAND	31759	2614	11.0	16.3	34.5	28.0	10.1	83990	85763	93	72	2070	1.7	2.8	13.2	71.5	10.8	244869
01545	SHREWSBURY	38720	13087	11.6	14.6	33.8	22.3	17.7	82736	84233	93	70	9471	0.5	0.9	8.1	54.8	35.7	335572
01550	SOUTHBRIDGE	22297	7045	27.8	28.4	32.5	8.4	2.9	43721	47037	45	8	3230	0.7	2.7	48.4	46.6	1.7	173042
01560	SOUTH GRAFTON	26490	1496	16.4	26.3	41.2	13.2	2.8	57459	61236	75	24	745	1.1	0.8	20.8	59.6	17.7	255750
01562	SPENCER	27427	4726	18.5	22.1	36.3	17.0	6.1	60083	63400	77	28	2989	0.2	0.3	23.8	68.4	7.3	220757
01564	STERLING	37540	2822	9.2	10.6	36.4	27.0	16.9	89568	88771	95	78	2349	0.3	1.9	6.2	49.8	41.8	362694
01566	STURBRIDGE	33874	2438	10.0	20.3	35.6	23.4	10.6	76291	77291	90	58	1955	0.7	4.2	19.5	61.2	14.4	233677
01568	UPTON	42959	2251	12.1	9.4	26.7	24.2	27.6	103001	103991	97	86	1824	0.8	0.0	2.2	42.1	54.9	417451
01569	UXBRIDGE	31969	4595	11.2	17.1	32.9	29.0	9.7	81823	82888	93	68	3600	0.1	1.2	11.5	68.0	19.2	271598
01570	WEBSTER	25104	7308	26.7	24.5	33.8	10.6	4.5	48644	52057	58	14	4027	1.2	1.5	35.7	53.4	8.1	192066
01571	DUDLEY	27838	4025	16.9	22.3	36.5	17.8	6.5	62714	66090	81	34	2846	1.9	0.9	28.2	62.8	6.1	210154
01581	WESTBOROUGH	44887	6919	8.8	11.8	30.3	22.4	26.7	98151	97537	96	83	4442	1.5	1.1	5.9	33.1	58.4	440546
01583	WEST BOYLSTON	30393	2563	13.9	18.8	32.4	25.4	9.4	72628	75082	88	52	2051	0.1	0.6	11.9	63.9	23.5	252133
01585	WEST BROOKFIELD	25727	2381	17.8	25.9	37.0	14.5	4.8	56744	61181	74	23	1801	2.7	3.7	30.1	57.9	5.6	208983
01588	WHITINSVILLE	28839	3515	15.3	24.8	33.8	18.3	7.8	61869	65817	80	32	2121	0.6	0.5	13.2	67.3	18.4	255284
01590	SUTTON	37014	3017	7.4	12.4	28.7	34.8	16.8	102048	103525	97	85	2617	0.4	0.9	9.0	55.5	34.2	328212
01602	WORCESTER	31284	8469	15.0	20.1	38.3	19.0	7.6	65876	68443	84	40	5661	0.2	1.2	29.1	64.0	5.5	207500
01603	WORCESTER	21470	7548	27.9	25.8	33.9	9.4	3.0	46377	49201	52	10	3408	0.5	2.3	56.1	39.3	1.7	165520
01604	WORCESTER	25384	13652	22.1	28.4	33.8	11.7	4.1	49506	52298	60	15	6382	0.4	2.5	42.3	52.8	2.0	182012
01605	WORCESTER	22460	10507	34.4	25.9	24.9	9.5	5.3	38388	42233	28	6	3936	1.3	1.5	38.9	52.3	6.0	191516
01606	WORCESTER	27949	8649	17.2	25.4	39.4	13.4	4.5	56723	60499	74	23	5348	1.3	0.6	40.9	55.8	1.3	183712
01607	WORCESTER	21961	3777	26.4	32.6	31.9	7.3	1.8	42588	45361	41	7	1591	1.6	5.6	55.9	34.1	2.8	159252
01608	WORCESTER	11366	1444	61.4	23.4	11.9	2.7	0.6	17637	18040	1	1	76	21.1	13.2	26.3	27.6	11.8	125000
01609	WORCESTER	24052	7734	33.1	23.8	24.3	12.4	6.4	41007	44162	36	6	2702	1.2	2.2	20.2	52.3	24.2	251582
	MASSACHUSETTS	34904		17.4	19.0	33.1	18.1	12.4	68225	71891				0.7	1.2	13.3	53.8	31.0	297007
	UNITED STATES	27277		20.9	24.4	35.3	11.7	7.6	54719	56938				9.3	13.1	31.6	32.6	13.5	162279

#	POST OFFICE NAME	FINANCIAL SERVICES: Auto Loan	Home Loan	Invest-ments	Retire-ment Plans	THE HOME: Home Improvements: Home Repair	Lawn & Garden	Furnishings: Comput-ers & Hard-ware-Personal	Major Appli-ances	TV, Radio, Sound Equip-ment	Furni-ture	ENTERTAINMENT: Dine out/ Carry out	Sports Equip-ment	Fees & Tickets	Toys & Games	Travel	Cable TV	PERSONAL: Apparel & Services	Auto Repairs	Health Insur-ance	Pets & Supplies
01338	BUCKLAND	100	112	97	116	109	110	101	104	99	101	99	82	107	101	106	99	69	100	103	123
01339	CHARLEMONT	93	99	105	100	99	106	89	99	91	88	91	74	94	90	97	93	63	94	100	115
01340	COLRAIN	89	100	86	103	97	98	89	93	88	90	88	73	95	90	94	88	62	89	92	109
01341	CONWAY	116	144	148	148	148	137	123	130	118	131	119	96	140	117	138	115	85	123	123	148
01342	DEERFIELD	103	127	122	129	126	123	108	114	107	113	108	85	124	107	121	107	77	110	114	131
01343	DRURY	93	85	84	89	87	100	84	95	87	76	85	72	77	88	84	92	58	87	98	110
01344	ERVING	78	91	84	90	89	84	87	84	84	85	85	66	93	85	90	84	61	85	84	98
01346	HEATH	94	106	91	109	103	104	95	98	93	95	94	77	101	95	100	93	65	95	97	116
01349	MILLERS FALLS	72	84	79	83	83	77	82	78	79	79	80	62	87	80	85	79	58	80	78	91
01350	MONROE BRIDGE	82	102	91	102	98	101	87	91	88	88	89	68	100	89	96	90	63	89	96	106
01351	MONTAGUE	94	106	102	107	105	99	101	98	98	102	99	77	108	99	105	97	71	99	96	115
01354	GILL	93	115	103	115	111	113	98	102	99	100	100	77	113	101	109	101	71	100	108	119
01355	NEW SALEM	97	109	94	112	106	107	97	101	96	98	96	79	104	98	103	96	67	97	100	119
01360	NORTHFIELD	91	108	95	109	104	106	94	98	94	95	95	75	104	96	102	95	66	95	100	115
01364	ORANGE	76	72	70	73	72	80	75	77	77	70	76	58	72	77	73	80	53	76	83	90
01366	PETERSHAM	97	115	118	115	119	121	99	110	102	104	102	76	112	99	112	106	71	105	118	124
01367	ROWE	85	100	90	100	96	100	87	92	88	86	88	69	96	89	94	90	62	89	96	107
01368	ROYALSTON	92	103	89	106	100	101	92	96	91	92	91	75	98	93	97	91	64	92	95	113
01370	SHELBURNE FALLS	92	96	94	97	96	98	92	95	91	90	91	73	93	92	95	92	64	93	96	111
01373	SOUTH DEERFIELD	113	129	128	132	130	123	118	119	115	123	116	91	128	114	126	113	82	117	116	139
01375	SUNDERLAND	90	70	67	75	68	72	102	78	94	88	95	67	84	95	81	92	67	89	81	97
01376	TURNERS FALLS	60	58	57	59	58	61	63	61	65	60	64	46	62	63	61	67	45	63	67	72
01378	WARWICK	91	102	88	105	99	100	91	95	90	91	90	74	97	92	96	90	63	91	94	112
01379	WENDELL	90	101	87	104	98	99	91	94	89	91	90	74	97	91	96	89	63	91	93	111
01420	FITCHBURG	73	76	72	75	75	74	80	75	81	77	81	58	81	80	79	82	58	79	80	89
01430	ASHBURNHAM	108	132	116	133	127	122	113	116	109	116	111	90	126	113	122	108	79	112	112	135
01431	ASHBY	115	136	118	138	131	126	118	121	113	121	115	95	129	117	126	112	81	116	115	141
01432	AYER	105	125	117	121	124	112	115	113	111	116	113	88	125	113	121	110	81	113	109	130
01434	DEVENS	49	57	53	56	56	52	55	53	53	53	54	42	59	54	57	53	39	54	53	61
01436	BALDWINVILLE	85	102	94	100	100	96	95	93	93	93	94	72	104	94	100	94	67	94	95	108
01440	GARDNER	77	81	78	81	80	80	82	80	82	80	82	62	84	82	83	83	58	82	83	94
01450	GROTON	181	236	239	244	242	208	198	203	183	213	186	161	232	187	222	174	138	191	177	230
01451	HARVARD	196	279	341	290	312	261	228	245	212	254	209	182	290	208	274	202	162	224	216	266
01452	HUBBARDSTON	121	152	133	151	146	131	127	129	119	134	122	103	143	124	137	115	88	123	115	148
01453	LEOMINSTER	90	100	95	100	99	92	99	94	97	98	98	75	105	97	101	96	70	97	94	110
01460	LITTLETON	147	204	216	200	213	183	167	175	158	173	160	131	201	161	192	156	119	165	161	193
01462	LUNENBURG	119	151	145	151	150	141	127	133	124	132	125	100	146	125	142	123	90	127	129	152
01463	PEPPERELL	140	167	154	167	164	151	148	149	141	153	143	117	162	145	157	138	103	144	139	171
01464	SHIRLEY	106	125	116	125	123	113	116	113	111	117	113	89	125	113	121	109	81	113	109	132
01468	TEMPLETON	95	109	95	111	106	107	97	100	96	97	97	78	105	98	103	96	68	97	101	118
01469	TOWNSEND	120	149	132	148	144	130	128	129	121	132	123	102	143	125	137	117	88	124	117	148
01473	WESTMINSTER	115	139	122	140	135	129	120	123	116	123	117	96	133	119	129	114	83	118	118	143
01474	WEST TOWNSEND	127	159	140	159	153	137	133	135	125	140	128	108	150	130	144	120	92	129	121	155
01475	WINCHENDON	86	99	90	99	97	94	93	92	91	91	91	72	99	92	97	90	65	92	92	108
01501	AUBURN	98	116	116	115	117	117	104	109	105	104	105	80	115	104	114	107	74	107	114	125
01503	BERLIN	120	167	180	162	175	153	137	145	131	140	132	106	164	131	159	131	97	137	137	159
01504	BLACKSTONE	101	119	107	118	116	106	109	106	104	110	106	85	118	107	114	101	76	105	100	123
01505	BOYLSTON	134	158	156	160	159	149	143	144	139	148	140	111	158	140	154	137	101	141	140	167
01506	BROOKFIELD	92	98	101	96	101	102	92	98	92	94	92	72	95	90	98	94	64	96	102	114
01507	CHARLTON	120	149	132	148	144	130	128	129	121	133	123	102	143	125	137	117	89	124	117	148
01510	CLINTON	88	101	97	100	100	93	99	94	96	97	98	74	105	96	102	96	71	96	93	109
01515	EAST BROOKFIELD	103	123	108	124	119	121	106	111	107	108	108	84	119	109	116	108	76	108	115	130
01516	DOUGLAS	113	138	124	137	134	122	122	121	116	125	118	96	135	119	130	113	85	118	113	140
01518	FISKDALE	100	123	119	120	123	113	111	111	108	111	109	85	123	108	120	107	78	110	109	127
01519	GRAFTON	136	163	163	168	166	153	144	147	139	152	141	113	162	140	157	137	102	142	140	169
01520	HOLDEN	122	160	163	158	164	150	133	141	130	138	131	104	157	130	152	129	95	134	136	158
01521	HOLLAND	100	113	97	116	110	111	101	105	99	101	100	82	108	102	107	100	70	101	104	124
01522	JEFFERSON	134	162	149	163	159	145	141	142	134	147	136	111	156	137	151	130	97	137	132	164
01523	LANCASTER	120	153	156	151	157	141	132	136	127	135	128	102	151	128	147	126	93	132	130	154
01524	LEICESTER	99	122	111	121	119	114	106	108	104	109	105	83	119	105	115	104	75	105	109	125
01527	MILLBURY	97	122	120	118	123	112	109	110	106	108	107	84	122	107	119	106	78	109	108	125
01529	MILLVILLE	105	127	116	125	124	113	115	113	110	116	112	90	126	113	122	108	81	112	108	131
01531	NEW BRAINTREE	96	110	96	111	107	106	100	102	98	99	99	80	107	100	105	98	69	99	101	119
01532	NORTHBOROUGH	157	203	207	208	208	182	172	176	161	182	163	138	200	164	192	155	120	167	158	199
01534	NORTHBRIDGE	109	135	124	132	132	119	119	119	114	121	116	93	132	117	128	112	83	116	112	136
01535	NORTH BROOKFIELD	87	102	92	101	99	96	94	94	92	93	93	73	102	94	99	93	66	93	94	109
01536	NORTH GRAFTON	113	142	143	140	145	131	124	127	120	127	122	96	141	121	137	120	88	124	123	144
01537	NORTH OXFORD	96	111	101	110	109	104	105	103	102	102	103	81	112	103	109	102	73	103	102	120
01540	OXFORD	98	118	108	118	115	112	105	106	104	106	105	82	117	105	113	104	74	105	107	124
01541	PRINCETON	159	211	218	222	219	189	173	180	161	188	163	142	208	165	197	154	123	167	156	203
01542	ROCHDALE	104	124	114	122	121	112	115	112	111	114	113	89	125	113	121	110	81	112	109	130
01543	RUTLAND	117	145	129	144	140	132	125	127	121	128	123	99	141	124	135	120	88	123	123	147
01545	SHREWSBURY	129	153	153	152	155	141	141	139	137	143	138	107	155	138	150	135	100	138	135	159
01550	SOUTHBRIDGE	71	73	68	73	71	71	77	72	78	74	78	56	78	77	76	79	55	76	77	86
01560	SOUTH GRAFTON	80	94	88	91	92	86	90	87	88	88	89	68	97	88	94	88	64	88	87	101
01562	SPENCER	92	104	99	103	103	99	100	98	98	97	98	75	105	98	102	98	70	98	98	114
01564	STERLING	142	171	163	176	172	163	147	154	142	154	143	118	165	144	161	140	102	146	147	178
01566	STURBRIDGE	112	140	138	136	141	130	121	125	117	124	119	93	136	118	133	117	85	121	122	141
01568	UPTON	149	198	205	198	205	181	166	172	159	173	161	131	196	160	188	157	119	164	162	193
01569	UXBRIDGE	118	145	133	144	142	129	127	127	122	129	124	99	141	125	136	120	90	124	120	146
01570	WEBSTER	78	82	77	83	81	82	84	81	85	81	85	63	86	84	84	86	60	83	85	96
01571	DUDLEY	94	113	103	112	110	106	102	102	101	101	102	79	112	102	109	101	73	101	103	119
01581	WESTBOROUGH	156	193	200	198	199	174	173	173	163	182	165	136	196	164	189	157	122	168	159	197
01583	WEST BOYLSTON	112	133	135	135	137	133	117	124	116	123	117	90	131	115	129	117	83	119	126	142
01585	WEST BROOKFIELD	90	102	92	101	99	98	94	95	93	94	94	73	100	95	98	94	66	94	96	111
01588	WHITINSVILLE	96	114	112	111	114	107	107	106	105	104	106	81	116	105	113	105	76	106	105	122
01590	SUTTON	140	182	177	181	183	163	152	157	144	159	146	121	175	147	169	140	106	149	144	178
01602	WORCESTER	98	116	115	114	117	111	108	108	108	108	108	81	119	106	116	109	78	108	112	124
01603	WORCESTER	69	72	69	72	71	68	79	72	78	75	79	57	80	77	77	78	57	77	74	85
01604	WORCESTER	79	81	77	81	79	78	87	80	86	84	87	63	88	85	85	87	62	85	83	95
01605	WORCESTER	73	68	66	69	67	69	79	72	80	75	81	56	77	79	74	82	57	78	77	86
01606	WORCESTER	87	95	90	95	94	90	95	91	94	93	95	71	100	94	97	94	68	94	93	107
01607	WORCESTER	69	63	59	64	61	61	74	66	74	70	75	53	71	74	69	74	53	72	69	79
01608	WORCESTER	39	28	24	30	26	29	40	32	43	38	43	27	35	42	33	44	30	39	36	41
01609	WORCESTER	81	71	73	74	72	70	92	77	89	85	91	62	85	88	82	88	65	86	80	92
	MASSACHUSETTS	113	129	133	129	131	121	127	122	123	125	125	94	135	122	132	123	90	124	121	141
	UNITED STATES	100	100	100	100	100	100	100	100	100	100	100	100	100	100	100	100	100	100	100	100

ZIP CODE #	POST OFFICE NAME	COUNTY FIPS CODE	POPULATION 2000	POPULATION 2009	POPULATION 2014	2000-2009 ANNUAL RATE % Rate	2000-2009 ANNUAL RATE State Centile	HOUSEHOLDS 2000	HOUSEHOLDS 2009	HOUSEHOLDS 2014	HOUSEHOLDS % Annual Rate 2000-2009	HOUSEHOLDS 2009 Average HH Size	FAMILIES 2000	FAMILIES 2009	FAMILIES % Annual Rate 2000-2009
01610	WORCESTER	027	23133	23884	24079	0.3	58	7388	7635	7727	0.4	2.64	4210	4308	0.2
01611	CHERRY VALLEY	027	2229	2410	2490	0.8	84	828	895	929	0.8	2.67	608	653	0.8
01612	PAXTON	027	4322	4548	4617	0.6	76	1400	1475	1502	0.6	2.81	1133	1188	0.5
01701	FRAMINGHAM	017	31124	30656	30510	-0.2	14	12182	12109	12091	-0.1	2.49	8743	8655	-0.1
01702	FRAMINGHAM	017	36006	37001	37319	0.3	58	14069	14274	14385	0.2	2.40	7885	7950	0.1
01718	VILLAGE OF NAGOG WOO	017	420	422	423	0.1	41	174	174	174	0.0	2.43	101	100	-0.1
01719	BOXBOROUGH	017	4906	5192	5287	0.6	76	1864	1943	1976	0.4	2.67	1280	1326	0.4
01720	ACTON	017	19828	19862	19948	0.0	32	7296	7321	7356	0.0	2.69	5424	5425	0.0
01721	ASHLAND	017	14674	15848	16352	0.8	84	5721	6180	6386	0.8	2.56	4021	4333	0.8
01730	BEDFORD	017	12506	12923	13091	0.4	65	4590	4775	4853	0.4	2.58	3400	3523	0.4
01731	HANSCOM AFB	017	3047	2667	2549	-1.4	0	855	751	718	-1.4	3.36	825	722	-1.4
01740	BOLTON	027	4248	4624	4769	0.9	88	1458	1585	1642	0.9	2.92	1228	1329	0.9
01741	CARLISLE	017	4583	4708	4773	0.3	58	1578	1637	1664	0.4	2.88	1336	1383	0.4
01742	CONCORD	017	17074	17153	17217	0.0	32	5971	6059	6100	0.2	2.60	4452	4499	0.1
01745	FAYVILLE	027	271	305	319	1.3	95	107	120	126	1.2	2.54	75	83	1.1
01746	HOLLISTON	017	13815	13823	13840	0.0	32	4798	4838	4857	0.1	2.85	3844	3868	0.1
01747	HOPEDALE	027	5852	6093	6171	0.4	65	2215	2313	2354	0.5	2.58	1556	1613	0.4
01748	HOPKINTON	017	13346	14416	14922	0.8	84	4444	4789	4951	0.8	2.98	3624	3894	0.8
01749	HUDSON	017	18044	18914	19308	0.5	71	6969	7383	7561	0.6	2.54	4825	5093	0.6
01752	MARLBOROUGH	017	36317	37248	37691	0.3	58	14520	14910	15103	0.3	2.47	9306	9507	0.2
01754	MAYNARD	017	10372	10281	10260	-0.1	23	4274	4274	4277	0.0	2.40	2790	2779	0.0
01756	MENDON	027	5256	5770	5988	1.0	91	1804	1981	2063	1.0	2.90	1442	1577	1.0
01757	MILFORD	027	26995	27656	27831	0.3	58	10494	10722	10825	0.2	2.55	7255	7363	0.2
01760	NATICK	017	31915	31746	31731	-0.1	23	12967	13002	13040	0.0	2.40	8469	8457	0.0
01770	SHERBORN	017	4145	4336	4416	0.5	71	1403	1477	1508	0.6	2.94	1206	1267	0.5
01772	SOUTHBOROUGH	027	8547	9286	9540	0.9	88	2857	3090	3188	0.9	3.00	2360	2542	0.8
01773	LINCOLN	017	5138	5170	5186	0.1	41	1978	1997	2007	0.1	2.58	1464	1472	0.1
01775	STOW	017	5936	6129	6210	0.3	58	2088	2183	2222	0.5	2.79	1688	1759	0.4
01776	SUDBURY	017	16845	17293	17460	0.3	58	5505	5675	5745	0.3	3.01	4752	4889	0.3
01778	WAYLAND	017	13150	13063	13040	-0.1	23	4651	4645	4650	0.0	2.78	3743	3731	0.0
01801	WOBURN	017	37215	38285	38761	0.3	58	14984	15531	15767	0.4	2.45	9643	9945	0.3
01803	BURLINGTON	017	22852	23842	24247	0.5	71	8283	8751	8947	0.6	2.72	6366	6683	0.5
01810	ANDOVER	009	31276	32126	32265	0.3	58	11313	11611	11690	0.3	2.74	8496	8708	0.3
01821	BILLERICA	017	29364	30440	30868	0.4	65	9937	10447	10650	0.5	2.91	7931	8284	0.5
01824	CHELMSFORD	017	25282	24868	24884	-0.2	14	9318	9342	9378	0.0	2.64	6993	6983	0.0
01826	DRACUT	017	28683	29469	29855	0.3	58	10491	10882	11060	0.4	2.70	7763	8026	0.4
01827	DUNSTABLE	017	2841	2716	2674	-0.5	4	926	894	883	-0.4	3.04	800	770	-0.4
01830	HAVERHILL	009	24220	24580	24665	0.2	48	9359	9506	9561	0.2	2.49	5843	5904	0.1
01832	HAVERHILL	009	21176	21808	21995	0.3	58	8394	8608	8685	0.3	2.52	5497	5599	0.2
01833	GEORGETOWN	009	7350	7862	8018	0.7	81	2551	2718	2776	0.7	2.89	2014	2142	0.7
01834	GROVELAND	009	6038	6598	6790	1.0	91	2058	2253	2327	1.0	2.93	1707	1861	0.9
01835	HAVERHILL	009	13416	13783	13838	0.3	58	5172	5317	5347	0.3	2.53	3488	3568	0.2
01840	LAWRENCE	009	4573	4592	4585	0.0	32	2026	2013	2009	-0.1	2.21	932	915	-0.2
01841	LAWRENCE	009	44759	48099	49102	0.8	84	14226	15104	15408	0.6	3.14	10329	10944	0.6
01843	LAWRENCE	009	23189	24193	24393	0.5	71	8359	8586	8647	0.3	2.80	5740	5872	0.2
01844	METHUEN	009	43357	44385	44573	0.3	58	16396	16782	16893	0.3	2.62	11449	11636	0.2
01845	NORTH ANDOVER	009	27204	28490	28890	0.5	71	9724	10197	10364	0.5	2.61	6903	7249	0.5
01850	LOWELL	017	15652	15735	15763	0.1	41	5629	5669	5689	0.1	2.74	3785	3791	0.0
01851	LOWELL	017	29541	29702	29710	0.1	41	10126	10112	10112	0.0	2.91	6819	6774	-0.1
01852	LOWELL	017	32739	33167	33367	0.1	41	12820	13134	13271	0.3	2.49	7714	7800	0.1
01854	LOWELL	017	27069	27923	28267	0.3	58	9265	9597	9740	0.4	2.61	5630	5808	0.3
01860	MERRIMAC	009	6248	6566	6679	0.5	71	2271	2390	2437	0.6	2.73	1725	1806	0.5
01862	NORTH BILLERICA	017	9853	10108	10232	0.3	58	3092	3199	3247	0.4	2.80	2389	2472	0.4
01863	NORTH CHELMSFORD	017	8556	8897	9054	0.4	65	3477	3649	3723	0.5	2.43	2308	2408	0.5
01864	NORTH READING	017	13897	14116	14243	0.2	48	4816	4929	4989	0.3	2.84	3771	3847	0.2
01867	READING	017	23690	23655	23662	0.0	32	8684	8749	8785	0.1	2.69	6435	6446	0.0
01876	TEWKSBURY	017	28777	29403	29728	0.2	48	9906	10257	10420	0.4	2.79	7661	7881	0.3
01879	TYNGSBORO	017	11106	11602	11857	0.5	71	3736	3928	4019	0.5	2.95	2953	3095	0.5
01880	WAKEFIELD	017	24997	25064	25126	0.0	32	9816	9948	10011	0.1	2.49	6648	6706	0.1
01886	WESTFORD	017	20712	21473	21797	0.4	65	6798	7071	7190	0.4	3.02	5797	6013	0.4
01887	WILMINGTON	017	21296	21635	21843	0.2	48	7002	7183	7271	0.3	2.98	5758	5894	0.3
01890	WINCHESTER	017	20764	20481	20390	-0.1	23	7701	7666	7660	0.0	2.62	5710	5657	-0.1
01901	LYNN	009	1808	1875	1884	0.4	65	1120	1153	1160	0.3	1.56	357	359	0.1
01902	LYNN	009	45447	45702	45405	0.1	41	17190	17013	16899	-0.1	2.63	10066	9882	-0.2
01904	LYNN	009	17837	17794	17691	0.0	32	6699	6658	6635	-0.1	2.66	4856	4805	-0.1
01905	LYNN	009	23926	24403	24359	0.2	48	8487	8535	8522	0.1	2.83	5752	5744	0.0
01906	SAUGUS	009	26113	26571	26570	0.2	48	9987	10193	10230	0.2	2.59	7149	7260	0.2
01907	SWAMPSCOTT	009	14420	14223	14115	-0.1	23	5723	5646	5618	-0.1	2.48	3987	3906	-0.2
01908	NAHANT	009	3632	3586	3565	-0.1	23	1629	1610	1604	-0.1	2.19	971	951	-0.2
01913	AMESBURY	009	16474	17105	17321	0.4	65	6387	6629	6724	0.4	2.53	4233	4364	0.3
01915	BEVERLY	009	39851	39341	39039	-0.1	23	15747	15564	15481	-0.1	2.39	9905	9700	-0.2
01921	BOXFORD	009	7911	8291	8405	0.5	71	2569	2697	2740	0.5	3.07	2254	2360	0.5
01922	BYFIELD	009	2953	3148	3212	0.7	81	979	1046	1070	0.7	3.01	812	864	0.7
01923	DANVERS	009	25347	26773	27496	0.6	76	9598	10148	10457	0.6	2.53	6590	6986	0.6
01929	ESSEX	009	3275	3376	3412	0.3	58	1316	1360	1377	0.4	2.48	892	913	0.3
01930	GLOUCESTER	009	30275	30534	30301	0.1	41	12593	12718	12659	0.1	2.37	7897	7918	0.0
01938	IPSWICH	009	13016	13302	13351	0.2	48	5299	5417	5442	0.2	2.42	3469	3527	0.2
01940	LYNNFIELD	009	11589	11440	11365	-0.1	23	4203	4153	4134	-0.1	2.75	3365	3311	-0.2
01944	MANCHESTER	009	5224	5171	5135	-0.1	23	2167	2145	2136	-0.1	2.40	1435	1410	-0.2
01945	MARBLEHEAD	009	20361	19731	19467	-0.3	9	8537	8261	8165	-0.4	2.37	5680	5471	-0.4
01949	MIDDLETON	009	7377	7965	8138	0.8	84	2126	2320	2383	0.9	2.91	1625	1764	0.9
01950	NEWBURYPORT	009	17221	18037	18297	0.5	71	7542	7839	7946	0.4	2.25	4441	4646	0.5
01951	NEWBURY	009	3783	3958	4021	0.5	71	1531	1606	1635	0.5	2.44	1007	1047	0.4
01952	SALISBURY	009	7803	9122	9583	1.7	99	3075	3645	3849	1.9	2.49	1986	2295	1.6
01960	PEABODY	009	48053	51955	52983	0.8	84	18550	20262	20768	1.0	2.53	12957	14006	0.8
01966	ROCKPORT	009	7765	7562	7471	-0.3	9	3489	3400	3366	-0.3	2.20	2028	1960	-0.4
01969	ROWLEY	009	5491	5946	6106	0.9	88	1955	2125	2189	0.9	2.76	1466	1584	0.8
01970	SALEM	009	40425	41004	41066	0.2	48	17502	17821	17909	0.2	2.24	9714	9790	0.1
01982	SOUTH HAMILTON	009	8301	8323	8315	0.0	32	2664	2673	2676	0.0	2.87	2141	2138	0.0
01983	TOPSFIELD	009	6318	6247	6208	-0.1	23	2220	2205	2199	-0.1	2.73	1790	1767	-0.1
01984	WENHAM	009	4482	4540	4558	0.1	41	1298	1321	1330	0.2	2.71	967	978	0.1
01985	WEST NEWBURY	009	4149	4387	4465	0.6	76	1392	1474	1505	0.6	2.97	1183	1249	0.6
02019	BELLINGHAM	021	15295	16384	16790	0.7	81	5549	6035	6218	0.9	2.71	4276	4636	0.9
02021	CANTON	021	20773	21015	21072	0.1	41	7951	8153	8204	0.3	2.52	5548	5657	0.2
02025	COHASSET	021	7192	7096	7045	-0.1	23	2673	2666	2659	0.0	2.64	2014	2003	-0.1
	MASSACHUSETTS					0.3					0.3	2.50			0.3
	UNITED STATES					1.0					1.1	2.59			0.9

ZIP CODE #	POST OFFICE NAME	RACE (%) White 2000	White 2009	Black 2000	Black 2009	Asian/Pacific 2000	Asian/Pacific 2009	% Hispanic Origin 2000	% Hispanic Origin 2009	2009 AGE DISTRIBUTION (%) 0-4	5-9	10-14	15-19	20-24	25-44	45-64	65-84	85+	18+	MEDIAN AGE 2009	% 2009 Males	% 2009 Females
01610	WORCESTER	65.5	58.9	8.7	9.3	7.4	9.4	24.4	30.6	7.1	6.5	5.5	13.6	16.2	26.9	17.1	6.0	1.2	77.0	25.7	49.7	50.3
01611	CHERRY VALLEY	96.2	94.8	1.6	2.1	0.6	1.0	2.2	3.5	6.3	6.3	6.5	7.2	6.4	27.0	27.6	11.4	1.5	76.3	38.7	49.9	50.1
01612	PAXTON	96.7	95.1	0.7	0.9	1.1	1.7	1.6	2.4	4.7	5.6	6.7	10.4	8.6	19.1	29.9	12.7	2.2	78.6	41.2	47.2	52.8
01701	FRAMINGHAM	88.6	84.5	2.6	3.1	5.6	8.6	2.8	3.9	6.1	6.4	6.9	5.7	4.3	24.6	30.1	13.3	2.7	77.0	42.8	47.8	52.2
01702	FRAMINGHAM	72.1	66.6	7.3	8.0	5.1	7.1	17.8	22.4	6.4	5.6	5.2	7.2	9.6	32.6	22.6	8.6	2.2	79.2	34.5	48.0	52.0
01718	VILLAGE OF NAGOG WOO	80.4	73.0	1.7	1.9	14.1	20.6	3.3	4.3	4.7	5.0	5.2	6.9	6.9	27.3	35.1	8.3	0.7	81.3	41.5	49.8	50.2
01719	BOXBOROUGH	88.9	84.0	0.3	0.4	8.4	12.9	1.1	1.6	6.4	7.5	8.8	8.4	4.8	23.3	33.8	6.4	0.5	72.0	38.7	50.2	49.8
01720	ACTON	88.7	83.8	0.7	0.8	8.5	12.8	1.7	2.4	6.6	7.9	8.9	7.4	4.5	22.7	31.9	8.8	1.3	71.7	40.2	49.4	50.6
01721	ASHLAND	91.9	89.0	1.8	2.3	2.5	3.9	2.9	4.3	7.0	7.8	8.1	6.3	4.0	25.2	31.0	9.3	1.2	72.7	40.6	48.0	52.0
01730	BEDFORD	91.3	87.6	1.6	2.0	5.4	8.3	1.8	2.5	6.0	6.7	7.5	6.2	3.6	19.0	32.0	15.5	3.5	75.3	45.5	49.8	50.2
01731	HANSCOM AFB	79.0	73.8	11.0	13.2	2.7	4.0	6.3	8.6	14.9	11.2	9.5	4.9	8.7	44.5	5.7	0.6	0.1	60.8	25.3	51.4	48.6
01740	BOLTON	97.7	96.6	0.2	0.3	1.3	2.1	0.8	1.3	6.9	8.4	9.8	7.8	3.4	20.2	34.5	8.3	0.7	69.8	41.6	50.3	49.7
01741	CARLISLE	93.5	90.4	0.2	0.2	4.8	7.5	1.2	1.7	5.4	7.6	10.7	8.8	3.5	13.2	38.4	11.6	0.9	70.6	45.4	49.0	51.0
01742	CONCORD	91.6	88.4	2.2	2.7	3.0	4.6	2.8	4.0	5.1	6.1	7.7	7.1	4.4	19.3	32.7	14.3	3.2	76.2	45.1	50.2	49.8
01745	FAYVILLE	96.3	94.1	0.4	0.3	1.9	3.3	1.5	2.3	7.2	7.9	8.9	6.2	2.6	22.0	29.8	13.4	2.0	72.1	42.7	46.6	53.4
01746	HOLLISTON	96.7	95.4	0.9	1.1	1.2	1.9	1.4	2.0	6.7	7.8	8.9	7.9	4.1	21.1	32.3	10.1	1.1	71.5	41.0	48.8	51.2
01747	HOPEDALE	97.5	96.5	0.6	0.8	0.7	1.1	1.2	1.9	6.5	7.1	7.4	6.6	4.6	22.5	30.0	12.1	3.2	74.8	42.1	47.9	52.1
01748	HOPKINTON	96.3	94.6	0.7	0.9	1.7	2.7	1.3	2.0	8.2	9.9	11.1	8.4	3.5	20.5	31.2	6.2	1.0	64.8	38.4	49.5	50.5
01749	HUDSON	94.1	91.9	0.9	1.2	1.5	2.3	3.1	4.5	6.4	6.5	6.7	6.6	5.6	27.1	28.7	10.9	1.6	76.3	39.8	49.4	50.6
01752	MARLBOROUGH	87.7	83.8	2.2	2.6	3.8	5.6	6.0	8.3	6.7	6.6	6.6	6.0	5.4	29.1	27.3	10.3	2.0	76.3	38.9	49.0	51.0
01754	MAYNARD	94.8	92.8	0.9	1.2	1.5	2.4	2.8	4.1	6.5	6.7	7.0	6.4	4.9	26.1	30.2	10.3	1.9	75.7	41.0	48.2	51.8
01756	MENDON	98.0	97.0	0.4	0.6	0.6	1.0	1.0	1.6	7.2	8.3	9.1	7.4	4.1	23.5	31.5	7.7	1.3	71.7	40.0	49.5	50.5
01757	MILFORD	93.0	90.2	1.3	1.7	1.8	2.8	4.3	6.7	6.9	6.9	7.0	6.5	5.6	26.5	27.6	10.5	2.4	75.1	39.3	48.7	51.3
01760	NATICK	92.1	89.1	1.6	2.0	3.9	5.9	2.0	2.8	6.7	6.7	7.1	5.7	4.5	26.4	28.4	11.9	2.6	75.6	40.9	47.6	52.4
01770	SHERBORN	96.5	94.8	0.4	0.5	2.4	3.8	1.1	1.7	6.3	8.1	10.6	8.5	3.6	14.1	35.9	11.4	1.5	69.5	44.1	48.4	51.6
01772	SOUTHBOROUGH	94.3	91.5	0.5	0.7	3.7	5.7	1.5	2.5	8.4	10.0	10.8	7.5	2.8	21.0	30.7	7.9	0.9	65.8	39.0	49.8	50.2
01773	LINCOLN	92.1	88.6	1.1	1.4	5.1	7.9	1.0	1.5	5.7	7.4	9.5	7.3	3.0	15.2	34.1	15.3	2.5	72.3	46.0	47.2	52.8
01775	STOW	95.2	93.3	0.5	0.7	2.2	3.4	1.4	2.1	7.4	8.9	9.7	6.8	3.3	20.7	32.5	9.8	1.1	69.3	41.1	50.3	49.7
01776	SUDBURY	94.2	91.6	0.8	1.0	3.7	5.8	1.2	1.8	7.3	9.1	11.1	8.3	3.3	16.2	33.2	10.0	1.5	66.8	41.8	49.1	50.9
01778	WAYLAND	92.2	88.8	0.8	0.9	5.4	8.2	1.2	1.7	6.2	7.5	9.6	8.0	3.8	15.8	33.4	13.3	2.3	71.3	44.3	48.8	51.2
01801	WOBURN	90.6	86.8	1.9	2.3	4.9	7.4	3.1	4.3	5.8	5.7	5.7	5.9	5.8	29.5	27.2	12.3	2.3	79.2	40.0	49.1	50.9
01803	BURLINGTON	86.7	81.7	1.4	1.6	10.7	15.3	1.3	1.8	6.6	6.5	6.9	5.9	4.8	25.3	27.8	14.5	1.7	76.2	41.4	49.1	50.9
01810	ANDOVER	91.6	87.1	0.7	1.0	5.8	9.2	1.8	3.0	6.0	7.0	8.2	7.7	4.6	20.4	32.5	11.4	2.2	73.7	42.2	48.3	51.7
01821	BILLERICA	95.1	93.0	0.8	1.0	2.7	4.3	1.3	1.9	6.8	7.0	7.2	6.8	5.1	27.4	28.5	10.1	1.0	74.8	38.8	49.6	50.4
01824	CHELMSFORD	93.1	90.0	0.8	0.9	4.7	7.3	1.3	1.8	6.2	6.6	7.4	6.7	4.7	21.5	30.8	13.8	2.4	75.9	43.2	48.9	51.1
01826	DRACUT	95.1	93.0	0.8	1.0	2.6	4.1	1.6	2.3	6.6	6.7	6.8	6.8	5.6	28.2	27.7	10.0	1.5	75.5	38.4	49.1	50.9
01827	DUNSTABLE	97.5	96.3	0.1	0.1	1.5	2.5	0.5	0.7	7.3	8.9	10.1	7.9	3.3	21.2	32.0	8.7	0.8	68.7	40.8	48.0	52.0
01830	HAVERHILL	90.0	85.7	2.8	3.7	0.8	1.3	8.9	13.6	6.8	6.6	6.3	6.5	6.5	26.0	26.5	11.4	3.3	76.1	38.9	47.9	52.1
01832	HAVERHILL	86.9	81.2	2.4	3.0	1.8	2.7	11.7	18.0	7.8	7.5	7.1	6.5	6.3	29.3	24.3	9.3	1.8	73.6	35.8	48.4	51.6
01833	GEORGETOWN	98.5	97.8	0.1	0.2	0.4	0.7	0.6	1.2	7.4	8.5	9.1	7.1	3.6	22.5	31.5	8.9	1.3	70.2	40.6	50.2	49.8
01834	GROVELAND	98.4	97.7	0.3	0.5	0.6	1.0	0.5	0.8	6.6	7.3	8.0	7.8	5.2	21.8	31.8	10.0	1.4	73.2	40.9	49.2	50.8
01835	HAVERHILL	93.4	90.1	1.7	2.2	1.7	2.7	3.9	6.7	6.9	7.0	6.9	7.5	6.7	27.1	27.5	8.9	1.5	75.1	37.7	47.3	52.7
01840	LAWRENCE	41.4	34.6	6.5	6.3	1.3	1.4	72.7	81.8	8.3	7.3	6.1	6.3	7.1	25.8	22.8	13.7	2.5	75.2	36.1	49.8	50.2
01841	LAWRENCE	44.2	36.6	5.0	5.0	1.5	1.7	66.9	76.1	10.0	8.7	7.6	8.5	10.1	29.1	17.9	6.3	1.8	68.7	27.6	48.4	51.6
01843	LAWRENCE	59.8	49.6	4.3	4.6	5.5	6.5	41.8	53.8	8.4	8.3	7.6	7.7	8.2	28.3	21.3	8.6	1.6	71.1	31.4	48.0	52.0
01844	METHUEN	89.2	84.5	1.4	1.7	2.4	3.7	9.8	14.2	6.3	6.2	6.3	6.8	6.4	26.1	27.6	11.5	2.8	77.0	39.5	48.1	51.9
01845	NORTH ANDOVER	93.7	90.1	0.7	1.0	4.0	6.5	2.0	3.3	6.6	7.1	7.7	8.7	6.7	21.8	28.6	10.0	2.9	74.3	39.8	48.7	51.3
01850	LOWELL	77.3	71.2	4.6	5.2	6.6	9.2	15.6	20.3	8.4	7.5	6.9	7.6	8.7	30.1	22.0	7.4	1.3	72.6	31.6	49.3	50.7
01851	LOWELL	57.2	48.6	3.8	3.9	30.9	38.7	10.2	11.7	8.4	7.4	6.7	7.6	9.0	32.1	20.5	7.0	1.2	72.9	30.9	49.9	50.1
01852	LOWELL	74.3	67.9	3.6	4.1	9.9	13.4	15.3	19.5	7.1	6.7	6.4	7.1	7.4	29.9	23.3	10.2	1.8	75.5	34.8	49.2	50.8
01854	LOWELL	68.9	62.4	5.2	5.6	14.8	19.3	15.7	18.6	6.8	6.6	6.4	9.6	11.4	27.3	19.9	9.6	2.4	76.1	31.2	49.2	50.8
01860	MERRIMAC	98.3	97.4	0.4	0.6	0.3	0.5	0.9	1.6	6.7	7.4	8.1	8.0	5.3	22.6	30.5	10.1	1.4	72.2	40.4	48.6	51.4
01862	NORTH BILLERICA	93.5	90.9	2.0	2.8	3.0	4.5	2.2	3.4	6.1	6.5	6.9	7.1	6.4	29.3	26.6	9.5	1.7	76.4	38.1	53.5	46.5
01863	NORTH CHELMSFORD	93.1	89.9	0.8	1.0	4.5	7.1	1.1	1.6	6.3	6.5	6.6	6.4	5.2	26.6	29.8	11.0	1.7	76.5	40.7	47.4	52.6
01864	NORTH READING	97.5	96.4	0.4	0.5	1.3	2.1	0.7	1.1	6.8	7.6	8.6	7.5	4.0	22.0	31.1	10.8	1.6	71.9	41.2	49.0	51.0
01867	READING	96.5	94.7	0.4	0.5	2.2	3.6	0.8	1.2	6.5	7.1	7.9	6.9	4.5	22.1	30.8	11.8	2.4	73.9	42.0	48.4	51.6
01876	TEWKSBURY	96.4	94.9	0.7	0.9	1.6	2.6	1.2	1.8	6.5	6.7	7.1	6.7	4.9	25.2	29.5	11.8	1.6	75.4	40.9	48.8	51.2
01879	TYNGSBORO	95.6	93.6	0.5	0.6	2.5	4.1	1.1	1.6	8.4	8.7	8.7	6.9	4.6	27.5	28.0	6.4	0.9	69.6	36.4	49.6	50.4
01880	WAKEFIELD	96.9	95.6	0.4	0.6	1.4	2.3	0.8	1.2	6.1	6.2	6.5	6.0	5.4	26.1	29.6	11.3	2.8	77.3	41.3	47.6	52.4
01886	WESTFORD	93.7	90.4	0.3	0.4	4.8	7.7	1.1	1.6	8.1	9.1	9.6	7.7	3.6	22.8	30.5	7.6	1.2	68.1	38.7	49.9	50.1
01887	WILMINGTON	96.3	94.6	0.4	0.5	2.0	3.2	0.9	1.4	7.4	7.9	8.1	7.1	4.6	25.0	27.9	10.2	1.8	72.1	39.3	49.1	50.9
01890	WINCHESTER	93.1	90.0	0.7	0.9	4.6	7.2	1.0	1.4	6.6	7.6	8.8	6.8	3.8	19.7	30.4	12.8	3.6	72.4	43.0	47.9	52.1
01901	LYNN	58.6	50.6	16.3	17.5	2.1	2.6	24.7	32.5	5.3	5.2	4.4	4.5	4.2	22.5	24.2	24.1	5.7	82.9	48.5	45.9	54.1
01902	LYNN	61.4	53.0	13.2	14.4	7.0	8.7	23.0	30.8	7.8	7.1	6.4	7.4	8.4	28.4	23.1	9.4	2.0	74.3	33.4	48.7	51.3
01904	LYNN	88.0	83.5	3.9	4.9	2.4	3.4	6.2	9.5	6.1	6.3	6.4	6.4	5.8	26.0	28.6	11.9	2.5	77.2	40.3	48.2	51.8
01905	LYNN	65.9	57.6	10.1	11.3	8.9	11.3	18.4	25.1	8.0	7.3	6.9	7.8	8.0	28.2	22.9	9.2	1.7	73.1	32.7	48.8	51.2
01906	SAUGUS	97.3	95.8	0.5	0.6	1.2	2.1	1.0	1.7	5.0	5.3	5.7	5.9	4.8	25.0	29.9	15.4	2.9	80.3	43.8	47.9	52.1
01907	SWAMPSCOTT	97.4	96.1	0.7	1.1	0.7	1.2	1.3	2.3	5.7	6.2	7.1	6.3	4.7	20.4	31.7	13.5	4.3	76.9	44.7	46.5	53.5
01908	NAHANT	97.1	95.6	0.4	0.6	1.1	1.8	1.1	1.9	4.2	4.7	5.3	5.0	4.4	20.8	35.7	16.0	4.0	82.7	48.4	48.4	51.6
01913	AMESBURY	97.2	96.0	0.6	0.9	0.6	1.0	0.9	1.7	6.5	6.7	7.0	6.8	5.8	27.0	28.1	10.2	1.9	75.3	39.1	48.3	51.7
01915	BEVERLY	96.0	94.0	1.0	1.4	1.3	2.1	1.8	3.1	5.9	6.0	6.3	7.1	6.9	24.8	27.9	11.9	3.3	78.1	40.4	47.6	52.4
01921	BOXFORD	97.4	95.9	0.3	0.5	1.3	2.1	0.8	1.5	6.4	8.2	10.0	8.1	3.6	17.0	35.1	10.5	1.2	70.1	42.9	50.2	49.8
01922	BYFIELD	98.3	97.4	0.6	0.8	0.5	0.9	0.7	1.3	6.9	8.5	9.8	8.0	3.5	21.8	32.7	7.9	0.9	69.6	40.8	49.6	50.4
01923	DANVERS	97.7	96.4	0.4	0.6	1.1	1.9	0.9	1.6	5.4	5.6	6.2	6.8	6.0	22.7	30.2	13.9	3.2	78.4	43.2	46.8	53.2
01929	ESSEX	98.5	97.8	0.2	0.2	0.5	0.8	0.9	1.6	5.7	5.2	5.8	6.9	6.8	23.3	33.3	11.0	2.0	79.3	42.1	48.5	51.5
01930	GLOUCESTER	97.0	95.5	0.6	0.9	0.7	1.2	1.5	2.6	5.6	5.8	5.9	5.8	5.6	24.6	30.6	13.4	2.6	79.1	42.7	48.0	52.0
01938	IPSWICH	97.6	96.3	0.4	0.6	0.8	1.4	1.0	1.8	5.3	5.6	6.4	6.4	5.4	21.1	33.3	13.9	2.7	78.6	44.9	47.7	52.3
01940	LYNNFIELD	96.7	94.9	0.4	0.6	2.0	3.2	0.7	1.2	5.9	6.6	7.6	6.5	4.0	19.1	32.4	15.3	2.8	75.7	45.2	49.3	50.7
01944	MANCHESTER	98.9	98.4	0.1	0.1	0.4	0.6	0.8	1.4	4.8	5.1	6.1	6.4	5.2	19.8	33.7	16.2	2.7	80.0	46.5	47.3	52.7
01945	MARBLEHEAD	97.6	96.3	0.4	0.6	1.0	1.7	0.9	1.6	5.9	6.5	7.7	6.6	4.1	19.5	33.2	13.8	2.7	75.6	44.8	47.6	52.4
01949	MIDDLETON	95.6	94.0	1.5	2.0	1.2	1.9	5.8	8.7	5.8	6.3	7.0	7.3	6.7	28.4	27.8	9.3	1.3	76.5	38.2	57.2	42.8
01950	NEWBURYPORT	98.1	97.1	0.4	0.6	0.6	1.1	0.9	1.6	5.3	5.5	5.9	5.6	5.4	23.8	33.6	12.3	2.7	79.6	44.2	46.8	53.2
01951	NEWBURY	98.3	97.6	0.2	0.3	0.4	0.7	1.1	1.8	5.2	5.6	6.7	6.6	5.4	20.3	35.9	12.4	2.0	78.0	45.1	47.7	52.3
01952	SALISBURY	97.5	96.4	0.4	0.6	0.4	0.7	1.2	2.1	6.1	6.3	6.5	6.2	5.4	25.8	30.2	12.0	1.5	77.1	40.9	49.7	50.3
01960	PEABODY	93.9	91.3	1.0	1.3	1.4	2.3	3.4	5.5	5.7	5.8	6.2	6.3	5.1	23.9	29.4	14.7	2.9	78.3	43.0	47.9	52.1
01966	ROCKPORT	97.7	96.6	0.3	0.4	0.5	0.8	1.1	1.9	4.4	4.6	5.3	5.8	5.7	18.9	34.3	17.0	4.1	82.1	48.3	46.9	53.1
01969	ROWLEY	98.4	97.5	0.2	0.3	0.5	0.8	0.9	1.5	6.3	7.0	7.9	7.6	4.4	22.5	33.4	9.1	1.7	73.8	41.4	49.3	50.7
01970	SALEM	85.4	79.9	3.2	4.0	2.0	3.1	11.2	16.1	5.6	5.2	5.1	6.7	7.9	29.5	26.1	11.3	2.5	80.7	38.3	46.6	53.4
01982	SOUTH HAMILTON	94.2	90.9	0.5	0.7	4.3	6.9	1.0	1.7	6.2	6.7	7.6	7.7	6.0	25.4	29.5	9.4	1.5	74.3	38.2	48.6	51.4
01983	TOPSFIELD	97.5	96.4	0.5	0.7	0.8	1.4	1.4	2.4	5.6	6.5	8.3	8.3	4.2	17.5	33.5	13.3	2.8	74.2	44.8	49.0	51.0
01984	WENHAM	97.8	96.6	0.4	0.6	1.4	2.2	0.6	1.0	4.9	5.6	6.3	15.4	13.4	15.0	25.4	11.7	2.3	79.4	34.5	45.2	54.8
01985	WEST NEWBURY	98.5	97.7	0.2	0.3	0.5	0.9	0.7	1.2	6.5	8.0	9.6	7.8	3.6	18.6	35.3	9.4	1.2	70.7	42.3	50.4	49.6
02019	BELLINGHAM	96.9	95.8	0.9	1.2	0.9	1.4	1.2	1.7	6.8	7.2	7.5	7.0	4.7	27.0	28.9	9.8	1.1	74.1	39.5	48.9	51.1
02021	CANTON	92.5	89.4	2.9	3.7	3.0	4.9	1.4	2.1	6.2	6.2	6.9	6.4	4.8	24.2	28.9	12.9	3.4	76.5	42.1	47.5	52.5
02025	COHASSET	98.2	97.4	0.2	0.3	0.8	1.3	0.7	1.0	6.5	7.4	8.6	7.6	4.2	17.9	32.0	13.4	2.5	72.6	43.6	48.8	51.2
	MASSACHUSETTS	84.5	81.0	5.4	6.0	3.8	5.4	6.8	8.7	6.1	6.2	6.3	7.1	7.1	26.5	27.1	11.3	2.3	77.4	38.6	48.4	51.6
	UNITED STATES	75.1	72.0	12.3	12.7	3.8	4.6	12.5	15.7	6.8	6.7	6.6	7.1	6.9	27.0	26.0	10.9	1.9	75.7	36.9	49.2	50.8

ZIP CODE #	POST OFFICE NAME	2009 Per Capita Income	2009 HH Income Base	2009 HOUSEHOLD INCOME DISTRIBUTION (%) Less than $25,000	$25,000 to $49,999	$50,000 to $99,999	$100,000 to $149,999	$150,000 or More	MEDIAN HOUSEHOLD INCOME 2009	2014	2009 National Centile	2009 State Centile	2009 Home Value Base	2009 HOME VALUE DISTRIBUTION (%) Less than $50,000	$50,000 to $89,999	$90,000 to $174,999	$175,000 to $399,999	$400,000 or More	2009 Median Home Value
01610	WORCESTER	15522	7635	39.3	30.2	25.2	4.0	1.2	32252	34422	12	3	1750	1.8	5.7	54.2	37.0	1.3	158810
01611	CHERRY VALLEY	27193	895	10.9	22.3	44.9	17.4	4.4	65285	67267	84	39	663	0.0	0.3	45.4	53.5	0.8	180700
01612	PAXTON	37279	1475	4.9	13.9	32.9	30.8	17.4	96175	96134	96	81	1356	0.0	0.6	8.3	67.5	23.7	295306
01701	FRAMINGHAM	46330	12109	7.4	12.1	32.7	27.2	20.6	95647	101661	96	81	9475	0.0	0.2	2.8	71.1	25.9	332391
01702	FRAMINGHAM	31245	14274	20.3	21.7	32.2	16.4	9.4	59651	63047	77	27	5289	0.5	1.2	11.0	65.4	21.9	293316
01718	VILLAGE OF NAGOG WOO	51646	174	9.2	8.6	32.8	28.2	21.3	98954	104895	97	84	111	0.0	0.0	3.6	73.0	23.4	292500
01719	BOXBOROUGH	63639	1943	3.5	7.3	30.2	21.5	37.6	119545	126167	98	92	1381	0.0	1.8	12.2	18.7	67.3	513889
01720	ACTON	64244	7321	5.7	7.8	22.3	23.6	40.6	127988	134570	99	94	5556	0.2	0.3	4.1	25.9	69.5	489309
01721	ASHLAND	45940	6180	6.2	13.5	32.7	27.5	20.1	95649	101604	96	81	4882	0.1	0.1	2.5	69.1	28.1	321471
01730	BEDFORD	56125	4775	5.4	8.3	25.9	23.7	36.7	121623	127182	99	93	3780	1.0	0.7	0.7	24.9	72.6	495217
01731	HANSCOM AFB	22265	751	2.5	30.8	48.5	13.0	5.2	63942	65042	82	36	51	9.8	3.9	0.0	29.4	56.9	458333
01740	BOLTON	54462	1585	2.6	5.9	21.7	27.8	42.0	133418	139933	99	97	1432	0.0	0.0	0.5	17.1	82.4	593918
01741	CARLISLE	75973	1637	4.8	9.6	15.0	10.9	59.7	203287	211013	100	100	1487	0.6	0.3	0.1	4.4	94.6	729662
01742	CONCORD	70630	6059	6.5	5.9	23.3	18.6	45.7	136807	147581	99	97	4808	0.4	0.3	0.4	12.5	86.5	695084
01745	FAYVILLE	53799	120	13.3	4.2	26.7	24.2	31.7	114717	122051	98	91	89	0.0	0.0	0.0	23.6	76.4	550676
01746	HOLLISTON	46807	4838	7.5	8.0	29.7	27.2	27.6	107033	112182	98	89	4085	0.0	0.1	3.3	59.5	37.1	363292
01747	HOPEDALE	33139	2313	13.3	13.1	37.0	26.9	9.7	79511	82017	92	64	1782	0.0	0.0	10.5	64.0	25.4	298341
01748	HOPKINTON	64233	4789	5.3	5.4	23.9	26.2	39.1	125436	130983	99	94	4213	0.2	0.2	2.5	36.0	61.1	476179
01749	HUDSON	36996	7383	11.9	16.7	34.4	24.4	12.6	79076	83320	92	63	5196	0.2	0.8	8.2	74.6	16.3	275764
01752	MARLBOROUGH	38238	14910	13.6	16.0	35.5	22.0	12.8	77360	80892	91	59	9284	0.2	2.4	9.5	68.5	19.4	277696
01754	MAYNARD	36886	4274	13.1	17.0	32.6	27.0	10.2	80529	84324	92	66	2981	0.0	0.4	4.3	82.9	12.4	282152
01756	MENDON	37242	1981	9.0	11.5	32.6	24.4	22.5	93340	92651	96	80	1707	0.0	0.0	3.7	42.6	53.6	416142
01757	MILFORD	30958	10722	17.1	20.0	32.8	20.3	9.8	66301	70256	84	42	6990	0.2	1.2	9.3	70.2	19.1	283688
01760	NATICK	51016	13002	9.3	11.3	30.6	26.7	22.1	97665	103516	96	82	9226	0.4	0.2	2.8	53.9	42.6	373409
01770	SHERBORN	78369	1477	3.6	7.1	12.3	18.8	58.3	188595	204226	100	99	1327	0.0	0.0	0.0	6.0	94.0	795879
01772	SOUTHBOROUGH	54401	3090	5.0	7.6	21.9	22.4	43.0	134235	139592	99	97	2656	0.1	0.2	1.1	22.0	76.6	566705
01773	LINCOLN	88802	1997	3.0	7.1	17.9	19.9	52.1	157650	173723	100	99	1680	0.4	0.0	0.0	8.3	91.3	833691
01775	STOW	56753	2183	4.9	7.8	23.7	21.3	42.3	130743	137990	99	95	1855	0.5	0.0	0.4	37.6	61.5	447013
01776	SUDBURY	75218	5675	4.9	5.6	15.2	15.3	59.0	179453	192898	100	99	5060	0.0	0.0	0.3	14.0	85.7	669193
01778	WAYLAND	68234	4645	7.0	5.1	21.4	20.6	45.9	136385	147607	99	97	4135	0.3	0.0	0.4	15.4	83.9	628752
01801	WOBURN	35425	15531	12.9	17.1	37.7	22.7	9.5	76461	79417	90	58	9635	0.3	0.2	2.8	72.9	23.7	329839
01803	BURLINGTON	42589	8751	6.3	11.9	32.0	29.7	20.2	99766	104266	97	84	6815	0.3	1.0	1.7	59.8	37.2	368588
01810	ANDOVER	54086	11611	10.1	7.6	23.8	23.1	35.5	116179	121386	98	91	8978	0.3	0.7	1.7	19.6	77.7	563827
01821	BILLERICA	35244	10447	7.7	11.3	36.8	31.2	13.0	91001	96331	95	79	8721	0.1	0.6	6.3	72.6	20.4	303818
01824	CHELMSFORD	42918	9342	7.4	12.4	31.3	28.6	20.3	97902	103044	96	82	7839	1.7	0.9	3.5	65.8	28.1	333236
01826	DRACUT	32371	10882	10.5	15.8	42.2	22.9	8.6	77990	80401	91	61	8427	0.2	1.4	16.6	72.6	9.2	240935
01827	DUNSTABLE	45478	894	4.5	6.9	24.5	35.7	28.4	118292	121746	98	92	807	0.4	0.0	1.4	46.5	51.8	407513
01830	HAVERHILL	29372	9506	21.6	19.5	32.4	19.6	6.9	63524	67064	82	35	5435	0.3	0.9	11.2	74.6	13.0	251787
01832	HAVERHILL	28638	8608	17.7	19.8	38.9	18.1	5.5	64647	68013	83	38	5228	0.3	0.5	14.2	72.4	12.6	241685
01833	GEORGETOWN	40390	2718	11.4	8.6	25.2	31.9	22.8	105070	105556	97	88	2298	0.0	0.0	1.0	43.8	55.3	420755
01834	GROVELAND	34672	2253	6.3	15.5	31.9	32.6	13.7	93041	96701	96	80	1901	1.2	0.4	1.3	52.8	44.3	379126
01835	HAVERHILL	33047	5317	11.1	18.4	37.6	23.5	9.5	73205	76645	88	53	3609	0.0	0.5	9.9	75.9	13.7	256179
01840	LAWRENCE	12502	2013	63.4	20.7	13.2	1.7	1.0	15504	15672	1	1	93	2.2	10.8	49.5	18.3	19.4	149621
01841	LAWRENCE	15171	15104	36.0	28.5	26.0	7.1	2.4	35751	38798	20	5	5049	0.7	4.2	39.5	52.9	2.8	184785
01843	LAWRENCE	20523	8586	27.3	25.8	33.8	10.1	3.0	46140	49272	52	10	3618	0.2	1.6	23.9	72.8	1.5	208105
01844	METHUEN	29242	16782	17.1	20.2	35.1	20.0	7.6	66286	70308	84	41	11988	0.5	0.6	10.0	77.3	11.8	255186
01845	NORTH ANDOVER	46910	10197	10.4	13.1	25.6	21.9	29.0	101549	102695	97	85	7387	0.7	0.1	5.1	33.0	61.1	471534
01850	LOWELL	20763	5669	21.8	25.8	40.0	10.1	2.4	51651	52890	65	17	2759	0.3	2.2	47.8	48.4	1.2	174585
01851	LOWELL	23372	10112	19.3	23.9	38.7	13.0	5.1	56558	58490	73	22	4535	1.4	1.0	28.5	66.3	2.8	210495
01852	LOWELL	25514	13134	28.5	21.7	31.8	12.7	5.3	49743	51428	60	15	5920	0.8	2.1	32.0	57.3	7.8	208159
01854	LOWELL	21266	9597	30.7	23.9	31.1	10.9	3.4	44982	47126	48	9	3753	0.3	1.8	30.1	65.4	2.4	207796
01860	MERRIMAC	33241	2390	9.7	16.8	35.1	26.4	11.9	77198	81345	91	59	1948	1.3	2.5	8.6	49.9	37.7	342857
01862	NORTH BILLERICA	33081	3199	6.5	11.8	38.1	31.9	11.7	90414	95657	95	78	2534	1.2	1.8	4.1	74.1	18.9	316596
01863	NORTH CHELMSFORD	38907	3649	11.5	13.1	37.8	25.5	12.2	82402	86498	93	69	2855	0.2	0.8	7.2	81.1	10.7	265461
01864	NORTH READING	44338	4929	5.0	11.0	31.8	29.1	23.2	102993	107695	97	86	4338	0.8	0.4	4.4	45.0	49.4	397410
01867	READING	47077	8749	8.7	11.4	27.1	27.3	25.5	104274	109376	97	87	7073	0.3	0.0	1.8	47.4	50.5	402061
01876	TEWKSBURY	36562	10257	7.8	11.7	35.3	31.1	14.1	92083	97714	95	79	8865	0.5	0.6	3.5	78.3	17.1	299596
01879	TYNGSBORO	38170	3928	8.8	8.5	35.0	31.3	16.4	95374	101312	96	81	3249	0.7	0.3	11.2	62.9	24.9	310483
01880	WAKEFIELD	42055	9948	9.4	12.7	34.0	29.0	14.9	88376	94555	95	77	7117	0.2	0.2	2.3	60.2	37.2	365233
01886	WESTFORD	57008	7071	4.7	6.0	21.3	26.5	41.5	130882	135663	99	96	6305	0.6	0.1	2.3	44.0	52.9	415471
01887	WILMINGTON	36183	7183	7.5	8.3	34.5	35.8	13.9	99422	103168	97	84	6306	0.3	0.2	3.0	68.9	27.6	339173
01890	WINCHESTER	68683	7666	6.9	7.9	21.4	21.0	42.7	130681	137265	99	95	6065	0.1	0.0	1.3	16.7	81.9	645363
01901	LYNN	16251	1153	68.5	16.0	11.9	3.4	0.2	14661	14459	1	0	66	0.0	0.0	25.8	60.6	13.6	260000
01902	LYNN	20695	17013	29.7	26.6	30.0	10.3	3.5	43903	46811	45	8	6329	0.6	1.4	21.9	68.3	7.8	224723
01904	LYNN	31422	6658	12.5	17.1	35.7	27.3	7.4	75018	78385	89	56	5076	0.4	0.4	7.2	82.1	9.9	267084
01905	LYNN	20940	8535	26.4	24.4	34.2	11.0	4.0	49091	53305	59	14	4157	0.3	0.4	17.1	78.7	3.5	224893
01906	SAUGUS	32966	10193	13.3	17.1	36.2	24.1	9.4	74553	78511	89	55	8053	0.5	0.6	2.6	63.4	32.9	347265
01907	SWAMPSCOTT	46314	5646	9.3	12.2	30.5	24.5	23.5	95227	95832	96	80	4282	0.1	1.1	2.7	35.9	60.1	443042
01908	NAHANT	50361	1610	7.9	15.6	32.7	25.9	18.0	88176	90067	95	76	1106	0.0	0.2	1.1	30.6	68.2	478210
01913	AMESBURY	31831	6629	14.7	20.0	33.8	23.4	8.1	71051	76410	87	50	4406	0.2	1.0	10.6	65.5	22.8	288669
01915	BEVERLY	36289	15564	14.2	16.8	36.1	21.3	11.6	72880	77048	88	53	9395	0.4	0.6	2.9	54.9	41.3	371501
01921	BOXFORD	65285	2697	1.9	5.6	14.8	26.1	51.7	153201	161514	100	98	2512	0.0	0.0	3.2	7.4	89.4	659914
01922	BYFIELD	46342	1046	6.1	3.3	25.7	34.2	30.7	119417	122446	98	92	856	0.0	0.0	0.2	28.2	71.6	475820
01923	DANVERS	35355	10148	10.2	18.3	34.9	23.8	12.8	77178	80899	91	59	7650	1.3	0.7	4.2	50.4	43.5	379733
01929	ESSEX	40072	1360	14.8	12.1	32.1	27.5	13.5	83816	86110	93	71	959	0.0	0.4	0.8	35.6	63.2	454762
01930	GLOUCESTER	32735	12718	17.4	20.3	36.4	18.2	7.7	65370	69270	84	39	7694	0.0	0.7	5.0	57.4	36.9	343544
01938	IPSWICH	41309	5417	14.4	15.5	31.7	21.5	16.9	77910	81947	91	61	3935	0.2	0.0	2.9	39.3	57.6	435153
01940	LYNNFIELD	50219	4153	5.9	10.2	27.7	23.8	32.4	109847	111421	98	89	3776	0.2	0.0	1.0	20.5	78.3	530922
01944	MANCHESTER	55769	2145	10.5	12.7	23.8	22.1	31.0	104798	107488	97	88	1519	0.6	0.0	0.1	7.4	91.8	722748
01945	MARBLEHEAD	56730	8261	9.0	12.3	27.0	20.2	31.4	102877	104381	97	86	6184	0.1	0.0	0.7	19.3	79.9	572365
01949	MIDDLETON	37562	2320	10.8	9.7	25.4	26.0	28.0	106674	109159	98	89	1949	0.5	0.6	0.7	37.1	61.2	460526
01950	NEWBURYPORT	44378	7839	10.9	15.6	32.9	24.7	15.9	80377	83408	92	66	5320	0.1	0.1	3.3	44.5	52.1	408321
01951	NEWBURY	44558	1606	9.8	15.6	27.8	27.1	19.6	91852	95902	95	79	1258	0.0	0.0	1.5	39.4	59.1	438908
01952	SALISBURY	29257	3645	15.8	22.2	37.0	19.5	5.6	64961	68768	83	39	2461	1.7	1.2	13.7	60.8	22.6	282843
01960	PEABODY	33229	20262	14.0	18.8	34.0	23.2	9.9	72453	76226	88	52	14218	1.5	2.5	3.2	59.2	33.6	348134
01966	ROCKPORT	39146	3400	16.4	18.2	33.0	21.4	11.1	70329	75028	87	48	2214	0.3	0.0	0.2	33.6	65.9	458375
01969	ROWLEY	36532	2125	8.8	12.8	35.8	26.9	15.8	86378	87755	94	74	1627	0.0	0.0	1.9	34.7	63.4	462251
01970	SALEM	31941	17821	18.8	23.0	35.0	16.2	7.1	61770	65099	80	32	9032	0.1	0.3	4.9	71.3	23.4	313763
01982	SOUTH HAMILTON	41369	2673	7.2	9.3	34.7	23.8	25.0	97546	96900	96	82	2146	0.0	0.0	2.4	28.7	68.9	482353
01983	TOPSFIELD	50859	2205	5.9	8.7	23.2	20.0	42.1	125415	131237	99	94	1895	0.0	0.0	0.4	18.7	80.8	565652
01984	WENHAM	45114	1321	9.8	13.6	21.3	18.2	37.1	110955	116289	98	90	1098	0.0	0.8	0.3	18.6	80.3	613982
01985	WEST NEWBURY	50052	1474	7.3	6.7	22.7	26.4	36.8	123332	126669	99	94	1324	0.0	0.0	0.5	23.6	76.0	525057
02019	BELLINGHAM	34792	6035	9.9	10.9	38.0	31.7	9.4	87521	91939	94	76	4987	0.2	0.1	7.5	81.9	10.3	249422
02021	CANTON	45487	8153	11.3	11.8	29.3	27.7	19.9	95356	101904	96	80	6041	0.4	0.0	4.7	41.7	53.2	416181
02025	COHASSET	59260	2666	9.3	8.7	22.3	23.8	35.9	121861	128209	99	93	2238	0.0	0.0	0.5	16.4	83.0	672783
	MASSACHUSETTS	34904		17.4	19.0	33.1	18.1	12.4	68225	71891				0.7	1.2	13.3	53.8	31.0	297007
	UNITED STATES	27277		20.9	24.4	35.3	11.7	7.6	54719	56938				9.3	13.1	31.6	32.6	13.5	162279

ZIP CODE #	POST OFFICE NAME	FINANCIAL SERVICES: Auto Loan	Home Loan	Invest-ments	Retire-ment Plans	THE HOME: Home Improvements: Home Repair	Lawn & Garden	Furnishings: Comput-ers & Hard-ware-Personal	Major Appli-ances	TV, Radio, Sound Equip-ment	Furni-ture	ENTERTAINMENT: Dine out/ Carry out	Sports Equip-ment	Fees & Tickets	Toys & Games	Travel	Cable TV	PERSONAL: Apparel & Services	Auto Repairs	Health Insur-ance	Pets & Supplies
01610	WORCESTER	55	47	42	48	45	44	61	51	61	57	62	42	56	61	54	60	45	58	52	61
01611	CHERRY VALLEY	93	111	102	109	108	104	102	101	101	101	102	78	112	102	109	101	73	102	103	118
01612	PAXTON	144	179	184	183	185	174	151	162	148	161	149	119	175	147	171	147	107	153	159	183
01701	FRAMINGHAM	141	188	207	184	199	172	163	167	155	166	156	125	190	154	185	154	116	161	158	185
01702	FRAMINGHAM	98	103	108	104	106	93	114	103	109	110	112	83	116	108	114	107	82	110	100	119
01718	VILLAGE OF NAGOG WOO	170	189	182	192	187	176	179	175	173	182	175	136	190	175	185	170	124	175	170	205
01719	BOXBOROUGH	234	272	261	285	272	239	242	239	228	260	232	195	271	238	256	215	170	230	209	274
01720	ACTON	220	280	306	292	297	250	248	250	228	266	230	198	286	227	278	215	172	238	219	282
01721	ASHLAND	151	185	186	188	188	170	165	165	159	169	161	128	186	160	178	157	118	161	156	189
01730	BEDFORD	179	245	286	247	268	226	210	220	195	225	195	163	251	191	246	189	146	207	201	242
01731	HANSCOM AFB	132	73	56	83	66	62	125	88	117	117	123	87	97	140	92	108	87	111	80	107
01740	BOLTON	203	269	278	282	278	241	220	229	206	239	208	181	266	210	251	196	156	213	200	259
01741	CARLISLE	257	368	452	386	413	347	296	319	278	330	275	239	385	277	356	267	215	292	280	347
01742	CONCORD	235	324	392	334	362	298	276	291	252	306	250	219	336	244	327	238	189	271	256	319
01745	FAYVILLE	163	228	276	234	255	212	191	205	175	214	173	151	234	168	230	166	130	189	183	224
01746	HOLLISTON	164	225	242	227	237	203	186	194	174	196	175	148	223	175	214	169	131	182	175	215
01747	HOPEDALE	109	135	133	132	136	127	119	122	118	122	119	91	134	117	130	119	85	120	124	139
01748	HOPKINTON	242	322	335	334	334	290	267	276	252	284	255	215	320	256	303	243	191	259	246	311
01749	HUDSON	114	145	146	140	147	133	132	131	129	127	132	98	148	129	143	132	97	130	130	147
01752	MARLBOROUGH	123	143	139	142	143	130	136	131	131	135	133	102	146	132	142	129	96	132	128	152
01754	MAYNARD	103	138	146	132	142	127	122	122	121	117	123	90	141	120	135	124	91	121	122	137
01756	MENDON	142	177	179	183	181	163	151	156	144	161	145	120	174	145	168	139	106	148	143	178
01757	MILFORD	102	118	118	117	120	110	113	111	110	112	111	85	121	110	118	109	80	111	108	127
01760	NATICK	155	192	211	193	203	175	176	175	166	181	168	135	199	166	194	162	123	172	163	197
01770	SHERBORN	272	387	474	404	433	363	314	338	293	350	290	252	403	290	378	281	225	309	298	368
01772	SOUTHBOROUGH	205	276	302	288	294	249	227	238	211	251	211	185	277	213	262	200	160	220	207	264
01773	LINCOLN	276	386	459	402	427	359	316	338	294	352	292	254	397	290	377	281	224	311	298	370
01775	STOW	203	266	281	278	278	237	224	231	206	243	208	182	265	208	254	195	156	216	199	259
01776	SUDBURY	275	384	455	400	424	357	315	336	293	350	291	253	395	289	375	279	223	309	297	369
01778	WAYLAND	227	320	383	327	354	297	264	281	246	288	244	210	330	243	314	237	187	260	251	306
01801	WOBURN	104	133	139	128	137	123	121	120	119	117	121	89	137	119	132	122	89	120	121	135
01803	BURLINGTON	143	186	200	182	195	172	161	165	155	164	156	123	187	156	181	155	115	160	160	183
01810	ANDOVER	189	239	263	247	255	217	212	216	196	228	197	168	244	194	238	187	146	206	193	242
01821	BILLERICA	130	167	164	161	168	148	144	146	138	146	140	111	163	141	158	137	102	142	138	164
01824	CHELMSFORD	135	184	201	178	194	172	156	162	152	158	152	118	185	150	179	154	112	157	162	179
01826	DRACUT	113	138	131	134	137	123	125	123	119	125	121	96	137	122	132	118	87	122	117	141
01827	DUNSTABLE	177	234	241	246	242	210	191	199	179	208	181	157	231	183	218	170	136	185	173	225
01830	HAVERHILL	95	105	104	104	105	98	106	100	105	103	106	78	111	103	108	105	76	104	103	117
01832	HAVERHILL	94	104	97	103	102	95	104	98	101	102	103	78	109	102	105	100	74	101	96	115
01833	GEORGETOWN	144	192	203	193	201	177	160	167	154	168	155	126	191	154	183	152	115	159	158	187
01834	GROVELAND	126	172	171	165	175	152	141	147	134	144	136	111	166	137	160	133	100	140	136	163
01835	HAVERHILL	110	132	126	129	131	120	120	119	116	121	117	92	131	117	128	115	84	118	115	137
01840	LAWRENCE	34	25	26	27	25	26	40	32	42	36	43	25	35	38	34	43	31	39	38	39
01841	LAWRENCE	64	56	51	55	54	48	71	60	68	69	72	50	66	68	65	65	52	68	57	69
01843	LAWRENCE	74	75	70	74	73	66	85	75	81	81	84	61	84	82	82	79	61	82	72	87
01844	METHUEN	97	116	115	112	117	108	108	107	106	107	107	81	118	106	115	107	77	107	108	122
01845	NORTH ANDOVER	156	202	220	204	213	188	179	182	171	184	172	137	207	169	200	170	128	176	173	204
01850	LOWELL	73	77	72	76	75	70	83	76	81	80	83	61	84	81	82	80	60	80	75	89
01851	LOWELL	90	91	85	90	90	80	100	90	96	97	99	73	100	97	97	93	72	96	85	104
01852	LOWELL	80	82	82	82	82	77	92	83	92	87	93	65	92	90	90	93	68	90	86	97
01854	LOWELL	72	74	69	74	72	68	84	75	83	78	85	59	83	82	79	83	62	79	75	87
01860	MERRIMAC	113	153	150	146	155	134	127	131	121	129	123	99	147	124	143	120	90	126	122	146
01862	NORTH BILLERICA	121	166	169	157	171	147	138	143	131	139	133	106	161	133	156	131	98	137	134	158
01863	NORTH CHELMSFORD	121	150	150	147	152	137	133	134	128	135	130	102	149	130	145	128	94	132	129	153
01864	NORTH READING	155	213	225	209	222	193	175	184	166	181	168	137	209	168	201	165	124	174	171	203
01867	READING	153	209	231	207	222	190	177	183	167	183	168	137	210	167	204	164	125	175	170	202
01876	TEWKSBURY	128	168	171	161	172	151	145	147	139	145	141	110	166	141	161	139	103	144	141	165
01879	TYNGSBORO	152	186	168	187	182	161	160	161	151	169	154	129	179	158	171	145	111	154	144	183
01880	WAKEFIELD	122	164	179	159	172	150	147	146	143	142	145	109	170	142	164	145	108	145	143	163
01886	WESTFORD	223	291	290	300	297	257	241	249	226	259	229	197	285	233	270	216	171	233	219	280
01887	WILMINGTON	134	183	183	175	186	161	151	156	144	153	145	118	177	147	171	142	107	150	145	174
01890	WINCHESTER	216	298	350	302	327	274	254	265	238	271	238	198	308	233	297	231	180	250	241	291
01901	LYNN	29	23	26	26	23	26	37	29	40	31	40	22	33	35	32	42	29	35	38	37
01902	LYNN	70	68	65	68	67	62	80	70	79	76	81	57	78	77	76	78	59	77	71	83
01904	LYNN	102	133	135	126	136	120	117	118	113	116	115	88	133	114	129	114	84	117	115	132
01905	LYNN	74	80	77	79	79	74	85	78	84	81	86	61	88	83	85	85	62	83	80	91
01906	SAUGUS	103	138	143	130	143	129	117	123	115	116	116	89	136	115	133	118	85	119	123	136
01907	SWAMPSCOTT	138	182	206	180	196	171	161	166	155	167	155	123	188	150	184	154	114	161	162	185
01908	NAHANT	137	180	205	180	195	165	158	164	146	168	146	124	183	143	182	141	108	156	151	182
01913	AMESBURY	105	124	121	122	124	111	117	113	111	117	113	89	126	113	123	110	82	113	108	130
01915	BEVERLY	111	132	140	131	136	123	127	123	123	125	125	94	139	122	135	123	91	125	121	140
01921	BOXFORD	243	336	395	348	370	311	279	297	257	310	256	223	344	252	331	245	194	274	263	326
01922	BYFIELD	178	236	244	248	245	212	193	201	181	210	183	159	233	184	220	172	137	187	175	227
01923	DANVERS	107	147	157	140	153	135	126	129	123	123	125	94	148	123	143	126	92	126	128	143
01929	ESSEX	118	151	169	150	161	134	143	140	134	143	135	108	159	130	157	131	101	138	129	157
01930	GLOUCESTER	98	117	122	115	121	109	111	110	107	110	108	84	121	107	119	107	78	110	108	125
01938	IPSWICH	126	156	167	157	163	142	144	142	135	147	137	110	160	134	157	132	101	140	133	161
01940	LYNNFIELD	166	228	263	228	249	213	192	204	180	206	180	150	231	176	226	176	133	192	190	224
01944	MANCHESTER	164	217	258	222	241	194	194	199	173	212	173	153	224	167	225	162	129	188	172	220
01945	MARBLEHEAD	164	218	253	220	238	195	194	197	176	206	177	152	225	172	222	167	132	188	175	218
01949	MIDDLETON	159	199	195	202	201	177	172	176	160	182	162	137	193	162	189	154	117	167	158	201
01950	NEWBURYPORT	128	152	165	152	158	141	144	142	138	143	140	110	157	136	155	137	102	142	137	162
01951	NEWBURY	134	177	201	178	192	156	158	160	143	167	143	125	181	140	180	135	107	153	140	177
01952	SALISBURY	96	110	101	110	108	104	104	103	101	102	102	80	111	103	109	101	73	102	102	120
01960	PEABODY	101	131	139	125	136	123	117	119	116	113	117	86	133	114	129	119	85	117	120	133
01966	ROCKPORT	109	130	145	130	139	125	122	125	118	124	118	93	134	114	134	118	85	122	123	140
01969	ROWLEY	128	172	172	169	175	154	142	147	134	146	136	112	167	137	160	132	100	139	136	164
01970	SALEM	90	99	102	99	101	93	104	96	102	99	104	75	108	100	106	102	75	101	99	112
01982	SOUTH HAMILTON	152	207	228	207	221	185	176	182	163	185	164	139	208	163	202	158	122	172	163	201
01983	TOPSFIELD	169	238	282	240	263	219	199	212	183	217	182	157	242	178	238	176	137	197	191	231
01984	WENHAM	172	237	279	239	261	216	203	213	186	218	185	159	242	181	239	178	139	200	191	233
01985	WEST NEWBURY	190	252	261	265	261	226	206	215	193	224	195	170	249	197	235	183	146	199	187	243
02019	BELLINGHAM	121	158	149	153	157	138	133	136	126	136	128	105	152	130	146	123	93	130	125	153
02021	CANTON	141	186	205	184	198	170	164	166	155	166	156	126	190	154	185	152	115	161	156	185
02025	COHASSET	189	260	308	263	287	237	223	233	203	242	202	175	266	197	262	193	151	219	208	256
	MASSACHUSETTS	113	129	133	129	131	121	127	122	123	125	125	94	135	122	132	123	90	124	121	141
	UNITED STATES	100	100	100	100	100	100	100	100	100	100	100	100	100	100	100	100	100	100	100	100

ZIP CODE #	POST OFFICE NAME	COUNTY FIPS CODE	POPULATION 2000	POPULATION 2009	POPULATION 2014	2000-2009 ANNUAL RATE % Rate	2000-2009 ANNUAL RATE State Centile	HOUSEHOLDS 2000	HOUSEHOLDS 2009	HOUSEHOLDS 2014	HOUSEHOLDS % Annual Rate 2000-2009	HOUSEHOLDS 2009 Average HH Size	FAMILIES 2000	FAMILIES 2009	FAMILIES % Annual Rate 2000-2009
02026	DEDHAM	021	23471	23897	24064	0.2	48	8661	8931	9032	0.3	2.58	6153	6326	0.3
02030	DOVER	021	5579	5707	5746	0.2	48	1857	1907	1923	0.3	2.99	1575	1614	0.3
02032	EAST WALPOLE	021	3575	3923	4043	1.0	91	1308	1454	1506	1.2	2.70	931	1031	1.1
02035	FOXBORO	021	16180	16150	16109	0.0	32	6116	6197	6213	0.1	2.59	4375	4412	0.1
02038	FRANKLIN	021	29719	31354	31869	0.6	76	10215	10803	11001	0.6	2.85	7928	8384	0.6
02043	HINGHAM	023	19951	19838	19748	-0.1	23	7189	7239	7239	0.1	2.70	5479	5498	0.0
02045	HULL	023	11050	10835	10737	-0.2	14	4522	4507	4492	0.0	2.40	2821	2787	-0.1
02048	MANSFIELD	005	22447	23108	23199	0.3	58	7953	8212	8265	0.3	2.81	5868	6033	0.3
02050	MARSHFIELD	023	24764	26464	27058	0.7	81	9110	9824	10082	0.8	2.69	6726	7215	0.8
02052	MEDFIELD	021	12221	12519	12620	0.3	58	3988	4103	4144	0.3	3.01	3255	3341	0.3
02053	MEDWAY	021	12398	12888	13026	0.4	65	4168	4354	4410	0.5	2.93	3326	3472	0.5
02054	MILLIS	021	7915	8144	8217	0.3	58	3007	3138	3180	0.5	2.58	2166	2250	0.4
02056	NORFOLK	021	10414	10747	10856	0.3	58	2787	2910	2951	0.5	3.10	2393	2494	0.4
02061	NORWELL	023	9639	10263	10530	0.7	81	3209	3460	3561	0.8	2.91	2673	2876	0.8
02062	NORWOOD	021	28592	28487	28437	0.0	32	11625	11746	11771	0.1	2.38	7384	7419	0.1
02066	SCITUATE	023	17485	18157	18350	0.4	65	6507	6838	6942	0.5	2.63	4813	5030	0.5
02067	SHARON	021	17448	17339	17265	-0.1	23	5950	5968	5963	0.0	2.89	4943	4949	0.0
02071	SOUTH WALPOLE	021	691	765	813	1.1	93	216	244	262	1.3	2.94	188	211	1.3
02072	STOUGHTON	021	27192	27278	27303	0.0	32	10271	10443	10499	0.2	2.57	7279	7392	0.2
02081	WALPOLE	021	18594	19659	20019	0.6	76	6547	7002	7155	0.7	2.68	4863	5184	0.7
02090	WESTWOOD	021	14048	14380	14460	0.3	58	5095	5278	5327	0.4	2.70	3844	3972	0.4
02093	WRENTHAM	021	10521	11133	11376	0.6	76	3393	3662	3763	0.8	2.84	2645	2840	0.8
02108	BOSTON	025	3746	3560	3526	-0.5	4	2154	2078	2063	-0.4	1.50	601	572	-0.5
02109	BOSTON	025	3718	3698	3701	-0.1	23	2189	2201	2207	0.1	1.60	666	665	0.0
02110	BOSTON	025	1579	1778	1809	1.3	95	961	1042	1054	0.9	1.60	338	377	1.2
02111	BOSTON	025	4692	5894	6372	2.5	99	1737	2476	2721	3.9	2.05	789	1017	2.8
02113	BOSTON	025	6070	5951	5913	-0.2	14	3874	3846	3842	-0.1	1.54	835	822	-0.2
02114	BOSTON	025	11044	10965	10908	-0.1	23	6438	6431	6416	0.0	1.52	1532	1521	-0.1
02115	BOSTON	025	26221	25379	25327	-0.4	6	11077	10949	10944	-0.1	1.69	2452	2410	-0.2
02116	BOSTON	025	18853	18225	18156	-0.4	6	10745	10521	10515	-0.2	1.54	2965	2883	-0.3
02118	BOSTON	025	22945	23902	24409	0.4	65	10705	11387	11677	0.7	1.89	3516	3733	0.6
02119	BOSTON	025	23110	23310	23516	0.1	41	8576	8786	8899	0.3	2.57	5272	5374	0.2
02120	BOSTON	025	13342	13912	14164	0.5	71	5041	5356	5484	0.7	2.43	2151	2285	0.7
02121	BOSTON	025	24934	25056	25193	0.1	41	8906	9045	9120	0.2	2.76	6088	6158	0.1
02122	BOSTON	025	24433	24409	24446	0.0	32	8275	8240	8255	0.0	2.89	5376	5327	-0.1
02124	BOSTON	025	51414	51144	51208	-0.1	23	17583	17589	17643	0.0	2.89	12071	12049	0.0
02125	BOSTON	025	32617	32784	32962	0.1	41	11222	11359	11446	0.1	2.83	6971	7020	0.1
02126	MATTAPAN	025	28103	27639	27561	-0.2	14	9457	9408	9403	-0.1	2.90	6942	6885	-0.1
02127	BOSTON	025	29456	29900	30221	0.2	48	13791	14110	14287	0.2	2.09	6226	6324	0.2
02128	BOSTON	025	38413	40805	41528	0.7	81	14326	14875	15083	0.4	2.72	8672	8976	0.4
02129	CHARLESTOWN	025	15195	15420	15591	0.2	48	7350	7496	7589	0.2	2.04	3219	3265	0.2
02130	JAMAICA PLAIN	025	34411	34180	34286	-0.1	23	13869	13935	14002	0.1	2.32	6504	6517	0.0
02131	ROSLINDALE	025	30820	30726	30804	0.0	32	11683	11708	11753	0.0	2.59	7354	7335	0.0
02132	WEST ROXBURY	025	26931	26509	26375	-0.2	14	11008	10899	10853	-0.1	2.34	6573	6482	-0.2
02134	ALLSTON	025	22000	21851	21862	-0.1	23	9546	9567	9603	0.0	2.22	2773	2755	-0.1
02135	BRIGHTON	025	43974	43553	43569	-0.1	23	20304	20290	20346	0.0	2.10	6970	6909	-0.1
02136	HYDE PARK	025	27105	27175	27177	0.0	32	10173	10140	10128	0.0	2.65	6672	6622	-0.1
02138	CAMBRIDGE	017	34767	34784	34787	0.0	32	13819	13850	13881	0.0	1.87	5324	5281	-0.1
02139	CAMBRIDGE	017	35449	35904	36112	0.1	41	14410	14728	14870	0.2	2.13	5775	5855	0.1
02140	CAMBRIDGE	017	17517	18198	18486	0.4	65	8124	8458	8599	0.4	2.12	3693	3870	0.5
02141	CAMBRIDGE	017	12040	12495	12675	0.4	65	5458	5738	5852	0.5	2.14	2439	2531	0.4
02142	CAMBRIDGE	017	1783	1829	1850	0.3	58	908	946	962	0.4	1.44	400	413	0.3
02143	SOMERVILLE	017	25391	25554	25645	0.1	41	11133	11271	11336	0.1	2.22	4543	4557	0.0
02144	SOMERVILLE	017	23684	24093	24287	0.2	48	10458	10765	10894	0.3	2.15	4319	4408	0.2
02145	SOMERVILLE	017	26075	26677	26863	0.2	48	9706	9846	9911	0.2	2.70	5681	5724	0.1
02148	MALDEN	017	56539	57186	57477	0.1	41	23032	23368	23549	0.2	2.42	13582	13687	0.1
02149	EVERETT	017	38016	37975	37964	0.0	32	15424	15429	15446	0.0	2.45	9545	9489	-0.1
02150	CHELSEA	025	35032	36392	36778	0.4	65	11857	12071	12143	0.2	2.94	7595	7735	0.2
02151	REVERE	025	47299	48342	48848	0.2	48	19479	19990	20217	0.3	2.40	11875	12147	0.2
02152	WINTHROP	025	18303	17860	17733	-0.3	9	7843	7729	7690	-0.2	2.28	4584	4497	-0.2
02153	MEDFORD	017	1279	1325	1344	0.4	65	2	2	2	0.0	2.50	1	1	0.0
02155	MEDFORD	017	56455	56338	56365	0.0	32	22214	22339	22415	0.1	2.42	13577	13564	0.0
02163	BOSTON	025	1191	1279	1267	0.8	84	409	389	382	-0.5	2.53	197	186	-0.6
02169	QUINCY	021	52419	54157	54708	0.4	65	23891	24956	25320	0.5	2.13	12211	12654	0.4
02170	QUINCY	021	18811	18421	18258	-0.2	14	7701	7639	7600	-0.1	2.33	4279	4219	-0.2
02171	QUINCY	021	17689	18193	18382	0.3	58	7422	7828	7977	0.6	2.24	4119	4253	0.3
02176	MELROSE	017	27098	26778	26682	-0.1	23	10970	10958	10963	0.0	2.41	7097	7034	-0.1
02180	STONEHAM	017	22113	21725	21592	-0.2	14	9007	8931	8909	-0.1	2.40	5847	5767	-0.1
02184	BRAINTREE	021	33508	34511	34852	0.3	58	12474	13035	13231	0.5	2.59	8804	9163	0.4
02186	MILTON	021	26096	26382	26461	0.1	41	9004	9211	9279	0.2	2.75	6772	6905	0.2
02188	WEYMOUTH	021	13643	13894	13981	0.2	48	5579	5786	5857	0.4	2.31	3447	3551	0.3
02189	EAST WEYMOUTH	021	14899	14998	15031	0.1	41	6088	6225	6268	0.2	2.40	3805	3860	0.2
02190	SOUTH WEYMOUTH	021	16774	16676	16607	-0.1	23	6835	6868	6870	0.1	2.42	4332	4335	0.0
02191	NORTH WEYMOUTH	021	8696	8602	8551	-0.1	23	3548	3567	3562	0.1	2.41	2361	2362	0.0
02199	BOSTON	025	1005	1090	1125	0.9	88	732	789	811	0.8	1.38	186	200	0.8
02210	BOSTON	025	509	818	903	5.3	100	247	413	459	5.7	1.90	83	141	5.9
02215	BOSTON	025	19254	19813	20309	0.3	58	6611	7378	7715	1.2	1.54	881	970	1.0
02301	BROCKTON	023	62026	62699	62547	0.1	41	22678	22913	22890	0.1	2.68	14639	14663	0.0
02302	BROCKTON	023	32562	33117	33222	0.2	48	11100	11407	11486	0.3	2.87	8192	8368	0.2
02322	AVON	021	4416	4356	4317	-0.1	23	1695	1696	1690	0.0	2.57	1212	1207	0.0
02324	BRIDGEWATER	023	25244	26396	26838	0.5	71	7546	8048	8221	0.7	2.80	5602	5943	0.6
02330	CARVER	023	11191	11583	11679	0.4	65	3991	4174	4226	0.5	2.77	3016	3144	0.5
02332	DUXBURY	023	14273	15164	15493	0.7	81	4956	5315	5450	0.8	2.83	3950	4217	0.7
02333	EAST BRIDGEWATER	023	13056	14248	14708	0.9	88	4375	4830	5005	1.1	2.91	3416	3753	1.0
02338	HALIFAX	023	7417	7840	7951	0.6	76	2733	2902	2950	0.7	2.70	2036	2151	0.6
02339	HANOVER	023	13164	14102	14456	0.7	81	4349	4699	4830	0.8	3.00	3567	3848	0.8
02341	HANSON	023	9619	10303	10556	0.7	81	3164	3430	3530	0.9	3.00	2575	2779	0.8
02343	HOLBROOK	021	10738	10716	10697	0.0	32	4064	4115	4123	0.1	2.59	2846	2872	0.1
02346	MIDDLEBORO	023	19860	22559	23636	1.4	96	6951	8042	8478	1.6	2.74	5090	5896	1.6
02347	LAKEVILLE	023	9826	10877	11319	1.1	93	3296	3683	3849	1.2	2.89	2662	2961	1.2
02351	ABINGTON	023	14605	16114	16758	1.1	93	5263	5858	6111	1.2	2.72	3746	4145	1.1
02356	NORTH EASTON	005	11990	12312	12409	0.3	58	4189	4355	4410	0.4	2.80	3280	3402	0.4
02357	NORTH EASTON	005	1734	1663	1666	-0.5	4	25	28	29	1.2	3.00	9	10	1.1
02359	PEMBROKE	023	16988	18069	18461	0.7	81	5772	6221	6390	0.8	2.88	4573	4899	0.7
02360	PLYMOUTH	023	51677	57598	59906	1.2	94	18415	20814	21758	1.3	2.65	13262	14935	1.3
	MASSACHUSETTS					0.3					0.3	2.50			0.3
	UNITED STATES					1.0					1.1	2.59			0.9

ZIP CODE #	POST OFFICE NAME	RACE (%) White 2000	White 2009	Black 2000	Black 2009	Asian/Pacific 2000	Asian/Pacific 2009	% Hispanic Origin 2000	% Hispanic Origin 2009	2009 AGE DISTRIBUTION (%) 0-4	5-9	10-14	15-19	20-24	25-44	45-64	65-84	85+	18+	MEDIAN AGE 2009	% 2009 Males	% 2009 Females
02026	DEDHAM	94.5	92.4	1.5	2.0	1.9	3.0	2.4	3.4	6.0	6.2	6.6	6.1	5.2	25.4	28.3	13.5	2.7	77.5	41.8	48.5	51.5
02030	DOVER	95.2	92.8	0.4	0.5	3.6	5.8	1.2	1.6	6.7	8.4	11.0	9.0	3.2	15.9	33.4	11.1	1.3	68.1	42.3	49.0	51.0
02032	EAST WALPOLE	98.0	97.2	0.4	0.5	0.7	1.1	1.5	2.1	6.4	6.8	7.3	6.8	5.3	22.7	31.0	11.8	2.0	75.2	41.9	48.4	51.6
02035	FOXBORO	97.1	95.9	0.8	1.0	1.2	2.0	1.1	1.5	6.4	6.9	7.5	6.9	4.8	23.8	30.2	11.7	1.8	74.6	41.3	49.1	50.9
02038	FRANKLIN	96.0	94.4	1.1	1.3	1.7	2.7	1.1	1.5	9.4	9.0	8.0	7.2	4.4	29.0	25.0	7.1	1.1	69.5	36.0	49.1	50.9
02043	HINGHAM	97.5	96.4	0.4	0.5	0.9	1.5	0.7	1.2	6.8	7.5	8.4	7.0	4.2	18.9	31.3	13.1	2.7	72.4	43.1	47.8	52.2
02045	HULL	97.0	95.7	0.5	0.7	0.9	1.5	1.1	1.7	5.4	5.5	5.7	5.7	5.4	24.9	33.5	12.4	1.5	79.9	43.3	48.2	51.8
02048	MANSFIELD	94.3	92.4	2.2	2.7	1.9	2.9	1.4	2.1	9.0	9.3	8.8	7.1	5.0	28.8	25.3	5.7	0.9	68.2	34.6	49.9	50.1
02050	MARSHFIELD	97.7	96.8	0.5	0.7	0.4	0.6	0.7	1.1	7.0	7.6	8.1	7.0	4.9	23.4	30.4	10.2	1.3	72.8	40.2	48.7	51.3
02052	MEDFIELD	96.8	95.2	0.5	0.6	1.8	2.8	0.9	1.3	7.4	8.8	10.2	8.3	4.5	18.5	32.1	8.8	1.3	67.8	40.3	48.9	51.1
02053	MEDWAY	97.5	96.5	0.6	0.7	1.0	1.6	0.8	1.2	8.2	9.1	9.1	7.4	4.1	24.6	28.3	7.8	1.5	68.2	37.8	48.5	51.5
02054	MILLIS	96.9	95.8	0.7	0.9	1.1	1.8	0.9	1.3	7.1	7.6	8.0	6.9	4.6	23.4	31.1	10.1	1.2	72.9	40.4	48.5	51.5
02056	NORFOLK	88.9	86.7	4.9	5.4	1.2	1.9	4.9	6.2	6.2	7.6	8.8	7.4	4.2	26.5	32.0	6.8	0.6	72.8	39.6	58.7	41.3
02061	NORWELL	97.6	96.4	0.4	0.5	1.2	1.9	0.6	1.0	6.5	7.6	8.9	7.6	3.6	19.1	31.8	12.2	2.7	72.1	43.0	48.5	51.5
02062	NORWOOD	90.5	87.5	2.3	2.7	5.1	7.2	1.7	2.3	5.9	5.7	5.8	5.8	5.9	27.9	26.7	12.9	3.4	79.1	40.7	47.3	52.7
02066	SCITUATE	96.7	95.5	0.5	0.7	0.5	0.7	0.8	1.3	6.4	7.0	7.7	6.7	4.2	20.0	31.5	14.0	2.4	74.5	43.7	47.9	52.1
02067	SHARON	90.0	86.2	3.4	4.2	4.9	7.5	1.1	1.5	6.0	7.2	8.9	8.5	4.4	17.7	34.6	10.8	1.8	72.0	43.0	48.5	51.5
02071	SOUTH WALPOLE	94.1	91.9	2.7	3.5	0.7	1.2	2.3	3.3	7.1	7.3	8.0	7.5	5.1	24.8	29.8	9.5	0.9	72.2	39.1	51.9	48.1
02072	STOUGHTON	88.5	85.2	5.7	7.0	2.2	3.4	1.5	2.2	5.5	5.6	6.0	6.1	5.4	25.7	29.2	13.7	2.7	78.9	42.3	48.1	51.9
02081	WALPOLE	95.0	93.3	1.8	2.2	1.2	1.9	2.1	3.0	6.2	6.8	7.6	6.9	4.6	23.0	29.4	12.4	3.2	74.7	41.7	49.9	50.1
02090	WESTWOOD	96.0	94.0	0.5	0.7	2.5	4.0	0.9	1.3	7.0	8.2	9.3	7.4	3.5	17.5	30.3	13.1	3.8	70.3	43.2	48.5	51.5
02093	WRENTHAM	97.6	96.6	0.6	0.8	0.8	1.3	0.8	1.2	6.6	7.6	8.4	7.5	4.2	21.7	32.2	9.4	2.4	72.4	41.5	49.5	50.5
02108	BOSTON	89.8	85.8	4.0	5.3	4.3	6.5	3.2	4.6	2.8	2.4	1.5	2.3	6.0	37.3	35.6	10.4	1.6	92.7	43.0	53.6	46.4
02109	BOSTON	93.7	90.5	0.9	1.3	3.6	5.7	2.4	3.7	2.5	1.2	0.9	1.4	8.5	46.1	26.4	9.8	3.2	94.9	36.7	48.6	51.4
02110	BOSTON	87.5	74.6	3.4	4.9	6.9	17.2	4.9	7.1	3.4	1.9	1.6	2.3	3.7	29.9	39.2	15.2	2.9	91.8	49.5	50.0	50.0
02111	BOSTON	34.1	27.9	4.2	4.8	58.6	63.7	3.9	4.9	3.1	2.6	2.5	8.0	12.9	30.1	23.7	14.2	3.0	89.8	37.6	52.5	47.5
02113	BOSTON	96.3	94.6	0.4	0.6	1.3	2.1	2.0	3.1	1.8	0.7	0.7	1.0	13.5	51.8	15.8	11.4	3.4	96.4	31.8	45.3	54.7
02114	BOSTON	82.2	75.5	6.6	8.4	7.9	11.8	4.8	6.6	2.9	1.4	1.0	2.0	10.4	47.8	23.9	8.8	1.9	93.7	34.3	51.5	48.5
02115	BOSTON	69.7	61.2	10.2	12.4	12.2	16.7	9.6	12.4	1.9	1.6	1.3	18.1	27.9	32.2	11.2	5.0	0.8	94.2	24.9	50.8	49.2
02116	BOSTON	76.1	69.4	7.1	8.7	13.3	17.6	4.2	5.7	2.5	1.3	1.1	7.2	11.5	39.8	25.4	9.5	1.7	94.2	35.5	51.4	48.6
02118	BOSTON	46.9	39.4	25.6	28.2	12.8	15.5	19.1	22.6	4.4	3.7	3.4	4.3	9.6	42.2	22.8	8.3	1.2	86.4	35.2	55.3	44.7
02119	BOSTON	10.9	9.6	62.9	63.5	0.8	0.8	24.8	26.9	7.6	7.8	7.3	8.5	8.4	28.1	22.8	8.2	1.2	72.3	32.0	46.2	53.8
02120	BOSTON	41.5	34.3	32.2	34.8	9.4	11.5	20.7	24.3	5.2	5.1	4.6	9.6	20.6	29.7	17.3	6.8	1.2	82.0	27.2	51.8	48.2
02121	BOSTON	4.9	4.6	77.6	77.6	0.5	0.6	19.0	20.1	9.0	9.0	8.3	9.3	8.4	26.6	21.2	7.2	1.0	68.0	29.1	44.1	55.9
02122	BOSTON	41.2	35.6	28.2	30.3	13.6	16.7	10.5	12.3	7.7	7.2	6.7	7.7	8.5	31.1	21.5	7.9	1.8	73.7	32.3	48.0	52.0
02124	BOSTON	21.5	17.8	59.7	61.7	5.8	7.0	12.5	13.7	7.9	7.6	7.3	8.2	8.4	29.0	22.8	7.7	1.1	72.3	32.0	46.2	53.8
02125	BOSTON	34.9	29.1	31.0	32.9	11.4	14.5	16.3	18.7	7.5	6.7	6.1	7.6	10.6	33.4	20.5	6.6	1.0	75.1	30.0	48.7	51.3
02126	MATTAPAN	6.6	5.1	83.3	84.8	1.0	1.2	7.2	7.8	7.4	7.4	7.5	8.3	7.6	27.1	24.7	8.9	1.1	72.5	33.7	45.5	54.5
02127	BOSTON	86.8	83.5	3.2	3.7	3.9	5.4	7.5	9.4	5.2	4.9	4.5	4.8	7.6	36.2	23.8	10.8	2.2	82.6	37.0	47.0	53.0
02128	BOSTON	67.7	61.0	3.8	4.2	4.2	5.2	39.0	48.2	7.5	7.1	6.3	6.5	7.5	33.8	21.4	8.1	1.8	75.3	33.6	51.4	48.6
02129	CHARLESTOWN	82.9	79.6	4.8	5.1	5.0	6.7	11.6	13.5	5.7	4.7	4.4	4.2	6.3	40.6	22.8	9.8	1.4	82.7	34.7	46.0	54.0
02130	JAMAICA PLAIN	61.5	54.4	16.0	18.3	4.7	6.2	25.4	30.5	5.2	4.7	4.3	5.6	8.4	37.8	24.1	8.0	1.9	82.7	35.6	47.5	52.5
02131	ROSLINDALE	61.9	55.0	19.0	21.7	2.6	3.3	21.0	25.8	6.8	6.5	6.3	6.7	7.2	29.6	25.8	8.8	2.3	76.2	36.6	47.2	52.8
02132	WEST ROXBURY	89.4	85.1	3.4	4.4	3.8	5.9	3.7	5.4	5.7	5.6	5.7	4.8	4.4	26.3	27.8	14.8	5.0	80.0	43.6	46.2	53.8
02134	ALLSTON	67.0	57.8	5.3	6.4	16.9	22.8	12.5	16.1	2.8	2.2	1.8	5.3	32.5	39.0	11.5	4.2	0.7	91.9	26.4	51.5	48.5
02135	BRIGHTON	76.9	69.0	4.5	5.5	12.1	17.3	7.4	9.9	3.4	2.7	2.3	3.2	20.4	40.6	15.3	9.5	2.6	90.1	29.6	47.8	52.2
02136	HYDE PARK	53.2	45.4	33.5	38.4	1.7	2.3	13.6	17.1	7.2	6.9	6.8	7.1	7.2	26.7	25.7	10.1	2.3	74.8	36.5	46.7	53.3
02138	CAMBRIDGE	76.5	69.9	6.8	7.7	11.5	16.3	5.6	7.3	3.2	2.5	2.3	9.9	20.5	31.7	20.2	7.9	1.8	90.6	29.6	47.8	52.2
02139	CAMBRIDGE	60.2	53.2	16.7	18.2	13.4	17.7	8.8	11.0	4.3	3.2	2.9	7.0	16.2	40.2	19.0	6.0	1.1	87.4	30.5	51.0	49.0
02140	CAMBRIDGE	66.4	60.9	15.9	16.7	11.1	14.8	5.2	6.5	5.4	4.3	4.3	4.5	8.5	35.9	26.0	9.1	2.0	83.1	36.2	46.4	53.6
02141	CAMBRIDGE	70.0	63.3	8.0	8.7	8.6	12.3	11.1	14.4	4.4	3.4	3.1	4.4	9.7	42.2	21.4	9.8	1.7	87.0	34.9	52.2	47.8
02142	CAMBRIDGE	67.0	58.6	3.5	3.9	22.4	29.5	8.0	10.1	4.4	2.8	1.5	11.2	18.5	42.7	12.4	5.7	0.8	90.4	28.8	53.5	46.5
02143	SOMERVILLE	77.9	71.8	5.2	6.1	7.9	11.4	7.0	9.5	4.2	3.2	2.8	3.4	10.7	44.7	20.2	8.7	2.1	87.9	34.3	49.7	50.3
02144	SOMERVILLE	85.1	80.4	5.1	6.1	5.6	8.4	3.7	5.2	3.8	2.7	2.6	4.8	15.1	41.8	18.7	8.8	1.8	89.1	31.5	47.3	52.7
02145	SOMERVILLE	68.7	62.7	9.0	10.0	5.7	7.9	15.3	19.7	6.3	5.6	5.1	5.6	8.3	38.3	21.9	7.5	1.3	79.7	34.1	50.3	49.7
02148	MALDEN	72.2	64.7	8.1	9.2	14.0	19.5	4.8	6.3	5.8	5.5	5.2	5.4	6.6	32.8	25.5	10.8	2.3	80.2	38.2	48.5	51.5
02149	EVERETT	79.7	74.6	6.3	7.4	3.3	4.9	9.5	13.0	6.1	5.7	5.6	6.3	6.6	31.9	24.9	10.6	2.2	78.9	37.6	48.2	51.8
02150	CHELSEA	57.9	51.4	7.3	8.1	4.8	5.8	48.5	56.0	8.4	7.5	6.6	7.5	8.6	31.2	20.0	8.3	1.9	73.1	31.6	50.5	49.5
02151	REVERE	84.4	79.5	2.9	3.8	4.6	6.3	9.4	13.1	6.0	5.7	5.5	5.9	7.0	28.7	25.7	12.8	2.7	79.3	39.1	48.5	51.5
02152	WINTHROP	94.4	91.9	1.7	2.4	1.2	1.9	2.7	4.2	4.8	4.7	4.9	5.3	5.8	27.7	29.9	13.8	3.2	82.5	42.9	46.8	53.2
02153	MEDFORD	77.2	69.7	5.0	5.8	12.8	18.4	4.5	6.0	1.7	1.1	1.1	35.8	29.1	18.7	8.1	3.5	1.0	95.6	21.8	46.4	53.6
02155	MEDFORD	86.2	82.2	6.1	7.3	4.0	6.1	2.7	3.7	4.9	4.8	4.8	6.9	7.5	29.9	25.5	12.6	3.1	82.4	39.2	47.2	52.8
02163	BOSTON	63.6	53.9	7.6	9.1	20.7	27.4	11.4	14.6	7.0	4.1	2.9	3.1	13.2	56.6	8.3	4.1	0.5	84.2	28.1	55.1	44.9
02169	QUINCY	83.1	76.9	3.0	3.6	10.6	15.7	2.5	3.3	5.4	5.1	4.8	5.0	6.8	31.8	24.9	12.9	3.3	81.7	39.6	47.9	52.1
02170	QUINCY	77.0	68.4	1.0	1.1	20.3	28.4	1.5	2.0	4.4	4.3	4.4	5.8	6.9	30.8	27.2	13.4	2.8	84.1	40.8	47.7	52.3
02171	QUINCY	71.2	62.9	2.4	2.6	23.7	31.7	2.1	2.5	4.7	4.5	4.5	4.6	5.6	32.4	29.3	12.2	2.1	83.6	41.4	49.5	50.5
02176	MELROSE	95.2	93.2	0.9	1.2	2.0	3.2	1.0	1.5	6.2	6.3	6.6	5.6	4.5	24.9	29.6	12.8	3.4	77.2	42.6	47.3	52.7
02180	STONEHAM	95.0	92.9	0.9	1.1	2.6	4.0	1.8	2.6	5.6	5.7	6.1	5.7	5.0	25.0	28.7	14.7	3.7	79.0	43.1	47.1	52.9
02184	BRAINTREE	94.0	91.4	1.2	1.4	3.2	5.1	1.2	1.6	6.1	6.2	6.4	6.0	4.7	24.9	27.9	14.6	3.3	77.5	42.2	47.3	52.7
02186	MILTON	85.4	82.2	10.2	11.8	2.1	3.2	1.7	2.3	5.9	6.3	7.2	7.8	6.1	21.0	30.2	12.2	3.2	76.3	42.0	47.8	52.2
02188	WEYMOUTH	94.7	92.8	1.3	1.6	1.9	3.1	0.9	1.2	5.5	5.5	5.8	5.8	5.1	24.6	27.7	15.6	4.5	79.5	43.5	46.6	53.4
02189	EAST WEYMOUTH	94.8	93.0	1.8	2.3	1.3	2.1	1.7	2.4	6.2	6.1	6.3	6.5	6.3	26.9	28.0	11.6	2.1	77.5	39.7	48.4	51.6
02190	SOUTH WEYMOUTH	94.0	92.1	1.8	2.2	1.9	2.9	1.4	1.9	6.5	6.4	6.4	5.9	6.0	26.9	28.0	12.0	1.8	77.0	40.1	48.5	51.5
02191	NORTH WEYMOUTH	97.0	95.9	0.4	0.5	1.2	1.9	1.4	1.9	5.5	5.7	5.9	5.5	4.5	26.0	29.3	14.9	2.6	79.5	43.0	47.2	52.8
02199	BOSTON	85.3	79.1	2.6	3.6	7.9	11.9	2.4	3.6	0.8	0.9	0.4	0.6	4.7	33.5	31.3	20.4	7.5	97.6	52.4	46.3	53.7
02210	BOSTON	89.8	86.9	2.0	2.3	5.1	7.2	2.5	4.3	3.9	2.7	2.9	4.0	9.3	42.2	25.1	8.9	1.0	88.5	36.5	53.3	46.7
02215	BOSTON	74.4	65.0	4.1	5.2	15.3	21.6	7.3	10.1	0.6	0.4	0.3	28.3	37.2	23.4	5.8	3.4	0.6	98.4	22.7	45.6	54.4
02301	BROCKTON	57.3	50.6	18.7	21.9	2.6	3.6	8.7	11.3	7.8	7.1	6.8	7.5	7.9	27.9	23.2	9.7	2.1	73.8	33.8	48.1	51.9
02302	BROCKTON	69.9	63.1	16.1	19.8	1.5	2.2	6.7	9.2	6.8	6.9	6.9	7.4	6.4	26.6	25.9	11.3	1.7	74.7	37.2	48.4	51.6
02322	AVON	93.4	91.4	3.7	4.7	0.9	1.5	1.4	2.0	5.5	5.6	5.9	6.4	5.3	24.7	28.7	15.2	2.6	79.0	42.6	47.5	52.5
02324	BRIDGEWATER	87.3	84.8	4.0	4.7	1.1	1.7	2.7	3.7	6.0	6.2	6.4	8.9	9.5	29.0	25.1	7.8	1.2	77.6	34.7	52.6	47.4
02330	CARVER	95.8	94.3	1.2	1.7	0.3	0.5	0.8	1.3	6.4	6.8	7.2	7.0	4.7	25.8	28.8	11.1	2.1	75.1	39.9	48.7	51.3
02332	DUXBURY	97.8	96.8	0.6	0.9	0.7	1.1	0.7	1.1	6.4	7.6	9.0	7.7	3.6	18.6	33.2	11.5	2.3	71.7	43.0	48.3	51.7
02333	EAST BRIDGEWATER	96.9	95.7	1.0	1.4	0.5	0.8	0.8	1.2	6.9	7.2	7.4	7.2	5.1	26.8	28.2	9.6	1.7	73.8	38.4	48.9	51.1
02338	HALIFAX	98.1	97.4	0.3	0.4	0.3	0.4	0.6	0.9	6.5	7.0	7.2	6.5	4.4	25.0	29.5	12.1	1.8	75.3	41.3	48.6	51.4
02339	HANOVER	97.7	96.6	0.6	0.8	0.8	1.2	0.7	1.1	7.1	7.8	8.7	7.5	4.7	21.7	30.3	10.6	1.7	71.6	40.4	49.2	50.8
02341	HANSON	96.7	95.3	1.1	1.6	0.4	0.6	0.7	1.1	6.8	7.2	7.3	7.3	5.2	26.0	29.2	9.9	1.1	74.2	38.5	48.8	51.2
02343	HOLBROOK	91.9	89.5	4.0	5.0	1.5	2.4	2.4	3.3	6.0	6.2	6.4	6.3	5.1	26.3	28.2	13.3	2.1	77.5	40.9	48.7	51.3
02346	MIDDLEBORO	96.1	94.8	1.3	1.7	0.5	0.7	0.8	1.2	6.8	7.1	7.3	7.1	5.4	27.6	27.9	9.0	1.8	74.0	38.1	49.3	50.7
02347	LAKEVILLE	97.3	96.1	0.3	0.4	0.6	1.0	1.1	1.7	6.9	7.6	8.1	7.0	4.5	23.1	30.4	10.0	2.3	72.6	40.5	48.3	51.7
02351	ABINGTON	97.5	96.6	0.8	1.0	0.5	0.8	0.7	1.1	6.6	6.7	6.9	6.7	5.6	25.9	28.1	11.2	2.3	75.6	39.5	48.7	51.3
02356	NORTH EASTON	96.0	94.4	1.2	1.5	1.4	2.2	1.1	1.6	6.8	7.7	8.6	7.4	4.1	23.7	30.8	9.5	1.5	72.0	40.3	48.9	51.1
02357	NORTH EASTON	51.6	46.8	0.6	0.7	0.8	1.1	6.5	9.0	0.2	0.3	0.1	41.9	53.6	1.0	1.3	1.3	0.2	99.1	20.7	43.8	56.2
02359	PEMBROKE	97.9	97.0	0.5	0.7	0.5	0.8	0.5	0.8	7.4	7.9	8.3	7.1	4.6	25.3	28.9	9.6	1.1	71.9	38.9	49.6	50.4
02360	PLYMOUTH	94.8	93.1	1.9	2.4	0.6	1.0	1.7	2.5	6.7	6.8	7.0	6.8	5.3	28.0	27.6	9.9	2.1	75.2	38.4	49.7	50.3
	MASSACHUSETTS	84.5	81.0	5.4	6.0	3.8	5.4	6.8	8.7	6.1	6.2	6.3	7.1	7.1	26.5	27.1	11.3	2.3	77.4	38.6	48.4	51.6
	UNITED STATES	75.1	72.0	12.3	12.7	3.8	4.6	12.5	15.7	6.8	6.7	6.6	7.1	6.9	27.0	26.0	10.9	1.9	75.7	36.9	49.2	50.8

#	POST OFFICE NAME	2009 Per Capita Income	2009 HH Income Base	2009 Household Income Distribution (%) Less than $25,000	$25,000 to $49,999	$50,000 to $99,999	$100,000 to $149,999	$150,000 or More	Median Household Income 2009	2014	2009 National Centile	2009 State Centile	2009 Home Value Base	2009 Home Value Distribution (%) Less than $50,000	$50,000 to $89,999	$90,000 to $174,999	$175,000 to $399,999	$400,000 or More	2009 Median Home Value
02026	DEDHAM	39729	8931	12.0	13.6	33.2	26.9	14.3	85858	91025	94	74	7108	0.1	0.1	2.7	58.2	38.9	364462
02030	DOVER	79020	1907	3.0	3.7	16.9	9.8	66.6	209277	216614	100	100	1749	0.0	0.0	0.0	3.0	97.0	961516
02032	EAST WALPOLE	41268	1454	7.6	14.7	27.1	31.3	19.3	100768	105139	97	85	1159	0.2	0.0	3.2	60.4	36.2	358679
02035	FOXBORO	43520	6197	9.7	13.8	34.6	23.3	18.5	87740	91892	95	76	4426	0.8	0.5	3.7	59.4	35.6	351849
02038	FRANKLIN	39995	10803	8.5	10.2	32.0	30.0	19.3	98710	103376	96	83	8689	0.2	0.1	4.2	56.2	39.3	360825
02043	HINGHAM	51354	7239	6.4	9.8	27.3	22.6	33.9	111672	118310	98	90	6181	0.3	0.0	1.7	18.1	79.9	616964
02045	HULL	35005	4507	16.6	16.5	36.2	21.8	8.9	70977	76596	87	50	3270	0.0	0.0	8.6	59.5	31.9	301002
02048	MANSFIELD	36780	8212	9.8	12.3	37.5	22.4	18.0	86564	86646	94	74	5837	0.5	0.5	4.3	50.4	44.3	378603
02050	MARSHFIELD	38886	9824	10.4	12.8	32.3	27.0	17.5	89379	99034	95	77	7918	0.3	0.3	3.9	46.4	49.1	395759
02052	MEDFIELD	59347	4103	4.3	7.7	19.1	23.0	45.9	140063	146833	99	98	3448	0.4	0.5	1.2	15.6	82.3	602217
02053	MEDWAY	40256	4354	7.5	9.9	30.4	30.5	21.7	103195	108487	97	87	3619	0.3	0.2	3.3	52.9	43.3	374336
02054	MILLIS	39191	3138	7.9	13.5	35.5	30.4	12.7	88802	93265	95	77	2412	0.2	0.0	1.2	74.3	24.3	322914
02056	NORFOLK	47661	2910	4.5	6.4	22.5	33.0	33.6	120783	123671	99	92	2615	0.2	0.0	1.6	35.6	62.6	458011
02061	NORWELL	49284	3460	4.5	9.1	27.7	21.7	37.0	116838	122963	98	92	3142	0.1	0.2	0.7	19.4	79.5	587644
02062	NORWOOD	38149	11746	12.4	16.0	35.7	24.1	11.8	80680	84095	92	66	6881	0.5	0.1	3.7	60.6	35.1	352633
02066	SCITUATE	44601	6838	9.0	11.7	29.6	26.5	23.2	99391	105334	97	84	5654	0.1	0.1	1.0	27.5	71.4	486667
02067	SHARON	60326	5968	7.3	7.7	22.5	24.1	38.3	128447	133070	99	95	5225	0.2	0.1	2.2	39.8	57.7	444231
02071	SOUTH WALPOLE	38960	244	2.5	9.0	28.7	41.0	18.9	111489	113203	98	90	221	0.9	0.0	1.8	44.3	52.9	409848
02072	STOUGHTON	35063	10443	13.0	16.9	34.8	23.6	11.7	79590	82792	92	64	7756	0.4	0.5	7.0	75.5	16.6	275504
02081	WALPOLE	47244	7002	7.7	12.9	29.8	26.7	22.9	99177	104736	97	84	5913	0.2	0.1	2.1	49.0	48.6	395204
02090	WESTWOOD	61188	5278	8.1	6.9	24.9	23.3	36.8	122686	128882	99	93	4563	0.2	0.2	0.9	14.9	83.8	612409
02093	WRENTHAM	43267	3662	7.2	10.5	28.8	31.9	21.6	104556	108824	97	87	3039	0.1	0.0	2.2	52.7	44.9	379087
02108	BOSTON	94999	2078	13.1	12.4	22.2	20.1	32.2	104601	108735	97	87	859	0.0	0.0	3.5	20.0	76.5	1000001
02109	BOSTON	90311	2201	8.8	10.6	28.1	22.7	29.8	104606	107708	97	87	833	0.0	0.0	5.6	25.7	68.7	582682
02110	BOSTON	81769	1042	19.3	13.6	15.5	22.6	28.9	102379	105819	97	86	517	0.0	0.0	1.5	10.8	87.6	717061
02111	BOSTON	24555	2476	44.7	21.7	18.6	8.8	6.1	29708	35349	8	2	519	1.0	0.0	1.9	19.7	77.5	485843
02113	BOSTON	61178	3846	12.8	17.6	35.2	23.2	11.2	74508	75380	89	55	813	0.0	0.5	5.5	41.2	52.8	417045
02114	BOSTON	75902	6431	14.3	13.9	27.7	19.5	24.6	85391	87419	94	73	1923	0.0	0.0	1.7	41.8	56.5	467473
02115	BOSTON	34369	10949	35.9	19.8	23.8	10.9	9.6	43234	47231	43	8	1786	3.5	0.6	2.1	36.7	57.2	468617
02116	BOSTON	85696	10521	17.0	12.7	21.7	19.4	29.2	95621	100054	96	81	4078	0.4	0.1	0.9	15.9	82.7	737031
02118	BOSTON	42889	11387	31.6	17.5	20.8	16.1	14.0	51617	56226	65	17	2924	0.5	0.4	0.4	26.0	72.7	587182
02119	BOSTON	18046	8786	36.3	30.3	23.9	7.3	2.2	34965	37803	18	4	2188	0.3	0.6	14.6	64.8	19.7	258288
02120	BOSTON	18947	5356	37.5	29.0	23.9	7.0	2.6	37224	40330	24	5	732	1.2	0.7	7.1	57.4	33.6	295062
02121	BOSTON	16425	9045	36.0	30.2	25.6	6.4	1.9	34965	37961	18	4	2265	1.1	0.2	11.1	67.4	20.2	289428
02122	BOSTON	21488	8240	20.7	27.1	36.1	12.3	3.8	52063	55058	66	17	3319	0.9	0.7	9.0	73.6	15.8	295096
02124	BOSTON	20305	17589	27.2	25.7	31.5	11.7	3.8	47313	49782	55	12	6888	0.5	0.5	8.9	71.2	18.9	290969
02125	BOSTON	20889	11359	26.9	26.1	31.4	11.6	4.0	47510	49972	55	12	3423	0.4	1.0	9.6	68.4	20.6	281988
02126	MATTAPAN	21030	9408	22.8	27.1	34.8	11.7	3.6	50127	53142	61	15	4375	0.6	0.6	9.1	84.1	5.6	257171
02127	BOSTON	32982	14110	25.5	20.1	31.2	16.5	6.8	55528	59108	72	20	5104	0.5	0.5	6.6	56.4	36.0	342174
02128	BOSTON	19268	14875	29.3	27.5	32.9	8.0	2.3	43116	46609	43	8	4554	0.7	0.4	15.3	67.4	16.2	278075
02129	CHARLESTOWN	55430	7496	19.9	14.0	24.4	19.0	22.7	79997	82548	92	65	3298	0.3	0.0	1.0	35.9	62.8	495056
02130	JAMAICA PLAIN	37110	13935	16.8	18.1	33.9	18.9	12.2	68516	70239	86	46	5838	0.5	0.2	6.2	46.9	46.2	381175
02131	ROSLINDALE	27419	11708	19.0	21.7	35.9	17.5	5.9	60809	63244	79	30	5937	0.4	0.3	5.5	68.1	25.7	309906
02132	WEST ROXBURY	37387	10899	12.3	18.1	36.2	23.1	10.4	74681	76078	89	55	7577	1.4	0.2	3.6	55.2	39.6	365366
02134	ALLSTON	25323	9567	30.0	25.8	29.0	11.3	3.9	44557	47671	47	9	1369	2.4	0.7	12.7	55.0	29.1	312691
02135	BRIGHTON	35456	20290	23.4	16.9	32.8	18.7	8.2	62496	65025	81	34	5186	1.6	0.9	7.6	49.9	40.0	347411
02136	HYDE PARK	24439	10140	22.6	21.7	35.7	15.9	4.1	55317	58161	72	20	5614	0.6	0.6	6.5	82.6	9.8	272524
02138	CAMBRIDGE	54742	13850	15.7	14.1	27.2	20.3	22.7	84084	92158	94	72	5365	0.3	0.3	1.6	24.1	73.6	647663
02139	CAMBRIDGE	40612	14728	19.0	17.9	30.5	18.8	13.8	67817	73597	85	45	4399	0.3	0.4	4.2	36.6	58.6	451915
02140	CAMBRIDGE	50130	8458	15.5	18.6	28.8	19.1	18.0	77525	82313	91	60	3272	0.5	0.0	2.0	32.9	64.6	493372
02141	CAMBRIDGE	36932	5738	24.6	17.0	31.8	17.0	9.6	61163	65355	79	30	1749	0.8	0.4	1.7	46.6	50.5	402879
02142	CAMBRIDGE	61630	946	16.9	16.1	33.0	16.4	17.7	76331	80508	90	58	207	0.5	1.0	0.0	27.5	71.0	547727
02143	SOMERVILLE	36708	11271	18.4	18.1	34.6	19.4	9.5	67715	72634	85	45	3363	0.9	0.5	3.2	55.4	40.0	365452
02144	SOMERVILLE	43070	10765	14.2	13.9	35.0	23.3	13.7	79421	83390	92	64	3625	0.0	0.2	1.2	31.4	67.1	471651
02145	SOMERVILLE	26731	9846	20.9	20.7	37.8	14.1	6.5	58129	60585	75	25	3500	0.6	0.4	4.9	59.4	34.7	345897
02148	MALDEN	30249	23368	19.0	20.8	37.3	16.4	6.6	62408	65511	81	33	10445	1.3	0.4	7.2	77.4	13.8	280246
02149	EVERETT	26359	15429	21.8	23.8	37.7	12.3	4.5	54354	56679	70	19	6715	0.8	0.2	9.8	77.3	11.9	271431
02150	CHELSEA	18270	12071	31.6	27.2	28.9	9.0	3.3	41285	45627	37	7	3789	2.1	2.1	15.0	71.8	9.1	259625
02151	REVERE	25692	19990	25.3	25.1	33.2	11.7	4.7	49637	53013	60	15	10510	0.7	1.2	10.0	74.2	13.9	272089
02152	WINTHROP	36641	7729	13.7	17.2	39.1	21.4	8.5	71605	73148	88	51	4303	0.3	0.2	5.3	64.4	29.8	342198
02153	MEDFORD	8362	0	0.0	0.0	0.0	0.0	0.0	0	0	0	0	0	0.0	0.0	0.0	0.0	0.0	0
02155	MEDFORD	33910	22339	16.4	18.0	34.9	21.4	9.4	71607	75942	88	51	13225	0.3	0.2	2.8	62.9	33.8	345133
02163	BOSTON	21583	389	32.6	24.4	28.0	10.8	4.1	46745	48167	53	10	8	0.0	0.0	12.5	25.0	62.5	433333
02169	QUINCY	35676	24956	18.5	21.2	35.2	17.1	8.0	62028	65295	80	33	11613	1.0	0.4	7.6	71.4	19.6	279773
02170	QUINCY	34965	7639	13.0	19.2	37.1	21.9	8.8	73672	76598	89	53	4303	1.7	0.3	7.1	71.9	19.0	298039
02171	QUINCY	39009	7828	11.8	20.3	35.8	21.8	10.4	71644	76258	88	51	4642	2.1	0.1	9.2	64.4	24.2	297316
02176	MELROSE	41341	10958	13.1	13.5	32.8	25.6	15.0	84014	89168	94	72	7327	0.3	0.1	1.5	55.5	42.6	378129
02180	STONEHAM	37263	8931	11.9	19.8	32.7	24.9	10.7	78020	82185	91	62	6136	0.1	0.0	4.0	63.0	32.9	346295
02184	BRAINTREE	38631	13035	10.8	14.4	34.3	27.0	13.7	85134	89961	94	73	10084	0.2	0.1	2.6	65.1	32.0	343688
02186	MILTON	50642	9211	8.3	11.2	27.0	23.0	30.5	106602	113825	98	89	7635	0.2	0.0	0.9	33.8	65.1	471816
02188	WEYMOUTH	32492	5786	18.9	18.1	36.9	19.4	6.8	66196	69733	84	41	3825	0.4	1.8	5.7	76.5	15.6	289521
02189	EAST WEYMOUTH	30999	6225	16.0	20.8	39.3	18.3	5.7	64133	66742	82	37	3929	0.3	0.4	9.0	78.7	11.6	261718
02190	SOUTH WEYMOUTH	34845	6868	11.8	17.9	39.3	22.7	8.3	75916	78192	90	57	4563	0.0	0.6	7.8	70.1	21.6	311614
02191	NORTH WEYMOUTH	37448	3567	11.0	18.3	35.1	25.9	9.6	78009	81379	91	62	2853	0.1	0.1	8.6	78.0	13.1	261219
02199	BOSTON	101117	789	7.0	18.9	31.4	16.2	26.5	81575	85513	93	68	0	0.0	0.0	0.0	0.0	0.0	0
02210	BOSTON	48482	413	10.2	15.7	38.3	24.0	11.9	78307	78333	91	62	189	0.0	0.0	12.7	64.6	22.8	262209
02215	BOSTON	26584	7378	38.2	20.6	25.6	11.6	3.9	38333	43262	28	5	860	2.3	0.0	11.6	69.0	17.1	257895
02301	BROCKTON	21837	22913	28.1	24.5	31.0	11.9	4.4	47238	48859	55	11	10687	0.6	1.1	24.2	69.7	4.4	215770
02302	BROCKTON	23036	11407	20.0	22.3	37.9	15.2	4.6	59383	60858	77	27	8033	0.5	0.6	28.7	68.8	1.4	196944
02322	AVON	33555	1696	15.6	19.6	32.5	23.3	8.8	69934	75149	87	47	1297	0.0	0.0	8.1	83.2	8.7	252524
02324	BRIDGEWATER	32065	8048	10.9	12.6	34.0	28.6	13.9	87435	95253	94	75	6010	0.0	0.8	6.9	61.8	30.4	326654
02330	CARVER	27254	4174	17.5	18.2	36.1	22.9	5.3	71063	76525	87	51	3762	0.2	7.4	22.8	61.1	8.5	236536
02332	DUXBURY	53750	5315	5.1	8.5	19.6	24.5	42.3	133129	138134	99	96	4658	0.0	0.0	0.6	15.8	83.6	601055
02333	EAST BRIDGEWATER	32048	4830	10.7	15.3	36.1	25.9	12.2	81837	87747	93	69	3934	0.2	0.5	7.2	71.6	20.5	287318
02338	HALIFAX	31500	2902	11.6	16.0	39.5	24.5	8.3	77960	81910	91	61	2613	1.0	3.4	20.5	59.4	15.8	253185
02339	HANOVER	40518	4699	9.1	8.4	31.5	27.3	23.7	101447	107171	97	85	4061	0.4	0.0	0.2	37.5	62.0	454673
02341	HANSON	32193	3430	9.0	12.3	37.5	29.6	11.7	86985	93369	94	75	3005	0.2	0.0	2.3	70.9	26.5	319830
02343	HOLBROOK	31201	4115	16.7	16.7	37.3	21.5	7.8	75563	77798	90	57	3125	3.0	1.4	9.2	80.7	5.7	235067
02346	MIDDLEBORO	27901	8042	12.3	17.4	42.7	22.4	5.2	72558	77085	88	52	6047	0.9	0.8	8.4	76.8	13.0	259593
02347	LAKEVILLE	36291	3683	8.9	8.1	34.2	32.3	16.5	97625	103908	96	82	3276	0.3	0.9	9.5	60.8	28.4	314631
02351	ABINGTON	31398	5858	12.7	17.9	33.6	24.8	11.0	77882	83852	91	61	4217	0.1	0.4	6.5	70.5	22.6	301491
02356	NORTH EASTON	41986	4355	7.5	11.7	36.0	20.6	24.1	92833	93144	96	80	3636	0.2	0.2	2.2	43.6	53.8	416411
02357	NORTH EASTON	15751	28	0.0	50.0	39.3	0.0	10.7	47500	51404	55	12	13	0.0	0.0	0.0	100.0	0.0	225000
02359	PEMBROKE	35074	6221	10.7	12.7	32.5	29.9	14.3	88574	97971	95	77	5458	0.3	0.2	3.9	62.2	33.5	329121
02360	PLYMOUTH	32078	20814	12.8	17.1	36.0	24.2	9.9	76485	81413	90	59	16248	0.8	0.9	10.6	68.8	18.8	270987
	MASSACHUSETTS	34904		17.4	19.0	33.1	18.1	12.4	68225	71891				0.7	1.2	13.3	53.8	31.0	297007
	UNITED STATES	27277		20.9	24.4	35.3	11.7	7.6	54719	56938				9.3	13.1	31.6	32.6	13.5	162279

ZIP CODE #	POST OFFICE NAME	FINANCIAL SERVICES: Auto Loan	Home Loan	Invest-ments	Retire-ment Plans	THE HOME: Home Improvements: Home Repair	Lawn & Garden	Furnishings: Comput-ers & Hard-ware-Personal	Major Appli-ances	TV, Radio, Sound Equip-ment	Furni-ture	ENTERTAINMENT: Dine out/ Carry out	Sports Equip-ment	Fees & Tickets	Toys & Games	Travel	Cable TV	PERSONAL: Apparel & Services	Auto Repairs	Health Insur-ance	Pets & Supplies
02026	DEDHAM	122	170	185	163	179	154	145	149	140	144	141	110	171	139	166	141	105	144	143	164
02030	DOVER	279	398	490	418	447	375	320	345	301	358	298	259	417	299	386	289	233	316	303	375
02032	EAST WALPOLE	128	180	197	172	190	166	153	157	149	149	150	114	182	149	175	152	112	152	154	172
02035	FOXBORO	147	179	186	179	185	169	158	163	153	161	154	123	177	154	173	152	112	157	156	185
02038	FRANKLIN	155	185	171	186	182	162	163	163	156	171	158	130	181	162	171	151	115	156	148	185
02043	HINGHAM	170	230	266	232	251	211	197	206	182	212	182	154	234	178	230	175	135	194	187	227
02045	HULL	103	129	133	124	133	119	118	118	115	118	115	89	131	113	129	115	83	118	118	134
02048	MANSFIELD	140	164	156	168	163	144	148	145	139	156	142	118	163	145	156	133	103	141	130	167
02050	MARSHFIELD	130	172	176	167	177	154	146	150	139	149	141	113	169	142	163	138	104	144	140	167
02052	MEDFIELD	220	296	348	306	326	268	255	265	232	280	232	204	306	228	297	219	176	248	229	292
02053	MEDWAY	154	198	195	199	201	173	168	171	157	178	159	134	193	161	185	150	117	162	152	192
02054	MILLIS	131	162	162	160	164	147	143	144	137	146	139	110	160	139	155	135	101	141	137	164
02056	NORFOLK	210	282	293	290	293	253	231	241	217	247	219	187	278	221	264	209	164	225	213	270
02061	NORWELL	176	245	275	250	263	224	201	212	188	216	188	160	246	188	236	182	142	197	191	234
02062	NORWOOD	109	137	146	134	142	126	128	125	126	123	128	94	144	125	138	129	95	126	125	141
02066	SCITUATE	142	196	219	194	210	179	164	172	154	172	155	128	196	153	191	151	115	163	159	189
02067	SHARON	213	295	325	298	314	268	243	255	227	259	228	193	295	228	283	220	171	239	230	282
02071	SOUTH WALPOLE	138	202	226	194	216	185	163	173	155	165	156	126	200	157	193	156	117	164	165	187
02072	STOUGHTON	110	142	147	137	147	132	126	128	123	125	125	95	144	123	139	125	91	126	128	144
02081	WALPOLE	157	215	234	210	227	202	179	189	173	183	174	138	214	173	207	174	128	180	184	208
02090	WESTWOOD	197	278	331	281	308	258	232	247	214	253	212	182	284	208	277	206	160	230	224	270
02093	WRENTHAM	161	216	218	214	221	192	179	185	169	186	171	142	211	173	202	165	127	175	168	207
02108	BOSTON	203	198	230	220	206	186	237	200	225	230	232	173	240	221	233	219	171	218	196	240
02109	BOSTON	203	174	191	196	174	164	228	182	218	217	226	163	217	218	210	211	164	208	181	226
02110	BOSTON	172	180	212	198	190	164	205	177	190	201	197	153	213	188	208	182	147	188	165	209
02111	BOSTON	62	55	63	60	57	58	77	64	79	68	81	50	73	72	72	83	58	74	76	79
02113	BOSTON	133	100	104	115	96	96	146	110	141	135	146	101	130	142	126	136	104	132	114	141
02114	BOSTON	167	149	167	167	151	141	191	155	182	182	188	136	185	181	179	176	137	174	154	190
02115	BOSTON	97	65	68	76	63	66	118	79	109	98	112	74	94	107	89	106	81	99	84	103
02116	BOSTON	185	179	207	199	186	168	217	182	206	209	212	157	217	202	212	200	156	200	179	219
02118	BOSTON	108	97	107	108	98	91	131	105	127	120	131	89	124	123	120	126	97	119	106	129
02119	BOSTON	53	53	55	55	52	52	66	56	70	57	72	42	65	66	61	75	53	63	63	69
02120	BOSTON	62	45	46	50	44	46	77	55	73	62	74	48	62	70	59	73	54	66	59	69
02121	BOSTON	53	52	53	55	51	52	64	54	68	55	70	41	64	65	59	73	51	61	62	68
02122	BOSTON	72	81	83	80	82	75	89	80	90	80	92	61	93	87	88	93	69	86	82	93
02124	BOSTON	69	73	75	74	72	70	83	73	86	74	88	55	85	83	80	91	65	80	80	88
02125	BOSTON	73	72	72	74	71	65	87	74	86	79	89	60	85	84	82	87	66	82	75	88
02126	MATTAPAN	71	76	79	78	75	75	85	75	90	75	92	57	89	87	83	96	67	83	84	92
02127	BOSTON	84	86	92	89	87	80	102	88	100	93	103	71	101	96	99	101	75	96	90	104
02128	BOSTON	63	64	64	64	64	57	77	66	75	70	78	53	76	73	73	76	58	73	66	77
02129	CHARLESTOWN	138	140	159	153	146	128	169	143	161	159	167	120	170	157	165	159	125	155	137	169
02130	JAMAICA PLAIN	113	109	120	117	112	97	136	113	126	128	131	98	131	124	130	120	96	125	107	135
02131	ROSLINDALE	82	96	100	94	97	89	100	92	102	90	104	69	107	100	102	106	77	97	96	107
02132	WEST ROXBURY	107	135	147	132	142	128	125	124	122	123	123	92	141	119	137	124	90	124	127	140
02134	ALLSTON	83	51	53	59	49	52	104	65	90	82	92	64	76	89	73	84	66	83	65	85
02135	BRIGHTON	101	80	86	90	80	76	120	90	112	107	116	81	105	110	103	108	83	106	91	113
02136	HYDE PARK	75	89	94	88	91	84	91	84	93	83	94	63	98	90	93	97	69	89	90	99
02138	CAMBRIDGE	167	156	176	173	161	145	194	160	181	186	187	140	189	180	185	174	137	177	154	194
02139	CAMBRIDGE	123	112	125	124	115	101	146	117	134	137	139	105	138	133	137	127	101	132	111	143
02140	CAMBRIDGE	130	137	156	147	143	127	158	138	150	150	156	114	162	147	159	148	115	148	135	162
02141	CAMBRIDGE	102	96	106	104	98	85	122	100	113	115	118	89	117	112	117	108	86	112	95	121
02142	CAMBRIDGE	147	131	145	146	132	121	169	136	159	161	165	121	162	159	158	152	120	154	132	167
02143	SOMERVILLE	107	96	106	105	97	87	126	102	118	119	123	91	119	116	119	113	89	117	101	125
02144	SOMERVILLE	120	117	133	127	122	106	145	121	134	137	139	105	141	131	141	128	101	134	115	144
02145	SOMERVILLE	89	92	96	93	93	80	108	93	101	101	106	77	107	100	105	99	78	102	88	108
02148	MALDEN	87	102	107	100	104	94	105	97	103	97	106	74	112	102	108	105	78	102	99	111
02149	EVERETT	73	92	97	89	94	86	89	85	91	81	93	63	100	89	95	95	69	88	89	97
02150	CHELSEA	68	66	64	65	65	58	80	69	77	75	80	56	77	76	75	75	59	77	67	79
02151	REVERE	74	84	86	83	85	80	87	81	88	80	90	61	92	86	89	91	66	85	86	94
02152	WINTHROP	98	122	130	118	126	117	116	114	117	110	119	83	130	113	125	122	87	116	122	129
02153	MEDFORD	0	0	0	0	0	0	0	0	0	0	0	0	0	0	0	0	0	0	0	0
02155	MEDFORD	97	121	130	118	125	113	117	112	117	109	119	84	130	114	125	120	88	115	116	128
02163	BOSTON	84	62	64	71	60	60	92	69	89	85	92	63	81	89	79	86	65	83	72	89
02169	QUINCY	97	101	106	103	102	96	111	100	109	105	111	79	113	107	110	111	80	107	105	118
02170	QUINCY	99	121	127	117	124	115	115	113	116	110	117	84	127	113	123	119	85	115	118	129
02171	QUINCY	106	131	137	128	134	120	126	120	123	119	126	92	139	123	134	125	93	123	120	137
02176	MELROSE	117	155	169	150	163	147	138	140	137	135	138	102	160	134	155	140	101	139	145	156
02180	STONEHAM	107	140	149	134	146	132	124	126	123	121	124	92	143	121	138	126	90	125	129	141
02184	BRAINTREE	120	165	176	157	173	151	140	144	135	139	137	106	165	136	159	137	101	140	140	159
02186	MILTON	168	238	271	234	258	220	198	209	187	206	187	153	240	185	233	186	140	198	197	228
02188	WEYMOUTH	96	112	115	109	115	110	107	107	107	105	107	79	116	104	114	109	76	108	113	122
02189	EAST WEYMOUTH	95	110	110	108	111	102	106	102	103	104	105	79	114	103	111	103	75	104	102	118
02190	SOUTH WEYMOUTH	108	123	125	120	125	114	121	115	117	118	119	89	129	117	125	118	86	119	116	133
02191	NORTH WEYMOUTH	109	144	148	136	148	134	124	128	122	124	123	93	143	121	139	125	89	126	131	143
02199	BOSTON	197	146	152	168	140	141	216	162	209	200	216	149	191	211	185	202	154	195	169	209
02210	BOSTON	129	107	115	119	106	98	147	115	137	138	143	105	135	137	134	130	103	134	112	143
02215	BOSTON	78	51	52	59	48	51	91	61	83	77	86	58	72	83	69	79	61	77	63	80
02301	BROCKTON	75	78	75	77	77	72	85	77	84	81	86	61	86	83	83	84	62	83	79	90
02302	BROCKTON	84	95	89	95	93	92	93	89	94	90	95	69	100	93	96	96	68	92	95	106
02322	AVON	103	136	142	128	141	128	118	122	117	118	117	88	136	115	133	119	85	120	126	136
02324	BRIDGEWATER	126	151	148	151	152	135	140	136	132	141	135	108	153	134	148	129	98	135	128	156
02330	CARVER	107	117	114	116	115	119	103	112	105	104	105	85	109	106	110	107	73	107	113	130
02332	DUXBURY	187	257	292	266	278	236	212	224	197	232	197	170	260	196	249	189	149	208	199	248
02333	EAST BRIDGEWATER	119	155	148	150	155	137	132	134	126	134	128	103	151	129	145	124	93	130	125	152
02338	HALIFAX	113	136	138	131	138	131	117	125	115	122	116	92	130	115	129	116	82	120	124	142
02339	HANOVER	146	202	219	200	213	186	167	175	160	172	161	130	201	160	193	159	119	166	166	193
02341	HANSON	119	162	160	153	164	142	135	139	128	136	130	105	156	131	151	128	95	134	130	155
02343	HOLBROOK	101	129	124	125	129	120	112	115	110	112	112	86	128	112	124	111	80	113	114	130
02346	MIDDLEBORO	99	123	115	120	122	111	109	110	105	110	106	85	121	107	118	104	77	107	104	125
02347	LAKEVILLE	134	178	174	172	179	157	148	153	141	152	143	116	171	144	166	139	104	147	142	172
02351	ABINGTON	104	138	141	130	142	125	119	122	116	118	117	90	137	116	133	117	85	120	120	136
02356	NORTH EASTON	147	196	201	199	202	176	164	169	156	171	158	130	195	158	185	152	118	160	153	190
02357	NORTH EASTON	93	60	58	66	58	65	111	75	99	88	99	69	81	99	78	97	70	92	79	96
02359	PEMBROKE	129	170	167	166	172	151	142	146	135	146	137	112	165	138	159	133	100	140	135	164
02360	PLYMOUTH	116	136	128	135	134	124	123	123	119	126	121	96	134	121	130	117	86	121	118	142
	MASSACHUSETTS	113	129	133	129	131	121	127	122	123	125	125	94	135	122	132	123	90	124	121	141
	UNITED STATES	100	100	100	100	100	100	100	100	100	100	100	100	100	100	100	100	100	100	100	100

ZIP CODE #	POST OFFICE NAME	COUNTY FIPS CODE	POPULATION 2000	POPULATION 2009	POPULATION 2014	2000-2009 ANNUAL RATE % Rate	2000-2009 ANNUAL RATE State Centile	HOUSEHOLDS 2000	HOUSEHOLDS 2009	HOUSEHOLDS 2014	HOUSEHOLDS % Annual Rate 2000-2009	HOUSEHOLDS 2009 Average HH Size	FAMILIES 2000	FAMILIES 2009	FAMILIES % Annual Rate 2000-2009
02364	KINGSTON	023	11770	12478	12756	0.6	76	4244	4525	4636	0.7	2.70	3135	3324	0.6
02367	PLYMPTON	023	2700	2999	3127	1.1	93	874	980	1026	1.2	3.06	754	843	1.2
02368	RANDOLPH	021	31008	30739	30593	-0.1	23	11323	11315	11289	0.0	2.69	7988	7948	-0.1
02370	ROCKLAND	023	17670	17942	17954	0.2	48	6539	6719	6750	0.3	2.64	4584	4677	0.2
02375	SOUTH EASTON	005	8448	8701	8774	0.3	58	3244	3386	3431	0.5	2.57	2261	2339	0.4
02379	WEST BRIDGEWATER	023	6241	6697	6877	0.8	84	2303	2507	2586	0.9	2.62	1683	1824	0.9
02382	WHITMAN	023	13836	14304	14416	0.4	65	4982	5205	5269	0.5	2.74	3591	3726	0.4
02420	LEXINGTON	017	13735	13439	13346	-0.2	14	4938	4861	4836	-0.2	2.68	3879	3806	-0.2
02421	LEXINGTON	017	16640	16836	16945	0.1	41	6181	6319	6387	0.2	2.61	4553	4628	0.2
02445	BROOKLINE	021	21149	21336	21313	0.1	41	9081	9228	9243	0.2	2.26	4713	4760	0.1
02446	BROOKLINE	021	30153	30821	30968	0.2	48	14412	14782	14889	0.3	2.04	5815	5907	0.2
02451	WALTHAM	017	17672	17699	17726	0.0	32	7282	7360	7400	0.1	2.36	4322	4351	0.1
02452	WALTHAM	017	12328	12864	13114	0.5	71	4355	4647	4778	0.7	2.19	2468	2627	0.7
02453	WALTHAM	017	29195	29674	29873	0.2	48	11560	11833	11951	0.3	2.26	5661	5744	0.2
02458	NEWTON	017	13565	13411	13360	-0.1	23	5278	5271	5272	0.0	2.38	2988	2965	-0.1
02459	NEWTON CENTER	017	18404	18784	18739	0.2	48	6617	7001	7012	0.6	2.61	4852	5080	0.5
02460	NEWTONVILLE	017	8238	8078	8019	-0.2	14	3389	3341	3325	-0.2	2.41	2056	2015	-0.2
02461	NEWTON HIGHLANDS	017	6500	6315	6366	-0.3	9	2553	2510	2537	-0.2	2.42	1744	1704	-0.3
02462	NEWTON LOWER FALLS	017	2023	2296	2350	1.4	96	812	919	944	1.3	2.20	534	602	1.3
02464	NEWTON UPPER FALLS	017	2693	3154	3218	1.7	99	1137	1327	1357	1.7	2.32	663	778	1.7
02465	WEST NEWTON	017	11871	11786	11764	-0.1	23	4438	4443	4450	0.0	2.62	3104	3090	0.0
02466	AUBURNDALE	017	6495	6570	6654	0.1	41	2507	2542	2575	0.1	2.40	1577	1592	0.1
02467	CHESTNUT HILL	021	15492	15433	15578	0.0	32	5088	4855	4920	-0.5	2.51	3318	3287	-0.1
02468	WABAN	017	5772	5606	5550	-0.3	9	2018	1980	1969	-0.2	2.81	1564	1528	-0.3
02472	WATERTOWN	017	33139	32862	32810	-0.1	23	14673	14685	14715	0.0	2.15	7351	7293	-0.1
02474	ARLINGTON	017	26128	25749	25625	-0.2	14	11762	11731	11730	0.0	2.19	6590	6517	-0.1
02476	ARLINGTON	017	16393	16114	16034	-0.2	14	7297	7257	7251	-0.1	2.20	4230	4176	-0.1
02478	BELMONT	017	24055	23663	23529	-0.2	14	9695	9600	9573	-0.1	2.43	6428	6324	-0.2
02481	WELLESLEY HILLS	021	15082	14952	14896	-0.1	23	4876	4873	4871	0.0	2.85	3938	3923	0.0
02482	WELLESLEY	021	11630	11507	11467	-0.1	23	3743	3739	3727	0.0	2.48	2618	2606	0.0
02492	NEEDHAM	021	19799	19591	19497	-0.1	23	7121	7113	7103	0.0	2.65	5333	5319	0.0
02493	WESTON	017	11447	11489	11502	0.0	32	3710	3711	3718	0.0	2.87	2986	2979	0.0
02494	NEEDHAM HEIGHTS	021	8999	8894	8823	-0.1	23	3459	3449	3433	0.0	2.51	2424	2405	-0.1
02532	BUZZARDS BAY	001	12633	12763	12709	0.1	41	5112	5276	5285	0.3	2.27	3286	3373	0.3
02535	CHILMARK	007	1187	1341	1403	1.3	95	523	595	624	1.4	2.25	327	369	1.3
02536	EAST FALMOUTH	001	19368	20722	21063	0.7	81	7756	8489	8683	1.0	2.43	5430	5907	0.9
02537	EAST SANDWICH	001	6247	7004	7212	1.2	94	2327	2657	2751	1.4	2.63	1750	1990	1.4
02538	EAST WAREHAM	023	4619	4680	4656	0.1	41	1862	1907	1908	0.3	2.45	1167	1189	0.2
02539	EDGARTOWN	007	3766	3832	3881	0.2	48	1576	1611	1634	0.2	2.34	953	968	0.2
02540	FALMOUTH	001	9127	9246	9200	0.1	41	4346	4505	4509	0.4	1.93	2364	2436	0.3
02542	BUZZARDS BAY	001	1581	1476	1431	-0.7	1	504	483	472	-0.5	3.00	416	397	-0.5
02543	WOODS HOLE	001	788	781	769	-0.1	23	387	394	391	0.2	1.94	206	208	0.1
02554	NANTUCKET	019	9520	10763	11410	1.3	95	3699	4164	4412	1.3	2.40	2106	2357	1.2
02556	NORTH FALMOUTH	001	3365	3377	3338	0.0	32	1368	1410	1403	0.3	2.31	973	997	0.3
02559	POCASSET	001	4112	4010	3926	-0.3	9	1866	1868	1844	0.0	2.14	1195	1188	-0.1
02562	SAGAMORE BEACH	001	2882	2988	2996	0.4	65	1043	1105	1114	0.6	2.56	792	833	0.5
02563	SANDWICH	001	9966	10322	10333	0.4	65	3696	3906	3935	0.6	2.61	2718	2856	0.5
02568	VINEYARD HAVEN	007	9832	10454	10739	0.7	81	4228	4504	4627	0.7	2.29	2458	2609	0.6
02571	WAREHAM	023	10284	10831	11094	0.6	76	4069	4337	4461	0.7	2.45	2686	2841	0.6
02575	WEST TISBURY	007	116	135	142	1.7	99	48	56	59	1.7	2.39	31	36	1.6
02576	WEST WAREHAM	023	3171	3674	3832	1.6	97	1275	1483	1547	1.6	2.44	878	1021	1.6
02601	HYANNIS	001	15632	15208	14909	-0.3	9	6638	6510	6399	-0.2	2.23	3691	3583	-0.3
02630	BARNSTABLE	001	1997	2299	2297	1.5	97	861	888	890	0.3	2.35	618	633	0.3
02631	BREWSTER	001	10033	9950	9823	-0.1	23	4089	4132	4104	0.1	2.30	2823	2834	0.0
02632	CENTERVILLE	001	11464	10832	10617	-0.6	2	4700	4643	4581	-0.1	2.29	3206	3146	-0.2
02633	CHATHAM	001	4535	4685	4703	0.4	65	2214	2345	2372	0.6	1.93	1304	1371	0.5
02635	COTUIT	001	3287	3509	3566	0.7	81	1411	1534	1568	0.9	2.28	1027	1110	0.8
02638	DENNIS	001	3779	3929	3961	0.4	65	1721	1836	1864	0.7	2.14	1136	1203	0.6
02639	DENNIS PORT	001	3508	3700	3745	0.6	76	1695	1807	1834	0.7	2.01	917	968	0.6
02642	EASTHAM	001	5449	5502	5454	0.1	41	2394	2476	2472	0.4	2.19	1634	1678	0.3
02644	FORESTDALE	001	3788	4028	4089	0.7	81	1243	1343	1369	0.8	2.99	997	1073	0.8
02645	HARWICH	001	9107	9888	10081	0.9	88	3829	4269	4390	1.2	2.24	2658	2938	1.1
02646	HARWICH PORT	001	2298	2413	2431	0.5	71	1227	1307	1320	0.7	1.83	637	672	0.6
02648	MARSTONS MILLS	001	7238	7273	7182	0.1	41	2651	2723	2704	0.3	2.66	2039	2085	0.2
02649	MASHPEE	001	13301	15637	16361	1.8	99	5376	6437	6775	2.0	2.41	3742	4456	1.9
02650	NORTH CHATHAM	001	1014	969	949	-0.5	4	431	419	412	-0.3	1.95	270	262	-0.3
02652	NORTH TRURO	001	1206	1188	1152	-0.2	14	488	491	478	0.1	2.21	283	283	0.0
02653	ORLEANS	001	6298	6204	6125	-0.2	14	3070	3082	3058	0.0	1.96	1761	1752	-0.1
02655	OSTERVILLE	001	3999	3913	3837	-0.2	14	1810	1794	1767	-0.1	2.18	1232	1213	-0.2
02657	PROVINCETOWN	001	3431	3521	3521	0.3	58	1837	1938	1954	0.6	1.65	465	484	0.4
02659	SOUTH CHATHAM	001	1076	1022	999	-0.6	2	515	504	498	-0.2	2.00	313	304	-0.3
02660	SOUTH DENNIS	001	7109	7362	7387	0.4	65	3234	3429	3466	0.6	2.13	2061	2169	0.6
02664	SOUTH YARMOUTH	001	9631	9234	9022	-0.5	4	4636	4532	4452	-0.2	1.99	2632	2549	-0.3
02666	TRURO	001	772	749	736	-0.3	9	367	366	362	0.0	2.03	201	199	-0.1
02667	WELLFLEET	001	2863	2911	2896	0.2	48	1355	1414	1420	0.5	2.06	758	783	0.4
02668	WEST BARNSTABLE	001	3277	3459	3502	0.6	76	1201	1286	1309	0.7	2.64	913	974	0.7
02670	WEST DENNIS	001	1603	1842	1915	1.5	97	816	967	1017	1.9	1.86	446	523	1.7
02671	WEST HARWICH	001	1023	1091	1107	0.7	81	497	539	549	0.9	2.01	309	332	0.8
02673	WEST YARMOUTH	001	8935	8644	8449	-0.4	6	3958	3886	3817	-0.2	2.16	2365	2303	-0.3
02675	YARMOUTH PORT	001	6906	6821	6700	-0.1	23	3192	3225	3187	0.1	2.11	2116	2125	0.0
02702	ASSONET	005	4061	4296	4371	0.6	76	1393	1496	1531	0.8	2.82	1153	1232	0.7
02703	ATTLEBORO	005	41917	42467	42516	0.1	41	15930	16323	16408	0.3	2.55	10871	11083	0.2
02713	CUTTYHUNK	007	86	90	93	0.5	71	46	49	51	0.7	1.84	21	22	0.5
02715	DIGHTON	005	2374	2787	2943	1.7	99	830	991	1051	1.9	2.78	666	790	1.9
02717	EAST FREETOWN	005	4320	4331	4333	0.0	32	1501	1528	1536	0.2	2.81	1208	1225	0.2
02718	EAST TAUNTON	005	6799	7137	7229	0.5	71	2373	2514	2554	0.6	2.84	1856	1956	0.6
02719	FAIRHAVEN	005	16159	16247	16222	0.1	41	6622	6746	6770	0.2	2.36	4251	4302	0.1
02720	FALL RIVER	005	31685	31465	31283	-0.1	23	13299	13364	13337	0.1	2.26	7951	7931	0.0
02721	FALL RIVER	005	25932	26136	26140	0.1	41	10730	10909	10948	0.2	2.38	6720	6784	0.1
02723	FALL RIVER	005	16119	16154	16071	0.0	32	6774	6871	6867	0.2	2.32	4155	4179	0.1
02724	FALL RIVER	005	17624	17428	17287	-0.1	23	7772	7789	7766	0.0	2.23	4598	4565	-0.1
02725	SOMERSET	005	2665	2700	2710	0.1	41	942	973	981	0.4	2.64	709	729	0.3
02726	SOMERSET	005	15564	15709	15716	0.1	41	6042	6175	6201	0.2	2.52	4550	4625	0.2
02738	MARION	023	5123	5456	5591	0.7	81	1996	2155	2220	0.8	2.49	1442	1549	0.8
02739	MATTAPOISETT	023	6268	6485	6538	0.4	65	2532	2659	2696	0.5	2.42	1771	1847	0.5
	MASSACHUSETTS					0.3					0.3	2.50			0.3
	UNITED STATES					1.0					1.1	2.59			0.9

# ZIP CODE	POST OFFICE NAME	RACE (%) White 2000	White 2009	Black 2000	Black 2009	Asian/Pacific 2000	Asian/Pacific 2009	% Hispanic Origin 2000	% Hispanic Origin 2009	2009 AGE DISTRIBUTION (%) 0-4	5-9	10-14	15-19	20-24	25-44	45-64	65-84	85+	18+	MEDIAN AGE 2009	% 2009 Males	% 2009 Females
02364	KINGSTON	97.0	95.8	1.0	1.3	0.4	0.7	0.7	1.2	8.0	7.9	7.9	6.5	4.2	25.0	27.5	10.4	2.5	71.8	39.3	48.1	51.9
02367	PLYMPTON	96.9	95.8	1.0	1.4	0.3	0.5	0.4	0.7	5.9	6.6	7.3	7.7	4.6	24.8	32.8	9.2	0.9	75.4	40.9	48.2	51.8
02368	RANDOLPH	62.9	55.3	20.8	23.5	10.2	14.4	3.2	4.1	6.0	6.1	6.3	6.4	5.6	26.6	28.8	11.9	2.3	77.6	40.4	48.0	52.0
02370	ROCKLAND	94.8	92.8	1.7	2.4	1.1	1.7	1.0	1.5	7.3	7.0	6.7	6.4	5.6	27.6	26.8	10.6	2.0	75.0	38.0	48.1	51.9
02375	SOUTH EASTON	94.5	92.6	2.3	2.9	1.5	2.4	1.3	1.9	6.2	6.5	6.8	6.2	4.6	26.9	30.3	11.3	1.3	76.5	40.9	48.4	51.6
02379	WEST BRIDGEWATER	96.4	94.9	0.9	1.3	0.7	1.1	1.0	1.6	5.7	6.2	6.3	5.9	5.0	24.3	29.0	14.0	3.6	78.1	42.6	48.6	51.4
02382	WHITMAN	97.1	96.0	0.7	0.9	0.4	0.7	0.9	1.4	6.7	6.8	6.8	6.9	6.3	28.7	26.9	9.3	1.5	75.4	37.1	48.8	51.2
02420	LEXINGTON	86.4	80.4	0.9	1.1	11.0	16.5	1.4	1.9	4.7	5.9	7.6	7.8	3.8	15.5	34.1	16.5	4.1	76.4	47.7	47.3	52.7
02421	LEXINGTON	86.0	79.9	1.3	1.7	10.8	16.2	1.4	2.0	5.4	6.1	7.5	7.4	4.3	17.4	33.2	14.7	3.9	75.9	46.0	47.5	52.5
02445	BROOKLINE	82.1	75.9	3.5	4.0	10.6	15.6	3.6	4.6	4.5	4.2	4.6	5.3	9.1	32.9	27.3	9.9	2.2	83.6	36.9	45.5	54.5
02446	BROOKLINE	79.5	72.1	2.4	2.8	14.8	21.3	3.9	5.0	4.2	3.0	3.2	3.6	12.2	38.4	22.2	9.7	3.5	87.6	33.5	45.4	54.6
02451	WALTHAM	82.5	76.9	4.5	5.3	9.4	13.2	5.4	7.3	5.3	4.9	4.9	4.9	6.8	31.7	27.1	12.2	2.1	81.9	39.7	49.2	50.8
02452	WALTHAM	87.4	82.7	3.6	4.3	6.4	9.6	3.7	5.1	4.2	3.8	3.9	10.8	12.2	24.8	24.0	13.4	2.9	86.2	37.7	48.1	51.9
02453	WALTHAM	81.4	75.9	4.7	5.4	6.6	9.5	12.4	16.0	4.6	4.1	3.7	7.9	11.8	35.2	21.4	9.0	2.2	85.2	34.1	50.2	49.8
02458	NEWTON	88.6	83.8	1.6	2.0	7.3	11.1	2.8	3.9	4.8	4.7	5.1	9.5	5.9	31.3	25.4	10.4	3.0	82.1	37.9	47.2	52.8
02459	NEWTON CENTER	87.6	82.5	2.3	3.0	8.0	11.8	2.3	3.4	5.1	5.7	7.0	8.5	5.8	21.1	31.4	13.0	2.6	78.2	42.8	47.8	52.2
02460	NEWTONVILLE	89.6	85.1	1.4	1.8	7.1	10.8	1.9	2.7	5.2	5.1	6.2	5.4	4.2	30.7	29.9	10.7	2.5	79.8	40.9	47.6	52.4
02461	NEWTON HIGHLANDS	85.4	79.9	2.6	3.1	9.2	13.6	3.0	4.1	5.3	5.4	6.0	7.4	5.8	23.3	31.6	12.6	2.7	79.6	42.9	45.2	54.8
02462	NEWTON LOWER FALLS	84.9	77.6	2.8	3.7	10.8	16.8	2.2	3.3	4.8	5.1	6.0	10.1	8.4	21.1	28.4	12.3	3.9	79.8	40.7	44.9	55.1
02464	NEWTON UPPER FALLS	83.6	76.3	2.2	2.7	11.2	17.4	2.4	3.5	6.1	5.7	6.1	5.2	4.4	30.0	29.4	10.1	3.0	78.9	40.9	45.5	54.5
02465	WEST NEWTON	89.8	85.6	1.7	2.1	6.6	10.0	2.7	3.9	5.9	6.2	7.1	5.9	3.8	26.3	30.6	11.7	2.6	76.8	42.1	47.1	52.9
02466	AUBURNDALE	88.2	83.3	2.4	3.0	7.5	11.3	2.8	4.0	5.6	5.6	6.0	7.1	6.3	26.4	28.1	11.7	3.0	79.5	40.5	46.5	53.5
02467	CHESTNUT HILL	84.9	78.5	2.2	2.5	10.0	15.1	2.8	4.2	4.3	4.7	5.4	13.5	15.3	17.4	24.2	12.1	3.1	82.5	35.0	46.3	53.7
02468	WABAN	91.5	87.7	0.9	1.1	5.9	9.1	1.5	2.1	5.0	6.3	8.7	8.0	3.6	15.9	36.0	13.6	3.1	74.8	46.5	48.1	51.9
02472	WATERTOWN	91.4	88.1	1.7	2.2	3.9	6.0	2.7	3.8	4.7	4.1	3.9	4.8	6.9	35.7	25.4	11.5	3.0	84.9	39.1	47.3	52.7
02474	ARLINGTON	90.3	86.5	1.8	2.2	5.4	8.2	1.9	2.7	5.4	5.2	5.4	4.5	5.2	30.6	27.8	13.1	2.8	81.2	41.4	47.4	52.6
02476	ARLINGTON	92.1	88.9	1.5	1.8	4.4	6.7	1.8	2.5	5.9	6.1	6.2	4.5	4.4	26.3	30.5	13.0	3.2	78.9	43.1	46.4	53.6
02478	BELMONT	91.2	87.4	1.1	1.4	5.8	8.8	1.8	2.6	5.5	5.7	6.7	6.1	4.5	25.0	29.9	13.4	3.3	78.0	42.8	47.0	53.0
02481	WELLESLEY HILLS	92.6	89.4	1.1	1.4	4.6	7.2	2.2	3.0	7.1	8.5	10.0	9.2	6.8	15.3	30.3	10.4	2.3	69.5	40.1	48.8	51.2
02482	WELLESLEY	86.7	82.0	2.2	2.6	8.5	12.5	2.5	3.2	5.5	6.3	7.2	12.9	12.3	14.9	25.5	12.5	2.9	77.3	36.8	38.9	61.1
02492	NEEDHAM	95.4	93.3	0.6	0.8	3.1	4.9	1.2	1.7	6.7	7.7	8.8	7.7	4.6	17.3	29.8	13.1	4.5	72.2	43.3	47.8	52.2
02493	WESTON	90.3	86.1	1.2	1.4	6.9	10.4	1.9	2.7	6.2	7.7	9.7	9.1	6.2	13.8	30.9	13.2	3.2	71.0	42.9	46.9	53.1
02494	NEEDHAM HEIGHTS	93.4	90.3	0.9	1.1	4.6	7.2	1.2	1.6	6.7	6.9	7.5	6.1	5.0	20.8	29.7	13.1	4.2	74.8	43.0	47.7	52.3
02532	BUZZARDS BAY	94.4	93.2	1.3	1.6	0.6	0.9	1.1	1.6	5.2	5.2	5.3	7.0	8.0	21.1	29.5	16.1	2.6	80.9	43.6	49.7	50.3
02535	CHILMARK	84.9	83.4	0.3	0.4	0.3	0.4	0.9	1.3	4.5	5.5	5.1	5.7	5.3	21.5	35.9	14.2	2.4	81.2	46.5	48.8	51.2
02536	EAST FALMOUTH	92.3	90.6	2.1	2.6	0.7	1.1	1.5	2.1	5.0	5.5	6.0	6.3	5.0	21.7	31.6	16.9	2.0	79.4	45.3	47.5	52.5
02537	EAST SANDWICH	98.4	97.9	0.2	0.3	0.4	0.6	0.7	1.0	5.4	6.4	7.5	7.1	4.2	19.2	35.0	13.2	2.0	75.8	45.1	48.2	51.8
02538	EAST WAREHAM	85.4	81.5	4.1	5.4	0.6	1.0	1.8	2.7	6.2	5.9	6.0	6.9	7.6	25.2	29.0	11.5	1.8	77.7	39.3	48.7	51.3
02539	EDGARTOWN	93.3	92.2	1.8	2.1	0.6	0.9	1.2	1.6	5.4	5.3	5.6	5.5	5.3	24.4	34.5	12.4	1.6	80.2	44.0	51.0	49.0
02540	FALMOUTH	94.5	93.1	1.5	1.8	1.4	2.1	1.0	1.4	3.1	3.1	3.6	4.3	4.3	16.7	32.7	25.7	6.5	87.3	55.1	45.3	54.7
02542	BUZZARDS BAY	90.8	88.6	3.6	4.3	0.9	1.4	5.4	7.4	15.4	10.5	8.1	5.3	14.2	44.3	2.0	0.2	0.0	62.7	23.8	53.7	46.3
02543	WOODS HOLE	94.9	93.3	1.1	1.3	2.0	3.1	1.1	1.7	2.9	2.6	3.5	3.1	3.6	19.0	35.1	26.6	3.7	88.6	55.4	50.1	49.9
02554	NANTUCKET	87.8	85.3	8.3	9.8	0.7	1.0	2.2	3.0	5.4	5.4	5.3	4.6	6.1	34.4	28.2	9.1	1.4	80.9	38.8	51.2	48.8
02556	NORTH FALMOUTH	96.3	95.4	1.0	1.2	0.7	1.1	0.9	1.2	4.5	4.9	5.7	5.8	3.5	15.8	33.4	21.9	4.5	80.7	51.5	47.0	53.0
02559	POCASSET	96.2	95.2	1.0	1.2	0.6	0.9	0.6	0.8	3.8	4.2	4.6	4.8	3.9	18.8	35.2	21.6	3.2	84.4	51.9	48.4	51.6
02562	SAGAMORE BEACH	94.3	92.8	1.7	2.1	0.8	1.2	1.6	2.1	7.2	7.1	7.3	6.6	5.3	22.4	26.6	13.4	4.0	73.9	41.2	45.5	54.5
02563	SANDWICH	97.8	97.2	0.3	0.4	0.6	0.9	0.6	0.9	5.7	6.6	7.6	7.5	4.3	19.1	32.8	13.7	2.8	75.2	44.4	48.3	51.7
02568	VINEYARD HAVEN	90.3	88.6	2.9	3.5	0.6	0.8	1.0	1.4	5.2	5.1	5.8	6.0	5.7	24.2	33.7	12.0	2.4	79.9	43.7	48.4	51.6
02571	WAREHAM	87.4	83.9	2.9	4.0	0.5	0.7	1.5	2.3	6.4	6.2	6.4	6.3	5.5	24.2	28.6	14.0	2.4	77.0	41.5	48.0	52.0
02575	WEST TISBURY	96.5	95.6	0.9	0.7	0.0	1.5	0.9	0.7	5.2	4.4	5.9	7.4	7.4	23.0	35.6	9.6	1.5	78.5	42.5	47.4	52.6
02576	WEST WAREHAM	86.9	83.6	1.9	2.6	0.5	0.8	1.3	1.9	5.0	5.8	6.4	6.2	4.1	22.7	30.3	17.0	2.5	78.8	44.9	47.9	52.1
02601	HYANNIS	83.1	80.2	6.2	7.2	1.4	2.0	3.1	4.2	5.7	5.2	5.0	5.9	7.1	27.1	27.2	13.6	3.1	80.7	40.9	47.6	52.4
02630	BARNSTABLE	97.8	95.4	0.8	1.6	0.4	1.1	0.4	1.3	3.1	3.3	4.6	7.4	5.4	15.3	36.0	22.5	2.5	86.6	51.9	48.6	51.4
02631	BREWSTER	97.2	96.5	0.8	1.0	0.8	1.2	1.0	1.5	3.3	3.8	4.9	6.7	3.9	16.7	35.3	19.8	5.5	83.3	51.3	46.2	53.8
02632	CENTERVILLE	95.4	94.6	1.4	1.6	0.8	1.1	1.3	1.7	4.5	5.0	5.3	6.2	4.8	19.4	31.7	19.0	4.1	81.5	47.9	46.9	53.1
02633	CHATHAM	95.7	94.8	1.9	2.3	0.3	0.5	1.0	1.4	2.6	3.0	3.7	3.5	2.6	15.7	35.2	27.9	5.7	88.1	57.2	48.2	51.8
02635	COTUIT	97.1	96.5	0.6	0.7	0.2	0.4	0.8	1.1	4.5	5.2	5.7	5.6	3.9	17.2	36.1	19.3	2.5	80.6	49.5	49.2	50.8
02638	DENNIS	97.5	96.9	0.4	0.5	0.6	0.9	1.3	1.9	3.1	3.4	3.8	3.9	3.1	14.1	37.1	27.5	4.0	87.1	56.6	47.8	52.2
02639	DENNIS PORT	90.1	88.1	4.8	5.7	0.4	0.6	2.9	3.9	4.5	4.0	4.1	4.6	5.1	21.7	28.6	23.5	3.8	84.5	49.1	45.9	54.1
02642	EASTHAM	96.3	95.6	1.5	1.7	0.3	0.5	0.8	1.1	3.7	3.7	4.3	4.7	3.7	19.6	36.1	21.2	3.0	85.3	51.1	48.5	51.5
02644	FORESTDALE	96.6	95.6	0.9	1.2	0.6	0.9	1.4	2.1	7.2	7.9	8.6	8.6	5.4	24.8	28.9	7.7	0.9	70.1	37.4	49.7	50.3
02645	HARWICH	94.9	94.1	0.7	0.8	0.3	0.5	1.0	1.5	4.1	4.5	5.1	5.5	3.5	18.1	35.0	19.6	4.7	82.7	50.7	47.2	52.8
02646	HARWICH PORT	97.2	96.7	0.4	0.5	0.1	0.2	0.7	0.9	2.8	3.1	3.4	3.4	2.3	14.7	32.5	30.3	7.5	88.4	58.6	44.3	55.7
02648	MARSTONS MILLS	94.8	93.8	1.4	1.6	0.6	0.9	1.0	1.4	5.4	6.2	7.1	7.3	5.1	20.7	33.7	12.7	1.8	76.0	43.8	48.9	51.1
02649	MASHPEE	90.4	88.5	2.8	3.4	0.6	0.9	1.6	2.4	5.7	5.9	6.3	6.7	5.3	21.6	29.3	16.9	2.4	77.8	44.0	47.0	53.0
02650	NORTH CHATHAM	97.1	96.7	2.0	2.4	0.2	0.2	0.6	0.8	1.2	1.5	3.0	3.5	2.2	13.9	30.3	31.9	12.4	91.3	62.3	43.3	56.7
02652	NORTH TRURO	94.9	93.8	2.7	3.3	0.3	0.4	1.0	1.3	3.3	4.3	6.1	3.5	2.3	25.9	40.2	12.4	2.0	84.1	47.0	46.3	53.7
02653	ORLEANS	97.6	96.9	0.6	0.7	0.5	0.8	0.8	1.1	2.3	2.5	2.9	3.4	3.0	13.4	35.4	30.6	6.5	89.9	59.3	47.6	52.4
02655	OSTERVILLE	96.8	96.0	0.8	1.0	0.5	0.7	1.2	1.7	4.0	4.1	4.8	4.8	3.1	14.8	34.1	26.3	4.1	84.0	55.2	46.9	53.1
02657	PROVINCETOWN	87.6	85.2	7.5	8.9	0.5	0.7	2.2	2.9	1.9	2.0	2.2	2.9	5.5	26.7	40.4	15.2	3.3	92.4	49.1	52.8	47.2
02659	SOUTH CHATHAM	96.7	95.7	0.9	1.2	0.2	0.3	1.4	1.9	3.5	3.9	4.3	4.8	3.0	17.8	36.7	21.6	4.3	85.4	52.4	49.2	50.8
02660	SOUTH DENNIS	96.0	95.2	1.2	1.4	0.2	0.4	1.4	1.9	3.6	4.0	4.9	4.4	3.2	17.8	32.7	25.0	4.4	84.6	53.4	46.1	53.9
02664	SOUTH YARMOUTH	95.3	94.2	1.3	1.6	0.8	1.2	1.5	2.1	3.8	4.0	4.1	4.2	3.5	17.7	29.3	25.9	7.4	85.3	54.1	46.1	53.9
02666	TRURO	95.5	94.4	0.9	1.1	0.6	0.9	1.2	1.6	2.9	3.3	4.0	4.1	3.2	17.2	43.1	19.5	2.5	87.0	53.2	49.3	50.7
02667	WELLFLEET	96.6	95.9	0.9	1.1	0.4	0.7	0.8	1.1	3.7	4.2	4.5	3.8	3.2	18.4	41.4	18.3	2.5	85.2	52.1	47.0	53.0
02668	WEST BARNSTABLE	98.2	97.3	0.4	0.6	0.5	0.8	0.4	0.8	5.4	6.5	7.7	7.5	3.9	18.3	33.4	14.9	2.4	75.9	45.4	48.4	51.6
02670	WEST DENNIS	95.0	94.0	2.6	3.1	0.3	0.5	1.1	1.4	2.4	2.6	3.0	3.8	2.3	17.9	35.1	29.1	3.7	89.6	56.8	45.9	54.1
02671	WEST HARWICH	96.1	95.4	1.7	2.0	0.1	0.1	1.0	1.3	3.5	3.8	4.1	3.8	2.6	16.0	35.7	25.5	4.9	85.8	55.4	48.7	51.3
02673	WEST YARMOUTH	93.1	91.7	2.1	2.5	0.4	0.6	1.8	2.4	5.1	5.2	5.4	5.0	4.5	23.8	28.0	18.5	4.5	81.2	45.6	46.5	53.5
02675	YARMOUTH PORT	98.2	97.8	0.3	0.4	0.4	0.6	0.8	1.1	3.3	3.7	4.6	4.5	2.8	15.0	34.7	26.3	5.1	85.3	55.2	47.1	52.9
02702	ASSONET	97.0	96.1	0.4	0.6	0.7	1.1	0.7	1.0	4.8	5.4	6.6	7.4	5.7	26.0	34.6	8.5	1.2	78.7	41.5	49.9	50.1
02703	ATTLEBORO	91.3	88.6	1.6	2.0	3.3	4.7	4.3	5.7	6.9	6.8	6.8	6.4	5.7	28.1	26.5	10.7	2.1	75.5	38.5	48.8	51.2
02713	CUTTYHUNK	95.3	94.4	0.0	0.0	0.0	0.0	0.0	0.0	5.6	5.6	5.6	3.3	2.2	28.9	36.7	11.1	1.1	82.2	44.3	54.4	45.6
02715	DIGHTON	97.9	97.2	0.4	0.5	0.5	0.8	1.2	1.7	5.9	6.1	6.6	7.3	5.7	25.3	29.8	11.2	2.0	76.7	40.7	49.5	50.5
02717	EAST FREETOWN	95.3	94.1	1.0	1.2	0.6	0.9	0.8	1.2	5.5	6.1	6.7	6.8	5.0	25.6	31.5	11.3	1.4	77.1	41.5	50.2	49.8
02718	EAST TAUNTON	95.2	93.7	1.5	2.0	0.6	0.9	1.3	2.0	7.9	7.7	7.6	7.4	5.8	29.9	26.0	6.8	0.9	72.0	35.1	48.7	51.3
02719	FAIRHAVEN	96.3	95.3	0.6	0.8	0.5	0.7	0.8	1.2	5.0	5.0	5.3	6.1	6.0	24.6	29.2	14.7	4.2	80.9	43.6	47.4	52.6
02720	FALL RIVER	92.9	90.8	2.5	3.0	1.6	2.4	2.6	3.6	6.1	5.7	5.6	6.3	6.8	27.8	24.6	13.1	4.0	78.7	39.0	47.1	52.9
02721	FALL RIVER	90.0	87.1	2.7	3.2	2.2	3.3	4.2	5.8	6.9	6.5	6.3	7.1	7.6	28.1	22.8	12.0	2.7	76.1	35.4	47.6	52.4
02723	FALL RIVER	88.7	85.4	2.7	3.1	4.2	6.0	3.6	4.9	6.9	6.4	6.0	7.0	7.6	28.8	22.0	12.6	2.7	76.6	35.1	47.5	52.5
02724	FALL RIVER	91.8	89.5	2.1	2.5	1.3	2.0	3.2	4.4	7.0	6.0	5.6	6.7	7.9	28.4	23.9	11.8	2.6	77.4	36.6	47.0	53.0
02725	SOMERSET	98.0	97.4	0.2	0.3	0.7	1.0	0.6	0.8	4.8	4.9	5.3	5.3	4.6	22.6	29.0	17.9	5.7	81.6	46.6	45.2	54.8
02726	SOMERSET	98.2	97.6	0.2	0.2	0.5	0.8	0.5	0.7	4.7	5.0	5.4	6.2	5.1	23.6	29.9	16.9	3.3	81.1	45.0	48.2	51.8
02738	MARION	92.2	89.9	1.6	2.2	0.4	0.7	0.5	0.9	5.5	6.0	7.0	7.2	4.6	19.8	31.3	15.4	3.2	76.7	45.0	47.9	52.1
02739	MATTAPOISETT	96.5	95.2	0.6	0.9	0.7	1.1	0.6	0.9	5.0	5.5	6.5	6.7	4.3	20.4	33.0	15.9	2.6	78.2	45.8	47.6	52.4
	MASSACHUSETTS	84.5	81.0	5.4	6.0	3.8	5.4	6.8	8.7	6.1	6.2	6.3	7.1	7.1	26.5	27.1	11.3	2.3	77.4	38.6	48.4	51.6
	UNITED STATES	75.1	72.0	12.3	12.7	3.8	4.6	12.5	15.7	6.8	6.7	6.6	7.1	6.9	27.0	26.0	10.9	1.9	75.7	36.9	49.2	50.8

ZIP CODE #	POST OFFICE NAME	2009 Per Capita Income	2009 HH Income Base	2009 HOUSEHOLD INCOME DISTRIBUTION (%) Less than $25,000	$25,000 to $49,999	$50,000 to $99,999	$100,000 to $149,999	$150,000 or More	MEDIAN HOUSEHOLD INCOME 2009	2014	2009 National Centile	2009 State Centile	2009 Home Value Base	2009 HOME VALUE DISTRIBUTION (%) Less than $50,000	$50,000 to $89,999	$90,000 to $174,999	$175,000 to $399,999	$400,000 or More	2009 Median Home Value
02364	KINGSTON	31984	4525	12.9	17.3	37.2	21.4	11.2	73988	79256	89	54	3669	0.2	0.4	12.0	48.8	38.6	340527
02367	PLYMPTON	34397	980	4.8	9.7	36.5	35.2	13.8	98091	103268	96	83	922	0.0	0.4	3.0	56.2	40.3	363673
02368	RANDOLPH	31990	11315	13.1	16.0	37.3	24.3	9.3	78311	81464	91	63	8221	0.8	0.4	8.7	81.9	8.3	252639
02370	ROCKLAND	30547	6719	14.4	18.2	38.2	21.1	8.2	68840	74452	86	47	4893	0.5	0.6	8.1	82.2	8.6	257923
02375	SOUTH EASTON	37974	3386	8.4	15.1	40.8	20.4	15.4	81688	83142	93	68	2576	0.9	1.0	13.0	48.6	36.6	321005
02379	WEST BRIDGEWATER	31476	2507	14.4	17.6	33.8	26.6	7.6	74426	80350	89	55	2113	0.8	2.1	9.6	66.8	20.8	283353
02382	WHITMAN	30282	5205	11.7	20.5	37.3	22.0	8.4	72218	77000	88	52	3746	0.0	0.8	8.4	81.9	8.9	256243
02420	LEXINGTON	66585	4861	4.3	7.2	22.3	21.9	44.3	137015	143920	99	98	4193	0.3	0.5	0.2	13.1	85.9	653664
02421	LEXINGTON	66604	6319	6.6	8.5	22.1	18.2	44.6	133354	143085	99	96	4834	0.0	0.1	0.5	12.3	87.2	656034
02445	BROOKLINE	68421	9228	10.1	11.3	24.8	23.5	30.4	106142	112171	97	88	5002	0.7	0.3	1.2	24.7	73.2	667434
02446	BROOKLINE	66507	14782	15.1	11.5	24.0	20.2	29.3	98563	107191	96	83	5668	0.2	0.3	1.7	24.8	73.1	590114
02451	WALTHAM	40435	7360	13.0	15.6	33.5	24.7	13.2	81005	85430	92	67	4156	0.8	0.3	2.4	58.3	38.1	360528
02452	WALTHAM	43409	4647	7.8	15.3	32.9	26.6	17.3	89788	95801	95	78	2832	0.0	0.3	3.5	41.4	54.8	420455
02453	WALTHAM	35056	11833	15.8	19.6	33.9	20.7	10.1	70779	75700	87	49	4210	0.3	0.4	2.6	59.8	36.9	365631
02458	NEWTON	59869	5271	11.5	9.6	26.1	19.1	33.8	106101	113764	97	88	2819	1.1	0.1	0.4	22.5	75.8	602971
02459	NEWTON CENTER	67891	7001	8.0	7.7	20.1	19.3	45.0	136027	145371	99	97	5456	0.2	0.4	0.5	10.7	88.2	719498
02460	NEWTONVILLE	65345	3341	7.0	9.6	23.6	21.0	38.9	121120	128392	99	93	1997	0.3	0.6	0.3	14.8	84.1	601034
02461	NEWTON HIGHLANDS	69521	2510	9.7	8.2	19.6	19.4	43.1	128529	138267	99	95	1903	0.5	0.5	0.3	13.3	85.4	658442
02462	NEWTON LOWER FALLS	66484	919	11.1	10.4	20.3	21.9	36.2	122608	129372	99	93	632	0.0	0.0	0.2	8.4	91.5	644195
02464	NEWTON UPPER FALLS	55941	1327	6.5	13.0	28.6	23.1	28.9	102972	109053	97	86	878	1.6	0.8	1.1	29.2	67.3	464407
02465	WEST NEWTON	57873	4443	7.0	8.2	26.1	24.1	34.6	115843	122625	98	91	3185	0.5	0.5	1.1	21.5	76.4	561620
02466	AUBURNDALE	62310	2542	10.1	8.7	20.5	22.4	38.2	123906	130707	99	94	1600	0.4	0.4	0.6	17.7	80.9	619072
02467	CHESTNUT HILL	63644	4855	6.3	10.0	21.7	17.7	44.3	132729	142993	99	96	3678	0.0	0.4	2.1	13.5	84.0	774827
02468	WABAN	82068	1980	7.2	6.0	12.9	16.5	57.5	193096	208861	100	99	1650	0.2	0.3	0.3	3.0	96.2	834842
02472	WATERTOWN	49995	14685	12.4	14.4	31.1	23.9	18.4	85429	91851	94	73	7191	0.3	0.1	1.6	43.5	54.5	418154
02474	ARLINGTON	46799	11731	11.2	14.8	30.9	26.9	16.2	87084	93145	94	75	6449	0.2	0.1	2.6	41.6	55.5	424186
02476	ARLINGTON	54582	7257	10.8	13.0	26.0	26.9	23.3	100387	105999	97	85	4782	0.5	0.1	2.7	37.4	59.3	438749
02478	BELMONT	61711	9600	8.3	10.4	23.2	24.8	33.3	115411	121507	98	91	5873	0.2	0.2	0.2	11.5	87.9	644839
02481	WELLESLEY HILLS	75218	4873	4.3	6.3	16.4	17.4	55.6	178481	199658	100	99	4195	0.0	0.1	1.0	2.3	96.5	963015
02482	WELLESLEY	65749	3739	8.9	8.1	18.3	15.9	48.7	144391	158574	100	98	2841	0.0	0.1	0.4	5.2	94.2	774821
02492	NEEDHAM	64181	7113	7.4	7.8	22.3	18.7	43.7	132517	140144	99	96	5870	0.0	0.0	0.1	7.8	92.2	667534
02493	WESTON	88954	3711	5.9	5.0	13.8	10.0	65.3	223162	238868	100	100	3128	0.6	0.2	1.0	2.3	95.9	963228
02494	NEEDHAM HEIGHTS	56210	3449	7.9	10.7	24.1	22.2	35.1	113776	120603	98	91	2562	0.3	0.2	0.1	14.6	84.8	596205
02532	BUZZARDS BAY	28295	5276	21.1	22.9	36.7	15.6	3.8	56684	60405	74	23	3920	1.6	0.4	15.8	61.3	20.9	248622
02535	CHILMARK	34856	595	14.6	22.5	43.4	8.1	11.4	56999	57030	74	23	418	0.0	0.0	0.5	5.0	94.5	1000001
02536	EAST FALMOUTH	32042	8489	13.8	21.7	40.4	17.7	6.4	64664	67320	83	38	6998	0.3	0.3	9.0	65.0	25.3	273826
02537	EAST SANDWICH	43050	2657	5.8	14.4	34.0	28.9	16.9	92720	92745	96	79	2353	0.0	0.0	1.7	50.7	47.6	387251
02538	EAST WAREHAM	26229	1907	22.7	30.0	29.6	11.1	6.6	47215	49435	55	11	1456	10.6	5.6	33.3	46.9	3.6	175723
02539	EDGARTOWN	33256	1611	12.1	25.6	42.3	11.2	8.7	62730	62950	81	34	1165	0.0	0.0	0.0	17.3	82.7	634915
02540	FALMOUTH	44285	4505	17.0	21.8	30.1	20.2	10.9	65054	69225	83	39	3000	0.2	0.0	3.4	38.4	58.0	443934
02542	BUZZARDS BAY	18986	483	16.6	28.8	48.2	5.0	1.4	52337	54413	67	17	0	0.0	0.0	0.0	0.0	0.0	0
02543	WOODS HOLE	58816	394	9.4	17.5	31.2	26.6	15.2	82192	83769	93	69	276	0.0	0.0	0.0	11.6	88.4	782407
02554	NANTUCKET	40649	4164	10.1	17.4	34.7	21.1	16.8	79431	80272	92	64	2662	0.1	0.3	0.4	1.4	97.7	1000001
02556	NORTH FALMOUTH	45383	1410	7.7	16.3	31.5	30.1	14.4	86148	88090	94	74	1208	0.2	0.2	0.6	34.7	64.3	468651
02559	POCASSET	41387	1868	12.6	23.5	29.9	23.6	10.4	70962	75447	87	50	1539	2.8	0.1	5.7	58.0	33.4	317314
02562	SAGAMORE BEACH	31978	1105	10.4	21.4	38.1	23.2	7.0	70746	72783	87	49	888	0.0	0.0	5.5	62.2	32.3	322660
02563	SANDWICH	35776	3906	11.0	14.5	36.0	28.6	9.9	80910	82242	92	67	3356	0.3	0.3	2.1	66.4	31.0	320870
02568	VINEYARD HAVEN	33972	4504	16.5	23.0	40.2	12.0	8.3	60028	61164	77	28	3222	0.1	0.2	0.2	23.3	76.3	596983
02571	WAREHAM	26912	4337	22.8	24.8	32.6	14.2	5.6	52242	54422	66	17	3095	2.5	2.3	29.3	54.8	11.0	200184
02575	WEST TISBURY	41519	56	5.4	17.9	42.9	21.4	12.5	81704	81462	93	68	43	0.0	0.0	0.0	9.3	90.7	683824
02576	WEST WAREHAM	24920	1483	24.3	21.9	37.2	13.7	2.9	53308	55382	69	18	1278	4.3	12.0	30.2	49.1	4.5	180137
02601	HYANNIS	24106	6510	29.8	26.0	32.3	9.0	2.9	42766	46261	42	7	3496	0.5	0.2	18.9	66.6	13.8	232070
02630	BARNSTABLE	48481	888	10.8	10.0	31.0	27.3	20.9	96425	96384	96	82	787	0.0	0.3	4.4	24.3	71.0	545705
02631	BREWSTER	33959	4132	13.6	21.9	38.7	17.8	8.0	66183	69003	84	41	3464	0.0	0.1	0.7	52.8	46.4	384483
02632	CENTERVILLE	36639	4643	13.4	21.4	37.5	19.9	7.8	68079	70837	86	46	3938	0.2	0.0	7.0	63.3	29.5	299363
02633	CHATHAM	44499	2345	14.0	23.8	30.4	21.7	10.0	66865	69941	85	43	1854	0.3	0.0	1.5	29.0	69.3	520955
02635	COTUIT	42051	1534	9.5	17.5	34.5	27.5	11.1	80339	81137	92	65	1323	0.0	0.0	4.2	49.4	46.5	377644
02638	DENNIS	44087	1836	9.2	20.1	32.7	28.4	9.6	79705	80710	92	64	1563	0.3	0.0	3.3	43.8	52.7	414928
02639	DENNIS PORT	32084	1807	25.7	26.8	32.9	7.5	7.0	47494	49950	55	12	1088	0.2	0.9	29.0	57.0	13.0	230556
02642	EASTHAM	31984	2476	17.3	27.1	37.5	12.3	5.8	55757	60177	72	21	2029	0.0	0.0	1.6	54.8	43.6	373354
02644	FORESTDALE	31771	1343	4.5	9.2	47.2	32.2	6.8	83956	84600	93	72	1185	0.0	0.0	1.9	81.1	17.0	286733
02645	HARWICH	30813	4269	13.6	25.9	42.7	12.7	5.1	58902	61983	76	25	3639	0.2	0.0	4.8	62.8	32.2	316731
02646	HARWICH PORT	33993	1307	27.8	25.2	31.7	10.1	5.2	45654	50425	50	9	948	0.0	0.0	5.0	40.1	55.0	435606
02648	MARSTONS MILLS	34923	2723	8.4	19.6	37.1	23.4	11.5	75825	77505	90	57	2437	0.0	0.1	6.3	64.4	29.1	289168
02649	MASHPEE	34751	6437	11.6	17.9	43.8	18.7	8.0	70352	72517	87	48	5328	0.8	0.7	11.2	59.5	27.7	284611
02650	NORTH CHATHAM	42871	419	13.6	19.1	30.5	24.3	12.4	80568	81707	92	66	346	0.0	0.0	2.3	26.3	71.4	599315
02652	NORTH TRURO	26493	491	20.6	28.1	38.3	9.4	3.7	51397	55789	65	16	369	0.0	0.0	0.8	23.3	75.9	534515
02653	ORLEANS	42270	3082	22.6	19.7	28.7	18.3	10.6	60312	64766	78	29	2331	0.0	0.0	5.2	27.8	67.1	530482
02655	OSTERVILLE	52108	1794	10.9	16.4	33.2	22.4	17.1	77680	80438	91	60	1529	0.0	0.0	0.7	45.8	53.6	438112
02657	PROVINCETOWN	37084	1938	24.4	25.0	38.1	7.0	5.5	50533	54174	62	15	1065	0.0	0.0	0.8	19.2	79.9	624641
02659	SOUTH CHATHAM	35372	504	19.2	27.0	32.9	12.1	8.7	54724	60000	71	20	400	0.0	0.0	0.3	41.3	58.5	439535
02660	SOUTH DENNIS	33386	3429	14.6	26.6	36.4	18.0	4.4	60328	62980	78	29	2738	0.4	0.1	8.1	60.2	31.1	290241
02664	SOUTH YARMOUTH	29713	4532	20.4	27.8	38.2	10.8	2.8	51229	53398	64	16	3255	0.3	0.2	9.4	70.6	19.4	257418
02666	TRURO	34259	366	18.3	23.2	41.0	12.8	4.6	60171	62374	78	28	298	0.0	0.0	1.7	19.8	78.5	541667
02667	WELLFLEET	34908	1414	18.8	25.3	34.2	14.1	7.6	56177	60360	73	21	1075	0.6	0.8	3.6	31.7	63.3	479609
02668	WEST BARNSTABLE	40983	1286	7.2	11.7	37.0	30.0	14.1	88281	88355	95	76	1178	0.3	0.3	3.1	36.3	59.9	447755
02670	WEST DENNIS	40653	967	16.1	26.6	38.1	11.8	7.4	57612	61423	75	24	699	0.0	0.4	9.0	41.1	49.5	396023
02671	WEST HARWICH	37666	539	18.7	27.5	31.7	11.7	10.4	54231	58145	70	19	427	0.0	0.0	2.3	51.3	46.4	372321
02673	WEST YARMOUTH	26359	3886	20.9	29.9	35.2	11.4	2.6	49227	51553	59	14	2761	0.4	0.8	14.3	75.8	8.7	237050
02675	YARMOUTH PORT	43627	3225	9.5	20.1	35.8	23.7	11.0	73735	75425	89	54	2857	0.0	0.0	3.3	57.6	39.1	349350
02702	ASSONET	33380	1496	9.8	11.5	39.0	28.1	11.6	86911	87671	94	75	1321	0.5	0.0	9.3	70.2	20.0	283967
02703	ATTLEBORO	28946	16323	14.2	21.1	44.1	13.9	6.7	67012	69560	85	43	10544	1.0	2.7	13.2	73.9	9.1	246357
02713	CUTTYHUNK	22139	49	32.7	44.9	16.3	4.1	2.0	29058	28590	7	2	19	0.0	0.0	0.0	10.5	89.5	732143
02715	DIGHTON	31415	991	5.7	19.7	43.0	22.8	8.9	80347	81056	92	65	835	0.0	0.0	7.4	80.8	11.7	262452
02717	EAST FREETOWN	30247	1528	9.4	12.4	48.2	21.7	8.3	78350	79804	91	63	1303	0.3	0.0	11.7	71.3	16.7	270853
02718	EAST TAUNTON	28178	2514	10.2	17.8	48.2	16.4	7.3	75092	76168	89	56	2029	0.4	0.0	14.2	73.3	12.0	252736
02719	FAIRHAVEN	26769	6746	22.0	24.5	36.9	12.7	4.0	54490	58898	70	19	4864	0.5	0.5	23.7	65.7	9.6	220545
02720	FALL RIVER	23710	13364	28.7	26.5	34.2	7.4	3.1	45981	48522	51	9	5553	0.7	1.6	17.1	74.0	6.6	227074
02721	FALL RIVER	18535	10909	38.6	27.0	28.2	4.7	1.5	35257	38790	19	4	3889	0.8	0.0	21.7	75.0	2.4	213491
02723	FALL RIVER	18522	6871	39.0	28.3	27.3	4.1	1.4	33573	38826	15	3	2128	0.4	0.9	14.4	81.6	2.7	226055
02724	FALL RIVER	18236	7789	40.4	29.1	26.0	4.0	0.6	32242	36071	12	3	2609	0.3	1.8	21.5	75.3	1.1	216146
02725	SOMERSET	25743	973	16.4	23.3	42.0	13.5	4.7	64371	66716	83	37	789	0.0	0.0	12.8	80.9	6.3	233443
02726	SOMERSET	29835	6175	15.8	20.5	40.1	15.9	7.7	67529	69019	85	44	4981	0.4	0.0	7.0	83.5	9.0	244245
02738	MARION	45635	2155	9.0	14.8	34.6	23.7	18.0	84430	93089	94	73	1682	0.0	0.4	8.3	39.3	52.1	415217
02739	MATTAPOISETT	38523	2659	8.4	20.3	34.0	23.4	13.9	79708	85500	92	65	2051	0.4	0.2	6.0	54.8	38.5	350000
	MASSACHUSETTS	34904		17.4	19.0	33.1	18.1	12.4	68225	71891				0.7	1.2	13.3	53.8	31.0	297007
	UNITED STATES	27277		20.9	24.4	35.3	11.7	7.6	54719	56938				9.3	13.1	31.6	32.6	13.5	162279

ZIP CODE		FINANCIAL SERVICES				THE HOME						ENTERTAINMENT						PERSONAL			
						Home Improvements		Furnishings													
#	POST OFFICE NAME	Auto Loan	Home Loan	Invest-ments	Retire-ment Plans	Home Repair	Lawn & Garden	Comput-ers & Hard-ware-Personal	Major Appli-ances	TV, Radio, Sound Equip-ment	Furni-ture	Dine out/ Carry out	Sports Equip-ment	Fees & Tickets	Toys & Games	Travel	Cable TV	Apparel & Services	Auto Repairs	Health Insur-ance	Pets & Supplies
02364	KINGSTON	112	138	135	137	139	125	124	125	118	127	119	96	137	119	134	116	86	122	119	142
02367	PLYMPTON	142	178	156	178	172	154	149	152	140	157	143	121	168	146	161	135	103	144	135	174
02368	RANDOLPH	105	139	142	132	142	125	121	122	117	119	118	91	138	118	134	118	87	120	118	136
02370	ROCKLAND	102	127	126	122	128	117	114	115	111	113	112	86	126	111	123	111	81	113	113	129
02375	SOUTH EASTON	130	153	144	155	151	139	138	137	133	142	135	107	151	135	146	130	97	135	130	159
02379	WEST BRIDGEWATER	102	135	137	127	139	127	114	120	112	113	113	87	132	113	129	115	82	116	120	133
02382	WHITMAN	103	130	127	125	131	118	117	117	113	115	115	89	130	114	127	114	83	116	115	133
02420	LEXINGTON	217	305	367	312	340	283	255	273	234	282	232	201	313	227	306	224	175	252	245	298
02421	LEXINGTON	213	289	347	296	322	263	252	263	227	277	226	199	298	219	296	214	170	246	230	288
02445	BROOKLINE	198	206	240	225	217	189	234	204	218	230	224	173	242	215	236	210	166	216	192	240
02446	BROOKLINE	173	179	211	198	189	165	206	177	192	201	198	152	213	190	207	184	148	188	165	208
02451	WALTHAM	121	143	151	142	148	130	139	132	132	136	135	103	150	133	147	131	98	135	127	151
02452	WALTHAM	138	167	189	170	179	148	164	156	148	167	151	126	178	146	178	140	111	157	140	177
02453	WALTHAM	105	108	118	112	111	98	126	109	118	119	122	91	125	116	124	115	89	119	106	128
02458	NEWTON	184	215	251	227	231	194	219	204	202	222	206	167	239	199	234	193	154	207	185	233
02459	NEWTON CENTER	218	294	352	303	325	268	256	265	234	279	233	203	306	229	298	221	177	249	232	291
02460	NEWTONVILLE	195	242	286	251	265	215	231	225	208	244	209	180	258	203	256	195	157	220	196	253
02461	NEWTON HIGHLANDS	213	278	330	284	308	246	252	256	224	274	224	199	289	217	289	209	168	243	220	283
02462	NEWTON LOWER FALLS	200	255	300	260	281	222	239	238	210	257	210	188	265	203	269	193	156	228	201	264
02464	NEWTON UPPER FALLS	164	207	243	211	228	178	196	194	172	211	172	155	216	166	219	158	128	187	163	216
02465	WEST NEWTON	185	249	294	253	274	223	219	225	198	236	198	173	257	194	253	187	149	213	196	247
02466	AUBURNDALE	196	249	293	254	275	217	234	233	206	252	206	184	259	199	263	189	153	224	197	259
02467	CHESTNUT HILL	233	295	350	308	323	271	274	271	253	289	255	213	316	248	307	242	192	263	246	304
02468	WABAN	275	389	476	405	436	364	318	342	296	355	293	255	405	291	382	283	226	314	302	372
02472	WATERTOWN	137	148	165	154	154	131	165	146	153	159	158	123	169	150	168	146	116	155	137	170
02474	ARLINGTON	127	145	165	150	154	131	152	140	139	150	143	114	160	137	160	133	105	144	130	160
02476	ARLINGTON	147	182	208	184	196	167	174	170	162	178	163	132	193	158	192	157	120	169	160	191
02478	BELMONT	186	233	275	241	255	211	219	217	200	233	201	170	248	194	245	189	149	211	195	243
02481	WELLESLEY HILLS	270	379	461	393	424	352	315	335	291	350	288	252	394	285	376	277	221	309	295	366
02482	WELLESLEY	233	305	364	315	337	286	271	279	253	293	252	211	321	244	312	243	189	266	258	310
02492	NEEDHAM	208	281	333	287	310	265	243	254	229	262	228	189	293	222	283	223	171	240	238	281
02493	WESTON	322	455	558	476	510	426	371	397	347	413	344	299	476	344	444	331	267	365	348	433
02494	NEEDHAM HEIGHTS	178	228	268	233	252	199	212	212	187	228	187	167	237	181	239	172	139	203	180	235
02532	BUZZARDS BAY	93	95	107	94	98	102	91	98	93	90	92	72	93	90	96	95	64	96	102	114
02535	CHILMARK	120	111	161	111	122	128	109	128	107	107	107	96	103	102	119	109	73	119	120	146
02536	EAST FALMOUTH	107	119	145	115	127	124	106	119	106	107	106	86	114	103	119	109	75	113	117	134
02537	EAST SANDWICH	150	182	192	184	189	173	158	167	151	170	152	124	178	149	176	148	109	159	158	190
02538	EAST WAREHAM	90	90	96	88	90	95	90	94	91	85	91	72	89	91	92	94	64	93	96	109
02539	EDGARTOWN	117	113	141	113	117	123	109	121	109	108	109	91	107	107	116	111	75	116	117	140
02540	FALMOUTH	115	129	155	129	141	139	120	130	122	128	121	89	132	114	134	126	85	127	141	147
02542	BUZZARDS BAY	100	52	39	60	47	44	94	65	89	88	93	65	72	107	68	82	66	83	59	80
02543	WOODS HOLE	159	168	228	166	193	198	151	178	159	171	156	111	166	143	174	166	107	170	198	201
02554	NANTUCKET	135	159	180	161	171	142	150	151	135	160	136	119	161	133	164	127	99	145	131	169
02556	NORTH FALMOUTH	137	172	200	172	186	171	146	160	143	157	142	112	170	138	169	143	103	151	158	179
02559	POCASSET	115	137	159	133	148	143	119	132	120	126	120	89	135	115	136	124	85	126	139	148
02562	SAGAMORE BEACH	108	134	134	130	136	122	118	120	114	120	116	90	132	115	129	114	83	117	115	136
02563	SANDWICH	126	151	152	151	154	146	129	138	127	138	128	102	145	126	143	126	90	132	135	158
02568	VINEYARD HAVEN	109	116	145	116	125	116	112	120	106	114	106	92	114	103	122	104	75	115	110	136
02571	WAREHAM	87	100	96	98	98	97	93	94	92	92	93	72	100	93	98	93	66	93	96	109
02575	WEST TISBURY	125	157	183	160	172	135	149	147	130	160	131	117	163	126	166	119	97	142	124	164
02576	WEST WAREHAM	85	92	97	89	94	99	83	91	85	86	84	65	88	82	90	88	58	88	98	106
02601	HYANNIS	77	69	78	70	71	75	78	77	79	74	79	59	74	77	76	81	55	80	81	91
02630	BARNSTABLE	163	180	233	180	204	195	165	184	165	183	163	124	181	151	188	167	114	177	192	208
02631	BREWSTER	114	118	151	118	128	133	107	125	110	111	109	87	112	105	120	114	75	118	128	142
02632	CENTERVILLE	116	127	152	125	137	139	113	129	116	119	116	88	123	111	128	121	80	123	136	146
02633	CHATHAM	125	126	175	124	143	151	115	137	121	126	119	88	122	110	131	127	81	130	150	156
02635	COTUIT	126	147	181	142	163	157	128	145	130	139	129	95	144	122	147	135	91	138	153	162
02638	DENNIS	131	136	186	135	156	161	123	146	130	138	127	92	134	117	142	136	87	139	161	165
02639	DENNIS PORT	86	85	97	86	90	94	90	90	93	91	93	64	92	87	93	96	64	93	103	105
02642	EASTHAM	115	95	150	94	105	124	94	118	98	91	97	85	84	93	103	105	65	110	119	137
02644	FORESTDALE	128	161	141	161	155	139	135	137	127	142	129	109	152	132	146	122	93	130	122	157
02645	HARWICH	113	95	149	94	106	123	94	117	98	91	97	84	85	92	103	104	65	109	118	135
02646	HARWICH PORT	87	87	116	86	97	103	82	95	87	87	86	63	86	80	92	92	59	92	106	109
02648	MARSTONS MILLS	118	153	160	149	158	142	129	136	124	134	125	99	148	124	146	124	91	130	131	153
02649	MASHPEE	116	126	131	126	129	126	117	121	116	122	117	90	124	115	124	117	82	119	123	141
02650	NORTH CHATHAM	128	135	184	134	156	160	122	144	129	138	126	90	134	116	141	134	87	137	160	163
02652	NORTH TRURO	102	81	131	80	89	107	81	103	85	76	84	76	71	81	88	91	56	95	102	120
02653	ORLEANS	119	118	162	117	133	142	111	130	117	118	115	86	116	107	125	123	79	124	143	148
02655	OSTERVILLE	153	168	220	165	190	191	149	173	155	166	153	110	165	142	172	162	106	165	189	195
02657	PROVINCETOWN	82	93	107	96	100	80	98	90	87	101	88	76	102	84	104	80	65	92	78	103
02659	SOUTH CHATHAM	112	98	149	97	109	124	94	117	99	95	98	82	89	92	105	105	66	109	120	135
02660	SOUTH DENNIS	104	100	138	99	112	121	95	112	99	99	98	75	96	92	105	105	67	106	121	128
02664	SOUTH YARMOUTH	84	83	111	80	94	101	79	93	84	83	82	61	82	76	89	89	55	89	106	105
02666	TRURO	117	93	151	92	102	123	93	119	98	88	97	87	81	93	101	104	64	109	117	137
02667	WELLFLEET	120	96	155	94	105	127	96	122	100	90	99	89	83	95	104	107	66	113	120	141
02668	WEST BARNSTABLE	143	176	183	181	182	169	152	161	146	162	147	119	172	144	170	144	105	152	154	183
02670	WEST DENNIS	105	111	151	110	128	131	100	118	105	113	103	74	110	95	115	110	71	112	131	133
02671	WEST HARWICH	119	104	159	103	116	133	101	125	106	101	104	87	95	99	111	112	70	116	128	144
02673	WEST YARMOUTH	79	81	85	81	84	88	79	83	82	78	81	60	81	80	82	85	57	82	91	96
02675	YARMOUTH PORT	125	136	171	135	152	155	121	140	127	134	125	90	134	116	139	132	86	134	155	158
02702	ASSONET	119	158	163	155	163	144	132	138	126	137	127	103	154	127	150	124	93	131	129	154
02703	ATTLEBORO	98	114	110	112	113	103	106	105	102	108	104	81	114	104	111	101	75	104	100	120
02713	CUTTYHUNK	68	54	88	53	60	72	54	69	57	51	56	50	47	54	59	61	37	64	68	80
02715	DIGHTON	106	148	150	138	152	130	122	127	116	122	118	94	143	118	139	117	87	122	119	139
02717	EAST FREETOWN	106	142	146	137	146	128	118	124	113	121	114	91	138	114	134	113	84	118	117	138
02718	EAST TAUNTON	110	129	113	126	124	111	115	114	109	119	111	90	123	114	119	106	79	110	104	131
02719	FAIRHAVEN	79	97	97	94	98	92	89	89	88	87	88	67	98	87	95	89	64	89	91	102
02720	FALL RIVER	70	72	71	72	72	70	78	72	78	74	79	56	79	77	77	79	56	77	76	85
02721	FALL RIVER	56	55	54	56	55	54	64	57	64	59	65	45	63	63	61	65	47	62	61	68
02723	FALL RIVER	54	53	53	53	53	51	62	55	62	57	64	44	61	61	59	64	46	60	58	65
02724	FALL RIVER	53	49	49	50	49	50	59	53	60	53	60	41	56	59	54	63	43	57	57	63
02725	SOMERSET	87	110	112	106	113	108	94	101	95	95	95	72	108	94	106	97	68	97	104	113
02726	SOMERSET	93	123	126	116	127	115	104	109	102	104	102	79	120	102	117	104	74	105	109	121
02738	MARION	148	183	190	184	190	173	161	168	154	168	155	126	181	152	179	151	111	161	160	190
02739	MATTAPOISETT	120	151	158	150	157	143	130	137	125	136	126	100	148	124	146	125	91	131	133	155
	MASSACHUSETTS	113	129	133	129	131	121	127	122	123	125	125	94	135	122	132	123	90	124	121	141
	UNITED STATES	100	100	100	100	100	100	100	100	100	100	100	100	100	100	100	100	100	100	100	100

ZIP CODE			POPULATION			2000-2009 ANNUAL RATE		HOUSEHOLDS					FAMILIES		
#	POST OFFICE NAME	COUNTY FIPS CODE	2000	2009	2014	% Rate	State Centile	2000	2009	2014	% Annual Rate 2000-2009	2009 Average HH Size	2000	2009	% Annual Rate 2000-2009
02740	NEW BEDFORD	005	43700	44383	44504	0.2	48	17907	18421	18551	0.3	2.33	10892	11123	0.2
02743	ACUSHNET	005	10103	10459	10576	0.4	65	3773	3951	4013	0.5	2.64	2821	2946	0.5
02744	NEW BEDFORD	005	11739	12270	12424	0.5	71	4748	5029	5120	0.6	2.44	3060	3205	0.5
02745	NEW BEDFORD	005	24065	24626	24755	0.2	48	9738	10110	10211	0.4	2.40	6564	6765	0.3
02746	NEW BEDFORD	005	14742	15154	15242	0.3	58	5980	6210	6277	0.4	2.42	3715	3826	0.3
02747	NORTH DARTMOUTH	005	19282	20191	20558	0.5	71	5948	6428	6599	0.8	2.68	4608	4948	0.8
02748	SOUTH DARTMOUTH	005	11210	11340	11329	0.1	41	4516	4618	4632	0.2	2.43	3139	3195	0.2
02760	NORTH ATTLEBORO	005	25218	25870	26013	0.3	58	9738	10060	10149	0.4	2.56	6677	6882	0.3
02762	PLAINVILLE	021	7686	8529	8840	1.1	93	3010	3367	3500	1.2	2.52	2041	2273	1.2
02763	ATTLEBORO FALLS	005	1948	2031	2055	0.5	71	658	693	705	0.6	2.93	554	579	0.5
02764	NORTH DIGHTON	005	3702	4106	4257	1.1	93	1337	1501	1563	1.3	2.72	1024	1145	1.2
02766	NORTON	005	18187	19424	19836	0.7	81	5910	6396	6569	0.9	2.79	4503	4847	0.8
02767	RAYNHAM	005	11540	13054	13602	1.3	95	4042	4637	4856	1.5	2.78	3145	3591	1.4
02769	REHOBOTH	005	9805	10872	11255	1.1	93	3400	3824	3979	1.3	2.84	2770	3101	1.2
02770	ROCHESTER	023	4393	4922	5122	1.2	94	1515	1717	1794	1.4	2.86	1244	1405	1.3
02771	SEEKONK	005	13782	13833	13796	0.0	32	5006	5090	5102	0.2	2.72	3986	4034	0.1
02777	SWANSEA	005	16069	16283	16314	0.1	41	5944	6097	6137	0.3	2.64	4585	4682	0.2
02779	BERKLEY	005	5742	6105	6234	0.7	81	1835	1971	2021	0.8	3.09	1559	1669	0.7
02780	TAUNTON	005	49425	49767	49681	0.1	41	19800	20156	20217	0.2	2.43	12731	12873	0.1
02790	WESTPORT	005	14629	15696	16085	0.8	84	5527	6005	6181	0.9	2.60	4183	4519	0.8
	MASSACHUSETTS					0.3					0.3	2.50			0.3
	UNITED STATES					1.0					1.1	2.59			0.9

ZIP CODE		RACE (%)								2009 AGE DISTRIBUTION (%)										MEDIAN AGE		
#	POST OFFICE NAME	White		Black		Asian/Pacific		% Hispanic Origin														
		2000	2009	2000	2009	2000	2009	2000	2009	0-4	5-9	10-14	15-19	20-24	25-44	45-64	65-84	85+	18+	2009	% 2009 Males	% 2009 Females
02740	NEW BEDFORD	72.8	68.8	6.1	6.9	0.8	1.1	10.2	13.5	6.6	6.1	5.7	6.4	7.6	26.8	24.5	13.0	3.2	77.7	37.6	47.6	52.4
02743	ACUSHNET	97.2	96.4	0.4	0.5	0.2	0.3	0.8	1.2	5.3	5.5	6.0	6.4	5.8	25.0	30.8	13.1	2.1	79.4	42.3	48.8	51.2
02744	NEW BEDFORD	81.4	77.1	3.4	4.0	0.4	0.6	11.3	15.3	7.9	7.2	6.3	6.7	8.2	29.4	21.6	10.7	2.1	74.7	33.4	49.5	50.5
02745	NEW BEDFORD	91.1	88.8	1.9	2.3	0.7	1.0	4.9	6.9	6.2	6.1	6.0	6.4	6.2	26.8	26.1	13.2	3.1	77.7	39.5	47.4	52.6
02746	NEW BEDFORD	75.3	70.4	4.1	4.6	0.6	0.8	17.6	22.9	8.9	7.8	6.9	7.0	8.2	28.6	20.8	9.6	2.1	72.2	31.7	48.1	51.9
02747	NORTH DARTMOUTH	87.6	85.9	1.4	1.7	1.4	2.2	1.9	2.8	4.9	5.1	5.4	10.2	10.6	25.2	26.2	10.5	1.9	81.2	36.4	50.5	49.5
02748	SOUTH DARTMOUTH	96.2	95.0	0.6	0.7	0.9	1.4	0.8	1.2	4.2	4.5	5.3	6.0	4.3	21.0	32.0	18.2	4.5	82.4	47.9	48.0	52.0
02760	NORTH ATTLEBORO	95.9	94.3	1.0	1.2	1.7	2.6	1.3	1.9	6.8	7.1	7.2	6.8	5.4	27.7	28.3	9.1	1.6	74.6	38.3	48.7	51.3
02762	PLAINVILLE	96.8	95.4	0.7	0.9	1.6	2.6	0.9	1.3	6.4	6.6	6.7	6.8	5.5	25.9	28.5	12.0	1.7	75.9	40.2	48.9	51.1
02763	ATTLEBORO FALLS	96.9	95.4	0.4	0.5	2.1	3.2	1.2	1.8	7.3	8.6	9.3	8.0	4.2	24.1	30.6	7.0	0.9	69.5	38.2	48.7	51.3
02764	NORTH DIGHTON	97.7	97.0	0.6	0.8	0.5	0.8	1.0	1.5	6.0	6.4	6.7	7.3	5.6	24.6	29.8	11.7	2.0	76.4	40.9	49.1	50.9
02766	NORTON	92.2	90.7	1.2	1.4	1.0	1.5	1.1	1.7	7.5	7.8	7.7	9.7	8.1	24.6	25.6	7.7	1.3	72.4	35.1	48.0	52.0
02767	RAYNHAM	96.5	95.5	1.0	1.3	0.7	1.1	0.8	1.2	6.5	6.7	7.0	6.6	5.2	25.3	28.7	12.0	2.1	75.6	40.3	48.0	52.0
02769	REHOBOTH	97.7	96.9	0.4	0.5	0.5	0.8	0.5	0.8	5.5	6.3	7.2	7.0	4.4	22.7	34.4	11.1	1.4	76.6	43.1	49.8	50.2
02770	ROCHESTER	96.7	95.5	0.6	0.9	0.4	0.6	0.4	0.5	5.7	6.2	7.0	7.3	5.1	24.6	33.7	9.1	1.2	76.3	41.1	50.4	49.6
02771	SEEKONK	96.5	95.3	0.6	0.7	1.0	1.5	0.8	1.2	5.7	6.4	6.8	6.8	5.2	24.3	31.4	11.6	1.8	76.7	41.6	48.6	51.4
02777	SWANSEA	97.9	97.2	0.4	0.5	0.4	0.6	0.6	0.9	4.9	5.1	5.5	6.4	5.3	24.9	30.9	14.3	2.7	80.3	43.6	49.1	50.9
02779	BERKLEY	96.7	95.4	0.6	0.7	0.4	0.6	1.0	1.4	7.5	8.1	8.6	7.6	4.2	28.4	28.2	6.7	0.7	70.6	36.7	49.3	50.7
02780	TAUNTON	91.2	88.9	2.9	3.6	0.6	1.0	4.3	6.0	7.0	6.7	6.5	6.5	6.0	28.7	25.6	10.8	2.3	75.9	37.7	48.1	51.9
02790	WESTPORT	97.9	97.2	0.2	0.2	0.5	0.8	0.7	1.0	5.0	5.2	5.8	6.4	5.0	25.8	30.8	13.9	2.1	79.9	43.1	48.7	51.3
	MASSACHUSETTS	84.5	81.0	5.4	6.0	3.8	5.4	6.8	8.7	6.1	6.2	6.3	7.1	7.1	26.5	27.1	11.3	2.3	77.4	38.6	48.4	51.6
	UNITED STATES	75.1	72.0	12.3	12.7	3.8	4.6	12.5	15.7	6.8	6.7	6.6	7.1	6.9	27.0	26.0	10.9	1.9	75.7	36.9	49.2	50.8

ZIP CODE #	POST OFFICE NAME	2009 Per Capita Income	2009 HH Income Base	2009 HOUSEHOLD INCOME DISTRIBUTION (%) Less than $25,000	$25,000 to $49,999	$50,000 to $99,999	$100,000 to $149,999	$150,000 or More	MEDIAN HOUSEHOLD INCOME 2009	2014	2009 National Centile	2009 State Centile	2009 Home Value Base	2009 HOME VALUE DISTRIBUTION (%) Less than $50,000	$50,000 to $89,999	$90,000 to $174,999	$175,000 to $399,999	$400,000 or More	2009 Median Home Value
02740	NEW BEDFORD	18867	18421	37.2	28.7	27.9	4.8	1.4	35268	38853	19	5	8316	1.0	1.9	45.4	48.9	2.7	177638
02743	ACUSHNET	27596	3951	15.1	20.0	45.8	14.0	5.1	65918	67667	84	41	3264	1.9	1.8	18.1	68.8	9.3	228229
02744	NEW BEDFORD	16573	5029	43.2	27.0	24.2	4.3	1.3	29701	32231	8	2	1988	0.2	0.6	39.1	58.2	1.8	186038
02745	NEW BEDFORD	23270	10110	26.5	26.2	36.6	7.8	2.8	47630	50536	56	13	5975	1.5	0.6	27.8	68.8	1.3	198501
02746	NEW BEDFORD	13996	6210	51.3	25.3	20.4	2.3	0.7	23905	25523	3	2	1636	0.0	1.4	42.8	55.1	0.7	181864
02747	NORTH DARTMOUTH	26717	6428	13.9	19.6	45.1	15.1	6.4	69429	71416	86	47	5204	0.4	0.1	10.9	71.7	16.9	257689
02748	SOUTH DARTMOUTH	33110	4618	18.6	21.4	35.8	13.4	10.8	63517	66490	82	35	3542	0.8	0.5	12.7	50.8	35.2	298871
02760	NORTH ATTLEBORO	33362	10060	11.1	20.8	37.9	20.3	10.0	76155	77267	90	58	6814	3.1	1.6	8.0	61.7	25.7	296364
02762	PLAINVILLE	35404	3367	12.7	16.4	36.7	23.2	11.0	78417	81706	91	63	2456	0.2	3.2	11.2	68.2	17.3	276818
02763	ATTLEBORO FALLS	34350	693	6.9	14.3	40.4	19.3	19.0	82501	83823	93	70	583	0.0	0.0	4.6	61.9	33.4	337742
02764	NORTH DIGHTON	31344	1501	9.9	17.7	41.5	22.1	8.9	78099	79068	91	62	1220	0.0	0.2	8.9	77.7	13.2	258978
02766	NORTON	31349	6396	9.2	16.2	38.0	26.0	10.7	82332	83259	93	69	5172	0.2	0.5	6.8	68.1	24.3	296722
02767	RAYNHAM	31036	4637	9.9	17.1	43.6	19.6	9.7	77816	78509	91	60	3797	1.7	3.3	8.2	60.3	26.6	289116
02769	REHOBOTH	35652	3824	8.4	13.0	39.5	23.8	15.3	83762	85723	93	71	3325	0.4	0.1	3.0	56.5	40.0	363868
02770	ROCHESTER	34086	1717	7.1	15.0	36.6	27.5	13.7	85549	93058	94	74	1570	0.0	0.0	4.3	69.0	26.6	316591
02771	SEEKONK	31442	5090	8.9	20.6	43.6	16.5	10.4	75041	75889	89	56	4354	0.0	0.2	6.1	77.1	16.6	276259
02777	SWANSEA	28227	6097	14.3	20.4	44.0	14.4	6.9	69232	71714	86	47	5076	0.4	0.2	13.0	77.3	9.2	235376
02779	BERKLEY	28557	1971	8.0	9.9	47.7	27.0	7.4	82688	83374	93	70	1805	0.0	0.0	10.5	74.8	14.6	282955
02780	TAUNTON	25333	20156	20.0	26.3	40.3	9.6	3.7	53824	57445	69	19	12007	0.4	2.2	19.6	72.2	5.7	232653
02790	WESTPORT	32102	6005	13.0	17.4	42.0	18.0	9.6	74169	75604	89	54	4877	0.4	0.1	8.8	63.7	27.1	285674
	MASSACHUSETTS	34904		17.4	19.0	33.1	18.1	12.4	68225	71891				0.7	1.2	13.3	53.8	31.0	297007
	UNITED STATES	27277		20.9	24.4	35.3	11.7	7.6	54719	56938				9.3	13.1	31.6	32.6	13.5	162279

ZIP CODE	FINANCIAL SERVICES				THE HOME						ENTERTAINMENT						PERSONAL			
					Home Improvements		Furnishings													
# POST OFFICE NAME	Auto Loan	Home Loan	Invest-ments	Retire-ment Plans	Home Repair	Lawn & Garden	Comput-ers & Hard-ware-Personal	Major Appli-ances	TV, Radio, Sound Equip-ment	Furni-ture	Dine out/ Carry out	Sports Equip-ment	Fees & Tickets	Toys & Games	Travel	Cable TV	Apparel & Services	Auto Repairs	Health Insur-ance	Pets & Supplies
02740 NEW BEDFORD	57	57	53	57	55	56	64	58	65	59	65	45	63	63	61	67	46	62	63	69
02743 ACUSHNET	90	117	117	111	119	110	100	105	99	100	100	77	115	100	112	101	72	102	105	117
02744 NEW BEDFORD	52	49	45	49	47	48	59	51	60	54	60	41	56	58	54	61	43	57	56	62
02745 NEW BEDFORD	75	78	77	77	78	80	79	78	80	75	80	59	81	80	79	83	57	79	82	91
02746 NEW BEDFORD	45	38	35	39	37	38	49	42	50	46	51	34	46	50	44	51	37	48	45	51
02747 NORTH DARTMOUTH	101	123	117	121	123	114	107	111	104	110	106	83	119	106	116	104	75	107	108	126
02748 SOUTH DARTMOUTH	102	126	132	125	131	125	110	117	110	114	110	85	125	107	124	112	79	113	121	133
02760 NORTH ATTLEBORO	110	132	129	132	132	120	121	119	117	122	118	93	134	118	129	115	86	118	114	137
02762 PLAINVILLE	115	140	145	134	144	132	125	129	122	126	122	95	138	121	136	123	88	126	127	146
02763 ATTLEBORO FALLS	129	166	165	171	168	149	141	144	133	149	135	113	164	136	156	128	99	137	129	164
02764 NORTH DIGHTON	105	144	144	136	147	127	119	123	113	120	115	92	139	116	135	113	85	118	115	136
02766 NORTON	121	149	139	147	147	132	129	130	123	133	125	102	144	126	139	120	90	126	121	149
02767 RAYNHAM	111	140	143	135	144	130	121	126	117	121	118	94	136	119	134	118	86	121	121	141
02769 REHOBOTH	128	169	175	169	174	155	140	147	134	147	135	110	165	135	160	131	99	139	137	166
02770 ROCHESTER	126	162	153	158	162	145	137	141	131	139	132	108	155	134	151	129	96	135	132	160
02771 SEEKONK	105	143	146	137	147	127	119	123	113	121	114	92	139	115	134	112	84	118	115	137
02777 SWANSEA	93	120	119	115	122	115	102	108	102	102	102	78	117	102	114	104	74	104	110	121
02779 BERKLEY	119	149	131	149	144	129	125	127	117	132	120	101	141	123	135	113	86	121	114	146
02780 TAUNTON	80	91	86	89	89	83	89	85	86	87	88	67	94	87	91	86	63	87	84	98
02790 WESTPORT	102	139	144	132	144	123	118	121	111	119	112	91	136	112	133	110	83	116	112	134
MASSACHUSETTS	113	129	133	129	131	121	127	122	123	125	125	94	135	122	132	123	90	124	121	141
UNITED STATES	100	100	100	100	100	100	100	100	100	100	100	100	100	100	100	100	100	100	100	100

ZIP CODE #	POST OFFICE NAME	COUNTY FIPS CODE	POPULATION 2000	POPULATION 2009	POPULATION 2014	2000-2009 ANNUAL RATE % Rate	2000-2009 ANNUAL RATE State Centile	HOUSEHOLDS 2000	HOUSEHOLDS 2009	HOUSEHOLDS 2014	HOUSEHOLDS % Annual Rate 2000-2009	HOUSEHOLDS 2009 Average HH Size	FAMILIES 2000	FAMILIES 2009	FAMILIES % Annual Rate 2000-2009
48001	ALGONAC	147	13282	13632	13610	0.3	54	5263	5561	5598	0.6	2.45	3695	3852	0.5
48002	ALLENTON	147	3162	3321	3353	0.5	66	1050	1141	1165	0.9	2.91	873	941	0.8
48003	ALMONT	087	5581	6474	6828	1.6	94	1947	2341	2501	2.0	2.76	1555	1851	1.9
48005	ARMADA	099	5255	5384	5429	0.3	54	1720	1795	1826	0.5	2.93	1418	1462	0.3
48006	AVOCA	147	3782	4315	4528	1.4	92	1297	1520	1607	1.7	2.83	1076	1248	1.6
48009	BIRMINGHAM	125	19263	18684	18385	-0.3	21	9120	9055	8979	-0.1	2.06	5077	4926	-0.3
48014	CAPAC	147	3767	4113	4228	1.0	84	1292	1439	1489	1.2	2.86	1012	1113	1.0
48015	CENTER LINE	099	8531	8366	8279	-0.2	25	3821	3812	3803	0.0	2.14	2074	2002	-0.4
48017	CLAWSON	125	12817	12448	12240	-0.3	21	5624	5620	5572	0.0	2.19	3281	3203	-0.3
48021	EASTPOINTE	099	33435	32786	32462	-0.2	25	13244	13209	13189	0.0	2.48	8744	8506	-0.3
48022	EMMETT	147	2506	2893	3046	1.6	94	820	977	1040	1.9	2.96	683	807	1.8
48023	FAIR HAVEN	147	6966	6794	6756	-0.3	21	2677	2649	2649	-0.1	2.56	1833	1778	-0.3
48025	FRANKLIN	125	14750	14583	14446	-0.1	32	5733	5766	5748	0.1	2.50	4299	4271	-0.1
48026	FRASER	099	15297	15548	15565	0.2	48	6062	6212	6263	0.3	2.47	4124	4126	0.0
48027	GOODELLS	147	2963	3367	3534	1.4	92	1018	1196	1267	1.8	2.79	829	964	1.6
48028	HARSENS ISLAND	147	1284	1230	1210	-0.5	12	594	588	585	-0.1	2.09	397	386	-0.3
48030	HAZEL PARK	125	18963	18137	17790	-0.5	12	7284	7147	7066	-0.2	2.54	4669	4491	-0.4
48032	JEDDO	147	1966	2194	2276	1.2	88	666	760	795	1.4	2.86	541	612	1.3
48033	SOUTHFIELD	125	17339	16698	16423	-0.4	16	8253	8074	7983	-0.2	2.06	4334	4138	-0.5
48034	SOUTHFIELD	125	14096	14775	14883	0.5	66	7094	7406	7481	0.5	1.99	3315	3342	0.1
48035	CLINTON TOWNSHIP	099	34166	35041	35193	0.3	54	13746	14388	14583	0.5	2.42	9123	9310	0.2
48036	CLINTON TOWNSHIP	099	22140	22158	22015	0.0	37	9471	9637	9653	0.2	2.26	6062	6017	-0.1
48038	CLINTON TOWNSHIP	099	39495	41199	41931	0.5	66	17138	18261	18775	0.7	2.25	10406	10771	0.4
48039	MARINE CITY	147	8335	8570	8510	0.3	54	3192	3368	3369	0.6	2.54	2233	2326	0.4
48040	MARYSVILLE	147	9684	10195	10353	0.6	71	4025	4352	4444	0.8	2.34	2741	2924	0.7
48041	MEMPHIS	147	4181	4506	4653	0.8	80	1477	1643	1713	1.2	2.72	1179	1294	1.0
48042	MACOMB	099	16063	24595	28177	4.7	100	5408	8315	9572	4.8	2.95	4620	7082	4.7
48043	MOUNT CLEMENS	099	17347	17061	16892	-0.2	25	7085	7086	7069	0.0	2.17	3861	3736	-0.4
48044	MACOMB	099	34507	48290	53919	3.7	100	11569	16156	18103	3.7	2.99	9460	13171	3.6
48045	HARRISON TOWNSHIP	099	24370	25731	26216	0.6	71	10687	11472	11780	0.8	2.24	6407	6682	0.5
48047	NEW BALTIMORE	099	31219	38794	41996	2.4	98	11627	14666	15995	2.5	2.62	8438	10399	2.3
48048	NEW HAVEN	099	6700	8171	8782	2.2	98	1940	2517	2767	2.9	2.73	1453	1845	2.6
48049	NORTH STREET	147	5517	5801	5889	0.5	66	1931	2104	2157	0.9	2.74	1591	1716	0.8
48050	NEW HAVEN	099	1702	1784	1799	0.5	66	561	600	612	0.7	2.91	484	512	0.6
48051	NEW BALTIMORE	099	13499	17082	18480	2.6	99	4631	5821	6303	2.5	2.93	3617	4487	2.4
48054	EAST CHINA	147	6932	7614	7866	1.0	84	2558	2885	3009	1.3	2.57	1943	2173	1.2
48059	FORT GRATIOT	147	14583	15926	16345	1.0	84	5667	6336	6561	1.2	2.46	4057	4476	1.1
48060	PORT HURON	147	41033	42665	42789	0.4	60	16300	17267	17451	0.6	2.40	10506	10995	0.5
48062	RICHMOND	099	8302	9367	9851	1.3	90	2993	3451	3669	1.6	2.64	2172	2459	1.4
48063	COLUMBUS	147	4615	4700	4630	0.2	48	1533	1603	1592	0.5	2.92	1267	1313	0.4
48064	CASCO	147	4748	4720	4676	-0.1	32	1635	1680	1681	0.3	2.81	1294	1317	0.2
48065	ROMEO	099	10127	10859	11151	0.8	80	3647	3951	4077	0.9	2.72	2789	2998	0.8
48066	ROSEVILLE	099	48638	47884	47526	-0.2	25	20279	20362	20391	0.0	2.34	12907	12630	-0.2
48067	ROYAL OAK	125	25289	24759	24498	-0.2	25	12224	12337	12324	0.1	1.99	5806	5706	-0.2
48069	PLEASANT RIDGE	125	2514	2427	2391	-0.4	16	1079	1072	1065	-0.1	2.26	686	669	-0.3
48070	HUNTINGTON WOODS	125	6173	5974	5872	-0.4	16	2388	2375	2353	-0.1	2.51	1806	1771	-0.2
48071	MADISON HEIGHTS	125	31101	30346	29832	-0.3	21	13299	13239	13108	0.0	2.28	8001	7807	-0.3
48072	BERKLEY	125	15529	15063	14760	-0.3	21	6678	6665	6591	0.0	2.26	4018	3929	-0.2
48073	ROYAL OAK	125	34706	33631	33069	-0.3	21	16615	16554	16411	0.0	2.01	8628	8389	-0.3
48074	SMITHS CREEK	147	8685	9559	9800	1.0	84	3137	3575	3705	1.4	2.65	2397	2697	1.3
48075	SOUTHFIELD	125	22508	23332	23473	0.4	60	9289	9726	9823	0.5	2.34	5845	5981	0.2
48076	SOUTHFIELD	125	28647	27800	27297	-0.3	21	10989	10933	10823	-0.1	2.49	7503	7325	-0.3
48079	SAINT CLAIR	147	12257	13079	13344	0.7	76	4602	4995	5130	0.9	2.61	3451	3710	0.8
48080	SAINT CLAIR SHORES	099	23525	23193	22997	-0.2	25	10862	10908	10908	0.0	2.11	6211	6049	-0.3
48081	SAINT CLAIR SHORES	099	22005	21889	21713	-0.1	32	9108	9234	9242	0.1	2.34	6147	6086	-0.1
48082	SAINT CLAIR SHORES	099	17517	17437	17305	0.0	37	7445	7561	7572	0.2	2.30	4916	4873	-0.1
48083	TROY	125	22259	23062	23137	0.4	60	8971	9496	9602	0.6	2.43	5744	5969	0.4
48084	TROY	125	13763	14280	14081	0.4	60	6179	6541	6491	0.6	2.17	3475	3588	0.3
48085	TROY	125	24310	24644	24616	0.1	42	7968	8312	8378	0.5	2.96	6900	7143	0.4
48088	WARREN	099	23658	23273	23025	-0.2	25	9539	9563	9544	0.0	2.42	6877	6768	-0.2
48089	WARREN	099	34313	33394	33187	-0.3	21	12816	12728	12765	-0.1	2.59	8582	8310	-0.3
48091	WARREN	099	32168	31273	30916	-0.3	21	12955	12824	12785	-0.1	2.44	8197	7898	-0.4
48092	WARREN	099	25345	25608	25675	0.1	42	10081	10348	10455	0.3	2.46	7014	7050	0.1
48093	WARREN	099	22896	22527	22361	-0.2	25	10208	10211	10212	0.0	2.16	6077	5913	-0.3
48094	WASHINGTON	099	12938	16757	18373	2.8	99	4762	6275	6939	3.0	2.67	3660	4737	2.8
48095	WASHINGTON	099	3805	4800	5233	2.5	98	1270	1643	1809	2.8	2.90	1091	1397	2.7
48096	RAY	099	3731	3829	3845	0.3	54	1300	1361	1378	0.5	2.79	1058	1092	0.3
48097	YALE	147	5276	5637	5696	0.7	76	1823	1976	2009	0.9	2.78	1402	1502	0.7
48098	TROY	125	20633	20520	20347	-0.1	32	6902	7036	7035	0.2	2.90	5751	5822	0.1
48101	ALLEN PARK	163	29401	28191	27363	-0.5	12	11982	11549	11216	-0.4	2.42	8206	7792	-0.6
48103	ANN ARBOR	161	50158	53769	55377	0.8	80	21542	23370	24184	0.9	2.29	12711	13464	0.6
48104	ANN ARBOR	161	40003	41263	41651	0.3	54	15170	15881	16146	0.5	2.22	5316	5328	0.0
48105	ANN ARBOR	161	31570	34368	35567	0.9	82	13271	14680	15300	1.1	2.28	7875	8427	0.7
48108	ANN ARBOR	161	23870	26385	27557	1.1	86	10021	11148	11679	1.2	2.31	5932	6414	0.8
48109	ANN ARBOR	161	6706	6833	6830	0.2	48	615	611	610	-0.1	1.81	134	124	-0.8
48111	BELLEVILLE	163	39081	40873	40825	0.5	66	15714	16461	16415	0.5	2.48	10235	10665	0.4
48114	BRIGHTON	093	19902	22352	23361	1.3	90	6877	7987	8431	1.6	2.79	5660	6491	1.5
48116	BRIGHTON	093	24369	28676	30539	1.8	96	9315	11222	12025	2.0	2.54	6849	8195	2.0
48117	CARLETON	115	9866	10619	10915	0.8	80	3566	3991	4146	1.2	2.66	2746	3042	1.1
48118	CHELSEA	161	11678	13221	13870	1.4	92	4243	4991	5311	1.8	2.51	3111	3544	1.4
48120	DEARBORN	163	7480	7785	7690	0.4	60	2643	2628	2579	-0.1	2.96	1466	1446	-0.1
48122	MELVINDALE	163	10710	10435	10170	-0.3	21	4491	4378	4265	-0.3	2.38	2690	2583	-0.4
48124	DEARBORN	163	33180	31923	30971	-0.4	16	14169	13687	13290	-0.4	2.32	9004	8562	-0.5
48125	DEARBORN HEIGHTS	163	23274	22454	21793	-0.4	16	9088	8823	8575	-0.3	2.52	6310	6041	-0.5
48126	DEARBORN	163	46808	46245	44886	-0.1	32	15763	14993	14510	-0.5	3.07	10465	9757	-0.8
48127	DEARBORN HEIGHTS	163	35600	34406	33442	-0.4	16	14400	13925	13535	-0.4	2.44	9614	9159	-0.5
48128	DEARBORN	163	10371	10006	9713	-0.4	16	4204	4076	3960	-0.3	2.45	2926	2799	-0.5
48130	DEXTER	161	10501	13170	14240	2.5	98	3824	4864	5286	2.6	2.70	3005	3754	2.4
48131	DUNDEE	115	6469	7103	7318	1.0	84	2419	2702	2805	1.2	2.62	1757	1941	1.1
48133	ERIE	115	5311	5442	5460	0.3	54	1944	2072	2106	0.7	2.62	1472	1548	0.5
48134	FLAT ROCK	163	16750	19483	19961	1.6	94	6122	7107	7274	1.6	2.73	4557	5229	1.5
48135	GARDEN CITY	163	30047	28821	27952	-0.4	16	11479	11080	10760	-0.4	2.60	8234	7848	-0.5
48137	GREGORY	093	4327	5182	5618	2.0	97	1541	1910	2085	2.3	2.68	1183	1449	2.2
48138	GROSSE ILE	163	10894	10755	10548	-0.1	32	4122	4097	4026	-0.1	2.62	3295	3246	-0.2
48140	IDA	115	3272	3480	3563	0.7	76	1087	1191	1233	1.0	2.90	917	997	0.9
	MICHIGAN					0.3					0.4	2.52			0.3
	UNITED STATES					1.0					1.1	2.59			0.9

POPULATION COMPOSITION

ZIP CODE #	POST OFFICE NAME	RACE (%) White 2000	White 2009	Black 2000	Black 2009	Asian/Pacific 2000	Asian/Pacific 2009	% Hispanic Origin 2000	% Hispanic Origin 2009	2009 AGE DISTRIBUTION (%) 0-4	5-9	10-14	15-19	20-24	25-44	45-64	65-84	85+	18+	MEDIAN AGE 2009	% 2009 Males	% 2009 Females
48001	ALGONAC	97.7	97.3	0.2	0.2	0.2	0.2	1.0	1.3	5.8	5.9	6.2	6.6	5.1	25.7	30.4	12.6	1.8	78.1	41.6	50.1	49.9
48002	ALLENTON	97.2	96.5	0.9	1.0	0.3	0.4	2.8	3.7	7.0	7.6	7.9	7.0	4.4	27.3	30.1	7.6	1.0	73.0	38.5	50.8	49.2
48003	ALMONT	96.6	95.6	0.2	0.2	0.3	0.5	3.2	4.3	6.9	7.3	7.6	7.9	5.3	27.0	28.0	8.7	1.2	73.1	37.5	50.1	49.9
48005	ARMADA	98.1	97.6	0.1	0.1	0.1	0.2	1.5	2.0	6.4	7.3	7.7	7.1	4.7	25.9	30.1	9.3	1.5	74.1	39.0	50.8	49.2
48006	AVOCA	97.4	96.8	0.5	0.5	0.2	0.3	1.2	1.7	6.9	7.2	7.7	7.2	4.5	25.9	29.8	9.9	1.0	73.5	39.4	50.9	49.1
48009	BIRMINGHAM	96.1	94.5	0.9	1.2	1.5	2.5	1.2	1.6	6.2	6.3	6.8	5.1	4.0	26.7	30.5	12.0	2.3	77.4	42.0	48.4	51.6
48014	CAPAC	93.9	92.3	0.2	0.2	0.3	0.5	9.8	12.7	7.5	7.5	7.4	8.0	6.3	27.3	26.8	8.1	1.1	72.6	34.9	51.1	48.9
48015	CENTER LINE	93.8	92.3	3.1	3.6	1.0	1.6	1.5	1.9	6.3	6.0	5.5	5.4	5.8	25.0	25.7	15.4	4.8	78.9	42.0	45.8	54.2
48017	CLAWSON	96.1	94.6	0.8	1.1	1.3	2.2	1.1	1.6	5.3	5.4	5.9	5.6	4.7	30.2	27.3	12.9	2.6	79.9	40.6	48.6	51.4
48021	EASTPOINTE	92.1	90.4	4.8	5.5	0.9	1.4	1.3	1.7	6.3	6.4	6.4	6.4	5.6	27.9	27.2	11.2	2.7	76.9	39.2	49.0	51.0
48022	EMMETT	98.2	97.7	0.2	0.3	0.4	0.5	1.5	2.0	8.0	8.3	8.4	6.9	4.6	25.9	28.5	8.7	0.8	71.0	37.2	50.6	49.4
48023	FAIR HAVEN	96.9	96.3	0.8	1.0	0.3	0.4	1.3	1.6	7.4	7.3	7.4	6.8	6.0	28.1	27.1	8.9	1.1	73.7	37.1	50.4	49.6
48025	FRANKLIN	92.3	89.4	3.8	4.9	2.2	3.5	1.2	1.6	5.4	6.3	7.6	6.9	3.9	17.6	33.5	15.6	3.2	75.9	46.2	48.8	51.2
48026	FRASER	96.7	95.7	0.9	1.1	0.9	1.5	1.3	1.8	5.6	5.8	6.1	6.6	5.6	25.7	28.7	13.0	3.0	78.5	41.2	47.0	53.0
48027	GOODELLS	95.8	95.2	3.2	3.5	0.1	0.1	1.1	1.5	5.9	7.1	7.7	7.7	4.7	27.0	29.8	8.9	1.2	74.5	39.2	51.4	48.6
48028	HARSENS ISLAND	98.0	97.6	0.2	0.2	0.1	0.2	0.2	0.3	2.4	2.8	3.2	3.5	2.9	13.7	40.8	27.7	3.0	89.7	57.2	51.1	48.9
48030	HAZEL PARK	91.6	89.0	1.6	2.1	1.8	3.0	2.1	2.8	7.2	7.0	6.7	7.1	6.9	29.9	24.7	8.9	1.6	74.8	35.1	49.8	50.2
48032	JEDDO	98.0	97.5	0.2	0.1	0.2	0.2	2.1	2.8	6.2	6.5	7.0	7.8	5.6	26.4	30.7	8.8	1.0	75.3	39.4	51.5	48.5
48033	SOUTHFIELD	38.5	32.5	55.3	60.4	2.3	3.1	1.4	1.5	5.2	4.9	5.0	5.1	6.2	28.4	28.5	13.2	3.6	81.8	41.4	45.2	54.8
48034	SOUTHFIELD	39.4	32.1	48.9	53.7	6.6	9.0	1.4	1.5	5.5	4.6	4.4	5.2	9.7	32.9	22.8	11.2	3.6	82.6	36.9	46.8	53.2
48035	CLINTON TOWNSHIP	87.8	84.8	7.0	8.1	2.3	3.6	1.5	2.0	6.6	6.2	6.2	6.3	6.1	28.7	26.1	11.8	2.0	77.2	38.0	48.5	51.5
48036	CLINTON TOWNSHIP	89.4	87.3	6.8	7.7	1.0	1.6	1.5	1.9	5.9	5.8	5.7	5.5	5.0	25.5	28.3	15.6	2.7	79.2	42.5	47.8	52.2
48038	CLINTON TOWNSHIP	95.0	93.3	1.4	1.7	1.6	2.5	2.0	2.7	5.4	5.3	5.5	5.8	6.0	29.3	27.5	12.5	2.7	80.4	39.7	48.3	51.7
48039	MARINE CITY	97.9	97.4	0.1	0.1	0.3	0.4	1.1	1.5	6.5	6.3	6.4	7.3	6.7	26.2	28.0	10.8	1.7	76.4	38.1	48.8	51.2
48040	MARYSVILLE	98.2	97.7	0.2	0.2	0.4	0.7	1.2	1.6	5.6	5.9	6.2	6.6	5.2	24.5	29.1	14.2	2.8	78.2	42.2	48.6	51.4
48041	MEMPHIS	97.4	96.8	0.7	0.8	0.2	0.3	1.6	2.1	6.9	7.5	8.1	7.2	4.3	27.0	28.8	9.0	1.1	73.0	38.7	51.2	48.8
48042	MACOMB	96.7	95.4	0.7	0.8	1.1	1.9	1.4	2.0	9.3	9.4	8.7	6.4	3.4	30.1	23.6	8.4	0.8	68.5	35.9	49.3	50.7
48043	MOUNT CLEMENS	75.9	73.1	19.5	21.4	0.5	0.8	2.3	2.9	6.1	5.9	5.8	6.4	6.5	30.2	26.0	11.0	2.1	78.3	38.3	52.2	47.8
48044	MACOMB	95.8	94.3	0.9	1.1	1.6	2.5	1.5	1.9	9.2	9.1	8.7	6.8	4.4	31.0	24.3	6.0	0.7	68.8	34.5	50.0	50.0
48045	HARRISON TOWNSHIP	94.5	93.4	2.5	2.8	0.6	1.0	1.5	1.9	5.8	5.7	5.7	5.5	6.2	27.6	30.6	11.5	1.4	79.6	40.6	50.1	49.9
48047	NEW BALTIMORE	94.4	93.6	2.4	2.5	0.7	1.0	2.3	2.9	7.9	7.5	7.3	6.5	5.3	30.7	26.1	7.5	1.2	73.2	35.8	49.6	50.4
48048	NEW HAVEN	74.1	69.3	20.6	24.2	0.3	0.5	3.5	4.5	7.3	7.0	6.6	6.2	7.0	34.7	24.0	6.7	0.6	75.5	34.4	57.2	42.8
48049	NORTH STREET	97.8	97.2	0.3	0.3	0.4	0.6	1.3	1.7	5.8	6.3	7.0	6.7	4.4	24.9	32.6	11.1	1.2	76.4	41.5	50.3	49.7
48050	NEW HAVEN	97.9	97.5	0.9	1.1	0.1	0.2	0.4	0.6	6.8	7.2	7.6	6.9	4.3	25.4	30.2	10.8	0.8	73.7	40.7	52.0	48.0
48051	NEW BALTIMORE	93.1	90.6	2.9	4.0	0.9	1.3	2.3	3.1	9.8	9.3	8.6	7.5	6.2	30.4	22.9	4.8	0.5	67.6	31.2	48.6	51.4
48054	EAST CHINA	98.4	98.0	0.3	0.3	0.2	0.4	0.8	1.1	4.9	5.4	6.1	6.8	4.6	22.9	32.3	14.1	3.1	79.2	44.6	49.2	50.8
48059	FORT GRATIOT	95.9	94.7	1.1	1.3	1.1	1.8	1.8	2.3	6.1	6.2	6.4	6.3	5.0	25.8	28.9	12.9	2.4	77.3	40.9	47.6	52.4
48060	PORT HURON	88.2	86.2	6.8	7.7	0.5	0.8	3.9	5.1	7.5	7.1	6.7	6.8	7.0	26.9	24.6	11.0	2.4	74.6	36.0	48.4	51.6
48062	RICHMOND	96.0	95.0	0.5	0.6	0.7	1.1	3.2	3.9	6.2	6.4	6.6	6.8	5.3	26.9	28.1	11.2	2.4	76.4	39.2	49.4	50.6
48063	COLUMBUS	97.0	96.3	0.1	0.1	0.4	0.6	2.3	3.1	7.3	8.6	8.4	7.8	4.5	27.6	27.2	8.1	0.6	70.6	36.4	52.4	47.6
48064	CASCO	96.6	95.9	0.5	0.6	0.3	0.4	0.9	1.2	7.1	7.3	7.5	6.9	5.0	26.7	29.4	9.2	0.7	73.8	37.9	50.3	49.7
48065	ROMEO	95.7	94.9	1.9	2.1	0.5	0.8	2.0	2.5	6.8	7.2	7.5	7.5	5.5	25.7	29.7	8.8	1.3	73.6	38.3	49.8	50.2
48066	ROSEVILLE	93.5	91.8	2.6	3.0	1.7	2.6	1.5	1.9	6.4	6.4	6.3	6.0	5.6	28.7	26.2	12.1	2.3	77.3	38.9	48.5	51.5
48067	ROYAL OAK	95.6	94.0	1.1	1.5	1.1	1.8	1.5	2.0	5.0	4.4	4.3	4.6	6.7	36.6	25.7	10.4	2.4	83.6	38.5	49.6	50.4
48069	PLEASANT RIDGE	96.5	95.2	0.9	1.2	1.0	1.5	1.8	2.5	5.6	5.6	6.6	5.7	3.1	25.9	34.6	11.1	1.9	78.3	43.7	50.4	49.6
48070	HUNTINGTON WOODS	97.0	95.5	0.7	0.9	1.4	2.4	0.9	1.2	6.4	7.7	9.1	6.8	3.3	20.3	33.9	10.2	2.4	72.3	43.2	49.1	50.9
48071	MADISON HEIGHTS	89.6	85.9	1.8	2.2	5.0	7.7	1.6	2.1	6.0	5.7	5.7	5.6	5.8	30.4	26.0	12.4	2.1	79.1	39.0	48.9	51.1
48072	BERKLEY	96.1	94.7	0.7	0.9	1.0	1.7	1.3	1.8	6.5	6.2	6.2	5.6	5.6	32.3	25.7	9.7	2.2	77.6	38.2	48.7	51.3
48073	ROYAL OAK	94.2	92.1	1.8	2.4	2.0	3.2	1.2	1.6	5.1	4.7	4.8	4.5	6.0	31.5	28.1	12.2	3.0	82.6	41.0	48.6	51.4
48074	SMITHS CREEK	96.8	96.2	0.9	1.0	0.2	0.3	1.6	2.1	6.7	6.8	6.9	6.3	5.3	28.5	28.6	9.7	1.2	75.4	38.6	50.5	49.5
48075	SOUTHFIELD	23.7	20.1	71.6	74.7	1.7	2.3	1.1	1.2	5.2	5.2	5.8	6.4	6.6	25.0	29.5	13.7	2.6	80.1	41.7	46.2	53.8
48076	SOUTHFIELD	52.0	45.0	41.7	47.3	2.6	3.8	1.1	1.3	5.5	5.7	6.2	6.4	5.4	25.2	30.2	12.4	3.0	78.4	42.0	46.9	53.1
48079	SAINT CLAIR	97.8	97.2	0.2	0.2	0.6	0.9	1.1	1.5	6.5	6.7	7.2	7.4	5.7	24.2	29.4	11.1	1.8	74.9	39.7	48.7	51.3
48080	SAINT CLAIR SHORES	96.2	95.0	0.8	1.0	1.4	2.3	1.2	1.7	4.9	5.1	5.4	5.1	4.4	24.5	28.3	17.4	4.8	81.4	45.3	46.7	53.3
48081	SAINT CLAIR SHORES	97.7	97.0	0.3	0.4	0.6	1.0	1.0	1.3	4.6	5.1	5.7	5.7	4.2	23.2	31.0	16.9	3.7	81.0	45.9	48.3	51.7
48082	SAINT CLAIR SHORES	96.6	95.8	1.0	1.2	0.5	0.8	1.4	1.8	5.1	5.4	5.8	5.8	4.5	24.7	28.8	17.0	2.9	80.1	44.1	48.5	51.5
48083	TROY	81.3	73.8	2.2	2.6	13.4	20.1	1.8	2.3	6.9	6.5	6.7	5.8	5.2	29.3	26.0	11.3	2.3	76.3	38.5	48.6	51.4
48084	TROY	80.5	70.3	2.4	3.3	14.9	22.2	1.8	4.3	5.2	5.6	6.1	5.7	7.0	29.4	28.4	10.8	1.8	79.3	39.2	50.5	49.5
48085	TROY	84.8	77.9	1.7	2.1	11.4	17.4	1.3	1.6	5.8	6.8	7.9	7.6	3.9	22.6	33.0	11.3	1.0	74.3	41.9	50.0	50.0
48088	WARREN	95.5	94.0	1.0	1.1	1.9	3.0	1.0	1.3	5.2	5.4	5.7	5.5	4.5	24.3	27.0	19.4	3.1	80.2	44.6	48.1	51.9
48089	WARREN	90.8	88.2	2.7	3.1	2.9	4.6	1.7	2.1	7.9	7.6	7.2	6.9	6.3	29.4	22.9	9.8	2.0	73.1	35.2	49.8	50.2
48091	WARREN	88.2	85.1	4.4	4.9	3.5	5.4	1.6	2.0	6.7	6.5	6.4	6.4	6.1	27.8	25.8	12.1	2.2	76.4	38.2	49.9	50.1
48092	WARREN	89.9	86.7	2.6	2.8	4.6	7.1	1.2	1.5	5.9	6.0	6.2	5.7	5.0	26.3	26.8	15.7	2.4	78.4	41.7	49.6	50.4
48093	WARREN	93.5	91.3	2.0	2.3	2.6	4.1	1.1	1.5	4.9	5.0	5.2	5.1	4.4	23.5	27.0	19.6	5.2	81.8	46.2	46.1	53.9
48094	WASHINGTON	97.4	96.6	0.3	0.4	0.6	1.0	2.3	3.2	6.6	7.1	7.5	6.6	4.5	25.7	30.3	10.9	0.8	74.6	40.1	49.9	50.1
48095	WASHINGTON	97.8	97.1	0.1	0.1	0.7	1.0	2.7	3.8	6.4	7.3	8.0	7.7	4.3	23.9	31.0	10.6	0.8	73.0	40.4	50.5	49.5
48096	RAY	97.8	97.1	0.2	0.2	0.4	0.6	1.2	1.6	5.8	6.6	7.1	6.6	4.2	23.9	32.9	11.7	1.1	76.1	42.3	51.2	48.8
48097	YALE	97.3	96.4	0.5	0.6	0.1	0.2	1.9	2.6	7.9	7.8	7.6	7.1	5.4	26.3	25.2	10.0	2.6	72.3	36.4	48.8	51.2
48098	TROY	81.6	73.7	2.3	2.8	14.2	21.4	1.1	1.4	4.9	6.4	8.2	8.3	4.1	19.4	36.6	11.0	1.2	74.8	44.1	49.0	51.0
48101	ALLEN PARK	95.6	92.8	0.7	1.6	0.8	1.4	4.7	7.1	5.3	5.5	5.9	6.2	4.8	23.9	29.6	14.7	4.0	79.4	43.9	48.0	52.0
48103	ANN ARBOR	83.8	78.4	7.2	8.3	5.5	9.0	2.6	3.4	6.2	5.8	5.9	5.8	7.3	29.3	28.5	9.4	1.8	78.4	38.1	48.7	51.3
48104	ANN ARBOR	81.3	74.7	5.4	6.0	9.2	14.4	3.6	4.6	2.8	2.5	2.6	12.4	35.6	21.9	15.3	5.9	1.0	90.3	24.2	50.5	49.5
48105	ANN ARBOR	67.9	58.9	7.6	7.9	20.3	28.7	2.8	3.2	6.7	5.7	5.3	5.9	10.1	31.9	23.7	9.1	1.7	79.3	34.2	50.1	49.9
48108	ANN ARBOR	68.5	61.9	15.5	16.2	10.2	15.6	3.7	4.4	7.0	6.4	6.2	6.0	9.3	33.8	23.7	6.7	0.9	76.8	33.1	49.6	50.4
48109	ANN ARBOR	63.8	53.6	10.5	10.8	20.4	29.8	3.9	4.6	0.4	0.2	0.4	61.4	25.1	9.4	2.1	0.8	0.2	98.4	19.0	51.1	48.9
48111	BELLEVILLE	84.3	73.8	11.1	20.5	1.3	1.8	2.1	2.8	7.1	6.7	6.6	6.6	7.6	30.2	26.4	8.0	0.9	75.7	34.9	50.1	49.9
48114	BRIGHTON	97.5	96.5	0.4	0.6	0.8	1.3	1.0	1.3	6.7	7.6	8.4	7.4	4.3	23.9	31.5	9.4	0.8	72.4	39.8	50.5	49.5
48116	BRIGHTON	96.8	96.1	0.5	0.5	0.8	1.4	1.4	1.8	6.8	7.4	7.5	7.0	4.6	25.6	30.0	9.5	1.5	73.7	39.3	49.8	50.2
48117	CARLETON	95.6	94.8	1.9	2.2	0.3	0.4	1.5	2.0	6.1	6.4	6.9	7.4	5.6	25.4	31.3	9.7	1.1	76.1	39.5	50.6	49.4
48118	CHELSEA	95.8	94.6	1.8	2.1	0.5	0.8	1.5	2.0	4.7	5.1	6.1	8.1	6.2	21.8	31.8	12.4	3.8	79.3	43.6	50.0	50.0
48120	DEARBORN	75.5	65.2	2.9	5.4	3.9	5.9	1.9	2.4	9.7	8.2	7.5	8.8	8.8	24.0	20.2	9.3	3.5	69.2	29.3	55.4	44.6
48122	MELVINDALE	87.4	80.0	5.2	9.8	1.3	2.1	8.9	12.5	6.8	6.5	6.3	6.3	6.2	27.8	26.7	11.5	1.8	76.8	38.1	49.0	51.0
48124	DEARBORN	95.5	92.5	1.0	2.0	1.3	2.2	2.9	4.4	5.6	6.0	6.4	5.9	4.5	25.2	29.4	13.5	3.5	78.3	42.7	48.3	51.7
48125	DEARBORN HEIGHTS	92.9	89.4	2.6	3.9	1.1	1.9	4.0	6.0	6.5	6.5	6.6	6.1	5.2	28.2	26.3	12.8	2.0	76.7	39.1	48.8	51.2
48126	DEARBORN	80.3	72.5	1.4	3.0	1.4	2.2	3.2	4.4	10.6	9.2	7.7	7.3	7.3	27.0	18.4	9.6	2.9	68.1	30.1	50.5	49.5
48127	DEARBORN HEIGHTS	90.0	84.1	2.7	5.3	2.9	4.6	3.0	4.3	6.2	6.3	6.6	6.1	4.4	24.8	26.0	16.1	3.5	77.0	41.9	47.9	52.1
48128	DEARBORN	96.6	94.5	0.4	0.9	0.9	1.5	3.4	5.2	6.0	6.8	7.4	6.3	4.1	24.6	30.7	10.8	3.4	75.6	42.1	48.9	51.1
48130	DEXTER	97.3	96.1	0.4	0.5	0.9	1.6	1.1	1.6	6.1	6.8	7.6	7.4	5.3	22.4	33.9	9.5	1.0	74.5	41.3	50.3	49.7
48131	DUNDEE	97.2	96.5	0.5	0.6	0.3	0.5	1.4	1.9	7.4	7.4	7.3	6.8	5.8	27.9	27.0	9.2	1.3	73.8	35.9	50.5	49.5
48133	ERIE	95.4	94.3	1.0	1.1	0.3	0.6	4.2	5.5	5.7	6.2	6.6	7.4	5.6	26.0	30.0	11.4	1.1	76.8	40.3	50.3	49.7
48134	FLAT ROCK	93.9	89.0	1.6	4.1	1.5	2.7	3.1	4.5	8.0	7.7	7.4	7.0	6.2	29.8	25.9	7.0	0.9	72.4	33.8	49.7	50.3
48135	GARDEN CITY	96.2	93.5	1.1	2.4	0.7	1.2	2.0	3.1	6.1	6.4	6.8	6.8	5.0	27.7	27.3	12.4	1.5	76.4	39.7	49.2	50.8
48137	GREGORY	95.6	94.1	0.6	0.7	0.4	0.7	2.5	3.6	6.1	6.8	7.7	6.9	4.3	25.1	32.7	9.2	1.3	74.9	40.9	50.4	49.6
48138	GROSSE ILE	95.2	92.1	0.4	0.8	2.8	4.8	1.6	2.4	4.4	5.7	6.9	6.9	3.6	19.1	38.7	13.3	1.4	78.1	46.8	50.1	49.9
48140	IDA	98.6	98.1	0.1	0.1	0.2	0.4	1.0	1.4	6.6	7.2	7.6	7.0	5.0	25.5	30.7	9.3	1.0	74.1	39.0	50.6	49.4
	MICHIGAN	80.2	78.3	14.2	14.5	1.8	2.8	3.3	4.1	6.7	6.7	6.8	7.2	6.6	26.3	26.9	10.9	1.9	75.6	37.6	49.2	50.8
	UNITED STATES	75.1	72.0	12.3	12.7	3.8	4.6	12.5	15.7	6.8	6.7	6.6	7.1	6.9	27.0	26.0	10.9	1.9	75.7	36.9	49.2	50.8

ZIP CODE #	POST OFFICE NAME	2009 Per Capita Income	2009 HH Income Base	2009 Household Income Distribution (%) Less than $25,000	$25,000 to $49,999	$50,000 to $99,999	$100,000 to $149,999	$150,000 or More	Median Household Income 2009	2014	2009 National Centile	2009 State Centile	2009 Home Value Base	2009 Home Value Distribution (%) Less than $50,000	$50,000 to $89,999	$90,000 to $174,999	$175,000 to $399,999	$400,000 or More	2009 Median Home Value
48001	ALGONAC	28825	5561	17.8	20.5	44.1	11.5	6.2	58709	60484	76	73	4718	9.7	15.0	47.6	26.0	1.6	130065
48002	ALLENTON	23668	1141	12.7	19.9	54.1	11.1	2.2	65830	64974	84	86	1030	3.8	10.6	41.4	40.2	4.1	152985
48003	ALMONT	28329	2341	9.7	14.7	48.4	22.4	4.7	69663	75647	87	90	2109	14.2	5.2	41.2	34.7	4.8	157308
48005	ARMADA	28625	1795	10.9	16.2	40.2	24.0	8.6	77365	78742	91	93	1621	0.9	6.6	47.1	42.4	3.0	167998
48006	AVOCA	23038	1520	11.7	23.6	52.5	9.3	2.8	60215	61006	78	75	1392	9.6	19.5	43.1	26.2	1.5	124813
48009	BIRMINGHAM	69971	9055	8.1	12.9	31.4	19.0	28.7	95450	105754	96	98	6784	1.4	6.0	22.9	34.8	34.9	267094
48014	CAPAC	21648	1439	19.1	23.6	42.5	11.7	3.1	55162	57247	71	66	1166	8.0	16.4	57.1	18.3	0.3	116784
48015	CENTER LINE	23936	3812	33.0	23.8	31.4	8.9	2.8	41608	44831	38	23	2214	4.5	30.6	62.9	2.0	0.0	98970
48017	CLAWSON	32512	5620	15.1	22.3	42.3	16.3	4.1	63463	62179	82	82	4178	2.0	12.4	78.6	7.0	0.0	129693
48021	EASTPOINTE	25655	13209	18.6	22.4	44.3	11.9	2.8	60256	62904	78	75	11470	6.0	35.3	57.2	1.3	0.1	94235
48022	EMMETT	20728	977	13.0	21.1	58.6	6.8	0.5	61234	61707	79	78	904	9.1	17.9	40.9	30.5	1.5	142679
48023	FAIR HAVEN	25581	2649	16.5	23.9	47.3	9.6	2.8	55599	57344	72	67	2307	39.5	16.0	20.4	21.1	3.0	78659
48025	FRANKLIN	60830	5766	5.2	11.0	28.4	23.8	31.7	109833	116305	98	99	5352	0.9	5.2	15.2	55.6	23.2	277938
48026	FRASER	27706	6212	17.9	24.0	37.7	15.3	5.2	61506	65006	79	79	4503	4.7	14.3	61.8	19.3	0.0	131563
48027	GOODELLS	23203	1196	14.2	24.2	51.0	6.9	3.7	60523	61302	78	77	1087	6.3	10.9	52.6	28.5	1.7	130020
48028	HARSENS ISLAND	39125	588	10.0	21.1	47.3	12.1	9.5	65930	65806	84	86	546	5.3	20.1	36.1	30.4	8.1	140789
48030	HAZEL PARK	22589	7147	23.3	28.0	37.2	8.4	3.1	47792	50035	56	43	5190	12.9	70.2	16.4	0.5	0.1	73303
48032	JEDDO	22545	760	13.6	25.4	48.0	10.3	2.8	61572	61878	79	79	690	13.6	17.1	48.1	20.6	0.6	125781
48033	SOUTHFIELD	35433	8074	19.1	22.3	36.3	15.9	6.6	58876	56063	76	73	3761	4.9	24.9	52.4	17.6	0.3	122555
48034	SOUTHFIELD	37294	7406	17.8	25.3	36.5	12.7	7.7	56534	54851	73	69	1747	0.9	8.0	46.3	44.5	0.3	154432
48035	CLINTON TOWNSHIP	27539	14388	15.9	24.2	43.3	12.5	4.1	60383	62907	78	76	9305	3.9	21.0	63.2	11.4	0.5	114927
48036	CLINTON TOWNSHIP	31229	9637	16.2	25.9	37.1	14.1	6.7	57392	60312	74	70	7251	20.5	19.1	38.1	20.9	1.4	110815
48038	CLINTON TOWNSHIP	33273	18261	14.6	23.0	38.7	16.2	7.5	63610	66582	82	82	12080	7.2	6.8	52.1	33.4	0.5	153668
48039	MARINE CITY	25983	3368	18.5	25.5	40.0	10.5	5.6	53916	56650	69	62	2681	12.2	20.0	47.6	18.3	1.9	108941
48040	MARYSVILLE	27596	4352	19.6	21.2	44.3	10.9	4.0	59028	61083	76	73	3590	9.7	19.4	58.2	12.7	0.0	112703
48041	MEMPHIS	25993	1643	12.5	17.9	52.7	12.7	4.3	65529	67256	84	86	1449	2.8	8.2	51.2	36.0	1.8	157279
48042	MACOMB	39171	8315	4.6	8.2	33.2	31.5	22.4	104322	104690	97	99	7967	0.3	1.2	24.1	73.1	1.3	216820
48043	MOUNT CLEMENS	25310	7086	27.1	25.0	35.2	8.8	3.9	47832	49380	56	44	4228	13.6	33.8	46.5	5.6	0.5	92115
48044	MACOMB	34026	16156	6.2	12.9	38.1	26.8	16.0	87975	90765	95	96	15306	12.8	4.6	23.1	58.9	0.6	188284
48045	HARRISON TOWNSHIP	34458	11472	14.8	23.8	37.8	15.3	8.3	62695	65774	81	81	7901	10.0	11.5	41.3	32.9	4.2	142002
48047	NEW BALTIMORE	32306	14666	10.1	17.2	41.2	22.0	9.5	73487	77372	89	92	11142	2.2	10.2	50.2	35.1	2.3	152124
48048	NEW HAVEN	22754	2517	18.4	22.3	41.7	13.0	4.6	60100	62734	77	75	2161	45.2	27.1	18.6	8.4	0.7	54726
48049	NORTH STREET	24686	2104	11.0	22.9	51.3	12.6	2.2	62016	62403	80	80	1916	3.5	18.1	58.1	20.4	0.0	128769
48050	NEW HAVEN	23688	600	14.3	20.2	51.2	11.8	2.5	66727	72407	85	88	536	0.0	6.5	40.3	51.7	1.5	182083
48051	NEW BALTIMORE	26929	5821	11.9	18.5	38.7	24.4	6.4	73768	77371	89	92	5045	22.3	7.3	32.9	37.5	0.0	156160
48054	EAST CHINA	26922	2885	16.3	20.5	48.8	9.6	4.9	62957	63220	81	81	2451	3.6	6.9	45.1	40.5	3.9	162981
48059	FORT GRATIOT	28728	6336	16.1	22.1	43.8	12.0	6.0	59562	61317	77	74	5150	12.0	22.5	43.3	17.4	4.8	115302
48060	PORT HURON	21453	17267	29.5	26.1	35.9	5.6	3.0	43449	49517	44	30	10541	14.1	39.9	37.9	7.5	0.6	86333
48062	RICHMOND	26048	3451	17.0	22.8	41.2	14.3	4.7	62256	65612	80	80	2644	6.2	12.8	53.4	26.2	1.4	134419
48063	COLUMBUS	24965	1603	10.2	22.1	45.3	18.2	4.2	65460	66055	84	86	1513	22.9	15.9	29.4	29.5	2.2	123690
48064	CASCO	25306	1680	10.7	28.4	41.4	14.6	4.9	61359	62812	79	79	1585	27.8	6.6	34.3	28.6	2.7	129597
48065	ROMEO	32455	3951	13.2	17.9	37.4	17.2	14.3	72113	76861	88	91	3313	13.1	6.1	31.4	42.0	7.4	173619
48066	ROSEVILLE	25178	20362	19.7	27.1	41.4	9.3	2.6	52978	55041	68	59	15112	7.0	38.6	53.3	1.0	0.1	92605
48067	ROYAL OAK	39646	12337	14.6	21.3	37.3	20.3	6.5	66151	65511	84	87	8427	2.5	13.3	66.9	16.3	1.1	131191
48069	PLEASANT RIDGE	50535	1072	6.2	11.7	35.4	27.3	19.5	94533	105475	96	97	1002	2.7	2.2	35.2	45.9	14.0	198571
48070	HUNTINGTON WOODS	55320	2375	7.4	9.6	31.2	24.0	27.8	102463	108728	97	98	2308	1.1	2.8	18.7	64.6	12.8	232250
48071	MADISON HEIGHTS	27286	13239	20.0	25.9	37.9	13.6	2.6	53433	53778	69	61	9207	9.0	31.3	58.0	1.6	0.1	97955
48072	BERKLEY	34848	6665	12.2	17.3	44.1	22.4	4.1	73935	75336	89	92	5673	3.5	15.1	70.6	10.6	0.2	131016
48073	ROYAL OAK	39149	16554	14.5	22.4	36.8	19.5	6.8	65340	63361	84	85	11603	5.3	13.0	59.7	21.5	0.4	137363
48074	SMITHS CREEK	23192	3575	14.6	23.2	52.3	7.9	2.1	56768	58366	74	69	3102	14.8	34.9	37.4	12.2	0.8	90478
48075	SOUTHFIELD	32408	9726	17.5	19.3	37.4	18.5	7.3	66960	64384	85	88	6093	2.8	17.1	59.2	20.2	0.8	127847
48076	SOUTHFIELD	35116	10933	12.2	17.7	37.2	22.7	10.3	76769	79811	90	93	8565	3.5	11.4	50.2	34.5	0.4	152125
48079	SAINT CLAIR	28110	4995	15.4	21.0	43.1	14.4	6.1	63629	63659	82	83	4084	4.2	14.0	47.4	30.7	3.6	139377
48080	SAINT CLAIR SHORES	29780	10908	17.9	27.3	40.7	10.8	3.3	55501	59173	72	67	8615	4.7	20.2	64.8	9.3	1.0	111657
48081	SAINT CLAIR SHORES	30824	9234	14.7	20.6	44.4	15.0	5.4	64444	67980	83	84	8238	1.7	13.5	70.9	11.9	2.0	122443
48082	SAINT CLAIR SHORES	27501	7561	14.9	27.1	44.2	11.3	2.4	59161	61480	76	74	6597	1.8	15.7	77.1	4.1	1.3	115767
48083	TROY	33099	9496	16.8	15.0	39.3	21.1	7.8	75220	77159	89	92	6336	3.5	7.4	54.9	34.2	0.0	154839
48084	TROY	51953	6541	7.5	14.6	37.0	22.2	18.7	85730	97361	94	96	3267	0.9	1.5	25.4	61.1	11.2	237781
48085	TROY	42769	8312	4.5	8.3	33.0	31.5	22.8	105274	111206	97	99	7719	2.6	4.3	23.5	67.4	2.2	201401
48088	WARREN	29284	9563	13.4	23.7	43.8	14.7	4.4	63697	67108	82	83	8346	2.6	5.8	86.9	4.5	0.2	133807
48089	WARREN	21771	12728	20.1	28.8	40.3	8.6	2.1	50940	52283	63	52	9331	14.2	51.4	33.7	0.5	0.1	77773
48091	WARREN	23213	12824	21.6	29.1	38.1	8.8	2.4	49268	50896	59	48	10041	17.3	33.9	47.9	0.9	0.0	88987
48092	WARREN	28004	10348	14.8	24.1	40.9	16.1	4.1	62346	64610	80	80	8377	3.6	9.0	78.2	9.1	0.1	131987
48093	WARREN	29650	10211	16.9	25.8	43.5	9.9	3.9	57150	60347	74	70	8135	3.7	17.0	69.1	10.1	0.1	124861
48094	WASHINGTON	35635	6275	8.7	17.3	39.4	20.1	14.5	77841	80710	91	93	5560	13.4	6.9	22.2	49.1	8.4	201200
48095	WASHINGTON	37688	1643	9.5	7.7	42.5	25.3	15.0	85324	88172	94	96	1462	0.0	0.0	27.5	58.3	14.2	224096
48096	RAY	28982	1361	8.5	13.5	48.6	24.7	4.7	75380	77497	90	92	1225	5.1	1.3	29.8	51.2	12.6	189042
48097	YALE	21880	1976	19.4	24.1	44.5	9.0	3.0	54426	56425	70	63	1633	12.0	26.8	44.2	14.8	2.3	104068
48098	TROY	66396	7036	2.9	8.3	20.0	25.1	43.6	134310	134823	99	100	6749	1.2	3.6	19.4	56.2	19.6	264881
48101	ALLEN PARK	27604	11549	12.2	25.1	47.7	11.6	3.3	60860	61273	79	78	10115	5.0	22.8	68.1	4.1	0.0	105292
48103	ANN ARBOR	40417	23370	13.0	17.7	37.4	18.8	13.0	72137	76370	88	91	14968	5.7	6.2	28.9	50.8	8.4	196393
48104	ANN ARBOR	30013	15881	30.9	21.2	25.6	11.4	10.8	47726	48625	56	43	6213	1.0	9.5	29.0	39.8	20.7	207411
48105	ANN ARBOR	40088	14680	19.1	18.8	33.5	14.0	14.6	66460	70239	85	87	7081	2.8	5.6	24.5	49.5	17.6	234692
48108	ANN ARBOR	37479	11148	15.0	22.7	34.7	14.3	13.2	65637	68256	84	86	5463	6.8	5.9	39.2	34.8	13.4	170651
48109	ANN ARBOR	14912	611	57.3	15.4	21.6	3.1	2.6	19693	20316	1	1	41	0.0	12.2	24.4	51.2	12.2	225000
48111	BELLEVILLE	26518	16461	13.4	25.1	46.6	11.6	3.4	59185	60425	76	74	11568	27.7	16.5	37.0	17.6	1.2	100412
48114	BRIGHTON	42712	7987	7.1	13.7	29.4	28.8	20.9	99450	104456	97	98	7501	7.3	9.5	19.8	54.9	8.6	209767
48116	BRIGHTON	43655	11222	9.6	16.1	31.5	24.6	18.3	86204	95342	94	96	9259	2.4	8.2	31.0	50.2	8.3	195967
48117	CARLETON	28452	3991	12.5	22.1	45.9	12.2	7.3	64832	69469	83	85	3608	21.1	12.7	35.7	28.4	2.0	126923
48118	CHELSEA	33196	4991	11.6	16.5	42.6	19.8	9.5	73327	76978	89	91	3951	1.7	8.7	33.9	49.8	5.9	187072
48120	DEARBORN	20625	2628	31.1	23.2	29.6	10.2	5.8	45078	48870	48	35	967	10.4	7.4	51.1	24.9	6.1	128750
48122	MELVINDALE	22468	4378	23.1	28.3	41.0	5.8	1.8	48810	51861	58	47	2945	14.0	66.6	19.4	0.0	0.1	75131
48124	DEARBORN	32232	13687	13.8	20.6	45.1	13.6	6.9	64501	63974	83	84	11728	4.3	20.9	61.1	12.4	1.2	111175
48125	DEARBORN HEIGHTS	24324	8823	14.0	27.7	46.9	9.3	2.2	56505	57770	73	69	7716	7.8	58.9	31.7	1.5	0.1	82722
48126	DEARBORN	15857	14993	32.6	29.3	29.7	5.6	2.7	37094	41405	24	9	9014	4.4	26.7	61.1	7.3	0.5	106800
48127	DEARBORN HEIGHTS	26632	13925	15.1	26.5	44.6	9.9	3.8	57737	59316	75	71	11561	6.6	17.9	60.5	14.5	0.5	115505
48128	DEARBORN	33601	4076	8.2	18.1	48.9	16.9	7.9	69945	68112	87	90	3907	2.7	7.4	77.8	11.7	0.3	131302
48130	DEXTER	38845	4864	5.2	13.7	41.4	25.0	14.6	84049	86799	94	95	4072	2.3	5.0	21.2	59.1	12.4	230451
48131	DUNDEE	23972	2702	19.1	21.4	45.9	10.4	3.2	59183	62173	76	74	2061	17.2	18.5	50.7	13.1	0.5	110503
48133	ERIE	25824	2072	16.4	20.5	47.5	11.4	4.2	63090	67402	81	81	1827	19.0	23.8	42.4	14.5	0.4	98079
48134	FLAT ROCK	26389	7107	13.3	21.7	44.9	13.2	6.9	63412	63330	82	82	5423	21.0	22.8	40.5	15.2	0.5	99048
48135	GARDEN CITY	24978	11080	13.7	23.1	50.9	9.8	2.5	61289	61381	79	78	9490	3.6	29.8	65.9	0.7	0.0	98148
48137	GREGORY	28080	1910	9.8	23.1	46.6	15.0	5.4	66713	65316	85	88	1729	9.4	16.7	34.4	37.1	2.4	149357
48138	GROSSE ILE	46390	4097	6.0	10.1	36.5	20.8	26.6	95000	93879	96	97	3838	1.9	5.3	32.5	47.2	13.2	196678
48140	IDA	23942	1191	9.6	21.6	54.5	11.1	3.3	65015	69401	83	85	1065	3.2	10.4	56.2	29.8	0.5	147855
	MICHIGAN	26713		20.1	24.2	38.5	11.3	5.9	55536	56866				13.2	21.9	40.3	21.5	3.2	115137
	UNITED STATES	27277		20.9	24.4	35.3	11.7	7.6	54719	56938				9.3	13.1	31.6	32.6	13.5	162279

ZIP CODE		FINANCIAL SERVICES				THE HOME						ENTERTAINMENT						PERSONAL			
						Home Improvements		Furnishings													
#	POST OFFICE NAME	Auto Loan	Home Loan	Invest-ments	Retire-ment Plans	Home Repair	Lawn & Garden	Comput-ers & Hard-ware-Personal	Major Appli-ances	TV, Radio, Sound Equip-ment	Furni-ture	Dine out/ Carry out	Sports Equip-ment	Fees & Tickets	Toys & Games	Travel	Cable TV	Apparel & Services	Auto Repairs	Health Insur-ance	Pets & Supplies
48001	ALGONAC	98	108	96	109	105	107	99	101	99	99	99	78	105	100	103	99	69	99	103	119
48002	ALLENTON	96	108	93	111	105	106	97	100	95	97	95	78	103	97	102	95	67	97	99	118
48003	ALMONT	110	126	108	123	120	113	111	112	107	116	109	88	119	112	115	105	77	109	105	130
48005	ARMADA	116	138	120	140	133	129	119	123	116	122	117	96	131	119	128	115	83	118	118	143
48006	AVOCA	95	99	89	102	97	103	91	98	91	88	91	76	93	93	94	93	63	93	98	115
48009	BIRMINGHAM	185	219	241	226	231	203	207	203	195	216	196	159	230	193	223	188	144	200	189	232
48014	CAPAC	82	95	85	95	92	90	88	88	86	87	86	69	94	87	92	86	61	87	87	103
48015	CENTER LINE	69	64	59	67	62	71	73	68	77	68	76	53	71	73	69	80	52	73	81	84
48017	CLAWSON	91	107	100	107	105	105	99	99	100	99	101	75	109	99	106	101	71	100	105	116
48021	EASTPOINTE	86	93	80	94	89	97	88	89	91	85	90	68	93	91	90	94	63	89	100	106
48022	EMMETT	86	96	83	99	93	95	86	89	85	86	85	70	92	87	91	85	59	86	89	105
48023	FAIR HAVEN	95	99	86	98	95	96	93	94	92	95	93	72	95	95	93	93	65	93	93	111
48025	FRANKLIN	185	253	292	255	275	237	213	225	200	229	199	166	257	196	250	195	149	212	209	248
48026	FRASER	89	100	95	100	99	98	96	95	97	94	97	72	102	96	99	99	69	96	100	111
48027	GOODELLS	91	102	88	105	99	100	91	95	90	91	90	74	97	92	96	90	63	91	94	111
48028	HARSENS ISLAND	111	120	153	119	135	138	107	124	112	119	111	80	119	103	123	117	76	119	138	141
48030	HAZEL PARK	80	78	64	80	73	83	82	78	84	77	83	62	80	84	78	87	57	81	88	95
48032	JEDDO	97	98	87	98	96	100	90	96	92	91	92	72	90	94	91	93	63	92	96	113
48033	SOUTHFIELD	100	96	94	100	95	95	106	96	105	104	106	77	105	104	103	105	75	103	101	116
48034	SOUTHFIELD	108	87	84	93	85	88	110	94	110	107	111	76	101	110	99	109	78	106	101	116
48035	CLINTON TOWNSHIP	90	95	88	95	93	93	95	92	95	93	96	70	98	95	95	96	67	94	96	108
48036	CLINTON TOWNSHIP	99	105	99	105	104	105	100	102	100	100	101	77	104	101	103	102	70	101	105	119
48038	CLINTON TOWNSHIP	103	103	96	106	101	100	107	100	107	108	108	79	109	107	106	106	76	105	104	120
48039	MARINE CITY	92	98	88	98	95	97	94	94	93	93	93	72	96	95	95	94	65	93	97	111
48040	MARYSVILLE	84	96	92	96	95	95	89	91	90	90	90	68	97	89	95	91	64	91	96	106
48041	MEMPHIS	98	115	99	117	111	107	100	103	96	102	98	81	109	100	106	95	69	98	98	120
48042	MACOMB	161	193	178	197	191	170	163	168	154	179	156	133	184	161	175	146	113	156	150	190
48043	MOUNT CLEMENS	77	76	69	78	73	79	83	77	84	78	84	60	82	83	79	86	59	82	86	93
48044	MACOMB	143	166	145	167	160	145	145	145	138	155	140	117	158	145	151	132	100	139	131	166
48045	HARRISON TOWNSHIP	108	111	104	113	109	106	111	106	109	112	110	83	113	110	111	107	77	109	106	126
48047	NEW BALTIMORE	122	132	115	132	127	118	123	120	118	128	120	96	127	123	124	114	84	118	113	140
48048	NEW HAVEN	98	99	86	96	95	94	96	95	95	98	96	73	95	98	94	95	67	95	93	112
48049	NORTH STREET	93	107	95	110	105	105	94	99	93	96	94	76	103	95	101	93	66	95	98	115
48050	NEW HAVEN	97	109	94	112	106	107	98	101	96	98	96	79	104	98	103	96	67	98	100	119
48051	NEW BALTIMORE	118	125	106	121	119	110	114	114	110	122	111	89	115	117	112	106	78	110	104	131
48054	EAST CHINA	96	106	98	108	105	109	97	102	98	97	98	77	103	98	103	100	68	99	106	119
48059	FORT GRATIOT	103	108	103	107	106	109	100	105	100	101	100	79	102	102	103	102	70	102	106	122
48060	PORT HURON	73	69	63	70	67	73	74	71	76	71	76	55	72	76	71	79	53	74	79	86
48062	RICHMOND	92	106	96	105	104	102	98	99	97	96	98	76	105	98	103	98	69	98	101	115
48063	COLUMBUS	108	115	101	113	111	109	102	107	102	106	103	81	106	106	104	102	72	103	103	125
48064	CASCO	102	109	94	110	105	107	100	103	99	102	100	80	103	102	103	99	69	100	102	122
48065	ROMEO	123	136	125	137	133	131	125	126	124	128	124	97	133	126	129	123	88	124	125	148
48066	ROSEVILLE	81	83	74	84	80	87	83	82	85	80	85	63	85	85	83	87	59	84	90	98
48067	ROYAL OAK	106	111	107	113	109	108	113	107	113	113	114	84	117	112	113	113	80	111	112	127
48069	PLEASANT RIDGE	145	180	192	183	188	171	160	164	154	170	154	124	183	152	179	151	111	159	159	187
48070	HUNTINGTON WOODS	173	231	256	236	247	215	192	204	181	207	182	152	231	180	224	177	135	191	188	227
48071	MADISON HEIGHTS	86	87	75	88	82	87	89	84	90	87	90	66	90	91	87	91	63	88	91	101
48072	BERKLEY	103	122	113	120	119	114	110	110	109	111	110	84	121	110	117	109	78	109	112	128
48073	ROYAL OAK	106	113	109	115	112	111	112	108	112	112	113	84	118	111	115	112	79	111	113	128
48074	SMITHS CREEK	94	90	79	90	88	94	86	90	88	86	88	68	84	91	84	91	60	88	93	107
48075	SOUTHFIELD	102	112	106	113	111	110	108	106	108	108	109	80	115	107	112	109	76	108	112	125
48076	SOUTHFIELD	115	136	134	136	137	128	125	125	121	127	123	95	137	121	133	121	88	124	123	144
48079	SAINT CLAIR	99	111	103	112	110	109	103	105	102	102	103	81	110	103	108	103	72	103	106	123
48080	SAINT CLAIR SHORES	81	91	88	91	91	96	85	88	89	85	89	64	93	86	91	93	62	88	100	103
48081	SAINT CLAIR SHORES	94	112	106	112	111	115	98	104	100	99	101	76	110	99	108	104	71	101	112	120
48082	SAINT CLAIR SHORES	81	97	90	97	95	98	86	90	88	86	89	66	97	88	94	90	62	88	97	104
48083	TROY	108	120	114	121	119	113	113	111	111	116	112	86	121	112	118	110	80	111	111	130
48084	TROY	154	156	162	167	158	146	166	150	159	168	162	124	171	160	165	153	116	157	145	179
48085	TROY	164	211	216	217	217	194	176	184	167	188	168	141	206	168	199	162	123	173	169	209
48088	WARREN	91	108	100	108	106	109	96	100	99	97	99	74	108	98	105	102	70	99	109	116
48089	WARREN	80	79	67	79	75	82	81	78	82	78	82	61	80	83	78	84	57	80	85	94
48091	WARREN	80	79	71	79	76	82	80	79	82	78	81	60	80	82	78	84	56	80	86	94
48092	WARREN	90	102	96	102	100	101	96	96	97	95	98	72	104	96	101	99	69	97	102	112
48093	WARREN	85	93	92	92	93	98	89	92	92	88	91	67	94	90	93	95	64	91	101	106
48094	WASHINGTON	136	146	138	148	146	141	134	137	131	139	133	104	140	134	138	131	93	133	132	160
48095	WASHINGTON	148	180	163	184	177	166	154	159	147	160	149	125	172	152	167	144	107	151	148	184
48096	RAY	113	127	110	131	124	125	114	118	112	114	113	93	121	115	120	112	79	114	117	139
48097	YALE	86	92	77	94	88	94	87	88	87	84	87	69	89	89	88	88	60	86	92	105
48098	TROY	248	325	335	341	336	294	269	279	252	291	254	220	321	256	304	240	190	260	246	316
48101	ALLEN PARK	87	103	95	102	101	106	90	96	93	91	94	70	101	93	99	97	65	93	105	110
48103	ANN ARBOR	126	133	131	137	133	126	133	126	130	135	131	100	139	130	135	128	94	129	126	149
48104	ANN ARBOR	103	81	83	87	80	79	127	90	111	107	112	81	103	109	98	104	80	105	88	112
48105	ANN ARBOR	128	124	129	130	127	113	144	124	132	140	134	104	139	133	135	125	97	132	115	146
48108	ANN ARBOR	128	118	109	124	114	108	130	115	126	132	128	96	127	130	122	122	91	123	112	139
48109	ANN ARBOR	58	25	24	30	22	28	81	40	65	55	66	43	48	63	44	59	47	57	40	54
48111	BELLEVILLE	97	91	81	92	88	88	95	90	94	95	95	71	92	97	91	94	66	93	90	108
48114	BRIGHTON	165	197	185	199	195	176	168	173	160	180	162	135	188	166	180	154	117	163	155	198
48116	BRIGHTON	149	174	164	177	172	160	157	157	152	164	154	123	172	154	166	148	110	153	150	182
48117	CARLETON	108	116	102	116	113	114	106	109	106	108	106	83	110	108	109	106	74	107	110	129
48118	CHELSEA	113	135	127	135	134	126	120	122	117	124	118	94	133	118	129	116	84	119	120	141
48120	DEARBORN	83	78	73	76	77	72	88	81	86	89	89	63	85	85	85	84	64	88	81	92
48122	MELVINDALE	76	72	63	72	69	79	76	74	79	71	77	57	73	79	72	82	53	76	84	89
48124	DEARBORN	95	115	110	114	114	114	102	105	104	103	104	78	115	103	112	106	74	104	113	122
48125	DEARBORN HEIGHTS	84	90	75	90	85	94	86	86	88	82	88	66	89	89	87	91	61	87	97	103
48126	DEARBORN	68	69	64	64	69	64	70	69	69	72	69	51	69	68	69	68	49	70	69	78
48127	DEARBORN HEIGHTS	84	99	93	97	98	101	89	93	91	89	91	68	98	90	96	94	64	91	101	107
48128	DEARBORN	106	131	123	131	129	130	112	118	113	115	114	87	128	113	124	115	80	115	124	136
48130	DEXTER	140	167	162	171	167	154	148	150	142	155	144	116	165	144	159	138	103	145	141	173
48131	DUNDEE	83	96	87	96	94	90	89	89	87	88	88	70	95	88	94	87	62	88	88	104
48133	ERIE	94	106	94	105	102	104	93	97	94	95	95	73	101	96	99	96	66	95	100	114
48134	FLAT ROCK	105	109	95	108	105	101	104	103	102	106	102	80	105	106	102	100	72	101	99	120
48135	GARDEN CITY	84	100	89	100	96	99	89	91	90	89	91	69	99	91	96	92	64	90	97	107
48137	GREGORY	106	118	107	121	117	118	106	112	104	106	105	86	112	107	112	105	73	107	111	131
48138	GROSSE ILE	159	197	209	203	206	189	168	179	162	181	163	132	193	160	190	159	117	169	170	204
48140	IDA	97	110	95	113	107	107	98	101	96	98	96	79	105	98	103	96	68	98	100	119
	MICHIGAN	98	97	93	98	95	100	96	97	97	95	97	74	96	98	96	99	68	97	100	115
	UNITED STATES	100	100	100	100	100	100	100	100	100	100	100	100	100	100	100	100	100	100	100	100

#	POST OFFICE NAME	COUNTY FIPS CODE	POPULATION 2000	POPULATION 2009	POPULATION 2014	2000-2009 ANNUAL RATE % Rate	2000-2009 ANNUAL RATE State Centile	HOUSEHOLDS 2000	HOUSEHOLDS 2009	HOUSEHOLDS 2014	HOUSEHOLDS % Annual Rate 2000-2009	HOUSEHOLDS 2009 Average HH Size	FAMILIES 2000	FAMILIES 2009	FAMILIES % Annual Rate 2000-2009
48141	INKSTER	163	29701	28053	27147	-0.6	9	11042	10463	10133	-0.6	2.66	7368	6875	-0.7
48144	LAMBERTVILLE	115	9051	10025	10467	1.1	86	3223	3709	3915	1.5	2.70	2599	2964	1.4
48145	LA SALLE	115	3755	3767	3752	0.0	37	1327	1386	1395	0.5	2.72	1065	1102	0.4
48146	LINCOLN PARK	163	40008	37862	36602	-0.6	9	16204	15415	14916	-0.5	2.45	10575	9902	-0.7
48150	LIVONIA	163	27591	26803	26118	-0.3	21	10829	10590	10335	-0.2	2.50	7773	7500	-0.4
48152	LIVONIA	163	31820	31154	30473	-0.2	25	12341	12130	11873	-0.2	2.54	8720	8465	-0.3
48154	LIVONIA	163	41134	39873	38885	-0.3	21	14919	14530	14171	-0.3	2.66	11588	11176	-0.4
48157	LUNA PIER	115	1506	1585	1621	0.6	71	600	657	680	1.0	2.41	412	446	0.9
48158	MANCHESTER	161	6830	7595	7942	1.2	88	2564	2912	3066	1.4	2.57	1903	2108	1.1
48159	MAYBEE	115	2635	2894	3016	1.0	84	879	1002	1056	1.4	2.89	703	794	1.3
48160	MILAN	115	12814	14122	14666	1.1	86	4208	4792	5028	1.4	2.62	3112	3493	1.3
48161	MONROE	115	25174	26821	27400	0.7	76	9697	10606	10927	1.0	2.48	6681	7233	0.9
48162	MONROE	115	29427	30491	30898	0.4	60	11317	12123	12410	0.7	2.45	7832	8306	0.6
48164	NEW BOSTON	163	7634	8576	8738	1.3	90	2607	2949	3007	1.3	2.89	2104	2354	1.2
48165	NEW HUDSON	125	5228	5943	6220	1.4	92	1836	2140	2257	1.7	2.77	1415	1627	1.5
48166	NEWPORT	115	10488	12127	12795	1.6	94	3685	4350	4628	1.8	2.79	2856	3334	1.7
48167	NORTHVILLE	125	22359	23234	23337	0.4	60	9499	9914	9971	0.5	2.34	6456	6685	0.4
48168	NORTHVILLE	163	13792	19542	20963	3.8	100	4678	6741	7212	4.0	2.67	3555	5285	4.4
48169	PINCKNEY	093	18911	22581	24230	1.9	96	6554	8062	8724	2.3	2.78	5251	6398	2.2
48170	PLYMOUTH	163	40524	40691	40147	0.0	37	16517	16586	16347	0.0	2.38	11071	11046	0.0
48173	ROCKWOOD	163	10076	11847	12083	1.8	96	3921	4596	4681	1.7	2.57	2822	3280	1.6
48174	ROMULUS	163	29812	31116	31054	0.5	66	10980	11451	11417	0.5	2.70	7882	8152	0.4
48176	SALINE	161	17944	21440	22913	1.9	96	6264	7619	8200	2.1	2.76	4835	5812	2.0
48178	SOUTH LYON	125	23802	27680	29072	1.6	94	8985	10604	11182	1.8	2.60	6566	7688	1.7
48179	SOUTH ROCKWOOD	115	2740	3196	3387	1.7	95	969	1170	1255	2.1	2.73	746	890	1.9
48180	TAYLOR	163	65733	62924	61055	-0.5	12	24721	23784	23103	-0.4	2.62	17711	16816	-0.6
48182	TEMPERANCE	115	20634	23065	24089	1.2	88	7476	8652	9142	1.6	2.65	5809	6648	1.5
48183	TRENTON	163	41361	42908	42774	0.4	60	16198	16879	16821	0.4	2.52	11574	11910	0.3
48184	WAYNE	163	19206	18671	18244	-0.3	21	7430	7272	7114	-0.2	2.51	4889	4697	-0.4
48185	WESTLAND	163	48372	48086	47186	-0.1	32	22189	22022	21597	-0.1	2.16	12173	11798	-0.3
48186	WESTLAND	163	38230	37313	36454	-0.3	21	14344	14084	13781	-0.2	2.63	10071	9755	-0.3
48187	CANTON	163	44953	48071	48283	0.7	76	16337	17276	17263	0.6	2.78	12051	12785	0.6
48188	CANTON	163	31413	38293	39851	2.2	98	11153	13471	13940	2.1	2.84	8510	10201	2.0
48189	WHITMORE LAKE	161	14533	15440	15948	0.7	76	5398	5916	6173	1.0	2.56	3946	4242	0.8
48191	WILLIS	161	2646	3706	4143	3.7	100	956	1365	1537	3.9	2.71	766	1071	3.7
48192	WYANDOTTE	163	28006	26597	25715	-0.6	9	11816	11274	10911	-0.5	2.35	7422	6967	-0.7
48193	RIVERVIEW	163	16689	15699	15147	-0.7	7	6526	6175	5964	-0.6	2.46	4399	4096	-0.8
48195	SOUTHGATE	163	30136	29552	28859	-0.2	25	12836	12690	12421	-0.1	2.31	8043	7795	-0.3
48197	YPSILANTI	161	55134	62721	65793	1.4	92	21610	24780	26123	1.5	2.32	11359	13112	1.6
48198	YPSILANTI	161	39422	40993	41611	0.4	60	15998	16977	17365	0.6	2.40	9773	10048	0.3
48201	DETROIT	163	15181	14791	14452	-0.3	21	7579	7223	7013	-0.5	1.81	2320	2159	-0.8
48202	DETROIT	163	22643	21439	20725	-0.6	9	9316	8640	8325	-0.8	2.30	4274	3830	-1.2
48203	HIGHLAND PARK	163	45332	39562	37511	-1.5	1	16402	14256	13499	-1.5	2.71	10041	8551	-1.7
48204	DETROIT	163	42504	37623	35691	-1.3	2	15456	13681	12981	-1.3	2.72	10140	8837	-1.5
48205	DETROIT	163	65686	57903	55021	-1.4	1	19529	16705	15814	-1.7	3.45	14897	12587	-1.8
48206	DETROIT	163	32864	29053	27607	-1.3	2	12011	10483	9929	-1.5	2.69	7477	6416	-1.6
48207	DETROIT	163	25302	23432	22641	-0.8	6	11661	10942	10604	-0.7	2.00	5072	4572	-1.1
48208	DETROIT	163	11339	10384	9976	-0.9	5	4542	4115	3945	-1.1	2.42	2287	2013	-1.4
48209	DETROIT	163	38872	37230	35881	-0.5	12	11830	10903	10453	-0.9	3.39	8182	7435	-1.0
48210	DETROIT	163	39867	36939	35290	-0.8	6	12803	11420	10855	-1.2	3.22	8670	7624	-1.4
48211	DETROIT	163	10627	9402	8959	-1.3	2	3273	2818	2667	-1.6	3.03	2089	1769	-1.8
48212	HAMTRAMCK	163	46166	43230	41605	-0.7	7	15250	13834	13237	-1.0	2.95	9708	8632	-1.3
48213	DETROIT	163	44741	38846	36818	-1.5	1	14020	12165	11525	-1.5	3.14	10019	8577	-1.7
48214	DETROIT	163	33110	29596	28236	-1.2	2	13216	11771	11196	-1.2	2.36	6725	5840	-1.5
48215	DETROIT	163	19235	17658	16911	-0.9	5	6830	6256	5986	-0.9	2.77	4299	3869	-1.1
48216	DETROIT	163	6771	6689	6569	-0.1	32	2476	2395	2340	-0.4	2.65	1365	1298	-0.5
48217	DETROIT	163	10515	9582	9157	-1.0	4	3973	3631	3472	-1.0	2.64	2642	2379	-1.1
48218	RIVER ROUGE	163	9917	8804	8341	-1.3	2	3640	3219	3049	-1.3	2.73	2503	2185	-1.5
48219	DETROIT	163	59964	54284	51812	-1.1	3	21815	19795	18896	-1.0	2.69	14700	13158	-1.2
48220	FERNDALE	125	24929	23789	23311	-0.5	12	10919	10689	10564	-0.2	2.21	5762	5502	-0.5
48221	DETROIT	163	45886	42447	40740	-0.8	6	16804	15624	15008	-0.8	2.68	11677	10710	-0.9
48223	DETROIT	163	35348	31682	30255	-1.2	2	12125	10798	10305	-1.2	2.91	8466	7467	-1.3
48224	DETROIT	163	55931	51723	49585	-0.8	6	18818	17085	16325	-1.0	3.00	13278	11881	-1.2
48225	HARPER WOODS	163	14223	13314	12807	-0.7	7	6276	5876	5655	-0.7	2.24	3747	3448	-0.9
48226	DETROIT	163	6138	6062	5994	-0.1	32	2630	2594	2545	-0.1	1.47	612	577	-0.6
48227	DETROIT	163	61065	55314	52793	-1.1	3	20740	18883	18041	-1.0	2.91	14783	13279	-1.2
48228	DETROIT	163	65049	59210	56499	-1.0	4	23226	20913	19921	-1.1	2.82	15858	14065	-1.3
48229	ECORSE	163	11229	10387	9968	-0.8	6	4339	4028	3869	-0.8	2.57	2733	2496	-1.0
48230	GROSSE POINTE	163	17875	17039	16503	-0.5	12	7094	6778	6567	-0.5	2.51	4811	4539	-0.6
48234	DETROIT	163	46342	42664	40940	-0.9	5	15736	14426	13835	-0.9	2.93	11156	10083	-1.1
48235	DETROIT	163	52704	48756	46823	-0.8	6	19496	18138	17436	-0.8	2.66	13492	12371	-0.9
48236	GROSSE POINTE	163	31577	30045	29059	-0.5	12	12235	11691	11321	-0.5	2.56	9181	8682	-0.6
48237	OAK PARK	125	32495	31359	30862	-0.4	16	12599	12394	12274	-0.2	2.53	8262	7997	-0.4
48238	DETROIT	163	45127	40637	38726	-1.1	3	16445	14761	14055	-1.2	2.72	10856	9598	-1.3
48239	REDFORD	163	37571	36067	34980	-0.4	16	14864	14342	13924	-0.4	2.51	10082	9588	-0.5
48240	REDFORD	163	18920	18439	17985	-0.3	21	7205	7080	6914	-0.2	2.56	4819	4659	-0.4
48301	BLOOMFIELD HILLS	125	14690	14114	13850	-0.4	16	5647	5556	5491	-0.2	2.53	4429	4310	-0.3
48302	BLOOMFIELD HILLS	125	16507	15973	15679	-0.4	16	6431	6386	6323	-0.1	2.46	4769	4670	-0.2
48304	BLOOMFIELD HILLS	125	16829	16413	16170	-0.3	21	6651	6654	6615	0.0	2.41	4990	4931	-0.1
48306	ROCHESTER	125	22863	26163	27369	1.5	93	7629	8890	9347	1.7	2.94	6497	7545	1.6
48307	ROCHESTER	125	37997	40598	41336	0.7	76	15736	16953	17304	0.8	2.36	9984	10702	0.8
48309	ROCHESTER	125	28543	29694	30022	0.4	60	10446	11110	11303	0.7	2.53	7695	8071	0.5
48310	STERLING HEIGHTS	099	41953	42825	43004	0.2	48	14653	15199	15386	0.4	2.80	11140	11393	0.2
48312	STERLING HEIGHTS	099	32153	33437	33866	0.4	60	13016	13724	13989	0.6	2.40	8742	8989	0.3
48313	STERLING HEIGHTS	099	33549	35497	36220	0.6	71	12363	13311	13694	0.8	2.65	9155	9688	0.6
48314	STERLING HEIGHTS	099	16847	21446	23351	2.6	99	6299	7844	8514	2.4	2.72	4361	5441	2.4
48315	UTICA	099	22661	25972	27361	1.5	93	8091	9275	9796	1.5	2.78	6290	7194	1.5
48316	UTICA	099	21239	25258	26941	1.9	96	7783	9488	10220	2.2	2.66	6098	7317	2.0
48317	UTICA	099	25812	27498	27707	0.7	76	10555	11391	11562	0.8	2.40	6727	7148	0.7
48320	KEEGO HARBOR	125	4349	4293	4256	-0.1	32	1975	1997	1995	0.1	2.15	1089	1075	-0.1
48322	WEST BLOOMFIELD	125	30112	31665	31979	0.5	66	11206	11892	12072	0.6	2.62	8296	8668	0.5
48323	WEST BLOOMFIELD	125	17993	18092	17936	0.1	42	6267	6465	6465	0.3	2.78	5179	5293	0.2
48324	WEST BLOOMFIELD	125	18115	17975	17680	-0.1	32	6372	6406	6338	0.1	2.79	5115	5091	-0.1
48326	AUBURN HILLS	125	18995	19828	20070	0.5	66	8203	8767	8942	0.7	2.21	4716	4942	0.5
48327	WATERFORD	125	21220	21705	21772	0.2	48	8804	9252	9365	0.5	2.32	5498	5655	0.3
	MICHIGAN					0.3					0.4	2.52			0.3
	UNITED STATES					1.0					1.1	2.59			0.9

ZIP CODE #	POST OFFICE NAME	RACE (%) White 2000	White 2009	Black 2000	Black 2009	Asian/Pacific 2000	Asian/Pacific 2009	% Hispanic Origin 2000	% Hispanic Origin 2009	2009 AGE DISTRIBUTION (%) 0-4	5-9	10-14	15-19	20-24	25-44	45-64	65-84	85+	18+	MEDIAN AGE 2009	% 2009 Males	% 2009 Females
48141	INKSTER	25.3	15.5	67.3	77.1	3.5	4.1	1.6	1.6	8.0	7.6	7.4	8.0	7.2	27.0	23.9	9.6	1.4	72.0	33.3	47.7	52.3
48144	LAMBERTVILLE	97.9	97.2	0.3	0.3	0.6	0.9	1.6	2.1	5.7	6.3	7.1	7.4	4.8	24.0	32.6	10.9	1.2	76.3	41.7	49.4	50.6
48145	LA SALLE	97.8	97.3	0.4	0.4	0.3	0.5	2.5	3.2	4.9	5.7	6.3	7.9	5.0	26.1	31.4	11.7	1.1	77.8	41.3	50.9	49.1
48146	LINCOLN PARK	93.3	89.4	2.1	3.7	0.5	0.8	6.4	9.5	6.8	6.7	6.6	6.3	5.6	29.1	26.3	10.6	2.0	76.0	37.7	49.1	50.9
48150	LIVONIA	96.2	93.5	0.7	1.7	1.3	2.2	1.9	2.8	6.2	6.6	6.9	6.3	4.3	25.8	28.6	12.5	2.7	76.2	41.3	48.7	51.3
48152	LIVONIA	93.7	89.3	1.4	3.0	3.0	5.0	1.8	2.6	5.2	5.7	6.3	6.3	4.9	23.7	31.5	13.9	2.5	78.8	43.5	48.7	51.3
48154	LIVONIA	96.4	93.8	0.7	1.5	1.6	2.7	1.6	2.4	5.0	5.6	6.4	6.9	4.7	21.1	30.9	16.0	3.4	78.7	45.2	48.0	52.0
48157	LUNA PIER	95.5	94.6	0.2	0.2	0.0	0.0	3.1	3.9	7.3	7.4	8.9	5.7	4.7	28.0	28.5	8.4	1.1	72.5	37.7	49.5	50.5
48158	MANCHESTER	97.3	96.4	0.3	0.4	0.2	0.3	2.5	3.4	5.8	6.2	6.8	7.1	5.4	23.5	33.0	10.7	1.6	76.7	41.9	50.0	50.0
48159	MAYBEE	90.8	89.3	7.2	8.3	0.3	0.4	1.2	1.6	6.2	6.9	8.1	7.5	4.8	27.9	28.9	8.7	1.0	74.2	37.5	51.8	48.2
48160	MILAN	87.1	85.9	9.5	9.7	0.6	1.0	3.7	4.7	5.7	6.1	6.5	6.1	5.9	32.3	27.6	8.7	1.1	78.0	37.6	55.4	44.6
48161	MONROE	92.1	90.6	4.2	4.8	0.6	0.9	2.7	3.5	7.3	7.1	6.8	6.9	6.6	26.9	26.0	10.6	1.9	74.4	36.7	49.2	50.8
48162	MONROE	95.0	93.8	2.1	2.4	0.9	1.4	1.9	2.5	6.3	6.1	6.4	7.0	6.2	26.4	26.7	12.2	2.7	76.8	38.7	48.2	51.8
48164	NEW BOSTON	93.4	89.8	4.0	6.6	0.4	0.7	2.3	3.2	6.3	6.9	7.5	7.1	4.7	25.8	31.1	9.4	1.1	74.7	40.0	50.5	49.5
48165	NEW HUDSON	97.6	96.5	0.3	0.4	0.3	0.6	1.8	2.7	7.0	7.6	8.0	7.1	4.1	28.5	29.8	7.1	0.8	72.8	37.7	50.7	49.3
48166	NEWPORT	96.2	95.5	0.9	1.0	0.2	0.4	2.6	3.4	8.2	7.9	7.7	7.1	6.3	28.6	26.2	7.3	0.7	71.9	34.6	50.5	49.5
48167	NORTHVILLE	93.2	89.4	1.2	2.1	3.9	6.2	1.7	2.3	5.7	6.0	6.5	6.2	5.4	24.8	31.7	12.0	1.7	77.8	41.8	48.5	51.5
48168	NORTHVILLE	88.1	84.2	5.9	7.0	3.7	6.1	1.5	2.2	5.0	5.8	6.9	6.4	4.3	22.9	32.8	14.0	2.0	78.1	44.1	47.1	52.9
48169	PINCKNEY	97.3	96.6	0.8	0.9	0.4	0.7	1.0	1.3	6.7	7.2	7.8	7.3	4.5	27.6	30.2	8.0	0.7	73.6	38.6	50.4	49.6
48170	PLYMOUTH	93.6	89.7	2.2	3.7	2.3	4.0	1.5	2.3	5.5	5.9	6.4	5.8	4.6	25.7	30.8	13.1	2.3	78.5	42.6	49.4	50.6
48173	ROCKWOOD	96.3	91.9	0.6	2.9	0.5	0.7	2.3	4.0	6.0	6.2	6.5	6.3	4.8	27.1	30.6	11.3	1.1	77.3	40.1	50.1	49.9
48174	ROMULUS	71.2	58.8	23.9	35.5	1.0	1.4	2.2	2.7	7.5	7.3	7.3	7.6	6.4	27.8	26.6	8.5	0.9	73.0	35.4	48.6	51.4
48176	SALINE	94.9	92.8	1.4	1.6	2.0	3.5	1.4	2.0	6.4	7.3	8.0	7.6	5.2	24.5	30.9	8.3	1.7	73.4	39.4	49.0	51.0
48178	SOUTH LYON	97.0	95.9	0.4	0.5	0.9	1.4	1.4	1.9	7.4	7.7	7.7	6.5	4.3	25.5	28.5	10.4	1.9	73.1	39.4	49.3	50.7
48179	SOUTH ROCKWOOD	97.2	96.6	0.4	0.4	0.1	0.1	1.0	1.4	5.6	6.6	6.9	7.3	5.7	25.9	30.9	10.4	0.8	76.2	39.8	52.6	47.4
48180	TAYLOR	86.1	79.3	8.8	13.8	1.7	2.5	3.2	4.6	7.5	7.1	6.6	6.7	6.6	28.1	24.9	11.0	1.4	74.7	35.8	48.3	51.7
48182	TEMPERANCE	97.5	96.7	0.4	0.5	0.4	0.7	2.1	2.9	6.2	6.7	7.3	7.3	5.3	24.7	30.1	10.8	1.5	75.1	40.1	49.0	51.0
48183	TRENTON	94.4	90.3	1.5	3.5	1.6	2.7	2.8	4.1	6.3	6.2	6.4	6.4	5.4	26.5	28.9	12.3	1.8	77.2	39.9	48.3	51.7
48184	WAYNE	84.3	74.7	11.4	19.5	1.5	2.1	1.9	2.7	7.3	7.1	6.7	6.7	6.3	28.0	25.6	10.6	1.7	74.8	36.6	48.0	52.0
48185	WESTLAND	86.6	78.1	6.2	11.9	4.0	5.8	2.5	3.5	6.1	5.7	5.5	5.5	6.7	30.1	24.5	13.0	3.0	79.5	38.6	47.4	52.6
48186	WESTLAND	88.0	80.2	7.5	13.5	1.4	2.3	2.4	3.3	7.6	7.6	7.4	6.7	5.4	29.1	25.5	9.5	1.2	73.3	36.5	49.2	50.8
48187	CANTON	84.9	75.2	4.0	8.0	8.5	13.5	2.2	2.9	7.5	7.5	7.7	6.9	5.5	28.9	27.5	7.5	1.0	72.9	35.3	49.4	50.6
48188	CANTON	82.5	71.8	5.3	10.9	9.1	13.3	2.5	3.2	9.9	9.5	8.9	6.6	4.5	32.3	23.2	4.7	0.4	67.5	33.1	49.2	50.8
48189	WHITMORE LAKE	95.8	95.0	1.7	1.7	0.6	1.0	1.3	1.7	7.2	7.5	7.5	7.5	4.9	28.5	28.6	7.5	0.9	73.1	37.3	50.8	49.2
48191	WILLIS	91.3	90.3	6.5	6.9	0.2	0.5	0.8	1.1	5.6	6.2	6.8	6.8	4.8	25.5	32.6	10.4	1.3	77.1	41.3	50.1	49.9
48192	WYANDOTTE	96.3	94.1	0.5	1.1	0.4	0.6	2.9	4.5	5.7	5.6	5.7	6.1	6.0	28.0	28.7	11.8	2.5	79.4	40.2	49.2	50.8
48193	RIVERVIEW	91.6	86.0	3.3	6.6	3.0	4.5	2.6	3.7	5.7	5.8	5.8	6.1	5.7	25.1	27.2	15.3	3.3	78.9	41.6	47.2	52.8
48195	SOUTHGATE	93.7	89.2	2.1	4.4	1.7	2.7	4.0	5.8	5.4	5.4	5.6	5.9	5.7	27.8	27.7	13.8	2.8	80.1	40.9	48.0	52.0
48197	YPSILANTI	64.8	60.6	25.2	26.0	4.6	7.1	3.2	4.2	7.1	6.3	5.6	7.4	12.5	34.5	20.2	5.6	0.8	77.8	30.3	51.3	48.7
48198	YPSILANTI	65.0	60.5	29.1	31.9	1.4	2.4	2.4	3.1	7.8	7.2	6.7	7.1	8.7	29.0	24.1	8.2	1.3	74.3	33.3	48.4	51.6
48201	DETROIT	16.1	8.9	75.3	83.2	5.4	5.4	1.9	1.8	6.3	6.2	4.7	5.9	7.5	30.9	24.6	11.5	2.6	79.8	36.9	50.8	49.2
48202	DETROIT	9.1	5.3	85.0	89.3	3.0	3.3	1.1	1.1	6.6	6.4	6.1	7.0	7.9	28.4	25.3	10.2	2.2	77.1	36.2	49.3	50.7
48203	HIGHLAND PARK	9.3	4.9	86.6	91.9	0.3	0.3	0.8	0.8	8.2	8.9	8.0	7.8	7.0	25.0	23.3	10.3	1.6	70.2	33.0	46.6	53.4
48204	DETROIT	1.3	0.6	97.0	98.1	0.1	0.1	0.7	0.7	7.8	8.4	8.0	8.4	6.5	24.2	23.1	11.4	2.1	70.6	34.4	45.5	54.5
48205	DETROIT	10.0	5.3	84.1	89.9	3.6	3.1	0.8	0.8	9.6	10.3	9.9	10.5	8.2	26.2	20.0	4.4	0.7	63.5	26.0	46.6	53.4
48206	DETROIT	1.6	0.8	96.4	97.8	0.3	0.3	0.5	0.5	8.0	8.1	7.7	8.5	6.4	23.8	23.8	11.0	2.7	70.9	35.1	45.6	54.4
48207	DETROIT	7.4	3.8	90.1	94.2	0.5	0.5	0.9	0.8	5.6	5.7	5.5	6.4	6.9	25.8	28.0	13.8	2.4	79.1	40.4	45.5	54.5
48208	DETROIT	9.1	5.2	87.4	92.0	0.2	0.2	2.4	2.2	6.5	6.7	6.7	7.7	6.5	26.2	26.7	10.9	2.1	75.2	37.8	48.5	51.5
48209	DETROIT	52.1	43.1	8.9	12.7	0.6	0.7	58.6	64.8	10.4	9.5	8.2	8.3	8.5	30.5	17.8	6.0	0.8	67.0	27.8	52.8	47.2
48210	DETROIT	37.0	30.0	38.5	42.2	1.1	1.3	30.0	33.9	10.4	9.7	8.4	8.6	7.9	28.4	18.8	6.7	1.2	66.4	28.2	51.2	48.8
48211	DETROIT	15.6	9.1	74.7	81.1	2.0	2.3	1.0	1.0	8.4	8.8	7.5	8.2	7.8	27.2	21.8	8.7	1.6	70.5	31.4	52.3	47.7
48212	HAMTRAMCK	38.2	29.9	43.3	47.8	8.8	11.6	1.3	1.5	8.5	8.2	7.4	7.5	7.5	29.6	21.6	7.9	1.8	71.4	32.0	52.3	47.7
48213	DETROIT	2.1	1.0	96.1	97.8	0.1	0.1	0.6	0.6	9.0	9.8	9.0	9.2	7.5	25.1	21.4	7.9	1.1	66.5	28.9	45.9	54.1
48214	DETROIT	7.5	3.9	90.5	94.6	0.3	0.3	0.7	0.7	6.3	6.7	6.4	7.1	5.9	23.0	26.3	14.5	3.6	76.3	40.6	46.3	53.7
48215	DETROIT	8.0	4.4	89.3	93.5	0.4	0.4	1.0	0.9	8.4	8.6	8.3	8.4	7.4	24.8	24.2	8.8	1.1	69.4	31.5	46.2	53.8
48216	DETROIT	35.1	26.9	39.2	45.8	0.4	0.5	38.0	40.2	7.7	7.6	6.7	7.2	7.9	30.7	23.4	7.7	1.1	73.8	33.6	51.6	48.4
48217	DETROIT	10.3	7.9	85.1	87.2	0.4	0.6	5.6	6.3	6.2	6.7	7.0	7.8	6.1	23.3	26.6	13.5	2.8	75.4	39.3	46.6	53.4
48218	RIVER ROUGE	52.6	41.5	42.0	52.3	0.2	0.3	5.0	6.1	8.4	8.0	7.9	8.6	7.2	26.3	23.3	8.9	1.4	70.5	32.0	47.1	52.9
48219	DETROIT	12.0	6.6	84.8	90.7	0.6	0.6	1.0	0.9	7.1	8.1	8.0	8.0	6.8	26.6	26.3	7.8	1.3	71.8	34.2	46.0	54.0
48220	FERNDALE	81.3	78.7	13.9	15.0	1.2	2.0	1.7	2.3	5.9	5.5	5.3	5.6	7.5	34.8	24.8	8.8	1.7	80.0	36.0	49.4	50.6
48221	DETROIT	3.3	1.7	94.3	96.5	0.3	0.3	0.7	0.7	6.0	6.5	7.0	8.1	6.2	23.6	26.4	14.1	2.1	75.7	39.4	45.2	54.8
48223	DETROIT	12.8	6.4	83.2	90.5	1.0	1.0	1.2	1.1	8.8	9.3	8.8	8.9	7.1	26.9	24.0	5.6	0.6	67.6	30.2	46.2	53.8
48224	DETROIT	17.6	10.1	79.2	87.3	0.6	0.6	1.1	1.1	8.2	8.9	8.7	9.0	7.2	27.9	23.3	5.4	1.3	68.5	30.8	46.3	53.7
48225	HARPER WOODS	85.9	76.2	10.3	18.5	1.7	2.6	1.6	2.2	6.1	6.2	6.3	5.9	5.1	27.7	26.1	12.4	4.0	77.6	40.6	47.5	52.5
48226	DETROIT	22.4	12.2	73.2	84.0	1.4	1.2	2.6	2.5	1.7	1.6	1.3	5.6	11.6	38.5	27.6	10.5	1.5	93.5	39.0	64.6	35.4
48227	DETROIT	2.1	1.0	96.1	97.8	0.1	0.1	0.6	0.6	7.8	8.7	8.5	8.9	6.9	26.4	23.9	8.0	0.8	69.4	31.9	45.7	54.3
48228	DETROIT	23.5	16.4	69.7	76.6	0.6	0.7	3.3	3.8	8.8	9.0	8.5	8.6	7.0	27.8	22.3	6.9	1.1	68.4	30.8	47.0	53.0
48229	ECORSE	52.2	43.4	40.6	47.7	0.2	0.3	8.9	11.2	7.9	7.6	7.0	7.3	7.0	26.4	25.0	10.3	1.5	73.1	34.8	48.5	51.5
48230	GROSSE POINTE	94.0	89.7	2.2	4.7	1.6	2.7	1.6	2.5	6.0	6.4	7.4	7.2	6.2	22.3	31.6	11.1	1.9	75.8	41.1	48.3	51.7
48234	DETROIT	6.1	2.9	91.4	95.2	0.6	0.5	0.6	0.6	8.0	8.8	8.8	9.1	7.0	25.6	23.2	8.1	1.4	68.8	31.4	45.8	54.2
48235	DETROIT	1.7	0.8	96.3	97.7	0.2	0.2	0.6	0.6	6.2	7.1	7.3	8.0	6.2	24.3	26.9	12.3	1.7	74.5	38.1	44.2	55.8
48236	GROSSE POINTE	94.7	91.2	2.4	4.1	2.0	3.3	1.1	1.7	5.6	6.4	7.4	7.1	4.4	19.3	31.9	14.8	3.1	76.2	44.9	48.2	51.8
48237	OAK PARK	47.0	42.1	45.8	49.4	2.2	3.1	1.3	1.5	6.6	6.8	7.2	7.6	6.1	27.0	25.9	10.6	2.1	74.7	37.2	46.9	53.1
48238	DETROIT	1.2	0.6	97.1	98.1	0.1	0.1	0.7	0.7	8.0	8.6	8.0	8.7	7.1	24.8	22.8	10.5	1.6	70.2	32.9	45.7	54.3
48239	REDFORD	81.5	72.5	14.7	22.4	1.2	1.7	2.4	3.3	6.6	6.9	7.1	6.7	5.1	27.8	27.5	10.0	2.5	75.3	39.1	49.0	51.0
48240	REDFORD	93.4	88.5	2.9	6.2	0.7	1.1	1.9	2.9	6.9	6.9	7.0	6.5	5.5	28.8	25.3	9.8	3.3	75.2	37.9	49.0	51.0
48301	BLOOMFIELD HILLS	92.6	89.4	2.1	2.7	4.1	6.4	1.3	1.7	5.1	6.3	8.0	7.4	3.8	15.7	34.5	16.7	2.6	75.7	47.1	49.0	51.0
48302	BLOOMFIELD HILLS	83.7	77.6	6.1	7.6	8.4	12.8	1.3	1.7	4.1	4.9	6.1	6.0	4.0	18.9	33.9	19.3	2.9	81.1	49.1	47.7	52.3
48304	BLOOMFIELD HILLS	87.2	82.1	3.8	4.6	7.5	11.6	1.5	1.9	4.1	4.9	6.2	6.4	4.0	15.6	34.6	20.9	3.3	80.5	50.8	47.5	52.5
48306	ROCHESTER	92.3	88.5	1.9	2.7	4.6	7.4	1.3	1.8	6.7	8.2	8.8	7.8	3.3	22.9	33.9	7.5	0.9	70.8	40.7	49.5	50.5
48307	ROCHESTER	88.0	83.5	2.5	3.1	6.9	10.4	2.4	3.1	7.3	6.7	6.4	6.0	6.3	30.5	26.7	8.4	1.6	76.0	37.2	49.0	51.0
48309	ROCHESTER	88.4	83.6	3.9	4.9	6.0	9.5	2.4	3.1	5.4	6.0	6.7	8.3	5.7	21.6	30.8	13.0	2.7	77.9	42.4	48.0	52.0
48310	STERLING HEIGHTS	86.4	81.4	1.2	1.4	7.7	11.8	1.2	1.5	6.3	6.4	6.5	6.2	4.9	29.7	27.5	11.0	1.6	77.1	38.5	49.7	50.3
48312	STERLING HEIGHTS	92.4	89.7	1.7	1.9	4.1	6.2	1.2	1.6	5.6	5.5	5.7	5.6	5.3	25.7	27.3	16.0	3.2	79.7	42.6	48.3	51.7
48313	STERLING HEIGHTS	94.9	93.0	1.0	1.2	2.1	3.4	1.6	2.1	6.4	6.5	6.6	6.4	5.4	28.6	28.4	9.9	1.9	76.5	38.2	49.1	50.9
48314	STERLING HEIGHTS	89.7	84.3	1.3	1.5	5.5	9.9	1.4	1.7	7.1	7.0	7.2	6.8	4.9	30.1	26.2	8.9	1.7	74.3	36.9	48.7	51.3
48315	UTICA	95.9	94.2	0.7	0.8	1.9	3.1	1.4	1.8	5.7	6.1	7.0	7.0	4.5	22.8	31.3	13.3	2.3	76.8	42.8	48.0	52.0
48316	UTICA	96.5	95.2	0.5	0.6	1.3	2.1	1.2	1.6	6.1	6.3	6.7	6.5	5.0	26.5	29.8	12.1	1.0	76.8	40.2	49.4	50.6
48317	UTICA	92.7	90.3	1.2	1.4	3.1	4.7	2.5	3.2	6.6	6.2	6.0	6.1	7.4	32.6	25.5	8.4	1.2	77.6	35.7	50.8	49.2
48320	KEEGO HARBOR	94.6	92.9	0.8	1.1	0.9	1.6	3.2	4.3	5.6	5.8	6.0	6.3	6.3	31.3	28.0	9.4	1.3	78.8	39.1	50.9	49.1
48322	WEST BLOOMFIELD	80.1	72.9	6.5	8.0	9.8	15.0	1.4	1.8	5.7	6.3	7.1	6.7	4.1	21.5	30.5	14.5	3.6	76.5	44.1	48.1	51.9
48323	WEST BLOOMFIELD	86.6	81.4	4.3	5.4	6.8	10.5	1.3	1.6	5.6	6.6	7.4	6.9	3.7	21.6	33.0	13.8	1.5	75.7	43.8	49.3	50.7
48324	WEST BLOOMFIELD	90.4	86.7	3.7	4.7	4.2	6.6	1.5	1.9	7.2	8.4	9.0	7.1	3.5	23.8	30.7	9.2	1.2	70.7	39.7	50.3	49.7
48326	AUBURN HILLS	77.2	71.3	11.8	13.8	6.5	9.6	4.6	5.9	7.3	6.2	5.6	5.6	8.4	35.6	22.8	7.4	1.1	77.7	33.7	50.7	49.3
48327	WATERFORD	93.3	90.8	2.0	2.7	1.6	2.6	3.8	5.2	7.6	7.4	6.9	5.6	5.6	32.5	25.0	8.0	1.3	74.7	36.1	49.5	50.5
	MICHIGAN	80.2	78.3	14.2	14.5	1.8	2.8	3.3	4.1	6.7	6.7	6.8	7.2	6.6	26.3	26.9	10.9	1.9	75.6	37.6	49.2	50.8
	UNITED STATES	75.1	72.0	12.3	12.7	3.8	4.6	12.5	15.7	6.8	6.7	6.6	7.1	6.9	27.0	26.0	10.9	1.9	75.7	36.9	49.2	50.8

ZIP CODE #	POST OFFICE NAME	2009 Per Capita Income	2009 HH Income Base	2009 Household Income Distribution (%) Less than $25,000	$25,000 to $49,999	$50,000 to $99,999	$100,000 to $149,999	$150,000 or More	Median Household Income 2009	2014	2009 National Centile	2009 State Centile	2009 Home Value Base	2009 Home Value Distribution (%) Less than $50,000	$50,000 to $89,999	$90,000 to $174,999	$175,000 to $399,999	$400,000 or More	2009 Median Home Value
48141	INKSTER	19316	10463	28.1	26.6	36.8	6.3	2.2	45069	50019	48	35	5916	28.5	62.7	8.4	0.1	0.3	64719
48144	LAMBERTVILLE	27966	3709	12.1	20.8	46.8	13.4	7.0	66502	71323	85	87	3362	6.3	13.1	48.4	30.6	1.6	137809
48145	LA SALLE	27954	1386	12.3	19.8	48.5	13.6	5.8	69414	75943	86	89	1254	5.2	16.2	45.9	29.1	3.6	136675
48146	LINCOLN PARK	24038	15415	18.3	27.0	44.4	8.1	2.2	53579	55763	69	61	12085	8.9	62.6	28.3	0.2	0.0	79817
48150	LIVONIA	28870	10590	10.8	21.8	48.9	14.3	4.2	64803	63779	83	84	9424	1.5	13.1	77.6	7.7	0.1	130989
48152	LIVONIA	32219	12130	12.8	20.3	40.1	17.1	9.7	67984	66820	86	88	9932	1.1	13.0	50.4	34.6	0.9	143641
48154	LIVONIA	30577	14530	8.5	18.9	45.9	19.3	7.4	72600	71592	88	91	13576	2.1	10.7	56.6	30.6	0.1	151991
48157	LUNA PIER	23904	657	27.2	21.0	42.6	6.4	2.7	52374	57700	67	57	469	13.9	36.5	33.7	12.6	3.4	89583
48158	MANCHESTER	31134	2912	11.7	17.7	45.0	19.0	6.7	69030	72482	86	89	2420	4.2	10.4	37.9	40.9	6.7	169792
48159	MAYBEE	24882	1002	10.0	23.2	51.2	11.4	4.3	65558	70346	84	86	890	4.6	16.9	55.2	22.5	0.9	126818
48160	MILAN	27159	4792	13.2	19.3	44.7	17.9	4.9	68094	73083	86	89	3801	8.4	13.9	47.0	27.8	2.8	137543
48161	MONROE	25381	10606	25.0	21.3	37.5	11.0	5.1	54491	58195	70	64	7747	24.0	20.4	36.8	17.2	1.6	97741
48162	MONROE	26446	12123	19.3	22.5	43.1	10.3	4.8	59319	62018	77	74	8426	6.3	16.5	58.7	17.6	0.9	121925
48164	NEW BOSTON	26253	2949	11.6	23.7	41.7	16.7	6.3	65905	66026	84	86	2688	10.9	19.4	45.4	23.3	1.0	122601
48165	NEW HUDSON	32304	2140	9.0	13.5	43.8	24.9	8.8	80622	83901	92	94	1895	19.7	6.2	23.1	49.4	1.6	176477
48166	NEWPORT	26587	4350	10.1	26.1	43.0	15.1	5.7	63329	66684	82	82	3767	27.6	24.3	27.5	19.5	1.1	84596
48167	NORTHVILLE	49290	9914	8.5	15.5	35.5	19.9	20.7	83451	83859	93	95	7337	2.8	7.9	32.0	47.9	9.4	198704
48168	NORTHVILLE	46077	6741	6.6	14.1	30.3	19.5	29.5	97297	97794	96	98	5931	3.1	11.8	10.2	49.9	25.0	279254
48169	PINCKNEY	34692	8062	7.1	14.3	40.8	26.1	11.7	82099	87596	93	95	7235	1.9	6.7	33.8	52.1	5.5	190739
48170	PLYMOUTH	41464	16586	9.7	20.5	35.7	17.5	16.7	75941	73216	90	93	12983	7.0	10.7	35.5	37.4	9.5	168389
48173	ROCKWOOD	31164	4596	12.0	23.1	42.8	13.7	8.4	64468	64182	83	84	3540	3.8	19.6	59.4	16.3	0.9	115040
48174	ROMULUS	23250	11451	20.3	22.8	42.5	10.7	3.7	56084	57981	73	68	8445	19.5	35.6	37.3	7.2	0.4	86163
48176	SALINE	38479	7619	8.8	12.2	35.0	26.6	17.4	88674	88773	95	97	6243	2.5	5.9	23.9	54.2	13.4	217460
48178	SOUTH LYON	37750	10604	9.8	17.7	34.8	24.1	13.7	81508	87110	93	95	9001	8.9	13.9	29.0	41.5	6.7	170288
48179	SOUTH ROCKWOOD	24767	1170	15.6	24.4	44.0	10.9	5.0	62826	66871	81	81	1035	21.2	18.9	43.1	15.8	1.0	105682
48180	TAYLOR	22863	23784	19.0	27.3	41.4	9.5	2.8	52954	55141	68	59	16665	12.7	48.0	37.4	1.8	0.1	83713
48182	TEMPERANCE	28200	8652	13.3	19.1	45.4	16.4	5.8	66372	71028	84	87	7553	11.0	12.9	50.5	23.9	1.7	132409
48183	TRENTON	28608	16879	13.6	22.6	42.7	15.4	5.6	62792	63267	81	81	12805	7.0	17.6	61.8	13.5	0.1	126436
48184	WAYNE	24722	7272	20.1	24.3	40.9	10.9	3.7	55083	56740	71	65	4595	8.1	47.8	40.7	3.5	0.0	87288
48185	WESTLAND	26898	22022	18.9	28.1	42.3	8.7	1.9	52357	54932	67	57	11777	6.5	23.7	63.9	5.9	0.0	107609
48186	WESTLAND	24664	14084	14.6	22.9	48.0	11.9	2.5	60507	61013	78	76	10543	11.3	29.5	58.1	1.0	0.0	95783
48187	CANTON	34349	17276	8.5	15.3	39.8	22.6	13.8	79575	77956	92	94	12796	4.5	5.8	38.3	49.1	2.4	176844
48188	CANTON	37109	13471	7.8	15.4	36.6	22.0	18.3	83551	82897	93	95	11767	20.8	5.5	29.3	42.0	2.3	161506
48189	WHITMORE LAKE	34434	5916	8.2	17.6	40.9	24.3	8.9	75438	79243	90	92	5049	19.4	12.0	26.4	37.6	4.6	156833
48191	WILLIS	31155	1365	14.4	15.9	38.4	24.2	7.1	74360	77352	89	92	1211	3.4	11.4	47.0	37.5	0.7	154986
48192	WYANDOTTE	25515	11274	19.6	26.2	43.5	8.3	2.4	53689	55829	69	61	8143	5.7	41.3	48.0	5.0	0.1	91767
48193	RIVERVIEW	27072	6175	16.2	27.9	38.9	11.2	5.8	55366	57107	72	66	3959	11.3	16.8	51.7	19.9	0.3	119534
48195	SOUTHGATE	26424	12690	16.4	27.0	45.3	9.0	2.4	55642	57351	72	67	8802	3.5	34.8	57.1	4.5	0.1	96155
48197	YPSILANTI	29221	24780	23.5	20.7	33.0	15.3	7.4	61704	64281	80	79	12638	11.4	9.6	41.4	36.9	0.7	155583
48198	YPSILANTI	26725	16977	20.1	26.6	38.5	10.4	4.3	57217	60086	74	70	10214	16.3	37.2	40.3	3.7	2.4	87371
48201	DETROIT	14414	7223	63.1	23.0	11.3	1.5	1.1	16139	16715	1	0	253	31.2	23.7	28.5	15.4	1.2	81071
48202	DETROIT	16011	8640	48.2	26.4	20.3	3.4	1.7	25965	27141	4	1	2170	40.9	31.3	17.0	8.2	2.6	57615
48203	HIGHLAND PARK	14946	14256	47.2	24.6	21.4	4.3	2.6	26868	28510	5	2	5867	55.5	31.6	6.1	3.8	3.0	46569
48204	DETROIT	14540	13681	41.5	30.2	23.7	3.2	1.5	30545	32234	9	3	6857	57.0	36.6	6.3	0.1	0.0	44845
48205	DETROIT	13952	16705	31.6	26.8	34.0	5.8	1.8	40559	45758	35	20	10711	33.3	59.5	7.0	0.1	0.0	59908
48206	DETROIT	14959	10483	43.2	28.6	22.6	3.8	1.8	28877	30455	7	2	4260	52.1	31.7	12.2	3.5	0.4	48236
48207	DETROIT	20865	10942	42.1	24.3	27.1	4.5	2.0	30556	34369	9	3	2649	53.3	19.3	21.9	4.8	0.8	46457
48208	DETROIT	13404	4115	53.9	24.7	17.6	2.7	1.1	21739	23339	2	1	1321	63.7	23.8	11.3	1.1	0.1	35431
48209	DETROIT	12544	10903	39.4	28.7	26.3	3.7	2.0	32579	35195	13	4	4851	75.6	23.3	0.9	0.1	0.0	34544
48210	DETROIT	12475	11420	40.8	29.4	25.3	3.1	1.4	30318	31966	9	3	5622	74.5	23.5	1.9	0.1	0.0	35354
48211	DETROIT	11557	2818	47.6	30.2	17.5	3.9	0.8	26137	27055	4	1	1212	80.5	14.9	3.2	1.1	0.3	30648
48212	HAMTRAMCK	14055	13834	38.1	30.9	25.9	3.5	1.6	32046	34015	11	4	7346	47.5	44.0	8.1	0.4	0.0	51902
48213	DETROIT	12492	12165	43.2	28.9	22.9	3.6	1.5	29582	30791	7	2	5984	61.6	34.1	4.3	0.1	0.0	42426
48214	DETROIT	16512	11771	48.0	25.0	20.0	4.9	2.2	26045	27134	4	1	4550	62.9	20.8	5.1	8.9	2.4	37154
48215	DETROIT	14954	6256	43.5	26.6	24.0	4.1	1.8	30111	31726	8	2	2617	61.4	25.6	6.6	5.8	0.6	39117
48216	DETROIT	15620	2395	43.3	26.1	24.7	4.3	1.7	30454	32638	9	3	841	57.7	33.3	8.2	0.8	0.0	44625
48217	DETROIT	17692	3631	36.1	27.8	30.8	3.6	1.7	34266	37575	16	6	2518	58.1	39.6	2.2	0.1	0.0	45393
48218	RIVER ROUGE	16396	3219	34.4	29.7	29.1	4.9	1.8	35793	37924	20	7	1821	59.0	35.9	5.0	0.1	0.0	45148
48219	DETROIT	20624	19795	26.1	25.5	37.5	7.9	2.9	48279	51717	57	45	13010	18.8	57.4	22.1	1.7	0.0	73368
48220	FERNDALE	28917	10689	19.6	24.0	40.1	13.3	3.0	55263	54890	72	66	7188	7.7	39.5	47.4	5.3	0.0	91849
48221	DETROIT	22727	15624	23.2	26.4	35.8	9.8	4.8	50358	53223	62	50	11470	19.0	44.1	27.4	9.2	0.3	80932
48223	DETROIT	18667	10798	27.7	26.3	34.1	8.9	3.0	45828	50324	51	38	6575	27.8	36.6	31.5	4.0	0.1	76940
48224	DETROIT	19208	17085	22.2	27.1	38.6	9.5	2.7	50572	53304	63	51	12077	18.3	56.3	24.5	0.8	0.0	75027
48225	HARPER WOODS	27841	5876	16.2	25.0	47.9	8.5	2.3	56992	58209	74	70	4786	6.2	35.9	55.6	2.3	0.0	95149
48226	DETROIT	24908	2594	39.9	24.5	28.1	4.3	3.2	33743	36934	15	5	55	38.2	41.8	20.0	0.0	0.0	55417
48227	DETROIT	16705	18883	31.5	28.9	31.8	5.6	2.1	39483	44085	31	17	11257	35.2	52.1	12.5	0.2	0.0	61443
48228	DETROIT	16818	20913	30.2	29.6	33.7	5.1	1.5	40504	45396	34	20	13071	27.4	65.9	6.6	0.1	0.0	63028
48229	ECORSE	17327	4028	33.9	30.9	29.6	3.8	1.8	34068	37116	16	6	2429	65.8	31.8	2.3	0.1	0.1	41770
48230	GROSSE POINTE	48845	6778	8.1	12.3	36.6	17.9	25.1	86372	84901	94	96	5050	1.7	7.3	23.4	46.2	21.4	247006
48234	DETROIT	17071	14426	29.4	28.5	34.3	5.9	1.9	41373	45997	37	22	9523	46.2	49.8	4.0	0.1	0.0	52542
48235	DETROIT	21202	18138	25.1	25.9	38.6	7.4	3.0	48991	52163	59	47	12989	23.0	55.2	21.2	0.6	0.1	72580
48236	GROSSE POINTE	47279	11691	7.1	12.4	35.7	20.5	24.3	90344	88736	95	97	11044	2.4	6.6	26.9	44.2	19.9	212557
48237	OAK PARK	26466	12394	21.6	21.9	38.1	14.2	4.2	56201	55700	73	68	8192	4.8	26.7	64.3	4.1	0.1	102900
48238	DETROIT	15086	14761	41.0	27.3	26.3	3.9	1.4	31229	33581	10	3	7189	53.1	40.1	6.4	0.4	0.0	47747
48239	REDFORD	25806	14342	13.6	24.1	50.0	10.3	2.0	59952	60277	77	75	13010	5.0	31.1	62.7	1.2	0.0	97025
48240	REDFORD	24526	7080	10.9	27.2	51.7	8.1	2.1	59650	60363	77	74	6211	5.6	46.0	47.9	0.5	0.0	89219
48301	BLOOMFIELD HILLS	74088	5556	5.5	9.3	22.7	22.0	40.5	125936	128225	99	100	5052	0.0	2.1	7.3	48.9	41.7	351273
48302	BLOOMFIELD HILLS	75902	6386	6.8	10.3	24.0	17.7	41.1	121212	125185	99	99	5650	1.2	3.6	13.4	37.5	44.3	361905
48304	BLOOMFIELD HILLS	64342	6654	5.8	11.3	22.8	21.4	38.7	122590	125803	99	100	6020	0.0	4.5	11.4	50.4	33.7	291427
48306	ROCHESTER	63428	8890	5.7	6.7	20.0	24.0	43.6	135394	137767	99	100	8223	0.5	1.7	13.0	59.6	25.3	292633
48307	ROCHESTER	41157	16953	11.3	17.7	35.9	21.6	13.6	79096	83608	92	94	11717	12.4	9.4	35.1	38.6	4.5	158171
48309	ROCHESTER	46220	11110	9.7	11.1	30.7	25.0	23.5	96868	105209	96	98	9262	4.3	9.0	29.1	52.3	5.2	195974
48310	STERLING HEIGHTS	28481	15199	11.6	18.8	40.7	21.6	7.3	69597	74200	87	89	12387	7.2	4.4	58.3	30.0	0.1	159756
48312	STERLING HEIGHTS	29709	13724	15.0	21.1	41.8	16.9	5.3	64608	68479	83	84	10371	3.2	7.8	67.8	20.9	0.3	150472
48313	STERLING HEIGHTS	30566	13311	12.1	15.7	42.8	22.2	7.2	72596	76715	88	91	10158	1.3	6.8	63.4	27.9	0.6	149864
48314	STERLING HEIGHTS	34887	7844	10.9	17.4	35.5	20.0	16.1	77571	82746	91	93	6356	11.9	3.3	30.0	48.5	6.3	194501
48315	UTICA	40131	9275	12.3	13.9	29.2	21.1	23.5	87692	88200	95	96	8522	10.2	6.5	19.4	50.9	12.9	226548
48316	UTICA	40262	9488	6.6	13.6	35.9	25.1	18.7	88986	88425	95	97	7809	1.0	3.2	33.1	54.2	8.5	192802
48317	UTICA	30166	11391	13.2	23.1	43.7	14.7	5.2	63414	66909	82	82	6639	6.9	9.5	61.8	20.5	1.2	135026
48320	KEEGO HARBOR	44862	1997	12.2	17.9	41.9	16.5	11.5	67996	68506	86	89	1501	7.7	18.7	44.7	24.1	4.9	128879
48322	WEST BLOOMFIELD	54972	11892	8.4	12.8	28.4	23.7	26.7	100616	108341	97	98	9137	1.5	1.8	22.3	60.1	14.3	228478
48323	WEST BLOOMFIELD	61898	6465	5.9	8.8	24.9	23.9	36.5	120318	123888	98	99	6152	0.7	4.5	21.7	47.5	25.7	267508
48324	WEST BLOOMFIELD	56523	6406	3.9	8.9	29.9	27.6	29.6	110538	115442	98	99	5970	1.1	4.3	31.1	44.2	19.2	218919
48326	AUBURN HILLS	35796	8767	14.1	21.9	38.6	18.5	6.9	66096	63733	84	87	4485	18.8	16.7	45.4	15.4	3.6	111350
48327	WATERFORD	34067	9252	13.2	22.8	37.3	21.5	5.1	66993	64488	85	88	6503	1.9	15.6	62.0	18.8	1.7	128427
	MICHIGAN	26713		20.1	24.2	38.5	11.3	5.9	55536	56866				13.2	21.9	40.3	21.5	3.2	115137
	UNITED STATES	27277		20.9	24.4	35.3	11.7	7.6	54719	56938				9.3	13.1	31.6	32.6	13.5	162279

ZIP CODE #	POST OFFICE NAME	FINANCIAL SERVICES: Auto Loan	Home Loan	Invest-ments	Retire-ment Plans	THE HOME: Home Improvements: Home Repair	Lawn & Garden	Furnishings: Comput-ers & Hard-ware-Personal	Major Appli-ances	TV, Radio, Sound Equip-ment	Furni-ture	ENTERTAINMENT: Dine out/ Carry out	Sports Equip-ment	Fees & Tickets	Toys & Games	Travel	Cable TV	PERSONAL: Apparel & Services	Auto Repairs	Health Insur-ance	Pets & Supplies
48141	INKSTER	73	67	58	68	63	71	72	68	76	71	76	52	70	75	67	79	52	73	77	85
48144	LAMBERTVILLE	103	121	107	123	118	116	105	110	103	108	104	85	116	105	113	103	73	105	107	128
48145	LA SALLE	102	120	108	123	117	118	105	110	104	107	105	84	116	106	114	105	74	106	110	128
48146	LINCOLN PARK	82	84	70	85	79	88	83	82	85	79	85	64	84	86	82	88	58	83	91	98
48150	LIVONIA	94	116	104	115	112	112	99	103	100	101	101	77	113	101	109	101	71	101	107	119
48152	LIVONIA	108	126	123	127	126	123	114	117	113	117	114	87	126	113	123	114	81	115	120	135
48154	LIVONIA	105	132	130	131	133	128	113	119	112	116	113	87	130	112	127	114	81	115	121	135
48157	LUNA PIER	85	82	73	85	80	91	81	85	83	75	82	66	78	85	80	86	56	83	91	101
48158	MANCHESTER	107	125	114	126	123	119	114	115	111	114	112	90	123	113	121	111	79	113	114	134
48159	MAYBEE	97	113	99	115	110	111	100	104	99	100	100	80	109	101	107	100	70	100	105	122
48160	MILAN	103	115	104	116	112	110	107	107	105	107	106	83	114	107	111	104	74	106	106	125
48161	MONROE	90	91	82	91	88	93	89	90	91	89	91	68	90	92	89	93	63	90	95	106
48162	MONROE	89	96	88	96	94	94	92	92	92	92	93	70	96	93	94	93	65	92	96	108
48164	NEW BOSTON	104	120	107	122	117	116	106	110	104	108	105	84	115	107	113	105	74	106	109	129
48165	NEW HUDSON	120	151	135	151	147	132	127	129	119	133	122	102	143	124	137	115	87	123	116	148
48166	NEWPORT	108	109	94	109	105	108	105	105	105	106	105	82	105	108	104	105	73	105	106	125
48167	NORTHVILLE	155	179	176	182	180	166	164	163	157	170	159	127	179	160	173	154	114	160	155	188
48168	NORTHVILLE	163	211	237	214	227	201	180	190	172	193	172	141	214	171	206	169	127	179	180	211
48169	PINCKNEY	134	160	141	161	155	143	137	141	131	145	133	111	151	136	146	126	95	133	128	161
48170	PLYMOUTH	132	154	154	156	156	148	140	142	138	146	139	108	155	137	151	137	99	140	142	164
48173	ROCKWOOD	108	123	112	124	120	122	111	114	111	112	112	87	121	113	118	113	79	112	117	134
48174	ROMULUS	92	90	78	90	86	90	89	88	90	89	90	68	88	92	86	91	63	89	91	105
48176	SALINE	145	171	164	176	170	154	152	152	145	161	147	121	169	149	162	139	107	147	139	175
48178	SOUTH LYON	135	153	143	154	151	142	139	140	135	146	136	108	149	137	145	133	97	136	136	161
48179	SOUTH ROCKWOOD	93	105	93	106	102	106	93	98	94	93	94	75	100	96	99	96	66	95	101	115
48180	TAYLOR	83	84	73	85	80	85	85	82	87	83	87	64	86	87	84	88	60	85	89	98
48182	TEMPERANCE	101	120	106	120	116	112	105	107	103	107	104	83	115	106	112	102	73	104	105	125
48183	TRENTON	97	110	100	109	107	105	102	102	101	102	102	78	109	102	106	101	72	101	103	118
48184	WAYNE	87	87	75	88	82	90	89	86	91	86	91	67	89	92	86	93	63	89	94	104
48185	WESTLAND	80	77	72	79	75	77	84	77	84	81	85	61	83	84	81	85	60	83	83	93
48186	WESTLAND	89	95	84	95	91	94	91	90	92	90	93	69	95	93	92	94	65	91	95	107
48187	CANTON	132	146	135	149	143	132	137	133	131	143	133	106	146	135	140	127	95	132	126	155
48188	CANTON	153	168	145	169	162	144	152	150	144	164	147	122	161	153	153	136	105	144	131	172
48189	WHITMORE LAKE	127	140	123	139	135	127	127	128	123	133	125	100	133	128	130	120	88	124	120	148
48191	WILLIS	111	136	127	135	136	128	118	123	115	118	116	94	131	117	129	115	83	118	119	141
48192	WYANDOTTE	80	86	77	86	83	89	84	83	86	81	86	64	88	86	85	88	60	85	92	99
48193	RIVERVIEW	91	99	95	99	99	99	94	95	95	95	95	71	100	95	98	96	67	95	100	111
48195	SOUTHGATE	83	88	80	88	85	89	85	85	87	85	88	64	89	87	87	89	61	86	92	100
48197	YPSILANTI	106	89	81	94	85	85	109	92	105	106	106	77	99	107	95	101	75	101	90	112
48198	YPSILANTI	94	84	74	86	80	82	95	85	94	93	95	68	89	96	87	93	66	92	88	103
48201	DETROIT	36	24	26	28	24	28	39	31	41	36	41	25	33	38	32	42	29	37	38	40
48202	DETROIT	54	41	40	44	40	46	53	47	57	51	56	36	48	55	46	59	39	53	55	59
48203	HIGHLAND PARK	58	47	44	49	45	53	56	52	61	56	61	39	52	60	50	65	42	57	61	65
48204	DETROIT	58	48	45	49	46	57	53	53	60	54	59	38	50	58	49	65	40	56	63	66
48205	DETROIT	71	60	50	62	54	64	67	62	73	67	72	48	64	73	60	75	50	68	71	79
48206	DETROIT	59	47	44	48	45	55	54	53	62	55	60	38	51	60	49	66	41	57	63	66
48207	DETROIT	58	47	48	50	46	52	60	53	65	58	64	41	56	61	55	67	45	61	64	67
48208	DETROIT	45	37	37	38	36	43	44	42	50	43	48	30	41	47	40	53	34	46	50	52
48209	DETROIT	61	51	43	49	48	49	61	55	63	60	64	42	56	63	54	64	46	61	57	65
48210	DETROIT	57	46	41	47	44	50	57	51	61	54	61	39	52	60	50	64	43	57	58	63
48211	DETROIT	50	39	36	40	37	46	47	44	53	47	52	32	43	51	41	57	36	49	53	56
48212	HAMTRAMCK	59	50	44	52	47	55	59	54	63	56	62	42	55	63	52	66	43	59	62	67
48213	DETROIT	58	47	42	48	44	54	53	51	60	54	59	38	50	59	48	63	40	56	60	65
48214	DETROIT	54	43	44	45	43	51	54	50	60	53	59	37	50	56	49	64	41	56	62	63
48215	DETROIT	60	48	44	50	46	55	57	53	64	57	62	40	53	62	51	67	43	59	63	67
48216	DETROIT	57	47	41	48	44	50	60	52	64	56	63	41	55	63	51	67	45	59	59	65
48217	DETROIT	65	63	58	63	61	68	63	64	68	65	68	45	63	65	62	72	46	66	73	77
48218	RIVER ROUGE	66	56	49	57	52	62	63	60	68	61	66	46	59	68	57	71	46	64	68	74
48219	DETROIT	79	75	66	77	71	79	77	75	82	78	82	56	77	81	74	85	56	79	84	92
48220	FERNDALE	90	88	77	90	84	89	92	87	93	90	93	69	91	94	88	94	65	91	93	105
48221	DETROIT	83	88	83	88	86	93	82	85	87	85	87	60	88	85	85	91	60	86	95	102
48223	DETROIT	77	72	63	74	67	75	76	72	80	76	80	55	76	80	72	83	55	76	80	89
48224	DETROIT	84	78	65	80	72	81	81	77	85	80	84	60	80	86	76	87	58	81	85	96
48225	HARPER WOODS	82	92	83	92	89	92	88	87	88	86	89	66	94	88	91	90	62	88	94	102
48226	DETROIT	60	46	50	52	46	50	68	54	70	62	70	45	61	65	60	71	49	65	66	70
48227	DETROIT	71	64	55	66	59	69	67	64	72	68	72	48	66	72	62	75	49	68	73	81
48228	DETROIT	70	61	51	63	55	66	66	62	71	65	70	48	64	71	60	74	48	67	71	78
48229	ECORSE	66	55	49	56	53	63	63	60	67	60	66	46	57	67	56	71	46	64	68	74
48230	GROSSE POINTE	157	191	210	196	202	174	177	176	164	186	164	138	197	162	193	156	121	171	160	199
48234	DETROIT	72	66	57	68	61	71	68	66	74	70	74	49	68	73	65	77	50	70	76	83
48235	DETROIT	78	79	71	80	75	84	76	77	82	78	82	55	79	79	76	86	56	79	88	94
48236	GROSSE POINTE	148	201	221	200	214	186	168	177	159	178	159	132	201	158	195	157	118	167	166	196
48237	OAK PARK	90	96	87	96	92	96	93	91	95	93	96	69	98	95	95	97	67	94	98	109
48238	DETROIT	61	49	45	50	46	57	55	54	63	56	61	39	52	61	50	67	42	58	64	68
48239	REDFORD	87	98	85	98	94	98	90	91	91	89	92	69	97	92	94	93	64	91	97	107
48240	REDFORD	85	93	78	94	88	96	88	88	90	86	90	68	93	91	90	92	62	89	97	105
48301	BLOOMFIELD HILLS	222	316	378	321	350	293	260	278	241	285	240	206	323	236	312	233	182	257	251	303
48302	BLOOMFIELD HILLS	234	306	356	315	335	290	263	278	248	288	246	206	315	242	305	240	183	261	257	308
48304	BLOOMFIELD HILLS	228	295	341	303	321	283	252	269	240	276	239	198	299	233	293	234	176	253	253	300
48306	ROCHESTER	245	308	304	320	314	277	260	268	246	282	249	211	303	252	287	236	183	251	242	302
48307	ROCHESTER	137	143	133	147	140	133	142	135	137	145	139	108	146	140	141	134	99	137	131	159
48309	ROCHESTER	159	192	201	196	199	181	170	175	163	179	164	133	192	163	187	160	119	168	167	199
48310	STERLING HEIGHTS	106	127	118	125	125	115	113	113	109	115	111	88	124	112	120	108	79	111	109	131
48312	STERLING HEIGHTS	95	106	103	105	106	106	100	101	100	100	101	75	107	100	105	102	71	101	106	118
48313	STERLING HEIGHTS	109	125	113	125	121	114	115	113	112	118	114	88	124	114	119	111	81	113	111	132
48314	STERLING HEIGHTS	131	150	137	151	147	134	135	134	130	142	132	106	148	135	141	126	95	131	124	153
48315	UTICA	149	173	179	176	179	169	154	162	152	164	153	121	171	150	167	152	109	155	161	184
48316	UTICA	145	166	161	171	166	155	151	151	146	157	148	117	166	148	160	143	106	148	145	175
48317	UTICA	102	102	92	104	98	96	105	98	103	105	105	78	106	106	103	102	74	102	98	117
48320	KEEGO HARBOR	130	142	135	143	141	132	139	134	134	140	136	105	145	136	142	132	97	135	131	156
48322	WEST BLOOMFIELD	182	234	256	237	248	216	205	210	193	217	193	160	237	190	231	187	142	201	196	236
48323	WEST BLOOMFIELD	216	291	319	300	310	263	242	255	224	267	224	195	291	223	281	212	167	236	224	282
48324	WEST BLOOMFIELD	211	263	259	270	267	233	223	229	209	242	212	181	257	215	245	199	155	215	202	259
48326	AUBURN HILLS	118	105	95	109	100	97	119	105	116	119	118	87	113	120	109	113	83	113	103	127
48327	WATERFORD	113	118	104	118	113	107	115	110	112	117	113	87	118	116	114	109	80	111	106	129
	MICHIGAN	98	97	93	98	95	100	96	97	97	95	97	74	96	98	96	99	68	97	100	115
	UNITED STATES	100	100	100	100	100	100	100	100	100	100	100	100	100	100	100	100	100	100	100	100

ZIP CODE			POPULATION			2000-2009 ANNUAL RATE		HOUSEHOLDS					FAMILIES		
#	POST OFFICE NAME	COUNTY FIPS CODE	2000	2009	2014	% Rate	State Centile	2000	2009	2014	% Annual Rate 2000-2009	2009 Average HH Size	2000	2009	% Annual Rate 2000-2009
48328	WATERFORD	125	26733	25240	24968	-0.6	9	10956	11091	11066	0.1	2.24	6497	6427	-0.1
48329	WATERFORD	125	24997	24997	24847	0.0	37	9545	9812	9839	0.3	2.53	7069	7165	0.1
48331	FARMINGTON	125	22026	21393	21056	-0.3	21	7954	7906	7841	-0.1	2.69	6245	6164	-0.1
48334	FARMINGTON	125	17624	17336	17153	-0.2	25	7447	7446	7412	0.0	2.27	4858	4796	-0.1
48335	FARMINGTON	125	23818	23966	23731	0.1	42	11126	11365	11310	0.2	2.08	5976	5935	-0.1
48336	FARMINGTON	125	26601	26069	25689	-0.2	25	11006	11083	11018	0.1	2.29	6762	6671	-0.1
48340	PONTIAC	125	25244	25495	25433	0.1	42	9834	10166	10230	0.4	2.51	5980	6019	0.1
48341	PONTIAC	125	18720	19454	19008	0.4	60	6752	6737	6610	0.0	2.56	4173	4097	-0.2
48342	PONTIAC	125	22421	21755	21389	-0.3	21	7678	7569	7489	-0.2	2.82	5139	4977	-0.3
48346	CLARKSTON	125	22671	22885	22880	0.1	42	8615	8922	8989	0.4	2.54	6220	6367	0.3
48348	CLARKSTON	125	20378	22123	22737	0.9	82	6861	7617	7882	1.1	2.89	5767	6349	1.0
48350	DAVISBURG	125	8001	8260	8312	0.3	54	2757	2903	2944	0.6	2.83	2150	2244	0.5
48353	HARTLAND	093	5667	6512	6858	1.5	93	1979	2363	2515	1.9	2.75	1644	1945	1.8
48356	HIGHLAND	125	8606	8491	8376	-0.1	32	3051	3102	3087	0.2	2.73	2446	2459	0.1
48357	HIGHLAND	125	9070	9150	9122	0.1	42	3231	3333	3347	0.3	2.74	2494	2542	0.2
48359	LAKE ORION	125	8544	8852	8885	0.4	60	3308	3434	3461	0.4	2.55	2150	2192	0.2
48360	LAKE ORION	125	9977	10620	10846	0.7	76	3439	3720	3821	0.9	2.85	2828	3018	0.7
48362	LAKE ORION	125	14450	14630	14622	0.1	42	5360	5549	5587	0.4	2.61	3878	3971	0.3
48363	OAKLAND	125	4163	4739	4826	1.4	92	1502	1733	1774	1.6	2.73	1199	1392	1.6
48367	LEONARD	125	4773	5010	5052	0.5	66	1658	1782	1813	0.8	2.76	1332	1417	0.7
48370	OXFORD	125	1681	1797	1834	0.7	76	555	611	631	1.0	2.84	455	496	0.9
48371	OXFORD	125	19202	22436	23580	1.7	95	6821	8129	8603	1.9	2.74	5172	6138	1.9
48374	NOVI	125	11819	15005	16111	2.6	99	3499	4415	4750	2.5	3.40	3123	3910	2.5
48375	NOVI	125	20372	21215	21471	0.4	60	7938	8418	8565	0.6	2.49	5249	5486	0.5
48377	NOVI	125	11475	14707	15930	2.7	99	5726	7356	7983	2.7	2.00	2731	3511	2.8
48380	MILFORD	125	5224	6448	6877	2.3	98	1726	2192	2360	2.6	2.89	1480	1863	2.5
48381	MILFORD	125	12856	13466	13684	0.5	66	4679	5016	5133	0.8	2.66	3570	3774	0.6
48382	COMMERCE TOWNSHIP	125	18962	21285	22041	1.3	90	6541	7471	7786	1.4	2.85	5353	6069	1.4
48383	WHITE LAKE	125	12399	12800	12835	0.3	54	4207	4437	4478	0.6	2.87	3399	3547	0.5
48386	WHITE LAKE	125	15847	17724	18337	1.2	88	5894	6764	7048	1.5	2.59	4431	5015	1.3
48390	WALLED LAKE	125	19582	21676	22488	1.1	86	7861	8948	9369	1.4	2.42	5322	5908	1.1
48393	WIXOM	125	15979	17673	18129	1.1	86	6792	7395	7573	0.9	2.38	3913	4282	1.0
48401	APPLEGATE	151	1505	1544	1532	0.3	54	577	602	601	0.5	2.55	428	443	0.4
48412	ATTICA	087	6042	6520	6745	0.8	80	2076	2352	2466	1.4	2.74	1674	1877	1.2
48413	BAD AXE	063	8119	7718	7507	-0.5	12	3072	3000	2940	-0.3	2.45	2127	2058	-0.4
48414	BANCROFT	155	2446	2627	2627	0.8	80	861	950	958	1.1	2.76	693	757	1.0
48415	BIRCH RUN	145	9767	9533	9284	-0.3	21	3597	3559	3480	-0.1	2.66	2798	2739	-0.2
48416	BROWN CITY	151	5083	5304	5321	0.5	66	1772	1904	1926	0.8	2.78	1382	1471	0.7
48417	BURT	145	3302	3272	3202	-0.1	32	1129	1136	1118	0.1	2.87	918	916	0.0
48418	BYRON	155	4121	4523	4560	1.0	84	1406	1571	1593	1.2	2.88	1173	1299	1.1
48419	CARSONVILLE	151	2644	2631	2593	-0.1	32	1007	1025	1017	0.2	2.55	730	737	0.1
48420	CLIO	049	21079	21587	21393	0.3	54	7844	8280	8276	0.6	2.57	5891	6118	0.4
48421	COLUMBIAVILLE	087	6944	7269	7379	0.5	66	2428	2659	2734	1.0	2.73	1971	2135	0.9
48422	CROSWELL	151	6475	6645	6597	0.3	54	2345	2450	2447	0.5	2.70	1759	1820	0.4
48423	DAVISON	049	30839	31864	31622	0.4	60	12682	13272	13232	0.5	2.39	8369	8628	0.3
48426	DECKER	151	1179	1165	1145	-0.1	32	426	430	426	0.1	2.70	328	329	0.0
48427	DECKERVILLE	151	3163	3142	3100	-0.1	32	1221	1243	1234	0.2	2.45	854	859	0.1
48428	DRYDEN	087	4866	5742	6088	1.8	96	1652	2025	2172	2.2	2.82	1385	1684	2.1
48429	DURAND	155	10146	10080	9894	-0.1	32	3778	3863	3826	0.2	2.57	2832	2865	0.1
48430	FENTON	093	32771	36610	37705	1.2	88	12327	14155	14680	1.5	2.56	9152	10426	1.4
48432	FILION	063	872	813	784	-0.8	6	337	326	318	-0.4	2.48	258	247	-0.5
48433	FLUSHING	049	25141	26329	26258	0.5	66	9706	10406	10446	0.8	2.51	7205	7641	0.6
48435	FOSTORIA	157	1965	2098	2123	0.7	76	672	741	757	1.1	2.83	542	595	1.0
48436	GAINES	049	3529	3790	3796	0.8	80	1183	1297	1308	1.0	2.92	978	1062	0.9
48438	GOODRICH	049	6195	6618	6657	0.7	76	2086	2302	2337	1.1	2.85	1743	1905	1.0
48439	GRAND BLANC	049	40112	46179	47263	1.5	93	15846	18597	19146	1.7	2.46	11071	12770	1.6
48441	HARBOR BEACH	063	4471	4042	3858	-1.1	3	1776	1654	1596	-0.8	2.41	1250	1150	-0.9
48442	HOLLY	125	18431	20749	21268	1.3	90	6631	7605	7840	1.5	2.69	4987	5717	1.5
48444	IMLAY CITY	087	8869	9553	9699	0.8	80	3153	3478	3562	1.1	2.70	2306	2535	1.0
48445	KINDE	063	1487	1382	1328	-0.8	6	586	561	544	-0.5	2.45	415	392	-0.6
48446	LAPEER	087	30897	31542	31152	0.2	48	11042	11681	11671	0.6	2.56	8102	8474	0.5
48449	LENNON	155	3752	3493	3366	-0.8	6	1384	1329	1291	-0.4	2.62	1063	1009	-0.6
48450	LEXINGTON	151	4941	5074	5037	0.3	54	2205	2310	2308	0.5	2.19	1427	1476	0.4
48451	LINDEN	049	12085	14185	14473	1.7	95	4420	5320	5471	2.0	2.65	3421	4069	1.9
48453	MARLETTE	151	5451	5315	5215	-0.3	21	1922	1910	1885	-0.1	2.68	1422	1399	-0.2
48454	MELVIN	151	1276	1357	1357	0.7	76	458	498	503	0.9	2.72	363	392	0.8
48455	METAMORA	087	8399	8756	8772	0.5	66	2973	3236	3281	0.9	2.70	2432	2623	0.8
48456	MINDEN CITY	151	1128	1078	1051	-0.5	12	406	399	392	-0.2	2.68	301	292	-0.3
48457	MONTROSE	049	8540	8870	8828	0.4	60	2918	3119	3128	0.7	2.79	2328	2449	0.5
48458	MOUNT MORRIS	049	25208	23880	23136	-0.6	9	9771	9470	9237	-0.3	2.51	6753	6449	-0.5
48460	NEW LOTHROP	155	2446	2436	2386	0.0	37	890	910	899	0.2	2.66	701	711	0.2
48461	NORTH BRANCH	087	7947	8864	9212	1.2	88	2593	3007	3169	1.6	2.93	2119	2432	1.5
48462	ORTONVILLE	125	12523	13301	13525	0.7	76	4186	4553	4669	0.9	2.89	3492	3770	0.8
48463	OTISVILLE	049	4714	4799	4747	0.2	48	1709	1785	1780	0.5	2.68	1366	1412	0.4
48464	OTTER LAKE	087	2153	2307	2380	0.7	76	750	842	878	1.3	2.68	609	678	1.2
48465	PALMS	151	723	695	677	-0.4	16	288	284	279	-0.2	2.40	210	205	-0.3
48466	PECK	151	1652	1724	1719	0.5	66	596	640	643	0.8	2.65	460	489	0.7
48467	PORT AUSTIN	063	2661	2430	2327	-1.0	4	1234	1169	1131	-0.6	2.06	785	734	-0.7
48468	PORT HOPE	063	1391	1362	1341	-0.2	25	587	598	596	0.2	2.27	439	443	0.1
48469	PORT SANILAC	151	1374	1305	1268	-0.6	9	642	627	615	-0.3	2.07	411	395	-0.4
48470	RUTH	063	981	917	888	-0.7	7	354	343	336	-0.3	2.67	270	259	-0.4
48471	SANDUSKY	151	6067	5893	5773	-0.3	21	2305	2281	2245	-0.1	2.46	1586	1551	-0.2
48472	SNOVER	151	2060	2024	1984	-0.2	25	719	721	711	0.0	2.79	552	549	-0.1
48473	SWARTZ CREEK	049	19647	20599	20635	0.5	66	7573	8144	8216	0.8	2.52	5682	6031	0.6
48475	UBLY	151	2538	2532	2501	0.0	37	973	1002	1000	0.3	2.51	692	705	0.2
48502	FLINT	049	985	952	942	-0.4	16	222	206	199	-0.8	1.32	46	40	-1.5
48503	FLINT	049	29424	26871	25731	-1.0	4	12575	11711	11288	-0.8	2.24	6934	6267	-1.1
48504	FLINT	049	38650	36092	34766	-0.7	7	14176	13370	12924	-0.6	2.65	9659	8966	-0.8
48505	FLINT	049	35374	31414	29820	-1.3	2	12499	11268	10745	-1.1	2.74	8701	7725	-1.3
48506	FLINT	049	33496	31343	30272	-0.7	7	13042	12436	12087	-0.5	2.50	8560	8043	-0.7
48507	FLINT	049	32275	30940	29946	-0.5	12	13864	13549	13197	-0.2	2.26	8651	8329	-0.4
48509	BURTON	049	10148	9742	9476	-0.4	16	3828	3763	3688	-0.2	2.58	2855	2765	-0.3
48519	BURTON	049	7306	7543	7508	0.3	54	2864	3019	3025	0.6	2.50	1979	2055	0.4
48529	BURTON	049	11314	11051	10788	-0.3	21	4476	4399	4309	-0.2	2.50	2895	2800	-0.4
48532	FLINT	049	19793	19473	19068	-0.2	25	8396	8378	8243	0.0	2.28	5282	5184	-0.2
	MICHIGAN					0.3					0.4	2.52			0.3
	UNITED STATES					1.0					1.1	2.59			0.9

ZIP CODE #	POST OFFICE NAME	RACE (%) White 2000	White 2009	Black 2000	Black 2009	Asian/Pacific 2000	Asian/Pacific 2009	% Hispanic Origin 2000	% Hispanic Origin 2009	2009 AGE DISTRIBUTION (%) 0-4	5-9	10-14	15-19	20-24	25-44	45-64	65-84	85+	18+	MEDIAN AGE 2009	% 2009 Males	% 2009 Females
48328	WATERFORD	89.7	87.7	5.2	5.3	1.2	1.9	5.1	6.9	6.9	6.5	6.0	5.4	5.8	31.5	26.2	9.5	2.1	77.6	37.6	49.6	50.4
48329	WATERFORD	95.1	93.4	1.3	1.7	1.1	1.8	2.8	3.8	6.6	6.8	6.8	6.1	4.2	29.0	28.3	10.7	1.5	76.0	39.5	49.3	50.7
48331	FARMINGTON	84.3	78.3	5.1	6.3	8.4	12.9	1.3	1.6	5.8	6.4	7.1	6.8	4.4	23.8	32.5	11.8	1.4	76.3	42.1	48.9	51.1
48334	FARMINGTON	83.8	78.5	7.1	8.9	6.1	9.2	1.5	2.0	5.6	5.9	6.7	5.9	4.5	22.0	28.6	16.2	4.6	77.9	44.6	47.0	53.0
48335	FARMINGTON	77.8	70.4	6.7	8.0	13.4	19.2	1.7	2.1	5.4	4.9	4.6	4.8	8.0	32.1	25.0	11.6	3.5	82.2	37.8	48.3	51.7
48336	FARMINGTON	86.2	81.7	7.2	9.0	3.9	6.1	1.4	1.8	6.2	6.1	6.1	6.0	5.2	27.2	28.0	12.1	3.0	77.6	40.5	48.3	51.7
48340	PONTIAC	56.4	49.4	27.6	31.3	2.7	3.8	16.3	19.4	9.6	8.7	7.6	7.0	7.7	31.6	20.0	6.7	1.3	70.1	30.5	48.8	51.2
48341	PONTIAC	32.3	31.3	60.2	60.3	1.2	1.7	7.6	8.2	7.2	7.2	7.1	9.1	7.5	28.4	23.4	8.6	1.6	74.3	33.7	50.1	49.9
48342	PONTIAC	25.6	21.1	60.2	63.1	3.2	3.9	13.0	14.4	9.1	8.8	8.1	8.6	7.6	26.9	22.0	8.0	1.0	68.7	30.6	47.8	52.2
48346	CLARKSTON	95.5	93.8	0.9	1.2	1.2	2.0	2.8	3.9	6.7	6.9	7.2	6.4	4.7	28.3	28.1	10.4	1.3	75.1	38.7	49.5	50.5
48348	CLARKSTON	96.8	95.5	0.8	1.0	0.9	1.5	1.8	2.5	7.1	7.9	8.6	7.8	4.5	23.8	32.0	7.7	0.6	71.2	39.2	49.8	50.2
48350	DAVISBURG	96.5	95.4	1.2	1.6	0.4	0.7	2.1	2.8	7.3	7.7	7.8	7.4	5.0	26.4	30.2	7.7	0.6	72.4	37.8	49.5	50.5
48353	HARTLAND	98.0	97.4	0.3	0.4	0.3	0.4	1.1	1.5	6.7	7.1	7.6	7.3	4.3	25.3	30.7	10.0	1.0	74.0	39.4	49.6	50.4
48356	HIGHLAND	97.9	97.2	0.2	0.3	0.4	0.7	1.3	1.7	6.9	6.6	7.8	7.7	4.7	27.6	30.4	7.3	0.9	73.5	38.2	50.8	49.2
48357	HIGHLAND	97.0	96.2	0.4	0.5	0.4	0.6	1.3	1.8	7.2	7.5	7.7	7.7	5.8	26.3	29.5	7.6	0.8	72.8	36.9	50.6	49.4
48359	LAKE ORION	93.3	91.1	1.8	2.4	1.3	2.2	4.3	5.7	8.3	8.1	7.1	6.1	6.1	33.8	23.1	6.3	1.0	72.7	34.5	50.4	49.6
48360	LAKE ORION	95.4	93.4	1.7	2.2	1.6	2.6	2.0	2.8	9.7	9.8	8.8	6.5	3.3	30.9	24.8	5.8	0.5	67.3	35.1	50.9	49.1
48362	LAKE ORION	96.7	95.5	0.7	0.9	0.9	1.5	1.9	2.6	7.5	7.5	7.5	6.3	4.8	29.6	28.0	7.5	1.3	73.5	37.4	50.0	50.0
48363	OAKLAND	96.7	95.2	0.8	1.2	1.0	1.7	0.8	1.2	5.9	7.0	8.1	8.1	4.2	21.9	33.3	10.5	1.0	73.7	41.7	50.3	49.7
48367	LEONARD	97.2	96.4	0.9	1.2	0.2	0.3	2.3	3.1	6.4	7.0	8.0	8.1	4.1	25.4	31.0	9.2	0.9	72.9	39.4	51.3	48.7
48370	OXFORD	97.0	95.9	1.4	1.9	0.5	0.8	0.9	1.3	5.4	6.3	7.6	8.9	3.9	21.4	34.4	11.0	1.2	74.2	42.8	51.5	48.5
48371	OXFORD	97.0	95.8	0.5	0.6	0.5	0.8	2.1	2.8	7.9	8.0	8.0	7.1	5.1	28.8	27.2	7.0	0.9	71.3	36.2	49.4	50.6
48374	NOVI	87.9	81.8	1.0	1.3	9.4	14.7	1.5	2.0	8.9	10.4	10.4	8.3	3.7	28.9	26.1	3.1	0.2	64.1	33.0	50.2	49.8
48375	NOVI	85.4	78.6	2.1	2.6	10.4	16.4	1.9	2.5	6.9	6.9	7.1	6.1	4.6	29.6	28.3	8.8	1.8	74.9	38.9	48.6	51.4
48377	NOVI	88.3	82.9	2.8	3.6	5.6	9.5	2.1	2.7	6.5	6.0	5.6	5.4	7.4	34.9	24.4	8.5	1.4	79.0	35.5	49.7	50.3
48380	MILFORD	97.8	97.2	0.4	0.6	0.4	0.6	1.3	1.8	5.7	7.2	8.2	8.1	3.9	22.6	33.7	9.0	1.4	73.5	41.4	50.8	49.2
48381	MILFORD	97.4	96.5	0.4	0.6	0.5	0.8	1.2	1.6	7.0	7.2	7.4	7.4	4.9	25.8	29.9	9.1	1.3	73.6	38.8	49.1	50.9
48382	COMMERCE TOWNSHIP	97.4	96.3	0.4	0.5	0.8	1.4	1.1	1.5	7.2	8.3	9.1	7.8	3.9	24.0	31.5	7.7	0.7	70.2	39.1	50.1	49.9
48383	WHITE LAKE	97.0	96.0	0.5	0.7	0.4	0.7	1.7	2.5	7.9	7.8	8.0	7.5	4.8	29.1	28.1	6.3	0.7	71.5	35.6	49.6	50.4
48386	WHITE LAKE	96.2	94.9	1.0	1.3	0.7	1.2	1.9	2.5	6.0	6.8	7.5	6.7	4.0	24.9	33.0	10.0	1.1	75.2	41.3	50.3	49.7
48390	WALLED LAKE	95.6	93.4	0.6	0.9	2.0	3.5	1.4	1.9	6.8	7.2	7.4	6.5	4.4	27.1	29.4	10.0	1.3	74.3	39.7	49.1	50.9
48393	WIXOM	91.9	89.3	2.1	2.6	2.4	3.9	2.7	3.6	8.5	7.5	6.8	6.4	7.5	35.7	21.7	5.1	0.7	73.4	31.5	51.7	48.3
48401	APPLEGATE	97.7	97.6	0.1	0.1	0.1	0.1	1.7	1.7	6.2	6.6	7.1	6.9	4.3	21.6	29.9	15.7	1.7	75.4	43.1	49.0	51.0
48412	ATTICA	97.5	96.8	0.2	0.3	0.3	0.6	2.3	3.1	6.7	7.1	7.6	7.3	4.3	26.2	29.2	10.6	1.0	73.8	39.7	50.7	49.3
48413	BAD AXE	97.9	97.4	0.2	0.3	0.4	0.6	1.4	1.9	6.1	6.5	6.4	6.5	5.5	24.7	27.5	13.2	3.6	76.9	40.9	48.4	51.6
48414	BANCROFT	97.5	96.9	0.0	0.0	0.1	0.2	1.4	1.9	5.9	6.6	6.9	7.1	4.8	25.3	32.2	10.0	1.2	76.2	40.6	50.1	49.9
48415	BIRCH RUN	96.7	95.3	0.5	0.9	0.3	0.4	2.7	4.0	6.6	6.9	7.2	6.8	5.0	26.1	29.1	11.2	1.2	75.1	39.5	49.4	50.6
48416	BROWN CITY	98.2	97.9	0.2	0.2	0.2	0.3	2.6	3.0	7.6	8.1	8.1	7.1	5.5	26.0	26.7	9.7	1.3	71.8	36.5	50.2	49.8
48417	BURT	93.5	90.7	1.5	2.3	0.3	0.4	4.4	6.6	6.7	8.2	7.4	7.8	5.0	26.1	29.3	8.6	0.8	72.9	37.4	51.1	48.9
48418	BYRON	97.6	96.9	0.1	0.2	0.3	0.5	1.2	1.6	7.5	8.1	7.9	7.0	4.3	28.0	27.6	8.5	0.9	71.9	36.8	50.6	49.4
48419	CARSONVILLE	97.9	97.9	0.1	0.1	0.2	0.2	1.7	1.7	5.7	6.2	6.7	6.5	5.1	21.9	30.2	15.7	2.0	76.7	43.3	48.8	51.2
48420	CLIO	96.0	94.1	1.1	2.0	0.3	0.5	1.9	2.7	5.9	6.2	6.5	6.7	5.7	26.6	29.5	11.2	1.6	77.2	39.6	49.6	50.4
48421	COLUMBIAVILLE	97.3	96.7	0.4	0.5	0.2	0.3	1.9	2.6	6.0	6.9	7.6	7.9	4.9	26.1	31.3	8.9	0.6	74.5	39.1	50.8	49.2
48422	CROSWELL	94.8	94.8	0.1	0.1	0.1	0.1	6.2	6.2	7.2	7.2	7.5	7.4	5.8	25.3	27.4	10.6	1.4	73.2	37.5	50.9	49.1
48423	DAVISON	95.2	92.8	1.5	2.7	0.6	0.9	2.0	2.8	6.2	6.1	6.1	6.7	7.0	27.2	27.6	11.4	1.6	77.5	37.9	47.9	52.1
48426	DECKER	97.0	96.9	0.4	0.4	0.0	0.0	1.8	1.8	6.4	7.6	7.5	8.2	5.9	25.4	25.8	11.2	1.8	73.1	37.3	53.1	46.9
48427	DECKERVILLE	96.3	96.2	0.1	0.1	0.3	0.3	4.4	4.5	5.5	5.8	6.0	6.3	5.3	23.0	29.9	14.7	3.5	78.9	43.5	48.5	51.5
48428	DRYDEN	97.8	97.3	0.1	0.1	0.2	0.4	1.2	1.7	6.5	7.5	8.0	7.3	4.1	24.6	31.8	9.4	0.8	73.2	40.3	51.0	49.0
48429	DURAND	97.2	96.7	0.1	0.1	0.1	0.2	1.7	2.3	6.9	7.2	7.3	6.8	4.9	25.6	28.1	11.0	2.1	74.4	38.8	49.1	50.9
48430	FENTON	97.0	95.7	0.4	0.7	0.7	1.2	1.4	2.0	6.7	7.0	7.3	6.7	4.6	26.1	30.0	10.2	1.5	74.7	39.7	49.5	50.5
48432	FILION	98.2	97.7	0.2	0.2	0.3	0.6	0.6	0.7	5.5	6.2	6.5	6.9	4.3	23.6	31.9	12.9	2.2	76.9	42.9	51.9	48.1
48433	FLUSHING	94.6	91.4	2.4	4.4	0.7	1.2	1.8	2.4	5.2	5.9	6.5	7.1	4.9	23.0	31.4	13.9	2.2	78.1	43.2	47.6	52.4
48435	FOSTORIA	97.9	97.5	0.2	0.2	0.1	0.2	1.2	1.6	7.3	7.5	7.6	7.5	5.2	25.5	28.2	9.9	1.2	72.9	37.5	52.8	47.2
48436	GAINES	96.9	95.7	0.4	0.7	0.3	0.5	1.1	1.6	6.5	7.1	7.5	6.8	4.6	25.0	33.0	8.6	0.8	74.6	40.4	50.4	49.6
48438	GOODRICH	97.8	96.8	0.3	0.6	0.5	0.8	1.0	1.5	6.4	6.9	7.7	7.7	4.6	25.5	31.4	9.0	0.8	73.6	39.4	51.3	48.7
48439	GRAND BLANC	89.5	84.6	5.5	8.6	2.5	3.7	1.8	2.3	6.5	6.4	6.8	6.8	5.6	26.6	28.6	10.9	1.7	76.1	39.2	49.1	50.9
48441	HARBOR BEACH	97.3	96.5	0.0	0.0	0.9	1.4	1.0	1.3	6.1	6.2	6.5	6.7	5.6	22.2	28.1	15.7	3.0	76.5	42.4	50.5	49.5
48442	HOLLY	95.5	93.1	1.7	2.8	0.4	1.0	2.5	3.4	6.6	7.0	7.3	6.9	5.1	27.6	29.9	8.4	1.1	75.0	38.5	50.5	49.5
48444	IMLAY CITY	93.3	91.6	0.4	0.4	0.8	1.2	11.9	15.0	7.4	7.1	7.3	7.6	5.9	26.2	26.4	10.3	1.9	73.5	36.9	49.9	50.1
48445	KINDE	98.3	97.8	0.2	0.2	0.4	0.7	0.5	0.6	6.6	6.4	6.0	5.8	5.9	24.0	28.7	14.3	2.3	77.1	41.8	50.1	49.9
48446	LAPEER	95.1	94.0	1.9	2.2	0.5	0.7	2.3	3.1	6.4	6.6	6.7	6.8	5.8	28.1	28.1	10.0	1.6	76.1	38.3	51.0	49.0
48449	LENNON	96.3	95.2	0.3	0.7	0.2	0.2	3.0	4.0	6.5	6.5	6.8	7.5	5.7	25.8	28.6	11.3	1.3	76.2	38.9	49.6	50.4
48450	LEXINGTON	98.1	98.2	0.1	0.1	0.2	0.2	1.7	1.7	5.2	5.6	5.9	5.7	5.0	21.9	28.9	18.7	3.0	79.6	45.5	48.0	52.0
48451	LINDEN	97.5	96.4	0.2	0.3	0.5	0.8	1.1	1.6	7.2	7.4	7.7	6.8	4.6	25.9	29.4	10.0	1.1	73.4	38.8	49.4	50.6
48453	MARLETTE	96.4	96.3	1.0	1.0	0.2	0.2	1.9	2.0	7.2	7.4	7.8	8.3	5.1	24.1	26.8	10.7	2.6	72.0	37.1	50.1	49.9
48454	MELVIN	97.0	96.8	0.4	0.6	0.2	0.2	1.1	1.1	7.7	8.0	8.0	7.1	5.0	24.8	27.6	10.5	1.3	71.8	38.1	51.6	48.4
48455	METAMORA	97.6	97.0	0.1	0.1	0.4	0.6	1.3	1.9	5.8	6.8	7.5	7.1	4.3	24.2	33.3	10.1	0.9	75.2	41.2	50.5	49.5
48456	MINDEN CITY	98.0	97.9	0.0	0.0	0.1	0.1	1.5	1.6	6.7	7.1	7.2	7.1	4.4	24.3	27.9	13.0	2.2	74.0	40.3	51.5	48.5
48457	MONTROSE	95.8	93.8	1.6	2.6	0.1	0.1	2.2	3.2	6.3	7.2	7.7	7.8	5.3	27.2	27.7	9.4	1.4	73.6	37.3	50.5	49.5
48458	MOUNT MORRIS	75.4	69.8	20.6	25.2	0.3	0.4	2.5	3.1	7.3	7.4	7.2	7.4	6.3	26.3	25.5	11.2	1.3	73.6	35.5	48.4	51.6
48460	NEW LOTHROP	98.1	97.7	0.0	0.1	0.1	0.1	1.1	1.6	5.5	5.8	6.1	6.3	5.5	25.6	31.3	12.6	1.4	78.6	41.4	50.0	50.0
48461	NORTH BRANCH	97.2	96.6	0.1	0.1	0.2	0.3	2.5	3.3	7.6	8.2	8.0	8.2	5.9	26.9	26.5	7.8	0.9	70.9	34.7	50.5	49.5
48462	ORTONVILLE	97.6	96.7	0.4	0.5	0.5	0.8	1.3	1.9	6.4	7.3	7.9	7.8	4.4	25.4	32.8	7.3	0.6	73.2	39.8	50.3	49.7
48463	OTISVILLE	94.7	92.1	2.6	4.2	0.3	0.4	1.3	1.9	5.7	6.4	7.0	7.0	5.0	25.2	32.4	10.5	0.9	76.5	41.0	51.1	48.9
48464	OTTER LAKE	96.8	96.2	0.5	0.6	0.2	0.3	1.8	2.4	5.8	6.3	6.8	6.8	5.0	26.8	30.6	11.0	0.9	76.7	39.9	50.3	49.7
48465	PALMS	97.1	97.0	0.0	0.0	0.1	0.1	2.6	2.7	6.2	6.8	7.1	6.6	4.2	23.2	29.2	14.4	2.4	75.3	41.9	51.1	48.9
48466	PECK	97.0	96.9	0.4	0.4	0.2	0.2	2.4	2.4	7.2	7.5	7.5	6.8	4.8	25.6	27.1	11.9	1.6	73.5	39.1	50.4	49.6
48467	PORT AUSTIN	98.8	98.4	0.1	0.1	0.2	0.4	1.0	1.3	4.0	4.3	4.6	4.3	3.5	17.7	35.1	23.5	3.0	84.1	53.1	51.0	49.0
48468	PORT HOPE	98.6	98.4	0.0	0.0	0.1	0.3	0.8	1.0	4.8	5.1	5.6	6.5	4.7	19.9	30.9	19.9	2.6	80.1	47.3	51.8	48.2
48469	PORT SANILAC	97.2	97.1	0.1	0.1	0.5	0.5	1.2	1.3	5.1	5.7	5.6	4.8	3.6	20.0	32.5	19.9	2.8	80.2	48.3	47.3	52.7
48470	RUTH	98.6	98.1	0.0	0.0	0.4	0.7	0.8	1.1	7.3	7.6	7.9	7.0	4.4	23.9	26.8	13.0	2.2	72.4	39.8	52.3	47.7
48471	SANDUSKY	96.3	96.2	0.5	0.5	1.0	1.0	3.0	3.1	5.8	5.9	6.1	6.6	5.9	24.7	28.8	13.2	3.0	77.9	41.3	48.7	51.3
48472	SNOVER	98.0	97.9	0.0	0.0	0.0	0.0	1.3	1.2	7.3	7.7	7.7	6.6	4.6	26.3	27.2	11.1	1.6	73.1	38.2	50.4	49.6
48473	SWARTZ CREEK	96.4	94.5	1.0	1.8	0.5	0.8	1.7	2.5	5.5	6.0	6.5	6.3	4.7	24.5	31.2	13.7	1.7	78.2	42.5	48.5	51.5
48475	UBLY	98.6	98.5	0.1	0.1	0.1	0.2	0.7	0.9	7.0	7.1	7.1	6.8	5.2	24.4	27.1	13.0	2.2	73.9	39.8	49.9	50.1
48502	FLINT	44.8	31.0	48.9	63.0	0.4	0.4	3.8	3.9	1.2	1.8	1.1	6.5	15.5	52.0	18.4	3.3	0.3	95.3	34.3	78.0	22.0
48503	FLINT	49.0	42.1	45.2	51.4	0.7	0.9	2.7	3.2	8.1	8.0	7.3	6.5	6.2	26.2	24.6	11.0	2.0	72.7	35.7	46.6	53.4
48504	FLINT	29.6	23.7	65.6	71.6	0.4	0.5	2.0	2.2	8.2	8.5	8.5	9.4	7.3	25.6	23.2	8.0	1.2	69.4	31.2	46.5	53.5
48505	FLINT	11.5	7.6	84.2	88.7	0.1	0.1	2.0	2.0	9.2	9.7	8.5	9.3	7.4	23.8	21.4	9.8	1.1	67.1	29.7	46.2	53.8
48506	FLINT	88.2	83.1	5.5	8.9	0.6	0.8	5.4	7.1	8.3	7.8	7.2	7.2	6.6	27.2	24.8	9.4	1.4	72.3	34.7	49.2	50.8
48507	FLINT	81.9	75.5	13.2	18.3	0.9	1.3	3.1	4.0	7.5	6.9	6.5	6.5	6.3	27.8	25.3	11.4	1.9	75.3	36.9	47.6	52.4
48509	BURTON	93.8	90.5	3.0	5.2	0.5	0.8	2.3	3.2	5.9	6.1	6.5	6.8	5.2	25.3	29.7	12.7	1.8	77.2	40.9	48.4	51.6
48519	BURTON	93.2	89.4	2.9	5.3	0.6	0.9	1.9	2.7	6.6	6.4	6.6	6.8	5.9	26.1	27.6	12.4	1.6	75.9	39.2	48.3	51.7
48529	BURTON	89.6	84.9	4.6	7.5	1.0	1.4	2.7	3.6	8.3	7.7	7.1	7.5	7.4	29.8	23.3	7.7	1.0	72.0	32.7	49.1	50.9
48532	FLINT	75.2	65.3	17.6	25.6	3.2	4.3	2.2	2.7	5.6	5.5	5.7	6.6	5.9	25.4	28.4	13.8	3.1	79.3	41.3	47.0	53.0
	MICHIGAN	80.2	78.3	14.2	14.5	1.8	2.8	3.3	4.1	6.7	6.7	6.8	7.2	6.6	26.3	26.9	10.9	1.9	75.6	37.6	49.2	50.8
	UNITED STATES	75.1	72.0	12.3	12.7	3.8	4.6	12.5	15.7	6.8	6.7	6.6	7.1	6.9	27.0	26.0	10.9	1.9	75.7	36.9	49.2	50.8

ZIP CODE #	POST OFFICE NAME	2009 Per Capita Income	2009 HH Income Base	2009 HOUSEHOLD INCOME DISTRIBUTION (%) Less than $25,000	$25,000 to $49,999	$50,000 to $99,999	$100,000 to $149,999	$150,000 or More	MEDIAN HOUSEHOLD INCOME 2009	2014	2009 National Centile	2009 State Centile	2009 Home Value Base	2009 HOME VALUE DISTRIBUTION (%) Less than $50,000	$50,000 to $89,999	$90,000 to $174,999	$175,000 to $399,999	$400,000 or More	2009 Median Home Value
48328	WATERFORD	32605	11091	16.0	24.9	38.7	15.6	4.9	60276	57757	78	76	7405	8.5	19.6	56.8	12.7	2.5	116312
48329	WATERFORD	36797	9812	7.5	15.9	42.5	25.6	8.5	80274	86448	92	94	8846	2.4	13.3	63.4	18.7	2.2	130838
48331	FARMINGTON	57607	7906	4.7	8.0	27.9	27.0	32.4	115516	120115	98	99	6666	2.0	0.7	17.3	71.1	9.0	251257
48334	FARMINGTON	42082	7446	12.8	17.4	34.4	21.4	14.0	77511	82164	91	93	5147	0.3	8.0	26.3	61.4	3.9	199579
48335	FARMINGTON	45116	11365	13.4	18.5	36.0	17.9	14.1	72751	75196	88	91	4726	5.7	5.1	19.0	65.7	4.5	219464
48336	FARMINGTON	35944	11083	15.1	20.6	34.9	20.5	8.9	69642	70950	87	90	8103	6.6	13.5	49.8	29.8	0.3	141342
48340	PONTIAC	20204	10166	31.8	28.2	30.2	7.7	2.2	39650	40589	32	17	5171	20.1	60.9	16.5	2.6	0.0	71147
48341	PONTIAC	23150	6737	31.3	25.1	28.1	10.9	4.6	40840	42260	35	21	3968	19.6	44.9	30.5	4.3	0.8	76877
48342	PONTIAC	17227	7569	38.6	25.4	26.0	7.3	2.6	34649	35908	17	6	3668	34.9	56.8	7.8	0.5	0.0	57579
48346	CLARKSTON	39485	8922	8.4	16.0	36.3	26.8	12.5	83870	95977	93	95	6792	8.6	11.5	40.7	36.1	3.0	152821
48348	CLARKSTON	46034	7617	4.7	12.2	30.6	30.2	22.3	102740	108928	97	98	7220	8.7	9.6	27.2	44.1	10.5	187330
48350	DAVISBURG	33447	2903	6.3	16.1	40.0	25.1	12.6	81689	92006	93	95	2668	18.7	6.7	30.2	39.1	5.1	159700
48353	HARTLAND	37729	2363	5.5	9.9	42.2	26.4	16.0	88346	96062	95	96	2250	4.3	17.5	22.8	50.7	4.8	186131
48356	HIGHLAND	33203	3102	8.9	15.6	42.9	23.3	9.3	80572	86083	92	94	2818	1.2	10.3	58.1	27.3	3.2	146684
48357	HIGHLAND	32433	3333	12.5	17.4	39.9	20.3	10.0	74258	75236	89	92	3090	36.8	6.7	31.3	22.0	3.2	98670
48359	LAKE ORION	31891	3434	12.1	20.1	38.8	20.8	8.3	75452	77535	90	93	2554	13.5	12.1	46.0	26.8	1.5	135026
48360	LAKE ORION	48916	3720	5.3	8.2	27.8	27.6	31.1	112924	116224	98	99	3219	1.7	3.9	25.0	62.1	7.3	202901
48362	LAKE ORION	41806	5549	9.3	12.6	34.0	28.7	15.5	89523	101590	95	97	4487	4.1	10.6	45.8	32.9	6.7	156623
48363	OAKLAND	56246	1733	10.2	12.9	26.9	25.7	24.2	99941	107779	97	98	1660	24.2	3.7	16.9	31.8	23.4	194545
48367	LEONARD	36831	1782	8.9	15.5	37.9	24.3	13.4	81492	88004	93	95	1644	11.4	11.4	25.0	45.3	6.9	182627
48370	OXFORD	40715	611	8.8	17.5	29.1	24.1	20.5	90418	101527	95	97	551	0.0	11.6	34.3	42.1	12.0	186250
48371	OXFORD	33911	8129	8.5	16.2	38.3	27.7	9.2	80986	88158	92	94	7097	15.4	14.6	35.2	30.9	3.9	141240
48374	NOVI	59578	4415	2.7	6.2	18.5	20.7	51.9	153550	155922	100	100	4265	17.4	1.8	3.2	53.6	24.1	282849
48375	NOVI	45813	8418	5.8	13.0	36.2	27.8	17.2	91637	102353	95	97	5939	3.8	7.4	41.3	44.1	3.4	167988
48377	NOVI	37578	7356	12.0	29.1	37.8	14.7	6.3	58541	56640	76	73	3972	22.5	9.2	25.1	37.4	5.9	158478
48380	MILFORD	50256	2192	3.8	10.2	32.9	26.9	26.1	104381	109904	97	99	2072	0.3	7.3	33.7	43.4	15.2	206838
48381	MILFORD	36551	5016	11.2	15.1	34.0	27.5	12.2	81760	91770	93	95	4252	11.7	14.5	31.1	37.0	5.6	148744
48382	COMMERCE TOWNSHIP	45363	7471	6.7	10.4	35.4	26.6	21.0	95876	104542	96	98	7077	0.6	5.3	42.1	43.2	8.9	180920
48383	WHITE LAKE	35090	4437	5.9	14.4	36.4	30.2	13.0	88671	101357	95	96	4119	19.0	11.6	27.7	39.6	2.1	149079
48386	WHITE LAKE	34736	6764	11.0	17.3	37.4	24.1	10.1	78432	82908	91	94	6060	9.5	8.7	42.4	36.6	2.7	156075
48390	WALLED LAKE	35762	8948	12.7	16.0	41.6	20.9	8.8	74576	74611	89	92	6962	6.2	11.3	52.8	27.7	2.1	135668
48393	WIXOM	34305	7395	11.7	28.4	33.3	17.8	8.7	61245	58112	79	78	4068	26.8	7.6	26.7	37.1	1.7	147195
48401	APPLEGATE	20363	602	21.6	30.9	41.5	4.5	1.5	47887	48630	56	44	533	9.6	20.5	45.2	22.7	2.1	116888
48412	ATTICA	23947	2352	14.8	24.5	46.9	11.6	2.3	60379	65427	78	76	2151	6.8	15.5	48.6	27.8	1.3	141887
48413	BAD AXE	21064	3000	26.7	27.7	37.9	5.6	2.1	45732	46521	50	37	2350	17.9	35.8	37.5	8.2	0.6	86654
48414	BANCROFT	21777	950	16.0	28.0	46.0	7.7	2.3	53898	54364	69	62	846	6.9	11.3	54.3	26.2	1.3	137786
48415	BIRCH RUN	22911	3559	16.8	26.8	44.8	8.6	3.1	54972	55229	71	65	3018	13.7	24.3	49.4	12.2	0.4	101365
48416	BROWN CITY	19339	1904	21.7	30.0	39.8	6.4	2.1	48249	49556	57	45	1552	10.7	16.6	48.5	21.0	3.2	121273
48417	BURT	19739	1136	21.6	24.2	44.9	7.4	1.9	52903	53487	68	59	1028	11.5	35.6	45.8	6.3	0.8	93125
48418	BYRON	25067	1571	10.9	20.1	51.3	12.4	5.2	64191	63268	83	83	1441	1.9	9.0	50.1	37.6	1.4	154886
48419	CARSONVILLE	18422	1025	28.5	31.5	34.8	3.7	1.5	41270	44703	37	22	876	14.5	25.5	40.8	17.2	2.1	102911
48420	CLIO	24249	8280	17.4	24.6	44.8	10.1	3.1	55941	57105	73	67	6730	9.6	37.0	43.9	8.9	0.5	93532
48421	COLUMBIAVILLE	24526	2659	11.5	25.8	48.9	11.3	2.4	61137	64039	79	78	2372	5.0	19.6	53.2	21.2	1.1	122081
48422	CROSWELL	18314	2450	24.4	30.6	38.7	5.3	1.0	44933	46648	48	35	2058	10.9	18.7	49.5	19.7	1.2	115890
48423	DAVISON	26659	13272	18.2	26.7	39.6	11.4	4.1	55099	57424	71	66	9317	14.2	22.4	49.2	13.2	1.0	104806
48426	DECKER	19005	430	22.6	30.9	40.7	4.7	1.2	46620	47643	53	40	356	13.5	16.9	48.6	19.1	2.0	113272
48427	DECKERVILLE	19713	1243	28.9	31.8	32.9	4.2	2.3	40271	43566	34	19	1010	14.2	23.2	42.5	17.3	2.9	107000
48428	DRYDEN	32019	2025	4.6	13.7	49.6	23.8	8.2	72634	77391	88	91	1858	5.4	9.0	32.5	45.2	8.0	183529
48429	DURAND	22167	3863	20.2	27.0	41.4	9.1	2.4	52199	53495	66	56	3114	13.4	14.8	51.1	19.7	0.9	119211
48430	FENTON	33325	14155	12.0	17.4	39.5	21.3	9.8	70893	70162	87	90	11779	5.2	13.8	37.1	37.1	6.9	161254
48432	FILION	20262	326	21.8	31.9	40.8	4.3	1.2	46864	46999	54	41	288	14.9	35.4	38.5	9.7	1.4	89655
48433	FLUSHING	29190	10406	13.8	22.8	41.9	15.1	6.4	63405	63372	82	82	9048	8.1	21.5	52.1	17.3	1.0	115409
48435	FOSTORIA	21783	741	16.9	28.5	43.0	8.5	3.1	53092	53342	68	60	653	10.7	21.4	47.5	19.3	1.1	121447
48436	GAINES	25154	1297	9.3	21.4	48.6	15.8	4.9	65372	65520	84	85	1207	1.6	18.3	56.1	22.0	2.1	129423
48438	GOODRICH	33090	2302	7.6	11.2	47.7	20.0	13.6	76276	78181	90	93	2142	1.8	6.2	45.2	41.8	5.0	170802
48439	GRAND BLANC	32556	18597	12.2	19.1	44.5	15.7	8.5	66456	66744	85	87	13695	6.5	13.2	53.2	24.7	2.4	137007
48441	HARBOR BEACH	19063	1654	29.5	30.8	34.5	4.3	0.8	39236	42792	30	15	1337	18.3	34.0	34.3	12.0	1.4	87886
48442	HOLLY	29598	7605	12.4	20.0	38.7	22.0	6.9	72414	72672	88	91	6587	15.1	20.1	39.8	23.0	2.0	117616
48444	IMLAY CITY	21687	3478	22.5	24.8	40.4	9.0	3.2	52226	56161	66	56	2604	6.5	18.0	51.8	22.0	1.7	126663
48445	KINDE	18850	561	27.6	31.4	36.5	3.4	1.1	42264	45070	40	25	479	25.7	38.4	27.6	7.5	0.8	75204
48446	LAPEER	24802	11681	16.6	23.1	45.3	11.5	3.4	60242	62418	78	75	9187	11.1	15.2	50.8	21.6	1.4	123912
48449	LENNON	22746	1329	15.1	26.6	49.4	7.8	1.1	56545	56868	73	69	1220	27.9	13.4	43.0	15.3	0.3	100951
48450	LEXINGTON	24043	2310	24.6	30.2	37.2	5.9	2.1	45268	46995	49	36	1898	5.8	14.7	51.3	24.2	4.0	128210
48451	LINDEN	29896	5320	10.4	19.1	47.6	16.8	6.2	67168	66494	85	88	4696	10.0	14.4	40.8	32.0	2.6	142600
48453	MARLETTE	19206	1910	24.9	28.3	39.5	5.8	1.5	46659	47944	53	40	1427	9.7	20.0	50.3	17.9	2.2	115300
48454	MELVIN	20317	498	20.9	28.1	44.2	4.6	2.2	50764	50872	63	51	447	9.4	14.3	46.8	26.4	3.1	131836
48455	METAMORA	32001	3236	12.1	14.4	44.1	20.9	8.5	70007	75831	87	90	2967	11.2	6.7	31.5	41.0	9.6	176563
48456	MINDEN CITY	18173	399	26.3	30.6	37.6	4.3	1.3	42471	45000	41	26	355	14.6	25.6	39.2	16.3	4.2	100227
48457	MONTROSE	21445	3119	18.3	24.9	46.5	7.8	2.5	55043	56091	71	65	2689	16.0	44.2	34.7	5.0	0.1	84305
48458	MOUNT MORRIS	20887	9470	26.0	29.0	36.8	6.2	2.1	44575	49548	47	34	7415	44.6	37.5	15.7	2.0	0.1	55116
48460	NEW LOTHROP	25047	910	16.7	24.0	45.7	9.8	3.8	56420	55946	73	68	763	3.7	14.7	59.2	21.0	1.4	127461
48461	NORTH BRANCH	20742	3007	14.9	26.7	47.9	9.2	1.3	56391	60329	73	68	2578	10.1	23.8	47.1	18.1	0.8	114254
48462	ORTONVILLE	34525	4553	6.4	11.0	40.5	31.0	11.1	88278	99875	95	96	4208	5.1	8.2	40.5	43.2	2.9	167962
48463	OTISVILLE	23292	1785	12.4	27.9	48.5	9.7	1.6	58046	58823	75	71	1610	8.4	35.6	41.7	14.0	0.2	97823
48464	OTTER LAKE	21844	842	16.4	24.9	50.2	6.5	1.9	56203	57682	73	68	751	7.7	26.0	49.8	16.1	0.4	109395
48465	PALMS	20149	284	26.4	29.9	38.0	3.5	2.1	42909	45116	42	28	253	13.0	22.1	41.5	17.8	5.5	110577
48466	PECK	18569	640	25.5	30.3	38.9	4.2	1.1	44153	45992	46	33	530	13.8	19.8	45.8	18.1	2.5	111111
48467	PORT AUSTIN	23294	1169	29.4	30.2	32.9	6.0	1.5	40231	43158	33	18	1014	12.5	30.2	40.2	13.9	3.2	98132
48468	PORT HOPE	21768	598	25.3	32.1	36.0	4.8	1.8	41488	44082	38	22	538	20.6	34.4	33.6	8.7	2.6	85091
48469	PORT SANILAC	21650	627	31.7	30.3	33.5	3.5	1.0	40263	43290	34	19	528	14.4	15.0	48.9	18.9	2.8	118434
48470	RUTH	18598	343	23.9	32.7	37.9	4.4	1.2	41936	44354	39	24	305	16.1	26.6	39.0	16.1	2.3	99375
48471	SANDUSKY	20415	2281	26.4	27.1	39.7	5.2	1.6	45938	47544	51	38	1673	11.6	22.7	49.6	14.5	1.7	107883
48472	SNOVER	18744	721	22.9	32.0	38.6	4.4	2.1	44575	46538	47	34	603	13.3	22.4	49.6	13.3	1.5	104446
48473	SWARTZ CREEK	26525	8144	14.0	23.0	46.9	12.6	3.5	60603	60838	78	77	7106	13.1	19.1	54.1	13.3	0.5	110784
48475	UBLY	19879	1002	25.2	31.0	37.0	5.6	1.1	43589	45837	44	30	857	15.6	33.1	39.1	10.7	1.4	91154
48502	FLINT	16383	206	52.4	30.1	14.6	1.0	1.9	22868	24277	2	1	18	55.6	33.3	11.1	0.0	0.0	46667
48503	FLINT	21809	11711	37.0	25.2	27.9	6.1	3.7	36025	38201	21	7	6266	33.2	46.5	15.5	3.8	0.9	62924
48504	FLINT	18083	13370	34.2	26.7	30.8	6.3	1.9	38236	41207	27	12	8555	50.7	39.9	8.3	0.9	0.3	49634
48505	FLINT	14203	11268	47.6	25.0	21.8	3.9	1.7	26694	28089	4	2	6114	71.6	26.0	2.0	0.2	0.2	36888
48506	FLINT	19778	12436	30.1	27.5	33.7	6.7	1.9	41277	45679	37	22	8831	40.7	37.7	19.9	1.8	0.0	58233
48507	FLINT	24580	13549	23.9	26.4	39.7	7.2	2.9	49629	52647	60	49	9455	25.8	44.7	26.7	2.7	0.2	70257
48509	BURTON	26405	3763	12.5	25.3	49.2	8.6	4.4	60530	60716	78	77	3473	12.0	45.5	36.9	5.6	0.0	84893
48519	BURTON	23669	3019	21.3	22.7	45.4	7.5	3.0	54045	55435	70	62	2392	12.7	50.7	33.2	3.4	0.0	80912
48529	BURTON	20265	4399	24.7	29.1	39.4	5.0	1.7	45144	50359	49	36	2954	37.7	54.4	7.1	0.8	0.0	55593
48532	FLINT	26846	8378	24.8	26.2	36.5	7.2	5.3	48732	52158	58	46	5216	14.5	37.0	33.7	13.8	1.0	88554
	MICHIGAN	26713		20.1	24.2	38.5	11.3	5.9	55536	56866				13.2	21.9	40.3	21.5	3.2	115137
	UNITED STATES	27277		20.9	24.4	35.3	11.7	7.6	54719	56938				9.3	13.1	31.6	32.6	13.5	162279

ZIP CODE #	POST OFFICE NAME	FINANCIAL SERVICES: Auto Loan	Home Loan	Invest-ments	Retire-ment Plans	THE HOME: Home Improvements: Home Repair	Lawn & Garden	Furnishings: Comput-ers & Hard-ware-Personal	Major Appli-ances	TV, Radio, Sound Equip-ment	Furni-ture	ENTERTAINMENT: Dine out/ Carry out	Sports Equip-ment	Fees & Tickets	Toys & Games	Travel	Cable TV	PERSONAL: Apparel & Services	Auto Repairs	Health Insur-ance	Pets & Supplies
48328	WATERFORD	101	105	96	106	101	98	106	100	104	106	106	80	109	106	106	103	75	104	101	119
48329	WATERFORD	125	150	135	149	145	141	130	134	128	135	129	102	144	131	140	127	91	130	132	155
48331	FARMINGTON	205	247	258	257	256	223	221	221	207	236	209	174	251	211	241	198	154	213	199	252
48334	FARMINGTON	124	144	153	146	150	142	135	136	134	138	134	101	150	131	146	134	96	135	141	155
48335	FARMINGTON	131	123	121	130	120	118	138	123	136	136	139	100	136	137	132	135	98	132	127	148
48336	FARMINGTON	110	124	121	125	124	120	118	116	116	119	117	89	127	116	124	116	83	117	119	135
48340	PONTIAC	75	61	52	63	57	61	74	65	75	73	76	53	67	77	65	75	53	72	69	80
48341	PONTIAC	87	82	72	83	78	84	88	82	92	87	91	64	87	91	83	94	64	88	90	101
48342	PONTIAC	68	59	52	61	55	64	68	62	73	66	73	47	66	72	62	77	51	68	72	78
48346	CLARKSTON	139	159	149	161	157	146	142	144	138	150	139	112	155	141	150	134	99	140	136	166
48348	CLARKSTON	180	220	209	224	219	197	188	192	178	200	181	151	213	184	203	172	131	182	173	220
48350	DAVISBURG	134	151	136	150	147	138	135	137	130	141	132	106	143	135	140	128	93	133	128	159
48353	HARTLAND	142	172	159	173	169	153	147	151	139	157	141	117	163	143	158	134	101	143	137	173
48356	HIGHLAND	124	147	133	148	144	135	128	132	123	133	125	102	140	126	137	121	89	126	124	152
48357	HIGHLAND	127	139	127	137	136	129	126	128	123	132	124	98	132	127	130	121	88	125	122	149
48359	LAKE ORION	121	120	103	122	114	109	118	113	116	122	118	90	118	121	114	113	82	114	108	134
48360	LAKE ORION	193	236	214	243	233	200	198	201	184	218	188	164	225	196	211	172	138	186	171	226
48362	LAKE ORION	153	177	161	177	173	154	157	157	149	167	151	124	170	155	163	143	108	151	142	180
48363	OAKLAND	210	248	243	253	250	229	215	222	207	230	209	171	240	212	232	201	151	212	204	255
48367	LEONARD	137	172	160	173	169	154	145	149	137	153	139	116	164	140	158	133	100	142	136	171
48370	OXFORD	157	196	188	199	196	178	166	172	157	176	160	132	188	160	183	153	115	163	159	197
48371	OXFORD	127	150	133	149	145	132	133	133	127	139	129	106	145	132	139	123	93	129	122	153
48374	NOVI	287	349	301	359	339	286	290	293	267	325	272	244	328	289	305	244	200	267	239	327
48375	NOVI	158	182	168	186	179	162	164	162	156	173	159	130	178	162	171	150	114	158	150	187
48377	NOVI	111	95	88	100	91	89	112	96	109	111	111	80	105	112	102	107	78	106	96	118
48380	MILFORD	193	245	240	255	248	223	205	213	194	218	196	167	239	199	228	187	144	200	192	243
48381	MILFORD	137	157	139	155	152	143	138	141	134	144	136	109	149	140	143	132	96	135	133	162
48382	COMMERCE TOWNSHIP	172	216	201	220	214	193	181	187	171	192	174	147	207	177	199	165	126	176	169	214
48383	WHITE LAKE	145	167	143	164	159	144	145	147	137	154	140	115	154	145	149	132	99	139	132	168
48386	WHITE LAKE	130	142	143	143	141	142	125	136	124	128	125	104	132	126	134	124	87	128	130	157
48390	WALLED LAKE	116	135	126	135	133	124	123	123	119	125	120	96	133	121	129	117	86	120	117	142
48393	WIXOM	124	109	95	114	103	98	122	107	118	124	120	90	115	124	111	114	85	115	102	129
48401	APPLEGATE	89	69	100	67	73	93	69	87	75	65	73	65	58	73	71	81	49	80	88	102
48412	ATTICA	92	104	89	107	100	102	93	96	91	93	91	75	99	93	98	91	64	92	95	113
48413	BAD AXE	85	70	77	71	71	88	72	82	77	67	75	63	64	78	70	82	51	78	87	97
48414	BANCROFT	90	88	83	91	88	98	84	92	85	79	84	70	82	87	85	89	58	86	94	108
48415	BIRCH RUN	89	92	83	92	90	95	85	90	86	85	86	68	86	88	87	88	60	87	92	105
48416	BROWN CITY	87	75	76	76	75	90	74	84	78	69	77	64	67	80	73	83	52	78	87	99
48417	BURT	88	80	79	83	82	94	79	89	81	71	80	67	73	83	79	86	55	82	92	104
48418	BYRON	105	112	98	114	109	110	102	107	100	102	101	83	104	104	105	101	70	102	104	125
48419	CARSONVILLE	81	61	89	60	65	83	63	78	68	58	66	58	52	66	64	74	44	72	81	92
48420	CLIO	88	91	83	93	88	94	88	89	89	86	89	69	90	90	89	90	62	89	93	105
48421	COLUMBIAVILLE	92	105	93	107	102	104	93	97	92	93	93	75	101	94	99	93	65	94	98	114
48422	CROSWELL	81	67	68	67	66	81	69	75	73	65	71	58	60	75	65	77	49	72	79	90
48423	DAVISON	91	89	82	90	87	89	91	88	91	91	92	68	90	92	89	92	64	91	92	105
48426	DECKER	80	72	72	75	74	85	71	81	74	65	72	61	66	75	71	78	49	74	83	94
48427	DECKERVILLE	84	61	90	60	64	87	65	81	71	58	69	62	52	69	65	77	46	75	85	96
48428	DRYDEN	121	151	140	152	149	136	127	132	121	134	123	102	144	124	139	117	88	125	121	151
48429	DURAND	87	82	80	83	80	92	79	86	82	76	81	66	76	84	79	86	56	83	90	102
48430	FENTON	119	134	125	135	132	126	121	123	118	125	119	95	130	120	127	116	84	120	119	143
48432	FILION	85	66	87	67	68	90	69	83	72	59	71	66	56	71	69	77	47	77	86	99
48433	FLUSHING	100	112	108	114	112	113	102	106	102	103	102	80	110	102	109	103	72	103	108	123
48435	FOSTORIA	96	88	85	90	89	101	86	96	88	80	87	72	80	90	85	93	59	89	98	112
48436	GAINES	102	114	99	118	111	113	103	107	102	103	102	83	109	104	108	102	71	103	107	126
48438	GOODRICH	132	160	137	158	153	136	135	137	127	143	130	109	149	134	143	122	93	130	121	157
48439	GRAND BLANC	114	118	109	121	115	112	115	112	113	118	114	87	119	115	116	111	80	113	109	132
48441	HARBOR BEACH	81	57	84	56	60	84	62	77	67	54	66	59	48	66	60	74	43	71	82	92
48442	HOLLY	113	124	110	124	121	118	113	115	111	116	112	89	119	114	117	111	79	112	112	135
48444	IMLAY CITY	87	82	78	84	81	87	83	85	84	81	84	66	80	86	82	87	58	84	87	101
48445	KINDE	75	59	71	60	61	76	65	72	68	58	66	55	55	67	62	72	45	70	76	86
48446	LAPEER	93	95	85	96	92	95	92	93	92	91	92	72	93	94	92	93	64	92	94	110
48449	LENNON	87	89	81	89	87	92	83	88	84	82	84	67	84	86	85	86	58	85	90	103
48450	LEXINGTON	77	74	79	74	76	85	72	80	75	69	74	58	71	74	74	79	51	77	85	92
48451	LINDEN	111	126	115	126	123	119	112	115	109	116	110	88	120	112	117	108	78	111	112	133
48453	MARLETTE	87	68	88	68	70	91	71	84	75	64	74	65	59	75	70	81	49	79	88	100
48454	MELVIN	86	78	77	81	80	92	77	87	79	70	78	66	71	81	77	84	53	80	90	101
48455	METAMORA	122	138	125	139	135	131	121	126	118	126	119	97	130	122	128	117	84	121	121	147
48456	MINDEN CITY	87	60	96	60	63	92	67	83	69	54	68	68	49	68	66	76	44	77	87	102
48457	MONTROSE	91	86	79	88	85	96	84	91	87	78	85	69	80	89	83	91	58	87	95	107
48458	MOUNT MORRIS	78	74	66	73	71	78	74	75	76	73	76	57	71	77	71	79	52	75	80	90
48460	NEW LOTHROP	96	99	94	101	99	108	92	101	94	87	94	76	93	96	96	98	65	95	105	117
48461	NORTH BRANCH	85	93	83	94	91	91	86	88	85	85	85	68	89	87	89	85	60	86	87	103
48462	ORTONVILLE	135	169	153	170	165	148	142	145	133	150	136	115	161	138	154	128	98	137	130	166
48463	OTISVILLE	86	97	84	98	94	96	87	90	87	87	87	69	93	89	91	88	61	88	92	106
48464	OTTER LAKE	91	84	82	88	85	98	82	92	84	75	83	70	77	86	83	89	57	85	95	107
48465	PALMS	87	60	96	60	63	91	66	83	69	55	68	68	49	68	67	75	44	77	87	101
48466	PECK	78	69	69	72	70	82	69	78	71	62	70	59	63	73	68	76	48	72	80	91
48467	PORT AUSTIN	77	65	96	62	71	84	64	80	68	63	67	57	58	64	69	72	44	75	83	92
48468	PORT HOPE	88	62	93	61	65	91	66	83	71	58	70	65	51	71	65	78	46	77	87	100
48469	PORT SANILAC	75	60	97	59	66	79	60	76	63	56	62	56	52	60	65	67	41	70	75	88
48470	RUTH	89	61	98	61	64	94	68	84	71	55	70	70	50	69	68	77	45	79	89	104
48471	SANDUSKY	81	68	77	68	70	83	71	79	74	66	73	60	63	74	69	78	49	76	84	93
48472	SNOVER	87	70	87	71	72	93	72	85	75	62	74	67	60	75	72	80	49	79	89	102
48473	SWARTZ CREEK	90	103	93	104	100	103	93	96	93	93	93	73	100	94	98	94	65	94	100	112
48475	UBLY	86	62	89	62	65	90	68	83	72	58	71	65	53	71	66	79	47	77	89	99
48502	FLINT	37	27	32	31	28	32	43	35	46	39	46	28	38	41	38	49	32	43	47	45
48503	FLINT	68	62	56	64	59	66	70	64	73	67	73	50	68	72	65	76	51	70	73	80
48504	FLINT	70	63	55	64	59	69	66	65	72	66	71	49	65	71	62	75	49	68	73	80
48505	FLINT	58	47	43	48	44	54	53	51	59	54	58	38	50	58	48	63	40	55	61	64
48506	FLINT	70	67	59	68	64	71	71	68	73	67	72	53	69	74	67	75	50	70	74	82
48507	FLINT	78	76	67	77	73	80	79	76	81	76	81	59	78	82	76	84	56	79	84	92
48509	BURTON	93	103	92	104	100	108	94	99	96	91	96	74	99	97	99	99	66	96	106	116
48519	BURTON	79	85	77	85	83	87	82	82	84	81	84	61	86	83	84	87	59	83	90	97
48529	BURTON	77	66	57	67	63	70	74	70	75	71	75	55	67	77	66	77	52	73	74	85
48532	FLINT	85	86	79	88	84	89	88	85	89	85	88	66	89	89	87	90	62	87	92	102
	MICHIGAN	98	97	93	98	95	100	96	97	97	95	97	74	96	98	96	99	68	97	100	115
	UNITED STATES	100	100	100	100	100	100	100	100	100	100	100	100	100	100	100	100	100	100	100	100

ZIP CODE			POPULATION			2000-2009 ANNUAL RATE		HOUSEHOLDS					FAMILIES		
#	POST OFFICE NAME	COUNTY FIPS CODE	2000	2009	2014	% Rate	State Centile	2000	2009	2014	% Annual Rate 2000-2009	2009 Average HH Size	2000	2009	% Annual Rate 2000-2009
48601	SAGINAW	145	48133	43699	41652	-1.0	4	17274	15787	15099	-1.0	2.72	12392	11196	-1.1
48602	SAGINAW	145	32788	30364	29000	-0.8	6	13013	12039	11520	-0.8	2.44	8068	7349	-1.0
48603	SAGINAW	145	25283	26210	25924	0.4	60	10786	11286	11222	0.5	2.23	6698	6915	0.3
48604	SAGINAW	145	12248	12412	12191	0.1	42	4475	4551	4490	0.2	2.50	3108	3116	0.0
48607	SAGINAW	145	2528	2249	2132	-1.3	2	1037	888	836	-1.7	2.31	496	416	-1.9
48609	SAGINAW	145	12285	12105	11809	-0.2	25	4779	4773	4678	0.0	2.49	3592	3549	-0.1
48610	ALGER	051	3588	3643	3648	0.2	48	1524	1598	1615	0.5	2.26	1070	1111	0.4
48611	AUBURN	017	5984	6186	6154	0.4	60	2255	2410	2424	0.7	2.55	1667	1760	0.6
48612	BEAVERTON	051	9300	9447	9333	0.2	48	3744	3914	3900	0.5	2.40	2710	2803	0.4
48613	BENTLEY	017	1145	1161	1154	0.2	48	400	421	423	0.6	2.55	311	324	0.4
48614	BRANT	145	1272	1270	1253	0.0	37	453	460	457	0.2	2.75	354	356	0.1
48615	BRECKENRIDGE	057	3045	3125	3114	0.3	54	1175	1230	1233	0.5	2.53	857	886	0.4
48616	CHESANING	145	7429	7183	6960	-0.4	16	2814	2758	2687	-0.2	2.57	2118	2054	-0.3
48617	CLARE	035	8664	8643	8490	0.0	37	3315	3376	3337	0.2	2.51	2275	2304	0.1
48618	COLEMAN	111	5466	5695	5726	0.4	60	2080	2246	2281	0.8	2.53	1542	1646	0.7
48619	COMINS	135	688	739	742	0.8	80	284	312	315	1.0	2.37	207	224	0.9
48621	FAIRVIEW	135	1429	1463	1453	0.3	54	563	584	583	0.4	2.43	394	404	0.3
48622	FARWELL	035	6185	6420	6362	0.4	60	2404	2569	2567	0.7	2.45	1765	1867	0.6
48623	FREELAND	145	12354	13533	13568	1.0	84	4038	4465	4506	1.1	2.68	3192	3497	1.0
48624	GLADWIN	051	15988	16790	16740	0.5	66	6485	7036	7086	0.9	2.35	4677	5027	0.8
48625	HARRISON	035	13615	13664	13437	0.0	37	5617	5774	5720	0.3	2.33	3871	3927	0.2
48626	HEMLOCK	145	6312	6368	6291	0.1	42	2274	2336	2322	0.3	2.72	1804	1837	0.2
48628	HOPE	111	1944	1985	1978	0.2	48	780	828	833	0.6	2.39	588	618	0.5
48629	HOUGHTON LAKE	143	7854	8440	8502	0.8	80	3396	3673	3709	0.9	2.26	2309	2473	0.7
48631	KAWKAWLIN	017	4943	4887	4814	-0.1	32	1802	1845	1836	0.3	2.61	1395	1413	0.1
48632	LAKE	035	5455	5653	5604	0.4	60	2326	2476	2474	0.7	2.27	1627	1711	0.5
48634	LINWOOD	017	4625	4626	4574	0.0	37	1732	1798	1795	0.4	2.53	1354	1391	0.3
48635	LUPTON	129	1950	1806	1754	-0.8	6	849	808	792	-0.5	2.23	599	564	-0.6
48636	LUZERNE	135	826	821	808	-0.1	32	348	351	347	0.1	2.34	237	236	0.0
48637	MERRILL	145	3442	3574	3553	0.4	60	1277	1354	1356	0.6	2.63	996	1045	0.5
48638	SAGINAW	145	13577	12818	12297	-0.6	9	5990	5731	5534	-0.5	2.23	3745	3521	-0.7
48640	MIDLAND	111	32504	32446	32044	0.0	37	12461	12803	12745	0.3	2.45	8622	8741	0.1
48642	MIDLAND	111	31378	32236	32219	0.3	54	12075	12758	12848	0.6	2.50	8618	9040	0.5
48647	MIO	135	4817	4656	4546	-0.4	16	1946	1909	1871	-0.2	2.43	1351	1309	-0.3
48649	OAKLEY	145	2051	2014	1966	-0.2	25	754	753	740	0.0	2.67	568	561	-0.1
48650	PINCONNING	017	7595	7483	7374	-0.2	25	2926	2989	2976	0.2	2.49	2151	2171	0.1
48651	PRUDENVILLE	143	5010	5170	5147	0.3	54	2290	2412	2418	0.6	2.14	1569	1634	0.4
48652	RHODES	051	1575	1609	1594	0.2	48	591	624	624	0.6	2.57	441	461	0.5
48653	ROSCOMMON	143	10600	10862	10745	0.3	54	4512	4741	4726	0.5	2.25	3154	3276	0.4
48654	ROSE CITY	129	2789	2812	2799	0.1	42	1066	1102	1106	0.4	2.44	752	771	0.3
48655	SAINT CHARLES	145	6286	6063	5884	-0.4	16	2351	2304	2247	-0.2	2.62	1818	1766	-0.3
48656	SAINT HELEN	143	4421	4625	4632	0.5	66	2010	2148	2164	0.7	2.15	1320	1393	0.6
48657	SANFORD	111	8025	8084	7967	0.1	42	3147	3289	3273	0.5	2.46	2373	2451	0.4
48658	STANDISH	011	6007	5964	5917	-0.1	32	2104	2143	2142	0.2	2.48	1454	1465	0.1
48659	STERLING	011	3101	3154	3152	0.2	48	1156	1213	1225	0.5	2.53	841	875	0.4
48661	WEST BRANCH	129	9740	9533	9426	-0.2	25	3948	3968	3957	0.1	2.36	2762	2745	-0.1
48662	WHEELER	057	1484	1519	1513	0.3	54	546	577	579	0.6	2.62	429	450	0.5
48701	AKRON	157	1626	1614	1587	-0.1	32	633	648	644	0.3	2.46	464	469	0.1
48703	AU GRES	011	3382	3584	3636	0.6	71	1514	1654	1693	1.0	2.15	1030	1112	0.8
48705	BARTON CITY	001	667	654	650	-0.2	25	302	304	305	0.1	2.14	208	206	-0.1
48706	BAY CITY	017	40772	40341	39731	-0.1	32	16626	17003	16915	0.2	2.34	11366	11482	0.1
48708	BAY CITY	017	29220	27993	27269	-0.5	12	12022	11793	11587	-0.2	2.33	7527	7275	-0.4
48710	UNIVERSITY CENTER	017	7	8	8	1.5	93	1	1	1	0.0	3.00	1	1	0.0
48720	BAY PORT	063	1242	1228	1207	-0.1	32	496	508	505	0.3	2.40	346	350	0.1
48721	BLACK RIVER	001	483	509	519	0.6	71	201	217	222	0.8	2.35	146	155	0.6
48722	BRIDGEPORT	145	3179	3172	3106	0.0	37	1238	1255	1234	0.1	2.51	918	916	0.0
48723	CARO	157	12929	12469	12201	-0.4	16	4796	4757	4684	-0.1	2.47	3330	3265	-0.2
48725	CASEVILLE	063	2592	2496	2438	-0.4	16	1237	1229	1213	-0.1	2.01	790	771	-0.3
48726	CASS CITY	157	6196	5951	5803	-0.4	16	2394	2360	2321	-0.2	2.48	1708	1666	-0.3
48727	CLIFFORD	087	1276	1379	1416	0.8	80	458	518	539	1.3	2.66	345	385	1.2
48728	CURRAN	001	432	429	427	-0.1	32	215	219	220	0.2	1.95	144	146	0.1
48729	DEFORD	157	1776	1819	1805	0.3	54	633	664	664	0.5	2.73	494	513	0.4
48730	EAST TAWAS	069	5055	4725	4550	-0.7	7	2310	2261	2211	-0.2	2.09	1470	1413	-0.4
48731	ELKTON	063	1913	1760	1687	-0.9	5	737	700	677	-0.6	2.47	531	498	-0.7
48732	ESSEXVILLE	017	11630	11291	11079	-0.3	21	4687	4684	4633	0.0	2.35	3095	3042	-0.2
48733	FAIRGROVE	157	1920	1917	1886	0.0	37	730	749	744	0.3	2.52	547	556	0.2
48734	FRANKENMUTH	145	7244	7153	6989	-0.1	32	2961	2952	2895	0.0	2.32	2030	1995	-0.2
48735	GAGETOWN	157	845	824	808	-0.3	21	316	318	314	0.1	2.54	229	227	-0.1
48737	GLENNIE	001	1340	1298	1285	-0.3	21	598	598	597	0.0	2.15	413	408	-0.1
48738	GREENBUSH	001	1236	1173	1155	-0.6	9	587	571	566	-0.3	2.05	400	384	-0.4
48739	HALE	069	4640	4401	4266	-0.6	9	2016	1990	1956	-0.1	2.20	1396	1359	-0.3
48740	HARRISVILLE	001	2659	2695	2711	0.1	42	1120	1166	1183	0.4	2.21	758	779	0.3
48741	KINGSTON	157	2210	2292	2281	0.4	60	801	852	855	0.7	2.69	627	660	0.6
48742	LINCOLN	001	1819	1794	1786	-0.1	32	815	823	826	0.1	2.13	558	558	0.0
48743	LONG LAKE	069	29	28	27	-0.4	16	15	15	15	0.0	1.87	11	11	0.0
48744	MAYVILLE	157	4592	4644	4611	0.1	42	1634	1705	1707	0.5	2.69	1261	1304	0.4
48745	MIKADO	001	1460	1451	1447	-0.1	32	570	578	581	0.2	2.49	426	427	0.0
48746	MILLINGTON	157	9205	9351	9252	0.2	48	3286	3443	3437	0.5	2.71	2622	2722	0.4
48747	MUNGER	017	1595	1620	1609	0.2	48	555	586	588	0.6	2.59	431	451	0.5
48748	NATIONAL CITY	069	1733	1603	1536	-0.8	6	800	772	751	-0.4	2.07	560	532	-0.6
48749	OMER	011	963	990	995	0.3	54	392	416	422	0.6	2.37	277	291	0.5
48750	OSCODA	069	9030	9141	9049	0.1	42	3894	4086	4090	0.5	2.23	2559	2673	0.5
48754	OWENDALE	063	1319	1247	1206	-0.6	9	484	472	460	-0.3	2.51	353	341	-0.4
48755	PIGEON	063	3293	3254	3189	-0.1	32	1352	1376	1363	0.2	2.32	981	990	0.1
48756	PRESCOTT	129	4338	4328	4298	0.0	37	1798	1828	1827	0.2	2.36	1247	1253	0.1
48757	REESE	157	4058	3977	3893	-0.2	25	1566	1579	1559	0.1	2.51	1173	1168	0.0
48759	SEBEWAING	063	3523	3182	3034	-1.1	3	1505	1400	1348	-0.8	2.26	1009	926	-0.9
48760	SILVERWOOD	087	1063	1134	1151	0.7	76	385	426	437	1.1	2.65	305	334	1.0
48761	SOUTH BRANCH	001	1206	1118	1084	-0.8	6	555	536	526	-0.4	2.08	375	357	-0.5
48762	SPRUCE	001	1038	996	981	-0.4	16	453	447	443	-0.1	2.23	321	313	-0.3
48763	TAWAS CITY	069	5223	4909	4751	-0.7	7	2052	2014	1972	-0.2	2.27	1432	1387	-0.3
48765	TURNER	011	764	756	747	-0.1	32	300	305	303	0.2	2.47	218	220	0.1
48766	TWINING	011	1550	1534	1513	-0.1	32	565	572	570	0.1	2.68	415	417	0.1
48767	UNIONVILLE	157	2385	2309	2257	-0.3	21	902	900	887	0.0	2.53	680	672	-0.1
48768	VASSAR	157	10436	10246	10064	-0.2	25	3744	3792	3757	0.1	2.63	2854	2861	0.0
	MICHIGAN					0.3					0.4	2.52			0.3
	UNITED STATES					1.0					1.1	2.59			0.9

ZIP CODE #	POST OFFICE NAME	RACE (%) White 2000	White 2009	Black 2000	Black 2009	Asian/Pacific 2000	Asian/Pacific 2009	% Hispanic Origin 2000	% Hispanic Origin 2009	2009 AGE DISTRIBUTION (%) 0-4	5-9	10-14	15-19	20-24	25-44	45-64	65-84	85+	18+	MEDIAN AGE 2009	% 2009 Males	% 2009 Females
48601	SAGINAW	31.0	27.0	60.4	63.8	0.1	0.2	11.1	12.3	8.3	8.7	8.0	8.7	7.0	23.5	24.1	10.3	1.3	69.8	32.2	46.0	54.0
48602	SAGINAW	78.3	70.7	11.9	16.3	0.6	0.8	11.4	15.4	7.7	7.4	6.8	7.1	7.5	28.4	23.9	8.9	2.3	73.9	34.3	48.5	51.5
48603	SAGINAW	88.2	82.9	5.3	7.8	3.0	4.5	4.0	5.8	5.1	5.0	5.2	5.6	6.4	24.8	27.5	15.8	4.6	81.3	43.1	46.9	53.1
48604	SAGINAW	86.0	80.2	7.2	10.4	1.1	1.7	7.9	11.2	6.6	6.5	6.3	10.3	8.4	25.3	23.3	11.3	1.9	76.9	33.9	48.1	51.9
48607	SAGINAW	14.6	10.8	76.9	80.4	0.6	0.6	10.2	10.6	7.5	8.1	7.3	7.6	6.4	23.9	26.8	10.7	1.6	72.6	36.0	49.5	50.5
48609	SAGINAW	97.1	95.7	0.5	0.8	0.5	0.8	2.9	4.5	4.8	5.7	6.1	6.9	4.5	22.0	33.1	14.5	2.3	78.8	44.9	48.2	51.8
48610	ALGER	97.3	96.8	0.1	0.2	0.2	0.4	0.9	1.2	4.7	5.2	5.4	5.5	4.6	19.3	31.8	21.5	2.1	81.0	48.7	49.8	50.2
48611	AUBURN	97.8	97.3	0.3	0.3	0.3	0.4	1.8	2.4	6.3	6.5	6.7	6.6	5.5	25.7	29.7	11.4	1.6	76.5	40.0	50.4	49.6
48612	BEAVERTON	97.8	97.3	0.2	0.2	0.2	0.3	1.2	1.7	5.7	6.0	6.2	6.4	4.8	22.8	30.9	15.5	1.7	78.0	43.6	50.1	49.9
48613	BENTLEY	98.4	98.3	0.1	0.1	0.0	0.0	8.5	11.3	6.1	6.2	7.2	8.1	5.5	24.4	30.1	11.2	1.2	75.4	39.7	50.2	49.8
48614	BRANT	97.4	96.5	0.2	0.2	0.4	0.6	1.4	2.3	6.5	6.9	7.0	6.7	5.7	26.9	28.7	10.2	1.3	75.2	38.2	48.8	51.2
48615	BRECKENRIDGE	96.5	95.6	0.1	0.1	0.1	0.2	3.9	5.2	6.7	6.8	6.8	7.1	6.3	27.2	26.7	10.8	1.6	75.3	37.3	50.6	49.4
48616	CHESANING	97.4	96.1	0.3	0.4	0.1	0.2	3.6	5.5	6.2	6.5	6.7	6.2	4.9	25.7	28.8	12.8	2.2	76.7	40.8	49.4	50.6
48617	CLARE	97.4	96.9	0.3	0.3	0.3	0.4	1.2	1.6	7.5	7.1	6.9	7.0	6.6	24.2	25.7	12.6	2.3	74.3	37.3	48.3	51.7
48618	COLEMAN	97.4	97.0	0.1	0.1	0.1	0.2	1.1	1.5	6.6	6.7	6.8	7.0	5.4	26.8	27.6	11.6	1.5	75.5	38.6	50.6	49.4
48619	COMINS	98.7	98.4	0.1	0.1	0.0	0.0	0.6	0.7	3.4	5.1	5.1	6.8	2.8	17.5	37.8	20.4	1.1	81.7	50.7	50.6	49.4
48621	FAIRVIEW	98.1	97.8	0.1	0.1	0.0	0.0	0.4	0.6	5.1	5.6	6.0	6.4	4.9	18.9	30.2	18.9	4.1	79.1	47.2	46.3	53.7
48622	FARWELL	97.1	96.6	0.2	0.3	0.4	0.6	1.6	2.1	5.5	5.7	6.0	6.2	4.8	23.7	30.1	16.0	2.0	78.7	43.5	49.3	50.7
48623	FREELAND	91.2	88.1	5.7	7.6	0.6	0.9	2.6	3.8	6.0	6.3	6.5	6.7	5.1	31.0	28.5	9.0	1.0	77.1	38.3	55.2	44.8
48624	GLADWIN	97.6	97.0	0.1	0.1	0.4	0.5	0.8	1.0	5.4	5.6	5.9	5.7	4.5	20.7	29.4	20.4	2.4	79.3	46.7	50.0	50.0
48625	HARRISON	97.0	96.4	0.5	0.5	0.3	0.4	1.2	1.6	5.5	6.0	6.0	6.2	5.1	22.0	29.9	17.5	1.8	78.6	44.4	50.2	49.8
48626	HEMLOCK	98.0	97.0	0.1	0.2	0.2	0.4	2.0	3.1	6.5	7.0	7.3	7.0	5.2	24.2	29.6	11.7	1.4	74.9	39.9	49.3	50.7
48628	HOPE	98.3	98.0	0.3	0.4	0.2	0.2	0.5	0.7	5.2	5.7	6.3	6.2	4.1	23.7	32.2	15.3	1.3	78.9	44.2	50.1	49.9
48629	HOUGHTON LAKE	97.9	97.5	0.6	0.7	0.2	0.4	0.9	1.1	4.4	5.6	5.9	5.7	3.7	19.1	32.7	20.4	2.5	80.6	49.1	48.7	51.3
48631	KAWKAWLIN	96.8	96.1	0.3	0.4	0.3	0.4	2.0	2.7	6.1	6.4	6.7	6.3	4.7	24.5	30.7	12.6	2.0	77.0	41.4	49.4	50.6
48632	LAKE	97.7	97.3	0.2	0.2	0.1	0.2	1.3	1.7	4.6	5.1	5.3	5.7	4.4	19.5	33.2	20.5	1.8	81.3	48.8	50.4	49.6
48634	LINWOOD	97.3	96.7	0.6	0.6	0.3	0.5	1.7	2.3	5.7	6.2	6.5	6.2	4.6	24.7	31.4	12.9	1.8	77.9	42.2	50.6	49.4
48635	LUPTON	98.4	98.1	0.1	0.1	0.2	0.3	1.3	1.7	4.4	4.5	4.7	5.0	4.3	17.2	32.6	25.2	2.2	82.8	52.4	50.6	49.4
48636	LUZERNE	98.7	98.5	0.0	0.0	0.2	0.2	0.5	0.5	5.0	5.0	5.6	6.1	3.9	17.1	35.7	19.9	1.8	80.8	50.0	49.2	50.8
48637	MERRILL	97.8	96.8	0.1	0.1	0.1	0.2	2.6	3.9	5.9	6.4	6.8	6.7	5.0	25.5	29.9	12.1	1.8	76.8	41.0	49.6	50.4
48638	SAGINAW	89.6	84.9	5.5	8.3	1.9	2.8	4.6	6.6	5.0	5.0	5.4	5.9	5.8	23.6	29.6	16.4	3.4	81.1	44.5	47.3	52.7
48640	MIDLAND	94.8	93.2	1.3	1.4	2.0	3.1	1.6	2.1	6.1	6.3	6.8	8.3	7.3	24.5	27.6	11.0	2.1	76.3	38.4	49.3	50.7
48642	MIDLAND	94.9	93.3	1.3	1.5	1.8	2.9	1.8	2.4	6.7	7.1	7.3	7.2	5.6	26.3	27.5	10.4	1.9	74.3	38.0	48.2	51.8
48647	MIO	97.3	96.9	0.1	0.1	0.1	0.1	1.2	1.6	5.4	6.0	6.7	6.9	4.6	20.3	30.7	17.3	2.1	77.4	45.1	49.9	50.1
48649	OAKLEY	97.5	96.5	0.5	0.7	0.3	0.4	2.8	4.2	6.2	6.4	6.8	7.0	5.2	25.9	29.1	12.0	1.6	76.4	39.8	50.2	49.8
48650	PINCONNING	97.2	96.6	0.3	0.3	0.2	0.3	1.9	2.6	5.6	6.0	6.3	6.4	4.7	25.3	31.3	12.6	1.8	78.1	41.9	50.3	49.7
48651	PRUDENVILLE	98.0	97.9	0.1	0.1	0.1	0.2	0.7	0.9	4.1	4.5	4.7	5.1	4.1	16.9	32.7	25.5	2.5	83.7	52.7	48.9	51.1
48652	RHODES	97.8	97.3	0.1	0.1	0.1	0.2	1.2	1.7	5.0	5.4	6.0	6.6	4.8	23.5	32.7	14.7	1.3	79.5	44.2	49.8	50.2
48653	ROSCOMMON	98.1	97.7	0.3	0.3	0.3	0.4	0.8	1.1	4.2	4.5	5.0	5.7	4.2	17.5	33.3	22.8	2.8	82.8	50.9	50.6	49.4
48654	ROSE CITY	97.7	97.3	0.2	0.2	0.1	0.2	1.4	1.9	5.2	5.5	6.3	7.3	4.8	19.9	31.3	16.5	3.4	78.1	45.8	49.7	50.3
48655	SAINT CHARLES	97.0	95.8	0.3	0.5	0.2	0.3	2.7	4.1	6.4	7.0	7.2	6.5	5.2	25.4	29.1	11.6	1.5	75.3	39.7	49.7	50.3
48656	SAINT HELEN	98.3	98.0	0.1	0.1	0.2	0.4	0.7	1.0	4.2	4.4	4.6	5.4	4.5	17.6	30.5	26.0	2.7	83.4	51.8	49.6	50.4
48657	SANFORD	97.9	97.5	0.1	0.1	0.3	0.5	0.8	1.1	6.0	6.4	6.9	6.6	4.5	25.4	30.7	12.3	1.0	76.4	41.1	50.4	49.6
48658	STANDISH	91.8	90.4	4.9	5.7	0.4	0.6	2.2	2.9	5.6	5.7	5.6	6.2	6.9	28.5	27.3	12.3	2.0	79.4	39.2	53.3	46.7
48659	STERLING	98.1	97.8	0.0	0.0	0.2	0.3	1.6	2.3	5.6	6.3	6.7	7.3	5.0	23.3	30.0	13.4	2.2	76.7	42.1	50.5	49.5
48661	WEST BRANCH	97.7	97.1	0.1	0.1	0.7	1.2	0.9	1.2	5.5	6.1	6.4	6.7	4.7	22.6	30.0	15.7	2.3	77.6	43.5	49.5	50.5
48662	WHEELER	96.4	95.4	0.1	0.1	0.1	0.2	4.8	6.5	6.5	6.8	7.3	7.2	5.0	25.8	28.0	12.0	1.4	75.0	39.4	51.6	48.4
48701	AKRON	96.7	96.1	0.2	0.2	0.2	0.2	4.5	5.9	6.3	6.4	6.3	6.2	5.5	26.0	27.6	13.5	2.1	76.6	40.2	49.4	50.6
48703	AU GRES	97.2	96.5	0.1	0.1	0.4	0.6	1.0	1.3	4.5	4.9	5.0	5.0	4.0	18.2	33.0	23.2	2.2	82.6	50.8	50.6	49.4
48705	BARTON CITY	98.7	98.6	0.0	0.0	0.1	0.2	1.0	1.4	3.1	3.4	3.8	4.6	3.8	15.1	35.3	28.0	2.9	86.4	55.4	52.1	47.9
48706	BAY CITY	96.3	95.3	0.7	0.8	0.6	0.9	3.1	4.1	5.6	5.8	6.0	6.2	5.2	24.4	29.1	14.9	2.7	78.6	42.6	48.0	52.0
48708	BAY CITY	90.5	88.4	3.1	3.5	0.5	0.8	6.8	8.9	6.6	6.4	6.3	6.7	6.6	26.4	26.8	11.6	2.4	76.6	38.2	48.9	51.1
48710	UNIVERSITY CENTER	100.0	100.0	0.0	0.0	0.0	0.0	0.0	0.0	0.0	0.0	0.0	0.0	0.0	12.5	87.5	0.0	0.0	100.0	52.5	50.0	50.0
48720	BAY PORT	98.0	97.2	0.3	0.5	0.2	0.4	2.2	2.9	4.8	5.1	5.6	6.4	5.0	23.1	32.7	15.1	2.2	79.8	44.9	51.1	48.9
48721	BLACK RIVER	97.3	96.9	0.0	0.0	0.0	0.2	0.6	0.8	4.3	4.7	5.5	5.7	3.7	18.1	34.2	22.0	1.8	81.9	50.2	50.5	49.5
48722	BRIDGEPORT	88.3	83.0	7.5	11.3	0.4	0.6	5.9	8.7	5.6	5.8	6.1	5.7	4.6	25.0	29.9	15.5	1.8	79.0	43.0	48.4	51.6
48723	CARO	94.6	91.5	1.7	3.9	0.4	0.8	3.1	4.0	5.5	5.9	6.3	6.9	5.7	26.0	28.5	12.5	2.6	78.6	40.4	49.2	50.8
48725	CASEVILLE	98.5	98.1	0.1	0.1	0.2	0.3	1.2	1.6	3.1	3.5	3.8	4.2	4.2	16.6	34.8	26.2	3.6	86.8	55.2	50.0	50.0
48726	CASS CITY	97.5	97.0	0.2	0.3	0.3	0.5	1.5	1.9	6.1	6.4	6.4	6.7	5.9	24.0	28.2	13.6	2.7	76.8	40.5	49.8	50.2
48727	CLIFFORD	96.5	95.6	0.8	0.9	0.3	0.4	1.9	2.6	6.7	6.9	7.1	6.5	5.4	25.1	29.1	11.9	1.3	75.3	39.9	50.8	49.2
48728	CURRAN	99.3	99.1	0.0	0.0	0.0	0.0	0.9	1.2	2.3	2.8	3.0	4.2	3.5	12.1	35.9	33.1	3.0	88.6	58.8	51.3	48.7
48729	DEFORD	97.1	95.8	0.3	1.1	0.1	0.2	1.7	2.3	5.8	6.8	7.0	8.3	5.4	24.9	30.1	10.4	1.3	75.2	39.4	50.8	49.2
48730	EAST TAWAS	97.4	96.8	0.2	0.3	0.5	0.9	1.0	1.3	4.6	5.2	5.6	6.2	4.3	19.4	30.7	20.6	3.4	80.6	48.1	47.4	52.6
48731	ELKTON	97.4	96.9	0.3	0.3	0.4	0.6	3.7	4.9	7.0	7.2	7.7	6.8	4.4	25.5	27.3	12.1	2.2	73.5	38.8	50.1	49.9
48732	ESSEXVILLE	95.3	94.2	1.1	1.3	0.7	1.0	2.4	3.3	5.6	5.5	5.9	6.5	5.8	23.8	29.1	14.1	3.7	79.0	42.5	47.6	52.4
48733	FAIRGROVE	96.6	95.9	0.2	0.2	0.2	0.2	4.5	6.0	5.5	6.1	6.4	6.5	4.2	25.9	30.5	12.8	2.1	77.6	41.7	49.2	50.8
48734	FRANKENMUTH	98.4	97.6	0.3	0.6	0.4	0.6	1.3	1.9	4.8	4.8	5.2	6.4	5.5	19.1	29.0	18.6	6.5	80.9	48.0	46.7	53.3
48735	GAGETOWN	95.3	94.2	0.2	0.2	0.2	0.5	4.1	5.3	5.3	5.7	6.1	6.8	5.6	23.8	31.3	13.2	2.2	77.8	42.5	51.3	48.7
48737	GLENNIE	97.8	97.5	0.1	0.1	0.1	0.2	0.7	0.9	3.9	4.0	4.3	4.4	3.5	14.2	33.4	29.7	2.5	84.8	56.4	50.8	49.2
48738	GREENBUSH	97.8	97.4	0.4	0.4	0.4	0.7	0.3	0.4	3.8	4.3	4.8	4.1	2.9	15.7	31.7	29.8	2.9	84.2	55.9	50.4	49.6
48739	HALE	97.4	97.0	0.1	0.1	0.2	0.3	0.7	1.0	4.2	4.3	4.5	5.7	4.7	16.1	32.0	25.8	2.5	83.0	52.4	51.1	48.9
48740	HARRISVILLE	97.5	97.1	0.5	0.6	0.2	0.4	0.6	0.8	4.3	4.7	5.0	5.2	4.2	16.9	32.8	23.3	3.6	82.7	51.5	49.3	50.7
48741	KINGSTON	95.8	92.3	1.0	3.8	0.2	0.6	1.6	1.9	6.9	7.2	7.6	7.0	5.1	25.5	28.0	11.4	1.4	74.2	38.4	49.4	50.6
48742	LINCOLN	98.3	98.1	0.1	0.1	0.1	0.1	0.6	0.8	4.3	4.6	4.9	5.0	3.8	17.3	31.5	24.5	4.0	83.0	51.8	49.3	50.7
48743	LONG LAKE	100.0	100.0	0.0	0.0	0.0	0.0	0.0	0.0	7.1	7.1	7.1	7.1	7.1	10.7	28.6	25.0	0.0	71.4	47.5	46.4	53.6
48744	MAYVILLE	97.5	97.0	0.2	0.2	0.1	0.2	1.5	2.0	6.8	6.8	6.9	6.9	5.5	25.7	28.2	11.3	1.7	75.0	38.3	50.9	49.1
48745	MIKADO	97.3	96.9	0.0	0.0	0.2	0.3	1.1	1.4	5.4	5.9	6.3	6.5	4.3	20.1	32.3	17.2	2.0	77.4	45.9	52.2	47.8
48746	MILLINGTON	97.6	97.0	0.3	0.4	0.2	0.3	1.2	1.6	6.0	6.4	6.7	7.0	5.1	26.0	30.4	11.2	1.2	76.7	40.0	49.6	50.4
48747	MUNGER	97.2	96.6	0.1	0.1	0.3	0.4	9.1	11.7	5.7	6.2	7.2	6.9	4.7	23.1	31.7	12.7	1.8	76.4	42.1	51.7	48.3
48748	NATIONAL CITY	97.7	97.4	0.1	0.1	0.4	0.6	0.8	0.9	2.9	3.4	4.0	5.2	4.2	15.3	34.7	28.2	2.1	86.3	54.2	50.6	49.4
48749	OMER	97.1	96.6	0.0	0.1	0.1	0.2	1.0	1.4	5.3	5.5	5.9	6.1	4.7	22.4	32.4	16.0	1.8	79.7	45.1	49.6	50.4
48750	OSCODA	95.5	94.5	0.8	0.9	0.8	1.2	1.3	1.7	5.5	5.7	6.2	6.4	5.2	20.8	30.0	18.4	1.8	78.3	45.1	49.7	50.3
48754	OWENDALE	97.5	97.0	0.6	0.6	0.2	0.4	3.9	5.1	6.3	6.7	7.3	7.7	4.7	24.6	28.5	12.3	1.9	74.7	40.6	52.1	47.9
48755	PIGEON	97.3	96.6	0.4	0.5	0.4	0.7	2.0	2.6	3.9	4.2	4.7	5.8	4.4	18.0	31.5	23.8	3.7	83.1	51.0	49.9	50.1
48756	PRESCOTT	96.5	95.9	0.1	0.2	0.1	0.1	1.5	2.1	5.0	5.2	5.6	6.0	5.0	20.3	30.7	20.1	2.1	80.5	46.9	49.4	50.6
48757	REESE	97.8	97.1	0.1	0.1	0.6	0.9	2.3	3.2	5.9	6.2	6.5	6.5	5.2	25.5	29.8	12.5	1.8	77.4	40.7	50.0	50.0
48759	SEBEWAING	98.6	98.1	0.1	0.1	0.1	0.3	3.0	4.1	5.8	5.8	5.8	5.9	5.9	24.2	28.7	14.7	3.0	78.8	42.3	48.4	51.6
48760	SILVERWOOD	94.5	93.6	2.5	2.9	0.3	0.4	0.8	1.2	6.5	7.0	7.2	6.6	5.3	25.1	28.9	11.8	1.5	74.8	39.8	50.4	49.6
48761	SOUTH BRANCH	99.0	98.8	0.0	0.0	0.2	0.2	1.2	1.6	4.2	4.3	4.5	4.5	3.5	15.2	32.1	29.4	2.3	84.0	55.9	49.6	50.4
48762	SPRUCE	99.0	98.8	0.0	0.0	0.0	0.1	0.6	0.7	3.1	3.3	3.7	4.6	3.4	18.0	33.1	28.0	2.7	86.8	54.9	51.1	48.9
48763	TAWAS CITY	97.7	97.3	0.3	0.3	0.5	0.8	0.8	1.0	4.3	4.7	5.4	6.2	4.7	20.1	30.7	19.3	4.5	81.4	48.0	48.7	51.3
48765	TURNER	97.9	97.5	0.1	0.1	0.3	0.5	1.2	1.5	5.0	5.3	5.7	6.7	4.5	20.8	32.0	18.3	1.7	79.8	46.3	51.7	48.3
48766	TWINING	96.3	95.8	0.1	0.1	0.1	0.1	0.8	1.1	6.2	6.4	6.8	7.5	5.4	22.1	31.2	13.1	1.3	75.9	41.8	50.8	49.2
48767	UNIONVILLE	96.8	96.0	0.0	0.0	0.4	0.7	3.0	3.9	6.1	6.2	6.3	6.3	6.1	25.8	28.3	12.6	2.2	77.3	40.0	49.9	50.1
48768	VASSAR	94.5	93.5	2.6	3.0	0.5	0.8	2.3	3.0	6.4	6.9	7.2	9.3	5.5	25.7	27.1	10.5	1.4	72.9	36.9	50.8	49.2
	MICHIGAN	80.2	78.3	14.2	14.5	1.8	2.8	3.3	4.1	6.7	6.7	6.8	7.2	6.6	26.3	26.9	10.9	1.9	75.6	37.6	49.2	50.8
	UNITED STATES	75.1	72.0	12.3	12.7	3.8	4.6	12.5	15.7	6.8	6.7	6.6	7.1	6.9	27.0	26.0	10.9	1.9	75.7	36.9	49.2	50.8

#	POST OFFICE NAME	2009 Per Capita Income	2009 HH Income Base	2009 Household Income Distribution (%) Less than $25,000	$25,000 to $49,999	$50,000 to $99,999	$100,000 to $149,999	$150,000 or More	Median Household Income 2009	2014	2009 National Centile	2009 State Centile	2009 Home Value Base	2009 Home Value Distribution (%) Less than $50,000	$50,000 to $89,999	$90,000 to $174,999	$175,000 to $399,999	$400,000 or More	2009 Median Home Value
48601	SAGINAW	15889	15787	40.7	28.2	24.7	4.3	2.2	31667	34008	11	3	10393	59.8	26.5	12.4	1.3	0.1	42370
48602	SAGINAW	20542	12039	26.9	29.6	36.1	5.6	1.8	43066	47864	43	29	8468	35.2	46.7	16.3	1.7	0.1	59323
48603	SAGINAW	28070	11286	19.5	28.9	35.0	11.6	5.1	51485	52987	65	55	7054	7.9	17.4	55.7	17.9	1.1	116997
48604	SAGINAW	21812	4551	21.3	27.3	42.7	6.5	2.2	51096	52906	64	53	3504	19.0	53.3	24.5	3.0	0.2	73940
48607	SAGINAW	11381	888	67.1	18.6	10.7	3.2	0.5	14613	15141	1	0	306	79.4	14.1	5.6	1.0	0.0	27571
48609	SAGINAW	27611	4773	14.0	25.6	45.0	10.1	5.3	58444	57472	76	72	4249	10.0	25.8	49.1	13.7	1.4	102347
48610	ALGER	19671	1598	31.5	31.4	31.7	4.4	1.0	36786	39058	23	8	1432	23.5	28.1	34.9	11.8	1.6	87714
48611	AUBURN	25303	2410	16.2	24.4	45.5	10.9	2.9	58903	57859	76	73	2071	9.9	19.7	56.8	12.9	0.6	105940
48612	BEAVERTON	19630	3914	29.2	30.3	34.4	5.1	1.1	40290	42345	34	19	3293	17.2	24.0	39.1	18.7	1.0	103901
48613	BENTLEY	19330	421	26.4	30.4	35.2	6.2	1.9	42944	47003	42	29	379	23.5	33.8	34.8	7.7	0.3	81667
48614	BRANT	19455	460	21.5	30.2	40.2	5.9	2.2	48282	50944	57	45	407	15.0	33.7	39.6	10.3	1.5	91310
48615	BRECKENRIDGE	21248	1230	20.5	30.7	41.0	6.3	1.5	48819	51009	58	47	1004	16.1	29.6	45.2	8.7	0.4	93772
48616	CHESANING	22193	2758	22.4	26.5	41.0	7.8	2.3	50787	52362	63	52	2239	9.6	34.3	42.7	12.9	0.5	94523
48617	CLARE	19189	3376	30.5	30.3	33.1	4.5	1.6	41012	43940	36	21	2444	14.0	24.4	44.0	16.1	1.5	104212
48618	COLEMAN	20363	2246	24.2	26.9	42.3	5.1	1.5	47582	51029	56	42	1911	20.4	28.6	40.9	9.5	0.6	91291
48619	COMINS	21801	312	25.3	33.0	35.3	4.2	2.2	42924	45175	42	28	280	17.9	30.7	33.9	14.3	3.2	91905
48621	FAIRVIEW	17091	584	35.1	32.7	28.1	3.4	0.7	34118	35069	16	6	469	16.6	44.3	30.3	7.7	1.1	82197
48622	FARWELL	19245	2569	29.8	31.8	32.5	4.5	1.4	40045	43334	33	18	2199	16.3	26.6	42.5	13.8	0.9	100718
48623	FREELAND	25256	4465	13.2	20.6	45.4	15.9	4.9	63678	63387	82	83	3914	7.7	16.6	49.5	24.7	1.6	125687
48624	GLADWIN	19616	7036	30.0	33.1	31.1	4.4	1.3	38382	40375	28	12	5997	15.9	22.8	40.6	18.7	2.0	106597
48625	HARRISON	17984	5774	36.5	31.3	27.7	3.3	1.2	33482	34603	14	5	4871	27.6	30.8	30.7	10.0	0.9	78648
48626	HEMLOCK	22436	2336	17.4	24.9	47.0	7.6	3.2	54872	54883	71	65	2059	11.9	27.2	45.4	14.3	1.2	102292
48628	HOPE	24356	828	20.0	28.1	43.2	6.6	1.9	51084	52119	64	53	752	14.9	21.5	43.6	18.1	1.9	108688
48629	HOUGHTON LAKE	20184	3673	28.2	36.3	30.7	3.4	1.4	36916	38896	23	9	3106	14.2	27.5	40.7	15.3	2.4	99085
48631	KAWKAWLIN	23433	1845	16.0	30.7	39.2	10.8	3.3	52627	53642	67	58	1668	16.8	22.5	46.7	13.2	0.7	98599
48632	LAKE	20886	2476	27.3	35.9	31.0	4.3	1.6	38485	40580	28	13	2167	22.4	26.6	35.8	14.1	1.1	91215
48634	LINWOOD	23613	1798	17.1	28.5	42.7	9.1	2.6	53867	54695	69	62	1629	9.3	29.9	47.3	12.7	0.9	99241
48635	LUPTON	20650	808	30.1	35.1	30.0	3.3	1.5	36882	38459	23	9	737	19.5	32.4	34.7	12.6	0.7	87456
48636	LUZERNE	20141	351	27.9	32.8	35.3	3.4	0.6	42129	43486	40	25	297	23.6	32.7	32.0	11.1	0.7	79250
48637	MERRILL	21236	1354	19.7	29.1	43.6	5.5	2.1	50757	52275	63	51	1193	13.9	35.0	38.9	11.7	0.4	91238
48638	SAGINAW	30056	5731	19.7	23.8	40.1	11.1	5.3	55454	55621	72	67	3859	5.8	18.4	57.5	17.6	0.8	123066
48640	MIDLAND	30103	12803	20.9	21.5	37.7	11.1	8.9	55972	55555	73	67	9600	6.2	19.1	42.7	27.4	4.5	126805
48642	MIDLAND	29185	12758	18.7	21.7	38.5	13.2	8.0	58363	57773	76	72	9693	9.2	14.0	46.9	25.9	4.0	128235
48647	MIO	17015	1909	34.6	32.9	28.7	3.5	0.4	34492	35256	17	6	1607	21.6	41.1	27.4	9.3	0.7	75893
48649	OAKLEY	19614	753	21.4	30.1	42.0	5.4	1.1	48554	51189	58	46	637	17.6	33.6	39.4	9.4	0.0	88636
48650	PINCONNING	20902	2989	25.3	26.9	40.2	5.9	1.7	47115	50956	54	42	2572	15.3	35.8	42.0	6.7	0.2	89057
48651	PRUDENVILLE	22472	2412	31.8	28.7	33.3	4.6	1.5	37500	40826	25	10	2005	8.8	29.2	40.3	20.3	1.4	104267
48652	RHODES	18903	624	27.1	30.1	36.2	5.6	1.0	42207	46078	40	25	565	18.9	27.1	39.8	13.5	0.7	94327
48653	ROSCOMMON	21582	4741	25.0	33.9	35.1	4.5	1.5	42458	44510	41	26	4144	10.4	27.7	42.6	15.5	3.8	106200
48654	ROSE CITY	18423	1102	31.0	33.4	29.9	4.5	1.1	37516	38733	25	10	912	18.5	34.5	35.9	10.0	1.1	85556
48655	SAINT CHARLES	22120	2304	19.9	27.2	42.9	7.3	2.7	51991	53068	66	56	1958	10.8	37.3	39.7	11.5	0.7	91841
48656	SAINT HELEN	19443	2148	36.0	33.1	27.0	2.0	1.9	33507	36229	14	5	1862	23.5	37.6	30.1	8.3	0.5	76203
48657	SANFORD	22939	3289	20.3	28.0	42.8	6.6	2.3	50981	51876	64	52	2882	15.5	21.5	41.5	19.6	1.8	109277
48658	STANDISH	18226	2143	33.0	27.9	32.0	6.3	0.8	38085	40000	27	11	1678	17.8	29.4	42.3	9.2	1.3	93721
48659	STERLING	18813	1213	28.3	28.8	37.3	4.8	0.9	42632	45323	41	28	1058	19.4	28.0	40.5	10.4	1.8	93256
48661	WEST BRANCH	20717	3968	26.8	31.9	35.0	5.0	1.3	42925	45250	42	28	3206	13.8	31.6	41.9	11.7	1.0	95444
48662	WHEELER	18473	577	23.2	34.1	37.3	4.2	1.2	43502	47964	44	30	506	19.4	27.5	42.7	8.5	2.0	93636
48701	AKRON	21401	648	23.0	29.3	38.6	6.9	2.2	45986	50174	51	38	551	17.4	37.6	34.1	10.3	0.5	84712
48703	AU GRES	21720	1654	33.4	29.5	30.6	4.8	1.6	37641	38883	26	11	1377	8.9	21.2	42.2	23.5	4.2	116523
48705	BARTON CITY	21568	304	30.3	33.2	30.6	3.3	2.6	38359	39885	28	12	279	16.5	35.1	35.5	10.8	2.2	88200
48706	BAY CITY	25442	17003	22.0	27.2	37.3	9.6	3.9	50692	52472	63	51	13825	15.1	29.9	41.4	12.6	1.0	94850
48708	BAY CITY	21735	11793	29.6	28.5	32.6	6.8	2.5	41429	45756	37	22	8195	16.6	46.5	31.3	5.2	0.4	80918
48710	UNIVERSITY CENTER	0	0	0.0	0.0	0.0	0.0	0.0	0	0	0	0	0	0.0	0.0	0.0	0.0	0.0	0
48720	BAY PORT	19811	508	24.8	33.9	36.0	4.5	0.8	43000	45193	42	29	434	23.3	30.4	38.5	7.4	0.5	85294
48721	BLACK RIVER	22227	217	24.9	36.4	30.0	5.1	3.7	41751	41849	38	23	197	11.7	21.3	41.6	21.3	4.1	111149
48722	BRIDGEPORT	23635	1255	19.6	26.3	42.2	9.5	2.5	52283	52973	66	57	1090	11.9	39.8	42.5	5.3	0.5	88603
48723	CARO	20643	4757	23.9	30.8	36.2	7.4	1.7	43789	47791	45	31	3739	14.0	21.9	46.0	17.2	0.9	108571
48725	CASEVILLE	24603	1229	27.3	33.4	32.8	4.3	2.1	39450	43190	31	16	1037	17.1	25.8	38.5	16.2	2.4	97424
48726	CASS CITY	19793	2360	24.7	33.9	34.0	6.1	1.4	42165	45260	40	25	1938	14.3	24.1	44.8	16.2	0.6	105918
48727	CLIFFORD	19768	518	22.6	24.5	46.1	5.6	1.2	52250	53190	66	56	445	19.3	27.0	37.1	12.8	3.8	94125
48728	CURRAN	23465	219	31.5	32.9	30.1	3.2	2.3	38249	39335	27	12	202	16.3	33.7	34.7	11.9	3.5	90000
48729	DEFORD	18708	664	21.7	30.3	41.7	5.3	1.1	46942	50272	54	41	569	14.9	23.0	43.8	16.3	1.9	104073
48730	EAST TAWAS	21525	2261	30.6	33.6	30.4	4.6	0.8	36665	38873	23	8	1732	9.6	39.2	36.8	12.3	2.1	91329
48731	ELKTON	18241	700	28.7	30.6	37.0	3.3	0.4	40182	43893	33	18	559	22.7	38.6	30.1	7.5	1.1	79746
48732	ESSEXVILLE	25089	4684	25.2	28.3	33.1	9.3	4.1	45757	49266	51	38	3276	12.0	23.5	49.1	14.3	1.0	103041
48733	FAIRGROVE	21291	749	22.6	31.6	36.8	6.5	2.4	44724	48582	47	34	633	12.5	35.2	40.6	10.6	1.1	92042
48734	FRANKENMUTH	29892	2952	16.5	24.7	41.7	10.3	6.8	60554	59369	78	77	2156	1.4	8.4	56.9	30.8	2.5	149416
48735	GAGETOWN	19686	318	22.3	34.9	35.5	6.3	0.9	42992	45677	42	29	266	24.4	28.2	35.7	10.9	0.8	86500
48737	GLENNIE	19861	598	29.6	37.1	30.8	1.3	1.2	37154	38969	24	9	540	20.6	35.0	38.9	4.3	1.3	84340
48738	GREENBUSH	23149	571	24.2	39.4	31.7	3.7	1.1	40439	41283	34	19	512	11.1	23.0	41.2	22.7	2.0	110756
48739	HALE	21038	1990	30.4	32.5	31.1	3.8	2.2	36076	38893	21	7	1765	19.0	27.5	39.4	13.3	0.7	94583
48740	HARRISVILLE	21228	1166	31.0	34.3	28.4	3.5	2.8	38902	40278	29	15	978	13.3	30.0	40.8	13.2	2.8	97333
48741	KINGSTON	19199	852	22.8	29.1	41.1	6.0	1.1	46287	50179	52	39	714	9.9	18.8	48.0	21.4	1.8	117174
48742	LINCOLN	21920	823	32.1	32.8	29.6	3.5	1.9	36963	38815	23	9	726	14.3	32.8	37.6	12.8	2.5	92658
48743	LONG LAKE	21250	15	26.7	40.0	33.3	0.0	0.0	33972	36064	15	5	14	14.3	21.4	50.0	14.3	0.0	106250
48744	MAYVILLE	20898	1705	19.3	29.0	41.6	8.0	2.1	51214	51811	64	54	1439	10.5	17.4	47.4	23.2	1.5	121684
48745	MIKADO	18483	578	28.7	36.0	30.1	3.3	1.9	38338	39521	28	12	516	17.8	39.1	36.0	6.0	1.0	83455
48746	MILLINGTON	22105	3443	14.4	29.7	45.0	8.9	2.0	54753	54071	71	64	3018	9.3	16.1	54.3	19.6	0.6	118824
48747	MUNGER	22817	586	18.3	25.4	44.9	8.5	2.9	54842	55057	71	65	539	8.5	29.3	54.4	6.1	1.7	101786
48748	NATIONAL CITY	24484	772	24.1	38.2	31.6	4.4	1.7	40783	41629	35	21	725	14.6	29.8	39.9	14.8	1.0	97941
48749	OMER	20873	416	29.8	30.8	31.7	5.8	1.9	39038	40479	30	15	368	17.9	31.3	38.9	10.9	1.1	90789
48750	OSCODA	20686	4086	29.6	32.3	33.3	3.5	1.3	38867	41474	29	14	3096	15.6	41.6	32.9	9.3	0.7	82043
48754	OWENDALE	19431	472	20.1	34.7	40.3	4.0	0.8	45188	46559	49	36	406	21.2	40.4	27.6	10.1	0.7	81132
48755	PIGEON	25314	1376	20.3	30.5	39.2	6.6	3.3	49158	49157	59	48	1173	11.5	30.8	35.5	17.0	5.3	98153
48756	PRESCOTT	15835	1828	41.1	31.8	23.7	2.6	0.7	29243	30743	7	2	1539	36.3	32.7	24.6	5.7	0.7	65979
48757	REESE	23269	1579	19.4	26.8	43.6	8.0	2.2	53131	52978	68	60	1357	16.6	16.3	48.0	19.1	0.1	115650
48759	SEBEWAING	21450	1400	24.4	34.1	35.4	5.3	0.9	41572	43611	38	23	1115	18.9	44.3	30.3	6.1	0.4	79123
48760	SILVERWOOD	21628	426	18.8	28.6	42.5	7.5	2.6	51768	52504	65	55	376	10.9	19.7	47.3	20.7	1.3	121154
48761	SOUTH BRANCH	20699	536	32.3	33.8	28.9	3.9	1.1	34327	36324	16	6	494	20.9	38.9	31.4	8.3	0.6	77551
48762	SPRUCE	21732	447	27.7	32.9	32.9	4.3	2.2	42260	44485	40	25	409	9.3	29.6	38.6	19.1	3.4	100236
48763	TAWAS CITY	20497	2014	26.1	34.8	33.6	4.3	1.3	41902	42908	39	24	1731	11.7	37.4	37.7	11.6	1.6	91303
48765	TURNER	18655	305	30.5	27.2	36.7	4.6	1.0	43439	45354	44	30	265	21.1	29.4	34.3	12.8	2.3	89250
48766	TWINING	16747	572	33.7	26.6	35.3	3.3	1.0	38799	42026	29	14	502	21.9	33.9	35.5	8.0	0.8	82162
48767	UNIONVILLE	22083	900	16.0	34.6	40.0	8.0	1.4	49134	50779	59	48	779	13.1	30.3	42.9	12.6	1.2	97464
48768	VASSAR	21427	3792	17.2	29.5	44.6	6.4	2.2	52297	52552	66	57	3187	11.7	22.1	49.3	16.5	0.3	110454
	MICHIGAN	26713		20.1	24.2	38.5	11.3	5.9	55536	56866				13.2	21.9	40.3	21.5	3.2	115137
	UNITED STATES	27277		20.9	24.4	35.3	11.7	7.6	54719	56938				9.3	13.1	31.6	32.6	13.5	162279

ZIP CODE		FINANCIAL SERVICES				THE HOME						ENTERTAINMENT						PERSONAL			
						Home Improvements		Furnishings													
#	POST OFFICE NAME	Auto Loan	Home Loan	Invest-ments	Retire-ment Plans	Home Repair	Lawn & Garden	Comput-ers & Hard-ware-Personal	Major Appli-ances	TV, Radio, Sound Equip-ment	Furni-ture	Dine out/ Carry out	Sports Equip-ment	Fees & Tickets	Toys & Games	Travel	Cable TV	Apparel & Services	Auto Repairs	Health Insur-ance	Pets & Supplies
48601	SAGINAW	63	55	50	56	52	62	59	58	65	59	64	43	57	64	55	68	44	61	67	72
48602	SAGINAW	70	67	58	68	64	71	73	68	75	68	74	53	71	75	68	77	52	72	76	83
48603	SAGINAW	89	88	85	90	88	92	91	89	92	88	92	68	90	91	90	93	64	91	95	106
48604	SAGINAW	80	80	69	80	77	84	79	79	81	77	81	60	79	82	78	84	56	80	87	95
48607	SAGINAW	36	28	28	29	27	34	35	33	40	34	39	24	32	37	31	43	27	37	41	41
48609	SAGINAW	94	106	102	106	106	111	94	102	97	94	96	75	102	96	102	100	67	98	108	118
48610	ALGER	74	59	80	56	62	78	59	73	64	58	63	52	51	62	60	70	42	68	78	85
48611	AUBURN	95	93	88	95	93	99	91	95	92	89	91	72	90	93	91	94	63	93	98	112
48612	BEAVERTON	80	62	82	60	65	83	63	77	68	60	67	57	53	68	63	74	45	72	81	91
48613	BENTLEY	79	71	72	73	72	85	70	80	72	63	71	60	64	74	70	77	48	74	82	93
48614	BRANT	92	72	78	72	72	91	73	84	79	69	77	64	62	82	69	85	52	79	88	101
48615	BRECKENRIDGE	80	77	67	78	74	83	76	78	78	73	77	60	74	80	74	80	53	77	83	93
48616	CHESANING	84	82	80	83	83	93	79	87	82	74	81	64	77	82	80	86	55	82	93	101
48617	CLARE	76	62	68	62	63	75	68	72	72	63	70	54	59	72	64	76	48	71	78	86
48618	COLEMAN	84	71	71	72	71	84	71	79	75	68	74	60	64	77	69	80	50	75	83	94
48619	COMINS	76	72	92	67	80	86	69	81	73	74	71	53	68	67	75	77	48	78	90	93
48621	FAIRVIEW	71	53	74	51	56	74	55	69	61	52	59	50	46	60	55	67	40	64	74	81
48622	FARWELL	82	62	82	61	64	83	63	77	69	59	68	58	53	69	63	75	45	72	80	92
48623	FREELAND	103	112	99	112	108	108	101	105	100	103	100	81	105	102	104	99	70	101	103	122
48624	GLADWIN	76	61	85	59	65	81	62	76	66	59	65	55	53	64	63	72	43	71	80	88
48625	HARRISON	69	55	76	52	58	74	56	68	61	54	59	49	48	59	57	66	39	64	74	80
48626	HEMLOCK	90	90	79	92	88	95	86	90	87	83	86	69	85	89	86	89	59	87	93	106
48628	HOPE	92	82	89	84	84	97	81	92	83	75	82	69	74	84	81	88	56	86	94	107
48629	HOUGHTON LAKE	72	62	88	59	68	79	61	75	65	61	64	52	56	61	65	69	42	70	79	86
48631	KAWKAWLIN	91	91	85	91	90	98	84	92	88	83	87	68	85	89	86	91	60	88	96	107
48632	LAKE	75	65	85	60	70	82	63	76	68	65	66	53	58	64	67	73	44	72	83	88
48634	LINWOOD	91	86	84	89	87	99	83	93	86	77	85	70	79	87	84	90	58	87	96	108
48635	LUPTON	72	63	86	59	69	79	61	74	65	63	64	51	57	61	66	70	43	70	80	86
48636	LUZERNE	69	66	84	61	73	79	63	74	66	68	65	48	62	61	69	70	43	71	82	85
48637	MERRILL	86	79	78	82	81	93	78	88	80	71	79	66	72	82	78	85	54	81	90	102
48638	SAGINAW	95	95	94	96	96	101	94	97	96	93	95	71	94	95	95	98	66	96	103	113
48640	MIDLAND	108	109	103	111	108	111	106	108	106	106	106	82	107	108	106	108	74	106	110	126
48642	MIDLAND	104	108	101	108	105	106	103	104	103	104	104	80	106	105	104	104	73	104	105	122
48647	MIO	68	54	74	52	58	72	55	67	60	54	58	48	48	57	56	65	39	63	73	78
48649	OAKLEY	80	74	73	77	75	87	72	82	75	66	74	62	68	76	73	80	50	76	85	95
48650	PINCONNING	79	74	73	76	75	86	72	81	75	66	73	61	68	76	73	79	50	75	85	94
48651	PRUDENVILLE	74	66	88	62	73	82	64	77	68	67	67	52	61	63	69	73	45	73	84	89
48652	RHODES	81	66	83	66	69	83	66	79	70	62	69	58	58	69	67	74	46	73	80	92
48653	ROSCOMMON	79	65	92	62	70	85	65	80	70	64	68	57	58	66	68	75	46	75	85	93
48654	ROSE CITY	75	59	87	57	64	80	60	75	65	57	64	55	52	62	63	70	42	70	79	88
48655	SAINT CHARLES	87	82	76	85	81	93	81	87	84	75	82	67	77	85	80	88	56	84	92	103
48656	SAINT HELEN	66	55	74	52	60	72	56	67	60	56	58	47	50	57	58	65	39	64	74	78
48657	SANFORD	87	83	76	84	82	88	79	85	80	77	80	64	76	83	78	83	55	81	86	100
48658	STANDISH	76	59	77	59	62	78	63	74	68	58	67	55	53	67	62	74	45	70	79	87
48659	STERLING	84	62	87	60	65	86	63	79	70	60	68	59	52	69	63	76	45	73	83	94
48661	WEST BRANCH	78	64	83	64	67	81	68	77	71	63	70	57	60	69	67	76	47	74	81	91
48662	WHEELER	75	69	67	71	70	79	68	75	70	62	69	57	63	71	67	73	47	70	77	88
48701	AKRON	82	73	74	74	71	86	73	79	77	69	76	62	68	78	72	81	51	77	85	95
48703	AU GRES	77	61	93	60	66	82	62	78	67	59	65	57	54	64	66	72	44	73	81	91
48705	BARTON CITY	72	63	83	59	69	79	61	74	66	63	64	51	57	62	65	70	43	70	81	86
48706	BAY CITY	83	87	84	86	86	93	82	87	85	82	85	64	85	85	85	89	59	85	94	101
48708	BAY CITY	71	69	64	70	67	75	72	71	74	68	73	54	71	74	70	77	51	72	79	85
48710	UNIVERSITY CENTER	0	0	0	0	0	0	0	0	0	0	0	0	0	0	0	0	0	0	0	0
48720	BAY PORT	84	62	85	60	64	86	63	79	69	58	68	59	51	69	62	76	45	73	82	94
48721	BLACK RIVER	87	70	112	69	76	92	70	89	73	65	72	65	60	69	75	78	48	82	87	103
48722	BRIDGEPORT	82	89	78	90	86	93	83	85	84	80	84	66	87	85	86	86	58	84	91	101
48723	CARO	81	70	75	71	71	85	72	80	75	67	74	60	65	76	71	80	50	76	85	94
48725	CASEVILLE	73	70	88	65	77	83	66	78	70	71	68	51	66	64	72	74	46	75	87	89
48726	CASS CITY	79	65	73	66	67	81	68	77	72	63	70	58	60	72	66	77	48	73	81	90
48727	CLIFFORD	81	74	73	77	76	87	73	83	75	66	74	63	67	77	73	80	51	76	85	96
48728	CURRAN	66	64	82	59	72	77	61	72	65	66	63	47	61	59	67	68	42	69	81	82
48729	DEFORD	84	70	73	71	71	86	70	80	75	65	73	61	62	77	68	80	50	75	84	95
48730	EAST TAWAS	68	60	77	58	64	75	60	71	64	59	63	50	56	61	63	69	43	68	77	82
48731	ELKTON	73	59	70	60	61	78	61	73	66	55	64	55	53	66	60	71	43	67	77	85
48732	ESSEXVILLE	84	84	82	84	84	91	83	86	86	81	85	63	83	85	84	89	59	85	94	101
48733	FAIRGROVE	92	71	91	71	74	95	72	88	78	67	77	66	61	78	72	85	51	81	92	104
48734	FRANKENMUTH	93	104	105	105	106	106	98	100	99	100	99	74	106	96	104	101	70	99	108	116
48735	GAGETOWN	87	66	87	65	68	89	67	83	73	62	72	62	56	73	67	80	48	76	86	98
48737	GLENNIE	64	60	76	55	66	72	57	68	61	61	59	45	56	56	62	64	40	65	75	77
48738	GREENBUSH	80	63	100	62	69	84	63	80	67	60	66	59	54	64	68	72	44	74	80	93
48739	HALE	71	64	86	60	71	79	62	74	65	65	64	50	59	61	67	70	43	71	81	85
48740	HARRISVILLE	76	65	89	61	70	82	63	77	68	64	66	54	58	64	67	73	44	73	83	89
48741	KINGSTON	80	72	73	75	74	86	72	81	74	65	73	62	66	75	72	78	50	75	84	95
48742	LINCOLN	77	62	90	59	68	85	61	78	67	60	66	55	55	64	65	73	43	72	84	90
48743	LONG LAKE	58	56	71	51	62	66	53	62	56	57	54	41	52	51	58	59	37	60	69	71
48744	MAYVILLE	86	81	73	82	80	89	79	84	81	75	81	64	75	83	78	85	55	81	88	100
48745	MIKADO	82	59	84	57	61	84	60	77	67	56	66	58	48	67	60	74	44	71	80	91
48746	MILLINGTON	91	87	81	89	86	96	84	91	86	79	85	69	80	88	83	89	58	86	93	107
48747	MUNGER	94	86	85	90	88	101	85	95	87	77	86	72	78	89	85	92	58	88	98	111
48748	NATIONAL CITY	81	69	96	65	75	88	67	83	72	68	71	58	62	68	72	77	47	78	88	96
48749	OMER	87	64	94	62	67	89	65	83	72	61	70	62	53	71	66	78	47	76	86	98
48750	OSCODA	75	59	79	58	61	78	63	74	67	58	66	55	53	66	62	73	44	70	79	87
48754	OWENDALE	82	67	80	67	68	86	67	80	72	61	70	60	58	72	66	77	47	74	83	94
48755	PIGEON	92	80	103	78	86	102	79	94	85	78	83	66	73	81	82	91	56	88	102	109
48756	PRESCOTT	63	48	68	46	50	66	50	62	55	46	53	45	41	53	50	60	35	57	66	72
48757	REESE	89	83	80	84	83	91	82	88	84	79	83	66	77	85	81	87	57	84	91	103
48759	SEBEWAING	76	66	75	65	66	82	66	75	70	61	69	57	60	70	66	75	47	72	82	89
48760	SILVERWOOD	89	81	80	84	83	95	80	90	82	72	81	68	74	84	80	87	55	83	93	105
48761	SOUTH BRANCH	63	60	77	56	67	72	57	68	61	62	59	44	57	56	63	64	40	65	75	77
48762	SPRUCE	74	66	94	63	73	84	64	79	68	64	66	55	61	63	71	72	44	74	84	90
48763	TAWAS CITY	76	63	83	62	67	80	65	77	69	61	67	56	57	67	66	73	45	72	80	89
48765	TURNER	79	61	88	58	65	82	61	77	66	59	65	56	52	64	63	72	43	71	80	90
48766	TWINING	80	58	83	56	60	81	59	75	65	55	64	56	47	65	59	72	42	69	78	89
48767	UNIONVILLE	84	79	73	82	78	90	79	84	81	73	80	65	75	82	78	84	55	81	89	99
48768	VASSAR	85	82	76	83	80	90	79	84	82	76	81	64	77	83	79	85	55	81	89	100
	MICHIGAN	98	97	93	98	95	100	96	97	97	95	97	74	96	98	96	99	68	97	100	115
	UNITED STATES	100	100	100	100	100	100	100	100	100	100	100	100	100	100	100	100	100	100	100	100

ZIP CODE #	POST OFFICE NAME	COUNTY FIPS CODE	POPULATION 2000	POPULATION 2009	POPULATION 2014	2000-2009 ANNUAL RATE % Rate	2000-2009 ANNUAL RATE State Centile	HOUSEHOLDS 2000	HOUSEHOLDS 2009	HOUSEHOLDS 2014	HOUSEHOLDS % Annual Rate 2000-2009	HOUSEHOLDS 2009 Average HH Size	FAMILIES 2000	FAMILIES 2009	FAMILIES % Annual Rate 2000-2009
48770	WHITTEMORE	069	2066	2019	1972	-0.2	25	811	826	818	0.2	2.44	579	581	0.0
48801	ALMA	057	12617	12453	12249	-0.1	32	4472	4433	4377	-0.1	2.41	2993	2928	-0.2
48806	ASHLEY	057	1808	1871	1867	0.4	60	674	719	725	0.7	2.56	517	545	0.6
48807	BANNISTER	057	943	963	958	0.2	48	363	381	382	0.5	2.53	276	287	0.4
48808	BATH	037	3852	4325	4516	1.3	90	1419	1643	1731	1.6	2.63	1092	1257	1.5
48809	BELDING	067	11259	11692	11748	0.4	60	4031	4245	4289	0.6	2.69	2913	3038	0.5
48811	CARSON CITY	117	4908	5800	5826	1.8	96	1205	1287	1305	0.7	2.84	886	936	0.6
48813	CHARLOTTE	045	20214	21439	21838	0.6	71	7509	8177	8404	0.9	2.56	5531	5965	0.8
48815	CLARKSVILLE	067	1897	2098	2180	1.1	86	670	757	790	1.3	2.77	511	573	1.2
48817	CORUNNA	155	6658	6550	6424	-0.2	25	2531	2574	2546	0.2	2.44	1842	1852	0.1
48818	CRYSTAL	117	2392	2416	2394	0.1	42	947	980	976	0.4	2.45	657	671	0.2
48819	DANSVILLE	065	2652	2872	2907	0.9	82	924	1029	1051	1.2	2.78	759	836	1.1
48820	DEWITT	037	14377	16219	17119	1.3	90	5129	5866	6222	1.5	2.75	4088	4658	1.4
48821	DIMONDALE	045	5505	5816	5923	0.6	71	2094	2275	2337	0.9	2.47	1528	1629	0.7
48822	EAGLE	037	2453	2644	2702	0.8	80	889	988	1018	1.1	2.67	734	815	1.1
48823	EAST LANSING	065	44989	48388	49334	0.8	80	18947	21093	21654	1.2	2.22	7865	8983	1.4
48824	EAST LANSING	065	2688	1167	1167	-8.6	0	15	14	14	-0.7	2.57	1	0	-100.0
48825	EAST LANSING	065	10778	13127	13106	2.2	98	405	389	382	-0.4	2.12	192	179	-0.8
48827	EATON RAPIDS	045	15493	16412	16632	0.6	71	5607	6039	6156	0.8	2.70	4281	4567	0.7
48829	EDMORE	117	3706	3916	3933	0.6	71	1416	1528	1545	0.8	2.54	1042	1113	0.7
48831	ELSIE	037	3394	3488	3485	0.3	54	1262	1328	1336	0.6	2.62	943	987	0.5
48832	ELWELL	057	1573	1581	1564	0.1	42	582	603	603	0.4	2.60	446	457	0.3
48834	FENWICK	117	3456	2886	2870	-1.9	0	1007	1044	1046	0.4	2.68	794	816	0.3
48835	FOWLER	037	2745	2831	2852	0.3	54	928	989	1004	0.7	2.86	728	776	0.7
48836	FOWLERVILLE	093	11442	13650	14799	1.9	96	3955	4851	5309	2.2	2.80	3065	3742	2.2
48837	GRAND LEDGE	045	17757	18826	19059	0.6	71	6818	7385	7533	0.9	2.54	5014	5410	0.8
48838	GREENVILLE	117	16705	17272	17277	0.4	60	6445	6793	6830	0.6	2.51	4516	4711	0.5
48840	HASLETT	065	12105	12211	12173	0.1	42	5346	5491	5504	0.3	2.21	3083	3105	0.1
48841	HENDERSON	155	880	872	854	-0.1	32	299	304	300	0.2	2.87	241	242	0.0
48842	HOLT	065	18888	20223	20543	0.7	76	7251	7891	8065	0.9	2.54	5156	5542	0.8
48843	HOWELL	093	32438	44906	50803	3.6	99	11716	16744	19095	3.9	2.66	8726	12527	4.0
48845	HUBBARDSTON	067	1068	1140	1159	0.7	76	359	392	402	1.0	2.64	280	303	0.9
48846	IONIA	067	19738	20973	20890	0.7	76	5497	5754	5762	0.5	2.55	3864	3996	0.4
48847	ITHACA	057	6571	6481	6386	-0.1	32	2473	2492	2474	0.1	2.52	1794	1788	0.0
48848	LAINGSBURG	155	8278	8190	8060	-0.1	32	2907	2960	2935	0.2	2.76	2338	2366	0.1
48849	LAKE ODESSA	067	6283	6423	6395	0.2	48	2324	2414	2414	0.4	2.66	1742	1794	0.3
48850	LAKEVIEW	117	4690	4944	4981	0.6	71	1707	1826	1849	0.7	2.67	1269	1345	0.6
48851	LYONS	067	2283	2336	2302	0.2	48	847	890	882	0.5	2.62	622	647	0.4
48854	MASON	065	16849	17535	17615	0.4	60	6263	6707	6794	0.7	2.53	4628	4882	0.6
48855	HOWELL	093	11942	15047	16463	2.5	98	3940	5194	5745	3.0	2.89	3280	4263	2.9
48856	MIDDLETON	057	851	843	832	-0.1	32	306	310	308	0.1	2.70	230	230	0.0
48857	MORRICE	155	2451	2785	2821	1.4	92	850	992	1013	1.7	2.80	682	784	1.5
48858	MOUNT PLEASANT	073	44791	48815	49722	0.9	82	15494	17532	18119	1.3	2.41	7820	8730	1.2
48860	MUIR	067	1352	1440	1471	0.7	76	498	544	560	1.0	2.63	371	401	0.8
48861	MULLIKEN	045	1585	1738	1793	1.0	84	572	645	671	1.3	2.68	457	511	1.2
48864	OKEMOS	065	20173	19844	19657	-0.2	25	7980	8049	8027	0.1	2.43	5092	5056	-0.1
48865	ORLEANS	067	1547	1641	1675	0.6	71	563	613	632	0.9	2.68	430	464	0.8
48866	OVID	037	4416	4804	4904	0.9	82	1594	1770	1817	1.1	2.66	1201	1326	1.1
48867	OWOSSO	155	28543	28369	27831	-0.1	32	11214	11434	11311	0.2	2.46	7759	7821	0.1
48871	PERRINTON	057	2152	2142	2119	-0.1	32	787	802	798	0.2	2.61	610	616	0.1
48872	PERRY	155	7473	8039	8068	0.8	80	2668	2943	2977	1.1	2.72	2092	2286	1.0
48873	PEWAMO	067	1702	1691	1656	-0.1	32	567	580	571	0.2	2.92	441	447	0.1
48875	PORTLAND	067	9021	9815	10030	0.9	82	3252	3624	3730	1.2	2.71	2502	2764	1.1
48876	POTTERVILLE	045	3617	3926	4035	0.9	82	1332	1481	1535	1.2	2.64	1012	1109	1.0
48877	RIVERDALE	057	2587	2741	2741	0.6	71	910	991	999	0.9	2.73	718	775	0.8
48878	ROSEBUSH	073	1597	1684	1677	0.6	71	568	619	623	0.9	2.71	413	446	0.8
48879	SAINT JOHNS	037	17692	18009	18165	0.2	48	6395	6662	6767	0.4	2.63	4779	4987	0.5
48880	SAINT LOUIS	057	9890	10168	10074	0.3	54	2686	2725	2707	0.2	2.47	1886	1890	0.0
48881	SARANAC	067	4977	5528	5723	1.1	86	1866	2121	2211	1.4	2.58	1389	1559	1.3
48883	SHEPHERD	073	6633	7121	7192	0.8	80	2417	2675	2725	1.1	2.66	1809	1990	1.0
48884	SHERIDAN	117	4002	4241	4295	0.6	71	1489	1620	1653	0.9	2.57	1121	1204	0.8
48885	SIDNEY	117	1053	1110	1112	0.6	71	392	424	429	0.9	2.62	306	327	0.7
48886	SIX LAKES	117	2405	2557	2584	0.7	76	936	1006	1020	0.8	2.54	694	738	0.7
48888	STANTON	117	6874	7046	6991	0.3	54	2550	2670	2665	0.5	2.60	1876	1943	0.4
48889	SUMNER	057	1464	1474	1461	0.1	42	528	547	547	0.4	2.65	411	422	0.3
48890	SUNFIELD	067	2251	2368	2400	0.5	66	796	862	882	0.9	2.73	639	684	0.7
48891	VESTABURG	117	2812	2960	2971	0.6	71	1008	1085	1097	0.8	2.71	774	825	0.7
48892	WEBBERVILLE	065	4103	4313	4381	0.5	66	1488	1620	1661	0.9	2.66	1147	1241	0.9
48893	WEIDMAN	073	4595	4798	4797	0.5	66	1782	1928	1951	0.9	2.48	1316	1411	0.8
48894	WESTPHALIA	037	1702	1788	1810	0.5	66	597	648	662	0.9	2.76	472	512	0.9
48895	WILLIAMSTON	065	10879	11040	11010	0.2	48	4040	4168	4183	0.3	2.64	3053	3108	0.2
48897	WOODLAND	015	1585	1616	1594	0.2	48	584	611	609	0.5	2.64	441	458	0.4
48906	LANSING	037	26922	28207	28647	0.5	66	10594	11429	11741	0.8	2.45	6713	7200	0.8
48910	LANSING	065	35069	33960	33413	-0.3	21	15473	15326	15208	-0.1	2.20	8325	8033	-0.4
48911	LANSING	065	40080	39983	39540	0.0	37	15944	16220	16158	0.2	2.44	10453	10452	0.0
48912	LANSING	065	18318	17473	17120	-0.5	12	7975	7780	7681	-0.3	2.23	4009	3807	-0.6
48915	LANSING	065	10256	9488	9194	-0.8	6	4060	3843	3754	-0.6	2.46	2387	2203	-0.9
48917	LANSING	045	31231	31578	31559	0.1	42	13627	14139	14253	0.4	2.21	8301	8467	0.2
48933	LANSING	065	2227	2049	1984	-0.9	5	1368	1284	1252	-0.7	1.57	324	291	-1.2
49001	KALAMAZOO	077	22392	21308	20935	-0.5	12	9298	9029	8922	-0.3	2.30	5085	4801	-0.6
49002	PORTAGE	077	18431	19116	19473	0.4	60	7813	8296	8501	0.7	2.28	4899	5142	0.5
49004	KALAMAZOO	077	15157	16195	16622	0.7	76	5892	6362	6558	0.8	2.51	4233	4525	0.7
49006	KALAMAZOO	077	22658	23130	23439	0.2	48	9643	10242	10488	0.7	2.11	3891	4005	0.3
49007	KALAMAZOO	077	12692	12896	13028	0.2	48	4946	5199	5303	0.5	2.35	2251	2236	-0.1
49008	KALAMAZOO	077	21579	20682	20637	-0.5	12	7227	7322	7362	0.1	2.08	3636	3610	-0.1
49009	KALAMAZOO	077	32578	37166	39104	1.4	92	13305	15496	16405	1.7	2.37	8427	9741	1.6
49010	ALLEGAN	005	16569	18139	18760	1.0	84	6170	6921	7212	1.2	2.56	4488	4980	1.1
49011	ATHENS	025	2449	2500	2482	0.2	48	921	950	946	0.3	2.63	711	727	0.2
49012	AUGUSTA	077	3050	3300	3411	0.9	82	1197	1322	1376	1.1	2.49	869	943	0.9
49013	BANGOR	159	5664	5740	5732	0.1	42	2006	2049	2050	0.2	2.75	1467	1483	0.1
49014	BATTLE CREEK	025	23208	22869	22416	-0.2	25	8758	8629	8476	-0.2	2.52	5941	5797	-0.3
49015	BATTLE CREEK	025	25272	25810	25595	0.2	48	10396	10719	10666	0.3	2.39	6920	7046	0.2
49017	BATTLE CREEK	025	22508	22057	21663	-0.2	25	9193	9098	8961	-0.1	2.38	5946	5835	-0.2
49021	BELLEVUE	045	6240	6426	6428	0.3	54	2316	2449	2470	0.6	2.61	1802	1884	0.5
49022	BENTON HARBOR	021	35131	34002	33411	-0.4	16	13332	13088	12925	-0.2	2.55	8850	8546	-0.4
	MICHIGAN					0.3					0.4	2.52			0.3
	UNITED STATES					1.0					1.1	2.59			0.9

ZIP CODE #	POST OFFICE NAME	RACE (%) White 2000	White 2009	Black 2000	Black 2009	Asian/Pacific 2000	Asian/Pacific 2009	% Hispanic Origin 2000	% Hispanic Origin 2009	2009 AGE DISTRIBUTION (%) 0-4	5-9	10-14	15-19	20-24	25-44	45-64	65-84	85+	18+	MEDIAN AGE 2009	% 2009 Males	% 2009 Females
48770	WHITTEMORE	98.1	97.8	0.2	0.2	0.1	0.2	1.0	1.3	5.3	5.8	6.2	6.6	4.6	22.0	30.7	16.6	2.1	78.4	44.5	49.8	50.2
48801	ALMA	94.4	92.9	0.4	0.5	0.6	1.0	5.6	7.3	5.8	5.7	5.6	10.5	10.7	21.8	23.0	12.6	4.3	79.0	35.7	46.3	53.7
48806	ASHLEY	98.0	97.5	0.2	0.2	0.2	0.3	1.5	2.1	6.1	6.4	6.5	5.9	4.5	25.4	29.6	12.9	2.6	77.4	41.4	50.5	49.5
48807	BANNISTER	97.5	96.8	0.2	0.2	0.1	0.1	2.0	2.8	7.2	7.4	7.4	7.2	4.7	26.3	27.3	11.0	1.7	73.7	38.5	51.0	49.0
48808	BATH	96.1	95.1	0.6	0.7	0.5	0.8	2.3	3.1	6.4	7.0	7.7	7.3	4.3	26.2	31.1	9.0	1.0	74.2	40.0	49.2	50.8
48809	BELDING	96.7	95.9	0.5	0.5	0.3	0.6	2.6	3.6	7.9	7.6	7.4	7.4	6.1	26.8	25.2	9.7	1.8	72.2	35.4	49.6	50.4
48811	CARSON CITY	79.5	75.0	15.9	19.2	0.3	0.8	3.5	4.6	4.7	4.6	4.8	7.9	10.2	38.0	20.8	8.2	1.0	83.2	34.1	64.2	35.8
48813	CHARLOTTE	96.6	95.4	0.6	0.7	0.4	0.7	2.8	3.8	6.5	6.7	6.8	6.9	5.8	26.2	28.5	10.9	1.8	75.7	38.7	49.2	50.8
48815	CLARKSVILLE	98.1	97.8	0.2	0.2	0.1	0.1	1.6	2.1	6.5	6.9	7.4	7.1	4.9	25.9	29.3	10.6	1.4	74.8	39.5	51.0	49.0
48817	CORUNNA	97.1	96.7	0.5	0.6	0.2	0.3	1.8	2.3	5.7	6.0	6.2	6.5	5.2	26.1	29.1	13.2	1.9	78.1	40.6	50.1	49.9
48818	CRYSTAL	97.4	96.9	0.1	0.2	0.2	0.3	1.2	1.6	6.3	6.2	6.7	7.0	5.0	24.7	28.9	14.2	1.2	76.6	40.8	49.5	50.5
48819	DANSVILLE	97.3	96.4	0.3	0.3	0.4	0.6	1.7	2.4	6.7	7.3	7.7	6.9	4.5	26.1	30.8	9.1	1.0	73.9	39.6	50.0	50.0
48820	DEWITT	95.7	94.5	0.8	0.9	0.8	1.2	2.4	3.2	6.8	7.1	7.7	7.8	5.3	25.3	30.2	9.0	1.0	73.3	38.0	49.5	50.5
48821	DIMONDALE	92.4	91.0	3.7	4.1	0.7	1.1	3.3	4.4	4.6	5.1	5.9	6.4	4.9	20.6	33.9	15.0	3.5	80.3	46.4	47.5	52.5
48822	EAGLE	98.0	97.5	0.3	0.4	0.4	0.6	1.8	2.4	6.0	6.8	7.5	7.2	4.5	21.7	34.0	11.4	1.0	75.1	42.3	50.6	49.4
48823	EAST LANSING	82.9	79.3	6.0	6.4	7.5	10.2	2.9	3.7	3.9	3.7	3.8	6.4	30.3	21.8	19.2	8.7	2.2	86.1	26.1	48.7	51.3
48824	EAST LANSING	80.0	64.4	11.4	21.9	5.4	11.6	2.2	1.1	0.0	0.0	0.0	63.7	36.3	0.0	0.0	0.0	0.0	95.2	18.9	40.3	59.7
48825	EAST LANSING	78.9	70.6	9.5	14.2	8.9	11.4	2.5	3.5	0.8	0.6	0.7	51.8	32.0	10.4	2.9	0.7	0.2	95.1	19.6	51.3	48.7
48827	EATON RAPIDS	96.3	95.2	0.4	0.5	0.3	0.6	2.6	3.6	7.0	7.4	7.7	7.4	5.5	25.5	29.2	9.2	1.2	73.1	37.8	49.5	50.5
48829	EDMORE	96.6	95.9	0.3	0.3	0.1	0.2	2.9	4.0	7.0	7.0	7.2	7.3	5.3	25.3	26.4	12.5	2.1	73.6	38.3	49.3	50.7
48831	ELSIE	98.2	97.7	0.1	0.1	0.2	0.3	1.9	2.6	6.8	7.0	7.0	7.3	5.2	25.5	27.7	11.6	1.8	74.6	38.8	50.7	49.3
48832	ELWELL	97.8	97.2	0.2	0.2	0.1	0.1	2.2	3.0	6.7	6.7	6.9	7.1	6.0	27.0	26.5	11.8	1.3	75.1	38.1	49.7	50.3
48834	FENWICK	90.6	92.3	6.3	3.7	0.3	1.0	3.2	4.0	6.4	6.3	6.4	9.1	5.7	27.2	28.2	9.7	0.8	77.2	37.4	53.4	46.6
48835	FOWLER	99.1	98.9	0.0	0.0	0.2	0.3	1.2	1.6	8.2	8.6	8.5	7.6	4.8	25.9	24.8	10.1	1.4	70.0	35.3	51.2	48.8
48836	FOWLERVILLE	97.0	96.3	0.2	0.3	0.4	0.6	1.1	1.4	7.6	7.9	8.1	7.8	5.4	28.5	25.8	7.8	1.1	71.1	35.6	50.5	49.5
48837	GRAND LEDGE	96.6	95.6	0.6	0.8	0.5	0.9	2.2	3.0	5.8	6.1	6.7	6.9	5.5	24.8	31.1	11.5	1.7	77.1	41.0	48.7	51.3
48838	GREENVILLE	96.7	95.9	0.4	0.5	0.4	0.6	2.5	3.4	6.7	6.7	6.9	7.0	5.8	26.6	27.1	10.8	2.2	75.1	38.1	49.8	50.2
48840	HASLETT	93.1	90.6	2.1	2.6	2.2	3.6	2.5	3.4	5.4	5.2	6.3	6.7	8.3	27.0	29.0	9.9	2.1	80.7	38.7	47.0	53.0
48841	HENDERSON	98.2	97.9	0.1	0.1	0.1	0.1	1.4	1.8	5.6	6.1	6.8	7.5	5.3	24.0	31.1	12.2	1.6	76.8	41.4	50.0	50.0
48842	HOLT	92.9	90.7	2.5	2.9	1.1	1.9	3.5	4.8	6.5	6.5	6.8	7.1	6.5	26.3	29.3	9.5	1.7	75.9	38.0	48.1	51.9
48843	HOWELL	96.8	96.1	0.4	0.4	0.8	1.1	1.5	1.9	7.8	7.7	7.8	6.9	5.3	28.2	27.1	8.1	1.1	72.2	36.3	49.9	50.1
48845	HUBBARDSTON	93.5	92.7	4.1	4.4	0.3	0.4	2.1	2.6	7.3	7.1	7.2	7.4	6.4	26.3	26.8	10.8	0.7	74.4	36.7	54.1	45.9
48846	IONIA	81.4	78.2	13.2	15.0	0.5	0.9	4.1	5.2	5.3	5.2	5.2	8.9	15.7	30.4	20.7	7.1	1.5	81.1	29.8	61.8	38.2
48847	ITHACA	96.4	95.3	0.2	0.2	0.3	0.5	4.1	5.5	6.9	6.8	7.0	6.9	5.4	26.3	26.6	11.7	2.3	74.7	37.9	48.6	51.4
48848	LAINGSBURG	97.4	97.0	0.4	0.5	0.1	0.1	1.4	2.0	6.3	6.8	7.5	7.3	4.7	25.2	32.0	9.3	0.9	74.6	40.2	50.6	49.4
48849	LAKE ODESSA	96.3	95.4	0.1	0.2	0.4	0.6	3.6	4.7	7.6	7.6	7.5	7.0	5.8	26.6	26.7	9.9	1.4	73.0	36.5	49.3	50.7
48850	LAKEVIEW	96.8	96.2	0.2	0.2	0.2	0.3	2.1	2.8	7.0	7.1	7.1	7.1	5.4	24.7	26.0	13.2	2.3	74.2	38.3	49.8	50.2
48851	LYONS	96.8	96.3	0.2	0.2	0.1	0.2	2.1	2.7	6.0	6.5	7.0	7.1	5.1	26.6	30.2	10.3	1.1	75.9	39.3	51.3	48.7
48854	MASON	95.0	93.2	1.7	2.2	0.7	1.2	2.6	3.7	5.5	5.8	6.3	7.1	6.0	25.9	30.9	11.2	1.4	79.0	40.6	49.7	50.3
48855	HOWELL	97.8	97.1	0.1	0.1	0.4	0.7	1.0	1.3	7.0	7.5	8.1	7.4	4.6	26.0	30.2	8.4	0.8	72.5	38.7	50.9	49.1
48856	MIDDLETON	96.8	96.1	0.1	0.1	0.1	0.1	2.0	2.7	7.1	7.8	8.1	7.2	5.9	25.9	25.1	11.5	1.3	72.0	36.2	49.3	50.7
48857	MORRICE	97.1	96.3	0.3	0.4	0.2	0.4	1.6	2.1	7.7	7.9	8.0	7.1	4.4	28.5	26.7	8.8	0.9	72.0	36.6	51.1	48.9
48858	MOUNT PLEASANT	89.7	87.8	2.5	2.8	1.9	3.0	2.4	3.0	4.8	4.3	4.2	15.9	24.6	20.8	17.4	6.8	1.3	83.9	24.2	46.9	53.1
48860	MUIR	96.7	96.1	0.1	0.1	0.2	0.3	1.7	2.3	7.4	7.0	7.3	7.8	6.5	27.9	26.3	8.8	1.1	73.4	35.7	50.3	49.7
48861	MULLIKEN	96.7	95.7	0.4	0.5	0.1	0.2	2.1	2.9	5.8	6.4	6.8	6.8	4.9	26.1	31.3	10.4	1.5	76.8	40.0	51.0	49.0
48864	OKEMOS	84.2	77.9	4.1	4.6	8.7	13.9	2.2	2.8	5.0	5.0	5.8	6.9	9.8	26.3	29.8	9.6	1.8	80.4	37.2	48.3	51.7
48865	ORLEANS	98.1	97.5	0.1	0.1	0.1	0.2	1.7	2.4	7.2	7.3	7.2	6.9	6.1	28.3	27.6	8.5	0.8	74.1	35.9	51.4	48.6
48866	OVID	97.3	96.8	0.2	0.2	0.2	0.2	2.8	3.7	7.5	7.6	7.4	6.7	5.1	26.4	25.7	11.2	2.4	73.4	37.4	48.7	51.3
48867	OWOSSO	97.3	96.7	0.2	0.2	0.4	0.6	2.3	3.0	6.8	6.7	6.8	7.0	5.9	25.6	27.2	11.9	2.0	75.4	38.4	48.6	51.4
48871	PERRINTON	97.1	96.5	0.2	0.2	0.0	0.0	2.3	3.2	5.9	6.3	6.8	6.9	4.9	24.9	29.3	12.7	2.2	76.7	41.0	50.4	49.6
48872	PERRY	97.6	97.0	0.2	0.2	0.4	0.6	1.0	1.3	7.4	7.6	7.7	7.5	5.8	26.8	27.6	8.6	1.0	72.7	36.3	48.0	52.0
48873	PEWAMO	98.6	98.3	0.0	0.0	0.1	0.1	1.2	1.6	9.4	9.3	9.2	7.2	4.6	25.7	23.6	9.7	1.2	67.5	34.0	49.6	50.4
48875	PORTLAND	97.8	97.3	0.3	0.3	0.2	0.3	1.4	1.8	7.5	7.6	7.7	7.2	5.3	26.8	27.3	9.4	1.2	72.7	36.9	49.1	50.9
48876	POTTERVILLE	96.2	95.0	0.4	0.5	0.2	0.4	3.7	5.1	7.0	7.0	7.0	7.1	6.7	26.4	29.1	8.8	1.0	74.7	36.9	48.9	51.1
48877	RIVERDALE	97.6	97.0	0.2	0.3	0.1	0.1	2.2	3.0	7.6	7.7	7.6	6.7	5.6	26.3	26.9	10.7	0.9	72.7	36.5	51.1	48.9
48878	ROSEBUSH	95.2	94.6	0.6	0.7	0.4	0.6	1.3	1.7	7.7	7.5	7.4	7.1	5.6	27.0	27.3	9.0	1.4	73.0	35.9	48.2	51.8
48879	SAINT JOHNS	97.0	96.3	0.4	0.4	0.5	0.7	2.5	3.3	6.7	7.0	7.3	7.2	5.3	26.0	27.7	10.4	2.4	74.2	38.2	50.0	50.0
48880	SAINT LOUIS	79.2	76.8	15.0	16.4	0.4	0.6	5.2	6.6	4.3	4.2	4.4	5.4	8.9	39.8	22.6	9.0	1.4	84.1	35.6	65.8	34.2
48881	SARANAC	95.5	95.5	1.9	1.2	0.2	0.6	1.9	2.5	6.8	7.2	7.2	8.1	5.4	27.5	27.5	9.1	1.2	74.5	37.1	51.2	48.8
48883	SHEPHERD	95.3	94.6	0.4	0.5	0.3	0.4	2.2	2.9	6.9	6.9	6.9	7.1	6.2	27.7	28.0	9.3	1.1	75.0	36.7	49.5	50.5
48884	SHERIDAN	93.4	93.4	4.0	3.3	0.3	0.9	2.0	2.6	6.5	6.2	6.3	8.5	6.1	27.8	27.6	9.9	1.1	77.4	37.2	52.1	47.9
48885	SIDNEY	98.0	97.2	0.3	0.4	0.1	0.4	1.1	1.6	5.4	5.9	6.3	7.4	5.7	25.9	31.3	11.4	0.9	77.8	40.4	50.3	49.7
48886	SIX LAKES	96.4	95.8	0.4	0.5	0.1	0.2	1.6	2.2	7.1	7.0	7.2	7.2	5.3	24.3	26.2	13.9	1.7	74.0	38.8	49.4	50.6
48888	STANTON	97.2	96.6	0.2	0.2	0.3	0.5	2.4	3.2	6.4	6.6	6.9	7.5	5.9	25.5	27.8	11.8	1.6	75.2	38.5	49.8	50.2
48889	SUMNER	98.0	97.6	0.2	0.2	0.1	0.1	2.0	2.8	7.4	7.5	7.5	6.4	5.2	24.8	27.4	11.9	1.8	73.1	38.1	49.9	50.1
48890	SUNFIELD	97.4	96.6	0.3	0.3	0.2	0.3	2.0	2.7	6.7	7.3	7.6	7.2	4.8	25.7	29.5	9.7	1.6	74.2	38.8	49.3	50.7
48891	VESTABURG	97.9	97.4	0.2	0.3	0.2	0.3	1.6	2.2	6.8	6.7	7.0	7.7	6.2	25.8	27.6	11.0	1.2	74.2	37.6	50.9	49.1
48892	WEBBERVILLE	96.9	96.0	0.5	0.5	0.4	0.6	1.5	2.1	6.9	7.3	7.6	7.5	5.1	28.6	27.6	8.3	1.1	73.4	36.8	49.4	50.6
48893	WEIDMAN	96.2	95.6	0.4	0.5	0.2	0.3	1.4	1.9	6.5	6.8	6.9	6.5	4.4	24.5	28.9	14.1	1.3	75.7	41.5	50.3	49.7
48894	WESTPHALIA	99.3	99.1	0.0	0.0	0.1	0.2	0.3	0.4	9.3	9.1	8.9	7.1	4.6	24.6	22.4	12.6	1.5	68.3	35.7	49.6	50.4
48895	WILLIAMSTON	97.3	96.3	0.4	0.5	0.6	1.1	1.7	2.4	6.0	6.6	7.3	7.5	5.2	22.9	32.6	10.6	1.4	75.4	41.3	48.5	51.5
48897	WOODLAND	97.5	96.8	0.1	0.1	0.3	0.4	2.6	3.5	6.6	6.8	7.0	7.1	5.1	25.0	28.6	12.5	1.4	75.2	40.0	51.0	49.0
48906	LANSING	73.2	70.7	12.8	12.8	3.2	4.4	12.4	14.6	7.9	7.2	7.0	7.1	6.7	27.4	25.0	10.3	1.4	73.6	35.4	49.8	50.2
48910	LANSING	76.3	71.2	13.7	15.7	1.9	3.0	7.9	10.4	7.4	6.6	6.1	6.3	9.9	30.6	23.2	8.3	1.6	76.4	33.4	48.2	51.8
48911	LANSING	61.0	56.4	27.6	29.3	3.3	4.9	7.7	9.4	8.4	7.9	7.5	7.3	7.4	28.6	23.5	8.3	1.1	72.1	32.7	47.0	53.0
48912	LANSING	72.8	67.5	13.4	14.9	2.7	4.3	11.0	13.9	6.9	6.6	6.1	6.0	9.2	32.0	23.2	8.4	1.5	77.1	33.6	49.1	50.9
48915	LANSING	47.5	42.5	40.0	42.5	1.6	2.4	11.1	13.6	8.5	8.3	7.6	7.2	7.1	29.4	23.1	7.6	1.1	71.2	32.1	48.6	51.4
48917	LANSING	83.7	79.6	8.9	10.5	2.6	4.1	4.9	6.3	5.8	5.5	5.6	5.9	6.7	28.7	27.5	12.1	2.3	79.6	38.5	47.2	52.8
48933	LANSING	54.2	47.5	30.8	33.3	5.5	8.0	9.2	11.4	5.1	3.5	3.3	6.2	16.1	34.6	21.7	8.3	1.1	85.8	30.5	53.0	47.0
49001	KALAMAZOO	72.8	68.3	16.8	19.0	1.0	1.5	7.4	9.3	7.9	7.1	6.6	6.9	9.6	29.9	22.0	7.9	2.2	74.6	32.6	48.4	51.6
49002	PORTAGE	92.5	90.3	3.2	3.7	1.5	2.4	2.1	2.8	6.1	6.2	6.4	6.1	6.1	27.7	27.0	12.4	1.9	77.4	38.9	48.8	51.2
49004	KALAMAZOO	87.6	85.1	8.0	9.4	0.8	1.3	2.2	2.9	7.3	7.5	7.6	6.8	5.2	25.2	26.8	11.4	2.0	73.0	38.1	48.0	52.0
49006	KALAMAZOO	80.6	75.9	11.5	13.5	3.9	5.8	2.6	3.4	4.7	3.9	3.6	9.4	30.1	22.2	15.5	8.3	2.4	85.7	24.7	48.3	51.7
49007	KALAMAZOO	44.0	41.3	48.3	49.4	0.8	1.2	4.7	5.8	7.1	7.0	6.1	7.8	20.5	25.7	18.0	6.5	1.3	76.0	25.8	49.1	50.9
49008	KALAMAZOO	84.7	80.6	8.7	10.3	3.5	5.2	2.1	2.8	4.1	3.9	3.9	21.4	16.4	20.8	17.8	9.7	2.1	85.9	25.3	48.1	51.9
49009	KALAMAZOO	89.5	86.3	5.8	7.0	2.1	3.4	1.9	2.6	6.0	6.1	6.4	6.7	8.8	25.0	27.3	11.2	2.4	77.5	37.6	48.0	52.0
49010	ALLEGAN	94.6	93.4	2.3	2.6	0.4	0.7	2.3	3.2	6.7	6.7	6.8	6.8	6.0	25.8	28.1	11.4	1.7	77.7	38.7	50.0	50.0
49011	ATHENS	97.1	96.6	0.2	0.2	0.2	0.3	1.5	2.1	6.2	6.2	6.2	6.5	6.7	26.4	27.2	12.9	1.6	77.2	38.8	49.6	50.4
49012	AUGUSTA	96.6	95.5	0.5	0.6	0.4	0.6	1.4	1.9	5.2	6.2	6.8	7.6	4.7	21.8	34.3	11.9	1.5	76.7	43.4	49.6	50.4
49013	BANGOR	82.1	78.8	8.4	9.4	0.1	0.2	10.9	14.1	7.6	7.2	7.2	7.4	6.5	24.8	26.2	11.5	1.5	73.3	36.2	49.4	50.6
49014	BATTLE CREEK	86.1	83.7	8.6	9.7	0.9	1.3	4.0	5.1	6.3	6.3	6.4	7.6	6.7	27.3	27.5	10.4	1.6	76.4	37.5	50.6	49.4
49015	BATTLE CREEK	88.1	84.8	4.4	5.1	3.6	5.6	3.8	4.9	6.5	6.3	6.3	6.7	6.6	25.6	27.4	12.2	2.3	76.7	39.0	48.1	51.9
49017	BATTLE CREEK	85.7	83.2	9.7	11.2	0.6	0.8	2.8	3.6	6.4	6.1	6.4	6.7	6.3	24.6	28.7	12.9	2.0	77.0	40.1	48.5	51.5
49021	BELLEVUE	97.2	96.4	0.5	0.6	0.3	0.5	1.8	2.4	5.6	6.1	6.6	6.6	4.9	24.9	31.7	12.3	1.3	77.5	41.7	50.4	49.6
49022	BENTON HARBOR	39.8	36.2	56.9	60.2	0.3	0.4	2.7	3.4	8.8	8.4	7.7	7.9	6.8	23.7	24.4	10.6	1.7	70.2	33.6	47.2	52.8
	MICHIGAN	80.2	78.3	14.2	14.5	1.8	2.8	3.3	4.1	6.7	6.7	6.8	7.2	6.6	26.3	26.9	10.9	1.9	75.6	37.6	49.2	50.8
	UNITED STATES	75.1	72.0	12.3	12.7	3.8	4.6	12.5	15.7	6.8	6.7	6.6	7.1	6.9	27.0	26.0	10.9	1.9	75.7	36.9	49.2	50.8

ZIP CODE #	POST OFFICE NAME	2009 Per Capita Income	2009 HH Income Base	2009 Household Income Distribution (%): Less than $25,000	$25,000 to $49,999	$50,000 to $99,999	$100,000 to $149,999	$150,000 or More	Median Household Income: 2009	2014	2009 National Centile	2009 State Centile	2009 Home Value Base	2009 Home Value Distribution (%): Less than $50,000	$50,000 to $89,999	$90,000 to $174,999	$175,000 to $399,999	$400,000 or More	2009 Median Home Value
48770	WHITTEMORE	18099	826	31.7	30.5	33.4	3.1	1.2	39262	41823	31	16	701	21.5	35.9	32.8	8.4	1.3	78913
48801	ALMA	20818	4433	26.0	29.2	35.4	7.1	2.2	44452	48144	47	33	3087	13.3	31.7	40.6	13.7	0.7	96215
48806	ASHLEY	20708	719	20.4	32.0	40.2	5.7	1.7	47624	50636	56	43	605	15.9	27.6	42.3	12.6	1.7	98977
48807	BANNISTER	20510	381	23.9	32.8	36.7	4.2	2.4	43835	48132	45	31	311	15.8	28.6	39.9	14.5	1.3	97292
48808	BATH	27966	1643	11.6	19.3	54.0	10.8	4.3	65795	68831	84	86	1450	5.7	10.6	47.0	33.6	3.2	148298
48809	BELDING	20548	4245	22.2	27.6	41.6	6.7	1.9	50170	53737	62	50	3260	8.9	24.2	49.2	16.5	1.1	109298
48811	CARSON CITY	16756	1287	24.2	29.0	38.5	6.8	1.4	46204	47868	52	39	1011	11.7	29.2	45.3	13.5	0.4	100470
48813	CHARLOTTE	23986	8177	16.4	24.6	46.8	9.3	3.0	56841	60690	74	69	6543	10.2	20.7	47.2	20.6	1.2	117182
48815	CLARKSVILLE	22539	757	18.6	26.7	42.9	8.3	3.4	54327	57563	70	63	655	5.3	15.7	46.0	29.8	3.2	140755
48817	CORUNNA	22221	2574	23.5	27.4	38.7	9.0	1.4	49085	51277	59	48	1931	6.1	19.8	54.3	18.5	1.2	119857
48818	CRYSTAL	20258	980	24.7	35.8	31.6	6.2	1.6	40372	43483	34	19	823	15.2	25.9	39.5	14.9	4.5	101420
48819	DANSVILLE	23379	1029	12.5	23.1	53.4	8.5	2.4	61152	60684	79	78	937	3.9	14.5	56.2	23.9	1.4	130015
48820	DEWITT	31245	5866	8.6	15.2	45.9	21.7	8.6	75883	78050	90	93	4770	1.5	5.2	41.6	47.3	4.5	179464
48821	DIMONDALE	27050	2275	15.8	22.9	45.7	11.5	4.0	61438	64521	79	79	2028	24.8	9.1	35.4	29.4	1.3	128484
48822	EAGLE	30232	988	6.8	18.6	53.4	15.4	5.8	70014	73972	87	90	921	1.8	7.2	38.4	47.6	5.0	180021
48823	EAST LANSING	27419	21093	33.5	23.0	27.7	8.6	7.2	41583	46262	38	23	9589	4.6	11.0	45.7	34.5	4.2	148119
48824	EAST LANSING	13917	14	100.0	0.0	0.0	0.0	0.0	12857	12857	1	0	0	0.0	0.0	0.0	0.0	0.0	0
48825	EAST LANSING	13973	389	49.9	24.9	19.5	5.7	0.0	25059	26191	3	1	45	0.0	8.9	71.1	20.0	0.0	128409
48827	EATON RAPIDS	23832	6039	14.3	22.8	50.4	10.0	2.5	60599	63129	78	77	5030	5.8	16.9	51.2	25.6	0.5	127694
48829	EDMORE	18031	1528	30.4	31.6	32.6	4.4	1.0	38868	42189	29	15	1205	16.7	27.6	46.2	8.3	1.2	97092
48831	ELSIE	20939	1328	20.6	28.5	44.3	4.9	1.7	50714	52757	63	51	1080	15.4	26.5	41.7	14.8	1.7	100680
48832	ELWELL	20225	603	20.7	26.4	46.4	6.0	0.5	51290	52241	64	54	523	21.4	22.4	39.0	16.4	0.8	102214
48834	FENWICK	19423	1044	21.3	30.3	42.0	5.5	1.1	48409	50730	58	46	910	18.8	24.1	42.2	13.4	1.5	100667
48835	FOWLER	21793	989	15.7	25.0	49.0	8.7	1.6	60727	62955	78	77	850	7.1	12.7	47.9	29.2	3.2	138816
48836	FOWLERVILLE	27261	4851	12.0	20.8	44.1	17.4	5.7	66297	64808	84	87	4095	14.0	11.4	43.0	29.7	1.9	141365
48837	GRAND LEDGE	30031	7385	12.0	19.4	44.8	17.2	6.6	66442	71021	84	87	5889	7.6	9.4	46.9	33.8	2.3	147083
48838	GREENVILLE	20696	6793	22.6	31.9	37.8	6.3	1.3	45483	47776	50	37	5146	12.4	19.4	48.5	18.6	1.1	115836
48840	HASLETT	30791	5491	21.5	22.1	38.5	10.9	6.9	57211	57827	74	70	3308	2.3	13.9	45.8	35.2	2.7	143735
48841	HENDERSON	20263	304	17.4	28.6	44.1	7.2	2.6	52540	53438	67	58	270	6.7	19.3	46.7	25.9	1.5	123936
48842	HOLT	27115	7891	13.7	25.6	43.2	13.3	4.2	58422	58587	76	72	5897	17.2	12.7	50.5	18.6	1.0	116525
48843	HOWELL	34784	16744	9.7	16.1	38.1	24.6	11.6	79663	84382	92	94	13585	6.7	6.9	29.4	50.7	6.2	187415
48845	HUBBARDSTON	19502	392	20.7	30.1	42.1	6.1	1.0	49283	52669	59	48	340	17.9	23.5	40.9	16.8	0.9	100439
48846	IONIA	19238	5754	22.3	25.5	44.1	6.5	1.7	51463	54872	65	54	4347	19.0	28.9	39.3	11.6	1.2	92742
48847	ITHACA	20674	2492	23.6	28.5	39.8	6.9	1.2	47592	50619	56	43	1931	14.1	28.3	45.4	11.4	0.7	96896
48848	LAINGSBURG	25975	2960	13.7	23.5	47.2	10.4	5.1	62053	62618	80	80	2667	7.0	7.3	44.9	36.1	4.7	155489
48849	LAKE ODESSA	22515	2414	19.4	28.9	40.4	8.9	2.4	51455	55444	65	54	1963	12.5	21.0	45.0	18.8	2.7	114528
48850	LAKEVIEW	18871	1826	22.3	31.6	40.3	4.8	1.0	45920	47686	51	38	1482	12.2	24.1	43.9	18.4	1.4	106538
48851	LYONS	21528	890	17.4	25.3	49.3	6.7	1.2	53857	56611	69	62	760	11.2	28.8	44.5	14.9	0.7	102953
48854	MASON	25815	6707	12.9	25.7	47.3	11.0	3.2	60219	60174	78	75	5229	10.6	10.9	53.0	24.0	1.4	129028
48855	HOWELL	31779	5194	9.5	15.3	39.9	25.9	9.4	78447	81512	91	94	4741	5.7	9.4	32.3	47.1	5.4	180226
48856	MIDDLETON	20440	310	20.6	31.6	38.4	7.4	1.9	46973	50321	54	41	257	12.8	30.0	44.0	12.1	1.2	98409
48857	MORRICE	21212	992	12.0	30.2	49.5	5.6	2.6	54120	54448	70	63	896	6.5	16.1	52.7	22.8	2.0	132222
48858	MOUNT PLEASANT	19537	17532	33.3	27.4	30.9	6.0	2.4	39032	42356	30	15	9197	11.8	16.1	47.3	22.7	2.2	121202
48860	MUIR	19151	544	25.4	29.6	37.1	7.2	0.7	45452	50737	50	37	438	18.9	30.8	38.8	10.5	0.9	90303
48861	MULLIKEN	24111	645	12.7	24.0	50.2	9.8	3.3	60662	63245	78	77	580	7.2	22.9	48.4	19.5	1.9	113281
48864	OKEMOS	38874	8049	17.2	18.0	33.6	15.9	15.3	68152	67049	86	89	5229	1.5	3.8	32.2	54.0	8.5	194979
48865	ORLEANS	19688	613	21.4	30.8	40.9	5.9	1.0	47548	52032	56	42	515	19.8	26.0	40.8	11.7	1.7	97414
48866	OVID	21406	1770	17.8	28.1	44.9	7.4	1.8	53757	55230	69	62	1493	14.3	18.6	46.1	19.9	1.0	115545
48867	OWOSSO	21950	11434	22.3	30.4	38.4	7.1	1.9	47398	50555	55	42	8450	10.5	18.8	52.2	17.2	1.3	114654
48871	PERRINTON	22216	802	17.2	30.3	43.9	6.5	2.1	51765	52426	65	55	688	7.6	20.5	46.9	24.1	0.9	121639
48872	PERRY	24559	2943	12.7	22.9	49.7	11.2	3.4	61393	60896	79	79	2543	11.5	9.8	47.1	29.3	2.3	142493
48873	PEWAMO	18806	580	16.7	31.0	45.2	5.5	1.6	51117	53987	64	53	499	11.2	25.1	48.9	13.2	1.6	107969
48875	PORTLAND	24143	3624	14.1	23.1	48.8	11.2	2.8	60542	61534	78	77	3045	9.0	14.4	52.0	23.2	1.5	127360
48876	POTTERVILLE	24759	1481	15.0	24.4	45.6	11.3	3.8	58928	62163	76	73	1253	26.5	16.5	37.1	19.2	0.7	102140
48877	RIVERDALE	17769	991	22.8	32.5	39.9	4.0	0.8	45204	48610	49	36	850	18.4	28.4	40.8	11.5	0.9	95600
48878	ROSEBUSH	19102	619	23.6	29.2	40.7	4.8	1.6	46403	48838	53	40	520	13.8	22.7	45.0	17.3	1.2	107798
48879	SAINT JOHNS	24142	6662	15.4	25.1	48.1	8.9	2.6	60437	62158	78	76	5316	8.5	11.3	49.6	28.8	1.8	136189
48880	SAINT LOUIS	17970	2725	24.6	31.3	37.2	5.8	1.0	45095	48326	49	35	2142	19.4	34.0	36.5	9.7	0.4	86826
48881	SARANAC	21465	2121	20.6	26.4	44.9	6.5	1.7	51653	54765	66	56	1723	9.8	16.0	56.0	16.7	1.6	121722
48883	SHEPHERD	21008	2675	19.8	25.9	46.5	6.4	1.5	52611	52628	67	58	2218	11.7	22.0	49.7	15.4	1.2	110922
48884	SHERIDAN	18857	1620	24.6	32.2	37.8	4.8	0.6	43215	45779	43	30	1374	18.0	23.0	43.5	15.1	0.4	103326
48885	SIDNEY	20474	424	17.5	30.9	44.8	6.4	0.5	51013	50720	64	53	364	12.4	21.2	49.5	16.8	0.3	111000
48886	SIX LAKES	18457	1006	27.0	32.2	36.1	4.0	0.7	41505	44195	38	22	870	14.7	26.3	49.0	9.5	0.5	102273
48888	STANTON	18966	2670	23.5	31.4	39.1	5.1	0.9	44727	47057	47	34	2189	15.3	22.9	46.5	14.5	0.8	106294
48889	SUMNER	18753	547	22.7	32.4	39.5	4.4	1.1	45233	49343	49	36	461	13.9	30.6	43.4	11.1	1.1	99107
48890	SUNFIELD	22513	862	15.3	23.3	50.6	9.0	1.7	59090	61663	76	73	744	7.7	23.3	46.0	21.2	1.9	116270
48891	VESTABURG	17822	1085	23.9	35.5	35.5	4.1	1.1	41818	45244	39	24	924	18.6	27.3	42.1	11.0	1.0	95938
48892	WEBBERVILLE	22410	1620	16.4	25.7	49.2	7.4	1.4	56368	56283	73	68	1422	17.4	10.2	48.4	22.3	1.7	124057
48893	WEIDMAN	21124	1928	21.0	33.3	38.6	5.5	1.6	46433	47951	53	40	1729	14.5	22.1	41.9	19.5	2.0	112181
48894	WESTPHALIA	25278	648	11.4	19.6	55.4	11.9	1.7	66225	70385	84	87	573	3.7	8.4	51.5	35.6	0.9	149488
48895	WILLIAMSTON	29937	4168	12.2	19.9	43.9	16.1	7.9	67516	66687	85	88	3420	4.3	8.3	45.2	37.6	4.6	152980
48897	WOODLAND	21545	611	21.6	29.6	38.1	7.5	3.1	48338	53159	57	46	511	5.9	22.5	47.0	20.7	3.9	118364
48906	LANSING	22960	11429	25.1	26.8	37.7	7.6	2.9	47812	51469	56	43	7981	22.9	32.1	35.0	9.0	1.1	84388
48910	LANSING	22990	15326	23.9	30.6	39.0	5.3	1.2	45823	50090	51	38	9307	12.1	52.0	34.4	1.3	0.2	82151
48911	LANSING	23359	16220	21.4	27.2	40.4	8.1	2.9	50916	53172	63	52	9478	13.2	38.8	38.9	8.4	0.6	88623
48912	LANSING	22511	7780	28.7	27.5	36.3	5.5	2.0	43949	48773	45	32	4097	21.5	38.3	34.7	5.2	0.2	78942
48915	LANSING	21039	3843	29.0	28.6	32.7	7.3	2.4	42206	46439	40	25	2351	20.5	46.8	28.9	3.5	0.2	75160
48917	LANSING	31083	14139	15.1	24.1	43.3	12.2	5.3	59856	62194	77	75	8582	7.0	11.9	52.1	27.2	1.8	137843
48933	LANSING	20306	1284	54.3	23.4	19.2	2.1	1.0	20936	23150	2	1	126	10.3	51.6	32.5	5.6	0.0	84000
49001	KALAMAZOO	20752	9029	29.7	27.5	37.2	4.4	1.3	42434	47166	41	26	5134	21.7	41.0	35.8	1.3	0.2	78109
49002	PORTAGE	26348	8296	18.2	28.8	42.2	7.8	3.1	52672	54690	67	58	5843	8.3	18.2	52.0	19.4	2.1	119735
49004	KALAMAZOO	22639	6362	17.9	29.3	44.9	5.6	2.4	52218	54153	66	56	5227	12.3	28.6	45.6	12.1	1.4	101008
49006	KALAMAZOO	21956	10242	33.9	27.3	32.1	4.9	1.9	39305	43014	31	16	4100	9.1	20.8	62.8	6.9	0.3	109480
49007	KALAMAZOO	15829	5199	47.3	25.1	23.9	2.4	1.2	27265	29610	5	2	1535	39.3	37.0	20.1	2.6	1.0	59561
49008	KALAMAZOO	26811	7322	27.1	23.8	33.0	9.5	6.6	48892	51524	59	47	4304	6.2	22.8	44.1	24.4	2.5	128438
49009	KALAMAZOO	29343	15496	21.6	22.1	38.8	10.3	7.2	56685	58211	74	69	10551	14.2	11.8	33.1	36.5	4.4	147785
49010	ALLEGAN	21739	6921	19.5	27.3	44.3	6.9	2.0	52145	53332	66	56	5597	12.4	18.2	44.1	23.5	1.8	122714
49011	ATHENS	21704	950	20.2	24.6	45.4	8.1	1.7	53562	54811	69	61	805	13.7	33.8	42.6	9.6	0.4	92204
49012	AUGUSTA	29746	1322	13.3	25.0	43.1	11.3	7.2	63430	63286	82	82	1099	6.2	17.3	41.2	27.7	7.6	140234
49013	BANGOR	17340	2049	28.9	32.0	33.1	4.8	1.2	40304	42759	34	19	1584	23.4	34.8	35.6	5.5	0.7	82073
49014	BATTLE CREEK	21904	8629	22.9	28.7	39.2	6.2	2.9	47403	51532	55	42	6206	23.3	25.3	35.5	14.8	1.1	91805
49015	BATTLE CREEK	26363	10719	18.8	25.6	41.1	10.2	4.3	54832	55881	71	64	7726	8.2	28.9	44.1	16.4	2.4	109610
49017	BATTLE CREEK	23984	9098	21.0	28.1	40.3	7.6	3.0	50689	52937	63	51	6767	14.3	35.1	38.4	11.6	0.6	90560
49021	BELLEVUE	22250	2449	15.4	28.7	46.8	7.6	1.5	55281	58723	72	66	2165	10.6	23.6	45.6	18.9	1.2	111951
49022	BENTON HARBOR	16856	13088	40.2	25.3	28.7	4.0	1.7	33711	36444	15	5	7499	27.2	30.0	34.5	7.5	0.7	81510
	MICHIGAN	26713		20.1	24.2	38.5	11.3	5.9	55536	56866				13.2	21.9	40.3	21.5	3.2	115137
	UNITED STATES	27277		20.9	24.4	35.3	11.7	7.6	54719	56938				9.3	13.1	31.6	32.6	13.5	162279

ZIP CODE	FINANCIAL SERVICES				THE HOME						ENTERTAINMENT						PERSONAL			
					Home Improvements		Furnishings													
# POST OFFICE NAME	Auto Loan	Home Loan	Invest-ments	Retire-ment Plans	Home Repair	Lawn & Garden	Comput-ers & Hard-ware-Personal	Major Appli-ances	TV, Radio, Sound Equip-ment	Furni-ture	Dine out/ Carry out	Sports Equip-ment	Fees & Tickets	Toys & Games	Travel	Cable TV	Apparel & Services	Auto Repairs	Health Insur-ance	Pets & Supplies
48770 WHITTEMORE	78	57	83	55	59	80	58	74	64	54	63	55	47	63	58	70	42	68	76	88
48801 ALMA	77	72	69	72	71	79	75	76	77	72	76	58	71	77	73	80	52	77	83	91
48806 ASHLEY	88	72	84	73	74	92	72	86	77	66	76	65	63	78	72	83	51	79	89	101
48807 BANNISTER	85	71	74	72	72	87	71	81	75	66	74	62	63	78	69	81	50	76	85	96
48808 BATH	105	114	99	115	111	112	103	107	102	104	103	82	108	105	107	103	72	103	107	126
48809 BELDING	81	79	70	80	77	84	79	81	80	75	79	62	77	81	77	83	55	79	85	96
48811 CARSON CITY	79	72	71	73	71	83	74	78	76	69	75	60	69	76	72	79	51	76	84	93
48813 CHARLOTTE	87	92	79	94	88	93	87	88	88	85	88	69	90	90	88	89	61	87	92	105
48815 CLARKSVILLE	93	92	86	95	92	100	87	95	88	83	88	73	85	90	88	92	60	89	96	111
48817 CORUNNA	79	81	74	82	79	87	77	81	78	73	78	62	78	80	78	81	54	78	86	95
48818 CRYSTAL	85	65	95	64	69	87	66	83	71	62	70	61	56	70	68	77	47	77	84	97
48819 DANSVILLE	92	100	88	104	98	102	91	96	90	90	90	75	95	93	95	91	63	92	96	113
48820 DEWITT	119	139	124	139	135	126	122	124	117	127	119	97	132	121	129	115	84	119	117	143
48821 DIMONDALE	90	105	100	105	104	106	93	98	94	95	94	71	103	93	101	96	66	95	103	113
48822 EAGLE	112	128	111	132	125	124	114	118	111	115	112	92	122	114	120	110	78	113	115	138
48823 EAST LANSING	90	70	68	74	68	72	105	78	95	89	96	68	85	94	82	92	67	90	80	97
48824 EAST LANSING	19	8	8	10	8	10	27	13	22	18	22	15	16	21	15	20	16	19	13	18
48825 EAST LANSING	59	32	28	37	29	32	58	40	57	54	58	37	44	58	42	54	40	52	42	53
48827 EATON RAPIDS	92	96	85	98	94	98	91	94	91	89	91	73	93	93	93	92	63	91	96	111
48829 EDMORE	78	59	75	58	60	80	61	74	67	57	66	56	51	68	59	74	44	69	79	88
48831 ELSIE	83	78	71	80	76	88	77	82	79	72	78	63	73	81	75	83	54	79	87	97
48832 ELWELL	84	77	70	76	76	81	73	78	76	75	76	57	69	79	70	78	52	75	79	93
48834 FENWICK	87	72	75	73	73	87	72	82	77	68	75	62	64	79	70	82	51	77	85	97
48835 FOWLER	95	90	87	93	91	102	87	97	89	80	88	73	82	91	88	93	60	90	99	112
48836 FOWLERVILLE	107	121	105	121	117	111	109	110	105	112	107	86	115	109	113	104	75	107	105	128
48837 GRAND LEDGE	105	117	107	118	114	112	108	108	106	110	107	83	114	107	112	106	75	107	108	127
48838 GREENVILLE	79	72	70	73	71	79	74	77	76	70	75	59	69	77	71	78	51	75	80	91
48840 HASLETT	97	93	86	96	90	89	99	91	98	99	99	73	98	99	95	97	69	96	93	109
48841 HENDERSON	92	81	82	84	82	97	80	91	84	74	82	69	73	86	79	89	56	85	94	107
48842 HOLT	98	103	91	103	99	98	99	97	98	100	98	75	101	100	98	97	69	97	96	114
48843 HOWELL	129	145	132	147	142	131	133	131	127	139	129	104	142	132	137	124	92	128	123	152
48845 HUBBARDSTON	92	70	79	69	70	90	72	83	78	69	77	64	60	81	67	85	52	78	87	100
48846 IONIA	85	75	74	76	75	87	77	82	80	73	79	63	71	81	74	84	54	80	87	98
48847 ITHACA	82	73	71	75	72	86	73	80	76	68	75	61	68	78	71	80	51	76	84	95
48848 LAINGSBURG	104	111	96	113	108	110	100	105	100	102	101	81	104	103	104	101	70	101	104	124
48849 LAKE ODESSA	92	86	81	87	84	96	83	89	86	80	85	69	79	88	82	90	58	86	93	107
48850 LAKEVIEW	80	70	74	71	70	84	70	79	73	64	72	60	63	74	69	78	49	74	83	93
48851 LYONS	85	82	78	85	82	92	79	87	80	73	79	66	76	82	80	84	54	81	89	101
48854 MASON	94	100	92	101	99	100	93	96	93	94	93	72	96	95	95	94	65	94	97	112
48855 HOWELL	126	149	131	151	144	137	130	133	125	133	126	105	142	129	138	122	90	127	125	154
48856 MIDDLETON	86	76	79	77	74	91	77	84	79	70	78	67	70	80	76	83	53	81	90	101
48857 MORRICE	90	90	79	90	88	90	83	87	84	85	84	65	83	87	83	86	58	84	87	103
48858 MOUNT PLEASANT	74	57	54	59	55	59	82	64	75	71	76	54	66	76	64	74	53	72	65	79
48860 MUIR	90	66	75	64	65	86	68	79	75	66	74	61	55	78	62	82	50	75	83	96
48861 MULLIKEN	93	97	90	99	96	104	89	97	91	86	91	74	91	93	93	94	63	92	100	113
48864 OKEMOS	132	137	133	142	136	129	141	130	134	140	135	105	143	136	138	131	97	133	126	154
48865 ORLEANS	84	78	69	75	76	80	73	78	76	76	76	57	69	79	70	78	52	75	78	92
48866 OVID	83	84	72	86	81	89	81	83	82	77	81	65	81	84	81	84	56	82	88	99
48867 OWOSSO	78	77	70	78	75	82	76	78	78	73	77	60	75	79	75	81	53	77	83	93
48871 PERRINTON	83	88	78	90	85	91	82	85	82	80	82	67	85	84	85	83	57	83	87	101
48872 PERRY	97	104	87	103	98	98	95	96	94	98	94	74	98	97	95	93	66	94	94	113
48873 PEWAMO	84	78	76	81	79	90	76	85	78	70	77	65	71	80	76	83	53	79	88	99
48875 PORTLAND	93	99	86	100	96	100	91	94	92	91	92	72	95	94	93	94	64	92	97	111
48876 POTTERVILLE	98	99	85	96	95	96	93	95	93	95	93	72	92	96	91	94	65	93	94	112
48877 RIVERDALE	82	68	67	66	67	77	67	73	71	68	71	55	60	74	63	75	48	70	75	88
48878 ROSEBUSH	83	76	68	74	75	79	72	77	75	74	75	56	68	78	69	77	51	74	77	91
48879 SAINT JOHNS	92	96	86	97	94	98	90	94	90	89	90	72	92	92	92	92	63	91	95	110
48880 SAINT LOUIS	76	68	66	68	66	79	69	74	73	65	71	57	64	74	67	76	49	72	80	88
48881 SARANAC	86	82	75	82	81	87	77	84	79	76	79	62	74	82	77	82	54	79	84	98
48883 SHEPHERD	87	82	71	80	79	85	78	82	81	79	80	61	75	84	75	83	55	80	84	97
48884 SHERIDAN	84	65	70	65	65	82	66	76	72	64	71	58	56	74	62	77	48	72	79	91
48885 SIDNEY	84	77	72	78	77	85	75	82	77	72	76	61	70	79	73	80	52	77	83	96
48886 SIX LAKES	79	61	72	61	62	81	63	75	69	58	67	57	53	70	61	75	45	70	79	89
48888 STANTON	80	67	68	68	67	81	69	76	73	64	71	58	60	74	65	77	48	72	80	91
48889 SUMNER	82	68	71	69	69	84	69	78	73	64	71	60	60	75	66	78	48	73	81	93
48890 SUNFIELD	87	95	84	98	93	96	86	91	86	85	86	71	90	88	90	87	60	87	91	107
48891 VESTABURG	85	65	70	63	65	80	66	75	72	65	71	57	55	75	61	77	48	71	78	90
48892 WEBBERVILLE	91	90	79	89	88	90	83	87	84	86	85	65	83	88	83	86	58	84	87	103
48893 WEIDMAN	87	71	93	71	74	91	71	86	75	66	74	64	62	74	72	80	49	79	87	100
48894 WESTPHALIA	90	111	99	111	107	109	95	99	96	96	97	74	108	97	105	98	68	97	104	115
48895 WILLIAMSTON	110	121	114	125	121	118	112	114	109	115	110	88	118	111	117	108	77	111	112	134
48897 WOODLAND	88	80	80	84	82	95	79	90	82	72	80	68	73	83	79	87	55	83	92	104
48906 LANSING	79	77	67	77	73	79	81	77	83	78	82	60	79	83	77	84	58	80	82	92
48910 LANSING	74	64	54	67	60	66	74	67	75	71	75	54	69	77	67	76	52	72	72	82
48911 LANSING	82	77	66	79	73	77	83	77	84	81	84	61	81	85	78	84	58	81	81	93
48912 LANSING	70	63	57	66	61	65	73	66	74	69	74	52	70	74	67	76	52	71	72	81
48915 LANSING	75	68	58	69	63	69	74	69	76	73	76	54	71	77	68	78	53	73	74	85
48917 LANSING	96	99	93	101	97	95	99	95	97	100	98	74	102	98	99	96	69	97	95	112
48933 LANSING	42	30	32	33	30	34	50	38	50	43	50	32	41	46	40	51	35	46	46	48
49001 KALAMAZOO	68	59	52	61	56	62	71	62	72	66	72	50	66	72	63	73	50	68	69	77
49002 PORTAGE	86	86	76	87	82	85	86	83	86	86	87	65	86	88	85	86	60	85	86	100
49004 KALAMAZOO	81	84	72	86	81	86	80	81	81	79	81	63	82	83	81	83	56	81	85	97
49006 KALAMAZOO	68	51	49	54	49	54	80	59	74	67	74	51	64	73	61	73	52	69	63	74
49007 KALAMAZOO	55	38	34	41	35	41	61	45	59	52	59	39	48	59	46	60	41	54	50	58
49008 KALAMAZOO	90	83	81	86	82	85	100	86	96	92	97	69	93	95	90	96	68	94	92	104
49009 KALAMAZOO	97	98	94	101	97	96	103	96	99	101	100	77	102	100	100	98	71	99	97	114
49010 ALLEGAN	89	78	73	78	76	87	79	83	82	77	81	63	72	85	74	86	56	81	87	99
49011 ATHENS	85	81	74	84	79	91	80	85	82	74	81	66	77	84	79	86	56	82	90	101
49012 AUGUSTA	103	113	97	116	109	114	104	106	104	103	104	83	109	106	107	105	72	104	110	126
49013 BANGOR	78	64	63	64	63	77	67	72	71	63	69	55	58	73	62	75	47	70	77	87
49014 BATTLE CREEK	82	77	73	78	75	82	80	80	82	76	81	62	77	82	77	84	56	81	84	95
49015 BATTLE CREEK	89	87	80	89	85	91	90	88	91	87	91	68	89	92	88	93	63	90	94	105
49017 BATTLE CREEK	81	80	72	81	78	84	82	80	83	78	83	62	81	84	80	86	58	82	86	96
49021 BELLEVUE	86	85	82	87	85	95	81	89	83	75	82	67	79	84	83	87	56	83	92	104
49022 BENTON HARBOR	64	54	50	55	51	61	60	58	65	58	64	45	56	64	55	68	44	61	66	72
MICHIGAN	98	97	93	98	95	100	96	97	97	95	97	74	96	98	96	99	68	97	100	115
UNITED STATES	100	100	100	100	100	100	100	100	100	100	100	100	100	100	100	100	100	100	100	100

POPULATION CHANGE

ZIP CODE #	POST OFFICE NAME	COUNTY FIPS CODE	POPULATION 2000	POPULATION 2009	POPULATION 2014	2000-2009 ANNUAL RATE % Rate	2000-2009 ANNUAL RATE State Centile	HOUSEHOLDS 2000	HOUSEHOLDS 2009	HOUSEHOLDS 2014	HOUSEHOLDS % Annual Rate 2000-2009	HOUSEHOLDS 2009 Average HH Size	FAMILIES 2000	FAMILIES 2009	FAMILIES % Annual Rate 2000-2009
49024	PORTAGE	077	27599	28312	28637	0.3	54	10784	11374	11612	0.6	2.47	7553	7829	0.4
49026	BLOOMINGDALE	159	2264	2283	2264	0.1	42	801	815	811	0.2	2.70	601	606	0.1
49028	BRONSON	023	6852	6803	6683	-0.1	32	2442	2442	2407	0.0	2.73	1765	1748	-0.1
49029	BURLINGTON	025	1629	1692	1683	0.4	60	599	632	632	0.6	2.68	465	485	0.5
49030	BURR OAK	149	2766	2828	2821	0.2	48	985	1022	1024	0.4	2.76	726	746	0.3
49031	CASSOPOLIS	027	7554	7682	7585	0.2	48	2956	3034	3020	0.3	2.46	2083	2113	0.2
49032	CENTREVILLE	149	3364	3444	3442	0.3	54	1020	1065	1068	0.5	2.99	757	783	0.4
49033	CERESCO	025	1735	1767	1754	0.2	48	660	684	682	0.4	2.58	531	544	0.3
49034	CLIMAX	077	2467	2657	2744	0.8	80	906	1001	1040	1.1	2.65	710	774	0.9
49036	COLDWATER	023	24518	25653	25404	0.5	66	8724	8949	8879	0.3	2.44	5959	6052	0.2
49037	BATTLE CREEK	025	22338	22405	22102	0.0	37	8965	9062	8970	0.1	2.36	5472	5406	-0.1
49038	COLOMA	021	9891	9600	9439	-0.3	21	3980	3926	3882	-0.1	2.43	2772	2696	-0.3
49040	COLON	149	3256	3221	3187	-0.1	32	1298	1308	1301	0.1	2.46	924	922	0.0
49042	CONSTANTINE	149	5088	4940	4862	-0.3	21	1892	1876	1858	-0.1	2.63	1405	1380	-0.2
49043	COVERT	159	2765	2860	2868	0.4	60	968	1007	1013	0.4	2.81	668	686	0.3
49045	DECATUR	159	6548	6720	6707	0.3	54	2282	2376	2382	0.4	2.67	1637	1682	0.3
49046	DELTON	015	7630	7964	8051	0.5	66	2799	2979	3033	0.7	2.66	2118	2233	0.6
49047	DOWAGIAC	027	15167	14774	14519	-0.3	21	5741	5780	5720	0.1	2.47	4033	4018	0.0
49048	KALAMAZOO	077	24728	25101	25348	0.2	48	9431	9854	10036	0.5	2.51	6317	6468	0.3
49050	DOWLING	015	1428	1510	1530	0.6	71	561	607	619	0.9	2.48	434	466	0.8
49051	EAST LEROY	025	1920	2136	2166	1.2	88	692	780	793	1.3	2.72	538	601	1.2
49052	FULTON	077	819	872	892	0.7	76	293	319	329	0.9	2.73	237	256	0.8
49053	GALESBURG	077	5904	6363	6576	0.8	80	2199	2421	2517	1.0	2.58	1620	1759	0.9
49055	GOBLES	159	6304	6622	6687	0.5	66	2321	2494	2535	0.8	2.63	1719	1825	0.6
49056	GRAND JUNCTION	159	4302	4547	4602	0.6	71	1529	1634	1659	0.7	2.72	1137	1203	0.6
49057	HARTFORD	159	6643	6825	6870	0.3	54	2303	2411	2439	0.5	2.74	1684	1744	0.4
49058	HASTINGS	015	18262	19097	19340	0.5	66	6846	7289	7420	0.7	2.57	5035	5308	0.6
49060	HICKORY CORNERS	015	1741	1768	1763	0.2	48	680	703	706	0.4	2.49	518	531	0.3
49061	JONES	027	1727	1755	1739	0.2	48	646	674	674	0.5	2.60	472	487	0.3
49064	LAWRENCE	159	3888	4003	3981	0.3	54	1362	1419	1415	0.4	2.76	1021	1052	0.3
49065	LAWTON	159	5853	6297	6435	0.8	80	2043	2255	2322	1.1	2.68	1568	1713	1.0
49066	LEONIDAS	149	780	796	795	0.2	48	249	258	258	0.4	3.08	202	207	0.3
49067	MARCELLUS	027	4660	4635	4573	-0.1	32	1730	1763	1752	0.2	2.62	1294	1304	0.1
49068	MARSHALL	025	15058	14830	14561	-0.2	25	5945	5905	5819	-0.1	2.47	4147	4076	-0.2
49070	MARTIN	005	2229	2445	2539	1.0	84	777	879	922	1.3	2.76	598	670	1.2
49071	MATTAWAN	159	8717	10055	10502	1.6	94	3104	3667	3852	1.8	2.74	2481	2904	1.7
49072	MENDON	149	3289	3603	3654	1.0	84	1207	1344	1371	1.2	2.67	913	1008	1.1
49073	NASHVILLE	015	5207	5588	5741	0.8	80	1923	2117	2191	1.0	2.63	1454	1585	0.9
49076	OLIVET	045	4384	4633	4708	0.6	71	1400	1511	1548	0.8	2.68	1033	1099	0.7
49078	OTSEGO	005	8699	8904	8951	0.3	54	3227	3386	3430	0.5	2.61	2392	2481	0.4
49079	PAW PAW	159	12538	13007	13169	0.4	60	4781	5042	5127	0.6	2.54	3458	3611	0.5
49080	PLAINWELL	005	15054	15707	15927	0.5	66	5632	6046	6185	0.8	2.56	4235	4495	0.6
49082	QUINCY	023	6876	6894	6786	0.0	37	2433	2461	2432	0.1	2.76	1809	1813	0.0
49083	RICHLAND	077	6676	7373	7668	1.1	86	2544	2849	2979	1.2	2.59	1973	2180	1.1
49085	SAINT JOSEPH	021	23364	23983	23950	0.3	54	9654	9983	10004	0.4	2.32	6315	6498	0.3
49087	SCHOOLCRAFT	077	5500	6047	6279	1.0	84	1949	2191	2291	1.3	2.75	1516	1685	1.1
49088	SCOTTS	077	3146	3698	3885	1.8	96	1151	1383	1463	2.0	2.66	925	1098	1.9
49089	SHERWOOD	023	2011	1964	1921	-0.3	21	758	755	743	0.0	2.60	574	567	-0.1
49090	SOUTH HAVEN	159	15011	15591	15735	0.4	60	5905	6280	6388	0.7	2.42	3996	4193	0.5
49091	STURGIS	149	20656	20519	20314	-0.1	32	7704	7712	7659	0.0	2.61	5346	5295	-0.1
49092	TEKONSHA	025	2279	2307	2283	0.1	42	867	891	887	0.3	2.59	633	645	0.2
49093	THREE RIVERS	149	17778	17997	17936	0.1	42	6970	7196	7210	0.3	2.46	4832	4923	0.2
49094	UNION CITY	023	4204	4115	4034	-0.2	25	1614	1608	1584	0.0	2.55	1170	1155	-0.1
49095	VANDALIA	027	2298	2356	2339	0.3	54	905	945	944	0.5	2.49	664	686	0.4
49096	VERMONTVILLE	045	3117	3273	3290	0.5	66	1109	1197	1215	0.8	2.73	879	938	0.7
49097	VICKSBURG	077	9820	10321	10578	0.5	66	3653	3909	4028	0.7	2.64	2834	2997	0.6
49098	WATERVLIET	021	6307	6207	6140	-0.2	25	2421	2415	2398	0.0	2.51	1686	1661	-0.2
49099	WHITE PIGEON	149	5780	6030	6056	0.5	66	2209	2357	2380	0.7	2.55	1605	1694	0.6
49101	BARODA	021	3139	3114	3089	-0.1	32	1199	1205	1200	0.1	2.55	875	868	-0.1
49102	BERRIEN CENTER	021	1805	2003	2039	1.1	86	543	615	630	1.4	2.92	420	472	1.3
49103	BERRIEN SPRINGS	021	12292	12267	12168	0.0	37	4152	4201	4185	0.1	2.61	3012	3016	0.0
49106	BRIDGMAN	021	4852	4921	4902	0.2	48	1899	1957	1961	0.3	2.41	1351	1374	0.2
49107	BUCHANAN	021	10705	10659	10573	0.0	37	4186	4227	4214	0.1	2.50	2942	2938	0.0
49111	EAU CLAIRE	021	3787	4029	4061	0.7	76	1345	1460	1480	0.9	2.56	1022	1098	0.8
49112	EDWARDSBURG	027	9194	9740	9751	0.6	71	3649	3975	4014	0.9	2.45	2644	2846	0.8
49113	GALIEN	021	2166	2211	2210	0.2	48	826	858	862	0.4	2.56	602	618	0.3
49116	LAKESIDE	021	214	222	223	0.4	60	114	120	122	0.6	1.85	69	72	0.5
49117	NEW BUFFALO	021	4228	4350	4350	0.3	54	1855	1944	1957	0.5	2.22	1194	1231	0.3
49120	NILES	021	35562	35783	35515	0.1	42	14168	14464	14428	0.2	2.45	9753	9870	0.1
49125	SAWYER	021	2594	2477	2421	-0.5	12	1088	1054	1036	-0.3	2.34	759	727	-0.5
49126	SODUS	021	1443	1426	1413	-0.1	32	588	593	591	0.1	2.24	385	382	-0.1
49127	STEVENSVILLE	021	10204	10381	10354	0.2	48	4031	4156	4163	0.3	2.47	2888	2944	0.2
49128	THREE OAKS	021	4530	4360	4278	-0.4	16	1863	1824	1801	-0.2	2.39	1286	1241	-0.4
49129	UNION PIER	021	808	845	849	0.5	66	375	399	404	0.7	2.10	243	254	0.5
49130	UNION	027	1785	1868	1862	0.5	66	725	781	786	0.8	2.39	541	577	0.7
49201	JACKSON	075	46822	49876	50507	0.7	76	15146	16177	16487	0.7	2.55	10766	11418	0.6
49202	JACKSON	075	20180	20638	20703	0.2	48	8487	8734	8785	0.3	2.26	5098	5162	0.1
49203	JACKSON	075	38467	38574	38428	0.0	37	15175	15487	15526	0.2	2.47	10172	10210	0.0
49220	ADDISON	091	2414	2447	2459	0.1	42	928	966	981	0.4	2.53	679	695	0.3
49221	ADRIAN	091	40426	42189	42860	0.5	66	13971	14913	15274	0.7	2.53	9623	10185	0.6
49224	ALBION	025	14361	13968	13653	-0.3	21	5166	5000	4889	-0.4	2.48	3508	3366	-0.4
49227	ALLEN	059	1378	1431	1437	0.4	60	498	526	531	0.6	2.71	369	384	0.4
49228	BLISSFIELD	091	5533	5531	5506	0.0	37	2126	2176	2183	0.3	2.46	1545	1560	0.1
49229	BRITTON	091	3233	3587	3749	1.1	86	1127	1280	1348	1.4	2.80	911	1023	1.3
49230	BROOKLYN	075	9633	10148	10324	0.6	71	3844	4134	4230	0.8	2.44	2813	2981	0.6
49232	CAMDEN	059	2746	2858	2838	0.4	60	939	993	991	0.6	2.86	716	749	0.5
49233	CEMENT CITY	059	2842	3238	3375	1.4	92	1083	1263	1324	1.7	2.56	861	992	1.5
49234	CLARKLAKE	075	2684	2875	2951	0.7	76	1034	1130	1165	1.0	2.52	785	847	0.8
49235	CLAYTON	091	2137	2268	2316	0.6	71	780	847	873	0.9	2.67	603	646	0.7
49236	CLINTON	091	4872	5060	5153	0.4	60	1847	1962	2012	0.7	2.58	1389	1452	0.5
49237	CONCORD	075	3073	3279	3359	0.7	76	1121	1221	1257	0.9	2.67	857	921	0.8
49238	DEERFIELD	091	1653	1806	1871	1.0	84	559	621	648	1.1	2.87	436	479	1.0
49240	GRASS LAKE	075	7175	8015	8323	1.2	88	2521	2869	2998	1.4	2.73	1994	2237	1.3
49241	HANOVER	075	2420	2610	2678	0.8	80	888	979	1011	1.1	2.65	699	763	1.0
49242	HILLSDALE	059	15373	15236	14957	-0.1	32	5785	5841	5765	0.1	2.44	3853	3841	0.0
	MICHIGAN					0.3					0.4	2.52			0.3
	UNITED STATES					1.0					1.1	2.59			0.9

ZIP CODE #	POST OFFICE NAME	RACE (%) White 2000	White 2009	Black 2000	Black 2009	Asian/Pacific 2000	Asian/Pacific 2009	% Hispanic Origin 2000	% Hispanic Origin 2009	2009 AGE DISTRIBUTION (%) 0-4	5-9	10-14	15-19	20-24	25-44	45-64	65-84	85+	18+	MEDIAN AGE 2009	% 2009 Males	% 2009 Females
49024	PORTAGE	89.8	86.1	4.1	5.1	3.4	5.3	1.8	2.5	7.1	6.9	7.2	7.3	6.7	25.9	27.2	10.1	1.6	74.1	36.6	47.7	52.3
49026	BLOOMINGDALE	92.9	91.4	2.4	2.8	0.3	0.4	4.7	6.4	6.5	6.8	7.2	7.2	5.4	23.7	29.4	11.9	1.9	74.9	39.5	49.9	50.1
49028	BRONSON	93.8	92.2	0.3	0.3	0.1	0.2	6.5	8.5	7.0	7.0	6.9	7.0	6.2	27.2	26.2	10.7	1.7	74.9	36.7	51.1	48.9
49029	BURLINGTON	97.9	97.3	0.1	0.2	0.3	0.5	0.9	1.2	5.1	5.5	6.1	7.0	5.3	26.0	31.9	11.8	1.3	79.0	41.7	50.4	49.6
49030	BURR OAK	97.7	97.2	0.5	0.5	0.2	0.3	1.6	2.2	6.8	6.9	7.1	7.2	5.8	26.9	27.1	10.9	1.4	74.7	37.5	50.7	49.3
49031	CASSOPOLIS	78.5	75.2	15.1	16.9	1.2	1.8	1.7	2.1	6.3	6.4	6.7	6.9	5.3	23.9	29.8	12.8	1.9	76.9	41.0	50.1	49.9
49032	CENTREVILLE	95.5	94.8	2.2	2.4	0.2	0.3	1.2	1.7	7.3	7.3	7.1	7.1	7.0	26.2	25.7	10.6	1.8	74.0	36.1	50.5	49.5
49033	CERESCO	97.1	96.2	0.6	0.7	0.3	0.5	1.4	1.9	5.0	6.5	7.4	6.5	3.1	22.1	35.6	12.6	1.3	76.7	44.6	50.0	50.0
49034	CLIMAX	97.3	96.4	0.4	0.5	0.4	0.7	1.7	2.3	6.1	6.4	7.0	7.0	4.9	23.7	31.1	12.4	1.4	76.0	41.6	49.2	50.8
49036	COLDWATER	90.9	88.4	4.6	6.0	0.7	1.0	3.2	4.2	5.5	5.3	5.4	6.0	6.2	30.2	27.4	11.9	2.2	80.5	39.5	51.4	48.6
49037	BATTLE CREEK	64.8	61.4	28.8	31.0	0.6	1.0	3.2	4.0	7.1	7.0	6.7	7.0	6.7	26.1	25.1	11.9	2.5	74.9	36.7	48.4	51.6
49038	COLOMA	94.5	93.0	2.4	3.1	0.5	0.8	2.7	3.6	6.4	6.3	6.4	6.5	5.9	24.5	28.9	13.2	1.7	76.8	40.4	49.2	50.8
49040	COLON	97.6	97.1	0.4	0.4	0.2	0.3	0.7	1.0	7.1	6.9	7.0	6.8	5.5	24.6	27.6	12.4	2.0	74.7	38.7	49.6	50.4
49042	CONSTANTINE	95.3	94.3	1.2	1.4	0.6	1.0	1.7	2.3	6.9	6.8	7.2	7.1	5.5	26.7	27.7	10.8	1.3	74.6	37.5	50.1	49.9
49043	COVERT	53.5	49.5	32.6	34.3	0.1	0.1	15.4	18.9	8.2	8.2	7.9	7.7	6.1	22.5	26.7	11.2	1.5	70.6	36.1	50.2	49.8
49045	DECATUR	89.3	87.1	3.4	3.9	0.2	0.3	11.3	14.6	7.0	7.2	7.3	7.8	6.8	25.3	25.6	11.4	1.6	73.8	36.0	51.1	48.9
49046	DELTON	97.4	96.9	0.3	0.3	0.2	0.3	1.4	1.8	5.8	6.5	6.8	6.7	4.5	24.5	31.8	12.0	1.3	76.7	41.6	50.1	49.9
49047	DOWAGIAC	85.0	82.7	7.9	8.7	0.4	0.6	5.3	7.0	7.1	6.9	6.8	6.8	6.3	24.4	27.0	12.7	2.0	74.9	38.3	49.4	50.6
49048	KALAMAZOO	79.2	76.5	15.1	16.4	1.0	1.6	3.0	3.8	7.4	7.2	6.9	7.1	7.0	27.8	25.5	9.6	1.6	74.0	35.1	48.4	51.6
49050	DOWLING	98.0	97.7	0.2	0.2	0.1	0.1	1.1	1.5	5.4	6.1	6.6	5.9	4.2	23.8	33.1	13.5	1.3	78.1	43.4	50.7	49.3
49051	EAST LEROY	96.9	96.2	0.6	0.7	0.4	0.5	1.4	1.9	5.6	6.0	6.6	6.4	4.6	23.3	32.5	13.9	1.2	77.3	43.3	49.2	50.8
49052	FULTON	97.6	96.6	0.4	0.5	0.1	0.3	1.1	1.5	6.1	6.7	7.6	7.8	4.4	25.6	29.2	11.5	1.3	74.2	39.9	51.1	48.9
49053	GALESBURG	96.0	94.8	1.1	1.3	0.5	0.8	1.1	1.5	6.6	7.2	7.4	7.1	5.1	24.9	29.5	10.5	1.7	74.2	39.1	49.7	50.3
49055	GOBLES	95.1	94.1	1.0	1.2	0.3	0.4	2.7	3.6	6.6	6.7	7.1	6.9	6.2	23.9	30.4	11.0	1.3	75.3	39.6	50.6	49.4
49056	GRAND JUNCTION	85.5	82.5	4.7	5.3	0.2	0.3	9.7	12.7	7.6	7.7	7.7	7.7	6.2	25.4	26.1	10.6	1.0	71.9	35.5	50.3	49.7
49057	HARTFORD	86.8	83.9	1.0	1.1	0.2	0.3	15.3	19.8	7.6	7.3	7.4	7.4	6.9	26.1	26.0	10.1	1.2	73.1	35.3	50.8	49.2
49058	HASTINGS	97.6	97.1	0.2	0.2	0.3	0.4	1.6	2.2	6.9	6.9	7.1	6.9	5.3	25.3	27.7	11.5	2.3	74.7	38.7	49.3	50.7
49060	HICKORY CORNERS	97.6	96.9	0.1	0.1	0.8	1.3	1.5	2.0	5.2	5.8	6.4	6.6	4.7	22.6	33.0	14.0	1.6	78.4	44.0	49.6	50.4
49061	JONES	95.0	93.7	1.8	2.1	0.6	1.0	1.7	2.3	4.8	6.6	6.8	7.2	4.6	24.7	30.8	13.2	1.3	77.2	41.9	51.7	48.3
49064	LAWRENCE	85.0	81.6	2.8	3.2	0.3	0.4	13.6	17.7	6.8	6.8	7.2	7.4	6.1	24.7	28.4	10.9	1.5	74.4	38.1	49.6	50.4
49065	LAWTON	93.4	91.6	1.0	1.2	0.3	0.5	6.8	9.2	6.4	6.8	7.0	7.3	5.6	24.2	29.4	10.7	2.7	75.2	39.9	49.0	51.0
49066	LEONIDAS	97.7	97.2	0.6	0.8	0.0	0.0	0.5	0.8	8.3	8.0	8.3	7.7	5.7	24.0	24.7	11.7	1.6	70.5	35.5	49.5	50.5
49067	MARCELLUS	96.3	95.5	0.9	1.0	0.3	0.4	1.7	2.3	6.6	6.7	6.8	6.7	5.4	25.6	29.1	11.8	1.3	75.7	39.3	50.4	49.6
49068	MARSHALL	96.5	95.5	0.3	0.3	0.5	0.7	2.6	3.5	6.1	6.3	6.9	6.7	5.2	24.1	28.9	12.9	3.0	76.5	41.2	48.2	51.8
49070	MARTIN	97.1	96.3	0.2	0.2	0.4	0.7	2.2	3.0	7.4	7.6	7.5	7.4	5.4	26.6	26.6	10.3	1.3	72.7	36.7	50.4	49.6
49071	MATTAWAN	94.8	93.6	1.4	1.7	0.5	0.8	2.6	3.6	6.7	7.2	7.6	7.2	5.4	25.6	31.5	7.9	0.9	73.8	38.4	49.5	50.5
49072	MENDON	96.9	96.3	0.8	0.9	0.2	0.2	1.6	2.2	7.0	7.4	7.7	7.4	4.7	23.9	27.8	12.9	1.3	73.2	39.2	49.9	50.1
49073	NASHVILLE	97.5	96.9	0.3	0.3	0.4	0.6	0.7	1.0	6.3	6.9	7.5	7.6	5.2	25.8	28.5	10.7	1.3	74.2	37.9	50.0	50.0
49076	OLIVET	92.5	90.5	4.0	4.9	0.8	1.3	1.7	2.2	7.0	6.9	6.3	10.8	13.2	26.3	21.8	6.8	0.9	75.6	28.7	51.1	48.9
49078	OTSEGO	97.2	96.4	0.4	0.4	0.5	0.8	1.5	2.0	6.4	7.0	7.3	7.0	5.8	26.0	28.4	10.7	1.5	74.9	38.3	50.0	50.0
49079	PAW PAW	94.4	93.1	1.9	2.2	0.3	0.5	3.0	4.0	6.1	6.5	6.6	7.0	5.7	25.5	29.8	11.0	1.6	76.4	39.8	50.0	50.0
49080	PLAINWELL	97.1	96.3	0.4	0.5	0.4	0.6	1.5	2.0	6.3	6.6	7.0	6.8	5.3	25.0	30.3	11.0	1.6	75.5	40.2	49.7	50.3
49082	QUINCY	98.0	97.6	0.2	0.3	0.2	0.3	1.0	1.4	7.6	7.7	7.6	7.3	5.9	25.0	27.2	10.4	1.3	72.4	36.4	50.5	49.5
49083	RICHLAND	95.7	94.3	1.7	2.2	0.8	1.3	1.3	1.9	5.5	6.2	7.1	7.1	5.3	21.3	34.2	12.0	1.3	76.7	43.1	49.1	50.9
49085	SAINT JOSEPH	93.2	90.3	2.8	3.8	2.2	3.7	1.6	2.1	5.2	5.4	6.0	6.8	6.5	22.4	30.5	14.2	3.1	79.1	43.4	49.4	50.6
49087	SCHOOLCRAFT	96.9	95.9	0.5	0.5	0.7	1.1	1.0	1.4	6.0	6.4	7.2	8.0	5.6	23.9	31.6	10.1	1.1	74.7	40.3	50.2	49.8
49088	SCOTTS	97.9	97.3	0.4	0.5	0.4	0.6	1.0	1.4	5.5	6.2	6.9	6.9	4.4	22.7	34.2	12.0	1.1	76.6	43.2	50.1	49.9
49089	SHERWOOD	97.1	96.6	0.2	0.3	0.2	0.3	0.8	1.2	6.2	6.4	6.9	7.1	6.0	26.4	28.1	11.8	1.3	76.2	38.8	51.3	48.7
49090	SOUTH HAVEN	83.6	81.0	10.4	11.5	0.5	0.7	5.8	7.7	6.0	6.1	6.3	6.9	5.8	23.7	29.4	13.4	2.4	77.2	41.2	48.8	51.2
49091	STURGIS	93.7	92.1	0.9	1.0	0.8	1.1	8.6	11.2	8.0	7.5	6.9	6.7	6.1	26.1	25.0	11.1	2.5	73.5	35.9	49.0	51.0
49092	TEKONSHA	97.3	96.7	0.3	0.3	0.1	0.2	0.7	1.0	6.0	6.2	6.7	6.6	4.5	25.7	29.5	13.5	1.3	77.0	41.1	50.7	49.3
49093	THREE RIVERS	89.3	87.5	6.8	7.6	0.6	0.9	2.1	2.9	7.1	6.8	6.9	6.8	5.9	25.9	27.0	11.7	2.1	75.1	38.3	49.4	50.6
49094	UNION CITY	97.1	96.6	0.4	0.3	0.3	0.4	0.9	1.2	6.8	6.4	6.5	6.9	6.1	26.3	26.7	13.1	1.4	76.2	38.5	50.4	49.6
49095	VANDALIA	80.2	77.1	14.1	15.7	1.8	2.8	1.8	2.3	5.8	6.1	6.2	6.8	5.8	24.2	30.1	13.4	1.8	77.8	41.6	52.0	48.0
49096	VERMONTVILLE	97.5	96.7	0.2	0.3	0.3	0.5	1.1	1.5	6.1	6.4	6.8	6.9	5.6	24.5	31.2	11.2	1.2	75.9	40.5	50.6	49.4
49097	VICKSBURG	97.3	96.4	0.4	0.5	0.5	0.8	1.1	1.5	5.7	6.0	6.7	7.4	5.4	23.7	32.0	11.9	1.3	76.9	41.6	49.2	50.8
49098	WATERVLIET	94.7	93.0	1.1	1.5	0.3	0.6	4.9	6.7	7.1	6.9	6.9	6.8	5.8	25.9	28.0	11.1	1.7	74.9	38.1	49.3	50.7
49099	WHITE PIGEON	96.6	95.8	0.2	0.3	0.5	0.7	1.5	2.1	5.3	5.7	6.2	6.5	4.9	25.5	31.9	12.7	1.3	78.6	42.1	49.1	50.9
49101	BARODA	96.3	94.9	0.4	0.5	0.5	0.8	2.5	3.6	6.1	6.6	7.0	7.2	4.9	25.2	29.8	11.5	1.6	75.6	40.2	50.1	49.9
49102	BERRIEN CENTER	87.5	83.2	6.5	9.1	1.0	1.5	7.7	10.0	6.1	6.1	7.2	7.8	5.3	25.4	26.9	11.8	3.2	75.0	39.1	51.1	48.9
49103	BERRIEN SPRINGS	71.0	64.6	14.8	17.7	6.4	8.9	7.9	9.4	5.6	5.3	5.3	8.7	11.6	25.5	24.8	11.0	2.1	79.6	34.4	48.6	51.4
49106	BRIDGMAN	97.2	95.8	0.7	1.1	0.4	0.6	1.3	1.9	5.1	5.5	6.2	6.1	4.7	21.6	33.5	13.5	3.8	79.2	45.4	49.4	50.6
49107	BUCHANAN	91.6	89.1	5.1	6.7	0.4	0.7	1.7	2.2	6.2	6.3	6.4	6.6	5.8	26.1	28.6	12.1	2.0	77.1	39.8	49.9	50.1
49111	EAU CLAIRE	89.7	86.3	5.1	7.1	0.3	0.4	10.3	13.4	6.0	6.1	6.4	7.5	5.7	24.1	28.9	13.3	2.0	76.7	40.7	51.0	49.0
49112	EDWARDSBURG	96.3	95.3	0.8	1.0	0.4	0.6	1.2	1.6	5.6	6.0	7.0	6.9	4.6	24.5	31.4	12.6	1.4	77.0	41.9	50.4	49.6
49113	GALIEN	96.1	94.7	0.4	0.6	0.4	0.7	1.5	2.0	5.2	5.4	5.7	6.2	5.9	25.6	31.2	13.4	1.4	80.0	42.2	50.5	49.5
49116	LAKESIDE	91.6	88.7	6.5	9.0	0.5	0.5	0.5	0.5	3.2	3.6	4.5	4.5	3.2	15.3	40.1	22.5	3.2	86.0	53.9	50.9	49.1
49117	NEW BUFFALO	95.9	94.4	1.4	2.1	0.5	0.8	2.1	2.8	4.4	4.8	5.2	4.9	3.5	19.9	35.0	20.0	2.3	82.6	49.7	50.2	49.8
49120	NILES	89.7	86.8	6.3	8.1	0.5	0.8	2.5	3.2	6.2	6.2	6.4	6.6	5.8	25.1	28.5	12.9	2.3	77.1	40.3	48.7	51.3
49125	SAWYER	96.3	95.0	0.7	1.0	0.3	0.5	2.0	2.8	4.7	5.4	6.1	6.1	4.0	21.4	33.8	16.0	2.5	80.0	46.4	49.5	50.5
49126	SODUS	88.2	84.2	7.2	10.1	0.3	0.6	10.3	12.8	5.8	6.0	6.7	7.7	5.0	22.6	28.7	15.0	2.5	76.6	42.3	52.0	48.0
49127	STEVENSVILLE	95.7	93.8	1.1	1.6	1.2	2.0	1.3	1.7	5.7	5.6	6.0	6.7	6.2	23.6	30.8	13.1	2.2	78.3	42.2	48.7	51.3
49128	THREE OAKS	96.4	95.1	1.2	1.9	0.2	0.3	1.5	2.1	5.7	6.1	6.3	5.9	5.0	23.8	31.3	13.9	2.0	78.1	42.9	49.1	50.9
49129	UNION PIER	90.2	86.3	7.3	10.4	0.2	0.5	1.9	2.5	3.9	4.6	5.2	5.3	3.2	16.6	37.3	20.9	3.0	82.8	51.2	50.8	49.2
49130	UNION	97.2	96.5	0.5	0.6	0.3	0.5	1.1	1.4	4.8	6.2	6.6	6.7	4.2	24.4	33.2	12.6	1.3	78.0	43.2	50.5	49.5
49201	JACKSON	86.7	84.1	10.0	11.7	0.6	1.0	2.1	2.8	5.4	5.5	5.8	6.1	6.3	30.2	28.1	10.7	1.8	79.4	39.4	56.7	43.3
49202	JACKSON	88.3	85.7	6.8	8.1	0.7	1.0	3.2	4.3	8.2	7.1	6.4	6.2	6.9	28.1	22.8	11.2	3.1	74.6	35.5	47.9	52.1
49203	JACKSON	78.9	76.8	15.9	17.0	0.8	1.3	3.0	3.7	7.7	7.5	7.2	7.1	6.2	25.4	25.2	11.5	2.2	73.3	36.6	47.9	52.1
49220	ADDISON	97.9	97.1	0.1	0.2	0.4	0.6	1.4	2.0	6.3	6.8	7.0	6.7	4.7	23.7	30.5	13.0	1.3	75.7	41.3	50.4	49.6
49221	ADRIAN	86.4	83.7	4.8	5.3	0.7	1.0	12.1	15.3	6.5	6.3	6.3	7.6	7.3	27.6	25.2	11.1	2.3	77.1	36.6	50.6	49.4
49224	ALBION	71.9	69.1	23.1	25.0	0.5	0.8	3.7	4.7	6.4	6.3	6.3	11.3	10.6	22.0	23.6	11.5	2.0	75.8	33.1	47.8	52.2
49227	ALLEN	97.7	97.1	0.3	0.3	0.1	0.2	0.8	1.2	6.4	6.9	7.3	6.8	5.0	24.6	30.3	11.0	1.5	75.2	39.5	52.0	48.0
49228	BLISSFIELD	95.6	94.1	0.2	0.2	0.1	0.1	7.0	9.7	5.7	6.0	6.5	7.4	6.1	26.1	28.5	11.6	2.1	77.0	39.6	49.6	50.4
49229	BRITTON	97.2	96.3	0.3	0.4	0.2	0.4	2.8	4.0	6.1	6.4	7.2	7.9	5.0	25.8	29.8	10.5	1.3	75.2	39.9	49.5	50.5
49230	BROOKLYN	97.6	96.9	0.2	0.3	0.3	0.5	1.2	1.7	4.7	5.3	5.9	6.7	4.7	22.6	33.1	15.0	2.0	79.8	45.0	50.0	50.0
49232	CAMDEN	98.1	97.6	0.0	0.1	0.1	0.2	0.7	0.9	8.2	8.3	8.3	7.3	5.4	24.3	26.6	10.5	1.2	70.6	35.3	50.2	49.8
49233	CEMENT CITY	98.2	97.5	0.3	0.4	0.3	0.4	1.1	1.6	5.4	5.9	6.6	6.5	4.5	23.3	33.0	13.4	1.4	77.9	43.5	50.8	49.2
49234	CLARKLAKE	98.0	97.5	0.2	0.2	0.2	0.3	1.2	1.6	4.6	5.6	6.5	7.4	4.2	22.7	34.2	13.1	1.7	78.4	44.4	50.8	49.2
49235	CLAYTON	97.3	96.5	0.3	0.4	0.1	0.2	3.4	4.8	5.6	6.0	6.8	7.4	5.1	24.6	31.2	12.3	1.0	76.9	41.2	51.2	48.8
49236	CLINTON	98.2	97.6	0.2	0.3	0.2	0.3	1.5	2.2	5.9	6.6	6.9	6.7	4.7	25.0	30.8	12.0	1.4	76.4	41.2	49.1	50.9
49237	CONCORD	98.0	97.4	0.2	0.2	0.4	0.5	0.9	1.3	6.9	7.3	7.7	7.0	5.0	24.4	29.9	10.5	1.3	73.6	39.2	49.5	50.5
49238	DEERFIELD	96.5	95.5	0.4	0.6	0.2	0.3	3.9	5.3	7.6	8.0	8.0	6.7	5.0	26.0	26.9	10.4	1.4	72.4	37.2	49.3	50.7
49240	GRASS LAKE	97.1	96.5	1.6	1.8	0.1	0.2	1.0	1.3	6.2	6.8	7.4	6.8	4.5	25.8	31.1	10.2	1.3	75.2	40.6	51.0	49.0
49241	HANOVER	98.2	97.6	0.2	0.3	0.0	0.0	1.0	1.3	6.5	7.1	7.7	7.4	4.8	26.7	27.8	10.8	1.3	73.5	38.6	50.2	49.8
49242	HILLSDALE	97.1	96.3	0.6	0.6	0.6	0.9	1.3	1.8	6.4	6.2	6.4	8.6	8.7	24.7	25.6	11.4	2.1	76.9	36.0	49.1	50.9
	MICHIGAN	80.2	78.3	14.2	14.5	1.8	2.8	3.3	4.1	6.7	6.7	6.8	7.2	6.6	26.3	26.9	10.9	1.9	75.6	37.6	49.2	50.8
	UNITED STATES	75.1	72.0	12.3	12.7	3.8	4.6	12.5	15.7	6.8	6.7	6.6	7.1	6.9	27.0	26.0	10.9	1.9	75.7	36.9	49.2	50.8

ZIP CODE #	POST OFFICE NAME	2009 Per Capita Income	2009 HH Income Base	2009 HOUSEHOLD INCOME DISTRIBUTION (%) Less than $25,000	$25,000 to $49,999	$50,000 to $99,999	$100,000 to $149,999	$150,000 or More	MEDIAN HOUSEHOLD INCOME 2009	2014	2009 National Centile	2009 State Centile	2009 Home Value Base	2009 HOME VALUE DISTRIBUTION (%) Less than $50,000	$50,000 to $89,999	$90,000 to $174,999	$175,000 to $399,999	$400,000 or More	2009 Median Home Value
49024	PORTAGE	31225	11374	14.6	21.2	43.2	12.1	9.0	62618	62181	81	81	7605	1.2	8.6	55.4	31.5	3.2	147023
49026	BLOOMINGDALE	18988	815	24.4	25.9	42.0	6.7	1.0	49462	50490	60	49	673	13.5	30.8	37.4	17.5	0.7	99625
49028	BRONSON	18872	2442	21.9	31.2	40.7	5.0	1.2	45806	50043	51	38	1910	13.8	29.5	43.9	11.5	1.4	98477
49029	BURLINGTON	20892	632	22.3	24.8	45.6	5.1	2.2	51160	52382	64	53	546	18.9	31.3	37.5	11.2	1.1	89773
49030	BURR OAK	19807	1022	19.1	30.9	42.4	5.8	1.9	50000	51588	61	49	826	14.6	25.2	42.3	15.6	2.3	102500
49031	CASSOPOLIS	22382	3034	25.0	27.9	37.6	7.2	2.2	47835	50376	56	44	2349	14.9	25.5	39.1	14.1	6.4	103737
49032	CENTREVILLE	17517	1065	23.5	32.2	36.3	5.6	2.3	44660	48335	47	34	839	10.8	24.9	48.6	14.7	1.0	107420
49033	CERESCO	25063	684	15.8	25.7	46.9	8.5	3.1	57373	56817	74	70	640	4.1	16.6	51.6	25.5	2.3	132675
49034	CLIMAX	22516	1001	15.8	24.6	51.8	5.2	2.6	55972	56252	73	67	872	16.9	20.4	46.7	14.4	1.6	106786
49036	COLDWATER	21100	8949	20.7	31.1	39.4	7.2	1.7	47836	50514	56	44	6936	13.1	23.0	43.3	18.2	2.5	108704
49037	BATTLE CREEK	19165	9062	29.8	31.0	33.7	4.4	1.1	39546	42287	31	17	5757	31.3	48.5	18.3	1.8	0.1	63843
49038	COLOMA	22548	3926	22.7	28.1	40.4	6.2	2.6	49115	51645	59	48	3054	13.4	25.3	45.0	13.9	2.4	106990
49040	COLON	19509	1308	26.1	33.3	35.6	3.9	1.1	40000	45445	33	18	1046	14.0	30.3	42.9	11.3	1.5	100000
49042	CONSTANTINE	20790	1876	19.9	28.0	44.7	5.7	1.6	51453	52731	65	54	1502	13.9	18.6	52.5	13.8	1.1	109831
49043	COVERT	14320	1007	42.6	25.4	25.7	5.5	0.8	30247	32964	8	2	701	33.1	36.7	23.5	5.6	1.1	67651
49045	DECATUR	19130	2376	24.5	29.9	38.4	5.3	1.8	44510	47979	47	33	1846	18.7	30.8	34.8	14.1	1.5	90516
49046	DELTON	21570	2979	17.9	30.3	41.3	8.0	2.5	51084	53755	64	53	2516	8.3	20.0	49.2	21.6	0.9	117565
49047	DOWAGIAC	21171	5780	24.1	31.3	36.3	6.5	1.7	46386	49191	52	40	4363	13.5	32.4	38.7	12.9	2.5	95442
49048	KALAMAZOO	22332	9854	22.7	26.9	40.9	6.7	2.8	50302	52842	62	50	6791	17.5	35.3	37.2	9.5	0.5	87175
49050	DOWLING	24210	607	14.7	26.9	48.8	8.6	1.2	57589	60440	75	71	542	6.3	19.2	56.1	18.5	0.0	121154
49051	EAST LEROY	21986	780	17.7	23.1	50.6	5.6	2.9	57661	57570	75	71	709	13.4	25.0	41.3	17.2	3.1	107161
49052	FULTON	21721	319	19.1	22.3	49.8	6.6	2.2	57029	56901	74	70	286	11.5	27.6	40.2	19.2	1.4	108333
49053	GALESBURG	24902	2421	17.7	23.7	45.6	9.0	4.0	57390	57939	74	70	1981	18.5	16.0	44.6	18.4	2.5	119580
49055	GOBLES	21303	2494	21.3	27.8	42.2	6.5	2.2	50696	50937	63	51	2087	12.9	23.8	46.5	14.8	2.0	111032
49056	GRAND JUNCTION	17214	1634	27.8	31.9	34.0	4.9	1.3	40627	44273	35	20	1329	24.8	32.5	32.5	9.8	0.5	82280
49057	HARTFORD	17826	2411	28.2	29.1	35.9	5.1	1.7	42491	46525	41	27	1775	24.5	36.9	32.6	5.4	0.6	77045
49058	HASTINGS	23369	7289	16.7	27.3	44.3	8.4	3.3	54140	57490	70	63	5945	6.6	19.9	55.3	15.9	2.3	116852
49060	HICKORY CORNERS	35464	703	10.8	20.8	43.0	14.7	10.8	67559	66765	85	88	605	1.0	13.2	49.1	22.6	14.0	152885
49061	JONES	22507	674	22.1	24.0	44.4	7.0	2.5	53160	54613	68	60	558	14.0	23.7	40.1	17.7	4.5	106557
49064	LAWRENCE	18407	1419	25.8	28.1	39.2	5.5	1.4	43943	47721	45	31	1149	15.5	32.1	39.8	11.2	1.4	92412
49065	LAWTON	22340	2255	16.5	27.5	43.1	10.6	2.4	55295	53566	72	66	1875	8.6	18.8	42.5	29.2	0.9	131986
49066	LEONIDAS	16974	258	22.5	30.6	39.9	5.4	1.6	45928	50000	51	38	228	13.2	27.6	47.4	10.5	1.3	105319
49067	MARCELLUS	20801	1763	21.2	30.3	40.4	6.1	1.9	48809	51067	58	47	1464	11.0	28.9	42.6	16.3	1.2	104185
49068	MARSHALL	24310	5905	17.8	27.7	42.6	8.4	3.5	53994	55332	70	62	4551	6.9	22.1	48.9	20.9	1.3	117621
49070	MARTIN	19987	879	19.1	28.2	44.1	7.2	1.4	51624	52602	65	55	740	14.5	12.7	46.5	24.5	1.9	129318
49071	MATTAWAN	26068	3667	10.9	21.1	52.7	10.9	4.4	63773	63017	82	83	3279	14.2	11.6	43.1	27.9	3.2	136554
49072	MENDON	20031	1344	17.9	30.8	45.1	5.4	0.8	50888	52253	63	52	1155	9.9	22.7	52.6	14.5	0.3	108612
49073	NASHVILLE	20836	2117	17.6	31.1	43.5	6.0	1.9	50919	54565	63	52	1751	14.8	27.7	41.4	14.2	1.8	99962
49076	OLIVET	19956	1511	19.3	26.3	47.0	6.0	1.4	52573	54661	67	58	1082	7.1	30.5	45.5	15.4	1.5	106667
49078	OTSEGO	21879	3386	17.4	27.2	47.2	6.7	1.6	53361	54084	69	61	2697	11.4	13.8	52.7	20.8	1.2	125879
49079	PAW PAW	23056	5042	19.1	25.7	44.2	9.4	1.6	54805	53517	71	64	3947	8.5	18.2	51.7	19.7	1.9	123409
49080	PLAINWELL	23879	6046	17.9	25.7	43.7	9.2	3.6	55020	55208	71	65	5106	13.6	10.7	44.4	29.6	1.8	137925
49082	QUINCY	19559	2461	18.2	31.2	42.7	6.7	1.1	50331	51386	62	50	2019	9.6	23.8	46.1	18.4	2.1	109916
49083	RICHLAND	32103	2849	12.5	21.8	44.8	13.1	7.9	65101	64451	83	85	2380	3.7	3.0	45.3	32.4	15.6	170395
49085	SAINT JOSEPH	29581	9983	18.8	22.7	40.4	11.4	6.7	58322	58828	76	72	7585	3.6	6.3	49.4	35.2	5.5	155150
49087	SCHOOLCRAFT	27537	2191	14.3	17.7	48.3	13.5	6.2	64740	64946	83	84	1842	3.7	11.0	45.5	35.6	4.1	150131
49088	SCOTTS	24099	1383	12.0	26.3	49.2	10.3	2.1	59394	58002	77	74	1276	4.0	13.7	49.7	31.3	1.3	142028
49089	SHERWOOD	18631	755	20.7	38.7	35.4	4.5	0.8	42552	46316	41	27	606	16.2	33.7	39.4	9.7	1.0	90217
49090	SOUTH HAVEN	22216	6280	25.4	29.9	34.5	7.5	2.7	43945	47414	45	32	4828	15.7	19.9	38.4	20.3	5.7	115049
49091	STURGIS	21275	7712	21.5	29.6	40.3	5.7	2.9	48764	51057	58	47	5466	8.2	24.1	49.3	16.5	1.8	110183
49092	TEKONSHA	20755	891	19.9	28.4	44.9	5.8	1.0	51087	52601	64	53	722	13.0	30.2	42.2	12.7	1.8	95052
49093	THREE RIVERS	22922	7196	22.1	29.5	38.4	6.7	3.2	48564	50636	58	46	5535	12.0	25.1	44.8	16.6	1.5	106418
49094	UNION CITY	20705	1608	22.7	29.2	40.6	6.3	1.2	48050	50419	57	44	1272	14.9	30.9	43.2	10.5	0.5	95567
49095	VANDALIA	22495	945	21.4	27.6	42.0	7.2	1.8	50796	52527	63	52	745	14.4	21.5	37.4	23.4	3.4	116715
49096	VERMONTVILLE	21319	1197	18.1	25.3	46.6	8.6	1.3	54807	58883	71	64	1062	10.9	25.9	44.4	18.0	0.8	108644
49097	VICKSBURG	24491	3909	14.0	23.8	50.9	8.4	2.8	60258	58979	78	76	3325	5.9	19.7	45.0	26.9	2.4	134744
49098	WATERVLIET	21861	2415	23.7	26.3	41.9	6.0	2.1	50044	52120	61	49	1842	17.3	28.4	40.5	11.8	2.0	95411
49099	WHITE PIGEON	23915	2357	19.9	27.1	43.2	5.5	4.3	52315	53344	67	57	1924	12.1	23.8	40.7	18.9	4.5	110086
49101	BARODA	23405	1205	19.4	26.7	44.8	5.6	3.4	52452	53717	67	57	1018	27.5	8.3	39.6	20.8	3.8	125000
49102	BERRIEN CENTER	17135	615	22.8	29.4	40.2	6.5	1.1	47467	50834	55	42	500	25.4	26.0	28.8	19.2	0.6	87742
49103	BERRIEN SPRINGS	21106	4201	26.0	24.1	39.3	7.1	3.5	49899	52053	61	49	2577	7.3	11.1	43.9	33.6	4.1	148108
49106	BRIDGMAN	25770	1957	18.9	23.0	44.0	9.7	4.4	56608	56467	74	69	1540	9.7	15.3	40.3	28.1	6.6	138821
49107	BUCHANAN	21282	4227	22.2	31.7	38.5	5.2	2.4	46449	50077	53	40	3255	13.2	29.5	39.1	16.4	1.9	103804
49111	EAU CLAIRE	19471	1460	24.1	28.4	41.8	4.1	1.6	47438	51027	55	42	1207	16.1	23.6	39.6	18.3	2.4	109052
49112	EDWARDSBURG	23449	3975	19.3	31.7	39.1	7.3	2.5	49114	51296	59	48	3368	16.9	17.9	42.4	19.7	3.1	114342
49113	GALIEN	21316	858	19.3	30.7	41.1	7.8	1.0	50000	52254	61	49	729	9.9	32.6	41.4	13.7	2.3	99909
49116	LAKESIDE	38012	120	17.5	27.5	36.7	11.7	6.7	55000	57224	71	65	105	5.7	4.8	27.6	39.0	22.9	223214
49117	NEW BUFFALO	33021	1944	22.6	24.4	38.2	7.9	6.9	52582	53688	67	58	1522	3.7	12.0	36.9	30.0	17.5	166739
49120	NILES	21645	14464	23.6	29.4	39.6	5.6	1.8	46962	50599	54	41	11169	12.7	32.9	40.3	12.4	1.6	95052
49125	SAWYER	27556	1054	16.7	28.7	44.3	6.2	4.2	53700	54513	69	61	893	11.2	11.9	36.1	27.9	13.0	148214
49126	SODUS	22504	593	28.5	29.3	34.6	5.2	2.4	41871	47031	39	24	512	33.0	20.1	33.0	13.3	0.6	85429
49127	STEVENSVILLE	29380	4156	15.4	23.3	43.6	10.8	6.9	60776	60259	79	78	3201	11.1	4.7	47.0	30.7	6.5	151733
49128	THREE OAKS	24192	1824	21.4	27.4	41.4	6.7	3.0	50954	52998	63	52	1511	12.6	16.7	42.0	21.8	6.9	125282
49129	UNION PIER	33088	399	20.1	24.3	40.6	8.0	7.0	56217	57279	73	68	349	4.9	4.9	37.2	35.0	18.1	185938
49130	UNION	25663	781	13.3	31.1	46.2	7.7	1.7	54264	54852	70	63	664	6.6	13.7	37.2	36.6	5.9	146104
49201	JACKSON	23012	16177	20.9	23.4	41.8	9.8	4.0	55094	57315	71	65	12541	14.1	19.3	45.2	19.5	2.0	115037
49202	JACKSON	20870	8734	28.0	29.7	36.9	4.2	1.2	42552	47786	41	27	5415	24.3	51.3	22.5	1.8	0.1	70274
49203	JACKSON	23589	15487	23.2	24.6	40.7	8.2	3.3	51797	54594	66	56	10845	17.6	33.9	37.6	10.2	0.7	88407
49220	ADDISON	22630	966	21.6	29.5	37.6	8.1	3.2	48762	50956	58	46	778	7.8	19.2	35.5	31.9	5.7	142733
49221	ADRIAN	22329	14913	19.1	27.5	42.3	8.1	3.0	52328	53544	67	57	10588	12.2	16.0	46.0	24.3	1.5	120648
49224	ALBION	19023	5000	29.0	28.0	36.8	4.2	1.9	42332	46804	40	26	3416	16.4	47.2	30.2	5.9	0.4	78676
49227	ALLEN	20781	526	16.9	27.9	48.7	5.1	1.3	52635	51774	67	58	434	8.8	21.7	50.0	16.8	2.8	115179
49228	BLISSFIELD	23081	2176	21.3	26.9	41.2	8.7	1.9	51278	52525	64	54	1751	11.2	14.2	48.4	24.3	1.9	130550
49229	BRITTON	23817	1280	11.4	22.4	51.7	12.0	2.5	62106	60680	80	80	1095	2.9	9.2	46.1	38.7	3.0	157461
49230	BROOKLYN	26092	4134	16.6	25.2	45.0	9.2	4.0	58474	60083	76	72	3597	5.8	14.9	40.2	33.6	5.6	148059
49232	CAMDEN	18400	993	23.0	33.4	36.1	5.7	1.8	43893	46998	45	31	832	14.2	18.8	35.5	28.5	3.1	120575
49233	CEMENT CITY	23752	1263	16.4	29.5	42.0	10.3	1.8	54470	54624	70	64	1159	3.7	11.2	39.2	42.2	3.7	165021
49234	CLARKLAKE	31484	1130	13.4	22.2	47.0	10.0	7.4	62367	62600	80	80	991	5.9	15.1	34.3	34.2	10.5	160253
49235	CLAYTON	21490	847	19.0	24.8	48.3	6.7	1.2	54178	54650	70	63	729	9.7	18.5	41.7	28.5	1.5	127861
49236	CLINTON	25997	1962	12.3	21.1	52.0	11.7	2.9	62089	61180	80	80	1683	10.0	7.9	37.7	39.8	4.6	164342
49237	CONCORD	22117	1221	18.3	24.0	47.7	7.6	2.4	57532	59574	75	71	986	11.2	24.4	43.8	19.1	1.5	111378
49238	DEERFIELD	21146	621	15.9	25.8	46.7	9.3	2.3	56205	56001	73	68	504	3.2	9.9	56.0	28.0	3.0	141566
49240	GRASS LAKE	26062	2869	11.9	19.8	52.2	10.1	6.0	63345	63201	82	82	2485	4.8	9.6	39.6	41.4	4.5	164185
49241	HANOVER	20872	979	20.4	27.7	44.4	4.8	2.7	51466	54854	65	55	852	23.9	22.1	37.0	15.8	1.2	96667
49242	HILLSDALE	21143	5841	23.4	29.7	38.2	7.0	1.7	46048	48874	51	39	4106	11.4	24.9	43.4	18.3	2.0	109156
	MICHIGAN	26713		20.1	24.2	38.5	11.3	5.9	55536	56866				13.2	21.9	40.3	21.5	3.2	115137
	UNITED STATES	27277		20.9	24.4	35.3	11.7	7.6	54719	56938				9.3	13.1	31.6	32.6	13.5	162279

ZIP CODE #	POST OFFICE NAME	FINANCIAL SERVICES: Auto Loan	Home Loan	Invest-ments	Retire-ment Plans	THE HOME: Home Improvements: Home Repair	Lawn & Garden	Furnishings: Comput-ers & Hard-ware-Personal	Major Appli-ances	TV, Radio, Sound Equip-ment	Furni-ture	ENTERTAINMENT: Dine out/ Carry out	Sports Equip-ment	Fees & Tickets	Toys & Games	Travel	Cable TV	PERSONAL: Apparel & Services	Auto Repairs	Health Insur-ance	Pets & Supplies
49024	PORTAGE	107	109	103	113	107	103	112	105	109	113	111	84	115	111	111	107	78	109	105	125
49026	BLOOMINGDALE	83	74	71	74	74	83	72	79	75	70	74	59	66	77	70	78	50	75	81	93
49028	BRONSON	81	72	70	74	71	85	72	79	75	67	74	61	66	77	70	79	51	75	83	94
49029	BURLINGTON	94	76	81	77	76	94	76	87	82	73	80	67	67	84	73	87	55	82	90	104
49030	BURR OAK	92	74	79	75	75	92	75	86	80	70	79	66	65	83	72	86	53	80	90	102
49031	CASSOPOLIS	89	76	82	77	76	92	77	86	81	72	79	66	69	82	75	86	54	82	90	102
49032	CENTREVILLE	88	75	74	74	74	86	73	82	78	72	77	61	66	80	70	82	52	77	84	97
49033	CERESCO	94	98	94	101	97	103	90	97	90	88	90	75	92	91	95	92	62	93	97	114
49034	CLIMAX	89	86	84	89	87	98	83	92	85	76	84	69	80	86	84	89	58	86	95	107
49036	COLDWATER	83	74	78	76	74	86	77	82	79	71	78	63	71	79	75	83	53	80	87	97
49037	BATTLE CREEK	66	60	52	61	57	64	65	62	68	63	67	48	62	68	61	70	47	65	69	76
49038	COLOMA	81	78	71	78	75	86	77	80	79	73	78	62	75	81	75	82	54	79	86	96
49040	COLON	82	63	81	62	65	83	65	78	70	61	69	58	54	70	63	76	46	73	81	92
49042	CONSTANTINE	87	75	76	77	75	90	76	84	79	71	78	64	68	81	73	84	53	79	88	100
49043	COVERT	75	49	71	46	49	73	52	65	60	50	59	51	39	61	49	67	39	62	69	80
49045	DECATUR	81	71	67	72	69	83	73	77	76	68	75	60	66	78	69	80	51	75	83	93
49046	DELTON	88	82	84	84	84	95	79	90	82	73	81	67	75	83	81	86	55	84	93	104
49047	DOWAGIAC	80	71	70	73	71	82	75	79	77	69	76	60	68	78	71	81	52	77	83	93
49048	KALAMAZOO	84	77	68	77	73	79	81	78	82	79	82	61	77	84	76	83	57	80	82	94
49050	DOWLING	91	86	84	89	87	99	83	93	86	77	85	71	79	87	84	91	58	87	96	109
49051	EAST LEROY	93	85	92	88	87	100	83	95	85	77	84	71	78	86	85	89	57	88	96	110
49052	FULTON	92	84	83	87	85	99	82	93	85	75	84	70	76	87	82	90	57	86	96	108
49053	GALESBURG	92	98	86	99	95	99	91	94	91	91	91	72	94	93	93	92	63	92	95	110
49055	GOBLES	91	76	76	77	76	91	78	86	82	74	81	65	69	85	74	87	55	82	90	102
49056	GRAND JUNCTION	83	62	69	60	61	79	64	73	70	63	69	56	52	73	59	75	46	70	76	88
49057	HARTFORD	82	62	64	62	61	78	69	73	74	65	72	57	58	76	61	80	49	73	79	89
49058	HASTINGS	91	86	80	88	86	94	85	90	87	81	86	68	82	89	84	90	59	87	94	106
49060	HICKORY CORNERS	121	139	129	141	139	140	122	130	122	125	123	97	134	122	133	124	86	125	133	151
49061	JONES	98	79	107	78	82	103	79	97	84	73	82	72	68	83	81	90	55	89	98	113
49064	LAWRENCE	86	69	74	69	69	86	70	80	75	66	74	61	60	77	66	81	50	75	84	95
49065	LAWTON	89	91	80	92	88	93	86	89	86	84	86	68	86	89	86	88	59	86	90	105
49066	LEONIDAS	81	74	73	77	75	87	73	82	75	66	74	62	67	76	73	79	50	76	85	95
49067	MARCELLUS	82	77	73	80	77	88	76	83	79	70	77	64	72	80	76	82	53	79	87	98
49068	MARSHALL	86	87	83	89	87	92	84	87	86	82	86	66	85	86	86	88	59	86	92	103
49070	MARTIN	88	80	74	80	80	86	77	83	80	76	79	61	72	82	74	83	54	79	84	98
49071	MATTAWAN	102	112	100	113	109	106	101	104	98	105	99	79	106	101	104	97	70	100	99	121
49072	MENDON	85	74	78	77	76	90	74	85	77	67	76	64	67	78	73	82	51	78	88	99
49073	NASHVILLE	81	80	71	82	78	85	77	81	78	75	78	62	76	80	77	80	54	78	83	95
49076	OLIVET	86	77	72	79	77	83	80	82	81	77	80	63	74	83	76	82	55	80	83	97
49078	OTSEGO	86	83	75	85	82	90	80	86	82	76	81	65	77	84	79	85	56	82	89	101
49079	PAW PAW	89	83	79	84	82	91	83	87	85	80	84	66	79	86	81	88	58	85	90	103
49080	PLAINWELL	94	89	85	90	88	95	86	91	88	84	87	70	83	90	85	91	60	88	93	108
49082	QUINCY	84	76	76	77	75	88	76	83	78	70	77	64	70	79	75	82	53	79	87	98
49083	RICHLAND	110	131	125	134	132	125	117	121	113	120	113	93	128	113	127	111	81	116	116	140
49085	SAINT JOSEPH	96	101	98	103	101	102	98	99	98	99	99	75	102	98	101	99	69	99	102	116
49087	SCHOOLCRAFT	103	120	111	121	118	112	107	109	104	109	105	85	116	106	114	102	75	106	104	126
49088	SCOTTS	90	99	88	102	97	101	89	95	89	88	89	73	94	91	94	91	62	90	95	111
49089	SHERWOOD	86	63	71	62	63	83	66	76	72	63	71	58	54	75	60	78	48	72	80	92
49090	SOUTH HAVEN	86	74	82	74	75	88	74	83	78	72	78	63	68	79	73	83	53	80	87	99
49091	STURGIS	82	75	70	77	74	83	80	81	82	74	81	62	75	82	76	85	56	81	86	96
49092	TEKONSHA	83	76	75	79	77	89	75	84	77	68	76	64	69	79	75	82	52	78	87	98
49093	THREE RIVERS	86	77	75	79	76	88	80	84	83	75	81	64	74	84	77	87	56	82	89	100
49094	UNION CITY	81	74	68	75	71	84	74	78	77	70	76	61	70	79	72	80	52	76	84	94
49095	VANDALIA	93	74	105	73	78	96	76	91	80	71	79	68	65	78	77	86	53	86	93	107
49096	VERMONTVILLE	90	82	81	86	84	97	81	91	83	73	82	69	75	85	81	88	56	84	94	106
49097	VICKSBURG	92	97	92	99	95	101	90	95	90	88	90	74	93	91	94	92	63	92	97	112
49098	WATERVLIET	86	78	79	78	77	87	78	84	80	74	79	64	72	81	77	83	54	81	86	99
49099	WHITE PIGEON	99	85	95	86	87	103	84	97	88	79	86	73	76	89	84	93	59	90	99	114
49101	BARODA	92	90	80	89	88	92	84	89	85	85	85	66	82	88	83	87	59	85	89	105
49102	BERRIEN CENTER	88	68	75	68	69	87	70	80	75	66	74	61	59	78	66	81	50	75	84	96
49103	BERRIEN SPRINGS	83	78	72	80	76	80	83	80	83	80	83	63	79	84	79	84	58	82	83	96
49106	BRIDGMAN	97	90	94	93	93	106	87	99	90	82	89	73	83	91	89	95	61	92	103	115
49107	BUCHANAN	79	75	70	76	73	83	75	78	77	71	76	60	72	78	73	81	52	77	84	93
49111	EAU CLAIRE	84	70	74	71	71	86	70	81	74	65	73	61	62	76	68	79	49	75	84	95
49112	EDWARDSBURG	92	80	81	82	81	96	79	90	83	74	82	68	71	85	77	88	56	84	93	106
49113	GALIEN	81	78	71	80	76	87	77	82	79	71	78	63	73	80	76	82	53	78	87	97
49116	LAKESIDE	117	94	152	92	103	124	94	119	98	88	97	87	81	93	102	105	65	110	118	138
49117	NEW BUFFALO	110	103	126	105	111	123	100	115	104	99	102	82	97	100	106	109	70	109	122	133
49120	NILES	78	73	69	75	72	82	75	77	77	70	76	59	71	78	73	81	52	76	83	92
49125	SAWYER	100	92	112	92	95	109	88	103	91	83	90	76	84	90	93	96	61	96	105	119
49126	SODUS	93	65	98	64	68	96	69	87	75	61	74	68	53	74	69	82	48	81	91	105
49127	STEVENSVILLE	102	109	102	109	107	107	103	103	102	104	103	79	107	103	106	103	72	103	104	122
49128	THREE OAKS	89	79	94	79	80	96	79	90	83	74	82	67	73	82	81	88	55	86	96	106
49129	UNION PIER	106	99	134	98	106	119	93	112	97	92	96	80	91	93	103	102	65	105	115	129
49130	UNION	95	90	86	91	88	99	85	92	87	83	87	72	82	90	85	91	60	88	94	110
49201	JACKSON	89	94	85	95	92	94	89	91	90	89	90	69	92	91	91	91	63	90	93	107
49202	JACKSON	69	63	57	64	61	68	69	66	71	65	70	52	65	71	64	73	48	69	72	80
49203	JACKSON	82	81	74	82	79	86	82	81	85	80	84	62	82	85	81	87	58	83	88	98
49220	ADDISON	91	81	90	81	83	94	79	90	82	76	81	67	73	82	80	86	55	84	91	105
49221	ADRIAN	86	83	76	84	81	86	84	84	85	81	84	65	82	86	82	87	59	84	87	100
49224	ALBION	74	63	61	64	61	72	70	70	73	64	71	54	63	73	64	76	49	71	76	84
49227	ALLEN	88	79	79	83	81	94	78	89	81	71	80	67	72	83	78	86	54	82	91	103
49228	BLISSFIELD	89	82	78	84	81	93	80	87	83	76	82	67	76	85	79	87	56	83	91	103
49229	BRITTON	90	105	92	107	102	103	92	96	92	93	92	74	101	94	99	93	65	93	98	113
49230	BROOKLYN	93	94	97	95	95	102	88	96	89	86	89	72	88	90	92	92	61	92	99	112
49232	CAMDEN	87	72	76	73	73	89	72	83	77	67	75	63	64	79	70	82	51	77	86	98
49233	CEMENT CITY	89	91	87	94	91	97	85	92	85	82	85	71	86	86	88	87	59	87	92	108
49234	CLARKLAKE	108	124	115	126	124	125	110	117	110	112	110	87	120	110	119	111	77	112	120	135
49235	CLAYTON	89	81	80	85	83	96	80	90	82	72	81	68	74	84	80	87	55	83	93	105
49236	CLINTON	96	100	97	101	98	107	92	100	94	91	94	76	95	95	97	97	65	96	103	117
49237	CONCORD	91	85	82	87	86	97	82	92	85	76	84	69	77	87	82	89	57	86	94	107
49238	DEERFIELD	93	88	85	91	89	100	85	94	87	78	86	72	81	89	86	91	59	88	97	110
49240	GRASS LAKE	101	113	99	116	110	110	101	105	99	102	100	81	107	102	106	99	70	101	103	123
49241	HANOVER	86	80	77	82	81	90	77	86	79	72	78	65	73	81	77	83	54	80	88	100
49242	HILLSDALE	80	70	74	71	70	81	75	78	77	69	76	60	68	77	72	81	52	77	83	93
	MICHIGAN	98	97	93	98	95	100	96	97	97	95	97	74	96	98	96	99	68	97	100	115
	UNITED STATES	100	100	100	100	100	100	100	100	100	100	100	100	100	100	100	100	100	100	100	100

POPULATION CHANGE

49245-49436

ZIP CODE			POPULATION			2000-2009 ANNUAL RATE		HOUSEHOLDS					FAMILIES		
#	POST OFFICE NAME	COUNTY FIPS CODE	2000	2009	2014	% Rate	State Centile	2000	2009	2014	% Annual Rate 2000-2009	2009 Average HH Size	2000	2009	% Annual Rate 2000-2009
49245	HOMER	025	5082	5134	5083	0.1	42	1869	1918	1908	0.3	2.67	1387	1408	0.2
49246	HORTON	075	3459	3626	3659	0.5	66	1273	1366	1390	0.8	2.65	1041	1105	0.6
49247	HUDSON	091	5926	5956	5931	0.1	42	2221	2286	2296	0.3	2.57	1634	1658	0.2
49248	JASPER	091	969	1011	1024	0.5	66	356	379	387	0.7	2.65	280	294	0.5
49249	JEROME	059	3455	3715	3781	0.8	80	1344	1484	1521	1.1	2.50	1036	1131	1.0
49250	JONESVILLE	059	5835	5970	5936	0.2	48	2169	2247	2243	0.4	2.51	1604	1643	0.3
49251	LESLIE	065	6648	6805	6811	0.3	54	2375	2495	2518	0.5	2.71	1822	1890	0.4
49252	LITCHFIELD	059	2627	2824	2864	0.8	80	987	1084	1107	1.0	2.51	701	760	0.9
49253	MANITOU BEACH	091	2956	2923	2914	-0.1	32	1198	1208	1213	0.1	2.42	842	835	-0.1
49254	MICHIGAN CENTER	075	3418	3460	3442	0.1	42	1385	1426	1427	0.3	2.42	968	979	0.1
49255	MONTGOMERY	023	2013	2019	1999	0.0	37	654	670	668	0.3	2.99	488	495	0.2
49256	MORENCI	091	4325	4220	4171	-0.3	21	1582	1577	1572	0.0	2.64	1199	1179	-0.2
49259	MUNITH	075	2974	3098	3143	0.4	60	1063	1121	1141	0.6	2.64	825	859	0.4
49262	NORTH ADAMS	059	1411	1507	1518	0.7	76	538	588	596	1.0	2.56	408	441	0.8
49264	ONONDAGA	065	1916	1920	1917	0.0	37	651	668	671	0.3	2.84	518	525	0.1
49265	ONSTED	091	4530	5197	5473	1.5	93	1667	1955	2076	1.7	2.66	1331	1545	1.6
49266	OSSEO	059	3216	3381	3398	0.5	66	1205	1301	1318	0.8	2.59	903	964	0.7
49267	OTTAWA LAKE	115	4138	4270	4282	0.3	54	1488	1584	1604	0.7	2.68	1157	1218	0.6
49268	PALMYRA	091	1462	1482	1479	0.1	42	490	509	512	0.4	2.70	381	391	0.3
49269	PARMA	075	5756	6084	6195	0.6	71	2034	2181	2230	0.8	2.76	1622	1722	0.6
49270	PETERSBURG	115	5775	6058	6165	0.5	66	1971	2140	2201	0.9	2.81	1598	1719	0.8
49271	PITTSFORD	059	2215	2160	2106	-0.3	21	782	782	768	0.0	2.75	621	614	-0.1
49272	PLEASANT LAKE	075	2045	2086	2079	0.2	48	777	807	809	0.4	2.57	597	611	0.3
49274	READING	059	3264	3323	3312	0.2	48	1202	1247	1249	0.4	2.64	889	910	0.3
49276	RIGA	091	992	1021	1021	0.3	54	348	367	370	0.6	2.71	278	290	0.5
49277	RIVES JUNCTION	075	3184	3386	3465	0.7	76	1092	1183	1217	0.9	2.85	900	966	0.8
49279	SAND CREEK	091	1163	1191	1198	0.3	54	402	420	426	0.5	2.83	309	319	0.3
49283	SPRING ARBOR	075	4019	4355	4419	0.9	82	1293	1411	1447	0.9	2.49	891	957	0.8
49284	SPRINGPORT	075	3365	3515	3564	0.5	66	1267	1349	1373	0.7	2.61	954	1002	0.5
49285	STOCKBRIDGE	065	5194	5681	5812	1.0	84	1824	2048	2113	1.3	2.74	1409	1563	1.1
49286	TECUMSEH	091	14214	15124	15491	0.7	76	5471	5925	6105	0.9	2.54	3974	4273	0.8
49287	TIPTON	091	2054	2242	2284	1.0	84	754	841	864	1.2	2.67	602	663	1.0
49288	WALDRON	059	1392	1392	1351	0.0	37	512	525	513	0.3	2.64	370	374	0.1
49301	ADA	081	13806	15838	16651	1.5	93	4492	5267	5573	1.7	3.00	3885	4515	1.6
49302	ALTO	081	7444	8118	8423	0.9	82	2423	2690	2802	1.1	3.01	2060	2266	1.0
49303	BAILEY	121	785	843	867	0.8	80	260	285	295	1.0	2.93	205	223	0.9
49304	BALDWIN	085	4494	4538	4710	0.1	42	1824	1982	2078	0.9	2.12	1098	1174	0.7
49305	BARRYTON	107	2392	2392	2324	0.0	37	973	996	974	0.3	2.39	704	711	0.1
49306	BELMONT	081	8006	9204	9707	1.5	93	2784	3238	3426	1.6	2.84	2250	2603	1.6
49307	BIG RAPIDS	107	18827	19534	19609	0.4	60	6419	6881	6974	0.8	2.35	3627	3824	0.6
49309	BITELY	123	2009	2084	2069	0.4	60	832	880	879	0.6	2.34	586	612	0.5
49310	BLANCHARD	073	2773	2831	2793	0.2	48	1024	1082	1078	0.6	2.60	774	812	0.5
49315	BYRON CENTER	081	15062	19360	21045	2.8	99	5292	7033	7706	3.1	2.74	4078	5331	2.9
49316	CALEDONIA	081	12721	16756	18518	3.0	99	4422	5993	6676	3.3	2.79	3557	4736	3.1
49318	CASNOVIA	121	1650	1727	1760	0.5	66	565	605	620	0.7	2.76	450	476	0.6
49319	CEDAR SPRINGS	081	12786	14378	15133	1.3	90	4470	5140	5440	1.5	2.77	3456	3929	1.4
49321	COMSTOCK PARK	081	16057	16447	16626	0.3	54	6270	6515	6610	0.4	2.52	4004	4089	0.2
49322	CORAL	117	1125	1195	1190	0.7	76	406	440	443	0.9	2.71	312	335	0.8
49323	DORR	005	7785	9179	9771	1.8	96	2508	3048	3274	2.1	3.01	2096	2530	2.1
49325	FREEPORT	015	1779	1883	1917	0.6	71	580	625	640	0.8	3.01	478	512	0.7
49326	GOWEN	081	2833	3042	3134	0.8	80	1048	1152	1194	1.0	2.59	805	875	0.9
49327	GRANT	123	8193	8729	8912	0.7	76	2763	2981	3055	0.8	2.90	2112	2258	0.7
49328	HOPKINS	005	3659	4202	4434	1.5	93	1222	1434	1523	1.7	2.90	969	1125	1.6
49329	HOWARD CITY	117	6780	7923	8287	1.7	95	2404	2862	3014	1.9	2.76	1832	2160	1.8
49330	KENT CITY	081	4809	5185	5356	0.8	80	1556	1720	1788	1.1	2.99	1268	1387	1.0
49331	LOWELL	081	14963	16825	17601	1.3	90	5097	5842	6142	1.5	2.81	3943	4484	1.4
49332	MECOSTA	107	2842	2918	2878	0.3	54	1206	1266	1260	0.5	2.29	869	899	0.4
49333	MIDDLEVILLE	015	9921	11249	11732	1.4	92	3482	4045	4249	1.6	2.78	2783	3206	1.5
49336	MORLEY	107	3883	4339	4478	1.2	88	1337	1524	1583	1.4	2.84	1007	1134	1.3
49337	NEWAYGO	123	12042	12901	13110	0.7	76	4653	5044	5145	0.9	2.54	3415	3670	0.8
49338	PARIS	123	2052	2095	2053	0.2	48	781	817	808	0.5	2.56	543	560	0.3
49339	PIERSON	117	2268	2362	2351	0.4	60	792	846	850	0.7	2.79	614	650	0.6
49340	REMUS	107	2971	3031	3039	0.2	48	1099	1164	1181	0.6	2.60	810	847	0.5
49341	ROCKFORD	081	29314	33945	35810	1.6	94	9946	11717	12414	1.8	2.89	8112	9463	1.7
49342	RODNEY	107	1750	1780	1740	0.2	48	689	717	706	0.4	2.48	494	507	0.3
49343	SAND LAKE	081	5839	6069	6150	0.4	60	2086	2217	2260	0.7	2.73	1615	1696	0.5
49344	SHELBYVILLE	005	3216	3318	3333	0.3	54	1239	1311	1327	0.6	2.52	939	981	0.5
49345	SPARTA	081	12190	13115	13513	0.8	80	4409	4832	5002	1.0	2.70	3343	3635	0.9
49346	STANWOOD	107	4726	5372	5592	1.4	92	1916	2261	2384	1.8	2.37	1471	1715	1.7
49347	TRUFANT	117	1221	1297	1301	0.7	76	480	523	528	0.9	2.48	358	386	0.8
49348	WAYLAND	005	11644	12814	13201	1.0	84	4130	4611	4770	1.2	2.75	3173	3524	1.1
49349	WHITE CLOUD	123	8272	8950	9201	0.9	82	3035	3345	3459	1.1	2.61	2188	2386	0.9
49401	ALLENDALE	139	12464	16728	18273	3.2	99	3152	4403	4948	3.7	2.99	2130	2871	3.3
49402	BRANCH	085	1553	1651	1712	0.7	76	699	769	804	1.0	2.10	474	514	0.9
49403	CONKLIN	139	2617	2769	2816	0.6	71	839	909	932	0.9	2.85	682	732	0.8
49404	COOPERSVILLE	139	7898	8579	8835	0.9	82	2686	2999	3115	1.2	2.82	2086	2311	1.1
49405	CUSTER	105	1504	1592	1631	0.6	71	561	608	627	0.9	2.59	396	422	0.7
49408	FENNVILLE	005	9134	10333	10850	1.3	90	3394	3913	4131	1.6	2.60	2388	2725	1.4
49410	FOUNTAIN	105	1716	1799	1828	0.5	66	702	757	775	0.8	2.34	491	520	0.6
49411	FREE SOIL	105	1577	1648	1690	0.5	66	578	627	647	0.9	2.53	425	455	0.7
49412	FREMONT	123	11365	11634	11556	0.3	54	4194	4342	4327	0.4	2.62	3038	3117	0.3
49415	FRUITPORT	121	5540	6217	6469	1.3	90	1982	2274	2382	1.5	2.72	1560	1771	1.4
49417	GRAND HAVEN	139	27681	30356	31611	1.0	84	10633	11897	12465	1.2	2.50	7582	8426	1.1
49418	GRANDVILLE	081	25399	28645	30023	1.3	90	9186	10405	10910	1.4	2.73	6797	7633	1.3
49419	HAMILTON	005	6497	7628	8144	1.8	96	2174	2599	2792	1.9	2.93	1820	2160	1.9
49420	HART	127	6667	6698	6721	0.1	42	2255	2271	2283	0.1	2.74	1638	1637	0.0
49421	HESPERIA	127	5864	5890	5863	0.0	37	2213	2263	2262	0.2	2.59	1624	1644	0.1
49423	HOLLAND	005	46993	49394	50011	0.5	66	16325	17426	17783	0.7	2.63	11273	11894	0.6
49424	HOLLAND	139	40144	45884	48041	1.5	93	13871	16174	17076	1.7	2.78	10723	12374	1.6
49425	HOLTON	121	3651	3810	3860	0.5	66	1263	1344	1369	0.7	2.83	967	1017	0.5
49426	HUDSONVILLE	139	27172	32871	35232	2.1	97	8743	10796	11653	2.3	3.02	7262	8921	2.2
49428	JENISON	139	25042	26131	26660	0.5	66	8597	9224	9488	0.8	2.79	6754	7149	0.6
49431	LUDINGTON	105	16812	17537	17800	0.5	66	6942	7364	7506	0.6	2.35	4634	4879	0.6
49435	MARNE	139	3595	3872	3955	0.8	80	1148	1263	1302	1.0	2.90	926	1013	1.0
49436	MEARS	127	1647	1993	2160	2.1	97	654	802	873	2.2	2.45	499	606	2.1
	MICHIGAN					0.3					0.4	2.52			0.3
	UNITED STATES					1.0					1.1	2.59			0.9

ZIP CODE #	POST OFFICE NAME	RACE (%) White 2000	White 2009	Black 2000	Black 2009	Asian/Pacific 2000	Asian/Pacific 2009	% Hispanic Origin 2000	% Hispanic Origin 2009	2009 AGE DISTRIBUTION (%) 0-4	5-9	10-14	15-19	20-24	25-44	45-64	65-84	85+	18+	MEDIAN AGE 2009	% 2009 Males	% 2009 Females
49245	HOMER	97.6	97.0	0.2	0.3	0.0	0.1	1.5	2.1	7.0	6.8	6.8	7.3	6.8	26.0	27.3	10.8	1.4	74.7	37.2	49.5	50.5
49246	HORTON	98.1	97.5	0.2	0.2	0.4	0.6	0.9	1.2	5.3	6.3	7.3	6.9	4.5	23.7	33.7	11.4	0.9	76.8	42.3	51.3	48.7
49247	HUDSON	97.2	96.4	0.2	0.3	0.4	0.6	2.0	2.8	6.1	6.2	6.4	7.0	6.0	26.2	28.4	12.2	1.6	77.0	39.4	50.0	50.0
49248	JASPER	97.5	97.0	0.3	0.4	0.1	0.1	3.4	4.5	5.9	6.3	6.7	6.9	5.6	23.9	31.7	11.3	1.6	76.9	40.9	50.8	49.2
49249	JEROME	97.9	97.4	0.3	0.3	0.2	0.3	1.2	1.6	5.2	5.6	6.7	6.1	4.8	22.4	33.5	14.2	1.5	78.6	44.5	50.4	49.6
49250	JONESVILLE	97.0	96.3	1.0	1.1	0.4	0.7	1.4	1.8	6.4	6.5	7.2	8.4	6.3	24.5	26.8	11.4	2.5	75.1	37.9	49.4	50.6
49251	LESLIE	96.5	95.3	0.5	0.6	0.3	0.6	2.6	3.6	6.8	7.0	7.4	7.0	5.5	27.0	29.2	9.2	1.0	74.3	37.8	49.7	50.3
49252	LITCHFIELD	97.8	97.3	0.3	0.4	0.2	0.2	1.7	2.2	6.9	7.0	7.2	6.6	5.0	24.9	26.8	13.0	2.7	75.1	39.4	49.5	50.5
49253	MANITOU BEACH	98.1	97.6	0.2	0.2	0.2	0.4	1.6	2.3	4.9	5.2	5.9	6.6	4.6	23.5	33.8	14.2	1.4	79.8	44.6	51.0	49.0
49254	MICHIGAN CENTER	97.5	96.8	0.4	0.5	0.4	0.6	1.6	2.2	5.3	5.7	6.2	6.5	4.7	24.4	31.7	13.6	2.0	78.9	43.2	50.9	49.1
49255	MONTGOMERY	97.1	96.8	0.6	0.6	0.1	0.1	0.5	0.8	9.7	9.3	8.8	8.2	5.8	24.4	22.6	9.9	1.2	66.6	31.8	51.6	48.4
49256	MORENCI	96.9	96.1	0.2	0.3	0.2	0.4	3.4	4.8	6.8	6.7	6.5	6.9	5.9	25.7	27.0	11.9	2.5	75.9	38.5	50.6	49.4
49259	MUNITH	97.1	96.4	0.5	0.7	0.2	0.3	1.8	2.6	6.4	6.8	7.0	6.7	5.2	26.0	28.1	11.5	2.3	75.5	39.9	49.6	50.4
49262	NORTH ADAMS	98.4	98.1	0.3	0.3	0.2	0.3	1.3	1.7	6.6	7.1	7.4	6.5	4.7	25.3	28.1	12.8	1.5	74.8	40.1	50.2	49.8
49264	ONONDAGA	95.9	94.6	0.4	0.5	0.2	0.2	2.6	3.6	6.7	7.0	7.6	7.6	5.5	25.3	30.4	9.1	1.0	73.8	38.7	49.6	50.4
49265	ONSTED	97.2	96.3	0.2	0.2	0.3	0.6	2.1	2.9	5.7	6.3	7.1	7.3	4.3	24.3	31.9	12.0	1.0	76.3	41.7	49.1	50.9
49266	OSSEO	97.9	97.5	0.3	0.3	0.2	0.4	0.7	0.9	6.2	6.6	6.8	6.5	4.9	26.0	29.5	12.0	1.4	76.2	39.8	50.5	49.5
49267	OTTAWA LAKE	95.8	94.9	2.0	2.2	0.2	0.3	2.2	2.9	5.4	6.0	6.6	6.7	4.9	23.9	32.6	12.6	1.3	77.8	42.4	49.7	50.3
49268	PALMYRA	87.8	84.0	0.5	0.6	0.2	0.3	12.7	17.1	6.3	6.3	7.0	8.2	5.9	25.2	27.2	12.1	1.8	75.2	38.8	52.1	47.9
49269	PARMA	97.2	96.3	0.6	0.8	0.3	0.6	1.5	2.1	6.2	7.6	7.9	7.2	5.0	24.4	30.3	10.1	1.2	73.3	39.8	50.8	49.2
49270	PETERSBURG	98.0	97.5	0.2	0.2	0.1	0.2	2.0	2.7	6.4	6.7	7.1	7.4	5.2	26.4	29.8	10.0	1.0	75.1	38.9	51.3	48.7
49271	PITTSFORD	97.9	97.5	0.0	0.1	0.1	0.1	0.9	1.2	6.3	6.8	7.0	6.7	5.3	24.8	29.0	12.6	1.4	75.6	40.0	49.7	50.3
49272	PLEASANT LAKE	97.5	96.7	0.3	0.4	0.1	0.2	1.8	2.6	5.7	6.5	6.9	7.0	4.7	26.4	30.7	11.1	1.1	76.6	41.0	51.4	48.6
49274	READING	98.1	97.8	0.2	0.2	0.2	0.3	1.1	1.4	6.7	6.9	7.1	7.8	5.4	24.3	28.9	11.4	1.5	74.0	38.7	50.8	49.2
49276	RIGA	96.2	95.0	0.2	0.2	0.1	0.2	4.8	6.7	6.2	6.8	7.4	7.0	5.1	23.3	30.8	12.0	1.5	75.3	40.8	51.7	48.3
49277	RIVES JUNCTION	97.6	96.9	0.2	0.3	0.2	0.2	1.5	2.1	6.1	6.7	7.3	7.4	4.8	24.2	31.4	11.0	1.0	75.2	40.6	50.7	49.3
49279	SAND CREEK	97.1	96.4	0.3	0.3	0.1	0.2	3.3	4.5	5.6	6.0	6.4	7.2	5.6	24.4	31.7	11.6	1.4	77.6	41.0	51.1	48.9
49283	SPRING ARBOR	96.2	94.8	1.2	1.6	0.9	1.5	1.7	2.3	5.1	4.7	4.7	11.3	14.8	20.5	21.7	12.6	4.6	81.5	33.0	45.7	54.3
49284	SPRINGPORT	97.1	96.3	0.4	0.5	0.2	0.3	1.1	1.5	6.3	6.4	6.5	6.5	6.4	24.8	29.3	12.7	1.2	77.0	40.1	50.5	49.5
49285	STOCKBRIDGE	97.1	96.1	0.3	0.4	0.2	0.4	1.9	2.7	6.8	7.0	7.2	7.1	5.6	26.6	28.4	9.7	1.7	74.3	38.1	50.0	50.0
49286	TECUMSEH	96.3	95.2	0.3	0.3	0.6	0.9	3.9	5.3	6.4	6.5	6.8	6.6	5.7	25.4	29.2	11.2	2.0	75.9	39.8	48.8	51.2
49287	TIPTON	97.7	96.9	0.1	0.2	0.2	0.4	1.6	2.2	5.7	6.3	7.1	7.3	4.3	24.4	33.1	10.7	1.0	76.4	41.7	50.5	49.5
49288	WALDRON	98.1	97.7	0.2	0.2	0.0	0.1	0.9	1.2	6.8	7.0	7.5	7.4	5.6	25.1	27.1	12.2	1.3	73.7	37.7	49.8	50.2
49301	ADA	95.9	93.8	0.6	0.8	2.1	3.4	1.0	1.6	6.6	7.6	9.1	8.5	4.2	20.3	34.1	8.9	0.8	71.1	40.9	49.9	50.1
49302	ALTO	97.6	96.6	0.3	0.4	0.8	1.3	1.2	1.8	6.7	7.5	8.3	8.5	4.8	24.2	31.8	7.6	0.7	71.9	38.6	50.2	49.8
49303	BAILEY	94.5	92.4	0.3	0.4	0.0	0.1	5.6	7.8	6.4	6.5	6.8	8.1	6.6	27.3	28.0	9.4	0.9	75.0	37.3	52.1	47.9
49304	BALDWIN	75.6	72.7	19.4	21.7	0.2	0.3	2.1	2.7	4.5	4.2	5.0	9.3	4.3	17.3	32.1	20.3	2.8	81.8	49.2	53.1	46.9
49305	BARRYTON	97.2	96.6	0.7	0.8	0.1	0.2	1.1	1.6	5.5	5.6	5.7	5.9	5.2	21.2	30.0	19.0	1.9	79.4	45.7	49.5	50.5
49306	BELMONT	97.1	95.8	0.6	0.9	0.7	1.2	1.4	2.2	7.2	7.8	8.2	7.8	5.4	23.1	31.0	8.5	1.1	71.6	37.9	50.6	49.4
49307	BIG RAPIDS	88.6	84.3	6.7	9.3	1.7	2.7	1.5	2.3	5.7	4.9	4.8	11.7	20.1	23.3	19.5	8.5	1.7	81.4	27.0	52.4	47.6
49309	BITELY	89.6	87.9	5.8	6.5	0.2	0.3	2.8	3.6	6.6	6.7	7.1	6.8	4.7	22.4	29.0	15.4	1.4	75.1	41.3	51.5	48.5
49310	BLANCHARD	96.1	95.3	0.8	0.9	0.3	0.5	1.7	2.3	6.9	7.0	7.5	6.9	4.8	25.8	28.4	11.5	1.3	74.2	39.0	51.0	49.0
49315	BYRON CENTER	97.3	96.0	0.5	0.7	0.7	1.3	1.2	1.9	7.0	7.2	7.4	7.5	5.2	25.6	27.5	11.2	1.3	73.4	37.9	49.8	50.2
49316	CALEDONIA	95.8	93.7	1.1	1.7	1.3	2.2	1.5	2.3	7.4	7.3	7.6	7.3	5.0	25.4	27.7	11.3	1.0	73.0	38.0	49.5	50.5
49318	CASNOVIA	95.3	93.4	0.2	0.3	0.1	0.2	5.5	7.8	6.5	7.2	7.5	7.8	5.4	27.9	26.7	9.5	1.4	73.7	37.2	51.8	48.2
49319	CEDAR SPRINGS	96.9	95.7	0.2	0.3	0.4	0.7	2.1	3.2	7.6	7.7	7.7	7.5	5.8	27.0	27.3	8.3	1.1	72.2	35.8	49.7	50.3
49321	COMSTOCK PARK	90.6	87.7	2.7	3.3	1.5	2.2	5.5	7.8	7.9	7.1	6.6	6.5	8.3	32.6	22.4	7.7	0.8	74.8	31.2	50.6	49.4
49322	CORAL	97.5	96.9	0.2	0.2	0.3	0.5	0.7	0.9	6.4	7.9	9.2	8.8	5.3	24.7	25.9	10.7	1.1	71.0	36.5	50.5	49.5
49323	DORR	97.0	96.3	0.4	0.5	0.3	0.4	2.0	2.7	8.4	8.1	8.1	8.0	5.6	29.5	25.4	6.2	0.7	70.3	33.7	50.5	49.5
49325	FREEPORT	97.2	96.7	0.4	0.4	0.2	0.3	1.3	1.9	7.3	7.8	8.1	7.7	4.9	26.0	28.8	8.7	0.8	71.9	37.4	50.1	49.9
49326	GOWEN	97.3	96.4	0.8	1.1	0.2	0.4	1.3	2.0	5.7	6.1	6.6	7.1	5.8	25.2	30.9	11.5	1.2	77.1	40.7	51.3	48.7
49327	GRANT	93.8	92.2	0.4	0.4	0.2	0.3	8.4	11.0	7.9	7.7	7.9	7.9	6.4	26.2	26.1	8.7	1.2	71.5	34.5	50.8	49.2
49328	HOPKINS	94.3	92.6	0.4	0.4	0.4	0.7	4.0	5.5	7.5	7.8	7.9	7.8	5.6	25.8	28.1	8.4	1.1	71.8	36.3	51.5	48.5
49329	HOWARD CITY	96.4	95.5	0.3	0.4	0.3	0.5	1.8	2.4	8.0	7.9	8.0	7.5	5.7	27.2	25.7	9.2	0.9	71.2	35.5	49.5	50.5
49330	KENT CITY	96.6	95.1	0.2	0.2	0.2	0.3	5.1	7.9	7.7	7.8	8.4	8.1	6.8	28.2	25.0	7.0	0.9	70.9	33.2	50.3	49.7
49331	LOWELL	96.8	95.6	0.7	0.9	0.6	0.9	2.1	3.2	7.0	7.5	8.2	7.8	5.3	26.3	27.9	8.4	1.5	72.1	37.0	50.0	50.0
49332	MECOSTA	92.9	91.5	2.5	2.9	0.2	0.3	1.4	1.9	6.2	6.1	6.4	6.2	4.2	20.5	28.7	20.0	1.8	77.3	45.3	50.7	49.3
49333	MIDDLEVILLE	97.0	96.2	0.2	0.3	0.4	0.7	1.4	1.8	7.7	8.0	8.0	7.4	5.2	26.7	27.7	8.4	0.9	71.7	36.2	49.9	50.1
49336	MORLEY	96.3	95.6	0.4	0.5	0.2	0.4	0.9	1.3	8.0	7.8	8.0	7.6	5.4	26.3	25.1	10.7	1.1	71.5	35.8	49.6	50.4
49337	NEWAYGO	96.1	95.2	0.3	0.3	0.2	0.4	3.6	4.7	6.7	6.9	7.2	6.9	5.5	24.1	28.4	12.8	1.5	74.7	39.8	50.4	49.6
49338	PARIS	97.3	96.8	0.8	1.0	0.1	0.2	0.7	1.0	6.1	6.3	6.8	7.1	5.0	26.9	28.2	12.2	1.4	76.3	39.1	50.2	49.8
49339	PIERSON	96.9	96.1	0.1	0.1	0.4	0.6	1.1	1.4	7.0	7.7	8.1	7.5	5.2	25.5	28.1	10.1	0.8	72.5	37.5	50.2	49.8
49340	REMUS	95.0	93.9	1.7	2.0	0.1	0.3	1.4	1.8	6.0	6.1	6.5	6.3	4.6	22.4	29.7	16.7	1.6	77.2	43.5	49.8	50.2
49341	ROCKFORD	97.4	96.4	0.4	0.6	0.5	0.9	1.2	1.9	7.9	8.3	8.5	8.0	4.5	25.5	28.6	7.9	0.8	70.1	36.6	49.9	50.1
49342	RODNEY	97.1	96.5	0.3	0.3	0.5	0.8	0.5	0.6	5.0	5.1	5.6	6.3	4.4	21.8	32.1	18.0	1.6	80.1	46.2	51.6	48.4
49343	SAND LAKE	96.6	95.6	0.4	0.5	0.3	0.4	2.3	3.2	7.0	7.0	7.3	7.5	6.0	25.5	29.2	9.6	0.9	73.5	37.8	50.3	49.7
49344	SHELBYVILLE	96.9	96.4	0.3	0.4	0.2	0.4	2.2	3.0	6.1	6.7	7.6	6.2	4.5	24.8	29.6	12.9	1.6	75.4	41.0	51.2	48.8
49345	SPARTA	96.5	95.1	0.4	0.5	0.4	0.6	3.1	4.7	7.4	7.5	7.5	7.5	5.8	27.2	26.9	8.8	1.5	72.7	35.9	49.2	50.8
49346	STANWOOD	97.1	96.3	0.7	0.8	0.3	0.5	1.1	1.6	5.9	5.7	6.0	5.7	4.0	19.8	27.9	22.7	2.2	78.7	47.2	49.5	50.5
49347	TRUFANT	97.5	96.9	0.2	0.2	0.4	0.5	1.2	1.6	6.2	6.6	7.2	6.8	4.5	26.5	27.5	13.0	1.5	75.6	39.5	51.7	48.3
49348	WAYLAND	96.9	96.3	0.4	0.5	0.2	0.4	1.8	2.3	8.1	8.2	7.9	7.0	5.5	27.5	26.3	8.3	1.3	71.3	35.6	49.5	50.5
49349	WHITE CLOUD	93.2	92.0	2.6	2.9	0.2	0.4	2.7	3.5	6.7	6.7	7.5	7.5	6.5	24.3	27.8	11.7	1.3	74.5	38.3	50.7	49.3
49401	ALLENDALE	93.7	91.4	2.7	3.3	0.9	1.6	2.8	4.1	6.9	5.4	4.7	19.6	23.9	23.3	11.7	3.7	0.8	80.7	22.8	47.2	52.8
49402	BRANCH	93.4	92.6	3.1	3.2	0.3	0.4	3.2	4.2	4.4	4.5	5.1	5.6	4.5	21.5	32.8	19.5	2.1	82.6	47.9	51.3	48.7
49403	CONKLIN	94.2	91.9	0.5	0.5	0.2	0.4	6.7	9.6	6.8	7.3	8.0	8.2	5.3	27.0	25.6	9.6	2.2	72.6	36.7	51.0	49.0
49404	COOPERSVILLE	96.9	95.9	0.2	0.2	0.4	0.7	2.6	3.8	7.2	7.4	7.5	7.6	6.2	27.4	26.4	9.0	1.2	73.1	35.3	50.1	49.9
49405	CUSTER	96.8	96.0	0.3	0.4	0.3	0.4	2.5	3.3	4.8	5.1	5.5	6.3	5.0	23.2	31.5	16.6	2.0	80.7	45.1	50.4	49.6
49408	FENNVILLE	87.3	84.3	1.3	1.4	0.4	0.6	17.4	22.2	7.2	7.8	7.9	6.7	5.0	24.6	28.9	10.5	1.5	73.0	38.5	51.1	48.9
49410	FOUNTAIN	93.5	93.9	3.1	2.4	0.3	0.3	1.5	2.0	4.4	5.2	5.4	4.4	4.2	24.2	34.5	15.5	2.2	83.2	46.2	52.9	47.1
49411	FREE SOIL	95.0	93.3	1.5	2.5	0.3	0.4	1.4	2.1	5.0	5.6	6.1	7.3	5.2	23.4	32.8	13.2	1.6	81.6	43.2	52.4	47.6
49412	FREMONT	96.3	95.4	0.5	0.6	0.6	1.0	2.3	3.0	6.7	7.0	7.4	7.2	5.8	23.3	26.7	13.3	2.7	74.0	39.0	48.3	51.7
49415	FRUITPORT	97.3	96.3	0.4	0.5	0.3	0.6	1.7	2.4	5.9	6.6	7.1	7.0	4.6	26.0	30.9	10.6	1.3	75.8	40.3	50.3	49.7
49417	GRAND HAVEN	96.4	95.2	0.3	0.3	0.7	1.2	2.1	3.1	6.6	6.6	6.7	6.6	5.7	27.0	28.1	10.6	2.1	75.8	38.3	49.1	50.9
49418	GRANDVILLE	95.0	92.9	1.4	1.8	1.5	2.5	2.8	4.2	7.7	7.3	7.1	7.0	6.6	28.8	24.2	9.5	1.7	73.3	33.9	48.9	51.1
49419	HAMILTON	96.6	95.5	0.2	0.2	0.7	1.1	3.2	4.4	9.1	8.7	8.0	7.0	6.0	30.0	23.9	6.6	0.7	69.6	32.2	50.5	49.5
49420	HART	87.3	84.4	0.4	0.4	0.1	0.2	16.3	21.0	7.6	7.2	7.1	7.3	6.4	24.9	24.9	11.9	2.7	73.2	36.7	50.4	49.6
49421	HESPERIA	94.1	92.8	1.1	1.3	0.3	0.4	3.3	4.4	6.7	6.8	7.2	7.3	6.0	23.9	28.8	12.0	1.3	74.7	39.0	51.0	49.0
49423	HOLLAND	82.3	78.1	2.0	2.0	2.9	4.4	18.0	22.3	7.6	7.2	6.9	9.0	9.9	25.6	21.1	9.7	2.9	74.2	32.1	48.2	51.8
49424	HOLLAND	84.0	78.8	1.6	1.7	6.0	8.9	12.8	16.7	9.4	8.7	8.1	6.8	5.3	31.3	22.7	6.9	0.8	69.5	32.7	50.3	49.7
49425	HOLTON	96.1	95.0	0.4	0.6	0.2	0.4	1.9	2.6	6.5	6.5	6.9	7.3	6.3	25.7	29.8	10.2	0.9	75.7	38.5	51.5	48.5
49426	HUDSONVILLE	97.6	96.7	0.4	0.4	0.7	1.1	1.4	2.1	8.8	8.6	8.6	8.4	6.1	26.7	23.9	7.6	1.3	68.5	32.5	49.2	50.8
49428	JENISON	96.9	95.6	0.6	0.7	0.9	1.6	1.8	2.6	6.4	6.5	6.8	7.6	7.2	25.5	26.0	11.2	2.7	75.8	36.9	48.1	51.9
49431	LUDINGTON	96.0	95.2	0.6	0.6	0.3	0.5	3.3	4.3	5.6	5.8	6.1	6.6	5.5	22.7	29.9	15.0	2.9	78.4	43.3	48.5	51.5
49435	MARNE	97.4	96.5	0.4	0.5	0.2	0.4	1.9	2.7	6.6	6.9	7.5	7.8	5.1	23.8	29.1	10.7	2.6	74.1	39.7	50.0	50.0
49436	MEARS	89.4	86.7	0.3	0.3	0.2	0.3	12.3	16.2	5.0	5.8	6.7	7.2	5.2	20.9	34.4	13.5	1.3	77.4	44.3	51.9	48.1
	MICHIGAN	80.2	78.3	14.2	14.5	1.8	2.8	3.3	4.1	6.7	6.7	6.8	7.2	6.6	26.3	26.9	10.9	1.9	75.6	37.6	49.2	50.8
	UNITED STATES	75.1	72.0	12.3	12.7	3.8	4.6	12.5	15.7	6.8	6.7	6.6	7.1	6.9	27.0	26.0	10.9	1.9	75.7	36.9	49.2	50.8

ZIP CODE #	POST OFFICE NAME	2009 Per Capita Income	2009 HH Income Base	2009 HOUSEHOLD INCOME DISTRIBUTION (%) Less than $25,000	$25,000 to $49,999	$50,000 to $99,999	$100,000 to $149,999	$150,000 or More	MEDIAN HOUSEHOLD INCOME 2009	2014	2009 National Centile	2009 State Centile	2009 Home Value Base	2009 HOME VALUE DISTRIBUTION (%) Less than $50,000	$50,000 to $89,999	$90,000 to $174,999	$175,000 to $399,999	$400,000 or More	2009 Median Home Value
49245	HOMER	20363	1918	21.5	27.8	43.9	4.1	2.8	50433	52587	62	50	1527	24.8	33.4	31.3	8.6	2.0	80423
49246	HORTON	26922	1366	10.6	26.2	45.5	13.0	4.8	62786	63553	81	81	1236	3.6	11.7	46.4	35.2	3.1	145906
49247	HUDSON	21749	2286	19.8	27.7	43.6	7.2	1.7	51446	52285	65	54	1842	11.7	24.5	45.0	16.9	2.0	108210
49248	JASPER	21823	379	15.6	29.8	47.2	5.8	1.6	53226	53829	68	60	329	10.0	21.9	47.7	19.1	1.2	116598
49249	JEROME	23900	1484	17.8	28.6	42.7	8.0	2.9	52527	51966	67	58	1359	12.1	13.9	35.2	35.9	2.9	141925
49250	JONESVILLE	20965	2247	21.0	31.1	40.2	6.2	1.5	47663	49103	56	43	1799	15.6	23.3	45.6	14.1	1.3	102981
49251	LESLIE	23556	2495	15.2	25.4	47.4	9.4	2.6	58418	58838	76	72	2127	9.4	22.0	51.8	15.7	1.1	110914
49252	LITCHFIELD	20067	1084	24.0	27.4	41.1	6.5	1.0	48065	49521	57	44	805	13.5	26.5	46.8	12.9	0.2	99471
49253	MANITOU BEACH	25761	1208	20.9	26.2	36.2	12.3	4.3	53232	54424	68	60	1034	3.6	13.8	34.3	40.5	7.7	170545
49254	MICHIGAN CENTER	23404	1426	19.2	26.8	44.1	8.5	1.4	53171	55553	68	60	1204	7.7	28.9	54.7	8.5	0.2	100870
49255	MONTGOMERY	16981	670	24.0	30.0	40.0	4.2	1.8	46152	49080	52	39	554	17.1	22.6	40.3	16.4	3.6	105044
49256	MORENCI	21094	1577	18.2	28.2	46.2	5.4	2.0	52309	53556	67	57	1211	8.7	27.2	48.6	13.5	2.0	105572
49259	MUNITH	23420	1121	14.4	24.3	51.1	7.3	2.9	58341	60014	76	72	1009	21.7	17.4	37.0	22.6	1.3	110900
49262	NORTH ADAMS	20171	588	19.2	32.7	42.9	3.9	1.4	47983	49708	57	44	497	9.5	28.2	44.9	14.9	2.6	102060
49264	ONONDAGA	19676	668	18.3	27.8	46.3	6.3	1.3	53012	54895	68	59	585	12.3	22.1	47.9	17.4	0.3	110348
49265	ONSTED	27333	1955	13.5	22.4	44.6	14.1	5.4	63818	62444	82	83	1718	1.0	6.1	33.4	50.6	9.0	193836
49266	OSSEO	19995	1301	19.9	30.4	43.5	5.8	0.3	49492	50000	60	49	1102	14.5	22.2	44.6	16.4	2.3	110440
49267	OTTAWA LAKE	24638	1584	13.6	24.1	49.1	9.6	3.6	61972	65257	80	79	1370	6.4	17.0	43.0	26.8	6.8	132604
49268	PALMYRA	20967	509	13.6	32.8	43.0	10.0	0.6	53053	53951	68	59	417	5.8	17.0	51.6	24.5	1.2	133627
49269	PARMA	22669	2181	14.5	25.2	48.9	8.4	3.0	60269	60791	78	76	1913	13.2	18.2	46.6	20.5	1.5	121055
49270	PETERSBURG	25515	2140	13.8	20.8	47.9	12.1	5.3	64250	68449	83	83	1832	6.7	16.2	52.5	23.2	1.4	132353
49271	PITTSFORD	19274	782	18.8	30.6	43.6	6.3	0.8	50382	50518	62	50	690	14.1	23.0	44.2	16.1	2.6	107308
49272	PLEASANT LAKE	23634	807	13.0	26.6	52.2	5.8	2.4	60357	60866	78	76	723	7.5	16.9	49.5	23.9	2.2	131715
49274	READING	19427	1247	22.5	33.1	38.0	4.7	1.6	44085	47319	46	32	1036	14.5	27.2	42.6	13.8	1.9	99663
49276	RIGA	24902	367	14.4	23.7	46.9	10.1	4.9	60523	60464	78	77	327	2.1	13.8	47.1	32.7	4.3	149449
49277	RIVES JUNCTION	22104	1183	16.1	21.7	50.5	9.0	2.6	60574	61006	78	77	1078	7.8	23.0	50.1	18.1	1.0	118365
49279	SAND CREEK	19785	420	15.5	29.8	47.6	6.2	1.0	53062	53633	68	60	362	9.9	19.9	45.0	22.1	3.0	120769
49283	SPRING ARBOR	21292	1411	22.6	22.2	43.7	9.4	2.1	55543	57834	72	67	1004	24.2	14.2	41.6	19.0	0.9	117548
49284	SPRINGPORT	21874	1349	17.9	27.7	45.4	7.3	1.8	53055	55076	68	60	1096	12.6	33.2	36.2	16.2	1.7	97667
49285	STOCKBRIDGE	23295	2048	16.5	25.8	45.0	9.9	2.8	56049	56104	73	68	1698	5.0	12.6	53.6	27.4	1.4	135513
49286	TECUMSEH	26404	5925	14.3	23.2	46.9	11.6	3.9	60112	58716	77	75	4697	2.5	7.1	48.4	40.8	1.2	162649
49287	TIPTON	26249	841	11.5	20.6	55.2	8.8	3.9	63124	62241	81	82	768	6.8	6.4	30.7	50.5	5.6	187634
49288	WALDRON	17674	525	27.0	31.8	36.4	4.0	0.8	42493	46040	41	27	427	18.3	28.3	36.8	15.2	1.4	93372
49301	ADA	42078	5267	6.1	12.4	37.1	21.8	22.6	90859	91772	95	97	5029	1.4	1.4	30.5	50.4	16.3	222266
49302	ALTO	29326	2690	6.1	15.7	53.2	16.1	8.9	72002	73331	88	90	2504	2.4	5.4	29.9	55.7	6.5	195412
49303	BAILEY	19467	285	20.0	29.8	40.4	7.4	2.5	50126	52367	61	50	250	9.2	28.8	47.2	14.4	0.4	103261
49304	BALDWIN	17476	1982	42.5	30.9	23.2	2.2	1.2	27762	29195	5	2	1515	30.8	31.0	26.8	9.3	2.1	72670
49305	BARRYTON	18667	996	29.8	36.2	29.3	3.3	1.3	37490	39548	25	10	864	25.3	28.9	32.4	12.3	1.0	82745
49306	BELMONT	29555	3238	7.9	17.7	50.2	16.9	7.2	71517	73526	88	90	3133	16.3	7.9	35.5	36.5	3.7	154688
49307	BIG RAPIDS	18664	6881	36.3	26.1	30.2	5.5	2.0	36750	39401	23	8	3915	11.3	21.7	47.2	17.8	2.1	113114
49309	BITELY	17728	880	34.5	32.8	29.1	2.7	0.8	35536	39654	19	7	761	26.8	36.3	28.3	8.0	0.7	78264
49310	BLANCHARD	19840	1082	22.6	33.1	37.2	5.5	1.5	45207	46578	49	36	949	17.1	22.9	42.4	15.6	2.1	104115
49315	BYRON CENTER	27867	7033	10.7	21.8	51.1	11.3	5.1	64677	66289	83	84	5835	6.8	5.9	46.4	37.0	3.8	158297
49316	CALEDONIA	28283	5993	10.5	19.3	49.3	14.0	7.0	68200	69097	86	89	5319	11.6	9.4	35.2	38.5	5.3	159393
49318	CASNOVIA	22188	605	18.5	24.8	44.0	9.1	3.6	57312	58497	74	70	530	7.2	19.2	53.6	19.6	0.4	116741
49319	CEDAR SPRINGS	22234	5140	15.6	24.7	50.0	7.8	1.9	58220	60995	75	72	4410	15.2	20.1	44.5	19.3	0.9	114933
49321	COMSTOCK PARK	24989	6515	14.7	28.4	45.0	9.2	2.7	55960	59707	73	67	3826	10.2	10.0	57.2	21.4	1.2	133778
49322	CORAL	18612	440	18.2	36.8	40.0	3.9	1.1	45196	47465	49	36	378	8.2	25.4	47.4	17.2	1.9	110870
49323	DORR	23038	3048	10.0	20.9	52.8	14.6	1.7	65043	64018	83	85	2837	5.3	7.8	44.7	39.0	3.2	160233
49325	FREEPORT	20565	625	12.0	26.4	53.9	5.6	2.1	59148	60896	76	73	566	7.4	13.4	49.6	26.9	2.7	136000
49326	GOWEN	22200	1152	16.9	23.3	52.7	6.2	1.0	59034	60527	76	73	1048	16.7	19.2	43.1	20.6	0.4	110906
49327	GRANT	17841	2981	23.1	27.4	43.0	5.5	0.9	49358	50067	60	48	2513	14.1	25.3	45.0	14.2	1.4	103980
49328	HOPKINS	20551	1434	18.8	24.6	46.2	8.0	2.3	55009	54730	71	65	1246	7.5	12.9	49.7	27.3	2.6	137374
49329	HOWARD CITY	18759	2862	19.1	30.0	45.6	4.9	0.5	50484	50322	62	51	2439	11.9	19.5	48.4	19.1	1.1	116222
49330	KENT CITY	20492	1720	15.2	26.0	48.2	8.5	2.0	58000	60763	75	71	1497	18.9	18.4	47.0	14.1	1.6	105661
49331	LOWELL	23469	5842	15.0	21.2	50.5	10.7	2.6	62126	63958	80	80	4976	12.3	9.3	43.7	30.8	3.8	138233
49332	MECOSTA	21349	1266	27.2	32.4	35.0	3.5	2.0	40640	42733	35	20	1089	17.0	23.7	37.7	20.4	1.2	105787
49333	MIDDLEVILLE	24069	4045	10.7	25.1	50.8	9.8	3.5	61301	62105	79	79	3577	9.7	11.5	47.2	28.4	3.2	136715
49336	MORLEY	16968	1524	25.2	34.2	35.2	4.4	1.0	41815	43283	39	24	1249	20.7	24.8	36.8	16.2	1.5	97244
49337	NEWAYGO	20412	5044	23.0	29.8	40.2	5.8	1.2	46848	48704	54	41	4339	16.5	26.9	39.9	15.9	0.9	100316
49338	PARIS	17753	817	29.9	31.9	32.9	4.2	1.1	40894	43244	36	21	699	14.4	27.8	42.3	14.7	0.7	99237
49339	PIERSON	21463	846	13.9	27.2	49.2	7.7	2.0	55319	53903	72	66	764	4.3	16.8	49.1	25.8	4.1	135744
49340	REMUS	19497	1164	25.9	31.3	36.1	4.7	2.0	43600	45159	44	30	998	16.2	24.7	36.3	20.6	2.1	106475
49341	ROCKFORD	29154	11717	10.9	16.2	47.5	17.8	7.7	72319	75127	88	91	10349	7.0	5.5	41.6	41.6	4.3	165253
49342	RODNEY	21141	717	23.0	33.5	36.8	4.6	2.1	43526	45000	44	30	620	12.1	20.5	41.5	23.7	2.3	119837
49343	SAND LAKE	20915	2217	17.7	25.4	50.0	6.1	0.7	55175	56026	71	66	2013	14.3	19.8	47.9	17.0	0.9	114019
49344	SHELBYVILLE	24271	1311	15.0	28.9	45.8	7.7	2.6	54338	55520	70	63	1155	11.3	8.5	42.6	32.5	5.2	150260
49345	SPARTA	22524	4832	15.3	26.7	47.9	8.1	2.0	57106	60559	74	70	4004	15.9	18.2	45.7	18.2	2.0	114334
49346	STANWOOD	26362	2261	18.4	26.8	43.5	7.5	3.9	53717	53566	69	61	1964	9.1	15.6	40.9	31.5	2.9	136441
49347	TRUFANT	20220	523	19.5	35.9	39.2	4.2	1.2	44003	46444	45	32	461	7.4	21.9	57.0	12.4	1.3	114266
49348	WAYLAND	22835	4611	13.9	27.1	47.3	9.0	2.8	57991	57834	75	71	3849	15.1	8.8	42.0	30.6	3.4	140850
49349	WHITE CLOUD	17130	3345	31.4	30.8	32.4	4.7	0.7	40466	43763	34	19	2686	27.0	32.3	33.0	7.1	0.6	80421
49401	ALLENDALE	20924	4403	14.5	24.8	44.5	10.8	5.3	62243	63213	80	80	3070	19.0	8.4	43.1	28.2	1.3	139639
49402	BRANCH	20655	769	32.0	34.1	28.6	4.2	1.2	36141	38336	21	7	660	21.4	28.2	37.0	11.8	1.7	90714
49403	CONKLIN	21236	909	14.9	26.3	50.6	5.9	2.3	60205	62042	78	75	810	9.5	13.1	44.8	30.2	2.3	136310
49404	COOPERSVILLE	24130	2999	16.3	20.0	51.1	8.3	4.3	63679	66099	82	83	2508	16.7	9.8	46.9	23.3	3.3	131959
49405	CUSTER	17560	608	29.3	33.6	31.4	4.8	1.0	38712	41271	29	14	517	17.8	26.7	40.8	12.8	1.9	98143
49408	FENNVILLE	22658	3913	19.3	26.4	45.0	6.6	2.7	52851	53524	68	59	3304	13.3	12.6	37.9	29.4	6.8	141545
49410	FOUNTAIN	20305	757	29.6	31.3	33.0	4.1	2.0	38306	41197	28	12	667	20.5	24.9	39.0	14.1	1.5	97093
49411	FREE SOIL	19440	627	25.4	30.6	37.8	5.1	1.1	44913	45751	48	35	555	15.1	24.1	44.1	13.9	2.7	103496
49412	FREMONT	20650	4342	24.0	28.7	39.4	6.2	1.8	46742	48842	53	40	3497	13.3	27.6	44.9	13.3	0.9	100869
49415	FRUITPORT	23063	2274	15.8	27.4	46.0	7.7	3.0	57506	57807	75	71	2023	6.3	19.7	51.5	20.2	2.3	123149
49417	GRAND HAVEN	29046	11897	13.1	21.9	46.0	13.4	5.6	64934	67975	83	85	9617	9.4	9.6	43.2	34.4	3.5	145966
49418	GRANDVILLE	27789	10405	11.4	23.1	45.1	13.9	6.5	65119	67767	83	85	7778	4.6	7.4	51.5	34.2	2.2	151943
49419	HAMILTON	24282	2599	8.7	20.0	57.2	10.7	3.4	64210	64781	83	83	2346	8.4	8.5	30.7	48.8	3.6	179758
49420	HART	16111	2271	31.4	30.6	33.3	3.6	1.1	38191	41154	27	12	1740	16.7	29.8	40.5	11.2	1.8	93885
49421	HESPERIA	17704	2263	29.0	32.7	33.1	4.2	0.9	39354	42587	31	16	1941	20.7	28.0	40.0	10.4	1.0	91606
49423	HOLLAND	24480	17426	16.5	25.2	44.3	9.3	4.7	58390	59011	76	72	12515	5.9	14.4	45.5	29.8	4.3	140409
49424	HOLLAND	28594	16174	9.4	20.1	49.0	14.5	7.0	69626	74643	87	89	12589	12.6	6.0	41.2	34.9	5.4	154854
49425	HOLTON	18734	1344	20.8	31.6	40.0	5.9	1.6	47445	50644	55	42	1163	20.8	27.9	39.2	11.3	0.9	91505
49426	HUDSONVILLE	26090	10796	8.8	16.3	55.0	14.6	5.3	70987	75385	87	90	9542	6.2	6.0	42.2	43.5	2.2	167428
49428	JENISON	26766	9224	12.1	16.8	52.1	14.3	4.7	68738	72667	86	89	7771	3.1	6.7	61.7	26.6	2.0	148318
49431	LUDINGTON	21574	7364	27.8	29.0	35.3	6.0	1.9	42325	44701	40	26	5405	9.3	23.5	43.9	20.6	2.7	111713
49435	MARNE	24292	1263	13.2	17.4	55.9	9.2	4.3	66522	70758	85	88	1153	3.6	9.3	46.7	36.3	4.2	155857
49436	MEARS	21700	802	23.9	30.7	38.2	5.2	2.0	45635	46262	50	37	669	10.6	20.2	39.5	23.6	6.1	120668
	MICHIGAN	26713		20.1	24.2	38.5	11.3	5.9	55536	56866				13.2	21.9	40.3	21.5	3.2	115137
	UNITED STATES	27277		20.9	24.4	35.3	11.7	7.6	54719	56938				9.3	13.1	31.6	32.6	13.5	162279

ZIP CODE	FINANCIAL SERVICES				THE HOME						ENTERTAINMENT						PERSONAL			
					Home Improvements		Furnishings													
# POST OFFICE NAME	Auto Loan	Home Loan	Investments	Retirement Plans	Home Repair	Lawn & Garden	Computers & Hardware-Personal	Major Appliances	TV, Radio, Sound Equipment	Furniture	Dine out/ Carry out	Sports Equipment	Fees & Tickets	Toys & Games	Travel	Cable TV	Apparel & Services	Auto Repairs	Health Insurance	Pets & Supplies
49245 HOMER	85	73	69	75	72	86	77	81	80	71	78	62	69	82	72	84	54	79	87	97
49246 HORTON	98	113	105	116	112	111	100	105	97	102	98	80	108	99	107	97	69	100	102	122
49247 HUDSON	84	80	72	82	78	89	79	83	81	73	80	64	76	83	78	84	55	80	88	99
49248 JASPER	90	82	81	85	84	96	81	91	83	73	82	69	75	85	81	88	56	84	94	106
49249 JEROME	99	82	100	82	84	101	81	95	86	78	85	72	72	86	82	91	57	89	97	113
49250 JONESVILLE	86	75	74	75	75	86	75	82	78	72	77	61	68	80	72	82	52	78	85	97
49251 LESLIE	92	95	81	97	91	98	90	92	91	88	91	72	91	93	91	93	63	91	96	110
49252 LITCHFIELD	86	69	73	69	69	86	70	80	75	66	74	61	60	77	66	80	50	75	83	95
49253 MANITOU BEACH	95	89	97	91	90	102	86	97	88	81	87	73	82	88	89	92	59	91	98	113
49254 MICHIGAN CENTER	82	82	76	83	81	91	78	85	81	73	80	63	78	82	80	85	55	81	91	99
49255 MONTGOMERY	85	69	77	69	70	86	70	80	74	65	73	61	60	76	67	79	49	75	83	95
49256 MORENCI	83	80	71	82	78	89	79	83	81	73	80	64	76	82	78	84	55	80	88	98
49259 MUNITH	98	93	85	93	92	98	88	95	90	87	90	71	84	93	86	93	61	90	96	112
49262 NORTH ADAMS	80	73	72	76	74	86	72	81	74	65	73	61	66	76	72	79	50	75	84	94
49264 ONONDAGA	87	82	75	82	82	88	78	84	80	78	80	63	75	83	77	83	55	80	85	99
49265 ONSTED	103	112	101	116	110	113	102	107	101	101	101	83	106	103	107	101	70	103	106	126
49266 OSSEO	80	73	72	76	75	86	72	81	74	65	73	62	67	76	72	79	50	75	84	94
49267 OTTAWA LAKE	90	104	91	106	101	102	92	96	91	93	92	74	100	93	98	92	64	92	96	112
49268 PALMYRA	83	87	82	89	86	94	80	87	82	76	81	66	82	83	84	85	56	82	90	101
49269 PARMA	93	93	86	95	92	100	88	95	89	84	88	73	87	91	89	91	61	90	96	111
49270 PETERSBURG	98	112	98	114	109	107	101	103	99	101	100	81	109	101	107	99	70	101	102	121
49271 PITTSFORD	82	75	74	78	76	88	74	83	76	67	75	63	68	78	74	81	51	77	86	97
49272 PLEASANT LAKE	87	93	83	96	92	96	85	90	85	84	85	70	88	87	89	86	59	86	90	106
49274 READING	85	70	82	71	72	88	70	82	74	66	73	62	62	75	70	80	49	77	85	97
49276 RIGA	100	103	94	106	102	109	95	103	96	92	95	79	96	98	98	98	66	97	104	120
49277 RIVES JUNCTION	90	96	87	99	95	100	88	94	88	86	88	72	91	90	92	90	61	89	95	110
49279 SAND CREEK	84	81	79	84	82	92	78	86	80	72	79	65	75	81	79	84	54	81	89	100
49283 SPRING ARBOR	77	80	78	79	81	84	79	80	82	80	82	58	82	79	81	85	57	81	90	94
49284 SPRINGPORT	85	81	73	84	79	91	80	85	82	74	81	66	77	84	79	86	55	82	90	101
49285 STOCKBRIDGE	89	95	89	96	94	96	90	93	90	87	90	72	93	91	93	91	63	91	94	109
49286 TECUMSEH	93	100	91	101	98	100	95	96	94	93	94	74	98	95	97	95	66	95	98	113
49287 TIPTON	97	110	95	113	107	108	98	102	96	98	97	80	105	99	104	97	68	98	101	120
49288 WALDRON	80	62	68	62	63	79	64	73	69	60	67	56	54	71	60	74	46	69	77	88
49301 ADA	166	211	208	217	214	191	177	184	167	190	169	143	205	170	197	160	123	173	165	209
49302 ALTO	120	145	129	147	141	132	125	128	119	129	121	101	138	123	134	116	86	122	119	148
49303 BAILEY	97	77	83	77	77	97	78	90	84	74	82	68	67	87	74	90	56	84	94	107
49304 BALDWIN	59	50	66	47	54	64	50	60	54	50	53	42	46	51	52	58	35	57	66	70
49305 BARRYTON	76	59	81	56	62	79	59	73	65	57	63	53	50	63	60	70	42	68	78	86
49306 BELMONT	118	134	121	132	131	124	118	122	115	124	116	94	126	118	124	113	82	118	116	142
49307 BIG RAPIDS	70	55	53	57	54	59	73	62	70	65	70	51	61	70	61	70	49	67	64	76
49309 BITELY	74	53	76	52	55	75	55	69	61	51	60	52	44	60	54	67	39	64	72	83
49310 BLANCHARD	85	71	80	71	72	88	70	82	75	66	74	62	62	76	69	80	49	76	85	97
49315 BYRON CENTER	105	118	106	119	115	113	108	110	106	108	107	86	115	108	113	106	75	107	108	128
49316 CALEDONIA	114	122	106	123	118	113	113	113	110	117	111	89	117	114	115	107	78	111	107	132
49318 CASNOVIA	96	89	87	92	89	102	86	96	89	80	88	73	81	91	86	93	60	90	99	113
49319 CEDAR SPRINGS	94	92	80	91	89	93	87	90	88	88	88	68	85	91	85	90	61	88	91	107
49321 COMSTOCK PARK	91	84	75	86	80	81	92	84	91	90	92	68	89	94	87	90	65	89	85	101
49322 CORAL	78	71	70	74	73	84	70	79	72	64	71	60	65	74	70	77	49	73	82	92
49323 DORR	106	109	92	106	104	100	99	101	97	104	98	77	99	102	97	96	68	97	95	118
49325 FREEPORT	90	95	84	97	93	96	87	91	87	86	87	70	89	89	89	88	60	88	91	108
49326 GOWEN	91	84	85	84	84	92	80	89	82	79	82	66	76	84	80	86	56	84	89	104
49327 GRANT	87	73	71	71	72	82	71	78	76	72	75	58	64	79	67	80	51	75	80	94
49328 HOPKINS	91	88	82	89	87	95	83	91	85	80	85	69	80	87	83	88	58	86	92	107
49329 HOWARD CITY	83	76	68	74	75	79	72	77	75	74	75	56	68	78	69	77	51	74	77	91
49330 KENT CITY	92	91	81	91	89	94	87	91	87	86	87	70	85	90	86	89	60	88	91	107
49331 LOWELL	97	101	88	102	98	98	94	96	94	96	94	74	96	97	95	94	65	94	95	113
49332 MECOSTA	82	65	97	63	71	87	65	81	70	63	69	59	57	67	68	75	46	75	84	95
49333 MIDDLEVILLE	98	104	92	104	101	101	94	98	93	96	94	74	96	96	96	94	65	94	95	115
49336 MORLEY	83	65	70	64	65	81	66	75	71	64	70	57	56	74	61	76	47	71	78	90
49337 NEWAYGO	85	72	78	71	73	84	71	80	75	70	74	60	64	77	70	79	50	76	82	95
49338 PARIS	76	64	68	62	64	73	62	70	66	62	66	52	56	68	60	69	44	67	71	83
49339 PIERSON	94	86	81	87	86	96	83	92	86	80	85	68	78	89	82	90	58	86	93	107
49340 REMUS	87	67	97	65	71	90	67	85	72	63	71	63	57	71	69	78	47	78	86	99
49341 ROCKFORD	119	136	119	136	132	122	120	122	115	126	117	96	129	120	125	112	83	117	112	140
49342 RODNEY	88	71	98	70	74	92	70	86	75	67	74	64	61	73	73	80	49	80	87	101
49343 SAND LAKE	92	83	82	81	82	89	79	87	82	80	82	63	74	84	77	85	55	83	87	102
49344 SHELBYVILLE	91	89	88	91	91	101	85	95	87	80	86	70	82	88	87	91	59	88	98	109
49345 SPARTA	87	91	80	92	88	91	86	88	86	85	86	68	88	88	87	87	60	86	89	103
49346 STANWOOD	94	90	108	89	97	102	84	96	88	90	87	65	84	85	89	92	59	92	101	111
49347 TRUFANT	78	71	70	74	72	83	70	79	72	63	71	60	64	73	70	76	48	73	81	91
49348 WAYLAND	97	94	88	93	92	96	88	94	89	89	89	71	86	92	88	91	61	90	93	111
49349 WHITE CLOUD	79	58	68	56	58	76	61	70	67	58	66	54	50	69	56	73	44	67	75	85
49401 ALLENDALE	104	92	79	92	87	85	107	92	100	103	101	76	95	105	92	97	71	97	88	111
49402 BRANCH	74	57	79	55	61	77	58	72	63	56	62	52	49	61	59	68	41	67	76	84
49403 CONKLIN	90	94	85	97	93	98	87	93	87	84	87	72	88	89	90	89	60	88	93	109
49404 COOPERSVILLE	102	104	90	103	100	101	97	100	96	99	97	76	97	100	97	97	67	97	97	117
49405 CUSTER	79	59	80	58	61	81	60	75	66	56	65	57	49	66	60	73	43	69	79	89
49408 FENNVILLE	94	84	89	85	86	96	82	92	85	79	84	68	76	86	82	89	57	86	93	108
49410 FOUNTAIN	83	62	94	61	66	86	63	80	68	59	67	60	52	67	65	74	45	74	82	95
49411 FREE SOIL	87	64	96	63	68	89	66	83	72	61	70	62	54	70	67	78	47	77	85	98
49412 FREMONT	85	74	82	74	75	89	75	84	79	71	77	63	68	79	74	83	53	80	88	99
49415 FRUITPORT	91	96	85	98	94	98	88	93	88	87	88	72	90	90	91	89	61	89	93	109
49417 GRAND HAVEN	104	110	100	109	107	107	104	105	103	106	104	80	107	105	105	104	72	103	106	122
49418 GRANDVILLE	105	115	103	116	111	107	108	106	106	112	107	83	115	109	110	104	76	106	104	124
49419 HAMILTON	108	113	95	111	108	102	102	105	99	107	100	82	103	105	101	97	70	99	97	121
49420 HART	76	57	68	57	58	75	61	70	66	57	65	53	50	67	57	72	43	67	75	84
49421 HESPERIA	82	59	77	57	60	81	61	75	68	58	66	57	49	69	58	74	44	69	78	90
49423 HOLLAND	96	96	86	95	94	91	96	94	94	97	95	73	95	96	94	93	66	95	92	110
49424 HOLLAND	117	128	110	125	122	113	115	116	111	121	113	90	119	117	116	108	79	112	107	134
49425 HOLTON	93	71	79	70	70	90	72	83	78	70	77	64	61	81	67	85	52	78	87	100
49426 HUDSONVILLE	114	126	107	125	121	115	113	114	109	117	111	89	118	114	115	107	77	110	108	133
49428 JENISON	104	116	103	116	112	109	106	106	104	108	105	82	113	106	110	104	74	105	106	124
49431 LUDINGTON	77	69	77	69	70	80	71	77	74	67	73	57	66	73	71	77	50	75	81	90
49435 MARNE	104	110	99	113	108	114	101	108	101	98	101	83	103	103	105	103	70	102	108	126
49436 MEARS	89	71	115	70	78	94	71	91	75	67	74	66	62	71	77	80	49	84	90	105
MICHIGAN	98	97	93	98	95	100	96	97	97	95	97	74	96	98	96	99	68	97	100	115
UNITED STATES	100	100	100	100	100	100	100	100	100	100	100	100	100	100	100	100	100	100	100	100

POPULATION CHANGE

ZIP CODE #	POST OFFICE NAME	COUNTY FIPS CODE	POPULATION 2000	POPULATION 2009	POPULATION 2014	2000-2009 ANNUAL RATE % Rate	2000-2009 ANNUAL RATE State Centile	HOUSEHOLDS 2000	HOUSEHOLDS 2009	HOUSEHOLDS 2014	HOUSEHOLDS % Annual Rate 2000-2009	HOUSEHOLDS 2009 Average HH Size	FAMILIES 2000	FAMILIES 2009	FAMILIES % Annual Rate 2000-2009
49437	MONTAGUE	121	6791	7075	7187	0.4	60	2619	2780	2839	0.6	2.52	1915	2007	0.5
49440	MUSKEGON	121	1025	1041	1044	0.2	48	385	392	394	0.2	2.03	144	142	-0.2
49441	MUSKEGON	121	34899	35411	35522	0.2	48	14483	14905	15026	0.3	2.34	9442	9556	0.1
49442	MUSKEGON	121	45629	46150	46227	0.1	42	15752	16108	16206	0.2	2.60	10459	10541	0.1
49444	MUSKEGON	121	27173	27962	28047	0.3	54	10305	10730	10806	0.4	2.55	7138	7351	0.3
49445	MUSKEGON	121	20982	22423	22979	0.7	76	7761	8440	8700	0.9	2.64	5974	6429	0.8
49446	NEW ERA	127	2248	2329	2346	0.4	60	793	836	846	0.6	2.76	619	647	0.5
49448	NUNICA	139	3370	3492	3528	0.4	60	1232	1311	1336	0.7	2.65	956	1008	0.6
49449	PENTWATER	127	2789	3041	3185	0.9	82	1192	1337	1410	1.2	2.25	852	943	1.1
49450	PULLMAN	005	3498	3983	4186	1.4	92	1093	1234	1297	1.3	3.20	828	926	1.2
49451	RAVENNA	121	5559	5934	6086	0.7	76	1897	2066	2131	0.9	2.85	1528	1648	0.8
49452	ROTHBURY	127	1833	1962	2039	0.7	76	651	710	741	0.9	2.75	500	540	0.8
49453	SAUGATUCK	005	3020	3387	3558	1.2	88	1423	1633	1728	1.5	2.04	793	889	1.2
49454	SCOTTVILLE	105	4472	4479	4458	0.0	37	1691	1731	1730	0.3	2.54	1248	1256	0.1
49455	SHELBY	127	5396	5521	5603	0.2	48	1939	2016	2055	0.4	2.71	1447	1490	0.3
49456	SPRING LAKE	139	17984	19308	19934	0.8	80	7170	7910	8232	1.1	2.40	4965	5408	0.9
49457	TWIN LAKE	121	9018	10257	10755	1.4	92	3284	3815	4027	1.6	2.68	2501	2874	1.5
49459	WALKERVILLE	127	1440	1513	1566	0.5	66	505	543	566	0.8	2.60	373	397	0.7
49460	WEST OLIVE	139	8459	9277	9554	1.0	84	2723	3068	3192	1.3	2.91	2243	2515	1.2
49461	WHITEHALL	121	8234	8643	8763	0.5	66	3103	3304	3364	0.7	2.56	2253	2370	0.5
49464	ZEELAND	139	22935	27778	29928	2.1	97	7566	9318	10099	2.3	2.95	5872	7201	2.2
49503	GRAND RAPIDS	081	37896	39154	39505	0.4	60	14799	15290	15466	0.4	2.41	7115	7153	0.1
49504	GRAND RAPIDS	081	39854	41580	42225	0.5	66	15288	16188	16510	0.6	2.53	9515	9884	0.4
49505	GRAND RAPIDS	081	31932	32267	32396	0.1	42	12793	13193	13324	0.3	2.35	7917	7974	0.1
49506	GRAND RAPIDS	081	36248	35776	35581	-0.1	32	12318	12395	12392	0.1	2.58	8185	8081	-0.1
49507	GRAND RAPIDS	081	39793	39932	39790	0.0	37	12732	12771	12751	0.0	3.09	9044	8918	-0.2
49508	GRAND RAPIDS	081	38048	37993	38083	0.0	37	14538	14775	14885	0.2	2.54	9922	9886	0.0
49509	WYOMING	081	26131	26304	26389	0.1	42	9855	10052	10118	0.2	2.59	6615	6622	0.0
49512	GRAND RAPIDS	081	11911	14685	15816	2.3	98	5803	7063	7576	2.1	2.06	2820	3491	2.3
49519	WYOMING	081	27216	29007	29772	0.7	76	11026	11987	12370	0.9	2.41	6818	7194	0.6
49525	GRAND RAPIDS	081	26876	28577	29273	0.7	76	9872	10664	10977	0.8	2.61	7117	7587	0.7
49534	GRAND RAPIDS	081	19457	22195	23313	1.4	92	7448	8628	9114	1.6	2.56	5097	5808	1.4
49544	GRAND RAPIDS	081	8959	9084	9183	0.1	42	3614	3740	3802	0.4	2.37	2134	2157	0.1
49546	GRAND RAPIDS	081	28040	30637	31744	1.0	84	10735	11891	12373	1.1	2.50	7406	8101	1.0
49548	GRAND RAPIDS	081	32196	31756	31635	-0.1	32	12535	12512	12510	0.0	2.52	8229	8040	-0.3
49601	CADILLAC	165	20312	21074	21201	0.4	60	8017	8503	8612	0.6	2.44	5586	5853	0.5
49612	ALDEN	009	1037	1114	1123	0.8	80	440	487	493	1.1	2.29	310	340	1.0
49613	ARCADIA	101	773	828	840	0.7	76	348	378	386	0.9	2.18	248	267	0.8
49614	BEAR LAKE	101	2631	2836	2850	0.8	80	1061	1167	1182	1.0	2.39	748	812	0.9
49615	BELLAIRE	009	4025	4214	4272	0.5	66	1645	1773	1813	0.8	2.29	1181	1260	0.7
49616	BENZONIA	019	2041	2344	2483	1.5	93	815	959	1023	1.8	2.38	551	642	1.7
49617	BEULAH	019	3296	3681	3875	1.2	88	1322	1517	1606	1.5	2.39	926	1051	1.4
49618	BOON	165	602	672	701	1.2	88	226	256	268	1.4	2.62	171	191	1.2
49619	BRETHREN	101	1060	1115	1113	0.5	66	413	440	441	0.7	2.51	302	317	0.5
49620	BUCKLEY	055	1986	2473	2661	2.4	98	699	884	960	2.6	2.79	530	663	2.5
49621	CEDAR	089	2642	2800	2816	0.6	71	1037	1135	1153	1.0	2.46	767	832	0.9
49622	CENTRAL LAKE	009	2728	2861	2858	0.5	66	1096	1182	1190	0.8	2.39	794	846	0.7
49623	CHASE	085	1306	1452	1529	1.2	88	503	573	608	1.4	2.53	354	397	1.2
49625	COPEMISH	101	1240	1324	1333	0.7	76	473	516	524	0.9	2.57	341	368	0.8
49629	ELK RAPIDS	009	2155	2190	2172	0.2	48	969	1014	1014	0.5	2.15	663	686	0.4
49630	EMPIRE	089	1287	1416	1455	1.0	84	579	652	673	1.3	2.17	388	431	1.1
49631	EVART	133	6136	6158	6115	0.0	37	2403	2464	2465	0.3	2.45	1733	1755	0.1
49632	FALMOUTH	113	1164	1245	1265	0.7	76	448	491	503	1.0	2.53	344	373	0.9
49633	FIFE LAKE	079	3323	3759	3910	1.3	90	1306	1508	1587	1.6	2.42	952	1087	1.4
49635	FRANKFORT	019	3766	4239	4443	1.3	90	1623	1885	1998	1.6	2.18	1080	1235	1.5
49636	GLEN ARBOR	089	399	427	425	0.7	76	193	211	211	1.0	2.02	127	137	0.8
49637	GRAWN	055	3336	3694	3841	1.1	86	1223	1404	1476	1.5	2.60	883	1001	1.4
49638	HARRIETTA	165	882	1065	1137	2.1	97	341	422	453	2.3	2.52	240	293	2.2
49639	HERSEY	133	2627	2644	2606	0.1	42	990	1022	1014	0.3	2.57	712	726	0.2
49640	HONOR	019	1408	1703	1829	2.1	97	630	777	840	2.3	2.17	458	558	2.2
49642	IDLEWILD	085	733	876	940	1.9	96	316	384	414	2.1	2.27	206	247	2.0
49643	INTERLOCHEN	019	5036	5638	5889	1.2	88	1991	2305	2434	1.6	2.44	1454	1659	1.4
49644	IRONS	085	1611	1762	1843	1.0	84	749	847	893	1.3	2.08	492	551	1.2
49645	KALEVA	101	1590	1629	1615	0.3	54	656	684	683	0.5	2.37	461	476	0.3
49646	KALKASKA	079	8128	8590	8725	0.6	71	3173	3466	3557	1.0	2.43	2223	2399	0.8
49648	KEWADIN	009	1966	1915	1870	-0.3	21	818	819	807	0.0	2.33	611	606	-0.1
49649	KINGSLEY	055	5868	6845	7244	1.7	95	1926	2290	2449	1.9	2.91	1496	1760	1.8
49650	LAKE ANN	019	2378	2993	3260	2.5	98	894	1141	1252	2.7	2.62	675	853	2.6
49651	LAKE CITY	113	7256	7676	7756	0.6	71	2893	3133	3188	0.9	2.41	2077	2227	0.8
49653	LAKE LEELANAU	089	2130	2285	2314	0.8	80	816	904	925	1.1	2.49	605	665	1.0
49654	LELAND	089	559	591	587	0.6	71	258	282	282	1.0	2.02	186	201	0.8
49655	LEROY	133	3007	3117	3175	0.4	60	1127	1202	1235	0.7	2.58	849	897	0.6
49656	LUTHER	085	1761	1980	2108	1.3	90	737	861	925	1.7	2.30	506	585	1.6
49657	MC BAIN	113	3561	3822	3887	0.8	80	1209	1330	1364	1.0	2.82	944	1029	0.9
49659	MANCELONA	009	6697	7607	7810	1.4	92	2526	2920	3014	1.6	2.59	1851	2118	1.5
49660	MANISTEE	101	14450	14484	14280	0.0	37	5767	5817	5758	0.1	2.30	3826	3810	0.0
49663	MANTON	165	5476	6336	6692	1.6	94	2004	2358	2505	1.8	2.68	1482	1723	1.6
49664	MAPLE CITY	089	2103	2268	2323	0.8	80	817	906	935	1.1	2.48	617	678	1.0
49665	MARION	133	4396	4531	4600	0.3	54	1691	1790	1834	0.6	2.52	1223	1282	0.5
49667	MERRITT	113	640	673	676	0.5	66	238	256	259	0.8	2.63	178	189	0.7
49668	MESICK	165	3509	3907	4103	1.2	88	1337	1526	1615	1.4	2.56	983	1110	1.3
49670	NORTHPORT	089	2175	2343	2368	0.8	80	923	1023	1044	1.1	2.21	651	715	1.0
49675	ONEKAMA	101	1093	1172	1172	0.8	80	438	475	479	0.9	2.14	294	314	0.7
49676	RAPID CITY	009	3541	3567	3531	0.1	42	1441	1500	1500	0.4	2.37	1062	1094	0.3
49677	REED CITY	133	6564	6416	6412	-0.2	25	2501	2505	2521	0.0	2.49	1758	1743	-0.1
49679	SEARS	133	1363	1414	1440	0.4	60	513	547	562	0.7	2.53	374	394	0.6
49680	SOUTH BOARDMAN	079	1842	2035	2108	1.1	86	653	741	776	1.4	2.74	504	567	1.3
49682	SUTTONS BAY	089	4350	4618	4642	0.6	71	1627	1768	1793	0.9	2.59	1246	1342	0.8
49683	THOMPSONVILLE	019	1764	2163	2275	2.2	98	720	905	960	2.5	2.38	522	647	2.3
49684	TRAVERSE CITY	055	33683	38876	40697	1.6	94	13145	15570	16460	1.8	2.43	8974	10469	1.7
49686	TRAVERSE CITY	055	29282	32906	34454	1.3	90	12062	13812	14618	1.5	2.29	7886	8959	1.4
49688	TUSTIN	133	2470	2556	2556	0.4	60	920	981	989	0.7	2.59	701	739	0.6
49689	WELLSTON	101	1721	1931	1968	1.3	90	714	810	829	1.4	2.31	521	585	1.3
49690	WILLIAMSBURG	055	6456	7089	7327	1.0	84	2463	2782	2907	1.3	2.49	1830	2043	1.2
49701	MACKINAW CITY	047	1098	1160	1175	0.6	71	506	555	568	1.0	2.09	330	355	0.8
	MICHIGAN					0.3					0.4	2.52			0.3
	UNITED STATES					1.0					1.1	2.59			0.9

ZIP CODE #	POST OFFICE NAME	RACE (%) White 2000	White 2009	Black 2000	Black 2009	Asian/Pacific 2000	Asian/Pacific 2009	% Hispanic Origin 2000	% Hispanic Origin 2009	2009 AGE DISTRIBUTION (%) 0-4	5-9	10-14	15-19	20-24	25-44	45-64	65-84	85+	18+	MEDIAN AGE 2009	% 2009 Males	% 2009 Females
49437	MONTAGUE	96.3	95.2	0.6	0.9	0.3	0.4	3.2	4.3	6.0	6.0	6.2	6.7	5.8	24.3	30.0	13.4	1.5	77.6	41.1	49.3	50.7
49440	MUSKEGON	51.9	43.0	41.4	49.5	0.1	0.2	5.8	6.8	6.3	6.0	5.0	7.1	8.3	31.9	19.3	12.1	4.0	78.9	34.2	55.5	44.5
49441	MUSKEGON	88.2	85.3	7.1	8.8	0.7	1.1	3.5	4.7	6.1	6.0	6.1	6.7	5.9	24.4	27.6	14.1	3.0	77.7	41.0	48.3	51.7
49442	MUSKEGON	70.5	66.0	22.9	26.4	0.4	0.6	5.5	6.8	7.8	7.3	6.8	7.3	7.8	29.6	22.3	9.0	2.0	73.8	33.2	51.1	48.9
49444	MUSKEGON	59.6	58.5	36.2	36.7	0.5	0.8	3.2	3.9	7.7	7.9	7.6	7.4	6.1	25.5	25.7	10.4	1.6	72.0	35.6	48.5	51.5
49445	MUSKEGON	94.6	92.6	2.4	3.4	0.4	0.7	1.8	2.7	5.7	6.1	6.7	7.4	5.7	24.1	30.5	12.0	1.9	76.8	40.9	49.2	50.8
49446	NEW ERA	93.7	92.1	0.4	0.5	0.4	0.5	8.5	11.2	6.4	6.7	7.1	7.0	5.7	23.7	29.4	12.3	1.6	75.1	40.1	50.2	49.8
49448	NUNICA	96.7	95.8	0.7	0.8	0.1	0.3	1.8	2.6	6.2	7.0	7.5	7.2	5.0	26.3	29.4	10.3	1.0	74.5	38.9	51.6	48.4
49449	PENTWATER	96.0	95.0	0.2	0.2	0.4	0.6	4.1	5.3	4.0	4.3	4.7	4.9	4.4	17.0	35.4	22.8	2.6	83.7	52.8	49.5	50.5
49450	PULLMAN	75.1	70.8	6.6	7.0	0.3	0.5	22.6	28.2	9.5	9.0	8.5	8.9	7.4	28.8	20.1	7.0	0.7	67.4	29.3	51.7	48.3
49451	RAVENNA	96.5	95.3	0.4	0.6	0.1	0.2	2.6	3.8	6.7	7.2	8.2	8.0	5.6	27.4	26.2	9.5	1.2	72.8	36.7	49.8	50.2
49452	ROTHBURY	92.0	89.8	0.1	0.1	0.3	0.6	8.8	11.7	7.5	7.3	7.3	8.2	6.6	26.2	26.8	9.3	0.8	72.5	35.6	51.5	48.5
49453	SAUGATUCK	96.0	94.9	0.8	0.9	0.5	0.7	4.0	5.5	4.8	5.1	6.0	5.5	3.9	22.3	36.3	13.8	2.5	80.6	46.3	49.4	50.6
49454	SCOTTVILLE	95.7	94.7	0.5	0.7	0.3	0.5	3.6	4.8	6.0	6.3	6.5	6.8	5.5	23.8	29.5	13.2	2.4	77.1	41.2	49.4	50.6
49455	SHELBY	87.7	85.0	0.3	0.4	0.2	0.3	15.8	20.0	6.6	6.5	6.8	7.7	5.9	23.5	28.9	12.1	2.0	75.1	39.6	50.3	49.7
49456	SPRING LAKE	97.0	96.0	0.5	0.6	0.6	1.0	1.6	2.3	6.2	6.3	6.5	6.5	5.6	24.3	29.4	12.8	2.5	77.0	41.3	48.6	51.4
49457	TWIN LAKE	92.7	90.2	2.8	4.1	0.2	0.3	2.6	3.6	6.9	7.3	7.4	7.2	5.4	27.5	28.6	8.9	0.9	74.0	37.2	50.8	49.2
49459	WALKERVILLE	84.9	81.5	1.5	1.6	0.1	0.2	18.7	23.7	7.7	7.5	7.7	8.2	6.9	25.0	25.0	10.8	1.3	71.7	34.5	50.9	49.1
49460	WEST OLIVE	91.7	89.5	1.3	1.3	0.9	1.5	9.1	11.8	7.6	7.8	8.2	8.0	6.0	26.1	27.6	8.1	0.7	71.1	35.6	52.5	47.5
49461	WHITEHALL	96.7	95.6	0.8	1.2	0.3	0.4	1.5	2.2	6.1	6.4	6.9	6.9	5.3	23.8	30.7	11.7	2.2	76.0	41.0	49.1	50.9
49464	ZEELAND	92.6	89.4	0.8	0.9	2.1	3.6	5.3	7.8	8.9	8.5	7.9	7.2	5.5	30.3	21.4	8.4	1.8	70.1	32.7	48.8	51.2
49503	GRAND RAPIDS	61.9	55.6	21.1	23.9	1.3	1.8	20.9	25.4	8.4	7.0	6.0	6.9	10.4	34.9	18.9	6.3	1.3	75.0	29.9	52.2	47.8
49504	GRAND RAPIDS	84.5	80.3	3.1	3.6	1.1	1.7	13.2	17.7	8.1	7.6	6.9	6.7	6.9	28.9	22.8	9.5	2.6	73.5	34.3	49.9	50.1
49505	GRAND RAPIDS	83.7	79.6	9.9	11.9	1.5	2.3	3.9	5.6	7.8	7.0	6.7	6.4	6.8	28.4	22.8	11.4	2.8	74.5	35.8	48.5	51.5
49506	GRAND RAPIDS	74.9	71.3	20.0	22.0	1.2	1.9	3.7	4.9	6.9	6.7	7.0	11.1	9.9	23.7	22.9	8.7	3.1	75.1	32.2	47.0	53.0
49507	GRAND RAPIDS	40.8	36.7	42.2	43.6	1.4	1.9	22.8	26.5	10.2	9.4	8.6	8.9	8.1	29.5	19.3	5.3	0.9	66.4	28.1	49.6	50.4
49508	GRAND RAPIDS	77.2	71.0	13.1	15.8	5.1	7.6	4.0	5.4	7.4	7.0	6.8	7.0	7.6	28.9	24.1	9.3	1.8	74.3	34.1	47.6	52.4
49509	WYOMING	81.5	75.3	4.7	5.8	3.2	4.9	12.7	17.6	8.5	7.8	7.1	7.0	7.2	30.4	21.6	8.7	1.6	72.3	32.7	49.4	50.6
49512	GRAND RAPIDS	75.0	68.6	12.7	14.5	7.4	11.0	4.1	5.5	8.1	6.2	5.4	5.2	11.1	37.1	19.6	6.2	1.2	77.6	30.5	50.3	49.7
49519	WYOMING	86.5	81.5	5.3	6.9	2.4	3.8	7.2	10.4	7.4	6.6	6.1	6.6	8.6	33.3	22.7	7.6	1.0	76.0	32.5	49.0	51.0
49525	GRAND RAPIDS	94.3	92.1	1.9	2.6	1.3	2.1	1.8	2.7	6.4	6.4	6.7	8.4	7.5	25.3	28.1	10.0	1.2	76.0	36.3	48.6	51.4
49534	GRAND RAPIDS	96.1	94.6	0.9	1.2	0.7	1.1	2.0	2.9	7.1	7.0	6.9	7.1	6.5	28.9	26.1	9.1	1.4	74.7	35.3	50.1	49.9
49544	GRAND RAPIDS	93.2	90.5	1.9	2.5	1.2	2.0	3.7	5.5	6.6	5.6	5.6	6.8	11.2	29.1	23.4	9.4	2.1	78.0	33.3	49.6	50.4
49546	GRAND RAPIDS	87.9	84.2	5.4	6.4	3.8	5.9	2.0	2.8	6.3	6.5	7.0	7.1	5.7	22.8	27.6	13.1	3.9	75.6	40.8	47.5	52.5
49548	GRAND RAPIDS	84.0	78.6	5.8	7.4	3.2	4.8	7.8	10.9	8.6	8.1	7.5	6.9	6.6	31.1	22.9	7.1	1.2	71.5	32.8	49.4	50.6
49601	CADILLAC	97.3	96.7	0.2	0.2	0.6	0.9	0.9	1.1	6.3	6.3	6.3	6.5	6.3	24.8	28.2	12.9	2.3	76.9	40.0	49.2	50.8
49612	ALDEN	97.0	96.3	0.1	0.1	0.6	0.9	0.9	1.3	5.2	5.1	5.5	5.9	4.5	23.1	33.8	15.2	1.7	80.4	45.4	51.5	48.5
49613	ARCADIA	98.7	98.7	0.1	0.1	0.1	0.1	1.6	2.1	5.2	5.4	5.8	5.9	3.3	18.8	32.2	21.3	2.1	79.2	48.7	48.8	51.2
49614	BEAR LAKE	97.0	96.3	0.0	0.0	0.6	0.9	3.3	4.2	5.0	5.6	6.1	6.7	3.8	21.5	31.0	17.7	2.4	78.9	45.7	49.9	50.1
49615	BELLAIRE	97.5	97.0	0.1	0.1	0.3	0.5	1.0	1.3	5.2	5.5	5.7	5.6	3.8	20.3	31.9	18.9	3.1	79.7	47.5	49.2	50.8
49616	BENZONIA	94.2	93.5	0.7	0.8	0.1	0.2	2.4	3.3	5.5	5.8	5.8	5.9	4.5	20.7	32.9	16.6	2.2	79.0	46.1	49.6	50.4
49617	BEULAH	96.3	95.8	0.2	0.2	0.2	0.3	1.3	1.7	5.0	5.4	5.5	5.2	3.7	20.5	32.5	20.0	2.1	80.9	48.1	50.0	50.0
49618	BOON	98.0	97.6	0.2	0.1	0.2	0.3	0.8	0.9	6.3	6.5	7.0	7.0	5.1	23.8	30.2	12.6	1.5	75.6	41.1	51.3	48.7
49619	BRETHREN	97.5	96.9	0.3	0.4	0.1	0.2	1.7	2.2	4.9	5.3	5.9	5.7	3.9	18.8	36.6	17.0	1.8	80.4	48.2	49.9	50.1
49620	BUCKLEY	96.8	96.2	0.3	0.3	0.1	0.2	2.0	2.7	7.2	7.5	7.6	6.8	5.4	26.0	28.3	10.0	1.1	73.3	37.3	49.9	50.1
49621	CEDAR	97.4	96.7	0.3	0.3	0.5	0.7	1.3	1.8	5.0	5.8	6.4	6.1	4.6	21.6	35.2	13.6	1.8	79.0	45.3	50.6	49.4
49622	CENTRAL LAKE	97.7	97.4	0.1	0.2	0.1	0.1	0.5	0.7	5.0	5.5	5.7	5.9	4.2	21.6	32.6	17.4	2.1	80.1	46.2	49.9	50.1
49623	CHASE	86.3	83.0	10.3	12.7	0.2	0.3	1.5	1.9	6.3	6.5	6.8	6.9	5.6	23.0	29.1	14.3	1.6	76.0	41.1	49.7	50.3
49625	COPEMISH	96.3	95.7	0.3	0.4	0.0	0.0	2.1	2.7	6.3	6.6	6.9	6.5	5.7	25.2	30.3	11.2	1.2	75.9	39.7	52.6	47.4
49629	ELK RAPIDS	97.3	96.9	0.2	0.2	0.3	0.4	2.0	2.6	3.9	4.2	4.7	5.8	5.2	19.4	34.0	20.5	2.3	83.2	49.8	50.1	49.9
49630	EMPIRE	98.5	98.2	0.1	0.1	0.3	0.4	0.5	0.5	3.2	3.9	4.4	4.7	4.0	16.5	39.7	20.8	2.7	85.5	53.3	49.5	50.5
49631	EVART	97.0	96.4	0.5	0.6	0.3	0.4	1.1	1.5	6.1	6.1	6.6	7.3	6.0	21.9	29.4	14.8	1.8	76.8	41.6	49.2	50.8
49632	FALMOUTH	97.8	97.4	0.3	0.3	0.2	0.2	1.2	1.6	7.1	7.2	7.1	6.7	5.7	22.4	29.6	12.7	1.5	74.5	40.0	51.2	48.8
49633	FIFE LAKE	95.5	94.7	1.4	1.7	0.1	0.2	0.8	1.1	6.0	6.0	6.4	6.9	5.7	26.3	29.0	12.8	1.0	77.1	40.1	52.5	47.5
49635	FRANKFORT	96.9	96.4	0.2	0.2	0.3	0.4	1.5	2.0	4.5	4.7	5.0	5.3	4.2	18.5	31.5	22.0	4.3	82.3	50.4	48.1	51.9
49636	GLEN ARBOR	99.5	99.5	0.0	0.0	0.3	0.2	0.5	0.7	1.9	2.3	2.8	3.0	3.0	7.7	38.2	35.8	5.2	90.9	61.4	48.0	52.0
49637	GRAWN	95.6	95.0	0.1	0.1	0.4	0.6	1.4	1.9	6.2	6.1	6.5	7.2	6.1	27.6	30.0	9.4	0.9	76.7	38.7	49.5	50.5
49638	HARRIETTA	97.6	97.4	0.0	0.0	0.0	0.0	1.0	1.4	5.7	6.1	6.5	5.9	4.6	21.7	31.7	16.3	1.4	78.0	44.6	50.8	49.2
49639	HERSEY	97.8	97.3	0.2	0.2	0.3	0.4	0.9	1.2	6.7	6.7	7.0	7.0	5.9	25.4	27.5	12.5	1.4	75.3	38.5	48.7	51.3
49640	HONOR	96.0	95.5	0.4	0.4	0.1	0.2	1.0	1.3	5.0	5.5	5.7	5.0	3.5	20.6	34.9	17.9	1.8	80.6	48.0	50.1	49.9
49642	IDLEWILD	72.9	69.1	23.1	26.1	0.3	0.5	1.6	2.1	5.6	5.9	6.4	7.1	4.3	20.5	30.6	17.7	1.8	77.5	45.1	49.8	50.2
49643	INTERLOCHEN	96.8	96.4	0.1	0.1	0.2	0.3	1.0	1.3	6.5	6.7	6.9	6.3	5.3	27.2	30.1	9.9	1.2	76.0	39.7	49.9	50.1
49644	IRONS	96.5	95.8	0.3	0.3	0.2	0.3	1.2	1.5	4.8	4.8	4.5	3.6	3.5	15.3	32.4	29.1	2.1	83.7	55.7	50.6	49.4
49645	KALEVA	96.5	96.0	0.3	0.2	0.1	0.1	2.5	3.4	5.8	6.2	6.4	6.0	5.1	21.9	31.9	14.5	2.1	77.8	43.8	48.8	51.2
49646	KALKASKA	97.5	96.9	0.3	0.3	0.3	0.5	0.8	1.1	6.8	6.8	6.7	6.4	5.6	25.6	27.1	13.0	2.0	75.6	39.1	49.5	50.5
49648	KEWADIN	96.8	96.4	0.4	0.4	0.1	0.2	1.9	2.5	3.4	4.3	4.7	5.5	3.5	18.5	34.8	23.1	2.2	83.9	51.7	51.3	48.7
49649	KINGSLEY	96.4	95.9	0.8	0.9	0.2	0.3	1.3	1.7	8.2	8.2	8.1	7.3	5.9	29.1	24.5	7.9	0.9	70.6	34.1	51.0	49.0
49650	LAKE ANN	97.4	97.1	0.3	0.2	0.1	0.2	1.2	1.6	7.9	7.5	7.5	6.4	5.3	29.5	27.2	8.0	0.8	73.2	35.9	49.7	50.3
49651	LAKE CITY	97.5	97.1	0.1	0.1	0.3	0.3	1.1	1.5	6.1	6.4	6.7	6.7	4.9	23.2	28.7	15.3	2.1	76.5	42.0	50.1	49.9
49653	LAKE LEELANAU	92.7	91.9	0.7	0.7	0.4	0.5	3.8	5.0	4.8	6.2	6.8	5.6	3.9	20.5	31.9	17.7	2.6	78.5	46.3	50.7	49.3
49654	LELAND	94.8	93.4	0.0	0.0	0.5	0.8	5.0	6.8	3.0	4.7	4.9	5.6	4.6	14.6	35.0	23.2	4.4	83.4	52.6	49.2	50.8
49655	LEROY	97.9	97.5	0.2	0.2	0.2	0.4	0.8	1.1	5.9	6.2	6.5	6.9	5.6	24.4	29.6	13.5	1.5	77.1	40.9	48.4	51.6
49656	LUTHER	95.1	94.3	0.6	0.7	0.2	0.3	1.5	2.0	5.5	5.8	6.1	6.2	4.8	21.3	30.7	17.9	1.8	78.4	45.2	50.1	49.9
49657	MC BAIN	97.7	97.3	0.3	0.4	0.3	0.2	1.3	1.6	7.0	7.8	8.1	7.9	5.0	24.5	26.1	11.5	2.1	72.0	37.3	50.6	49.4
49659	MANCELONA	96.8	96.4	0.2	0.2	0.1	0.2	1.2	1.7	7.3	7.2	7.1	6.6	5.3	23.2	27.6	14.1	1.6	74.6	39.7	50.6	49.4
49660	MANISTEE	92.8	91.4	2.4	2.8	0.5	0.7	2.2	2.9	4.9	5.1	5.4	5.9	6.4	24.3	29.1	15.5	3.3	81.0	43.4	51.3	48.7
49663	MANTON	97.4	97.0	0.2	0.2	0.3	0.4	1.1	1.4	6.4	6.5	6.8	7.4	5.7	24.9	29.0	11.9	1.5	75.5	39.3	50.1	49.9
49664	MAPLE CITY	97.8	97.4	0.1	0.1	0.3	0.4	1.0	1.2	5.0	5.7	6.4	6.7	5.2	20.3	35.8	13.0	1.9	78.3	45.4	49.9	50.1
49665	MARION	98.0	97.6	0.3	0.3	0.1	0.1	1.3	1.7	6.2	6.4	6.7	7.3	5.6	23.6	28.6	14.0	1.6	76.3	40.7	50.5	49.5
49667	MERRITT	97.5	97.2	0.2	0.1	0.2	0.1	0.6	0.9	6.2	6.5	6.4	6.5	5.5	23.2	29.1	15.0	1.5	76.8	41.6	51.4	48.6
49668	MESICK	97.2	96.7	0.1	0.2	0.2	0.3	1.0	1.3	6.7	6.9	7.3	7.0	5.5	23.9	28.9	12.4	1.4	74.8	39.9	52.3	47.7
49670	NORTHPORT	93.2	92.1	0.3	0.3	0.1	0.1	6.9	8.9	3.0	4.7	5.9	5.0	3.5	15.9	36.4	21.6	3.9	83.0	52.1	49.6	50.4
49675	ONEKAMA	91.9	89.7	0.1	0.1	0.0	0.0	11.3	14.8	5.2	5.8	5.4	6.0	4.8	19.9	30.0	19.5	3.4	79.5	47.2	51.0	49.0
49676	RAPID CITY	97.4	97.0	0.1	0.1	0.3	0.5	1.2	1.6	5.2	5.4	5.8	6.3	4.4	23.2	32.2	15.5	1.9	79.3	44.8	50.9	49.1
49677	REED CITY	96.7	95.9	0.8	1.0	0.2	0.3	1.0	1.3	6.5	6.4	6.6	6.9	6.4	25.2	27.2	12.7	2.2	76.0	38.6	48.6	51.4
49679	SEARS	97.6	97.2	0.4	0.4	0.2	0.3	0.5	0.7	6.2	6.1	7.0	7.2	5.3	22.6	28.5	15.7	1.3	76.2	41.3	52.3	47.7
49680	SOUTH BOARDMAN	97.7	97.3	0.2	0.2	0.2	0.3	0.9	1.2	7.5	7.4	7.6	8.0	6.1	25.6	27.4	9.5	0.9	72.5	36.3	50.6	49.4
49682	SUTTONS BAY	82.9	81.7	0.1	0.1	0.1	0.2	5.8	7.3	5.8	6.6	7.5	6.9	4.5	21.0	32.4	13.9	1.4	75.7	43.1	50.6	49.4
49683	THOMPSONVILLE	96.7	96.3	0.1	0.1	0.1	0.1	1.8	2.3	5.8	6.4	6.8	6.8	4.5	25.0	30.5	12.9	1.2	76.9	41.5	50.3	49.7
49684	TRAVERSE CITY	96.5	95.7	0.3	0.4	0.6	0.8	1.6	2.1	6.1	6.1	6.5	6.6	5.8	26.8	28.7	11.1	2.3	77.1	39.6	48.5	51.5
49686	TRAVERSE CITY	96.8	96.1	0.3	0.3	0.6	0.8	1.6	2.1	5.4	5.6	6.0	6.6	5.8	24.8	29.7	13.4	2.7	79.1	41.8	48.5	51.5
49688	TUSTIN	98.1	97.6	0.1	0.1	0.3	0.5	0.7	0.9	6.5	6.6	6.7	6.7	6.1	25.3	28.3	12.4	1.4	75.8	39.4	51.7	48.3
49689	WELLSTON	94.7	94.1	1.9	2.1	0.2	0.2	0.8	1.0	5.2	5.5	6.0	6.1	5.4	22.1	31.7	16.6	1.4	79.8	44.8	52.8	47.2
49690	WILLIAMSBURG	97.1	96.4	0.3	0.3	0.5	0.7	1.8	2.3	4.9	5.4	6.2	6.8	4.7	22.4	35.0	12.9	1.8	78.7	44.8	49.8	50.2
49701	MACKINAW CITY	93.0	92.4	0.3	0.3	0.0	0.1	0.4	0.4	5.0	5.7	5.8	4.8	3.0	21.1	34.7	17.8	2.2	80.3	48.2	49.2	50.8
	MICHIGAN	80.2	78.3	14.2	14.5	1.8	2.8	3.3	4.1	6.7	6.7	6.8	7.2	6.6	26.3	26.9	10.9	1.9	75.6	37.6	49.2	50.8
	UNITED STATES	75.1	72.0	12.3	12.7	3.8	4.6	12.5	15.7	6.8	6.7	6.6	7.1	6.9	27.0	26.0	10.9	1.9	75.7	36.9	49.2	50.8

ZIP CODE #	POST OFFICE NAME	2009 Per Capita Income	2009 HH Income Base	2009 Household Income Distribution (%): Less than $25,000	$25,000 to $49,999	$50,000 to $99,999	$100,000 to $149,999	$150,000 or More	Median Household Income: 2009	2014	2009 National Centile	2009 State Centile	2009 Home Value Base	2009 Home Value Distribution (%): Less than $50,000	$50,000 to $89,999	$90,000 to $174,999	$175,000 to $399,999	$400,000 or More	2009 Median Home Value
49437	MONTAGUE	22781	2780	21.2	26.6	43.1	6.9	2.2	51638	52810	65	55	2355	7.6	27.8	46.8	15.8	2.1	107880
49440	MUSKEGON	14546	392	54.6	24.7	18.1	2.6	0.0	22768	23377	2	1	88	58.0	25.0	17.0	0.0	0.0	46500
49441	MUSKEGON	23729	14905	22.9	28.8	39.0	6.3	2.9	47599	51403	56	43	11126	11.4	32.2	40.3	14.2	1.7	98278
49442	MUSKEGON	17655	16108	31.4	28.6	34.2	4.5	1.3	40033	43329	33	18	11021	27.9	42.3	27.1	2.7	0.0	71762
49444	MUSKEGON	19917	10730	30.5	26.5	35.5	5.3	2.3	41776	46671	39	24	7945	28.9	25.5	36.2	8.1	1.4	82937
49445	MUSKEGON	24466	8440	13.7	25.2	48.1	10.1	3.0	59267	58302	77	74	7374	7.5	19.5	53.0	17.6	2.4	118667
49446	NEW ERA	19046	836	21.2	27.4	45.0	5.3	1.2	50845	50000	63	52	735	13.5	28.0	41.4	15.4	1.8	104500
49448	NUNICA	22088	1311	18.5	28.1	44.6	6.0	2.7	54661	56771	71	64	1121	15.1	17.0	39.7	23.6	4.5	125083
49449	PENTWATER	26258	1337	19.1	26.4	42.3	9.9	2.3	53441	53388	69	61	1134	6.3	10.9	46.0	29.1	7.6	138559
49450	PULLMAN	15054	1234	27.6	29.1	38.4	4.1	0.8	43033	48151	42	29	889	26.0	22.2	36.3	14.1	1.5	92426
49451	RAVENNA	19377	2066	20.2	28.2	45.2	4.9	1.5	51192	53195	64	53	1811	9.0	22.9	51.5	15.8	0.7	113309
49452	ROTHBURY	17700	710	26.3	33.0	36.1	2.8	1.8	41281	44363	37	22	605	21.5	26.0	39.3	12.7	0.5	93229
49453	SAUGATUCK	32496	1633	18.6	27.3	38.5	9.5	6.1	52760	53530	67	59	1217	6.7	3.9	23.4	48.7	17.3	218152
49454	SCOTTVILLE	19000	1731	26.1	31.0	36.7	5.3	0.9	44525	45508	47	33	1406	12.8	25.2	44.1	15.5	2.4	105181
49455	SHELBY	19685	2016	24.5	29.9	37.8	5.4	2.4	45465	46179	50	37	1629	14.1	30.8	38.9	13.7	2.5	95935
49456	SPRING LAKE	32122	7910	14.0	24.8	40.2	11.5	9.5	62962	65202	81	81	6232	11.0	8.9	37.4	35.6	7.2	155656
49457	TWIN LAKE	19902	3815	20.2	26.0	47.5	5.7	0.7	52467	53589	67	57	3392	17.0	26.0	43.8	12.7	0.6	98129
49459	WALKERVILLE	16310	543	34.6	31.5	30.0	3.1	0.7	35740	37946	20	7	443	25.3	28.2	33.9	11.5	1.1	85811
49460	WEST OLIVE	27505	3068	7.8	17.1	56.7	11.8	6.6	69648	73537	87	90	2817	14.0	11.0	24.4	42.6	8.0	176389
49461	WHITEHALL	24068	3304	18.2	23.9	46.1	8.4	3.5	56904	56927	74	69	2659	7.1	21.8	49.8	19.3	2.0	119411
49464	ZEELAND	23882	9318	11.8	21.3	52.8	10.1	4.0	64709	67245	83	84	7867	11.7	13.3	42.2	31.1	1.7	144270
49503	GRAND RAPIDS	19349	15290	32.9	30.6	29.4	4.8	2.2	38064	40090	27	11	6399	17.7	39.1	32.1	9.3	1.8	83796
49504	GRAND RAPIDS	22526	16188	21.7	28.0	41.0	6.9	2.4	50258	53666	62	50	10524	9.8	31.7	50.6	7.7	0.2	98735
49505	GRAND RAPIDS	24162	13193	19.0	28.8	42.6	7.5	2.1	51797	55195	66	56	8902	4.7	26.1	60.8	8.0	0.5	106589
49506	GRAND RAPIDS	30836	12395	16.6	19.3	40.7	12.1	11.1	64529	66520	83	84	9118	4.4	18.6	40.3	30.3	6.4	143004
49507	GRAND RAPIDS	17597	12771	26.2	26.3	38.0	7.3	2.2	47456	51194	55	42	8255	16.4	41.2	40.3	2.1	0.1	83052
49508	GRAND RAPIDS	26741	14775	15.2	24.4	44.3	11.8	4.4	60776	62684	79	78	9115	2.7	7.5	69.0	20.2	0.7	139500
49509	WYOMING	22246	10052	17.9	27.0	46.9	6.1	2.1	53774	56996	69	62	7237	8.5	33.1	55.4	3.0	0.0	95558
49512	GRAND RAPIDS	31110	7063	19.2	27.9	37.4	10.9	4.6	52519	56349	67	58	2652	13.4	6.6	45.6	33.2	1.2	148028
49519	WYOMING	25454	11987	15.7	29.6	43.5	8.6	2.7	54221	57954	70	63	6558	8.7	16.8	60.1	13.9	0.4	115513
49525	GRAND RAPIDS	27458	10664	14.1	22.9	44.6	12.7	5.7	61344	63270	79	79	8116	4.6	8.8	55.4	27.0	4.2	142503
49534	GRAND RAPIDS	25387	8628	16.6	23.8	46.0	10.7	2.9	60872	62891	79	78	6348	7.7	10.7	51.6	28.4	1.6	140749
49544	GRAND RAPIDS	24542	3740	15.9	32.3	43.5	6.1	2.2	51969	56720	66	56	2181	18.1	12.4	52.3	16.6	0.7	119863
49546	GRAND RAPIDS	35532	11891	16.6	20.6	33.9	15.7	13.3	65685	67571	84	86	8109	0.7	4.3	34.1	50.8	10.1	199087
49548	GRAND RAPIDS	21990	12512	16.6	31.2	45.8	5.2	1.2	51608	54951	65	55	9269	32.3	27.5	38.7	1.5	0.0	81251
49601	CADILLAC	21724	8503	24.8	30.9	35.6	6.4	2.2	45338	47756	49	37	6434	15.4	23.7	38.5	19.6	2.8	117704
49612	ALDEN	23062	487	20.9	30.8	42.1	4.7	1.4	48182	47964	57	45	422	9.2	19.7	43.4	21.6	6.2	118987
49613	ARCADIA	24230	378	25.9	33.1	33.6	5.3	2.1	40718	43580	35	21	337	7.7	24.6	38.9	23.1	5.6	119612
49614	BEAR LAKE	20468	1167	26.3	31.7	36.6	4.1	1.3	42363	43818	41	26	1022	12.1	20.7	43.2	20.5	3.5	115250
49615	BELLAIRE	24410	1773	21.2	30.1	40.1	6.2	2.4	48314	47849	57	45	1515	4.0	13.5	45.4	26.9	10.1	144960
49616	BENZONIA	20224	959	25.5	35.0	33.6	3.9	2.0	41030	44090	36	21	770	10.9	20.0	40.9	21.4	6.8	124048
49617	BEULAH	23238	1517	19.8	32.7	39.9	5.2	2.4	45283	49381	49	36	1304	7.4	15.6	36.0	29.8	11.3	146599
49618	BOON	18690	256	25.4	32.4	35.5	5.1	1.6	42982	45900	42	29	224	18.3	26.8	37.9	15.6	1.3	97857
49619	BRETHREN	19218	440	24.5	32.0	37.7	4.3	1.4	44612	45621	47	34	392	15.3	24.5	40.1	17.9	2.3	102273
49620	BUCKLEY	17621	884	19.9	36.2	40.4	2.4	1.1	45816	48701	51	38	755	13.8	18.9	44.0	22.0	1.3	118851
49621	CEDAR	24011	1135	15.7	27.9	47.4	6.9	2.1	53814	53977	69	62	972	2.0	7.3	38.9	39.9	11.9	179128
49622	CENTRAL LAKE	22772	1182	21.1	30.4	41.4	5.6	1.6	48289	47881	57	45	998	6.6	20.9	41.0	23.0	8.4	125455
49623	CHASE	17421	573	31.9	29.5	34.0	3.7	0.9	40179	43009	33	18	491	21.2	30.8	35.6	11.4	1.0	87500
49625	COPEMISH	17036	516	27.1	37.0	32.6	3.3	0.0	38355	40440	28	12	444	18.9	30.6	35.4	14.2	0.9	90625
49629	ELK RAPIDS	26443	1014	22.8	30.4	36.0	8.3	2.6	44811	45765	48	35	792	4.0	7.1	33.3	37.6	17.9	195755
49630	EMPIRE	28247	652	15.6	33.0	41.4	6.9	3.1	51037	52888	64	53	542	0.9	7.4	33.4	36.7	21.6	196226
49631	EVART	18610	2464	29.2	33.1	32.7	3.7	1.3	38546	40573	28	13	1943	20.6	33.9	34.6	9.7	1.2	85084
49632	FALMOUTH	19328	491	23.4	36.3	34.4	4.7	1.2	42624	43981	41	28	424	15.3	29.0	41.7	11.8	2.1	95106
49633	FIFE LAKE	20596	1508	23.5	32.5	38.5	3.7	1.9	44382	46746	46	33	1310	13.8	27.0	41.0	15.6	2.5	105303
49635	FRANKFORT	25285	1885	22.4	30.3	39.3	5.1	2.8	44671	48905	47	34	1489	6.9	14.4	40.1	29.3	9.3	146510
49636	GLEN ARBOR	36448	211	12.8	23.7	46.0	11.8	5.7	62449	62608	81	81	194	0.0	2.1	10.8	35.1	52.1	425000
49637	GRAWN	20096	1404	15.9	31.1	47.8	4.8	0.4	51509	52632	65	55	1166	10.5	22.5	48.2	17.8	1.1	111373
49638	HARRIETTA	16699	422	28.2	37.9	31.3	2.6	0.0	37235	39649	24	10	354	23.4	33.6	35.9	6.5	0.6	80741
49639	HERSEY	18558	1022	25.1	31.9	37.9	4.0	1.1	45000	45700	48	35	858	16.3	32.4	40.3	9.6	1.4	91325
49640	HONOR	24249	777	19.6	34.5	39.6	4.4	1.9	44212	48138	46	33	692	5.5	11.4	41.0	35.0	7.1	154478
49642	IDLEWILD	17846	384	39.6	27.6	28.9	3.4	0.5	32875	34705	13	4	312	22.4	36.5	28.2	12.2	0.6	79259
49643	INTERLOCHEN	22795	2305	14.9	32.5	47.1	3.6	1.9	51294	52253	64	54	2020	7.4	12.3	47.7	27.4	5.2	141191
49644	IRONS	20390	847	31.9	32.8	31.2	2.8	1.3	37499	39388	25	10	747	20.1	27.2	33.5	17.5	1.7	95395
49645	KALEVA	20061	684	26.5	30.0	38.3	4.5	0.7	43688	44942	44	31	581	16.2	31.8	36.3	13.9	1.7	92674
49646	KALKASKA	19862	3466	23.6	32.3	38.6	4.4	1.0	43437	45910	44	30	2789	14.3	21.1	50.9	12.5	1.1	107823
49648	KEWADIN	26090	819	17.9	31.5	39.7	8.1	2.8	50366	49515	62	50	726	4.3	7.3	34.7	29.5	24.2	191071
49649	KINGSLEY	19304	2290	16.3	29.0	48.1	4.8	1.7	53215	53739	68	60	1941	13.2	11.0	47.4	26.0	2.3	135194
49650	LAKE ANN	24008	1141	12.4	26.0	52.0	7.4	2.2	59686	58339	77	74	1033	4.8	7.6	51.2	33.5	2.8	151098
49651	LAKE CITY	19614	3133	25.4	35.6	33.9	3.8	1.3	39916	42826	32	17	2561	15.5	24.6	42.6	15.6	1.7	102396
49653	LAKE LEELANAU	25736	904	15.3	28.8	44.9	7.2	3.9	53554	54410	69	61	759	3.2	4.6	29.1	41.8	21.3	221914
49654	LELAND	39787	282	9.6	21.6	46.5	16.0	6.4	65141	65651	83	85	249	1.6	2.0	14.5	46.2	35.7	315476
49655	LEROY	18745	1202	25.2	31.9	37.2	5.0	0.7	42556	43945	41	27	1084	21.3	32.3	35.9	9.0	1.5	86214
49656	LUTHER	18601	861	33.0	32.3	29.5	4.1	1.2	36344	37588	22	8	757	29.3	26.8	31.7	10.7	1.5	79327
49657	MC BAIN	17974	1330	20.4	32.3	42.0	4.1	1.1	47637	47431	56	43	1120	9.7	23.8	48.0	15.7	2.8	109756
49659	MANCELONA	18222	2920	25.9	34.3	35.1	3.6	1.1	41306	43918	37	22	2432	18.5	28.8	38.7	12.8	1.2	93702
49660	MANISTEE	20971	5817	28.6	28.6	36.5	4.6	1.7	42365	44376	41	26	4451	9.5	34.6	38.9	15.4	1.6	98663
49663	MANTON	17454	2358	25.9	34.5	34.3	4.2	1.1	40480	44330	34	20	1956	17.9	26.8	40.6	14.1	0.5	98226
49664	MAPLE CITY	23787	906	16.4	29.1	44.7	7.2	2.5	52788	53747	68	59	765	3.7	8.1	33.5	40.9	13.9	185369
49665	MARION	17867	1790	30.7	32.2	33.0	2.8	1.3	37878	39964	26	11	1439	22.9	35.0	31.1	10.1	0.9	80927
49667	MERRITT	18283	256	26.2	36.7	31.6	3.9	1.6	39776	41887	32	17	217	18.0	24.0	41.9	13.8	2.3	97292
49668	MESICK	17920	1526	27.0	35.5	33.0	3.4	1.0	40131	43678	33	18	1339	19.8	27.3	38.7	13.0	1.2	95000
49670	NORTHPORT	28453	1023	19.1	26.9	41.6	7.8	4.6	52701	53441	67	59	847	4.1	7.2	24.1	39.7	24.9	227292
49675	ONEKAMA	25187	475	27.4	24.8	37.7	6.7	3.4	46974	47369	54	41	388	7.7	17.0	42.5	20.1	12.6	124315
49676	RAPID CITY	24109	1500	19.5	32.5	39.4	6.1	2.5	48045	47847	57	44	1323	6.6	17.1	37.1	26.5	12.7	142817
49677	REED CITY	19399	2505	25.7	29.5	39.0	4.8	0.9	44734	46012	47	34	1947	18.2	33.8	39.8	7.2	1.0	87787
49679	SEARS	17496	547	30.3	32.7	33.1	2.9	0.9	37810	39593	26	11	482	23.2	31.7	36.7	7.7	0.6	84783
49680	SOUTH BOARDMAN	17491	741	22.0	37.5	35.6	3.9	0.9	40643	43975	35	20	648	13.7	28.4	43.7	13.0	1.2	101010
49682	SUTTONS BAY	25945	1768	17.3	22.1	47.1	9.2	4.4	58142	56900	75	71	1434	4.5	4.1	28.0	43.2	20.2	216667
49683	THOMPSONVILLE	19879	905	23.5	35.8	36.6	3.2	0.9	42221	45117	40	25	800	14.6	23.9	40.9	18.9	1.8	108740
49684	TRAVERSE CITY	26334	15570	16.7	25.6	46.0	7.3	4.4	55422	55669	72	66	11872	8.1	7.1	37.5	40.7	6.6	169657
49686	TRAVERSE CITY	29439	13812	17.6	27.1	41.1	8.2	6.1	54369	55173	70	63	10417	6.3	8.6	35.7	38.2	11.2	173811
49688	TUSTIN	18793	981	23.8	31.8	38.9	4.6	0.9	44812	45633	48	35	843	21.8	30.5	35.2	10.7	1.8	87214
49689	WELLSTON	20137	810	27.5	32.5	34.6	4.2	1.2	39826	42391	32	17	683	23.3	28.4	38.7	7.9	1.8	87653
49690	WILLIAMSBURG	26105	2782	14.8	27.0	44.6	8.5	5.0	56702	55657	74	69	2299	1.3	4.1	30.7	50.8	13.1	199502
49701	MACKINAW CITY	25488	555	24.1	32.1	36.9	4.7	2.2	43706	46780	44	31	456	4.8	17.8	40.8	27.6	9.0	138265
	MICHIGAN	26713		20.1	24.2	38.5	11.3	5.9	55536	56866				13.2	21.9	40.3	21.5	3.2	115137
	UNITED STATES	27277		20.9	24.4	35.3	11.7	7.6	54719	56938				9.3	13.1	31.6	32.6	13.5	162279

ZIP CODE #	POST OFFICE NAME	FINANCIAL SERVICES: Auto Loan	Home Loan	Invest-ments	Retire-ment Plans	THE HOME: Home Improvements: Home Repair	Lawn & Garden	Furnishings: Comput-ers & Hard-ware-Personal	Major Appli-ances	TV, Radio, Sound Equip-ment	Furni-ture	ENTERTAINMENT: Dine out/ Carry out	Sports Equip-ment	Fees & Tickets	Toys & Games	Travel	Cable TV	PERSONAL: Apparel & Services	Auto Repairs	Health Insur-ance	Pets & Supplies
49437	MONTAGUE	89	80	83	82	81	92	80	88	83	76	82	66	75	83	80	87	56	84	92	103
49440	MUSKEGON	39	30	34	32	30	35	43	37	46	39	45	29	38	42	38	48	31	43	47	46
49441	MUSKEGON	77	79	74	80	78	84	78	79	80	76	80	59	79	80	79	83	55	79	86	93
49442	MUSKEGON	70	62	54	63	58	65	67	64	69	65	69	50	63	70	62	71	47	67	69	78
49444	MUSKEGON	77	68	62	69	65	76	71	72	75	69	74	55	67	76	67	79	51	73	79	88
49445	MUSKEGON	90	99	90	100	97	100	89	94	90	90	91	71	95	92	94	92	63	91	96	110
49446	NEW ERA	82	75	73	77	76	86	73	82	76	68	75	62	68	77	72	80	51	76	84	96
49448	NUNICA	89	87	79	88	86	91	82	87	83	81	83	66	80	86	82	85	57	83	88	103
49449	PENTWATER	89	83	114	82	92	102	78	93	83	83	82	63	78	78	86	88	55	88	101	108
49450	PULLMAN	77	69	64	65	67	69	69	71	69	71	69	54	63	72	65	70	48	70	69	83
49451	RAVENNA	87	78	78	80	79	92	77	86	80	71	78	65	71	82	76	84	54	80	89	101
49452	ROTHBURY	86	65	71	63	64	82	66	76	72	65	71	58	55	75	61	78	48	72	79	92
49453	SAUGATUCK	103	94	131	94	102	114	90	108	93	89	92	77	86	88	98	97	62	101	110	125
49454	SCOTTVILLE	78	66	74	66	67	82	66	77	70	61	69	58	58	71	65	75	46	72	81	91
49455	SHELBY	87	73	86	72	73	90	73	84	77	69	76	64	65	77	72	82	51	80	87	100
49456	SPRING LAKE	112	114	106	116	112	116	109	112	110	110	110	85	111	112	111	111	77	110	114	131
49457	TWIN LAKE	84	77	73	78	76	85	74	81	77	73	76	62	70	79	73	79	52	77	82	95
49459	WALKERVILLE	77	55	66	54	55	74	58	68	64	56	63	52	46	66	53	70	42	64	71	82
49460	WEST OLIVE	116	128	116	128	125	122	115	119	113	120	113	91	121	115	120	112	80	115	114	138
49461	WHITEHALL	91	90	83	92	89	95	87	91	89	85	88	69	86	90	87	91	61	89	94	108
49464	ZEELAND	102	112	95	110	107	104	100	103	98	103	99	79	104	102	102	97	69	99	99	119
49503	GRAND RAPIDS	67	55	51	57	53	55	72	60	71	67	72	50	64	71	62	71	51	68	64	74
49504	GRAND RAPIDS	78	76	68	78	73	79	82	77	84	77	84	60	81	84	78	86	59	81	85	93
49505	GRAND RAPIDS	79	78	69	80	74	78	84	77	84	80	84	62	83	84	80	85	59	82	83	94
49506	GRAND RAPIDS	115	124	120	126	123	119	120	118	119	123	119	91	127	119	123	118	85	118	118	138
49507	GRAND RAPIDS	79	73	61	73	68	71	78	73	79	78	80	57	75	80	73	80	56	77	75	88
49508	GRAND RAPIDS	99	97	85	97	93	88	99	93	97	101	99	74	98	100	95	95	69	96	90	110
49509	WYOMING	83	79	67	79	75	78	85	79	84	82	84	62	81	86	79	85	59	82	83	95
49512	GRAND RAPIDS	100	72	64	78	67	68	98	79	97	97	99	68	85	100	82	94	69	92	80	99
49519	WYOMING	90	81	72	84	77	78	90	81	89	89	90	66	86	92	84	88	63	87	83	99
49525	GRAND RAPIDS	99	110	101	110	107	103	104	102	101	105	102	80	109	103	106	100	72	102	100	119
49534	GRAND RAPIDS	93	95	85	97	92	91	93	91	92	94	93	72	95	94	93	91	65	92	90	108
49544	GRAND RAPIDS	88	73	65	77	69	71	87	75	87	86	88	62	81	89	78	86	61	84	78	93
49546	GRAND RAPIDS	121	132	132	136	134	127	127	125	125	132	126	96	136	125	132	124	90	126	126	145
49548	GRAND RAPIDS	84	80	68	78	76	79	80	79	80	81	80	61	76	83	76	80	55	79	79	94
49601	CADILLAC	80	72	72	73	72	82	75	78	78	71	76	59	70	78	72	81	52	77	84	93
49612	ALDEN	87	72	103	71	77	90	71	87	74	69	74	63	63	72	75	79	49	81	86	101
49613	ARCADIA	88	71	114	70	78	93	71	90	74	66	73	66	61	70	77	79	49	83	89	104
49614	BEAR LAKE	82	66	94	65	70	86	66	82	70	61	69	61	57	68	69	75	46	76	83	96
49615	BELLAIRE	95	76	122	75	83	100	76	96	80	71	79	70	66	76	82	85	52	89	95	112
49616	BENZONIA	78	65	97	63	72	84	65	80	68	64	67	57	58	64	70	73	45	75	83	93
49617	BEULAH	91	75	110	73	82	98	74	92	79	73	78	65	67	75	79	84	52	86	95	107
49618	BOON	86	64	86	62	66	87	65	80	71	61	70	60	53	71	64	78	47	74	83	96
49619	BRETHREN	81	65	104	64	71	85	65	82	68	61	67	60	56	64	70	72	44	76	81	95
49620	BUCKLEY	80	72	65	70	70	75	68	73	71	71	71	53	64	74	65	73	48	70	73	87
49621	CEDAR	90	86	104	87	88	98	81	93	82	79	82	70	78	81	87	85	56	88	92	109
49622	CENTRAL LAKE	89	75	103	75	80	94	74	90	77	69	76	67	66	75	78	82	51	83	91	105
49623	CHASE	79	57	73	55	58	78	59	71	65	56	64	54	47	66	56	71	43	67	75	86
49625	COPEMISH	78	57	69	55	57	76	59	70	65	57	64	53	47	67	55	71	43	65	73	84
49629	ELK RAPIDS	92	76	111	75	82	97	77	93	81	73	79	68	68	77	81	85	53	88	94	109
49630	EMPIRE	95	86	121	85	94	105	82	99	85	82	84	70	79	81	90	89	57	93	101	114
49631	EVART	76	59	70	59	60	76	63	72	68	58	66	54	53	68	60	73	45	68	76	85
49632	FALMOUTH	87	63	90	61	65	89	64	82	71	60	70	61	51	71	63	78	46	75	85	97
49633	FIFE LAKE	84	70	81	68	71	83	68	79	73	67	72	58	60	74	67	77	48	75	80	94
49635	FRANKFORT	85	76	101	76	83	94	75	88	79	76	78	61	72	75	80	84	53	84	94	101
49636	GLEN ARBOR	101	107	145	106	123	126	96	113	101	109	99	71	105	91	111	106	68	108	126	128
49637	GRAWN	84	76	79	73	75	80	73	79	75	75	75	59	68	76	72	76	51	77	78	94
49638	HARRIETTA	75	54	78	52	56	76	55	70	61	52	60	53	45	61	55	67	40	65	73	84
49639	HERSEY	82	63	71	62	63	79	65	74	71	64	70	56	55	73	61	76	47	71	77	89
49640	HONOR	88	71	114	70	78	93	71	90	74	66	73	65	62	70	77	79	49	83	89	104
49642	IDLEWILD	70	52	74	50	55	72	53	67	59	51	58	49	44	58	54	64	38	62	71	79
49643	INTERLOCHEN	90	82	79	79	80	86	77	84	80	79	80	62	72	83	75	82	54	80	83	99
49644	IRONS	62	59	76	55	66	71	56	67	60	61	58	44	56	55	62	63	39	64	74	76
49645	KALEVA	81	61	86	59	64	84	63	79	69	58	67	59	52	68	63	75	45	73	83	92
49646	KALKASKA	78	67	69	65	66	77	67	73	71	65	70	55	61	72	64	74	47	71	77	88
49648	KEWADIN	101	81	131	80	89	107	81	103	85	76	84	75	70	81	88	91	56	95	102	120
49649	KINGSLEY	91	83	77	80	82	86	79	84	81	81	81	61	74	84	76	84	55	81	84	100
49650	LAKE ANN	99	99	88	95	95	91	90	93	88	95	89	72	88	93	88	87	61	89	86	108
49651	LAKE CITY	81	62	82	60	65	84	63	77	69	60	68	57	53	68	63	75	45	72	82	91
49653	LAKE LEELANAU	104	88	134	87	97	112	86	107	90	84	89	76	79	85	94	95	60	99	108	123
49654	LELAND	113	119	162	118	137	141	107	127	113	121	111	79	118	102	124	118	76	121	141	143
49655	LEROY	86	63	81	61	64	85	65	78	71	62	70	59	53	72	62	78	47	73	82	94
49656	LUTHER	73	56	76	54	59	75	56	70	62	55	61	51	48	61	57	68	40	65	74	83
49657	MC BAIN	86	68	84	68	70	89	69	83	74	63	72	62	59	74	68	80	48	76	86	98
49659	MANCELONA	80	62	75	61	64	79	64	74	69	62	68	55	55	70	62	75	46	71	79	88
49660	MANISTEE	76	66	78	65	67	80	68	76	72	64	71	56	62	71	68	77	48	74	82	89
49663	MANTON	77	64	69	63	65	77	64	73	68	62	67	54	57	69	62	72	45	69	75	86
49664	MAPLE CITY	85	90	92	91	91	95	82	89	82	82	82	67	85	82	88	83	57	85	90	104
49665	MARION	81	58	78	56	60	80	60	74	66	56	65	56	48	67	58	73	43	68	77	89
49667	MERRITT	86	61	88	60	64	87	63	80	70	59	69	60	50	70	62	77	45	74	84	95
49668	MESICK	82	59	77	58	61	81	61	74	67	58	66	56	49	68	58	74	44	69	77	89
49670	NORTHPORT	106	86	137	85	95	113	86	108	90	81	88	78	75	85	93	95	59	100	108	125
49675	ONEKAMA	96	77	122	76	84	102	77	98	81	72	80	72	67	77	83	86	53	90	97	113
49676	RAPID CITY	95	77	118	76	84	99	77	96	80	73	79	70	67	77	82	85	53	89	95	111
49677	REED CITY	76	66	69	66	67	78	67	74	71	64	70	54	61	72	65	76	48	71	78	87
49679	SEARS	79	58	67	57	58	76	60	70	66	58	65	54	49	68	56	72	43	66	74	85
49680	SOUTH BOARDMAN	82	66	68	64	65	78	66	73	71	66	70	55	57	74	61	75	47	70	76	88
49682	SUTTONS BAY	111	92	130	91	98	114	91	111	95	88	94	81	81	93	95	100	63	103	110	129
49683	THOMPSONVILLE	82	64	79	62	65	81	64	76	69	62	68	56	54	69	62	74	45	71	78	90
49684	TRAVERSE CITY	93	96	91	96	94	94	92	93	91	94	92	71	93	92	93	91	64	92	92	109
49686	TRAVERSE CITY	99	100	103	100	102	103	97	101	97	98	96	75	97	96	99	98	67	99	103	117
49688	TUSTIN	84	66	73	64	66	81	66	76	71	65	71	57	57	74	63	76	47	72	79	91
49689	WELLSTON	84	60	87	58	63	85	62	79	68	58	67	59	50	68	62	75	44	72	82	93
49690	WILLIAMSBURG	98	99	105	100	99	105	91	101	91	90	91	77	91	92	96	93	63	95	99	118
49701	MACKINAW CITY	89	71	115	70	78	94	71	90	74	67	74	66	62	71	77	79	49	83	89	105
	MICHIGAN	98	97	93	98	95	100	96	97	97	95	97	74	96	98	96	99	68	97	100	115
	UNITED STATES	100	100	100	100	100	100	100	100	100	100	100	100	100	100	100	100	100	100	100	100

ZIP CODE			POPULATION			2000-2009 ANNUAL RATE		HOUSEHOLDS					FAMILIES		
#	POST OFFICE NAME	COUNTY FIPS CODE	2000	2009	2014	% Rate	State Centile	2000	2009	2014	% Annual Rate 2000-2009	2009 Average HH Size	2000	2009	% Annual Rate 2000-2009
49705	AFTON	031	760	849	898	1.2	88	255	297	318	1.7	2.79	194	223	1.5
49706	ALANSON	047	4596	5075	5244	1.1	86	1833	2085	2175	1.4	2.43	1338	1499	1.2
49707	ALPENA	007	24324	22703	21829	-0.7	7	10123	9734	9446	-0.4	2.28	6656	6313	-0.6
49709	ATLANTA	119	3769	3827	3836	0.2	48	1683	1759	1779	0.5	2.16	1175	1214	0.4
49710	BARBEAU	033	425	422	413	-0.1	32	196	198	196	0.1	2.13	147	147	0.0
49712	BOYNE CITY	029	7793	8027	8229	0.3	54	3160	3332	3443	0.6	2.40	2177	2276	0.5
49713	BOYNE FALLS	029	2110	2349	2476	1.2	88	810	928	988	1.5	2.51	599	679	1.4
49715	BRIMLEY	033	2607	2652	2620	0.2	48	1020	1075	1074	0.6	2.47	739	769	0.4
49716	BRUTUS	031	835	916	939	1.0	84	331	368	378	1.2	2.49	240	264	1.0
49718	CARP LAKE	047	615	624	614	0.2	48	272	286	284	0.5	2.18	186	192	0.3
49719	CEDARVILLE	097	1593	1532	1526	-0.4	16	701	696	700	-0.1	2.20	496	486	-0.2
49720	CHARLEVOIX	029	9696	9784	9802	0.1	42	3968	4098	4135	0.3	2.36	2754	2812	0.2
49721	CHEBOYGAN	031	15368	15288	15212	-0.1	32	6301	6477	6515	0.3	2.31	4330	4400	0.2
49724	DAFTER	033	1067	1098	1089	0.3	54	392	416	416	0.6	2.63	292	306	0.5
49725	DE TOUR VILLAGE	033	864	987	1000	1.4	92	402	474	486	1.8	2.08	259	301	1.6
49726	DRUMMOND ISLAND	033	992	1158	1180	1.7	95	467	560	576	2.0	2.07	307	362	1.8
49727	EAST JORDAN	009	7461	7797	7888	0.5	66	2765	2939	2989	0.7	2.61	2044	2146	0.5
49728	ECKERMAN	033	404	363	346	-1.2	2	163	151	145	-0.8	2.40	112	103	-0.9
49729	ELLSWORTH	009	1585	1712	1729	0.8	80	610	678	693	1.1	2.48	468	515	1.0
49730	ELMIRA	009	2132	2426	2554	1.4	92	769	902	960	1.7	2.68	593	689	1.6
49733	FREDERIC	039	1909	2176	2240	1.4	92	760	873	908	1.5	2.41	555	630	1.4
49735	GAYLORD	137	18687	19729	19794	0.6	71	7175	7799	7898	0.9	2.50	5182	5579	0.8
49736	GOETZVILLE	033	644	694	693	0.8	80	303	336	339	1.1	2.07	210	230	1.0
49738	GRAYLING	039	10353	10766	10693	0.4	60	4073	4298	4312	0.6	2.35	2873	3000	0.5
49740	HARBOR SPRINGS	047	7135	7600	7717	0.7	76	2964	3275	3358	1.1	2.27	2025	2204	0.9
49743	HAWKS	141	864	873	863	0.1	42	343	365	366	0.7	2.37	243	255	0.5
49744	HERRON	007	1000	968	942	-0.4	16	366	367	361	0.0	2.62	287	284	-0.1
49745	HESSEL	097	582	558	551	-0.5	12	247	245	244	-0.1	2.28	176	172	-0.2
49746	HILLMAN	119	3789	3737	3714	-0.1	32	1527	1552	1560	0.2	2.34	1052	1059	0.1
49747	HUBBARD LAKE	007	1890	1842	1812	-0.3	21	788	787	782	0.0	2.33	578	572	-0.1
49749	INDIAN RIVER	031	4195	4287	4369	0.2	48	1837	1942	2002	0.6	2.20	1282	1337	0.5
49751	JOHANNESBURG	137	2066	2138	2097	0.4	60	858	910	899	0.6	2.35	638	668	0.5
49752	KINROSS	033	183	192	192	0.5	66	66	71	72	0.8	2.70	49	53	0.9
49753	LACHINE	007	1999	2035	2016	0.2	48	786	830	831	0.6	2.44	593	619	0.5
49755	LEVERING	047	2022	2134	2152	0.6	71	804	877	893	0.9	2.42	566	608	0.8
49756	LEWISTON	135	4070	3968	3929	-0.3	21	1863	1856	1851	0.0	2.14	1241	1219	-0.2
49757	MACKINAC ISLAND	097	523	479	479	-0.9	5	252	239	242	-0.6	2.00	144	134	-0.8
49759	MILLERSBURG	141	1732	1757	1737	0.2	48	746	788	789	0.6	2.20	529	552	0.5
49760	MORAN	097	801	753	749	-0.7	7	334	325	327	-0.3	2.31	238	229	-0.4
49762	NAUBINWAY	097	881	834	840	-0.6	9	396	390	396	-0.2	2.13	268	261	-0.3
49765	ONAWAY	141	4242	4152	4096	-0.2	25	1735	1752	1748	0.1	2.33	1182	1178	0.0
49766	OSSINEKE	007	2557	2435	2353	-0.5	12	1016	1000	976	-0.2	2.42	748	727	-0.3
49768	PARADISE	033	588	520	494	-1.3	2	285	261	250	-0.9	1.99	195	176	-1.1
49769	PELLSTON	047	1715	1966	2041	1.5	93	558	654	684	1.7	2.97	425	492	1.6
49770	PETOSKEY	047	15553	16677	16971	0.8	80	6212	6898	7084	1.1	2.36	4062	4467	1.0
49774	PICKFORD	033	1862	1863	1848	0.0	37	715	738	739	0.3	2.52	529	540	0.2
49775	POINTE AUX PINS	097	71	68	69	-0.5	12	42	41	42	-0.3	1.66	17	16	-0.7
49776	POSEN	141	2165	2107	2069	-0.3	21	872	889	883	0.2	2.35	616	620	0.1
49777	PRESQUE ISLE	141	1345	1561	1595	1.6	94	621	742	767	1.9	2.10	459	543	1.8
49779	ROGERS CITY	141	5193	5012	4893	-0.4	16	2245	2268	2244	0.1	2.16	1482	1479	0.0
49780	RUDYARD	033	2069	2182	2178	0.6	71	782	853	858	0.9	2.55	588	634	0.8
49781	SAINT IGNACE	097	4924	4717	4679	-0.5	12	1996	1967	1972	-0.2	2.33	1313	1278	-0.3
49782	BEAVER ISLAND	029	551	600	631	0.9	82	258	289	306	1.2	2.08	155	170	1.0
49783	SAULT SAINTE MARIE	033	21621	19242	18862	-1.3	2	7756	7858	7759	0.1	2.28	4826	4817	0.0
49788	KINCHELOE	033	5322	8057	8038	4.6	100	930	999	1001	0.8	2.95	720	765	0.7
49792	TOWER	031	29	27	27	-0.8	6	16	15	15	-0.7	1.80	12	11	-0.9
49795	VANDERBILT	137	1954	2154	2233	1.1	86	748	850	888	1.4	2.51	535	600	1.2
49799	WOLVERINE	031	2374	2633	2746	1.1	86	908	1041	1098	1.5	2.52	657	744	1.4
49801	IRON MOUNTAIN	043	12243	11990	11742	-0.2	25	5107	5109	5038	0.0	2.30	3335	3298	-0.1
49802	KINGSFORD	043	6626	6461	6330	-0.3	21	2792	2798	2762	0.0	2.24	1796	1774	-0.1
49806	AU TRAIN	003	396	392	387	-0.1	32	175	180	180	0.3	2.11	117	119	0.2
49807	BARK RIVER	041	3585	3593	3537	0.0	37	1378	1433	1428	0.4	2.50	1030	1056	0.3
49812	CARNEY	109	1244	1283	1279	0.3	54	513	545	548	0.7	2.27	355	372	0.5
49814	CHAMPION	103	1926	1831	1793	-0.5	12	767	760	755	-0.1	2.41	578	566	-0.2
49815	CHANNING	043	529	531	524	0.0	37	219	227	226	0.4	2.34	154	158	0.3
49816	CHATHAM	003	449	450	445	0.0	37	185	194	195	0.5	2.19	130	135	0.4
49817	COOKS	153	554	530	517	-0.5	12	208	206	203	-0.1	2.57	153	150	-0.2
49818	CORNELL	041	789	827	823	0.5	66	311	339	341	0.9	2.44	240	258	0.8
49820	CURTIS	097	889	886	884	0.0	37	392	405	408	0.4	2.13	266	271	0.2
49821	DAGGETT	109	1289	1289	1275	0.0	37	519	532	530	0.3	2.36	360	365	0.1
49822	DEERTON	003	310	307	303	-0.1	32	146	151	150	0.4	2.02	103	105	0.2
49825	EBEN JUNCTION	003	172	170	168	-0.1	32	71	73	73	0.3	2.32	50	51	0.2
49826	RUMELY	003	371	368	362	-0.1	32	154	159	158	0.3	2.30	108	111	0.3
49827	ENGADINE	097	853	840	840	-0.2	25	359	366	370	0.2	2.25	244	247	0.1
49829	ESCANABA	041	17941	17227	16738	-0.4	16	7548	7468	7324	-0.1	2.24	4713	4590	-0.3
49831	FELCH	043	439	438	432	0.0	37	163	168	167	0.3	2.59	119	121	0.2
49833	LITTLE LAKE	103	294	280	275	-0.5	12	120	120	119	0.0	2.33	83	81	-0.3
49834	FOSTER CITY	043	419	432	429	0.3	54	170	180	180	0.6	2.40	119	125	0.5
49835	GARDEN	041	860	869	858	0.1	42	370	390	389	0.6	2.23	259	269	0.4
49836	GERMFASK	153	583	558	543	-0.5	12	239	233	228	-0.3	2.27	178	171	-0.4
49837	GLADSTONE	041	10018	9949	9761	-0.1	32	3976	4075	4039	0.3	2.43	2843	2889	0.2
49838	GOULD CITY	097	341	332	332	-0.3	21	164	166	168	0.1	1.96	111	111	0.0
49839	GRAND MARAIS	003	480	491	487	0.2	48	243	258	259	0.6	1.69	170	178	0.5
49840	GULLIVER	153	875	790	754	-1.1	3	358	334	322	-0.7	2.36	271	250	-0.9
49841	GWINN	103	5579	6535	6944	1.7	95	2279	2716	2901	1.9	2.41	1629	1916	1.8
49847	HERMANSVILLE	109	1020	1044	1037	0.3	54	433	457	458	0.6	2.19	294	306	0.4
49848	INGALLS	109	203	202	200	-0.1	32	76	78	78	0.3	2.56	48	48	0.0
49849	ISHPEMING	103	12159	11716	11490	-0.4	16	4981	4962	4935	0.0	2.31	3337	3279	-0.2
49853	MC MILLAN	095	1233	1301	1294	0.6	71	524	577	582	1.0	2.20	394	429	0.9
49854	MANISTIQUE	153	6915	6653	6470	-0.4	16	2828	2759	2700	-0.3	2.27	1912	1846	-0.4
49855	MARQUETTE	103	31970	32104	31909	0.0	37	12358	12737	12836	0.3	2.20	7218	7333	0.2
49858	MENOMINEE	109	12890	12471	12199	-0.4	16	5604	5551	5473	-0.1	2.22	3571	3489	-0.3
49861	MICHIGAMME	103	1284	1246	1221	-0.3	21	600	606	603	0.1	2.04	415	418	0.1
49862	MUNISING	003	4647	4634	4569	0.0	37	1903	1960	1952	0.3	2.20	1254	1276	0.2
49866	NEGAUNEE	103	8250	8159	8097	-0.1	32	3368	3434	3452	0.2	2.33	2277	2289	0.1
	MICHIGAN					0.3					0.4	2.52			0.3
	UNITED STATES					1.0					1.1	2.59			0.9

# ZIP CODE	POST OFFICE NAME	RACE (%) White 2000	White 2009	Black 2000	Black 2009	Asian/Pacific 2000	Asian/Pacific 2009	% Hispanic Origin 2000	% Hispanic Origin 2009	2009 AGE DISTRIBUTION (%) 0-4	5-9	10-14	15-19	20-24	25-44	45-64	65-84	85+	18+	MEDIAN AGE 2009	% 2009 Males	% 2009 Females
49705	AFTON	96.6	96.0	0.5	0.7	0.0	0.1	0.4	0.4	6.4	6.6	6.8	6.4	4.7	22.0	30.7	15.2	1.2	75.6	42.8	51.0	49.0
49706	ALANSON	94.7	94.1	0.3	0.3	0.2	0.3	0.6	0.9	6.5	6.6	7.1	6.4	4.8	25.7	30.5	11.0	1.3	75.8	39.8	51.0	49.0
49707	ALPENA	98.1	97.7	0.3	0.3	0.4	0.6	0.6	0.7	5.6	5.7	5.8	6.3	5.9	23.3	29.5	15.0	2.8	79.1	42.9	48.5	51.5
49709	ATLANTA	98.0	98.0	0.4	0.4	0.2	0.2	0.5	0.5	4.4	4.6	4.9	4.9	4.4	18.3	33.2	22.9	2.4	82.8	50.8	49.1	50.9
49710	BARBEAU	84.0	82.9	0.7	0.7	0.2	0.2	0.7	0.9	5.2	5.5	6.2	5.9	3.8	21.3	35.1	15.4	1.7	79.6	46.2	50.7	49.3
49712	BOYNE CITY	97.5	97.1	0.1	0.1	0.2	0.4	0.7	0.8	6.4	6.6	6.9	6.6	5.0	23.8	30.3	12.8	1.6	75.8	41.3	50.1	49.9
49713	BOYNE FALLS	97.6	97.2	0.1	0.1	0.2	0.3	0.6	0.8	6.6	7.1	7.2	6.8	5.0	24.7	28.7	12.7	1.2	74.5	40.4	50.5	49.5
49715	BRIMLEY	60.4	59.8	0.1	0.1	0.3	0.5	0.8	0.9	7.5	7.7	7.5	6.6	5.7	27.0	26.1	10.9	1.0	73.2	36.2	49.1	50.9
49716	BRUTUS	92.6	91.7	0.2	0.3	0.4	0.4	0.5	0.7	7.0	6.8	6.8	6.1	4.8	24.5	27.8	14.2	2.1	75.5	40.9	50.4	49.6
49718	CARP LAKE	93.3	92.8	0.8	0.8	0.0	0.2	0.8	0.8	5.3	5.1	7.2	6.3	3.5	22.6	35.7	13.1	1.1	78.0	45.0	51.3	48.7
49719	CEDARVILLE	92.5	91.6	0.1	0.1	0.3	0.5	0.7	0.8	4.0	4.3	5.0	5.4	4.1	18.8	34.1	21.9	2.3	83.6	50.4	50.3	49.7
49720	CHARLEVOIX	95.6	94.8	0.2	0.3	0.5	0.7	1.3	1.7	5.7	6.2	6.6	6.6	4.7	23.1	31.2	13.7	2.3	77.0	43.0	48.8	51.2
49721	CHEBOYGAN	93.8	93.0	0.2	0.3	0.3	0.4	0.8	1.0	5.6	6.0	6.2	5.9	4.8	22.5	30.1	16.3	2.7	78.3	44.3	49.3	50.7
49724	DAFTER	84.4	82.9	0.5	0.5	0.4	0.5	0.8	1.1	6.5	6.6	6.4	5.6	5.0	24.5	31.8	12.4	1.2	77.0	41.8	51.7	48.3
49725	DE TOUR VILLAGE	88.4	87.1	0.0	0.0	0.2	0.3	1.5	2.0	4.0	4.4	4.4	4.0	3.3	17.1	33.9	26.5	2.4	84.9	53.4	50.2	49.8
49726	DRUMMOND ISLAND	89.1	87.9	0.2	0.3	0.1	0.1	0.6	0.8	4.0	4.3	4.7	4.2	3.2	18.1	35.2	24.0	2.2	84.5	52.6	51.4	48.6
49727	EAST JORDAN	95.4	94.7	0.2	0.3	0.3	0.3	1.3	1.7	7.2	7.3	7.4	6.6	4.9	24.2	26.8	13.4	2.2	73.8	39.7	49.4	50.6
49728	ECKERMAN	92.6	91.7	0.0	0.0	0.0	0.0	0.5	0.6	2.8	2.8	3.3	4.4	4.4	14.3	38.3	27.3	2.5	88.4	55.9	52.3	47.7
49729	ELLSWORTH	97.5	97.0	0.3	0.3	0.3	0.4	1.5	2.0	6.4	6.7	7.0	6.7	5.2	21.8	31.2	13.2	1.9	75.5	42.2	50.3	49.7
49730	ELMIRA	96.8	96.2	0.2	0.2	0.4	0.6	0.8	1.2	6.6	6.9	7.2	6.8	4.9	24.1	29.3	13.1	1.1	74.7	40.5	50.3	49.7
49733	FREDERIC	97.4	97.0	0.1	0.1	0.2	0.2	0.9	1.3	4.8	5.6	6.7	7.6	3.8	21.2	32.4	16.4	1.7	77.4	45.2	51.9	48.1
49735	GAYLORD	97.4	96.8	0.2	0.2	0.4	0.6	0.8	1.1	6.3	6.6	7.1	7.2	5.0	25.1	28.9	12.1	1.7	75.3	39.9	49.6	50.4
49736	GOETZVILLE	91.5	90.9	0.2	0.1	0.2	0.1	1.1	1.6	4.6	5.2	5.2	4.2	3.3	18.3	38.5	18.3	2.4	82.4	50.6	50.3	49.7
49738	GRAYLING	95.8	95.0	2.0	2.3	0.3	0.5	1.0	1.3	5.3	5.4	5.4	6.5	5.9	23.1	29.4	16.6	2.4	79.8	43.8	51.9	48.1
49740	HARBOR SPRINGS	93.8	93.1	0.9	1.1	0.4	0.7	0.9	1.2	5.2	5.7	6.3	5.4	3.5	22.5	34.6	15.1	1.8	79.0	45.8	50.6	49.4
49743	HAWKS	98.5	98.4	0.2	0.2	0.1	0.1	0.2	0.2	4.8	5.0	5.7	5.6	4.1	20.5	34.5	17.1	2.6	80.8	47.5	50.9	49.1
49744	HERRON	98.6	98.1	0.3	0.3	0.0	0.1	0.6	0.9	5.6	6.2	6.7	6.9	5.1	22.6	31.2	14.0	1.7	77.2	42.8	51.0	49.0
49745	HESSEL	86.2	85.3	0.0	0.0	0.3	0.5	0.9	1.1	4.7	4.8	5.6	5.9	4.1	19.9	34.4	18.6	2.0	81.2	48.1	50.7	49.3
49746	HILLMAN	98.7	98.6	0.1	0.1	0.1	0.1	0.6	0.7	4.7	5.1	5.4	5.5	4.5	20.4	31.3	19.6	3.6	81.3	48.1	49.5	50.5
49747	HUBBARD LAKE	98.7	98.4	0.1	0.1	0.1	0.2	0.5	0.7	4.1	4.6	5.0	5.5	4.1	17.5	32.0	24.8	2.4	83.0	51.4	50.7	49.3
49749	INDIAN RIVER	96.5	95.9	0.4	0.4	0.1	0.2	1.2	1.6	5.2	5.6	5.7	5.0	3.5	20.6	31.8	20.3	2.4	80.2	48.1	50.2	49.8
49751	JOHANNESBURG	98.5	98.4	0.2	0.2	0.1	0.1	0.2	0.2	5.1	5.4	5.8	6.0	4.0	21.7	31.4	19.2	1.5	79.8	46.4	51.2	48.8
49752	KINROSS	80.9	79.7	0.0	0.0	0.5	1.0	1.1	1.6	6.3	6.3	6.8	6.8	4.7	24.5	31.3	12.5	1.0	76.0	40.5	50.5	49.5
49753	LACHINE	98.3	97.7	0.3	0.3	0.1	0.1	0.9	1.3	4.7	5.4	6.3	7.4	4.5	22.6	31.5	15.5	2.0	79.0	44.3	50.2	49.8
49755	LEVERING	93.9	93.4	0.6	0.7	0.1	0.2	0.7	0.9	6.2	6.2	7.3	6.7	4.2	23.0	32.4	12.6	1.4	75.4	42.2	50.5	49.5
49756	LEWISTON	98.4	98.2	0.1	0.2	0.0	0.1	0.9	1.1	4.1	4.2	4.6	5.2	3.7	17.4	31.9	26.4	2.6	83.8	53.4	49.3	50.7
49757	MACKINAC ISLAND	75.7	74.3	0.0	0.0	0.4	0.6	0.6	0.6	3.5	3.1	3.3	5.2	8.8	27.3	35.3	11.9	1.5	87.1	44.0	51.8	48.2
49759	MILLERSBURG	98.2	98.2	0.2	0.2	0.2	0.2	0.6	0.6	4.7	4.8	5.1	4.7	3.7	18.6	33.1	22.4	2.8	82.1	50.6	49.4	50.6
49760	MORAN	68.8	67.2	0.5	0.5	0.2	0.4	0.6	0.7	4.4	6.8	8.6	6.9	4.1	24.3	31.7	11.6	1.6	75.8	41.7	50.7	49.3
49762	NAUBINWAY	83.5	82.1	0.0	0.1	0.1	0.2	1.1	1.3	3.4	3.8	5.3	5.8	3.6	16.8	36.1	23.0	2.3	83.7	53.3	49.9	50.1
49765	ONAWAY	96.8	96.5	0.3	0.3	0.3	0.3	0.8	0.9	5.7	5.8	5.8	6.0	5.7	21.8	29.7	17.0	2.5	78.8	44.3	49.5	50.5
49766	OSSINEKE	98.4	98.0	0.2	0.2	0.2	0.3	0.5	0.7	5.2	5.7	6.0	5.6	4.9	23.0	33.1	14.6	1.9	79.6	44.7	50.6	49.4
49768	PARADISE	94.2	93.7	0.0	0.0	0.0	0.0	0.5	0.6	2.1	2.5	2.9	4.2	4.4	13.1	39.2	28.8	2.7	89.8	57.2	52.7	47.3
49769	PELLSTON	90.5	89.6	1.2	1.2	0.3	0.4	0.9	1.1	8.0	8.0	8.1	7.7	5.6	26.4	26.4	8.6	1.1	70.8	35.6	51.3	48.7
49770	PETOSKEY	95.3	94.6	0.2	0.2	0.6	1.0	1.0	1.3	5.8	6.3	6.7	6.6	5.3	25.1	29.2	12.1	2.8	77.0	40.7	48.0	52.0
49774	PICKFORD	87.3	86.6	0.4	0.5	0.2	0.3	1.0	1.3	5.4	5.9	6.2	5.8	3.9	20.9	34.6	15.6	1.8	79.0	46.2	50.6	49.4
49775	POINTE AUX PINS	100.0	100.0	0.0	0.0	0.0	0.0	0.0	0.0	0.0	1.5	1.5	2.9	1.5	5.9	45.6	38.2	2.9	95.6	63.0	50.0	50.0
49776	POSEN	98.5	98.4	0.5	0.5	0.0	0.0	0.4	0.4	5.3	5.6	6.1	5.8	4.8	21.7	32.8	15.3	2.6	79.6	45.5	50.9	49.1
49777	PRESQUE ISLE	98.7	98.7	0.2	0.3	0.2	0.2	0.4	0.3	3.1	3.7	4.3	4.8	2.9	14.2	36.3	27.9	2.9	86.0	55.1	51.7	48.3
49779	ROGERS CITY	98.3	98.2	0.2	0.2	0.2	0.2	0.4	0.4	4.7	4.9	5.2	5.6	4.6	20.7	30.9	19.7	3.7	81.6	47.9	48.5	51.5
49780	RUDYARD	89.7	88.5	0.1	0.2	0.4	0.7	1.2	1.5	6.5	6.9	7.1	6.7	4.9	23.2	31.3	11.9	1.4	74.8	40.7	50.0	50.0
49781	SAINT IGNACE	73.4	71.7	0.3	0.3	0.5	0.7	0.8	1.0	5.1	6.0	6.6	6.8	5.4	23.5	29.6	14.0	3.1	78.1	42.6	49.7	50.3
49782	BEAVER ISLAND	98.4	98.2	0.0	0.0	0.0	0.0	0.2	0.2	3.8	4.5	4.8	4.7	4.3	13.2	38.8	23.8	2.0	83.8	52.9	49.0	51.0
49783	SAULT SAINTE MARIE	75.8	75.5	5.0	2.5	0.6	0.9	1.6	1.5	5.4	5.2	5.2	8.3	10.6	26.5	24.9	11.5	2.4	80.8	35.9	50.7	49.3
49788	KINCHELOE	61.6	59.2	19.2	23.5	0.6	1.6	2.9	4.1	4.5	3.8	3.5	10.2	13.3	43.2	17.9	3.2	0.4	85.6	31.4	71.8	28.2
49792	TOWER	100.0	96.3	0.0	0.0	0.0	0.0	0.0	0.0	7.4	7.4	7.4	7.4	7.4	25.9	29.6	7.4	0.0	74.1	33.8	51.9	48.1
49795	VANDERBILT	97.2	96.7	0.2	0.2	0.2	0.3	0.8	1.0	6.5	6.8	6.8	6.8	4.6	24.9	27.3	14.8	1.4	75.8	40.5	49.4	50.6
49799	WOLVERINE	96.5	96.1	0.0	0.0	0.0	0.1	0.7	0.9	7.1	7.3	7.3	6.5	4.8	24.3	27.5	13.8	1.4	74.0	40.1	50.4	49.6
49801	IRON MOUNTAIN	97.9	97.3	0.1	0.2	0.6	0.9	0.9	1.1	5.4	5.8	6.3	7.0	5.5	22.4	30.2	14.2	3.2	78.1	43.3	50.0	50.0
49802	KINGSFORD	97.9	97.4	0.2	0.2	0.4	0.6	0.5	0.7	6.0	6.0	6.1	6.6	6.0	23.3	28.7	13.4	4.0	77.0	41.9	48.8	51.2
49806	AU TRAIN	93.7	93.6	0.0	0.0	0.0	0.0	0.8	1.0	4.8	4.8	5.6	6.4	3.8	20.7	34.4	16.1	3.3	80.9	47.1	49.2	50.8
49807	BARK RIVER	96.2	95.7	0.1	0.1	0.3	0.4	0.4	0.5	5.3	5.8	6.0	6.0	4.7	24.4	33.4	13.0	1.6	79.2	43.3	51.2	48.8
49812	CARNEY	88.7	88.3	0.1	0.2	0.1	0.1	1.1	1.3	6.0	6.2	6.5	6.3	4.9	22.0	29.5	15.5	3.0	77.0	43.6	50.3	49.7
49814	CHAMPION	98.7	98.5	0.1	0.1	0.1	0.2	0.3	0.4	5.1	5.1	5.6	6.1	4.7	23.4	34.1	14.5	1.5	80.3	45.1	51.2	48.8
49815	CHANNING	97.5	97.4	0.0	0.0	0.2	0.2	0.8	0.9	5.5	6.0	6.4	6.2	4.7	21.3	31.6	16.4	1.9	78.7	44.9	49.7	50.3
49816	CHATHAM	91.8	91.1	4.2	4.7	0.0	0.0	0.9	0.9	4.4	4.7	5.6	6.0	5.1	22.2	35.1	14.7	2.2	81.8	46.1	52.9	47.1
49817	COOKS	91.0	89.8	0.2	0.2	0.4	0.6	0.5	0.6	4.0	4.5	5.1	5.5	3.4	19.1	36.8	19.6	2.1	83.0	50.3	50.8	49.2
49818	CORNELL	96.6	96.1	0.0	0.0	0.1	0.2	0.5	0.7	4.8	5.6	6.2	6.3	4.7	23.5	34.7	13.1	1.2	79.4	44.3	52.1	47.9
49820	CURTIS	89.1	88.3	0.2	0.2	0.1	0.2	1.3	1.7	3.6	3.8	4.0	4.5	4.4	16.7	34.4	26.7	1.8	85.6	54.3	49.7	50.3
49821	DAGGETT	94.2	93.8	0.2	0.2	0.2	0.2	0.5	0.8	5.7	6.3	6.7	6.2	4.7	21.0	31.4	15.4	2.6	77.0	44.5	51.7	48.3
49822	DEERTON	95.1	95.1	0.0	0.0	0.0	0.0	0.6	0.3	4.6	3.9	5.9	7.2	4.2	20.5	37.5	14.0	2.3	81.1	46.6	51.5	48.5
49825	EBEN JUNCTION	95.3	95.3	0.0	0.0	0.0	0.0	0.6	0.6	4.7	4.1	5.9	7.1	4.1	20.0	38.2	13.5	2.4	80.6	46.7	51.2	48.8
49826	RUMELY	95.1	95.1	0.0	0.0	0.0	0.0	0.5	0.5	4.6	4.1	5.7	7.1	4.3	20.7	37.5	13.9	2.2	81.3	46.5	50.5	49.5
49827	ENGADINE	85.4	84.4	0.1	0.1	0.1	0.2	1.5	2.0	4.0	4.3	5.6	5.8	3.8	19.0	34.8	20.6	2.0	82.5	50.5	50.7	49.3
49829	ESCANABA	95.9	95.4	0.1	0.1	0.4	0.5	0.6	0.8	5.7	5.7	6.1	6.8	5.7	24.3	27.6	14.3	3.8	78.4	41.6	48.2	51.8
49831	FELCH	97.7	97.5	0.0	0.0	0.5	0.5	0.5	0.7	5.3	5.7	6.4	6.6	5.3	21.9	33.1	14.2	1.6	78.5	44.1	50.7	49.3
49833	LITTLE LAKE	97.6	97.5	0.3	0.4	0.0	0.0	0.3	0.0	4.3	4.3	4.3	5.0	4.6	20.7	37.5	17.1	2.1	83.9	48.5	46.8	53.2
49834	FOSTER CITY	98.3	97.9	0.0	0.0	0.0	0.2	0.5	0.9	4.9	5.3	6.0	6.5	4.9	22.0	34.0	14.6	1.9	79.6	45.3	50.2	49.8
49835	GARDEN	90.2	89.2	0.1	0.1	0.2	0.3	0.3	0.5	4.4	4.8	4.9	4.8	3.3	17.8	35.1	22.4	2.3	82.9	50.7	51.3	48.7
49836	GERMFASK	90.1	88.4	0.2	0.2	0.0	0.2	0.5	0.5	6.3	6.6	6.8	5.4	3.2	21.1	28.9	19.7	2.0	77.1	45.4	50.2	49.8
49837	GLADSTONE	96.5	96.0	0.1	0.1	0.4	0.6	0.4	0.5	5.6	6.0	6.4	6.5	5.3	22.8	31.6	13.8	2.1	77.8	43.0	49.2	50.8
49838	GOULD CITY	88.0	87.3	0.3	0.3	0.0	0.3	1.2	1.2	3.3	3.3	3.6	4.2	4.2	14.8	35.2	29.2	2.1	86.4	56.4	48.5	51.5
49839	GRAND MARAIS	79.8	79.2	14.6	15.1	0.2	0.2	1.3	1.2	2.6	2.9	3.5	4.3	6.7	26.5	31.8	19.1	2.6	88.0	47.3	60.9	39.1
49840	GULLIVER	89.1	88.0	0.2	0.3	0.0	0.0	1.4	1.6	4.7	4.8	6.3	7.5	3.0	23.3	32.7	16.1	1.6	79.2	45.2	52.5	47.5
49841	GWINN	94.3	92.9	0.6	0.7	0.6	0.8	1.1	1.6	7.7	6.5	6.2	7.1	8.8	24.7	28.2	9.8	1.0	75.5	36.1	49.9	50.1
49847	HERMANSVILLE	96.0	95.7	0.1	0.2	0.1	0.2	0.7	0.9	6.1	6.3	6.5	5.9	4.6	21.7	29.0	16.2	3.5	77.3	44.0	50.0	50.0
49848	INGALLS	98.0	97.5	0.0	0.0	0.5	0.5	0.0	0.5	4.5	4.5	5.4	5.9	5.4	21.8	32.7	16.8	3.0	81.2	46.5	49.0	51.0
49849	ISHPEMING	97.8	97.6	0.1	0.1	0.2	0.3	0.6	0.8	5.6	5.8	5.9	6.0	6.1	24.6	29.2	13.7	3.2	79.0	41.9	48.3	51.7
49853	MC MILLAN	93.3	93.1	0.2	0.2	0.3	0.4	0.3	0.2	4.3	5.0	6.0	6.0	3.5	18.2	35.0	20.4	1.6	80.2	49.7	50.6	49.4
49854	MANISTIQUE	88.2	86.6	2.0	2.3	0.5	0.8	1.0	1.2	5.5	5.4	5.6	6.2	6.1	22.8	29.2	16.0	3.1	79.5	43.6	50.2	49.8
49855	MARQUETTE	93.3	92.2	2.5	2.7	0.8	1.4	0.8	1.2	4.3	4.3	4.5	10.8	12.6	25.2	25.9	10.4	2.0	83.6	34.9	50.6	49.4
49858	MENOMINEE	97.8	97.4	0.1	0.1	0.3	0.4	0.9	1.1	5.7	5.9	5.9	6.2	5.8	23.6	30.3	14.0	2.6	78.9	42.6	49.0	51.0
49861	MICHIGAMME	96.0	95.7	0.1	0.1	0.2	0.2	0.5	0.5	3.7	4.3	5.1	5.1	3.5	20.6	39.8	16.5	1.4	83.5	48.6	52.0	48.0
49862	MUNISING	89.7	89.4	3.1	3.3	0.6	0.6	1.0	1.0	4.9	5.2	5.5	5.9	5.4	23.8	30.8	15.6	3.0	80.7	44.5	51.4	48.6
49866	NEGAUNEE	97.1	96.7	0.2	0.2	0.3	0.4	0.4	0.6	5.2	5.6	5.7	5.8	5.4	25.1	30.5	13.3	3.3	79.9	42.8	49.0	51.0
	MICHIGAN	80.2	78.3	14.2	14.5	1.8	2.8	3.3	4.1	6.7	6.7	6.8	7.2	6.6	26.3	26.9	10.9	1.9	75.6	37.6	49.2	50.8
	UNITED STATES	75.1	72.0	12.3	12.7	3.8	4.6	12.5	15.7	6.8	6.7	6.6	7.1	6.9	27.0	26.0	10.9	1.9	75.7	36.9	49.2	50.8

INCOME

#	POST OFFICE NAME	2009 Per Capita Income	2009 HH Income Base	2009 Household Income Distribution (%) Less than $25,000	$25,000 to $49,999	$50,000 to $99,999	$100,000 to $149,999	$150,000 or More	Median Household Income 2009	2014	2009 National Centile	2009 State Centile	2009 Home Value Base	2009 Home Value Distribution (%) Less than $50,000	$50,000 to $89,999	$90,000 to $174,999	$175,000 to $399,999	$400,000 or More	2009 Median Home Value
49705	AFTON	16725	297	27.6	37.4	29.0	4.7	1.3	38768	39665	29	14	257	11.3	29.6	45.1	10.5	3.5	103250
49706	ALANSON	21481	2085	21.4	33.6	38.4	4.8	1.7	44727	48640	47	34	1698	10.2	17.2	47.2	22.7	2.7	118648
49707	ALPENA	21605	9734	28.6	27.8	37.3	4.9	1.4	42973	46088	42	29	7407	12.4	38.6	39.4	9.0	0.6	89174
49709	ATLANTA	20858	1759	30.4	33.7	32.1	2.6	1.3	37242	39384	24	10	1538	20.4	30.9	37.6	10.1	0.9	88551
49710	BARBEAU	23032	198	23.2	32.8	38.9	4.5	0.5	45640	47755	50	37	178	7.9	28.7	45.5	16.9	1.1	107031
49712	BOYNE CITY	23751	3332	20.4	30.3	40.2	6.4	2.6	48933	51077	59	47	2688	9.1	15.0	44.3	23.6	8.1	134543
49713	BOYNE FALLS	21668	928	21.4	29.8	40.4	6.3	2.0	48398	50854	58	46	791	12.8	18.6	43.0	21.5	4.2	119193
49715	BRIMLEY	20684	1075	24.0	27.7	42.0	5.1	1.2	48288	49801	57	45	894	15.1	25.7	47.8	10.4	1.0	101684
49716	BRUTUS	21465	368	18.8	36.4	38.9	3.3	2.7	44633	48420	47	34	322	12.1	18.0	43.5	17.4	9.0	117742
49718	CARP LAKE	23860	286	26.2	31.5	33.9	5.2	3.1	42531	46447	41	27	242	14.0	24.4	34.3	22.3	5.0	110000
49719	CEDARVILLE	23571	696	25.4	31.0	35.9	5.9	1.7	43090	44837	43	29	587	5.8	16.0	42.9	29.5	5.8	143432
49720	CHARLEVOIX	24665	4098	20.0	29.3	40.1	7.8	2.9	50455	51784	62	50	3268	7.1	13.2	42.0	29.2	8.5	149380
49721	CHEBOYGAN	20853	6477	29.2	32.8	31.9	4.2	1.9	39401	41039	31	16	5162	10.8	23.0	45.0	17.8	3.4	111747
49724	DAFTER	19104	416	24.5	28.4	42.1	4.1	1.0	47632	48357	56	43	370	13.0	30.0	43.2	12.4	1.4	100347
49725	DE TOUR VILLAGE	24283	474	31.2	26.8	35.0	4.4	2.5	42827	46109	42	28	431	12.8	15.1	39.2	28.1	4.9	132102
49726	DRUMMOND ISLAND	23778	560	30.0	27.5	36.3	3.6	2.7	42052	46167	39	25	481	11.9	23.9	35.1	25.6	3.5	112897
49727	EAST JORDAN	19812	2939	22.6	30.6	40.1	5.1	1.6	46265	49189	52	39	2403	10.8	20.1	42.1	20.7	6.2	117763
49728	ECKERMAN	19316	151	30.5	30.5	34.4	3.3	1.3	38389	43655	28	12	135	17.8	22.2	44.4	12.6	3.0	101786
49729	ELLSWORTH	21184	678	16.5	31.3	46.9	4.6	0.7	51458	51032	65	54	595	11.9	14.8	41.0	23.2	9.1	133135
49730	ELMIRA	20304	902	19.5	31.7	40.9	6.1	1.8	48329	49065	57	45	803	11.5	20.7	48.7	17.4	1.7	113260
49733	FREDERIC	19877	873	23.0	36.9	34.0	5.2	0.9	41511	43785	38	23	757	20.7	26.4	36.5	14.7	1.7	94300
49735	GAYLORD	23017	7799	19.5	29.6	41.0	7.3	2.6	50583	51808	63	51	6257	6.7	12.9	49.0	28.2	3.3	137568
49736	GOETZVILLE	22880	336	28.3	33.9	32.4	3.6	1.8	39217	43159	30	15	306	13.4	26.1	45.8	11.8	2.9	105392
49738	GRAYLING	20342	4298	23.4	38.0	32.4	4.5	1.7	40071	41738	33	18	3428	13.1	32.4	42.9	10.2	1.4	94709
49740	HARBOR SPRINGS	29071	3275	17.9	26.7	39.6	10.2	5.6	54766	55133	71	64	2678	6.1	6.1	29.0	40.8	18.0	203846
49743	HAWKS	17794	365	28.2	38.4	29.9	3.0	0.5	38007	40000	27	11	324	19.1	39.2	34.6	5.9	1.2	80690
49744	HERRON	18790	367	24.5	33.0	37.3	3.5	1.6	43398	46389	44	30	337	15.1	33.5	39.8	11.0	0.6	91324
49745	HESSEL	20394	245	29.4	33.9	31.0	4.5	1.2	37095	38621	24	9	209	11.5	23.9	41.1	18.7	4.8	112500
49746	HILLMAN	18067	1552	33.2	32.9	30.0	2.8	1.1	35341	37360	19	6	1309	22.5	32.3	32.6	11.2	1.4	84469
49747	HUBBARD LAKE	21749	787	25.7	31.8	35.3	5.3	1.9	43870	45797	45	31	713	11.9	28.3	42.8	14.6	2.4	99026
49749	INDIAN RIVER	22221	1942	25.7	34.1	34.3	3.9	1.9	41686	43378	38	23	1648	8.3	17.0	40.3	26.1	8.4	131696
49751	JOHANNESBURG	23076	910	19.8	34.2	37.4	6.5	2.2	44065	50198	46	32	832	8.8	16.6	49.3	20.4	4.9	124522
49752	KINROSS	18304	71	28.2	29.6	36.6	4.2	1.4	44311	47932	46	33	62	22.6	27.4	38.7	11.3	0.0	90000
49753	LACHINE	19711	830	25.1	33.5	35.7	4.6	1.2	41066	44379	36	21	754	18.0	35.3	35.3	10.6	0.8	86951
49755	LEVERING	20862	877	24.7	33.1	35.1	4.8	2.3	42529	46201	41	27	755	13.6	20.9	38.8	22.5	4.1	116288
49756	LEWISTON	21666	1856	28.7	36.5	28.9	4.1	1.7	38543	39401	28	13	1599	14.7	34.0	36.9	13.0	1.4	91213
49757	MACKINAC ISLAND	32459	239	11.7	40.6	36.8	5.4	5.4	46471	46554	53	40	142	2.1	8.5	33.1	29.6	26.8	207143
49759	MILLERSBURG	20631	788	27.5	37.7	30.2	3.6	1.0	39414	40550	31	16	696	19.3	28.6	38.8	11.4	2.0	92273
49760	MORAN	21344	325	25.8	32.3	36.6	3.7	1.5	41902	43570	39	24	258	16.7	26.4	40.3	15.5	1.2	102660
49762	NAUBINWAY	22237	390	31.0	29.5	33.1	5.1	1.3	39311	41090	31	16	332	18.4	27.7	37.7	13.9	2.4	95909
49765	ONAWAY	18400	1752	32.8	35.1	28.5	2.6	1.0	33847	36514	15	5	1421	27.6	30.7	31.2	9.3	1.3	79947
49766	OSSINEKE	20401	1000	26.2	30.5	36.7	4.7	1.9	42371	45549	41	26	842	14.0	36.3	38.4	10.6	0.7	89667
49768	PARADISE	23205	261	30.3	29.9	35.6	3.1	1.1	38480	42599	28	13	233	16.3	22.3	45.9	12.4	3.0	104063
49769	PELLSTON	16411	654	21.6	35.5	37.5	3.8	1.7	42929	48316	42	28	560	15.5	25.7	41.8	14.6	2.3	103947
49770	PETOSKEY	24947	6898	22.0	28.2	38.0	8.7	3.1	49587	51598	60	49	4755	6.3	8.5	38.5	38.2	8.5	166900
49774	PICKFORD	18850	738	26.6	32.1	36.7	3.7	0.9	42296	45557	40	26	663	12.1	28.4	45.4	12.2	2.0	102671
49775	POINTE AUX PINS	39191	41	12.2	31.7	46.3	0.0	9.8	54468	55492	70	64	39	10.3	28.2	15.4	25.6	20.5	117500
49776	POSEN	19631	889	27.1	31.9	36.3	3.8	0.8	41755	44798	39	23	791	18.7	34.3	39.1	7.6	0.4	87330
49777	PRESQUE ISLE	24353	742	22.5	32.3	38.9	4.7	1.5	46068	48230	52	39	706	4.1	19.4	42.4	30.9	3.3	132813
49779	ROGERS CITY	19490	2268	34.1	33.9	27.7	3.7	0.7	34568	37540	17	6	1818	19.7	38.9	34.5	6.4	0.6	78978
49780	RUDYARD	19394	853	25.7	28.1	40.7	4.5	1.1	46799	47753	54	41	738	17.3	28.9	43.9	9.5	0.4	94746
49781	SAINT IGNACE	20989	1967	24.9	31.6	38.7	3.6	1.2	44079	45487	46	32	1429	11.8	22.0	48.6	16.2	1.5	109345
49782	BEAVER ISLAND	26673	289	25.6	40.5	25.3	5.2	3.5	37529	38908	25	10	261	3.8	12.3	36.4	37.9	9.6	166875
49783	SAULT SAINTE MARIE	20702	7858	30.3	25.8	37.1	5.4	1.4	42267	46175	40	25	5361	18.2	30.9	37.4	12.7	0.8	91309
49788	KINCHELOE	14757	999	24.6	29.0	40.9	5.1	0.3	46107	48023	52	39	453	23.6	22.5	51.0	2.6	0.2	92431
49792	TOWER	20185	15	26.7	46.7	26.7	0.0	0.0	32320	37166	12	4	13	15.4	30.8	46.2	7.7	0.0	95000
49795	VANDERBILT	18774	850	26.4	34.9	34.2	3.5	0.9	40973	43016	36	21	660	9.2	28.5	46.8	13.3	2.1	107331
49799	WOLVERINE	17277	1041	29.5	35.4	31.8	2.3	1.0	37520	38920	25	10	881	16.5	26.7	43.2	11.8	1.8	102021
49801	IRON MOUNTAIN	22540	5109	27.1	28.7	35.6	6.3	2.3	44140	46910	46	32	4026	23.7	34.9	28.6	11.5	1.3	79186
49802	KINGSFORD	21372	2798	29.1	28.2	36.5	4.8	1.3	41903	46388	39	24	2083	20.5	51.7	21.1	5.7	1.1	69715
49806	AU TRAIN	23509	180	26.1	27.8	39.4	5.6	1.1	46939	46479	54	41	148	15.5	31.1	39.2	12.2	2.0	93571
49807	BARK RIVER	21202	1433	21.0	30.7	40.9	5.9	1.5	48443	49903	58	46	1238	14.2	27.2	42.2	14.5	1.9	97571
49812	CARNEY	19418	545	31.2	31.7	31.9	4.6	0.6	37585	40000	25	10	446	27.1	33.9	29.6	7.6	1.8	77429
49814	CHAMPION	21761	760	20.4	31.1	42.6	4.9	1.1	48645	50628	58	46	700	24.6	33.1	35.1	5.9	1.3	80182
49815	CHANNING	20306	227	28.6	32.2	33.5	4.4	1.3	40479	43447	34	19	206	25.7	38.8	30.1	5.3	0.0	77500
49816	CHATHAM	20877	194	27.3	33.0	34.5	4.6	0.5	39662	42614	32	17	174	20.7	32.8	35.6	10.3	0.6	86250
49817	COOKS	19657	206	27.2	30.6	36.4	3.9	1.9	43524	46745	44	30	190	20.5	27.9	34.7	16.3	0.5	92727
49818	CORNELL	20796	339	22.4	29.5	41.6	5.9	0.6	48166	49895	57	45	314	12.4	30.6	43.6	13.1	0.3	98462
49820	CURTIS	22856	405	30.1	32.6	30.4	4.9	2.0	38765	40966	29	14	354	21.2	24.3	39.0	13.0	2.5	95714
49821	DAGGETT	19379	532	29.1	31.8	34.8	3.6	0.8	40755	43871	35	21	445	25.6	34.8	30.1	7.9	1.6	80700
49822	DEERTON	24539	151	23.8	31.1	38.4	5.3	1.3	45757	44191	51	38	134	12.7	32.8	39.6	12.7	2.2	95455
49825	EBEN JUNCTION	21423	73	24.7	32.9	35.6	5.5	1.4	44096	43035	46	32	65	12.3	32.3	43.1	12.3	0.0	97000
49826	RUMELY	21602	159	25.2	32.7	35.8	5.0	1.3	43095	44243	43	29	141	13.5	32.6	39.0	12.8	2.1	95000
49827	ENGADINE	20405	366	31.7	29.2	33.3	4.6	1.1	39464	41332	31	16	316	21.5	25.9	39.9	11.1	1.6	94000
49829	ESCANABA	21396	7468	31.8	27.3	34.1	4.8	1.9	40070	43455	33	18	5220	12.5	30.9	43.5	12.2	0.8	96897
49831	FELCH	18937	168	25.0	30.4	39.3	4.8	0.6	44445	47553	47	33	154	20.1	32.5	37.7	9.1	0.6	87333
49833	LITTLE LAKE	17271	120	40.0	29.2	27.5	2.5	0.8	32691	36142	13	4	107	28.0	26.2	42.1	3.7	0.0	84375
49834	FOSTER CITY	19810	180	28.3	31.1	35.0	5.0	0.6	41864	45589	39	24	162	25.3	34.6	31.5	8.6	0.0	80588
49835	GARDEN	20525	390	31.3	32.1	31.5	3.8	1.3	38441	41747	28	13	359	20.6	29.5	29.2	19.5	1.1	89762
49836	GERMFASK	19677	233	33.0	29.6	32.2	3.9	1.3	38941	40000	30	15	210	32.9	30.5	27.6	8.1	1.0	74167
49837	GLADSTONE	21626	4075	24.4	27.2	39.4	8.0	1.0	47908	50273	56	44	3462	12.2	30.9	39.1	16.5	1.3	97796
49838	GOULD CITY	25306	166	29.5	32.5	30.1	5.4	2.4	38715	40404	29	14	144	20.1	25.0	36.8	15.3	2.8	95833
49839	GRAND MARAIS	30149	258	26.7	35.3	32.2	3.5	2.3	38010	40738	27	11	237	16.5	32.5	35.0	12.2	3.8	91250
49840	GULLIVER	21140	334	23.4	36.2	33.2	6.0	1.2	42572	45266	41	28	307	20.5	29.3	34.9	12.7	2.6	90156
49841	GWINN	19370	2716	26.5	32.4	36.1	4.2	0.8	40615	45150	35	20	1504	21.9	29.1	41.4	7.6	0.0	88532
49847	HERMANSVILLE	20639	457	31.7	30.4	32.2	5.0	0.7	38536	40831	28	13	373	30.0	31.9	31.4	6.2	0.5	74130
49848	INGALLS	16530	78	32.1	35.9	28.2	3.8	0.0	35897	40000	20	7	66	19.7	37.9	37.9	4.5	0.0	82857
49849	ISHPEMING	21403	4962	25.7	29.5	38.2	5.9	0.6	45017	48069	48	35	3833	22.7	41.0	31.6	4.6	0.2	75014
49853	MC MILLAN	19877	577	27.6	35.7	32.8	3.3	0.7	39608	41437	32	17	512	20.9	21.9	43.0	12.3	2.0	96607
49854	MANISTIQUE	19502	2759	34.5	29.5	30.8	4.2	1.1	35709	37750	20	7	2195	31.8	32.9	25.3	9.2	0.9	72005
49855	MARQUETTE	23417	12737	28.2	25.4	36.2	7.5	2.8	45448	49025	50	37	7923	5.9	20.4	54.6	17.4	1.7	116533
49858	MENOMINEE	21262	5551	28.4	30.2	36.5	3.9	1.0	41675	44946	38	23	4141	28.9	37.1	27.9	5.9	0.1	71657
49861	MICHIGAMME	26339	606	23.9	29.4	39.8	4.6	2.3	46554	49305	53	40	551	27.4	24.5	31.9	12.0	4.2	86250
49862	MUNISING	21358	1960	28.1	28.1	38.6	4.3	0.9	44031	45378	45	32	1482	17.7	35.8	35.6	9.0	1.9	85487
49866	NEGAUNEE	22097	3434	23.5	29.8	40.2	5.5	1.1	46777	49401	53	41	2717	16.0	35.1	40.2	8.4	0.4	88634
	MICHIGAN	26713		20.1	24.2	38.5	11.3	5.9	55536	56866				13.2	21.9	40.3	21.5	3.2	115137
	UNITED STATES	27277		20.9	24.4	35.3	11.7	7.6	54719	56938				9.3	13.1	31.6	32.6	13.5	162279

ZIP CODE #	POST OFFICE NAME	FINANCIAL SERVICES: Auto Loan	Home Loan	Invest-ments	Retire-ment Plans	THE HOME: Home Improvements: Home Repair	Lawn & Garden	Furnishings: Comput-ers & Hard-ware-Personal	Major Appli-ances	TV, Radio, Sound Equip-ment	Furni-ture	ENTERTAINMENT: Dine out/ Carry out	Sports Equip-ment	Fees & Tickets	Toys & Games	Travel	Cable TV	PERSONAL: Apparel & Services	Auto Repairs	Health Insur-ance	Pets & Supplies
49705	AFTON	84	60	86	58	62	85	62	78	68	57	67	59	49	68	61	75	44	72	82	93
49706	ALANSON	85	73	95	71	76	87	71	84	74	69	73	62	64	73	73	78	49	79	84	98
49707	ALPENA	76	66	74	67	68	79	69	75	72	64	71	57	63	71	68	76	48	73	80	89
49709	ATLANTA	73	60	86	57	65	79	60	74	65	58	63	53	53	61	63	69	42	70	78	86
49710	BARBEAU	80	66	102	64	73	86	66	82	69	63	68	59	58	65	71	73	45	76	83	95
49712	BOYNE CITY	89	80	91	79	82	92	79	88	82	77	81	65	73	81	80	85	55	85	91	104
49713	BOYNE FALLS	88	75	84	76	77	93	74	87	79	68	77	66	66	79	74	84	52	80	90	102
49715	BRIMLEY	81	72	73	71	73	79	71	77	74	71	73	56	66	75	69	76	50	74	78	91
49716	BRUTUS	88	75	95	73	78	88	73	85	76	72	75	62	66	75	74	79	51	80	85	100
49718	CARP LAKE	87	69	112	68	76	92	69	88	73	65	72	64	60	69	75	77	48	81	87	102
49719	CEDARVILLE	87	69	111	68	76	92	69	88	73	65	72	64	60	69	75	78	48	81	87	102
49720	CHARLEVOIX	90	82	97	82	85	94	80	91	83	79	82	67	76	82	83	86	56	87	92	106
49721	CHEBOYGAN	78	63	87	63	67	82	66	78	70	61	69	58	58	68	67	75	46	74	81	91
49724	DAFTER	82	72	82	70	73	81	69	78	72	69	72	57	63	72	69	75	48	75	78	92
49725	DE TOUR VILLAGE	84	68	109	66	74	89	68	86	71	63	70	63	59	67	73	75	46	79	85	99
49726	DRUMMOND ISLAND	82	66	106	65	72	87	66	84	69	62	68	61	57	65	71	73	45	77	82	97
49727	EAST JORDAN	84	71	81	71	72	87	71	82	75	67	74	61	64	75	71	80	50	77	85	96
49728	ECKERMAN	69	65	82	60	72	78	62	73	66	66	64	48	61	60	67	69	43	70	81	84
49729	ELLSWORTH	87	74	94	72	77	88	72	85	75	70	74	62	65	74	74	79	50	80	84	99
49730	ELMIRA	92	74	89	72	75	93	73	87	79	70	78	65	63	80	72	85	52	81	90	103
49733	FREDERIC	83	64	98	62	69	86	64	82	69	60	68	60	54	66	67	74	45	75	82	95
49735	GAYLORD	89	82	88	83	84	91	80	88	82	79	82	66	77	82	81	85	56	85	89	103
49736	GOETZVILLE	79	63	102	62	69	83	63	80	66	59	65	59	55	63	68	70	43	74	79	93
49738	GRAYLING	76	65	79	65	68	79	67	76	71	63	69	56	60	69	67	75	47	73	80	89
49740	HARBOR SPRINGS	102	94	131	94	103	114	89	107	93	90	92	76	87	88	98	97	62	101	110	124
49743	HAWKS	73	55	83	54	59	76	56	71	60	52	60	53	46	59	58	66	39	65	72	84
49744	HERRON	79	68	77	70	71	84	68	79	71	62	69	59	61	71	68	75	47	73	81	92
49745	HESSEL	79	61	95	60	66	83	62	78	66	58	65	58	52	64	65	71	43	72	79	92
49746	HILLMAN	72	55	80	53	58	75	56	71	61	53	60	52	47	59	58	67	40	66	74	83
49747	HUBBARD LAKE	81	68	93	65	74	90	67	83	72	66	71	58	62	69	71	78	47	77	90	96
49749	INDIAN RIVER	82	65	103	64	71	87	65	83	69	61	68	61	56	66	70	74	45	76	82	96
49751	JOHANNESBURG	87	74	99	74	79	93	74	89	77	69	75	65	66	75	77	81	51	82	90	103
49752	KINROSS	85	66	85	63	68	86	66	80	72	64	71	59	56	72	65	78	47	75	83	95
49753	LACHINE	82	63	96	62	68	86	64	81	68	60	67	60	54	66	67	74	45	74	82	95
49755	LEVERING	83	70	94	69	74	85	69	82	72	66	71	60	61	70	71	75	48	77	82	96
49756	LEWISTON	68	65	83	60	72	78	62	73	65	66	64	48	61	60	67	69	43	70	81	83
49757	MACKINAC ISLAND	90	92	87	94	89	88	94	88	92	94	93	70	95	92	92	92	66	91	90	106
49759	MILLERSBURG	75	61	92	59	66	80	61	76	64	59	63	55	54	61	65	69	42	71	78	88
49760	MORAN	84	65	95	63	69	88	65	82	71	62	69	60	55	68	67	77	46	76	85	96
49762	NAUBINWAY	69	66	85	61	74	79	63	74	67	68	65	49	62	61	69	71	44	72	83	85
49765	ONAWAY	73	55	73	53	57	75	58	70	63	54	62	52	48	62	56	69	41	66	74	82
49766	OSSINEKE	82	67	86	67	70	86	67	81	71	62	70	60	58	70	68	76	47	75	83	95
49768	PARADISE	68	65	83	60	72	77	62	73	65	67	64	48	61	60	67	69	43	70	81	83
49769	PELLSTON	79	71	71	69	71	76	67	74	70	69	70	54	63	72	66	72	47	71	74	87
49770	PETOSKEY	84	85	84	86	85	89	84	85	84	82	84	65	84	84	85	86	58	85	90	101
49774	PICKFORD	80	63	95	63	68	84	64	80	67	59	66	59	55	65	67	72	44	74	80	93
49775	POINTE AUX PINS	89	94	128	93	108	111	84	100	89	96	88	62	93	80	98	93	60	95	111	113
49776	POSEN	81	60	87	59	63	83	61	77	67	57	66	58	50	66	62	73	44	71	80	91
49777	PRESQUE ISLE	86	68	109	67	75	91	68	87	72	64	71	64	59	68	74	77	47	80	86	101
49779	ROGERS CITY	72	53	77	52	56	75	56	70	62	51	60	52	46	61	56	68	40	65	74	82
49780	RUDYARD	80	68	74	70	70	84	68	79	71	62	70	59	61	72	67	76	47	73	81	92
49781	SAINT IGNACE	79	65	83	65	68	81	68	78	71	64	70	57	60	70	68	75	47	74	81	91
49782	BEAVER ISLAND	92	74	119	73	81	98	74	94	77	69	77	69	64	74	80	83	51	87	93	109
49783	SAULT SAINTE MARIE	71	65	62	66	64	71	70	69	71	66	70	53	65	71	66	73	48	70	74	82
49788	KINCHELOE	70	61	52	63	58	64	73	64	73	66	72	52	66	74	64	74	50	70	70	79
49792	TOWER	65	46	67	45	48	66	48	61	53	44	52	46	38	53	47	58	34	56	63	72
49795	VANDERBILT	84	61	84	59	63	85	62	78	69	58	68	59	50	69	61	76	45	72	81	93
49799	WOLVERINE	78	56	72	55	57	76	58	70	64	56	63	53	47	66	55	70	42	66	73	84
49801	IRON MOUNTAIN	75	74	73	74	74	82	72	77	75	71	74	57	72	74	73	78	51	75	83	90
49802	KINGSFORD	73	66	66	67	65	76	67	72	70	64	69	55	63	70	66	74	47	70	78	85
49806	AU TRAIN	84	67	108	66	74	89	67	85	70	63	69	62	58	67	73	75	46	79	84	99
49807	BARK RIVER	85	73	85	74	76	91	73	85	76	66	75	64	65	76	74	81	50	79	88	100
49812	CARNEY	77	57	78	56	59	79	59	74	65	54	64	55	48	65	58	71	42	68	78	87
49814	CHAMPION	78	76	78	73	78	84	71	79	75	72	74	56	70	74	73	78	50	76	85	92
49815	CHANNING	85	61	87	59	63	86	62	79	69	58	68	60	50	69	62	76	45	73	83	94
49816	CHATHAM	81	60	90	59	64	84	62	78	67	57	66	58	51	66	63	73	44	72	80	92
49817	COOKS	84	68	109	66	74	89	68	86	71	63	70	63	59	67	73	75	46	79	85	100
49818	CORNELL	79	72	71	74	73	84	71	80	73	64	71	60	65	74	70	77	49	74	82	93
49820	CURTIS	72	69	88	63	76	82	65	77	69	71	68	51	65	63	72	73	45	74	86	88
49821	DAGGETT	82	59	84	57	61	83	60	77	67	56	66	58	48	67	60	74	44	71	80	91
49822	DEERTON	83	66	107	65	73	88	66	84	70	62	69	62	58	66	72	74	46	78	83	98
49825	EBEN JUNCTION	83	66	107	65	73	88	66	84	70	62	69	62	57	66	72	74	46	78	83	98
49826	RUMELY	83	67	107	65	73	88	67	85	70	62	69	62	58	66	72	74	46	78	84	98
49827	ENGADINE	68	65	83	60	72	77	62	73	65	67	64	48	61	60	67	69	43	70	81	83
49829	ESCANABA	70	64	67	65	65	74	67	71	71	63	69	53	64	69	66	74	48	70	78	84
49831	FELCH	81	67	78	67	68	85	67	79	71	61	70	60	58	71	66	76	47	73	82	93
49833	LITTLE LAKE	72	52	74	50	54	73	53	67	59	49	58	51	42	58	52	65	38	62	70	80
49834	FOSTER CITY	80	64	78	64	66	83	64	77	69	59	68	58	55	69	64	74	45	71	80	91
49835	GARDEN	76	61	99	60	67	81	61	78	64	57	63	57	53	61	66	68	42	72	77	90
49836	GERMFASK	78	59	83	57	62	81	60	75	66	57	64	55	50	64	60	72	43	69	79	88
49837	GLADSTONE	81	74	78	73	74	87	71	81	76	68	75	60	67	76	72	80	51	77	86	95
49838	GOULD CITY	73	70	89	65	78	84	67	79	71	72	69	51	66	64	73	75	46	76	88	90
49839	GRAND MARAIS	85	68	111	67	75	90	68	87	72	64	71	64	59	68	74	76	47	80	86	101
49840	GULLIVER	84	66	107	65	73	88	67	85	70	62	69	62	57	67	72	75	46	78	84	98
49841	GWINN	75	56	68	57	57	67	66	68	69	63	68	53	56	68	61	71	47	70	71	82
49847	HERMANSVILLE	81	58	82	56	60	82	60	76	67	56	66	57	48	66	59	74	43	70	80	90
49848	INGALLS	72	52	72	50	54	75	56	70	63	50	61	52	45	62	55	69	41	65	76	82
49849	ISHPEMING	75	68	69	67	67	78	69	73	73	65	72	55	65	73	67	76	49	72	79	87
49853	MC MILLAN	75	58	91	57	63	78	59	74	62	55	62	55	50	60	62	67	41	69	75	87
49854	MANISTIQUE	73	56	79	55	59	75	61	72	66	56	64	53	52	63	61	71	43	69	76	84
49855	MARQUETTE	78	70	68	73	70	75	82	75	80	76	80	59	75	80	75	81	56	79	79	90
49858	MENOMINEE	73	62	66	62	62	75	66	71	70	61	68	53	60	70	63	74	47	69	77	84
49861	MICHIGAMME	87	73	108	70	80	94	72	89	76	71	75	63	65	72	77	81	50	83	92	103
49862	MUNISING	80	64	87	63	67	84	65	79	69	59	68	59	56	68	66	75	45	73	82	93
49866	NEGAUNEE	76	72	71	73	71	82	72	77	75	68	74	58	70	75	72	78	50	75	83	91
	MICHIGAN	98	97	93	98	95	100	96	97	97	95	97	74	96	98	96	99	68	97	100	115
	UNITED STATES	100	100	100	100	100	100	100	100	100	100	100	100	100	100	100	100	100	100	100	100

ZIP CODE			POPULATION			2000-2009 ANNUAL RATE		HOUSEHOLDS					FAMILIES		
#	POST OFFICE NAME	COUNTY FIPS CODE	2000	2009	2014	% Rate	State Centile	2000	2009	2014	% Annual Rate 2000-2009	2009 Average HH Size	2000	2009	% Annual Rate 2000-2009
49868	NEWBERRY	095	6079	5935	5806	-0.3	21	2097	2076	2038	-0.1	2.34	1443	1411	-0.2
49870	NORWAY	043	3365	3258	3183	-0.3	21	1431	1420	1397	-0.1	2.29	949	926	-0.3
49873	PERRONVILLE	109	115	119	118	0.4	60	51	54	54	0.6	2.17	35	37	0.6
49874	POWERS	109	1350	1387	1380	0.3	54	462	490	492	0.6	2.69	331	347	0.5
49876	QUINNESEC	043	1187	1186	1173	0.0	37	436	449	447	0.3	2.63	356	364	0.2
49878	RAPID RIVER	041	4304	4368	4314	0.2	48	1822	1925	1924	0.6	2.22	1292	1345	0.4
49879	REPUBLIC	103	1023	974	958	-0.5	12	454	451	450	-0.1	2.15	318	311	-0.2
49880	ROCK	103	1253	1240	1220	-0.1	32	522	538	535	0.3	2.30	373	378	0.1
49881	SAGOLA	043	347	348	343	0.0	37	142	147	147	0.4	2.37	100	102	0.2
49883	SENEY	153	180	160	152	-1.3	2	56	50	48	-1.2	2.90	42	37	-1.4
49884	SHINGLETON	003	878	896	889	0.2	48	212	223	223	0.5	3.54	161	166	0.3
49885	SKANDIA	103	2379	2308	2272	-0.3	21	943	956	954	0.1	2.41	698	698	0.0
49886	SPALDING	109	350	361	359	0.3	54	130	138	139	0.6	2.56	91	96	0.6
49887	STEPHENSON	109	2569	2550	2516	-0.1	32	1109	1134	1130	0.2	2.20	739	745	0.1
49891	TRENARY	003	624	619	609	-0.1	32	279	288	287	0.3	2.13	192	196	0.2
49892	VULCAN	043	2268	2341	2324	0.3	54	912	970	972	0.7	2.39	636	669	0.5
49893	WALLACE	109	2115	2107	2081	0.0	37	851	874	870	0.3	2.41	624	633	0.2
49894	WELLS	041	732	713	696	-0.3	21	308	311	308	0.1	2.29	216	214	-0.1
49895	WETMORE	041	1042	1107	1111	0.7	76	209	233	237	1.2	3.35	153	169	1.1
49896	WILSON	109	1585	1658	1656	0.5	66	546	589	594	0.8	2.80	398	423	0.7
49905	ATLANTIC MINE	061	3526	3406	3323	-0.4	16	1318	1294	1267	-0.2	2.54	853	828	-0.3
49908	BARAGA	013	1915	2162	2168	1.3	90	790	867	880	1.0	1.82	498	541	0.9
49910	BERGLAND	131	499	433	401	-1.5	1	235	212	199	-1.1	2.04	153	136	-1.3
49911	BESSEMER	053	3388	3119	2964	-0.9	5	1533	1433	1372	-0.7	2.12	912	839	-0.9
49912	BRUCE CROSSING	131	1059	1069	1041	0.1	42	459	480	474	0.5	2.20	299	308	0.3
49913	CALUMET	083	8693	8534	8373	-0.2	25	3615	3652	3599	0.1	2.26	2173	2139	-0.2
49916	CHASSELL	061	3344	3206	3113	-0.5	12	1348	1298	1262	-0.4	2.39	891	850	-0.5
49919	COVINGTON	013	243	230	223	-0.6	9	95	91	89	-0.5	2.40	67	64	-0.5
49920	CRYSTAL FALLS	071	4881	4661	4542	-0.5	12	2151	2089	2048	-0.3	2.12	1359	1303	-0.5
49921	DODGEVILLE	061	403	387	377	-0.4	16	148	145	142	-0.2	2.67	90	86	-0.5
49925	EWEN	131	716	646	609	-1.1	3	318	296	282	-0.8	2.18	203	186	-0.9
49927	GAASTRA	071	356	327	314	-0.9	5	137	127	122	-0.8	2.45	94	87	-0.8
49930	HANCOCK	061	7233	7336	7248	0.2	48	2930	3019	2993	0.3	2.29	1684	1727	0.3
49931	HOUGHTON	061	8572	8594	8466	0.0	37	2701	2686	2642	-0.1	2.41	1270	1247	-0.2
49935	IRON RIVER	071	7962	7609	7382	-0.5	12	3478	3365	3279	-0.4	2.15	2173	2076	-0.5
49938	IRONWOOD	053	8801	8128	7719	-0.9	5	3932	3662	3501	-0.8	2.14	2374	2182	-0.9
49945	LAKE LINDEN	061	3963	3787	3686	-0.5	12	1650	1609	1573	-0.3	2.30	1114	1074	-0.4
49946	LANSE	013	4074	3880	3783	-0.5	12	1669	1613	1584	-0.4	2.30	1102	1053	-0.5
49947	MARENISCO	053	1097	1231	1202	1.3	90	283	272	264	-0.4	2.73	199	189	-0.6
49948	MASS CITY	131	692	674	649	-0.3	21	310	309	301	0.0	2.18	202	199	-0.2
49950	MOHAWK	083	1342	1304	1282	-0.3	21	542	554	547	0.2	2.24	332	334	0.1
49952	NISULA	061	92	96	95	0.5	66	40	43	43	0.8	2.23	25	26	0.4
49953	ONTONAGON	131	4426	3851	3617	-1.5	1	1938	1726	1632	-1.2	2.14	1240	1091	-1.4
49958	PELKIE	013	2169	2234	2208	0.3	54	601	593	583	-0.1	3.26	403	393	-0.3
49962	SKANEE	013	334	301	290	-1.1	3	163	152	148	-0.8	1.98	114	105	-0.9
49965	TOIVOLA	061	327	345	345	0.6	71	140	151	151	0.8	2.12	92	97	0.6
49967	TROUT CREEK	061	655	655	641	0.0	37	319	328	323	0.3	1.98	202	205	0.2
49968	WAKEFIELD	053	2663	2519	2407	-0.6	9	1148	1085	1041	-0.6	2.13	725	674	-0.8
49969	WATERSMEET	053	1472	1596	1544	0.9	82	552	510	487	-0.9	1.94	386	353	-1.0
49970	WATTON	013	326	308	300	-0.6	9	143	137	134	-0.5	2.13	101	96	-0.5
	MICHIGAN					0.3					0.4	2.52			0.3
	UNITED STATES					1.0					1.1	2.59			0.9

ZIP CODE		RACE (%)								2009 AGE DISTRIBUTION (%)										MEDIAN AGE		
#	POST OFFICE NAME	White		Black		Asian/Pacific		% Hispanic Origin														
		2000	2009	2000	2009	2000	2009	2000	2009	0-4	5-9	10-14	15-19	20-24	25-44	45-64	65-84	85+	18+	2009	% 2009 Males	% 2009 Females
49868	NEWBERRY	81.2	79.9	8.7	9.3	0.4	0.7	2.0	2.0	4.6	4.9	5.4	10.8	8.6	26.2	24.4	12.7	2.3	81.3	37.2	54.4	45.6
49870	NORWAY	97.7	97.2	0.0	0.0	0.2	0.4	0.6	0.8	6.2	6.3	6.4	6.8	5.5	24.4	27.2	14.1	2.9	76.5	41.1	49.4	50.6
49873	PERRONVILLE	94.8	95.0	0.0	0.0	0.0	0.0	0.9	0.8	6.7	6.7	6.7	6.7	5.0	23.5	28.6	14.3	1.7	75.6	40.9	50.4	49.6
49874	POWERS	97.3	97.0	0.0	0.0	0.0	0.0	0.5	0.8	6.0	6.2	6.3	5.7	4.7	22.9	29.0	15.6	3.7	77.7	43.8	50.8	49.2
49876	QUINNESEC	98.5	98.1	0.0	0.0	0.3	0.5	0.3	0.3	4.6	6.8	6.9	9.7	3.1	26.6	30.7	10.1	1.4	75.0	40.7	50.3	49.7
49878	RAPID RIVER	93.1	92.4	1.5	1.6	0.3	0.4	0.4	0.5	4.3	4.9	5.7	5.6	4.2	21.6	34.6	17.2	1.9	81.4	47.2	52.7	47.3
49879	REPUBLIC	97.5	97.3	0.0	0.0	0.0	0.0	0.1	0.1	3.2	4.9	4.5	5.6	2.5	18.7	36.9	20.9	2.8	83.4	51.5	52.2	47.8
49880	ROCK	96.6	96.1	0.1	0.1	0.5	0.7	0.4	0.6	4.6	4.8	5.1	5.6	5.0	22.0	35.5	15.6	1.8	82.1	46.6	50.4	49.6
49881	SAGOLA	97.7	97.1	0.0	0.0	0.0	0.3	0.9	0.9	5.5	6.0	6.3	6.3	4.6	21.3	31.6	16.4	2.0	78.2	45.0	50.3	49.7
49883	SENEY	93.9	93.8	0.0	0.0	0.0	0.0	0.0	0.0	7.5	7.5	6.3	5.6	2.5	20.0	26.3	21.9	2.5	75.6	45.6	48.8	51.2
49884	SHINGLETON	84.7	84.5	7.5	7.7	0.3	0.3	1.3	1.1	4.6	4.9	5.4	5.6	6.1	24.7	31.4	15.3	2.1	81.4	44.1	56.1	43.9
49885	SKANDIA	95.7	95.3	0.2	0.2	0.2	0.3	0.8	1.0	5.3	5.6	6.1	6.7	4.9	23.6	34.6	12.0	1.3	78.8	43.5	51.8	48.2
49886	SPALDING	95.7	95.0	0.0	0.3	0.0	0.3	0.6	0.6	6.4	6.6	6.9	6.1	4.4	23.3	29.4	14.1	2.8	75.9	42.3	51.0	49.0
49887	STEPHENSON	95.7	95.1	0.1	0.1	0.3	0.5	0.4	0.5	5.0	5.4	5.8	5.8	4.9	20.5	32.9	16.4	3.3	79.8	46.6	49.8	50.2
49891	TRENARY	95.7	95.5	1.1	1.3	0.0	0.0	1.1	1.0	4.7	5.3	6.0	5.5	4.2	18.7	36.7	16.5	2.4	80.6	48.5	50.1	49.9
49892	VULCAN	98.5	98.2	0.1	0.1	0.2	0.2	0.4	0.5	4.8	5.2	5.8	6.6	5.2	22.2	33.8	13.8	2.7	80.1	45.2	50.4	49.6
49893	WALLACE	98.5	98.3	0.0	0.0	0.2	0.4	0.5	0.7	5.3	5.7	6.4	6.5	4.9	22.1	33.4	14.0	1.7	78.6	44.4	50.7	49.3
49894	WELLS	95.9	95.1	0.0	0.0	0.4	0.7	0.7	0.7	5.9	6.0	6.5	6.7	4.8	23.7	30.0	14.2	2.2	77.3	42.5	50.5	49.5
49895	WETMORE	72.9	72.4	22.7	23.4	0.2	0.2	1.2	1.2	3.2	3.4	3.8	4.7	8.9	36.5	26.3	12.0	1.2	87.0	38.2	65.8	34.2
49896	WILSON	88.7	88.6	0.1	0.1	0.1	0.1	1.0	1.3	6.5	6.8	7.0	6.6	4.8	24.1	30.0	12.6	1.6	75.4	41.0	51.8	48.2
49905	ATLANTIC MINE	95.9	95.0	2.0	2.4	0.4	0.7	0.5	0.6	6.5	6.5	6.5	6.5	6.0	24.7	28.1	13.1	2.3	76.4	39.4	53.0	47.0
49908	BARAGA	61.1	61.8	15.5	14.8	0.5	0.5	1.3	1.2	4.7	4.8	5.0	5.6	8.5	35.7	23.3	10.2	2.3	82.2	36.3	61.8	38.2
49910	BERGLAND	98.0	97.5	0.0	0.0	0.4	0.7	0.2	0.2	2.3	3.9	4.2	5.5	3.5	17.6	38.3	21.5	3.2	86.6	52.6	51.7	48.3
49911	BESSEMER	97.1	96.7	0.2	0.2	0.4	0.6	0.6	0.7	4.6	4.6	4.9	6.6	6.3	21.4	29.8	17.6	3.9	81.7	45.9	50.5	49.5
49912	BRUCE CROSSING	97.3	96.8	0.1	0.1	0.3	0.4	0.8	0.8	4.0	4.2	5.1	5.2	5.1	20.2	33.2	19.6	3.2	82.9	48.7	51.5	48.5
49913	CALUMET	98.1	97.7	0.4	0.4	0.2	0.3	0.8	1.0	6.4	6.2	6.3	6.8	7.3	20.9	27.2	15.3	3.6	77.0	41.5	49.8	50.2
49916	CHASSELL	94.8	93.5	1.8	2.0	1.5	2.3	0.6	0.8	5.5	5.4	5.8	6.8	9.0	24.0	27.8	13.7	2.1	79.0	39.6	53.4	46.6
49919	COVINGTON	94.7	94.8	0.4	0.4	0.0	0.0	1.2	0.9	5.2	5.2	6.1	6.1	5.2	20.9	33.9	14.3	3.0	79.1	45.9	53.0	47.0
49920	CRYSTAL FALLS	97.9	97.5	0.2	0.2	0.2	0.3	0.8	1.0	3.7	4.2	4.6	6.2	4.3	17.1	33.9	20.9	5.2	83.6	51.4	50.0	50.0
49921	DODGEVILLE	94.8	92.2	0.2	0.3	3.2	5.4	0.7	1.0	5.9	5.7	7.2	9.0	14.2	24.0	25.1	8.3	0.5	76.2	31.7	54.8	45.2
49925	EWEN	96.9	96.0	0.0	0.0	0.4	0.9	0.7	0.9	4.0	4.2	4.6	5.4	5.0	20.4	33.0	20.7	2.6	83.9	49.8	49.8	50.2
49927	GAASTRA	96.6	95.4	1.1	1.2	0.0	0.3	0.8	1.2	4.6	4.9	4.6	4.3	6.4	19.0	32.1	21.1	3.1	83.2	48.8	49.5	50.5
49930	HANCOCK	97.1	96.3	0.5	0.6	0.7	1.2	0.7	0.9	5.5	5.4	5.3	6.1	9.3	23.9	25.7	14.0	4.7	80.5	39.9	50.6	49.4
49931	HOUGHTON	90.8	87.2	1.5	1.7	5.7	8.8	0.8	1.0	3.5	3.3	3.9	19.4	31.7	15.4	14.4	6.4	1.9	85.4	23.1	60.2	39.8
49935	IRON RIVER	95.3	94.4	1.7	1.9	0.2	0.3	0.5	0.7	4.7	4.7	4.9	5.7	5.9	21.6	30.3	17.9	4.4	82.2	46.7	49.6	50.4
49938	IRONWOOD	97.6	97.1	0.1	0.1	0.2	0.3	0.9	1.2	5.3	5.2	5.5	6.2	5.2	21.5	28.0	17.6	5.6	80.4	45.8	47.3	52.7
49945	LAKE LINDEN	98.1	97.6	0.4	0.4	0.2	0.4	0.7	0.9	6.2	6.4	6.4	5.8	4.6	20.3	29.3	17.5	3.5	77.2	45.2	50.3	49.7
49946	LANSE	83.7	84.2	0.2	0.2	0.2	0.2	0.7	0.7	5.6	5.5	6.2	6.8	4.8	23.0	28.2	15.7	4.1	78.5	43.5	47.9	52.1
49947	MARENISCO	80.1	79.0	15.3	14.8	0.3	0.4	1.9	2.6	1.9	2.3	2.5	6.1	12.1	29.4	22.5	18.4	4.8	90.6	41.4	67.2	32.8
49948	MASS CITY	97.3	96.9	0.0	0.0	0.1	0.1	1.2	1.5	5.5	6.1	6.2	5.3	4.0	20.0	32.6	17.7	2.5	78.9	46.7	53.0	47.0
49950	MOHAWK	94.9	94.5	3.8	4.1	0.1	0.1	0.8	0.8	4.0	4.5	4.8	8.2	4.6	18.0	34.4	18.4	3.1	80.9	48.8	51.3	48.7
49952	NISULA	95.7	94.8	0.0	0.0	1.1	1.0	0.0	1.0	4.2	5.2	6.3	6.3	5.2	21.9	30.2	18.8	2.1	82.3	45.8	54.2	45.8
49953	ONTONAGON	97.2	96.5	0.0	0.0	0.1	0.2	0.7	1.0	4.4	4.7	4.9	5.2	4.7	18.3	32.4	21.5	3.9	82.4	50.3	49.7	50.3
49958	PELKIE	81.2	80.2	6.4	6.6	0.5	0.5	1.0	1.0	4.9	5.2	5.6	5.7	6.6	27.4	28.4	13.6	2.6	80.9	40.8	57.0	43.0
49962	SKANEE	89.2	89.4	0.0	0.0	0.3	0.3	0.3	0.0	4.7	3.0	6.0	5.6	2.3	17.9	41.5	15.9	3.0	82.4	50.6	52.2	47.8
49965	TOIVOLA	92.0	90.4	4.0	4.3	0.3	0.6	0.6	0.6	4.9	5.2	5.2	5.8	6.1	25.2	30.1	15.4	2.0	80.9	42.3	55.7	44.3
49967	TROUT CREEK	96.5	95.7	0.0	0.0	0.9	1.4	0.6	0.9	4.1	4.4	5.0	5.3	4.6	20.0	33.1	20.0	3.4	83.1	49.3	53.9	46.1
49968	WAKEFIELD	97.9	97.5	0.0	0.0	0.2	0.2	0.3	0.4	3.7	3.8	4.0	4.9	4.4	20.8	31.1	21.4	6.1	85.5	50.8	49.3	50.7
49969	WATERSMEET	71.7	70.1	8.2	8.3	0.2	0.3	1.6	2.0	3.8	3.9	4.3	13.5	14.1	26.4	19.4	13.3	1.3	82.5	31.4	66.7	33.3
49970	WATTON	94.8	95.1	0.3	0.3	0.0	0.0	0.9	0.6	5.2	5.5	6.2	6.2	5.2	20.8	32.8	15.3	2.9	79.2	45.7	52.6	47.4
	MICHIGAN	80.2	78.3	14.2	14.5	1.8	2.8	3.3	4.1	6.7	6.7	6.8	7.2	6.6	26.3	26.9	10.9	1.9	75.6	37.6	49.2	50.8
	UNITED STATES	75.1	72.0	12.3	12.7	3.8	4.6	12.5	15.7	6.8	6.7	6.6	7.1	6.9	27.0	26.0	10.9	1.9	75.7	36.9	49.2	50.8

ZIP CODE #	POST OFFICE NAME	2009 Per Capita Income	2009 HH Income Base	2009 HOUSEHOLD INCOME DISTRIBUTION (%) Less than $25,000	$25,000 to $49,999	$50,000 to $99,999	$100,000 to $149,999	$150,000 or More	MEDIAN HOUSEHOLD INCOME 2009	2014	2009 National Centile	2009 State Centile	2009 Home Value Base	2009 HOME VALUE DISTRIBUTION (%) Less than $50,000	$50,000 to $89,999	$90,000 to $174,999	$175,000 to $399,999	$400,000 or More	2009 Median Home Value
49868	NEWBERRY	18097	2076	31.4	33.6	30.9	3.2	0.9	37466	38975	25	10	1620	28.6	34.5	32.0	4.3	0.6	74141
49870	NORWAY	20869	1420	30.8	32.5	30.0	4.6	2.0	38154	41293	27	11	1103	27.5	42.6	23.6	5.9	0.5	67120
49873	PERRONVILLE	21576	54	31.5	31.5	31.5	5.6	0.0	38616	41541	28	14	44	29.5	29.5	36.4	4.5	0.0	80000
49874	POWERS	16315	490	31.0	33.3	31.4	3.7	0.6	37180	39676	24	9	408	28.4	33.1	32.4	4.9	1.2	76765
49876	QUINNESEC	19193	449	17.8	33.6	43.4	4.7	0.4	49090	50217	59	48	417	14.1	60.0	23.0	2.4	0.5	76964
49878	RAPID RIVER	22782	1925	26.6	31.4	34.8	5.2	2.0	42571	45859	41	27	1722	14.5	28.1	37.1	18.3	2.0	102059
49879	REPUBLIC	21435	451	31.0	32.8	31.5	3.1	1.6	38164	41714	27	11	397	38.3	38.5	18.9	4.0	0.3	62386
49880	ROCK	20898	538	28.8	31.2	33.6	4.8	1.5	42603	45644	41	28	486	20.2	35.8	36.6	5.6	1.9	83830
49881	SAGOLA	20091	147	28.6	32.7	32.7	4.1	2.0	40247	43489	33	19	133	25.6	38.3	30.8	5.3	0.0	77500
49883	SENEY	14274	50	36.0	32.0	30.0	2.0	0.0	36527	36525	22	8	47	36.2	36.2	21.3	6.4	0.0	65000
49884	SHINGLETON	14048	223	23.8	30.0	41.7	3.6	0.9	46350	46392	52	39	190	20.5	34.2	35.8	8.4	1.1	81818
49885	SKANDIA	21667	956	22.6	28.5	41.4	5.6	1.9	48801	50450	58	47	841	16.2	25.7	43.3	14.6	0.2	101328
49886	SPALDING	17862	138	29.7	32.6	33.3	4.3	0.0	38886	40981	29	15	114	29.8	32.5	31.6	6.1	0.0	75000
49887	STEPHENSON	20218	1134	30.6	32.4	33.0	3.3	0.8	39281	41969	31	16	949	21.8	35.2	34.4	7.6	1.1	83000
49891	TRENARY	20100	288	29.9	34.4	30.9	4.5	0.3	37012	39407	24	9	259	23.2	37.1	33.2	6.6	0.0	80536
49892	VULCAN	20084	970	28.1	29.3	35.9	5.6	1.1	43757	46763	45	31	848	24.8	31.8	32.5	9.7	1.2	81385
49893	WALLACE	20662	874	22.8	31.0	41.4	4.1	0.7	46308	47737	52	39	769	17.8	29.0	40.2	12.5	0.5	94900
49894	WELLS	19896	311	32.8	28.0	32.5	5.8	1.0	40504	43369	34	20	261	11.5	44.8	35.6	8.0	0.0	85541
49895	WETMORE	14709	233	24.9	30.5	36.9	6.0	1.7	45173	46149	49	36	212	21.2	25.5	36.8	16.0	0.5	95833
49896	WILSON	16202	589	27.8	34.1	33.4	4.1	0.5	38584	40948	28	13	485	24.1	32.8	33.8	7.6	1.6	82717
49905	ATLANTIC MINE	17261	1294	30.6	32.3	32.8	3.5	0.9	38643	42492	29	14	1062	42.5	27.1	22.1	7.4	0.8	57547
49908	BARAGA	20724	867	34.8	32.8	28.0	3.8	0.6	36331	37548	22	8	555	27.0	40.9	28.1	3.6	0.4	74831
49910	BERGLAND	20541	212	28.3	38.7	29.2	3.3	0.5	33880	34276	15	5	181	45.3	28.7	16.6	8.8	0.6	56071
49911	BESSEMER	20412	1433	35.9	32.2	27.6	2.9	1.3	33793	35654	15	5	1105	54.1	28.1	14.7	3.0	0.2	47593
49912	BRUCE CROSSING	18890	480	35.4	33.1	27.5	3.1	0.8	34200	34653	16	6	421	43.7	32.5	19.7	3.8	0.2	56463
49913	CALUMET	17794	3652	39.2	32.1	24.2	3.1	1.3	31437	33213	10	3	2846	47.3	32.6	15.9	3.7	0.6	52644
49916	CHASSELL	19589	1298	31.4	29.1	33.2	5.2	1.2	41095	44638	36	22	1051	25.2	35.5	27.4	10.0	1.9	77841
49919	COVINGTON	20987	91	22.0	28.6	45.1	4.4	0.0	49451	48283	60	49	83	30.1	28.9	32.5	8.4	0.0	69444
49920	CRYSTAL FALLS	20129	2089	31.8	31.4	32.8	3.4	0.7	38396	41279	28	13	1798	34.4	32.5	25.7	6.6	0.8	67230
49921	DODGEVILLE	16987	145	36.6	21.4	35.2	6.2	0.7	38647	46895	29	14	99	25.3	40.4	22.2	12.1	0.0	71250
49925	EWEN	18137	296	39.9	31.8	24.3	3.4	0.7	31092	31886	10	3	245	44.5	35.5	17.1	2.0	0.8	57500
49927	GAASTRA	17741	127	33.9	29.1	33.9	1.6	1.6	39601	41881	32	17	109	50.5	22.0	19.3	7.3	0.9	49688
49930	HANCOCK	18650	3019	33.1	32.6	29.0	4.3	1.0	36201	38700	21	8	2039	28.9	36.6	27.6	6.2	0.7	71677
49931	HOUGHTON	16512	2686	43.0	22.6	28.1	5.4	0.9	31856	33708	11	4	1245	14.7	30.8	41.4	12.4	0.7	96975
49935	IRON RIVER	19070	3365	37.5	30.3	28.5	2.6	1.2	33209	34472	14	4	2652	42.6	33.0	18.3	5.2	0.8	56331
49938	IRONWOOD	18156	3662	40.6	29.5	25.8	3.2	0.9	30931	32290	10	3	2797	50.8	28.9	16.9	3.3	0.1	49410
49945	LAKE LINDEN	19070	1609	31.6	31.6	32.1	3.7	0.9	37193	40536	24	9	1322	37.8	30.9	20.5	9.2	1.6	63897
49946	LANSE	19483	1613	30.1	28.3	37.0	4.0	0.6	40514	41418	34	20	1265	25.1	36.7	31.5	6.2	0.6	78852
49947	MARENISCO	15418	272	25.7	35.7	36.0	1.8	0.7	41694	46521	38	23	251	34.3	24.3	19.5	18.3	3.6	72692
49948	MASS CITY	20952	309	25.9	35.9	34.6	2.6	1.0	39071	40189	30	15	280	50.7	33.2	13.6	1.8	0.7	49444
49950	MOHAWK	19921	554	27.4	39.0	28.3	3.4	1.8	36522	38284	22	8	489	41.9	28.4	18.6	8.2	2.9	57453
49952	NISULA	16817	43	37.2	34.9	25.6	2.3	0.0	32317	35741	12	4	37	43.2	35.1	21.6	0.0	0.0	56250
49953	ONTONAGON	20577	1726	32.2	32.2	30.6	3.7	1.3	36772	38759	23	8	1440	47.9	34.9	13.2	3.7	0.3	52174
49958	PELKIE	14391	593	27.5	31.4	35.9	4.4	0.8	42509	45228	41	27	517	31.5	33.7	28.0	6.0	0.8	68839
49962	SKANEE	23480	152	31.6	23.7	40.8	3.3	0.7	43669	42992	44	31	140	20.0	27.9	43.6	8.6	0.0	92500
49965	TOIVOLA	18397	151	34.4	33.8	28.5	2.6	0.7	35547	38483	19	7	131	33.6	35.9	26.0	4.6	0.0	67500
49967	TROUT CREEK	20244	328	35.4	35.4	26.2	2.4	0.6	33718	34557	15	5	289	43.9	32.5	20.1	3.1	0.3	55645
49968	WAKEFIELD	19088	1085	37.3	31.9	26.8	2.9	1.0	32168	33726	12	4	929	57.4	28.4	11.8	2.3	0.1	44563
49969	WATERSMEET	21036	510	26.9	37.8	27.6	5.1	2.5	38405	39547	28	13	415	31.1	26.3	21.4	15.9	5.3	78103
49970	WATTON	23573	137	22.6	28.5	43.1	5.1	0.7	48977	49066	59	47	125	29.6	30.4	32.0	7.2	0.8	68929
	MICHIGAN	26713		20.1	24.2	38.5	11.3	5.9	55536	56866				13.2	21.9	40.3	21.5	3.2	115137
	UNITED STATES	27277		20.9	24.4	35.3	11.7	7.6	54719	56938				9.3	13.1	31.6	32.6	13.5	162279

ZIP CODE	FINANCIAL SERVICES				THE HOME						ENTERTAINMENT						PERSONAL			
					Home Improvements		Furnishings													
# POST OFFICE NAME	Auto Loan	Home Loan	Invest-ments	Retire-ment Plans	Home Repair	Lawn & Garden	Comput-ers & Hard-ware-Personal	Major Appli-ances	TV, Radio, Sound Equip-ment	Furni-ture	Dine out/ Carry out	Sports Equip-ment	Fees & Tickets	Toys & Games	Travel	Cable TV	Apparel & Services	Auto Repairs	Health Insur-ance	Pets & Supplies
49868 NEWBERRY	76	56	79	54	59	79	59	74	65	54	64	55	48	64	58	72	42	68	79	87
49870 NORWAY	80	59	80	57	61	84	64	78	71	57	68	58	51	70	62	78	46	73	85	92
49873 PERRONVILLE	84	60	87	59	63	86	62	79	69	58	68	59	50	68	61	76	45	72	82	94
49874 POWERS	73	58	70	59	60	76	60	71	64	54	63	54	51	65	59	70	42	66	75	84
49876 QUINNESEC	78	71	70	74	73	84	70	79	72	64	71	60	65	74	70	77	49	73	82	92
49878 RAPID RIVER	85	68	104	67	74	90	68	86	72	64	71	63	59	69	72	77	47	79	86	100
49879 REPUBLIC	68	65	82	59	72	77	61	72	65	66	63	47	61	59	67	69	43	70	81	83
49880 ROCK	84	63	85	61	65	86	64	80	70	59	69	60	52	70	63	77	46	73	83	94
49881 SAGOLA	85	61	87	59	63	86	62	79	69	58	68	60	50	69	62	76	45	73	83	94
49883 SENEY	75	53	77	52	55	76	55	70	61	51	60	52	44	60	54	67	39	64	73	83
49884 SHINGLETON	79	69	79	71	72	84	69	80	71	63	70	60	62	71	70	75	47	74	81	93
49885 SKANDIA	85	71	95	72	75	90	71	86	74	65	73	64	63	73	74	79	49	79	86	100
49886 SPALDING	79	59	80	58	61	82	61	76	67	56	66	57	50	67	60	73	44	70	79	89
49887 STEPHENSON	77	57	81	55	59	80	59	74	65	54	64	55	48	64	59	72	42	69	78	88
49891 TRENARY	77	55	79	53	57	78	56	72	63	52	61	54	45	62	56	69	41	66	75	85
49892 VULCAN	77	65	72	66	67	81	66	77	70	59	68	58	59	70	65	75	46	71	80	89
49893 WALLACE	79	68	75	70	70	84	69	79	72	62	70	60	62	72	69	76	48	73	82	92
49894 WELLS	74	60	71	60	61	78	62	73	66	56	65	55	53	66	61	72	44	68	78	85
49895 WETMORE	89	65	96	64	69	91	67	85	73	62	72	63	54	72	67	80	48	78	87	100
49896 WILSON	77	60	76	60	62	80	61	74	66	56	65	56	52	66	61	71	43	68	77	88
49905 ATLANTIC MINE	74	57	77	55	59	76	59	72	64	55	63	53	50	63	59	70	42	67	76	84
49908 BARAGA	73	52	73	51	54	75	56	70	63	51	61	52	45	62	55	69	40	65	75	82
49910 BERGLAND	65	56	73	52	61	72	56	67	60	56	59	46	51	57	58	65	39	64	74	77
49911 BESSEMER	71	52	70	52	54	73	59	69	65	53	63	51	48	63	56	71	42	66	76	81
49912 BRUCE CROSSING	66	54	72	51	58	72	55	67	60	54	59	48	49	58	56	66	39	63	74	78
49913 CALUMET	66	49	65	48	51	67	55	64	60	50	58	47	46	59	52	66	39	61	70	75
49916 CHASSELL	75	61	77	61	63	76	66	74	69	61	67	55	57	67	64	73	46	71	77	86
49919 COVINGTON	91	66	94	64	68	93	67	86	75	63	73	64	54	74	67	82	48	79	89	102
49920 CRYSTAL FALLS	68	58	79	55	63	75	58	70	62	57	60	49	52	58	61	67	40	66	76	81
49921 DODGEVILLE	68	60	62	61	62	69	64	67	66	62	65	49	59	65	62	69	44	66	72	78
49925 EWEN	66	49	67	47	51	69	52	64	58	48	56	47	43	57	51	64	37	60	70	75
49927 GAASTRA	66	60	78	56	66	74	59	70	63	61	61	47	56	58	63	67	41	67	77	80
49930 HANCOCK	68	52	63	52	53	67	62	64	65	55	64	49	52	64	57	69	43	65	71	77
49931 HOUGHTON	63	47	46	49	46	51	69	55	65	59	64	46	55	65	54	64	45	62	58	68
49935 IRON RIVER	68	52	75	51	55	72	56	68	61	51	59	50	47	59	56	66	39	64	72	79
49938 IRONWOOD	64	48	65	47	50	66	53	62	58	48	56	46	44	57	51	63	38	60	68	73
49945 LAKE LINDEN	74	56	82	54	59	78	59	73	64	54	62	54	49	62	59	70	41	68	77	85
49946 LANSE	74	58	74	57	60	79	61	74	67	56	65	54	52	66	60	72	43	69	79	86
49947 MARENISCO	75	58	88	57	63	79	60	75	64	56	63	55	51	62	62	70	42	70	78	87
49948 MASS CITY	80	57	81	55	59	82	60	76	67	55	65	57	48	66	59	74	43	70	80	90
49950 MOHAWK	73	58	80	57	62	79	60	73	66	57	64	52	53	63	61	72	43	69	80	85
49952 NISULA	65	46	65	45	48	67	50	62	55	45	54	46	40	55	48	61	36	57	67	73
49953 ONTONAGON	75	57	81	55	60	79	59	74	65	55	63	54	50	63	60	71	42	69	78	86
49958 PELKIE	83	60	86	58	62	85	62	79	69	57	68	59	50	68	61	76	45	72	83	93
49962 SKANEE	68	65	83	60	72	78	62	73	66	67	64	48	61	60	68	69	43	70	81	84
49965 TOIVOLA	67	49	72	48	52	70	53	66	58	48	56	49	43	57	53	64	38	61	70	77
49967 TROUT CREEK	68	51	71	49	54	71	53	66	58	50	57	48	44	57	53	64	38	61	71	77
49968 WAKEFIELD	68	53	72	51	56	73	55	68	61	52	59	49	47	59	56	67	39	64	74	79
49969 WATERSMEET	86	64	96	63	68	89	65	83	71	61	70	62	54	70	67	77	46	76	85	98
49970 WATTON	92	66	94	64	68	93	67	86	75	63	74	64	54	74	67	82	49	79	89	102
MICHIGAN	98	97	93	98	95	100	96	97	97	95	97	74	96	98	96	99	68	97	100	115
UNITED STATES	100	100	100	100	100	100	100	100	100	100	100	100	100	100	100	100	100	100	100	100

55001-55129

ZIP CODE #	POST OFFICE NAME	COUNTY FIPS CODE	POPULATION 2000	POPULATION 2009	POPULATION 2014	2000-2009 ANNUAL RATE % Rate	2000-2009 ANNUAL RATE State Centile	HOUSEHOLDS 2000	HOUSEHOLDS 2009	HOUSEHOLDS 2014	HOUSEHOLDS % Annual Rate 2000-2009	HOUSEHOLDS 2009 Average HH Size	FAMILIES 2000	FAMILIES 2009	FAMILIES % Annual Rate 2000-2009
55001	AFTON	163	2911	3115	3243	0.7	69	1023	1136	1196	1.1	2.74	855	926	0.9
55003	BAYPORT	163	2875	3071	3134	0.7	69	660	727	763	1.1	2.13	422	439	0.4
55005	BETHEL	003	4036	4813	5256	1.9	90	1293	1589	1753	2.3	3.03	1078	1287	1.9
55006	BRAHAM	065	2737	3169	3309	1.6	86	1057	1250	1316	1.8	2.53	752	864	1.5
55007	BROOK PARK	065	2150	2264	2296	0.6	67	777	839	858	0.8	2.70	588	617	0.5
55008	CAMBRIDGE	059	12274	16319	18164	3.1	95	4539	6154	6898	3.3	2.58	3236	4238	3.0
55009	CANNON FALLS	049	7814	8339	8514	0.7	69	2939	3235	3327	1.0	2.55	2150	2292	0.7
55011	CEDAR	003	8727	10077	10618	1.6	86	2831	3369	3592	1.9	2.99	2354	2723	1.6
55012	CENTER CITY	025	1881	2545	2736	3.3	96	586	769	836	3.0	3.16	450	573	2.6
55013	CHISAGO CITY	025	4613	5490	5740	1.9	90	1694	1995	2096	1.8	2.62	1244	1426	1.5
55014	CIRCLE PINES	003	26564	29517	30745	1.1	79	8407	9545	10045	1.4	2.95	6739	7387	1.0
55016	COTTAGE GROVE	163	30112	33987	36114	1.3	83	9777	11444	12292	1.7	2.96	8317	9477	1.4
55017	DALBO	059	701	787	824	1.3	83	249	288	304	1.6	2.73	186	210	1.3
55018	DENNISON	049	941	1042	1081	1.1	79	330	374	390	1.4	2.78	268	297	1.1
55019	DUNDAS	131	1026	1394	1544	3.4	96	387	546	607	3.8	2.55	287	382	3.1
55020	ELKO	139	2126	4055	5001	7.2	100	676	1282	1586	7.2	3.16	578	1075	6.9
55021	FARIBAULT	131	27278	29420	30035	0.8	72	9777	10743	11002	1.0	2.55	6782	7166	0.6
55024	FARMINGTON	037	21397	31055	35040	4.1	97	7069	10437	11845	4.3	2.97	5664	8181	4.1
55025	FOREST LAKE	003	19370	22946	24702	1.8	89	7063	8681	9456	2.3	2.62	5302	6320	1.9
55026	FRONTENAC	049	476	515	521	0.9	74	199	219	224	1.0	2.34	153	163	0.7
55027	GOODHUE	049	2562	2953	3080	1.5	85	909	1076	1131	1.8	2.74	712	819	1.5
55030	GRASSTON	065	583	618	626	0.6	67	223	245	251	1.0	2.51	172	183	0.7
55031	HAMPTON	037	1808	2114	2262	1.7	88	598	727	785	2.1	2.90	475	561	1.8
55032	HARRIS	025	3033	3533	3740	1.7	88	1039	1233	1313	1.9	2.85	807	937	1.6
55033	HASTINGS	037	25684	30805	33039	2.0	91	9089	11291	12222	2.4	2.67	6799	8188	2.0
55036	HENRIETTE	115	101	108	111	0.7	69	37	41	42	1.1	2.63	28	30	0.7
55037	HINCKLEY	115	3668	3822	3818	0.4	61	1436	1527	1536	0.7	2.48	976	1003	0.3
55038	HUGO	163	10769	17619	20492	5.5	99	3587	6045	7105	5.8	2.91	2957	4856	5.5
55040	ISANTI	059	9544	13591	15507	3.9	97	3233	4761	5490	4.3	2.85	2532	3635	4.0
55041	LAKE CITY	157	7171	7764	7885	0.9	74	2860	3166	3237	1.1	2.40	2010	2159	0.8
55042	LAKE ELMO	163	7390	8730	9395	1.8	89	2512	3047	3310	2.1	2.85	2073	2460	1.9
55043	LAKELAND	163	3701	3856	3958	0.4	61	1379	1494	1553	0.9	2.58	1036	1078	0.4
55044	LAKEVILLE	037	35069	45383	50114	2.8	94	11054	14621	16264	3.1	3.10	9410	12161	2.8
55045	LINDSTROM	025	5377	6809	7281	2.6	93	2045	2602	2800	2.6	2.49	1520	1880	2.3
55046	LONSDALE	131	2837	4316	4939	4.6	98	1004	1567	1806	4.9	2.74	765	1162	4.6
55047	MARINE ON SAINT CROI	163	2620	2853	2995	0.9	74	969	1098	1166	1.4	2.59	763	835	1.0
55049	MEDFORD	147	2174	2584	2788	1.9	90	808	985	1072	2.2	2.60	615	727	1.8
55051	MORA	065	9640	10536	10788	1.0	77	3801	4241	4370	1.2	2.46	2673	2883	0.8
55052	MORRISTOWN	131	2049	2457	2638	2.0	91	754	926	999	2.2	2.63	568	676	1.9
55053	NERSTRAND	131	956	1061	1100	1.1	79	316	358	372	1.4	2.96	261	290	1.1
55054	NEW MARKET	139	317	1048	1328	13.8	100	127	406	516	13.4	2.58	109	341	13.1
55055	NEWPORT	163	3703	3646	3673	-0.2	39	1412	1447	1475	0.3	2.50	965	939	-0.3
55056	NORTH BRANCH	025	10970	15004	16970	3.4	96	3839	5329	6060	3.6	2.81	2984	4033	3.3
55057	NORTHFIELD	131	21981	25161	26457	1.5	85	6505	7760	8297	1.9	2.61	4553	5252	1.6
55060	OWATONNA	147	26658	29748	31155	1.2	81	10202	11591	12202	1.4	2.52	7119	7826	1.0
55063	PINE CITY	115	9140	10054	10329	1.0	77	3493	3932	4066	1.3	2.51	2448	2653	0.9
55065	RANDOLPH	037	894	1025	1091	1.5	85	301	359	385	1.9	2.85	239	277	1.6
55066	RED WING	049	18280	19031	19213	0.4	61	7306	7750	7860	0.6	2.36	4779	4869	0.2
55067	ROCK CREEK	115	426	413	399	-0.3	35	145	145	142	0.0	2.85	113	111	-0.2
55068	ROSEMOUNT	037	20460	26129	28458	2.7	93	6631	8894	9816	3.2	2.94	5505	7088	2.8
55069	RUSH CITY	025	4185	5245	5542	2.5	93	1471	1790	1911	2.1	2.58	1061	1249	1.8
55070	SAINT FRANCIS	003	5078	7375	8284	4.1	97	1701	2579	2936	4.6	2.86	1349	1966	4.2
55071	SAINT PAUL PARK	163	5377	5680	5854	0.6	67	1947	2125	2218	1.0	2.64	1439	1506	0.5
55072	SANDSTONE	115	4620	5166	5161	1.2	81	1441	1540	1548	0.7	2.44	984	1017	0.4
55073	SCANDIA	163	2761	3004	3163	0.9	74	954	1079	1147	1.3	2.78	811	894	1.1
55074	SHAFER	025	895	1481	1682	5.6	99	319	556	635	6.2	2.66	246	414	5.8
55075	SOUTH SAINT PAUL	037	20176	20579	20691	0.2	54	8125	8511	8621	0.5	2.41	5240	5239	0.0
55076	INVER GROVE HEIGHTS	037	18509	21753	22992	1.8	89	7027	8621	9220	2.2	2.51	5136	6026	1.7
55077	INVER GROVE HEIGHTS	037	11288	12493	13143	1.1	79	4245	4770	5031	1.3	2.59	2824	3096	1.0
55079	STACY	025	7081	8154	8587	1.5	85	2399	2847	3027	1.9	2.85	1941	2238	1.6
55080	STANCHFIELD	059	2592	3100	3324	2.0	91	947	1158	1250	2.2	2.66	721	857	1.9
55082	STILLWATER	163	31101	36189	38814	1.7	88	11280	13472	14566	1.9	2.62	8490	9879	1.7
55084	TAYLORS FALLS	025	1461	1926	2226	3.0	95	540	700	813	2.8	2.75	396	500	2.6
55087	WARSAW	131	193	200	207	0.4	61	65	70	73	0.8	2.84	52	54	0.4
55088	WEBSTER	131	1566	1827	1973	1.7	88	527	632	683	2.0	2.88	443	522	1.8
55089	WELCH	049	1876	2037	2099	0.9	74	638	716	745	1.3	2.84	507	553	0.9
55092	WYOMING	003	9468	10911	11464	1.5	85	3243	3796	4007	1.7	2.86	2612	2983	1.4
55101	SAINT PAUL	123	3968	4671	4825	1.8	89	2674	3231	3353	2.1	1.29	482	528	1.0
55102	SAINT PAUL	123	18389	19328	19438	0.5	63	8789	9457	9551	0.8	1.92	3336	3387	0.2
55103	SAINT PAUL	123	13276	13097	12822	-0.1	44	4448	4294	4197	-0.4	3.00	2612	2406	-0.9
55104	SAINT PAUL	123	48343	47742	47222	-0.1	44	17994	17797	17599	-0.1	2.48	9280	8702	-0.7
55105	SAINT PAUL	123	26453	25568	25094	-0.4	30	11087	10884	10704	-0.2	2.14	5750	5351	-0.8
55106	SAINT PAUL	123	54327	54159	53388	0.0	48	18550	18163	17834	-0.2	2.94	11869	11147	-0.7
55107	SAINT PAUL	123	16133	15950	15725	-0.1	44	5564	5473	5380	-0.2	2.86	3477	3281	-0.6
55108	SAINT PAUL	123	16370	16168	15972	-0.1	44	6749	6748	6675	0.0	2.11	3421	3242	-0.6
55109	SAINT PAUL	123	29174	28811	28494	-0.1	44	11386	11528	11433	0.1	2.45	7655	7468	-0.3
55110	SAINT PAUL	123	40172	40961	41143	0.2	54	15113	15782	15895	0.5	2.57	11066	11233	0.2
55112	SAINT PAUL	123	44721	44030	43486	-0.2	39	17049	17195	17049	0.1	2.40	11551	11218	-0.3
55113	SAINT PAUL	123	37632	37375	36989	-0.1	44	16298	16608	16511	0.2	2.14	9656	9403	-0.3
55114	SAINT PAUL	123	1309	2171	2239	5.6	99	713	1095	1131	4.7	1.87	249	370	4.4
55115	SAINT PAUL	163	9283	10419	11047	1.3	83	3151	3612	3862	1.5	2.88	2508	2787	1.1
55116	SAINT PAUL	123	22871	22686	22431	-0.1	44	10990	11068	10966	0.1	1.99	5409	5138	-0.6
55117	SAINT PAUL	123	41201	40507	39923	-0.2	39	16487	16380	16164	-0.1	2.46	9726	9241	-0.6
55118	SAINT PAUL	037	27324	28140	28379	0.3	58	11667	12319	12515	0.6	2.25	7227	7281	0.1
55119	SAINT PAUL	123	37774	37263	36750	-0.1	44	15179	15139	14937	0.0	2.42	9656	9278	-0.4
55120	SAINT PAUL	037	4722	4865	4908	0.3	58	1732	1842	1874	0.7	2.62	1225	1248	0.2
55121	SAINT PAUL	037	7451	7978	8206	0.7	69	3139	3494	3634	1.2	2.28	1780	1870	0.5
55122	SAINT PAUL	037	29400	31723	32580	0.8	72	11732	12971	13408	1.1	2.44	7685	8158	0.6
55123	SAINT PAUL	037	26696	28342	28761	0.6	67	8899	9513	9704	0.7	2.97	6967	7228	0.4
55124	SAINT PAUL	037	45622	51802	54364	1.4	84	16357	19590	20863	2.0	2.63	12410	14013	1.3
55125	SAINT PAUL	163	40104	45360	48212	1.3	83	14472	16876	18116	1.7	2.66	10896	12327	1.3
55126	SAINT PAUL	123	25940	25662	25374	-0.1	44	10129	10330	10273	0.2	2.47	7171	7078	-0.1
55127	SAINT PAUL	123	17030	17370	17336	0.2	54	6445	6767	6785	0.5	2.55	4686	4816	0.3
55128	SAINT PAUL	163	27398	29112	30159	0.7	69	10550	11582	12130	1.0	2.50	7306	7641	0.5
55129	SAINT PAUL	163	6351	16172	20412	10.6	100	2201	5801	7401	11.0	2.78	1766	4557	10.8
	MINNESOTA					0.9					1.1	2.48			0.7
	UNITED STATES					1.0					1.1	2.59			0.9

ZIP CODE #	POST OFFICE NAME	RACE (%) White 2000	White 2009	Black 2000	Black 2009	Asian/Pacific 2000	Asian/Pacific 2009	% Hispanic Origin 2000	% Hispanic Origin 2009	2009 AGE DISTRIBUTION (%) 0-4	5-9	10-14	15-19	20-24	25-44	45-64	65-84	85+	18+	MEDIAN AGE 2009	% 2009 Males	% 2009 Females
55001	AFTON	96.7	95.4	0.2	0.4	1.0	1.4	1.0	1.5	4.4	5.6	7.1	7.5	4.1	18.4	39.3	12.5	1.1	78.0	46.6	50.0	50.0
55003	BAYPORT	70.5	66.1	19.8	24.0	0.7	0.9	3.5	4.3	2.5	2.6	3.0	3.9	11.8	46.0	20.9	7.5	1.7	89.7	35.6	74.1	25.9
55005	BETHEL	97.0	96.2	0.2	0.4	0.3	0.5	1.0	1.5	8.8	8.1	8.2	7.9	5.7	32.3	24.2	4.6	0.3	70.1	31.9	51.9	48.1
55006	BRAHAM	97.5	97.0	0.2	0.3	0.2	0.3	0.5	0.9	7.0	6.8	6.8	6.7	5.9	26.6	27.4	11.1	1.8	75.3	38.2	51.0	49.0
55007	BROOK PARK	97.9	97.4	0.3	0.4	0.2	0.3	0.7	0.9	6.1	7.0	7.1	7.1	5.2	24.5	30.0	11.9	1.2	75.4	40.4	51.2	48.8
55008	CAMBRIDGE	97.4	96.8	0.3	0.3	0.5	0.8	0.8	1.2	6.9	6.6	6.8	7.3	6.5	25.9	26.5	10.4	3.0	75.0	37.5	48.5	51.5
55009	CANNON FALLS	98.3	97.9	0.1	0.2	0.5	0.6	0.9	1.3	6.2	6.6	7.0	7.4	5.9	25.6	29.1	10.5	1.8	75.5	39.0	50.1	49.9
55011	CEDAR	97.6	96.8	0.2	0.3	0.4	0.6	0.9	1.4	7.1	7.6	8.0	8.1	5.1	27.8	29.8	6.0	0.4	72.1	36.6	51.2	48.8
55012	CENTER CITY	97.8	97.0	0.4	0.5	0.5	0.9	1.1	1.6	7.1	7.1	7.5	7.5	5.5	26.8	27.9	9.4	1.3	73.2	37.1	51.6	48.4
55013	CHISAGO CITY	97.6	96.9	0.4	0.4	0.4	0.5	1.1	1.7	6.8	6.8	7.0	6.8	5.4	25.9	27.6	10.1	3.7	75.2	39.3	50.0	50.0
55014	CIRCLE PINES	94.2	92.4	1.8	2.5	1.4	1.9	1.5	2.3	7.8	8.3	8.2	7.8	5.5	32.3	24.6	5.2	0.4	70.7	34.1	52.4	47.6
55016	COTTAGE GROVE	93.5	91.3	2.4	3.3	1.5	2.0	2.6	3.8	8.4	8.3	8.3	7.6	5.0	30.1	25.3	6.6	0.4	70.1	34.4	49.2	50.8
55017	DALBO	98.7	98.3	0.0	0.0	0.6	0.6	0.6	1.0	5.6	6.2	6.7	6.7	5.2	24.3	33.3	10.5	1.4	77.4	42.1	50.1	49.9
55018	DENNISON	97.3	96.8	0.1	0.1	0.4	0.6	0.5	0.9	6.5	7.2	7.5	6.6	5.0	22.7	32.9	10.4	1.2	74.5	40.9	51.9	48.1
55019	DUNDAS	97.5	95.9	0.7	1.1	0.6	0.8	1.5	2.7	5.7	6.2	7.3	7.6	5.8	27.5	29.7	9.0	1.2	75.9	38.4	50.7	49.3
55020	ELKO	98.5	98.1	0.1	0.2	0.3	0.4	0.8	1.6	7.4	8.0	8.7	8.3	4.6	25.8	30.2	6.4	0.5	70.7	37.3	51.1	48.9
55021	FARIBAULT	92.0	88.9	2.1	2.8	1.5	2.1	7.1	11.0	6.6	6.6	7.0	7.4	6.4	27.3	25.6	10.8	2.3	75.1	37.3	51.6	48.4
55024	FARMINGTON	95.2	93.2	0.7	1.1	1.9	2.9	1.6	2.5	11.2	9.9	8.6	6.7	4.8	35.8	18.5	3.9	0.7	65.9	30.5	50.6	49.4
55025	FOREST LAKE	97.5	96.7	0.3	0.4	0.6	0.8	0.9	1.5	6.5	6.9	7.3	7.2	5.1	25.9	30.3	9.4	1.4	74.7	39.1	49.8	50.2
55026	FRONTENAC	98.5	98.1	0.2	0.4	0.4	0.6	0.4	0.8	5.2	6.2	7.4	7.4	4.3	19.0	36.3	12.6	1.6	76.5	45.2	48.2	51.8
55027	GOODHUE	97.6	96.8	0.0	0.0	0.4	0.5	1.6	2.5	6.3	6.8	7.1	7.2	4.7	25.2	30.2	11.2	1.4	75.4	39.8	52.3	47.7
55030	GRASSTON	98.1	97.6	0.3	0.3	0.0	0.2	0.9	1.1	5.8	6.0	6.8	6.8	4.4	25.6	29.9	13.8	1.0	77.0	41.5	52.6	47.4
55031	HAMPTON	98.3	97.6	0.1	0.2	0.3	0.4	1.0	1.6	6.7	7.0	7.4	7.6	5.3	26.2	29.6	9.4	0.9	73.7	38.5	51.0	49.0
55032	HARRIS	98.3	97.9	0.3	0.3	0.2	0.3	1.0	1.4	6.1	7.5	8.0	8.0	4.4	26.7	28.9	9.5	0.8	72.9	38.5	51.7	48.3
55033	HASTINGS	97.3	96.3	0.4	0.6	0.6	0.9	1.1	1.7	6.7	6.7	6.8	7.0	5.8	27.9	27.9	9.7	1.6	75.4	37.2	50.0	50.0
55036	HENRIETTE	98.0	97.2	0.0	0.9	0.0	0.0	1.0	0.0	6.5	5.6	7.4	7.4	3.7	25.9	27.8	14.8	0.9	75.0	40.6	50.0	50.0
55037	HINCKLEY	90.8	89.6	0.5	0.6	0.5	0.8	1.3	1.9	6.0	6.6	7.7	8.3	5.6	24.2	28.4	11.6	1.6	74.0	39.1	50.2	49.8
55038	HUGO	96.8	95.9	0.2	0.3	1.3	1.7	1.3	2.0	9.5	9.1	8.7	7.0	4.9	31.7	23.6	5.0	0.4	68.2	32.9	50.6	49.4
55040	ISANTI	97.9	97.4	0.3	0.4	0.3	0.4	0.8	1.1	7.6	7.2	7.4	7.7	7.4	28.4	26.4	7.3	0.7	72.7	34.2	51.3	48.7
55041	LAKE CITY	97.4	96.6	0.5	0.7	1.0	1.3	1.7	2.3	5.3	5.5	5.8	6.4	5.4	23.5	30.3	14.6	3.2	79.3	43.6	49.1	50.9
55042	LAKE ELMO	95.9	94.7	0.4	0.5	1.7	2.3	1.3	2.0	6.5	7.6	8.4	7.5	4.6	22.0	33.4	9.3	0.7	72.4	40.7	50.1	49.9
55043	LAKELAND	97.2	96.2	0.1	0.2	0.5	0.7	1.2	2.0	5.7	6.0	7.2	7.1	4.0	25.2	34.2	9.8	0.9	76.6	41.8	49.7	50.3
55044	LAKEVILLE	95.0	93.0	1.1	1.6	1.6	2.4	1.9	3.0	9.7	9.7	9.3	7.7	4.4	31.0	23.6	4.3	0.3	66.2	32.6	50.5	49.5
55045	LINDSTROM	97.9	97.4	0.5	0.6	0.3	0.4	1.2	1.7	6.3	6.4	7.2	7.7	5.5	25.0	28.7	11.4	2.0	74.9	39.7	50.5	49.5
55046	LONSDALE	98.7	98.3	0.1	0.2	0.2	0.2	0.6	1.0	7.4	7.8	8.3	7.3	4.2	28.0	27.1	8.7	1.2	71.8	37.2	51.7	48.3
55047	MARINE ON SAINT CROI	98.1	97.4	0.3	0.4	0.5	0.6	0.8	1.3	4.8	6.1	7.6	6.5	3.6	18.7	38.2	13.1	1.4	77.3	46.3	50.4	49.6
55049	MEDFORD	95.5	93.5	0.1	0.1	0.5	0.7	4.6	7.2	7.7	7.9	7.8	6.9	4.9	29.6	25.4	8.7	1.0	72.1	35.4	50.8	49.2
55051	MORA	97.2	96.6	0.2	0.3	0.4	0.6	1.0	1.6	6.2	6.6	6.8	6.6	5.5	24.3	28.0	13.5	2.5	76.1	40.4	50.3	49.7
55052	MORRISTOWN	98.7	98.2	0.1	0.2	0.0	0.0	4.2	6.7	6.4	6.6	7.2	8.1	5.0	25.5	28.6	11.1	1.5	75.3	39.0	50.9	49.1
55053	NERSTRAND	98.7	98.5	0.1	0.2	0.4	0.5	0.7	1.3	7.5	8.0	8.1	7.8	5.0	23.8	29.6	9.0	1.0	71.3	37.9	50.1	49.9
55054	NEW MARKET	98.1	98.0	0.3	0.2	0.3	0.3	0.9	1.5	7.5	8.3	8.9	8.3	4.4	26.1	29.6	6.3	0.6	70.0	37.0	51.0	49.0
55055	NEWPORT	91.7	88.8	1.7	2.4	1.6	2.1	4.2	6.4	7.5	7.2	6.9	6.7	6.3	28.7	26.4	8.8	1.5	74.1	35.7	48.4	51.6
55056	NORTH BRANCH	97.5	96.8	0.2	0.2	0.9	1.2	1.2	1.8	8.9	8.3	8.0	7.3	5.0	31.5	22.8	7.1	1.1	70.1	33.0	50.0	50.0
55057	NORTHFIELD	93.9	91.7	0.7	1.1	2.0	2.8	4.7	6.5	5.4	5.5	5.7	13.2	16.4	20.6	22.7	8.4	2.0	79.4	28.6	48.6	51.4
55060	OWATONNA	94.7	93.0	1.3	1.8	1.0	1.2	3.9	5.6	7.1	6.8	6.9	7.4	6.2	26.4	26.4	10.6	2.1	74.4	37.0	49.4	50.6
55063	PINE CITY	97.9	97.4	0.2	0.3	0.2	0.3	0.9	1.2	6.1	5.9	6.5	7.3	5.8	25.4	27.5	13.2	2.3	76.8	40.0	50.7	49.3
55065	RANDOLPH	98.4	97.9	0.1	0.2	0.2	0.4	0.9	1.4	6.5	7.2	7.6	7.7	5.3	25.6	30.0	9.3	0.9	73.3	38.8	51.0	49.0
55066	RED WING	95.1	93.9	1.2	1.6	0.7	1.0	1.2	1.8	6.0	6.0	6.2	7.0	6.1	24.8	28.0	12.8	3.1	77.4	40.3	48.5	51.5
55067	ROCK CREEK	98.4	97.8	0.0	0.0	0.5	0.7	0.5	0.7	7.0	7.5	7.7	7.7	4.6	24.5	28.8	11.1	1.0	72.9	38.6	52.1	47.9
55068	ROSEMOUNT	92.9	90.7	2.0	2.6	2.2	3.2	1.8	2.8	9.1	9.2	9.0	7.7	4.6	32.2	22.1	5.5	0.6	67.6	32.6	49.8	50.2
55069	RUSH CITY	94.1	92.9	2.4	2.7	0.9	1.2	1.8	2.7	6.2	6.2	6.5	6.5	7.7	28.9	25.6	10.1	2.3	76.9	36.7	54.6	45.4
55070	SAINT FRANCIS	95.7	94.7	0.2	0.3	1.3	1.5	1.0	1.6	11.3	9.6	8.1	6.3	5.8	36.5	18.1	4.0	0.3	66.9	29.9	49.6	50.4
55071	SAINT PAUL PARK	94.1	91.7	2.2	3.3	1.1	1.5	2.7	4.0	7.1	7.0	7.1	7.5	6.1	26.7	27.3	10.1	1.1	74.2	37.1	49.5	50.5
55072	SANDSTONE	85.5	83.3	5.2	6.8	0.7	0.9	5.7	7.4	4.3	4.7	5.9	7.7	6.8	32.2	24.9	10.5	2.9	79.8	37.8	60.6	39.4
55073	SCANDIA	97.8	97.0	0.2	0.3	0.8	1.1	0.7	1.1	5.1	6.5	7.9	7.8	3.7	22.7	36.5	9.0	0.9	75.5	42.5	51.3	48.7
55074	SHAFER	96.4	94.9	0.0	0.1	2.7	3.8	0.9	1.4	6.9	6.8	6.9	7.8	7.3	26.2	27.9	8.8	1.4	74.2	36.1	49.6	50.4
55075	SOUTH SAINT PAUL	92.8	89.9	1.3	1.8	0.8	1.2	6.3	9.6	7.2	6.9	6.5	6.2	6.3	28.8	26.0	10.1	1.9	75.5	36.6	48.8	51.2
55076	INVER GROVE HEIGHTS	92.4	89.6	1.8	2.3	1.4	2.1	4.7	7.1	6.8	7.0	7.2	6.8	5.6	28.5	27.8	9.3	1.0	74.7	37.3	48.7	51.3
55077	INVER GROVE HEIGHTS	90.6	87.4	2.7	3.5	3.1	4.4	3.6	5.3	7.5	7.3	7.2	7.4	7.4	31.3	24.3	6.5	1.1	73.5	33.3	50.8	49.2
55079	STACY	97.6	96.9	0.3	0.4	0.3	0.5	1.3	2.0	7.8	8.0	8.0	7.2	5.0	29.6	28.0	6.0	0.5	71.5	35.8	51.9	48.1
55080	STANCHFIELD	98.0	97.5	0.2	0.2	0.3	0.4	1.1	1.6	6.0	6.4	7.0	6.7	4.5	25.4	31.7	11.2	1.1	76.1	41.3	51.8	48.2
55082	STILLWATER	96.7	95.6	0.8	1.1	0.9	1.3	1.2	1.7	6.0	6.7	7.5	7.5	5.3	23.3	32.2	9.9	1.6	74.9	40.9	50.0	50.0
55084	TAYLORS FALLS	95.6	94.1	0.1	0.1	3.4	4.5	0.8	1.2	6.9	6.5	6.5	7.4	7.8	26.2	27.6	9.7	1.5	75.1	36.3	49.6	50.4
55087	WARSAW	99.5	99.5	0.0	0.0	0.0	0.0	1.0	2.0	6.0	6.5	7.0	7.0	4.5	24.5	31.5	12.0	1.0	76.5	41.6	52.0	48.0
55088	WEBSTER	98.5	98.2	0.1	0.1	0.3	0.4	0.8	1.4	7.2	7.9	8.4	7.7	4.4	23.3	31.3	9.1	0.7	71.3	39.2	51.6	48.4
55089	WELCH	94.7	94.2	0.5	0.7	0.2	0.2	0.9	1.4	5.9	6.5	7.1	6.6	5.2	24.0	33.3	10.1	1.2	76.0	41.1	51.0	49.0
55092	WYOMING	97.5	96.9	0.2	0.3	0.6	0.9	0.8	1.1	8.0	8.1	8.2	7.3	4.7	29.1	27.1	6.6	0.9	71.0	35.8	50.8	49.2
55101	SAINT PAUL	71.9	63.2	16.8	21.9	5.6	7.7	6.2	8.8	2.5	1.9	1.9	3.1	8.7	38.1	28.8	12.2	2.7	92.4	41.1	53.9	46.1
55102	SAINT PAUL	78.0	71.0	10.8	14.4	3.9	5.2	6.1	9.3	5.0	4.3	4.2	5.3	9.3	33.8	25.8	9.9	2.3	83.4	36.7	49.1	50.9
55103	SAINT PAUL	38.4	31.6	21.2	23.1	29.2	33.4	9.1	11.0	9.2	8.8	8.6	9.2	10.0	27.6	18.9	6.2	1.3	67.6	27.2	50.0	50.0
55104	SAINT PAUL	62.9	55.5	20.3	24.4	9.7	12.2	4.2	5.8	6.9	5.8	5.7	9.9	12.9	30.0	21.2	6.3	1.4	77.7	29.7	48.4	51.6
55105	SAINT PAUL	93.0	89.6	1.8	2.8	2.4	3.9	2.0	3.3	5.1	4.8	4.9	8.8	11.7	28.6	26.4	8.0	1.7	82.0	34.8	45.7	54.3
55106	SAINT PAUL	58.2	48.5	10.7	13.0	19.9	25.5	10.4	13.4	9.8	8.5	7.6	8.2	8.7	28.3	20.1	7.1	1.7	69.1	29.1	49.6	50.4
55107	SAINT PAUL	58.5	49.9	6.7	7.9	8.1	9.6	32.6	41.5	9.0	8.2	7.7	8.1	8.1	27.9	20.1	7.8	3.1	70.1	30.7	49.4	50.6
55108	SAINT PAUL	80.9	74.5	5.1	6.9	10.4	14.2	3.1	4.5	6.0	4.2	3.7	8.4	14.5	31.9	19.5	7.9	3.9	83.3	30.9	47.4	52.6
55109	SAINT PAUL	90.7	86.2	2.9	4.4	3.4	5.3	2.1	3.4	6.3	6.3	6.5	6.7	5.6	26.1	27.6	12.1	2.9	76.6	39.5	48.3	51.7
55110	SAINT PAUL	95.8	93.6	0.9	1.4	1.5	2.5	1.5	2.5	6.3	6.5	6.8	6.8	5.5	25.9	28.9	11.6	1.8	76.2	39.6	48.6	51.4
55112	SAINT PAUL	90.1	85.6	2.6	3.8	3.9	6.1	1.9	3.1	5.8	5.7	5.9	7.7	8.1	26.1	26.5	11.9	2.2	78.9	37.4	48.2	51.8
55113	SAINT PAUL	89.4	84.4	2.7	3.9	5.1	7.9	1.9	3.0	4.7	4.4	4.6	6.1	6.4	26.2	26.7	16.5	4.3	83.1	43.0	46.5	53.5
55114	SAINT PAUL	74.4	67.5	11.9	14.7	7.8	8.9	5.0	9.1	5.3	4.3	4.0	4.2	8.2	36.3	26.4	7.8	3.5	84.2	37.2	49.3	50.7
55115	SAINT PAUL	96.7	95.3	0.8	1.2	0.8	1.1	1.1	1.8	6.3	7.7	8.7	9.0	5.1	21.0	32.2	9.0	1.1	71.4	39.6	49.1	50.9
55116	SAINT PAUL	87.3	81.9	4.5	6.3	3.5	5.4	4.9	7.3	5.6	5.2	5.2	5.3	6.8	28.6	26.5	12.2	4.5	80.8	40.4	46.4	53.6
55117	SAINT PAUL	69.9	62.2	10.1	12.7	13.1	16.9	5.3	7.2	8.1	7.1	6.4	6.7	8.3	29.4	23.3	8.7	2.0	74.3	33.1	48.4	51.6
55118	SAINT PAUL	90.0	86.4	2.1	2.9	1.7	2.4	7.7	11.2	5.6	5.6	5.9	5.9	5.4	23.6	28.7	15.4	3.9	79.2	43.3	46.9	53.1
55119	SAINT PAUL	78.9	71.8	9.0	11.9	6.3	9.2	4.3	6.3	7.7	7.2	6.8	6.9	7.0	28.8	24.1	9.5	1.8	74.2	34.8	48.8	51.2
55120	SAINT PAUL	94.0	91.5	1.5	2.2	2.8	4.1	1.4	2.2	5.7	6.4	7.7	8.0	4.9	21.7	33.0	11.0	1.6	74.6	41.5	47.6	52.4
55121	SAINT PAUL	84.8	79.5	4.3	5.7	6.5	9.1	3.5	5.1	7.3	6.5	5.8	5.1	9.9	35.9	22.4	6.4	0.8	77.3	32.3	50.0	50.0
55122	SAINT PAUL	86.8	82.4	3.5	4.7	6.4	8.8	2.2	3.3	6.9	7.0	7.3	6.4	5.8	32.4	27.0	6.7	0.4	74.9	36.1	48.8	51.2
55123	SAINT PAUL	90.3	86.6	3.1	4.3	4.0	5.7	1.9	2.9	9.0	10.3	9.2	7.1	4.0	32.6	24.3	3.3	0.3	66.6	33.3	49.6	50.4
55124	SAINT PAUL	91.8	88.2	1.9	2.7	3.4	5.2	2.0	3.1	7.2	7.2	7.6	7.2	5.5	29.3	28.7	6.5	0.8	73.4	36.7	48.9	51.1
55125	SAINT PAUL	89.8	85.9	2.7	3.9	5.1	6.9	2.2	3.3	9.5	8.5	7.7	6.4	4.6	32.7	23.6	6.0	1.0	69.8	34.1	48.4	51.6
55126	SAINT PAUL	93.3	89.8	1.0	1.5	3.7	5.9	1.3	2.1	5.2	5.7	6.7	7.0	5.4	24.6	33.2	11.0	1.2	77.8	41.8	48.3	51.7
55127	SAINT PAUL	92.4	88.6	1.1	1.6	4.4	7.0	1.4	2.3	5.5	6.2	7.1	7.1	5.1	23.6	33.5	10.6	1.2	76.5	41.6	47.6	52.4
55128	SAINT PAUL	92.2	89.3	2.2	3.2	2.4	3.3	2.8	4.2	7.8	7.5	7.4	7.0	5.9	29.8	25.9	7.7	1.0	72.6	35.3	48.2	51.8
55129	SAINT PAUL	91.5	88.4	1.6	2.3	4.8	6.5	2.0	3.1	9.6	9.7	9.3	6.6	3.5	31.3	25.1	4.6	0.3	66.7	34.3	49.1	50.9
	MINNESOTA	89.4	86.8	3.5	4.3	2.9	3.9	2.9	4.1	6.8	6.7	6.7	7.2	6.8	27.2	26.3	10.2	2.1	75.6	36.9	49.6	50.4
	UNITED STATES	75.1	72.0	12.3	12.7	3.8	4.6	12.5	15.7	6.8	6.7	6.6	7.1	6.9	27.0	26.0	10.9	1.9	75.7	36.9	49.2	50.8

ZIP CODE #	POST OFFICE NAME	2009 Per Capita Income	2009 HH Income Base	2009 Household Income Distribution (%): Less than $25,000	$25,000 to $49,999	$50,000 to $99,999	$100,000 to $149,999	$150,000 or More	Median Household Income: 2009	2014	2009 National Centile	2009 State Centile	2009 Home Value Base	2009 Home Value Distribution (%): Less than $50,000	$50,000 to $89,999	$90,000 to $174,999	$175,000 to $399,999	$400,000 or More	2009 Median Home Value
55001	AFTON	48605	1136	4.1	10.2	22.4	30.3	32.9	120586	125000	98	100	1090	1.3	0.4	3.9	54.7	39.8	356126
55003	BAYPORT	24702	727	16.0	22.4	38.9	16.1	6.6	62960	66512	81	82	531	0.0	0.6	44.6	47.3	7.5	184961
55005	BETHEL	29080	1589	5.9	14.7	46.3	25.9	7.2	78391	82504	91	91	1515	15.8	5.0	25.3	51.0	2.8	182224
55006	BRAHAM	23472	1250	21.1	26.8	39.1	9.4	3.5	51533	53540	65	60	1008	10.3	12.6	47.5	27.4	2.2	136957
55007	BROOK PARK	19675	839	21.5	28.1	42.8	6.1	1.5	50219	50957	62	54	754	13.1	19.1	38.7	26.4	2.7	129945
55008	CAMBRIDGE	26761	6154	16.7	24.0	41.5	11.8	6.0	60441	64403	78	78	4831	3.3	8.1	41.2	43.9	3.5	170324
55009	CANNON FALLS	29541	3235	15.5	20.9	40.7	15.5	7.3	64760	67754	83	84	2633	8.1	4.5	26.4	50.4	10.6	203490
55011	CEDAR	29507	3369	5.1	13.2	46.5	29.1	6.1	79927	84333	92	92	3284	6.7	4.1	28.3	56.5	4.4	200435
55012	CENTER CITY	22792	769	12.1	19.9	47.1	16.0	4.9	64699	68690	83	84	665	4.1	5.7	27.7	54.0	8.6	209000
55013	CHISAGO CITY	29227	1995	14.2	18.8	42.2	17.7	7.2	66415	71242	84	86	1592	3.8	3.4	25.2	54.1	13.4	229150
55014	CIRCLE PINES	34180	9545	6.3	11.3	38.1	29.7	14.6	90564	95860	95	94	8718	5.9	1.7	32.9	54.7	4.8	195439
55016	COTTAGE GROVE	32965	11444	4.5	12.5	39.2	33.4	10.4	90336	95379	95	94	10336	0.9	1.0	31.5	64.1	2.5	196560
55017	DALBO	22080	288	17.7	23.6	48.3	6.6	3.8	55538	58392	72	71	261	6.9	6.1	43.3	39.1	4.6	163851
55018	DENNISON	30006	374	8.3	19.5	46.5	18.2	7.5	70184	73153	87	87	336	1.5	4.2	18.2	54.8	21.4	251000
55019	DUNDAS	32311	546	9.9	22.0	44.5	15.9	7.7	75805	76128	90	90	443	2.7	5.0	25.5	51.5	15.3	227431
55020	ELKO	36459	1282	4.3	9.4	33.9	34.0	18.3	102789	106314	97	97	1214	0.3	0.9	8.7	55.8	34.2	339048
55021	FARIBAULT	23914	10743	17.5	26.3	44.1	9.2	2.9	55475	57535	72	71	8167	8.1	7.0	39.9	38.7	6.3	165960
55024	FARMINGTON	33085	10437	5.3	11.5	42.4	31.8	9.0	88390	93229	95	94	9498	5.3	1.9	20.2	68.8	3.9	215804
55025	FOREST LAKE	33515	8681	10.3	17.1	37.2	26.9	8.5	78341	82744	91	91	7104	3.2	1.2	23.2	62.5	9.9	226930
55026	FRONTENAC	30438	219	10.0	27.9	46.1	11.9	4.1	62461	64875	81	81	198	4.0	6.1	29.3	45.5	15.2	202941
55027	GOODHUE	24370	1076	12.4	25.1	49.2	9.5	3.9	60609	62723	78	78	916	5.3	6.7	35.0	41.2	11.8	185887
55030	GRASSTON	22938	245	16.3	33.9	40.4	6.1	3.3	49771	51150	60	52	225	9.3	11.6	47.1	28.0	4.0	143561
55031	HAMPTON	29009	727	8.5	20.8	41.3	22.6	6.9	70508	76466	87	88	634	2.8	1.4	26.2	53.8	15.8	232407
55032	HARRIS	25290	1233	11.6	21.7	48.2	14.2	4.3	64011	68016	82	83	1136	1.5	3.9	34.7	53.0	7.0	198156
55033	HASTINGS	32050	11291	9.2	18.3	37.9	26.6	8.0	76901	81740	91	90	8978	6.1	2.0	30.9	53.7	7.3	199314
55036	HENRIETTE	21768	41	17.1	34.1	41.5	4.9	2.4	48654	51350	58	50	38	5.3	13.2	50.0	26.3	5.3	150000
55037	HINCKLEY	21083	1527	25.7	28.7	37.1	6.4	2.2	44974	47598	48	33	1176	9.5	21.3	45.7	20.6	3.0	122297
55038	HUGO	36817	6045	3.6	11.3	37.2	33.6	14.4	96882	100814	96	96	5640	2.2	0.9	16.5	66.7	13.7	234107
55040	ISANTI	24525	4761	11.0	22.1	51.3	11.8	3.8	63212	66786	81	82	4319	3.9	3.7	42.8	45.1	4.5	174442
55041	LAKE CITY	25890	3166	17.4	25.6	45.0	8.2	3.8	54996	57408	71	70	2523	8.9	8.4	47.3	30.9	4.5	145689
55042	LAKE ELMO	41691	3047	7.7	13.9	27.0	26.0	25.3	101940	106784	97	97	2911	16.2	1.7	9.4	42.8	29.9	300085
55043	LAKELAND	37385	1494	8.4	11.5	36.3	34.9	8.8	89636	94957	95	94	1382	1.7	1.7	29.8	58.1	8.8	208311
55044	LAKEVILLE	42169	14621	4.6	8.7	27.4	33.5	25.8	111462	114155	98	99	13263	4.9	0.6	8.4	68.0	18.1	271204
55045	LINDSTROM	29420	2602	12.7	20.6	44.6	15.6	6.6	65588	70875	84	85	2210	6.0	2.8	32.7	50.3	8.3	197826
55046	LONSDALE	26602	1567	13.1	18.1	51.3	12.8	4.7	66706	67553	85	86	1385	2.1	4.5	31.8	49.7	11.8	206323
55047	MARINE ON SAINT CROI	42336	1098	6.9	14.2	28.3	34.2	16.4	100647	104288	97	97	993	0.7	0.4	12.0	61.0	25.9	310634
55049	MEDFORD	23561	985	14.4	25.5	51.5	6.3	2.3	57747	59460	75	74	850	9.4	11.9	36.7	34.6	7.4	160593
55051	MORA	22301	4241	22.2	29.0	40.7	5.6	2.5	48513	50403	58	49	3411	11.7	14.5	42.6	28.9	2.3	135448
55052	MORRISTOWN	23062	926	17.4	27.2	44.7	8.4	2.3	54780	56549	71	69	803	13.4	11.6	35.9	30.0	9.1	144559
55053	NERSTRAND	24143	358	10.9	25.4	48.3	10.9	4.5	62888	64513	81	81	312	1.6	4.2	23.4	51.0	19.9	241000
55054	NEW MARKET	45792	406	4.4	8.9	33.0	33.3	20.4	104427	107754	97	97	384	0.5	1.0	10.7	52.9	34.9	339583
55055	NEWPORT	27111	1447	13.3	29.9	39.2	12.8	4.8	57173	59326	74	73	922	0.0	9.1	52.7	33.9	4.2	153543
55056	NORTH BRANCH	27558	5329	12.0	19.9	47.6	13.7	6.9	67508	71320	85	86	4685	9.3	3.0	32.1	51.8	3.6	185869
55057	NORTHFIELD	27778	7760	12.6	18.5	43.6	15.7	9.6	69693	72059	87	87	5732	3.7	1.2	22.1	62.2	10.8	233347
55060	OWATONNA	26754	11591	14.3	23.9	46.3	10.6	4.9	60314	61912	78	78	9003	3.7	5.1	48.9	38.4	3.9	165222
55063	PINE CITY	22022	3932	22.1	28.8	39.9	6.5	2.7	48839	50274	59	50	3228	9.6	13.0	48.7	25.4	3.3	135400
55065	RANDOLPH	29066	359	8.6	20.1	42.9	21.7	6.7	69952	75629	87	87	312	2.9	1.6	24.7	54.8	16.0	237736
55066	RED WING	28139	7750	18.2	22.9	43.5	9.9	5.5	58627	61305	76	75	5669	5.8	8.2	45.2	36.3	4.6	158549
55067	ROCK CREEK	20430	145	16.6	26.9	46.2	8.3	2.1	54445	55589	70	68	129	3.9	8.5	52.7	31.0	3.9	150625
55068	ROSEMOUNT	34104	8894	7.2	10.6	38.0	32.1	12.2	91272	95678	95	94	7784	2.9	1.0	25.2	66.3	4.6	213050
55069	RUSH CITY	22852	1790	18.8	26.4	40.3	11.0	3.5	53698	56080	69	66	1398	7.7	10.3	43.7	34.2	4.1	149000
55070	SAINT FRANCIS	28510	2579	6.6	18.0	48.7	21.1	5.6	71137	75827	87	88	2176	6.1	15.9	33.4	43.2	1.4	165378
55071	SAINT PAUL PARK	28117	2125	8.0	27.1	41.2	19.1	4.6	65587	69174	84	85	1793	9.4	3.6	59.3	26.3	1.3	147756
55072	SANDSTONE	20652	1540	22.5	26.4	41.5	6.8	2.8	50717	51897	63	57	1167	13.5	23.7	41.4	19.3	2.2	112500
55073	SCANDIA	37102	1079	6.4	12.9	31.7	39.3	9.7	98051	101680	96	96	1028	1.3	0.2	13.4	67.1	18.0	273077
55074	SHAFER	29853	556	12.1	18.9	41.9	20.0	7.2	70137	75694	87	87	475	4.6	5.7	31.2	48.0	10.5	201056
55075	SOUTH SAINT PAUL	29321	8511	15.2	24.7	39.4	16.4	4.2	61009	63527	79	79	5947	1.6	3.9	64.9	29.1	0.5	155220
55076	INVER GROVE HEIGHTS	36254	8621	8.2	17.7	36.3	27.6	10.2	79088	85609	92	91	7432	8.4	3.0	35.9	48.5	4.3	181096
55077	INVER GROVE HEIGHTS	38366	4770	5.5	20.5	36.2	21.6	16.2	81399	86508	93	92	3014	12.0	3.2	14.6	47.7	22.5	276768
55079	STACY	31067	2847	5.7	15.6	45.1	26.2	7.4	77018	80909	91	90	2682	9.4	1.6	28.7	57.6	2.8	199298
55080	STANCHFIELD	24980	1158	13.0	25.2	46.3	12.0	3.5	60000	62951	77	77	1061	2.4	9.4	35.8	47.9	4.5	180958
55082	STILLWATER	39480	13472	10.2	14.4	30.8	25.6	19.0	88675	96052	95	94	11119	1.0	0.7	16.6	56.9	24.8	267053
55084	TAYLORS FALLS	25866	700	15.1	22.3	42.9	14.4	5.3	60148	64282	78	77	585	6.2	6.0	38.3	43.4	6.2	173992
55087	WARSAW	26367	70	11.4	21.4	51.4	11.4	4.3	67180	71173	85	86	63	1.6	6.3	25.4	50.8	15.9	221154
55088	WEBSTER	31042	632	6.5	14.7	50.2	18.5	10.1	78082	78972	91	91	593	1.3	1.3	11.8	57.2	28.3	310140
55089	WELCH	30574	716	9.2	19.8	41.8	20.1	9.1	70966	74578	87	88	603	4.8	4.0	21.7	54.6	14.9	236340
55092	WYOMING	29561	3796	8.8	14.9	43.0	26.8	6.5	76360	81864	90	90	3468	8.5	4.8	25.1	56.2	5.4	202252
55101	SAINT PAUL	43685	3231	30.6	25.5	28.1	9.7	6.0	43935	46111	45	29	443	18.7	21.9	28.4	29.1	1.8	114500
55102	SAINT PAUL	33470	9457	22.4	27.5	31.1	13.1	5.9	50063	52086	61	53	4169	3.4	14.9	55.2	18.4	8.1	130298
55103	SAINT PAUL	16589	4294	32.6	26.3	30.6	8.5	2.0	41144	42568	36	19	1748	5.7	29.3	54.6	9.6	0.7	106801
55104	SAINT PAUL	26538	17797	21.6	26.3	32.3	13.4	6.4	52004	55025	66	62	9219	1.9	12.7	53.6	27.4	4.4	138820
55105	SAINT PAUL	45199	10884	10.2	19.8	32.8	20.4	16.8	74287	79438	89	89	7059	0.3	1.5	26.3	58.5	13.3	232328
55106	SAINT PAUL	19780	18163	21.5	29.3	35.9	10.5	2.9	49272	51131	59	51	10976	1.5	16.3	72.0	9.9	0.3	121966
55107	SAINT PAUL	21400	5473	20.9	24.8	40.1	11.0	3.2	53909	57370	69	67	3157	2.3	16.4	68.0	12.4	0.8	117136
55108	SAINT PAUL	33650	6748	18.5	25.9	31.9	14.0	9.7	56368	60724	73	72	3117	0.4	2.1	40.8	52.3	4.2	190307
55109	SAINT PAUL	32214	11528	13.5	19.7	39.7	19.4	7.7	67456	71905	85	86	8342	2.3	1.5	54.4	40.1	1.7	163567
55110	SAINT PAUL	36632	15782	9.2	16.1	37.4	25.8	11.5	78102	81581	91	91	12642	0.2	1.1	41.1	49.0	8.6	190133
55112	SAINT PAUL	36928	17195	10.8	20.2	36.6	20.2	12.3	70751	75900	87	88	12217	8.8	2.1	35.8	48.9	4.4	181719
55113	SAINT PAUL	37614	16608	12.5	22.5	35.7	19.4	9.8	66137	70423	84	85	11243	1.3	3.7	37.5	53.7	3.8	189431
55114	SAINT PAUL	27762	1095	32.9	25.7	30.7	7.3	3.5	41499	44542	38	20	361	0.6	5.8	59.0	34.6	0.0	151875
55115	SAINT PAUL	38269	3612	7.2	12.8	32.9	26.8	20.3	93739	100765	96	95	3130	0.7	0.7	17.9	59.0	21.8	270903
55116	SAINT PAUL	41343	11068	18.9	20.4	33.4	15.8	11.5	61486	64849	79	80	6029	0.6	3.3	33.1	54.4	8.6	204237
55117	SAINT PAUL	26483	16380	20.2	26.9	35.4	12.7	4.7	52828	55677	68	65	9673	5.7	13.6	52.4	26.7	1.7	137280
55118	SAINT PAUL	40140	12319	15.5	23.0	31.5	17.5	12.5	65585	71498	84	85	8078	0.3	1.8	36.0	49.3	12.5	205734
55119	SAINT PAUL	30188	15139	15.4	25.0	36.1	17.0	6.5	60817	64051	79	79	10433	5.7	6.5	56.9	30.0	1.0	144466
55120	SAINT PAUL	48111	1842	6.1	8.8	35.0	26.5	23.6	100153	105870	97	96	1466	0.0	0.0	20.1	57.4	22.5	267801
55121	SAINT PAUL	36114	3494	9.4	19.2	42.3	21.5	7.6	68896	72985	86	87	1459	0.0	4.8	21.7	66.9	6.6	220146
55122	SAINT PAUL	41151	12971	5.5	15.8	39.4	25.5	13.7	82485	87989	93	93	9878	0.6	1.4	33.2	55.1	9.6	208352
55123	SAINT PAUL	44829	9513	4.2	9.7	25.5	33.2	27.4	113469	116816	98	99	7689	0.4	1.5	14.8	69.7	13.6	270360
55124	SAINT PAUL	41368	19590	5.4	13.8	34.6	29.2	16.9	92862	97728	96	95	16675	4.5	2.4	24.2	59.6	9.3	217508
55125	SAINT PAUL	43826	16876	3.3	11.1	35.2	29.5	21.0	100517	103727	97	96	14133	0.7	0.5	21.2	64.4	13.2	246440
55126	SAINT PAUL	45714	10330	6.8	12.4	32.6	27.7	20.6	96054	96039	96	96	8983	4.0	1.9	28.9	58.0	7.3	213077
55127	SAINT PAUL	54557	6767	4.6	14.2	29.0	24.8	27.4	103483	104977	97	97	5990	4.5	2.3	29.0	38.6	25.6	224967
55128	SAINT PAUL	32638	11582	10.0	20.5	37.3	24.4	7.7	72532	77503	88	88	9121	7.5	2.0	34.7	53.2	2.6	186197
55129	SAINT PAUL	54743	5801	2.9	7.2	23.2	26.3	40.4	131547	135017	99	100	5109	0.0	0.2	21.4	57.5	20.9	258410
	MINNESOTA	31285		15.9	22.3	36.8	16.4	8.6	62767	65994				6.5	9.7	37.4	39.4	7.0	167369
	UNITED STATES	27277		20.9	24.4	35.3	11.7	7.6	54719	56938				9.3	13.1	31.6	32.6	13.5	162279

#	POST OFFICE NAME	FINANCIAL SERVICES: Auto Loan	FINANCIAL SERVICES: Home Loan	FINANCIAL SERVICES: Invest-ments	FINANCIAL SERVICES: Retire-ment Plans	THE HOME: Home Improvements: Home Repair	THE HOME: Home Improvements: Lawn & Garden	THE HOME: Furnishings: Comput-ers & Hard-ware-Personal	THE HOME: Furnishings: Major Appli-ances	THE HOME: Furnishings: TV, Radio, Sound Equip-ment	THE HOME: Furnishings: Furni-ture	ENTERTAINMENT: Dine out/ Carry out	ENTERTAINMENT: Sports Equip-ment	ENTERTAINMENT: Fees & Tickets	ENTERTAINMENT: Toys & Games	ENTERTAINMENT: Travel	ENTERTAINMENT: Cable TV	PERSONAL: Apparel & Services	PERSONAL: Auto Repairs	PERSONAL: Health Insur-ance	PERSONAL: Pets & Supplies
55001	AFTON	172	223	228	232	230	204	185	193	174	199	176	150	218	177	209	168	130	181	174	220
55003	BAYPORT	96	120	107	119	115	118	102	106	103	103	104	80	117	105	113	105	73	104	112	124
55005	BETHEL	128	146	122	142	138	123	127	127	120	136	122	101	134	128	129	114	86	121	113	146
55006	BRAHAM	88	83	82	85	84	93	84	89	85	80	84	67	80	86	83	88	58	86	93	104
55007	BROOK PARK	85	75	84	75	77	88	73	84	76	69	75	62	67	76	74	80	51	78	85	98
55008	CAMBRIDGE	98	104	95	105	101	101	99	99	98	100	99	76	102	99	101	98	69	99	101	116
55009	CANNON FALLS	109	116	106	115	114	112	106	110	106	109	107	84	110	109	109	106	75	107	107	129
55011	CEDAR	125	145	125	143	139	129	125	128	120	131	122	100	135	125	131	117	86	122	118	148
55012	CENTER CITY	103	117	100	116	112	108	104	106	101	107	102	83	111	105	108	100	72	102	102	123
55013	CHISAGO CITY	107	121	109	122	119	115	110	112	108	113	109	86	118	110	115	108	77	109	113	130
55014	CIRCLE PINES	148	170	146	170	163	146	149	149	141	160	143	119	160	149	153	134	102	142	132	170
55016	COTTAGE GROVE	136	163	140	161	156	141	139	141	132	148	135	111	153	139	146	127	96	134	128	161
55017	DALBO	92	87	84	90	88	99	84	94	86	77	85	71	80	88	85	90	58	87	96	109
55018	DENNISON	116	133	115	136	129	127	117	121	114	119	115	95	127	118	125	114	81	117	118	142
55019	DUNDAS	106	126	122	126	126	118	117	116	113	117	114	90	128	114	125	112	82	115	114	134
55020	ELKO	155	195	171	195	188	168	163	166	153	172	157	132	184	160	176	147	113	158	148	191
55021	FARIBAULT	89	92	83	93	90	93	89	90	89	87	89	69	90	90	90	90	62	89	92	106
55024	FARMINGTON	143	161	134	156	152	135	143	142	135	152	137	113	149	143	143	128	97	135	126	162
55025	FOREST LAKE	123	139	129	140	137	129	125	127	121	130	122	99	134	124	131	118	87	123	119	147
55026	FRONTENAC	101	110	102	113	108	112	100	106	99	99	99	82	104	100	105	99	69	101	105	124
55027	GOODHUE	111	89	119	90	91	119	92	109	94	80	93	88	77	94	93	100	62	102	112	132
55030	GRASSTON	92	80	100	82	84	98	79	93	82	73	81	70	72	81	82	86	54	87	94	108
55031	HAMPTON	117	133	115	137	129	129	118	123	116	119	117	96	127	119	125	116	82	118	120	144
55032	HARRIS	101	113	98	117	110	111	101	105	100	102	100	82	108	102	107	100	70	101	104	124
55033	HASTINGS	117	136	121	135	132	123	123	123	119	126	121	97	133	122	129	116	86	120	117	142
55036	HENRIETTE	96	77	124	75	84	101	77	97	80	72	79	71	66	76	83	85	53	90	96	113
55037	HINCKLEY	84	70	96	70	75	87	72	84	75	68	74	62	64	72	74	79	49	80	86	98
55038	HUGO	159	179	150	175	170	148	156	156	146	170	149	124	164	157	157	137	105	146	134	176
55040	ISANTI	101	103	89	106	99	98	101	98	98	101	99	78	101	102	100	97	69	99	96	117
55041	LAKE CITY	100	86	100	86	89	102	87	98	90	83	89	73	78	90	87	94	60	93	101	115
55042	LAKE ELMO	159	196	196	202	199	179	166	172	158	179	160	134	191	162	183	153	117	163	155	197
55043	LAKELAND	129	157	143	159	154	147	135	140	130	139	132	108	150	133	146	129	94	134	134	162
55044	LAKEVILLE	182	216	193	220	212	184	187	187	175	202	178	152	208	185	196	165	130	177	162	212
55045	LINDSTROM	105	117	104	117	113	113	105	109	104	107	105	83	112	107	110	105	73	105	109	126
55046	LONSDALE	101	117	101	119	113	111	103	106	100	104	101	83	111	103	109	99	71	102	103	124
55047	MARINE ON SAINT CROI	143	181	186	188	187	169	152	160	145	164	147	122	177	145	172	141	107	151	148	183
55049	MEDFORD	95	92	81	91	90	93	86	90	88	88	88	67	84	91	84	90	60	87	90	107
55051	MORA	85	76	84	76	78	87	76	84	79	74	78	62	71	78	76	82	53	81	87	98
55052	MORRISTOWN	91	93	81	92	90	93	85	89	86	87	86	67	85	89	85	87	59	86	89	106
55053	NERSTRAND	99	113	98	116	110	109	100	104	98	101	99	81	108	101	106	98	69	100	101	122
55054	NEW MARKET	159	200	175	200	193	173	167	170	157	176	160	136	189	164	181	151	115	162	152	195
55055	NEWPORT	86	103	95	101	101	96	96	94	94	94	96	73	105	95	102	95	68	95	96	110
55056	NORTH BRANCH	116	120	100	118	113	107	112	111	109	117	110	87	112	115	110	105	77	108	103	129
55057	NORTHFIELD	114	121	109	123	118	113	117	113	113	119	115	90	121	116	118	111	81	114	110	134
55060	OWATONNA	95	102	90	102	98	98	97	96	96	97	96	74	100	98	98	96	67	96	97	113
55063	PINE CITY	85	77	86	79	79	88	78	85	79	74	79	65	73	79	76	82	54	82	87	100
55065	RANDOLPH	116	130	112	134	126	128	116	121	114	117	115	94	124	117	123	114	80	116	120	142
55066	RED WING	95	95	92	97	94	99	96	96	97	93	96	74	96	96	96	99	67	97	101	114
55067	ROCK CREEK	81	91	79	94	89	90	82	85	80	82	81	66	87	82	86	80	56	82	84	100
55068	ROSEMOUNT	141	163	141	161	157	139	144	143	136	152	139	114	155	144	148	130	99	137	128	164
55069	RUSH CITY	93	90	87	90	87	97	87	91	89	85	88	70	85	90	87	91	60	90	95	109
55070	SAINT FRANCIS	124	135	109	130	126	110	119	118	112	129	114	94	122	121	117	105	80	112	103	135
55071	SAINT PAUL PARK	95	116	106	115	113	110	104	105	103	104	104	80	116	104	112	104	74	104	107	122
55072	SANDSTONE	91	75	103	75	80	94	77	91	81	73	79	67	69	78	80	85	53	86	93	106
55073	SCANDIA	138	172	162	174	170	155	145	150	137	153	139	116	164	140	159	133	100	142	137	172
55074	SHAFER	102	122	113	120	120	110	114	111	109	113	111	87	123	111	119	108	80	111	107	128
55075	SOUTH SAINT PAUL	91	104	98	102	103	98	100	98	99	98	100	76	107	100	104	99	71	99	99	114
55076	INVER GROVE HEIGHTS	128	145	126	144	139	131	130	130	125	135	128	101	139	130	134	123	90	127	123	151
55077	INVER GROVE HEIGHTS	147	137	126	144	133	126	147	133	143	151	145	109	145	148	139	138	103	140	126	158
55079	STACY	125	148	126	146	141	127	127	128	120	134	122	102	138	126	133	115	87	122	115	147
55080	STANCHFIELD	96	102	99	104	101	105	93	100	92	92	92	77	96	93	98	93	64	95	99	117
55082	STILLWATER	138	170	163	173	169	154	148	149	141	154	143	117	167	144	160	137	104	144	139	172
55084	TAYLORS FALLS	91	106	99	105	105	99	102	99	99	99	100	78	109	100	106	99	72	100	98	115
55087	WARSAW	105	118	101	121	114	116	105	109	103	105	104	85	112	106	111	104	73	105	108	129
55088	WEBSTER	123	145	126	147	140	135	126	130	122	129	123	102	138	126	134	120	87	124	123	151
55089	WELCH	123	133	123	136	131	133	122	127	120	122	121	99	127	123	127	121	84	123	126	149
55092	WYOMING	120	138	120	137	133	125	120	123	116	125	117	96	129	121	125	113	83	117	114	142
55101	SAINT PAUL	82	61	66	70	60	63	92	70	92	84	94	62	82	89	80	92	66	86	81	91
55102	SAINT PAUL	90	80	80	85	78	79	99	84	97	93	99	70	94	96	91	97	70	94	90	103
55103	SAINT PAUL	72	57	52	60	54	56	75	63	75	71	76	52	67	75	65	74	53	72	65	77
55104	SAINT PAUL	93	89	85	91	86	87	100	90	99	96	100	72	98	98	95	99	71	96	94	109
55105	SAINT PAUL	139	145	144	149	144	137	150	139	145	149	147	112	154	145	150	143	105	144	139	165
55106	SAINT PAUL	80	77	68	78	74	75	85	77	85	82	86	62	83	86	80	85	60	83	81	93
55107	SAINT PAUL	86	82	74	81	80	75	90	83	89	89	90	65	87	89	85	87	63	87	82	97
55108	SAINT PAUL	110	91	89	98	89	90	114	97	113	111	114	80	106	113	103	111	80	109	102	119
55109	SAINT PAUL	103	121	113	120	119	116	111	111	111	111	112	85	122	111	119	111	79	111	115	129
55110	SAINT PAUL	126	148	139	149	146	138	133	134	129	137	131	103	147	131	142	128	93	131	131	155
55112	SAINT PAUL	127	134	129	137	133	128	132	127	129	134	130	99	137	130	134	127	92	129	127	150
55113	SAINT PAUL	109	120	120	121	121	120	116	115	116	117	117	86	124	114	121	118	82	117	123	135
55114	SAINT PAUL	73	66	65	70	65	66	79	69	78	76	79	56	75	77	74	77	55	76	74	85
55115	SAINT PAUL	148	183	172	185	181	161	156	159	147	165	149	125	176	152	169	141	108	151	143	181
55116	SAINT PAUL	112	115	116	117	116	112	120	113	119	120	120	88	123	117	121	119	85	118	118	134
55117	SAINT PAUL	90	87	79	89	84	85	94	87	94	92	95	69	93	95	90	95	67	92	92	104
55118	SAINT PAUL	116	133	134	133	135	131	127	127	127	127	128	95	138	124	135	129	91	128	134	147
55119	SAINT PAUL	103	104	94	105	101	100	107	100	105	106	106	80	107	107	104	104	74	104	102	120
55120	SAINT PAUL	168	201	202	206	204	190	178	183	171	187	173	138	198	171	194	168	123	176	175	211
55121	SAINT PAUL	123	110	99	116	105	99	122	108	118	125	121	90	117	124	113	114	85	115	102	130
55122	SAINT PAUL	143	151	136	155	146	134	146	138	139	151	142	112	152	145	145	134	101	139	128	162
55123	SAINT PAUL	190	211	185	217	204	181	193	186	182	206	185	154	206	193	196	171	134	181	164	215
55124	SAINT PAUL	150	171	158	174	168	153	156	154	149	163	151	122	169	154	162	144	108	151	142	178
55125	SAINT PAUL	167	185	166	191	180	159	170	164	160	182	163	135	182	169	172	151	118	159	145	189
55126	SAINT PAUL	152	179	174	184	179	164	160	160	153	168	155	126	177	156	171	149	112	156	149	186
55127	SAINT PAUL	186	222	220	226	224	200	199	198	188	209	190	156	222	192	212	181	138	192	181	227
55128	SAINT PAUL	118	129	110	128	123	113	118	116	113	125	115	92	123	119	119	109	81	113	107	134
55129	SAINT PAUL	216	263	227	270	256	215	218	221	201	245	205	184	247	218	230	184	151	202	180	246
	MINNESOTA	113	113	112	114	112	114	112	113	111	111	112	88	112	113	112	112	78	112	113	133
	UNITED STATES	100	100	100	100	100	100	100	100	100	100	100	100	100	100	100	100	100	100	100	100

ZIP CODE			POPULATION			2000-2009 ANNUAL RATE		HOUSEHOLDS					FAMILIES		
#	POST OFFICE NAME	COUNTY FIPS CODE	2000	2009	2014	% Rate	State Centile	2000	2009	2014	% Annual Rate 2000-2009	2009 Average HH Size	2000	2009	% Annual Rate 2000-2009
55130	SAINT PAUL	123	17886	17962	17698	0.0	48	5729	5562	5447	-0.3	3.16	3664	3417	-0.8
55301	ALBERTVILLE	171	3991	9575	11961	9.9	100	1395	3464	4366	10.3	2.76	1142	2800	10.2
55302	ANNANDALE	171	6618	7582	8133	1.5	85	2581	3109	3376	2.0	2.41	1831	2117	1.6
55303	ANOKA	003	41380	46579	48653	1.3	83	14663	16824	17686	1.5	2.71	10823	12143	1.3
55304	ANDOVER	003	39300	46794	49790	1.9	90	12247	14935	16038	2.2	3.13	10623	12662	1.9
55305	HOPKINS	053	18755	19343	19426	0.3	58	8650	9189	9298	0.7	2.08	5025	5042	0.0
55306	BURNSVILLE	037	15518	16770	17155	0.8	72	5981	6707	6931	1.2	2.50	4092	4362	0.7
55307	ARLINGTON	143	3124	3131	3100	0.0	48	1211	1244	1239	0.3	2.46	832	823	-0.1
55308	BECKER	141	6095	8210	9817	3.3	96	1971	2748	3313	3.7	2.99	1639	2226	3.4
55309	BIG LAKE	141	12399	18365	21147	4.3	98	4083	6131	7105	4.5	2.99	3256	4790	4.3
55310	BIRD ISLAND	129	1745	1576	1504	-1.1	7	696	650	625	-0.7	2.36	455	409	-1.1
55311	OSSEO	053	20728	27622	30422	3.2	95	6895	9412	10432	3.4	2.93	5769	7764	3.3
55312	BROWNTON	085	1669	1773	1795	0.7	69	631	689	704	1.0	2.56	462	487	0.6
55313	BUFFALO	171	18154	23723	26825	2.9	94	6332	8648	9890	3.4	2.70	4803	6342	3.1
55314	BUFFALO LAKE	129	1415	1368	1332	-0.4	30	552	547	536	-0.1	2.39	396	380	-0.4
55315	CARVER	019	2310	3781	4451	5.5	99	789	1346	1594	5.9	2.81	635	1057	5.7
55316	CHAMPLIN	053	22182	23822	24498	0.8	72	7420	8176	8449	1.1	2.91	5919	6325	0.7
55317	CHANHASSEN	019	16729	21281	23402	2.6	93	5728	7333	8045	2.7	2.90	4478	5667	2.6
55318	CHASKA	019	19613	27116	30520	3.6	97	6850	9529	10735	3.6	2.82	5107	6847	3.2
55319	CLEAR LAKE	141	4518	5554	6229	2.3	92	1529	1964	2225	2.7	2.81	1264	1581	2.4
55320	CLEARWATER	145	3949	4648	5032	1.8	89	1354	1679	1839	2.4	2.77	1064	1279	2.0
55321	COKATO	171	5051	6509	7303	2.8	94	1650	2211	2516	3.2	2.89	1202	1551	2.8
55322	COLOGNE	019	2924	3977	4393	3.4	96	1005	1429	1588	3.9	2.78	780	1086	3.6
55324	DARWIN	093	1180	1188	1178	0.1	51	473	489	488	0.4	2.43	374	376	0.1
55325	DASSEL	093	4019	4470	4575	1.2	81	1494	1695	1746	1.4	2.60	1095	1202	1.0
55327	DAYTON	053	3697	3712	3742	0.0	48	1181	1221	1238	0.4	3.04	993	1003	0.1
55328	DELANO	171	7019	8518	9320	2.1	92	2395	3005	3318	2.5	2.81	1875	2282	2.1
55329	EDEN VALLEY	093	1883	2086	2161	1.1	79	698	801	838	1.5	2.59	507	561	1.1
55330	ELK RIVER	141	26859	38212	43755	3.9	97	9011	13144	15159	4.2	2.88	7194	10051	3.7
55331	EXCELSIOR	053	18054	18685	19053	0.4	61	6660	7001	7149	0.5	2.66	5044	5172	0.3
55332	FAIRFAX	129	2197	2132	2088	-0.3	35	865	858	843	-0.1	2.41	588	563	-0.5
55333	FRANKLIN	129	784	746	725	-0.5	26	308	298	290	-0.4	2.40	196	182	-0.8
55334	GAYLORD	143	2947	2801	2727	-0.5	26	1130	1100	1078	-0.3	2.47	779	732	-0.7
55335	GIBBON	143	1841	1848	1832	0.0	48	692	710	708	0.3	2.52	488	485	-0.1
55336	GLENCOE	085	8496	8822	8884	0.4	61	3167	3343	3386	0.6	2.60	2289	2332	0.2
55337	BURNSVILLE	037	44677	45925	46485	0.3	58	17697	18873	19282	0.7	2.42	11531	11681	0.1
55338	GREEN ISLE	143	932	977	980	0.5	63	344	369	373	0.8	2.65	272	286	0.5
55339	HAMBURG	019	944	1184	1329	2.5	93	339	445	503	3.0	2.65	268	340	2.6
55340	HAMEL	053	5266	6291	6648	1.9	90	1696	2056	2173	2.1	3.06	1424	1678	1.8
55341	HANOVER	171	1296	2032	2452	5.0	98	422	695	849	5.5	2.92	361	576	5.2
55342	HECTOR	129	2114	1970	1895	-0.8	15	884	849	823	-0.4	2.32	604	559	-0.8
55343	HOPKINS	053	24274	24406	24622	0.1	51	11568	11930	12106	0.3	2.01	5672	5415	-0.5
55344	EDEN PRAIRIE	053	10397	12464	13323	2.0	91	4771	5839	6268	2.2	2.11	2528	2913	1.5
55345	MINNETONKA	053	22707	22113	21915	-0.3	35	8496	8506	8479	0.0	2.57	6485	6280	-0.3
55346	EDEN PRAIRIE	053	18673	18373	18261	-0.2	39	6632	6679	6667	0.1	2.75	5154	5040	-0.2
55347	EDEN PRAIRIE	053	25831	30116	31716	1.7	88	9054	10614	11181	1.7	2.84	6897	7862	1.4
55349	HOWARD LAKE	171	3775	4706	5231	2.4	93	1386	1811	2041	2.9	2.60	1018	1282	2.5
55350	HUTCHINSON	085	17234	18504	19083	0.8	72	6786	7486	7782	1.1	2.44	4620	4924	0.7
55352	JORDAN	139	6919	9032	10204	2.9	94	2326	3116	3548	3.2	2.86	1801	2350	2.9
55353	KIMBALL	145	3090	3379	3479	1.0	77	1089	1246	1303	1.5	2.70	833	914	1.0
55354	LESTER PRAIRIE	085	2211	2738	2934	2.3	92	812	1024	1107	2.5	2.67	618	760	2.3
55355	LITCHFIELD	093	9597	9630	9509	0.0	48	3743	3837	3811	0.3	2.42	2541	2508	-0.1
55356	LONG LAKE	053	5343	5321	5347	0.0	48	1909	1951	1972	0.2	2.70	1477	1466	-0.1
55357	LORETTO	053	3001	3388	3631	1.3	83	990	1138	1226	1.5	2.98	816	916	1.3
55358	MAPLE LAKE	171	4881	6046	6732	2.3	92	1791	2328	2622	2.9	2.59	1329	1649	2.4
55359	MAPLE PLAIN	053	5887	6144	6331	0.5	63	2031	2173	2249	0.7	2.79	1599	1659	0.4
55360	MAYER	019	1500	2529	2929	5.8	99	521	962	1124	6.9	2.62	413	746	6.6
55362	MONTICELLO	171	13722	18857	21797	3.5	96	4827	6999	8185	4.1	2.67	3638	5086	3.7
55363	MONTROSE	171	2669	3564	4112	3.2	95	972	1382	1614	3.9	2.57	709	970	3.4
55364	MOUND	053	14312	14841	15030	0.4	61	5713	6055	6159	0.6	2.45	3971	4064	0.3
55366	NEW AUBURN	143	5	5	5	0.0	48	1	1	1	0.0	5.00	1	1	0.0
55367	NEW GERMANY	019	950	1168	1310	2.3	92	348	419	471	2.0	2.79	277	325	1.7
55368	NORWOOD YOUNG AMERIC	019	2171	2803	3110	2.8	94	800	1055	1173	3.0	2.65	612	784	2.7
55369	OSSEO	053	33075	34237	34714	0.4	61	12038	12832	13109	0.7	2.65	9081	9338	0.3
55370	PLATO	085	731	776	798	0.6	67	286	312	324	0.9	2.49	219	232	0.6
55371	PRINCETON	095	12208	16515	18252	3.3	96	4489	6161	6852	3.5	2.65	3328	4474	3.3
55372	PRIOR LAKE	139	22627	31529	36529	3.7	97	7807	11148	12998	3.9	2.83	6283	8683	3.6
55373	ROCKFORD	053	4723	5575	5966	1.8	89	1737	2118	2285	2.2	2.63	1299	1532	1.8
55374	ROGERS	053	8070	12244	13967	4.6	98	2588	4050	4648	5.0	3.02	2187	3348	4.7
55375	SAINT BONIFACIUS	053	1913	2962	3394	4.8	98	695	1105	1272	5.1	2.68	556	857	4.8
55376	SAINT MICHAEL	171	8805	15476	18874	6.3	99	2823	5106	6287	6.6	3.03	2276	4020	6.3
55378	SAVAGE	139	20600	28473	32709	3.6	97	6634	9098	10446	3.5	3.13	5567	7556	3.4
55379	SHAKOPEE	139	23987	39065	46724	5.4	99	8656	14372	17289	5.6	2.68	6259	10256	5.5
55381	SILVER LAKE	085	1890	2053	2118	0.9	74	720	803	837	1.2	2.56	526	564	0.8
55382	SOUTH HAVEN	145	3662	4163	4336	1.4	84	1308	1538	1622	1.8	2.71	1032	1176	1.4
55384	SPRING PARK	053	1717	1654	1640	-0.4	30	930	913	907	-0.2	1.58	416	378	-1.0
55385	STEWART	085	1416	1453	1455	0.3	58	545	579	585	0.7	2.48	379	388	0.3
55386	VICTORIA	019	2974	4528	5321	4.6	98	1023	1619	1914	5.1	2.75	832	1293	4.9
55387	WACONIA	019	8946	11647	13189	2.9	94	3138	4201	4787	3.2	2.66	2336	3031	2.9
55388	WATERTOWN	019	4534	5892	6569	2.9	94	1595	2152	2420	3.3	2.67	1206	1577	2.9
55389	WATKINS	093	2363	2532	2570	0.7	69	841	932	955	1.1	2.64	622	668	0.8
55390	WAVERLY	171	1980	2634	2936	3.1	95	703	985	1113	3.7	2.64	534	726	3.4
55391	WAYZATA	053	15130	15257	15355	0.1	51	5941	6088	6152	0.3	2.45	4019	3947	-0.2
55395	WINSTED	085	2825	3284	3526	1.6	86	1061	1272	1377	2.0	2.52	750	868	1.6
55396	WINTHROP	143	2505	2503	2474	0.0	48	1012	1040	1034	0.3	2.33	686	676	-0.2
55397	YOUNG AMERICA	019	2521	2808	3039	1.2	81	879	991	1074	1.3	2.83	644	698	0.9
55398	ZIMMERMAN	141	10226	16279	19755	5.2	99	3410	5585	6840	5.5	2.91	2745	4382	5.2
55401	MINNEAPOLIS	053	3531	5472	6128	4.8	98	2557	3893	4378	4.6	1.17	474	673	3.9
55402	MINNEAPOLIS	053	176	180	181	0.2	54	154	160	162	0.4	1.13	16	15	-0.7
55403	MINNEAPOLIS	053	15317	15506	15609	0.1	51	10375	10678	10810	0.3	1.39	1864	1708	-0.9
55404	MINNEAPOLIS	053	27634	29580	30161	0.7	69	11439	12184	12473	0.7	2.11	3726	3571	-0.5
55405	MINNEAPOLIS	053	15452	15847	16069	0.3	58	6919	7100	7165	0.3	2.12	2617	2503	-0.5
55406	MINNEAPOLIS	053	32513	32182	32147	-0.1	44	14871	15005	15038	0.1	2.13	7471	7037	-0.6
55407	MINNEAPOLIS	053	36073	38960	40098	0.8	72	13463	14346	14721	0.7	2.67	7374	7332	-0.1
55408	MINNEAPOLIS	053	31437	32203	32477	0.3	58	14808	15105	15205	0.2	2.09	4759	4466	-0.7
	MINNESOTA					0.9					1.1	2.48			0.7
	UNITED STATES					1.0					1.1	2.59			0.9

ZIP CODE #	POST OFFICE NAME	RACE (%) White 2000	White 2009	Black 2000	Black 2009	Asian/Pacific 2000	Asian/Pacific 2009	% Hispanic Origin 2000	% Hispanic Origin 2009	2009 AGE DISTRIBUTION (%) 0-4	5-9	10-14	15-19	20-24	25-44	45-64	65-84	85+	18+	MEDIAN AGE 2009	% 2009 Males	% 2009 Females
55130	SAINT PAUL	42.5	33.8	15.0	16.9	30.2	35.9	11.3	13.9	11.1	9.7	8.6	9.3	10.1	28.2	17.2	5.0	0.8	65.1	25.7	50.9	49.1
55301	ALBERTVILLE	98.6	98.2	0.1	0.1	0.4	0.7	0.8	1.1	10.9	10.1	9.2	7.0	4.8	32.9	20.3	4.4	0.4	65.2	31.2	50.2	49.8
55302	ANNANDALE	98.3	97.9	0.3	0.3	0.2	0.3	0.8	1.2	6.7	6.6	6.8	7.2	5.8	24.9	27.5	12.1	2.3	75.4	39.2	50.2	49.8
55303	ANOKA	95.3	93.9	1.3	1.7	0.9	1.3	1.4	2.2	7.9	7.5	7.4	7.1	6.0	29.9	25.7	7.5	1.1	72.8	35.2	50.8	49.2
55304	ANDOVER	96.6	95.3	0.5	0.8	1.0	1.4	1.1	1.7	8.7	8.8	8.6	7.7	4.6	29.9	26.3	4.9	0.5	68.9	34.1	51.0	49.0
55305	HOPKINS	93.4	89.9	2.2	3.6	2.4	3.7	1.3	2.3	4.5	4.7	5.3	5.6	5.1	26.8	30.7	13.8	3.7	81.7	43.6	47.0	53.0
55306	BURNSVILLE	89.6	85.3	2.9	4.3	3.4	5.1	2.6	4.0	7.6	6.7	6.6	6.6	7.8	33.2	25.2	6.0	0.3	74.9	32.7	50.1	49.9
55307	ARLINGTON	96.3	94.4	0.2	0.2	0.4	0.5	4.5	7.0	7.4	7.4	7.0	7.1	5.4	26.0	24.0	12.5	3.3	73.5	37.8	49.7	50.3
55308	BECKER	98.1	97.4	0.2	0.3	0.3	0.6	0.7	1.2	10.8	9.4	8.4	7.1	5.8	34.5	19.1	4.6	0.3	67.3	29.8	50.5	49.5
55309	BIG LAKE	97.5	96.5	0.1	0.2	0.4	0.7	1.3	2.1	9.9	9.2	8.6	7.2	5.4	32.0	22.2	5.0	0.5	67.9	31.7	50.3	49.7
55310	BIRD ISLAND	97.5	96.4	0.0	0.0	0.3	0.4	2.8	4.3	5.5	6.3	6.6	6.6	6.0	21.8	28.4	15.0	3.9	77.0	42.9	51.4	48.6
55311	OSSEO	94.7	91.4	1.1	2.1	2.7	4.3	0.9	1.6	8.8	9.0	9.0	7.5	3.6	30.8	27.2	3.9	0.2	68.1	35.7	49.4	50.6
55312	BROWNTON	96.0	94.0	0.2	0.3	0.6	0.8	3.4	5.2	6.3	6.7	7.1	6.7	5.0	25.2	29.3	11.8	2.0	75.5	40.0	49.8	50.2
55313	BUFFALO	97.3	96.5	0.4	0.5	0.6	0.9	1.0	1.5	8.0	7.6	7.5	7.0	5.9	28.6	25.2	8.6	1.6	72.3	35.1	49.6	50.4
55314	BUFFALO LAKE	95.5	93.6	0.0	0.0	0.4	0.5	5.2	7.9	6.1	6.6	6.7	6.4	4.3	23.8	26.4	14.3	5.3	76.6	42.4	49.3	50.7
55315	CARVER	98.1	97.3	0.1	0.1	0.3	0.5	1.1	1.8	6.7	7.4	7.9	7.4	4.7	27.8	30.1	7.4	0.6	73.3	38.4	50.9	49.1
55316	CHAMPLIN	95.0	92.3	1.4	2.5	1.7	2.6	1.1	1.8	8.4	8.6	8.5	8.0	5.1	31.5	25.3	4.3	0.3	69.5	33.3	49.8	50.2
55317	CHANHASSEN	94.4	92.3	0.8	0.9	3.2	4.7	2.2	3.4	9.2	10.1	10.4	8.1	3.7	26.5	27.2	4.3	0.4	64.6	34.4	50.1	49.9
55318	CHASKA	94.2	92.6	0.9	0.9	1.6	2.2	5.3	7.4	9.1	8.8	8.8	7.7	5.3	29.5	24.4	5.3	1.0	68.4	33.1	49.9	50.1
55319	CLEAR LAKE	98.5	97.9	0.3	0.4	0.2	0.4	0.5	0.8	7.7	8.0	8.1	7.1	4.6	27.2	28.1	8.6	0.8	72.3	36.9	51.6	48.4
55320	CLEARWATER	98.5	98.0	0.1	0.2	0.3	0.4	0.6	0.9	7.5	8.0	8.2	7.3	5.1	25.4	29.1	8.6	0.7	71.6	37.4	50.6	49.4
55321	COKATO	97.4	96.5	0.2	0.2	0.3	0.5	1.9	3.0	8.7	8.3	8.7	9.5	5.6	21.9	23.1	11.1	3.0	67.8	34.2	50.0	50.0
55322	COLOGNE	98.0	97.1	0.0	0.1	1.0	1.6	0.9	1.6	8.9	8.5	7.9	6.5	4.6	32.6	22.6	7.4	1.1	70.6	34.1	51.5	48.5
55324	DARWIN	98.1	97.5	0.1	0.2	0.1	0.2	1.1	1.6	4.9	5.5	7.1	6.6	4.3	21.2	35.7	13.3	1.5	78.3	45.3	51.4	48.6
55325	DASSEL	98.1	97.4	0.0	0.0	0.6	0.9	1.1	1.7	6.8	7.1	7.4	6.7	5.0	23.1	28.8	12.3	2.7	74.3	40.3	51.3	48.7
55327	DAYTON	95.9	93.7	0.6	1.1	0.7	1.1	2.2	3.8	7.3	7.9	8.2	7.5	4.7	26.5	30.5	7.0	0.4	71.9	37.6	50.3	49.7
55328	DELANO	98.2	96.7	0.3	1.4	0.5	0.7	0.9	1.3	7.9	7.7	7.9	7.3	4.9	28.1	27.1	7.7	1.3	73.2	36.6	50.1	49.9
55329	EDEN VALLEY	98.6	98.0	0.3	0.5	0.4	0.6	1.1	1.7	7.0	7.3	7.2	6.8	5.5	26.6	26.5	11.3	2.0	74.5	37.1	50.1	49.9
55330	ELK RIVER	97.3	96.3	0.4	0.4	0.5	0.8	1.3	1.9	8.2	8.1	8.0	7.5	6.0	29.5	25.5	6.3	0.9	70.8	33.9	50.4	49.6
55331	EXCELSIOR	97.2	95.8	0.5	0.7	1.1	1.6	1.3	2.1	6.2	7.5	8.7	8.1	4.5	20.8	33.5	9.5	1.2	72.2	41.2	49.6	50.4
55332	FAIRFAX	94.5	92.4	0.1	0.2	0.0	0.0	5.5	8.0	7.1	7.3	7.0	6.4	4.9	21.3	26.5	14.6	4.9	74.5	41.2	48.6	51.4
55333	FRANKLIN	95.1	93.7	0.0	0.0	0.1	0.4	2.0	3.1	6.3	6.4	6.8	7.2	5.9	19.4	29.4	15.0	3.5	75.3	43.2	50.7	49.3
55334	GAYLORD	90.5	86.9	0.2	0.2	0.6	0.7	13.6	19.8	6.5	6.6	7.0	6.9	5.4	24.4	25.2	14.1	4.0	75.8	39.6	50.6	49.4
55335	GIBBON	97.1	96.0	0.1	0.1	0.4	0.6	2.0	3.2	6.8	7.0	7.3	6.9	5.1	22.2	27.2	15.0	2.5	74.4	40.7	51.9	48.1
55336	GLENCOE	94.6	92.5	0.2	0.2	0.6	0.8	9.4	14.0	7.3	7.2	7.3	6.9	5.9	25.5	25.8	11.7	2.5	73.8	37.9	49.9	50.1
55337	BURNSVILLE	86.8	82.3	4.5	6.2	4.4	6.1	3.0	4.3	7.2	6.3	6.0	6.0	7.6	32.5	24.0	9.3	1.2	76.8	34.2	49.0	51.0
55338	GREEN ISLE	98.7	98.0	0.1	0.2	0.3	0.5	1.2	1.9	6.0	6.7	7.2	7.8	4.4	24.9	30.4	11.1	1.6	75.3	40.7	52.3	47.7
55339	HAMBURG	98.1	97.6	0.1	0.1	0.8	1.1	1.4	2.2	7.1	7.3	7.7	7.2	4.6	27.8	28.0	9.0	1.2	73.6	38.0	51.1	48.9
55340	HAMEL	96.8	95.2	0.3	0.6	1.7	2.6	0.8	1.3	7.6	8.5	8.2	7.9	4.6	25.4	29.8	7.5	0.6	70.5	37.0	50.4	49.6
55341	HANOVER	98.7	98.3	0.1	0.1	0.4	0.5	0.5	0.7	9.1	8.8	8.4	7.4	4.2	30.1	26.2	5.4	0.4	68.9	35.0	50.0	50.0
55342	HECTOR	96.6	95.2	0.0	0.0	0.1	0.2	3.7	5.5	5.9	6.3	6.7	6.6	5.2	23.8	28.2	14.1	3.2	76.9	41.8	48.5	51.5
55343	HOPKINS	85.6	79.3	4.2	6.3	5.1	7.4	4.4	6.8	5.4	4.7	4.8	5.1	8.4	32.6	24.8	10.9	3.3	82.4	37.6	47.4	52.6
55344	EDEN PRAIRIE	84.0	76.6	5.0	7.9	6.8	9.9	3.3	5.1	6.7	5.2	4.8	5.7	9.6	36.1	23.3	7.2	1.4	79.9	33.5	49.2	50.8
55345	MINNETONKA	95.6	93.4	0.9	1.5	1.9	2.9	1.1	1.9	5.5	6.3	7.5	7.5	4.1	20.8	34.5	11.9	1.9	75.5	43.9	49.1	50.9
55346	EDEN PRAIRIE	92.0	88.2	2.1	3.3	4.0	6.0	1.1	1.8	7.3	7.9	8.7	7.6	5.0	25.6	31.4	6.1	0.5	71.0	37.7	48.8	51.2
55347	EDEN PRAIRIE	92.4	88.8	1.3	1.9	4.7	6.8	1.2	2.0	7.9	8.6	8.9	7.2	4.3	29.2	28.9	4.7	0.3	69.8	36.1	49.3	50.7
55349	HOWARD LAKE	97.9	97.3	0.4	0.4	0.4	0.6	1.0	1.5	7.7	7.9	8.0	7.5	5.7	25.6	26.3	9.8	1.5	71.7	35.8	50.0	50.0
55350	HUTCHINSON	96.8	95.5	0.3	0.4	0.8	1.1	1.8	2.8	7.3	6.9	6.8	7.1	7.1	26.9	25.2	10.4	2.3	74.3	36.0	49.4	50.6
55352	JORDAN	95.6	95.0	0.6	0.5	0.4	0.5	4.0	5.6	7.8	8.0	8.0	7.8	5.7	27.1	26.9	7.6	1.2	71.4	35.5	50.9	49.1
55353	KIMBALL	98.5	98.0	0.2	0.3	0.4	0.6	0.6	0.9	7.1	7.7	7.9	7.5	4.7	25.8	27.8	10.1	1.3	72.5	37.6	51.6	48.4
55354	LESTER PRAIRIE	97.4	96.3	0.0	0.0	0.1	0.2	4.2	6.2	7.4	7.7	7.8	7.2	5.1	26.2	26.9	10.4	1.3	72.6	37.5	51.2	48.8
55355	LITCHFIELD	95.8	94.0	0.3	0.4	0.3	0.4	3.8	5.8	6.4	6.2	6.5	6.9	5.4	23.9	26.9	13.6	4.1	76.5	40.8	49.7	50.3
55356	LONG LAKE	97.4	96.0	0.6	1.1	0.8	1.2	0.9	1.5	5.4	6.6	7.7	7.5	4.6	21.3	35.1	10.4	1.5	75.3	43.0	49.5	50.5
55357	LORETTO	97.5	96.3	0.4	0.6	1.0	1.5	0.8	1.3	8.0	8.9	8.9	7.6	4.2	25.4	28.9	7.6	0.5	69.3	36.7	50.4	49.6
55358	MAPLE LAKE	98.9	98.7	0.2	0.2	0.2	0.3	0.6	0.9	6.9	6.9	6.9	7.0	6.3	25.8	28.7	10.1	1.5	74.9	38.3	50.7	49.3
55359	MAPLE PLAIN	97.7	96.5	0.2	0.4	0.9	1.5	0.8	1.3	6.1	7.0	7.8	7.6	4.9	22.4	32.9	9.3	1.8	73.9	41.0	49.5	50.5
55360	MAYER	98.3	97.9	0.4	0.5	0.5	0.6	0.5	0.8	6.3	6.8	7.3	7.4	4.3	26.8	29.9	9.6	1.6	74.9	39.2	51.3	48.7
55362	MONTICELLO	97.4	96.5	0.3	0.3	0.5	0.7	1.6	2.5	9.0	8.3	7.8	7.2	6.5	30.2	23.0	6.9	1.2	70.5	32.7	49.2	50.8
55363	MONTROSE	98.3	97.5	0.3	0.8	0.2	0.2	0.9	1.2	7.1	6.8	7.0	7.2	6.3	29.0	26.2	8.9	1.4	74.6	36.0	51.6	48.4
55364	MOUND	96.7	95.0	0.5	0.9	1.3	2.0	0.8	1.4	5.8	6.5	7.4	6.8	4.4	25.7	32.9	9.3	1.1	75.9	41.2	51.5	48.5
55366	NEW AUBURN	100.0	100.0	0.0	0.0	0.0	0.0	0.0	0.0	0.0	0.0	0.0	0.0	0.0	60.0	40.0	0.0	0.0	100.0	37.5	20.0	80.0
55367	NEW GERMANY	98.2	97.7	0.4	0.5	0.5	0.8	0.4	0.6	6.3	6.9	7.4	7.1	4.1	27.3	29.5	9.8	1.5	74.8	39.1	51.9	48.1
55368	NORWOOD YOUNG AMERIC	98.0	97.5	0.1	0.1	0.8	1.1	1.7	2.6	6.9	6.9	7.1	7.0	5.5	27.9	28.0	9.3	1.3	74.8	37.5	50.4	49.6
55369	OSSEO	94.8	92.0	1.0	1.7	2.3	3.5	1.2	2.1	6.3	6.7	7.2	7.2	5.4	29.4	29.7	7.2	0.9	75.2	37.2	49.3	50.7
55370	PLATO	98.4	97.8	0.1	0.1	0.5	0.6	1.2	2.1	7.1	7.3	7.6	6.2	4.3	26.0	29.6	10.7	1.2	74.2	39.7	51.0	49.0
55371	PRINCETON	98.0	97.4	0.2	0.2	0.3	0.5	0.9	1.3	7.4	7.1	7.1	6.8	5.6	28.1	26.6	9.5	1.8	74.5	36.8	49.4	50.6
55372	PRIOR LAKE	95.8	93.8	0.7	0.9	0.9	1.2	1.0	1.8	8.5	8.3	8.1	6.9	5.3	29.3	27.0	6.0	0.5	70.7	34.8	50.0	50.0
55373	ROCKFORD	97.7	97.0	0.3	0.4	0.6	0.8	1.1	1.7	9.2	8.6	8.1	7.6	7.0	29.0	24.3	5.6	0.4	69.4	31.8	49.4	50.6
55374	ROGERS	97.5	96.4	0.3	0.5	0.7	1.0	0.8	1.4	10.5	9.5	8.6	6.8	3.7	32.0	23.6	4.9	0.4	67.0	33.6	50.0	50.0
55375	SAINT BONIFACIUS	97.0	95.6	0.2	0.3	0.9	1.4	1.7	2.9	10.0	9.6	8.6	5.5	4.2	35.4	21.0	4.9	0.7	68.2	33.0	51.7	48.3
55376	SAINT MICHAEL	98.5	98.1	0.1	0.1	0.4	0.5	0.9	1.2	9.9	9.6	8.9	7.6	5.0	31.3	21.7	5.4	0.6	66.7	32.2	50.1	49.9
55378	SAVAGE	90.6	88.2	1.6	1.6	5.5	7.2	1.6	2.8	12.0	11.2	9.3	6.2	3.6	34.6	20.1	2.8	0.2	63.5	31.5	50.6	49.4
55379	SHAKOPEE	90.9	88.6	1.2	1.1	2.3	3.9	5.8	7.4	9.4	8.7	7.9	6.2	4.4	36.3	20.6	5.6	0.8	70.1	33.4	49.4	50.6
55381	SILVER LAKE	98.9	98.5	0.3	0.4	0.2	0.2	0.4	0.6	6.5	6.7	7.0	6.6	4.6	27.6	27.9	11.1	2.0	75.8	39.3	51.3	48.7
55382	SOUTH HAVEN	98.7	98.3	0.3	0.4	0.2	0.3	0.7	1.1	6.7	7.4	7.8	7.4	4.8	24.5	29.9	10.6	0.9	73.4	39.1	51.5	48.5
55384	SPRING PARK	96.4	94.6	1.2	2.1	0.8	1.3	0.9	1.5	3.5	3.5	3.6	3.1	2.9	25.6	27.5	16.2	14.1	87.7	50.3	47.8	52.2
55385	STEWART	97.9	97.1	0.1	0.2	0.3	0.3	2.1	3.4	6.1	6.4	6.7	6.6	5.6	26.3	28.3	11.9	2.1	76.7	39.5	52.8	47.2
55386	VICTORIA	98.0	97.3	0.2	0.2	0.8	1.1	0.8	1.2	8.7	9.3	9.4	7.3	3.6	27.8	26.5	6.8	0.6	67.8	36.8	50.2	49.8
55387	WACONIA	97.1	96.1	0.3	0.4	0.9	1.3	1.2	1.9	8.5	8.3	7.9	7.2	6.1	28.7	22.2	8.4	2.7	71.2	34.3	48.0	52.0
55388	WATERTOWN	98.1	97.2	0.3	0.6	0.5	0.8	1.1	1.8	7.1	7.1	7.2	7.1	5.7	27.1	27.0	9.3	2.4	74.3	37.4	49.1	50.9
55389	WATKINS	99.2	99.0	0.2	0.3	0.1	0.1	0.3	0.6	6.5	7.0	7.0	7.3	5.4	24.4	26.5	12.8	3.1	74.6	39.6	50.9	49.1
55390	WAVERLY	98.0	97.5	0.4	0.4	0.2	0.3	1.6	2.5	7.6	7.5	7.6	7.0	5.3	27.8	27.4	8.9	1.1	72.7	36.8	52.6	47.4
55391	WAYZATA	96.6	94.7	0.4	0.7	1.5	2.4	1.2	2.0	5.3	6.1	7.1	6.5	4.0	22.1	33.2	13.1	2.7	77.1	44.3	48.4	51.6
55395	WINSTED	98.5	98.0	0.1	0.2	0.3	0.5	0.8	1.3	7.4	7.2	7.2	7.0	5.8	27.1	25.1	10.3	3.0	73.7	36.9	49.3	50.7
55396	WINTHROP	95.9	93.9	0.1	0.2	0.1	0.2	4.2	6.7	6.4	6.6	7.0	6.2	4.9	22.3	28.2	14.4	4.0	75.5	42.0	50.4	49.6
55397	YOUNG AMERICA	98.0	97.4	0.3	0.3	0.4	0.6	2.5	3.9	7.2	6.7	6.5	6.8	7.3	28.1	26.8	8.9	1.8	75.6	35.1	49.2	50.8
55398	ZIMMERMAN	98.1	97.5	0.1	0.2	0.3	0.5	0.8	1.3	8.9	8.5	8.2	7.4	5.5	31.2	24.4	5.5	0.5	69.9	33.0	50.4	49.6
55401	MINNEAPOLIS	75.5	67.7	15.3	20.1	4.4	5.4	2.5	4.4	2.9	2.3	1.8	2.4	8.8	45.2	25.0	9.6	2.0	92.3	37.5	55.3	44.7
55402	MINNEAPOLIS	75.0	67.2	17.0	21.7	6.3	7.8	2.8	4.4	1.7	1.7	1.1	4.4	10.0	42.8	27.8	9.4	1.1	95.0	39.2	62.2	37.8
55403	MINNEAPOLIS	80.0	72.5	10.1	14.5	3.4	4.7	5.4	7.9	2.1	1.5	1.3	2.9	14.6	42.2	22.8	10.2	2.4	94.2	35.2	54.3	45.7
55404	MINNEAPOLIS	43.2	35.3	28.3	34.4	4.5	5.1	15.2	18.8	7.3	5.4	4.4	7.2	14.5	36.7	16.3	5.3	2.8	80.0	29.0	53.7	46.3
55405	MINNEAPOLIS	67.7	59.8	16.1	20.6	9.5	11.8	4.5	6.2	6.4	5.5	4.8	4.9	11.1	37.9	22.6	6.0	0.8	80.6	31.7	52.4	47.6
55406	MINNEAPOLIS	78.2	70.9	8.8	12.5	2.8	3.8	5.8	8.6	5.7	5.1	4.9	5.1	7.8	29.9	29.7	9.4	2.2	81.3	39.6	48.5	51.5
55407	MINNEAPOLIS	51.8	42.7	22.0	26.9	5.3	6.2	17.9	23.0	8.3	7.3	6.5	7.2	9.2	32.4	21.7	5.8	1.6	73.6	31.2	50.2	49.8
55408	MINNEAPOLIS	62.4	55.1	16.5	20.0	5.6	6.7	15.7	19.9	6.4	4.7	3.9	4.9	13.4	44.1	16.8	4.3	1.4	82.3	29.6	52.2	47.8
	MINNESOTA	89.4	86.8	3.5	4.3	2.9	3.9	2.9	4.1	6.8	6.7	6.7	7.2	6.8	27.2	26.3	10.2	2.1	75.6	36.9	49.6	50.4
	UNITED STATES	75.1	72.0	12.3	12.7	3.8	4.6	12.5	15.7	6.8	6.7	6.6	7.1	6.9	27.0	26.0	10.9	1.9	75.7	36.9	49.2	50.8

ZIP CODE #	POST OFFICE NAME	2009 Per Capita Income	2009 HH Income Base	2009 Household Income Distribution (%) Less than $25,000	$25,000 to $49,999	$50,000 to $99,999	$100,000 to $149,999	$150,000 or More	Median Household Income 2009	2014	2009 National Centile	2009 State Centile	2009 Home Value Base	2009 Home Value Distribution (%) Less than $50,000	$50,000 to $89,999	$90,000 to $174,999	$175,000 to $399,999	$400,000 or More	2009 Median Home Value
55130	SAINT PAUL	16324	5562	29.5	28.5	31.6	8.5	2.0	43033	45154	42	25	2360	2.8	24.2	64.9	7.9	0.2	112481
55301	ALBERTVILLE	36574	3464	4.5	11.6	36.6	34.8	12.4	94662	97924	96	95	3087	0.3	1.5	16.7	74.6	6.9	229899
55302	ANNANDALE	28404	3109	18.6	22.4	39.0	15.5	4.6	58366	61209	76	75	2604	10.8	9.7	27.5	42.2	9.9	182314
55303	ANOKA	32866	16824	10.5	15.0	38.4	27.1	8.9	78566	83823	91	91	12966	1.9	1.4	31.1	61.0	4.6	202131
55304	ANDOVER	36657	14935	4.0	7.6	32.5	39.7	16.2	104993	107019	97	98	14067	2.2	1.4	17.1	70.7	8.5	233058
55305	HOPKINS	57403	9189	9.1	17.9	32.9	20.8	19.3	76879	81772	91	90	5775	0.3	4.3	18.9	53.9	22.6	253134
55306	BURNSVILLE	38741	6707	6.2	16.4	39.6	24.6	13.2	81163	86103	92	92	4749	14.6	3.6	18.3	56.0	7.5	216143
55307	ARLINGTON	23410	1244	20.6	27.7	41.6	7.3	2.8	51208	52332	64	59	950	7.1	18.4	52.3	18.4	3.8	119920
55308	BECKER	31429	2748	5.3	11.3	49.1	24.6	9.8	79717	84390	92	92	2256	2.6	2.8	24.2	64.1	6.3	219044
55309	BIG LAKE	28637	6131	7.0	15.3	47.9	23.3	6.5	75088	78507	89	90	5501	2.7	3.2	23.7	62.6	7.8	216826
55310	BIRD ISLAND	22914	650	22.2	30.9	38.9	6.2	1.8	46660	48988	53	41	545	22.2	30.6	38.0	6.1	3.1	86477
55311	OSSEO	50683	9412	1.9	5.3	24.7	34.0	34.1	121059	125414	99	100	9106	0.3	0.8	13.0	64.9	21.1	284404
55312	BROWNTON	23342	689	18.1	29.2	40.6	8.4	3.6	52314	53394	67	63	590	4.9	19.5	45.4	23.9	6.3	135795
55313	BUFFALO	30223	8648	11.4	19.0	39.2	22.9	7.5	72249	76937	88	88	6879	5.1	3.2	23.8	56.7	11.3	218689
55314	BUFFALO LAKE	22108	547	17.0	31.3	44.8	6.0	0.9	50990	52259	64	58	468	14.1	26.9	39.7	16.0	3.2	105128
55315	CARVER	36917	1346	5.1	10.1	33.6	40.1	11.1	100777	103175	97	97	1178	2.3	2.0	16.7	62.1	16.9	254450
55316	CHAMPLIN	35106	8176	3.8	11.8	38.0	36.0	10.4	94239	96260	96	95	7126	0.2	0.8	41.0	54.3	3.7	183974
55317	CHANHASSEN	51199	7333	3.6	10.0	24.6	29.2	32.7	120319	126262	98	99	6472	0.0	0.2	9.6	58.0	32.2	320592
55318	CHASKA	35747	9529	9.9	16.0	34.1	25.9	14.0	83869	89030	93	93	7372	12.9	1.8	17.0	54.2	14.0	225828
55319	CLEAR LAKE	31281	1964	6.3	16.0	42.4	28.3	7.0	78731	83412	91	91	1789	0.7	2.8	26.9	61.2	8.3	220626
55320	CLEARWATER	24893	1679	13.2	21.6	49.0	12.3	4.0	60399	62580	78	78	1466	1.8	8.0	37.7	46.2	6.2	181250
55321	COKATO	23283	2211	17.9	22.0	40.1	15.9	4.1	57682	60930	75	74	1675	7.7	9.9	35.9	41.1	5.5	167354
55322	COLOGNE	31761	1429	9.0	13.1	43.9	26.9	7.1	81074	85316	92	92	1238	1.7	0.9	24.2	60.3	12.9	226299
55324	DARWIN	26731	489	15.5	25.6	43.8	11.7	3.5	56816	58950	74	73	449	3.8	11.1	34.7	43.7	6.7	176071
55325	DASSEL	24601	1695	16.1	24.5	45.4	10.4	3.5	58208	60624	75	75	1407	4.7	10.7	41.4	38.5	4.8	159189
55327	DAYTON	36684	1221	5.4	14.7	35.0	30.9	14.0	89542	90483	95	94	1170	10.3	2.2	25.7	52.7	9.0	198785
55328	DELANO	32036	3005	9.0	16.0	36.9	29.5	8.6	79702	82867	92	91	2494	1.1	1.7	21.4	57.9	17.8	239781
55329	EDEN VALLEY	18492	801	30.0	25.8	38.5	3.9	1.9	44691	46736	47	32	640	10.8	19.7	44.5	22.0	3.0	119200
55330	ELK RIVER	29621	13144	10.8	15.3	39.6	26.8	7.5	77245	81502	91	90	11049	3.3	1.9	22.2	65.8	6.8	223254
55331	EXCELSIOR	61397	7001	6.2	11.6	24.2	23.1	34.9	113342	119181	98	99	5823	0.3	0.3	7.7	46.2	45.5	375330
55332	FAIRFAX	21022	858	25.9	32.2	35.3	4.3	2.3	43705	45339	44	28	674	21.2	36.6	32.6	6.4	3.1	80364
55333	FRANKLIN	20228	298	20.8	37.9	35.9	4.7	0.7	43304	45222	43	26	227	31.3	36.6	24.7	4.8	2.6	65000
55334	GAYLORD	21801	1100	23.7	26.1	41.7	6.2	2.3	50097	50847	61	54	816	5.5	24.1	52.3	14.7	3.3	115240
55335	GIBBON	20484	710	24.9	30.8	36.2	5.9	2.1	44910	46775	48	33	585	12.5	33.3	36.1	12.3	5.8	94804
55336	GLENCOE	24503	3343	15.9	25.5	46.3	9.4	3.0	59622	60260	77	76	2693	7.2	7.9	47.5	33.2	4.2	152178
55337	BURNSVILLE	36160	18873	10.3	20.3	36.7	22.7	10.0	72167	78062	88	88	11798	2.3	4.4	24.3	65.1	3.9	212383
55338	GREEN ISLE	25544	369	15.4	21.1	50.9	8.7	3.8	61521	62745	79	80	331	5.4	5.7	36.9	42.3	9.7	180242
55339	HAMBURG	26552	445	13.5	20.4	47.4	15.7	2.9	64104	66336	82	83	385	0.0	3.1	40.8	47.8	8.3	189688
55340	HAMEL	46174	2056	3.7	7.0	30.7	31.6	27.0	110115	113090	98	98	1862	4.6	2.4	10.7	58.1	24.2	274739
55341	HANOVER	39777	695	3.6	6.6	32.2	43.2	14.4	106558	107788	97	98	666	0.0	0.0	14.3	73.0	12.8	255556
55342	HECTOR	22649	849	24.0	31.7	36.9	4.8	2.6	44316	46047	46	31	713	19.6	29.2	39.8	7.7	3.6	91604
55343	HOPKINS	37871	11930	13.3	28.1	36.4	16.0	6.2	60864	63046	79	79	5584	1.5	7.1	39.8	44.1	7.5	178160
55344	EDEN PRAIRIE	42692	5839	10.2	19.4	37.2	22.9	10.3	74904	78075	89	89	2514	1.5	1.4	31.5	53.1	12.4	214725
55345	MINNETONKA	50117	8506	5.8	11.2	29.1	27.2	26.7	104736	106326	97	98	7333	0.1	0.0	10.9	72.9	16.1	257651
55346	EDEN PRAIRIE	49370	6679	4.8	8.4	28.4	28.7	29.6	110829	112488	98	98	5744	0.1	0.1	15.7	73.5	10.6	252264
55347	EDEN PRAIRIE	60577	10614	3.5	6.5	26.3	24.7	39.0	122925	128325	99	100	9491	0.3	0.0	14.7	52.0	33.0	307052
55349	HOWARD LAKE	25238	1811	16.0	24.4	42.3	13.7	3.7	57973	60985	75	74	1414	9.1	9.3	33.5	39.5	8.7	169758
55350	HUTCHINSON	27182	7486	15.5	24.4	44.9	11.1	4.0	59175	60000	76	76	5481	5.8	5.4	43.1	40.6	5.0	167724
55352	JORDAN	27414	3116	10.9	21.0	43.4	19.1	5.6	70556	75159	87	88	2613	8.8	6.0	20.7	48.6	15.9	225173
55353	KIMBALL	22431	1246	15.7	27.4	47.0	7.2	2.6	54560	56750	71	69	1047	5.2	11.4	41.6	38.0	3.8	156084
55354	LESTER PRAIRIE	22793	1024	15.9	27.8	44.1	9.8	2.3	55508	56680	72	71	847	5.1	6.5	47.3	36.8	4.3	159654
55355	LITCHFIELD	24381	3837	21.6	28.6	37.4	8.6	3.8	49815	51029	61	52	2936	8.4	13.6	52.1	22.4	3.5	130971
55356	LONG LAKE	58959	1951	6.2	13.7	27.5	24.7	28.0	103300	105238	97	97	1641	0.2	0.6	17.9	43.1	38.2	294107
55357	LORETTO	44806	1138	4.0	9.5	28.8	33.8	23.8	108323	110057	98	98	1008	3.8	2.0	10.5	53.4	30.4	294776
55358	MAPLE LAKE	28580	2328	12.5	21.1	42.4	19.5	4.6	65190	68424	83	85	1994	3.8	4.8	33.8	48.7	9.0	191776
55359	MAPLE PLAIN	43306	2173	6.1	13.8	32.5	28.6	19.1	94705	97993	96	95	1799	0.0	0.9	17.5	51.0	30.6	271286
55360	MAYER	28477	962	12.9	22.3	42.7	16.8	5.2	63575	66765	82	83	838	3.8	1.3	29.6	50.6	14.7	224419
55362	MONTICELLO	28136	6999	11.4	19.5	43.0	21.7	4.5	66185	69953	84	85	5543	10.3	3.6	22.3	57.8	6.0	202050
55363	MONTROSE	27095	1382	15.5	21.9	42.3	17.4	2.9	63330	65774	82	82	1110	14.5	10.8	27.7	36.7	10.3	167130
55364	MOUND	47412	6055	7.4	13.5	33.0	27.6	18.5	92053	92869	95	95	5070	0.6	3.8	27.4	42.2	26.0	236589
55366	NEW AUBURN	0	0	0.0	0.0	0.0	0.0	0.0	0	0	0	0	0	0.0	0.0	0.0	0.0	0.0	0
55367	NEW GERMANY	25490	419	13.8	25.1	41.8	14.6	4.8	60292	62119	78	77	356	3.1	2.5	29.5	46.3	18.5	223636
55368	NORWOOD YOUNG AMERIC	26710	1055	14.4	21.9	43.2	17.2	3.3	64141	67567	82	84	854	2.7	2.0	41.1	44.5	9.7	185714
55369	OSSEO	38277	12832	4.0	11.9	38.0	34.3	11.8	92481	93253	95	95	11034	1.2	0.6	40.4	56.4	1.5	186435
55370	PLATO	27066	312	16.3	18.3	51.0	12.2	2.2	64177	63974	82	84	280	2.1	6.4	33.9	49.6	7.9	197826
55371	PRINCETON	27134	6161	13.4	22.0	43.2	16.7	4.6	63363	66083	82	82	5240	5.7	4.5	36.8	48.6	4.4	181772
55372	PRIOR LAKE	42122	11148	6.2	11.2	29.8	32.6	20.2	103148	105951	97	97	9924	0.6	1.7	10.3	61.6	25.7	289242
55373	ROCKFORD	32967	2118	7.7	19.1	40.0	24.1	9.1	74196	77304	89	89	1741	19.7	14.2	12.7	41.9	11.5	188523
55374	ROGERS	39600	4050	4.0	5.5	31.5	42.7	16.3	107156	107783	98	98	3815	1.6	0.7	12.8	76.6	8.3	253307
55375	SAINT BONIFACIUS	37883	1105	7.2	11.1	34.9	34.1	12.6	93728	94148	96	95	925	0.0	0.1	30.9	66.9	2.1	210446
55376	SAINT MICHAEL	34438	5106	6.4	10.7	33.6	35.8	13.6	98669	99363	96	96	4504	0.3	0.2	17.0	72.1	10.5	237454
55378	SAVAGE	38911	9098	4.5	8.9	28.5	37.2	21.0	109610	112236	98	98	8159	0.6	0.6	7.2	75.7	15.9	275044
55379	SHAKOPEE	36777	14372	6.6	13.3	38.2	30.4	11.5	86216	94252	94	93	11691	3.4	2.1	16.0	70.3	8.2	232266
55381	SILVER LAKE	22451	803	19.7	26.2	43.2	9.3	1.6	52810	53715	68	65	661	3.9	8.9	51.6	30.6	5.0	147029
55382	SOUTH HAVEN	24682	1538	13.3	25.7	44.8	12.7	3.5	59021	61573	76	76	1416	5.1	10.2	31.9	44.2	8.6	183333
55384	SPRING PARK	48682	913	21.0	25.7	29.0	14.6	9.6	55089	60158	71	70	344	0.3	2.6	18.0	36.0	43.0	344186
55385	STEWART	23739	579	18.0	26.6	44.9	7.8	2.8	53786	54871	69	67	494	11.1	19.2	42.1	21.7	5.9	124074
55386	VICTORIA	47322	1619	3.8	10.1	26.6	34.3	25.2	111031	114595	98	99	1448	0.2	0.3	7.1	65.7	26.7	290189
55387	WACONIA	35952	4201	11.5	15.9	33.8	26.3	12.5	81846	88438	93	92	3322	1.5	0.7	17.6	64.6	15.6	245711
55388	WATERTOWN	27282	2152	16.9	22.7	36.3	18.7	5.3	62591	66927	81	81	1764	14.0	4.1	29.3	40.7	11.9	183099
55389	WATKINS	21391	932	23.2	24.5	40.8	9.8	1.8	51786	53648	65	61	790	10.4	16.1	45.4	23.7	4.4	128512
55390	WAVERLY	24678	985	16.1	26.0	40.9	13.8	3.1	58277	60852	75	75	856	23.1	8.6	22.8	36.6	8.9	159524
55391	WAYZATA	68701	6088	7.6	12.5	26.9	18.5	34.6	106470	112889	97	98	4664	0.3	1.1	11.2	41.6	45.9	371907
55395	WINSTED	25242	1272	15.6	25.7	45.8	8.8	4.2	57046	58103	74	73	977	2.9	6.0	47.4	38.2	5.5	165509
55396	WINTHROP	22021	1040	24.7	30.0	38.4	4.7	2.2	45090	47088	49	34	846	11.3	21.3	48.2	13.1	6.0	111655
55397	YOUNG AMERICA	24044	991	15.2	26.4	37.7	17.0	3.6	60282	63724	78	77	726	5.0	1.5	47.7	39.8	6.1	169048
55398	ZIMMERMAN	31040	5585	5.5	14.7	43.8	28.5	7.6	80266	85155	92	92	5174	3.1	2.5	28.1	58.5	7.8	213321
55401	MINNEAPOLIS	62105	3893	20.9	22.2	30.0	18.2	8.7	61602	65956	80	80	1649	0.5	9.2	41.4	38.9	10.0	172756
55402	MINNEAPOLIS	66461	160	21.9	16.9	36.9	16.3	8.1	60452	62892	78	78	54	1.9	24.1	61.1	13.0	0.0	120455
55403	MINNEAPOLIS	52027	10678	28.3	28.3	25.2	8.5	9.7	44213	46854	46	30	1945	1.2	5.2	25.6	35.0	33.0	265240
55404	MINNEAPOLIS	17406	12184	44.7	31.0	18.9	4.0	1.3	28376	28673	6	2	1166	8.8	22.5	48.3	18.2	2.2	119307
55405	MINNEAPOLIS	39686	7100	18.2	26.6	28.6	15.7	11.0	59969	61985	77	77	2676	4.6	10.1	21.9	37.3	26.1	226912
55406	MINNEAPOLIS	31918	15005	16.6	26.2	37.8	15.1	4.3	59075	61581	76	76	10556	0.5	12.1	63.6	22.5	1.3	138057
55407	MINNEAPOLIS	22625	14346	20.4	29.2	35.6	11.8	3.0	50546	53588	62	56	8220	3.2	18.5	62.2	15.6	0.4	124876
55408	MINNEAPOLIS	31027	15105	20.4	31.4	31.0	11.7	5.5	48255	50545	57	48	3468	4.1	9.7	35.6	39.5	11.1	176820
	MINNESOTA	31285		15.9	22.3	36.8	16.4	8.6	62767	65994				6.5	9.7	37.4	39.4	7.0	167369
	UNITED STATES	27277		20.9	24.4	35.3	11.7	7.6	54719	56938				9.3	13.1	31.6	32.6	13.5	162279

ZIP CODE		FINANCIAL SERVICES				THE HOME						ENTERTAINMENT						PERSONAL			
						Home Improvements		Furnishings													
#	POST OFFICE NAME	Auto Loan	Home Loan	Invest-ments	Retire-ment Plans	Home Repair	Lawn & Garden	Comput-ers & Hard-ware-Personal	Major Appli-ances	TV, Radio, Sound Equip-ment	Furni-ture	Dine out/ Carry out	Sports Equip-ment	Fees & Tickets	Toys & Games	Travel	Cable TV	Apparel & Services	Auto Repairs	Health Insur-ance	Pets & Supplies
55130	SAINT PAUL	70	62	56	63	59	58	76	66	77	72	78	52	71	76	68	77	56	73	68	79
55301	ALBERTVILLE	149	169	139	164	159	139	147	146	137	158	140	117	154	148	148	130	99	138	127	166
55302	ANNANDALE	101	102	91	102	100	103	98	100	98	98	97	77	97	100	98	99	67	98	101	118
55303	ANOKA	125	139	122	139	133	123	130	126	125	134	127	100	136	129	131	121	90	125	119	147
55304	ANDOVER	161	193	167	193	186	165	164	166	154	175	157	133	181	163	172	146	113	156	146	189
55305	HOPKINS	157	174	178	180	177	168	171	165	167	174	168	129	183	165	178	165	121	168	167	194
55306	BURNSVILLE	143	143	124	146	135	124	142	132	136	148	139	109	142	143	137	130	98	134	121	156
55307	ARLINGTON	92	78	87	80	80	96	81	91	84	74	82	69	72	84	80	89	56	86	95	107
55308	BECKER	143	156	125	149	145	126	137	136	129	149	132	109	140	140	135	121	92	129	118	155
55309	BIG LAKE	129	138	114	134	130	119	124	124	119	132	121	97	126	126	122	114	84	119	112	143
55310	BIRD ISLAND	94	67	96	65	69	98	73	90	80	64	78	69	57	79	71	88	52	84	98	107
55311	OSSEO	205	251	226	258	247	214	211	214	197	231	200	174	240	209	226	184	146	199	184	242
55312	BROWNTON	94	84	91	87	85	101	83	94	85	75	84	73	76	86	84	89	57	88	97	111
55313	BUFFALO	116	128	112	128	123	115	118	117	114	122	115	92	124	118	120	111	81	114	110	135
55314	BUFFALO LAKE	88	72	87	74	74	94	74	87	77	65	76	68	63	77	74	82	51	81	91	104
55315	CARVER	140	175	154	175	169	152	147	149	138	154	141	119	166	144	159	133	101	142	134	171
55316	CHAMPLIN	148	169	142	166	160	142	147	147	139	158	142	117	157	147	150	132	100	140	130	169
55317	CHANHASSEN	206	254	222	258	247	213	211	215	196	231	200	175	240	209	226	184	146	199	182	242
55318	CHASKA	145	161	141	164	156	139	146	143	138	157	140	117	156	146	148	131	101	138	126	165
55319	CLEAR LAKE	124	143	124	144	138	131	125	128	120	130	122	101	135	125	131	117	86	122	120	149
55320	CLEARWATER	102	106	92	106	103	105	96	101	97	98	97	77	98	100	98	98	67	97	100	119
55321	COKATO	93	99	93	100	99	99	96	97	95	94	96	75	99	96	99	96	67	96	98	113
55322	COLOGNE	130	146	120	142	137	123	128	128	121	137	123	102	133	129	129	115	87	122	113	146
55324	DARWIN	100	94	116	94	97	108	89	103	90	86	90	78	85	89	95	94	61	97	102	120
55325	DASSEL	95	92	94	94	93	101	90	97	91	88	90	73	88	91	92	94	62	93	99	113
55327	DAYTON	152	184	161	186	178	165	157	161	150	163	152	128	175	156	169	146	109	154	149	186
55328	DELANO	125	148	131	146	143	129	129	130	123	135	125	102	140	128	135	118	89	125	119	149
55329	EDEN VALLEY	74	68	67	71	69	80	67	75	69	61	68	57	62	70	67	72	46	69	77	87
55330	ELK RIVER	124	135	117	133	129	120	123	123	119	129	120	96	127	124	124	116	85	119	113	142
55331	EXCELSIOR	215	266	268	277	271	242	230	234	217	245	220	184	265	221	252	209	162	222	211	267
55332	FAIRFAX	89	63	94	63	66	93	69	85	74	59	72	67	54	73	68	81	48	80	91	103
55333	FRANKLIN	82	62	81	61	64	86	66	80	72	59	70	60	54	72	64	79	47	75	87	94
55334	GAYLORD	85	73	81	75	75	89	76	84	79	70	77	64	68	79	75	83	52	81	89	99
55335	GIBBON	88	66	91	65	68	93	70	86	76	62	74	66	57	75	69	83	49	80	92	102
55336	GLENCOE	96	91	88	92	90	101	90	96	92	85	91	74	86	94	89	95	63	92	99	113
55337	BURNSVILLE	124	124	115	128	121	114	128	119	124	130	126	96	129	127	125	121	89	123	116	141
55338	GREEN ISLE	100	101	94	104	100	108	94	102	95	90	94	79	94	97	97	98	65	97	103	120
55339	HAMBURG	98	111	95	114	107	109	99	103	97	99	98	80	105	100	104	97	68	99	102	121
55340	HAMEL	192	240	214	243	234	205	200	204	187	216	190	164	228	197	216	177	138	191	177	232
55341	HANOVER	163	196	168	195	188	165	167	168	156	178	159	135	183	165	175	148	114	158	147	191
55342	HECTOR	90	64	94	63	67	95	70	87	77	61	75	68	55	75	69	84	49	81	94	104
55343	HOPKINS	109	95	91	101	93	91	114	99	112	111	114	81	108	113	105	110	80	109	102	120
55344	EDEN PRAIRIE	135	115	110	123	112	105	136	117	131	137	134	99	128	135	125	126	94	128	113	142
55345	MINNETONKA	170	208	209	214	212	194	181	186	174	191	176	142	205	174	199	170	127	179	177	214
55346	EDEN PRAIRIE	185	220	206	227	218	195	193	193	182	206	185	155	215	189	205	174	134	185	173	221
55347	EDEN PRAIRIE	238	284	261	294	281	244	245	246	229	267	233	200	275	241	259	215	170	231	212	279
55349	HOWARD LAKE	92	98	81	101	93	99	93	93	93	90	93	73	96	95	94	94	64	92	98	111
55350	HUTCHINSON	92	97	88	98	94	91	96	92	94	96	95	73	98	96	96	93	67	94	91	109
55352	JORDAN	108	125	110	125	121	115	112	113	108	114	109	89	120	112	117	107	78	110	108	132
55353	KIMBALL	89	91	83	94	90	97	85	92	85	81	85	71	85	87	87	88	59	87	93	107
55354	LESTER PRAIRIE	90	90	84	93	90	98	85	93	86	80	85	71	84	88	87	89	59	87	94	108
55355	LITCHFIELD	89	83	82	84	83	92	84	89	87	80	86	67	80	87	83	90	59	87	93	104
55356	LONG LAKE	208	260	267	269	267	238	224	229	213	238	215	178	259	216	248	206	158	219	210	262
55357	LORETTO	180	226	206	230	222	195	188	193	176	203	179	154	216	184	205	167	131	181	168	219
55358	MAPLE LAKE	99	114	102	115	111	109	105	106	103	104	103	83	112	104	110	102	73	104	104	123
55359	MAPLE PLAIN	161	200	192	205	200	179	172	174	162	181	165	137	195	166	187	157	120	167	159	200
55360	MAYER	105	118	101	121	114	114	105	109	103	106	104	85	112	106	110	103	73	105	107	128
55362	MONTICELLO	107	115	100	114	110	102	109	106	105	112	107	84	112	109	109	102	75	105	100	123
55363	MONTROSE	98	104	96	101	102	100	99	99	98	99	99	75	101	100	100	99	70	98	99	116
55364	MOUND	154	184	178	187	184	170	164	166	157	169	159	129	182	160	176	154	115	160	156	191
55366	NEW AUBURN	0	0	0	0	0	0	0	0	0	0	0	0	0	0	0	0	0	0	0	0
55367	NEW GERMANY	99	111	96	115	108	109	100	104	98	100	98	81	106	101	105	98	69	100	102	122
55368	NORWOOD YOUNG AMERIC	96	109	97	111	107	105	100	102	98	99	99	80	107	100	105	98	70	99	101	119
55369	OSSEO	139	163	147	164	159	145	145	145	138	151	141	115	158	143	152	134	101	141	134	167
55370	PLATO	94	106	91	109	103	104	94	98	93	95	93	77	101	95	100	93	65	94	97	115
55371	PRINCETON	107	110	98	110	107	107	103	106	101	105	102	81	103	105	103	101	71	102	103	123
55372	PRIOR LAKE	170	194	170	195	187	165	171	170	161	183	165	137	185	171	176	153	118	163	149	194
55373	ROCKFORD	129	133	113	130	126	118	126	123	122	132	123	97	126	128	123	118	86	122	114	144
55374	ROGERS	173	203	171	202	193	167	172	173	160	189	164	141	187	173	177	150	118	162	147	196
55375	SAINT BONIFACIUS	154	169	136	161	157	137	149	148	139	162	143	117	152	151	146	131	100	140	127	167
55376	SAINT MICHAEL	151	173	145	171	164	147	150	151	142	160	144	121	160	151	154	135	102	143	134	173
55378	SAVAGE	173	205	176	207	198	170	175	176	163	192	166	144	193	175	182	152	120	163	149	198
55379	SHAKOPEE	144	162	137	161	155	137	144	142	135	155	138	115	152	144	145	128	98	136	126	162
55381	SILVER LAKE	85	85	79	88	85	92	80	87	81	76	80	67	79	83	82	84	55	82	89	102
55382	SOUTH HAVEN	94	104	91	107	101	104	94	98	92	93	93	76	98	95	98	93	65	94	98	115
55384	SPRING PARK	105	119	127	119	125	123	116	118	119	118	118	86	126	111	125	122	83	119	133	136
55385	STEWART	90	82	85	84	80	97	83	89	84	76	84	71	77	85	82	88	57	87	95	108
55386	VICTORIA	180	225	209	234	225	192	186	191	173	207	175	155	216	183	202	160	130	175	160	213
55387	WACONIA	142	159	135	154	151	134	142	141	135	151	137	112	148	143	143	129	97	135	126	161
55388	WATERTOWN	98	113	102	113	110	107	104	105	102	103	103	82	112	104	110	102	73	103	104	122
55389	WATKINS	90	78	86	79	79	96	78	90	82	72	81	68	71	83	78	88	55	84	94	105
55390	WAVERLY	103	98	86	96	95	99	91	96	94	94	94	71	88	97	89	96	64	93	96	114
55391	WAYZATA	218	277	297	287	291	256	240	247	226	256	227	191	279	225	269	218	168	235	227	279
55395	WINSTED	84	97	89	97	95	91	91	90	89	90	90	71	98	90	96	89	64	90	90	105
55396	WINTHROP	87	67	88	67	69	92	71	85	75	61	73	66	58	75	70	81	49	79	90	101
55397	YOUNG AMERICA	89	103	94	102	101	96	97	95	95	95	96	75	104	96	101	94	68	95	94	111
55398	ZIMMERMAN	130	151	127	148	143	127	130	131	122	139	125	104	139	130	134	117	89	124	116	150
55401	MINNEAPOLIS	117	86	92	99	84	86	129	99	127	120	131	88	115	126	111	125	93	119	108	127
55402	MINNEAPOLIS	106	78	81	90	75	75	115	87	112	107	116	80	102	113	99	108	83	105	91	112
55403	MINNEAPOLIS	106	78	81	89	75	76	114	87	112	107	115	78	102	112	98	109	82	105	92	112
55404	MINNEAPOLIS	54	37	37	41	35	38	58	44	58	53	59	38	49	57	48	58	41	54	49	57
55405	MINNEAPOLIS	119	104	107	113	103	102	130	108	127	125	129	92	124	127	119	125	93	122	113	134
55406	MINNEAPOLIS	92	94	89	95	92	91	99	92	98	96	98	73	100	97	97	98	69	96	96	110
55407	MINNEAPOLIS	84	78	71	79	75	74	90	79	89	86	90	64	86	89	83	88	64	86	81	95
55408	MINNEAPOLIS	93	69	70	77	67	66	100	77	98	94	101	69	89	98	86	95	72	93	81	98
	MINNESOTA	113	113	112	114	112	114	112	113	111	111	112	88	112	113	112	112	78	112	113	133
	UNITED STATES	100	100	100	100	100	100	100	100	100	100	100	100	100	100	100	100	100	100	100	100

ZIP CODE #	POST OFFICE NAME	COUNTY FIPS CODE	POPULATION 2000	POPULATION 2009	POPULATION 2014	2000-2009 ANNUAL RATE % Rate	2000-2009 ANNUAL RATE State Centile	HOUSEHOLDS 2000	HOUSEHOLDS 2009	HOUSEHOLDS 2014	HOUSEHOLDS % Annual Rate 2000-2009	HOUSEHOLDS 2009 Average HH Size	FAMILIES 2000	FAMILIES 2009	FAMILIES % Annual Rate 2000-2009
55409	MINNEAPOLIS	053	12821	13082	13189	0.2	54	5219	5372	5417	0.3	2.31	2571	2494	-0.3
55410	MINNEAPOLIS	053	18707	18181	18050	-0.3	35	8825	8809	8790	0.0	2.06	4818	4515	-0.7
55411	MINNEAPOLIS	053	31699	31679	31231	0.0	48	9343	9140	8988	-0.2	3.40	6454	6057	-0.7
55412	MINNEAPOLIS	053	24918	24524	24249	-0.2	39	8794	8442	8325	-0.4	2.90	5504	5000	-1.0
55413	MINNEAPOLIS	053	12280	12617	12704	0.3	58	5710	5969	6036	0.5	2.07	2386	2286	-0.5
55414	MINNEAPOLIS	053	22217	24765	25838	1.2	81	9253	10379	10860	1.2	2.17	2604	2700	0.4
55415	MINNEAPOLIS	053	2066	2468	2588	1.9	90	545	742	810	3.4	2.14	83	159	7.3
55416	MINNEAPOLIS	053	26981	27972	28454	0.4	61	13745	14688	15058	0.7	1.88	6144	6089	-0.1
55417	MINNEAPOLIS	053	24997	24830	24859	-0.1	44	10724	10865	10919	0.1	2.20	6147	5846	-0.5
55418	MINNEAPOLIS	053	30784	30067	29990	-0.3	35	13498	13495	13504	0.0	2.21	7163	6712	-0.7
55419	MINNEAPOLIS	053	26361	25768	25582	-0.2	39	11118	11078	11050	0.0	2.27	6668	6279	-0.6
55420	MINNEAPOLIS	053	21417	21781	22000	0.2	54	9191	9583	9725	0.5	2.24	5617	5535	-0.2
55421	MINNEAPOLIS	003	25220	25967	26054	0.3	58	11234	11865	12023	0.6	2.16	6379	6235	-0.2
55422	MINNEAPOLIS	053	27672	27443	27468	-0.1	44	11658	11841	11916	0.2	2.24	7190	6922	-0.4
55423	MINNEAPOLIS	053	34563	34162	34154	-0.1	44	15122	15307	15378	0.1	2.21	8757	8340	-0.5
55424	MINNEAPOLIS	053	9936	9814	9776	-0.1	44	3727	3727	3722	0.0	2.63	2775	2673	-0.4
55425	MINNEAPOLIS	053	8925	9050	9152	0.2	54	3918	4042	4100	0.3	2.21	2084	2009	-0.4
55426	MINNEAPOLIS	053	25472	25667	25810	0.1	51	11384	11775	11919	0.4	2.11	6243	6063	-0.3
55427	MINNEAPOLIS	053	23596	23419	23477	-0.1	44	9933	10119	10194	0.2	2.26	6342	6160	-0.3
55428	MINNEAPOLIS	053	30417	30094	30029	-0.1	44	12253	12351	12374	0.1	2.35	7738	7381	-0.5
55429	MINNEAPOLIS	053	24539	23874	23690	-0.3	35	9914	9810	9767	-0.1	2.41	6164	5791	-0.7
55430	MINNEAPOLIS	053	21313	20986	20889	-0.2	39	8130	8097	8079	0.0	2.55	5191	4907	-0.6
55431	MINNEAPOLIS	053	18542	18265	18193	-0.2	39	7874	7972	7983	0.1	2.25	5117	4934	-0.4
55432	MINNEAPOLIS	003	30507	30563	30426	0.0	48	12487	12907	13002	0.4	2.35	8156	7960	-0.3
55433	MINNEAPOLIS	003	34981	35720	35783	0.2	54	13152	13876	14068	0.6	2.56	9383	9408	0.0
55434	MINNEAPOLIS	003	27586	29827	30717	0.8	72	10117	11319	11797	1.2	2.63	7493	7997	0.7
55435	MINNEAPOLIS	053	11294	10998	10944	-0.3	35	6388	6326	6305	-0.1	1.70	2514	2298	-1.0
55436	MINNEAPOLIS	053	13095	13039	13035	0.0	48	5605	5729	5765	0.2	2.27	3693	3588	-0.3
55437	MINNEAPOLIS	053	18711	19320	19685	0.3	58	8026	8537	8754	0.7	2.22	5201	5255	0.1
55438	MINNEAPOLIS	053	17563	17753	17839	0.1	51	7387	7642	7717	0.4	2.28	4747	4660	-0.2
55439	MINNEAPOLIS	053	8884	8795	8782	-0.1	44	3521	3598	3619	0.2	2.44	2670	2631	-0.2
55441	MINNEAPOLIS	053	17904	18181	18327	0.2	54	7223	7528	7641	0.4	2.35	4667	4626	-0.1
55442	MINNEAPOLIS	053	13017	14547	15182	1.2	81	4741	5439	5712	1.5	2.67	3675	4065	1.1
55443	MINNEAPOLIS	053	26525	30618	32018	1.6	86	9444	10971	11479	1.6	2.78	6872	7828	1.4
55444	MINNEAPOLIS	053	15408	15091	15107	-0.2	39	5059	5062	5088	0.0	2.98	4021	3914	-0.3
55445	MINNEAPOLIS	053	8828	9295	9477	0.6	67	3229	3366	3426	0.5	2.76	2313	2319	0.0
55446	MINNEAPOLIS	053	12983	18579	20666	4.0	97	4654	6773	7569	4.1	2.74	3468	5006	4.0
55447	MINNEAPOLIS	053	22351	22126	22218	-0.1	44	8359	8368	8412	0.0	2.53	5937	5718	-0.4
55448	MINNEAPOLIS	003	26647	28840	29624	0.9	74	9436	10460	10835	1.1	2.74	7197	7748	0.8
55449	MINNEAPOLIS	003	11887	21785	25758	6.8	100	3968	7456	8902	7.1	2.92	3235	5939	6.8
55454	MINNEAPOLIS	053	7545	8661	8709	1.5	85	2838	3040	3093	0.7	2.13	1097	1038	-0.6
55455	MINNEAPOLIS	053	3047	3413	3554	1.2	81	35	160	202	17.9	3.66	5	20	16.2
55602	BRIMSON	137	240	225	220	-0.7	18	124	123	122	-0.1	1.83	81	77	-0.5
55603	FINLAND	075	637	675	676	0.6	67	261	285	288	1.0	2.34	180	189	0.5
55604	GRAND MARAIS	031	3467	3676	3797	0.6	67	1578	1724	1799	1.0	2.10	959	1000	0.5
55605	GRAND PORTAGE	031	557	558	549	0.0	48	247	256	254	0.4	2.18	147	145	-0.1
55606	HOVLAND	031	214	214	211	0.0	48	98	102	101	0.4	2.10	58	58	0.0
55607	ISABELLA	075	254	264	264	0.4	61	115	124	124	0.8	2.13	78	81	0.4
55612	LUTSEN	031	496	527	549	0.7	69	232	253	266	0.9	2.08	149	157	0.6
55613	SCHROEDER	031	187	199	207	0.7	69	84	92	97	1.0	2.16	54	57	0.6
55614	SILVER BAY	075	2648	2588	2540	-0.2	39	1080	1084	1072	0.0	2.30	738	712	-0.4
55615	TOFTE	031	226	239	249	0.6	67	102	111	117	0.9	2.15	66	69	0.5
55616	TWO HARBORS	075	7217	7283	7196	0.1	51	3016	3105	3087	0.3	2.29	2037	2023	-0.1
55702	ALBORN	137	412	421	417	0.2	54	159	169	169	0.7	2.42	118	119	0.1
55703	ANGORA	137	705	678	665	-0.4	30	278	281	278	0.1	2.39	198	192	-0.3
55704	ASKOV	115	1224	1464	1550	2.0	91	475	587	628	2.3	2.49	323	386	1.9
55705	AURORA	137	3444	3187	3078	-0.8	15	1456	1398	1361	-0.4	2.21	964	886	-0.9
55706	BABBITT	137	2096	1985	1926	-0.6	22	917	896	878	-0.3	2.16	661	620	-0.7
55707	BARNUM	017	3146	3500	3653	1.2	81	1196	1378	1455	1.5	2.53	885	987	1.2
55709	BOVEY	061	6143	6215	6151	0.1	51	2489	2581	2577	0.4	2.40	1753	1756	0.0
55710	BRITT	137	1401	1332	1302	-0.5	26	539	537	530	0.0	2.47	426	413	-0.3
55711	BROOKSTON	137	588	650	655	1.1	79	201	230	235	1.5	2.79	155	171	1.1
55712	BRUNO	115	330	350	356	0.6	67	132	145	149	1.0	2.41	90	95	0.6
55717	CANYON	137	285	276	271	-0.3	35	123	126	125	0.3	2.19	91	89	-0.2
55718	CARLTON	017	3045	3351	3484	1.0	77	1116	1267	1330	1.4	2.58	841	926	1.0
55719	CHISHOLM	137	7104	6675	6459	-0.7	18	3045	2946	2874	-0.4	2.18	1877	1725	-0.9
55720	CLOQUET	017	15021	15963	16195	0.7	69	6060	6583	6728	0.9	2.40	4047	4226	0.5
55721	COHASSET	061	2834	2984	3028	0.6	67	1056	1153	1183	1.0	2.57	812	862	0.6
55723	COOK	137	2595	2607	2586	0.0	48	1105	1164	1168	0.6	2.19	761	768	0.1
55724	COTTON	137	840	804	786	-0.5	26	336	335	331	0.0	2.37	243	234	-0.4
55725	CRANE LAKE	137	105	101	99	-0.4	30	50	50	50	0.0	2.00	35	33	-0.6
55726	CROMWELL	017	849	949	990	1.2	81	352	406	426	1.6	2.29	254	283	1.2
55731	ELY	137	6214	5884	5714	-0.6	22	2794	2719	2662	-0.3	2.03	1654	1530	-0.8
55732	EMBARRASS	137	1557	1426	1377	-0.9	12	625	603	588	-0.4	2.36	447	414	-0.8
55733	ESKO	017	4155	4694	4948	1.3	83	1458	1686	1792	1.6	2.78	1181	1334	1.3
55734	EVELETH	137	6441	5945	5716	-0.9	12	2774	2632	2549	-0.6	2.17	1748	1582	-1.1
55735	FINLAYSON	001	2067	1975	1912	-0.5	26	848	835	816	-0.2	2.34	577	551	-0.5
55736	FLOODWOOD	137	1518	1491	1463	-0.2	39	626	635	629	0.2	2.29	393	377	-0.4
55738	FORBES	137	574	538	525	-0.7	18	215	211	208	-0.2	2.55	169	160	-0.6
55741	GILBERT	137	4298	4191	4113	-0.3	35	1878	1919	1902	0.2	2.18	1208	1172	-0.3
55742	GOODLAND	061	429	442	441	0.3	58	180	191	193	0.6	2.31	131	134	0.2
55744	GRAND RAPIDS	061	20022	20057	19840	0.0	48	8144	8436	8426	0.4	2.32	5563	5560	0.0
55746	HIBBING	137	17975	17089	16622	-0.5	26	7789	7665	7523	-0.2	2.17	4871	4563	-0.7
55748	HILL CITY	001	1251	1204	1168	-0.4	30	502	496	486	-0.1	2.43	337	321	-0.5
55749	HOLYOKE	017	267	271	271	0.2	54	121	127	128	0.5	2.13	84	84	0.0
55750	HOYT LAKES	137	2082	1910	1846	-0.9	12	916	888	868	-0.3	2.15	649	604	-0.8
55751	IRON	137	1555	1497	1468	-0.4	30	618	626	619	0.1	2.36	462	452	-0.2
55752	JACOBSON	001	402	400	387	-0.1	44	168	173	168	0.3	2.31	113	113	0.0
55756	KERRICK	115	511	542	551	0.6	67	216	237	244	1.0	2.29	147	156	0.6
55757	KETTLE RIVER	017	869	893	890	0.3	58	362	384	387	0.6	2.32	250	255	0.2
55760	MCGREGOR	001	2904	3217	3322	1.1	79	1309	1494	1553	1.4	2.15	870	960	1.1
55763	MAKINEN	137	645	608	593	-0.6	22	265	263	260	-0.1	2.30	179	169	-0.6
55765	MEADOWLANDS	137	827	777	753	-0.7	18	333	325	318	-0.3	2.32	241	226	-0.7
55767	MOOSE LAKE	017	3617	4073	4231	1.3	83	1099	1294	1380	1.8	2.25	696	784	1.3
55768	MOUNTAIN IRON	137	2824	2688	2622	-0.5	26	1211	1206	1187	0.0	2.20	785	746	-0.5
	MINNESOTA					0.9					1.1	2.48			0.7
	UNITED STATES					1.0					1.1	2.59			0.9

ZIP CODE #	POST OFFICE NAME	RACE (%) White 2000	White 2009	Black 2000	Black 2009	Asian/Pacific 2000	Asian/Pacific 2009	% Hispanic Origin 2000	% Hispanic Origin 2009	2009 AGE DISTRIBUTION (%) 0-4	5-9	10-14	15-19	20-24	25-44	45-64	65-84	85+	18+	MEDIAN AGE 2009	% 2009 Males	% 2009 Females
55409	MINNEAPOLIS	66.3	58.7	20.7	25.8	2.6	3.3	8.8	11.3	6.5	5.4	5.4	5.8	7.8	34.2	22.9	8.0	4.0	79.2	35.5	47.8	52.2
55410	MINNEAPOLIS	93.6	90.5	1.5	2.4	2.3	3.4	1.6	2.7	6.0	5.7	5.6	4.3	5.1	31.1	31.1	9.2	1.9	79.9	41.0	47.6	52.4
55411	MINNEAPOLIS	18.8	14.8	55.9	60.1	15.1	15.4	5.1	5.8	10.8	10.6	9.8	10.3	9.3	25.0	18.1	5.2	0.9	62.2	24.5	47.5	52.5
55412	MINNEAPOLIS	48.9	38.6	31.1	38.8	11.2	13.2	3.6	4.6	8.6	8.7	8.1	8.3	7.6	28.2	22.9	6.3	1.2	69.4	30.8	48.2	51.8
55413	MINNEAPOLIS	77.3	69.4	7.0	10.0	4.0	5.7	9.1	13.2	5.3	4.5	4.3	5.2	9.1	34.2	25.5	8.9	3.1	83.3	36.6	51.5	48.5
55414	MINNEAPOLIS	77.8	69.3	5.7	8.5	10.6	14.6	3.6	5.4	3.3	2.2	1.8	11.0	37.2	27.8	12.1	4.0	0.8	91.6	24.3	52.6	47.4
55415	MINNEAPOLIS	54.8	43.8	33.7	42.6	3.3	3.9	5.3	7.7	2.5	2.1	2.4	6.2	12.3	39.5	22.6	8.1	4.3	92.1	36.7	62.9	37.1
55416	MINNEAPOLIS	91.9	87.9	3.1	4.9	2.8	4.2	1.6	2.6	5.1	4.6	4.6	4.1	6.8	33.9	26.7	10.4	3.8	83.0	39.3	48.1	51.9
55417	MINNEAPOLIS	85.5	79.9	6.7	9.9	2.4	3.3	3.6	5.2	6.3	6.0	5.6	5.0	5.4	30.1	27.6	11.5	2.5	79.1	40.3	50.2	49.8
55418	MINNEAPOLIS	83.5	76.5	5.2	8.1	3.6	5.1	5.4	8.3	5.9	5.6	5.4	5.3	6.3	29.9	27.1	11.5	3.0	80.0	39.7	49.3	50.7
55419	MINNEAPOLIS	85.3	80.2	7.9	10.7	2.5	3.6	2.8	4.2	6.4	6.5	6.6	5.4	5.3	29.4	28.9	9.1	2.5	77.2	40.0	47.9	52.1
55420	MINNEAPOLIS	84.4	77.5	4.1	6.1	7.2	10.4	3.3	5.2	5.8	5.7	5.8	5.6	5.5	28.4	26.5	14.3	2.6	79.3	40.6	49.1	50.9
55421	MINNEAPOLIS	86.9	82.6	3.8	5.4	3.7	5.2	3.1	4.6	5.7	5.4	5.3	5.4	6.4	28.3	25.6	14.3	3.5	80.7	40.3	47.9	52.1
55422	MINNEAPOLIS	89.8	84.8	4.7	7.3	2.4	3.6	1.9	3.1	5.9	6.0	6.2	5.4	4.8	25.9	28.3	13.5	4.0	78.4	42.4	48.4	51.6
55423	MINNEAPOLIS	81.3	74.5	6.7	9.3	5.3	7.3	6.2	9.2	6.0	5.7	5.6	5.3	6.2	29.9	26.1	11.9	3.2	79.6	39.2	49.2	50.8
55424	MINNEAPOLIS	96.5	94.8	0.6	1.0	1.7	2.6	1.3	2.2	7.2	8.0	8.7	7.5	3.9	19.5	31.8	11.1	2.3	71.0	41.9	48.3	51.7
55425	MINNEAPOLIS	77.7	69.5	9.1	12.8	6.0	8.3	7.6	10.8	6.3	5.3	5.0	5.3	8.2	31.9	24.2	11.7	2.2	80.3	36.8	51.2	48.8
55426	MINNEAPOLIS	87.1	81.8	5.1	7.5	3.6	5.1	3.9	5.8	5.5	5.0	5.1	5.1	7.3	30.6	25.2	12.5	3.7	81.2	39.3	48.0	52.0
55427	MINNEAPOLIS	89.4	84.4	4.1	6.3	3.5	5.3	2.0	3.3	5.7	5.6	5.8	5.5	5.0	27.2	28.2	14.8	2.4	79.3	42.0	47.8	52.2
55428	MINNEAPOLIS	80.1	72.7	9.7	13.7	4.6	6.3	4.4	6.5	6.7	6.2	6.0	6.1	6.6	28.0	23.4	12.8	4.3	77.4	38.1	48.0	52.0
55429	MINNEAPOLIS	70.7	61.4	15.2	20.3	8.3	11.1	3.1	4.4	6.9	6.5	6.3	6.6	6.8	29.2	23.7	12.0	1.9	76.3	36.5	48.6	51.4
55430	MINNEAPOLIS	65.9	55.5	17.1	23.2	10.1	13.1	3.7	5.1	7.5	6.8	6.6	7.0	7.2	29.3	23.1	9.8	2.6	74.8	34.7	49.0	51.0
55431	MINNEAPOLIS	91.3	87.0	2.7	4.3	3.6	5.5	1.7	2.7	5.1	5.3	5.7	5.3	4.2	24.9	29.0	17.5	3.0	80.6	44.7	48.3	51.7
55432	MINNEAPOLIS	89.2	85.5	2.9	4.1	3.0	4.2	2.7	4.1	6.4	6.0	5.9	5.9	6.4	29.2	25.6	13.1	1.5	78.3	37.8	48.9	51.1
55433	MINNEAPOLIS	92.5	89.8	2.5	3.6	1.7	2.4	1.7	2.6	7.6	7.2	6.8	6.8	6.9	29.4	25.2	9.0	1.1	74.4	34.7	48.4	51.6
55434	MINNEAPOLIS	94.1	91.9	0.7	1.0	2.2	3.2	1.6	2.5	7.0	7.0	6.9	6.6	5.7	30.8	27.0	8.5	0.6	74.9	35.9	49.6	50.4
55435	MINNEAPOLIS	90.4	86.1	2.4	3.8	5.3	7.6	1.2	2.0	3.4	3.5	3.7	3.7	4.7	19.7	24.7	24.8	11.7	87.2	54.4	41.2	58.8
55436	MINNEAPOLIS	95.8	93.6	0.8	1.2	2.1	3.2	1.1	1.8	4.6	5.2	6.4	6.5	4.6	17.4	32.7	18.4	4.3	79.6	48.4	46.6	53.4
55437	MINNEAPOLIS	91.0	86.5	2.2	3.5	4.3	6.4	2.2	3.5	4.7	4.9	5.3	5.6	5.0	23.5	30.0	18.2	2.9	81.8	45.7	47.1	52.9
55438	MINNEAPOLIS	91.6	87.3	1.9	3.0	4.6	6.9	1.0	1.7	4.6	4.9	5.5	5.9	5.8	24.8	33.3	12.5	2.8	81.3	43.9	46.7	53.3
55439	MINNEAPOLIS	94.6	91.7	1.1	1.8	2.9	4.5	1.0	1.6	4.4	5.6	6.6	6.8	3.7	15.2	35.4	19.8	2.6	78.8	49.7	47.8	52.2
55441	MINNEAPOLIS	90.3	85.7	3.0	4.8	3.6	5.3	2.0	3.3	5.4	5.4	5.7	6.3	6.6	29.3	29.8	10.6	1.0	79.6	38.7	49.5	50.5
55442	MINNEAPOLIS	92.7	88.8	1.7	2.8	3.9	5.9	1.3	2.1	6.9	7.7	8.2	6.7	4.1	25.6	31.7	8.2	0.9	72.8	39.4	48.9	51.1
55443	MINNEAPOLIS	71.8	65.2	14.9	18.0	8.7	11.5	2.6	3.4	8.2	8.0	7.8	6.9	5.5	30.9	25.0	7.1	0.5	71.5	34.4	49.6	50.4
55444	MINNEAPOLIS	76.8	68.0	8.1	11.6	11.8	16.2	1.6	2.4	7.3	7.8	7.9	7.5	4.9	31.0	27.3	5.9	0.4	72.2	35.4	50.1	49.9
55445	MINNEAPOLIS	77.1	68.2	9.5	13.2	9.6	13.8	1.6	2.3	8.6	8.4	7.6	5.7	4.9	33.3	25.1	6.0	0.3	71.9	35.2	48.8	51.2
55446	MINNEAPOLIS	91.2	86.3	1.7	2.7	5.4	8.5	1.7	2.8	8.5	8.8	8.7	7.3	4.0	31.0	26.2	4.9	0.4	69.1	35.2	48.6	51.4
55447	MINNEAPOLIS	91.6	87.8	3.6	5.3	3.0	4.5	1.5	2.4	6.4	7.1	7.5	6.6	5.6	27.9	27.5	10.5	1.0	74.7	38.4	49.8	50.2
55448	MINNEAPOLIS	94.2	92.0	1.8	2.5	1.5	2.3	1.3	1.9	7.2	7.4	7.6	7.4	5.2	29.2	27.4	7.8	0.7	73.0	36.2	48.6	51.4
55449	MINNEAPOLIS	91.3	89.0	1.4	1.9	3.6	5.0	2.1	2.6	9.1	8.7	8.1	6.9	5.1	32.1	24.6	5.0	0.4	69.5	32.9	49.7	50.3
55454	MINNEAPOLIS	42.1	36.1	32.2	36.2	15.8	17.3	5.6	6.7	7.2	3.4	3.1	18.0	24.5	24.9	12.7	5.5	0.7	83.8	23.7	51.0	49.0
55455	MINNEAPOLIS	88.0	82.3	3.2	5.0	5.4	8.0	2.4	3.8	0.4	0.2	0.2	63.7	30.3	3.8	1.0	0.3	0.1	98.9	18.9	50.7	49.3
55602	BRIMSON	97.9	97.8	0.0	0.0	0.0	0.0	0.0	0.0	3.6	3.6	4.9	7.6	3.1	20.4	39.1	16.9	0.9	82.7	48.0	54.7	45.3
55603	FINLAND	97.7	97.6	0.3	0.3	0.3	0.3	0.6	0.7	5.2	5.8	6.2	6.2	5.9	21.2	33.6	14.4	1.5	79.1	44.6	52.1	47.9
55604	GRAND MARAIS	91.8	90.9	0.1	0.1	0.4	0.5	0.7	1.1	4.4	5.0	5.4	5.4	3.8	22.4	35.0	15.2	3.4	81.7	47.0	49.4	50.6
55605	GRAND PORTAGE	69.5	66.8	0.7	0.7	0.4	0.5	1.6	2.2	5.9	6.6	5.2	5.6	4.1	23.1	37.6	9.9	2.0	78.7	44.6	51.8	48.2
55606	HOVLAND	69.6	66.8	0.5	0.5	0.5	0.5	1.4	1.9	5.6	6.5	5.1	5.6	3.7	22.9	38.3	9.8	2.3	79.0	45.2	50.9	49.1
55607	ISABELLA	98.0	98.1	0.0	0.0	0.4	0.4	0.8	0.4	3.0	3.8	4.9	6.1	3.4	18.9	42.8	15.5	1.5	84.8	49.6	53.0	47.0
55612	LUTSEN	97.6	97.0	0.4	0.4	0.2	0.4	0.2	0.2	2.8	4.6	5.9	4.7	2.7	20.1	43.8	14.2	1.1	83.9	49.4	52.0	48.0
55613	SCHROEDER	96.8	96.5	0.5	0.5	0.5	0.5	0.0	0.0	3.0	4.5	6.0	4.5	3.0	20.6	42.7	14.6	1.0	83.9	48.9	50.8	49.2
55614	SILVER BAY	97.7	97.5	0.2	0.2	0.2	0.2	0.6	0.6	5.0	5.3	6.3	6.4	4.8	18.2	28.2	23.1	2.6	79.1	47.5	51.6	48.4
55615	TOFTE	97.3	96.7	0.4	0.4	0.4	0.4	0.0	0.0	2.9	4.6	5.9	4.6	2.5	20.5	42.7	15.1	1.3	83.7	49.3	51.5	48.5
55616	TWO HARBORS	98.2	98.1	0.1	0.1	0.2	0.2	0.6	0.6	5.4	5.5	6.2	6.0	5.0	22.3	31.4	15.0	3.2	79.1	44.7	49.2	50.8
55702	ALBORN	93.9	93.1	0.0	0.0	0.5	0.7	1.2	1.9	5.2	5.7	6.4	7.4	5.2	22.8	30.6	14.7	1.9	78.1	42.9	50.8	49.2
55703	ANGORA	96.5	96.0	0.0	0.0	0.3	0.4	0.7	0.9	4.4	5.0	5.9	7.2	3.4	22.7	36.4	12.7	2.2	80.1	45.8	51.8	48.2
55704	ASKOV	96.5	95.7	0.3	0.3	0.2	0.3	0.7	1.2	5.8	6.1	6.4	7.0	5.6	21.7	30.0	15.5	1.8	77.3	43.0	50.5	49.5
55705	AURORA	98.2	97.7	0.0	0.0	0.3	0.5	0.4	0.6	4.6	5.4	5.4	5.6	5.1	20.5	32.2	17.2	4.0	81.1	47.2	49.6	50.4
55706	BABBITT	98.9	98.5	0.1	0.1	0.1	0.2	0.0	0.1	4.1	4.4	5.2	6.2	4.6	18.6	28.5	24.4	4.0	82.5	49.3	49.1	50.9
55707	BARNUM	97.4	96.7	0.2	0.2	0.3	0.4	0.8	1.2	5.6	6.1	6.4	6.1	4.7	23.4	34.0	12.1	1.6	78.0	43.2	51.2	48.8
55709	BOVEY	97.3	96.7	0.0	0.1	0.2	0.3	0.7	1.0	5.6	5.6	6.0	6.4	5.4	24.2	31.0	13.7	2.0	78.7	42.5	50.5	49.5
55710	BRITT	97.1	96.5	0.1	0.1	0.5	0.7	0.9	1.4	4.1	4.6	5.6	7.5	4.1	22.0	37.8	13.1	1.4	80.9	46.3	51.4	48.6
55711	BROOKSTON	74.2	72.3	0.2	0.3	0.0	0.0	0.7	1.1	8.2	8.3	7.5	8.5	5.4	26.2	24.2	10.5	1.4	70.5	36.0	52.6	47.4
55712	BRUNO	97.0	96.6	0.6	0.9	0.3	0.3	0.3	0.3	3.1	3.7	4.3	4.9	4.0	19.7	38.6	19.7	2.0	85.7	51.0	52.9	47.1
55717	CANYON	98.9	98.9	0.0	0.0	0.0	0.0	0.4	0.4	2.9	3.3	5.8	6.5	3.6	18.5	45.3	13.0	1.1	83.7	48.7	52.5	47.5
55718	CARLTON	94.9	94.2	0.2	0.4	0.2	0.2	0.6	0.9	5.6	5.8	6.2	6.5	5.6	24.3	31.5	12.3	2.1	78.1	42.1	50.2	49.8
55719	CHISHOLM	97.8	97.3	0.1	0.1	0.3	0.4	0.6	0.9	5.3	5.0	5.6	6.3	5.2	24.5	29.6	14.2	4.3	80.2	43.4	49.9	50.1
55720	CLOQUET	87.9	86.8	0.2	0.2	0.3	0.5	0.7	1.0	6.4	6.4	6.6	6.9	6.0	24.7	27.3	13.0	2.6	76.2	39.6	48.4	51.6
55721	COHASSET	95.9	95.3	0.2	0.3	0.2	0.3	0.5	0.8	5.3	6.0	6.6	6.4	4.8	22.0	33.3	13.7	1.8	78.1	44.1	49.3	50.7
55723	COOK	96.4	95.9	0.1	0.1	0.2	0.2	0.3	0.6	3.4	4.3	5.4	6.6	3.2	19.7	37.7	17.0	2.7	82.4	49.6	51.9	48.1
55724	COTTON	98.6	98.4	0.1	0.1	0.0	0.0	0.5	0.7	3.9	4.5	6.7	7.0	3.2	20.9	39.1	12.2	2.6	80.7	46.6	51.1	48.9
55725	CRANE LAKE	83.7	83.2	0.0	0.0	1.0	1.0	0.0	0.0	3.0	4.0	4.0	5.0	4.0	15.8	45.5	17.8	1.0	84.2	51.9	52.5	47.5
55726	CROMWELL	97.4	96.6	0.0	0.1	0.1	0.2	0.5	0.6	5.7	6.1	6.3	6.0	4.8	21.0	31.1	15.8	3.2	77.9	45.0	50.4	49.6
55731	ELY	97.0	96.3	0.5	0.7	0.2	0.3	0.7	1.1	3.4	3.9	4.7	9.2	6.7	19.8	31.6	16.7	3.8	84.3	46.3	51.7	48.3
55732	EMBARRASS	98.0	97.8	0.1	0.1	0.1	0.2	0.3	0.5	4.7	5.4	6.0	6.3	4.0	20.8	36.5	14.5	1.7	79.8	46.5	53.0	47.0
55733	ESKO	97.9	97.2	0.2	0.3	0.6	0.9	0.4	0.6	6.1	6.5	7.8	7.7	4.6	23.9	32.4	9.9	0.9	74.5	40.9	50.0	50.0
55734	EVELETH	97.0	96.4	0.1	0.2	0.4	0.6	0.3	0.5	4.6	5.3	5.9	6.4	5.0	22.7	31.4	14.4	4.4	80.3	45.1	48.8	51.2
55735	FINLAYSON	97.1	96.6	0.3	0.5	0.4	0.6	0.9	1.4	5.0	6.5	6.6	7.2	3.7	22.5	32.1	15.0	1.4	77.3	43.9	52.7	47.3
55736	FLOODWOOD	97.7	97.3	0.1	0.1	0.3	0.3	0.7	0.9	6.1	6.5	6.3	6.3	5.2	21.3	30.7	15.1	2.5	77.1	43.5	51.0	49.0
55738	FORBES	94.8	93.1	0.5	0.7	0.3	0.6	1.6	2.4	3.5	6.5	6.7	9.9	4.5	24.0	34.2	9.5	1.3	82.0	42.2	52.8	47.2
55741	GILBERT	98.3	98.0	0.1	0.1	0.3	0.4	0.3	0.4	4.6	5.0	5.6	6.9	4.5	22.9	32.9	15.0	2.6	80.3	45.3	51.1	48.9
55742	GOODLAND	97.9	97.1	0.0	0.0	0.0	0.2	0.7	1.1	5.4	5.9	6.1	5.4	5.0	21.3	33.5	16.1	1.4	79.0	45.5	51.6	48.4
55744	GRAND RAPIDS	97.0	96.3	0.2	0.3	0.4	0.6	0.6	0.9	5.1	5.4	5.8	6.5	5.7	23.1	31.0	14.1	3.2	79.5	43.6	49.2	50.8
55746	HIBBING	97.3	96.7	0.5	0.6	0.3	0.4	0.7	1.0	5.2	5.1	5.4	6.4	6.0	23.6	29.3	15.0	4.0	80.6	43.6	48.4	51.6
55748	HILL CITY	97.5	97.2	0.2	0.2	0.1	0.1	1.0	1.6	5.4	5.5	5.8	6.9	5.9	22.0	30.6	16.0	1.8	79.2	43.9	49.8	50.2
55749	HOLYOKE	95.9	94.5	0.4	0.7	0.7	1.1	0.0	0.0	5.5	6.3	6.6	6.3	4.8	21.8	36.5	10.7	1.5	77.5	44.1	53.1	46.9
55750	HOYT LAKES	99.1	99.0	0.3	0.4	0.1	0.1	0.2	0.2	4.1	4.4	4.9	5.4	4.7	22.0	30.0	22.0	2.5	83.3	48.5	49.0	51.0
55751	IRON	97.0	96.3	0.3	0.4	0.3	0.3	1.0	1.4	4.7	5.4	6.8	8.4	4.3	21.9	34.3	13.1	1.2	77.8	43.8	53.8	46.2
55752	JACOBSON	97.0	96.8	0.2	0.3	0.2	0.3	0.5	0.5	2.8	3.0	3.0	3.0	3.3	16.8	35.3	30.5	2.5	89.3	55.7	51.3	48.7
55756	KERRICK	97.1	96.7	0.6	0.7	0.2	0.4	0.2	0.4	3.3	4.1	4.4	4.8	3.9	19.7	38.0	19.7	2.0	85.1	50.8	52.6	47.4
55757	KETTLE RIVER	98.8	98.4	0.0	0.0	0.2	0.3	0.8	1.2	5.3	6.0	6.2	6.3	4.8	22.4	33.0	14.1	1.9	78.7	44.3	52.4	47.6
55760	MCGREGOR	92.7	92.1	0.3	0.4	0.2	0.2	0.5	0.7	4.0	4.2	4.4	5.5	4.3	17.7	33.3	24.2	2.4	84.1	51.7	50.4	49.6
55763	MAKINEN	98.4	98.2	0.0	0.0	0.0	0.0	0.2	0.3	3.9	4.1	5.8	7.7	3.0	21.2	37.8	14.6	1.8	81.1	46.8	53.5	46.5
55765	MEADOWLANDS	97.0	96.3	0.0	0.0	0.1	0.1	0.7	1.0	5.0	6.8	6.7	6.2	3.5	24.1	31.9	13.9	1.9	77.7	43.5	52.5	47.5
55767	MOOSE LAKE	86.9	83.9	7.2	9.3	0.5	0.7	2.4	3.3	5.0	4.8	4.7	5.3	9.0	31.9	23.1	12.9	3.3	82.5	37.7	60.3	39.7
55768	MOUNTAIN IRON	98.1	97.7	0.1	0.1	0.1	0.1	0.5	0.7	5.3	4.8	5.3	7.3	6.3	22.5	31.3	15.0	2.2	80.1	43.7	49.9	50.1
	MINNESOTA	89.4	86.8	3.5	4.3	2.9	3.9	2.9	4.1	6.8	6.7	6.7	7.2	6.8	27.2	26.3	10.2	2.1	75.6	36.9	49.6	50.4
	UNITED STATES	75.1	72.0	12.3	12.7	3.8	4.6	12.5	15.7	6.8	6.7	6.6	7.1	6.9	27.0	26.0	10.9	1.9	75.7	36.9	49.2	50.8

ZIP CODE #	POST OFFICE NAME	2009 Per Capita Income	2009 HH Income Base	2009 HOUSEHOLD INCOME DISTRIBUTION (%) Less than $25,000	$25,000 to $49,999	$50,000 to $99,999	$100,000 to $149,999	$150,000 or More	MEDIAN HOUSEHOLD INCOME 2009	2014	2009 National Centile	2009 State Centile	2009 Home Value Base	2009 HOME VALUE DISTRIBUTION (%) Less than $50,000	$50,000 to $89,999	$90,000 to $174,999	$175,000 to $399,999	$400,000 or More	2009 Median Home Value
55409	MINNEAPOLIS	32726	5372	12.8	24.9	36.6	17.5	8.2	64145	67121	82	84	3209	1.8	11.5	45.1	38.8	2.7	156655
55410	MINNEAPOLIS	53431	8809	7.1	15.4	33.7	26.9	17.0	87817	89832	95	93	6860	0.2	0.6	16.5	69.8	12.8	239444
55411	MINNEAPOLIS	13621	9140	34.8	30.7	26.8	5.8	1.9	35845	36851	20	5	4438	4.3	32.4	54.2	8.4	0.7	103610
55412	MINNEAPOLIS	21286	8442	18.8	29.2	38.0	11.0	3.0	52704	56930	67	64	6478	2.5	28.8	60.4	7.9	0.4	107447
55413	MINNEAPOLIS	27132	5969	29.8	25.8	31.5	9.4	3.5	45046	47189	48	34	2445	0.9	13.4	56.8	25.0	3.9	139281
55414	MINNEAPOLIS	24379	10379	34.3	27.9	25.8	7.0	5.0	37351	39140	25	8	2361	1.4	7.6	48.1	37.3	5.6	161134
55415	MINNEAPOLIS	20016	742	37.5	18.7	34.5	6.1	3.2	38400	40273	28	11	272	0.4	12.1	46.7	35.3	5.5	160795
55416	MINNEAPOLIS	53831	14688	9.0	20.0	34.7	21.9	14.3	76175	79257	90	90	8446	0.6	4.8	28.0	53.0	13.6	217185
55417	MINNEAPOLIS	37310	10865	9.6	21.0	39.8	21.5	8.1	69529	73424	87	87	9087	0.6	5.4	51.9	41.2	0.8	163964
55418	MINNEAPOLIS	29729	13495	16.9	27.7	37.0	14.2	4.2	57426	60769	75	73	9371	1.7	10.2	58.7	29.2	0.2	144531
55419	MINNEAPOLIS	48016	11078	7.8	14.6	34.5	23.5	19.7	85815	88179	94	93	8622	0.3	2.0	26.7	57.8	13.2	220761
55420	MINNEAPOLIS	31815	9583	12.5	25.3	41.2	16.8	4.2	63639	66673	82	83	6433	4.1	1.9	52.4	41.0	0.6	166490
55421	MINNEAPOLIS	28623	11865	19.3	29.5	36.1	11.4	3.7	51073	52247	64	58	7328	3.7	7.5	62.2	25.5	1.1	146898
55422	MINNEAPOLIS	37321	11841	9.7	22.4	39.3	19.6	9.0	69017	72818	86	87	9206	0.6	4.5	54.3	37.8	2.8	162817
55423	MINNEAPOLIS	32711	15307	13.8	26.9	37.0	16.9	5.3	62025	64800	80	81	10135	0.9	1.4	54.5	42.8	0.3	168450
55424	MINNEAPOLIS	60284	3727	4.8	10.1	26.4	22.9	35.9	115268	120185	98	99	3331	0.1	0.5	6.2	49.3	43.9	362008
55425	MINNEAPOLIS	31437	4042	12.3	28.6	40.5	14.0	4.6	61393	63184	79	80	1730	1.4	5.5	44.3	47.1	1.7	173442
55426	MINNEAPOLIS	34913	11775	13.5	24.0	38.7	18.1	5.7	63658	66332	82	83	7568	0.6	4.9	51.8	41.3	1.4	166776
55427	MINNEAPOLIS	36865	10119	9.4	21.4	40.1	21.0	8.1	70189	74881	87	88	7067	0.4	3.5	38.2	56.7	1.1	184247
55428	MINNEAPOLIS	28447	12351	16.0	25.6	38.0	16.3	4.2	60810	62928	79	79	7299	1.7	2.9	62.6	32.4	0.4	157160
55429	MINNEAPOLIS	27770	9810	14.8	26.4	40.7	14.4	3.8	60942	63352	79	79	6244	0.1	4.0	78.4	16.9	0.5	143089
55430	MINNEAPOLIS	24912	8097	16.3	28.3	39.0	13.7	2.8	57889	61187	75	74	5588	1.1	9.3	77.9	11.2	0.5	129706
55431	MINNEAPOLIS	38388	7972	11.4	19.1	36.3	24.5	8.7	73185	77422	88	89	5844	0.4	0.7	28.4	68.6	2.0	201333
55432	MINNEAPOLIS	31572	12907	12.8	22.5	42.3	16.0	6.3	63404	65736	82	83	8581	6.5	3.8	48.5	40.1	1.1	165508
55433	MINNEAPOLIS	29799	13876	11.7	21.2	41.4	19.8	5.9	66576	70093	85	86	9992	2.8	1.6	51.6	42.6	1.4	168172
55434	MINNEAPOLIS	29741	11319	7.2	19.5	48.1	20.2	5.0	69957	74053	87	87	9854	12.5	5.3	49.2	32.8	0.2	155983
55435	MINNEAPOLIS	46350	6326	20.7	24.4	31.6	13.1	10.2	58045	61477	75	75	3344	1.8	8.2	36.7	38.5	14.7	189193
55436	MINNEAPOLIS	58578	5729	7.6	13.8	30.2	21.0	27.3	95768	96684	96	96	4513	0.2	1.1	13.0	51.8	33.9	317889
55437	MINNEAPOLIS	44282	8537	8.2	19.9	35.6	22.7	13.6	74928	79385	89	89	6269	0.3	2.1	22.9	66.3	8.4	220368
55438	MINNEAPOLIS	50942	7642	5.3	14.3	36.3	22.8	21.2	88155	90409	95	94	5832	0.2	1.2	30.8	52.2	15.6	235314
55439	MINNEAPOLIS	68926	3598	5.0	10.5	25.5	21.9	37.1	118904	124958	98	99	3122	0.0	0.2	6.0	48.4	45.5	378852
55441	MINNEAPOLIS	44270	7528	6.9	19.4	32.6	24.8	16.3	79840	83632	92	92	4639	1.6	1.1	19.9	64.0	13.4	239977
55442	MINNEAPOLIS	54341	5439	3.6	9.9	25.2	29.7	31.6	115190	117902	98	99	4566	0.7	5.7	12.5	66.0	15.2	270068
55443	MINNEAPOLIS	35234	10971	8.0	14.6	36.4	27.9	13.2	83719	86623	93	93	8278	0.5	2.9	35.8	57.1	3.7	193641
55444	MINNEAPOLIS	32447	5062	2.7	13.4	41.3	33.6	9.0	88331	91400	95	94	4644	0.2	4.7	50.9	42.8	1.4	169231
55445	MINNEAPOLIS	35439	3366	4.1	14.4	42.1	29.1	10.4	83959	86999	93	93	3109	0.6	10.7	41.8	46.6	0.3	169331
55446	MINNEAPOLIS	62736	6773	3.3	5.5	22.7	27.2	41.3	132812	138549	99	100	5522	0.2	0.1	13.1	54.7	31.9	328735
55447	MINNEAPOLIS	48991	8368	4.8	13.0	32.0	27.3	22.9	100273	99955	97	96	6681	0.5	0.3	22.8	64.9	11.5	240026
55448	MINNEAPOLIS	33977	10460	6.5	13.3	43.3	26.2	10.7	80913	85986	92	92	8983	0.8	1.4	41.4	55.3	1.0	187733
55449	MINNEAPOLIS	37691	7456	5.5	7.4	39.2	32.0	15.9	96387	101465	96	96	6928	8.1	2.5	25.8	57.9	5.6	207034
55454	MINNEAPOLIS	14574	3040	59.8	21.8	13.0	4.2	1.3	19027	19242	1	1	307	1.6	14.0	65.1	18.6	0.7	138449
55455	MINNEAPOLIS	12990	160	68.8	22.5	5.0	3.8	0.0	19565	20109	1	1	18	0.0	0.0	50.0	50.0	0.0	175000
55602	BRIMSON	25658	123	30.9	26.0	38.2	3.3	1.6	41789	44213	39	21	116	21.6	32.8	36.2	9.5	0.0	84444
55603	FINLAND	21985	285	22.5	31.6	38.2	5.3	2.5	45528	47918	50	36	247	13.4	26.3	36.4	20.2	3.6	107328
55604	GRAND MARAIS	26009	1724	21.5	30.7	38.3	6.3	3.2	47442	48183	55	44	1315	7.5	11.4	45.0	28.5	7.5	146684
55605	GRAND PORTAGE	23837	256	28.5	25.4	37.1	5.9	3.1	44161	46036	46	30	200	17.5	24.0	26.0	20.5	12.0	109211
55606	HOVLAND	24660	102	28.4	25.5	37.3	5.9	2.9	44298	46768	46	30	80	15.0	23.8	31.3	18.8	11.3	110417
55607	ISABELLA	27381	124	19.4	28.2	42.7	8.1	1.6	52646	52646	67	64	112	8.9	17.9	40.2	24.1	8.9	136538
55612	LUTSEN	29843	253	17.8	37.5	33.2	7.5	4.0	46135	46910	52	39	212	6.6	9.0	29.2	39.6	15.6	192188
55613	SCHROEDER	28689	92	18.5	37.0	32.6	7.6	4.3	45753	47318	51	37	77	5.2	9.1	29.9	39.0	16.9	193750
55614	SILVER BAY	24299	1084	17.3	30.7	42.0	8.7	1.3	51426	52505	65	60	927	17.4	46.8	27.2	7.6	1.1	75282
55615	TOFTE	28834	111	18.0	37.8	32.4	7.2	4.5	45844	46433	51	38	93	6.5	8.6	31.2	39.8	14.0	187500
55616	TWO HARBORS	26632	3105	19.8	24.8	42.8	9.4	3.2	54501	55969	70	69	2518	7.2	23.7	48.5	18.3	2.3	116766
55702	ALBORN	20779	169	18.3	33.1	40.8	7.1	0.6	48329	49723	57	49	153	15.7	17.0	40.5	26.8	0.0	117262
55703	ANGORA	21360	281	23.5	31.7	38.1	4.6	2.1	45882	47595	51	38	249	13.3	26.1	46.2	11.6	2.8	104808
55704	ASKOV	20998	587	25.7	31.7	34.6	6.5	1.5	41468	42954	38	19	485	12.0	20.6	44.5	21.9	1.0	116618
55705	AURORA	24673	1398	22.4	31.0	36.2	8.3	2.1	47156	49347	55	43	1206	22.6	39.1	33.9	3.6	0.7	76846
55706	BABBITT	26068	896	18.0	36.5	36.9	5.6	3.0	46586	48893	53	41	802	15.6	45.8	27.8	6.6	4.2	77174
55707	BARNUM	22270	1378	19.5	28.9	42.8	7.1	1.7	51233	53190	64	59	1217	12.6	12.9	43.2	29.0	2.3	137250
55709	BOVEY	21550	2581	25.3	28.5	38.2	6.3	1.7	45806	47067	51	37	2178	16.9	28.5	42.1	11.4	1.1	95952
55710	BRITT	25623	537	14.0	29.8	41.5	11.9	2.8	56287	59498	73	72	507	9.7	12.8	45.8	26.4	5.3	144970
55711	BROOKSTON	18773	230	25.2	25.7	40.4	8.7	0.0	48558	50910	59	51	179	10.1	12.3	50.8	26.3	0.6	139453
55712	BRUNO	22705	145	25.5	26.2	38.6	7.6	2.1	47391	50255	55	44	135	14.8	14.8	41.5	25.9	3.0	128676
55717	CANYON	30124	126	15.1	31.7	40.5	7.9	4.8	52670	56091	67	64	120	5.8	7.5	39.2	40.8	6.7	169231
55718	CARLTON	23786	1267	16.3	28.8	42.5	9.7	2.6	54447	57859	70	68	1092	8.7	12.9	43.8	33.6	1.0	148175
55719	CHISHOLM	22198	2946	26.9	32.2	33.7	5.6	1.6	41445	43882	38	19	2371	22.6	35.4	32.5	8.9	0.6	78521
55720	CLOQUET	24296	6583	23.8	25.3	38.2	9.5	3.2	50736	53374	63	57	5033	7.1	15.0	53.1	23.8	1.0	131379
55721	COHASSET	23096	1153	19.9	22.6	46.1	9.5	1.9	55672	56317	72	71	1026	10.3	12.6	42.7	27.7	6.7	135588
55723	COOK	23548	1164	24.1	27.5	41.4	4.7	2.2	47948	50103	56	46	1014	10.2	24.2	38.9	17.9	9.0	118898
55724	COTTON	24702	335	19.1	30.4	42.1	6.0	2.4	50363	52874	62	55	314	11.8	19.4	40.1	25.5	3.2	125714
55725	CRANE LAKE	35880	50	14.0	22.0	48.0	10.0	6.0	64683	64683	83	84	46	0.0	4.3	21.7	41.3	32.6	311111
55726	CROMWELL	21359	406	29.3	29.8	34.0	5.2	1.7	42146	45000	40	21	361	15.5	20.8	39.1	23.8	0.8	119345
55731	ELY	24333	2719	28.0	32.7	31.7	4.9	2.7	40616	43057	35	17	2117	8.1	30.4	37.5	17.6	6.4	109478
55732	EMBARRASS	22950	603	19.2	32.8	39.5	7.0	1.5	48182	50329	57	48	574	16.4	35.5	38.0	9.4	0.7	87963
55733	ESKO	25438	1686	12.8	19.9	48.4	15.4	3.6	62902	65458	81	82	1592	2.9	7.1	47.2	39.4	3.4	164748
55734	EVELETH	22686	2632	28.3	29.3	34.5	6.9	0.9	42831	45306	42	24	2068	15.6	34.1	38.0	11.3	1.1	90467
55735	FINLAYSON	21661	835	25.6	28.1	40.0	4.4	1.8	44731	47103	47	32	737	14.0	15.6	49.7	18.2	2.6	123152
55736	FLOODWOOD	19054	635	36.4	29.4	28.0	4.3	1.9	37432	38278	25	8	541	18.9	28.8	38.8	13.5	0.0	93378
55738	FORBES	20542	211	22.3	26.1	46.4	4.3	0.9	51155	53855	64	59	191	22.0	26.7	43.5	7.9	0.0	91471
55741	GILBERT	23255	1919	26.6	28.1	38.2	5.6	1.5	46342	48117	52	40	1635	19.1	37.2	33.6	8.4	1.6	82083
55742	GOODLAND	20873	191	26.2	27.2	43.5	2.1	1.0	46290	47350	52	40	175	12.6	27.4	49.1	10.9	0.0	103716
55744	GRAND RAPIDS	24018	8436	22.0	28.0	39.7	7.6	2.7	50000	50532	61	53	6484	8.4	18.2	47.5	22.8	3.1	125334
55746	HIBBING	24113	7665	28.0	27.3	35.3	7.1	2.4	44355	47220	46	31	5672	14.9	31.2	46.1	7.0	0.8	94129
55748	HILL CITY	20309	496	30.0	31.5	30.6	5.0	2.8	40702	41979	35	17	414	27.1	22.9	32.4	15.2	2.4	90000
55749	HOLYOKE	26771	127	18.1	30.7	43.3	4.7	3.1	50818	53505	63	57	118	8.5	15.3	45.8	22.9	7.6	135000
55750	HOYT LAKES	28267	888	15.8	30.0	41.2	10.5	2.6	53073	55501	68	65	805	21.5	63.6	13.8	1.1	0.0	62580
55751	IRON	24771	626	15.3	27.3	47.3	9.3	0.8	54916	57085	71	70	592	15.4	23.8	48.6	11.0	1.2	104255
55752	JACOBSON	21763	173	28.9	29.5	33.5	5.8	2.3	40223	41751	33	16	158	14.6	16.5	36.7	28.5	3.8	129348
55756	KERRICK	23989	237	24.1	26.2	39.7	8.0	2.1	49662	50634	60	52	220	14.5	15.9	40.9	25.9	2.7	129464
55757	KETTLE RIVER	21122	384	24.5	33.3	37.2	4.2	0.8	43056	45631	43	25	336	17.9	15.2	42.0	22.3	2.7	125000
55760	MCGREGOR	22231	1494	30.7	32.9	30.3	3.7	2.3	38229	39277	27	10	1295	14.5	21.5	36.0	24.5	3.5	119577
55763	MAKINEN	21401	263	26.2	26.6	42.2	3.8	1.1	46166	49019	52	39	248	20.2	32.3	37.5	10.1	0.0	87000
55765	MEADOWLANDS	20500	325	30.2	27.4	36.0	4.9	1.5	42209	44579	40	22	285	18.6	31.9	40.7	8.8	0.0	88636
55767	MOOSE LAKE	21365	1294	24.0	29.1	38.5	5.4	2.9	46902	49480	54	42	922	7.7	17.4	50.0	23.0	2.0	130072
55768	MOUNTAIN IRON	23397	1206	26.8	28.9	35.7	6.7	1.9	43898	46804	45	29	875	12.9	29.5	42.7	14.7	0.1	99925
	MINNESOTA	31285		15.9	22.3	36.8	16.4	8.6	62767	65994				6.5	9.7	37.4	39.4	7.0	167369
	UNITED STATES	27277		20.9	24.4	35.3	11.7	7.6	54719	56938				9.3	13.1	31.6	32.6	13.5	162279

ZIP CODE		FINANCIAL SERVICES				THE HOME						ENTERTAINMENT						PERSONAL			
						Home Improvements		Furnishings													
#	POST OFFICE NAME	Auto Loan	Home Loan	Invest-ments	Retire-ment Plans	Home Repair	Lawn & Garden	Comput-ers & Hard-ware-Personal	Major Appli-ances	TV, Radio, Sound Equip-ment	Furni-ture	Dine out/ Carry out	Sports Equip-ment	Fees & Tickets	Toys & Games	Travel	Cable TV	Apparel & Services	Auto Repairs	Health Insur-ance	Pets & Supplies
55409	MINNEAPOLIS	107	103	100	107	101	97	115	103	111	113	113	84	113	112	110	109	80	110	103	124
55410	MINNEAPOLIS	145	166	170	168	169	152	159	154	151	163	152	122	171	151	167	146	110	154	146	179
55411	MINNEAPOLIS	65	55	47	58	51	58	66	58	70	63	70	46	62	69	58	73	49	65	66	74
55412	MINNEAPOLIS	88	85	71	86	80	86	88	84	90	86	90	66	87	91	83	92	62	87	90	102
55413	MINNEAPOLIS	78	69	66	73	67	70	84	73	84	80	84	60	79	83	77	84	59	81	79	90
55414	MINNEAPOLIS	81	52	51	58	50	54	101	65	88	79	89	61	74	87	69	83	63	81	66	83
55415	MINNEAPOLIS	64	55	58	59	55	57	73	61	74	68	75	50	68	70	67	76	53	70	71	76
55416	MINNEAPOLIS	135	136	143	144	138	131	148	134	144	147	147	109	152	143	147	143	105	142	136	160
55417	MINNEAPOLIS	112	124	116	124	121	118	119	116	118	119	119	90	126	118	123	117	84	117	118	136
55418	MINNEAPOLIS	89	90	84	91	88	91	94	89	95	91	95	69	95	94	92	96	66	93	97	107
55419	MINNEAPOLIS	147	167	169	171	169	157	158	155	152	163	153	121	172	152	167	149	110	154	150	180
55420	MINNEAPOLIS	94	105	98	105	103	102	101	99	101	100	102	76	108	101	105	101	72	101	103	116
55421	MINNEAPOLIS	83	85	80	86	84	87	88	84	89	86	89	65	90	88	88	91	62	88	93	100
55422	MINNEAPOLIS	109	126	123	126	126	125	118	119	119	119	119	90	129	117	126	121	85	119	126	139
55423	MINNEAPOLIS	96	103	97	104	101	101	102	99	103	102	104	76	108	102	105	104	73	102	105	116
55424	MINNEAPOLIS	196	258	292	263	278	240	222	232	208	238	208	174	263	205	255	201	155	219	212	258
55425	MINNEAPOLIS	96	89	86	92	87	88	101	91	101	99	103	72	99	101	97	101	72	99	97	110
55426	MINNEAPOLIS	102	100	97	102	99	99	108	99	108	106	109	78	108	107	106	108	77	106	106	119
55427	MINNEAPOLIS	111	124	121	125	124	121	118	117	118	119	119	89	127	117	124	119	84	118	122	137
55428	MINNEAPOLIS	91	96	90	96	94	93	97	92	97	96	98	71	100	96	97	97	69	96	98	109
55429	MINNEAPOLIS	93	92	84	93	89	91	96	91	96	95	97	71	97	97	94	96	68	95	94	108
55430	MINNEAPOLIS	88	91	79	92	87	90	92	87	92	89	92	69	93	93	90	92	64	90	93	105
55431	MINNEAPOLIS	114	130	129	131	131	130	120	123	121	123	122	91	132	119	129	123	86	122	130	142
55432	MINNEAPOLIS	101	107	98	107	104	103	106	102	105	105	107	79	110	107	107	106	75	105	105	120
55433	MINNEAPOLIS	108	112	99	112	108	103	110	105	108	112	109	83	112	111	109	106	77	107	103	124
55434	MINNEAPOLIS	113	122	104	120	116	111	111	111	109	116	111	86	115	113	112	108	77	109	107	130
55435	MINNEAPOLIS	98	109	124	108	117	115	110	111	112	113	112	79	119	104	119	115	79	113	126	126
55436	MINNEAPOLIS	162	205	234	207	223	201	184	192	178	194	177	140	213	170	210	178	129	185	194	215
55437	MINNEAPOLIS	129	149	153	151	153	146	139	141	137	143	138	105	152	134	150	137	98	139	144	162
55438	MINNEAPOLIS	158	181	180	186	183	169	167	166	161	174	162	129	182	162	177	157	116	163	159	192
55439	MINNEAPOLIS	208	271	331	273	302	262	233	252	220	257	218	181	275	210	275	215	161	237	238	278
55441	MINNEAPOLIS	146	156	153	162	156	145	152	146	146	157	149	116	160	149	156	142	106	148	140	172
55442	MINNEAPOLIS	196	235	232	243	238	215	204	209	194	217	196	164	230	199	221	188	143	198	191	239
55443	MINNEAPOLIS	141	151	132	153	145	133	141	137	136	149	138	110	148	142	141	130	98	135	126	159
55444	MINNEAPOLIS	133	160	140	159	154	139	137	139	130	145	133	109	151	136	145	126	95	133	126	160
55445	MINNEAPOLIS	146	153	128	149	144	131	143	139	136	151	139	109	144	144	139	130	97	136	126	161
55446	MINNEAPOLIS	240	288	257	297	283	244	245	247	229	270	232	202	276	243	258	213	170	229	211	277
55447	MINNEAPOLIS	175	199	193	206	199	182	181	180	174	191	176	142	199	178	191	168	127	176	168	208
55448	MINNEAPOLIS	130	150	131	148	144	134	132	133	128	138	130	104	143	133	138	125	92	129	126	154
55449	MINNEAPOLIS	162	183	152	178	173	152	159	159	150	172	153	127	168	160	161	142	108	151	139	182
55454	MINNEAPOLIS	41	28	31	32	28	33	50	37	49	42	49	31	40	45	39	51	34	45	46	47
55455	MINNEAPOLIS	47	21	20	25	19	24	66	33	53	45	54	36	39	52	36	48	38	47	33	45
55602	BRIMSON	78	63	101	62	69	83	63	80	66	59	65	58	54	62	68	70	43	74	79	92
55603	FINLAND	80	73	72	76	74	86	72	81	74	65	73	61	66	76	72	79	50	75	84	94
55604	GRAND MARAIS	89	73	107	73	79	93	75	90	78	70	77	66	66	75	78	82	51	85	91	105
55605	GRAND PORTAGE	87	69	112	68	76	92	69	88	73	65	72	64	60	69	75	77	48	81	87	102
55606	HOVLAND	86	69	112	68	76	91	69	88	72	65	71	64	60	69	75	77	47	81	87	102
55607	ISABELLA	96	79	117	78	85	102	79	98	82	73	81	72	69	79	84	87	54	90	97	113
55612	LUTSEN	104	83	134	82	91	110	83	106	87	78	86	77	72	83	90	93	57	97	104	122
55613	SCHROEDER	103	83	134	82	91	109	83	105	87	78	86	77	72	82	90	92	57	97	104	122
55614	SILVER BAY	79	83	88	80	86	93	76	85	80	77	79	59	79	77	82	85	54	82	96	98
55615	TOFTE	104	83	134	82	91	110	83	105	87	78	86	77	72	82	90	93	57	97	104	122
55616	TWO HARBORS	92	84	100	84	87	100	84	94	88	80	87	69	80	86	87	93	59	91	100	110
55702	ALBORN	79	72	71	75	73	84	71	80	73	64	72	60	65	74	71	77	49	74	82	93
55703	ANGORA	85	69	94	68	73	89	69	85	73	64	72	63	60	72	71	78	48	78	86	99
55704	ASKOV	93	67	98	65	70	94	69	88	76	64	75	65	56	75	69	83	49	80	90	104
55705	AURORA	83	75	82	75	76	90	75	84	80	70	79	61	71	79	76	86	54	81	92	98
55706	BABBITT	79	83	90	81	85	94	76	86	80	74	80	61	79	78	82	86	55	82	95	99
55707	BARNUM	88	80	93	81	83	94	77	90	80	73	79	68	72	79	80	83	54	84	90	105
55709	BOVEY	82	69	80	69	69	87	71	81	75	65	74	62	63	75	70	81	50	77	87	96
55710	BRITT	93	95	96	97	95	102	88	96	88	86	88	74	88	89	92	90	61	91	96	113
55711	BROOKSTON	84	77	70	75	76	81	73	79	76	74	75	58	69	78	70	78	51	75	79	93
55712	BRUNO	91	73	118	72	80	97	73	93	77	69	76	68	63	73	79	82	50	86	92	108
55717	CANYON	109	89	138	88	97	115	89	111	92	83	91	81	78	88	96	98	61	103	109	129
55718	CARLTON	89	92	80	94	89	97	87	90	88	83	87	70	88	90	88	90	60	88	94	107
55719	CHISHOLM	73	67	67	66	66	79	68	73	72	63	70	55	64	72	66	76	48	71	80	86
55720	CLOQUET	83	83	77	84	81	90	81	84	84	78	83	64	82	84	82	87	58	83	91	99
55721	COHASSET	90	86	91	89	88	98	82	93	84	78	83	70	79	85	85	88	57	86	94	108
55723	COOK	88	69	97	69	73	92	70	86	74	65	73	64	60	73	72	80	49	80	88	101
55724	COTTON	99	78	123	77	85	104	79	100	83	73	82	73	67	79	84	89	54	92	99	116
55725	CRANE LAKE	100	104	142	103	120	123	94	111	99	106	97	70	103	89	108	104	67	106	124	126
55726	CROMWELL	88	63	90	61	66	89	65	82	72	60	71	62	52	71	64	79	47	75	86	98
55731	ELY	80	67	88	66	70	84	69	80	73	65	72	59	62	71	70	78	48	77	84	94
55732	EMBARRASS	90	73	89	73	75	94	73	88	78	67	77	66	63	79	73	85	52	81	91	103
55733	ESKO	96	112	97	114	108	109	98	102	97	99	98	79	107	100	105	98	69	99	103	120
55734	EVELETH	78	66	76	66	67	82	68	77	73	63	71	58	61	72	67	78	48	74	83	91
55735	FINLAYSON	85	68	108	67	74	90	68	86	72	64	71	63	59	68	73	76	47	80	86	100
55736	FLOODWOOD	72	56	72	56	59	76	59	71	64	53	62	53	50	64	58	70	42	66	76	84
55738	FORBES	82	74	76	76	75	87	73	83	75	66	74	62	67	76	73	79	50	76	85	96
55741	GILBERT	82	66	86	65	69	88	68	82	74	62	72	61	59	72	69	80	48	77	88	96
55742	GOODLAND	78	66	74	67	68	83	66	77	70	60	68	58	58	70	66	75	46	71	80	91
55744	GRAND RAPIDS	84	77	86	77	79	89	77	85	81	74	80	62	74	79	78	85	55	82	90	99
55746	HIBBING	78	71	75	71	72	83	73	78	77	69	76	58	70	76	72	81	52	77	85	92
55748	HILL CITY	85	62	88	60	64	88	65	82	72	59	70	61	53	71	64	79	47	76	87	96
55749	HOLYOKE	88	81	80	84	82	95	79	90	82	72	80	68	73	84	79	87	55	83	93	104
55750	HOYT LAKES	80	91	86	89	91	99	80	88	86	79	85	62	88	84	88	91	59	85	101	101
55751	IRON	91	83	82	87	85	98	82	92	84	74	83	70	76	86	82	89	57	85	95	107
55752	JACOBSON	85	67	107	66	73	89	67	85	71	63	70	62	58	67	72	76	46	79	85	99
55756	KERRICK	91	73	117	72	80	97	73	93	77	69	76	68	64	73	79	82	50	86	92	108
55757	KETTLE RIVER	83	64	84	65	66	88	67	81	70	58	69	64	55	70	67	75	46	75	84	97
55760	MCGREGOR	78	64	93	61	70	84	64	79	68	63	67	56	56	65	67	73	44	74	82	92
55763	MAKINEN	82	66	103	66	72	87	66	83	69	62	68	61	58	66	71	74	46	77	82	96
55765	MEADOWLANDS	83	63	88	61	65	86	64	80	69	59	68	60	53	69	64	76	45	73	82	94
55767	MOOSE LAKE	82	73	78	75	75	84	77	82	79	74	78	61	72	79	76	82	53	80	87	96
55768	MOUNTAIN IRON	75	70	74	70	70	81	71	77	75	67	74	57	68	74	71	79	51	75	83	90
	MINNESOTA	113	113	112	114	112	114	112	113	111	111	112	88	112	113	112	112	78	112	113	133
	UNITED STATES	100	100	100	100	100	100	100	100	100	100	100	100	100	100	100	100	100	100	100	100

POPULATION CHANGE

ZIP CODE #	POST OFFICE NAME	COUNTY FIPS CODE	POPULATION 2000	POPULATION 2009	POPULATION 2014	2000-2009 ANNUAL RATE % Rate	2000-2009 ANNUAL RATE State Centile	HOUSEHOLDS 2000	HOUSEHOLDS 2009	HOUSEHOLDS 2014	HOUSEHOLDS % Annual Rate 2000-2009	HOUSEHOLDS 2009 Average HH Size	FAMILIES 2000	FAMILIES 2009	FAMILIES % Annual Rate 2000-2009
55769	NASHWAUK	061	3398	3339	3264	-0.2	39	1467	1490	1472	0.2	2.23	947	925	-0.3
55771	ORR	137	1733	1744	1726	0.1	51	738	775	776	0.5	2.25	494	495	0.0
55775	PENGILLY	061	1329	1363	1368	0.3	58	568	599	608	0.6	2.28	405	413	0.2
55779	SAGINAW	137	3571	3674	3652	0.3	58	1244	1336	1343	0.8	2.61	964	1002	0.4
55780	SAWYER	017	318	344	349	0.9	74	120	132	135	1.0	2.61	87	92	0.6
55781	SIDE LAKE	137	503	509	506	0.1	51	210	221	222	0.6	2.26	160	163	0.2
55783	STURGEON LAKE	115	2519	2470	2445	-0.2	39	1017	1036	1037	0.2	2.34	702	691	-0.2
55784	SWAN RIVER	061	315	328	330	0.4	61	117	126	128	0.8	2.60	85	88	0.4
55785	SWATARA	001	232	240	236	0.4	61	87	93	92	0.7	2.58	63	64	0.2
55787	TAMARACK	001	573	695	722	2.1	92	251	311	325	2.3	2.22	166	198	1.9
55790	TOWER	137	2434	2351	2301	-0.4	30	1089	1099	1088	0.1	2.12	725	697	-0.4
55792	VIRGINIA	137	10910	10566	10316	-0.3	35	5061	5031	4953	-0.1	1.98	2789	2619	-0.7
55793	WARBA	061	523	529	523	0.1	51	217	227	227	0.5	2.33	160	162	0.1
55795	WILLOW RIVER	115	1213	1140	1109	-0.7	18	492	476	467	-0.4	2.33	346	325	-0.7
55797	WRENSHALL	017	1244	1337	1375	0.8	72	448	498	518	1.2	2.51	319	341	0.7
55798	WRIGHT	017	645	684	690	0.6	67	239	261	266	1.0	2.50	169	177	0.5
55801	DULUTH	137	40	40	40	0.0	48	14	15	15	0.7	2.67	11	11	0.0
55802	DULUTH	137	2478	2406	2344	-0.3	35	1406	1365	1335	-0.3	1.45	372	332	-1.2
55803	DULUTH	137	16841	16601	16298	-0.2	39	6454	6575	6517	0.2	2.50	4711	4644	-0.2
55804	DULUTH	137	14293	14169	13932	-0.1	44	5497	5622	5582	0.2	2.46	3938	3873	-0.2
55805	DULUTH	137	10599	9957	9593	-0.7	18	5140	4903	4760	-0.5	1.98	1923	1696	-1.3
55806	DULUTH	137	9786	9148	8828	-0.7	18	4425	4246	4135	-0.4	2.11	2230	2014	-1.1
55807	DULUTH	137	10122	9599	9323	-0.6	22	4377	4278	4192	-0.2	2.18	2615	2421	-0.8
55808	DULUTH	137	5818	5613	5487	-0.4	30	2445	2450	2419	0.0	2.26	1539	1463	-0.5
55810	DULUTH	137	8710	8652	8530	-0.1	44	3378	3479	3464	0.3	2.43	2423	2408	-0.1
55811	DULUTH	137	24711	26734	26707	0.9	74	8970	9749	9833	0.9	2.32	6014	6261	0.4
55812	DULUTH	137	10615	10686	10463	0.1	51	3507	3441	3378	-0.2	2.30	1781	1642	-0.9
55901	ROCHESTER	109	42372	53136	57520	2.5	93	16513	20738	22499	2.5	2.50	10673	13153	2.3
55902	ROCHESTER	109	18412	20955	22147	1.4	84	7370	8567	9087	1.6	2.40	4782	5392	1.3
55904	ROCHESTER	109	23718	25048	25896	0.6	67	9065	10047	10480	1.1	2.46	5932	6237	0.5
55906	ROCHESTER	109	16576	19228	20006	1.6	86	6459	7372	7731	1.4	2.46	4413	4785	0.9
55909	ADAMS	099	1480	1422	1381	-0.4	30	544	542	531	0.0	2.53	400	383	-0.5
55910	ALTURA	169	2595	2596	2563	0.0	48	929	970	968	0.5	2.68	716	721	0.1
55912	AUSTIN	099	27677	27646	27191	0.0	48	11511	11620	11438	0.1	2.32	7327	7115	-0.3
55917	BLOOMING PRAIRIE	147	3578	3690	3741	0.3	58	1330	1416	1451	0.7	2.54	974	999	0.3
55918	BROWNSDALE	099	1039	988	960	-0.5	26	407	395	385	-0.3	2.50	290	271	-0.7
55919	BROWNSVILLE	055	1156	1129	1104	-0.3	35	451	454	447	0.1	2.49	335	327	-0.3
55920	BYRON	109	5678	6606	7096	1.6	86	1971	2362	2561	2.0	2.80	1622	1871	1.6
55921	CALEDONIA	055	5245	5170	5063	-0.2	39	2009	2029	2000	0.1	2.47	1340	1303	-0.3
55922	CANTON	045	1355	1284	1256	-0.6	22	437	416	407	-0.5	3.07	324	300	-0.8
55923	CHATFIELD	045	4756	4803	4830	0.1	51	1778	1850	1874	0.4	2.53	1297	1302	0.0
55924	CLAREMONT	039	1405	1454	1452	0.4	61	513	543	547	0.6	2.66	391	402	0.3
55925	DAKOTA	169	747	780	781	0.5	63	273	296	300	0.9	2.59	212	223	0.5
55926	DEXTER	099	594	630	631	0.6	67	222	240	242	0.8	2.50	169	177	0.5
55927	DODGE CENTER	039	3535	4060	4257	1.5	85	1265	1494	1581	1.8	2.67	962	1105	1.5
55929	DOVER	109	945	970	984	0.3	58	342	367	376	0.8	2.64	261	267	0.2
55932	ELGIN	157	1985	2068	2065	0.4	61	710	758	761	0.7	2.73	531	547	0.3
55933	ELKTON	099	308	306	301	-0.1	44	108	110	109	0.2	2.68	80	79	-0.1
55934	EYOTA	109	2880	3142	3302	0.9	74	1061	1208	1283	1.4	2.60	830	903	0.9
55935	FOUNTAIN	045	659	698	716	0.6	67	251	272	280	0.9	2.56	193	204	0.6
55936	GRAND MEADOW	099	1701	1638	1601	-0.4	30	646	638	626	-0.1	2.50	444	420	-0.6
55939	HARMONY	045	2349	2400	2417	0.2	54	875	903	912	0.3	2.59	598	596	0.0
55940	HAYFIELD	039	2476	2859	3013	1.6	86	889	1061	1131	1.9	2.61	658	761	1.6
55941	HOKAH	055	1302	1271	1240	-0.3	35	507	509	501	0.0	2.50	384	376	-0.2
55943	HOUSTON	055	3347	3303	3237	-0.1	44	1287	1300	1282	0.1	2.49	932	911	-0.2
55944	KASSON	039	5637	6801	7200	2.1	92	2103	2521	2679	2.0	2.69	1528	1780	1.7
55945	KELLOGG	157	1389	1451	1488	0.5	63	512	557	578	0.9	2.61	380	401	0.6
55946	KENYON	049	3429	3691	3754	0.8	72	1285	1398	1426	0.9	2.60	935	981	0.5
55947	LA CRESCENT	055	7450	7383	7242	-0.1	44	2828	2863	2830	0.1	2.54	2077	2041	-0.2
55949	LANESBORO	045	1497	1581	1612	0.6	67	653	714	736	1.0	2.21	419	441	0.6
55951	LE ROY	099	1475	1399	1355	-0.6	22	608	593	578	-0.3	2.35	413	385	-0.8
55952	LEWISTON	169	2172	2150	2164	-0.1	44	762	775	788	0.2	2.73	587	576	-0.2
55953	LYLE	099	1237	1229	1203	-0.1	44	457	461	454	0.1	2.67	341	334	-0.2
55954	MABEL	045	1567	1747	1811	1.2	81	639	741	778	1.6	2.27	418	468	1.2
55955	MANTORVILLE	039	2274	2648	2897	1.7	88	756	933	1022	2.3	2.84	632	762	2.0
55956	MAZEPPA	157	1831	1898	1883	0.4	61	685	727	727	0.6	2.61	508	522	0.3
55957	MILLVILLE	157	585	584	569	0.0	48	201	206	202	0.3	2.83	146	144	-0.1
55959	MINNESOTA CITY	169	1108	1192	1206	0.8	72	413	462	472	1.2	2.58	321	348	0.9
55960	ORONOCO	109	2764	2989	3125	0.8	72	1046	1178	1243	1.3	2.54	793	844	0.7
55961	OSTRANDER	045	586	570	561	-0.3	35	233	229	226	-0.2	2.49	178	171	-0.4
55962	PETERSON	045	979	969	967	-0.1	44	342	348	350	0.2	2.73	259	257	-0.1
55963	PINE ISLAND	049	4383	5031	5234	1.5	85	1563	1852	1941	1.9	2.66	1204	1396	1.6
55964	PLAINVIEW	157	3913	4395	4566	1.3	83	1397	1618	1695	1.6	2.64	1013	1133	1.2
55965	PRESTON	045	1603	1481	1440	-0.9	12	657	618	603	-0.7	2.28	456	414	-1.0
55967	RACINE	099	1015	978	954	-0.4	30	351	347	340	-0.1	2.82	274	263	-0.4
55968	READS LANDING	157	141	130	126	-0.9	12	55	52	50	-0.6	2.50	43	39	-1.0
55969	ROLLINGSTONE	169	1080	1056	1044	-0.2	39	404	411	411	0.2	2.57	314	309	-0.2
55970	ROSE CREEK	099	1022	1005	984	-0.2	39	365	366	360	0.0	2.73	280	272	-0.3
55971	RUSHFORD	169	2923	2898	2910	-0.1	44	1156	1177	1189	0.2	2.37	795	779	-0.2
55972	SAINT CHARLES	169	4660	5110	5173	1.0	77	1663	1894	1944	1.4	2.66	1227	1342	1.0
55973	SARGEANT	099	392	416	417	0.6	67	126	136	137	0.8	2.90	96	100	0.4
55974	SPRING GROVE	055	2332	2520	2525	0.8	72	952	1060	1071	1.2	2.32	661	712	0.8
55975	SPRING VALLEY	045	4567	4618	4636	0.1	51	1784	1830	1847	0.3	2.49	1252	1243	-0.1
55976	STEWARTVILLE	109	7075	7653	7959	0.9	74	2619	2951	3100	1.3	2.54	1912	2034	0.7
55977	TAOPI	099	347	293	271	-1.8	2	120	103	96	-1.6	2.84	101	85	-1.8
55979	UTICA	169	570	834	853	4.2	98	186	287	297	4.8	2.83	146	217	4.4
55981	WABASHA	157	4039	4218	4281	0.5	63	1645	1755	1794	0.7	2.30	1097	1129	0.3
55982	WALTHAM	099	551	540	529	-0.2	39	192	189	185	-0.2	2.84	157	151	-0.4
55983	WANAMINGO	049	1476	1548	1561	0.5	63	559	600	609	0.8	2.55	399	414	0.4
55985	WEST CONCORD	039	2065	2201	2228	0.7	69	782	850	866	0.9	2.57	589	623	0.6
55987	WINONA	169	36046	35711	35230	-0.1	44	13751	13841	13758	0.1	2.28	7890	7533	-0.5
55990	WYKOFF	045	945	885	864	-0.7	18	385	368	362	-0.5	2.40	281	261	-0.8
55991	ZUMBRO FALLS	157	1835	1909	1897	0.4	61	702	750	752	0.7	2.55	522	540	0.4
55992	ZUMBROTA	049	4408	4412	4401	0.0	48	1708	1758	1768	0.3	2.48	1213	1201	-0.1
56001	MANKATO	013	39633	43326	45122	1.0	77	14959	17060	17983	1.4	2.32	8089	8788	0.9
	MINNESOTA					0.9					1.1	2.48			0.7
	UNITED STATES					1.0					1.1	2.59			0.9

ZIP CODE #	POST OFFICE NAME	RACE (%) White 2000	White 2009	Black 2000	Black 2009	Asian/Pacific 2000	Asian/Pacific 2009	% Hispanic Origin 2000	% Hispanic Origin 2009	2009 AGE DISTRIBUTION (%) 0-4	5-9	10-14	15-19	20-24	25-44	45-64	65-84	85+	18+	MEDIAN AGE 2009	% 2009 Males	% 2009 Females
55769	NASHWAUK	97.9	97.5	0.2	0.2	0.2	0.2	0.3	0.4	5.0	5.1	5.6	6.7	5.1	23.2	31.0	15.6	2.8	80.1	44.5	50.0	50.0
55771	ORR	76.8	75.1	0.0	0.0	0.6	0.8	0.9	1.3	5.2	5.6	5.8	5.8	4.2	20.8	34.1	17.0	1.5	79.8	46.6	52.1	47.9
55775	PENGILLY	97.6	97.1	0.2	0.3	0.1	0.1	0.2	0.2	4.8	5.2	5.6	5.4	4.0	20.0	34.5	17.7	2.8	81.1	48.7	49.0	51.0
55779	SAGINAW	95.4	94.2	0.4	0.6	0.3	0.5	1.1	1.8	5.2	6.0	6.6	6.5	5.0	25.1	34.4	9.9	1.2	78.0	41.8	53.2	46.8
55780	SAWYER	65.7	64.8	0.0	0.0	0.3	0.3	1.3	1.7	7.8	7.8	8.1	7.8	6.4	24.4	26.2	10.2	1.2	71.2	34.8	51.7	48.3
55781	SIDE LAKE	97.8	97.2	0.0	0.2	0.0	0.2	0.6	0.8	4.1	3.9	6.3	9.0	2.6	20.6	36.9	14.5	2.0	81.7	46.8	52.3	47.7
55783	STURGEON LAKE	96.1	95.4	1.1	1.4	0.2	0.2	0.8	1.2	4.9	5.3	5.6	5.4	5.0	22.1	33.3	16.7	1.7	80.9	46.0	52.1	47.9
55784	SWAN RIVER	97.8	97.3	0.0	0.0	0.0	0.3	0.6	0.9	5.2	6.4	6.4	6.4	4.9	21.3	31.7	15.9	1.8	77.7	44.6	52.7	47.3
55785	SWATARA	97.4	97.1	0.4	0.4	0.0	0.0	0.9	1.3	5.4	5.8	5.8	5.8	4.6	20.4	33.3	17.1	1.7	78.8	46.2	50.8	49.2
55787	TAMARACK	92.7	91.9	0.2	0.3	0.2	0.1	0.5	0.9	4.3	4.5	4.6	5.6	4.7	17.3	32.2	23.9	2.9	83.0	51.1	49.8	50.2
55790	TOWER	93.4	92.7	0.2	0.3	0.5	0.6	0.8	1.1	3.6	4.2	4.7	5.0	3.6	18.4	40.9	17.7	2.0	84.2	50.6	51.6	48.4
55792	VIRGINIA	95.6	94.7	0.4	0.6	0.5	0.8	0.8	1.1	4.6	4.6	4.9	6.0	6.2	23.1	29.3	16.1	5.2	82.5	45.4	47.5	52.5
55793	WARBA	97.9	97.2	0.2	0.2	0.0	0.2	0.8	1.5	5.1	5.7	5.9	5.1	5.5	21.7	35.7	14.0	1.3	80.0	45.6	52.0	48.0
55795	WILLOW RIVER	96.0	95.3	1.2	1.5	0.2	0.2	1.1	1.5	5.6	6.4	6.9	6.1	5.2	23.6	30.8	14.0	1.3	77.5	42.3	51.7	48.3
55797	WRENSHALL	95.8	95.1	0.2	0.2	0.3	0.4	0.3	0.4	5.3	5.6	6.0	6.2	5.6	23.5	31.7	11.9	4.2	79.2	43.5	51.3	48.7
55798	WRIGHT	97.5	97.1	0.2	0.1	0.2	0.1	0.6	0.9	6.4	6.7	6.9	5.8	4.2	19.9	28.4	17.1	4.5	75.9	45.0	50.3	49.7
55801	DULUTH	100.0	100.0	0.0	0.0	0.0	0.0	0.0	0.0	5.0	7.5	7.5	7.5	2.5	27.5	37.5	5.0	0.0	72.5	41.3	57.5	42.5
55802	DULUTH	91.7	90.1	1.7	2.2	1.0	1.5	1.2	1.7	1.7	2.3	2.1	3.3	3.9	18.1	33.2	24.3	11.1	92.1	55.8	44.6	55.4
55803	DULUTH	97.4	96.7	0.3	0.4	0.7	1.0	0.5	0.8	5.3	6.2	6.9	7.4	4.7	23.4	32.3	11.5	2.2	76.6	42.4	50.4	49.6
55804	DULUTH	97.1	96.2	0.3	0.5	0.7	1.1	0.6	1.0	5.6	6.2	6.8	6.7	4.7	22.3	32.0	12.5	3.1	76.9	43.3	48.1	51.9
55805	DULUTH	84.0	81.0	4.4	5.8	2.0	2.8	1.7	2.3	6.6	4.8	4.5	5.9	17.9	29.7	20.4	8.0	2.4	81.5	30.2	49.8	50.2
55806	DULUTH	86.2	84.0	3.1	4.1	1.1	1.6	1.4	2.0	7.4	6.0	5.6	6.7	10.5	29.5	24.5	8.1	1.8	77.3	33.0	49.5	50.5
55807	DULUTH	94.2	93.0	0.8	1.1	0.6	0.9	0.8	1.1	5.9	5.5	6.0	6.6	6.0	27.2	26.5	12.8	3.3	78.6	39.4	48.3	51.7
55808	DULUTH	95.4	94.6	0.3	0.3	0.3	0.4	0.7	1.0	6.9	6.4	6.4	6.9	7.0	26.1	25.5	12.1	2.8	76.1	37.8	49.3	50.7
55810	DULUTH	97.0	96.4	0.1	0.1	0.4	0.6	0.6	0.9	5.5	6.0	6.5	7.0	4.8	24.0	29.6	13.8	2.8	77.5	42.2	48.6	51.4
55811	DULUTH	95.1	93.7	1.5	2.2	0.9	1.3	1.1	1.6	4.4	4.6	5.2	9.0	9.5	23.3	26.5	13.5	4.0	82.2	40.2	49.2	50.8
55812	DULUTH	94.1	92.3	0.9	1.3	1.9	2.8	1.1	1.6	3.6	3.3	3.7	22.0	22.4	19.7	18.1	6.0	1.3	86.6	23.9	49.8	50.2
55901	ROCHESTER	88.5	84.5	2.7	3.6	6.0	8.3	2.4	3.4	7.9	7.5	7.2	6.3	6.4	29.9	23.4	9.0	2.4	73.1	35.4	48.2	51.8
55902	ROCHESTER	91.9	89.1	1.7	2.3	4.0	5.5	2.6	3.8	6.3	6.6	7.2	6.7	5.6	25.7	28.8	11.0	2.1	75.3	39.8	48.8	51.2
55904	ROCHESTER	85.1	81.2	5.8	7.3	4.8	6.3	4.1	5.9	7.3	6.7	6.7	7.2	7.6	29.0	25.4	8.8	1.3	75.5	34.9	49.9	50.1
55906	ROCHESTER	90.4	86.7	2.5	3.8	4.8	6.5	1.8	2.8	5.8	5.9	6.6	7.2	6.0	25.3	30.0	11.4	1.8	77.1	40.3	50.9	49.1
55909	ADAMS	99.2	99.0	0.1	0.1	0.3	0.4	0.6	0.9	6.3	6.7	6.9	7.3	4.5	22.2	26.9	14.8	4.5	75.7	42.2	50.1	49.9
55910	ALTURA	98.8	98.4	0.3	0.3	0.3	0.4	0.5	0.7	6.8	7.8	8.2	7.3	4.5	24.1	29.0	10.8	1.5	72.6	39.3	53.1	46.9
55912	AUSTIN	93.2	90.6	0.7	1.0	2.0	2.8	5.6	8.2	6.5	6.1	6.0	6.4	5.8	23.8	25.7	15.5	4.2	77.5	41.1	49.0	51.0
55917	BLOOMING PRAIRIE	97.1	95.7	0.2	0.3	0.5	0.7	3.4	5.5	6.7	6.7	6.9	6.9	5.4	24.2	26.5	12.9	3.9	75.1	39.8	48.9	51.1
55918	BROWNSDALE	96.1	94.5	0.1	0.1	0.0	0.0	3.4	5.1	6.3	6.1	6.0	6.6	6.8	25.8	27.0	13.2	2.3	77.8	38.6	51.5	48.5
55919	BROWNSVILLE	99.0	99.0	0.2	0.2	0.2	0.2	0.5	0.5	6.0	7.1	7.6	7.4	5.4	24.2	30.9	10.0	1.3	74.5	40.3	52.0	48.0
55920	BYRON	98.0	97.1	0.3	0.4	0.7	1.0	0.7	1.2	7.5	7.3	7.6	8.2	6.2	28.3	27.4	6.8	0.7	72.5	34.0	49.3	50.7
55921	CALEDONIA	98.6	98.5	0.3	0.3	0.2	0.2	0.7	0.7	5.8	6.2	6.8	7.1	5.7	22.8	27.2	14.6	3.9	76.4	41.8	49.0	51.0
55922	CANTON	98.9	98.4	0.1	0.1	0.1	0.2	1.2	1.9	9.4	9.9	9.3	7.7	4.9	21.5	24.9	10.9	1.4	66.3	32.5	50.5	49.5
55923	CHATFIELD	98.5	98.0	0.5	0.7	0.2	0.2	0.7	1.0	6.2	6.7	7.2	6.8	4.6	25.0	27.5	12.5	3.5	75.5	40.5	49.5	50.5
55924	CLAREMONT	92.8	89.3	0.0	0.0	0.1	0.1	7.7	11.8	7.4	7.7	8.9	7.8	4.2	27.0	24.4	11.1	1.4	71.0	36.7	52.3	47.7
55925	DAKOTA	98.8	98.1	0.0	0.1	0.1	0.3	1.1	1.4	5.5	6.3	7.1	7.1	4.6	23.5	33.6	11.5	0.9	76.4	42.2	51.5	48.5
55926	DEXTER	97.3	96.8	0.3	0.3	0.5	0.6	0.7	1.0	7.8	8.6	8.3	7.1	4.3	23.2	26.5	12.9	1.4	70.3	39.2	47.3	52.7
55927	DODGE CENTER	94.6	91.8	0.2	0.3	0.4	0.5	4.7	7.7	7.7	7.7	7.5	6.8	5.5	27.3	25.8	9.5	2.2	72.8	36.4	49.7	50.3
55929	DOVER	98.1	97.0	0.3	0.5	0.2	0.3	1.2	2.0	5.7	6.2	8.4	9.1	5.6	24.1	29.8	9.8	1.4	73.1	38.4	52.0	48.0
55932	ELGIN	98.7	98.1	0.1	0.1	0.2	0.3	0.8	1.2	7.4	8.1	8.2	8.4	5.5	26.7	26.0	8.4	1.4	70.9	34.4	51.5	48.5
55933	ELKTON	99.4	99.0	0.0	0.0	0.3	0.7	0.6	1.0	6.2	6.9	6.9	7.2	4.6	22.9	27.1	13.7	4.6	75.5	41.7	50.3	49.7
55934	EYOTA	98.1	97.2	0.2	0.4	0.4	0.6	0.8	1.2	7.2	7.4	7.8	7.7	5.7	27.4	27.2	8.3	1.2	72.6	35.5	49.7	50.3
55935	FOUNTAIN	99.1	98.9	0.2	0.1	0.2	0.1	0.5	0.7	6.9	7.6	7.4	5.6	3.9	27.2	28.1	11.6	1.7	74.4	38.7	52.9	47.1
55936	GRAND MEADOW	98.9	98.5	0.0	0.0	0.2	0.2	0.5	0.7	6.7	6.7	6.8	6.6	6.0	25.0	26.5	12.2	3.5	75.6	39.3	50.2	49.8
55939	HARMONY	99.2	98.8	0.1	0.1	0.1	0.3	0.5	0.8	6.0	6.7	8.0	7.6	5.0	20.4	25.7	16.1	4.5	73.8	41.8	50.1	49.9
55940	HAYFIELD	97.9	97.0	0.2	0.3	0.7	1.0	1.7	2.8	6.9	6.9	6.8	7.1	5.8	25.4	26.6	11.2	3.4	74.6	37.7	50.1	49.9
55941	HOKAH	98.8	98.7	0.2	0.2	0.2	0.2	0.4	0.3	5.7	6.3	7.2	7.6	5.0	24.9	32.9	9.4	1.2	76.2	40.9	51.5	48.5
55943	HOUSTON	98.7	98.7	0.3	0.3	0.2	0.2	0.5	0.6	5.2	5.9	6.4	7.2	4.6	24.5	31.2	12.0	2.9	77.6	42.5	51.2	48.8
55944	KASSON	97.5	96.7	0.3	0.4	0.6	0.8	2.1	2.8	7.9	7.7	8.0	7.2	5.6	26.6	25.4	9.9	1.7	71.6	35.8	48.7	51.3
55945	KELLOGG	99.1	98.7	0.0	0.0	0.2	0.3	0.8	1.2	5.0	6.1	7.1	7.6	4.5	22.3	31.9	13.9	1.6	76.8	43.2	51.6	48.4
55946	KENYON	97.3	96.4	0.1	0.2	0.7	0.9	1.8	2.7	7.0	7.2	7.2	6.7	5.1	25.2	27.3	11.4	3.0	74.4	39.1	50.6	49.4
55947	LA CRESCENT	98.0	97.8	0.4	0.4	0.7	0.7	0.7	0.8	6.2	6.3	6.7	7.1	6.5	22.8	30.2	11.8	2.2	76.0	40.5	49.3	50.7
55949	LANESBORO	99.1	98.8	0.1	0.2	0.2	0.3	0.2	0.4	5.2	5.9	5.9	5.8	5.3	21.9	29.3	17.3	3.3	79.3	44.9	50.7	49.3
55951	LE ROY	99.3	99.0	0.1	0.1	0.1	0.3	0.7	1.0	5.4	5.7	6.0	7.5	6.1	23.4	29.2	13.8	2.9	78.1	41.2	51.2	48.8
55952	LEWISTON	98.8	98.2	0.3	0.5	0.1	0.2	1.2	1.6	8.6	8.5	8.3	7.2	5.4	26.2	24.7	9.3	1.8	70.0	35.0	50.3	49.7
55953	LYLE	99.3	99.0	0.0	0.0	0.2	0.2	0.2	0.4	5.5	6.7	7.1	8.5	4.2	24.6	27.5	14.2	1.8	75.2	40.8	52.2	47.8
55954	MABEL	99.0	98.7	0.0	0.0	0.1	0.2	0.4	0.7	4.9	6.6	7.6	7.2	4.5	19.7	27.0	17.9	4.7	75.8	44.7	47.9	52.1
55955	MANTORVILLE	98.4	97.8	0.0	0.0	0.1	0.2	0.8	1.3	8.8	9.2	8.6	7.7	3.3	28.5	26.0	6.5	1.5	68.2	35.0	50.3	49.7
55956	MAZEPPA	98.3	97.8	0.4	0.6	0.2	0.2	0.5	0.7	5.6	6.2	6.7	8.1	5.3	24.2	31.2	11.2	1.6	76.6	40.9	50.3	49.7
55957	MILLVILLE	98.1	97.6	0.0	0.0	0.2	0.2	1.5	2.2	6.3	9.6	10.4	8.7	5.3	25.9	23.5	9.1	1.2	67.5	34.5	52.7	47.3
55959	MINNESOTA CITY	97.3	96.5	0.5	0.6	1.1	1.5	0.6	0.8	6.3	6.6	7.0	6.4	4.7	27.5	30.5	9.7	1.2	76.1	38.9	51.4	48.6
55960	ORONOCO	95.3	93.3	1.3	2.0	1.6	2.3	1.8	2.8	6.6	6.9	7.3	7.0	5.3	24.5	32.0	9.4	1.0	74.9	39.8	50.9	49.1
55961	OSTRANDER	99.1	99.1	0.2	0.2	0.3	0.4	0.5	0.9	6.8	7.7	7.7	6.5	3.9	23.5	27.7	13.3	2.8	73.7	41.3	53.5	46.5
55962	PETERSON	99.1	98.8	0.0	0.0	0.2	0.3	0.4	0.5	5.5	6.1	6.5	6.4	4.3	22.2	31.4	14.9	2.8	77.9	44.2	51.9	48.1
55963	PINE ISLAND	98.1	97.4	0.2	0.3	0.4	0.5	0.6	1.0	6.1	6.6	7.0	6.9	5.1	23.8	31.3	10.7	2.4	75.7	40.7	49.9	50.1
55964	PLAINVIEW	97.2	96.0	0.0	0.0	0.1	0.1	4.4	6.7	7.9	7.8	7.5	6.9	6.2	27.8	22.9	9.8	3.1	72.4	34.7	49.0	51.0
55965	PRESTON	98.9	98.4	0.1	0.1	0.1	0.2	0.6	1.0	5.3	6.2	6.1	6.5	5.7	21.7	26.7	17.3	4.4	77.7	43.5	51.0	49.0
55967	RACINE	98.5	98.1	0.3	0.4	0.1	0.1	0.4	0.5	6.3	6.9	7.7	8.8	4.7	24.9	29.9	9.3	1.5	73.7	39.4	48.7	51.3
55968	READS LANDING	100.0	99.2	0.0	0.0	0.0	0.8	1.4	2.3	4.6	7.7	8.5	8.5	3.1	22.3	30.8	13.1	1.5	73.8	42.0	52.3	47.7
55969	ROLLINGSTONE	98.8	98.2	0.2	0.3	0.3	0.5	0.6	0.9	6.7	7.3	7.6	6.8	4.2	25.2	29.8	10.9	1.5	74.1	39.7	53.1	46.9
55970	ROSE CREEK	98.0	97.2	0.0	0.0	0.4	0.6	1.8	2.8	5.6	6.2	6.6	7.2	4.5	24.0	30.8	12.8	2.4	77.2	41.9	50.8	49.2
55971	RUSHFORD	99.0	98.8	0.2	0.2	0.2	0.3	0.2	0.2	5.7	5.9	6.2	6.5	5.3	22.8	27.9	14.7	4.9	77.8	42.9	47.9	52.1
55972	SAINT CHARLES	93.7	91.3	0.7	1.0	2.7	4.0	3.8	5.0	8.2	7.9	7.6	7.2	6.7	25.6	24.1	10.2	2.5	71.5	34.5	49.2	50.8
55973	SARGEANT	97.7	96.6	0.3	0.2	0.3	0.7	0.8	1.0	7.7	8.7	8.2	7.2	4.6	23.3	26.4	12.5	1.4	70.7	38.9	47.6	52.4
55974	SPRING GROVE	99.0	98.9	0.2	0.2	0.3	0.3	0.7	0.8	5.2	5.7	6.2	7.1	4.6	22.9	30.8	13.3	4.2	78.2	43.6	51.2	48.8
55975	SPRING VALLEY	99.0	98.7	0.2	0.2	0.1	0.1	0.5	0.7	5.8	6.1	6.4	7.0	5.7	24.8	27.7	13.5	3.0	77.3	40.4	49.0	51.0
55976	STEWARTVILLE	97.6	96.5	0.6	0.9	0.5	0.7	0.9	1.5	7.9	7.6	7.2	7.1	6.8	26.8	24.6	9.7	2.4	72.9	35.0	48.3	51.7
55977	TAOPI	99.1	99.0	0.3	0.3	0.0	0.0	0.0	0.0	7.2	7.8	7.8	8.2	5.5	21.5	29.0	11.6	1.4	71.7	38.8	52.9	47.1
55979	UTICA	98.4	97.8	0.5	0.7	0.2	0.2	1.4	2.2	9.6	9.4	8.9	7.3	5.4	26.0	22.3	9.2	1.9	67.4	32.6	49.4	50.6
55981	WABASHA	98.4	98.1	0.4	0.6	0.1	0.2	0.3	0.5	5.1	5.2	5.5	6.1	5.1	20.8	29.9	17.9	4.3	80.0	46.4	48.5	51.5
55982	WALTHAM	98.0	96.9	0.4	0.6	0.2	0.4	2.2	3.3	5.4	6.5	8.9	8.9	4.6	23.1	26.1	14.8	1.7	73.3	40.1	51.9	48.1
55983	WANAMINGO	98.6	98.1	0.1	0.1	0.4	0.6	0.3	0.5	7.4	7.6	7.5	6.2	5.0	24.7	27.2	11.6	2.7	73.4	39.3	50.8	49.2
55985	WEST CONCORD	96.7	95.1	0.1	0.1	0.2	0.4	3.2	5.0	7.0	7.0	7.5	7.4	5.6	26.6	25.7	11.2	1.9	73.4	36.9	49.3	50.7
55987	WINONA	95.4	93.8	0.9	1.2	2.2	3.1	1.2	1.6	4.8	4.7	4.8	11.1	14.3	23.3	23.2	10.7	3.0	82.2	32.8	47.7	52.3
55990	WYKOFF	98.5	98.1	0.3	0.5	0.1	0.1	0.5	0.8	4.6	5.3	5.6	6.0	4.3	25.1	30.8	15.6	2.6	80.7	44.2	50.8	49.2
55991	ZUMBRO FALLS	98.2	97.6	0.4	0.5	0.4	0.7	0.6	0.8	5.4	6.1	7.2	8.4	5.0	26.3	31.0	9.7	0.8	75.6	39.8	51.4	48.6
55992	ZUMBROTA	97.1	96.4	0.6	0.8	0.6	0.7	1.0	1.5	6.5	6.5	6.6	6.9	6.5	24.1	28.7	11.0	3.1	76.0	39.6	49.3	50.7
56001	MANKATO	93.6	91.3	1.6	2.1	2.5	3.5	2.0	3.0	5.3	4.6	4.7	10.6	18.3	24.6	20.6	9.1	2.3	82.4	28.8	49.6	50.4
	MINNESOTA	89.4	86.8	3.5	4.3	2.9	3.9	2.9	4.1	6.8	6.7	6.7	7.2	6.8	27.2	26.3	10.2	2.1	75.6	36.9	49.6	50.4
	UNITED STATES	75.1	72.0	12.3	12.7	3.8	4.6	12.5	15.7	6.8	6.7	6.6	7.1	6.9	27.0	26.0	10.9	1.9	75.7	36.9	49.2	50.8

ZIP CODE #	POST OFFICE NAME	2009 Per Capita Income	2009 HH Income Base	2009 HOUSEHOLD INCOME DISTRIBUTION (%) Less than $25,000	$25,000 to $49,999	$50,000 to $99,999	$100,000 to $149,999	$150,000 or More	MEDIAN HOUSEHOLD INCOME 2009	2014	2009 National Centile	2009 State Centile	2009 Home Value Base	2009 HOME VALUE DISTRIBUTION (%) Less than $50,000	$50,000 to $89,999	$90,000 to $174,999	$175,000 to $399,999	$400,000 or More	2009 Median Home Value
55769	NASHWAUK	19650	1490	31.2	32.4	31.5	4.5	0.3	38693	39889	29	11	1245	27.4	34.5	30.4	7.3	0.5	70938
55771	ORR	21376	775	29.2	30.1	34.2	4.3	2.3	41642	44357	38	20	643	14.2	23.3	36.9	18.5	7.2	108654
55775	PENGILLY	28557	599	21.0	19.4	45.9	8.5	5.2	58039	58513	75	75	557	9.5	28.2	40.8	19.9	1.6	109853
55779	SAGINAW	24937	1336	13.3	24.9	47.2	11.2	3.4	60438	62773	78	78	1246	6.4	12.1	41.2	37.4	2.9	157910
55780	SAWYER	16949	132	33.3	31.1	30.3	5.3	0.0	35557	36787	19	5	99	10.1	14.1	43.4	30.3	2.0	130682
55781	SIDE LAKE	26353	221	14.5	31.2	44.3	6.3	3.6	53661	56074	69	66	211	6.2	21.8	39.3	28.0	4.7	133854
55783	STURGEON LAKE	22557	1036	25.2	27.6	38.5	6.4	2.3	46197	48782	52	39	938	15.8	18.8	41.2	22.2	2.1	119960
55784	SWAN RIVER	18703	126	26.2	25.4	45.2	2.4	0.8	48221	48196	57	48	117	10.3	24.8	51.3	13.7	0.0	111413
55785	SWATARA	19360	93	28.0	33.3	29.0	5.4	4.3	40371	40000	34	16	83	25.3	19.3	42.2	12.0	1.2	99000
55787	TAMARACK	21810	311	30.5	33.1	29.9	3.9	2.6	38307	39881	28	10	269	15.2	21.6	35.7	25.3	2.2	118534
55790	TOWER	28179	1099	22.4	25.5	40.3	7.9	3.9	51842	54391	66	62	963	9.6	19.5	30.7	24.2	16.0	139423
55792	VIRGINIA	24699	5031	30.6	28.0	32.5	6.7	2.2	41779	44164	39	21	3203	11.5	40.3	39.8	7.6	0.8	88268
55793	WARBA	21022	227	24.7	29.1	41.9	3.1	1.3	46351	46883	52	40	205	14.1	27.8	48.3	9.8	0.0	99706
55795	WILLOW RIVER	21850	476	25.4	28.6	38.7	5.0	2.3	45000	47684	48	34	425	16.5	20.9	42.1	18.1	2.4	112708
55797	WRENSHALL	21377	498	18.3	31.1	43.2	6.2	1.2	50395	51789	62	55	429	10.0	14.2	43.1	29.1	3.5	139375
55798	WRIGHT	19503	261	26.1	34.1	33.3	4.2	2.3	40704	42558	35	17	224	12.5	18.8	44.2	24.1	0.4	128261
55801	DULUTH	23249	15	13.3	26.7	46.7	13.3	0.0	63080	63080	81	82	14	0.0	14.3	42.9	42.9	0.0	166667
55802	DULUTH	24865	1365	55.4	15.1	22.1	5.2	2.3	20828	21240	2	1	351	0.0	2.6	24.8	65.8	6.8	226750
55803	DULUTH	29858	6575	12.9	23.1	41.6	16.3	6.1	65018	68653	83	84	5785	3.4	8.9	48.8	34.5	4.3	156163
55804	DULUTH	30471	5622	14.5	23.1	40.2	13.7	8.4	61846	65699	80	80	4996	1.2	9.0	55.5	28.6	5.7	148357
55805	DULUTH	19532	4903	42.5	30.7	22.1	3.0	1.6	29992	30478	8	2	1626	6.9	42.0	43.8	5.7	1.6	90960
55806	DULUTH	19545	4246	39.3	30.8	25.0	3.5	1.3	32440	34041	12	3	1934	7.9	38.1	45.6	8.2	0.2	93645
55807	DULUTH	23357	4278	25.7	32.4	34.1	5.9	1.9	43922	46121	45	29	2940	6.2	36.7	51.3	5.2	0.6	95547
55808	DULUTH	22809	2450	24.0	32.6	35.4	6.5	1.5	44311	46782	46	31	1780	20.3	25.5	48.5	5.7	0.0	95474
55810	DULUTH	25643	3479	18.1	26.9	40.4	10.8	3.7	53700	56163	69	67	3069	10.1	16.9	51.7	19.4	1.9	124136
55811	DULUTH	26670	9749	17.2	23.9	42.4	11.4	5.1	57986	60992	75	74	7553	3.0	8.1	55.9	29.0	4.0	148136
55812	DULUTH	26916	3441	24.4	23.2	31.4	11.1	9.9	52060	54115	66	63	1781	0.4	7.2	51.5	33.4	7.6	158914
55901	ROCHESTER	34597	20738	12.6	18.5	36.0	23.2	9.8	72802	77609	88	89	14768	1.6	5.2	52.6	37.8	2.8	159623
55902	ROCHESTER	50146	8567	10.7	15.2	31.3	20.3	22.4	82044	86104	93	93	6484	3.7	3.3	30.2	45.8	17.1	214293
55904	ROCHESTER	27618	10047	16.8	23.9	40.9	14.2	4.2	61883	63874	80	81	7213	9.7	11.9	56.9	20.2	1.3	124358
55906	ROCHESTER	35149	7372	13.6	21.8	34.5	18.0	12.1	68716	73443	86	87	5775	6.7	8.1	41.0	37.7	6.4	158176
55909	ADAMS	20186	542	23.4	34.1	35.1	5.4	2.0	44070	46103	46	29	440	10.2	23.9	46.4	15.0	4.5	111688
55910	ALTURA	22648	970	17.5	29.4	42.1	8.1	2.9	52065	54217	66	63	818	6.2	10.4	42.9	31.7	8.8	150000
55912	AUSTIN	25029	11620	23.5	29.3	35.7	7.7	3.8	46762	49724	53	42	8701	10.9	27.5	47.3	13.0	1.3	103158
55917	BLOOMING PRAIRIE	23028	1416	17.5	27.3	45.7	7.1	2.4	53729	55466	69	67	1190	5.0	16.0	50.0	24.9	4.2	135000
55918	BROWNSDALE	22288	395	25.6	24.3	39.5	9.9	0.8	50092	52133	61	54	329	15.2	20.1	54.4	9.1	1.2	106944
55919	BROWNSVILLE	22895	454	19.2	29.3	42.7	5.5	3.3	50982	53719	64	58	393	10.9	22.4	37.2	23.7	5.9	119133
55920	BYRON	29992	2362	8.6	19.3	41.8	25.4	5.0	73121	75751	88	89	1974	3.0	4.4	51.3	37.2	4.2	159375
55921	CALEDONIA	22576	2029	22.7	28.3	40.2	5.8	3.1	48812	51818	58	50	1573	10.4	26.8	43.7	15.9	3.2	106748
55922	CANTON	15343	416	31.3	31.0	29.3	5.5	2.9	39534	40085	31	14	346	23.1	17.6	39.3	16.2	3.8	105000
55923	CHATFIELD	25302	1850	16.8	25.7	44.4	9.7	3.3	58052	60520	75	75	1459	6.4	8.9	52.0	26.7	6.0	141998
55924	CLAREMONT	21886	543	19.5	28.4	42.5	6.8	2.8	51676	53557	65	61	448	11.6	16.1	43.1	24.8	4.5	128521
55925	DAKOTA	24866	296	15.9	27.7	44.3	8.1	4.1	55454	58060	72	70	265	8.3	12.5	38.5	30.9	9.8	152315
55926	DEXTER	23037	240	24.2	27.9	37.9	5.8	4.2	47791	50764	56	46	205	12.2	16.1	46.3	18.0	7.3	122635
55927	DODGE CENTER	21689	1494	17.5	28.4	45.7	6.5	1.9	53302	55872	69	66	1184	10.7	18.8	51.4	18.0	1.1	120500
55929	DOVER	23240	367	17.2	30.8	39.2	10.6	2.2	52454	54408	67	64	285	6.3	10.5	38.9	34.0	10.2	155357
55932	ELGIN	25518	758	13.3	21.9	48.4	12.3	4.1	60775	62607	78	79	610	6.4	12.1	47.2	28.0	6.2	139175
55933	ELKTON	20936	110	20.9	32.7	37.3	7.3	1.8	47001	48965	54	43	89	7.9	21.3	46.1	18.0	6.7	119167
55934	EYOTA	27739	1208	11.8	25.8	39.5	18.5	4.4	63903	65954	82	83	974	6.3	10.9	52.4	26.6	3.9	138102
55935	FOUNTAIN	24553	272	12.1	31.3	43.8	11.4	1.5	55978	58382	73	72	231	4.3	16.0	39.4	31.6	8.7	150543
55936	GRAND MEADOW	25955	638	15.7	25.9	43.3	10.0	5.2	56665	58826	74	72	523	5.5	18.5	50.3	20.1	5.5	120173
55939	HARMONY	18442	903	29.3	31.1	33.1	4.8	1.7	40820	41837	35	18	725	13.0	24.4	44.4	15.4	2.8	106206
55940	HAYFIELD	24022	1061	14.9	26.4	46.0	9.3	3.4	57488	60560	75	74	874	10.0	14.8	47.0	23.6	4.7	130993
55941	HOKAH	25364	509	15.3	25.1	48.7	8.1	2.8	57599	61745	75	74	428	6.8	13.1	45.3	30.6	4.2	142460
55943	HOUSTON	21330	1300	21.8	31.2	39.3	5.5	2.2	47416	49737	55	44	1054	11.4	16.9	40.6	23.6	7.5	127518
55944	KASSON	25984	2521	13.0	24.4	44.7	13.1	4.8	62594	65910	81	81	2092	9.0	9.6	49.5	29.3	2.6	142559
55945	KELLOGG	24064	557	16.2	29.6	42.4	8.4	3.4	53199	55286	68	66	489	8.6	16.0	40.5	28.8	6.1	138908
55946	KENYON	24993	1398	15.4	23.2	48.6	8.6	4.2	59424	61544	77	76	1169	7.2	10.5	41.7	31.6	9.0	151589
55947	LA CRESCENT	27558	2863	12.7	24.1	45.7	12.8	4.7	61240	64813	79	80	2319	6.6	5.7	52.3	31.0	4.5	147440
55949	LANESBORO	24169	714	26.1	25.9	38.8	6.4	2.8	47470	49544	55	44	551	8.5	20.0	47.7	19.1	4.7	120678
55951	LE ROY	22901	593	20.1	36.3	36.6	4.4	2.7	45380	46964	49	35	488	15.6	27.5	43.6	10.0	3.3	96182
55952	LEWISTON	20963	775	18.3	26.3	47.2	5.5	2.6	52662	54059	67	64	620	11.3	10.8	43.2	29.0	5.6	138947
55953	LYLE	22581	461	16.3	31.5	41.0	6.9	4.3	51528	53291	65	60	387	9.6	16.3	54.8	14.7	4.7	118324
55954	MABEL	19299	741	30.2	36.2	28.1	4.6	0.9	36613	37642	22	7	615	18.7	33.2	39.0	6.7	2.4	87500
55955	MANTORVILLE	31314	933	7.7	17.0	45.9	19.1	10.3	76558	78324	90	90	839	3.2	4.4	35.4	47.3	9.7	198589
55956	MAZEPPA	23884	727	17.1	27.4	44.0	8.1	3.4	54430	56980	70	68	628	13.4	10.7	41.6	29.6	4.8	139904
55957	MILLVILLE	19145	206	17.5	34.5	40.8	6.3	1.0	47659	50835	56	45	161	6.8	11.8	42.9	28.0	10.6	143056
55959	MINNESOTA CITY	25885	462	14.3	25.1	45.0	12.1	3.5	58510	61485	76	75	408	14.7	11.3	38.7	34.3	1.0	141204
55960	ORONOCO	33809	1178	11.3	20.3	39.8	20.0	8.6	67265	69385	85	86	1058	18.4	6.3	25.0	41.8	8.4	175610
55961	OSTRANDER	24407	229	20.5	26.6	43.2	5.7	3.9	52125	53521	66	63	194	13.4	16.5	41.2	24.2	4.6	124107
55962	PETERSON	19549	348	19.0	32.8	39.7	6.0	2.6	48216	49747	57	48	280	9.3	13.9	40.4	28.2	8.2	143571
55963	PINE ISLAND	26149	1852	14.8	23.1	41.9	15.5	4.8	63069	65842	81	82	1584	9.2	7.1	37.1	41.2	5.4	166118
55964	PLAINVIEW	22366	1618	18.6	28.4	42.5	8.3	2.2	52785	55836	68	65	1300	12.2	13.5	53.8	18.8	1.8	123193
55965	PRESTON	24150	618	22.7	25.6	42.7	6.6	2.4	51267	52728	64	60	489	8.0	19.6	48.1	19.8	4.5	121994
55967	RACINE	23763	347	9.8	27.4	48.4	12.1	2.3	60745	62188	78	78	304	2.6	7.6	52.0	31.6	6.3	151282
55968	READS LANDING	25916	52	11.5	30.8	44.2	7.7	5.8	60000	61249	77	77	46	2.2	13.0	47.8	28.3	8.7	139286
55969	ROLLINGSTONE	24221	411	18.7	24.8	43.6	9.7	3.2	53759	55929	69	67	364	5.8	7.7	48.4	33.5	4.7	153922
55970	ROSE CREEK	23432	366	15.3	28.1	43.2	10.9	2.5	55208	57615	72	70	312	5.1	19.6	49.7	21.5	4.2	127451
55971	RUSHFORD	22408	1177	22.8	26.1	43.7	5.8	1.7	50614	51447	63	56	926	7.9	21.3	48.7	19.5	2.6	117045
55972	SAINT CHARLES	24345	1894	16.5	25.9	43.1	10.4	4.0	57683	60985	75	74	1385	8.3	9.2	48.1	30.5	3.8	141185
55973	SARGEANT	19898	136	24.3	27.9	38.2	5.9	3.7	47729	50970	56	45	116	12.9	16.4	45.7	18.1	6.9	122500
55974	SPRING GROVE	21344	1060	26.9	33.6	32.6	4.7	2.2	41825	43595	39	21	846	11.6	32.6	32.6	19.4	3.8	97778
55975	SPRING VALLEY	22587	1830	19.6	30.9	41.2	5.7	2.6	49382	51238	60	51	1457	10.6	18.3	47.8	19.8	3.6	123634
55976	STEWARTVILLE	26588	2951	15.8	24.1	40.6	16.2	3.4	62327	63947	80	81	2343	15.9	7.1	50.6	24.5	2.0	132557
55977	TAOPI	21603	103	17.5	30.1	40.8	7.8	3.9	51461	54460	65	60	93	7.5	16.1	37.6	25.8	12.9	141250
55979	UTICA	20525	287	18.1	26.8	46.7	5.6	2.8	52616	53851	67	64	226	13.7	10.2	36.3	31.9	8.0	142593
55981	WABASHA	25369	1755	22.6	27.3	38.9	7.3	4.0	50092	51698	61	54	1386	8.8	20.9	44.3	23.2	2.7	120507
55982	WALTHAM	21485	189	17.5	31.7	41.8	3.7	5.3	50437	51820	62	55	170	7.1	13.5	55.3	21.8	2.4	130357
55983	WANAMINGO	22701	600	22.5	23.7	42.3	8.7	2.8	52459	53885	67	64	493	10.3	9.1	48.3	27.4	4.9	142154
55985	WEST CONCORD	24018	850	18.9	23.8	45.4	9.1	2.8	56909	60759	74	73	728	5.1	22.1	44.6	23.8	4.4	129481
55987	WINONA	23863	13841	24.2	27.6	36.9	7.8	3.5	47793	50490	56	46	9124	7.6	12.4	51.4	26.4	2.1	134275
55990	WYKOFF	23562	368	18.8	36.1	37.5	4.6	3.0	45648	47344	50	36	313	13.4	22.7	40.6	17.9	5.4	113281
55991	ZUMBRO FALLS	26749	750	17.1	22.9	43.2	11.5	5.3	60098	62462	77	77	636	9.4	13.7	33.0	36.8	7.1	151220
55992	ZUMBROTA	28789	1758	14.7	23.8	44.4	10.8	6.3	61582	63941	79	80	1392	6.4	4.8	45.6	37.7	5.5	160606
56001	MANKATO	24858	17060	22.3	28.4	36.5	8.3	4.5	49218	51242	59	51	9926	11.9	9.1	42.4	33.0	3.5	150130
	MINNESOTA	31285		15.9	22.3	36.8	16.4	8.6	62767	65994				6.5	9.7	37.4	39.4	7.0	167369
	UNITED STATES	27277		20.9	24.4	35.3	11.7	7.6	54719	56938				9.3	13.1	31.6	32.6	13.5	162279

ZIP CODE #	POST OFFICE NAME	FINANCIAL SERVICES: Auto Loan	Home Loan	Invest-ments	Retire-ment Plans	THE HOME: Home Improvements: Home Repair	Lawn & Garden	Furnishings: Comput-ers & Hard-ware-Personal	Major Appli-ances	TV, Radio, Sound Equip-ment	Furni-ture	ENTERTAINMENT: Dine out/ Carry out	Sports Equip-ment	Fees & Tickets	Toys & Games	Travel	Cable TV	PERSONAL: Apparel & Services	Auto Repairs	Health Insur-ance	Pets & Supplies
55769	NASHWAUK	72	56	73	56	58	76	59	71	64	53	62	53	50	64	58	70	42	66	76	83
55771	ORR	82	63	96	62	68	86	64	81	68	60	67	59	54	66	67	74	45	74	82	94
55775	PENGILLY	96	92	114	90	96	110	86	102	92	83	91	73	85	88	94	98	61	96	108	118
55779	SAGINAW	93	104	90	107	101	103	93	97	92	93	92	76	99	94	98	92	65	93	96	114
55780	SAWYER	71	65	58	63	64	67	61	65	64	64	64	47	58	66	59	66	43	63	65	77
55781	SIDE LAKE	89	88	108	87	90	100	81	94	83	79	83	69	82	82	89	87	57	89	95	109
55783	STURGEON LAKE	91	70	109	69	76	95	71	90	75	66	74	66	60	73	74	81	49	83	90	105
55784	SWAN RIVER	75	69	68	72	70	81	68	76	70	61	69	58	62	71	68	74	47	71	79	89
55785	SWATARA	86	65	91	62	69	89	66	82	72	63	71	60	55	71	66	79	47	76	87	97
55787	TAMARACK	78	65	89	62	70	84	64	79	69	65	68	55	58	66	67	75	45	74	84	92
55790	TOWER	94	83	121	82	91	104	80	98	84	79	82	69	75	79	87	89	56	91	101	113
55792	VIRGINIA	68	67	65	67	66	73	70	70	73	66	73	52	69	71	69	77	50	71	80	83
55793	WARBA	82	66	80	66	68	85	66	80	71	61	70	60	57	71	66	77	47	73	82	94
55795	WILLOW RIVER	89	67	103	66	72	92	68	87	73	64	72	64	57	71	71	79	48	80	88	102
55797	WRENSHALL	85	78	77	81	79	91	76	86	79	69	77	65	71	80	76	83	53	80	89	100
55798	WRIGHT	87	64	88	63	66	89	65	82	72	61	71	61	53	72	65	79	47	75	85	97
55801	DULUTH	86	97	84	100	94	95	87	90	85	87	86	71	93	88	92	86	60	87	89	106
55802	DULUTH	47	42	48	45	44	49	55	49	59	51	58	36	53	52	52	62	41	56	64	60
55803	DULUTH	101	117	111	119	117	117	103	109	103	105	103	82	114	103	112	104	73	105	111	127
55804	DULUTH	99	119	109	121	117	118	104	108	104	106	105	82	117	105	114	106	74	105	112	126
55805	DULUTH	55	41	40	44	40	44	62	48	60	54	60	40	51	58	50	60	42	56	54	60
55806	DULUTH	58	49	44	51	46	51	62	53	62	57	62	43	56	62	54	63	44	59	59	66
55807	DULUTH	72	69	62	70	67	75	73	72	76	69	75	55	71	75	70	79	51	74	80	86
55808	DULUTH	74	71	63	70	68	75	74	72	76	71	75	55	71	76	70	78	52	74	79	86
55810	DULUTH	89	94	85	95	92	98	87	92	89	86	89	69	90	90	90	91	61	89	96	107
55811	DULUTH	91	99	94	100	98	102	94	96	95	93	95	71	99	94	97	97	66	95	102	111
55812	DULUTH	102	92	89	97	91	92	113	95	107	104	107	79	103	107	99	105	76	103	97	116
55901	ROCHESTER	125	129	116	131	124	118	127	121	123	131	125	97	130	127	125	120	88	122	117	142
55902	ROCHESTER	166	182	177	187	181	169	174	169	169	179	171	133	185	171	179	165	122	169	163	197
55904	ROCHESTER	97	95	85	97	91	94	99	94	98	97	99	74	97	100	95	98	69	97	97	112
55906	ROCHESTER	124	133	124	135	131	130	127	127	125	128	126	97	132	126	129	125	88	126	128	149
55909	ADAMS	92	64	101	64	67	97	70	87	73	57	72	72	52	72	70	80	47	82	92	108
55910	ALTURA	103	79	113	80	82	109	83	100	85	72	85	81	68	84	84	92	56	94	104	121
55912	AUSTIN	84	81	77	82	80	89	82	84	85	78	84	63	80	85	81	89	58	84	93	100
55917	BLOOMING PRAIRIE	92	81	89	83	83	97	83	92	85	76	83	71	75	85	82	89	57	87	96	109
55918	BROWNSDALE	80	79	67	81	74	86	79	79	80	74	80	63	78	82	77	83	55	79	87	96
55919	BROWNSVILLE	89	80	86	83	81	96	79	89	81	72	80	70	72	82	80	85	54	84	92	106
55920	BYRON	123	135	114	133	128	119	120	122	115	127	117	94	124	121	121	112	82	116	112	141
55921	CALEDONIA	87	76	82	77	75	91	79	85	81	73	80	67	72	81	78	85	54	83	91	102
55922	CANTON	84	58	93	58	61	89	64	80	67	52	66	66	47	66	64	73	43	75	84	98
55923	CHATFIELD	97	92	96	94	92	103	91	98	91	86	91	76	87	92	92	94	62	94	101	116
55924	CLAREMONT	93	81	90	83	82	100	81	93	83	72	82	72	72	84	81	88	55	86	96	110
55925	DAKOTA	91	101	89	104	99	100	91	95	90	91	90	74	96	92	96	90	63	91	94	112
55926	DEXTER	105	72	115	72	76	111	80	100	83	65	82	82	59	82	80	91	53	93	105	123
55927	DODGE CENTER	90	86	79	86	85	92	81	88	83	80	83	66	78	86	80	86	57	83	89	103
55929	DOVER	103	81	111	82	83	110	84	100	87	73	86	82	69	86	85	92	57	94	104	122
55932	ELGIN	107	107	96	105	102	102	99	102	97	102	99	78	97	101	98	96	68	98	97	120
55933	ELKTON	96	75	102	76	77	102	78	93	80	68	80	76	65	80	79	85	53	87	96	113
55934	EYOTA	110	111	101	109	107	107	102	106	100	105	102	82	101	104	102	100	70	102	101	125
55935	FOUNTAIN	89	98	86	100	95	98	88	92	87	88	87	72	93	89	93	87	61	89	92	109
55936	GRAND MEADOW	96	93	90	95	93	100	93	97	94	90	93	73	90	94	93	97	64	95	101	113
55939	HARMONY	83	59	88	58	61	88	65	80	70	55	68	63	50	69	63	77	45	75	86	96
55940	HAYFIELD	89	95	77	97	89	96	90	90	90	88	90	71	93	92	91	91	62	89	95	108
55941	HOKAH	90	97	87	100	95	99	89	94	88	87	88	73	92	90	93	89	61	89	94	110
55943	HOUSTON	88	72	89	74	74	94	74	86	76	65	75	69	63	76	74	81	50	81	90	103
55944	KASSON	101	109	93	107	104	102	99	100	98	103	99	76	102	102	100	97	69	98	98	118
55945	KELLOGG	107	82	125	81	88	112	85	105	88	76	88	80	70	86	88	95	58	98	106	125
55946	KENYON	96	94	88	96	90	103	92	95	93	87	93	76	90	94	92	96	63	94	102	115
55947	LA CRESCENT	97	104	97	105	103	103	100	101	99	98	99	78	103	100	103	100	70	100	102	118
55949	LANESBORO	85	69	84	70	71	87	75	83	77	68	76	64	65	76	73	82	51	80	88	99
55951	LE ROY	90	67	92	66	70	95	72	88	79	64	77	67	59	78	71	86	51	82	95	104
55952	LEWISTON	89	86	79	85	84	89	80	85	81	81	82	65	78	84	80	83	56	82	86	101
55953	LYLE	96	80	94	81	78	102	84	93	86	74	85	76	73	86	83	91	57	90	100	114
55954	MABEL	76	54	79	53	56	80	59	74	65	51	63	57	46	64	58	71	42	69	79	88
55955	MANTORVILLE	132	145	119	142	137	125	128	129	122	137	124	102	133	130	129	117	87	123	116	148
55956	MAZEPPA	92	93	86	96	92	100	87	95	88	83	87	73	86	90	89	91	60	89	96	110
55957	MILLVILLE	97	67	106	67	70	102	74	92	77	60	76	76	55	76	74	84	50	86	97	113
55959	MINNESOTA CITY	95	104	90	106	101	103	94	97	93	94	93	75	98	95	97	93	65	94	97	115
55960	ORONOCO	122	133	119	135	130	129	121	124	119	124	119	96	127	122	125	118	84	121	121	146
55961	OSTRANDER	109	75	119	75	78	115	83	103	86	67	85	85	61	85	83	94	55	96	109	127
55962	PETERSON	96	66	105	66	69	101	73	91	76	60	76	75	54	75	73	83	49	85	96	112
55963	PINE ISLAND	102	109	94	110	106	108	98	103	98	100	99	79	102	101	101	99	68	99	102	121
55964	PLAINVIEW	92	86	79	85	82	92	84	87	86	82	86	67	79	88	81	89	58	86	92	105
55965	PRESTON	93	71	96	72	74	97	78	90	81	69	80	71	64	80	77	86	53	86	96	108
55967	RACINE	93	105	90	108	102	103	94	98	92	94	93	76	100	95	99	92	65	94	97	115
55968	READS LANDING	116	80	127	80	83	122	88	110	92	72	91	91	65	90	88	100	59	103	116	135
55969	ROLLINGSTONE	88	97	86	99	94	97	87	91	86	87	86	72	92	88	92	86	60	88	91	108
55970	ROSE CREEK	103	88	99	90	90	110	89	103	92	78	90	80	78	93	89	98	61	95	107	121
55971	RUSHFORD	87	69	87	69	71	91	74	85	78	67	77	65	63	77	73	83	51	81	91	101
55972	SAINT CHARLES	100	90	88	90	91	99	92	96	95	90	93	71	86	95	88	98	64	95	101	113
55973	SARGEANT	105	72	115	72	76	111	80	100	83	65	83	82	59	82	80	91	54	93	105	123
55974	SPRING GROVE	89	61	98	61	64	94	68	85	71	55	70	70	50	70	68	77	46	79	90	104
55975	SPRING VALLEY	87	77	85	78	77	92	79	86	81	73	80	67	72	81	78	84	54	84	91	103
55976	STEWARTVILLE	97	104	90	102	99	97	98	97	96	99	97	75	100	99	98	95	68	96	95	114
55977	TAOPI	108	78	117	78	81	114	84	103	87	70	86	85	64	86	84	94	56	96	108	126
55979	UTICA	96	84	82	82	83	91	81	88	84	82	84	66	75	87	78	87	57	85	89	105
55981	WABASHA	92	81	100	81	83	98	81	93	85	77	84	69	75	83	83	90	57	89	97	109
55982	WALTHAM	109	75	120	75	79	116	84	104	87	68	86	86	61	85	83	95	56	97	110	128
55983	WANAMINGO	89	83	83	86	84	96	81	91	83	74	82	69	76	84	82	87	56	84	93	106
55985	WEST CONCORD	90	90	82	92	86	97	87	90	88	83	87	72	87	89	88	90	60	89	95	109
55987	WINONA	81	77	72	79	76	81	84	79	84	80	83	62	80	83	79	85	58	82	85	95
55990	WYKOFF	101	70	111	70	73	107	77	96	80	63	80	80	57	79	77	88	52	90	102	118
55991	ZUMBRO FALLS	103	99	98	102	100	111	95	105	96	89	95	81	91	98	97	100	65	98	107	123
55992	ZUMBROTA	98	105	99	105	104	105	102	103	101	100	101	79	105	102	104	102	71	102	104	120
56001	MANKATO	87	76	70	78	73	78	92	80	89	85	89	65	83	90	81	89	62	86	83	97
	MINNESOTA	113	113	112	114	112	114	112	113	111	111	112	88	112	113	112	112	78	112	113	133
	UNITED STATES	100	100	100	100	100	100	100	100	100	100	100	100	100	100	100	100	100	100	100	100

 56003-56141

ZIP CODE #	POST OFFICE NAME	COUNTY FIPS CODE	POPULATION 2000	POPULATION 2009	POPULATION 2014	2000-2009 ANNUAL RATE % Rate	2000-2009 ANNUAL RATE State Centile	HOUSEHOLDS 2000	HOUSEHOLDS 2009	HOUSEHOLDS 2014	HOUSEHOLDS % Annual Rate 2000-2009	HOUSEHOLDS 2009 Average HH Size	FAMILIES 2000	FAMILIES 2009	FAMILIES % Annual Rate 2000-2009
56003	MANKATO	103	12778	14119	14719	1.1	79	5094	5811	6104	1.4	2.43	3467	3820	1.1
56007	ALBERT LEA	047	22644	21875	21240	-0.4	30	9395	9292	9078	-0.1	2.30	6065	5770	-0.5
56009	ALDEN	047	1879	1806	1754	-0.4	30	744	738	722	-0.1	2.45	552	530	-0.4
56010	AMBOY	013	1294	1334	1349	0.3	58	528	555	565	0.5	2.39	387	391	0.1
56011	BELLE PLAINE	139	5777	9242	10957	5.2	99	2048	3333	3981	5.4	2.71	1485	2325	5.0
56013	BLUE EARTH	043	4937	4561	4361	-0.9	12	2046	1927	1851	-0.6	2.26	1322	1197	-1.1
56014	BRICELYN	043	883	802	761	-1.0	9	372	344	328	-0.8	2.33	245	218	-1.3
56016	CLARKS GROVE	047	933	883	854	-0.6	22	361	353	344	-0.2	2.39	272	259	-0.5
56017	CLEVELAND	079	1520	1814	1945	1.9	90	576	705	762	2.2	2.57	431	508	1.8
56019	COMFREY	033	798	766	747	-0.4	30	329	323	316	-0.2	2.36	251	239	-0.5
56020	CONGER	047	34	31	29	-1.0	9	15	14	13	-0.7	2.21	11	10	-1.0
56021	COURTLAND	103	1253	1377	1447	1.0	77	423	483	513	1.4	2.85	338	376	1.2
56022	DARFUR	165	277	251	239	-1.1	7	122	112	108	-0.9	2.24	93	83	-1.2
56023	DELAVAN	043	620	578	552	-0.8	15	259	247	239	-0.5	2.34	193	178	-0.9
56024	EAGLE LAKE	013	2285	3146	3478	3.5	96	822	1170	1308	3.9	2.69	609	835	3.5
56025	EASTON	043	591	539	512	-1.0	9	219	206	197	-0.7	2.62	168	153	-1.0
56026	ELLENDALE	147	1566	1602	1621	0.2	54	594	623	635	0.5	2.57	440	447	0.2
56027	ELMORE	043	1014	982	952	-0.3	35	413	410	400	-0.1	2.19	274	262	-0.5
56028	ELYSIAN	079	1317	1586	1707	2.0	91	515	645	703	2.5	2.46	370	443	2.0
56029	EMMONS	047	578	531	506	-0.9	12	238	226	218	-0.6	2.35	181	168	-0.8
56030	ESSIG	015	142	134	129	-0.6	22	48	47	45	-0.2	2.83	38	36	-0.6
56031	FAIRMONT	091	12956	12364	12003	-0.5	26	5473	5345	5225	-0.3	2.25	3571	3360	-0.7
56032	FREEBORN	047	574	527	501	-0.9	12	231	218	210	-0.6	2.42	173	158	-1.0
56033	FROST	043	389	366	350	-0.7	18	176	169	163	-0.4	2.17	120	111	-0.8
56034	GARDEN CITY	013	448	514	546	1.5	85	178	211	226	1.9	2.43	135	154	1.4
56035	GENEVA	047	523	474	450	-1.1	7	209	195	187	-0.7	2.42	153	138	-1.1
56036	GLENVILLE	047	1475	1361	1298	-0.9	12	616	589	567	-0.5	2.31	433	397	-0.9
56037	GOOD THUNDER	013	1047	1105	1126	0.6	67	384	412	424	0.8	2.68	289	299	0.4
56039	GRANADA	091	1097	1074	1056	-0.2	39	428	433	431	0.1	2.48	304	296	-0.3
56041	HANSKA	015	1127	1081	1051	-0.4	30	439	434	426	-0.1	2.49	325	311	-0.5
56042	HARTLAND	047	599	547	523	-1.0	9	250	236	227	-0.6	2.31	184	168	-1.0
56043	HAYWARD	047	593	713	732	2.0	91	237	294	304	2.4	2.40	179	215	2.0
56044	HENDERSON	143	2094	2237	2254	0.7	69	731	794	802	0.9	2.80	524	551	0.5
56045	HOLLANDALE	047	1302	1160	1097	-1.2	5	509	466	445	-0.9	2.48	391	349	-1.2
56047	HUNTLEY	043	33	30	29	-1.0	9	16	15	14	-0.7	2.00	12	11	-0.9
56048	JANESVILLE	161	3692	3673	3714	-0.1	44	1335	1428	1454	0.7	2.55	992	1028	0.4
56050	KASOTA	079	2164	2403	2534	1.1	79	837	962	1024	1.5	2.49	645	721	1.2
56051	KIESTER	043	778	736	707	-0.6	22	344	331	320	-0.4	2.22	241	224	-0.8
56052	KILKENNY	079	707	783	818	1.1	79	277	317	334	1.5	2.47	209	231	1.1
56054	LAFAYETTE	103	1674	1768	1802	0.6	67	601	658	679	1.0	2.62	462	489	0.6
56055	LAKE CRYSTAL	013	3812	4030	4127	0.6	67	1454	1575	1629	0.9	2.52	1041	1082	0.4
56057	LE CENTER	079	3539	3542	3553	0.0	48	1311	1338	1352	0.2	2.59	925	910	-0.2
56058	LE SUEUR	079	6042	6529	6748	0.8	72	2328	2590	2701	1.2	2.48	1646	1771	0.8
56060	LEWISVILLE	165	561	507	484	-1.1	7	222	203	194	-1.0	2.50	158	140	-1.3
56062	MADELIA	165	3016	2943	2889	-0.3	35	1154	1144	1127	-0.1	2.49	758	724	-0.5
56063	MADISON LAKE	013	2520	2586	2647	0.3	58	962	1015	1048	0.6	2.55	720	735	0.2
56065	MAPLETON	013	2470	2571	2619	0.4	61	927	1000	1030	0.8	2.51	689	716	0.4
56068	MINNESOTA LAKE	043	1010	933	893	-0.9	12	414	394	380	-0.5	2.36	287	264	-0.9
56069	MONTGOMERY	079	4053	4713	5021	1.6	86	1545	1843	1978	1.9	2.55	1030	1179	1.5
56071	NEW PRAGUE	079	9318	12962	14867	3.6	97	3207	4532	5227	3.8	2.82	2471	3386	3.5
56072	NEW RICHLAND	161	2330	2262	2217	-0.3	35	900	901	889	0.0	2.44	638	616	-0.4
56073	NEW ULM	015	16357	15890	15604	-0.3	35	6474	6531	6464	0.1	2.32	4347	4235	-0.3
56074	NICOLLET	103	1806	1944	2013	0.8	72	673	755	792	1.3	2.57	503	545	0.9
56075	NORTHROP	091	13	13	13	0.0	48	4	4	4	0.0	3.25	3	3	0.0
56078	PEMBERTON	013	903	927	937	0.3	58	320	338	344	0.6	2.70	241	245	0.2
56080	SAINT CLAIR	013	913	980	1010	0.8	72	322	355	370	1.1	2.76	245	261	0.7
56081	SAINT JAMES	165	6656	6211	5982	-0.7	18	2584	2420	2329	-0.7	2.53	1750	1579	-1.1
56082	SAINT PETER	103	11525	12363	12549	0.8	72	3593	3913	4023	0.9	2.47	2331	2438	0.5
56083	SANBORN	127	820	732	695	-1.2	5	317	293	280	-0.8	2.50	235	210	-1.2
56085	SLEEPY EYE	015	5858	5776	5684	-0.2	39	2270	2302	2279	0.2	2.46	1555	1517	-0.3
56087	SPRINGFIELD	015	3268	3106	3027	-0.5	26	1273	1238	1210	-0.3	2.42	837	783	-0.7
56088	TRUMAN	091	2033	1927	1863	-0.6	22	801	780	760	-0.3	2.33	542	509	-0.7
56089	TWIN LAKES	047	740	675	642	-1.0	9	303	285	273	-0.7	2.37	230	210	-1.0
56090	VERNON CENTER	013	907	947	962	0.5	63	335	357	366	0.7	2.65	262	270	0.3
56091	WALDORF	161	444	432	422	-0.3	35	175	176	173	0.1	2.45	136	132	-0.3
56093	WASECA	161	12989	13216	13206	0.2	54	4619	4762	4782	0.3	2.52	3204	3196	0.0
56096	WATERVILLE	079	2800	2969	3062	0.6	67	1114	1211	1254	0.9	2.38	787	826	0.5
56097	WELLS	043	4000	3630	3453	-1.0	9	1576	1446	1377	-0.9	2.45	1087	962	-1.3
56098	WINNEBAGO	043	2311	2069	1966	-1.2	5	966	880	840	-1.0	2.27	645	565	-1.4
56101	WINDOM	033	5787	5523	5321	-0.5	26	2423	2355	2279	-0.3	2.26	1605	1504	-0.7
56110	ADRIAN	105	1953	1964	1944	0.1	51	724	745	740	0.3	2.57	508	506	0.0
56111	ALPHA	063	643	626	610	-0.3	35	250	249	244	0.0	2.51	198	192	-0.3
56113	ARCO	081	368	315	294	-1.7	2	154	136	128	-1.3	2.26	119	102	-1.7
56114	AVOCA	101	438	408	391	-0.8	15	186	179	173	-0.4	2.28	135	125	-0.8
56115	BALATON	083	1322	1236	1193	-0.7	18	537	517	502	-0.4	2.39	391	364	-0.8
56116	BEAVER CREEK	133	641	619	613	-0.4	30	247	248	248	0.0	2.50	200	197	-0.2
56117	BIGELOW	105	482	455	442	-0.6	22	173	167	163	-0.4	2.72	135	127	-0.7
56118	BINGHAM LAKE	033	615	575	550	-0.7	18	226	211	202	-0.7	2.63	180	164	-1.0
56119	BREWSTER	105	898	858	838	-0.5	26	338	331	324	-0.2	2.59	253	241	-0.5
56120	BUTTERFIELD	165	894	849	821	-0.6	22	347	336	326	-0.3	2.53	245	229	-0.7
56121	CEYLON	091	753	631	592	-1.9	1	314	272	258	-1.5	2.32	221	185	-1.9
56122	CHANDLER	101	656	601	572	-0.9	12	238	223	215	-0.7	2.70	182	167	-0.9
56123	CURRIE	101	778	716	683	-0.9	12	339	324	313	-0.5	2.21	259	240	-0.8
56125	DOVRAY	101	9	8	8	-1.3	4	3	3	3	0.0	2.67	2	2	0.0
56127	DUNNELL	091	451	371	346	-2.1	1	184	156	147	-1.8	2.38	128	104	-2.2
56128	EDGERTON	117	2124	2082	2048	-0.2	39	842	858	852	0.2	2.36	609	599	-0.2
56129	ELLSWORTH	105	731	695	677	-0.5	26	297	289	282	-0.3	2.27	193	181	-0.7
56131	FULDA	101	2365	2350	2317	-0.1	44	928	947	939	0.2	2.40	633	622	-0.2
56132	GARVIN	083	488	480	469	-0.2	39	199	202	199	0.2	2.38	156	154	-0.1
56134	HARDWICK	133	448	429	424	-0.5	26	177	176	175	-0.1	2.44	130	125	-0.4
56136	HENDRICKS	081	1259	1178	1124	-0.7	18	509	484	465	-0.5	2.25	330	301	-1.0
56137	HERON LAKE	063	1310	1273	1245	-0.3	35	484	479	470	-0.1	2.55	330	313	-0.6
56138	HILLS	133	1016	1068	1080	0.5	63	378	411	419	0.9	2.50	277	288	0.4
56139	HOLLAND	117	655	551	513	-1.9	1	265	230	216	-1.5	2.40	206	175	-1.7
56141	IONA	101	389	373	361	-0.5	26	149	148	144	-0.1	2.52	104	100	-0.4
	MINNESOTA					0.9					1.1	2.48			0.7
	UNITED STATES					1.0					1.1	2.59			0.9

ZIP CODE #	POST OFFICE NAME	RACE (%) White 2000	White 2009	Black 2000	Black 2009	Asian/Pacific 2000	Asian/Pacific 2009	% Hispanic Origin 2000	% Hispanic Origin 2009	2009 AGE DISTRIBUTION (%) 0-4	5-9	10-14	15-19	20-24	25-44	45-64	65-84	85+	18+	MEDIAN AGE 2009	% 2009 Males	% 2009 Females
56003	MANKATO	96.6	95.4	0.6	0.8	1.3	1.9	1.5	2.3	7.2	6.6	6.3	6.1	6.7	31.2	25.7	9.0	1.2	76.3	34.9	49.5	50.5
56007	ALBERT LEA	93.9	91.5	0.3	0.4	0.7	1.0	8.2	11.9	6.1	6.0	5.9	6.0	5.6	23.1	27.4	15.8	4.1	78.3	42.7	48.4	51.6
56009	ALDEN	98.3	97.3	0.1	0.1	0.4	0.6	1.9	3.0	6.0	6.5	6.4	6.3	4.7	23.6	29.5	14.5	2.7	77.3	42.5	51.7	48.3
56010	AMBOY	99.0	98.7	0.1	0.1	0.1	0.1	0.9	1.3	4.9	5.5	5.8	6.7	5.0	22.5	32.2	13.9	3.4	79.5	44.6	51.9	48.1
56011	BELLE PLAINE	97.5	96.8	0.1	0.1	0.6	0.7	1.1	2.3	7.2	7.2	7.2	7.2	5.9	26.3	26.6	10.2	2.2	73.8	37.5	50.1	49.9
56013	BLUE EARTH	97.0	95.8	0.2	0.2	0.4	0.6	3.8	5.3	5.2	5.3	5.7	6.7	5.2	21.0	28.5	16.6	5.8	79.5	45.6	48.2	51.8
56014	BRICELYN	98.0	97.3	0.6	0.7	0.1	0.1	2.8	4.0	5.2	6.4	6.4	6.2	4.2	20.3	29.6	18.3	3.4	78.1	45.8	52.2	47.8
56016	CLARKS GROVE	98.6	98.2	0.2	0.3	0.3	0.3	2.8	4.4	4.8	6.0	7.2	8.8	4.3	22.0	27.9	16.1	2.9	75.7	42.9	51.4	48.6
56017	CLEVELAND	97.8	96.9	0.1	0.1	1.2	1.8	1.1	1.9	6.0	6.5	7.1	6.9	4.7	25.0	31.4	10.7	1.5	76.1	40.6	51.8	48.2
56019	COMFREY	98.1	97.3	0.0	0.1	0.9	1.2	1.1	1.8	5.9	6.4	6.5	7.2	4.4	22.8	29.2	15.1	2.3	76.0	42.8	51.8	48.2
56020	CONGER	100.0	100.0	0.0	0.0	0.0	0.0	3.0	0.0	6.5	6.5	6.5	6.5	6.5	25.8	29.0	12.9	0.0	74.2	38.8	51.6	48.4
56021	COURTLAND	98.4	97.7	0.0	0.0	0.4	0.6	1.6	2.5	6.8	7.8	7.9	7.5	5.0	24.7	30.9	8.4	1.1	72.8	38.3	50.6	49.4
56022	DARFUR	96.0	94.4	0.0	0.0	0.4	0.8	2.9	4.4	5.6	6.4	6.4	6.4	4.4	19.5	32.7	15.9	2.8	77.7	45.7	52.6	47.4
56023	DELAVAN	98.7	98.1	0.2	0.3	0.2	0.2	1.5	2.1	4.0	5.7	6.2	6.9	3.3	21.3	33.2	17.1	2.2	79.6	46.7	52.9	47.1
56024	EAGLE LAKE	97.3	96.4	0.5	0.8	0.6	0.9	1.2	1.7	7.9	8.1	7.9	7.0	5.6	29.9	25.9	7.0	0.7	71.7	33.9	49.7	50.3
56025	EASTON	97.6	96.8	0.5	0.6	0.2	0.2	1.2	1.7	3.3	6.5	7.2	8.5	3.0	21.5	32.3	16.3	1.3	77.4	44.9	51.9	48.1
56026	ELLENDALE	99.1	98.8	0.1	0.1	0.3	0.4	1.2	1.9	5.6	6.1	6.3	6.8	5.3	23.7	32.1	11.5	2.7	77.7	42.3	51.9	48.1
56027	ELMORE	93.8	91.8	1.4	1.8	0.9	1.2	3.8	5.4	5.6	5.8	7.6	12.0	3.9	17.6	27.3	16.9	3.3	71.8	42.4	51.4	48.6
56028	ELYSIAN	99.2	98.9	0.0	0.0	0.2	0.2	0.8	1.3	5.9	6.5	6.8	6.2	4.0	24.2	30.6	13.9	1.8	76.9	42.3	50.8	49.2
56029	EMMONS	97.6	96.4	0.3	0.6	0.2	0.2	2.4	4.0	4.9	5.5	5.8	6.2	4.0	23.2	32.6	15.3	2.6	79.8	45.3	49.2	50.8
56030	ESSIG	100.0	98.5	0.0	0.0	0.0	0.7	0.7	0.7	7.5	9.0	8.2	6.7	5.2	23.1	28.4	10.4	1.5	70.9	37.9	56.0	44.0
56031	FAIRMONT	96.1	94.6	0.4	0.5	0.6	0.9	2.7	4.0	5.7	5.6	6.0	6.6	5.8	21.9	29.2	15.2	4.1	78.5	43.8	48.5	51.5
56032	FREEBORN	98.8	98.5	0.0	0.0	0.3	0.4	0.5	0.8	6.3	6.3	6.5	6.6	4.4	23.3	30.0	14.2	2.5	77.0	42.8	52.6	47.4
56033	FROST	96.9	95.6	0.0	0.0	0.5	0.5	3.6	5.2	5.7	6.3	6.0	6.6	4.4	23.2	32.8	13.1	1.9	78.4	43.3	55.5	44.5
56034	GARDEN CITY	98.0	97.1	0.2	0.2	0.2	0.4	1.6	2.3	5.3	5.8	6.6	6.4	4.5	23.2	33.3	13.2	1.8	78.0	43.8	50.0	50.0
56035	GENEVA	98.7	98.1	0.0	0.0	0.2	0.2	2.9	4.4	6.3	7.2	7.4	6.8	4.6	23.8	30.6	11.0	2.3	74.3	40.6	50.0	50.0
56036	GLENVILLE	98.8	98.2	0.0	0.0	0.3	0.6	1.0	1.5	5.7	6.2	6.5	6.2	3.9	24.8	29.8	14.6	2.3	77.8	42.8	52.2	47.8
56037	GOOD THUNDER	98.3	97.6	0.1	0.2	0.4	0.5	0.8	1.0	8.0	8.0	8.1	7.2	5.6	25.6	25.8	10.0	1.7	71.6	36.6	50.2	49.8
56039	GRANADA	98.1	97.1	0.0	0.0	0.1	0.2	2.0	3.0	5.5	6.2	6.8	6.8	4.1	21.7	32.8	13.9	2.2	77.1	44.0	51.6	48.4
56041	HANSKA	98.9	98.5	0.2	0.3	0.2	0.3	1.0	1.4	6.8	6.9	6.9	6.6	4.2	26.7	27.1	12.8	2.0	75.2	39.4	51.3	48.7
56042	HARTLAND	98.3	97.3	0.0	0.0	0.0	0.0	1.3	2.2	5.1	5.5	6.0	6.6	5.1	23.8	31.4	14.4	2.0	79.3	43.4	51.2	48.8
56043	HAYWARD	98.0	97.1	0.0	0.0	0.0	0.0	1.9	2.9	6.2	6.9	7.0	7.3	3.5	21.5	31.1	14.6	2.0	74.9	43.2	50.6	49.4
56044	HENDERSON	97.6	96.6	0.0	0.0	0.4	0.6	3.2	4.8	6.9	7.2	7.5	7.8	5.1	25.9	27.9	10.6	1.2	73.7	38.4	51.5	48.5
56045	HOLLANDALE	98.0	97.0	0.1	0.1	0.2	0.3	2.7	4.3	5.6	6.2	6.6	6.8	5.2	23.1	31.6	12.8	2.2	77.3	42.5	50.8	49.2
56047	HUNTLEY	97.0	96.7	0.0	0.0	0.0	0.0	6.1	6.7	6.7	6.7	6.7	6.7	6.7	26.7	26.7	13.3	0.0	73.3	37.5	50.0	50.0
56048	JANESVILLE	97.2	97.1	0.9	0.7	0.3	0.5	1.3	1.5	7.3	7.8	7.6	5.9	5.1	27.7	26.1	10.2	2.3	73.4	37.0	50.7	49.3
56050	KASOTA	98.2	97.7	0.2	0.3	0.2	0.2	1.0	1.6	5.3	5.7	6.7	6.7	4.7	24.2	34.9	10.7	1.2	78.5	42.7	51.9	48.1
56051	KIESTER	98.6	98.2	0.3	0.4	0.1	0.1	1.4	1.9	5.6	6.0	6.5	6.5	3.9	20.7	30.2	17.1	3.5	77.9	45.5	52.0	48.0
56052	KILKENNY	98.4	97.7	0.0	0.0	0.3	0.4	1.4	2.3	5.6	6.1	6.4	6.5	4.7	24.5	31.2	13.5	1.4	77.9	42.6	51.0	49.0
56054	LAFAYETTE	99.2	98.8	0.0	0.1	0.1	0.2	0.7	1.1	6.7	7.4	7.6	7.2	4.6	23.0	29.1	11.5	2.9	73.5	40.5	51.2	48.8
56055	LAKE CRYSTAL	98.2	97.5	0.3	0.5	0.3	0.5	0.8	1.1	6.9	7.0	7.1	6.4	5.0	26.0	27.3	11.2	3.1	74.6	39.0	50.6	49.4
56057	LE CENTER	95.5	93.4	0.0	0.0	0.4	0.5	6.5	9.8	6.7	6.6	6.6	6.8	5.9	25.9	26.7	11.8	3.0	76.1	38.9	49.5	50.5
56058	LE SUEUR	94.4	92.0	0.2	0.3	0.3	0.4	6.6	10.0	6.3	6.3	6.5	7.4	6.2	24.8	27.8	12.1	2.7	76.1	39.8	49.4	50.6
56060	LEWISVILLE	94.7	92.3	0.7	1.0	0.2	0.2	4.8	7.5	7.5	8.1	8.3	7.1	4.3	19.1	28.2	15.2	2.2	71.8	41.7	49.9	50.1
56062	MADELIA	88.3	83.6	0.5	0.7	0.4	0.5	16.6	23.6	7.1	6.7	7.1	7.1	5.2	24.0	24.4	14.0	4.4	74.2	39.2	48.3	51.7
56063	MADISON LAKE	98.5	97.9	0.2	0.3	0.5	0.8	1.1	1.6	5.9	6.5	6.9	6.4	4.1	25.5	31.2	12.2	1.2	76.7	41.5	50.6	49.4
56065	MAPLETON	97.9	97.2	0.0	0.0	0.4	0.5	2.3	3.4	7.0	6.3	6.5	7.4	5.0	23.5	25.5	14.3	4.6	75.7	40.8	50.1	49.9
56068	MINNESOTA LAKE	99.4	99.4	0.0	0.0	0.0	0.0	0.7	1.0	4.7	5.1	5.6	6.1	5.9	23.2	31.7	14.4	3.3	80.7	44.5	51.8	48.2
56069	MONTGOMERY	95.0	92.7	0.2	0.3	0.3	0.4	7.2	11.1	7.5	7.3	7.7	7.1	5.5	26.4	26.1	10.8	1.7	73.1	36.9	50.8	49.2
56071	NEW PRAGUE	98.6	98.2	0.1	0.1	0.3	0.4	0.8	1.3	7.6	8.2	8.2	7.7	4.8	25.7	25.5	10.2	2.2	70.8	37.0	49.1	50.9
56072	NEW RICHLAND	99.0	98.9	0.0	0.0	0.2	0.2	1.1	1.2	6.0	6.9	7.5	6.7	4.8	21.8	27.4	14.5	4.5	75.2	42.1	50.9	49.1
56073	NEW ULM	98.3	96.1	0.1	1.3	0.5	0.7	1.1	2.1	5.1	5.4	5.8	8.2	8.1	23.6	28.4	13.1	2.3	79.8	40.1	49.9	50.1
56074	NICOLLET	98.7	98.4	0.1	0.1	0.4	0.6	0.6	0.8	5.7	6.3	6.8	7.1	4.7	26.1	31.4	10.3	1.5	76.8	40.1	51.1	48.9
56075	NORTHROP	100.0	100.0	0.0	0.0	0.0	0.0	0.0	0.0	0.0	0.0	0.0	7.7	0.0	23.1	69.2	0.0	0.0	92.3	49.2	69.2	30.8
56078	PEMBERTON	98.6	98.1	0.0	0.0	0.2	0.3	2.0	2.8	6.6	7.1	7.2	6.4	4.1	24.8	29.2	11.8	2.8	75.0	40.6	52.4	47.6
56080	SAINT CLAIR	99.8	99.6	0.1	0.2	0.0	0.0	0.5	0.8	7.2	7.7	7.8	7.1	4.7	28.3	27.2	8.6	1.4	72.8	36.9	51.1	48.9
56081	SAINT JAMES	87.3	82.8	0.3	0.4	0.5	0.7	17.4	23.9	7.6	7.6	7.5	7.1	5.3	23.2	24.8	13.6	3.3	72.8	37.7	48.6	51.4
56082	SAINT PETER	94.9	93.1	1.4	1.9	1.4	1.9	2.6	3.8	5.0	4.9	5.2	13.2	16.7	21.9	21.3	9.2	2.5	82.2	29.1	49.7	50.3
56083	SANBORN	98.8	98.4	0.0	0.1	0.1	0.3	0.6	0.8	5.9	5.9	6.7	6.4	3.8	23.9	29.9	14.6	2.9	77.5	43.2	53.1	46.9
56085	SLEEPY EYE	96.0	94.3	0.2	0.2	0.3	0.4	4.9	7.3	6.5	6.6	6.8	7.4	5.4	22.4	27.1	13.6	4.1	74.9	41.1	49.8	50.2
56087	SPRINGFIELD	98.5	98.0	0.0	0.0	0.5	0.6	1.6	2.4	6.1	6.1	6.4	7.1	5.6	20.7	27.5	15.4	5.0	76.6	43.2	48.7	51.3
56088	TRUMAN	99.1	98.8	0.1	0.2	0.0	0.1	0.8	1.2	4.9	5.4	5.8	6.6	4.9	18.8	29.8	17.2	6.6	79.6	47.4	48.1	51.9
56089	TWIN LAKES	98.8	98.4	0.1	0.1	0.1	0.1	1.5	2.2	4.4	5.0	5.3	6.2	5.0	22.4	34.4	15.3	1.9	81.3	46.0	51.0	49.0
56090	VERNON CENTER	99.6	99.4	0.0	0.0	0.1	0.2	0.8	1.2	6.5	6.9	7.4	7.0	4.2	23.9	28.5	13.3	2.3	74.9	41.0	51.7	48.3
56091	WALDORF	98.9	98.8	0.0	0.0	0.2	0.2	1.3	1.4	6.3	7.6	7.6	5.6	3.5	23.8	30.1	13.7	1.9	75.0	41.3	52.8	47.2
56093	WASECA	93.0	92.5	3.1	3.4	0.6	0.7	3.8	3.9	6.7	6.8	6.7	6.2	6.6	28.9	26.1	9.6	2.4	76.4	36.5	52.5	47.5
56096	WATERVILLE	97.9	97.4	0.1	0.1	0.3	0.4	0.4	0.7	5.7	5.9	6.1	6.0	4.8	23.9	30.1	14.4	3.1	78.3	43.3	49.4	50.6
56097	WELLS	97.1	95.9	0.1	0.1	0.5	0.7	3.9	5.5	6.6	7.0	6.7	6.0	5.0	21.0	27.7	15.4	4.7	75.9	43.0	49.8	50.2
56098	WINNEBAGO	97.0	96.0	0.0	0.0	0.5	0.7	4.8	6.7	4.9	5.3	5.5	5.8	4.9	21.5	29.7	17.6	4.8	80.8	46.5	50.0	50.0
56101	WINDOM	97.5	96.7	0.3	0.4	0.6	0.9	1.5	2.2	5.4	5.7	6.2	6.6	5.8	21.6	28.6	15.6	4.3	78.5	43.9	48.5	51.5
56110	ADRIAN	97.1	95.5	0.2	0.3	0.4	0.7	2.4	4.0	6.3	6.7	7.3	7.6	4.1	23.7	26.4	13.7	4.1	74.6	41.0	50.3	49.7
56111	ALPHA	99.4	98.9	0.0	0.0	0.3	0.6	0.6	1.0	5.6	6.1	6.5	6.2	4.2	22.0	32.7	14.2	2.4	78.0	44.5	52.2	47.8
56113	ARCO	98.9	98.7	0.0	0.0	0.0	0.0	0.5	1.0	5.7	6.3	6.7	5.4	3.8	22.9	29.8	16.2	3.2	77.8	44.3	51.1	48.9
56114	AVOCA	99.1	99.0	0.0	0.0	0.0	0.0	0.0	0.0	4.9	6.6	8.3	7.6	2.7	22.5	30.9	15.0	1.5	74.3	43.1	54.2	45.8
56115	BALATON	98.6	98.2	0.1	0.1	0.2	0.2	0.8	1.3	7.3	7.5	7.2	6.5	4.8	23.9	27.6	12.3	2.9	73.9	39.0	49.9	50.1
56116	BEAVER CREEK	99.2	98.9	0.0	0.0	0.2	0.3	0.2	0.3	6.3	7.3	7.1	5.8	4.2	23.4	31.5	12.8	1.6	75.6	40.9	50.6	49.4
56117	BIGELOW	97.7	96.5	0.0	0.0	0.4	0.4	2.1	3.3	7.7	8.1	7.9	6.4	4.2	23.5	28.8	11.6	1.8	72.1	38.8	51.4	48.6
56118	BINGHAM LAKE	95.9	94.4	0.8	1.0	1.5	1.9	2.0	3.0	5.9	7.7	9.7	8.5	4.0	23.3	26.4	13.0	1.4	71.0	39.5	51.5	48.5
56119	BREWSTER	97.4	96.2	0.1	0.2	0.3	0.5	1.8	3.0	7.7	8.0	7.8	6.5	4.3	24.6	27.5	11.3	2.2	72.3	39.0	51.4	48.6
56120	BUTTERFIELD	88.7	84.7	0.0	0.0	5.6	7.3	11.6	16.8	6.9	5.9	7.8	8.6	5.8	20.7	28.5	13.9	1.9	73.7	40.7	51.7	48.3
56121	CEYLON	98.5	98.1	0.0	0.0	0.5	0.6	1.2	1.7	4.8	5.5	5.9	6.0	4.1	21.9	34.2	15.1	2.5	80.0	46.1	52.8	47.2
56122	CHANDLER	98.5	98.0	0.0	0.0	0.0	0.0	6.3	9.5	5.8	6.5	7.2	7.7	4.5	22.1	31.4	12.1	2.7	75.7	41.8	53.9	46.1
56123	CURRIE	99.1	98.7	0.1	0.1	0.0	0.3	0.5	0.6	4.5	4.9	5.7	5.6	3.8	20.5	32.4	20.8	1.8	81.4	48.3	51.1	48.9
56125	DOVRAY	100.0	100.0	0.0	0.0	0.0	0.0	0.0	0.0	0.0	0.0	0.0	0.0	0.0	12.5	87.5	0.0	0.0	100.0	50.0	62.5	37.5
56127	DUNNELL	98.4	97.6	0.0	0.0	0.4	0.5	1.3	2.2	4.9	5.7	5.9	6.2	4.3	21.8	34.0	14.6	2.7	79.5	45.7	52.8	47.2
56128	EDGERTON	98.5	97.9	0.0	0.0	0.4	0.7	0.8	1.3	5.3	5.9	6.3	6.5	4.9	20.4	27.5	18.0	5.3	77.7	45.5	50.2	49.8
56129	ELLSWORTH	98.5	97.8	0.1	0.1	0.0	0.0	0.8	1.4	5.9	6.5	6.3	6.0	3.9	22.6	26.9	15.5	6.3	77.3	43.9	49.6	50.4
56131	FULDA	97.5	96.5	0.1	0.2	0.2	0.3	2.2	3.2	5.5	6.3	6.5	7.0	5.3	20.3	28.6	15.5	4.9	76.8	44.2	48.5	51.5
56132	GARVIN	98.6	98.1	0.0	0.0	0.2	0.4	1.2	1.9	5.0	5.6	6.3	6.0	3.8	23.3	33.1	15.6	1.3	79.2	45.0	51.9	48.1
56134	HARDWICK	96.9	96.3	0.0	0.0	0.2	0.5	1.1	1.6	6.3	6.8	7.5	7.7	4.9	21.9	29.6	13.3	2.1	74.6	40.7	51.5	48.5
56136	HENDRICKS	99.4	99.2	0.1	0.1	0.3	0.4	0.2	0.3	4.6	5.3	5.9	5.6	3.1	17.7	23.7	25.6	8.6	79.8	51.2	47.2	52.8
56137	HERON LAKE	95.5	93.4	0.0	0.0	0.3	0.5	6.6	10.0	6.0	6.9	7.1	6.6	4.4	22.8	27.8	13.4	4.9	75.4	42.2	51.5	48.5
56138	HILLS	98.4	97.6	0.2	0.2	0.3	0.6	1.1	1.7	5.9	6.4	6.7	7.4	4.2	24.1	27.2	13.1	5.0	75.9	41.0	48.9	51.1
56139	HOLLAND	98.9	98.7	0.0	0.0	0.0	0.0	0.5	0.7	5.4	6.2	6.5	8.2	4.5	21.8	31.0	14.3	2.0	76.8	43.2	50.6	49.4
56141	IONA	97.7	97.1	0.0	0.0	0.5	0.8	1.5	2.4	5.6	6.4	6.7	8.0	5.6	22.5	30.6	12.1	2.4	76.1	41.0	50.4	49.6
	MINNESOTA	89.4	86.8	3.5	4.3	2.9	3.9	2.9	4.1	6.8	6.7	6.7	7.2	6.8	27.2	26.3	10.2	2.1	75.6	36.9	49.6	50.4
	UNITED STATES	75.1	72.0	12.3	12.7	3.8	4.6	12.5	15.7	6.8	6.7	6.6	7.1	6.9	27.0	26.0	10.9	1.9	75.7	36.9	49.2	50.8

ZIP CODE #	POST OFFICE NAME	2009 Per Capita Income	2009 HH Income Base	2009 HOUSEHOLD INCOME DISTRIBUTION (%) Less than $25,000	$25,000 to $49,999	$50,000 to $99,999	$100,000 to $149,999	$150,000 or More	MEDIAN HOUSEHOLD INCOME 2009	2014	2009 National Centile	2009 State Centile	2009 Home Value Base	2009 HOME VALUE DISTRIBUTION (%) Less than $50,000	$50,000 to $89,999	$90,000 to $174,999	$175,000 to $399,999	$400,000 or More	2009 Median Home Value
56003	MANKATO	31792	5811	11.9	24.4	41.8	14.0	7.8	65086	68821	83	85	4284	6.0	6.2	37.9	45.1	4.7	174741
56007	ALBERT LEA	23640	9292	24.8	28.7	37.1	6.6	2.9	45844	48830	51	38	6930	12.6	26.7	45.3	14.1	1.4	103094
56009	ALDEN	23086	738	18.6	29.9	43.1	6.0	2.4	50854	52402	63	58	634	11.4	26.5	46.7	12.5	3.0	107243
56010	AMBOY	21981	555	25.0	29.5	38.0	5.2	2.2	46145	47915	52	39	462	10.2	25.3	45.9	14.7	3.9	107000
56011	BELLE PLAINE	25471	3333	15.2	23.2	40.4	18.3	2.9	64757	69146	83	84	2735	8.9	1.6	26.4	54.7	8.3	207931
56013	BLUE EARTH	22046	1927	24.2	33.0	35.9	4.7	2.3	44623	46178	47	32	1457	15.7	34.7	40.8	8.2	0.5	89472
56014	BRICELYN	19796	344	27.9	33.7	33.7	3.5	1.2	40000	40567	33	15	289	40.5	27.7	22.1	7.3	2.4	58871
56016	CLARKS GROVE	23426	353	16.4	31.7	43.3	6.2	2.3	51213	52948	64	59	302	12.6	19.2	46.0	18.5	3.6	114500
56017	CLEVELAND	25779	705	12.1	25.8	49.6	9.6	2.8	60977	61519	79	79	615	1.8	10.9	48.6	32.7	6.0	153006
56019	COMFREY	22767	323	23.2	32.2	36.2	5.6	2.8	45753	47760	51	37	276	17.4	27.2	35.5	17.4	2.5	97500
56020	CONGER	21855	14	21.4	35.7	35.7	7.1	0.0	45000	47338	48	34	12	0.0	33.3	41.7	25.0	0.0	125000
56021	COURTLAND	24792	483	12.0	21.7	51.1	11.2	3.9	63454	65473	82	83	415	4.3	12.8	35.9	41.0	6.0	166987
56022	DARFUR	25168	112	13.4	32.1	46.4	6.3	1.8	51774	51669	65	61	97	24.7	28.9	32.0	10.3	4.1	83000
56023	DELAVAN	23167	247	19.4	30.8	42.1	5.3	2.4	49771	50950	60	52	208	29.3	26.4	28.8	12.0	3.4	80769
56024	EAGLE LAKE	24587	1170	12.2	25.0	48.8	10.7	3.2	60322	62245	78	78	983	16.7	7.4	39.6	33.9	2.4	154371
56025	EASTON	19915	206	22.3	35.0	34.5	6.3	1.9	43169	43626	43	25	181	17.1	29.3	41.4	6.1	6.1	94333
56026	ELLENDALE	21652	623	21.2	26.2	44.5	5.5	2.7	52215	54067	66	63	531	5.8	18.8	45.8	24.7	4.9	132853
56027	ELMORE	20921	410	28.8	36.3	30.0	3.2	1.7	36458	37859	22	7	342	50.6	29.8	15.2	3.8	0.6	49556
56028	ELYSIAN	24293	645	18.6	25.7	45.3	7.3	3.1	53972	54122	70	67	561	8.0	13.2	32.1	36.2	10.5	169071
56029	EMMONS	22509	226	21.2	30.1	39.8	7.1	1.8	48397	50296	58	49	192	9.4	36.5	36.5	13.5	4.2	95000
56030	ESSIG	26306	47	6.4	25.5	53.2	10.6	4.3	63796	65502	82	83	41	2.4	14.6	48.8	31.7	2.4	145833
56031	FAIRMONT	23866	5345	26.0	28.1	37.7	5.3	2.9	44693	47623	47	32	3964	13.9	33.1	41.2	11.1	0.7	94855
56032	FREEBORN	24141	218	16.5	30.3	43.6	5.5	4.1	51933	52407	66	62	189	15.3	22.8	47.6	9.0	5.3	109274
56033	FROST	22274	169	28.4	34.9	29.6	5.3	1.8	40509	41139	34	17	138	35.5	29.7	27.5	5.8	1.4	65000
56034	GARDEN CITY	26442	211	14.2	25.6	47.4	10.0	2.8	58340	60242	76	75	185	6.5	10.3	43.8	35.1	4.3	155500
56035	GENEVA	21930	195	24.6	26.7	39.5	7.2	2.1	48511	49724	58	49	168	6.5	22.6	53.0	16.1	1.8	116667
56036	GLENVILLE	21687	589	19.7	34.6	40.9	4.1	0.7	46148	48497	52	39	477	13.2	29.8	44.9	9.6	2.5	96569
56037	GOOD THUNDER	18801	412	20.4	30.1	44.9	3.4	1.2	49615	50326	60	52	347	4.3	18.7	52.4	19.9	4.6	127206
56039	GRANADA	20125	433	21.2	34.6	39.7	3.2	1.2	45400	46743	49	35	353	28.9	29.5	27.2	11.3	3.1	75250
56041	HANSKA	23376	434	17.7	29.0	44.0	6.5	2.8	51931	53744	66	62	365	16.2	24.1	35.1	19.5	5.2	105068
56042	HARTLAND	23790	236	17.4	31.8	43.2	6.4	1.3	50479	52010	62	56	199	12.1	20.1	50.8	11.6	5.5	118750
56043	HAYWARD	24169	294	15.6	29.3	46.6	6.8	1.7	55328	58659	72	70	242	11.2	14.5	36.0	30.6	7.9	137121
56044	HENDERSON	21348	794	16.8	23.4	49.2	8.6	2.0	55824	56903	72	71	651	5.8	14.9	45.8	28.1	5.4	142522
56045	HOLLANDALE	22470	466	18.5	30.5	43.6	5.6	1.9	50600	52117	63	56	401	8.7	19.2	47.4	21.7	3.0	120719
56047	HUNTLEY	24167	15	26.7	26.7	40.0	6.7	0.0	47351	45000	55	44	12	25.0	33.3	33.3	8.3	0.0	80000
56048	JANESVILLE	22578	1428	18.3	27.5	44.5	7.8	2.0	53048	55291	68	65	1200	8.6	13.4	54.3	21.4	2.3	130610
56050	KASOTA	29408	962	11.6	23.7	46.3	11.5	6.9	62339	62259	80	81	850	6.9	12.0	31.3	41.3	8.5	174425
56051	KIESTER	20492	331	26.3	35.6	34.1	2.7	1.2	41250	42226	37	19	269	43.5	32.0	17.5	4.1	3.0	56731
56052	KILKENNY	24477	317	18.0	26.5	45.7	7.3	2.5	54497	54833	70	69	287	7.0	7.0	28.2	49.1	8.7	196635
56054	LAFAYETTE	22300	658	17.2	27.8	44.2	9.0	1.8	53102	54220	68	65	538	8.9	18.2	38.3	26.6	8.0	133333
56055	LAKE CRYSTAL	23881	1575	16.4	27.0	45.5	8.6	2.5	54630	56815	71	69	1280	8.5	15.2	50.0	22.4	3.9	128315
56057	LE CENTER	23048	1338	22.0	23.8	43.2	8.1	2.8	53422	53901	69	66	1074	5.0	10.9	47.9	31.8	4.5	150817
56058	LE SUEUR	26332	2590	17.5	24.2	45.5	9.2	3.7	57025	57039	74	73	2004	7.5	9.6	41.4	36.9	4.5	154545
56060	LEWISVILLE	20538	203	20.2	42.4	31.0	3.9	2.5	41443	42703	37	19	175	26.9	22.3	36.6	12.0	2.3	92143
56062	MADELIA	22331	1144	21.7	27.4	41.3	6.6	3.1	50601	52102	63	56	808	13.5	37.9	38.6	8.0	2.0	88358
56063	MADISON LAKE	30876	1015	10.0	21.9	48.8	11.6	7.8	65563	67100	84	85	875	4.5	6.3	28.9	48.8	11.5	206588
56065	MAPLETON	23964	1000	18.1	27.4	42.9	8.6	3.0	53462	55591	69	66	819	3.3	14.9	54.6	21.4	5.4	133691
56068	MINNESOTA LAKE	22101	394	20.3	33.5	38.3	6.6	1.3	45766	47725	51	37	323	20.7	31.0	35.6	11.1	1.5	87800
56069	MONTGOMERY	21937	1843	22.6	26.2	41.9	7.2	2.1	51219	52430	64	59	1477	7.0	9.4	47.2	32.1	4.3	147139
56071	NEW PRAGUE	26014	4532	13.9	20.4	43.4	16.8	5.5	65563	67240	84	85	3746	0.3	4.4	26.6	54.0	14.2	230192
56072	NEW RICHLAND	22130	901	18.2	33.5	41.4	5.1	1.8	48234	50607	57	48	755	9.3	20.9	47.2	20.9	1.7	118558
56073	NEW ULM	26045	6531	20.3	26.0	41.3	8.7	3.7	52906	55334	68	65	5121	10.0	14.5	53.7	19.9	2.0	126068
56074	NICOLLET	24112	755	16.6	26.8	46.5	7.9	2.3	55936	58942	73	71	636	7.4	9.9	40.7	33.8	8.2	158861
56075	NORTHROP	20678	4	0.0	0.0	100.0	0.0	0.0	60000	60000	77	77	0	0.0	0.0	0.0	0.0	0.0	0
56078	PEMBERTON	21089	338	16.9	29.6	43.5	7.1	3.0	52021	52828	66	62	293	7.8	13.0	44.7	24.9	9.6	142969
56080	SAINT CLAIR	23361	355	12.4	29.9	45.4	8.7	3.7	55741	58381	72	71	307	4.6	5.5	52.8	34.2	2.9	154847
56081	SAINT JAMES	20728	2420	21.4	33.2	38.4	5.2	1.8	45000	47178	48	34	1848	20.5	30.8	38.7	8.5	1.6	87830
56082	SAINT PETER	22950	3913	16.8	28.4	40.6	10.1	4.0	54147	56979	70	68	2790	8.5	6.1	45.7	36.1	3.5	158218
56083	SANBORN	21760	293	18.4	32.4	43.7	3.4	2.0	49147	49416	59	51	244	44.3	27.5	19.3	8.2	0.8	56087
56085	SLEEPY EYE	23364	2302	20.1	29.1	42.8	5.5	2.4	50631	52897	63	57	1815	9.9	19.3	48.7	19.7	2.5	120498
56087	SPRINGFIELD	20371	1238	28.0	33.3	31.8	4.8	2.1	42440	44011	41	23	1037	23.3	31.5	39.1	4.9	1.2	82887
56088	TRUMAN	22051	780	22.3	33.1	36.8	5.8	2.1	44682	46802	47	32	592	16.9	40.9	31.4	7.6	3.2	81481
56089	TWIN LAKES	26155	285	15.4	28.1	46.0	8.1	2.5	54752	57976	71	69	256	7.4	21.1	42.2	25.0	4.3	130488
56090	VERNON CENTER	21976	357	17.9	30.5	41.7	5.9	3.9	51329	54249	64	60	297	10.8	16.5	52.9	15.2	4.7	121065
56091	WALDORF	20560	176	21.0	30.7	43.2	4.5	0.6	48009	50411	57	47	156	12.8	18.6	46.8	17.3	4.5	125000
56093	WASECA	23524	4762	17.1	28.3	42.8	8.1	3.7	53920	56559	69	67	3677	4.7	12.7	56.1	23.7	2.7	134677
56096	WATERVILLE	23900	1211	22.8	25.8	40.4	8.7	2.4	51112	51730	64	59	973	8.0	8.6	46.6	31.4	5.3	146371
56097	WELLS	19447	1446	29.3	30.2	34.2	4.8	1.5	39385	40484	31	13	1168	23.4	33.7	32.6	8.6	1.7	79770
56098	WINNEBAGO	21023	880	25.5	34.0	35.0	4.1	1.5	42003	43555	39	21	699	32.9	35.5	24.2	6.3	1.1	65750
56101	WINDOM	21729	2355	25.1	32.9	35.6	4.3	2.2	41553	43363	38	20	1801	17.0	27.0	46.0	8.6	1.4	96891
56110	ADRIAN	19245	745	25.6	31.1	36.5	5.0	1.7	44219	46375	46	30	642	21.7	34.3	35.7	7.6	0.8	80732
56111	ALPHA	22807	249	11.2	28.5	55.0	3.2	2.0	55788	56949	72	71	200	18.5	29.0	34.0	13.5	5.0	94167
56113	ARCO	22141	136	25.7	28.7	41.2	3.7	0.7	45652	46741	50	36	116	22.4	24.1	38.8	13.8	0.9	101250
56114	AVOCA	21762	179	17.9	35.2	44.1	2.2	0.6	45995	48330	51	38	151	31.8	18.5	33.1	11.9	4.6	89375
56115	BALATON	20223	517	22.2	33.3	40.2	4.1	0.2	44927	46801	48	33	427	29.3	32.6	27.6	10.1	0.5	73409
56116	BEAVER CREEK	21879	248	19.4	29.8	44.4	4.4	2.0	51017	52215	64	58	206	14.1	22.3	43.2	16.5	3.9	112931
56117	BIGELOW	17942	167	25.7	31.1	38.3	3.6	1.2	43405	46144	44	27	135	21.5	37.0	26.7	14.1	0.7	79667
56118	BINGHAM LAKE	19321	211	21.3	35.1	37.9	3.3	2.4	44768	46211	48	33	176	24.4	36.9	25.6	10.8	2.3	75000
56119	BREWSTER	19649	331	24.2	27.2	42.0	6.6	0.0	48775	49756	58	50	279	26.9	29.7	34.8	7.5	1.1	78529
56120	BUTTERFIELD	17560	336	29.5	33.6	34.2	2.1	0.6	40732	41645	35	17	265	38.1	35.1	16.6	6.0	4.2	59844
56121	CEYLON	20999	272	24.6	38.6	31.3	3.7	1.8	41196	42082	37	19	227	39.2	27.8	22.0	7.0	4.0	61471
56122	CHANDLER	18399	223	22.9	37.2	32.7	5.4	1.8	42678	44311	41	24	183	23.5	32.2	34.4	8.7	1.1	83824
56123	CURRIE	25151	324	19.1	35.8	35.5	6.5	3.1	46245	47738	52	40	281	22.8	22.8	32.7	19.9	1.8	100391
56125	DOVRAY	0	0	0.0	0.0	0.0	0.0	0.0	0	0	0	0	0	0.0	0.0	0.0	0.0	0.0	0
56127	DUNNELL	19298	156	25.0	41.7	30.8	2.6	0.0	40502	41936	34	16	132	46.2	28.0	19.7	3.0	3.0	53571
56128	EDGERTON	19390	858	28.0	34.0	33.6	3.3	1.2	40000	41121	33	15	749	21.6	28.4	39.8	8.7	1.5	89881
56129	ELLSWORTH	19821	289	29.4	33.2	31.1	5.2	1.0	36067	37579	21	6	245	55.5	22.9	15.1	3.7	2.9	47672
56131	FULDA	19144	947	29.3	33.3	32.1	3.7	1.7	39422	40045	31	13	781	26.8	36.1	27.5	7.3	2.3	73689
56132	GARVIN	22998	202	17.8	31.7	42.1	6.9	1.5	50193	50541	62	54	167	26.9	18.0	34.1	18.0	3.0	101705
56134	HARDWICK	19197	176	22.7	38.1	34.7	4.0	0.6	44596	45878	47	31	147	32.7	23.1	31.3	11.6	1.4	80556
56136	HENDRICKS	18574	484	34.3	32.9	28.1	3.3	1.4	34451	35947	16	4	392	31.1	34.2	26.0	8.7	0.0	68605
56137	HERON LAKE	19023	479	24.2	34.4	34.4	4.8	2.1	42689	43993	41	24	389	40.1	29.6	22.4	5.1	2.8	61806
56138	HILLS	20201	411	20.9	29.9	44.3	3.9	1.0	49230	50066	59	51	348	13.8	33.9	42.5	8.6	1.1	91860
56139	HOLLAND	19497	230	26.1	34.8	33.9	4.3	0.9	41180	41847	37	19	183	24.0	29.5	29.5	14.2	2.7	82778
56141	IONA	17571	148	28.4	29.7	37.8	2.7	1.4	39486	41888	31	13	129	30.2	25.6	29.5	10.1	4.7	83182
	MINNESOTA	31285		15.9	22.3	36.8	16.4	8.6	62767	65994				6.5	9.7	37.4	39.4	7.0	167369
	UNITED STATES	27277		20.9	24.4	35.3	11.7	7.6	54719	56938				9.3	13.1	31.6	32.6	13.5	162279

ZIP CODE #	POST OFFICE NAME	FINANCIAL SERVICES: Auto Loan	Home Loan	Invest-ments	Retire-ment Plans	THE HOME: Home Improvements: Home Repair	Lawn & Garden	Furnishings: Comput-ers & Hard-ware-Personal	Major Appli-ances	TV, Radio, Sound Equip-ment	Furni-ture	ENTERTAINMENT: Dine out/ Carry out	Sports Equip-ment	Fees & Tickets	Toys & Games	Travel	Cable TV	PERSONAL: Apparel & Services	Auto Repairs	Health Insur-ance	Pets & Supplies
56003	MANKATO	110	114	104	115	111	107	111	108	108	113	109	85	113	111	111	106	77	108	106	127
56007	ALBERT LEA	78	74	72	75	73	84	76	78	80	72	79	59	74	79	75	84	54	78	87	93
56009	ALDEN	92	76	90	78	78	98	78	91	81	68	80	71	67	81	78	86	53	85	95	108
56010	AMBOY	94	65	103	65	68	99	72	89	75	58	74	74	53	73	71	81	48	83	94	110
56011	BELLE PLAINE	93	107	96	107	104	101	99	99	97	98	98	78	106	98	104	96	69	98	98	116
56013	BLUE EARTH	84	64	83	64	65	88	69	81	74	61	72	63	57	73	67	80	48	77	88	97
56014	BRICELYN	83	57	91	57	59	87	63	78	66	51	65	65	46	64	63	72	42	73	83	96
56016	CLARKS GROVE	97	74	100	75	77	103	79	94	81	66	80	75	63	81	78	88	53	88	99	114
56017	CLEVELAND	92	104	91	107	102	102	93	97	91	94	92	75	100	93	98	91	64	93	95	114
56019	COMFREY	96	66	106	66	69	102	73	91	76	60	76	76	54	75	73	83	49	85	96	112
56020	CONGER	75	68	68	71	70	80	67	76	69	61	68	58	62	71	67	73	47	70	78	88
56021	COURTLAND	98	111	95	114	108	109	99	103	97	99	98	80	106	100	105	98	68	99	102	121
56022	DARFUR	101	69	111	69	73	106	77	96	80	62	79	79	56	79	77	87	51	89	101	118
56023	DELAVAN	97	67	106	67	70	102	74	92	77	60	76	76	54	76	74	84	49	86	97	113
56024	EAGLE LAKE	99	104	86	102	98	93	94	95	92	100	94	72	95	97	93	90	65	92	89	111
56025	EASTON	93	64	102	64	67	98	71	88	74	58	73	73	52	73	71	81	47	83	93	109
56026	ELLENDALE	91	75	90	77	77	97	77	90	80	67	78	71	66	80	77	85	52	84	94	107
56027	ELMORE	81	58	83	56	60	85	63	78	69	55	67	60	50	68	62	76	45	73	85	93
56028	ELYSIAN	91	86	83	89	87	98	83	92	85	77	84	70	79	87	84	89	57	86	94	108
56029	EMMONS	94	65	104	65	68	100	72	90	75	59	74	74	53	74	72	82	48	84	95	110
56030	ESSIG	104	118	101	121	114	115	105	109	103	105	104	85	112	106	111	103	73	105	108	129
56031	FAIRMONT	83	72	81	73	73	87	75	82	79	70	77	62	69	78	74	83	53	80	89	97
56032	FREEBORN	104	72	115	72	75	110	80	99	83	65	82	82	58	81	79	90	53	92	105	122
56033	FROST	86	59	95	59	62	91	66	82	69	53	68	68	48	67	66	75	44	76	86	101
56034	GARDEN CITY	90	101	87	103	98	99	90	94	89	90	89	73	96	91	95	89	62	90	93	111
56035	GENEVA	82	75	74	78	76	88	74	83	76	67	75	63	68	78	74	81	51	77	86	97
56036	GLENVILLE	82	68	79	70	70	87	69	81	72	61	71	63	60	72	69	77	47	75	84	96
56037	GOOD THUNDER	79	70	73	73	72	85	70	80	72	63	71	61	64	73	70	76	48	74	82	93
56039	GRANADA	89	61	98	61	64	94	68	85	71	55	70	70	50	69	68	77	45	79	89	104
56041	HANSKA	93	80	89	82	82	100	81	93	83	71	82	72	71	84	80	89	55	86	97	110
56042	HARTLAND	86	77	78	80	79	92	76	87	79	69	77	66	70	80	76	84	53	80	89	101
56043	HAYWARD	104	72	114	71	75	110	80	99	83	64	82	82	58	81	79	90	53	92	104	122
56044	HENDERSON	88	90	82	93	89	96	84	91	84	80	84	70	84	86	86	87	58	85	91	106
56045	HOLLANDALE	86	79	78	82	80	93	78	88	80	70	79	66	72	82	78	85	54	81	90	102
56047	HUNTLEY	86	59	95	59	62	91	66	82	69	53	68	68	48	67	66	75	44	77	87	101
56048	JANESVILLE	90	82	85	85	83	96	80	90	82	73	81	70	74	83	81	86	55	84	93	106
56050	KASOTA	108	109	104	113	110	118	102	112	103	98	102	85	102	105	106	106	71	105	113	130
56051	KIESTER	81	56	89	56	59	86	62	77	65	50	64	64	46	63	62	71	42	72	82	95
56052	KILKENNY	91	88	84	92	89	98	84	93	86	79	85	71	82	87	86	89	58	87	94	108
56054	LAFAYETTE	97	80	102	81	81	104	81	95	83	72	82	77	70	83	83	88	55	89	98	115
56055	LAKE CRYSTAL	87	89	83	90	86	96	84	88	86	80	85	69	85	87	86	89	59	87	94	106
56057	LE CENTER	90	85	83	88	86	95	84	91	86	80	85	69	81	87	84	89	58	87	94	106
56058	LE SUEUR	95	97	90	98	96	99	93	96	93	92	93	73	94	94	94	94	65	94	97	112
56060	LEWISVILLE	92	63	101	63	66	97	70	87	73	57	72	72	51	71	70	79	47	81	92	107
56062	MADELIA	85	77	77	78	75	89	80	83	81	74	80	65	74	82	77	85	55	82	90	100
56063	MADISON LAKE	108	125	112	128	123	121	110	115	108	112	108	89	119	110	118	107	76	110	112	134
56065	MAPLETON	96	81	92	82	79	102	85	93	87	75	86	75	75	87	83	92	58	91	100	114
56068	MINNESOTA LAKE	89	64	92	62	66	94	70	86	77	61	74	66	55	75	68	84	49	81	93	103
56069	MONTGOMERY	83	81	73	83	79	89	79	84	80	73	79	65	76	82	78	83	54	80	88	99
56071	NEW PRAGUE	100	116	102	117	112	109	105	105	102	105	103	83	113	104	110	101	73	103	103	123
56072	NEW RICHLAND	93	68	96	68	71	97	74	90	79	64	77	70	59	78	72	86	51	84	96	107
56073	NEW ULM	88	90	83	91	88	95	86	89	88	85	88	68	88	89	87	91	61	88	94	106
56074	NICOLLET	94	91	95	93	90	102	86	95	86	82	86	75	84	87	90	89	59	90	96	113
56075	NORTHROP	120	83	132	82	87	127	92	114	95	74	94	94	67	93	91	104	61	106	120	140
56078	PEMBERTON	103	70	113	70	74	108	78	97	81	63	80	80	57	80	78	89	52	91	103	120
56080	SAINT CLAIR	90	101	87	104	98	99	90	94	89	91	89	73	96	91	95	89	62	90	93	111
56081	SAINT JAMES	84	68	83	67	69	88	73	82	77	65	75	63	62	76	71	83	51	79	89	98
56082	SAINT PETER	88	90	84	91	89	90	89	88	89	89	90	68	91	90	90	90	63	89	90	105
56083	SANBORN	97	67	107	67	70	103	74	92	77	60	76	76	54	76	74	84	50	86	97	114
56085	SLEEPY EYE	88	81	84	82	80	96	80	88	83	74	82	69	75	83	81	87	56	85	94	105
56087	SPRINGFIELD	86	61	88	60	63	90	67	83	73	58	71	64	52	72	65	80	47	77	89	98
56088	TRUMAN	90	64	94	63	67	95	70	87	77	61	75	67	55	75	69	84	49	81	94	104
56089	TWIN LAKES	97	86	89	90	88	104	86	98	89	77	87	75	78	90	86	94	59	91	101	114
56090	VERNON CENTER	104	72	114	72	75	110	80	99	83	65	82	82	59	81	79	90	53	92	104	122
56091	WALDORF	90	62	99	62	65	95	69	86	72	56	71	71	50	70	69	78	46	80	90	105
56093	WASECA	93	89	84	90	87	96	86	91	88	84	88	70	84	90	86	91	60	88	94	108
56096	WATERVILLE	88	81	95	82	84	93	80	89	81	77	81	67	76	80	83	84	55	85	90	104
56097	WELLS	83	59	88	58	61	87	65	80	70	55	68	63	50	68	63	76	45	75	86	96
56098	WINNEBAGO	83	59	87	58	61	87	65	80	70	56	69	62	50	69	63	77	45	75	87	96
56101	WINDOM	78	63	76	64	65	81	69	77	73	62	71	59	60	72	67	78	48	74	83	91
56110	ADRIAN	80	68	77	70	70	86	69	80	71	60	70	62	60	72	69	76	47	74	83	94
56111	ALPHA	103	71	113	70	74	108	78	97	81	63	81	80	57	80	78	89	52	91	103	120
56113	ARCO	90	62	99	62	65	95	69	86	72	56	71	71	51	70	69	78	46	80	91	106
56114	AVOCA	89	61	97	61	64	94	68	84	70	55	70	70	50	69	67	77	45	79	89	104
56115	BALATON	84	59	88	58	62	88	65	81	70	56	69	63	50	69	64	77	45	75	87	97
56116	BEAVER CREEK	98	67	107	67	70	103	75	93	78	60	77	77	55	76	74	85	50	87	98	114
56117	BIGELOW	87	60	96	60	63	92	67	83	69	54	69	69	49	68	66	76	45	77	88	102
56118	BINGHAM LAKE	92	63	100	63	66	97	70	87	73	57	72	72	51	72	70	80	47	81	92	107
56119	BREWSTER	82	69	79	71	71	87	71	82	73	62	72	63	62	74	70	78	48	76	85	96
56120	BUTTERFIELD	80	57	67	56	57	76	60	70	66	58	65	54	48	69	55	72	44	66	74	85
56121	CEYLON	87	60	96	60	63	92	67	83	69	54	68	68	49	68	66	75	44	77	87	102
56122	CHANDLER	89	61	97	61	64	94	68	84	70	55	70	70	50	69	67	77	45	79	89	104
56123	CURRIE	99	68	109	68	72	105	76	94	79	62	78	78	56	77	76	86	51	88	100	116
56125	DOVRAY	0	0	0	0	0	0	0	0	0	0	0	0	0	0	0	0	0	0	0	0
56127	DUNNELL	82	56	90	56	59	87	63	78	65	51	64	64	46	64	62	71	42	73	82	96
56128	EDGERTON	80	56	83	55	59	84	62	77	67	53	65	60	48	66	61	74	43	72	83	92
56129	ELLSWORTH	82	56	90	56	59	86	62	78	65	51	64	64	46	64	62	71	42	73	82	96
56131	FULDA	80	57	83	56	59	84	62	77	68	54	66	60	48	66	61	74	43	72	83	92
56132	GARVIN	98	67	107	67	70	103	75	93	78	60	77	77	55	76	74	85	50	87	98	114
56134	HARDWICK	84	58	92	57	60	88	64	79	66	52	66	66	47	65	64	73	43	74	84	98
56136	HENDRICKS	74	52	76	51	54	77	57	71	62	49	61	55	44	61	56	68	40	66	76	85
56137	HERON LAKE	88	60	96	60	63	93	67	83	70	54	69	69	49	68	67	76	45	78	88	103
56138	HILLS	91	63	100	63	66	96	70	87	73	57	72	72	51	71	69	79	47	81	92	107
56139	HOLLAND	84	57	92	57	60	88	64	79	66	52	66	66	47	65	63	72	43	74	84	98
56141	IONA	79	54	87	54	57	84	60	75	63	49	62	62	44	62	60	69	40	70	79	93
	MINNESOTA	113	113	112	114	112	114	112	113	111	111	112	88	112	113	112	112	78	112	113	133
	UNITED STATES	100	100	100	100	100	100	100	100	100	100	100	100	100	100	100	100	100	100	100	100

ZIP CODE #	POST OFFICE NAME	COUNTY FIPS CODE	POPULATION 2000	POPULATION 2009	POPULATION 2014	2000-2009 ANNUAL RATE % Rate	2000-2009 ANNUAL RATE State Centile	HOUSEHOLDS 2000	HOUSEHOLDS 2009	HOUSEHOLDS 2014	HOUSEHOLDS % Annual Rate 2000-2009	HOUSEHOLDS 2009 Average HH Size	FAMILIES 2000	FAMILIES 2009	FAMILIES % Annual Rate 2000-2009
56142	IVANHOE	081	1518	1296	1208	-1.7	2	621	546	512	-1.4	2.28	408	345	-1.8
56143	JACKSON	063	4890	4606	4435	-0.6	22	2051	1975	1914	-0.4	2.24	1317	1218	-0.8
56144	JASPER	133	1192	1138	1097	-0.5	26	497	488	476	-0.2	2.33	345	328	-0.5
56145	JEFFERS	033	799	738	704	-0.9	12	338	321	308	-0.6	2.30	235	215	-1.0
56146	KANARANZI	133	286	277	274	-0.3	35	95	95	95	0.0	2.91	69	66	-0.5
56147	KENNETH	133	542	516	508	-0.5	26	191	189	187	-0.1	2.73	140	134	-0.5
56149	LAKE BENTON	081	1361	1327	1290	-0.3	35	571	578	570	0.1	2.28	385	374	-0.3
56150	LAKEFIELD	063	3159	3157	3104	0.0	48	1265	1301	1291	0.3	2.36	872	863	-0.1
56151	LAKE WILSON	101	896	784	738	-1.4	3	373	337	321	-1.1	2.33	280	246	-1.4
56152	LAMBERTON	127	1605	1412	1333	-1.4	3	666	599	569	-1.1	2.24	432	375	-1.5
56153	LEOTA	105	49	46	45	-0.7	18	24	23	22	-0.5	2.00	19	18	-0.6
56155	LISMORE	105	547	498	479	-1.0	9	208	194	187	-0.8	2.57	160	146	-1.0
56156	LUVERNE	133	5633	5437	5369	-0.4	30	2328	2293	2279	-0.2	2.29	1573	1497	-0.5
56157	LYND	083	779	816	827	0.5	63	283	312	318	1.1	2.62	219	236	0.8
56158	MAGNOLIA	133	543	520	512	-0.5	26	195	193	191	-0.1	2.69	142	135	-0.5
56159	MOUNTAIN LAKE	033	2872	2795	2721	-0.3	35	1041	1013	987	-0.3	2.62	714	672	-0.7
56160	ODIN	165	427	389	373	-1.0	9	179	166	159	-0.8	2.34	132	118	-1.2
56161	OKABENA	063	464	448	435	-0.4	30	177	175	170	-0.1	2.56	140	134	-0.5
56162	ORMSBY	091	344	317	304	-0.9	12	142	134	130	-0.6	2.37	107	99	-0.8
56164	PIPESTONE	117	5657	5250	5018	-0.8	15	2360	2244	2160	-0.5	2.26	1497	1364	-1.0
56165	READING	105	429	418	413	-0.3	35	153	153	152	0.0	2.73	126	123	-0.3
56166	REVERE	033	320	293	279	-0.9	12	127	119	115	-0.7	2.34	92	83	-1.1
56167	ROUND LAKE	063	1076	1036	1007	-0.4	30	454	448	437	-0.1	2.31	344	330	-0.4
56168	RUSHMORE	105	1026	977	952	-0.5	26	382	373	364	-0.3	2.62	290	275	-0.6
56169	RUSSELL	083	769	729	707	-0.6	22	295	289	283	-0.2	2.52	221	209	-0.6
56170	RUTHTON	117	1048	936	885	-1.2	5	404	373	355	-0.9	2.51	305	274	-1.2
56171	SHERBURN	091	1877	1731	1669	-0.9	12	783	739	716	-0.6	2.33	518	469	-1.1
56172	SLAYTON	101	2991	2735	2610	-1.0	9	1269	1187	1139	-0.7	2.24	825	743	-1.1
56173	STEEN	133	474	477	476	0.1	51	172	179	181	0.4	2.61	125	125	0.0
56174	STORDEN	033	377	348	333	-0.9	12	167	159	153	-0.5	2.19	121	111	-0.9
56175	TRACY	083	3255	3157	3077	-0.3	35	1294	1268	1239	-0.2	2.41	819	771	-0.7
56176	TRIMONT	091	1178	1146	1127	-0.3	35	483	483	478	0.0	2.29	326	314	-0.4
56178	TYLER	081	1806	1653	1571	-1.0	9	745	698	667	-0.7	2.30	508	462	-1.0
56180	WALNUT GROVE	127	1172	1024	977	-1.4	3	498	437	418	-1.4	2.33	346	297	-1.6
56181	WELCOME	091	1172	1053	1006	-1.2	5	482	447	431	-0.8	2.36	338	304	-1.1
56183	WESTBROOK	033	1329	1247	1199	-0.7	18	577	553	534	-0.5	2.20	385	355	-0.9
56185	WILMONT	105	764	730	711	-0.5	26	285	280	274	-0.2	2.61	218	209	-0.5
56186	WOODSTOCK	117	486	460	447	-0.6	22	180	178	175	-0.1	2.58	136	131	-0.4
56187	WORTHINGTON	105	12529	12281	12031	-0.2	39	4774	4669	4563	-0.2	2.57	3177	2989	-0.7
56201	WILLMAR	067	22144	22177	22087	0.0	48	8625	8857	8878	0.3	2.43	5534	5458	-0.1
56207	ALBERTA	149	292	268	256	-0.9	12	105	99	96	-0.6	2.71	89	83	-0.8
56208	APPLETON	151	3570	3625	3508	0.2	54	1016	911	859	-1.2	2.07	595	508	-1.7
56209	ATWATER	067	2463	2444	2412	-0.1	44	972	1005	1001	0.4	2.41	685	682	0.0
56210	BARRY	011	112	103	98	-0.9	12	41	38	37	-0.3	2.63	28	25	-1.2
56211	BEARDSLEY	011	549	459	427	-1.9	1	218	185	173	-1.3	2.48	150	124	-2.0
56212	BELLINGHAM	073	563	478	442	-1.8	2	231	201	188	-1.5	2.38	169	144	-1.7
56214	BELVIEW	127	846	802	769	-0.6	22	317	308	298	-0.3	2.54	230	217	-0.6
56215	BENSON	151	4905	4659	4480	-0.6	22	1996	1920	1855	-0.4	2.34	1319	1221	-0.8
56216	BLOMKEST	067	842	808	790	-0.4	30	282	275	271	-0.3	2.94	233	222	-0.5
56218	BOYD	073	611	519	479	-1.7	2	243	210	195	-1.6	2.47	167	140	-1.9
56219	BROWNS VALLEY	155	899	828	793	-0.9	12	370	345	332	-0.8	2.29	236	211	-1.2
56220	CANBY	173	2965	2662	2527	-1.2	5	1218	1114	1061	-1.0	2.26	751	657	-1.4
56221	CHOKIO	149	790	624	597	-2.5	0	294	278	269	-0.6	2.24	208	190	-1.0
56222	CLARA CITY	023	2072	1994	1934	-0.4	30	822	797	775	-0.3	2.38	570	533	-0.7
56223	CLARKFIELD	173	1771	1685	1626	-0.5	26	676	655	634	-0.3	2.41	462	432	-0.7
56224	CLEMENTS	127	396	360	343	-1.0	9	151	143	137	-0.6	2.52	113	104	-0.9
56225	CLINTON	011	733	589	546	-2.3	1	285	228	212	-2.4	2.42	188	145	-2.8
56226	CLONTARF	151	203	197	191	-0.3	35	75	74	72	-0.1	2.66	60	58	-0.4
56227	CORRELL	011	320	255	235	-2.4	0	129	105	97	-2.2	2.43	98	78	-2.4
56228	COSMOS	093	1003	1019	987	0.2	54	393	412	403	0.5	2.39	282	286	0.2
56229	COTTONWOOD	083	1601	1536	1496	-0.4	30	603	593	580	-0.2	2.55	436	414	-0.6
56230	DANUBE	129	858	793	762	-0.8	15	331	314	303	-0.6	2.53	259	240	-0.8
56231	DANVERS	151	474	413	387	-1.5	2	178	160	150	-1.1	2.58	133	115	-1.6
56232	DAWSON	073	2208	2121	2044	-0.4	30	928	913	888	-0.2	2.24	598	566	-0.6
56235	DONNELLY	149	476	441	425	-0.8	15	204	198	193	-0.3	2.23	142	133	-0.7
56236	DUMONT	155	573	524	500	-1.0	9	214	201	194	-0.7	2.61	162	148	-1.0
56237	ECHO	173	622	583	558	-0.7	18	255	244	235	-0.5	2.39	183	170	-0.8
56239	GHENT	083	561	529	512	-0.6	22	205	200	195	-0.3	2.64	160	152	-0.6
56240	GRACEVILLE	011	941	906	882	-0.4	30	362	353	346	-0.3	2.42	236	222	-0.7
56241	GRANITE FALLS	173	4314	4116	3980	-0.5	26	1813	1765	1715	-0.3	2.29	1165	1087	-0.7
56243	GROVE CITY	093	1669	1752	1763	0.5	63	634	687	697	0.9	2.55	457	478	0.5
56244	HANCOCK	149	1240	1236	1217	0.0	48	463	480	477	0.4	2.50	319	317	-0.1
56245	HANLEY FALLS	173	687	645	620	-0.7	18	248	235	226	-0.6	2.74	184	170	-0.9
56248	HERMAN	051	849	878	870	0.4	61	356	378	377	0.7	2.28	236	241	0.2
56249	HOLLOWAY	151	407	350	327	-1.6	2	156	139	131	-1.2	2.52	116	100	-1.6
56251	KANDIYOHI	067	967	1041	1066	0.8	72	373	418	432	1.2	2.48	290	315	0.9
56252	KERKHOVEN	151	1144	1029	971	-1.1	7	444	409	388	-0.9	2.52	310	275	-1.3
56253	LAKE LILLIAN	067	1190	1223	1231	0.3	58	474	508	517	0.8	2.41	331	342	0.4
56255	LUCAN	127	485	445	426	-0.9	12	189	177	170	-0.7	2.51	140	127	-1.0
56256	MADISON	073	3740	3325	3128	-1.3	4	1511	1369	1291	-1.1	2.33	1012	884	-1.5
56257	MARIETTA	073	776	717	687	-0.9	12	337	321	311	-0.5	2.23	232	214	-0.9
56258	MARSHALL	083	14564	14503	14247	0.0	48	5527	5628	5555	0.2	2.40	3402	3320	-0.3
56260	MAYNARD	023	947	925	905	-0.3	35	357	359	355	0.1	2.58	278	271	-0.3
56262	MILAN	023	743	690	661	-0.8	15	320	305	294	-0.5	2.26	212	194	-1.0
56263	MILROY	127	691	624	594	-1.1	7	261	242	232	-0.8	2.58	193	173	-1.2
56264	MINNEOTA	083	2571	2447	2371	-0.5	26	994	974	950	-0.2	2.41	697	658	-0.6
56265	MONTEVIDEO	023	7678	7315	7077	-0.5	26	3183	3102	3019	-0.3	2.29	2090	1960	-0.7
56266	MORGAN	127	2043	1923	1851	-0.7	18	803	780	757	-0.3	2.41	568	534	-0.7
56267	MORRIS	149	7262	7003	6804	-0.4	30	2687	2653	2593	-0.1	2.32	1611	1521	-0.6
56270	MORTON	129	1015	1022	1008	0.1	51	394	410	408	0.4	2.49	274	273	0.0
56271	MURDOCK	151	1228	1110	1050	-1.1	7	470	438	418	-0.8	2.53	342	309	-1.1
56273	NEW LONDON	067	4717	5016	5110	0.7	69	1743	1935	1992	1.1	2.54	1319	1416	0.8
56274	NORCROSS	051	242	213	200	-1.4	3	107	96	91	-1.2	2.20	75	65	-1.5
56276	ODESSA	011	364	290	267	-2.4	0	151	123	114	-2.2	2.36	113	90	-2.4
56277	OLIVIA	129	3487	3211	3093	-0.9	12	1389	1323	1283	-0.5	2.35	901	826	-0.9
	MINNESOTA					0.9					1.1	2.48			0.7
	UNITED STATES					1.0					1.1	2.59			0.9

ZIP CODE #	POST OFFICE NAME	RACE (%) White 2000	White 2009	Black 2000	Black 2009	Asian/Pacific 2000	Asian/Pacific 2009	% Hispanic Origin 2000	% Hispanic Origin 2009	2009 AGE DISTRIBUTION (%) 0-4	5-9	10-14	15-19	20-24	25-44	45-64	65-84	85+	18+	MEDIAN AGE 2009	% 2009 Males	% 2009 Females
56142	IVANHOE	99.4	99.2	0.0	0.0	0.0	0.0	0.4	0.6	4.9	5.5	6.0	5.9	5.0	22.6	27.3	17.4	5.3	79.5	45.1	49.2	50.8
56143	JACKSON	95.5	93.6	0.2	0.2	2.9	4.2	1.4	2.0	5.4	5.5	5.5	5.9	5.9	24.4	28.2	14.4	4.8	80.0	42.8	50.7	49.3
56144	JASPER	98.2	97.8	0.2	0.2	0.2	0.3	0.7	1.0	6.2	6.5	7.0	6.9	4.3	21.8	29.8	14.5	2.9	75.8	42.9	48.8	51.2
56145	JEFFERS	98.5	97.8	0.3	0.4	0.3	0.4	1.1	1.5	4.7	5.3	5.7	5.8	4.1	22.5	32.4	16.5	3.0	80.5	46.1	51.1	48.9
56146	KANARANZI	94.1	92.4	1.0	1.4	1.7	2.5	1.7	2.2	6.9	7.2	7.2	7.2	4.7	24.2	29.2	11.6	1.8	74.0	39.3	51.3	48.7
56147	KENNETH	96.7	95.9	0.0	0.0	0.6	0.8	1.3	1.7	6.4	6.8	7.6	7.9	4.7	21.9	29.7	13.2	1.9	74.2	40.8	51.6	48.4
56149	LAKE BENTON	98.4	98.0	0.1	0.2	0.2	0.3	0.7	1.0	6.2	6.3	6.3	6.3	4.9	21.2	26.3	18.7	3.8	76.7	44.0	49.7	50.3
56150	LAKEFIELD	99.1	98.8	0.0	0.0	0.2	0.3	0.8	1.3	5.2	5.6	6.2	6.5	5.0	21.8	29.2	16.2	4.2	78.9	44.7	49.1	50.9
56151	LAKE WILSON	98.2	97.6	0.1	0.1	0.2	0.3	1.7	2.6	6.1	6.6	7.1	6.8	4.2	22.8	31.0	13.3	2.0	75.9	41.9	51.8	48.2
56152	LAMBERTON	99.4	99.2	0.0	0.0	0.1	0.1	0.6	0.9	4.9	5.1	6.7	5.9	3.7	19.5	25.7	20.8	7.8	78.9	48.4	49.6	50.4
56153	LEOTA	98.0	97.8	0.0	0.0	2.0	2.2	0.0	0.0	4.3	4.3	4.3	8.7	4.3	17.4	37.0	17.4	2.2	78.3	48.8	52.2	47.8
56155	LISMORE	97.8	96.8	0.0	0.0	1.1	1.8	1.5	2.2	6.2	7.4	8.2	8.2	3.4	22.9	26.1	15.1	2.4	72.5	40.8	50.2	49.8
56156	LUVERNE	97.5	96.7	0.7	0.9	0.6	0.8	1.4	2.1	5.8	5.7	6.8	7.2	4.7	21.1	25.7	17.8	5.3	77.0	44.0	48.0	52.0
56157	LYND	96.5	95.2	0.3	0.4	0.4	0.6	3.3	5.3	6.1	7.7	8.6	8.9	5.4	25.2	29.2	8.0	0.9	71.6	36.8	52.2	47.8
56158	MAGNOLIA	94.6	92.9	0.9	1.2	1.7	2.5	1.7	2.5	6.7	7.3	7.5	7.3	4.4	24.6	28.3	11.9	1.9	73.7	39.3	51.3	48.7
56159	MOUNTAIN LAKE	87.1	82.8	0.6	0.8	5.4	7.4	4.8	6.8	7.1	7.7	8.6	7.6	4.7	21.6	23.2	13.8	5.7	71.9	39.0	49.4	50.6
56160	ODIN	97.7	96.7	0.0	0.0	1.2	1.8	0.5	0.5	4.4	5.1	5.9	6.2	4.1	18.8	35.0	17.7	2.8	80.7	48.4	50.6	49.4
56161	OKABENA	98.7	98.4	0.2	0.2	0.0	0.0	2.8	4.2	6.3	6.7	6.9	7.1	4.7	22.3	29.2	14.7	2.0	75.7	41.7	49.6	50.4
56162	ORMSBY	98.0	97.5	0.0	0.0	0.9	0.9	0.3	0.6	4.7	5.4	6.0	6.3	4.1	19.2	35.6	16.1	2.5	80.1	47.4	50.5	49.5
56164	PIPESTONE	95.3	94.3	0.2	0.3	0.7	0.9	0.9	1.2	6.3	6.1	6.2	6.6	6.3	23.7	25.0	15.1	4.8	77.3	40.9	47.6	52.4
56165	READING	97.4	95.9	0.2	0.5	0.5	1.0	0.9	1.7	7.9	8.4	8.1	6.2	4.1	21.3	30.9	11.7	1.4	72.0	39.3	48.1	51.9
56166	REVERE	99.4	99.0	0.0	0.0	0.3	0.3	0.6	1.0	4.1	5.5	7.2	6.1	3.4	20.8	30.7	18.1	4.1	78.2	47.4	52.2	47.8
56167	ROUND LAKE	98.3	97.6	0.0	0.0	0.1	0.1	1.7	2.7	5.2	5.8	6.3	6.8	4.2	22.4	33.2	14.1	2.0	78.6	44.5	51.3	48.7
56168	RUSHMORE	97.8	96.4	0.0	0.0	0.4	0.6	1.9	3.3	6.7	7.2	7.4	6.9	4.1	22.3	30.4	13.1	2.0	74.4	41.4	49.9	50.1
56169	RUSSELL	97.1	96.2	0.1	0.1	0.8	1.1	2.3	3.6	6.3	7.1	7.3	6.6	4.1	23.5	30.0	13.0	2.1	75.3	41.7	51.0	49.0
56170	RUTHTON	98.7	98.3	0.3	0.3	0.1	0.1	0.4	0.6	7.5	8.1	8.1	6.5	4.1	23.2	28.6	12.0	1.9	72.1	39.3	51.0	49.0
56171	SHERBURN	99.0	98.7	0.0	0.0	0.2	0.3	0.7	1.1	6.0	6.2	6.5	7.2	5.1	21.8	28.8	15.3	2.9	76.9	42.9	49.3	50.7
56172	SLAYTON	99.0	98.7	0.1	0.1	0.3	0.4	0.5	0.7	5.2	5.6	5.9	5.9	4.3	20.7	27.8	19.9	4.8	79.3	46.7	47.3	52.7
56173	STEEN	96.2	94.8	0.6	0.8	1.1	1.7	1.3	2.1	6.3	6.7	6.9	7.3	4.4	24.5	28.3	12.2	3.4	75.3	40.2	50.3	49.7
56174	STORDEN	98.4	97.4	0.0	0.0	0.0	0.0	2.1	3.2	5.7	6.3	6.3	5.7	3.7	21.8	32.2	15.5	2.6	78.2	45.2	52.9	47.1
56175	TRACY	90.9	87.7	0.2	0.3	5.8	8.1	2.1	3.0	6.4	6.4	6.4	6.7	4.9	21.2	25.5	17.1	5.4	76.6	43.2	47.5	52.5
56176	TRIMONT	98.6	98.2	0.3	0.4	0.1	0.1	0.3	0.5	4.9	5.2	5.8	6.7	5.0	19.7	31.2	16.1	5.4	79.4	46.9	47.6	52.4
56178	TYLER	98.3	97.7	0.1	0.1	0.3	0.5	1.8	2.7	6.8	7.0	6.9	5.7	4.2	21.8	26.3	16.5	4.8	75.4	43.0	49.7	50.3
56180	WALNUT GROVE	98.5	97.9	0.3	0.5	0.9	1.3	0.3	0.3	5.7	6.0	6.3	6.3	4.6	22.0	29.6	16.4	3.3	78.1	44.4	49.4	50.6
56181	WELCOME	98.6	98.1	0.0	0.0	0.2	0.3	0.9	1.5	6.1	6.2	6.7	6.5	5.6	21.4	31.3	13.8	2.5	77.0	42.9	51.7	48.3
56183	WESTBROOK	98.6	98.2	0.1	0.1	0.2	0.3	0.6	0.9	5.2	6.0	5.5	5.4	3.0	17.5	28.1	21.2	8.2	79.6	51.1	48.1	51.9
56185	WILMONT	99.1	98.9	0.0	0.0	0.3	0.4	0.4	0.5	6.0	7.1	7.5	7.9	4.1	22.2	30.1	12.7	2.2	74.4	41.4	52.5	47.5
56186	WOODSTOCK	98.1	97.6	0.0	0.0	0.6	0.9	0.4	0.7	5.7	6.5	7.0	6.5	4.1	23.0	31.3	14.1	1.7	76.7	42.9	50.4	49.6
56187	WORTHINGTON	79.0	72.1	1.7	2.2	6.5	8.6	17.5	24.1	7.5	6.7	6.4	6.4	6.6	25.2	24.3	13.2	3.7	75.5	37.6	50.0	50.0
56201	WILLMAR	89.7	85.7	0.8	1.1	0.6	0.8	13.6	19.7	6.9	6.6	6.8	8.1	7.6	24.9	24.6	11.4	3.1	75.4	36.2	48.6	51.4
56207	ALBERTA	97.6	97.0	0.0	0.0	0.0	0.0	1.4	1.5	6.3	7.1	7.5	7.1	4.5	20.9	31.7	13.4	1.5	74.6	42.9	50.7	49.3
56208	APPLETON	73.6	67.3	8.6	10.9	9.5	11.8	4.3	6.0	2.5	2.7	3.3	4.4	7.4	40.9	24.1	10.6	4.1	88.9	39.6	71.3	28.7
56209	ATWATER	98.3	97.5	0.1	0.1	0.2	0.4	1.3	2.1	5.2	5.7	7.0	6.7	5.3	23.7	30.2	13.5	2.7	77.5	42.2	50.7	49.3
56210	BARRY	99.1	99.0	0.0	0.0	0.9	1.0	0.0	0.0	5.8	5.8	5.8	6.8	5.8	20.4	28.2	17.5	3.9	77.7	44.6	48.5	51.5
56211	BEARDSLEY	99.3	99.1	0.0	0.0	0.4	0.4	0.7	1.1	6.1	6.8	6.3	5.7	5.0	19.2	30.9	17.0	3.1	77.1	45.5	51.2	48.8
56212	BELLINGHAM	99.5	99.4	0.2	0.2	0.2	0.2	0.2	0.4	5.4	5.9	6.1	7.7	4.6	21.5	29.5	16.7	2.5	77.8	44.1	53.8	46.2
56214	BELVIEW	98.6	98.3	0.0	0.0	0.6	0.7	0.6	0.9	6.2	6.7	6.9	6.4	4.9	21.7	28.9	14.3	4.0	75.8	43.1	52.7	47.3
56215	BENSON	98.3	97.8	0.2	0.2	0.2	0.3	1.5	2.3	6.4	6.3	6.4	7.0	4.9	22.8	25.6	15.6	4.9	76.0	42.1	48.6	51.4
56216	BLOMKEST	97.5	96.3	0.1	0.1	1.2	1.7	2.5	4.1	8.0	8.4	8.4	7.5	4.3	22.6	29.6	9.4	1.6	70.2	37.5	53.2	46.8
56218	BOYD	98.9	98.7	0.0	0.0	0.7	0.8	0.0	0.0	4.6	7.3	8.5	8.3	3.5	21.2	31.6	12.9	2.1	74.6	43.1	49.3	50.7
56219	BROWNS VALLEY	86.5	84.8	0.0	0.0	0.4	0.5	1.6	1.9	6.5	5.4	6.5	7.0	4.3	16.5	24.3	22.7	6.6	77.3	47.2	48.1	51.9
56220	CANBY	98.7	98.2	0.1	0.2	0.1	0.2	0.9	1.4	5.2	5.2	5.8	6.9	5.6	20.4	26.1	18.9	5.9	79.8	45.6	49.1	50.9
56221	CHOKIO	99.2	96.3	0.0	0.0	0.1	2.9	0.3	0.5	5.6	4.6	5.1	4.6	3.8	14.3	25.6	22.8	13.5	83.2	54.4	44.2	55.8
56222	CLARA CITY	98.2	97.4	0.3	0.4	0.1	0.2	1.7	2.7	6.0	6.9	7.1	6.6	4.2	21.1	25.4	16.6	6.1	75.7	43.5	50.0	50.0
56223	CLARKFIELD	98.5	98.0	0.1	0.1	0.2	0.3	1.1	1.7	6.0	6.2	6.4	6.6	4.5	21.0	27.5	15.5	6.3	76.9	44.4	49.8	50.2
56224	CLEMENTS	99.5	99.4	0.0	0.0	0.0	0.0	1.3	1.9	6.1	6.7	7.2	6.4	4.4	22.8	30.3	14.7	1.4	75.8	42.5	53.1	46.9
56225	CLINTON	98.2	98.0	0.0	0.0	0.8	1.0	0.0	0.0	6.3	6.8	6.6	6.3	5.1	21.7	24.1	15.6	7.5	75.9	42.5	48.4	51.6
56226	CLONTARF	100.0	100.0	0.0	0.0	0.0	0.0	1.5	2.5	6.1	7.1	7.1	7.1	4.6	22.8	31.5	12.7	1.0	75.1	42.2	54.8	45.2
56227	CORRELL	99.1	98.8	0.0	0.0	0.3	0.4	0.0	0.0	3.9	5.9	6.7	6.3	3.5	22.0	31.0	18.4	2.4	79.2	46.1	53.7	46.3
56228	COSMOS	98.4	97.7	0.0	0.0	0.8	1.2	0.4	0.7	6.3	6.6	6.7	6.0	4.5	23.8	27.8	14.6	3.7	76.3	42.2	49.9	50.1
56229	COTTONWOOD	97.3	96.4	0.1	0.1	0.5	0.7	1.2	1.8	7.0	8.0	8.3	7.4	4.6	24.9	26.3	10.9	2.6	71.8	37.7	52.9	47.1
56230	DANUBE	96.7	95.6	0.0	0.0	0.3	0.4	5.1	7.4	5.8	7.2	7.8	6.8	4.3	24.2	30.4	11.2	2.3	74.8	40.3	52.8	47.2
56231	DANVERS	99.2	98.8	0.0	0.0	0.0	0.0	0.8	1.2	5.8	6.5	6.5	7.3	4.8	21.5	33.7	11.6	2.2	76.8	43.2	54.0	46.0
56232	DAWSON	98.5	98.3	0.2	0.2	0.3	0.3	0.4	0.6	5.8	6.1	5.9	5.8	5.5	19.4	28.9	16.8	5.9	78.5	46.1	48.2	51.8
56235	DONNELLY	98.5	98.0	0.0	0.0	0.2	0.5	0.4	0.7	4.8	5.4	5.4	5.2	5.2	20.2	35.1	15.9	2.7	81.4	46.7	51.2	48.8
56236	DUMONT	99.0	98.9	0.2	0.2	0.2	0.2	1.0	1.5	6.3	6.7	6.9	7.1	5.2	20.6	29.2	16.2	1.9	76.0	42.9	52.3	47.7
56237	ECHO	97.6	97.1	0.0	0.0	0.2	0.2	0.8	1.2	6.2	6.7	6.9	6.5	4.5	22.3	29.7	14.8	2.6	76.2	42.9	51.6	48.4
56239	GHENT	97.5	97.0	0.5	0.8	0.2	0.2	0.5	0.8	7.8	8.5	8.1	6.6	4.2	25.9	27.6	9.8	1.5	71.3	36.0	51.2	48.8
56240	GRACEVILLE	99.1	99.2	0.0	0.0	0.5	0.4	0.1	0.2	5.7	6.1	6.3	6.8	5.1	18.9	26.9	18.2	6.0	77.4	45.8	48.5	51.5
56241	GRANITE FALLS	91.3	89.6	0.1	0.1	0.2	0.5	2.0	3.0	5.9	6.1	6.2	6.7	5.5	22.2	28.3	15.1	4.1	77.7	42.8	48.0	52.0
56243	GROVE CITY	98.2	97.4	0.1	0.1	0.6	0.9	1.3	1.9	6.4	6.8	7.1	7.0	4.5	24.1	29.6	12.7	1.8	75.4	40.6	51.8	48.2
56244	HANCOCK	98.5	98.1	0.1	0.2	0.2	0.2	0.4	0.6	6.2	7.1	7.0	6.3	4.5	26.1	29.4	10.8	2.5	75.6	38.8	53.9	46.1
56245	HANLEY FALLS	92.1	89.3	0.3	0.3	0.1	0.2	10.0	14.7	8.1	8.7	8.2	6.4	4.2	25.1	27.4	10.4	1.6	70.7	36.6	53.2	46.8
56248	HERMAN	98.7	98.5	0.1	0.1	0.4	0.5	0.5	0.7	5.9	5.9	5.6	5.7	5.5	21.2	29.5	16.2	4.6	79.3	45.1	47.8	52.2
56249	HOLLOWAY	97.3	96.0	0.0	0.0	1.0	1.4	2.5	3.7	4.0	4.9	5.7	8.9	4.6	21.7	32.6	16.3	1.4	80.0	45.2	53.4	46.6
56251	KANDIYOHI	97.8	96.6	0.5	0.8	0.5	0.9	1.1	1.8	5.6	6.5	6.9	8.1	4.7	26.0	29.0	11.9	1.2	76.0	39.1	49.7	50.3
56252	KERKHOVEN	95.7	94.0	0.2	0.2	0.0	0.0	4.1	6.0	7.3	7.8	7.9	7.0	5.0	22.8	28.0	11.6	2.7	72.9	39.3	50.0	50.0
56253	LAKE LILLIAN	97.8	97.0	0.2	0.2	0.2	0.2	2.4	3.9	5.8	6.3	7.8	7.7	4.2	22.2	30.4	13.2	2.5	75.1	41.9	53.0	47.0
56255	LUCAN	98.6	98.2	0.0	0.0	0.4	0.4	0.8	1.1	5.8	6.3	6.7	7.2	4.5	24.3	30.3	12.6	2.2	76.6	41.3	51.9	48.1
56256	MADISON	98.9	98.6	0.2	0.3	0.3	0.3	0.2	0.3	4.6	5.5	5.8	7.1	4.9	19.1	28.7	18.1	6.1	79.4	46.8	49.3	50.7
56257	MARIETTA	99.2	99.2	0.1	0.1	0.4	0.4	0.3	0.1	5.2	6.1	6.6	6.3	4.5	19.5	32.2	16.9	2.8	78.4	46.2	53.6	46.4
56258	MARSHALL	92.1	89.3	2.5	3.2	1.5	2.1	5.4	7.9	6.5	6.1	6.2	9.5	12.8	24.9	22.3	9.2	2.5	77.6	31.6	48.7	51.3
56260	MAYNARD	98.2	95.9	0.1	0.1	0.2	2.3	1.3	1.7	5.0	6.6	6.9	7.5	4.0	20.8	32.3	13.4	3.6	76.8	44.5	51.5	48.5
56262	MILAN	95.8	93.8	0.0	0.0	0.4	0.7	3.5	5.2	5.7	6.4	6.7	6.2	4.2	21.4	32.6	13.8	3.0	77.4	44.5	52.8	47.2
56263	MILROY	98.3	97.6	0.1	0.2	0.4	0.8	0.7	1.1	6.4	7.2	7.2	7.1	4.5	24.7	28.8	12.2	1.9	74.7	39.6	52.9	47.1
56264	MINNEOTA	97.9	97.0	0.2	0.2	0.2	0.2	2.4	3.6	6.4	7.0	7.0	6.7	4.6	23.0	26.6	13.4	5.3	75.5	41.5	49.6	50.4
56265	MONTEVIDEO	97.5	96.3	0.1	0.3	0.4	0.8	1.6	2.5	6.0	5.7	6.1	7.0	6.3	23.1	27.9	14.4	3.5	78.4	41.5	49.1	50.9
56266	MORGAN	92.5	91.4	0.0	0.1	0.1	0.1	1.5	2.1	6.9	7.2	7.0	6.7	5.5	21.9	26.7	14.3	3.8	74.6	41.0	49.6	50.4
56267	MORRIS	95.2	93.5	1.2	1.8	1.1	1.7	1.1	1.6	5.4	5.0	4.8	11.6	13.1	24.2	22.1	11.0	3.0	82.4	31.3	48.1	51.9
56270	MORTON	81.5	79.3	0.1	0.1	0.2	0.4	4.5	6.8	7.3	8.0	8.0	7.7	5.7	23.5	28.3	9.9	1.6	71.6	37.0	52.2	47.8
56271	MURDOCK	97.3	96.4	0.3	0.5	0.1	0.1	2.4	3.6	7.0	7.6	7.8	7.4	4.1	22.6	28.7	12.3	2.3	72.9	40.3	52.0	48.0
56273	NEW LONDON	98.9	98.4	0.1	0.1	0.2	0.2	0.7	1.2	5.4	6.4	7.2	7.5	4.5	23.7	29.9	12.9	2.5	76.0	41.7	50.5	49.5
56274	NORCROSS	99.2	99.1	0.0	0.0	0.4	0.5	0.0	0.0	5.2	5.6	6.1	5.6	4.2	18.8	35.2	16.9	2.3	79.8	47.4	48.8	51.2
56276	ODESSA	99.2	99.0	0.0	0.0	0.3	0.3	0.3	0.3	4.1	5.5	6.2	6.2	3.4	21.4	31.4	19.0	2.8	80.0	46.8	52.8	47.2
56277	OLIVIA	96.6	95.3	0.1	0.2	0.2	0.2	6.3	9.0	6.0	6.6	7.0	6.6	5.0	23.1	27.1	14.8	3.7	75.9	41.6	49.6	50.4
	MINNESOTA	89.4	86.8	3.5	4.3	2.9	3.9	2.9	4.1	6.8	6.7	6.7	7.2	6.8	27.2	26.3	10.2	2.1	75.6	36.9	49.6	50.4
	UNITED STATES	75.1	72.0	12.3	12.7	3.8	4.6	12.5	15.7	6.8	6.7	6.6	7.1	6.9	27.0	26.0	10.9	1.9	75.7	36.9	49.2	50.8

INCOME

ZIP CODE #	POST OFFICE NAME	2009 Per Capita Income	2009 HH Income Base	2009 HOUSEHOLD INCOME DISTRIBUTION (%) Less than $25,000	$25,000 to $49,999	$50,000 to $99,999	$100,000 to $149,999	$150,000 or More	MEDIAN HOUSEHOLD INCOME 2009	2014	2009 National Centile	2009 State Centile	2009 Home Value Base	2009 HOME VALUE DISTRIBUTION (%) Less than $50,000	$50,000 to $89,999	$90,000 to $174,999	$175,000 to $399,999	$400,000 or More	2009 Median Home Value
56142	IVANHOE	18829	546	31.0	33.2	31.3	3.8	0.7	38510	40143	28	11	436	28.9	36.5	26.4	7.6	0.7	72222
56143	JACKSON	23750	1975	21.2	29.9	41.0	5.6	2.3	48741	50753	58	50	1441	13.0	32.5	41.2	11.5	1.8	95864
56144	JASPER	20248	488	27.3	32.6	35.7	2.5	2.0	41534	42694	38	20	398	35.4	31.9	26.6	4.8	1.3	67727
56145	JEFFERS	22651	321	25.5	34.0	33.6	2.8	4.0	41488	42353	38	20	269	43.9	24.5	16.7	12.6	2.2	56875
56146	KANARANZI	17917	95	23.2	30.5	40.0	4.2	2.1	47342	49647	55	44	74	16.2	23.0	37.8	17.6	5.4	107692
56147	KENNETH	17181	189	23.3	36.5	35.4	4.2	0.5	44798	45885	48	33	158	31.0	22.8	32.3	12.7	1.3	84000
56149	LAKE BENTON	17813	578	29.4	39.8	28.7	2.1	0.0	35842	37439	20	5	445	31.5	34.2	25.6	7.9	0.9	68370
56150	LAKEFIELD	19680	1301	25.6	32.3	37.3	4.3	0.5	42621	43791	41	23	1082	25.3	29.3	35.2	8.0	2.1	83421
56151	LAKE WILSON	22132	337	26.4	37.4	31.2	2.4	2.7	38813	39755	29	11	294	35.7	28.2	22.8	12.2	1.0	69474
56152	LAMBERTON	19763	599	32.4	28.5	34.2	4.0	0.8	39457	40792	31	13	475	42.9	29.9	20.8	5.3	1.1	57614
56153	LEOTA	19511	23	30.4	43.5	26.1	0.0	0.0	36108	40000	21	6	20	30.0	20.0	30.0	20.0	0.0	90000
56155	LISMORE	18230	194	26.8	33.0	35.6	2.6	2.1	41937	43502	39	21	171	31.6	21.1	33.3	12.9	1.2	84375
56156	LUVERNE	24444	2293	24.8	25.0	39.2	7.6	3.4	50179	51472	62	54	1698	8.5	27.4	51.8	10.8	1.5	106778
56157	LYND	24700	312	15.7	25.6	45.2	8.0	5.4	55905	58537	73	71	257	7.8	18.3	44.0	27.6	2.3	136944
56158	MAGNOLIA	19224	193	23.3	29.0	42.0	3.6	2.1	48132	49127	57	47	152	16.4	23.7	39.5	16.4	3.9	105172
56159	MOUNTAIN LAKE	15930	1013	31.8	35.9	28.6	2.9	0.8	36824	37849	23	7	814	31.7	39.6	24.9	3.7	0.1	65625
56160	ODIN	23234	166	19.9	31.3	39.2	7.8	1.8	49001	49782	59	51	144	29.9	19.4	31.3	16.0	3.5	91250
56161	OKABENA	18938	175	18.3	38.9	38.9	2.9	1.1	43951	45000	45	29	151	26.5	23.2	37.1	9.3	4.0	90625
56162	ORMSBY	24069	134	17.9	32.1	40.3	7.5	2.2	50000	50000	61	53	115	20.9	22.6	34.8	15.7	6.1	102083
56164	PIPESTONE	21338	2244	28.7	31.7	32.9	4.7	2.0	40155	41474	33	15	1592	23.6	37.5	32.0	6.0	0.8	74453
56165	READING	18770	153	16.3	39.2	39.9	3.9	0.7	46576	48517	53	41	126	18.3	23.0	44.4	11.1	3.2	105682
56166	REVERE	20396	119	29.4	31.1	31.9	5.9	1.7	39066	40575	30	12	97	29.9	30.9	25.8	11.3	2.1	75000
56167	ROUND LAKE	22559	448	18.3	35.3	40.0	4.9	1.6	46676	48591	53	41	360	21.9	22.8	36.9	13.3	5.0	97600
56168	RUSHMORE	18854	373	24.7	34.6	33.8	5.9	1.1	41833	44390	39	21	314	20.1	37.9	27.7	13.1	1.3	79394
56169	RUSSELL	19533	289	21.1	31.8	41.9	4.5	0.7	46362	48653	52	40	249	18.1	26.5	34.5	20.1	0.8	97105
56170	RUTHTON	17567	373	29.8	33.8	31.9	4.0	0.5	37558	38511	25	9	318	27.0	31.1	24.2	15.4	2.2	76800
56171	SHERBURN	19945	739	30.2	32.6	31.4	4.2	1.6	39017	40000	30	12	582	22.9	32.3	30.9	11.0	2.9	83478
56172	SLAYTON	23102	1187	23.1	29.4	41.4	4.2	1.9	47785	49678	56	45	958	25.2	31.5	35.7	6.6	1.0	82289
56173	STEEN	19652	179	21.8	29.6	43.6	3.9	1.1	48858	49811	59	50	145	13.8	29.0	41.4	13.1	2.8	98077
56174	STORDEN	24004	159	25.2	30.2	37.1	5.0	2.5	42678	44545	41	24	134	44.0	22.4	16.4	14.2	3.0	57273
56175	TRACY	19253	1268	28.3	32.1	33.0	5.2	1.3	41680	42610	38	20	982	32.8	33.2	25.7	7.6	0.7	72000
56176	TRIMONT	21512	483	28.0	31.7	34.6	3.5	2.3	42266	43744	40	22	397	32.0	30.5	26.4	7.8	3.3	72742
56178	TYLER	19591	698	29.4	33.8	30.5	4.9	1.4	40300	41030	34	16	548	20.4	41.8	30.3	6.2	1.3	76462
56180	WALNUT GROVE	19662	437	30.7	30.9	32.7	4.6	1.1	39302	40214	31	13	360	40.0	30.3	21.4	7.5	0.8	59730
56181	WELCOME	20958	447	24.4	33.6	37.1	3.1	1.8	43897	45486	45	29	364	23.1	36.5	29.7	8.0	2.7	74839
56183	WESTBROOK	20667	553	34.4	31.3	28.0	4.3	2.0	36746	37933	23	7	460	42.2	29.1	18.5	8.3	2.0	60541
56185	WILMONT	18025	280	24.6	40.0	30.0	3.9	1.4	39436	41142	31	13	242	26.0	27.3	26.4	15.7	4.5	83846
56186	WOODSTOCK	18412	178	30.9	31.5	33.1	2.2	2.2	40339	41619	34	16	156	29.5	21.8	28.2	17.3	3.2	87143
56187	WORTHINGTON	22604	4669	23.8	26.3	39.1	6.9	4.0	49954	51776	61	53	3130	14.2	29.9	44.0	11.2	0.7	97023
56201	WILLMAR	24672	8857	22.8	27.5	35.8	9.2	4.6	49590	51811	60	52	5802	5.9	11.8	57.6	21.8	2.9	130206
56207	ALBERTA	20582	99	15.2	33.3	46.5	4.0	1.0	51025	51520	64	58	85	14.1	34.1	32.9	16.5	2.4	93750
56208	APPLETON	17635	911	37.1	26.3	31.4	4.1	1.1	37164	37776	24	8	654	31.5	35.5	27.2	4.7	1.1	69231
56209	ATWATER	24930	1005	19.3	25.8	45.3	6.5	3.2	53516	55791	69	66	840	10.1	20.1	48.3	15.6	5.8	117857
56210	BARRY	16065	38	34.2	31.6	31.6	2.6	0.0	37351	34054	25	8	33	33.3	27.3	27.3	12.1	0.0	72500
56211	BEARDSLEY	18082	185	31.9	30.3	32.4	3.8	1.6	38271	38747	27	10	163	51.5	20.2	17.2	9.8	1.2	48529
56212	BELLINGHAM	19459	201	29.9	35.3	29.9	3.5	1.5	36819	37396	23	7	166	36.7	19.9	27.1	15.1	1.2	74000
56214	BELVIEW	20699	308	18.8	34.4	39.9	5.2	1.6	47353	49492	55	44	253	23.7	25.7	33.2	13.8	3.6	91250
56215	BENSON	21286	1920	21.9	33.1	39.1	4.4	1.5	43749	46371	45	28	1435	13.5	32.3	45.4	7.7	1.0	93914
56216	BLOMKEST	20446	275	16.0	33.5	40.4	6.2	4.0	50292	51787	62	54	239	12.6	21.8	43.9	17.2	4.6	113603
56218	BOYD	21604	210	23.8	33.8	32.4	7.1	2.9	43383	45186	44	26	176	38.6	30.1	19.9	6.8	4.5	66667
56219	BROWNS VALLEY	18669	345	39.4	29.0	26.7	2.3	2.6	31985	32028	11	3	253	64.4	18.6	11.9	4.7	0.4	36711
56220	CANBY	19708	1114	34.5	28.9	31.6	3.3	1.7	37770	38715	26	9	828	30.4	30.2	31.6	7.1	0.6	71220
56221	CHOKIO	21792	278	27.7	28.1	38.8	4.7	0.7	44266	45817	46	30	229	25.8	36.7	30.6	6.6	0.4	75952
56222	CLARA CITY	20422	797	21.6	37.4	35.0	3.9	2.1	42633	43512	41	24	647	14.5	35.4	37.4	10.5	2.2	90100
56223	CLARKFIELD	19764	655	26.1	30.5	38.2	3.1	2.1	43786	45229	45	28	524	29.8	33.2	25.6	10.1	1.3	70541
56224	CLEMENTS	20748	143	21.0	33.6	38.5	5.6	1.4	45324	46444	49	35	123	27.6	20.3	36.6	10.6	4.9	94167
56225	CLINTON	18767	228	27.6	32.9	34.2	4.4	0.9	42053	43332	39	21	194	44.8	25.8	24.2	4.1	1.0	60000
56226	CLONTARF	23912	74	16.2	29.7	44.6	5.4	4.1	53289	55251	69	66	66	13.6	27.3	43.9	13.6	1.5	102778
56227	CORRELL	17557	105	29.5	36.2	30.5	3.8	0.0	40214	40832	33	15	96	37.5	22.9	27.1	9.4	3.1	68750
56228	COSMOS	21270	412	23.1	31.8	39.1	4.9	1.2	46307	47550	52	40	344	13.1	25.9	39.2	15.4	6.4	103704
56229	COTTONWOOD	23126	593	19.9	27.8	42.5	6.4	3.4	51666	53136	65	61	454	11.7	25.6	47.4	14.1	1.3	113426
56230	DANUBE	24901	314	15.3	32.5	39.5	8.3	4.5	51580	53103	65	60	270	17.4	31.5	38.5	10.0	2.6	91500
56231	DANVERS	21905	160	18.1	28.8	44.4	5.6	3.1	51694	52673	65	61	138	23.2	24.6	35.5	14.5	2.2	93000
56232	DAWSON	21817	913	29.8	29.6	33.3	4.9	2.4	40600	41802	35	17	719	24.5	31.0	36.4	6.8	1.3	82404
56235	DONNELLY	25825	198	23.2	24.2	43.9	6.1	2.5	51586	53625	65	61	177	17.5	33.9	37.9	9.0	1.7	88438
56236	DUMONT	19433	201	26.4	31.8	37.3	1.5	3.0	42333	44081	40	22	170	37.6	21.8	27.6	12.4	0.6	75000
56237	ECHO	20982	244	24.6	32.8	36.5	3.7	2.5	44073	45872	46	29	205	30.7	24.4	33.2	8.8	2.9	81250
56239	GHENT	21023	200	19.0	27.5	44.0	7.5	2.0	52167	53872	66	63	167	15.0	24.0	44.3	15.0	1.8	107386
56240	GRACEVILLE	16556	353	34.8	35.1	27.2	1.7	1.1	34742	35672	17	4	298	32.6	33.6	27.9	4.7	1.3	68529
56241	GRANITE FALLS	23821	1765	25.0	28.8	37.5	5.6	3.1	44742	48191	47	32	1308	15.3	31.6	43.1	9.0	1.0	94271
56243	GROVE CITY	20524	687	23.1	31.1	37.8	6.1	1.7	46206	47639	52	39	545	11.6	21.1	41.8	20.9	4.6	119918
56244	HANCOCK	23011	480	20.8	34.8	34.6	6.9	2.9	46397	47490	53	40	379	30.9	32.2	26.6	6.9	3.4	72292
56245	HANLEY FALLS	17389	235	20.9	35.3	40.0	3.8	0.0	45658	46353	50	37	193	26.4	22.3	34.7	14.5	2.1	92083
56248	HERMAN	20472	378	31.0	27.2	36.8	4.2	0.8	39302	41496	31	13	319	33.5	36.1	24.5	5.0	0.9	66500
56249	HOLLOWAY	20251	139	21.6	34.5	37.4	3.6	2.9	44762	45750	48	33	117	25.6	27.4	27.4	14.5	5.1	85000
56251	KANDIYOHI	24801	418	14.4	28.0	50.7	4.8	2.2	57263	60731	74	73	338	2.7	11.2	55.6	26.3	4.1	140541
56252	KERKHOVEN	20239	409	25.7	32.8	35.7	3.2	2.7	43290	45152	43	26	329	20.1	31.3	37.7	9.1	1.8	88200
56253	LAKE LILLIAN	21830	508	21.1	33.1	38.8	4.5	2.6	46934	48283	54	43	443	15.6	16.7	46.0	16.7	5.0	125753
56255	LUCAN	20032	177	20.3	38.4	35.6	4.0	1.7	44208	45586	46	30	137	23.4	32.1	34.3	9.5	0.7	83182
56256	MADISON	19560	1369	30.2	33.2	31.1	4.2	1.2	38697	39522	29	11	1075	32.7	33.5	25.1	7.1	1.6	67670
56257	MARIETTA	19987	321	30.8	33.6	30.2	3.7	1.6	37128	37940	24	8	272	44.5	22.4	19.5	12.5	1.1	58333
56258	MARSHALL	23633	5628	24.4	23.8	39.4	8.9	3.5	51561	53515	65	60	3319	5.2	15.4	56.0	22.0	1.5	130176
56260	MAYNARD	20554	359	19.8	32.3	41.8	4.2	1.9	47670	49345	56	45	312	18.3	21.5	39.7	16.0	4.5	106667
56262	MILAN	22494	305	22.3	30.5	41.3	4.9	1.0	46364	47875	52	40	248	35.9	28.6	24.6	9.7	1.2	65789
56263	MILROY	20271	242	19.4	36.8	37.2	5.0	1.7	45526	47201	50	35	191	22.5	31.4	34.0	11.0	1.0	85313
56264	MINNEOTA	20781	974	24.4	26.9	42.6	4.8	1.2	48385	50069	58	49	768	18.0	30.1	40.8	10.4	0.8	93061
56265	MONTEVIDEO	23654	3102	22.6	30.5	37.5	7.2	2.3	46116	48635	52	38	2301	14.1	32.5	41.6	10.6	1.2	94906
56266	MORGAN	22423	780	24.2	28.3	38.1	6.3	3.1	47101	49384	54	43	655	22.7	31.3	34.4	8.9	2.7	84592
56267	MORRIS	22935	2653	30.3	21.3	38.3	6.1	4.0	48102	50457	57	47	1701	8.5	28.6	44.1	17.1	1.6	107169
56270	MORTON	22220	410	19.0	31.0	42.7	5.1	2.2	50000	51836	61	53	328	27.1	28.0	33.5	9.1	2.1	82609
56271	MURDOCK	20549	438	22.8	33.1	37.9	3.4	2.7	44800	46649	48	33	361	19.7	28.5	34.9	11.6	5.3	92241
56273	NEW LONDON	23702	1935	17.4	28.4	44.4	7.1	2.7	53133	55611	68	65	1669	10.8	9.2	46.0	29.7	4.3	143215
56274	NORCROSS	22338	96	27.1	27.1	38.5	6.3	1.0	45000	45573	48	34	83	26.5	27.7	37.3	7.2	1.2	85000
56276	ODESSA	17928	123	30.9	35.8	29.3	4.1	0.0	38640	40000	29	11	113	38.9	23.0	23.0	11.5	3.5	67222
56277	OLIVIA	22980	1323	23.1	30.2	36.4	7.3	3.1	46880	48820	54	42	1002	15.7	30.0	43.4	8.8	2.1	95309
	MINNESOTA	31285		15.9	22.3	36.8	16.4	8.6	62767	65994				6.5	9.7	37.4	39.4	7.0	167369
	UNITED STATES	27277		20.9	24.4	35.3	11.7	7.6	54719	56938				9.3	13.1	31.6	32.6	13.5	162279

ZIP CODE #	POST OFFICE NAME	FINANCIAL SERVICES: Auto Loan	Home Loan	Invest-ments	Retire-ment Plans	THE HOME: Home Improvements: Home Repair	Lawn & Garden	Furnishings: Comput-ers & Hard-ware-Personal	Major Appli-ances	TV, Radio, Sound Equip-ment	Furni-ture	ENTERTAINMENT: Dine out/ Carry out	Sports Equip-ment	Fees & Tickets	Toys & Games	Travel	Cable TV	PERSONAL: Apparel & Services	Auto Repairs	Health Insur-ance	Pets & Supplies
56142	IVANHOE	75	53	79	52	55	79	58	72	63	50	61	57	45	62	57	69	40	67	78	87
56143	JACKSON	83	73	83	73	73	90	74	83	78	68	77	64	68	77	74	83	52	80	91	99
56144	JASPER	84	58	93	58	61	89	64	80	67	52	66	66	47	66	64	73	43	75	85	99
56145	JEFFERS	93	64	102	64	67	98	71	88	74	58	73	73	52	73	71	81	47	82	93	109
56146	KANARANZI	93	64	102	64	67	98	71	88	74	58	73	73	52	73	71	81	47	83	93	109
56147	KENNETH	84	58	92	58	60	89	64	80	67	52	66	66	47	65	64	73	43	74	84	98
56149	LAKE BENTON	70	50	73	49	52	74	55	68	59	47	58	52	42	58	53	65	38	63	73	81
56150	LAKEFIELD	81	57	84	56	60	85	63	78	68	54	67	61	49	67	61	75	44	73	84	93
56151	LAKE WILSON	92	63	101	63	66	97	70	87	73	57	72	72	52	72	70	80	47	82	92	108
56152	LAMBERTON	78	55	82	54	57	82	60	75	65	52	64	59	47	64	59	72	42	70	80	90
56153	LEOTA	70	48	77	48	50	74	53	66	55	43	55	55	39	54	53	60	36	62	70	82
56155	LISMORE	84	58	92	57	60	88	64	79	66	52	66	66	47	65	64	73	43	74	84	98
56156	LUVERNE	82	79	85	79	80	92	78	85	81	74	80	64	76	80	80	85	55	83	93	100
56157	LYND	96	96	97	98	95	105	90	98	90	86	90	78	89	91	94	92	62	93	99	117
56158	MAGNOLIA	92	64	102	63	67	98	71	88	73	57	73	73	52	72	70	80	47	82	93	108
56159	MOUNTAIN LAKE	73	51	75	50	53	76	56	70	61	49	60	54	44	60	55	67	39	65	75	83
56160	ODIN	97	67	107	67	70	103	74	92	77	60	77	76	55	76	74	84	50	86	98	114
56161	OKABENA	87	60	95	60	62	91	66	82	69	54	68	68	48	68	66	75	44	77	87	101
56162	ORMSBY	102	70	112	70	73	107	78	97	81	63	80	80	57	79	77	88	52	90	102	119
56164	PIPESTONE	78	61	75	61	62	80	68	76	72	61	70	58	57	71	64	77	47	73	83	90
56165	READING	92	63	101	63	66	97	70	87	73	57	72	72	51	71	70	79	47	81	92	107
56166	REVERE	87	60	95	59	62	91	66	82	69	54	68	68	48	68	66	75	44	77	87	101
56167	ROUND LAKE	93	64	102	64	67	98	71	89	74	58	73	73	52	73	71	81	48	83	94	109
56168	RUSHMORE	88	61	97	61	64	93	67	84	70	55	69	69	49	69	67	77	45	78	89	103
56169	RUSSELL	88	61	96	61	64	93	67	83	70	55	69	69	50	69	67	76	45	78	88	103
56170	RUTHTON	79	54	86	54	57	83	60	75	63	49	62	62	44	61	60	68	40	70	79	92
56171	SHERBURN	80	57	83	56	59	84	62	77	68	54	66	60	49	67	61	75	44	72	83	92
56172	SLAYTON	83	68	88	67	70	92	70	83	76	63	74	63	61	74	71	82	50	79	91	99
56173	STEEN	92	64	101	63	66	97	71	88	73	57	73	72	52	72	70	80	47	82	93	108
56174	STORDEN	94	65	103	64	68	99	72	89	75	58	74	74	53	73	71	81	48	83	94	110
56175	TRACY	80	57	83	56	60	84	63	78	69	55	67	60	49	67	61	75	44	72	84	92
56176	TRIMONT	86	61	89	60	63	90	67	83	73	58	71	64	52	72	65	80	47	77	89	99
56178	TYLER	79	56	82	55	58	83	61	76	66	52	64	59	47	65	60	73	42	71	81	91
56180	WALNUT GROVE	80	56	83	55	58	83	62	77	67	53	65	60	48	66	60	73	43	71	82	92
56181	WELCOME	85	60	88	59	63	89	66	82	72	57	70	63	51	71	65	79	46	76	88	98
56183	WESTBROOK	80	56	83	55	58	83	62	76	67	53	65	60	47	65	60	73	43	71	82	92
56185	WILMONT	84	58	92	58	61	89	64	80	67	52	66	66	47	65	64	73	43	74	84	98
56186	WOODSTOCK	85	59	93	58	61	90	65	81	68	53	67	67	48	66	65	74	43	75	85	99
56187	WORTHINGTON	84	79	78	79	78	87	83	84	85	79	84	63	79	84	80	88	58	85	92	99
56201	WILLMAR	86	82	77	83	80	84	87	83	88	85	88	65	85	88	84	89	61	87	88	100
56207	ALBERTA	100	69	109	68	72	105	76	95	79	62	78	78	56	78	76	86	51	88	100	116
56208	APPLETON	75	53	78	52	55	79	58	72	64	51	62	56	46	63	57	70	41	68	78	86
56209	ATWATER	97	79	102	79	83	100	84	95	87	77	85	72	73	85	84	92	57	91	100	113
56210	BARRY	74	52	77	51	54	77	57	71	61	48	60	56	44	60	56	67	39	66	76	85
56211	BEARDSLEY	80	55	88	55	58	85	61	76	64	50	63	63	45	62	61	70	41	71	80	94
56212	BELLINGHAM	83	57	91	57	60	87	63	79	66	51	65	65	46	64	63	72	42	73	83	97
56214	BELVIEW	95	65	104	65	68	100	72	90	75	59	74	74	53	74	72	82	48	84	95	111
56215	BENSON	81	66	81	66	68	88	68	81	73	61	71	61	59	73	68	79	48	76	87	95
56216	BLOMKEST	107	74	118	74	77	113	82	102	85	66	84	84	60	84	82	93	55	95	108	125
56218	BOYD	95	66	105	66	69	101	73	91	76	59	75	75	53	74	73	83	49	85	96	112
56219	BROWNS VALLEY	74	53	75	52	55	77	58	71	64	51	62	54	46	63	56	70	41	67	78	85
56220	CANBY	78	55	80	54	57	81	61	75	66	53	64	58	47	65	59	73	43	70	81	89
56221	CHOKIO	87	60	96	60	63	92	67	83	69	54	69	69	49	68	66	76	45	78	88	102
56222	CLARA CITY	86	60	90	59	63	90	66	82	72	57	70	64	51	71	65	79	46	77	89	99
56223	CLARKFIELD	84	59	88	58	62	88	65	81	71	56	69	63	50	69	64	78	45	75	87	97
56224	CLEMENTS	93	64	103	64	67	99	71	89	74	58	73	73	52	73	71	81	48	83	94	109
56225	CLINTON	79	56	80	55	59	82	62	76	68	54	66	58	49	67	60	75	44	71	83	90
56226	CLONTARF	114	78	125	78	82	120	87	108	90	70	89	89	64	89	86	99	58	101	114	133
56227	CORRELL	76	52	84	52	55	80	58	72	61	47	60	60	43	59	58	66	39	68	76	89
56228	COSMOS	78	74	71	77	75	85	72	80	73	66	72	61	67	75	72	77	49	74	82	93
56229	COTTONWOOD	97	80	94	82	82	103	82	96	85	72	83	75	70	85	82	91	56	89	99	113
56230	DANUBE	112	77	123	77	81	119	86	107	89	70	88	88	63	88	85	97	57	100	113	131
56231	DANVERS	101	70	111	69	73	107	77	96	80	63	79	79	57	79	77	88	52	90	101	118
56232	DAWSON	85	60	87	59	63	89	66	82	73	58	70	63	52	71	65	80	47	76	89	97
56235	DONNELLY	103	71	113	71	74	109	79	98	82	64	81	81	58	80	78	89	52	91	103	120
56236	DUMONT	91	62	99	62	65	96	69	86	72	56	71	71	51	71	69	78	46	80	91	106
56237	ECHO	90	62	98	62	65	95	68	85	71	55	70	70	50	70	68	78	46	79	90	105
56239	GHENT	99	68	109	68	71	105	76	94	79	61	78	78	56	77	75	86	51	88	100	116
56240	GRACEVILLE	69	49	71	48	51	72	54	67	60	47	58	51	43	59	53	66	38	62	73	79
56241	GRANITE FALLS	84	74	87	73	75	92	75	85	79	69	78	64	68	78	76	85	53	82	93	100
56243	GROVE CITY	91	66	98	67	69	96	72	87	74	60	73	71	55	73	72	80	48	82	92	107
56244	HANCOCK	104	72	114	71	75	110	79	99	83	64	82	82	58	81	79	90	53	92	104	122
56245	HANLEY FALLS	85	59	94	59	61	90	65	81	68	53	67	67	48	66	65	74	43	76	86	100
56248	HERMAN	80	57	83	56	60	84	63	78	69	55	67	59	49	68	61	76	44	72	84	92
56249	HOLLOWAY	91	63	100	63	66	96	70	87	72	56	72	72	51	71	69	79	46	81	91	107
56251	KANDIYOHI	93	89	86	93	90	101	86	95	88	80	87	73	82	89	87	92	59	89	97	111
56252	KERKHOVEN	91	65	95	63	67	93	67	85	74	61	73	65	53	73	67	81	48	79	89	102
56253	LAKE LILLIAN	94	65	103	65	68	99	72	89	75	58	74	74	53	73	71	81	48	83	94	110
56255	LUCAN	90	62	99	62	65	95	69	85	72	56	71	71	50	70	68	78	46	80	90	105
56256	MADISON	80	56	84	55	59	84	62	77	67	53	65	60	48	66	61	74	43	72	83	92
56257	MARIETTA	80	55	88	55	57	84	61	76	63	49	63	63	45	62	61	69	41	71	80	93
56258	MARSHALL	84	77	73	80	75	80	87	80	85	82	85	65	81	86	80	85	59	84	83	97
56260	MAYNARD	95	65	104	65	68	100	72	90	75	59	74	74	53	74	72	82	48	84	95	111
56262	MILAN	91	63	100	62	66	96	70	86	72	56	71	71	51	71	69	79	46	81	91	106
56263	MILROY	93	64	103	64	67	99	71	89	74	58	73	73	52	73	71	81	48	83	94	109
56264	MINNEOTA	85	66	86	66	68	90	69	83	73	60	72	65	57	73	69	79	48	77	88	99
56265	MONTEVIDEO	86	72	82	72	73	89	77	84	80	70	78	64	68	79	74	84	53	82	90	100
56266	MORGAN	94	68	99	67	70	99	74	90	79	63	77	71	58	78	73	86	51	85	97	109
56267	MORRIS	83	70	80	72	71	83	81	80	82	74	81	64	72	80	77	85	56	82	88	97
56270	MORTON	90	75	87	77	77	96	77	89	79	67	78	69	66	80	76	84	52	82	92	105
56271	MURDOCK	93	64	102	64	67	98	71	88	74	58	73	73	52	73	71	81	47	83	93	109
56273	NEW LONDON	99	82	105	84	86	105	83	99	86	74	85	76	72	86	85	92	57	92	101	116
56274	NORCROSS	88	61	97	61	64	93	67	84	70	55	69	69	49	69	67	77	45	78	89	103
56276	ODESSA	76	52	83	52	54	80	58	72	60	47	59	59	42	59	57	65	39	67	76	88
56277	OLIVIA	84	76	85	74	76	93	73	84	79	69	78	63	69	78	75	85	53	80	92	99
	MINNESOTA	113	113	112	114	112	114	112	113	111	111	112	88	112	113	112	112	78	112	113	133
	UNITED STATES	100	100	100	100	100	100	100	100	100	100	100	100	100	100	100	100	100	100	100	100

ZIP CODE #	POST OFFICE NAME	COUNTY FIPS CODE	POPULATION 2000	POPULATION 2009	POPULATION 2014	2000-2009 ANNUAL RATE % Rate	2000-2009 ANNUAL RATE State Centile	HOUSEHOLDS 2000	HOUSEHOLDS 2009	HOUSEHOLDS 2014	HOUSEHOLDS % Annual Rate 2000-2009	HOUSEHOLDS 2009 Average HH Size	FAMILIES 2000	FAMILIES 2009	FAMILIES % Annual Rate 2000-2009
56278	ORTONVILLE	011	2886	2892	2821	0.0	48	1218	1233	1204	0.1	2.28	818	798	-0.3
56279	PENNOCK	067	1237	1271	1278	0.3	58	427	454	461	0.7	2.80	340	351	0.3
56280	PORTER	173	382	354	338	-0.8	15	158	150	144	-0.6	2.36	116	107	-0.9
56281	PRINSBURG	067	643	680	692	0.6	67	249	272	279	1.0	2.50	197	209	0.6
56282	RAYMOND	067	1835	1815	1786	-0.1	44	650	659	653	0.1	2.75	504	497	-0.2
56283	REDWOOD FALLS	127	7095	6736	6491	-0.6	22	2857	2774	2688	-0.3	2.32	1823	1701	-0.7
56284	RENVILLE	129	2209	2119	2063	-0.4	30	817	795	776	-0.3	2.56	576	543	-0.6
56285	SACRED HEART	129	1395	1268	1213	-1.0	9	551	512	492	-0.3	2.48	389	350	-1.1
56287	SEAFORTH	127	107	102	98	-0.5	26	46	45	44	-0.2	2.20	33	32	-0.3
56288	SPICER	067	4490	4628	4665	0.3	58	1862	1996	2031	0.8	2.32	1330	1375	0.4
56289	SUNBURG	067	712	674	656	-0.6	22	286	281	276	-0.2	2.40	217	206	-0.6
56291	TAUNTON	083	330	312	303	-0.6	22	114	111	109	-0.3	2.68	85	80	-0.7
56292	VESTA	127	710	622	586	-1.4	3	255	228	216	-1.2	2.72	189	163	-1.6
56293	WABASSO	127	1256	1219	1189	-0.3	35	473	473	466	0.0	2.48	334	322	-0.4
56294	WANDA	127	108	98	93	-1.0	9	47	44	42	-0.7	2.23	38	35	-0.9
56295	WATSON	023	321	302	291	-0.7	18	127	123	120	-0.3	2.46	89	84	-0.6
56296	WHEATON	155	2330	2109	2011	-1.1	7	1007	934	897	-0.8	2.18	635	565	-1.3
56297	WOOD LAKE	173	907	845	807	-0.8	15	364	345	331	-0.6	2.45	259	237	-1.0
56301	SAINT CLOUD	145	29639	32413	33626	1.0	77	10152	11559	12166	1.4	2.57	5805	6430	1.1
56303	SAINT CLOUD	145	23865	26268	27337	1.0	77	9692	11015	11532	1.4	2.33	5880	6357	0.8
56304	SAINT CLOUD	141	15581	17476	18374	1.2	81	6129	7083	7541	1.6	2.26	3232	3508	0.9
56307	ALBANY	145	4241	4782	5028	1.3	83	1471	1740	1855	1.8	2.68	1073	1211	1.3
56308	ALEXANDRIA	041	21750	24120	25022	1.1	79	8934	10174	10636	1.4	2.32	5878	6473	1.0
56309	ASHBY	051	1107	1030	988	-0.8	15	427	401	386	-0.7	2.50	318	292	-0.9
56310	AVON	145	5386	5740	5903	0.7	69	1881	2132	2228	1.4	2.53	1510	1654	1.0
56311	BARRETT	051	768	681	643	-1.3	4	284	254	239	-1.2	2.48	207	179	-1.6
56312	BELGRADE	145	2584	2819	2928	0.9	74	938	1076	1136	1.5	2.57	660	720	0.9
56313	BOCK	095	106	107	122	0.1	51	46	47	54	0.2	2.28	37	37	0.0
56314	BOWLUS	097	1025	997	980	-0.3	35	355	358	355	0.1	2.78	263	255	-0.3
56315	BRANDON	041	1514	1565	1580	0.4	61	602	648	661	0.8	2.41	449	468	0.4
56316	BROOTEN	145	1108	1201	1240	0.9	74	439	500	524	1.4	2.40	302	326	0.8
56318	BURTRUM	153	1539	1551	1545	0.1	51	577	602	606	0.5	2.58	404	405	0.0
56319	CARLOS	041	1233	1392	1461	1.3	83	483	563	597	1.7	2.46	354	398	1.3
56320	COLD SPRING	145	7287	8419	8915	1.6	86	2551	3099	3335	2.1	2.68	1977	2306	1.7
56323	CYRUS	121	938	952	955	0.2	54	356	375	381	0.6	2.54	260	265	0.2
56324	DALTON	111	1100	1288	1354	1.7	88	447	535	564	2.0	2.41	338	392	1.6
56326	EVANSVILLE	041	1450	1483	1496	0.2	54	566	605	619	0.7	2.34	377	384	0.2
56327	FARWELL	121	843	899	920	0.7	69	320	352	364	1.0	2.55	237	254	0.8
56328	FLENSBURG	097	32	33	32	0.3	58	11	12	12	0.9	2.75	9	9	0.0
56329	FOLEY	009	6856	8060	8639	1.8	89	2338	2813	3041	2.0	2.80	1783	2080	1.7
56330	FORESTON	095	1055	1499	1713	3.9	97	381	557	641	4.2	2.69	298	423	3.9
56331	FREEPORT	145	2093	2444	2585	1.7	88	693	849	912	2.2	2.86	557	659	1.8
56332	GARFIELD	041	1187	1302	1338	1.0	77	435	487	504	1.2	2.67	335	364	0.9
56334	GLENWOOD	121	6231	6071	6030	-0.3	35	2545	2546	2548	0.0	2.30	1680	1621	-0.4
56336	GREY EAGLE	153	2308	2360	2382	0.2	54	871	919	935	0.6	2.56	636	648	0.2
56338	HILLMAN	097	1573	1725	1774	1.0	77	605	692	722	1.5	2.49	449	495	1.1
56339	HOFFMAN	051	1025	943	901	-0.9	12	404	374	357	-0.8	2.34	266	239	-1.2
56340	HOLDINGFORD	145	2326	2524	2600	0.9	74	814	926	968	1.4	2.70	627	689	1.0
56341	HOLMES CITY	041	35	38	39	0.9	74	11	12	13	0.9	3.17	9	10	1.1
56342	ISLE	065	2044	2445	2604	2.0	91	902	1106	1188	2.2	2.21	596	703	1.8
56343	KENSINGTON	041	712	758	769	0.7	69	296	326	335	1.0	2.33	224	239	0.7
56345	LITTLE FALLS	097	14744	15175	15171	0.3	58	5611	5949	6003	0.6	2.48	3864	3964	0.3
56347	LONG PRAIRIE	153	7057	6994	6945	-0.1	44	2601	2627	2624	0.1	2.60	1827	1779	-0.3
56349	LOWRY	121	517	520	512	0.1	51	197	204	202	0.4	2.55	152	154	0.1
56350	MC GRATH	001	538	565	575	0.5	63	232	251	257	0.9	2.25	153	160	0.5
56352	MELROSE	145	5571	5851	5978	0.5	63	2001	2186	2263	1.0	2.65	1474	1543	0.5
56353	MILACA	095	7282	9417	10383	2.8	94	2725	3616	4022	3.1	2.55	1921	2464	2.7
56354	MILTONA	041	1034	990	978	-0.5	26	416	412	411	-0.1	2.40	313	301	-0.4
56355	NELSON	041	560	618	636	1.1	79	209	239	249	1.5	2.56	163	181	1.1
56357	OAK PARK	009	694	852	928	2.2	92	236	295	323	2.4	2.89	189	230	2.1
56358	OGILVIE	065	2648	2998	3156	1.4	84	949	1096	1159	1.6	2.74	708	794	1.2
56359	ONAMIA	095	3673	3870	3921	0.6	67	1368	1487	1520	0.9	2.49	930	971	0.5
56360	OSAKIS	041	3245	4313	4797	3.1	95	1325	1872	2120	3.8	2.25	909	1216	3.2
56361	PARKERS PRAIRIE	111	2646	2608	2570	-0.2	39	1020	1025	1015	0.1	2.45	716	694	-0.3
56362	PAYNESVILLE	145	5926	6456	6685	0.9	74	2217	2541	2673	1.5	2.50	1629	1785	1.0
56363	PEASE	095	137	132	147	-0.4	30	53	53	59	0.0	2.49	42	41	-0.3
56364	PIERZ	097	5087	5346	5400	0.5	63	1781	1949	1989	1.0	2.69	1319	1394	0.6
56367	RICE	009	5468	6723	7308	2.3	92	1859	2339	2559	2.5	2.87	1479	1799	2.1
56368	RICHMOND	145	4074	4488	4682	1.1	79	1509	1756	1862	1.7	2.55	1175	1315	1.2
56373	ROYALTON	097	2720	3243	3462	1.9	90	959	1195	1292	2.4	2.71	748	901	2.0
56374	SAINT JOSEPH	145	9857	10479	10782	0.7	69	2305	2654	2800	1.5	2.89	1703	1867	1.0
56375	SAINT STEPHEN	145	891	924	938	0.4	61	300	329	339	1.0	2.81	244	259	0.6
56377	SARTELL	145	11586	16120	17877	3.6	97	4084	5896	6615	4.0	2.71	3067	4329	3.8
56378	SAUK CENTRE	145	6402	6870	7061	0.8	72	2434	2728	2842	1.2	2.48	1695	1804	0.7
56379	SAUK RAPIDS	009	13581	15939	17062	1.7	88	5112	6159	6662	2.0	2.54	3536	4091	1.6
56381	STARBUCK	121	2369	2539	2609	0.8	72	971	1068	1109	1.0	2.29	649	686	0.6
56382	SWANVILLE	097	1383	1473	1494	0.7	69	492	535	547	0.9	2.75	373	392	0.5
56384	UPSALA	097	178	180	175	0.1	51	86	89	88	0.4	2.02	59	58	-0.2
56385	VILLARD	121	999	988	995	-0.1	44	366	377	383	0.3	2.62	278	278	0.0
56386	WAHKON	095	965	1026	1063	0.7	69	417	453	473	0.9	2.26	276	288	0.5
56387	WAITE PARK	145	6020	6788	7136	1.3	83	2777	3330	3561	2.0	2.02	1444	1594	1.1
56389	WEST UNION	153	88	88	88	0.0	48	32	33	33	0.3	2.67	27	27	0.0
56401	BRAINERD	035	27384	30799	32151	1.3	83	10833	12441	13062	1.5	2.41	7128	7981	1.2
56425	BAXTER	035	5561	6623	6955	1.9	90	1922	2419	2571	2.5	2.71	1519	1794	1.8
56431	AITKIN	001	8015	8587	8673	0.7	69	3489	3822	3892	1.0	2.20	2318	2436	0.5
56433	AKELEY	057	1471	1601	1650	0.9	74	614	685	712	1.2	2.31	440	472	0.8
56434	ALDRICH	159	71	69	68	-0.3	35	32	32	32	0.0	2.16	22	21	-0.5
56435	BACKUS	021	2723	2879	2931	0.6	67	1064	1163	1194	1.0	2.40	764	806	0.6
56437	BERTHA	153	1253	1231	1188	-0.2	39	459	464	451	0.1	2.65	333	324	-0.3
56438	BROWERVILLE	153	2323	2735	2899	1.8	89	868	1068	1145	2.3	2.54	618	732	1.8
56440	CLARISSA	153	1425	1378	1355	-0.4	30	533	531	527	0.0	2.43	353	337	-0.5
56441	CROSBY	035	4752	5049	5089	0.7	69	1964	2144	2183	1.0	2.32	1263	1321	0.5
56442	CROSSLAKE	035	2033	2254	2326	1.1	79	971	1120	1167	1.6	2.01	683	755	1.1
56443	CUSHING	097	1638	1613	1583	-0.2	39	675	687	680	0.2	2.35	497	491	-0.1
56444	DEERWOOD	035	3101	3090	3037	0.0	48	1297	1324	1314	0.2	2.29	941	927	-0.2
	MINNESOTA					0.9					1.1	2.48			0.7
	UNITED STATES					1.0					1.1	2.59			0.9

ZIP CODE #	POST OFFICE NAME	RACE (%) White 2000	White 2009	Black 2000	Black 2009	Asian/Pacific 2000	Asian/Pacific 2009	% Hispanic Origin 2000	% Hispanic Origin 2009	2009 AGE DISTRIBUTION (%) 0-4	5-9	10-14	15-19	20-24	25-44	45-64	65-84	85+	18+	MEDIAN AGE 2009	% 2009 Males	% 2009 Females
56278	ORTONVILLE	97.9	97.6	0.3	0.4	0.3	0.3	0.5	0.7	4.7	4.9	5.3	6.5	6.2	19.1	29.1	19.1	5.0	81.0	47.4	47.0	53.0
56279	PENNOCK	95.4	93.0	0.1	0.2	0.3	0.5	4.4	7.2	6.3	6.9	7.5	7.9	4.8	25.7	29.5	10.1	1.3	74.4	39.1	51.0	49.0
56280	PORTER	99.2	99.2	0.3	0.3	0.0	0.0	0.0	0.0	6.8	7.3	7.6	6.5	4.0	22.9	31.6	11.3	2.0	74.0	40.5	51.4	48.6
56281	PRINSBURG	98.6	98.1	0.2	0.3	0.3	0.3	0.8	1.2	6.5	7.1	6.9	6.5	5.1	23.7	27.4	14.3	2.6	75.4	41.3	50.1	49.9
56282	RAYMOND	96.7	95.2	0.5	0.8	0.2	0.2	3.7	6.0	7.2	7.9	8.2	8.0	4.6	24.4	27.3	10.6	1.9	71.6	37.8	50.8	49.2
56283	REDWOOD FALLS	93.0	91.3	0.2	0.3	0.5	0.7	1.9	2.7	6.3	6.3	6.6	6.8	5.8	22.7	27.7	13.6	4.3	76.2	41.4	49.6	50.4
56284	RENVILLE	94.3	92.1	0.0	0.0	0.3	0.4	6.8	9.9	6.8	7.6	7.6	6.7	4.8	22.4	24.5	14.6	4.8	73.4	40.4	50.2	49.8
56285	SACRED HEART	97.6	96.5	0.1	0.1	0.2	0.4	4.2	6.4	5.3	6.9	7.1	7.2	4.8	23.0	28.2	15.5	2.0	75.7	41.9	51.0	49.0
56287	SEAFORTH	99.1	99.0	0.0	0.0	0.9	1.0	0.9	0.0	5.9	5.9	5.9	5.9	4.9	21.6	32.4	13.7	3.9	78.4	45.0	53.9	46.1
56288	SPICER	98.7	98.0	0.1	0.2	0.2	0.3	0.9	1.5	4.9	5.8	6.6	7.1	4.9	22.9	32.2	13.8	1.8	78.1	43.4	50.0	50.0
56289	SUNBURG	99.0	98.5	0.3	0.4	0.1	0.1	0.3	0.6	4.5	4.9	6.2	7.6	3.9	24.6	31.6	15.0	1.8	79.7	43.9	53.7	46.3
56291	TAUNTON	97.3	95.8	0.0	0.0	0.3	0.6	1.8	2.2	7.1	7.7	8.0	8.0	4.2	23.1	26.3	12.2	3.5	71.8	39.1	52.9	47.1
56292	VESTA	98.7	98.4	0.3	0.3	0.1	0.2	0.4	0.8	8.5	9.2	8.4	7.2	4.3	23.2	24.3	13.3	1.6	69.3	36.1	53.1	46.9
56293	WABASSO	99.1	98.9	0.0	0.0	0.2	0.2	0.6	0.8	6.6	6.3	7.8	7.3	5.2	22.2	25.9	13.8	4.9	73.9	41.1	49.3	50.7
56294	WANDA	99.1	99.0	0.0	0.0	0.0	0.0	0.9	2.0	4.1	5.1	10.2	9.2	3.1	21.4	32.7	12.2	2.0	73.5	42.9	53.1	46.9
56295	WATSON	97.8	96.7	0.0	0.0	0.6	1.0	1.2	2.0	5.3	6.0	7.0	7.0	4.3	21.2	34.4	12.9	2.0	77.2	44.5	51.3	48.7
56296	WHEATON	99.2	99.1	0.0	0.0	0.3	0.4	1.2	1.8	5.2	5.6	5.7	6.3	5.0	18.8	26.5	19.9	6.9	79.2	47.5	48.2	51.8
56297	WOOD LAKE	96.0	94.8	0.1	0.1	0.1	0.1	3.5	5.1	6.5	7.1	7.0	6.5	4.5	23.7	29.2	13.0	2.5	75.4	41.2	51.7	48.3
56301	SAINT CLOUD	92.8	90.2	1.8	2.8	3.3	4.4	1.5	2.4	5.7	5.6	5.5	10.5	18.1	26.1	20.8	6.7	1.0	79.4	27.9	50.7	49.3
56303	SAINT CLOUD	93.6	91.2	1.4	2.1	2.6	3.9	1.2	1.8	6.2	6.2	6.3	7.4	7.8	28.8	25.6	10.1	1.4	77.1	35.5	49.9	50.1
56304	SAINT CLOUD	90.0	87.2	3.6	4.3	2.7	4.0	1.5	2.3	6.0	5.2	4.8	7.7	16.1	26.1	20.8	9.8	3.5	80.8	31.0	50.2	49.8
56307	ALBANY	98.8	98.3	0.1	0.2	0.1	0.2	0.6	0.9	7.9	7.6	7.3	6.7	6.0	25.5	24.7	11.0	3.2	72.7	36.6	50.4	49.6
56308	ALEXANDRIA	98.4	97.8	0.2	0.3	0.5	0.7	0.7	1.0	5.7	5.6	5.5	6.2	6.3	24.5	27.9	14.8	3.5	79.8	41.8	49.2	50.8
56309	ASHBY	98.4	97.9	0.1	0.1	0.0	0.1	0.3	0.5	4.6	4.9	5.3	6.6	4.8	20.5	32.2	17.6	3.6	80.8	47.1	50.5	49.5
56310	AVON	98.7	98.2	0.1	0.2	0.4	0.6	1.2	1.8	6.9	7.4	7.4	8.5	7.2	24.7	27.7	9.1	1.0	74.1	36.5	53.2	46.8
56311	BARRETT	98.6	98.2	0.7	0.7	0.1	0.1	0.4	0.6	5.3	5.6	5.9	6.0	4.1	22.0	28.2	16.9	6.0	79.7	45.7	51.2	48.8
56312	BELGRADE	99.3	99.0	0.0	0.0	0.0	0.1	0.6	0.9	6.2	7.2	7.3	7.8	4.8	24.2	25.3	13.6	3.6	73.8	39.5	51.4	48.6
56313	BOCK	99.0	99.1	0.0	0.0	0.0	0.0	1.0	0.9	6.5	6.5	7.5	7.5	4.7	25.2	30.8	10.3	0.9	73.8	39.7	53.3	46.7
56314	BOWLUS	99.4	99.2	0.1	0.1	0.2	0.2	0.4	0.5	7.1	7.6	7.3	6.5	4.9	27.7	26.7	10.7	1.4	73.8	37.7	53.3	46.7
56315	BRANDON	98.7	98.1	0.0	0.0	0.7	1.0	0.5	0.6	5.0	5.3	7.7	7.7	4.4	21.9	32.8	13.3	1.9	77.0	43.6	51.1	48.9
56316	BROOTEN	99.0	98.5	0.1	0.2	0.1	0.2	1.5	2.4	7.0	7.1	7.5	7.8	4.7	23.9	26.8	13.0	2.2	72.8	39.1	52.1	47.9
56318	BURTRUM	99.1	98.6	0.1	0.1	0.1	0.3	0.6	0.8	6.1	6.7	7.1	7.0	4.3	24.7	28.9	13.6	1.5	75.6	40.4	52.4	47.6
56319	CARLOS	99.1	98.6	0.2	0.3	0.3	0.5	0.5	0.6	5.3	6.1	6.8	6.5	4.5	25.2	29.8	14.0	1.8	77.7	42.2	52.5	47.5
56320	COLD SPRING	97.9	96.8	0.4	0.5	0.2	0.3	2.1	3.2	7.1	7.6	7.8	7.4	4.8	24.9	27.7	10.7	2.1	72.6	38.9	50.5	49.5
56323	CYRUS	98.3	98.2	0.6	0.7	0.2	0.2	0.2	0.2	4.8	6.1	7.9	8.2	4.1	22.5	30.9	13.7	1.9	75.6	42.4	50.9	49.1
56324	DALTON	99.1	98.7	0.2	0.2	0.3	0.5	0.4	0.5	4.6	5.1	6.4	7.8	3.9	20.2	35.2	14.8	1.9	78.7	46.1	52.0	48.0
56326	EVANSVILLE	99.3	99.2	0.0	0.0	0.2	0.2	0.1	0.1	5.9	6.3	6.5	6.1	4.0	22.7	28.4	15.1	5.0	77.0	43.8	50.8	49.2
56327	FARWELL	98.6	98.3	0.2	0.2	0.4	0.4	0.4	0.6	5.7	6.3	6.3	7.0	4.2	23.1	31.9	13.5	1.9	76.9	43.0	51.2	48.8
56328	FLENSBURG	100.0	100.0	0.0	0.0	0.0	0.0	0.0	0.0	6.1	6.1	6.1	9.1	6.1	24.2	36.4	6.1	0.0	72.7	38.8	48.5	51.5
56329	FOLEY	98.2	97.8	0.5	0.6	0.3	0.4	0.4	0.6	7.5	7.3	7.3	7.3	5.9	27.2	25.2	10.1	2.2	73.3	35.6	51.9	48.1
56330	FORESTON	98.9	98.4	0.1	0.1	0.1	0.1	1.4	2.2	7.1	7.5	7.9	7.8	5.0	26.6	27.1	9.8	1.1	72.4	37.1	52.0	48.0
56331	FREEPORT	99.4	99.3	0.1	0.2	0.0	0.0	0.2	0.4	7.0	7.2	7.3	7.4	5.0	26.0	26.9	11.1	2.2	73.8	38.1	51.8	48.2
56332	GARFIELD	98.5	98.1	0.0	0.0	0.3	0.5	0.3	0.5	6.0	6.5	7.0	7.5	4.7	23.8	31.3	12.2	1.2	76.0	41.2	49.8	50.2
56334	GLENWOOD	98.9	98.9	0.2	0.2	0.0	0.0	0.6	0.6	5.0	4.8	5.6	7.2	5.0	21.2	28.6	17.6	4.9	79.8	45.8	49.3	50.7
56336	GREY EAGLE	99.0	98.8	0.1	0.1	0.2	0.3	0.3	0.6	5.4	5.9	6.7	8.3	4.7	22.4	29.5	15.1	1.9	76.5	42.5	51.7	48.3
56338	HILLMAN	97.5	97.0	0.1	0.2	0.2	0.3	0.8	1.2	6.7	6.4	6.7	6.5	5.0	22.8	29.6	15.0	1.3	76.1	41.9	52.1	47.9
56339	HOFFMAN	98.6	98.4	0.4	0.4	0.1	0.1	0.2	0.2	5.5	5.7	5.6	5.9	5.2	21.2	26.0	17.7	7.1	79.6	45.6	48.3	51.7
56340	HOLDINGFORD	99.2	98.9	0.0	0.0	0.2	0.4	0.2	0.4	6.9	7.3	7.4	7.4	5.3	26.1	27.7	10.2	1.7	73.6	37.8	51.5	48.5
56341	HOLMES CITY	100.0	100.0	0.0	0.0	0.0	0.0	0.0	0.0	5.3	5.3	5.3	5.3	5.3	21.1	42.1	10.5	0.0	78.9	46.0	50.0	50.0
56342	ISLE	93.7	91.9	0.2	0.2	0.3	0.4	1.0	1.5	5.4	6.0	6.1	5.3	3.7	20.2	31.9	19.3	2.2	79.1	47.1	50.5	49.5
56343	KENSINGTON	98.6	98.0	0.1	0.1	0.4	0.7	0.6	0.9	4.7	5.9	6.1	7.3	4.5	21.1	34.4	14.1	1.8	78.4	45.3	51.2	48.8
56345	LITTLE FALLS	98.0	97.5	0.3	0.4	0.4	0.6	0.7	1.1	6.5	6.4	6.8	7.1	6.0	23.9	26.9	13.1	3.2	75.7	39.8	49.2	50.8
56347	LONG PRAIRIE	96.2	94.8	0.1	0.1	0.4	0.6	4.5	6.5	6.5	6.6	7.2	7.5	5.4	22.6	26.9	13.8	3.4	75.0	40.1	50.1	49.9
56349	LOWRY	98.5	98.1	0.0	0.0	0.2	0.4	0.2	0.2	5.2	5.8	6.2	7.5	4.8	23.5	31.2	14.0	1.9	78.3	42.7	53.1	46.9
56350	MC GRATH	97.2	96.8	0.2	0.2	0.4	0.5	1.5	1.8	5.8	6.2	6.4	6.5	4.4	19.5	32.6	17.0	1.6	77.5	45.8	52.7	47.3
56352	MELROSE	97.5	96.6	0.3	0.4	0.3	0.5	6.7	9.5	7.5	7.7	7.7	6.9	5.0	25.4	25.3	11.7	2.8	72.4	37.7	50.8	49.2
56353	MILACA	97.7	97.1	0.3	0.3	0.2	0.3	0.8	1.2	6.5	6.5	6.9	7.4	5.7	24.4	27.5	12.3	2.8	75.4	39.6	49.7	50.3
56354	MILTONA	98.8	98.4	0.0	0.0	0.3	0.4	0.7	1.1	5.3	5.4	6.7	7.6	3.4	22.3	31.2	17.1	1.1	77.6	44.6	52.9	47.1
56355	NELSON	98.7	98.2	0.2	0.2	0.0	0.2	0.9	1.5	4.7	6.8	8.1	7.6	5.7	25.4	30.4	10.4	1.0	75.4	40.2	52.6	47.4
56357	OAK PARK	98.3	97.7	0.1	0.1	0.1	0.2	0.9	1.2	7.3	7.5	7.4	6.5	5.3	26.4	28.6	10.1	0.9	73.9	37.9	50.5	49.5
56358	OGILVIE	97.5	96.8	0.1	0.2	0.8	1.2	0.7	1.1	6.0	7.4	8.2	7.9	5.4	26.5	27.8	9.8	1.0	73.1	37.0	51.7	48.3
56359	ONAMIA	78.6	75.9	0.4	0.5	0.1	0.2	1.1	1.6	6.4	6.2	6.2	8.1	5.9	21.0	27.8	15.6	2.7	75.6	41.7	49.4	50.6
56360	OSAKIS	98.1	97.8	0.1	0.2	0.5	0.6	0.8	1.0	6.3	6.7	6.9	6.6	4.6	21.7	27.5	15.9	3.9	75.9	42.8	50.1	49.9
56361	PARKERS PRAIRIE	98.9	98.6	0.0	0.0	0.1	0.2	0.5	0.7	5.3	5.3	5.8	6.5	5.4	21.9	29.3	16.6	3.8	79.4	44.8	50.2	49.8
56362	PAYNESVILLE	98.8	98.2	0.1	0.2	0.4	0.6	0.9	1.4	6.6	6.9	7.2	6.4	4.6	24.4	27.2	13.6	3.1	75.3	40.6	50.6	49.4
56363	PEASE	96.4	96.2	1.4	1.5	0.7	0.8	0.7	0.8	6.1	6.8	7.6	7.6	5.3	24.2	29.5	11.4	1.5	75.0	38.9	50.8	49.2
56364	PIERZ	99.2	99.0	0.0	0.0	0.1	0.1	0.4	0.5	7.4	6.9	7.3	7.4	5.5	25.9	24.8	11.9	2.8	73.7	37.4	51.0	49.0
56367	RICE	98.8	98.4	0.1	0.1	0.2	0.3	0.6	0.9	7.6	7.5	7.9	7.7	5.8	27.6	27.1	7.9	0.8	71.8	35.2	51.5	48.5
56368	RICHMOND	98.7	98.1	0.2	0.2	0.2	0.4	0.8	1.2	6.2	6.8	7.0	6.8	4.5	26.4	28.1	12.6	1.6	75.6	40.5	51.5	48.5
56373	ROYALTON	99.0	98.8	0.0	0.0	0.3	0.4	0.5	0.8	7.9	7.4	7.8	7.6	6.0	27.3	26.8	8.1	1.1	72.0	34.7	52.2	47.8
56374	SAINT JOSEPH	97.2	95.9	0.7	1.0	1.1	1.6	1.0	1.5	5.0	4.8	5.0	15.4	21.9	20.5	18.7	7.7	1.0	81.6	24.5	48.0	52.0
56375	SAINT STEPHEN	99.3	98.9	0.0	0.0	0.2	0.3	0.4	0.8	6.5	8.9	7.8	9.2	5.7	31.0	24.6	5.5	0.9	70.1	34.4	52.6	47.4
56377	SARTELL	97.5	96.4	0.3	0.5	1.2	1.8	0.8	1.3	9.3	8.5	7.9	6.8	6.5	31.5	21.6	6.1	1.9	70.1	31.8	48.6	51.4
56378	SAUK CENTRE	98.7	98.3	0.2	0.3	0.2	0.3	0.7	1.1	6.6	6.6	6.9	8.0	6.1	23.3	25.4	14.1	3.1	74.6	39.0	48.9	51.1
56379	SAUK RAPIDS	97.5	96.8	0.5	0.5	0.7	1.0	0.9	1.3	7.5	7.0	6.7	6.9	7.3	30.1	24.4	8.2	2.0	74.5	34.3	48.8	51.2
56381	STARBUCK	98.9	98.8	0.2	0.2	0.0	0.1	0.5	0.5	5.0	5.8	6.5	6.4	5.2	18.8	28.0	18.3	6.0	78.0	46.6	48.6	51.4
56382	SWANVILLE	98.7	98.2	0.0	0.0	0.8	1.2	0.9	1.3	7.8	8.4	8.4	7.9	4.6	22.2	27.6	11.3	1.8	70.3	37.1	50.6	49.4
56384	UPSALA	98.9	98.9	0.0	0.0	0.0	0.0	0.6	0.6	6.7	6.7	7.2	8.3	5.0	23.3	29.4	11.1	2.2	73.3	39.5	52.8	47.2
56385	VILLARD	99.0	98.9	0.1	0.1	0.2	0.2	0.7	0.8	6.0	6.6	6.5	7.8	5.0	22.3	30.5	13.7	1.8	75.8	41.5	50.9	49.1
56386	WAHKON	94.2	92.7	0.2	0.2	0.1	0.2	1.0	1.6	4.9	5.4	5.5	4.8	3.5	20.0	32.9	21.0	2.1	81.2	48.8	51.1	48.9
56387	WAITE PARK	93.1	90.5	0.7	1.0	3.3	4.7	1.9	2.9	6.9	4.9	4.1	5.1	13.9	33.6	16.9	11.6	2.8	81.9	30.2	48.9	51.1
56389	WEST UNION	100.0	100.0	0.0	0.0	0.0	0.0	0.0	0.0	5.7	8.0	8.0	10.2	3.4	21.6	29.5	11.4	2.3	71.6	40.0	53.4	46.6
56401	BRAINERD	96.8	96.2	0.4	0.6	0.3	0.5	0.8	1.2	6.6	6.3	6.6	7.2	6.4	25.3	26.7	12.2	2.6	76.8	38.5	49.5	50.5
56425	BAXTER	98.5	97.7	0.1	0.2	0.4	0.7	0.6	1.1	6.8	7.3	8.2	8.2	4.5	24.8	27.8	10.6	1.9	72.3	38.2	48.3	51.7
56431	AITKIN	97.5	97.1	0.2	0.3	0.2	0.4	0.5	0.8	4.6	4.7	4.9	5.3	4.0	17.5	31.3	23.4	4.4	82.5	51.4	49.5	50.5
56433	AKELEY	97.1	96.8	0.1	0.2	0.2	0.2	0.7	1.0	4.9	5.6	6.1	6.1	3.6	19.2	34.0	18.9	1.7	79.5	48.1	51.5	48.5
56434	ALDRICH	97.2	97.1	0.0	0.0	0.0	0.0	1.4	1.4	7.2	7.2	7.2	5.8	5.8	23.2	29.0	11.6	2.9	75.4	39.4	49.3	50.7
56435	BACKUS	97.7	97.0	0.1	0.1	0.4	0.6	0.3	0.4	4.3	4.6	5.1	5.8	4.1	18.3	32.0	21.8	4.0	82.2	50.4	49.8	50.2
56437	BERTHA	98.9	98.5	0.0	0.0	0.1	0.1	0.4	0.6	6.2	6.4	6.4	6.7	5.6	22.5	28.6	14.7	2.8	76.8	41.3	46.6	53.4
56438	BROWERVILLE	97.2	96.6	0.0	0.0	0.3	0.5	1.2	1.8	6.2	6.6	7.0	7.7	5.2	22.6	28.4	13.8	2.4	75.0	40.9	50.7	49.3
56440	CLARISSA	98.3	97.9	0.2	0.3	0.3	0.4	0.6	0.9	5.2	5.5	5.9	6.7	5.4	20.8	27.6	16.8	6.0	78.6	45.3	49.9	50.1
56441	CROSBY	98.1	97.6	0.2	0.3	0.2	0.3	0.6	0.9	6.0	5.9	5.9	5.9	5.8	21.3	29.2	16.6	3.4	78.5	44.3	48.2	51.8
56442	CROSSLAKE	99.1	98.8	0.3	0.4	0.1	0.2	0.5	0.8	3.2	3.6	4.2	4.2	2.4	13.9	34.2	31.4	2.9	86.2	57.2	51.0	49.0
56443	CUSHING	98.4	97.8	0.4	0.6	0.1	0.1	0.8	1.2	4.2	6.1	6.7	7.8	4.2	20.1	32.6	17.0	1.4	77.6	45.6	52.6	47.4
56444	DEERWOOD	98.3	97.8	0.3	0.4	0.1	0.2	0.7	1.1	5.0	5.2	5.6	5.7	4.3	16.7	33.5	20.7	3.2	80.6	49.9	49.2	50.8
	MINNESOTA	89.4	86.8	3.5	4.3	2.9	3.9	2.9	4.1	6.8	6.7	6.7	7.2	6.8	27.2	26.3	10.2	2.1	75.6	36.9	49.6	50.4
	UNITED STATES	75.1	72.0	12.3	12.7	3.8	4.6	12.5	15.7	6.8	6.7	6.6	7.1	6.9	27.0	26.0	10.9	1.9	75.7	36.9	49.2	50.8

ZIP CODE #	POST OFFICE NAME	2009 Per Capita Income	2009 HH Income Base	2009 Household Income Distribution (%) Less than $25,000	$25,000 to $49,999	$50,000 to $99,999	$100,000 to $149,999	$150,000 or More	Median Household Income 2009	2014	2009 National Centile	2009 State Centile	2009 Home Value Base	2009 Home Value Distribution (%) Less than $50,000	$50,000 to $89,999	$90,000 to $174,999	$175,000 to $399,999	$400,000 or More	2009 Median Home Value
56278	ORTONVILLE	18975	1233	32.0	35.4	28.1	3.2	1.3	36746	37895	23	7	1024	27.0	38.2	27.7	5.9	1.3	68900
56279	PENNOCK	21888	454	14.3	26.4	47.8	8.8	2.6	54730	56168	71	69	392	10.2	12.2	43.9	28.8	4.8	143750
56280	PORTER	21356	150	24.0	29.3	42.7	4.0	0.0	46752	47635	53	42	123	19.5	29.3	31.7	17.1	2.4	91875
56281	PRINSBURG	24947	272	18.0	33.5	37.5	5.9	5.1	48644	50425	58	49	247	6.5	30.8	49.0	11.7	2.0	103989
56282	RAYMOND	19677	659	19.7	31.3	41.9	4.4	2.7	48962	50284	59	50	528	11.2	24.4	45.8	15.2	3.4	114655
56283	REDWOOD FALLS	25347	2774	19.3	30.1	39.2	8.3	3.1	50479	52324	62	56	2074	15.2	26.4	46.0	11.6	0.9	101521
56284	RENVILLE	19941	795	20.9	32.3	40.0	5.9	0.9	46617	48441	53	41	626	20.3	34.8	36.3	6.7	1.9	84576
56285	SACRED HEART	21244	512	18.0	33.4	43.2	3.9	1.6	48551	50187	58	49	413	25.7	35.4	30.5	7.7	0.7	78143
56287	SEAFORTH	23841	45	17.8	35.6	42.2	4.4	0.0	47351	50000	55	44	37	27.0	24.3	32.4	13.5	2.7	87500
56288	SPICER	29869	1996	16.7	24.6	43.3	9.5	5.8	59061	62208	76	76	1657	4.2	7.8	41.6	36.9	9.6	167866
56289	SUNBURG	21973	281	20.6	32.0	40.9	4.6	1.8	46995	49633	54	43	248	12.1	14.9	47.2	21.8	4.0	131122
56291	TAUNTON	20758	111	19.8	24.3	48.6	4.5	2.7	54105	54475	70	68	88	14.8	30.7	34.1	17.0	3.4	100000
56292	VESTA	19093	228	23.2	33.8	34.6	5.3	3.1	44341	46854	46	31	193	35.2	30.6	26.4	7.3	0.5	68846
56293	WABASSO	20801	473	24.9	32.3	35.9	4.0	2.7	44424	46260	47	31	386	35.8	22.0	34.5	6.2	1.6	75000
56294	WANDA	22674	44	25.0	34.1	31.8	6.8	2.3	42313	43187	40	22	37	29.7	24.3	29.7	10.8	5.4	82500
56295	WATSON	22724	123	17.1	30.1	43.9	7.3	1.6	52124	54523	66	63	101	31.7	22.8	24.8	16.8	4.0	81000
56296	WHEATON	21038	934	33.3	29.4	29.9	5.1	2.2	37687	38578	26	9	742	36.7	29.2	28.6	4.9	0.7	63333
56297	WOOD LAKE	20457	345	23.5	31.6	39.7	3.8	1.4	46235	47240	52	39	286	29.7	30.4	28.0	10.5	1.4	70000
56301	SAINT CLOUD	25400	11559	21.4	23.1	39.4	9.6	6.5	54037	56921	70	68	6874	4.5	5.0	44.3	40.6	5.6	167877
56303	SAINT CLOUD	27745	11015	17.8	26.1	40.5	10.3	5.5	54615	57653	71	69	7381	1.3	6.8	66.7	23.5	1.7	139351
56304	SAINT CLOUD	26266	7083	21.3	30.3	32.5	10.8	5.0	47847	49866	56	46	3238	7.8	8.9	46.6	32.6	4.1	148372
56307	ALBANY	21224	1740	24.7	26.2	39.5	5.7	3.9	48667	51471	58	50	1396	6.1	10.5	49.6	29.0	4.8	144538
56308	ALEXANDRIA	25295	10174	23.6	25.9	39.0	7.5	4.1	50413	52803	62	55	7348	5.3	8.1	43.1	37.6	5.9	162617
56309	ASHBY	20959	401	22.2	33.9	36.4	4.5	3.0	43981	45650	45	29	343	16.6	23.6	43.1	14.0	2.6	106250
56310	AVON	27116	2132	13.1	22.0	48.2	11.5	5.2	61598	64177	79	80	1883	2.8	5.0	41.7	43.9	6.6	175988
56311	BARRETT	20672	254	23.6	27.6	41.7	5.5	1.6	48026	49103	57	47	217	22.6	22.6	35.0	14.7	5.1	98750
56312	BELGRADE	18647	1076	31.7	29.1	33.2	4.3	1.8	39034	40241	30	12	886	18.1	28.4	30.5	18.2	4.9	100694
56313	BOCK	23509	47	23.4	23.4	44.7	6.4	2.1	52098	53749	66	63	44	4.5	11.4	43.2	40.9	0.0	165000
56314	BOWLUS	18695	358	25.1	24.6	42.5	6.4	1.4	50160	50901	62	54	313	4.8	20.8	46.0	23.3	5.1	127679
56315	BRANDON	22813	648	24.5	28.5	37.3	7.3	2.3	47357	49467	55	44	567	10.2	16.6	41.6	30.7	0.9	133160
56316	BROOTEN	21243	500	25.2	30.8	37.6	3.6	2.8	43332	45000	43	26	418	21.8	27.3	31.3	17.5	2.2	94000
56318	BURTRUM	20078	602	25.1	28.7	37.9	6.6	1.7	45821	47959	51	38	513	14.2	20.3	42.3	20.7	2.5	114495
56319	CARLOS	25117	563	18.7	25.4	41.7	10.3	3.9	53794	55133	69	67	505	10.3	15.6	32.9	34.3	6.9	154009
56320	COLD SPRING	24809	3099	13.3	25.7	48.5	8.7	3.8	59163	61573	76	76	2524	4.3	4.7	44.6	41.5	5.0	168223
56323	CYRUS	20825	375	23.7	30.4	38.4	4.5	2.9	45635	46320	50	36	313	15.3	26.8	35.8	17.6	4.5	104847
56324	DALTON	24034	535	16.6	32.5	41.5	6.5	2.8	50497	50576	62	56	478	12.1	15.7	45.0	24.5	2.7	127985
56326	EVANSVILLE	19732	605	34.0	26.4	32.2	6.0	1.3	40210	42188	33	15	482	17.6	22.2	36.1	21.0	3.1	109333
56327	FARWELL	21549	352	23.6	28.4	39.5	5.1	3.4	47548	49180	56	45	303	11.9	15.8	37.3	31.0	4.0	139453
56328	FLENSBURG	16212	12	33.3	33.3	25.0	8.3	0.0	40000	40000	33	15	10	0.0	10.0	80.0	10.0	0.0	125000
56329	FOLEY	21782	2813	18.9	24.8	44.4	8.5	3.4	55386	58412	72	70	2405	8.8	12.4	40.3	34.1	4.4	150911
56330	FORESTON	20846	557	16.0	32.0	44.5	6.1	1.4	51060	51317	64	58	497	6.2	9.1	40.0	42.1	2.6	163578
56331	FREEPORT	20767	849	21.2	25.2	42.4	7.2	4.0	51750	52978	65	61	749	6.7	12.1	42.3	30.7	8.1	148892
56332	GARFIELD	19503	487	18.7	30.8	45.4	4.3	0.8	50270	51467	62	54	441	12.5	10.4	43.3	31.3	2.5	148438
56334	GLENWOOD	25142	2546	23.6	29.0	37.9	5.5	3.9	47059	48096	54	43	1969	8.4	22.5	45.8	20.7	2.6	117537
56336	GREY EAGLE	22008	919	22.5	30.3	37.1	6.9	3.3	46702	48905	53	42	824	11.0	18.0	41.9	26.7	2.4	129318
56338	HILLMAN	19757	692	27.6	28.8	37.0	4.9	1.7	43408	45000	44	27	637	9.7	13.8	44.0	28.9	3.6	138625
56339	HOFFMAN	19442	374	33.4	26.5	33.7	5.3	1.1	39796	41395	32	14	296	20.9	34.8	29.7	12.2	2.4	81905
56340	HOLDINGFORD	20772	926	19.7	29.3	43.0	5.5	2.6	50535	51468	62	56	816	5.5	16.8	45.0	30.3	2.5	143371
56341	HOLMES CITY	14803	12	25.0	33.3	33.3	8.3	0.0	40000	37321	33	15	11	0.0	0.0	45.5	54.5	0.0	187500
56342	ISLE	22587	1106	26.3	31.0	35.4	5.2	2.2	43188	44474	43	26	930	9.6	18.3	38.9	29.5	3.8	133523
56343	KENSINGTON	23972	326	21.8	26.7	42.0	6.4	3.1	50786	52234	63	57	291	13.1	13.1	30.6	39.5	3.8	161071
56345	LITTLE FALLS	21816	5949	24.7	27.1	38.7	6.9	2.7	47943	49726	56	46	4517	7.5	19.0	51.4	20.4	1.7	123564
56347	LONG PRAIRIE	18542	2627	27.4	31.1	35.7	4.2	1.6	42743	44693	42	24	2067	12.5	24.4	47.2	14.8	1.2	108190
56349	LOWRY	21202	204	20.1	33.8	38.2	5.4	2.5	45509	46146	50	35	181	6.6	13.3	49.2	27.1	3.9	131548
56350	MC GRATH	22234	251	30.3	33.1	28.7	4.4	3.6	37189	37796	24	8	226	15.5	17.3	47.8	17.7	1.8	123333
56352	MELROSE	19852	2186	24.1	28.7	39.9	4.3	2.9	45217	49474	49	34	1785	9.3	18.3	43.5	25.4	3.5	125384
56353	MILACA	20141	3616	25.9	28.2	38.4	5.5	2.0	45558	47015	50	36	2922	7.8	12.6	43.1	33.9	2.6	149383
56354	MILTONA	22392	412	25.5	27.2	39.3	5.3	2.7	48020	49437	57	47	365	4.9	13.4	39.2	36.7	5.8	159012
56355	NELSON	21962	239	17.6	32.6	40.2	7.5	2.1	49787	52240	61	52	210	7.1	10.0	47.6	28.6	6.7	150781
56357	OAK PARK	21134	295	14.6	26.1	47.5	8.8	3.1	56193	57447	73	72	275	8.0	14.9	35.3	37.5	4.4	157955
56358	OGILVIE	19476	1096	20.8	27.7	44.3	5.6	1.6	50647	51068	63	57	938	15.4	19.8	38.9	24.1	1.8	116949
56359	ONAMIA	19580	1487	30.3	28.2	32.8	6.5	2.3	40977	41761	36	18	1108	11.6	17.8	36.9	29.3	4.4	134007
56360	OSAKIS	20717	1872	32.2	28.4	32.6	5.0	1.8	40000	41180	33	15	1470	8.9	18.8	46.3	23.3	2.7	121000
56361	PARKERS PRAIRIE	19178	1025	32.1	30.3	31.4	3.9	2.2	38041	39219	27	10	882	17.5	24.9	40.0	16.0	1.6	100591
56362	PAYNESVILLE	23555	2541	20.3	25.2	43.6	7.3	3.6	52775	54641	68	64	2082	5.0	14.9	48.3	26.0	5.8	134364
56363	PEASE	22867	53	13.2	35.8	43.4	5.7	1.9	50327	47983	62	55	48	2.1	10.4	43.8	37.5	6.3	162500
56364	PIERZ	18303	1949	28.7	27.8	36.8	4.8	2.0	44379	46017	46	31	1648	7.5	15.7	44.3	28.2	4.4	137547
56367	RICE	22869	2339	12.1	24.7	52.2	8.3	2.7	60195	61947	78	77	2153	11.1	7.6	39.9	36.9	4.5	156424
56368	RICHMOND	23427	1756	15.9	26.4	48.2	7.2	2.3	54274	55894	70	68	1553	3.4	7.4	48.4	36.1	4.7	158353
56373	ROYALTON	20799	1195	19.8	29.5	41.6	6.4	2.7	50458	51404	62	55	997	5.5	14.9	48.1	28.5	2.9	139985
56374	SAINT JOSEPH	20981	2654	13.0	23.1	49.5	10.1	4.3	59275	61935	77	76	2140	3.4	4.1	50.5	38.7	3.4	163642
56375	SAINT STEPHEN	28421	329	6.4	18.8	56.8	11.6	6.4	68132	70913	86	86	299	2.0	3.3	45.8	40.5	8.4	173349
56377	SARTELL	30811	5896	12.3	13.8	48.6	17.2	8.1	73370	76606	89	89	4712	9.2	4.6	33.3	47.5	5.4	180284
56378	SAUK CENTRE	22617	2728	21.2	27.6	42.6	5.9	2.7	50845	52503	63	57	2086	7.3	21.9	44.9	23.1	2.9	122175
56379	SAUK RAPIDS	27240	6159	13.4	23.4	45.2	13.5	4.6	62302	65183	80	81	4234	3.9	6.0	49.9	37.6	2.6	160590
56381	STARBUCK	21170	1068	29.5	26.5	36.6	6.2	1.2	43869	45336	45	28	863	11.5	27.1	43.2	14.9	3.2	108700
56382	SWANVILLE	18241	535	25.8	28.8	38.5	4.7	2.2	45837	47561	51	38	450	9.8	17.3	52.4	18.0	2.4	117268
56384	UPSALA	26369	89	23.6	32.6	37.1	4.5	2.2	45372	46295	49	35	73	8.2	19.2	39.7	28.8	4.1	137500
56385	VILLARD	19553	377	25.2	32.4	34.5	4.8	3.2	43644	44581	44	28	330	10.9	21.8	48.2	16.4	2.7	117727
56386	WAHKON	22368	453	25.6	31.1	34.9	6.0	2.4	43265	44195	43	26	384	9.9	16.7	35.4	33.1	4.9	145139
56387	WAITE PARK	25497	3330	21.1	32.4	41.7	2.7	2.2	45296	48642	49	34	1325	4.0	16.0	49.6	29.1	1.3	140479
56389	WEST UNION	21504	33	18.2	30.3	39.4	9.1	3.0	51025	46145	64	58	31	3.2	12.9	48.4	32.3	3.2	140625
56401	BRAINERD	22827	12441	25.7	28.0	36.5	6.9	2.9	46701	48985	53	41	8991	9.1	14.7	42.1	28.3	5.8	139128
56425	BAXTER	24850	2419	12.8	23.3	48.4	11.0	4.5	61162	63084	79	79	1973	3.0	3.3	50.0	42.0	1.7	165540
56431	AITKIN	24213	3822	26.5	29.7	35.0	5.8	3.0	43778	46227	45	28	3080	8.0	17.5	43.1	27.9	3.6	132417
56433	AKELEY	20704	685	26.7	32.0	35.3	4.8	1.2	41835	43119	39	21	600	18.5	18.0	30.5	28.0	5.0	125417
56434	ALDRICH	16087	32	40.6	31.3	28.1	0.0	0.0	31479	40000	11	2	24	25.0	41.7	25.0	8.3	0.0	70000
56435	BACKUS	19392	1163	29.0	32.1	33.2	4.4	1.4	40946	41972	36	18	1034	11.3	19.4	40.3	25.4	3.5	128879
56437	BERTHA	15148	464	39.9	30.0	24.4	5.4	0.4	33627	35381	15	3	378	24.6	35.7	27.8	11.1	0.8	74667
56438	BROWERVILLE	18332	1068	32.8	27.1	33.4	5.3	1.4	40000	40774	33	15	887	11.0	31.8	47.1	9.5	0.6	98819
56440	CLARISSA	19106	531	34.7	33.9	24.1	3.8	3.6	36973	37540	24	7	441	20.4	30.2	40.1	8.2	1.1	89306
56441	CROSBY	20320	2144	33.0	28.6	31.7	4.9	1.8	39091	40745	30	12	1693	12.2	26.6	35.7	21.0	4.5	109230
56442	CROSSLAKE	34776	1120	16.4	28.7	37.9	10.1	6.9	53978	56566	70	67	1034	2.8	7.4	22.1	41.3	26.5	261739
56443	CUSHING	22776	687	24.3	30.3	37.0	5.5	2.9	45677	46904	50	37	626	8.9	17.6	44.4	25.4	3.7	125000
56444	DEERWOOD	26276	1324	21.7	25.5	40.0	9.7	3.1	52426	55254	67	63	1127	7.9	8.4	31.1	44.5	8.1	182500
	MINNESOTA	31285		15.9	22.3	36.8	16.4	8.6	62767	65994				6.5	9.7	37.4	39.4	7.0	167369
	UNITED STATES	27277		20.9	24.4	35.3	11.7	7.6	54719	56938				9.3	13.1	31.6	32.6	13.5	162279

ZIP CODE #	POST OFFICE NAME	FINANCIAL SERVICES: Auto Loan	Home Loan	Invest-ments	Retire-ment Plans	THE HOME: Home Improvements: Home Repair	Lawn & Garden	Furnishings: Comput-ers & Hard-ware-Personal	Major Appli-ances	TV, Radio, Sound Equip-ment	Furni-ture	ENTERTAINMENT: Dine out/ Carry out	Sports Equip-ment	Fees & Tickets	Toys & Games	Travel	Cable TV	PERSONAL: Apparel & Services	Auto Repairs	Health Insur-ance	Pets & Supplies
56278	ORTONVILLE	74	53	76	52	55	78	58	72	64	51	62	55	46	63	56	71	41	67	78	85
56279	PENNOCK	89	93	94	95	92	98	85	93	85	84	85	71	87	85	90	86	59	88	92	109
56280	PORTER	90	62	99	62	65	95	69	86	72	56	71	71	50	70	68	78	46	80	90	105
56281	PRINSBURG	112	77	122	77	80	118	85	106	89	69	88	88	62	87	85	97	57	99	112	130
56282	RAYMOND	94	69	102	69	71	100	74	90	77	62	76	74	57	76	74	83	50	85	95	111
56283	REDWOOD FALLS	93	79	90	80	81	97	83	92	87	76	85	70	75	86	82	92	58	89	98	109
56284	RENVILLE	89	63	93	62	66	94	69	86	75	60	73	67	54	74	68	83	48	80	93	103
56285	SACRED HEART	92	64	97	64	67	96	71	88	76	60	74	70	54	75	70	84	49	82	94	106
56287	SEAFORTH	95	65	104	65	68	100	73	90	75	59	75	75	53	74	72	82	48	84	95	111
56288	SPICER	105	97	111	98	100	110	96	106	98	93	97	79	92	97	99	101	66	102	108	124
56289	SUNBURG	92	67	107	66	71	97	71	89	74	61	74	71	56	72	73	81	48	83	92	108
56291	TAUNTON	101	69	111	69	73	107	77	96	80	63	79	79	57	79	77	88	51	90	101	118
56292	VESTA	93	64	102	64	67	98	71	88	74	58	73	73	52	72	71	81	47	82	93	109
56293	WABASSO	90	64	94	63	67	95	70	87	76	60	74	68	54	75	69	84	49	81	94	104
56294	WANDA	90	62	99	62	65	95	69	86	72	56	71	71	51	70	69	78	46	80	91	105
56295	WATSON	100	69	110	68	72	105	76	95	79	62	78	78	56	78	76	86	51	88	100	117
56296	WHEATON	80	57	82	55	59	83	62	77	68	54	66	59	49	67	60	75	44	72	83	91
56297	WOOD LAKE	90	62	98	61	65	95	68	85	71	55	70	70	50	70	68	78	46	79	90	105
56301	SAINT CLOUD	98	89	79	92	85	86	108	90	100	98	101	76	97	101	93	97	71	97	90	109
56303	SAINT CLOUD	92	89	79	91	85	88	96	88	94	92	95	71	93	95	91	94	66	92	92	106
56304	SAINT CLOUD	90	74	70	78	72	75	96	80	93	89	93	66	85	93	82	92	65	89	84	98
56307	ALBANY	87	77	84	78	76	91	80	86	83	73	82	68	73	82	79	87	56	84	92	103
56308	ALEXANDRIA	87	80	88	81	82	91	83	88	85	79	84	66	79	84	83	89	58	87	94	103
56309	ASHBY	95	65	104	65	68	100	72	90	75	59	74	74	53	74	72	82	48	84	95	111
56310	AVON	100	111	100	113	109	110	99	104	97	99	98	81	105	100	105	98	68	100	103	122
56311	BARRETT	94	65	103	65	68	99	72	89	75	58	74	74	53	73	71	82	48	83	94	110
56312	BELGRADE	83	60	87	59	62	88	65	80	69	55	68	63	50	68	64	76	45	75	85	96
56313	BOCK	75	84	72	86	81	82	75	78	74	75	74	61	80	76	79	74	52	75	77	92
56314	BOWLUS	83	71	79	74	73	89	72	83	75	64	73	64	64	75	72	79	50	77	86	98
56315	BRANDON	93	72	117	71	79	98	74	93	77	67	76	70	62	74	79	83	50	86	93	110
56316	BROOTEN	82	70	77	72	72	87	71	81	73	62	72	63	62	74	70	78	48	75	84	96
56318	BURTRUM	84	70	80	73	72	89	72	83	74	63	73	65	62	75	71	79	49	77	86	98
56319	CARLOS	93	90	96	93	93	102	86	97	87	81	86	73	83	88	89	90	59	90	97	112
56320	COLD SPRING	97	101	93	105	100	106	93	100	93	90	93	77	95	96	97	96	65	95	101	117
56323	CYRUS	95	65	104	65	68	100	72	90	75	59	74	74	53	74	72	82	48	84	95	110
56324	DALTON	99	75	121	75	82	104	78	98	81	70	80	75	64	78	82	87	53	91	99	116
56326	EVANSVILLE	83	58	93	58	61	88	64	79	66	52	66	65	48	65	64	72	43	74	83	97
56327	FARWELL	95	71	114	70	76	100	74	93	77	65	77	72	60	75	78	83	50	87	95	111
56328	FLENSBURG	80	55	88	55	57	84	61	76	63	49	63	63	45	62	61	69	41	71	80	93
56329	FOLEY	92	88	85	90	86	99	86	92	87	81	87	72	83	89	87	90	59	89	96	110
56330	FORESTON	85	81	78	84	82	92	78	87	80	72	79	66	75	81	79	83	54	81	89	101
56331	FREEPORT	99	80	105	81	81	106	82	96	84	72	83	79	69	83	83	89	55	91	100	117
56332	GARFIELD	83	72	86	74	75	88	72	84	74	65	73	63	65	74	73	79	49	78	85	98
56334	GLENWOOD	93	78	95	78	80	97	82	91	84	75	83	70	72	83	81	89	56	88	96	109
56336	GREY EAGLE	91	77	87	79	79	97	78	90	81	69	79	70	68	81	78	86	53	84	94	107
56338	HILLMAN	85	64	102	63	69	89	66	84	69	59	68	64	54	67	70	75	45	78	85	99
56339	HOFFMAN	79	57	84	56	60	83	62	77	68	55	66	58	50	66	61	75	44	72	83	91
56340	HOLDINGFORD	90	78	89	80	79	96	78	89	80	70	79	70	70	80	79	84	53	84	92	106
56341	HOLMES CITY	78	63	101	62	69	83	63	80	66	59	65	58	54	62	68	70	43	73	79	92
56342	ISLE	82	67	100	67	73	87	67	84	70	62	69	61	59	68	71	75	46	77	83	97
56343	KENSINGTON	93	74	120	73	82	98	74	95	78	70	77	69	65	74	81	83	51	87	93	110
56345	LITTLE FALLS	80	75	75	77	75	85	76	81	79	72	78	62	73	79	76	82	53	79	86	95
56347	LONG PRAIRIE	81	61	80	61	63	83	66	77	71	59	69	60	54	70	64	76	46	74	83	93
56349	LOWRY	96	67	107	67	71	101	74	92	77	61	76	75	55	75	74	83	49	86	96	112
56350	MC GRATH	88	65	95	63	68	90	66	84	72	61	71	63	54	71	66	79	47	77	86	99
56352	MELROSE	90	69	88	70	71	93	72	86	76	64	75	67	59	76	71	82	50	80	89	103
56353	MILACA	79	72	74	73	73	82	72	79	74	69	73	59	68	75	71	78	50	75	82	92
56354	MILTONA	92	70	113	69	76	97	72	91	76	65	75	69	60	73	76	81	49	85	92	108
56355	NELSON	87	80	79	84	82	93	79	88	81	72	79	67	73	82	79	85	54	82	91	102
56357	OAK PARK	94	86	85	90	88	101	85	96	87	77	86	72	79	89	85	92	59	88	98	111
56358	OGILVIE	89	74	77	73	74	86	73	82	78	73	77	61	65	80	70	82	52	78	84	98
56359	ONAMIA	78	63	92	63	68	81	67	79	71	63	70	58	59	68	69	76	47	76	81	92
56360	OSAKIS	81	59	87	59	62	85	63	78	68	55	66	61	50	66	63	74	44	73	83	94
56361	PARKERS PRAIRIE	83	58	87	57	61	87	64	79	69	55	67	62	49	68	63	76	44	74	85	95
56362	PAYNESVILLE	88	85	91	86	86	99	81	91	84	76	83	69	79	83	85	88	57	86	96	107
56363	PEASE	88	80	80	84	82	95	79	89	82	72	80	68	73	83	79	86	55	83	92	104
56364	PIERZ	83	64	87	64	66	88	67	81	71	59	70	64	56	70	67	76	46	76	85	97
56367	RICE	100	99	91	99	96	102	92	98	93	92	93	75	91	95	92	95	64	94	98	116
56368	RICHMOND	89	89	85	91	88	96	83	91	84	79	83	70	82	86	86	86	57	86	92	107
56373	ROYALTON	87	83	79	83	82	89	79	85	80	78	80	64	76	82	78	82	55	81	85	101
56374	SAINT JOSEPH	95	100	89	101	97	93	98	95	96	99	97	75	100	98	98	94	68	96	92	112
56375	SAINT STEPHEN	111	125	108	129	122	123	112	116	110	112	111	91	119	113	118	110	77	112	115	137
56377	SARTELL	124	132	110	129	124	113	122	119	116	129	119	95	124	123	120	112	83	116	109	137
56378	SAUK CENTRE	85	77	83	76	78	91	78	85	82	73	81	63	73	81	77	86	55	83	92	100
56379	SAUK RAPIDS	102	101	84	102	95	96	101	97	100	102	100	77	100	103	97	98	70	98	97	116
56381	STARBUCK	80	62	81	62	65	83	67	78	71	61	70	59	56	70	66	77	47	75	84	93
56382	SWANVILLE	88	63	94	63	66	93	69	84	71	57	71	69	52	70	68	78	46	79	89	103
56384	UPSALA	95	66	105	65	69	101	73	91	76	59	75	75	53	74	72	83	49	85	96	111
56385	VILLARD	90	64	103	64	68	95	70	87	72	59	72	70	53	70	71	79	47	81	90	105
56386	WAHKON	84	68	109	67	74	89	68	86	71	63	70	63	59	67	73	75	46	79	85	100
56387	WAITE PARK	77	59	54	63	56	60	77	65	77	75	78	53	69	78	67	77	54	74	70	80
56389	WEST UNION	103	71	113	70	74	108	78	97	81	63	81	80	57	80	78	89	52	91	103	120
56401	BRAINERD	82	76	79	77	76	83	79	81	80	76	79	62	75	80	77	82	55	81	84	96
56425	BAXTER	98	106	91	106	102	100	96	99	94	98	95	77	99	97	98	93	66	95	95	115
56431	AITKIN	83	71	98	70	77	88	73	85	77	71	75	60	67	73	76	81	51	81	90	98
56433	AKELEY	80	64	104	63	71	85	64	82	67	60	66	60	56	64	70	72	44	75	81	95
56434	ALDRICH	62	44	64	43	46	63	46	58	51	42	50	43	36	50	45	56	33	53	60	69
56435	BACKUS	78	63	96	62	68	83	63	79	66	58	65	58	55	63	67	70	43	73	79	92
56437	BERTHA	69	49	71	48	51	72	54	67	59	47	57	51	42	58	52	65	38	62	72	79
56438	BROWERVILLE	79	58	81	57	60	83	63	77	68	55	66	59	50	67	62	74	44	72	82	91
56440	CLARISSA	80	58	81	57	61	84	63	78	70	56	67	59	51	68	62	76	45	72	84	92
56441	CROSBY	75	59	78	59	62	77	65	74	69	59	68	55	56	67	63	74	46	71	79	87
56442	CROSSLAKE	106	98	144	96	110	121	92	113	97	96	95	76	91	89	103	102	65	106	119	129
56443	CUSHING	87	73	92	74	76	92	73	87	76	66	75	66	64	75	75	81	50	81	89	102
56444	DEERWOOD	100	81	124	80	88	105	82	101	85	77	84	74	72	82	87	91	56	94	101	117
	MINNESOTA	113	113	112	114	112	114	112	113	111	111	112	88	112	113	112	112	78	112	113	133
	UNITED STATES	100	100	100	100	100	100	100	100	100	100	100	100	100	100	100	100	100	100	100	100

ZIP CODE #	POST OFFICE NAME	COUNTY FIPS CODE	POPULATION 2000	POPULATION 2009	POPULATION 2014	2000-2009 ANNUAL RATE % Rate	2000-2009 ANNUAL RATE State Centile	HOUSEHOLDS 2000	HOUSEHOLDS 2009	HOUSEHOLDS 2014	HOUSEHOLDS % Annual Rate 2000-2009	HOUSEHOLDS 2009 Average HH Size	FAMILIES 2000	FAMILIES 2009	FAMILIES % Annual Rate 2000-2009
56446	EAGLE BEND	153	1543	1464	1425	-0.6	22	614	600	589	-0.2	2.44	433	407	-0.7
56447	EMILY	035	964	986	983	0.2	54	419	447	452	0.7	2.21	287	293	0.2
56448	FIFTY LAKES	035	355	351	348	-0.1	44	174	178	178	0.2	1.97	119	116	-0.3
56449	FORT RIPLEY	035	1202	1583	1767	3.0	95	427	584	658	3.4	2.71	339	449	3.1
56450	GARRISON	035	933	1014	1060	0.9	74	442	493	520	1.2	2.06	305	327	0.8
56452	HACKENSACK	021	1764	1852	1883	0.5	63	828	896	919	0.9	2.05	593	620	0.5
56453	HEWITT	153	1143	1105	1081	-0.4	30	424	422	417	-0.1	2.61	323	312	-0.4
56455	IRONTON	035	695	761	771	1.0	77	302	340	348	1.3	2.24	206	222	0.8
56456	JENKINS	035	216	244	272	1.3	83	89	105	118	1.8	2.32	64	73	1.4
56458	LAKE GEORGE	057	171	185	190	0.9	74	67	74	77	1.1	2.50	51	54	0.6
56461	LAPORTE	057	2727	3098	3226	1.4	84	1024	1198	1260	1.7	2.59	797	903	1.4
56464	MENAHGA	159	3659	3788	3764	0.4	61	1401	1490	1493	0.7	2.46	964	986	0.2
56465	MERRIFIELD	035	1462	1772	1892	2.1	92	591	734	787	2.4	2.41	432	516	1.9
56466	MOTLEY	021	2670	3003	3134	1.3	83	1089	1256	1320	1.6	2.38	782	872	1.2
56467	NEVIS	057	2118	2180	2202	0.3	58	917	966	983	0.6	2.25	678	690	0.2
56468	NISSWA	035	4300	4470	4581	0.4	61	1822	1965	2031	0.8	2.27	1338	1381	0.3
56469	PALISADE	001	1338	1464	1496	1.0	77	558	630	650	1.3	2.32	417	457	1.0
56470	PARK RAPIDS	057	9750	9536	9437	-0.2	39	4048	4071	4062	0.1	2.30	2755	2659	-0.4
56472	PEQUOT LAKES	035	5540	7046	7622	2.6	93	2357	3079	3362	2.9	2.29	1617	2013	2.4
56473	PILLAGER	021	2825	3415	3682	2.1	92	1038	1289	1403	2.4	2.64	797	961	2.0
56474	PINE RIVER	021	3737	4052	4166	0.9	74	1508	1686	1749	1.2	2.39	1003	1082	0.8
56475	RANDALL	097	1396	1490	1507	0.7	69	501	558	571	1.2	2.67	375	404	0.8
56477	SEBEKA	159	2873	2786	2726	-0.3	35	1129	1129	1114	0.0	2.45	806	780	-0.4
56479	STAPLES	153	5493	5119	4985	-0.8	15	2124	2017	1973	-0.6	2.49	1382	1271	-0.9
56481	VERNDALE	159	1995	1974	1938	-0.1	44	769	784	778	0.2	2.51	565	559	-0.1
56482	WADENA	159	6834	6503	6322	-0.5	26	2716	2646	2589	-0.3	2.38	1737	1620	-0.8
56484	WALKER	021	3666	3960	4074	0.8	72	1450	1607	1667	1.1	2.33	1006	1074	0.7
56501	DETROIT LAKES	005	15558	16273	16391	0.5	63	6411	6841	6934	0.7	2.33	4215	4337	0.3
56510	ADA	107	2273	2100	1995	-0.9	12	980	922	880	-0.7	2.25	601	542	-1.1
56511	AUDUBON	005	1652	1899	1993	1.5	85	657	780	828	1.9	2.38	483	553	1.5
56514	BARNESVILLE	027	3460	3669	3792	0.6	67	1337	1472	1541	1.0	2.44	968	1022	0.6
56515	BATTLE LAKE	111	2837	3060	3116	0.8	72	1193	1323	1355	1.1	2.25	873	938	0.8
56516	BEJOU	087	289	253	241	-1.4	3	109	98	95	-1.1	2.58	84	74	-1.4
56517	BELTRAMI	119	450	422	410	-0.7	18	173	168	165	-0.3	2.51	125	118	-0.6
56518	BLUFFTON	111	426	394	383	-0.8	15	151	143	140	-0.6	2.74	119	110	-0.8
56519	BORUP	107	267	209	192	-2.6	0	105	84	78	-2.4	2.49	80	62	-2.7
56520	BRECKENRIDGE	167	4524	4245	4093	-0.7	18	1774	1708	1657	-0.4	2.40	1178	1091	-0.8
56521	CALLAWAY	005	1608	1764	1836	1.0	77	561	631	662	1.3	2.80	427	465	0.9
56522	CAMPBELL	167	781	718	689	-0.9	12	283	268	260	-0.6	2.65	217	201	-0.8
56523	CLIMAX	119	675	636	620	-0.6	22	261	255	251	-0.3	2.49	188	177	-0.6
56524	CLITHERALL	111	738	772	777	0.5	63	304	324	328	0.7	2.38	225	233	0.4
56525	COMSTOCK	027	54	57	58	0.6	67	20	22	23	1.0	2.59	17	18	0.6
56527	DEER CREEK	111	895	879	870	-0.2	39	336	335	332	0.0	2.62	254	245	-0.4
56528	DENT	111	1673	1678	1660	0.0	48	686	706	703	0.3	2.37	512	511	0.0
56529	DILWORTH	027	3127	3844	4303	2.3	92	1182	1492	1683	2.5	2.53	791	934	1.8
56531	ELBOW LAKE	051	2178	2179	2138	0.0	48	898	913	899	0.2	2.36	597	585	-0.2
56533	ELIZABETH	111	444	406	391	-1.0	9	160	149	144	-0.8	2.72	123	111	-1.1
56534	ERHARD	111	1230	1195	1178	-0.3	35	502	499	495	-0.1	2.39	375	361	-0.4
56535	ERSKINE	119	1099	1250	1278	1.4	84	417	500	517	2.0	2.36	261	298	1.4
56536	FELTON	027	421	447	459	0.6	67	165	182	189	1.1	2.41	120	128	0.7
56537	FERGUS FALLS	111	18848	19107	19113	0.1	51	7566	7795	7826	0.3	2.35	4853	4811	-0.1
56540	FERTILE	119	1775	1790	1777	0.1	51	737	765	765	0.4	2.26	487	484	-0.1
56542	FOSSTON	119	2497	2591	2593	0.4	61	1044	1116	1126	0.7	2.24	651	666	0.2
56543	FOXHOME	167	245	220	209	-1.2	5	95	88	85	-0.8	2.48	72	66	-0.9
56544	FRAZEE	005	4660	5201	5438	1.2	81	1701	1962	2073	1.6	2.59	1235	1372	1.1
56545	GARY	107	707	599	558	-1.8	2	267	234	219	-1.4	2.56	195	167	-1.7
56546	GEORGETOWN	027	465	472	478	0.2	54	176	187	191	0.7	2.52	139	143	0.3
56547	GLYNDON	027	2467	2870	3069	1.6	86	841	1017	1101	2.1	2.82	672	789	1.8
56548	HALSTAD	107	834	781	744	-0.7	18	329	312	299	-0.6	2.40	223	203	-1.0
56549	HAWLEY	027	3403	3791	3997	1.2	81	1255	1440	1536	1.5	2.59	938	1033	1.0
56550	HENDRUM	107	491	474	456	-0.4	30	186	184	178	-0.1	2.57	134	128	-0.5
56551	HENNING	111	2241	2253	2226	0.1	51	942	966	961	0.3	2.26	632	624	-0.1
56552	HITTERDAL	027	419	507	549	2.1	92	159	197	214	2.3	2.57	128	154	2.0
56553	KENT	167	176	160	153	-1.0	9	65	61	59	-0.7	2.62	52	48	-0.9
56554	LAKE PARK	005	2496	2786	2898	1.2	81	1027	1169	1225	1.4	2.38	729	799	1.0
56556	MCINTOSH	119	1030	974	953	-0.6	22	411	403	397	-0.2	2.08	269	253	-0.7
56557	MAHNOMEN	087	2845	2622	2547	-0.9	12	1147	1077	1053	-0.7	2.38	761	691	-1.0
56560	MOORHEAD	027	32182	35955	37664	1.2	81	12727	14657	15497	1.5	2.34	7966	8849	1.1
56562	MOORHEAD	027	1607	1646	1653	0.3	58	2	2	2	0.0	2.50	1	1	0.0
56563	MOORHEAD	027	1429	1433	1434	0.0	48	0	0	0	0.0	0.00	0	0	0.0
56565	NASHUA	167	142	127	121	-1.2	5	57	53	51	-0.8	2.38	44	39	-1.3
56566	NAYTAHWAUSH	087	1072	987	958	-0.9	12	322	299	291	-0.8	3.25	246	223	-1.1
56567	NEW YORK MILLS	111	3159	3076	3019	-0.3	35	1188	1183	1168	0.0	2.52	836	801	-0.5
56568	NIELSVILLE	119	199	185	179	-0.8	15	85	82	80	-0.4	2.26	57	53	-0.8
56569	OGEMA	005	865	986	1040	1.4	84	308	357	379	1.6	2.76	216	241	1.2
56570	OSAGE	005	1386	1461	1463	0.6	67	544	591	598	0.9	2.47	406	427	0.5
56571	OTTERTAIL	111	1778	1860	1882	0.5	63	734	789	803	0.8	2.33	549	570	0.4
56572	PELICAN RAPIDS	111	5397	5320	5242	-0.2	39	2058	2035	2011	-0.1	2.57	1466	1398	-0.5
56573	PERHAM	111	5539	5587	5545	0.1	51	2175	2233	2225	0.3	2.46	1471	1455	-0.1
56574	PERLEY	107	222	215	207	-0.3	35	91	90	87	-0.1	2.39	66	64	-0.3
56575	PONSFORD	005	791	779	771	-0.2	39	291	296	296	0.2	2.63	218	214	-0.2
56576	RICHVILLE	111	971	999	1003	0.3	58	416	439	443	0.6	2.27	308	314	0.2
56577	RICHWOOD	005	9	10	10	1.1	79	4	5	5	2.4	2.00	3	4	3.2
56578	ROCHERT	005	727	808	845	1.1	79	306	350	369	1.5	2.31	237	263	1.1
56579	ROTHSAY	167	1024	993	975	-0.3	35	391	386	382	-0.1	2.57	291	279	-0.5
56580	SABIN	027	1246	1278	1371	0.3	58	455	500	542	1.0	2.56	370	396	0.7
56581	SHELLY	107	405	379	361	-0.7	18	165	156	150	-0.6	2.33	112	102	-1.0
56583	TINTAH	155	240	220	210	-0.9	12	95	90	87	-0.6	2.44	73	67	-0.9
56584	TWIN VALLEY	107	1977	1782	1693	-1.1	7	778	722	688	-0.8	2.32	518	461	-1.3
56585	ULEN	027	1114	1136	1147	0.2	54	419	440	448	0.5	2.42	287	289	0.1
56586	UNDERWOOD	111	1754	2024	2121	1.6	86	710	826	872	1.6	2.45	525	590	1.3
56587	VERGAS	111	1310	1458	1502	1.2	81	546	622	646	1.4	2.34	414	457	1.1
56588	VINING	111	465	468	463	0.1	51	194	198	197	0.2	2.36	145	143	-0.2
56589	WAUBUN	087	1198	1419	1467	1.8	89	472	586	613	2.4	2.42	337	397	1.8
56590	WENDELL	051	415	372	350	-1.2	5	168	152	144	-1.1	2.37	125	110	-1.4
	MINNESOTA					0.9					1.1	2.48			0.7
	UNITED STATES					1.0					1.1	2.59			0.9

ZIP CODE #	POST OFFICE NAME	RACE (%) White 2000	White 2009	Black 2000	Black 2009	Asian/Pacific 2000	Asian/Pacific 2009	% Hispanic Origin 2000	% Hispanic Origin 2009	2009 AGE DISTRIBUTION (%) 0-4	5-9	10-14	15-19	20-24	25-44	45-64	65-84	85+	18+	MEDIAN AGE 2009	% 2009 Males	% 2009 Females
56446	EAGLE BEND	99.1	98.8	0.1	0.1	0.2	0.3	1.0	1.5	6.2	6.4	6.2	6.2	5.4	22.3	29.6	15.1	2.5	77.3	42.1	51.4	48.6
56447	EMILY	98.1	97.5	0.3	0.5	0.3	0.4	0.7	1.2	4.4	4.7	5.2	5.3	3.3	17.8	31.7	25.2	2.4	82.4	51.8	51.7	48.3
56448	FIFTY LAKES	98.3	97.4	0.3	0.6	0.3	0.3	0.6	0.9	4.3	4.6	5.1	4.8	2.8	16.8	30.8	28.2	2.6	82.6	53.7	52.7	47.3
56449	FORT RIPLEY	98.3	97.9	0.1	0.1	0.2	0.3	0.7	1.3	5.6	5.6	6.8	7.6	5.0	24.9	30.6	12.8	1.1	77.2	41.3	51.5	48.5
56450	GARRISON	81.5	79.9	0.1	0.1	0.3	0.5	0.5	0.8	5.6	5.7	6.0	6.1	4.0	21.3	31.4	18.3	1.5	78.7	45.8	50.2	49.8
56452	HACKENSACK	97.5	96.9	0.1	0.1	0.2	0.3	0.3	0.4	3.5	3.7	4.1	4.2	2.9	14.3	33.4	31.2	2.7	86.0	57.1	50.9	49.1
56453	HEWITT	98.6	98.2	0.1	0.1	0.2	0.3	0.6	1.0	6.6	7.3	8.8	9.6	4.8	22.2	27.5	11.5	1.7	71.5	37.6	51.3	48.7
56455	IRONTON	98.3	97.8	0.1	0.3	0.4	0.5	0.7	0.9	5.8	6.0	6.6	6.3	5.3	23.1	30.6	14.1	2.2	77.7	42.6	49.7	50.3
56456	JENKINS	98.6	98.4	0.0	0.0	0.5	0.4	0.5	0.4	5.3	6.1	5.7	5.3	3.7	20.1	32.4	19.3	2.0	79.1	47.0	50.4	49.6
56458	LAKE GEORGE	96.5	96.2	0.0	0.0	0.0	0.5	1.2	1.1	3.8	4.3	4.9	4.3	3.2	18.4	35.1	24.3	1.6	84.9	52.3	51.9	48.1
56461	LAPORTE	93.5	93.1	0.1	0.2	0.3	0.4	0.6	0.9	5.4	6.4	7.8	8.1	4.6	22.9	31.2	12.2	1.3	75.0	41.3	51.4	48.6
56464	MENAHGA	97.8	97.4	0.2	0.2	0.1	0.2	0.5	0.8	6.5	6.7	6.9	6.9	5.1	20.5	27.0	16.7	3.6	75.4	42.7	49.7	50.3
56465	MERRIFIELD	98.6	98.3	0.1	0.2	0.1	0.1	0.3	0.5	4.9	5.4	5.9	5.9	3.6	22.2	33.9	16.9	1.4	80.2	46.2	51.3	48.7
56466	MOTLEY	98.1	97.6	0.1	0.1	0.3	0.5	1.0	1.5	6.4	6.7	6.7	6.6	5.1	24.0	27.6	14.9	2.0	76.2	40.7	49.8	50.2
56467	NEVIS	97.7	97.2	0.3	0.4	0.1	0.2	0.6	1.0	3.6	4.7	5.2	6.1	3.3	18.1	35.5	21.5	2.0	82.6	50.9	50.4	49.6
56468	NISSWA	98.8	98.4	0.2	0.3	0.2	0.3	0.6	0.9	4.4	4.9	5.8	6.0	3.4	20.0	35.0	18.7	1.8	80.7	48.1	51.7	48.3
56469	PALISADE	98.1	97.6	0.4	0.5	0.1	0.1	0.4	0.5	4.3	4.8	5.3	6.1	3.1	20.1	33.9	20.4	1.8	81.6	49.3	51.6	48.4
56470	PARK RAPIDS	97.2	96.9	0.2	0.2	0.3	0.5	0.7	1.1	5.7	5.6	5.8	5.8	4.9	19.6	29.8	19.2	3.6	79.3	46.8	48.9	51.1
56472	PEQUOT LAKES	98.7	98.3	0.3	0.4	0.2	0.3	0.5	0.7	5.2	5.4	5.6	5.9	4.1	20.1	31.9	19.6	2.2	79.9	47.3	48.9	51.1
56473	PILLAGER	98.1	97.5	0.0	0.0	0.5	0.7	0.7	1.1	5.7	6.2	8.1	7.6	5.2	25.5	29.5	11.3	0.9	75.0	39.7	51.1	48.9
56474	PINE RIVER	97.8	97.1	0.3	0.3	0.2	0.3	0.6	0.9	5.5	5.8	6.2	7.3	5.6	21.7	30.5	14.6	2.9	77.6	43.3	49.3	50.7
56475	RANDALL	98.0	97.3	0.4	0.6	0.3	0.4	0.2	0.3	6.2	6.8	7.1	7.3	5.2	24.2	30.0	11.7	1.5	75.2	40.6	51.5	48.5
56477	SEBEKA	97.9	97.3	0.4	0.5	0.3	0.4	1.1	1.8	6.7	7.0	7.2	6.5	4.5	22.0	28.9	15.1	2.0	74.7	41.7	51.1	48.9
56479	STAPLES	97.4	96.8	0.2	0.3	0.3	0.4	1.3	2.0	6.5	6.6	6.5	7.0	6.6	23.9	26.8	13.2	3.0	76.2	39.2	49.8	50.2
56481	VERNDALE	97.6	96.9	0.2	0.3	0.3	0.5	1.2	1.8	6.6	7.5	7.7	6.8	5.0	22.5	29.4	12.6	1.7	74.0	39.7	50.2	49.8
56482	WADENA	98.0	97.4	0.7	1.0	0.2	0.2	0.6	0.9	6.3	6.0	6.5	6.8	6.2	21.1	26.2	16.4	4.4	77.1	42.4	49.5	50.5
56484	WALKER	82.1	80.0	0.2	0.4	0.2	0.3	1.1	1.5	4.4	4.7	5.6	6.4	4.8	19.5	31.5	20.1	3.0	80.6	48.0	50.9	49.1
56501	DETROIT LAKES	92.9	91.8	0.3	0.4	0.4	0.6	0.8	1.2	6.0	6.0	6.4	6.6	5.4	22.5	29.7	14.3	3.1	77.2	42.8	49.1	50.9
56510	ADA	96.0	94.7	0.1	0.1	0.5	0.7	3.0	4.5	6.3	6.3	6.9	7.0	5.2	21.2	27.6	15.9	3.7	75.9	42.8	48.8	51.2
56511	AUDUBON	96.1	95.5	0.0	0.1	0.1	0.1	0.8	1.3	5.9	6.2	6.2	5.3	3.8	21.7	33.2	15.4	2.3	77.9	45.6	51.9	48.1
56514	BARNESVILLE	99.1	98.9	0.1	0.1	0.1	0.2	0.6	1.0	6.3	6.7	7.2	6.9	5.3	23.7	28.9	12.2	2.7	75.3	40.5	51.0	49.0
56515	BATTLE LAKE	98.6	98.2	0.2	0.3	0.4	0.5	0.6	0.9	4.2	4.7	5.0	5.4	3.9	17.5	33.0	22.3	4.0	82.7	51.5	50.0	50.0
56516	BEJOU	82.0	79.1	0.0	0.0	0.0	0.0	0.3	0.8	7.5	8.3	7.9	7.5	4.3	21.7	27.7	13.0	2.0	71.5	38.3	50.6	49.4
56517	BELTRAMI	97.3	96.7	0.0	0.0	0.0	0.0	2.7	4.0	5.0	5.5	6.2	7.1	4.5	22.0	32.2	14.5	3.1	78.9	44.8	50.7	49.3
56518	BLUFFTON	99.1	98.7	0.0	0.0	0.0	0.0	0.2	0.3	6.6	7.1	7.1	6.3	4.6	22.8	30.7	12.9	1.8	74.9	41.5	53.3	46.7
56519	BORUP	94.8	93.3	0.7	1.0	0.4	0.5	1.9	2.4	5.7	4.8	8.1	7.7	4.3	22.0	28.7	17.7	1.0	76.1	43.0	52.6	47.4
56520	BRECKENRIDGE	97.7	97.1	0.1	0.2	0.2	0.3	1.7	2.6	6.4	6.9	6.5	7.0	7.1	23.1	26.3	13.1	3.8	75.7	39.6	47.3	52.7
56521	CALLAWAY	61.1	58.6	0.1	0.1	0.2	0.3	1.0	1.3	7.8	7.7	8.2	7.7	5.8	22.1	28.2	11.3	1.3	71.6	36.6	50.0	50.0
56522	CAMPBELL	97.6	96.9	0.3	0.3	0.0	0.0	1.3	1.9	6.4	7.1	6.8	6.5	4.9	21.6	31.8	13.2	1.7	74.8	42.5	51.3	48.7
56523	CLIMAX	97.0	96.1	0.3	0.5	0.0	0.0	3.1	5.0	5.3	5.8	6.4	7.5	4.6	22.3	32.1	13.4	2.5	77.7	43.5	50.9	49.1
56524	CLITHERALL	98.8	98.6	0.0	0.0	0.1	0.1	0.3	0.5	4.8	5.4	6.0	6.3	4.5	19.8	32.8	18.0	2.3	79.9	47.0	51.6	48.4
56525	COMSTOCK	98.1	98.2	0.0	0.0	0.0	0.0	0.0	0.0	3.5	3.5	7.0	8.8	3.5	17.5	35.1	17.5	3.5	78.9	47.5	52.6	47.4
56527	DEER CREEK	98.2	97.5	0.1	0.2	0.0	0.0	0.7	1.1	7.1	7.4	7.7	7.1	5.0	21.7	27.9	14.4	1.7	73.3	39.8	52.2	47.8
56528	DENT	99.2	98.9	0.1	0.1	0.0	0.0	0.4	0.7	4.6	5.1	5.4	5.8	4.2	17.3	35.4	20.7	1.5	81.2	49.5	52.4	47.6
56529	DILWORTH	92.0	89.5	0.0	0.1	0.2	0.3	7.4	10.8	8.0	7.7	7.6	8.1	6.7	26.4	24.2	9.3	2.1	71.7	33.5	48.1	51.9
56531	ELBOW LAKE	97.8	97.1	0.0	0.0	0.3	0.5	0.9	1.4	5.9	5.9	6.1	6.6	5.5	21.7	28.0	16.3	4.0	78.2	43.6	48.6	51.4
56533	ELIZABETH	98.4	98.0	0.0	0.0	0.5	0.5	0.5	0.5	5.4	7.9	8.4	8.4	3.9	23.9	28.3	13.1	0.7	73.2	39.8	52.0	48.0
56534	ERHARD	97.6	96.9	0.2	0.3	0.7	1.1	0.6	0.9	5.5	5.7	7.4	7.3	3.5	22.7	31.7	14.3	1.9	76.5	43.4	52.1	47.9
56535	ERSKINE	95.5	94.7	0.1	0.2	0.0	0.1	0.4	0.5	6.6	6.6	6.8	6.1	4.6	19.0	26.4	17.9	5.8	75.5	45.1	49.0	51.0
56536	FELTON	97.4	96.4	0.2	0.4	0.2	0.4	1.4	2.0	6.9	7.6	8.1	8.1	4.7	21.3	29.8	11.6	2.0	71.6	40.4	50.8	49.2
56537	FERGUS FALLS	97.5	96.7	0.5	0.7	0.5	0.8	0.7	1.1	5.7	5.9	6.2	7.3	5.8	23.3	27.3	14.2	4.3	78.0	41.8	48.5	51.5
56540	FERTILE	97.7	97.0	0.0	0.0	0.2	0.3	1.0	1.7	5.4	5.3	5.9	6.1	3.7	19.6	25.3	21.5	7.4	79.3	48.3	48.2	51.8
56542	FOSSTON	96.2	95.2	0.3	0.4	0.5	0.8	0.6	1.0	6.4	6.1	5.8	6.0	6.4	21.9	25.7	16.8	5.0	77.6	42.8	47.9	52.1
56543	FOXHOME	97.2	96.4	0.4	0.5	0.0	0.0	1.6	2.3	6.8	7.3	6.8	6.4	5.0	21.4	31.4	13.2	1.8	74.1	42.3	51.4	48.6
56544	FRAZEE	96.1	95.2	0.2	0.3	0.6	0.9	0.6	0.9	5.9	6.3	6.5	6.7	5.1	22.8	29.7	14.1	2.9	77.0	42.4	49.9	50.1
56545	GARY	96.3	95.3	0.0	0.0	0.0	0.0	1.1	1.7	6.5	7.0	6.5	6.3	4.5	23.9	27.9	15.4	2.0	75.8	41.4	51.8	48.2
56546	GEORGETOWN	97.6	97.0	0.4	0.4	0.4	0.6	1.9	2.8	5.1	7.2	7.6	7.4	4.0	23.5	31.6	11.7	1.9	74.8	41.9	52.1	47.9
56547	GLYNDON	96.8	95.5	0.1	0.2	0.2	0.2	4.1	6.3	8.2	8.5	8.5	7.7	5.5	25.3	27.2	8.3	0.8	69.7	35.1	51.1	48.9
56548	HALSTAD	94.1	92.7	0.1	0.1	0.6	0.8	6.7	9.6	6.0	6.5	6.8	6.7	4.4	19.7	28.6	16.3	5.1	75.7	44.9	48.9	51.1
56549	HAWLEY	98.6	98.2	0.1	0.1	0.2	0.3	0.6	0.8	6.4	6.4	6.7	7.3	6.6	23.6	27.9	12.1	3.1	75.9	39.9	50.2	49.8
56550	HENDRUM	95.3	93.7	0.0	0.0	0.4	0.4	2.7	3.8	5.9	6.5	7.6	8.9	4.9	23.6	31.6	9.3	1.7	73.8	41.1	51.7	48.3
56551	HENNING	98.6	98.0	0.0	0.1	0.6	0.8	0.5	0.8	5.0	5.1	5.6	5.5	4.2	17.9	29.4	21.8	5.5	80.8	50.2	48.6	51.4
56552	HITTERDAL	98.3	97.6	0.0	0.0	0.2	0.6	0.5	1.0	5.3	5.9	6.3	7.3	6.3	22.5	32.0	12.6	1.8	77.9	42.3	52.5	47.5
56553	KENT	98.9	98.8	0.0	0.0	0.0	0.0	1.7	2.5	6.3	6.9	7.5	8.1	6.3	20.0	31.9	11.9	1.3	73.8	41.0	50.6	49.4
56554	LAKE PARK	98.0	97.5	0.2	0.3	0.2	0.4	0.5	0.7	5.5	5.8	5.7	5.7	4.5	20.5	32.7	17.6	1.9	79.5	46.5	52.2	47.8
56556	MCINTOSH	98.2	97.6	0.0	0.0	0.2	0.3	1.3	2.1	5.0	5.1	5.3	5.2	4.3	18.1	25.6	22.1	9.2	80.9	51.0	47.9	52.1
56557	MAHNOMEN	71.5	67.3	0.1	0.1	0.1	0.1	0.9	1.3	6.5	6.8	7.1	7.1	5.0	21.0	27.6	15.0	3.9	75.0	42.0	50.7	49.3
56560	MOORHEAD	92.8	90.8	0.6	0.8	1.1	1.6	4.2	6.1	6.3	6.3	6.6	8.7	11.5	24.0	23.2	11.0	2.4	76.6	34.0	48.2	51.8
56562	MOORHEAD	94.2	92.0	2.0	2.7	2.4	3.5	1.4	2.1	1.1	1.0	0.8	45.7	42.1	4.2	2.8	2.1	0.3	96.7	20.2	37.0	63.0
56563	MOORHEAD	86.0	82.4	1.5	2.1	2.0	3.0	6.2	8.9	2.6	2.9	2.5	38.5	36.8	10.3	4.3	1.7	0.3	90.5	20.5	41.0	59.0
56565	NASHUA	97.9	96.1	0.0	0.0	0.0	0.0	1.4	2.4	7.1	7.1	7.1	6.3	4.7	21.3	32.3	12.6	1.6	73.2	42.5	51.2	48.8
56566	NAYTAHWAUSH	25.0	21.2	0.4	0.6	0.0	0.0	1.0	1.0	8.4	8.7	8.1	10.8	7.0	20.3	25.2	10.5	0.9	68.1	30.6	50.5	49.5
56567	NEW YORK MILLS	98.4	97.8	0.1	0.2	0.2	0.3	0.8	1.2	6.1	6.3	6.6	6.6	5.1	22.5	27.3	15.2	4.2	76.8	42.4	49.6	50.4
56568	NIELSVILLE	97.0	95.7	0.0	0.0	0.0	0.0	3.5	5.4	4.3	4.9	5.9	7.0	4.3	21.1	32.4	15.7	4.3	80.5	46.6	50.3	49.7
56569	OGEMA	40.7	38.1	0.0	0.0	0.0	0.0	1.5	1.8	8.8	8.7	8.6	8.0	6.5	22.3	25.5	10.4	1.1	69.0	32.5	51.1	48.9
56570	OSAGE	96.0	95.4	0.0	0.0	0.5	0.8	0.3	0.5	6.8	7.0	7.0	6.1	4.6	21.6	30.5	14.9	1.5	75.4	42.3	52.6	47.4
56571	OTTERTAIL	98.9	98.7	0.1	0.1	0.3	0.4	0.5	0.6	4.3	4.8	5.5	5.8	3.8	19.3	33.5	21.2	1.8	81.8	49.4	51.9	48.1
56572	PELICAN RAPIDS	87.6	82.8	0.3	0.4	1.7	2.2	10.9	15.8	5.8	5.8	6.8	7.3	4.9	21.1	28.5	16.0	4.0	76.9	43.8	50.7	49.3
56573	PERHAM	97.7	97.0	0.3	0.4	0.3	0.4	1.4	2.0	6.1	6.3	6.6	7.3	5.4	22.1	28.7	14.1	3.5	76.3	42.2	50.5	49.5
56574	PERLEY	95.1	94.0	0.0	0.0	0.4	0.5	2.2	3.3	5.6	6.5	7.9	9.3	4.7	24.2	31.2	9.3	1.4	73.5	40.8	52.1	47.9
56575	PONSFORD	53.2	52.1	0.0	0.0	0.3	0.4	0.9	1.4	7.3	6.7	9.5	7.7	4.0	19.8	28.9	14.6	1.5	71.4	41.1	51.3	48.7
56576	RICHVILLE	98.9	98.5	0.1	0.1	0.3	0.5	0.5	0.8	4.2	4.9	5.6	6.1	3.7	19.2	34.0	20.6	1.6	81.4	49.0	52.7	47.3
56577	RICHWOOD	100.0	100.0	0.0	0.0	0.0	0.0	0.0	0.0	0.0	0.0	0.0	10.0	0.0	20.0	70.0	0.0	0.0	90.0	52.5	60.0	40.0
56578	ROCHERT	86.2	85.0	0.0	0.1	0.1	0.2	0.6	0.6	5.6	6.2	7.8	7.4	5.0	22.6	32.4	11.4	1.6	75.4	41.8	51.1	48.9
56579	ROTHSAY	97.7	97.0	0.2	0.2	0.4	0.6	0.8	1.3	6.6	7.4	8.1	7.3	3.6	23.9	28.8	12.5	1.9	73.3	40.7	51.3	48.7
56580	SABIN	97.2	96.6	0.2	0.2	0.3	0.4	1.3	1.7	6.4	6.7	7.2	7.7	5.0	26.1	30.2	9.6	1.0	74.7	38.2	51.9	48.1
56581	SHELLY	94.3	92.6	0.0	0.3	0.5	0.8	6.7	9.8	6.1	6.3	6.6	6.6	4.2	19.5	29.0	16.4	5.3	76.0	45.4	49.3	50.7
56583	TINTAH	99.2	98.6	0.0	0.0	0.4	0.5	0.4	0.9	5.9	6.8	6.8	7.3	5.5	19.1	27.3	18.6	2.7	76.8	43.6	51.4	48.6
56584	TWIN VALLEY	94.5	93.0	0.2	0.2	0.1	0.1	2.1	3.3	6.2	5.7	6.0	6.6	4.8	18.6	25.3	20.1	6.6	77.9	46.4	49.3	50.7
56585	ULEN	98.3	98.0	0.1	0.1	0.2	0.3	0.5	0.8	5.4	6.0	6.3	6.8	4.4	21.1	29.7	14.1	6.3	77.6	45.0	50.4	49.6
56586	UNDERWOOD	98.6	98.3	0.2	0.2	0.4	0.5	0.7	1.0	5.2	5.5	5.7	5.2	4.0	20.3	34.9	17.1	2.2	80.4	47.8	52.1	47.9
56587	VERGAS	98.2	97.7	0.1	0.1	0.2	0.3	0.5	0.8	4.7	5.3	5.6	6.9	4.5	19.4	34.6	17.4	1.6	79.6	47.0	52.5	47.5
56588	VINING	98.7	98.5	0.0	0.0	0.0	0.0	0.4	0.6	4.9	5.6	6.2	6.4	4.5	19.9	32.5	17.9	2.1	79.5	46.6	51.9	48.1
56589	WAUBUN	69.6	66.2	0.0	0.0	0.1	0.1	0.8	1.1	7.0	7.4	8.1	7.5	3.9	20.7	28.8	14.4	2.1	72.7	41.3	52.7	47.3
56590	WENDELL	98.6	97.8	0.0	0.0	0.0	0.0	0.2	0.5	4.0	4.6	5.1	6.5	4.6	20.4	32.8	18.0	4.0	82.0	47.8	49.7	50.3
	MINNESOTA	89.4	86.8	3.5	4.3	2.9	3.9	2.9	4.1	6.8	6.7	6.7	7.2	6.8	27.2	26.3	10.2	2.1	75.6	36.9	49.6	50.4
	UNITED STATES	75.1	72.0	12.3	12.7	3.8	4.6	12.5	15.7	6.8	6.7	6.6	7.1	6.9	27.0	26.0	10.9	1.9	75.7	36.9	49.2	50.8

ZIP CODE				2009 HOUSEHOLD INCOME DISTRIBUTION (%)					MEDIAN HOUSEHOLD INCOME					2009 HOME VALUE DISTRIBUTION (%)					
#	POST OFFICE NAME	2009 Per Capita Income	2009 HH Income Base	Less than $25,000	$25,000 to $49,999	$50,000 to $99,999	$100,000 to $149,999	$150,000 or More	2009	2014	2009 National Centile	2009 State Centile	2009 Home Value Base	Less than $50,000	$50,000 to $89,999	$90,000 to $174,999	$175,000 to $399,999	$400,000 or More	2009 Median Home Value
56446	EAGLE BEND	18317	600	31.5	35.2	27.7	3.8	1.8	37264	37906	24	8	498	21.9	33.7	32.3	10.0	2.0	80000
56447	EMILY	23330	447	26.8	32.9	31.8	4.9	3.6	43264	45223	43	26	404	4.0	14.4	39.4	34.7	7.7	156548
56448	FIFTY LAKES	27313	178	24.7	34.3	31.5	5.6	3.9	44200	45548	46	30	161	2.5	11.2	35.4	40.4	10.6	178750
56449	FORT RIPLEY	20441	584	20.5	28.9	43.2	5.5	1.9	50304	51533	62	54	545	6.8	14.5	40.6	34.1	4.0	151964
56450	GARRISON	24839	493	28.8	29.6	33.3	5.5	2.8	41506	43269	38	20	423	13.7	13.0	38.5	29.6	5.2	140691
56452	HACKENSACK	25796	896	21.9	34.6	34.0	6.8	2.7	44144	45755	46	30	807	5.9	12.5	35.1	37.9	8.6	165240
56453	HEWITT	16109	422	32.0	36.3	27.7	3.1	0.9	37796	38570	26	9	379	19.5	27.7	41.2	9.2	2.4	93387
56455	IRONTON	21199	340	28.2	30.9	34.4	5.3	1.2	43627	45439	44	27	296	12.5	27.7	43.2	15.5	1.0	106633
56456	JENKINS	22646	105	21.9	31.4	39.0	4.8	2.9	46396	48456	53	40	91	12.1	8.8	38.5	29.7	11.0	151389
56458	LAKE GEORGE	21961	74	24.3	33.8	32.4	6.8	2.7	43413	46378	44	27	68	8.8	13.2	42.6	30.9	4.4	144444
56461	LAPORTE	20670	1198	23.0	29.3	39.4	6.3	2.1	48042	48963	57	47	1062	13.5	20.0	37.8	24.8	4.0	122872
56464	MENAHGA	18239	1490	34.0	32.1	28.8	3.2	1.9	36375	37374	22	6	1244	19.7	23.2	43.4	12.5	1.2	98990
56465	MERRIFIELD	25396	734	19.3	30.9	38.1	8.6	3.0	49748	52929	60	52	672	3.3	10.9	37.8	38.8	9.2	170423
56466	MOTLEY	19618	1256	27.9	31.4	35.8	3.7	1.1	42504	43982	41	23	1039	16.9	21.6	41.8	16.8	2.9	111568
56467	NEVIS	23509	966	22.8	32.7	36.3	5.9	2.3	45000	46571	48	34	867	8.8	15.9	35.6	33.1	6.6	148363
56468	NISSWA	30713	1965	18.3	22.6	42.5	9.8	6.8	57352	60021	74	73	1749	2.9	7.0	30.0	38.4	21.7	219920
56469	PALISADE	20606	630	27.3	34.3	32.4	4.0	2.1	41151	42225	37	19	588	10.5	21.1	43.9	21.1	3.4	118687
56470	PARK RAPIDS	22746	4071	27.8	29.4	33.2	6.5	3.1	42541	44257	41	23	3075	10.7	20.0	39.6	24.7	5.0	125663
56472	PEQUOT LAKES	26165	3079	24.1	27.2	36.4	7.3	5.0	48798	50591	58	50	2556	4.9	8.3	33.3	37.5	16.0	188012
56473	PILLAGER	20973	1289	18.6	28.4	46.0	5.1	1.9	51807	52668	66	61	1141	13.6	15.6	42.4	23.7	4.7	131151
56474	PINE RIVER	19109	1686	32.1	29.2	33.8	3.2	1.6	39878	40925	32	14	1344	10.9	25.7	42.1	18.4	2.9	111290
56475	RANDALL	19625	558	22.6	31.4	39.1	5.0	2.0	46959	47803	54	43	483	12.8	24.2	43.5	17.8	1.7	112148
56477	SEBEKA	18363	1129	31.4	32.2	31.4	4.0	1.1	39674	40403	32	14	960	20.9	26.5	37.2	14.7	0.7	93425
56479	STAPLES	18608	2017	32.0	30.0	31.6	4.2	2.2	38975	40062	30	12	1520	20.9	27.0	40.7	10.3	1.3	93267
56481	VERNDALE	17385	784	31.8	33.0	30.9	3.6	0.8	37758	39504	26	9	652	17.6	30.5	38.2	12.7	0.9	92727
56482	WADENA	19231	2646	34.8	27.2	31.3	4.6	2.1	39499	40737	31	14	1873	18.5	33.4	37.3	10.4	0.5	87649
56484	WALKER	23571	1607	26.8	25.0	38.1	6.3	3.7	47682	50083	56	45	1283	7.6	10.1	38.0	30.5	13.9	156314
56501	DETROIT LAKES	23464	6841	25.6	27.9	36.1	7.0	3.3	45755	47014	51	37	5247	10.9	18.6	42.8	22.6	5.1	128530
56510	ADA	20077	922	32.9	31.3	29.1	5.3	1.4	37215	38132	24	8	690	29.7	31.6	33.3	4.8	0.6	75606
56511	AUDUBON	22734	780	22.6	27.3	42.8	4.1	3.2	50068	49874	61	53	653	10.4	16.4	44.1	25.7	3.4	132031
56514	BARNESVILLE	24156	1472	19.2	29.4	42.3	5.5	3.6	50982	53315	64	58	1256	9.5	16.0	52.9	19.7	1.9	123790
56515	BATTLE LAKE	23253	1323	26.5	29.8	36.0	5.0	2.7	43657	44968	44	28	1148	8.9	15.3	45.6	25.7	4.4	130690
56516	BEJOU	17104	98	26.5	41.8	25.5	6.1	0.0	39292	39642	31	12	78	19.2	15.4	34.6	19.2	11.5	120833
56517	BELTRAMI	20046	168	23.8	35.7	33.3	5.4	1.8	40404	40857	34	16	144	32.6	22.9	29.9	12.5	2.1	78750
56518	BLUFFTON	19941	143	18.2	33.6	39.2	6.3	2.8	48494	48029	58	49	128	10.9	18.0	54.7	16.4	0.0	126786
56519	BORUP	19914	84	20.2	29.8	45.2	4.8	0.0	50000	51103	61	53	69	21.7	24.6	42.0	7.2	4.3	94167
56520	BRECKENRIDGE	23469	1708	23.1	26.5	40.9	6.8	2.8	50379	52584	62	55	1275	18.0	29.1	42.3	10.0	0.5	93174
56521	CALLAWAY	16149	631	33.0	29.3	31.7	4.8	1.3	40042	40431	33	15	536	22.4	29.3	28.9	14.2	5.2	87805
56522	CAMPBELL	20341	268	17.5	35.8	38.8	6.0	1.9	47592	48987	56	45	248	30.2	21.8	38.7	8.1	1.2	85833
56523	CLIMAX	21953	255	20.8	31.0	39.2	7.1	2.0	47838	49319	56	46	212	22.6	23.6	35.4	16.0	2.4	96667
56524	CLITHERALL	20610	324	28.1	31.2	34.3	4.6	1.9	41139	42350	36	18	284	16.5	16.5	43.0	21.5	2.5	117857
56525	COMSTOCK	22849	22	13.6	31.8	45.5	9.1	0.0	54545	52174	70	69	21	9.5	14.3	52.4	23.8	0.0	145833
56527	DEER CREEK	16839	335	29.6	34.0	32.5	2.7	1.2	39646	40860	32	14	283	17.3	25.8	40.3	14.5	2.1	103274
56528	DENT	22588	706	25.1	31.0	36.7	5.0	2.3	45380	46346	49	35	647	9.7	18.2	41.9	27.5	2.6	133654
56529	DILWORTH	19566	1492	30.2	25.8	34.8	7.5	1.7	44051	46762	46	29	1026	12.7	19.0	49.7	17.5	1.1	114013
56531	ELBOW LAKE	19981	913	29.6	34.0	30.0	4.9	1.5	39402	39962	31	13	702	21.8	35.2	36.5	5.8	0.7	80755
56533	ELIZABETH	20296	149	16.1	30.2	46.3	6.7	0.7	51854	51755	66	62	133	18.0	21.8	39.8	18.8	1.5	110156
56534	ERHARD	23565	499	21.2	30.5	38.9	6.0	3.4	48249	48325	57	48	445	15.3	19.8	38.0	23.8	3.1	122877
56535	ERSKINE	19622	500	32.2	36.2	24.6	4.4	2.6	35921	37000	20	5	375	33.3	31.2	25.9	7.5	2.1	68871
56536	FELTON	25483	182	19.2	29.1	37.9	9.9	3.8	51183	53113	64	59	153	13.1	18.3	46.4	19.0	3.3	126389
56537	FERGUS FALLS	23542	7795	24.9	28.1	36.0	7.5	3.5	46534	47739	53	41	5537	9.4	22.2	48.0	18.8	1.6	116405
56540	FERTILE	19514	765	33.3	33.7	27.5	3.7	1.8	34956	36058	17	4	605	26.6	32.4	29.4	9.8	1.8	77941
56542	FOSSTON	20705	1116	35.2	28.9	27.9	5.5	2.6	36100	37963	21	6	818	24.3	31.2	37.8	6.2	0.5	81509
56543	FOXHOME	21787	88	17.0	35.2	39.8	6.8	1.1	48198	48813	57	48	82	34.1	23.2	34.1	7.3	1.2	75000
56544	FRAZEE	19328	1962	26.8	30.2	36.6	4.0	2.5	43113	44259	43	25	1565	17.2	19.8	41.0	19.0	3.0	111932
56545	GARY	17952	234	25.6	32.9	37.2	3.4	0.9	42893	43633	42	25	205	32.2	30.7	29.3	6.3	1.5	72647
56546	GEORGETOWN	25770	187	16.0	26.7	42.8	11.2	3.2	57141	60222	74	73	167	6.6	20.4	45.5	24.6	3.0	134914
56547	GLYNDON	22181	1017	14.9	27.3	47.2	7.7	2.9	56722	59841	74	72	892	13.1	14.5	46.6	24.0	1.8	130906
56548	HALSTAD	19958	312	29.2	32.4	31.1	5.4	1.9	40446	41593	34	16	245	32.2	30.6	31.8	3.3	2.0	70789
56549	HAWLEY	22710	1440	19.6	27.1	42.3	7.8	3.2	52870	55771	68	65	1153	13.7	16.4	49.2	19.0	1.7	119563
56550	HENDRUM	19695	184	20.1	34.8	38.6	6.0	0.5	45827	46938	51	38	159	31.4	27.7	33.3	6.3	1.3	75500
56551	HENNING	19576	966	34.9	29.5	31.0	3.1	1.6	36052	37088	21	6	782	14.7	25.3	39.6	16.8	3.6	106391
56552	HITTERDAL	21233	197	19.3	33.0	40.6	3.6	3.6	47991	50000	57	47	179	22.3	20.1	39.7	15.6	2.2	102315
56553	KENT	23382	61	14.8	37.7	37.7	4.9	4.9	47986	49437	57	47	54	22.2	20.4	42.6	13.0	1.9	100000
56554	LAKE PARK	24779	1169	21.8	26.5	40.8	6.9	3.9	51093	51758	64	59	1015	10.6	16.9	35.1	31.6	5.7	142139
56556	MCINTOSH	22567	403	28.8	34.2	31.0	3.2	2.7	39131	40278	30	12	301	28.2	37.5	26.6	7.3	0.3	70893
56557	MAHNOMEN	17318	1077	33.3	33.1	29.1	4.0	0.5	35117	36059	18	4	827	25.2	29.1	35.3	7.5	2.9	82755
56560	MOORHEAD	25364	14657	23.9	26.4	35.8	9.4	4.4	49563	52091	60	51	9601	5.1	10.8	59.6	23.3	1.3	135030
56562	MOORHEAD	11476	0	0.0	0.0	0.0	0.0	0.0	0	0	0	0	0	0.0	0.0	0.0	0.0	0.0	0
56563	MOORHEAD	7595	0	0.0	0.0	0.0	0.0	0.0	0	0	0	0	0	0.0	0.0	0.0	0.0	0.0	0
56565	NASHUA	22641	53	17.0	35.8	39.6	5.7	1.9	47974	47971	57	46	49	34.7	22.4	38.8	4.1	0.0	72500
56566	NAYTAHWAUSH	12550	299	36.1	31.1	29.1	2.7	1.0	33038	33349	13	3	203	22.2	31.5	35.0	9.4	2.0	85313
56567	NEW YORK MILLS	18443	1183	28.7	31.7	34.2	3.8	1.6	42168	42945	40	22	888	13.3	23.3	44.6	16.1	2.7	113750
56568	NIELSVILLE	19979	82	28.0	37.8	29.3	3.7	1.2	35738	37323	20	5	68	39.7	26.5	20.6	10.3	2.9	66667
56569	OGEMA	14503	357	41.5	27.7	24.9	5.0	0.8	33057	34229	13	3	242	31.0	28.9	28.5	8.7	2.9	78182
56570	OSAGE	19412	591	23.7	35.9	36.0	3.2	1.2	42799	43891	42	24	527	13.3	19.4	42.3	21.6	3.4	125457
56571	OTTERTAIL	23235	789	22.7	33.0	37.0	4.3	3.0	45927	46328	51	38	698	10.9	14.3	43.8	23.8	7.2	135000
56572	PELICAN RAPIDS	19656	2035	26.7	28.3	37.3	5.7	2.0	44975	46052	48	33	1594	11.2	21.0	40.3	23.8	3.7	120714
56573	PERHAM	21021	2233	26.5	29.1	36.7	5.0	2.7	44503	45644	47	31	1611	8.6	20.2	45.6	22.3	3.2	122067
56574	PERLEY	21403	90	18.9	34.4	40.0	6.7	0.0	46871	47768	54	42	79	30.4	30.4	31.6	6.3	1.3	73000
56575	PONSFORD	15714	296	40.5	29.4	26.0	2.7	1.4	32825	34340	13	3	231	19.5	26.4	38.5	14.7	0.9	95278
56576	RICHVILLE	23686	439	23.5	31.9	36.4	5.2	3.0	45585	46453	50	36	392	11.2	16.1	43.4	24.7	4.6	132273
56577	RICHWOOD	30585	5	0.0	20.0	80.0	0.0	0.0	56580	56580	73	72	5	0.0	0.0	100.0	0.0	0.0	112500
56578	ROCHERT	24137	350	20.0	31.7	40.0	5.7	2.6	48217	48430	57	48	324	12.3	16.4	46.0	20.7	4.6	127551
56579	ROTHSAY	20079	386	21.8	33.7	37.0	5.7	1.8	46134	47032	52	39	337	21.7	27.9	34.1	15.1	1.2	90682
56580	SABIN	27352	500	13.6	23.0	46.0	12.4	5.0	63199	66067	81	82	446	6.3	8.7	52.2	30.7	2.0	148795
56581	SHELLY	20608	156	28.8	32.7	31.4	5.1	1.9	40446	41745	34	16	122	32.0	31.1	31.1	4.1	1.6	71000
56583	TINTAH	19117	90	28.9	30.0	34.4	5.6	1.1	40748	41379	35	17	81	27.2	30.9	28.4	11.1	2.5	75000
56584	TWIN VALLEY	18229	722	34.2	28.9	33.0	2.5	1.4	37506	38450	25	9	591	41.3	30.6	23.5	3.7	0.8	58583
56585	ULEN	19730	440	25.2	33.0	35.0	5.7	1.1	43584	45523	44	27	349	25.5	20.6	42.4	10.9	0.6	95870
56586	UNDERWOOD	22240	826	22.9	28.9	40.3	5.3	2.5	47958	48758	56	46	704	12.6	18.8	43.5	22.6	2.6	119512
56587	VERGAS	23946	622	19.9	32.3	39.1	5.9	2.7	47749	48046	56	45	557	10.6	16.7	44.0	26.6	2.2	129006
56588	VINING	20467	198	29.3	30.3	34.3	4.0	2.0	40752	42143	35	18	175	17.1	18.3	40.0	21.7	2.9	116477
56589	WAUBUN	18282	586	26.3	35.5	34.8	3.1	0.3	40949	41929	36	18	474	19.2	27.4	39.2	12.0	2.1	95161
56590	WENDELL	22271	152	21.7	34.9	35.5	4.6	3.3	43619	45567	44	27	130	16.9	26.2	43.8	11.5	1.5	101389
	MINNESOTA	31285		15.9	22.3	36.8	16.4	8.6	62767	65994				6.5	9.7	37.4	39.4	7.0	167369
	UNITED STATES	27277		20.9	24.4	35.3	11.7	7.6	54719	56938				9.3	13.1	31.6	32.6	13.5	162279

ZIP CODE #	POST OFFICE NAME	FINANCIAL SERVICES: Auto Loan	Home Loan	Invest-ments	Retire-ment Plans	THE HOME: Home Improvements: Home Repair	Lawn & Garden	Furnishings: Comput-ers & Hard-ware-Personal	Major Appli-ances	TV, Radio, Sound Equip-ment	Furni-ture	ENTERTAINMENT: Dine out/ Carry out	Sports Equip-ment	Fees & Tickets	Toys & Games	Travel	Cable TV	PERSONAL: Apparel & Services	Auto Repairs	Health Insur-ance	Pets & Supplies
56446	EAGLE BEND	77	55	79	53	57	80	60	74	65	52	63	57	47	64	58	72	42	69	80	88
56447	EMILY	86	69	111	68	75	91	69	87	72	64	71	64	60	68	75	77	47	81	86	101
56448	FIFTY LAKES	90	72	116	71	79	95	72	91	75	67	74	67	62	72	78	80	49	84	90	106
56449	FORT RIPLEY	85	80	93	81	82	92	76	87	78	73	77	66	73	77	80	81	53	82	87	102
56450	GARRISON	85	68	110	67	75	90	68	87	71	64	71	63	59	68	74	76	47	80	86	101
56452	HACKENSACK	83	73	111	72	82	93	70	87	74	71	73	60	67	69	78	78	49	81	90	100
56453	HEWITT	75	52	83	52	54	79	57	71	60	47	59	59	42	59	57	65	38	67	75	88
56455	IRONTON	77	62	74	62	64	82	64	76	69	58	67	57	55	69	63	75	45	71	81	89
56456	JENKINS	88	70	113	69	77	93	70	89	74	66	73	65	61	70	76	78	48	82	88	104
56458	LAKE GEORGE	92	73	118	72	81	97	73	93	77	69	76	68	64	73	79	82	50	86	92	108
56461	LAPORTE	85	76	95	75	79	88	73	85	75	71	75	63	68	74	76	78	51	80	84	99
56464	MENAHGA	79	56	82	55	59	82	60	75	66	53	64	58	47	65	59	72	42	70	80	90
56465	MERRIFIELD	99	85	122	84	91	105	83	101	85	79	85	75	75	83	89	90	57	94	100	117
56466	MOTLEY	77	63	75	62	64	78	64	74	68	60	66	55	56	68	63	72	45	70	77	87
56467	NEVIS	88	71	114	70	78	93	71	90	74	66	73	66	61	70	77	79	49	83	89	104
56468	NISSWA	114	95	145	94	103	121	94	117	97	89	96	86	84	93	101	103	64	108	115	135
56469	PALISADE	80	64	102	63	70	85	64	81	67	60	66	59	55	64	69	72	44	75	81	94
56470	PARK RAPIDS	84	67	95	67	72	87	72	84	76	67	75	62	63	73	73	81	50	80	87	98
56472	PEQUOT LAKES	95	80	115	80	87	102	81	97	84	78	83	70	73	81	86	89	56	91	100	113
56473	PILLAGER	90	77	97	76	80	92	76	89	79	73	78	65	68	78	77	83	53	83	89	104
56474	PINE RIVER	78	58	81	57	60	82	62	76	66	54	65	58	50	65	61	72	43	70	80	90
56475	RANDALL	83	73	78	75	74	89	73	83	75	65	74	64	66	76	73	79	50	77	86	97
56477	SEBEKA	79	56	84	55	58	82	61	75	65	52	64	59	47	64	60	71	42	70	80	91
56479	STAPLES	74	60	70	60	61	74	65	71	68	60	67	54	56	68	62	73	45	69	76	85
56481	VERNDALE	77	56	82	54	58	79	58	73	63	53	62	56	46	62	58	69	41	67	76	87
56482	WADENA	73	58	73	57	60	76	63	72	68	57	66	54	54	66	62	73	45	69	79	85
56484	WALKER	90	75	106	74	80	94	77	91	80	73	79	67	68	77	80	84	53	86	92	106
56501	DETROIT LAKES	85	73	91	73	76	88	76	85	79	72	78	63	69	78	77	84	53	82	89	100
56510	ADA	78	55	79	54	57	81	61	75	67	53	65	57	48	65	59	73	43	70	81	89
56511	AUDUBON	91	73	117	72	80	96	73	93	76	68	75	68	63	73	79	81	50	86	92	108
56514	BARNESVILLE	89	85	80	88	83	95	83	89	85	78	84	70	80	86	83	88	58	86	93	106
56515	BATTLE LAKE	89	70	113	69	77	94	71	90	74	66	73	67	60	71	76	79	49	83	89	105
56516	BEJOU	79	54	87	54	57	83	60	75	63	49	62	62	44	62	60	68	40	70	79	92
56517	BELTRAMI	89	62	98	62	65	94	69	85	71	56	71	70	51	70	69	78	46	80	90	105
56518	BLUFFTON	98	67	107	67	70	103	75	93	78	61	77	77	55	76	74	85	50	87	98	114
56519	BORUP	89	61	97	61	64	93	68	84	70	55	70	70	50	69	67	77	45	79	89	103
56520	BRECKENRIDGE	89	77	84	77	76	93	80	86	83	74	82	67	72	83	78	87	55	84	93	104
56521	CALLAWAY	80	57	86	56	60	83	60	76	65	54	64	59	47	64	60	71	42	70	79	91
56522	CAMPBELL	97	67	106	66	70	102	74	92	77	60	76	76	54	75	74	84	49	86	97	113
56523	CLIMAX	97	68	107	68	71	103	75	93	78	61	77	76	55	76	75	85	50	86	98	114
56524	CLITHERALL	86	61	98	61	65	91	67	83	69	56	69	67	51	68	68	75	45	78	87	101
56525	COMSTOCK	106	73	116	73	76	112	81	100	84	66	83	83	59	82	80	92	54	94	106	124
56527	DEER CREEK	78	56	84	55	59	80	59	74	64	53	63	57	47	63	59	70	41	68	77	89
56528	DENT	89	72	116	70	79	95	72	91	75	67	74	67	62	71	78	80	49	84	90	106
56529	DILWORTH	75	69	58	69	65	71	72	70	73	70	72	54	67	75	66	74	50	71	73	84
56531	ELBOW LAKE	81	58	84	57	60	85	63	78	69	55	67	61	49	68	62	76	44	73	85	94
56533	ELIZABETH	92	74	98	74	75	98	76	90	78	66	77	73	64	77	77	83	51	85	93	109
56534	ERHARD	95	75	105	75	77	101	77	93	79	68	79	74	64	78	79	85	52	87	95	112
56535	ERSKINE	80	58	83	57	61	83	63	78	69	56	67	58	50	68	61	76	45	72	84	91
56536	FELTON	109	77	119	77	81	116	85	104	88	70	87	86	64	86	85	95	57	97	110	128
56537	FERGUS FALLS	81	76	80	77	76	85	79	82	81	75	80	62	75	80	78	84	55	82	88	97
56540	FERTILE	76	55	81	54	58	80	60	74	65	52	63	57	47	63	59	71	42	69	79	88
56542	FOSSTON	76	56	74	56	58	77	64	73	70	57	68	55	53	68	61	76	46	71	80	87
56543	FOXHOME	97	67	106	66	70	102	74	92	77	60	76	76	54	75	74	84	49	86	97	113
56544	FRAZEE	85	67	91	66	70	89	68	83	72	62	71	63	57	71	69	78	47	77	85	98
56545	GARY	82	56	90	56	59	87	63	78	65	51	64	64	46	64	62	71	42	73	82	96
56546	GEORGETOWN	116	80	128	80	84	123	89	110	92	72	91	91	65	90	88	101	59	103	116	136
56547	GLYNDON	98	92	88	91	90	97	87	93	89	88	89	71	83	91	86	91	61	90	93	111
56548	HALSTAD	87	60	95	60	63	92	66	82	69	54	68	68	49	68	66	75	44	77	87	101
56549	HAWLEY	88	83	82	84	84	91	84	88	85	80	84	66	80	85	83	88	58	86	92	103
56550	HENDRUM	90	62	99	62	65	95	69	86	72	56	71	71	51	70	69	78	46	80	91	106
56551	HENNING	76	57	87	56	61	80	60	75	64	54	63	56	49	62	61	70	42	69	78	88
56552	HITTERDAL	86	76	79	79	78	92	76	87	78	68	77	66	69	80	76	83	52	80	89	101
56553	KENT	110	75	120	75	79	116	84	104	87	68	86	86	61	85	83	95	56	97	110	128
56554	LAKE PARK	95	79	105	79	82	100	81	94	84	74	83	73	72	82	83	88	55	90	98	112
56556	MCINTOSH	85	61	87	59	63	89	67	82	74	59	71	63	53	72	65	81	47	77	89	97
56557	MAHNOMEN	72	51	75	50	53	75	55	69	60	48	59	53	43	59	54	66	39	64	74	82
56560	MOORHEAD	87	81	75	83	78	81	91	82	88	86	89	66	85	89	83	88	62	86	84	99
56562	MOORHEAD	0	0	0	0	0	0	0	0	0	0	0	0	0	0	0	0	0	0	0	0
56563	MOORHEAD	0	0	0	0	0	0	0	0	0	0	0	0	0	0	0	0	0	0	0	0
56565	NASHUA	96	66	106	66	69	102	74	92	77	60	76	76	54	75	73	84	49	85	97	113
56566	NAYTAHWAUSH	71	51	72	49	53	73	54	67	60	49	58	50	43	59	53	66	39	62	72	79
56567	NEW YORK MILLS	80	59	82	59	61	84	63	77	68	55	66	60	51	67	63	74	44	72	82	92
56568	NIELSVILLE	81	55	89	55	58	85	62	76	64	50	63	63	45	63	61	70	41	71	81	94
56569	OGEMA	72	51	74	50	53	73	53	67	58	48	57	51	42	58	52	64	38	62	70	80
56570	OSAGE	83	61	98	61	66	88	65	81	68	56	67	64	51	65	67	73	44	76	84	98
56571	OTTERTAIL	90	73	113	72	80	95	73	92	76	68	75	67	64	73	78	81	50	85	91	106
56572	PELICAN RAPIDS	81	65	88	65	68	84	70	81	73	63	72	61	60	71	70	78	48	77	85	95
56573	PERHAM	84	68	91	68	71	88	71	84	75	65	73	63	61	73	71	80	49	79	87	98
56574	PERLEY	91	63	100	63	66	96	70	87	73	57	72	72	51	71	69	79	47	81	92	107
56575	PONSFORD	74	53	77	51	55	76	55	69	60	50	59	53	43	59	54	66	39	64	72	83
56576	RICHVILLE	90	72	116	71	79	95	72	91	75	67	74	67	62	71	78	80	49	84	90	106
56577	RICHWOOD	102	82	132	80	90	108	82	104	86	77	84	76	71	81	89	91	56	96	103	120
56578	ROCHERT	94	74	109	73	79	98	75	93	79	69	78	69	64	77	78	85	52	86	94	109
56579	ROTHSAY	92	64	101	63	67	97	71	88	73	57	73	72	52	72	70	80	47	82	93	108
56580	SABIN	115	99	112	97	97	112	98	109	98	94	99	86	86	100	96	101	66	103	108	130
56581	SHELLY	87	60	96	60	63	92	67	83	69	54	68	68	49	68	66	75	44	77	87	102
56583	TINTAH	84	57	92	57	60	88	64	79	66	52	66	66	47	65	63	72	43	74	84	98
56584	TWIN VALLEY	74	52	78	52	55	78	58	72	62	49	61	56	44	61	57	68	40	67	77	86
56585	ULEN	85	62	91	62	64	90	67	81	69	55	68	67	51	68	67	75	45	76	85	99
56586	UNDERWOOD	91	73	117	72	80	96	73	93	76	68	75	68	63	72	79	81	50	85	91	107
56587	VERGAS	94	75	121	74	82	99	75	95	78	70	78	70	65	75	81	84	52	88	94	110
56588	VINING	86	60	96	60	64	90	66	82	69	55	68	67	50	67	66	75	44	77	86	100
56589	WAUBUN	79	55	86	54	57	83	60	75	63	50	62	61	45	62	60	69	41	70	79	92
56590	WENDELL	96	66	105	66	69	101	73	91	76	59	75	75	53	74	73	83	49	85	96	112
	MINNESOTA	113	113	112	114	112	114	112	113	111	111	112	88	112	113	112	112	78	112	113	133
	UNITED STATES	100	100	100	100	100	100	100	100	100	100	100	100	100	100	100	100	100	100	100	100

ZIP CODE #	POST OFFICE NAME	COUNTY FIPS CODE	POPULATION 2000	POPULATION 2009	POPULATION 2014	2000-2009 ANNUAL RATE % Rate	2000-2009 ANNUAL RATE State Centile	HOUSEHOLDS 2000	HOUSEHOLDS 2009	HOUSEHOLDS 2014	HOUSEHOLDS % Annual Rate 2000-2009	HOUSEHOLDS 2009 Average HH Size	FAMILIES 2000	FAMILIES 2009	FAMILIES % Annual Rate 2000-2009
56592	WINGER	119	382	369	361	-0.4	30	161	160	158	-0.1	2.31	113	109	-0.4
56593	WOLF LAKE	005	10	11	10	1.0	77	1	1	1	0.0	3.00	1	1	0.0
56594	WOLVERTON	167	801	764	744	-0.5	26	307	300	294	-0.2	2.55	237	226	-0.5
56601	BEMIDJI	007	29780	32686	34073	1.0	77	11071	12491	13151	1.3	2.47	7341	7992	0.9
56621	BAGLEY	029	4115	4521	4644	1.0	77	1585	1830	1908	1.6	2.41	1088	1202	1.1
56623	BAUDETTE	077	3311	3099	2982	-0.7	18	1402	1359	1323	-0.3	2.25	919	857	-0.8
56626	BENA	021	467	488	493	0.5	63	172	183	186	0.7	2.67	127	131	0.3
56627	BIG FALLS	071	460	425	408	-0.9	12	228	220	214	-0.4	1.93	151	139	-0.9
56628	BIGFORK	061	1719	1797	1815	0.5	63	746	806	824	0.8	2.17	523	546	0.5
56629	BIRCHDALE	071	26	25	24	-0.4	30	13	13	13	0.0	1.92	9	9	0.0
56630	BLACKDUCK	061	1515	1661	1730	1.0	77	621	705	743	1.4	2.28	424	456	0.8
56633	CASS LAKE	021	3493	3788	3836	0.9	74	1212	1322	1345	0.9	2.86	868	920	0.6
56634	CLEARBROOK	029	1241	1121	1062	-1.1	7	515	466	441	-1.1	2.27	323	283	-1.4
56636	DEER RIVER	061	4868	4848	4814	0.0	48	1807	1861	1870	0.3	2.57	1290	1282	-0.1
56637	TALMOON	061	176	181	181	0.3	58	65	68	69	0.5	2.65	46	47	0.2
56639	EFFIE	061	384	416	427	0.9	74	162	183	190	1.3	2.11	110	120	0.9
56641	FEDERAL DAM	021	348	388	404	1.2	81	136	156	163	1.5	2.46	89	98	1.0
56644	GONVICK	029	899	813	772	-1.1	7	383	350	334	-1.0	2.32	255	226	-1.3
56646	GULLY	119	445	420	409	-0.6	22	187	183	180	-0.2	2.30	132	123	-0.8
56647	HINES	007	1234	1357	1426	1.0	77	457	519	551	1.4	2.60	341	373	1.0
56649	INTERNATIONAL FALLS	071	10616	10092	9781	-0.5	26	4525	4483	4400	-0.1	2.21	2926	2787	-0.5
56650	KELLIHER	007	1173	1293	1362	1.1	79	450	511	544	1.4	2.49	315	341	0.9
56651	LENGBY	119	508	491	482	-0.4	30	207	207	206	0.0	2.36	148	142	-0.4
56652	LEONARD	029	1032	936	890	-1.0	9	403	371	354	-0.9	2.51	291	261	-1.2
56653	LITTLEFORK	071	1615	1498	1445	-0.8	15	616	593	578	-0.4	2.45	433	402	-0.8
56654	LOMAN	071	186	177	171	-0.5	26	75	74	73	-0.1	2.39	53	50	-0.6
56655	LONGVILLE	021	1533	1685	1749	1.0	77	722	818	855	1.4	2.06	496	540	0.9
56657	MARCELL	061	260	264	264	0.2	54	126	132	134	0.5	1.99	97	99	0.2
56659	MAX	061	161	159	155	-0.1	44	67	67	66	0.0	2.37	49	48	-0.2
56660	MIZPAH	071	291	277	268	-0.5	26	114	112	110	-0.2	2.37	74	70	-0.6
56661	NORTHOME	071	898	869	841	-0.4	30	351	351	344	0.0	2.40	240	230	-0.5
56662	OUTING	021	553	573	576	0.4	61	276	295	300	0.7	1.94	180	185	0.3
56663	PENNINGTON	007	200	235	251	1.8	89	79	93	100	1.8	2.53	60	68	1.4
56666	PONEMAH	007	1029	1206	1290	1.7	88	247	295	317	1.9	4.06	207	241	1.7
56667	PUPOSKY	007	1008	1110	1164	1.0	77	402	457	484	1.4	2.43	293	319	0.9
56668	RANIER	071	88	90	89	0.2	54	29	31	31	0.7	2.87	21	21	0.0
56669	KABETOGAMA	071	308	307	304	0.0	48	144	150	150	0.4	2.05	101	101	0.0
56670	REDBY	007	2124	2488	2662	1.7	88	527	629	677	1.9	3.93	442	513	1.6
56671	REDLAKE	007	1862	2171	2323	1.7	88	534	639	689	2.0	3.37	423	489	1.6
56672	REMER	021	1692	1745	1752	0.3	58	743	793	804	0.7	2.18	489	501	0.3
56673	ROOSEVELT	135	1284	1240	1207	-0.4	30	469	467	460	0.0	2.66	357	347	-0.3
56676	SHEVLIN	029	928	842	796	-1.0	9	357	329	314	-0.9	2.53	267	241	-1.1
56678	SOLWAY	007	1416	1579	1656	1.2	81	532	611	647	1.5	2.58	404	447	1.1
56680	SPRING LAKE	061	182	185	184	0.2	54	84	87	88	0.4	2.11	59	59	0.0
56681	SQUAW LAKE	061	248	246	238	-0.1	44	95	95	93	0.0	2.59	69	67	-0.3
56682	SWIFT	135	940	936	919	0.0	48	303	311	309	0.3	3.01	243	243	0.0
56683	TENSTRIKE	007	210	213	218	0.2	54	89	93	97	0.5	2.28	64	65	0.2
56684	TRAIL	119	316	298	291	-0.6	22	130	127	125	-0.3	2.35	91	86	-0.6
56685	WASKISH	007	116	127	133	1.0	77	61	69	73	1.3	1.78	38	41	0.8
56686	WILLIAMS	077	975	903	868	-0.8	15	405	389	378	-0.4	2.32	283	263	-0.8
56688	WIRT	061	125	123	119	-0.2	39	47	48	47	0.2	2.56	34	33	-0.3
56701	THIEF RIVER FALLS	113	12198	12447	12565	0.2	54	4972	5207	5302	0.5	2.31	3142	3157	0.1
56710	ALVARADO	089	589	559	541	-0.6	22	223	213	207	-0.5	2.62	164	153	-0.7
56711	ANGLE INLET	077	118	106	100	-1.2	5	53	49	48	-0.8	2.16	36	33	-0.9
56713	ARGYLE	089	981	921	891	-0.7	18	377	363	354	-0.4	2.50	267	249	-0.8
56714	BADGER	135	1264	1219	1187	-0.4	30	500	497	489	-0.1	2.45	369	357	-0.4
56715	BROOKS	125	266	248	238	-0.8	15	109	106	103	-0.3	2.34	70	66	-0.6
56716	CROOKSTON	119	9912	9433	9235	-0.5	26	3638	3589	3541	-0.1	2.36	2269	2132	-0.7
56720	DONALDSON	069	89	75	70	-1.8	2	37	32	30	-1.6	2.34	26	21	-2.3
56721	EAST GRAND FORKS	119	8629	8749	8696	0.1	51	3328	3455	3458	0.4	2.51	2246	2273	0.1
56722	EUCLID	119	354	337	329	-0.5	26	130	126	124	-0.3	2.67	102	96	-0.7
56723	FISHER	119	1529	1462	1435	-0.5	26	533	526	521	-0.1	2.78	431	415	-0.4
56724	GATZKE	089	139	130	126	-0.7	18	63	62	60	-0.2	2.10	43	41	-0.5
56725	GOODRIDGE	113	798	750	736	-0.7	18	308	298	294	-0.4	2.51	228	214	-0.7
56726	GREENBUSH	135	1424	1325	1277	-0.8	15	565	543	527	-0.4	2.34	385	356	-0.8
56727	GRYGLA	089	1075	1048	1036	-0.3	35	443	447	447	0.1	2.33	303	294	-0.3
56728	HALLOCK	069	1560	1369	1273	-1.4	3	620	550	513	-1.3	2.34	408	349	-1.7
56729	HALMA	069	172	154	145	-1.2	5	72	66	62	-0.9	2.33	54	48	-1.3
56732	KARLSTAD	069	1396	1320	1276	-0.6	22	561	545	530	-0.3	2.30	374	349	-0.7
56733	KENNEDY	069	555	473	438	-1.7	2	227	198	184	-1.5	2.39	158	133	-1.8
56734	LAKE BRONSON	069	518	456	423	-1.4	3	238	213	199	-1.2	2.14	147	127	-1.6
56735	LANCASTER	069	788	697	649	-1.3	4	326	294	275	-1.1	2.37	219	190	-1.5
56736	MENTOR	119	1302	1282	1267	-0.2	39	535	545	544	0.2	2.35	399	394	-0.1
56737	MIDDLE RIVER	089	849	996	1018	1.7	88	366	446	460	2.2	2.23	238	281	1.8
56738	NEWFOLDEN	089	1589	1481	1427	-0.8	15	630	609	593	-0.4	2.43	465	436	-0.7
56740	NOYES	069	75	66	61	-1.4	3	28	25	24	-1.2	2.64	20	18	-1.1
56741	OAK ISLAND	077	31	28	26	-1.1	7	16	15	14	-0.7	1.87	11	10	-1.0
56742	OKLEE	125	629	588	564	-0.7	18	286	279	271	-0.3	2.11	185	174	-0.7
56744	OSLO	089	491	448	431	-1.0	9	206	194	188	-0.6	2.31	143	130	-1.0
56748	PLUMMER	125	729	690	663	-0.6	22	306	303	295	-0.1	2.28	201	192	-0.5
56750	RED LAKE FALLS	125	2699	2636	2568	-0.3	35	1032	1040	1023	0.1	2.38	679	658	-0.3
56751	ROSEAU	135	5925	5850	5729	-0.1	44	2329	2347	2314	0.1	2.44	1622	1580	-0.3
56754	SAINT HILAIRE	113	748	736	734	-0.2	39	298	302	304	0.1	2.41	225	222	-0.1
56755	SAINT VINCENT	069	177	156	145	-1.4	3	74	67	63	-1.1	2.33	53	46	-1.5
56756	SALOL	135	704	711	702	0.1	51	254	265	265	0.5	2.68	194	198	0.2
56757	STEPHEN	089	1179	1097	1057	-0.8	15	471	447	434	-0.6	2.45	315	288	-1.0
56758	STRANDQUIST	089	725	670	645	-0.8	15	287	275	267	-0.5	2.44	200	184	-0.9
56759	STRATHCONA	135	467	444	431	-0.5	26	192	190	186	-0.1	2.29	135	128	-0.6
56760	VIKING	089	441	413	398	-0.7	18	185	179	175	-0.4	2.29	137	129	-0.6
56761	WANNASKA	135	662	630	610	-0.5	26	248	242	237	-0.3	2.60	182	173	-0.5
56762	WARREN	119	2573	2459	2398	-0.5	26	1046	1023	1006	-0.2	2.30	704	663	-0.6
56763	WARROAD	135	4077	4238	4207	0.4	61	1494	1614	1619	0.8	2.58	1064	1111	0.5
	MINNESOTA					0.9					1.1	2.48			0.7
	UNITED STATES					1.0					1.1	2.59			0.9

ZIP CODE #	POST OFFICE NAME	RACE (%) White 2000	White 2009	Black 2000	Black 2009	Asian/Pacific 2000	Asian/Pacific 2009	% Hispanic Origin 2000	% Hispanic Origin 2009	2009 AGE DISTRIBUTION (%) 0-4	5-9	10-14	15-19	20-24	25-44	45-64	65-84	85+	18+	MEDIAN AGE 2009	% 2009 Males	% 2009 Females
56592	WINGER	96.6	95.9	0.0	0.0	0.0	0.0	0.5	1.1	6.0	6.5	6.8	6.5	4.3	23.0	30.6	13.6	2.7	76.7	42.9	52.0	48.0
56593	WOLF LAKE	100.0	90.9	0.0	0.0	0.0	0.0	0.0	0.0	0.0	0.0	0.0	0.0	0.0	9.1	90.9	0.0	0.0	100.0	50.8	63.6	36.4
56594	WOLVERTON	98.1	97.1	0.3	0.4	0.3	0.4	1.0	1.6	6.8	7.2	7.9	6.9	4.5	24.2	27.9	13.0	1.7	73.8	41.0	51.2	48.8
56601	BEMIDJI	87.0	86.2	0.4	0.5	0.8	1.1	0.9	1.3	6.5	6.2	6.6	8.6	10.1	24.9	24.7	10.3	2.0	76.3	33.9	49.4	50.6
56621	BAGLEY	83.7	84.3	0.3	0.3	0.3	0.3	0.9	0.8	6.5	6.9	6.8	6.7	5.4	23.0	27.7	13.8	3.3	75.9	40.5	49.0	51.0
56623	BAUDETTE	96.6	96.2	0.3	0.4	0.2	0.4	0.7	0.9	4.4	5.0	5.8	6.8	6.0	21.7	31.8	15.1	3.5	80.1	45.2	49.7	50.3
56626	BENA	46.0	42.2	0.0	0.0	0.4	0.4	1.1	1.4	7.6	7.6	7.4	7.0	4.9	23.4	24.6	16.2	1.4	73.0	39.0	49.6	50.4
56627	BIG FALLS	97.0	96.2	0.0	0.0	0.2	0.2	0.0	0.0	4.0	4.7	4.7	4.5	4.0	17.9	36.0	21.6	2.6	83.8	50.7	52.9	47.1
56628	BIGFORK	97.3	96.7	0.3	0.4	0.1	0.2	0.4	0.6	3.5	3.9	4.8	6.5	3.4	19.2	34.9	20.8	3.0	83.3	50.6	51.2	48.8
56629	BIRCHDALE	100.0	96.0	0.0	0.0	0.0	0.0	0.0	0.0	8.0	8.0	8.0	4.0	8.0	20.0	32.0	12.0	0.0	72.0	41.3	52.0	48.0
56630	BLACKDUCK	94.1	93.3	0.4	0.5	0.2	0.2	0.6	0.8	5.1	5.2	5.8	7.2	5.5	22.0	28.8	15.8	4.4	79.2	44.2	47.3	52.7
56633	CASS LAKE	38.4	38.4	0.0	0.0	0.1	0.2	1.8	2.1	8.9	9.2	8.7	8.5	6.6	22.4	24.0	10.2	1.5	67.5	32.0	47.7	52.3
56634	CLEARBROOK	93.2	93.0	0.1	0.1	0.2	0.2	0.8	0.9	5.0	5.2	5.6	6.5	6.0	21.1	26.2	18.1	6.3	79.8	45.5	49.7	50.3
56636	DEER RIVER	78.7	77.4	0.1	0.1	0.2	0.3	0.9	1.1	7.0	7.1	7.3	7.7	4.9	21.0	28.9	13.8	2.2	73.6	40.8	50.0	50.0
56637	TALMOON	98.3	98.3	0.6	0.6	0.0	0.0	0.0	0.0	3.3	3.9	4.4	6.1	3.3	19.9	35.9	21.0	2.2	85.1	50.7	49.2	50.8
56639	EFFIE	95.6	94.7	0.0	0.0	0.5	0.7	0.8	0.7	3.6	4.1	5.3	6.5	2.6	20.7	32.9	19.5	4.8	82.0	50.2	52.9	47.1
56641	FEDERAL DAM	77.0	73.2	0.0	0.3	0.3	0.3	0.6	1.0	4.6	5.4	6.2	6.4	4.1	18.6	35.1	17.8	1.8	79.1	48.1	50.5	49.5
56644	GONVICK	92.1	92.1	0.0	0.0	0.0	0.0	1.3	1.5	4.6	4.9	4.9	5.8	5.3	22.0	31.1	18.8	2.6	82.3	46.6	53.0	47.0
56646	GULLY	96.6	95.5	0.0	0.0	0.4	0.7	1.1	1.9	5.2	5.7	6.2	6.7	4.0	22.4	31.7	15.2	2.9	78.6	44.8	54.0	46.0
56647	HINES	96.8	96.2	0.2	0.2	0.1	0.2	0.9	1.3	4.9	5.8	8.0	8.5	4.4	21.8	31.0	13.6	1.9	75.5	42.6	51.9	48.1
56649	INTERNATIONAL FALLS	96.1	95.3	0.2	0.3	0.3	0.4	0.6	0.8	5.4	5.7	6.1	6.6	5.3	22.1	30.3	15.5	3.0	78.8	44.0	49.1	50.9
56650	KELLIHER	87.5	86.5	0.3	0.3	0.1	0.1	0.4	0.6	6.5	7.0	7.4	8.0	5.5	19.4	28.6	14.8	2.7	73.9	41.8	51.5	48.5
56651	LENGBY	97.6	96.9	0.2	0.2	0.2	0.4	0.8	1.0	6.7	6.9	6.7	5.5	4.9	20.4	28.9	17.5	2.4	76.2	44.0	48.9	51.1
56652	LEONARD	98.2	98.2	0.2	0.2	0.3	0.3	0.4	0.4	6.1	6.6	6.9	6.4	4.9	22.2	28.3	16.1	2.4	76.4	42.5	53.8	46.2
56653	LITTLEFORK	96.6	96.1	0.1	0.1	0.0	0.0	0.7	1.1	4.7	5.7	6.7	7.1	4.1	21.7	33.1	13.6	3.3	78.1	45.0	50.9	49.1
56654	LOMAN	98.4	97.7	0.0	0.0	0.0	0.0	0.0	0.0	4.5	5.1	5.6	5.6	5.1	18.6	36.7	16.4	2.3	81.4	48.0	54.2	45.8
56655	LONGVILLE	88.0	85.7	0.1	0.1	0.2	0.3	0.4	0.5	3.2	3.6	4.0	4.5	3.3	14.7	35.4	29.1	2.4	86.5	56.1	51.3	48.7
56657	MARCELL	96.5	96.6	0.4	0.4	0.0	0.0	0.4	0.8	4.5	3.8	4.9	6.8	3.8	18.2	36.7	19.7	1.5	82.2	49.4	50.4	49.6
56659	MAX	56.5	54.1	0.6	0.6	0.0	0.0	1.9	1.9	8.2	6.9	8.8	7.5	4.4	17.6	30.2	14.5	1.9	71.7	41.6	50.3	49.7
56660	MIZPAH	95.2	94.6	0.0	0.0	0.3	0.4	0.7	0.7	5.8	6.1	6.9	6.5	5.1	18.1	32.1	15.9	3.6	76.9	46.0	50.9	49.1
56661	NORTHOME	95.1	94.2	0.0	0.0	0.3	0.3	0.8	1.0	5.3	5.5	6.3	6.8	4.8	17.5	32.9	17.7	3.1	78.4	47.4	50.5	49.5
56662	OUTING	97.1	96.7	0.0	0.0	0.4	0.5	0.5	0.7	3.5	5.1	4.5	5.2	3.1	15.7	35.1	25.1	2.6	83.4	53.1	51.0	49.0
56663	PENNINGTON	49.5	49.4	0.0	0.0	0.0	0.0	1.0	1.3	7.2	7.7	9.8	9.4	5.5	20.4	30.2	8.9	0.9	68.9	37.3	49.8	50.2
56666	PONEMAH	2.6	2.6	0.2	0.2	0.1	0.1	1.7	1.8	14.6	13.4	11.1	10.8	8.8	23.2	14.0	3.8	0.2	53.6	20.0	48.3	51.7
56667	PUPOSKY	94.2	93.5	0.0	0.0	0.4	0.5	0.7	1.0	4.4	5.3	6.2	6.8	5.0	21.9	34.0	14.4	1.9	79.8	45.2	50.8	49.2
56668	RANIER	97.7	97.8	0.0	0.0	0.0	0.0	0.0	0.0	4.4	4.4	4.4	4.4	3.3	17.8	40.0	18.9	2.2	82.2	52.0	51.1	48.9
56669	KABETOGAMA	76.5	74.6	0.0	0.0	0.0	0.0	1.0	1.0	4.9	5.9	6.2	6.2	3.6	21.2	34.5	15.6	2.0	79.2	46.2	51.8	48.2
56670	REDBY	2.6	2.6	0.2	0.2	0.0	0.1	1.7	1.7	14.6	13.4	11.1	10.4	8.8	23.3	14.2	3.9	0.2	53.9	20.3	48.4	51.6
56671	REDLAKE	3.0	3.1	0.3	0.4	0.0	0.0	1.5	1.6	12.1	11.5	10.0	9.5	9.1	23.5	18.1	5.8	0.4	60.6	23.8	47.2	52.8
56672	REMER	94.9	93.7	0.1	0.1	0.4	0.5	0.6	1.0	3.6	5.4	5.6	6.4	3.1	16.6	35.7	20.9	2.6	80.6	50.9	51.5	48.5
56673	ROOSEVELT	98.3	98.0	0.2	0.2	0.1	0.1	0.3	0.5	6.8	7.4	7.6	6.9	6.0	23.7	30.3	10.2	1.1	73.9	39.1	52.4	47.6
56676	SHEVLIN	96.5	96.6	0.0	0.0	0.1	0.1	0.2	0.2	5.6	5.8	6.3	6.8	5.2	22.7	32.5	13.3	1.8	77.7	43.0	50.4	49.6
56678	SOLWAY	96.3	95.8	0.1	0.1	0.4	0.6	0.6	0.9	6.2	6.4	6.5	7.0	6.8	26.0	30.4	9.5	1.1	76.8	38.1	52.8	47.2
56680	SPRING LAKE	94.0	94.1	0.5	0.5	0.0	0.0	0.5	0.5	4.3	4.9	4.9	6.5	4.3	20.5	33.0	19.5	2.2	82.7	48.0	50.3	49.7
56681	SQUAW LAKE	53.8	51.2	0.4	0.8	0.0	0.0	1.6	2.0	8.1	6.1	8.9	8.1	4.5	17.5	29.3	15.4	2.0	72.0	41.9	51.2	48.8
56682	SWIFT	97.2	96.9	0.2	0.2	0.3	0.4	0.2	0.3	8.2	8.2	7.8	7.4	7.4	24.5	27.4	8.3	0.9	71.3	34.0	51.9	48.1
56683	TENSTRIKE	95.7	95.3	0.5	0.5	0.0	0.0	1.0	0.9	5.2	4.7	8.0	8.0	4.2	23.9	33.8	11.3	0.9	76.1	42.8	53.1	46.9
56684	TRAIL	96.8	96.0	0.0	0.0	0.3	0.7	0.9	1.7	5.4	5.7	6.4	6.7	4.0	22.5	31.9	14.8	2.7	77.9	44.4	54.4	45.6
56685	WASKISH	95.7	96.1	0.9	0.8	0.0	0.0	0.0	0.0	5.5	5.5	6.3	6.3	4.7	17.3	31.5	18.9	3.9	79.5	48.4	50.4	49.6
56686	WILLIAMS	98.5	98.1	0.2	0.3	0.2	0.3	0.5	0.7	4.1	6.2	7.8	6.3	3.8	22.0	33.4	14.7	1.7	77.3	44.9	52.3	47.7
56688	WIRT	95.2	95.1	0.0	0.0	0.0	0.0	0.8	1.6	4.1	4.1	4.1	5.7	4.9	17.9	35.8	22.0	1.6	83.7	51.0	52.0	48.0
56701	THIEF RIVER FALLS	96.8	96.0	0.2	0.3	0.7	0.9	1.4	2.0	6.3	5.8	5.7	6.5	7.0	25.6	26.5	13.0	3.6	78.6	39.0	49.2	50.8
56710	ALVARADO	94.7	92.3	0.0	0.0	0.0	0.0	7.3	10.9	7.2	7.5	7.5	6.3	4.1	24.3	27.9	13.2	2.0	74.1	40.2	48.1	51.9
56711	ANGLE INLET	100.0	100.0	0.0	0.0	0.0	0.0	0.9	0.9	3.8	5.7	6.6	5.7	2.8	21.7	37.7	14.2	1.9	79.2	47.0	52.8	47.2
56713	ARGYLE	95.4	93.7	0.1	0.1	0.1	0.1	4.8	7.3	6.0	6.6	6.6	6.9	4.8	21.1	29.9	15.0	3.1	75.5	43.5	50.2	49.8
56714	BADGER	99.1	98.8	0.2	0.3	0.1	0.1	0.6	0.9	8.0	7.9	7.6	6.2	5.5	25.6	26.7	10.8	1.6	72.6	38.2	52.8	47.2
56715	BROOKS	99.6	99.6	0.0	0.0	0.0	0.0	0.0	0.0	5.2	5.2	5.2	6.0	6.5	21.8	28.6	18.1	3.2	81.0	45.0	51.2	48.8
56716	CROOKSTON	92.4	89.7	0.5	0.6	0.5	0.6	7.6	11.3	5.7	6.1	6.2	9.5	9.0	21.7	24.1	13.3	4.4	77.3	38.1	48.8	51.2
56720	DONALDSON	98.9	98.7	0.0	0.0	0.0	0.0	3.4	5.3	6.7	6.7	6.7	6.7	4.0	17.3	34.7	14.7	2.7	74.7	46.3	52.0	48.0
56721	EAST GRAND FORKS	91.9	89.5	0.5	0.6	0.3	0.4	6.8	9.8	6.7	6.8	7.3	8.6	7.2	24.6	25.8	11.2	1.9	74.1	36.6	49.9	50.1
56722	EUCLID	98.0	97.9	0.0	0.0	0.0	0.0	0.3	0.6	6.2	8.0	7.1	10.1	4.5	24.0	26.4	12.2	1.5	72.1	38.8	52.2	47.8
56723	FISHER	96.8	95.6	0.3	0.5	0.1	0.1	3.0	4.8	6.0	6.5	7.0	7.8	5.5	22.9	32.1	11.0	1.1	75.6	40.8	51.2	48.8
56724	GATZKE	98.6	98.5	0.0	0.0	0.7	0.8	0.0	0.0	4.6	6.2	6.2	6.9	3.8	21.5	32.3	15.4	3.1	79.2	45.5	52.3	47.7
56725	GOODRIDGE	98.7	98.5	0.1	0.1	0.5	0.7	0.4	0.5	6.5	7.6	7.2	6.8	4.3	23.5	31.2	11.2	1.7	74.3	39.6	52.9	47.1
56726	GREENBUSH	98.9	98.6	0.2	0.3	0.1	0.2	0.2	0.2	7.3	7.6	7.5	5.9	3.8	23.3	25.5	14.6	4.5	74.0	41.3	51.2	48.8
56727	GRYGLA	96.2	95.3	0.1	0.2	0.5	0.7	0.2	0.2	5.4	6.0	6.4	6.2	4.4	20.9	31.2	16.1	3.3	78.3	45.4	52.2	47.8
56728	HALLOCK	97.6	96.8	0.1	0.1	0.3	0.4	1.7	2.6	6.0	6.9	6.9	6.1	4.2	17.8	30.2	15.6	6.3	76.1	46.3	49.1	50.9
56729	HALMA	97.7	97.4	0.0	0.0	0.6	0.6	1.2	1.3	5.8	5.8	7.1	7.1	3.9	22.7	29.9	14.9	2.6	76.6	43.0	50.6	49.4
56732	KARLSTAD	98.0	97.5	0.0	0.0	0.1	0.2	0.7	1.1	6.1	6.6	7.2	6.1	4.2	21.4	26.8	16.0	5.6	76.4	43.6	48.3	51.7
56733	KENNEDY	98.7	98.5	0.0	0.0	0.2	0.2	3.1	4.7	5.7	6.3	6.6	7.0	4.2	20.1	33.0	14.6	2.5	77.0	45.1	51.0	49.0
56734	LAKE BRONSON	98.5	98.2	1.0	1.1	0.0	0.0	0.4	0.7	5.7	6.1	6.1	5.7	5.0	17.3	32.9	18.2	2.9	78.5	47.3	53.1	46.9
56735	LANCASTER	98.6	98.1	0.1	0.1	0.4	0.6	0.8	1.0	6.3	7.0	7.3	6.2	4.6	19.8	31.6	14.5	2.7	75.2	43.8	52.4	47.6
56736	MENTOR	98.2	97.8	0.1	0.1	0.2	0.2	0.5	0.8	5.3	5.8	6.2	5.8	4.4	19.2	34.1	17.3	2.0	79.1	47.3	51.7	48.3
56737	MIDDLE RIVER	98.7	98.3	0.0	0.0	0.2	0.4	0.5	0.8	6.2	6.4	6.4	5.5	4.4	22.7	30.3	16.1	1.9	77.6	43.8	49.0	51.0
56738	NEWFOLDEN	98.6	98.2	0.1	0.2	0.3	0.3	0.6	0.9	5.9	6.5	6.4	5.6	4.6	23.8	31.3	14.2	1.8	77.8	42.7	52.3	47.7
56740	NOYES	98.6	97.0	0.0	0.0	0.0	1.5	1.4	1.5	6.1	7.6	7.6	6.1	4.5	21.2	28.8	15.2	3.0	72.7	42.5	50.0	50.0
56741	OAK ISLAND	100.0	100.0	0.0	0.0	0.0	0.0	0.0	0.0	0.0	7.1	7.1	7.1	0.0	21.4	42.9	14.3	0.0	78.6	47.5	53.6	46.4
56742	OKLEE	99.4	99.3	0.2	0.2	0.0	0.0	0.2	0.2	5.1	5.4	5.4	6.1	6.1	21.4	30.1	17.2	3.1	80.3	45.2	50.5	49.5
56744	OSLO	94.7	92.4	0.2	0.2	0.0	0.0	7.3	11.2	6.5	6.9	6.9	6.7	4.0	22.5	30.4	13.6	2.5	75.4	42.3	53.3	46.7
56748	PLUMMER	98.9	98.4	0.8	1.3	0.0	0.0	0.1	0.1	7.4	7.7	7.4	5.8	3.6	24.2	28.6	12.5	2.9	74.1	39.9	51.7	48.3
56750	RED LAKE FALLS	96.4	96.1	0.0	0.0	0.1	0.2	0.4	0.6	5.7	6.1	5.8	6.0	5.3	22.9	28.8	15.9	3.5	78.4	43.3	50.2	49.8
56751	ROSEAU	98.4	98.1	0.1	0.1	0.5	0.6	0.5	0.7	7.1	7.1	7.3	7.0	5.6	24.5	26.9	11.3	3.2	74.2	39.0	50.6	49.4
56754	SAINT HILAIRE	98.5	98.0	0.3	0.3	0.3	0.4	0.4	0.7	5.7	6.0	6.5	6.9	5.2	21.9	32.9	13.9	1.1	77.2	43.2	52.4	47.6
56755	SAINT VINCENT	98.3	97.4	0.0	0.0	0.6	0.6	1.1	1.3	5.8	7.1	7.1	6.4	4.5	20.5	32.1	14.1	2.6	76.3	44.0	50.6	49.4
56756	SALOL	96.0	95.5	0.0	0.0	1.7	2.0	0.4	0.6	7.9	7.6	7.6	8.6	6.6	28.4	25.9	6.8	0.7	71.7	33.9	51.5	48.5
56757	STEPHEN	94.1	91.6	0.1	0.1	0.1	0.1	7.7	11.7	5.9	6.0	6.2	6.7	5.6	21.6	29.4	15.3	3.3	77.9	43.3	51.1	48.9
56758	STRANDQUIST	99.0	98.8	0.1	0.1	0.0	0.0	0.6	0.7	5.2	6.0	7.3	9.1	4.3	21.6	30.3	14.5	1.6	75.4	41.7	53.0	47.0
56759	STRATHCONA	99.1	98.9	0.0	0.2	0.2	0.2	0.0	0.2	6.5	7.0	7.0	5.9	3.8	23.0	28.6	14.9	3.4	76.1	42.8	53.6	46.4
56760	VIKING	97.3	96.4	0.2	0.2	0.2	0.2	1.8	2.7	5.8	6.3	7.0	7.3	4.6	22.5	31.2	13.1	2.2	76.5	42.4	53.5	46.5
56761	WANNASKA	99.1	98.9	0.0	0.0	0.2	0.2	0.3	0.5	6.0	6.8	6.8	6.3	4.8	23.2	31.4	12.9	1.7	76.3	42.4	54.4	45.6
56762	WARREN	98.1	97.3	0.2	0.2	0.0	0.0	2.3	3.5	5.0	5.1	6.0	7.0	5.7	21.0	28.5	16.6	5.1	79.3	45.1	49.9	50.1
56763	WARROAD	88.7	87.0	0.1	0.2	5.8	7.2	0.6	0.9	8.0	7.6	7.3	7.8	7.6	26.7	25.8	7.6	1.7	72.1	33.8	50.7	49.3
	MINNESOTA	89.4	86.8	3.5	4.3	2.9	3.9	2.9	4.1	6.8	6.7	6.7	7.2	6.8	27.2	26.3	10.2	2.1	75.6	36.9	49.6	50.4
	UNITED STATES	75.1	72.0	12.3	12.7	3.8	4.6	12.5	15.7	6.8	6.7	6.6	7.1	6.9	27.0	26.0	10.9	1.9	75.7	36.9	49.2	50.8

ZIP CODE #	POST OFFICE NAME	2009 Per Capita Income	2009 HH Income Base	2009 Household Income Distribution (%): Less than $25,000	$25,000 to $49,999	$50,000 to $99,999	$100,000 to $149,999	$150,000 or More	Median Household Income: 2009	2014	2009 National Centile	2009 State Centile	2009 Home Value Base	2009 Home Value Distribution (%): Less than $50,000	$50,000 to $89,999	$90,000 to $174,999	$175,000 to $399,999	$400,000 or More	2009 Median Home Value
56592	WINGER	21225	160	30.6	31.3	33.1	4.4	0.6	39382	41539	31	13	132	34.8	28.0	22.0	12.1	3.0	66923
56593	WOLF LAKE	0	0	0.0	0.0	0.0	0.0	0.0	0	0	0	0	0	0.0	0.0	0.0	0.0	0.0	0
56594	WOLVERTON	20293	300	20.3	34.3	37.7	6.7	1.0	46803	47909	54	42	262	18.7	26.3	39.7	14.9	0.4	95200
56601	BEMIDJI	21907	12491	24.9	29.0	35.7	7.2	3.2	45689	48225	50	37	9065	15.9	18.4	42.8	20.0	3.0	120710
56621	BAGLEY	18890	1830	34.4	27.3	30.7	5.8	1.7	37765	38743	26	9	1386	22.8	22.7	43.1	10.0	1.3	96327
56623	BAUDETTE	23921	1359	25.9	28.8	36.1	6.0	3.2	45415	47448	49	35	1119	19.4	34.0	38.2	7.1	1.4	83182
56626	BENA	15492	183	42.6	23.0	29.0	4.4	1.1	30220	31140	8	2	142	35.2	19.7	33.1	10.6	1.4	83000
56627	BIG FALLS	21857	220	36.4	35.5	23.2	3.6	1.4	36203	37496	21	6	181	43.6	30.9	20.4	4.4	0.6	54107
56628	BIGFORK	23162	806	25.2	31.0	36.6	4.5	2.7	43222	44892	43	26	707	13.4	22.2	41.4	20.1	2.8	112500
56629	BIRCHDALE	22814	13	30.8	30.8	38.5	0.0	0.0	42330	42330	40	22	12	25.0	33.3	41.7	0.0	0.0	80000
56630	BLACKDUCK	18334	705	36.5	32.8	25.8	4.1	0.9	35143	35902	18	5	565	27.4	23.0	37.5	11.3	0.7	88913
56633	CASS LAKE	14733	1322	35.9	28.5	30.9	3.6	1.1	35689	36760	20	5	935	25.0	29.3	30.4	11.4	3.9	83468
56634	CLEARBROOK	17181	466	40.3	27.3	29.2	2.8	0.4	31512	32777	11	2	360	28.9	30.6	28.3	10.8	1.4	77667
56636	DEER RIVER	17597	1861	31.9	32.4	29.6	4.6	1.5	38331	39684	28	10	1552	18.2	27.6	36.5	14.2	3.4	97558
56637	TALMOON	19527	68	29.4	27.9	33.8	5.9	2.9	42840	42987	42	25	61	16.4	21.3	41.0	19.7	1.6	109722
56639	EFFIE	22645	183	20.8	35.0	39.3	2.7	2.2	43621	44569	44	27	147	9.5	26.5	43.5	18.4	2.0	107500
56641	FEDERAL DAM	18497	156	35.9	30.8	27.6	3.8	1.9	35000	36447	18	4	137	11.7	24.8	29.2	25.5	8.8	120536
56644	GONVICK	19567	350	37.4	24.9	32.6	3.1	2.0	36146	37671	21	6	307	26.7	32.6	31.6	8.5	0.7	76042
56646	GULLY	18030	183	33.9	37.2	23.5	3.8	1.6	33741	35311	15	4	155	38.7	23.2	29.7	7.1	1.3	68636
56647	HINES	18668	519	28.9	29.9	34.5	5.4	1.3	42533	44225	41	23	476	19.7	21.8	39.1	16.4	2.9	106250
56649	INTERNATIONAL FALLS	24239	4483	27.2	25.8	37.6	6.6	2.8	46836	47726	54	42	3472	18.8	27.9	42.1	10.5	0.8	94979
56650	KELLIHER	15683	511	42.5	28.0	24.9	3.7	1.0	31393	31682	10	2	437	30.0	24.9	32.5	10.1	2.5	82321
56651	LENGBY	18756	207	31.9	35.7	26.6	4.8	1.0	36263	37759	21	6	176	19.9	28.4	39.2	11.4	1.1	93000
56652	LEONARD	18985	371	29.9	29.1	33.2	5.9	1.9	41312	42955	37	19	340	17.9	33.2	36.8	10.6	1.5	88667
56653	LITTLEFORK	22109	593	25.8	27.2	36.6	8.8	1.7	46402	47210	53	41	515	20.2	27.0	44.9	7.4	0.6	93372
56654	LOMAN	18590	74	33.8	23.0	37.8	4.1	1.4	42359	42991	40	23	67	23.9	31.3	37.3	7.5	0.0	84167
56655	LONGVILLE	25249	818	27.0	32.3	31.2	5.9	3.7	42208	43958	40	22	742	6.3	15.9	30.7	37.6	9.4	165517
56657	MARCELL	28062	132	17.4	31.8	41.7	6.8	2.3	50505	49384	62	56	125	9.6	16.8	46.4	24.0	3.2	126786
56659	MAX	15050	67	46.3	34.3	14.9	1.5	3.0	27946	26111	6	1	56	21.4	35.7	26.8	8.9	7.1	80000
56660	MIZPAH	17202	112	39.3	28.6	27.7	3.6	0.9	33427	34073	14	3	92	37.0	33.7	21.7	6.5	1.1	60000
56661	NORTHOME	17098	351	37.3	30.2	28.5	2.8	1.1	33988	35672	15	4	305	28.5	29.2	34.1	7.2	1.0	78043
56662	OUTING	24140	295	30.8	32.2	29.5	5.8	1.7	39026	40000	30	12	266	12.4	17.3	33.1	30.1	7.1	135417
56663	PENNINGTON	17404	93	31.2	31.2	33.3	4.3	0.0	38372	40000	28	11	80	23.8	12.5	40.0	20.0	3.8	114583
56666	PONEMAH	8897	295	48.8	25.1	22.0	3.4	0.7	25911	26374	4	1	170	25.3	41.2	29.4	4.1	0.0	74375
56667	PUPOSKY	20308	457	28.0	28.2	36.8	4.8	2.2	42941	45546	42	25	414	16.7	25.4	40.3	14.5	3.1	103390
56668	RANIER	23897	31	9.7	29.0	45.2	12.9	3.2	60911	58502	79	79	28	3.6	3.6	60.7	32.1	0.0	141667
56669	KABETOGAMA	23142	150	29.3	33.3	28.7	6.7	2.0	37839	39486	26	9	131	16.8	24.4	42.0	13.7	3.1	101442
56670	REDBY	9210	629	48.0	25.4	22.1	3.5	1.0	26524	26935	4	1	363	25.9	41.6	27.8	4.7	0.0	73286
56671	REDLAKE	12538	639	42.1	26.9	25.5	2.7	2.8	31634	32545	11	2	433	17.6	43.9	34.9	3.7	0.0	82143
56672	REMER	20785	793	31.7	31.7	30.3	5.2	1.3	38102	39080	27	10	716	13.8	20.9	35.6	23.5	6.1	118367
56673	ROOSEVELT	18921	467	21.0	34.0	39.6	3.9	1.5	45587	47196	50	36	436	17.9	28.4	44.0	9.2	0.5	96667
56676	SHEVLIN	20295	329	27.1	30.7	35.6	3.6	3.0	42339	44386	40	23	303	23.1	25.1	39.6	11.2	1.0	93056
56678	SOLWAY	20713	611	20.6	28.2	44.5	5.1	1.6	50631	51582	63	57	562	13.2	24.6	43.1	16.9	2.3	114244
56680	SPRING LAKE	22763	87	32.2	28.7	32.2	3.4	3.4	39312	40000	31	13	76	17.1	23.7	36.8	18.4	3.9	107500
56681	SQUAW LAKE	13595	95	48.4	35.8	11.6	2.1	2.1	26109	26108	4	1	79	21.5	31.6	29.1	8.9	8.9	85000
56682	SWIFT	17272	311	17.0	38.6	38.9	3.5	1.9	45751	47425	51	37	290	15.2	29.3	45.2	10.0	0.3	100446
56683	TENSTRIKE	23880	93	20.4	37.6	35.5	5.4	1.1	44680	47646	47	32	85	10.6	16.5	56.5	14.1	2.4	128289
56684	TRAIL	17665	127	34.6	37.8	23.6	3.9	0.0	33061	32764	13	3	108	39.8	23.1	29.6	6.5	0.9	67143
56685	WASKISH	21698	69	44.9	29.0	23.2	2.9	0.0	29291	28584	7	2	59	30.5	28.8	30.5	8.5	1.7	78750
56686	WILLIAMS	19701	389	27.8	34.4	32.1	4.4	1.3	41046	42128	36	18	360	22.5	30.6	37.8	7.2	1.9	82667
56688	WIRT	16457	48	31.3	35.4	31.3	2.1	0.0	38188	39074	27	10	44	20.5	22.7	50.0	6.8	0.0	102778
56701	THIEF RIVER FALLS	22516	5207	26.8	28.3	36.9	5.5	2.5	43847	45908	45	28	3744	21.5	26.2	42.2	9.5	0.5	92925
56710	ALVARADO	20348	213	20.2	21.6	52.1	6.1	0.0	54869	55051	71	70	179	22.3	29.1	39.7	7.3	1.7	87500
56711	ANGLE INLET	21052	49	32.7	26.5	36.7	2.0	2.0	37950	38607	27	10	45	20.0	26.7	48.9	4.4	0.0	95000
56713	ARGYLE	19817	363	29.2	26.4	36.4	6.3	1.7	44603	45786	47	32	301	28.2	37.9	30.6	2.7	0.7	68939
56714	BADGER	20978	497	24.7	28.6	39.6	5.4	1.6	47196	48252	55	43	433	24.7	23.3	39.3	11.3	1.4	93864
56715	BROOKS	18042	106	35.8	31.1	28.3	4.7	0.0	35000	34593	18	4	84	41.7	29.8	26.2	2.4	0.0	58750
56716	CROOKSTON	23417	3589	23.9	27.7	37.9	6.1	4.3	48254	50386	57	48	2349	19.3	27.9	41.3	10.6	0.9	94119
56720	DONALDSON	23100	32	15.6	40.6	34.4	6.3	3.1	43162	47351	43	25	27	51.9	22.2	25.9	0.0	0.0	47500
56721	EAST GRAND FORKS	22243	3455	24.2	27.4	38.0	7.6	2.8	47818	51070	56	46	2407	7.3	10.6	55.7	25.8	0.6	139701
56722	EUCLID	22980	126	16.7	27.0	45.2	7.9	3.2	54145	55081	70	68	114	14.0	21.9	44.7	18.4	0.9	117647
56723	FISHER	23274	526	12.4	28.3	46.6	9.5	3.2	56754	59338	74	72	445	6.3	16.4	50.3	24.7	2.2	134968
56724	GATZKE	20758	62	25.8	35.5	35.5	1.6	1.6	38880	38878	29	11	52	38.5	23.1	32.7	5.8	0.0	70000
56725	GOODRIDGE	19965	298	27.2	30.2	34.6	4.7	3.4	42334	43843	40	23	254	19.3	25.6	39.4	14.6	1.2	95909
56726	GREENBUSH	20769	543	26.2	32.0	36.3	3.9	1.7	43167	45165	43	25	462	27.1	25.5	39.0	8.0	0.4	85556
56727	GRYGLA	18479	447	30.9	34.5	30.6	2.9	1.1	36297	37036	21	6	375	33.6	24.3	33.9	7.2	1.1	77381
56728	HALLOCK	21590	550	23.1	31.6	38.5	5.1	1.6	45606	47354	50	36	451	32.6	35.3	29.0	2.9	0.2	69125
56729	HALMA	18831	66	27.3	31.8	37.9	1.5	1.5	42351	41136	40	23	59	32.2	32.2	32.2	3.4	0.0	73000
56732	KARLSTAD	17138	545	35.4	31.0	31.0	2.2	0.4	35417	35940	19	5	415	34.0	33.7	30.4	1.9	0.0	66714
56733	KENNEDY	22349	198	19.2	38.9	33.8	4.5	3.5	42765	43729	42	24	170	44.1	25.3	26.5	2.9	1.2	59091
56734	LAKE BRONSON	18796	213	40.4	32.9	24.4	1.4	0.9	31917	32148	11	2	178	58.4	25.8	10.1	4.5	1.1	43750
56735	LANCASTER	19590	294	27.9	34.4	33.0	4.1	0.7	39752	40995	32	14	250	42.0	32.0	22.4	3.2	0.4	57407
56736	MENTOR	23265	545	20.7	32.3	39.3	4.8	2.9	46824	49467	54	42	485	19.6	20.6	33.2	21.9	4.7	113771
56737	MIDDLE RIVER	20147	446	30.7	32.1	32.7	2.7	1.8	38314	39429	28	10	371	33.2	27.0	31.3	7.8	0.8	74048
56738	NEWFOLDEN	19117	609	25.5	31.5	39.4	3.1	0.5	43600	45171	44	27	531	25.6	24.3	39.5	8.7	1.9	90143
56740	NOYES	19082	25	24.0	36.0	36.0	4.0	0.0	41122	50000	36	18	22	27.3	50.0	22.7	0.0	0.0	60000
56741	OAK ISLAND	20625	15	33.3	26.7	40.0	0.0	0.0	37333	35000	25	8	14	7.1	21.4	71.4	0.0	0.0	108333
56742	OKLEE	20051	279	35.5	31.5	27.6	4.7	0.7	35122	35617	18	4	223	41.7	28.3	26.9	2.7	0.4	59737
56744	OSLO	21448	194	29.9	26.3	36.1	6.7	1.0	43635	46255	44	27	167	27.5	32.3	32.9	6.6	0.6	76538
56748	PLUMMER	19635	303	27.7	32.3	34.7	4.6	0.7	40746	40936	35	17	249	28.9	22.9	40.2	8.0	0.0	86250
56750	RED LAKE FALLS	18654	1040	29.7	29.3	36.7	3.4	0.9	41513	42690	38	20	815	27.1	35.0	32.4	4.9	0.6	75411
56751	ROSEAU	22111	2347	19.1	31.3	41.4	6.6	1.6	49677	50345	60	52	1906	20.9	16.9	46.3	15.4	0.5	108871
56754	SAINT HILAIRE	22753	302	22.2	26.2	43.4	5.0	3.3	51265	51842	64	60	270	16.7	25.6	43.3	13.3	1.1	102717
56755	SAINT VINCENT	21336	67	23.9	32.8	37.3	4.5	1.5	44439	47988	47	31	58	29.3	39.7	25.9	5.2	0.0	66250
56756	SALOL	20352	265	12.5	34.0	48.3	4.9	0.4	52005	52693	66	62	239	31.4	17.2	39.3	12.1	0.0	93889
56757	STEPHEN	19761	447	28.2	32.4	32.7	5.4	1.3	40520	41475	34	17	372	30.1	38.4	27.7	3.2	0.5	66250
56758	STRANDQUIST	17357	275	32.0	31.3	33.1	3.6	0.0	36603	37530	22	7	243	39.9	30.5	25.9	3.7	0.0	59423
56759	STRATHCONA	20315	190	27.4	32.1	35.3	4.2	1.1	42334	43518	40	23	169	27.2	23.7	37.3	10.7	1.2	88333
56760	VIKING	21911	179	23.5	30.2	39.7	5.0	1.7	45327	47370	49	35	161	32.9	19.9	38.5	6.2	2.5	85500
56761	WANNASKA	19454	242	21.1	24.0	50.0	4.5	0.4	52017	52542	66	62	226	21.7	22.6	42.0	13.3	0.4	98667
56762	WARREN	24222	1023	21.7	25.8	43.3	6.7	2.4	51820	53464	66	62	776	19.7	31.3	40.7	7.3	0.9	88667
56763	WARROAD	21128	1614	16.2	32.7	44.3	4.8	1.9	50647	51226	63	57	1229	22.2	19.0	46.0	12.0	0.8	106417
	MINNESOTA	31285		15.9	22.3	36.8	16.4	8.6	62767	65994				6.5	9.7	37.4	39.4	7.0	167369
	UNITED STATES	27277		20.9	24.4	35.3	11.7	7.6	54719	56938				9.3	13.1	31.6	32.6	13.5	162279

ZIP CODE		FINANCIAL SERVICES				THE HOME						ENTERTAINMENT						PERSONAL			
						Home Improvements		Furnishings													
#	POST OFFICE NAME	Auto Loan	Home Loan	Invest-ments	Retire-ment Plans	Home Repair	Lawn & Garden	Comput-ers & Hard-ware-Personal	Major Appli-ances	TV, Radio, Sound Equip-ment	Furni-ture	Dine out/ Carry out	Sports Equip-ment	Fees & Tickets	Toys & Games	Travel	Cable TV	Apparel & Services	Auto Repairs	Health Insur-ance	Pets & Supplies
56592	WINGER	87	61	98	61	64	91	67	83	69	55	69	67	50	68	67	75	45	77	87	101
56593	WOLF LAKE	0	0	0	0	0	0	0	0	0	0	0	0	0	0	0	0	0	0	0	0
56594	WOLVERTON	92	64	101	63	67	98	71	88	73	57	73	73	52	72	70	80	47	82	93	108
56601	BEMIDJI	83	76	70	77	74	78	80	78	80	78	80	60	75	82	75	81	55	79	80	93
56621	BAGLEY	79	58	80	57	61	81	61	76	67	56	65	57	50	66	60	73	44	70	80	89
56623	BAUDETTE	87	71	87	71	74	89	74	85	78	70	77	63	65	77	73	83	52	81	89	99
56626	BENA	74	53	76	51	55	75	54	69	60	50	59	52	43	60	54	66	39	63	72	82
56627	BIG FALLS	75	54	77	52	56	77	55	71	62	52	60	53	44	61	55	68	40	65	73	84
56628	BIGFORK	85	68	109	67	74	90	68	86	71	64	70	63	59	67	74	76	47	80	85	100
56629	BIRCHDALE	78	56	80	54	58	80	58	73	64	54	63	55	46	63	57	70	41	67	76	87
56630	BLACKDUCK	74	54	80	53	57	76	56	71	61	51	60	53	45	60	56	66	39	65	73	84
56633	CASS LAKE	65	55	52	56	52	61	58	59	62	58	62	45	54	63	54	65	42	61	64	73
56634	CLEARBROOK	68	49	68	47	50	70	52	65	58	47	56	49	42	57	51	64	37	60	70	77
56636	DEER RIVER	78	58	87	57	62	81	60	76	65	56	64	56	50	64	62	71	43	70	78	89
56637	TALMOON	87	69	112	68	76	92	69	88	73	65	72	64	60	69	75	77	48	81	87	102
56639	EFFIE	82	66	106	65	72	87	66	84	69	62	68	61	57	65	71	73	45	77	82	97
56641	FEDERAL DAM	76	61	99	60	67	81	61	78	64	57	63	57	53	61	66	68	42	72	77	90
56644	GONVICK	78	56	79	55	58	81	60	75	67	54	65	56	48	66	59	74	43	70	81	88
56646	GULLY	74	51	81	51	53	78	57	70	59	46	58	58	41	58	56	64	38	66	74	86
56647	HINES	86	62	93	61	65	88	64	82	70	59	69	62	52	69	65	76	45	75	84	97
56649	INTERNATIONAL FALLS	82	73	81	73	74	88	74	83	78	69	77	62	68	77	74	83	52	79	89	97
56650	KELLIHER	69	49	71	49	51	70	52	64	57	47	56	51	41	56	52	62	37	60	68	78
56651	LENGBY	79	57	81	55	59	80	58	74	65	54	63	55	47	64	58	71	42	68	77	88
56652	LEONARD	85	59	93	59	62	90	65	81	68	53	67	66	48	67	65	74	44	75	85	99
56653	LITTLEFORK	94	72	94	71	74	97	73	90	79	67	78	68	61	80	72	87	52	83	93	106
56654	LOMAN	79	57	82	55	59	81	58	74	65	54	64	56	47	64	58	71	42	68	77	88
56655	LONGVILLE	83	71	110	70	79	91	69	86	72	68	71	61	64	68	76	77	48	80	88	99
56657	MARCELL	94	75	121	74	82	99	75	95	78	70	77	70	65	74	81	84	51	88	94	110
56659	MAX	60	47	75	47	52	63	48	61	50	45	50	44	41	48	51	54	33	56	60	70
56660	MIZPAH	73	53	75	51	55	75	54	69	60	50	59	52	43	59	53	66	39	63	71	82
56661	NORTHOME	72	54	81	52	57	74	55	69	59	51	58	52	45	58	56	64	39	64	71	82
56662	OUTING	73	64	92	61	71	80	63	77	66	63	65	53	58	61	68	70	43	72	80	88
56663	PENNINGTON	71	63	66	62	64	69	61	67	63	62	63	49	56	64	60	65	43	64	67	79
56666	PONEMAH	54	45	37	47	41	49	50	46	54	50	54	36	48	55	45	56	37	51	53	59
56667	PUPOSKY	87	64	89	62	66	89	65	82	72	61	70	62	53	71	64	79	47	75	85	97
56668	RANIER	115	92	149	91	101	122	92	117	96	86	95	86	80	92	100	103	63	108	116	136
56669	KABETOGAMA	82	62	94	60	66	85	63	80	68	59	67	59	52	66	65	73	44	73	81	94
56670	REDBY	54	46	37	47	41	49	50	47	54	50	54	37	48	55	45	56	37	51	53	60
56671	REDLAKE	63	53	43	55	48	57	59	55	64	59	63	43	56	64	53	66	43	59	62	70
56672	REMER	72	62	90	59	69	78	61	75	64	61	63	52	56	60	66	68	42	70	78	86
56673	ROOSEVELT	82	71	77	70	72	81	69	78	72	69	72	57	63	73	68	75	48	74	78	92
56676	SHEVLIN	92	66	97	64	69	93	68	86	75	63	74	65	55	74	68	82	49	79	89	102
56678	SOLWAY	86	79	70	76	77	81	74	79	77	78	77	57	70	80	71	79	53	76	79	94
56680	SPRING LAKE	81	64	102	63	70	86	64	82	68	60	67	60	55	65	69	73	45	75	81	95
56681	SQUAW LAKE	59	47	76	46	52	62	47	60	49	44	49	44	41	47	51	52	32	55	59	69
56682	SWIFT	83	77	68	74	75	78	72	77	75	75	75	56	68	78	69	77	51	74	77	91
56683	TENSTRIKE	91	73	118	72	80	96	73	93	76	68	75	68	63	72	79	81	50	85	91	107
56684	TRAIL	74	51	81	51	53	78	57	70	59	46	58	58	41	58	56	64	38	66	74	87
56685	WASKISH	70	50	72	49	52	71	51	65	57	48	56	49	41	57	51	63	37	60	68	78
56686	WILLIAMS	80	59	89	58	63	82	60	77	66	56	65	57	50	64	62	71	43	71	78	91
56688	WIRT	70	56	91	55	62	74	56	72	59	53	58	52	49	56	61	63	39	66	71	83
56701	THIEF RIVER FALLS	80	70	70	70	70	79	75	78	77	70	76	58	68	77	71	81	52	77	82	92
56710	ALVARADO	96	66	105	66	69	101	73	91	76	59	75	75	53	74	73	83	49	85	96	112
56711	ANGLE INLET	76	61	98	60	67	80	61	77	64	57	63	56	53	60	66	68	42	71	76	90
56713	ARGYLE	87	62	96	62	65	93	68	84	71	56	70	69	51	69	68	77	46	78	89	103
56714	BADGER	93	65	86	64	66	92	70	83	75	63	74	66	54	77	66	82	49	78	88	102
56715	BROOKS	71	51	72	50	53	75	56	69	62	50	60	52	45	61	54	69	40	65	76	82
56716	CROOKSTON	84	77	75	78	75	86	83	82	85	77	83	64	77	84	79	88	58	84	90	99
56720	DONALDSON	97	67	106	66	70	102	74	92	77	60	76	76	54	75	74	84	49	86	97	113
56721	EAST GRAND FORKS	84	73	74	75	72	79	80	79	81	77	81	63	74	81	76	83	56	81	83	95
56722	EUCLID	110	76	121	75	79	116	84	104	87	68	86	86	61	86	84	95	56	97	110	128
56723	FISHER	107	87	114	88	88	114	89	105	91	78	90	85	76	91	91	97	60	99	108	127
56724	GATZKE	78	54	85	53	56	82	59	74	62	48	61	61	44	61	59	68	40	69	78	91
56725	GOODRIDGE	87	64	92	65	67	92	69	84	72	57	71	68	54	71	69	77	46	78	88	102
56726	GREENBUSH	88	61	95	61	64	93	67	83	70	55	69	69	50	69	67	77	45	78	88	102
56727	GRYGLA	77	54	82	53	56	80	58	72	62	49	61	58	44	61	58	67	40	68	76	88
56728	HALLOCK	92	64	101	63	66	97	71	88	73	57	73	72	52	72	70	80	47	82	93	108
56729	HALMA	79	54	86	54	57	83	60	75	62	49	62	62	44	61	60	68	40	70	79	92
56732	KARLSTAD	69	49	72	48	51	73	54	66	58	46	57	52	41	57	53	64	37	62	71	80
56733	KENNEDY	95	66	105	66	69	101	73	91	76	59	75	75	53	74	73	83	49	85	96	112
56734	LAKE BRONSON	68	49	69	48	51	71	54	66	59	47	57	50	43	58	52	66	38	62	72	78
56735	LANCASTER	82	57	89	57	60	87	63	78	66	52	65	64	47	65	63	73	43	73	83	96
56736	MENTOR	93	71	115	70	77	98	73	93	77	66	76	70	61	74	78	83	50	86	93	109
56737	MIDDLE RIVER	80	58	83	56	60	82	59	75	66	55	64	57	47	65	58	72	42	69	78	89
56738	NEWFOLDEN	83	58	88	57	61	86	62	78	67	54	66	62	48	66	62	73	43	73	82	95
56740	NOYES	90	62	99	62	65	95	69	85	72	56	71	71	50	70	68	78	46	80	90	105
56741	OAK ISLAND	64	51	83	51	56	68	51	65	54	48	53	48	45	51	56	57	35	60	65	76
56742	OKLEE	72	52	73	50	53	75	56	70	62	50	60	53	45	61	55	69	40	65	76	82
56744	OSLO	89	61	97	61	64	93	68	84	70	55	70	70	50	69	67	77	45	78	89	103
56748	PLUMMER	80	55	87	55	58	84	61	76	64	50	63	63	45	62	61	69	41	71	80	93
56750	RED LAKE FALLS	76	58	76	58	60	80	61	74	65	53	64	57	50	65	61	71	42	69	78	88
56751	ROSEAU	87	76	77	77	75	89	75	83	79	72	78	64	69	81	73	83	53	79	86	99
56754	SAINT HILAIRE	85	78	77	81	79	92	77	87	79	69	78	66	71	81	77	84	53	80	89	101
56755	SAINT VINCENT	89	61	98	61	64	94	68	84	71	55	70	70	50	69	68	77	45	79	89	104
56756	SALOL	87	80	70	77	78	81	77	80	79	80	79	59	73	82	73	80	54	78	80	95
56757	STEPHEN	84	59	87	58	62	88	65	81	71	56	69	62	51	70	64	78	46	75	87	96
56758	STRANDQUIST	76	52	82	52	55	79	57	72	60	48	60	58	43	59	57	66	39	67	75	88
56759	STRATHCONA	84	58	91	58	61	88	64	79	67	53	66	65	47	66	63	73	43	74	84	97
56760	VIKING	88	63	97	63	66	94	69	85	72	57	71	69	52	70	69	78	46	79	90	104
56761	WANNASKA	83	68	81	70	70	88	70	82	72	61	71	64	60	73	70	77	48	76	85	97
56762	WARREN	84	78	86	78	80	93	77	86	81	73	80	64	74	80	79	86	55	83	94	101
56763	WARROAD	87	81	71	78	78	81	77	80	79	80	79	59	73	83	73	81	54	79	80	95
	MINNESOTA	113	113	112	114	112	114	112	113	111	111	112	88	112	113	112	112	78	112	113	133
	UNITED STATES	100	100	100	100	100	100	100	100	100	100	100	100	100	100	100	100	100	100	100	100

38601-38849

ZIP CODE #	POST OFFICE NAME	COUNTY FIPS CODE	POPULATION 2000	POPULATION 2009	POPULATION 2014	2000-2009 ANNUAL RATE % Rate	2000-2009 ANNUAL RATE State Centile	HOUSEHOLDS 2000	HOUSEHOLDS 2009	HOUSEHOLDS 2014	HOUSEHOLDS % Annual Rate 2000-2009	HOUSEHOLDS 2009 Average HH Size	FAMILIES 2000	FAMILIES 2009	FAMILIES % Annual Rate 2000-2009
38601	ABBEVILLE	071	1977	2168	2246	1.0	86	759	861	899	1.4	2.52	547	603	1.1
38603	ASHLAND	009	3563	3685	3720	0.4	69	1368	1477	1513	0.8	2.42	988	1042	0.6
38606	BATESVILLE	107	14869	15858	16295	0.7	79	5406	5953	6177	1.0	2.63	3936	4229	0.8
38610	BLUE MOUNTAIN	139	3341	3583	3655	0.8	82	1231	1370	1414	1.2	2.54	921	1000	0.9
38611	BYHALIA	093	14556	16339	17173	1.3	90	5187	6015	6396	1.6	2.72	3965	4495	1.4
38614	CLARKSDALE	027	24292	22557	21761	-0.8	14	8444	8055	7814	-0.5	2.72	5960	5538	-0.8
38617	COAHOMA	027	2975	2682	2558	-1.1	7	948	878	844	-0.8	3.03	668	602	-1.1
38618	COLDWATER	137	10955	12178	12664	1.2	89	3967	4592	4830	1.6	2.65	3037	3438	1.3
38619	COMO	107	4863	4770	4758	-0.2	41	1756	1796	1816	0.2	2.66	1276	1268	-0.1
38620	COURTLAND	107	3803	4259	4445	1.2	89	1203	1402	1482	1.7	2.86	935	1066	1.4
38621	CRENSHAW	107	2314	2284	2260	-0.1	47	803	821	821	0.2	2.78	602	601	0.0
38625	DUMAS	139	1241	1300	1327	0.5	72	473	511	525	0.8	2.54	354	373	0.6
38626	DUNDEE	143	1429	1345	1307	-0.7	16	492	486	477	-0.1	2.77	335	330	-0.2
38627	ETTA	145	933	991	1024	0.7	79	354	386	402	0.9	2.56	274	293	0.7
38629	FALKNER	139	1502	1487	1473	-0.1	47	581	599	601	0.3	2.48	433	436	0.1
38631	FRIARS POINT	027	1453	1299	1233	-1.2	5	466	430	412	-0.9	3.02	339	306	-1.1
38632	HERNANDO	033	16860	24825	29337	4.3	99	6062	9150	10934	4.6	2.67	4740	6978	4.3
38633	HICKORY FLAT	009	2260	2308	2333	0.2	59	873	908	925	0.4	2.54	661	672	0.2
38635	HOLLY SPRINGS	093	15680	15913	15972	0.2	59	5205	5506	5595	0.6	2.60	3822	3948	0.4
38637	HORN LAKE	033	19662	28825	34201	4.2	98	6884	10363	12405	4.5	2.78	5294	7757	4.2
38641	LAKE CORMORANT	033	1648	1859	2046	1.3	90	568	647	718	1.4	2.87	437	483	1.1
38642	LAMAR	009	2653	2842	2959	0.7	79	913	1023	1076	1.2	2.78	705	774	1.0
38643	LAMBERT	119	3507	3180	3015	-1.1	7	1225	1141	1090	-0.8	2.72	844	766	-1.0
38645	LYON	027	1355	1279	1241	-0.6	21	458	449	439	-0.2	2.84	346	332	-0.4
38646	MARKS	119	4205	3790	3578	-1.1	7	1533	1420	1354	-0.8	2.60	1073	967	-1.1
38647	MICHIGAN CITY	009	1059	1047	1052	-0.1	47	390	405	412	0.4	2.59	287	290	0.1
38650	MYRTLE	145	3836	4222	4424	1.0	86	1451	1625	1711	1.2	2.60	1112	1219	1.0
38651	NESBIT	033	4914	6466	8148	3.0	97	1783	2336	2979	3.0	2.76	1480	1893	2.7
38652	NEW ALBANY	145	15394	16083	16487	0.5	72	5976	6376	6571	0.7	2.49	4327	4500	0.4
38654	OLIVE BRANCH	033	28509	45452	55377	5.2	99	10101	16492	20260	5.4	2.75	8235	13156	5.2
38655	OXFORD	071	28878	31856	32893	1.1	87	12009	13652	14206	1.4	2.22	6754	7373	1.0
38658	POPE	107	2086	2150	2171	0.3	64	775	825	842	0.7	2.61	601	625	0.4
38659	POTTS CAMP	093	2530	2848	2991	1.3	90	916	1079	1149	1.8	2.55	676	778	1.5
38661	RED BANKS	093	1586	1674	1713	0.6	76	583	643	666	1.1	2.60	453	488	0.8
38663	RIPLEY	139	11031	11068	10967	0.0	52	4288	4456	4463	0.4	2.42	3076	3122	0.2
38664	ROBINSONVILLE	143	1285	2953	3611	9.4	100	524	1253	1548	9.9	2.36	321	770	9.9
38665	SARAH	137	2026	2235	2330	1.1	87	736	845	892	1.5	2.64	554	621	1.2
38666	SARDIS	107	7347	7391	7435	0.1	54	2702	2823	2872	0.5	2.58	1938	1978	0.2
38668	SENATOBIA	137	12723	14103	14575	1.1	87	4265	4919	5156	1.6	2.63	3212	3629	1.3
38670	SLEDGE	119	1628	1518	1445	-0.8	14	555	532	512	-0.5	2.85	401	375	-0.7
38671	SOUTHAVEN	033	26451	35301	40351	3.2	97	10147	14018	16199	3.6	2.51	7396	9922	3.2
38672	SOUTHAVEN	033	2992	8910	11340	12.5	100	1055	3381	4336	13.4	2.63	890	2800	13.2
38673	TAYLOR	071	666	631	657	-0.6	21	253	253	267	0.0	2.47	146	142	-0.3
38674	TIPLERSVILLE	139	1072	1068	1062	0.0	52	412	424	426	0.3	2.51	311	313	0.1
38676	TUNICA	143	6699	6816	6904	0.2	59	2321	2469	2514	0.7	2.72	1585	1645	0.4
38677	UNIVERSITY	071	4331	3933	3871	-1.0	9	177	152	143	-1.6	6.07	47	35	-3.1
38680	WALLS	033	4569	5136	5625	1.3	90	1662	1935	2141	1.7	2.65	1224	1377	1.3
38683	WALNUT	139	4719	4858	4901	0.3	64	1935	2066	2109	0.7	2.35	1411	1465	0.4
38685	WATERFORD	093	1082	1166	1206	0.8	82	406	459	481	1.3	2.44	304	336	1.1
38701	GREENVILLE	151	30596	27928	26634	-1.0	9	10978	10349	9963	-0.6	2.67	7655	7037	-0.9
38703	GREENVILLE	151	18775	17480	16794	-0.8	14	6434	6223	6044	-0.4	2.74	4745	4461	-0.7
38720	ALLIGATOR	027	535	520	513	-0.3	36	205	205	204	0.0	2.48	153	149	-0.3
38721	ANGUILLA	125	2403	2211	2115	-0.9	11	758	739	716	-0.3	2.99	565	538	-0.5
38725	BENOIT	011	1341	1270	1234	-0.6	21	465	463	456	0.0	2.71	359	349	-0.3
38726	BEULAH	011	151	145	142	-0.4	31	45	44	44	-0.2	2.11	32	30	-0.7
38730	BOYLE	011	2000	1945	1901	-0.3	36	738	740	732	0.0	2.56	560	550	-0.2
38731	CHATHAM	151	56	54	52	-0.4	31	24	24	24	0.0	2.25	18	18	0.0
38732	CLEVELAND	011	20104	19311	18906	-0.4	31	6924	6924	6851	0.0	2.55	4691	4562	-0.3
38733	CLEVELAND	011	148	143	141	-0.4	31	4	4	4	0.0	2.50	3	2	-4.3
38736	DODDSVILLE	133	1807	1754	1727	-0.3	36	272	278	275	0.2	4.21	203	203	0.0
38737	DREW	133	8706	7993	7861	-0.9	11	1404	1349	1307	-0.4	2.86	1028	964	-0.7
38740	DUNCAN	011	788	745	722	-0.6	21	258	251	245	-0.3	2.75	183	173	-0.6
38744	GLEN ALLAN	151	477	434	412	-1.0	9	165	157	151	-0.5	2.76	123	114	-0.8
38746	GUNNISON	011	1127	1037	998	-0.9	11	372	357	348	-0.4	2.90	262	245	-0.7
38748	HOLLANDALE	151	6082	5843	5669	-0.4	31	2041	2032	1993	0.0	2.87	1550	1508	-0.3
38751	INDIANOLA	133	13445	12926	12531	-0.4	31	4383	4287	4166	-0.2	2.98	3350	3207	-0.5
38753	INVERNESS	133	1816	1651	1573	-1.0	9	627	584	558	-0.8	2.77	479	436	-1.0
38754	ISOLA	053	1599	1436	1351	-1.2	5	588	542	514	-0.9	2.65	425	382	-1.1
38756	LELAND	151	7443	7159	6924	-0.4	31	2674	2679	2620	0.0	2.66	1962	1914	-0.3
38759	MERIGOLD	011	1176	1124	1099	-0.5	25	470	468	462	0.0	2.38	337	327	-0.3
38761	MOORHEAD	133	3145	2944	2840	-0.7	16	844	807	777	-0.5	3.25	655	614	-0.7
38762	MOUND BAYOU	011	3522	3485	3437	-0.1	47	1171	1220	1217	0.4	2.85	855	869	0.2
38769	ROSEDALE	011	3499	3242	3124	-0.8	14	1123	1078	1051	-0.4	2.92	816	763	-0.7
38771	RULEVILLE	133	3496	3162	3004	-1.1	7	1117	1021	970	-1.0	2.99	847	757	-1.2
38773	SHAW	011	4069	3899	3802	-0.5	25	1400	1396	1377	0.0	2.76	1051	1024	-0.3
38774	SHELBY	011	3099	2926	2829	-0.6	21	978	951	931	-0.3	2.99	718	680	-0.6
38778	SUNFLOWER	133	1939	1814	1737	-0.7	16	608	583	562	-0.5	3.11	451	423	-0.7
38801	TUPELO	081	28708	30285	31189	0.6	76	11089	11728	12106	0.6	2.55	7749	7987	0.3
38804	TUPELO	081	17583	17929	18232	0.2	59	6955	7146	7300	0.3	2.41	4770	4761	0.0
38821	AMORY	095	12707	12437	12176	-0.2	41	5107	5151	5088	0.1	2.38	3640	3580	-0.2
38824	BALDWYN	117	7856	8195	8296	0.5	72	3020	3218	3277	0.7	2.52	2213	2298	0.4
38826	BELDEN	115	4351	4857	5105	1.2	89	1555	1762	1858	1.4	2.75	1242	1380	1.1
38827	BELMONT	141	2704	2668	2638	-0.1	47	1091	1096	1089	0.0	2.43	796	781	-0.2
38828	BLUE SPRINGS	145	3171	3653	3892	1.5	91	1213	1438	1541	1.9	2.54	931	1078	1.6
38829	BOONEVILLE	117	17989	17726	17446	-0.2	41	6912	7072	7013	0.2	2.41	4978	4968	0.0
38833	BURNSVILLE	141	2578	2651	2666	0.3	64	1027	1084	1098	0.6	2.45	751	774	0.3
38834	CORINTH	003	27447	28165	28542	0.3	64	11445	12111	12394	0.6	2.28	7789	8009	0.3
38838	DENNIS	141	1633	1574	1547	-0.4	31	641	631	623	-0.2	2.49	494	476	-0.4
38841	ECRU	115	3547	4135	4398	1.7	93	1364	1611	1716	1.8	2.54	1022	1177	1.5
38843	FULTON	057	11553	11764	11654	0.2	59	4378	4519	4503	0.3	2.40	3179	3202	0.1
38844	GATTMAN	095	313	307	302	-0.2	41	132	134	133	0.2	2.28	100	99	-0.1
38846	GLEN	003	2454	2501	2532	0.2	59	950	1004	1028	0.6	2.49	726	750	0.4
38847	GOLDEN	057	3563	3423	3344	-0.4	31	1392	1370	1347	-0.2	2.50	1053	1014	-0.4
38848	GREENWOOD SPRINGS	095	857	843	828	-0.2	41	338	346	343	0.3	2.43	254	254	0.0
38849	GUNTOWN	081	4396	4886	5130	1.1	87	1639	1843	1942	1.3	2.64	1246	1365	1.0
	MISSISSIPPI					0.5					0.8	2.56			0.5
	UNITED STATES					1.0					1.1	2.59			0.9

ZIP CODE #	POST OFFICE NAME	RACE (%) White 2000	White 2009	Black 2000	Black 2009	Asian/Pacific 2000	Asian/Pacific 2009	% Hispanic Origin 2000	% Hispanic Origin 2009	2009 AGE DISTRIBUTION (%) 0-4	5-9	10-14	15-19	20-24	25-44	45-64	65-84	85+	18+	MEDIAN AGE 2009	% 2009 Males	% 2009 Females
38601	ABBEVILLE	44.0	40.6	55.4	58.6	0.1	0.0	1.0	1.1	7.3	7.1	6.3	7.6	8.9	25.0	26.7	9.2	2.0	74.2	34.9	48.1	51.9
38603	ASHLAND	64.7	62.6	32.9	35.0	0.1	0.1	1.2	1.2	6.3	6.4	6.5	6.6	5.3	24.5	27.0	14.8	2.7	76.8	40.9	48.6	51.4
38606	BATESVILLE	58.2	54.4	40.4	43.7	0.3	0.4	1.2	1.7	7.8	7.8	7.7	7.3	6.2	25.5	25.1	10.8	1.9	72.3	35.1	48.6	51.4
38610	BLUE MOUNTAIN	71.4	68.2	26.2	28.3	0.1	0.2	2.4	3.7	6.8	6.4	6.5	8.2	8.2	24.8	26.4	10.7	2.1	75.7	36.3	48.3	51.7
38611	BYHALIA	62.6	59.2	35.6	38.3	0.1	0.2	1.9	2.6	7.1	7.2	7.2	6.7	5.4	25.6	28.4	11.3	1.1	74.3	38.4	49.8	50.2
38614	CLARKSDALE	32.1	29.5	66.4	68.4	0.6	0.8	0.8	1.1	8.6	8.3	8.0	8.5	7.3	23.2	23.5	10.4	2.1	70.0	32.8	46.1	53.9
38617	COAHOMA	13.8	11.4	84.8	86.7	0.2	0.3	0.7	0.9	12.0	10.8	8.8	8.7	8.5	23.0	19.1	7.6	1.7	62.8	25.9	45.7	54.3
38618	COLDWATER	64.6	61.5	34.3	37.0	0.0	0.1	1.0	1.4	7.2	7.2	7.3	6.8	6.2	25.6	27.2	11.2	1.4	74.2	37.2	49.2	50.8
38619	COMO	43.9	42.7	55.3	56.0	0.0	0.0	1.0	1.4	7.5	8.0	7.9	6.7	5.2	23.0	27.1	12.9	1.7	72.4	38.0	48.4	51.6
38620	COURTLAND	52.2	47.6	46.6	50.7	0.2	0.3	1.3	1.8	7.8	7.3	7.7	12.3	7.4	25.6	22.7	8.0	1.2	70.3	30.7	48.7	51.3
38621	CRENSHAW	35.5	32.5	63.7	66.4	0.1	0.2	1.0	1.2	7.7	8.0	7.8	8.0	6.5	27.0	24.0	9.7	1.3	71.6	33.5	47.3	52.7
38625	DUMAS	94.0	92.9	5.0	5.6	0.1	0.2	1.0	1.6	6.7	6.5	6.7	6.8	5.4	28.3	26.0	12.0	1.5	75.8	38.4	51.3	48.7
38626	DUNDEE	25.7	21.5	71.6	75.2	0.2	0.3	1.6	1.9	7.6	8.5	8.8	8.9	5.7	24.0	23.7	10.9	1.9	69.3	33.4	48.2	51.8
38627	ETTA	96.2	95.7	3.4	3.8	0.0	0.0	1.1	1.7	6.5	6.4	6.5	6.8	5.8	29.4	25.1	11.6	2.1	76.7	37.1	48.3	51.7
38629	FALKNER	77.6	74.8	20.9	23.0	0.1	0.1	1.3	2.0	6.7	6.5	6.7	6.5	5.7	28.9	26.5	11.1	1.4	76.4	37.5	49.2	50.8
38631	FRIARS POINT	6.9	5.4	92.7	94.1	0.1	0.1	1.4	1.5	11.3	11.2	9.8	8.5	7.0	23.0	20.6	7.3	1.2	62.4	26.7	44.6	55.4
38632	HERNANDO	81.4	80.2	16.8	17.0	0.5	0.8	1.8	3.0	6.7	7.1	7.3	6.8	4.9	26.1	28.6	11.1	1.3	74.5	39.2	50.5	49.5
38633	HICKORY FLAT	88.9	88.3	10.4	11.0	0.0	0.0	0.5	0.6	8.5	8.4	8.4	6.8	5.1	26.6	23.8	11.1	1.4	70.5	34.9	49.4	50.6
38635	HOLLY SPRINGS	33.2	30.0	65.9	68.8	0.1	0.2	0.7	0.9	6.7	7.0	7.0	8.3	9.4	26.7	23.8	9.6	1.5	74.9	33.0	49.6	50.4
38637	HORN LAKE	84.9	82.1	10.8	11.5	0.8	1.2	3.8	6.0	8.8	8.1	7.7	7.3	6.7	31.5	22.3	7.0	0.7	70.9	32.3	49.1	50.9
38641	LAKE CORMORANT	78.7	76.0	18.1	19.4	1.0	1.4	2.7	4.0	7.0	7.3	7.3	6.7	5.2	26.5	27.9	11.0	1.2	74.3	38.5	51.7	48.3
38642	LAMAR	39.1	36.5	60.3	62.8	0.0	0.1	1.0	1.2	8.2	8.6	8.2	7.1	5.3	25.2	25.9	10.2	1.2	70.5	35.1	47.0	53.0
38643	LAMBERT	36.7	33.2	62.1	65.2	0.2	0.3	0.7	0.9	8.6	8.9	8.0	8.7	7.0	23.0	22.8	11.4	1.6	69.1	32.8	48.1	51.9
38645	LYON	26.5	22.8	71.9	75.1	0.1	0.1	2.4	2.7	8.7	8.7	8.2	7.6	6.4	23.8	25.9	9.7	1.1	69.7	32.9	46.8	53.2
38646	MARKS	33.6	31.6	65.5	67.2	0.2	0.3	0.4	0.5	7.1	7.8	7.6	7.9	6.4	23.0	23.8	13.4	3.0	72.5	36.6	46.5	53.5
38647	MICHIGAN CITY	41.0	39.4	57.7	59.3	0.2	0.2	1.3	1.4	7.8	8.0	7.6	7.3	5.4	26.2	24.1	12.1	1.4	71.9	35.3	49.3	50.7
38650	MYRTLE	91.1	89.4	8.0	9.2	0.1	0.1	0.7	1.2	7.7	7.5	7.4	6.7	5.5	27.8	25.7	10.5	1.2	73.4	36.2	49.0	51.0
38651	NESBIT	83.7	81.2	14.5	16.3	0.7	0.9	1.2	1.9	6.0	6.6	7.3	6.8	4.1	24.3	32.0	11.6	1.1	75.4	41.8	49.7	50.3
38652	NEW ALBANY	77.5	74.5	20.4	22.5	0.3	0.4	2.2	3.3	7.6	7.2	7.0	6.4	5.7	26.6	25.4	12.1	2.1	74.3	37.4	48.7	51.3
38654	OLIVE BRANCH	86.4	84.0	11.7	13.1	0.4	0.6	1.4	2.2	8.0	7.8	7.7	6.8	4.8	29.8	25.4	8.8	0.9	72.0	35.8	49.2	50.8
38655	OXFORD	71.9	68.8	25.5	27.4	1.3	2.0	1.1	1.7	5.9	5.4	5.1	7.3	16.7	27.5	21.1	9.2	1.8	80.3	30.7	49.8	50.2
38658	POPE	67.6	64.1	31.7	34.8	0.2	0.2	0.5	0.7	7.3	7.1	7.0	6.4	5.9	26.9	27.2	10.9	1.3	74.6	37.0	49.9	50.1
38659	POTTS CAMP	66.0	61.4	33.4	37.6	0.1	0.1	0.6	0.7	5.9	6.2	7.4	7.4	7.0	26.6	27.0	10.7	1.7	75.7	37.1	50.8	49.2
38661	RED BANKS	61.3	56.2	36.8	41.0	0.2	0.3	2.0	2.7	7.2	7.2	7.3	6.5	5.4	26.8	26.9	11.4	1.3	74.3	37.3	49.5	50.5
38663	RIPLEY	81.5	78.7	15.7	17.1	0.2	0.2	2.7	4.2	6.9	6.6	6.6	6.4	6.1	27.4	24.7	12.7	2.7	76.1	37.9	49.1	50.9
38664	ROBINSONVILLE	34.7	30.1	60.1	64.1	1.2	1.3	4.7	5.4	8.6	7.9	7.2	7.1	7.8	29.7	23.7	7.3	0.6	72.1	31.9	50.6	49.4
38665	SARAH	80.8	79.5	18.4	19.3	0.0	0.1	1.2	1.8	7.9	7.7	7.7	6.9	5.3	26.6	25.8	11.3	1.0	72.4	36.9	50.0	50.0
38666	SARDIS	39.1	36.4	59.9	62.3	0.1	0.2	1.0	1.3	8.1	8.1	7.9	7.6	6.3	25.0	23.7	11.2	2.1	71.1	34.7	47.3	52.7
38668	SENATOBIA	67.8	64.9	31.0	33.5	0.2	0.3	0.8	1.1	6.6	6.6	6.8	10.2	8.1	25.4	24.7	9.9	1.7	75.6	34.1	48.2	51.8
38670	SLEDGE	15.7	13.8	83.9	85.6	0.0	0.0	0.7	0.8	9.0	9.3	8.8	8.9	7.2	26.1	21.5	7.8	1.4	67.5	29.6	44.9	55.1
38671	SOUTHAVEN	90.7	88.3	6.1	6.9	0.8	1.2	2.4	3.8	7.7	7.2	6.9	6.8	6.5	30.2	23.9	9.6	1.0	74.0	34.6	48.7	51.3
38672	SOUTHAVEN	86.1	83.3	12.1	14.0	0.8	1.1	1.0	1.6	6.0	6.6	7.3	6.9	4.2	24.5	32.3	11.3	1.0	75.6	41.7	49.5	50.5
38673	TAYLOR	73.7	70.8	24.7	26.6	0.9	1.3	0.8	1.3	5.5	5.4	5.4	7.4	20.4	24.6	20.6	8.7	1.9	79.9	29.1	50.4	49.6
38674	TIPLERSVILLE	84.5	82.9	14.5	15.8	0.0	0.0	0.7	0.9	5.9	5.9	6.4	6.8	5.6	28.4	27.7	11.8	1.5	77.9	38.9	49.3	50.7
38676	TUNICA	27.4	24.4	70.9	73.6	0.4	0.4	2.3	2.6	8.6	8.2	8.3	8.4	7.8	24.7	22.8	9.5	1.8	69.7	31.2	46.8	53.2
38677	UNIVERSITY	73.5	68.9	17.7	18.6	5.9	8.6	1.2	1.7	1.2	1.0	0.5	39.2	42.4	12.6	2.5	0.5	0.1	96.8	20.9	45.0	55.0
38680	WALLS	82.3	78.4	11.3	12.0	1.2	1.6	6.6	10.5	7.1	7.1	7.3	6.4	4.7	32.0	26.9	7.9	0.7	74.7	36.9	52.7	47.3
38683	WALNUT	93.4	92.3	5.6	6.2	0.0	0.1	0.8	1.3	6.1	6.2	6.4	6.5	5.1	27.1	27.6	13.3	1.7	77.4	39.9	48.7	51.3
38685	WATERFORD	62.6	59.1	36.7	40.1	0.1	0.2	0.6	0.7	6.1	6.2	6.6	6.7	6.4	26.4	28.6	11.6	1.5	77.0	38.6	51.2	48.8
38701	GREENVILLE	35.9	33.9	62.5	63.9	0.8	1.0	0.8	1.1	8.4	8.3	7.8	7.9	7.0	25.1	24.1	9.7	1.8	70.7	32.9	47.3	52.7
38703	GREENVILLE	28.5	25.1	70.0	72.9	0.5	0.7	0.7	0.9	8.2	8.4	8.0	8.2	6.7	25.0	23.2	10.3	2.0	70.2	33.0	46.8	53.2
38720	ALLIGATOR	39.1	33.5	58.9	63.8	0.6	0.8	1.3	1.9	8.5	8.5	8.3	7.3	5.6	22.5	25.2	12.1	2.1	70.0	36.6	47.5	52.5
38721	ANGUILLA	27.2	24.6	71.4	73.4	0.2	0.3	2.0	2.7	8.6	8.8	8.7	9.5	7.3	24.1	23.7	8.0	1.4	67.8	30.1	47.5	52.5
38725	BENOIT	29.5	25.6	68.5	71.7	0.1	0.2	1.7	2.3	8.9	8.5	8.2	8.0	7.2	25.4	22.4	10.1	1.3	69.8	31.9	49.8	50.2
38726	BEULAH	46.1	40.7	52.0	57.2	0.7	0.7	1.3	1.4	3.4	3.4	3.4	9.0	15.9	35.2	19.3	9.0	1.4	85.5	31.6	70.3	29.7
38730	BOYLE	67.3	62.2	31.1	35.3	0.4	0.6	1.3	2.0	7.0	6.8	6.8	7.5	6.1	29.1	25.8	9.7	1.1	74.8	35.3	50.2	49.8
38731	CHATHAM	47.3	38.9	52.7	61.1	0.0	0.0	1.8	0.0	5.6	5.6	7.4	7.4	5.6	20.4	33.3	13.0	1.9	75.9	43.3	42.6	57.4
38732	CLEVELAND	46.3	44.1	51.9	53.4	0.8	1.0	1.3	4.3	6.7	6.9	6.8	8.9	11.2	25.5	22.7	9.3	2.0	75.7	31.5	47.1	52.9
38733	CLEVELAND	76.9	80.4	21.8	17.5	0.7	0.7	0.7	27.3	2.1	1.4	2.1	22.4	42.7	11.2	9.1	7.7	1.4	94.4	22.6	39.9	60.1
38736	DODDSVILLE	33.0	29.1	65.8	69.4	0.2	0.2	1.2	1.5	5.5	5.9	5.3	5.9	13.3	37.2	18.4	7.4	1.1	80.0	31.1	66.3	33.7
38737	DREW	29.1	26.5	69.7	72.0	0.4	0.5	0.9	1.1	3.9	4.1	4.2	7.0	13.5	42.4	18.6	5.3	0.9	84.3	32.6	74.6	25.4
38740	DUNCAN	22.2	18.7	75.4	78.1	0.1	0.1	1.8	2.3	8.2	7.9	7.8	7.9	6.6	21.2	24.2	12.6	3.6	70.5	37.3	47.5	52.5
38744	GLEN ALLAN	48.3	42.4	50.2	56.0	0.0	0.0	1.0	1.2	6.2	6.2	6.0	8.1	6.7	23.3	29.7	12.2	1.6	76.7	40.3	47.5	52.5
38746	GUNNISON	21.7	18.5	76.5	79.2	0.4	0.5	1.1	1.4	8.7	8.2	8.7	10.0	6.0	20.8	24.3	11.6	1.7	67.7	32.7	47.9	52.1
38748	HOLLANDALE	37.5	33.9	61.5	64.8	0.1	0.1	1.0	1.2	8.0	8.0	7.7	9.4	6.9	23.6	25.0	9.7	1.5	70.3	33.2	46.5	53.5
38751	INDIANOLA	28.1	26.0	70.7	72.3	0.5	0.6	1.2	1.6	8.5	8.8	8.6	8.6	7.4	26.9	21.4	8.2	1.6	68.8	30.3	45.7	54.3
38753	INVERNESS	36.9	33.1	61.8	65.1	0.6	0.8	1.5	1.8	7.2	7.1	7.0	9.0	6.9	24.7	25.3	11.2	1.6	74.0	35.3	46.5	53.5
38754	ISOLA	34.3	31.2	63.0	65.0	0.2	0.3	3.3	4.7	8.1	8.2	7.9	7.7	5.9	25.3	26.0	9.2	1.7	71.1	33.8	47.8	52.2
38756	LELAND	36.5	32.7	62.2	65.4	0.2	0.2	1.1	1.4	8.5	8.7	8.1	8.2	6.7	25.5	23.4	9.4	1.5	69.7	31.8	48.3	51.7
38759	MERIGOLD	42.7	38.5	55.8	59.5	0.2	0.3	0.9	1.2	6.7	6.7	6.8	6.9	6.0	25.5	28.3	11.1	2.1	75.7	38.3	48.1	51.9
38761	MOORHEAD	21.9	19.0	77.1	79.6	0.2	0.3	1.6	1.9	8.5	8.3	8.1	15.8	12.1	21.0	19.1	6.0	1.3	69.6	23.9	47.7	52.3
38762	MOUND BAYOU	2.9	2.4	96.1	96.4	0.1	0.2	0.4	0.4	9.0	8.4	8.2	9.7	7.7	24.0	22.9	8.5	1.6	68.8	29.9	44.7	55.3
38769	ROSEDALE	15.7	13.3	82.7	84.7	0.4	0.6	1.1	1.3	8.4	9.9	9.5	9.7	6.1	25.2	20.7	9.0	1.5	66.0	29.2	46.4	53.6
38771	RULEVILLE	21.1	18.7	78.1	80.3	0.4	0.6	1.1	1.2	8.4	8.3	7.6	9.0	7.2	22.4	22.8	10.9	3.4	70.1	32.4	45.6	54.4
38773	SHAW	19.3	17.7	79.6	80.8	0.3	0.4	1.0	1.4	8.3	8.4	7.7	8.0	7.4	26.1	23.9	8.7	1.5	70.7	31.9	48.6	51.4
38774	SHELBY	9.9	8.3	88.5	89.7	0.1	0.1	1.3	1.6	9.8	9.6	8.6	11.0	7.2	22.0	19.2	9.9	2.6	64.7	28.2	45.6	54.4
38778	SUNFLOWER	30.6	27.7	66.2	67.9	0.3	0.4	3.7	5.2	9.0	9.4	8.4	9.3	9.1	24.5	19.2	8.6	2.5	67.4	28.5	48.7	51.3
38801	TUPELO	65.0	61.1	32.7	35.7	0.7	1.0	1.3	1.9	7.9	7.6	7.3	7.2	6.6	26.9	24.9	9.9	1.7	72.7	35.2	47.2	52.8
38804	TUPELO	74.3	72.9	23.6	24.1	0.6	1.0	1.4	2.1	6.8	6.8	6.9	6.8	5.9	26.8	26.2	11.6	2.3	75.4	38.2	49.1	50.9
38821	AMORY	80.1	78.4	19.1	20.4	0.1	0.2	0.6	0.9	6.5	6.5	6.6	7.1	5.5	25.1	26.2	13.8	2.7	76.0	39.6	47.2	52.8
38824	BALDWYN	74.1	71.2	24.6	26.9	0.1	0.2	0.7	1.0	7.6	7.3	7.1	6.9	6.1	26.3	24.9	11.7	2.1	73.9	36.8	48.0	52.0
38826	BELDEN	77.9	75.1	21.2	23.6	0.4	0.6	0.6	0.9	7.1	7.5	7.9	7.0	4.7	25.3	29.6	9.8	1.1	73.0	38.6	49.3	50.7
38827	BELMONT	94.0	90.7	0.7	0.8	0.0	0.0	6.5	10.5	7.0	7.0	7.1	6.1	4.8	28.2	25.5	12.6	1.7	75.1	38.3	49.7	50.3
38828	BLUE SPRINGS	91.7	89.8	7.3	8.8	0.1	0.1	0.8	1.3	6.4	6.5	6.8	6.5	5.2	27.0	28.4	11.8	1.5	76.4	38.8	49.9	50.1
38829	BOONEVILLE	87.5	85.8	11.3	12.5	0.2	0.3	0.6	1.0	6.6	6.5	6.5	8.5	6.9	25.4	25.0	12.5	2.1	76.4	37.3	49.0	51.0
38833	BURNSVILLE	98.1	97.4	0.4	0.5	0.1	0.2	1.0	1.6	7.0	6.6	6.7	7.5	6.5	26.1	26.1	12.1	1.4	75.1	37.2	49.1	50.9
38834	CORINTH	85.5	83.5	12.9	14.2	0.3	0.4	1.3	2.0	6.3	6.4	6.5	6.2	5.1	25.9	27.4	13.9	2.4	77.1	40.4	48.8	51.2
38838	DENNIS	95.8	94.8	3.3	3.8	0.0	0.0	0.9	1.5	6.3	6.2	6.7	6.7	5.3	26.5	28.3	12.5	1.7	76.7	40.2	49.3	50.7
38841	ECRU	88.2	86.2	9.6	10.7	0.1	0.1	3.0	4.6	7.4	7.4	7.5	6.7	5.7	27.2	26.1	10.0	1.9	73.6	36.9	49.8	50.2
38843	FULTON	89.4	87.7	9.5	10.7	0.3	0.4	1.2	1.7	5.8	5.8	6.3	9.5	7.1	23.9	25.3	13.7	2.6	78.1	38.3	48.3	51.7
38844	GATTMAN	92.3	90.2	7.4	9.1	0.0	0.0	0.6	0.7	6.5	6.5	6.5	6.5	5.5	28.7	27.4	11.4	1.0	76.5	37.7	50.2	49.8
38846	GLEN	98.7	98.2	0.3	0.3	0.1	0.2	0.6	1.0	7.4	7.6	7.5	6.4	5.4	27.3	26.5	10.8	1.2	73.6	37.2	51.2	48.8
38847	GOLDEN	97.6	96.5	0.4	0.4	0.0	0.0	2.0	3.2	6.9	6.9	7.1	6.5	5.1	27.6	26.5	12.2	1.3	75.1	38.4	50.2	49.8
38848	GREENWOOD SPRINGS	92.1	90.0	7.1	8.9	0.0	0.0	0.5	0.7	6.3	6.3	6.4	6.5	5.6	27.6	27.8	12.1	1.4	77.0	39.0	50.1	49.9
38849	GUNTOWN	89.2	87.2	9.8	11.3	0.2	0.2	0.7	1.1	7.4	7.4	7.4	7.1	5.7	26.9	26.7	9.7	1.6	73.5	36.8	49.7	50.3
	MISSISSIPPI	61.4	59.6	36.3	37.4	0.7	0.9	1.4	2.0	7.2	7.1	7.0	7.5	7.1	26.4	25.3	10.6	1.7	74.3	35.6	48.6	51.4
	UNITED STATES	75.1	72.0	12.3	12.7	3.8	4.6	12.5	15.7	6.8	6.7	6.6	7.1	6.9	27.0	26.0	10.9	1.9	75.7	36.9	49.2	50.8

ZIP CODE #	POST OFFICE NAME	2009 Per Capita Income	2009 HH Income Base	2009 HOUSEHOLD INCOME DISTRIBUTION (%) Less than $25,000	$25,000 to $49,999	$50,000 to $99,999	$100,000 to $149,999	$150,000 or More	MEDIAN HOUSEHOLD INCOME 2009	2014	2009 National Centile	2009 State Centile	2009 Home Value Base	2009 HOME VALUE DISTRIBUTION (%) Less than $50,000	$50,000 to $89,999	$90,000 to $174,999	$175,000 to $399,999	$400,000 or More	2009 Median Home Value
38601	ABBEVILLE	15379	861	41.9	31.5	22.0	3.6	1.0	30404	30349	9	39	696	34.1	29.0	25.7	5.2	6.0	72642
38603	ASHLAND	14382	1477	48.7	28.6	18.6	3.5	0.6	26219	27001	4	17	1269	39.2	33.6	23.9	3.1	0.2	63870
38606	BATESVILLE	16608	5953	39.4	29.1	24.2	5.3	2.0	32358	32039	12	55	4436	34.6	29.5	28.1	6.6	1.1	69205
38610	BLUE MOUNTAIN	16671	1370	34.6	30.7	30.1	3.7	0.9	35000	35359	18	69	1066	36.4	34.1	21.8	7.4	0.4	66744
38611	BYHALIA	17571	6015	31.3	28.9	33.0	4.8	2.0	41134	40430	36	86	5005	26.1	30.8	29.8	12.3	1.1	80243
38614	CLARKSDALE	14421	8055	47.5	25.4	20.7	4.5	2.0	26814	27366	4	20	4503	35.6	36.1	22.1	5.1	1.1	62388
38617	COAHOMA	10586	878	56.4	26.7	12.8	2.6	1.6	20144	21780	1	4	513	52.0	29.6	14.8	2.9	0.6	48359
38618	COLDWATER	17436	4592	32.6	29.9	30.3	6.3	0.8	39148	41449	30	81	3760	24.7	32.7	30.9	10.7	1.0	83381
38619	COMO	14510	1796	44.3	26.1	24.3	4.5	0.8	29734	30204	8	34	1402	37.1	31.2	25.3	5.8	0.5	67642
38620	COURTLAND	14601	1402	35.9	32.9	25.8	3.8	1.6	35331	34880	19	71	1220	39.9	31.6	23.0	5.0	0.5	60536
38621	CRENSHAW	12079	821	51.3	27.9	17.7	2.2	1.0	23971	26023	3	9	633	52.0	27.2	19.4	1.4	0.0	48418
38625	DUMAS	17244	511	32.9	30.3	31.1	5.1	0.6	39198	38712	30	81	448	35.5	26.3	29.2	7.4	1.6	71290
38626	DUNDEE	14742	486	47.3	25.1	19.1	7.0	1.4	27056	28109	5	22	342	45.9	27.8	21.1	5.0	0.3	54516
38627	ETTA	17616	386	31.9	31.6	32.6	2.6	1.3	40612	40333	35	84	326	33.4	27.9	19.6	12.0	7.1	71053
38629	FALKNER	17543	599	34.6	34.6	25.7	3.8	1.3	36643	36491	22	75	484	31.0	30.2	31.6	6.6	0.6	73415
38631	FRIARS POINT	10751	430	58.1	29.8	9.5	1.2	1.4	20694	22184	2	5	253	70.4	24.9	4.7	0.0	0.0	38977
38632	HERNANDO	22014	9150	20.6	25.7	42.8	7.7	3.1	52826	54639	68	97	7600	10.5	11.7	39.7	33.7	4.3	145860
38633	HICKORY FLAT	16442	908	38.1	27.6	28.1	5.4	0.8	35888	36246	20	73	721	24.8	36.9	34.1	4.2	0.0	76277
38635	HOLLY SPRINGS	15449	5506	43.3	29.1	21.6	3.8	2.2	28270	30022	6	27	4092	29.5	34.2	27.8	7.4	1.1	73591
38637	HORN LAKE	20539	10363	17.9	32.7	40.4	6.9	2.1	49507	48466	60	95	7613	1.7	23.7	63.1	10.4	1.1	107913
38641	LAKE CORMORANT	18160	647	26.6	30.8	35.2	4.6	2.8	43568	41861	44	90	499	15.8	16.0	39.1	27.1	2.0	119167
38642	LAMAR	14350	1023	43.3	34.2	19.6	1.6	1.4	29298	31777	7	31	883	24.8	43.8	26.3	3.7	1.4	75414
38643	LAMBERT	11836	1141	54.0	23.9	18.6	2.5	1.0	21681	22463	2	6	776	58.9	28.2	11.7	1.0	0.1	44153
38645	LYON	14296	449	45.9	26.7	19.4	4.9	3.1	28260	28100	6	27	318	43.4	37.7	14.2	4.4	0.3	55122
38646	MARKS	13610	1420	49.9	27.7	18.6	2.5	1.3	25056	25714	3	14	958	54.1	31.1	12.9	1.5	0.4	47532
38647	MICHIGAN CITY	13274	405	47.2	31.6	18.5	2.5	0.2	28234	28406	6	26	346	28.3	38.7	27.5	5.2	0.3	72941
38650	MYRTLE	17007	1625	28.1	32.8	34.4	4.4	0.4	38782	38887	29	80	1347	28.3	30.7	32.6	8.4	0.1	78853
38651	NESBIT	23380	2336	18.8	23.5	41.2	12.7	3.7	59098	61258	76	98	2135	11.1	6.4	37.5	41.9	3.1	163167
38652	NEW ALBANY	18892	6376	32.6	31.0	30.3	3.9	2.2	37183	37745	24	76	4618	18.9	34.0	35.6	10.2	1.3	86543
38654	OLIVE BRANCH	26749	16492	12.0	21.2	47.0	14.4	5.4	63393	65007	82	99	14087	3.6	5.7	41.6	44.1	4.9	173119
38655	OXFORD	20033	13652	41.7	24.9	25.6	5.1	2.6	31559	31616	11	50	7786	20.2	19.1	31.3	24.4	5.1	113653
38658	POPE	16041	825	32.0	37.1	26.4	3.5	1.0	33814	33097	15	62	730	38.1	37.1	19.3	4.9	0.5	63521
38659	POTTS CAMP	15678	1079	38.6	31.7	26.0	2.2	1.5	33284	35308	14	59	906	36.2	36.6	23.7	3.2	0.2	66579
38661	RED BANKS	18771	643	29.9	30.6	33.7	3.6	2.2	41954	40774	39	87	530	34.2	28.7	31.3	4.7	1.1	71905
38663	RIPLEY	16693	4456	36.4	33.5	25.2	3.9	1.0	34069	34413	16	63	3362	29.5	34.2	28.4	6.9	1.0	72551
38664	ROBINSONVILLE	18675	1253	34.0	33.5	27.2	4.4	0.9	34929	34461	17	68	393	23.7	35.6	30.0	7.1	3.6	77105
38665	SARAH	15755	845	32.2	42.7	19.1	3.9	2.1	35028	34170	18	69	706	44.1	25.4	22.9	5.4	2.3	66296
38666	SARDIS	14439	2823	47.2	26.2	21.8	3.3	1.5	26719	27829	4	19	2110	44.1	30.2	19.4	5.4	0.9	56510
38668	SENATOBIA	20135	4919	25.5	27.9	36.5	7.1	3.0	45570	46660	50	92	3611	16.0	22.6	41.8	19.1	0.5	105562
38670	SLEDGE	11279	532	53.9	28.0	14.5	2.1	1.5	22371	23431	2	7	364	65.9	23.4	9.1	1.1	0.5	39571
38671	SOUTHAVEN	23834	14018	17.6	26.8	45.3	7.8	2.4	54257	57090	70	97	9662	2.6	12.9	64.7	17.8	1.9	121779
38672	SOUTHAVEN	27316	3381	15.2	21.0	43.8	14.9	5.1	63171	64408	81	99	3174	6.3	5.1	37.0	46.3	5.3	179262
38673	TAYLOR	16502	253	40.3	26.1	28.1	4.7	0.8	32481	32517	12	56	158	27.2	21.5	27.8	21.5	1.9	92222
38674	TIPLERSVILLE	17403	424	34.0	33.3	28.1	3.8	0.9	37643	37346	26	78	361	34.1	30.5	26.9	7.8	0.8	70156
38676	TUNICA	13109	2469	53.6	24.1	18.1	2.6	1.7	22581	24804	2	7	1491	36.6	33.7	23.8	5.2	0.7	62952
38677	UNIVERSITY	8831	152	66.4	23.0	9.2	1.3	0.0	16675	17271	1	2	12	50.0	16.7	33.3	0.0	0.0	32500
38680	WALLS	21423	1935	22.5	27.6	39.5	8.5	1.9	49927	49667	61	95	1236	17.2	7.0	51.1	21.0	3.7	140702
38683	WALNUT	16366	2066	40.9	31.7	23.7	2.9	0.9	30945	30408	10	43	1696	39.1	30.7	22.6	6.7	0.9	61429
38685	WATERFORD	15515	459	41.4	27.7	27.5	2.8	0.7	31979	34220	11	52	395	37.0	34.4	23.0	5.6	0.0	67000
38701	GREENVILLE	16579	10349	43.8	26.0	22.4	4.8	3.0	29838	30281	8	34	5779	34.6	29.7	24.5	9.1	2.2	70557
38703	GREENVILLE	14860	6223	40.8	28.0	26.5	3.2	1.4	31353	31328	10	48	3835	30.1	50.1	16.7	2.7	0.3	63127
38720	ALLIGATOR	16828	205	44.4	22.4	26.8	4.4	2.0	30221	29038	8	37	153	58.8	28.8	11.8	0.7	0.0	43571
38721	ANGUILLA	11486	739	51.3	23.1	21.8	3.4	0.4	24185	25070	3	9	518	45.9	36.5	17.4	0.2	0.0	52692
38725	BENOIT	14410	463	47.1	25.9	20.1	4.5	2.4	27222	27680	5	22	261	42.1	28.7	21.8	7.3	0.0	58542
38726	BEULAH	14179	44	40.9	40.9	15.9	2.3	0.0	31095	28832	10	45	28	32.1	46.4	17.9	0.0	3.6	60000
38730	BOYLE	19552	740	33.1	32.2	23.1	7.6	4.1	37111	35939	24	76	529	22.1	28.0	34.6	13.2	2.1	89821
38731	CHATHAM	17788	24	50.0	29.2	12.5	4.2	4.2	25000	26430	3	13	18	44.4	22.2	33.3	0.0	0.0	60000
38732	CLEVELAND	16273	6924	40.8	28.6	24.0	4.6	2.0	31955	31076	11	52	4196	27.2	32.0	30.8	9.6	0.4	78487
38733	CLEVELAND	8417	4	0.0	0.0	100.0	0.0	0.0	75000	75000	89	100	3	0.0	0.0	100.0	0.0	0.0	112500
38736	DODDSVILLE	10059	278	40.3	27.7	27.0	3.2	1.8	31177	30651	10	45	198	38.4	32.3	24.2	5.1	0.0	59583
38737	DREW	10934	1349	49.3	27.1	21.2	2.0	0.4	25416	26716	4	15	791	48.5	36.5	11.8	2.7	0.5	51139
38740	DUNCAN	13483	251	52.2	22.3	20.3	3.2	2.0	23497	24835	2	8	172	55.8	30.8	9.9	1.2	2.3	46429
38744	GLEN ALLAN	14323	157	50.3	28.0	14.6	3.8	3.2	24829	26674	3	11	118	48.3	21.2	22.9	5.1	2.5	52857
38746	GUNNISON	11876	357	54.3	25.5	16.8	1.4	2.0	22397	23762	2	7	229	62.0	25.8	9.6	1.3	1.3	38750
38748	HOLLANDALE	13028	2032	48.1	29.6	16.8	3.2	2.2	25957	27158	4	16	1411	46.1	31.0	17.9	4.0	1.1	53447
38751	INDIANOLA	14575	4287	41.4	28.5	23.3	4.2	2.6	31144	30805	10	45	2693	25.2	46.0	23.2	5.4	0.1	69365
38753	INVERNESS	16339	584	38.5	27.1	27.2	5.5	1.7	34309	34845	16	64	373	23.6	32.7	34.9	4.8	4.0	80208
38754	ISOLA	14129	542	45.8	32.1	18.5	2.6	1.1	27672	27156	5	24	354	45.5	35.6	15.8	3.1	0.0	53556
38756	LELAND	14558	2679	43.0	31.0	20.2	4.8	1.1	29457	29415	7	32	1672	33.8	38.2	21.7	5.6	0.7	65679
38759	MERIGOLD	15439	468	49.1	25.0	22.2	2.8	0.9	25560	26817	4	15	317	48.6	30.9	18.0	1.9	0.6	52045
38761	MOORHEAD	11462	807	49.9	25.9	17.8	5.3	1.0	25035	26329	3	13	458	40.2	44.3	14.2	1.3	0.0	57143
38762	MOUND BAYOU	9993	1220	57.5	28.0	12.5	1.6	0.4	20985	22423	2	5	724	44.9	43.2	11.3	0.6	0.0	53136
38769	ROSEDALE	10355	1078	55.3	31.4	10.3	1.5	1.5	21611	24035	2	5	626	51.0	35.0	12.5	1.3	0.3	49277
38771	RULEVILLE	12599	1021	46.9	28.6	21.3	2.1	1.2	27021	27890	5	21	635	44.1	40.9	13.5	1.4	0.0	53606
38773	SHAW	12262	1396	51.6	28.1	16.5	2.5	1.4	23946	25514	3	8	912	47.3	33.6	15.8	2.9	0.5	52976
38774	SHELBY	10253	951	61.7	24.0	11.1	1.6	1.6	17574	19142	1	2	529	55.2	34.4	9.1	0.6	0.8	46014
38778	SUNFLOWER	13380	583	46.3	32.6	15.4	3.1	2.6	27294	28104	5	23	341	41.1	43.4	10.6	4.4	0.6	58472
38801	TUPELO	22115	11728	27.9	29.9	31.1	6.9	4.3	43144	42839	43	90	7355	9.8	24.6	46.9	16.6	2.2	111169
38804	TUPELO	21488	7146	30.9	30.6	28.5	6.3	3.7	39886	40375	32	83	4722	15.9	26.7	37.1	16.1	4.3	102337
38821	AMORY	18098	5151	33.9	31.9	28.8	4.2	1.3	36601	36450	22	74	3952	22.3	34.3	34.6	7.9	1.0	81553
38824	BALDWYN	16300	3218	38.8	29.7	27.2	3.5	0.8	33725	34431	15	61	2467	29.2	32.5	30.6	7.5	0.0	74055
38826	BELDEN	26493	1762	20.8	26.5	33.7	10.3	8.7	52137	51212	66	96	1502	13.4	17.1	34.0	30.2	5.3	129310
38827	BELMONT	18018	1096	36.3	31.6	26.3	4.2	1.6	35264	35636	19	70	817	22.0	38.4	30.7	8.2	0.6	80500
38828	BLUE SPRINGS	17494	1438	31.9	30.5	32.8	4.0	0.8	34799	34974	17	67	1234	30.6	33.1	29.9	6.4	0.0	74286
38829	BOONEVILLE	16802	7072	38.4	32.8	23.3	4.3	1.2	32529	32767	12	56	5392	29.9	38.6	24.9	6.0	0.6	68527
38833	BURNSVILLE	15910	1084	46.8	26.5	20.7	4.7	1.4	27843	28115	5	25	821	36.1	39.7	20.0	4.3	0.0	64844
38834	CORINTH	18366	12111	39.8	29.2	25.0	4.5	1.5	32594	32584	13	57	8556	25.0	33.1	31.1	9.3	1.6	80470
38838	DENNIS	17464	631	32.5	34.9	27.3	4.3	1.1	37276	37385	24	77	549	27.5	36.8	26.8	8.9	0.0	70625
38841	ECRU	18696	1611	27.1	34.9	32.0	4.3	1.7	40075	39883	33	84	1262	27.3	31.8	33.2	7.5	0.2	80952
38843	FULTON	18510	4519	34.6	31.5	25.9	5.7	2.3	36354	36964	22	74	3633	24.2	38.1	29.6	7.5	0.7	78271
38844	GATTMAN	18341	134	41.8	27.6	27.6	3.0	0.0	30552	31579	9	40	118	46.6	19.5	22.0	11.9	0.0	58000
38846	GLEN	17739	1004	33.6	33.2	28.2	3.4	1.7	34751	34487	17	67	827	38.9	32.5	22.5	5.4	0.6	63125
38847	GOLDEN	17182	1370	33.9	33.0	27.7	4.3	1.1	37998	37125	27	79	1170	33.2	42.1	19.1	5.5	0.1	63972
38848	GREENWOOD SPRINGS	16733	346	38.7	29.8	27.7	2.9	0.9	35000	34834	18	69	308	41.2	23.1	26.3	8.8	0.6	60000
38849	GUNTOWN	18358	1843	30.0	33.5	29.9	5.3	1.2	37485	37236	25	77	1506	28.3	25.6	35.2	10.4	0.5	82625
	MISSISSIPPI	18363		35.3	29.0	27.5	5.7	2.5	36311	37046				25.4	28.2	31.6	12.7	2.1	84642
	UNITED STATES	27277		20.9	24.4	35.3	11.7	7.6	54719	56938				9.3	13.1	31.6	32.6	13.5	162279

ZIP CODE #	POST OFFICE NAME	FINANCIAL SERVICES: Auto Loan	Home Loan	Invest-ments	Retire-ment Plans	THE HOME: Home Improvements: Home Repair	Lawn & Garden	Furnishings: Comput-ers & Hard-ware-Personal	Major Appli-ances	TV, Radio, Sound Equip-ment	Furni-ture	ENTERTAINMENT: Dine out/ Carry out	Sports Equip-ment	Fees & Tickets	Toys & Games	Travel	Cable TV	PERSONAL: Apparel & Services	Auto Repairs	Health Insur-ance	Pets & Supplies
38601	ABBEVILLE	70	48	66	46	48	69	51	62	58	49	56	48	40	59	48	63	38	59	65	76
38603	ASHLAND	65	43	62	40	43	64	46	57	53	43	51	45	34	54	43	59	34	54	60	70
38606	BATESVILLE	74	56	67	55	55	73	59	67	65	57	64	51	50	66	56	70	43	65	72	82
38610	BLUE MOUNTAIN	79	53	72	51	53	76	56	69	64	54	63	53	44	66	52	71	42	65	73	84
38611	BYHALIA	85	62	76	60	62	82	64	75	71	63	70	57	52	73	60	77	47	71	78	91
38614	CLARKSDALE	59	50	48	50	48	58	54	54	59	53	58	41	51	59	50	63	40	57	62	67
38617	COAHOMA	49	32	33	34	30	39	45	41	51	42	49	32	38	50	37	54	34	46	48	52
38618	COLDWATER	81	60	67	59	59	77	62	71	69	61	68	54	52	71	57	74	46	68	75	86
38619	COMO	68	49	69	45	50	69	50	62	57	50	55	47	41	56	49	63	37	59	67	75
38620	COURTLAND	78	53	73	50	53	76	56	69	64	53	62	53	43	65	52	70	41	65	73	84
38621	CRENSHAW	59	41	53	40	40	57	44	52	50	43	49	40	36	51	41	55	33	50	55	64
38625	DUMAS	79	57	65	55	57	75	59	69	66	58	64	53	47	68	54	72	43	65	73	84
38626	DUNDEE	73	50	70	47	49	72	53	66	61	50	59	51	42	62	50	67	40	62	70	80
38627	ETTA	82	59	67	57	58	77	61	71	68	59	66	54	49	70	55	74	45	67	75	86
38629	FALKNER	79	56	65	55	56	75	59	68	65	57	64	53	47	68	53	71	43	65	72	83
38631	FRIARS POINT	49	38	37	38	37	47	43	44	50	44	48	31	39	48	39	54	33	47	53	55
38632	HERNANDO	92	87	82	87	86	93	82	89	84	82	84	67	79	87	82	87	58	85	90	105
38633	HICKORY FLAT	75	54	62	53	54	72	56	66	62	55	61	50	45	65	51	68	41	62	69	80
38635	HOLLY SPRINGS	72	52	62	51	50	69	56	63	62	54	61	49	46	63	51	68	41	62	68	78
38637	HORN LAKE	84	83	69	83	78	80	82	80	82	83	82	63	81	85	79	81	57	81	81	95
38641	LAKE CORMORANT	82	78	69	76	76	79	73	77	75	75	75	57	70	78	71	76	51	74	77	91
38642	LAMAR	74	48	71	45	48	73	52	65	60	49	58	51	39	61	48	67	39	61	69	80
38643	LAMBERT	53	38	45	38	37	51	42	47	49	43	48	34	36	48	39	54	32	48	54	58
38645	LYON	74	49	69	47	49	71	53	65	61	51	60	50	41	62	50	68	40	62	69	80
38646	MARKS	59	43	53	42	43	58	47	54	54	46	52	40	40	53	44	59	35	53	60	65
38647	MICHIGAN CITY	64	42	62	39	41	63	45	56	51	42	50	44	33	52	42	57	33	53	59	69
38650	MYRTLE	80	57	66	56	57	76	60	69	66	58	65	53	48	69	54	72	44	66	73	84
38651	NESBIT	90	101	87	104	98	99	91	94	89	91	90	74	96	91	96	89	63	91	93	111
38652	NEW ALBANY	81	61	67	60	60	78	65	72	71	62	69	56	54	73	59	76	47	70	78	88
38654	OLIVE BRANCH	108	120	101	118	114	105	106	107	101	112	103	84	111	107	108	98	72	102	98	123
38655	OXFORD	70	54	53	56	53	58	73	61	69	65	69	51	60	70	59	69	48	67	63	75
38658	POPE	75	54	66	52	54	73	56	67	62	54	61	51	45	64	52	68	41	63	70	81
38659	POTTS CAMP	75	49	72	46	49	74	53	66	61	50	59	51	39	62	49	68	39	62	70	81
38661	RED BANKS	89	62	77	60	62	85	65	77	73	63	72	60	51	76	60	80	48	73	82	95
38663	RIPLEY	71	52	60	51	52	68	55	63	61	53	60	48	45	63	51	66	40	61	68	76
38664	ROBINSONVILLE	68	64	54	61	61	61	63	63	64	66	64	48	60	66	59	63	44	63	62	75
38665	SARAH	75	54	64	52	53	72	56	66	62	54	61	50	45	64	51	68	41	62	69	80
38666	SARDIS	65	45	61	43	45	65	49	59	56	47	55	45	39	56	46	62	36	57	64	72
38668	SENATOBIA	87	77	74	76	74	86	77	81	81	76	80	62	71	83	73	84	54	80	86	98
38670	SLEDGE	52	40	42	40	37	49	44	46	48	43	48	36	39	49	40	52	32	47	50	57
38671	SOUTHAVEN	88	87	73	87	82	82	87	83	85	88	86	66	85	89	83	84	60	84	82	99
38672	SOUTHAVEN	100	114	102	117	112	109	101	105	98	104	99	81	109	101	107	98	70	100	102	122
38673	TAYLOR	65	44	45	46	43	52	67	54	64	56	64	47	50	65	51	65	44	61	57	68
38674	TIPLERSVILLE	79	57	65	55	56	75	59	69	65	57	64	53	47	68	54	71	43	65	72	84
38676	TUNICA	53	44	40	45	41	49	50	48	54	49	53	36	46	54	45	57	36	51	54	59
38677	UNIVERSITY	41	18	17	22	16	20	58	29	46	39	47	31	34	45	31	42	33	41	29	39
38680	WALLS	91	84	74	81	82	86	79	84	82	82	82	61	75	85	76	84	56	81	84	99
38683	WALNUT	70	49	61	47	49	67	51	61	58	49	56	47	40	59	47	63	38	58	65	75
38685	WATERFORD	70	47	69	44	47	70	50	63	57	48	56	48	38	58	47	64	37	59	66	77
38701	GREENVILLE	67	56	55	56	55	64	61	62	66	61	65	46	56	66	57	70	45	64	69	75
38703	GREENVILLE	61	55	50	55	52	62	56	57	61	56	60	43	54	61	54	64	41	59	64	70
38720	ALLIGATOR	78	51	74	48	51	76	55	68	63	52	62	53	41	64	51	70	41	65	73	84
38721	ANGUILLA	59	42	51	42	40	56	46	52	52	44	51	40	38	52	42	56	34	51	56	64
38725	BENOIT	73	47	70	45	47	71	51	64	59	48	57	50	38	60	47	65	38	60	68	79
38726	BEULAH	65	42	62	40	42	63	45	57	52	43	51	44	34	53	42	58	34	54	60	70
38730	BOYLE	84	72	71	69	71	80	70	76	74	71	73	56	63	76	66	77	50	73	77	91
38731	CHATHAM	74	49	72	46	48	73	52	65	60	49	58	51	39	61	48	67	39	62	69	80
38732	CLEVELAND	67	54	59	54	54	65	59	62	64	58	63	46	53	63	55	68	43	63	68	75
38733	CLEVELAND	99	116	120	116	121	123	101	111	104	106	104	77	114	100	114	107	72	106	120	126
38736	DODDSVILLE	77	53	76	50	54	77	55	70	62	52	61	53	43	62	53	69	40	65	73	84
38737	DREW	55	40	49	39	40	55	44	50	51	43	49	37	37	50	41	56	33	50	57	61
38740	DUNCAN	67	45	62	44	45	66	49	59	57	48	56	46	39	57	46	63	37	57	65	73
38744	GLEN ALLAN	74	48	71	45	48	72	51	65	59	49	58	50	38	60	48	66	38	61	68	80
38746	GUNNISON	54	40	44	40	40	53	45	49	53	46	51	35	40	51	41	58	35	50	57	60
38748	HOLLANDALE	62	45	54	45	45	61	50	56	56	48	55	42	42	56	46	62	37	56	63	69
38751	INDIANOLA	66	57	54	58	53	65	60	61	65	59	64	47	57	65	56	68	44	62	67	75
38753	INVERNESS	79	58	73	57	57	79	61	72	68	58	66	56	50	69	57	74	44	68	76	88
38754	ISOLA	69	46	66	43	45	68	49	61	56	46	55	47	37	57	45	62	36	57	64	75
38756	LELAND	60	50	48	50	47	58	53	54	58	52	57	42	49	58	49	62	39	56	61	67
38759	MERIGOLD	69	45	66	42	45	67	48	60	55	46	54	47	36	56	45	62	36	57	64	74
38761	MOORHEAD	57	48	39	49	43	52	52	49	57	52	56	38	50	57	47	59	39	53	55	63
38762	MOUND BAYOU	43	34	32	35	32	40	38	38	43	39	42	28	36	43	35	46	29	41	45	48
38769	ROSEDALE	51	33	42	33	32	45	41	43	47	39	46	34	33	47	36	51	31	45	48	55
38771	RULEVILLE	59	47	45	48	44	55	52	52	57	51	56	40	48	57	47	60	38	54	58	65
38773	SHAW	55	42	47	41	40	53	45	49	51	45	50	37	40	51	42	55	34	50	55	61
38774	SHELBY	49	36	41	36	35	48	40	44	47	41	45	32	35	46	37	51	31	45	51	55
38778	SUNFLOWER	69	49	60	48	49	67	54	61	63	54	61	46	46	62	50	70	41	62	70	76
38801	TUPELO	84	77	71	78	74	80	81	78	83	80	82	61	78	84	77	84	57	81	82	95
38804	TUPELO	81	71	70	72	70	81	74	77	78	72	76	59	69	78	70	81	53	76	82	92
38821	AMORY	70	58	59	58	57	71	59	65	64	57	63	50	53	65	56	69	43	63	71	79
38824	BALDWYN	70	53	60	52	53	69	56	63	62	54	60	48	47	63	52	67	41	61	68	77
38826	BELDEN	113	108	113	108	108	117	100	110	103	103	102	84	98	105	102	106	71	104	109	130
38827	BELMONT	79	57	65	55	56	75	59	69	66	58	64	53	47	68	54	72	43	65	73	84
38828	BLUE SPRINGS	80	58	66	56	57	76	60	70	66	58	65	54	48	69	54	72	44	66	74	85
38829	BOONEVILLE	72	52	63	51	52	70	55	65	61	53	60	49	45	63	51	67	40	61	69	78
38833	BURNSVILLE	66	49	52	49	48	62	54	58	59	51	57	45	45	61	48	63	39	57	63	71
38834	CORINTH	70	54	62	54	55	70	57	65	63	54	61	49	49	63	54	68	41	62	70	78
38838	DENNIS	78	56	66	55	56	75	59	69	65	57	64	53	47	67	54	71	43	65	73	83
38841	ECRU	86	62	71	60	61	82	64	75	71	63	70	57	52	74	58	78	47	71	79	91
38843	FULTON	81	59	70	58	60	78	62	72	69	60	67	55	51	71	58	75	45	69	76	87
38844	GATTMAN	76	54	62	53	54	72	56	66	63	55	61	50	45	65	51	68	41	62	69	80
38846	GLEN	80	57	66	56	57	76	60	69	66	58	65	53	48	69	54	72	44	66	73	84
38847	GOLDEN	77	56	64	54	55	74	58	67	64	56	63	52	46	67	53	70	42	64	71	82
38848	GREENWOOD SPRINGS	73	53	61	51	52	70	55	64	61	53	60	49	44	63	50	66	40	60	67	78
38849	GUNTOWN	86	63	72	62	63	83	65	76	72	64	71	58	54	75	60	79	48	72	80	92
	MISSISSIPPI	77	63	67	62	62	74	66	70	70	65	69	54	59	71	62	74	47	70	74	85
	UNITED STATES	100	100	100	100	100	100	100	100	100	100	100	100	100	100	100	100	100	100	100	100

ZIP CODE #	POST OFFICE NAME	COUNTY FIPS CODE	POPULATION 2000	POPULATION 2009	POPULATION 2014	2000-2009 ANNUAL RATE % Rate	2000-2009 ANNUAL RATE State Centile	HOUSEHOLDS 2000	HOUSEHOLDS 2009	HOUSEHOLDS 2014	HOUSEHOLDS % Annual Rate 2000-2009	HOUSEHOLDS 2009 Average HH Size	FAMILIES 2000	FAMILIES 2009	FAMILIES % Annual Rate 2000-2009
38850	HOULKA	017	3182	3408	3443	0.7	79	1173	1291	1315	1.0	2.63	870	933	0.8
38851	HOUSTON	017	9366	9230	9105	-0.2	41	3517	3574	3555	0.2	2.55	2572	2551	-0.1
38852	IUKA	141	9140	9268	9287	0.2	59	3873	4062	4106	0.5	2.22	2617	2668	0.2
38855	MANTACHIE	057	4626	4895	4900	0.6	76	1826	1975	1988	0.9	2.48	1371	1449	0.6
38856	MARIETTA	117	1452	1519	1515	0.5	72	558	599	602	0.8	2.54	432	454	0.5
38857	MOOREVILLE	081	2499	2860	3023	1.5	91	926	1071	1138	1.6	2.64	716	808	1.3
38858	NETTLETON	095	7184	7187	7140	0.0	52	2757	2831	2834	0.3	2.54	2040	2044	0.0
38859	NEW SITE	117	876	906	901	0.4	69	333	355	356	0.7	2.55	261	273	0.5
38860	OKOLONA	017	6407	6085	5938	-0.6	21	2415	2365	2327	-0.2	2.54	1733	1655	-0.5
38862	PLANTERSVILLE	081	2894	3070	3181	0.6	76	1073	1150	1197	0.8	2.65	789	821	0.4
38863	PONTOTOC	115	17019	18391	18999	0.8	82	6462	7085	7344	1.0	2.57	4774	5114	0.7
38864	RANDOLPH	115	1524	1595	1626	0.5	72	567	602	616	0.6	2.65	444	462	0.4
38865	RIENZI	003	4550	4872	4989	0.7	79	1762	1957	2025	1.1	2.49	1379	1498	0.9
38866	SALTILLO	081	8651	9384	9711	0.9	83	3391	3708	3855	1.0	2.51	2458	2611	0.7
38868	SHANNON	081	5066	5545	5797	1.0	86	1919	2124	2227	1.1	2.61	1420	1526	0.8
38870	SMITHVILLE	095	2786	2841	2816	0.2	59	1090	1152	1153	0.6	2.47	797	820	0.3
38871	THAXTON	115	1884	2012	2054	0.7	79	694	748	765	0.8	2.69	546	577	0.6
38873	TISHOMINGO	141	2598	2667	2674	0.3	64	1074	1132	1143	0.6	2.36	767	788	0.3
38876	TREMONT	057	1207	1250	1246	0.4	69	490	520	522	0.6	2.40	366	379	0.4
38878	VARDAMAN	013	3103	3045	2988	-0.2	41	1198	1209	1197	0.1	2.51	849	832	-0.2
38901	GRENADA	043	19356	19159	18985	-0.1	47	7312	7512	7527	0.3	2.48	5125	5123	0.0
38913	BANNER	013	676	652	636	-0.4	31	270	267	263	-0.1	2.44	200	192	-0.4
38914	BIG CREEK	013	417	414	410	-0.1	47	180	186	186	0.4	2.21	136	137	0.1
38915	BRUCE	013	4209	3988	3877	-0.6	21	1742	1707	1678	-0.2	2.31	1193	1142	-0.5
38916	CALHOUN CITY	013	5304	4949	4798	-0.7	16	2126	2052	2007	-0.4	2.35	1513	1420	-0.7
38917	CARROLLTON	015	3240	3451	3425	0.7	79	1188	1283	1286	0.8	2.47	913	969	0.6
38920	CASCILLA	135	2152	2067	1983	-0.4	31	781	776	753	-0.1	2.66	606	590	-0.3
38921	CHARLESTON	135	6852	6314	6068	-0.9	11	2464	2376	2312	-0.4	2.63	1758	1650	-0.7
38922	COFFEEVILLE	161	3846	3969	4033	0.3	64	1606	1722	1769	0.8	2.30	1114	1159	0.4
38923	COILA	015	1718	1634	1588	-0.5	25	626	621	612	-0.1	2.63	483	469	-0.3
38924	CRUGER	051	970	940	918	-0.3	36	349	349	344	0.0	2.69	243	237	-0.3
38925	DUCK HILL	097	2485	2474	2436	0.0	52	976	1011	1006	0.4	2.45	721	729	0.1
38927	ENID	135	1123	1083	1045	-0.4	31	423	423	413	0.0	2.56	324	318	-0.2
38929	GORE SPRINGS	043	996	1076	1098	0.8	82	370	416	430	1.3	2.58	285	313	1.0
38930	GREENWOOD	083	28526	27082	26351	-0.6	21	10523	10258	10051	-0.3	2.56	7122	6743	-0.6
38940	HOLCOMB	043	1752	1759	1751	0.0	52	665	698	703	0.5	2.52	527	542	0.3
38941	ITTA BENA	083	6546	6277	6151	-0.5	25	1827	1815	1787	-0.1	2.87	1327	1284	-0.4
38943	MC CARLEY	015	1085	1032	997	-0.5	25	420	415	407	-0.1	2.49	315	302	-0.5
38944	MINTER CITY	083	895	867	854	-0.3	36	289	291	290	0.1	2.98	223	219	-0.2
38948	OAKLAND	161	1810	1883	1921	0.4	69	736	801	827	0.9	2.35	498	526	0.6
38949	PARIS	071	290	297	293	0.3	64	111	118	118	0.7	2.52	81	85	0.5
38950	PHILIPP	135	481	440	418	-1.0	9	182	174	167	-0.5	2.53	136	127	-0.7
38951	PITTSBORO	013	1212	1208	1198	0.0	52	439	455	455	0.4	2.53	323	326	0.1
38952	SCHLATER	083	676	640	631	-0.6	21	249	239	233	-0.4	1.69	178	166	-0.8
38953	SCOBEY	161	565	599	614	0.6	76	223	247	256	1.1	2.43	159	171	0.8
38954	SIDON	083	2242	2206	2172	-0.2	41	817	837	834	0.3	2.62	620	619	0.0
38961	TILLATOBA	161	630	666	686	0.6	76	255	281	293	1.1	2.37	175	187	0.7
38963	TUTWILER	135	4439	4113	3922	-0.8	14	1469	1395	1342	-0.6	2.92	1042	965	-0.8
38964	VANCE	119	110	93	87	-1.8	3	42	37	35	-1.4	2.51	31	27	-1.5
38965	WATER VALLEY	161	8573	8895	9030	0.4	69	3375	3593	3678	0.7	2.44	2350	2441	0.4
38967	WINONA	097	7491	7282	7104	-0.3	36	2860	2864	2820	0.0	2.49	2042	1993	-0.3
39038	BELZONI	053	7268	6605	6248	-1.0	9	2384	2222	2116	-0.8	2.93	1731	1574	-1.0
39039	BENTON	163	2105	2252	2229	0.7	79	765	794	789	0.4	2.47	574	581	0.1
39040	BENTONIA	163	3570	3578	3522	0.0	52	1280	1308	1292	0.2	2.74	958	956	0.0
39041	BOLTON	049	3349	3495	3514	0.5	72	1141	1224	1238	0.8	2.84	856	890	0.4
39042	BRANDON	121	28106	33574	37202	1.9	95	10343	12737	14261	2.3	2.61	7924	9548	2.0
39044	BRAXTON	127	3128	3350	3421	0.7	79	1159	1286	1325	1.1	2.59	873	947	0.9
39045	CAMDEN	089	1312	1423	1507	0.9	83	418	464	493	1.1	3.05	321	346	0.8
39046	CANTON	089	22623	26985	29666	1.9	95	7206	9090	10140	2.5	2.89	5497	6781	2.3
39047	BRANDON	121	24154	34814	40372	4.0	98	9224	13716	16019	4.4	2.53	6889	9990	4.1
39051	CARTHAGE	079	17257	18985	19288	1.0	86	6181	6581	6720	0.7	2.63	4550	4733	0.4
39056	CLINTON	049	25182	26600	26916	0.6	76	8915	9726	9906	0.9	2.57	6571	6977	0.7
39057	CONEHATTA	101	2298	2395	2431	0.4	69	803	859	878	0.7	2.79	600	628	0.5
39059	CRYSTAL SPRINGS	029	11761	11970	12028	0.2	59	4257	4456	4515	0.5	2.63	3151	3222	0.2
39063	DURANT	051	3950	3838	3734	-0.3	36	1419	1391	1359	-0.2	2.65	999	953	-0.5
39066	EDWARDS	049	4745	4829	4826	0.2	59	1613	1688	1697	0.5	2.86	1221	1237	0.1
39067	ETHEL	007	2039	2056	2062	0.1	54	802	825	834	0.3	2.48	589	591	0.0
39069	FAYETTE	063	7190	6741	6498	-0.7	16	2349	2297	2235	-0.2	2.65	1659	1579	-0.5
39071	FLORA	089	4373	5309	5919	2.1	95	1488	1879	2109	2.6	2.82	1166	1431	2.2
39073	FLORENCE	121	17505	20558	22479	1.8	94	6375	7653	8440	2.0	2.67	4944	5828	1.8
39074	FOREST	123	14600	14624	14490	0.0	52	5198	5294	5264	0.2	2.73	3821	3799	-0.1
39078	GEORGETOWN	029	936	1021	1055	0.9	83	352	397	414	1.3	2.57	255	281	1.1
39079	GOODMAN	051	1874	2013	1969	0.8	82	487	475	463	-0.3	2.89	352	335	-0.5
39082	HARRISVILLE	127	1172	1253	1275	0.7	79	436	485	497	1.2	2.58	322	350	0.9
39083	HAZLEHURST	029	10488	10799	10896	0.3	64	3773	3989	4054	0.6	2.65	2757	2843	0.3
39086	HERMANVILLE	021	2511	2381	2331	-0.6	21	900	896	886	0.0	2.60	639	620	-0.3
39088	HOLLY BLUFF	163	156	146	140	-0.7	16	60	58	56	-0.4	2.52	47	44	-0.7
39090	KOSCIUSKO	007	12347	12279	12267	-0.1	47	4813	4904	4928	0.2	2.44	3328	3297	-0.1
39092	LAKE	123	2946	2986	2949	0.1	54	1057	1092	1083	0.4	2.73	799	806	0.1
39094	LENA	079	3832	4217	4397	1.0	86	1402	1578	1655	1.3	2.67	1047	1148	1.0
39095	LEXINGTON	051	7817	7934	7804	0.2	59	2782	2866	2835	0.3	2.69	1957	1965	0.0
39096	LORMAN	063	804	818	809	0.2	59	297	320	320	0.8	2.56	211	222	0.6
39097	LOUISE	053	1393	1218	1140	-1.4	4	473	426	402	-1.1	2.86	327	286	-1.4
39108	MC COOL	007	1641	1663	1660	0.1	54	664	694	700	0.5	2.40	471	480	0.2
39110	MADISON	089	24192	33466	38463	3.6	98	8361	11721	13545	3.7	2.80	6961	9518	3.4
39111	MAGEE	127	10514	10435	10252	-0.1	47	3844	3928	3890	0.2	2.50	2714	2703	0.0
39113	MAYERSVILLE	055	1889	1638	1505	-1.5	3	586	512	468	-1.4	2.65	410	349	-1.7
39114	MENDENHALL	127	10681	11105	11150	0.4	69	3846	4106	4159	0.7	2.63	2897	3024	0.5
39116	MIZE	129	3154	3113	3050	-0.1	47	1159	1176	1161	0.2	2.65	867	861	-0.1
39117	MORTON	123	8667	9448	9616	0.9	83	3136	3510	3595	1.2	2.65	2317	2535	1.0
39119	MOUNT OLIVE	031	3687	3859	3938	0.5	72	1383	1496	1542	0.9	2.58	998	1052	0.6
39120	NATCHEZ	001	34745	32122	30690	-0.8	14	13813	13277	12824	-0.4	2.38	9504	8883	-0.7
39140	NEWHEBRON	077	1602	1668	1674	0.4	69	595	640	648	0.8	2.61	439	461	0.5
39144	PATTISON	021	937	1008	1031	0.8	82	337	381	393	1.3	2.65	232	255	1.0
39145	PELAHATCHIE	121	5318	6160	6691	1.6	92	1915	2262	2477	1.8	2.72	1487	1720	1.6
	MISSISSIPPI					0.5					0.8	2.56			0.5
	UNITED STATES					1.0					1.1	2.59			0.9

ZIP CODE #	POST OFFICE NAME	RACE (%) White 2000	White 2009	Black 2000	Black 2009	Asian/Pacific 2000	Asian/Pacific 2009	% Hispanic Origin 2000	% Hispanic Origin 2009	2009 AGE DISTRIBUTION (%) 0-4	5-9	10-14	15-19	20-24	25-44	45-64	65-84	85+	18+	MEDIAN AGE 2009	% 2009 Males	% 2009 Females
38850	HOULKA	70.9	67.8	27.6	30.2	0.0	0.0	1.9	2.9	7.0	6.7	7.5	7.3	6.0	25.9	25.9	11.7	2.0	74.2	37.8	49.0	51.0
38851	HOUSTON	62.9	59.4	34.5	37.0	0.3	0.4	3.2	4.7	7.6	7.5	7.5	7.1	6.0	25.5	24.7	11.7	2.3	73.2	36.3	49.3	50.7
38852	IUKA	95.9	95.1	2.9	3.1	0.2	0.2	0.8	1.2	5.3	5.4	5.8	6.0	4.6	24.0	28.7	17.1	3.2	80.0	44.2	48.5	51.5
38855	MANTACHIE	97.6	96.9	1.4	1.7	0.1	0.2	0.7	1.1	6.5	6.6	7.2	7.2	5.6	27.7	25.9	11.7	1.6	75.1	37.7	49.0	51.0
38856	MARIETTA	98.1	97.4	0.6	0.7	0.1	0.1	0.8	1.3	6.1	6.2	6.5	6.3	5.0	28.5	27.4	12.4	1.6	77.4	39.1	50.8	49.2
38857	MOOREVILLE	97.0	96.1	2.2	2.7	0.2	0.3	1.0	1.6	6.6	6.7	7.0	6.6	5.3	27.9	28.0	10.6	1.3	75.6	38.6	51.5	48.5
38858	NETTLETON	73.7	69.8	25.4	29.0	0.3	0.4	0.8	1.2	6.9	7.0	7.1	7.0	5.4	26.8	27.0	11.3	1.6	74.7	37.9	48.2	51.8
38859	NEW SITE	98.6	97.8	0.3	0.4	0.0	0.0	1.4	2.3	7.5	7.7	7.9	5.8	4.6	27.4	26.9	10.7	1.3	73.1	37.1	53.8	46.2
38860	OKOLONA	44.9	41.6	54.3	57.3	0.1	0.1	0.7	0.9	8.1	8.1	8.0	7.5	5.7	25.0	24.6	11.1	2.0	71.2	35.5	47.4	52.6
38862	PLANTERSVILLE	67.8	63.1	30.6	34.6	0.0	0.1	1.9	2.8	7.2	6.9	7.0	7.4	6.7	28.0	26.4	9.2	1.2	74.3	35.6	49.3	50.7
38863	PONTOTOC	84.3	82.1	13.9	15.4	0.1	0.2	1.8	2.7	7.2	7.0	7.0	7.0	6.1	26.6	26.1	10.9	2.0	74.6	37.3	48.6	51.4
38864	RANDOLPH	94.7	93.3	3.9	4.3	0.1	0.1	1.7	2.7	8.0	7.8	7.8	7.3	5.7	28.0	23.9	10.2	1.4	71.8	35.2	49.8	50.2
38865	RIENZI	90.5	88.1	8.2	9.9	0.1	0.1	1.1	1.8	6.7	6.8	7.0	6.5	4.8	28.1	26.4	12.2	1.5	75.3	38.5	50.8	49.2
38866	SALTILLO	91.4	88.9	6.9	8.7	0.5	0.7	0.9	1.5	7.2	7.2	7.2	6.4	5.1	28.8	26.7	10.0	1.4	74.5	37.5	48.6	51.4
38868	SHANNON	60.3	55.4	38.5	42.9	0.1	0.1	0.8	1.2	7.7	7.6	7.6	6.8	5.7	27.9	26.2	9.5	1.0	72.9	35.8	49.7	50.3
38870	SMITHVILLE	91.0	88.5	8.0	10.1	0.2	0.3	0.7	1.2	6.3	6.5	6.6	6.5	5.4	27.2	27.6	12.2	1.7	76.6	39.2	49.9	50.1
38871	THAXTON	93.2	92.6	6.1	6.3	0.0	0.0	1.0	1.5	6.8	6.7	6.9	6.9	5.9	27.4	27.4	10.6	1.4	75.4	37.6	50.0	50.0
38873	TISHOMINGO	89.6	87.9	9.3	10.4	0.0	0.0	0.7	1.1	6.2	6.2	6.4	6.0	4.9	24.6	28.7	15.2	1.8	77.5	42.1	48.4	51.6
38876	TREMONT	98.8	98.2	0.4	0.5	0.1	0.2	0.4	0.7	6.6	6.4	6.5	6.6	5.1	29.0	25.8	12.5	1.6	76.4	38.7	50.9	49.1
38878	VARDAMAN	71.3	67.2	24.7	26.9	0.1	0.1	6.2	9.2	6.3	6.1	6.4	7.4	6.4	26.0	26.9	12.4	2.1	76.7	38.1	48.6	51.4
38901	GRENADA	56.0	54.7	42.8	44.0	0.4	0.4	0.7	0.7	7.2	7.1	7.1	7.2	6.2	25.3	25.4	12.0	2.5	74.1	37.3	46.8	53.2
38913	BANNER	90.4	88.2	8.6	10.3	0.1	0.2	1.2	1.8	6.3	6.6	6.4	5.8	5.1	26.4	27.5	14.0	2.0	77.0	40.4	51.1	48.9
38914	BIG CREEK	80.8	77.8	18.7	21.5	0.0	0.0	0.2	0.0	5.6	6.0	6.0	5.8	5.1	24.6	30.9	13.8	2.2	79.0	42.7	49.3	50.7
38915	BRUCE	68.2	66.0	29.7	31.2	0.1	0.1	1.4	2.0	6.8	7.1	6.9	6.3	5.4	25.8	25.9	13.5	2.3	75.1	38.9	49.6	50.4
38916	CALHOUN CITY	65.8	62.7	33.1	35.7	0.1	0.1	0.9	1.4	6.7	6.6	7.3	6.6	5.3	24.3	26.4	13.4	3.5	75.3	39.9	46.7	53.3
38917	CARROLLTON	67.8	66.3	31.5	32.9	0.3	0.5	0.7	1.0	5.4	5.6	6.1	7.2	7.4	25.4	28.8	12.2	1.8	79.1	39.1	52.4	47.6
38920	CASCILLA	64.8	60.6	34.5	38.3	0.1	0.2	0.9	1.2	7.1	6.9	7.0	7.4	5.9	24.7	27.8	11.7	1.5	74.5	37.9	47.9	52.1
38921	CHARLESTON	36.9	34.4	62.3	64.6	0.2	0.3	1.2	1.4	7.3	7.3	7.7	7.8	6.7	24.0	24.8	12.0	2.4	72.9	36.1	46.5	53.5
38922	COFFEEVILLE	56.4	53.2	43.0	46.0	0.0	0.1	0.8	0.9	6.0	5.9	6.2	6.6	5.5	24.6	28.7	14.1	2.2	77.9	41.4	48.0	52.0
38923	COILA	53.0	48.7	46.3	50.2	0.1	0.1	0.9	1.3	6.4	6.5	6.5	6.4	5.7	23.8	29.4	13.5	1.7	76.7	41.0	48.7	51.3
38924	CRUGER	21.3	18.8	77.9	80.4	0.1	0.1	1.8	1.9	8.1	8.4	8.1	7.9	5.6	22.8	25.7	11.3	2.1	70.6	35.3	47.3	52.7
38925	DUCK HILL	58.0	54.9	41.6	44.6	0.0	0.0	0.4	0.5	7.0	7.2	7.3	6.7	5.3	25.0	28.0	11.7	1.7	74.3	38.3	48.1	51.9
38927	ENID	70.3	65.7	29.0	33.4	0.1	0.1	0.4	0.6	6.3	6.4	6.6	7.8	5.7	25.6	26.5	13.3	1.9	76.0	38.8	50.1	49.9
38929	GORE SPRINGS	56.4	53.1	43.1	46.5	0.0	0.0	0.6	0.7	5.0	5.2	5.8	7.6	5.2	23.5	31.3	14.6	1.8	79.3	43.3	47.4	52.6
38930	GREENWOOD	35.4	33.1	62.9	64.6	0.8	1.1	0.9	1.2	8.3	8.2	7.6	7.9	7.1	24.9	23.0	10.6	2.5	71.1	33.4	46.3	53.7
38940	HOLCOMB	70.6	67.6	28.7	31.7	0.1	0.1	0.2	0.2	6.8	6.7	7.2	7.5	5.7	27.6	25.1	11.9	1.5	74.6	37.3	48.9	51.1
38941	ITTA BENA	14.8	12.4	80.2	80.4	0.3	0.4	6.2	8.6	7.3	7.5	6.9	11.3	15.9	24.3	19.3	6.4	1.1	74.1	25.7	49.4	50.6
38943	MC CARLEY	68.1	63.8	31.3	35.3	0.0	0.0	0.9	1.4	4.8	5.1	5.6	6.2	5.0	25.2	32.1	14.0	1.9	80.7	43.6	49.3	50.7
38944	MINTER CITY	39.6	33.9	58.4	63.3	0.1	0.1	2.2	3.0	8.4	8.7	9.3	8.0	4.6	21.9	27.7	10.1	1.3	68.6	35.8	47.8	52.2
38948	OAKLAND	53.9	52.2	45.4	46.8	0.1	0.1	1.0	1.3	6.6	7.0	6.8	7.1	5.4	23.0	28.7	13.9	1.5	75.3	40.7	50.5	49.5
38949	PARIS	97.6	96.6	1.7	2.0	0.0	0.3	0.3	0.7	6.7	7.1	7.1	6.1	4.4	27.6	28.3	11.4	1.3	75.1	38.5	48.5	51.5
38950	PHILIPP	40.1	35.2	59.3	64.1	0.0	0.0	1.5	1.6	6.4	6.6	6.6	7.0	6.4	22.3	27.7	15.2	1.8	75.9	40.6	48.2	51.8
38951	PITTSBORO	64.8	60.8	34.5	38.2	0.0	0.0	0.7	1.2	6.5	6.5	6.6	6.6	5.2	25.7	26.1	13.5	3.3	76.3	39.6	48.4	51.6
38952	SCHLATER	26.3	21.9	72.8	77.0	0.1	0.2	0.7	0.9	4.1	3.9	3.4	4.8	19.1	45.8	14.5	3.9	0.5	86.7	29.6	77.7	22.3
38953	SCOBEY	76.8	74.1	22.3	24.9	0.2	0.2	0.7	1.0	7.2	7.2	7.0	6.2	5.0	26.9	26.7	12.5	1.3	74.6	38.4	48.2	51.8
38954	SIDON	53.8	48.5	44.9	49.6	0.4	0.5	1.1	1.6	7.8	7.8	7.3	8.3	5.4	25.5	26.2	10.6	1.3	72.3	35.5	49.4	50.6
38961	TILLATOBA	70.5	67.0	28.7	32.0	0.2	0.3	0.8	1.1	8.0	8.0	7.5	6.3	4.8	25.2	25.5	13.1	1.7	72.7	37.4	46.5	53.5
38963	TUTWILER	23.8	20.5	74.7	77.5	0.8	1.1	0.5	0.6	7.7	7.7	7.6	8.8	7.2	24.5	24.7	10.1	1.8	71.6	33.6	46.8	53.2
38964	VANCE	41.3	37.6	57.8	61.3	0.0	0.0	0.9	0.0	9.7	7.5	6.5	8.6	5.4	20.4	26.9	15.1	0.0	71.0	37.5	50.5	49.5
38965	WATER VALLEY	67.2	64.1	31.8	34.5	0.2	0.3	1.0	1.4	6.4	6.6	6.9	6.8	5.3	25.6	27.5	13.0	2.1	76.2	39.3	48.8	51.2
38967	WINONA	50.0	46.8	49.0	52.0	0.4	0.5	0.8	1.0	6.6	6.6	6.5	7.6	6.4	23.2	25.6	14.8	2.8	75.8	39.7	45.6	54.4
39038	BELZONI	26.9	24.7	71.9	73.7	0.2	0.3	1.3	1.7	8.5	8.5	8.7	9.3	7.5	25.1	21.1	8.8	2.5	68.4	30.2	47.0	53.0
39039	BENTON	51.6	47.3	47.2	51.2	0.1	0.2	5.2	7.0	6.0	6.0	6.1	6.3	6.2	30.5	27.2	10.3	1.5	78.1	37.3	55.0	45.0
39040	BENTONIA	62.4	58.1	36.5	40.5	0.1	0.1	0.5	0.7	6.9	7.1	7.0	6.6	5.4	25.3	27.9	12.0	1.7	74.9	38.5	48.9	51.1
39041	BOLTON	33.2	25.2	66.0	73.8	0.0	0.0	0.6	0.7	6.7	7.1	7.1	6.7	5.9	25.3	29.6	10.2	1.5	75.1	37.6	48.5	51.5
39042	BRANDON	83.2	81.3	15.4	16.6	0.5	0.7	1.3	1.9	6.7	6.8	6.8	6.7	6.1	26.8	28.1	10.6	1.4	75.5	38.0	49.0	51.0
39044	BRAXTON	70.2	67.2	28.2	30.6	0.2	0.2	0.7	1.0	7.0	6.8	7.1	7.2	5.7	26.3	28.0	10.5	1.3	74.6	37.4	49.5	50.5
39045	CAMDEN	14.9	10.5	83.9	88.3	0.5	0.5	0.4	0.3	7.7	8.4	10.1	8.2	7.0	21.2	24.2	11.4	1.8	68.7	33.4	47.9	52.1
39046	CANTON	24.8	23.5	74.2	75.3	0.2	0.3	1.1	1.2	8.4	8.7	8.2	8.1	6.7	24.5	23.9	9.8	1.6	69.7	33.0	47.2	52.8
39047	BRANDON	85.0	82.3	12.8	14.7	1.1	1.5	1.0	1.6	7.3	7.0	7.0	6.3	5.4	31.2	27.0	8.0	0.8	74.7	36.3	48.6	51.4
39051	CARTHAGE	56.0	52.4	37.2	38.9	0.2	0.3	2.3	3.4	7.0	7.0	6.6	6.8	6.8	27.6	24.4	11.7	2.2	75.4	35.9	51.8	48.2
39056	CLINTON	73.3	67.2	24.3	29.3	1.4	2.0	0.9	1.4	6.2	6.3	6.5	8.3	8.8	26.7	25.4	10.1	1.7	76.9	35.1	47.7	52.3
39057	CONEHATTA	55.8	49.7	10.8	10.9	0.0	0.1	1.2	1.5	9.1	8.6	8.2	7.6	6.5	27.2	22.4	9.3	1.1	69.4	32.5	48.8	51.2
39059	CRYSTAL SPRINGS	47.8	44.2	51.2	54.5	0.1	0.2	0.9	1.2	6.9	6.8	6.7	8.8	6.8	25.2	26.4	10.7	1.7	74.6	36.2	48.0	52.0
39063	DURANT	31.7	29.3	67.3	69.3	0.2	0.3	0.7	0.9	7.0	7.3	7.5	8.0	7.2	24.0	23.9	12.1	3.0	73.2	35.3	47.4	52.6
39066	EDWARDS	25.3	19.1	73.9	79.9	0.1	0.1	0.9	1.0	7.7	8.0	7.8	7.5	6.1	24.7	27.2	9.7	1.3	71.6	34.8	47.4	52.6
39067	ETHEL	68.9	65.4	29.4	32.3	0.3	0.4	1.5	2.1	6.3	6.5	6.8	6.6	5.3	25.1	28.0	13.8	1.8	76.3	40.2	50.0	50.0
39069	FAYETTE	8.2	7.3	91.3	92.1	0.1	0.2	0.6	0.6	7.2	7.8	7.4	7.8	8.4	27.5	23.9	8.1	1.8	73.1	32.7	51.0	49.0
39071	FLORA	49.3	41.6	50.0	57.5	0.1	0.1	0.4	0.5	7.9	8.0	7.7	6.5	5.2	28.6	26.2	9.0	1.0	72.4	35.4	48.3	51.7
39073	FLORENCE	82.3	79.5	16.6	18.9	0.2	0.3	0.9	1.4	7.1	7.0	7.0	6.6	5.9	28.1	27.5	9.7	1.1	74.9	36.8	49.6	50.4
39074	FOREST	47.5	43.6	47.9	50.0	0.3	0.4	6.2	8.6	7.9	7.9	7.7	7.4	5.8	25.9	25.5	10.3	1.6	71.9	35.5	48.5	51.5
39078	GEORGETOWN	54.2	50.1	44.8	48.4	0.0	0.0	1.0	1.4	7.1	7.1	7.2	7.8	5.7	24.6	27.5	11.7	1.4	73.8	37.9	49.3	50.7
39079	GOODMAN	28.0	24.9	71.1	74.0	0.0	0.0	0.6	0.6	6.7	6.8	6.3	25.5	15.7	17.4	14.1	6.5	1.1	75.0	21.5	49.9	50.1
39082	HARRISVILLE	64.2	60.9	35.1	38.1	0.2	0.2	1.4	1.5	7.9	8.0	7.7	6.8	4.9	25.2	27.0	11.1	1.4	72.1	37.0	50.8	49.2
39083	HAZLEHURST	38.7	36.1	59.8	61.9	0.3	0.3	1.4	2.0	6.8	7.2	7.1	7.4	6.3	24.4	27.2	11.4	2.1	74.6	37.1	48.3	51.7
39086	HERMANVILLE	26.4	23.6	73.0	75.6	0.0	0.1	0.8	1.0	7.8	8.3	8.0	8.4	6.8	23.5	24.7	10.6	1.9	71.1	33.7	46.9	53.1
39088	HOLLY BLUFF	58.1	53.4	41.9	46.6	0.0	0.0	6.5	6.8	7.5	7.5	8.9	8.2	6.2	27.4	24.0	8.9	1.4	70.5	33.9	50.7	49.3
39090	KOSCIUSKO	57.5	54.3	40.7	43.2	0.3	0.4	1.4	2.0	6.5	6.5	6.4	6.9	6.0	24.1	25.5	14.9	3.2	76.5	39.7	47.9	52.1
39092	LAKE	62.4	58.0	36.6	40.4	0.0	0.1	1.3	2.1	7.6	7.9	7.8	7.3	5.8	25.8	25.4	10.9	1.5	72.1	35.5	48.8	51.2
39094	LENA	55.5	52.0	43.7	46.8	0.0	0.0	0.9	1.3	7.0	7.1	7.1	7.3	5.8	24.9	27.3	11.7	1.8	74.3	38.2	49.3	50.7
39095	LEXINGTON	20.6	18.4	78.5	80.4	0.3	0.4	1.2	1.2	7.3	8.3	8.1	8.9	6.9	23.4	23.6	11.2	2.3	70.8	33.9	46.6	53.4
39096	LORMAN	16.8	15.0	83.2	85.0	0.0	0.0	1.2	1.3	6.5	6.5	6.5	6.7	7.0	24.4	27.9	12.3	2.2	76.3	38.4	48.0	52.0
39097	LOUISE	21.0	18.6	78.0	80.1	0.6	0.8	0.6	0.7	7.5	7.1	7.2	8.5	6.7	26.1	24.4	10.8	1.6	72.9	35.1	47.6	52.4
39108	MC COOL	66.0	62.7	32.2	34.9	0.5	0.7	1.6	2.4	6.6	6.7	6.9	6.4	4.9	24.0	27.4	15.1	2.0	75.9	40.7	49.0	51.0
39110	MADISON	87.6	81.2	10.4	16.0	1.3	1.8	0.7	1.2	7.6	8.1	8.6	7.1	4.0	26.6	28.6	8.0	1.5	71.0	37.9	48.3	51.7
39111	MAGEE	68.5	65.1	29.8	32.4	0.2	0.2	1.8	2.7	6.7	6.8	7.5	7.2	5.9	25.6	26.1	12.1	2.2	74.5	37.4	48.9	51.1
39113	MAYERSVILLE	33.4	30.6	65.6	68.2	0.0	0.0	0.4	0.5	6.2	5.9	5.7	7.8	10.2	30.9	21.9	10.2	1.3	77.7	34.1	55.4	44.6
39114	MENDENHALL	61.1	58.3	37.9	40.3	0.1	0.2	0.8	1.2	7.5	7.6	7.4	7.3	5.8	25.5	25.7	11.3	1.8	73.0	36.4	48.2	51.8
39116	MIZE	83.2	81.0	16.2	18.2	0.1	0.1	0.6	0.9	7.2	7.0	7.2	7.3	6.0	26.3	26.4	11.1	1.5	74.2	36.9	49.3	50.7
39117	MORTON	71.1	68.1	24.6	25.6	0.2	0.2	7.8	11.3	6.6	7.0	6.8	7.0	6.1	26.7	26.3	11.3	2.2	75.2	37.6	49.8	50.2
39119	MOUNT OLIVE	52.7	46.2	46.2	52.3	0.1	0.2	0.6	0.8	7.6	7.7	7.6	7.6	5.4	24.6	26.4	11.5	1.5	72.3	36.7	48.4	51.6
39120	NATCHEZ	45.1	42.0	53.7	56.4	0.3	0.4	0.8	1.0	6.7	6.7	6.7	6.8	6.1	22.9	28.1	13.8	2.3	75.8	40.0	46.4	53.6
39140	NEWHEBRON	59.9	57.1	39.6	42.3	0.1	0.2	0.5	0.7	7.1	7.3	7.5	7.6	5.3	24.9	27.2	11.1	2.0	73.4	37.4	47.7	52.3
39144	PATTISON	23.4	20.5	76.0	78.6	0.1	0.2	0.9	1.0	8.3	8.1	7.7	6.8	6.3	26.3	25.0	9.7	1.6	71.7	33.8	49.6	50.4
39145	PELAHATCHIE	78.2	75.2	20.4	22.9	0.2	0.3	2.1	3.4	7.7	7.7	7.5	6.1	5.2	27.4	26.3	11.0	1.1	73.5	36.7	49.8	50.2
	MISSISSIPPI	61.4	59.6	36.3	37.4	0.7	0.9	1.4	2.0	7.2	7.1	7.0	7.5	7.1	26.4	25.3	10.6	1.7	74.3	35.6	48.6	51.4
	UNITED STATES	75.1	72.0	12.3	12.7	3.8	4.6	12.5	15.7	6.8	6.7	6.6	7.1	6.9	27.0	26.0	10.9	1.9	75.7	36.9	49.2	50.8

ZIP CODE #	POST OFFICE NAME	2009 Per Capita Income	2009 HH Income Base	2009 HOUSEHOLD INCOME DISTRIBUTION (%) Less than $25,000	$25,000 to $49,999	$50,000 to $99,999	$100,000 to $149,999	$150,000 or More	MEDIAN HOUSEHOLD INCOME 2009	2014	2009 National Centile	2009 State Centile	2009 Home Value Base	2009 HOME VALUE DISTRIBUTION (%) Less than $50,000	$50,000 to $89,999	$90,000 to $174,999	$175,000 to $399,999	$400,000 or More	2009 Median Home Value
38850	HOULKA	14607	1291	39.0	33.5	24.3	2.7	0.5	32001	32016	11	52	1035	41.6	33.4	20.1	3.6	1.3	59010
38851	HOUSTON	15294	3574	40.5	31.8	23.4	3.7	0.6	31209	31210	10	46	2777	38.5	35.6	21.4	4.4	0.2	61498
38852	IUKA	18927	4062	37.8	34.8	21.1	4.2	2.1	33011	33221	13	58	3166	29.8	34.6	28.6	5.9	1.2	69647
38855	MANTACHIE	17106	1975	33.5	34.0	28.1	3.3	1.1	35847	36271	20	73	1590	26.7	35.0	29.4	8.7	0.3	78599
38856	MARIETTA	15757	599	37.7	31.4	25.9	4.5	0.5	34077	35214	16	63	524	35.7	31.9	26.3	4.6	1.5	67273
38857	MOOREVILLE	19139	1071	25.8	35.9	29.3	6.8	2.2	41250	41475	37	86	838	23.3	31.5	32.7	10.6	1.9	83548
38858	NETTLETON	17259	2831	35.0	29.8	30.2	3.5	1.4	35311	35571	19	71	2297	39.4	28.4	25.0	6.5	0.7	65340
38859	NEW SITE	14151	355	37.5	38.6	20.3	3.7	0.0	32952	34526	13	57	325	40.3	34.8	21.5	3.4	0.0	59545
38860	OKOLONA	16064	2365	41.3	29.6	23.9	3.5	1.7	32341	33358	12	55	1781	39.0	32.2	22.3	4.8	1.6	65345
38862	PLANTERSVILLE	16635	1150	31.0	35.0	28.1	5.2	0.7	36563	35842	22	74	868	32.1	29.8	27.8	10.0	0.2	77105
38863	PONTOTOC	17767	7085	33.2	32.1	28.1	4.6	2.0	35063	35977	18	69	5331	21.2	34.1	34.7	8.5	1.6	83567
38864	RANDOLPH	17375	602	29.9	36.0	27.2	6.5	0.3	35640	36435	20	73	521	28.4	41.7	22.5	6.5	1.0	73481
38865	RIENZI	18615	1957	32.2	31.4	29.9	5.0	1.5	39523	38808	31	83	1677	31.2	30.9	26.5	9.1	2.3	72852
38866	SALTILLO	20371	3708	26.9	29.8	35.4	6.2	1.7	42825	42146	42	89	2738	21.4	25.2	38.7	12.1	2.6	96159
38868	SHANNON	17604	2124	30.9	33.1	30.7	4.3	0.9	39111	39389	30	81	1690	34.4	29.6	30.6	5.2	0.2	72819
38870	SMITHVILLE	17302	1152	31.9	34.7	28.2	4.7	0.5	39433	38855	31	82	973	29.9	32.4	28.3	7.6	1.8	74236
38871	THAXTON	18957	748	25.8	29.9	37.2	4.8	2.3	45706	44140	50	92	639	23.5	37.9	29.0	7.7	2.0	77308
38873	TISHOMINGO	17920	1132	39.0	33.0	22.7	3.4	1.9	32146	32071	12	53	971	30.5	35.9	30.1	3.5	0.0	68941
38876	TREMONT	16723	520	34.0	36.7	25.0	3.8	0.4	34731	35000	17	67	417	39.1	31.2	22.8	3.6	3.4	63472
38878	VARDAMAN	15998	1209	43.0	27.5	24.2	3.8	1.5	31385	31059	10	48	944	44.5	35.4	17.3	2.6	0.2	55532
38901	GRENADA	16230	7512	40.2	30.5	23.8	4.1	1.4	31555	31817	11	50	4964	18.5	36.8	33.6	10.1	1.0	84924
38913	BANNER	17203	267	39.7	30.7	23.2	6.0	0.4	35521	36221	19	72	231	34.6	35.9	23.4	5.6	0.4	62241
38914	BIG CREEK	20114	186	33.9	29.0	31.7	4.3	1.1	40000	39386	33	83	159	35.8	27.7	30.8	5.0	0.6	67188
38915	BRUCE	17448	1707	42.8	27.9	23.8	3.9	1.7	31461	32062	10	49	1240	37.7	32.7	23.6	5.1	0.8	62266
38916	CALHOUN CITY	16539	2052	43.9	26.8	25.2	3.1	1.1	29538	29225	7	33	1537	38.8	38.1	19.9	3.0	0.2	59857
38917	CARROLLTON	17724	1283	39.3	30.6	22.8	4.1	3.3	31395	31037	10	48	1043	39.3	27.1	20.8	11.3	1.4	62134
38920	CASCILLA	13713	776	42.5	29.8	24.6	2.8	0.3	30282	29451	9	38	663	45.1	42.7	9.0	2.6	0.6	54392
38921	CHARLESTON	12594	2376	50.5	27.8	18.5	2.5	0.7	24710	25666	3	10	1812	55.8	28.4	13.6	1.9	0.2	45093
38922	COFFEEVILLE	17032	1722	42.0	31.1	22.4	3.4	1.2	30624	31048	9	41	1435	40.7	35.6	18.8	4.5	0.3	58613
38923	COILA	16392	621	37.2	33.7	24.5	3.5	1.1	33711	34302	15	61	555	34.1	31.7	27.0	6.8	0.4	65182
38924	CRUGER	13201	349	55.6	27.2	12.0	3.2	2.0	20303	21137	1	4	266	54.5	30.1	11.3	3.4	0.8	45385
38925	DUCK HILL	16279	1011	40.3	30.1	24.9	3.6	1.2	34680	35371	17	66	845	35.5	37.0	21.9	4.5	1.1	64494
38927	ENID	14171	423	38.1	37.1	22.2	2.1	0.5	31035	29947	10	44	367	42.2	33.2	15.5	9.0	0.0	59828
38929	GORE SPRINGS	15889	416	39.2	30.5	24.8	4.1	1.4	34781	35807	17	67	357	42.6	20.4	30.3	6.7	0.0	58833
38930	GREENWOOD	14900	10258	48.5	26.3	18.7	4.6	1.9	26008	26889	4	16	5605	28.0	39.6	23.5	7.7	1.1	69957
38940	HOLCOMB	16874	698	29.8	42.4	22.2	4.4	1.1	34710	35042	17	66	572	33.9	32.2	24.3	7.7	1.9	71452
38941	ITTA BENA	12732	1815	51.5	27.4	15.3	3.5	2.3	24021	25936	3	9	970	37.6	46.7	13.6	1.8	0.3	58955
38943	MC CARLEY	14953	415	40.5	28.0	28.0	2.7	1.0	31455	30416	10	49	364	38.2	40.4	10.2	11.3	0.0	66757
38944	MINTER CITY	13833	291	34.0	35.4	25.4	4.5	0.7	31487	30723	11	49	169	30.2	36.7	29.6	3.0	0.6	72647
38948	OAKLAND	16146	801	42.2	31.8	22.1	2.4	1.5	28685	29043	6	29	640	44.5	33.3	12.5	8.8	0.9	55469
38949	PARIS	18571	118	28.8	33.9	29.7	5.9	1.7	37601	37290	26	78	98	38.8	27.6	22.4	5.1	6.1	66667
38950	PHILIPP	13709	174	51.1	28.2	16.7	2.9	1.1	24105	25139	3	9	142	43.7	36.6	14.1	5.6	0.0	55000
38951	PITTSBORO	17435	455	36.7	31.4	26.8	3.5	1.5	34249	34898	16	63	375	47.5	27.5	19.7	4.5	0.8	52436
38952	SCHLATER	22850	239	46.9	23.8	21.3	5.9	2.1	26502	26844	4	19	137	51.1	28.5	13.1	7.3	0.0	48500
38953	SCOBEY	15647	247	38.9	35.2	20.6	3.6	1.6	30487	30410	9	40	205	31.7	37.6	22.0	6.8	2.0	71250
38954	SIDON	14888	837	44.2	29.7	22.2	2.4	1.4	29417	29077	7	32	588	42.2	35.2	13.4	8.5	0.7	57419
38961	TILLATOBA	15854	281	41.6	34.5	18.9	2.8	2.1	28745	29087	6	30	236	34.7	36.0	21.2	5.5	2.5	70286
38963	TUTWILER	11979	1395	52.3	27.9	15.6	2.5	1.7	23457	25100	2	8	893	56.2	29.2	11.8	2.2	0.6	45088
38964	VANCE	14086	37	43.2	27.0	27.0	2.7	0.0	31130	28608	10	45	26	61.5	23.1	15.4	0.0	0.0	44000
38965	WATER VALLEY	17868	3593	37.1	30.1	26.8	4.6	1.4	33434	33694	14	59	2745	32.8	33.7	23.5	8.6	1.5	69934
38967	WINONA	15999	2864	46.3	26.6	20.3	4.9	1.9	30122	30841	8	36	2074	29.6	40.3	24.1	4.9	1.2	67167
39038	BELZONI	11303	2222	53.9	25.2	17.9	1.9	1.1	22087	23215	2	6	1314	40.0	39.7	17.4	2.7	0.2	58973
39039	BENTON	17301	794	42.1	27.0	23.4	5.5	2.0	30855	30887	9	43	657	40.9	30.3	22.7	5.8	0.3	61771
39040	BENTONIA	15299	1308	33.6	33.0	29.1	3.8	0.5	34577	34434	17	65	1041	38.1	32.0	24.6	4.8	0.5	62260
39041	BOLTON	19171	1224	33.6	23.9	32.6	6.4	3.5	40975	42284	36	85	992	27.3	33.2	26.6	11.6	1.3	74054
39042	BRANDON	24410	12737	16.9	26.4	41.5	11.8	3.4	55364	60266	72	98	10103	15.3	13.4	38.8	29.9	2.6	138595
39044	BRAXTON	17927	1286	33.7	29.4	28.9	6.1	1.9	37925	37664	26	79	1098	33.9	28.4	29.3	7.6	0.8	67662
39045	CAMDEN	12699	464	42.5	31.3	21.8	3.0	1.5	29275	29138	7	31	400	52.5	26.3	17.5	2.5	1.3	47297
39046	CANTON	15838	9090	39.6	25.5	27.0	5.6	2.3	34849	35162	17	68	6306	31.4	31.7	20.0	11.6	5.3	71109
39047	BRANDON	31108	13716	14.2	21.2	40.7	16.0	7.9	63272	65669	81	99	11233	7.7	9.0	40.1	37.9	5.3	159552
39051	CARTHAGE	14947	6581	40.5	31.4	22.4	4.5	1.3	31662	31989	11	51	5278	36.1	32.9	22.4	7.1	1.6	67270
39056	CLINTON	22984	9726	18.7	28.6	40.3	9.0	3.4	51848	50652	66	96	7004	7.5	17.6	53.3	19.8	1.7	118076
39057	CONEHATTA	14844	859	33.5	34.3	28.8	2.6	0.8	36950	36855	23	75	720	37.9	30.0	26.4	5.7	0.0	62381
39059	CRYSTAL SPRINGS	14687	4456	44.5	28.2	22.1	4.2	1.0	29669	32059	8	33	3523	31.6	34.5	24.6	8.2	1.1	67817
39063	DURANT	12917	1391	49.8	29.2	18.3	1.3	1.4	25088	25094	3	14	1004	45.7	31.2	21.3	0.4	1.4	54943
39066	EDWARDS	15309	1688	39.0	28.8	25.7	4.5	2.0	33125	33137	14	58	1326	37.6	32.4	19.5	9.4	1.1	65447
39067	ETHEL	16579	825	43.5	29.3	21.8	3.4	1.9	30100	29647	8	36	690	40.4	33.8	20.1	3.5	2.2	60313
39069	FAYETTE	10579	2297	58.6	24.8	14.7	1.7	0.3	19385	19619	1	3	1772	47.2	37.2	13.7	1.9	0.0	52768
39071	FLORA	19880	1879	28.6	23.4	36.3	8.5	3.3	47244	44671	55	94	1453	24.2	32.9	21.1	18.0	3.9	78510
39073	FLORENCE	20203	7653	23.6	29.3	36.8	8.6	1.7	46762	43975	53	93	6286	26.3	17.7	40.0	15.0	1.0	100123
39074	FOREST	15180	5294	41.8	30.4	22.9	2.5	2.4	30604	30923	9	41	4017	46.5	28.2	19.8	4.5	1.1	53909
39078	GEORGETOWN	16015	397	46.1	28.7	19.6	3.5	2.0	27917	29786	6	25	334	47.6	25.7	22.5	3.6	0.6	52963
39079	GOODMAN	10414	475	56.6	24.6	14.9	3.2	0.6	19123	19469	1	3	298	60.7	28.9	9.4	0.3	0.7	38750
39082	HARRISVILLE	17726	485	32.8	31.3	27.2	8.7	0.0	38930	38141	30	81	433	44.6	18.5	29.6	7.4	0.0	61400
39083	HAZLEHURST	14633	3989	41.3	31.2	21.8	4.7	1.0	30503	32049	9	40	3060	35.8	31.7	24.4	7.0	1.1	69865
39086	HERMANVILLE	14835	896	47.0	28.9	17.4	4.6	2.1	27634	28017	5	24	742	52.3	24.3	17.4	5.1	0.9	47385
39088	HOLLY BLUFF	13476	58	41.4	34.5	22.4	1.7	0.0	31230	31464	10	46	36	30.6	30.6	30.6	8.3	0.0	67500
39090	KOSCIUSKO	14990	4904	47.7	26.9	20.7	3.6	1.1	26827	28196	4	20	3540	34.2	37.4	21.7	6.2	0.5	64624
39092	LAKE	15107	1092	37.6	31.4	26.6	2.3	2.0	31187	30818	10	46	935	41.9	33.6	19.3	4.4	0.9	56398
39094	LENA	14912	1578	42.5	27.8	23.3	5.9	0.6	30878	31226	9	43	1378	43.0	29.2	19.7	5.5	2.6	58205
39095	LEXINGTON	12670	2866	55.2	25.4	14.7	3.2	1.5	20293	20571	1	4	2188	47.6	28.6	18.9	4.1	0.8	53118
39096	LORMAN	12850	320	59.1	19.7	15.3	5.9	0.0	18690	19282	1	3	270	43.3	30.4	15.9	3.0	7.4	60000
39097	LOUISE	11202	426	53.3	28.4	13.8	2.8	1.6	21882	23207	2	6	290	62.8	29.3	7.6	0.3	0.0	31538
39108	MC COOL	17466	694	42.5	32.0	20.7	2.6	2.2	30437	30082	9	39	609	41.9	29.1	22.8	3.8	2.5	59340
39110	MADISON	36679	11721	8.0	15.3	38.3	20.5	17.9	82109	85799	93	100	10966	4.6	5.0	34.4	45.0	10.9	189270
39111	MAGEE	15282	3928	42.9	30.1	22.5	2.8	1.8	30250	31869	8	37	2941	35.3	28.8	27.1	8.2	0.6	70211
39113	MAYERSVILLE	11679	512	56.4	23.8	15.8	2.1	1.8	21070	21696	2	5	339	54.3	22.4	14.5	6.8	2.1	44821
39114	MENDENHALL	15826	4106	38.3	31.1	25.7	3.8	1.0	33889	35963	15	62	3346	32.4	30.6	28.8	7.3	0.9	70931
39116	MIZE	15251	1176	34.4	35.7	26.5	2.5	0.9	35380	35517	19	72	1025	38.1	32.4	26.7	1.6	1.2	67389
39117	MORTON	16393	3510	37.6	30.6	26.2	4.1	1.4	33803	34843	15	62	2729	38.5	38.1	18.1	4.4	0.8	59921
39119	MOUNT OLIVE	16304	1496	43.2	27.7	23.3	3.5	2.2	30649	31036	9	42	1216	37.1	33.6	23.8	4.8	0.8	62818
39120	NATCHEZ	17781	13277	43.9	29.2	20.4	4.0	2.5	29265	29342	7	31	9322	29.0	36.8	25.1	7.1	2.1	70377
39140	NEWHEBRON	15973	640	37.7	31.9	25.6	3.4	1.4	32082	32208	12	53	544	34.0	46.0	12.3	7.0	0.7	59667
39144	PATTISON	12711	381	49.3	29.9	15.7	5.0	0.0	25397	26244	3	14	323	45.8	31.9	18.0	2.2	2.2	53971
39145	PELAHATCHIE	18043	2262	28.4	30.9	34.2	4.9	1.6	41512	39370	38	86	1810	31.2	28.0	29.6	9.5	1.8	75379
	MISSISSIPPI	18363		35.3	29.0	27.5	5.7	2.5	36311	37046				25.4	28.2	31.6	12.7	2.1	84642
	UNITED STATES	27277		20.9	24.4	35.3	11.7	7.6	54719	56938				9.3	13.1	31.6	32.6	13.5	162279

ZIP CODE #	POST OFFICE NAME	FINANCIAL SERVICES: Auto Loan	FINANCIAL SERVICES: Home Loan	FINANCIAL SERVICES: Invest-ments	FINANCIAL SERVICES: Retire-ment Plans	THE HOME: Home Improvements: Home Repair	THE HOME: Home Improvements: Lawn & Garden	THE HOME: Furnishings: Comput-ers & Hard-ware-Personal	THE HOME: Furnishings: Major Appli-ances	THE HOME: Furnishings: TV, Radio, Sound Equip-ment	THE HOME: Furnishings: Furni-ture	ENTERTAINMENT: Dine out/ Carry out	ENTERTAINMENT: Sports Equip-ment	ENTERTAINMENT: Fees & Tickets	ENTERTAINMENT: Toys & Games	ENTERTAINMENT: Travel	ENTERTAINMENT: Cable TV	PERSONAL: Apparel & Services	PERSONAL: Auto Repairs	PERSONAL: Health Insur-ance	PERSONAL: Pets & Supplies
38850	HOULKA	71	47	66	45	47	69	50	62	58	48	56	48	38	59	47	64	37	59	66	76
38851	HOUSTON	71	49	64	47	49	69	52	63	58	49	57	48	41	60	48	64	38	59	67	76
38852	IUKA	75	54	71	52	55	75	57	69	63	53	61	52	45	63	54	69	41	64	73	83
38855	MANTACHIE	77	55	63	53	55	73	57	66	63	56	62	51	46	66	52	69	42	63	70	81
38856	MARIETTA	72	52	60	50	51	68	54	63	60	52	59	48	43	62	49	65	39	59	66	76
38857	MOOREVILLE	90	67	75	66	67	87	69	80	75	66	74	61	57	78	64	82	50	75	84	96
38858	NETTLETON	79	55	71	53	55	77	58	70	65	56	64	54	45	67	54	72	43	66	74	85
38859	NEW SITE	65	47	54	45	47	62	49	57	54	47	53	44	39	56	44	59	36	54	60	69
38860	OKOLONA	72	51	63	50	50	69	55	63	61	53	60	49	44	63	50	67	40	61	68	78
38862	PLANTERSVILLE	75	60	61	58	59	70	61	66	65	61	64	51	53	68	56	69	44	65	68	80
38863	PONTOTOC	80	59	67	57	58	77	62	71	68	60	67	54	51	71	57	74	45	68	76	86
38864	RANDOLPH	83	60	69	58	59	79	62	72	69	60	67	55	50	72	56	75	45	68	76	88
38865	RIENZI	81	61	68	60	61	79	63	73	69	60	67	56	52	71	58	75	45	68	76	88
38866	SALTILLO	87	71	72	69	70	84	70	79	75	70	74	59	61	78	66	80	50	75	81	94
38868	SHANNON	83	59	69	58	59	79	62	72	69	60	67	55	50	72	56	75	45	68	76	88
38870	SMITHVILLE	77	55	64	54	55	73	58	67	64	56	63	51	46	67	52	70	42	63	71	81
38871	THAXTON	92	66	76	64	66	87	69	80	76	67	75	61	55	79	62	83	50	76	84	97
38873	TISHOMINGO	74	53	66	52	54	73	57	67	63	53	61	51	45	64	53	69	41	63	72	81
38876	TREMONT	73	52	60	51	52	69	54	63	60	53	59	48	43	63	49	66	40	60	67	77
38878	VARDAMAN	74	50	67	48	50	71	53	65	60	51	59	50	41	62	49	66	39	61	68	79
38901	GRENADA	67	51	56	51	51	64	55	60	61	54	60	45	48	61	51	66	40	60	66	73
38913	BANNER	76	54	66	53	54	73	56	67	62	54	61	51	45	64	52	68	41	63	70	81
38914	BIG CREEK	81	57	69	55	57	77	60	70	67	58	65	54	47	69	55	73	44	67	74	86
38915	BRUCE	74	51	70	49	51	72	53	66	60	51	59	51	41	61	50	66	39	62	69	80
38916	CALHOUN CITY	71	49	68	47	49	70	52	64	58	49	57	49	40	59	49	65	38	60	68	77
38917	CARROLLTON	83	57	82	55	58	83	59	75	67	56	66	57	46	67	57	74	43	70	79	91
38920	CASCILLA	67	45	61	43	45	65	48	59	55	46	53	46	37	56	44	60	36	55	62	72
38921	CHARLESTON	60	40	57	38	40	59	43	53	50	41	49	41	33	50	40	55	32	51	57	65
38922	COFFEEVILLE	73	48	69	45	48	71	51	64	59	49	57	50	39	60	48	65	38	60	68	79
38923	COILA	79	54	76	51	54	78	57	70	64	54	63	54	44	65	53	71	42	66	74	86
38924	CRUGER	66	43	64	41	43	65	46	58	53	44	52	45	35	54	43	59	34	55	61	71
38925	DUCK HILL	73	50	64	48	50	70	53	64	60	51	58	49	41	61	49	66	39	60	67	78
38927	ENID	67	44	64	42	44	66	47	59	54	45	53	46	36	55	44	60	35	56	62	72
38929	GORE SPRINGS	76	50	72	48	50	74	54	67	61	51	60	52	40	63	50	68	40	63	71	82
38930	GREENWOOD	57	47	44	48	45	54	53	52	58	52	57	39	50	57	49	61	39	55	59	64
38940	HOLCOMB	75	57	61	55	56	71	58	66	63	57	62	50	49	66	53	68	42	63	68	79
38941	ITTA BENA	62	47	50	47	44	58	51	54	57	51	56	42	45	58	47	61	38	55	59	68
38943	MC CARLEY	69	45	67	42	45	68	48	61	56	46	54	47	36	57	45	62	36	57	64	75
38944	MINTER CITY	74	51	80	50	53	78	56	70	59	46	58	57	41	58	56	64	38	65	74	86
38948	OAKLAND	66	49	68	46	50	68	50	62	56	49	54	46	41	55	49	61	36	58	66	74
38949	PARIS	79	65	72	63	65	77	63	73	68	63	67	54	56	69	61	72	45	69	74	87
38950	PHILIPP	64	42	62	40	42	63	45	57	52	43	51	44	34	53	42	58	34	53	60	70
38951	PITTSBORO	83	56	77	53	55	81	59	73	67	56	66	56	45	69	55	75	44	68	77	89
38952	SCHLATER	85	56	82	52	55	84	60	75	68	56	67	59	45	70	56	76	44	70	79	92
38953	SCOBEY	70	47	63	45	47	67	50	61	57	48	56	47	39	58	46	63	37	58	64	75
38954	SIDON	71	48	71	46	49	71	51	64	58	48	57	49	39	58	49	64	37	60	68	78
38961	TILLATOBA	70	46	67	43	45	69	49	61	56	46	55	48	36	57	45	63	36	58	65	76
38963	TUTWILER	55	41	45	41	40	54	46	49	54	47	52	36	41	52	42	59	35	51	58	61
38964	VANCE	66	43	64	40	43	65	46	58	53	44	52	45	34	54	43	59	34	54	61	71
38965	WATER VALLEY	78	56	73	54	57	77	58	70	65	56	64	53	47	66	55	71	42	66	75	85
38967	WINONA	69	50	61	49	49	67	55	62	60	51	59	48	44	61	50	66	40	60	67	76
39038	BELZONI	51	41	39	42	39	49	46	46	50	44	49	35	41	50	42	53	33	48	52	57
39039	BENTON	84	55	81	52	55	83	59	74	68	56	66	58	44	69	55	76	44	70	78	91
39040	BENTONIA	77	52	75	49	52	76	55	69	62	52	61	53	42	63	52	69	40	64	72	84
39041	BOLTON	94	73	86	71	73	92	73	85	80	72	79	65	63	82	70	86	53	81	88	103
39042	BRANDON	94	94	88	95	93	94	91	92	90	93	91	70	91	93	90	91	63	91	91	109
39044	BRAXTON	83	61	71	59	60	79	63	73	69	61	68	56	51	72	58	75	46	69	76	89
39045	CAMDEN	71	47	69	45	47	70	50	63	58	48	57	49	38	59	47	64	37	59	67	77
39046	CANTON	71	59	62	60	57	70	63	66	68	62	68	50	58	68	60	73	46	67	72	81
39047	BRANDON	115	123	110	123	119	111	113	113	109	119	111	89	117	114	114	106	78	109	104	131
39051	CARTHAGE	72	50	65	48	50	70	54	64	61	51	59	49	43	62	50	67	40	61	68	78
39056	CLINTON	87	91	83	91	89	89	86	87	86	88	87	66	89	87	87	86	60	86	87	102
39057	CONEHATTA	75	53	62	52	53	71	56	65	62	54	61	50	45	64	51	68	41	62	69	79
39059	CRYSTAL SPRINGS	67	48	59	47	48	65	52	60	58	50	57	45	43	59	48	64	38	58	65	73
39063	DURANT	57	41	51	40	41	56	45	52	52	44	51	38	38	51	42	57	34	51	59	63
39066	EDWARDS	74	55	66	54	53	72	58	66	65	56	64	51	49	66	55	70	43	65	71	82
39067	ETHEL	75	51	75	49	52	75	54	68	61	51	60	52	42	61	52	67	39	63	71	82
39069	FAYETTE	46	33	40	33	33	45	37	41	43	37	41	31	31	42	34	47	28	42	47	51
39071	FLORA	90	83	73	80	81	85	78	83	81	81	81	60	74	84	75	83	55	80	83	98
39073	FLORENCE	89	78	72	75	76	83	75	81	79	77	78	60	69	82	71	82	53	78	81	96
39074	FOREST	75	52	70	50	51	74	55	67	62	52	61	52	43	63	51	69	40	63	71	82
39078	GEORGETOWN	76	51	71	48	50	74	54	67	62	51	60	52	41	63	50	68	40	63	70	82
39079	GOODMAN	49	36	40	36	35	47	40	44	47	40	45	32	35	45	37	51	30	45	51	54
39082	HARRISVILLE	85	55	82	52	55	83	59	75	68	56	67	58	44	70	55	76	44	70	79	92
39083	HAZLEHURST	66	49	60	48	48	66	52	60	58	50	57	46	43	58	49	64	38	58	65	73
39086	HERMANVILLE	72	47	70	44	47	71	50	63	58	48	57	49	38	59	47	65	38	60	67	78
39088	HOLLY BLUFF	63	41	61	39	41	62	44	55	51	42	50	43	33	52	41	57	33	52	59	68
39090	KOSCIUSKO	61	45	56	45	46	61	49	56	55	47	54	43	41	55	46	60	36	55	62	68
39092	LAKE	76	51	69	49	51	73	54	66	62	52	60	51	42	63	50	68	40	63	70	81
39094	LENA	74	48	71	45	48	73	52	65	60	49	58	51	39	61	48	66	39	61	69	80
39095	LEXINGTON	60	41	54	40	41	58	45	53	52	44	50	40	36	52	41	57	34	52	58	65
39096	LORMAN	61	40	59	37	40	60	43	54	49	40	48	42	32	50	40	55	32	51	57	66
39097	LOUISE	60	39	57	37	39	58	42	52	48	39	47	41	31	49	39	53	31	49	55	64
39108	MC COOL	76	53	76	51	54	76	55	69	61	51	60	53	43	61	53	68	40	64	73	83
39110	MADISON	146	174	155	177	170	151	148	151	139	161	141	121	165	147	157	132	102	141	133	172
39111	MAGEE	66	49	61	47	49	66	53	60	58	50	57	46	43	59	49	63	38	58	65	73
39113	MAYERSVILLE	53	38	47	37	38	52	42	48	48	41	47	35	35	47	39	53	31	47	53	58
39114	MENDENHALL	72	53	65	52	53	71	56	65	63	54	61	50	46	63	52	68	41	63	70	79
39116	MIZE	73	51	63	50	51	70	54	64	60	52	59	49	42	62	49	66	40	61	68	78
39117	MORTON	78	55	68	53	54	75	58	68	65	56	64	53	46	67	53	72	43	65	72	84
39119	MOUNT OLIVE	78	51	75	48	51	77	55	69	63	52	61	54	41	64	51	70	41	65	73	84
39120	NATCHEZ	68	54	62	54	54	68	57	63	63	56	62	47	51	63	55	68	42	63	70	77
39140	NEWHEBRON	77	51	72	49	51	75	54	67	62	52	61	52	41	64	51	69	40	64	71	83
39144	PATTISON	63	41	60	38	41	61	44	55	50	41	49	43	33	51	41	56	33	52	58	68
39145	PELAHATCHIE	85	66	71	64	66	81	67	76	73	66	72	57	57	75	62	78	48	72	78	91
	MISSISSIPPI	77	63	67	62	62	74	66	70	70	65	69	54	59	71	62	74	47	70	74	85
	UNITED STATES	100	100	100	100	100	100	100	100	100	100	100	100	100	100	100	100	100	100	100	100

POPULATION CHANGE

ZIP CODE #	POST OFFICE NAME	COUNTY FIPS CODE	POPULATION 2000	POPULATION 2009	POPULATION 2014	2000-2009 ANNUAL RATE % Rate	2000-2009 ANNUAL RATE State Centile	HOUSEHOLDS 2000	HOUSEHOLDS 2009	HOUSEHOLDS 2014	HOUSEHOLDS % Annual Rate 2000-2009	HOUSEHOLDS 2009 Average HH Size	FAMILIES 2000	FAMILIES 2009	FAMILIES % Annual Rate 2000-2009
39146	PICKENS	089	3130	3232	3234	0.3	64	1053	1117	1126	0.6	2.89	780	806	0.4
39149	PINOLA	127	1810	1858	1838	0.3	64	655	693	692	0.6	2.68	487	503	0.4
39150	PORT GIBSON	021	8769	8569	8547	-0.2	41	2590	2687	2693	0.4	2.65	1767	1782	0.1
39152	PULASKI	123	564	571	557	0.1	54	213	221	216	0.4	2.58	154	155	0.1
39153	RALEIGH	129	8801	8675	8492	-0.2	41	3313	3367	3325	0.2	2.54	2503	2488	-0.1
39154	RAYMOND	049	9608	9929	10012	0.4	69	2991	3229	3278	0.8	2.59	2316	2437	0.6
39156	REDWOOD	149	282	291	290	0.3	64	118	126	127	0.7	2.31	86	89	0.4
39157	RIDGELAND	089	20909	26554	29763	2.6	97	9503	12317	13878	2.8	2.12	5202	6457	2.4
39159	ROLLING FORK	125	4177	3865	3722	-0.8	14	1405	1374	1340	-0.2	2.74	1024	978	-0.5
39160	SALLIS	007	2839	2799	2793	-0.2	41	999	1018	1024	0.2	2.75	759	757	0.0
39162	SATARTIA	163	544	550	545	0.1	54	187	196	196	0.5	2.81	141	144	0.2
39166	SILVER CITY	053	961	824	767	-1.6	3	323	288	270	-1.2	2.86	219	189	-1.6
39168	TAYLORSVILLE	129	4818	4891	4893	0.2	59	1728	1801	1812	0.4	2.71	1307	1333	0.2
39169	TCHULA	051	3767	3458	3307	-0.9	11	1168	1101	1059	-0.6	3.13	866	797	-0.9
39170	TERRY	049	7035	7803	7944	1.1	87	2515	2880	2952	1.5	2.70	2023	2259	1.2
39175	UTICA	049	5186	5326	5329	0.3	64	1690	1778	1790	0.6	2.91	1274	1299	0.2
39176	VAIDEN	015	2667	2561	2495	-0.4	31	1045	1034	1017	-0.1	2.36	741	713	-0.4
39177	VALLEY PARK	055	198	161	144	-2.2	2	71	60	54	-1.8	2.68	49	40	-2.2
39179	VAUGHAN	163	1353	1387	1377	0.3	64	435	458	458	0.6	3.03	327	336	0.3
39180	VICKSBURG	149	33291	32650	32096	-0.2	41	12677	12762	12635	0.1	2.52	8844	8668	-0.2
39183	VICKSBURG	149	15816	15564	15314	-0.2	41	5881	5956	5906	0.1	2.59	4230	4171	-0.2
39189	WALNUT GROVE	079	2226	2094	2045	-0.7	16	848	805	787	-0.6	2.56	614	567	-0.9
39191	WESSON	029	8171	8750	8985	0.7	79	2773	3076	3190	1.1	2.67	2121	2302	0.9
39192	WEST	007	2116	2052	2017	-0.3	36	801	799	791	0.0	2.55	592	577	-0.3
39194	YAZOO CITY	163	20513	21090	20589	0.3	64	6468	6312	6153	-0.3	2.79	4612	4383	-0.5
39201	JACKSON	049	1097	1005	989	-0.9	11	98	85	80	-1.5	3.31	32	26	-2.2
39202	JACKSON	049	8976	8196	7967	-1.0	9	4080	3749	3636	-0.9	1.90	1610	1364	-1.8
39203	JACKSON	049	9452	8264	7896	-1.4	4	2777	2431	2310	-1.4	2.76	1716	1431	-1.9
39204	JACKSON	049	19497	18587	18147	-0.5	25	7339	6979	6814	-0.5	2.60	4662	4221	-1.1
39206	JACKSON	049	26660	26472	26151	-0.1	47	9910	9775	9664	-0.1	2.65	6563	6233	-0.6
39208	PEARL	121	29369	33100	34939	1.3	90	9836	11320	12163	1.5	2.50	6943	7835	1.3
39209	JACKSON	049	34738	33189	32483	-0.5	25	11553	11207	11014	-0.3	2.94	8450	7929	-0.7
39210	JACKSON	049	733	670	654	-1.0	9	0	0	0	0.0	0.00	0	0	0.0
39211	JACKSON	049	24316	23376	22979	-0.4	31	10713	10538	10411	-0.2	2.18	6670	6245	-0.7
39212	JACKSON	049	31798	31467	31205	-0.1	47	11537	11591	11540	0.1	2.71	8573	8378	-0.2
39213	JACKSON	049	28393	26648	25997	-0.7	16	9984	9613	9427	-0.4	2.68	6923	6430	-0.8
39216	JACKSON	049	3928	3708	3619	-0.6	21	1648	1537	1491	-0.8	2.08	827	724	-1.4
39217	JACKSON	049	104	91	87	-1.4	4	0	0	0	0.0	0.00	0	0	0.0
39218	RICHLAND	121	5900	6806	7282	1.6	92	2256	2654	2862	1.8	2.56	1672	1920	1.5
39232	FLOWOOD	121	4807	8201	9690	5.9	99	2141	3486	4150	5.4	2.33	1263	2037	5.3
39272	BYRAM	049	7417	12110	13490	5.4	99	2744	4607	5169	5.8	2.63	2191	3582	5.5
39301	MERIDIAN	075	26907	26022	25586	-0.4	31	10578	10598	10504	0.0	2.38	6953	6737	-0.3
39305	MERIDIAN	075	19336	19413	19293	0.0	52	7761	8072	8087	0.4	2.29	5339	5405	0.1
39307	MERIDIAN	075	18182	17436	17054	-0.5	25	6751	6568	6459	-0.3	2.41	4532	4273	-0.6
39309	MERIDIAN	075	658	691	691	0.5	72	13	15	15	1.6	2.53	10	12	2.0
39320	BAILEY	075	1393	1441	1442	0.4	69	526	565	571	0.8	2.55	394	411	0.5
39322	BUCKATUNNA	153	1940	2067	2103	0.7	79	686	756	777	1.1	2.72	535	577	0.8
39323	CHUNKY	101	1058	1252	1324	1.8	94	406	491	523	2.1	2.55	308	363	1.8
39325	COLLINSVILLE	075	4653	4824	4824	0.4	69	1755	1888	1908	0.8	2.56	1374	1444	0.5
39326	DALEVILLE	075	450	484	488	0.8	82	164	185	189	1.3	2.62	127	140	1.1
39327	DECATUR	101	4269	4397	4453	0.3	64	1520	1624	1662	0.7	2.45	1109	1157	0.5
39328	DE KALB	069	5040	4801	4612	-0.5	25	1956	1910	1855	-0.3	2.44	1388	1320	-0.5
39330	ENTERPRISE	023	2736	2614	2551	-0.5	25	1070	1055	1038	-0.2	2.48	767	736	-0.4
39332	HICKORY	101	1667	1791	1837	0.8	82	660	728	753	1.1	2.46	498	537	0.8
39335	LAUDERDALE	075	3245	3371	3387	0.4	69	1274	1396	1416	1.0	2.37	946	1008	0.7
39336	LAWRENCE	101	902	881	871	-0.3	36	337	341	340	0.1	2.58	254	251	-0.1
39337	LITTLE ROCK	101	1717	1739	1745	0.1	54	686	722	733	0.6	2.41	514	528	0.3
39338	LOUIN	061	2638	2542	2474	-0.4	31	989	989	973	0.0	2.56	707	688	-0.3
39339	LOUISVILLE	159	16612	16290	15914	-0.2	41	6203	6263	6172	0.1	2.51	4459	4390	-0.2
39341	MACON	103	6838	6569	6404	-0.4	31	2450	2451	2418	0.0	2.61	1734	1693	-0.3
39342	MARION	075	1287	1517	1565	1.8	94	464	574	600	2.3	2.58	331	398	2.0
39345	NEWTON	101	6666	6605	6578	-0.1	47	2571	2621	2629	0.2	2.44	1827	1814	-0.1
39346	NOXAPATER	159	2381	2364	2319	-0.1	47	932	958	950	0.3	2.47	683	684	0.0
39347	PACHUTA	023	928	891	869	-0.4	31	358	357	351	0.0	2.50	256	249	-0.3
39348	PAULDING	061	513	513	506	0.0	52	184	192	191	0.5	2.67	137	139	0.2
39350	PHILADELPHIA	099	28213	29710	30536	0.6	76	10467	11389	11825	0.9	2.55	7592	8061	0.7
39352	PORTERVILLE	069	980	914	875	-0.8	14	364	356	345	-0.2	2.57	258	245	-0.6
39354	PRESTON	069	2413	2415	2371	0.0	52	933	971	966	0.4	2.49	685	697	0.2
39355	QUITMAN	023	8103	8088	7995	0.0	52	3128	3243	3240	0.4	2.44	2267	2292	0.1
39356	ROSE HILL	061	1532	1548	1527	0.1	54	602	627	625	0.4	2.46	428	433	0.1
39358	SCOOBA	069	2193	2177	2085	-0.1	47	742	698	670	-0.7	2.42	529	485	-0.9
39359	SEBASTOPOL	123	233	227	224	-0.3	36	107	106	104	-0.1	2.14	76	73	-0.4
39360	SHUBUTA	023	4343	4214	4111	-0.3	36	1624	1626	1604	0.0	2.59	1172	1143	-0.3
39361	SHUQUALAK	103	1313	1218	1178	-0.8	14	491	481	472	-0.2	2.53	360	344	-0.5
39362	STATE LINE	041	2853	2950	3005	0.4	69	994	1073	1106	0.8	2.70	760	799	0.5
39363	STONEWALL	023	1839	1794	1756	-0.3	36	733	736	727	0.0	2.44	531	519	-0.2
39364	TOOMSUBA	075	3120	3191	3195	0.2	59	1143	1232	1246	0.8	2.55	874	917	0.5
39365	UNION	101	3744	3971	4058	0.6	76	1437	1561	1610	0.9	2.46	1019	1077	0.6
39366	VOSSBURG	061	1619	1610	1587	-0.1	47	555	579	577	0.5	2.78	427	435	0.2
39367	WAYNESBORO	153	15950	15892	15809	0.0	52	5956	6146	6180	0.3	2.55	4388	4427	0.1
39401	HATTIESBURG	035	40775	43276	44754	0.6	76	16119	17526	18267	0.9	2.35	9350	9691	0.4
39402	HATTIESBURG	073	27773	34833	38653	2.5	96	10840	13844	15438	2.7	2.49	7508	9446	2.5
39406	HATTIESBURG	035	4046	4011	4058	-0.1	47	490	530	558	0.9	2.00	177	175	-0.1
39421	BASSFIELD	065	4032	3911	3818	-0.3	36	1414	1446	1432	0.2	2.69	1064	1063	0.0
39422	BAY SPRINGS	061	5967	5962	5868	0.0	52	2194	2264	2251	0.3	2.57	1600	1612	0.1
39423	BEAUMONT	111	2798	2690	2655	-0.4	31	1024	1017	1013	-0.1	2.65	775	754	-0.3
39425	BROOKLYN	111	1597	1747	1828	1.0	86	600	675	711	1.3	2.59	454	496	1.0
39426	CARRIERE	109	13492	16930	18787	2.5	96	4950	6415	7182	2.8	2.63	3913	4966	2.6
39427	CARSON	065	1483	1438	1404	-0.3	36	576	590	584	0.3	2.44	404	402	-0.1
39428	COLLINS	031	10704	11005	11166	0.3	64	3848	4126	4235	0.8	2.61	2842	2976	0.5
39429	COLUMBIA	091	17496	17521	17489	0.0	52	6392	6555	6593	0.3	2.52	4622	4625	0.0
39437	ELLISVILLE	067	11793	12347	12560	0.5	72	4075	4399	4516	0.8	2.54	3027	3184	0.5
39439	HEIDELBERG	061	4902	4913	4872	0.0	52	1770	1850	1854	0.5	2.65	1331	1358	0.2
39440	LAUREL	067	20942	20620	20432	-0.2	41	8016	7986	7948	0.0	2.52	5220	5014	-0.4
39443	LAUREL	067	22377	23355	23801	0.5	72	8554	9223	9470	0.8	2.53	6510	6844	0.5
	MISSISSIPPI					0.5					0.8	2.56			0.5
	UNITED STATES					1.0					1.1	2.59			0.9

ZIP CODE #	POST OFFICE NAME	RACE (%) White 2000	White 2009	Black 2000	Black 2009	Asian/Pacific 2000	Asian/Pacific 2009	% Hispanic Origin 2000	% Hispanic Origin 2009	2009 AGE DISTRIBUTION (%) 0-4	5-9	10-14	15-19	20-24	25-44	45-64	65-84	85+	18+	MEDIAN AGE 2009	% 2009 Males	% 2009 Females
39146	PICKENS	14.9	12.6	84.5	86.7	0.2	0.2	1.0	1.0	8.6	8.5	8.1	8.0	6.4	25.0	23.7	10.1	1.5	69.8	33.1	47.5	52.5
39149	PINOLA	47.5	44.0	51.8	55.1	0.1	0.2	0.5	0.6	7.7	7.5	7.5	7.7	5.7	25.5	26.0	10.9	1.6	72.6	35.4	48.3	51.7
39150	PORT GIBSON	12.4	11.2	86.9	87.8	0.2	0.2	0.8	0.9	6.2	6.6	6.8	12.1	15.6	20.5	22.2	8.1	1.9	76.2	27.3	46.3	53.7
39152	PULASKI	73.8	70.1	25.4	28.4	0.0	0.0	2.7	4.4	6.0	5.8	6.3	7.2	5.8	26.4	28.5	12.6	1.4	77.8	39.9	48.3	51.7
39153	RALEIGH	77.9	75.5	21.2	23.3	0.2	0.3	0.6	0.8	7.3	7.2	7.2	6.8	5.7	25.6	25.3	13.0	1.9	74.1	37.7	48.9	51.1
39154	RAYMOND	66.4	58.6	32.8	40.2	0.2	0.3	0.7	1.1	4.9	5.2	5.5	14.3	7.9	23.1	25.8	11.5	1.9	77.7	35.8	51.2	48.8
39156	REDWOOD	82.2	78.7	16.4	19.2	0.4	0.7	0.7	1.0	5.2	5.8	6.2	5.8	4.1	25.1	32.6	14.1	1.0	78.7	43.3	50.9	49.1
39157	RIDGELAND	75.1	68.4	20.6	25.5	2.9	4.1	1.5	2.3	6.9	6.6	6.1	5.7	7.6	34.9	23.2	6.9	2.1	77.0	34.3	47.5	52.5
39159	ROLLING FORK	30.6	28.1	68.1	70.2	0.3	0.4	0.9	1.1	8.4	8.5	8.3	8.3	6.7	22.5	25.0	10.0	2.3	69.9	33.2	47.5	52.5
39160	SALLIS	39.9	36.7	59.4	62.4	0.0	0.0	1.2	1.6	7.4	7.4	7.9	7.5	6.4	25.0	25.0	11.5	1.9	72.7	35.6	48.4	51.6
39162	SATARTIA	80.0	76.2	18.9	22.4	0.0	0.0	0.6	0.7	7.1	7.5	7.3	6.0	4.4	23.8	29.6	12.9	1.5	74.4	40.5	50.5	49.5
39166	SILVER CITY	27.0	24.2	72.0	74.6	0.1	0.1	1.0	1.2	6.6	6.3	6.3	8.6	7.8	22.7	27.8	12.1	1.8	75.5	37.4	48.1	51.9
39168	TAYLORSVILLE	56.9	51.4	42.3	47.5	0.0	0.0	0.6	0.8	6.7	6.7	6.9	7.4	5.9	25.6	27.5	11.8	1.5	75.1	37.7	48.9	51.1
39169	TCHULA	8.0	7.1	91.3	91.9	0.0	0.0	0.4	0.5	9.9	10.2	9.7	9.8	8.7	22.7	20.0	7.8	1.3	64.5	26.3	45.0	55.0
39170	TERRY	63.8	59.5	35.5	39.5	0.2	0.2	0.5	0.7	5.7	6.2	6.7	6.3	4.5	24.3	32.1	12.8	1.3	77.6	42.1	48.7	51.3
39175	UTICA	39.5	31.8	59.3	66.7	0.1	0.1	1.4	1.7	6.8	7.4	7.6	8.2	6.8	24.3	26.2	10.5	2.1	73.6	35.7	49.7	50.3
39176	VAIDEN	48.9	44.6	50.0	54.0	0.1	0.1	0.9	1.2	5.3	6.5	6.3	7.7	6.7	25.2	26.8	13.5	1.9	77.6	39.1	50.2	49.8
39177	VALLEY PARK	50.5	47.8	49.0	51.6	0.0	0.0	0.5	0.6	7.5	6.8	6.8	7.5	5.0	21.1	29.2	14.3	1.9	73.9	40.3	46.0	54.0
39179	VAUGHAN	38.7	33.7	60.8	65.5	0.0	0.0	1.0	1.1	7.4	7.6	7.4	6.9	6.1	24.2	28.1	10.0	2.2	73.2	36.7	50.3	49.7
39180	VICKSBURG	57.0	53.2	41.0	44.3	0.7	0.9	1.2	1.7	7.6	7.4	7.1	7.2	6.3	25.7	26.3	10.4	2.0	73.5	36.3	46.8	53.2
39183	VICKSBURG	49.8	47.9	48.7	49.9	0.4	0.6	0.7	1.0	7.2	7.6	7.7	7.7	5.9	24.6	27.7	10.2	1.4	72.7	36.4	47.6	52.4
39189	WALNUT GROVE	60.3	56.2	31.9	34.0	0.1	0.1	1.4	2.1	7.1	7.0	7.2	7.0	5.8	24.1	27.6	12.1	2.1	74.5	38.5	48.0	52.0
39191	WESSON	69.6	65.9	29.2	32.4	0.1	0.2	0.9	1.4	6.3	6.5	6.5	10.4	7.6	24.7	26.3	10.3	1.3	76.5	35.2	49.5	50.5
39192	WEST	53.1	49.8	45.0	47.7	0.1	0.1	1.6	2.0	7.1	6.9	7.6	8.0	5.7	24.3	25.8	12.9	1.9	73.3	37.8	48.1	51.9
39194	YAZOO CITY	40.8	39.7	57.8	58.5	0.5	0.6	5.2	7.5	7.2	7.4	6.9	7.0	6.7	30.4	23.0	9.7	1.9	74.4	34.4	54.6	45.4
39201	JACKSON	16.9	12.1	80.9	85.4	0.2	0.2	1.0	1.3	1.8	1.5	1.4	9.0	22.6	43.5	14.6	5.1	0.6	92.2	29.7	78.4	21.6
39202	JACKSON	49.1	45.4	48.8	51.7	0.7	1.0	0.9	1.2	5.8	5.1	4.9	8.8	13.5	30.2	22.5	6.8	2.3	81.0	31.8	50.1	49.9
39203	JACKSON	2.3	1.6	96.7	97.2	0.1	0.1	1.2	1.3	7.1	7.1	6.2	13.1	14.9	21.6	20.6	7.9	1.6	75.7	26.4	47.3	52.7
39204	JACKSON	25.3	19.5	72.9	78.3	0.6	0.8	0.7	0.9	9.5	8.8	7.5	7.4	9.2	27.6	19.9	8.0	2.1	69.9	29.4	46.6	53.4
39206	JACKSON	14.5	11.3	83.7	86.6	0.7	0.9	0.7	0.7	7.6	7.4	7.2	8.1	9.1	28.3	24.0	6.9	1.5	73.2	31.5	46.0	54.0
39208	PEARL	74.2	70.4	23.5	26.4	0.7	0.9	1.7	2.7	6.7	6.3	6.0	6.2	7.4	32.1	24.0	9.9	1.3	77.3	35.6	49.7	50.3
39209	JACKSON	10.0	8.4	88.9	90.4	0.1	0.1	0.9	0.9	9.4	9.7	9.1	9.2	7.4	25.9	22.1	6.3	0.8	66.1	28.5	45.9	54.1
39210	JACKSON	50.6	40.6	46.4	55.5	1.0	1.3	0.8	1.3	3.7	3.9	4.8	27.0	27.5	14.6	10.4	6.0	2.1	83.7	21.9	45.7	54.3
39211	JACKSON	80.8	74.8	16.7	21.6	1.5	2.2	1.0	1.6	5.5	5.7	6.1	5.7	4.9	26.4	27.4	15.2	3.1	79.1	41.8	47.5	52.5
39212	JACKSON	44.0	37.0	54.5	61.1	0.5	0.6	0.7	1.0	8.3	8.0	7.6	7.5	6.5	30.0	23.4	7.7	1.1	71.5	32.9	47.7	52.3
39213	JACKSON	2.0	1.5	97.3	97.7	0.2	0.2	0.5	0.5	7.3	7.4	7.2	8.8	8.5	23.1	24.5	11.0	2.2	73.3	33.6	45.2	54.8
39216	JACKSON	61.0	54.3	35.5	40.6	2.6	3.7	0.4	0.6	6.1	5.4	4.9	5.0	6.9	31.2	22.1	13.6	4.9	80.5	38.2	47.7	52.3
39217	JACKSON	0.0	0.0	98.1	97.8	0.0	0.0	0.0	0.0	6.6	6.6	5.5	7.7	16.5	20.9	22.0	11.0	3.3	78.0	31.5	54.9	45.1
39218	RICHLAND	89.6	87.3	7.7	8.9	1.5	2.1	0.9	1.4	8.4	8.3	7.7	6.1	5.3	31.0	24.1	8.3	0.8	71.9	34.6	49.7	50.3
39232	FLOWOOD	85.0	83.1	12.1	12.9	1.4	2.0	1.6	2.3	8.4	7.4	6.5	5.4	6.3	38.2	20.9	6.0	1.0	74.5	33.2	47.6	52.4
39272	BYRAM	83.9	77.2	14.7	20.4	0.6	0.9	0.7	1.2	7.8	7.6	7.3	6.3	5.3	32.9	24.7	7.5	0.7	73.4	35.0	47.9	52.1
39301	MERIDIAN	49.4	47.4	49.3	50.9	0.4	0.5	1.0	1.4	7.7	7.5	7.2	7.1	6.4	25.8	24.6	11.1	2.5	73.2	35.8	47.0	53.0
39305	MERIDIAN	79.9	75.7	17.9	21.2	0.9	1.1	1.5	2.2	6.4	5.9	5.9	7.0	6.9	26.0	25.6	12.9	3.6	78.1	38.5	48.0	52.0
39307	MERIDIAN	46.9	43.0	51.5	54.8	0.5	0.6	1.0	1.3	6.9	6.7	6.7	8.2	6.9	25.4	24.3	12.6	2.3	75.2	36.7	48.6	51.4
39309	MERIDIAN	61.2	54.4	28.8	32.1	2.7	3.2	7.3	10.4	11.6	8.4	6.2	15.8	15.9	35.5	5.4	1.3	0.0	71.1	22.5	57.0	43.0
39320	BAILEY	78.8	74.7	20.2	23.9	0.1	0.1	0.7	1.1	6.0	6.2	6.5	6.7	5.4	28.6	28.4	11.0	1.2	77.2	38.7	48.5	51.5
39322	BUCKATUNNA	56.3	51.6	43.0	47.3	0.0	0.0	0.8	1.1	8.7	8.8	8.1	7.3	5.7	25.8	24.6	9.7	1.3	70.1	34.0	47.5	52.5
39323	CHUNKY	83.5	80.5	13.1	14.4	0.3	0.5	3.0	4.6	6.3	6.5	6.8	7.0	5.2	26.3	27.9	12.4	1.7	76.2	39.4	50.5	49.5
39325	COLLINSVILLE	91.2	88.7	8.0	10.0	0.3	0.5	0.7	1.0	6.7	6.9	7.1	7.0	5.3	26.2	29.0	10.5	1.2	75.0	38.7	49.6	50.4
39326	DALEVILLE	67.8	62.0	31.1	36.6	0.4	0.4	0.7	1.0	5.8	5.8	6.4	7.0	4.8	26.4	29.5	13.2	1.0	77.7	41.2	48.8	51.2
39327	DECATUR	71.5	68.2	27.5	30.4	0.2	0.2	0.7	1.1	6.7	6.7	6.7	12.1	7.7	24.0	23.7	11.0	1.5	76.4	33.9	49.8	50.2
39328	DE KALB	40.1	36.8	58.5	61.5	0.2	0.2	0.8	1.0	7.0	7.1	6.8	7.8	6.5	23.2	25.8	12.3	3.6	74.6	38.1	47.6	52.4
39330	ENTERPRISE	72.0	67.8	27.3	31.3	0.1	0.2	0.5	0.7	6.2	6.3	6.6	7.2	5.2	25.2	28.8	12.7	1.8	76.5	40.2	49.1	50.9
39332	HICKORY	69.4	66.8	28.8	30.7	0.2	0.2	1.4	2.3	7.1	7.3	7.3	7.2	5.4	25.3	26.3	12.2	2.0	74.0	38.3	50.1	49.9
39335	LAUDERDALE	65.1	61.7	33.1	35.9	0.5	0.6	1.1	1.6	6.6	6.5	6.5	6.6	6.0	26.9	28.2	11.8	1.0	76.9	38.2	50.0	50.0
39336	LAWRENCE	62.2	58.0	35.0	38.6	0.1	0.1	0.6	0.8	6.7	6.8	6.9	6.7	5.1	27.0	26.8	12.3	1.7	75.5	38.4	48.6	51.4
39337	LITTLE ROCK	91.6	90.1	8.0	9.3	0.0	0.0	0.5	0.7	6.4	6.7	6.9	6.1	4.3	26.7	27.9	13.4	1.7	76.3	39.8	51.6	48.4
39338	LOUIN	48.0	45.6	51.3	53.7	0.0	0.0	0.6	0.6	7.4	7.5	7.4	7.1	5.7	25.4	25.9	11.6	1.9	73.3	37.3	48.2	51.8
39339	LOUISVILLE	53.7	50.6	44.7	47.3	0.1	0.1	1.2	1.8	6.9	6.8	6.8	6.7	6.6	24.9	26.1	12.8	2.4	75.4	37.8	48.8	51.2
39341	MACON	31.9	28.9	66.9	69.6	0.2	0.2	1.1	1.3	7.7	7.7	7.5	7.4	6.4	24.8	25.2	11.0	2.1	72.5	35.6	48.2	51.8
39342	MARION	52.0	45.2	46.8	53.3	0.4	0.5	1.6	2.2	9.2	8.8	7.6	7.7	7.4	28.4	20.4	8.4	2.0	69.8	30.7	45.6	54.4
39345	NEWTON	47.7	43.8	51.3	54.8	0.3	0.5	0.8	1.1	7.6	7.6	7.4	7.4	5.6	24.1	25.2	12.2	3.0	73.2	36.9	46.9	53.1
39346	NOXAPATER	60.7	57.2	38.6	41.9	0.0	0.0	1.0	1.4	6.6	6.6	6.9	7.0	5.8	23.7	28.0	13.5	1.9	75.5	40.0	49.3	50.7
39347	PACHUTA	50.9	46.9	48.7	52.6	0.0	0.0	0.6	0.8	6.6	6.8	6.8	6.8	4.9	24.7	28.8	12.3	2.0	75.6	40.0	47.5	52.5
39348	PAULDING	31.0	29.4	68.8	70.4	0.0	0.0	0.4	0.6	7.0	7.8	7.6	9.4	6.2	23.8	24.4	11.3	2.5	71.5	35.5	48.7	51.3
39350	PHILADELPHIA	64.8	60.6	19.7	20.7	0.2	0.3	1.2	1.6	7.7	7.7	7.6	7.1	5.7	25.4	25.0	11.6	2.2	72.5	36.3	47.9	52.1
39352	PORTERVILLE	29.0	26.1	70.0	72.3	0.1	0.1	0.9	1.1	7.9	7.8	7.8	7.1	5.4	25.9	25.6	10.8	1.8	72.0	36.2	47.9	52.1
39354	PRESTON	49.3	47.2	43.3	45.0	0.1	0.1	0.7	1.0	5.9	6.1	6.3	6.7	5.3	24.3	29.1	13.9	2.4	77.6	41.5	48.1	51.9
39355	QUITMAN	69.7	66.8	29.5	32.2	0.1	0.2	0.7	1.0	6.5	6.6	6.7	6.6	5.2	24.0	27.2	14.4	2.8	76.2	40.5	47.9	52.1
39356	ROSE HILL	52.4	50.3	47.0	49.1	0.0	0.0	1.4	1.4	6.7	6.9	6.9	6.8	4.8	25.1	27.8	12.4	2.4	75.3	39.4	50.4	49.6
39358	SCOOBA	39.5	36.0	59.7	63.0	0.0	0.0	0.6	0.7	5.5	5.6	5.6	17.2	10.9	22.3	20.3	10.2	2.4	78.6	29.3	50.0	50.0
39359	SEBASTOPOL	89.3	87.2	9.4	11.0	0.0	0.0	1.3	2.2	7.0	7.0	7.0	7.0	7.0	26.9	26.0	10.6	1.3	75.3	35.9	51.1	48.9
39360	SHUBUTA	45.1	41.3	54.2	57.8	0.1	0.1	0.7	0.9	7.2	7.4	7.5	7.3	5.4	24.6	27.7	11.1	1.8	73.3	37.5	47.7	52.3
39361	SHUQUALAK	33.7	31.2	64.5	66.5	0.0	0.0	1.1	1.6	7.8	7.7	7.6	7.9	5.7	25.0	26.4	10.1	1.7	71.9	35.3	50.3	49.7
39362	STATE LINE	52.4	48.6	47.2	50.9	0.0	0.0	0.3	0.3	8.4	8.4	8.1	7.8	6.7	25.5	24.5	9.3	1.3	70.3	33.5	48.5	51.5
39363	STONEWALL	74.7	71.0	24.5	27.8	0.1	0.1	0.7	1.1	7.9	7.9	7.9	7.6	5.0	25.3	25.1	11.9	1.3	71.5	36.7	47.8	52.2
39364	TOOMSUBA	59.2	53.2	39.8	45.4	0.2	0.3	0.5	0.8	6.2	6.2	7.2	8.4	6.1	25.6	28.1	10.2	1.9	75.2	37.5	47.9	52.1
39365	UNION	76.3	72.8	22.6	25.6	0.1	0.1	0.7	0.9	6.7	6.5	6.9	6.9	5.5	23.5	26.0	14.7	3.3	75.3	40.1	48.0	52.0
39366	VOSSBURG	20.8	19.1	79.0	80.7	0.0	0.0	0.2	0.2	7.1	8.0	7.8	10.6	6.8	23.4	23.8	10.3	2.2	70.2	33.2	47.8	52.2
39367	WAYNESBORO	59.9	57.3	39.3	41.7	0.2	0.3	0.7	0.9	7.5	7.7	7.5	7.5	6.1	25.1	25.7	11.1	1.7	72.6	35.9	47.7	52.3
39401	HATTIESBURG	49.2	45.7	48.6	51.3	0.8	1.2	1.4	1.9	7.5	6.6	6.0	7.2	12.9	27.7	21.0	9.0	2.1	76.1	30.5	47.6	52.4
39402	HATTIESBURG	82.8	79.6	14.8	17.1	1.1	1.5	1.2	1.7	7.0	6.7	6.6	6.7	7.5	28.6	25.3	10.1	1.4	75.7	35.1	47.5	52.5
39406	HATTIESBURG	57.3	49.2	39.0	45.5	2.6	3.9	1.6	2.3	2.6	0.9	0.3	31.0	52.8	10.8	1.2	0.4	0.0	95.8	21.4	39.3	60.7
39421	BASSFIELD	46.2	43.1	52.9	55.7	0.3	0.3	0.8	1.0	7.7	7.8	7.5	6.9	5.7	26.6	25.5	10.4	2.0	72.7	35.4	48.9	51.1
39422	BAY SPRINGS	48.8	47.0	50.5	52.2	0.1	0.1	0.6	0.6	7.0	7.1	7.1	7.3	5.5	24.7	26.3	12.2	2.7	74.1	38.1	47.0	53.0
39423	BEAUMONT	61.2	60.0	37.4	38.6	0.0	0.0	0.6	0.6	7.6	8.3	7.2	8.0	6.2	26.9	24.9	10.0	1.0	71.7	34.6	48.3	51.7
39425	BROOKLYN	86.5	84.2	12.6	14.7	0.0	0.0	1.3	1.7	7.0	7.0	7.0	6.4	5.3	27.1	27.0	11.8	1.2	74.9	37.4	50.0	50.0
39426	CARRIERE	94.1	92.4	3.6	4.4	0.2	0.3	1.5	2.3	7.0	7.0	7.3	6.7	5.3	25.9	27.6	12.0	1.1	74.5	38.0	49.4	50.6
39427	CARSON	48.8	45.8	49.9	52.6	0.2	0.2	0.4	0.5	6.9	7.2	7.1	6.7	5.6	24.5	27.7	12.4	1.9	74.7	38.3	48.3	51.7
39428	COLLINS	53.0	50.1	46.0	48.5	0.2	0.2	1.0	1.3	7.8	8.0	8.0	7.7	5.8	24.7	24.1	12.0	2.0	71.7	35.5	48.2	51.8
39429	COLUMBIA	63.0	59.9	35.8	38.4	0.3	0.4	0.6	0.8	6.8	6.8	7.8	7.3	6.2	24.8	25.7	12.2	2.5	74.1	37.3	49.0	51.0
39437	ELLISVILLE	82.6	79.1	16.0	18.8	0.2	0.3	1.1	1.7	6.2	6.4	6.4	8.9	6.5	26.2	26.1	11.8	1.6	77.2	37.0	49.9	50.1
39439	HEIDELBERG	43.6	41.7	54.3	55.8	0.0	0.0	0.6	0.7	7.2	7.3	7.3	7.2	5.8	25.0	26.9	11.6	1.7	73.9	36.7	48.0	52.0
39440	LAUREL	47.6	43.9	47.9	49.5	0.6	0.8	3.8	5.8	7.6	7.2	7.0	7.1	6.3	25.4	23.4	13.1	2.9	73.8	36.4	47.0	53.0
39443	LAUREL	82.6	79.3	15.8	18.5	0.1	0.2	1.1	1.8	6.7	7.0	7.0	6.4	5.1	26.0	28.0	12.3	1.5	75.4	38.8	49.1	50.9
	MISSISSIPPI	61.4	59.6	36.3	37.4	0.7	0.9	1.4	2.0	7.2	7.1	7.0	7.5	7.1	26.4	25.3	10.6	1.7	74.3	35.6	48.6	51.4
	UNITED STATES	75.1	72.0	12.3	12.7	3.8	4.6	12.5	15.7	6.8	6.7	6.6	7.1	6.9	27.0	26.0	10.9	1.9	75.7	36.9	49.2	50.8

ZIP CODE #	POST OFFICE NAME	2009 Per Capita Income	2009 HH Income Base	2009 HOUSEHOLD INCOME DISTRIBUTION (%) Less than $25,000	$25,000 to $49,999	$50,000 to $99,999	$100,000 to $149,999	$150,000 or More	MEDIAN HOUSEHOLD INCOME 2009	2014	2009 National Centile	2009 State Centile	2009 Home Value Base	2009 HOME VALUE DISTRIBUTION (%) Less than $50,000	$50,000 to $89,999	$90,000 to $174,999	$175,000 to $399,999	$400,000 or More	2009 Median Home Value
39146	PICKENS	11812	1117	52.6	27.3	15.8	2.7	1.7	22887	23294	2	8	888	51.5	33.7	12.4	1.7	0.8	48713
39149	PINOLA	14800	693	40.4	34.5	18.9	4.9	1.3	30257	31482	8	37	612	47.2	32.4	16.0	3.4	1.0	52152
39150	PORT GIBSON	13756	2687	48.5	26.0	18.8	5.3	1.4	26484	26821	4	19	2095	38.5	35.0	20.3	5.2	1.0	59179
39152	PULASKI	18026	221	27.6	37.1	27.6	7.7	0.0	42170	41418	40	88	183	37.7	31.1	23.5	6.0	1.6	63214
39153	RALEIGH	17803	3367	35.0	29.1	29.6	4.2	2.1	35350	35840	19	71	2900	39.3	27.2	25.2	7.1	1.2	65257
39154	RAYMOND	20743	3229	20.7	29.3	37.4	9.9	2.7	49986	48348	61	95	2630	18.3	21.3	36.5	21.6	2.3	110135
39156	REDWOOD	21615	126	32.5	31.0	26.2	7.9	2.4	39302	39685	31	82	105	34.3	21.9	30.5	10.5	2.9	79286
39157	RIDGELAND	33579	12317	18.0	27.8	37.6	9.0	7.6	54171	54564	70	97	5890	6.2	10.1	42.1	31.6	10.1	151066
39159	ROLLING FORK	14471	1374	48.7	25.8	19.9	3.3	2.2	25809	26310	4	16	870	40.5	35.4	21.4	2.8	0.0	58469
39160	SALLIS	13950	1018	45.8	27.6	23.4	2.4	0.9	27976	28473	6	26	869	54.0	30.0	12.4	3.0	0.6	45893
39162	SATARTIA	15034	196	36.7	33.2	24.0	5.1	1.0	33265	33417	14	58	163	42.3	25.8	27.0	4.9	0.0	62083
39166	SILVER CITY	13599	288	44.1	33.3	16.7	4.5	1.4	27239	26854	5	22	191	37.2	31.9	21.5	9.4	0.0	73800
39168	TAYLORSVILLE	16265	1801	35.8	33.1	24.9	4.4	1.8	34336	34329	16	64	1530	34.3	34.7	24.1	6.7	0.1	66667
39169	TCHULA	8501	1101	68.0	19.9	8.0	2.0	2.1	13714	15311	1	1	654	52.3	36.7	9.8	0.2	1.1	47458
39170	TERRY	22547	2880	27.0	26.4	33.2	9.4	4.0	46816	46739	54	94	2575	13.7	25.7	33.2	24.3	3.0	116744
39175	UTICA	16541	1778	31.6	33.1	26.7	6.9	1.7	37685	39942	26	78	1479	34.3	30.7	20.4	12.3	2.2	68673
39176	VAIDEN	19154	1034	47.9	22.3	20.1	5.9	3.8	27029	27994	5	21	830	43.0	29.2	21.7	5.8	0.4	58406
39177	VALLEY PARK	14970	60	48.3	18.3	30.0	1.7	1.7	27345	28592	5	23	39	41.0	23.1	23.1	12.8	0.0	58750
39179	VAUGHAN	14185	458	43.0	27.7	22.1	4.6	2.6	30320	29865	9	38	387	38.2	33.6	22.0	6.2	0.0	67969
39180	VICKSBURG	20986	12762	30.3	27.6	31.0	8.2	2.9	42951	42543	42	89	8726	24.5	27.7	35.5	10.7	1.6	87210
39183	VICKSBURG	18036	5956	35.9	29.9	24.1	7.9	2.2	34499	34637	17	65	3980	34.0	20.9	30.4	13.1	1.6	79952
39189	WALNUT GROVE	15720	805	39.5	32.3	25.0	2.2	1.0	31507	31674	11	50	663	29.9	44.3	23.4	2.1	0.3	66438
39191	WESSON	16101	3076	35.8	30.3	27.0	5.6	1.3	34332	35481	16	64	2589	36.1	28.9	27.3	5.9	1.8	68701
39192	WEST	17884	799	40.1	31.8	19.5	5.5	3.1	31055	30430	10	44	679	42.4	33.3	19.7	3.2	1.3	57153
39194	YAZOO CITY	13030	6312	48.6	26.2	19.9	3.7	1.6	26135	27500	4	17	3971	37.7	33.8	22.4	5.7	0.3	62549
39201	JACKSON	9000	85	68.2	25.9	5.9	0.0	0.0	14716	15639	1	1	15	73.3	26.7	0.0	0.0	0.0	35833
39202	JACKSON	20754	3749	46.0	28.2	17.7	4.2	3.9	27187	27139	5	22	1126	21.4	12.5	38.4	23.1	4.6	127273
39203	JACKSON	9224	2431	66.1	23.2	8.8	1.6	0.3	16858	17771	1	2	886	60.6	33.0	4.9	0.8	0.8	43856
39204	JACKSON	14405	6979	47.1	29.8	19.4	2.3	1.5	26872	26942	5	20	3178	26.0	55.4	17.1	1.4	0.1	65353
39206	JACKSON	18621	9775	31.9	33.0	26.6	5.8	2.6	37583	40049	25	77	5351	8.6	51.2	34.4	4.4	1.3	82267
39208	PEARL	18935	11320	25.7	29.9	35.8	7.1	1.5	44150	42060	46	90	7742	20.6	29.9	37.0	11.2	1.3	89372
39209	JACKSON	12433	11207	44.4	31.7	20.6	2.5	0.8	28643	28131	6	28	5934	31.0	52.0	13.8	2.6	0.6	60978
39210	JACKSON	5921	0	0.0	0.0	0.0	0.0	0.0	0	0	0	0	0	0.0	0.0	0.0	0.0	0.0	0
39211	JACKSON	41607	10538	15.8	25.1	34.2	11.3	13.6	60853	59977	79	99	7502	1.3	12.0	49.2	27.8	9.7	143964
39212	JACKSON	18529	11591	24.8	32.8	36.1	5.0	1.3	44498	44590	47	91	8646	11.9	49.1	34.3	4.5	0.1	81141
39213	JACKSON	12756	9613	50.5	28.0	17.6	2.9	1.0	24618	25586	3	10	5348	35.7	42.2	19.3	2.7	0.1	59387
39216	JACKSON	21871	1537	40.5	29.0	18.9	6.0	5.7	31271	29908	10	47	756	6.2	25.1	41.4	19.6	7.7	120413
39217	JACKSON	1190	0	0.0	0.0	0.0	0.0	0.0	0	0	0	0	0	0.0	0.0	0.0	0.0	0.0	0
39218	RICHLAND	19433	2654	24.5	31.6	37.2	5.8	1.0	45287	42406	49	91	1963	30.1	24.4	38.8	6.7	0.1	83024
39232	FLOWOOD	28097	3486	14.7	25.0	44.3	13.1	3.0	57512	61571	75	98	2192	8.8	6.9	58.8	22.5	2.9	135063
39272	BYRAM	24433	4607	12.7	24.2	49.4	11.7	1.9	60181	59399	78	98	4209	5.3	16.2	65.8	11.6	1.2	115087
39301	MERIDIAN	14758	10598	48.8	27.2	19.4	3.6	1.0	25926	26978	4	16	6551	37.8	32.1	24.4	5.2	0.5	64469
39305	MERIDIAN	26247	8072	25.5	27.3	33.0	9.2	5.0	47688	45998	56	95	5389	11.9	22.8	42.5	18.2	4.5	110855
39307	MERIDIAN	15225	6568	45.0	28.3	22.6	3.1	1.0	28688	28677	6	29	4409	27.4	49.0	19.9	3.4	0.3	65867
39309	MERIDIAN	3991	15	40.0	26.7	26.7	6.7	0.0	32320	32320	12	55	9	22.2	33.3	44.4	0.0	0.0	85000
39320	BAILEY	20127	565	26.4	31.5	31.7	9.7	0.7	42739	42305	42	89	490	20.0	36.1	31.0	11.6	1.2	85238
39322	BUCKATUNNA	12970	756	45.5	32.0	18.3	3.6	0.7	26563	27234	4	19	672	57.4	17.9	18.8	5.4	0.6	42647
39323	CHUNKY	17337	491	33.4	27.3	33.8	5.5	0.0	37836	36829	26	78	432	38.2	25.9	29.4	5.3	1.2	66667
39325	COLLINSVILLE	19807	1888	27.6	25.6	39.0	6.2	1.6	46392	42516	53	93	1662	17.2	29.9	33.3	17.2	2.4	95714
39326	DALEVILLE	21882	185	26.5	25.4	30.3	16.2	1.6	45585	45585	50	92	168	22.6	19.6	34.5	17.9	5.4	103571
39327	DECATUR	16694	1624	39.5	27.0	28.0	4.4	1.2	34632	35578	17	66	1287	31.2	34.0	29.1	4.9	0.8	73000
39328	DE KALB	14637	1910	48.3	29.6	18.0	3.3	0.7	26462	27314	4	18	1571	41.4	38.2	17.6	2.1	0.7	58018
39330	ENTERPRISE	16246	1055	41.0	30.0	23.2	4.9	0.8	30377	30785	9	39	878	43.7	27.1	24.3	4.7	0.2	59649
39332	HICKORY	16809	728	36.7	31.0	27.6	4.0	0.7	32294	31904	12	54	620	42.1	27.4	24.7	3.7	2.1	60426
39335	LAUDERDALE	19043	1396	29.1	34.5	30.5	4.6	1.3	40728	41315	35	85	1152	30.9	39.4	25.2	3.6	0.9	68047
39336	LAWRENCE	14635	341	33.7	40.5	23.5	1.8	0.6	32419	31776	12	55	302	40.7	34.1	22.2	3.0	0.0	59655
39337	LITTLE ROCK	18306	722	35.5	27.7	32.4	2.9	1.5	36253	36110	21	74	651	35.5	35.3	22.7	5.2	1.2	67315
39338	LOUIN	14973	989	49.2	27.4	19.4	2.3	1.6	25649	26608	4	15	873	49.5	24.7	20.7	3.7	1.4	50692
39339	LOUISVILLE	16698	6263	39.2	30.2	24.7	4.3	1.6	32535	32818	12	56	4846	29.6	35.6	26.2	7.0	1.7	72783
39341	MACON	14320	2451	49.1	26.8	18.3	4.0	1.8	25723	26353	4	15	1879	45.3	30.8	15.3	3.7	0.9	54116
39342	MARION	13047	574	50.2	24.6	23.2	1.2	0.9	24898	26081	3	11	247	20.2	42.1	32.4	5.3	0.0	78478
39345	NEWTON	16530	2621	41.1	30.2	23.1	4.2	1.4	30998	30823	10	44	1960	35.7	35.8	24.4	4.1	0.0	64688
39346	NOXAPATER	15906	958	38.9	33.8	22.3	4.4	0.5	31408	31352	10	49	808	34.5	33.0	27.1	4.7	0.6	69848
39347	PACHUTA	13795	357	50.1	26.6	18.2	3.6	1.4	24911	25945	3	12	306	33.0	37.3	27.8	1.6	0.3	68857
39348	PAULDING	14062	192	48.4	24.0	23.4	2.6	1.6	26721	27474	4	20	173	50.3	23.1	22.0	4.6	0.0	49792
39350	PHILADELPHIA	16729	11389	39.2	30.2	24.6	4.2	1.8	32874	33281	13	57	9005	28.9	36.0	24.9	8.1	2.1	73071
39352	PORTERVILLE	14770	356	43.5	26.7	24.4	5.3	0.0	31325	31179	10	47	321	38.6	37.4	21.5	1.6	0.9	56887
39354	PRESTON	15197	971	46.9	28.7	19.8	2.1	2.6	27879	28255	5	25	862	36.8	37.1	19.8	5.8	0.5	61429
39355	QUITMAN	17518	3243	38.2	30.4	26.6	3.4	1.4	33636	34575	15	60	2669	38.0	31.3	25.4	5.1	0.2	64912
39356	ROSE HILL	15032	627	45.9	28.7	20.7	2.7	1.9	28006	28019	6	26	546	31.9	36.1	26.6	4.8	0.7	72807
39358	SCOOBA	14390	698	45.7	28.4	20.1	5.3	0.6	28608	28443	6	28	547	35.5	34.9	26.3	2.0	1.3	60104
39359	SEBASTOPOL	20198	106	38.7	34.9	21.7	1.9	2.8	30589	30703	9	41	82	51.2	25.6	19.5	3.7	0.0	48889
39360	SHUBUTA	13663	1626	46.9	29.6	18.5	3.7	1.2	26902	28248	5	21	1409	47.4	30.9	16.7	4.2	0.8	54620
39361	SHUQUALAK	18047	481	42.2	25.6	23.7	6.2	2.3	31988	31030	11	52	390	48.2	26.9	17.4	4.1	3.3	51556
39362	STATE LINE	13008	1073	43.2	32.4	21.5	2.3	0.5	28695	28560	6	30	924	48.8	27.3	20.7	2.6	0.6	51594
39363	STONEWALL	16939	736	41.7	26.8	26.6	3.5	1.4	30687	30812	9	42	592	45.8	30.7	19.9	2.5	1.0	54630
39364	TOOMSUBA	17123	1232	33.0	34.0	27.9	3.8	1.3	36668	36306	23	75	1011	38.0	27.0	22.5	10.9	1.7	62500
39365	UNION	17671	1561	40.2	28.1	25.4	3.6	2.8	31575	31268	11	51	1232	36.6	33.0	25.6	4.4	0.3	67653
39366	VOSSBURG	13144	579	47.7	25.6	22.6	3.3	0.9	27426	27742	5	23	525	51.2	26.7	18.3	3.2	0.6	48968
39367	WAYNESBORO	15690	6146	41.0	32.8	20.0	4.3	1.9	30305	30482	9	38	5065	46.3	27.3	20.1	5.7	0.6	54607
39401	HATTIESBURG	14660	17526	47.8	30.5	17.9	2.7	1.0	26441	27880	4	18	8640	29.2	32.7	28.2	9.5	0.5	74013
39402	HATTIESBURG	27260	13844	23.5	25.7	34.1	10.0	6.7	50640	50395	63	96	9692	11.5	12.0	37.9	30.3	8.4	144907
39406	HATTIESBURG	10091	530	66.8	27.9	5.3	0.0	0.0	14206	16225	1	1	11	9.1	72.7	18.2	0.0	0.0	68333
39421	BASSFIELD	12926	1446	50.1	29.9	16.6	2.6	0.8	24929	25137	3	12	1246	46.9	33.7	17.1	1.8	0.5	53071
39422	BAY SPRINGS	15122	2264	46.7	25.9	22.7	3.4	1.2	29460	29591	7	32	1897	39.5	32.7	19.3	7.2	1.2	61442
39423	BEAUMONT	14216	1017	41.0	37.2	17.6	3.6	0.6	29722	30721	8	34	856	47.1	25.2	22.0	5.6	0.1	54630
39425	BROOKLYN	14993	675	44.4	28.9	20.7	5.8	0.1	28676	29951	6	29	588	32.3	27.7	32.1	5.6	2.2	76458
39426	CARRIERE	19315	6415	29.1	30.5	31.6	6.5	2.3	41904	40746	39	87	5503	16.4	21.1	39.5	20.4	2.6	114586
39427	CARSON	12994	590	50.0	32.7	14.4	2.0	0.8	25000	25366	3	13	508	47.0	33.7	17.3	1.8	0.2	52941
39428	COLLINS	16939	4126	42.6	30.9	20.5	3.2	2.8	30000	29980	8	36	3417	38.9	30.3	24.8	5.5	0.6	64442
39429	COLUMBIA	15126	6555	46.9	27.1	20.4	3.9	1.7	27924	27977	6	26	5021	30.2	32.5	28.9	7.2	1.2	72475
39437	ELLISVILLE	17129	4399	33.1	32.6	27.9	4.4	2.0	35130	35384	18	70	3575	31.9	32.7	24.6	9.3	1.4	70729
39439	HEIDELBERG	13465	1850	45.7	31.3	20.1	2.4	0.6	28795	28714	6	30	1573	39.5	37.6	18.8	2.5	1.7	61076
39440	LAUREL	17479	7986	43.1	29.6	20.2	4.2	3.0	29683	29576	8	34	4780	34.6	34.1	21.9	7.2	2.2	64792
39443	LAUREL	17377	9223	32.4	35.3	26.3	4.8	1.2	34916	35268	17	68	7729	33.3	29.1	28.1	8.3	1.2	73395
	MISSISSIPPI	18363		35.3	29.0	27.5	5.7	2.5	36311	37046				25.4	28.2	31.6	12.7	2.1	84642
	UNITED STATES	27277		20.9	24.4	35.3	11.7	7.6	54719	56938				9.3	13.1	31.6	32.6	13.5	162279

ZIP CODE #	POST OFFICE NAME	FINANCIAL SERVICES: Auto Loan	FINANCIAL SERVICES: Home Loan	FINANCIAL SERVICES: Invest-ments	FINANCIAL SERVICES: Retire-ment Plans	THE HOME: Home Improvements: Home Repair	THE HOME: Home Improvements: Lawn & Garden	THE HOME: Furnishings: Computers & Hardware-Personal	THE HOME: Furnishings: Major Appli-ances	THE HOME: Furnishings: TV, Radio, Sound Equip-ment	THE HOME: Furnishings: Furni-ture	ENTERTAINMENT: Dine out/ Carry out	ENTERTAINMENT: Sports Equip-ment	ENTERTAINMENT: Fees & Tickets	ENTERTAINMENT: Toys & Games	ENTERTAINMENT: Travel	ENTERTAINMENT: Cable TV	PERSONAL: Apparel & Services	PERSONAL: Auto Repairs	PERSONAL: Health Insur-ance	PERSONAL: Pets & Supplies
39146	PICKENS	63	41	61	39	41	62	44	56	51	42	50	43	33	52	41	57	33	52	59	68
39149	PINOLA	73	49	68	46	49	71	52	64	59	50	58	50	40	61	48	66	39	61	68	79
39150	PORT GIBSON	67	48	62	46	47	66	50	60	57	49	56	46	41	58	47	63	37	58	65	74
39152	PULASKI	84	60	69	59	60	80	63	73	70	61	68	56	50	73	57	76	46	69	77	89
39153	RALEIGH	82	58	71	56	58	79	61	72	68	58	66	55	48	70	56	75	45	68	77	88
39154	RAYMOND	89	86	83	86	86	90	82	87	84	83	83	65	80	85	82	86	57	84	88	103
39156	REDWOOD	84	67	84	66	68	87	67	80	72	64	71	61	58	73	66	78	48	75	82	95
39157	RIDGELAND	108	96	85	100	91	87	107	94	104	109	106	78	102	108	98	100	74	101	91	114
39159	ROLLING FORK	69	48	64	47	48	68	52	62	60	50	58	47	42	60	49	66	39	60	69	76
39160	SALLIS	71	47	68	44	47	70	50	62	57	47	56	49	38	58	46	64	37	59	66	77
39162	SATARTIA	77	53	77	51	54	77	55	70	62	52	61	53	43	62	53	69	40	65	73	84
39166	SILVER CITY	72	47	70	44	47	71	50	64	58	48	57	50	38	59	47	65	38	60	67	78
39168	TAYLORSVILLE	80	55	75	53	55	78	58	71	66	55	64	55	45	67	55	72	43	67	76	87
39169	TCHULA	43	29	32	30	28	38	36	36	41	35	40	28	30	41	31	45	28	39	42	46
39170	TERRY	95	89	89	89	87	99	84	92	87	83	86	71	80	89	84	90	59	88	93	110
39175	UTICA	81	65	76	63	64	82	65	75	72	64	71	56	57	72	62	77	47	72	80	91
39176	VAIDEN	85	57	81	54	57	84	60	75	69	57	67	58	46	70	57	77	45	71	80	92
39177	VALLEY PARK	72	51	74	50	53	73	53	67	59	49	57	50	42	58	52	64	38	62	70	80
39179	VAUGHAN	80	52	77	49	52	78	56	70	64	53	63	55	42	65	52	72	42	66	74	86
39180	VICKSBURG	82	72	70	71	70	79	75	77	78	74	77	58	69	79	71	81	53	77	81	92
39183	VICKSBURG	70	63	59	64	61	70	64	66	69	65	68	50	62	69	62	72	47	67	71	80
39189	WALNUT GROVE	75	49	72	46	49	74	53	66	61	50	59	51	40	62	49	68	39	62	70	81
39191	WESSON	80	56	72	53	56	78	58	70	66	56	64	54	46	68	54	72	43	66	74	86
39192	WEST	83	57	81	54	58	83	60	75	68	56	66	58	46	68	57	75	44	70	79	91
39194	YAZOO CITY	60	47	50	47	46	58	51	54	57	51	56	40	46	56	47	61	38	55	61	66
39201	JACKSON	23	17	21	20	18	21	28	23	30	25	30	18	25	26	25	32	21	28	32	29
39202	JACKSON	62	47	45	51	45	49	62	53	64	61	64	43	56	64	54	65	45	60	57	66
39203	JACKSON	37	28	27	29	27	34	33	33	38	34	37	23	30	37	29	42	25	35	40	41
39204	JACKSON	56	44	38	46	40	47	54	48	57	53	57	38	49	58	47	59	39	54	53	60
39206	JACKSON	73	64	56	66	59	65	71	65	73	71	74	51	68	74	65	74	51	71	70	81
39208	PEARL	76	71	61	71	68	72	74	71	74	72	74	55	70	76	69	75	51	73	74	86
39209	JACKSON	55	45	39	46	41	49	51	48	55	51	55	37	48	55	45	58	38	52	54	60
39210	JACKSON	0	0	0	0	0	0	0	0	0	0	0	0	0	0	0	0	0	0	0	0
39211	JACKSON	124	134	134	137	136	133	129	129	128	133	129	97	137	127	135	128	91	129	132	150
39212	JACKSON	74	72	60	72	68	70	72	70	73	72	73	54	70	75	68	73	50	71	72	84
39213	JACKSON	50	41	39	42	39	46	47	45	52	48	51	33	44	50	43	55	35	49	53	56
39216	JACKSON	67	65	62	67	64	69	68	66	72	69	71	50	70	70	67	74	50	69	75	80
39217	JACKSON	0	0	0	0	0	0	0	0	0	0	0	0	0	0	0	0	0	0	0	0
39218	RICHLAND	79	73	64	70	71	74	70	73	72	73	72	54	66	75	66	73	49	71	73	87
39232	FLOWOOD	100	94	81	95	88	83	97	89	94	101	96	73	94	99	91	90	67	92	84	106
39272	BYRAM	99	103	85	99	96	89	93	93	89	99	91	72	92	95	90	87	63	89	85	108
39301	MERIDIAN	57	43	45	43	42	52	49	50	53	48	53	38	42	53	44	57	36	51	56	62
39305	MERIDIAN	88	86	83	87	85	89	87	87	89	87	89	65	87	89	86	91	62	88	92	102
39307	MERIDIAN	59	47	49	47	46	58	52	55	57	50	56	41	46	57	48	61	38	55	61	67
39309	MERIDIAN	65	52	45	52	50	52	57	54	58	58	59	43	51	63	51	58	40	56	53	65
39320	BAILEY	82	76	67	73	74	77	71	76	74	74	74	55	68	77	68	76	50	73	76	90
39322	BUCKATUNNA	65	44	59	42	44	63	47	57	53	45	52	44	36	54	43	59	34	54	60	70
39323	CHUNKY	80	57	67	56	57	76	59	70	66	58	65	53	48	68	55	72	43	66	74	85
39325	COLLINSVILLE	84	71	75	69	71	81	69	78	73	70	73	57	62	75	67	77	49	74	79	92
39326	DALEVILLE	76	90	80	89	87	89	78	82	79	79	80	61	87	81	84	81	56	80	85	95
39327	DECATUR	75	54	71	52	54	74	57	69	63	53	62	52	46	63	54	69	41	65	72	83
39328	DE KALB	63	44	58	42	43	62	47	56	54	46	53	42	38	54	44	60	35	54	61	69
39330	ENTERPRISE	74	50	71	47	50	73	53	66	60	50	59	51	40	61	49	67	39	62	69	80
39332	HICKORY	75	52	66	50	52	73	55	66	62	53	61	51	43	64	50	68	40	62	70	80
39335	LAUDERDALE	78	61	66	59	60	72	62	69	67	62	66	52	54	70	58	71	45	67	70	83
39336	LAWRENCE	68	49	56	48	49	65	51	59	57	50	55	46	41	59	46	62	37	56	63	72
39337	LITTLE ROCK	79	56	79	55	58	80	58	73	64	54	63	55	46	64	57	71	42	67	76	87
39338	LOUIN	71	47	69	44	46	70	50	63	57	47	56	49	37	58	46	64	37	59	66	77
39339	LOUISVILLE	73	53	66	52	53	71	57	66	63	54	62	50	47	64	54	69	42	64	71	80
39341	MACON	67	45	61	43	45	65	49	59	57	48	55	45	39	57	45	63	37	57	64	72
39342	MARION	48	40	37	40	37	43	49	44	52	44	51	35	44	51	42	54	36	48	48	54
39345	NEWTON	72	50	66	48	50	71	54	65	61	51	60	49	43	61	50	67	40	62	70	78
39346	NOXAPATER	73	48	71	45	48	72	51	64	59	48	57	50	38	60	48	65	38	60	68	79
39347	PACHUTA	64	42	62	39	42	63	45	56	52	42	50	44	33	52	42	57	33	53	59	69
39348	PAULDING	70	46	67	43	45	68	49	61	56	46	55	48	36	57	45	63	36	58	65	75
39350	PHILADELPHIA	73	55	63	54	54	70	58	65	64	57	63	49	50	65	54	69	43	64	70	79
39352	PORTERVILLE	71	46	68	43	46	69	49	62	57	47	55	48	37	58	46	63	37	58	65	76
39354	PRESTON	70	46	67	43	46	69	49	62	57	47	55	48	37	58	46	63	37	58	65	76
39355	QUITMAN	76	55	71	53	55	76	57	69	64	54	63	53	46	65	54	70	42	65	74	83
39356	ROSE HILL	69	45	66	42	45	68	48	61	55	46	54	47	36	56	45	62	36	57	64	75
39358	SCOOBA	70	46	68	43	46	69	49	62	57	47	55	48	37	57	46	63	37	58	65	76
39359	SEBASTOPOL	78	56	64	54	56	74	58	68	65	57	63	52	47	67	53	71	43	64	72	83
39360	SHUBUTA	66	43	63	41	43	64	46	58	53	44	52	45	35	54	43	59	34	54	61	71
39361	SHUQUALAK	85	55	82	52	55	83	59	75	68	56	67	58	44	70	55	76	44	70	79	92
39362	STATE LINE	65	43	62	41	43	64	46	57	53	44	52	45	35	54	43	59	34	54	61	71
39363	STONEWALL	76	50	74	48	51	75	54	68	62	51	60	53	41	62	50	69	40	63	71	83
39364	TOOMSUBA	78	57	70	55	57	75	59	69	65	58	64	53	48	67	55	71	43	66	72	84
39365	UNION	79	55	76	53	56	79	58	72	66	55	64	55	45	66	55	72	43	67	76	87
39366	VOSSBURG	68	44	66	42	44	67	47	60	55	45	53	47	35	56	44	61	35	56	63	73
39367	WAYNESBORO	73	50	67	48	50	71	53	64	60	51	59	50	42	62	49	66	39	61	68	79
39401	HATTIESBURG	54	40	38	41	38	45	53	46	54	49	53	37	44	54	44	55	37	51	50	57
39402	HATTIESBURG	99	98	92	99	97	95	99	96	97	100	98	74	98	99	96	96	69	96	94	113
39406	HATTIESBURG	30	13	13	16	12	15	42	21	34	29	34	23	25	33	23	31	24	30	21	28
39421	BASSFIELD	65	42	62	40	42	63	45	57	52	43	51	44	34	53	42	58	34	53	60	70
39422	BAY SPRINGS	71	48	69	45	48	71	51	64	58	48	57	49	39	59	48	65	38	60	68	78
39423	BEAUMONT	69	47	62	45	47	66	50	60	56	48	55	47	39	58	46	62	37	57	64	74
39425	BROOKLYN	70	50	60	49	50	67	52	61	58	50	57	47	42	60	48	63	38	58	65	74
39426	CARRIERE	80	74	71	72	73	81	70	76	73	71	73	56	67	76	69	76	50	73	78	90
39427	CARSON	59	38	57	36	38	58	41	52	47	39	46	40	31	48	38	53	31	49	55	64
39428	COLLINS	79	55	73	53	55	78	59	71	67	56	65	54	47	67	55	73	43	67	76	86
39429	COLUMBIA	67	49	63	47	49	67	51	61	58	49	56	46	42	58	49	63	38	58	66	74
39437	ELLISVILLE	79	59	71	58	59	78	61	72	67	59	66	54	50	69	57	73	44	68	76	86
39439	HEIDELBERG	66	44	61	42	44	64	47	58	53	45	52	45	36	55	43	59	35	54	61	71
39440	LAUREL	69	54	60	55	54	68	61	65	67	58	65	48	54	66	57	72	44	65	72	78
39443	LAUREL	77	57	70	56	58	76	59	70	65	57	64	53	48	66	56	71	43	66	73	84
	MISSISSIPPI	77	63	67	62	62	74	66	70	70	65	69	54	59	71	62	74	47	70	74	85
	UNITED STATES	100	100	100	100	100	100	100	100	100	100	100	100	100	100	100	100	100	100	100	100

ZIP CODE			POPULATION			2000-2009 ANNUAL RATE		HOUSEHOLDS					FAMILIES		
#	POST OFFICE NAME	COUNTY FIPS CODE	2000	2009	2014	% Rate	State Centile	2000	2009	2014	% Annual Rate 2000-2009	2009 Average HH Size	2000	2009	% Annual Rate 2000-2009
39451	LEAKESVILLE	041	7291	7099	7037	-0.3	36	1981	1975	1976	0.0	2.50	1469	1428	-0.3
39452	LUCEDALE	039	20940	24118	25616	1.5	91	7340	8564	9168	1.7	2.73	5818	6662	1.5
39455	LUMBERTON	073	7914	8743	9327	1.1	87	2906	3302	3550	1.4	2.64	2210	2453	1.1
39456	MC LAIN	041	1458	1399	1365	-0.4	31	517	511	506	-0.1	2.74	387	373	-0.4
39459	MOSELLE	067	3252	3623	3781	1.2	89	1207	1396	1468	1.6	2.57	911	1028	1.3
39461	NEELY	041	1085	1100	1109	0.1	54	403	427	436	0.6	2.44	311	322	0.4
39462	NEW AUGUSTA	111	1339	1329	1318	-0.1	47	469	478	478	0.2	2.73	357	357	0.0
39464	OVETT	067	2102	2289	2370	0.9	83	787	886	924	1.3	2.57	620	682	1.0
39465	PETAL	035	18685	21605	23054	1.6	92	6741	7940	8521	1.8	2.70	5189	5972	1.5
39466	PICAYUNE	109	25096	29652	32153	1.8	94	9476	11538	12640	2.2	2.55	6981	8281	1.9
39470	POPLARVILLE	109	11086	13219	14400	1.9	95	4012	4960	5474	2.3	2.53	3001	3621	2.1
39474	PRENTISS	065	8516	8123	7866	-0.5	25	3206	3178	3116	-0.1	2.53	2320	2242	-0.4
39475	PURVIS	073	9221	10794	11910	1.7	93	3311	3985	4437	2.0	2.66	2619	3079	1.8
39476	RICHTON	111	7402	7780	7894	0.5	72	2726	2971	3046	0.9	2.59	2093	2237	0.7
39478	SANDY HOOK	091	1910	1870	1852	-0.2	41	725	737	738	0.2	2.53	530	524	-0.1
39479	SEMINARY	031	5324	5827	6039	1.0	86	2024	2282	2388	1.3	2.55	1542	1699	1.1
39480	SOSO	067	2406	2719	2833	1.3	90	952	1108	1163	1.7	2.45	741	842	1.4
39481	STRINGER	061	1676	1722	1702	0.3	64	633	673	673	0.7	2.56	501	521	0.4
39482	SUMRALL	073	7143	8326	9148	1.7	93	2566	3061	3394	1.9	2.71	2010	2340	1.7
39483	FOXWORTH	091	5643	5908	6012	0.5	72	2050	2215	2274	0.8	2.67	1584	1672	0.6
39501	GULFPORT	047	25887	23683	22789	-1.0	9	9487	8813	8507	-0.8	2.49	5895	5230	-1.3
39503	GULFPORT	047	36136	44341	44988	2.2	95	12676	16367	16759	2.8	2.65	9708	11979	2.3
39507	GULFPORT	047	19337	16040	15171	-2.0	2	8459	7121	6776	-1.8	2.19	4933	3914	-2.5
39520	BAY SAINT LOUIS	045	17649	12854	12422	-3.4	1	6976	5284	5151	-3.0	2.39	4591	3275	-3.6
39525	DIAMONDHEAD	045	5886	8335	9162	3.8	98	2548	3696	4096	4.1	2.24	1908	2653	3.6
39530	BILOXI	047	14125	7850	7146	-6.2	0	6180	3599	3300	-5.7	2.15	3296	1759	-6.6
39531	BILOXI	047	19721	17835	17084	-1.1	7	8060	7650	7385	-0.6	2.26	4992	4282	-1.6
39532	BILOXI	047	25587	26511	26100	0.4	69	9423	10112	10040	0.8	2.62	7237	7438	0.3
39534	BILOXI	047	3666	2895	2852	-2.5	1	343	149	136	-8.6	3.03	330	142	-8.7
39540	DIBERVILLE	047	7639	7192	6914	-0.6	21	2842	2767	2678	-0.3	2.60	1982	1815	-0.9
39553	GAUTIER	059	16239	17835	18274	1.0	86	5891	6652	6873	1.3	2.67	4502	4936	1.0
39556	KILN	045	5979	6992	7436	1.7	93	2150	2605	2796	2.1	2.68	1636	1910	1.7
39560	LONG BEACH	047	19777	16891	16360	-1.7	3	7455	6420	6261	-1.6	2.59	5381	4592	-1.7
39561	MC HENRY	131	1162	1430	1517	2.3	96	424	514	555	2.1	2.26	327	387	1.8
39562	MOSS POINT	059	16723	17683	17825	0.6	76	5821	6313	6414	0.9	2.79	4711	4989	0.6
39563	MOSS POINT	059	15816	15491	15128	-0.2	41	5700	5718	5622	0.0	2.68	4214	4092	-0.3
39564	OCEAN SPRINGS	059	31874	34941	35672	1.0	86	12004	13347	13689	1.2	2.60	8807	9565	0.9
39565	VANCLEAVE	059	14466	18500	19756	2.7	97	4828	6322	6801	3.0	2.92	3960	5047	2.7
39567	PASCAGOULA	059	13927	11171	10667	-2.4	2	5362	4640	4456	-1.6	2.31	3408	2828	-2.0
39571	PASS CHRISTIAN	047	14909	12248	11966	-2.1	2	5725	4694	4612	-2.1	2.58	4091	3306	-2.3
39572	PEARLINGTON	045	1782	1300	1247	-3.4	1	684	528	513	-2.8	2.46	480	353	-3.3
39573	PERKINSTON	131	6372	8037	8626	2.5	96	2128	2766	3000	2.9	2.73	1669	2115	2.6
39574	SAUCIER	047	11012	13267	13323	2.0	95	3817	4809	4871	2.5	2.74	3019	3645	2.1
39576	WAVELAND	045	6656	4529	4330	-4.1	1	2725	1891	1825	-3.9	2.39	1790	1173	-4.5
39577	WIGGINS	131	8781	9658	10048	1.0	86	3176	3532	3692	1.2	2.66	2399	2607	0.9
39581	PASCAGOULA	059	12333	11060	10621	-1.2	5	4518	4145	4007	-0.9	2.65	3331	2952	-1.3
39601	BROOKHAVEN	085	22736	23310	23628	0.3	64	8681	9139	9330	0.6	2.48	6197	6360	0.3
39629	BOGUE CHITTO	085	5672	5974	6110	0.6	76	2123	2288	2356	0.8	2.60	1663	1753	0.6
39630	BUDE	037	1162	1140	1117	-0.2	41	485	490	484	0.1	2.29	309	302	-0.2
39631	CENTREVILLE	157	3851	3688	3608	-0.5	25	1420	1422	1409	0.0	2.52	1018	994	-0.3
39633	CROSBY	157	1055	970	939	-0.9	11	409	396	387	-0.3	2.45	285	269	-0.6
39638	GLOSTER	005	3747	3528	3447	-0.6	21	1483	1460	1443	-0.2	2.42	1058	1015	-0.4
39641	JAYESS	077	4268	4350	4338	0.2	59	1615	1707	1720	0.6	2.55	1254	1298	0.4
39643	KOKOMO	091	1219	1310	1346	0.8	82	445	495	513	1.2	2.65	349	379	0.9
39645	LIBERTY	005	5493	5450	5375	-0.1	47	2136	2166	2162	0.2	2.47	1572	1557	-0.1
39647	MC CALL CREEK	037	1979	1956	1922	-0.1	47	783	794	785	0.2	2.45	575	569	-0.1
39648	MCCOMB	113	21260	21255	21255	0.0	52	8228	8434	8501	0.3	2.46	5635	5611	0.0
39652	MAGNOLIA	113	8399	8603	8683	0.3	64	3115	3314	3380	0.7	2.54	2297	2378	0.4
39653	MEADVILLE	037	1635	1590	1556	-0.3	36	610	608	599	0.0	2.51	443	431	-0.3
39654	MONTICELLO	077	4376	4555	4593	0.4	69	1701	1823	1857	0.8	2.45	1207	1256	0.4
39656	OAK VALE	077	344	365	369	0.6	76	133	147	150	1.1	2.48	103	111	0.8
39657	OSYKA	113	2195	2259	2287	0.3	64	794	845	864	0.7	2.62	589	611	0.4
39661	ROXIE	037	3563	3533	3477	-0.1	47	1280	1303	1291	0.2	2.71	955	949	-0.1
39662	RUTH	085	1174	1268	1310	0.8	82	440	491	511	1.2	2.58	339	369	0.9
39663	SILVER CREEK	077	3101	3155	3146	0.2	59	1165	1232	1242	0.6	2.56	870	899	0.4
39664	SMITHDALE	005	2181	2103	2063	-0.4	31	879	876	869	0.0	2.40	673	656	-0.3
39665	SONTAG	077	1712	1581	1528	-0.9	11	642	609	593	-0.6	2.60	500	470	-0.7
39666	SUMMIT	113	8506	9143	9397	0.8	82	3173	3532	3671	1.2	2.53	2370	2573	0.9
39667	TYLERTOWN	147	12475	12894	12973	0.4	69	4596	4932	5018	0.8	2.58	3365	3527	0.5
39668	UNION CHURCH	063	767	729	712	-0.5	25	307	309	306	0.1	2.36	214	209	-0.3
39669	WOODVILLE	157	6410	6340	6221	-0.1	47	2103	2133	2114	0.2	2.48	1473	1454	-0.1
39701	COLUMBUS	087	16619	15802	15389	-0.5	25	6128	5960	5830	-0.3	2.49	3989	3777	-0.6
39702	COLUMBUS	087	22206	22240	21968	0.0	52	8145	8345	8290	0.3	2.61	6159	6176	0.0
39705	COLUMBUS	087	14150	13445	13102	-0.6	21	5538	5444	5354	-0.2	2.40	3915	3702	-0.6
39710	COLUMBUS	087	277	246	233	-1.3	4	8	7	7	-1.4	2.57	7	7	0.0
39730	ABERDEEN	095	12646	12353	12090	-0.3	36	4674	4716	4660	0.1	2.57	3416	3364	-0.2
39735	ACKERMAN	019	5327	5016	4868	-0.6	21	2069	2032	1997	-0.2	2.43	1475	1411	-0.5
39739	BROOKSVILLE	103	4377	4149	4037	-0.6	21	1518	1518	1498	0.0	2.73	1124	1093	-0.3
39740	CALEDONIA	087	4961	5179	5172	0.5	72	1797	1918	1926	0.7	2.70	1405	1468	0.5
39741	CEDARBLUFF	025	1085	1035	1007	-0.5	25	394	394	388	0.0	2.62	294	287	-0.3
39743	CRAWFORD	087	2299	2210	2174	-0.4	31	776	777	773	0.0	2.84	595	583	-0.2
39744	EUPORA	155	5563	5771	5782	0.4	69	2089	2202	2214	0.6	2.55	1508	1553	0.3
39745	FRENCH CAMP	019	1656	1539	1492	-0.8	14	542	523	511	-0.4	2.53	407	384	-0.6
39746	HAMILTON	095	3236	3252	3205	0.1	54	1223	1273	1268	0.4	2.55	921	936	0.2
39747	KILMICHAEL	097	2455	2516	2494	0.3	64	934	989	989	0.6	2.54	682	704	0.3
39750	MABEN	105	2192	2097	2067	-0.5	25	859	860	859	0.0	2.43	626	610	-0.3
39751	MANTEE	155	2019	1902	1857	-0.6	21	788	758	743	-0.4	2.51	609	574	-0.6
39752	MATHISTON	155	2600	2489	2439	-0.5	25	1022	1006	992	-0.2	2.45	751	722	-0.4
39755	PHEBA	025	762	720	695	-0.6	21	281	278	272	-0.1	2.58	205	198	-0.4
39756	PRAIRIE	095	527	493	477	-0.7	16	187	183	179	-0.2	2.69	138	132	-0.5
39759	STARKVILLE	105	37728	39408	40448	0.5	72	14549	15972	16608	1.0	2.24	8244	8723	0.6
39762	MISSISSIPPI STATE	105	1643	1580	1585	-0.4	31	11	11	11	0.0	2.55	3	3	0.0
39766	STEENS	087	2025	2057	2038	0.2	59	797	829	827	0.4	2.48	595	603	0.1
39767	STEWART	155	550	537	528	-0.3	36	225	226	223	0.0	2.38	167	163	-0.3
39769	STURGIS	105	1767	1750	1755	-0.1	47	704	728	741	0.4	2.34	516	518	0.0
	MISSISSIPPI					0.5					0.8	2.56			0.5
	UNITED STATES					1.0					1.1	2.59			0.9

ZIP CODE #	POST OFFICE NAME	RACE (%) White 2000	White 2009	Black 2000	Black 2009	Asian/Pacific 2000	Asian/Pacific 2009	% Hispanic Origin 2000	% Hispanic Origin 2009	2009 AGE DISTRIBUTION (%) 0-4	5-9	10-14	15-19	20-24	25-44	45-64	65-84	85+	18+	MEDIAN AGE 2009	% 2009 Males	% 2009 Females
39451	LEAKESVILLE	68.9	66.5	29.6	32.0	0.1	0.1	1.0	1.1	5.5	5.5	5.4	6.3	10.9	35.0	20.6	9.2	1.7	80.5	33.9	62.6	37.4
39452	LUCEDALE	90.2	88.5	8.1	9.0	0.2	0.3	1.5	2.3	7.8	7.7	7.6	7.6	6.0	27.2	24.4	10.1	1.5	72.0	34.8	50.3	49.7
39455	LUMBERTON	80.3	78.9	18.5	19.5	0.1	0.2	1.0	1.5	7.3	7.3	7.4	7.2	5.6	25.8	26.7	11.4	1.3	73.5	37.3	48.9	51.1
39456	MC LAIN	68.2	65.8	31.1	33.5	0.1	0.1	0.7	0.6	9.1	8.9	8.6	8.0	6.3	25.6	23.5	8.9	1.1	68.3	32.5	48.5	51.5
39459	MOSELLE	87.1	83.2	11.4	14.3	0.2	0.2	1.3	2.2	7.0	7.0	7.0	5.7	4.9	26.8	28.0	12.3	1.4	75.8	39.1	50.6	49.4
39461	NEELY	93.2	92.8	6.5	6.8	0.1	0.1	0.5	0.4	7.5	7.5	7.4	6.4	6.3	30.0	23.8	10.2	1.0	73.9	34.7	52.2	47.8
39462	NEW AUGUSTA	68.9	67.3	29.7	31.2	0.1	0.2	0.9	1.0	8.6	8.7	8.1	7.1	5.9	26.3	25.5	9.0	1.0	69.8	33.6	51.4	48.6
39464	OVETT	95.3	93.5	3.0	3.9	0.1	0.1	0.9	1.4	7.3	7.2	7.2	6.3	5.7	27.7	26.8	10.8	1.0	74.5	37.3	50.5	49.5
39465	PETAL	90.9	88.2	7.8	9.9	0.2	0.3	1.1	1.7	7.3	7.2	7.2	7.5	6.0	27.2	26.0	10.1	1.3	73.7	36.1	48.6	51.4
39466	PICAYUNE	81.0	78.8	16.6	17.8	0.4	0.5	1.5	2.1	7.1	7.2	7.2	6.9	5.5	25.0	26.9	12.6	1.7	74.3	38.1	48.1	51.9
39470	POPLARVILLE	86.2	83.7	11.9	13.8	0.3	0.5	1.1	1.6	6.8	6.8	7.0	8.4	6.1	24.3	26.4	12.5	1.8	75.3	37.6	49.3	50.7
39474	PRENTISS	39.7	36.6	59.3	62.1	0.2	0.2	0.8	1.0	7.1	7.5	7.3	7.4	5.7	23.8	26.4	12.5	2.2	73.5	37.6	47.6	52.4
39475	PURVIS	90.3	88.7	8.4	9.4	0.2	0.3	1.1	1.8	7.9	7.7	7.4	6.6	5.3	29.2	25.0	9.6	1.4	73.0	35.4	48.4	51.6
39476	RICHTON	87.6	87.2	11.3	11.7	0.2	0.2	0.9	1.0	7.6	7.6	7.4	6.6	5.4	27.2	25.5	11.3	1.3	73.1	35.9	48.6	51.4
39478	SANDY HOOK	69.6	66.6	29.1	31.6	0.1	0.1	1.6	2.1	5.1	5.4	5.7	6.7	5.5	25.7	29.9	14.3	1.7	79.8	41.8	50.2	49.8
39479	SEMINARY	91.7	89.0	7.3	9.6	0.1	0.1	0.7	1.1	7.0	7.0	7.1	7.1	6.0	27.4	26.0	11.2	1.3	74.7	37.2	49.4	50.6
39480	SOSO	72.1	66.1	26.9	32.5	0.1	0.2	0.6	0.9	6.8	6.9	7.0	6.9	5.2	26.1	27.7	12.0	1.5	75.3	38.7	49.3	50.7
39481	STRINGER	84.4	83.5	14.4	15.4	0.5	0.5	0.7	0.7	6.2	6.4	6.6	6.9	4.8	27.8	27.5	12.6	1.4	76.7	39.4	49.9	50.1
39482	SUMRALL	89.0	86.8	10.0	11.8	0.1	0.1	0.6	1.0	7.2	7.3	7.3	7.4	6.1	28.5	26.0	9.1	1.1	73.6	35.4	49.4	50.6
39483	FOXWORTH	77.8	75.0	21.3	23.8	0.1	0.1	0.6	0.8	7.4	7.5	7.5	6.8	5.3	26.8	27.0	10.3	1.3	73.4	36.5	49.3	50.7
39501	GULFPORT	44.0	35.5	52.2	59.8	1.1	1.5	2.3	2.6	8.1	7.6	6.7	8.2	9.3	25.7	22.7	9.9	1.8	73.5	32.0	49.4	50.6
39503	GULFPORT	75.3	70.7	20.3	23.5	1.5	2.3	2.3	2.9	7.6	7.4	7.2	7.2	6.6	29.4	25.6	8.4	0.7	73.4	34.7	49.8	50.2
39507	GULFPORT	78.0	73.2	18.0	21.5	1.2	1.9	2.9	3.6	5.5	5.4	5.6	6.1	6.6	25.9	27.3	15.5	2.1	79.8	41.1	48.7	51.3
39520	BAY SAINT LOUIS	87.2	84.0	9.0	11.2	1.2	1.4	1.8	2.3	6.1	5.8	6.1	6.7	6.5	24.8	29.8	12.4	1.8	77.8	40.4	50.1	49.9
39525	DIAMONDHEAD	95.3	94.2	1.8	2.2	0.9	1.2	2.9	3.7	4.2	4.5	4.9	4.4	2.9	15.9	35.6	25.2	2.5	83.6	53.5	48.6	51.4
39530	BILOXI	56.8	49.4	29.5	33.8	10.8	13.0	2.6	3.7	6.3	5.8	5.4	6.4	7.1	25.4	26.0	14.7	2.9	79.0	40.1	49.0	51.0
39531	BILOXI	72.0	65.2	19.6	23.4	3.3	5.2	4.3	5.2	8.0	6.9	6.0	6.2	8.2	30.1	21.4	11.3	1.8	75.5	33.6	49.3	50.7
39532	BILOXI	88.1	84.4	5.9	7.4	3.5	5.1	2.1	2.7	6.7	6.8	6.9	6.6	5.3	27.4	28.7	10.9	0.9	75.5	38.8	49.8	50.2
39534	BILOXI	66.9	57.6	19.2	23.5	3.0	4.7	9.0	11.5	3.2	1.9	0.9	37.9	41.5	13.8	0.6	0.0	0.0	93.0	20.7	68.6	31.4
39540	DIBERVILLE	77.7	68.4	11.9	15.5	7.1	11.7	2.6	3.3	7.2	6.9	6.7	6.7	6.7	30.1	25.6	9.3	0.7	75.2	35.6	49.9	50.1
39553	GAUTIER	70.3	64.6	25.8	30.7	1.2	1.4	2.6	3.2	8.3	8.0	7.5	7.0	6.2	27.8	25.2	9.2	0.8	71.9	34.4	49.3	50.7
39556	KILN	96.8	95.8	1.9	2.6	0.2	0.2	1.2	1.5	8.1	7.6	7.3	7.2	7.0	27.6	25.7	8.8	0.6	72.5	34.1	50.8	49.2
39560	LONG BEACH	85.2	79.8	9.9	13.0	2.4	4.1	2.2	2.7	6.7	6.6	6.6	7.2	6.9	26.2	27.8	10.8	1.2	75.5	37.0	47.8	52.2
39561	MC HENRY	89.5	87.1	8.5	10.4	0.4	0.5	1.9	2.5	5.9	6.0	6.1	14.5	12.2	23.5	22.9	8.2	0.8	78.5	29.6	52.4	47.6
39562	MOSS POINT	91.4	88.1	7.1	10.0	0.4	0.5	0.6	0.9	6.9	6.9	7.1	7.2	5.8	27.6	27.2	10.6	0.8	74.6	36.9	50.3	49.7
39563	MOSS POINT	28.4	22.7	70.1	75.8	0.2	0.3	1.0	1.0	6.3	6.9	7.0	7.5	6.1	23.5	28.0	13.0	1.8	75.3	39.0	47.3	52.7
39564	OCEAN SPRINGS	87.8	83.0	6.7	9.4	3.0	4.3	2.3	3.2	6.4	6.4	6.5	6.7	5.7	27.3	28.3	11.2	1.5	76.5	38.7	48.2	51.8
39565	VANCLEAVE	93.9	91.5	3.5	5.0	0.6	1.0	1.3	1.9	7.5	7.4	7.5	7.3	5.8	29.1	26.4	8.4	0.6	72.9	35.6	50.5	49.5
39567	PASCAGOULA	70.6	65.1	26.6	32.0	0.5	0.5	2.4	2.6	6.8	6.4	6.0	6.3	6.9	24.9	26.1	14.0	2.6	77.1	39.3	49.5	50.5
39571	PASS CHRISTIAN	77.9	77.0	17.7	17.6	2.2	2.7	1.6	2.1	6.8	6.8	6.7	6.5	5.9	26.1	28.1	11.6	1.5	75.7	38.5	49.2	50.8
39572	PEARLINGTON	80.0	72.4	17.6	24.4	0.3	0.4	1.5	1.9	5.4	5.6	6.0	6.2	5.7	22.6	33.2	13.9	1.5	79.5	43.9	50.0	50.0
39573	PERKINSTON	91.6	89.8	6.6	7.7	0.3	0.4	1.3	1.8	6.7	6.7	6.8	9.3	7.9	26.0	25.9	9.7	0.9	75.7	34.8	50.8	49.2
39574	SAUCIER	93.7	91.5	4.1	5.5	0.4	0.7	1.3	1.6	8.1	7.8	7.6	7.3	6.6	27.9	26.2	7.9	0.5	71.9	34.2	51.4	48.6
39576	WAVELAND	85.9	80.7	10.9	15.0	1.4	2.1	1.9	2.2	6.1	6.0	6.2	7.4	6.8	24.4	28.3	13.1	1.7	77.1	39.6	47.2	52.8
39577	WIGGINS	74.0	70.8	24.9	27.6	0.1	0.2	1.1	1.6	7.2	7.1	7.0	7.2	6.2	25.6	25.9	11.9	1.9	74.3	36.8	48.5	51.5
39581	PASCAGOULA	62.3	54.8	32.6	39.3	1.5	1.9	5.6	6.1	9.1	8.4	7.6	7.1	7.8	27.7	22.7	8.8	0.8	70.7	31.4	49.2	50.8
39601	BROOKHAVEN	64.0	61.3	34.9	37.2	0.3	0.5	0.7	1.0	7.1	7.2	7.0	6.9	5.7	25.4	26.1	12.4	2.3	74.6	37.8	47.5	52.5
39629	BOGUE CHITTO	83.6	80.4	15.7	18.7	0.1	0.1	0.7	1.1	6.8	7.0	7.0	6.5	5.3	27.0	27.7	11.3	1.4	75.1	38.0	49.9	50.1
39630	BUDE	46.7	43.1	52.7	56.1	0.0	0.0	0.9	1.0	7.3	7.5	7.3	7.0	6.1	22.9	27.0	12.5	2.4	73.7	37.6	45.9	54.1
39631	CENTREVILLE	41.1	38.4	58.6	61.3	0.0	0.0	0.2	0.2	6.9	6.9	6.9	6.8	5.8	23.2	27.7	12.6	3.2	75.2	39.3	47.5	52.5
39633	CROSBY	54.1	50.8	44.6	47.3	0.1	0.2	1.1	1.5	6.3	6.6	6.9	6.4	5.5	23.4	29.8	12.9	2.3	76.3	41.0	49.1	50.9
39638	GLOSTER	48.4	46.0	50.7	52.7	0.0	0.1	1.0	1.2	6.3	7.0	6.7	7.5	5.6	23.6	27.9	13.4	2.1	75.1	39.8	47.4	52.6
39641	JAYESS	78.2	75.3	20.9	23.5	0.2	0.3	0.9	1.3	7.0	7.1	7.2	6.3	4.7	25.9	28.0	12.4	1.4	74.8	38.6	49.6	50.4
39643	KOKOMO	67.8	64.4	31.4	34.7	0.0	0.0	0.4	0.5	7.4	7.6	7.6	6.6	5.4	24.5	28.3	11.0	1.5	73.1	37.2	48.7	51.3
39645	LIBERTY	58.4	54.9	40.5	43.6	0.1	0.2	0.8	1.0	6.0	6.2	6.4	6.9	5.6	24.6	28.3	14.0	2.0	77.1	40.4	49.8	50.2
39647	MC CALL CREEK	82.3	80.3	17.3	19.3	0.0	0.0	0.4	0.6	6.9	7.3	6.9	5.1	4.8	24.4	27.5	14.7	2.5	75.9	40.8	49.3	50.7
39648	MCCOMB	46.5	43.3	52.1	54.8	0.4	0.6	0.8	1.0	7.7	7.7	7.0	7.4	6.2	24.1	24.8	12.2	2.9	73.2	36.2	46.2	53.8
39652	MAGNOLIA	44.2	39.8	54.7	58.9	0.1	0.2	0.8	1.0	6.7	7.0	7.1	7.3	5.8	24.7	27.7	11.9	1.8	74.7	37.8	49.0	51.0
39653	MEADVILLE	72.7	69.6	26.1	28.9	0.2	0.2	0.6	0.9	5.5	5.8	5.9	6.0	5.8	23.1	29.9	14.1	3.8	79.1	43.2	48.4	51.6
39654	MONTICELLO	73.2	69.5	25.5	28.7	0.5	0.7	0.6	0.8	6.6	6.6	6.8	7.0	5.8	24.5	26.5	13.8	2.5	75.8	39.1	47.7	52.3
39656	OAK VALE	59.7	57.0	40.0	42.7	0.0	0.0	0.3	0.5	6.8	7.1	7.1	6.0	6.6	26.8	27.7	10.4	1.4	75.6	36.1	49.0	51.0
39657	OSYKA	56.9	52.0	42.2	46.8	0.1	0.1	0.7	0.9	7.9	7.9	7.5	6.7	5.4	23.2	26.0	13.4	2.0	72.4	37.3	47.9	52.1
39661	ROXIE	46.5	42.4	52.6	56.4	0.1	0.1	0.6	0.7	6.9	7.4	8.1	8.0	5.9	24.0	27.9	10.2	1.6	72.4	36.7	48.6	51.4
39662	RUTH	89.3	86.7	10.2	12.7	0.0	0.0	0.5	0.7	6.8	6.9	7.0	7.1	5.4	26.9	28.1	10.8	1.1	74.9	37.7	50.5	49.5
39663	SILVER CREEK	50.2	47.5	49.0	51.5	0.3	0.3	0.4	0.6	6.9	7.0	7.2	7.4	6.1	25.1	27.4	11.4	1.5	74.3	37.5	48.4	51.6
39664	SMITHDALE	77.9	75.2	20.9	23.0	0.1	0.2	0.8	1.2	5.7	6.0	6.2	6.0	4.9	24.6	30.4	14.4	1.9	78.5	42.5	50.6	49.4
39665	SONTAG	54.0	50.7	45.1	47.9	0.2	0.4	1.2	1.5	6.5	7.5	7.0	8.0	6.6	25.0	26.9	11.0	1.5	74.0	36.3	47.8	52.2
39666	SUMMIT	70.5	67.4	28.5	31.3	0.3	0.5	0.7	1.0	6.3	6.7	6.7	8.0	5.7	24.6	28.1	12.3	1.6	76.1	38.8	48.3	51.7
39667	TYLERTOWN	52.3	49.0	46.3	49.0	0.3	0.4	1.3	1.6	7.3	7.3	7.2	7.5	6.3	23.9	26.0	12.2	2.2	73.5	37.1	47.6	52.4
39668	UNION CHURCH	43.1	39.6	55.6	58.8	0.3	0.3	0.8	0.8	6.2	5.9	6.3	6.7	6.6	23.5	29.9	12.6	2.3	77.5	40.2	46.8	53.2
39669	WOODVILLE	25.6	23.3	73.8	75.9	0.0	0.0	0.4	0.5	5.1	5.3	5.6	7.2	9.9	29.5	25.2	10.4	1.8	79.7	35.3	56.2	43.8
39701	COLUMBUS	28.4	26.1	70.0	71.8	0.4	0.5	1.1	1.4	7.6	7.6	7.4	9.0	9.5	24.8	22.6	9.6	1.8	72.6	31.6	45.6	54.4
39702	COLUMBUS	64.3	60.2	34.3	38.0	0.2	0.3	0.7	1.0	7.6	7.7	7.4	7.2	6.2	26.0	25.0	10.5	2.3	72.7	35.8	46.7	53.3
39705	COLUMBUS	70.7	65.8	25.6	29.1	1.5	1.9	1.9	2.8	7.9	7.0	6.5	5.7	7.7	29.8	24.4	9.6	1.4	75.1	34.6	50.5	49.5
39710	COLUMBUS	75.8	71.1	16.2	18.3	2.5	3.3	4.7	6.9	15.4	8.9	6.1	5.3	21.5	39.0	3.7	0.0	0.0	67.5	23.3	56.5	43.5
39730	ABERDEEN	50.3	46.5	48.9	52.4	0.3	0.4	0.5	0.7	7.2	7.3	7.5	8.0	6.5	25.2	24.6	11.4	2.3	72.9	35.7	47.0	53.0
39735	ACKERMAN	69.8	67.3	28.7	30.7	0.2	0.3	0.9	1.4	6.8	6.5	6.7	6.4	5.9	24.0	27.4	13.7	2.7	76.0	39.8	47.9	52.1
39739	BROOKSVILLE	24.4	22.5	74.6	76.0	0.0	0.0	1.2	1.4	8.7	8.8	8.7	7.7	6.7	24.2	23.6	9.7	1.8	69.1	32.0	47.5	52.5
39740	CALEDONIA	85.4	82.7	13.2	15.3	0.3	0.4	1.0	1.5	7.6	7.6	7.6	7.2	5.7	27.9	26.5	9.0	0.9	72.8	35.7	49.8	50.2
39741	CEDARBLUFF	52.6	49.2	46.7	49.9	0.0	0.0	0.8	1.2	7.5	7.2	7.2	7.0	6.4	26.6	26.7	10.3	1.1	73.8	35.4	48.7	51.3
39743	CRAWFORD	14.9	12.9	84.3	86.1	0.1	0.1	0.3	0.4	8.8	8.4	8.5	8.0	6.8	25.4	24.6	8.2	1.2	69.4	32.3	47.1	52.9
39744	EUPORA	71.4	70.9	26.6	27.2	0.1	0.1	2.3	2.3	6.8	6.8	6.5	6.6	6.1	22.8	26.7	14.2	3.5	75.8	40.4	48.4	51.6
39745	FRENCH CAMP	71.7	68.7	26.9	29.0	0.1	0.1	0.8	1.5	6.3	6.5	9.6	11.0	5.5	21.7	25.0	12.4	2.1	69.7	34.4	49.6	50.4
39746	HAMILTON	81.3	78.0	17.8	20.7	0.1	0.1	1.6	2.4	6.2	6.2	6.5	6.9	6.0	28.1	27.6	11.1	1.4	76.9	38.2	49.7	50.3
39747	KILMICHAEL	61.4	57.8	38.0	41.4	0.1	0.2	1.2	1.5	6.9	7.0	7.0	6.5	5.0	23.4	27.3	14.6	2.4	75.3	40.5	49.2	50.8
39750	MABEN	68.8	66.5	30.5	32.6	0.1	0.1	0.6	0.8	7.3	7.5	7.4	6.9	5.4	26.3	25.9	11.6	1.5	73.6	36.8	47.2	52.8
39751	MANTEE	90.5	89.7	8.8	9.5	0.2	0.2	0.8	0.8	6.7	6.9	7.0	6.4	5.2	26.3	27.2	12.5	1.7	75.3	39.2	51.4	48.6
39752	MATHISTON	82.0	80.4	17.0	18.4	0.3	0.3	0.9	1.0	6.8	7.4	7.0	7.3	6.4	24.7	27.0	11.9	1.5	74.6	37.2	47.8	52.2
39755	PHEBA	53.2	49.7	46.0	49.3	0.1	0.1	0.4	0.4	7.6	7.6	7.6	6.7	5.6	25.7	26.9	10.6	1.7	73.1	36.5	50.0	50.0
39756	PRAIRIE	19.0	15.6	80.5	83.6	0.2	0.2	0.4	0.4	7.5	7.5	7.3	5.9	5.7	26.6	28.6	9.3	1.6	74.0	37.3	49.9	50.1
39759	STARKVILLE	57.7	54.0	38.1	40.1	2.8	3.9	1.1	1.6	6.1	5.3	5.2	10.3	20.8	24.2	19.0	7.9	1.3	80.2	26.4	50.2	49.8
39762	MISSISSIPPI STATE	71.7	67.4	24.8	27.6	2.6	3.6	1.0	1.4	2.6	2.8	2.7	19.1	41.9	14.1	11.1	5.1	0.7	89.7	22.7	50.0	50.0
39766	STEENS	74.4	70.0	24.5	28.4	0.2	0.3	0.4	0.6	5.3	6.1	6.6	7.4	5.1	26.3	29.1	12.7	1.5	77.3	40.0	48.0	52.0
39767	STEWART	79.4	77.8	19.1	20.3	0.0	0.2	1.8	1.9	6.7	7.1	6.9	6.5	4.8	23.6	28.5	13.8	2.0	75.4	40.6	50.1	49.9
39769	STURGIS	74.5	71.1	24.6	27.7	0.1	0.1	0.6	0.9	5.8	6.1	6.1	5.8	5.8	27.9	28.3	12.6	1.7	78.7	39.8	52.5	47.5
	MISSISSIPPI	61.4	59.6	36.3	37.4	0.7	0.9	1.4	2.0	7.2	7.1	7.0	7.5	7.1	26.4	25.3	10.6	1.7	74.3	35.6	48.6	51.4
	UNITED STATES	75.1	72.0	12.3	12.7	3.8	4.6	12.5	15.7	6.8	6.7	6.6	7.1	6.9	27.0	26.0	10.9	1.9	75.7	36.9	49.2	50.8

#	POST OFFICE NAME	2009 Per Capita Income	2009 HH Income Base	2009 HOUSEHOLD INCOME DISTRIBUTION (%) Less than $25,000	$25,000 to $49,999	$50,000 to $99,999	$100,000 to $149,999	$150,000 or More	MEDIAN HOUSEHOLD INCOME 2009	2014	2009 National Centile	2009 State Centile	2009 Home Value Base	2009 HOME VALUE DISTRIBUTION (%) Less than $50,000	$50,000 to $89,999	$90,000 to $174,999	$175,000 to $399,999	$400,000 or More	2009 Median Home Value
39451	LEAKESVILLE	14678	1975	38.8	31.4	24.6	4.0	1.1	33628	34282	15	60	1657	33.1	31.7	27.8	6.2	1.1	69247
39452	LUCEDALE	16925	8564	30.8	30.2	32.6	5.0	1.5	39821	41375	32	83	7331	23.3	26.6	33.1	14.7	2.3	90097
39455	LUMBERTON	14564	3302	42.0	31.7	21.7	3.5	1.2	29589	28793	7	33	2726	30.0	31.8	26.6	9.3	2.3	74563
39456	MC LAIN	13638	511	43.4	33.5	19.6	2.3	1.2	30487	31011	9	40	446	49.8	26.5	19.3	3.8	0.7	50370
39459	MOSELLE	16234	1396	39.5	34.7	18.7	4.9	2.1	30173	29878	8	37	1222	35.5	25.7	29.3	8.3	1.2	71481
39461	NEELY	17460	427	34.2	33.5	26.2	4.9	1.2	37239	37618	24	76	382	35.6	29.3	26.2	7.1	1.8	70000
39462	NEW AUGUSTA	13648	478	42.1	28.9	25.5	3.3	0.2	29849	30777	8	35	366	31.4	39.1	25.1	3.0	1.4	71667
39464	OVETT	15775	886	35.9	34.8	24.2	4.2	1.0	32479	32021	12	56	797	38.3	30.1	21.0	10.0	0.6	66339
39465	PETAL	17103	7940	32.6	29.5	31.1	5.7	1.1	40290	39740	34	84	6365	20.8	27.9	38.7	12.0	0.6	92163
39466	PICAYUNE	16889	11538	38.2	29.9	25.6	4.4	1.9	32709	32108	13	57	8697	22.7	27.7	33.1	14.6	2.0	89515
39470	POPLARVILLE	17037	4960	35.0	33.1	25.2	4.9	1.8	35560	35765	19	72	4038	25.6	25.3	30.1	15.3	3.8	88819
39474	PRENTISS	14880	3178	49.5	25.2	20.1	3.3	1.9	25371	25577	3	14	2608	39.6	34.4	22.8	2.8	0.5	60617
39475	PURVIS	18919	3985	25.2	34.9	31.3	6.9	1.7	42652	45060	41	89	3292	18.8	23.8	38.0	17.6	1.8	105700
39476	RICHTON	16079	2971	36.9	31.3	26.4	4.2	1.2	34281	35164	16	63	2558	37.1	33.0	23.4	6.0	0.6	65809
39478	SANDY HOOK	14137	737	44.5	31.6	20.9	2.6	0.4	30321	29683	9	38	657	47.8	22.1	20.5	8.7	0.9	54394
39479	SEMINARY	16645	2282	37.1	33.0	24.7	4.1	1.1	33555	34246	14	60	2009	36.4	27.5	26.0	8.3	1.8	70514
39480	SOSO	17434	1108	32.8	36.6	24.7	4.3	1.5	33788	33928	15	61	945	33.0	33.0	22.8	10.5	0.7	67857
39481	STRINGER	17842	673	37.7	29.1	24.8	6.5	1.8	35627	36244	20	72	609	36.8	30.0	23.0	8.2	2.0	67614
39482	SUMRALL	17190	3061	33.2	33.1	27.9	3.8	2.1	37396	37490	25	77	2612	24.8	28.1	30.6	12.9	3.6	86465
39483	FOXWORTH	13306	2215	46.0	29.2	22.1	2.1	0.5	28467	28391	6	28	1909	38.0	34.8	20.2	6.7	0.4	63115
39501	GULFPORT	14474	8813	46.4	30.6	18.6	3.1	1.3	27248	26898	5	23	4321	19.3	44.8	30.8	4.1	0.9	77934
39503	GULFPORT	20339	16367	26.2	29.4	34.1	7.5	2.9	44475	46390	47	91	11785	13.3	22.5	45.3	15.7	3.2	107763
39507	GULFPORT	23462	7121	31.0	30.8	27.9	7.4	2.9	36855	36703	23	75	3830	3.1	16.6	51.7	24.3	4.2	127664
39520	BAY SAINT LOUIS	17961	5284	39.8	32.3	22.0	3.9	2.0	31777	32010	11	51	3718	23.0	28.2	37.1	9.9	1.7	88351
39525	DIAMONDHEAD	27917	3696	21.2	25.5	39.1	9.1	5.1	52387	50614	67	97	3299	2.2	8.4	45.5	39.6	4.4	162277
39530	BILOXI	18752	3599	45.0	29.8	19.0	3.9	2.4	28390	27729	6	27	1462	14.5	38.1	32.7	10.0	4.7	87008
39531	BILOXI	21095	7650	30.1	34.3	27.6	5.4	2.6	35301	35459	19	70	2586	4.6	17.9	49.2	23.1	5.3	118889
39532	BILOXI	21120	10112	22.1	30.4	37.8	7.4	2.3	47657	47946	56	94	7996	12.8	14.8	47.9	22.1	2.4	122420
39534	BILOXI	10738	149	19.5	56.4	20.1	3.4	0.7	33385	33605	14	59	4	0.0	0.0	100.0	0.0	0.0	137500
39540	DIBERVILLE	17771	2767	27.4	37.5	30.2	3.8	1.0	38440	40876	28	80	1938	23.5	26.5	43.2	4.7	2.0	89950
39553	GAUTIER	20304	6652	27.0	27.8	34.6	7.5	3.1	46207	46655	52	93	4797	15.3	25.9	41.0	16.4	1.5	107859
39556	KILN	16750	2605	38.0	29.8	25.1	4.9	2.1	33951	35182	15	62	2183	34.7	28.1	24.1	11.8	1.2	70478
39560	LONG BEACH	20902	6420	25.8	29.2	34.6	7.6	2.9	46079	47094	52	92	4362	6.1	19.1	54.6	17.1	3.0	118704
39561	MC HENRY	19399	514	26.7	33.3	33.7	4.3	2.1	42206	41785	40	88	446	22.9	19.5	38.6	14.3	4.7	101538
39562	MOSS POINT	17785	6313	26.9	32.8	32.1	6.7	1.4	41548	43354	38	87	5299	19.8	26.0	39.5	13.2	1.5	96157
39563	MOSS POINT	16747	5718	35.6	31.6	25.8	5.0	1.9	35263	34519	19	70	4102	13.6	41.3	36.0	7.9	1.0	84756
39564	OCEAN SPRINGS	24081	13347	18.4	29.5	36.9	11.0	4.3	51704	51121	65	96	10184	4.8	11.9	52.2	26.7	4.3	141394
39565	VANCLEAVE	17192	6322	23.5	33.4	36.1	6.2	0.8	44540	45685	47	91	5648	18.1	21.9	39.0	19.4	1.7	106612
39567	PASCAGOULA	18530	4640	41.5	28.3	22.7	5.0	2.5	31408	30454	10	49	2684	8.0	34.8	39.4	14.0	3.8	100467
39571	PASS CHRISTIAN	20575	4694	30.2	29.3	29.8	7.0	3.7	42064	45266	39	87	3700	14.4	26.0	35.6	19.7	4.3	104688
39572	PEARLINGTON	15267	528	44.5	32.8	18.4	3.0	1.3	29164	29828	7	30	419	38.4	30.1	27.2	2.9	1.4	64697
39573	PERKINSTON	17026	2766	33.4	29.0	30.5	5.4	1.8	39399	40027	31	82	2395	29.7	19.5	31.4	16.4	3.1	91560
39574	SAUCIER	17713	4809	29.2	33.1	31.1	4.3	2.3	40579	41716	35	84	4081	19.2	28.4	34.4	15.4	2.5	93339
39576	WAVELAND	18565	1891	36.3	32.4	25.7	3.6	2.0	34656	35925	17	66	1299	11.5	28.6	43.3	14.5	2.0	101206
39577	WIGGINS	15886	3532	42.5	26.6	24.1	4.7	2.1	30990	30194	10	44	2741	25.5	25.7	32.2	12.6	4.0	88017
39581	PASCAGOULA	17564	4145	36.7	29.2	26.0	6.1	2.1	35861	35748	20	73	2190	3.6	34.6	49.0	11.6	1.2	101478
39601	BROOKHAVEN	16387	9139	41.6	28.9	22.3	5.7	1.5	30712	30595	9	42	6682	30.1	29.9	29.4	9.4	1.2	76843
39629	BOGUE CHITTO	16198	2288	35.9	33.8	24.8	4.9	0.6	34565	35088	17	65	1999	32.7	31.8	28.4	6.7	0.5	67941
39630	BUDE	12594	490	61.6	21.6	14.5	1.8	0.4	20542	21056	2	4	347	51.6	32.3	15.3	0.6	0.3	48721
39631	CENTREVILLE	13943	1422	50.3	26.4	19.3	2.6	1.3	24761	25533	3	11	1184	41.9	31.5	18.5	7.1	1.0	58496
39633	CROSBY	12835	396	57.8	21.7	15.7	3.8	1.0	20129	20529	1	3	330	55.5	23.9	16.4	1.8	2.4	38929
39638	GLOSTER	14495	1460	47.9	31.0	17.3	2.7	1.0	26351	27868	4	18	1198	46.3	26.7	20.7	5.0	1.3	53667
39641	JAYESS	15221	1707	46.6	24.2	24.7	3.7	0.8	28404	28591	6	28	1495	28.4	30.0	34.1	5.8	1.8	77439
39643	KOKOMO	13402	495	45.5	28.7	23.8	2.0	0.0	29645	29618	8	33	425	39.5	33.2	20.9	6.4	0.0	62561
39645	LIBERTY	16150	2166	43.4	29.7	21.7	4.0	1.3	29485	30137	7	32	1846	38.7	27.6	24.4	7.4	1.8	64335
39647	MC CALL CREEK	16220	794	46.9	23.9	25.1	2.8	1.4	27877	28017	5	25	712	40.4	30.1	22.9	6.5	0.1	63492
39648	MCCOMB	15515	8434	46.7	29.5	18.7	3.1	1.9	27039	27840	5	21	5583	34.1	36.1	23.6	5.4	0.8	64494
39652	MAGNOLIA	14784	3314	45.8	31.7	17.8	3.3	1.5	27559	28228	5	24	2736	34.9	33.9	23.6	6.1	1.5	63576
39653	MEADVILLE	17368	608	35.5	33.9	25.0	3.8	1.8	38017	40059	27	79	523	38.4	32.9	21.8	6.5	0.4	60804
39654	MONTICELLO	18573	1823	37.7	24.4	30.6	5.3	2.1	35108	34912	18	69	1407	27.9	33.8	32.2	5.4	0.7	77439
39656	OAK VALE	16822	147	33.3	29.3	35.4	0.7	1.4	34336	33882	16	64	130	26.2	49.2	19.2	5.4	0.0	66667
39657	OSYKA	15604	845	43.3	32.0	17.4	5.0	2.4	30760	30880	9	43	707	33.7	25.6	28.1	10.6	2.0	69746
39661	ROXIE	13637	1303	50.5	23.9	21.6	2.8	1.2	24750	26335	3	11	1133	50.6	28.7	16.3	3.8	0.6	49561
39662	RUTH	17421	491	31.2	33.8	30.8	3.7	0.6	40739	40184	35	85	433	33.3	27.5	22.6	15.5	1.2	73125
39663	SILVER CREEK	14680	1232	43.2	26.9	26.2	3.5	0.2	29931	29585	8	35	1070	34.5	35.5	22.5	6.1	1.4	64234
39664	SMITHDALE	17904	876	33.7	35.0	26.0	3.8	1.5	33443	34152	14	60	768	36.8	33.9	19.4	7.8	2.1	66333
39665	SONTAG	17607	609	35.5	29.6	26.1	7.7	1.1	38056	39105	27	79	534	44.6	33.7	16.3	5.4	0.0	55088
39666	SUMMIT	18857	3532	39.0	26.3	26.6	4.9	3.2	33218	33082	14	58	2926	26.5	27.1	28.7	13.9	3.7	84673
39667	TYLERTOWN	14792	4932	48.3	26.1	20.9	2.9	1.8	26340	27132	4	17	4012	33.2	29.8	27.5	7.3	2.2	70588
39668	UNION CHURCH	15727	309	43.7	33.0	19.1	1.3	2.9	30734	30843	9	42	286	53.8	34.3	9.8	0.0	2.1	47963
39669	WOODVILLE	14325	2133	52.8	25.0	17.3	2.4	2.4	22423	22902	2	7	1805	51.1	27.5	16.5	3.4	1.6	48781
39701	COLUMBUS	14825	5960	50.0	26.5	17.6	4.0	2.0	24987	26132	3	13	3059	33.8	32.1	22.5	9.2	2.5	68887
39702	COLUMBUS	17660	8345	33.2	29.7	30.3	5.1	1.7	38290	37851	28	80	6379	14.5	39.3	37.7	8.2	0.3	86641
39705	COLUMBUS	24678	5444	25.7	28.1	31.9	9.2	5.1	46791	44718	54	93	3241	12.7	19.6	45.2	19.4	3.1	113882
39710	COLUMBUS	2627	7	0.0	71.4	28.6	0.0	0.0	42248	51787	40	88	0	0.0	0.0	0.0	0.0	0.0	0
39730	ABERDEEN	15440	4716	39.9	30.9	24.6	3.4	1.3	32306	32263	12	54	3516	32.7	31.5	25.8	8.5	1.5	71821
39735	ACKERMAN	16409	2032	41.1	31.6	21.5	4.2	1.6	31911	32336	11	51	1553	30.3	35.5	26.7	6.4	1.0	71443
39739	BROOKSVILLE	13059	1518	50.7	28.3	16.8	2.9	1.4	24518	25393	3	10	1237	48.8	30.2	15.6	3.3	2.1	51295
39740	CALEDONIA	18578	1918	23.0	34.8	35.0	5.6	1.6	44261	41962	46	90	1546	20.7	29.9	35.8	13.1	0.6	89514
39741	CEDARBLUFF	16254	394	39.8	20.8	34.3	4.3	0.8	33801	33562	15	61	327	27.2	49.2	15.9	7.6	0.0	69082
39743	CRAWFORD	12256	777	50.7	26.4	18.4	3.6	0.9	24542	26280	3	10	661	57.2	24.1	10.9	7.0	0.9	40865
39744	EUPORA	15051	2202	41.4	28.9	25.9	3.2	0.5	31504	31166	11	50	1607	34.3	31.6	28.6	4.5	0.9	72290
39745	FRENCH CAMP	13847	650	42.4	33.8	20.8	2.5	0.4	29927	30227	8	35	442	36.4	34.8	21.7	5.0	2.0	64750
39746	HAMILTON	18052	1273	28.7	29.0	37.5	4.4	0.5	41221	40274	37	86	1080	27.0	32.1	30.1	9.7	1.0	78737
39747	KILMICHAEL	14815	989	50.1	27.4	18.3	2.6	1.6	24977	27080	3	12	809	45.1	31.4	22.0	1.5	0.0	56810
39750	MABEN	16944	860	42.6	32.3	20.3	2.1	2.7	30000	29843	8	36	680	38.1	29.1	25.3	6.3	1.2	66964
39751	MANTEE	19204	758	34.0	33.9	23.5	6.2	2.4	38345	38154	28	80	673	39.5	33.4	21.0	5.2	0.9	59038
39752	MATHISTON	16506	1006	38.6	36.1	20.9	2.6	1.9	32272	32765	12	54	826	41.4	28.2	25.5	4.8	0.0	62222
39755	PHEBA	16337	278	38.1	28.1	28.8	3.2	1.8	32101	31485	12	53	228	28.5	43.9	20.2	7.0	0.4	66333
39756	PRAIRIE	15319	183	38.3	36.1	18.0	4.4	3.3	31220	30116	10	46	144	52.1	29.9	11.1	6.9	0.0	48000
39759	STARKVILLE	17943	15972	45.8	24.8	20.7	6.7	2.0	28383	28892	6	27	8431	24.4	21.0	34.2	17.3	3.1	98770
39762	MISSISSIPPI STATE	2669	11	63.6	18.2	18.2	0.0	0.0	17207	17207	1	2	0	0.0	0.0	0.0	0.0	0.0	0
39766	STEENS	18446	829	25.1	34.0	35.8	4.9	0.1	41069	40204	36	85	683	15.2	31.8	40.7	11.0	1.3	94271
39767	STEWART	16228	226	48.7	29.6	19.0	0.9	1.8	26118	27587	4	17	191	44.5	29.3	24.1	2.1	0.0	61364
39769	STURGIS	16642	728	40.1	31.7	22.9	4.5	0.7	30549	29905	9	40	592	40.4	27.2	24.2	8.3	0.0	59661
	MISSISSIPPI	18363		35.3	29.0	27.5	5.7	2.5	36311	37046				25.4	28.2	31.6	12.7	2.1	84642
	UNITED STATES	27277		20.9	24.4	35.3	11.7	7.6	54719	56938				9.3	13.1	31.6	32.6	13.5	162279

ZIP CODE #	POST OFFICE NAME	FINANCIAL SERVICES: Auto Loan	Home Loan	Invest-ments	Retire-ment Plans	THE HOME: Home Improvements: Home Repair	Lawn & Garden	Furnishings: Computers & Hardware-Personal	Major Appli-ances	TV, Radio, Sound Equip-ment	Furni-ture	ENTERTAINMENT: Dine out/ Carry out	Sports Equip-ment	Fees & Tickets	Toys & Games	Travel	Cable TV	PERSONAL: Apparel & Services	Auto Repairs	Health Insur-ance	Pets & Supplies
39451	LEAKESVILLE	74	53	66	52	54	72	56	67	62	53	60	51	45	63	52	68	40	63	71	80
39452	LUCEDALE	81	63	68	61	62	77	64	72	69	63	68	54	54	72	59	74	46	69	75	87
39455	LUMBERTON	69	49	63	47	50	67	51	61	57	49	56	47	41	58	48	62	37	58	65	74
39456	MC LAIN	68	47	61	45	47	66	49	60	56	47	55	46	38	57	45	62	36	56	63	73
39459	MOSELLE	75	54	75	52	55	75	55	69	61	52	60	52	44	61	54	67	40	64	72	83
39461	NEELY	79	56	66	55	56	75	59	69	65	57	64	53	47	68	54	71	43	65	72	83
39462	NEW AUGUSTA	69	47	64	44	46	67	49	60	56	47	55	47	38	57	46	62	36	57	63	74
39464	OVETT	73	53	60	51	52	69	55	63	61	53	59	49	44	63	50	66	40	60	67	77
39465	PETAL	71	67	60	66	65	70	65	67	67	65	67	50	63	69	63	69	46	66	70	80
39466	PICAYUNE	72	57	68	55	57	72	58	67	63	56	62	51	50	64	56	68	42	64	71	81
39470	POPLARVILLE	76	58	73	56	59	76	59	71	64	56	63	53	50	65	57	70	42	66	74	84
39474	PRENTISS	70	46	67	43	46	69	49	62	57	46	55	48	37	57	46	63	37	58	65	76
39475	PURVIS	83	73	75	71	72	80	70	78	73	71	73	58	65	75	68	75	49	74	77	91
39476	RICHTON	74	54	64	52	54	71	56	66	62	55	61	50	46	64	52	67	41	62	69	79
39478	SANDY HOOK	66	43	64	41	43	65	46	58	53	44	52	46	35	54	43	60	35	55	62	72
39479	SEMINARY	76	55	64	54	55	73	57	67	63	55	62	51	46	65	53	69	42	63	70	81
39480	SOSO	77	55	74	52	55	76	56	69	63	54	62	53	45	64	54	69	41	65	72	84
39481	STRINGER	82	59	75	57	59	80	61	74	68	58	66	56	48	69	57	74	44	69	77	89
39482	SUMRALL	79	65	67	62	63	75	64	71	68	64	68	53	56	71	60	73	46	68	73	86
39483	FOXWORTH	65	44	59	42	44	63	47	57	53	45	52	44	36	55	43	59	35	54	60	70
39501	GULFPORT	55	45	41	47	43	50	52	49	55	50	55	38	48	56	47	58	38	53	55	61
39503	GULFPORT	84	79	69	78	76	78	77	78	78	79	79	59	74	81	73	79	54	77	78	93
39507	GULFPORT	73	70	69	71	70	74	74	73	75	72	75	55	73	74	73	77	52	75	79	86
39520	BAY SAINT LOUIS	68	58	65	58	59	68	60	65	63	58	62	49	55	63	59	66	42	64	68	77
39525	DIAMONDHEAD	92	89	127	88	101	108	82	100	87	88	85	66	85	79	93	91	58	94	107	114
39530	BILOXI	59	50	49	51	49	56	58	55	61	55	60	42	53	60	53	63	41	59	62	67
39531	BILOXI	70	58	55	61	57	58	72	62	71	70	72	51	66	72	65	71	50	69	65	76
39532	BILOXI	84	83	73	81	80	84	77	80	79	79	79	60	76	81	76	81	54	79	82	95
39534	BILOXI	73	38	28	44	34	32	69	48	65	64	68	48	52	78	50	60	48	61	43	58
39540	DIBERVILLE	72	65	58	64	63	68	66	67	67	66	67	50	61	69	62	69	46	66	68	80
39553	GAUTIER	82	79	68	78	76	78	77	77	78	79	78	58	75	81	74	79	54	77	78	92
39556	KILN	71	65	61	62	63	66	64	66	65	66	65	50	60	67	61	65	44	65	65	78
39560	LONG BEACH	78	79	69	80	76	81	77	78	78	76	78	60	78	79	77	79	54	78	81	93
39561	MC HENRY	80	70	65	68	69	75	67	73	71	69	71	53	62	74	64	74	48	70	74	87
39562	MOSS POINT	83	69	69	67	68	80	68	75	73	68	72	57	61	76	64	77	49	72	78	90
39563	MOSS POINT	65	63	60	63	61	70	60	64	65	61	65	46	62	64	61	69	44	64	72	77
39564	OCEAN SPRINGS	90	95	86	94	93	93	88	90	88	91	89	68	91	90	89	89	62	88	91	105
39565	VANCLEAVE	82	73	67	71	71	77	70	75	73	72	73	55	65	76	66	75	49	72	75	89
39567	PASCAGOULA	63	55	57	56	55	65	60	62	65	57	63	46	56	63	57	69	43	63	70	74
39571	PASS CHRISTIAN	83	76	75	75	75	81	75	79	77	75	76	59	70	78	73	79	52	77	80	94
39572	PEARLINGTON	69	47	68	44	47	68	49	62	56	46	54	48	38	56	47	62	36	58	65	75
39573	PERKINSTON	78	68	64	66	67	74	66	71	69	68	69	53	61	72	62	72	47	69	72	85
39574	SAUCIER	77	71	62	69	69	71	69	71	70	71	70	52	65	73	65	71	48	70	70	84
39576	WAVELAND	67	59	64	60	61	69	62	66	64	59	63	50	58	64	61	67	43	65	71	78
39577	WIGGINS	71	55	62	54	55	69	59	65	63	56	62	49	50	64	55	68	42	63	69	78
39581	PASCAGOULA	68	60	53	62	57	62	68	62	69	65	69	50	63	70	62	70	48	67	67	76
39601	BROOKHAVEN	66	53	56	53	53	65	56	61	61	55	60	45	50	62	52	66	41	60	66	73
39629	BOGUE CHITTO	76	54	67	52	54	73	56	67	63	54	61	51	45	64	52	68	41	63	70	81
39630	BUDE	54	35	52	33	35	53	37	47	43	36	42	37	28	44	35	48	28	44	50	58
39631	CENTREVILLE	65	43	64	41	44	64	46	58	53	44	51	45	35	53	43	59	34	54	61	71
39633	CROSBY	58	38	56	36	38	57	41	51	47	39	46	40	31	48	38	52	30	48	54	63
39638	GLOSTER	65	43	63	40	43	64	45	57	52	43	51	45	34	53	43	58	34	54	61	70
39641	JAYESS	70	49	70	47	50	70	51	64	57	48	56	49	40	57	49	63	37	59	67	77
39643	KOKOMO	65	44	63	41	44	64	46	58	53	44	52	45	35	54	43	59	34	54	61	71
39645	LIBERTY	73	50	72	47	50	73	53	66	60	49	58	51	41	60	50	66	39	62	70	80
39647	MC CALL CREEK	73	50	72	48	51	72	52	66	59	49	58	50	40	59	50	65	38	61	69	79
39648	MCCOMB	60	48	52	48	47	59	52	55	58	51	56	42	47	57	49	61	38	56	62	68
39652	MAGNOLIA	69	46	65	44	46	68	49	61	57	47	55	47	38	57	46	63	37	58	65	75
39653	MEADVILLE	81	55	80	53	56	81	58	73	66	54	64	56	45	66	56	73	42	68	77	89
39654	MONTICELLO	80	57	75	56	58	80	61	74	68	57	66	56	49	69	58	75	44	70	80	88
39656	OAK VALE	75	54	62	53	54	72	56	65	62	55	61	50	45	65	51	68	41	62	69	80
39657	OSYKA	76	50	74	47	50	75	53	67	61	51	60	52	40	62	50	68	40	63	71	83
39661	ROXIE	69	45	66	42	45	67	48	60	55	46	54	47	36	56	45	62	36	57	64	74
39662	RUTH	80	59	71	57	59	78	60	72	67	58	65	55	49	68	56	73	44	67	75	86
39663	SILVER CREEK	70	46	65	44	46	68	49	61	56	47	55	47	37	57	46	62	36	57	64	75
39664	SMITHDALE	78	55	72	53	56	76	57	70	64	54	62	53	45	65	54	70	42	65	73	84
39665	SONTAG	85	55	82	52	55	83	59	75	68	56	67	58	44	70	55	76	44	70	79	92
39666	SUMMIT	84	63	80	61	63	83	64	77	71	62	70	58	53	72	61	77	47	72	80	92
39667	TYLERTOWN	69	47	65	45	47	68	50	62	57	48	56	47	39	58	47	63	37	58	66	75
39668	UNION CHURCH	69	45	67	42	45	68	48	61	56	46	54	47	36	56	45	62	36	57	64	75
39669	WOODVILLE	67	45	63	43	45	66	49	59	57	47	55	46	38	57	45	63	37	57	64	73
39701	COLUMBUS	58	46	47	47	45	55	51	52	57	51	56	39	47	56	47	60	38	54	59	64
39702	COLUMBUS	73	64	61	63	62	72	64	68	68	63	67	51	59	70	61	72	46	67	72	82
39705	COLUMBUS	89	83	75	85	80	82	87	83	87	87	87	66	85	90	83	86	61	86	84	99
39710	COLUMBUS	79	41	31	48	37	35	74	51	70	69	74	51	56	84	54	64	52	66	46	63
39730	ABERDEEN	66	50	54	49	48	63	54	58	60	53	59	45	47	61	50	65	40	58	64	72
39735	ACKERMAN	67	50	60	50	51	66	55	62	60	51	58	47	45	60	51	65	39	60	66	74
39739	BROOKSVILLE	66	44	62	41	44	64	47	58	53	44	52	45	35	54	43	59	35	54	61	71
39740	CALEDONIA	81	73	66	71	71	76	70	74	73	72	73	54	65	76	66	75	49	72	75	88
39741	CEDARBLUFF	77	55	65	53	55	74	57	67	64	56	63	52	46	66	52	70	42	64	71	82
39743	CRAWFORD	66	42	62	40	42	64	45	57	52	43	51	44	34	53	42	58	34	54	60	70
39744	EUPORA	66	47	63	45	47	65	52	60	58	49	56	46	42	57	48	64	38	58	65	73
39745	FRENCH CAMP	67	45	61	43	45	65	48	59	55	46	53	46	37	56	44	60	36	55	62	72
39746	HAMILTON	83	59	70	58	59	80	62	73	69	60	68	56	49	72	56	75	45	69	77	88
39747	KILMICHAEL	70	46	67	43	45	69	49	61	56	46	55	48	37	57	46	63	36	58	65	76
39750	MABEN	75	52	67	50	52	73	55	66	62	53	60	51	43	64	50	68	40	62	69	80
39751	MANTEE	87	62	72	61	62	83	65	76	72	63	71	58	52	75	59	79	47	72	80	92
39752	MATHISTON	74	51	65	49	51	71	54	65	61	52	59	50	42	63	49	67	40	61	68	79
39755	PHEBA	77	54	65	53	54	73	57	67	63	55	62	51	45	66	52	69	42	63	70	81
39756	PRAIRIE	77	50	74	47	50	75	54	67	62	51	60	53	40	63	50	69	40	63	71	83
39759	STARKVILLE	64	48	49	50	47	53	68	56	64	59	64	47	54	65	54	64	45	62	58	69
39762	MISSISSIPPI STATE	39	20	19	23	18	22	52	29	43	37	43	29	33	42	30	40	31	38	29	38
39766	STEENS	74	63	68	64	64	78	63	72	66	57	65	55	56	68	62	71	44	67	75	85
39767	STEWART	72	47	69	44	47	70	50	63	58	48	56	49	37	59	47	64	37	59	67	78
39769	STURGIS	71	50	72	48	51	71	51	65	58	48	57	49	40	58	50	64	37	60	68	78
	MISSISSIPPI	77	63	67	62	62	74	66	70	70	65	69	54	59	71	62	74	47	70	74	85
	UNITED STATES	100	100	100	100	100	100	100	100	100	100	100	100	100	100	100	100	100	100	100	100

ZIP CODE #	POST OFFICE NAME	COUNTY FIPS CODE	POPULATION 2000	POPULATION 2009	POPULATION 2014	2000-2009 ANNUAL RATE % Rate	2000-2009 ANNUAL RATE State Centile	HOUSEHOLDS 2000	HOUSEHOLDS 2009	HOUSEHOLDS 2014	HOUSEHOLDS % Annual Rate 2000-2009	HOUSEHOLDS 2009 Average HH Size	FAMILIES 2000	FAMILIES 2009	FAMILIES % Annual Rate 2000-2009
39772	WEIR	019	1558	1562	1543	0.0	52	577	598	598	0.4	2.61	418	423	0.1
39773	WEST POINT	025	20391	19549	18978	-0.5	25	7565	7561	7422	0.0	2.54	5455	5317	-0.3
39776	WOODLAND	017	1890	2020	2037	0.7	79	673	735	745	1.0	2.75	522	558	0.7
	MISSISSIPPI					0.5					0.8	2.56			0.5
	UNITED STATES					1.0					1.1	2.59			0.9

ZIP CODE #	POST OFFICE NAME	RACE (%) White 2000	White 2009	Black 2000	Black 2009	Asian/Pacific 2000	Asian/Pacific 2009	% Hispanic Origin 2000	% Hispanic Origin 2009	2009 AGE DISTRIBUTION (%) 0-4	5-9	10-14	15-19	20-24	25-44	45-64	65-84	85+	18+	MEDIAN AGE 2009	% 2009 Males	% 2009 Females
39772	WEIR	53.8	50.3	45.2	48.5	0.1	0.1	0.5	0.6	7.4	7.4	7.4	7.5	6.0	22.9	27.3	12.2	2.0	73.1	37.1	48.0	52.0
39773	WEST POINT	41.6	38.6	57.6	60.2	0.2	0.3	0.9	1.2	7.5	7.7	7.6	7.7	6.8	24.8	25.1	10.7	2.0	72.6	34.9	47.6	52.4
39776	WOODLAND	56.5	52.0	41.3	45.0	0.4	0.5	2.5	3.5	7.4	7.3	7.4	7.7	6.4	25.3	26.5	10.4	1.5	73.2	36.2	50.0	50.0
	MISSISSIPPI	61.4	59.6	36.3	37.4	0.7	0.9	1.4	2.0	7.2	7.1	7.0	7.5	7.1	26.4	25.3	10.6	1.7	74.3	35.6	48.6	51.4
	UNITED STATES	75.1	72.0	12.3	12.7	3.8	4.6	12.5	15.7	6.8	6.7	6.6	7.1	6.9	27.0	26.0	10.9	1.9	75.7	36.9	49.2	50.8

39772-39776

#	POST OFFICE NAME	2009 Per Capita Income	2009 HH Income Base	2009 Household Income Distribution (%): Less than $25,000	$25,000 to $49,999	$50,000 to $99,999	$100,000 to $149,999	$150,000 or More	Median Household Income: 2009	2014	2009 National Centile	2009 State Centile	2009 Home Value Base	2009 Home Value Distribution (%): Less than $50,000	$50,000 to $89,999	$90,000 to $174,999	$175,000 to $399,999	$400,000 or More	2009 Median Home Value
39772	WEIR	15629	598	44.6	30.6	19.1	3.3	2.3	29232	29667	7	31	505	36.6	36.0	21.0	5.3	1.0	62255
39773	WEST POINT	17111	7561	40.1	28.5	23.8	5.4	2.2	32198	32522	12	54	5453	24.7	39.0	28.0	7.2	1.2	76244
39776	WOODLAND	15571	735	43.4	27.6	23.8	2.7	2.4	31253	31200	10	47	635	45.4	29.9	18.4	5.5	0.8	57763
	MISSISSIPPI	18363		35.3	29.0	27.5	5.7	2.5	36311	37046				25.4	28.2	31.6	12.7	2.1	84642
	UNITED STATES	27277		20.9	24.4	35.3	11.7	7.6	54719	56938				9.3	13.1	31.6	32.6	13.5	162279

ZIP CODE	FINANCIAL SERVICES				THE HOME						ENTERTAINMENT						PERSONAL			
					Home Improvements		Furnishings													
# POST OFFICE NAME	Auto Loan	Home Loan	Invest-ments	Retire-ment Plans	Home Repair	Lawn & Garden	Comput-ers & Hard-ware-Personal	Major Appli-ances	TV, Radio, Sound Equip-ment	Furni-ture	Dine out/ Carry out	Sports Equip-ment	Fees & Tickets	Toys & Games	Travel	Cable TV	Apparel & Services	Auto Repairs	Health Insur-ance	Pets & Supplies
39772 WEIR	76	49	73	47	49	74	53	67	61	50	60	52	40	62	49	68	39	63	70	82
39773 WEST POINT	72	55	60	55	54	69	60	65	66	57	64	50	51	66	55	71	44	64	70	79
39776 WOODLAND	79	53	72	51	53	76	56	69	64	54	63	53	43	66	52	71	42	65	73	84
MISSISSIPPI	77	63	67	62	62	74	66	70	70	65	69	54	59	71	62	74	47	70	74	85
UNITED STATES	100	100	100	100	100	100	100	100	100	100	100	100	100	100	100	100	100	100	100	100

ZIP CODE #	POST OFFICE NAME	COUNTY FIPS CODE	POPULATION 2000	POPULATION 2009	POPULATION 2014	2000-2009 ANNUAL RATE % Rate	2000-2009 ANNUAL RATE State Centile	HOUSEHOLDS 2000	HOUSEHOLDS 2009	HOUSEHOLDS 2014	HOUSEHOLDS % Annual Rate 2000-2009	HOUSEHOLDS 2009 Average HH Size	FAMILIES 2000	FAMILIES 2009	FAMILIES % Annual Rate 2000-2009
63005	CHESTERFIELD	189	16613	18259	18564	1.0	76	5469	6101	6233	1.2	2.99	4558	4998	1.0
63010	ARNOLD	099	34226	36803	37971	0.8	69	12583	13728	14243	0.9	2.66	9527	10071	0.6
63011	BALLWIN	189	38555	37487	36979	-0.3	21	14129	14085	13995	0.0	2.65	11151	10792	-0.4
63012	BARNHART	099	10080	11148	11776	1.1	79	3290	3705	3946	1.3	2.99	2772	3052	1.0
63013	BEAUFORT	071	1624	1899	2005	1.7	89	551	655	697	1.9	2.90	445	516	1.6
63014	BERGER	071	1113	1200	1231	0.8	69	416	456	470	1.0	2.63	317	336	0.6
63015	CATAWISSA	071	1930	2190	2322	1.4	86	691	801	854	1.6	2.72	541	608	1.3
63016	CEDAR HILL	099	7864	8607	8938	1.0	76	2695	3008	3148	1.2	2.82	2113	2285	0.8
63017	CHESTERFIELD	189	41911	42075	41871	0.0	37	16055	16514	16549	0.3	2.44	11670	11559	-0.1
63019	CRYSTAL CITY	099	3876	4340	4562	1.2	82	1567	1779	1882	1.4	2.35	1076	1170	0.9
63020	DE SOTO	099	19932	22025	22979	1.1	79	7310	8230	8641	1.3	2.64	5486	5983	0.9
63021	BALLWIN	189	55643	56390	56178	0.1	42	20455	21073	21112	0.3	2.66	15389	15339	0.0
63023	DITTMER	099	5228	5906	6252	1.3	83	1883	2164	2306	1.5	2.73	1469	1634	1.2
63025	EUREKA	189	11129	14182	14987	2.7	96	3673	4601	4881	2.5	3.03	3068	3750	2.2
63026	FENTON	189	41110	44469	45783	0.9	72	14877	16432	17045	1.1	2.69	11429	12241	0.7
63028	FESTUS	099	22851	26568	28281	1.6	89	8323	9811	10498	1.8	2.65	6200	7073	1.4
63030	FLETCHER	221	257	290	305	1.3	83	89	102	109	1.5	2.84	72	80	1.1
63031	FLORISSANT	189	50520	49373	48752	-0.2	27	19278	19298	19194	0.0	2.51	13664	13129	-0.4
63033	FLORISSANT	189	44300	43107	42633	-0.3	21	17312	17284	17218	0.0	2.47	11937	11394	-0.5
63034	FLORISSANT	189	16798	18141	18292	0.8	69	5798	6456	6568	1.2	2.79	4802	5199	0.9
63036	FRENCH VILLAGE	187	715	817	888	1.5	87	294	340	373	1.6	2.40	231	259	1.2
63037	GERALD	071	3136	3534	3734	1.3	83	1195	1373	1460	1.5	2.55	883	978	1.1
63038	GLENCOE	189	5104	5560	5632	0.9	72	1644	1817	1852	1.1	3.05	1440	1565	0.9
63039	GRAY SUMMIT	071	827	940	996	1.4	86	307	356	380	1.6	2.64	245	276	1.3
63040	GROVER	189	7805	8064	8031	0.4	53	2756	2933	2957	0.7	2.75	2186	2257	0.3
63041	GRUBVILLE	071	331	378	398	1.4	86	116	135	144	1.7	2.80	92	105	1.4
63042	HAZELWOOD	189	19493	19144	18938	-0.2	27	8573	8624	8589	0.1	2.21	5021	4768	-0.6
63043	MARYLAND HEIGHTS	189	22339	21945	21705	-0.2	27	9476	9549	9515	0.1	2.28	5837	5564	-0.5
63044	BRIDGETON	189	14686	13732	13442	-0.7	8	5827	5576	5499	-0.5	2.37	3988	3658	-0.9
63048	HERCULANEUM	099	2737	3300	3502	2.0	92	1001	1212	1294	2.1	2.64	691	812	1.8
63049	HIGH RIDGE	099	14068	15961	16689	1.4	86	5098	5922	6237	1.6	2.69	3869	4327	1.2
63050	HILLSBORO	099	13383	15358	16415	1.5	87	4689	5490	5915	1.7	2.76	3725	4246	1.4
63051	HOUSE SPRINGS	099	12542	13268	13632	0.6	63	4442	4776	4939	0.8	2.78	3427	3570	0.4
63052	IMPERIAL	099	22296	27825	30256	2.4	95	7678	9647	10515	2.5	2.88	6200	7668	2.3
63055	LABADIE	071	2077	2370	2498	1.4	86	742	863	916	1.6	2.75	586	662	1.3
63056	LESLIE	071	2171	2386	2522	1.0	76	811	909	967	1.2	2.62	628	681	0.9
63060	LONEDELL	071	2500	2649	2707	0.6	63	874	942	968	0.8	2.81	689	721	0.5
63061	LUEBBERING	071	239	272	286	1.4	86	81	94	100	1.6	2.89	64	73	1.4
63068	NEW HAVEN	071	4256	4447	4540	0.5	58	1567	1664	1708	0.7	2.63	1172	1202	0.3
63069	PACIFIC	071	15475	16828	17422	0.9	72	5322	5890	6140	1.1	2.64	3971	4256	0.8
63070	PEVELY	099	5576	6836	7460	2.2	94	2070	2572	2818	2.4	2.65	1561	1871	2.0
63071	RICHWOODS	221	1439	1539	1592	0.7	66	529	579	604	1.0	2.66	396	420	0.6
63072	ROBERTSVILLE	071	3010	3315	3468	1.0	76	1036	1170	1233	1.3	2.82	833	914	1.0
63074	SAINT ANN	189	15164	14662	14427	-0.4	18	6902	6832	6768	-0.1	2.14	3895	3628	-0.8
63077	SAINT CLAIR	071	10988	12066	12522	1.0	76	4170	4656	4857	1.2	2.57	3013	3243	0.8
63080	SULLIVAN	071	12212	13330	13818	1.0	76	4724	5200	5410	1.0	2.52	3358	3572	0.7
63084	UNION	071	14369	16267	17102	1.4	86	5282	6111	6475	1.6	2.62	3862	4323	1.2
63087	VALLES MINES	187	699	851	924	2.1	93	252	313	342	2.4	2.71	197	238	2.1
63088	VALLEY PARK	189	7727	8430	8596	0.9	72	3245	3687	3806	1.4	2.25	1832	1949	0.7
63089	VILLA RIDGE	071	5870	6397	6640	0.9	72	2098	2333	2437	1.2	2.74	1634	1760	0.8
63090	WASHINGTON	071	20247	22171	22934	1.0	76	7641	8469	8802	1.1	2.58	5455	5859	0.8
63091	ROSEBUD	073	1149	1257	1292	1.0	76	457	507	524	1.1	2.41	350	376	0.8
63101	SAINT LOUIS	510	809	1103	1213	3.4	97	429	567	624	3.1	1.94	189	206	0.9
63102	SAINT LOUIS	510	1258	1369	1389	0.9	72	654	714	730	1.0	1.24	66	61	-0.8
63103	SAINT LOUIS	510	4656	4978	5036	0.7	66	2939	3095	3137	0.6	1.41	427	421	-0.2
63104	SAINT LOUIS	510	18457	19671	19976	0.7	66	8014	8387	8510	0.5	2.28	3855	3853	0.0
63105	SAINT LOUIS	189	14523	17156	16936	1.8	90	6332	6186	6103	-0.3	2.01	3199	2913	-1.0
63106	SAINT LOUIS	510	10657	10856	10998	0.2	46	4247	4233	4288	0.0	2.47	2359	2247	-0.5
63107	SAINT LOUIS	510	16395	14800	14624	-1.1	2	5654	4996	4933	-1.3	2.90	3719	3164	-1.7
63108	SAINT LOUIS	510	19622	20676	20951	0.6	63	10168	10677	10847	0.5	1.66	2829	2718	-0.4
63109	SAINT LOUIS	510	29613	30813	30912	0.4	53	14361	14638	14676	0.2	2.09	7162	6918	-0.4
63110	SAINT LOUIS	510	20621	20178	20164	-0.2	27	8275	7968	7964	-0.4	2.43	4391	3996	-1.0
63111	SAINT LOUIS	510	21137	20323	20206	-0.4	18	8797	8170	8107	-0.8	2.40	4760	4200	-1.3
63112	SAINT LOUIS	510	23068	23715	23864	0.3	50	10045	10210	10279	0.2	2.29	4911	4691	-0.5
63113	SAINT LOUIS	510	16840	16097	16095	-0.5	14	6253	5869	5870	-0.7	2.67	3693	3299	-1.2
63114	SAINT LOUIS	189	39176	36993	36105	-0.6	11	16248	15695	15428	-0.4	2.34	10081	9224	-1.0
63115	SAINT LOUIS	510	25268	24576	24500	-0.3	21	9998	9541	9505	-0.5	2.57	6246	5718	-1.0
63116	SAINT LOUIS	510	47667	49374	49479	0.4	53	20495	20604	20619	0.1	2.38	11377	10886	-0.5
63117	SAINT LOUIS	189	9528	9018	8812	-0.6	11	4548	4399	4326	-0.4	2.02	2164	1950	-1.1
63118	SAINT LOUIS	510	30466	28111	27802	-0.9	4	11413	10062	9936	-1.4	2.77	6668	5606	-1.9
63119	SAINT LOUIS	189	34338	32974	32386	-0.4	18	14732	14488	14329	-0.2	2.21	8773	8169	-0.8
63120	SAINT LOUIS	510	13278	12972	12887	-0.3	21	4432	4264	4239	-0.4	2.95	3153	2939	-0.8
63121	SAINT LOUIS	189	29299	27237	26538	-0.8	6	11749	11122	10909	-0.6	2.41	7411	6688	-1.1
63122	SAINT LOUIS	189	38244	37475	37011	-0.2	27	15850	15947	15868	0.1	2.30	10303	9854	-0.5
63123	SAINT LOUIS	189	49835	48949	48396	-0.2	27	22161	22228	22121	0.0	2.19	13567	12913	-0.5
63124	SAINT LOUIS	189	9907	9565	9413	-0.4	18	4245	4182	4145	-0.2	2.26	2831	2666	-0.6
63125	SAINT LOUIS	189	33150	32053	31524	-0.4	18	14194	14033	13899	-0.1	2.24	8808	8254	-0.7
63126	SAINT LOUIS	189	14814	14426	14240	-0.3	21	6389	6391	6358	0.0	2.25	4384	4196	-0.5
63127	SAINT LOUIS	189	5226	5306	5296	0.2	46	2083	2182	2197	0.5	2.34	1429	1429	0.0
63128	SAINT LOUIS	189	29287	29643	29560	0.1	42	11934	12401	12458	0.4	2.36	8350	8311	-0.1
63129	SAINT LOUIS	189	51191	53308	53507	0.4	53	19197	20386	20591	0.7	2.59	14141	14548	0.3
63130	SAINT LOUIS	189	34501	29849	29161	-1.6	0	13179	12764	12555	-0.3	2.29	7735	7104	-0.9
63131	SAINT LOUIS	189	16416	15838	15599	-0.4	18	5974	5918	5869	-0.1	2.66	4832	4657	-0.4
63132	SAINT LOUIS	189	14087	13479	13196	-0.5	14	6174	6074	5997	-0.2	2.20	3779	3504	-0.8
63133	SAINT LOUIS	189	8259	8139	7956	-0.2	27	2791	2887	2843	0.4	2.77	1991	1932	-0.3
63134	SAINT LOUIS	189	15097	14290	13957	-0.6	11	5610	5413	5321	-0.4	2.62	3850	3566	-0.8
63135	SAINT LOUIS	189	22322	21077	20536	-0.6	11	8391	7995	7823	-0.5	2.61	5772	5255	-1.0
63136	SAINT LOUIS	189	53901	51475	50408	-0.5	14	20063	19368	19051	-0.4	2.64	14073	13023	-0.8
63137	SAINT LOUIS	189	21029	19965	19571	-0.6	11	8296	8019	7886	-0.4	2.42	5572	5154	-0.8
63138	SAINT LOUIS	189	21879	21397	21124	-0.2	27	8561	8426	8335	-0.2	2.52	5812	5465	-0.7
63139	SAINT LOUIS	510	24094	25019	25129	0.4	53	11617	11830	11863	0.2	2.07	5515	5312	-0.4
63140	SAINT LOUIS	189	449	410	396	-1.0	3	157	147	143	-0.7	2.78	112	100	-1.2
63141	SAINT LOUIS	189	20090	20095	19972	0.0	37	8089	8304	8317	0.3	2.31	5578	5474	-0.2
63143	SAINT LOUIS	189	11010	10326	10059	-0.7	8	5596	5346	5238	-0.5	1.93	2464	2184	-1.3
63144	SAINT LOUIS	189	9056	8991	8918	-0.1	32	4643	4642	4611	0.0	1.93	2154	2031	-0.6
	MISSOURI					0.7					0.8	2.45			0.4
	UNITED STATES					1.0					1.1	2.59			0.9

ZIP CODE #	POST OFFICE NAME	RACE (%) White 2000	White 2009	Black 2000	Black 2009	Asian/Pacific 2000	Asian/Pacific 2009	% Hispanic Origin 2000	% Hispanic Origin 2009	2009 AGE DISTRIBUTION (%) 0-4	5-9	10-14	15-19	20-24	25-44	45-64	65-84	85+	18+	MEDIAN AGE 2009	% 2009 Males	% 2009 Females
63005	CHESTERFIELD	93.4	90.4	1.9	2.7	3.5	5.3	1.6	2.3	6.9	8.4	9.6	8.1	4.0	23.2	32.2	7.1	0.5	69.6	38.8	49.9	50.1
63010	ARNOLD	97.9	97.4	0.2	0.3	0.4	0.6	1.1	1.5	7.2	7.1	7.0	6.5	5.4	28.4	26.8	10.5	1.2	74.8	37.2	48.9	51.1
63011	BALLWIN	93.3	90.5	1.7	2.3	3.4	5.2	1.7	2.3	6.3	7.0	7.7	7.0	4.7	22.1	30.2	13.2	2.0	74.5	41.8	48.5	51.5
63012	BARNHART	98.0	97.6	0.3	0.4	0.3	0.5	1.2	1.6	7.7	7.8	7.7	7.1	6.1	28.9	27.1	7.0	0.6	72.2	34.3	50.3	49.7
63013	BEAUFORT	98.8	98.6	0.2	0.3	0.2	0.3	0.7	0.9	6.1	6.5	7.1	7.4	5.3	24.8	30.8	11.1	1.0	75.7	40.6	51.0	49.0
63014	BERGER	98.4	98.1	0.4	0.4	0.2	0.3	0.4	0.5	6.1	6.7	7.1	6.9	4.7	23.3	31.7	12.4	1.3	75.8	41.7	51.2	48.8
63015	CATAWISSA	98.4	97.9	0.3	0.3	0.4	0.5	0.8	1.1	6.1	6.3	6.9	7.5	5.9	26.1	30.9	9.4	0.8	76.0	39.2	49.9	50.1
63016	CEDAR HILL	98.3	97.8	0.1	0.1	0.3	0.4	0.7	1.0	6.7	6.9	7.2	7.4	5.7	26.5	29.4	9.2	1.1	74.6	38.1	49.7	50.3
63017	CHESTERFIELD	91.0	86.8	1.9	2.6	5.8	9.0	1.4	1.9	4.6	5.3	6.5	6.3	4.3	19.8	32.5	16.4	4.3	79.4	47.0	47.3	52.7
63019	CRYSTAL CITY	94.0	92.9	3.6	4.1	0.4	0.7	0.5	0.8	7.0	6.7	6.2	6.4	5.8	24.5	25.9	14.3	3.2	76.3	40.2	47.7	52.3
63020	DE SOTO	97.5	97.0	0.9	1.0	0.2	0.4	0.9	1.2	6.6	6.7	6.7	6.4	5.4	26.5	28.4	11.5	1.9	76.0	38.9	49.4	50.6
63021	BALLWIN	92.5	89.3	1.9	2.6	4.0	6.1	1.5	2.1	7.5	8.0	8.2	7.0	4.6	27.1	28.6	7.9	1.0	71.7	37.3	48.4	51.6
63023	DITTMER	98.5	98.1	0.1	0.1	0.2	0.4	0.6	0.8	6.1	6.4	7.2	7.4	5.1	27.0	30.6	9.2	0.9	75.6	39.2	50.2	49.8
63025	EUREKA	97.7	96.7	0.5	0.7	0.6	1.0	1.0	1.5	8.1	8.2	8.3	7.1	4.6	27.8	27.4	7.1	1.4	70.5	35.6	49.1	50.9
63026	FENTON	97.1	96.0	0.7	0.9	0.8	1.3	1.1	1.6	7.4	7.5	7.5	6.9	5.7	27.7	28.6	7.8	1.0	73.4	36.2	49.6	50.4
63028	FESTUS	95.9	95.1	2.2	2.4	0.6	0.9	0.8	1.0	6.8	6.8	6.9	6.8	5.5	26.5	27.5	11.3	1.9	75.3	38.3	49.0	51.0
63030	FLETCHER	97.7	97.6	0.4	0.3	0.0	0.0	1.2	1.4	8.3	8.3	7.6	6.2	5.5	27.6	26.2	9.7	0.7	72.1	35.0	50.7	49.3
63031	FLORISSANT	85.3	80.7	11.8	15.6	0.8	1.2	1.4	1.9	6.5	6.6	6.9	6.9	5.7	26.5	27.1	11.8	2.2	75.7	38.5	47.7	52.3
63033	FLORISSANT	53.3	46.6	43.9	50.1	0.8	1.0	1.2	1.4	6.2	6.1	6.3	6.7	6.1	25.4	27.0	13.7	2.5	77.4	39.7	46.6	53.4
63034	FLORISSANT	67.0	57.6	29.8	38.7	1.4	1.9	1.0	1.2	5.2	6.0	6.9	7.1	5.1	23.0	34.0	11.3	1.5	77.4	42.7	48.2	51.8
63036	FRENCH VILLAGE	98.3	97.9	0.0	0.0	0.0	0.0	0.4	0.6	5.4	5.8	6.2	6.6	4.9	22.5	33.0	14.3	1.2	78.5	44.0	51.0	49.0
63037	GERALD	99.0	98.6	0.0	0.0	0.2	0.4	0.7	1.0	5.3	5.7	6.1	6.6	5.1	24.3	31.0	13.9	2.1	78.7	42.7	50.9	49.1
63038	GLENCOE	95.8	93.6	1.7	2.4	1.4	2.2	1.6	2.4	6.8	8.3	9.4	8.4	3.8	21.0	33.8	8.0	0.5	69.8	40.4	49.6	50.4
63039	GRAY SUMMIT	96.5	95.7	1.6	1.8	0.4	0.5	0.5	0.7	6.9	7.4	7.8	6.6	4.4	25.2	30.5	10.3	0.9	73.7	39.1	50.1	49.9
63040	GROVER	94.6	91.9	1.2	1.8	2.9	4.7	1.3	1.8	9.6	10.0	10.0	7.8	3.8	28.3	25.7	4.6	0.4	65.4	33.7	48.8	51.2
63041	GRUBVILLE	98.8	98.7	0.3	0.3	0.0	0.0	0.6	0.5	7.4	7.1	7.7	7.9	5.6	25.9	28.8	8.5	1.1	73.3	36.9	51.6	48.4
63042	HAZELWOOD	79.1	74.3	17.0	20.9	1.3	1.9	1.8	2.4	6.1	6.0	5.8	6.2	7.2	30.3	25.3	11.6	1.5	78.4	36.6	48.6	51.4
63043	MARYLAND HEIGHTS	86.6	81.6	5.2	6.9	6.4	9.4	1.8	2.4	6.0	5.5	5.6	5.8	7.3	30.6	26.6	11.3	1.2	79.5	37.9	48.8	51.2
63044	BRIDGETON	87.6	83.6	8.1	10.6	2.2	3.3	2.1	2.7	4.9	5.0	5.4	6.1	5.7	24.2	29.3	16.4	3.1	80.8	44.0	48.0	52.0
63048	HERCULANEUM	95.1	94.6	3.6	3.7	0.3	0.6	0.5	0.8	7.4	7.4	7.1	6.3	5.5	26.1	25.5	11.9	2.9	74.1	37.6	47.7	52.3
63049	HIGH RIDGE	98.1	97.6	0.2	0.3	0.3	0.5	1.1	1.5	6.7	6.9	7.1	6.9	5.1	29.0	29.2	8.3	0.8	75.0	37.5	49.9	50.1
63050	HILLSBORO	98.0	97.6	0.4	0.5	0.2	0.3	0.9	1.3	6.4	6.7	7.2	7.4	5.2	26.7	29.5	10.0	0.8	74.9	38.3	50.4	49.6
63051	HOUSE SPRINGS	97.8	97.3	0.2	0.2	0.2	0.3	1.1	1.5	7.2	7.2	7.3	7.3	6.1	28.2	28.2	7.8	0.6	73.6	35.8	49.9	50.1
63052	IMPERIAL	98.0	97.5	0.2	0.2	0.4	0.6	1.3	1.7	8.1	8.0	8.1	7.2	5.6	31.5	25.0	6.1	0.5	71.3	33.5	50.5	49.5
63055	LABADIE	97.1	96.5	1.3	1.4	0.3	0.4	0.7	1.0	7.0	7.6	8.0	7.0	4.3	25.5	30.2	9.5	0.8	72.9	38.7	50.1	49.9
63056	LESLIE	98.7	98.4	0.2	0.2	0.2	0.3	0.5	0.7	5.7	5.9	6.4	7.0	5.7	24.6	30.6	12.9	1.3	77.7	41.6	50.8	49.2
63060	LONEDELL	97.6	97.3	0.7	0.8	0.2	0.2	0.5	0.6	6.8	7.1	7.3	7.3	5.4	25.7	28.7	10.9	0.9	74.3	38.8	50.2	49.8
63061	LUEBBERING	99.6	98.5	0.0	0.4	0.0	0.0	0.4	0.4	7.4	7.4	7.7	7.4	5.5	25.4	29.0	9.2	1.1	73.2	37.2	51.1	48.9
63068	NEW HAVEN	98.4	98.2	0.5	0.6	0.1	0.1	0.6	0.9	7.0	7.0	7.0	6.9	5.7	25.1	26.7	12.2	2.4	74.7	38.9	49.9	50.1
63069	PACIFIC	93.1	91.9	4.9	5.5	0.4	0.6	0.9	1.2	6.4	6.7	6.8	6.8	6.1	28.4	28.3	9.3	1.2	75.8	37.7	53.2	46.8
63070	PEVELY	96.6	95.8	1.1	1.2	0.3	0.5	1.1	1.6	7.9	7.5	7.1	6.7	6.5	27.5	26.3	9.7	0.8	73.5	35.2	50.0	50.0
63071	RICHWOODS	98.2	97.8	0.1	0.2	0.1	0.2	0.6	0.9	7.7	7.2	7.1	6.4	6.6	24.8	26.7	12.5	1.0	74.0	36.8	50.7	49.3
63072	ROBERTSVILLE	93.7	92.6	3.9	4.6	0.1	0.2	1.0	1.3	6.8	6.8	7.1	7.2	5.9	26.7	29.9	8.8	0.8	74.7	37.8	51.2	48.8
63074	SAINT ANN	83.0	78.0	11.4	14.7	2.0	2.9	3.8	5.0	6.2	6.0	5.9	6.0	6.7	27.8	27.0	11.9	2.5	78.3	38.6	48.6	51.4
63077	SAINT CLAIR	97.6	97.2	0.8	1.0	0.2	0.3	0.6	0.8	7.1	7.0	7.0	6.9	5.8	27.2	27.0	10.5	1.5	74.7	37.3	50.0	50.0
63080	SULLIVAN	98.4	97.9	0.1	0.2	0.5	0.8	0.9	1.3	6.9	6.9	6.9	6.8	5.7	26.0	26.5	12.2	2.1	75.2	38.5	49.5	50.5
63084	UNION	97.2	96.6	1.1	1.3	0.2	0.3	0.9	1.2	7.1	7.1	7.2	7.2	5.7	27.4	26.8	10.2	1.4	74.3	36.9	49.7	50.3
63087	VALLES MINES	98.4	98.1	0.0	0.0	0.0	0.0	0.6	0.7	5.9	6.0	6.5	6.7	5.1	23.1	32.1	13.6	1.1	77.6	42.7	51.4	48.6
63088	VALLEY PARK	90.2	86.3	3.8	5.2	3.6	5.5	2.2	3.1	8.9	8.1	7.0	4.9	5.2	36.4	20.7	7.3	1.4	72.9	34.1	48.6	51.4
63089	VILLA RIDGE	95.8	95.1	2.0	2.3	0.3	0.4	0.7	0.9	7.0	7.1	7.2	6.9	5.6	26.4	28.7	10.2	1.0	74.5	38.1	50.4	49.6
63090	WASHINGTON	98.1	97.7	0.6	0.6	0.4	0.6	0.6	0.9	7.2	7.3	7.3	6.7	5.1	26.4	27.0	10.8	2.2	74.0	38.2	49.6	50.4
63091	ROSEBUD	98.1	97.6	0.0	0.0	0.5	0.8	0.3	0.3	6.1	6.5	6.7	6.1	4.9	22.7	29.2	14.6	3.3	76.8	42.7	50.0	50.0
63101	SAINT LOUIS	10.1	7.3	88.8	91.7	0.0	0.0	0.6	0.6	8.0	6.5	5.9	6.3	7.8	35.4	23.8	5.8	0.5	75.9	32.8	45.5	54.5
63102	SAINT LOUIS	57.3	46.8	37.7	46.8	2.4	3.4	1.0	1.4	1.5	0.9	0.6	1.7	9.0	48.6	28.2	8.7	0.9	96.6	39.4	69.2	30.8
63103	SAINT LOUIS	44.4	35.2	48.2	55.8	3.6	4.9	3.1	3.7	2.4	1.7	1.3	3.4	21.1	20.4	22.1	20.9	6.7	93.5	44.7	48.6	51.4
63104	SAINT LOUIS	39.8	32.3	56.5	63.7	0.9	1.1	2.0	2.1	8.3	7.7	6.8	6.6	8.3	30.4	23.0	7.3	1.4	73.0	31.9	48.6	51.4
63105	SAINT LOUIS	85.2	77.3	7.3	9.2	5.5	7.8	1.5	2.6	3.0	3.8	4.4	17.1	13.3	23.9	21.8	9.7	2.9	85.1	30.7	50.3	49.7
63106	SAINT LOUIS	4.6	3.4	93.7	95.0	0.1	0.1	0.8	0.8	10.9	11.1	9.2	8.5	7.2	22.5	19.1	9.4	2.0	63.3	27.3	42.7	57.3
63107	SAINT LOUIS	8.4	6.0	90.0	92.3	0.4	0.4	0.6	0.6	8.0	8.9	8.4	8.9	7.0	22.7	23.5	10.4	2.0	69.0	32.1	45.9	54.1
63108	SAINT LOUIS	49.9	42.8	43.3	48.3	4.4	6.4	2.0	2.4	3.0	2.8	2.4	8.3	15.3	27.2	25.3	12.6	3.0	89.7	36.9	48.4	51.6
63109	SAINT LOUIS	93.4	90.9	2.8	3.9	1.2	2.0	2.1	3.0	5.9	5.6	5.3	5.2	6.7	30.0	26.8	11.4	3.1	80.1	39.7	47.4	52.6
63110	SAINT LOUIS	41.1	35.5	54.1	59.0	1.2	1.7	1.8	2.1	7.5	7.4	6.9	9.2	9.0	28.9	22.3	7.0	1.7	73.5	30.9	47.3	52.7
63111	SAINT LOUIS	68.6	60.1	23.7	30.2	2.1	3.1	4.1	5.3	7.7	6.9	6.3	6.9	7.5	27.7	23.1	10.0	3.8	75.0	35.3	48.5	51.5
63112	SAINT LOUIS	17.2	14.2	78.5	80.7	2.1	3.0	0.9	1.1	6.5	6.6	6.1	6.8	10.0	27.9	22.5	11.4	2.2	76.7	33.3	45.9	54.1
63113	SAINT LOUIS	0.9	0.6	97.9	98.3	0.1	0.1	0.6	0.6	6.6	7.0	7.4	8.2	6.8	22.2	25.0	13.5	3.3	74.1	38.0	45.6	54.4
63114	SAINT LOUIS	74.0	68.1	20.9	25.5	1.7	2.5	2.4	3.2	6.9	6.6	6.4	6.7	7.1	27.6	26.3	10.4	1.9	76.0	36.7	48.2	51.8
63115	SAINT LOUIS	0.7	0.5	98.0	98.3	0.1	0.1	0.5	0.5	6.8	7.2	7.2	8.2	6.3	22.1	25.4	14.1	2.6	73.7	38.3	44.6	55.4
63116	SAINT LOUIS	72.8	66.3	17.7	21.5	4.6	6.5	3.6	4.6	7.2	6.8	6.2	6.3	7.3	29.5	25.0	9.4	2.2	76.0	36.0	48.8	51.2
63117	SAINT LOUIS	81.7	78.0	13.5	15.5	2.7	4.1	1.7	2.3	5.0	4.5	4.4	4.9	9.5	32.2	26.0	10.5	2.9	83.2	38.0	47.4	52.6
63118	SAINT LOUIS	38.7	30.7	52.3	59.0	4.0	5.1	3.7	4.2	9.1	8.7	7.5	8.5	8.9	28.8	20.9	6.4	1.3	69.6	29.3	48.2	51.8
63119	SAINT LOUIS	88.9	86.3	7.8	9.2	1.6	2.5	1.3	1.8	5.3	5.8	6.5	6.9	6.0	23.1	28.5	12.8	5.1	78.5	42.4	46.3	53.7
63120	SAINT LOUIS	3.7	2.7	95.1	96.2	0.1	0.1	0.5	0.5	7.7	9.2	9.0	11.2	7.4	21.9	21.8	10.5	1.4	66.9	29.5	45.4	54.6
63121	SAINT LOUIS	17.8	13.8	79.4	83.4	0.7	0.9	1.1	1.2	6.5	6.9	6.9	7.8	7.8	24.9	25.9	11.6	1.7	75.2	36.6	45.2	54.8
63122	SAINT LOUIS	92.4	90.0	5.4	6.9	1.0	1.5	1.1	1.5	5.9	6.4	7.0	6.1	4.8	22.0	29.6	13.9	4.3	76.8	43.4	46.2	53.8
63123	SAINT LOUIS	95.8	94.2	0.8	1.1	1.8	2.7	1.2	1.7	5.3	5.5	5.5	5.5	5.4	25.6	27.4	16.2	3.5	80.3	43.0	47.4	52.6
63124	SAINT LOUIS	94.2	89.7	2.6	5.5	2.3	3.5	1.0	1.4	4.4	5.3	6.7	7.4	5.1	15.8	30.9	18.9	5.6	79.5	48.7	47.1	52.9
63125	SAINT LOUIS	95.7	94.0	1.5	2.1	1.0	1.5	1.8	2.6	5.8	5.6	5.6	5.8	5.8	26.0	26.3	15.8	3.3	79.5	41.6	47.4	52.6
63126	SAINT LOUIS	96.2	94.7	0.8	1.1	1.7	2.6	1.1	1.5	4.5	4.9	5.5	5.6	4.1	21.7	30.2	19.9	3.4	81.5	47.2	46.9	53.1
63127	SAINT LOUIS	96.3	94.9	1.0	1.3	1.3	2.1	1.1	1.5	3.6	4.4	5.7	6.7	3.8	15.8	30.8	20.5	8.7	81.5	51.3	47.0	53.0
63128	SAINT LOUIS	97.6	96.5	0.4	0.5	1.1	1.8	0.9	1.3	4.5	4.7	5.1	5.6	5.1	20.9	30.3	20.0	3.8	82.2	47.8	47.4	52.6
63129	SAINT LOUIS	97.1	96.0	0.6	0.7	1.2	1.9	1.1	1.5	5.7	6.1	6.7	6.9	5.6	25.8	30.4	11.2	1.7	77.2	40.0	48.8	51.2
63130	SAINT LOUIS	50.5	43.5	42.8	50.2	2.6	3.4	1.7	1.8	6.0	6.0	5.9	6.8	9.1	27.6	25.4	11.3	1.9	78.8	36.3	46.2	53.8
63131	SAINT LOUIS	94.4	91.9	1.0	1.3	3.6	5.5	1.0	1.4	5.1	6.2	7.9	7.2	3.9	16.0	33.9	17.1	2.7	76.0	47.3	48.5	51.5
63132	SAINT LOUIS	56.1	49.7	36.9	41.3	4.3	6.0	1.9	2.3	5.6	5.6	5.9	6.2	7.2	24.6	27.3	14.5	3.2	79.6	41.0	46.4	53.6
63133	SAINT LOUIS	10.4	8.4	87.4	89.3	0.3	0.5	0.8	0.9	7.6	7.4	7.8	9.1	9.1	22.4	24.9	10.1	1.4	71.7	32.6	44.4	55.6
63134	SAINT LOUIS	37.9	33.1	58.7	63.0	0.5	0.8	2.1	2.5	7.7	7.8	7.6	8.5	7.4	26.8	23.2	9.6	1.4	71.8	32.9	45.6	54.4
63135	SAINT LOUIS	54.1	46.9	42.9	49.8	0.6	0.8	1.1	1.3	6.8	7.2	7.3	7.9	6.9	25.5	25.8	10.6	2.1	73.7	36.0	46.4	53.6
63136	SAINT LOUIS	17.3	13.1	80.9	85.0	0.4	0.4	0.6	0.7	8.2	8.1	7.6	8.5	7.8	25.3	23.7	9.2	1.6	71.0	32.2	44.5	55.5
63137	SAINT LOUIS	52.0	43.6	46.0	54.2	0.3	0.4	0.9	1.1	6.8	6.9	6.9	7.9	6.7	26.7	24.7	11.1	2.3	74.4	36.3	46.8	53.2
63138	SAINT LOUIS	43.2	35.7	53.8	61.1	0.7	0.9	1.0	1.2	8.9	8.4	7.0	7.1	8.2	27.5	21.6	9.3	2.1	71.4	31.5	46.4	53.6
63139	SAINT LOUIS	88.8	84.7	6.5	8.7	2.1	3.3	1.9	2.7	5.5	5.1	5.0	5.0	7.2	31.6	26.7	10.9	2.9	81.6	38.9	49.1	50.9
63140	SAINT LOUIS	21.2	15.9	76.8	82.0	0.4	0.5	0.7	1.0	9.8	9.5	9.0	9.8	8.0	24.4	21.5	7.3	0.7	65.9	28.0	43.7	56.3
63141	SAINT LOUIS	89.2	84.9	3.3	4.4	5.9	8.8	1.7	2.2	4.7	5.4	6.2	7.1	5.9	19.8	30.7	17.3	3.0	79.7	45.7	48.0	52.0
63143	SAINT LOUIS	77.5	71.1	15.2	19.6	3.7	5.2	2.4	3.2	6.1	5.2	4.7	5.0	9.1	34.0	26.5	8.1	1.3	81.3	35.8	50.0	50.0
63144	SAINT LOUIS	89.3	85.8	4.7	5.8	3.8	5.7	1.8	2.6	5.7	5.3	5.2	5.2	7.9	33.1	25.0	10.4	2.2	80.6	37.2	47.0	53.0
	MISSOURI	84.9	83.3	11.2	11.7	1.2	1.7	2.1	2.8	6.6	6.6	6.6	7.0	6.7	26.1	26.5	11.7	2.1	76.1	37.7	48.8	51.2
	UNITED STATES	75.1	72.0	12.3	12.7	3.8	4.6	12.5	15.7	6.8	6.7	6.6	7.1	6.9	27.0	26.0	10.9	1.9	75.7	36.9	49.2	50.8

#	POST OFFICE NAME	2009 Per Capita Income	2009 HH Income Base	2009 HOUSEHOLD INCOME DISTRIBUTION (%) Less than $25,000	$25,000 to $49,999	$50,000 to $99,999	$100,000 to $149,999	$150,000 or More	MEDIAN HOUSEHOLD INCOME 2009	2014	2009 National Centile	2009 State Centile	2009 Home Value Base	2009 HOME VALUE DISTRIBUTION (%) Less than $50,000	$50,000 to $89,999	$90,000 to $174,999	$175,000 to $399,999	$400,000 or More	2009 Median Home Value
63005	CHESTERFIELD	75753	6101	3.7	6.3	22.4	12.7	54.9	162824	167771	100	100	5339	1.5	0.4	2.2	29.4	66.5	483857
63010	ARNOLD	26449	13728	11.7	24.4	45.4	14.3	4.2	63346	68421	82	92	11237	11.5	5.1	52.3	29.9	1.1	145036
63011	BALLWIN	43804	14085	7.1	12.8	34.4	24.7	21.0	92656	95288	96	99	12035	0.4	1.8	22.7	68.3	6.9	219694
63012	BARNHART	25675	3705	6.3	18.5	54.3	16.5	4.6	71607	76573	88	96	3443	8.4	5.1	50.7	32.8	3.1	151196
63013	BEAUFORT	21875	655	12.8	29.8	47.6	7.2	2.6	55898	58281	73	86	597	8.2	14.4	31.2	38.4	7.9	161919
63014	BERGER	22139	456	17.5	32.0	39.9	8.6	2.0	50341	52071	62	80	383	13.1	20.6	35.0	24.8	6.5	124679
63015	CATAWISSA	23858	801	13.9	26.7	42.6	14.6	2.2	59332	61473	77	89	688	10.8	14.4	42.0	30.2	2.6	135586
63016	CEDAR HILL	23077	3008	14.6	24.4	49.6	8.0	3.5	61352	64161	79	91	2728	16.8	13.1	40.1	28.7	1.2	135753
63017	CHESTERFIELD	51994	16514	6.0	12.4	32.7	18.1	30.8	97805	101629	96	99	12761	0.6	0.9	7.8	68.1	22.7	300979
63019	CRYSTAL CITY	22751	1779	28.2	25.2	37.1	5.6	3.9	46767	48597	53	73	1308	8.1	14.8	55.5	19.9	1.7	124796
63020	DE SOTO	21684	8230	22.2	27.5	40.9	6.3	3.0	50234	52413	62	79	6511	10.1	21.6	42.5	23.4	2.4	121357
63021	BALLWIN	39275	21073	6.3	13.7	42.9	20.4	16.7	83332	85619	93	98	17635	0.4	1.9	37.3	53.5	6.9	193012
63023	DITTMER	22076	2164	15.9	27.1	46.1	9.6	1.4	56207	59585	73	87	1917	10.4	17.3	41.4	28.2	2.8	132116
63025	EUREKA	40180	4601	3.9	9.0	38.7	25.4	23.0	97163	99297	96	99	4194	3.3	5.7	28.5	43.7	18.8	222854
63026	FENTON	30695	16432	10.0	20.2	42.5	18.7	8.6	72504	76929	88	96	13697	17.0	4.2	36.7	39.6	2.5	154879
63028	FESTUS	23258	9811	19.4	27.2	41.5	8.1	3.7	53185	56598	68	83	7613	12.8	13.4	42.8	28.0	2.9	135303
63030	FLETCHER	17382	102	30.4	29.4	35.3	2.9	2.0	40000	41764	33	54	88	23.9	18.2	35.2	18.2	4.5	108333
63031	FLORISSANT	27500	19298	11.1	25.3	48.3	11.8	3.4	63752	66190	82	92	15606	1.1	29.9	60.0	8.7	0.3	98342
63033	FLORISSANT	28007	17284	12.4	25.5	46.3	11.4	4.4	62444	64585	81	92	12719	0.9	16.5	76.6	5.9	0.1	112900
63034	FLORISSANT	35690	6456	3.4	14.3	43.9	26.5	12.0	85255	87123	94	98	6290	0.3	4.1	51.0	41.6	3.0	166772
63036	FRENCH VILLAGE	20929	340	28.2	31.2	32.6	6.5	1.5	42406	44323	41	62	307	15.0	18.2	42.7	16.9	7.2	122256
63037	GERALD	22923	1373	23.1	27.8	38.0	7.5	3.6	49134	52477	59	78	1146	13.4	16.0	44.9	22.9	2.7	122137
63038	GLENCOE	57280	1817	3.2	6.8	21.6	27.5	40.9	132528	135344	99	100	1706	0.9	2.1	6.6	46.1	44.3	377336
63039	GRAY SUMMIT	26565	356	12.1	25.0	47.8	11.0	4.2	60768	61826	78	90	277	9.7	11.9	27.4	42.2	8.7	178676
63040	GROVER	48256	2933	3.4	9.4	24.1	32.9	30.1	117735	119721	98	100	2510	0.0	1.3	16.7	75.8	6.2	256498
63041	GRUBVILLE	24103	135	9.6	24.4	50.4	11.9	3.7	62311	63211	80	92	120	10.8	14.2	47.5	25.8	1.7	120455
63042	HAZELWOOD	28179	8624	13.9	27.9	46.3	9.5	2.3	57851	59288	75	88	5044	5.8	32.8	57.3	4.1	0.0	95389
63043	MARYLAND HEIGHTS	31258	9549	10.9	22.7	50.1	11.9	4.4	64812	67284	83	93	6767	0.4	4.4	73.4	21.3	0.5	136464
63044	BRIDGETON	29268	5576	13.7	23.1	44.7	13.9	4.5	63120	65528	81	92	4080	5.0	11.8	55.5	27.5	0.2	136937
63048	HERCULANEUM	21144	1212	27.9	24.9	38.4	5.1	3.6	47399	50198	55	75	859	9.1	17.1	45.1	26.7	2.1	131618
63049	HIGH RIDGE	25959	5922	12.2	24.1	46.2	13.1	4.4	63451	69559	82	92	5137	18.6	6.9	47.3	23.4	3.7	135609
63050	HILLSBORO	24214	5490	14.7	26.4	44.5	10.5	3.9	58602	63058	76	88	4644	12.7	9.5	32.8	40.8	4.2	162607
63051	HOUSE SPRINGS	24188	4776	12.2	26.0	48.2	9.7	3.9	60080	64046	77	90	4124	29.0	13.2	35.1	20.8	1.9	109375
63052	IMPERIAL	26811	9647	9.3	18.9	50.6	15.5	5.7	69295	75829	86	95	8253	13.3	6.9	40.6	36.4	3.0	158511
63055	LABADIE	29607	863	11.1	21.4	47.6	11.7	8.1	66132	65979	84	94	702	13.7	8.5	23.2	37.2	17.4	194048
63056	LESLIE	21516	909	16.7	32.3	43.1	6.4	1.4	50691	53666	63	80	819	9.8	19.7	34.1	31.3	5.3	133059
63060	LONEDELL	23880	942	9.8	26.5	48.3	11.1	4.2	60119	60846	77	90	832	15.4	20.0	33.2	26.4	5.0	116587
63061	LUEBBERING	23951	94	9.6	24.5	47.9	13.8	4.3	62237	62796	80	91	84	15.5	14.3	41.7	25.0	3.6	114286
63068	NEW HAVEN	23412	1664	15.6	30.9	41.6	9.4	2.5	53494	56742	69	84	1342	8.9	15.0	42.6	27.8	5.7	135983
63069	PACIFIC	29455	5890	15.5	19.5	42.1	12.9	10.1	65628	66799	84	94	4542	12.2	11.7	30.6	32.4	13.1	159673
63070	PEVELY	21508	2572	21.7	25.6	42.6	8.0	2.1	52041	54569	66	82	2023	31.8	14.5	38.6	13.5	1.6	95731
63071	RICHWOODS	17556	579	35.8	31.6	27.5	2.6	2.6	32991	35109	13	21	473	34.9	18.6	31.9	12.1	2.5	79773
63072	ROBERTSVILLE	25036	1170	11.6	23.8	51.7	9.1	3.8	62993	64791	81	92	1048	15.4	18.8	34.6	28.3	2.9	129063
63074	SAINT ANN	24538	6832	23.6	33.5	35.7	5.7	1.5	43770	46042	45	66	3988	1.9	63.5	32.4	1.8	0.4	82614
63077	SAINT CLAIR	22202	4656	22.6	28.3	38.6	8.7	1.8	49323	52841	60	78	3480	15.1	23.1	42.2	17.5	2.2	105499
63080	SULLIVAN	21664	5200	26.9	29.5	35.4	5.5	2.8	44725	48720	47	68	3863	14.5	23.3	39.0	20.3	3.0	109519
63084	UNION	23594	6111	17.5	27.9	43.0	8.0	3.6	53514	56001	69	84	4775	14.5	15.2	38.3	28.5	3.5	135019
63087	VALLES MINES	18709	313	27.8	31.3	32.6	6.7	1.6	42730	45451	42	64	279	16.8	18.6	40.1	17.9	6.5	119097
63088	VALLEY PARK	28511	3687	14.9	26.1	45.2	10.7	3.2	58863	60266	76	89	2350	0.7	6.1	51.8	41.1	0.3	161472
63089	VILLA RIDGE	23050	2333	16.3	27.7	42.2	10.5	3.3	54813	57083	71	85	1971	24.7	13.7	26.7	29.5	5.4	128380
63090	WASHINGTON	26504	8469	14.0	26.9	44.3	10.6	4.3	58892	60773	76	89	6374	5.0	4.6	46.6	38.2	5.6	163351
63091	ROSEBUD	21899	507	21.7	32.0	39.3	5.5	1.6	46577	46909	53	73	443	15.6	13.1	41.1	23.3	7.0	135179
63101	SAINT LOUIS	20064	567	36.2	31.2	31.4	0.7	0.5	33226	32964	14	23	18	0.0	0.0	100.0	0.0	0.0	120455
63102	SAINT LOUIS	36769	714	22.0	25.4	43.7	5.9	3.1	52468	53047	67	82	11	0.0	27.3	54.5	18.2	0.0	135417
63103	SAINT LOUIS	19265	3095	60.2	26.9	11.1	0.8	1.0	18969	20020	1	1	39	59.0	20.5	0.0	12.8	7.7	46818
63104	SAINT LOUIS	23495	8387	33.9	28.2	25.8	7.2	4.9	38120	41616	27	46	2995	9.3	14.5	40.2	29.1	6.8	140061
63105	SAINT LOUIS	49253	6186	10.6	18.3	32.4	14.0	24.7	81102	84969	92	97	3339	0.6	0.2	5.3	30.5	63.4	500127
63106	SAINT LOUIS	10049	4233	68.4	19.6	10.1	1.2	0.7	15058	15043	1	0	616	37.2	28.7	23.1	10.1	1.0	68780
63107	SAINT LOUIS	11338	4996	52.5	30.4	13.5	2.5	1.1	23281	23889	2	1	2220	39.1	38.2	19.5	2.2	1.1	62109
63108	SAINT LOUIS	31250	10677	39.5	23.6	23.1	6.2	7.6	34656	37768	17	29	2756	4.2	14.6	27.2	33.5	20.5	189231
63109	SAINT LOUIS	29640	14638	17.2	30.9	38.6	9.6	3.8	51506	53240	65	81	9032	1.4	9.5	63.1	24.9	1.1	140806
63110	SAINT LOUIS	20039	7968	31.5	32.7	27.5	4.9	3.3	37292	39849	24	41	3115	9.3	23.4	51.8	14.9	0.6	108327
63111	SAINT LOUIS	16131	8170	40.4	32.2	23.4	3.0	1.0	30487	32116	9	13	3646	22.1	45.7	30.6	1.4	0.2	73447
63112	SAINT LOUIS	18959	10210	47.2	23.6	21.5	4.1	3.6	26969	28739	5	4	3521	22.8	26.4	29.7	14.5	6.6	91228
63113	SAINT LOUIS	12498	5869	50.3	29.2	17.5	2.4	0.6	24780	25304	3	2	2681	37.3	37.7	23.1	1.6	0.2	61094
63114	SAINT LOUIS	23340	15695	20.8	34.1	37.0	5.9	2.1	45736	48093	50	71	10491	6.5	65.4	26.3	1.6	0.2	78191
63115	SAINT LOUIS	15330	9541	42.7	31.1	21.4	3.6	1.2	30052	31574	8	11	5300	22.2	50.3	26.6	0.8	0.1	71669
63116	SAINT LOUIS	20145	20604	29.7	32.7	31.2	4.4	2.0	40045	43280	33	54	12016	7.2	38.3	48.4	5.9	0.2	93232
63117	SAINT LOUIS	43877	4399	17.4	20.4	37.8	11.6	12.8	64721	67749	83	93	2508	1.2	9.0	43.9	30.6	15.3	164575
63118	SAINT LOUIS	14208	10062	41.5	32.3	21.5	2.8	1.8	30156	31891	8	12	3759	26.2	37.6	29.6	6.3	0.3	73615
63119	SAINT LOUIS	38392	14488	13.0	19.5	41.5	14.6	11.3	69241	74377	86	95	11015	0.8	5.6	43.9	38.1	11.6	174484
63120	SAINT LOUIS	11889	4264	48.9	29.5	17.6	2.8	1.2	25563	26473	4	2	2474	34.4	51.1	12.6	1.6	0.4	59530
63121	SAINT LOUIS	21165	11122	29.1	32.4	29.8	6.2	2.5	39845	41616	32	53	6698	14.6	56.3	23.6	5.4	0.1	74053
63122	SAINT LOUIS	43460	15947	10.4	18.9	35.5	18.7	16.4	77215	80829	91	96	12739	0.7	3.7	28.0	49.7	18.0	226391
63123	SAINT LOUIS	29179	22228	14.9	30.4	41.4	9.8	3.5	55107	57194	71	86	16808	1.0	10.5	70.3	17.2	0.9	124474
63124	SAINT LOUIS	78219	4182	12.0	10.5	25.6	10.2	41.6	107287	115509	98	100	3233	0.0	1.4	3.7	22.6	72.3	677561
63125	SAINT LOUIS	25531	14033	20.5	29.6	40.5	6.9	2.5	49891	52102	61	79	10332	4.1	24.7	61.9	8.9	0.4	109174
63126	SAINT LOUIS	33960	6391	9.4	24.6	45.4	15.3	5.3	68863	74257	86	95	5452	0.6	3.0	54.2	39.4	2.9	163421
63127	SAINT LOUIS	46730	2182	10.5	20.0	32.4	17.8	19.2	78614	82957	91	97	1730	0.2	3.8	26.2	39.3	30.5	250962
63128	SAINT LOUIS	37915	12401	8.6	20.9	41.7	17.9	10.9	73145	77242	88	96	9721	0.6	5.0	32.1	52.3	10.1	194962
63129	SAINT LOUIS	33715	20386	7.7	18.6	42.6	21.8	9.4	76367	79549	90	96	16099	0.2	5.0	40.2	50.8	3.9	182375
63130	SAINT LOUIS	33711	12764	21.8	25.3	31.8	10.0	11.1	53782	56345	69	84	7721	3.5	28.5	23.8	31.9	12.3	138214
63131	SAINT LOUIS	64387	5918	5.2	8.3	25.4	16.0	45.0	134849	139573	99	100	5692	0.3	1.0	10.3	36.0	52.4	417918
63132	SAINT LOUIS	36045	6074	16.9	24.8	35.1	11.6	11.6	61046	62976	79	91	3640	1.2	22.0	30.0	34.9	11.9	161991
63133	SAINT LOUIS	14253	2887	38.9	34.2	22.1	3.5	1.2	29991	30657	8	11	1779	39.9	51.2	8.7	0.2	0.1	56516
63134	SAINT LOUIS	18816	5413	25.9	34.6	32.6	5.8	1.1	41954	43853	39	61	3351	12.2	74.5	12.5	0.7	0.0	71535
63135	SAINT LOUIS	21992	7995	21.7	29.4	39.4	7.0	2.6	48993	51369	59	78	6071	8.0	53.3	33.1	5.2	0.3	82864
63136	SAINT LOUIS	18384	19368	29.7	33.1	30.4	5.2	1.6	39235	41089	30	50	12584	10.8	64.0	24.3	0.7	0.2	75635
63137	SAINT LOUIS	22735	8019	21.4	32.3	37.0	7.1	2.2	46600	49264	53	73	6396	4.2	72.5	21.3	1.7	0.3	77680
63138	SAINT LOUIS	23406	8426	18.8	34.0	37.0	7.4	2.8	47584	49886	56	75	4572	1.6	32.9	58.6	6.3	0.5	102033
63139	SAINT LOUIS	25628	11830	22.2	32.7	37.1	5.7	2.4	45383	49959	49	70	7309	3.8	26.2	61.8	8.1	0.1	103693
63140	SAINT LOUIS	13759	147	44.9	31.3	17.0	5.4	1.4	29058	30216	7	7	74	29.7	66.2	2.7	1.4	0.0	57895
63141	SAINT LOUIS	56831	8304	7.2	12.5	34.8	18.6	26.9	91958	95688	95	99	6372	0.7	1.2	12.6	42.7	42.8	354154
63143	SAINT LOUIS	24531	5346	31.5	30.7	30.9	5.1	1.8	38503	40724	28	47	2365	4.5	39.0	50.3	5.9	0.3	93997
63144	SAINT LOUIS	41174	4642	13.1	22.7	43.0	12.7	8.6	65580	69692	84	93	3434	0.4	4.9	58.7	28.2	7.7	147904
	MISSOURI	25286		22.8	27.7	35.3	9.1	5.2	49522	52035				12.8	19.4	39.1	24.2	4.6	122064
	UNITED STATES	27277		20.9	24.4	35.3	11.7	7.6	54719	56938				9.3	13.1	31.6	32.6	13.5	162279

ZIP CODE #	POST OFFICE NAME	FINANCIAL SERVICES: Auto Loan	Home Loan	Invest-ments	Retire-ment Plans	THE HOME: Home Improvements: Home Repair	Lawn & Garden	Furnishings: Comput-ers & Hard-ware-Personal	Major Appli-ances	TV, Radio, Sound Equip-ment	Furni-ture	ENTERTAINMENT: Dine out/ Carry out	Sports Equip-ment	Fees & Tickets	Toys & Games	Travel	Cable TV	PERSONAL: Apparel & Services	Auto Repairs	Health Insur-ance	Pets & Supplies
63005	CHESTERFIELD	309	369	355	387	371	323	321	321	301	348	306	260	365	315	344	284	226	305	279	366
63010	ARNOLD	106	106	97	105	103	106	99	104	100	101	100	79	99	103	99	101	69	100	103	121
63011	BALLWIN	153	187	186	191	190	176	162	168	156	171	158	127	184	158	178	153	114	160	160	192
63012	BARNHART	118	119	100	115	113	110	110	112	109	115	110	84	108	114	106	108	76	108	106	131
63013	BEAUFORT	95	94	88	97	93	102	88	96	89	85	89	74	87	92	90	92	61	91	97	113
63014	BERGER	94	80	91	82	82	100	81	94	83	72	82	72	71	84	81	89	55	87	97	110
63015	CATAWISSA	103	97	86	94	95	98	91	96	93	94	94	70	87	97	87	96	64	93	95	114
63016	CEDAR HILL	104	96	88	95	95	102	91	98	94	91	94	73	86	97	88	97	64	94	99	116
63017	CHESTERFIELD	168	206	223	213	217	195	183	188	175	195	176	143	209	173	204	171	128	181	179	214
63019	CRYSTAL CITY	78	76	72	76	73	83	75	77	78	72	78	59	75	79	75	82	54	77	84	92
63020	DE SOTO	88	81	78	82	80	90	80	85	83	77	82	65	76	84	78	86	56	83	90	102
63021	BALLWIN	143	169	155	172	166	150	149	148	141	157	144	119	165	147	158	136	104	143	135	171
63023	DITTMER	93	88	81	89	88	94	84	91	86	83	86	68	80	89	83	89	59	86	91	107
63025	EUREKA	173	209	181	212	202	175	176	178	164	192	167	145	196	175	185	153	121	165	151	201
63026	FENTON	119	128	112	127	123	118	118	118	115	122	117	92	122	120	119	113	82	116	113	138
63028	FESTUS	92	90	81	90	88	94	87	90	89	87	89	68	86	91	86	92	61	89	94	107
63030	FLETCHER	86	67	71	65	66	81	67	76	73	67	72	57	57	76	62	78	49	72	79	92
63031	FLORISSANT	96	105	91	104	101	103	98	98	98	98	99	75	102	100	100	100	69	98	103	116
63033	FLORISSANT	94	102	92	102	99	104	97	98	99	96	99	73	102	99	99	101	69	98	106	115
63034	FLORISSANT	132	163	150	164	160	153	138	144	135	143	137	110	157	138	152	134	97	138	140	166
63036	FRENCH VILLAGE	89	65	91	63	67	91	66	84	73	62	72	63	53	73	66	80	48	77	87	99
63037	GERALD	96	80	92	81	82	101	80	95	85	73	83	71	70	85	79	91	56	87	98	111
63038	GLENCOE	231	298	294	312	304	261	245	253	228	269	231	203	291	237	273	215	172	234	216	285
63039	GRAY SUMMIT	98	110	95	113	107	108	98	102	97	99	97	80	104	99	103	97	68	98	101	120
63040	GROVER	188	228	197	235	222	187	190	192	175	213	178	160	215	189	200	160	131	175	157	214
63041	GRUBVILLE	107	98	90	97	97	105	94	101	97	94	97	75	88	101	91	101	66	97	102	120
63042	HAZELWOOD	89	84	73	86	79	83	90	83	91	89	91	66	88	92	86	91	63	88	89	101
63043	MARYLAND HEIGHTS	100	101	92	104	97	96	103	96	102	103	103	77	105	104	102	101	73	100	98	115
63044	BRIDGETON	92	106	99	105	105	105	98	100	99	97	100	75	107	99	104	101	70	99	105	116
63048	HERCULANEUM	85	77	75	78	75	89	79	83	82	74	81	65	74	83	77	86	55	82	90	99
63049	HIGH RIDGE	107	107	92	105	103	102	99	102	99	103	99	76	98	103	97	99	68	98	99	120
63050	HILLSBORO	101	101	90	101	99	103	94	99	95	95	95	75	94	98	94	97	66	96	100	117
63051	HOUSE SPRINGS	103	100	88	97	97	100	94	98	96	97	96	72	92	100	92	98	66	96	98	116
63052	IMPERIAL	116	122	101	119	115	111	111	112	108	116	109	87	112	114	110	106	76	108	106	131
63055	LABADIE	116	126	109	129	123	125	114	119	113	115	114	92	119	116	118	114	79	114	118	140
63056	LESLIE	93	77	81	78	78	95	78	89	82	72	81	67	68	85	75	88	55	83	92	105
63060	LONEDELL	103	100	90	100	98	104	93	100	96	94	95	75	91	99	93	98	65	96	100	118
63061	LUEBBERING	109	103	91	101	101	105	96	102	99	100	100	75	93	103	93	102	68	99	102	121
63068	NEW HAVEN	91	89	79	92	87	98	87	92	89	81	88	71	85	91	87	92	60	89	97	109
63069	PACIFIC	122	120	109	121	118	121	115	118	116	116	115	91	113	120	112	117	80	115	117	139
63070	PEVELY	89	82	73	79	79	85	81	84	83	81	82	63	75	86	77	85	56	82	84	99
63071	RICHWOODS	84	60	69	59	60	80	63	73	70	61	68	56	50	73	57	76	46	69	77	89
63072	ROBERTSVILLE	114	104	93	101	102	107	98	105	102	102	102	76	93	106	94	105	70	101	105	124
63074	SAINT ANN	74	70	60	71	66	73	76	71	77	71	77	56	73	78	71	79	53	75	79	86
63077	SAINT CLAIR	93	78	77	79	77	92	80	86	84	76	83	66	71	87	75	89	56	83	91	103
63080	SULLIVAN	88	74	74	75	74	88	77	83	81	72	79	63	68	83	72	86	54	80	88	99
63084	UNION	94	90	81	91	87	97	87	92	90	85	89	70	84	92	86	93	61	89	96	109
63087	VALLES MINES	90	66	88	64	67	90	67	83	74	64	73	63	54	75	65	81	49	77	87	99
63088	VALLEY PARK	97	94	81	95	89	82	96	88	91	99	93	72	94	97	90	87	66	90	81	104
63089	VILLA RIDGE	96	92	86	93	91	99	89	95	90	86	89	73	85	92	88	93	61	91	96	112
63090	WASHINGTON	99	100	91	103	99	105	97	101	98	94	97	78	97	99	98	100	67	98	104	119
63091	ROSEBUD	83	75	75	78	77	89	74	84	77	67	75	64	68	78	74	81	51	77	87	98
63101	SAINT LOUIS	57	39	38	43	38	39	58	46	59	55	61	39	51	60	49	58	43	56	48	58
63102	SAINT LOUIS	87	64	66	73	61	62	94	71	92	88	95	65	83	93	81	89	68	86	74	92
63103	SAINT LOUIS	34	26	32	29	28	32	40	34	43	37	43	25	36	37	36	46	30	40	46	43
63104	SAINT LOUIS	75	65	61	68	62	66	79	69	81	75	81	55	74	80	71	83	57	76	75	85
63105	SAINT LOUIS	158	175	203	188	186	163	184	168	173	185	177	138	198	171	192	167	131	173	159	195
63106	SAINT LOUIS	35	23	22	26	22	27	35	28	39	33	38	22	30	37	28	41	27	34	35	37
63107	SAINT LOUIS	48	36	34	37	34	43	44	42	51	45	49	31	40	49	39	55	34	46	51	53
63108	SAINT LOUIS	77	60	64	67	59	62	86	68	85	79	87	58	77	83	75	85	61	80	76	86
63109	SAINT LOUIS	86	83	75	85	80	84	90	83	90	87	90	66	88	90	86	91	63	88	90	101
63110	SAINT LOUIS	70	58	53	61	56	61	72	63	74	67	74	50	66	74	64	76	52	70	70	78
63111	SAINT LOUIS	54	46	41	47	43	48	57	50	59	51	59	40	52	59	50	61	42	55	56	61
63112	SAINT LOUIS	62	47	47	51	46	52	63	54	67	60	66	43	57	65	55	69	46	62	62	69
63113	SAINT LOUIS	48	40	38	40	38	47	44	44	51	45	49	31	42	48	41	55	34	47	54	55
63114	SAINT LOUIS	77	74	62	76	69	77	79	74	80	75	80	59	77	81	74	82	55	78	82	90
63115	SAINT LOUIS	57	49	47	49	47	57	52	53	60	54	58	38	50	57	49	64	40	56	64	66
63116	SAINT LOUIS	68	62	53	63	58	65	70	64	72	65	71	51	66	72	64	74	50	68	71	78
63117	SAINT LOUIS	123	118	117	123	116	115	131	118	129	129	130	95	129	127	126	127	92	126	122	143
63118	SAINT LOUIS	54	45	40	47	42	47	57	49	60	53	60	39	53	59	50	62	42	55	55	61
63119	SAINT LOUIS	112	129	128	131	130	128	119	121	120	122	120	90	132	117	128	121	85	120	127	140
63120	SAINT LOUIS	51	41	38	43	39	48	47	46	53	48	52	33	44	52	42	57	36	49	54	57
63121	SAINT LOUIS	73	66	61	67	63	70	72	68	76	72	76	51	70	75	67	78	52	73	76	84
63122	SAINT LOUIS	132	155	163	157	161	151	142	145	138	147	139	108	157	137	154	138	99	142	145	166
63123	SAINT LOUIS	85	92	87	92	91	96	88	90	91	87	91	66	93	90	92	94	63	90	99	105
63124	SAINT LOUIS	217	275	326	286	302	265	248	254	237	266	236	191	293	230	282	231	176	245	244	284
63125	SAINT LOUIS	79	82	73	82	79	87	80	81	83	78	83	61	82	83	81	86	57	82	90	96
63126	SAINT LOUIS	101	115	115	115	117	122	103	111	107	106	106	79	113	104	113	111	74	108	122	128
63127	SAINT LOUIS	140	168	182	169	178	174	152	162	154	158	153	114	172	147	170	158	109	157	175	183
63128	SAINT LOUIS	119	135	137	137	139	137	124	129	124	128	125	94	136	122	134	126	88	126	136	148
63129	SAINT LOUIS	119	136	126	138	133	126	124	123	120	128	122	96	135	123	131	119	87	122	120	144
63130	SAINT LOUIS	107	107	105	110	107	106	114	106	112	113	112	83	114	110	111	111	79	111	109	127
63131	SAINT LOUIS	210	286	332	295	313	268	237	254	222	262	221	189	291	218	281	214	166	235	231	280
63132	SAINT LOUIS	108	110	113	114	112	112	114	110	113	114	113	84	117	111	115	114	80	112	115	129
63133	SAINT LOUIS	58	48	43	49	45	54	55	52	60	55	59	39	51	59	49	63	41	56	60	65
63134	SAINT LOUIS	71	65	53	67	60	69	69	65	73	68	73	51	68	74	64	76	50	70	74	82
63135	SAINT LOUIS	81	81	68	82	76	85	80	79	84	79	83	60	82	84	78	86	57	81	88	96
63136	SAINT LOUIS	70	62	53	64	58	66	67	63	72	68	72	48	66	72	63	75	50	68	72	80
63137	SAINT LOUIS	79	77	63	78	72	82	79	76	82	76	81	59	78	82	75	84	56	79	85	93
63138	SAINT LOUIS	86	75	65	77	71	75	87	78	87	84	88	63	81	89	79	88	61	85	83	95
63139	SAINT LOUIS	75	70	60	72	66	72	79	71	79	73	79	57	75	79	73	80	55	76	78	87
63140	SAINT LOUIS	56	40	34	44	36	45	54	46	60	52	59	37	48	60	45	63	41	54	54	60
63141	SAINT LOUIS	181	208	231	214	220	200	190	195	184	204	184	146	213	182	208	180	134	189	187	222
63143	SAINT LOUIS	67	56	51	59	54	57	72	60	71	66	71	50	65	71	63	71	50	68	65	75
63144	SAINT LOUIS	106	108	109	112	108	102	117	105	113	114	115	86	118	113	116	110	82	112	106	126
	MISSOURI	94	86	87	87	85	93	89	91	91	87	90	70	84	92	86	93	62	90	94	108
	UNITED STATES	100	100	100	100	100	100	100	100	100	100	100	100	100	100	100	100	100	100	100	100

63146-63540

ZIP CODE #	POST OFFICE NAME	COUNTY FIPS CODE	POPULATION 2000	POPULATION 2009	POPULATION 2014	2000-2009 ANNUAL RATE % Rate	2000-2009 ANNUAL RATE State Centile	HOUSEHOLDS 2000	HOUSEHOLDS 2009	HOUSEHOLDS 2014	HOUSEHOLDS % Annual Rate 2000-2009	HOUSEHOLDS 2009 Average HH Size	FAMILIES 2000	FAMILIES 2009	FAMILIES % Annual Rate 2000-2009
63146	SAINT LOUIS	189	29631	29075	28720	-0.2	27	13761	13735	13640	0.0	2.10	7610	7181	-0.6
63147	SAINT LOUIS	510	13081	13106	13058	0.0	37	4433	4344	4322	-0.2	2.73	2892	2729	-0.6
63301	SAINT CHARLES	183	46002	48860	50882	0.7	66	18312	20256	21332	1.1	2.29	11723	12254	0.5
63303	SAINT CHARLES	183	41959	46469	48848	1.1	79	16274	18719	19901	1.5	2.47	11166	12100	0.9
63304	SAINT CHARLES	183	37296	41318	43872	1.1	79	12316	14206	15245	1.6	2.89	10327	11513	1.2
63330	ANNADA	163	111	117	119	0.6	63	56	60	61	0.7	1.95	41	42	0.3
63332	AUGUSTA	183	1133	1180	1287	0.4	53	438	473	519	0.8	2.49	336	345	0.3
63333	BELLFLOWER	139	854	847	835	-0.1	32	316	316	313	0.0	2.68	234	228	-0.3
63334	BOWLING GREEN	163	7938	8069	8090	0.2	46	2324	2404	2419	0.4	2.52	1604	1602	0.0
63336	CLARKSVILLE	163	1378	1426	1429	0.4	53	566	590	593	0.4	2.42	377	376	0.0
63339	CURRYVILLE	163	1625	1690	1709	0.4	53	551	585	596	0.6	2.78	440	454	0.3
63341	DEFIANCE	183	3295	3708	4032	1.3	83	1144	1330	1464	1.6	2.79	960	1088	1.4
63343	ELSBERRY	113	4464	5056	5611	1.4	86	1643	1865	2071	1.4	2.67	1192	1301	1.0
63344	EOLIA	113	1165	1315	1402	1.3	83	461	525	561	1.4	2.46	328	358	1.0
63345	FARBER	007	530	559	564	0.6	63	218	234	238	0.8	2.39	161	167	0.4
63347	FOLEY	113	2306	3183	3727	3.5	97	795	1099	1291	3.6	2.89	626	839	3.2
63348	FORISTELL	183	4591	6999	8594	4.7	99	1602	2482	3073	4.8	2.82	1331	2005	4.5
63349	HAWK POINT	113	1390	1851	2151	3.1	97	515	685	798	3.1	2.70	388	496	2.7
63350	HIGH HILL	139	738	807	830	1.0	76	300	331	342	1.1	2.39	203	216	0.7
63351	JONESBURG	139	1473	1744	1862	1.8	90	590	716	768	2.1	2.39	401	468	1.7
63352	LADDONIA	007	1089	1060	1046	-0.3	21	433	427	424	-0.2	2.48	314	298	-0.6
63353	LOUISIANA	163	5183	5084	5016	-0.2	27	2083	2056	2035	-0.1	2.40	1390	1315	-0.6
63357	MARTHASVILLE	219	4843	6502	7353	3.2	97	1733	2378	2711	3.5	2.69	1383	1851	3.2
63359	MIDDLETOWN	163	1344	1366	1358	0.2	46	524	539	537	0.3	2.53	399	396	-0.1
63361	MONTGOMERY CITY	139	4067	4088	4050	0.1	42	1666	1692	1681	0.2	2.37	1151	1126	-0.2
63362	MOSCOW MILLS	113	3473	5429	6661	4.9	99	1198	1883	2312	5.0	2.88	935	1424	4.7
63363	NEW FLORENCE	139	1502	1675	1721	1.2	82	544	615	635	1.3	2.57	396	432	0.9
63366	O FALLON	183	32499	45061	51673	3.6	97	11444	16472	19098	4.0	2.72	8865	12187	3.5
63367	LAKE SAINT LOUIS	183	11459	17894	20578	4.9	99	4349	6887	7978	5.1	2.60	3425	5237	4.7
63368	O FALLON	183	23238	40276	48374	6.1	99	7441	13114	15811	6.3	3.07	6362	10961	6.1
63369	OLD MONROE	113	1887	2507	2896	3.1	97	678	906	1049	3.2	2.77	516	668	2.8
63373	PORTAGE DES SIOUX	183	690	694	694	0.1	42	257	266	269	0.4	2.61	194	192	-0.1
63376	SAINT PETERS	183	68577	77696	82338	1.4	86	23535	27720	29630	1.8	2.79	18835	21475	1.4
63377	SILEX	113	2263	2802	3164	2.3	94	812	1010	1144	2.4	2.71	624	749	2.0
63379	TROY	113	16574	24221	28832	4.2	98	5893	8633	10298	4.2	2.76	4478	6381	3.9
63381	TRUXTON	219	603	660	712	1.0	76	226	251	272	1.1	2.63	174	188	0.8
63382	VANDALIA	007	4828	5147	5108	0.7	66	1499	1476	1466	-0.2	2.22	961	902	-0.7
63383	WARRENTON	219	12335	15893	17934	2.8	96	4638	6040	6838	2.9	2.61	3401	4292	2.5
63384	WELLSVILLE	139	2046	1901	1844	-0.8	6	768	714	694	-0.8	2.52	527	472	-1.2
63385	WENTZVILLE	183	13449	30392	37106	9.2	100	4666	10916	13464	9.6	2.77	3682	8434	9.4
63386	WEST ALTON	183	598	676	708	1.3	83	221	256	271	1.6	2.64	159	174	1.0
63388	WILLIAMSBURG	027	674	687	690	0.2	46	267	276	279	0.4	2.49	194	193	-0.1
63389	WINFIELD	113	4638	5961	6970	2.8	96	1650	2161	2533	3.0	2.75	1270	1612	2.6
63390	WRIGHT CITY	219	6860	9654	11156	3.8	98	2569	3665	4252	3.9	2.63	1934	2674	3.6
63401	HANNIBAL	127	21579	21727	21684	0.1	42	8534	8665	8668	0.2	2.40	5678	5528	-0.3
63430	ALEXANDRIA	045	617	627	622	0.2	46	242	250	250	0.4	2.51	179	179	0.0
63431	ANABEL	121	384	397	396	0.4	53	133	140	140	0.6	2.84	103	105	0.2
63432	ARBELA	199	571	573	571	0.0	37	206	202	200	-0.2	2.84	152	144	-0.6
63433	ASHBURN	163	201	210	212	0.5	58	84	89	91	0.6	2.33	58	59	0.2
63434	BETHEL	205	541	599	609	1.1	79	206	227	231	1.1	2.64	158	169	0.7
63435	CANTON	111	3974	3830	3756	-0.4	18	1347	1275	1245	-0.6	2.52	888	805	-1.1
63436	CENTER	173	1275	1303	1316	0.2	46	502	516	523	0.3	2.44	360	358	-0.1
63437	CLARENCE	205	1570	1518	1482	-0.4	18	643	625	612	-0.3	2.35	436	406	-0.8
63438	DURHAM	111	649	629	619	-0.3	21	233	229	225	-0.2	2.74	182	174	-0.5
63439	EMDEN	205	238	260	264	1.0	76	78	85	87	0.9	3.01	59	62	0.5
63440	EWING	111	1243	1203	1184	-0.4	18	496	484	477	-0.3	2.46	381	362	-0.6
63441	FRANKFORD	163	919	931	932	0.1	42	370	382	385	0.3	2.41	269	267	-0.1
63443	HUNNEWELL	205	383	365	356	-0.5	14	157	151	148	-0.4	2.38	106	98	-0.8
63445	KAHOKA	045	4080	3991	3921	-0.2	27	1594	1587	1568	0.0	2.44	1083	1036	-0.5
63446	KNOX CITY	103	495	443	419	-1.2	1	220	197	187	-1.2	2.24	148	127	-1.6
63447	LA BELLE	111	1145	1071	1046	-0.7	8	453	425	414	-0.7	2.39	289	260	-1.1
63448	LA GRANGE	111	1755	1845	1848	0.5	58	732	783	788	0.7	2.35	487	500	0.3
63450	LENTNER	205	138	134	131	-0.3	21	54	53	52	-0.2	2.43	35	33	-0.6
63451	LEONARD	205	267	259	254	-0.3	21	102	99	97	-0.3	2.56	73	68	-0.8
63452	LEWISTOWN	111	990	891	858	-1.1	2	391	354	341	-1.1	2.45	268	233	-1.5
63453	LURAY	045	507	481	467	-0.6	11	197	191	187	-0.3	2.52	150	141	-0.7
63454	MAYWOOD	127	973	971	967	0.0	37	353	356	356	0.1	2.72	281	277	-0.2
63456	MONROE CITY	173	4171	4307	4332	0.3	50	1650	1727	1744	0.5	2.44	1132	1143	0.1
63457	MONTICELLO	111	393	374	366	-0.5	14	157	151	148	-0.4	2.28	120	112	-0.7
63458	NEWARK	103	240	215	203	-1.2	1	98	88	84	-1.2	2.44	66	56	-1.8
63459	NEW LONDON	173	4047	4168	4238	0.3	50	1537	1597	1629	0.4	2.60	1163	1172	0.1
63460	NOVELTY	103	481	445	427	-0.8	6	200	186	178	-0.8	2.39	142	127	-1.2
63461	PALMYRA	127	5458	5453	5433	0.0	37	2088	2104	2103	0.1	2.47	1489	1448	-0.3
63462	PERRY	173	1276	1334	1362	0.5	58	540	570	583	0.6	2.28	353	358	0.2
63463	PHILADELPHIA	127	624	658	667	0.6	63	222	235	239	0.6	2.78	178	184	0.4
63464	PLEVNA	103	132	122	117	-0.8	6	61	57	54	-0.7	2.14	43	39	-1.0
63466	SAINT PATRICK	045	450	452	447	0.0	37	178	183	182	0.3	2.47	140	141	0.1
63468	SHELBINA	205	2643	2468	2383	-0.7	8	1107	1038	1005	-0.7	2.28	714	641	-1.2
63469	SHELBYVILLE	205	1165	1189	1182	0.2	46	454	463	459	0.2	2.37	307	301	-0.2
63471	TAYLOR	127	559	573	575	0.3	50	226	234	236	0.4	2.45	181	183	0.1
63472	WAYLAND	045	1227	1264	1257	0.3	50	516	544	545	0.6	2.32	356	361	0.2
63473	WILLIAMSTOWN	111	318	298	290	-0.7	8	137	128	125	-0.7	2.33	96	87	-1.1
63474	WYACONDA	045	535	492	472	-0.9	4	239	224	217	-0.7	2.20	172	156	-1.0
63501	KIRKSVILLE	001	21054	20930	20817	-0.1	32	8156	8172	8145	0.0	2.22	4196	3965	-0.6
63530	ATLANTA	121	986	1029	1034	0.5	58	364	380	381	0.5	2.71	279	283	0.2
63531	BARING	103	426	396	380	-0.8	6	159	148	142	-0.8	2.68	113	101	-1.2
63532	BEVIER	121	1339	1294	1269	-0.4	18	548	536	527	-0.2	2.41	377	354	-0.7
63533	BRASHEAR	001	1517	1499	1490	-0.1	32	571	574	574	0.1	2.61	443	432	-0.3
63534	CALLAO	121	813	777	762	-0.5	14	334	323	318	-0.4	2.41	239	223	-0.7
63535	COATSVILLE	197	136	134	132	-0.2	27	56	55	54	-0.2	2.44	42	40	-0.5
63536	DOWNING	197	1012	982	958	-0.3	21	405	394	385	-0.3	2.49	283	265	-0.7
63537	EDINA	103	2013	1885	1814	-0.7	8	828	776	746	-0.7	2.32	546	490	-1.2
63538	ELMER	121	291	305	306	0.5	58	129	136	137	0.6	2.24	94	95	0.1
63539	ETHEL	121	324	337	337	0.4	53	145	152	152	0.5	2.22	105	106	0.1
63540	GIBBS	001	415	425	427	0.3	50	155	161	163	0.4	2.64	112	112	0.0
	MISSOURI					0.7					0.8	2.45			0.4
	UNITED STATES					1.0					1.1	2.59			0.9

#	POST OFFICE NAME	RACE (%) White 2000	White 2009	Black 2000	Black 2009	Asian/Pacific 2000	Asian/Pacific 2009	% Hispanic Origin 2000	% Hispanic Origin 2009	2009 AGE DISTRIBUTION (%) 0-4	5-9	10-14	15-19	20-24	25-44	45-64	65-84	85+	18+	MEDIAN AGE 2009	% 2009 Males	% 2009 Females
63146	SAINT LOUIS	84.9	79.3	6.1	8.1	6.9	10.0	2.1	2.7	4.9	4.8	5.1	5.3	6.1	28.1	27.7	15.2	2.8	81.9	42.0	47.7	52.3
63147	SAINT LOUIS	9.3	6.5	89.2	92.2	0.1	0.1	0.5	0.5	5.9	6.3	6.5	8.7	8.2	26.4	25.3	10.7	1.9	76.4	35.7	48.7	51.3
63301	SAINT CHARLES	94.0	92.8	3.0	3.3	0.7	1.0	2.1	2.8	5.9	5.7	5.7	7.2	8.4	26.0	26.6	12.5	2.0	79.1	38.0	49.1	50.9
63303	SAINT CHARLES	93.8	92.1	3.2	3.6	1.3	2.1	1.4	2.0	6.7	6.6	6.6	6.7	6.4	29.3	27.2	9.3	1.1	76.0	36.4	49.0	51.0
63304	SAINT CHARLES	95.0	93.6	2.4	2.8	1.0	1.6	1.2	1.7	8.5	8.6	8.8	7.6	4.5	28.2	26.0	6.8	1.0	68.9	34.8	48.9	51.1
63330	ANNADA	96.4	94.9	2.7	3.4	0.0	0.0	0.0	0.9	5.1	6.8	6.0	6.8	3.4	24.8	29.9	14.5	2.6	77.8	43.5	52.1	47.9
63332	AUGUSTA	98.4	97.8	0.3	0.4	0.4	0.5	0.5	0.8	4.7	5.5	6.1	6.9	4.7	22.3	34.2	13.7	1.9	79.7	44.8	50.8	49.2
63333	BELLFLOWER	97.9	97.5	0.4	0.4	0.4	0.5	0.9	1.3	6.1	6.0	6.6	7.8	7.2	21.6	30.5	12.6	1.5	76.7	40.8	52.9	47.1
63334	BOWLING GREEN	82.6	80.4	15.4	17.3	0.2	0.3	1.0	1.3	4.8	4.6	4.7	6.3	9.1	32.7	25.1	10.2	2.4	82.1	37.1	60.5	39.5
63336	CLARKSVILLE	92.0	90.7	5.4	6.3	0.2	0.2	1.5	2.0	5.6	6.5	6.5	6.9	4.5	24.0	28.3	15.3	2.6	77.3	42.3	48.8	51.2
63339	CURRYVILLE	94.1	93.2	4.4	5.0	0.1	0.1	0.3	0.4	7.5	7.3	7.8	8.5	6.7	24.7	24.1	12.2	1.2	72.4	35.8	51.7	48.3
63341	DEFIANCE	97.6	97.1	1.1	1.2	0.3	0.5	0.8	1.1	6.0	6.8	7.6	8.1	5.2	21.4	34.7	9.4	0.8	76.2	41.4	49.7	50.3
63343	ELSBERRY	95.1	94.1	2.1	2.3	0.2	0.3	2.3	3.2	6.8	6.9	7.4	7.8	6.1	24.0	26.9	12.0	2.1	73.6	38.6	48.8	51.2
63344	EOLIA	93.2	92.2	4.7	5.3	0.3	0.3	0.9	1.3	5.8	6.0	6.4	6.8	5.3	23.2	30.9	13.6	2.1	77.6	42.2	49.5	50.5
63345	FARBER	98.9	98.9	0.0	0.0	0.2	0.2	0.0	0.0	4.5	4.8	5.7	6.3	3.4	25.2	32.2	15.9	2.0	81.2	45.1	50.4	49.6
63347	FOLEY	96.7	96.0	0.8	0.9	0.2	0.3	1.0	1.5	7.0	6.8	6.9	8.0	7.6	26.0	28.3	8.6	0.8	74.3	35.6	50.0	50.0
63348	FORISTELL	95.6	95.4	2.8	2.7	0.2	0.3	1.0	1.4	6.4	6.9	7.5	7.4	4.7	24.7	31.4	9.9	0.9	74.5	40.1	50.4	49.6
63349	HAWK POINT	97.8	97.2	0.9	1.1	0.2	0.4	0.2	0.4	7.1	7.2	7.3	7.2	6.3	24.3	28.8	10.5	1.4	74.1	37.6	50.8	49.2
63350	HIGH HILL	95.4	94.4	1.1	1.2	0.8	1.1	1.5	2.0	5.8	5.8	6.1	6.7	5.2	23.7	28.9	14.6	3.2	78.2	42.0	49.9	50.1
63351	JONESBURG	96.0	94.9	0.9	1.0	0.7	1.2	1.2	1.5	5.6	5.7	6.0	6.5	5.2	23.2	29.6	14.7	3.4	78.8	43.1	49.8	50.2
63352	LADDONIA	98.3	98.2	0.6	0.7	0.0	0.0	0.2	0.1	6.6	7.7	7.6	6.1	5.0	23.3	28.0	14.3	1.2	74.1	39.9	50.2	49.8
63353	LOUISIANA	92.0	90.2	4.2	4.9	0.3	0.5	3.6	4.9	6.2	6.4	6.4	6.4	5.3	22.7	27.2	15.7	3.7	77.1	42.3	49.0	51.0
63357	MARTHASVILLE	98.1	97.8	0.6	0.7	0.3	0.5	0.7	0.9	5.9	6.2	6.6	7.1	5.0	24.9	31.7	11.3	1.3	76.9	41.0	50.9	49.1
63359	MIDDLETOWN	98.3	98.1	0.9	1.0	0.1	0.1	0.4	0.6	5.7	6.1	6.7	6.8	4.2	21.9	30.5	15.8	2.2	77.5	44.0	51.5	48.5
63361	MONTGOMERY CITY	95.5	94.7	2.7	3.2	0.1	0.2	0.4	0.6	5.8	5.8	6.2	7.1	6.0	24.5	29.4	13.0	2.2	77.7	40.9	49.8	50.2
63362	MOSCOW MILLS	96.0	95.1	1.5	1.8	0.2	0.3	1.2	1.7	8.6	8.3	7.8	7.5	6.6	27.8	24.9	7.7	0.8	70.6	33.1	50.5	49.5
63363	NEW FLORENCE	96.7	95.9	1.7	2.1	0.1	0.1	1.1	1.6	5.2	5.6	6.5	6.7	4.5	22.5	29.9	14.1	4.9	78.0	44.1	49.3	50.7
63366	O FALLON	95.6	94.5	1.9	2.3	0.6	1.0	1.6	2.1	8.9	8.4	7.8	6.7	5.2	30.9	23.2	8.0	0.9	70.6	33.8	48.9	51.1
63367	LAKE SAINT LOUIS	95.6	94.3	2.1	2.6	0.8	1.2	1.3	1.8	6.6	6.8	7.1	6.7	5.0	25.1	30.0	11.8	1.0	75.4	40.0	49.2	50.8
63368	O FALLON	95.4	94.3	2.1	2.2	0.9	1.5	1.3	1.9	11.0	10.6	9.9	7.4	4.3	30.8	21.2	4.4	0.3	63.6	30.9	49.4	50.6
63369	OLD MONROE	98.6	98.3	0.3	0.4	0.1	0.1	0.9	1.2	7.1	7.5	7.7	7.2	5.0	26.8	28.0	9.4	1.3	73.2	37.1	49.9	50.1
63373	PORTAGE DES SIOUX	98.3	98.0	0.1	0.1	0.1	0.3	0.9	1.3	5.5	6.1	6.8	7.3	4.6	24.8	31.6	11.7	1.7	76.9	41.5	52.7	47.3
63376	SAINT PETERS	95.0	93.7	2.4	2.7	1.0	1.6	1.4	2.1	7.7	7.6	7.7	7.3	5.8	29.2	26.7	7.2	0.8	72.2	34.9	48.9	51.1
63377	SILEX	97.8	97.3	0.9	1.1	0.1	0.2	0.7	1.0	6.5	6.8	6.8	6.9	5.7	23.8	29.0	12.6	1.9	75.6	40.0	51.1	48.9
63379	TROY	95.1	94.3	2.6	2.8	0.2	0.3	1.2	1.7	7.8	7.4	7.3	7.7	6.8	26.6	25.7	9.2	1.5	72.7	35.1	49.0	51.0
63381	TRUXTON	96.7	96.4	0.5	0.6	0.5	0.8	0.3	0.5	5.5	6.2	6.5	6.5	4.7	23.6	31.2	14.1	1.7	78.2	42.4	51.5	48.5
63382	VANDALIA	81.6	80.0	15.9	17.5	0.3	0.4	1.0	1.0	4.0	4.0	3.9	4.5	6.7	40.2	21.5	11.4	3.8	85.4	38.0	31.8	68.2
63383	WARRENTON	96.5	95.9	1.4	1.5	0.3	0.5	1.1	1.5	6.8	7.0	7.2	6.8	5.2	24.9	27.4	12.9	1.8	74.5	39.3	49.0	51.0
63384	WELLSVILLE	94.3	93.4	3.5	4.1	0.0	0.1	0.8	1.0	6.4	6.3	7.3	6.8	5.0	22.3	24.7	16.3	5.0	75.9	41.6	49.0	51.0
63385	WENTZVILLE	90.7	91.0	7.0	6.4	0.4	0.6	1.0	1.4	7.5	7.5	7.6	7.5	5.9	26.0	27.8	9.1	1.1	72.8	36.5	49.2	50.8
63386	WEST ALTON	99.2	98.8	0.0	0.0	0.2	0.3	0.5	0.7	5.0	5.6	6.2	7.7	4.7	24.7	33.6	11.2	1.2	78.4	42.2	54.1	45.9
63388	WILLIAMSBURG	95.1	94.2	1.8	2.2	0.0	0.0	1.9	2.6	5.5	5.4	6.1	6.6	5.8	24.0	30.0	15.0	1.6	78.7	42.5	51.1	48.9
63389	WINFIELD	97.9	97.4	0.5	0.6	0.3	0.4	0.6	0.8	7.4	7.2	7.5	8.0	6.3	26.3	27.1	9.3	1.1	73.0	36.0	49.3	50.7
63390	WRIGHT CITY	94.2	93.0	3.2	4.0	0.1	0.1	2.1	2.6	6.8	6.7	7.2	6.5	5.4	25.1	30.0	10.9	1.3	75.2	39.6	50.5	49.5
63401	HANNIBAL	91.9	90.6	5.6	6.4	0.4	0.6	1.0	1.3	6.8	6.4	6.4	7.4	6.9	24.6	26.4	12.1	2.9	76.0	37.9	47.4	52.6
63430	ALEXANDRIA	99.0	99.0	0.2	0.2	0.2	0.2	0.5	0.8	6.2	6.5	6.7	6.2	4.5	23.9	30.0	14.2	1.8	76.7	42.0	50.9	49.1
63431	ANABEL	97.7	97.2	1.3	1.5	0.0	0.0	1.3	1.8	6.3	6.8	7.1	6.3	4.8	23.4	30.7	13.1	1.5	76.1	41.7	51.9	48.1
63432	ARBELA	99.3	99.3	0.0	0.0	0.2	0.2	1.4	1.4	8.2	8.4	8.4	6.8	4.4	23.6	25.8	12.7	1.7	70.7	37.7	51.1	48.9
63433	ASHBURN	92.1	90.5	5.9	7.1	0.0	0.5	0.5	0.5	5.7	5.7	6.2	5.7	5.2	21.9	29.5	17.6	2.4	78.6	44.6	50.0	50.0
63434	BETHEL	97.8	97.2	1.1	1.3	0.0	0.0	1.1	1.5	5.8	6.3	6.5	8.0	4.7	22.0	31.9	11.9	2.8	76.1	42.2	51.1	48.9
63435	CANTON	95.8	94.9	1.8	2.0	0.5	0.8	1.2	1.6	7.2	6.7	6.6	10.4	13.7	20.0	19.9	12.0	3.4	75.6	30.0	48.3	51.7
63436	CENTER	99.1	98.8	0.2	0.2	0.0	0.0	0.8	1.1	6.2	7.8	7.1	6.4	4.4	23.6	27.2	13.9	3.4	74.9	40.9	52.5	47.5
63437	CLARENCE	98.4	98.2	0.6	0.7	0.1	0.1	0.5	0.7	5.7	6.1	6.9	7.4	4.3	21.1	28.6	15.6	4.3	76.5	43.7	47.4	52.6
63438	DURHAM	99.4	99.4	0.2	0.2	0.0	0.0	0.2	0.3	6.2	6.7	6.8	6.0	5.7	25.0	30.0	12.2	1.3	76.3	39.9	52.3	47.7
63439	EMDEN	97.9	97.7	1.3	1.2	0.0	0.0	0.8	1.5	6.2	6.5	6.5	7.3	4.6	21.9	31.5	12.3	3.1	75.8	42.5	51.2	48.8
63440	EWING	99.3	99.2	0.2	0.2	0.1	0.1	0.2	0.2	6.3	6.8	6.9	6.6	5.3	23.8	29.6	12.6	2.1	75.7	40.6	51.7	48.3
63441	FRANKFORD	96.8	96.2	2.8	3.3	0.0	0.0	0.0	0.0	4.7	5.0	5.4	6.4	5.6	24.3	32.4	14.4	1.7	81.1	43.9	53.2	46.8
63443	HUNNEWELL	97.4	96.7	1.8	2.2	0.0	0.3	0.5	0.8	7.1	7.4	7.1	5.8	4.9	21.4	29.3	13.7	3.3	74.8	42.1	49.3	50.7
63445	KAHOKA	98.6	98.3	0.0	0.1	0.1	0.1	0.9	1.2	6.3	6.4	6.6	6.6	5.1	23.3	27.1	14.8	3.9	76.4	41.7	48.8	51.2
63446	KNOX CITY	98.8	98.6	0.2	0.2	0.2	0.2	1.2	1.6	5.6	6.1	6.3	5.9	4.1	20.5	31.8	17.2	2.5	78.3	45.8	48.1	51.9
63447	LA BELLE	95.2	94.5	3.5	3.7	0.1	0.3	1.0	1.6	6.7	6.8	6.7	6.6	4.9	21.0	26.1	15.3	5.9	75.9	42.7	48.4	51.6
63448	LA GRANGE	91.0	89.8	7.4	8.4	0.0	0.0	0.4	0.6	7.2	6.9	7.0	5.9	5.1	24.7	26.9	14.0	2.3	75.3	40.1	49.1	50.9
63450	LENTNER	98.6	97.8	0.7	0.7	0.0	0.0	0.7	0.7	4.5	5.2	6.0	6.7	4.5	19.4	32.1	16.4	5.2	79.9	47.3	48.5	51.5
63451	LEONARD	98.1	98.1	0.7	0.8	0.0	0.0	0.4	0.4	6.9	7.7	8.1	7.7	3.9	23.6	26.6	12.4	3.1	71.4	39.0	47.1	52.9
63452	LEWISTOWN	98.4	98.2	1.2	1.3	0.0	0.0	0.3	0.4	7.6	7.6	7.5	5.9	4.2	21.0	25.7	16.7	3.7	73.6	41.0	48.1	51.9
63453	LURAY	99.2	99.2	0.2	0.2	0.0	0.0	0.4	0.6	6.7	6.9	6.9	6.2	4.4	24.7	28.1	14.8	1.5	75.9	41.6	52.6	47.4
63454	MAYWOOD	97.7	97.5	1.0	1.0	0.2	0.2	0.4	0.5	6.8	7.3	7.3	6.2	5.3	24.2	29.2	12.5	1.2	74.4	40.0	50.7	49.3
63456	MONROE CITY	93.0	92.7	5.5	5.9	0.1	0.1	0.5	0.6	6.1	6.8	6.8	6.9	5.1	22.7	29.7	12.9	3.1	75.8	41.8	48.9	51.1
63457	MONTICELLO	98.7	98.7	0.3	0.3	0.0	0.0	0.0	0.0	5.3	5.6	5.9	6.4	4.5	22.5	29.7	15.0	5.1	79.7	44.8	52.4	47.6
63458	NEWARK	99.2	98.6	0.0	0.0	0.0	0.5	1.3	1.9	5.6	6.0	6.0	5.6	3.7	20.5	33.0	17.2	2.3	78.6	46.3	48.8	51.2
63459	NEW LONDON	96.8	96.2	2.1	2.4	0.1	0.2	0.3	0.5	6.2	6.6	6.8	6.4	5.0	23.8	30.8	12.7	1.7	76.2	41.1	50.8	49.2
63460	NOVELTY	98.8	98.7	0.0	0.0	0.2	0.2	0.8	1.1	4.5	4.9	5.6	6.1	4.3	20.4	33.7	17.8	2.7	81.1	46.9	49.7	50.3
63461	PALMYRA	97.1	96.6	1.9	2.2	0.2	0.4	0.5	0.7	6.5	6.6	6.6	6.5	5.4	24.7	27.1	13.1	3.5	76.4	40.1	48.6	51.4
63462	PERRY	98.7	98.4	0.5	0.5	0.1	0.1	0.6	0.8	4.1	5.9	5.6	6.4	4.5	23.2	31.2	15.1	4.0	80.4	45.2	48.6	51.4
63463	PHILADELPHIA	99.4	99.2	0.2	0.2	0.0	0.0	0.0	0.0	6.7	7.1	7.0	6.5	5.5	24.5	30.5	10.8	1.4	74.3	38.9	50.9	49.1
63464	PLEVNA	99.2	99.2	0.0	0.0	0.0	0.0	0.8	0.8	4.9	4.9	4.9	6.6	4.1	19.7	34.4	18.0	2.5	81.1	47.0	51.6	48.4
63466	SAINT PATRICK	99.6	99.6	0.0	0.0	0.2	0.2	0.9	1.3	5.8	6.4	6.0	5.3	3.8	22.8	31.6	16.6	1.8	78.3	45.0	50.0	50.0
63468	SHELBINA	97.8	97.5	1.2	1.4	0.0	0.0	0.3	0.4	5.9	6.0	6.1	6.4	5.1	22.2	27.2	15.2	5.8	77.9	43.3	46.4	53.6
63469	SHELBYVILLE	97.5	96.8	0.8	0.8	0.4	0.7	1.2	1.7	5.6	5.9	5.8	10.4	6.1	21.4	28.2	13.8	2.8	74.9	40.6	49.2	50.8
63471	TAYLOR	99.1	99.0	0.0	0.0	0.7	0.9	0.7	0.9	6.5	7.0	7.0	6.3	5.4	24.1	28.6	13.8	1.4	75.6	40.9	51.3	48.7
63472	WAYLAND	98.8	98.6	0.1	0.1	0.1	0.1	0.6	0.7	6.2	6.2	6.6	6.4	5.1	25.5	29.4	12.8	1.9	77.3	40.8	51.0	49.0
63473	WILLIAMSTOWN	97.5	96.6	0.9	1.0	0.0	0.0	1.6	2.3	9.4	9.4	10.1	7.7	4.0	21.1	24.8	11.7	1.7	66.1	35.0	51.3	48.7
63474	WYACONDA	99.3	99.2	0.0	0.0	0.0	0.0	0.2	0.2	5.9	6.5	6.9	6.5	4.1	21.1	32.7	14.4	1.8	76.2	44.1	51.0	49.0
63501	KIRKSVILLE	95.2	91.6	1.4	3.8	1.7	2.5	1.4	1.8	5.0	4.7	4.6	11.1	18.8	22.6	20.5	10.0	2.5	82.5	29.6	47.6	52.4
63530	ATLANTA	99.3	99.1	0.0	0.0	0.0	0.0	0.2	0.3	6.7	7.0	7.6	7.8	5.4	26.7	25.5	11.9	1.5	73.9	37.3	50.7	49.3
63531	BARING	99.5	99.5	0.0	0.0	0.0	0.0	0.2	0.3	7.8	7.8	7.3	7.1	4.0	21.7	28.3	13.9	2.0	72.5	40.6	50.5	49.5
63532	BEVIER	97.6	97.2	0.1	0.2	0.2	0.2	0.4	0.5	6.3	6.6	6.6	7.3	4.5	24.0	28.5	14.2	2.0	75.8	41.3	49.4	50.6
63533	BRASHEAR	99.0	98.8	0.1	0.1	0.1	0.1	0.3	0.4	5.9	6.8	7.5	8.0	3.8	22.7	30.8	13.1	1.5	74.6	41.6	51.4	48.6
63534	CALLAO	97.4	97.0	0.1	0.1	0.0	0.0	0.6	0.9	4.1	4.5	4.6	5.9	5.5	24.5	34.0	14.8	2.1	83.4	45.5	51.6	48.4
63535	COATSVILLE	99.3	99.3	0.0	0.0	0.0	0.0	0.0	0.0	6.0	6.7	6.7	6.7	4.5	21.6	28.4	17.2	2.2	76.1	43.5	50.7	49.3
63536	DOWNING	97.4	97.1	0.1	0.1	0.2	0.3	1.0	1.5	6.6	6.7	7.1	7.5	4.2	23.9	27.2	14.6	2.1	74.6	40.7	49.6	50.4
63537	EDINA	97.8	97.5	0.1	0.2	0.1	0.2	0.5	0.6	6.6	6.6	6.6	6.3	4.7	20.2	25.9	18.0	5.1	75.9	44.0	47.0	53.0
63538	ELMER	99.0	98.4	0.0	0.3	0.0	0.0	0.3	0.3	8.2	8.2	7.9	6.6	3.9	25.6	24.9	13.1	1.6	71.5	36.8	52.5	47.5
63539	ETHEL	98.8	98.5	0.0	0.3	0.0	0.0	0.3	0.3	8.0	7.7	7.7	6.5	3.9	24.9	25.8	13.6	1.8	72.4	37.7	52.5	47.5
63540	GIBBS	98.6	98.4	0.0	0.0	0.0	0.0	0.7	0.7	6.1	7.1	7.1	6.4	4.9	21.2	31.8	13.6	1.9	75.8	42.9	49.2	50.8
	MISSOURI	84.9	83.3	11.2	11.7	1.2	1.7	2.1	2.8	6.6	6.6	6.6	7.0	6.7	26.1	26.5	11.7	2.1	76.1	37.7	48.8	51.2
	UNITED STATES	75.1	72.0	12.3	12.7	3.8	4.6	12.5	15.7	6.8	6.7	6.6	7.1	6.9	27.0	26.0	10.9	1.9	75.7	36.9	49.2	50.8

ZIP CODE #	POST OFFICE NAME	2009 Per Capita Income	2009 HH Income Base	2009 HOUSEHOLD INCOME DISTRIBUTION (%) Less than $25,000	$25,000 to $49,999	$50,000 to $99,999	$100,000 to $149,999	$150,000 or More	MEDIAN HOUSEHOLD INCOME 2009	2014	2009 National Centile	2009 State Centile	2009 Home Value Base	2009 HOME VALUE DISTRIBUTION (%) Less than $50,000	$50,000 to $89,999	$90,000 to $174,999	$175,000 to $399,999	$400,000 or More	2009 Median Home Value
63146	SAINT LOUIS	37587	13735	11.8	22.9	41.7	15.8	7.8	66556	70339	85	94	8455	0.9	3.9	41.7	51.5	1.9	179767
63147	SAINT LOUIS	16080	4344	35.5	29.2	29.7	4.4	1.3	35232	38470	18	32	2893	12.0	50.6	35.3	1.8	0.3	83036
63301	SAINT CHARLES	29444	20256	16.5	26.1	37.3	15.3	4.8	56501	55394	73	87	13103	11.1	5.3	44.9	35.3	3.4	152034
63303	SAINT CHARLES	34051	18719	8.1	21.1	39.8	22.8	8.2	69488	70075	86	95	13174	4.9	4.0	31.6	55.3	4.2	193105
63304	SAINT CHARLES	35776	14206	5.2	12.9	38.3	29.0	14.6	90253	100755	95	98	12740	1.0	2.1	27.2	61.2	8.5	209611
63330	ANNADA	28366	60	26.7	30.0	33.3	8.3	1.7	45000	42365	48	69	46	21.7	15.2	32.6	19.6	10.9	129167
63332	AUGUSTA	30163	473	10.6	29.0	33.8	21.1	5.5	61592	58194	79	91	382	1.3	12.8	24.6	40.1	21.2	218478
63333	BELLFLOWER	16194	316	27.5	36.1	33.5	2.2	0.6	38987	42171	30	49	258	29.5	25.6	24.8	16.3	3.9	81333
63334	BOWLING GREEN	17573	2404	30.0	28.6	34.7	5.2	1.6	42347	43900	40	62	1709	18.9	25.7	34.1	19.1	2.1	97148
63336	CLARKSVILLE	19118	590	33.7	32.5	26.3	5.3	2.2	36673	37977	23	38	428	24.1	25.0	32.2	12.4	6.3	91111
63339	CURRYVILLE	14878	585	30.9	33.3	33.2	2.6	0.0	34903	37884	17	30	493	26.4	11.6	36.7	21.5	3.9	129219
63341	DEFIANCE	35662	1330	7.2	17.1	31.8	30.5	13.4	88412	99633	95	98	1221	9.7	4.8	8.8	44.7	32.1	318773
63343	ELSBERRY	20149	1865	24.2	29.5	37.6	6.3	2.3	46277	50847	52	72	1416	18.4	17.8	40.8	19.8	3.2	111304
63344	EOLIA	18760	525	27.2	34.1	33.7	4.6	0.4	42394	43722	41	62	417	18.9	22.8	32.1	20.4	5.8	104808
63345	FARBER	21084	234	22.6	32.1	39.7	4.3	1.3	47079	47779	54	74	183	39.9	30.6	20.8	8.7	0.0	60417
63347	FOLEY	21405	1099	16.9	24.5	47.2	8.8	2.5	56846	59488	74	88	934	18.5	17.2	31.8	26.7	5.8	120085
63348	FORISTELL	29517	2482	7.9	20.3	41.7	23.9	6.2	72418	75622	88	96	2261	6.0	5.3	25.0	54.4	9.3	209851
63349	HAWK POINT	18649	685	24.8	35.5	32.1	6.4	1.2	40519	43208	34	55	520	15.0	14.0	31.7	33.3	6.0	145339
63350	HIGH HILL	19152	331	32.0	26.9	36.6	3.9	0.6	40820	43099	35	56	248	21.8	29.8	34.3	11.7	2.4	87647
63351	JONESBURG	19545	716	32.3	29.2	32.0	4.7	1.8	38567	40784	28	47	549	20.0	25.3	33.7	18.2	2.7	96375
63352	LADDONIA	20685	427	23.4	37.9	31.4	5.4	1.9	41644	43311	38	59	342	31.3	29.2	26.3	11.4	1.8	76154
63353	LOUISIANA	20267	2056	30.6	30.8	32.1	4.3	2.2	39545	40093	31	52	1464	23.5	29.2	29.6	14.4	3.3	85979
63357	MARTHASVILLE	26236	2378	14.5	24.6	41.3	15.0	4.7	58951	60654	76	89	2096	5.7	6.5	32.2	44.0	11.6	193671
63359	MIDDLETOWN	16896	539	30.8	34.5	31.2	2.8	0.7	37349	39744	25	42	464	22.4	18.8	36.0	17.0	5.8	107292
63361	MONTGOMERY CITY	20106	1692	27.2	31.9	34.0	5.7	1.2	42974	45048	42	64	1299	12.5	27.2	37.0	18.2	5.2	106686
63362	MOSCOW MILLS	22305	1883	13.6	26.3	47.4	10.0	2.7	60696	62027	78	90	1579	20.4	17.5	25.5	31.4	5.1	130413
63363	NEW FLORENCE	17212	615	34.3	29.8	31.5	2.9	1.5	39297	40051	31	50	505	22.6	22.6	29.9	20.2	4.8	101179
63366	O FALLON	27810	16472	9.7	22.9	43.6	19.3	4.5	66292	66512	84	94	13832	9.6	5.7	36.0	44.7	3.9	171738
63367	LAKE SAINT LOUIS	39984	6887	6.3	16.6	35.2	26.5	15.4	85696	93462	94	98	5768	5.9	4.0	20.5	53.4	16.3	226895
63368	O FALLON	38313	13114	3.5	9.2	34.9	33.0	19.5	102527	110031	97	99	12383	7.4	2.1	22.1	63.2	5.2	214702
63369	OLD MONROE	22492	906	18.3	24.0	43.2	12.3	2.3	58940	60992	76	89	751	7.7	15.4	37.4	32.5	6.9	146108
63373	PORTAGE DES SIOUX	24497	266	15.4	24.4	47.0	10.2	3.0	59572	55650	77	89	213	1.4	19.2	46.5	28.6	4.2	135357
63376	SAINT PETERS	31779	27720	5.7	16.4	43.8	26.1	8.0	79650	86895	92	97	24091	1.9	2.5	44.8	49.0	1.8	175973
63377	SILEX	19954	1010	23.5	28.7	39.4	6.6	1.8	48296	52001	57	76	836	15.6	16.3	25.7	32.5	9.9	150000
63379	TROY	22846	8633	16.8	26.1	43.2	10.5	3.3	56928	60182	74	88	6741	10.3	7.8	37.4	35.8	8.6	162599
63381	TRUXTON	22729	251	25.1	21.9	39.0	9.6	4.4	52387	55576	67	82	217	5.1	11.1	32.7	43.3	7.8	180208
63382	VANDALIA	16830	1476	33.8	33.1	29.7	2.7	0.7	34695	37000	17	29	1124	30.8	30.8	29.2	7.4	1.9	70784
63383	WARRENTON	21572	6040	20.2	33.1	36.5	7.1	3.0	46807	51279	54	73	4884	15.4	10.1	37.5	32.9	4.2	150000
63384	WELLSVILLE	16016	714	32.8	37.1	27.5	2.0	0.7	36467	37872	22	37	529	31.9	28.5	27.4	9.5	2.6	72273
63385	WENTZVILLE	28594	10916	11.4	18.1	44.1	19.5	6.9	66890	66692	85	94	9096	4.1	5.7	31.1	49.8	9.3	193829
63386	WEST ALTON	21616	256	17.6	39.1	31.3	8.2	3.9	43968	47517	45	66	221	19.0	30.8	40.7	9.5	0.0	90294
63388	WILLIAMSBURG	19965	276	25.4	35.5	34.4	2.2	2.5	43551	45873	44	65	239	33.5	26.8	26.8	8.4	4.6	73696
63389	WINFIELD	23012	2161	18.5	22.7	46.0	9.1	3.7	58958	61013	76	89	1787	17.0	13.3	35.5	30.6	3.7	140982
63390	WRIGHT CITY	25735	3665	18.6	25.6	41.4	10.2	4.1	55063	57968	71	85	2991	15.4	11.1	30.2	32.6	10.7	156013
63401	HANNIBAL	21350	8665	29.1	29.4	32.9	5.7	2.9	41168	43363	37	58	5955	21.6	27.7	33.5	15.2	2.0	91231
63430	ALEXANDRIA	19200	250	26.0	31.2	38.8	2.8	1.2	43396	50000	44	65	205	25.9	27.8	30.7	13.7	2.0	84231
63431	ANABEL	15919	140	17.1	48.6	30.7	2.9	0.7	39378	40000	31	51	121	15.7	26.4	40.5	15.7	1.7	109167
63432	ARBELA	15196	202	36.1	39.6	17.8	2.5	4.0	33782	35000	15	25	160	43.8	19.4	25.6	11.3	0.0	63636
63433	ASHBURN	17546	89	39.3	31.5	23.6	3.4	2.2	28768	28019	6	7	69	27.5	31.9	14.5	21.7	4.3	71250
63434	BETHEL	15484	227	30.4	35.2	32.2	2.2	0.0	39747	41746	32	53	166	19.9	24.7	30.7	15.7	9.0	100000
63435	CANTON	19884	1275	31.1	32.5	28.0	4.9	3.5	40993	42023	36	57	883	28.2	23.3	37.4	8.3	2.8	87955
63436	CENTER	17679	516	31.0	33.1	31.0	4.7	0.2	38825	41419	29	48	397	24.9	21.7	31.2	13.4	8.8	92872
63437	CLARENCE	18204	625	34.7	34.9	24.6	3.8	1.9	36632	37208	22	38	472	34.7	23.5	25.8	14.2	1.7	74839
63438	DURHAM	16892	229	24.0	37.6	34.1	3.5	0.9	41383	42679	37	59	198	21.7	25.8	39.9	10.6	2.0	94167
63439	EMDEN	14649	85	28.2	32.9	35.3	3.5	0.0	41130	43001	36	58	63	19.0	22.2	36.5	15.9	6.3	106944
63440	EWING	18266	484	27.5	35.3	32.6	3.9	0.6	39785	41180	32	53	398	24.4	23.1	34.2	14.3	4.0	94545
63441	FRANKFORD	18532	382	29.1	32.5	32.7	5.8	0.0	38952	40597	30	48	313	29.4	25.6	28.1	15.3	1.6	68721
63443	HUNNEWELL	19168	151	35.1	25.8	31.8	6.0	1.3	38832	40927	29	48	110	30.9	10.0	40.9	16.4	1.8	105952
63445	KAHOKA	17519	1587	33.6	33.7	27.5	4.0	1.2	33418	34403	14	24	1199	30.4	28.0	32.6	7.6	1.3	78355
63446	KNOX CITY	15339	197	41.1	39.6	15.2	4.1	0.0	28808	28366	6	7	156	46.2	18.6	19.9	14.1	1.3	58571
63447	LA BELLE	15241	425	40.9	31.5	24.7	2.4	0.5	29152	31660	7	8	323	53.3	21.4	18.6	5.9	0.9	47500
63448	LA GRANGE	18321	783	29.9	36.4	30.3	2.6	0.9	39465	40380	31	51	613	35.4	30.0	26.9	7.5	0.2	65119
63450	LENTNER	16955	53	39.6	32.1	20.8	5.7	1.9	33640	38194	15	25	37	32.4	16.2	35.1	16.2	0.0	91667
63451	LEONARD	17365	99	30.3	40.4	24.2	4.0	1.0	37328	38809	25	42	81	34.6	30.9	23.5	9.9	1.2	67500
63452	LEWISTOWN	16968	354	34.7	31.4	29.7	3.7	0.6	31025	32921	10	15	266	39.8	33.1	19.5	3.0	4.5	60000
63453	LURAY	20746	191	30.4	34.0	27.7	3.1	4.7	37868	37718	26	45	156	38.5	16.0	28.8	12.2	4.5	83636
63454	MAYWOOD	17691	356	22.5	35.1	37.6	3.4	1.4	43727	46818	45	65	310	28.7	14.8	35.5	17.7	3.2	105114
63456	MONROE CITY	19028	1727	26.2	35.0	33.2	4.4	1.2	41165	42734	37	58	1321	17.0	25.0	41.1	13.9	3.0	102488
63457	MONTICELLO	22396	151	19.2	41.7	31.1	4.0	4.0	38307	40000	28	46	138	26.8	17.4	26.8	19.6	9.4	98000
63458	NEWARK	13912	88	43.2	39.8	13.6	3.4	0.0	27752	27922	5	5	70	45.7	20.0	21.4	11.4	1.4	60000
63459	NEW LONDON	19300	1597	23.5	33.7	36.6	5.2	1.1	44190	45142	46	67	1313	19.9	25.4	35.5	16.5	2.7	97102
63460	NOVELTY	14214	186	35.5	46.2	17.2	1.1	0.0	30561	31545	9	13	152	44.7	15.8	23.0	11.2	5.3	60000
63461	PALMYRA	20105	2104	27.8	26.6	39.0	5.4	1.3	44668	48722	47	68	1553	13.3	23.3	39.3	21.7	2.3	111161
63462	PERRY	20349	570	29.5	30.0	36.1	3.9	0.5	42122	43507	40	61	450	24.4	22.9	36.2	11.3	5.1	91791
63463	PHILADELPHIA	15677	235	27.2	37.9	31.1	3.4	0.4	37734	39862	26	44	192	15.6	23.4	39.6	17.2	4.2	114474
63464	PLEVNA	15560	57	35.1	47.4	15.8	1.8	0.0	29655	32357	8	10	47	48.9	12.8	21.3	10.6	6.4	52500
63466	SAINT PATRICK	23550	183	15.8	28.4	50.8	3.3	1.6	51492	52373	65	81	155	20.6	17.4	34.8	23.2	3.9	125431
63468	SHELBINA	19100	1038	36.6	33.7	23.6	4.4	1.6	33187	33873	14	23	777	34.4	30.2	27.5	7.3	0.5	71985
63469	SHELBYVILLE	16781	463	31.1	36.9	28.9	3.0	0.0	36360	37019	22	36	343	32.4	32.1	23.3	7.6	4.7	71618
63471	TAYLOR	23311	234	16.7	35.0	40.6	4.7	3.0	48455	50771	58	77	193	13.5	19.7	34.7	28.0	4.1	118359
63472	WAYLAND	17405	544	34.4	36.0	25.9	2.8	0.9	32563	33575	13	20	441	32.9	32.2	26.5	6.8	1.6	71571
63473	WILLIAMSTOWN	16639	128	47.7	22.7	27.3	1.6	0.8	30718	31574	9	14	101	37.6	20.8	29.7	5.0	6.9	79167
63474	WYACONDA	19434	224	34.4	29.0	33.0	3.6	0.0	34291	35250	16	27	175	33.1	41.1	17.7	5.7	2.3	66167
63501	KIRKSVILLE	20689	8172	39.7	28.1	23.8	4.8	3.6	33129	35242	14	22	4533	17.0	23.4	36.3	19.9	3.5	107913
63530	ATLANTA	16146	380	26.6	35.8	33.7	2.6	1.3	41733	45851	38	60	309	37.5	22.7	30.4	8.7	0.6	65938
63531	BARING	16559	148	32.4	30.4	31.8	3.4	2.0	39380	42724	31	51	123	33.3	37.4	15.4	8.9	4.9	65000
63532	BEVIER	18824	536	32.3	37.1	25.7	2.6	2.2	37114	38008	24	41	442	38.7	29.2	22.9	7.5	1.8	62813
63533	BRASHEAR	19065	574	24.2	35.7	33.3	5.1	1.7	41184	44802	37	58	490	20.6	18.8	35.1	19.6	5.9	112500
63534	CALLAO	18135	323	31.3	33.7	32.8	1.2	0.9	37767	41560	26	44	266	45.9	20.3	22.2	10.2	1.5	60000
63535	COATSVILLE	22879	55	32.7	36.4	25.5	1.8	3.6	31701	35000	11	16	45	28.9	13.3	40.0	15.6	2.2	109375
63536	DOWNING	18293	394	35.0	33.8	25.1	2.5	3.6	35767	36931	20	34	313	35.8	18.5	25.2	14.4	6.1	81563
63537	EDINA	15494	776	36.9	39.8	21.4	1.8	0.1	32548	33217	12	19	565	26.5	26.9	29.4	15.0	2.1	85244
63538	ELMER	17031	136	33.8	42.6	19.9	2.2	1.5	30561	31676	9	13	113	33.6	19.5	28.3	16.8	1.8	85000
63539	ETHEL	17356	152	33.6	41.4	21.7	2.0	1.3	31277	32256	10	15	126	34.9	17.5	31.0	15.1	1.6	85714
63540	GIBBS	16180	161	33.5	33.5	29.8	3.1	0.0	36314	37791	21	36	130	29.2	23.1	27.7	13.8	6.2	85714
	MISSOURI	25286		22.8	27.7	35.3	9.1	5.2	49522	52035				12.8	19.4	39.1	24.2	4.6	122064
	UNITED STATES	27277		20.9	24.4	35.3	11.7	7.6	54719	56938				9.3	13.1	31.6	32.6	13.5	162279

ZIP CODE #	POST OFFICE NAME	FINANCIAL SERVICES: Auto Loan	Home Loan	Invest-ments	Retire-ment Plans	THE HOME: Home Improvements: Home Repair	Lawn & Garden	Furnishings: Comput-ers & Hard-ware-Personal	Major Appli-ances	TV, Radio, Sound Equip-ment	Furni-ture	ENTERTAINMENT: Dine out/ Carry out	Sports Equip-ment	Fees & Tickets	Toys & Games	Travel	Cable TV	PERSONAL: Apparel & Services	Auto Repairs	Health Insur-ance	Pets & Supplies
63146	SAINT LOUIS	110	108	107	112	108	107	113	107	113	114	114	83	115	112	113	112	80	112	112	128
63147	SAINT LOUIS	64	60	53	61	56	65	60	60	66	62	65	44	61	65	58	69	45	63	69	75
63301	SAINT CHARLES	97	99	90	99	96	98	99	96	99	98	99	74	100	100	97	100	69	98	100	114
63303	SAINT CHARLES	119	126	113	126	121	113	123	117	118	125	120	93	126	121	122	114	85	118	110	137
63304	SAINT CHARLES	147	173	151	172	166	148	148	150	140	159	142	119	162	148	154	133	102	142	133	171
63330	ANNADA	92	74	119	73	81	98	74	94	77	69	76	69	64	73	80	82	51	87	93	109
63332	AUGUSTA	116	109	134	110	112	125	103	119	105	100	104	90	99	103	110	108	71	112	118	139
63333	BELLFLOWER	78	56	70	54	57	76	58	70	64	56	63	53	47	66	54	70	42	65	73	84
63334	BOWLING GREEN	75	61	68	62	62	76	67	73	71	60	69	55	58	70	63	75	47	71	78	86
63336	CLARKSVILLE	78	59	86	57	62	82	61	77	67	56	65	57	51	65	62	73	43	71	80	90
63339	CURRYVILLE	75	54	63	53	54	72	56	65	62	54	61	50	45	64	51	67	41	62	69	80
63341	DEFIANCE	140	161	150	160	157	147	140	145	135	146	137	114	151	139	149	132	97	139	134	168
63343	ELSBERRY	89	72	77	71	72	86	75	82	80	72	78	62	65	81	70	84	53	80	86	98
63344	EOLIA	83	60	82	58	61	83	61	76	68	57	67	58	49	68	60	74	44	71	80	91
63345	FARBER	90	64	93	62	67	91	66	84	73	61	72	63	53	73	66	81	48	77	88	100
63347	FOLEY	98	91	79	87	88	90	87	90	89	91	90	67	83	93	83	91	61	89	89	107
63348	FORISTELL	120	129	112	131	125	128	116	122	116	118	116	94	121	119	121	117	81	117	121	144
63349	HAWK POINT	87	67	74	67	67	86	69	79	74	65	73	61	58	77	65	80	49	74	83	95
63350	HIGH HILL	80	58	74	56	59	80	62	74	69	57	67	56	49	69	58	75	45	70	80	88
63351	JONESBURG	81	58	79	57	60	83	62	77	69	57	67	58	50	69	60	76	45	71	82	91
63352	LADDONIA	86	65	87	64	67	91	69	84	75	61	73	64	56	74	68	82	49	78	90	99
63353	LOUISIANA	82	62	81	61	64	86	66	80	72	59	70	60	54	71	64	79	47	74	86	94
63357	MARTHASVILLE	105	108	99	109	106	111	99	106	100	99	100	81	100	102	102	102	69	101	106	125
63359	MIDDLETOWN	77	54	80	53	56	79	57	72	62	50	61	56	44	61	57	68	40	67	75	87
63361	MONTGOMERY CITY	73	64	67	65	64	76	67	71	70	62	69	54	61	70	65	74	47	70	77	85
63362	MOSCOW MILLS	102	94	82	91	91	94	91	94	93	94	93	69	86	97	86	94	64	92	93	111
63363	NEW FLORENCE	78	59	84	57	62	80	59	75	65	55	63	56	49	64	60	70	42	69	77	88
63366	O FALLON	113	119	100	117	113	107	109	110	106	114	107	86	110	112	108	103	74	106	103	127
63367	LAKE SAINT LOUIS	146	165	155	165	163	151	147	150	142	156	144	114	157	145	154	138	101	145	141	173
63368	O FALLON	173	197	166	197	189	163	170	170	159	187	162	139	183	171	173	148	116	159	144	192
63369	OLD MONROE	97	89	85	91	90	101	87	96	89	82	88	72	80	92	85	94	60	90	98	112
63373	PORTAGE DES SIOUX	99	90	89	94	92	106	89	100	92	80	90	76	82	93	89	97	61	93	103	117
63376	SAINT PETERS	127	143	122	141	136	124	128	127	122	134	124	100	135	128	130	118	88	123	116	146
63377	SILEX	94	74	85	72	74	92	74	86	80	72	79	64	63	81	71	85	53	81	89	103
63379	TROY	98	91	81	91	89	92	90	91	91	91	92	69	86	94	87	93	63	91	92	109
63381	TRUXTON	92	87	92	88	87	98	82	92	84	80	84	71	79	85	84	88	57	87	93	109
63382	VANDALIA	74	51	74	49	52	76	55	69	62	50	60	53	43	61	53	68	40	65	74	83
63383	WARRENTON	86	82	80	82	82	89	78	85	80	78	80	63	76	81	78	83	55	81	87	100
63384	WELLSVILLE	67	50	62	50	51	68	57	63	60	50	59	50	46	60	53	65	39	62	69	76
63385	WENTZVILLE	116	120	105	121	117	117	112	114	111	114	112	88	115	115	113	112	78	112	113	135
63386	WEST ALTON	88	81	80	84	82	95	79	90	82	72	80	68	73	83	79	87	55	83	92	104
63388	WILLIAMSBURG	89	64	91	62	66	90	65	83	72	61	71	62	52	72	65	80	47	76	86	99
63389	WINFIELD	101	93	81	89	90	93	89	92	91	93	92	68	84	95	85	93	63	91	92	110
63390	WRIGHT CITY	107	94	103	93	95	105	94	102	97	93	97	76	87	98	92	101	66	100	103	121
63401	HANNIBAL	79	69	66	70	68	79	74	76	77	69	75	58	67	77	69	81	52	76	82	90
63430	ALEXANDRIA	87	61	82	60	62	86	65	78	70	59	69	62	50	72	62	77	46	74	83	96
63431	ANABEL	78	59	77	59	61	80	60	74	65	56	64	56	50	66	60	71	43	68	77	88
63432	ARBELA	77	53	85	53	55	81	59	73	61	48	61	60	43	60	59	67	39	68	77	90
63433	ASHBURN	73	52	75	51	54	74	54	68	60	50	59	51	43	59	53	66	39	63	71	81
63434	BETHEL	73	50	80	50	53	77	56	69	58	45	57	57	41	57	56	63	37	65	73	85
63435	CANTON	83	69	71	71	69	83	76	80	78	69	77	61	66	79	71	83	52	78	85	95
63436	CENTER	78	56	74	55	57	77	59	70	64	54	63	55	47	65	56	69	42	66	74	85
63437	CLARENCE	75	53	78	52	55	78	58	72	63	50	61	56	45	62	57	69	40	67	77	86
63438	DURHAM	82	61	68	60	61	79	63	73	69	60	67	56	52	71	58	75	45	69	76	88
63439	EMDEN	76	57	80	57	59	81	61	74	63	51	62	59	48	62	60	68	41	68	77	89
63440	EWING	79	58	75	58	59	80	61	73	66	55	65	57	49	67	58	71	43	68	77	88
63441	FRANKFORD	80	58	81	56	60	81	59	75	65	55	64	56	48	65	58	72	42	68	78	89
63443	HUNNEWELL	80	60	81	59	62	82	61	76	67	56	65	57	50	67	60	73	43	70	79	90
63445	KAHOKA	73	54	72	54	56	76	58	70	63	52	61	53	47	63	56	69	41	65	75	83
63446	KNOX CITY	61	42	67	42	44	65	47	58	49	38	48	48	34	48	47	53	31	54	62	72
63447	LA BELLE	63	45	65	44	47	66	49	61	54	43	52	47	38	53	48	59	35	57	66	72
63448	LA GRANGE	74	54	70	52	55	75	57	70	64	53	62	52	46	64	55	70	42	65	75	83
63450	LENTNER	71	51	71	50	53	74	55	69	62	49	59	51	44	60	54	68	40	64	74	81
63451	LEONARD	80	55	87	55	57	84	61	76	63	49	63	63	45	62	61	69	41	71	80	93
63452	LEWISTOWN	71	51	72	50	53	74	56	69	62	49	60	52	44	61	54	68	40	64	75	81
63453	LURAY	93	64	103	64	67	99	71	89	74	58	73	73	52	73	71	81	48	83	94	109
63454	MAYWOOD	78	66	69	68	67	81	66	76	70	61	69	57	59	72	64	75	47	70	78	89
63456	MONROE CITY	76	60	74	61	62	78	64	74	68	58	67	56	55	68	63	73	45	70	78	87
63457	MONTICELLO	94	68	97	65	70	96	69	88	77	65	76	66	56	77	69	85	50	81	92	105
63458	NEWARK	61	42	67	42	44	64	46	58	48	38	48	48	34	47	46	53	31	54	61	71
63459	NEW LONDON	85	67	78	67	68	86	69	80	73	63	72	62	58	74	67	78	48	75	83	96
63460	NOVELTY	61	42	67	42	44	64	46	58	48	38	48	48	34	47	46	53	31	54	61	71
63461	PALMYRA	78	70	71	71	71	82	70	77	73	66	72	58	65	74	69	77	49	73	81	90
63462	PERRY	80	58	87	57	61	84	63	78	68	55	66	60	50	66	63	74	44	73	83	93
63463	PHILADELPHIA	68	62	61	64	63	73	61	69	63	55	62	52	56	64	61	66	42	63	71	80
63464	PLEVNA	60	41	65	41	43	63	45	57	47	37	47	47	33	46	45	52	30	53	60	70
63466	SAINT PATRICK	104	72	113	71	75	109	79	98	83	65	82	81	58	81	79	90	53	92	104	121
63468	SHELBINA	76	54	77	53	57	78	58	73	65	53	63	54	47	64	57	72	42	68	78	86
63469	SHELBYVILLE	70	50	73	49	52	73	54	67	59	47	57	52	42	58	53	65	38	63	72	80
63471	TAYLOR	88	81	80	84	82	95	79	90	82	72	80	68	73	83	79	87	55	83	92	104
63472	WAYLAND	73	52	65	51	52	71	55	65	60	51	59	51	43	61	51	65	39	61	68	79
63473	WILLIAMSTOWN	69	48	76	47	50	73	53	66	55	43	54	54	39	54	53	60	35	61	69	81
63474	WYACONDA	76	55	78	53	57	77	56	71	62	52	61	54	45	62	55	68	40	65	74	85
63501	KIRKSVILLE	73	58	60	60	58	65	75	67	73	66	72	54	63	73	64	74	50	71	70	81
63530	ATLANTA	78	56	68	55	57	76	59	69	65	56	64	54	47	67	55	71	42	66	73	85
63531	BARING	79	54	87	54	57	84	61	75	63	49	62	62	44	62	60	69	40	70	79	93
63532	BEVIER	82	57	80	55	57	82	60	74	67	56	66	57	47	68	57	74	44	69	78	90
63533	BRASHEAR	89	62	96	61	65	93	67	84	71	57	70	67	50	70	67	78	46	78	88	102
63534	CALLAO	78	56	79	54	58	79	57	73	63	53	62	55	46	63	57	70	41	67	76	87
63535	COATSVILLE	100	69	109	68	72	105	76	95	79	62	78	78	56	78	76	86	51	88	100	116
63536	DOWNING	82	56	89	56	59	86	62	77	65	51	64	64	46	64	62	71	42	72	82	95
63537	EDINA	62	44	64	43	46	65	48	60	53	42	51	46	38	52	47	58	34	56	65	71
63538	ELMER	68	47	75	47	49	72	52	65	54	42	54	54	38	53	52	59	35	61	68	80
63539	ETHEL	69	47	75	47	50	72	52	65	55	43	54	54	39	54	52	60	35	61	69	80
63540	GIBBS	76	55	78	53	57	77	56	71	62	52	61	54	45	62	56	68	40	65	74	85
	MISSOURI	94	86	87	87	85	93	89	91	91	87	90	70	84	92	86	93	62	90	94	108
	UNITED STATES	100	100	100	100	100	100	100	100	100	100	100	100	100	100	100	100	100	100	100	100

POPULATION CHANGE

ZIP CODE #	POST OFFICE NAME	COUNTY FIPS CODE	POPULATION 2000	POPULATION 2009	POPULATION 2014	2000-2009 ANNUAL RATE % Rate	2000-2009 ANNUAL RATE State Centile	HOUSEHOLDS 2000	HOUSEHOLDS 2009	HOUSEHOLDS 2014	HOUSEHOLDS % Annual Rate 2000-2009	HOUSEHOLDS 2009 Average HH Size	FAMILIES 2000	FAMILIES 2009	FAMILIES % Annual Rate 2000-2009
63541	GLENWOOD	197	370	365	359	-0.1	32	146	145	142	-0.1	2.52	110	105	-0.5
63543	GORIN	199	407	415	416	0.2	46	152	151	151	-0.1	2.75	106	101	-0.5
63544	GREEN CASTLE	211	428	413	403	-0.4	18	177	168	163	-0.6	2.46	128	117	-1.0
63545	GREEN CITY	211	1210	1137	1102	-0.7	8	538	501	484	-0.8	2.27	349	311	-1.2
63546	GREENTOP	001	892	1054	1104	1.8	90	363	440	464	2.1	2.40	272	316	1.6
63547	HURDLAND	103	571	531	509	-0.8	6	223	208	199	-0.7	2.55	158	142	-1.1
63548	LANCASTER	197	1014	983	956	-0.3	21	419	404	393	-0.4	2.43	278	256	-0.9
63549	LA PLATA	121	2310	2391	2386	0.4	53	910	942	941	0.4	2.49	596	589	-0.1
63551	LIVONIA	171	371	365	362	-0.2	27	150	148	147	-0.1	2.47	113	108	-0.5
63552	MACON	121	7879	7615	7476	-0.4	18	3355	3283	3237	-0.2	2.24	2161	2024	-0.7
63555	MEMPHIS	199	3667	3618	3592	-0.1	32	1445	1387	1366	-0.4	2.52	970	892	-0.9
63556	MILAN	211	3926	3731	3624	-0.5	14	1531	1428	1378	-0.8	2.51	1011	907	-1.2
63557	NEW BOSTON	115	185	186	186	0.1	42	75	76	76	0.1	2.45	58	57	-0.2
63558	NEW CAMBRIA	121	717	675	658	-0.7	8	292	278	272	-0.5	2.40	209	192	-0.9
63559	NOVINGER	001	1685	1630	1610	-0.4	18	680	668	663	-0.2	2.44	504	476	-0.6
63560	POLLOCK	211	485	456	444	-0.7	8	202	189	183	-0.7	2.41	143	129	-1.1
63561	QUEEN CITY	197	1154	1200	1207	0.4	53	486	509	511	0.5	2.25	328	331	0.1
63563	RUTLEDGE	199	338	345	345	0.2	46	99	98	98	-0.1	3.52	75	71	-0.6
63565	UNIONVILLE	171	3720	3762	3766	0.1	42	1600	1612	1612	0.1	2.30	1047	1010	-0.4
63566	WINIGAN	115	250	246	243	-0.2	27	106	104	102	-0.2	2.37	81	77	-0.5
63567	WORTHINGTON	171	475	468	465	-0.2	27	202	199	198	-0.2	2.35	149	142	-0.5
63601	PARK HILLS	187	15602	17033	17887	1.0	76	6205	6833	7217	1.0	2.44	4260	4515	0.6
63620	ANNAPOLIS	093	1383	1379	1364	0.0	37	550	559	555	0.2	2.41	392	384	-0.2
63621	ARCADIA	093	1345	1335	1312	-0.1	32	507	506	498	0.0	2.43	368	355	-0.4
63622	BELGRADE	221	1128	1201	1267	0.7	66	445	484	514	0.9	2.48	335	353	0.6
63623	BELLEVIEW	093	1007	975	956	-0.3	21	385	380	374	-0.1	2.38	275	262	-0.5
63624	BISMARCK	187	2983	3332	3493	1.2	82	1164	1297	1366	1.2	2.52	869	938	0.8
63625	BLACK	179	703	695	685	-0.1	32	241	244	242	0.1	2.65	181	178	-0.2
63626	BLACKWELL	221	1378	1390	1405	0.1	42	467	483	492	0.4	2.88	361	363	0.1
63627	BLOOMSDALE	186	2947	3135	3187	0.7	66	1076	1158	1183	0.8	2.70	818	852	0.4
63628	BONNE TERRE	187	11864	13020	13654	1.0	76	4601	5092	5375	1.1	2.52	3406	3645	0.7
63629	BUNKER	179	836	832	819	-0.1	32	345	352	350	0.2	2.28	245	241	-0.2
63630	CADET	221	3230	3198	3211	-0.1	32	1174	1193	1208	0.2	2.67	882	866	-0.2
63631	CALEDONIA	221	910	959	984	0.6	63	359	386	400	0.8	2.48	269	280	0.4
63633	CENTERVILLE	179	492	485	476	-0.2	27	205	207	205	0.1	2.22	150	147	-0.2
63636	DES ARC	093	665	653	640	-0.2	27	270	269	265	0.0	2.43	188	181	-0.4
63637	DOE RUN	187	973	1189	1290	2.2	94	357	437	478	2.2	2.68	263	310	1.8
63638	ELLINGTON	179	3415	3397	3333	-0.1	32	1390	1414	1399	0.2	2.38	962	942	-0.2
63640	FARMINGTON	187	23019	28248	29705	2.2	94	7971	9293	9947	1.7	2.40	5512	6191	1.3
63645	FREDERICKTOWN	123	10972	11321	11510	0.3	50	4385	4570	4664	0.4	2.43	3102	3118	0.1
63648	IRONDALE	221	1656	1715	1757	0.4	53	616	655	677	0.7	2.59	478	493	0.3
63650	IRONTON	093	4649	4568	4491	-0.2	27	1837	1831	1811	0.0	2.43	1275	1224	-0.4
63653	LEADWOOD	187	1099	1106	1131	0.1	42	396	406	418	0.3	2.72	300	297	-0.1
63654	LESTERVILLE	179	682	678	668	-0.1	32	294	300	298	0.2	2.24	207	204	-0.2
63655	MARQUAND	123	1448	1499	1519	0.4	53	562	590	601	0.5	2.54	416	422	0.2
63656	MIDDLE BROOK	093	539	531	524	-0.2	27	218	219	218	0.0	2.42	151	146	-0.4
63660	MINERAL POINT	221	4474	4644	4727	0.4	53	1289	1371	1415	0.7	2.73	995	1027	0.3
63662	PATTON	017	1836	1826	1795	-0.1	32	706	710	701	0.1	2.54	536	523	-0.3
63664	POTOSI	221	8321	8904	9143	0.7	66	3225	3523	3646	1.0	2.45	2287	2421	0.6
63665	REDFORD	179	425	403	390	-0.6	11	180	175	170	-0.3	2.25	125	116	-0.8
63670	SAINTE GENEVIEVE	186	11130	11104	11014	0.0	37	4145	4203	4191	0.2	2.56	3054	3000	-0.2
63673	SAINT MARY	186	2009	1980	1966	-0.2	27	751	755	753	0.1	2.59	566	551	-0.3
63675	VULCAN	093	138	135	133	-0.2	27	65	65	64	0.0	2.08	45	44	-0.2
63701	CAPE GIRARDEAU	031	31787	34668	35592	0.9	72	13020	14100	14610	0.9	2.27	8262	8539	0.4
63703	CAPE GIRARDEAU	031	9965	8277	8232	-2.0	0	3725	3707	3717	-0.1	2.09	1872	1704	-1.0
63730	ADVANCE	207	2885	2975	3005	0.3	50	1200	1254	1272	0.5	2.33	836	839	0.0
63732	ALTENBURG	157	773	828	860	0.7	66	311	342	357	1.0	2.42	231	244	0.6
63735	BELL CITY	207	847	806	789	-0.5	14	343	330	325	-0.4	2.44	238	221	-0.8
63736	BENTON	201	3084	3467	3620	1.3	83	1098	1256	1319	1.5	2.73	849	943	1.1
63739	BURFORDVILLE	031	699	731	756	0.5	58	262	286	299	1.0	2.56	213	225	0.6
63740	CHAFFEE	201	5497	5479	5482	0.0	37	2207	2237	2249	0.1	2.42	1529	1487	-0.3
63743	DAISY	031	90	103	109	1.5	87	29	35	37	2.1	2.89	23	27	1.7
63744	DELTA	031	180	189	195	0.5	58	74	81	84	1.0	2.33	58	61	0.5
63747	FRIEDHEIM	031	439	501	531	1.4	86	161	192	205	1.9	2.56	130	149	1.5
63748	FROHNA	157	1061	1099	1125	0.4	53	406	429	442	0.6	2.56	303	310	0.2
63750	GIPSY	017	80	77	75	-0.4	18	30	29	29	-0.4	2.66	23	22	-0.5
63751	GLENALLEN	017	1208	1176	1151	-0.3	21	436	427	418	-0.2	2.75	347	331	-0.5
63755	JACKSON	031	20783	23563	24900	1.4	86	7905	9239	9842	1.7	2.53	5984	6710	1.2
63760	LEOPOLD	017	315	311	305	-0.1	32	111	110	109	-0.1	2.83	89	86	-0.4
63763	MC GEE	223	334	326	321	-0.3	21	130	129	128	-0.1	2.53	90	86	-0.5
63764	MARBLE HILL	017	5878	5845	5758	-0.1	32	2233	2237	2208	0.0	2.55	1656	1606	-0.3
63766	MILLERSVILLE	031	818	927	977	1.4	86	300	353	377	1.8	2.63	243	276	1.4
63769	OAK RIDGE	031	1478	1661	1748	1.3	83	559	655	697	1.7	2.53	441	498	1.3
63770	OLD APPLETON	031	158	170	176	0.8	69	65	72	75	1.1	2.36	50	53	0.6
63771	ORAN	201	3803	3955	4026	0.4	53	1467	1551	1587	0.6	2.55	1072	1093	0.2
63775	PERRYVILLE	157	15635	16340	16719	0.5	58	5941	6287	6462	0.6	2.54	4232	4321	0.2
63780	SCOTT CITY	201	6935	7058	7098	0.2	46	2658	2741	2771	0.3	2.57	1964	1960	0.0
63781	SEDGEWICKVILLE	017	911	1031	1048	1.3	83	352	404	412	1.5	2.55	270	302	1.2
63782	STURDIVANT	017	238	234	230	-0.2	27	88	88	86	0.0	2.66	67	65	-0.3
63783	UNIONTOWN	157	302	303	305	0.0	37	108	110	112	0.2	2.75	82	82	0.0
63785	WHITEWATER	031	840	883	911	0.5	58	313	342	356	1.0	2.58	247	259	0.5
63787	ZALMA	017	1076	1050	1028	-0.3	21	437	433	425	-0.1	2.42	333	320	-0.4
63801	SIKESTON	201	24523	24750	24793	0.1	42	9635	9849	9910	0.2	2.46	6789	6688	-0.2
63821	ARBYRD	069	944	937	927	-0.1	32	395	398	396	0.1	2.35	267	258	-0.4
63822	BERNIE	207	2741	2855	2893	0.4	53	1168	1235	1257	0.6	2.31	816	829	0.2
63823	BERTRAND	133	1335	1447	1452	0.9	72	570	605	612	0.6	2.24	395	403	0.2
63825	BLOOMFIELD	207	4452	4640	4702	0.4	53	1743	1837	1870	0.6	2.43	1274	1298	0.2
63827	BRAGG CITY	155	1155	1054	1010	-1.0	3	429	398	383	-0.8	2.65	307	274	-1.2
63829	CARDWELL	069	1308	1245	1207	-0.5	14	568	548	534	-0.4	2.27	370	341	-0.9
63830	CARUTHERSVILLE	155	7850	7276	7017	-0.8	6	3054	2863	2773	-0.7	2.51	2034	1835	-1.1
63833	CATRON	143	226	206	198	-1.0	3	89	83	80	-0.8	2.48	68	62	-1.0
63834	CHARLESTON	133	6448	6582	6497	0.2	46	2522	2461	2447	-0.3	2.43	1712	1606	-0.7
63837	CLARKTON	069	1840	1787	1741	-0.3	21	744	727	709	-0.2	2.46	530	499	-0.6
63841	DEXTER	207	12989	12968	12939	0.0	37	5401	5456	5468	0.1	2.33	3717	3620	-0.3
63845	EAST PRAIRIE	133	6004	6076	6026	0.1	42	2426	2437	2437	0.0	2.39	1674	1620	-0.4
	MISSOURI					0.7					0.8	2.45			0.4
	UNITED STATES					1.0					1.1	2.59			0.9

ZIP CODE #	POST OFFICE NAME	RACE (%) White 2000	White 2009	Black 2000	Black 2009	Asian/Pacific 2000	Asian/Pacific 2009	% Hispanic Origin 2000	% Hispanic Origin 2009	2009 AGE DISTRIBUTION (%) 0-4	5-9	10-14	15-19	20-24	25-44	45-64	65-84	85+	18+	MEDIAN AGE 2009	% 2009 Males	% 2009 Females
63541	GLENWOOD	99.2	99.2	0.0	0.0	0.0	0.0	0.0	0.0	5.8	6.0	6.6	6.6	4.1	20.8	32.6	15.3	2.2	77.3	45.1	50.4	49.6
63543	GORIN	99.3	99.0	0.2	0.5	0.0	0.0	1.2	1.2	7.7	8.2	7.7	6.3	4.1	24.3	26.5	13.3	1.9	72.5	38.7	51.8	48.2
63544	GREEN CASTLE	99.3	99.0	0.0	0.0	0.0	0.2	0.2	0.0	7.5	8.2	8.5	6.8	4.4	20.3	27.6	14.3	2.4	71.2	40.5	49.4	50.6
63545	GREEN CITY	98.2	97.4	0.0	0.0	0.6	0.9	4.1	6.0	5.6	5.8	6.0	6.2	4.7	22.8	28.3	17.1	3.5	78.6	44.0	47.1	52.9
63546	GREENTOP	98.7	98.5	0.1	0.1	0.7	0.9	0.3	0.5	5.7	6.1	6.3	6.4	4.2	22.1	31.0	15.8	2.5	78.0	44.5	49.6	50.4
63547	HURDLAND	99.5	99.4	0.0	0.0	0.0	0.0	0.2	0.4	7.7	7.9	8.1	7.0	4.0	21.5	27.9	13.9	2.1	71.8	40.2	50.5	49.5
63548	LANCASTER	98.9	98.8	0.0	0.0	0.2	0.2	0.5	0.7	6.8	7.1	7.2	6.7	5.2	23.1	25.5	15.1	3.3	74.7	39.5	46.2	53.8
63549	LA PLATA	98.7	98.4	0.1	0.1	0.1	0.1	1.2	1.6	7.3	7.3	7.1	6.4	4.8	22.9	24.3	15.6	4.3	74.3	40.2	48.4	51.6
63551	LIVONIA	99.2	99.2	0.0	0.0	0.0	0.0	0.3	0.3	5.8	6.0	6.6	6.8	5.2	21.6	32.1	14.2	1.6	77.0	43.3	51.2	48.8
63552	MACON	94.2	93.3	4.1	4.8	0.3	0.3	0.8	1.1	6.3	6.2	6.1	5.9	5.0	22.5	27.8	15.5	4.7	77.6	43.3	48.6	51.4
63555	MEMPHIS	98.8	98.8	0.1	0.1	0.1	0.1	0.8	0.8	7.1	7.1	7.1	7.0	5.1	22.1	24.6	15.2	4.6	74.2	40.2	48.0	52.0
63556	MILAN	92.0	89.6	0.2	0.2	0.2	0.2	14.1	18.8	7.4	7.1	6.9	6.3	5.6	25.6	25.2	12.3	3.7	74.4	38.5	51.1	48.9
63557	NEW BOSTON	100.0	98.9	0.0	0.0	0.0	0.0	0.5	1.1	8.1	8.1	7.5	7.0	3.8	22.6	25.3	15.6	2.2	71.5	39.2	49.5	50.5
63558	NEW CAMBRIA	98.7	98.5	0.1	0.1	0.0	0.0	0.3	0.3	4.4	4.7	5.6	6.4	4.6	20.9	33.2	17.3	2.8	81.2	47.3	49.8	50.2
63559	NOVINGER	99.2	99.1	0.0	0.0	0.1	0.2	0.9	1.3	6.6	6.6	7.0	6.1	4.5	23.4	29.8	14.2	1.7	75.9	41.9	50.7	49.3
63560	POLLOCK	98.8	98.7	0.2	0.2	0.0	0.0	1.0	1.3	6.4	7.0	7.0	5.5	2.9	22.8	29.6	16.4	2.4	75.9	43.9	48.5	51.5
63561	QUEEN CITY	98.5	98.5	0.0	0.0	0.1	0.2	0.9	1.1	5.6	5.9	6.1	5.8	4.4	20.6	27.7	18.8	5.3	78.7	46.1	48.2	51.8
63563	RUTLEDGE	97.6	97.7	1.5	1.4	0.0	0.0	0.0	0.0	9.3	9.3	9.3	8.1	4.6	25.5	21.2	11.0	1.7	67.0	33.1	55.4	44.6
63565	UNIONVILLE	99.1	99.1	0.1	0.1	0.2	0.2	0.7	0.7	6.8	6.1	6.3	5.6	4.7	21.3	26.8	18.3	4.1	77.4	44.3	48.4	51.6
63566	WINIGAN	99.6	99.6	0.0	0.0	0.0	0.0	0.4	0.8	8.1	8.1	7.7	6.9	4.1	22.0	26.0	14.6	2.4	71.1	40.0	49.2	50.8
63567	WORTHINGTON	99.8	99.8	0.0	0.0	0.0	0.0	0.2	0.4	6.4	6.6	7.3	7.5	4.1	22.2	28.2	15.8	1.9	74.8	41.7	51.9	48.1
63601	PARK HILLS	98.0	97.7	0.4	0.4	0.3	0.4	0.7	1.0	7.1	6.8	6.5	7.0	6.7	26.4	25.2	12.2	2.0	75.5	36.8	48.3	51.7
63620	ANNAPOLIS	94.7	94.0	3.3	3.8	0.0	0.0	0.3	0.4	5.4	5.5	6.6	6.8	5.1	22.8	30.6	15.4	1.7	77.8	43.1	49.4	50.6
63621	ARCADIA	97.5	97.2	0.7	0.9	0.1	0.1	0.5	0.7	5.4	5.8	5.8	5.5	4.4	21.0	27.9	17.5	6.7	79.4	46.7	45.4	54.6
63622	BELGRADE	97.8	97.6	0.4	0.3	0.4	0.6	0.3	0.3	6.6	6.7	6.9	6.4	5.2	24.9	28.2	13.4	1.6	75.9	39.5	50.5	49.5
63623	BELLEVIEW	98.1	97.7	0.6	0.7	0.0	0.0	0.6	0.8	4.5	4.4	5.2	7.4	4.5	23.2	30.8	16.3	3.7	81.0	45.5	50.5	49.5
63624	BISMARCK	98.5	98.3	0.1	0.1	0.1	0.2	0.9	1.2	6.4	6.5	6.5	6.5	5.4	25.2	29.2	12.7	1.6	76.5	40.3	49.7	50.3
63625	BLACK	94.6	94.4	1.6	1.7	0.1	0.1	0.6	0.6	4.9	5.2	6.9	7.5	4.7	23.0	29.5	16.8	1.4	77.6	43.2	53.1	46.9
63626	BLACKWELL	97.3	97.0	0.4	0.5	0.1	0.1	0.6	0.9	7.7	7.4	7.3	7.0	6.5	28.6	25.8	9.0	0.7	73.5	34.9	49.9	50.1
63627	BLOOMSDALE	98.7	98.4	0.1	0.1	0.1	0.1	0.5	0.7	7.1	7.2	7.3	7.0	5.3	25.9	27.5	11.7	1.1	74.1	38.5	49.8	50.2
63628	BONNE TERRE	98.5	98.3	0.2	0.2	0.2	0.2	0.4	0.6	6.0	6.1	6.3	6.5	5.5	24.2	28.6	14.6	2.2	77.6	41.5	50.0	50.0
63629	BUNKER	93.2	93.1	0.7	0.7	0.1	0.1	1.1	1.1	5.5	5.6	6.7	6.6	5.2	24.6	29.7	14.9	1.1	77.6	41.5	52.5	47.5
63630	CADET	97.4	97.1	0.6	0.7	0.1	0.1	0.6	0.9	7.6	7.5	7.3	7.2	6.4	28.7	25.8	8.7	0.7	73.2	34.8	50.7	49.3
63631	CALEDONIA	98.1	98.0	0.1	0.1	0.0	0.0	0.8	1.0	6.3	6.7	6.8	6.3	4.2	25.8	28.4	14.3	1.5	76.2	40.1	49.2	50.8
63633	CENTERVILLE	95.1	95.3	1.2	1.2	0.2	0.2	0.6	0.6	5.2	5.4	6.6	6.6	4.3	22.5	30.5	17.3	1.6	78.1	44.6	52.4	47.6
63636	DES ARC	98.8	98.6	0.2	0.2	0.0	0.0	0.5	0.6	5.4	5.7	6.0	6.7	5.1	22.5	31.7	15.6	1.4	78.9	44.1	48.5	51.5
63637	DOE RUN	98.7	98.2	0.0	0.0	0.3	0.4	0.9	1.3	6.4	6.6	6.9	6.6	5.1	23.5	30.7	12.6	1.4	75.4	40.9	50.5	49.5
63638	ELLINGTON	96.1	96.0	0.2	0.2	0.3	0.3	0.9	0.9	6.3	6.2	6.9	6.6	4.4	23.2	28.8	15.9	1.7	76.2	42.2	50.1	49.9
63640	FARMINGTON	93.2	92.1	4.5	5.0	0.5	0.8	1.0	1.4	4.9	4.9	5.2	6.1	7.1	31.3	25.2	12.5	2.8	81.5	38.8	56.3	43.7
63645	FREDERICKTOWN	98.4	98.0	0.1	0.2	0.3	0.4	0.5	0.7	6.0	6.0	6.5	6.5	5.5	24.2	27.8	14.5	3.0	77.4	41.4	48.2	51.8
63648	IRONDALE	98.0	97.8	0.1	0.1	0.1	0.2	0.7	1.0	6.1	6.8	7.0	7.9	5.5	24.6	28.0	12.4	1.7	75.0	38.6	48.5	51.5
63650	IRONTON	96.0	95.3	2.2	2.4	0.2	0.3	0.8	1.1	6.4	6.5	6.5	6.5	5.3	23.5	27.6	14.9	2.8	76.4	41.0	48.3	51.7
63653	LEADWOOD	97.9	97.7	0.2	0.2	0.0	0.0	1.0	1.3	6.5	6.0	5.9	8.3	8.6	27.9	24.5	10.8	1.5	76.9	35.9	48.9	51.1
63654	LESTERVILLE	97.4	97.2	0.3	0.4	0.0	0.0	0.3	0.1	5.3	5.6	6.0	4.9	3.5	22.6	31.4	18.6	2.1	79.8	46.3	50.4	49.6
63655	MARQUAND	97.4	97.2	0.1	0.1	0.2	0.3	0.7	1.0	6.1	6.3	6.7	6.6	4.7	23.9	29.9	14.1	1.6	76.9	41.5	49.3	50.7
63656	MIDDLE BROOK	97.4	97.0	0.9	0.9	0.0	0.0	0.7	0.9	5.1	4.7	6.0	9.0	4.9	23.7	31.8	11.7	3.0	78.5	42.4	53.3	46.7
63660	MINERAL POINT	88.0	86.3	9.3	10.8	0.2	0.2	0.6	0.9	5.6	5.6	5.6	6.2	8.2	32.3	24.9	10.1	1.5	79.6	36.7	58.2	41.8
63662	PATTON	97.7	97.6	0.4	0.4	0.1	0.1	0.4	0.4	6.0	6.0	6.4	7.2	5.6	25.4	27.4	14.6	1.5	77.2	40.3	49.9	50.1
63664	POTOSI	96.6	96.0	1.5	1.7	0.2	0.3	0.9	1.2	6.7	6.4	6.4	6.5	6.6	25.5	27.0	13.1	1.8	76.4	38.6	49.6	50.4
63665	REDFORD	96.0	95.8	0.5	0.5	0.0	0.0	1.2	1.2	5.7	5.7	6.2	6.2	4.2	21.1	29.5	18.4	3.0	77.9	45.6	50.1	49.9
63670	SAINTE GENEVIEVE	97.8	97.4	1.0	1.1	0.2	0.4	0.8	1.1	6.0	6.3	6.6	6.7	5.3	24.3	28.7	13.2	2.7	76.7	40.8	50.1	49.9
63673	SAINT MARY	97.8	97.2	1.0	1.2	0.1	0.2	0.6	0.9	6.1	6.7	8.5	8.0	5.3	24.5	28.4	11.5	1.1	73.6	38.9	52.3	47.7
63675	VULCAN	99.3	99.3	0.0	0.0	0.0	0.0	0.7	0.0	5.9	5.9	5.9	6.7	5.2	22.2	30.4	16.3	1.5	78.5	43.8	46.7	53.3
63701	CAPE GIRARDEAU	91.6	88.4	5.4	7.5	1.1	1.8	1.0	1.4	5.3	5.2	5.4	7.7	9.9	26.3	25.7	12.0	2.5	80.6	37.1	49.4	50.6
63703	CAPE GIRARDEAU	79.6	72.5	16.8	22.8	0.8	1.1	1.3	1.8	6.2	5.5	4.8	8.6	12.3	26.1	19.9	11.4	5.1	80.2	32.9	45.5	54.5
63730	ADVANCE	98.2	97.8	0.1	0.1	0.1	0.2	0.8	1.1	5.2	5.1	5.3	5.8	5.2	24.1	28.6	16.9	3.7	80.9	44.5	47.4	52.6
63732	ALTENBURG	97.8	97.5	1.0	1.2	0.0	0.0	0.4	0.6	5.8	6.3	6.9	6.2	4.1	25.5	30.0	13.0	2.3	77.2	41.8	51.8	48.2
63735	BELL CITY	93.2	91.9	5.4	6.6	0.0	0.0	0.7	1.0	5.6	7.4	7.4	7.4	5.3	23.7	28.3	12.8	2.0	74.4	39.4	49.5	50.5
63736	BENTON	98.2	97.8	0.7	1.0	0.0	0.0	0.9	1.3	6.8	6.8	7.0	7.0	5.6	28.1	27.4	9.9	1.3	75.3	36.7	49.8	50.2
63739	BURFORDVILLE	98.7	98.4	0.0	0.0	0.0	0.0	0.3	0.3	7.0	7.4	7.5	5.7	4.8	25.9	29.0	11.5	1.2	74.4	39.9	52.0	48.0
63740	CHAFFEE	98.7	98.4	0.1	0.1	0.1	0.1	0.8	1.1	6.7	6.4	6.4	7.0	6.3	25.1	26.7	12.9	2.4	76.1	38.4	48.7	51.3
63743	DAISY	97.8	98.1	1.1	1.0	0.0	0.0	0.0	0.0	5.8	5.8	6.8	7.8	4.9	25.2	29.1	12.6	1.9	77.7	40.4	49.5	50.5
63744	DELTA	97.8	97.4	0.0	0.0	0.0	0.0	0.6	0.5	5.8	5.8	6.9	6.3	4.8	23.3	30.7	14.8	1.6	77.2	42.9	51.3	48.7
63747	FRIEDHEIM	97.7	97.2	0.9	1.0	0.2	0.2	0.2	0.4	5.8	6.2	6.8	7.4	4.4	25.7	29.3	12.4	2.0	77.2	40.6	50.1	49.9
63748	FROHNA	98.3	97.9	0.7	0.7	0.2	0.3	0.3	0.4	5.6	6.2	7.6	6.4	4.8	24.4	29.7	13.2	2.3	76.7	41.4	52.5	47.5
63750	GIPSY	97.5	97.4	1.3	1.3	0.0	0.0	0.0	0.0	6.5	6.5	6.5	5.2	5.2	20.8	32.5	14.3	2.6	75.3	44.4	53.2	46.8
63751	GLENALLEN	97.4	97.4	0.4	0.4	0.2	0.2	0.9	0.9	6.7	6.5	6.8	6.8	6.5	23.3	28.2	13.6	1.5	75.8	40.2	50.1	49.9
63755	JACKSON	97.1	96.3	1.0	1.2	0.4	0.7	0.8	1.1	6.7	6.8	7.1	7.0	5.6	26.6	28.1	10.5	1.7	75.0	38.5	49.0	51.0
63760	LEOPOLD	99.0	99.0	0.0	0.0	0.3	0.3	0.6	0.3	5.5	5.5	6.1	7.1	5.8	22.8	32.2	13.5	1.6	78.8	42.3	47.3	52.7
63763	MC GEE	98.2	97.2	0.0	0.0	0.0	0.3	0.3	0.3	6.1	6.4	6.7	6.4	4.3	19.9	30.1	18.1	1.8	76.4	45.0	50.0	50.0
63764	MARBLE HILL	97.7	97.6	0.1	0.1	0.3	0.3	0.7	0.7	6.4	6.2	6.4	6.7	6.2	25.0	27.8	13.0	2.2	76.7	39.5	49.2	50.8
63766	MILLERSVILLE	99.3	99.1	0.4	0.4	0.0	0.0	0.5	0.8	6.4	6.7	7.2	6.5	4.6	24.7	31.0	11.7	1.3	75.8	41.3	49.9	50.1
63769	OAK RIDGE	97.9	97.3	0.7	0.8	0.0	0.1	0.5	0.8	6.2	6.7	7.1	6.9	4.4	26.5	29.0	11.7	1.6	75.8	40.2	49.5	50.5
63770	OLD APPLETON	97.5	97.1	0.6	0.6	0.0	0.0	0.6	0.6	6.5	6.5	7.1	6.5	4.1	27.6	28.2	11.8	1.8	75.9	40.0	50.0	50.0
63771	ORAN	94.1	92.7	4.5	5.5	0.0	0.1	1.4	2.0	7.4	7.2	7.5	7.2	5.5	25.9	26.4	11.2	1.8	73.4	37.9	50.4	49.6
63775	PERRYVILLE	98.2	97.6	0.1	0.2	0.7	1.2	0.6	0.8	6.8	6.9	7.0	6.5	5.4	25.7	26.6	12.3	2.8	75.3	38.9	49.3	50.7
63780	SCOTT CITY	98.4	98.0	0.3	0.4	0.0	0.1	0.7	0.9	6.4	6.4	6.6	7.2	5.8	27.2	27.3	11.5	1.6	75.9	38.2	49.6	50.4
63781	SEDGEWICKVILLE	98.7	98.5	0.1	0.2	0.3	0.4	0.3	0.4	6.6	6.6	6.9	6.9	6.1	26.3	26.7	12.2	1.7	75.9	38.7	50.3	49.7
63782	STURDIVANT	98.7	98.7	0.0	0.0	0.0	0.0	0.4	0.0	6.0	6.0	6.8	7.3	5.6	26.5	28.2	12.4	1.3	76.5	39.7	51.7	48.3
63783	UNIONTOWN	99.0	98.7	0.0	0.0	0.7	1.0	0.3	0.0	6.3	6.9	7.3	6.3	5.0	23.8	29.7	12.5	2.3	75.2	40.4	52.8	47.2
63785	WHITEWATER	98.0	97.3	0.0	0.0	0.1	0.1	0.6	0.8	5.8	6.1	6.5	6.0	4.5	23.2	31.4	15.1	1.5	77.9	43.5	51.4	48.6
63787	ZALMA	98.0	97.9	0.5	0.5	0.1	0.1	0.2	0.3	6.1	6.1	6.6	6.6	5.5	24.2	29.6	13.7	1.6	77.2	41.1	51.4	48.6
63801	SIKESTON	81.3	78.4	16.6	18.9	0.4	0.6	1.3	1.7	7.2	7.0	6.7	6.7	6.2	24.7	26.4	12.8	2.3	74.9	38.2	47.8	52.2
63821	ARBYRD	98.7	98.6	0.1	0.1	0.0	0.0	1.3	1.6	6.3	6.5	6.5	6.2	5.0	23.4	28.4	15.6	2.1	76.8	42.0	50.2	49.8
63822	BERNIE	96.8	96.3	1.7	2.0	0.0	0.0	0.5	0.6	6.0	5.8	5.8	6.0	6.1	24.7	28.1	15.1	2.3	78.7	41.6	47.6	52.4
63823	BERTRAND	92.1	89.4	7.0	9.5	0.0	0.0	0.4	0.5	5.0	5.3	5.6	5.6	5.0	24.6	28.8	17.0	3.1	80.4	44.2	49.7	50.3
63825	BLOOMFIELD	98.1	97.7	0.4	0.5	0.0	0.0	0.7	0.9	5.5	5.9	6.3	6.7	4.9	24.5	28.8	14.9	2.5	78.1	42.1	49.1	50.9
63827	BRAGG CITY	84.1	80.3	13.8	17.2	0.2	0.3	2.1	2.8	5.3	6.2	6.6	8.3	6.0	23.8	29.4	12.4	2.0	76.7	39.9	49.7	50.3
63829	CARDWELL	98.1	97.8	0.5	0.6	0.0	0.0	1.1	1.6	5.9	6.1	5.9	5.9	5.5	24.2	29.2	14.7	2.7	78.4	42.6	49.2	50.8
63830	CARUTHERSVILLE	69.7	66.8	27.9	30.1	0.5	0.8	1.6	2.1	9.3	8.3	8.0	7.6	6.2	23.4	23.7	11.3	2.1	69.7	33.8	47.5	52.5
63833	CATRON	90.7	88.8	8.9	10.7	0.0	0.0	0.4	0.0	5.8	5.8	6.3	6.8	5.3	24.8	28.6	15.0	1.5	77.7	41.2	51.5	48.5
63834	CHARLESTON	60.6	56.9	38.0	41.5	0.2	0.3	1.0	1.2	7.4	7.0	7.0	7.5	6.3	24.0	24.4	13.2	3.2	73.8	37.9	48.1	51.9
63837	CLARKTON	94.0	93.1	3.2	3.5	0.1	0.1	2.4	3.4	7.0	7.3	7.6	7.2	5.1	24.8	27.0	12.6	1.4	73.7	38.3	48.3	51.7
63841	DEXTER	97.6	97.1	0.4	0.4	0.2	0.2	0.9	1.2	6.2	5.9	6.1	6.0	5.3	24.1	28.3	15.3	2.8	78.2	42.2	47.4	52.6
63845	EAST PRAIRIE	94.6	93.0	3.6	4.8	0.0	0.1	1.1	1.5	6.8	6.6	6.2	6.2	6.6	26.8	25.4	13.4	2.1	76.7	38.0	49.5	50.5
	MISSOURI	84.9	83.3	11.2	11.7	1.2	1.7	2.1	2.8	6.6	6.6	6.6	7.0	6.7	26.1	26.5	11.7	2.1	76.1	37.7	48.8	51.2
	UNITED STATES	75.1	72.0	12.3	12.7	3.8	4.6	12.5	15.7	6.8	6.7	6.6	7.1	6.9	27.0	26.0	10.9	1.9	75.7	36.9	49.2	50.8

63541-63845

ZIP CODE #	POST OFFICE NAME	2009 Per Capita Income	2009 HH Income Base	2009 Household Income Distribution (%) Less than $25,000	$25,000 to $49,999	$50,000 to $99,999	$100,000 to $149,999	$150,000 or More	Median Household Income 2009	2014	2009 National Centile	2009 State Centile	2009 Home Value Base	2009 Home Value Distribution (%) Less than $50,000	$50,000 to $89,999	$90,000 to $174,999	$175,000 to $399,999	$400,000 or More	2009 Median Home Value
63541	GLENWOOD	21975	145	30.3	37.9	28.3	2.1	1.4	31252	35759	10	15	120	25.0	11.7	41.7	16.7	5.0	127381
63543	GORIN	13145	151	43.0	37.1	14.6	3.3	2.0	28297	29773	6	6	119	48.7	23.5	21.8	5.0	0.8	52500
63544	GREEN CASTLE	15744	168	41.1	31.5	24.4	3.0	0.0	29631	31946	7	9	135	44.4	17.8	23.7	12.6	1.5	61000
63545	GREEN CITY	17308	501	40.5	31.1	25.5	2.0	0.8	29938	30000	8	11	377	34.5	27.6	28.1	8.2	1.6	70577
63546	GREENTOP	17863	440	31.6	33.6	30.9	3.2	0.7	39041	40952	30	49	353	21.0	29.7	29.5	15.6	4.2	88913
63547	HURDLAND	17219	208	32.7	30.8	30.3	3.8	2.4	39078	41822	30	49	172	34.3	34.9	15.7	9.3	5.8	65882
63548	LANCASTER	17342	404	36.6	29.5	29.7	2.5	1.7	33670	34097	15	25	285	32.3	35.1	24.6	6.7	1.4	70208
63549	LA PLATA	17004	942	32.8	36.9	25.9	3.3	1.1	35645	37141	20	33	667	32.2	27.4	30.6	8.7	1.0	75341
63551	LIVONIA	16593	148	30.4	37.8	28.4	2.7	0.7	38017	41158	27	45	127	35.4	27.6	29.1	6.3	1.6	69583
63552	MACON	20212	3283	32.2	33.5	27.7	4.9	1.8	36638	38059	22	38	2388	19.6	26.0	40.1	11.8	2.5	96753
63555	MEMPHIS	17720	1387	36.2	33.1	24.9	3.0	2.8	35025	36406	18	31	1043	32.0	26.1	30.1	11.2	0.6	73727
63556	MILAN	15930	1428	37.1	31.5	27.6	2.5	1.3	32041	32563	11	17	968	31.5	32.2	26.4	8.5	1.3	72317
63557	NEW BOSTON	17914	76	27.6	42.1	25.0	2.6	2.6	36842	36842	23	39	65	26.2	27.7	30.8	12.3	3.1	81667
63558	NEW CAMBRIA	18318	278	27.0	34.5	34.5	2.9	1.1	41951	45606	39	61	226	31.9	23.9	31.4	12.4	0.4	80714
63559	NOVINGER	17769	668	34.6	36.2	24.1	2.7	2.4	35166	36865	18	32	558	36.9	28.0	18.3	14.9	2.0	63906
63560	POLLOCK	17185	189	34.9	30.7	31.7	1.6	1.1	33626	38093	15	24	143	28.0	23.1	30.1	9.8	9.1	88636
63561	QUEEN CITY	17784	509	41.3	31.6	24.8	1.6	0.8	30140	32132	8	11	378	41.0	25.7	23.3	7.7	2.4	62333
63563	RUTLEDGE	10018	98	46.9	29.6	18.4	5.1	0.0	26675	30635	4	3	82	31.7	30.5	28.0	7.3	2.4	69000
63565	UNIONVILLE	16123	1612	41.9	33.5	22.3	1.6	0.7	29295	29815	7	8	1195	28.2	34.0	30.1	5.6	2.1	76888
63566	WINIGAN	18104	104	31.7	37.5	26.0	3.8	1.0	36294	38192	21	36	87	32.2	25.3	27.6	12.6	2.3	75000
63567	WORTHINGTON	16170	199	33.7	42.7	19.1	4.5	0.0	35794	38513	20	34	168	42.3	35.1	17.3	3.0	2.4	57647
63601	PARK HILLS	17907	6833	35.1	30.6	29.0	4.2	1.1	36670	39164	23	38	4583	21.2	32.4	36.4	9.2	0.8	86281
63620	ANNAPOLIS	14813	559	39.9	34.9	22.9	1.6	0.7	30805	31858	9	14	455	32.3	25.7	29.2	9.7	3.1	80395
63621	ARCADIA	18247	506	33.4	30.2	29.8	4.9	1.6	35164	38459	18	32	365	12.1	33.2	41.4	13.2	0.3	96250
63622	BELGRADE	17137	484	32.2	34.1	29.5	3.7	0.4	38363	39179	28	46	406	26.1	24.1	33.7	12.6	3.4	89615
63623	BELLEVIEW	18994	380	34.7	38.4	22.4	3.2	1.3	31111	31603	10	15	323	30.3	21.1	25.7	16.4	6.5	87857
63624	BISMARCK	15354	1297	38.6	32.5	25.6	2.6	0.6	32818	35523	13	20	1021	33.1	30.9	25.8	8.8	1.5	68813
63625	BLACK	14712	244	36.9	34.8	25.0	2.5	0.8	31633	31134	11	16	207	32.4	24.2	32.9	8.7	1.9	81563
63626	BLACKWELL	14816	483	31.3	34.4	31.3	1.9	1.2	40177	41542	33	54	411	30.2	24.1	29.0	12.7	4.1	83269
63627	BLOOMSDALE	20746	1158	21.7	26.2	43.3	6.5	2.4	51721	52978	65	81	974	14.9	14.6	37.7	31.7	1.1	132927
63628	BONNE TERRE	19752	5092	27.8	29.1	36.4	5.4	1.4	43876	47069	45	66	4091	15.8	22.3	41.2	18.1	2.7	110784
63629	BUNKER	15703	352	42.0	35.5	20.2	1.4	0.9	29610	28777	7	9	292	34.2	26.7	26.4	10.3	2.4	73750
63630	CADET	14302	1193	36.4	35.1	25.9	2.5	0.1	35956	36755	20	35	983	37.7	24.7	26.0	8.9	2.6	70071
63631	CALEDONIA	16654	386	33.4	38.9	22.8	4.7	0.3	37154	37458	24	41	329	28.0	24.3	32.5	13.4	1.8	86053
63633	CENTERVILLE	17231	207	39.1	32.9	24.2	2.9	1.0	30672	31802	9	14	170	30.6	24.1	34.7	8.8	1.8	83333
63636	DES ARC	14762	269	42.4	36.1	18.6	2.6	0.4	28960	28893	7	7	220	30.0	31.4	32.3	5.0	1.4	73750
63637	DOE RUN	16728	437	29.5	33.9	33.0	1.6	2.1	39687	43397	32	52	347	31.4	24.5	23.9	13.5	6.6	71071
63638	ELLINGTON	15643	1414	39.2	32.9	25.0	2.5	0.4	32271	33920	12	18	1045	28.6	31.7	27.7	11.0	1.1	77378
63640	FARMINGTON	19875	9293	28.2	29.7	34.2	5.1	2.8	42576	46197	41	63	6626	12.5	18.2	41.2	23.7	4.4	120908
63645	FREDERICKTOWN	16081	4570	38.4	33.2	24.9	2.6	0.8	32136	33952	12	18	3471	21.3	31.3	35.0	11.0	1.5	86462
63648	IRONDALE	16146	655	33.7	32.4	30.8	2.3	0.8	35728	36362	20	34	558	34.4	22.9	29.7	9.9	3.0	75714
63650	IRONTON	16194	1831	41.2	30.7	24.2	2.6	1.3	29545	30133	7	9	1315	24.1	36.0	31.0	8.3	0.5	79159
63653	LEADWOOD	14927	406	34.2	36.9	24.9	3.4	0.5	34391	35281	16	28	324	39.8	44.8	12.7	2.8	0.0	55500
63654	LESTERVILLE	17646	300	39.7	31.0	24.0	4.0	1.3	31253	32362	10	15	233	27.5	22.3	39.5	8.2	2.6	90217
63655	MARQUAND	15304	590	37.3	35.3	23.7	2.0	1.7	32198	33546	12	18	469	25.8	22.2	34.3	14.9	2.8	93276
63656	MIDDLE BROOK	17353	219	33.3	37.9	24.7	3.2	0.9	31722	32631	11	17	182	28.6	22.0	27.5	18.1	3.8	88889
63660	MINERAL POINT	14472	1371	43.7	28.0	23.6	2.8	1.8	28824	31665	6	7	1153	44.4	18.6	25.4	11.6	0.0	63125
63662	PATTON	17711	710	26.5	37.9	30.4	3.5	1.7	40722	41872	35	56	613	24.5	23.0	31.6	19.4	1.5	93605
63664	POTOSI	16385	3523	41.3	29.0	25.2	3.3	1.1	29732	32058	8	10	2552	29.3	24.9	35.0	10.1	0.7	82411
63665	REDFORD	15729	175	45.7	30.3	21.1	2.3	0.6	29065	32360	7	8	137	29.2	27.0	32.8	10.9	0.0	83929
63670	SAINTE GENEVIEVE	21624	4203	20.0	30.4	40.3	7.6	1.7	49672	51040	60	78	3349	11.6	17.7	44.5	23.7	2.4	122929
63673	SAINT MARY	20496	755	18.7	34.8	40.8	3.3	2.4	46720	49938	53	73	665	22.9	14.4	38.8	22.0	2.0	113494
63675	VULCAN	17190	65	44.6	33.8	18.5	3.1	0.0	27692	28363	5	5	53	30.2	32.1	30.2	5.7	1.9	73750
63701	CAPE GIRARDEAU	26096	14100	23.7	28.0	35.7	7.7	4.9	48057	50693	57	76	9064	8.4	12.9	42.2	30.9	5.6	146201
63703	CAPE GIRARDEAU	18351	3707	42.7	30.6	22.7	2.4	1.6	30262	31642	8	12	1640	33.4	33.0	29.3	4.1	0.1	68197
63730	ADVANCE	18041	1254	34.8	30.6	30.0	3.3	1.2	35820	37504	20	34	971	22.9	28.0	38.9	8.3	1.9	88583
63732	ALTENBURG	21825	342	21.1	29.5	43.0	5.3	1.2	49449	50346	60	78	300	21.7	21.7	35.3	19.3	2.0	98696
63735	BELL CITY	16382	330	41.5	31.2	21.8	3.0	2.4	29608	30825	7	9	229	50.7	21.8	22.3	4.4	0.9	49531
63736	BENTON	19992	1256	22.5	32.0	35.4	7.7	2.4	45366	49147	49	70	1056	20.8	17.5	36.6	21.4	3.6	115455
63739	BURFORDVILLE	25944	286	16.8	27.3	49.3	1.4	5.2	55859	56532	72	86	262	16.0	13.7	31.3	28.2	10.7	127941
63740	CHAFFEE	19987	2237	33.8	27.8	32.2	4.6	1.7	37948	40552	27	45	1651	24.1	33.2	30.3	11.3	1.0	80871
63743	DAISY	16885	35	22.9	31.4	42.9	2.9	0.0	47327	51203	55	74	29	24.1	20.7	24.1	24.1	6.9	104167
63744	DELTA	20039	81	30.9	27.2	35.8	4.9	1.2	39441	43227	31	51	71	19.7	32.4	26.8	21.1	0.0	86250
63747	FRIEDHEIM	19238	192	22.4	29.7	42.7	4.7	0.5	48442	49849	58	77	160	24.4	20.6	26.3	23.1	5.6	103571
63748	FROHNA	18976	429	25.4	31.7	36.8	5.4	0.7	44918	47007	48	69	377	22.3	19.9	39.8	15.1	2.9	99833
63750	GIPSY	14376	29	48.3	24.1	24.1	3.4	0.0	25702	29028	4	2	25	32.0	32.0	28.0	8.0	0.0	72500
63751	GLENALLEN	15542	427	33.7	32.1	30.0	2.8	1.4	34302	36969	16	27	358	27.4	25.7	31.8	12.0	3.1	85600
63755	JACKSON	23176	9239	19.7	28.0	41.9	6.6	3.8	51668	52482	65	81	7307	12.8	11.3	40.6	31.0	4.3	142107
63760	LEOPOLD	17438	110	24.5	36.4	33.6	2.7	2.7	42049	44539	39	61	95	20.0	13.7	44.2	18.9	3.2	121250
63763	MC GEE	14777	129	34.1	44.2	20.2	1.6	0.0	32317	33617	12	19	109	27.5	39.4	24.8	8.3	0.0	66389
63764	MARBLE HILL	16475	2237	33.8	33.3	28.7	3.0	1.3	35792	37108	20	34	1724	26.9	25.7	33.6	11.5	2.3	86809
63766	MILLERSVILLE	20401	353	26.6	27.8	38.2	4.0	3.4	46359	47511	52	72	317	13.9	13.6	36.9	31.5	4.1	148047
63769	OAK RIDGE	20450	655	23.1	30.1	40.0	4.7	2.1	47620	49229	56	75	563	19.0	17.1	32.9	25.8	5.3	123566
63770	OLD APPLETON	21444	72	23.6	27.8	41.7	5.6	1.4	48901	48804	59	77	62	17.7	16.1	38.7	21.0	6.5	121875
63771	ORAN	17313	1551	33.8	30.4	31.0	3.2	1.5	36814	39622	23	39	1213	31.2	35.2	22.4	9.6	1.5	72669
63775	PERRYVILLE	20033	6287	24.8	31.4	37.7	4.1	2.0	44485	46561	47	67	4932	14.0	20.6	43.3	20.7	1.4	118455
63780	SCOTT CITY	20363	2741	24.0	32.5	37.0	4.5	2.0	44527	47313	47	68	2110	18.9	26.0	38.0	16.4	0.7	97200
63781	SEDGEWICKVILLE	16757	404	30.0	30.7	35.9	3.0	0.5	42423	47380	41	62	341	14.7	23.8	43.7	17.3	0.6	108255
63782	STURDIVANT	14505	88	31.8	37.5	29.5	1.1	0.0	37360	37849	25	42	69	33.3	33.3	26.1	7.2	0.0	65833
63783	UNIONTOWN	17783	110	26.4	24.5	45.5	3.6	0.0	49305	49482	60	78	98	12.2	16.3	49.0	16.3	6.1	122222
63785	WHITEWATER	18395	342	29.8	28.7	35.1	4.7	1.8	39490	42963	31	51	300	19.3	29.0	28.0	22.3	1.3	92778
63787	ZALMA	15828	433	38.6	31.4	26.3	2.5	1.2	31377	33858	10	16	356	30.1	30.6	28.4	9.3	1.7	75556
63801	SIKESTON	18939	9849	33.0	29.3	30.6	5.1	2.0	38125	41393	27	46	6192	23.1	24.0	35.7	14.6	2.7	94877
63821	ARBYRD	15445	398	43.7	38.7	14.3	0.8	2.5	30170	30502	8	12	299	46.5	31.1	17.4	3.7	1.3	53182
63822	BERNIE	17334	1235	37.7	34.7	24.1	2.2	1.3	32570	34097	13	20	903	31.5	35.8	26.4	5.9	0.6	67718
63823	BERTRAND	20953	605	38.8	28.9	25.3	3.5	3.5	35220	36479	18	32	440	30.5	26.8	34.5	6.8	1.4	78077
63825	BLOOMFIELD	16953	1837	35.4	35.0	25.5	2.8	1.3	33660	34914	15	25	1407	29.5	24.7	33.5	10.0	2.3	83533
63827	BRAGG CITY	14177	398	43.7	29.4	22.9	4.0	0.0	30243	30834	8	12	274	43.1	35.4	17.5	3.3	0.7	55938
63829	CARDWELL	16301	548	45.4	31.9	19.2	1.5	2.0	29781	30401	8	10	402	46.8	30.3	20.6	1.7	0.5	52955
63830	CARUTHERSVILLE	15280	2863	48.2	26.1	19.7	4.0	2.0	26422	28556	4	3	1578	25.3	37.6	28.5	8.1	0.5	74419
63833	CATRON	18222	83	33.7	36.1	22.9	4.8	2.4	36389	38174	22	37	65	41.5	16.9	33.8	7.7	0.0	68333
63834	CHARLESTON	17478	2461	44.7	26.3	22.1	2.8	4.1	29020	31128	7	7	1531	29.1	29.7	28.9	11.2	1.0	77440
63837	CLARKTON	13592	727	52.3	26.4	17.7	3.0	0.6	23574	25046	3	1	469	46.1	28.6	19.4	5.8	0.2	54405
63841	DEXTER	19269	5456	35.9	31.3	26.3	4.2	2.2	34499	36190	17	28	3749	17.0	26.4	38.5	15.2	2.9	99595
63845	EAST PRAIRIE	15147	2437	42.7	32.2	20.8	3.2	1.1	28417	29202	6	6	1555	37.9	30.9	25.1	5.3	0.8	64883
	MISSOURI	25286		22.8	27.7	35.3	9.1	5.2	49522	52035				12.8	19.4	39.1	24.2	4.6	122064
	UNITED STATES	27277		20.9	24.4	35.3	11.7	7.6	54719	56938				9.3	13.1	31.6	32.6	13.5	162279

#	POST OFFICE NAME	FINANCIAL SERVICES: Auto Loan	FINANCIAL SERVICES: Home Loan	FINANCIAL SERVICES: Invest-ments	FINANCIAL SERVICES: Retire-ment Plans	THE HOME: Home Improvements: Home Repair	THE HOME: Home Improvements: Lawn & Garden	THE HOME: Furnishings: Comput-ers & Hard-ware-Personal	THE HOME: Furnishings: Major Appli-ances	THE HOME: Furnishings: TV, Radio, Sound Equip-ment	THE HOME: Furnishings: Furni-ture	ENTERTAINMENT: Dine out/ Carry out	ENTERTAINMENT: Sports Equip-ment	ENTERTAINMENT: Fees & Tickets	ENTERTAINMENT: Toys & Games	ENTERTAINMENT: Travel	ENTERTAINMENT: Cable TV	PERSONAL: Apparel & Services	PERSONAL: Auto Repairs	PERSONAL: Health Insur-ance	PERSONAL: Pets & Supplies
63541	GLENWOOD	99	68	109	68	71	104	76	94	79	61	78	78	55	77	75	86	50	88	99	116
63543	GORIN	65	44	71	44	47	68	49	61	51	40	51	51	36	50	49	56	33	57	65	75
63544	GREEN CASTLE	69	49	71	48	51	70	51	65	56	47	55	49	40	56	50	62	36	59	67	77
63545	GREEN CITY	68	48	69	47	50	70	52	65	58	46	56	49	41	57	51	64	37	60	70	77
63546	GREENTOP	76	54	80	53	56	79	57	72	62	51	61	56	44	61	56	68	40	66	75	86
63547	HURDLAND	78	54	86	54	57	83	60	74	62	49	62	61	44	61	60	68	40	70	79	92
63548	LANCASTER	72	51	74	50	54	76	56	70	62	49	60	53	44	61	55	68	40	65	76	83
63549	LA PLATA	73	52	74	51	54	76	57	70	62	50	61	53	45	61	55	69	40	65	76	83
63551	LIVONIA	73	52	75	51	54	74	54	68	60	50	59	51	43	59	53	66	39	63	71	81
63552	MACON	74	59	70	59	60	76	63	72	67	58	66	54	54	67	61	72	44	68	77	85
63555	MEMPHIS	78	55	81	54	57	81	60	75	66	52	64	58	47	65	59	72	42	70	81	89
63556	MILAN	67	50	56	50	50	65	56	61	60	51	59	48	46	61	51	65	40	60	66	74
63557	NEW BOSTON	78	54	86	54	56	83	60	74	62	49	62	62	44	61	60	68	40	69	79	92
63558	NEW CAMBRIA	79	56	82	55	58	81	58	74	64	53	63	57	46	63	58	70	41	68	77	88
63559	NOVINGER	77	55	80	54	57	79	57	73	63	53	62	55	45	63	57	69	41	67	76	86
63560	POLLOCK	74	51	81	51	53	78	57	70	59	46	58	58	42	58	56	64	38	66	74	86
63561	QUEEN CITY	70	50	72	49	52	73	54	67	59	48	58	51	42	58	53	65	38	62	72	80
63563	RUTLEDGE	63	43	69	43	45	67	48	60	50	39	50	49	35	49	48	55	32	56	63	74
63565	UNIONVILLE	65	46	67	45	48	67	50	62	54	43	53	48	39	53	49	60	35	58	66	74
63566	WINIGAN	77	54	82	53	56	80	58	72	61	49	61	57	44	61	57	67	40	67	76	88
63567	WORTHINGTON	68	49	70	47	50	69	50	64	55	46	54	48	40	55	49	61	36	58	66	76
63601	PARK HILLS	70	55	61	55	55	69	61	66	66	57	64	50	53	66	57	70	44	65	71	79
63620	ANNAPOLIS	64	46	66	44	48	65	47	60	52	44	51	45	38	52	46	57	34	55	62	71
63621	ARCADIA	81	58	83	56	60	82	60	76	66	55	65	57	48	66	59	73	43	69	79	90
63622	BELGRADE	76	55	71	53	56	75	57	69	63	54	62	52	45	64	54	69	41	64	72	83
63623	BELLEVIEW	83	59	85	57	61	84	61	77	67	56	66	58	49	67	60	74	44	71	80	92
63624	BISMARCK	71	48	69	46	49	70	51	64	57	48	56	49	39	58	48	64	37	59	67	77
63625	BLACK	70	50	72	49	52	71	51	66	57	48	56	49	41	57	51	63	37	60	68	78
63626	BLACKWELL	75	57	61	55	56	70	58	66	63	58	62	50	49	66	53	68	42	63	68	79
63627	BLOOMSDALE	88	82	76	82	81	88	78	85	81	77	80	63	74	83	77	84	55	81	86	100
63628	BONNE TERRE	84	65	81	65	67	85	68	79	73	64	72	60	58	74	66	79	48	75	83	94
63629	BUNKER	65	46	58	45	47	63	48	58	53	46	52	44	38	55	45	58	35	54	61	70
63630	CADET	67	50	59	47	49	64	52	60	57	51	56	46	42	58	48	61	37	57	62	72
63631	CALEDONIA	74	53	75	51	55	75	54	69	60	51	59	52	44	60	54	66	39	63	72	82
63633	CENTERVILLE	69	50	71	48	51	70	51	65	57	48	56	49	41	56	50	62	37	59	67	77
63636	DES ARC	64	46	66	44	48	65	47	60	52	44	51	45	38	52	47	57	34	55	62	71
63637	DOE RUN	80	57	82	56	60	82	59	75	66	55	64	56	47	65	58	72	42	69	78	89
63638	ELLINGTON	64	49	61	47	51	64	50	59	55	49	54	44	42	55	48	59	36	56	63	71
63640	FARMINGTON	81	70	75	70	71	82	72	79	76	69	74	58	65	76	70	80	51	76	83	92
63645	FREDERICKTOWN	66	49	63	48	50	66	53	62	58	49	56	47	44	57	51	63	38	59	66	74
63648	IRONDALE	75	54	69	52	54	74	56	67	62	53	61	51	44	63	52	68	41	63	71	81
63650	IRONTON	69	48	69	47	50	70	52	65	58	47	57	49	41	58	50	65	38	60	70	77
63653	LEADWOOD	63	50	45	51	48	59	59	57	62	54	60	44	51	63	51	65	41	59	64	70
63654	LESTERVILLE	71	51	73	49	53	72	52	66	58	48	57	50	42	57	51	63	37	61	69	79
63655	MARQUAND	70	50	69	48	51	70	51	64	57	48	56	48	41	57	50	62	37	59	67	77
63656	MIDDLE BROOK	75	53	76	52	55	76	55	70	61	51	60	53	44	61	54	68	40	64	73	83
63660	MINERAL POINT	74	50	68	47	50	72	53	65	60	51	59	50	40	62	49	67	39	61	69	80
63662	PATTON	81	58	74	57	59	79	60	73	67	58	66	55	48	68	57	73	44	68	76	88
63664	POTOSI	69	50	63	49	50	67	54	63	60	51	59	48	44	61	51	66	40	61	68	76
63665	REDFORD	63	46	64	44	47	64	47	59	52	44	51	44	38	52	46	57	34	54	61	70
63670	SAINTE GENEVIEVE	85	79	79	80	79	90	78	85	80	74	79	64	74	81	78	84	54	81	89	100
63673	SAINT MARY	91	71	84	71	72	92	72	85	78	67	76	64	61	79	70	84	51	79	89	101
63675	VULCAN	64	46	65	44	47	65	47	60	52	44	51	45	37	52	46	57	34	55	62	71
63701	CAPE GIRARDEAU	88	84	78	86	82	86	91	85	89	86	90	67	87	90	86	90	63	88	89	102
63703	CAPE GIRARDEAU	58	45	45	47	45	52	59	53	60	53	59	42	50	59	50	62	41	57	59	64
63730	ADVANCE	73	53	74	51	54	75	56	70	62	51	61	52	45	62	54	69	40	65	75	82
63732	ALTENBURG	81	75	74	78	76	87	74	83	76	67	74	63	69	77	74	80	51	76	85	96
63735	BELL CITY	74	49	72	47	50	73	52	66	59	49	58	51	40	60	49	66	39	61	69	80
63736	BENTON	87	79	74	79	79	86	76	83	79	75	78	61	71	81	74	82	53	79	84	98
63739	BURFORDVILLE	107	97	88	94	95	101	92	98	96	95	96	72	87	99	88	99	65	95	99	117
63740	CHAFFEE	79	61	67	60	60	77	68	73	73	63	71	55	57	74	61	78	48	72	79	88
63743	DAISY	76	69	68	72	70	81	68	77	70	62	69	58	63	72	68	74	47	71	79	89
63744	DELTA	84	60	86	58	62	85	61	78	68	57	67	59	49	68	61	75	44	72	81	93
63747	FRIEDHEIM	77	70	69	73	71	82	69	78	71	62	70	59	64	72	69	75	48	72	80	90
63748	FROHNA	78	67	74	69	68	83	67	78	70	60	68	60	59	70	67	74	46	72	81	92
63750	GIPSY	68	49	70	47	51	69	50	64	56	47	55	48	40	55	50	61	36	58	66	76
63751	GLENALLEN	77	55	70	54	56	75	57	69	63	55	62	52	46	65	54	69	41	64	72	83
63755	JACKSON	87	85	77	86	83	89	83	86	84	81	84	66	81	86	82	86	58	84	89	102
63760	LEOPOLD	88	63	89	61	65	89	65	82	72	61	71	62	52	72	64	79	47	75	85	98
63763	MC GEE	64	49	68	47	51	67	49	62	54	47	53	45	41	53	50	59	35	57	65	73
63764	MARBLE HILL	73	53	63	52	53	71	57	66	63	54	62	50	47	64	53	69	41	63	70	79
63766	MILLERSVILLE	83	76	74	78	77	88	75	84	77	69	76	63	69	79	74	81	52	78	86	97
63769	OAK RIDGE	80	73	72	76	74	86	72	81	74	65	73	61	66	76	72	79	50	75	84	94
63770	OLD APPLETON	78	71	71	74	73	84	70	80	73	64	71	60	65	74	70	77	49	73	82	92
63771	ORAN	79	57	67	55	57	76	59	69	66	58	64	53	48	68	54	72	43	66	73	84
63775	PERRYVILLE	84	68	77	68	69	87	70	81	75	64	73	61	61	76	68	81	49	76	86	95
63780	SCOTT CITY	83	72	73	72	71	85	73	80	76	68	75	61	65	78	70	81	51	76	84	95
63781	SEDGEWICKVILLE	77	55	64	54	55	73	58	67	64	56	63	52	46	67	52	70	42	64	71	82
63782	STURDIVANT	70	50	57	49	50	66	52	60	58	51	57	46	42	60	47	63	38	57	64	74
63783	UNIONTOWN	76	69	68	72	70	81	68	77	70	62	69	58	63	72	68	74	47	71	79	89
63785	WHITEWATER	85	61	86	59	63	86	62	79	69	58	68	59	50	69	62	76	45	73	82	94
63787	ZALMA	69	49	63	48	50	68	51	62	57	49	56	47	41	58	48	62	37	58	65	75
63801	SIKESTON	71	62	63	62	61	70	65	68	69	63	68	52	61	69	62	72	47	68	73	81
63821	ARBYRD	67	45	65	43	45	66	47	60	54	45	53	46	36	55	45	60	35	56	63	73
63822	BERNIE	66	50	57	49	49	65	56	61	60	51	58	47	46	61	51	65	39	60	67	74
63823	BERTRAND	83	59	85	57	61	86	64	79	71	56	69	61	50	70	62	78	45	74	86	95
63825	BLOOMFIELD	72	52	70	51	53	73	55	68	61	51	60	51	44	61	53	68	40	63	73	81
63827	BRAGG CITY	70	45	67	43	45	68	49	61	56	46	55	48	37	57	45	63	36	58	65	75
63829	CARDWELL	68	46	67	43	46	67	48	61	55	46	54	47	37	56	46	61	36	57	64	74
63830	CARUTHERSVILLE	59	47	46	48	46	56	54	54	58	51	57	41	48	58	48	62	39	56	61	66
63833	CATRON	82	58	70	57	58	78	61	72	67	58	66	55	48	70	56	73	44	68	75	87
63834	CHARLESTON	72	50	61	51	50	67	60	63	66	55	64	50	49	65	54	71	43	65	71	79
63837	CLARKTON	62	41	60	39	41	61	43	55	50	41	49	42	33	51	41	56	32	51	58	67
63841	DEXTER	73	57	67	57	58	74	62	70	67	57	65	53	53	67	59	72	44	67	75	83
63845	EAST PRAIRIE	61	45	52	44	44	59	50	55	55	47	53	43	41	56	46	59	36	54	60	67
	MISSOURI	94	86	87	87	85	93	89	91	91	87	90	70	84	92	86	93	62	90	94	108
	UNITED STATES	100	100	100	100	100	100	100	100	100	100	100	100	100	100	100	100	100	100	100	100

ZIP CODE #	POST OFFICE NAME	COUNTY FIPS CODE	POPULATION 2000	POPULATION 2009	POPULATION 2014	2000-2009 ANNUAL RATE % Rate	2000-2009 ANNUAL RATE State Centile	HOUSEHOLDS 2000	HOUSEHOLDS 2009	HOUSEHOLDS 2014	HOUSEHOLDS % Annual Rate 2000-2009	HOUSEHOLDS 2009 Average HH Size	FAMILIES 2000	FAMILIES 2009	FAMILIES % Annual Rate 2000-2009
63846	ESSEX	207	1561	1563	1559	0.0	37	613	623	624	0.2	2.50	454	446	-0.2
63848	GIDEON	143	1687	1714	1702	0.2	46	647	673	674	0.4	2.45	460	463	0.1
63849	GOBLER	155	174	171	168	-0.2	27	69	69	68	0.0	2.48	50	48	-0.4
63851	HAYTI	155	4527	4315	4209	-0.5	14	1796	1742	1706	-0.3	2.41	1158	1074	-0.8
63852	HOLCOMB	069	1661	1663	1635	0.0	37	655	650	638	-0.1	2.56	481	461	-0.5
63855	HORNERSVILLE	069	1577	1500	1454	-0.5	14	642	615	598	-0.5	2.44	442	406	-0.9
63857	KENNETT	069	13070	12587	12242	-0.4	18	5251	5090	4961	-0.3	2.40	3588	3346	-0.8
63862	LILBOURN	143	1771	1628	1565	-0.9	4	703	660	639	-0.7	2.45	490	442	-1.1
63863	MALDEN	069	6537	6303	6134	-0.4	18	2621	2545	2483	-0.3	2.41	1769	1650	-0.8
63866	MARSTON	143	689	624	598	-1.1	2	293	271	262	-0.8	2.30	192	170	-1.3
63867	MATTHEWS	143	2006	1844	1767	-0.9	4	770	726	701	-0.6	2.53	585	537	-0.9
63868	MOREHOUSE	143	205	193	186	-0.6	11	71	68	66	-0.5	2.84	58	54	-0.8
63869	NEW MADRID	143	4335	4038	3902	-0.8	6	1676	1583	1536	-0.6	2.44	1165	1058	-1.0
63870	PARMA	143	1989	1794	1715	-1.1	2	782	721	694	-0.9	2.49	573	512	-1.2
63873	PORTAGEVILLE	143	5186	4816	4639	-0.8	6	2046	1935	1877	-0.6	2.45	1433	1306	-1.0
63876	SENATH	069	2141	1916	1823	-1.2	1	877	791	754	-1.1	2.30	583	504	-1.6
63877	STEELE	155	4891	4696	4561	-0.4	18	1941	1887	1843	-0.3	2.46	1355	1268	-0.7
63879	WARDELL	155	909	818	782	-1.1	2	360	327	314	-1.0	2.50	259	227	-1.4
63901	POPLAR BLUFF	023	33041	32946	32977	0.0	37	13491	13624	13694	0.1	2.35	9019	8736	-0.3
63931	BRIAR	181	657	672	670	0.2	46	253	263	263	0.4	2.56	176	176	0.0
63932	BROSELEY	023	1844	1796	1779	-0.3	21	744	738	736	-0.1	2.42	536	510	-0.5
63933	CAMPBELL	069	4062	3922	3816	-0.4	18	1655	1624	1586	-0.2	2.37	1132	1068	-0.6
63934	CLUBB	223	109	104	102	-0.5	14	40	39	38	-0.3	2.64	28	26	-0.8
63935	DONIPHAN	181	8832	8941	8884	0.1	42	3557	3637	3627	0.2	2.42	2478	2440	-0.2
63936	DUDLEY	207	965	1010	1022	0.5	58	371	391	397	0.6	2.58	282	287	0.2
63937	ELLSINORE	035	1732	2008	2071	1.6	89	691	816	847	1.8	2.42	515	590	1.5
63939	FAIRDEALING	181	550	578	581	0.5	58	229	244	246	0.7	2.36	172	178	0.4
63940	FISK	023	921	855	832	-0.8	6	386	365	357	-0.6	2.33	275	248	-1.1
63941	FREMONT	035	510	509	506	0.0	37	199	203	203	0.2	2.46	139	136	-0.2
63942	GATEWOOD	181	374	384	383	0.3	50	145	151	152	0.4	2.54	113	114	0.1
63943	GRANDIN	035	2639	2677	2637	0.2	46	971	993	982	0.2	2.69	737	731	-0.1
63944	GREENVILLE	223	1659	1594	1561	-0.4	18	678	657	646	-0.3	2.40	484	453	-0.7
63945	HARVIELL	023	1170	1398	1458	1.9	91	453	545	571	2.0	2.57	339	397	1.7
63950	LODI	223	59	56	55	-0.6	11	22	21	21	-0.5	2.67	16	15	-0.7
63951	LOWNDES	223	134	129	127	-0.4	18	51	50	49	-0.2	2.58	36	34	-0.6
63952	MILL SPRING	223	855	839	826	-0.2	27	331	329	325	-0.1	2.55	238	227	-0.5
63953	NAYLOR	181	1098	1117	1112	0.2	46	450	460	459	0.2	2.43	327	323	-0.1
63954	NEELYVILLE	023	1527	1531	1531	0.0	37	614	625	629	0.2	2.45	413	402	-0.3
63955	OXLY	181	613	626	624	0.2	46	259	268	268	0.4	2.34	185	184	-0.1
63956	PATTERSON	223	1511	1445	1416	-0.5	14	619	596	585	-0.4	2.41	458	428	-0.7
63957	PIEDMONT	223	3973	3859	3806	-0.3	21	1687	1669	1655	-0.1	2.27	1129	1072	-0.6
63960	PUXICO	207	3074	3135	3145	0.2	46	1146	1187	1199	0.4	2.35	808	806	0.0
63961	QULIN	023	1639	1721	1752	0.5	58	678	726	744	0.7	2.36	485	499	0.3
63963	SHOOK	223	280	271	267	-0.4	18	121	119	118	-0.2	2.28	86	82	-0.5
63964	SILVA	223	1003	965	945	-0.4	18	420	407	400	-0.3	2.32	294	274	-0.8
63965	VAN BUREN	035	2608	2620	2590	0.0	37	1121	1148	1140	0.3	2.22	741	727	-0.2
63966	WAPPAPELLO	223	2182	2191	2184	0.0	37	1007	1028	1030	0.2	2.13	664	650	-0.2
63967	WILLIAMSVILLE	223	1996	1959	1937	-0.2	27	837	834	831	0.0	2.33	586	563	-0.4
64001	ALMA	107	698	686	678	-0.2	27	282	281	279	0.0	2.44	207	198	-0.5
64011	BATES CITY	107	3552	3883	3950	1.0	76	1283	1411	1441	1.0	2.75	1027	1104	0.8
64012	BELTON	037	25859	28893	30430	1.2	82	9553	10833	11473	1.4	2.64	7051	7678	0.9
64014	BLUE SPRINGS	095	22983	24708	25575	0.8	69	8200	8958	9316	1.0	2.73	6327	6684	0.6
64015	BLUE SPRINGS	095	28568	31294	32585	1.0	76	10432	11668	12213	1.2	2.68	8053	8692	0.8
64016	BUCKNER	095	4208	4673	4907	1.1	79	1551	1756	1852	1.4	2.66	1198	1298	0.9
64017	CAMDEN	177	474	528	545	1.2	82	182	206	214	1.3	2.55	136	149	1.0
64018	CAMDEN POINT	165	826	865	899	0.5	58	304	326	342	0.8	2.65	245	256	0.5
64019	CENTERVIEW	101	2114	2348	2454	1.1	79	768	858	899	1.2	2.73	607	658	0.9
64020	CONCORDIA	107	3651	3908	3967	0.7	66	1393	1504	1528	0.8	2.51	978	1015	0.4
64021	CORDER	107	667	636	623	-0.5	14	272	262	258	-0.4	2.43	193	178	-0.9
64022	DOVER	107	311	287	278	-0.9	4	122	115	112	-0.6	2.33	90	81	-1.1
64024	EXCELSIOR SPRINGS	047	16202	17013	17596	0.5	58	6005	6411	6698	0.7	2.55	4372	4430	0.1
64029	GRAIN VALLEY	095	8098	14085	16330	6.2	99	2945	5270	6170	6.5	2.67	2322	3975	6.0
64030	GRANDVIEW	095	24849	25249	25508	0.2	46	9701	10070	10244	0.4	2.48	6479	6344	-0.2
64034	GREENWOOD	095	5805	7515	8204	2.8	96	2035	2673	2940	3.0	2.81	1711	2184	2.7
64035	HARDIN	177	1194	1195	1166	0.0	37	471	473	461	0.0	2.52	349	339	-0.3
64036	HENRIETTA	177	468	554	581	1.8	90	130	161	171	2.3	2.91	92	109	1.8
64037	HIGGINSVILLE	107	5944	5870	5823	-0.1	32	2252	2244	2228	0.0	2.45	1565	1499	-0.5
64040	HOLDEN	101	6113	6511	6692	0.7	66	2283	2426	2492	0.7	2.67	1694	1746	0.3
64048	HOLT	047	3966	4383	4732	1.1	79	1407	1582	1719	1.3	2.76	1173	1278	0.9
64050	INDEPENDENCE	095	23495	22594	22362	-0.4	18	9831	9631	9584	-0.2	2.30	6026	5542	-0.9
64052	INDEPENDENCE	095	20857	20141	19964	-0.4	18	9462	9333	9306	-0.1	2.15	5429	4958	-1.0
64053	INDEPENDENCE	095	5763	5160	4983	-1.2	1	2474	2264	2200	-1.0	2.25	1399	1179	-1.8
64054	INDEPENDENCE	095	4369	3904	3774	-1.2	1	1938	1774	1724	-1.0	2.20	1140	971	-1.7
64055	INDEPENDENCE	095	33808	33576	33604	-0.1	32	14710	14984	15122	0.2	2.23	9596	9167	-0.5
64056	INDEPENDENCE	095	15203	16194	16702	0.7	66	5372	5863	6092	1.0	2.75	4217	4437	0.6
64057	INDEPENDENCE	095	11591	14193	15306	2.2	94	4424	5632	6154	2.6	2.47	3170	3810	2.0
64058	INDEPENDENCE	095	6133	6445	6633	0.5	58	2099	2266	2349	0.8	2.83	1734	1812	0.5
64060	KEARNEY	047	9648	12579	14191	2.9	96	3308	4360	4955	3.0	2.87	2724	3480	2.7
64061	KINGSVILLE	101	2579	3036	3245	1.8	90	968	1150	1230	1.9	2.63	775	894	1.6
64062	LAWSON	177	5932	6589	6775	1.1	79	2078	2341	2421	1.3	2.79	1678	1837	1.0
64063	LEES SUMMIT	095	20227	20644	20908	0.2	46	7807	8128	8280	0.4	2.54	5488	5419	-0.1
64064	LEES SUMMIT	095	11311	14288	15561	2.6	95	4158	5392	5924	2.8	2.63	3367	4206	2.4
64067	LEXINGTON	107	5887	5154	4924	-1.4	1	2344	2065	1974	-1.4	2.42	1647	1398	-1.8
64068	LIBERTY	047	33188	35918	38310	0.9	72	12137	13300	14300	1.0	2.60	8926	9336	0.5
64070	LONE JACK	095	2399	3022	3286	2.5	95	870	1125	1233	2.8	2.69	722	900	2.4
64071	MAYVIEW	107	905	970	983	0.8	69	333	361	367	0.9	2.67	257	270	0.5
64074	NAPOLEON	107	685	711	713	0.4	53	253	268	270	0.6	2.61	200	205	0.3
64075	OAK GROVE	095	9211	11149	12049	2.1	93	3258	4050	4414	2.4	2.73	2560	3042	1.9
64076	ODESSA	107	8711	9338	9464	0.8	69	3267	3533	3587	0.8	2.63	2412	2519	0.5
64077	ORRICK	177	1808	1953	1982	0.8	69	678	745	760	1.0	2.62	525	558	0.7
64078	PECULIAR	037	6891	9264	10482	3.3	97	2380	3262	3709	3.5	2.84	1968	2620	3.1
64079	PLATTE CITY	165	8110	11641	13248	4.0	98	2966	4232	4816	3.9	2.71	2254	3108	3.5
64080	PLEASANT HILL	037	9967	12715	14126	2.7	96	3646	4694	5237	2.8	2.69	2814	3488	2.3
64081	LEES SUMMIT	095	18089	24116	26773	3.2	97	7082	8830	9626	2.4	2.66	4721	5931	2.5
64082	LEES SUMMIT	095	5537	11659	13889	8.4	100	1874	3965	4740	8.4	2.94	1623	3388	8.3
	MISSOURI					0.7					0.8	2.45			0.4
	UNITED STATES					1.0					1.1	2.59			0.9

ZIP CODE #	POST OFFICE NAME	RACE (%) White 2000	White 2009	Black 2000	Black 2009	Asian/Pacific 2000	Asian/Pacific 2009	% Hispanic Origin 2000	% Hispanic Origin 2009	2009 AGE DISTRIBUTION (%) 0-4	5-9	10-14	15-19	20-24	25-44	45-64	65-84	85+	18+	MEDIAN AGE 2009	% 2009 Males	% 2009 Females
63846	ESSEX	95.0	94.2	3.7	4.2	0.1	0.1	0.6	0.8	6.7	6.7	6.8	6.9	5.8	26.4	26.2	12.6	1.9	75.3	38.7	48.4	51.6
63848	GIDEON	97.6	97.3	0.6	0.7	0.0	0.0	0.8	1.2	6.9	6.5	6.8	7.6	6.7	23.7	24.3	13.9	3.6	75.0	38.2	48.1	51.9
63849	GOBLER	84.0	81.3	13.1	15.2	0.0	0.6	3.4	4.1	4.7	5.8	6.4	8.2	5.3	21.1	33.9	12.9	1.8	77.8	43.8	50.9	49.1
63851	HAYTI	49.8	45.7	48.7	52.6	0.2	0.3	1.1	1.3	8.6	7.9	7.5	8.1	6.3	21.9	23.0	13.1	3.5	70.8	35.8	44.8	55.2
63852	HOLCOMB	96.1	94.9	0.7	0.7	0.1	0.2	3.3	4.6	7.3	7.6	7.5	6.4	5.1	23.1	29.3	11.7	2.0	73.5	39.2	50.5	49.5
63855	HORNERSVILLE	94.3	92.9	3.0	3.5	0.3	0.5	4.2	5.8	5.5	5.6	6.0	6.7	5.7	22.9	30.7	14.7	2.3	78.9	43.2	50.6	49.4
63857	KENNETT	85.5	84.0	11.8	12.5	0.5	0.7	2.3	3.1	7.8	7.1	6.9	6.8	6.2	24.1	24.8	13.4	2.7	73.9	37.5	46.7	53.3
63862	LILBOURN	64.9	59.4	33.6	38.7	0.1	0.1	1.0	1.3	6.3	6.4	6.6	8.6	6.2	23.5	27.1	13.1	2.2	75.5	39.0	48.0	52.0
63863	MALDEN	79.3	74.9	18.2	22.2	0.3	0.4	1.3	1.8	7.2	7.3	7.1	6.8	5.1	23.5	25.2	15.0	2.9	74.2	39.4	46.8	53.2
63866	MARSTON	77.9	73.6	21.1	25.3	0.0	0.0	2.0	2.7	8.2	8.0	8.2	6.4	4.2	23.2	27.2	12.8	1.8	71.5	38.3	48.7	51.3
63867	MATTHEWS	97.2	96.3	1.1	1.4	0.0	0.1	1.1	1.6	6.3	6.9	7.2	6.7	4.4	26.4	28.3	12.4	1.4	75.0	39.0	51.2	48.8
63868	MOREHOUSE	99.0	98.4	0.0	0.5	0.0	0.0	1.5	1.6	6.7	6.7	7.3	6.7	4.7	27.5	26.9	12.4	1.0	74.6	37.5	53.4	46.6
63869	NEW MADRID	71.7	68.4	27.1	30.2	0.2	0.3	0.6	0.8	6.9	7.1	7.1	6.9	5.6	24.3	26.6	13.0	2.5	74.6	38.4	48.2	51.8
63870	PARMA	79.5	76.6	19.1	21.7	0.0	0.0	0.6	0.8	5.8	6.2	6.4	7.0	5.1	26.2	28.1	13.2	2.1	77.3	39.8	48.9	51.1
63873	PORTAGEVILLE	85.3	82.2	13.3	16.0	0.2	0.3	0.7	1.0	6.6	6.3	6.5	7.5	6.0	23.8	27.4	13.7	2.3	76.0	39.9	47.7	52.3
63876	SENATH	92.9	90.8	0.6	0.6	0.1	0.1	9.5	13.2	6.7	6.9	6.8	5.6	4.0	22.9	24.9	17.3	4.7	76.0	42.6	49.1	50.9
63877	STEELE	87.4	84.6	10.7	13.0	0.0	0.1	1.9	2.6	7.5	7.5	7.6	7.6	5.6	24.7	24.7	12.4	2.4	72.8	36.6	48.0	52.0
63879	WARDELL	84.3	80.3	14.1	17.6	0.1	0.1	0.9	1.2	5.9	6.1	6.1	7.1	6.1	24.9	28.6	13.1	2.1	77.8	39.9	49.8	50.2
63901	POPLAR BLUFF	91.5	90.0	5.8	6.7	0.5	0.8	1.1	1.5	6.5	6.3	6.1	6.3	5.7	24.7	27.4	14.3	2.8	77.3	40.5	47.6	52.4
63931	BRIAR	96.2	95.5	0.0	0.0	0.2	0.3	0.8	1.0	6.5	6.1	6.7	7.9	5.5	23.2	27.4	15.3	1.3	75.9	40.3	51.8	48.2
63932	BROSELEY	96.4	95.9	1.6	1.8	0.2	0.2	0.5	0.6	5.9	6.1	5.9	5.9	5.1	23.9	28.7	16.4	2.2	78.4	43.0	49.9	50.1
63933	CAMPBELL	98.4	98.1	0.1	0.2	0.1	0.1	1.1	1.4	6.3	6.6	6.1	5.8	4.7	24.0	27.7	15.5	3.3	77.4	42.1	48.3	51.7
63934	CLUBB	97.3	97.1	0.9	1.0	0.0	0.0	0.9	1.0	5.8	5.8	5.8	6.7	5.8	21.2	26.0	20.2	2.9	78.8	44.2	49.0	51.0
63935	DONIPHAN	97.6	97.1	0.0	0.0	0.3	0.4	1.0	1.3	6.2	6.1	6.3	6.5	5.3	22.9	28.1	16.0	2.7	77.5	42.3	48.3	51.7
63936	DUDLEY	97.8	97.3	0.1	0.1	0.1	0.2	1.0	1.5	6.0	6.0	6.3	6.5	5.6	26.6	27.9	13.2	1.7	77.5	39.2	50.1	49.9
63937	ELLSINORE	97.5	96.8	0.2	0.4	0.2	0.4	0.4	0.5	5.9	6.2	6.4	7.7	5.4	24.0	29.3	13.7	1.4	76.3	40.5	48.3	51.7
63939	FAIRDEALING	97.6	97.4	0.2	0.2	0.4	0.5	0.9	1.0	5.7	5.9	6.2	6.4	5.0	23.5	29.9	15.7	1.6	77.9	42.8	47.8	52.2
63940	FISK	97.8	97.3	0.3	0.4	0.0	0.1	1.2	1.5	6.1	6.2	6.4	6.0	4.8	23.4	29.8	15.2	2.1	77.5	42.9	49.6	50.4
63941	FREMONT	93.3	92.9	0.2	0.2	0.2	0.2	2.7	3.3	5.7	5.9	6.3	6.3	4.1	21.8	31.8	16.5	1.6	78.4	44.9	50.1	49.9
63942	GATEWOOD	98.4	97.9	0.0	0.0	0.0	0.3	1.1	1.6	4.9	4.9	5.5	6.0	5.7	23.4	33.3	14.6	1.6	81.0	44.5	51.8	48.2
63943	GRANDIN	97.8	97.4	0.0	0.0	0.1	0.2	0.5	0.6	7.1	7.0	7.1	7.0	6.0	23.5	27.5	13.4	1.4	74.7	39.0	49.2	50.8
63944	GREENVILLE	97.7	97.3	0.2	0.2	0.2	0.3	0.7	0.9	5.4	5.5	5.6	5.8	5.2	21.2	29.5	19.1	2.6	79.9	45.8	50.7	49.3
63945	HARVIELL	96.5	96.1	0.5	0.6	0.3	0.3	0.7	0.9	6.2	6.3	6.5	6.1	5.4	26.0	29.3	13.0	1.2	77.3	40.5	50.1	49.9
63950	LODI	98.3	98.2	0.0	0.0	0.0	0.0	0.0	0.0	3.6	7.1	7.1	7.1	5.4	17.9	28.6	21.4	1.8	75.0	46.3	50.0	50.0
63951	LOWNDES	98.5	97.7	0.0	0.0	0.0	0.0	0.0	0.0	7.0	7.0	7.0	6.2	3.9	20.2	29.5	17.8	1.6	75.2	43.8	49.6	50.4
63952	MILL SPRING	96.8	96.2	0.0	0.0	0.2	0.6	0.4	0.5	6.7	6.9	6.3	6.4	5.5	22.3	27.3	16.7	1.9	76.2	41.3	50.1	49.9
63953	NAYLOR	94.1	93.4	0.1	0.1	0.4	0.5	1.7	2.4	6.6	6.8	6.8	6.1	5.1	23.9	26.4	16.0	2.2	76.0	40.0	47.6	52.4
63954	NEELYVILLE	87.1	84.5	10.3	12.3	0.3	0.5	0.3	0.4	6.6	6.7	6.7	7.3	5.6	26.5	26.7	12.4	1.6	75.6	38.7	50.4	49.6
63955	OXLY	96.6	96.0	0.0	0.0	0.0	0.2	1.1	1.4	6.2	6.4	6.4	5.6	4.3	24.3	29.2	15.7	1.9	77.3	42.7	51.0	49.0
63956	PATTERSON	97.2	96.8	0.5	0.5	0.0	0.0	0.6	0.8	5.6	6.0	6.0	6.0	5.2	20.1	29.6	19.2	2.4	78.8	45.7	50.0	50.0
63957	PIEDMONT	97.7	97.2	0.2	0.2	0.2	0.4	0.5	0.6	5.4	5.5	5.6	6.4	5.4	22.0	27.0	18.8	3.8	79.5	44.7	48.0	52.0
63960	PUXICO	96.9	96.3	1.7	1.9	0.0	0.1	0.8	1.1	4.8	4.9	5.1	13.0	6.3	22.7	25.4	14.8	3.0	77.1	39.6	52.2	47.8
63961	QULIN	97.7	97.4	0.5	0.6	0.0	0.0	0.6	0.9	5.6	5.8	6.2	7.0	5.3	25.0	27.5	15.3	2.3	78.0	41.7	50.6	49.4
63963	SHOOK	98.2	97.0	0.0	0.0	0.0	0.4	0.4	0.4	5.9	5.9	6.3	5.9	4.4	19.9	31.4	18.5	1.8	78.2	46.0	50.6	49.4
63964	SILVA	97.8	97.5	0.3	0.3	0.1	0.1	0.8	0.9	5.6	5.6	5.7	6.1	5.4	21.6	27.5	19.3	3.3	79.3	45.0	49.9	50.1
63965	VAN BUREN	95.6	95.0	0.2	0.2	0.1	0.2	1.8	2.6	5.5	5.7	6.1	6.0	4.8	22.3	29.8	17.2	2.7	79.0	44.7	48.9	51.1
63966	WAPPAPELLO	97.9	97.5	0.3	0.3	0.1	0.1	0.6	0.9	4.7	4.2	5.4	6.2	4.1	18.1	36.8	18.9	1.5	81.7	49.9	51.3	48.7
63967	WILLIAMSVILLE	98.0	97.7	0.2	0.2	0.1	0.2	0.5	0.6	5.4	5.7	5.8	5.6	4.5	22.7	32.2	16.6	1.6	79.8	45.2	50.9	49.1
64001	ALMA	99.4	99.3	0.0	0.0	0.1	0.1	0.3	0.3	5.7	6.1	6.3	6.7	3.8	23.0	29.3	17.1	2.0	77.7	43.8	49.9	50.1
64011	BATES CITY	96.7	95.9	0.8	1.0	0.2	0.3	1.4	2.0	6.1	6.5	7.2	7.2	5.8	26.5	30.7	9.3	0.8	75.8	38.9	51.8	48.2
64012	BELTON	93.5	92.2	2.5	2.8	0.7	1.0	4.1	5.7	7.7	7.6	7.3	7.0	6.1	27.8	25.4	9.6	1.6	73.1	35.6	48.9	51.1
64014	BLUE SPRINGS	93.4	90.1	2.6	4.2	1.1	1.9	3.0	4.7	7.6	7.6	7.4	7.1	6.2	30.0	25.5	7.5	1.2	73.1	34.5	48.5	51.5
64015	BLUE SPRINGS	93.4	89.9	3.0	4.7	1.0	1.7	2.4	3.7	6.9	6.8	6.9	7.1	6.3	28.0	28.2	8.8	1.0	75.1	36.0	49.1	50.9
64016	BUCKNER	96.7	95.2	0.2	0.3	0.3	0.5	1.4	2.3	6.2	6.5	7.1	7.6	5.7	26.4	28.8	10.7	1.0	75.5	37.7	49.7	50.3
64017	CAMDEN	98.1	97.5	0.4	0.6	0.0	0.0	1.3	1.9	6.3	6.3	6.8	7.4	6.1	26.5	27.8	11.7	1.1	76.1	38.7	49.8	50.2
64018	CAMDEN POINT	98.4	98.3	0.0	0.0	0.0	0.0	0.6	0.8	6.6	7.5	7.9	5.5	3.9	24.7	32.5	10.2	1.2	74.5	41.5	49.9	50.1
64019	CENTERVIEW	96.6	95.7	0.6	0.7	0.5	0.8	1.6	2.2	6.2	6.5	6.8	6.8	5.5	25.6	30.3	11.3	1.0	76.1	39.6	50.6	49.4
64020	CONCORDIA	98.3	97.9	0.5	0.7	0.2	0.3	0.7	1.0	6.0	6.4	6.4	6.6	5.1	23.2	26.6	14.9	4.9	77.0	42.1	48.0	52.0
64021	CORDER	96.7	95.9	1.2	1.4	0.3	0.3	0.9	1.4	5.0	5.3	5.7	6.6	5.3	22.3	30.8	16.5	2.4	80.2	44.8	50.3	49.7
64022	DOVER	91.9	89.5	5.2	6.6	0.3	0.3	1.6	2.1	5.9	5.6	5.9	6.6	6.6	26.1	27.5	13.9	1.7	78.4	39.9	50.5	49.5
64024	EXCELSIOR SPRINGS	94.6	93.4	2.4	2.8	0.4	0.6	1.7	2.4	7.2	6.8	6.6	7.7	6.4	25.3	26.2	12.0	1.9	74.8	37.4	49.5	50.5
64029	GRAIN VALLEY	96.2	94.2	0.9	1.3	0.6	1.0	2.4	3.9	9.4	8.7	8.0	6.4	4.7	34.2	21.8	6.2	0.6	69.9	33.2	50.3	49.7
64030	GRANDVIEW	59.8	50.3	33.6	41.6	1.2	1.6	4.3	5.8	7.3	6.8	6.5	6.7	7.6	28.6	24.8	10.4	1.3	75.4	34.7	48.2	51.8
64034	GREENWOOD	95.8	93.7	1.8	2.9	0.5	0.8	1.9	3.0	9.5	9.1	8.5	6.6	4.3	30.9	23.1	7.3	0.6	68.7	35.0	49.3	50.7
64035	HARDIN	97.7	97.2	0.4	0.5	0.1	0.2	0.6	0.8	6.5	6.7	7.1	7.5	5.6	22.5	29.0	12.8	2.3	75.2	40.4	51.4	48.6
64036	HENRIETTA	91.7	90.3	4.7	5.4	0.0	0.0	2.1	2.9	6.3	6.3	6.1	7.8	8.5	30.1	23.6	10.1	1.1	77.4	35.0	55.4	44.6
64037	HIGGINSVILLE	92.8	91.2	4.2	5.0	0.5	0.8	1.3	1.9	6.3	6.1	6.0	6.5	6.2	23.9	26.5	14.3	4.2	77.5	41.1	47.5	52.5
64040	HOLDEN	96.1	95.3	0.9	1.0	0.3	0.4	1.3	1.9	6.1	6.3	6.5	7.2	6.4	25.1	28.3	12.4	1.8	76.8	39.3	49.9	50.1
64048	HOLT	97.9	97.4	0.5	0.5	0.1	0.2	1.1	1.6	5.4	6.2	6.9	7.4	4.4	23.7	33.7	11.5	0.8	76.7	42.4	50.2	49.8
64050	INDEPENDENCE	90.9	86.9	2.8	4.4	1.2	1.8	3.9	6.1	7.3	6.3	6.2	6.5	7.0	26.4	24.5	12.7	2.9	76.3	37.4	47.4	52.6
64052	INDEPENDENCE	90.9	86.9	2.5	3.8	1.2	1.9	4.5	7.0	6.6	6.2	5.9	5.3	5.5	25.6	28.0	14.1	2.7	78.1	41.2	48.7	51.3
64053	INDEPENDENCE	89.8	85.4	2.8	4.3	1.2	1.7	5.2	8.2	7.2	6.8	6.3	5.7	7.0	27.4	27.5	10.5	1.7	76.4	37.4	51.2	48.8
64054	INDEPENDENCE	91.2	87.5	1.9	2.9	1.8	2.7	3.8	6.0	6.1	6.2	6.2	5.7	5.0	27.4	28.5	13.1	1.9	78.0	40.5	50.3	49.7
64055	INDEPENDENCE	94.0	91.0	2.0	3.2	1.0	1.6	3.0	4.7	5.2	5.2	5.3	5.7	5.6	25.4	27.6	17.2	2.8	80.8	43.1	47.1	52.9
64056	INDEPENDENCE	89.8	85.6	3.8	5.6	1.2	1.9	3.9	6.0	8.3	7.6	7.2	7.7	7.1	27.1	24.2	9.9	1.0	72.1	33.6	48.8	51.2
64057	INDEPENDENCE	93.5	89.5	2.1	3.7	1.1	2.0	3.4	5.5	6.3	6.2	6.1	6.6	6.7	26.2	27.6	11.2	3.1	77.6	38.7	46.6	53.4
64058	INDEPENDENCE	94.8	92.2	0.8	1.6	1.5	2.3	2.2	3.6	6.7	6.9	6.7	7.1	6.1	27.2	28.6	9.7	1.1	75.1	36.4	48.6	51.4
64060	KEARNEY	97.2	96.5	0.6	0.7	0.4	0.5	1.6	2.2	8.4	8.0	8.0	7.4	5.6	28.7	25.2	7.6	1.1	70.6	34.6	48.9	51.1
64061	KINGSVILLE	97.4	96.8	0.5	0.6	0.1	0.2	0.9	1.3	5.6	6.3	6.8	6.5	4.1	25.3	31.7	12.5	1.3	77.2	42.1	50.3	49.7
64062	LAWSON	97.3	96.8	0.5	0.6	0.4	0.6	1.1	1.4	6.7	6.8	7.0	7.3	6.1	24.5	29.4	10.9	1.3	74.7	39.0	50.4	49.6
64063	LEES SUMMIT	93.4	90.0	3.0	4.8	0.8	1.4	2.1	3.3	8.9	8.2	7.7	6.7	6.0	31.4	23.0	7.1	1.0	71.0	33.0	47.4	52.6
64064	LEES SUMMIT	92.1	87.4	4.4	7.3	1.6	2.7	1.8	2.7	6.9	7.4	7.9	6.3	3.9	25.5	30.9	10.2	1.0	73.6	40.1	49.0	51.0
64067	LEXINGTON	92.7	91.1	4.8	5.7	0.4	0.7	1.9	2.5	5.4	5.6	6.0	6.8	5.5	24.3	28.2	15.3	2.9	78.5	42.1	47.9	52.1
64068	LIBERTY	94.2	92.7	2.3	2.6	0.6	1.0	2.6	3.6	6.7	6.5	6.6	7.8	7.0	27.2	26.7	9.8	1.7	75.8	36.5	48.3	51.7
64070	LONE JACK	97.1	95.6	1.2	2.0	0.3	0.4	1.5	2.3	5.7	6.3	6.9	7.0	4.8	23.0	33.5	11.9	0.9	76.7	42.5	50.9	49.1
64071	MAYVIEW	94.5	93.5	3.8	4.5	0.0	0.0	1.0	1.3	6.1	6.1	6.6	7.4	5.4	25.8	28.2	12.9	1.5	75.6	40.1	50.0	50.0
64074	NAPOLEON	96.5	95.8	1.0	1.3	0.1	0.3	0.9	1.4	6.3	6.6	7.0	6.6	5.3	23.5	30.1	13.4	1.1	76.1	41.4	52.0	48.0
64075	OAK GROVE	97.2	95.8	0.2	0.4	0.5	0.8	1.4	2.4	7.3	7.4	7.5	7.5	5.7	26.8	26.5	9.9	1.4	73.0	36.4	49.6	50.4
64076	ODESSA	97.0	96.3	1.1	1.3	0.2	0.3	0.8	1.1	7.1	7.0	7.0	7.2	5.9	26.5	26.5	11.1	1.7	74.6	37.5	49.0	51.0
64077	ORRICK	98.2	97.8	0.2	0.2	0.0	0.1	1.4	1.9	6.2	6.3	6.7	7.1	5.8	25.6	28.9	12.2	1.1	76.4	39.6	50.3	49.7
64078	PECULIAR	96.5	95.6	0.9	1.1	0.6	0.9	1.2	1.8	7.0	7.4	7.7	7.4	5.4	24.3	30.3	9.7	0.8	73.3	38.3	49.7	50.3
64079	PLATTE CITY	94.3	93.2	1.9	2.2	0.7	1.0	2.0	2.7	7.4	7.5	7.3	6.8	5.5	28.8	27.3	8.1	1.3	73.4	36.4	50.2	49.8
64080	PLEASANT HILL	97.6	97.0	0.4	0.5	0.3	0.5	1.3	1.9	7.7	7.3	7.3	7.1	5.3	27.7	25.9	10.2	1.5	73.0	36.5	49.5	50.5
64081	LEES SUMMIT	93.2	88.1	4.0	7.6	1.0	2.0	1.7	2.8	7.8	7.8	7.8	6.6	4.1	24.9	23.9	11.3	5.7	72.2	38.9	46.9	53.1
64082	LEES SUMMIT	95.8	91.5	2.0	5.0	0.8	1.7	1.4	2.6	7.2	7.9	8.3	7.6	4.4	25.1	30.4	8.5	0.6	71.8	38.6	48.8	51.2
	MISSOURI	84.9	83.3	11.2	11.7	1.2	1.7	2.1	2.8	6.6	6.6	6.6	7.0	6.7	26.1	26.5	11.7	2.1	76.1	37.7	48.8	51.2
	UNITED STATES	75.1	72.0	12.3	12.7	3.8	4.6	12.5	15.7	6.8	6.7	6.6	7.1	6.9	27.0	26.0	10.9	1.9	75.7	36.9	49.2	50.8

ZIP CODE #	POST OFFICE NAME	2009 Per Capita Income	2009 HH Income Base	2009 HOUSEHOLD INCOME DISTRIBUTION (%) Less than $25,000	$25,000 to $49,999	$50,000 to $99,999	$100,000 to $149,999	$150,000 or More	MEDIAN HOUSEHOLD INCOME 2009	2014	2009 National Centile	2009 State Centile	2009 Home Value Base	2009 HOME VALUE DISTRIBUTION (%) Less than $50,000	$50,000 to $89,999	$90,000 to $174,999	$175,000 to $399,999	$400,000 or More	2009 Median Home Value
63846	ESSEX	16300	623	37.6	35.0	23.1	2.4	1.9	31994	33462	11	17	467	42.4	26.3	24.0	6.2	1.1	58068
63848	GIDEON	17320	673	40.7	29.4	23.6	4.0	2.2	31012	32675	10	14	461	46.0	35.6	16.5	1.5	0.4	53854
63849	GOBLER	16380	69	40.6	30.4	24.6	4.3	0.0	31346	35000	10	15	49	40.8	28.6	22.4	6.1	2.0	59000
63851	HAYTI	13750	1742	57.5	26.4	13.1	1.5	1.5	20297	20731	1	1	934	45.2	38.0	13.8	2.9	0.1	55294
63852	HOLCOMB	15041	650	43.1	31.4	22.5	2.2	0.9	29321	31089	7	8	493	35.7	30.6	27.2	5.9	0.6	66705
63855	HORNERSVILLE	16275	615	40.3	30.9	23.7	2.9	2.1	31793	34044	11	17	452	35.4	39.2	21.7	3.1	0.7	62656
63857	KENNETT	18040	5090	41.0	24.5	27.8	4.8	1.8	34285	37186	16	27	3175	18.2	27.8	43.4	8.9	1.7	95080
63862	LILBOURN	16393	660	43.8	28.9	21.5	4.2	1.5	28217	28670	6	6	466	42.7	39.3	16.7	1.3	0.0	57727
63863	MALDEN	15914	2545	43.3	29.7	23.3	2.8	0.9	29724	31255	8	10	1622	28.4	37.3	28.7	5.5	0.1	71615
63866	MARSTON	18114	271	47.6	27.7	18.8	2.2	3.7	26988	28804	5	4	176	59.1	26.1	13.6	1.1	0.0	43333
63867	MATTHEWS	15070	726	34.7	39.9	23.1	2.1	0.1	34652	36545	17	29	525	33.0	32.0	29.9	4.6	0.6	73065
63868	MOREHOUSE	12827	68	30.9	45.6	22.1	1.5	0.0	35000	38629	18	31	52	28.8	25.0	40.4	5.8	0.0	85000
63869	NEW MADRID	16713	1583	41.8	28.7	23.1	4.1	2.2	30531	31128	9	13	1012	22.7	37.2	32.7	7.0	0.4	81803
63870	PARMA	15498	721	44.2	28.7	22.9	2.9	1.2	29440	30198	7	9	505	49.5	27.9	17.6	4.2	0.8	50581
63873	PORTAGEVILLE	17678	1935	39.5	28.1	26.9	3.4	2.1	35052	36824	18	31	1233	30.7	26.6	33.8	8.7	0.2	78803
63876	SENATH	15687	791	43.1	30.8	23.1	2.5	0.4	30103	31258	8	11	557	28.9	36.4	30.2	4.3	0.2	71442
63877	STEELE	17857	1887	40.8	27.8	23.9	5.6	2.0	33873	36092	15	26	1204	31.1	33.1	27.8	7.1	0.9	73924
63879	WARDELL	14413	327	46.2	29.1	21.4	3.4	0.0	29398	29532	7	8	228	45.6	35.5	15.8	3.1	0.0	54167
63901	POPLAR BLUFF	20207	13624	36.2	30.5	25.7	4.6	3.0	35235	37677	18	32	9096	22.0	26.9	34.6	13.1	3.3	91658
63931	BRIAR	11635	263	54.8	30.0	13.3	1.5	0.4	22705	23589	2	1	213	40.4	24.4	27.2	8.0	0.0	63214
63932	BROSELEY	17792	738	40.2	30.9	23.0	3.8	2.0	31979	34091	11	17	584	33.6	31.5	27.4	7.2	0.3	69000
63933	CAMPBELL	17332	1624	38.1	30.4	27.8	2.8	1.0	33005	35557	13	21	1161	28.4	43.3	22.0	4.7	1.6	66580
63934	CLUBB	11473	39	48.7	38.5	12.8	0.0	0.0	25720	23541	4	3	31	38.7	29.0	25.8	6.5	0.0	61667
63935	DONIPHAN	15295	3637	46.4	31.3	18.6	2.3	1.4	27123	28199	5	4	2764	30.4	27.1	30.8	9.4	2.4	79290
63936	DUDLEY	15191	391	38.6	31.5	26.1	3.6	0.3	29560	30472	7	9	294	27.6	21.8	35.0	13.9	1.7	91250
63937	ELLSINORE	17864	816	38.5	29.9	26.1	3.3	2.2	33732	36638	15	25	670	31.0	22.8	34.6	9.1	2.4	82353
63939	FAIRDEALING	15052	244	44.3	34.4	18.4	2.0	0.8	27970	28517	6	6	206	38.3	25.2	25.2	8.3	2.9	70909
63940	FISK	19159	365	41.1	28.5	24.9	3.0	2.5	33064	36000	13	22	290	33.1	33.8	25.2	5.9	2.1	66000
63941	FREMONT	17048	203	40.4	33.5	20.2	3.0	3.0	31170	33231	10	15	160	25.0	24.4	34.4	14.4	1.9	91429
63942	GATEWOOD	16074	151	43.0	30.5	21.9	4.6	0.0	31589	35561	11	16	130	21.5	31.5	32.3	11.5	3.1	86364
63943	GRANDIN	13607	993	46.2	31.9	17.6	2.5	1.7	27559	28631	5	5	794	34.5	29.8	24.2	8.4	3.0	71552
63944	GREENVILLE	15408	657	46.7	32.9	16.9	1.7	1.8	26947	28196	5	4	518	43.8	26.4	20.8	5.8	3.1	57619
63945	HARVIELL	17512	545	36.1	27.0	31.7	2.4	2.8	36061	39907	21	35	447	26.4	21.7	34.7	14.3	2.9	91932
63950	LODI	13430	21	47.6	28.6	23.8	0.0	0.0	27327	32344	5	4	17	17.6	29.4	41.2	11.8	0.0	95000
63951	LOWNDES	13703	50	36.0	44.0	18.0	2.0	0.0	32304	30740	12	18	43	27.9	41.9	23.3	7.0	0.0	65625
63952	MILL SPRING	13239	329	45.3	36.2	15.8	1.8	0.9	27449	27283	5	5	255	51.4	24.3	16.5	6.3	1.6	47500
63953	NAYLOR	16207	460	45.9	33.0	17.4	2.0	1.7	27773	28068	5	5	343	52.5	27.7	15.2	2.9	1.7	47167
63954	NEELYVILLE	13754	625	43.5	38.1	15.8	1.8	0.8	28229	28505	6	6	441	49.9	31.5	15.6	1.8	1.1	50143
63955	OXLY	13401	268	47.4	34.3	17.2	1.1	0.0	26338	26656	4	3	222	30.6	35.6	29.3	3.2	1.4	65217
63956	PATTERSON	18831	596	40.6	23.2	32.0	1.3	2.9	32480	36067	12	19	483	23.6	21.1	35.0	18.2	2.1	100636
63957	PIEDMONT	15366	1669	48.1	30.2	18.2	2.9	0.7	25927	26288	4	3	1226	32.5	33.0	27.2	5.9	1.5	69124
63960	PUXICO	15643	1187	41.1	32.9	22.8	2.4	0.8	29608	30557	7	9	892	32.6	26.5	30.5	9.9	0.6	74364
63961	QULIN	15562	726	44.2	32.4	20.2	2.3	0.8	29185	30000	7	8	549	39.0	31.1	23.3	6.6	0.0	66771
63963	SHOOK	17870	119	38.7	39.5	18.5	2.5	0.8	30730	32954	9	14	100	35.0	34.0	21.0	7.0	3.0	63750
63964	SILVA	13704	407	49.4	31.9	17.2	0.7	0.7	25332	26493	3	2	310	40.6	28.1	24.8	6.5	0.0	59355
63965	VAN BUREN	18129	1148	44.0	30.4	20.6	2.5	2.4	29917	31598	8	11	855	25.7	28.3	32.7	10.5	2.7	84344
63966	WAPPAPELLO	20928	1028	31.2	36.0	26.2	5.5	1.1	39520	41353	31	52	829	35.3	30.6	25.7	8.0	0.4	65000
63967	WILLIAMSVILLE	20619	834	36.5	29.4	28.3	3.5	2.4	33888	36905	15	26	683	33.1	26.4	27.5	11.0	2.0	72500
64001	ALMA	24478	281	20.3	30.6	40.9	3.2	5.0	49092	51314	59	78	223	15.2	30.9	34.5	17.0	2.2	94048
64011	BATES CITY	24370	1411	15.6	20.7	47.3	12.7	3.8	61712	61290	80	91	1268	24.0	8.8	35.4	28.3	3.5	130808
64012	BELTON	25535	10833	14.1	23.9	47.8	10.2	4.1	60375	62507	78	90	8296	17.3	17.5	45.8	16.0	3.4	115475
64014	BLUE SPRINGS	28768	8958	9.2	19.9	48.9	15.7	6.3	69597	69934	87	95	6746	0.9	6.1	67.8	24.2	0.9	133052
64015	BLUE SPRINGS	30937	11668	8.9	21.9	45.6	14.4	9.1	69039	69125	86	95	8755	4.2	5.2	57.9	29.6	3.0	146338
64016	BUCKNER	23018	1756	15.5	27.2	47.6	7.5	2.2	55837	57042	72	86	1379	7.8	29.9	43.8	16.7	1.8	99016
64017	CAMDEN	20811	206	21.4	32.0	40.3	5.8	0.5	46949	50957	54	74	165	24.2	33.3	34.5	7.3	0.6	81667
64018	CAMDEN POINT	27293	326	8.6	27.6	45.7	15.0	3.1	64122	65601	82	93	287	3.5	9.1	49.1	32.4	5.9	154063
64019	CENTERVIEW	22046	858	17.5	29.0	42.9	7.6	3.0	52513	53001	67	82	734	14.6	17.0	35.1	28.7	4.5	144231
64020	CONCORDIA	20721	1504	25.9	30.9	35.4	5.9	1.9	44581	47164	47	68	1058	11.2	31.8	42.0	12.9	2.3	99259
64021	CORDER	20409	262	30.5	33.2	29.8	3.1	3.4	40698	42548	35	56	197	24.4	37.1	27.4	10.2	1.0	74333
64022	DOVER	22614	115	27.8	27.0	35.7	7.0	2.6	44685	50000	47	68	79	26.6	15.2	35.4	19.0	3.8	103125
64024	EXCELSIOR SPRINGS	23691	6411	20.0	27.5	40.1	9.2	3.2	52247	55052	66	82	4622	11.7	19.1	50.3	17.6	1.1	113536
64029	GRAIN VALLEY	29929	5270	7.3	21.9	48.0	16.4	6.3	72524	71671	88	96	4145	7.2	14.0	49.3	28.2	1.3	140600
64030	GRANDVIEW	23805	10070	17.2	32.3	39.2	8.6	2.8	50416	52874	62	80	5971	4.0	35.7	54.2	5.7	0.4	97822
64034	GREENWOOD	33260	2673	5.6	12.5	49.3	21.7	11.0	81461	81698	93	97	2513	3.3	5.5	50.6	33.0	7.5	161351
64035	HARDIN	21247	473	21.8	28.3	44.0	4.7	1.3	49897	52317	61	79	373	19.8	35.4	33.0	11.3	0.5	82500
64036	HENRIETTA	16663	161	22.4	29.2	42.2	5.0	1.2	48103	51696	57	76	114	26.3	44.7	16.7	12.3	0.0	72500
64037	HIGGINSVILLE	22694	2244	23.9	31.0	36.1	5.7	3.3	46231	48709	52	72	1589	16.4	31.7	35.7	14.0	2.2	92944
64040	HOLDEN	19855	2426	22.2	32.0	38.3	5.5	1.9	46097	49021	52	72	1963	16.6	24.8	31.1	25.3	2.3	111853
64048	HOLT	29954	1582	8.4	20.9	47.7	16.6	6.4	67851	70151	85	94	1434	6.1	8.2	37.1	42.5	6.2	172139
64050	INDEPENDENCE	20835	9631	28.6	32.2	33.7	4.1	1.5	41543	43570	38	59	5265	14.5	51.7	30.6	3.0	0.2	79278
64052	INDEPENDENCE	22926	9333	22.2	37.1	35.3	4.0	1.5	43002	45869	42	64	6315	11.1	54.6	30.8	3.2	0.3	80465
64053	INDEPENDENCE	20029	2264	28.1	37.8	29.9	2.5	1.7	39201	41798	30	50	1280	39.1	54.5	6.3	0.2	0.0	55833
64054	INDEPENDENCE	23122	1774	22.8	34.3	36.5	4.8	1.6	43301	47748	43	64	1025	20.0	45.3	31.0	3.7	0.0	75083
64055	INDEPENDENCE	27674	14984	15.3	30.0	43.6	8.0	3.1	53416	55370	69	83	10861	7.1	17.6	63.8	11.1	0.4	110787
64056	INDEPENDENCE	21991	5863	17.8	24.2	48.2	7.3	2.4	56446	58732	73	87	4240	7.5	25.7	60.4	5.9	0.4	102858
64057	INDEPENDENCE	29909	5632	14.0	23.4	41.4	14.1	7.1	62974	61750	81	92	3632	0.7	12.0	56.6	28.8	2.0	137865
64058	INDEPENDENCE	23147	2266	11.0	24.4	52.4	10.0	2.1	61036	62204	79	91	1872	5.6	29.5	51.1	13.0	0.7	107239
64060	KEARNEY	31259	4360	6.3	15.3	46.2	23.6	8.5	79007	81076	92	97	3562	3.0	2.0	49.9	39.1	6.0	168566
64061	KINGSVILLE	23702	1150	15.3	28.1	44.2	9.1	3.3	54983	54529	71	85	1045	11.3	14.4	29.6	40.2	4.6	160190
64062	LAWSON	23437	2341	13.8	26.9	45.0	11.7	2.7	59919	61263	77	90	2001	6.2	13.2	47.2	31.0	2.3	137071
64063	LEES SUMMIT	30361	8128	12.7	21.1	44.8	14.1	7.3	67930	67202	86	95	5590	0.9	10.3	63.8	24.5	0.5	136114
64064	LEES SUMMIT	48361	5392	4.2	12.8	31.4	22.2	29.3	103913	105898	97	99	4802	1.7	0.9	22.6	58.6	16.3	232468
64067	LEXINGTON	21794	2065	27.0	29.6	34.4	6.7	2.2	43803	47069	45	66	1453	22.6	30.3	35.3	9.4	2.4	87233
64068	LIBERTY	30453	13300	11.3	22.5	42.1	16.2	7.8	66184	71603	84	94	9876	7.5	6.4	48.4	33.6	4.0	152345
64070	LONE JACK	26946	1125	11.8	21.6	48.7	13.5	4.4	65779	64202	84	94	987	6.5	8.6	32.9	44.2	7.8	179974
64071	MAYVIEW	20338	361	14.1	38.0	41.6	4.7	1.7	47900	50305	56	75	290	27.6	18.3	33.4	14.1	6.6	93333
64074	NAPOLEON	25698	268	15.3	25.4	47.0	9.0	3.4	61162	59621	79	91	222	20.3	21.2	32.4	22.5	3.6	109848
64075	OAK GROVE	24088	4050	15.5	25.0	47.4	9.0	3.2	59877	59670	77	90	3022	4.6	14.8	52.1	25.7	2.9	120165
64076	ODESSA	23604	3533	19.6	30.1	37.6	8.4	4.2	50291	52771	62	80	2696	14.8	17.7	43.1	21.9	2.6	115693
64077	ORRICK	21574	745	18.1	30.3	43.4	7.0	1.2	51167	53824	64	80	621	20.0	28.0	39.0	12.4	0.6	92404
64078	PECULIAR	25272	3262	11.7	21.2	51.4	10.7	5.0	64268	67005	83	93	2756	3.6	6.3	48.5	38.2	3.3	160938
64079	PLATTE CITY	29743	4232	11.2	19.0	42.2	19.9	7.8	71549	75410	88	95	3076	1.9	6.4	47.5	36.5	7.8	164744
64080	PLEASANT HILL	28345	4694	11.2	23.4	46.7	11.7	6.9	65395	69389	84	93	3719	5.8	10.8	40.7	37.8	4.9	155487
64081	LEES SUMMIT	35959	8830	12.9	16.3	37.6	16.3	17.0	77878	79366	91	97	6571	1.0	3.4	36.4	50.7	8.4	192011
64082	LEES SUMMIT	39106	3965	2.6	7.4	48.0	20.9	21.1	90027	90082	95	98	3703	0.3	0.5	23.0	66.0	10.3	220969
	MISSOURI	25286		22.8	27.7	35.3	9.1	5.2	49522	52035				12.8	19.4	39.1	24.2	4.6	122064
	UNITED STATES	27277		20.9	24.4	35.3	11.7	7.6	54719	56938				9.3	13.1	31.6	32.6	13.5	162279

ZIP CODE #	POST OFFICE NAME	FINANCIAL SERVICES: Auto Loan	Home Loan	Investments	Retirement Plans	THE HOME: Home Improvements: Home Repair	Lawn & Garden	Furnishings: Computers & Hardware-Personal	Major Appliances	TV, Radio, Sound Equipment	Furniture	ENTERTAINMENT: Dine out/Carry out	Sports Equipment	Fees & Tickets	Toys & Games	Travel	Cable TV	PERSONAL: Apparel & Services	Auto Repairs	Health Insurance	Pets & Supplies
63846	ESSEX	74	53	62	51	52	70	55	64	61	53	60	49	44	63	50	66	40	61	68	78
63848	GIDEON	69	53	57	53	52	67	61	63	64	54	62	50	51	65	55	68	42	64	70	78
63849	GOBLER	74	50	73	48	51	74	53	67	60	50	59	51	41	61	50	67	39	62	70	81
63851	HAYTI	54	38	44	38	37	50	44	47	51	44	50	36	37	51	39	55	34	49	53	59
63852	HOLCOMB	71	47	69	45	48	70	50	63	57	47	56	49	38	58	48	63	37	59	67	77
63855	HORNERSVILLE	69	50	67	48	51	70	53	65	59	49	57	49	42	59	51	64	38	60	69	77
63857	KENNETT	68	55	58	55	55	67	61	64	65	57	64	49	54	65	56	69	44	64	69	77
63862	LILBOURN	75	49	71	46	49	73	52	65	60	50	59	51	40	61	49	67	39	62	69	80
63863	MALDEN	66	48	63	47	49	67	51	61	57	48	56	46	42	57	49	63	37	58	66	73
63866	MARSTON	77	51	73	48	51	76	54	68	62	52	61	53	41	64	51	69	40	64	72	83
63867	MATTHEWS	68	49	62	48	50	67	51	61	57	49	55	47	41	58	48	62	37	57	64	74
63868	MOREHOUSE	66	47	54	46	47	62	49	57	54	48	53	44	39	57	45	59	36	54	60	69
63869	NEW MADRID	69	52	62	52	52	69	55	64	61	52	60	48	46	61	52	67	40	61	70	77
63870	PARMA	70	48	65	46	48	69	51	62	57	48	56	49	39	59	48	63	37	59	66	76
63873	PORTAGEVILLE	71	55	60	56	55	71	60	66	65	56	63	50	51	66	55	70	43	64	72	79
63876	SENATH	63	46	59	44	46	63	49	59	54	45	53	44	39	55	46	59	35	55	63	70
63877	STEELE	78	55	66	54	54	74	60	68	66	57	65	53	48	68	54	72	44	66	73	83
63879	WARDELL	67	44	64	41	44	65	47	59	54	45	53	46	35	55	44	60	35	55	62	72
63901	POPLAR BLUFF	75	63	65	63	63	74	67	71	71	64	70	53	60	71	63	75	47	70	76	85
63931	BRIAR	55	36	53	34	36	54	39	49	44	37	43	38	29	45	36	50	29	46	51	60
63932	BROSELEY	77	54	78	52	56	78	56	71	63	53	62	54	44	63	55	70	41	66	75	86
63933	CAMPBELL	70	52	67	50	53	71	56	66	61	51	59	50	45	61	53	66	40	62	71	79
63934	CLUBB	53	38	54	37	40	54	40	50	44	37	43	38	32	44	39	49	29	46	53	59
63935	DONIPHAN	65	46	64	45	47	66	49	61	55	45	53	46	39	55	47	60	35	56	65	72
63936	DUDLEY	70	51	59	50	51	67	53	62	59	51	57	47	43	61	48	64	39	58	65	75
63937	ELLSINORE	77	57	73	54	57	76	57	70	64	55	63	53	47	64	55	69	42	65	72	84
63939	FAIRDEALING	64	46	64	44	47	64	47	59	52	44	51	44	37	52	46	57	34	54	62	70
63940	FISK	82	55	81	52	55	82	58	74	67	55	65	57	44	67	55	74	43	69	77	90
63941	FREMONT	75	54	77	52	56	76	55	70	61	51	60	53	44	61	55	68	40	65	73	84
63942	GATEWOOD	73	52	75	51	54	74	54	68	60	50	58	51	43	59	53	66	39	63	71	81
63943	GRANDIN	67	46	62	44	46	65	48	59	55	46	53	46	37	56	45	60	36	55	62	72
63944	GREENVILLE	65	47	66	45	48	66	49	61	54	45	53	46	39	54	48	60	35	57	65	73
63945	HARVIELL	76	62	67	60	62	73	61	70	65	61	65	52	54	67	58	69	44	66	71	83
63950	LODI	64	46	66	44	48	65	47	60	52	44	51	45	38	52	47	57	34	55	62	71
63951	LOWNDES	63	45	65	44	47	64	46	59	52	43	51	44	37	51	46	57	33	54	61	70
63952	MILL SPRING	62	41	60	39	41	61	44	55	50	41	49	43	33	51	41	56	33	52	58	68
63953	NAYLOR	73	48	71	46	49	72	51	65	59	48	57	50	39	59	48	65	38	60	68	79
63954	NEELYVILLE	63	41	60	39	41	61	44	55	50	42	49	43	33	51	41	56	33	52	58	68
63955	OXLY	56	40	57	39	42	57	41	52	46	38	45	39	33	45	41	50	30	48	54	62
63956	PATTERSON	81	58	82	56	60	82	60	76	66	55	65	57	48	66	59	73	43	70	79	90
63957	PIEDMONT	61	42	60	41	44	62	46	57	52	42	50	43	36	52	44	57	33	53	62	68
63960	PUXICO	65	47	66	46	49	67	49	62	55	45	54	46	40	55	48	60	36	57	66	73
63961	QULIN	67	46	60	44	46	65	49	59	55	47	54	45	38	57	45	60	36	55	62	72
63963	SHOOK	71	53	74	51	55	73	54	67	59	51	58	50	44	58	54	65	38	62	71	80
63964	SILVA	55	40	56	39	41	57	42	53	47	38	46	39	34	46	41	52	30	49	56	62
63965	VAN BUREN	71	51	72	49	52	73	53	67	60	49	58	50	43	59	52	66	39	62	71	80
63966	WAPPAPELLO	66	62	80	57	69	75	59	70	63	64	61	46	58	58	65	67	41	67	78	80
63967	WILLIAMSVILLE	83	64	84	62	66	84	64	78	70	62	69	58	54	69	64	76	46	73	82	93
64001	ALMA	107	74	117	73	77	113	82	101	85	66	84	84	60	83	81	93	54	95	107	125
64011	BATES CITY	102	101	87	100	98	100	94	98	95	97	96	74	93	99	93	96	66	95	97	116
64012	BELTON	102	100	87	99	96	97	96	97	96	98	97	74	95	100	94	97	67	96	96	114
64014	BLUE SPRINGS	117	121	103	120	115	107	114	111	110	120	112	87	115	116	112	106	78	110	103	130
64015	BLUE SPRINGS	122	129	109	127	122	115	119	118	115	125	117	91	121	121	118	112	82	116	110	138
64016	BUCKNER	89	92	78	93	88	92	87	88	87	86	87	69	88	89	87	87	60	86	90	105
64017	CAMDEN	94	70	79	69	70	91	72	83	79	69	77	64	59	82	66	86	52	79	88	101
64018	CAMDEN POINT	102	112	98	116	110	113	101	106	100	101	101	83	107	103	106	101	70	102	106	125
64019	CENTERVIEW	94	88	81	88	87	95	84	91	86	82	86	68	79	89	82	90	59	86	92	107
64020	CONCORDIA	88	67	87	66	69	92	71	86	77	63	75	65	58	77	69	84	50	80	92	101
64021	CORDER	85	60	87	59	63	89	66	82	73	58	71	62	52	71	64	80	47	76	89	97
64022	DOVER	86	70	85	71	73	88	76	84	78	69	77	64	66	77	74	83	52	81	89	100
64024	EXCELSIOR SPRINGS	89	86	77	89	84	91	88	88	89	84	88	69	85	90	85	90	61	88	92	105
64029	GRAIN VALLEY	118	131	107	128	123	112	116	116	110	123	112	92	120	117	116	105	78	110	104	133
64030	GRANDVIEW	86	82	72	82	78	81	86	82	86	85	86	63	83	87	81	86	60	84	84	97
64034	GREENWOOD	137	154	131	150	147	131	135	136	128	145	130	107	141	135	137	122	91	129	121	155
64035	HARDIN	91	66	93	65	69	96	72	88	79	63	76	68	57	77	70	86	51	82	95	105
64036	HENRIETTA	91	65	75	63	65	86	68	79	75	66	74	61	54	78	62	82	50	75	83	96
64037	HIGGINSVILLE	91	74	81	74	75	91	80	86	84	74	82	65	70	84	75	89	56	85	93	103
64040	HOLDEN	81	73	69	75	72	84	75	79	77	69	76	61	69	79	72	81	52	77	84	94
64048	HOLT	118	127	118	131	126	131	116	124	115	114	115	95	120	117	121	117	80	117	123	144
64050	INDEPENDENCE	69	63	55	64	60	68	69	66	72	65	71	51	65	72	64	74	49	69	74	80
64052	INDEPENDENCE	71	66	61	66	64	73	70	69	73	65	71	53	67	72	67	76	49	71	77	83
64053	INDEPENDENCE	70	54	50	56	52	63	66	62	69	61	67	49	57	70	57	72	46	66	69	76
64054	INDEPENDENCE	75	68	65	68	66	79	71	74	75	66	73	56	67	75	68	79	50	74	82	88
64055	INDEPENDENCE	85	88	84	88	87	94	85	88	88	84	88	65	88	88	88	91	61	88	96	103
64056	INDEPENDENCE	90	85	71	86	80	83	88	84	87	87	88	66	84	90	83	87	61	86	85	100
64057	INDEPENDENCE	106	105	92	107	100	101	108	101	107	107	108	81	108	110	104	107	76	105	103	121
64058	INDEPENDENCE	99	103	85	100	97	92	94	95	92	99	93	72	94	96	92	90	64	92	89	111
64060	KEARNEY	132	145	122	142	137	123	131	129	124	139	126	102	135	131	131	118	89	124	116	148
64061	KINGSVILLE	92	93	86	96	92	100	87	94	88	83	87	73	87	90	90	90	60	89	96	110
64062	LAWSON	92	99	83	102	95	100	93	94	92	91	92	74	97	94	95	93	64	92	97	112
64063	LEES SUMMIT	113	113	97	113	108	106	112	108	110	113	110	85	111	114	108	108	77	108	106	127
64064	LEES SUMMIT	172	212	202	219	212	188	180	184	169	195	172	146	205	175	196	161	126	173	163	209
64067	LEXINGTON	88	69	84	69	70	91	72	86	78	65	76	64	61	78	70	85	51	80	91	101
64068	LIBERTY	115	122	110	121	119	116	116	116	113	117	114	90	118	116	116	112	80	114	113	134
64070	LONE JACK	101	114	98	117	110	111	101	105	100	102	100	82	108	102	107	100	70	101	104	124
64071	MAYVIEW	91	74	92	73	75	95	73	88	78	69	77	67	64	78	73	84	52	82	90	104
64074	NAPOLEON	105	96	92	98	97	109	95	104	97	88	96	79	88	99	93	102	65	98	107	122
64075	OAK GROVE	98	99	89	99	97	97	94	96	93	96	93	73	93	95	93	93	64	93	94	112
64076	ODESSA	96	89	81	88	87	93	87	91	90	88	89	67	83	92	84	93	61	89	93	107
64077	ORRICK	97	76	82	76	76	96	77	89	83	73	82	68	66	86	73	90	55	83	93	106
64078	PECULIAR	107	109	96	109	107	109	100	105	101	102	101	80	101	105	101	103	70	101	105	124
64079	PLATTE CITY	117	127	109	126	121	113	117	116	112	122	114	92	121	118	117	109	80	113	107	134
64080	PLEASANT HILL	113	120	107	119	115	113	109	113	106	112	107	88	111	111	110	105	75	107	108	130
64081	LEES SUMMIT	134	152	148	149	155	147	135	143	133	146	133	105	148	134	145	132	94	136	143	161
64082	LEES SUMMIT	156	194	173	196	189	168	163	166	153	174	156	132	184	160	176	146	112	157	147	190
	MISSOURI	94	86	87	87	85	93	89	91	91	87	90	70	84	92	86	93	62	90	94	108
	UNITED STATES	100	100	100	100	100	100	100	100	100	100	100	100	100	100	100	100	100	100	100	100

ZIP CODE			POPULATION			2000-2009 ANNUAL RATE		HOUSEHOLDS					FAMILIES		
#	POST OFFICE NAME	COUNTY FIPS CODE	2000	2009	2014	% Rate	State Centile	2000	2009	2014	% Annual Rate 2000-2009	2009 Average HH Size	2000	2009	% Annual Rate 2000-2009
64083	RAYMORE	037	12586	19006	22095	4.6	99	4565	6992	8164	4.7	2.69	3595	5418	4.5
64084	RAYVILLE	177	1576	1657	1642	0.5	58	578	615	612	0.7	2.69	471	489	0.4
64085	RICHMOND	177	8752	8741	8608	0.0	37	3479	3514	3473	0.1	2.43	2359	2282	-0.4
64086	LEES SUMMIT	095	19906	22127	23116	1.2	82	7226	8204	8629	1.4	2.69	5602	6105	0.9
64088	SIBLEY	095	1341	1438	1492	0.8	69	475	523	546	1.0	2.75	388	412	0.7
64089	SMITHVILLE	047	8243	10566	11821	2.7	96	3008	3904	4398	2.9	2.68	2337	2936	2.5
64093	WARRENSBURG	101	24330	26436	27316	0.9	72	8943	9764	10122	1.0	2.42	5269	5505	0.5
64096	WAVERLY	107	1133	1073	1050	-0.6	11	426	408	400	-0.5	2.47	297	275	-0.8
64097	WELLINGTON	107	1345	1401	1410	0.4	53	538	565	569	0.5	2.44	373	375	0.1
64098	WESTON	165	2928	3034	3136	0.4	53	1151	1217	1264	0.6	2.48	841	860	0.2
64101	KANSAS CITY	095	335	350	357	0.5	58	14	17	18	2.1	5.18	2	2	0.0
64105	KANSAS CITY	095	2417	2930	3160	2.1	93	1760	2250	2459	2.7	1.23	235	241	0.3
64106	KANSAS CITY	095	6573	7552	7961	1.5	87	2520	3153	3438	2.5	2.01	1042	1080	0.4
64108	KANSAS CITY	095	6712	7490	7676	1.2	82	2634	3104	3230	1.8	2.20	1343	1447	0.8
64109	KANSAS CITY	095	12215	11350	11107	-0.8	6	5148	4767	4672	-0.8	2.23	2358	2006	-1.7
64110	KANSAS CITY	095	17591	16712	16476	-0.6	11	7148	6939	6887	-0.3	2.24	3662	3272	-1.2
64111	KANSAS CITY	095	17734	16720	16432	-0.6	11	10301	9801	9667	-0.5	1.64	2665	2237	-1.9
64112	KANSAS CITY	095	8527	8485	8533	-0.1	32	5531	5551	5598	0.0	1.52	1334	1191	-1.2
64113	KANSAS CITY	095	11506	11334	11283	-0.2	27	4850	4888	4906	0.1	2.32	3216	3054	-0.6
64114	KANSAS CITY	095	23312	22974	22922	-0.2	27	11862	11996	12068	0.1	1.87	5683	5231	-0.9
64116	KANSAS CITY	047	16434	16815	17351	0.2	46	7797	8000	8292	0.3	2.10	4049	3810	-0.7
64117	KANSAS CITY	047	13571	14268	14962	0.5	58	5644	6001	6339	0.7	2.38	3662	3623	-0.1
64118	KANSAS CITY	047	38363	40288	42132	0.5	58	16465	17552	18517	0.7	2.29	10532	10406	-0.1
64119	KANSAS CITY	047	25639	27959	29599	0.9	72	10135	11119	11829	1.0	2.49	7159	7486	0.5
64120	KANSAS CITY	095	527	487	474	-0.8	6	234	221	217	-0.6	2.20	124	108	-1.5
64123	KANSAS CITY	095	10826	10716	10637	-0.1	32	3902	3769	3732	-0.4	2.78	2475	2235	-1.1
64124	KANSAS CITY	095	13080	13293	13328	0.2	46	4635	4610	4615	-0.1	2.85	2870	2660	-0.8
64125	KANSAS CITY	095	2269	2176	2145	-0.5	14	806	766	755	-0.5	2.82	524	468	-1.2
64126	KANSAS CITY	095	6769	6501	6422	-0.4	18	2403	2309	2283	-0.4	2.81	1579	1423	-1.1
64127	KANSAS CITY	095	21052	20081	19856	-0.5	14	7818	7532	7483	-0.4	2.61	4782	4283	-1.2
64128	KANSAS CITY	095	14865	13723	13408	-0.9	4	5742	5423	5336	-0.6	2.52	3609	3184	-1.3
64129	KANSAS CITY	095	10215	9983	9934	-0.2	27	4259	4255	4263	0.0	2.31	2625	2445	-0.8
64130	KANSAS CITY	095	26528	25383	25078	-0.5	14	10150	9966	9926	-0.2	2.51	6689	6164	-0.9
64131	KANSAS CITY	095	23503	22596	22391	-0.4	18	10275	10065	10040	-0.2	2.18	5781	5243	-1.1
64132	KANSAS CITY	095	16099	15377	15176	-0.5	14	6375	6196	6150	-0.3	2.47	4032	3673	-1.0
64133	KANSAS CITY	095	32507	32475	32625	0.0	37	13765	14054	14206	0.2	2.28	8774	8409	-0.5
64134	KANSAS CITY	095	22932	22604	22583	-0.2	27	8478	8536	8584	0.1	2.63	6067	5789	-0.5
64136	KANSAS CITY	095	1176	2303	2712	7.5	99	442	927	1113	8.3	2.29	317	632	7.7
64137	KANSAS CITY	095	10589	11050	11251	0.5	58	4376	4681	4803	0.7	2.30	2699	2682	-0.1
64138	KANSAS CITY	095	25974	25942	26003	0.0	37	10712	10933	11036	0.2	2.34	7035	6753	-0.4
64139	KANSAS CITY	095	1057	1523	1765	4.0	98	277	424	497	4.7	3.35	197	287	4.2
64145	KANSAS CITY	095	4613	5041	5194	1.0	76	1934	2182	2269	1.3	2.26	1308	1385	0.6
64146	KANSAS CITY	095	1328	1418	1489	0.7	66	655	722	769	1.1	1.81	382	391	0.3
64147	KANSAS CITY	095	743	750	757	0.1	42	266	270	273	0.2	2.78	232	232	0.0
64149	KANSAS CITY	095	377	375	440	-0.1	32	136	136	161	0.0	2.76	119	117	-0.2
64150	RIVERSIDE	165	3094	3173	3259	0.3	50	1270	1323	1369	0.4	2.24	744	738	-0.1
64151	KANSAS CITY	165	22295	24303	25706	0.9	72	9506	10587	11273	1.2	2.29	6212	6611	0.7
64152	KANSAS CITY	165	23397	25866	27472	1.1	79	8621	9661	10309	1.2	2.65	6410	7021	1.0
64153	KANSAS CITY	165	3598	4483	4955	2.4	95	1456	1809	2004	2.4	2.48	960	1139	1.9
64154	KANSAS CITY	165	4628	7575	8941	5.5	99	2056	3459	4119	5.8	2.14	1147	1866	5.4
64155	KANSAS CITY	047	16818	21805	24623	2.8	96	6093	7933	9030	2.9	2.73	4715	5871	2.4
64156	KANSAS CITY	047	1111	2861	3534	10.8	100	424	1197	1495	11.9	2.38	306	823	11.3
64157	KANSAS CITY	047	3181	12443	15643	15.9	100	1037	4056	5119	15.9	3.07	889	3349	15.4
64158	KANSAS CITY	047	2405	4658	5622	7.4	99	786	1501	1810	7.2	3.10	657	1210	6.8
64161	KANSAS CITY	047	427	393	382	-0.9	4	174	163	160	-0.7	2.41	121	106	-1.4
64163	KANSAS CITY	165	559	607	639	0.9	72	294	327	348	1.2	1.86	142	148	0.4
64164	KANSAS CITY	165	400	438	464	1.0	76	152	171	183	1.3	2.56	95	103	0.9
64165	KANSAS CITY	047	56	68	75	2.1	93	24	30	33	2.4	2.27	21	25	1.9
64166	KANSAS CITY	047	228	277	305	2.1	93	81	100	111	2.3	2.77	71	86	2.1
64167	KANSAS CITY	047	396	374	444	-0.6	11	128	127	152	-0.1	2.94	111	107	-0.4
64401	AGENCY	021	1473	1541	1574	0.5	58	536	568	582	0.6	2.71	435	450	0.4
64402	ALBANY	075	2568	2345	2237	-1.0	3	1104	1008	960	-1.0	2.24	702	613	-1.5
64421	AMAZONIA	003	1079	1233	1297	1.5	87	428	496	523	1.6	2.49	309	346	1.2
64422	AMITY	063	511	491	482	-0.4	18	196	190	186	-0.3	2.58	150	141	-0.7
64423	BARNARD	147	796	817	825	0.3	50	314	330	336	0.5	2.29	237	241	0.2
64424	BETHANY	081	4140	4169	4192	0.1	42	1733	1717	1719	-0.1	2.32	1118	1061	-0.6
64426	BLYTHEDALE	081	445	466	474	0.5	58	184	192	194	0.5	2.43	126	125	-0.1
64427	BOLCKOW	003	636	624	620	-0.2	27	235	233	232	-0.1	2.68	180	173	-0.4
64428	BURLINGTON JUNCTION	147	894	885	881	-0.1	32	367	369	370	0.1	2.39	255	246	-0.4
64429	CAMERON	063	10359	11931	12241	1.5	87	3019	3348	3477	1.1	2.47	2039	2179	0.7
64430	CLARKSDALE	063	736	777	781	0.6	63	294	313	315	0.7	2.48	225	233	0.4
64431	CLEARMONT	147	443	436	436	-0.2	27	205	207	208	0.1	2.11	141	136	-0.4
64432	CLYDE	147	211	209	208	-0.1	32	61	62	62	0.2	3.02	46	45	-0.2
64433	CONCEPTION	147	274	271	270	-0.1	32	48	49	49	0.2	4.96	36	35	-0.3
64434	CONCEPTION JUNCTION	147	303	300	299	-0.1	32	113	114	115	0.1	2.35	85	83	-0.3
64436	COSBY	003	832	833	829	0.0	37	322	326	326	0.1	2.54	250	245	-0.2
64437	CRAIG	087	961	887	858	-0.9	4	401	375	364	-0.7	2.37	281	252	-1.2
64438	DARLINGTON	075	235	215	205	-1.0	3	70	64	61	-1.0	3.23	53	47	-1.3
64439	DEARBORN	165	1909	2092	2193	1.0	76	752	843	890	1.2	2.48	547	591	0.8
64440	DE KALB	021	659	666	672	0.1	42	244	249	251	0.2	2.66	187	185	-0.1
64441	DENVER	227	195	176	167	-1.1	2	87	78	74	-1.2	2.24	65	57	-1.4
64442	EAGLEVILLE	081	748	771	779	0.3	50	318	325	328	0.2	2.37	226	223	-0.1
64443	EASTON	021	1429	1605	1681	1.3	83	553	629	661	1.4	2.55	422	467	1.1
64444	EDGERTON	165	1238	1360	1442	1.0	76	481	541	578	1.3	2.51	382	418	1.0
64445	ELMO	147	450	438	433	-0.3	21	183	180	179	-0.2	2.42	124	117	-0.6
64446	FAIRFAX	005	1177	1144	1124	-0.3	21	523	517	512	-0.1	2.21	352	334	-0.6
64448	FAUCETT	021	868	939	968	0.9	72	332	364	377	1.0	2.58	256	271	0.6
64449	FILLMORE	003	460	481	491	0.5	58	190	201	206	0.6	2.39	135	138	0.2
64451	FOREST CITY	087	485	447	432	-0.9	4	196	183	177	-0.7	2.44	135	121	-1.2
64453	GENTRY	075	241	242	238	0.0	37	88	87	86	-0.1	2.76	67	65	-0.3
64454	GOWER	049	2387	2497	2548	0.5	58	870	927	951	0.7	2.61	654	676	0.4
64455	GRAHAM	147	492	483	482	-0.2	27	207	209	210	0.1	2.31	151	146	-0.4
64456	GRANT CITY	227	1370	1243	1179	-1.0	3	577	518	489	-1.2	2.31	370	318	-1.6
64457	GUILFORD	147	372	368	366	-0.1	32	130	132	132	0.2	2.51	98	95	-0.3
64458	HATFIELD	081	207	207	207	0.0	37	72	71	71	-0.2	2.92	59	57	-0.4
	MISSOURI					0.7					0.8	2.45			0.4
	UNITED STATES					1.0					1.1	2.59			0.9

ZIP CODE #	POST OFFICE NAME	RACE (%) White 2000	White 2009	Black 2000	Black 2009	Asian/Pacific 2000	Asian/Pacific 2009	% Hispanic Origin 2000	% Hispanic Origin 2009	2009 AGE DISTRIBUTION (%) 0-4	5-9	10-14	15-19	20-24	25-44	45-64	65-84	85+	18+	MEDIAN AGE 2009	% 2009 Males	% 2009 Females
64083	RAYMORE	95.3	94.3	1.7	2.0	0.7	1.1	1.8	2.6	7.5	7.2	7.2	6.7	5.2	26.2	25.1	11.4	3.6	73.8	38.0	48.1	51.9
64084	RAYVILLE	97.3	96.7	0.4	0.4	0.2	0.3	0.8	1.1	5.9	6.3	6.8	6.6	4.5	22.4	33.3	13.3	1.0	76.9	43.2	50.4	49.6
64085	RICHMOND	94.9	93.9	3.0	3.5	0.1	0.2	1.0	1.4	7.0	6.6	6.6	6.7	6.6	24.6	25.9	13.1	2.9	75.7	38.4	48.8	51.2
64086	LEES SUMMIT	93.8	90.6	2.7	4.4	0.9	1.5	2.3	3.7	7.9	7.5	7.8	7.2	5.7	31.0	26.6	5.7	0.6	72.2	34.8	49.7	50.3
64088	SIBLEY	96.7	95.1	0.4	0.8	0.1	0.4	1.7	3.0	6.1	6.3	7.0	7.3	5.3	24.1	30.0	12.6	1.3	76.2	40.3	50.9	49.1
64089	SMITHVILLE	96.8	95.8	0.2	0.3	0.5	0.9	1.7	2.4	7.9	7.6	7.3	6.4	5.2	28.3	26.8	9.2	1.3	73.1	36.6	48.9	51.1
64093	WARRENSBURG	89.2	86.5	5.1	5.9	2.2	3.4	2.2	3.1	5.8	5.2	5.1	11.1	19.1	24.6	19.3	8.0	1.7	80.5	27.2	49.4	50.6
64096	WAVERLY	97.5	97.0	0.6	0.7	0.2	0.3	1.2	1.8	5.3	5.3	6.2	9.3	4.7	21.3	28.5	16.5	2.8	75.7	43.1	49.8	50.2
64097	WELLINGTON	97.8	97.3	0.7	0.9	0.1	0.2	1.3	1.7	6.3	6.5	6.9	6.4	4.3	24.5	29.2	13.9	2.1	75.9	41.6	51.0	49.0
64098	WESTON	97.7	97.2	0.1	0.1	0.2	0.3	0.9	1.2	5.2	5.6	6.2	7.1	5.0	23.1	33.5	12.6	1.8	78.4	43.4	49.1	50.9
64101	KANSAS CITY	64.0	51.4	33.6	45.7	0.6	0.9	0.9	1.4	0.6	0.6	0.3	0.3	14.0	69.7	14.0	0.6	0.0	98.6	34.6	81.4	18.6
64105	KANSAS CITY	71.6	61.0	17.7	25.5	1.9	2.7	8.5	11.2	2.2	0.9	0.9	1.6	13.4	47.3	20.2	11.1	2.5	95.6	34.8	56.7	43.3
64106	KANSAS CITY	33.7	31.0	48.0	47.6	9.7	12.4	7.5	9.1	7.7	6.3	5.2	6.2	10.1	35.3	19.9	7.6	1.7	77.7	32.1	56.2	43.8
64108	KANSAS CITY	44.0	36.9	32.0	38.0	1.2	1.4	39.4	39.1	7.4	6.8	6.4	7.1	8.9	31.6	22.8	7.7	1.3	75.0	32.3	52.8	47.2
64109	KANSAS CITY	24.5	19.5	70.2	74.7	0.6	0.8	4.7	5.9	6.8	5.9	5.7	7.6	9.0	28.1	26.3	9.0	1.6	77.0	36.1	50.1	49.9
64110	KANSAS CITY	39.6	33.5	54.4	59.4	1.6	2.3	3.4	4.3	6.5	6.3	6.0	9.6	10.9	27.8	24.6	7.5	0.9	77.4	32.0	46.9	53.1
64111	KANSAS CITY	73.2	64.9	14.0	18.0	1.7	2.5	15.8	21.7	3.9	3.2	2.7	3.8	11.2	41.0	23.0	8.7	2.4	88.5	35.0	53.7	46.3
64112	KANSAS CITY	86.8	81.6	3.9	5.8	5.9	8.3	3.7	5.5	2.5	2.3	2.4	3.9	12.9	37.4	24.2	11.2	3.1	91.5	36.3	50.5	49.5
64113	KANSAS CITY	95.8	93.5	1.6	2.6	0.9	1.6	1.8	2.9	6.6	7.7	8.2	5.6	2.9	23.3	33.1	10.5	2.1	73.9	42.9	49.0	51.0
64114	KANSAS CITY	88.1	82.4	6.6	9.9	2.1	3.5	3.5	5.4	4.8	4.7	4.7	4.1	4.6	27.8	27.4	16.1	5.9	83.4	44.6	46.2	53.8
64116	KANSAS CITY	86.4	82.4	3.9	4.5	4.2	6.4	6.0	7.9	6.2	5.8	5.5	5.5	7.5	29.9	26.3	11.2	2.0	79.2	37.6	48.8	51.2
64117	KANSAS CITY	88.2	84.5	4.9	6.0	2.1	3.5	5.3	7.4	7.9	6.8	6.5	6.6	7.2	28.7	24.7	10.2	1.4	74.8	35.3	47.4	52.6
64118	KANSAS CITY	90.7	88.1	3.3	3.8	1.8	2.8	4.4	6.0	6.7	6.2	6.0	5.9	6.7	29.9	25.7	11.3	1.6	77.6	37.0	49.2	50.8
64119	KANSAS CITY	93.6	91.5	1.9	2.3	1.3	2.3	3.8	5.3	6.6	6.5	6.5	6.2	5.7	27.7	27.4	11.7	1.8	76.5	38.5	48.1	51.9
64120	KANSAS CITY	80.1	72.7	6.1	8.2	3.8	5.7	11.8	16.8	8.2	7.8	6.2	5.1	6.4	26.9	25.1	11.9	2.5	74.7	36.5	52.4	47.6
64123	KANSAS CITY	65.9	56.3	8.0	10.1	5.5	7.4	30.3	39.1	8.2	7.7	7.0	7.1	7.2	28.0	23.7	9.3	1.8	72.9	34.1	50.7	49.3
64124	KANSAS CITY	49.0	39.7	18.4	21.7	7.2	9.1	30.0	36.3	9.3	8.5	7.3	7.2	7.8	29.5	22.0	7.3	1.1	70.7	31.1	51.4	48.6
64125	KANSAS CITY	78.0	70.5	6.1	8.2	1.9	2.7	19.6	26.7	9.5	8.6	7.6	7.1	7.4	28.4	22.7	7.7	1.0	70.0	31.5	51.2	48.8
64126	KANSAS CITY	53.5	45.3	25.5	28.1	3.9	5.1	22.1	28.4	9.8	10.1	8.7	7.9	7.0	26.7	20.7	7.9	1.2	66.5	29.3	48.6	51.4
64127	KANSAS CITY	24.8	18.8	60.9	65.1	1.4	1.7	15.6	17.9	8.7	8.6	8.0	8.1	7.6	24.9	22.8	9.4	1.8	69.9	31.9	46.9	53.1
64128	KANSAS CITY	6.0	4.5	90.1	91.6	0.3	0.4	2.9	3.3	7.7	7.7	7.3	8.1	7.5	23.0	24.1	12.2	2.5	72.4	35.6	45.6	54.4
64129	KANSAS CITY	59.9	49.9	34.5	43.3	0.6	0.8	4.5	6.0	7.2	6.9	6.3	6.7	7.7	30.2	24.8	9.2	1.2	75.6	34.4	49.4	50.6
64130	KANSAS CITY	3.4	2.4	94.1	95.4	0.2	0.2	1.2	1.3	7.2	7.4	7.4	8.5	7.0	23.3	24.0	13.3	1.8	72.7	36.0	44.9	55.1
64131	KANSAS CITY	53.0	46.5	41.2	46.6	1.8	2.4	3.1	4.1	6.8	6.4	5.9	5.9	7.5	28.0	25.7	11.1	2.7	77.4	37.5	46.0	54.0
64132	KANSAS CITY	17.1	12.5	79.1	83.7	0.5	0.6	1.7	2.0	8.7	8.3	7.8	8.2	8.4	26.8	22.1	8.6	0.9	70.1	30.0	44.9	55.1
64133	KANSAS CITY	82.2	75.0	13.4	19.1	1.0	1.6	2.7	4.0	6.0	5.7	5.9	5.8	5.9	24.8	27.6	15.1	3.2	78.9	41.9	47.6	52.4
64134	KANSAS CITY	47.7	37.0	46.7	56.7	0.9	1.2	3.0	3.8	7.6	7.3	7.1	7.8	7.5	27.7	24.4	9.6	1.0	73.2	33.8	48.1	51.9
64136	KANSAS CITY	92.2	87.9	4.3	6.7	0.6	1.0	2.9	4.6	6.3	6.6	6.8	6.6	4.6	24.6	28.4	12.5	3.5	75.8	41.4	47.9	52.1
64137	KANSAS CITY	67.9	57.4	27.1	36.6	1.3	1.8	3.4	4.6	6.6	6.1	6.1	6.2	7.5	30.4	23.9	11.4	1.7	77.7	35.5	48.4	51.6
64138	KANSAS CITY	68.2	59.1	27.0	35.0	1.2	1.7	2.9	3.9	6.2	5.8	5.8	6.6	6.7	26.2	27.1	13.3	2.2	78.2	39.5	47.0	53.0
64139	KANSAS CITY	87.3	83.3	8.7	11.2	0.8	1.1	2.8	4.4	6.2	6.5	6.6	6.4	4.7	25.6	28.4	12.4	3.2	76.4	41.1	48.3	51.7
64145	KANSAS CITY	87.9	82.5	8.2	12.0	1.5	2.4	3.1	5.0	4.7	4.6	5.2	5.7	4.6	18.0	31.7	21.5	3.9	81.8	50.5	47.3	52.7
64146	KANSAS CITY	84.3	77.7	11.5	16.4	1.1	1.8	3.8	5.6	5.7	5.1	5.6	6.6	6.1	23.7	26.1	15.9	5.1	79.6	42.5	46.9	53.1
64147	KANSAS CITY	30.4	22.8	65.8	73.2	0.4	0.5	3.0	3.6	27.6	15.1	7.5	4.9	16.0	18.7	7.1	2.9	0.3	47.2	14.9	42.5	57.5
64149	KANSAS CITY	93.9	90.7	2.4	4.3	0.8	1.6	2.1	3.2	6.9	7.5	8.5	8.0	4.3	24.5	29.9	9.6	0.8	72.0	38.3	48.5	51.5
64150	RIVERSIDE	84.5	80.9	6.0	6.8	2.5	3.8	7.1	9.7	7.6	6.5	5.6	5.4	8.8	28.8	24.1	10.4	2.8	77.3	35.3	50.3	49.7
64151	KANSAS CITY	90.8	88.3	4.2	4.9	1.9	3.0	3.0	4.1	6.6	6.1	5.8	5.8	6.5	29.7	28.5	9.7	1.3	78.0	37.3	49.1	50.9
64152	KANSAS CITY	91.5	89.5	3.4	3.8	2.0	3.0	3.3	4.4	6.8	6.9	7.2	7.2	5.9	27.0	29.2	8.9	0.8	74.8	37.2	49.4	50.6
64153	KANSAS CITY	90.0	87.1	3.1	3.5	2.3	3.7	3.9	5.3	7.8	7.3	7.0	6.3	6.9	36.6	23.2	4.4	0.4	74.0	33.3	49.4	50.6
64154	KANSAS CITY	86.0	84.8	7.4	7.3	2.4	3.2	3.1	4.0	6.5	5.5	5.3	4.8	6.3	31.1	23.7	12.9	3.9	79.9	38.1	47.0	53.0
64155	KANSAS CITY	93.3	91.4	2.5	2.8	1.4	2.1	3.9	5.4	8.2	7.9	7.6	6.5	4.8	32.1	25.3	6.5	0.9	72.1	34.9	48.9	51.1
64156	KANSAS CITY	94.8	92.2	1.4	2.3	0.5	1.4	2.8	4.2	8.2	7.7	7.0	6.2	6.2	31.6	24.9	7.5	0.7	73.2	33.6	49.7	50.3
64157	KANSAS CITY	95.5	94.0	1.8	2.3	0.5	0.8	2.5	3.6	10.1	9.1	8.3	7.0	5.4	33.1	22.0	4.8	0.3	68.2	31.5	49.2	50.8
64158	KANSAS CITY	91.1	88.3	4.3	5.0	1.9	3.1	3.9	5.4	11.9	11.2	9.8	6.6	4.4	35.7	18.7	1.7	0.1	62.9	30.5	48.1	51.9
64161	KANSAS CITY	96.3	95.7	0.7	0.8	0.2	0.3	0.7	0.8	4.8	5.1	6.1	7.6	6.4	29.8	29.8	9.4	1.0	79.6	38.2	55.0	45.0
64163	KANSAS CITY	90.3	88.1	2.9	3.3	0.7	1.3	3.2	4.4	6.6	6.4	6.4	7.2	6.1	29.5	28.8	8.2	0.7	76.1	37.7	54.0	46.0
64164	KANSAS CITY	91.5	90.0	2.0	2.3	0.7	1.1	3.0	3.9	6.2	6.4	6.6	7.3	5.7	27.6	30.6	8.9	0.7	76.3	38.8	53.0	47.0
64165	KANSAS CITY	98.2	97.1	0.0	0.0	0.0	0.0	1.8	1.5	5.9	7.4	7.4	5.9	5.9	26.5	30.9	10.3	0.0	75.0	40.0	51.5	48.5
64166	KANSAS CITY	97.4	97.1	0.0	0.4	0.4	0.4	1.3	1.8	5.8	6.1	7.2	6.9	4.3	24.5	35.4	9.0	0.7	76.5	41.9	50.9	49.1
64167	KANSAS CITY	96.5	95.5	1.5	1.9	0.5	0.8	2.3	3.2	8.8	8.3	7.8	7.0	5.3	32.4	24.6	5.3	0.5	70.6	33.5	50.0	50.0
64401	AGENCY	98.6	98.2	0.1	0.2	0.3	0.5	1.1	1.5	5.7	6.2	6.6	6.4	5.2	24.5	32.2	12.1	1.2	77.6	41.8	51.5	48.5
64402	ALBANY	98.9	98.7	0.1	0.1	0.2	0.3	0.5	0.7	6.0	6.1	6.2	5.9	5.1	21.6	26.2	18.1	4.9	77.7	44.2	48.6	51.4
64421	AMAZONIA	98.8	98.5	0.3	0.3	0.1	0.2	1.2	1.6	5.9	6.4	6.8	6.4	4.5	23.5	33.8	11.2	1.5	77.0	42.6	52.1	47.9
64422	AMITY	98.4	98.2	0.0	0.0	0.2	0.2	0.6	0.8	6.3	7.1	7.5	7.5	3.9	20.6	30.1	15.3	1.6	74.5	42.7	52.7	47.3
64423	BARNARD	98.0	97.3	0.1	0.1	0.8	1.1	0.9	1.1	6.2	6.6	6.9	6.9	5.3	26.4	26.6	13.1	2.1	75.9	39.3	53.2	46.8
64424	BETHANY	98.8	98.6	0.2	0.2	0.1	0.3	0.8	1.1	6.5	6.7	6.5	5.4	4.4	21.9	25.3	17.5	5.8	77.0	43.7	47.6	52.4
64426	BLYTHEDALE	98.0	97.9	0.2	0.2	0.7	0.9	0.4	0.9	6.9	7.3	7.9	6.7	3.6	22.3	26.8	16.1	2.4	73.4	41.9	53.4	46.6
64427	BOLCKOW	98.6	98.6	0.2	0.2	0.2	0.2	0.8	0.8	7.1	7.2	7.1	6.9	4.6	25.6	29.2	11.2	1.1	74.2	38.3	50.5	49.5
64428	BURLINGTON JUNCTION	99.0	99.0	0.1	0.1	0.1	0.1	0.3	0.5	6.1	6.1	6.2	6.8	5.9	24.9	27.7	13.8	2.6	77.4	40.0	49.4	50.6
64429	CAMERON	87.4	83.7	10.2	13.0	0.3	0.7	1.3	1.7	5.3	4.9	4.8	7.3	8.6	33.5	22.1	10.9	2.6	81.9	36.5	59.1	40.9
64430	CLARKSDALE	98.6	98.1	0.0	0.0	0.1	0.3	0.8	1.2	5.4	6.2	6.6	6.3	5.1	22.4	32.3	13.9	1.8	78.0	43.5	50.6	49.4
64431	CLEARMONT	98.9	98.9	0.0	0.0	0.2	0.2	0.5	0.5	6.4	6.0	5.7	5.5	5.7	20.9	28.0	18.8	3.0	78.2	44.8	48.4	51.6
64432	CLYDE	97.6	97.1	0.0	0.0	0.9	1.4	0.9	1.4	6.2	6.2	6.7	7.2	5.7	27.8	24.9	12.9	2.4	76.6	37.9	53.6	46.4
64433	CONCEPTION	97.8	97.0	0.0	0.0	1.1	1.5	1.1	1.5	6.3	6.3	6.6	7.4	5.9	27.3	25.1	13.3	1.8	75.6	37.9	53.5	46.5
64434	CONCEPTION JUNCTION	97.4	96.7	0.3	0.3	1.0	1.3	1.0	1.3	6.3	6.3	6.7	7.3	5.7	27.3	25.0	13.0	2.3	76.7	38.0	53.0	47.0
64436	COSBY	98.8	98.4	0.1	0.1	0.4	0.6	1.1	1.6	4.9	6.1	8.4	6.6	4.6	25.3	27.9	14.5	1.7	75.6	40.8	51.1	48.9
64437	CRAIG	98.0	97.6	0.1	0.1	0.1	0.1	0.5	0.7	4.7	5.1	5.7	6.7	4.6	21.1	31.9	17.6	2.6	80.4	46.3	51.5	48.5
64438	DARLINGTON	97.9	97.7	0.4	0.5	0.9	0.9	1.7	2.3	6.0	6.0	6.5	7.0	4.7	22.3	27.9	15.8	3.7	76.3	42.9	53.0	47.0
64439	DEARBORN	97.7	97.1	0.2	0.3	0.3	0.5	1.5	2.1	5.6	6.6	7.0	6.5	4.5	24.9	29.7	13.5	1.7	76.7	41.2	50.9	49.1
64440	DE KALB	98.6	98.0	0.0	0.0	0.0	0.3	0.3	0.6	7.4	7.7	7.8	6.2	4.4	26.3	26.6	12.5	1.4	73.1	38.4	50.0	50.0
64441	DENVER	99.0	98.9	0.5	0.6	0.0	0.0	0.5	0.6	3.4	4.5	5.1	7.4	4.0	19.9	34.7	18.2	2.8	81.8	47.8	52.3	47.7
64442	EAGLEVILLE	97.9	97.1	0.1	0.1	0.4	0.6	1.1	1.4	6.7	7.3	7.8	6.4	3.9	22.0	27.1	16.5	2.3	74.2	42.1	52.7	47.3
64443	EASTON	97.2	96.3	0.1	0.2	0.5	0.7	1.5	2.1	5.4	5.8	6.4	6.4	4.9	22.2	31.9	15.1	1.9	78.5	44.1	49.2	50.8
64444	EDGERTON	97.3	96.3	0.0	0.0	0.2	0.3	1.8	2.6	5.3	5.9	6.7	7.3	4.5	23.8	32.9	12.0	1.6	77.6	42.8	51.0	49.0
64445	ELMO	99.6	99.5	0.0	0.0	0.0	0.0	0.2	0.5	6.4	6.2	6.2	7.1	6.4	24.4	26.3	14.4	2.7	76.9	39.0	49.3	50.7
64446	FAIRFAX	99.0	98.9	0.3	0.3	0.0	0.0	0.3	0.3	4.5	5.0	5.3	6.5	4.9	20.6	32.9	16.6	3.7	81.1	46.9	47.4	52.6
64448	FAUCETT	97.8	97.0	0.3	0.4	0.2	0.4	1.6	2.2	4.5	6.4	7.6	7.6	5.3	25.5	30.5	11.7	1.1	76.8	40.3	51.1	48.9
64449	FILLMORE	98.0	97.7	0.2	0.2	0.2	0.4	0.9	1.2	7.7	7.7	7.7	6.9	5.2	25.6	27.2	10.8	1.2	72.8	37.2	51.4	48.6
64451	FOREST CITY	97.9	97.3	0.2	0.4	0.0	0.0	0.2	0.2	5.4	6.0	6.7	6.9	4.0	23.3	30.4	14.5	2.7	77.6	43.3	53.0	47.0
64453	GENTRY	98.3	97.1	0.0	0.0	0.0	0.8	0.4	0.4	7.4	7.4	7.4	8.7	5.4	21.9	26.0	13.6	2.1	72.3	38.9	52.9	47.1
64454	GOWER	99.1	98.9	0.2	0.2	0.1	0.1	0.6	0.9	6.1	6.2	6.4	6.5	5.3	25.7	28.4	12.0	3.4	76.9	40.6	47.9	52.1
64455	GRAHAM	99.0	98.8	0.2	0.2	0.0	0.0	0.0	0.0	5.2	5.6	6.0	5.8	3.9	22.8	29.0	19.3	2.5	79.5	45.5	52.6	47.4
64456	GRANT CITY	99.1	99.0	0.2	0.2	0.1	0.1	0.2	0.2	5.6	5.7	5.8	6.0	4.7	21.4	27.8	17.4	5.6	79.1	45.5	47.5	52.5
64457	GUILFORD	97.6	96.7	0.3	0.3	0.8	1.4	1.1	1.1	6.3	6.3	6.5	7.1	6.0	26.9	25.5	13.3	2.2	76.6	38.8	52.7	47.3
64458	HATFIELD	95.7	94.7	0.0	0.0	0.0	0.0	2.9	3.4	6.3	7.2	7.2	6.3	3.4	21.3	27.5	18.8	1.9	74.4	43.7	49.8	50.2
	MISSOURI	84.9	83.3	11.2	11.7	1.2	1.7	2.1	2.8	6.6	6.6	6.6	7.0	6.7	26.1	26.5	11.7	2.1	76.1	37.7	48.8	51.2
	UNITED STATES	75.1	72.0	12.3	12.7	3.8	4.6	12.5	15.7	6.8	6.7	6.6	7.1	6.9	27.0	26.0	10.9	1.9	75.7	36.9	49.2	50.8

ZIP CODE #	POST OFFICE NAME	2009 Per Capita Income	2009 HH Income Base	2009 Household Income Distribution (%) Less than $25,000	$25,000 to $49,999	$50,000 to $99,999	$100,000 to $149,999	$150,000 or More	Median Household Income 2009	2014	2009 National Centile	2009 State Centile	2009 Home Value Base	2009 Home Value Distribution (%) Less than $50,000	$50,000 to $89,999	$90,000 to $174,999	$175,000 to $399,999	$400,000 or More	2009 Median Home Value
64083	RAYMORE	30904	6992	7.6	18.8	46.6	19.0	8.0	77259	79959	91	97	5780	2.3	4.5	49.0	42.3	1.9	168058
64084	RAYVILLE	22375	615	15.9	28.9	43.1	9.4	2.6	54279	57438	70	84	544	14.2	13.1	42.8	28.5	1.5	124725
64085	RICHMOND	23411	3514	24.3	29.9	33.2	8.9	3.8	45942	50458	51	71	2411	12.5	26.7	43.3	14.8	2.7	103194
64086	LEES SUMMIT	33421	8204	6.8	15.5	49.4	17.9	10.5	78498	78298	91	97	6393	1.0	2.7	59.6	32.2	4.5	159044
64088	SIBLEY	22329	523	12.8	29.6	48.4	7.6	1.5	56237	57301	73	87	439	8.4	23.0	46.5	19.6	2.5	110901
64089	SMITHVILLE	32559	3904	9.3	17.2	43.7	20.8	8.9	76197	78929	90	96	3203	2.4	5.9	43.6	44.0	4.1	171579
64093	WARRENSBURG	21433	9764	30.8	24.6	33.8	7.5	3.3	43704	47514	44	65	5089	10.4	15.7	45.1	25.5	3.3	133513
64096	WAVERLY	20237	408	28.4	28.4	35.8	4.4	2.9	44073	47258	46	67	302	36.4	27.8	28.8	5.3	1.7	66800
64097	WELLINGTON	22081	565	25.7	28.5	37.9	6.0	1.9	46425	48398	53	73	445	14.8	37.3	33.7	12.6	1.6	88100
64098	WESTON	26286	1217	18.2	20.4	46.9	11.6	3.0	58937	59172	76	89	877	4.8	19.5	42.9	27.7	5.1	139302
64101	KANSAS CITY	12612	17	5.9	23.5	70.6	0.0	0.0	54747	54529	71	85	0	0.0	0.0	0.0	0.0	0.0	0
64105	KANSAS CITY	38954	2250	30.8	32.4	29.6	4.4	2.9	41149	43407	36	58	201	4.0	14.4	58.7	21.4	1.5	119363
64106	KANSAS CITY	18638	3153	42.7	30.8	21.5	3.7	1.3	30928	32716	10	14	440	23.4	20.0	41.4	13.2	2.0	97250
64108	KANSAS CITY	20875	3104	35.1	31.8	25.8	4.1	3.2	33809	36032	15	25	1134	35.5	24.3	20.1	18.3	1.9	70308
64109	KANSAS CITY	17131	4767	46.4	26.9	20.9	3.9	1.8	27010	27678	5	4	1699	35.2	28.7	20.5	14.2	1.4	69207
64110	KANSAS CITY	22242	6939	33.9	27.8	29.7	5.2	3.4	39268	41284	31	50	3430	17.5	29.5	41.2	9.9	1.9	94333
64111	KANSAS CITY	28286	9801	31.2	34.3	27.9	4.1	2.6	36689	39539	23	39	2366	5.8	24.0	48.4	19.3	2.5	115249
64112	KANSAS CITY	47927	5551	23.8	26.4	32.9	7.6	9.3	49788	52756	61	79	1606	0.7	6.5	34.1	33.9	24.8	204694
64113	KANSAS CITY	59669	4888	4.1	9.0	34.2	21.4	31.2	106931	107852	98	99	4592	0.6	3.7	18.7	57.2	19.8	237794
64114	KANSAS CITY	34635	11996	16.0	27.4	43.0	9.0	4.6	55539	56888	72	86	7617	2.9	20.8	52.0	22.4	2.0	122921
64116	KANSAS CITY	31485	8000	18.5	35.4	31.8	7.5	6.9	46312	48662	52	72	3550	4.5	20.5	46.1	22.3	6.7	122376
64117	KANSAS CITY	23016	6001	19.2	32.9	39.8	6.3	1.8	47916	49882	56	76	3443	4.2	23.7	68.8	3.1	0.3	105667
64118	KANSAS CITY	30179	17552	11.0	29.2	43.7	11.6	4.5	58433	60374	76	88	10894	5.9	10.2	63.8	19.1	0.9	130728
64119	KANSAS CITY	30107	11119	9.9	24.7	45.4	13.3	6.6	62848	66096	81	92	8531	1.4	13.6	59.6	24.0	1.4	124656
64120	KANSAS CITY	17053	221	35.7	37.1	25.8	1.4	0.0	33015	34583	13	21	128	95.3	3.9	0.8	0.0	0.0	18548
64123	KANSAS CITY	16671	3769	30.9	31.8	31.4	4.5	1.4	39505	42310	31	51	2233	45.8	39.4	13.3	0.9	0.5	53316
64124	KANSAS CITY	13556	4610	40.2	33.5	22.6	2.7	1.1	30814	31513	9	14	2038	49.4	36.3	11.3	2.6	0.4	50502
64125	KANSAS CITY	16509	766	33.3	33.7	27.0	3.1	2.9	34927	36573	17	30	429	74.8	15.6	7.0	2.6	0.0	37964
64126	KANSAS CITY	13122	2309	40.6	33.7	23.0	2.5	0.1	30356	31504	9	12	1239	67.2	28.6	3.8	0.4	0.0	37476
64127	KANSAS CITY	14048	7532	46.7	31.4	18.5	2.1	1.3	26755	27221	4	4	3079	67.6	21.9	10.0	0.3	0.2	38040
64128	KANSAS CITY	14439	5423	47.9	28.0	20.7	2.2	1.2	26482	27316	4	3	3024	52.4	37.4	9.3	0.5	0.5	48528
64129	KANSAS CITY	22229	4255	21.5	36.2	35.6	5.1	1.6	43741	47092	45	65	2543	22.5	46.6	29.5	1.1	0.4	74062
64130	KANSAS CITY	15019	9966	43.1	31.4	21.6	2.9	0.9	29202	30192	7	8	6020	43.3	45.5	10.2	0.7	0.3	54754
64131	KANSAS CITY	26243	10065	20.7	31.1	37.7	7.6	2.9	48097	51591	57	76	5617	8.1	25.8	48.6	17.2	0.3	114067
64132	KANSAS CITY	16017	6196	36.4	35.7	24.8	2.3	0.8	32807	34287	13	20	3105	34.6	47.7	16.8	0.9	0.0	60792
64133	KANSAS CITY	27363	14054	16.2	28.7	43.0	8.8	3.3	54403	56127	70	85	9997	3.2	31.3	55.1	10.1	0.3	102505
64134	KANSAS CITY	21143	8536	18.2	31.9	42.1	6.0	1.8	49882	52275	61	79	6087	6.2	53.1	36.6	3.7	0.4	84134
64136	KANSAS CITY	29881	927	19.8	17.8	41.9	15.6	4.9	64261	65209	83	93	695	2.6	11.8	54.7	30.6	0.3	136352
64137	KANSAS CITY	25251	4681	16.1	32.3	41.7	7.8	2.1	51324	53397	64	81	2762	1.4	34.2	57.8	6.0	0.5	101159
64138	KANSAS CITY	26091	10933	15.8	30.0	43.6	7.8	2.8	53202	55183	68	83	7655	2.6	33.1	56.8	7.1	0.4	100491
64139	KANSAS CITY	20881	424	18.2	19.3	42.5	14.4	5.7	63466	64421	82	92	304	3.0	10.9	52.3	32.9	1.0	142045
64145	KANSAS CITY	36699	2182	13.2	22.2	40.0	12.3	12.4	67814	67898	85	94	1613	1.2	7.6	27.3	50.8	13.0	206424
64146	KANSAS CITY	35187	722	15.7	32.3	38.1	8.6	5.4	51450	53431	65	81	479	3.5	12.7	58.9	23.0	1.9	132344
64147	KANSAS CITY	11294	270	51.1	27.4	18.9	0.7	1.9	23787	23189	3	1	33	24.2	15.2	3.0	30.3	27.3	241667
64149	KANSAS CITY	39758	136	2.9	6.6	55.1	16.9	18.4	82935	84416	93	98	127	0.0	11.0	16.5	53.5	18.9	244048
64150	RIVERSIDE	22810	1323	23.8	31.9	35.8	5.6	2.9	43831	46489	45	66	424	11.8	16.5	49.5	21.2	0.9	118675
64151	KANSAS CITY	36610	10587	9.9	20.6	41.6	20.1	7.7	72304	75589	88	96	6966	1.7	4.1	44.0	46.2	4.0	175371
64152	KANSAS CITY	37717	9661	7.1	16.1	40.5	21.8	14.6	82092	85477	93	97	7464	1.1	3.3	49.7	37.0	8.9	168226
64153	KANSAS CITY	32919	1809	8.7	22.7	43.3	18.1	7.2	71283	74585	87	95	1188	0.5	1.3	45.2	49.7	3.3	178409
64154	KANSAS CITY	36659	3459	13.9	24.0	37.1	16.5	8.4	63876	66287	82	93	1537	2.3	3.3	37.4	50.8	6.2	188997
64155	KANSAS CITY	31929	7933	5.6	15.7	47.2	24.1	7.3	78530	80382	91	97	6574	0.9	4.1	60.4	34.1	0.4	156245
64156	KANSAS CITY	31365	1197	9.4	30.3	40.2	13.5	6.7	56207	57204	73	87	962	18.4	9.0	35.7	34.3	2.6	134337
64157	KANSAS CITY	31564	4056	4.3	11.6	48.5	24.0	11.5	82349	83912	93	98	3749	3.5	3.8	31.0	54.8	7.0	192615
64158	KANSAS CITY	35092	1501	2.3	0.9	48.6	36.6	11.7	97868	102813	96	99	1317	2.8	2.1	25.1	70.1	0.0	197491
64161	KANSAS CITY	26242	163	14.1	23.3	55.2	5.5	1.8	61562	64868	79	91	121	9.1	34.7	47.1	3.3	5.8	94688
64163	KANSAS CITY	31515	327	13.8	32.7	46.5	5.5	1.5	53055	53593	68	83	189	53.4	12.2	19.6	14.3	0.5	44091
64164	KANSAS CITY	28920	171	11.7	24.6	44.4	13.5	5.8	64697	65264	83	93	120	27.5	7.5	28.3	35.0	1.7	138636
64165	KANSAS CITY	47377	30	0.0	10.0	46.7	30.0	13.3	91774	88673	95	99	28	0.0	0.0	25.0	75.0	0.0	218750
64166	KANSAS CITY	39253	100	3.0	9.0	44.0	30.0	14.0	91626	91202	95	99	93	0.0	1.1	23.7	71.0	4.3	225000
64167	KANSAS CITY	33016	127	3.1	12.6	44.1	30.7	9.4	87564	88310	94	98	117	0.0	1.7	42.7	47.9	7.7	185156
64401	AGENCY	24518	568	14.6	27.5	46.5	7.7	3.7	55290	54601	72	86	494	9.3	10.3	42.7	32.0	5.7	147945
64402	ALBANY	19924	1008	33.2	35.6	25.1	3.5	2.6	32595	33740	13	20	730	31.8	26.8	32.2	7.8	1.4	78444
64421	AMAZONIA	22753	496	25.0	26.6	40.7	3.6	4.0	48598	51573	58	77	420	32.1	20.7	29.0	13.3	4.8	84000
64422	AMITY	18874	190	24.2	37.4	31.6	4.7	2.1	38187	40656	27	46	151	20.5	25.2	31.8	20.5	2.0	96500
64423	BARNARD	19814	330	26.1	35.2	34.2	3.3	1.2	41452	44328	38	59	263	31.9	19.0	27.0	19.8	2.3	87727
64424	BETHANY	17068	1717	35.9	35.6	24.3	3.1	1.0	34976	36683	18	30	1181	26.8	26.4	38.0	8.2	0.5	85860
64426	BLYTHEDALE	15766	192	37.5	35.9	25.0	0.5	1.0	30879	32936	9	14	155	40.0	25.8	22.6	9.7	1.9	66111
64427	BOLCKOW	19519	233	25.8	33.0	34.3	4.7	2.1	43326	45378	43	64	197	39.1	26.4	24.4	8.6	1.5	66765
64428	BURLINGTON JUNCTION	18942	369	30.9	35.5	26.8	5.7	1.1	36836	38343	23	39	286	38.8	27.6	20.3	11.5	1.7	60000
64429	CAMERON	18794	3348	25.1	30.3	36.6	5.3	2.7	45607	49264	50	71	2270	11.3	27.5	44.6	14.9	1.7	104867
64430	CLARKSDALE	19177	313	24.3	35.1	34.8	5.1	0.6	41943	45595	39	61	266	16.9	25.9	36.5	18.4	2.3	103704
64431	CLEARMONT	20160	207	37.2	27.1	31.4	2.9	1.4	34431	36247	16	28	152	31.6	24.3	33.6	7.2	3.3	82500
64432	CLYDE	14795	62	25.8	35.5	35.5	3.2	0.0	42305	43887	40	61	49	38.8	24.5	20.4	14.3	2.0	63750
64433	CONCEPTION	9529	49	26.5	34.7	36.7	2.0	0.0	41711	45756	38	60	39	35.9	25.6	23.1	15.4	0.0	68333
64434	CONCEPTION JUNCTION	18808	114	25.4	36.0	33.3	4.4	0.9	41825	44070	39	60	90	34.4	24.4	23.3	15.6	2.2	70000
64436	COSBY	27363	326	17.8	27.0	41.4	8.0	5.8	60000	61068	77	90	289	20.1	12.8	41.5	22.8	2.8	125278
64437	CRAIG	17332	375	37.9	35.7	22.9	1.9	1.6	32430	33117	12	19	288	38.5	25.0	26.4	9.0	1.0	61765
64438	DARLINGTON	16069	64	23.4	39.1	31.3	4.7	1.6	38882	40760	29	48	53	32.1	17.0	28.3	17.0	5.7	95000
64439	DEARBORN	24422	843	18.4	28.2	41.9	8.7	2.8	52817	53541	68	83	656	10.7	20.4	38.7	26.5	3.7	123158
64440	DE KALB	20386	249	17.7	34.9	39.8	6.0	1.6	48305	49876	57	76	204	23.5	27.9	32.4	15.7	0.5	87273
64441	DENVER	18743	78	28.2	41.0	26.9	3.8	0.0	37321	40000	25	41	63	33.3	28.6	23.8	12.7	1.6	66250
64442	EAGLEVILLE	16721	325	34.2	37.2	26.2	1.2	1.2	33119	35247	14	22	263	36.1	25.9	23.6	11.4	3.0	70833
64443	EASTON	23588	629	14.0	28.9	48.6	5.2	3.2	55098	54340	71	85	520	12.1	14.8	40.2	21.2	11.7	138846
64444	EDGERTON	25106	541	16.3	24.0	46.6	10.5	2.6	57740	57619	75	88	457	10.7	18.4	45.7	21.2	3.9	121955
64445	ELMO	17892	180	36.1	35.0	23.9	4.4	0.6	35000	36344	18	31	137	50.4	30.7	13.1	5.1	0.7	49643
64446	FAIRFAX	21412	517	27.9	37.1	30.0	2.7	2.3	38353	39824	28	46	371	33.7	33.2	26.7	5.4	1.1	70172
64448	FAUCETT	23672	364	15.9	26.6	47.5	7.4	2.5	55785	55183	72	86	309	10.4	15.5	37.2	33.3	3.6	142279
64449	FILLMORE	22878	201	25.4	30.3	35.8	3.5	5.0	46054	50305	51	72	168	34.5	25.0	32.7	6.0	1.8	73333
64451	FOREST CITY	20723	183	26.8	39.3	26.8	3.8	3.3	39000	39240	30	49	149	30.2	31.5	22.8	11.4	4.0	74091
64453	GENTRY	15949	87	33.3	32.2	31.0	3.4	0.0	35366	37849	19	33	72	29.2	15.3	30.6	23.6	1.4	108333
64454	GOWER	24980	927	16.6	23.5	45.0	11.2	3.7	58989	59511	76	89	745	7.8	22.8	42.0	24.2	3.2	117842
64455	GRAHAM	19971	209	28.7	33.5	32.5	3.3	1.9	40171	43640	33	54	163	41.7	12.3	21.5	16.0	8.6	77000
64456	GRANT CITY	16357	518	40.3	34.6	22.0	2.3	0.8	30000	30366	8	11	383	47.8	30.3	17.2	3.9	0.8	52500
64457	GUILFORD	17648	132	25.8	36.4	33.3	3.8	0.8	41502	44438	38	59	105	37.1	22.9	23.8	14.3	1.9	66875
64458	HATFIELD	15615	71	21.1	40.8	35.2	1.4	1.4	41117	47381	36	57	59	18.6	23.7	30.5	18.6	8.5	102500
	MISSOURI	25286		22.8	27.7	35.3	9.1	5.2	49522	52035				12.8	19.4	39.1	24.2	4.6	122064
	UNITED STATES	27277		20.9	24.4	35.3	11.7	7.6	54719	56938				9.3	13.1	31.6	32.6	13.5	162279

ZIP CODE #	POST OFFICE NAME	FINANCIAL SERVICES Auto Loan	Home Loan	Investments	Retirement Plans	THE HOME Home Improvements Home Repair	Lawn & Garden	Furnishings Computers & Hardware Personal	Major Appliances	TV, Radio, Sound Equipment	Furniture	ENTERTAINMENT Dine out/ Carry out	Sports Equipment	Fees & Tickets	Toys & Games	Travel	Cable TV	PERSONAL Apparel & Services	Auto Repairs	Health Insurance	Pets & Supplies
64083	RAYMORE	119	132	124	128	132	123	118	123	115	127	116	91	125	117	124	113	81	117	120	139
64084	RAYVILLE	90	88	83	91	88	98	84	93	85	79	85	71	81	87	85	89	58	86	94	108
64085	RICHMOND	87	77	77	78	75	90	81	85	84	75	83	66	74	84	78	88	56	84	92	102
64086	LEES SUMMIT	130	141	124	140	135	123	131	128	124	138	126	101	135	130	131	119	89	125	117	148
64088	SIBLEY	89	91	82	94	89	97	86	91	87	82	86	71	86	89	88	89	60	87	94	107
64089	SMITHVILLE	129	140	120	137	134	124	126	128	121	133	123	100	130	128	127	117	86	122	117	147
64093	WARRENSBURG	82	66	60	68	63	67	87	72	82	77	82	60	73	83	71	80	57	78	73	88
64096	WAVERLY	87	62	90	61	65	92	68	84	75	59	73	65	54	74	66	82	48	79	91	100
64097	WELLINGTON	89	70	86	70	72	93	73	87	79	66	77	66	63	79	72	86	52	81	93	102
64098	WESTON	99	94	92	94	93	102	92	97	93	90	93	74	88	94	91	96	63	95	100	115
64101	KANSAS CITY	77	57	59	65	55	55	84	63	81	78	84	58	74	82	72	79	60	76	66	81
64105	KANSAS CITY	70	52	54	60	50	50	77	58	74	71	77	53	68	75	66	72	55	70	60	74
64106	KANSAS CITY	55	39	40	44	38	43	58	47	61	54	61	39	51	59	49	62	43	56	55	60
64108	KANSAS CITY	68	53	48	55	50	53	70	59	72	67	72	47	62	71	60	72	51	67	63	73
64109	KANSAS CITY	54	43	43	45	42	50	54	50	59	52	58	37	50	56	49	62	40	55	60	62
64110	KANSAS CITY	74	62	56	65	59	65	75	66	77	71	77	53	69	77	66	79	53	73	73	82
64111	KANSAS CITY	70	50	48	55	48	50	73	57	72	68	73	49	63	72	61	70	51	68	61	72
64112	KANSAS CITY	103	83	86	92	81	81	113	89	108	105	111	79	103	109	99	105	79	103	91	112
64113	KANSAS CITY	175	224	241	230	236	209	193	200	183	207	183	152	226	181	218	177	135	190	186	226
64114	KANSAS CITY	89	91	88	92	90	94	93	91	94	91	94	69	95	92	93	96	65	93	99	107
64116	KANSAS CITY	94	85	81	88	84	86	97	88	97	94	97	70	93	97	90	97	68	94	93	106
64117	KANSAS CITY	78	73	61	76	69	76	79	73	80	75	80	58	77	81	74	81	55	77	81	90
64118	KANSAS CITY	99	95	86	97	92	93	100	94	99	99	100	74	98	101	96	99	70	98	97	112
64119	KANSAS CITY	106	112	96	113	106	108	108	105	107	107	107	83	111	109	107	106	75	105	107	125
64120	KANSAS CITY	58	45	40	46	43	53	55	51	58	50	56	40	47	58	47	61	39	55	58	63
64123	KANSAS CITY	70	58	51	58	56	64	68	64	70	64	69	50	60	71	60	73	48	68	70	78
64124	KANSAS CITY	55	46	40	47	43	48	57	50	59	52	58	40	51	59	49	61	41	55	55	62
64125	KANSAS CITY	72	57	51	58	55	67	68	65	71	62	69	51	58	72	58	75	48	68	73	79
64126	KANSAS CITY	57	45	38	44	43	49	53	50	56	51	55	38	46	57	45	58	38	53	54	61
64127	KANSAS CITY	53	43	39	44	40	48	51	47	56	49	55	35	47	55	45	60	39	52	55	59
64128	KANSAS CITY	54	43	40	44	41	51	49	48	56	50	54	35	46	54	44	60	37	52	57	60
64129	KANSAS CITY	74	69	58	70	65	71	75	70	76	71	76	55	71	77	69	77	52	74	76	85
64130	KANSAS CITY	55	46	43	47	44	53	51	50	57	52	56	36	48	56	47	61	38	54	59	63
64131	KANSAS CITY	83	75	70	77	72	77	83	78	85	82	85	60	80	85	78	86	59	83	84	94
64132	KANSAS CITY	59	47	41	50	43	51	56	50	60	55	59	40	52	60	49	61	41	56	57	64
64133	KANSAS CITY	86	87	81	88	85	92	88	87	91	85	90	66	89	90	88	93	63	89	97	103
64134	KANSAS CITY	79	77	63	79	72	79	80	75	81	77	81	60	79	82	76	83	56	79	83	92
64136	KANSAS CITY	92	114	102	114	110	112	97	101	98	99	100	76	112	100	108	100	70	99	107	118
64137	KANSAS CITY	84	78	69	80	75	78	85	79	85	84	86	62	82	87	80	86	60	83	83	95
64138	KANSAS CITY	86	86	75	88	81	86	87	83	88	86	89	65	89	90	86	89	62	87	89	100
64139	KANSAS CITY	93	113	103	113	110	110	98	101	99	100	100	76	111	100	108	100	70	100	105	118
64145	KANSAS CITY	116	119	132	121	126	130	116	122	118	120	117	86	120	114	122	122	82	121	131	142
64146	KANSAS CITY	100	87	87	89	88	98	96	96	99	91	97	73	88	98	91	102	67	98	104	114
64147	KANSAS CITY	48	29	24	33	26	31	47	36	50	44	50	31	39	52	36	51	35	44	41	47
64149	KANSAS CITY	148	184	169	187	181	162	155	159	145	166	148	125	175	151	168	139	107	149	142	181
64150	RIVERSIDE	81	60	56	63	58	60	78	67	78	77	80	55	68	80	68	77	55	76	69	83
64151	KANSAS CITY	119	125	115	127	122	114	121	116	117	124	119	92	125	120	121	114	84	117	111	137
64152	KANSAS CITY	142	159	142	160	154	141	144	143	138	152	140	112	153	143	148	133	99	139	132	165
64153	KANSAS CITY	123	120	102	121	113	104	120	112	115	125	118	92	118	122	114	110	83	113	102	132
64154	KANSAS CITY	109	108	107	111	108	105	113	107	113	115	114	83	115	112	112	113	80	111	112	126
64155	KANSAS CITY	128	143	119	138	135	121	126	126	120	135	122	99	131	128	127	115	86	121	114	144
64156	KANSAS CITY	115	116	96	111	109	103	109	108	106	115	107	84	106	112	104	103	74	105	100	125
64157	KANSAS CITY	148	161	129	154	150	130	142	141	133	154	136	112	144	144	139	125	95	133	121	160
64158	KANSAS CITY	166	181	145	173	168	147	159	158	149	173	153	126	162	162	156	141	107	150	137	180
64161	KANSAS CITY	88	91	71	93	84	94	90	87	92	86	91	70	91	93	88	93	63	89	97	106
64163	KANSAS CITY	90	87	74	83	83	82	84	84	84	88	84	64	81	87	80	83	58	84	81	99
64164	KANSAS CITY	108	116	101	113	112	106	106	106	103	111	104	82	109	107	107	101	73	104	100	124
64165	KANSAS CITY	145	182	159	181	175	157	152	155	143	160	146	123	172	149	164	137	105	147	138	178
64166	KANSAS CITY	146	184	161	184	177	159	154	157	145	162	148	125	174	151	166	139	106	149	140	180
64167	KANSAS CITY	148	161	129	154	150	131	142	141	133	155	137	112	145	145	140	126	95	134	122	160
64401	AGENCY	102	95	93	99	96	110	93	104	95	85	94	79	87	97	93	100	64	96	106	121
64402	ALBANY	77	55	79	54	57	81	60	75	67	53	64	57	48	65	59	73	43	70	81	89
64421	AMAZONIA	101	72	104	70	75	103	74	94	82	69	81	71	59	82	73	91	53	87	98	112
64422	AMITY	87	60	96	60	63	92	67	83	69	54	68	68	49	68	66	76	44	77	87	102
64423	BARNARD	83	57	92	57	60	88	64	79	66	52	65	65	47	65	63	72	42	74	84	97
64424	BETHANY	69	49	70	48	51	72	53	66	59	47	57	51	42	58	52	65	38	62	72	79
64426	BLYTHEDALE	68	47	75	47	49	72	52	65	54	42	54	53	38	53	52	59	35	61	69	80
64427	BOLCKOW	94	67	92	65	69	94	69	86	77	65	75	65	55	77	67	84	50	80	90	103
64428	BURLINGTON JUNCTION	75	58	73	57	59	79	61	74	67	55	64	55	51	66	60	73	43	68	79	86
64429	CAMERON	77	69	67	70	69	77	75	75	77	70	76	57	69	77	71	80	52	76	82	89
64430	CLARKSDALE	76	66	71	68	67	81	66	76	68	59	67	58	59	69	66	73	45	70	78	89
64431	CLEARMONT	72	52	72	50	54	75	56	70	63	50	61	52	45	62	55	69	40	65	76	82
64432	CLYDE	81	56	89	55	58	85	62	77	64	50	63	63	45	63	61	70	41	72	81	94
64433	CONCEPTION	80	55	88	55	58	85	61	76	64	50	63	63	45	63	61	70	41	71	81	94
64434	CONCEPTION JUNCTION	82	56	89	56	59	86	62	77	65	51	64	64	46	64	62	71	42	72	82	95
64436	COSBY	122	88	132	88	91	129	95	117	99	79	98	96	73	97	95	107	64	109	123	143
64437	CRAIG	73	51	79	50	53	76	55	69	59	47	58	56	42	58	55	64	38	64	73	84
64438	DARLINGTON	94	64	103	64	67	99	71	89	74	58	73	73	52	73	71	81	48	83	94	109
64439	DEARBORN	91	88	84	91	89	99	84	93	86	79	85	71	81	88	86	90	58	87	95	109
64440	DE KALB	84	77	76	80	78	90	76	85	78	68	77	65	70	80	76	83	52	79	88	99
64441	DENVER	75	52	83	52	54	80	58	72	60	47	59	59	42	59	57	65	38	67	76	88
64442	EAGLEVILLE	70	49	77	48	51	74	54	67	57	44	56	55	40	56	54	62	36	63	71	82
64443	EASTON	93	85	84	88	87	100	84	95	86	76	85	72	77	88	84	91	58	87	97	110
64444	EDGERTON	96	90	88	94	92	104	88	98	90	81	89	75	83	92	88	95	61	91	101	114
64445	ELMO	73	53	74	51	55	77	58	71	64	51	62	53	46	63	56	71	41	66	78	84
64446	FAIRFAX	81	58	83	56	60	85	63	78	69	55	67	60	50	68	61	76	45	73	85	93
64448	FAUCETT	91	89	84	93	90	99	85	94	87	80	86	72	83	88	87	90	59	88	95	109
64449	FILLMORE	99	71	82	69	71	94	74	86	82	72	80	66	59	85	67	89	54	81	91	105
64451	FOREST CITY	91	62	99	62	65	95	69	86	72	56	71	70	51	71	69	79	46	80	91	105
64453	GENTRY	79	54	87	54	57	83	60	75	63	49	62	62	44	61	60	68	40	70	79	92
64454	GOWER	105	96	89	95	95	104	92	100	95	91	95	74	86	98	89	99	64	95	101	118
64455	GRAHAM	83	57	91	57	59	87	63	78	66	51	65	65	46	64	63	72	42	73	83	96
64456	GRANT CITY	65	46	67	45	48	68	51	63	56	44	54	48	40	55	50	61	36	59	68	75
64457	GUILFORD	81	56	89	56	58	86	62	77	65	50	64	64	45	63	62	70	41	72	81	95
64458	HATFIELD	81	56	89	56	59	86	62	77	65	50	64	64	46	63	62	71	41	72	82	95
	MISSOURI	94	86	87	87	85	93	89	91	91	87	90	70	84	92	86	93	62	90	94	108
	UNITED STATES	100	100	100	100	100	100	100	100	100	100	100	100	100	100	100	100	100	100	100	100

ZIP CODE #	POST OFFICE NAME	COUNTY FIPS CODE	POPULATION 2000	POPULATION 2009	POPULATION 2014	2000-2009 ANNUAL RATE % Rate	2000-2009 ANNUAL RATE State Centile	HOUSEHOLDS 2000	HOUSEHOLDS 2009	HOUSEHOLDS 2014	HOUSEHOLDS % Annual Rate 2000-2009	HOUSEHOLDS 2009 Average HH Size	FAMILIES 2000	FAMILIES 2009	FAMILIES % Annual Rate 2000-2009
64459	HELENA	003	595	582	577	-0.2	27	233	230	229	-0.1	2.36	178	171	-0.4
64461	HOPKINS	147	846	830	825	-0.2	27	340	341	340	0.0	2.43	231	221	-0.5
64463	KING CITY	075	1620	1632	1618	0.1	42	636	639	634	0.1	2.51	452	437	-0.4
64465	LATHROP	049	3975	4626	4960	1.7	89	1500	1778	1916	1.9	2.57	1143	1311	1.5
64466	MAITLAND	087	564	517	497	-0.9	4	235	219	212	-0.8	2.36	164	147	-1.2
64467	MARTINSVILLE	081	248	243	242	-0.2	27	91	88	88	-0.4	2.74	68	64	-0.7
64468	MARYVILLE	147	14243	14472	14553	0.2	46	5097	5293	5369	0.4	2.22	2677	2631	-0.2
64469	MAYSVILLE	063	2307	2221	2180	-0.4	18	853	822	806	-0.4	2.63	618	582	-0.6
64470	MOUND CITY	087	1712	1609	1562	-0.7	8	767	730	712	-0.5	2.15	476	431	-1.1
64471	NEW HAMPTON	081	527	520	520	-0.1	32	219	215	215	-0.2	2.31	154	146	-0.6
64473	OREGON	087	1629	1615	1599	-0.1	32	638	636	632	0.0	2.45	447	430	-0.4
64474	OSBORN	063	749	748	744	0.0	37	297	299	297	0.1	2.50	213	207	-0.3
64475	PARNELL	147	387	379	377	-0.2	27	168	168	168	0.0	2.26	114	109	-0.5
64476	PICKERING	147	495	493	493	0.0	37	206	212	213	0.3	2.30	152	150	-0.1
64477	PLATTSBURG	049	3572	3841	3985	0.8	69	1377	1503	1566	1.0	2.50	990	1039	0.5
64479	RAVENWOOD	147	958	1002	1019	0.5	58	376	405	416	0.8	2.47	267	276	0.4
64480	REA	003	434	428	427	-0.2	27	173	173	173	0.0	2.47	132	128	-0.3
64481	RIDGEWAY	081	1153	1153	1153	0.0	37	468	463	462	-0.1	2.49	339	324	-0.5
64482	ROCK PORT	005	2319	2186	2127	-0.6	11	1045	999	974	-0.5	2.14	660	602	-1.0
64483	ROSENDALE	003	675	654	646	-0.3	21	249	244	242	-0.2	2.68	193	183	-0.6
64484	RUSHVILLE	021	1133	1139	1147	0.1	42	454	462	468	0.2	2.46	329	322	-0.2
64485	SAVANNAH	003	7635	7905	7977	0.4	53	2919	3049	3089	0.5	2.52	2067	2081	0.1
64486	SHERIDAN	227	627	577	550	-0.9	4	266	244	232	-0.9	2.36	183	161	-1.4
64487	SKIDMORE	147	759	727	717	-0.5	14	327	322	319	-0.2	2.26	208	193	-0.8
64489	STANBERRY	075	1852	1742	1677	-0.7	8	707	660	633	-0.7	2.55	500	450	-1.1
64490	STEWARTSVILLE	049	2056	2119	2131	0.3	50	775	807	814	0.4	2.62	593	600	0.1
64491	TARKIO	005	2269	2071	1987	-1.0	3	891	812	778	-1.0	2.25	563	490	-1.5
64492	TRIMBLE	049	1167	1561	1743	3.2	97	459	618	694	3.3	2.53	350	456	2.9
64493	TURNEY	049	390	473	511	2.1	93	155	191	207	2.3	2.47	127	153	2.0
64494	UNION STAR	063	908	915	913	0.1	42	364	370	369	0.2	2.47	259	254	-0.2
64496	WATSON	005	193	183	177	-0.6	11	72	70	68	-0.3	2.61	51	47	-0.9
64497	WEATHERBY	063	432	435	430	0.1	42	166	166	164	0.0	2.62	128	125	-0.3
64498	WESTBORO	005	472	436	418	-0.9	4	191	179	173	-0.7	2.42	152	139	-1.0
64499	WORTH	227	211	191	181	-1.1	2	90	81	77	-1.1	2.36	67	58	-1.5
64501	SAINT JOSEPH	021	12348	11890	11731	-0.4	18	5080	4877	4815	-0.4	2.30	2829	2568	-1.0
64503	SAINT JOSEPH	021	12272	12434	12503	0.1	42	4847	4936	4977	0.2	2.48	3346	3274	-0.2
64504	SAINT JOSEPH	021	11196	11019	10980	-0.2	27	4338	4299	4294	-0.1	2.55	3037	2891	-0.5
64505	SAINT JOSEPH	003	12479	12700	12790	0.2	46	4736	4852	4897	0.3	2.57	3397	3359	-0.1
64506	SAINT JOSEPH	021	21374	22380	22791	0.5	58	8269	8748	8948	0.6	2.25	5201	5251	0.1
64507	SAINT JOSEPH	021	13522	13712	13817	0.2	46	5170	5275	5326	0.2	2.44	3276	3190	-0.3
64601	CHILLICOTHE	117	11786	11535	11395	-0.2	27	4651	4591	4546	-0.1	2.31	3014	2848	-0.6
64620	ALTAMONT	061	368	410	419	1.2	82	145	163	167	1.3	2.52	111	121	0.9
64622	BOGARD	033	935	963	957	0.3	50	351	360	358	0.3	2.68	260	257	-0.1
64623	BOSWORTH	033	661	669	663	0.1	42	265	270	268	0.2	2.48	197	195	-0.1
64624	BRAYMER	025	1774	1792	1798	0.1	42	696	704	707	0.1	2.46	476	463	-0.3
64625	BRECKENRIDGE	025	672	677	680	0.1	42	276	280	282	0.2	2.42	192	188	-0.2
64628	BROOKFIELD	115	6173	5744	5501	-0.8	6	2601	2416	2311	-0.8	2.30	1634	1450	-1.3
64630	BROWNING	115	415	391	376	-0.6	11	173	164	158	-0.6	2.38	115	104	-1.1
64631	BUCKLIN	115	1027	980	949	-0.5	14	444	427	413	-0.4	2.30	292	268	-0.9
64632	CAINSVILLE	129	730	705	694	-0.4	18	315	302	296	-0.5	2.33	213	196	-0.9
64633	CARROLLTON	033	5354	5167	5028	-0.4	18	2179	2108	2052	-0.4	2.36	1438	1332	-0.8
64635	CHULA	117	700	740	743	0.6	63	267	287	290	0.8	2.56	197	204	0.4
64636	COFFEY	061	291	290	288	0.0	37	115	116	115	0.1	2.49	80	77	-0.4
64637	COWGILL	025	658	705	722	0.7	66	259	281	288	0.9	2.51	194	203	0.5
64638	DAWN	117	349	346	342	-0.1	32	148	148	146	0.0	2.34	101	96	-0.5
64639	DE WITT	033	453	443	432	-0.2	27	180	178	174	-0.1	2.49	145	139	-0.5
64640	GALLATIN	061	3190	3144	3103	-0.2	27	1331	1316	1300	-0.1	2.35	917	874	-0.5
64641	GALT	079	575	575	572	0.0	37	240	242	241	0.1	2.38	172	167	-0.3
64642	GILMAN CITY	081	902	960	984	0.7	66	373	395	405	0.6	2.43	264	269	0.2
64643	HALE	033	694	691	677	0.0	37	282	282	277	0.0	2.45	199	192	-0.4
64644	HAMILTON	025	2882	2835	2827	-0.2	27	1140	1127	1124	-0.1	2.46	790	750	-0.6
64645	HARRIS	211	158	149	144	-0.6	11	70	65	63	-0.8	2.29	49	43	-1.4
64646	HUMPHREYS	211	473	449	437	-0.6	11	186	175	169	-0.7	2.57	130	117	-1.1
64647	JAMESON	061	349	344	340	-0.2	27	149	148	147	-0.1	2.32	112	107	-0.5
64648	JAMESPORT	061	2169	2164	2147	0.0	37	709	714	710	0.1	3.03	522	507	-0.3
64649	KIDDER	025	1023	1103	1136	0.8	69	387	420	433	0.9	2.63	303	318	0.5
64650	KINGSTON	025	891	895	894	0.0	37	346	351	353	0.2	2.55	252	245	-0.3
64651	LACLEDE	115	733	722	702	-0.2	27	297	294	286	-0.1	2.45	218	208	-0.5
64652	LAREDO	079	454	480	485	0.6	63	194	208	211	0.8	2.31	143	149	0.4
64653	LINNEUS	115	863	813	788	-0.6	11	326	309	299	-0.6	2.63	240	221	-0.9
64654	LOCK SPRINGS	061	141	135	131	-0.5	14	55	53	51	-0.4	2.55	44	41	-0.8
64655	LUCERNE	171	200	199	199	-0.1	32	85	85	85	0.0	2.34	64	62	-0.3
64656	LUDLOW	117	412	405	398	-0.2	27	168	166	164	-0.1	2.44	108	101	-0.7
64657	MC FALL	075	614	573	552	-0.7	8	235	218	209	-0.8	2.48	178	160	-1.1
64658	MARCELINE	041	3483	3094	2929	-1.3	1	1402	1240	1173	-1.3	2.44	934	794	-1.7
64659	MEADVILLE	115	943	841	794	-1.2	1	370	329	310	-1.3	2.56	261	224	-1.6
64660	MENDON	041	530	502	485	-0.6	11	222	214	208	-0.4	2.35	158	147	-0.8
64661	MERCER	129	1045	966	923	-0.8	6	446	411	392	-0.9	2.35	318	283	-1.3
64664	MOORESVILLE	117	304	299	296	-0.2	27	129	128	127	-0.1	2.34	98	94	-0.4
64667	NEWTOWN	211	388	365	354	-0.7	8	150	139	134	-0.8	2.63	105	93	-1.3
64668	NORBORNE	033	1643	1603	1561	-0.3	21	698	687	671	-0.2	2.33	480	454	-0.6
64670	PATTONSBURG	061	973	959	950	-0.2	27	413	411	409	-0.1	2.32	291	279	-0.5
64671	POLO	025	1813	2072	2180	1.5	87	717	823	869	1.5	2.52	526	585	1.2
64672	POWERSVILLE	171	268	266	267	-0.1	32	113	113	113	0.0	2.35	86	83	-0.4
64673	PRINCETON	129	2527	2396	2305	-0.6	11	1073	1019	981	-0.6	2.29	715	652	-1.0
64674	PURDIN	115	505	481	467	-0.5	14	217	208	202	-0.5	2.31	151	139	-0.9
64676	ROTHVILLE	041	327	310	299	-0.6	11	125	121	117	-0.4	2.56	89	83	-0.8
64679	SPICKARD	079	701	692	685	-0.1	32	292	292	290	0.0	2.37	202	194	-0.4
64681	SUMNER	041	260	246	238	-0.6	11	118	114	110	-0.4	2.16	84	78	-0.8
64682	TINA	033	431	438	435	0.2	46	168	172	171	0.3	2.55	127	126	-0.1
64683	TRENTON	079	8439	8337	8255	-0.1	32	3585	3575	3552	0.0	2.23	2319	2215	-0.5
64686	UTICA	117	323	318	314	-0.2	27	122	122	121	0.0	2.61	92	89	-0.4
64688	WHEELING	117	433	411	401	-0.6	11	173	167	164	-0.4	2.46	123	114	-0.8
64689	WINSTON	061	751	842	860	1.2	82	288	326	334	1.3	2.58	218	239	1.0
64701	HARRISONVILLE	037	13769	15479	16315	1.3	83	5146	5881	6228	1.5	2.57	3725	4092	1.0
	MISSOURI					0.7					0.8	2.45			0.4
	UNITED STATES					1.0					1.1	2.59			0.9

#	POST OFFICE NAME	RACE (%) White 2000	White 2009	Black 2000	Black 2009	Asian/Pacific 2000	Asian/Pacific 2009	% Hispanic Origin 2000	% Hispanic Origin 2009	2009 AGE DISTRIBUTION (%) 0-4	5-9	10-14	15-19	20-24	25-44	45-64	65-84	85+	18+	MEDIAN AGE 2009	% 2009 Males	% 2009 Females
64459	HELENA	99.5	99.3	0.3	0.3	0.0	0.2	0.8	1.0	6.5	6.7	7.0	6.2	4.1	21.8	29.6	14.3	3.8	75.4	43.2	48.8	51.2
64461	HOPKINS	98.6	98.2	0.1	0.1	0.1	0.2	0.4	0.5	6.7	6.6	6.6	6.0	5.9	24.9	27.0	13.9	2.3	76.4	38.3	51.2	48.8
64463	KING CITY	98.6	98.2	0.2	0.2	0.2	0.4	0.9	1.3	6.9	6.9	7.4	7.3	5.5	23.2	24.3	14.5	4.1	74.5	39.9	48.7	51.3
64465	LATHROP	96.9	96.3	1.3	1.6	0.1	0.1	1.3	1.8	6.9	7.1	7.0	6.9	5.6	26.0	27.8	11.1	1.7	74.7	38.3	49.2	50.8
64466	MAITLAND	99.8	99.8	0.0	0.0	0.0	0.0	0.4	0.6	3.7	5.4	7.7	9.5	4.6	21.7	31.1	12.4	3.9	77.2	43.3	54.7	45.3
64467	MARTINSVILLE	98.4	97.9	0.0	0.0	0.0	0.0	1.6	2.1	7.0	7.0	7.0	6.2	4.5	22.6	26.3	16.9	2.5	74.9	41.3	51.4	48.6
64468	MARYVILLE	95.5	94.3	2.0	2.2	1.2	1.9	0.9	1.2	4.1	3.8	4.0	13.6	21.7	20.9	19.4	9.7	2.8	85.0	27.3	49.3	50.7
64469	MAYSVILLE	98.7	98.4	0.0	0.0	0.2	0.3	0.6	0.9	7.4	7.4	7.2	7.1	5.8	22.2	26.4	13.2	3.2	73.5	39.5	48.8	51.2
64470	MOUND CITY	98.7	98.6	0.1	0.1	0.1	0.1	0.5	0.6	5.1	5.2	5.5	5.9	4.9	21.3	27.7	18.5	5.9	80.3	46.4	47.9	52.1
64471	NEW HAMPTON	99.2	99.2	0.2	0.2	0.2	0.2	1.1	1.5	6.7	6.9	6.3	5.6	5.0	21.7	27.3	15.8	4.6	76.5	42.9	51.2	48.8
64473	OREGON	98.3	98.0	0.1	0.2	0.2	0.2	0.3	0.4	5.7	6.1	6.4	7.2	4.4	24.6	27.9	13.1	4.5	77.0	42.0	50.8	49.2
64474	OSBORN	98.0	97.5	0.5	0.7	0.0	0.0	0.5	0.8	6.7	7.0	7.1	6.8	4.4	25.5	27.8	12.8	1.9	75.0	40.1	47.6	52.4
64475	PARNELL	98.4	98.2	0.0	0.0	0.3	0.3	0.3	0.3	6.9	6.9	6.9	6.1	6.1	25.6	26.1	13.2	2.4	75.5	37.2	51.2	48.8
64476	PICKERING	97.2	96.6	1.0	1.2	0.6	0.8	0.2	0.2	5.9	6.5	6.3	5.7	3.0	28.8	27.6	13.8	2.4	77.9	40.4	52.5	47.5
64477	PLATTSBURG	93.1	91.9	4.6	5.3	0.2	0.3	1.1	1.5	6.5	6.7	6.7	6.0	5.5	22.9	29.5	13.2	3.1	76.2	41.8	48.8	51.2
64479	RAVENWOOD	99.3	99.1	0.0	0.0	0.1	0.2	0.0	0.0	6.9	6.7	6.4	6.1	6.6	27.5	27.4	10.6	1.8	76.4	36.8	52.4	47.6
64480	REA	97.9	97.4	0.9	1.2	0.5	0.7	0.7	0.9	5.6	6.1	6.3	5.1	4.0	25.7	30.1	15.0	2.1	78.5	43.3	53.0	47.0
64481	RIDGEWAY	97.9	97.2	0.1	0.1	0.1	0.2	1.1	1.6	6.7	6.7	6.9	6.7	4.6	22.6	26.5	17.0	2.4	75.5	41.6	51.1	48.9
64482	ROCK PORT	99.0	98.8	0.1	0.1	0.2	0.3	0.7	1.1	4.6	4.8	5.1	5.9	4.9	21.5	30.6	18.0	4.7	82.6	47.2	49.2	50.8
64483	ROSENDALE	99.0	98.5	0.0	0.0	0.0	0.2	0.7	1.1	7.0	7.2	7.2	7.0	4.4	25.7	29.4	11.0	1.1	74.2	38.2	50.0	50.0
64484	RUSHVILLE	98.6	98.2	0.0	0.0	0.2	0.3	0.7	1.0	6.0	6.4	6.8	6.6	4.8	25.4	29.7	12.9	1.5	76.6	41.2	50.7	49.3
64485	SAVANNAH	98.6	98.3	0.2	0.3	0.2	0.3	0.7	0.9	6.3	6.4	6.7	6.9	5.5	24.6	27.1	12.9	3.6	76.4	40.0	47.4	52.6
64486	SHERIDAN	98.7	98.4	0.0	0.0	0.0	0.0	0.5	0.5	6.9	7.8	7.1	5.2	4.0	21.7	27.9	16.3	3.1	74.9	43.0	53.0	47.0
64487	SKIDMORE	99.3	99.3	0.4	0.4	0.0	0.0	0.0	0.0	5.6	6.3	6.5	6.5	3.4	23.2	31.6	15.0	1.8	77.7	43.8	52.3	47.7
64489	STANBERRY	98.4	98.0	0.1	0.1	0.3	0.5	0.2	0.3	6.6	6.8	7.1	7.1	4.7	21.8	26.2	15.5	4.4	75.1	41.9	49.4	50.6
64490	STEWARTSVILLE	97.9	97.2	0.7	0.9	0.1	0.2	0.8	1.2	5.9	6.1	6.2	6.5	5.5	24.2	30.2	13.5	1.9	77.7	41.9	49.3	50.7
64491	TARKIO	93.3	92.2	5.5	6.4	0.2	0.3	0.7	1.0	4.8	4.7	7.2	11.8	5.8	20.7	25.7	15.2	4.2	74.6	40.0	51.9	48.1
64492	TRIMBLE	97.5	96.8	0.5	0.6	0.3	0.6	1.0	1.5	6.4	7.2	7.6	6.3	4.5	22.9	32.2	11.5	1.3	74.6	41.4	51.0	49.0
64493	TURNEY	97.2	96.6	0.3	0.4	0.3	0.2	1.3	1.5	5.5	6.1	6.6	6.6	4.7	22.8	32.6	14.0	1.3	77.6	43.4	50.5	49.5
64494	UNION STAR	97.7	97.0	0.3	0.4	0.1	0.1	1.1	1.5	5.6	5.7	8.5	7.7	3.6	24.9	26.4	14.5	3.1	75.4	41.1	52.1	47.9
64496	WATSON	99.0	98.9	0.5	0.5	0.0	0.0	1.0	1.1	4.9	5.5	4.9	6.0	3.8	26.2	30.6	15.8	2.2	80.9	44.0	51.9	48.1
64497	WEATHERBY	97.7	97.2	0.0	0.0	0.2	0.2	0.7	0.9	7.6	7.8	8.0	6.7	4.4	23.7	27.6	13.1	1.1	72.4	38.2	51.7	48.3
64498	WESTBORO	98.7	98.4	0.2	0.2	0.0	0.0	0.8	1.4	4.6	5.0	5.5	6.4	3.9	22.7	33.3	16.3	2.3	80.5	46.1	49.3	50.7
64499	WORTH	99.1	99.0	0.5	0.5	0.0	0.0	0.5	0.5	4.2	4.7	5.2	6.8	4.7	20.4	33.0	18.3	2.6	81.2	47.2	53.4	46.6
64501	SAINT JOSEPH	85.7	83.4	10.3	11.8	0.3	0.4	3.0	4.1	7.9	7.0	6.4	7.2	8.3	28.5	22.4	9.8	2.4	74.4	33.7	49.8	50.2
64503	SAINT JOSEPH	94.9	93.9	2.2	2.5	0.3	0.4	3.2	4.4	7.3	7.1	6.7	6.4	6.0	26.2	25.3	12.6	2.4	74.9	37.3	47.7	52.3
64504	SAINT JOSEPH	95.8	95.0	1.4	1.6	0.2	0.2	2.6	3.7	6.4	6.1	6.5	7.5	6.6	26.5	26.8	11.8	1.7	76.3	38.2	49.7	50.3
64505	SAINT JOSEPH	95.8	94.9	1.9	2.2	0.3	0.4	1.7	2.3	6.6	6.7	6.7	7.2	6.3	26.3	26.9	10.9	2.5	75.7	38.0	47.9	52.1
64506	SAINT JOSEPH	91.1	89.3	6.1	6.9	1.0	1.5	2.2	3.0	5.1	4.9	5.2	7.0	8.8	26.6	25.3	13.6	3.4	81.3	39.4	51.3	48.7
64507	SAINT JOSEPH	93.1	91.9	4.1	4.6	0.5	0.7	2.3	3.1	6.5	6.2	6.1	8.4	8.1	26.6	24.8	11.1	2.3	77.6	35.7	48.7	51.3
64601	CHILLICOTHE	95.1	94.2	2.9	3.3	0.3	0.5	0.8	1.0	6.2	6.1	6.0	6.2	5.8	24.4	26.1	15.1	4.1	77.9	41.1	45.6	54.4
64620	ALTAMONT	99.2	99.3	0.0	0.0	0.0	0.0	0.5	0.5	6.1	6.3	6.6	5.6	3.9	21.2	31.5	17.1	1.7	77.3	45.2	48.8	51.2
64622	BOGARD	98.9	98.7	0.1	0.1	0.1	0.1	0.4	0.6	5.8	7.1	7.7	7.8	4.3	22.4	29.1	13.5	2.4	74.5	40.7	52.4	47.6
64623	BOSWORTH	99.1	99.0	0.2	0.1	0.2	0.3	0.2	0.3	5.2	5.8	6.3	7.0	4.8	22.3	30.9	15.1	2.5	78.3	43.8	50.7	49.3
64624	BRAYMER	98.6	98.3	0.1	0.1	0.2	0.3	0.5	0.7	6.6	6.7	7.0	7.3	5.3	22.2	26.1	14.4	4.4	74.9	40.8	48.7	51.3
64625	BRECKENRIDGE	97.6	97.3	0.0	0.0	0.3	0.4	0.9	1.2	6.6	6.8	7.4	7.7	4.6	22.9	28.2	13.9	1.9	74.3	40.7	52.4	47.6
64628	BROOKFIELD	97.4	97.0	1.0	1.2	0.2	0.2	0.8	1.1	6.2	5.9	6.0	6.5	5.5	21.0	26.3	17.7	4.8	77.9	43.9	46.7	53.3
64630	BROWNING	98.6	98.5	0.2	0.3	0.0	0.0	0.7	1.0	6.6	6.1	6.4	6.4	4.9	23.8	25.3	17.9	2.6	76.5	41.3	47.3	52.7
64631	BUCKLIN	98.5	98.3	0.1	0.1	0.0	0.0	0.9	1.2	5.4	5.4	6.0	6.6	5.1	23.0	27.9	17.0	3.6	79.0	43.9	49.1	50.9
64632	CAINSVILLE	97.9	97.6	0.1	0.1	0.4	0.4	0.7	0.9	5.8	6.0	6.0	5.8	5.2	21.6	28.7	18.0	3.0	78.6	44.7	49.6	50.4
64633	CARROLLTON	95.7	94.8	2.6	3.0	0.1	0.2	0.9	1.3	6.7	6.7	6.4	6.2	4.9	21.7	26.1	16.4	4.9	76.5	42.7	47.8	52.2
64635	CHULA	99.4	99.2	0.0	0.1	0.1	0.3	0.1	0.3	7.7	8.1	7.4	6.4	4.3	23.1	27.3	13.4	2.3	72.6	39.0	50.3	49.7
64636	COFFEY	97.3	96.9	0.0	0.0	0.7	0.7	1.7	2.1	7.2	7.2	7.2	6.9	4.8	22.8	24.5	16.9	2.4	73.8	39.7	46.9	53.1
64637	COWGILL	98.6	98.4	0.2	0.3	0.0	0.0	0.5	0.4	6.2	6.4	7.0	7.5	5.2	22.3	29.1	14.2	2.1	75.7	41.6	53.6	46.4
64638	DAWN	99.1	98.6	0.0	0.0	0.0	0.3	0.0	0.0	6.1	6.4	6.4	6.4	5.2	22.5	29.8	15.0	2.3	77.5	42.2	49.4	50.6
64639	DE WITT	97.1	96.8	1.8	2.0	0.2	0.2	0.2	0.2	4.7	5.0	5.6	5.9	4.3	23.3	33.4	15.8	2.0	81.0	45.7	51.2	48.8
64640	GALLATIN	99.1	99.1	0.1	0.1	0.1	0.1	0.5	0.5	6.7	6.7	6.7	6.4	4.6	22.2	27.5	15.6	3.6	75.7	42.3	47.6	52.4
64641	GALT	98.3	98.3	0.7	0.7	0.0	0.0	1.0	1.2	7.5	7.7	7.8	5.7	4.5	21.0	28.2	15.5	2.1	73.6	41.5	49.6	50.4
64642	GILMAN CITY	97.5	96.8	0.0	0.0	0.2	0.3	1.2	1.7	6.5	6.5	6.8	6.3	3.8	26.3	26.5	15.3	2.3	76.3	40.7	49.5	50.5
64643	HALE	99.7	99.6	0.0	0.0	0.1	0.1	0.6	0.9	7.7	7.7	7.5	7.1	5.4	23.2	26.0	12.9	2.6	72.5	38.1	47.9	52.1
64644	HAMILTON	98.8	98.6	0.1	0.1	0.1	0.1	0.7	1.1	7.2	6.9	6.9	6.8	5.5	22.9	25.3	14.6	4.0	74.7	40.4	48.5	51.5
64645	HARRIS	98.7	97.3	0.0	0.0	0.0	0.0	2.5	3.4	9.4	9.4	6.7	6.0	5.4	23.5	24.8	12.1	2.7	70.5	37.5	53.7	46.3
64646	HUMPHREYS	98.5	98.2	0.2	0.2	0.2	0.2	1.5	2.2	7.8	7.8	7.8	5.8	4.5	22.7	27.4	14.0	2.2	72.8	40.4	53.0	47.0
64647	JAMESON	98.9	98.8	0.0	0.0	0.9	0.9	0.3	0.0	7.3	7.6	7.8	7.3	4.4	24.1	26.2	14.0	1.5	73.0	38.3	49.4	50.6
64648	JAMESPORT	98.5	98.4	0.0	0.0	0.5	0.5	0.6	0.6	7.7	7.7	7.5	7.5	5.1	23.4	25.7	13.3	1.9	72.4	36.8	49.0	51.0
64649	KIDDER	99.0	98.7	0.3	0.4	0.1	0.2	1.7	2.3	7.6	7.6	7.8	7.2	6.3	21.4	29.0	11.9	1.3	72.6	38.7	50.8	49.2
64650	KINGSTON	98.7	98.4	0.1	0.1	0.1	0.1	0.6	0.8	6.1	6.4	6.7	7.4	4.9	22.7	30.6	13.7	1.5	76.1	41.3	51.6	48.4
64651	LACLEDE	97.7	97.2	1.1	1.2	0.1	0.3	1.2	1.8	5.4	5.8	6.2	6.8	4.4	23.0	31.0	14.8	2.5	78.4	43.7	50.8	49.2
64652	LAREDO	98.5	98.3	0.0	0.0	0.0	0.0	1.1	1.3	5.2	6.0	6.5	6.5	4.6	21.3	33.8	14.2	2.1	78.5	45.0	50.2	49.8
64653	LINNEUS	98.8	98.8	0.3	0.4	0.1	0.1	0.2	0.2	7.1	7.5	7.3	5.7	4.4	22.6	29.3	13.5	2.6	74.4	41.1	49.9	50.1
64654	LOCK SPRINGS	99.3	99.3	0.0	0.0	0.0	0.0	0.0	0.0	11.9	11.9	10.4	8.1	4.4	23.7	20.0	8.9	0.7	60.7	28.2	49.6	50.4
64655	LUCERNE	99.5	99.5	0.0	0.0	0.0	0.0	0.5	0.5	6.0	6.0	6.0	5.0	3.5	19.6	32.2	19.1	2.5	78.9	46.9	51.8	48.2
64656	LUDLOW	98.5	98.5	0.2	0.2	0.2	0.2	0.0	0.0	5.9	5.9	6.2	6.2	5.4	22.2	30.9	14.8	2.5	78.0	42.9	49.1	50.9
64657	MC FALL	98.4	97.6	0.3	0.5	0.7	1.0	1.6	2.3	6.1	6.3	6.5	6.8	4.2	21.8	26.9	16.2	5.2	76.1	43.6	51.7	48.3
64658	MARCELINE	98.2	98.0	0.1	0.1	0.2	0.3	0.6	0.8	5.9	5.9	6.5	7.1	5.4	22.8	27.1	15.0	4.3	76.9	41.9	46.8	53.2
64659	MEADVILLE	99.4	99.3	0.2	0.2	0.1	0.1	0.4	0.6	7.8	8.2	7.7	6.2	3.2	24.1	27.2	12.5	3.0	72.4	39.8	49.6	50.4
64660	MENDON	99.1	99.0	0.2	0.2	0.0	0.0	0.2	0.4	6.8	7.2	7.0	6.0	3.6	22.7	26.9	17.3	2.6	75.3	42.3	50.4	49.6
64661	MERCER	98.8	98.7	0.5	0.5	0.0	0.0	0.2	0.2	4.7	5.3	5.8	6.2	4.1	20.3	32.7	18.2	2.7	80.5	47.2	50.4	49.6
64664	MOORESVILLE	100.0	100.0	0.0	0.0	0.0	0.0	0.3	0.3	6.0	6.4	6.7	6.7	4.3	22.4	31.4	13.7	2.3	76.3	43.0	51.2	48.8
64667	NEWTOWN	97.9	97.5	0.3	0.3	0.0	0.3	2.6	3.6	9.6	9.3	9.0	6.0	4.9	23.0	24.1	11.8	2.2	68.2	36.2	54.0	46.0
64668	NORBORNE	97.1	96.7	1.8	2.1	0.0	0.1	0.7	1.0	6.3	6.8	6.9	5.5	4.9	22.6	29.2	15.0	2.9	76.5	42.5	49.0	51.0
64670	PATTONSBURG	97.6	97.6	0.0	0.0	0.2	0.2	1.6	1.8	7.4	7.3	7.2	6.5	4.9	22.5	25.4	16.5	2.3	74.1	40.0	47.2	52.8
64671	POLO	98.0	97.6	0.3	0.3	0.1	0.2	0.9	1.1	5.1	6.3	6.9	7.7	4.8	22.5	32.0	13.1	1.7	76.7	42.9	49.6	50.4
64672	POWERSVILLE	99.3	99.2	0.0	0.0	0.0	0.0	0.4	0.4	5.6	6.4	6.0	4.9	3.8	19.9	31.6	19.9	1.9	78.6	46.9	50.8	49.2
64673	PRINCETON	98.7	98.6	0.0	0.0	0.1	0.1	0.4	0.4	6.0	6.4	6.3	5.6	4.5	22.1	27.7	17.1	4.3	78.0	44.2	48.8	51.2
64674	PURDIN	98.8	98.8	0.2	0.2	0.0	0.0	0.8	1.0	6.9	6.9	7.1	6.4	4.6	23.7	25.2	16.8	2.5	75.5	40.3	47.6	52.4
64676	ROTHVILLE	99.1	99.0	0.0	0.0	0.0	0.0	0.3	0.3	6.8	7.4	7.1	6.1	3.2	22.6	27.1	17.1	2.6	74.8	42.4	51.0	49.0
64679	SPICKARD	98.3	98.3	0.3	0.3	0.1	0.1	0.4	0.4	5.8	6.2	6.2	5.5	4.8	23.0	30.5	15.9	2.2	78.6	44.0	50.3	49.7
64681	SUMNER	99.2	99.2	0.0	0.0	0.0	0.0	0.4	0.4	6.5	7.3	7.3	6.1	3.3	22.0	28.0	17.1	2.4	74.4	42.9	49.6	50.4
64682	TINA	98.6	98.4	0.0	0.0	0.5	0.7	0.5	0.7	5.3	5.9	6.4	7.1	4.6	23.1	29.5	15.5	2.7	77.9	43.2	49.8	50.2
64683	TRENTON	97.5	97.4	0.4	0.5	0.2	0.2	1.8	1.8	6.1	5.8	5.9	7.0	5.7	21.1	26.7	17.2	4.5	78.4	43.6	47.2	52.8
64686	UTICA	99.1	99.1	0.3	0.3	0.0	0.0	0.3	0.6	6.0	6.3	6.9	6.3	4.4	22.3	30.8	14.2	2.8	76.7	43.3	51.3	48.7
64688	WHEELING	99.8	99.8	0.0	0.0	0.0	0.0	0.2	0.5	7.3	8.0	7.8	6.8	3.9	21.2	28.7	13.9	2.4	72.5	41.1	51.8	48.2
64689	WINSTON	99.1	99.0	0.1	0.1	0.0	0.0	0.5	0.5	6.2	6.5	6.8	5.7	3.9	21.7	31.0	16.5	1.7	76.8	44.4	49.2	50.8
64701	HARRISONVILLE	96.4	95.5	0.8	1.0	0.5	0.8	1.3	1.8	7.3	7.2	7.1	6.9	5.8	25.4	26.5	11.7	2.1	73.9	38.0	48.6	51.4
	MISSOURI	84.9	83.3	11.2	11.7	1.2	1.7	2.1	2.8	6.6	6.6	6.6	7.0	6.7	26.1	26.5	11.7	2.1	76.1	37.7	48.8	51.2
	UNITED STATES	75.1	72.0	12.3	12.7	3.8	4.6	12.5	15.7	6.8	6.7	6.6	7.1	6.9	27.0	26.0	10.9	1.9	75.7	36.9	49.2	50.8

ZIP CODE #	POST OFFICE NAME	2009 Per Capita Income	2009 HH Income Base	2009 HOUSEHOLD INCOME DISTRIBUTION (%) Less than $25,000	$25,000 to $49,999	$50,000 to $99,999	$100,000 to $149,999	$150,000 or More	MEDIAN HOUSEHOLD INCOME 2009	2014	2009 National Centile	2009 State Centile	2009 Home Value Base	2009 HOME VALUE DISTRIBUTION (%) Less than $50,000	$50,000 to $89,999	$90,000 to $174,999	$175,000 to $399,999	$400,000 or More	2009 Median Home Value
64459	HELENA	23185	230	16.5	34.8	40.0	5.2	3.5	48536	52587	58	77	208	19.7	14.9	32.2	30.8	2.4	126136
64461	HOPKINS	17346	341	33.1	32.0	32.0	2.1	0.9	37127	39298	24	41	252	55.6	19.8	15.1	7.9	1.6	37941
64463	KING CITY	17025	639	34.4	35.4	25.8	2.7	1.7	33983	35879	15	26	467	39.8	22.3	28.5	7.5	1.9	65167
64465	LATHROP	24769	1778	19.2	25.6	41.3	10.3	3.6	55015	57760	71	85	1411	9.0	16.4	46.8	24.0	3.8	126854
64466	MAITLAND	18463	219	35.6	29.2	28.3	5.0	1.8	37141	40917	24	41	156	43.6	25.6	17.9	9.6	3.2	60000
64467	MARTINSVILLE	15961	88	25.0	42.0	29.5	3.4	0.0	38420	40909	28	47	71	31.0	22.5	32.4	11.3	2.8	81667
64468	MARYVILLE	20862	5293	31.0	27.1	33.6	5.3	2.9	41533	45168	38	59	2937	9.7	17.6	43.3	26.6	2.8	129242
64469	MAYSVILLE	16125	822	29.4	36.3	30.0	3.9	0.4	37812	41189	26	44	652	31.6	22.9	31.1	10.3	4.1	78529
64470	MOUND CITY	18640	730	41.1	30.1	24.4	3.2	1.2	30378	31821	9	12	508	29.9	28.3	34.1	6.9	0.8	76774
64471	NEW HAMPTON	18614	215	24.2	41.4	31.2	2.8	0.5	38624	38355	29	47	169	34.9	21.3	31.4	12.4	0.0	80455
64473	OREGON	19602	636	25.6	35.7	32.7	4.2	1.7	41685	44060	38	60	499	26.7	30.5	33.5	7.6	1.8	82604
64474	OSBORN	21820	299	20.1	34.4	38.5	4.3	2.7	45455	50232	50	70	227	15.9	28.2	37.4	17.6	0.9	94821
64475	PARNELL	18668	168	32.1	32.7	32.1	2.4	0.6	37513	40568	25	43	124	59.7	20.2	12.1	7.3	0.8	34231
64476	PICKERING	21942	212	22.2	28.8	43.4	3.8	1.9	48919	50879	59	77	172	25.0	16.3	30.2	22.1	6.4	127000
64477	PLATTSBURG	24147	1503	22.1	27.3	37.5	8.7	4.4	50407	53156	62	80	1145	10.0	17.1	44.2	24.9	3.8	127417
64479	RAVENWOOD	21240	405	22.7	36.5	33.1	5.7	2.0	42585	45000	41	63	301	26.2	33.9	25.6	12.6	1.7	73409
64480	REA	21284	173	22.0	30.1	41.6	4.6	1.7	47930	50900	56	76	143	32.9	16.1	33.6	12.6	4.9	92143
64481	RIDGEWAY	15181	463	36.3	40.0	19.9	3.5	0.4	32599	33628	13	20	361	41.0	22.4	23.0	10.2	3.3	63611
64482	ROCK PORT	21804	999	34.4	30.4	28.1	5.2	1.8	37496	38584	25	43	701	22.5	28.1	38.7	9.1	1.6	89151
64483	ROSENDALE	19296	244	27.0	34.0	32.0	4.9	2.0	41684	44022	38	60	207	40.6	27.5	23.2	8.2	0.5	64474
64484	RUSHVILLE	23072	462	21.4	32.3	37.9	5.6	2.8	47411	49141	55	75	381	23.4	25.2	34.1	15.0	2.4	92200
64485	SAVANNAH	22376	3049	23.8	28.1	38.4	6.1	3.5	47784	51461	56	75	2286	14.1	19.0	48.2	17.1	1.6	111508
64486	SHERIDAN	18596	244	30.7	36.9	26.2	4.1	2.0	36847	38521	23	39	192	38.5	24.5	19.8	10.9	6.3	64444
64487	SKIDMORE	19022	322	29.8	35.1	32.0	2.5	0.6	38363	40834	28	46	243	45.7	26.3	17.7	7.4	2.9	53750
64489	STANBERRY	16211	660	32.4	35.6	28.0	2.9	1.1	36665	38595	23	38	520	35.0	24.0	28.1	10.8	2.1	70000
64490	STEWARTSVILLE	19995	807	23.0	31.6	36.7	6.8	1.9	45999	50047	51	72	654	18.5	24.6	33.5	22.2	1.2	98824
64491	TARKIO	18288	812	33.9	34.9	25.7	4.3	1.2	34492	35557	17	28	548	30.3	32.8	31.9	4.6	0.4	74524
64492	TRIMBLE	30752	618	17.6	26.4	38.3	8.9	8.7	55947	58977	73	86	527	2.3	17.1	40.6	31.1	8.9	147837
64493	TURNEY	24427	191	15.7	32.5	38.2	11.0	2.6	51772	55113	65	81	170	10.0	13.5	37.1	34.7	4.7	148529
64494	UNION STAR	19044	370	27.8	34.3	32.2	3.5	2.2	40193	44343	33	54	303	29.4	25.7	27.4	15.5	2.0	80882
64496	WATSON	18794	70	28.6	30.0	31.4	7.1	2.9	42843	45000	42	64	46	39.1	26.1	30.4	4.3	0.0	66667
64497	WEATHERBY	18618	166	19.9	38.6	36.7	4.2	0.6	42572	46757	41	63	140	29.3	15.0	34.3	15.0	6.4	105000
64498	WESTBORO	21955	179	26.8	33.0	29.1	6.7	4.5	40861	41451	36	57	121	36.4	25.6	30.6	5.8	1.7	62778
64499	WORTH	17340	81	29.6	39.5	27.2	3.7	0.0	36913	37985	23	40	65	36.9	29.2	23.1	10.8	0.0	63750
64501	SAINT JOSEPH	17159	4877	39.3	32.2	24.7	2.4	1.4	31718	33174	11	17	2384	23.9	41.9	29.5	4.5	0.3	74770
64503	SAINT JOSEPH	21920	4936	23.5	30.4	36.5	6.8	2.7	45180	50237	49	69	3591	21.6	30.9	40.2	6.9	0.4	87075
64504	SAINT JOSEPH	19944	4299	26.1	29.9	38.5	4.2	1.3	43976	47224	45	66	3303	30.3	35.3	26.1	7.8	0.5	69810
64505	SAINT JOSEPH	23724	4852	20.6	29.2	38.0	8.3	4.0	50199	52159	62	79	3594	15.7	28.3	38.3	16.0	1.7	98816
64506	SAINT JOSEPH	28368	8748	21.0	25.4	37.4	10.1	6.1	53816	55910	69	84	5453	3.4	8.3	53.8	31.6	2.9	146732
64507	SAINT JOSEPH	21001	5275	24.9	33.0	34.3	5.6	2.3	42662	46041	41	63	3637	15.6	34.8	38.0	9.7	1.9	89652
64601	CHILLICOTHE	21076	4591	30.0	30.5	31.8	4.7	3.0	40746	43265	35	56	3174	23.5	26.1	34.1	13.8	2.6	90751
64620	ALTAMONT	19756	163	20.9	38.7	33.7	5.5	1.2	42498	43752	41	63	137	20.4	19.7	34.3	23.4	2.2	111719
64622	BOGARD	16269	360	34.2	30.6	31.4	2.5	1.4	36759	40709	23	39	292	26.4	23.6	32.5	12.7	4.8	90000
64623	BOSWORTH	18664	270	27.4	34.1	31.9	5.9	0.7	39702	42603	32	52	227	39.2	23.8	25.6	6.6	4.8	66458
64624	BRAYMER	16796	704	34.4	34.4	27.0	3.7	0.6	34596	37220	17	29	525	35.0	31.8	22.9	9.0	1.3	66705
64625	BRECKENRIDGE	16874	280	38.2	31.1	25.7	5.0	0.0	32192	34338	12	18	209	43.1	24.4	19.6	12.0	1.0	60455
64628	BROOKFIELD	18881	2416	33.7	33.3	28.4	3.3	1.3	34406	35213	16	28	1792	30.3	31.2	29.0	9.1	0.4	70603
64630	BROWNING	15036	164	42.7	33.5	21.3	1.8	0.6	30670	30616	9	13	129	53.5	18.6	22.5	5.4	0.0	43571
64631	BUCKLIN	18127	427	37.9	33.7	24.4	2.6	1.4	31464	32525	10	16	346	45.7	27.2	19.9	6.1	1.2	55556
64632	CAINSVILLE	15972	302	37.7	37.1	22.2	2.0	1.0	31724	32804	11	17	245	46.5	32.7	15.1	4.9	0.8	53542
64633	CARROLLTON	20105	2108	33.3	36.1	22.7	3.9	4.0	36360	37649	22	36	1445	26.3	29.5	35.6	6.7	1.9	82339
64635	CHULA	17583	287	34.1	31.4	29.6	2.4	2.4	38904	39558	29	48	216	38.9	19.4	29.2	12.0	0.5	70000
64636	COFFEY	16401	116	39.7	31.9	24.1	2.6	1.7	33902	36246	15	26	88	34.1	30.7	22.7	11.4	1.1	68571
64637	COWGILL	17690	281	31.0	34.5	28.5	5.0	1.1	34891	37063	17	30	220	28.2	21.4	30.9	17.7	1.8	90909
64638	DAWN	21311	148	33.8	29.7	29.1	5.4	2.0	37349	39379	25	42	105	45.7	17.1	21.0	13.3	2.9	57500
64639	DE WITT	19102	178	20.2	39.3	36.0	3.4	1.1	45238	47955	49	69	144	21.5	27.8	31.3	13.9	5.6	95000
64640	GALLATIN	20570	1316	28.0	34.1	31.3	4.5	2.1	39617	41825	32	52	969	22.2	25.7	33.1	17.2	1.8	93661
64641	GALT	16231	242	31.4	40.5	26.4	1.7	0.0	34597	36644	17	29	185	48.6	16.8	20.0	9.2	5.4	52273
64642	GILMAN CITY	16437	395	35.7	31.6	29.1	3.0	0.5	34859	38635	17	30	320	49.4	25.9	17.2	5.9	1.6	50667
64643	HALE	17064	282	30.5	37.2	27.7	4.6	0.0	36906	38723	23	40	231	42.0	30.3	21.6	4.8	1.3	60172
64644	HAMILTON	18384	1127	33.3	34.3	26.8	3.5	2.1	34388	37157	16	28	809	24.7	30.4	30.7	12.5	1.7	83083
64645	HARRIS	16275	65	41.5	30.8	24.6	1.5	1.5	29511	34078	7	9	49	65.3	10.2	16.3	6.1	2.0	41667
64646	HUMPHREYS	16793	175	36.0	32.0	26.9	3.4	1.7	34717	37365	17	29	131	45.0	15.3	27.5	9.9	2.3	62500
64647	JAMESON	22001	148	29.7	40.5	22.3	2.0	5.4	35000	37902	18	31	111	31.5	18.0	34.2	11.7	4.5	90714
64648	JAMESPORT	13603	714	35.6	38.2	20.6	3.9	1.7	32837	34144	13	21	564	28.4	25.0	32.4	12.1	2.1	79032
64649	KIDDER	19687	420	21.9	31.4	40.7	4.0	1.9	46951	47327	54	74	349	18.9	23.5	31.5	23.2	2.9	104500
64650	KINGSTON	17378	351	27.9	37.3	29.3	4.3	1.1	36830	38427	23	39	289	28.7	24.9	24.2	14.9	7.3	79800
64651	LACLEDE	15810	294	37.8	29.6	28.9	3.4	0.3	33215	34675	14	23	218	45.9	16.1	26.1	10.1	1.8	55625
64652	LAREDO	17447	208	28.8	38.9	30.3	1.9	0.0	40000	42326	33	54	162	44.4	21.0	20.4	12.3	1.9	60625
64653	LINNEUS	17728	309	30.4	32.4	31.4	3.2	2.6	40286	41212	34	55	246	32.5	24.0	30.5	11.0	2.0	78571
64654	LOCK SPRINGS	14905	53	32.1	43.4	22.6	1.9	0.0	33317	32679	14	24	44	22.7	22.7	29.5	22.7	2.3	108333
64655	LUCERNE	22298	85	25.9	36.5	29.4	4.7	3.5	41130	46384	36	58	70	22.9	27.1	30.0	14.3	5.7	90000
64656	LUDLOW	19865	166	40.4	25.3	27.7	5.4	1.2	32359	36008	12	19	106	57.5	16.0	17.9	7.5	0.9	40000
64657	MC FALL	20826	218	22.0	39.0	33.0	3.7	2.3	40000	44094	33	54	179	30.7	15.6	30.2	18.4	5.0	101630
64658	MARCELINE	17737	1240	34.7	32.3	28.6	2.7	1.8	34508	36532	17	28	948	31.2	31.9	26.7	9.1	1.2	71972
64659	MEADVILLE	17749	329	24.9	38.6	31.9	3.3	1.2	41077	42482	36	57	277	22.0	32.9	30.0	10.5	4.7	81563
64660	MENDON	17473	214	35.0	34.6	28.0	2.3	0.0	32972	35634	13	21	183	36.1	20.8	25.1	14.8	3.3	75625
64661	MERCER	16545	411	36.5	34.1	25.3	3.4	0.7	32455	33968	12	19	349	48.4	27.2	16.3	6.3	1.7	51410
64664	MOORESVILLE	19859	128	28.1	32.0	33.6	4.7	1.6	39433	39759	31	51	108	50.9	25.9	18.5	2.8	1.9	48333
64667	NEWTOWN	16033	139	38.1	30.9	27.3	2.2	1.4	33066	35000	13	22	104	62.5	9.6	17.3	8.7	1.9	42353
64668	NORBORNE	20673	687	33.3	33.3	26.5	3.3	3.5	37365	39268	25	42	522	25.7	28.2	32.2	11.3	2.7	82308
64670	PATTONSBURG	19018	411	36.3	34.5	23.1	2.9	3.2	34871	36258	17	30	311	35.7	26.7	22.2	13.5	1.9	70227
64671	POLO	21687	823	21.6	32.6	35.6	6.8	3.4	46829	47460	54	74	702	21.9	17.0	33.3	25.1	2.7	109239
64672	POWERSVILLE	22177	113	27.4	35.4	30.1	3.5	3.5	40275	45320	34	55	93	20.4	29.0	31.2	15.1	4.3	90625
64673	PRINCETON	18542	1019	32.3	33.7	29.3	3.1	1.6	37468	38828	25	42	740	34.9	29.3	24.6	6.9	4.3	69649
64674	PURDIN	16363	208	39.9	36.1	21.2	1.9	1.0	32159	32635	12	18	169	48.5	21.3	22.5	6.5	1.2	52778
64676	ROTHVILLE	15932	121	34.7	35.5	27.3	2.5	0.0	33058	35274	13	21	103	35.9	21.4	25.2	14.6	2.9	75000
64679	SPICKARD	16618	292	39.4	32.2	25.7	1.4	1.4	29812	31678	8	10	219	52.5	21.9	18.3	5.0	2.3	47500
64681	SUMNER	18952	114	35.1	35.1	27.2	2.6	0.0	32694	34470	13	20	97	37.1	20.6	23.7	15.5	3.1	73750
64682	TINA	16641	172	29.7	34.9	32.0	2.9	0.6	38718	41672	29	48	140	26.4	26.4	31.4	10.7	5.0	83333
64683	TRENTON	19165	3575	34.9	33.5	26.1	3.2	2.3	33283	34977	14	23	2518	33.0	26.6	28.4	10.0	1.9	71884
64686	UTICA	17659	122	27.9	32.8	34.4	4.9	0.0	38879	41396	29	48	104	49.0	28.8	18.3	2.9	1.0	50769
64688	WHEELING	22544	167	28.1	28.1	34.1	6.0	3.6	46123	48516	52	72	130	27.7	20.8	36.9	13.8	0.8	91818
64689	WINSTON	18553	326	22.4	38.7	33.1	4.6	1.2	41451	42803	38	59	272	23.2	19.9	32.7	22.1	2.2	105833
64701	HARRISONVILLE	24001	5881	15.8	26.1	47.1	8.0	3.0	56546	58772	73	87	4360	10.8	14.2	46.4	26.0	2.7	125000
	MISSOURI	25286		22.8	27.7	35.3	9.1	5.2	49522	52035				12.8	19.4	39.1	24.2	4.6	122064
	UNITED STATES	27277		20.9	24.4	35.3	11.7	7.6	54719	56938				9.3	13.1	31.6	32.6	13.5	162279

ZIP CODE #	POST OFFICE NAME	FINANCIAL SERVICES: Auto Loan	Home Loan	Invest-ments	Retire-ment Plans	THE HOME: Home Improvements: Home Repair	Lawn & Garden	Furnishings: Comput-ers & Hard-ware-Personal	Major Appli-ances	TV, Radio, Sound Equip-ment	Furni-ture	ENTERTAINMENT: Dine out/ Carry out	Sports Equip-ment	Fees & Tickets	Toys & Games	Travel	Cable TV	PERSONAL: Apparel & Services	Auto Repairs	Health Insur-ance	Pets & Supplies
64459	HELENA	87	79	79	83	81	94	78	89	81	71	79	67	72	82	78	86	54	82	91	103
64461	HOPKINS	76	54	64	53	54	73	57	67	63	55	62	51	45	65	52	69	41	63	71	81
64463	KING CITY	74	52	76	51	54	77	57	71	63	50	61	55	45	62	56	69	40	66	77	84
64465	LATHROP	95	94	85	95	92	99	90	94	91	88	91	72	89	93	90	93	62	91	97	112
64466	MAITLAND	78	54	86	53	56	82	60	74	62	48	61	61	44	61	59	68	40	69	78	91
64467	MARTINSVILLE	78	55	83	54	57	81	59	74	63	51	62	58	45	62	58	69	41	68	77	89
64468	MARYVILLE	75	59	60	61	58	65	80	67	76	69	76	55	66	76	66	76	53	74	71	82
64469	MAYSVILLE	73	54	72	52	56	75	57	70	63	52	61	52	46	62	55	68	41	65	74	82
64470	MOUND CITY	69	49	71	48	51	72	54	67	59	48	57	51	42	58	52	65	38	62	72	79
64471	NEW HAMPTON	78	55	81	54	57	80	58	73	63	52	62	56	45	63	57	69	41	67	76	87
64473	OREGON	87	60	95	60	63	92	66	82	69	54	68	68	49	68	66	75	44	77	87	101
64474	OSBORN	98	67	107	67	70	103	75	93	78	60	77	77	55	76	74	85	50	87	98	114
64475	PARNELL	76	55	63	53	54	72	57	66	63	55	62	51	45	66	52	69	41	63	70	80
64476	PICKERING	90	63	98	63	66	95	69	85	72	57	71	70	52	71	69	78	46	80	90	105
64477	PLATTSBURG	93	85	96	85	85	103	83	95	87	77	86	72	78	87	85	92	58	90	100	111
64479	RAVENWOOD	95	68	78	66	68	90	71	82	78	69	77	63	57	82	64	85	52	78	87	100
64480	REA	94	65	103	65	68	99	72	89	75	58	74	74	53	73	72	82	48	83	94	110
64481	RIDGEWAY	66	46	71	46	48	70	51	63	54	43	53	51	39	53	50	60	35	59	68	77
64482	ROCK PORT	80	57	82	56	60	84	63	78	69	55	67	59	50	68	61	76	45	73	84	92
64483	ROSENDALE	92	66	93	64	68	93	68	86	75	63	74	65	54	75	67	83	49	79	89	102
64484	RUSHVILLE	95	76	87	77	77	98	78	90	82	71	81	70	66	84	76	89	55	84	94	108
64485	SAVANNAH	89	79	81	79	80	92	79	87	83	75	81	65	73	83	77	87	55	83	92	102
64486	SHERIDAN	79	54	86	54	57	83	60	75	62	49	62	62	44	61	60	68	40	70	79	92
64487	SKIDMORE	76	53	83	53	56	81	59	73	61	48	60	60	43	60	58	66	39	68	77	89
64489	STANBERRY	73	51	77	50	53	76	56	70	60	48	59	55	43	59	55	66	39	65	75	84
64490	STEWARTSVILLE	84	70	80	71	72	90	72	84	76	64	74	63	63	76	71	82	50	78	88	98
64491	TARKIO	72	52	73	51	54	76	57	70	63	50	61	53	45	62	55	69	41	65	76	83
64492	TRIMBLE	118	113	111	117	114	127	108	120	110	101	109	91	103	112	110	115	75	112	122	140
64493	TURNEY	90	89	84	92	89	98	84	92	85	79	85	71	82	87	86	89	58	87	94	108
64494	UNION STAR	84	58	92	58	61	89	64	80	67	52	66	66	47	66	64	73	43	74	84	98
64496	WATSON	88	60	96	60	63	93	67	83	70	54	69	69	49	68	67	76	45	78	88	103
64497	WEATHERBY	80	69	73	67	69	78	67	75	70	67	70	56	61	72	65	73	47	72	76	89
64498	WESTBORO	95	66	105	65	69	100	73	90	76	59	75	75	53	74	72	83	49	84	95	111
64499	WORTH	73	50	80	50	53	77	56	69	58	45	57	57	41	57	56	63	37	65	73	85
64501	SAINT JOSEPH	57	48	43	50	46	52	58	52	61	53	60	42	53	60	51	63	42	57	60	65
64503	SAINT JOSEPH	82	75	71	75	72	85	77	80	80	72	79	62	72	81	74	84	54	79	87	96
64504	SAINT JOSEPH	78	68	65	68	66	78	72	75	75	68	74	58	65	76	67	79	51	74	80	89
64505	SAINT JOSEPH	90	87	79	88	84	92	87	88	89	85	88	67	85	90	85	91	61	88	93	105
64506	SAINT JOSEPH	94	93	91	95	93	96	96	94	98	95	98	71	97	97	96	100	68	97	102	112
64507	SAINT JOSEPH	77	70	64	71	68	78	75	74	77	70	76	58	70	78	71	80	52	76	81	90
64601	CHILLICOTHE	78	65	75	65	66	82	69	77	74	63	72	58	61	73	67	79	49	75	85	91
64620	ALTAMONT	87	63	101	62	67	92	67	84	70	58	69	67	52	68	69	76	45	78	87	102
64622	BOGARD	78	54	85	53	56	82	59	74	62	49	61	60	44	61	59	68	40	69	78	90
64623	BOSWORTH	83	57	89	57	60	86	63	78	66	53	65	63	47	65	62	72	43	73	82	95
64624	BRAYMER	71	52	73	51	54	74	56	69	61	49	59	52	44	60	54	67	39	64	74	81
64625	BRECKENRIDGE	73	52	75	50	54	74	54	68	59	49	58	52	43	59	53	65	38	63	71	81
64628	BROOKFIELD	69	56	66	55	56	72	60	67	65	55	63	51	52	64	58	70	43	65	74	80
64630	BROWNING	62	44	63	43	45	64	48	59	53	42	51	46	38	52	47	58	34	55	64	71
64631	BUCKLIN	72	51	74	50	53	75	56	69	61	49	59	53	44	60	54	67	39	64	74	82
64632	CAINSVILLE	64	46	65	45	48	66	49	61	55	44	53	46	39	54	48	60	35	57	66	73
64633	CARROLLTON	82	59	81	58	61	84	66	78	71	57	69	61	51	70	63	77	46	74	84	94
64635	CHULA	80	58	82	56	60	82	60	75	65	55	64	57	48	65	59	72	43	69	78	89
64636	COFFEY	70	50	72	49	52	73	55	68	60	48	58	52	43	59	53	66	39	63	73	80
64637	COWGILL	77	57	80	57	60	80	59	74	64	54	63	56	48	64	59	70	42	68	77	88
64638	DAWN	86	61	89	60	63	90	67	83	73	58	71	64	52	72	65	80	47	77	89	99
64639	DE WITT	85	58	93	58	61	90	65	81	68	53	67	67	48	66	65	74	43	75	85	99
64640	GALLATIN	83	60	90	59	64	87	65	81	71	58	69	61	52	69	65	77	46	75	86	96
64641	GALT	69	49	71	48	51	70	51	64	56	47	55	48	40	56	50	62	36	59	67	77
64642	GILMAN CITY	71	49	77	49	51	75	54	67	57	45	56	55	40	56	54	62	37	63	72	83
64643	HALE	71	51	72	50	53	74	55	69	62	50	60	51	44	61	54	68	40	64	75	81
64644	HAMILTON	78	57	78	56	59	80	61	75	67	54	65	57	49	66	59	73	43	70	80	88
64645	HARRIS	67	48	68	46	50	68	49	62	54	46	53	47	39	54	48	60	35	57	65	74
64646	HUMPHREYS	77	54	82	53	56	80	58	73	62	50	61	57	44	61	57	68	40	67	76	88
64647	JAMESON	91	63	100	63	66	96	70	87	73	57	72	71	51	71	69	79	47	81	92	107
64648	JAMESPORT	71	52	73	52	54	74	56	68	60	48	58	53	44	59	55	65	39	63	73	81
64649	KIDDER	84	74	72	72	73	81	72	78	75	72	74	58	66	77	69	77	50	75	79	93
64650	KINGSTON	79	57	82	55	59	80	58	74	64	54	63	55	47	64	58	71	42	68	77	88
64651	LACLEDE	69	50	71	48	51	70	51	65	56	47	55	49	41	56	50	62	37	59	67	77
64652	LAREDO	72	50	79	49	52	76	55	68	57	45	57	56	40	56	55	62	37	64	72	84
64653	LINNEUS	83	57	91	57	60	88	64	79	66	52	66	65	47	65	63	72	43	74	84	97
64654	LOCK SPRINGS	68	47	75	47	49	72	52	64	54	42	53	53	38	53	52	59	35	60	68	79
64655	LUCERNE	93	64	103	64	67	99	71	89	74	58	73	73	52	73	71	81	48	83	94	109
64656	LUDLOW	82	59	82	57	61	85	64	80	72	57	69	59	52	71	62	79	46	74	87	93
64657	MC FALL	94	65	103	65	68	100	72	90	75	58	74	74	53	74	72	82	48	84	95	110
64658	MARCELINE	71	55	67	55	56	74	60	69	64	53	62	53	50	64	57	69	42	65	74	82
64659	MEADVILLE	81	56	89	56	58	86	62	77	64	50	64	64	45	63	62	70	41	72	81	95
64660	MENDON	73	50	80	50	53	77	56	70	58	45	58	58	41	57	56	64	37	65	73	86
64661	MERCER	69	49	72	48	51	71	51	65	56	47	55	50	40	56	51	62	37	60	68	78
64664	MOORESVILLE	83	59	85	57	62	84	61	78	68	57	66	58	49	67	60	74	44	71	81	92
64667	NEWTOWN	75	54	77	52	56	76	55	70	61	51	60	53	44	61	55	67	40	65	73	84
64668	NORBORNE	83	59	87	58	61	88	65	80	70	56	68	63	50	69	63	77	45	75	86	96
64670	PATTONSBURG	76	54	78	53	56	79	59	73	65	52	63	56	46	64	58	71	42	68	79	87
64671	POLO	90	72	102	71	76	95	73	90	78	68	76	67	64	76	76	84	51	84	92	105
64672	POWERSVILLE	93	64	103	64	67	99	71	89	74	58	73	73	52	73	71	81	48	83	94	109
64673	PRINCETON	75	52	78	52	55	78	58	71	62	49	61	56	44	61	57	68	40	67	77	86
64674	PURDIN	65	46	68	45	48	69	51	63	55	44	54	49	39	54	50	61	35	59	68	75
64676	ROTHVILLE	73	50	80	50	53	77	56	69	58	45	57	57	41	57	55	63	37	65	73	85
64679	SPICKARD	68	49	68	47	50	70	52	65	58	47	56	49	42	57	51	64	37	60	70	77
64681	SUMNER	73	50	80	50	53	77	56	69	58	45	57	57	41	57	56	63	37	65	73	85
64682	TINA	75	53	79	52	55	77	56	71	61	50	60	55	44	61	56	67	40	66	75	85
64683	TRENTON	71	54	69	53	55	73	59	69	64	53	62	52	49	63	56	70	42	66	74	81
64686	UTICA	82	59	84	57	61	83	60	77	67	56	66	58	48	67	60	74	43	71	80	91
64688	WHEELING	99	68	109	68	71	105	76	94	79	61	78	78	55	77	75	86	51	88	99	116
64689	WINSTON	84	60	96	60	64	89	65	81	68	55	67	65	50	66	66	74	44	76	85	99
64701	HARRISONVILLE	90	91	80	92	88	93	88	89	89	86	88	69	88	90	88	90	61	89	93	106
	MISSOURI	94	86	87	87	85	93	89	91	91	87	90	70	84	92	86	93	62	90	94	108
	UNITED STATES	100	100	100	100	100	100	100	100	100	100	100	100	100	100	100	100	100	100	100	100

#	POST OFFICE NAME	COUNTY FIPS CODE	POPULATION 2000	POPULATION 2009	POPULATION 2014	2000-2009 ANNUAL RATE % Rate	2000-2009 ANNUAL RATE State Centile	HOUSEHOLDS 2000	HOUSEHOLDS 2009	HOUSEHOLDS 2014	HOUSEHOLDS % Annual Rate 2000-2009	HOUSEHOLDS 2009 Average HH Size	FAMILIES 2000	FAMILIES 2009	FAMILIES % Annual Rate 2000-2009
64720	ADRIAN	013	2764	3405	3658	2.3	94	1018	1269	1364	2.4	2.63	745	893	2.0
64722	AMORET	013	449	458	458	0.2	46	167	170	170	0.2	2.69	126	124	-0.2
64723	AMSTERDAM	013	759	779	782	0.3	50	280	288	289	0.3	2.70	202	199	-0.2
64724	APPLETON CITY	185	1602	1476	1421	-0.9	4	665	611	586	-0.9	2.30	427	375	-1.4
64725	ARCHIE	037	1678	1940	2057	1.6	89	646	756	806	1.7	2.57	492	555	1.3
64726	BLAIRSTOWN	083	590	636	655	0.8	69	224	243	251	0.9	2.62	184	194	0.6
64728	BRONAUGH	217	583	576	564	-0.1	32	231	230	226	0.0	2.50	169	162	-0.5
64730	BUTLER	013	9053	8981	8973	-0.1	32	3612	3568	3564	-0.1	2.46	2481	2361	-0.5
64733	CHILHOWEE	101	990	1145	1211	1.6	89	388	450	476	1.6	2.54	284	318	1.2
64734	CLEVELAND	037	1834	2047	2143	1.2	82	669	761	801	1.4	2.69	552	611	1.1
64735	CLINTON	083	13118	13415	13559	0.2	46	5500	5675	5753	0.3	2.31	3669	3634	-0.1
64738	COLLINS	185	953	894	860	-0.7	8	395	374	362	-0.6	2.39	292	268	-0.9
64739	CREIGHTON	037	921	1103	1190	2.0	92	346	417	450	2.0	2.65	265	308	1.6
64740	DEEPWATER	083	1657	1655	1650	0.0	37	708	716	716	0.1	2.31	531	520	-0.2
64741	DEERFIELD	217	1060	1056	1040	0.0	37	424	427	422	0.1	2.47	316	307	-0.3
64742	DREXEL	037	2057	2391	2570	1.6	89	781	920	993	1.8	2.60	585	661	1.3
64744	EL DORADO SPRINGS	039	7165	7261	7230	0.1	42	2962	3016	3005	0.2	2.35	1990	1944	-0.3
64745	FOSTER	013	419	422	424	0.1	42	170	170	170	0.0	2.48	126	121	-0.4
64746	FREEMAN	037	1441	1831	2038	2.6	95	517	670	750	2.8	2.73	405	509	2.5
64747	GARDEN CITY	037	3672	4415	4790	2.0	92	1379	1681	1830	2.2	2.63	1046	1227	1.7
64748	GOLDEN CITY	011	1460	1592	1618	0.9	72	589	630	638	0.7	2.51	399	413	0.4
64750	HARWOOD	217	167	163	159	-0.3	21	69	68	67	-0.2	2.40	48	45	-0.7
64752	HUME	217	781	783	782	0.0	37	295	293	292	-0.1	2.67	219	210	-0.5
64755	JASPER	097	3428	3940	4219	1.5	87	1299	1489	1595	1.5	2.61	962	1061	1.1
64756	JERICO SPRINGS	039	1016	973	953	-0.5	14	406	391	384	-0.4	2.49	301	280	-0.8
64759	LAMAR	011	8339	8474	8388	0.2	46	3270	3293	3247	0.1	2.53	2279	2209	-0.3
64761	LEETON	101	1425	1572	1639	1.1	79	548	606	631	1.1	2.59	408	435	0.7
64762	LIBERAL	011	1779	1831	1814	0.3	50	684	696	688	0.2	2.63	498	490	-0.2
64763	LOWRY CITY	185	1396	1422	1412	0.2	46	584	598	595	0.3	2.27	375	366	-0.3
64767	MILO	217	560	569	568	0.2	46	211	214	213	0.2	2.64	163	160	-0.2
64769	MINDENMINES	011	558	580	577	0.4	53	207	213	212	0.3	2.71	154	154	0.0
64770	MONTROSE	083	780	833	855	0.7	66	346	375	387	0.9	2.22	217	224	0.3
64771	MOUNDVILLE	217	469	463	454	-0.1	32	192	191	188	-0.1	2.42	140	135	-0.4
64772	NEVADA	217	12580	12245	12008	-0.3	21	4893	4792	4704	-0.2	2.35	3128	2931	-0.7
64776	OSCEOLA	185	5678	5784	5733	0.2	46	2388	2442	2421	0.2	2.35	1691	1666	-0.2
64778	RICHARDS	217	852	847	831	-0.1	32	309	303	297	-0.2	2.79	231	219	-0.6
64779	RICH HILL	013	1837	1782	1772	-0.3	21	740	715	709	-0.4	2.49	484	445	-0.9
64780	ROCKVILLE	013	424	423	425	0.0	37	175	175	176	0.0	2.42	128	123	-0.4
64783	SCHELL CITY	217	877	887	879	0.1	42	345	351	349	0.2	2.53	251	246	-0.2
64784	SHELDON	217	1519	1540	1538	0.1	42	583	590	587	0.1	2.59	452	443	-0.2
64788	URICH	083	1003	1106	1147	1.1	79	411	458	477	1.2	2.41	291	312	0.8
64790	WALKER	217	569	600	603	0.6	63	220	235	236	0.7	2.55	171	176	0.3
64801	JOPLIN	097	33048	35925	37679	0.9	72	13435	14545	15268	0.9	2.38	8500	8789	0.4
64804	JOPLIN	145	34315	36384	37498	0.6	63	14227	15039	15488	0.6	2.38	9429	9565	0.2
64831	ANDERSON	119	6655	6937	7058	0.4	53	2461	2563	2608	0.4	2.66	1805	1817	0.1
64832	ASBURY	097	703	806	858	1.5	87	265	302	322	1.4	2.65	207	228	1.1
64833	AVILLA	097	91	101	107	1.1	79	35	39	41	1.2	2.59	28	30	0.7
64834	CARL JUNCTION	097	7277	8858	9650	2.1	93	2580	3128	3406	2.1	2.82	2080	2448	1.8
64835	CARTERVILLE	097	1829	1912	1977	0.5	58	691	720	745	0.4	2.66	497	488	-0.2
64836	CARTHAGE	097	22186	24459	25844	1.1	79	8383	9233	9773	1.0	2.57	5950	6291	0.6
64840	DIAMOND	145	2578	2832	2946	1.0	76	946	1048	1094	1.1	2.70	738	795	0.8
64842	FAIRVIEW	145	779	846	874	0.9	72	287	314	326	1.0	2.66	214	227	0.6
64843	GOODMAN	119	2718	2699	2694	-0.1	32	1056	1050	1048	-0.1	2.56	764	735	-0.4
64844	GRANBY	145	4464	4895	5060	1.0	76	1695	1873	1943	1.1	2.59	1268	1353	0.7
64847	LANAGAN	119	767	814	832	0.6	63	301	321	328	0.7	2.54	208	213	0.3
64848	LA RUSSELL	109	831	874	901	0.5	58	283	297	306	0.5	2.94	221	225	0.2
64850	NEOSHO	145	21115	21979	22307	0.4	53	8055	8414	8552	0.5	2.56	5786	5835	0.1
64854	NOEL	119	3651	4372	4655	2.0	92	1302	1532	1624	1.8	2.85	910	1033	1.4
64855	ORONOGO	097	2311	2659	2851	1.5	87	873	1002	1074	1.5	2.63	674	744	1.1
64856	PINEVILLE	119	3470	3575	3653	0.3	50	1352	1391	1420	0.3	2.55	976	975	0.0
64859	REEDS	097	891	1016	1086	1.4	86	338	384	410	1.4	2.65	265	291	1.0
64861	ROCKY COMFORT	119	843	877	886	0.4	53	318	333	337	0.5	2.63	230	233	0.1
64862	SARCOXIE	097	2563	2912	3106	1.4	86	1009	1141	1217	1.3	2.52	703	759	0.8
64863	SOUTH WEST CITY	119	1534	1777	1880	1.6	89	551	630	665	1.5	2.82	402	445	1.1
64865	SENECA	145	5065	5460	5661	0.8	69	1875	2040	2120	0.9	2.63	1413	1485	0.5
64866	STARK CITY	145	1317	1502	1583	1.4	86	495	567	598	1.5	2.65	377	418	1.1
64867	STELLA	119	1666	1788	1833	0.8	69	621	667	684	0.8	2.67	471	490	0.4
64868	TIFF CITY	119	44	46	47	0.5	58	19	20	20	0.6	2.30	15	15	0.0
64870	WEBB CITY	097	11416	13634	14607	1.9	91	4313	5035	5374	1.7	2.67	3010	3378	1.3
64873	WENTWORTH	145	1243	1490	1589	2.0	92	473	574	616	2.1	2.59	368	432	1.7
64874	WHEATON	009	1138	1190	1185	0.5	58	434	453	450	0.5	2.63	317	320	0.1
65001	ARGYLE	151	400	396	394	-0.1	32	144	146	146	0.1	2.71	106	104	-0.2
65010	ASHLAND	019	4100	4565	4854	1.2	82	1562	1781	1908	1.4	2.53	1145	1249	0.9
65011	BARNETT	141	2036	2385	2532	1.7	89	713	833	884	1.7	2.86	551	626	1.4
65013	BELLE	125	3252	3299	3308	0.2	46	1343	1381	1390	0.3	2.38	910	899	-0.1
65014	BLAND	073	2430	2570	2608	0.6	63	1006	1080	1102	0.8	2.33	704	724	0.3
65016	BONNOTS MILL	151	1483	1424	1397	-0.4	18	556	549	544	-0.1	2.59	427	410	-0.4
65017	BRUMLEY	131	1717	1885	1954	1.0	76	618	688	716	1.2	2.71	434	464	0.7
65018	CALIFORNIA	135	7318	7588	7648	0.4	53	2835	2946	2973	0.4	2.53	2042	2052	0.1
65020	CAMDENTON	029	11559	13781	14872	1.9	91	4880	5877	6372	2.0	2.31	3471	4015	1.6
65023	CENTERTOWN	051	1596	1766	1852	1.1	79	617	693	732	1.3	2.55	461	496	0.8
65024	CHAMOIS	151	1119	1072	1051	-0.5	14	426	414	408	-0.3	2.59	287	270	-0.7
65025	CLARKSBURG	135	912	897	887	-0.2	27	333	332	330	0.0	2.70	238	228	-0.5
65026	ELDON	131	10808	11390	11634	0.6	63	4417	4681	4791	0.6	2.40	2926	2980	0.2
65032	EUGENE	131	1331	1500	1578	1.3	83	469	540	572	1.5	2.78	369	410	1.1
65034	FORTUNA	141	587	623	640	0.6	63	202	213	218	0.6	2.87	153	157	0.3
65035	FREEBURG	151	1577	1599	1587	0.1	42	575	597	598	0.4	2.67	437	441	0.1
65037	GRAVOIS MILLS	141	3951	4580	4845	1.6	89	1800	2111	2242	1.7	2.13	1215	1361	1.2
65039	HARTSBURG	019	2103	2461	2659	1.7	89	805	973	1061	2.1	2.49	626	729	1.7
65040	HENLEY	051	1290	1456	1535	1.3	83	455	527	560	1.6	2.76	362	405	1.2
65041	HERMANN	073	5469	5458	5428	0.0	37	2277	2289	2281	0.1	2.32	1553	1505	-0.3
65042	HIGH POINT	135	100	112	116	1.2	82	28	32	33	1.5	3.50	22	24	0.9
65043	HOLTS SUMMIT	027	8566	9370	9731	1.0	76	3183	3538	3693	1.1	2.64	2411	2593	0.8
65046	JAMESTOWN	135	1111	1168	1187	0.5	58	461	491	500	0.7	2.38	309	314	0.2
65047	KAISER	131	1040	1104	1129	0.6	63	454	486	498	0.7	2.24	304	312	0.3
	MISSOURI					0.7					0.8	2.45			0.4
	UNITED STATES					1.0					1.1	2.59			0.9

ZIP CODE #	POST OFFICE NAME	RACE (%) White 2000	White 2009	Black 2000	Black 2009	Asian/Pacific 2000	Asian/Pacific 2009	% Hispanic Origin 2000	% Hispanic Origin 2009	2009 AGE DISTRIBUTION (%) 0-4	5-9	10-14	15-19	20-24	25-44	45-64	65-84	85+	18+	MEDIAN AGE 2009	% 2009 Males	% 2009 Females
64720	ADRIAN	98.6	98.2	0.1	0.1	0.1	0.2	1.2	1.7	6.6	6.6	6.7	6.8	5.6	24.4	26.4	14.0	3.0	75.9	39.7	49.1	50.9
64722	AMORET	98.2	97.8	0.0	0.0	0.0	0.2	2.0	2.6	5.5	5.9	6.3	6.1	5.0	23.4	30.8	15.3	1.7	78.4	43.4	50.7	49.3
64723	AMSTERDAM	96.4	95.8	0.1	0.1	0.1	0.1	0.8	1.2	5.0	7.7	8.6	7.8	4.6	25.0	28.8	11.0	1.4	73.6	38.5	51.6	48.4
64724	APPLETON CITY	98.2	98.1	0.0	0.0	0.1	0.1	0.5	0.5	6.4	6.2	6.4	6.6	5.3	20.7	24.0	16.8	7.6	76.4	43.5	47.1	52.9
64725	ARCHIE	98.1	97.7	0.4	0.5	0.1	0.2	0.7	1.0	6.9	6.9	7.1	7.5	5.8	25.7	25.9	12.5	1.8	74.6	38.4	49.0	51.0
64726	BLAIRSTOWN	97.1	96.5	0.8	0.9	0.0	0.0	1.5	2.2	5.5	6.0	6.8	7.2	3.6	23.9	32.1	13.7	1.3	77.4	42.8	50.2	49.8
64728	BRONAUGH	98.6	98.4	0.0	0.0	0.2	0.2	0.2	0.3	6.1	6.4	6.8	6.4	4.0	24.3	29.7	14.2	2.1	76.7	42.3	50.9	49.1
64730	BUTLER	97.1	96.4	1.0	1.2	0.2	0.3	0.9	1.3	6.1	6.2	6.3	6.6	5.6	23.2	27.5	14.9	3.6	77.3	41.7	48.6	51.4
64733	CHILHOWEE	97.9	97.4	0.3	0.3	0.3	0.4	0.5	0.6	6.5	6.6	7.1	6.8	5.2	23.1	29.9	13.2	1.7	75.6	40.6	50.1	49.9
64734	CLEVELAND	96.7	95.9	0.6	0.7	0.2	0.3	1.0	1.4	5.1	6.0	6.8	6.7	4.5	22.7	34.0	13.1	1.0	77.9	43.6	51.4	48.6
64735	CLINTON	96.1	95.4	1.4	1.6	0.3	0.4	1.0	1.4	6.1	5.5	6.0	6.4	5.7	23.3	28.0	15.5	3.6	78.5	42.6	48.7	51.3
64738	COLLINS	95.8	95.7	0.1	0.1	0.5	0.6	1.3	1.3	5.7	6.3	6.4	5.5	4.8	18.7	30.4	20.0	2.2	78.2	46.6	50.9	49.1
64739	CREIGHTON	97.5	97.0	0.9	1.1	0.1	0.1	0.9	1.2	6.5	6.9	7.0	7.1	5.1	23.5	29.8	12.8	1.4	75.2	40.8	51.4	48.6
64740	DEEPWATER	97.5	97.0	0.5	0.6	0.3	0.5	0.6	0.7	4.7	4.7	4.5	4.2	4.5	19.5	39.6	16.9	1.3	83.1	49.6	52.2	47.8
64741	DEERFIELD	98.7	98.5	0.1	0.1	0.2	0.3	0.4	0.6	5.8	6.4	7.0	6.9	4.7	22.9	31.2	13.1	2.0	76.5	42.2	49.5	50.5
64742	DREXEL	98.0	97.5	0.8	1.0	0.1	0.2	1.0	1.3	8.0	8.1	7.9	6.9	5.5	24.2	27.6	10.2	1.5	71.6	36.8	50.6	49.4
64744	EL DORADO SPRINGS	96.2	95.4	0.5	0.6	0.4	0.6	1.3	1.8	6.1	5.9	5.9	7.0	5.9	21.9	27.2	16.7	3.3	77.6	42.9	48.5	51.5
64745	FOSTER	96.4	95.7	0.0	0.0	0.0	0.2	1.9	2.4	7.3	7.1	7.3	7.3	5.5	23.5	27.0	13.3	1.7	73.9	39.6	50.7	49.3
64746	FREEMAN	96.9	96.2	0.5	0.6	0.3	0.4	1.2	1.7	7.0	7.6	7.8	6.5	4.4	23.2	30.6	11.6	1.2	73.4	40.5	50.6	49.4
64747	GARDEN CITY	97.5	96.9	0.4	0.5	0.1	0.2	1.3	1.9	7.3	7.5	7.5	6.8	5.2	25.5	26.9	11.9	1.3	73.5	37.7	50.3	49.7
64748	GOLDEN CITY	96.3	95.7	0.3	0.3	0.3	0.6	1.5	1.9	6.3	7.5	6.2	7.1	5.2	23.5	26.5	15.0	2.7	75.9	40.8	50.4	49.6
64750	HARWOOD	98.2	98.2	0.0	0.0	0.0	0.0	0.6	1.2	5.5	5.5	6.1	6.1	4.3	22.7	30.1	17.8	1.8	79.1	44.8	49.1	50.9
64752	HUME	96.8	96.0	0.3	0.4	0.1	0.1	1.3	1.8	7.4	7.4	7.7	7.2	5.1	22.9	27.5	13.2	1.8	73.2	39.7	50.4	49.6
64755	JASPER	96.8	96.1	0.2	0.3	0.2	0.3	1.3	2.0	6.6	6.8	7.0	7.6	5.4	23.4	28.9	12.4	1.9	75.0	39.4	50.3	49.7
64756	JERICO SPRINGS	98.1	97.7	0.0	0.0	0.4	0.6	0.5	0.6	6.7	7.1	7.6	6.7	4.4	19.8	28.8	16.8	2.2	74.4	43.0	51.0	49.0
64759	LAMAR	97.0	96.4	0.3	0.4	0.4	0.6	1.0	1.3	7.3	7.4	7.5	6.7	5.2	23.1	26.9	12.9	3.0	73.6	39.0	49.2	50.8
64761	LEETON	97.4	96.6	0.2	0.3	0.3	0.5	0.9	1.4	7.1	7.3	7.4	6.9	6.0	24.0	28.9	11.3	1.2	74.0	38.4	49.9	50.1
64762	LIBERAL	96.9	96.3	0.2	0.2	0.2	0.4	0.7	1.1	9.2	7.4	7.4	6.9	5.2	23.5	25.4	12.4	2.6	71.6	36.8	48.4	51.6
64763	LOWRY CITY	98.1	98.2	0.1	0.1	0.1	0.1	1.7	1.7	5.3	5.3	5.5	5.3	4.2	20.4	28.6	20.2	5.2	80.2	47.8	49.2	50.8
64767	MILO	97.7	97.4	0.0	0.0	0.2	0.2	0.2	0.4	6.9	7.2	7.0	6.3	4.9	23.9	28.3	13.9	1.6	74.3	39.9	48.9	51.1
64769	MINDENMINES	98.0	97.6	0.0	0.0	0.0	0.2	0.2	0.3	8.3	9.1	8.6	7.1	3.8	23.3	26.7	11.7	1.4	69.8	38.0	50.2	49.8
64770	MONTROSE	98.5	98.1	0.1	0.1	0.5	0.7	0.1	0.0	6.0	6.6	6.4	5.3	4.0	23.5	30.3	14.9	3.1	77.8	43.7	54.0	46.0
64771	MOUNDVILLE	98.5	98.5	0.0	0.0	0.2	0.2	0.2	0.2	6.0	6.3	6.9	6.5	4.1	24.2	29.8	14.3	1.9	76.5	42.3	51.6	48.4
64772	NEVADA	96.4	95.7	0.8	1.0	0.5	0.7	1.1	1.5	6.5	6.3	6.8	9.2	6.2	23.1	25.5	13.2	3.2	75.5	38.2	47.4	52.6
64776	OSCEOLA	97.2	97.1	0.3	0.4	0.1	0.2	0.9	0.9	5.3	5.6	6.2	5.9	4.2	20.0	32.4	18.2	2.2	79.0	46.9	50.7	49.3
64778	RICHARDS	97.4	97.2	0.9	1.1	0.2	0.2	0.1	0.1	7.9	8.1	8.1	7.1	4.1	21.6	28.0	12.9	2.1	71.2	39.2	50.6	49.4
64779	RICH HILL	97.4	97.0	0.2	0.2	0.1	0.2	1.0	1.2	6.6	6.4	6.6	6.7	5.8	23.5	27.6	14.3	2.5	76.4	40.8	47.3	52.7
64780	ROCKVILLE	97.4	96.7	0.7	0.9	0.0	0.0	0.7	0.9	7.3	7.8	7.3	5.9	4.0	21.5	28.1	15.4	2.6	73.8	41.7	49.6	50.4
64783	SCHELL CITY	97.9	97.6	0.1	0.1	0.1	0.2	0.8	1.1	6.4	6.7	7.1	6.4	5.1	24.1	28.4	13.9	1.9	75.8	40.2	49.8	50.2
64784	SHELDON	97.8	97.1	0.1	0.1	0.1	0.3	0.3	0.4	6.8	7.1	7.0	6.7	4.9	24.2	27.9	13.8	1.6	74.4	39.6	49.4	50.6
64788	URICH	96.8	96.2	0.3	0.3	0.3	0.5	2.1	2.9	5.7	6.0	6.4	6.6	4.8	23.5	29.6	14.6	2.6	77.8	42.7	50.0	50.0
64790	WALKER	97.2	96.7	0.2	0.2	0.4	0.5	1.1	1.3	7.7	7.7	8.0	6.7	5.8	25.2	27.3	10.2	1.5	72.5	35.8	48.7	51.3
64801	JOPLIN	91.7	90.0	2.6	2.9	0.7	1.2	2.3	3.2	7.1	6.6	6.4	7.5	8.0	26.7	24.7	11.0	2.0	76.2	35.4	48.7	51.3
64804	JOPLIN	93.2	91.8	1.4	1.7	0.7	1.0	2.1	3.0	6.7	6.5	6.6	6.2	5.6	25.7	27.1	13.3	2.3	76.5	39.3	48.2	51.8
64831	ANDERSON	90.6	89.1	0.3	0.3	0.3	0.4	3.7	4.8	7.6	7.5	7.5	6.9	5.4	25.6	25.4	12.1	1.9	73.1	37.1	50.0	50.0
64832	ASBURY	95.9	94.9	0.3	0.4	0.3	0.4	1.1	1.6	7.3	7.6	7.8	7.1	5.2	25.6	28.5	9.7	1.2	72.7	37.4	51.6	48.4
64833	AVILLA	97.8	97.0	0.0	0.0	0.0	0.0	1.1	2.0	6.9	6.9	7.9	6.9	4.0	24.8	28.7	11.9	2.0	72.3	39.6	50.5	49.5
64834	CARL JUNCTION	95.9	95.1	0.3	0.4	0.3	0.4	1.4	2.0	6.5	6.7	7.2	7.8	5.5	26.4	28.7	9.9	1.2	74.5	38.1	49.7	50.3
64835	CARTERVILLE	96.7	96.0	0.2	0.2	0.3	0.4	0.9	1.3	6.9	6.4	6.4	7.8	7.7	26.9	27.0	9.7	1.2	75.6	35.8	49.2	50.8
64836	CARTHAGE	90.2	87.8	1.1	1.2	1.2	1.7	8.4	10.9	7.0	7.0	6.7	6.7	6.1	25.8	26.1	12.1	2.4	75.2	37.6	50.0	50.0
64840	DIAMOND	95.2	94.1	0.5	0.7	0.2	0.4	1.4	2.0	7.7	7.9	7.6	6.5	5.7	26.3	25.9	11.2	1.2	72.9	36.0	48.9	51.1
64842	FAIRVIEW	96.4	95.7	0.3	0.2	0.4	0.6	1.5	2.1	7.9	8.0	7.7	7.1	6.7	25.1	24.1	12.1	1.3	71.6	36.2	51.7	48.3
64843	GOODMAN	91.0	89.4	0.3	0.3	1.0	1.5	1.8	2.4	6.9	6.7	7.2	8.1	5.9	25.4	26.6	11.9	1.3	74.0	37.4	51.4	48.6
64844	GRANBY	95.4	94.5	0.2	0.2	0.3	0.4	1.1	1.6	7.5	7.4	7.5	7.0	5.3	25.6	25.9	11.8	2.0	73.0	37.2	49.4	50.6
64847	LANAGAN	90.0	88.6	0.1	0.1	0.1	0.1	8.2	10.9	6.9	7.1	7.1	6.1	4.8	25.7	28.1	12.7	1.5	75.2	39.3	50.6	49.4
64848	LA RUSSELL	96.9	95.9	0.1	0.2	0.0	0.1	1.8	2.5	6.6	7.2	8.2	7.6	4.7	25.1	27.7	11.6	1.4	73.1	38.2	51.0	49.0
64850	NEOSHO	92.3	90.7	0.6	0.7	0.9	1.3	3.2	4.3	7.4	7.1	7.1	7.4	6.1	25.1	25.2	12.2	2.3	74.2	37.2	49.0	51.0
64854	NOEL	81.5	78.8	0.2	0.2	0.1	0.1	32.0	39.0	9.2	7.9	8.1	6.7	5.7	28.1	23.7	9.7	1.0	70.6	34.2	51.9	48.1
64855	ORONOGO	96.4	95.6	0.1	0.1	0.2	0.3	1.1	1.7	7.3	7.5	7.7	7.6	5.5	25.6	27.7	10.1	1.1	73.1	36.9	50.2	49.8
64856	PINEVILLE	94.6	93.6	0.1	0.1	0.1	0.2	2.0	2.6	7.3	7.0	6.8	7.3	7.4	25.1	26.5	11.5	1.2	74.7	37.1	50.9	49.1
64859	REEDS	96.2	94.7	0.2	0.4	0.3	0.7	1.8	2.8	7.2	7.7	7.7	7.0	3.8	24.7	28.0	12.7	1.3	73.1	39.3	50.6	49.4
64861	ROCKY COMFORT	96.1	95.6	0.0	0.0	0.1	0.2	0.9	1.1	5.2	7.8	8.4	8.1	5.1	25.3	29.2	8.7	2.2	73.7	39.1	50.5	49.5
64862	SARCOXIE	95.8	94.8	0.2	0.3	0.2	0.3	1.4	2.1	7.6	7.4	7.5	7.3	5.6	25.9	23.7	12.6	2.4	72.7	36.8	47.4	52.6
64863	SOUTH WEST CITY	77.1	73.7	0.2	0.2	0.1	0.2	28.0	34.0	10.0	9.6	9.1	7.4	5.6	28.2	21.5	7.5	1.0	66.6	31.5	51.4	48.6
64865	SENECA	90.0	88.7	0.2	0.2	0.4	0.5	1.0	1.3	6.5	6.7	7.3	7.1	5.4	24.9	27.5	12.5	2.2	75.0	39.2	48.8	51.2
64866	STARK CITY	93.8	92.5	0.0	0.1	0.1	0.1	2.8	3.9	7.1	7.0	7.0	6.6	6.6	25.2	27.8	11.2	1.7	74.9	37.2	51.7	48.3
64867	STELLA	96.0	95.4	0.1	0.2	0.2	0.4	1.1	1.6	7.6	7.6	7.9	7.7	6.4	24.6	26.2	10.7	1.3	72.1	36.6	51.4	48.6
64868	TIFF CITY	90.9	91.3	0.0	0.0	0.0	0.0	0.0	0.0	8.7	8.7	8.7	6.5	4.3	30.4	23.9	8.7	0.0	67.4	37.0	50.0	50.0
64870	WEBB CITY	93.8	92.1	0.7	0.8	0.8	1.2	2.4	3.6	8.4	7.6	6.9	7.1	8.1	27.2	23.3	9.8	1.7	73.0	32.6	48.5	51.5
64873	WENTWORTH	97.8	97.3	0.0	0.0	0.4	0.6	1.0	1.4	6.0	6.1	6.4	7.0	6.1	22.6	30.7	13.6	1.5	77.2	41.7	49.9	50.1
64874	WHEATON	93.8	91.4	0.1	0.1	0.0	0.0	8.0	11.4	8.5	8.2	8.2	7.1	5.6	26.2	23.9	10.6	1.7	70.7	34.0	47.1	52.9
65001	ARGYLE	99.3	99.0	0.0	0.0	0.0	0.0	0.8	1.3	7.1	7.3	7.6	7.1	5.6	26.3	26.3	11.1	1.8	73.5	37.3	50.5	49.5
65010	ASHLAND	97.0	96.3	0.9	1.1	0.3	0.5	1.1	1.6	6.4	6.6	7.2	7.1	5.3	26.0	29.7	9.8	1.9	75.0	39.1	48.3	51.7
65011	BARNETT	97.5	97.1	0.1	0.2	0.2	0.3	0.9	1.2	8.2	8.3	8.2	6.9	4.7	21.7	28.1	12.6	1.3	70.9	38.7	49.6	50.4
65013	BELLE	97.4	97.0	0.2	0.2	0.1	0.1	0.9	1.2	6.7	6.4	6.3	6.1	5.8	25.6	26.9	14.3	1.8	76.9	40.0	50.9	49.1
65014	BLAND	98.1	97.8	0.1	0.2	0.1	0.2	0.7	0.9	5.6	5.7	6.0	6.0	5.6	23.1	30.0	15.6	2.5	78.7	43.5	51.2	48.8
65016	BONNOTS MILL	99.0	98.9	0.4	0.4	0.1	0.1	0.5	0.6	6.3	6.4	6.7	6.6	4.6	27.5	27.9	12.4	1.6	76.6	39.6	51.2	48.8
65017	BRUMLEY	96.7	96.2	0.3	0.4	0.1	0.2	1.6	2.2	8.0	7.1	7.0	6.3	6.4	26.7	26.4	10.8	1.2	74.1	36.5	50.6	49.4
65018	CALIFORNIA	95.1	93.7	0.6	0.7	0.4	0.5	4.9	6.5	7.4	7.2	7.1	6.8	6.0	25.8	25.3	11.8	2.7	74.1	37.2	49.5	50.5
65020	CAMDENTON	97.1	96.4	0.2	0.2	0.4	0.7	1.2	1.6	5.1	5.2	5.4	5.7	5.1	20.5	30.8	20.1	2.1	80.8	47.1	49.9	50.1
65023	CENTERTOWN	99.1	98.6	0.1	0.2	0.1	0.2	0.4	0.6	5.8	6.2	6.6	6.8	4.7	25.6	31.0	12.1	1.2	77.1	41.4	51.7	48.3
65024	CHAMOIS	98.6	98.2	0.0	0.0	0.0	0.1	1.2	1.7	6.3	6.3	6.4	6.8	5.5	25.1	27.0	14.1	2.6	76.9	39.4	50.0	50.0
65025	CLARKSBURG	98.6	98.2	0.2	0.2	0.1	0.2	2.0	2.8	7.9	8.5	8.2	7.4	5.8	26.2	25.1	9.6	1.3	70.8	34.5	49.8	50.2
65026	ELDON	98.2	97.8	0.3	0.3	0.2	0.3	1.0	1.4	6.6	6.6	6.7	6.6	5.7	24.7	26.8	13.5	2.8	75.9	39.5	48.2	51.8
65032	EUGENE	98.3	97.9	0.1	0.1	0.2	0.3	0.6	0.9	7.5	8.2	7.4	8.0	5.3	27.2	25.3	9.9	1.2	71.9	36.2	50.2	49.8
65034	FORTUNA	98.5	98.1	0.3	0.3	0.2	0.2	1.0	1.3	8.2	8.2	8.2	7.7	5.1	23.8	25.5	11.4	1.9	70.6	35.9	50.7	49.3
65035	FREEBURG	99.9	99.9	0.0	0.0	0.0	0.0	0.8	1.3	7.9	8.1	8.0	6.9	3.9	28.7	25.0	10.2	1.3	71.6	36.1	50.5	49.5
65037	GRAVOIS MILLS	97.9	97.5	0.2	0.3	0.1	0.1	0.6	0.8	3.5	3.6	3.9	4.2	3.3	15.0	33.8	29.5	3.3	86.2	56.7	49.3	50.7
65039	HARTSBURG	97.2	96.7	0.5	0.6	0.1	0.1	1.1	1.5	6.1	6.7	7.4	6.7	4.3	26.0	31.5	9.7	1.6	75.2	40.1	49.1	50.9
65040	HENLEY	98.8	98.4	0.0	0.0	0.3	0.5	0.5	0.8	8.2	8.5	7.8	7.6	5.6	27.7	25.2	8.4	1.0	70.6	34.9	49.9	50.1
65041	HERMANN	98.7	98.5	0.4	0.4	0.1	0.2	0.4	0.6	5.3	5.6	5.8	6.1	4.9	21.5	29.1	17.2	4.5	79.3	45.5	48.6	51.4
65042	HIGH POINT	98.0	98.2	0.0	0.0	0.0	0.0	1.0	0.9	8.0	8.0	6.3	7.1	5.4	26.8	25.9	10.7	1.8	72.3	35.8	50.0	50.0
65043	HOLTS SUMMIT	95.4	94.2	2.1	2.7	0.3	0.4	1.3	1.8	7.8	7.9	7.7	7.0	5.5	28.8	26.5	8.0	0.8	72.2	35.3	49.9	50.1
65046	JAMESTOWN	96.6	95.6	0.5	0.7	0.4	0.7	0.7	0.9	6.3	6.6	7.0	6.6	4.7	24.3	30.8	11.8	1.9	76.2	41.0	52.1	47.9
65047	KAISER	96.1	95.5	0.5	0.5	0.2	0.2	1.6	2.2	8.1	6.7	6.7	6.3	6.6	26.9	26.2	11.1	1.4	74.6	36.8	50.7	49.3
	MISSOURI	84.9	83.3	11.2	11.7	1.2	1.7	2.1	2.8	6.6	6.6	6.6	7.0	6.7	26.1	26.5	11.7	2.1	76.1	37.7	48.8	51.2
	UNITED STATES	75.1	72.0	12.3	12.7	3.8	4.6	12.5	15.7	6.8	6.7	6.6	7.1	6.9	27.0	26.0	10.9	1.9	75.7	36.9	49.2	50.8

ZIP CODE				2009 HOUSEHOLD INCOME DISTRIBUTION (%)					MEDIAN HOUSEHOLD INCOME					2009 HOME VALUE DISTRIBUTION (%)					
#	POST OFFICE NAME	2009 Per Capita Income	2009 HH Income Base	Less than $25,000	$25,000 to $49,999	$50,000 to $99,999	$100,000 to $149,999	$150,000 or More	2009	2014	2009 National Centile	2009 State Centile	2009 Home Value Base	Less than $50,000	$50,000 to $89,999	$90,000 to $174,999	$175,000 to $399,999	$400,000 or More	2009 Median Home Value
64720	ADRIAN	18870	1269	25.5	31.8	35.5	5.5	1.7	43357	44375	43	65	942	14.2	35.0	37.3	11.5	2.0	90843
64722	AMORET	20018	170	24.1	32.9	33.5	7.1	2.4	44661	45000	47	68	144	27.8	15.3	29.9	24.3	2.8	104688
64723	AMSTERDAM	17010	288	27.4	35.4	31.6	4.2	1.4	39156	40116	30	49	241	24.1	18.3	35.3	16.6	5.8	108929
64724	APPLETON CITY	17022	611	38.5	36.2	21.8	2.6	1.0	29637	29672	8	10	422	29.1	34.4	25.1	10.2	1.2	68800
64725	ARCHIE	22184	756	19.4	28.2	44.2	5.8	2.4	51630	53094	65	81	590	7.6	20.7	49.5	17.5	4.7	113178
64726	BLAIRSTOWN	21293	243	14.8	37.0	41.2	4.1	2.9	48148	51232	57	76	203	20.7	17.7	27.6	22.7	11.3	128125
64728	BRONAUGH	18087	230	33.0	32.6	28.7	3.5	2.2	38066	40919	27	45	189	24.3	27.5	26.5	17.5	4.2	86500
64730	BUTLER	18567	3568	30.0	34.4	29.4	4.2	1.9	37059	39790	24	40	2619	20.2	28.2	31.9	16.6	3.1	92643
64733	CHILHOWEE	18801	450	27.1	34.7	31.6	5.3	1.3	40697	43197	35	55	364	24.7	21.7	31.0	20.9	1.6	97222
64734	CLEVELAND	27837	761	9.6	22.9	49.7	12.9	5.0	66412	70151	84	94	685	8.0	10.5	29.5	43.6	8.3	179623
64735	CLINTON	20708	5675	32.2	31.5	29.2	4.2	2.9	37676	40133	26	43	3918	15.8	23.8	40.9	16.8	2.7	104606
64738	COLLINS	13905	374	43.3	35.3	20.3	1.1	0.0	27167	27162	5	4	318	36.2	19.2	27.0	17.0	0.6	81053
64739	CREIGHTON	22267	417	21.3	29.7	40.3	5.3	3.4	48936	50709	59	78	356	21.6	22.2	32.9	18.0	5.3	99167
64740	DEEPWATER	21644	716	27.4	35.5	29.9	5.6	1.7	39319	40355	31	50	602	26.7	23.6	33.4	15.8	0.5	89500
64741	DEERFIELD	19117	427	35.6	27.6	30.0	4.4	2.3	37246	37766	24	41	351	17.9	20.8	33.6	23.6	4.0	112260
64742	DREXEL	21866	920	18.5	28.8	43.4	7.6	1.7	52086	53606	66	82	688	14.2	23.5	36.2	21.7	4.4	107609
64744	EL DORADO SPRINGS	16438	3016	37.4	35.1	24.0	2.8	0.6	31249	32143	10	15	2240	24.2	30.7	32.1	11.4	1.6	83889
64745	FOSTER	17407	170	33.5	32.9	32.4	1.2	0.0	36535	37906	22	37	136	33.8	20.6	27.2	14.7	3.7	80000
64746	FREEMAN	25504	670	13.1	25.8	47.0	10.1	3.9	58701	60577	76	88	590	12.2	19.5	36.9	26.6	4.7	120522
64747	GARDEN CITY	22918	1681	18.6	27.1	45.6	6.2	2.5	53045	54761	68	83	1335	15.1	20.3	38.7	22.0	3.9	114015
64748	GOLDEN CITY	15817	630	34.8	35.7	26.3	1.9	1.3	33023	34123	13	21	448	31.7	33.9	22.8	10.7	0.9	68182
64750	HARWOOD	14674	68	42.6	36.8	20.6	0.0	0.0	30000	30791	8	11	55	45.5	34.5	9.1	10.9	0.0	55000
64752	HUME	15729	293	35.8	31.7	30.7	1.7	0.0	34863	36793	17	30	234	34.6	20.9	27.8	13.2	3.4	78000
64755	JASPER	18192	1489	28.3	36.5	29.9	3.7	1.6	38496	41732	28	47	1150	22.1	34.1	28.8	12.7	2.3	83238
64756	JERICO SPRINGS	15368	391	32.0	41.4	24.3	2.0	0.3	38081	37708	27	45	347	27.1	36.0	19.0	17.3	0.6	77794
64759	LAMAR	17695	3293	33.6	30.8	30.2	3.9	1.5	37861	40306	26	45	2377	19.4	28.4	38.0	12.6	1.7	93323
64761	LEETON	18235	606	24.4	36.1	34.5	4.1	0.8	42168	45048	40	61	488	24.6	26.6	29.1	17.6	2.0	88500
64762	LIBERAL	15639	696	30.7	36.4	30.3	2.2	0.4	37077	38478	24	40	545	32.5	37.1	20.9	8.8	0.7	67157
64763	LOWRY CITY	17166	598	40.3	30.6	26.1	1.8	1.2	30666	31298	9	13	446	32.5	23.8	34.5	9.0	0.2	78125
64767	MILO	17003	214	24.8	40.7	29.9	2.8	1.9	38251	39008	27	46	167	35.9	24.6	29.9	7.2	2.4	68846
64769	MINDENMINES	15556	213	31.5	33.3	31.9	2.3	0.9	38119	40000	27	46	174	25.9	28.2	31.0	11.5	3.4	82222
64770	MONTROSE	18808	375	35.7	29.6	30.4	4.0	0.3	34353	36074	16	28	290	30.3	25.5	30.3	10.3	3.4	81500
64771	MOUNDVILLE	18797	191	31.4	33.0	30.4	3.1	2.1	39243	41757	30	50	157	24.2	27.4	28.0	16.6	3.8	86875
64772	NEVADA	19301	4792	35.5	27.6	29.8	4.5	2.7	37006	39657	24	40	3172	19.2	28.6	35.2	15.0	2.0	92734
64776	OSCEOLA	17431	2442	36.9	33.6	25.3	3.0	1.1	32168	33716	12	18	1998	32.2	20.5	33.4	11.4	2.6	85221
64778	RICHARDS	14174	303	39.9	28.4	27.7	3.3	0.7	32183	33479	12	18	241	32.0	19.9	32.8	10.8	4.6	86538
64779	RICH HILL	14673	715	43.2	36.1	18.5	1.4	0.8	28902	30231	7	7	535	56.1	27.5	12.7	3.2	0.6	42442
64780	ROCKVILLE	15865	175	29.7	44.0	24.0	2.3	0.0	34487	38785	16	28	124	36.3	36.3	12.9	10.5	4.0	63571
64783	SCHELL CITY	15097	351	39.6	34.2	24.2	1.1	0.9	32039	33311	11	17	286	39.9	28.0	21.7	9.1	1.4	62593
64784	SHELDON	17396	590	24.7	40.7	30.2	2.7	1.7	38397	39212	28	47	463	34.1	24.8	30.5	8.2	2.4	71591
64788	URICH	19503	458	26.4	35.8	31.0	6.1	0.7	40000	40222	33	54	343	32.4	20.7	32.7	10.8	3.5	85000
64790	WALKER	16531	235	34.9	31.9	30.2	2.1	0.9	36594	39450	22	38	194	30.4	23.2	38.7	6.2	1.5	83000
64801	JOPLIN	21318	14545	28.9	31.3	31.4	5.3	3.1	40710	45052	35	56	8870	19.4	29.1	36.7	13.4	1.4	92368
64804	JOPLIN	24642	15039	24.8	31.0	34.1	5.8	4.3	44413	47284	47	67	10260	13.1	25.9	42.1	15.0	3.9	104189
64831	ANDERSON	15769	2563	36.7	35.5	24.1	2.1	1.6	33858	35518	15	26	1882	21.2	24.2	36.7	15.8	2.1	96350
64832	ASBURY	20344	302	19.9	29.8	41.7	7.9	0.7	50246	51742	62	79	256	21.9	21.1	39.1	14.1	3.9	107317
64833	AVILLA	17570	39	25.6	35.9	35.9	2.6	0.0	42330	45747	40	62	32	25.0	28.1	28.1	12.5	6.3	85000
64834	CARL JUNCTION	21744	3128	18.2	30.1	38.5	10.2	3.1	51291	53622	64	80	2602	9.0	29.8	41.2	18.7	1.2	104402
64835	CARTERVILLE	16288	720	27.8	38.6	30.0	3.1	0.6	37683	41158	26	43	552	30.3	48.4	17.9	3.1	0.4	63735
64836	CARTHAGE	19138	9233	27.2	35.6	30.9	4.5	1.9	39895	42275	32	53	6611	17.2	29.5	36.9	14.3	2.2	95913
64840	DIAMOND	19218	1048	18.9	37.1	37.0	5.3	1.6	44054	46337	46	67	795	19.1	31.8	33.1	12.6	3.4	88611
64842	FAIRVIEW	16625	314	32.5	37.9	25.5	2.2	1.9	34792	36502	17	29	261	25.7	27.2	32.2	12.6	2.3	86429
64843	GOODMAN	14970	1050	34.9	37.0	25.6	1.9	0.7	32389	33838	12	19	820	25.9	32.0	27.4	9.6	5.1	81899
64844	GRANBY	16286	1873	28.2	36.6	32.7	1.9	0.6	37639	39800	26	43	1476	35.0	28.1	24.4	10.4	2.0	70217
64847	LANAGAN	13410	321	43.3	35.5	19.9	0.6	0.6	28392	29146	6	6	217	36.9	22.6	21.7	16.1	2.8	68056
64848	LA RUSSELL	15760	297	31.3	32.0	31.3	4.0	1.3	36480	39347	22	37	237	28.7	19.8	30.8	16.0	4.6	93182
64850	NEOSHO	19626	8414	26.1	31.6	35.3	4.9	2.1	42031	45328	39	61	6046	15.3	30.4	38.8	13.2	2.3	96667
64854	NOEL	15026	1532	32.6	38.8	24.5	2.5	1.6	36157	37037	21	36	874	23.7	27.7	29.9	17.3	1.5	88095
64855	ORONOGO	19438	1002	24.6	32.5	36.9	4.7	1.3	45594	47788	50	71	850	21.2	30.6	36.5	9.1	2.7	87761
64856	PINEVILLE	17434	1391	32.9	32.2	28.8	4.5	1.7	38162	40190	27	46	1063	29.3	30.1	26.1	10.4	4.1	76500
64859	REEDS	17440	384	29.7	33.9	31.5	3.1	1.8	38810	41776	29	48	326	20.6	23.6	35.9	16.6	3.4	101163
64861	ROCKY COMFORT	21862	333	40.2	30.0	21.0	2.7	6.0	32980	34176	13	21	269	20.8	25.7	23.4	19.0	11.2	95588
64862	SARCOXIE	16610	1141	35.1	32.6	28.0	3.0	1.3	33219	35645	14	23	840	28.2	27.6	32.6	10.6	1.0	82687
64863	SOUTH WEST CITY	11986	630	47.8	33.7	17.0	0.6	1.0	25711	26064	4	2	375	27.7	25.1	37.1	8.3	1.9	83438
64865	SENECA	19048	2040	25.8	32.7	34.8	4.6	2.1	40799	44763	35	56	1617	20.8	29.3	36.3	12.3	1.2	89840
64866	STARK CITY	16632	567	32.1	34.4	28.9	3.4	1.2	35684	38756	20	34	460	37.4	19.1	30.2	10.9	2.4	71304
64867	STELLA	16459	667	31.9	35.5	28.5	2.7	1.3	35453	37425	19	33	562	24.4	22.4	32.6	16.9	3.7	95806
64868	TIFF CITY	14837	20	45.0	30.0	25.0	0.0	0.0	30000	35000	8	11	16	25.0	12.5	43.8	18.8	0.0	106250
64870	WEBB CITY	18197	5035	28.8	33.6	31.1	4.6	2.0	39227	41667	30	50	3321	15.6	27.6	47.1	9.0	0.7	99515
64873	WENTWORTH	18103	574	28.6	42.3	24.2	2.6	2.3	37552	39025	25	43	490	28.6	15.7	35.7	18.8	1.2	100610
64874	WHEATON	13462	453	38.0	40.6	19.2	2.0	0.2	30289	31258	9	12	313	23.0	32.3	31.0	9.9	3.8	82826
65001	ARGYLE	17714	146	25.3	30.1	39.0	4.1	1.4	45500	47473	50	70	128	21.9	26.6	32.0	17.2	2.3	94000
65010	ASHLAND	25726	1781	13.3	27.0	49.5	7.0	3.3	58862	57754	76	88	1319	10.9	11.8	30.9	37.4	9.0	164583
65011	BARNETT	19063	833	25.7	33.6	31.9	4.2	4.6	41456	42700	38	59	729	20.0	24.1	34.2	17.1	4.5	100884
65013	BELLE	19723	1381	29.2	33.3	31.9	4.3	1.2	39200	40513	30	49	1060	22.0	29.2	35.0	12.4	1.5	88681
65014	BLAND	20269	1080	25.8	35.3	32.9	5.3	0.7	41297	42783	37	58	892	22.1	25.4	31.8	15.2	5.4	94583
65016	BONNOTS MILL	21825	549	21.9	27.5	41.3	7.5	1.8	50436	50402	62	80	481	14.3	20.2	40.1	20.6	4.8	122098
65017	BRUMLEY	17746	688	32.3	33.1	28.6	4.1	1.9	36555	38353	22	37	538	24.9	21.7	30.9	19.1	3.3	96429
65018	CALIFORNIA	21628	2946	22.2	29.2	40.7	5.7	2.3	48495	50350	58	77	2207	15.9	25.8	39.4	17.0	1.9	100993
65020	CAMDENTON	21893	5877	25.9	32.9	34.5	4.5	2.1	42576	44291	41	63	4668	13.4	16.3	36.9	27.4	5.9	132626
65023	CENTERTOWN	23475	693	19.5	23.2	47.5	7.9	1.9	55347	57045	72	86	573	14.0	17.3	44.0	23.0	1.7	125772
65024	CHAMOIS	17327	414	30.2	30.9	35.0	2.9	1.0	41050	42768	36	57	346	43.1	19.7	25.1	9.5	2.6	60000
65025	CLARKSBURG	17932	332	28.0	31.0	36.4	2.7	1.8	42500	43806	41	63	257	29.2	22.2	27.6	14.8	6.2	87941
65026	ELDON	18947	4681	32.9	32.3	29.1	3.5	2.2	35441	38621	19	33	3236	19.5	27.8	36.1	14.2	2.3	93891
65032	EUGENE	21314	540	21.1	21.3	47.6	6.9	3.1	54817	55538	71	85	485	16.3	13.8	42.9	22.9	4.1	128783
65034	FORTUNA	18660	213	24.4	31.9	37.6	3.3	2.8	44403	46336	47	67	177	22.6	19.8	32.8	22.0	2.8	108553
65035	FREEBURG	20036	597	18.1	31.3	44.2	5.2	1.2	50282	50520	62	80	511	14.9	20.0	39.9	22.3	2.9	112639
65037	GRAVOIS MILLS	24483	2111	26.7	37.0	28.0	4.4	3.9	39916	41555	32	53	1770	16.3	15.5	36.9	27.7	3.6	129694
65039	HARTSBURG	27881	973	11.0	25.1	49.9	9.9	4.1	62278	61381	80	91	788	9.9	7.7	31.2	42.0	9.1	177557
65040	HENLEY	22969	527	20.3	22.4	46.1	6.3	4.9	55714	57098	72	86	472	24.2	15.7	39.2	17.4	3.6	112281
65041	HERMANN	22614	2289	22.6	32.8	36.9	5.1	2.7	45848	46143	51	71	1806	11.6	20.7	44.0	18.3	5.4	118290
65042	HIGH POINT	16112	32	18.8	25.0	46.9	6.3	3.1	56250	56483	73	87	28	14.3	10.7	32.1	35.7	7.1	150000
65043	HOLTS SUMMIT	23155	3538	15.0	28.0	46.4	8.5	2.1	56389	56620	73	87	2910	20.1	12.2	49.4	17.0	1.3	116497
65046	JAMESTOWN	20460	491	22.2	36.5	36.5	3.3	1.6	43149	45767	43	64	402	25.6	26.4	32.6	13.7	1.7	87143
65047	KAISER	21751	486	30.2	34.2	29.2	4.5	1.9	37520	38930	25	43	350	25.4	20.0	31.4	19.4	3.7	100000
	MISSOURI	25286		22.8	27.7	35.3	9.1	5.2	49522	52035				12.8	19.4	39.1	24.2	4.6	122064
	UNITED STATES	27277		20.9	24.4	35.3	11.7	7.6	54719	56938				9.3	13.1	31.6	32.6	13.5	162279

ZIP CODE #	POST OFFICE NAME	FINANCIAL SERVICES: Auto Loan	Home Loan	Invest-ments	Retire-ment Plans	THE HOME: Home Improvements: Home Repair	Lawn & Garden	Furnishings: Comput-ers & Hard-ware-Personal	Major Appli-ances	TV, Radio, Sound Equip-ment	Furni-ture	ENTERTAINMENT: Dine out/ Carry out	Sports Equip-ment	Fees & Tickets	Toys & Games	Travel	Cable TV	PERSONAL: Apparel & Services	Auto Repairs	Health Insur-ance	Pets & Supplies
64720	ADRIAN	82	64	79	64	66	85	67	80	73	62	71	60	57	73	65	80	48	75	86	94
64722	AMORET	96	69	99	67	72	98	71	90	79	66	77	68	57	78	70	86	51	83	94	107
64723	AMSTERDAM	81	60	82	58	62	82	61	76	67	57	66	57	50	67	60	73	44	70	79	90
64724	APPLETON CITY	67	48	68	47	50	70	53	65	58	46	56	49	42	57	51	64	37	61	71	77
64725	ARCHIE	81	83	68	85	78	87	81	81	82	77	81	64	81	83	80	84	56	81	87	97
64726	BLAIRSTOWN	99	69	109	69	72	105	76	94	79	62	78	78	56	78	76	86	51	88	100	116
64728	BRONAUGH	81	56	87	56	59	85	61	77	65	51	64	62	46	64	61	71	42	71	81	93
64730	BUTLER	76	58	76	57	60	78	62	74	67	56	66	55	52	66	60	73	44	69	79	87
64733	CHILHOWEE	84	63	85	61	64	85	63	79	69	59	68	59	52	69	63	76	45	73	82	94
64734	CLEVELAND	104	117	101	121	114	115	105	109	103	105	104	85	112	106	111	103	73	105	108	128
64735	CLINTON	76	62	70	62	63	78	67	73	71	62	69	55	59	71	64	76	47	71	79	87
64738	COLLINS	59	43	61	41	44	60	44	55	48	41	48	41	35	48	43	53	31	51	58	66
64739	CREIGHTON	94	81	89	84	83	100	82	94	84	72	83	72	72	85	81	90	56	87	97	110
64740	DEEPWATER	79	68	90	64	74	86	66	80	71	68	70	55	61	67	70	76	47	76	87	93
64741	DEERFIELD	80	64	81	63	65	82	63	76	68	60	67	58	55	68	64	73	45	71	79	91
64742	DREXEL	88	85	75	84	83	86	79	83	81	82	81	62	78	84	78	83	56	81	83	99
64744	EL DORADO SPRINGS	63	50	63	48	51	65	52	61	57	50	55	45	45	56	51	62	37	58	66	72
64745	FOSTER	77	55	79	54	57	78	57	72	63	53	62	54	45	63	56	69	41	66	75	86
64746	FREEMAN	106	100	97	104	101	114	97	108	99	89	98	82	92	101	98	104	67	100	110	126
64747	GARDEN CITY	87	88	76	91	85	94	85	88	86	81	85	68	85	88	85	88	59	85	92	104
64748	GOLDEN CITY	65	49	52	50	48	62	57	59	60	51	58	46	47	61	50	64	40	59	64	72
64750	HARWOOD	63	45	64	44	47	64	46	59	51	43	50	44	37	51	46	56	33	54	61	70
64752	HUME	75	53	79	52	55	77	56	71	61	50	60	55	43	60	55	67	39	65	74	85
64755	JASPER	82	61	79	60	62	84	64	77	70	58	68	59	52	70	62	76	46	72	82	92
64756	JERICO SPRINGS	68	49	70	47	51	69	50	64	56	47	55	48	40	55	50	61	36	59	66	76
64759	LAMAR	77	57	73	56	58	78	61	72	66	55	64	56	49	66	58	72	43	68	77	87
64761	LEETON	83	63	69	62	63	79	64	73	70	63	69	56	54	73	59	75	47	70	77	89
64762	LIBERAL	68	51	62	51	51	68	58	63	61	50	59	51	46	61	54	65	40	63	69	78
64763	LOWRY CITY	66	50	74	49	53	69	52	66	57	48	55	49	43	55	53	62	37	61	69	77
64767	MILO	80	58	83	56	60	82	59	75	66	55	64	57	47	65	59	72	43	69	78	90
64769	MINDENMINES	75	52	83	52	54	80	58	72	60	47	59	59	42	59	57	65	38	67	76	88
64770	MONTROSE	75	52	82	51	54	79	57	71	59	47	59	58	42	58	57	65	38	66	75	87
64771	MOUNDVILLE	81	56	89	56	59	85	62	77	65	51	64	63	46	64	61	71	42	72	81	94
64772	NEVADA	72	60	66	60	59	72	65	69	69	60	67	54	58	68	62	72	46	69	74	83
64776	OSCEOLA	68	53	75	51	57	72	54	67	59	52	58	49	47	57	56	64	38	63	72	79
64778	RICHARDS	71	49	78	49	51	75	54	67	56	44	56	56	40	55	54	61	36	63	71	83
64779	RICH HILL	62	45	63	43	46	65	49	60	54	43	52	45	39	53	47	59	35	56	65	71
64780	ROCKVILLE	69	47	75	47	49	72	52	65	54	42	54	54	38	53	52	59	35	61	69	80
64783	SCHELL CITY	68	49	65	48	50	68	51	62	56	48	55	47	41	57	48	62	37	58	65	75
64784	SHELDON	81	58	83	56	60	82	59	75	66	55	65	57	47	65	59	72	43	69	79	90
64788	URICH	84	60	87	58	62	86	62	79	68	57	67	60	49	68	62	75	44	73	82	94
64790	WALKER	76	55	63	53	54	72	57	66	63	55	62	51	46	66	52	69	42	63	70	81
64801	JOPLIN	77	68	63	69	66	74	74	73	76	70	75	56	68	77	68	79	52	74	78	87
64804	JOPLIN	90	80	79	81	80	90	83	87	86	79	85	66	77	87	79	90	58	86	92	103
64831	ANDERSON	75	54	67	52	54	73	56	67	62	53	61	51	45	64	53	68	41	63	71	81
64832	ASBURY	88	78	76	76	77	85	75	81	78	76	78	61	69	80	72	81	53	78	82	97
64833	AVILLA	81	56	89	56	59	86	62	77	65	50	64	64	46	63	62	71	41	72	82	95
64834	CARL JUNCTION	91	91	79	92	87	95	86	89	88	85	87	69	85	90	85	90	60	87	92	107
64835	CARTERVILLE	71	54	54	54	53	67	61	63	66	57	64	49	51	67	54	70	44	64	69	77
64836	CARTHAGE	77	66	67	66	65	78	69	74	73	65	72	56	62	74	66	77	49	73	80	88
64840	DIAMOND	81	73	71	72	71	82	72	77	75	70	75	59	67	77	70	79	51	75	82	93
64842	FAIRVIEW	80	57	66	56	57	76	60	70	66	58	65	53	48	69	54	72	44	66	73	85
64843	GOODMAN	69	50	59	48	50	66	51	61	57	50	56	46	41	59	47	62	38	57	64	73
64844	GRANBY	76	55	65	53	55	73	57	67	63	55	62	51	45	65	52	69	41	63	70	81
64847	LANAGAN	61	44	60	42	45	61	45	56	50	42	49	42	36	50	44	55	32	52	58	67
64848	LA RUSSELL	83	59	82	58	61	84	62	76	68	57	67	59	49	68	60	74	44	71	80	92
64850	NEOSHO	80	67	69	68	67	81	70	76	74	66	73	58	63	75	67	79	50	74	81	91
64854	NOEL	74	55	60	54	54	70	59	65	64	56	63	51	49	66	53	69	42	64	70	79
64855	ORONOGO	84	72	72	71	72	82	71	78	74	70	74	59	63	77	67	78	50	74	80	93
64856	PINEVILLE	73	61	65	58	60	70	62	68	65	61	64	52	54	66	59	68	44	66	70	81
64859	REEDS	81	59	84	59	61	84	62	77	66	54	65	61	49	66	62	72	43	71	81	93
64861	ROCKY COMFORT	103	71	110	71	74	107	78	97	82	65	81	80	58	81	77	90	53	91	102	119
64862	SARCOXIE	73	53	62	53	53	70	58	65	63	54	61	50	47	64	53	68	41	63	69	79
64863	SOUTH WEST CITY	61	44	50	43	44	58	46	53	51	44	50	41	37	53	41	55	33	50	56	65
64865	SENECA	88	67	80	65	67	87	68	81	74	65	73	61	56	75	65	80	49	75	84	96
64866	STARK CITY	79	57	66	55	57	75	59	69	66	58	65	53	48	69	54	72	43	65	73	84
64867	STELLA	79	57	67	55	57	76	59	69	65	57	64	54	47	68	54	71	43	66	73	85
64868	TIFF CITY	61	44	53	43	44	59	46	54	51	44	50	41	37	52	42	55	33	51	57	66
64870	WEBB CITY	72	65	57	66	62	69	71	67	72	67	71	52	66	73	65	74	49	70	73	82
64873	WENTWORTH	84	60	76	59	61	82	63	75	69	60	68	58	50	71	59	76	45	71	79	91
64874	WHEATON	64	45	55	44	46	62	48	56	52	45	51	44	38	54	44	57	34	53	59	69
65001	ARGYLE	82	65	70	65	65	81	66	75	71	62	69	58	56	73	62	76	47	71	79	90
65010	ASHLAND	97	96	88	97	95	100	92	96	93	92	93	73	91	95	92	95	64	94	98	113
65011	BARNETT	93	72	98	69	75	97	72	90	79	70	77	66	61	77	73	86	51	83	94	106
65013	BELLE	75	61	63	62	61	75	66	71	70	60	68	54	58	71	62	74	46	69	76	85
65014	BLAND	85	62	76	60	62	82	64	76	70	61	69	58	52	72	60	77	46	71	79	91
65016	BONNOTS MILL	95	76	92	76	78	99	76	92	82	70	80	69	66	82	76	89	54	85	95	108
65017	BRUMLEY	83	65	68	63	64	77	67	73	71	66	70	56	57	74	61	75	48	71	76	89
65018	CALIFORNIA	90	73	80	71	73	89	76	85	81	72	80	63	66	82	71	87	54	82	90	101
65020	CAMDENTON	78	69	82	68	72	82	70	78	73	70	72	56	65	71	70	77	49	76	83	91
65023	CENTERTOWN	93	85	82	87	86	97	83	93	86	78	85	69	77	88	82	90	58	86	95	108
65024	CHAMOIS	77	56	78	54	58	80	59	74	66	54	64	55	48	65	58	73	43	69	79	87
65025	CLARKSBURG	85	64	71	63	64	82	66	76	72	63	70	58	55	74	61	78	47	72	80	92
65026	ELDON	73	59	67	58	59	73	63	69	68	59	66	52	54	68	59	72	45	68	75	83
65032	EUGENE	90	88	80	89	87	93	83	89	84	81	84	67	80	86	83	87	57	85	90	105
65034	FORTUNA	97	69	92	67	70	96	72	88	79	67	78	68	57	80	69	86	52	82	92	106
65035	FREEBURG	83	76	75	79	77	89	74	84	77	67	75	64	69	78	74	81	52	78	87	98
65037	GRAVOIS MILLS	77	74	98	70	83	89	69	82	74	75	72	54	70	67	77	78	49	79	91	94
65039	HARTSBURG	98	109	94	112	106	107	98	102	97	99	97	80	104	99	103	97	68	98	101	120
65040	HENLEY	100	93	84	92	92	97	88	94	91	90	91	70	84	95	85	94	62	91	95	112
65041	HERMANN	87	68	91	68	71	91	72	86	77	65	75	65	61	76	72	83	50	81	90	101
65042	HIGH POINT	90	83	74	80	81	85	78	83	81	82	81	60	74	85	75	84	55	80	83	99
65043	HOLTS SUMMIT	95	92	80	90	89	90	86	89	87	90	88	67	84	91	83	88	60	87	88	106
65046	JAMESTOWN	86	64	86	62	65	86	64	80	71	61	70	60	53	71	63	77	46	74	83	95
65047	KAISER	81	68	65	66	66	75	69	73	72	70	71	55	61	75	64	74	49	71	73	87
	MISSOURI	94	86	87	87	85	93	89	91	91	87	90	70	84	92	86	93	62	90	94	108
	UNITED STATES	100	100	100	100	100	100	100	100	100	100	100	100	100	100	100	100	100	100	100	100

ZIP CODE #	POST OFFICE NAME	COUNTY FIPS CODE	POPULATION 2000	POPULATION 2009	POPULATION 2014	2000-2009 ANNUAL RATE % Rate	2000-2009 ANNUAL RATE State Centile	HOUSEHOLDS 2000	HOUSEHOLDS 2009	HOUSEHOLDS 2014	HOUSEHOLDS % Annual Rate 2000-2009	HOUSEHOLDS 2009 Average HH Size	FAMILIES 2000	FAMILIES 2009	FAMILIES % Annual Rate 2000-2009
65048	KOELTZTOWN	151	217	214	212	-0.2	27	78	79	79	0.1	2.67	58	57	-0.2
65049	LAKE OZARK	131	5813	7042	7631	2.1	93	2605	3219	3514	2.3	2.18	1809	2162	1.9
65050	LATHAM	135	649	666	670	0.3	50	180	187	188	0.4	3.56	141	142	0.1
65051	LINN	151	4541	5090	5305	1.2	82	1753	1997	2093	1.4	2.49	1210	1326	1.0
65052	LINN CREEK	029	3586	3547	3587	-0.1	32	1375	1383	1403	0.1	2.55	1051	1030	-0.2
65053	LOHMAN	051	1221	1383	1460	1.4	86	437	502	533	1.5	2.75	358	398	1.2
65054	LOOSE CREEK	151	846	820	805	-0.3	21	302	299	296	-0.1	2.70	239	231	-0.4
65058	META	125	1051	1050	1045	0.0	37	414	421	422	0.2	2.49	311	307	-0.1
65059	MOKANE	027	1022	1220	1309	1.9	91	381	461	497	2.1	2.62	302	354	1.7
65061	MORRISON	073	867	856	845	-0.1	32	356	356	353	0.0	2.40	247	235	-0.5
65062	MOUNT STERLING	073	93	103	106	1.1	79	40	45	46	1.3	2.29	30	32	0.7
65063	NEW BLOOMFIELD	027	2987	3442	3638	1.5	87	1102	1282	1361	1.6	2.67	843	949	1.3
65064	OLEAN	131	764	845	882	1.1	79	278	312	327	1.3	2.68	219	239	0.9
65065	OSAGE BEACH	029	4909	5549	5928	1.3	83	2199	2535	2728	1.5	2.14	1442	1602	1.1
65066	OWENSVILLE	073	6430	6753	6809	0.5	58	2498	2638	2664	0.6	2.53	1744	1773	0.2
65067	PORTLAND	027	447	539	578	2.0	92	184	225	243	2.2	2.40	132	155	1.8
65068	PRAIRIE HOME	053	617	632	639	0.3	50	252	261	265	0.4	2.42	191	192	0.1
65069	RHINELAND	139	654	629	617	-0.4	18	260	253	249	-0.3	2.49	184	173	-0.7
65072	ROCKY MOUNT	141	1519	1789	1905	1.8	90	702	836	894	1.9	2.14	499	571	1.5
65074	RUSSELLVILLE	051	2627	2944	3080	1.2	82	993	1125	1181	1.4	2.62	756	821	0.9
65075	SAINT ELIZABETH	131	885	894	895	0.1	42	296	303	305	0.3	2.79	229	229	0.0
65076	SAINT THOMAS	051	741	784	808	0.6	63	241	262	273	0.9	2.99	200	212	0.6
65077	STEEDMAN	027	506	618	666	2.2	94	194	241	261	2.4	2.56	139	165	1.9
65078	STOVER	141	3364	3607	3702	0.8	69	1428	1538	1580	0.8	2.32	988	1022	0.4
65079	SUNRISE BEACH	029	3444	3457	3508	0.0	37	1615	1645	1680	0.2	2.10	1171	1157	-0.1
65080	TEBBETTS	027	988	1074	1106	0.9	72	365	403	418	1.1	2.66	299	322	0.8
65081	TIPTON	135	3828	3794	3762	-0.1	32	1084	1066	1054	-0.2	2.39	718	675	-0.7
65082	TUSCUMBIA	131	1316	1329	1332	0.1	42	455	467	470	0.3	2.63	332	326	-0.2
65083	ULMAN	131	536	605	634	1.3	83	201	230	242	1.5	2.60	148	163	1.0
65084	VERSAILLES	141	6484	6875	7019	0.6	63	2475	2614	2661	0.6	2.57	1727	1767	0.2
65085	WESTPHALIA	151	1224	1221	1205	0.0	37	418	427	424	0.2	2.75	326	326	0.0
65101	JEFFERSON CITY	051	28803	29324	29972	0.2	46	10346	10957	11265	0.6	2.36	6544	6686	0.2
65109	JEFFERSON CITY	051	35496	37966	39301	0.7	66	14102	15587	16273	1.1	2.35	9375	9876	0.6
65201	COLUMBIA	019	33910	36862	39057	0.9	72	12485	14412	15441	1.6	2.08	5122	5563	0.9
65202	COLUMBIA	019	35219	44113	48663	2.5	95	14038	18181	20216	2.8	2.39	8935	10952	2.2
65203	COLUMBIA	019	45080	51288	54801	1.4	86	18560	21702	23326	1.7	2.34	11464	12735	1.1
65211	COLUMBIA	019	229	1104	1117	18.5	100	146	152	156	0.4	3.85	19	17	-1.2
65215	COLUMBIA	019	301	295	294	-0.2	27	20	20	20	0.0	5.50	4	3	-3.1
65216	COLUMBIA	019	242	229	226	-0.6	11	15	14	14	-0.7	2.57	6	5	-2.0
65230	ARMSTRONG	089	721	741	736	0.3	50	267	280	279	0.5	2.54	196	197	0.1
65231	AUXVASSE	027	3230	3447	3554	0.7	66	1237	1340	1385	0.9	2.55	892	927	0.4
65232	BENTON CITY	007	245	244	243	0.0	37	103	104	104	0.1	2.35	82	81	-0.1
65233	BOONVILLE	053	10974	11622	11903	0.6	63	3700	3989	4119	0.8	2.40	2507	2597	0.4
65236	BRUNSWICK	041	1440	1363	1313	-0.6	11	631	601	581	-0.5	2.21	390	354	-1.0
65237	BUNCETON	053	1027	1081	1107	0.6	63	416	445	458	0.7	2.43	300	309	0.3
65239	CAIRO	175	1242	1076	1033	-1.5	1	480	422	407	-1.4	2.55	364	310	-1.7
65240	CENTRALIA	007	6718	7138	7336	0.7	66	2573	2790	2888	0.9	2.53	1909	1997	0.5
65243	CLARK	175	3412	3605	3713	0.6	63	1159	1257	1302	0.9	2.50	918	966	0.6
65244	CLIFTON HILL	175	404	429	440	0.7	66	161	173	178	0.8	2.48	125	131	0.5
65246	DALTON	041	155	134	126	-1.6	0	68	59	56	-1.5	2.25	42	35	-2.0
65247	EXCELLO	121	606	619	615	0.2	46	240	249	249	0.4	2.49	182	183	0.1
65248	FAYETTE	089	4669	4496	4397	-0.4	18	1671	1602	1562	-0.5	2.39	1113	1025	-0.9
65250	FRANKLIN	089	738	746	737	0.1	42	284	288	286	0.2	2.59	208	204	-0.2
65251	FULTON	027	20724	21893	22548	0.6	63	6887	7541	7835	1.0	2.45	4648	4901	0.6
65254	GLASGOW	089	1761	1643	1583	-0.7	8	687	647	625	-0.6	2.47	462	416	-1.1
65255	HALLSVILLE	019	3605	4074	4363	1.3	83	1397	1633	1765	1.7	2.49	1072	1207	1.3
65256	HARRISBURG	019	1389	1478	1534	0.7	66	527	576	602	1.0	2.56	405	426	0.5
65257	HIGBEE	089	1248	1314	1336	0.6	63	512	547	558	0.7	2.38	356	365	0.3
65258	HOLLIDAY	137	293	298	294	0.2	46	117	119	118	0.2	2.49	85	83	-0.3
65259	HUNTSVILLE	175	3353	3717	3866	1.1	79	1257	1417	1483	1.3	2.58	909	987	0.9
65260	JACKSONVILLE	175	708	768	793	0.9	72	265	290	300	1.0	2.65	204	217	0.7
65261	KEYTESVILLE	041	1234	1091	1032	-1.3	1	551	491	466	-1.2	2.21	353	302	-1.7
65262	KINGDOM CITY	027	624	694	727	1.2	82	229	260	274	1.4	2.66	184	202	1.0
65263	MADISON	137	2178	2256	2244	0.4	53	824	862	861	0.5	2.59	622	631	0.2
65264	MARTINSBURG	007	796	817	817	0.3	50	309	321	322	0.4	2.54	241	243	0.1
65265	MEXICO	007	15537	14944	14670	-0.4	18	6376	6175	6091	-0.3	2.31	4246	3928	-0.8
65270	MOBERLY	175	16140	16160	16238	0.0	37	5928	6021	6072	0.2	2.41	3806	3698	-0.3
65274	NEW FRANKLIN	089	1773	1791	1772	0.1	42	713	727	722	0.2	2.43	494	484	-0.2
65275	PARIS	137	3263	3285	3245	0.1	42	1271	1285	1271	0.1	2.46	874	849	-0.3
65276	PILOT GROVE	053	1625	1725	1774	0.6	63	616	662	683	0.8	2.56	431	447	0.4
65279	ROCHEPORT	019	1521	1607	1665	0.6	63	591	647	676	1.0	2.48	452	477	0.6
65280	RUSH HILL	007	274	270	269	-0.2	27	109	110	110	0.1	2.45	88	86	-0.2
65281	SALISBURY	041	3523	3319	3195	-0.6	11	1402	1343	1299	-0.5	2.38	977	901	-0.9
65282	SANTA FE	137	717	733	728	0.2	46	278	290	290	0.5	2.52	223	225	0.1
65283	STOUTSVILLE	137	430	468	472	0.9	72	174	193	195	1.1	2.40	134	143	0.7
65284	STURGEON	019	2342	2584	2725	1.1	79	872	988	1049	1.4	2.60	634	688	0.9
65285	THOMPSON	007	953	972	965	0.2	46	349	358	357	0.3	2.72	279	277	-0.1
65286	TRIPLETT	041	200	188	180	-0.7	8	83	78	76	-0.7	2.41	58	53	-1.0
65287	WOOLDRIDGE	053	388	442	465	1.4	86	148	170	180	1.5	2.60	113	126	1.2
65301	SEDALIA	159	32025	32834	33303	0.3	50	12855	13201	13402	0.3	2.44	8511	8377	-0.2
65305	WHITEMAN AIR FORCE B	101	3843	3333	3166	-1.5	1	940	796	750	-1.8	3.50	910	767	-1.8
65321	BLACKBURN	195	785	744	722	-0.6	11	293	279	271	-0.5	2.67	216	200	-0.8
65322	BLACKWATER	053	720	783	812	0.9	72	296	327	341	1.1	2.30	221	235	0.7
65323	CALHOUN	083	927	983	1009	0.6	63	366	392	404	0.7	2.51	272	281	0.4
65324	CLIMAX SPRINGS	029	2498	2529	2591	0.1	42	1150	1182	1216	0.3	2.14	835	833	0.0
65325	COLE CAMP	015	2594	3209	3502	2.3	94	1048	1346	1486	2.7	2.34	731	904	2.3
65326	EDWARDS	015	1720	1782	1811	0.4	53	797	836	852	0.5	2.13	561	567	0.1
65329	FLORENCE	141	749	832	854	1.1	79	269	298	306	1.1	2.79	211	227	0.8
65330	GILLIAM	195	492	471	457	-0.5	14	204	197	192	-0.4	2.39	140	130	-0.8
65332	GREEN RIDGE	159	1466	1525	1563	0.4	53	542	570	585	0.5	2.67	414	421	0.2
65333	HOUSTONIA	159	935	992	1018	0.6	63	339	363	373	0.7	2.68	261	270	0.4
65334	HUGHESVILLE	159	864	946	984	1.0	76	304	337	352	1.1	2.76	233	250	0.8
65335	IONIA	159	257	255	256	-0.1	32	107	107	107	0.0	2.37	82	79	-0.4
65336	KNOB NOSTER	101	5328	5692	5887	0.7	66	2038	2179	2253	0.7	2.61	1431	1472	0.3
65337	LA MONTE	159	1876	1997	2062	0.7	66	716	771	798	0.8	2.56	517	532	0.3
	MISSOURI					0.7					0.8	2.45			0.4
	UNITED STATES					1.0					1.1	2.59			0.9

ZIP CODE #	POST OFFICE NAME	RACE (%) White 2000	White 2009	Black 2000	Black 2009	Asian/Pacific 2000	Asian/Pacific 2009	% Hispanic Origin 2000	% Hispanic Origin 2009	2009 AGE DISTRIBUTION (%) 0-4	5-9	10-14	15-19	20-24	25-44	45-64	65-84	85+	18+	MEDIAN AGE 2009	% 2009 Males	% 2009 Females
65048	KOELTZTOWN	99.1	99.1	0.0	0.0	0.0	0.0	0.9	0.9	7.0	7.0	7.0	7.0	5.6	26.2	25.7	11.7	2.8	73.8	38.5	50.0	50.0
65049	LAKE OZARK	97.8	97.4	0.3	0.3	0.3	0.4	0.9	1.2	4.6	4.6	4.8	5.3	4.2	19.1	40.4	16.0	0.9	82.5	49.3	50.1	49.9
65050	LATHAM	95.2	94.1	2.5	3.0	0.2	0.2	1.2	1.8	10.4	9.8	9.6	9.2	6.9	24.5	21.5	7.5	0.8	64.7	28.1	52.4	47.6
65051	LINN	98.1	97.8	0.2	0.3	0.2	0.3	0.3	0.3	6.5	6.7	7.0	7.4	6.3	25.5	25.5	12.3	2.8	75.8	37.8	51.4	48.6
65052	LINN CREEK	98.0	97.7	0.2	0.3	0.3	0.3	1.2	1.6	6.4	6.8	6.9	6.0	4.4	23.8	30.6	14.0	1.1	75.9	41.8	50.4	49.6
65053	LOHMAN	96.3	95.4	2.0	2.6	0.4	0.6	0.8	1.1	7.1	7.6	7.8	7.3	5.4	24.3	30.3	8.7	1.5	72.9	38.2	50.3	49.7
65054	LOOSE CREEK	99.2	99.1	0.4	0.4	0.0	0.0	0.2	0.2	7.9	8.0	7.9	6.5	4.5	26.2	25.6	11.2	2.1	72.0	37.7	50.0	50.0
65058	META	98.3	98.1	0.1	0.2	0.1	0.1	0.9	1.1	7.0	7.1	7.3	7.0	5.2	24.2	28.1	12.5	1.6	74.2	39.5	51.0	49.0
65059	MOKANE	98.3	97.9	0.5	0.7	0.1	0.2	0.2	0.3	6.9	7.0	7.2	6.6	5.7	26.4	29.1	9.9	1.2	74.7	38.5	48.9	51.1
65061	MORRISON	98.5	98.1	0.1	0.1	0.2	0.5	0.5	0.6	5.6	5.8	6.4	7.0	4.9	21.8	29.4	16.9	2.0	77.6	43.9	49.6	50.4
65062	MOUNT STERLING	100.0	100.0	0.0	0.0	0.0	0.0	0.0	0.0	4.9	5.8	5.8	7.8	3.9	21.4	35.0	13.6	1.9	77.7	45.4	50.5	49.5
65063	NEW BLOOMFIELD	97.1	96.5	0.8	1.0	0.2	0.3	0.5	0.7	7.3	7.3	7.4	7.0	5.5	26.8	27.8	9.8	1.2	73.6	37.3	48.2	51.8
65064	OLEAN	98.7	98.6	0.3	0.4	0.0	0.0	0.5	0.7	5.8	6.7	7.1	6.9	5.7	25.3	29.5	11.8	1.2	75.6	39.6	49.9	50.1
65065	OSAGE BEACH	97.3	96.7	0.8	0.9	0.6	0.8	0.9	1.2	3.9	4.0	4.5	4.1	3.0	21.9	36.8	19.5	2.3	85.1	50.3	49.8	50.2
65066	OWENSVILLE	98.6	98.3	0.1	0.1	0.2	0.3	0.4	0.5	6.6	6.7	6.8	6.6	5.4	23.7	28.1	13.4	2.7	75.7	40.5	48.9	51.1
65067	PORTLAND	96.9	96.1	0.2	0.4	0.0	0.2	0.9	1.3	6.3	6.7	6.5	6.1	5.9	24.5	31.7	11.1	1.1	76.8	40.2	50.5	49.5
65068	PRAIRIE HOME	97.9	97.3	0.8	0.9	0.0	0.2	0.3	0.5	6.2	7.1	7.6	6.6	4.6	23.7	30.9	11.4	1.9	74.8	40.7	49.5	50.5
65069	RHINELAND	98.8	98.4	0.2	0.3	0.0	0.0	0.9	1.3	6.7	7.3	7.8	7.3	5.4	23.1	27.5	12.7	2.2	73.4	39.8	48.5	51.5
65072	ROCKY MOUNT	98.1	97.9	0.1	0.1	0.1	0.1	1.0	1.3	2.9	3.2	3.7	3.5	2.2	14.6	37.9	30.1	1.7	87.9	57.2	50.9	49.1
65074	RUSSELLVILLE	98.2	97.7	0.1	0.1	0.1	0.1	1.1	1.5	7.5	7.5	7.8	7.7	5.6	25.5	27.2	9.6	1.5	72.3	36.8	50.1	49.9
65075	SAINT ELIZABETH	99.5	99.4	0.0	0.0	0.0	0.0	0.8	1.1	6.5	6.9	7.2	7.0	4.6	24.4	27.1	12.2	4.1	74.7	40.5	49.9	50.1
65076	SAINT THOMAS	98.9	98.1	0.4	0.6	0.3	0.5	0.4	0.5	9.3	9.2	8.8	6.0	4.7	28.1	25.5	7.4	1.0	68.8	34.3	49.5	50.5
65077	STEEDMAN	96.6	96.3	0.2	0.2	0.2	0.2	1.0	1.3	6.3	6.6	6.5	6.0	5.8	24.8	32.2	10.8	1.0	76.7	40.3	50.2	49.8
65078	STOVER	97.5	97.1	0.3	0.3	0.1	0.2	0.8	1.1	5.5	5.5	6.2	6.2	4.4	20.6	31.1	18.1	2.6	79.1	46.2	50.1	49.9
65079	SUNRISE BEACH	98.1	97.9	0.1	0.1	0.2	0.2	0.7	0.9	2.5	2.9	3.3	3.2	2.3	11.5	37.0	35.1	2.2	89.4	60.2	50.0	50.0
65080	TEBBETTS	97.1	96.3	0.7	0.8	0.2	0.3	1.7	2.4	6.9	7.1	7.2	7.0	5.6	24.5	30.4	10.3	1.0	74.5	39.7	49.8	50.2
65081	TIPTON	84.0	81.3	12.9	15.1	0.4	0.7	0.9	1.2	4.6	4.8	4.9	5.1	6.0	39.9	22.6	9.4	2.7	82.5	37.3	64.3	35.7
65082	TUSCUMBIA	97.8	97.5	0.3	0.3	0.2	0.4	0.6	0.8	6.3	6.5	6.4	6.5	5.3	26.0	26.3	13.5	3.1	76.8	40.2	50.9	49.1
65083	ULMAN	97.6	96.9	0.2	0.2	0.0	0.2	1.5	2.0	7.6	7.4	7.1	6.4	6.0	26.6	26.8	10.7	1.3	73.9	36.7	50.6	49.4
65084	VERSAILLES	96.4	95.8	1.2	1.4	0.2	0.3	1.0	1.3	7.3	7.4	7.2	6.8	5.4	21.8	26.1	14.8	3.1	73.7	40.0	47.5	52.5
65085	WESTPHALIA	99.0	98.9	0.1	0.1	0.0	0.0	0.5	0.7	7.4	7.7	7.5	6.6	4.6	25.2	25.6	12.0	3.4	73.1	39.2	49.5	50.5
65101	JEFFERSON CITY	80.8	78.7	16.1	17.4	0.8	1.3	1.2	1.5	6.0	5.9	5.9	8.1	8.1	29.8	25.4	9.3	1.5	79.0	35.8	52.9	47.1
65109	JEFFERSON CITY	89.9	87.0	6.8	8.6	1.1	1.8	1.5	2.1	6.6	6.4	6.3	6.3	6.1	28.1	26.9	11.0	2.2	76.7	38.0	48.5	51.5
65201	COLUMBIA	85.4	81.7	7.4	8.8	4.3	6.3	1.9	2.6	4.0	3.5	3.3	16.4	28.1	23.6	14.9	4.9	1.4	87.2	24.1	48.6	51.4
65202	COLUMBIA	82.3	79.2	11.7	13.1	2.3	3.4	1.9	2.5	7.7	6.8	6.3	6.6	8.8	32.1	22.8	7.5	1.3	75.4	32.7	48.9	51.1
65203	COLUMBIA	82.7	79.2	10.4	11.3	3.8	5.9	1.9	2.5	6.8	6.1	6.3	7.2	10.3	28.1	25.5	8.5	1.2	76.6	33.3	47.8	52.2
65211	COLUMBIA	85.2	71.8	1.7	14.8	10.9	10.1	3.5	3.4	1.0	0.9	0.9	14.3	39.7	32.6	7.5	2.4	0.6	96.6	24.1	57.2	42.8
65215	COLUMBIA	87.7	84.4	8.0	9.5	2.3	3.7	3.3	4.7	1.0	1.0	0.7	32.5	40.3	14.9	7.1	2.0	0.3	96.3	21.8	25.1	74.9
65216	COLUMBIA	60.7	55.5	31.0	34.5	3.3	4.8	2.1	2.2	3.9	3.9	3.5	20.1	33.6	21.4	10.0	3.1	0.4	84.7	22.8	46.3	53.7
65230	ARMSTRONG	96.9	96.2	1.7	2.2	0.1	0.3	0.7	1.1	5.9	6.3	6.3	5.9	4.3	24.2	32.1	12.1	2.7	77.3	42.1	51.6	48.4
65231	AUXVASSE	95.8	94.7	2.2	2.8	0.2	0.3	0.6	0.8	6.2	6.1	6.9	8.1	5.5	26.4	27.5	11.9	1.4	75.3	39.0	48.2	51.8
65232	BENTON CITY	98.4	98.4	0.4	0.4	0.0	0.0	0.8	0.8	6.6	7.4	7.0	5.7	4.1	23.0	28.7	16.0	1.6	75.4	42.0	50.8	49.2
65233	BOONVILLE	84.6	82.4	13.0	14.7	0.3	0.5	1.0	1.2	5.2	5.4	5.6	8.1	12.9	24.2	23.7	12.0	2.9	79.9	34.5	56.2	43.8
65236	BRUNSWICK	89.7	88.0	9.2	10.6	0.2	0.4	1.2	1.6	5.2	5.3	5.4	5.8	5.6	20.2	28.8	19.0	4.8	80.5	46.7	48.1	51.9
65237	BUNCETON	95.8	94.7	2.9	3.6	0.1	0.2	0.3	0.5	5.7	6.3	6.7	6.1	5.6	24.4	31.1	12.3	1.9	77.7	40.8	50.9	49.1
65239	CAIRO	98.6	98.1	0.0	0.0	0.2	0.5	0.6	0.7	5.6	5.8	6.5	7.7	5.5	24.9	30.1	12.6	1.3	77.2	40.7	49.5	50.5
65240	CENTRALIA	97.4	97.0	0.8	1.0	0.1	0.1	0.7	0.9	7.6	7.4	7.5	7.1	5.6	24.4	26.4	11.5	2.5	72.9	37.7	48.7	51.3
65243	CLARK	91.7	90.8	6.2	6.7	0.2	0.2	0.7	1.0	7.7	7.1	7.1	6.7	6.6	28.1	25.9	9.3	1.2	73.6	36.0	55.5	44.5
65244	CLIFTON HILL	97.3	97.0	1.2	1.4	0.0	0.0	1.2	1.4	5.1	5.8	6.1	7.2	5.4	22.4	32.4	13.8	1.9	78.6	43.5	50.1	49.9
65246	DALTON	95.5	94.8	3.9	4.5	0.0	0.0	0.6	0.7	5.2	5.2	5.2	6.0	4.5	20.9	31.3	17.9	3.7	80.6	47.0	46.3	53.7
65247	EXCELLO	96.7	96.1	1.5	1.8	0.2	0.2	1.5	1.9	6.1	6.8	6.6	6.3	4.7	22.8	32.5	13.1	1.1	76.3	42.4	51.5	48.5
65248	FAYETTE	86.0	83.8	11.7	13.5	0.2	0.3	0.7	0.9	5.4	5.3	5.3	10.7	12.3	21.7	23.8	12.4	3.1	80.3	34.4	48.2	51.8
65250	FRANKLIN	97.6	96.9	0.4	0.5	0.1	0.1	1.2	1.7	7.0	6.8	7.0	7.1	5.9	26.4	28.8	9.8	1.2	74.8	37.7	50.4	49.6
65251	FULTON	87.7	85.1	9.5	10.7	0.8	1.6	0.9	1.2	5.3	5.4	5.7	9.7	10.6	26.6	24.0	10.5	2.2	80.2	35.3	51.4	48.6
65254	GLASGOW	92.0	90.5	6.4	7.5	0.1	0.2	0.6	0.7	6.2	6.3	6.2	6.6	6.2	25.7	27.7	12.1	3.0	77.0	38.9	48.8	51.2
65255	HALLSVILLE	96.8	96.1	0.9	1.2	0.1	0.1	1.0	1.4	6.8	7.0	7.3	7.0	5.3	26.9	29.9	9.0	0.9	74.5	38.3	49.7	50.3
65256	HARRISBURG	97.0	96.4	0.6	0.7	0.2	0.3	1.2	1.6	6.4	6.5	6.8	6.7	6.0	26.7	31.3	8.8	0.9	76.2	39.0	49.9	50.1
65257	HIGBEE	97.0	96.5	1.7	2.0	0.1	0.1	1.2	1.6	6.1	6.1	6.2	6.3	5.6	24.0	30.7	12.9	2.2	77.7	41.6	49.2	50.8
65258	HOLLIDAY	99.0	99.0	0.3	0.3	0.0	0.0	1.0	0.7	9.1	8.4	7.7	5.7	5.7	23.8	25.2	12.4	2.0	71.8	36.6	50.3	49.7
65259	HUNTSVILLE	93.9	92.9	3.6	4.2	0.1	0.2	0.7	1.0	6.5	6.6	7.1	7.3	6.6	25.0	27.8	11.3	1.8	75.4	37.7	49.6	50.4
65260	JACKSONVILLE	97.6	97.0	0.1	0.1	0.6	0.9	0.6	0.9	6.1	6.5	6.8	7.0	4.9	24.5	29.4	13.3	1.4	76.0	40.8	52.1	47.9
65261	KEYTESVILLE	96.2	95.7	3.0	3.4	0.0	0.0	0.6	0.9	5.7	6.0	5.9	5.9	4.8	21.8	28.2	18.2	3.6	78.6	45.0	47.8	52.2
65262	KINGDOM CITY	96.8	95.7	1.8	2.3	0.2	0.3	0.8	1.3	6.8	6.8	7.1	6.6	5.6	25.8	28.8	11.4	1.2	75.2	38.9	50.3	49.7
65263	MADISON	98.8	98.7	0.3	0.3	0.1	0.1	1.0	1.0	8.2	8.1	7.7	5.9	5.3	23.0	25.7	14.0	2.2	72.9	38.5	51.0	49.0
65264	MARTINSBURG	98.4	98.3	0.5	0.6	0.4	0.4	0.5	0.5	7.0	7.3	7.5	6.9	5.3	24.6	28.8	11.5	1.2	73.7	39.1	48.1	51.9
65265	MEXICO	91.3	90.9	6.9	7.3	0.5	0.5	0.8	0.8	6.3	6.2	6.4	6.8	5.2	23.5	26.9	14.9	3.8	76.8	41.5	47.5	52.5
65270	MOBERLY	88.9	87.1	8.6	9.9	0.5	0.8	1.3	1.8	6.7	6.1	6.0	6.6	6.6	27.9	24.9	12.2	2.9	77.5	37.8	51.8	48.2
65274	NEW FRANKLIN	96.8	96.1	0.9	1.1	0.3	0.4	1.5	2.1	6.1	6.0	6.3	7.3	5.6	24.2	27.4	13.5	3.6	76.7	41.3	46.4	53.6
65275	PARIS	95.0	94.6	3.6	4.0	0.1	0.1	0.5	0.5	6.3	6.6	6.7	6.5	4.4	21.9	26.1	16.7	4.8	76.3	43.1	49.1	50.9
65276	PILOT GROVE	98.0	97.5	0.9	1.1	0.1	0.1	0.8	1.1	6.6	6.8	7.0	6.7	4.5	23.9	27.9	13.6	3.0	75.4	40.9	49.7	50.3
65279	ROCHEPORT	96.1	95.0	1.4	1.8	0.7	1.1	1.0	1.4	5.5	6.7	7.2	7.3	4.9	24.4	34.0	9.1	1.0	75.8	41.3	50.2	49.8
65280	RUSH HILL	97.8	97.8	0.7	0.7	0.0	0.0	0.7	0.7	6.7	7.4	6.7	5.2	3.7	21.9	29.3	17.8	1.5	75.9	43.7	52.6	47.4
65281	SALISBURY	96.7	96.2	2.5	2.9	0.1	0.2	0.5	0.6	5.1	5.5	5.5	5.9	5.0	21.5	30.8	16.0	4.6	80.0	45.9	48.6	51.4
65282	SANTA FE	97.5	97.4	1.0	1.1	0.3	0.3	0.1	0.1	4.4	4.4	7.6	8.6	3.8	22.2	35.5	11.9	1.6	77.6	44.4	52.0	48.0
65283	STOUTSVILLE	97.4	97.2	0.9	1.1	0.2	0.2	0.2	0.2	3.6	5.8	7.9	7.7	4.7	21.6	32.7	14.1	1.9	77.8	44.3	52.1	47.9
65284	STURGEON	97.1	96.6	0.6	0.7	0.2	0.3	0.7	1.0	6.8	6.7	6.7	6.7	6.2	26.4	28.4	10.5	1.7	76.0	38.6	48.7	51.3
65285	THOMPSON	98.3	98.3	0.5	0.6	0.1	0.1	0.6	0.6	6.6	6.6	7.4	6.7	5.0	23.4	31.1	11.7	1.5	75.2	40.8	51.9	48.1
65286	TRIPLETT	96.5	96.3	2.0	2.1	1.0	1.1	0.5	0.5	4.8	4.8	5.3	6.4	4.8	22.3	30.3	18.6	2.7	80.9	46.1	48.9	51.1
65287	WOOLDRIDGE	97.9	97.7	0.5	0.7	0.3	0.2	0.3	0.5	5.2	6.1	6.6	5.9	4.3	26.0	33.7	10.6	1.6	78.1	42.2	49.5	50.5
65301	SEDALIA	91.2	89.3	3.6	4.1	0.5	0.7	4.1	5.5	7.2	6.9	6.7	6.8	6.0	26.0	25.5	12.4	2.5	75.1	37.7	48.5	51.5
65305	WHITEMAN AIR FORCE B	81.8	77.5	9.7	11.3	2.2	3.4	5.7	7.7	15.7	10.4	8.1	9.0	22.4	32.9	1.5	0.1	0.0	63.2	21.5	56.4	43.6
65321	BLACKBURN	96.0	95.0	1.1	1.3	0.4	0.5	2.0	3.0	6.2	6.6	6.6	6.2	4.3	24.3	30.1	13.4	2.3	76.7	42.0	48.5	51.5
65322	BLACKWATER	98.9	98.3	0.8	1.1	0.0	0.1	0.8	1.0	6.0	6.5	6.9	6.6	3.8	23.2	30.0	13.5	3.3	76.5	42.8	49.9	50.1
65323	CALHOUN	97.8	97.3	0.1	0.2	0.3	0.4	0.4	0.5	4.8	4.8	5.8	6.7	4.9	23.9	32.0	15.5	1.6	80.6	44.4	51.1	48.9
65324	CLIMAX SPRINGS	98.4	98.1	0.4	0.5	0.1	0.1	0.7	0.9	2.6	2.9	3.2	3.3	2.8	14.4	34.0	34.6	2.1	89.2	59.2	50.1	49.9
65325	COLE CAMP	98.6	98.4	0.0	0.1	0.2	0.3	0.6	0.7	6.0	6.1	6.2	6.3	5.1	23.0	27.5	16.1	3.6	77.8	42.8	48.9	51.1
65326	EDWARDS	97.8	97.4	0.3	0.4	0.1	0.2	1.0	1.5	3.1	3.2	3.5	4.3	4.3	12.6	33.7	33.6	1.7	87.6	58.2	50.4	49.6
65329	FLORENCE	97.3	96.9	0.0	0.0	0.1	0.1	0.4	0.7	7.3	7.9	8.3	7.0	4.6	21.9	28.5	13.1	1.4	72.0	39.8	48.6	51.4
65330	GILLIAM	96.5	96.0	2.0	2.3	0.2	0.2	0.4	0.6	5.7	5.7	5.7	6.4	5.9	21.9	28.7	16.6	3.4	79.0	43.9	49.5	50.5
65332	GREEN RIDGE	96.6	95.6	0.5	0.6	0.1	0.2	2.5	3.4	7.1	7.3	7.5	6.4	4.9	25.4	28.3	11.7	1.4	74.0	38.3	50.8	49.2
65333	HOUSTONIA	98.0	97.2	0.2	0.3	0.5	0.8	0.9	1.2	6.6	6.7	6.7	7.0	5.7	23.7	28.0	13.4	2.3	75.7	40.4	49.8	50.2
65334	HUGHESVILLE	97.8	97.1	0.2	0.3	0.5	0.7	0.8	1.2	7.0	7.0	7.2	7.3	5.8	23.9	27.2	12.6	2.1	74.2	38.9	49.7	50.3
65335	IONIA	98.0	97.3	0.4	0.4	0.0	0.4	1.6	1.6	6.7	6.7	6.7	6.7	5.1	23.1	29.8	14.1	1.2	76.1	41.1	51.4	48.6
65336	KNOB NOSTER	81.8	77.6	7.3	8.4	1.6	2.3	9.1	12.3	7.4	7.0	6.6	7.3	8.9	31.0	23.2	7.9	0.6	74.5	32.1	52.0	48.0
65337	LA MONTE	92.2	89.8	0.9	1.0	0.9	1.3	7.1	9.9	6.5	6.8	6.9	6.8	6.0	26.6	27.2	11.6	1.7	75.8	37.8	50.8	49.2
	MISSOURI	84.9	83.3	11.2	11.7	1.2	1.7	2.1	2.8	6.6	6.6	6.6	7.0	6.7	26.1	26.5	11.7	2.1	76.1	37.7	48.8	51.2
	UNITED STATES	75.1	72.0	12.3	12.7	3.8	4.6	12.5	15.7	6.8	6.7	6.6	7.1	6.9	27.0	26.0	10.9	1.9	75.7	36.9	49.2	50.8

#	ZIP CODE / POST OFFICE NAME	2009 Per Capita Income	2009 HH Income Base	2009 HOUSEHOLD INCOME DISTRIBUTION (%) Less than $25,000	$25,000 to $49,999	$50,000 to $99,999	$100,000 to $149,999	$150,000 or More	MEDIAN HOUSEHOLD INCOME 2009	2014	2009 National Centile	2009 State Centile	2009 Home Value Base	2009 HOME VALUE DISTRIBUTION (%) Less than $50,000	$50,000 to $89,999	$90,000 to $174,999	$175,000 to $399,999	$400,000 or More	2009 Median Home Value
65048	KOELTZTOWN	18403	79	24.1	29.1	40.5	5.1	1.3	47355	48443	55	75	69	15.9	27.5	37.7	17.4	1.4	105208
65049	LAKE OZARK	38041	3219	15.0	26.0	36.4	12.9	9.6	59777	59146	77	89	2577	4.7	7.2	29.1	41.4	17.7	202628
65050	LATHAM	14056	187	20.3	39.6	33.7	4.3	2.1	43458	45385	44	65	156	24.4	17.9	30.1	22.4	5.1	101852
65051	LINN	20780	1997	23.7	26.8	41.5	6.6	1.4	49275	50806	59	78	1526	10.2	24.6	40.4	23.2	1.6	114258
65052	LINN CREEK	22690	1383	20.5	32.0	38.0	6.4	3.1	47045	48257	54	74	1152	16.2	17.3	30.9	29.6	6.0	134449
65053	LOHMAN	22135	502	14.5	28.5	46.6	8.4	2.0	54663	56451	71	85	414	5.3	8.9	46.1	37.0	2.7	147872
65054	LOOSE CREEK	21517	299	15.7	29.8	45.5	7.4	1.7	53157	51716	68	83	264	5.3	18.2	49.2	23.9	3.4	128947
65058	META	18886	421	27.1	31.6	35.6	4.8	1.0	41928	45000	39	61	371	20.8	21.8	35.3	18.3	3.8	105324
65059	MOKANE	24633	461	11.1	30.4	44.9	10.8	2.8	56332	56925	73	87	398	15.3	21.1	33.4	26.4	3.8	119565
65061	MORRISON	20122	356	24.4	35.7	35.1	2.5	2.2	42472	44101	41	62	311	28.6	20.6	28.6	17.4	4.8	91923
65062	MOUNT STERLING	20653	45	24.4	31.1	42.2	2.2	0.0	42399	46537	41	62	41	19.5	17.1	36.6	22.0	4.9	121875
65063	NEW BLOOMFIELD	23759	1282	16.6	27.9	41.3	9.4	4.8	54319	55783	70	84	1046	15.9	21.3	33.0	23.0	6.8	114962
65064	OLEAN	19201	312	29.5	24.4	38.1	5.8	2.2	46711	48249	53	73	265	11.3	21.1	38.5	24.9	4.2	125338
65065	OSAGE BEACH	29705	2535	16.6	33.2	36.8	8.5	4.8	50112	51097	61	79	1850	6.9	8.9	32.3	40.6	11.4	181667
65066	OWENSVILLE	18596	2638	28.7	31.6	33.9	4.4	1.4	39613	41618	32	52	2079	15.9	24.4	40.2	15.2	4.3	106800
65067	PORTLAND	19524	225	28.4	34.7	30.2	6.7	0.0	37669	40876	26	43	191	26.7	29.8	34.6	8.4	0.5	84318
65068	PRAIRIE HOME	20975	261	22.2	32.6	40.2	3.8	1.1	45758	47215	51	71	213	13.1	16.9	35.7	26.8	7.5	136932
65069	RHINELAND	20971	253	19.8	37.2	36.4	4.7	2.0	45349	45669	49	70	212	18.9	12.7	33.0	23.1	12.3	131429
65072	ROCKY MOUNT	28077	836	23.0	29.8	34.7	9.1	3.5	47196	47862	55	74	749	6.9	20.2	28.0	41.1	3.7	163404
65074	RUSSELLVILLE	23620	1125	17.8	28.4	42.9	6.8	4.1	52745	54462	67	83	930	14.9	16.8	39.9	23.4	4.9	123022
65075	SAINT ELIZABETH	19862	303	17.8	28.1	44.2	5.3	4.6	52027	51874	66	82	261	13.4	16.9	39.1	24.1	6.5	132250
65076	SAINT THOMAS	20786	262	17.2	20.6	53.8	6.9	1.5	57843	58173	75	88	235	9.8	14.0	50.6	25.5	0.0	124250
65077	STEEDMAN	18193	241	27.8	34.9	30.7	6.6	0.0	37490	40173	25	42	205	25.4	31.2	34.6	8.8	0.0	85000
65078	STOVER	18847	1538	33.4	33.7	28.5	3.3	1.0	36108	37579	21	36	1242	30.3	20.6	33.4	14.3	1.4	88333
65079	SUNRISE BEACH	27371	1645	22.9	33.9	33.4	6.2	3.6	43938	45572	45	66	1481	10.8	12.0	32.2	35.7	9.3	163712
65080	TEBBETTS	25494	403	15.6	21.8	45.4	13.9	3.2	62076	62445	80	91	365	13.7	11.0	49.0	24.7	1.6	136473
65081	TIPTON	18143	1066	30.2	29.7	34.0	4.1	2.0	41004	43144	36	57	821	22.0	30.2	36.4	10.4	1.0	87109
65082	TUSCUMBIA	16676	467	28.7	34.0	33.0	2.8	1.5	35890	39083	20	35	382	24.9	18.3	38.7	13.9	4.2	99630
65083	ULMAN	18122	230	33.9	32.6	28.3	3.5	1.7	35000	38070	18	31	193	24.4	22.8	31.1	18.7	3.1	95000
65084	VERSAILLES	18331	2614	32.4	33.0	27.7	4.4	2.5	37480	39033	25	42	2011	20.3	27.6	33.4	15.9	2.8	94235
65085	WESTPHALIA	20093	427	14.5	31.9	45.2	6.6	1.9	52662	51517	67	83	369	6.2	16.3	54.5	20.3	2.7	126059
65101	JEFFERSON CITY	24291	10957	21.4	25.6	41.3	8.5	3.2	52687	55628	67	83	7070	6.3	15.8	49.3	26.5	2.1	130581
65109	JEFFERSON CITY	28630	15587	16.2	27.0	41.2	10.5	5.1	56900	59502	74	88	10443	6.2	11.5	52.8	26.0	3.5	132563
65201	COLUMBIA	22250	14412	35.2	27.1	28.5	5.4	3.8	36147	39709	21	36	5413	22.4	9.3	39.2	23.1	6.0	131061
65202	COLUMBIA	24794	18181	18.8	29.0	41.0	7.9	3.3	51587	53223	65	81	11066	16.9	12.1	51.1	17.8	2.2	123626
65203	COLUMBIA	30969	21702	22.0	24.3	32.3	13.0	8.5	53987	54452	70	84	12789	3.4	7.1	32.5	47.7	9.3	190886
65211	COLUMBIA	10392	152	62.5	16.4	18.4	2.0	0.7	17037	17409	1	0	3	0.0	0.0	100.0	0.0	0.0	131250
65215	COLUMBIA	10251	20	60.0	25.0	15.0	0.0	0.0	17832	17071	1	0	2	0.0	50.0	50.0	0.0	0.0	90000
65216	COLUMBIA	6560	14	64.3	28.6	7.1	0.0	0.0	20000	17143	1	1	3	0.0	33.3	66.7	0.0	0.0	95000
65230	ARMSTRONG	17616	280	31.8	28.9	35.0	3.2	1.1	40000	41757	33	54	243	29.2	22.2	29.2	15.2	4.1	88158
65231	AUXVASSE	20446	1340	22.4	31.6	39.8	5.0	1.3	46563	50330	53	73	1037	19.8	25.6	34.1	16.7	3.9	98661
65232	BENTON CITY	20966	104	27.9	32.7	35.6	2.9	1.0	41872	45000	39	60	82	25.6	28.0	26.8	18.3	1.2	84000
65233	BOONVILLE	19548	3989	25.2	30.5	38.4	4.4	1.5	45320	46700	49	70	2795	10.3	21.3	43.0	23.1	2.3	116456
65236	BRUNSWICK	19026	601	37.1	32.3	26.1	2.8	1.7	33145	35274	14	22	430	46.5	27.2	20.7	4.7	0.9	55172
65237	BUNCETON	18466	445	25.2	39.6	31.9	2.2	1.1	39593	41754	31	52	358	23.7	23.5	24.9	21.5	6.4	95263
65239	CAIRO	19907	422	24.2	30.6	37.4	6.4	1.4	45412	49624	49	70	354	24.9	24.6	29.9	16.9	3.7	91250
65240	CENTRALIA	21519	2790	22.4	29.6	40.6	5.3	2.0	47446	50880	55	75	2153	16.2	26.8	37.1	17.6	2.3	98091
65243	CLARK	19929	1257	25.4	31.6	35.1	5.5	2.5	43741	46627	45	65	1077	19.4	22.3	36.9	17.4	4.1	103327
65244	CLIFTON HILL	22699	173	23.1	32.4	34.7	6.4	3.5	45942	49570	51	71	144	28.5	17.4	34.0	14.6	5.6	100000
65246	DALTON	17559	59	37.3	35.6	23.7	3.4	0.0	32550	34159	12	19	44	43.2	25.0	25.0	6.8	0.0	60000
65247	EXCELLO	19725	249	19.3	47.0	29.7	2.8	1.2	38543	40172	28	47	214	21.0	23.8	37.4	15.4	2.3	101786
65248	FAYETTE	19588	1602	28.5	28.9	34.7	6.4	1.5	40521	42849	34	55	1147	20.7	26.1	34.6	14.7	3.9	96048
65250	FRANKLIN	17508	288	24.7	41.0	30.6	2.8	1.0	36689	38786	23	39	228	34.6	14.9	34.2	14.0	2.2	90769
65251	FULTON	21751	7541	23.0	29.2	37.6	6.8	3.5	46994	51040	54	74	5265	15.2	23.8	38.3	19.6	3.2	110173
65254	GLASGOW	18874	647	27.8	34.5	32.5	3.6	1.7	39937	40976	32	53	486	28.4	30.2	26.7	10.3	4.3	80000
65255	HALLSVILLE	23921	1633	16.1	30.4	42.3	8.6	2.6	52548	52966	67	82	1364	18.1	19.0	36.4	22.9	3.6	112267
65256	HARRISBURG	25312	576	15.1	27.6	45.5	7.3	4.5	56583	57820	73	87	497	11.1	20.3	39.0	26.8	2.8	124395
65257	HIGBEE	18835	547	32.5	31.3	32.0	3.5	0.7	36212	37783	21	36	451	46.6	21.1	22.0	7.1	3.3	55741
65258	HOLLIDAY	16105	119	31.9	37.0	27.7	2.5	0.8	34275	37332	16	27	97	34.0	33.0	22.7	10.3	0.0	68636
65259	HUNTSVILLE	18043	1417	29.4	31.3	33.9	4.5	0.8	41151	43735	37	58	1078	29.1	29.3	26.9	12.2	2.5	78182
65260	JACKSONVILLE	17635	290	23.1	37.6	34.8	3.1	1.4	42340	45201	40	62	245	23.3	15.9	35.1	20.4	5.3	124342
65261	KEYTESVILLE	18238	491	35.6	35.8	24.6	3.1	0.8	33006	34367	13	21	383	42.3	25.1	23.0	7.8	1.8	62206
65262	KINGDOM CITY	22651	260	16.2	34.6	34.6	11.2	3.5	49465	51800	60	78	209	8.1	21.1	36.4	30.6	3.8	134375
65263	MADISON	16568	862	29.7	36.0	29.7	3.0	1.6	36457	38704	22	37	704	26.7	26.4	27.4	17.0	2.4	84359
65264	MARTINSBURG	21196	321	22.7	24.3	47.0	4.0	1.9	52053	51987	66	82	272	16.2	18.0	36.4	26.1	3.3	117143
65265	MEXICO	21603	6175	26.9	32.7	31.4	6.8	2.2	41378	43141	37	58	4375	18.1	27.5	36.9	15.6	2.0	95175
65270	MOBERLY	19157	6021	30.5	30.9	32.2	4.5	1.8	39232	42276	30	50	3987	27.6	31.5	28.9	10.9	1.2	78481
65274	NEW FRANKLIN	19402	727	29.6	31.4	33.0	4.8	1.2	40151	41895	33	54	522	21.3	34.3	29.7	11.9	2.9	85606
65275	PARIS	17734	1285	28.1	38.0	30.2	2.6	1.2	38034	39193	27	45	1008	23.8	31.1	30.4	13.0	1.8	83099
65276	PILOT GROVE	17597	662	31.4	32.8	30.5	3.6	1.7	39118	41528	30	49	533	13.3	29.6	34.1	19.7	3.2	99375
65279	ROCHEPORT	31074	647	12.2	24.0	43.6	14.4	5.9	63776	62493	82	93	569	6.7	12.8	34.3	37.4	8.8	159191
65280	RUSH HILL	19386	110	30.0	33.6	32.7	2.7	0.9	39204	41876	30	50	85	29.4	29.4	22.4	18.8	0.0	75000
65281	SALISBURY	19881	1343	28.4	28.7	37.8	2.8	2.3	44675	45427	47	68	1099	24.7	28.9	34.6	11.6	0.3	85063
65282	SANTA FE	17516	290	21.0	37.2	39.7	1.7	0.3	45485	50193	50	70	242	7.4	19.0	34.3	26.4	12.8	122596
65283	STOUTSVILLE	18697	193	26.9	33.7	34.7	4.1	0.5	41224	43645	37	58	163	9.8	15.3	39.3	28.2	7.4	133654
65284	STURGEON	21009	988	22.3	28.6	40.7	5.7	2.7	48763	51053	58	77	790	20.6	27.1	36.5	14.6	1.3	92535
65285	THOMPSON	19162	358	16.2	34.9	44.1	3.4	1.4	48912	50329	59	77	313	18.2	15.0	35.5	25.6	5.8	134274
65286	TRIPLETT	17351	78	33.3	35.9	24.4	5.1	1.3	34181	35000	16	27	63	25.4	19.0	39.7	14.3	1.6	95833
65287	WOOLDRIDGE	19890	170	19.4	31.8	41.8	6.5	0.6	48796	50000	58	77	149	10.7	18.1	37.6	32.2	1.3	134375
65301	SEDALIA	20283	13201	26.6	34.4	32.2	4.7	2.2	40558	43597	35	55	9293	16.0	25.3	41.5	14.8	2.3	101212
65305	WHITEMAN AIR FORCE B	14504	796	11.4	51.5	32.2	3.0	1.9	43251	45649	43	64	14	0.0	14.3	57.1	28.6	0.0	133333
65321	BLACKBURN	17207	279	33.7	30.1	29.7	4.7	1.8	38724	43994	29	48	195	35.9	25.1	26.7	9.2	3.1	66538
65322	BLACKWATER	19289	327	29.4	32.7	32.7	3.7	1.5	40288	42513	34	55	273	17.6	24.2	30.8	22.7	4.8	104924
65323	CALHOUN	18799	392	30.9	26.8	35.5	6.4	0.5	42479	45616	41	63	334	29.0	22.2	30.8	16.5	1.5	88462
65324	CLIMAX SPRINGS	23877	1182	27.7	30.5	35.6	3.0	3.1	42408	44473	41	62	1061	14.4	14.3	29.3	35.7	6.2	145346
65325	COLE CAMP	20265	1346	31.9	34.0	27.4	4.0	2.7	36410	36963	22	37	1041	16.9	22.0	44.5	13.8	2.8	105432
65326	EDWARDS	19115	836	39.2	33.3	22.4	3.7	1.4	31378	32024	10	16	733	27.0	18.4	34.0	16.1	4.5	97614
65329	FLORENCE	16128	298	31.2	30.2	32.9	5.7	0.0	37786	41965	26	44	255	15.7	17.3	43.9	18.0	5.1	114031
65330	GILLIAM	15899	197	33.0	43.7	20.8	2.5	0.0	35318	36755	19	33	153	38.6	24.2	30.1	7.2	0.0	68125
65332	GREEN RIDGE	18609	570	26.1	32.3	34.9	4.0	2.6	41836	44683	39	60	464	17.7	17.2	41.4	18.8	5.0	113333
65333	HOUSTONIA	18657	363	24.5	29.8	39.7	4.1	1.9	45634	48088	50	71	299	20.7	23.7	36.8	15.7	3.0	97174
65334	HUGHESVILLE	17302	337	27.0	30.0	38.0	3.6	1.5	42765	45988	42	64	281	21.4	22.8	37.0	16.0	2.8	97174
65335	IONIA	19377	107	26.2	37.4	31.8	3.7	0.9	38633	38633	29	47	82	19.5	12.2	37.8	28.0	2.4	135000
65336	KNOB NOSTER	21467	2179	19.8	36.8	34.1	5.8	3.6	44950	47895	48	69	1323	20.0	15.9	43.5	17.3	3.3	111798
65337	LA MONTE	17744	771	30.0	33.1	33.7	2.1	1.2	39113	40757	30	49	546	18.5	24.4	44.5	9.7	2.9	94937
	MISSOURI	25286		22.8	27.7	35.3	9.1	5.2	49522	52035				12.8	19.4	39.1	24.2	4.6	122064
	UNITED STATES	27277		20.9	24.4	35.3	11.7	7.6	54719	56938				9.3	13.1	31.6	32.6	13.5	162279

ZIP CODE		FINANCIAL SERVICES				THE HOME						ENTERTAINMENT						PERSONAL			
						Home Improvements		Furnishings													
#	POST OFFICE NAME	Auto Loan	Home Loan	Invest-ments	Retire-ment Plans	Home Repair	Lawn & Garden	Comput-ers & Hard-ware-Personal	Major Appli-ances	TV, Radio, Sound Equip-ment	Furni-ture	Dine out/ Carry out	Sports Equip-ment	Fees & Tickets	Toys & Games	Travel	Cable TV	Apparel & Services	Auto Repairs	Health Insur-ance	Pets & Supplies
65048	KOELTZTOWN	85	66	72	66	66	84	67	77	73	64	71	59	57	75	63	79	48	73	81	93
65049	LAKE OZARK	121	118	159	117	132	140	110	129	115	119	114	86	113	107	122	120	78	123	138	148
65050	LATHAM	90	65	75	63	64	86	67	78	75	66	73	60	54	78	61	82	49	74	83	96
65051	LINN	84	71	76	71	72	86	72	82	76	67	74	61	64	77	70	81	50	77	85	96
65052	LINN CREEK	95	80	105	79	84	97	79	93	82	77	82	68	71	81	81	86	55	88	93	109
65053	LOHMAN	86	93	80	96	90	90	87	87	85	87	86	69	90	87	89	84	60	86	86	103
65054	LOOSE CREEK	91	83	82	86	84	97	81	92	84	74	82	70	75	86	81	89	56	85	95	107
65058	META	78	64	70	65	65	80	64	75	68	60	67	57	56	70	62	74	45	69	78	88
65059	MOKANE	105	95	86	92	93	99	90	96	94	93	94	70	84	98	86	97	64	93	97	114
65061	MORRISON	86	62	87	61	65	87	64	81	70	59	69	60	52	70	63	77	46	74	84	96
65062	MOUNT STERLING	79	63	102	62	69	83	63	80	66	59	65	59	55	63	68	70	43	74	79	93
65063	NEW BLOOMFIELD	103	90	89	87	89	100	88	96	92	88	92	71	80	95	84	97	62	92	99	114
65064	OLEAN	85	73	76	71	73	84	71	80	75	70	74	59	64	76	69	79	50	75	81	94
65065	OSAGE BEACH	102	88	135	87	98	112	85	107	90	84	88	75	79	84	94	95	59	99	108	123
65066	OWENSVILLE	79	62	74	62	64	81	64	75	69	59	68	57	55	70	62	75	46	70	79	89
65067	PORTLAND	84	61	71	59	60	80	63	74	70	61	68	56	50	73	58	76	46	70	78	90
65068	PRAIRIE HOME	77	74	70	77	74	83	71	78	72	66	71	60	68	74	72	75	49	73	80	91
65069	RHINELAND	81	74	73	77	75	87	73	82	75	66	73	62	67	76	72	79	50	76	84	95
65072	ROCKY MOUNT	85	86	118	84	98	103	79	94	83	87	81	60	83	75	90	87	56	89	103	107
65074	RUSSELLVILLE	96	92	81	91	90	94	86	91	88	89	89	67	84	92	84	90	61	88	91	108
65075	SAINT ELIZABETH	101	69	111	69	73	107	77	96	80	63	79	79	57	79	77	88	51	90	101	118
65076	SAINT THOMAS	89	96	85	99	93	97	87	91	86	87	87	71	91	89	91	87	60	88	91	108
65077	STEEDMAN	84	61	69	59	60	80	63	73	70	61	68	56	51	73	57	76	46	69	77	89
65078	STOVER	71	57	75	55	61	76	58	71	63	56	62	51	51	61	59	69	41	66	76	83
65079	SUNRISE BEACH	86	81	115	79	91	99	76	92	80	80	78	61	76	73	85	84	53	87	98	105
65080	TEBBETTS	109	100	89	97	98	102	94	100	98	98	98	73	89	102	90	101	67	97	100	119
65081	TIPTON	84	61	84	59	63	87	65	81	72	59	70	60	52	72	63	80	47	75	86	95
65082	TUSCUMBIA	79	57	82	55	59	81	59	74	65	54	64	57	47	64	58	71	42	69	77	89
65083	ULMAN	84	62	71	60	62	80	64	74	70	63	69	57	53	73	59	76	46	70	77	90
65084	VERSAILLES	78	60	79	58	62	81	64	76	70	59	68	57	53	68	63	76	45	72	82	90
65085	WESTPHALIA	87	79	78	82	81	93	78	88	80	71	79	67	72	82	78	85	54	81	91	102
65101	JEFFERSON CITY	86	83	76	86	81	84	87	83	87	86	88	65	86	88	85	88	61	86	87	100
65109	JEFFERSON CITY	98	100	92	100	98	98	97	96	97	99	98	73	98	99	97	98	68	97	98	114
65201	COLUMBIA	76	55	51	59	53	56	87	64	78	73	79	56	68	79	65	76	55	74	64	79
65202	COLUMBIA	89	79	70	80	76	76	88	80	87	87	88	64	82	90	80	86	61	85	81	97
65203	COLUMBIA	104	98	92	102	96	94	109	97	105	106	106	79	105	107	101	103	75	103	97	117
65211	COLUMBIA	46	19	19	24	18	23	64	32	51	44	52	34	38	50	34	47	37	45	32	43
65215	COLUMBIA	41	27	26	29	26	29	49	34	44	39	44	31	36	44	35	43	31	41	35	43
65216	COLUMBIA	32	21	20	23	20	22	38	26	34	30	34	24	28	34	27	33	24	32	27	33
65230	ARMSTRONG	81	57	85	56	59	83	60	76	65	53	64	59	47	65	60	72	42	70	79	91
65231	AUXVASSE	85	72	76	70	72	84	71	80	76	71	75	59	64	78	68	80	51	77	83	95
65232	BENTON CITY	85	64	85	63	67	88	65	81	71	60	70	61	54	71	65	78	47	74	84	96
65233	BOONVILLE	77	68	74	69	69	81	69	76	72	65	71	57	64	72	69	76	49	73	81	90
65236	BRUNSWICK	73	52	75	51	54	76	57	70	62	49	60	54	44	61	55	68	40	65	76	83
65237	BUNCETON	77	60	66	60	60	76	61	71	66	58	65	54	52	68	58	71	44	66	74	84
65239	CAIRO	79	72	71	75	73	84	71	80	73	64	72	60	65	74	71	77	49	74	82	93
65240	CENTRALIA	83	76	72	78	75	87	77	82	79	71	78	63	71	81	75	83	53	79	86	97
65243	CLARK	92	68	86	67	69	91	70	84	77	66	75	65	57	78	67	83	50	79	88	101
65244	CLIFTON HILL	101	72	98	70	74	101	74	93	83	70	81	70	60	83	72	91	54	86	97	111
65246	DALTON	67	48	68	47	50	70	53	65	59	47	57	49	42	57	51	65	38	61	71	77
65247	EXCELLO	87	63	90	61	65	89	64	82	72	60	70	61	52	71	64	79	46	75	85	97
65248	FAYETTE	80	64	74	62	65	80	67	76	73	64	71	56	58	73	64	78	48	73	81	90
65250	FRANKLIN	82	59	68	57	58	78	61	71	68	59	66	55	49	71	56	74	45	67	75	87
65251	FULTON	86	78	75	77	77	85	80	82	83	78	83	62	76	84	77	86	57	82	88	98
65254	GLASGOW	78	58	72	58	58	78	66	73	69	58	68	59	53	69	61	74	45	72	79	89
65255	HALLSVILLE	93	89	78	87	87	90	83	88	85	86	85	65	81	88	81	87	58	85	88	104
65256	HARRISBURG	104	95	85	92	93	98	90	96	94	94	94	70	85	97	86	96	64	93	96	114
65257	HIGBEE	78	56	75	55	58	79	60	73	67	55	65	55	48	67	57	73	43	68	78	87
65258	HOLLIDAY	72	52	62	50	52	70	54	64	60	52	59	49	43	62	50	65	39	60	67	77
65259	HUNTSVILLE	81	61	72	60	62	80	63	74	69	60	68	56	52	70	60	75	45	70	78	88
65260	JACKSONVILLE	73	66	66	68	67	78	65	74	67	59	66	56	59	68	65	71	45	68	76	86
65261	KEYTESVILLE	69	49	71	48	51	72	54	67	59	47	57	51	42	58	53	65	38	62	72	79
65262	KINGDOM CITY	96	89	79	87	87	91	84	89	87	87	87	65	80	90	81	89	59	86	89	105
65263	MADISON	77	55	74	54	56	77	57	70	63	53	62	54	45	64	55	69	41	65	74	85
65264	MARTINSBURG	84	76	75	79	77	88	75	84	77	69	76	63	69	79	74	81	52	78	86	98
65265	MEXICO	81	65	74	65	66	83	70	79	75	64	73	59	61	75	67	81	50	76	85	93
65270	MOBERLY	71	62	62	63	62	71	68	69	71	63	69	52	62	70	63	74	48	69	75	82
65274	NEW FRANKLIN	79	61	75	59	62	80	64	75	70	59	68	56	53	70	61	76	46	71	81	89
65275	PARIS	77	54	81	53	56	80	59	73	64	50	62	58	45	63	58	70	41	69	79	88
65276	PILOT GROVE	77	57	78	57	59	81	61	75	66	54	64	57	49	65	60	72	43	69	79	89
65279	ROCHEPORT	110	123	113	123	121	115	108	112	106	114	107	85	115	108	114	104	75	108	107	130
65280	RUSH HILL	85	61	88	59	63	87	63	80	69	58	68	60	50	69	62	76	45	73	83	95
65281	SALISBURY	84	59	89	58	62	88	64	80	69	56	68	63	49	68	63	76	45	74	85	96
65282	SANTA FE	70	61	66	63	62	75	61	70	63	54	62	54	55	64	61	67	42	65	73	83
65283	STOUTSVILLE	81	55	88	55	58	85	62	76	64	50	63	63	45	63	61	70	41	71	81	94
65284	STURGEON	90	74	82	72	74	89	74	85	80	72	79	63	65	81	71	85	53	81	89	100
65285	THOMPSON	81	73	74	76	74	87	72	82	75	65	73	62	66	76	72	79	50	76	85	96
65286	TRIPLETT	75	51	82	51	54	79	57	71	59	46	59	59	42	58	57	65	38	66	75	87
65287	WOOLDRIDGE	76	78	75	80	77	82	72	77	72	71	72	60	73	73	75	74	50	74	77	91
65301	SEDALIA	76	66	67	66	65	77	70	73	73	66	72	56	64	74	66	77	49	73	79	88
65305	WHITEMAN AIR FORCE B	91	47	35	55	42	40	85	59	80	79	84	59	65	96	62	74	59	75	53	72
65321	BLACKBURN	82	57	89	57	59	86	63	78	65	51	64	64	46	64	62	71	42	73	82	96
65322	BLACKWATER	78	57	83	58	59	83	62	75	64	51	63	61	48	63	61	69	41	70	79	91
65323	CALHOUN	84	60	86	58	63	85	62	79	69	58	67	59	49	68	61	76	45	72	82	94
65324	CLIMAX SPRINGS	79	70	100	68	78	88	68	83	72	70	70	57	64	67	74	76	47	78	88	95
65325	COLE CAMP	80	60	80	60	62	84	64	78	70	57	68	59	53	69	63	76	45	73	84	92
65326	EDWARDS	60	57	73	53	63	68	54	64	57	59	56	42	54	53	59	61	38	62	71	73
65329	FLORENCE	81	56	87	55	58	84	61	76	64	51	63	63	45	63	61	70	41	71	80	93
65330	GILLIAM	64	46	65	45	48	67	50	62	56	45	54	47	40	55	49	62	36	58	68	73
65332	GREEN RIDGE	80	69	74	70	70	83	69	78	71	64	70	60	61	72	68	75	48	73	80	92
65333	HOUSTONIA	85	68	73	68	68	85	69	79	74	65	72	60	59	76	65	79	49	74	83	94
65334	HUGHESVILLE	83	63	73	63	64	82	65	76	70	61	69	59	54	72	62	76	46	71	79	92
65335	IONIA	79	62	75	61	63	78	62	74	67	60	66	55	53	68	61	72	44	69	76	87
65336	KNOB NOSTER	87	79	69	78	76	77	81	79	81	82	82	61	75	84	75	81	56	80	78	95
65337	LA MONTE	75	56	65	57	56	74	65	69	68	57	66	55	53	68	59	72	45	69	75	85
	MISSOURI	94	86	87	87	85	93	89	91	91	87	90	70	84	92	86	93	62	90	94	108
	UNITED STATES	100	100	100	100	100	100	100	100	100	100	100	100	100	100	100	100	100	100	100	100

ZIP CODE #	POST OFFICE NAME	COUNTY FIPS CODE	POPULATION 2000	POPULATION 2009	POPULATION 2014	2000-2009 ANNUAL RATE % Rate	2000-2009 ANNUAL RATE State Centile	HOUSEHOLDS 2000	HOUSEHOLDS 2009	HOUSEHOLDS 2014	HOUSEHOLDS % Annual Rate 2000-2009	HOUSEHOLDS 2009 Average HH Size	FAMILIES 2000	FAMILIES 2009	FAMILIES % Annual Rate 2000-2009
65338	LINCOLN	015	2101	2170	2190	0.3	50	835	860	868	0.3	2.46	591	587	-0.1
65339	MALTA BEND	195	605	574	558	-0.6	11	232	222	216	-0.5	2.59	172	159	-0.8
65340	MARSHALL	195	15383	14783	14435	-0.4	18	5688	5480	5340	-0.4	2.45	3709	3425	-0.9
65344	MIAMI	195	557	537	523	-0.4	18	215	209	204	-0.3	2.53	157	148	-0.6
65345	MORA	015	638	658	667	0.3	50	241	250	254	0.4	2.63	193	199	0.3
65347	NELSON	195	940	913	895	-0.3	21	367	359	353	-0.2	2.49	275	262	-0.5
65348	OTTERVILLE	053	1198	1323	1375	1.1	79	452	505	528	1.2	2.62	338	365	0.8
65349	SLATER	195	2753	2613	2535	-0.6	11	1159	1107	1076	-0.5	2.31	733	668	-1.0
65350	SMITHTON	159	1441	1612	1687	1.2	82	525	592	621	1.3	2.67	413	451	1.0
65351	SWEET SPRINGS	195	2418	2457	2455	0.2	46	914	925	920	0.1	2.55	656	640	-0.3
65354	SYRACUSE	141	624	694	728	1.2	82	235	262	275	1.2	2.65	182	197	0.9
65355	WARSAW	015	10497	11544	11951	1.0	76	4689	5222	5432	1.2	2.18	3233	3466	0.8
65360	WINDSOR	083	4304	4408	4461	0.3	50	1705	1743	1763	0.2	2.50	1177	1156	-0.2
65401	ROLLA	161	27191	29418	30604	0.9	72	11068	12132	12687	1.0	2.29	6993	7332	0.5
65409	ROLLA	161	1007	996	992	-0.1	32	1	1	1	0.0	3.00	0	0	0.0
65436	BEULAH	161	134	141	145	0.6	63	55	59	61	0.8	2.39	41	43	0.5
65438	BIRCH TREE	203	3569	3659	3683	0.3	50	1365	1419	1436	0.4	2.54	1014	1020	0.1
65439	BIXBY	093	493	486	479	-0.2	27	193	194	192	0.1	2.39	143	139	-0.3
65440	BOSS	065	433	407	396	-0.7	8	171	162	159	-0.6	2.50	138	129	-0.7
65441	BOURBON	055	4656	4836	4911	0.4	53	1709	1793	1828	0.5	2.65	1246	1263	0.1
65443	BRINKTOWN	125	1126	1183	1215	0.5	58	407	434	447	0.7	2.73	305	315	0.3
65444	BUCYRUS	215	1012	1005	1005	-0.1	32	407	411	413	0.1	2.42	304	297	-0.3
65446	CHERRYVILLE	055	646	696	716	0.8	69	243	264	273	0.9	2.64	187	197	0.6
65449	COOK STATION	055	327	350	361	0.7	66	125	135	140	0.8	2.59	94	98	0.5
65452	CROCKER	169	2721	2737	2747	0.1	42	1109	1126	1134	0.2	2.42	802	792	-0.1
65453	CUBA	055	8191	8630	8803	0.6	63	3242	3445	3526	0.7	2.46	2322	2382	0.3
65456	DAVISVILLE	055	474	515	530	0.9	72	186	203	210	0.9	2.54	144	152	0.6
65457	DEVILS ELBOW	169	544	548	547	0.1	42	202	204	205	0.1	2.62	134	130	-0.3
65459	DIXON	169	6272	6761	6968	0.8	69	2425	2649	2744	1.0	2.53	1770	1882	0.7
65461	DUKE	161	154	162	167	0.5	58	62	66	69	0.7	2.45	47	48	0.2
65462	EDGAR SPRINGS	161	1484	1566	1615	0.6	63	585	628	652	0.8	2.49	432	447	0.4
65463	ELDRIDGE	105	992	1152	1246	1.6	89	380	452	491	1.9	2.55	300	347	1.6
65464	ELK CREEK	215	421	414	413	-0.2	27	170	170	170	0.0	2.44	124	120	-0.4
65466	EMINENCE	203	2448	2487	2498	0.2	46	1047	1078	1087	0.3	2.29	698	688	-0.2
65468	EUNICE	215	111	119	123	0.8	69	49	53	55	0.9	2.25	37	39	0.6
65470	FALCON	105	785	827	843	0.6	63	296	316	323	0.7	2.62	235	244	0.4
65473	FORT LEONARD WOOD	169	13877	14994	14551	0.8	69	2723	2321	2199	-1.7	3.23	2390	2021	-1.8
65479	HARTSHORN	215	271	292	302	0.8	69	110	120	125	0.9	2.43	83	88	0.6
65483	HOUSTON	215	4499	4459	4464	-0.1	32	1937	1951	1964	0.1	2.24	1291	1247	-0.4
65484	HUGGINS	215	245	244	244	0.0	37	85	86	86	0.1	2.73	65	64	-0.2
65486	IBERIA	131	3443	3825	3970	1.1	79	1339	1518	1586	1.4	2.52	987	1074	0.9
65501	JADWIN	065	417	397	387	-0.5	14	149	143	141	-0.4	2.78	118	111	-0.7
65529	JEROME	161	267	320	344	2.0	92	113	138	149	2.2	2.32	77	90	1.7
65534	LAQUEY	169	894	947	967	0.6	63	335	359	368	0.8	2.63	257	268	0.5
65535	LEASBURG	055	1468	1719	1824	1.7	89	562	663	705	1.8	2.59	411	470	1.5
65536	LEBANON	105	26194	28593	29694	1.0	76	10329	11334	11796	1.0	2.49	7320	7748	0.6
65541	LENOX	065	755	718	700	-0.5	14	276	265	259	-0.4	2.65	218	205	-0.7
65542	LICKING	215	4439	4569	4637	0.3	50	1848	1931	1971	0.5	2.34	1294	1303	0.1
65543	LYNCHBURG	105	270	286	291	0.6	63	105	112	115	0.7	2.55	81	84	0.4
65548	MOUNTAIN VIEW	091	4864	5183	5313	0.7	66	2002	2157	2220	0.8	2.36	1399	1448	0.4
65550	NEWBURG	161	2937	3225	3381	1.0	76	1242	1385	1459	1.2	2.33	882	946	0.8
65552	PLATO	215	1673	1719	1748	0.3	50	666	695	711	0.5	2.47	488	492	0.1
65555	RAYMONDVILLE	215	1281	1325	1346	0.4	53	487	511	522	0.5	2.58	354	360	0.2
65556	RICHLAND	169	4634	4718	4761	0.2	46	1893	1958	1988	0.4	2.38	1338	1348	0.1
65557	ROBY	215	235	246	251	0.5	58	102	109	112	0.7	2.26	76	79	0.4
65559	SAINT JAMES	161	8399	8975	9309	0.7	66	3269	3534	3680	0.8	2.43	2284	2372	0.4
65560	SALEM	065	13169	13504	13567	0.3	50	5290	5488	5536	0.4	2.42	3737	3740	0.0
65564	SOLO	215	211	207	207	-0.2	27	92	92	92	0.0	2.25	67	65	-0.3
65565	STEELVILLE	055	4968	5219	5333	0.5	58	1964	2081	2132	0.6	2.46	1371	1401	0.2
65566	VIBURNUM	055	1000	1001	993	0.0	37	374	382	381	0.2	2.55	278	275	-0.1
65567	STOUTLAND	029	1381	1522	1616	1.1	79	526	589	628	1.2	2.57	399	435	0.9
65570	SUCCESS	215	360	376	384	0.5	58	139	147	151	0.6	2.56	104	107	0.3
65571	SUMMERSVILLE	215	1568	1713	1774	1.0	76	621	684	711	1.1	2.50	440	466	0.6
65580	VICHY	125	796	840	862	0.6	63	341	364	375	0.7	2.31	254	262	0.3
65582	VIENNA	125	2098	2169	2182	0.4	53	801	844	857	0.6	2.47	557	565	0.2
65583	WAYNESVILLE	169	8026	8781	9033	1.0	76	3103	3403	3506	1.0	2.53	2207	2358	0.7
65584	SAINT ROBERT	169	5884	7068	7507	2.0	92	2316	2794	2978	2.0	2.52	1560	1838	1.8
65586	WESCO	055	127	135	139	0.7	66	55	59	61	0.8	2.29	41	43	0.5
65588	WINONA	203	2460	2550	2595	0.4	53	977	1025	1047	0.5	2.49	698	707	0.1
65589	YUKON	215	326	341	348	0.5	58	120	127	131	0.6	2.68	90	93	0.4
65590	LONG LANE	059	1755	1892	1978	0.8	69	666	717	748	0.8	2.64	520	545	0.5
65591	MONTREAL	029	1111	1287	1390	1.6	89	432	509	552	1.8	2.53	326	374	1.5
65601	ALDRICH	167	731	811	864	1.1	79	302	337	360	1.2	2.41	230	251	0.9
65603	ARCOLA	057	519	484	471	-0.8	6	224	209	204	-0.7	2.32	170	154	-1.1
65604	ASH GROVE	077	2785	3275	3515	1.8	90	1072	1296	1405	2.1	2.49	780	892	1.5
65605	AURORA	009	11942	12650	13042	0.6	63	4688	4948	5100	0.6	2.53	3311	3375	0.2
65606	ALTON	149	3495	3308	3203	-0.6	11	1455	1391	1352	-0.5	2.38	1029	952	-0.8
65608	AVA	067	8581	9006	9205	0.5	58	3471	3677	3772	0.6	2.42	2368	2413	0.2
65609	BAKERSFIELD	153	782	791	782	0.1	42	291	297	295	0.2	2.66	218	216	-0.1
65610	BILLINGS	043	3234	4463	5233	3.5	97	1274	1780	2097	3.7	2.51	970	1315	3.3
65611	BLUE EYE	209	1879	2008	2102	0.7	66	814	873	917	0.8	2.30	615	641	0.4
65612	BOIS D ARC	077	1860	2084	2203	1.2	82	683	784	836	1.5	2.66	547	606	1.1
65613	BOLIVAR	167	14997	17227	18469	1.5	87	5388	6246	6731	1.6	2.53	3727	4162	1.2
65614	BRADLEYVILLE	213	555	668	729	2.0	92	214	259	283	2.1	2.58	165	194	1.8
65616	BRANSON	213	16708	19968	21832	1.9	91	6962	8309	9088	1.9	2.38	4707	5399	1.5
65617	BRIGHTON	167	1159	1295	1378	1.2	82	405	459	491	1.4	2.77	315	345	1.0
65618	BRIXEY	153	276	276	272	0.0	37	113	114	113	0.1	2.42	85	83	-0.3
65619	BROOKLINE STATION	077	3983	6158	7132	4.8	99	1509	2432	2844	5.3	2.53	1225	1921	5.0
65620	BRUNER	043	487	594	678	2.2	94	180	219	251	2.1	2.71	140	166	1.9
65622	BUFFALO	059	8408	9377	9894	1.2	82	3265	3643	3841	1.2	2.55	2323	2500	0.8
65623	BUTTERFIELD	009	916	968	964	0.6	63	339	360	359	0.7	2.69	249	256	0.3
65624	CAPE FAIR	209	1437	1711	1858	1.9	91	621	736	800	1.9	2.31	454	520	1.5
65625	CASSVILLE	009	6361	6681	6768	0.5	58	2518	2658	2695	0.6	2.46	1757	1785	0.2
65626	CAULFIELD	091	1291	1344	1361	0.4	53	520	546	554	0.5	2.46	391	399	0.2
65627	CEDARCREEK	213	510	535	562	0.5	58	220	230	242	0.5	2.33	147	148	0.1
	MISSOURI					0.7					0.8	2.45			0.4
	UNITED STATES					1.0					1.1	2.59			0.9

# ZIP CODE	POST OFFICE NAME	RACE (%) White 2000	White 2009	Black 2000	Black 2009	Asian/Pacific 2000	Asian/Pacific 2009	% Hispanic Origin 2000	% Hispanic Origin 2009	2009 AGE DISTRIBUTION (%) 0-4	5-9	10-14	15-19	20-24	25-44	45-64	65-84	85+	18+	MEDIAN AGE 2009	% 2009 Males	% 2009 Females
65338	LINCOLN	98.4	98.1	0.1	0.1	0.0	0.1	0.9	1.3	6.5	6.5	6.6	6.5	5.0	20.9	27.6	17.0	3.5	76.0	43.3	49.2	50.8
65339	MALTA BEND	97.0	95.8	0.8	1.0	0.5	0.9	1.7	2.3	5.1	5.9	6.4	6.4	4.2	25.4	31.4	13.1	2.1	78.6	42.6	53.1	46.9
65340	MARSHALL	87.7	85.3	6.6	7.4	0.7	1.0	6.2	8.3	6.6	6.2	6.0	8.3	8.8	24.3	25.0	12.1	2.6	77.3	36.0	49.2	50.8
65344	MIAMI	98.6	98.1	0.4	0.6	0.0	0.0	1.4	1.9	6.7	7.6	7.4	6.5	3.9	20.5	30.4	15.1	1.9	74.5	43.0	48.8	51.2
65345	MORA	97.7	97.1	0.3	0.3	0.3	0.6	0.6	0.9	5.9	6.2	6.7	7.4	4.7	23.6	30.2	14.0	1.2	76.6	42.1	51.7	48.3
65347	NELSON	97.6	97.0	1.4	1.6	0.1	0.1	0.5	0.8	5.0	5.4	5.9	6.5	4.7	22.6	31.5	15.1	3.3	79.4	45.0	50.4	49.6
65348	OTTERVILLE	97.7	97.1	0.6	0.8	0.1	0.2	0.8	1.3	7.2	7.3	7.2	6.5	4.8	25.0	28.1	12.2	1.7	74.3	39.0	49.0	51.0
65349	SLATER	89.7	87.8	7.6	8.8	0.2	0.3	1.3	1.9	6.2	6.0	5.9	5.9	5.9	23.5	27.4	14.4	4.7	78.3	42.0	49.6	50.4
65350	SMITHTON	96.2	95.3	0.9	1.0	0.2	0.3	1.6	2.3	7.3	7.0	6.8	7.9	6.9	24.8	25.9	11.2	2.2	74.1	36.6	49.3	50.7
65351	SWEET SPRINGS	96.0	94.9	0.9	1.1	0.7	1.1	1.2	1.7	6.1	6.3	6.3	6.3	5.4	22.8	28.4	15.2	3.1	77.0	42.6	49.9	50.1
65354	SYRACUSE	98.4	98.0	0.2	0.3	0.3	0.3	1.1	1.7	5.8	5.8	6.5	7.5	5.6	26.8	28.0	13.0	1.2	77.2	40.5	53.5	46.5
65355	WARSAW	97.7	97.3	0.2	0.2	0.1	0.2	1.0	1.4	3.8	3.8	4.7	4.9	4.0	16.4	34.5	25.5	2.4	84.6	53.7	49.6	50.4
65360	WINDSOR	97.0	96.5	0.6	0.7	0.3	0.4	0.7	0.9	7.0	6.7	6.9	6.8	5.6	23.9	26.0	13.9	3.2	75.2	39.3	49.4	50.6
65401	ROLLA	92.6	90.3	1.8	2.1	3.0	4.6	1.4	1.9	5.8	5.6	5.9	8.1	10.9	24.2	25.2	12.2	2.1	79.0	35.7	50.9	49.1
65409	ROLLA	82.4	75.8	2.9	3.1	11.0	17.0	1.5	2.0	3.6	2.9	2.5	24.2	35.3	19.0	6.8	3.8	1.8	89.2	22.4	67.8	32.2
65436	BEULAH	98.5	97.9	0.0	0.0	0.0	0.7	0.8	1.4	5.7	6.4	6.4	6.4	4.3	22.7	33.3	13.5	1.4	77.3	43.8	48.2	51.8
65438	BIRCH TREE	94.9	94.2	0.2	0.2	0.1	0.1	1.5	2.0	6.3	6.4	6.6	7.1	5.7	23.5	27.4	15.0	1.9	76.1	41.1	49.4	50.6
65439	BIXBY	98.4	98.1	0.2	0.2	0.0	0.2	0.4	0.6	6.6	6.8	7.0	6.8	4.3	23.0	27.4	15.0	3.1	75.1	41.5	48.4	51.6
65440	BOSS	97.9	97.3	0.2	0.2	0.5	0.7	1.2	1.7	5.7	6.1	6.1	5.4	4.9	22.4	33.7	14.7	1.0	78.9	44.5	50.9	49.1
65441	BOURBON	98.7	98.5	0.0	0.0	0.1	0.1	0.8	1.1	7.2	7.2	7.4	6.9	5.9	25.2	26.9	11.6	1.7	73.6	37.9	51.0	49.0
65443	BRINKTOWN	95.4	94.5	1.7	1.9	0.2	0.3	2.6	3.5	6.6	6.8	7.2	7.6	5.7	21.6	28.7	14.4	1.4	74.6	40.9	52.1	47.9
65444	BUCYRUS	97.4	96.8	0.1	0.1	0.8	1.3	1.0	1.3	6.2	6.4	6.4	5.8	4.7	22.0	30.7	15.8	2.1	77.6	44.0	49.5	50.5
65446	CHERRYVILLE	98.1	97.8	0.0	0.0	0.3	0.3	0.3	0.3	6.5	6.6	7.0	6.9	5.0	22.7	29.3	14.8	1.1	75.6	41.0	49.4	50.6
65449	COOK STATION	96.6	96.0	0.6	0.9	0.3	0.6	0.9	1.1	6.0	6.3	6.9	6.6	4.9	22.9	31.7	13.4	1.4	76.9	42.1	50.3	49.7
65452	CROCKER	96.1	95.4	0.4	0.5	0.6	0.9	1.1	1.4	5.9	6.2	6.9	7.1	4.9	23.6	30.1	13.9	1.4	76.5	41.4	50.1	49.9
65453	CUBA	98.0	97.6	0.3	0.3	0.2	0.3	1.0	1.3	6.2	6.3	6.3	6.3	5.4	23.8	27.7	15.2	2.7	77.0	41.5	49.2	50.8
65456	DAVISVILLE	98.3	98.1	0.0	0.0	0.0	0.2	0.2	0.2	6.2	6.6	7.0	6.6	4.7	21.9	30.5	15.3	1.2	75.9	42.4	48.9	51.1
65457	DEVILS ELBOW	84.9	81.6	6.4	7.1	5.0	6.9	1.7	2.0	6.2	6.0	6.0	5.8	6.2	24.1	31.4	10.9	3.3	77.9	41.6	48.4	51.6
65459	DIXON	93.6	92.0	2.1	2.5	1.1	1.7	1.9	2.6	6.4	6.5	6.8	6.7	5.4	24.7	28.9	12.7	1.8	76.1	40.0	48.5	51.5
65461	DUKE	98.7	97.5	0.0	0.0	0.0	0.6	1.3	1.2	5.6	6.2	6.2	6.2	4.3	22.8	32.1	14.8	1.9	78.4	44.1	48.1	51.9
65462	EDGAR SPRINGS	97.3	96.8	0.1	0.1	0.4	0.7	0.8	1.1	5.5	5.9	6.1	6.0	4.5	22.8	32.6	15.2	1.5	78.9	44.5	49.0	51.0
65463	ELDRIDGE	98.3	98.0	0.2	0.2	0.1	0.2	0.7	1.0	6.6	6.6	6.9	6.6	6.1	25.1	29.3	11.6	1.2	75.4	39.3	50.6	49.4
65464	ELK CREEK	96.0	95.4	0.0	0.0	0.2	0.5	1.4	1.7	5.6	6.0	6.5	6.5	4.8	20.8	30.7	17.1	1.7	78.0	44.6	49.5	50.5
65466	EMINENCE	95.8	95.4	0.2	0.2	0.0	0.0	0.6	0.8	5.2	4.9	6.5	6.4	4.6	21.9	32.0	16.2	2.2	79.4	45.3	49.3	50.7
65468	EUNICE	96.4	95.8	0.0	0.0	0.0	0.0	0.0	0.8	5.0	5.0	5.9	5.9	6.7	21.8	31.1	16.8	1.7	80.7	44.6	47.9	52.1
65470	FALCON	97.6	97.1	0.3	0.2	0.1	0.1	0.9	1.2	6.3	6.7	6.8	6.7	5.8	23.1	30.4	13.2	1.2	76.3	40.7	51.1	48.9
65473	FORT LEONARD WOOD	65.1	61.2	21.3	22.3	2.9	4.0	11.3	14.5	8.2	6.8	4.6	21.4	26.4	30.8	1.6	0.2	0.1	77.7	21.7	64.8	35.2
65479	HARTSHORN	96.3	95.9	0.0	0.0	0.0	0.0	0.4	0.7	5.1	5.5	5.8	6.5	6.2	22.6	30.5	16.1	1.7	79.5	43.5	48.6	51.4
65483	HOUSTON	96.5	96.0	0.1	0.1	0.2	0.3	1.2	1.5	5.4	5.8	6.1	6.4	5.5	21.2	29.6	17.0	3.1	78.7	44.7	47.7	52.3
65484	HUGGINS	97.6	97.1	0.0	0.0	0.4	0.4	0.8	0.8	5.3	5.3	6.1	6.1	4.1	20.5	30.7	17.2	4.5	79.1	46.7	46.7	53.3
65486	IBERIA	99.0	98.9	0.1	0.1	0.1	0.1	0.6	0.8	7.2	7.3	7.3	7.2	5.0	24.7	26.4	13.1	2.0	73.9	38.4	50.1	49.9
65501	JADWIN	95.9	95.2	0.2	0.3	0.2	0.5	0.5	0.5	6.3	6.8	7.1	7.1	4.8	21.9	29.2	15.1	1.8	75.3	42.2	48.9	51.1
65529	JEROME	95.9	95.0	0.4	0.3	0.4	0.9	1.1	1.6	3.8	5.9	5.9	7.2	4.7	22.2	36.3	12.2	1.9	79.1	45.2	53.8	46.2
65534	LAQUEY	92.3	90.6	2.3	2.7	1.2	1.8	3.0	4.0	6.8	6.9	6.9	6.4	5.3	25.0	29.8	11.9	1.1	75.3	40.1	49.3	50.7
65535	LEASBURG	98.4	98.0	0.1	0.2	0.1	0.2	0.4	0.5	6.6	6.9	7.0	6.4	6.1	24.0	29.3	12.4	1.3	75.5	39.1	48.9	51.1
65536	LEBANON	97.0	96.3	0.5	0.5	0.4	0.6	1.3	1.8	7.0	6.9	6.7	6.6	5.9	25.5	26.6	12.6	2.3	75.3	38.3	48.8	51.2
65541	LENOX	97.7	97.4	0.3	0.3	0.0	0.0	0.7	0.8	5.4	5.7	6.1	6.3	5.0	20.3	31.6	16.6	2.9	79.0	45.7	50.1	49.9
65542	LICKING	97.1	96.7	0.0	0.0	0.2	0.4	1.2	1.6	5.7	6.3	6.6	6.5	4.6	23.7	28.1	15.9	2.6	77.6	42.5	48.1	51.9
65543	LYNCHBURG	95.9	94.8	0.4	0.7	0.4	0.3	1.1	1.4	6.6	7.3	7.0	5.6	5.2	21.7	31.1	14.3	1.0	75.5	42.2	52.4	47.6
65548	MOUNTAIN VIEW	96.1	95.4	0.0	0.0	0.3	0.5	1.1	1.6	6.5	6.7	6.8	6.5	4.6	23.1	26.1	16.5	3.2	75.8	41.5	48.3	51.7
65550	NEWBURG	96.7	96.0	0.3	0.3	0.4	0.7	0.6	0.9	5.5	6.2	6.6	6.3	5.0	24.0	31.4	13.1	1.8	77.7	42.2	49.7	50.3
65552	PLATO	92.2	90.6	1.9	2.2	1.2	1.8	1.6	2.3	5.6	5.9	6.5	7.2	5.1	23.4	32.3	12.4	1.5	77.6	42.3	49.0	51.0
65555	RAYMONDVILLE	97.2	96.5	0.1	0.2	0.2	0.3	0.5	0.7	5.8	6.0	6.0	6.3	6.0	22.3	30.3	15.5	2.0	78.6	43.2	50.0	50.0
65556	RICHLAND	95.8	95.1	0.6	0.7	0.6	0.8	1.5	1.9	6.2	6.1	6.3	6.3	5.6	23.2	29.0	15.1	2.2	77.4	42.1	48.6	51.4
65557	ROBY	96.2	95.1	0.4	0.4	0.4	0.8	0.9	1.2	4.9	5.3	5.7	6.9	4.5	21.5	34.1	15.4	1.6	79.3	45.8	50.8	49.2
65559	SAINT JAMES	95.2	94.3	0.8	0.9	0.3	0.6	0.8	1.1	5.7	5.9	6.8	7.4	5.5	21.9	28.1	15.6	3.0	76.7	42.3	49.2	50.8
65560	SALEM	97.0	96.4	0.4	0.5	0.2	0.4	0.7	1.0	6.4	6.6	6.7	6.4	4.9	22.6	27.6	15.7	3.2	76.3	42.1	48.3	51.7
65564	SOLO	95.3	94.7	0.0	0.0	0.5	0.5	1.4	1.9	5.3	5.8	6.8	6.8	4.8	20.8	30.9	16.9	1.9	77.3	44.8	49.8	50.2
65565	STEELVILLE	98.1	97.8	0.1	0.1	0.3	0.4	0.5	0.7	6.6	6.4	6.6	6.9	5.4	23.8	26.7	15.2	2.4	76.1	40.5	47.8	52.2
65566	VIBURNUM	98.4	98.1	0.1	0.1	0.1	0.2	0.4	0.6	6.9	7.1	7.3	7.1	4.5	23.0	27.6	14.1	2.5	74.0	40.3	48.2	51.8
65567	STOUTLAND	97.7	97.2	0.0	0.0	0.2	0.3	0.7	0.9	5.3	5.3	5.7	6.6	6.7	24.4	30.7	13.8	1.4	79.2	42.0	53.0	47.0
65570	SUCCESS	96.9	96.3	0.0	0.0	0.6	1.1	0.6	0.8	6.1	6.4	6.1	6.4	5.1	23.1	30.9	14.6	1.3	77.4	42.5	50.0	50.0
65571	SUMMERSVILLE	97.0	96.6	0.1	0.1	0.1	0.2	0.4	0.6	7.0	7.0	7.1	6.4	5.7	22.7	26.5	15.6	1.9	75.1	39.7	49.2	50.8
65580	VICHY	97.1	96.5	0.3	0.2	0.3	0.4	1.8	2.5	5.6	5.8	6.3	6.2	4.6	22.0	31.4	16.3	1.7	78.3	44.5	52.3	47.7
65582	VIENNA	98.4	98.0	0.0	0.0	0.1	0.2	0.4	0.5	6.8	7.1	7.1	6.3	4.7	22.8	27.0	15.1	3.1	75.4	41.3	48.7	51.3
65583	WAYNESVILLE	82.4	78.1	8.7	10.5	2.8	4.3	3.4	4.7	6.4	6.5	6.9	7.1	6.3	25.1	29.5	11.0	1.3	75.5	38.8	48.0	52.0
65584	SAINT ROBERT	68.9	65.0	17.6	18.6	4.9	6.7	5.6	7.0	7.9	7.8	8.5	7.7	5.5	31.4	24.1	6.5	0.6	70.7	33.3	49.2	50.8
65586	WESCO	96.1	95.6	0.8	0.7	0.0	0.7	0.8	1.5	5.9	6.7	6.7	6.7	5.2	22.2	30.4	14.8	1.5	77.0	42.2	50.4	49.6
65588	WINONA	94.2	93.3	0.1	0.1	0.0	0.1	0.9	1.1	7.1	7.3	7.4	7.7	5.8	23.4	27.5	12.3	1.5	73.5	38.0	48.5	51.5
65589	YUKON	96.6	95.9	0.0	0.0	0.0	0.0	0.6	0.6	5.3	5.9	5.9	6.2	5.9	22.3	31.7	15.5	1.5	79.5	43.9	49.3	50.7
65590	LONG LANE	97.5	97.1	0.1	0.2	0.3	0.4	0.5	0.7	6.2	6.4	6.9	6.6	5.6	22.8	30.7	13.4	1.4	76.3	41.5	51.6	48.4
65591	MONTREAL	98.4	98.1	0.0	0.0	0.0	0.0	0.7	1.1	5.4	5.7	5.9	6.2	5.4	24.6	31.9	13.3	1.6	79.3	42.5	51.9	48.1
65601	ALDRICH	98.1	97.8	0.1	0.1	0.1	0.1	1.4	1.8	5.3	5.7	6.2	6.4	4.1	21.6	32.6	16.4	1.8	78.8	45.4	50.3	49.7
65603	ARCOLA	97.3	97.1	0.2	0.2	0.2	0.2	1.7	2.5	5.8	6.4	6.6	5.6	3.9	20.2	31.2	18.4	1.9	77.5	45.9	52.7	47.3
65604	ASH GROVE	97.6	97.1	0.2	0.3	0.1	0.2	0.7	1.0	6.1	6.5	6.9	6.4	4.9	23.3	30.3	12.7	2.9	75.9	41.7	49.9	50.1
65605	AURORA	96.2	95.3	0.2	0.2	0.2	0.3	2.3	3.1	7.5	7.1	7.1	7.3	6.2	24.5	25.3	12.6	2.4	73.8	37.5	49.6	50.4
65606	ALTON	92.8	92.7	0.1	0.2	0.1	0.1	0.9	1.0	6.0	6.2	6.4	6.0	4.6	21.9	29.7	17.1	2.0	77.7	44.1	49.5	50.5
65608	AVA	97.3	96.7	0.1	0.1	0.2	0.4	0.9	1.3	6.1	6.1	6.1	6.6	5.7	21.5	27.9	16.8	3.2	77.5	43.1	48.3	51.7
65609	BAKERSFIELD	95.9	95.7	0.1	0.3	0.0	0.0	1.0	1.1	8.2	8.0	8.2	6.6	5.2	25.4	25.3	11.8	1.4	71.4	36.0	50.8	49.2
65610	BILLINGS	97.2	96.6	0.3	0.3	0.3	0.4	0.4	0.6	6.2	6.3	6.6	6.6	5.2	24.3	29.8	13.2	1.8	76.9	41.2	49.7	50.3
65611	BLUE EYE	97.6	97.1	0.0	0.0	0.2	0.2	0.4	0.5	4.2	4.3	4.4	4.2	3.4	16.4	32.5	28.6	2.1	84.5	54.9	47.0	53.0
65612	BOIS D ARC	98.1	97.7	0.1	0.1	0.0	0.0	0.6	0.8	5.5	6.0	6.5	6.4	4.8	23.9	31.9	13.7	1.3	77.9	42.8	50.6	49.4
65613	BOLIVAR	96.9	96.2	0.6	0.7	0.3	0.5	1.4	2.0	6.7	6.2	6.0	9.4	11.7	22.2	22.0	13.0	2.8	77.1	33.5	47.5	52.5
65614	BRADLEYVILLE	97.3	96.9	0.0	0.0	0.4	0.4	0.9	1.3	5.8	6.3	6.6	5.4	4.6	23.7	31.1	14.2	2.2	78.1	43.0	51.2	48.8
65616	BRANSON	95.4	94.4	0.4	0.5	0.6	0.9	3.5	4.6	6.0	5.9	6.2	5.9	5.3	24.6	28.1	15.8	2.2	78.3	41.9	47.3	52.7
65617	BRIGHTON	97.7	97.4	0.2	0.2	0.1	0.2	1.5	2.1	7.3	7.3	7.6	7.6	5.4	25.9	27.2	10.6	1.1	72.7	36.8	51.1	48.9
65618	BRIXEY	98.2	98.2	0.0	0.0	0.0	0.0	0.7	0.7	5.4	6.2	5.4	4.7	5.1	19.2	33.3	19.2	1.4	79.7	47.5	49.6	50.4
65619	BROOKLINE STATION	96.5	95.4	0.4	0.5	0.8	1.3	1.1	1.6	7.5	7.8	7.9	6.6	4.7	27.6	28.0	9.1	0.8	72.6	37.3	49.0	51.0
65620	BRUNER	97.5	97.3	0.0	0.0	0.2	0.2	2.1	2.7	5.7	5.7	6.4	6.9	5.7	26.6	30.6	11.4	0.8	78.1	39.9	50.5	49.5
65622	BUFFALO	97.6	97.2	0.1	0.1	0.0	0.0	1.1	1.4	6.8	6.7	6.8	7.0	6.2	23.4	27.6	13.4	2.3	75.5	39.4	48.7	51.3
65623	BUTTERFIELD	90.3	86.8	0.2	0.2	0.4	0.6	12.5	17.5	8.2	8.2	8.2	7.5	5.4	26.3	25.2	10.1	0.9	70.8	34.9	49.2	50.8
65624	CAPE FAIR	97.1	96.7	0.1	0.1	0.2	0.3	1.4	1.9	5.1	5.5	6.0	5.8	4.1	21.7	30.7	19.5	1.5	79.7	46.1	51.0	49.0
65625	CASSVILLE	96.2	95.2	0.1	0.2	0.5	0.7	2.0	3.0	6.1	6.1	6.4	6.7	5.7	23.8	27.2	15.1	2.9	77.4	41.1	49.2	50.8
65626	CAULFIELD	97.9	97.6	0.3	0.4	0.1	0.1	1.3	1.8	6.1	6.1	6.3	5.8	5.6	23.9	28.6	16.0	1.7	78.1	41.8	51.2	48.8
65627	CEDARCREEK	95.1	94.2	0.4	0.4	0.4	0.6	3.7	4.5	6.5	6.2	5.8	6.2	6.9	25.0	29.2	12.9	1.3	77.6	39.3	49.0	51.0
	MISSOURI	84.9	83.3	11.2	11.7	1.2	1.7	2.1	2.8	6.6	6.6	6.6	7.0	6.7	26.1	26.5	11.7	2.1	76.1	37.7	48.8	51.2
	UNITED STATES	75.1	72.0	12.3	12.7	3.8	4.6	12.5	15.7	6.8	6.7	6.6	7.1	6.9	27.0	26.0	10.9	1.9	75.7	36.9	49.2	50.8

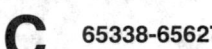

ZIP CODE #	POST OFFICE NAME	2009 Per Capita Income	2009 HH Income Base	2009 HOUSEHOLD INCOME DISTRIBUTION (%) Less than $25,000	$25,000 to $49,999	$50,000 to $99,999	$100,000 to $149,999	$150,000 or More	MEDIAN HOUSEHOLD INCOME 2009	2014	2009 National Centile	2009 State Centile	2009 Home Value Base	2009 HOME VALUE DISTRIBUTION (%) Less than $50,000	$50,000 to $89,999	$90,000 to $174,999	$175,000 to $399,999	$400,000 or More	2009 Median Home Value
65338	LINCOLN	16762	860	34.3	35.2	26.2	3.7	0.6	33160	34197	14	22	652	12.7	21.6	44.0	21.0	0.6	112113
65339	MALTA BEND	20672	222	23.9	31.5	38.7	4.1	1.8	45000	46854	48	69	161	26.1	19.3	28.6	21.1	5.0	101875
65340	MARSHALL	21788	5480	24.9	30.7	34.4	6.6	3.4	44765	47453	48	68	3595	18.6	25.7	37.0	16.6	2.2	98568
65344	MIAMI	21340	209	25.4	30.6	36.8	4.8	2.4	45480	47651	50	70	150	26.0	18.0	39.3	10.7	6.0	101667
65345	MORA	18895	250	24.0	36.8	32.4	3.6	3.2	39648	41701	32	52	216	21.3	14.4	37.0	24.1	3.2	120000
65347	NELSON	21132	359	20.9	36.2	34.0	6.1	2.8	44861	46917	48	69	301	24.6	18.9	32.9	18.3	5.3	104018
65348	OTTERVILLE	18608	505	28.7	35.0	30.9	2.8	2.6	39769	42527	32	53	407	21.9	24.1	36.9	14.5	2.7	96875
65349	SLATER	17279	1107	34.5	35.5	27.0	1.7	1.3	35196	37708	18	32	819	45.5	30.3	17.3	5.7	1.1	55069
65350	SMITHTON	19341	592	18.1	39.2	35.8	5.1	1.9	44238	46306	46	67	507	14.2	28.0	40.4	15.0	2.4	100142
65351	SWEET SPRINGS	19289	925	25.5	31.8	37.7	3.5	1.5	44226	46519	46	67	701	23.7	34.1	32.8	7.6	1.9	81866
65354	SYRACUSE	21134	262	22.5	34.7	36.6	2.3	3.8	45603	46867	50	71	223	26.0	19.3	28.3	24.2	2.2	99545
65355	WARSAW	21033	5222	33.9	31.8	28.6	3.7	2.1	35291	36367	19	32	4346	19.8	24.9	36.1	16.8	2.4	98121
65360	WINDSOR	18606	1743	31.8	30.2	32.7	3.8	1.4	38380	40026	28	47	1311	22.6	33.5	33.2	9.8	0.9	83484
65401	ROLLA	21430	12132	31.7	28.9	30.8	5.4	3.1	39591	41965	31	52	7501	16.1	19.7	39.8	21.3	3.1	115706
65409	ROLLA	5908	0	0.0	0.0	0.0	0.0	0.0	0	0	0	0	0	0.0	0.0	0.0	0.0	0.0	0
65436	BEULAH	16600	59	35.6	33.9	28.8	1.7	0.0	35553	36721	19	33	52	30.8	23.1	25.0	19.2	1.9	80000
65438	BIRCH TREE	11522	1419	52.2	33.1	12.8	1.4	0.6	23434	24130	2	1	1133	39.5	29.3	23.7	5.1	2.4	62969
65439	BIXBY	17957	194	33.0	34.0	28.4	3.1	1.5	35000	37637	18	31	152	28.9	33.6	32.2	3.9	1.3	75385
65440	BOSS	18754	162	25.3	37.7	29.0	6.2	1.9	40816	44546	35	56	144	15.3	29.2	33.3	19.4	2.8	108333
65441	BOURBON	17213	1793	29.2	31.2	35.2	3.2	1.2	41773	43315	39	60	1405	15.7	25.1	38.2	18.2	2.8	102683
65443	BRINKTOWN	14727	434	29.3	42.6	24.7	3.5	0.0	34638	36045	17	29	384	24.7	16.4	38.3	13.8	6.8	106633
65444	BUCYRUS	17881	411	41.6	29.7	23.8	2.4	2.4	30594	32579	9	13	354	27.7	23.2	33.6	13.0	2.5	88571
65446	CHERRYVILLE	15315	264	39.0	33.3	23.5	2.3	1.9	33145	35281	14	22	226	20.4	33.2	32.3	11.5	2.7	84667
65449	COOK STATION	14783	135	36.3	35.6	25.2	3.0	0.0	35974	38290	20	35	115	23.5	13.0	36.5	21.7	5.2	120192
65452	CROCKER	18119	1126	28.0	36.9	30.8	3.7	0.6	37698	39290	26	43	858	25.5	29.7	30.8	12.1	1.9	81818
65453	CUBA	18247	3445	32.1	31.5	31.3	3.8	1.4	37900	39805	26	45	2575	15.0	23.9	40.7	16.8	3.7	110490
65456	DAVISVILLE	15821	203	39.9	35.0	20.2	2.5	2.5	33103	34245	13	22	176	20.5	36.9	28.4	10.8	3.4	79375
65457	DEVILS ELBOW	19136	204	25.0	30.4	39.7	3.9	1.0	42390	47379	41	62	137	12.4	21.9	48.9	16.8	0.0	121875
65459	DIXON	18164	2649	26.2	36.7	32.3	3.3	1.5	39033	41873	30	49	1991	22.1	27.2	37.4	12.2	1.1	91134
65461	DUKE	16287	66	37.9	33.3	25.8	3.0	0.0	33196	37978	14	23	59	30.5	28.8	22.0	16.9	1.7	69000
65462	EDGAR SPRINGS	15619	628	36.5	32.6	28.2	2.2	0.5	33387	36349	14	24	549	30.1	22.8	29.3	15.1	2.7	81842
65463	ELDRIDGE	15467	452	31.2	42.9	21.9	4.0	0.0	34118	34378	16	27	392	25.5	26.8	32.7	10.5	4.6	83571
65464	ELK CREEK	20872	170	34.7	33.5	23.5	3.5	4.7	33406	34437	14	24	146	28.1	24.7	25.3	17.8	4.1	82000
65466	EMINENCE	14880	1078	46.9	31.4	18.4	2.3	0.9	26537	27817	4	3	868	26.4	26.2	31.9	13.5	2.1	85417
65468	EUNICE	14958	53	41.5	37.7	17.0	3.8	0.0	30544	32948	9	13	47	40.4	17.0	29.8	12.8	0.0	72500
65470	FALCON	16905	316	31.0	34.5	29.7	4.1	0.6	36347	37973	22	36	265	17.4	20.4	28.3	19.2	14.7	118145
65473	FORT LEONARD WOOD	14605	2321	8.9	51.9	33.8	3.8	1.6	42747	45941	42	64	66	9.1	12.1	65.2	13.6	0.0	132143
65479	HARTSHORN	13609	120	45.8	36.7	15.0	2.5	0.0	27572	29050	5	5	104	40.4	18.3	29.8	10.6	1.0	70000
65483	HOUSTON	17730	1951	41.3	32.4	21.6	2.6	2.1	29162	30653	7	8	1409	21.3	25.6	36.9	14.3	2.0	94944
65484	HUGGINS	16943	86	31.4	36.0	26.7	3.5	2.3	35000	38898	18	31	74	20.3	27.0	31.1	17.6	4.1	95000
65486	IBERIA	16645	1518	32.7	35.6	28.0	3.3	0.5	36675	37885	23	38	1251	22.4	26.2	37.0	11.7	2.7	92431
65501	JADWIN	15931	143	32.9	34.3	27.3	3.5	2.1	35846	37355	20	34	120	20.8	26.7	38.3	12.5	1.7	94286
65529	JEROME	16074	138	42.0	28.3	26.8	2.9	0.0	29513	30196	7	9	100	18.0	33.0	34.0	15.0	0.0	88000
65534	LAQUEY	17370	359	28.4	35.1	32.3	3.1	1.1	37408	39394	25	42	301	31.2	14.3	33.2	18.3	3.0	100893
65535	LEASBURG	17569	663	33.9	33.8	26.7	3.3	2.3	33144	36165	14	22	514	20.4	25.1	38.7	14.4	1.4	94792
65536	LEBANON	19520	11334	31.2	32.1	29.4	4.5	2.7	37796	39044	26	44	7979	21.3	21.5	36.0	17.7	3.4	103414
65541	LENOX	15341	265	34.3	34.0	28.7	1.9	1.1	36323	37750	21	36	228	23.2	21.9	36.4	16.2	2.2	97857
65542	LICKING	15960	1931	44.1	31.3	20.8	2.8	1.0	28689	30797	6	6	1426	28.5	24.7	32.6	11.3	2.9	84773
65543	LYNCHBURG	16716	112	31.3	37.5	27.7	3.6	0.0	37327	38464	25	42	95	25.3	16.8	33.7	9.5	14.7	105833
65548	MOUNTAIN VIEW	15112	2157	44.4	35.8	16.2	2.8	0.8	27952	27951	6	5	1561	21.8	31.1	35.6	10.2	1.3	84888
65550	NEWBURG	19308	1385	32.0	33.9	29.8	3.1	1.2	35745	39780	20	34	1086	30.1	24.3	32.3	11.2	2.0	81273
65552	PLATO	19722	695	31.4	29.2	32.5	4.5	2.4	38566	42230	28	47	590	19.5	19.5	44.2	10.8	5.9	108841
65555	RAYMONDVILLE	13710	511	45.0	34.8	17.2	2.0	1.0	27314	28096	5	4	414	33.6	21.7	29.7	12.3	2.7	79231
65556	RICHLAND	17714	1958	29.6	38.6	28.4	2.6	0.8	36099	38777	21	35	1514	26.4	27.7	30.1	13.6	2.3	83146
65557	ROBY	19258	109	42.2	27.5	22.9	4.6	2.8	30312	31524	9	12	93	22.6	24.7	35.5	10.8	6.5	93125
65559	SAINT JAMES	18051	3534	35.5	32.5	26.4	4.0	1.6	34644	37161	17	29	2590	17.0	23.2	38.9	17.2	3.6	105062
65560	SALEM	16563	5488	37.3	33.1	25.3	3.0	1.3	32727	34632	13	20	3984	20.3	27.1	37.8	12.8	2.0	93985
65564	SOLO	19795	92	32.6	32.6	28.3	2.2	4.3	35000	41566	18	31	79	27.8	25.3	24.1	17.7	5.1	81667
65565	STEELVILLE	17004	2081	37.6	30.7	25.9	4.1	1.7	33535	36707	14	24	1594	21.5	26.6	34.1	14.4	3.5	93069
65566	VIBURNUM	16504	382	32.5	33.0	29.3	3.7	1.6	36597	38769	22	38	297	26.9	37.0	33.3	2.4	0.3	74464
65567	STOUTLAND	17987	589	24.4	40.2	32.3	2.0	1.0	40803	43353	35	56	508	32.1	21.9	35.0	7.5	3.5	82308
65570	SUCCESS	15626	147	47.6	26.5	21.1	3.4	1.4	26572	27875	4	3	125	26.4	21.6	34.4	12.8	4.8	92500
65571	SUMMERSVILLE	12071	684	53.4	33.3	11.0	1.2	1.2	23069	22914	2	1	502	35.5	23.3	29.5	9.4	2.4	74000
65580	VICHY	20104	364	30.8	30.2	33.2	4.9	0.8	40900	41432	36	57	306	17.3	19.6	36.9	20.3	5.9	112963
65582	VIENNA	18349	844	30.8	30.8	32.3	5.0	1.1	37766	38759	26	44	664	19.1	21.4	34.2	21.1	4.2	106044
65583	WAYNESVILLE	22435	3403	21.7	26.0	41.9	7.9	2.4	51536	52559	65	81	2364	14.8	17.0	41.9	24.4	2.0	126466
65584	SAINT ROBERT	21427	2794	21.1	31.8	39.3	5.7	2.1	47300	50213	55	74	1643	20.9	12.9	48.6	17.2	0.4	119787
65586	WESCO	16487	59	37.3	33.9	25.4	3.4	0.0	35754	38593	20	34	50	22.0	14.0	36.0	22.0	6.0	125000
65588	WINONA	13140	1025	50.8	30.8	15.6	2.0	0.7	24302	26076	3	2	784	33.8	34.8	23.7	5.9	1.8	69681
65589	YUKON	13037	127	44.9	36.2	15.7	2.4	0.8	28054	28057	6	6	111	37.8	19.8	28.8	12.6	0.9	71000
65590	LONG LANE	17269	717	31.9	31.4	32.9	2.4	1.4	40284	42232	34	55	615	30.2	23.7	31.2	14.0	0.8	78913
65591	MONTREAL	17479	509	23.2	41.5	32.4	2.9	0.0	40965	43326	36	57	438	35.6	19.2	24.0	15.8	5.5	78500
65601	ALDRICH	18560	337	23.7	36.8	35.6	3.9	0.0	39449	43727	31	51	276	15.6	25.4	29.7	25.7	3.6	108621
65603	ARCOLA	17907	209	33.0	33.5	30.1	2.4	1.0	37109	41141	24	40	173	22.5	21.4	41.0	12.1	2.9	102717
65604	ASH GROVE	19100	1296	30.4	30.2	34.9	2.8	1.8	41105	44635	36	57	932	12.9	26.4	41.4	17.3	2.0	105690
65605	AURORA	17154	4948	33.6	33.9	27.1	3.4	2.0	33799	36290	15	25	3624	21.3	24.3	38.5	13.5	2.5	95649
65606	ALTON	14653	1391	49.1	33.5	13.9	1.9	1.5	25454	26030	4	2	1104	36.0	22.4	30.3	10.1	1.2	70476
65608	AVA	16785	3677	37.9	35.8	22.4	2.2	1.6	31529	32648	11	16	2791	21.5	27.1	33.5	15.6	2.2	91638
65609	BAKERSFIELD	16926	297	41.4	32.7	22.9	1.7	1.3	29124	29702	7	8	221	36.2	20.4	25.8	14.5	3.2	79167
65610	BILLINGS	20110	1780	25.9	33.4	33.7	5.3	1.7	42677	45291	41	63	1426	9.9	15.0	39.3	30.0	5.8	142021
65611	BLUE EYE	23623	873	18.7	38.3	37.5	3.9	1.7	45656	46586	50	71	716	14.1	20.8	29.5	30.7	4.9	137500
65612	BOIS D ARC	19555	784	21.3	32.4	39.4	5.4	1.5	46273	48507	52	72	663	11.2	22.0	33.6	29.7	3.5	126884
65613	BOLIVAR	17542	6246	33.1	30.9	29.9	4.0	2.0	37792	41311	26	44	4070	12.0	22.3	43.4	19.1	3.2	115129
65614	BRADLEYVILLE	16585	259	30.5	43.6	21.2	2.7	1.9	35294	37533	19	32	223	30.5	15.7	28.7	18.8	6.3	97083
65616	BRANSON	24208	8309	23.4	32.2	33.1	6.8	4.5	44779	47573	48	68	5283	9.4	12.8	37.8	32.2	7.9	153974
65617	BRIGHTON	18962	459	19.8	32.7	40.1	5.7	1.7	48115	50394	57	76	367	13.4	18.8	38.7	24.8	4.4	122955
65618	BRIXEY	14436	114	41.2	36.8	20.2	0.9	0.9	29465	29730	7	9	99	28.3	21.2	32.3	13.1	5.1	90714
65619	BROOKLINE STATION	26584	2432	12.8	25.9	47.7	9.0	4.5	59869	58858	77	90	2084	8.0	9.6	56.0	24.8	1.7	131944
65620	BRUNER	15640	219	29.7	35.2	33.3	1.4	0.5	38710	42898	29	48	191	24.1	24.6	33.0	14.1	4.2	93125
65622	BUFFALO	16992	3643	36.3	31.6	27.3	2.7	2.1	33583	35275	15	24	2738	20.4	23.2	38.6	14.1	3.8	100441
65623	BUTTERFIELD	17072	360	27.5	37.8	29.4	0.6	4.7	34674	38437	17	29	268	21.6	31.3	27.6	14.9	4.5	85294
65624	CAPE FAIR	21898	736	33.7	31.8	29.5	2.4	2.6	36499	37832	22	37	600	18.5	20.0	37.5	21.8	2.2	108807
65625	CASSVILLE	19653	2658	33.1	32.0	30.0	3.2	1.8	36401	37216	22	37	1952	15.7	27.2	40.1	13.7	3.3	96950
65626	CAULFIELD	16330	546	38.8	38.8	19.8	1.5	1.1	30266	30749	8	12	462	32.5	19.7	34.8	11.5	1.5	85000
65627	CEDARCREEK	20027	230	28.7	31.7	33.5	5.7	0.4	37131	42395	24	41	190	40.0	30.5	19.5	6.8	3.2	62800
	MISSOURI	25286		22.8	27.7	35.3	9.1	5.2	49522	52035				12.8	19.4	39.1	24.2	4.6	122064
	UNITED STATES	27277		20.9	24.4	35.3	11.7	7.6	54719	56938				9.3	13.1	31.6	32.6	13.5	162279

ZIP CODE #	POST OFFICE NAME	FINANCIAL SERVICES: Auto Loan	Home Loan	Invest-ments	Retire-ment Plans	THE HOME: Home Improvements: Home Repair	Lawn & Garden	Furnishings: Comput-ers & Hard-ware-Personal	Major Appli-ances	TV, Radio, Sound Equip-ment	Furni-ture	ENTERTAINMENT: Dine out/ Carry out	Sports Equip-ment	Fees & Tickets	Toys & Games	Travel	Cable TV	PERSONAL: Apparel & Services	Auto Repairs	Health Insur-ance	Pets & Supplies
65338	LINCOLN	72	52	73	50	54	74	55	69	61	50	59	51	44	60	54	67	39	64	73	81
65339	MALTA BEND	96	66	105	66	69	101	73	91	76	59	75	75	53	74	73	83	49	85	96	112
65340	MARSHALL	84	73	73	73	72	85	78	81	82	73	80	62	71	82	74	86	55	81	88	97
65344	MIAMI	97	67	105	67	70	102	74	92	77	61	76	76	55	76	74	84	50	86	97	113
65345	MORA	85	64	87	65	67	90	68	82	71	58	70	66	55	71	68	76	46	76	86	99
65347	NELSON	93	68	97	67	70	97	72	88	76	62	75	70	56	75	71	83	49	82	93	107
65348	OTTERVILLE	87	62	88	61	64	88	65	81	71	59	70	62	52	71	64	78	46	75	84	97
65349	SLATER	67	49	62	48	50	68	55	63	60	49	58	48	44	59	51	65	39	61	69	75
65350	SMITHTON	78	73	68	74	70	83	73	76	75	67	74	61	69	76	72	78	50	75	83	92
65351	SWEET SPRINGS	82	64	80	64	66	87	67	81	73	60	71	61	56	72	66	79	47	75	86	95
65354	SYRACUSE	101	72	85	70	72	96	75	88	84	73	82	68	60	87	69	91	55	83	93	107
65355	WARSAW	70	63	82	59	69	78	61	73	66	64	64	49	58	61	65	70	43	70	81	84
65360	WINDSOR	78	59	73	58	60	79	63	74	69	58	67	56	53	69	60	75	45	70	80	88
65401	ROLLA	75	66	69	67	66	75	72	73	73	68	73	56	66	73	68	76	50	73	77	87
65409	ROLLA	0	0	0	0	0	0	0	0	0	0	0	0	0	0	0	0	0	0	0	0
65436	BEULAH	71	51	73	49	53	72	52	66	58	48	57	50	42	57	52	64	37	61	69	79
65438	BIRCH TREE	53	37	51	36	38	53	39	48	43	36	42	37	30	44	37	48	28	45	50	58
65439	BIXBY	78	56	80	54	58	79	57	73	63	53	62	55	46	63	56	70	41	67	76	86
65440	BOSS	84	60	86	58	62	85	62	78	68	57	67	59	49	68	61	75	44	72	82	93
65441	BOURBON	81	60	69	59	60	78	62	72	68	60	67	55	51	71	57	74	45	68	76	87
65443	BRINKTOWN	72	51	73	50	53	73	53	67	58	49	57	50	42	58	52	64	38	61	70	80
65444	BUCYRUS	77	55	79	54	58	79	57	72	63	53	62	54	46	63	56	69	41	66	75	86
65446	CHERRYVILLE	72	52	71	50	53	72	53	67	59	50	58	50	43	59	52	65	38	61	69	80
65449	COOK STATION	68	49	69	47	51	69	50	64	56	47	55	48	40	56	49	61	36	58	66	76
65452	CROCKER	78	56	80	54	58	80	58	73	64	54	63	55	46	64	57	70	42	67	76	87
65453	CUBA	75	58	73	57	60	76	61	72	66	57	65	54	52	66	59	72	43	68	76	85
65456	DAVISVILLE	72	51	74	50	53	73	53	67	58	49	57	50	42	58	52	64	38	62	70	80
65457	DEVILS ELBOW	79	66	74	67	68	79	71	76	74	68	73	57	63	73	68	77	49	75	81	90
65459	DIXON	77	61	74	59	62	77	62	73	67	60	66	55	53	68	60	72	44	69	76	87
65461	DUKE	71	51	73	50	53	72	52	67	58	49	57	50	42	58	52	64	38	61	69	79
65462	EDGAR SPRINGS	70	50	71	48	52	71	51	65	57	48	56	49	41	56	51	62	37	60	68	77
65463	ELDRIDGE	71	51	59	50	51	68	53	62	59	52	58	47	43	61	48	64	39	59	65	75
65464	ELK CREEK	91	65	93	63	67	92	67	85	74	62	73	64	53	74	66	81	48	78	88	101
65466	EMINENCE	60	43	61	42	45	61	45	57	50	41	49	42	36	49	44	55	32	52	60	67
65468	EUNICE	60	43	62	42	45	61	44	56	49	41	48	42	35	49	44	54	32	51	58	67
65470	FALCON	79	57	75	55	58	79	59	72	65	55	64	55	47	66	56	71	42	67	76	87
65473	FORT LEONARD WOOD	90	48	36	55	43	41	84	59	79	78	84	58	64	95	61	73	59	75	54	72
65479	HARTSHORN	59	42	60	41	44	60	43	55	48	40	47	41	35	48	43	53	31	51	58	66
65483	HOUSTON	66	49	66	48	51	67	54	63	59	50	58	47	44	58	52	64	39	60	68	75
65484	HUGGINS	83	60	86	58	62	85	61	78	68	57	67	59	49	68	61	75	44	72	81	93
65486	IBERIA	74	53	75	51	55	76	55	70	61	50	60	53	44	61	54	67	40	64	74	83
65501	JADWIN	79	57	81	55	59	80	58	74	64	54	63	55	46	64	57	71	42	68	77	88
65529	JEROME	67	48	68	46	49	68	49	62	54	46	53	47	39	54	48	60	35	57	65	74
65534	LAQUEY	79	62	75	60	63	78	61	73	66	60	66	54	53	67	60	71	44	68	75	87
65535	LEASBURG	82	59	70	57	59	79	61	72	68	59	67	55	49	70	56	74	45	68	76	87
65536	LEBANON	79	64	66	63	63	76	68	73	72	65	71	55	59	74	63	77	48	72	78	87
65541	LENOX	73	52	75	50	54	74	53	68	59	50	58	51	43	59	53	65	39	62	71	81
65542	LICKING	65	47	67	46	49	67	49	62	55	45	53	46	39	54	48	60	35	57	66	73
65543	LYNCHBURG	76	55	78	53	57	77	56	71	62	52	61	54	45	62	55	68	40	65	74	85
65548	MOUNTAIN VIEW	62	44	63	43	46	64	47	59	53	43	51	44	38	52	46	58	34	55	63	70
65550	NEWBURG	77	58	76	56	60	78	60	73	66	56	64	54	50	66	58	72	43	68	77	86
65552	PLATO	81	68	73	66	68	79	66	75	71	67	70	55	60	72	64	74	47	71	77	89
65555	RAYMONDVILLE	63	45	65	44	47	64	46	59	52	43	51	44	37	51	46	57	33	54	61	70
65556	RICHLAND	72	54	69	52	55	72	57	68	63	53	61	51	47	62	54	68	41	64	72	80
65557	ROBY	77	56	78	55	58	78	57	72	63	54	62	54	47	63	57	69	41	66	75	85
65559	SAINT JAMES	75	56	75	55	58	77	59	72	65	55	63	54	49	64	58	71	42	67	77	85
65560	SALEM	69	50	69	49	52	70	53	66	59	49	58	49	43	58	52	65	38	61	70	77
65564	SOLO	80	57	82	55	59	81	58	74	65	54	64	56	47	64	58	71	42	68	77	88
65565	STEELVILLE	71	52	66	51	53	70	57	66	62	53	61	50	46	63	53	68	41	63	71	79
65566	VIBURNUM	76	54	78	52	56	77	56	71	62	52	61	53	44	61	55	68	40	65	74	84
65567	STOUTLAND	83	60	73	58	60	81	62	74	69	60	67	56	50	71	58	75	45	69	78	89
65570	SUCCESS	71	51	73	50	53	72	52	67	58	49	57	50	42	58	52	64	38	61	69	79
65571	SUMMERSVILLE	52	38	53	37	39	54	40	50	44	36	43	37	32	44	39	49	29	46	53	59
65580	VICHY	81	60	88	59	63	83	61	78	67	57	66	58	50	66	62	73	44	71	80	92
65582	VIENNA	74	61	70	62	63	78	62	73	67	56	65	55	55	67	62	72	44	68	77	86
65583	WAYNESVILLE	88	82	77	81	80	87	80	84	83	80	82	62	77	84	78	85	56	82	87	99
65584	SAINT ROBERT	84	76	66	74	73	73	78	76	78	81	79	59	73	82	73	78	54	77	75	91
65586	WESCO	67	48	69	47	50	68	49	63	55	46	54	47	40	55	49	60	36	58	66	75
65588	WINONA	60	41	57	39	41	59	43	53	49	41	48	41	33	50	40	54	32	50	56	65
65589	YUKON	62	45	64	43	46	63	46	58	51	43	50	44	37	51	45	56	33	54	61	69
65590	LONG LANE	79	60	68	60	61	78	62	72	67	59	66	55	52	69	58	73	44	67	75	86
65591	MONTREAL	78	57	80	55	59	79	58	73	64	55	63	55	47	64	57	71	42	67	76	87
65601	ALDRICH	80	56	85	55	58	83	60	75	64	52	63	59	46	63	59	70	41	70	79	91
65603	ARCOLA	74	51	81	51	53	78	57	70	59	46	58	58	41	58	56	64	38	66	74	87
65604	ASH GROVE	83	62	84	61	64	85	63	79	69	59	68	59	52	69	63	76	45	72	82	93
65605	AURORA	73	56	61	55	56	71	60	66	65	57	63	51	50	66	55	70	43	64	71	80
65606	ALTON	61	44	63	43	46	63	46	58	51	42	50	43	37	50	45	56	33	53	61	69
65608	AVA	69	51	64	50	52	68	55	64	60	51	59	48	46	60	52	66	40	61	69	77
65609	BAKERSFIELD	81	58	69	57	58	78	61	71	67	59	66	55	49	70	56	73	44	67	75	87
65610	BILLINGS	83	67	82	66	68	86	69	80	73	63	72	62	59	73	68	78	48	76	84	95
65611	BLUE EYE	81	75	100	70	84	92	72	86	77	77	75	58	70	71	79	81	50	82	95	99
65612	BOIS D ARC	81	73	73	76	75	86	72	82	75	66	73	62	67	76	72	79	50	75	84	95
65613	BOLIVAR	71	56	60	57	56	65	67	65	68	61	67	51	57	68	59	70	46	67	69	78
65614	BRADLEYVILLE	76	55	78	53	57	77	56	71	62	52	61	54	45	62	55	69	40	65	74	85
65616	BRANSON	87	78	83	78	80	88	81	86	84	79	83	63	76	83	79	87	57	85	92	101
65617	BRIGHTON	84	77	70	76	76	82	73	79	76	74	76	58	69	79	71	79	52	76	80	93
65618	BRIXEY	62	45	64	43	46	63	46	58	51	43	50	44	37	51	45	56	33	54	61	69
65619	BROOKLINE STATION	103	103	93	101	99	100	95	99	95	98	95	75	94	98	94	95	66	95	96	117
65620	BRUNER	77	55	63	53	55	73	57	66	63	56	62	51	46	66	52	69	42	63	70	81
65622	BUFFALO	74	54	71	53	55	75	58	69	64	54	63	52	47	64	55	70	42	66	74	83
65623	BUTTERFIELD	83	59	69	58	59	79	62	72	69	60	67	55	50	71	56	75	45	68	76	88
65624	CAPE FAIR	90	65	93	63	67	92	66	85	74	62	72	64	53	73	66	81	48	78	88	101
65625	CASSVILLE	83	62	78	61	64	83	66	78	72	62	70	58	54	72	63	78	47	73	82	92
65626	CAULFIELD	72	52	68	50	53	71	53	65	59	51	58	50	43	60	51	65	39	61	68	78
65627	CEDARCREEK	73	68	59	64	64	66	67	67	67	69	67	51	63	70	63	67	46	67	66	80
	MISSOURI	94	86	87	87	85	93	89	91	91	87	90	70	84	92	86	93	62	90	94	108
	UNITED STATES	100	100	100	100	100	100	100	100	100	100	100	100	100	100	100	100	100	100	100	100

ZIP CODE #	POST OFFICE NAME	COUNTY FIPS CODE	POPULATION 2000	POPULATION 2009	POPULATION 2014	2000-2009 ANNUAL RATE % Rate	2000-2009 ANNUAL RATE State Centile	HOUSEHOLDS 2000	HOUSEHOLDS 2009	HOUSEHOLDS 2014	HOUSEHOLDS % Annual Rate 2000-2009	HOUSEHOLDS 2009 Average HH Size	FAMILIES 2000	FAMILIES 2009	FAMILIES % Annual Rate 2000-2009
65629	CHADWICK	043	532	595	648	1.2	82	211	239	261	1.4	2.49	156	170	0.9
65630	CHESTNUTRIDGE	043	259	294	331	1.4	86	103	118	133	1.5	2.49	80	89	1.2
65631	CLEVER	043	3091	4633	5583	4.5	98	1143	1713	2067	4.5	2.70	886	1288	4.1
65632	CONWAY	105	2495	2795	2948	1.2	82	956	1078	1140	1.3	2.59	723	790	1.0
65633	CRANE	209	3195	3553	3779	1.2	82	1171	1301	1385	1.1	2.66	835	896	0.8
65634	CROSS TIMBERS	085	667	697	697	0.5	58	284	297	296	0.5	2.34	200	202	0.1
65635	DADEVILLE	057	983	941	921	-0.5	14	398	382	374	-0.4	2.46	292	272	-0.8
65637	DORA	153	1577	1647	1660	0.5	58	635	671	678	0.6	2.45	462	472	0.2
65638	DRURY	067	850	902	927	0.6	63	328	352	364	0.8	2.55	243	252	0.4
65640	DUNNEGAN	167	651	808	889	2.4	95	242	300	330	2.3	2.69	187	224	2.0
65641	EAGLE ROCK	009	1383	1471	1490	0.7	66	607	646	656	0.7	2.28	441	453	0.3
65644	ELKLAND	225	1226	1407	1502	1.5	87	447	516	550	1.6	2.73	342	383	1.2
65646	EVERTON	057	2128	2153	2163	0.1	42	840	852	857	0.2	2.53	631	621	-0.2
65647	EXETER	009	2626	2787	2856	0.6	63	1043	1113	1141	0.7	2.50	768	792	0.3
65648	FAIR GROVE	077	3814	4224	4473	1.1	79	1417	1625	1741	1.5	2.60	1129	1239	1.0
65649	FAIR PLAY	039	1528	1701	1791	1.2	82	633	706	741	1.2	2.41	450	482	0.7
65650	FLEMINGTON	167	679	777	833	1.5	87	282	323	347	1.5	2.40	226	252	1.2
65652	FORDLAND	225	3306	3551	3702	0.8	69	1022	1120	1175	1.0	2.70	757	805	0.7
65653	FORSYTH	213	4604	5417	5891	1.8	90	2020	2383	2594	1.8	2.20	1382	1568	1.4
65654	FREISTATT	109	289	316	333	1.0	76	121	130	136	0.8	2.43	97	101	0.4
65655	GAINESVILLE	153	2117	2101	2068	-0.1	32	886	882	869	0.0	2.33	623	598	-0.4
65656	GALENA	209	4527	5305	5743	1.7	89	1727	2015	2180	1.7	2.62	1332	1512	1.4
65657	GARRISON	043	207	229	248	1.1	79	68	76	83	1.2	3.01	50	53	0.6
65658	GOLDEN	009	1203	1312	1363	0.9	72	562	616	642	1.0	2.13	400	423	0.6
65660	GRAFF	229	285	286	288	0.0	37	107	109	110	0.2	2.62	88	87	-0.1
65661	GREENFIELD	057	2167	2094	2063	-0.4	18	902	868	853	-0.4	2.28	577	531	-0.9
65662	GROVESPRING	229	1335	1373	1393	0.3	50	509	530	539	0.4	2.59	375	377	0.1
65663	HALF WAY	167	2264	2627	2847	1.6	89	789	918	995	1.7	2.86	619	696	1.3
65666	HARDENVILLE	153	299	295	290	-0.1	32	117	116	114	-0.1	2.54	85	81	-0.5
65667	HARTVILLE	229	2910	3064	3128	0.6	63	1161	1239	1269	0.7	2.42	805	825	0.3
65668	HERMITAGE	085	3196	3424	3489	0.7	66	1445	1515	1547	0.5	2.20	1010	1020	0.1
65669	HIGHLANDVILLE	043	1508	2114	2491	3.7	98	556	782	923	3.8	2.70	448	613	3.4
65672	HOLLISTER	213	7785	9427	10352	2.1	93	2953	3686	4094	2.4	2.28	1926	2307	2.0
65674	HUMANSVILLE	167	1586	1674	1728	0.6	63	644	679	700	0.6	2.30	419	425	0.2
65675	HURLEY	209	66	76	82	1.5	87	24	28	30	1.7	2.71	18	20	1.1
65676	ISABELLA	153	681	681	670	0.0	37	294	297	293	0.1	2.27	208	203	-0.3
65679	KIRBYVILLE	213	2475	3203	3550	2.8	96	956	1226	1356	2.7	2.61	674	833	2.3
65680	KISSEE MILLS	213	986	1185	1297	2.0	92	431	520	571	2.1	2.28	314	366	1.7
65681	LAMPE	209	2542	2587	2625	0.2	46	1088	1105	1120	0.2	2.34	820	807	-0.2
65682	LOCKWOOD	057	2412	2413	2393	0.0	37	958	960	953	0.0	2.51	696	674	-0.3
65685	LOUISBURG	059	2007	2141	2223	0.7	66	778	825	855	0.6	2.58	562	575	0.2
65686	KIMBERLING CITY	209	3976	4608	4955	1.6	89	1774	2062	2218	1.6	2.21	1336	1509	1.3
65688	BRANDSVILLE	091	95	92	91	-0.3	21	39	38	38	-0.3	2.42	30	29	-0.4
65689	CABOOL	215	4089	4264	4345	0.5	58	1646	1741	1784	0.6	2.37	1133	1153	0.2
65690	COUCH	149	1125	1068	1038	-0.6	11	459	441	430	-0.4	2.42	354	330	-0.8
65692	KOSHKONONG	149	1215	1176	1153	-0.4	18	492	480	471	-0.3	2.45	369	349	-0.6
65702	MACOMB	229	346	352	354	0.2	46	127	129	129	0.2	2.73	103	101	-0.2
65704	MANSFIELD	229	3619	3548	3530	-0.2	27	1402	1385	1381	-0.1	2.53	1017	971	-0.5
65705	MARIONVILLE	109	4080	4388	4567	0.8	69	1616	1733	1803	0.8	2.46	1148	1187	0.4
65706	MARSHFIELD	225	12748	14941	16101	1.7	89	4827	5689	6140	1.8	2.59	3623	4135	1.4
65707	MILLER	109	2177	2328	2418	0.7	66	874	938	974	0.8	2.48	627	649	0.4
65708	MONETT	009	11086	12011	12419	0.9	72	4207	4526	4672	0.8	2.61	2933	3042	0.4
65710	MORRISVILLE	167	960	1015	1060	0.6	63	364	387	404	0.7	2.59	275	284	0.3
65711	MOUNTAIN GROVE	229	9073	9161	9202	0.1	42	3706	3765	3791	0.2	2.40	2598	2549	-0.2
65712	MOUNT VERNON	109	8079	8940	9365	1.1	79	3103	3422	3588	1.1	2.49	2207	2346	0.7
65713	NIANGUA	225	2767	3140	3338	1.4	86	1053	1203	1281	1.5	2.60	817	907	1.1
65714	NIXA	043	21014	30826	37111	4.2	98	7937	11773	14233	4.4	2.60	6068	8731	4.0
65715	NOBLE	153	99	99	98	0.0	37	35	35	35	0.0	2.83	26	25	-0.4
65717	NORWOOD	229	2484	2637	2689	0.6	63	883	947	971	0.8	2.78	678	704	0.4
65720	OLDFIELD	043	432	550	609	2.6	95	165	217	242	3.0	2.53	125	160	2.7
65721	OZARK	043	18935	28472	34166	4.5	98	6990	10703	12927	4.7	2.63	5358	7984	4.4
65722	PHILLIPSBURG	105	1378	1542	1625	1.2	82	511	578	610	1.3	2.64	407	448	1.0
65723	PIERCE CITY	109	3094	3126	3164	0.1	42	1181	1200	1216	0.2	2.60	864	847	-0.2
65724	PITTSBURG	085	864	942	977	0.9	72	412	449	466	0.9	2.10	287	301	0.5
65725	PLEASANT HOPE	167	2410	2621	2768	0.9	72	905	1000	1062	1.1	2.62	703	748	0.7
65727	POLK	167	259	302	326	1.7	89	93	108	117	1.6	2.80	76	86	1.3
65728	PONCE DE LEON	209	237	293	324	2.3	94	96	118	131	2.3	2.48	77	92	1.9
65729	PONTIAC	153	412	413	407	0.0	37	166	168	166	0.1	2.38	118	115	-0.3
65730	POWELL	119	1480	1604	1657	0.9	72	558	608	630	0.9	2.64	405	427	0.6
65731	POWERSITE	213	312	348	388	1.2	82	134	148	165	1.1	2.35	95	101	0.7
65732	PRESTON	085	823	850	845	0.3	50	317	328	325	0.4	2.57	252	254	0.1
65733	PROTEM	213	353	408	445	1.6	89	153	176	192	1.5	2.32	114	127	1.2
65734	PURDY	009	3425	3592	3617	0.5	58	1281	1342	1350	0.5	2.67	943	956	0.1
65735	QUINCY	085	274	286	286	0.5	58	111	116	116	0.5	2.47	74	74	0.0
65737	REEDS SPRING	209	6792	7685	8243	1.3	83	2828	3221	3459	1.4	2.36	2103	2319	1.1
65738	REPUBLIC	077	11389	15493	17426	3.4	97	4256	5992	6813	3.8	2.56	3274	4400	3.2
65739	RIDGEDALE	213	1075	1156	1233	0.8	69	459	496	529	0.8	2.33	348	366	0.5
65740	ROCKAWAY BEACH	213	2692	3473	3897	2.8	96	1087	1422	1599	2.9	2.38	748	949	2.6
65742	ROGERSVILLE	077	9371	11433	12641	2.2	94	3595	4484	4990	2.4	2.54	2848	3430	2.0
65744	RUETER	213	161	191	209	1.9	91	70	83	91	1.9	2.30	53	62	1.7
65745	SELIGMAN	009	2040	2168	2253	0.7	66	744	795	827	0.7	2.73	523	538	0.3
65746	SEYMOUR	225	7540	8263	8626	1.0	76	2447	2685	2803	1.0	3.01	1894	2025	0.7
65747	SHELL KNOB	009	3711	4116	4304	1.1	79	1742	1930	2018	1.1	2.13	1261	1350	0.7
65752	SOUTH GREENFIELD	057	268	242	232	-1.1	2	109	98	94	-1.1	2.47	82	72	-1.4
65753	SPARTA	043	3567	4226	4825	1.8	90	1388	1663	1905	2.0	2.54	1055	1225	1.6
65754	SPOKANE	043	766	1113	1339	4.1	98	280	412	498	4.3	2.70	229	329	4.0
65755	SQUIRES	067	558	586	600	0.5	58	228	242	249	0.6	2.40	174	180	0.4
65756	STOTTS CITY	109	586	648	682	1.1	79	220	242	254	1.0	2.68	163	174	0.7
65757	STRAFFORD	077	5832	6761	7282	1.6	89	2216	2649	2880	1.9	2.52	1713	1959	1.5
65759	TANEYVILLE	213	1246	1432	1555	1.5	87	471	540	588	1.5	2.65	344	381	1.1
65760	TECUMSEH	153	678	662	646	-0.3	21	276	270	264	-0.2	2.45	205	195	-0.5
65761	THEODOSIA	153	1105	1117	1111	0.1	42	510	520	518	0.2	2.15	361	355	-0.2
65762	THORNFIELD	153	688	689	679	0.0	37	274	277	274	0.1	2.47	200	195	-0.3
65764	TUNAS	059	1135	1220	1269	0.8	69	402	430	447	0.7	2.83	306	317	0.4
65766	UDALL	153	171	164	160	-0.5	14	72	69	67	-0.5	2.38	53	49	-0.8
	MISSOURI					0.7					0.8	2.45			0.4
	UNITED STATES					1.0					1.1	2.59			0.9

ZIP CODE #	POST OFFICE NAME	RACE (%) White 2000	White 2009	Black 2000	Black 2009	Asian/Pacific 2000	Asian/Pacific 2009	% Hispanic Origin 2000	% Hispanic Origin 2009	2009 AGE DISTRIBUTION (%) 0-4	5-9	10-14	15-19	20-24	25-44	45-64	65-84	85+	18+	MEDIAN AGE 2009	% 2009 Males	% 2009 Females
65629	CHADWICK	97.6	97.1	0.0	0.0	0.2	0.2	0.6	0.8	5.9	5.5	5.9	7.1	6.6	25.4	30.3	12.3	1.2	78.5	39.9	47.7	52.3
65630	CHESTNUTRIDGE	98.1	97.3	0.0	0.0	0.0	0.3	1.2	1.7	6.5	6.5	6.8	6.8	6.1	26.2	29.3	10.9	1.0	75.9	38.4	49.7	50.3
65631	CLEVER	97.5	96.9	0.1	0.2	0.2	0.3	1.1	1.5	8.2	8.4	8.3	6.8	4.7	26.5	27.0	9.0	1.0	70.8	36.6	49.5	50.5
65632	CONWAY	96.8	96.1	0.2	0.2	0.4	0.5	1.6	2.2	7.4	7.6	7.4	6.7	5.2	25.2	26.9	12.3	1.3	73.3	38.2	50.4	49.6
65633	CRANE	97.2	96.8	0.1	0.1	0.1	0.2	0.7	0.8	7.4	7.5	7.3	7.3	5.0	24.0	26.1	12.7	2.7	73.1	38.0	49.7	50.3
65634	CROSS TIMBERS	97.9	97.6	0.0	0.0	0.0	0.0	0.6	0.9	5.6	5.9	6.3	6.6	4.6	19.7	29.3	19.5	2.6	78.2	46.0	50.5	49.5
65635	DADEVILLE	97.4	96.9	0.4	0.4	0.1	0.1	0.6	0.9	5.0	5.3	5.6	5.5	5.2	21.4	30.3	19.4	2.2	80.6	46.3	50.5	49.5
65637	DORA	95.6	95.3	0.4	0.5	0.2	0.2	1.0	1.0	5.1	5.8	6.3	6.4	4.0	21.7	30.7	17.7	2.1	78.7	45.4	50.3	49.7
65638	DRURY	95.8	95.1	0.2	0.3	0.4	0.4	0.8	1.0	5.7	6.1	6.5	6.3	4.5	21.4	31.7	16.3	1.4	77.5	44.5	52.1	47.9
65640	DUNNEGAN	98.2	97.6	0.0	0.0	0.0	0.0	0.8	1.1	7.3	7.3	7.3	6.3	4.8	20.8	28.7	15.8	1.6	74.0	41.6	48.6	51.4
65641	EAGLE ROCK	96.7	96.0	0.1	0.1	0.1	0.1	1.6	2.4	4.6	4.8	5.2	6.2	4.7	17.6	32.5	22.3	2.0	81.6	49.6	50.1	49.9
65644	ELKLAND	95.4	94.5	0.7	0.9	0.5	0.8	0.7	0.9	6.8	6.9	7.2	7.7	6.5	25.3	28.8	9.7	1.1	74.5	37.7	51.7	48.3
65646	EVERTON	98.4	98.0	0.1	0.1	0.0	0.1	0.8	1.0	5.9	6.5	6.7	6.4	4.4	22.6	30.9	14.9	1.7	76.8	43.0	50.3	49.7
65647	EXETER	95.4	94.3	0.3	0.3	0.2	0.2	3.1	4.5	7.1	7.1	7.3	6.7	5.7	24.8	26.9	13.1	1.3	74.3	38.0	49.4	50.6
65648	FAIR GROVE	97.3	96.6	0.2	0.3	0.1	0.2	0.9	1.3	6.6	7.0	7.1	6.9	5.4	25.8	30.2	10.1	0.9	75.1	38.8	50.2	49.8
65649	FAIR PLAY	97.3	96.8	0.3	0.4	0.1	0.1	0.7	1.1	5.6	5.9	6.5	6.4	4.8	20.0	32.9	16.2	1.7	78.0	45.5	51.1	48.9
65650	FLEMINGTON	98.1	97.8	0.1	0.1	0.3	0.4	1.2	1.5	5.8	6.4	6.9	6.6	4.6	20.1	31.1	16.7	1.7	76.6	44.6	49.0	51.0
65652	FORDLAND	89.2	87.1	7.0	8.3	0.5	0.8	1.1	1.5	5.7	5.9	5.9	6.4	6.4	33.8	25.5	9.3	1.0	78.4	37.2	57.7	42.3
65653	FORSYTH	97.7	97.2	0.3	0.4	0.1	0.2	0.8	1.2	5.7	5.8	5.9	5.5	4.6	20.7	28.1	20.4	3.3	79.4	46.3	48.7	51.3
65654	FREISTATT	96.9	95.9	0.3	0.6	0.3	0.3	2.1	2.5	9.2	9.5	9.5	8.5	3.8	24.4	23.7	10.4	0.9	65.8	34.2	52.8	47.2
65655	GAINESVILLE	98.0	98.0	0.1	0.1	0.0	0.0	1.2	1.3	5.6	5.7	5.9	5.8	4.7	21.5	29.6	17.7	3.6	79.2	45.6	48.4	51.6
65656	GALENA	97.2	96.7	0.1	0.1	0.2	0.3	0.9	1.1	5.9	6.2	6.3	6.2	4.4	22.6	30.7	16.3	1.3	77.7	43.6	50.2	49.8
65657	GARRISON	98.1	96.9	0.0	0.0	0.0	0.0	0.5	0.4	5.7	5.2	5.7	7.4	7.0	24.5	29.7	13.5	1.3	79.0	40.5	47.2	52.8
65658	GOLDEN	98.3	98.1	0.0	0.0	0.2	0.2	1.2	1.7	3.7	4.0	4.2	4.1	3.7	13.3	35.0	29.9	2.1	85.6	56.9	50.7	49.3
65660	GRAFF	98.6	98.6	0.0	0.0	0.0	0.0	0.4	0.3	6.3	6.3	7.0	6.3	4.2	23.1	30.4	15.0	1.4	76.2	42.6	50.3	49.7
65661	GREENFIELD	96.8	96.2	0.3	0.4	0.1	0.3	1.1	1.5	6.0	6.1	6.0	5.9	4.9	19.7	26.2	18.1	7.0	78.6	46.0	46.8	53.2
65662	GROVESPRING	98.0	97.5	0.1	0.1	0.1	0.1	1.1	1.6	6.6	6.6	7.0	6.6	5.2	23.7	29.5	13.3	1.7	75.7	40.8	52.1	47.9
65663	HALF WAY	97.4	96.9	0.4	0.5	0.1	0.2	1.0	1.4	7.8	8.2	8.3	7.7	4.3	24.6	25.7	12.3	1.1	70.8	36.7	51.9	48.1
65666	HARDENVILLE	97.3	97.3	0.3	0.3	0.0	0.0	1.3	1.4	5.4	5.8	6.1	6.1	4.7	21.7	29.5	18.3	2.4	78.6	45.1	49.8	50.2
65667	HARTVILLE	97.0	96.5	0.8	1.0	0.1	0.1	0.9	1.3	6.7	7.0	7.2	6.9	5.3	22.8	26.9	14.6	2.6	74.8	40.3	49.2	50.8
65668	HERMITAGE	97.3	96.3	0.0	0.7	0.1	0.2	0.8	1.1	3.3	3.4	3.7	4.9	4.4	13.7	31.8	31.6	3.3	88.4	57.5	48.9	51.1
65669	HIGHLANDVILLE	97.9	97.4	0.0	0.0	0.1	0.1	1.0	1.3	6.7	6.9	6.9	6.8	5.9	27.2	29.0	9.8	0.9	75.4	38.0	49.8	50.2
65672	HOLLISTER	96.1	95.2	0.4	0.4	0.4	0.7	2.6	3.7	5.4	5.0	4.7	8.2	11.7	24.3	25.0	13.6	2.2	82.1	36.8	48.8	51.2
65674	HUMANSVILLE	98.3	97.9	0.3	0.3	0.1	0.2	0.6	0.9	6.2	6.2	6.2	6.3	5.0	20.9	25.6	19.1	4.7	77.5	44.5	47.9	52.1
65675	HURLEY	97.0	97.4	0.0	0.0	0.0	0.0	0.0	0.0	6.6	6.6	6.6	6.6	3.9	27.6	28.9	11.8	1.3	75.0	40.0	50.0	50.0
65676	ISABELLA	97.9	97.9	0.0	0.0	0.1	0.1	0.7	0.7	4.1	4.4	4.3	4.1	3.8	16.6	29.7	30.7	2.3	84.6	55.2	50.4	49.6
65679	KIRBYVILLE	96.5	95.5	0.3	0.4	0.4	0.6	2.1	2.9	6.8	7.0	7.1	6.1	4.4	25.4	27.3	14.3	1.5	75.3	39.9	48.6	51.4
65680	KISSEE MILLS	97.5	97.0	0.0	0.0	0.1	0.2	0.5	0.7	4.7	4.6	5.3	6.6	4.5	21.5	33.1	18.1	1.5	81.1	46.8	50.6	49.4
65681	LAMPE	98.8	98.5	0.0	0.0	0.0	0.1	0.7	0.9	4.5	4.8	5.2	5.2	3.4	19.5	31.3	24.3	1.8	82.3	50.1	48.4	51.6
65682	LOCKWOOD	97.6	97.2	0.3	0.3	0.3	0.5	0.7	1.0	6.2	6.7	6.5	6.0	5.2	22.5	28.5	15.8	2.6	77.0	42.3	48.9	51.1
65685	LOUISBURG	97.2	96.7	0.2	0.3	0.1	0.1	0.9	1.4	6.4	6.5	6.7	6.6	5.3	23.0	28.4	15.2	2.0	76.4	41.2	50.2	49.8
65686	KIMBERLING CITY	98.1	97.7	0.1	0.2	0.3	0.3	1.0	1.2	3.0	3.3	3.8	3.7	2.9	13.9	34.5	31.4	3.5	87.5	57.9	47.7	52.3
65688	BRANDSVILLE	96.8	96.7	0.0	0.0	0.0	0.0	1.1	2.2	6.5	6.5	6.5	7.6	6.5	25.0	25.0	14.1	2.2	76.1	38.3	50.0	50.0
65689	CABOOL	96.4	95.6	0.2	0.2	0.6	0.9	0.9	1.4	6.4	6.5	6.7	7.0	5.0	21.1	26.8	16.7	3.8	76.0	42.6	47.7	52.3
65690	COUCH	93.7	93.4	0.0	0.0	0.4	0.5	0.9	0.9	4.8	5.2	5.8	6.7	4.9	20.6	32.3	17.7	2.0	80.1	46.2	51.6	48.4
65692	KOSHKONONG	96.0	95.7	0.1	0.1	0.2	0.2	0.8	0.9	5.1	5.2	5.6	7.0	5.5	23.7	31.9	14.2	1.8	79.8	43.4	50.1	49.9
65702	MACOMB	97.1	96.3	0.3	0.3	0.3	0.6	0.9	1.1	7.1	7.7	7.7	6.8	5.4	22.7	28.7	12.8	1.1	73.3	38.3	50.0	50.0
65704	MANSFIELD	97.6	97.1	0.2	0.3	0.2	0.4	0.7	1.0	7.3	6.7	7.0	7.0	6.0	23.1	25.8	15.1	2.1	74.7	39.3	48.3	51.7
65705	MARIONVILLE	97.6	97.1	0.1	0.1	0.2	0.3	0.7	1.0	6.8	6.9	6.8	6.4	5.5	23.6	26.5	13.8	3.6	75.4	39.9	49.3	50.7
65706	MARSHFIELD	97.8	97.3	0.2	0.3	0.3	0.4	1.5	2.0	7.3	7.2	7.3	6.9	5.8	25.2	26.1	12.0	2.2	74.0	37.8	48.7	51.3
65707	MILLER	98.1	97.8	0.0	0.0	0.0	0.0	0.7	1.0	6.0	6.4	6.9	7.6	4.9	24.4	27.5	14.2	2.2	75.9	40.8	50.4	49.6
65708	MONETT	91.2	88.8	0.2	0.2	0.6	0.9	9.1	11.9	8.0	7.7	7.5	7.0	5.6	25.2	24.3	11.9	2.8	72.5	36.5	49.2	50.8
65710	MORRISVILLE	97.8	97.4	0.1	0.1	0.2	0.2	1.7	2.4	6.9	7.0	7.3	7.6	5.6	23.3	29.5	11.5	1.4	74.0	38.8	50.2	49.8
65711	MOUNTAIN GROVE	97.7	97.2	0.1	0.1	0.1	0.2	0.7	1.0	6.8	6.3	6.2	6.8	6.1	22.2	26.8	15.8	3.0	76.5	41.3	47.5	52.5
65712	MOUNT VERNON	96.9	96.2	0.4	0.5	0.3	0.4	1.4	2.0	6.2	6.5	6.8	6.8	4.9	23.3	27.1	15.1	3.3	76.3	41.5	50.3	49.7
65713	NIANGUA	97.8	97.3	0.1	0.1	0.2	0.3	1.4	1.8	6.5	6.8	6.9	6.5	5.1	23.5	30.6	12.9	1.2	75.7	40.8	50.5	49.5
65714	NIXA	97.4	96.8	0.4	0.4	0.4	0.7	1.4	1.9	7.9	7.6	7.4	7.0	6.6	28.1	25.1	9.0	1.3	72.8	35.0	48.6	51.4
65715	NOBLE	99.0	99.0	0.0	0.0	0.0	0.0	1.0	0.0	6.1	6.1	6.1	6.1	4.0	21.2	29.3	19.2	2.0	77.8	45.3	50.5	49.5
65717	NORWOOD	97.2	96.7	0.3	0.3	0.3	0.5	0.5	0.7	6.9	7.1	7.3	6.8	5.6	23.4	28.2	13.2	1.4	74.3	39.3	51.3	48.7
65720	OLDFIELD	97.7	97.5	0.0	0.0	0.0	0.0	1.2	1.6	6.0	5.8	6.2	7.1	6.0	25.5	30.0	12.2	1.3	77.6	40.0	49.6	50.4
65721	OZARK	96.9	96.3	0.2	0.3	0.3	0.5	1.5	2.0	8.2	7.6	7.0	6.4	6.2	31.0	23.7	8.5	1.3	73.2	33.9	48.4	51.6
65722	PHILLIPSBURG	97.9	97.3	0.3	0.4	0.2	0.3	0.9	1.3	7.2	7.2	7.3	7.2	5.9	24.8	27.4	11.5	1.5	73.9	38.0	50.9	49.1
65723	PIERCE CITY	95.9	94.9	0.2	0.2	0.0	0.1	2.5	3.6	7.5	7.7	7.5	6.6	5.5	25.0	26.8	11.6	1.7	73.2	37.0	50.4	49.6
65724	PITTSBURG	98.1	97.9	0.0	0.0	0.1	0.1	0.7	1.0	3.6	3.6	3.8	4.6	3.9	14.2	32.7	31.1	2.4	86.2	57.0	49.6	50.4
65725	PLEASANT HOPE	97.6	97.0	0.1	0.2	0.0	0.1	0.9	1.4	6.6	6.6	6.9	7.1	6.0	26.1	29.2	10.4	1.1	75.4	38.7	50.4	49.6
65727	POLK	98.1	96.7	0.4	0.3	0.4	1.0	1.6	2.3	6.0	6.6	7.0	6.3	4.3	19.2	31.1	17.9	1.7	76.5	45.4	49.0	51.0
65728	PONCE DE LEON	97.5	97.6	0.0	0.0	0.4	0.3	0.4	0.7	6.5	6.8	7.2	6.8	4.8	25.3	30.7	10.9	1.0	75.4	39.1	49.8	50.2
65729	PONTIAC	98.1	98.1	0.0	0.0	0.0	0.0	0.7	0.7	4.4	4.8	4.8	4.4	3.9	17.9	29.5	26.6	3.6	83.3	52.7	48.2	51.8
65730	POWELL	97.0	96.3	0.0	0.0	0.3	0.6	0.9	1.4	6.5	7.3	7.6	7.5	5.7	26.4	28.6	9.5	0.9	74.0	38.3	52.2	47.8
65731	POWERSITE	96.8	95.7	0.3	0.3	0.3	0.6	1.9	2.9	6.9	6.9	7.2	6.0	4.3	25.6	27.0	14.7	1.4	75.3	40.0	48.6	51.4
65732	PRESTON	97.1	96.5	0.1	0.1	0.0	0.0	1.3	1.9	6.0	6.6	6.8	6.8	5.1	20.2	29.8	16.8	1.9	76.1	43.7	48.7	51.3
65733	PROTEM	98.3	98.3	0.0	0.0	0.0	0.0	0.6	0.7	4.7	5.1	5.4	5.6	3.7	23.0	31.1	19.1	2.2	81.1	46.7	52.9	47.1
65734	PURDY	90.4	87.3	0.1	0.1	0.2	0.3	9.3	12.8	7.7	7.5	7.6	7.3	5.5	25.7	25.9	11.3	1.6	72.7	36.2	50.4	49.6
65735	QUINCY	98.5	98.3	0.0	0.0	0.0	0.0	0.4	0.3	5.6	5.2	5.9	6.3	4.5	18.5	30.4	19.6	3.8	79.4	48.2	50.3	49.7
65737	REEDS SPRING	97.4	96.9	0.1	0.1	0.3	0.4	1.7	2.3	5.3	5.5	5.8	5.4	4.0	21.4	31.3	19.3	1.9	79.8	46.8	48.7	51.3
65738	REPUBLIC	97.4	96.5	0.2	0.3	0.4	0.7	1.0	1.5	6.9	6.9	7.0	6.9	5.7	27.8	26.9	10.1	1.9	74.7	37.4	48.3	51.7
65739	RIDGEDALE	97.1	96.7	0.7	0.8	0.4	0.4	1.4	2.0	5.1	5.5	5.7	4.4	2.9	21.2	35.5	18.3	1.5	80.8	48.4	47.9	52.1
65740	ROCKAWAY BEACH	96.4	95.8	0.1	0.1	0.0	0.1	1.3	1.8	6.1	6.0	6.6	7.9	4.6	22.3	29.5	15.3	1.6	77.4	42.2	48.7	51.3
65742	ROGERSVILLE	97.3	96.7	0.2	0.3	0.4	0.6	1.0	1.4	6.1	6.4	7.0	7.1	5.0	24.3	31.1	11.8	1.3	76.1	41.1	49.9	50.1
65744	RUETER	98.1	97.4	0.0	0.0	0.0	0.5	0.6	1.0	5.2	5.8	6.3	5.2	4.2	23.6	31.4	16.2	2.1	79.6	44.8	51.8	48.2
65745	SELIGMAN	94.6	93.0	0.0	0.1	0.2	0.3	2.8	4.0	7.0	7.0	7.3	8.0	5.6	25.3	27.4	11.6	0.9	73.8	37.6	50.6	49.4
65746	SEYMOUR	95.8	94.9	1.0	1.3	0.2	0.4	1.2	1.6	9.3	8.5	8.3	8.2	6.6	25.1	22.7	9.7	1.6	68.8	32.0	49.8	50.2
65747	SHELL KNOB	98.0	97.6	0.0	0.0	0.1	0.1	1.1	1.6	3.4	3.6	3.9	4.4	3.4	14.8	34.4	29.1	2.9	86.4	56.2	50.3	49.7
65752	SOUTH GREENFIELD	97.8	97.1	0.0	0.0	0.4	0.4	0.4	0.8	6.2	7.0	6.6	6.6	4.5	21.9	31.0	14.5	1.7	76.0	42.9	50.0	50.0
65753	SPARTA	97.8	97.4	0.1	0.1	0.2	0.3	1.1	1.6	6.4	6.4	6.9	7.5	6.2	26.7	28.1	10.6	1.2	75.7	38.0	48.8	51.2
65754	SPOKANE	97.9	97.5	0.0	0.0	0.1	0.2	0.8	1.1	7.3	7.5	7.4	6.6	5.6	27.0	27.7	10.1	1.0	73.9	37.3	48.9	51.1
65755	SQUIRES	96.9	96.6	0.0	0.0	0.0	0.0	0.2	0.2	4.8	4.9	5.6	6.3	5.5	19.5	34.3	17.1	2.0	80.4	47.4	51.2	48.8
65756	STOTTS CITY	94.4	93.4	0.3	0.5	0.0	0.0	3.8	4.9	8.0	7.6	7.7	7.9	6.0	26.7	24.7	10.3	1.1	71.8	35.2	52.2	47.8
65757	STRAFFORD	97.8	97.2	0.2	0.3	0.1	0.2	1.2	1.9	6.3	6.7	7.0	6.6	4.9	26.4	29.5	11.3	1.4	75.9	39.8	50.5	49.5
65759	TANEYVILLE	98.0	97.6	0.1	0.1	0.1	0.2	1.0	1.4	8.4	8.4	7.9	6.2	5.3	25.6	24.5	12.0	1.7	71.5	36.7	49.0	51.0
65760	TECUMSEH	97.5	97.4	0.1	0.2	0.1	0.2	0.9	0.8	5.6	6.0	6.0	5.3	4.4	23.0	30.4	17.5	1.8	79.2	44.7	51.2	48.8
65761	THEODOSIA	97.9	97.9	0.0	0.0	0.1	0.1	1.0	1.0	2.9	3.1	3.2	4.2	3.8	15.4	33.5	31.8	2.1	88.4	55.9	49.9	50.1
65762	THORNFIELD	98.1	98.1	0.0	0.0	0.1	0.1	0.6	0.6	5.5	6.0	6.1	5.8	3.9	20.9	29.2	20.5	2.2	78.8	46.2	50.5	49.5
65764	TUNAS	97.0	96.2	0.1	0.2	0.2	0.3	1.3	1.8	8.5	8.9	8.9	7.1	4.1	22.1	25.5	13.5	1.4	69.1	38.0	49.6	50.4
65766	UDALL	98.2	98.2	0.0	0.0	0.0	0.0	0.6	0.6	6.1	6.1	6.1	5.5	4.9	24.4	28.7	16.5	1.8	78.7	42.5	51.2	48.8
	MISSOURI	84.9	83.3	11.2	11.7	1.2	1.7	2.1	2.8	6.6	6.6	6.6	7.0	6.7	26.1	26.5	11.7	2.1	76.1	37.7	48.8	51.2
	UNITED STATES	75.1	72.0	12.3	12.7	3.8	4.6	12.5	15.7	6.8	6.7	6.6	7.1	6.9	27.0	26.0	10.9	1.9	75.7	36.9	49.2	50.8

#	POST OFFICE NAME	2009 Per Capita Income	2009 HH Income Base	2009 Household Income Distribution (%): Less than $25,000	$25,000 to $49,999	$50,000 to $99,999	$100,000 to $149,999	$150,000 or More	Median Household Income: 2009	2014	2009 National Centile	2009 State Centile	2009 Home Value Base	2009 Home Value Distribution (%): Less than $50,000	$50,000 to $89,999	$90,000 to $174,999	$175,000 to $399,999	$400,000 or More	2009 Median Home Value
65629	CHADWICK	17653	239	32.6	38.5	23.4	3.8	1.7	35128	35924	18	31	196	18.4	21.4	39.8	16.8	3.6	107609
65630	CHESTNUTRIDGE	22557	118	26.3	30.5	33.9	7.6	1.7	44212	46666	46	67	99	16.2	17.2	31.3	30.3	5.1	142188
65631	CLEVER	19888	1713	19.0	35.4	37.5	6.9	1.2	46501	49806	53	73	1412	10.0	17.3	44.7	23.6	4.5	127619
65632	CONWAY	16418	1078	32.7	31.6	31.6	3.4	0.6	36556	38090	22	38	858	24.7	22.5	34.1	16.1	2.6	95455
65633	CRANE	15714	1301	36.2	33.6	25.6	3.2	1.5	35252	36811	19	32	968	23.7	23.5	31.7	18.3	2.9	97000
65634	CROSS TIMBERS	16259	297	42.1	31.3	21.2	3.7	1.7	28750	28683	6	7	252	25.4	19.4	31.0	20.2	4.0	95909
65635	DADEVILLE	17619	382	22.5	46.3	28.3	2.1	0.8	38115	39328	27	45	322	14.9	24.5	47.5	11.2	1.9	102273
65637	DORA	15708	671	38.5	38.5	19.5	2.2	1.3	31485	31698	11	16	555	15.7	25.4	37.7	15.7	5.6	104770
65638	DRURY	14199	352	38.4	41.8	17.9	1.7	0.3	28652	28595	6	6	296	19.3	23.6	31.8	19.3	6.1	107292
65640	DUNNEGAN	14486	300	38.0	34.7	25.0	1.7	0.7	33587	36631	15	24	257	25.3	24.1	27.2	23.0	0.4	91250
65641	EAGLE ROCK	19072	646	28.6	39.2	28.0	3.4	0.8	35823	36440	20	34	548	17.0	25.2	38.0	14.1	5.8	101812
65644	ELKLAND	15049	516	33.3	34.9	27.5	4.1	0.2	36689	38417	23	39	438	28.5	14.6	43.2	11.2	2.5	96000
65646	EVERTON	17835	852	29.9	35.1	30.3	3.4	1.3	40128	41367	33	54	733	18.7	22.1	33.8	22.4	3.0	108006
65647	EXETER	18015	1113	36.7	37.9	21.3	1.4	2.6	32535	32989	12	19	853	27.0	30.1	29.9	10.3	2.7	80970
65648	FAIR GROVE	23245	1625	16.9	27.5	46.2	6.6	2.8	53517	53869	69	84	1382	11.9	20.5	40.6	22.6	4.4	120616
65649	FAIR PLAY	17272	706	31.2	41.4	24.9	1.1	1.4	32207	33744	12	18	579	28.7	21.8	30.4	17.8	1.4	89242
65650	FLEMINGTON	19473	323	28.8	32.2	34.4	3.7	0.9	40712	44860	35	56	282	26.2	22.0	31.9	19.1	0.7	93333
65652	FORDLAND	17495	1120	28.4	33.9	30.7	4.4	2.6	39581	41676	31	52	920	19.8	21.0	35.1	19.1	5.0	105577
65653	FORSYTH	22026	2383	26.5	33.7	34.0	3.8	2.0	40422	43985	34	55	1858	17.2	17.9	43.9	18.4	2.6	119980
65654	FREISTATT	20406	130	27.7	30.0	37.7	2.3	2.3	42005	44217	39	61	101	13.9	19.8	35.6	24.8	5.9	118750
65655	GAINESVILLE	17530	882	40.5	33.6	22.4	1.4	2.2	31255	32496	10	15	667	27.9	30.0	28.8	9.4	3.9	78714
65656	GALENA	18320	2015	29.3	35.7	28.7	4.2	2.2	39345	40864	31	51	1685	21.7	18.5	30.4	23.4	5.9	111163
65657	GARRISON	12923	76	38.2	40.8	18.4	2.6	0.0	31937	33027	11	17	61	18.0	23.0	44.3	13.1	1.6	104167
65658	GOLDEN	21624	616	28.9	34.3	31.7	3.1	2.1	40772	41820	35	56	542	13.7	19.0	44.3	20.5	2.6	116011
65660	GRAFF	16149	109	40.4	34.9	20.2	1.8	2.8	28871	29090	7	7	92	18.5	22.8	31.5	20.7	6.5	115000
65661	GREENFIELD	16221	868	40.8	34.7	21.2	2.4	0.9	30458	31731	9	13	607	19.4	36.2	34.4	9.4	0.5	82813
65662	GROVESPRING	16594	530	36.6	34.3	23.0	4.3	1.7	35133	36207	18	31	435	23.7	18.4	37.0	15.2	5.7	104948
65663	HALF WAY	15729	918	30.0	34.6	30.2	3.2	2.1	37159	41058	24	41	761	20.1	26.8	30.9	17.7	4.5	95875
65666	HARDENVILLE	18025	116	40.5	30.2	24.1	1.7	3.4	33902	35638	15	26	90	27.8	28.9	27.8	10.0	5.6	80000
65667	HARTVILLE	17390	1239	43.0	30.7	20.7	3.3	2.3	29712	30091	8	10	966	22.9	23.2	31.7	17.3	5.0	95588
65668	HERMITAGE	19027	1515	30.5	42.8	22.2	3.2	1.3	35441	36463	19	33	1317	18.9	30.8	37.5	11.4	1.4	90337
65669	HIGHLANDVILLE	20001	782	21.7	30.7	40.7	5.8	1.2	47962	50644	57	76	657	12.9	12.6	36.7	32.3	5.5	153125
65672	HOLLISTER	18891	3686	30.2	37.6	27.2	3.5	1.4	35336	37480	19	33	2246	18.7	19.4	36.6	20.5	4.9	112954
65674	HUMANSVILLE	14665	679	46.2	32.1	19.4	1.2	1.0	27930	29683	6	5	509	35.6	31.2	19.8	11.8	1.6	62500
65675	HURLEY	15614	28	25.0	46.4	28.6	0.0	0.0	37238	40000	24	41	23	17.4	17.4	39.1	26.1	0.0	112500
65676	ISABELLA	20885	297	35.7	32.3	23.9	5.4	2.7	33852	34857	15	26	243	17.3	23.9	32.9	22.2	3.7	108500
65679	KIRBYVILLE	18993	1226	22.3	36.1	36.3	3.4	1.8	43713	47342	44	65	901	19.2	19.2	41.7	15.5	4.3	111272
65680	KISSEE MILLS	18562	520	29.4	41.2	24.8	3.8	0.8	34231	37012	16	27	443	21.7	27.3	36.6	10.4	4.1	91364
65681	LAMPE	21581	1105	24.0	40.5	27.5	5.6	2.4	39973	41672	32	53	895	9.2	15.8	39.6	30.3	5.3	142199
65682	LOCKWOOD	17761	960	31.7	37.8	26.7	1.6	2.3	35000	36588	18	31	732	29.0	28.4	28.6	10.8	3.3	81000
65685	LOUISBURG	16293	825	36.2	32.7	27.3	1.2	2.5	30050	32013	8	11	667	25.8	27.0	32.5	13.3	1.3	86224
65686	KIMBERLING CITY	27153	2062	17.7	32.1	39.6	6.5	4.1	50122	51476	61	79	1760	3.5	8.1	49.4	34.0	5.0	155062
65688	BRANDSVILLE	16902	38	39.5	28.9	26.3	2.6	2.6	32338	37351	12	19	32	21.9	18.8	34.4	18.8	6.3	110000
65689	CABOOL	16444	1741	41.9	35.7	17.8	2.4	2.3	29026	29848	7	7	1226	28.4	22.3	32.1	14.5	2.7	88163
65690	COUCH	15950	441	45.8	29.5	20.9	2.7	1.1	27354	27951	5	4	362	35.6	18.5	33.7	10.8	1.4	81176
65692	KOSHKONONG	18221	480	36.3	35.6	22.1	3.1	2.9	34232	36159	16	27	402	25.1	20.9	30.6	16.4	7.0	97619
65702	MACOMB	14722	129	37.2	32.6	27.1	3.1	0.0	32766	33632	13	20	99	20.2	24.2	33.3	17.2	5.1	94583
65704	MANSFIELD	15890	1385	38.8	31.6	25.3	2.7	1.6	33272	34648	14	23	1016	23.4	29.2	30.9	12.6	3.8	85781
65705	MARIONVILLE	16867	1733	33.4	35.3	27.8	3.0	0.6	34084	36836	16	26	1276	22.7	21.4	37.6	16.3	2.0	98824
65706	MARSHFIELD	18963	5689	24.2	35.6	33.8	4.6	1.8	41670	44235	38	59	4182	10.4	20.2	46.9	21.0	1.5	117904
65707	MILLER	17565	938	35.7	31.6	27.6	3.2	1.9	33924	36731	15	26	715	21.4	29.9	32.6	13.4	2.7	88681
65708	MONETT	19682	4526	28.1	32.9	32.0	4.5	2.4	41854	43404	39	60	3140	9.8	24.8	42.5	19.6	3.2	111181
65710	MORRISVILLE	16309	387	30.2	33.6	32.0	3.9	0.3	39368	43129	31	51	309	26.2	23.6	34.3	14.9	1.0	90250
65711	MOUNTAIN GROVE	16443	3765	40.7	34.7	19.9	2.5	2.2	29643	30441	8	10	2619	23.1	23.3	34.2	15.8	3.5	96126
65712	MOUNT VERNON	19898	3422	27.2	33.3	32.1	4.6	2.8	41575	42849	38	59	2535	9.3	17.5	48.2	21.6	3.4	121669
65713	NIANGUA	17498	1203	28.8	36.7	28.8	4.2	1.6	37493	39023	25	43	1003	21.2	22.1	30.4	23.2	3.0	103152
65714	NIXA	23937	11773	19.3	28.2	40.7	8.0	3.8	52513	53971	67	82	8668	10.8	6.3	43.9	35.0	4.0	152912
65715	NOBLE	13941	35	40.0	28.6	28.6	2.9	0.0	32297	36136	12	18	29	27.6	20.7	20.7	24.1	6.9	95000
65717	NORWOOD	14261	947	37.5	37.3	22.0	1.5	1.8	29825	30039	8	10	757	24.7	22.7	28.5	18.8	5.3	94063
65720	OLDFIELD	16342	217	32.3	36.4	28.6	1.8	0.9	36047	38959	21	35	184	22.8	23.4	35.3	14.1	4.3	97000
65721	OZARK	25622	10703	17.2	28.8	38.9	9.7	5.5	53719	55537	69	84	7862	6.7	8.2	42.1	35.0	8.1	162737
65722	PHILLIPSBURG	20654	578	22.7	36.5	34.9	2.8	3.1	42488	44788	41	63	483	19.3	21.3	40.6	15.1	3.7	103125
65723	PIERCE CITY	17202	1200	31.1	34.6	30.1	3.0	1.3	39067	41138	30	49	897	25.4	24.2	30.3	17.1	3.0	90673
65724	PITTSBURG	20408	449	30.1	38.3	26.5	4.0	1.1	36102	37579	21	35	388	22.4	28.6	35.8	11.1	2.1	88788
65725	PLEASANT HOPE	19980	1000	22.0	33.8	37.1	4.4	2.7	45149	48625	49	69	831	11.8	27.8	34.9	20.3	5.2	112117
65727	POLK	17785	108	25.0	31.5	36.1	6.5	0.9	44208	46658	46	67	98	22.4	24.5	37.8	15.3	0.0	94286
65728	PONCE DE LEON	21301	118	30.5	25.4	32.2	8.5	3.4	45000	45669	48	69	102	21.6	14.7	21.6	37.3	4.9	135000
65729	PONTIAC	19124	168	36.9	32.7	23.2	4.8	2.4	33166	33888	14	23	137	18.2	25.5	32.1	19.7	4.4	102679
65730	POWELL	17757	608	32.9	30.9	31.4	2.5	2.3	33769	36193	15	25	508	27.6	28.7	28.7	10.2	4.7	80303
65731	POWERSITE	21043	148	22.3	35.8	36.5	3.4	2.0	43897	47136	45	66	109	19.3	18.3	43.1	14.7	4.6	111607
65732	PRESTON	17282	328	30.5	31.4	31.1	4.6	2.4	36848	39865	23	39	285	9.1	17.2	41.1	26.3	6.3	127155
65733	PROTEM	16910	176	35.2	37.5	22.2	4.0	1.1	31608	33305	11	16	160	23.8	21.9	39.4	10.0	5.0	97000
65734	PURDY	15297	1342	33.1	38.8	24.6	2.6	0.9	35467	36171	19	33	988	16.5	33.6	31.7	15.1	3.1	89881
65735	QUINCY	14531	116	50.0	28.4	19.0	2.6	0.0	25000	26789	3	2	90	31.1	22.2	25.6	17.8	3.3	84000
65737	REEDS SPRING	22186	3221	27.9	37.4	26.4	4.6	3.7	37821	39204	26	44	2497	15.2	17.7	28.7	29.6	8.8	135738
65738	REPUBLIC	21106	5992	21.0	32.4	38.9	6.3	1.4	46768	50180	53	73	4715	10.8	18.9	53.4	15.5	1.4	109331
65739	RIDGEDALE	24225	496	20.6	34.3	40.3	2.8	2.0	46030	49134	51	72	400	14.3	11.8	27.8	37.5	8.8	168534
65740	ROCKAWAY BEACH	17838	1422	31.6	39.7	24.6	2.7	1.4	34225	36630	16	27	1114	34.3	35.2	24.9	4.5	1.2	65161
65742	ROGERSVILLE	29120	4484	18.1	27.5	36.6	9.7	8.0	54351	54743	70	84	3707	7.4	12.0	33.2	34.2	13.2	167383
65744	RUETER	18149	83	31.3	43.4	21.7	2.4	1.2	33790	37321	15	25	73	27.4	17.8	31.5	16.4	6.8	98750
65745	SELIGMAN	14760	795	34.8	36.6	24.4	3.4	0.8	33411	34344	14	24	609	25.8	26.3	36.3	8.9	2.8	87159
65746	SEYMOUR	13897	2685	36.4	32.7	26.6	3.0	1.3	34592	36083	17	28	2192	21.1	22.3	38.1	15.8	2.7	99542
65747	SHELL KNOB	22308	1930	31.9	35.3	27.5	3.1	2.3	36841	37864	23	39	1714	12.7	16.3	43.2	22.7	5.1	129289
65752	SOUTH GREENFIELD	17471	98	32.7	35.7	29.6	1.0	1.0	37858	41532	26	44	79	15.2	26.6	31.6	17.7	8.9	116071
65753	SPARTA	19361	1663	29.2	33.3	31.1	4.1	2.3	40020	42889	33	54	1299	14.5	20.2	37.2	24.3	3.7	117239
65754	SPOKANE	19267	412	23.5	33.5	36.7	5.8	0.5	45285	47561	49	69	345	12.2	9.3	37.4	37.4	3.8	161384
65755	SQUIRES	15500	242	38.4	36.8	21.1	2.9	0.8	33235	34190	14	23	214	19.6	15.9	36.4	22.4	5.6	111364
65756	STOTTS CITY	17552	242	36.4	32.6	23.1	5.0	2.9	33262	35276	14	23	195	30.3	22.6	32.8	10.8	3.6	82143
65757	STRAFFORD	22524	2649	19.2	33.4	38.6	6.0	2.8	47860	50015	56	75	2095	8.8	16.9	43.9	25.5	4.9	126947
65759	TANEYVILLE	15578	540	34.3	39.8	21.9	1.9	2.2	33000	35000	13	21	426	22.8	27.2	34.5	14.6	0.9	90000
65760	TECUMSEH	16185	270	40.0	37.4	18.1	1.5	3.0	30412	30486	9	13	226	27.9	27.9	30.5	10.6	3.1	81875
65761	THEODOSIA	18416	520	38.3	32.7	26.9	1.2	1.0	33073	34470	13	22	454	30.6	24.2	27.3	13.9	4.0	84634
65762	THORNFIELD	16162	277	39.7	29.6	27.4	2.5	0.7	31968	33540	11	17	227	26.4	19.4	26.0	22.0	6.2	100694
65764	TUNAS	12830	430	50.9	28.1	15.8	3.3	1.9	24344	26538	3	2	376	25.5	30.6	25.5	13.3	5.1	83947
65766	UDALL	15225	69	42.0	40.6	14.5	1.4	1.4	28212	27452	6	6	58	34.5	27.6	27.6	10.3	0.0	72500
	MISSOURI	25286		22.8	27.7	35.3	9.1	5.2	49522	52035				12.8	19.4	39.1	24.2	4.6	122064
	UNITED STATES	27277		20.9	24.4	35.3	11.7	7.6	54719	56938				9.3	13.1	31.6	32.6	13.5	162279

ZIP CODE #	POST OFFICE NAME	FINANCIAL SERVICES: Auto Loan	Home Loan	Investments	Retirement Plans	THE HOME: Home Improvements: Home Repair	Lawn & Garden	Furnishings: Computers & Hardware-Personal	Major Appliances	TV, Radio, Sound Equipment	Furniture	ENTERTAINMENT: Dine out/ Carry out	Sports Equipment	Fees & Tickets	Toys & Games	Travel	Cable TV	PERSONAL: Apparel & Services	Auto Repairs	Health Insurance	Pets & Supplies
65629	CHADWICK	78	58	64	57	58	74	60	68	65	59	64	52	49	68	55	71	43	65	71	83
65630	CHESTNUTRIDGE	94	80	76	77	78	88	77	84	82	79	82	62	70	85	73	86	55	81	86	101
65631	CLEVER	83	81	71	80	79	82	75	79	76	77	77	59	74	79	74	78	53	76	79	94
65632	CONWAY	74	56	70	55	57	74	57	69	62	54	61	52	48	63	55	67	41	64	71	82
65633	CRANE	71	54	70	52	55	73	56	68	62	52	60	51	46	61	54	67	40	64	72	80
65634	CROSS TIMBERS	67	49	70	47	51	69	50	63	55	47	54	47	40	55	50	61	36	58	66	75
65635	DADEVILLE	76	56	81	54	59	78	57	72	63	54	62	54	47	62	57	69	41	67	75	86
65637	DORA	69	49	73	48	51	71	51	65	56	45	55	51	40	55	51	61	36	60	68	78
65638	DRURY	65	45	69	45	47	67	49	61	52	42	51	49	37	51	48	57	33	57	64	74
65640	DUNNEGAN	69	50	71	48	52	71	51	65	57	48	56	49	41	56	51	63	37	60	68	77
65641	EAGLE ROCK	73	57	76	55	61	76	58	70	63	57	62	51	50	62	58	68	41	66	75	83
65644	ELKLAND	74	54	61	52	53	70	55	64	61	54	60	49	45	64	50	67	40	61	68	78
65646	EVERTON	78	59	79	58	61	81	61	74	65	54	64	58	49	65	60	71	42	69	78	89
65647	EXETER	81	58	68	57	58	78	61	71	67	59	66	55	49	70	56	73	44	67	75	86
65648	FAIR GROVE	96	89	80	87	87	92	84	89	87	87	87	66	80	90	81	89	59	86	90	106
65649	FAIR PLAY	67	54	73	51	58	72	55	67	60	54	59	48	49	58	57	65	39	63	73	78
65650	FLEMINGTON	83	60	86	58	62	85	61	78	68	57	67	59	49	68	61	75	44	72	81	93
65652	FORDLAND	87	65	77	63	65	84	66	78	73	64	71	59	55	75	62	79	48	73	81	94
65653	FORSYTH	79	64	87	62	69	83	66	78	71	64	69	56	58	68	68	76	46	75	84	92
65654	FREISTATT	89	61	97	61	64	94	68	84	70	55	70	70	50	69	67	77	45	79	89	104
65655	GAINESVILLE	72	52	73	50	54	74	54	68	60	50	59	51	43	60	53	66	39	63	72	81
65656	GALENA	83	64	87	62	66	84	64	79	69	61	68	58	54	69	64	75	45	73	81	93
65657	GARRISON	70	50	58	49	50	67	52	61	58	51	57	47	42	61	48	63	38	58	64	74
65658	GOLDEN	68	64	82	59	72	77	61	72	65	66	63	47	61	59	67	69	42	70	81	83
65660	GRAFF	76	52	83	52	55	80	58	72	60	47	60	59	42	59	58	66	39	67	76	89
65661	GREENFIELD	64	46	65	44	47	67	50	62	55	44	53	47	39	54	48	60	35	57	67	73
65662	GROVESPRING	77	55	71	54	55	76	58	69	63	54	62	55	45	65	55	69	41	65	73	85
65663	HALF WAY	80	57	83	56	59	82	60	75	65	54	64	59	47	65	59	71	42	70	79	91
65666	HARDENVILLE	81	58	82	56	60	82	60	76	67	56	66	57	48	66	59	74	43	70	80	90
65667	HARTVILLE	74	53	72	52	54	75	57	69	62	52	61	53	45	63	54	68	40	65	74	83
65668	HERMITAGE	62	59	75	54	65	71	56	66	60	60	58	44	55	55	61	63	39	64	74	76
65669	HIGHLANDVILLE	87	80	71	77	78	81	75	80	78	78	78	58	71	81	72	80	53	77	80	95
65672	HOLLISTER	67	57	65	57	58	66	64	65	65	60	64	49	58	64	61	68	44	66	69	77
65674	HUMANSVILLE	58	42	59	41	44	60	45	56	50	41	49	42	36	49	44	55	32	52	60	66
65675	HURLEY	75	55	75	53	57	75	56	70	62	53	61	52	46	62	55	67	40	64	72	83
65676	ISABELLA	72	66	86	61	72	81	63	76	67	67	66	51	60	63	68	72	44	72	83	87
65679	KIRBYVILLE	87	65	87	62	66	88	66	82	72	62	71	61	54	72	65	79	47	75	84	97
65680	KISSEE MILLS	67	57	76	54	62	73	56	68	60	58	59	47	52	57	59	65	39	64	74	79
65681	LAMPE	86	67	105	66	73	90	67	85	71	63	70	63	57	68	71	77	47	79	85	100
65682	LOCKWOOD	78	55	82	54	57	82	60	75	65	51	63	59	46	64	59	71	42	70	80	90
65685	LOUISBURG	73	53	73	52	55	74	56	69	62	52	61	52	46	61	55	68	40	64	72	82
65686	KIMBERLING CITY	88	85	118	83	96	103	79	95	84	86	82	62	81	76	89	88	56	90	103	109
65688	BRANDSVILLE	74	53	61	52	53	70	55	64	61	54	60	49	44	64	50	67	40	61	68	78
65689	CABOOL	68	49	69	47	50	70	52	65	58	47	56	49	41	57	51	63	37	60	70	77
65690	COUCH	69	49	71	48	51	70	51	65	56	47	55	48	41	56	50	62	36	59	67	77
65692	KOSHKONONG	80	57	77	56	59	79	59	73	66	56	64	55	47	66	57	72	43	68	76	87
65702	MACOMB	72	51	74	50	53	73	53	67	59	49	57	50	42	58	52	64	38	62	70	80
65704	MANSFIELD	67	51	60	50	51	66	56	62	60	51	59	48	46	60	52	65	39	60	67	75
65705	MARIONVILLE	71	53	63	52	53	70	57	65	62	53	61	49	47	63	53	67	41	62	70	78
65706	MARSHFIELD	80	65	68	65	65	78	69	74	73	65	72	57	60	74	64	77	49	72	78	89
65707	MILLER	76	54	79	53	56	79	58	73	63	51	62	56	45	62	57	70	41	68	77	87
65708	MONETT	80	70	72	70	69	82	72	78	75	67	74	60	65	76	70	79	51	75	82	93
65710	MORRISVILLE	73	57	71	55	58	73	57	68	62	55	61	51	48	62	55	66	41	64	70	81
65711	MOUNTAIN GROVE	65	49	62	49	50	65	55	61	58	49	57	47	45	58	52	63	38	60	66	74
65712	MOUNT VERNON	84	65	82	65	67	87	69	81	73	62	72	62	57	73	67	79	48	76	86	96
65713	NIANGUA	82	58	81	57	60	82	60	75	67	56	65	57	48	67	59	73	43	70	79	90
65714	NIXA	92	89	77	90	86	85	90	87	89	91	90	68	89	92	87	88	62	88	85	103
65715	NOBLE	69	50	76	49	52	73	54	66	56	46	55	53	41	54	54	61	36	62	70	81
65717	NORWOOD	71	51	68	49	52	71	53	65	58	49	57	49	42	59	51	64	38	60	68	78
65720	OLDFIELD	74	53	63	52	53	71	55	65	62	54	60	50	44	64	51	67	40	62	69	79
65721	OZARK	103	102	86	100	96	93	98	96	96	102	97	75	96	101	94	94	67	95	92	113
65722	PHILLIPSBURG	97	73	81	70	72	92	74	85	81	73	80	65	61	84	68	88	54	81	89	103
65723	PIERCE CITY	77	58	71	56	58	77	60	71	66	56	64	54	49	67	57	71	43	67	76	86
65724	PITTSBURG	63	60	77	55	67	72	57	67	60	62	59	44	56	55	62	64	40	65	75	77
65725	PLEASANT HOPE	87	74	72	72	72	83	72	79	76	72	76	59	64	79	68	80	51	76	81	95
65727	POLK	89	64	91	62	66	90	65	83	72	61	71	62	52	72	65	80	47	76	86	99
65728	PONCE DE LEON	85	78	69	75	76	80	74	78	76	77	76	57	70	79	70	78	52	76	78	93
65729	PONTIAC	72	63	83	59	68	79	61	74	66	63	64	51	57	62	65	70	43	70	80	85
65730	POWELL	76	67	66	65	66	73	65	71	68	65	67	53	59	70	62	70	46	68	71	84
65731	POWERSITE	88	63	91	61	66	90	65	83	72	60	71	62	52	72	64	79	47	76	86	98
65732	PRESTON	79	57	82	55	59	80	58	74	65	55	64	55	47	64	58	71	42	68	77	88
65733	PROTEM	70	50	72	49	52	71	51	65	57	48	56	49	41	57	51	63	37	60	68	78
65734	PURDY	73	53	64	52	53	71	55	65	60	53	59	50	44	62	51	66	40	61	68	79
65735	QUINCY	64	46	66	44	48	65	47	60	52	44	51	45	38	52	47	57	34	55	62	71
65737	REEDS SPRING	90	69	104	67	74	94	70	88	75	66	74	65	59	73	72	81	49	81	90	104
65738	REPUBLIC	85	78	72	77	76	84	75	80	78	75	78	60	71	80	73	81	53	78	84	96
65739	RIDGEDALE	94	75	122	74	83	100	75	96	79	71	78	70	65	75	82	84	52	88	95	111
65740	ROCKAWAY BEACH	63	60	76	55	67	72	57	67	60	62	59	44	56	55	62	64	39	65	75	77
65742	ROGERSVILLE	112	113	107	111	113	113	103	109	104	108	105	80	104	107	104	106	72	105	108	128
65744	RUETER	75	53	77	52	55	76	55	70	61	51	60	52	44	60	54	67	39	64	73	83
65745	SELIGMAN	73	52	60	51	52	69	54	63	60	53	59	48	44	63	49	66	40	60	67	77
65746	SEYMOUR	73	53	61	52	53	70	57	65	63	54	61	50	46	64	52	68	41	62	69	79
65747	SHELL KNOB	76	65	93	62	71	82	63	78	67	63	66	55	58	63	68	71	44	73	81	90
65752	SOUTH GREENFIELD	77	53	85	53	56	81	59	73	61	48	61	60	43	60	59	67	39	68	77	90
65753	SPARTA	85	67	71	65	66	81	67	76	72	67	72	58	57	76	62	77	48	72	78	91
65754	SPOKANE	84	77	68	74	75	78	72	77	75	75	75	56	69	78	69	77	51	74	77	91
65755	SQUIRES	66	48	68	46	49	68	49	62	54	45	53	47	39	54	48	60	35	57	65	74
65756	STOTTS CITY	85	61	70	59	61	81	63	74	70	62	69	57	51	73	58	77	46	70	78	90
65757	STRAFFORD	90	84	76	83	83	88	79	85	82	80	82	63	76	85	77	85	56	82	86	101
65759	TANEYVILLE	74	53	66	52	54	72	55	66	61	53	60	50	44	63	52	67	40	62	69	80
65760	TECUMSEH	71	51	73	49	53	72	52	66	58	48	57	50	42	57	52	64	37	61	69	79
65761	THEODOSIA	60	54	72	51	60	67	53	63	56	55	55	43	50	52	57	59	36	60	69	73
65762	THORNFIELD	69	51	76	50	54	73	54	67	57	48	56	52	43	55	55	62	37	63	71	81
65764	TUNAS	65	45	71	45	47	68	50	62	52	41	51	51	37	51	49	56	33	57	65	76
65766	UDALL	65	46	66	45	48	66	48	60	53	44	52	45	38	52	47	58	34	55	63	72
	MISSOURI	94	86	87	87	85	93	89	91	91	87	90	70	84	92	86	93	62	90	94	108
	UNITED STATES	100	100	100	100	100	100	100	100	100	100	100	100	100	100	100	100	100	100	100	100

ZIP CODE			POPULATION			2000-2009 ANNUAL RATE		HOUSEHOLDS					FAMILIES		
#	POST OFFICE NAME	COUNTY FIPS CODE	2000	2009	2014	% Rate	State Centile	2000	2009	2014	% Annual Rate 2000-2009	2009 Average HH Size	2000	2009	% Annual Rate 2000-2009
65767	URBANA	059	1315	1412	1469	0.8	69	521	554	577	0.7	2.51	375	386	0.3
65768	VANZANT	067	1167	1225	1250	0.5	58	446	474	486	0.7	2.58	351	363	0.4
65769	VERONA	009	2824	3111	3253	1.1	79	991	1078	1123	0.9	2.88	762	806	0.6
65770	WALNUT GROVE	077	2447	2896	3149	1.8	90	945	1153	1267	2.2	2.47	714	830	1.6
65771	WALNUT SHADE	213	1133	1271	1362	1.3	83	423	478	514	1.3	2.63	328	361	1.0
65772	WASHBURN	009	1875	2227	2357	1.9	91	715	854	906	1.9	2.61	528	610	1.6
65773	WASOLA	153	737	735	726	0.0	37	291	294	291	0.1	2.49	218	213	-0.3
65774	WEAUBLEAU	085	977	1086	1132	1.2	82	392	433	450	1.1	2.51	261	277	0.6
65775	WEST PLAINS	091	22736	23691	24079	0.4	53	9022	9469	9647	0.5	2.44	6425	6514	0.1
65777	MOODY	091	336	341	342	0.2	46	118	121	122	0.3	2.82	94	95	0.1
65778	MYRTLE	149	420	396	382	-0.6	11	169	161	157	-0.5	2.46	124	114	-0.9
65779	WHEATLAND	085	2138	2167	2202	0.1	42	949	1010	1028	0.7	2.14	653	669	0.3
65781	WILLARD	077	6737	8338	9092	2.3	94	2399	3068	3382	2.7	2.65	1914	2348	2.2
65783	WINDYVILLE	059	992	1070	1115	0.8	69	370	396	413	0.7	2.68	272	282	0.4
65784	ZANONI	153	261	259	255	-0.1	32	107	107	106	0.0	2.42	81	79	-0.3
65785	STOCKTON	039	5801	6009	6014	0.4	53	2382	2467	2471	0.4	2.35	1659	1656	0.0
65786	MACKS CREEK	029	1942	1880	1918	-0.4	18	754	741	759	-0.2	2.53	567	542	-0.5
65787	ROACH	029	2454	2810	2991	1.5	87	931	1090	1172	1.7	2.34	687	783	1.4
65788	PEACE VALLEY	091	358	397	413	1.1	79	125	140	147	1.2	2.84	102	111	0.9
65789	POMONA	091	1570	1730	1794	1.1	79	590	658	686	1.2	2.62	464	502	0.9
65790	POTTERSVILLE	091	643	701	724	0.9	72	263	288	298	1.0	2.43	206	219	0.7
65791	THAYER	149	3777	4067	4093	0.8	69	1560	1677	1685	0.8	2.36	1051	1087	0.4
65793	WILLOW SPRINGS	091	5938	6111	6162	0.3	50	2335	2428	2458	0.4	2.46	1676	1679	0.0
65802	SPRINGFIELD	077	38938	41329	42911	0.6	63	15684	17167	18008	1.0	2.25	9391	9701	0.4
65803	SPRINGFIELD	077	38716	40901	42388	0.6	63	15282	16714	17517	1.0	2.34	10008	10304	0.3
65804	SPRINGFIELD	077	36629	37217	38425	0.2	46	17141	18111	18907	0.6	2.04	9890	9626	-0.3
65806	SPRINGFIELD	077	10885	10679	10741	-0.2	27	5231	5280	5365	0.1	1.78	1548	1369	-1.3
65807	SPRINGFIELD	077	49431	54494	57611	1.1	79	20318	23587	25339	1.6	2.11	11654	12562	0.8
65809	SPRINGFIELD	077	9550	11436	12389	2.0	92	3453	4297	4708	2.4	2.61	2871	3462	2.0
65810	SPRINGFIELD	077	14758	20835	23576	3.8	98	5195	7678	8785	4.3	2.69	4271	6026	3.8
	MISSOURI					0.7					0.8	2.45			0.4
	UNITED STATES					1.0					1.1	2.59			0.9

ZIP CODE #	POST OFFICE NAME	RACE (%) White 2000	White 2009	Black 2000	Black 2009	Asian/Pacific 2000	Asian/Pacific 2009	% Hispanic Origin 2000	% Hispanic Origin 2009	2009 AGE DISTRIBUTION (%) 0-4	5-9	10-14	15-19	20-24	25-44	45-64	65-84	85+	18+	MEDIAN AGE 2009	% 2009 Males	% 2009 Females
65767	URBANA	97.6	97.1	0.2	0.1	0.0	0.0	0.7	0.9	6.0	6.4	6.8	6.7	5.0	22.2	28.4	16.0	2.4	76.5	42.4	49.9	50.1
65768	VANZANT	95.5	94.8	0.1	0.2	0.1	0.2	0.8	1.1	5.2	6.0	6.4	6.1	4.2	21.1	33.4	16.1	1.5	78.4	45.5	50.7	49.3
65769	VERONA	86.6	82.9	0.4	0.5	0.2	0.4	16.5	21.7	8.9	8.6	8.3	6.9	5.6	25.6	24.8	10.3	1.0	70.0	34.6	51.3	48.7
65770	WALNUT GROVE	97.9	97.4	0.2	0.2	0.1	0.1	0.6	0.8	6.0	6.3	6.6	6.7	4.7	24.1	29.7	13.5	2.5	76.8	41.9	49.9	50.1
65771	WALNUT SHADE	97.2	96.6	0.0	0.0	0.7	1.0	0.7	1.0	6.0	6.3	6.6	6.6	5.0	23.8	30.8	13.5	1.4	76.5	42.1	50.2	49.8
65772	WASHBURN	97.7	97.3	0.1	0.0	0.0	0.0	1.0	1.5	7.1	7.1	7.5	7.3	6.2	25.1	27.2	11.5	1.0	73.8	36.9	50.2	49.8
65773	WASOLA	98.2	98.2	0.0	0.0	0.0	0.0	0.7	0.8	5.7	6.1	5.9	5.2	4.6	20.3	31.8	18.5	1.9	79.0	46.4	49.7	50.3
65774	WEAUBLEAU	96.0	95.4	0.5	0.6	0.0	0.0	0.9	1.4	6.3	6.2	6.3	6.5	6.2	22.7	27.6	15.7	2.5	77.4	41.6	47.5	52.5
65775	WEST PLAINS	96.6	95.8	0.4	0.5	0.5	0.7	1.3	1.8	7.0	6.9	6.8	6.7	5.7	24.0	26.1	14.2	2.6	75.2	39.3	48.6	51.4
65777	MOODY	95.5	95.6	1.2	1.2	0.3	0.3	1.8	2.6	7.6	7.6	7.3	6.2	5.0	23.2	27.6	14.4	1.2	73.6	39.5	50.7	49.3
65778	MYRTLE	94.7	94.4	0.0	0.0	0.0	0.0	0.5	0.5	4.8	5.3	6.1	6.3	4.5	19.4	31.6	19.7	2.3	79.8	47.5	51.5	48.5
65779	WHEATLAND	98.1	98.0	0.0	0.0	0.2	0.3	0.5	0.6	3.8	3.8	4.2	4.8	4.2	15.1	32.4	27.8	3.8	85.7	55.8	49.0	51.0
65781	WILLARD	98.0	97.5	0.1	0.2	0.1	0.1	0.7	1.0	7.1	6.9	6.9	6.7	5.8	26.4	26.8	11.0	2.4	74.5	38.1	48.5	51.5
65783	WINDYVILLE	97.2	96.5	0.2	0.2	0.3	0.6	0.9	1.3	6.5	6.5	6.8	6.6	6.4	22.4	29.5	13.6	1.5	75.5	40.5	50.7	49.3
65784	ZANONI	96.9	96.9	0.4	0.4	0.0	0.0	1.1	1.2	5.8	5.8	5.8	5.0	4.2	21.2	31.3	19.3	1.5	79.2	46.3	49.8	50.2
65785	STOCKTON	96.8	96.0	0.2	0.2	0.6	1.0	1.0	1.4	5.4	5.6	5.9	8.1	4.5	18.8	29.4	19.6	2.8	77.6	46.4	49.9	50.1
65786	MACKS CREEK	98.2	97.9	0.1	0.1	0.2	0.2	1.0	1.3	5.7	6.1	6.2	6.5	5.1	23.2	30.3	15.1	1.7	77.4	42.7	51.0	49.0
65787	ROACH	97.6	97.1	0.2	0.2	0.4	0.5	0.7	1.0	4.6	5.1	4.8	5.3	5.0	19.5	34.8	19.1	1.8	82.2	49.0	50.2	49.8
65788	PEACE VALLEY	97.8	97.2	0.3	0.3	0.6	0.8	0.3	0.5	5.3	5.8	6.8	7.8	6.3	23.7	29.2	14.1	1.0	77.3	41.5	51.4	48.6
65789	POMONA	96.7	96.1	0.1	0.1	0.4	0.5	1.0	1.4	6.3	6.5	6.6	6.5	5.5	24.2	29.9	13.2	1.2	76.5	40.6	50.7	49.3
65790	POTTERSVILLE	95.0	94.4	0.0	0.0	0.2	0.1	0.6	0.9	7.4	7.4	7.3	6.8	6.1	25.2	27.8	11.0	0.9	73.9	37.0	48.9	51.1
65791	THAYER	96.4	96.3	0.1	0.1	0.1	0.1	1.3	1.3	6.5	6.5	6.5	6.4	4.9	22.9	26.0	16.5	3.9	76.5	42.0	47.2	52.8
65793	WILLOW SPRINGS	95.9	95.2	0.2	0.2	0.3	0.4	0.9	1.3	6.2	6.2	6.4	6.3	5.6	22.2	27.5	16.6	2.9	77.1	42.4	48.3	51.7
65802	SPRINGFIELD	91.6	89.8	3.5	4.1	1.0	1.5	2.5	3.5	6.7	6.3	5.9	7.7	9.9	28.2	23.4	10.2	1.7	77.7	34.2	49.0	51.0
65803	SPRINGFIELD	93.1	91.7	2.9	3.4	0.5	0.8	1.9	2.7	6.4	6.2	6.0	7.3	7.9	26.2	26.6	11.3	2.0	77.5	37.0	49.1	50.9
65804	SPRINGFIELD	94.6	92.9	1.4	1.8	1.5	2.2	1.6	2.3	5.0	4.8	4.9	5.3	7.6	26.4	26.2	16.3	3.5	82.3	41.5	47.3	52.7
65806	SPRINGFIELD	85.9	82.2	5.6	7.0	2.0	2.9	3.4	4.8	5.0	4.0	4.0	9.0	27.0	25.5	17.3	6.5	1.6	84.6	25.5	50.6	49.4
65807	SPRINGFIELD	91.9	89.7	3.1	3.5	2.0	3.1	2.3	3.1	5.8	5.2	4.9	8.5	10.3	29.7	22.0	10.9	2.8	81.2	34.3	48.7	51.3
65809	SPRINGFIELD	96.3	95.1	0.8	1.0	1.3	2.1	0.6	0.9	5.0	6.1	7.0	6.7	3.8	19.0	35.1	14.8	2.4	77.5	46.2	49.0	51.0
65810	SPRINGFIELD	95.3	93.5	0.8	1.1	1.9	3.0	1.3	1.9	6.8	7.1	7.4	6.8	4.7	28.0	28.2	9.7	1.3	74.4	38.1	49.4	50.6
	MISSOURI	84.9	83.3	11.2	11.7	1.2	1.7	2.1	2.8	6.6	6.6	6.6	7.0	6.7	26.1	26.5	11.7	2.1	76.1	37.7	48.8	51.2
	UNITED STATES	75.1	72.0	12.3	12.7	3.8	4.6	12.5	15.7	6.8	6.7	6.6	7.1	6.9	27.0	26.0	10.9	1.9	75.7	36.9	49.2	50.8

INCOME

ZIP CODE #	POST OFFICE NAME	2009 Per Capita Income	2009 HH Income Base	2009 HOUSEHOLD INCOME DISTRIBUTION (%) Less than $25,000	$25,000 to $49,999	$50,000 to $99,999	$100,000 to $149,999	$150,000 or More	MEDIAN HOUSEHOLD INCOME 2009	2014	2009 National Centile	2009 State Centile	2009 Home Value Base	2009 HOME VALUE DISTRIBUTION (%) Less than $50,000	$50,000 to $89,999	$90,000 to $174,999	$175,000 to $399,999	$400,000 or More	2009 Median Home Value
65767	URBANA	18216	554	33.4	32.3	28.5	2.5	3.2	35337	37900	19	33	434	27.6	21.9	29.0	16.4	5.1	91333
65768	VANZANT	19185	474	31.2	41.8	20.9	1.9	4.2	33859	34704	15	26	381	11.0	19.7	42.5	18.9	7.9	124219
65769	VERONA	15524	1078	31.8	34.7	28.0	4.2	1.3	36999	38746	24	40	820	20.4	24.9	32.2	18.2	4.4	96290
65770	WALNUT GROVE	19841	1153	23.9	33.6	36.9	4.5	1.1	43860	47356	45	66	946	16.7	25.6	35.9	18.6	3.2	106061
65771	WALNUT SHADE	20206	478	26.4	33.5	31.0	5.6	3.6	41216	44054	37	58	402	10.2	25.6	34.3	23.9	6.0	122170
65772	WASHBURN	16174	854	32.2	35.9	27.8	2.3	1.8	35198	37130	18	32	703	19.6	22.9	43.0	10.1	4.4	103942
65773	WASOLA	14176	294	40.8	34.7	23.1	1.0	0.3	30243	31367	8	12	251	29.5	21.1	28.7	15.5	5.2	89250
65774	WEAUBLEAU	12981	433	47.1	33.9	16.6	1.6	0.7	25929	25805	4	3	319	33.2	32.0	22.6	10.0	2.2	68370
65775	WEST PLAINS	18034	9469	36.2	33.1	25.2	3.4	2.0	34250	36175	16	27	6779	17.9	21.3	40.4	16.5	3.9	105549
65777	MOODY	12573	121	43.0	33.1	21.5	2.5	0.0	29136	30000	7	8	101	19.8	25.7	33.7	17.8	3.0	105682
65778	MYRTLE	14214	161	51.6	29.8	16.1	1.9	0.6	24019	24121	3	2	129	36.4	23.3	27.1	12.4	0.8	72143
65779	WHEATLAND	18560	1010	38.2	34.2	23.6	3.1	1.0	30735	31483	9	14	839	22.2	24.3	35.4	15.3	2.9	95463
65781	WILLARD	20595	3068	21.4	28.5	42.9	5.1	2.1	50048	51382	61	79	2492	4.0	16.1	54.9	21.8	3.3	125236
65783	WINDYVILLE	18261	396	40.7	23.7	31.1	1.5	3.0	36084	38325	21	35	336	23.5	33.0	33.9	8.9	0.6	83714
65784	ZANONI	17989	107	41.1	30.8	24.3	0.9	2.8	33368	33898	14	24	90	27.8	23.3	32.2	12.2	4.4	88000
65785	STOCKTON	18487	2467	32.8	34.2	27.9	3.1	2.0	35980	37699	21	35	1992	19.9	24.8	34.8	16.7	3.7	98966
65786	MACKS CREEK	16962	741	31.6	36.8	27.3	3.0	1.3	36996	39598	24	40	619	27.3	26.8	26.7	16.3	2.9	84457
65787	ROACH	23021	1090	25.8	30.7	32.4	7.2	3.9	43889	45524	45	66	920	13.3	16.3	25.3	36.6	8.5	152941
65788	PEACE VALLEY	15402	140	29.3	41.4	25.7	2.9	0.7	37731	39292	26	44	119	23.5	16.0	34.5	23.5	2.5	109868
65789	POMONA	16552	658	40.3	36.3	18.7	2.4	2.3	30749	31178	9	14	541	23.3	20.7	37.3	15.0	3.7	100850
65790	POTTERSVILLE	16481	288	37.5	36.1	22.6	2.8	1.0	31611	31992	11	16	243	20.2	15.6	39.5	18.5	6.2	110326
65791	THAYER	15131	1677	47.8	31.5	16.5	2.7	1.4	26284	27519	4	3	1237	29.2	30.1	29.3	8.8	2.7	75448
65793	WILLOW SPRINGS	14478	2428	45.6	31.6	20.0	1.9	0.9	27622	28184	5	5	1828	25.3	27.1	33.3	12.1	2.2	85810
65802	SPRINGFIELD	19371	17167	33.2	33.9	27.5	3.9	1.4	36513	39289	22	37	9952	16.4	32.0	40.5	9.4	1.7	91871
65803	SPRINGFIELD	19280	16714	32.0	33.7	28.9	3.7	1.7	37010	39992	24	40	10254	15.7	30.4	37.4	14.6	1.8	95116
65804	SPRINGFIELD	31037	18111	20.9	32.4	33.8	7.3	5.6	47007	49935	54	74	11011	4.8	11.0	49.7	29.9	4.6	142308
65806	SPRINGFIELD	14691	5280	63.6	24.2	10.5	1.1	0.6	18967	19532	1	1	874	18.6	57.3	19.1	4.2	0.7	69892
65807	SPRINGFIELD	23993	23587	23.8	33.3	35.8	4.7	2.4	44530	47450	47	68	12853	4.9	14.4	66.6	13.9	0.3	120042
65809	SPRINGFIELD	47357	4297	6.1	14.6	34.1	19.8	25.4	89287	89931	95	98	3878	0.6	1.2	20.4	55.3	22.4	262556
65810	SPRINGFIELD	34086	7678	7.6	18.2	46.8	14.9	12.5	72837	72367	88	96	6596	0.2	1.8	47.1	47.6	3.3	176680
	MISSOURI	25286		22.8	27.7	35.3	9.1	5.2	49522	52035				12.8	19.4	39.1	24.2	4.6	122064
	UNITED STATES	27277		20.9	24.4	35.3	11.7	7.6	54719	56938				9.3	13.1	31.6	32.6	13.5	162279

ZIP CODE	FINANCIAL SERVICES				THE HOME						ENTERTAINMENT						PERSONAL			
					Home Improvements		Furnishings													
# POST OFFICE NAME	Auto Loan	Home Loan	Invest-ments	Retire-ment Plans	Home Repair	Lawn & Garden	Comput-ers & Hard-ware-Personal	Major Appli-ances	TV, Radio, Sound Equip-ment	Furni-ture	Dine out/ Carry out	Sports Equip-ment	Fees & Tickets	Toys & Games	Travel	Cable TV	Apparel & Services	Auto Repairs	Health Insur-ance	Pets & Supplies
65767 URBANA	82	59	84	57	61	83	60	77	67	56	66	58	48	67	60	74	43	70	80	91
65768 VANZANT	89	61	97	61	64	93	67	84	71	55	70	69	50	69	67	77	45	78	89	103
65769 VERONA	81	58	67	57	58	77	60	70	67	59	65	54	49	69	55	73	44	67	74	86
65770 WALNUT GROVE	78	68	73	70	70	83	68	78	71	61	69	60	61	71	68	75	47	72	81	92
65771 WALNUT SHADE	90	74	82	72	74	87	72	83	77	72	77	61	64	79	70	82	52	79	85	99
65772 WASHBURN	76	55	63	53	54	72	57	66	63	55	62	51	46	66	52	69	42	63	70	81
65773 WASOLA	63	45	66	44	46	65	47	59	51	42	50	45	37	51	46	56	33	54	62	71
65774 WEAUBLEAU	57	42	60	40	44	59	43	54	47	40	46	40	35	47	43	52	31	50	57	64
65775 WEST PLAINS	73	57	65	57	58	71	61	68	66	58	64	51	53	66	58	70	44	66	72	81
65777 MOODY	63	45	65	44	47	64	46	59	52	43	51	44	37	51	46	57	33	54	62	70
65778 MYRTLE	62	45	64	43	46	63	46	58	51	43	50	44	37	51	45	56	33	54	61	69
65779 WHEATLAND	63	54	72	51	58	69	53	64	57	54	56	45	48	54	55	61	37	60	69	75
65781 WILLARD	82	80	71	82	78	86	78	82	79	73	78	63	75	81	77	81	54	79	85	97
65783 WINDYVILLE	88	63	76	62	63	85	66	78	73	63	72	60	53	76	61	79	48	73	82	95
65784 ZANONI	78	56	80	54	58	79	57	73	63	53	62	55	46	63	57	70	41	67	76	86
65785 STOCKTON	74	57	81	55	61	78	58	72	63	55	62	53	49	61	59	69	41	67	76	85
65786 MACKS CREEK	76	56	74	55	58	75	57	70	63	55	62	52	47	63	56	68	41	65	72	83
65787 ROACH	88	77	112	76	85	97	75	91	79	75	78	64	70	74	81	83	52	86	94	105
65788 PEACE VALLEY	79	56	69	55	57	76	58	70	65	56	64	53	47	67	54	71	43	65	73	84
65789 POMONA	78	56	76	54	57	78	57	71	64	54	62	54	46	64	56	70	41	66	74	85
65790 POTTERSVILLE	72	52	60	51	52	69	54	63	60	53	59	48	43	63	49	65	40	60	66	77
65791 THAYER	62	44	62	43	46	64	47	59	53	43	51	44	38	52	46	58	34	55	64	70
65793 WILLOW SPRINGS	63	45	61	44	46	63	47	58	53	44	51	44	38	53	46	58	34	54	62	69
65802 SPRINGFIELD	67	56	53	57	54	62	66	62	67	61	66	49	58	67	58	68	45	64	66	75
65803 SPRINGFIELD	69	59	57	60	58	67	65	65	68	61	67	51	59	68	60	71	46	67	71	79
65804 SPRINGFIELD	90	83	84	85	84	89	93	88	93	89	92	68	88	92	88	94	64	92	94	105
65806 SPRINGFIELD	39	25	24	27	24	27	46	32	42	37	42	29	34	42	33	41	30	39	34	41
65807 SPRINGFIELD	77	70	66	70	68	72	78	73	77	74	77	57	72	78	71	78	54	76	76	87
65809 SPRINGFIELD	160	203	219	208	214	191	175	184	166	189	166	137	202	164	199	161	121	174	171	208
65810 SPRINGFIELD	132	146	128	147	141	131	132	132	126	139	128	104	139	132	135	123	91	128	123	153
MISSOURI	94	86	87	87	85	93	89	91	91	87	90	70	84	92	86	93	62	90	94	108
UNITED STATES	100	100	100	100	100	100	100	100	100	100	100	100	100	100	100	100	100	100	100	100

POPULATION CHANGE

ZIP CODE #	POST OFFICE NAME	COUNTY FIPS CODE	POPULATION 2000	POPULATION 2009	POPULATION 2014	2000-2009 ANNUAL RATE % Rate	2000-2009 ANNUAL RATE State Centile	HOUSEHOLDS 2000	HOUSEHOLDS 2009	HOUSEHOLDS 2014	HOUSEHOLDS % Annual Rate 2000-2009	HOUSEHOLDS 2009 Average HH Size	FAMILIES 2000	FAMILIES 2009	FAMILIES % Annual Rate 2000-2009
59001	ABSAROKEE	095	1526	1628	1703	0.7	71	630	685	721	0.9	2.35	438	460	0.5
59002	ACTON	111	79	105	120	3.1	99	31	43	49	3.6	2.44	25	34	3.4
59003	ASHLAND	087	432	432	429	0.0	52	166	169	170	0.2	2.56	115	114	-0.1
59006	BALLANTINE	111	859	969	1034	1.3	87	322	369	396	1.5	2.63	235	258	1.0
59007	BEARCREEK	009	291	308	317	0.6	66	129	141	146	1.0	2.18	93	98	0.6
59008	BELFRY	009	164	175	180	0.7	71	68	74	77	0.9	2.36	49	52	0.6
59010	BIGHORN	103	149	135	127	-1.1	11	57	53	50	-0.8	2.55	39	35	-1.2
59011	BIG TIMBER	097	2921	3095	3190	0.6	66	1227	1308	1350	0.7	2.32	809	836	0.4
59012	BIRNEY	087	96	96	96	0.0	52	45	46	46	0.2	2.09	31	31	0.0
59014	BRIDGER	009	1606	1692	1726	0.6	66	669	721	740	0.8	2.34	460	479	0.4
59015	BROADVIEW	111	546	600	676	1.0	79	204	229	260	1.3	2.62	164	179	1.0
59016	BUSBY	003	1542	1663	1703	0.8	73	401	432	443	0.8	3.84	340	360	0.6
59019	COLUMBUS	095	3373	3669	3834	0.9	77	1320	1454	1527	1.1	2.48	934	1000	0.7
59022	CROW AGENCY	003	2583	2587	2578	0.0	52	635	645	646	0.2	3.91	555	556	0.0
59024	CUSTER	111	350	392	417	1.2	86	144	164	175	1.4	2.39	104	113	0.9
59025	DECKER	003	145	149	150	0.3	58	65	68	69	0.5	2.19	44	44	0.0
59027	EMIGRANT	067	484	510	522	0.6	66	191	208	216	0.9	2.45	123	130	0.6
59028	FISHTAIL	095	611	628	646	0.3	58	243	256	265	0.6	2.27	169	173	0.3
59029	FROMBERG	009	890	945	964	0.7	71	354	381	390	0.8	2.48	245	256	0.5
59030	GARDINER	067	1644	1638	1655	0.0	52	805	832	849	0.4	1.97	428	421	-0.2
59031	GARRYOWEN	003	353	355	356	0.1	53	103	106	106	0.3	3.16	93	95	0.2
59032	GRASS RANGE	027	451	439	431	-0.3	42	179	178	176	-0.1	2.31	131	126	-0.4
59033	GREYCLIFF	097	402	424	436	0.6	66	142	150	154	0.6	2.83	102	104	0.2
59034	HARDIN	003	4325	4261	4234	-0.2	45	1659	1660	1655	0.0	2.52	1139	1101	-0.4
59037	HUNTLEY	111	1202	1397	1501	1.6	92	453	535	579	1.8	2.61	339	386	1.4
59038	HYSHAM	103	119	108	101	-1.0	13	48	44	42	-0.9	2.45	33	29	-1.4
59039	INGOMAR	087	111	109	108	-0.2	45	48	49	49	0.2	2.22	36	35	-0.3
59041	JOLIET	009	1601	1686	1708	0.6	66	653	700	714	0.8	2.41	474	494	0.4
59043	LAME DEER	087	2880	2873	2856	0.0	52	774	784	784	0.1	3.62	590	584	-0.1
59044	LAUREL	111	9785	10659	11103	0.9	77	3811	4226	4431	1.1	2.50	2760	2943	0.7
59046	LAVINA	037	505	554	577	1.0	79	222	249	261	1.2	1.98	160	175	1.0
59047	LIVINGSTON	067	12434	12821	13025	0.3	58	5385	5708	5860	0.6	2.21	3356	3427	0.2
59050	LODGE GRASS	003	3060	3104	3113	0.2	57	863	894	902	0.4	3.44	705	715	0.2
59052	MC LEOD	097	238	252	259	0.6	66	91	97	100	0.7	2.60	65	67	0.3
59053	MARTINSDALE	059	213	232	234	0.9	77	98	107	108	1.0	2.17	68	72	0.6
59055	MELVILLE	097	66	69	71	0.5	63	27	29	30	0.8	2.38	20	20	0.0
59057	MOLT	095	578	692	774	2.0	96	207	255	287	2.3	2.71	166	199	2.0
59058	MOSBY	033	10	9	9	-1.1	11	3	3	3	0.0	3.00	2	2	0.0
59059	MUSSELSHELL	065	451	446	444	-0.1	48	178	179	179	0.1	2.39	129	126	-0.3
59061	NYE	095	225	233	240	0.4	61	106	112	117	0.6	1.95	74	76	0.3
59062	OTTER	075	409	390	378	-0.5	32	172	167	162	-0.3	2.34	124	117	-0.6
59063	PARK CITY	095	1691	1833	1902	0.9	77	635	704	735	1.1	2.58	503	546	0.9
59064	POMPEYS PILLAR	111	244	272	288	1.2	86	102	116	123	1.4	2.34	74	80	0.8
59065	PRAY	067	107	114	117	0.7	71	50	55	58	1.0	2.07	36	39	0.9
59067	RAPELJE	095	179	214	230	1.9	95	73	88	95	2.0	2.43	56	66	1.8
59068	RED LODGE	009	3441	3608	3677	0.5	63	1549	1665	1709	0.8	2.11	914	946	0.4
59069	REED POINT	095	386	450	479	1.7	93	154	182	194	1.8	2.47	117	135	1.6
59070	ROBERTS	009	833	870	877	0.5	63	345	371	378	0.8	2.35	252	263	0.5
59071	ROSCOE	009	119	124	125	0.4	61	52	56	57	0.8	2.21	38	40	0.6
59072	ROUNDUP	065	3992	4023	4041	0.1	53	1670	1703	1718	0.2	2.30	1084	1068	-0.2
59074	RYEGATE	037	635	694	723	1.0	79	192	215	226	1.2	2.77	138	150	0.9
59075	SAINT XAVIER	003	194	197	199	0.2	57	57	59	60	0.4	3.32	44	45	0.2
59076	SANDERS	103	120	108	102	-1.1	11	46	43	40	-0.7	2.51	31	28	-1.1
59077	SAND SPRINGS	033	76	70	68	-0.9	14	30	29	28	-0.4	2.38	20	19	-0.6
59078	SHAWMUT	107	313	295	286	-0.6	27	81	77	74	-0.5	3.23	60	56	-0.7
59079	SHEPHERD	111	2843	3254	3503	1.5	90	988	1155	1252	1.7	2.82	808	917	1.4
59085	TWO DOT	107	1646	1528	1473	-0.8	18	653	607	584	-0.8	2.09	393	352	-1.2
59086	WILSALL	067	996	1122	1177	1.3	87	387	452	480	1.7	2.41	272	308	1.4
59087	WINNETT	069	506	502	499	-0.1	48	215	218	219	0.1	2.30	140	137	-0.2
59088	WORDEN	111	1162	1354	1457	1.7	93	467	555	602	1.9	2.44	335	381	1.4
59089	WYOLA	003	437	464	474	0.7	71	130	141	145	0.9	3.20	105	111	0.6
59101	BILLINGS	111	36557	37945	38869	0.4	61	15346	15981	16416	0.4	2.31	8797	8768	0.0
59102	BILLINGS	111	44563	47343	48889	0.7	71	18951	20402	21208	0.8	2.23	11926	12153	0.2
59105	BILLINGS	111	23571	27757	29898	1.8	94	8690	10411	11293	2.0	2.65	6469	7481	1.6
59106	BILLINGS	111	7891	11338	12799	4.0	99	2707	3970	4518	4.2	2.83	2269	3250	4.0
59201	WOLF POINT	085	4975	4820	4677	-0.3	42	1746	1697	1649	-0.3	2.78	1273	1203	-0.6
59211	ANTELOPE	091	165	151	138	-1.0	13	70	66	61	-0.6	2.29	51	46	-1.1
59212	BAINVILLE	085	323	309	299	-0.5	32	139	135	131	-0.3	2.29	94	88	-0.7
59213	BROCKTON	085	922	880	854	-0.5	32	279	270	263	-0.4	3.26	232	221	-0.5
59214	BROCKWAY	055	179	148	135	-2.0	3	74	63	58	-1.7	2.35	61	51	-1.9
59215	CIRCLE	055	1166	1007	936	-1.6	6	483	431	404	-1.2	2.34	341	295	-1.6
59218	CULBERTSON	085	839	781	751	-0.8	18	338	318	307	-0.7	2.41	216	196	-1.0
59219	DAGMAR	091	224	181	163	-2.3	2	85	71	64	-1.9	2.55	59	48	-2.2
59221	FAIRVIEW	083	1453	1318	1293	-1.0	13	599	560	554	-0.7	2.35	401	363	-1.1
59222	FLAXVILLE	019	263	233	218	-1.3	9	117	107	100	-1.0	2.18	81	71	-1.4
59223	FORT PECK	105	562	480	446	-1.7	4	232	202	189	-1.5	2.37	173	147	-1.7
59225	FRAZER	105	733	625	578	-1.7	4	210	181	168	-1.6	3.43	171	145	-1.8
59226	FROID	085	416	393	379	-0.6	27	190	182	176	-0.5	2.07	125	115	-0.9
59230	GLASGOW	105	4924	4624	4422	-0.7	21	2095	1986	1904	-0.6	2.24	1348	1237	-0.9
59241	HINSDALE	105	561	464	426	-2.0	3	234	198	183	-1.8	2.34	159	130	-2.2
59242	HOMESTEAD	091	60	47	42	-2.6	1	27	22	20	-2.2	2.14	19	15	-2.5
59243	LAMBERT	083	600	551	540	-0.9	14	220	207	205	-0.7	2.66	167	153	-0.9
59244	LARSLAN	105	137	110	102	-2.3	2	54	44	41	-2.2	2.45	44	35	-2.4
59247	MEDICINE LAKE	091	425	328	293	-2.8	1	181	144	129	-2.4	2.28	126	97	-2.8
59248	NASHUA	105	420	357	331	-1.7	4	170	147	137	-1.6	2.40	130	110	-1.8
59250	OPHEIM	105	247	204	187	-2.0	3	114	96	89	-1.8	2.13	77	64	-2.0
59252	OUTLOOK	091	190	168	153	-1.3	9	82	74	68	-1.1	2.26	57	50	-1.4
59253	PEERLESS	019	317	282	265	-1.3	9	130	119	113	-1.0	2.37	90	80	-1.3
59254	PLENTYWOOD	091	2433	2012	1810	-2.0	3	1018	848	763	-2.0	2.23	635	508	-2.4
59255	POPLAR	085	3474	3304	3198	-0.5	32	1013	974	945	-0.4	3.25	771	723	-0.7
59256	RAYMOND	091	4	3	3	-3.1	0	3	2	2	-4.3	1.50	2	1	-7.2
59257	REDSTONE	091	106	98	90	-0.8	18	47	45	41	-0.5	2.18	34	32	-0.7
59258	RESERVE	091	116	104	96	-1.2	10	50	47	43	-0.7	2.21	35	32	-1.0
59259	RICHEY	021	379	373	366	-0.2	45	166	165	164	-0.1	2.25	121	117	-0.4
59260	RICHLAND	105	135	112	102	-2.0	3	61	51	48	-1.9	2.20	41	34	-2.0
	MONTANA					0.8					0.9	2.43			0.5
	UNITED STATES					1.0					1.1	2.59			0.9

ZIP CODE #	POST OFFICE NAME	RACE (%) White 2000	White 2009	Black 2000	Black 2009	Asian/Pacific 2000	Asian/Pacific 2009	% Hispanic Origin 2000	% Hispanic Origin 2009	2009 AGE DISTRIBUTION (%) 0-4	5-9	10-14	15-19	20-24	25-44	45-64	65-84	85+	18+	MEDIAN AGE 2009	% 2009 Males	% 2009 Females
59001	ABSAROKEE	97.1	96.6	0.1	0.1	0.2	0.2	2.6	3.4	5.8	6.3	6.8	6.9	4.7	22.2	31.1	13.9	2.3	76.0	43.0	49.9	50.1
59002	ACTON	97.4	94.3	0.0	0.0	0.0	1.0	2.6	2.9	5.7	6.7	6.7	7.6	4.8	21.9	37.1	9.5	0.0	75.2	42.8	53.3	46.7
59003	ASHLAND	72.9	66.0	0.2	0.2	0.2	0.2	4.2	5.3	7.9	7.9	8.6	8.3	6.3	25.2	27.1	8.1	0.7	70.1	33.8	51.2	48.8
59006	BALLANTINE	95.2	93.8	0.2	0.4	0.1	0.2	4.7	6.6	6.0	6.1	7.0	7.3	5.4	23.8	31.0	12.1	1.3	76.3	41.1	50.4	49.6
59007	BEARCREEK	97.6	97.4	0.0	0.0	0.3	0.3	1.4	2.3	5.5	5.2	6.5	6.8	2.9	23.7	32.5	14.9	1.9	77.9	44.6	51.3	48.7
59008	BELFRY	98.8	97.7	0.0	0.0	0.0	0.0	1.2	1.7	5.1	5.1	6.9	6.3	2.9	22.9	34.3	14.9	1.7	78.3	45.5	50.9	49.1
59010	BIGHORN	96.6	96.3	0.0	0.0	0.7	0.7	1.3	1.5	5.9	5.9	6.7	5.9	5.2	18.5	32.6	16.3	3.0	77.0	46.0	52.6	47.4
59011	BIG TIMBER	97.0	96.4	0.1	0.1	0.3	0.4	1.5	2.1	5.8	6.0	6.4	6.7	4.8	21.5	30.7	14.8	3.3	77.4	44.0	50.4	49.6
59012	BIRNEY	81.1	72.9	0.0	0.0	0.0	0.0	4.2	6.3	7.3	7.3	8.3	8.3	5.2	26.0	28.1	9.4	0.0	70.8	35.8	53.1	46.9
59014	BRIDGER	97.6	97.2	0.1	0.1	0.1	0.1	2.6	3.5	5.6	5.7	6.7	7.0	4.7	22.0	30.9	15.1	2.4	77.2	43.7	49.6	50.4
59015	BROADVIEW	96.0	94.8	0.2	0.3	0.4	0.5	2.0	2.7	5.5	6.3	7.3	7.7	4.8	22.7	34.5	10.2	1.0	76.3	42.0	51.7	48.3
59016	BUSBY	7.2	6.0	0.0	0.0	0.0	0.0	3.0	2.6	12.9	11.7	11.8	9.3	5.0	24.0	20.9	3.7	0.7	57.8	24.3	49.4	50.6
59019	COLUMBUS	96.7	96.3	0.1	0.2	0.2	0.3	1.8	2.3	5.3	6.1	7.3	7.8	4.0	23.0	32.9	11.3	2.3	75.8	42.8	51.0	49.0
59022	CROW AGENCY	16.1	13.6	0.0	0.0	0.1	0.2	1.5	1.5	11.0	10.4	9.1	8.9	9.3	25.3	19.1	6.5	0.5	63.7	25.7	50.1	49.9
59024	CUSTER	95.7	94.4	0.0	0.3	0.0	0.0	4.3	6.4	5.9	5.1	7.7	8.4	4.3	23.5	32.9	11.7	0.5	75.3	41.7	51.8	48.2
59025	DECKER	95.2	94.0	0.0	0.0	0.7	0.7	2.8	4.0	4.0	5.4	5.4	6.7	2.7	20.8	38.9	14.1	2.0	81.2	47.2	51.0	49.0
59027	EMIGRANT	95.9	94.9	1.2	1.4	0.4	0.6	1.9	2.5	6.9	6.1	5.9	6.1	3.3	24.1	36.3	10.4	1.0	77.3	43.7	49.2	50.8
59028	FISHTAIL	96.7	96.2	0.3	0.3	0.3	0.3	2.8	3.7	2.9	3.3	4.0	4.8	3.0	21.0	39.0	20.1	1.9	86.6	51.4	52.9	47.1
59029	FROMBERG	94.8	93.7	0.0	0.0	0.3	0.3	3.9	5.2	4.3	6.0	8.0	9.3	3.5	21.8	30.9	13.0	3.1	74.6	43.2	49.9	50.1
59030	GARDINER	97.3	96.8	0.4	0.4	0.3	0.4	1.2	1.7	5.7	5.1	4.8	4.3	6.1	26.3	37.5	9.5	0.7	81.7	43.8	48.5	51.5
59031	GARRYOWEN	21.0	17.7	0.0	0.0	0.3	0.3	1.1	1.1	8.7	8.5	8.2	7.9	6.8	24.8	23.4	10.4	1.4	69.0	32.4	47.6	52.4
59032	GRASS RANGE	98.7	98.4	0.0	0.0	0.0	0.0	0.4	0.7	5.0	6.6	7.7	8.0	3.0	21.4	33.3	13.7	1.4	74.5	43.9	51.9	48.1
59033	GREYCLIFF	97.0	96.2	0.0	0.0	0.5	0.7	1.7	2.1	5.9	6.6	6.8	7.1	4.7	19.6	33.5	14.2	1.7	75.9	44.5	49.8	50.2
59034	HARDIN	67.4	63.4	0.1	0.1	0.5	0.6	5.1	6.2	7.4	7.1	7.6	7.7	5.9	23.5	26.7	11.5	2.7	72.5	37.9	48.3	51.7
59037	HUNTLEY	95.1	93.7	0.2	0.4	0.2	0.3	4.2	5.7	5.9	6.4	6.9	7.2	5.7	23.7	31.4	11.6	1.3	76.5	40.9	49.9	50.1
59038	HYSHAM	96.6	96.3	0.0	0.0	0.0	0.0	1.7	1.9	5.6	6.5	6.5	6.5	4.6	19.4	33.3	14.8	2.8	76.9	45.6	51.9	48.1
59039	INGOMAR	97.3	95.4	0.0	0.0	0.0	0.0	1.8	3.7	5.5	6.4	7.3	5.5	4.6	17.4	36.7	14.7	1.8	76.1	46.9	53.2	46.8
59041	JOLIET	97.1	96.8	0.4	0.5	0.7	0.7	1.3	1.5	5.9	6.8	7.7	6.6	3.3	21.7	33.1	12.5	2.6	75.3	43.9	51.1	48.9
59043	LAME DEER	8.0	5.2	0.0	0.0	0.1	0.1	2.0	1.9	12.4	11.3	9.5	9.8	9.5	24.3	18.0	5.0	0.3	60.3	23.7	48.0	52.0
59044	LAUREL	96.5	95.6	0.2	0.2	0.4	0.5	2.2	3.0	6.5	6.8	7.0	6.7	5.2	24.2	29.5	12.0	2.3	75.4	40.2	49.1	50.9
59046	LAVINA	98.6	98.6	0.0	0.0	0.2	0.2	1.0	0.9	5.1	6.5	5.4	6.5	4.3	20.4	35.4	15.0	1.4	78.3	46.1	51.4	48.6
59047	LIVINGSTON	96.5	95.9	0.4	0.5	0.4	0.5	1.9	2.5	5.8	5.4	6.0	6.3	5.9	23.8	32.0	12.1	2.7	78.7	42.7	49.7	50.3
59050	LODGE GRASS	24.1	21.1	0.0	0.0	0.1	0.1	3.9	4.1	9.9	9.7	10.0	9.7	6.2	24.0	23.1	6.8	0.6	63.7	28.9	49.7	50.3
59052	MC LEOD	97.1	96.0	0.0	0.0	0.4	0.8	1.7	2.4	5.6	6.3	6.7	6.7	4.8	19.8	34.9	13.5	1.6	77.0	45.0	50.4	49.6
59053	MARTINSDALE	97.7	97.8	0.0	0.0	0.0	0.0	1.4	1.3	4.7	5.6	6.5	7.3	3.9	19.4	33.2	17.7	1.7	78.4	47.0	53.4	46.6
59055	MELVILLE	97.0	97.1	0.0	0.0	0.0	0.0	1.5	1.4	5.8	5.8	7.2	7.2	2.9	21.7	31.9	15.9	1.4	73.9	44.4	50.7	49.3
59057	MOLT	95.8	94.5	0.2	0.3	0.3	0.6	2.3	3.0	5.6	6.4	7.2	7.7	4.9	22.4	34.1	10.7	1.0	76.0	42.0	51.7	48.3
59058	MOSBY	100.0	100.0	0.0	0.0	0.0	0.0	0.0	0.0	0.0	0.0	0.0	0.0	0.0	0.0	100.0	0.0	0.0	100.0	55.6	66.7	33.3
59059	MUSSELSHELL	97.1	96.9	0.0	0.0	0.2	0.2	0.9	1.1	4.0	5.2	6.1	7.6	3.1	21.1	37.0	14.3	1.6	80.0	46.6	50.4	49.6
59061	NYE	96.9	96.6	0.4	0.4	0.0	0.0	2.7	3.9	3.0	3.4	4.3	4.7	3.0	20.2	39.1	20.2	2.1	86.3	51.6	53.6	46.4
59062	OTTER	96.6	96.2	0.0	0.0	0.2	0.3	0.0	0.0	6.4	7.2	7.7	6.2	3.6	18.7	33.6	15.4	1.3	74.6	45.2	49.7	50.3
59063	PARK CITY	97.4	96.8	0.1	0.2	0.2	0.3	1.1	1.6	5.3	5.8	6.4	6.7	5.7	22.6	34.4	12.0	1.0	77.9	42.7	49.9	50.1
59064	POMPEYS PILLAR	95.5	94.5	0.0	0.0	0.0	0.0	4.5	6.3	5.9	4.8	7.7	8.1	4.0	23.5	33.5	11.8	0.7	76.1	42.3	52.2	47.8
59065	PRAY	98.1	97.4	0.0	0.0	0.9	0.9	1.9	2.6	4.4	2.6	7.9	5.3	3.5	21.9	43.0	10.5	0.9	81.6	46.7	51.8	48.2
59067	RAPELJE	95.0	94.4	0.0	0.0	0.0	0.5	2.8	3.3	5.6	6.5	7.0	7.5	4.2	20.6	32.7	14.5	1.4	75.7	43.8	51.9	48.1
59068	RED LODGE	97.2	96.8	0.3	0.4	0.4	0.4	1.4	1.9	4.7	4.7	5.5	5.7	4.9	24.1	32.7	14.7	3.1	81.2	45.3	49.9	50.1
59069	REED POINT	95.6	94.7	0.0	0.0	0.3	0.4	2.6	3.1	5.1	6.0	7.1	7.3	4.2	21.1	33.1	14.4	1.6	77.1	44.3	52.2	47.8
59070	ROBERTS	98.1	97.6	0.0	0.0	0.2	0.2	0.7	1.1	4.3	5.6	7.8	7.1	2.3	22.8	33.6	13.9	2.6	77.2	45.1	52.1	47.9
59071	ROSCOE	98.3	97.6	0.0	0.0	0.0	0.0	0.8	0.8	4.8	5.6	8.1	7.3	2.4	23.4	32.3	13.7	2.4	75.8	44.2	52.4	47.6
59072	ROUNDUP	96.9	96.8	0.1	0.1	0.2	0.2	1.7	1.7	4.9	5.6	6.1	6.6	4.1	20.8	34.7	14.2	3.1	78.9	46.2	48.6	51.4
59074	RYEGATE	99.1	99.1	0.0	0.0	0.2	0.1	1.3	1.2	5.6	6.9	5.2	6.6	4.9	20.0	32.9	16.0	1.9	77.5	45.5	51.2	48.8
59075	SAINT XAVIER	47.7	43.7	0.0	0.0	0.0	0.0	9.2	10.7	8.6	8.6	8.6	9.1	5.6	25.4	25.4	8.6	0.0	67.5	33.1	50.8	49.2
59076	SANDERS	96.7	96.3	0.0	0.0	0.0	0.0	1.7	1.9	5.6	6.5	6.5	6.5	5.6	19.4	32.4	14.8	2.8	78.7	45.0	50.9	49.1
59077	SAND SPRINGS	98.7	98.6	0.0	0.0	0.0	0.0	0.0	0.0	5.7	8.6	7.1	4.3	2.9	22.9	31.4	12.9	4.3	75.7	43.8	51.4	48.6
59078	SHAWMUT	96.5	95.9	0.3	0.3	0.6	1.0	0.3	0.0	7.8	7.8	6.4	6.8	4.4	23.4	29.2	12.9	1.4	72.5	39.9	51.9	48.1
59079	SHEPHERD	96.3	95.4	0.1	0.2	0.1	0.2	1.9	2.7	6.7	6.9	7.5	8.0	5.8	25.4	31.2	7.8	0.6	73.9	37.5	51.4	48.6
59085	TWO DOT	97.4	97.1	0.1	0.1	0.2	0.2	1.4	1.8	5.5	5.8	7.1	6.0	4.8	19.0	30.8	17.3	3.7	77.3	46.6	48.8	51.2
59086	WILSALL	97.4	96.9	0.0	0.0	0.2	0.3	2.0	2.6	5.0	5.3	6.7	7.6	4.4	21.0	34.8	13.6	1.7	77.7	45.0	50.9	49.1
59087	WINNETT	99.2	99.2	0.0	0.0	0.0	0.0	1.2	1.2	6.6	7.0	7.6	6.0	3.4	20.7	32.1	14.7	2.0	74.9	44.1	53.6	46.4
59088	WORDEN	96.6	95.7	0.3	0.4	0.0	0.1	3.5	4.9	5.5	6.1	6.6	6.8	5.1	22.0	32.9	13.4	1.6	77.7	43.4	50.6	49.4
59089	WYOLA	28.7	24.6	0.0	0.0	0.2	0.2	2.5	2.6	9.1	9.5	8.8	7.1	4.7	26.3	25.0	8.6	0.9	67.9	32.6	51.9	48.1
59101	BILLINGS	87.1	84.9	0.8	1.0	0.5	0.6	7.0	8.9	7.4	6.8	6.4	6.6	7.2	29.3	26.3	8.7	1.4	75.5	35.0	50.1	49.9
59102	BILLINGS	94.9	93.8	0.4	0.5	0.6	0.8	2.3	3.2	5.8	5.5	5.7	6.7	6.3	23.8	26.3	15.7	4.2	79.3	41.8	46.7	53.3
59105	BILLINGS	94.0	92.6	0.4	0.4	0.7	0.9	2.7	3.7	6.7	6.8	7.0	7.1	6.2	25.9	29.4	9.7	1.1	75.0	37.7	49.4	50.6
59106	BILLINGS	96.3	95.2	0.2	0.2	0.9	1.1	1.9	2.7	5.5	6.6	8.0	8.7	4.9	20.6	35.1	9.8	0.9	73.9	41.9	50.8	49.2
59201	WOLF POINT	49.6	44.4	0.0	0.0	0.7	0.9	1.6	1.7	8.3	7.8	8.2	8.4	6.6	21.4	25.9	10.9	2.6	70.2	35.7	49.3	50.7
59211	ANTELOPE	97.0	96.7	0.0	0.0	0.0	0.0	1.2	1.3	5.3	6.6	6.0	5.3	4.0	19.2	33.8	17.2	2.6	78.8	47.5	51.7	48.3
59212	BAINVILLE	92.3	90.6	0.0	0.0	0.0	0.0	0.6	1.0	5.2	6.1	6.5	5.5	4.5	17.2	36.2	15.5	3.2	78.6	47.6	53.7	46.3
59213	BROCKTON	20.2	16.7	0.0	0.0	0.4	0.5	0.7	0.7	7.7	10.6	11.0	10.3	4.5	22.0	26.5	6.7	0.6	63.5	30.4	49.0	51.0
59214	BROCKWAY	98.9	98.6	0.0	0.0	0.0	0.0	0.6	0.7	3.4	4.1	5.4	6.8	4.7	20.9	37.2	14.9	2.7	83.1	46.8	51.4	48.6
59215	CIRCLE	97.3	96.9	0.4	0.5	0.1	0.1	0.9	1.1	5.6	5.6	6.3	6.8	5.5	19.6	31.4	16.4	3.1	78.5	45.5	48.6	51.4
59218	CULBERTSON	90.1	88.0	0.2	0.3	0.2	0.3	1.2	1.4	4.4	4.6	5.1	7.0	5.4	18.8	33.3	17.2	4.2	81.3	47.6	49.7	50.3
59219	DAGMAR	96.4	95.6	0.0	0.0	0.0	0.0	0.4	0.6	4.4	5.5	5.5	7.7	3.3	18.2	33.7	17.1	4.4	79.0	48.0	53.0	47.0
59221	FAIRVIEW	97.4	97.0	0.1	0.2	0.0	0.0	1.9	2.5	5.5	6.1	6.4	7.5	5.0	20.9	30.7	15.3	2.6	77.5	43.7	51.2	48.8
59222	FLAXVILLE	96.2	95.7	0.0	0.0	0.4	0.4	0.4	0.9	5.2	5.2	7.7	6.0	3.4	18.0	34.8	17.2	2.6	78.1	47.4	53.2	46.8
59223	FORT PECK	97.5	96.9	0.0	0.0	0.0	0.0	0.2	0.2	3.8	5.2	6.0	7.5	2.1	19.4	38.5	15.6	1.9	79.2	48.6	52.1	47.9
59225	FRAZER	34.7	29.4	0.1	0.2	0.0	0.0	0.3	0.3	9.0	9.0	8.6	8.8	7.5	25.1	22.9	8.3	0.8	67.8	29.6	49.9	50.1
59226	FROID	92.5	91.1	0.0	0.0	0.0	0.0	1.0	1.0	4.3	4.8	5.1	6.1	4.8	16.8	34.6	18.1	5.3	81.4	49.6	52.2	47.8
59230	GLASGOW	93.7	91.2	0.2	0.2	0.4	0.5	1.0	1.2	5.2	5.5	5.8	6.3	5.2	19.9	30.9	17.3	4.1	79.5	46.4	48.3	51.7
59241	HINSDALE	97.7	96.8	0.0	0.0	0.0	0.0	1.1	1.5	4.7	5.4	6.3	7.1	3.7	20.5	32.5	17.0	2.8	79.3	46.5	51.5	48.5
59242	HOMESTEAD	95.0	93.6	0.0	0.0	0.0	0.0	0.0	0.0	6.4	4.3	6.4	8.5	4.3	21.3	34.0	10.6	4.3	74.5	44.4	53.2	46.8
59243	LAMBERT	99.2	99.1	0.0	0.0	0.0	0.0	0.7	0.9	5.8	6.7	7.4	8.2	5.1	23.4	29.8	11.6	2.0	75.1	40.4	54.3	45.7
59244	LARSLAN	93.4	91.8	0.0	0.0	0.0	0.0	0.0	0.0	5.5	5.5	6.4	6.4	5.5	19.1	34.5	14.5	2.7	78.2	46.4	52.7	47.3
59247	MEDICINE LAKE	93.9	92.4	0.2	0.3	0.5	0.6	0.2	0.3	5.2	5.5	5.8	9.1	3.0	18.6	34.1	14.9	3.7	77.4	46.3	52.1	47.9
59248	NASHUA	81.4	78.7	0.0	0.0	0.0	0.0	0.2	0.3	5.3	6.4	6.7	7.6	4.5	21.8	32.5	13.4	1.7	75.9	43.2	49.6	50.4
59250	OPHEIM	98.0	96.6	0.0	0.0	0.0	0.0	0.8	1.5	4.4	5.4	5.9	6.9	3.4	20.1	33.8	17.2	2.9	79.9	47.5	52.0	48.0
59252	OUTLOOK	97.4	96.4	0.0	0.0	0.0	0.6	1.6	1.8	4.8	6.0	6.0	5.4	4.2	19.6	33.3	18.5	2.4	79.8	47.7	50.6	49.4
59253	PEERLESS	96.8	96.5	0.0	0.0	0.3	0.4	0.6	0.7	5.0	5.3	6.0	6.7	3.2	19.1	34.4	17.4	2.8	78.7	48.0	52.8	47.2
59254	PLENTYWOOD	97.3	96.6	0.1	0.1	0.4	0.5	1.2	1.4	4.4	4.7	4.9	6.0	5.5	17.6	32.3	19.1	5.6	81.7	49.3	48.7	51.3
59255	POPLAR	16.4	13.6	0.0	0.0	0.3	0.4	0.9	0.9	9.9	9.7	9.9	10.5	8.0	24.5	21.2	5.6	0.8	63.8	26.4	48.9	51.1
59256	RAYMOND	100.0	100.0	0.0	0.0	0.0	0.0	0.0	0.0	0.0	0.0	0.0	0.0	0.0	0.0	100.0	0.0	0.0	100.0	48.8	66.7	33.3
59257	REDSTONE	97.2	96.9	0.0	0.0	0.0	0.0	1.9	2.0	6.1	6.1	6.1	5.1	4.1	19.4	33.7	17.3	2.0	78.6	47.1	51.0	49.0
59258	RESERVE	98.3	98.1	0.0	0.0	0.0	0.0	3.4	4.8	4.8	6.7	5.8	6.7	1.9	12.5	42.3	17.3	1.9	77.9	51.3	52.9	47.1
59259	RICHEY	99.5	99.5	0.0	0.0	0.0	0.0	0.5	0.8	4.8	5.1	6.2	6.4	4.0	18.0	35.7	17.2	2.7	79.9	48.3	48.8	51.2
59260	RICHLAND	97.8	97.3	0.0	0.0	0.0	0.0	0.7	0.9	4.5	5.4	6.3	6.3	3.6	21.4	32.1	17.9	2.7	79.5	46.9	50.0	50.0
	MONTANA	90.6	89.7	0.3	0.4	0.6	0.7	2.0	2.6	6.0	6.1	6.5	7.3	7.0	24.2	29.0	11.8	2.1	77.1	39.4	49.8	50.2
	UNITED STATES	75.1	72.0	12.3	12.7	3.8	4.6	12.5	15.7	6.8	6.7	6.6	7.1	6.9	27.0	26.0	10.9	1.9	75.7	36.9	49.2	50.8

59001-59260

#	POST OFFICE NAME	2009 Per Capita Income	2009 HH Income Base	2009 Household Income Distribution (%): Less than $25,000	$25,000 to $49,999	$50,000 to $99,999	$100,000 to $149,999	$150,000 or More	Median Household Income: 2009	2014	2009 National Centile	2009 State Centile	2009 Home Value Base	2009 Home Value Distribution (%): Less than $50,000	$50,000 to $89,999	$90,000 to $174,999	$175,000 to $399,999	$400,000 or More	2009 Median Home Value
59001	ABSAROKEE	23404	685	22.9	27.4	39.3	8.9	1.5	49662	48054	60	92	495	8.5	5.5	28.5	44.4	13.1	193382
59002	ACTON	29174	43	16.3	25.6	44.2	7.0	7.0	58542	55311	76	99	40	2.5	5.0	17.5	60.0	15.0	227778
59003	ASHLAND	16932	169	33.7	30.2	31.4	3.0	1.8	36715	36755	23	58	96	26.0	10.4	29.2	25.0	9.4	113636
59006	BALLANTINE	19298	369	29.0	29.3	32.8	7.6	1.4	42217	45616	40	82	299	10.4	10.4	37.5	31.4	10.4	157986
59007	BEARCREEK	19219	141	34.0	28.4	34.0	3.5	0.0	38383	39525	28	69	113	5.3	5.3	22.1	46.9	20.4	230882
59008	BELFRY	19171	74	29.7	31.1	35.1	4.1	0.0	40000	41746	33	76	60	1.7	1.7	20.0	51.7	25.0	283333
59010	BIGHORN	15104	53	35.8	41.5	18.9	3.8	0.0	29614	32354	7	16	38	34.2	21.1	23.7	15.8	5.3	75000
59011	BIG TIMBER	21104	1308	30.1	34.5	27.9	4.8	2.7	38460	38999	28	69	978	9.2	8.1	36.8	32.3	13.6	163095
59012	BIRNEY	20883	46	34.8	32.6	28.3	2.2	2.2	35000	36108	18	48	27	25.9	11.1	29.6	25.9	7.4	112500
59014	BRIDGER	19317	721	33.0	32.7	29.5	3.7	1.0	36236	37387	21	55	538	9.7	13.0	35.9	31.0	10.4	151042
59015	BROADVIEW	25069	229	19.7	27.9	39.7	7.0	5.7	51954	52961	66	96	203	10.3	5.9	20.2	48.8	14.8	208871
59016	BUSBY	9308	432	35.9	43.3	18.8	2.1	0.0	33874	34343	15	39	231	26.4	20.3	31.6	9.5	12.1	95000
59019	COLUMBUS	20639	1454	23.3	32.4	36.2	5.8	2.2	45053	45193	48	87	1126	7.2	7.2	34.1	38.7	12.8	179775
59022	CROW AGENCY	11374	645	34.7	22.0	38.0	4.8	0.5	39313	40000	31	73	482	36.7	14.5	34.2	6.4	8.1	85714
59024	CUSTER	19057	164	31.1	32.9	28.7	6.1	1.2	37141	37997	24	61	129	12.4	7.8	26.4	24.8	28.7	193750
59025	DECKER	14178	68	54.4	27.9	17.6	0.0	0.0	23849	23730	3	3	41	9.8	48.8	26.8	12.2	2.4	86111
59027	EMIGRANT	21527	208	29.3	35.6	25.5	5.8	3.8	40294	41391	34	77	148	11.5	7.4	18.2	38.5	24.3	246429
59028	FISHTAIL	23366	256	22.3	26.6	42.2	6.6	2.3	50549	48636	62	93	183	4.4	2.2	25.7	45.4	22.4	242391
59029	FROMBERG	18946	381	30.7	33.6	30.4	3.1	2.1	37019	38010	24	60	301	13.6	13.6	36.9	25.2	10.6	137500
59030	GARDINER	26300	832	25.7	33.3	34.5	4.9	1.6	42301	44318	40	82	457	14.0	3.7	18.2	48.1	16.0	238500
59031	GARRYOWEN	13468	106	34.9	25.5	34.9	4.7	0.0	37369	37369	25	64	84	33.3	10.7	27.4	9.5	19.0	107692
59032	GRASS RANGE	17375	178	42.1	33.1	18.0	4.5	2.2	30307	30575	9	19	136	30.1	18.4	22.8	14.7	14.0	92857
59033	GREYCLIFF	19698	150	24.7	38.0	27.3	4.7	5.3	41234	42362	37	79	110	7.3	8.2	18.2	35.5	30.9	270833
59034	HARDIN	17228	1660	33.2	33.8	25.8	5.4	1.7	35038	35513	18	48	1030	14.4	19.3	46.3	15.4	4.6	116384
59037	HUNTLEY	21088	535	25.6	27.5	36.4	8.4	2.1	47428	48858	55	89	445	8.8	9.2	39.1	37.5	5.4	164063
59038	HYSHAM	15899	44	36.4	38.6	20.5	4.5	0.0	30000	30000	8	19	32	28.1	25.0	25.0	15.6	6.3	80000
59039	INGOMAR	24135	49	28.6	24.5	36.7	6.1	4.1	46164	45553	52	88	39	10.3	10.3	23.1	30.8	25.6	195833
59041	JOLIET	17785	700	33.3	33.7	28.6	3.6	0.9	36130	37751	21	54	552	8.9	7.4	30.6	39.3	13.8	184239
59043	LAME DEER	9830	784	46.0	26.3	24.0	3.1	0.6	27566	28334	5	7	371	40.4	20.2	31.8	7.5	0.0	70294
59044	LAUREL	21960	4226	28.0	28.4	34.6	6.3	2.7	44925	46866	48	86	3237	5.6	6.9	42.7	39.9	5.0	167188
59046	LAVINA	19108	249	41.4	30.5	23.7	2.8	1.6	31331	31810	10	23	197	10.7	21.3	31.0	24.9	12.2	141964
59047	LIVINGSTON	21458	5708	32.0	31.4	29.2	4.2	3.2	38469	38982	28	70	3888	8.8	7.7	40.2	33.0	10.3	156549
59050	LODGE GRASS	10667	894	41.2	32.9	23.6	1.2	1.1	29119	29692	7	12	588	28.4	15.6	34.9	12.2	8.8	99722
59052	MC LEOD	21880	97	23.7	37.1	28.9	5.2	5.2	42336	45388	40	83	71	8.5	7.0	16.9	36.6	31.0	282143
59053	MARTINSDALE	17706	107	36.4	38.3	20.6	3.7	0.9	34311	33641	16	42	76	18.4	13.2	30.3	31.6	6.6	125000
59055	MELVILLE	18587	29	27.6	41.4	24.1	3.4	3.4	34385	33802	16	42	22	4.5	4.5	22.7	27.3	40.9	300000
59057	MOLT	23019	255	21.2	30.2	37.6	6.3	4.7	48806	49660	58	91	220	12.3	7.3	21.8	45.0	13.6	195652
59058	MOSBY	0	0	0.0	0.0	0.0	0.0	0.0	0	0	0	0	0	0.0	0.0	0.0	0.0	0.0	0
59059	MUSSELSHELL	19700	179	33.0	39.1	20.7	3.4	3.9	32585	33257	13	30	152	18.4	8.6	32.9	28.3	11.8	147500
59061	NYE	27089	112	22.3	29.5	39.3	6.3	2.7	47883	45847	56	91	81	3.7	1.2	23.5	39.5	32.1	275000
59062	OTTER	19164	167	30.5	36.5	26.9	3.6	2.4	36569	37126	22	58	124	21.0	16.1	26.6	18.5	17.7	131250
59063	PARK CITY	19519	704	22.0	33.0	38.8	4.5	1.7	45664	45452	50	88	592	11.8	9.5	30.9	40.9	6.9	169758
59064	POMPEYS PILLAR	19440	116	31.0	34.5	26.7	6.0	1.7	36878	37285	23	60	91	9.9	7.7	29.7	24.2	28.6	190625
59065	PRAY	28449	55	20.0	36.4	32.7	7.3	3.6	46350	46436	52	89	41	2.4	2.4	14.6	46.3	34.1	327778
59067	RAPELJE	15374	88	36.4	37.5	23.9	2.3	0.0	33409	33799	14	35	64	26.6	10.9	35.9	20.3	6.3	125000
59068	RED LODGE	24224	1665	26.0	30.5	34.5	6.7	2.4	43887	45500	45	85	1151	4.9	5.0	24.2	47.2	18.8	227560
59069	REED POINT	17782	182	33.5	36.8	24.7	3.3	1.6	35000	35866	18	48	134	21.6	11.2	29.9	23.1	14.2	136538
59070	ROBERTS	18849	371	29.9	39.6	24.3	5.1	1.1	35716	36847	20	53	295	14.2	7.1	23.4	32.9	22.4	195395
59071	ROSCOE	20112	56	30.4	39.3	25.0	5.4	0.0	35715	36091	20	52	45	17.8	6.7	24.4	28.9	22.2	179167
59072	ROUNDUP	17733	1703	41.4	31.7	22.1	2.8	1.9	29713	30504	8	16	1291	20.6	18.7	31.9	22.3	6.5	112323
59074	RYEGATE	14039	215	40.0	31.6	23.3	3.3	1.9	32098	31241	12	26	167	9.6	27.5	31.7	19.2	12.0	122500
59075	SAINT XAVIER	11897	59	39.0	22.0	39.0	0.0	0.0	32954	32320	13	32	41	0.0	17.1	48.8	17.1	17.1	145833
59076	SANDERS	15237	43	37.2	37.2	20.9	4.7	0.0	32375	32341	12	28	31	29.0	25.8	22.6	16.1	6.5	77500
59077	SAND SPRINGS	16399	29	41.4	34.5	20.7	3.4	0.0	29028	30000	7	11	21	33.3	19.0	19.0	9.5	19.0	85000
59078	SHAWMUT	9384	77	51.9	32.5	14.3	1.3	0.0	24163	25000	3	3	57	19.3	35.1	26.3	10.5	8.8	83750
59079	SHEPHERD	19123	1155	23.5	28.8	37.5	8.7	1.4	47501	49503	55	90	978	6.6	8.3	29.8	45.9	9.4	185400
59085	TWO DOT	16379	607	41.2	34.6	20.8	3.0	0.5	29945	30294	8	18	441	20.4	32.9	34.2	8.2	4.3	86548
59086	WILSALL	18837	452	32.1	37.4	23.0	4.4	3.1	36522	36983	22	57	333	7.8	11.4	27.6	34.5	18.6	186413
59087	WINNETT	17279	218	46.3	32.1	16.1	2.8	2.8	27467	28094	5	7	164	29.3	18.3	32.9	12.8	6.7	94444
59088	WORDEN	18963	555	34.8	31.9	25.9	4.3	3.1	36248	36911	21	55	426	10.1	13.6	32.4	37.3	6.6	165441
59089	WYOLA	11288	141	45.4	31.9	18.4	3.5	0.7	27086	27257	5	6	106	34.0	13.2	37.7	11.3	3.8	101923
59101	BILLINGS	18499	15981	36.4	32.0	26.2	3.8	1.6	34725	35354	17	45	9061	12.3	8.5	47.5	28.0	3.8	145454
59102	BILLINGS	26991	20402	21.0	28.2	38.0	7.8	5.0	50608	51750	63	93	14101	4.6	3.2	35.7	52.8	3.8	184135
59105	BILLINGS	22915	10411	19.4	29.4	38.9	8.7	3.7	50991	51704	64	95	7640	5.0	4.9	26.3	59.4	4.5	195284
59106	BILLINGS	36662	3970	11.9	20.5	35.1	14.6	17.9	71210	71504	87	100	3603	4.9	2.1	12.5	59.0	21.5	288466
59201	WOLF POINT	15268	1697	36.5	32.0	25.2	4.2	2.1	33599	34250	15	36	1128	22.7	28.0	40.0	6.1	3.2	89012
59211	ANTELOPE	22390	66	28.8	42.4	21.2	4.5	3.0	37645	36579	26	65	54	46.3	14.8	31.5	7.4	0.0	60000
59212	BAINVILLE	20494	135	34.1	37.8	20.7	3.7	3.7	32097	33899	12	26	113	38.9	25.7	20.4	7.1	8.0	65000
59213	BROCKTON	11648	270	49.3	23.7	21.1	4.4	1.5	25406	25931	3	4	198	28.8	27.8	30.8	10.1	2.5	80000
59214	BROCKWAY	18764	63	34.9	36.5	22.2	3.2	3.2	34296	33610	16	41	50	34.0	28.0	26.0	4.0	8.0	73333
59215	CIRCLE	17576	431	34.3	35.5	27.1	1.9	1.2	34636	35821	17	44	324	37.3	30.2	23.5	4.9	4.0	66400
59218	CULBERTSON	16927	318	34.6	33.6	27.7	3.8	0.3	33704	34833	15	38	239	32.2	32.2	28.9	5.4	1.3	68393
59219	DAGMAR	16495	71	32.4	43.7	18.3	4.2	1.4	34520	34045	17	44	57	56.1	15.8	21.1	5.3	1.8	41250
59221	FAIRVIEW	17402	560	34.5	34.6	26.3	3.6	1.1	33342	33878	14	34	412	26.7	35.0	24.3	12.1	1.9	73125
59222	FLAXVILLE	16910	107	40.2	36.4	19.6	2.8	0.9	29260	30000	7	14	86	31.4	27.9	19.8	12.8	8.1	70000
59223	FORT PECK	20085	202	23.3	38.6	35.1	2.5	0.5	41537	45090	38	80	173	6.9	13.3	52.6	24.3	2.9	133203
59225	FRAZER	10953	181	42.5	37.6	16.0	1.7	2.2	27669	28090	5	8	127	49.6	16.5	16.5	10.2	7.1	50385
59226	FROID	20925	182	36.3	33.5	23.1	4.9	2.2	33301	35446	14	33	156	38.5	28.8	25.0	3.2	4.5	62500
59230	GLASGOW	20262	1986	32.5	31.1	30.0	4.1	2.3	37971	38426	27	68	1477	24.4	29.2	38.5	7.1	0.7	85420
59241	HINSDALE	20294	198	35.4	30.8	27.3	3.0	3.5	33503	33741	14	36	157	34.4	22.9	22.3	12.1	8.3	74500
59242	HOMESTEAD	19470	22	31.8	45.5	18.2	4.5	0.0	35000	35000	18	48	17	70.6	11.8	17.6	0.0	0.0	28750
59243	LAMBERT	15760	207	36.7	35.7	22.7	2.4	2.4	32277	32614	12	27	164	31.1	19.5	23.8	18.9	6.7	89000
59244	LARSLAN	16393	44	40.9	40.9	9.1	4.5	4.5	26858	26835	5	6	34	41.2	11.8	20.6	5.9	20.6	57500
59247	MEDICINE LAKE	18523	144	34.7	40.3	18.1	5.6	1.4	35281	35454	19	50	111	61.3	13.5	18.0	4.5	2.7	37500
59248	NASHUA	20301	147	27.9	39.5	26.5	2.7	3.4	38092	38829	27	68	119	22.7	16.8	37.0	17.6	5.9	115179
59250	OPHEIM	22431	96	35.4	33.3	24.0	3.1	4.2	33176	33358	14	33	76	32.9	23.7	21.1	13.2	9.2	76000
59252	OUTLOOK	18793	74	33.8	37.8	23.0	4.1	1.4	35733	38159	20	53	60	38.3	20.0	33.3	8.3	0.0	75000
59253	PEERLESS	16648	119	35.3	37.8	23.5	2.5	0.8	32873	32868	13	31	95	31.6	23.2	21.1	14.7	9.5	79286
59254	PLENTYWOOD	18359	848	36.0	34.1	24.4	3.9	1.7	33590	35048	15	36	669	29.6	31.2	33.9	4.5	0.7	75196
59255	POPLAR	10698	974	48.3	30.0	17.6	3.4	0.8	25779	26739	4	5	528	30.1	28.4	33.7	6.1	1.7	74286
59256	RAYMOND	0	0	0.0	0.0	0.0	0.0	0.0	0	0	0	0	0	0.0	0.0	0.0	0.0	0.0	0
59257	REDSTONE	20306	45	31.1	42.2	20.0	4.4	2.2	37278	36825	24	63	37	43.2	16.2	32.4	8.1	0.0	67500
59258	RESERVE	17276	47	36.2	44.7	14.9	2.1	2.1	31310	31678	10	23	43	41.9	4.7	44.2	9.3	0.0	97500
59259	RICHEY	18487	165	41.8	32.1	18.8	4.8	2.4	31701	31902	11	25	129	65.1	11.6	16.3	7.0	0.0	37750
59260	RICHLAND	21862	51	37.3	29.4	27.5	3.9	2.0	32330	33176	12	27	40	37.5	27.5	15.0	12.5	7.5	67500
	MONTANA	21013		28.7	31.3	31.1	5.8	3.0	40864	42494				10.4	9.4	31.4	38.6	10.1	171793
	UNITED STATES	27277		20.9	24.4	35.3	11.7	7.6	54719	56938				9.3	13.1	31.6	32.6	13.5	162279

ZIP CODE #	POST OFFICE NAME	FINANCIAL SERVICES: Auto Loan	FINANCIAL SERVICES: Home Loan	FINANCIAL SERVICES: Invest-ments	FINANCIAL SERVICES: Retire-ment Plans	THE HOME: Home Improvements: Home Repair	THE HOME: Home Improvements: Lawn & Garden	THE HOME: Furnishings: Comput-ers & Hard-ware-Personal	THE HOME: Furnishings: Major Appli-ances	THE HOME: Furnishings: TV, Radio, Sound Equip-ment	THE HOME: Furnishings: Furni-ture	ENTERTAINMENT: Dine out/ Carry out	ENTERTAINMENT: Sports Equip-ment	ENTERTAINMENT: Fees & Tickets	ENTERTAINMENT: Toys & Games	ENTERTAINMENT: Travel	ENTERTAINMENT: Cable TV	PERSONAL: Apparel & Services	PERSONAL: Auto Repairs	PERSONAL: Health Insur-ance	PERSONAL: Pets & Supplies
59001	ABSAROKEE	87	77	85	79	79	93	76	88	79	69	78	67	69	80	77	84	53	82	91	103
59002	ACTON	99	112	96	115	108	110	100	104	98	100	99	81	107	101	105	98	69	100	103	122
59003	ASHLAND	69	64	56	62	62	65	60	64	62	63	63	46	57	65	57	64	43	62	64	76
59006	BALLANTINE	85	70	78	69	70	83	70	79	73	68	73	60	61	74	67	77	49	75	80	94
59007	BEARCREEK	70	56	91	55	62	74	56	71	59	53	58	52	49	56	61	63	39	66	70	83
59008	BELFRY	76	61	98	60	66	80	61	77	63	57	63	56	53	60	66	68	42	71	76	89
59010	BIGHORN	69	47	76	47	50	73	53	65	55	43	54	54	38	54	52	60	35	61	69	80
59011	BIG TIMBER	84	64	91	63	67	87	67	81	71	61	70	62	55	69	68	76	46	76	84	97
59012	BIRNEY	70	64	57	62	63	66	61	64	63	63	63	47	57	65	58	65	43	62	64	76
59014	BRIDGER	77	57	84	56	61	80	60	75	66	55	64	56	50	64	61	72	43	70	79	88
59015	BROADVIEW	96	99	96	101	97	105	92	99	91	89	91	78	92	93	96	93	63	94	99	117
59016	BUSBY	53	45	37	47	40	49	50	46	54	50	53	36	48	54	45	56	37	50	52	59
59019	COLUMBUS	85	70	91	70	74	89	70	84	73	65	72	63	61	73	72	78	49	78	86	98
59022	CROW AGENCY	67	66	59	59	65	57	65	65	62	70	63	49	61	63	63	59	44	65	58	72
59024	CUSTER	81	56	89	56	59	86	62	77	65	50	64	64	46	63	62	71	42	72	82	95
59025	DECKER	56	38	61	38	40	59	42	53	44	34	44	44	31	43	42	48	28	49	56	65
59027	EMIGRANT	88	70	114	69	77	93	70	90	74	66	73	65	61	70	76	79	48	83	88	104
59028	FISHTAIL	92	74	119	73	81	98	74	94	77	69	76	69	64	73	80	82	51	87	93	109
59029	FROMBERG	83	60	88	59	63	85	62	79	68	58	67	59	50	67	62	75	44	72	81	93
59030	GARDINER	78	71	88	72	73	79	72	78	73	71	73	59	69	71	74	75	50	76	78	92
59031	GARRYOWEN	72	58	70	54	59	69	59	68	61	58	61	52	50	62	58	64	41	65	67	80
59032	GRASS RANGE	74	51	81	51	53	78	56	70	58	46	58	58	41	57	56	64	38	65	74	86
59033	GREYCLIFF	100	68	109	68	72	105	76	94	79	62	78	78	56	78	76	86	51	88	100	116
59034	HARDIN	70	54	65	54	54	69	61	66	65	54	63	52	51	64	57	69	43	66	72	80
59037	HUNTLEY	88	80	78	79	79	87	76	83	79	77	79	62	72	81	74	82	54	79	84	98
59038	HYSHAM	70	48	77	48	50	74	53	66	55	43	55	55	39	54	53	60	36	62	70	82
59039	INGOMAR	96	66	105	66	69	101	73	91	76	59	75	75	54	75	73	83	49	85	96	112
59041	JOLIET	75	55	84	54	58	78	57	72	61	51	60	56	46	60	58	67	40	67	74	86
59043	LAME DEER	54	47	38	47	42	49	50	47	53	50	53	37	48	54	45	54	36	50	51	59
59044	LAUREL	84	78	80	78	79	88	76	84	79	74	78	62	72	80	76	82	53	80	87	98
59046	LAVINA	71	49	77	49	52	74	54	67	57	45	56	54	40	56	54	62	37	63	71	82
59047	LIVINGSTON	76	63	77	62	65	76	66	74	69	63	68	55	59	68	65	73	46	72	77	87
59050	LODGE GRASS	61	47	56	47	47	60	50	56	54	47	53	43	43	54	48	57	36	54	59	68
59052	MC LEOD	100	71	114	71	75	106	77	96	81	64	80	78	59	78	78	87	52	90	101	117
59053	MARTINSDALE	69	47	75	47	49	72	52	65	55	42	54	54	38	53	52	59	35	61	69	80
59055	MELVILLE	79	54	87	54	57	83	60	75	63	49	62	62	44	62	60	69	40	70	79	92
59057	MOLT	94	92	95	94	91	102	87	95	87	82	87	76	84	88	90	89	60	91	96	114
59058	MOSBY	0	0	0	0	0	0	0	0	0	0	0	0	0	0	0	0	0	0	0	0
59059	MUSSELSHELL	86	59	94	59	62	90	65	81	68	53	67	67	48	67	65	74	44	76	86	100
59061	NYE	93	72	117	71	79	98	74	93	77	68	76	69	62	73	79	82	50	86	93	109
59062	OTTER	80	55	88	55	58	84	61	76	64	50	63	63	45	62	61	69	41	71	80	93
59063	PARK CITY	81	75	66	72	73	76	70	74	73	73	73	54	67	76	67	75	50	72	75	88
59064	POMPEYS PILLAR	82	56	90	56	59	86	62	77	65	50	64	64	46	63	62	71	42	72	82	95
59065	PRAY	98	79	127	77	86	104	79	100	82	74	81	73	68	78	85	88	54	92	99	116
59067	RAPELJE	67	46	73	46	48	71	51	63	53	41	53	52	37	52	51	58	34	59	67	78
59068	RED LODGE	79	70	84	70	72	81	72	79	74	70	73	59	67	73	73	77	50	77	82	93
59069	REED POINT	78	54	87	54	57	83	60	75	62	49	62	61	44	61	60	68	40	70	79	92
59070	ROBERTS	79	54	87	54	57	83	60	75	63	49	62	62	44	62	60	68	40	70	79	92
59071	ROSCOE	79	55	88	55	58	84	61	76	63	50	63	62	45	62	61	69	41	71	80	93
59072	ROUNDUP	72	51	74	50	53	75	55	69	60	48	59	53	43	59	54	66	39	64	73	82
59074	RYEGATE	72	50	79	49	52	76	55	68	57	45	57	57	40	56	55	62	37	64	72	84
59075	SAINT XAVIER	64	58	53	56	57	60	55	59	57	57	57	43	51	59	52	59	39	57	59	70
59076	SANDERS	68	47	75	47	49	72	52	65	54	42	54	54	38	53	52	59	35	61	69	80
59077	SAND SPRINGS	70	48	77	48	50	74	53	66	56	43	55	55	39	54	53	61	36	62	70	82
59078	SHAWMUT	53	36	58	36	38	55	40	50	42	33	41	41	29	41	40	46	27	47	53	61
59079	SHEPHERD	87	78	75	76	77	84	75	81	77	76	77	60	69	80	72	80	52	78	82	97
59085	TWO DOT	64	45	67	44	47	67	49	61	53	42	52	48	38	52	48	58	34	57	65	73
59086	WILSALL	80	58	92	58	62	85	62	78	65	53	64	62	49	63	64	70	42	72	81	94
59087	WINNETT	71	49	78	49	51	75	54	68	57	44	56	56	40	55	54	62	36	63	71	83
59088	WORDEN	82	60	82	58	62	82	61	76	67	58	66	57	50	67	60	73	44	70	79	91
59089	WYOLA	65	44	71	44	46	68	49	61	51	40	51	51	36	51	49	56	33	57	65	75
59101	BILLINGS	63	55	50	57	53	58	63	58	64	60	64	46	58	64	57	65	44	62	62	71
59102	BILLINGS	85	86	85	87	87	91	86	87	88	85	88	64	87	87	87	91	61	88	95	102
59105	BILLINGS	89	88	79	88	85	85	87	86	87	88	87	66	86	89	85	86	61	86	85	102
59106	BILLINGS	144	168	157	173	168	160	146	152	141	152	142	118	161	145	156	139	102	144	143	176
59201	WOLF POINT	70	53	64	53	52	70	59	65	63	53	62	51	49	63	55	68	42	64	71	79
59211	ANTELOPE	92	63	101	63	66	97	70	87	73	57	72	72	51	71	70	79	47	81	92	107
59212	BAINVILLE	84	58	92	58	60	89	64	80	67	52	66	66	47	65	64	73	43	74	84	98
59213	BROCKTON	68	47	75	47	49	72	52	64	54	42	53	53	38	53	52	59	35	60	68	79
59214	BROCKWAY	79	54	87	54	57	83	60	75	63	49	62	62	44	61	60	68	40	70	79	92
59215	CIRCLE	71	50	73	49	52	74	55	68	60	48	58	53	43	59	54	66	39	64	74	81
59218	CULBERTSON	71	51	72	49	53	73	54	68	60	49	59	51	43	60	53	67	39	63	73	80
59219	DAGMAR	75	52	83	52	54	79	57	71	60	47	59	59	42	59	57	65	38	67	75	88
59221	FAIRVIEW	71	50	74	49	52	74	55	68	60	47	58	53	42	59	54	65	38	64	73	82
59222	FLAXVILLE	66	45	72	45	47	69	50	62	52	41	52	52	37	51	50	57	34	58	66	77
59223	FORT PECK	80	63	102	62	69	85	64	81	67	59	66	60	54	64	68	71	44	75	81	95
59225	FRAZER	59	47	48	49	44	56	52	53	56	50	55	42	47	56	48	59	37	55	58	67
59226	FROID	79	56	83	55	58	81	59	74	64	52	63	57	46	63	58	70	41	68	77	89
59230	GLASGOW	74	60	75	59	61	79	63	73	67	56	66	56	54	66	62	73	44	69	80	86
59241	HINSDALE	85	58	93	58	61	90	65	81	68	53	67	67	48	66	65	74	43	75	85	99
59242	HOMESTEAD	74	51	82	51	54	78	57	71	59	46	58	58	42	58	57	64	38	66	75	87
59243	LAMBERT	75	52	82	51	54	79	57	71	60	46	59	59	42	58	57	65	38	66	75	88
59244	LARSLAN	72	50	80	50	52	76	55	69	58	45	57	57	41	56	55	63	37	64	73	85
59247	MEDICINE LAKE	75	52	83	52	54	80	58	72	60	47	59	59	42	59	57	65	38	67	76	88
59248	NASHUA	83	63	93	63	66	86	67	80	70	60	69	62	55	68	68	75	46	76	83	96
59250	OPHEIM	85	59	94	58	61	90	65	81	68	53	67	67	48	66	65	74	43	76	85	100
59252	OUTLOOK	76	52	84	52	55	80	58	72	60	47	60	60	43	59	58	66	39	67	76	89
59253	PEERLESS	67	46	74	46	48	71	51	64	53	41	53	53	37	52	51	58	34	59	67	78
59254	PLENTYWOOD	73	51	77	51	54	77	57	70	61	48	60	55	43	60	56	67	39	65	75	84
59255	POPLAR	53	44	41	45	40	50	48	47	52	47	51	37	44	52	44	54	35	50	53	60
59256	RAYMOND	0	0	0	0	0	0	0	0	0	0	0	0	0	0	0	0	0	0	0	0
59257	REDSTONE	79	54	87	54	57	83	60	75	63	49	62	62	44	62	60	69	40	70	79	92
59258	RESERVE	65	45	72	45	47	69	50	62	52	41	51	51	37	51	50	57	33	58	66	76
59259	RICHEY	75	51	82	51	54	79	57	71	59	46	59	59	42	58	57	65	38	66	75	87
59260	RICHLAND	86	59	94	59	62	91	66	81	68	53	67	67	48	67	65	74	44	76	86	100
	MONTANA	80	69	77	69	70	79	73	77	75	69	74	59	67	74	71	77	51	76	80	92
	UNITED STATES	100	100	100	100	100	100	100	100	100	100	100	100	100	100	100	100	100	100	100	100

#	POST OFFICE NAME	COUNTY FIPS CODE	POPULATION 2000	POPULATION 2009	POPULATION 2014	2000-2009 ANNUAL RATE % Rate	2000-2009 ANNUAL RATE State Centile	HOUSEHOLDS 2000	HOUSEHOLDS 2009	HOUSEHOLDS 2014	HOUSEHOLDS % Annual Rate 2000-2009	HOUSEHOLDS 2009 Average HH Size	FAMILIES 2000	FAMILIES 2009	FAMILIES % Annual Rate 2000-2009
59261	SACO	071	192	184	180	-0.5	32	69	68	67	-0.2	2.68	46	44	-0.5
59262	SAVAGE	083	1034	948	932	-0.9	14	392	370	367	-0.6	2.56	287	264	-0.9
59263	SCOBEY	019	1305	1172	1102	-1.2	10	587	541	513	-0.9	2.10	350	310	-1.3
59270	SIDNEY	083	6586	6484	6473	-0.2	45	2668	2700	2722	0.1	2.36	1799	1767	-0.2
59274	VIDA	055	257	246	236	-0.5	32	108	107	103	-0.1	2.30	83	81	-0.3
59275	WESTBY	091	382	331	300	-1.5	6	178	159	145	-1.2	2.08	123	106	-1.6
59276	WHITETAIL	019	132	116	108	-1.4	7	58	53	50	-1.0	2.19	40	35	-1.4
59301	MILES CITY	017	10563	10138	9929	-0.4	37	4347	4223	4149	-0.3	2.30	2774	2603	-0.7
59311	ALZADA	011	95	89	85	-0.7	21	37	35	34	-0.6	2.54	28	26	-0.8
59312	ANGELA	087	42	41	41	-0.3	42	20	20	20	0.0	2.05	15	15	0.0
59313	BAKER	025	2403	2344	2330	-0.3	42	965	966	969	0.0	2.38	670	651	-0.3
59314	BIDDLE	075	459	420	402	-1.0	13	175	163	157	-0.8	2.58	137	125	-1.0
59315	BLOOMFIELD	021	229	225	222	-0.2	45	85	85	85	0.0	2.62	64	63	-0.2
59316	BOYES	011	85	79	76	-0.8	18	29	27	26	-0.8	2.93	22	20	-1.0
59317	BROADUS	075	858	809	783	-0.6	27	339	322	312	-0.6	2.41	227	208	-0.9
59318	BRUSETT	033	182	170	163	-0.7	21	79	77	75	-0.3	2.21	55	52	-0.6
59322	COHAGEN	033	279	258	248	-0.8	18	109	105	102	-0.4	2.42	74	70	-0.6
59324	EKALAKA	011	874	834	807	-0.5	32	357	343	332	-0.4	2.38	241	225	-0.7
59326	FALLON	079	289	256	240	-1.3	9	126	115	109	-1.0	2.23	94	84	-1.2
59327	FORSYTH	087	3148	3050	2998	-0.3	42	1339	1329	1316	-0.1	2.25	876	840	-0.5
59330	GLENDIVE	021	8353	7890	7725	-0.6	27	3332	3214	3170	-0.4	2.30	2258	2108	-0.7
59332	HAMMOND	011	257	240	229	-0.7	21	97	92	88	-0.6	2.61	74	68	-0.9
59336	ISMAY	017	340	328	321	-0.4	37	122	121	119	-0.1	2.71	100	96	-0.4
59337	JORDAN	033	726	676	649	-0.8	18	309	301	293	-0.3	2.23	213	202	-0.6
59338	KINSEY	017	378	365	356	-0.4	37	135	133	131	-0.2	2.74	111	107	-0.4
59339	LINDSAY	021	92	90	90	-0.2	45	41	41	41	0.0	2.17	32	31	-0.3
59341	MILDRED	079	76	67	63	-1.4	7	28	26	24	-0.8	2.58	21	19	-1.1
59343	OLIVE	075	56	53	52	-0.6	27	22	21	21	-0.5	2.52	16	15	-0.7
59344	PLEVNA	025	373	363	360	-0.3	42	152	152	152	0.0	2.39	117	114	-0.3
59345	POWDERVILLE	075	18	17	17	-0.6	27	9	9	8	0.0	1.89	7	6	-1.7
59347	ROSEBUD	087	3142	3000	2944	-0.5	32	1120	1097	1086	-0.2	2.73	893	857	-0.4
59349	TERRY	079	834	745	699	-1.2	10	383	352	333	-0.9	2.05	240	212	-1.3
59351	VOLBORG	017	494	475	463	-0.4	37	192	189	185	-0.2	2.51	129	122	-0.6
59353	WIBAUX	109	1068	976	931	-1.0	13	421	389	372	-0.9	2.41	287	257	-1.2
59354	WILLARD	025	42	41	41	-0.3	42	16	16	16	0.0	2.56	12	12	0.0
59401	GREAT FALLS	013	14665	14115	13913	-0.4	37	6563	6311	6229	-0.4	2.19	3533	3259	-0.9
59402	MALMSTROM A F B	013	2128	1828	1728	-1.6	6	679	575	542	-1.8	2.81	597	498	-1.9
59404	GREAT FALLS	013	24827	25799	26178	0.4	61	9527	10000	10186	0.5	2.56	7071	7244	0.3
59405	GREAT FALLS	013	29239	29627	29725	0.1	53	12037	12352	12479	0.3	2.30	7534	7384	-0.2
59410	AUGUSTA	049	896	955	992	0.7	71	358	390	410	0.9	2.32	236	245	0.4
59411	BABB	035	538	567	573	0.6	66	178	186	188	0.5	3.05	136	138	0.2
59412	BELT	013	1649	1796	1847	0.9	77	656	714	735	0.9	2.52	455	479	0.6
59414	BLACK EAGLE	013	924	922	925	0.0	52	422	428	433	0.2	2.15	283	277	-0.2
59416	BRADY	073	322	301	290	-0.7	21	131	123	118	-0.7	2.45	100	92	-0.9
59417	BROWNING	035	7832	7823	7803	0.0	52	2286	2288	2282	0.0	3.36	1839	1805	-0.2
59418	BUFFALO	027	99	98	97	-0.1	48	36	36	36	0.0	2.58	28	27	-0.4
59419	BYNUM	099	147	142	138	-0.4	37	49	47	45	-0.4	3.02	39	36	-0.9
59420	CARTER	015	260	216	198	-2.0	3	112	95	88	-1.8	2.27	82	67	-2.2
59421	CASCADE	013	2759	2841	2870	0.3	58	1107	1155	1173	0.5	2.41	808	815	0.1
59422	CHOTEAU	099	3012	2836	2729	-0.6	27	1202	1130	1088	-0.7	2.45	779	705	-1.1
59424	COFFEE CREEK	027	117	113	111	-0.4	37	50	50	49	0.0	2.12	37	36	-0.3
59425	CONRAD	073	3550	3363	3238	-0.6	27	1448	1377	1328	-0.5	2.40	986	906	-0.9
59427	CUT BANK	035	4937	5024	5024	0.2	57	1850	1880	1879	0.2	2.65	1288	1271	-0.1
59430	DENTON	027	578	560	548	-0.3	42	233	231	228	-0.1	2.28	174	168	-0.4
59433	DUTTON	099	725	746	742	0.3	58	295	308	308	0.5	2.42	213	216	0.2
59434	EAST GLACIER PARK	035	47	49	49	0.5	63	23	24	24	0.5	2.04	14	14	0.0
59436	FAIRFIELD	099	1878	1780	1730	-0.6	27	727	697	679	-0.5	2.55	527	490	-0.8
59440	FLOWEREE	015	183	163	156	-1.2	10	76	69	66	-1.0	2.36	54	47	-1.5
59441	FOREST GROVE	027	88	86	84	-0.2	45	37	37	36	0.0	2.16	27	26	-0.4
59442	FORT BENTON	015	1987	1709	1592	-1.6	6	789	688	642	-1.5	2.33	536	449	-1.9
59443	FORT SHAW	013	730	710	702	-0.3	42	274	271	269	-0.1	2.62	208	200	-0.4
59444	GALATA	101	68	60	58	-1.3	9	28	25	24	-1.2	2.40	21	19	-1.1
59446	GERALDINE	015	642	557	521	-1.5	6	253	225	211	-1.3	2.48	187	159	-1.7
59447	GEYSER	045	431	420	411	-0.3	42	152	147	143	-0.4	2.86	113	106	-0.7
59448	HEART BUTTE	073	756	770	768	0.2	57	184	189	189	0.3	3.99	157	158	0.1
59450	HIGHWOOD	015	478	446	423	-0.7	21	172	164	157	-0.5	2.72	131	120	-0.9
59451	HILGER	027	773	750	733	-0.3	42	260	258	255	-0.1	2.72	194	187	-0.4
59452	HOBSON	045	698	672	659	-0.4	37	288	278	273	-0.4	2.41	211	198	-0.7
59453	JUDITH GAP	107	300	283	274	-0.6	27	119	113	109	-0.6	2.12	88	82	-0.8
59454	KEVIN	101	228	217	210	-0.5	32	95	87	84	-0.9	2.49	70	63	-1.1
59456	LEDGER	073	39	38	37	-0.3	42	12	12	11	0.0	3.17	10	10	0.0
59457	LEWISTOWN	027	8420	8101	7924	-0.4	37	3583	3520	3467	-0.2	2.20	2247	2127	-0.6
59460	LOMA	015	217	231	231	0.7	71	91	99	99	0.9	2.26	71	75	0.6
59462	MOCCASIN	045	174	167	164	-0.4	37	66	64	63	-0.3	2.61	48	45	-0.7
59463	MONARCH	013	93	104	108	1.2	86	42	47	49	1.2	2.21	32	35	1.0
59464	MOORE	027	578	570	565	-0.2	45	199	201	201	0.1	2.69	153	151	-0.1
59465	NEIHART	013	193	212	219	1.0	79	94	104	108	1.1	2.04	72	78	0.9
59466	OILMONT	101	96	86	82	-1.2	10	39	35	33	-1.2	2.46	29	25	-1.6
59467	PENDROY	099	109	100	95	-0.9	14	44	40	38	-1.0	2.50	34	31	-1.0
59468	POWER	099	669	682	680	0.2	57	253	262	263	0.4	2.60	192	194	0.1
59469	RAYNESFORD	045	203	199	196	-0.2	45	80	77	76	-0.4	2.58	59	56	-0.6
59471	ROY	027	409	398	391	-0.3	42	124	123	122	-0.1	3.04	91	87	-0.5
59472	SAND COULEE	013	594	603	604	0.2	57	209	211	211	0.1	2.86	153	149	-0.3
59474	SHELBY	101	3813	3827	3753	0.0	52	1428	1366	1336	-0.5	2.36	911	841	-0.9
59479	STANFORD	045	864	815	797	-0.6	27	381	361	353	-0.6	2.26	242	221	-1.0
59480	STOCKETT	013	541	542	541	0.0	52	201	203	204	0.1	2.67	148	144	-0.3
59482	SUNBURST	101	815	746	716	-1.0	13	288	258	247	-1.2	2.89	215	188	-1.4
59483	SUN RIVER	013	839	834	830	-0.1	48	308	307	307	0.0	2.45	237	230	-0.3
59484	SWEET GRASS	101	247	235	227	-0.5	32	84	77	74	-0.9	3.05	62	56	-1.1
59486	VALIER	073	1661	1465	1398	-1.3	9	606	535	512	-1.3	2.74	458	395	-1.6
59487	VAUGHN	013	1166	1139	1130	-0.3	42	431	428	427	-0.1	2.66	324	313	-0.4
59489	WINIFRED	027	312	304	298	-0.3	42	134	133	132	-0.1	2.14	98	95	-0.3
59501	HAVRE	041	13074	13037	13079	0.0	52	5308	5318	5363	0.0	2.36	3376	3268	-0.4
59520	BIG SANDY	015	2223	2314	2291	0.4	61	739	752	741	0.2	2.96	556	557	0.0
59521	BOX ELDER	041	2066	2022	2009	-0.2	45	531	530	530	0.0	3.82	451	443	-0.2
	MONTANA					0.8					0.9	2.43			0.5
	UNITED STATES					1.0					1.1	2.59			0.9

ZIP CODE		RACE (%)						% Hispanic Origin		2009 AGE DISTRIBUTION (%)										MEDIAN AGE		
#	POST OFFICE NAME	White		Black		Asian/Pacific																
		2000	2009	2000	2009	2000	2009	2000	2009	0-4	5-9	10-14	15-19	20-24	25-44	45-64	65-84	85+	18+	2009	% 2009 Males	% 2009 Females
59261	SACO	91.1	89.7	0.0	0.0	0.0	0.0	1.0	0.5	6.5	6.5	7.6	7.1	4.9	21.2	30.4	13.6	2.2	74.5	41.5	53.3	46.7
59262	SAVAGE	98.5	98.2	0.0	0.0	0.0	0.0	1.8	2.4	5.0	6.1	9.4	9.1	3.2	22.4	31.1	11.9	1.9	73.0	42.2	52.0	48.0
59263	SCOBEY	95.9	95.0	0.0	0.0	0.3	0.4	2.1	2.8	4.2	4.7	5.0	5.5	4.5	17.5	31.8	21.4	5.4	82.4	51.2	47.8	52.2
59270	SIDNEY	95.9	95.1	0.1	0.1	0.3	0.3	2.4	3.2	6.0	6.4	6.4	7.1	6.4	22.8	29.2	12.9	2.7	76.7	41.0	49.2	50.8
59274	VIDA	96.1	95.5	0.0	0.0	0.8	0.8	1.2	1.2	4.9	5.7	6.5	6.5	4.1	16.3	36.2	17.9	2.0	78.9	48.8	52.4	47.6
59275	WESTBY	99.0	98.8	0.0	0.0	0.0	0.0	0.5	0.9	3.9	5.1	5.1	5.4	3.9	16.6	35.0	20.2	4.5	82.2	51.1	55.3	44.7
59276	WHITETAIL	96.9	96.6	0.0	0.0	0.0	0.0	0.8	0.9	5.2	5.2	6.0	6.9	3.4	18.1	34.5	18.1	2.6	80.2	48.3	53.4	46.6
59301	MILES CITY	96.8	96.3	0.1	0.1	0.3	0.4	1.6	2.1	5.9	6.2	6.2	7.3	5.4	23.3	28.0	14.7	3.1	77.2	41.4	48.8	51.2
59311	ALZADA	97.9	97.8	0.0	0.0	0.0	0.0	1.1	0.0	3.4	5.6	5.6	6.7	4.5	23.6	31.5	16.9	2.2	82.0	45.3	48.3	51.7
59312	ANGELA	97.6	97.6	0.0	0.0	0.0	0.0	2.4	2.4	4.9	4.9	4.9	4.9	4.9	19.5	39.0	17.1	0.0	80.5	47.5	51.2	48.8
59313	BAKER	98.5	98.4	0.2	0.2	0.4	0.4	0.4	0.5	5.0	5.0	5.8	7.6	5.8	21.3	30.5	15.8	3.1	79.0	44.6	50.3	49.7
59314	BIDDLE	97.8	97.1	0.0	0.0	0.0	0.0	1.1	1.7	3.1	6.7	9.8	8.3	2.4	18.8	33.8	16.2	1.0	74.8	45.4	50.7	49.3
59315	BLOOMFIELD	99.1	99.1	0.0	0.0	0.0	0.0	0.4	0.4	4.4	4.9	5.8	7.1	4.4	18.7	36.4	15.6	2.7	80.0	47.8	48.9	51.1
59316	BOYES	97.6	97.5	0.0	0.0	0.0	0.0	1.2	0.0	3.8	3.8	6.3	7.6	5.1	24.1	30.4	16.5	2.5	79.7	44.6	49.4	50.6
59317	BROADUS	97.8	97.2	0.0	0.0	0.1	0.4	0.7	0.9	5.9	7.2	7.3	6.3	3.8	19.0	29.8	15.6	5.1	75.2	45.3	48.6	51.4
59318	BRUSETT	99.4	99.4	0.0	0.0	0.0	0.0	0.6	0.6	5.9	7.1	7.1	5.3	3.5	22.4	32.9	12.9	2.9	77.6	44.0	54.7	45.3
59322	COHAGEN	99.3	99.2	0.0	0.0	0.0	0.0	0.0	0.0	7.0	7.8	7.4	5.4	3.9	20.5	30.6	13.6	3.9	74.0	43.2	52.3	47.7
59324	EKALAKA	99.1	99.0	0.1	0.1	0.0	0.0	0.6	0.6	4.3	4.7	5.4	6.5	5.4	19.7	33.3	16.2	4.6	80.1	47.2	46.6	53.4
59326	FALLON	98.3	97.7	0.0	0.0	0.0	0.0	0.3	0.8	4.3	5.1	5.9	5.5	3.1	20.3	37.5	15.6	2.7	81.6	48.4	53.1	46.9
59327	FORSYTH	95.8	94.3	0.2	0.2	0.6	0.8	1.5	1.9	5.5	5.9	6.2	6.2	5.4	18.3	33.0	16.6	3.0	78.6	46.6	49.6	50.4
59330	GLENDIVE	97.3	96.7	0.3	0.3	0.2	0.2	0.9	1.2	5.1	5.3	5.6	7.1	6.3	22.8	29.6	15.2	3.1	80.1	43.2	49.5	50.5
59332	HAMMOND	97.3	97.1	0.0	0.0	0.4	0.4	0.8	0.8	3.8	4.6	5.4	7.1	4.6	22.5	34.2	16.3	1.7	81.3	46.2	50.8	49.2
59336	ISMAY	98.8	98.8	0.0	0.0	0.3	0.3	0.9	1.2	6.7	5.8	8.5	7.9	4.0	23.2	31.1	12.2	0.6	73.2	41.0	51.5	48.5
59337	JORDAN	99.2	99.1	0.1	0.1	0.1	0.1	0.4	0.6	6.7	7.1	7.1	5.3	3.7	22.2	31.1	13.6	3.3	75.9	43.3	53.0	47.0
59338	KINSEY	98.4	98.4	0.0	0.0	0.3	0.3	1.1	1.4	6.8	6.0	8.8	7.7	3.8	23.6	31.0	11.8	0.5	73.2	40.6	52.1	47.9
59339	LINDSAY	97.8	97.8	0.0	0.0	0.0	0.0	0.0	0.0	4.4	4.4	5.6	7.8	5.6	20.0	34.4	15.6	2.2	80.0	46.4	47.8	52.2
59341	MILDRED	97.4	97.0	0.0	0.0	0.0	0.0	0.0	0.0	3.0	4.5	6.0	6.0	3.0	17.9	41.8	14.9	3.0	80.6	50.4	56.7	43.3
59343	OLIVE	96.4	96.2	0.0	0.0	0.0	0.0	0.0	0.0	7.5	7.5	7.5	7.5	3.8	18.9	32.1	15.1	0.0	69.8	43.1	50.9	49.1
59344	PLEVNA	99.2	99.2	0.0	0.0	0.5	0.6	0.3	0.0	4.4	4.4	6.6	9.1	3.3	22.3	33.3	15.4	1.1	78.5	44.9	52.6	47.4
59345	POWDERVILLE	100.0	94.1	0.0	0.0	0.0	0.0	0.0	0.0	5.9	11.8	11.8	11.8	0.0	11.8	47.1	0.0	0.0	58.8	43.8	41.2	58.8
59347	ROSEBUD	86.2	81.2	0.5	0.6	0.2	0.2	3.1	4.0	6.1	6.7	7.3	8.2	6.8	21.8	34.7	8.0	0.5	75.1	39.0	50.6	49.4
59349	TERRY	98.0	97.6	0.0	0.0	0.2	0.3	0.8	0.8	3.2	3.5	4.2	4.2	3.6	15.0	37.4	23.8	5.1	86.0	56.3	50.5	49.5
59351	VOLBORG	98.6	98.5	0.0	0.0	0.2	0.2	0.6	0.8	4.4	5.1	5.3	4.4	3.4	22.9	37.5	14.9	2.1	82.5	47.6	51.2	48.8
59353	WIBAUX	98.0	97.8	0.2	0.2	0.2	0.2	0.4	0.4	5.5	5.7	7.1	7.4	5.2	19.1	29.3	16.0	4.7	76.5	45.0	47.4	52.6
59354	WILLARD	100.0	100.0	0.0	0.0	0.0	0.0	0.0	0.0	4.9	4.9	4.9	9.8	2.4	26.8	34.1	12.2	0.0	75.6	43.5	51.2	48.8
59401	GREAT FALLS	89.1	87.2	0.9	1.2	1.0	1.2	2.7	3.6	6.8	5.9	5.6	6.4	8.3	27.4	25.9	10.7	3.0	78.0	36.7	48.9	51.1
59402	MALMSTROM A F B	83.2	79.5	6.6	8.1	2.5	3.1	7.8	10.3	15.3	10.7	7.3	10.6	18.7	35.4	2.0	0.1	0.0	63.7	21.7	55.0	45.0
59404	GREAT FALLS	92.8	91.6	0.4	0.5	0.8	1.0	1.7	2.4	5.7	6.1	6.6	7.2	5.8	23.0	31.2	13.1	1.4	77.0	41.8	50.2	49.8
59405	GREAT FALLS	88.8	86.9	1.6	2.0	1.1	1.3	2.9	3.7	7.2	6.3	6.0	6.5	7.4	24.8	24.4	14.2	3.3	76.8	37.9	48.0	52.0
59410	AUGUSTA	96.9	96.2	0.0	0.0	0.0	0.0	1.3	1.8	5.8	5.9	6.2	8.5	6.5	19.2	30.3	15.7	2.1	78.0	43.0	49.5	50.5
59411	BABB	23.4	17.1	0.0	0.0	0.0	0.0	1.5	1.4	7.1	7.1	11.5	8.1	6.2	24.9	27.7	6.7	0.9	68.4	35.5	51.0	49.0
59412	BELT	96.8	96.2	0.8	1.1	0.2	0.2	1.4	2.1	5.1	5.6	6.1	6.8	5.0	22.2	33.1	14.2	1.9	79.0	44.4	50.4	49.6
59414	BLACK EAGLE	91.1	89.6	0.2	0.3	0.3	0.4	1.5	2.0	6.4	6.7	7.0	6.3	5.5	25.9	31.0	10.0	1.1	75.9	39.3	52.1	47.9
59416	BRADY	95.7	94.7	0.3	0.3	0.3	0.3	0.6	1.0	4.7	6.0	6.6	7.0	5.0	18.3	36.2	14.3	2.0	78.4	46.3	54.2	45.8
59417	BROWNING	10.7	8.0	0.1	0.1	0.1	0.1	1.4	1.2	9.7	9.3	9.2	9.8	8.1	25.2	22.1	6.0	0.6	65.2	27.6	49.8	50.2
59418	BUFFALO	98.0	96.9	0.0	0.0	0.0	0.0	1.0	0.0	5.1	6.1	6.1	6.1	4.1	19.4	32.7	17.3	3.1	78.6	46.9	50.0	50.0
59419	BYNUM	97.3	96.5	0.0	0.0	0.0	0.0	1.4	1.4	7.7	8.5	8.5	7.7	4.2	22.5	26.1	13.4	1.4	70.4	36.9	50.7	49.3
59420	CARTER	99.2	98.6	0.0	0.5	0.4	0.5	0.0	0.0	4.6	5.6	5.6	5.1	3.7	20.8	35.6	16.2	2.8	81.0	47.5	52.3	47.7
59421	CASCADE	96.2	95.4	0.3	0.3	0.1	0.2	0.9	1.2	4.4	5.0	5.4	6.7	5.0	19.5	35.3	17.0	1.8	80.7	47.3	51.4	48.6
59422	CHOTEAU	95.1	94.4	0.1	0.1	0.1	0.1	1.2	1.6	6.1	6.2	6.6	6.9	5.7	19.8	28.4	15.9	4.4	76.4	43.9	47.7	52.3
59424	COFFEE CREEK	97.4	97.3	0.0	0.0	0.0	0.0	1.7	1.8	5.3	5.3	6.2	7.1	5.3	22.1	32.7	14.2	1.8	77.9	43.9	52.2	47.8
59425	CONRAD	96.0	94.9	0.1	0.1	0.3	0.3	0.9	1.1	5.8	6.1	6.3	6.7	6.6	21.3	28.7	14.6	3.9	77.4	42.8	48.2	51.8
59427	CUT BANK	75.4	69.7	0.1	0.1	0.2	0.3	0.9	1.0	6.8	6.6	7.8	7.3	6.5	21.8	27.7	13.1	2.3	74.1	39.2	48.8	51.2
59430	DENTON	97.6	97.1	0.0	0.0	0.2	0.2	1.6	2.0	5.2	5.5	6.1	6.8	5.2	21.3	33.4	14.6	2.0	78.4	45.0	52.7	47.3
59433	DUTTON	95.9	95.3	0.3	0.4	0.3	0.3	2.1	2.4	5.5	6.2	6.6	6.2	4.2	17.4	36.5	15.5	2.0	77.7	47.0	50.8	49.2
59434	EAST GLACIER PARK	87.2	83.7	0.0	0.0	0.0	0.0	0.0	0.0	4.1	4.1	6.1	6.1	4.1	34.7	38.8	2.0	0.0	81.6	42.8	57.1	42.9
59436	FAIRFIELD	98.4	98.2	0.1	0.1	0.0	0.0	0.4	0.5	6.6	6.9	7.1	6.8	4.6	23.4	30.2	12.8	1.7	75.1	40.9	51.3	48.7
59440	FLOWEREE	96.2	94.5	0.0	0.6	0.5	0.6	0.5	0.6	5.5	6.1	6.1	5.5	4.3	22.1	35.6	12.9	1.8	78.5	45.2	52.1	47.9
59441	FOREST GROVE	98.9	98.8	0.0	0.0	0.0	0.0	0.0	0.0	4.7	7.0	7.0	8.1	3.5	22.1	31.4	15.1	1.2	74.4	43.6	52.3	47.7
59442	FORT BENTON	97.8	97.4	0.2	0.3	0.4	0.6	0.5	0.5	4.4	5.1	5.6	6.1	5.3	20.0	30.8	17.1	5.6	80.6	47.2	48.7	51.3
59443	FORT SHAW	96.3	95.2	0.3	0.4	0.3	0.6	0.8	1.0	4.9	5.6	6.3	7.5	4.9	19.9	33.2	15.8	1.8	77.5	45.5	52.7	47.3
59444	GALATA	98.5	98.3	0.0	0.0	0.0	0.0	1.5	0.0	5.0	6.7	8.3	6.7	3.3	20.0	33.3	13.3	3.3	73.3	45.0	56.7	43.3
59446	GERALDINE	98.3	98.2	0.0	0.0	0.2	0.2	0.6	0.5	5.0	5.9	6.6	7.4	4.5	21.9	32.0	14.4	2.3	77.9	44.1	50.4	49.6
59447	GEYSER	97.2	97.1	0.0	0.0	0.2	0.2	0.7	0.7	6.7	7.1	7.4	6.9	4.5	20.5	31.7	13.3	1.9	74.5	42.5	54.5	45.5
59448	HEART BUTTE	5.7	4.3	0.1	0.1	0.3	0.3	1.1	0.9	10.9	10.4	9.0	9.5	10.4	25.2	18.4	5.8	0.4	63.5	24.9	47.3	52.7
59450	HIGHWOOD	97.5	96.9	0.2	0.2	1.3	1.8	0.4	0.7	4.3	6.3	8.5	9.4	2.0	22.2	31.2	14.1	2.0	74.9	43.5	51.8	48.2
59451	HILGER	97.5	97.2	0.0	0.0	0.1	0.1	1.4	2.1	5.1	5.5	6.1	6.9	5.1	21.3	33.2	14.7	2.1	78.3	45.0	52.5	47.5
59452	HOBSON	98.9	98.7	0.0	0.0	0.1	0.1	0.9	0.9	5.8	6.3	7.1	7.0	4.2	18.2	32.6	16.8	2.1	76.3	45.8	51.8	48.2
59453	JUDITH GAP	96.3	95.8	0.3	0.4	0.7	1.1	0.3	0.0	7.4	7.8	6.4	6.7	4.6	23.3	29.0	13.4	1.4	73.1	40.1	52.3	47.7
59454	KEVIN	96.1	96.3	0.0	0.0	0.4	0.5	1.8	1.4	7.4	7.8	7.8	7.4	5.1	22.6	30.9	9.7	1.4	71.4	37.5	49.8	50.2
59456	LEDGER	100.0	100.0	0.0	0.0	0.0	0.0	0.0	0.0	5.3	5.3	5.3	5.3	5.3	21.1	36.8	15.8	0.0	78.9	46.3	50.0	50.0
59457	LEWISTOWN	96.7	96.2	0.1	0.1	0.2	0.3	0.7	1.0	5.3	5.4	5.6	6.1	5.6	20.7	29.4	17.3	4.5	79.5	45.9	47.5	52.5
59460	LOMA	99.1	99.1	0.0	0.0	0.0	0.0	0.0	0.0	4.8	5.2	6.1	6.9	4.3	22.5	33.3	15.2	1.7	79.2	45.1	55.4	44.6
59462	MOCCASIN	99.4	99.4	0.0	0.0	0.0	0.0	0.6	0.6	6.0	6.0	7.2	7.2	4.2	18.6	32.3	16.8	1.8	76.0	45.5	50.9	49.1
59463	MONARCH	96.8	97.1	0.0	0.0	0.0	0.0	1.1	1.0	5.8	5.8	5.8	5.8	3.8	23.1	34.6	13.5	1.9	79.8	45.0	51.9	48.1
59464	MOORE	97.6	97.2	0.0	0.0	0.0	0.0	0.7	0.7	5.1	5.4	6.0	6.3	4.0	19.1	33.0	17.9	3.2	79.1	47.6	50.2	49.8
59465	NEIHART	96.9	96.7	0.0	0.0	0.0	0.0	1.0	1.9	4.7	5.7	5.7	5.7	4.2	20.3	36.8	15.1	1.9	80.2	46.8	52.4	47.6
59466	OILMONT	94.8	95.3	0.0	0.0	0.0	0.0	0.0	0.0	5.8	7.0	7.0	8.1	3.5	23.3	29.1	14.0	2.3	73.3	41.7	50.0	50.0
59467	PENDROY	97.2	97.0	0.0	0.0	0.0	0.0	1.8	2.0	7.0	8.0	8.0	8.0	5.0	20.0	29.0	13.0	2.0	72.0	40.0	52.0	48.0
59468	POWER	95.4	94.4	0.7	1.0	0.0	0.0	1.6	2.2	6.3	6.9	6.7	5.7	4.3	21.3	33.6	13.5	1.8	76.4	44.1	51.6	48.4
59469	RAYNESFORD	97.5	97.5	0.0	0.0	0.0	0.0	0.5	0.5	7.0	7.0	7.0	6.5	4.5	20.1	32.2	13.6	2.0	74.4	43.1	55.8	44.2
59471	ROY	98.5	98.5	0.0	0.0	0.0	0.0	0.5	0.8	5.0	6.5	7.8	8.3	3.0	21.4	32.7	13.8	1.5	74.4	43.7	51.5	48.5
59472	SAND COULEE	97.8	97.3	0.0	0.2	0.0	0.0	1.0	1.3	4.6	7.3	7.1	6.3	4.1	23.7	31.3	12.9	2.5	77.4	42.8	51.1	48.9
59474	SHELBY	93.3	92.7	0.2	0.2	0.4	0.4	1.2	1.3	4.8	4.8	4.9	6.1	8.1	26.2	28.4	13.5	3.2	81.5	41.3	53.1	46.9
59479	STANFORD	99.2	99.1	0.1	0.1	0.0	0.0	0.2	0.2	3.1	3.7	4.8	7.1	4.8	18.2	37.8	17.4	3.2	84.2	49.5	54.0	46.0
59480	STOCKETT	98.1	97.6	0.0	0.0	0.0	0.0	0.9	1.3	4.6	7.4	7.0	6.3	4.1	23.6	31.4	13.1	2.6	77.5	43.0	51.8	48.2
59482	SUNBURST	95.0	95.3	0.0	0.0	0.1	0.1	0.9	0.7	6.2	7.1	7.5	7.5	4.2	21.8	30.4	13.3	2.0	74.4	41.6	50.5	49.5
59483	SUN RIVER	92.6	91.0	0.5	0.7	0.4	0.4	1.3	1.7	5.5	6.4	6.5	7.9	6.2	26.6	29.0	11.0	0.8	76.6	39.0	55.6	44.4
59484	SWEET GRASS	95.6	96.2	0.0	0.0	0.4	0.4	1.6	1.3	7.2	7.7	7.7	7.7	4.7	22.6	30.6	10.6	1.3	72.3	38.0	50.2	49.8
59486	VALIER	93.3	91.6	0.0	0.0	0.0	0.0	0.8	1.0	6.1	6.7	6.8	7.1	5.5	19.9	31.3	14.6	2.0	76.1	43.1	51.0	49.0
59487	VAUGHN	94.4	93.5	0.6	0.7	0.5	0.6	0.9	1.1	6.8	7.1	7.6	7.8	5.6	24.4	27.7	11.9	1.1	73.6	38.9	51.0	49.0
59489	WINIFRED	99.0	98.4	0.0	0.0	0.0	0.0	0.3	1.0	5.3	6.6	7.6	8.2	3.0	21.4	32.9	13.8	1.3	74.0	43.7	51.3	48.7
59501	HAVRE	88.3	84.9	0.1	0.1	0.5	0.6	1.3	1.7	6.9	6.5	6.3	7.5	7.7	25.7	26.3	10.8	2.3	76.2	35.3	49.7	50.3
59520	BIG SANDY	60.5	58.6	0.0	0.0	0.1	0.1	1.0	1.0	9.8	9.3	9.1	7.2	5.5	22.6	23.6	10.8	2.1	67.2	32.3	50.4	49.6
59521	BOX ELDER	10.3	8.8	0.0	0.0	0.1	0.2	1.5	1.3	10.4	10.8	11.0	10.7	8.1	22.9	19.4	6.4	0.3	60.9	24.4	49.6	50.4
	MONTANA	90.6	89.7	0.3	0.4	0.6	0.7	2.0	2.6	6.0	6.1	6.5	7.3	7.0	24.2	29.0	11.8	2.1	77.1	39.4	49.8	50.2
	UNITED STATES	75.1	72.0	12.3	12.7	3.8	4.6	12.5	15.7	6.8	6.7	6.6	7.1	6.9	27.0	26.0	10.9	1.9	75.7	36.9	49.2	50.8

ZIP CODE #	POST OFFICE NAME	2009 Per Capita Income	2009 HH Income Base	2009 HOUSEHOLD INCOME DISTRIBUTION (%) Less than $25,000	$25,000 to $49,999	$50,000 to $99,999	$100,000 to $149,999	$150,000 or More	MEDIAN HOUSEHOLD INCOME 2009	2014	2009 National Centile	2009 State Centile	2009 Home Value Base	2009 HOME VALUE DISTRIBUTION (%) Less than $50,000	$50,000 to $89,999	$90,000 to $174,999	$175,000 to $399,999	$400,000 or More	2009 Median Home Value
59261	SACO	14256	68	44.1	27.9	22.1	4.4	1.5	27618	27987	5	8	50	46.0	20.0	22.0	10.0	2.0	56667
59262	SAVAGE	15291	370	32.4	41.1	22.4	4.1	0.0	35000	35043	18	48	291	21.3	25.8	38.5	10.7	3.8	94048
59263	SCOBEY	19348	541	39.7	33.5	20.0	5.2	1.7	31640	32437	11	24	421	33.5	26.6	29.7	9.3	1.0	73906
59270	SIDNEY	20473	2700	27.3	33.0	33.9	3.7	2.1	41501	42682	38	80	1920	18.5	22.6	46.3	12.2	0.5	102817
59274	VIDA	21182	107	29.9	37.4	26.2	4.7	1.9	34770	34360	17	45	88	25.0	23.9	28.4	14.8	8.0	93333
59275	WESTBY	20215	159	28.3	46.5	19.5	3.1	2.5	33635	33256	15	37	134	57.5	18.7	20.9	3.0	0.0	39286
59276	WHITETAIL	15517	53	41.5	35.8	20.8	1.9	0.0	29413	31516	7	14	41	31.7	17.1	26.8	14.6	9.8	92500
59301	MILES CITY	19271	4223	33.5	31.9	28.1	5.2	1.4	36384	37122	22	56	2976	22.4	21.3	42.1	11.8	2.4	99082
59311	ALZADA	14742	35	42.9	28.6	25.7	2.9	0.0	33622	30000	15	37	26	23.1	11.5	3.8	11.5	50.0	400000
59312	ANGELA	26735	20	25.0	25.0	40.0	5.0	5.0	50000	47309	61	92	16	12.5	12.5	18.8	37.5	18.8	200000
59313	BAKER	18926	966	33.4	30.2	31.1	3.6	1.7	36243	36910	21	55	740	23.9	26.1	32.7	11.8	5.5	90000
59314	BIDDLE	16372	163	39.3	33.7	22.7	1.8	2.5	29254	29847	7	13	129	35.7	12.4	16.3	16.3	19.4	100962
59315	BLOOMFIELD	15084	85	38.8	35.3	20.0	4.7	1.2	31605	31605	11	24	67	41.8	14.9	31.3	9.0	3.0	71667
59316	BOYES	13017	27	40.7	33.3	25.9	0.0	0.0	33606	35000	15	36	20	15.0	15.0	0.0	5.0	65.0	625000
59317	BROADUS	17222	322	34.2	40.7	22.7	1.2	1.2	31521	30997	11	24	233	23.6	30.5	30.0	9.9	6.0	84722
59318	BRUSETT	15576	77	42.9	27.3	27.3	1.3	1.3	29516	30437	7	15	60	33.3	16.7	20.0	8.3	21.7	90000
59322	COHAGEN	16150	105	42.9	32.4	21.0	2.9	1.0	28571	30000	6	11	75	32.0	17.3	20.0	9.3	21.3	91667
59324	EKALAKA	15017	343	44.3	32.7	19.5	2.6	0.9	28166	28529	6	9	258	41.5	10.5	17.1	14.3	16.7	75000
59326	FALLON	16990	115	40.0	33.9	19.1	5.2	1.7	29751	30237	8	17	85	21.2	25.9	29.4	11.8	11.8	95000
59327	FORSYTH	20528	1329	31.2	31.8	31.3	3.9	1.9	39102	39784	30	72	945	23.2	23.6	35.1	11.7	6.3	95351
59330	GLENDIVE	18995	3214	33.6	30.2	30.1	4.4	1.6	38841	39589	29	71	2368	19.9	25.6	43.0	10.1	1.4	96057
59332	HAMMOND	14332	92	41.3	30.4	23.9	3.3	1.1	33173	34063	14	33	69	23.2	15.9	7.2	10.1	43.5	237500
59336	ISMAY	16318	121	28.1	37.2	29.8	4.1	0.8	38819	39281	29	71	95	11.6	10.5	27.4	32.6	17.9	176563
59337	JORDAN	16259	301	42.5	30.6	24.3	2.0	0.7	29220	29002	7	13	226	32.7	17.7	19.0	7.5	23.0	88889
59338	KINSEY	16362	133	27.1	36.8	29.3	5.3	1.5	39776	39379	32	74	104	10.6	11.5	29.8	30.8	17.3	170000
59339	LINDSAY	17558	41	39.0	39.0	19.5	2.4	0.0	30532	30532	9	21	32	25.0	21.9	34.4	12.5	6.3	95000
59341	MILDRED	14426	26	46.2	30.8	19.2	3.8	0.0	26441	27282	4	5	19	10.5	31.6	42.1	5.3	10.5	104167
59343	OLIVE	12925	21	42.9	33.3	23.8	0.0	0.0	28571	28596	6	11	16	12.5	25.0	25.0	25.0	12.5	125000
59344	PLEVNA	16428	152	34.9	36.2	25.7	2.0	1.3	33136	33576	14	32	122	26.2	8.2	19.7	26.2	19.7	146875
59345	POWDERVILLE	19853	9	22.2	55.6	22.2	0.0	0.0	37278	30000	24	63	7	28.6	0.0	14.3	28.6	28.6	212500
59347	ROSEBUD	22940	1097	16.0	25.7	44.3	11.7	2.3	57855	56592	75	98	884	26.0	16.6	39.4	12.2	5.8	106723
59349	TERRY	17761	352	40.9	36.9	18.5	3.7	0.0	29820	30669	8	18	281	44.1	27.4	24.2	2.1	2.1	57857
59351	VOLBORG	16806	189	32.8	37.0	25.4	3.7	1.1	36447	35281	22	56	114	11.4	16.7	15.8	21.1	35.1	218750
59353	WIBAUX	18087	389	35.0	34.7	24.7	3.9	1.8	33644	34082	15	38	286	37.1	18.2	24.5	13.6	6.6	79091
59354	WILLARD	15311	16	31.3	37.5	31.3	0.0	0.0	35000	32248	18	48	13	23.1	0.0	23.1	15.4	38.5	275000
59401	GREAT FALLS	19505	6311	36.2	32.5	26.0	3.2	2.0	34390	34841	16	43	3262	4.0	8.5	68.5	17.9	1.2	137243
59402	MALMSTROM A F B	15904	575	17.7	48.0	29.6	4.0	0.7	40375	40822	34	77	9	0.0	0.0	22.2	77.8	0.0	187500
59404	GREAT FALLS	24325	10000	19.8	30.6	36.4	8.3	5.0	49680	49490	60	92	8181	6.5	7.4	41.2	40.2	4.7	166499
59405	GREAT FALLS	21456	12352	30.3	29.6	33.0	4.6	2.6	40795	42107	35	78	7057	9.6	7.1	52.3	28.5	2.5	148224
59410	AUGUSTA	14976	390	43.8	38.5	13.6	1.5	2.6	28127	28677	6	8	271	15.1	8.5	55.4	13.3	7.7	122421
59411	BABB	12922	186	40.9	37.6	14.5	2.7	4.3	27870	28323	5	8	133	45.1	15.8	28.6	5.3	5.3	72143
59412	BELT	19654	714	31.1	35.6	26.1	3.9	3.4	35979	36690	21	54	544	9.7	18.9	30.9	28.9	11.6	144048
59414	BLACK EAGLE	20597	428	31.1	37.6	27.3	2.8	1.2	37226	37712	24	62	308	14.0	21.1	41.2	20.8	2.9	120192
59416	BRADY	21400	123	22.8	34.1	35.0	5.7	2.4	44229	45000	46	86	93	15.1	12.9	32.3	35.5	4.3	133929
59417	BROWNING	11235	2288	41.2	33.3	20.7	3.7	1.1	28262	28724	6	10	1247	20.9	20.1	41.6	13.3	4.1	105260
59418	BUFFALO	18637	36	27.8	33.3	33.3	5.6	0.0	40000	40000	33	76	30	10.0	10.0	26.7	33.3	20.0	187500
59419	BYNUM	15173	47	36.2	36.2	19.1	6.4	2.1	32933	34282	13	31	36	11.1	13.9	38.9	19.4	16.7	133333
59420	CARTER	22311	95	32.6	32.6	27.4	3.2	4.2	35567	36147	19	52	69	17.4	13.0	40.6	17.4	11.6	115833
59421	CASCADE	19594	1155	31.0	35.6	27.4	3.6	2.4	37852	38574	26	67	924	8.2	9.4	37.0	34.8	10.5	165652
59422	CHOTEAU	17161	1130	36.5	32.6	25.8	3.6	1.5	33390	34061	14	35	823	12.4	23.2	43.4	14.6	6.4	110725
59424	COFFEE CREEK	16806	50	38.0	38.0	22.0	2.0	0.0	32304	34286	12	27	37	29.7	18.9	27.0	16.2	8.1	92500
59425	CONRAD	19685	1377	33.5	27.4	31.4	5.6	2.2	38987	39716	30	71	988	17.4	24.4	43.8	13.0	1.4	101904
59427	CUT BANK	18168	1880	30.4	30.4	31.2	5.8	2.2	41298	42683	37	79	1364	15.9	21.8	45.5	14.5	2.2	106765
59430	DENTON	18089	231	33.8	37.2	23.4	3.9	1.7	35113	35000	18	48	169	29.6	20.7	24.9	15.4	9.5	89286
59433	DUTTON	17439	308	28.9	39.3	28.6	2.9	0.3	37787	38986	26	66	243	19.8	23.5	37.9	14.8	4.1	97174
59434	EAST GLACIER PARK	24239	24	37.5	4.2	58.3	0.0	0.0	62038	61132	80	99	12	41.7	8.3	50.0	0.0	0.0	92500
59436	FAIRFIELD	18215	697	26.5	36.6	30.7	4.9	1.3	37958	38460	27	67	532	8.8	16.9	38.5	30.8	4.9	135119
59440	FLOWEREE	20377	69	31.9	34.8	27.5	2.9	2.9	36730	38629	23	59	50	16.0	18.0	42.0	16.0	8.0	113889
59441	FOREST GROVE	15535	37	43.2	35.1	18.9	2.7	0.0	29043	30000	7	12	28	32.1	17.9	21.4	14.3	14.3	90000
59442	FORT BENTON	18045	688	32.0	37.1	25.7	3.6	1.6	35459	35971	19	51	527	14.6	25.4	43.1	13.7	3.2	103184
59443	FORT SHAW	16893	271	31.0	36.9	28.4	3.3	0.4	38431	39139	28	69	224	9.8	11.2	33.9	38.4	6.7	158824
59444	GALATA	14500	25	40.0	36.0	24.0	0.0	0.0	31106	32300	10	22	19	15.8	26.3	15.8	26.3	15.8	112500
59446	GERALDINE	17618	225	35.1	35.1	23.1	4.0	2.7	33667	34519	15	38	165	27.3	21.8	24.8	13.9	12.1	91500
59447	GEYSER	14828	147	38.8	37.4	16.3	4.1	3.4	33637	35164	15	37	118	33.9	11.9	27.1	15.3	11.9	106250
59448	HEART BUTTE	8756	189	42.3	35.4	18.5	3.7	0.0	28233	29573	6	10	84	31.0	19.0	26.2	19.0	4.8	90000
59450	HIGHWOOD	17883	164	25.0	34.8	31.7	6.7	1.8	42680	44170	41	84	127	11.8	12.6	30.7	33.1	11.8	156944
59451	HILGER	15170	258	34.9	36.8	22.9	3.9	1.6	34476	34605	16	43	189	29.1	20.1	24.9	15.9	10.1	91667
59452	HOBSON	19260	278	32.4	38.1	22.7	3.2	3.6	35163	35925	18	49	214	18.7	15.9	25.2	22.4	17.8	130882
59453	JUDITH GAP	15498	113	48.7	31.0	15.0	2.7	2.7	25718	28433	4	4	84	20.2	33.3	26.2	11.9	8.3	84000
59454	KEVIN	16191	87	41.4	33.3	17.2	5.7	2.3	30363	30733	9	20	64	35.9	26.6	28.1	7.8	1.6	72000
59456	LEDGER	14868	12	33.3	25.0	33.3	8.3	0.0	45000	42313	48	87	10	0.0	0.0	50.0	50.0	0.0	175000
59457	LEWISTOWN	20451	3520	32.2	33.3	28.0	4.5	2.0	37660	38260	26	65	2562	12.6	19.3	43.1	19.8	5.2	116890
59460	LOMA	23745	99	33.3	34.3	23.2	5.1	4.0	35369	36133	19	51	74	24.3	17.6	31.1	17.6	9.5	105000
59462	MOCCASIN	17740	64	32.8	35.9	23.4	3.1	4.7	36490	36100	22	57	49	18.4	16.3	26.5	22.4	16.3	128125
59463	MONARCH	20240	47	34.0	29.8	29.8	4.3	2.1	37337	37340	25	64	38	2.6	7.9	36.8	36.8	15.8	183333
59464	MOORE	17809	201	26.9	34.3	30.8	6.0	2.0	40251	41976	34	76	166	10.8	8.4	25.3	35.5	19.9	197500
59465	NEIHART	25873	104	32.7	27.9	30.8	4.8	3.8	40000	40000	33	76	85	4.7	5.9	34.1	38.8	16.5	189063
59466	OILMONT	18856	35	22.9	37.1	37.1	2.9	0.0	44064	43636	46	86	27	25.9	37.0	18.5	11.1	7.4	83000
59467	PENDROY	19165	40	30.0	42.5	20.0	2.5	5.0	35000	38170	18	48	31	16.1	12.9	29.0	22.6	19.4	137500
59468	POWER	17303	262	26.0	40.1	28.2	5.7	0.0	40000	40139	33	76	211	11.8	14.7	37.0	29.9	6.6	122756
59469	RAYNESFORD	16354	77	39.0	39.0	14.3	3.9	3.9	32355	35000	12	28	62	33.9	9.7	29.0	14.5	12.9	112500
59471	ROY	13438	123	42.3	33.3	17.9	4.9	1.6	30214	30431	8	19	94	30.9	18.1	23.4	13.8	13.8	92000
59472	SAND COULEE	17061	211	33.2	32.7	27.0	2.8	4.3	36560	37796	22	57	176	16.5	15.9	35.2	26.1	6.3	132407
59474	SHELBY	17821	1366	33.4	31.2	31.3	2.2	1.9	36721	37680	23	59	952	15.9	29.5	37.9	14.0	2.7	96027
59479	STANFORD	16120	361	42.4	34.1	20.8	2.5	0.3	29514	30521	7	15	273	27.5	27.5	34.8	4.8	5.5	82500
59480	STOCKETT	18354	203	33.5	32.0	27.1	3.0	4.4	36804	37159	23	59	169	14.2	14.8	36.7	27.8	6.5	137500
59482	SUNBURST	15588	258	31.0	36.8	26.0	3.9	2.3	39008	40148	30	72	196	29.6	31.6	21.9	9.2	7.7	80435
59483	SUN RIVER	18937	307	30.6	36.2	28.0	3.6	1.6	37680	38313	26	66	255	10.2	13.7	37.6	32.5	5.9	148162
59484	SWEET GRASS	13332	77	41.6	32.5	18.2	5.2	2.6	30438	30887	9	20	57	31.6	24.6	33.3	8.8	1.8	78750
59486	VALIER	14602	535	37.8	36.4	21.7	2.8	1.3	32391	33252	12	29	413	15.3	24.0	37.8	15.5	7.5	108167
59487	VAUGHN	16694	428	31.8	35.7	28.0	3.3	1.2	36689	37055	23	58	352	9.7	16.5	42.0	28.1	3.7	138839
59489	WINIFRED	18727	133	40.6	34.6	18.0	4.5	2.3	30999	31207	10	22	101	31.7	17.8	21.8	13.9	14.9	91000
59501	HAVRE	19573	5318	33.4	29.9	29.9	4.5	2.3	38578	39446	28	70	3399	11.5	17.2	46.6	23.5	1.3	128944
59520	BIG SANDY	14418	752	40.4	31.5	22.7	3.5	1.9	31203	31996	10	23	436	26.1	23.2	35.8	10.6	4.4	91071
59521	BOX ELDER	11156	530	35.3	32.3	25.8	5.1	1.5	35251	36126	19	49	305	45.9	29.5	17.4	7.2	0.0	58929
	MONTANA	21013		28.7	31.3	31.1	5.8	3.0	40864	42494				10.4	9.4	31.4	38.6	10.1	171793
	UNITED STATES	27277		20.9	24.4	35.3	11.7	7.6	54719	56938				9.3	13.1	31.6	32.6	13.5	162279

ZIP CODE #	POST OFFICE NAME	FINANCIAL SERVICES: Auto Loan	Home Loan	Invest-ments	Retire-ment Plans	THE HOME: Home Improvements: Home Repair	Lawn & Garden	Furnishings: Comput-ers & Hard-ware-Personal	Major Appli-ances	TV, Radio, Sound Equip-ment	Furni-ture	ENTERTAINMENT: Dine out/ Carry out	Sports Equip-ment	Fees & Tickets	Toys & Games	Travel	Cable TV	PERSONAL: Apparel & Services	Auto Repairs	Health Insur-ance	Pets & Supplies
59261	SACO	69	47	75	47	49	72	52	65	54	42	54	54	38	53	52	59	35	61	69	80
59262	SAVAGE	70	48	77	48	50	74	54	66	56	43	55	55	39	55	53	61	36	62	70	82
59263	SCOBEY	72	50	76	50	53	76	56	69	59	47	58	55	42	58	55	65	38	64	74	83
59270	SIDNEY	78	63	76	63	64	81	67	76	71	62	69	58	58	70	66	75	47	73	81	90
59274	VIDA	87	60	96	60	63	92	67	83	69	54	68	68	49	68	66	75	44	77	87	102
59275	WESTBY	75	52	83	52	54	79	57	71	60	47	59	59	42	59	57	65	38	67	75	88
59276	WHITETAIL	61	42	67	42	44	64	46	58	48	38	48	48	34	47	46	53	31	54	61	71
59301	MILES CITY	70	59	69	58	60	74	62	69	66	57	65	52	55	65	61	71	44	67	76	82
59311	ALZADA	67	46	74	46	48	71	51	64	53	41	53	53	38	52	51	58	34	59	67	78
59312	ANGELA	98	67	108	67	71	103	75	93	78	61	77	77	55	76	74	85	50	87	98	114
59313	BAKER	78	55	79	54	58	81	61	75	67	53	65	57	48	66	59	73	43	70	81	89
59314	BIDDLE	75	52	83	52	54	80	58	72	60	47	59	59	42	59	57	65	38	67	76	88
59315	BLOOMFIELD	71	49	78	49	51	75	54	67	56	44	56	56	40	55	54	62	36	63	71	83
59316	BOYES	68	47	75	47	49	72	52	65	54	42	53	53	38	53	52	59	35	60	68	80
59317	BROADUS	75	52	83	52	54	80	58	72	60	47	59	59	42	59	57	65	38	67	76	88
59318	BRUSETT	62	42	68	42	44	65	47	58	49	38	48	48	34	48	47	53	31	55	62	72
59322	COHAGEN	70	48	77	48	50	74	54	67	56	43	55	55	39	55	53	61	36	62	70	82
59324	EKALAKA	64	44	71	44	46	68	49	61	51	40	51	50	36	50	49	56	33	57	64	75
59326	FALLON	68	47	74	46	49	71	52	64	54	42	53	53	38	53	51	59	34	60	68	79
59327	FORSYTH	80	58	82	57	60	83	63	77	68	55	66	59	50	67	62	74	44	72	82	91
59330	GLENDIVE	75	57	72	56	59	76	61	71	66	56	64	54	51	65	59	71	43	68	76	85
59332	HAMMOND	67	46	73	46	48	71	51	63	53	41	53	52	37	52	51	58	34	59	67	78
59336	ISMAY	79	54	87	54	57	83	60	75	63	49	62	62	44	62	60	69	40	70	79	92
59337	JORDAN	65	45	71	45	47	69	50	62	52	40	51	51	36	51	49	56	33	58	65	76
59338	KINSEY	80	55	88	55	58	85	61	76	64	50	63	63	45	63	61	70	41	71	81	94
59339	LINDSAY	68	47	75	47	49	72	52	65	54	42	54	54	38	53	52	59	35	61	69	80
59341	MILDRED	66	46	73	46	48	70	51	63	53	41	52	52	37	52	51	58	34	59	67	78
59343	OLIVE	58	40	64	40	42	62	45	55	46	36	46	46	33	45	44	51	30	52	58	68
59344	PLEVNA	70	48	77	48	51	74	54	67	56	43	55	55	39	55	53	61	36	62	70	82
59345	POWDERVILLE	67	46	74	46	48	71	51	64	53	41	53	53	38	52	51	58	34	59	67	78
59347	ROSEBUD	100	93	90	89	89	94	89	94	89	90	89	73	83	92	86	89	61	91	91	111
59349	TERRY	56	50	67	47	55	63	49	59	52	51	51	41	46	48	53	55	34	56	65	68
59351	VOLBORG	76	52	83	52	54	80	58	72	60	47	59	59	42	59	57	65	38	67	76	88
59353	WIBAUX	77	54	80	53	56	80	60	74	65	51	63	57	46	63	58	71	42	69	79	88
59354	WILLARD	70	48	77	48	51	74	54	67	56	43	55	55	39	55	53	61	36	62	70	82
59401	GREAT FALLS	60	54	51	56	53	59	62	58	64	57	63	45	58	63	57	66	44	62	66	71
59402	MALMSTROM A F B	82	42	32	49	38	36	77	53	72	71	76	53	58	87	55	66	53	68	48	65
59404	GREAT FALLS	90	91	90	91	90	97	86	92	89	86	88	68	87	89	88	92	61	89	96	108
59405	GREAT FALLS	74	64	65	65	65	72	72	71	74	68	73	54	66	74	68	76	50	73	77	85
59410	AUGUSTA	63	43	69	43	45	67	48	60	50	39	49	49	35	49	48	55	32	56	63	74
59411	BABB	73	48	71	45	48	72	51	64	59	48	57	50	38	60	48	66	38	61	68	79
59412	BELT	88	62	93	61	65	91	66	83	71	58	70	65	51	70	65	78	46	77	87	100
59414	BLACK EAGLE	71	65	58	63	64	67	62	65	64	64	64	48	58	67	59	66	44	63	66	78
59416	BRADY	94	64	103	64	67	99	72	89	74	58	74	73	52	73	71	81	48	83	94	109
59417	BROWNING	60	49	51	49	47	57	52	54	56	50	55	42	47	56	49	58	37	55	59	67
59418	BUFFALO	88	61	97	60	63	93	67	84	70	54	69	69	49	69	67	76	45	78	88	103
59419	BYNUM	82	56	90	56	59	86	63	78	65	51	64	64	46	64	62	71	42	73	82	96
59420	CARTER	91	62	100	62	65	96	69	86	72	56	71	71	51	71	69	79	46	80	91	106
59421	CASCADE	82	62	95	61	66	86	63	80	68	58	67	60	52	66	66	73	44	74	82	95
59422	CHOTEAU	70	54	70	53	56	72	58	68	62	52	60	52	48	61	57	66	40	65	73	81
59424	COFFEE CREEK	65	45	72	45	47	69	50	62	52	40	51	51	36	51	50	56	33	58	65	76
59425	CONRAD	78	61	78	60	63	80	65	75	69	59	68	57	55	68	64	74	45	72	81	90
59427	CUT BANK	74	66	70	65	66	76	67	72	70	64	69	55	62	70	66	73	47	71	77	86
59430	DENTON	76	52	83	52	54	80	58	72	60	47	59	59	42	59	57	65	38	67	76	88
59433	DUTTON	76	52	83	52	54	80	58	72	60	47	59	59	42	59	57	65	38	67	76	88
59434	EAST GLACIER PARK	80	72	72	70	72	77	68	75	71	70	71	54	64	73	67	73	48	72	75	88
59436	FAIRFIELD	83	57	91	57	60	88	64	79	66	51	65	65	47	65	63	72	42	74	83	97
59440	FLOWEREE	83	64	83	63	65	84	66	78	69	59	68	62	54	69	65	73	45	73	81	94
59441	FOREST GROVE	62	42	68	42	44	65	47	59	49	38	48	48	35	48	47	53	31	55	62	72
59442	FORT BENTON	76	53	80	52	55	79	58	72	62	49	61	58	44	61	57	68	40	67	77	87
59443	FORT SHAW	79	54	87	54	57	83	60	75	63	49	62	62	44	62	60	69	40	70	79	92
59444	GALATA	62	43	68	43	45	66	48	59	49	39	49	49	35	48	47	54	32	55	62	73
59446	GERALDINE	78	54	86	54	56	82	60	74	62	48	61	61	44	61	59	68	40	69	78	91
59447	GEYSER	76	52	83	52	55	80	58	72	60	47	59	59	42	59	58	66	39	67	76	88
59448	HEART BUTTE	52	44	36	46	39	47	48	45	52	48	52	35	46	53	43	54	36	49	51	58
59450	HIGHWOOD	87	60	95	60	63	92	66	83	69	54	68	68	49	68	66	75	44	77	87	102
59451	HILGER	75	52	83	52	54	80	58	72	60	47	59	59	42	59	57	65	38	67	76	88
59452	HOBSON	83	57	91	57	60	88	64	79	66	51	65	65	47	65	63	72	42	74	83	97
59453	JUDITH GAP	62	42	68	42	44	65	47	59	49	38	48	48	35	48	47	53	31	55	62	72
59454	KEVIN	72	50	79	50	52	76	55	69	57	45	57	57	40	56	55	63	37	64	72	84
59456	LEDGER	84	58	92	58	61	89	64	80	67	52	66	66	47	66	64	73	43	75	84	98
59457	LEWISTOWN	76	57	76	57	60	79	63	74	67	56	66	56	51	66	61	73	44	70	80	87
59460	LOMA	98	67	107	67	70	103	75	93	78	60	77	77	55	76	74	85	50	87	98	114
59462	MOCCASIN	83	57	91	57	60	87	63	79	66	51	65	65	46	64	63	72	42	73	83	97
59463	MONARCH	80	55	88	55	58	85	61	76	64	50	63	63	45	62	61	69	41	71	80	94
59464	MOORE	87	60	96	60	63	92	67	83	69	54	69	69	49	68	66	76	45	77	88	102
59465	NEIHART	94	65	104	65	68	100	72	90	75	58	74	74	53	73	72	82	48	84	95	110
59466	OILMONT	83	57	91	57	60	87	63	79	66	51	65	65	46	65	63	72	42	73	83	97
59467	PENDROY	86	59	94	59	62	90	65	81	68	53	67	67	48	67	65	74	44	76	86	100
59468	POWER	79	57	84	57	59	82	62	75	64	52	64	61	47	64	61	69	42	70	79	92
59469	RAYNESFORD	76	52	83	52	54	80	58	72	60	47	59	59	42	59	57	65	39	67	76	88
59471	ROY	74	51	81	51	53	78	56	70	59	46	58	58	41	57	56	64	38	65	74	86
59472	SAND COULEE	87	62	91	60	64	89	64	82	71	58	70	63	51	70	64	78	46	75	85	98
59474	SHELBY	72	56	69	55	57	74	62	70	66	55	65	53	52	65	59	72	44	68	77	83
59479	STANFORD	65	45	71	45	47	69	50	62	52	40	51	51	36	51	49	56	33	58	65	76
59480	STOCKETT	88	62	92	61	65	90	65	82	71	58	70	63	51	70	64	78	46	76	86	99
59482	SUNBURST	81	55	89	55	58	85	62	76	64	50	63	63	45	63	61	70	41	71	81	94
59483	SUN RIVER	83	65	80	64	66	83	66	78	70	63	70	59	56	71	64	75	46	73	80	93
59484	SWEET GRASS	73	50	80	50	52	77	56	69	58	45	57	57	41	57	55	63	37	64	73	85
59486	VALIER	71	50	76	49	52	74	54	67	57	46	57	53	41	57	53	63	37	62	70	81
59487	VAUGHN	72	64	62	62	63	69	62	67	64	62	64	50	57	66	59	66	43	64	68	80
59489	WINIFRED	74	51	81	51	53	78	56	70	59	46	58	58	41	57	56	64	38	65	74	86
59501	HAVRE	70	63	61	63	62	69	67	67	69	64	68	51	62	69	63	71	47	68	72	80
59520	BIG SANDY	72	49	67	50	50	67	60	65	63	53	62	53	47	62	56	66	42	65	69	80
59521	BOX ELDER	66	55	51	55	51	62	58	59	63	58	63	45	54	64	54	66	43	61	65	73
	MONTANA	80	69	77	69	70	79	73	77	75	69	74	59	67	74	71	77	51	76	80	92
	UNITED STATES	100	100	100	100	100	100	100	100	100	100	100	100	100	100	100	100	100	100	100	100

ZIP CODE #	POST OFFICE NAME	COUNTY FIPS CODE	POPULATION 2000	POPULATION 2009	POPULATION 2014	2000-2009 ANNUAL RATE % Rate	2000-2009 ANNUAL RATE State Centile	HOUSEHOLDS 2000	HOUSEHOLDS 2009	HOUSEHOLDS 2014	HOUSEHOLDS % Annual Rate 2000-2009	HOUSEHOLDS 2009 Average HH Size	FAMILIES 2000	FAMILIES 2009	FAMILIES % Annual Rate 2000-2009
59522	CHESTER	051	1403	1304	1254	-0.8	18	570	536	515	-0.7	2.32	376	341	-1.1
59523	CHINOOK	005	2561	2407	2321	-0.7	21	1081	1019	983	-0.6	2.32	692	628	-1.0
59524	DODSON	071	158	152	148	-0.4	37	51	50	49	-0.2	3.04	42	40	-0.5
59525	GILDFORD	041	315	301	300	-0.5	32	123	119	119	-0.4	2.53	86	81	-0.6
59526	HARLEM	005	2400	2314	2251	-0.4	37	787	757	735	-0.4	3.03	599	562	-0.7
59527	HAYS	005	1538	1493	1459	-0.3	42	430	419	410	-0.3	3.55	349	334	-0.5
59528	HINGHAM	041	311	295	294	-0.6	27	114	110	110	-0.4	2.68	79	74	-0.7
59529	HOGELAND	005	131	124	120	-0.6	27	50	48	46	-0.4	2.58	38	36	-0.6
59530	INVERNESS	041	203	188	186	-0.8	18	79	75	74	-0.6	2.51	54	49	-1.0
59531	JOPLIN	051	381	359	345	-0.6	27	155	148	142	-0.5	2.41	122	114	-0.7
59532	KREMLIN	041	300	286	285	-0.5	32	122	118	118	-0.4	2.42	85	80	-0.7
59535	LLOYD	005	177	170	164	-0.4	37	72	69	67	-0.5	2.46	54	50	-0.8
59537	LORING	071	218	208	204	-0.5	32	76	75	73	-0.1	2.76	51	48	-0.7
59538	MALTA	071	3696	3491	3413	-0.6	27	1518	1463	1440	-0.4	2.33	1000	931	-0.8
59540	RUDYARD	041	395	366	363	-0.8	18	177	167	167	-0.6	2.19	121	110	-1.0
59542	TURNER	005	211	200	193	-0.6	27	84	80	77	-0.5	2.50	64	60	-0.7
59544	WHITEWATER	071	95	91	89	-0.5	32	30	29	29	-0.4	3.10	20	19	-0.6
59545	WHITLASH	051	374	361	349	-0.4	37	108	105	101	-0.3	3.44	86	81	-0.6
59546	ZORTMAN	071	244	229	224	-0.7	21	105	100	98	-0.5	2.29	82	76	-0.8
59601	HELENA	049	27566	28143	28767	0.2	57	12426	12911	13291	0.4	2.12	7079	6957	-0.2
59602	HELENA	049	18409	22373	24183	2.1	97	6856	8535	9299	2.4	2.61	5259	6317	2.0
59625	HELENA	049	480	523	523	0.9	77	1	1	1	0.0	3.00	0	0	0.0
59632	BOULDER	043	1918	2160	2312	1.3	87	714	818	882	1.5	2.42	472	525	1.2
59633	CANYON CREEK	049	325	391	417	2.0	96	139	169	182	2.1	2.31	105	124	1.8
59634	CLANCY	043	4945	5462	5752	1.1	83	1760	1966	2079	1.2	2.76	1457	1597	1.0
59635	EAST HELENA	049	5926	6518	6907	1.0	79	2136	2403	2569	1.3	2.71	1642	1784	0.9
59639	LINCOLN	049	1316	1449	1524	1.0	79	580	655	694	1.3	2.21	381	410	0.8
59641	RADERSBURG	007	101	110	114	0.9	77	40	44	46	1.0	2.50	32	34	0.7
59642	RINGLING	059	38	41	42	0.8	73	17	19	19	1.2	2.16	12	13	0.9
59643	TOSTON	007	372	412	431	1.1	83	157	176	186	1.2	2.33	125	137	1.0
59644	TOWNSEND	007	3375	3596	3722	0.7	71	1355	1472	1534	0.9	2.40	954	1006	0.6
59645	WHITE SULPHUR SPRING	059	1681	1627	1587	-0.4	37	688	668	652	-0.3	2.40	449	422	-0.7
59647	WINSTON	007	345	375	390	0.9	77	125	137	144	1.0	2.74	100	107	0.7
59648	WOLF CREEK	049	646	704	748	0.9	77	292	324	347	1.1	2.17	212	226	0.7
59701	BUTTE	093	33600	31982	31216	-0.5	32	14066	13552	13274	-0.4	2.28	8644	8023	-0.8
59711	ANACONDA	023	9511	9005	8704	-0.6	27	4028	3818	3697	-0.6	2.26	2554	2335	-1.0
59714	BELGRADE	031	10933	17787	21528	5.4	100	4069	6764	8232	5.6	2.63	3005	4776	5.1
59715	BOZEMAN	031	29187	32602	35576	1.2	86	11639	13109	14411	1.3	2.30	6153	6571	0.7
59717	BOZEMAN	031	808	863	879	0.7	71	33	38	42	1.5	4.00	23	25	0.9
59718	BOZEMAN	031	16272	25862	31840	5.1	100	6323	10142	12541	5.2	2.55	4119	6182	4.5
59720	CAMERON	057	313	355	369	1.4	89	144	168	176	1.7	2.11	88	99	1.3
59721	CARDWELL	043	353	403	427	1.4	89	143	165	175	1.6	2.44	104	117	1.3
59722	DEER LODGE	077	5846	5925	5793	0.1	53	1887	1822	1774	-0.4	2.31	1240	1155	-0.8
59724	DELL	001	34	32	31	-0.7	21	15	14	14	-0.7	2.29	11	11	0.0
59725	DILLON	001	8114	7780	7566	-0.5	32	3201	3137	3071	-0.2	2.32	2052	1943	-0.6
59727	DIVIDE	093	319	295	286	-0.8	18	130	122	118	-0.7	2.30	102	93	-1.0
59729	ENNIS	057	2073	2294	2406	1.1	83	947	1076	1139	1.4	2.10	576	630	1.0
59730	GALLATIN GATEWAY	031	2169	2722	3114	2.5	98	927	1189	1372	2.7	2.29	582	691	1.9
59731	GARRISON	077	822	850	850	0.4	61	329	341	341	0.4	2.49	237	238	0.0
59733	GOLD CREEK	077	109	116	117	0.7	71	45	49	49	0.9	2.37	33	35	0.6
59735	HARRISON	057	397	440	455	1.1	83	154	173	181	1.3	2.53	113	124	1.0
59736	JACKSON	001	236	222	214	-0.7	21	94	91	89	-0.4	2.40	58	54	-0.8
59739	LIMA	001	370	319	300	-1.6	6	160	141	134	-1.4	2.26	101	86	-1.7
59741	MANHATTAN	031	3953	4871	5573	2.3	97	1478	1861	2149	2.5	2.60	1105	1326	2.0
59745	NORRIS	057	274	304	314	1.1	83	107	121	125	1.3	2.50	79	86	0.9
59747	PONY	057	170	188	195	1.1	83	66	74	77	1.2	2.54	49	53	0.9
59748	RAMSAY	093	93	89	86	-0.5	32	35	34	33	-0.3	2.62	27	26	-0.4
59749	SHERIDAN	057	1696	1812	1899	0.7	71	741	811	857	1.0	2.19	465	491	0.6
59750	BUTTE	093	466	445	432	-0.5	32	155	151	148	-0.3	2.95	121	114	-0.6
59751	SILVER STAR	057	252	268	280	0.7	71	95	103	108	0.9	2.59	68	71	0.5
59752	THREE FORKS	031	3041	3881	4493	2.7	98	1193	1538	1786	2.8	2.52	839	1022	2.2
59754	TWIN BRIDGES	057	977	1056	1112	0.8	73	404	440	466	0.9	2.40	277	293	0.6
59755	VIRGINIA CITY	057	263	284	298	0.8	73	123	136	144	1.1	2.09	81	87	0.8
59756	WARM SPRINGS	023	23	24	24	0.5	63	11	11	11	0.0	1.64	7	7	0.0
59758	WEST YELLOWSTONE	031	1683	2126	2462	2.6	98	741	956	1116	2.8	2.16	431	515	1.9
59759	WHITEHALL	043	3221	3805	4126	1.8	94	1288	1534	1667	1.9	2.48	927	1079	1.7
59761	WISDOM	001	221	208	200	-0.7	21	105	102	99	-0.3	2.00	65	61	-0.7
59762	WISE RIVER	001	272	256	247	-0.7	21	131	126	122	-0.4	1.94	85	78	-0.9
59801	MISSOULA	063	28859	29964	30714	0.4	61	12249	12778	13171	0.5	2.14	5804	5598	-0.4
59802	MISSOULA	063	17699	18663	19293	0.6	66	7997	8514	8847	0.7	2.13	3907	3912	0.0
59803	MISSOULA	063	14105	16244	17338	1.5	90	5127	5915	6325	1.6	2.72	3828	4256	1.2
59804	MISSOULA	063	7324	7403	7517	0.1	53	2818	2885	2948	0.3	2.50	1968	1927	-0.2
59808	MISSOULA	063	11486	16145	18334	3.7	99	4143	6083	7016	4.2	2.58	2946	4108	3.7
59820	ALBERTON	061	1171	1217	1250	0.4	61	465	493	510	0.6	2.47	347	357	0.3
59821	ARLEE	047	2133	2323	2414	0.9	77	816	900	938	1.1	2.58	587	628	0.7
59823	BONNER	063	1738	1850	1927	0.7	71	684	737	772	0.8	2.51	500	518	0.4
59824	CHARLO	047	1390	1530	1591	1.0	79	519	579	604	1.2	2.55	373	403	0.8
59825	CLINTON	063	2073	2360	2518	1.4	89	798	920	986	1.5	2.56	604	670	1.1
59826	CONDON	063	585	584	594	0.0	52	251	254	260	0.1	2.30	173	168	-0.3
59827	CONNER	081	476	536	567	1.3	87	207	242	260	1.7	1.90	145	164	1.3
59828	CORVALLIS	081	4461	5431	5886	2.1	97	1684	2071	2254	2.3	2.61	1285	1543	2.0
59829	DARBY	081	2666	2998	3176	1.3	87	981	1124	1198	1.5	2.53	710	789	1.1
59831	DIXON	089	469	519	549	1.1	83	187	210	224	1.3	2.47	118	128	0.9
59832	DRUMMOND	039	803	802	797	0.0	52	338	343	342	0.2	2.34	232	228	-0.2
59833	FLORENCE	081	4983	5678	6015	1.4	89	1747	2024	2156	1.6	2.81	1424	1613	1.4
59834	FRENCHTOWN	063	1874	2174	2368	1.6	92	641	757	828	1.8	2.87	519	597	1.5
59837	HALL	039	230	227	225	-0.1	48	98	98	98	0.0	2.32	67	65	-0.3
59840	HAMILTON	081	12744	14360	15181	1.3	87	5435	6182	6553	1.4	2.28	3504	3852	1.0
59843	HELMVILLE	077	252	249	248	-0.1	48	102	102	102	0.0	2.44	76	74	-0.3
59844	HERON	089	639	704	741	1.1	83	259	294	313	1.4	2.39	187	206	1.1
59845	HOT SPRINGS	089	1054	1161	1223	1.1	83	496	562	599	1.4	2.03	284	310	1.0
59846	HUSON	063	1357	1605	1735	1.8	94	526	631	685	2.0	2.54	428	501	1.7
59847	LOLO	063	4881	5571	5963	1.4	89	1749	2023	2174	1.6	2.75	1383	1551	1.2
59848	LONEPINE	089	203	225	238	1.1	83	82	94	100	1.5	2.35	47	51	0.9
59853	NOXON	089	624	688	726	1.1	83	265	301	321	1.4	2.28	194	215	1.1
	MONTANA					0.8					0.9	2.43			0.5
	UNITED STATES					1.0					1.1	2.59			0.9

ZIP CODE		RACE (%)						% Hispanic Origin		2009 AGE DISTRIBUTION (%)										MEDIAN AGE		
#	POST OFFICE NAME	White		Black		Asian/Pacific															% 2009 Males	% 2009 Females
		2000	2009	2000	2009	2000	2009	2000	2009	0-4	5-9	10-14	15-19	20-24	25-44	45-64	65-84	85+	18+	2009		
59522	CHESTER	99.1	98.8	0.0	0.0	0.4	0.5	0.1	0.2	4.2	4.2	5.6	6.6	5.3	19.2	31.2	18.3	5.3	81.2	48.3	47.8	52.2
59523	CHINOOK	92.9	89.7	0.2	0.3	0.1	0.1	0.8	1.0	6.1	6.0	5.7	7.6	5.2	20.7	31.3	14.0	3.4	77.2	43.9	48.8	51.2
59524	DODSON	10.8	8.6	0.0	0.0	0.0	0.0	0.0	0.0	4.6	4.6	7.9	12.5	6.6	23.0	22.4	17.8	0.7	75.0	38.2	50.7	49.3
59525	GILDFORD	98.7	98.3	0.0	0.0	0.0	0.0	0.3	0.7	5.0	6.0	6.3	6.0	4.7	21.6	34.6	13.6	2.3	78.7	45.3	52.5	47.5
59526	HARLEM	31.5	25.8	0.2	0.2	0.2	0.2	1.4	1.4	10.1	9.6	8.5	7.8	7.5	22.1	23.7	9.1	1.7	66.8	29.7	48.4	51.6
59527	HAYS	4.4	2.8	0.1	0.1	0.0	0.0	0.9	0.9	10.4	11.1	12.3	10.4	6.1	24.0	18.6	6.7	0.5	59.1	24.8	50.2	49.8
59528	HINGHAM	98.7	98.3	0.0	0.0	0.0	0.0	0.3	0.7	5.1	6.1	6.4	6.1	4.4	21.0	34.6	14.2	2.0	78.3	45.5	52.2	47.8
59529	HOGELAND	93.9	91.9	0.0	0.0	0.0	0.0	0.8	0.8	4.8	6.5	7.3	7.3	4.0	24.2	29.8	13.7	2.4	75.8	41.9	52.4	47.6
59530	INVERNESS	98.5	98.4	0.0	0.0	0.0	0.0	0.0	0.0	5.3	6.4	6.9	6.4	4.3	18.1	34.6	16.0	2.1	77.1	46.2	52.7	47.3
59531	JOPLIN	99.5	99.2	0.0	0.0	0.0	0.3	0.5	0.3	6.4	6.1	8.9	8.6	4.2	22.3	28.1	13.1	2.2	72.7	40.5	51.5	48.5
59532	KREMLIN	98.7	98.3	0.0	0.0	0.0	0.0	0.3	0.7	4.9	5.9	6.6	5.9	4.5	21.3	35.3	13.3	2.1	78.7	45.4	52.1	47.9
59535	LLOYD	95.5	93.5	0.0	0.0	0.0	0.0	1.1	1.2	6.5	6.5	5.9	10.6	2.9	21.2	35.9	9.4	1.2	74.1	42.3	51.8	48.2
59537	LORING	90.8	88.9	0.5	0.5	0.0	0.0	0.9	0.5	6.3	6.7	7.2	7.2	4.3	21.2	32.2	13.0	1.9	74.5	42.5	54.8	45.2
59538	MALTA	92.3	90.8	0.1	0.1	0.4	0.5	1.2	1.6	4.9	5.4	6.2	7.7	5.0	20.1	32.1	15.0	3.5	78.0	45.3	49.9	50.1
59540	RUDYARD	98.7	98.6	0.0	0.0	0.0	0.0	0.3	0.3	5.5	6.8	7.1	6.6	4.4	18.3	33.1	16.4	1.9	76.2	45.7	52.2	47.8
59542	TURNER	94.3	91.5	0.0	0.0	0.0	0.0	0.5	0.5	6.0	6.0	7.0	8.5	4.0	23.5	30.0	13.0	2.0	75.5	40.8	52.0	48.0
59544	WHITEWATER	91.5	89.0	0.0	0.0	0.0	0.0	1.1	0.0	5.5	7.7	7.7	6.6	4.4	20.9	33.0	12.1	2.2	73.6	42.5	56.0	44.0
59545	WHITLASH	99.2	98.9	0.0	0.0	0.3	0.6	0.0	0.0	7.2	8.0	7.8	6.6	4.4	23.3	30.2	11.1	1.4	72.6	40.1	52.4	47.6
59546	ZORTMAN	93.9	92.6	0.4	0.4	0.0	0.0	2.0	2.6	5.2	6.6	9.2	8.7	2.2	22.7	32.8	11.4	1.3	72.5	42.5	51.5	48.5
59601	HELENA	94.8	93.9	0.2	0.3	0.8	0.9	1.6	2.1	5.7	5.4	5.7	6.2	7.3	24.6	29.7	12.4	3.0	79.5	41.0	48.0	52.0
59602	HELENA	96.0	95.2	0.1	0.2	0.4	0.5	1.4	1.9	6.3	6.7	7.3	7.5	5.0	24.9	32.4	9.0	0.9	74.6	39.8	50.1	49.9
59625	HELENA	94.4	92.7	0.0	0.0	3.8	5.0	1.7	2.3	0.2	0.0	0.2	45.9	46.5	3.1	2.9	1.0	0.4	98.5	20.4	45.5	54.5
59632	BOULDER	93.7	92.9	0.3	0.4	0.8	0.9	1.5	1.9	5.1	5.0	5.8	9.0	8.3	23.4	31.8	10.2	1.4	77.5	39.8	50.0	50.0
59633	CANYON CREEK	94.8	94.4	0.3	0.3	0.3	0.3	1.5	1.8	4.6	5.4	6.6	6.1	4.6	23.0	40.9	7.9	0.8	78.8	44.8	50.4	49.6
59634	CLANCY	96.9	96.3	0.1	0.1	0.4	0.6	1.4	1.9	5.1	6.1	7.5	7.9	4.3	21.5	37.6	9.1	0.8	75.8	43.4	49.4	50.6
59635	EAST HELENA	94.4	93.3	0.3	0.4	0.3	0.5	1.6	2.1	7.9	7.8	7.9	8.1	6.5	26.2	27.3	7.6	0.7	71.3	34.5	50.2	49.8
59639	LINCOLN	95.4	94.8	0.0	0.0	0.2	0.1	0.6	0.8	4.1	4.8	7.9	7.5	1.6	20.7	38.0	14.9	0.4	77.6	46.8	51.4	48.6
59641	RADERSBURG	97.0	96.4	1.0	0.9	0.0	0.0	1.0	1.8	4.5	6.4	8.2	7.3	1.8	27.3	32.7	11.8	0.0	74.5	41.7	51.8	48.2
59642	RINGLING	100.0	100.0	0.0	0.0	0.0	0.0	0.0	0.0	4.9	4.9	4.9	7.3	4.9	24.4	31.7	17.1	0.0	78.0	44.4	51.2	48.8
59643	TOSTON	96.8	96.4	0.5	0.5	0.3	0.5	0.8	1.2	4.6	6.6	7.8	7.0	1.7	24.3	35.9	11.2	1.0	75.7	43.8	51.9	48.1
59644	TOWNSEND	97.2	96.7	0.2	0.2	0.1	0.2	1.4	1.9	5.4	6.2	6.5	6.6	3.9	21.3	32.6	14.5	3.0	77.3	45.1	50.8	49.2
59645	WHITE SULPHUR SPRING	97.1	96.9	0.0	0.0	0.2	0.2	1.5	1.6	5.0	6.1	6.3	8.1	4.5	19.2	31.3	17.0	2.6	77.6	45.5	49.5	50.5
59647	WINSTON	96.5	95.7	0.6	0.8	0.3	0.5	1.2	1.3	5.1	6.9	8.5	7.2	1.3	25.9	32.5	12.3	0.3	73.6	42.0	51.7	48.3
59648	WOLF CREEK	96.1	95.6	0.2	0.1	0.2	0.1	1.5	2.0	3.1	5.0	5.3	6.0	1.8	18.8	42.2	16.9	1.0	82.0	49.3	52.6	47.4
59701	BUTTE	95.3	94.5	0.2	0.2	0.5	0.6	2.8	3.7	5.7	5.8	6.2	6.8	6.2	24.5	28.4	13.8	2.8	78.5	41.0	49.3	50.7
59711	ANACONDA	96.0	95.4	0.2	0.2	0.4	0.5	1.6	2.1	4.7	4.8	5.2	7.5	6.5	21.0	30.9	16.3	3.2	81.0	45.3	50.2	49.8
59714	BELGRADE	97.0	96.4	0.1	0.2	0.4	0.5	1.5	1.9	7.6	7.3	7.1	6.9	7.2	29.8	26.4	7.0	0.8	73.7	34.2	50.8	49.2
59715	BOZEMAN	95.6	94.7	0.3	0.3	1.4	1.9	1.4	1.9	4.4	4.2	4.5	9.3	18.1	25.4	23.9	8.3	1.9	83.7	30.4	52.2	47.8
59717	BOZEMAN	91.3	89.1	0.9	0.9	4.1	5.6	1.6	2.1	2.4	0.7	0.5	55.5	31.2	8.3	1.4	0.0	0.0	96.2	19.2	57.2	42.8
59718	BOZEMAN	96.5	95.6	0.3	0.4	0.7	1.0	1.4	2.0	6.6	6.2	6.5	7.0	12.3	29.2	23.7	7.6	1.0	76.9	32.0	51.1	48.9
59720	CAMERON	97.8	96.9	0.0	0.0	0.6	0.8	2.2	2.8	3.1	3.7	5.1	5.1	5.1	26.2	36.9	13.8	1.1	83.9	46.0	51.5	48.5
59721	CARDWELL	97.2	96.8	0.0	0.0	0.3	0.2	2.3	3.0	5.2	6.0	9.4	7.7	2.2	22.6	33.0	11.9	2.0	73.4	43.0	52.4	47.6
59722	DEER LODGE	91.4	89.9	0.6	0.7	0.5	0.6	2.2	2.8	4.1	4.1	4.4	6.3	8.0	30.3	28.6	11.9	2.4	83.8	40.6	63.0	37.0
59724	DELL	97.0	96.9	0.0	0.0	0.0	0.0	6.1	6.3	9.4	9.4	6.3	6.3	6.3	25.0	25.0	12.5	0.0	68.8	35.0	43.8	56.2
59725	DILLON	95.8	95.1	0.2	0.2	0.2	0.3	2.5	3.3	5.5	5.9	6.2	10.3	6.9	23.4	28.1	11.4	2.3	76.9	38.1	50.7	49.3
59727	DIVIDE	96.6	95.9	0.0	0.0	0.3	0.3	1.3	1.4	4.7	5.8	10.5	9.2	3.1	20.0	35.9	9.8	1.0	71.9	42.7	51.2	48.8
59729	ENNIS	97.7	97.4	0.0	0.0	0.3	0.3	1.7	2.3	4.1	4.5	5.4	5.2	4.2	23.6	35.6	14.8	2.5	82.1	46.7	49.7	50.3
59730	GALLATIN GATEWAY	97.7	97.2	0.1	0.1	0.6	0.9	1.5	2.1	5.2	5.1	5.5	5.2	5.7	29.5	33.2	9.5	1.2	81.0	41.2	52.2	47.8
59731	GARRISON	97.7	97.6	0.0	0.0	0.2	0.4	0.7	0.9	6.2	7.2	8.4	7.8	3.2	18.1	36.0	11.9	1.3	73.1	44.3	50.4	49.6
59733	GOLD CREEK	95.4	94.8	0.0	0.0	0.9	0.9	2.8	4.3	2.6	6.0	6.0	6.9	3.4	19.8	41.4	12.1	1.7	81.0	48.0	54.3	45.7
59735	HARRISON	97.2	96.8	0.0	0.0	0.3	0.2	3.0	4.1	5.0	5.7	8.2	8.2	2.0	22.7	33.4	11.8	3.0	75.0	43.7	52.0	48.0
59736	JACKSON	96.6	96.4	0.0	0.0	0.4	0.5	5.1	6.3	5.0	5.9	5.9	5.0	2.3	18.0	41.4	15.8	0.9	79.7	49.7	52.7	47.3
59739	LIMA	94.3	93.1	0.0	0.0	0.0	0.0	2.2	2.8	7.2	7.2	7.5	6.3	4.1	19.7	27.6	18.5	1.9	74.3	43.0	49.8	50.2
59741	MANHATTAN	97.9	97.4	0.0	0.0	0.4	0.5	1.1	1.5	5.7	6.5	7.8	7.6	5.4	25.0	30.2	10.0	1.7	75.0	39.4	51.1	48.9
59745	NORRIS	97.1	97.0	0.0	0.0	0.4	0.3	2.9	4.3	5.3	5.6	8.2	7.9	2.0	22.4	34.2	11.5	3.0	74.7	44.0	53.0	47.0
59747	PONY	97.6	96.8	0.0	0.0	0.0	0.0	3.0	4.3	5.3	5.3	8.0	8.0	2.1	22.9	34.0	11.2	3.2	75.5	43.8	52.7	47.3
59748	RAMSAY	98.9	98.9	0.0	0.0	0.0	0.0	1.1	1.1	4.5	5.6	6.7	7.9	5.6	23.6	32.6	12.4	1.1	78.7	42.1	50.6	49.4
59749	SHERIDAN	96.0	95.4	0.1	0.1	0.1	0.2	1.4	1.8	4.2	5.0	5.8	6.6	2.2	19.3	35.5	18.3	3.2	80.0	48.7	50.2	49.8
59750	BUTTE	98.3	98.2	0.0	0.0	0.2	0.2	1.1	1.6	4.5	5.4	6.1	8.1	5.8	22.2	35.3	11.5	1.1	79.1	43.2	51.9	48.1
59751	SILVER STAR	96.4	95.9	0.0	0.0	0.4	0.7	3.2	4.1	5.2	6.7	7.1	6.3	3.7	19.8	34.0	15.7	1.5	76.5	45.8	51.5	48.5
59752	THREE FORKS	96.5	95.8	0.2	0.2	0.5	0.6	1.8	2.4	6.3	6.8	7.4	7.6	4.9	23.4	30.7	11.6	1.4	74.6	40.7	50.5	49.5
59754	TWIN BRIDGES	97.2	96.7	0.0	0.0	0.3	0.5	1.5	2.0	5.5	6.0	6.4	7.1	4.8	19.5	34.1	15.1	1.5	77.7	45.4	48.7	51.3
59755	VIRGINIA CITY	96.2	95.4	0.0	0.0	0.0	0.4	1.1	1.8	4.2	4.6	6.3	6.3	1.8	20.4	40.8	14.1	1.4	79.6	47.9	53.2	46.8
59756	WARM SPRINGS	95.7	95.8	0.0	0.0	0.0	0.0	0.0	0.0	0.0	0.0	4.2	4.2	4.2	33.3	41.7	12.5	0.0	95.8	47.5	62.5	37.5
59758	WEST YELLOWSTONE	93.9	92.4	0.3	0.3	0.7	0.9	5.6	7.5	4.8	5.0	5.8	5.5	5.2	31.6	36.0	5.8	0.2	80.7	40.8	55.3	44.7
59759	WHITEHALL	96.1	95.6	0.1	0.1	0.4	0.6	1.7	2.3	5.0	5.9	7.6	7.1	3.6	20.5	35.3	13.1	1.8	76.8	45.1	51.1	48.9
59761	WISDOM	96.4	96.2	0.0	0.0	0.5	0.5	5.0	6.7	4.8	5.3	6.3	4.8	2.4	18.3	40.9	16.3	1.0	80.3	50.0	51.9	48.1
59762	WISE RIVER	96.0	95.7	0.0	0.0	0.4	0.4	4.4	5.9	4.7	5.5	5.5	8.6	3.9	17.2	38.7	14.8	1.2	78.9	47.9	53.1	46.9
59801	MISSOULA	92.7	91.3	0.4	0.5	1.8	2.3	1.9	2.5	5.1	4.3	4.1	10.4	18.6	27.3	19.9	8.4	1.9	83.7	28.6	49.2	50.8
59802	MISSOULA	93.4	92.2	0.3	0.4	0.8	0.9	1.8	2.4	5.2	4.5	4.5	5.6	12.4	31.3	24.9	9.6	2.0	82.8	34.5	51.1	48.9
59803	MISSOULA	96.0	95.4	0.3	0.4	0.8	1.1	1.4	1.8	6.3	6.3	6.8	7.0	6.1	27.1	29.5	9.6	1.2	76.2	37.8	49.0	51.0
59804	MISSOULA	95.6	94.8	0.1	0.2	1.1	1.4	1.2	1.6	5.1	5.3	5.8	6.3	5.9	24.3	31.1	13.1	3.1	79.9	42.7	48.8	51.2
59808	MISSOULA	92.9	91.9	0.1	0.2	1.3	1.6	1.6	2.0	7.0	6.9	7.0	7.5	6.5	27.9	27.0	8.8	1.4	74.4	35.8	50.1	49.9
59820	ALBERTON	95.9	95.5	0.4	0.5	0.3	0.3	0.7	0.7	5.0	5.9	7.5	7.9	4.2	22.8	35.9	10.1	0.7	76.4	42.6	50.8	49.2
59821	ARLEE	59.6	54.6	0.0	0.0	0.3	0.4	3.6	4.0	7.2	6.9	7.4	7.5	5.9	25.7	28.8	9.5	1.0	73.6	36.7	51.4	48.6
59823	BONNER	95.9	95.4	0.1	0.1	0.7	0.8	1.3	1.6	5.1	5.7	6.5	6.4	4.0	25.7	35.3	10.5	0.9	78.4	43.2	51.0	49.0
59824	CHARLO	77.0	73.5	0.4	0.4	0.0	0.0	1.5	1.8	7.8	7.8	7.8	9.7	6.8	23.3	24.8	10.5	1.4	70.8	33.9	49.4	50.6
59825	CLINTON	95.5	94.7	0.1	0.2	0.4	0.5	1.5	2.0	5.9	6.1	6.6	6.4	5.7	25.0	32.8	10.6	0.9	77.3	41.1	50.9	49.1
59826	CONDON	96.9	96.1	0.2	0.2	0.2	0.3	1.7	2.4	3.6	3.9	7.4	7.2	2.2	18.2	39.6	16.6	1.4	79.8	49.1	51.7	48.3
59827	CONNER	95.0	93.8	0.2	0.2	0.4	0.6	3.2	3.9	3.2	3.5	4.7	13.8	6.0	15.5	37.5	14.9	0.9	80.4	46.9	55.6	44.4
59828	CORVALLIS	96.9	96.3	0.1	0.1	0.5	0.6	2.1	2.8	5.5	6.6	7.3	7.6	3.7	21.9	32.7	13.1	1.6	75.4	43.2	50.1	49.9
59829	DARBY	94.1	93.2	0.1	0.2	0.2	0.2	2.5	3.2	4.4	5.2	6.7	9.7	4.5	18.7	36.7	12.8	1.2	77.5	45.4	52.6	47.4
59831	DIXON	56.2	52.2	0.0	0.0	0.0	0.0	3.6	4.0	7.3	7.5	7.5	6.2	5.2	24.3	28.5	11.9	1.5	74.0	38.9	51.3	48.7
59832	DRUMMOND	96.1	95.9	0.0	0.0	0.1	0.1	0.7	0.9	5.9	6.5	7.0	6.0	4.2	20.7	32.7	15.0	2.1	76.8	44.8	51.4	48.6
59833	FLORENCE	96.9	96.3	0.1	0.2	0.4	0.5	1.3	1.7	6.3	7.1	8.2	7.1	4.6	24.2	33.2	8.5	0.9	73.8	39.9	50.8	49.2
59834	FRENCHTOWN	96.1	95.4	0.1	0.1	0.5	0.6	1.3	1.7	6.1	6.7	7.6	7.7	5.0	23.8	33.6	8.9	0.7	74.8	40.6	51.0	49.0
59837	HALL	96.1	96.0	0.0	0.0	0.0	0.0	0.9	0.9	6.2	6.6	7.0	6.2	4.4	20.7	30.4	16.3	2.2	75.8	44.0	51.1	48.9
59840	HAMILTON	96.8	96.4	0.1	0.1	0.5	0.6	1.9	2.5	5.6	5.7	6.5	6.5	4.9	19.7	31.3	16.2	3.5	77.8	45.7	48.4	51.6
59843	HELMVILLE	97.2	97.2	0.0	0.0	0.4	0.4	1.2	1.2	4.8	6.8	8.0	5.6	2.4	21.7	36.1	12.9	1.6	75.9	45.4	52.2	47.8
59844	HERON	97.0	96.4	0.0	0.1	0.2	0.1	0.5	0.7	4.4	5.4	7.2	7.5	2.0	17.6	41.5	12.6	1.7	77.0	47.9	51.4	48.6
59845	HOT SPRINGS	79.0	75.3	0.2	0.3	0.2	0.3	2.4	3.0	4.4	4.7	4.9	5.7	5.0	15.3	35.1	21.4	3.4	82.1	52.1	49.4	50.6
59846	HUSON	96.4	95.6	0.1	0.1	0.4	0.6	1.0	1.4	5.8	6.5	7.2	7.3	4.7	22.7	35.3	9.8	0.8	75.8	42.3	51.2	48.8
59847	LOLO	96.6	96.0	0.2	0.3	0.4	0.6	1.1	1.5	7.5	7.6	7.8	7.3	5.8	27.6	28.8	7.0	0.6	72.5	35.9	49.8	50.2
59848	LONEPINE	79.3	75.1	0.5	0.4	0.0	0.4	2.5	3.6	4.0	3.6	4.4	5.8	5.3	14.7	35.6	23.1	3.6	83.6	53.4	48.9	51.1
59853	NOXON	96.2	95.6	0.2	0.1	0.3	0.3	0.5	0.6	3.6	5.5	7.1	8.1	2.2	17.6	40.7	13.5	1.6	77.3	47.7	52.0	48.0
	MONTANA	90.6	89.7	0.3	0.4	0.6	0.7	2.0	2.6	6.0	6.1	6.5	7.3	7.0	24.2	29.0	11.8	2.1	77.1	39.4	49.8	50.2
	UNITED STATES	75.1	72.0	12.3	12.7	3.8	4.6	12.5	15.7	6.8	6.7	6.6	7.1	6.9	27.0	26.0	10.9	1.9	75.7	36.9	49.2	50.8

#	POST OFFICE NAME	2009 Per Capita Income	2009 HH Income Base	2009 Household Income Distribution (%): Less than $25,000	$25,000 to $49,999	$50,000 to $99,999	$100,000 to $149,999	$150,000 or More	Median Household Income: 2009	2014	2009 National Centile	2009 State Centile	2009 Home Value Base	2009 Home Value Distribution (%): Less than $50,000	$50,000 to $89,999	$90,000 to $174,999	$175,000 to $399,999	$400,000 or More	2009 Median Home Value
59522	CHESTER	18901	536	35.4	28.7	29.9	4.1	1.9	35179	36381	18	49	378	17.7	29.9	35.2	14.8	2.4	95625
59523	CHINOOK	18040	1019	37.6	30.9	24.8	5.2	1.5	33938	34668	15	40	709	19.5	23.4	36.5	16.8	3.8	104066
59524	DODSON	12697	50	46.0	20.0	32.0	2.0	0.0	28163	28294	6	9	43	11.6	30.2	46.5	11.6	0.0	97000
59525	GILDFORD	18009	119	26.1	34.5	36.1	2.5	0.8	41689	42033	38	81	96	22.9	27.1	27.1	21.9	1.0	90000
59526	HARLEM	13621	757	38.7	30.0	25.4	4.9	1.1	32605	33487	13	30	415	28.0	32.8	31.1	7.5	0.7	76125
59527	HAYS	9202	419	47.7	28.9	20.8	2.4	0.2	25811	25962	4	5	227	28.6	31.3	31.3	7.9	0.9	76563
59528	HINGHAM	17032	110	28.2	34.5	33.6	2.7	0.9	40434	40000	34	77	88	23.9	27.3	28.4	19.3	1.1	88000
59529	HOGELAND	16559	48	35.4	33.3	22.9	8.3	0.0	35000	36791	18	48	28	21.4	21.4	25.0	32.1	0.0	112500
59530	INVERNESS	18525	75	33.3	38.7	18.7	6.7	2.7	35263	36088	19	50	57	22.8	31.6	26.3	12.3	7.0	85000
59531	JOPLIN	20318	148	29.1	33.1	31.1	4.1	2.7	40000	40765	33	76	113	22.1	26.5	28.3	16.8	6.2	93000
59532	KREMLIN	18800	118	26.3	34.7	35.6	2.5	0.8	41490	41728	38	79	95	23.2	26.3	27.4	22.1	1.1	91250
59535	LLOYD	16699	69	37.7	36.2	18.8	5.8	1.4	32965	34298	13	32	49	24.5	12.2	22.4	30.6	10.2	137500
59537	LORING	13894	75	42.7	28.0	24.0	4.0	1.3	28222	28219	6	9	55	45.5	20.0	23.6	9.1	1.8	56250
59538	MALTA	18492	1463	35.9	30.4	29.2	2.7	1.8	35787	36605	20	53	1032	25.8	21.1	42.5	9.0	1.6	95246
59540	RUDYARD	21319	167	32.9	38.3	19.2	7.2	2.4	35401	36089	19	51	126	23.8	31.0	27.8	12.7	4.8	84000
59542	TURNER	17248	80	35.0	33.8	22.5	8.8	0.0	35536	35810	19	52	47	25.5	21.3	19.1	34.0	0.0	104167
59544	WHITEWATER	10447	29	51.7	24.1	20.7	3.4	0.0	24012	25702	3	3	21	42.9	23.8	23.8	9.5	0.0	62500
59545	WHITLASH	11483	105	39.0	34.3	24.8	1.9	0.0	32000	32619	11	25	77	31.2	10.4	27.3	23.4	7.8	112500
59546	ZORTMAN	20015	100	35.0	33.0	25.0	5.0	2.0	30741	30000	9	22	73	31.5	20.5	27.4	17.8	2.7	82500
59601	HELENA	26464	12911	25.3	28.4	34.8	7.6	3.9	45723	47102	50	88	7421	5.1	3.8	39.0	45.4	6.7	178771
59602	HELENA	22343	8535	17.4	32.9	38.7	8.4	2.6	49676	49347	60	92	7288	10.0	6.2	29.4	46.6	7.9	183644
59625	HELENA	9713	0	0.0	0.0	0.0	0.0	0.0	0	0	0	0	0	0.0	0.0	0.0	0.0	0.0	0
59632	BOULDER	19033	818	28.0	30.3	35.6	4.4	1.7	41537	42936	38	80	601	18.3	12.1	39.1	24.6	5.8	127724
59633	CANYON CREEK	24468	169	21.3	31.4	36.1	7.1	4.1	45464	48219	50	87	145	5.5	4.1	38.6	46.9	4.8	178676
59634	CLANCY	26799	1966	11.5	20.3	46.7	16.0	5.5	64238	64720	83	100	1756	3.2	2.6	14.0	66.9	13.3	261326
59635	EAST HELENA	19883	2403	19.5	32.8	40.5	5.6	1.5	47766	48444	56	90	1953	5.6	5.2	52.8	31.8	4.5	159789
59639	LINCOLN	18135	655	38.3	38.3	19.5	1.8	2.0	32337	33863	12	28	492	10.8	11.0	47.4	26.0	4.9	134722
59641	RADERSBURG	24330	44	18.2	27.3	45.5	6.8	2.3	53513	51689	69	97	36	5.6	11.1	19.4	36.1	27.8	237500
59642	RINGLING	17380	19	31.6	42.1	26.3	0.0	0.0	37351	28562	25	64	14	7.1	7.1	42.9	42.9	0.0	150000
59643	TOSTON	24811	176	20.5	32.4	36.9	6.3	4.0	47584	47593	56	90	145	6.9	7.6	21.4	38.6	25.5	227941
59644	TOWNSEND	18722	1472	28.8	40.7	24.3	3.7	2.5	36207	36676	21	54	1151	10.3	9.7	44.1	25.8	10.1	140682
59645	WHITE SULPHUR SPRING	16318	668	36.2	36.1	23.2	3.3	1.2	34338	35221	16	42	496	16.5	21.8	38.7	18.1	4.8	107836
59647	WINSTON	22302	137	19.7	29.2	40.9	6.6	3.6	50767	51036	63	94	113	8.0	10.6	16.8	39.8	24.8	228333
59648	WOLF CREEK	21621	324	27.2	37.0	29.0	4.3	2.5	40000	40630	33	76	263	7.2	8.4	31.2	37.6	15.6	182589
59701	BUTTE	21213	13552	31.7	31.9	28.7	4.8	2.9	37665	38141	26	65	9474	14.8	22.2	40.4	20.5	2.1	112205
59711	ANACONDA	18866	3818	35.7	31.6	27.9	3.2	1.5	34522	35428	17	44	2819	15.9	24.4	44.9	13.3	1.5	105036
59714	BELGRADE	22289	6764	16.8	30.3	43.1	7.1	2.7	51933	51340	66	96	4933	6.9	2.6	10.7	66.4	13.4	240635
59715	BOZEMAN	25486	13109	26.7	28.1	29.9	9.3	5.9	44762	46527	48	86	7045	5.5	1.4	7.0	50.1	36.0	319171
59717	BOZEMAN	10187	38	55.3	36.8	7.9	0.0	0.0	22230	20000	2	2	2	0.0	0.0	0.0	100.0	0.0	300000
59718	BOZEMAN	23935	10142	17.3	31.3	39.9	7.6	4.0	50994	50824	64	95	6613	5.6	2.9	8.0	56.3	27.2	287979
59720	CAMERON	24455	168	26.8	39.3	24.4	6.0	3.6	37748	36391	26	66	114	2.6	4.4	11.4	51.8	29.8	278571
59721	CARDWELL	17341	165	36.4	34.5	23.6	3.0	2.4	34160	35221	16	41	135	6.7	10.4	35.6	33.3	14.1	168269
59722	DEER LODGE	17100	1822	28.4	36.9	29.1	4.1	1.4	38568	39558	28	70	1280	14.2	24.1	35.2	19.8	6.6	109420
59724	DELL	11875	14	50.0	35.7	14.3	0.0	0.0	25000	25000	3	4	8	0.0	0.0	37.5	25.0	37.5	225000
59725	DILLON	18883	3137	36.1	27.3	30.2	4.7	1.8	36343	37027	22	56	2015	13.5	13.2	44.4	23.4	5.6	131782
59727	DIVIDE	28160	122	23.0	26.2	36.1	8.2	6.6	50954	50952	63	94	109	1.8	9.2	26.6	44.0	18.3	226563
59729	ENNIS	22726	1076	29.0	37.5	25.1	5.4	3.1	37263	37083	24	62	722	4.6	3.5	26.6	46.5	18.8	220385
59730	GALLATIN GATEWAY	34138	1189	16.6	28.3	36.4	9.2	9.6	54645	54307	71	97	802	2.7	0.9	7.1	42.5	46.8	381560
59731	GARRISON	18478	341	31.7	36.7	26.4	3.2	2.1	37036	36772	24	61	269	9.7	16.7	27.9	34.2	11.5	163500
59733	GOLD CREEK	15862	49	36.7	38.8	22.4	2.0	0.0	36854	37686	23	60	35	22.9	14.3	20.0	25.7	17.1	154167
59735	HARRISON	16751	173	31.2	38.7	26.0	2.9	1.2	37539	38402	25	64	135	5.2	9.6	33.3	31.9	20.0	181944
59736	JACKSON	17619	91	36.3	34.1	22.0	4.4	3.3	30714	31735	9	21	57	17.5	14.0	22.8	28.1	17.5	154167
59739	LIMA	15448	141	40.4	34.0	24.8	0.7	0.0	29408	30000	7	14	105	21.0	23.8	41.0	6.7	7.6	95000
59741	MANHATTAN	19431	1861	23.3	37.7	32.3	5.0	1.8	42226	43490	40	82	1388	4.0	3.6	17.0	59.4	16.0	247551
59745	NORRIS	16845	121	32.2	38.0	24.8	3.3	1.7	37025	37890	24	61	94	6.4	9.6	34.0	30.9	19.1	175000
59747	PONY	16754	74	31.1	39.2	25.7	2.7	1.4	37838	38360	26	67	58	5.2	10.3	36.2	31.0	17.2	168750
59748	RAMSAY	20590	34	17.6	29.4	47.1	5.9	0.0	52941	54545	68	96	29	3.4	10.3	31.0	44.8	10.3	193750
59749	SHERIDAN	18076	811	41.7	33.0	20.8	3.3	1.1	29558	30025	7	16	565	6.7	9.2	37.7	33.3	13.1	166734
59750	BUTTE	20484	151	17.2	29.1	44.4	6.6	2.6	53230	53834	68	97	129	6.2	9.3	32.6	44.2	7.8	180682
59751	SILVER STAR	17487	103	33.0	31.1	30.1	3.9	1.9	36633	37959	22	58	75	1.3	6.7	29.3	28.0	34.7	227500
59752	THREE FORKS	18753	1538	25.0	39.3	31.3	2.7	1.7	39789	39970	32	74	1151	5.4	5.1	35.2	45.4	8.9	182783
59754	TWIN BRIDGES	17595	440	32.7	33.0	30.2	3.2	0.9	34854	35357	17	46	325	9.2	5.8	42.2	26.8	16.0	153241
59755	VIRGINIA CITY	19092	136	39.0	35.3	20.6	4.4	0.7	32094	33391	12	26	98	2.0	6.1	32.7	36.7	22.4	231250
59756	WARM SPRINGS	23556	11	36.4	18.2	45.5	0.0	0.0	42313	28490	40	83	7	0.0	0.0	42.9	57.1	0.0	187500
59758	WEST YELLOWSTONE	26221	956	23.8	34.7	31.4	6.1	4.0	42853	45039	42	84	395	13.4	0.5	3.5	48.1	34.4	325904
59759	WHITEHALL	17081	1534	34.6	31.7	30.4	2.0	1.4	37306	38142	24	63	1221	5.2	11.5	31.7	44.3	7.3	179643
59761	WISDOM	20966	102	39.2	32.4	21.6	3.9	2.9	29501	30639	7	15	64	15.6	15.6	23.4	28.1	17.2	160000
59762	WISE RIVER	21984	126	38.1	32.5	23.0	4.0	2.4	30000	31201	8	19	83	14.5	13.3	27.7	28.9	15.7	158929
59801	MISSOULA	20228	12778	36.4	31.4	24.7	5.0	2.5	34345	34937	16	42	5636	5.8	1.8	22.5	65.2	4.8	206859
59802	MISSOULA	22069	8514	39.4	28.1	23.0	6.0	3.4	33389	33950	14	34	4223	8.9	3.4	20.5	53.8	13.4	214438
59803	MISSOULA	27014	5915	12.8	23.6	45.1	12.3	6.2	62889	63472	81	99	4652	1.0	0.3	7.4	78.1	13.2	265739
59804	MISSOULA	23100	2885	19.8	29.2	41.9	6.2	2.9	50760	50393	63	94	2028	7.3	2.7	8.6	63.6	17.9	266938
59808	MISSOULA	21941	6083	23.2	27.6	38.0	7.7	3.5	49062	48687	59	91	4546	19.2	9.4	16.4	42.7	12.4	195714
59820	ALBERTON	24220	493	27.2	26.4	35.5	6.5	4.5	47036	47614	54	89	402	5.7	4.5	22.4	41.3	26.1	240816
59821	ARLEE	17340	900	35.4	31.9	24.6	6.7	1.4	34713	35215	17	45	681	15.4	7.6	28.5	38.2	10.3	171591
59823	BONNER	21531	737	24.6	35.1	30.8	6.2	3.3	42524	44248	41	83	593	4.6	2.9	18.4	54.1	20.1	242010
59824	CHARLO	14936	579	37.5	35.1	24.0	2.9	0.5	32456	33479	12	29	425	13.6	7.5	25.6	43.1	10.1	185547
59825	CLINTON	19865	920	23.2	37.7	32.6	4.6	2.0	41810	42944	39	81	739	6.4	2.8	19.9	58.9	12.0	230962
59826	CONDON	19756	254	34.6	31.5	26.8	3.9	3.1	37195	37301	24	62	204	7.8	1.5	20.1	39.7	30.9	275000
59827	CONNER	23503	242	35.1	35.1	19.8	5.4	4.5	35899	37030	20	53	194	5.2	2.6	28.9	29.4	34.0	207692
59828	CORVALLIS	18213	2071	28.6	34.5	28.6	6.3	2.0	38090	38528	27	68	1661	7.9	3.1	16.7	48.8	23.4	247624
59829	DARBY	16516	1124	33.1	41.3	19.3	3.7	2.6	32469	32528	12	29	818	6.0	4.3	28.5	33.4	27.9	223881
59831	DIXON	14554	210	51.9	19.5	23.3	3.3	1.9	23774	23718	3	3	155	20.0	27.7	28.4	18.1	5.8	95000
59832	DRUMMOND	18498	343	34.7	35.6	23.3	4.4	2.0	32901	33502	13	31	256	14.8	18.8	28.1	26.2	12.1	122000
59833	FLORENCE	21084	2024	16.8	32.5	39.7	7.9	3.0	50477	49679	62	93	1694	6.3	2.9	17.2	61.5	12.0	231865
59834	FRENCHTOWN	21443	757	16.0	26.7	48.2	7.1	2.0	56812	56281	74	98	661	7.3	2.9	14.4	56.0	19.5	259247
59837	HALL	17902	98	34.7	35.7	23.5	4.1	2.0	32784	32784	13	31	72	18.1	22.2	27.8	20.8	11.1	103571
59840	HAMILTON	21865	6182	32.2	34.9	23.8	5.6	3.5	35319	35966	19	50	4368	6.5	5.2	28.2	45.1	15.0	208067
59843	HELMVILLE	15507	102	41.2	34.3	20.6	3.9	0.0	30542	31695	9	21	74	6.8	8.1	28.4	36.5	20.3	200000
59844	HERON	18077	294	34.4	40.1	19.0	4.4	2.0	33930	35070	15	40	232	9.1	9.1	20.7	41.4	19.8	223438
59845	HOT SPRINGS	15424	562	57.1	24.2	15.8	1.4	1.4	20702	20726	2	2	372	12.6	16.1	35.2	26.3	9.7	140086
59846	HUSON	24449	631	16.0	26.9	48.3	6.5	2.2	56917	56389	74	98	549	5.6	2.7	9.7	58.1	23.9	292083
59847	LOLO	21755	2023	14.8	33.0	42.0	6.7	3.4	51321	50789	64	95	1646	6.4	1.8	15.2	67.6	8.9	215455
59848	LONEPINE	13164	94	60.6	21.3	14.9	2.1	1.1	19038	19512	1	1	62	14.5	16.1	35.5	25.8	8.1	137500
59853	NOXON	18895	301	32.9	39.9	20.9	4.7	1.7	34404	34892	16	43	234	8.1	9.4	21.8	38.5	22.2	221667
	MONTANA	21013		28.7	31.3	31.1	5.8	3.0	40864	42494				10.4	9.4	31.4	38.6	10.1	171793
	UNITED STATES	27277		20.9	24.4	35.3	11.7	7.6	54719	56938				9.3	13.1	31.6	32.6	13.5	162279

ZIP CODE #	POST OFFICE NAME	FINANCIAL SERVICES: Auto Loan	Home Loan	Invest-ments	Retire-ment Plans	THE HOME: Home Improvements: Home Repair	Lawn & Garden	Furnishings: Computers & Hardware-Personal	Major Appli-ances	TV, Radio, Sound Equip-ment	Furni-ture	ENTERTAINMENT: Dine out/ Carry out	Sports Equip-ment	Fees & Tickets	Toys & Games	Travel	Cable TV	PERSONAL: Apparel & Services	Auto Repairs	Health Insur-ance	Pets & Supplies
59522	CHESTER	77	55	80	54	57	81	60	74	65	52	64	57	47	64	58	72	42	69	80	88
59523	CHINOOK	70	51	71	50	53	72	58	67	62	50	60	52	46	60	55	67	40	65	73	80
59524	DODSON	63	45	65	44	47	64	47	59	52	43	51	45	37	51	46	57	34	54	62	71
59525	GILDFORD	81	56	89	56	59	86	62	77	65	50	64	64	46	63	62	71	42	72	82	95
59526	HARLEM	67	51	59	52	50	66	56	62	61	52	60	48	49	61	53	66	41	61	68	75
59527	HAYS	49	41	33	43	37	44	45	42	49	45	49	33	43	50	41	51	33	46	48	54
59528	HINGHAM	82	56	90	56	59	86	62	78	65	51	64	64	46	64	62	71	42	72	82	95
59529	HOGELAND	77	53	84	53	55	81	58	73	61	47	60	60	43	60	58	66	39	68	77	89
59530	INVERNESS	83	57	91	57	60	88	63	79	66	51	65	65	46	65	63	72	42	74	83	97
59531	JOPLIN	88	60	97	60	63	93	67	83	70	54	69	69	49	68	67	76	45	78	88	103
59532	KREMLIN	81	56	89	56	59	86	62	77	65	50	64	64	46	63	62	71	42	72	82	95
59535	LLOYD	74	51	81	50	53	78	56	70	58	46	58	58	41	57	56	64	37	65	74	86
59537	LORING	68	47	75	47	49	72	52	65	54	42	54	54	38	53	52	59	35	61	69	80
59538	MALTA	76	53	80	53	56	80	59	73	63	50	62	57	45	62	58	69	41	68	78	88
59540	RUDYARD	84	57	92	57	60	88	64	79	66	52	66	66	47	65	63	72	43	74	84	98
59542	TURNER	77	53	85	53	56	81	59	73	61	48	61	61	43	60	59	67	39	68	77	90
59544	WHITEWATER	58	40	64	40	42	61	44	55	46	36	46	46	33	45	44	50	30	52	58	68
59545	WHITLASH	71	49	78	48	51	74	54	67	56	44	55	55	39	55	54	61	36	63	71	82
59546	ZORTMAN	82	56	90	56	59	86	63	78	65	51	64	64	46	64	62	71	42	73	82	96
59601	HELENA	79	77	75	79	77	78	82	78	82	81	82	61	81	81	80	82	57	81	82	93
59602	HELENA	91	86	88	85	86	91	81	89	83	82	83	66	79	84	82	84	56	85	87	104
59625	HELENA	0	0	0	0	0	0	0	0	0	0	0	0	0	0	0	0	0	0	0	0
59632	BOULDER	73	69	62	67	67	70	68	69	69	69	69	52	65	71	66	70	47	69	70	82
59633	CANYON CREEK	92	77	115	77	83	98	76	94	79	72	78	69	68	76	82	83	52	87	93	109
59634	CLANCY	105	118	110	119	117	112	104	108	102	109	103	82	111	104	110	101	72	104	103	126
59635	EAST HELENA	83	80	74	78	77	78	77	79	76	79	77	59	74	79	75	76	53	77	77	93
59639	LINCOLN	67	53	86	53	59	71	54	68	56	50	55	50	46	53	58	60	37	63	67	79
59641	RADERSBURG	109	75	119	75	78	115	83	103	86	67	85	85	61	85	83	94	55	96	109	127
59642	RINGLING	67	46	74	46	48	71	51	64	53	42	53	53	38	52	51	58	34	59	67	78
59643	TOSTON	102	73	117	73	78	107	79	98	82	67	81	78	61	80	80	89	53	92	102	119
59644	TOWNSEND	77	57	84	56	60	80	60	75	66	54	64	56	49	64	61	72	43	70	80	89
59645	WHITE SULPHUR SPRING	69	48	73	48	50	72	53	66	57	45	56	53	40	56	52	62	36	62	70	80
59647	WINSTON	109	75	120	75	79	115	83	104	87	68	86	86	61	85	83	95	56	97	109	128
59648	WOLF CREEK	78	63	101	62	69	83	63	80	66	59	65	58	54	62	68	70	43	74	79	92
59701	BUTTE	72	65	70	65	66	76	68	72	72	65	71	54	64	71	67	76	48	72	79	85
59711	ANACONDA	66	56	69	55	58	72	58	67	63	54	62	49	53	62	59	68	42	64	74	78
59714	BELGRADE	89	84	74	84	81	80	85	82	84	86	85	64	81	87	80	83	59	83	81	98
59715	BOZEMAN	90	76	79	80	76	79	96	83	91	87	91	68	84	91	84	90	64	89	84	100
59717	BOZEMAN	40	17	17	21	16	20	57	28	45	38	46	30	34	44	30	41	33	40	28	38
59718	BOZEMAN	91	85	78	86	83	83	89	85	88	89	88	67	85	90	84	87	61	87	85	101
59720	CAMERON	86	69	111	68	76	91	69	88	72	65	71	64	60	69	75	77	47	81	87	102
59721	CARDWELL	76	52	83	52	55	80	58	72	60	47	59	59	42	59	58	66	39	67	76	88
59722	DEER LODGE	72	58	74	58	60	77	61	72	66	56	64	54	53	65	61	71	43	68	78	84
59724	DELL	49	33	53	33	35	51	37	46	39	30	38	38	27	38	37	42	25	43	49	57
59725	DILLON	72	58	73	58	60	73	63	70	65	58	64	53	54	64	61	69	43	68	74	84
59727	DIVIDE	111	89	144	88	98	118	89	113	93	84	92	83	77	89	97	100	61	105	112	131
59729	ENNIS	80	64	104	63	71	85	64	82	67	60	66	60	56	64	70	72	44	75	81	95
59730	GALLATIN GATEWAY	113	113	110	115	111	114	111	111	110	111	111	86	111	111	111	111	77	111	112	132
59731	GARRISON	80	59	94	58	63	84	62	78	65	54	64	61	49	63	64	70	42	73	80	94
59733	GOLD CREEK	63	50	81	49	55	66	50	64	53	47	52	47	43	50	54	56	34	59	63	74
59735	HARRISON	76	52	83	52	55	80	58	72	60	47	60	60	42	59	58	66	39	67	76	89
59736	JACKSON	71	57	92	56	62	75	57	72	59	53	59	53	49	56	62	63	39	67	71	84
59739	LIMA	63	43	69	43	45	66	48	59	50	39	49	49	35	49	47	54	32	55	63	73
59741	MANHATTAN	85	69	81	68	69	85	70	80	73	66	72	62	59	74	68	77	48	76	82	96
59745	NORRIS	75	52	83	52	54	80	58	72	60	47	59	59	42	59	57	65	38	67	76	88
59747	PONY	76	52	84	52	55	80	58	72	60	47	60	60	43	59	58	66	39	67	76	89
59748	RAMSAY	75	85	73	87	82	83	76	79	74	76	75	61	81	76	80	74	52	76	78	92
59749	SHERIDAN	63	54	79	52	60	69	53	65	56	53	55	46	49	53	58	60	37	61	68	75
59750	BUTTE	84	94	83	97	92	93	85	88	83	85	84	69	90	85	89	83	58	85	87	104
59751	SILVER STAR	81	56	89	56	59	86	62	77	65	50	64	64	46	63	62	70	41	72	81	95
59752	THREE FORKS	78	65	75	64	65	80	65	75	68	60	67	58	56	69	64	72	45	71	77	90
59754	TWIN BRIDGES	75	54	80	52	56	77	56	71	61	50	60	55	44	60	56	67	39	65	74	85
59755	VIRGINIA CITY	66	53	86	52	58	70	53	68	56	50	55	49	46	53	58	59	37	62	67	78
59756	WARM SPRINGS	74	60	96	59	65	79	60	76	62	56	62	55	52	59	65	66	41	70	75	88
59758	WEST YELLOWSTONE	83	70	81	73	71	76	83	79	84	79	84	62	77	81	79	85	58	84	84	96
59759	WHITEHALL	74	54	83	53	58	77	56	71	60	51	60	54	45	59	58	66	39	66	73	85
59761	WISDOM	71	57	91	56	62	75	57	72	59	53	58	53	49	56	61	63	39	66	71	83
59762	WISE RIVER	73	58	94	57	64	77	58	74	61	55	60	54	50	58	63	65	40	68	73	86
59801	MISSOULA	65	51	49	54	50	53	72	58	69	64	69	49	61	69	59	68	48	65	61	71
59802	MISSOULA	69	59	57	61	58	61	73	63	71	68	71	51	65	71	64	71	50	69	67	77
59803	MISSOULA	101	117	106	117	114	107	105	105	101	108	103	82	113	104	110	99	73	102	100	122
59804	MISSOULA	86	84	89	83	85	90	81	87	83	80	83	64	80	82	83	85	57	85	90	102
59808	MISSOULA	89	86	74	83	83	83	82	83	82	86	82	63	79	86	79	82	57	82	81	98
59820	ALBERTON	91	87	104	88	89	99	82	94	83	80	83	71	80	82	88	86	56	89	93	110
59821	ARLEE	72	66	59	64	64	68	62	66	65	65	65	48	59	67	59	66	44	64	66	79
59823	BONNER	88	76	100	74	79	90	73	87	76	72	76	64	67	75	76	80	51	82	86	102
59824	CHARLO	65	53	60	52	53	64	53	60	55	51	55	46	46	56	51	58	37	57	62	73
59825	CLINTON	82	75	69	72	73	78	71	76	73	73	73	55	67	76	68	76	50	73	76	90
59826	CONDON	76	61	98	60	67	80	61	77	64	57	63	56	53	60	66	68	42	71	76	89
59827	CONNER	81	65	105	64	71	86	65	82	68	61	67	60	56	64	70	72	45	76	81	96
59828	CORVALLIS	81	63	98	61	68	85	63	81	68	59	67	59	54	65	67	73	44	74	81	94
59829	DARBY	73	56	87	55	60	76	57	72	60	53	60	53	48	58	59	65	39	66	72	84
59831	DIXON	61	46	58	46	46	61	48	57	53	46	52	43	41	53	47	57	35	54	60	68
59832	DRUMMOND	76	54	86	54	57	81	59	73	61	49	61	60	44	60	59	67	39	68	77	89
59833	FLORENCE	90	87	94	87	88	95	82	91	83	81	83	68	80	83	85	85	57	86	90	107
59834	FRENCHTOWN	89	95	82	96	92	94	86	90	86	87	86	69	89	89	89	87	60	87	89	106
59837	HALL	74	51	82	51	54	78	57	70	59	46	58	58	42	58	56	64	38	66	74	87
59840	HAMILTON	77	66	87	66	70	81	69	79	72	66	71	57	63	70	70	76	48	76	83	91
59843	HELMVILLE	64	50	81	49	55	67	51	64	53	47	52	47	43	50	55	57	35	59	64	75
59844	HERON	72	58	93	57	63	76	58	73	60	54	60	54	50	57	63	64	40	68	72	85
59845	HOT SPRINGS	46	43	56	40	48	52	41	49	44	44	43	33	40	40	45	46	29	47	54	56
59846	HUSON	88	97	87	99	94	97	87	92	86	87	86	71	92	88	92	86	60	88	91	108
59847	LOLO	96	89	78	86	86	90	83	88	86	87	86	64	79	90	80	89	59	85	88	105
59848	LONEPINE	45	43	55	40	48	52	41	49	44	45	43	32	41	40	45	46	29	47	54	56
59853	NOXON	72	58	93	57	63	76	58	73	60	54	60	53	50	57	62	64	40	67	72	85
	MONTANA	80	69	77	69	70	79	73	77	75	69	74	59	67	74	71	77	51	76	80	92
	UNITED STATES	100	100	100	100	100	100	100	100	100	100	100	100	100	100	100	100	100	100	100	100

ZIP CODE #	POST OFFICE NAME	COUNTY FIPS CODE	POPULATION 2000	POPULATION 2009	POPULATION 2014	2000-2009 ANNUAL RATE % Rate	2000-2009 ANNUAL RATE State Centile	HOUSEHOLDS 2000	HOUSEHOLDS 2009	HOUSEHOLDS 2014	HOUSEHOLDS % Annual Rate 2000-2009	HOUSEHOLDS 2009 Average HH Size	FAMILIES 2000	FAMILIES 2009	FAMILIES % Annual Rate 2000-2009
59854	OVANDO	077	268	265	264	-0.1	48	112	112	112	0.0	2.37	84	82	-0.3
59858	PHILIPSBURG	039	1545	1571	1575	0.2	57	645	662	666	0.3	2.33	401	398	-0.1
59859	PLAINS	089	3371	3612	3736	0.7	71	1383	1519	1584	1.0	2.31	939	1000	0.7
59860	POLSON	047	9532	10215	10522	0.8	73	3856	4189	4337	0.9	2.40	2659	2802	0.6
59864	RONAN	047	6906	7287	7448	0.6	66	2343	2487	2550	0.6	2.77	1708	1767	0.4
59865	SAINT IGNATIUS	047	2872	3050	3142	0.7	71	1061	1147	1186	0.8	2.66	748	786	0.5
59866	SAINT REGIS	061	1099	1118	1103	0.2	57	469	487	485	0.4	2.29	308	309	0.0
59868	SEELEY LAKE	063	1853	2013	2137	0.9	77	762	839	894	1.0	2.40	533	562	0.6
59870	STEVENSVILLE	081	8326	9297	9771	1.2	86	3196	3612	3810	1.3	2.55	2376	2612	1.0
59871	SULA	081	165	191	205	1.6	92	83	98	106	1.8	1.91	55	63	1.5
59872	SUPERIOR	061	2232	2284	2270	0.2	57	891	929	929	0.5	2.39	603	609	0.1
59873	THOMPSON FALLS	089	2705	2960	3096	1.0	79	1137	1282	1355	1.3	2.27	779	852	1.0
59874	TROUT CREEK	089	1250	1397	1479	1.2	86	490	565	605	1.6	2.44	365	410	1.3
59875	VICTOR	081	3394	3939	4223	1.6	92	1341	1572	1690	1.7	2.51	995	1133	1.4
59901	KALISPELL	029	41560	49423	53978	1.9	95	16499	19216	21025	1.7	2.54	11223	12710	1.4
59910	BIG ARM	047	392	436	456	1.2	86	171	193	203	1.3	2.26	125	137	1.0
59911	BIGFORK	047	6875	8002	8654	1.7	93	2896	3356	3642	1.6	2.36	2070	2321	1.2
59912	COLUMBIA FALLS	029	11466	14095	15690	2.3	97	4283	5176	5780	2.1	2.69	3197	3748	1.7
59914	DAYTON	047	233	258	269	1.1	83	106	119	125	1.3	2.17	73	80	1.0
59915	ELMO	047	254	282	295	1.1	83	98	110	116	1.3	2.56	69	75	0.9
59916	ESSEX	029	219	239	251	0.9	77	74	83	90	1.2	1.89	36	38	0.6
59917	EUREKA	053	4532	4502	4472	-0.1	48	1843	1889	1899	0.3	2.35	1268	1258	-0.1
59920	KILA	029	1289	1510	1651	1.7	93	475	548	601	1.6	2.73	362	406	1.2
59922	LAKESIDE	029	1862	2310	2569	2.4	97	785	950	1058	2.1	2.43	578	677	1.7
59923	LIBBY	053	10161	10209	10219	0.1	53	4178	4301	4343	0.3	2.34	2872	2874	0.0
59925	MARION	029	616	670	709	0.9	77	250	268	284	0.8	2.44	190	198	0.4
59928	POLEBRIDGE	029	90	104	112	1.6	92	47	57	63	2.1	1.54	27	31	1.5
59929	PROCTOR	047	107	124	132	1.6	92	46	54	57	1.7	2.30	33	38	1.5
59930	REXFORD	053	851	877	887	0.3	58	333	355	363	0.7	2.45	240	248	0.4
59931	ROLLINS	047	327	378	402	1.6	92	147	172	183	1.7	2.20	106	120	1.4
59932	SOMERS	029	1374	1631	1796	1.9	95	590	688	760	1.7	2.37	410	461	1.3
59935	TROY	053	3293	3475	3543	0.6	66	1410	1536	1581	0.9	2.26	955	1006	0.6
59937	WHITEFISH	029	11673	13389	14427	1.5	90	4790	5397	5826	1.3	2.46	3123	3380	0.9
	MONTANA					0.8					0.9	2.43			0.5
	UNITED STATES					1.0					1.1	2.59			0.9

# POST OFFICE NAME	RACE (%) White 2000	White 2009	Black 2000	Black 2009	Asian/Pacific 2000	Asian/Pacific 2009	% Hispanic Origin 2000	% Hispanic Origin 2009	2009 AGE DISTRIBUTION (%) 0-4	5-9	10-14	15-19	20-24	25-44	45-64	65-84	85+	18+	MEDIAN AGE 2009	% 2009 Males	% 2009 Females
59854 OVANDO	96.7	96.6	0.4	0.4	0.4	0.4	1.1	1.9	4.5	6.4	7.9	5.3	2.3	21.9	37.4	12.5	1.9	76.6	46.2	52.5	47.5
59858 PHILIPSBURG	96.1	95.9	0.0	0.0	0.3	0.3	1.7	1.7	4.1	4.7	5.9	6.0	5.0	20.1	34.6	17.1	2.6	80.8	47.7	50.4	49.6
59859 PLAINS	94.5	93.7	0.1	0.1	0.5	0.6	2.1	2.8	4.9	5.1	6.2	7.2	4.3	19.2	35.2	15.4	2.5	79.1	47.0	49.9	50.1
59860 POLSON	77.2	73.9	0.1	0.1	0.5	0.6	2.2	2.8	6.4	6.2	6.9	6.8	5.9	20.9	29.9	14.4	2.6	76.1	42.5	48.7	51.3
59864 RONAN	58.1	53.5	0.1	0.1	0.3	0.3	3.3	3.7	7.9	7.7	7.9	9.2	7.9	23.9	24.1	9.6	1.7	70.6	32.1	49.4	50.6
59865 SAINT IGNATIUS	60.9	57.8	0.1	0.1	0.2	0.2	2.8	3.0	7.0	7.2	7.3	7.4	6.7	23.6	28.6	10.6	1.5	73.6	37.1	48.9	51.1
59866 SAINT REGIS	95.5	95.3	0.0	0.0	0.6	0.6	2.5	2.4	5.1	5.0	6.8	7.4	3.4	21.8	36.9	12.8	0.8	77.8	45.3	52.7	47.3
59868 SEELEY LAKE	96.4	95.9	0.1	0.1	0.2	0.2	1.5	2.0	5.1	5.6	7.3	6.8	3.2	23.6	35.5	11.9	1.0	77.1	44.1	52.6	47.4
59870 STEVENSVILLE	97.2	96.8	0.3	0.4	0.3	0.4	1.5	2.0	5.9	6.5	7.1	6.9	4.5	23.4	32.2	11.8	1.8	75.8	42.2	49.5	50.5
59871 SULA	95.1	93.7	0.0	0.0	0.6	1.0	4.3	5.2	3.7	4.2	4.7	4.7	3.1	16.8	40.3	20.9	1.6	83.2	53.8	50.8	49.2
59872 SUPERIOR	93.8	93.5	0.1	0.1	0.5	0.5	1.4	1.4	4.7	5.1	5.8	6.6	4.5	21.4	33.6	16.3	2.0	80.0	46.2	51.1	48.9
59873 THOMPSON FALLS	96.6	96.0	0.1	0.2	0.2	0.3	1.0	1.4	4.7	5.0	6.3	6.2	4.4	19.9	35.2	16.5	1.8	79.8	47.2	50.9	49.1
59874 TROUT CREEK	95.8	94.9	0.1	0.1	0.3	0.4	0.8	1.1	3.6	4.9	7.8	7.2	2.8	18.4	41.0	13.1	1.2	78.7	47.4	53.3	46.7
59875 VICTOR	96.6	96.0	0.1	0.1	0.3	0.3	2.4	3.2	5.9	6.6	7.1	7.2	3.7	21.0	33.0	14.2	1.4	75.6	44.0	50.2	49.8
59901 KALISPELL	96.1	95.5	0.2	0.2	0.5	0.6	1.4	1.8	6.1	6.4	6.9	7.1	5.6	24.0	30.2	11.6	2.2	76.3	40.5	48.8	51.2
59910 BIG ARM	75.3	71.1	0.0	0.0	0.3	0.5	1.0	1.4	5.5	5.5	6.4	6.2	3.4	17.9	35.1	18.1	1.8	78.7	47.8	47.2	52.8
59911 BIGFORK	96.7	96.1	0.1	0.2	0.4	0.5	1.9	2.5	3.6	5.0	6.2	6.1	3.5	19.5	38.2	15.8	2.1	81.0	48.4	49.8	50.2
59912 COLUMBIA FALLS	96.1	95.4	0.1	0.2	0.5	0.6	1.3	1.8	6.3	6.6	6.9	7.5	5.4	24.5	30.1	11.3	1.3	75.3	39.7	50.2	49.8
59914 DAYTON	72.6	68.2	0.0	0.0	0.0	0.0	0.4	0.8	5.0	5.4	5.8	5.0	3.1	16.7	33.3	23.3	2.3	80.2	51.6	47.3	52.7
59915 ELMO	72.2	67.7	0.0	0.0	0.0	0.0	0.8	1.1	5.3	5.7	5.7	5.7	3.2	17.0	35.1	20.6	1.8	79.8	49.8	46.8	53.2
59916 ESSEX	92.2	90.4	0.0	0.0	5.0	6.3	1.8	2.1	2.1	0.8	3.8	10.0	17.6	27.6	28.9	8.4	0.8	91.6	35.2	49.4	50.6
59917 EUREKA	97.0	96.5	0.1	0.1	0.4	0.5	1.4	1.9	5.4	5.7	7.1	7.2	4.2	20.8	33.3	14.6	1.8	77.0	44.8	50.3	49.7
59920 KILA	96.4	95.8	0.1	0.1	0.3	0.3	1.2	1.7	5.6	6.3	7.1	8.1	4.9	23.4	35.0	9.0	0.5	75.3	41.0	52.1	47.9
59922 LAKESIDE	97.5	97.0	0.1	0.1	0.6	0.9	1.2	1.6	5.3	6.0	6.3	5.5	3.4	18.1	36.5	17.2	1.7	78.8	48.4	49.2	50.8
59923 LIBBY	95.8	95.2	0.1	0.1	0.4	0.5	1.4	1.9	4.9	5.9	7.2	7.2	4.0	20.9	34.5	13.7	1.8	77.1	45.0	50.4	49.6
59925 MARION	94.8	93.9	0.0	0.0	0.5	0.6	1.3	1.8	4.6	5.2	6.9	9.6	3.7	20.9	39.4	9.1	0.6	76.1	44.4	54.0	46.0
59928 POLEBRIDGE	96.7	95.2	0.0	0.0	0.0	0.0	1.1	1.0	3.8	2.9	3.8	1.0	3.8	22.1	48.1	14.4	0.0	89.4	53.8	63.5	36.5
59929 PROCTOR	98.1	96.8	1.9	1.6	0.0	0.0	0.0	0.0	3.2	3.2	4.8	4.0	3.2	14.5	39.5	24.2	3.2	86.3	56.3	50.8	49.2
59930 REXFORD	96.7	96.0	0.1	0.2	0.1	0.1	2.0	2.6	5.6	5.9	6.2	5.8	5.2	20.9	34.2	15.2	1.0	78.0	45.2	51.4	48.6
59931 ROLLINS	97.6	96.8	1.8	2.1	0.0	0.0	0.3	0.3	3.2	3.4	4.8	4.5	3.4	15.3	38.1	24.3	2.9	85.7	55.9	51.9	48.1
59932 SOMERS	96.9	96.3	0.1	0.1	0.3	0.4	1.8	2.3	4.8	5.6	6.4	6.4	3.6	21.0	34.9	15.4	1.8	78.6	46.1	50.1	49.9
59935 TROY	95.7	95.1	0.2	0.3	0.3	0.4	1.3	1.8	4.2	4.9	6.5	7.3	3.7	18.2	37.9	15.9	1.4	78.7	47.6	51.6	48.4
59937 WHITEFISH	96.4	95.8	0.1	0.1	0.7	0.8	1.6	2.1	5.1	5.5	6.8	6.7	5.3	26.1	32.7	10.2	1.6	78.1	41.6	50.3	49.7
MONTANA	90.6	89.7	0.3	0.4	0.6	0.7	2.0	2.6	6.0	6.1	6.5	7.3	7.0	24.2	29.0	11.8	2.1	77.1	39.4	49.8	50.2
UNITED STATES	75.1	72.0	12.3	12.7	3.8	4.6	12.5	15.7	6.8	6.7	6.6	7.1	6.9	27.0	26.0	10.9	1.9	75.7	36.9	49.2	50.8

ZIP CODE #	POST OFFICE NAME	2009 Per Capita Income	2009 HH Income Base	2009 Household Income Distribution (%): Less than $25,000	$25,000 to $49,999	$50,000 to $99,999	$100,000 to $149,999	$150,000 or More	Median Household Income: 2009	2014	2009 National Centile	2009 State Centile	2009 Home Value Base	2009 Home Value Distribution (%): Less than $50,000	$50,000 to $89,999	$90,000 to $174,999	$175,000 to $399,999	$400,000 or More	2009 Median Home Value
59854	OVANDO	15757	112	42.9	33.9	19.6	3.6	0.0	30000	30978	8	19	81	7.4	6.2	27.2	37.0	22.2	207500
59858	PHILIPSBURG	19536	662	37.3	31.3	24.9	3.9	2.6	33321	34175	14	34	491	15.7	15.1	35.0	23.8	10.4	136318
59859	PLAINS	16962	1519	37.9	33.8	24.4	2.7	1.1	31881	32306	11	25	1199	10.8	10.4	30.8	33.4	14.7	168683
59860	POLSON	19358	4189	35.2	31.7	26.8	3.7	2.7	34088	35285	16	41	2874	5.7	6.5	29.1	42.2	16.5	202306
59864	RONAN	15590	2487	34.9	35.1	24.6	3.2	2.2	33806	34456	15	39	1720	11.1	8.5	32.2	38.1	10.0	170628
59865	SAINT IGNATIUS	15291	1147	38.8	30.5	26.0	3.9	0.8	30422	32553	9	20	873	9.2	7.4	37.1	34.5	11.8	162103
59866	SAINT REGIS	18526	487	42.7	33.3	17.2	3.7	3.1	28427	28896	6	10	358	16.8	10.6	35.2	28.8	8.7	143750
59868	SEELEY LAKE	20717	839	26.7	38.5	27.1	4.4	3.3	39278	39579	31	73	675	7.7	5.5	24.9	47.6	14.4	209069
59870	STEVENSVILLE	20139	3612	24.9	35.1	32.5	4.3	3.2	41813	43370	39	81	2846	2.7	3.8	24.6	56.6	12.2	224213
59871	SULA	26955	98	23.5	35.7	32.7	3.1	5.1	43962	45000	45	85	75	2.7	2.7	24.0	18.7	52.0	413636
59872	SUPERIOR	17060	929	36.7	36.1	21.7	4.1	1.4	32626	33206	13	30	695	11.8	12.4	38.7	29.5	7.6	140530
59873	THOMPSON FALLS	19069	1282	32.0	38.8	23.8	3.1	2.3	33777	34573	15	39	998	6.4	11.8	38.1	32.1	11.6	161875
59874	TROUT CREEK	18288	565	32.7	35.9	23.9	5.1	2.3	34035	35332	16	40	461	6.9	6.7	28.0	35.6	22.8	209722
59875	VICTOR	19557	1572	27.0	38.0	29.3	3.3	2.3	39478	40368	31	73	1241	5.0	4.8	30.5	42.5	17.3	218443
59901	KALISPELL	20277	19216	27.7	33.4	30.6	4.9	3.4	40771	41872	35	78	13891	7.1	4.2	30.8	46.9	11.0	197687
59910	BIG ARM	19297	193	37.8	29.0	25.4	4.1	3.6	29218	28986	7	13	158	11.4	8.9	10.1	44.9	24.7	240000
59911	BIGFORK	22101	3356	27.8	33.2	29.7	6.3	3.0	40071	41266	33	76	2604	3.3	4.0	20.1	43.9	28.7	249601
59912	COLUMBIA FALLS	18241	5176	26.7	31.5	34.9	5.4	1.4	43531	45466	44	84	4024	7.0	4.3	35.2	44.1	9.3	183846
59914	DAYTON	20645	119	40.3	26.9	24.4	4.2	4.2	29752	29785	8	17	95	8.4	5.3	10.5	41.1	34.7	246250
59915	ELMO	17390	110	40.0	27.3	24.5	3.6	4.5	29090	28819	7	12	88	10.2	6.8	10.2	42.0	30.7	239474
59916	ESSEX	24945	83	16.9	28.9	48.2	3.6	2.4	53420	54495	69	97	40	7.5	5.0	27.5	30.0	30.0	212500
59917	EUREKA	16131	1889	37.7	35.2	23.6	3.1	0.4	31811	32509	11	25	1502	11.4	11.5	34.8	34.6	7.7	152362
59920	KILA	17697	548	29.4	35.6	27.4	4.6	3.1	39182	39484	30	72	449	5.1	4.5	29.2	49.0	12.2	210915
59922	LAKESIDE	22027	950	30.2	28.7	30.7	6.5	3.8	40686	41104	35	78	739	4.7	1.5	19.9	44.2	29.6	267857
59923	LIBBY	16880	4301	37.5	33.7	24.6	3.2	0.9	33390	33912	14	35	3185	15.4	12.4	37.6	30.5	4.3	130372
59925	MARION	18818	268	33.6	31.3	29.9	3.4	1.9	38208	38744	27	69	217	3.7	5.5	29.0	47.9	13.8	217424
59928	POLEBRIDGE	24422	57	61.4	12.3	15.8	10.5	0.0	19343	19384	1	2	53	0.0	0.0	0.0	73.6	26.4	310714
59929	PROCTOR	22287	54	35.2	37.0	20.4	5.6	1.9	29314	29655	7	14	44	9.1	2.3	18.2	43.2	27.3	316667
59930	REXFORD	14594	355	44.5	32.4	19.4	3.4	0.3	27006	27613	5	6	305	8.9	12.8	28.5	38.7	11.1	174537
59931	ROLLINS	23364	172	36.6	33.1	20.9	5.8	3.5	29744	31149	8	17	140	7.1	4.3	19.3	42.9	26.4	308333
59932	SOMERS	24044	688	27.2	31.8	31.5	4.1	5.4	42121	43534	40	81	548	5.1	3.5	22.4	41.6	27.4	253571
59935	TROY	14721	1536	45.2	35.4	16.2	2.7	0.5	27101	27702	5	7	1222	14.2	18.5	33.6	25.9	7.8	131008
59937	WHITEFISH	23491	5397	25.6	30.7	33.3	5.9	4.4	43698	45547	44	85	3780	6.4	3.0	23.3	44.8	22.5	238978
	MONTANA	21013		28.7	31.3	31.1	5.8	3.0	40864	42494				10.4	9.4	31.4	38.6	10.1	171793
	UNITED STATES	27277		20.9	24.4	35.3	11.7	7.6	54719	56938				9.3	13.1	31.6	32.6	13.5	162279

ZIP CODE	FINANCIAL SERVICES				THE HOME						ENTERTAINMENT						PERSONAL			
					Home Improvements		Furnishings													
# POST OFFICE NAME	Auto Loan	Home Loan	Invest-ments	Retire-ment Plans	Home Repair	Lawn & Garden	Comput-ers & Hard-ware-Personal	Major Appli-ances	TV, Radio, Sound Equip-ment	Furni-ture	Dine out/ Carry out	Sports Equip-ment	Fees & Tickets	Toys & Games	Travel	Cable TV	Apparel & Services	Auto Repairs	Health Insur-ance	Pets & Supplies
59854 OVANDO	62	50	80	49	55	66	50	63	52	47	52	46	43	49	54	56	34	58	62	73
59858 PHILIPSBURG	77	58	85	56	61	81	61	76	67	55	65	56	50	65	62	73	43	71	80	89
59859 PLAINS	67	52	82	51	57	70	53	67	56	49	55	49	45	54	56	60	37	62	67	78
59860 POLSON	73	62	80	62	65	75	65	73	67	62	66	54	59	65	66	70	45	70	75	85
59864 RONAN	71	59	63	58	59	69	61	67	64	59	63	51	54	65	58	67	43	65	69	80
59865 SAINT IGNATIUS	65	56	59	55	57	64	56	62	59	56	58	45	51	59	54	61	39	59	64	73
59866 SAINT REGIS	76	54	78	53	56	77	56	71	62	52	61	53	45	62	55	68	40	65	74	84
59868 SEELEY LAKE	83	66	107	65	73	88	66	84	69	62	69	62	58	66	72	74	46	78	83	98
59870 STEVENSVILLE	79	73	88	73	75	84	71	81	72	68	72	60	67	71	74	75	49	77	81	94
59871 SULA	87	69	112	68	76	92	70	88	73	65	72	65	60	69	75	78	48	82	87	102
59872 SUPERIOR	71	54	84	53	58	73	55	70	59	51	58	51	46	57	57	63	38	64	70	81
59873 THOMPSON FALLS	73	57	88	56	61	77	58	73	62	54	61	54	49	60	61	67	41	68	75	85
59874 TROUT CREEK	75	60	97	59	66	79	60	76	63	56	62	56	52	60	65	67	41	70	75	88
59875 VICTOR	84	64	99	63	69	87	65	83	70	61	69	61	55	67	68	75	46	76	83	97
59901 KALISPELL	78	72	76	72	73	79	72	76	74	71	74	57	69	74	72	76	51	75	79	90
59910 BIG ARM	73	58	94	57	64	77	58	74	61	55	60	54	50	58	63	65	40	68	73	86
59911 BIGFORK	87	70	113	69	77	93	70	89	73	66	72	65	61	70	76	78	48	82	88	103
59912 COLUMBIA FALLS	76	70	70	70	70	77	69	74	71	67	70	55	65	72	68	73	48	71	76	87
59914 DAYTON	75	60	96	59	66	79	60	76	63	56	62	55	52	59	65	67	41	70	75	88
59915 ELMO	74	60	96	59	65	79	60	76	62	56	62	55	52	59	65	66	41	70	75	88
59916 ESSEX	90	81	115	84	88	92	86	92	85	82	86	72	82	82	90	86	60	90	89	107
59917 EUREKA	65	49	73	48	52	68	51	64	55	47	54	47	42	54	51	60	36	59	66	75
59920 KILA	80	68	87	66	71	80	66	78	69	65	68	57	59	68	68	72	46	73	77	91
59922 LAKESIDE	89	71	115	70	79	94	72	91	75	67	74	66	62	71	78	80	49	84	90	105
59923 LIBBY	68	51	74	49	53	70	53	66	58	49	56	49	44	56	53	63	38	61	68	77
59925 MARION	77	62	100	61	68	82	62	79	65	58	64	58	54	62	67	69	43	73	78	91
59928 POLEBRIDGE	65	52	84	51	57	69	52	66	55	49	54	48	45	52	57	58	36	61	66	77
59929 PROCTOR	85	68	110	67	75	90	68	87	72	64	71	63	59	68	74	76	47	80	86	101
59930 REXFORD	64	46	66	44	48	65	47	60	52	44	51	45	38	52	47	57	34	55	62	71
59931 ROLLINS	86	69	111	67	75	91	69	87	72	64	71	64	59	68	74	77	47	80	86	101
59932 SOMERS	95	76	123	75	84	101	76	97	80	71	79	71	66	76	83	85	52	89	96	112
59935 TROY	54	45	64	43	48	58	44	55	47	44	46	39	39	45	47	51	31	51	57	64
59937 WHITEFISH	88	81	90	82	83	89	81	87	82	80	82	66	77	82	82	84	56	85	88	103
MONTANA	80	69	77	69	70	79	73	77	75	69	74	59	67	74	71	77	51	76	80	92
UNITED STATES	100	100	100	100	100	100	100	100	100	100	100	100	100	100	100	100	100	100	100	100

ZIP CODE #	POST OFFICE NAME	COUNTY FIPS CODE	POPULATION 2000	POPULATION 2009	POPULATION 2014	2000-2009 ANNUAL RATE % Rate	2000-2009 ANNUAL RATE State Centile	HOUSEHOLDS 2000	HOUSEHOLDS 2009	HOUSEHOLDS 2014	HOUSEHOLDS % Annual Rate 2000-2009	HOUSEHOLDS 2009 Average HH Size	FAMILIES 2000	FAMILIES 2009	FAMILIES % Annual Rate 2000-2009
68001	ABIE	023	176	169	163	-0.4	49	61	60	58	-0.2	2.82	45	44	-0.2
68002	ARLINGTON	177	2154	2260	2298	0.5	81	797	852	871	0.7	2.65	609	647	0.7
68003	ASHLAND	155	4248	4681	4830	1.1	92	1668	1864	1933	1.2	2.46	1191	1323	1.1
68004	BANCROFT	039	983	925	893	-0.7	34	403	384	371	-0.5	2.36	292	277	-0.6
68005	BELLEVUE	153	23636	24485	25615	0.4	78	9460	10255	10885	0.9	2.37	6328	6833	0.8
68007	BENNINGTON	055	2335	4581	5467	7.6	99	828	1636	1961	7.6	2.79	665	1291	7.4
68008	BLAIR	177	11006	12157	12628	1.1	92	4083	4575	4771	1.2	2.54	2893	3235	1.2
68010	BOYS TOWN	055	775	861	889	1.1	92	54	71	79	3.0	3.30	49	65	3.1
68014	BRUNO	023	285	274	264	-0.4	49	113	111	108	-0.2	2.47	84	82	-0.3
68015	CEDAR BLUFFS	155	1037	1029	1030	-0.1	63	411	418	420	0.2	2.46	296	299	0.1
68017	CERESCO	155	1596	1666	1685	0.5	81	585	625	636	0.7	2.67	464	492	0.6
68018	COLON	155	545	610	637	1.2	93	193	220	231	1.4	2.77	150	170	1.4
68019	CRAIG	021	631	599	577	-0.6	37	243	232	224	-0.5	2.58	191	182	-0.5
68020	DECATUR	021	895	803	764	-1.2	13	393	357	339	-1.0	2.25	287	260	-1.1
68022	ELKHORN	055	9165	12780	14364	3.7	98	3035	4426	5037	4.2	2.87	2538	3566	3.7
68023	FORT CALHOUN	177	2650	2897	3002	1.0	90	966	1086	1134	1.3	2.67	779	873	1.2
68025	FREMONT	053	29346	29847	29915	0.2	73	11816	12214	12297	0.4	2.37	7922	8152	0.3
68028	GRETNA	153	5056	8701	10463	6.0	99	1750	2909	3516	5.6	2.97	1392	2282	5.5
68029	HERMAN	177	965	981	982	0.2	73	375	388	389	0.4	2.53	288	296	0.3
68030	HOMER	043	530	513	505	-0.4	49	189	184	181	-0.3	2.71	140	136	-0.3
68031	HOOPER	053	2156	2099	2075	-0.3	54	849	843	836	-0.1	2.43	608	602	-0.1
68033	ITHACA	155	493	547	570	1.1	92	175	196	205	1.2	2.79	137	152	1.1
68034	KENNARD	177	920	966	982	0.5	81	333	357	366	0.8	2.71	271	288	0.7
68036	LINWOOD	023	326	313	302	-0.4	49	131	129	125	-0.2	2.43	97	95	-0.2
68037	LOUISVILLE	025	2300	2507	2653	0.9	89	891	995	1059	1.2	2.46	649	714	1.0
68038	LYONS	021	1473	1382	1326	-0.7	34	600	572	551	-0.5	2.40	407	386	-0.6
68039	MACY	173	1471	1460	1450	-0.1	63	339	333	329	-0.2	4.32	287	281	-0.2
68040	MALMO	155	414	471	493	1.4	94	165	192	202	1.7	2.45	127	147	1.6
68041	MEAD	155	869	975	1020	1.3	94	299	338	355	1.3	2.88	236	266	1.3
68044	NICKERSON	053	821	835	829	0.2	73	287	297	296	0.4	2.81	230	238	0.4
68045	OAKLAND	021	2104	2015	1949	-0.5	42	830	796	768	-0.5	2.46	579	552	-0.5
68046	PAPILLION	153	18976	23038	25577	2.1	96	6398	8059	9083	2.5	2.80	5131	6444	2.5
68047	PENDER	173	1851	1840	1823	-0.1	63	733	726	717	-0.1	2.45	515	507	-0.2
68048	PLATTSMOUTH	025	11872	12744	13046	0.8	87	4434	4851	4992	1.0	2.59	3249	3555	1.0
68050	PRAGUE	155	754	783	780	0.4	78	287	305	305	0.7	2.57	210	222	0.6
68055	ROSALIE	173	391	397	396	0.2	73	146	147	146	0.1	2.70	108	108	0.0
68057	SCRIBNER	053	1868	1901	1903	0.2	73	709	734	737	0.4	2.47	482	496	0.3
68059	SPRINGFIELD	153	2978	3338	3651	1.2	93	1084	1295	1440	1.9	2.58	870	1031	1.9
68061	TEKAMAH	021	2824	2588	2468	-0.9	26	1134	1051	1004	-0.8	2.42	811	748	-0.9
68062	THURSTON	173	360	369	368	0.3	75	134	136	135	0.2	2.71	110	111	0.1
68064	VALLEY	055	3393	3884	4156	1.5	95	1352	1594	1719	1.8	2.40	937	1074	1.5
68065	VALPARAISO	155	1592	1697	1781	0.7	84	536	582	610	0.9	2.86	395	423	0.7
68066	WAHOO	155	4957	5007	4965	0.1	69	1922	1951	1937	0.2	2.49	1270	1282	0.1
68067	WALTHILL	173	1342	1380	1378	0.3	75	402	401	398	0.0	3.44	300	299	0.0
68069	WATERLOO	055	2041	2368	2541	1.6	95	857	1026	1113	2.0	2.30	603	701	1.6
68070	WESTON	155	796	857	885	0.8	87	304	334	345	1.0	2.56	217	236	0.9
68071	WINNEBAGO	173	1701	1792	1804	0.6	83	478	496	496	0.4	3.58	390	403	0.4
68073	YUTAN	155	1853	2055	2138	1.1	92	620	702	735	1.4	2.93	496	559	1.3
68102	OMAHA	055	5358	5705	5847	0.7	84	2287	2506	2633	1.0	1.47	443	458	0.4
68104	OMAHA	055	34744	34182	34285	-0.2	58	13760	13866	14007	0.1	2.42	8729	8514	-0.3
68105	OMAHA	055	24130	23315	23130	-0.4	49	10145	9771	9720	-0.4	2.29	5097	4746	-0.8
68106	OMAHA	055	20016	19533	19517	-0.3	54	9272	9290	9349	0.0	2.05	4826	4637	-0.4
68107	OMAHA	055	27157	27605	27844	0.2	73	9689	9759	9850	0.1	2.82	6285	6130	-0.3
68108	OMAHA	055	13825	14101	14276	0.2	73	5162	5245	5334	0.2	2.58	2921	2846	-0.3
68110	OMAHA	055	8522	8333	8319	-0.2	58	2932	2902	2918	-0.1	2.48	1854	1767	-0.5
68111	OMAHA	055	26928	25680	25460	-0.5	42	9508	9280	9264	-0.3	2.75	6605	6269	-0.6
68112	OMAHA	055	12001	11655	11607	-0.3	54	4413	4402	4420	0.0	2.58	3026	2933	-0.3
68113	OFFUTT A F B	153	1453	1400	1364	-0.4	49	322	277	267	-1.6	2.62	300	258	-1.6
68114	OMAHA	055	17263	17581	17836	0.2	73	8268	8662	8870	0.5	1.99	4292	4269	-0.1
68116	OMAHA	055	8851	20052	24108	9.2	100	3199	7740	9438	10.0	2.57	2446	5694	9.6
68117	OMAHA	055	8016	7813	7791	-0.3	54	3103	3116	3134	0.0	2.48	2134	2083	-0.3
68118	OMAHA	055	8520	9184	9646	0.8	87	2583	2942	3156	1.4	3.08	2246	2450	0.9
68122	OMAHA	055	5328	8366	9658	5.0	98	1923	3040	3535	5.1	2.75	1532	2367	4.8
68123	BELLEVUE	153	24413	28958	32075	1.9	96	7993	10128	11436	2.6	2.86	6542	8137	2.4
68124	OMAHA	055	15826	15924	16060	0.1	69	6494	6687	6795	0.3	2.28	4282	4269	0.0
68127	OMAHA	055	22801	22878	23100	0.0	66	9981	10295	10479	0.3	2.21	5593	5551	-0.1
68128	LA VISTA	153	11797	16617	18895	3.8	98	4432	6460	7427	4.2	2.57	3155	4476	3.9
68130	OMAHA	055	10927	16972	19181	4.9	98	3769	6054	6902	5.3	2.80	3175	5170	5.4
68131	OMAHA	055	14219	13674	13528	-0.4	49	5775	5489	5435	-0.5	2.17	2236	2021	-1.1
68132	OMAHA	055	13404	13092	13051	-0.3	54	6189	6177	6202	0.0	2.05	3083	2958	-0.4
68133	PAPILLION	153	5013	9498	11537	7.2	99	1604	3070	3749	7.3	3.09	1404	2664	7.2
68134	OMAHA	055	27828	27734	27990	0.0	66	12083	12315	12509	0.2	2.23	7195	7054	-0.2
68135	OMAHA	055	13225	25629	30287	7.4	99	3792	7142	8451	7.1	3.59	3561	6682	7.0
68136	OMAHA	153	2303	10686	13977	18.0	100	819	3995	5285	18.7	2.67	703	3312	18.2
68137	OMAHA	055	25049	26155	26846	0.5	81	9329	9989	10324	0.7	2.61	6854	7173	0.5
68138	OMAHA	153	12029	13694	14940	1.4	94	4142	4999	5545	2.1	2.74	3271	3820	1.7
68142	OMAHA	055	1632	2957	3378	6.6	99	613	993	1125	5.4	2.98	453	717	5.1
68144	OMAHA	055	25271	24992	25191	-0.1	63	10044	10213	10373	0.2	2.43	6985	6905	-0.1
68147	BELLEVUE	153	9851	10601	11415	0.8	87	3655	4055	4422	1.1	2.61	2704	2963	1.0
68152	OMAHA	055	7007	7228	7370	0.3	75	2554	2723	2810	0.7	2.48	1927	2001	0.4
68154	OMAHA	055	23498	23668	23929	0.1	69	9851	10174	10367	0.3	2.30	6122	6184	0.1
68157	OMAHA	153	5055	5148	5354	0.2	73	1744	1882	1988	0.8	2.70	1418	1523	0.8
68164	OMAHA	055	24985	27520	28993	1.1	92	9756	10880	11507	1.2	2.53	6710	7299	0.9
68182	OMAHA	055	556	564	566	0.2	73	0	0	0	0.0	0.00	0	0	0.0
68198	OMAHA	055	66	64	63	-0.3	54	0	0	0	0.0	0.00	0	0	0.0
68301	ADAMS	067	1385	1409	1419	0.2	73	503	522	528	0.4	2.59	391	403	0.3
68303	ALEXANDRIA	169	378	327	306	-1.6	4	159	141	133	-1.3	2.32	105	93	-1.3
68304	ALVO	025	374	404	421	0.8	87	140	155	162	1.1	2.61	111	122	1.0
68305	AUBURN	127	4325	4284	4215	-0.1	63	1812	1846	1828	0.2	2.25	1184	1197	0.1
68307	AVOCA	025	624	644	642	0.3	75	240	251	251	0.5	2.57	180	187	0.4
68309	BARNESTON	067	122	120	119	-0.2	58	49	49	49	0.0	2.39	34	34	0.0
68310	BEATRICE	067	14977	15264	15276	0.2	73	6149	6365	6395	0.4	2.25	3873	3983	0.3
68313	BEAVER CROSSING	159	951	884	859	-0.8	30	362	346	339	-0.5	2.55	268	256	-0.5
68314	BEE	159	445	465	469	0.5	81	164	176	179	0.8	2.64	123	131	0.7
68315	BELVIDERE	169	179	154	143	-1.6	4	77	68	64	-1.3	2.26	56	49	-1.4
	NEBRASKA					0.6					0.8	2.46			0.7
	UNITED STATES					1.0					1.1	2.59			0.9

ZIP CODE #	POST OFFICE NAME	RACE (%) White 2000	White 2009	Black 2000	Black 2009	Asian/Pacific 2000	Asian/Pacific 2009	% Hispanic Origin 2000	% Hispanic Origin 2009	2009 AGE DISTRIBUTION (%) 0-4	5-9	10-14	15-19	20-24	25-44	45-64	65-84	85+	18+	MEDIAN AGE 2009	% 2009 Males	% 2009 Females
68001	ABIE	97.2	95.9	0.0	0.0	0.0	0.0	3.4	5.3	6.5	7.1	7.7	6.5	4.1	24.9	28.4	13.6	1.2	74.6	39.8	55.0	45.0
68002	ARLINGTON	98.7	98.2	0.1	0.1	0.3	0.4	1.0	1.5	6.4	6.9	7.3	7.5	4.7	23.1	30.1	12.4	1.6	74.6	40.7	50.8	49.2
68003	ASHLAND	98.2	97.8	0.1	0.1	0.3	0.3	1.5	2.1	6.0	6.3	6.3	6.0	5.5	23.3	30.1	13.8	2.6	77.3	42.3	49.0	51.0
68004	BANCROFT	97.6	96.8	0.0	0.0	0.3	0.4	1.5	2.4	6.5	7.0	7.1	6.9	3.9	21.8	27.9	14.9	3.9	74.7	42.7	51.7	48.3
68005	BELLEVUE	85.6	81.1	6.3	7.6	2.5	3.9	5.1	7.9	7.1	6.5	6.1	6.4	6.9	29.0	24.5	11.9	1.6	76.4	36.0	49.2	50.8
68007	BENNINGTON	98.2	93.8	0.5	2.3	0.5	1.5	1.5	2.8	7.5	7.5	7.5	7.3	4.8	27.5	27.8	9.3	0.8	72.9	37.0	49.4	50.6
68008	BLAIR	97.8	97.1	0.4	0.4	0.5	0.8	1.2	1.8	6.5	6.5	6.8	8.2	7.3	24.5	27.1	10.8	2.3	75.6	37.0	49.4	50.6
68010	BOYS TOWN	66.1	56.3	21.2	26.8	0.5	0.7	7.6	12.8	5.1	4.3	26.6	51.2	1.2	9.6	1.5	0.5	0.0	20.0	16.4	67.4	32.6
68014	BRUNO	97.5	96.0	0.0	0.0	0.0	0.0	3.5	5.5	6.9	6.9	7.3	6.9	4.4	23.7	28.8	13.5	1.5	74.5	40.0	55.5	44.5
68015	CEDAR BLUFFS	98.9	98.6	0.3	0.3	0.0	0.1	0.5	0.8	5.5	5.7	6.4	7.2	5.7	21.8	31.5	14.3	1.8	78.0	43.3	52.0	48.0
68017	CERESCO	98.7	98.3	0.1	0.1	0.0	0.0	1.1	1.7	7.4	8.0	8.3	7.4	4.5	24.0	29.4	9.7	1.3	71.5	39.0	51.3	48.7
68018	COLON	97.8	97.4	0.0	0.0	0.2	0.3	1.7	2.6	5.9	7.4	8.0	7.5	4.3	22.1	29.8	13.4	1.5	73.6	41.4	51.8	48.2
68019	CRAIG	99.0	99.0	0.0	0.0	0.3	0.3	0.2	0.2	6.5	6.8	7.3	7.3	4.3	21.2	29.5	15.2	1.7	74.8	42.4	51.6	48.4
68020	DECATUR	90.5	88.9	0.4	0.5	0.2	0.2	0.9	1.4	5.6	6.5	7.1	6.8	4.2	19.2	31.3	17.3	2.0	76.6	45.3	51.3	48.7
68022	ELKHORN	98.0	96.9	0.2	0.3	0.4	0.6	1.8	3.2	7.3	7.5	7.7	7.6	5.3	25.5	29.2	8.9	1.1	72.8	37.1	49.3	50.7
68023	FORT CALHOUN	98.5	98.2	0.6	0.6	0.1	0.2	0.9	1.4	5.7	6.5	7.5	7.7	4.8	21.5	34.2	10.8	1.2	75.5	41.7	50.1	49.9
68025	FREMONT	95.5	94.0	0.5	0.6	0.7	0.9	4.2	6.2	6.3	6.2	6.1	7.2	6.5	25.0	26.0	13.7	3.0	77.6	39.0	48.4	51.6
68028	GRETNA	98.4	97.8	0.1	0.1	0.3	0.4	0.9	1.3	7.3	7.7	7.8	7.3	5.4	26.9	27.8	8.7	1.2	72.7	37.1	50.0	50.0
68029	HERMAN	99.5	99.1	0.1	0.2	0.0	0.1	0.5	0.8	5.9	6.6	7.1	6.8	4.3	21.0	32.9	13.7	1.6	75.9	43.5	51.7	48.3
68030	HOMER	95.3	93.4	0.0	0.0	0.0	0.0	3.0	4.7	6.0	6.4	7.0	7.6	4.7	22.8	29.2	12.9	3.3	75.4	41.3	50.7	49.3
68031	HOOPER	98.0	97.1	0.1	0.1	0.2	0.3	2.4	3.6	5.5	5.9	6.5	6.8	4.9	22.3	30.4	14.1	3.7	77.9	43.7	50.0	50.0
68033	ITHACA	99.0	98.5	0.0	0.0	0.0	0.2	0.8	1.3	6.6	6.9	7.1	7.3	5.1	22.9	30.3	12.6	1.1	75.0	40.9	50.3	49.7
68034	KENNARD	98.3	97.6	0.1	0.1	0.5	0.8	0.7	1.1	6.3	7.3	8.1	8.1	4.5	22.4	31.4	10.8	1.2	73.1	40.2	51.3	48.7
68036	LINWOOD	97.5	96.2	0.0	0.0	0.0	0.0	3.4	5.1	6.7	7.0	7.3	6.7	4.5	23.6	30.0	12.8	1.3	74.8	40.1	55.9	44.1
68037	LOUISVILLE	98.4	98.0	0.1	0.1	0.3	0.6	1.2	1.8	6.0	6.3	6.5	6.8	5.9	23.9	29.8	11.7	3.0	76.8	40.9	48.3	51.7
68038	LYONS	96.2	95.4	0.3	0.4	0.2	0.3	3.7	5.4	5.6	5.8	6.2	6.9	5.6	19.0	28.8	18.2	3.9	77.6	45.7	48.1	51.9
68039	MACY	9.4	6.4	0.1	0.1	0.1	0.1	2.4	2.3	14.9	13.2	10.7	10.5	8.4	22.5	13.8	5.8	0.4	54.5	20.5	48.4	51.6
68040	MALMO	98.3	97.7	0.0	0.0	0.2	0.6	1.0	1.5	6.8	7.4	7.9	7.9	4.7	19.7	29.1	14.4	2.1	72.6	42.0	50.3	49.7
68041	MEAD	98.5	98.4	0.1	0.1	0.1	0.1	1.1	1.6	6.9	7.3	7.6	7.7	5.2	23.8	28.4	12.0	1.1	73.4	39.2	49.8	50.2
68044	NICKERSON	94.2	92.0	0.4	0.4	0.0	0.1	7.7	11.1	8.1	6.5	7.9	7.8	5.4	24.4	28.0	11.1	0.7	72.0	38.1	51.7	48.3
68045	OAKLAND	98.6	98.4	0.0	0.0	0.2	0.2	0.7	1.0	5.8	6.1	6.4	6.9	5.5	19.0	28.2	17.3	4.9	77.2	45.2	48.9	51.1
68046	PAPILLION	93.6	91.0	2.2	2.7	1.4	2.2	2.7	4.4	6.8	7.2	8.0	8.4	6.1	27.2	27.7	7.5	1.3	72.7	35.7	49.3	50.7
68047	PENDER	97.5	96.5	0.2	0.3	0.1	0.1	1.4	2.2	5.7	6.1	6.4	6.6	4.8	22.2	26.3	17.6	4.3	77.6	43.6	50.4	49.6
68048	PLATTSMOUTH	97.5	96.9	0.3	0.3	0.4	0.7	1.7	2.6	7.0	7.1	7.2	6.9	5.3	25.3	28.0	11.1	2.0	74.4	38.3	48.6	51.4
68050	PRAGUE	98.7	98.5	0.0	0.0	0.1	0.1	1.1	1.5	6.5	6.9	7.4	7.2	4.2	19.8	30.3	15.2	2.6	75.0	43.6	51.3	48.7
68055	ROSALIE	80.1	73.3	0.0	0.0	0.3	0.3	2.6	3.5	8.3	9.1	8.6	8.3	4.5	24.9	22.9	11.8	1.5	68.8	36.1	48.9	51.1
68057	SCRIBNER	98.2	97.6	0.2	0.2	0.2	0.3	1.1	1.8	6.4	6.6	7.0	7.0	4.8	20.8	27.0	15.1	5.3	75.6	42.9	47.2	52.8
68059	SPRINGFIELD	98.5	97.8	0.2	0.4	0.3	0.6	1.2	2.1	5.7	6.5	6.9	6.7	4.9	25.2	32.5	10.5	1.1	76.6	40.3	50.3	49.7
68061	TEKAMAH	98.7	98.4	0.2	0.2	0.2	0.2	0.9	1.3	5.8	6.5	6.7	6.1	4.0	21.0	31.1	15.7	3.2	77.2	45.0	49.9	50.1
68062	THURSTON	98.3	97.6	0.0	0.0	0.0	0.0	0.6	1.1	7.0	7.6	7.0	6.2	3.8	25.7	27.4	13.3	1.9	74.3	40.3	49.9	50.1
68064	VALLEY	97.3	95.8	0.4	0.6	0.2	0.4	1.4	2.5	5.6	6.2	6.7	7.4	6.0	23.9	28.4	13.6	2.2	76.9	40.5	50.3	49.7
68065	VALPARAISO	98.2	97.6	0.2	0.3	0.1	0.2	1.0	1.5	6.1	6.5	7.7	8.6	5.2	23.3	30.3	10.7	1.5	73.8	39.9	51.0	49.0
68066	WAHOO	98.4	98.0	0.1	0.1	0.4	0.6	0.8	1.2	6.4	6.8	7.1	7.5	5.4	22.2	26.9	13.5	4.3	74.7	40.9	49.0	51.0
68067	WALTHILL	31.8	24.3	0.0	0.0	0.1	0.1	4.8	5.2	11.9	10.7	9.9	9.1	7.0	22.3	18.7	9.0	1.4	61.7	26.0	48.7	51.3
68069	WATERLOO	98.2	97.0	0.4	0.6	0.2	0.4	1.9	3.3	5.7	6.3	6.8	6.2	4.0	21.2	33.7	15.0	1.1	77.0	44.8	50.3	49.7
68070	WESTON	98.5	97.9	0.1	0.2	0.1	0.1	0.9	1.3	6.2	6.7	7.0	7.8	5.4	22.1	29.9	13.0	2.1	74.8	41.3	50.3	49.7
68071	WINNEBAGO	14.2	11.0	0.3	0.3	0.0	0.0	1.9	2.2	11.4	11.5	11.1	10.9	7.3	23.2	17.0	7.0	0.6	59.2	23.4	49.1	50.9
68073	YUTAN	97.6	97.2	0.1	0.1	0.3	0.5	1.1	1.6	7.2	7.4	7.4	8.6	6.4	27.0	26.4	8.6	1.0	72.7	34.1	51.2	48.8
68102	OMAHA	61.8	54.1	24.2	28.0	4.5	5.7	8.9	13.1	3.5	2.8	1.9	6.6	16.1	41.4	20.6	6.2	0.9	90.8	32.9	60.4	39.6
68104	OMAHA	67.9	61.2	27.0	32.0	1.0	1.5	3.1	5.3	8.0	7.4	7.2	7.2	7.0	28.0	24.1	9.0	2.0	72.9	34.4	47.8	52.2
68105	OMAHA	79.8	72.8	5.1	6.1	1.5	2.1	20.1	29.1	7.6	6.6	6.1	6.4	8.2	31.3	22.4	9.2	2.1	75.9	33.6	51.4	48.6
68106	OMAHA	92.8	89.1	2.3	3.2	2.1	3.2	3.5	6.2	6.0	5.6	5.3	5.6	6.6	29.9	24.1	13.2	3.6	80.1	38.4	46.2	53.8
68107	OMAHA	67.8	57.9	6.5	7.0	0.7	0.9	34.1	47.2	9.6	9.0	7.8	7.1	6.8	29.3	20.5	8.2	1.7	69.3	31.2	50.8	49.2
68108	OMAHA	73.3	62.4	3.3	3.8	1.2	1.5	27.7	41.0	8.3	7.5	6.6	7.2	8.8	30.3	21.0	8.3	2.1	73.8	31.9	51.0	49.0
68110	OMAHA	37.2	32.7	55.3	58.0	0.2	0.3	5.7	8.5	7.3	7.5	6.8	7.5	8.2	28.6	23.3	9.2	1.5	73.8	33.8	53.3	46.7
68111	OMAHA	23.7	18.5	70.0	74.4	0.5	0.6	4.0	5.8	9.0	9.2	9.0	9.4	7.8	24.5	21.5	8.3	1.3	67.0	28.8	46.6	53.4
68112	OMAHA	75.6	69.2	19.5	24.2	0.4	0.5	4.0	6.5	6.5	6.5	6.6	7.4	7.0	24.5	26.9	11.9	2.7	75.8	38.0	47.2	52.8
68113	OFFUTT A F B	72.8	65.2	14.0	16.3	2.8	4.0	8.7	13.5	8.3	3.4	2.4	18.2	47.0	19.4	1.0	0.2	0.0	84.6	21.9	61.8	38.2
68114	OMAHA	91.6	87.5	3.3	4.6	2.9	4.6	2.0	3.7	5.2	5.2	5.4	5.3	5.9	24.5	25.0	18.4	5.1	80.9	43.7	46.2	53.8
68116	OMAHA	93.5	91.2	1.6	2.3	3.0	3.9	1.6	3.2	9.6	9.5	8.4	5.5	4.1	34.5	22.5	5.2	0.6	68.8	33.8	49.2	50.8
68117	OMAHA	91.2	85.7	1.2	1.7	1.1	1.8	8.2	14.7	6.9	6.9	6.8	6.3	5.6	28.1	25.3	11.9	2.2	75.5	37.9	49.7	50.3
68118	OMAHA	95.1	92.7	1.1	1.5	2.2	3.4	1.4	2.7	6.7	9.5	11.0	10.5	3.5	26.2	28.2	3.9	0.4	65.1	35.5	49.8	50.2
68122	OMAHA	86.6	80.7	9.4	13.4	1.7	2.7	1.5	2.7	9.7	9.0	8.0	5.8	4.9	32.8	23.8	5.8	0.4	69.7	33.2	48.9	51.1
68123	BELLEVUE	82.7	78.3	8.5	9.8	3.0	4.6	5.2	7.9	9.9	9.4	8.2	6.7	7.2	33.7	20.5	4.3	0.2	68.4	29.7	49.8	50.2
68124	OMAHA	94.8	92.3	2.0	2.8	1.5	2.4	1.9	3.5	4.9	4.9	5.5	6.1	5.9	20.9	29.0	19.0	4.0	81.0	46.4	46.6	53.4
68127	OMAHA	90.8	86.4	2.3	3.1	3.0	4.4	5.1	8.8	5.9	5.4	5.4	6.1	9.5	33.8	25.0	8.2	0.7	79.8	33.4	50.8	49.2
68128	LA VISTA	90.5	87.7	2.9	3.0	2.4	3.7	4.1	6.3	8.5	7.6	7.4	7.1	7.6	33.7	22.4	5.3	0.4	72.1	31.5	48.5	51.5
68130	OMAHA	96.3	95.0	0.9	1.1	1.4	2.1	1.4	2.3	7.2	7.7	8.2	7.5	4.4	23.9	32.1	8.1	1.0	72.1	39.0	49.2	50.8
68131	OMAHA	64.6	56.2	21.1	24.3	4.7	6.6	10.7	16.1	7.1	5.5	5.0	12.2	14.4	31.6	17.0	5.8	1.4	79.2	27.6	51.0	49.0
68132	OMAHA	86.1	81.2	6.5	8.2	2.4	3.7	4.5	7.5	6.0	5.5	5.5	7.7	10.8	29.3	24.9	8.9	1.4	79.8	33.3	50.0	50.0
68133	PAPILLION	91.5	88.0	2.2	3.0	2.9	4.5	3.3	5.1	9.2	9.4	9.5	7.9	4.6	26.7	26.6	5.6	0.5	66.9	33.7	49.3	50.7
68134	OMAHA	87.6	82.5	7.3	9.9	2.2	3.4	2.5	4.4	7.0	6.2	6.0	5.8	7.5	29.4	24.0	11.8	2.3	77.5	35.7	47.5	52.5
68135	OMAHA	96.3	94.7	0.4	0.4	2.1	3.1	1.3	2.1	9.6	10.6	10.4	8.3	3.6	27.8	26.2	3.3	0.2	63.7	32.8	50.1	49.9
68136	OMAHA	97.8	96.6	0.3	0.4	0.7	1.3	1.7	2.5	9.3	8.7	8.4	6.9	4.6	30.7	24.6	6.3	0.5	69.2	33.7	49.1	50.9
68137	OMAHA	95.3	92.8	1.2	1.7	1.4	2.4	2.7	4.9	7.1	7.1	7.1	7.1	6.1	29.0	27.2	8.4	1.0	74.5	35.7	48.9	51.1
68138	OMAHA	95.4	93.2	0.8	1.0	1.0	1.7	2.8	4.6	10.8	8.9	7.8	6.5	6.4	37.2	19.5	2.7	0.2	68.5	29.5	49.9	50.1
68142	OMAHA	92.7	88.1	3.1	4.8	1.4	2.5	2.6	4.5	10.2	9.5	8.5	6.3	4.2	35.5	19.9	5.6	0.4	67.8	32.7	49.3	50.7
68144	OMAHA	94.8	92.2	1.4	2.0	1.6	2.5	2.4	4.4	6.0	6.0	6.5	6.7	6.8	25.0	27.6	13.9	1.6	77.5	39.7	48.8	51.2
68147	BELLEVUE	86.0	80.9	5.0	6.1	1.8	3.0	8.6	13.2	7.5	7.3	7.0	6.6	5.9	30.0	24.9	10.1	0.9	74.1	35.7	50.2	49.8
68152	OMAHA	72.5	67.4	23.8	28.1	0.5	0.7	1.8	2.9	6.9	5.6	5.6	6.5	5.9	20.5	29.1	16.0	4.0	77.9	44.1	46.6	53.4
68154	OMAHA	93.2	89.9	2.2	3.1	2.7	4.2	1.8	3.3	5.6	5.7	6.6	6.8	8.1	26.1	28.0	11.2	2.0	77.6	37.5	47.2	52.8
68157	OMAHA	92.4	88.9	2.4	3.0	0.7	1.2	5.9	9.7	6.8	7.2	7.0	6.7	6.4	27.7	26.7	11.0	0.6	74.7	35.7	48.9	51.1
68164	OMAHA	89.2	85.2	5.7	7.1	2.6	4.3	2.1	3.6	9.3	8.4	7.2	5.5	5.7	33.2	23.7	6.5	0.6	71.8	33.6	48.3	51.7
68182	OMAHA	91.9	87.6	2.2	3.0	3.6	5.9	1.8	3.0	2.7	3.2	4.3	29.8	14.4	10.8	21.8	11.0	2.1	88.1	23.5	48.4	51.6
68198	OMAHA	93.8	89.1	3.1	4.7	1.5	3.1	3.1	7.8	3.1	3.1	3.1	9.4	15.6	28.1	18.8	15.6	3.1	90.6	35.0	46.9	53.1
68301	ADAMS	98.8	98.4	0.1	0.1	0.2	0.4	0.5	0.8	7.2	7.7	8.0	6.8	3.4	23.1	27.9	11.6	4.3	72.1	41.1	47.8	52.2
68303	ALEXANDRIA	98.9	98.5	0.0	0.0	0.0	0.0	2.1	3.1	5.8	6.1	6.7	6.7	4.3	21.7	30.0	15.0	3.7	77.1	44.0	47.4	52.6
68304	ALVO	97.6	97.0	0.0	0.0	0.0	0.2	1.6	2.0	5.9	6.4	6.9	6.4	4.5	22.3	32.4	13.6	1.5	76.5	43.3	50.5	49.5
68305	AUBURN	97.5	96.7	0.3	0.3	0.9	1.4	0.9	1.3	5.4	5.3	5.6	6.5	6.2	21.7	30.1	14.8	4.5	79.6	44.4	47.1	52.9
68307	AVOCA	99.7	99.2	0.0	0.0	0.0	0.2	1.0	1.4	6.4	7.0	7.8	7.9	4.0	22.5	30.4	12.3	1.7	74.1	40.9	51.1	48.9
68309	BARNESTON	97.5	96.7	0.0	0.0	0.0	0.0	1.7	1.7	6.7	6.7	6.7	5.8	5.8	20.8	25.8	16.7	5.0	75.0	42.5	47.5	52.5
68310	BEATRICE	97.5	96.9	0.5	0.5	0.4	0.6	0.9	1.3	5.8	5.8	5.9	6.6	6.1	24.4	26.8	14.6	4.0	78.8	41.4	48.4	51.6
68313	BEAVER CROSSING	98.0	97.5	0.5	0.6	0.1	0.1	0.5	0.8	7.0	7.7	7.6	6.4	4.3	22.4	29.5	13.3	1.7	73.5	40.6	51.1	48.9
68314	BEE	98.2	97.8	0.0	0.0	0.4	0.4	0.9	1.5	5.8	6.5	7.1	6.9	4.3	25.4	30.8	11.8	1.5	76.1	41.2	52.7	47.3
68315	BELVIDERE	98.9	98.7	0.0	0.0	0.0	0.0	0.6	0.6	5.8	6.5	7.1	5.8	5.2	18.8	29.9	17.5	3.2	76.6	45.5	50.0	50.0
	NEBRASKA	89.6	86.9	4.0	4.4	1.3	2.1	5.5	7.9	6.9	6.8	6.8	7.3	6.9	26.3	25.7	11.0	2.3	75.3	36.5	49.4	50.6
	UNITED STATES	75.1	72.0	12.3	12.7	3.8	4.6	12.5	15.7	6.8	6.7	6.6	7.1	6.9	27.0	26.0	10.9	1.9	75.7	36.9	49.2	50.8

#	POST OFFICE NAME	2009 Per Capita Income	2009 HH Income Base	2009 Household Income Distribution (%) Less than $25,000	$25,000 to $49,999	$50,000 to $99,999	$100,000 to $149,999	$150,000 or More	Median Household Income 2009	2014	2009 National Centile	2009 State Centile	2009 Home Value Base	2009 Home Value Distribution (%) Less than $50,000	$50,000 to $89,999	$90,000 to $174,999	$175,000 to $399,999	$400,000 or More	2009 Median Home Value
68001	ABIE	16686	60	28.3	31.7	35.0	5.0	0.0	38878	43628	29	38	48	37.5	22.9	22.9	14.6	2.1	70000
68002	ARLINGTON	23571	852	13.0	30.9	43.4	10.7	2.0	55365	57931	72	88	664	15.2	18.1	40.8	20.3	5.6	113158
68003	ASHLAND	25872	1864	18.6	22.0	43.7	12.9	2.8	60840	61839	79	92	1442	14.4	23.7	43.4	16.4	2.1	105297
68004	BANCROFT	18852	384	27.9	37.0	32.6	1.3	1.3	39450	40809	31	42	284	27.1	29.6	31.0	9.9	2.5	77500
68005	BELLEVUE	27889	10255	14.1	29.2	40.5	12.5	3.7	56666	57034	74	89	5845	9.0	13.4	60.4	16.4	0.8	120457
68007	BENNINGTON	27527	1636	8.5	19.9	54.7	11.7	5.2	68575	70584	86	96	1400	1.5	13.5	58.4	22.0	4.6	130746
68008	BLAIR	25073	4575	17.1	25.2	41.4	12.3	4.0	58933	62379	76	90	3413	11.8	14.4	49.1	21.5	3.2	123038
68010	BOYS TOWN	14327	71	5.6	14.1	80.3	0.0	0.0	65652	65698	84	95	0	0.0	0.0	0.0	0.0	0.0	0
68014	BRUNO	19066	111	27.9	32.4	36.0	3.6	0.0	39682	43444	32	43	89	37.1	23.6	24.7	12.4	2.2	69167
68015	CEDAR BLUFFS	19218	418	23.4	36.6	36.1	2.6	1.2	43069	46157	43	62	345	27.2	35.1	28.1	9.3	0.3	71731
68017	CERESCO	23271	625	10.6	28.8	52.2	6.4	2.1	58647	60171	76	90	530	9.8	20.2	50.9	15.5	3.6	116193
68018	COLON	20793	220	18.6	32.3	40.5	5.9	2.7	49305	52782	60	79	186	13.4	19.9	44.1	19.4	3.2	113333
68019	CRAIG	18297	232	25.0	37.5	31.5	5.6	0.4	40758	41146	35	50	175	20.6	24.6	30.9	17.7	6.3	97083
68020	DECATUR	19683	357	29.1	31.7	35.0	3.1	1.1	39751	41005	32	44	278	38.8	24.1	23.4	9.0	4.7	70000
68022	ELKHORN	35773	4426	5.4	17.6	37.7	22.6	16.7	83250	83984	93	99	3768	4.1	11.7	44.4	31.1	8.7	153985
68023	FORT CALHOUN	31016	1086	12.6	19.0	42.5	16.1	9.8	68511	75753	86	96	916	9.4	10.8	33.2	40.2	6.4	167890
68025	FREMONT	23903	12214	21.5	29.0	39.6	7.1	2.9	49564	51673	60	80	8134	9.0	17.2	52.8	19.5	1.5	119207
68028	GRETNA	28222	2909	11.1	21.3	38.0	22.1	7.5	69830	75627	87	96	2388	8.0	5.5	42.8	35.2	8.4	162459
68029	HERMAN	22966	388	17.5	33.0	38.7	8.5	2.3	49625	50843	60	80	300	21.3	22.0	30.3	23.3	3.0	99524
68030	HOMER	19432	184	24.5	29.9	38.6	5.4	1.6	45916	50524	51	72	143	19.6	30.1	36.4	13.3	0.7	90833
68031	HOOPER	20593	843	21.0	34.4	39.5	4.0	1.1	46096	47764	52	73	635	15.9	26.9	43.6	11.0	2.5	101827
68033	ITHACA	21099	196	18.9	27.0	42.3	10.2	1.5	53541	56960	69	86	161	14.3	24.2	36.0	21.7	3.7	107237
68034	KENNARD	25689	357	14.8	20.4	49.3	12.3	3.1	64574	70519	83	95	303	7.6	15.5	39.6	31.7	5.6	150321
68036	LINWOOD	19346	129	27.1	31.8	35.7	3.9	1.6	40457	42899	34	48	104	38.5	24.0	22.1	12.5	2.9	67143
68037	LOUISVILLE	28115	995	11.9	26.5	44.7	12.9	4.0	61639	64758	80	93	793	9.3	25.0	42.7	21.4	1.5	110625
68038	LYONS	17804	572	32.5	34.8	28.3	3.0	1.4	36288	38570	21	26	436	37.4	39.2	18.8	3.2	1.4	63111
68039	MACY	8555	333	39.9	32.4	25.2	1.8	0.6	30757	32467	9	5	143	34.3	25.9	30.8	7.0	2.1	71667
68040	MALMO	20342	192	21.4	34.4	39.6	4.2	0.5	44003	47877	45	65	165	13.9	20.0	47.9	15.2	3.0	106250
68041	MEAD	20596	338	19.5	27.2	40.2	10.9	2.1	52823	55681	68	85	275	15.6	24.7	37.1	20.0	2.5	99464
68044	NICKERSON	19024	297	17.8	34.3	40.7	5.1	2.0	48884	50119	59	79	218	15.6	19.7	37.2	21.6	6.0	116964
68045	OAKLAND	19211	796	27.8	35.2	30.7	4.4	2.0	39156	40125	30	39	588	22.6	33.0	34.2	8.5	1.7	81750
68046	PAPILLION	33739	8059	7.9	16.6	39.7	23.9	11.9	81019	83318	92	98	6104	3.3	1.5	45.7	46.2	3.3	174431
68047	PENDER	19018	726	26.2	38.0	31.0	3.0	1.8	39531	40453	31	42	530	12.1	31.7	42.8	13.0	0.4	101053
68048	PLATTSMOUTH	25403	4851	14.8	26.7	44.4	9.9	4.2	58503	61737	76	89	3719	17.2	21.2	39.2	19.8	2.6	105187
68050	PRAGUE	16626	305	27.2	37.7	32.1	2.3	0.7	38545	41141	28	37	251	25.1	27.1	29.1	15.9	2.8	86071
68055	ROSALIE	12715	147	35.4	42.9	20.4	1.4	0.0	29357	30697	7	2	108	45.4	22.2	20.4	11.1	0.9	58333
68057	SCRIBNER	18670	734	27.1	36.6	32.3	2.9	1.1	41084	44477	36	52	579	24.9	32.6	33.5	7.6	1.4	79625
68059	SPRINGFIELD	32644	1295	10.1	20.2	41.0	21.6	7.0	70595	73701	87	97	1037	15.1	10.0	38.9	28.4	7.5	138728
68061	TEKAMAH	20309	1051	26.6	34.1	33.6	3.3	2.4	42198	42595	40	59	806	19.0	31.9	32.9	14.5	1.7	88814
68062	THURSTON	15699	136	27.2	35.3	34.6	2.9	0.0	41317	44326	37	53	107	30.8	16.8	40.2	10.3	1.9	92273
68064	VALLEY	25736	1594	20.4	26.1	41.2	8.0	4.3	53854	57459	69	87	1121	24.0	30.2	30.2	13.0	2.5	85682
68065	VALPARAISO	20018	582	17.2	28.5	46.7	5.7	1.9	53041	55451	68	86	479	20.7	25.3	38.2	14.6	1.3	95909
68066	WAHOO	20392	1951	24.3	30.0	38.0	6.2	1.5	46615	50660	53	74	1399	12.4	32.0	43.6	10.4	1.6	95304
68067	WALTHILL	12342	401	34.9	29.9	29.7	5.0	0.5	35942	37019	20	24	256	32.0	41.8	21.1	5.1	0.0	62703
68069	WATERLOO	32053	1026	15.8	23.9	41.6	11.8	6.9	61153	62905	79	92	845	16.1	24.1	32.1	23.2	4.5	106618
68070	WESTON	20279	334	20.4	32.0	42.2	4.2	1.2	48122	51282	57	77	273	24.5	28.2	35.2	11.0	1.1	84231
68071	WINNEBAGO	10909	496	36.3	35.7	23.6	4.2	0.2	32480	33599	12	9	226	54.9	11.9	26.5	5.3	1.3	46071
68073	YUTAN	23458	702	11.0	26.9	46.7	11.7	3.7	60812	61323	79	91	602	6.6	29.9	46.8	15.0	1.7	97105
68102	OMAHA	20124	2506	46.2	30.8	19.2	2.2	1.5	27102	27237	5	1	138	43.5	24.6	28.3	3.6	0.0	56429
68104	OMAHA	22334	13866	21.7	31.6	38.8	6.1	1.9	47339	50606	55	75	9118	18.0	61.9	17.8	2.2	0.1	69908
68105	OMAHA	20813	9771	29.6	31.3	33.2	4.6	1.3	41432	43036	37	54	4339	16.7	51.9	29.8	1.5	0.0	76872
68106	OMAHA	28217	9290	20.4	29.9	39.1	7.6	2.9	49626	52963	60	80	5973	12.3	42.4	42.0	3.0	0.3	87162
68107	OMAHA	16699	9759	30.1	30.9	34.0	3.8	1.2	40741	42271	35	50	6193	28.7	58.9	11.9	0.4	0.1	64227
68108	OMAHA	17322	5245	29.1	36.4	29.5	3.9	1.2	38618	40141	28	37	2504	42.8	47.2	9.7	0.2	0.0	55279
68110	OMAHA	14803	2902	43.0	33.6	19.5	3.0	0.9	28818	28358	6	2	1485	71.0	24.3	4.6	0.1	0.0	33721
68111	OMAHA	13418	9280	41.6	33.0	22.5	1.9	1.0	29691	29401	8	3	4573	68.1	28.3	3.1	0.3	0.1	39775
68112	OMAHA	21965	4402	22.1	27.9	40.1	7.5	2.4	49919	53579	61	81	3396	34.6	45.4	13.9	5.5	0.6	60951
68113	OFFUTT A F B	13554	277	25.3	54.9	18.1	1.4	0.4	35251	35412	19	21	5	0.0	0.0	100.0	0.0	0.0	137500
68114	OMAHA	35448	8662	16.9	32.9	34.3	7.9	8.0	50154	53310	62	81	4414	1.8	25.5	43.9	21.3	7.5	115153
68116	OMAHA	40157	7740	4.3	11.9	47.7	21.2	14.9	83170	83468	93	99	6039	0.9	4.0	45.5	46.9	2.8	174608
68117	OMAHA	23395	3116	19.0	26.5	45.1	7.5	1.9	53275	55631	68	86	2389	12.3	55.4	31.1	0.9	0.3	79959
68118	OMAHA	41060	2942	5.2	13.3	25.8	26.0	29.6	112092	112807	98	100	2569	3.7	1.5	30.7	52.2	12.0	195607
68122	OMAHA	30627	3040	5.5	13.8	59.0	15.5	6.3	75980	76512	90	98	2729	6.9	11.7	66.0	11.8	3.7	123008
68123	BELLEVUE	28108	10128	5.9	23.0	46.5	17.6	6.9	70122	75189	87	97	5899	2.9	3.1	54.5	37.2	2.2	165097
68124	OMAHA	32763	6687	16.6	24.6	38.5	12.1	8.2	61484	63031	79	93	4588	1.0	16.1	56.0	23.0	4.0	130343
68127	OMAHA	31131	10295	12.0	30.9	42.3	9.7	5.1	57773	60446	75	89	4696	1.9	16.5	68.3	13.2	0.1	116193
68128	LA VISTA	28480	6460	9.1	25.9	47.1	12.9	5.0	62732	64212	81	94	3836	4.6	6.9	68.2	19.3	1.0	126206
68130	OMAHA	48964	6054	3.7	9.2	34.7	23.2	29.2	104743	109874	97	100	5426	0.2	2.9	42.2	41.9	12.8	188449
68131	OMAHA	18552	5489	35.5	34.8	25.3	3.1	1.4	33167	33807	14	11	1390	29.6	48.4	17.5	2.9	1.5	67371
68132	OMAHA	30851	6177	22.6	30.4	31.3	8.9	6.8	47570	50426	56	76	3032	7.0	25.5	37.9	24.2	5.4	122819
68133	PAPILLION	34734	3070	4.0	7.7	42.0	33.2	13.2	95313	100417	96	99	2639	0.9	1.7	20.1	75.5	1.8	207572
68134	OMAHA	27721	12315	16.5	27.7	45.0	8.0	2.7	55452	58234	72	88	6832	2.7	24.2	68.2	4.6	0.2	102397
68135	OMAHA	42508	7142	1.0	5.9	26.7	31.7	34.8	127042	128612	99	100	6765	0.7	0.9	26.8	60.3	11.4	221102
68136	OMAHA	40619	3995	0.1	7.8	47.2	31.3	13.7	92871	98480	96	99	3697	0.6	1.5	41.7	47.3	8.9	187781
68137	OMAHA	30165	9989	6.9	19.1	53.4	15.6	5.0	72604	75080	88	98	7267	2.7	14.2	74.7	7.9	0.4	116414
68138	OMAHA	28413	4999	5.6	15.2	58.8	16.5	3.8	74484	76329	89	98	4061	1.0	2.7	75.4	20.1	0.8	151101
68142	OMAHA	25246	993	4.8	17.4	61.4	13.4	2.9	68178	69176	86	96	881	36.8	8.7	45.5	6.7	2.3	102291
68144	OMAHA	31834	10213	11.0	23.1	45.2	13.8	7.0	67523	69610	85	96	7219	4.4	11.4	69.2	14.1	0.8	128814
68147	BELLEVUE	24969	4055	12.6	28.6	46.6	9.1	3.1	56421	57760	73	89	2919	1.5	22.4	64.0	11.6	0.5	111707
68152	OMAHA	27585	2723	18.8	24.8	35.9	14.3	6.2	60163	62052	78	90	2089	6.4	25.4	43.8	21.8	2.6	116840
68154	OMAHA	38937	10174	9.2	22.9	40.7	15.2	12.0	71270	73424	87	97	6022	0.7	6.4	58.8	29.8	4.2	155634
68157	OMAHA	28225	1882	8.0	21.0	47.9	19.1	3.9	67442	68837	85	95	1498	0.0	3.8	80.7	15.4	0.1	139490
68164	OMAHA	32918	10880	8.7	19.1	49.2	14.1	8.9	72395	74300	88	97	7807	8.9	5.9	63.9	20.3	1.0	126708
68182	OMAHA	4647	0	0.0	0.0	0.0	0.0	0.0	0	0	0	0	0	0.0	0.0	0.0	0.0	0.0	0
68198	OMAHA	2036	0	0.0	0.0	0.0	0.0	0.0	0	0	0	0	0	0.0	0.0	0.0	0.0	0.0	0
68301	ADAMS	21481	522	18.4	32.0	41.4	5.4	2.9	49632	51368	60	80	413	9.2	11.4	38.3	39.2	1.9	149760
68303	ALEXANDRIA	19193	141	29.8	33.3	32.6	2.8	1.4	36653	41772	23	28	114	46.5	28.1	18.4	3.5	3.5	54444
68304	ALVO	21819	155	19.4	27.1	43.2	7.1	3.2	52803	54464	68	85	133	16.5	21.1	37.6	21.1	3.8	103676
68305	AUBURN	23121	1846	27.5	29.5	33.3	7.6	2.1	42277	44615	40	60	1303	20.7	32.2	36.4	9.5	1.2	86150
68307	AVOCA	21294	251	17.5	29.5	46.2	6.4	0.4	52731	55318	67	85	193	21.8	24.4	32.6	18.7	2.6	98333
68309	BARNESTON	18021	49	32.7	38.8	22.4	4.1	2.0	35546	37950	19	22	39	41.0	25.6	25.6	7.7	0.0	58750
68310	BEATRICE	22318	6365	24.9	32.3	35.0	5.5	2.3	44268	46862	46	66	4275	12.9	29.1	41.8	15.2	1.0	101103
68313	BEAVER CROSSING	17358	346	26.6	35.0	33.8	4.0	0.6	40715	43880	35	49	277	38.3	26.4	27.1	6.9	1.4	73929
68314	BEE	21876	176	19.3	29.0	41.5	6.8	3.4	51060	54188	64	83	137	29.9	22.6	35.0	10.9	1.5	85625
68315	BELVIDERE	19151	68	27.9	36.8	30.9	2.9	1.5	37831	45000	26	34	54	50.0	22.2	20.4	3.7	3.7	50000
	NEBRASKA	24998		20.5	28.3	37.5	9.0	4.6	50953	53316				15.1	21.8	43.3	17.4	2.4	109174
	UNITED STATES	27277		20.9	24.4	35.3	11.7	7.6	54719	56938				9.3	13.1	31.6	32.6	13.5	162279

ZIP CODE #	POST OFFICE NAME	FINANCIAL SERVICES: Auto Loan	Home Loan	Invest-ments	Retire-ment Plans	THE HOME: Home Improvements: Home Repair	Lawn & Garden	Furnishings: Comput-ers & Hard-ware-Personal	Major Appli-ances	TV, Radio, Sound Equip-ment	Furni-ture	ENTERTAINMENT: Dine out/ Carry out	Sports Equip-ment	Fees & Tickets	Toys & Games	Travel	Cable TV	PERSONAL: Apparel & Services	Auto Repairs	Health Insur-ance	Pets & Supplies
68001	ABIE	84	58	92	58	61	89	64	80	67	52	66	66	47	65	64	73	43	74	84	98
68002	ARLINGTON	98	88	93	90	89	105	87	99	89	78	88	76	79	90	87	94	60	92	102	116
68003	ASHLAND	100	87	99	87	87	105	90	98	92	83	91	76	81	92	89	97	62	96	105	118
68004	BANCROFT	80	55	88	55	58	85	61	76	64	50	63	63	45	62	61	69	41	71	80	94
68005	BELLEVUE	95	92	85	94	90	93	95	93	95	94	95	72	93	96	92	96	66	95	96	110
68007	BENNINGTON	109	123	104	123	118	114	109	112	106	113	107	87	116	111	113	104	75	107	107	129
68008	BLAIR	92	95	85	97	92	96	93	93	92	90	92	73	94	94	93	93	64	92	95	110
68010	BOYS TOWN	101	88	78	93	83	79	99	86	96	101	98	73	94	101	91	92	69	93	82	105
68014	BRUNO	84	58	92	58	61	89	64	80	67	52	66	66	47	66	64	73	43	75	84	98
68015	CEDAR BLUFFS	84	61	87	59	63	86	63	79	69	57	67	60	50	68	62	75	45	73	82	94
68017	CERESCO	95	89	87	92	90	102	86	97	88	79	87	74	81	90	87	93	60	90	99	112
68018	COLON	102	71	112	71	75	108	79	97	82	64	81	80	58	80	78	89	53	91	103	120
68019	CRAIG	84	58	93	58	61	89	65	80	67	52	66	66	47	66	64	73	43	75	85	99
68020	DECATUR	79	54	87	54	57	83	60	75	63	49	62	62	44	62	60	69	40	70	79	92
68022	ELKHORN	144	168	159	168	168	151	146	150	139	157	141	116	160	144	154	135	101	142	137	171
68023	FORT CALHOUN	117	131	123	133	130	128	116	123	113	116	114	95	123	116	123	113	80	116	118	142
68025	FREMONT	82	79	73	80	77	85	81	81	83	78	83	62	79	83	79	86	57	82	89	97
68028	GRETNA	115	135	120	137	131	123	119	120	114	124	116	95	131	119	126	112	83	116	113	139
68029	HERMAN	104	71	114	71	75	109	79	98	82	64	81	81	58	81	79	90	53	92	104	121
68030	HOMER	95	66	104	66	69	100	73	90	76	59	75	74	54	74	72	83	49	84	95	111
68031	HOOPER	83	68	81	69	70	88	70	82	72	61	71	64	60	73	69	77	48	76	85	97
68033	ITHACA	96	80	92	82	82	102	81	95	84	71	83	74	70	85	81	90	56	88	98	112
68034	KENNARD	97	110	95	113	107	107	98	101	95	98	96	79	105	98	103	95	67	97	99	119
68036	LINWOOD	84	58	92	58	60	89	64	80	67	52	66	66	47	65	64	73	43	74	84	98
68037	LOUISVILLE	99	103	86	106	97	106	99	99	100	96	100	78	102	102	99	102	69	99	106	119
68038	LYONS	73	52	75	51	54	76	57	71	63	50	61	54	45	61	55	69	40	66	76	84
68039	MACY	57	46	44	48	43	53	51	50	55	49	54	40	47	55	47	57	37	53	56	64
68040	MALMO	89	61	98	61	64	94	68	85	71	55	70	70	50	69	68	77	45	79	89	104
68041	MEAD	93	83	86	86	85	100	83	94	85	74	84	72	75	87	82	90	57	87	97	110
68044	NICKERSON	89	75	81	73	74	87	74	83	77	71	77	63	65	78	71	80	51	79	85	100
68045	OAKLAND	82	58	85	57	61	86	64	79	70	55	68	61	50	69	62	77	45	74	85	94
68046	PAPILLION	134	150	132	152	145	134	137	134	131	143	133	107	146	137	140	127	95	132	125	156
68047	PENDER	74	62	79	61	64	82	63	75	68	57	67	57	56	67	64	74	45	71	82	89
68048	PLATTSMOUTH	95	98	84	99	94	100	93	95	94	92	94	73	95	96	93	96	65	93	99	113
68050	PRAGUE	76	52	84	52	55	81	58	72	61	47	60	60	43	59	58	66	39	68	77	89
68055	ROSALIE	61	42	67	42	44	65	47	58	49	38	48	48	34	48	47	53	31	54	62	72
68057	SCRIBNER	81	58	84	57	60	85	63	78	68	54	67	61	49	67	62	75	44	73	84	93
68059	SPRINGFIELD	122	132	123	132	131	126	118	123	116	124	117	91	123	119	122	116	82	118	118	143
68061	TEKAMAH	89	61	97	61	64	93	68	84	70	55	70	69	50	69	67	77	45	78	89	103
68062	THURSTON	76	52	84	52	55	80	58	72	61	47	60	60	43	59	58	66	39	68	76	89
68064	VALLEY	93	86	84	88	86	98	88	93	90	82	89	71	82	91	86	94	61	90	99	110
68065	VALPARAISO	87	83	80	87	84	94	80	89	82	74	81	68	77	84	81	86	56	83	91	104
68066	WAHOO	81	69	75	71	70	86	71	80	74	64	73	61	63	75	70	79	49	76	85	95
68067	WALTHILL	71	52	70	51	53	74	57	68	63	51	61	52	46	62	54	69	41	65	75	81
68069	WATERLOO	106	112	113	116	115	118	103	112	102	102	102	84	106	103	109	104	71	105	111	129
68070	WESTON	82	72	77	74	74	88	72	83	74	64	73	63	64	75	72	79	50	76	86	97
68071	WINNEBAGO	59	49	44	51	45	55	54	52	58	53	58	41	51	59	49	61	39	56	58	66
68073	YUTAN	107	105	94	102	100	100	98	101	96	101	98	77	94	100	95	95	67	97	96	119
68102	OMAHA	47	35	38	40	35	38	53	42	55	48	55	35	47	51	46	56	39	51	51	54
68104	OMAHA	77	74	62	75	69	77	78	74	80	75	79	58	76	81	74	82	55	77	81	90
68105	OMAHA	69	59	53	61	56	61	71	63	72	67	72	51	66	72	64	73	50	69	69	77
68106	OMAHA	82	78	72	80	76	82	84	80	85	81	85	62	82	85	81	87	59	83	87	95
68107	OMAHA	68	62	52	62	59	64	68	64	69	66	69	50	64	70	62	71	48	67	68	77
68108	OMAHA	66	55	49	56	52	61	67	61	69	61	67	48	59	69	58	71	47	65	67	74
68110	OMAHA	57	45	41	46	43	52	52	50	58	52	56	38	47	57	46	61	39	54	58	63
68111	OMAHA	55	44	38	46	41	49	51	47	56	51	55	36	48	56	45	59	38	52	55	61
68112	OMAHA	81	81	71	81	77	85	80	80	83	79	82	61	81	83	79	86	57	81	88	96
68113	OFFUTT A F B	68	36	27	41	32	30	64	45	61	60	64	44	49	73	46	56	45	57	40	54
68114	OMAHA	97	96	96	99	97	99	101	97	102	101	102	73	103	100	101	104	72	101	106	115
68116	OMAHA	152	164	141	168	157	138	151	146	142	163	145	121	159	152	150	133	104	141	127	167
68117	OMAHA	81	85	67	86	78	87	83	80	84	79	83	64	85	86	82	86	58	82	89	98
68118	OMAHA	176	213	201	218	213	186	181	185	170	198	172	148	205	178	194	160	126	172	160	209
68122	OMAHA	127	138	113	134	130	116	122	122	116	132	118	97	125	124	121	110	83	116	108	140
68123	BELLEVUE	122	115	99	117	109	100	119	110	114	123	117	91	116	123	112	108	82	112	100	128
68124	OMAHA	102	110	112	111	112	114	106	108	108	108	108	79	113	105	112	110	76	108	117	125
68127	OMAHA	102	87	78	92	83	84	102	89	101	101	103	73	96	104	92	100	72	98	91	109
68128	LA VISTA	110	107	89	108	101	94	108	101	104	112	106	81	105	109	101	100	74	102	94	119
68130	OMAHA	187	229	213	235	227	199	194	197	182	210	185	158	220	190	209	173	135	186	172	224
68131	OMAHA	64	42	39	47	39	43	65	50	65	61	66	43	54	66	52	65	46	61	55	64
68132	OMAHA	92	80	77	85	79	81	96	84	95	93	95	68	90	95	88	94	67	92	88	102
68133	PAPILLION	152	179	158	179	174	155	153	156	144	166	147	124	168	152	160	137	105	146	138	176
68134	OMAHA	89	82	75	85	79	82	89	83	90	89	91	65	88	91	86	90	63	88	88	100
68135	OMAHA	210	261	238	270	259	220	216	221	200	240	204	181	249	213	233	186	150	203	184	247
68136	OMAHA	159	181	153	176	172	151	157	158	148	170	151	125	166	157	160	140	106	149	139	179
68137	OMAHA	116	121	104	119	115	109	113	112	110	118	112	86	115	114	112	108	78	110	106	130
68138	OMAHA	118	125	102	120	117	105	113	112	108	121	110	87	114	115	110	103	77	108	100	129
68142	OMAHA	112	124	101	120	116	104	109	109	103	117	105	86	113	111	109	98	74	104	97	124
68144	OMAHA	108	112	107	114	111	110	110	108	109	112	110	83	114	110	112	109	77	110	111	127
68147	BELLEVUE	93	98	79	98	91	95	93	91	93	92	93	72	95	96	92	93	64	91	95	109
68152	OMAHA	95	102	99	103	102	107	97	100	101	98	100	73	103	98	102	104	70	100	110	117
68154	OMAHA	129	123	118	129	122	118	131	121	128	133	130	97	131	130	126	126	92	127	120	144
68157	OMAHA	110	122	103	119	115	111	108	110	107	113	108	82	114	111	110	106	75	107	107	128
68164	OMAHA	122	124	110	125	119	111	120	116	116	126	118	92	122	121	118	113	83	116	109	135
68182	OMAHA	0	0	0	0	0	0	0	0	0	0	0	0	0	0	0	0	0	0	0	0
68198	OMAHA	0	0	0	0	0	0	0	0	0	0	0	0	0	0	0	0	0	0	0	0
68301	ADAMS	98	73	106	73	75	104	78	94	80	65	79	77	61	79	78	86	52	88	99	115
68303	ALEXANDRIA	79	55	87	55	57	84	61	75	63	49	63	62	45	62	60	69	41	70	80	93
68304	ALVO	102	70	112	70	73	107	78	97	81	63	80	80	57	79	77	88	52	90	102	119
68305	AUBURN	86	67	84	66	69	88	72	83	77	66	75	63	61	76	70	83	51	80	90	98
68307	AVOCA	98	67	107	67	70	103	75	93	78	61	77	77	55	76	74	85	50	87	98	114
68309	BARNESTON	73	53	73	51	55	76	57	71	64	51	62	53	46	63	55	71	41	66	77	83
68310	BEATRICE	78	69	70	70	68	81	73	77	76	67	74	59	67	76	70	80	51	75	83	91
68313	BEAVER CROSSING	79	54	87	54	57	84	61	75	63	49	62	62	44	62	60	69	40	70	79	93
68314	BEE	100	74	108	75	77	106	79	96	82	67	81	79	62	81	80	88	53	90	100	117
68315	BELVIDERE	78	53	85	53	56	82	59	74	62	48	61	61	43	60	59	67	40	69	78	90
	NEBRASKA	95	85	88	86	84	94	89	91	90	85	90	72	83	91	86	92	62	91	94	109
	UNITED STATES	100	100	100	100	100	100	100	100	100	100	100	100	100	100	100	100	100	100	100	100

POPULATION CHANGE

ZIP CODE #	POST OFFICE NAME	COUNTY FIPS CODE	POPULATION 2000	POPULATION 2009	POPULATION 2014	2000-2009 ANNUAL RATE % Rate	2000-2009 ANNUAL RATE State Centile	HOUSEHOLDS 2000	HOUSEHOLDS 2009	HOUSEHOLDS 2014	HOUSEHOLDS % Annual Rate 2000-2009	HOUSEHOLDS 2009 Average HH Size	FAMILIES 2000	FAMILIES 2009	FAMILIES % Annual Rate 2000-2009
68316	BENEDICT	185	575	564	556	-0.2	58	208	208	206	0.0	2.71	160	159	-0.1
68317	BENNET	109	1583	1690	1761	0.7	84	599	656	690	1.0	2.58	491	529	0.8
68318	BLUE SPRINGS	067	637	641	642	0.1	69	260	266	267	0.2	2.41	173	175	0.1
68319	BRADSHAW	185	614	580	567	-0.6	37	240	232	229	-0.4	2.50	193	186	-0.4
68320	BROCK	127	360	324	309	-1.1	17	147	135	130	-0.9	2.40	95	87	-0.9
68321	BROWNVILLE	127	421	381	365	-1.1	17	179	166	159	-0.8	2.30	122	113	-0.8
68322	BRUNING	169	444	384	358	-1.6	4	197	175	164	-1.3	2.19	130	115	-1.3
68323	BURCHARD	133	418	359	338	-1.6	4	171	150	142	-1.4	2.39	125	110	-1.4
68324	BURR	131	210	193	188	-0.9	26	95	88	86	-0.8	2.19	70	65	-0.8
68325	BYRON	169	332	293	275	-1.3	10	133	119	112	-1.2	2.36	90	80	-1.3
68326	CARLETON	169	274	237	220	-1.6	4	108	96	90	-1.3	2.47	72	64	-1.3
68327	CHESTER	169	442	383	356	-1.5	6	198	174	163	-1.4	2.19	134	118	-1.4
68328	CLATONIA	067	484	487	486	0.1	69	193	199	200	0.3	2.45	150	154	0.3
68329	COOK	097	699	687	678	-0.2	58	297	297	293	0.0	2.31	212	211	-0.1
68330	CORDOVA	159	141	131	127	-0.8	30	68	65	64	-0.5	2.02	50	48	-0.4
68331	CORTLAND	067	829	882	898	0.7	84	327	357	366	1.0	2.46	253	275	0.9
68332	CRAB ORCHARD	097	141	138	136	-0.2	58	65	65	64	0.0	2.12	43	43	0.0
68333	CRETE	151	7576	7932	7970	0.5	81	2643	2776	2787	0.5	2.58	1750	1833	0.5
68335	DAVENPORT	169	442	379	353	-1.6	4	195	172	161	-1.3	2.20	143	125	-1.4
68336	DAVEY	109	475	528	596	1.2	93	174	196	221	1.3	2.69	140	154	1.0
68337	DAWSON	147	378	326	304	-1.6	4	149	131	122	-1.4	2.49	103	90	-1.4
68338	DAYKIN	095	300	276	267	-0.9	26	128	121	118	-0.6	2.28	94	88	-0.7
68339	DENTON	109	905	1184	1318	2.9	97	343	457	514	3.2	2.59	278	364	3.0
68340	DESHLER	169	1072	946	885	-1.3	10	452	405	380	-1.2	2.24	307	274	-1.2
68341	DE WITT	067	1007	1017	1011	0.1	69	407	416	414	0.2	2.44	272	277	0.2
68342	DILLER	095	598	575	563	-0.4	49	231	228	225	-0.1	2.52	168	165	-0.2
68343	DORCHESTER	151	929	943	933	0.2	73	362	370	368	0.2	2.55	274	278	0.2
68344	DOUGLAS	131	424	389	377	-0.9	26	159	147	143	-0.8	2.65	117	108	-0.9
68345	DU BOIS	133	292	289	287	-0.1	63	127	128	128	0.1	2.26	80	80	0.0
68346	DUNBAR	131	558	640	670	1.5	95	201	228	238	1.4	2.81	156	176	1.3
68347	EAGLE	025	2236	2479	2597	1.1	92	781	880	924	1.3	2.82	628	702	1.2
68348	ELK CREEK	097	318	390	383	2.2	97	139	134	132	-0.4	2.16	93	89	-0.5
68349	ELMWOOD	025	1090	1176	1190	0.8	87	409	442	448	0.8	2.66	304	325	0.7
68350	ENDICOTT	095	253	241	234	-0.5	42	110	108	106	-0.2	2.23	79	76	-0.4
68351	EXETER	059	895	832	800	-0.8	30	345	323	310	-0.7	2.45	222	206	-0.8
68352	FAIRBURY	095	5563	5197	5035	-0.7	34	2407	2277	2213	-0.6	2.21	1526	1433	-0.7
68354	FAIRMONT	059	936	868	835	-0.8	30	368	345	331	-0.7	2.40	242	226	-0.7
68355	FALLS CITY	147	5886	5371	5091	-1.0	21	2465	2258	2138	-0.9	2.31	1552	1412	-1.0
68357	FILLEY	067	427	429	425	0.1	69	172	177	177	0.3	2.42	132	136	0.3
68358	FIRTH	109	1225	1353	1422	1.1	92	415	469	497	1.3	2.77	330	367	1.2
68359	FRIEND	151	1735	1678	1642	-0.4	49	669	647	632	-0.4	2.51	476	458	-0.4
68360	GARLAND	159	596	640	653	0.8	87	227	251	257	1.1	2.55	170	187	1.0
68361	GENEVA	059	2998	2844	2751	-0.6	37	1218	1179	1144	-0.4	2.28	808	778	-0.4
68362	GILEAD	169	156	148	141	-0.6	37	66	63	61	-0.5	2.19	41	40	-0.3
68365	GRAFTON	059	233	206	195	-1.3	10	95	86	82	-1.1	2.40	72	65	-1.1
68366	GREENWOOD	025	928	1010	1054	0.9	89	357	399	419	1.2	2.53	261	290	1.1
68367	GRESHAM	185	520	513	508	-0.1	63	204	205	204	0.1	2.50	154	154	0.0
68368	HALLAM	109	601	643	682	0.7	84	232	258	276	1.2	2.49	185	202	1.0
68370	HEBRON	169	2143	2003	1907	-0.7	34	874	833	797	-0.5	2.27	557	528	-0.6
68371	HENDERSON	185	1707	1695	1681	-0.1	63	647	654	653	0.1	2.42	470	473	0.1
68372	HICKMAN	109	2174	2080	2057	-0.5	42	743	731	730	-0.2	2.84	596	577	-0.3
68375	HUBBELL	169	186	163	152	-1.4	7	80	72	67	-1.1	2.24	53	48	-1.1
68376	HUMBOLDT	147	1633	1645	1628	0.1	69	694	709	705	0.2	2.26	438	446	0.2
68377	JANSEN	095	489	473	462	-0.4	49	195	193	191	-0.1	2.45	148	146	-0.1
68378	JOHNSON	127	779	702	669	-1.1	17	341	314	301	-0.9	2.24	231	211	-1.0
68379	JULIAN	127	81	73	69	-1.1	17	37	34	33	-0.9	2.15	24	22	-0.9
68380	LEWISTON	133	181	155	147	-1.7	2	73	64	61	-1.4	2.42	53	47	-1.3
68381	LIBERTY	067	234	232	230	-0.1	63	86	86	86	0.0	2.62	60	59	-0.2
68401	MC COOL JUNCTION	185	727	714	708	-0.2	58	294	299	299	0.2	2.39	217	220	0.1
68402	MALCOLM	109	1061	1193	1266	1.3	94	366	428	461	1.7	2.60	303	348	1.5
68404	MARTELL	109	977	1180	1303	2.1	96	377	475	529	2.5	2.48	292	359	2.3
68405	MILFORD	159	3383	3379	3321	0.0	66	1180	1207	1194	0.2	2.50	803	817	0.2
68406	MILLIGAN	059	477	422	400	-1.3	10	216	193	184	-1.2	2.19	137	122	-1.2
68407	MURDOCK	025	824	898	939	0.9	89	318	355	373	1.2	2.53	251	279	1.1
68409	MURRAY	025	825	889	912	0.8	87	313	348	359	1.2	2.55	239	264	1.1
68410	NEBRASKA CITY	131	8558	8683	8668	0.2	73	3370	3420	3407	0.2	2.46	2243	2262	0.1
68413	NEHAWKA	025	464	485	486	0.5	81	183	195	196	0.7	2.49	139	146	0.5
68414	NEMAHA	127	381	345	330	-1.1	17	158	146	141	-0.9	2.36	108	100	-0.8
68415	ODELL	067	736	772	786	0.5	81	282	301	308	0.7	2.56	219	233	0.7
68416	OHIOWA	059	265	234	222	-1.3	10	123	110	105	-1.2	2.13	78	69	-1.3
68417	OTOE	131	406	428	438	0.6	83	155	165	169	0.7	2.59	115	122	0.6
68418	PALMYRA	131	995	1086	1122	1.0	90	379	419	434	1.1	2.59	287	315	1.0
68420	PAWNEE CITY	133	1438	1352	1311	-0.7	34	629	595	576	-0.6	2.18	375	353	-0.7
68421	PERU	127	1229	1092	1056	-1.3	10	373	337	322	-1.1	2.31	216	194	-1.2
68422	PICKRELL	067	622	655	664	0.6	83	237	256	262	0.8	2.52	183	197	0.8
68423	PLEASANT DALE	159	837	847	838	0.1	69	327	340	339	0.4	2.39	247	256	0.4
68424	PLYMOUTH	095	870	835	816	-0.4	49	332	327	322	-0.2	2.55	251	246	-0.2
68428	RAYMOND	109	1210	1268	1519	0.5	81	436	442	534	0.1	2.80	361	360	0.0
68429	REYNOLDS	095	134	127	123	-0.6	37	60	59	57	-0.2	2.15	43	41	-0.5
68430	ROCA	109	1082	1190	1248	1.0	90	405	462	490	1.4	2.58	329	366	1.2
68431	RULO	147	349	299	279	-1.7	2	148	129	120	-1.5	2.32	106	92	-1.5
68433	SALEM	147	250	214	199	-1.7	2	112	97	91	-1.5	2.21	78	68	-1.5
68434	SEWARD	159	8232	8644	8695	0.5	81	2963	3185	3228	0.8	2.43	2020	2162	0.7
68436	SHICKLEY	059	665	587	554	-1.3	10	260	234	223	-1.1	2.50	198	178	-1.1
68437	SHUBERT	147	342	299	280	-1.4	7	133	118	111	-1.3	2.53	91	81	-1.3
68439	STAPLEHURST	159	563	584	587	0.4	78	219	233	237	0.7	2.51	164	174	0.6
68440	STEELE CITY	095	156	148	145	-0.6	37	74	72	71	-0.3	2.06	53	51	-0.4
68441	STEINAUER	133	308	291	284	-0.6	37	125	121	119	-0.4	2.40	83	79	-0.5
68442	STELLA	147	303	265	248	-1.4	7	134	119	112	-1.3	2.23	92	81	-1.4
68443	STERLING	097	1037	1013	995	-0.3	54	424	422	416	-0.1	2.40	287	284	-0.1
68444	STRANG	059	131	116	110	-1.3	10	53	48	45	-1.1	2.42	36	32	-1.3
68445	SWANTON	151	210	219	218	0.5	81	89	93	93	0.5	2.35	66	69	0.5
68446	SYRACUSE	131	2403	2629	2722	1.0	90	992	1103	1146	1.2	2.31	709	781	1.1
68447	TABLE ROCK	133	450	446	442	-0.1	63	214	216	216	0.1	2.06	134	135	0.1
68448	TALMAGE	131	515	534	535	0.4	78	199	207	208	0.4	2.58	148	152	0.3
	NEBRASKA					0.6					0.8	2.46			0.7
	UNITED STATES					1.0					1.1	2.59			0.9

ZIP CODE #	POST OFFICE NAME	RACE (%) White 2000	White 2009	Black 2000	Black 2009	Asian/Pacific 2000	Asian/Pacific 2009	% Hispanic Origin 2000	% Hispanic Origin 2009	2009 AGE DISTRIBUTION (%) 0-4	5-9	10-14	15-19	20-24	25-44	45-64	65-84	85+	18+	MEDIAN AGE 2009	% 2009 Males	% 2009 Females
68316	BENEDICT	98.3	97.5	0.5	0.7	0.0	0.0	0.7	1.1	5.7	6.4	6.9	7.6	4.8	21.3	32.8	12.6	2.0	76.4	42.8	50.4	49.6
68317	BENNET	98.1	97.2	0.1	0.1	0.3	0.7	0.9	1.4	5.6	6.7	7.6	7.4	4.4	20.9	34.0	12.2	1.2	75.5	43.3	50.9	49.1
68318	BLUE SPRINGS	96.9	96.1	0.2	0.2	0.5	0.8	0.8	1.1	6.6	6.6	6.6	6.1	5.1	21.5	27.8	17.0	2.8	76.6	43.0	48.7	51.3
68319	BRADSHAW	98.2	97.9	0.2	0.2	0.0	0.0	0.5	0.7	5.3	6.2	6.9	7.9	4.3	22.2	32.6	12.8	1.7	76.6	42.6	50.9	49.1
68320	BROCK	97.8	97.5	0.0	0.0	0.3	0.3	0.6	0.6	4.0	4.9	5.6	7.4	4.0	21.6	35.5	13.9	3.1	80.6	46.4	50.9	49.1
68321	BROWNVILLE	99.1	98.7	0.0	0.0	0.2	0.5	0.7	1.0	4.7	5.0	5.2	6.8	5.8	19.4	34.1	16.0	2.9	80.6	46.6	51.2	48.8
68322	BRUNING	98.9	98.4	0.0	0.0	0.0	0.0	2.0	3.1	6.0	6.3	6.8	6.8	4.2	22.1	29.7	14.8	3.4	76.3	43.6	47.1	52.9
68323	BURCHARD	98.6	97.8	0.0	0.0	0.7	1.1	0.0	0.0	5.8	6.4	6.7	5.8	4.5	20.3	30.9	16.2	3.3	77.4	45.3	51.0	49.0
68324	BURR	97.6	96.9	0.5	0.5	0.5	1.0	0.5	1.0	4.7	7.3	6.7	6.7	3.6	23.8	30.6	14.5	2.1	76.7	43.3	50.8	49.2
68325	BYRON	97.9	97.3	0.0	0.0	0.3	0.3	1.2	2.0	6.5	6.8	6.8	6.5	3.4	20.1	27.3	16.0	6.5	75.4	44.8	48.5	51.5
68326	CARLETON	98.9	98.3	0.0	0.0	0.0	0.0	1.8	3.0	5.9	5.9	6.8	6.8	4.2	21.5	30.8	14.8	3.4	76.4	44.2	47.3	52.7
68327	CHESTER	98.4	97.9	0.2	0.3	0.2	0.5	0.9	1.0	4.7	5.5	6.3	6.3	3.9	19.3	31.3	19.6	3.1	79.4	48.1	51.2	48.8
68328	CLATONIA	98.3	97.5	0.0	0.0	0.2	0.4	0.6	1.0	5.3	6.4	8.8	8.0	3.5	24.0	30.4	12.5	1.0	73.1	41.1	50.5	49.5
68329	COOK	98.4	97.7	0.0	0.0	1.1	1.7	0.4	0.7	4.8	5.4	6.1	6.3	4.5	19.8	33.2	16.6	3.3	79.6	46.9	51.4	48.6
68330	CORDOVA	97.9	96.9	0.7	0.8	0.0	0.0	0.7	0.8	6.9	7.6	7.6	6.1	4.6	22.1	30.5	13.0	1.5	73.3	40.9	51.1	48.9
68331	CORTLAND	99.3	99.1	0.1	0.1	0.1	0.2	0.5	0.8	6.5	7.1	7.7	6.7	3.9	22.2	30.7	12.9	2.3	74.3	42.0	51.4	48.6
68332	CRAB ORCHARD	99.3	98.6	0.0	0.0	0.0	0.7	0.7	0.7	5.1	6.5	6.5	6.5	4.3	21.7	32.6	14.5	2.2	77.5	44.5	47.8	52.2
68333	CRETE	88.7	84.9	0.6	0.7	2.9	3.9	11.0	15.5	7.0	6.6	6.4	9.2	9.9	23.9	23.8	10.0	3.1	76.0	33.3	50.1	49.9
68335	DAVENPORT	98.6	98.4	0.0	0.0	0.0	0.0	0.7	1.1	5.5	6.3	6.6	5.3	5.0	18.2	33.8	16.6	2.6	78.4	46.4	51.7	48.3
68336	DAVEY	98.1	97.2	0.4	0.8	0.0	0.2	1.9	2.8	5.5	6.3	7.0	7.8	4.9	22.7	32.4	12.1	1.3	76.5	41.9	50.9	49.1
68337	DAWSON	97.1	95.7	0.5	0.6	0.3	0.6	1.1	1.2	4.0	4.6	5.8	7.4	4.3	21.8	33.4	16.6	2.1	81.0	46.3	52.1	47.9
68338	DAYKIN	98.7	98.2	0.0	0.0	0.3	0.4	1.0	1.4	4.3	5.1	5.8	5.8	4.7	20.3	34.8	16.3	2.9	80.8	47.9	49.3	50.7
68339	DENTON	98.1	97.6	0.1	0.2	0.2	0.3	0.9	1.4	5.6	6.5	7.6	6.5	4.1	21.6	36.0	11.2	0.8	76.2	43.6	50.4	49.6
68340	DESHLER	97.9	97.5	0.0	0.0	0.3	0.4	1.2	1.9	6.3	6.9	7.0	6.2	3.6	20.3	27.0	16.5	6.2	75.7	44.7	48.2	51.8
68341	DE WITT	98.8	98.4	0.0	0.0	0.3	0.4	0.8	1.1	5.5	6.1	7.0	7.0	4.6	23.9	30.2	13.3	2.5	76.7	42.0	50.7	49.3
68342	DILLER	99.0	98.8	0.0	0.0	0.2	0.2	0.8	1.0	5.4	6.1	6.4	5.9	4.0	21.0	32.9	15.8	2.4	78.3	45.6	52.5	47.5
68343	DORCHESTER	98.2	97.5	0.1	0.1	0.0	0.0	2.3	3.5	6.0	6.6	6.8	7.3	4.3	24.5	29.2	13.4	1.9	75.9	41.0	51.6	48.4
68344	DOUGLAS	97.4	96.4	0.7	0.8	0.5	1.0	0.7	1.0	5.1	7.5	6.4	6.9	3.3	24.2	29.6	14.7	2.3	76.3	42.8	51.4	48.6
68345	DU BOIS	99.0	98.3	0.0	0.0	0.0	0.3	1.4	2.1	4.8	5.2	5.9	6.6	3.8	19.4	30.4	20.8	3.1	80.3	47.6	52.6	47.4
68346	DUNBAR	98.9	98.6	0.2	0.2	0.0	0.2	0.2	0.3	6.6	7.7	8.0	8.1	4.4	21.7	29.4	12.8	1.4	72.7	40.1	51.6	48.4
68347	EAGLE	98.3	97.8	0.0	0.0	0.1	0.2	1.7	2.5	7.9	8.2	8.1	7.7	5.9	25.7	27.6	7.8	0.9	70.9	35.1	50.3	49.7
68348	ELK CREEK	91.8	88.7	0.3	0.3	5.0	7.2	2.8	4.1	4.1	3.3	4.6	7.2	6.9	29.7	24.6	14.1	5.4	82.3	41.8	58.7	41.3
68349	ELMWOOD	99.1	98.9	0.1	0.1	0.3	0.4	0.4	0.5	7.5	8.1	8.5	7.5	4.2	23.0	28.4	10.7	2.2	71.1	39.4	52.0	48.0
68350	ENDICOTT	99.2	98.3	0.0	0.0	0.0	0.4	0.8	1.2	5.4	6.2	6.2	5.8	3.7	21.2	32.4	16.6	2.5	78.0	45.8	52.3	47.7
68351	EXETER	97.3	96.6	0.1	0.1	0.1	0.1	1.9	2.9	5.4	5.9	6.7	7.5	4.3	20.1	29.0	15.9	5.3	76.6	45.1	49.3	50.7
68352	FAIRBURY	98.1	97.6	0.1	0.1	0.2	0.3	1.6	2.3	5.5	5.7	5.9	5.7	5.1	21.2	28.9	16.5	5.5	79.2	45.6	48.3	51.7
68354	FAIRMONT	97.3	96.7	0.1	0.1	0.1	0.1	1.7	2.8	5.5	6.1	6.8	7.6	4.1	20.3	28.9	15.7	5.0	76.0	44.6	49.2	50.8
68355	FALLS CITY	94.9	93.9	0.1	0.1	0.2	0.3	0.9	1.2	5.9	6.0	6.3	6.8	5.7	20.8	27.1	16.6	4.8	77.3	43.6	47.9	52.1
68357	FILLEY	99.3	98.8	0.0	0.2	0.2	0.5	0.5	0.9	4.9	5.1	7.9	8.2	3.3	24.7	29.1	15.6	1.2	76.5	42.6	52.2	47.8
68358	FIRTH	98.6	98.0	0.2	0.2	0.4	0.7	0.2	0.4	7.8	8.3	8.6	8.0	3.9	23.4	26.0	9.8	4.1	69.8	38.2	47.3	52.7
68359	FRIEND	98.6	98.2	0.1	0.1	0.0	0.0	1.0	1.6	5.8	6.1	6.4	7.0	5.4	19.8	27.9	16.5	5.0	76.6	44.5	48.7	51.3
68360	GARLAND	97.5	96.7	0.2	0.2	0.0	0.2	2.2	3.1	5.2	6.1	6.9	6.6	4.7	22.8	35.3	11.3	1.3	77.7	43.4	51.6	48.4
68361	GENEVA	97.5	96.7	0.4	0.4	0.0	0.0	1.7	2.5	5.9	6.3	6.6	8.3	4.3	19.9	28.1	15.3	5.4	75.0	44.0	48.3	51.7
68362	GILEAD	99.4	98.6	0.0	0.0	0.0	0.0	0.6	1.4	6.1	6.1	6.1	6.1	4.7	17.6	28.4	18.9	6.1	77.0	47.5	48.6	51.4
68365	GRAFTON	99.1	98.5	0.0	0.0	0.0	0.0	0.9	1.5	6.8	7.3	7.8	6.8	3.9	20.9	30.1	14.6	1.9	72.3	42.5	51.9	48.1
68366	GREENWOOD	97.8	97.4	0.2	0.2	0.3	0.6	0.8	1.0	6.2	7.0	7.2	6.2	4.0	23.4	32.1	12.6	1.3	75.4	42.1	52.0	48.0
68367	GRESHAM	98.1	97.9	0.6	0.8	0.0	0.0	0.6	1.0	6.0	6.4	6.8	7.8	4.9	21.2	31.8	13.1	1.9	76.0	42.3	49.5	50.5
68368	HALLAM	96.3	94.4	0.0	0.0	1.8	3.0	0.7	1.2	5.6	5.8	6.5	7.2	4.4	26.4	31.4	11.4	1.4	77.8	41.7	49.9	50.1
68370	HEBRON	99.0	98.8	0.0	0.0	0.0	0.0	0.6	0.9	5.6	5.9	6.0	5.9	4.8	18.3	28.8	18.9	5.6	78.3	47.4	50.0	50.0
68371	HENDERSON	98.9	98.5	0.1	0.2	0.2	0.4	0.4	0.6	4.6	5.5	7.2	7.6	3.7	18.9	29.5	16.6	6.3	77.0	46.7	49.0	51.0
68372	HICKMAN	98.3	97.8	0.4	0.5	0.1	0.1	1.1	1.7	7.2	7.8	8.0	7.9	5.9	24.2	29.7	8.3	1.0	72.2	36.4	51.5	48.5
68375	HUBBELL	98.4	98.2	0.0	0.0	0.5	0.6	0.5	1.2	4.9	5.5	5.5	6.1	4.3	19.6	30.7	19.6	3.7	79.8	48.0	51.5	48.5
68376	HUMBOLDT	96.7	96.0	0.4	0.5	0.1	0.2	1.7	2.2	4.9	5.0	5.4	6.6	5.7	19.2	29.5	18.7	5.0	80.3	47.1	48.6	51.4
68377	JANSEN	99.2	98.9	0.0	0.0	0.2	0.2	0.6	1.1	5.3	5.7	6.6	7.2	4.7	21.8	33.0	13.3	2.5	78.0	44.1	52.4	47.6
68378	JOHNSON	98.3	97.9	0.0	0.0	0.1	0.3	0.6	0.7	4.3	5.0	5.8	7.0	4.4	20.7	36.0	13.8	3.0	80.6	46.6	50.6	49.4
68379	JULIAN	97.5	97.3	0.0	0.0	0.0	0.0	0.0	0.0	4.1	4.1	5.5	6.8	4.1	20.5	37.0	13.7	4.1	82.2	47.9	54.8	45.2
68380	LEWISTON	98.3	97.4	0.0	0.0	0.6	1.3	0.0	0.0	5.8	6.5	6.5	5.8	4.5	20.0	30.3	16.8	3.9	78.1	45.8	51.0	49.0
68381	LIBERTY	97.0	96.6	0.0	0.0	0.0	0.0	1.7	1.7	6.0	6.0	6.0	6.0	5.6	21.1	27.2	17.7	4.3	76.7	44.2	48.7	51.3
68401	MC COOL JUNCTION	97.8	96.9	0.0	0.0	0.7	1.0	1.6	2.7	5.7	7.7	7.8	7.8	3.4	23.5	31.4	11.1	1.5	72.7	40.1	51.1	48.9
68402	MALCOLM	98.1	97.7	0.5	0.6	0.3	0.4	0.6	0.9	5.1	6.0	8.9	10.6	4.4	23.7	32.5	8.0	0.7	72.6	39.2	53.1	46.9
68404	MARTELL	97.8	96.7	0.1	0.2	0.2	0.4	1.1	1.9	5.6	6.5	7.5	6.5	3.8	22.6	34.5	11.4	1.5	76.3	43.4	50.6	49.4
68405	MILFORD	97.9	97.4	0.2	0.2	0.2	0.3	1.4	2.2	5.3	5.3	6.1	13.4	10.0	21.3	24.3	12.1	2.2	79.3	35.0	54.6	45.4
68406	MILLIGAN	98.5	97.9	0.0	0.2	0.2	0.2	1.9	3.1	5.7	5.9	6.4	6.4	4.7	21.1	31.5	15.2	3.1	78.0	44.8	52.1	47.9
68407	MURDOCK	97.6	97.0	0.0	0.0	0.1	0.2	1.5	2.2	5.9	6.6	7.0	6.3	4.3	22.3	33.1	13.0	1.4	76.5	43.3	50.3	49.7
68409	MURRAY	98.2	97.3	0.0	0.0	0.7	1.3	1.5	2.1	6.1	6.4	7.1	7.3	4.5	24.2	30.6	12.0	1.8	76.2	41.6	49.5	50.5
68410	NEBRASKA CITY	96.5	95.2	0.4	0.4	0.4	0.6	3.8	5.6	6.7	6.8	6.7	6.6	5.7	23.1	26.8	13.9	3.6	75.5	40.1	48.7	51.3
68413	NEHAWKA	97.4	96.5	0.0	0.0	0.6	1.0	2.2	3.3	6.0	6.6	7.0	7.2	4.5	22.5	31.8	13.0	1.4	75.7	42.6	50.5	49.5
68414	NEMAHA	99.5	99.4	0.0	0.0	0.3	0.3	0.5	0.9	4.9	4.9	5.2	7.0	5.5	18.8	35.4	15.4	2.9	81.2	45.8	50.7	49.3
68415	ODELL	98.8	98.8	0.0	0.0	0.0	0.0	0.4	0.5	5.6	6.2	6.7	7.6	4.5	21.1	31.9	14.4	1.9	76.7	43.6	51.2	48.8
68416	OHIOWA	98.5	98.3	0.0	0.0	0.0	0.0	1.9	3.0	5.6	6.0	6.4	6.4	4.7	21.4	30.3	15.8	3.4	77.4	44.7	51.7	48.3
68417	OTOE	99.0	98.4	0.0	0.0	0.0	0.2	0.5	0.7	6.1	6.8	7.2	7.0	4.7	23.1	31.3	12.1	1.6	75.2	41.3	52.3	47.7
68418	PALMYRA	98.4	97.8	0.2	0.2	0.1	0.1	1.7	2.6	6.5	7.4	7.5	6.4	4.1	24.2	30.8	11.4	1.6	74.6	40.9	52.6	47.4
68420	PAWNEE CITY	99.1	98.9	0.0	0.0	0.1	0.2	0.6	0.8	5.6	5.5	5.7	6.7	4.7	18.1	27.2	19.3	7.2	78.6	47.8	46.3	53.7
68421	PERU	96.4	95.3	1.2	1.4	0.4	0.6	2.1	3.0	3.4	4.2	5.1	17.1	25.3	16.0	18.6	8.5	1.7	84.2	24.0	50.9	49.1
68422	PICKRELL	99.2	98.9	0.0	0.2	0.2	0.3	0.5	0.9	6.6	7.3	7.6	6.6	3.7	22.3	30.7	12.5	2.7	74.2	42.2	51.0	49.0
68423	PLEASANT DALE	98.1	97.5	0.1	0.1	0.4	0.6	1.2	1.8	5.3	6.0	6.8	6.6	4.3	23.6	32.7	12.8	1.9	77.6	43.1	51.2	48.8
68424	PLYMOUTH	99.2	98.8	0.0	0.0	0.1	0.2	0.7	1.1	5.3	5.7	6.3	6.9	4.6	21.7	33.4	13.5	2.5	78.4	44.6	52.0	48.0
68428	RAYMOND	97.4	96.1	0.2	0.3	0.2	0.4	1.8	3.0	5.5	6.4	7.9	8.8	4.7	23.4	33.4	9.1	0.9	74.4	40.7	51.6	48.4
68429	REYNOLDS	99.3	99.2	0.0	0.0	0.0	0.0	0.7	0.8	5.5	6.3	6.3	5.5	3.9	20.5	32.3	17.3	2.4	78.0	46.1	53.5	46.5
68430	ROCA	98.2	97.2	0.1	0.2	0.3	0.4	1.2	1.9	6.0	6.9	7.8	7.3	4.2	22.0	33.4	11.2	1.3	74.7	42.3	49.9	50.1
68431	RULO	93.7	92.3	0.0	0.0	0.0	0.0	0.6	1.0	6.4	7.0	7.4	7.4	4.3	19.7	30.4	15.4	2.0	74.6	43.1	51.2	48.8
68433	SALEM	96.8	95.8	0.4	0.5	0.4	0.5	0.8	1.4	4.2	4.7	5.6	7.0	4.2	21.5	34.1	16.4	2.3	81.3	46.7	52.3	47.7
68434	SEWARD	97.9	97.4	0.4	0.4	0.5	0.7	1.1	1.6	5.6	5.4	5.6	10.1	10.6	22.9	24.6	11.7	3.4	79.2	34.9	48.8	51.2
68436	SHICKLEY	98.9	98.5	0.0	0.0	0.0	0.2	0.9	1.4	6.5	7.2	7.2	6.6	3.7	21.0	31.2	14.7	2.0	74.1	43.4	51.8	48.2
68437	SHUBERT	97.7	97.3	0.0	0.0	0.0	0.0	1.2	1.7	3.7	7.0	7.7	10.4	3.3	22.1	30.4	13.0	2.3	73.9	42.2	50.2	49.8
68439	STAPLEHURST	98.6	97.9	0.0	0.0	0.4	0.5	0.7	1.2	6.0	6.5	7.2	7.0	4.3	26.0	29.3	11.8	1.9	75.7	40.5	52.7	47.3
68440	STEELE CITY	99.4	99.3	0.0	0.0	0.0	0.0	0.6	1.4	5.4	6.1	6.1	5.4	4.1	20.9	32.4	16.9	2.7	79.1	46.1	51.4	48.6
68441	STEINAUER	98.7	98.3	0.0	0.0	0.3	0.3	1.0	1.4	5.2	5.5	6.2	6.2	4.1	19.9	30.2	19.2	3.4	79.4	46.8	51.2	48.8
68442	STELLA	98.0	97.4	0.0	0.0	0.0	0.0	1.3	1.9	4.2	7.2	7.9	7.9	3.0	22.6	30.9	14.0	2.3	75.5	43.1	50.2	49.8
68443	STERLING	98.3	97.7	0.2	0.2	0.6	1.0	0.5	0.8	5.2	5.8	6.3	6.8	3.9	21.5	32.8	14.8	2.8	78.4	45.2	49.2	50.8
68444	STRANG	98.5	98.3	0.0	0.0	0.0	0.0	1.5	2.6	6.0	6.9	6.9	6.0	4.3	21.6	30.2	15.5	2.6	75.0	43.8	51.7	48.3
68445	SWANTON	98.6	97.7	0.0	0.0	0.0	0.0	1.4	2.3	4.1	6.4	8.7	8.7	3.7	20.5	32.9	12.8	2.3	74.4	43.4	53.9	46.1
68446	SYRACUSE	98.9	98.4	0.0	0.0	0.2	0.3	0.5	0.8	5.6	5.5	5.5	5.4	3.6	20.1	26.1	21.5	6.8	79.8	48.0	48.0	52.0
68447	TABLE ROCK	99.1	98.4	0.0	0.0	0.0	0.2	1.3	1.8	4.9	5.2	6.1	6.5	3.8	19.3	30.0	20.9	3.4	79.8	47.6	52.0	48.0
68448	TALMAGE	98.8	98.7	0.8	0.9	0.0	0.0	0.6	0.7	7.3	7.5	7.7	6.4	4.3	21.5	28.8	14.4	2.1	73.4	40.8	53.6	46.4
	NEBRASKA	89.6	86.9	4.0	4.4	1.3	2.1	5.5	7.9	6.9	6.8	6.8	7.3	6.9	26.3	25.7	11.0	2.3	75.3	36.5	49.4	50.6
	UNITED STATES	75.1	72.0	12.3	12.7	3.8	4.6	12.5	15.7	6.8	6.7	6.6	7.1	6.9	27.0	26.0	10.9	1.9	75.7	36.9	49.2	50.8

ZIP CODE #	POST OFFICE NAME	2009 Per Capita Income	2009 HH Income Base	2009 HOUSEHOLD INCOME DISTRIBUTION (%) Less than $25,000	$25,000 to $49,999	$50,000 to $99,999	$100,000 to $149,999	$150,000 or More	MEDIAN HOUSEHOLD INCOME 2009	2014	2009 National Centile	2009 State Centile	2009 Home Value Base	2009 HOME VALUE DISTRIBUTION (%) Less than $50,000	$50,000 to $89,999	$90,000 to $174,999	$175,000 to $399,999	$400,000 or More	2009 Median Home Value
68316	BENEDICT	20093	208	19.7	35.1	37.5	4.8	2.9	45412	48209	49	69	160	24.4	25.0	34.4	13.1	3.1	91667
68317	BENNET	27112	656	11.3	24.2	50.8	9.9	3.8	60954	62728	79	92	564	14.0	17.7	37.8	26.1	4.4	120055
68318	BLUE SPRINGS	17418	266	32.7	35.0	27.8	3.8	0.8	35915	38804	20	24	200	40.5	26.0	25.0	6.5	2.0	65833
68319	BRADSHAW	21791	232	16.8	34.1	44.4	3.9	0.9	49307	50649	60	79	179	15.1	17.3	37.4	20.1	10.1	121196
68320	BROCK	19480	135	28.9	31.9	34.1	4.4	0.7	39686	43215	32	43	107	26.2	23.4	29.0	19.6	1.9	92500
68321	BROWNVILLE	20677	166	30.7	28.3	33.7	4.8	2.4	40568	43095	35	49	134	32.8	29.9	17.9	13.4	6.0	69091
68322	BRUNING	20192	175	29.1	33.7	33.1	2.9	1.1	37352	41893	25	31	142	50.0	26.8	17.6	2.8	2.8	50000
68323	BURCHARD	19663	150	24.0	37.3	33.3	4.0	1.3	41666	45769	38	56	126	31.7	23.8	28.6	14.3	1.6	80000
68324	BURR	21928	88	21.6	42.0	28.4	6.8	1.1	41489	43746	38	55	75	20.0	16.0	34.7	24.0	5.3	121250
68325	BYRON	17699	119	31.9	37.0	28.6	2.5	0.0	36420	38909	22	27	95	54.7	28.4	11.6	3.2	2.1	45909
68326	CARLETON	17877	96	29.2	33.3	33.3	3.1	1.0	37857	41565	26	34	78	50.0	26.9	17.9	2.6	2.6	50000
68327	CHESTER	18247	174	33.9	37.9	23.0	4.0	1.1	33254	34484	14	12	143	51.7	25.2	18.2	3.5	1.4	47222
68328	CLATONIA	21556	199	14.6	36.7	43.7	4.5	0.5	48768	50551	58	78	161	11.2	21.1	30.4	37.3	0.0	148958
68329	COOK	19921	297	30.3	34.0	30.3	3.0	2.4	39750	40624	32	43	230	24.8	26.5	32.6	10.9	5.2	87692
68330	CORDOVA	21649	65	27.7	35.4	32.3	4.6	0.0	39303	45000	31	40	52	38.5	26.9	26.9	7.7	0.0	73333
68331	CORTLAND	21890	357	16.8	31.1	46.5	5.0	0.6	51530	51558	65	84	292	7.2	12.7	48.3	30.5	1.4	139881
68332	CRAB ORCHARD	21159	65	27.7	33.8	32.3	4.6	1.5	40440	41550	34	48	52	25.0	26.9	28.8	17.3	1.9	87500
68333	CRETE	20369	2776	23.8	28.2	38.4	7.7	1.9	47957	49759	56	77	1799	14.6	18.2	50.0	14.6	2.6	112288
68335	DAVENPORT	19663	172	28.5	36.6	29.7	4.1	1.2	37329	42388	25	30	136	48.5	23.5	19.1	4.4	4.4	51818
68336	DAVEY	25410	196	10.2	25.5	52.0	9.7	2.6	63525	62833	82	94	166	10.8	12.7	35.5	36.7	4.2	160577
68337	DAWSON	16660	131	28.2	40.5	27.5	3.8	0.0	37572	36992	25	32	104	52.9	22.1	17.3	7.7	0.0	46667
68338	DAYKIN	21925	121	24.0	38.0	31.4	4.1	2.5	40277	41879	34	47	90	35.6	17.8	35.6	7.8	3.3	80000
68339	DENTON	26897	457	9.6	20.4	56.0	11.2	2.8	64809	62780	83	95	384	7.0	6.3	42.2	41.1	3.4	166102
68340	DESHLER	18588	405	31.4	37.3	27.4	3.0	1.0	36677	38569	23	28	322	53.4	28.3	12.7	3.4	2.2	46452
68341	DE WITT	20396	416	24.5	29.6	40.6	4.6	0.7	45687	47864	50	71	321	17.1	28.7	35.5	17.8	0.9	94655
68342	DILLER	20115	228	27.2	31.6	36.0	3.1	2.2	42053	44312	39	59	193	39.9	24.9	21.2	11.4	2.6	61250
68343	DORCHESTER	17980	370	23.2	38.1	34.9	3.0	0.8	41462	44038	38	54	287	15.3	29.3	39.0	12.5	3.8	95962
68344	DOUGLAS	18200	147	21.1	41.5	30.6	6.1	0.7	41648	43685	38	56	125	19.2	14.4	36.8	24.8	4.8	122917
68345	DU BOIS	18321	128	32.0	41.4	21.9	3.9	0.8	35000	35556	18	20	106	49.1	24.5	17.9	6.6	1.9	51111
68346	DUNBAR	19237	228	18.9	30.3	42.1	7.5	1.3	50577	51829	63	82	171	9.9	21.1	24.0	39.2	5.8	153750
68347	EAGLE	27112	880	8.5	23.1	50.3	13.1	5.0	65424	68240	84	95	749	15.6	19.4	45.9	15.6	3.5	105019
68348	ELK CREEK	19243	134	28.4	33.6	30.6	5.2	2.2	42333	46145	40	61	100	20.0	34.0	32.0	14.0	0.0	85000
68349	ELMWOOD	21644	442	19.7	24.7	47.3	5.4	2.9	54387	56445	70	87	373	15.3	22.3	50.1	7.8	4.6	104332
68350	ENDICOTT	23179	108	27.8	30.6	37.0	1.9	2.8	42047	43204	39	58	92	46.7	22.8	18.5	10.9	1.1	53333
68351	EXETER	18887	323	28.8	30.7	35.9	3.7	0.9	43043	45337	43	62	251	44.6	30.3	19.9	4.0	1.2	56136
68352	FAIRBURY	20547	2277	32.7	33.4	28.2	3.4	2.3	35838	38380	20	24	1663	40.0	29.6	23.3	6.1	1.0	58444
68354	FAIRMONT	19862	345	27.8	30.4	36.2	4.1	1.4	44485	45875	47	67	267	43.8	30.0	21.0	4.1	1.1	57174
68355	FALLS CITY	18238	2258	35.9	31.0	27.6	4.1	1.3	35160	35968	18	20	1634	34.8	36.0	22.3	5.3	1.6	61712
68357	FILLEY	19052	177	21.5	38.4	36.7	3.4	0.0	39597	43982	31	43	142	13.4	21.1	41.5	21.8	2.1	115217
68358	FIRTH	20542	469	18.6	27.3	45.6	6.0	2.6	53011	54989	68	85	383	13.3	20.1	39.9	24.0	2.6	114718
68359	FRIEND	19704	647	25.2	34.8	35.2	2.8	2.0	43056	45361	43	62	509	17.1	26.7	41.5	13.4	1.4	99265
68360	GARLAND	27554	251	15.1	21.1	50.6	8.8	4.4	62011	62602	80	93	210	14.8	12.9	36.7	29.0	6.7	150000
68361	GENEVA	20400	1179	23.8	41.1	29.3	4.2	1.7	39497	40000	31	42	869	23.5	35.2	32.0	8.9	0.5	76875
68362	GILEAD	20341	63	31.7	36.5	23.8	6.3	1.6	35556	37355	19	22	49	30.6	32.7	32.7	4.1	0.0	71250
68365	GRAFTON	23255	86	20.9	36.0	34.9	7.0	1.2	45633	46110	50	71	63	28.6	28.6	27.0	14.3	1.6	81000
68366	GREENWOOD	23809	399	15.5	29.8	46.4	6.3	2.0	53818	57498	69	87	345	24.9	22.3	37.7	11.9	3.2	93393
68367	GRESHAM	21714	205	20.0	34.6	37.6	4.9	2.9	45620	48529	50	70	157	25.5	28.7	33.8	10.2	1.9	82778
68368	HALLAM	24479	258	16.3	28.3	47.3	5.8	2.3	53038	54265	68	85	208	15.4	28.8	45.7	9.6	0.5	95714
68370	HEBRON	19556	833	30.4	37.1	25.5	5.3	1.8	36329	37416	22	27	656	33.2	33.2	27.4	5.0	1.1	68254
68371	HENDERSON	21175	654	20.9	34.9	37.2	5.0	2.0	45612	48279	50	70	527	13.7	27.9	45.4	11.2	1.9	98396
68372	HICKMAN	22454	731	13.8	21.6	55.3	7.7	1.6	59497	60741	77	90	601	15.0	17.3	51.2	14.1	2.3	110061
68375	HUBBELL	18176	72	33.3	37.5	23.6	4.2	1.4	33391	33773	14	12	59	49.2	27.1	20.3	1.7	1.7	51250
68376	HUMBOLDT	18867	709	30.2	35.8	29.3	3.8	0.8	36432	37712	22	27	550	50.5	24.7	20.7	4.0	0.0	49412
68377	JANSEN	18140	193	24.9	36.8	33.7	4.1	0.5	41589	49118	38	56	161	26.1	30.4	31.7	8.1	3.7	79000
68378	JOHNSON	21523	314	28.0	31.5	34.4	4.5	1.6	40301	42760	34	47	247	25.1	21.9	30.4	19.4	3.2	100431
68379	JULIAN	21762	34	29.4	32.4	35.3	2.9	0.0	40000	43636	33	46	27	29.6	25.9	25.9	18.5	0.0	77500
68380	LEWISTON	19442	64	25.0	35.9	32.8	4.7	1.6	41837	46171	39	57	54	29.6	24.1	29.6	14.8	1.9	83333
68381	LIBERTY	16245	86	34.9	37.2	22.1	3.5	2.3	35000	37675	18	20	67	38.8	29.9	23.9	7.5	0.0	61250
68401	MC COOL JUNCTION	19901	299	20.7	34.4	41.8	2.3	0.7	45141	48643	49	68	220	16.4	21.4	35.5	18.2	8.6	112857
68402	MALCOLM	25879	428	11.9	21.0	53.7	9.1	4.2	60880	60741	79	92	350	9.1	11.4	44.3	33.1	2.0	142647
68404	MARTELL	26693	475	12.6	22.7	53.7	8.2	2.7	61849	61780	80	93	399	11.3	18.8	42.9	24.6	2.5	127035
68405	MILFORD	23239	1207	20.5	25.3	42.4	7.0	4.9	53980	56624	70	87	829	10.3	25.1	49.9	13.0	1.7	105015
68406	MILLIGAN	18994	193	29.0	40.4	26.4	3.6	0.5	36458	39619	22	27	144	37.5	26.4	16.7	14.6	4.9	71538
68407	MURDOCK	23144	355	18.6	27.0	43.4	8.2	2.8	53605	56913	69	86	302	14.9	20.2	37.7	23.2	4.0	110526
68409	MURRAY	25864	348	12.1	21.8	53.4	10.1	2.6	62189	63870	80	94	281	17.1	21.0	48.8	12.1	1.1	100947
68410	NEBRASKA CITY	20805	3420	26.0	30.7	35.6	5.5	2.2	44544	47059	47	67	2377	17.7	24.9	37.1	19.0	1.3	101624
68413	NEHAWKA	23314	195	14.9	32.8	44.1	6.2	2.1	52308	54794	67	84	162	19.8	24.1	37.0	14.2	4.9	96667
68414	NEMAHA	20189	146	29.5	28.1	37.7	4.1	0.7	42013	43089	39	58	118	32.2	30.5	18.6	13.6	5.1	69000
68415	ODELL	20299	301	22.6	32.9	36.5	5.3	2.7	43552	47878	44	64	250	13.2	33.2	30.8	21.6	1.2	96923
68416	OHIOWA	19505	110	28.2	41.8	25.5	3.6	0.9	36533	39644	22	28	82	37.8	28.0	15.9	13.4	4.9	70000
68417	OTOE	19264	165	22.4	32.7	38.2	6.7	0.0	46033	48122	51	72	124	17.7	22.6	33.9	21.8	4.0	107692
68418	PALMYRA	23106	419	16.2	33.7	38.9	6.9	4.3	50116	51192	61	81	353	10.5	16.4	37.4	25.8	9.9	131686
68420	PAWNEE CITY	18626	595	39.8	33.8	22.2	2.4	1.8	31410	33114	10	6	457	49.5	29.5	16.8	3.9	0.2	50610
68421	PERU	16475	337	32.9	36.8	24.9	3.9	1.5	33535	35675	14	13	223	42.6	34.1	17.9	5.4	0.0	56346
68422	PICKRELL	21445	256	17.2	31.3	45.7	5.1	0.8	51100	51673	64	84	208	7.2	12.0	47.1	32.2	1.4	142742
68423	PLEASANT DALE	26687	340	12.4	26.8	48.5	8.5	3.8	60300	61183	78	90	277	15.9	11.9	44.8	23.8	3.6	133681
68424	PLYMOUTH	17664	327	24.2	37.0	33.6	4.0	1.2	42005	45785	39	58	270	27.8	28.5	31.9	7.8	4.1	79130
68428	RAYMOND	25614	442	10.2	17.9	56.8	11.1	4.1	66889	64763	85	95	387	7.0	9.8	45.0	35.7	2.6	151302
68429	REYNOLDS	23743	59	28.8	30.5	37.3	1.7	1.7	41351	42361	37	54	50	48.0	24.0	16.0	10.0	2.0	52000
68430	ROCA	27243	462	11.9	21.9	53.0	9.3	3.9	63210	63035	81	94	392	13.5	14.5	40.8	26.5	4.6	134615
68431	RULO	18131	129	31.0	35.7	29.5	2.3	1.6	35660	36991	20	23	97	24.7	19.6	29.9	15.5	10.3	102083
68433	SALEM	18841	97	28.9	42.3	24.7	4.1	0.0	37005	38371	24	30	77	51.9	22.1	16.9	9.1	0.0	47857
68434	SEWARD	24461	3185	18.4	26.2	42.0	9.7	3.7	55528	58096	72	88	2208	10.4	24.6	50.5	13.4	1.0	105713
68436	SHICKLEY	22364	234	20.1	36.3	33.8	8.1	1.7	46285	46618	52	73	172	30.2	29.1	25.6	12.8	2.3	79091
68437	SHUBERT	16557	118	33.1	31.4	30.5	5.1	0.0	33868	34271	15	15	96	56.3	21.9	14.6	7.3	0.0	44000
68439	STAPLEHURST	22069	233	19.7	30.5	40.3	6.4	3.0	49851	52496	61	80	178	33.7	25.3	33.1	7.9	0.0	73333
68440	STEELE CITY	25392	72	29.2	29.2	37.5	2.8	1.4	42322	44311	40	60	61	49.2	23.0	16.4	9.8	1.6	50833
68441	STEINAUER	17851	121	29.8	39.7	25.6	4.1	0.8	36644	38638	22	28	101	45.5	23.8	19.8	8.9	2.0	56429
68442	STELLA	18822	119	33.6	31.1	30.3	5.0	0.0	33596	34511	15	13	97	56.7	21.6	14.4	7.2	0.0	43500
68443	STERLING	18827	422	28.7	33.6	32.9	3.6	1.2	38926	40430	30	38	335	24.2	27.5	31.3	14.6	2.4	87609
68444	STRANG	19143	48	25.0	39.6	31.3	4.2	0.0	41118	42951	36	52	36	38.9	25.0	19.4	11.1	5.6	70000
68445	SWANTON	19917	93	29.0	32.3	33.3	3.2	2.2	38625	42359	29	37	75	16.0	24.0	29.3	25.3	5.3	114773
68446	SYRACUSE	23981	1103	19.1	33.8	36.4	8.7	2.0	48077	49891	57	77	870	9.7	19.4	50.8	17.4	2.8	119667
68447	TABLE ROCK	20003	216	31.9	41.7	21.8	4.2	0.5	35000	35689	18	20	179	50.3	24.0	17.9	6.1	1.7	49706
68448	TALMAGE	19294	207	29.5	30.4	31.9	5.8	2.4	41968	45295	39	57	158	29.1	19.0	24.1	24.7	3.2	93750
	NEBRASKA	24998		20.5	28.3	37.5	9.0	4.6	50953	53316				15.1	21.8	43.3	17.4	2.4	109174
	UNITED STATES	27277		20.9	24.4	35.3	11.7	7.6	54719	56938				9.3	13.1	31.6	32.6	13.5	162279

ZIP CODE		FINANCIAL SERVICES				THE HOME						ENTERTAINMENT						PERSONAL			
						Home Improvements		Furnishings													
#	POST OFFICE NAME	Auto Loan	Home Loan	Investments	Retirement Plans	Home Repair	Lawn & Garden	Computers & Hardware-Personal	Major Appliances	TV, Radio, Sound Equipment	Furniture	Dine out/ Carry out	Sports Equipment	Fees & Tickets	Toys & Games	Travel	Cable TV	Apparel & Services	Auto Repairs	Health Insurance	Pets & Supplies
68316	BENEDICT	97	67	107	67	70	103	74	92	77	60	77	76	54	76	74	84	50	86	98	114
68317	BENNET	100	106	103	110	107	111	97	106	97	95	97	80	100	98	102	99	67	99	105	122
68318	BLUE SPRINGS	71	51	72	50	53	74	56	69	62	49	60	52	44	61	54	68	40	64	75	81
68319	BRADSHAW	97	67	107	67	70	103	74	92	77	60	77	76	54	76	74	84	50	86	98	114
68320	BROCK	84	58	92	57	60	88	64	79	66	52	66	66	47	65	64	72	43	74	84	98
68321	BROWNVILLE	85	61	87	59	63	86	62	79	69	58	68	59	50	69	62	76	45	73	82	94
68322	BRUNING	79	54	87	54	57	84	61	75	63	49	62	62	44	62	60	69	40	70	79	93
68323	BURCHARD	84	58	92	58	61	89	64	80	67	52	66	66	47	66	64	73	43	75	84	98
68324	BURR	86	59	94	59	62	91	66	82	68	53	68	67	48	67	65	75	44	76	86	100
68325	BYRON	76	52	83	52	54	80	58	72	60	47	59	59	42	59	58	66	39	67	76	88
68326	CARLETON	79	54	87	54	57	83	60	75	63	49	62	62	44	61	60	68	40	70	79	92
68327	CHESTER	72	49	79	49	52	76	55	68	57	44	56	56	40	56	54	62	37	63	72	84
68328	CLATONIA	94	65	104	65	68	100	72	90	75	58	74	74	53	73	72	82	48	84	95	110
68329	COOK	82	57	90	57	59	87	63	78	65	51	65	65	46	64	63	71	42	73	83	96
68330	CORDOVA	78	54	86	54	56	82	60	74	62	48	61	61	44	61	59	68	40	69	78	91
68331	CORTLAND	96	66	106	66	69	102	74	91	77	60	76	76	54	75	73	84	49	85	97	113
68332	CRAB ORCHARD	80	55	88	55	58	85	61	76	64	50	63	63	45	63	61	70	41	71	81	94
68333	CRETE	85	74	77	74	75	85	77	82	80	74	78	62	70	80	74	83	54	80	86	97
68335	DAVENPORT	77	53	85	53	56	82	59	74	62	48	61	61	43	60	59	67	39	69	78	91
68336	DAVEY	95	107	92	110	104	105	96	100	94	96	95	78	102	97	101	95	66	96	99	117
68337	DAWSON	74	51	81	51	53	78	57	70	59	46	58	58	42	58	56	64	38	66	74	86
68338	DAYKIN	89	62	98	61	64	94	68	85	71	55	70	70	50	70	68	77	46	79	90	104
68339	DENTON	97	109	94	113	106	107	98	102	96	98	97	79	104	99	103	96	68	98	100	119
68340	DESHLER	76	52	83	52	54	80	58	72	60	47	59	59	42	59	57	66	39	67	76	88
68341	DE WITT	80	68	77	70	70	86	69	80	71	61	70	62	60	72	69	76	47	74	83	94
68342	DILLER	91	62	100	62	65	96	69	86	72	56	71	71	51	71	69	79	46	80	91	106
68343	DORCHESTER	82	56	90	56	59	86	63	78	65	51	64	64	46	64	62	71	42	73	82	96
68344	DOUGLAS	86	59	95	59	62	91	66	82	68	53	68	68	48	67	65	75	44	76	86	101
68345	DU BOIS	74	51	81	51	53	78	56	70	59	46	58	58	41	58	56	64	38	66	74	86
68346	DUNBAR	97	66	106	66	70	102	74	92	77	60	76	76	54	75	73	84	49	86	97	113
68347	EAGLE	116	119	102	116	113	109	109	111	107	114	108	85	108	111	107	105	75	107	104	130
68348	ELK CREEK	84	58	92	58	61	89	64	80	67	52	66	66	47	65	64	73	43	75	84	98
68349	ELMWOOD	102	72	111	72	75	107	79	97	82	65	81	80	59	80	78	89	53	91	102	119
68350	ENDICOTT	93	64	102	63	67	98	71	88	73	57	73	73	52	72	70	80	47	82	93	108
68351	EXETER	84	58	92	58	61	89	64	80	67	52	66	66	47	66	64	73	43	75	84	98
68352	FAIRBURY	80	57	82	56	59	83	61	76	67	54	66	58	48	66	60	74	43	71	82	91
68354	FAIRMONT	87	60	95	60	62	92	66	82	69	54	68	68	49	68	66	75	44	77	87	101
68355	FALLS CITY	72	52	74	51	54	76	57	70	63	50	61	53	45	62	55	69	40	65	76	83
68357	FILLEY	83	57	91	57	59	87	63	78	66	51	65	65	46	64	63	72	42	73	83	96
68358	FIRTH	84	88	83	91	86	92	81	86	80	79	80	68	83	82	85	81	56	82	86	102
68359	FRIEND	86	61	89	60	64	90	67	83	73	58	71	64	52	72	65	81	47	77	90	99
68360	GARLAND	98	110	95	113	107	108	98	102	97	99	97	80	105	99	104	97	68	98	101	120
68361	GENEVA	83	58	89	58	61	88	64	80	69	54	67	64	49	67	63	75	44	74	85	96
68362	GILEAD	78	56	78	54	58	81	61	75	68	54	66	56	49	67	59	75	44	70	82	88
68365	GRAFTON	100	69	109	68	72	105	76	95	79	62	78	78	56	78	76	86	51	88	100	116
68366	GREENWOOD	93	85	85	88	87	100	84	95	86	76	85	72	77	88	84	91	58	88	97	110
68367	GRESHAM	97	67	107	67	70	102	74	92	77	60	76	76	54	76	74	84	49	86	97	113
68368	HALLAM	93	87	85	91	88	101	85	95	87	78	86	72	80	89	85	92	59	88	98	111
68370	HEBRON	77	55	78	54	57	81	60	75	67	53	65	56	48	66	59	74	43	70	81	88
68371	HENDERSON	94	65	104	65	68	100	72	90	75	58	74	74	53	73	72	82	48	84	95	110
68372	HICKMAN	93	101	84	100	96	93	91	92	89	94	90	71	93	92	92	87	62	89	88	108
68375	HUBBELL	72	50	78	50	52	76	55	69	59	46	58	56	41	57	55	64	38	64	73	84
68376	HUMBOLDT	73	52	74	51	54	77	57	71	63	51	61	54	45	62	56	70	41	66	77	84
68377	JANSEN	80	55	87	55	57	84	61	75	63	49	62	62	44	62	60	69	41	70	80	93
68378	JOHNSON	86	59	94	59	62	91	66	82	68	53	68	68	48	67	65	75	44	76	86	101
68379	JULIAN	84	57	92	57	60	88	64	79	66	52	66	66	47	65	63	72	43	74	84	98
68380	LEWISTON	84	58	92	58	61	89	64	80	67	52	66	66	47	66	64	73	43	75	84	98
68381	LIBERTY	73	52	73	51	54	76	57	70	64	51	61	53	46	63	55	70	41	66	77	83
68401	MC COOL JUNCTION	85	58	93	58	61	90	65	81	68	53	67	67	48	66	65	74	43	75	85	99
68402	MALCOLM	97	110	94	113	106	108	98	102	96	98	97	80	104	99	103	96	68	98	101	120
68404	MARTELL	92	104	90	107	101	102	93	97	91	93	92	75	99	94	98	92	64	93	96	114
68405	MILFORD	92	84	86	86	86	95	87	91	88	83	87	69	82	88	86	91	60	90	96	107
68406	MILLIGAN	74	51	82	51	53	78	57	70	59	46	58	58	42	58	56	64	38	66	74	87
68407	MURDOCK	102	74	112	74	77	108	80	98	83	67	82	80	62	81	81	90	54	92	103	120
68409	MURRAY	100	95	92	99	96	108	92	102	94	85	93	78	88	96	93	98	64	95	105	119
68410	NEBRASKA CITY	82	68	74	69	69	84	72	79	76	65	74	61	64	76	69	81	50	76	85	94
68413	NEHAWKA	103	72	112	72	75	109	79	98	82	65	81	81	59	81	79	90	53	91	103	120
68414	NEMAHA	85	61	88	59	63	87	63	80	69	58	68	60	50	69	62	76	45	73	83	95
68415	ODELL	93	64	102	64	67	98	71	88	74	58	73	73	52	73	71	81	47	83	93	109
68416	OHIOWA	74	51	81	51	53	78	57	70	59	46	58	58	42	58	56	64	38	66	74	87
68417	OTOE	89	61	98	61	64	94	68	85	71	55	70	70	50	70	68	77	46	79	90	104
68418	PALMYRA	87	91	86	94	89	95	84	89	83	82	83	70	86	85	88	84	58	85	89	106
68420	PAWNEE CITY	70	50	72	49	52	74	55	68	61	48	59	52	43	60	53	67	39	63	74	81
68421	PERU	72	51	73	50	53	75	56	69	62	49	60	52	44	61	54	68	40	65	75	82
68422	PICKRELL	97	67	107	67	70	103	74	92	77	60	76	76	54	76	74	84	50	86	98	114
68423	PLEASANT DALE	91	102	88	106	99	101	92	95	90	92	91	74	98	92	97	90	63	92	94	112
68424	PLYMOUTH	81	55	89	55	58	85	62	77	64	50	63	63	45	63	61	70	41	71	81	94
68428	RAYMOND	101	114	98	117	111	112	102	106	100	102	101	83	109	103	108	100	70	102	105	125
68429	REYNOLDS	91	63	100	63	66	96	70	87	73	57	72	72	51	71	69	79	47	81	92	107
68430	ROCA	97	111	98	114	108	108	98	102	96	99	97	79	106	98	105	96	68	98	101	120
68431	RULO	75	52	83	52	54	79	57	71	60	47	59	59	42	59	57	65	38	67	75	88
68433	SALEM	74	51	82	51	54	78	57	71	59	46	58	58	42	58	56	64	38	66	75	87
68434	SEWARD	94	85	91	87	87	97	89	93	90	85	89	71	83	90	88	93	61	92	98	110
68436	SHICKLEY	100	69	110	69	72	106	77	95	80	62	79	79	56	78	76	87	51	89	101	117
68437	SHUBERT	75	54	77	52	56	76	55	70	61	51	60	53	44	61	55	67	40	64	73	83
68439	STAPLEHURST	99	68	109	68	71	104	76	94	79	61	78	78	55	77	75	86	50	88	99	116
68440	STEELE CITY	93	64	102	64	67	98	71	89	74	58	73	73	52	73	71	81	48	83	94	109
68441	STEINAUER	77	53	84	53	55	81	59	73	61	48	60	60	43	60	58	67	39	68	77	90
68442	STELLA	75	54	77	52	56	76	55	70	61	51	60	53	44	61	54	67	40	64	73	83
68443	STERLING	81	56	89	55	58	85	62	77	64	50	63	63	45	63	61	70	41	72	81	94
68444	STRANG	83	57	91	57	60	87	63	79	66	51	65	65	46	64	63	72	42	73	83	97
68445	SWANTON	84	58	92	58	60	89	64	80	67	52	66	66	47	65	64	73	43	74	84	98
68446	SYRACUSE	84	78	91	77	80	97	75	87	80	69	79	66	72	78	79	85	53	83	96	103
68447	TABLE ROCK	74	51	81	51	53	78	56	70	59	46	58	58	41	58	56	64	38	65	74	86
68448	TALMAGE	89	61	98	61	64	94	68	84	71	55	70	70	50	69	68	77	45	79	89	104
	NEBRASKA	95	85	88	86	84	94	89	91	90	85	90	72	83	91	86	92	62	91	94	109
	UNITED STATES	100	100	100	100	100	100	100	100	100	100	100	100	100	100	100	100	100	100	100	100

ZIP CODE			POPULATION			2000-2009 ANNUAL RATE		HOUSEHOLDS					FAMILIES		
#	POST OFFICE NAME	COUNTY FIPS CODE	2000	2009	2014	% Rate	State Centile	2000	2009	2014	% Annual Rate 2000-2009	2009 Average HH Size	2000	2009	% Annual Rate 2000-2009
68450	TECUMSEH	097	2406	2653	2631	1.1	92	1001	1004	994	0.0	2.34	648	646	0.0
68452	ONG	035	117	115	114	-0.2	58	54	54	53	0.0	2.06	35	35	0.0
68453	TOBIAS	151	446	437	429	-0.2	58	180	178	175	-0.1	2.46	128	126	-0.2
68454	UNADILLA	131	662	730	757	1.1	92	272	303	315	1.2	2.41	206	228	1.1
68455	UNION	025	777	839	846	0.8	87	290	320	324	1.1	2.62	221	242	1.0
68456	UTICA	159	1143	1106	1085	-0.4	49	429	421	415	-0.2	2.57	315	307	-0.3
68457	VERDON	147	390	341	319	-1.4	7	158	140	132	-1.3	2.44	108	96	-1.3
68458	VIRGINIA	067	149	150	148	0.1	69	63	65	65	0.3	2.31	48	49	0.2
68460	WACO	185	806	797	789	-0.1	63	302	304	303	0.1	2.62	229	229	0.0
68461	WALTON	109	610	725	783	1.9	96	220	269	293	2.2	2.70	183	220	2.0
68462	WAVERLY	109	3095	3453	3661	1.2	93	1071	1240	1328	1.6	2.74	860	978	1.4
68463	WEEPING WATER	025	1911	2003	2013	0.5	81	729	775	783	0.7	2.58	526	553	0.5
68464	WESTERN	151	579	569	559	-0.2	58	245	242	238	-0.1	2.35	173	170	-0.2
68465	WILBER	151	2239	2279	2261	0.2	73	906	926	920	0.2	2.39	616	626	0.2
68466	WYMORE	067	2110	2101	2091	0.0	66	890	897	896	0.1	2.30	611	612	0.0
68467	YORK	185	9755	9661	9529	-0.1	63	3856	3843	3814	0.0	2.31	2532	2508	-0.1
68502	LINCOLN	109	27293	26659	26646	-0.3	54	11320	11291	11372	0.0	2.17	6015	5784	-0.4
68503	LINCOLN	109	15835	15740	15796	-0.1	63	6248	6272	6334	0.0	2.37	3053	2935	-0.4
68504	LINCOLN	109	14547	16427	17388	1.3	94	6474	7649	8228	1.8	2.03	3011	3368	1.2
68505	LINCOLN	109	13701	14761	15480	0.8	87	5867	6507	6873	1.1	2.26	3811	4169	1.0
68506	LINCOLN	109	27389	28767	29740	0.5	81	11600	12522	13048	0.8	2.23	7371	7725	0.5
68507	LINCOLN	109	13036	13562	13985	0.4	78	5338	5702	5918	0.7	2.37	3480	3633	0.5
68508	LINCOLN	109	13756	13963	13972	0.2	73	4902	4838	4847	-0.1	1.68	1241	1159	-0.7
68510	LINCOLN	109	20923	20407	20370	-0.3	54	9450	9439	9504	0.0	2.14	5243	5053	-0.4
68512	LINCOLN	109	6890	9221	10206	3.2	97	2832	3973	4434	3.7	2.32	1938	2674	3.5
68514	LINCOLN	109	162	188	204	1.6	95	59	70	77	1.9	2.69	45	53	1.8
68516	LINCOLN	109	32908	40436	44204	2.3	97	11976	14954	16406	2.4	2.69	8938	11231	2.5
68517	LINCOLN	109	444	514	564	1.6	95	154	184	203	1.9	2.79	119	140	1.8
68520	LINCOLN	109	1248	1258	1532	0.1	69	459	496	612	0.8	2.53	373	400	0.8
68521	LINCOLN	109	25363	29866	31802	1.8	96	9739	11702	12536	2.0	2.54	6363	7598	1.9
68522	LINCOLN	109	8317	11581	13162	3.6	98	2712	4010	4655	4.3	2.64	1919	2757	4.0
68523	LINCOLN	109	1078	1504	1767	3.7	98	375	481	570	2.7	3.11	299	377	2.5
68524	LINCOLN	109	4976	5099	5361	0.3	75	1493	1624	1737	0.9	2.98	1178	1239	0.5
68526	LINCOLN	109	1067	3764	4613	14.6	100	350	1323	1640	15.5	2.84	290	1071	15.2
68527	LINCOLN	109	708	798	893	1.3	94	256	302	341	1.8	2.64	213	248	1.7
68528	LINCOLN	109	3598	5783	6638	5.3	99	1577	2532	2938	5.3	2.28	959	1485	4.8
68531	LINCOLN	109	158	173	213	1.0	90	57	58	73	0.2	2.98	47	47	0.0
68532	LINCOLN	109	451	605	653	3.2	97	170	238	260	3.7	2.54	137	188	3.5
68583	LINCOLN	109	112	119	123	0.7	84	40	43	45	0.8	2.74	22	22	0.0
68588	LINCOLN	109	187	198	198	0.6	83	3	3	3	0.0	1.33	0	0	0.0
68601	COLUMBUS	141	26339	26797	27023	0.2	73	10218	10597	10748	0.4	2.50	7046	7273	0.3
68620	ALBION	011	3527	3309	3182	-0.7	34	1363	1301	1256	-0.5	2.50	945	893	-0.6
68621	AMES	053	365	363	361	-0.1	63	148	151	151	0.2	2.40	114	115	0.1
68622	BARTLETT	183	227	208	203	-0.9	26	93	89	87	-0.5	2.34	64	61	-0.5
68623	BELGRADE	125	239	201	185	-1.9	1	104	89	83	-1.7	2.26	76	65	-1.7
68624	BELLWOOD	023	1160	1103	1063	-0.5	42	437	424	411	-0.3	2.60	322	312	-0.3
68626	BRAINARD	023	665	599	569	-1.1	17	261	240	229	-0.9	2.50	180	163	-1.1
68627	CEDAR RAPIDS	011	688	576	530	-1.9	1	284	242	224	-1.7	2.38	194	165	-1.7
68628	CLARKS	121	726	722	708	-0.1	63	312	316	312	0.1	2.28	220	222	0.1
68629	CLARKSON	037	1525	1508	1514	-0.1	63	577	562	562	-0.3	2.60	392	380	-0.3
68631	CRESTON	141	703	645	626	-0.9	26	250	237	232	-0.6	2.72	197	186	-0.6
68632	DAVID CITY	023	3851	3794	3706	-0.2	58	1528	1529	1500	0.0	2.41	968	963	-0.1
68633	DODGE	053	1749	1722	1690	-0.2	58	674	675	665	0.0	2.48	478	475	-0.1
68635	DWIGHT	023	622	568	542	-1.0	21	249	232	223	-0.8	2.45	173	160	-0.8
68636	ELGIN	003	1303	1215	1174	-0.8	30	526	498	483	-0.6	2.43	360	338	-0.7
68637	ERICSON	183	311	285	279	-0.9	26	135	128	127	-0.6	2.23	94	89	-0.6
68638	FULLERTON	125	2001	1819	1732	-1.0	21	779	717	686	-0.9	2.44	548	504	-0.9
68640	GENOA	125	1994	1840	1752	-0.9	26	763	724	694	-0.6	2.49	533	501	-0.7
68641	HOWELLS	037	1031	1083	1088	0.5	81	413	428	428	0.4	2.53	298	306	0.3
68642	HUMPHREY	141	1839	1799	1791	-0.2	58	639	645	648	0.1	2.78	481	483	0.0
68643	LEIGH	037	1003	1005	1009	0.0	66	387	385	385	-0.1	2.61	282	278	-0.2
68644	LINDSAY	141	1008	971	957	-0.4	49	342	340	338	-0.1	2.85	255	252	-0.1
68647	MONROE	141	954	1063	1108	1.2	93	364	422	445	1.6	2.52	265	306	1.6
68648	MORSE BLUFF	155	464	482	480	0.4	78	191	203	203	0.7	2.37	140	147	0.5
68649	NORTH BEND	053	1867	1846	1833	-0.1	63	719	730	729	0.2	2.46	515	521	0.1
68651	OSCEOLA	143	1393	1362	1332	-0.2	58	568	565	554	-0.1	2.31	384	380	-0.1
68652	PETERSBURG	011	678	706	702	0.4	78	274	291	291	0.7	2.42	193	205	0.7
68653	PLATTE CENTER	141	976	972	975	0.0	66	358	369	374	0.3	2.63	280	288	0.3
68654	POLK	143	1018	990	967	-0.3	54	415	410	403	-0.1	2.41	300	295	-0.2
68655	PRIMROSE	011	235	195	179	-2.0	0	93	79	73	-1.7	2.47	66	56	-1.8
68658	RISING CITY	023	803	787	765	-0.2	58	309	309	302	0.0	2.55	229	228	0.0
68659	ROGERS	037	214	210	212	-0.2	58	78	75	75	-0.4	2.77	63	60	-0.5
68660	SAINT EDWARD	011	1058	900	834	-1.7	2	415	353	326	-1.7	2.41	283	241	-1.7
68661	SCHUYLER	037	6811	7074	7160	0.4	78	2244	2212	2222	-0.2	3.16	1588	1560	-0.2
68662	SHELBY	143	1515	1495	1473	-0.1	63	601	605	599	0.1	2.47	432	432	0.0
68663	SILVER CREEK	121	626	634	625	0.1	69	264	273	271	0.4	2.32	177	183	0.4
68665	SPALDING	077	962	857	809	-1.2	13	366	335	319	-1.0	2.50	249	226	-1.0
68666	STROMSBURG	143	1731	1689	1648	-0.3	54	672	664	650	-0.1	2.39	452	444	-0.2
68667	SURPRISE	023	191	207	207	0.9	89	72	80	80	1.1	2.59	55	60	0.9
68669	ULYSSES	023	500	539	540	0.8	87	183	202	203	1.1	2.66	138	152	1.1
68701	NORFOLK	119	30321	29440	28977	-0.3	54	11666	11510	11369	-0.1	2.47	7711	7572	-0.2
68710	ALLEN	051	813	846	848	0.4	78	317	333	334	0.5	2.54	230	241	0.5
68711	AMELIA	089	204	186	175	-1.0	21	77	73	70	-0.6	2.55	60	57	-0.6
68713	ATKINSON	089	2105	1881	1776	-1.2	13	864	801	763	-0.8	2.27	583	538	-0.9
68714	BASSETT	149	1463	1320	1257	-1.1	17	644	609	587	-0.6	2.12	412	387	-0.7
68715	BATTLE CREEK	119	1559	1526	1504	-0.2	58	575	572	567	-0.1	2.67	437	429	-0.2
68716	BEEMER	039	1165	1108	1074	-0.5	42	445	428	416	-0.4	2.53	318	304	-0.5
68717	BELDEN	027	238	208	192	-1.4	7	92	82	76	-1.2	2.54	72	64	-1.3
68718	BLOOMFIELD	107	2018	1896	1825	-0.7	34	848	810	782	-0.5	2.23	539	512	-0.6
68719	BRISTOW	015	288	261	247	-1.1	17	113	104	99	-0.9	2.51	75	69	-0.9
68720	BRUNSWICK	003	524	480	458	-0.9	26	176	164	158	-0.8	2.93	141	132	-0.7
68722	BUTTE	015	552	492	464	-1.2	13	215	194	184	-1.1	2.41	141	127	-1.1
68723	CARROLL	179	550	530	514	-0.4	49	220	215	210	-0.2	2.47	166	163	-0.2
68724	CENTER	107	222	220	215	-0.1	63	84	83	82	-0.1	2.61	57	56	-0.2
68725	CHAMBERS	089	804	726	689	-1.1	17	328	308	295	-0.7	2.36	238	223	-0.7
	NEBRASKA					0.6					0.8	2.46			0.7
	UNITED STATES					1.0					1.1	2.59			0.9

ZIP CODE #	POST OFFICE NAME	RACE (%) White 2000	White 2009	Black 2000	Black 2009	Asian/Pacific 2000	Asian/Pacific 2009	% Hispanic Origin 2000	% Hispanic Origin 2009	2009 AGE DISTRIBUTION (%) 0-4	5-9	10-14	15-19	20-24	25-44	45-64	65-84	85+	18+	MEDIAN AGE 2009	% 2009 Males	% 2009 Females
68450	TECUMSEH	90.3	86.8	0.1	0.1	3.8	5.7	4.6	6.5	5.3	4.9	5.6	6.8	6.0	24.9	26.7	15.3	4.4	79.5	42.6	52.2	47.8
68452	ONG	98.3	98.3	0.0	0.0	0.0	0.0	0.9	0.9	5.2	6.1	6.1	6.1	3.5	22.6	27.0	19.1	4.3	78.3	45.3	52.2	47.8
68453	TOBIAS	98.0	97.7	0.2	0.2	0.2	0.2	0.4	0.7	5.3	6.2	7.1	7.3	4.1	21.3	30.4	14.9	3.4	76.7	44.0	51.5	48.5
68454	UNADILLA	98.5	97.7	0.2	0.1	0.0	0.1	1.7	2.7	6.6	7.3	7.5	6.4	4.2	24.1	30.8	11.5	1.5	74.4	40.8	52.5	47.5
68455	UNION	97.2	96.2	0.0	0.0	0.6	1.1	2.2	3.3	6.0	6.6	7.0	7.2	4.6	22.4	32.2	12.9	1.2	76.0	42.6	50.7	49.3
68456	UTICA	99.2	99.1	0.1	0.1	0.2	0.3	0.3	0.5	5.6	6.1	6.7	7.5	4.8	21.2	30.7	14.4	3.1	76.3	43.6	51.2	48.8
68457	VERDON	97.7	97.4	0.0	0.0	0.0	0.0	1.3	1.8	3.8	7.0	7.3	9.1	3.5	22.3	31.1	13.5	2.3	75.4	43.0	51.0	49.0
68458	VIRGINIA	98.7	98.7	0.0	0.0	0.7	0.7	0.7	0.7	5.3	5.3	8.0	8.0	4.0	24.0	28.7	15.3	1.3	76.0	42.1	51.3	48.7
68460	WACO	98.1	97.4	0.6	0.8	0.0	0.1	0.7	1.3	5.9	6.5	7.0	7.8	4.8	21.3	32.0	12.8	1.9	75.5	42.3	49.8	50.2
68461	WALTON	97.7	97.0	0.0	0.0	0.8	1.1	1.1	1.7	4.7	5.8	6.9	7.3	4.1	19.9	36.1	13.7	1.5	78.1	45.7	50.2	49.8
68462	WAVERLY	98.1	97.4	0.1	0.2	0.2	0.4	0.9	1.5	7.8	7.8	7.7	7.4	5.6	26.3	26.3	9.4	1.8	71.6	35.6	48.1	51.9
68463	WEEPING WATER	99.1	98.9	0.1	0.0	0.2	0.3	0.6	0.9	7.1	7.4	7.7	6.9	4.9	23.5	29.5	11.2	1.8	73.5	39.2	48.1	51.9
68464	WESTERN	98.3	97.7	0.2	0.2	0.2	0.4	0.3	0.7	5.3	6.0	7.0	7.2	4.2	21.1	31.3	14.8	3.2	77.2	44.4	51.8	48.2
68465	WILBER	97.5	96.6	0.0	0.0	0.8	1.2	1.5	2.2	6.5	6.8	7.1	6.8	4.6	24.4	26.9	12.8	4.3	75.5	40.7	49.5	50.5
68466	WYMORE	96.9	96.2	0.1	0.1	0.3	0.4	1.3	1.9	6.4	6.3	6.2	6.1	5.5	21.3	27.3	17.0	3.8	76.8	43.4	48.5	51.5
68467	YORK	96.0	95.0	1.3	1.4	0.8	1.1	1.7	2.5	5.5	5.7	6.1	8.1	7.5	23.6	26.7	13.1	3.5	78.2	39.3	46.9	53.1
68502	LINCOLN	88.1	84.6	4.3	4.9	1.9	2.9	5.1	7.6	6.0	5.4	5.0	7.0	11.7	31.7	23.1	8.2	1.9	80.5	33.0	51.3	48.7
68503	LINCOLN	71.3	64.3	8.9	9.6	10.0	14.5	6.8	9.7	7.4	6.5	5.4	8.0	16.7	32.5	17.2	5.2	0.9	77.1	27.5	52.8	47.2
68504	LINCOLN	90.4	87.0	3.1	3.7	1.9	3.1	3.4	5.5	6.6	5.0	4.3	7.7	15.7	34.0	17.6	7.7	1.4	81.5	29.3	49.3	50.7
68505	LINCOLN	94.3	92.2	1.2	1.3	2.2	3.5	2.0	3.0	6.2	6.0	6.0	5.9	6.7	29.0	24.7	13.4	1.9	78.4	37.3	48.7	51.3
68506	LINCOLN	94.8	92.8	1.3	1.5	1.6	2.7	1.8	2.9	5.2	5.1	5.4	6.3	6.9	25.3	27.6	14.6	3.6	80.9	41.4	47.2	52.8
68507	LINCOLN	94.8	92.9	1.1	1.3	1.2	2.0	2.2	3.5	6.4	6.2	6.2	6.1	5.8	28.8	26.6	11.6	2.5	77.6	38.0	48.3	51.7
68508	LINCOLN	82.9	77.9	4.7	5.2	4.2	6.3	7.7	11.1	3.0	2.4	1.7	25.0	28.8	23.4	10.1	4.5	1.1	91.8	23.1	52.8	47.2
68510	LINCOLN	89.7	86.4	2.6	3.0	3.2	4.9	3.4	5.2	6.4	5.7	5.3	5.3	7.4	27.6	24.7	13.2	4.3	79.4	38.5	47.4	52.6
68512	LINCOLN	89.5	87.3	4.9	4.6	2.1	3.6	2.9	4.2	5.6	5.2	5.3	8.5	7.3	30.7	27.8	8.8	0.8	81.0	35.8	49.8	50.2
68514	LINCOLN	98.1	97.3	0.6	1.1	0.0	0.0	1.9	2.7	5.3	5.9	6.4	7.4	5.3	22.9	33.5	12.2	1.1	78.7	42.5	51.6	48.4
68516	LINCOLN	94.8	92.2	1.0	1.3	2.4	4.3	1.7	2.5	7.4	7.8	8.0	7.3	6.1	27.8	27.8	6.9	0.9	72.0	35.5	48.9	51.1
68517	LINCOLN	97.7	97.3	0.7	1.0	0.2	0.2	1.6	2.5	5.4	6.0	6.8	7.6	5.3	22.8	32.7	12.1	1.4	77.0	42.0	50.6	49.4
68520	LINCOLN	97.4	96.5	0.3	0.3	0.9	1.4	1.0	1.4	5.3	6.3	7.3	7.4	4.0	21.9	35.1	11.6	1.1	76.9	43.5	49.4	50.6
68521	LINCOLN	88.0	84.4	2.8	3.0	4.6	6.9	3.6	5.2	8.8	7.6	6.9	6.7	9.3	32.7	20.5	6.5	1.0	72.8	30.8	50.2	49.8
68522	LINCOLN	87.8	83.2	3.5	4.2	4.0	6.2	3.4	5.2	8.0	7.1	6.5	6.6	7.0	39.4	20.2	4.8	0.4	74.9	32.1	53.5	46.5
68523	LINCOLN	96.9	95.6	0.5	0.5	0.6	0.9	1.8	2.8	5.1	5.9	6.7	7.0	4.5	24.6	35.3	9.9	1.0	77.7	42.4	48.3	51.7
68524	LINCOLN	82.8	78.7	7.1	7.8	1.7	2.8	5.2	7.9	10.1	8.5	7.7	8.1	9.7	33.2	17.7	4.7	0.4	69.0	28.2	52.6	47.4
68526	LINCOLN	97.5	96.5	0.5	0.5	0.8	1.4	0.9	1.5	5.4	6.4	7.6	7.5	3.9	21.8	35.0	11.3	1.0	76.3	43.2	49.4	50.6
68527	LINCOLN	97.6	96.7	0.1	0.1	0.8	1.3	1.1	1.6	5.1	6.0	6.9	7.3	4.5	21.2	36.1	11.8	1.1	77.7	44.2	50.0	50.0
68528	LINCOLN	87.3	82.4	2.6	3.1	5.0	7.7	5.3	8.0	8.3	7.4	6.5	5.1	4.5	40.3	20.9	6.3	0.6	74.6	33.3	51.6	48.4
68531	LINCOLN	98.1	96.0	0.0	0.0	0.0	0.6	1.9	3.5	5.8	6.4	6.9	7.5	4.6	23.1	34.7	9.8	1.2	75.7	42.3	49.7	50.3
68532	LINCOLN	98.9	98.3	0.0	0.0	0.0	0.2	0.7	1.0	5.3	6.3	7.3	6.9	4.0	21.5	36.0	11.6	1.2	76.7	44.1	52.6	47.4
68583	LINCOLN	68.5	59.7	5.4	6.7	11.7	16.8	10.8	15.1	9.2	6.7	4.2	5.9	20.2	38.7	10.9	3.4	0.8	78.2	26.1	53.8	46.2
68588	LINCOLN	95.7	93.9	1.6	2.0	0.5	1.0	2.1	3.5	0.0	0.0	0.0	72.7	26.8	0.5	0.0	0.0	0.0	100.0	18.4	43.4	56.6
68601	COLUMBUS	93.2	90.5	0.4	0.5	0.5	0.7	7.8	11.5	7.4	7.3	7.5	7.3	5.9	25.5	26.0	10.8	2.3	73.2	36.7	49.5	50.5
68620	ALBION	99.2	99.0	0.0	0.0	0.1	0.1	0.9	1.4	6.4	7.2	7.8	7.1	4.8	21.0	27.0	15.0	3.6	73.4	41.5	49.4	50.6
68621	AMES	95.9	94.5	0.0	0.0	0.5	0.8	5.5	7.7	5.5	6.6	7.7	7.4	3.6	24.2	30.6	13.2	1.1	75.2	41.3	52.1	47.9
68622	BARTLETT	99.1	99.0	0.0	0.0	0.0	0.0	0.4	0.5	7.7	8.2	8.2	6.7	3.8	19.2	28.8	15.4	1.9	70.7	41.0	49.0	51.0
68623	BELGRADE	99.6	99.5	0.0	0.0	0.0	0.0	0.0	0.0	7.0	8.0	7.5	6.0	4.5	19.9	33.3	12.4	1.5	73.6	42.5	51.7	48.3
68624	BELLWOOD	98.5	97.8	0.1	0.1	0.2	0.2	2.0	3.1	7.3	7.8	7.7	6.3	4.2	22.8	29.8	12.4	1.7	73.3	40.3	51.8	48.2
68626	BRAINARD	98.6	98.3	0.2	0.2	0.0	0.0	1.4	2.0	7.0	7.8	7.8	6.3	4.2	21.2	29.5	13.9	2.2	73.1	41.3	52.4	47.6
68627	CEDAR RAPIDS	99.4	99.3	0.0	0.0	0.1	0.2	0.7	1.0	5.2	5.7	6.4	7.1	4.7	21.5	31.1	15.1	3.1	78.5	44.5	52.8	47.2
68628	CLARKS	98.8	98.2	0.1	0.1	0.0	0.0	0.8	1.5	6.5	6.9	7.5	6.6	3.9	20.9	29.2	15.7	2.8	74.9	43.1	49.2	50.8
68629	CLARKSON	98.8	98.1	0.0	0.0	0.1	0.1	1.7	2.9	6.2	6.7	7.0	7.4	4.6	21.8	26.3	15.6	4.3	74.9	42.1	49.1	50.9
68631	CRESTON	99.4	99.1	0.1	0.3	0.1	0.3	1.0	1.4	6.2	6.7	7.3	8.4	5.7	21.2	32.2	10.9	1.4	74.6	40.3	52.4	47.6
68632	DAVID CITY	98.5	98.1	0.1	0.1	0.3	0.3	1.3	2.0	6.6	6.5	6.7	6.8	5.6	21.9	27.0	14.8	4.1	75.3	41.6	50.1	49.9
68633	DODGE	98.1	97.4	0.0	0.0	0.2	0.2	1.4	2.1	6.5	7.0	7.4	7.6	3.9	22.2	27.4	14.2	3.8	73.8	41.9	49.5	50.5
68635	DWIGHT	98.7	98.4	0.2	0.2	0.0	0.0	1.3	1.9	7.0	7.7	7.9	6.3	4.4	21.3	29.4	13.7	2.1	73.1	41.1	51.9	48.1
68636	ELGIN	99.5	99.4	0.0	0.0	0.0	0.0	0.2	0.2	6.3	6.4	6.9	7.4	5.0	19.8	28.4	16.4	3.4	75.1	43.6	49.5	50.5
68637	ERICSON	99.0	98.9	0.0	0.0	0.0	0.0	0.6	0.7	7.7	8.4	8.4	6.7	3.9	19.3	29.1	14.7	1.8	71.6	40.2	48.4	51.6
68638	FULLERTON	97.8	97.1	0.0	0.0	0.0	0.1	1.7	2.6	5.8	6.0	6.4	6.8	5.1	20.2	30.6	15.6	3.4	77.2	44.7	49.8	50.2
68640	GENOA	98.9	98.6	0.0	0.0	0.1	0.1	0.8	1.1	6.4	6.7	7.0	7.0	5.4	22.0	29.2	13.8	2.6	75.3	40.4	51.4	48.6
68641	HOWELLS	97.9	97.1	0.0	0.0	0.4	0.6	1.6	2.3	5.8	6.6	6.9	8.1	4.9	21.4	27.9	15.5	2.9	75.5	42.4	50.8	49.2
68642	HUMPHREY	99.3	99.2	0.2	0.2	0.2	0.3	0.7	1.1	8.3	8.8	8.8	8.6	5.2	20.7	25.9	11.8	1.8	68.1	36.1	52.9	47.1
68643	LEIGH	98.0	97.0	0.1	0.1	0.1	0.1	2.6	4.2	5.8	6.5	6.9	8.3	5.2	21.6	28.8	14.4	2.7	75.0	41.9	51.2	48.8
68644	LINDSAY	98.5	97.7	0.0	0.0	0.1	0.1	2.0	3.0	5.8	6.6	7.3	8.1	5.6	21.7	30.5	12.3	2.2	75.4	40.9	53.5	46.5
68647	MONROE	98.6	98.2	0.1	0.1	0.4	0.7	0.7	1.0	6.5	6.8	7.1	5.9	4.4	24.7	29.4	13.1	2.2	75.7	41.0	50.1	49.9
68648	MORSE BLUFF	98.9	98.5	0.0	0.0	0.0	0.2	1.1	1.7	6.4	6.8	7.5	7.1	4.1	19.7	30.5	15.4	2.5	74.9	43.8	51.2	48.8
68649	NORTH BEND	99.1	98.9	0.1	0.1	0.1	0.1	1.1	1.7	4.9	5.4	6.0	7.5	6.0	21.1	30.1	14.8	4.3	78.8	44.3	48.5	51.5
68651	OSCEOLA	99.3	99.1	0.0	0.0	0.0	0.0	0.8	1.2	5.4	6.1	6.2	7.3	3.7	21.0	30.4	14.5	5.4	77.6	45.2	47.9	52.1
68652	PETERSBURG	99.0	98.6	0.0	0.0	0.0	0.0	1.0	1.4	6.1	6.5	7.1	7.9	5.5	20.4	29.7	13.7	3.0	73.2	42.4	52.8	47.2
68653	PLATTE CENTER	98.3	97.5	0.1	0.2	0.5	0.9	0.9	1.4	7.4	7.5	8.5	7.8	4.2	23.6	29.1	10.4	1.4	71.5	38.4	52.7	47.3
68654	POLK	99.0	98.8	0.0	0.0	0.0	0.0	1.2	1.7	4.7	5.4	6.0	7.3	4.2	21.0	34.3	14.5	2.5	79.3	45.8	53.1	46.9
68655	PRIMROSE	99.1	99.0	0.0	0.0	0.0	0.0	0.9	1.5	5.6	6.7	8.2	7.2	4.1	23.1	28.2	14.4	2.6	74.4	41.8	52.3	47.7
68658	RISING CITY	98.6	98.1	0.0	0.0	0.1	0.1	1.7	2.7	7.1	7.6	7.5	6.2	4.3	23.1	29.6	12.8	1.7	73.7	40.4	51.6	48.4
68659	ROGERS	96.3	94.3	0.0	0.0	0.5	0.5	5.6	9.0	5.7	8.1	8.1	11.0	2.9	24.8	27.6	10.5	1.4	70.5	39.7	53.3	46.7
68660	SAINT EDWARD	99.3	99.2	0.3	0.3	0.0	0.0	0.9	1.3	5.6	5.9	6.2	6.9	6.6	18.4	26.9	17.7	5.9	77.4	45.3	49.4	50.6
68661	SCHUYLER	73.5	65.1	0.1	0.1	0.4	0.5	38.3	50.6	8.2	8.6	7.8	8.0	5.6	27.8	21.7	10.1	2.4	70.3	33.7	52.9	47.1
68662	SHELBY	98.3	97.9	0.1	0.1	0.2	0.3	1.6	2.3	6.5	7.2	7.2	7.5	3.6	23.2	30.5	12.4	1.9	74.0	40.8	50.8	49.2
68663	SILVER CREEK	98.9	98.6	0.2	0.2	0.0	0.0	0.8	1.4	6.6	7.1	7.4	6.3	3.6	20.7	28.9	16.4	3.0	74.9	43.4	48.9	51.1
68665	SPALDING	98.5	98.1	0.1	0.1	0.0	0.0	0.8	1.3	6.4	6.9	7.0	7.0	4.3	20.4	27.1	17.0	3.9	75.0	43.3	48.9	51.1
68666	STROMSBURG	99.2	99.1	0.0	0.0	0.1	0.1	0.7	1.1	5.9	6.3	6.5	6.5	4.8	20.3	25.2	16.8	7.6	77.3	44.6	49.1	50.9
68667	SURPRISE	98.4	98.6	0.0	0.0	0.0	0.0	1.6	1.9	6.8	7.2	7.2	6.3	4.8	24.2	29.0	13.0	1.4	74.4	40.5	51.7	48.3
68669	ULYSSES	98.4	98.3	0.0	0.0	0.0	0.0	1.4	1.9	6.9	7.1	7.1	6.3	4.8	24.3	28.2	13.5	1.9	75.0	40.5	51.6	48.4
68701	NORFOLK	92.2	89.7	1.1	1.2	0.4	0.7	6.9	9.9	7.2	6.9	6.6	7.4	7.2	26.9	25.1	10.4	2.3	75.7	34.9	49.7	50.3
68710	ALLEN	97.8	96.7	0.1	0.1	0.1	0.4	1.8	3.0	6.9	7.6	7.6	6.6	4.3	22.5	29.2	13.2	2.2	73.9	40.8	50.1	49.9
68711	AMELIA	99.0	98.9	0.0	0.0	0.5	0.5	0.5	0.5	5.4	5.9	6.5	7.5	4.8	20.4	31.2	16.1	2.2	76.9	44.6	50.5	49.5
68713	ATKINSON	99.0	98.7	0.1	0.1	0.3	0.4	0.6	0.7	5.0	5.6	6.3	6.9	4.6	21.1	30.7	14.8	5.2	78.6	45.4	49.1	50.9
68714	BASSETT	98.9	98.6	0.0	0.0	0.2	0.3	0.5	0.8	5.3	5.8	5.7	5.0	4.7	20.5	30.5	17.6	5.0	79.9	47.1	47.4	52.6
68715	BATTLE CREEK	97.6	97.1	0.1	0.1	0.0	0.0	1.0	1.8	6.7	7.5	8.5	8.5	5.0	23.7	28.5	10.2	1.5	71.9	38.5	51.2	48.8
68716	BEEMER	97.4	96.5	0.0	0.0	0.3	0.4	1.6	2.6	6.9	7.1	7.3	6.7	4.2	21.4	27.1	15.3	4.1	74.2	42.5	51.4	48.6
68717	BELDEN	99.2	98.6	0.0	0.0	0.0	0.0	0.4	1.0	6.3	8.7	11.1	8.7	4.3	22.6	25.5	12.0	1.0	67.8	36.0	52.4	47.6
68718	BLOOMFIELD	94.9	94.1	0.0	0.0	0.2	0.3	0.7	1.1	4.8	5.1	5.4	5.8	4.9	19.5	28.7	19.7	6.2	80.9	46.4	47.4	52.6
68719	BRISTOW	98.6	98.5	0.0	0.0	0.3	0.4	0.0	0.0	5.4	6.1	6.5	7.3	4.6	19.2	30.3	16.9	3.8	77.4	45.6	47.1	52.9
68720	BRUNSWICK	98.9	98.5	0.0	0.0	0.2	0.2	0.0	0.0	7.3	7.7	9.2	7.9	4.2	21.7	27.5	13.1	1.5	70.4	38.8	50.4	49.6
68722	BUTTE	99.3	99.2	0.0	0.0	0.0	0.0	0.2	0.4	5.3	5.9	5.9	5.1	4.3	18.5	30.3	18.1	6.7	79.7	48.4	49.0	51.0
68723	CARROLL	97.8	97.4	0.2	0.2	0.5	0.9	0.0	0.0	6.6	7.4	7.4	7.7	4.5	20.8	30.0	14.0	1.7	73.8	41.2	52.5	47.5
68724	CENTER	79.6	77.3	0.0	0.0	0.0	0.0	1.4	1.4	7.3	6.8	7.3	7.3	5.5	19.5	26.4	16.4	3.6	73.2	41.7	49.1	50.9
68725	CHAMBERS	99.3	98.9	0.0	0.0	0.0	0.1	1.0	1.4	6.5	7.6	7.6	6.3	4.3	19.4	29.9	15.8	2.6	74.5	43.4	49.9	50.1
	NEBRASKA	89.6	86.9	4.0	4.4	1.3	2.1	5.5	7.9	6.9	6.8	6.8	7.3	6.9	26.3	25.7	11.0	2.3	75.3	36.5	49.4	50.6
	UNITED STATES	75.1	72.0	12.3	12.7	3.8	4.6	12.5	15.7	6.8	6.7	6.6	7.1	6.9	27.0	26.0	10.9	1.9	75.7	36.9	49.2	50.8

#	POST OFFICE NAME	2009 Per Capita Income	2009 HH Income Base	2009 Household Income Distribution (%) Less than $25,000	$25,000 to $49,999	$50,000 to $99,999	$100,000 to $149,999	$150,000 or More	Median Household Income 2009	2014	2009 National Centile	2009 State Centile	2009 Home Value Base	2009 Home Value Distribution (%) Less than $50,000	$50,000 to $89,999	$90,000 to $174,999	$175,000 to $399,999	$400,000 or More	2009 Median Home Value
68450	TECUMSEH	18254	1004	32.6	31.4	30.1	4.3	1.7	38054	40445	27	36	736	25.8	32.7	32.2	8.7	0.5	78065
68452	ONG	23001	54	27.8	35.2	31.5	3.7	1.9	42817	44300	42	61	41	34.1	31.7	24.4	9.8	0.0	64167
68453	TOBIAS	20052	178	24.7	38.2	32.0	2.8	2.2	41112	44118	36	52	145	37.9	28.3	15.2	16.6	2.1	66500
68454	UNADILLA	25087	303	16.5	33.0	39.3	6.9	4.3	50485	51777	62	81	255	9.8	16.9	36.5	26.3	10.6	133468
68455	UNION	22383	320	14.4	33.4	43.4	6.3	2.5	52173	55476	66	84	269	17.1	22.7	37.2	17.8	5.2	102083
68456	UTICA	20180	421	21.9	28.5	43.7	4.8	1.2	49728	52962	60	80	316	19.6	32.9	40.5	7.0	0.0	87241
68457	VERDON	17189	140	33.6	32.9	29.3	4.3	0.0	33595	35000	15	13	114	55.3	21.9	15.8	7.0	0.0	44545
68458	VIRGINIA	19651	65	23.1	38.5	35.4	3.1	0.0	38916	42369	29	38	52	17.3	19.2	44.2	17.3	1.9	110000
68460	WACO	20591	304	20.4	35.5	36.5	4.6	3.0	44324	47072	46	66	232	25.9	27.2	31.9	12.1	3.0	84167
68461	WALTON	31181	269	7.4	17.1	53.9	13.8	7.8	70801	71419	87	97	231	9.5	3.0	32.9	48.1	6.5	185500
68462	WAVERLY	24523	1240	11.7	22.3	53.8	9.6	2.7	62873	63459	81	94	937	5.8	11.3	66.1	15.8	1.1	122239
68463	WEEPING WATER	22656	775	19.7	27.0	42.6	9.0	1.7	53281	57324	68	86	590	19.0	26.9	38.0	12.5	3.6	95217
68464	WESTERN	20965	242	24.8	38.0	31.8	2.5	2.9	41217	43729	37	53	197	38.6	28.9	15.2	15.2	2.0	65357
68465	WILBER	21592	926	23.7	29.7	41.5	3.5	1.7	47270	48777	55	75	721	16.9	30.2	36.6	13.7	2.5	92847
68466	WYMORE	18505	897	32.6	37.5	24.4	4.0	1.6	35794	38001	20	24	696	38.4	28.2	24.4	7.2	1.9	64762
68467	YORK	22315	3843	22.0	34.5	35.5	5.5	2.6	45228	47356	49	68	2539	12.2	27.8	43.5	15.5	1.0	103929
68502	LINCOLN	25532	11291	23.9	28.5	37.1	6.7	3.7	46280	51096	52	73	5442	4.0	22.6	56.2	15.8	1.4	116354
68503	LINCOLN	17668	6272	35.4	31.5	29.0	3.0	1.2	34097	36101	16	17	1946	5.4	49.3	42.4	2.5	0.4	86118
68504	LINCOLN	22519	7649	26.4	34.8	34.3	3.3	1.2	40179	42813	33	46	3170	17.7	24.3	54.4	3.2	0.3	95546
68505	LINCOLN	29189	6507	15.4	27.1	43.7	9.5	4.2	56346	58708	73	88	4355	1.2	13.1	72.8	10.9	2.0	118700
68506	LINCOLN	32230	12522	11.7	24.8	45.0	12.4	6.0	60746	61272	78	91	8580	0.7	8.7	65.8	23.8	1.0	138481
68507	LINCOLN	27948	5702	15.7	24.3	46.2	10.1	3.7	58537	60180	76	89	3881	5.2	21.5	63.1	9.7	0.4	112436
68508	LINCOLN	17071	4838	50.0	28.2	19.0	2.0	0.9	25010	25130	3	1	630	27.5	43.2	26.7	2.2	0.5	68214
68510	LINCOLN	27579	9439	21.9	27.6	39.7	7.3	3.5	50389	52873	62	81	5159	0.6	14.2	70.9	13.0	1.2	122331
68512	LINCOLN	32376	3973	12.2	24.9	41.7	13.9	7.3	61162	61943	79	92	2705	4.8	4.9	53.9	30.0	6.4	146882
68514	LINCOLN	24568	70	10.0	27.1	52.9	8.6	1.4	61325	61200	79	92	56	12.5	16.1	30.4	35.7	5.4	157143
68516	LINCOLN	36979	14954	5.6	15.4	43.9	20.4	14.7	82456	82679	93	98	11316	1.9	1.7	46.9	44.4	5.0	174257
68517	LINCOLN	24894	184	10.3	27.2	48.9	9.2	4.3	62014	62239	80	93	151	11.3	12.6	35.1	35.8	5.3	162019
68520	LINCOLN	43289	496	9.5	12.9	38.1	21.0	18.5	84382	85072	94	99	437	2.7	4.8	33.2	46.9	12.4	214881
68521	LINCOLN	25728	11702	16.5	23.2	46.6	10.0	3.7	59151	60560	76	90	7658	13.9	10.3	60.7	14.7	0.5	122080
68522	LINCOLN	24255	4010	10.7	25.1	50.5	10.6	3.0	60626	63228	78	91	3055	16.5	9.4	63.9	9.4	0.9	112985
68523	LINCOLN	24933	481	12.7	15.8	47.2	17.3	7.1	69792	67129	87	96	425	11.8	10.8	20.9	47.5	8.9	201923
68524	LINCOLN	19938	1624	13.4	28.0	49.5	5.9	3.2	54155	56618	70	87	711	8.2	24.2	49.9	16.0	1.7	108635
68526	LINCOLN	40246	1323	8.2	10.5	38.6	23.1	19.6	88805	88850	95	99	1179	1.4	4.7	31.3	49.0	13.5	234491
68527	LINCOLN	30237	302	11.9	22.8	44.4	11.9	8.9	60705	61155	78	91	256	8.6	8.6	35.9	40.6	6.3	168750
68528	LINCOLN	31456	2532	14.3	24.4	44.1	10.9	6.3	60739	63389	78	91	1702	11.2	8.7	61.7	16.2	2.2	118406
68531	LINCOLN	24580	58	8.6	15.5	58.6	12.1	5.2	73101	65349	88	98	52	3.8	7.7	48.1	38.5	1.9	157143
68532	LINCOLN	26224	238	13.0	23.5	50.4	10.5	2.5	61337	61527	79	93	195	6.2	4.6	40.5	45.6	3.1	172845
68583	LINCOLN	13946	43	44.2	32.6	18.6	4.7	0.0	27241	28717	5	1	9	11.1	11.1	66.7	11.1	0.0	112500
68588	LINCOLN	12054	3	100.0	0.0	0.0	0.0	0.0	11833	11833	1	1	0	0.0	0.0	0.0	0.0	0.0	0
68601	COLUMBUS	23074	10597	19.6	29.6	41.0	6.9	2.9	50770	51740	63	82	7624	8.5	20.2	52.0	17.6	1.6	112218
68620	ALBION	19084	1301	28.5	35.3	29.8	4.2	2.2	38921	40207	30	38	961	20.9	31.5	32.3	13.1	2.2	87063
68621	AMES	21251	151	20.5	34.4	39.7	4.6	0.7	46140	48752	52	73	121	25.6	15.7	40.5	16.5	1.7	106250
68622	BARTLETT	16970	89	37.1	39.3	18.0	3.4	2.2	32740	34306	13	10	63	41.3	23.8	23.8	3.2	7.9	60833
68623	BELGRADE	18276	89	36.0	37.1	22.5	2.2	2.2	37993	39529	27	35	59	50.8	30.5	10.2	6.8	1.7	49167
68624	BELLWOOD	19133	424	19.3	40.1	34.0	5.0	1.7	43036	45552	43	62	345	22.0	25.8	36.8	13.0	2.3	92885
68626	BRAINARD	21008	240	21.7	36.7	32.9	6.7	2.1	44574	46281	47	67	184	25.0	23.4	38.0	10.3	3.3	92000
68627	CEDAR RAPIDS	18884	242	33.1	36.8	24.8	2.9	2.5	35257	37327	19	21	193	47.7	24.4	15.0	11.4	1.6	52368
68628	CLARKS	19836	316	26.3	36.4	33.5	2.5	1.3	40500	44033	34	48	248	37.1	25.4	25.4	8.9	3.2	66842
68629	CLARKSON	15980	562	31.5	34.3	30.8	2.5	0.9	36901	39351	23	29	450	32.7	28.0	28.0	9.8	1.6	74545
68631	CRESTON	17899	237	24.9	29.1	41.8	3.4	0.8	45625	48832	50	70	178	11.8	27.0	41.6	15.2	4.5	100625
68632	DAVID CITY	19552	1529	27.7	31.6	35.3	3.7	1.8	40997	44014	36	51	1103	22.3	30.9	37.4	8.7	0.7	86223
68633	DODGE	20275	675	25.0	39.3	29.3	3.4	3.0	39862	43134	32	44	537	23.3	33.0	27.9	12.1	3.7	80694
68635	DWIGHT	21383	232	21.1	36.2	35.3	6.0	1.3	45464	46277	50	70	177	24.3	23.7	37.3	10.7	4.0	92333
68636	ELGIN	16628	498	32.9	36.5	27.5	2.6	0.4	36472	39088	22	27	385	34.3	30.9	23.6	8.1	3.1	67121
68637	ERICSON	17978	128	36.7	39.1	18.8	3.9	1.6	33617	33815	15	14	90	44.4	22.2	22.2	3.3	7.8	57143
68638	FULLERTON	18083	717	31.7	36.3	26.8	3.9	1.4	37439	39869	25	32	544	40.4	36.4	19.1	3.3	0.7	58387
68640	GENOA	19144	724	30.8	35.1	28.2	4.0	1.9	37284	38596	24	30	547	27.2	29.3	29.1	10.4	4.0	79643
68641	HOWELLS	18552	428	24.5	39.7	29.9	3.3	2.6	39583	42130	31	43	351	27.1	30.5	25.6	14.5	2.3	78600
68642	HUMPHREY	18050	645	25.1	32.2	35.8	5.4	1.4	44799	47813	48	68	527	8.5	22.4	46.7	19.9	2.5	115745
68643	LEIGH	17866	385	28.6	31.2	36.9	2.3	1.0	41504	44224	38	55	317	27.4	32.8	28.1	9.8	1.9	77292
68644	LINDSAY	17856	340	25.6	35.9	31.8	4.1	2.6	40582	43273	35	49	273	14.3	18.7	41.8	19.4	5.9	112760
68647	MONROE	20384	422	23.5	32.7	36.5	5.9	1.4	45953	47829	51	72	354	15.8	30.2	37.6	13.0	3.4	94000
68648	MORSE BLUFF	17974	203	27.1	37.9	33.0	2.0	0.0	38498	41338	28	37	167	24.6	26.9	30.5	16.2	1.8	87222
68649	NORTH BEND	19771	730	20.1	38.1	37.1	3.4	1.2	45969	48425	51	72	561	14.3	34.6	37.4	12.7	1.1	91300
68651	OSCEOLA	21956	565	26.9	29.7	37.3	3.5	2.5	43186	43536	43	63	442	23.3	31.4	35.3	8.1	1.8	85435
68652	PETERSBURG	17250	291	29.2	39.5	26.8	2.7	1.7	34497	35187	17	17	221	45.2	25.8	14.0	9.5	5.4	54375
68653	PLATTE CENTER	21010	369	20.6	35.8	35.5	5.4	2.7	46194	48022	52	73	307	14.0	23.1	45.3	14.3	3.3	105410
68654	POLK	20012	410	22.2	37.8	35.9	2.4	1.7	42237	43464	40	59	321	37.4	19.0	27.1	12.8	3.7	75476
68655	PRIMROSE	18142	79	30.4	38.0	26.6	2.5	2.5	35443	36360	19	22	62	41.9	25.8	17.7	14.5	0.0	58333
68658	RISING CITY	19333	309	19.7	38.2	36.2	4.5	1.3	45087	46110	49	68	248	23.0	25.8	35.5	12.9	2.8	91667
68659	ROGERS	19246	75	18.7	34.7	40.0	4.0	2.7	47755	46076	56	77	60	16.7	20.0	38.3	21.7	3.3	112500
68660	SAINT EDWARD	16615	353	34.8	36.8	23.5	3.7	1.1	35352	35951	19	21	272	53.3	22.8	16.9	5.1	1.8	47750
68661	SCHUYLER	16464	2212	21.6	34.4	35.3	7.0	1.8	45611	46140	50	70	1585	19.3	30.2	42.2	7.9	0.4	90644
68662	SHELBY	21275	605	21.8	32.7	39.7	3.6	2.1	45873	45880	51	71	469	21.5	23.5	39.4	10.7	4.9	97121
68663	SILVER CREEK	18746	273	28.6	35.2	32.6	1.8	1.8	39405	42968	31	41	217	40.1	29.0	22.6	6.0	2.3	60789
68665	SPALDING	15739	335	34.9	39.1	21.2	3.9	0.9	34143	34655	16	17	267	43.4	28.1	18.4	6.7	3.4	59211
68666	STROMSBURG	20279	664	25.5	33.4	34.2	4.7	2.3	42022	45045	39	58	502	27.1	33.3	34.1	4.8	0.8	78723
68667	SURPRISE	18541	80	20.0	32.5	42.5	3.8	1.3	48427	47961	58	78	61	27.9	26.2	27.9	13.1	4.9	81667
68669	ULYSSES	18104	202	21.8	32.2	41.6	4.0	0.5	47602	47715	56	77	154	26.6	25.3	31.8	11.7	4.5	85714
68701	NORFOLK	21513	11510	23.3	30.3	36.8	7.3	2.2	46235	48763	52	73	7523	9.6	23.3	48.9	17.3	0.9	108997
68710	ALLEN	18990	333	22.8	36.3	35.7	3.3	1.8	44816	45089	48	68	263	28.5	34.2	31.6	5.7	0.0	74130
68711	AMELIA	15632	73	30.1	37.0	30.1	2.7	0.0	35560	40000	19	22	53	28.3	15.1	35.8	7.5	13.2	98750
68713	ATKINSON	19003	801	33.0	37.0	25.7	3.0	1.4	35732	37053	20	23	589	32.1	28.9	30.1	6.3	2.7	76143
68714	BASSETT	17543	609	39.2	37.1	19.9	2.8	1.0	30265	31257	8	5	452	43.1	29.0	21.0	5.1	1.8	57750
68715	BATTLE CREEK	20287	572	20.6	28.1	43.4	6.8	1.0	51029	51566	64	83	478	14.0	25.5	51.0	9.0	0.4	101136
68716	BEEMER	17638	428	29.2	36.7	30.8	1.6	1.6	39148	41051	30	39	324	26.9	29.6	28.1	11.4	4.0	77391
68717	BELDEN	17878	82	22.0	41.5	32.9	3.7	0.0	42569	43594	41	61	60	18.3	28.3	33.3	18.3	1.7	94000
68718	BLOOMFIELD	17433	810	38.4	33.1	24.9	2.6	1.0	32750	35105	13	10	607	42.8	29.8	21.3	5.6	0.5	57250
68719	BRISTOW	15954	104	38.5	35.6	22.1	2.9	1.0	32308	34441	12	8	84	54.8	21.4	17.9	6.0	0.0	43333
68720	BRUNSWICK	14285	164	32.9	37.8	25.6	1.8	1.8	34587	36230	17	18	121	22.3	22.3	27.3	26.4	1.7	99286
68722	BUTTE	14023	194	43.8	39.2	13.4	3.6	0.0	28340	28243	6	2	153	62.1	16.3	13.7	3.3	4.6	34833
68723	CARROLL	18522	215	20.9	41.9	34.0	3.3	0.0	41570	43331	38	55	160	23.1	33.1	33.1	10.6	0.0	85000
68724	CENTER	14488	83	37.3	36.1	21.7	3.6	1.2	33607	32343	15	14	59	39.0	33.9	20.3	6.8	0.0	62500
68725	CHAMBERS	16424	308	37.0	39.3	19.8	2.3	1.6	31053	32113	10	6	234	33.8	25.6	28.2	6.4	6.0	70667
	NEBRASKA	24998		20.5	28.3	37.5	9.0	4.6	50953	53316				15.1	21.8	43.3	17.4	2.4	109174
	UNITED STATES	27277		20.9	24.4	35.3	11.7	7.6	54719	56938				9.3	13.1	31.6	32.6	13.5	162279

ZIP CODE #	POST OFFICE NAME	FINANCIAL SERVICES: Auto Loan	Home Loan	Invest-ments	Retire-ment Plans	THE HOME: Home Improvements: Home Repair	Lawn & Garden	Furnishings: Computers & Hardware-Personal	Major Appliances	TV, Radio, Sound Equipment	Furniture	ENTERTAINMENT: Dine out/ Carry out	Sports Equipment	Fees & Tickets	Toys & Games	Travel	Cable TV	PERSONAL: Apparel & Services	Auto Repairs	Health Insurance	Pets & Supplies
68450	TECUMSEH	78	55	82	54	57	81	60	74	65	51	63	59	46	64	59	71	42	69	80	90
68452	ONG	86	59	94	59	62	91	66	82	68	53	68	68	48	67	65	75	44	76	86	100
68453	TOBIAS	88	61	97	60	63	93	67	84	70	54	69	69	49	69	67	76	45	78	88	103
68454	UNADILLA	87	93	85	95	91	95	85	90	84	83	84	70	87	85	89	84	58	86	89	106
68455	UNION	104	73	113	73	76	110	80	99	83	66	82	82	60	82	80	90	54	92	104	121
68456	UTICA	94	64	103	64	67	99	71	89	74	58	73	73	52	73	71	81	48	83	94	109
68457	VERDON	75	53	77	52	55	76	55	70	61	51	60	53	44	60	55	67	39	64	73	84
68458	VIRGINIA	81	56	88	55	58	85	62	77	65	51	64	63	46	64	61	71	42	72	81	94
68460	WACO	97	66	106	66	69	102	74	92	77	60	76	76	54	75	73	84	49	86	97	113
68461	WALTON	113	135	132	139	137	130	117	123	113	122	114	93	131	114	129	112	81	117	118	142
68462	WAVERLY	101	107	89	105	101	96	97	98	94	102	96	74	98	99	96	92	66	95	92	114
68463	WEEPING WATER	91	83	86	86	84	98	81	92	83	74	82	71	75	85	82	88	56	85	94	108
68464	WESTERN	88	61	96	61	64	93	67	83	70	55	69	69	50	69	67	76	45	78	88	102
68465	WILBER	82	73	76	76	75	88	73	83	75	65	74	63	66	76	73	80	50	77	86	97
68466	WYMORE	73	52	73	51	54	76	57	70	63	51	61	53	45	62	55	70	41	66	77	83
68467	YORK	82	70	76	71	71	85	75	81	78	69	77	62	67	78	72	82	52	79	86	96
68502	LINCOLN	84	72	66	75	70	73	88	76	86	82	86	62	80	87	78	86	60	83	80	93
68503	LINCOLN	63	48	42	51	45	48	65	53	65	61	65	45	57	66	55	64	46	61	56	66
68504	LINCOLN	70	52	46	56	49	53	74	58	72	67	72	50	62	73	60	71	50	68	62	74
68505	LINCOLN	93	90	84	92	88	92	95	90	95	93	96	70	94	96	92	96	67	94	95	108
68506	LINCOLN	100	105	101	106	104	107	103	103	103	103	104	78	106	103	105	105	72	103	109	121
68507	LINCOLN	93	97	83	98	93	97	94	93	95	92	95	72	96	96	93	96	66	93	98	111
68508	LINCOLN	52	34	32	38	32	35	55	41	54	49	54	36	44	54	43	53	38	50	44	53
68510	LINCOLN	83	77	75	78	77	81	85	81	86	82	86	61	82	85	81	88	60	85	89	96
68512	LINCOLN	105	113	101	114	109	106	107	105	105	110	106	82	111	107	108	104	75	105	103	124
68514	LINCOLN	93	100	87	104	97	99	93	95	92	93	92	75	97	94	96	92	65	93	94	112
68516	LINCOLN	140	156	142	159	152	139	143	140	136	151	139	112	153	142	146	131	99	137	129	162
68517	LINCOLN	97	107	94	111	104	105	98	100	96	98	97	79	104	99	102	96	68	98	99	118
68520	LINCOLN	146	178	178	183	181	169	152	161	147	161	148	120	172	147	170	144	106	153	153	185
68521	LINCOLN	95	95	81	94	90	85	96	90	93	97	95	72	94	97	92	91	66	92	87	106
68522	LINCOLN	101	101	84	100	95	87	99	94	94	104	96	76	97	100	94	90	67	94	85	109
68523	LINCOLN	108	122	105	126	118	120	109	113	107	109	108	89	116	110	115	107	75	109	112	133
68524	LINCOLN	92	86	73	86	81	76	90	83	87	92	88	67	86	91	84	83	61	86	78	98
68526	LINCOLN	150	186	191	192	191	177	159	168	152	169	154	125	181	151	178	149	110	159	159	192
68527	LINCOLN	110	126	114	130	124	123	112	117	109	114	110	90	121	111	120	109	77	112	114	136
68528	LINCOLN	108	112	91	109	105	96	106	102	101	110	102	82	105	107	101	97	71	100	93	118
68531	LINCOLN	102	115	99	118	112	113	103	107	101	103	102	84	110	104	109	101	71	103	106	126
68532	LINCOLN	93	105	90	108	102	103	93	97	92	94	92	76	100	94	99	92	65	93	96	114
68583	LINCOLN	63	35	31	41	31	34	60	43	60	58	61	39	47	62	45	58	42	56	45	57
68588	LINCOLN	15	6	6	8	6	7	21	11	17	14	17	11	13	17	11	15	12	15	11	14
68601	COLUMBUS	85	82	76	83	80	89	82	83	83	78	83	65	80	84	80	86	57	83	89	100
68620	ALBION	85	59	91	58	61	89	65	81	69	54	68	65	49	68	64	75	44	75	86	98
68621	AMES	85	68	83	69	70	90	70	83	73	61	72	65	59	74	70	79	48	77	86	99
68622	BARTLETT	71	49	78	49	51	75	54	67	56	44	56	56	40	55	54	61	36	63	71	83
68623	BELGRADE	74	51	81	51	53	78	56	70	59	46	58	58	41	57	56	64	38	65	74	86
68624	BELLWOOD	89	62	97	61	64	94	68	84	71	55	70	70	50	69	68	77	45	79	89	104
68626	BRAINARD	94	64	103	64	68	99	72	89	74	58	74	74	52	73	71	81	48	83	94	110
68627	CEDAR RAPIDS	80	55	88	55	58	85	61	76	64	50	63	63	45	63	61	70	41	71	81	94
68628	CLARKS	81	56	89	56	58	86	62	77	64	50	64	64	45	63	62	70	41	72	81	95
68629	CLARKSON	72	51	75	50	53	76	56	70	61	48	59	54	44	60	55	67	39	65	75	83
68631	CRESTON	87	60	96	60	63	92	67	83	69	54	68	68	49	68	66	75	44	77	87	102
68632	DAVID CITY	82	58	84	57	61	86	64	79	70	56	68	60	50	69	62	77	45	74	85	94
68633	DODGE	91	62	100	62	65	96	69	86	72	56	71	71	51	71	69	79	46	81	91	106
68635	DWIGHT	94	64	103	64	67	99	71	89	74	58	74	73	52	73	71	81	48	83	94	109
68636	ELGIN	72	50	79	50	52	76	55	69	57	45	57	57	40	56	55	63	37	64	73	85
68637	ERICSON	72	49	79	49	52	76	55	68	57	44	56	56	40	56	54	62	36	63	72	84
68638	FULLERTON	78	55	84	54	57	82	60	75	64	51	63	60	46	63	60	71	41	70	80	91
68640	GENOA	83	59	86	58	61	87	64	80	70	55	68	62	50	69	63	77	45	74	86	95
68641	HOWELLS	84	58	92	58	60	89	64	80	67	52	66	66	47	65	64	73	43	74	84	98
68642	HUMPHREY	90	62	99	62	65	95	69	85	71	56	71	71	50	70	68	78	46	80	90	105
68643	LEIGH	83	57	91	57	60	88	64	79	66	52	65	65	47	65	63	72	42	74	84	97
68644	LINDSAY	91	63	100	63	66	96	70	86	72	56	72	71	51	71	69	79	46	81	91	106
68647	MONROE	83	70	79	72	72	88	71	82	73	63	72	64	62	74	71	78	49	76	85	97
68648	MORSE BLUFF	76	52	84	52	55	81	58	72	61	47	60	60	43	59	58	66	39	68	77	89
68649	NORTH BEND	84	60	87	59	62	88	66	81	72	57	70	62	52	71	64	79	46	76	88	97
68651	OSCEOLA	93	64	102	64	67	98	71	88	74	57	73	73	52	72	70	80	47	82	93	108
68652	PETERSBURG	75	51	82	51	54	79	57	71	59	46	59	59	42	58	57	65	38	66	75	87
68653	PLATTE CENTER	94	72	100	73	74	100	76	91	78	65	77	74	61	77	76	84	51	85	95	111
68654	POLK	86	59	95	59	62	91	66	82	69	53	68	68	48	67	66	75	44	77	87	101
68655	PRIMROSE	80	55	88	55	58	85	61	76	64	50	63	63	45	62	61	69	41	71	80	94
68658	RISING CITY	88	61	97	60	63	93	67	84	70	54	69	69	49	69	67	76	45	78	88	103
68659	ROGERS	96	66	105	66	69	101	73	91	76	59	75	75	54	75	73	83	49	85	96	112
68660	SAINT EDWARD	70	50	71	49	52	73	54	67	60	48	58	51	43	59	53	66	39	63	73	80
68661	SCHUYLER	88	71	78	69	71	86	72	82	76	68	75	63	62	78	69	80	51	77	84	97
68662	SHELBY	94	65	103	64	68	99	72	89	75	58	74	74	53	73	71	81	48	83	94	110
68663	SILVER CREEK	78	54	85	53	56	82	59	74	62	48	61	61	44	61	59	67	40	69	78	91
68665	SPALDING	71	49	78	48	51	75	54	67	56	44	55	55	40	55	54	61	36	63	71	83
68666	STROMSBURG	85	61	87	59	63	89	66	82	73	58	71	63	52	72	65	80	47	77	89	98
68667	SURPRISE	86	59	94	59	62	91	66	81	68	53	67	67	48	67	65	74	44	76	86	100
68669	ULYSSES	86	59	95	59	62	91	66	82	69	53	68	68	48	67	66	75	44	77	87	101
68701	NORFOLK	80	74	67	75	72	78	78	76	79	75	78	59	73	80	73	81	54	77	80	92
68710	ALLEN	86	59	95	59	62	91	66	82	69	53	68	68	48	67	66	75	44	76	86	101
68711	AMELIA	71	49	78	49	51	75	54	68	57	44	56	56	40	55	54	62	36	63	71	83
68713	ATKINSON	78	54	86	54	56	82	60	74	62	48	61	61	44	61	59	68	40	69	78	91
68714	BASSETT	64	46	67	45	48	68	50	62	55	43	53	48	39	54	49	60	35	58	67	74
68715	BATTLE CREEK	86	75	81	77	76	92	75	86	78	67	76	66	67	78	75	82	52	80	89	101
68716	BEEMER	80	55	88	55	58	85	61	76	64	50	63	63	45	63	61	70	41	71	81	94
68717	BELDEN	81	56	89	56	58	86	62	77	64	50	64	64	45	63	62	70	41	72	81	95
68718	BLOOMFIELD	68	48	70	47	50	71	53	65	58	46	56	50	41	57	52	64	37	61	71	78
68719	BRISTOW	72	49	79	49	52	76	55	68	57	44	56	56	40	56	54	62	36	63	72	84
68720	BRUNSWICK	75	51	82	51	54	79	57	71	59	46	59	59	42	58	57	65	38	66	75	87
68722	BUTTE	61	42	67	42	44	64	46	58	48	38	48	48	34	47	46	53	31	54	61	71
68723	CARROLL	82	56	90	56	59	86	62	77	65	51	64	64	46	64	62	71	42	72	82	95
68724	CENTER	67	47	71	46	49	70	51	64	55	43	54	51	39	54	51	60	35	59	68	77
68725	CHAMBERS	69	48	76	48	50	73	53	66	55	43	54	54	39	54	53	60	35	61	69	81
	NEBRASKA	95	85	88	86	84	94	89	91	90	85	90	72	83	91	86	92	62	91	94	109
	UNITED STATES	100	100	100	100	100	100	100	100	100	100	100	100	100	100	100	100	100	100	100	100

ZIP CODE			POPULATION			2000-2009 ANNUAL RATE		HOUSEHOLDS					FAMILIES		
#	POST OFFICE NAME	COUNTY FIPS CODE	2000	2009	2014	% Rate	State Centile	2000	2009	2014	% Annual Rate 2000-2009	2009 Average HH Size	2000	2009	% Annual Rate 2000-2009
68726	CLEARWATER	003	1220	1119	1065	-0.9	26	469	441	423	-0.7	2.54	336	314	-0.7
68727	COLERIDGE	027	873	813	762	-0.8	30	351	335	316	-0.5	2.28	213	201	-0.6
68728	CONCORD	051	288	278	273	-0.4	49	116	113	111	-0.3	2.46	88	86	-0.2
68729	CREIGHTON	107	1804	1710	1646	-0.6	37	740	709	685	-0.5	2.35	492	468	-0.5
68730	CROFTON	107	2134	1938	1831	-1.0	21	816	761	724	-0.8	2.54	616	572	-0.8
68731	DAKOTA CITY	043	2531	2659	2708	0.5	81	846	888	902	0.5	2.97	644	674	0.5
68732	DIXON	051	300	291	285	-0.3	54	121	119	117	-0.2	2.45	91	89	-0.2
68733	EMERSON	043	1433	1385	1361	-0.4	49	543	527	519	-0.3	2.60	395	382	-0.4
68734	EMMET	089	185	164	155	-1.3	10	65	60	57	-0.9	2.73	45	42	-0.7
68735	EWING	089	1090	979	928	-1.2	13	416	389	373	-0.7	2.52	289	269	-0.8
68736	FORDYCE	027	738	671	622	-1.0	21	242	227	212	-0.7	2.96	194	181	-0.7
68739	HARTINGTON	027	3132	2968	2823	-0.6	37	1149	1121	1075	-0.3	2.60	792	767	-0.3
68740	HOSKINS	179	823	819	809	-0.1	63	304	308	306	0.1	2.66	225	228	0.1
68741	HUBBARD	043	1108	1096	1091	-0.1	63	409	407	405	-0.1	2.66	305	303	-0.1
68742	INMAN	089	374	335	315	-1.2	13	152	142	135	-0.7	2.36	106	99	-0.7
68743	JACKSON	043	672	682	687	0.2	73	244	249	251	0.2	2.74	184	187	0.2
68745	LAUREL	027	1678	1489	1377	-1.3	10	652	586	543	-1.1	2.47	452	405	-1.2
68746	LYNCH	015	445	404	382	-1.0	21	202	186	177	-0.9	2.17	134	123	-0.9
68747	MCLEAN	139	204	193	186	-0.6	37	74	72	70	-0.3	2.68	60	58	-0.4
68748	MADISON	119	3542	3393	3323	-0.5	42	1135	1087	1065	-0.5	2.94	841	802	-0.5
68749	MAGNET	027	101	85	77	-1.8	1	47	40	37	-1.7	2.13	36	31	-1.6
68751	MASKELL	051	165	160	157	-0.3	54	61	60	59	-0.2	2.67	45	44	-0.2
68752	MEADOW GROVE	119	887	872	860	-0.2	58	346	345	341	0.0	2.52	256	253	-0.1
68753	MILLS	103	325	314	310	-0.4	49	118	116	115	-0.2	2.71	84	83	-0.1
68755	NAPER	015	395	352	331	-1.2	13	173	156	148	-1.1	2.13	113	102	-1.1
68756	NELIGH	003	2128	1992	1919	-0.7	34	892	859	832	-0.4	2.23	591	566	-0.5
68757	NEWCASTLE	051	774	727	703	-0.7	34	308	295	286	-0.5	2.46	213	204	-0.5
68758	NEWMAN GROVE	119	1215	1309	1325	0.8	87	478	523	531	1.0	2.40	314	341	0.9
68759	NEWPORT	149	295	258	245	-1.4	7	120	111	106	-0.8	2.32	90	83	-0.9
68760	NIOBRARA	107	1329	1368	1364	0.3	75	523	542	540	0.4	2.50	366	377	0.3
68761	OAKDALE	003	489	453	433	-0.8	30	193	182	175	-0.6	2.49	140	132	-0.6
68763	ONEILL	089	5359	5036	4846	-0.7	34	2152	2072	2011	-0.4	2.37	1447	1385	-0.5
68764	ORCHARD	003	801	743	713	-0.8	30	328	312	302	-0.5	2.36	230	218	-0.6
68765	OSMOND	139	1607	1536	1493	-0.5	42	612	594	578	-0.3	2.57	447	432	-0.4
68766	PAGE	089	425	379	357	-1.2	13	174	162	154	-0.8	2.34	121	112	-0.8
68767	PIERCE	139	3018	2949	2886	-0.2	58	1106	1093	1071	-0.1	2.63	805	792	-0.2
68768	PILGER	167	1038	1034	1019	0.0	66	399	409	406	0.3	2.45	293	298	0.2
68769	PLAINVIEW	139	2278	2186	2120	-0.4	49	908	879	855	-0.4	2.43	615	592	-0.4
68770	PONCA	051	1657	1599	1563	-0.4	49	610	595	582	-0.3	2.60	445	432	-0.3
68771	RANDOLPH	027	1763	1579	1475	-1.2	13	667	602	562	-1.1	2.56	477	430	-1.1
68773	ROYAL	003	294	271	258	-0.9	26	115	108	104	-0.7	2.50	93	87	-0.7
68774	SAINT HELENA	027	387	361	337	-0.7	34	144	139	131	-0.4	2.60	113	108	-0.5
68776	SOUTH SIOUX CITY	043	14781	15182	15275	0.3	75	5175	5274	5291	0.2	2.84	3643	3695	0.2
68777	SPENCER	015	758	687	649	-1.1	17	311	286	271	-0.9	2.40	207	189	-1.0
68778	SPRINGVIEW	103	648	626	618	-0.4	49	287	282	280	-0.2	2.22	205	201	-0.2
68779	STANTON	167	2687	2854	2862	0.7	84	1004	1083	1091	0.8	2.55	744	801	0.8
68780	STUART	089	1228	1123	1064	-1.0	21	452	426	407	-0.6	2.55	330	309	-0.7
68781	TILDEN	003	1643	1478	1412	-1.1	17	620	560	535	-1.1	2.54	426	380	-1.2
68783	VERDIGRE	107	1043	1023	1000	-0.2	58	432	431	421	0.0	2.26	287	285	-0.1
68784	WAKEFIELD	051	2213	2113	2056	-0.5	42	802	764	742	-0.5	2.69	563	532	-0.6
68785	WATERBURY	051	250	260	260	0.4	78	94	99	99	0.6	2.63	68	71	0.5
68786	WAUSA	107	1114	1019	973	-1.0	21	460	425	406	-0.9	2.33	332	306	-0.9
68787	WAYNE	179	6810	6558	6401	-0.4	49	2294	2229	2168	-0.3	2.42	1343	1294	-0.4
68788	WEST POINT	039	5426	5158	4997	-0.5	42	2051	1966	1906	-0.5	2.54	1426	1358	-0.5
68789	WINNETOON	107	225	215	208	-0.5	42	89	86	83	-0.4	2.43	59	56	-0.6
68790	WINSIDE	179	809	768	746	-0.6	37	317	307	298	-0.3	2.50	227	220	-0.3
68791	WISNER	039	1950	1868	1813	-0.5	42	804	786	767	-0.2	2.32	533	519	-0.3
68792	WYNOT	027	457	432	406	-0.6	37	179	175	166	-0.2	2.47	136	132	-0.3
68801	GRAND ISLAND	079	27633	28014	28323	0.1	69	10407	10566	10685	0.2	2.60	7063	7072	0.0
68803	GRAND ISLAND	079	20227	22317	23333	1.1	92	7844	8724	9119	1.2	2.48	5450	6091	1.2
68810	ALDA	079	1024	1105	1149	0.8	87	371	410	428	1.1	2.69	286	312	0.9
68812	AMHERST	019	748	804	835	0.8	87	282	309	323	1.0	2.60	214	231	0.8
68813	ANSELMO	041	518	504	496	-0.3	54	188	187	185	-0.1	2.70	145	143	-0.2
68814	ANSLEY	041	1090	1044	1020	-0.5	42	425	414	407	-0.3	2.52	307	298	-0.3
68815	ARCADIA	175	543	503	483	-0.8	30	223	209	200	-0.7	2.41	160	149	-0.8
68816	ARCHER	121	225	213	205	-0.6	37	76	73	70	-0.4	2.92	61	58	-0.5
68817	ASHTON	163	496	474	459	-0.5	42	207	208	204	0.1	2.28	145	143	-0.2
68818	AURORA	081	5241	5309	5282	0.1	69	2011	2054	2047	0.2	2.51	1454	1478	0.2
68820	BOELUS	093	465	506	523	0.9	89	184	203	211	1.1	2.49	135	148	1.0
68821	BREWSTER	009	230	211	205	-0.9	26	89	83	81	-0.8	2.54	63	59	-0.7
68822	BROKEN BOW	041	4693	4381	4207	-0.7	34	1949	1844	1774	-0.6	2.29	1263	1186	-0.7
68823	BURWELL	071	1902	1727	1637	-1.0	21	813	758	724	-0.8	2.20	529	490	-0.8
68824	CAIRO	079	1297	1353	1390	0.5	81	488	520	537	0.7	2.60	378	399	0.6
68825	CALLAWAY	041	1152	1071	1025	-0.8	30	454	423	405	-0.8	2.44	318	294	-0.8
68826	CENTRAL CITY	121	3944	3691	3545	-0.7	34	1538	1455	1400	-0.6	2.46	1074	1010	-0.7
68827	CHAPMAN	121	855	825	801	-0.4	49	314	310	302	-0.1	2.66	243	239	-0.2
68828	COMSTOCK	041	323	286	271	-1.3	10	138	123	117	-1.2	2.33	102	90	-1.3
68831	DANNEBROG	093	879	950	980	0.8	87	328	360	372	1.0	2.64	244	266	0.9
68832	DONIPHAN	079	1865	1992	2065	0.7	84	689	751	781	0.9	2.62	529	570	0.8
68833	DUNNING	009	178	164	158	-0.9	26	81	76	74	-0.7	2.16	58	54	-0.8
68834	EDDYVILLE	047	180	186	188	0.4	78	77	79	80	0.3	2.35	57	58	0.2
68835	ELBA	093	609	604	602	-0.1	63	226	227	228	0.0	2.66	166	166	0.0
68836	ELM CREEK	019	1734	1813	1863	0.5	81	659	707	733	0.8	2.56	472	496	0.5
68837	ELYRIA	175	265	246	236	-0.8	30	110	103	99	-0.7	2.39	78	73	-0.7
68838	FARWELL	093	349	349	351	0.0	66	134	136	137	0.2	2.57	98	98	0.0
68840	GIBBON	019	2661	2873	2993	0.8	87	982	1072	1123	1.0	2.65	731	789	0.8
68841	GILTNER	081	709	690	680	-0.3	54	250	246	243	-0.2	2.80	203	199	-0.2
68842	GREELEY	077	773	737	710	-0.5	42	302	295	286	-0.3	2.44	207	201	-0.3
68843	HAMPTON	081	955	910	890	-0.5	42	346	335	330	-0.3	2.72	278	268	-0.4
68844	HAZARD	163	264	254	247	-0.4	49	113	114	113	0.1	2.23	83	84	0.1
68845	KEARNEY	019	16507	18055	18869	1.0	90	6282	7071	7439	1.3	2.38	3895	4370	1.3
68846	HORDVILLE	081	409	388	379	-0.6	37	142	137	134	-0.4	2.83	120	116	-0.4
68847	KEARNEY	019	14568	15747	16318	0.8	87	5989	6583	6853	1.0	2.35	3667	4012	1.0
68849	KEARNEY	019	1505	1454	1458	-0.4	49	8	8	8	0.0	2.50	3	3	0.0
68850	LEXINGTON	047	11884	12531	12667	0.6	83	3763	3792	3800	0.1	3.23	2746	2755	0.0
	NEBRASKA					0.6					0.8	2.46			0.7
	UNITED STATES					1.0					1.1	2.59			0.9

ZIP CODE #	POST OFFICE NAME	RACE (%) White 2000	White 2009	Black 2000	Black 2009	Asian/Pacific 2000	Asian/Pacific 2009	% Hispanic Origin 2000	% Hispanic Origin 2009	2009 AGE DISTRIBUTION (%) 0-4	5-9	10-14	15-19	20-24	25-44	45-64	65-84	85+	18+	MEDIAN AGE 2009	% 2009 Males	% 2009 Females
68726	CLEARWATER	99.0	98.7	0.1	0.1	0.1	0.2	0.6	0.8	7.0	7.4	7.6	7.3	4.9	21.0	28.9	13.3	2.6	73.4	40.0	51.3	48.7
68727	COLERIDGE	98.9	98.6	0.0	0.0	0.0	0.0	0.5	0.5	5.4	6.0	6.8	6.8	4.9	19.9	26.7	17.0	6.5	76.9	45.1	49.9	50.1
68728	CONCORD	97.6	96.0	0.0	0.0	0.0	0.0	3.5	5.4	7.6	7.9	7.2	5.0	4.3	21.6	27.3	16.9	2.2	73.7	42.2	52.9	47.1
68729	CREIGHTON	98.3	98.0	0.3	0.3	0.2	0.2	0.6	0.9	5.3	5.7	6.3	7.1	4.7	18.3	29.1	18.4	5.0	77.2	46.4	48.7	51.3
68730	CROFTON	98.2	97.9	0.0	0.1	0.1	0.1	0.7	0.9	5.9	6.6	7.0	7.1	5.1	20.9	32.1	13.3	2.1	75.5	42.7	50.8	49.2
68731	DAKOTA CITY	75.5	68.6	0.5	0.6	4.2	5.7	28.1	36.3	9.0	8.3	7.8	7.9	7.8	27.7	23.2	7.4	0.9	70.0	30.8	51.2	48.8
68732	DIXON	98.3	96.9	0.0	0.0	0.0	0.0	2.7	4.1	6.9	7.6	6.9	5.5	4.8	22.0	28.5	15.8	2.1	74.9	42.2	51.9	48.1
68733	EMERSON	92.8	89.7	0.0	0.0	0.6	0.8	4.1	6.2	6.0	7.1	7.5	7.5	4.7	23.9	27.0	13.7	2.5	74.2	39.7	50.8	49.2
68734	EMMET	99.5	99.4	0.0	0.0	0.5	0.6	0.5	0.6	4.9	5.5	6.1	7.3	4.9	21.3	32.9	14.6	2.4	78.7	45.0	51.8	48.2
68735	EWING	99.1	99.0	0.0	0.0	0.3	0.3	0.5	0.7	5.7	6.7	6.9	6.6	4.5	19.8	31.5	15.4	2.8	76.3	44.7	51.4	48.6
68736	FORDYCE	98.6	98.5	0.3	0.3	0.0	0.0	0.7	0.9	6.9	7.5	8.0	10.1	5.4	20.4	30.3	9.8	1.6	71.2	38.3	51.7	48.3
68739	HARTINGTON	99.1	99.0	0.1	0.1	0.0	0.0	0.4	0.6	7.0	7.1	7.4	8.1	6.3	20.9	25.1	14.0	4.1	73.1	39.4	51.5	48.5
68740	HOSKINS	99.0	98.8	0.0	0.0	0.1	0.2	0.7	1.0	5.9	7.0	8.4	9.8	3.7	23.9	27.0	12.9	1.5	71.9	39.9	50.4	49.6
68741	HUBBARD	96.1	94.4	0.0	0.0	0.5	0.8	2.2	3.4	5.9	6.4	6.8	7.7	5.2	23.2	30.0	12.4	2.4	76.1	40.7	51.7	48.3
68742	INMAN	99.5	99.1	0.0	0.0	0.3	0.6	0.3	0.3	4.8	6.0	6.3	6.9	4.5	20.6	32.5	15.8	2.7	78.5	45.6	52.8	47.2
68743	JACKSON	96.7	95.5	0.0	0.0	1.0	1.8	1.3	2.1	5.9	6.2	6.7	7.8	5.7	23.3	30.9	12.0	1.5	76.5	40.3	52.1	47.9
68745	LAUREL	99.3	99.1	0.1	0.1	0.1	0.2	0.4	0.5	5.1	5.7	6.7	7.7	5.8	21.8	26.9	14.6	5.7	77.2	42.2	49.2	50.8
68746	LYNCH	98.7	98.5	0.0	0.0	0.2	0.2	0.0	0.0	5.4	5.9	6.4	7.2	4.5	19.1	30.9	17.1	3.5	77.7	45.9	48.0	52.0
68747	MCLEAN	98.5	98.4	0.0	0.0	0.0	0.0	0.5	0.5	5.7	9.3	9.8	8.8	4.1	23.3	29.5	7.8	1.6	68.9	37.3	53.9	46.1
68748	MADISON	82.1	75.4	0.5	0.6	0.2	0.3	24.2	33.4	7.7	6.9	8.3	10.2	6.0	24.2	21.4	11.6	3.8	70.9	35.0	52.7	47.3
68749	MAGNET	98.0	97.6	0.0	0.0	0.0	0.0	1.0	1.2	7.1	7.1	7.1	8.2	4.7	23.5	28.2	11.8	2.4	75.3	41.4	51.8	48.2
68751	MASKELL	100.0	98.8	0.0	0.0	0.0	0.0	0.6	1.3	5.6	6.9	6.9	6.9	5.0	23.1	29.4	14.4	1.9	76.3	41.5	48.1	51.9
68752	MEADOW GROVE	97.7	96.7	0.1	0.2	0.2	0.3	1.5	2.5	5.0	6.8	9.1	8.5	4.0	22.6	28.6	13.2	2.3	73.9	41.6	50.5	49.5
68753	MILLS	99.4	99.4	0.0	0.0	0.0	0.0	4.0	4.1	6.7	6.7	7.3	6.7	3.5	21.7	27.4	16.9	3.2	75.2	42.8	50.0	50.0
68755	NAPER	99.0	98.9	0.0	0.0	0.0	0.0	0.3	0.3	5.1	6.0	6.0	5.1	4.3	18.2	30.4	17.9	7.1	79.3	48.7	48.9	51.1
68756	NELIGH	98.8	98.3	0.0	0.0	0.0	0.0	1.3	2.0	5.8	6.3	6.3	5.8	5.0	19.9	29.8	15.7	5.5	78.0	45.7	47.5	52.5
68757	NEWCASTLE	99.5	99.2	0.0	0.0	0.1	0.3	0.5	0.8	5.8	6.2	7.0	8.0	5.2	21.5	31.5	12.2	2.6	76.2	42.2	52.5	47.5
68758	NEWMAN GROVE	92.3	88.4	0.0	0.0	0.7	0.8	10.0	15.4	6.3	6.2	6.3	6.9	6.5	19.6	26.4	15.6	6.1	76.0	43.4	48.9	51.1
68759	NEWPORT	99.7	99.6	0.0	0.0	0.0	0.0	0.3	0.4	5.4	6.2	6.6	5.8	5.4	20.2	35.7	13.2	1.6	77.5	45.2	52.7	47.3
68760	NIOBRARA	62.4	59.6	0.0	0.0	0.4	0.4	1.9	2.3	8.3	8.0	7.8	6.9	5.9	21.0	25.5	13.8	2.6	71.4	37.3	49.3	50.7
68761	OAKDALE	99.2	99.1	0.2	0.2	0.0	0.0	0.4	0.4	7.3	7.5	7.9	6.4	4.6	20.1	30.5	13.7	2.0	73.3	42.0	49.4	50.6
68763	ONEILL	98.7	98.3	0.0	0.0	0.2	0.3	0.9	1.3	6.5	7.2	7.6	6.9	4.4	20.8	28.9	14.2	3.5	74.1	42.2	48.4	51.6
68764	ORCHARD	99.4	99.1	0.0	0.0	0.0	0.1	0.3	0.3	5.4	6.2	7.1	6.2	4.2	19.5	31.0	17.0	3.5	77.4	45.8	49.0	51.0
68765	OSMOND	98.8	98.4	0.1	0.1	0.3	0.5	0.6	0.8	6.3	7.3	7.8	7.9	4.6	22.3	28.1	13.3	2.4	73.0	40.1	50.8	49.2
68766	PAGE	99.3	99.2	0.0	0.0	0.2	0.3	0.2	0.3	4.7	5.8	6.9	7.1	4.2	20.6	33.0	14.8	2.9	78.1	45.4	53.3	46.7
68767	PIERCE	99.0	98.7	0.0	0.0	0.1	0.2	0.7	1.1	6.6	7.4	7.6	7.4	5.0	24.6	26.9	11.2	3.4	73.6	38.4	49.6	50.4
68768	PILGER	98.3	98.2	0.2	0.2	0.1	0.1	1.0	1.0	5.6	7.0	7.8	6.9	3.9	21.4	29.1	14.6	3.8	74.9	43.1	51.5	48.5
68769	PLAINVIEW	98.2	97.8	0.1	0.1	0.3	0.5	0.3	0.4	6.3	6.6	6.8	6.9	5.5	21.7	25.7	15.3	5.2	75.7	41.6	48.6	51.4
68770	PONCA	97.7	97.1	0.0	0.0	0.1	0.1	1.9	2.9	6.2	6.7	7.1	7.2	4.4	23.0	29.5	12.3	3.7	75.9	41.5	49.9	50.1
68771	RANDOLPH	98.7	98.4	0.1	0.1	0.3	0.4	0.3	0.4	6.3	7.5	7.7	6.9	4.4	20.8	27.5	14.6	4.2	74.0	42.4	50.4	49.6
68773	ROYAL	99.0	98.9	0.0	0.0	0.3	0.4	0.0	0.0	5.5	5.5	11.1	9.6	3.3	22.5	28.0	12.9	1.5	70.5	40.1	50.9	49.1
68774	SAINT HELENA	99.2	99.2	0.3	0.3	0.0	0.0	0.3	0.3	6.6	7.8	8.3	10.5	4.7	19.9	28.8	11.4	1.9	70.4	39.0	52.4	47.6
68776	SOUTH SIOUX CITY	76.0	68.8	0.8	0.8	3.5	4.9	25.7	34.2	9.2	8.3	7.8	7.4	6.9	28.2	22.3	8.3	1.5	70.0	31.8	49.3	50.7
68777	SPENCER	98.7	98.5	0.0	0.0	0.3	0.3	0.0	0.0	5.4	6.1	6.4	7.0	4.4	18.6	31.1	17.2	3.8	77.6	46.3	48.5	51.5
68778	SPRINGVIEW	99.4	99.4	0.0	0.0	0.0	0.0	3.9	4.0	6.5	6.7	7.0	6.7	3.5	21.7	28.0	16.9	2.9	75.4	43.0	50.2	49.8
68779	STANTON	97.9	97.8	0.1	0.1	0.2	0.2	1.6	1.7	6.2	7.0	7.2	6.5	4.9	23.2	27.1	14.1	3.8	75.5	40.9	49.2	50.8
68780	STUART	98.7	98.4	0.0	0.0	0.3	0.4	0.3	0.5	5.4	5.9	6.0	7.3	5.4	21.2	28.6	15.6	4.6	77.6	44.0	49.7	50.3
68781	TILDEN	96.7	95.5	0.1	0.1	0.1	0.1	4.7	7.1	5.8	6.0	6.2	6.6	5.8	22.3	28.1	14.3	4.9	77.8	42.2	48.7	51.3
68783	VERDIGRE	95.0	94.3	0.0	0.0	0.0	0.0	0.8	1.2	5.4	5.9	6.2	5.7	4.0	18.2	30.9	17.9	6.0	78.9	47.9	51.2	48.8
68784	WAKEFIELD	88.9	83.9	0.0	0.0	0.4	0.5	11.8	17.7	6.8	6.7	6.4	6.5	6.2	23.0	26.6	13.5	4.3	76.1	40.5	48.7	51.3
68785	WATERBURY	98.0	97.3	0.0	0.0	0.0	0.4	1.6	2.7	6.9	7.3	7.7	6.9	4.2	22.7	28.8	13.1	2.3	73.5	40.6	49.6	50.4
68786	WAUSA	98.2	97.7	0.2	0.2	0.3	0.3	0.9	1.4	6.7	7.3	7.3	6.1	4.3	19.7	29.0	15.7	3.9	74.5	43.8	51.3	48.7
68787	WAYNE	96.3	95.5	1.3	1.4	0.4	0.6	1.6	2.4	5.0	4.5	4.3	13.3	17.6	23.3	18.7	10.0	3.2	83.5	28.6	46.9	53.1
68788	WEST POINT	93.9	91.3	0.1	0.2	0.2	0.3	9.2	13.4	7.0	7.1	7.0	6.7	5.3	22.2	26.7	13.8	4.3	74.5	40.9	51.2	48.8
68789	WINNETOON	98.2	98.1	0.0	0.0	0.0	0.0	0.4	0.9	5.1	5.6	6.0	7.0	4.2	18.1	30.2	18.1	5.6	77.7	47.1	49.8	50.2
68790	WINSIDE	98.6	98.2	0.2	0.3	0.2	0.5	0.5	0.7	7.3	7.8	7.8	7.4	4.0	22.4	28.6	12.9	1.7	72.1	39.9	49.5	50.5
68791	WISNER	98.6	98.2	0.3	0.3	0.3	0.4	0.7	1.0	6.1	6.7	7.0	6.7	4.1	23.2	27.5	14.7	3.9	75.9	42.0	51.1	48.9
68792	WYNOT	99.8	99.8	0.2	0.2	0.0	0.0	0.2	0.5	7.2	7.9	7.9	8.1	4.9	20.6	27.8	13.9	1.9	72.2	40.2	53.0	47.0
68801	GRAND ISLAND	83.7	77.4	0.4	0.4	1.5	2.2	20.9	29.4	8.4	8.0	7.4	7.0	6.4	27.0	23.8	10.2	1.9	72.0	34.3	50.3	49.7
68803	GRAND ISLAND	92.9	89.7	0.4	0.5	1.1	1.7	7.3	11.0	6.6	6.6	6.7	6.5	5.6	24.6	27.4	13.3	2.8	76.1	39.8	48.7	51.3
68810	ALDA	95.8	93.8	0.3	0.4	0.1	0.2	5.8	9.0	6.4	6.7	7.1	7.5	5.2	25.3	30.6	10.2	0.8	75.0	39.2	51.2	48.8
68812	AMHERST	99.5	99.4	0.1	0.1	0.1	0.2	0.0	0.1	5.2	7.3	8.8	7.2	3.7	24.9	26.9	14.3	1.6	73.6	40.4	53.1	46.9
68813	ANSELMO	99.2	98.8	0.0	0.0	0.4	0.8	0.4	0.4	6.5	6.9	7.3	6.7	5.2	20.2	31.3	13.1	2.6	75.0	42.4	52.6	47.4
68814	ANSLEY	99.0	98.8	0.0	0.0	0.0	0.0	1.1	1.7	7.3	7.5	7.7	6.9	4.2	21.6	27.7	14.8	2.4	73.2	40.8	50.8	49.2
68815	ARCADIA	99.1	98.6	0.2	0.2	0.0	0.0	0.9	1.4	7.6	7.6	7.6	6.4	4.0	22.5	25.6	16.5	2.4	73.0	41.0	50.1	49.9
68816	ARCHER	98.7	98.1	0.0	0.0	0.0	0.0	1.3	1.4	6.6	7.0	7.5	7.5	4.7	22.5	28.2	14.1	1.9	73.2	41.3	49.8	50.2
68817	ASHTON	99.0	98.9	0.0	0.0	0.2	0.2	0.6	0.8	5.5	5.9	6.1	6.3	4.2	20.9	31.2	17.3	2.5	78.5	45.7	51.9	48.1
68818	AURORA	98.1	98.1	0.2	0.2	0.4	0.4	1.4	1.4	6.9	7.1	7.2	7.1	5.4	22.8	26.3	13.3	4.0	74.0	40.1	48.7	51.3
68820	BOELUS	98.7	98.4	0.2	0.2	0.2	0.4	1.3	1.8	4.9	5.3	6.1	7.9	4.5	23.1	31.8	14.0	2.2	78.7	43.5	49.0	51.0
68821	BREWSTER	99.1	99.1	0.0	0.0	0.0	0.0	0.0	0.0	5.7	6.6	6.6	7.6	1.9	22.3	31.3	14.2	3.8	74.9	44.3	51.2	48.8
68822	BROKEN BOW	98.5	98.3	0.1	0.2	0.1	0.1	0.8	1.1	6.0	6.3	6.8	6.7	4.5	20.8	27.8	16.2	4.9	76.5	44.1	47.9	52.1
68823	BURWELL	98.8	98.6	0.0	0.0	0.1	0.2	1.0	1.1	4.9	5.3	5.7	6.6	5.3	16.6	30.0	19.8	5.8	80.1	48.9	47.9	52.1
68824	CAIRO	98.8	98.0	0.1	0.1	0.0	0.0	1.8	3.1	7.2	7.7	7.8	6.6	4.4	22.7	30.6	11.4	1.7	73.1	39.7	49.6	50.4
68825	CALLAWAY	97.8	97.3	0.0	0.0	0.5	0.7	1.0	1.5	4.9	5.2	6.0	7.6	4.9	18.7	29.6	17.9	5.2	79.0	46.7	48.9	51.1
68826	CENTRAL CITY	98.3	97.9	0.3	0.4	0.4	0.6	1.2	1.7	6.6	6.4	6.7	7.4	5.8	22.2	26.5	14.4	4.0	75.2	40.6	47.8	52.2
68827	CHAPMAN	98.2	97.7	0.0	0.0	0.0	0.0	2.6	3.4	6.4	6.9	7.4	7.8	4.6	22.7	30.5	12.5	1.2	74.3	40.8	52.2	47.8
68828	COMSTOCK	99.4	99.3	0.0	0.0	0.0	0.0	0.9	1.4	7.0	7.0	7.3	7.3	4.5	19.9	26.9	17.5	2.4	73.8	42.0	52.1	47.9
68831	DANNEBROG	98.7	98.4	0.2	0.2	0.2	0.3	1.1	1.7	5.4	5.7	6.3	7.7	4.6	23.4	31.3	13.6	2.1	78.0	42.8	49.8	50.2
68832	DONIPHAN	98.2	97.2	0.1	0.2	0.1	0.1	2.5	4.1	6.5	7.0	7.6	7.3	5.2	24.3	29.9	10.5	1.7	74.0	39.0	49.8	50.2
68833	DUNNING	98.9	98.8	0.0	0.0	0.0	0.0	0.0	0.0	5.5	6.7	6.7	7.9	2.4	22.6	29.3	15.2	3.7	75.0	43.3	50.6	49.4
68834	EDDYVILLE	97.2	96.2	0.6	1.1	0.0	0.0	3.9	6.5	8.1	8.1	8.6	5.9	3.8	24.2	26.9	11.8	2.7	71.5	39.2	50.5	49.5
68835	ELBA	97.7	97.0	0.3	0.3	0.0	0.0	1.5	2.5	6.1	6.3	6.6	6.6	5.3	23.7	29.6	13.7	2.0	77.0	41.7	52.3	47.7
68836	ELM CREEK	98.0	97.1	0.0	0.0	0.1	0.2	2.5	4.0	6.8	7.3	7.9	7.7	5.4	24.8	28.0	10.7	1.3	73.1	37.6	50.2	49.8
68837	ELYRIA	98.9	98.4	0.0	0.0	0.0	0.0	1.1	1.6	7.3	7.3	7.3	6.5	4.1	22.4	26.0	16.3	2.8	73.6	41.5	50.4	49.6
68838	FARWELL	97.7	97.4	0.3	0.3	0.0	0.0	1.7	2.6	6.0	6.0	6.6	6.6	4.9	23.5	30.4	13.8	2.3	77.1	42.4	51.9	48.1
68840	GIBBON	89.3	85.0	0.2	0.1	0.2	0.2	15.0	21.2	7.7	7.7	7.8	7.3	5.2	24.7	26.6	10.8	2.1	72.0	37.2	49.4	50.6
68841	GILTNER	98.7	98.7	0.6	0.6	0.0	0.0	0.8	0.9	6.8	9.7	7.7	7.4	3.6	23.8	28.3	11.4	1.3	71.3	38.3	50.7	49.3
68842	GREELEY	97.3	96.6	1.2	1.2	0.1	0.3	0.8	1.4	6.0	6.4	6.9	7.7	4.3	20.4	28.2	15.5	4.6	75.0	43.4	51.8	48.2
68843	HAMPTON	99.2	99.1	0.1	0.1	0.0	0.0	0.3	0.3	5.1	6.0	6.9	7.9	4.9	20.1	35.2	12.3	1.5	77.3	44.2	52.0	48.0
68844	HAZARD	98.1	96.9	0.0	0.0	0.0	0.4	1.5	2.4	5.5	6.3	6.7	6.7	4.3	21.3	29.9	16.9	2.4	77.2	44.4	51.2	48.8
68845	KEARNEY	94.8	93.2	0.8	0.9	1.0	1.3	3.7	5.6	6.6	5.8	6.3	10.2	15.3	25.1	22.5	6.8	1.4	76.1	29.0	49.7	50.3
68846	HORDVILLE	99.0	99.0	0.2	0.3	0.0	0.0	0.2	0.3	5.7	6.7	7.2	7.7	4.4	20.1	34.0	13.1	1.0	75.3	43.5	54.4	45.6
68847	KEARNEY	95.9	94.6	0.4	0.5	0.6	0.9	4.5	6.5	7.4	6.4	5.7	6.4	9.5	28.9	22.8	10.1	2.7	76.8	33.6	48.7	51.3
68849	KEARNEY	93.4	91.3	1.5	1.6	2.7	3.7	2.4	3.6	1.0	1.1	0.9	50.3	34.1	6.8	3.4	1.6	0.8	96.4	19.7	46.4	53.6
68850	LEXINGTON	68.1	59.5	0.4	0.4	1.1	1.4	45.3	57.3	9.8	9.1	8.3	7.6	6.6	27.2	21.6	8.1	1.8	68.5	31.2	52.1	47.9
	NEBRASKA	89.6	86.9	4.0	4.4	1.3	2.1	5.5	7.9	6.9	6.8	6.8	7.3	6.9	26.3	25.7	11.0	2.3	75.3	36.5	49.4	50.6
	UNITED STATES	75.1	72.0	12.3	12.7	3.8	4.6	12.5	15.7	6.8	6.7	6.6	7.1	6.9	27.0	26.0	10.9	1.9	75.7	36.9	49.2	50.8

ZIP CODE				2009 HOUSEHOLD INCOME DISTRIBUTION (%)					MEDIAN HOUSEHOLD INCOME					2009 HOME VALUE DISTRIBUTION (%)					
#	POST OFFICE NAME	2009 Per Capita Income	2009 HH Income Base	Less than $25,000	$25,000 to $49,999	$50,000 to $99,999	$100,000 to $149,999	$150,000 or More	2009	2014	2009 National Centile	2009 State Centile	2009 Home Value Base	Less than $50,000	$50,000 to $89,999	$90,000 to $174,999	$175,000 to $399,999	$400,000 or More	2009 Median Home Value
68726	CLEARWATER	15931	441	36.1	33.8	25.6	3.6	0.9	36183	38235	21	26	335	43.0	21.2	21.2	10.4	4.2	59038
68727	COLERIDGE	18085	335	33.4	35.2	27.5	2.1	1.8	35139	38099	18	20	247	41.7	35.6	15.0	7.3	0.4	58913
68728	CONCORD	16996	113	30.1	33.6	32.7	3.5	0.0	38473	38846	28	36	87	28.7	28.7	35.6	6.9	0.0	79000
68729	CREIGHTON	16447	709	37.2	36.5	22.6	2.4	1.3	34085	36348	16	16	562	41.1	29.9	21.4	7.1	0.5	61273
68730	CROFTON	17232	761	24.3	42.2	29.3	3.3	0.9	37920	41388	26	34	609	19.9	32.0	35.1	12.3	0.7	87500
68731	DAKOTA CITY	20497	888	17.6	28.0	43.6	7.5	3.3	53815	55062	69	86	716	41.6	18.6	31.6	7.7	0.6	71515
68732	DIXON	18026	119	28.6	34.5	32.8	3.4	0.8	39281	40243	31	40	93	32.3	28.0	35.5	4.3	0.0	74167
68733	EMERSON	18447	527	27.1	31.9	35.7	4.4	0.9	43306	45434	43	63	405	23.5	31.4	32.3	10.9	2.0	81522
68734	EMMET	16017	60	31.7	35.0	30.0	3.3	0.0	40000	40757	33	46	43	32.6	32.6	30.2	4.7	0.0	72500
68735	EWING	15797	389	36.5	35.2	23.9	3.3	1.0	33660	34897	15	14	303	44.6	27.4	20.1	4.6	3.3	56111
68736	FORDYCE	15533	227	22.5	39.2	33.5	3.5	1.3	42061	44647	39	59	187	29.9	29.4	28.9	10.2	1.6	78214
68739	HARTINGTON	17774	1121	27.1	35.6	32.1	3.5	1.7	41208	43492	37	53	924	28.8	31.4	29.3	9.5	1.0	77922
68740	HOSKINS	17416	308	26.9	30.2	38.6	4.2	0.0	42345	45000	40	61	247	14.2	29.1	42.9	13.8	0.0	99167
68741	HUBBARD	21694	407	19.9	29.0	41.8	6.9	2.5	51094	53642	64	83	321	19.6	24.9	38.9	15.3	1.2	98750
68742	INMAN	17477	142	35.2	33.1	27.5	3.5	0.7	36312	38644	21	26	112	48.2	25.9	18.8	3.6	3.6	52000
68743	JACKSON	23036	249	15.3	28.1	45.4	8.8	2.4	56795	57579	74	89	200	20.0	18.5	43.5	16.5	1.5	103804
68745	LAUREL	18221	586	28.0	40.1	26.8	3.4	1.7	36829	39183	23	29	451	25.9	34.8	30.2	8.9	0.2	77927
68746	LYNCH	18454	186	38.2	34.9	22.6	2.7	1.6	32670	34717	13	9	150	55.3	20.7	18.7	5.3	0.0	42727
68747	MCLEAN	21025	72	25.0	38.9	26.4	5.6	4.2	40000	41845	33	46	53	13.2	18.9	41.5	24.5	1.9	113542
68748	MADISON	16821	1087	21.5	33.9	38.5	4.8	1.2	44771	48196	48	67	823	22.8	34.3	32.7	8.1	2.1	79316
68749	MAGNET	18265	40	27.5	37.5	35.0	0.0	0.0	40000	45742	33	46	32	37.5	12.5	21.9	21.9	6.3	90000
68751	MASKELL	18319	60	28.3	35.0	30.0	5.0	1.7	41134	42321	36	53	48	39.6	25.0	35.4	0.0	0.0	70000
68752	MEADOW GROVE	17754	345	29.9	33.3	31.3	5.5	0.0	39414	42560	31	41	269	32.7	26.8	29.4	10.4	0.7	76765
68753	MILLS	12163	116	47.4	39.7	11.2	0.9	0.9	28630	29526	6	2	85	48.2	14.1	16.5	5.9	15.3	53000
68755	NAPER	15541	156	44.9	39.1	12.8	3.2	0.0	27634	27086	5	1	123	62.6	16.3	13.8	3.3	4.1	34423
68756	NELIGH	19516	859	32.5	34.7	26.3	5.5	1.0	37869	40245	26	34	678	33.0	32.9	27.3	5.5	1.3	69818
68757	NEWCASTLE	17419	295	28.1	37.6	30.2	2.7	1.4	37419	38980	25	31	232	39.7	26.3	24.6	8.2	1.3	66250
68758	NEWMAN GROVE	19595	523	31.0	36.5	26.6	3.8	2.1	37870	40873	26	34	386	41.7	27.5	23.6	5.7	1.6	62308
68759	NEWPORT	16751	111	37.8	36.9	18.9	4.5	1.8	30190	30000	8	4	75	45.3	22.7	14.7	12.0	5.3	58750
68760	NIOBRARA	14570	542	43.0	34.9	18.5	3.0	0.7	29000	29228	7	2	338	37.3	31.4	20.4	8.0	3.0	66897
68761	OAKDALE	13938	182	35.7	45.6	17.6	0.0	1.1	30266	31708	8	5	150	70.0	17.3	8.7	1.3	2.7	30000
68763	ONEILL	18926	2072	31.2	32.8	30.4	3.9	1.7	38780	41664	29	38	1512	21.5	24.5	42.3	8.5	3.2	94586
68764	ORCHARD	15533	312	40.4	41.7	14.1	2.2	1.6	29628	29428	7	3	243	53.5	24.7	11.9	9.1	0.8	45526
68765	OSMOND	19195	594	29.8	35.5	28.1	3.7	2.9	35568	38461	19	23	452	27.4	28.1	30.3	12.6	1.5	80385
68766	PAGE	17277	162	35.8	32.7	26.5	4.3	0.6	35563	37985	19	22	128	45.3	28.1	17.2	6.3	3.1	55455
68767	PIERCE	18815	1093	26.3	32.5	34.2	5.0	1.9	42946	45092	42	62	854	17.7	32.1	38.4	11.2	0.6	90385
68768	PILGER	18841	409	23.5	37.4	34.0	3.9	1.2	39380	44748	31	41	300	20.3	23.7	39.3	12.3	4.3	100000
68769	PLAINVIEW	17783	879	33.9	35.4	25.7	2.8	2.2	33081	35713	13	11	689	30.3	33.8	25.8	9.4	0.6	71827
68770	PONCA	18484	595	22.9	34.3	37.3	3.9	1.7	44139	43910	46	66	457	20.1	29.5	44.4	5.0	0.9	90319
68771	RANDOLPH	18174	602	26.7	39.5	28.7	3.2	1.8	37901	39372	26	34	470	33.0	29.1	28.9	8.3	0.6	71481
68773	ROYAL	17310	108	33.3	36.1	23.1	3.7	3.7	35430	36498	19	21	78	29.5	20.5	23.1	25.6	1.3	90000
68774	SAINT HELENA	18959	139	23.0	32.4	38.1	4.3	2.2	45281	47911	49	69	113	33.6	27.4	25.7	10.6	2.7	72778
68776	SOUTH SIOUX CITY	20970	5274	20.5	28.4	38.4	9.5	3.3	50917	53267	63	83	3334	24.0	29.1	38.5	8.4	0.1	86958
68777	SPENCER	16575	286	38.1	35.7	21.7	3.1	1.4	32672	34072	13	10	231	54.5	21.2	17.7	5.2	1.3	43824
68778	SPRINGVIEW	14839	282	46.1	39.7	11.0	1.8	1.4	30000	30356	8	4	206	47.6	15.0	15.5	5.8	16.0	54167
68779	STANTON	17706	1083	25.7	35.5	33.6	4.2	1.0	38741	45090	29	37	808	19.8	25.5	40.8	11.9	2.0	96441
68780	STUART	18406	426	31.0	37.3	26.5	2.8	2.3	39389	40292	31	41	311	34.1	19.0	35.4	6.1	5.5	84063
68781	TILDEN	17276	560	31.4	33.2	30.7	3.2	1.4	40094	42128	33	46	413	31.0	32.9	27.1	7.7	1.2	71774
68783	VERDIGRE	16206	431	43.6	35.5	17.9	2.1	0.9	27896	27973	5	1	333	41.4	30.0	17.7	10.2	0.6	63088
68784	WAKEFIELD	17174	764	28.3	34.2	32.6	3.9	1.0	40000	40845	33	46	548	25.2	35.6	31.0	7.8	0.4	77907
68785	WATERBURY	18412	99	23.2	35.4	35.4	4.0	2.0	45241	44537	49	69	78	29.5	34.6	29.5	6.4	0.0	72857
68786	WAUSA	17667	425	31.3	39.1	25.2	3.1	1.4	35760	37613	20	23	335	39.1	23.0	20.9	14.0	3.0	67115
68787	WAYNE	19826	2229	27.5	30.1	33.2	6.7	2.5	41482	43473	38	55	1329	7.2	26.7	50.2	15.8	0.1	107397
68788	WEST POINT	19525	1966	24.8	38.7	29.1	4.8	2.6	40234	41758	33	47	1405	12.7	27.5	43.6	13.1	3.0	100727
68789	WINNETOON	15761	86	37.2	37.2	22.1	2.3	1.2	34062	35444	16	16	68	39.7	30.9	20.6	8.8	0.0	62857
68790	WINSIDE	17216	307	31.3	32.6	32.2	3.9	0.0	36146	38550	21	25	230	20.9	33.9	37.4	7.0	0.9	84500
68791	WISNER	19572	786	23.9	41.1	31.4	2.5	1.0	39786	41178	32	44	549	24.0	35.0	30.2	9.7	1.1	75625
68792	WYNOT	19650	175	23.4	36.6	34.3	4.0	1.7	42721	45000	42	61	149	35.6	30.2	22.8	10.1	1.3	68500
68801	GRAND ISLAND	21432	10566	22.9	30.7	37.4	5.4	3.6	46787	50009	54	74	6468	9.1	27.4	46.0	16.0	1.5	106358
68803	GRAND ISLAND	23042	8724	21.2	27.9	40.2	7.7	3.0	50721	52631	63	82	6131	5.2	13.1	59.9	20.5	1.4	129681
68810	ALDA	21799	410	16.6	35.1	39.8	5.9	2.7	48362	50779	57	78	314	20.1	15.3	29.3	30.3	5.1	125758
68812	AMHERST	19467	309	22.3	30.7	40.5	4.9	1.6	47588	50327	56	76	240	17.9	22.5	38.8	19.2	1.7	112500
68813	ANSELMO	14806	187	29.4	41.7	26.7	1.6	0.5	34837	36722	17	18	138	41.3	21.0	21.7	10.1	5.8	66667
68814	ANSLEY	16789	414	30.2	40.1	26.1	2.2	1.4	34498	34829	17	18	318	57.2	18.6	13.2	5.3	5.7	39722
68815	ARCADIA	16986	209	37.8	33.0	24.9	2.4	1.9	31719	35000	11	7	161	48.4	21.7	21.1	6.8	1.9	51923
68816	ARCHER	17026	73	19.2	39.7	35.6	5.5	0.0	45309	46295	49	69	55	27.3	16.4	30.9	16.4	9.1	101389
68817	ASHTON	17758	208	25.0	50.0	20.7	2.9	1.4	36620	37407	22	28	168	38.1	29.2	17.9	12.5	2.4	68462
68818	AURORA	21202	2054	20.1	33.8	38.9	5.3	1.9	47352	48138	55	76	1502	12.6	20.8	51.9	13.3	1.3	107792
68820	BOELUS	17056	203	29.1	33.5	36.0	1.5	0.0	40225	43128	33	46	166	18.7	27.1	29.5	22.3	2.4	96364
68821	BREWSTER	13748	83	34.9	45.8	16.9	2.4	0.0	29760	30305	8	4	54	55.6	22.2	7.4	1.9	13.0	40000
68822	BROKEN BOW	20091	1844	30.4	34.5	29.0	4.6	1.4	37373	40070	25	31	1304	24.0	37.7	28.8	8.2	1.3	76636
68823	BURWELL	16965	758	40.4	32.1	23.4	3.7	0.5	31830	32687	11	7	551	41.0	25.8	25.2	6.7	1.3	60152
68824	CAIRO	18877	520	23.5	36.3	34.6	3.8	1.7	41485	44175	38	55	413	10.2	24.9	45.8	18.6	0.5	106722
68825	CALLAWAY	17392	423	31.2	35.7	28.8	2.8	1.4	39442	42742	31	42	326	26.4	23.6	34.7	12.0	3.4	90000
68826	CENTRAL CITY	20068	1455	25.1	36.7	32.1	4.6	1.5	42136	44665	40	59	1025	22.8	31.7	38.5	5.5	1.5	84655
68827	CHAPMAN	17165	310	19.0	40.6	36.5	3.2	0.6	43441	46247	44	64	234	20.1	25.6	32.5	16.2	5.6	100714
68828	COMSTOCK	20625	123	32.5	39.0	21.1	2.4	4.9	36113	36247	21	25	89	41.6	20.2	16.9	15.7	5.6	58333
68831	DANNEBROG	16597	360	28.1	34.4	35.0	1.7	0.8	40503	43502	34	48	292	17.5	24.3	32.2	22.9	3.1	104412
68832	DONIPHAN	21286	751	18.6	34.9	39.1	4.4	2.9	47391	49769	55	76	564	14.5	20.0	42.0	20.7	2.7	114560
68833	DUNNING	16099	76	36.8	44.7	15.8	2.6	0.0	29445	30000	7	3	50	56.0	22.0	8.0	2.0	12.0	37500
68834	EDDYVILLE	20100	79	26.6	39.2	30.4	2.5	1.3	38034	42333	27	35	59	37.3	25.4	25.4	10.2	1.7	74167
68835	ELBA	16436	227	26.9	41.4	26.9	3.1	1.8	38396	40972	28	36	176	27.3	23.9	22.7	21.0	5.1	87778
68836	ELM CREEK	19260	707	23.1	38.2	32.8	4.2	1.7	42283	45616	40	60	530	17.9	23.6	39.8	16.0	2.6	102035
68837	ELYRIA	16920	103	36.9	35.9	22.3	2.9	1.9	31621	33618	11	7	79	46.8	22.8	21.5	6.3	2.5	54167
68838	FARWELL	16820	136	27.2	39.7	28.7	2.9	1.5	38488	41438	28	37	107	28.0	24.3	24.3	20.6	2.8	85000
68840	GIBBON	18421	1072	24.5	33.9	36.0	4.6	1.0	43853	46496	45	64	768	13.8	22.0	50.5	12.0	1.7	108503
68841	GILTNER	22239	246	18.7	30.1	38.2	8.5	4.5	50784	51021	63	82	194	22.2	17.5	41.8	12.9	5.7	107143
68842	GREELEY	15749	295	34.2	37.6	25.4	2.0	0.7	34061	35000	16	16	228	43.9	29.4	17.1	5.7	3.9	55385
68843	HAMPTON	21172	335	13.7	33.1	44.2	6.0	3.0	51630	51039	65	84	266	14.7	22.2	42.1	17.3	3.8	107212
68844	HAZARD	18207	114	31.6	46.5	19.3	0.9	1.8	35000	35965	18	20	93	29.0	22.6	33.3	8.6	6.5	87857
68845	KEARNEY	24159	7071	22.1	29.1	37.2	7.5	4.1	48794	51379	58	78	4136	8.5	7.3	43.9	35.4	4.9	157517
68846	HORDVILLE	22138	137	13.9	32.8	40.9	8.8	3.6	52400	50912	67	84	102	14.7	15.7	42.2	23.5	3.9	122059
68847	KEARNEY	22940	6583	22.7	29.7	37.6	7.7	2.3	47245	50617	55	75	4123	15.3	10.5	49.7	23.7	0.8	127746
68849	KEARNEY	9230	8	25.0	25.0	37.5	0.0	12.5	50000	55627	61	81	3	0.0	0.0	100.0	0.0	0.0	112500
68850	LEXINGTON	17649	3792	21.2	29.4	39.7	6.1	3.5	49337	51452	60	79	2508	16.1	34.7	38.4	10.0	0.8	89197
	NEBRASKA	24998		20.5	28.3	37.5	9.0	4.6	50953	53316				15.1	21.8	43.3	17.4	2.4	109174
	UNITED STATES	27277		20.9	24.4	35.3	11.7	7.6	54719	56938				9.3	13.1	31.6	32.6	13.5	162279

ZIP CODE #	POST OFFICE NAME	FINANCIAL SERVICES: Auto Loan	Home Loan	Invest-ments	Retire-ment Plans	THE HOME: Home Improvements: Home Repair	Lawn & Garden	Furnishings: Comput-ers & Hard-ware-Personal	Major Appli-ances	TV, Radio, Sound Equip-ment	Furni-ture	ENTERTAINMENT: Dine out/ Carry out	Sports Equip-ment	Fees & Tickets	Toys & Games	Travel	Cable TV	PERSONAL: Apparel & Services	Auto Repairs	Health Insur-ance	Pets & Supplies
68726	CLEARWATER	72	50	79	50	52	76	55	69	57	45	57	57	40	56	55	63	37	64	72	84
68727	COLERIDGE	72	51	74	50	53	76	56	70	62	49	60	53	44	61	55	68	40	65	75	83
68728	CONCORD	75	51	82	51	54	79	57	71	59	46	59	59	42	58	57	65	38	66	75	87
68729	CREIGHTON	70	48	76	48	50	73	53	66	55	43	55	55	39	54	53	60	35	62	70	81
68730	CROFTON	78	54	86	54	56	83	60	74	62	48	61	61	44	61	59	68	40	69	78	91
68731	DAKOTA CITY	95	89	78	86	85	89	87	89	88	88	88	68	82	91	83	89	60	88	88	105
68732	DIXON	79	54	87	54	57	83	60	75	63	49	62	62	44	61	60	68	40	70	79	92
68733	EMERSON	86	60	91	60	62	89	66	81	69	55	68	66	49	68	65	75	44	75	85	99
68734	EMMET	78	54	86	54	56	83	60	74	62	48	61	61	44	61	59	68	40	69	78	91
68735	EWING	71	49	78	49	51	75	54	67	56	44	56	56	40	55	54	62	36	63	71	83
68736	FORDYCE	82	56	90	56	59	87	63	78	65	51	64	64	46	64	62	71	42	73	82	96
68739	HARTINGTON	80	57	83	56	59	84	62	77	68	54	66	60	48	67	61	75	44	72	83	92
68740	HOSKINS	83	57	91	57	60	87	63	79	66	51	65	65	46	65	63	72	42	73	83	97
68741	HUBBARD	97	76	98	78	79	103	80	95	83	68	82	75	66	83	80	89	54	88	99	114
68742	INMAN	74	51	81	51	53	78	56	70	59	46	58	58	41	57	56	64	38	65	74	86
68743	JACKSON	98	89	88	93	91	105	88	99	91	79	89	75	81	92	88	96	61	92	102	115
68745	LAUREL	78	55	81	54	58	82	61	75	66	53	65	58	47	65	59	73	43	70	81	90
68746	LYNCH	72	49	79	49	52	76	55	68	57	44	56	56	40	56	54	62	37	64	72	84
68747	MCLEAN	101	69	111	69	73	106	77	96	80	62	79	79	56	79	77	87	51	89	101	118
68748	MADISON	85	68	76	65	68	81	70	79	73	68	72	61	59	75	66	76	49	75	79	93
68749	MAGNET	69	48	76	48	50	73	53	66	55	43	55	54	39	54	53	60	35	62	70	81
68751	MASKELL	87	60	96	60	63	92	67	83	69	54	69	69	49	68	66	76	45	77	88	102
68752	MEADOW GROVE	80	55	88	55	58	84	61	76	64	50	63	63	45	63	61	70	41	71	80	93
68753	MILLS	59	40	65	40	42	62	45	56	47	36	46	46	33	46	45	51	30	52	59	69
68755	NAPER	60	41	66	41	43	63	46	57	48	37	47	47	34	47	46	52	31	53	60	70
68756	NELIGH	77	54	81	53	56	81	59	74	64	51	63	58	46	63	58	70	41	69	79	89
68757	NEWCASTLE	77	53	84	53	55	81	59	73	61	48	60	60	43	60	58	67	39	68	77	90
68758	NEWMAN GROVE	81	58	83	57	60	85	64	79	70	56	68	59	51	69	62	78	45	73	86	93
68759	NEWPORT	70	48	76	48	50	73	53	66	55	43	55	55	39	54	53	60	35	62	70	81
68760	NIOBRARA	62	44	64	43	46	65	49	60	54	43	52	46	38	53	47	59	34	56	65	71
68761	OAKDALE	62	43	68	43	45	65	47	59	49	38	49	49	35	48	47	54	32	55	62	72
68763	ONEILL	80	56	86	55	58	84	61	76	65	51	64	62	46	64	61	71	42	71	81	93
68764	ORCHARD	66	45	72	45	47	69	50	62	52	41	52	52	37	51	50	57	33	58	66	77
68765	OSMOND	88	61	97	61	64	93	67	84	70	55	69	69	49	69	67	77	45	78	89	103
68766	PAGE	72	50	79	50	52	76	55	69	57	45	57	57	40	56	55	63	37	64	72	84
68767	PIERCE	80	69	75	71	70	85	69	79	72	62	71	61	61	73	69	76	48	74	82	94
68768	PILGER	83	57	92	57	60	88	64	79	66	52	66	65	47	65	63	72	43	74	84	97
68769	PLAINVIEW	75	53	77	52	55	78	58	72	64	51	62	56	46	63	57	70	41	67	78	86
68770	PONCA	87	60	95	60	63	91	66	82	69	54	68	68	49	68	66	75	44	77	87	101
68771	RANDOLPH	84	58	92	58	60	88	64	80	67	52	66	66	47	65	64	73	43	74	84	98
68773	ROYAL	78	53	85	53	56	82	59	74	62	48	61	61	43	60	59	67	39	69	78	91
68774	SAINT HELENA	88	61	97	60	63	93	67	84	70	54	69	69	49	69	67	76	45	78	88	103
68776	SOUTH SIOUX CITY	89	83	74	82	80	82	86	84	86	87	87	64	82	88	82	86	60	86	85	99
68777	SPENCER	71	49	78	49	51	75	54	67	56	44	56	56	40	55	54	62	36	63	71	83
68778	SPRINGVIEW	59	41	65	40	42	62	45	56	47	36	46	46	33	46	45	51	30	52	59	69
68779	STANTON	77	58	77	59	60	81	62	75	66	54	65	58	51	66	61	72	43	70	80	89
68780	STUART	85	58	93	58	61	90	65	81	67	53	67	67	48	66	65	74	43	75	85	99
68781	TILDEN	77	54	81	54	57	81	60	74	64	51	63	58	46	63	59	71	41	69	80	89
68783	VERDIGRE	66	46	72	45	48	70	51	63	53	41	52	52	37	52	50	58	34	59	66	77
68784	WAKEFIELD	81	57	84	56	59	84	63	77	68	54	66	60	48	67	61	75	44	72	83	93
68785	WATERBURY	86	59	95	59	62	91	66	82	69	54	68	68	48	67	66	75	44	77	87	101
68786	WAUSA	74	51	82	51	53	78	57	70	59	46	58	58	42	58	56	64	38	66	74	87
68787	WAYNE	80	62	69	64	63	74	79	74	78	70	77	59	66	77	69	80	53	77	79	90
68788	WEST POINT	84	64	81	64	65	87	69	80	73	60	72	63	56	73	67	79	48	76	86	97
68789	WINNETOON	69	47	76	47	50	73	53	65	55	43	54	54	38	54	52	60	35	61	69	80
68790	WINSIDE	77	53	85	53	55	81	59	73	61	48	60	60	43	60	59	67	39	68	77	90
68791	WISNER	82	56	90	56	59	87	63	78	65	51	64	64	46	64	62	71	42	73	82	96
68792	WYNOT	87	60	95	60	62	92	66	82	69	54	68	68	49	68	66	75	44	77	87	101
68801	GRAND ISLAND	80	78	69	79	75	79	81	78	81	78	81	61	79	82	78	82	57	80	81	93
68803	GRAND ISLAND	83	82	77	82	81	85	82	83	83	81	83	63	81	84	81	85	57	83	87	98
68810	ALDA	85	89	81	91	87	91	83	86	82	82	82	68	84	84	85	82	57	83	86	102
68812	AMHERST	91	62	99	62	65	96	69	86	72	56	71	71	51	71	69	78	46	80	91	106
68813	ANSELMO	71	49	78	49	51	75	55	68	57	44	56	56	40	56	54	62	36	63	72	83
68814	ANSLEY	76	52	83	52	55	80	58	72	60	47	59	59	42	59	58	66	39	67	76	88
68815	ARCADIA	73	50	80	50	53	77	56	69	58	45	57	57	41	57	56	63	37	65	73	85
68816	ARCHER	89	61	98	61	64	94	68	84	71	55	70	70	50	69	68	77	45	79	89	104
68817	ASHTON	72	50	79	50	52	76	55	69	57	45	57	57	40	56	55	63	37	64	73	85
68818	AURORA	81	77	74	78	75	84	76	80	77	73	77	62	73	78	75	79	52	78	83	95
68820	BOELUS	76	52	83	52	55	80	58	72	60	47	60	60	43	59	58	66	39	67	76	89
68821	BREWSTER	63	43	69	43	45	66	48	59	50	39	49	49	35	49	47	54	32	55	63	73
68822	BROKEN BOW	81	57	86	56	60	85	63	78	68	53	66	62	48	66	62	74	44	73	84	94
68823	BURWELL	65	46	67	45	48	68	51	63	55	44	54	48	39	54	49	61	36	58	68	75
68824	CAIRO	88	60	96	60	63	93	67	83	70	54	69	69	49	68	67	76	45	78	88	103
68825	CALLAWAY	77	53	84	53	55	81	59	73	61	47	60	60	43	60	58	66	39	68	77	90
68826	CENTRAL CITY	82	63	80	63	64	86	68	79	73	61	71	61	57	73	66	79	48	75	87	95
68827	CHAPMAN	80	57	86	58	60	85	63	77	65	51	64	63	47	64	62	71	42	72	81	94
68828	COMSTOCK	86	59	94	59	62	90	66	81	68	53	67	67	48	67	65	74	44	76	86	100
68831	DANNEBROG	78	54	86	54	56	83	60	74	62	48	62	61	44	61	60	68	40	69	79	91
68832	DONIPHAN	86	83	77	83	82	87	78	83	79	79	80	63	76	82	78	81	54	80	83	99
68833	DUNNING	62	43	68	43	45	66	47	59	49	38	49	49	35	48	47	54	32	55	62	73
68834	EDDYVILLE	85	58	93	58	61	89	65	80	67	52	66	66	47	66	64	73	43	75	85	99
68835	ELBA	78	54	86	54	56	83	60	74	62	48	61	61	44	61	59	68	40	69	78	91
68836	ELM CREEK	87	64	78	63	65	86	67	78	73	63	71	61	54	75	63	79	48	74	82	95
68837	ELYRIA	72	50	79	50	52	76	55	69	57	45	57	57	40	56	55	63	37	64	72	84
68838	FARWELL	77	53	85	53	56	81	59	73	61	48	61	61	43	60	59	67	39	68	77	90
68840	GIBBON	86	64	80	63	65	86	67	79	72	61	70	62	54	73	64	78	47	74	83	96
68841	GILTNER	112	77	122	77	80	118	85	106	89	69	88	88	62	87	85	97	57	99	112	130
68842	GREELEY	69	48	76	47	50	73	53	66	55	43	54	54	39	54	52	60	35	61	69	81
68843	HAMPTON	103	71	113	71	74	109	79	98	82	64	81	81	58	80	78	89	52	91	103	120
68844	HAZARD	73	50	80	50	52	77	55	69	58	45	57	57	41	57	55	63	37	64	73	85
68845	KEARNEY	86	82	75	84	80	79	90	82	86	86	87	66	85	88	83	85	61	85	81	98
68846	HORDVILLE	112	77	123	77	81	118	86	106	89	69	88	88	63	87	85	97	57	99	112	131
68847	KEARNEY	79	74	69	75	72	76	79	76	79	76	78	59	75	80	75	80	54	78	79	91
68849	KEARNEY	96	62	60	68	60	67	115	78	103	91	103	71	84	103	80	100	72	95	82	100
68850	LEXINGTON	90	81	80	77	80	84	82	86	82	81	82	66	74	83	79	83	56	84	85	100
	NEBRASKA	95	85	88	86	84	94	89	91	90	85	90	72	83	91	86	92	62	91	94	109
	UNITED STATES	100	100	100	100	100	100	100	100	100	100	100	100	100	100	100	100	100	100	100	100

POPULATION CHANGE

68852-69030

ZIP CODE #	POST OFFICE NAME	COUNTY FIPS CODE	POPULATION 2000	POPULATION 2009	POPULATION 2014	2000-2009 ANNUAL RATE % Rate	2000-2009 ANNUAL RATE State Centile	HOUSEHOLDS 2000	HOUSEHOLDS 2009	HOUSEHOLDS 2014	HOUSEHOLDS % Annual Rate 2000-2009	HOUSEHOLDS 2009 Average HH Size	FAMILIES 2000	FAMILIES 2009	FAMILIES % Annual Rate 2000-2009
68852	LITCHFIELD	163	544	520	505	-0.5	42	217	217	214	0.0	2.40	157	157	0.0
68853	LOUP CITY	163	1556	1448	1388	-0.8	30	676	650	630	-0.4	2.14	420	402	-0.5
68854	MARQUETTE	081	789	804	801	0.2	73	296	306	306	0.4	2.63	247	254	0.3
68855	MASON CITY	041	478	441	421	-0.9	26	191	179	171	-0.7	2.46	146	136	-0.8
68856	MERNA	041	924	852	816	-0.9	26	367	344	330	-0.7	2.47	278	259	-0.8
68858	MILLER	019	321	322	326	0.0	66	130	134	136	0.3	2.40	94	96	0.2
68859	NORTH LOUP	175	562	527	508	-0.7	34	241	230	222	-0.5	2.29	165	157	-0.5
68860	OCONTO	041	509	470	450	-0.9	26	214	200	192	-0.7	2.35	159	148	-0.8
68861	ODESSA	019	132	157	169	1.9	96	53	65	70	2.2	2.42	43	52	2.1
68862	ORD	175	3277	3130	3034	-0.5	42	1391	1350	1314	-0.3	2.26	896	863	-0.4
68863	OVERTON	047	1207	1217	1224	0.1	69	469	471	471	0.0	2.58	348	347	0.0
68864	PALMER	121	1002	996	983	-0.1	63	386	388	384	0.1	2.51	277	277	0.0
68865	PHILLIPS	081	933	1023	1036	1.0	90	343	383	390	1.2	2.67	283	314	1.1
68866	PLEASANTON	019	1023	1037	1051	0.1	69	381	395	403	0.4	2.63	289	297	0.3
68869	RAVENNA	019	2035	2173	2240	0.7	84	814	882	914	0.9	2.40	555	593	0.7
68870	RIVERDALE	019	467	551	592	1.8	96	172	209	226	2.1	2.64	142	171	2.0
68871	ROCKVILLE	163	469	450	437	-0.4	49	185	186	184	0.1	2.42	132	132	0.0
68872	SAINT LIBORY	093	940	985	1007	0.5	81	319	341	350	0.7	2.89	253	269	0.7
68873	SAINT PAUL	093	3186	3294	3286	0.4	78	1299	1356	1355	0.5	2.40	861	893	0.4
68874	SARGENT	041	929	851	816	-0.9	26	387	356	342	-0.9	2.28	256	234	-1.0
68875	SCOTIA	077	637	610	589	-0.5	42	256	252	244	-0.2	2.37	175	172	-0.2
68876	SHELTON	019	1803	1952	2034	0.9	89	662	716	746	0.9	2.72	488	521	0.7
68878	SUMNER	047	452	467	472	0.4	78	179	184	185	0.3	2.54	132	135	0.2
68879	TAYLOR	115	712	724	731	0.2	73	289	297	300	0.3	2.44	207	212	0.3
68881	WESTERVILLE	041	175	157	149	-1.2	13	66	60	57	-1.0	2.62	50	45	-1.1
68882	WOLBACH	077	513	471	450	-0.9	26	218	205	197	-0.7	2.25	152	142	-0.7
68883	WOOD RIVER	079	2406	2455	2499	0.2	73	910	948	970	0.4	2.53	666	686	0.3
68901	HASTINGS	001	26536	28002	28812	0.6	83	10431	11085	11415	0.7	2.39	6639	7010	0.6
68920	ALMA	083	1580	1470	1408	-0.8	30	666	626	601	-0.7	2.28	430	402	-0.7
68922	ARAPAHOE	065	1334	1453	1477	0.9	89	571	628	640	1.0	2.26	370	403	0.9
68923	ATLANTA	137	160	157	152	-0.2	58	64	64	62	0.0	2.44	50	49	-0.2
68924	AXTELL	099	1296	1242	1207	-0.5	42	427	416	405	-0.3	2.83	320	310	-0.3
68925	AYR	001	514	511	513	-0.1	63	191	193	195	0.1	2.65	150	151	0.1
68926	BEAVER CITY	065	788	712	690	-1.1	17	345	315	305	-1.0	2.15	214	194	-1.1
68927	BERTRAND	137	1318	1266	1230	-0.4	49	490	480	469	-0.2	2.57	350	340	-0.3
68928	BLADEN	181	532	488	468	-0.9	26	206	191	184	-0.8	2.55	156	144	-0.9
68929	BLOOMINGTON	061	382	340	320	-1.3	10	162	145	136	-1.2	2.31	112	100	-1.2
68930	BLUE HILL	181	1453	1413	1391	-0.3	54	556	547	540	-0.2	2.44	390	383	-0.2
68932	CAMPBELL	061	481	413	384	-1.6	4	190	162	149	-1.7	2.37	139	118	-1.8
68933	CLAY CENTER	035	1105	1107	1104	0.0	66	430	434	433	0.1	2.53	309	310	0.0
68934	DEWEESE	035	283	281	280	-0.1	63	112	113	113	0.1	2.49	82	82	0.0
68935	EDGAR	035	755	730	720	-0.4	49	316	310	307	-0.2	2.27	206	201	-0.3
68936	EDISON	065	282	254	245	-1.1	17	109	98	94	-1.1	2.53	76	68	-1.2
68937	ELWOOD	073	2016	2013	1983	0.0	66	849	854	841	0.1	2.30	634	633	0.0
68938	FAIRFIELD	035	567	620	641	1.0	90	221	245	253	1.1	2.53	164	181	1.1
68939	FRANKLIN	061	1194	1240	1235	0.4	78	507	528	525	0.4	2.22	327	341	0.5
68940	FUNK	137	526	503	486	-0.5	42	194	189	183	-0.3	2.66	153	149	-0.3
68941	GLENVIL	035	737	736	736	0.0	66	278	282	282	0.2	2.61	209	211	0.1
68942	GUIDE ROCK	181	455	417	400	-0.9	26	222	207	200	-0.8	1.91	136	126	-0.8
68943	HARDY	129	410	356	333	-1.5	6	156	140	132	-1.2	2.54	115	102	-1.3
68944	HARVARD	035	1376	1362	1351	-0.1	63	521	524	522	0.1	2.56	384	384	0.0
68945	HEARTWELL	099	236	222	215	-0.7	34	91	88	85	-0.4	2.52	68	65	-0.5
68946	HENDLEY	065	192	172	166	-1.2	13	70	64	62	-1.0	2.69	51	46	-1.1
68947	HILDRETH	061	625	539	499	-1.6	4	266	228	211	-1.7	2.36	193	165	-1.7
68948	HOLBROOK	065	357	319	308	-1.2	13	153	138	133	-1.1	2.31	105	95	-1.1
68949	HOLDREGE	137	6869	6483	6224	-0.6	37	2750	2626	2526	-0.5	2.39	1850	1754	-0.6
68950	HOLSTEIN	001	415	436	450	0.5	81	158	168	174	0.7	2.60	125	132	0.6
68952	INAVALE	181	263	237	225	-1.1	17	105	96	92	-1.0	2.35	66	60	-1.0
68954	INLAND	035	113	112	112	-0.1	63	45	45	45	0.0	2.44	32	33	0.3
68955	JUNIATA	001	1514	1700	1795	1.3	94	543	619	656	1.4	2.73	428	483	1.3
68956	KENESAW	001	1161	1243	1291	0.7	84	427	463	483	0.9	2.58	320	343	0.8
68957	LAWRENCE	129	596	515	480	-1.6	4	244	218	205	-1.2	2.36	170	151	-1.3
68958	LOOMIS	137	654	631	610	-0.4	49	255	250	243	-0.2	2.50	198	193	-0.3
68959	MINDEN	099	4161	4065	3964	-0.3	54	1640	1615	1577	-0.2	2.42	1152	1129	-0.2
68960	NAPONEE	061	324	284	265	-1.4	7	136	120	112	-1.3	2.36	94	83	-1.3
68961	NELSON	129	987	855	796	-1.5	6	426	378	355	-1.3	2.18	273	241	-1.3
68964	OAK	129	270	234	218	-1.5	6	110	98	92	-1.2	2.30	70	62	-1.3
68966	ORLEANS	083	689	638	611	-0.8	30	297	278	267	-0.7	2.29	184	171	-0.8
68967	OXFORD	065	1291	1176	1133	-1.0	21	542	494	476	-1.0	2.33	377	342	-1.0
68969	RAGAN	083	99	91	87	-0.9	26	37	35	33	-0.6	2.60	26	24	-0.9
68970	RED CLOUD	181	1521	1467	1437	-0.4	49	682	673	664	-0.1	2.10	419	410	-0.2
68971	REPUBLICAN CITY	083	513	477	457	-0.8	30	243	228	219	-0.7	2.03	160	150	-0.7
68972	RIVERTON	061	248	225	214	-1.0	21	102	93	89	-1.0	2.39	69	63	-1.0
68973	ROSELAND	001	560	558	561	0.0	66	219	222	224	0.1	2.51	172	173	0.1
68974	RUSKIN	129	292	251	234	-1.6	4	117	104	98	-1.3	2.41	87	77	-1.3
68975	SARONVILLE	035	225	220	218	-0.2	58	80	79	79	-0.1	2.78	65	64	-0.2
68976	SMITHFIELD	073	287	243	225	-1.8	1	121	105	98	-1.5	2.30	93	80	-1.6
68977	STAMFORD	083	408	374	358	-0.9	26	167	156	149	-0.7	2.39	118	109	-0.9
68978	SUPERIOR	129	2413	2239	2124	-0.8	30	1129	1080	1034	-0.5	2.07	708	674	-0.5
68979	SUTTON	035	1828	1802	1790	-0.2	58	726	722	720	-0.1	2.45	518	513	-0.1
68980	TRUMBULL	035	407	403	400	-0.1	63	143	144	143	0.1	2.75	104	104	0.0
68981	UPLAND	061	272	234	217	-1.6	4	104	89	82	-1.7	2.61	75	65	-1.5
68982	WILCOX	099	560	537	522	-0.5	42	220	214	209	-0.3	2.40	165	160	-0.3
69001	MC COOK	145	9345	8833	8507	-0.6	37	3875	3729	3609	-0.4	2.30	2574	2465	-0.5
69020	BARTLEY	145	514	493	477	-0.4	49	193	187	181	-0.3	2.64	138	133	-0.4
69021	BENKELMAN	057	1510	1447	1418	-0.5	42	662	640	627	-0.4	2.16	424	407	-0.4
69022	CAMBRIDGE	065	1360	1292	1273	-0.6	37	596	573	564	-0.4	2.19	375	358	-0.5
69023	CHAMPION	029	569	514	488	-1.1	17	231	216	207	-0.7	2.38	174	162	-0.8
69024	CULBERTSON	087	1208	1180	1151	-0.3	54	487	488	480	0.0	2.42	363	362	0.0
69025	CURTIS	063	1212	1129	1080	-0.8	30	445	416	398	-0.7	2.39	282	262	-0.8
69026	DANBURY	145	251	218	205	-1.5	6	105	93	87	-1.3	2.34	81	72	-1.3
69027	ENDERS	029	212	193	183	-1.0	21	89	84	80	-0.6	2.26	64	60	-0.7
69028	EUSTIS	063	842	755	711	-1.2	13	341	309	292	-1.1	2.44	240	217	-1.1
69029	FARNAM	047	284	267	263	-0.7	34	120	112	110	-0.7	2.38	89	83	-0.8
69030	HAIGLER	057	418	384	369	-0.9	26	157	146	140	-0.8	2.54	114	106	-0.8
	NEBRASKA					0.6					0.8	2.46			0.7
	UNITED STATES					1.0					1.1	2.59			0.9

#	POST OFFICE NAME	RACE (%) White 2000	White 2009	Black 2000	Black 2009	Asian/Pacific 2000	Asian/Pacific 2009	% Hispanic Origin 2000	% Hispanic Origin 2009	2009 AGE DISTRIBUTION (%) 0-4	5-9	10-14	15-19	20-24	25-44	45-64	65-84	85+	18+	MEDIAN AGE 2009	% 2009 Males	% 2009 Females
68852	LITCHFIELD	99.6	99.4	0.0	0.0	0.0	0.0	0.9	1.3	5.6	6.7	6.3	6.5	4.0	19.8	32.5	15.4	3.1	77.1	45.6	49.6	50.4
68853	LOUP CITY	98.0	97.2	0.1	0.1	0.5	0.9	1.1	1.5	5.6	5.5	5.8	6.6	5.7	20.0	25.8	19.1	6.0	78.9	45.6	46.6	53.4
68854	MARQUETTE	98.5	98.4	0.1	0.1	0.1	0.1	1.1	1.1	6.7	8.1	8.7	7.6	3.7	22.4	30.5	10.9	1.4	71.1	39.6	52.9	47.1
68855	MASON CITY	98.3	98.2	0.0	0.0	0.0	0.0	1.0	1.4	7.5	7.5	7.7	7.3	4.8	22.4	27.9	12.9	2.0	72.8	39.4	50.6	49.4
68856	MERNA	99.0	98.8	0.1	0.1	0.1	0.2	0.8	1.1	4.9	6.1	6.6	7.3	4.3	21.2	32.6	14.6	2.3	77.7	44.6	51.8	48.2
68858	MILLER	100.0	100.0	0.0	0.0	0.0	0.0	0.0	0.3	6.2	6.8	6.8	6.8	4.3	23.6	31.7	11.8	1.9	75.8	41.3	55.0	45.0
68859	NORTH LOUP	97.9	97.2	0.0	0.0	0.0	0.0	1.2	2.1	5.1	6.1	6.6	7.0	4.6	20.1	30.7	16.7	3.0	77.6	45.3	51.4	48.6
68860	OCONTO	99.0	98.5	0.0	0.0	0.0	0.0	1.2	1.9	5.3	7.2	7.7	7.0	3.8	21.9	30.4	14.9	1.7	74.7	43.0	53.4	46.6
68861	ODESSA	96.9	94.3	0.0	0.0	0.8	1.3	4.6	7.6	7.0	7.0	8.3	7.6	5.1	24.2	31.8	8.3	0.6	72.6	37.8	49.7	50.3
68862	ORD	98.0	97.5	0.2	0.2	0.2	0.3	1.8	2.6	5.5	5.8	6.1	6.4	4.7	19.6	29.1	17.7	5.1	78.2	46.4	47.6	52.4
68863	OVERTON	94.7	91.1	0.2	0.3	0.2	0.4	6.3	10.7	6.7	7.2	7.6	7.6	4.4	23.7	29.7	11.3	1.8	73.7	40.0	54.2	45.8
68864	PALMER	98.5	97.8	0.1	0.1	0.1	0.2	1.6	2.5	5.5	6.1	6.5	7.5	4.8	21.8	28.8	15.7	3.2	76.4	43.1	49.0	51.0
68865	PHILLIPS	99.0	99.1	0.0	0.0	0.0	0.0	1.3	1.3	6.5	7.4	8.1	7.6	3.5	22.5	31.7	11.6	1.1	72.9	41.2	51.6	48.4
68866	PLEASANTON	98.8	98.5	0.1	0.1	0.2	0.3	0.9	1.4	6.0	6.6	7.0	6.8	4.3	23.1	30.0	14.5	1.6	76.2	42.0	51.7	48.3
68869	RAVENNA	98.8	98.3	0.0	0.0	0.2	0.3	0.8	1.2	6.1	6.2	6.5	7.4	5.7	22.5	26.8	14.4	4.4	76.6	41.6	47.4	52.6
68870	RIVERDALE	99.6	99.6	0.2	0.2	0.0	0.0	0.2	0.4	4.5	5.3	6.0	6.7	4.9	26.9	32.7	11.6	1.5	79.9	41.9	51.5	48.5
68871	ROCKVILLE	98.5	98.0	0.0	0.0	0.2	0.2	1.1	1.6	5.3	6.0	6.4	6.4	4.2	21.1	30.7	17.3	2.4	78.0	45.3	52.2	47.8
68872	SAINT LIBORY	98.5	98.1	0.1	0.1	0.0	0.0	1.3	1.9	7.6	7.8	8.1	7.3	4.3	24.0	28.1	11.5	1.3	71.8	39.6	51.5	48.5
68873	SAINT PAUL	99.0	98.8	0.3	0.4	0.1	0.2	0.8	1.2	6.7	6.8	6.9	7.2	4.9	22.4	25.2	15.8	4.1	74.9	41.3	49.9	50.1
68874	SARGENT	98.3	97.8	0.0	0.0	0.3	0.6	1.6	2.2	5.3	5.5	5.9	6.8	5.8	18.1	28.6	16.7	7.4	78.5	46.7	49.6	50.4
68875	SCOTIA	97.2	96.7	1.3	1.3	0.2	0.2	0.8	1.1	5.9	6.2	6.9	7.5	4.4	20.7	28.4	15.4	4.6	75.4	43.4	52.0	48.0
68876	SHELTON	91.5	87.8	0.6	0.6	0.0	0.0	12.5	18.3	7.9	7.7	7.9	7.9	5.5	23.2	26.8	11.0	2.0	71.2	37.7	50.8	49.2
68878	SUMNER	96.9	95.7	0.7	1.1	0.2	0.2	4.2	7.1	8.1	8.1	8.6	6.2	3.6	24.4	26.1	12.2	2.6	71.1	38.8	51.2	48.8
68879	TAYLOR	98.9	98.9	0.0	0.0	0.1	0.1	1.7	1.7	6.2	6.8	7.0	6.2	4.7	18.2	31.2	17.1	2.5	76.0	45.5	51.5	48.5
68881	WESTERVILLE	99.4	99.4	0.0	0.0	0.0	0.0	0.6	1.3	6.4	7.0	7.0	7.0	4.5	20.4	29.3	15.9	2.5	75.2	43.1	52.2	47.8
68882	WOLBACH	98.6	97.9	0.4	0.4	0.0	0.0	0.8	1.3	6.2	6.6	6.8	7.0	4.5	21.2	28.2	16.1	3.4	76.0	43.3	49.9	50.1
68883	WOOD RIVER	97.6	96.3	0.2	0.2	0.2	0.2	7.4	11.9	6.5	6.8	7.2	7.0	4.1	22.9	28.0	14.4	3.2	74.7	41.8	50.7	49.3
68901	HASTINGS	93.9	91.4	0.7	0.8	1.9	2.9	5.2	7.6	6.4	5.9	5.8	7.8	7.7	25.1	25.0	12.9	3.3	78.2	37.5	49.0	51.0
68920	ALMA	99.1	99.0	0.1	0.1	0.1	0.1	0.6	0.7	4.8	5.2	5.8	6.4	4.0	17.9	31.4	19.5	5.0	79.9	49.2	48.8	51.2
68922	ARAPAHOE	97.8	97.5	0.0	0.0	0.5	0.5	1.4	2.1	5.6	5.8	6.4	7.0	5.1	20.0	27.4	17.1	5.6	77.6	45.1	45.6	54.4
68923	ATLANTA	98.8	98.7	0.0	0.0	0.0	0.0	0.6	0.6	5.7	6.4	7.0	7.6	4.5	20.4	32.5	14.6	1.3	74.5	43.8	51.0	49.0
68924	AXTELL	98.1	97.6	0.2	0.2	0.3	0.4	1.5	2.2	6.6	7.2	7.8	7.3	4.3	24.9	30.6	9.7	1.6	72.8	39.0	52.3	47.7
68925	AYR	97.5	96.7	0.0	0.0	0.6	0.8	1.4	2.2	6.5	7.0	7.4	6.7	3.9	23.3	31.5	12.1	1.6	74.8	41.7	52.1	47.9
68926	BEAVER CITY	98.1	97.9	0.3	0.3	0.0	0.0	1.8	2.7	4.8	5.1	5.5	6.6	5.5	17.4	30.1	18.3	6.9	79.9	49.0	46.1	53.9
68927	BERTRAND	99.2	99.0	0.1	0.1	0.2	0.2	0.6	0.9	5.5	6.2	6.6	6.8	4.5	20.5	32.8	13.0	4.2	77.1	44.9	50.1	49.9
68928	BLADEN	98.7	98.6	0.0	0.0	0.4	0.4	0.2	0.4	7.4	7.6	7.8	8.0	4.3	21.3	28.3	13.9	1.4	72.1	40.9	50.4	49.6
68929	BLOOMINGTON	99.2	98.8	0.0	0.0	0.0	0.3	0.5	0.9	5.9	6.5	7.1	7.1	3.8	20.0	28.2	18.5	2.9	76.2	44.8	50.0	50.0
68930	BLUE HILL	98.0	97.4	0.2	0.2	0.5	0.7	0.7	1.0	5.6	5.6	6.0	6.9	4.8	19.9	28.6	17.6	5.1	78.3	45.8	47.9	52.1
68932	CAMPBELL	98.8	98.5	0.0	0.0	0.0	0.0	0.4	0.5	5.8	6.3	6.3	5.6	3.4	23.2	25.9	17.7	5.8	77.7	44.5	48.9	51.1
68933	CLAY CENTER	96.7	96.7	0.5	0.5	0.7	0.7	2.5	2.4	6.5	7.0	7.0	6.7	5.1	20.6	31.0	14.5	1.8	75.1	42.5	49.0	51.0
68934	DEWEESE	98.2	98.2	0.0	0.0	0.7	0.7	0.7	0.4	6.8	6.8	7.1	6.0	4.3	25.6	30.6	11.0	1.8	75.4	40.6	51.2	48.8
68935	EDGAR	98.4	98.4	0.3	0.3	0.1	0.1	0.9	1.0	5.6	6.2	6.3	6.2	3.6	21.6	27.4	18.4	4.8	77.5	45.4	50.8	49.2
68936	EDISON	97.9	97.6	0.0	0.0	0.4	0.4	0.7	1.2	6.3	6.7	7.1	5.5	3.5	19.7	31.5	16.9	2.8	76.0	45.8	51.6	48.4
68937	ELWOOD	98.4	97.8	0.0	0.0	0.2	0.4	2.1	3.4	4.8	5.3	5.7	6.4	4.0	19.4	31.7	18.6	4.1	79.7	47.5	50.4	49.6
68938	FAIRFIELD	98.8	98.7	0.2	0.2	0.0	0.0	1.2	1.1	5.6	6.5	6.8	6.9	5.2	21.5	31.3	13.7	2.6	76.9	43.2	50.0	50.0
68939	FRANKLIN	99.5	99.4	0.0	0.0	0.1	0.2	0.8	1.1	5.2	5.5	5.6	6.5	4.8	17.8	27.9	19.9	6.8	78.7	48.1	45.2	54.8
68940	FUNK	98.1	97.4	0.0	0.0	0.4	0.4	1.5	2.4	5.6	7.6	7.6	7.6	4.2	23.5	31.0	11.9	1.2	74.2	40.7	52.3	47.7
68941	GLENVIL	98.6	98.6	0.0	0.0	0.4	0.4	0.5	0.7	6.0	6.1	6.5	6.7	4.3	24.6	31.8	12.2	1.8	77.3	42.1	51.0	49.0
68942	GUIDE ROCK	98.5	98.3	0.2	0.2	0.2	0.2	0.0	0.0	4.8	5.0	5.0	4.8	4.1	18.0	34.1	20.4	3.8	81.8	49.7	51.3	48.7
68943	HARDY	98.5	97.8	0.0	0.0	0.2	0.6	1.2	2.0	5.6	5.6	6.2	6.5	4.5	21.9	31.2	16.0	2.5	78.7	44.7	50.6	49.4
68944	HARVARD	96.9	96.8	0.1	0.1	0.1	0.1	7.0	7.3	5.9	6.8	7.4	8.0	4.1	22.6	29.4	13.3	2.5	74.5	41.5	49.3	50.7
68945	HEARTWELL	95.7	93.2	0.0	0.0	0.4	0.9	3.8	5.9	5.9	6.3	7.2	7.2	3.6	23.0	31.5	13.5	1.8	75.7	42.5	51.8	48.2
68946	HENDLEY	98.4	98.3	0.0	0.0	0.0	0.0	1.6	1.7	6.4	7.0	7.6	7.0	3.5	23.8	29.1	14.0	1.7	74.4	41.3	52.9	47.1
68947	HILDRETH	99.2	98.9	0.0	0.0	0.0	0.0	0.6	1.1	5.6	5.9	6.5	6.7	4.5	22.1	32.1	14.3	2.4	78.1	44.2	51.0	49.0
68948	HOLBROOK	98.0	97.5	0.0	0.0	0.3	0.3	1.1	1.6	6.3	6.9	6.9	5.6	3.8	22.3	28.5	17.2	2.5	76.2	43.6	51.7	48.3
68949	HOLDREGE	97.4	96.6	0.1	0.2	0.3	0.3	2.8	4.2	6.4	6.6	6.8	6.5	5.4	22.3	27.3	14.6	4.2	76.0	41.7	48.5	51.5
68950	HOLSTEIN	98.8	97.7	0.0	0.2	0.0	0.2	1.2	2.1	6.7	7.1	7.3	6.9	4.4	22.9	30.5	12.2	2.1	74.8	41.4	52.8	47.2
68952	INAVALE	98.5	98.3	0.0	0.0	0.4	0.4	0.0	0.0	5.1	5.1	5.5	5.5	3.8	18.6	32.1	21.1	3.4	80.6	48.9	51.1	48.9
68954	INLAND	97.3	97.3	0.0	0.0	0.0	0.0	6.2	6.3	7.1	7.1	7.1	7.1	4.5	22.3	28.6	13.4	2.7	74.1	40.7	49.1	50.9
68955	JUNIATA	98.7	98.2	0.2	0.4	0.1	0.2	0.9	1.5	6.9	7.1	7.6	7.7	5.8	23.4	30.8	9.5	1.2	73.4	38.2	49.5	50.5
68956	KENESAW	98.9	98.5	0.0	0.0	0.0	0.0	1.3	2.0	6.3	7.0	7.6	7.1	3.6	22.8	28.4	13.9	3.4	73.7	42.2	50.9	49.1
68957	LAWRENCE	99.0	98.6	0.0	0.0	0.0	0.0	0.7	1.0	6.2	7.0	6.6	6.0	4.7	19.0	30.7	17.1	2.7	76.5	45.3	53.0	47.0
68958	LOOMIS	98.8	98.3	0.0	0.0	0.2	0.2	0.9	1.4	6.0	6.8	7.3	7.6	4.6	21.4	30.7	13.5	2.1	74.5	42.1	51.0	49.0
68959	MINDEN	97.9	97.2	0.1	0.1	0.2	0.3	2.6	3.8	5.9	6.1	6.3	6.4	5.0	22.9	27.9	14.8	4.6	77.3	42.9	48.8	51.2
68960	NAPONEE	99.4	98.9	0.0	0.0	0.0	0.4	0.6	0.7	5.6	6.7	7.0	7.0	3.9	20.1	29.6	18.0	2.1	76.4	44.8	51.8	48.2
68961	NELSON	99.1	98.8	0.0	0.0	0.1	0.1	1.1	1.8	4.6	5.0	5.3	5.8	4.6	20.9	31.0	17.7	5.1	80.9	47.2	50.9	49.1
68964	OAK	99.3	99.1	0.0	0.0	0.0	0.0	1.1	1.7	4.3	5.1	5.1	6.0	4.3	21.4	30.8	17.5	5.6	80.8	47.3	50.4	49.6
68966	ORLEANS	98.3	98.0	0.3	0.3	0.1	0.2	1.0	1.4	4.7	5.2	5.5	6.1	4.1	19.6	33.5	17.9	3.4	80.7	48.1	50.6	49.4
68967	OXFORD	98.3	97.7	0.0	0.0	0.2	0.3	0.8	1.2	6.0	6.6	7.0	6.0	4.2	19.6	31.4	16.2	2.9	76.3	45.3	51.5	48.5
68969	RAGAN	99.0	98.9	0.0	0.0	0.0	0.0	1.0	1.1	5.5	6.6	6.6	6.6	5.5	18.7	33.0	15.4	2.2	76.9	45.3	52.7	47.3
68970	RED CLOUD	97.8	97.3	0.1	0.1	0.7	1.2	0.7	1.1	5.0	5.3	5.7	6.1	4.5	17.5	30.5	19.3	6.1	79.6	48.6	49.6	50.4
68971	REPUBLICAN CITY	99.6	99.4	0.0	0.0	0.0	0.0	0.6	0.6	4.8	5.5	5.9	6.5	4.2	17.8	31.9	18.7	4.8	79.7	48.8	49.3	50.7
68972	RIVERTON	99.2	99.1	0.0	0.0	0.0	0.0	0.8	0.9	5.8	6.7	6.7	7.1	4.0	19.1	28.4	19.1	3.1	75.6	45.4	49.8	50.2
68973	ROSELAND	97.7	96.6	0.0	0.0	0.5	0.9	1.4	2.2	6.6	7.3	7.5	6.8	3.9	23.3	31.0	11.8	1.6	74.2	41.2	52.2	47.8
68974	RUSKIN	98.3	97.6	0.0	0.0	0.3	0.4	1.4	2.0	5.2	5.6	6.0	6.8	4.4	21.9	32.3	15.5	2.4	78.9	45.1	51.4	48.6
68975	SARONVILLE	97.3	97.3	0.0	0.0	0.0	0.0	3.6	3.6	4.1	7.3	9.5	10.0	2.3	25.9	30.0	10.5	0.5	70.9	40.8	52.3	47.7
68976	SMITHFIELD	99.3	99.2	0.0	0.0	0.3	0.4	0.7	1.2	5.3	6.2	6.2	5.3	3.7	19.8	32.1	18.9	2.5	78.6	47.2	51.0	49.0
68977	STAMFORD	99.0	98.1	0.0	0.0	0.0	0.3	1.2	1.9	5.6	6.1	6.7	7.0	5.1	20.3	32.9	13.9	2.4	77.0	44.3	52.1	47.9
68978	SUPERIOR	98.9	98.3	0.0	0.0	0.2	0.4	1.0	1.4	5.5	5.6	5.6	5.4	5.4	18.7	28.4	20.8	4.6	79.6	47.7	46.8	53.2
68979	SUTTON	98.0	97.9	0.1	0.1	0.3	0.3	3.2	3.4	6.3	6.5	6.8	7.1	4.8	20.3	28.1	15.8	4.3	75.5	43.5	48.0	52.0
68980	TRUMBULL	97.1	97.0	0.0	0.0	0.0	0.0	7.4	7.4	6.5	6.9	6.9	7.4	4.5	21.8	29.5	13.6	2.7	74.7	41.7	49.4	50.6
68981	UPLAND	98.9	98.7	0.0	0.0	0.0	0.0	0.7	0.9	5.6	6.0	6.4	6.8	4.3	21.4	32.9	14.1	2.6	77.8	44.7	51.3	48.7
68982	WILCOX	98.4	97.8	0.2	0.2	0.2	0.4	1.3	1.9	6.5	7.1	7.6	7.4	4.5	24.2	30.9	10.1	1.7	73.2	39.5	52.3	47.7
69001	MC COOK	97.4	96.6	0.1	0.2	0.2	0.3	2.6	3.9	6.2	6.1	6.4	7.0	5.4	22.6	27.2	15.5	3.6	77.4	41.5	48.0	52.0
69020	BARTLEY	97.9	97.0	0.4	0.4	0.2	0.4	1.8	2.8	5.9	6.3	6.7	7.3	5.1	21.9	29.0	15.8	2.0	76.5	42.6	50.1	49.9
69021	BENKELMAN	97.4	96.5	0.0	0.0	0.7	1.1	1.7	2.6	4.7	5.5	5.7	5.5	4.3	19.8	31.4	17.5	5.6	80.5	47.9	47.3	52.7
69022	CAMBRIDGE	98.8	98.5	0.0	0.0	0.1	0.2	0.7	1.0	5.0	5.5	5.9	6.2	4.9	20.1	28.4	18.6	5.4	79.6	46.9	49.1	50.9
69023	CHAMPION	98.2	97.5	0.2	0.2	0.0	0.0	1.2	1.9	5.3	5.1	8.0	7.2	3.3	21.4	34.4	13.4	1.9	76.5	44.8	50.4	49.6
69024	CULBERTSON	98.4	98.3	0.2	0.2	0.1	0.1	1.5	2.2	5.4	5.8	6.0	6.4	5.0	20.4	31.5	16.5	3.0	78.9	45.6	49.9	50.1
69025	CURTIS	97.6	97.1	0.2	0.2	0.3	0.5	1.1	1.5	5.8	5.7	5.3	11.2	7.8	23.6	23.4	12.7	4.5	78.7	34.6	47.7	52.3
69026	DANBURY	99.6	99.5	0.0	0.0	0.0	0.0	0.4	0.5	5.5	6.4	6.4	6.4	5.0	17.9	31.2	19.3	1.8	77.1	46.2	47.7	52.3
69027	ENDERS	97.6	96.9	0.0	0.0	0.0	0.0	1.9	3.1	4.7	5.2	6.7	6.2	3.6	21.2	33.2	15.5	3.6	79.3	46.4	49.2	50.8
69028	EUSTIS	99.0	98.5	0.0	0.0	0.2	0.4	1.1	1.6	5.3	6.2	6.5	6.2	4.6	20.8	32.8	15.2	2.3	78.1	45.2	51.8	48.2
69029	FARNAM	98.2	97.0	0.0	0.0	0.0	0.0	1.4	3.0	6.0	6.4	6.7	6.4	4.1	21.7	33.3	13.9	1.5	76.8	43.9	52.4	47.6
69030	HAIGLER	95.9	94.5	0.0	0.0	0.2	0.3	7.7	11.5	5.7	7.0	7.0	6.8	4.4	22.9	32.0	12.2	1.8	75.5	41.9	54.2	45.8
	NEBRASKA	89.6	86.9	4.0	4.4	1.3	2.1	5.5	7.9	6.9	6.8	6.8	7.3	6.9	26.3	25.7	11.0	2.3	75.3	36.5	49.4	50.6
	UNITED STATES	75.1	72.0	12.3	12.7	3.8	4.6	12.5	15.7	6.8	6.7	6.6	7.1	6.9	27.0	26.0	10.9	1.9	75.7	36.9	49.2	50.8

ZIP CODE #	POST OFFICE NAME	2009 Per Capita Income	2009 HH Income Base	2009 Household Income Distribution (%) Less than $25,000	$25,000 to $49,999	$50,000 to $99,999	$100,000 to $149,999	$150,000 or More	Median Household Income 2009	2014	2009 National Centile	2009 State Centile	2009 Home Value Base	2009 Home Value Distribution (%) Less than $50,000	$50,000 to $89,999	$90,000 to $174,999	$175,000 to $399,999	$400,000 or More	2009 Median Home Value
68852	LITCHFIELD	17044	217	32.3	42.9	22.1	0.5	2.3	36127	37052	21	25	182	44.5	23.6	20.3	7.7	3.8	59091
68853	LOUP CITY	17385	650	38.5	34.5	24.2	2.3	0.6	29920	31477	8	4	500	40.2	35.6	19.0	3.8	1.4	59423
68854	MARQUETTE	21664	306	16.7	32.0	41.5	8.2	1.6	50911	50358	63	82	234	21.8	18.8	32.1	21.8	5.6	108088
68855	MASON CITY	19433	179	24.6	36.3	34.1	3.4	1.7	41669	44656	38	56	140	37.1	20.0	20.7	14.3	7.9	70000
68856	MERNA	19517	344	27.0	37.5	30.2	3.2	2.0	40525	43413	34	49	256	30.9	23.8	28.5	11.3	5.5	80000
68858	MILLER	19578	134	25.4	31.3	36.6	4.5	2.2	44381	48200	46	66	92	28.3	12.0	35.9	21.7	2.2	113636
68859	NORTH LOUP	16403	230	34.3	44.8	17.8	1.7	1.3	31099	30726	10	6	173	43.9	20.2	26.0	7.5	2.3	62273
68860	OCONTO	18760	200	31.0	35.5	28.5	3.5	1.5	40407	41250	34	48	145	34.5	11.0	33.8	11.7	9.0	101563
68861	ODESSA	26264	65	13.8	30.8	46.2	7.7	1.5	54504	53532	70	88	54	11.1	13.0	27.8	38.9	9.3	170000
68862	ORD	17825	1350	33.9	35.2	27.0	2.7	1.3	33552	35083	14	13	1019	36.2	29.8	27.6	5.4	1.0	67800
68863	OVERTON	17680	471	27.4	37.6	29.5	4.5	1.1	40746	44207	35	50	340	22.9	31.8	34.4	8.8	2.1	84839
68864	PALMER	17624	388	24.5	41.5	30.2	2.8	1.0	39099	42496	30	39	300	25.7	28.3	27.7	12.7	5.7	83333
68865	PHILLIPS	21160	383	15.7	37.3	38.1	6.0	2.9	47460	47934	55	76	308	28.2	20.1	36.0	14.3	1.3	93125
68866	PLEASANTON	18245	395	23.0	34.7	39.0	3.0	0.3	44136	47798	46	65	318	18.2	19.8	39.3	17.3	5.3	112273
68869	RAVENNA	19009	882	27.1	37.2	31.7	2.8	1.1	39876	43806	32	44	671	22.2	29.5	37.0	8.8	2.5	87500
68870	RIVERDALE	22628	209	13.9	30.6	47.8	4.8	2.9	54498	53729	70	87	171	11.1	15.2	33.9	33.9	5.8	142361
68871	ROCKVILLE	16746	186	27.4	48.9	19.9	2.2	1.6	36309	37308	21	26	151	33.8	26.5	25.2	10.6	4.0	76818
68872	SAINT LIBORY	17555	341	21.1	39.0	34.9	3.2	1.8	44219	45567	46	66	270	13.3	12.6	49.6	20.4	4.1	119203
68873	SAINT PAUL	20462	1356	28.4	31.3	32.8	5.3	2.1	41130	43367	36	52	1002	16.0	26.9	38.3	15.3	3.5	101786
68874	SARGENT	15592	356	36.5	41.3	19.9	1.7	0.6	30991	31946	10	5	277	62.1	18.8	14.1	3.6	1.4	36618
68875	SCOTIA	16203	252	34.1	37.7	25.8	2.0	0.4	34061	35257	16	16	194	44.8	27.3	17.0	6.7	4.1	55263
68876	SHELTON	18574	716	23.7	36.3	33.8	4.2	2.0	44095	46393	46	65	538	16.9	30.5	37.4	13.8	1.5	94242
68878	SUMNER	18611	184	26.6	39.1	28.8	2.7	2.7	37944	41959	27	35	138	36.2	25.4	23.2	12.3	2.9	75000
68879	TAYLOR	14662	297	38.7	40.1	18.2	2.4	0.7	30256	30888	8	4	233	39.9	19.7	15.5	15.0	9.9	67500
68881	WESTERVILLE	18772	60	30.0	38.3	26.7	1.7	3.3	37819	37963	26	33	44	40.9	20.5	20.5	13.6	4.5	60000
68882	WOLBACH	17971	205	32.2	39.5	23.9	3.4	1.0	35688	36123	20	23	162	37.0	25.9	20.4	9.9	6.8	69167
68883	WOOD RIVER	20808	948	24.1	32.4	36.7	4.3	2.5	45398	48704	49	69	688	16.0	24.7	39.1	16.6	3.6	103448
68901	HASTINGS	23543	11085	21.3	30.7	38.0	6.9	3.1	48359	50981	57	78	7202	10.9	22.0	48.2	17.0	2.0	110144
68920	ALMA	17985	626	32.9	38.3	24.6	2.6	1.6	34475	34695	16	17	508	41.3	28.3	22.0	7.9	0.4	62500
68922	ARAPAHOE	19007	628	30.3	38.7	25.2	4.1	1.8	35956	36605	20	25	479	37.8	26.5	27.6	7.3	0.8	65192
68923	ATLANTA	21325	64	21.9	35.9	34.4	6.3	1.6	43889	47839	45	64	50	18.0	28.0	44.0	8.0	2.0	95000
68924	AXTELL	18024	416	22.1	34.6	36.5	4.6	2.2	44319	46593	46	66	313	20.8	22.7	37.4	14.7	4.5	102744
68925	AYR	20340	193	18.1	34.2	42.0	3.1	2.6	47990	50469	57	77	153	16.3	19.6	37.3	20.9	5.9	115441
68926	BEAVER CITY	19208	315	33.3	38.1	23.5	3.2	1.9	32899	32984	13	10	250	52.0	30.8	12.8	3.2	1.2	47917
68927	BERTRAND	19522	480	23.3	37.9	31.7	4.6	2.5	42307	44554	40	60	373	20.1	34.0	31.6	11.8	2.4	84464
68928	BLADEN	18382	191	22.0	40.8	30.9	4.2	2.1	41860	46763	39	57	158	33.5	25.3	32.3	7.0	1.9	73636
68929	BLOOMINGTON	16653	145	37.2	39.3	18.6	2.8	2.1	32889	32531	13	10	118	55.1	22.9	13.6	6.8	1.7	43333
68930	BLUE HILL	18365	547	29.3	32.7	32.7	3.7	1.6	39619	42376	32	43	435	22.1	32.2	34.3	10.3	1.1	84714
68932	CAMPBELL	16788	162	30.9	42.6	21.6	3.1	1.9	33783	38648	15	15	133	52.6	19.5	21.1	5.3	1.5	47500
68933	CLAY CENTER	19851	434	26.7	32.5	32.9	5.5	2.3	41818	43798	39	57	337	28.8	25.8	37.4	7.7	0.3	84464
68934	DEWEESE	18996	113	23.9	40.7	31.9	1.8	1.8	42327	43962	40	60	87	31.0	28.7	29.9	10.3	0.0	75000
68935	EDGAR	20688	310	27.7	37.4	29.7	3.5	1.6	41390	43206	37	54	236	37.7	30.1	24.2	7.6	0.4	62414
68936	EDISON	17729	98	28.6	35.7	31.6	3.1	1.0	36290	38902	21	26	74	44.6	31.1	20.3	1.4	2.7	53636
68937	ELWOOD	22354	854	23.7	35.1	34.2	4.4	2.6	43417	45076	44	63	663	15.8	24.9	42.2	15.4	1.7	103208
68938	FAIRFIELD	18961	245	27.8	37.1	28.6	4.9	1.6	38031	41145	27	35	196	31.1	38.3	23.0	7.7	0.0	70000
68939	FRANKLIN	17902	528	35.2	41.3	19.5	2.3	1.7	32030	32861	11	8	428	46.5	30.4	19.4	3.7	0.0	55172
68940	FUNK	19669	189	19.6	34.9	37.0	7.4	1.1	46040	47881	51	72	134	15.7	22.4	41.0	15.7	5.2	108333
68941	GLENVIL	18893	282	23.8	38.3	32.6	2.5	2.8	42557	44440	41	61	214	28.0	22.9	29.4	15.9	3.7	88333
68942	GUIDE ROCK	19475	207	39.6	40.6	15.9	2.4	1.4	29610	30699	7	3	164	54.9	18.3	15.9	8.5	2.4	43846
68943	HARDY	16859	140	30.7	42.9	20.0	5.0	1.4	36014	37541	21	25	114	55.3	14.9	18.4	10.5	0.9	42500
68944	HARVARD	18166	524	26.9	36.6	29.8	4.6	2.1	39434	41532	31	41	409	34.7	26.7	31.5	5.6	1.5	68448
68945	HEARTWELL	21656	88	22.7	30.7	37.5	5.7	3.4	46869	47866	54	74	66	18.2	19.7	40.9	19.7	1.5	111364
68946	HENDLEY	18532	64	25.0	42.2	28.1	3.1	1.6	40000	41136	33	46	48	35.4	27.1	20.8	10.4	6.3	75000
68947	HILDRETH	21941	228	23.7	34.2	34.2	5.3	2.6	43308	47467	43	63	182	35.7	28.0	22.0	9.3	4.9	67692
68948	HOLBROOK	19364	138	33.3	35.5	23.9	5.1	2.2	35000	35276	18	20	115	46.1	25.2	19.1	7.8	1.7	55000
68949	HOLDREGE	23809	2626	23.0	30.1	36.7	6.7	3.4	47111	49071	54	75	1926	15.6	33.2	41.8	8.3	1.1	91326
68950	HOLSTEIN	21689	168	21.4	33.3	35.7	5.4	4.2	46770	48815	53	74	129	18.6	24.0	31.8	21.7	3.9	106250
68952	INAVALE	15497	96	40.6	40.6	14.6	2.1	2.1	29409	30000	7	3	77	58.4	18.2	14.3	7.8	1.3	39375
68954	INLAND	19058	45	26.7	37.8	28.9	4.4	2.2	39288	42343	31	40	35	34.3	28.6	34.3	2.9	0.0	68333
68955	JUNIATA	18939	619	17.8	38.8	37.6	4.0	1.8	45445	47666	50	69	513	12.5	16.6	42.1	28.1	0.8	124851
68956	KENESAW	19087	463	20.7	35.9	38.4	3.7	1.3	45681	48239	50	71	363	16.8	27.3	41.3	14.3	0.3	97414
68957	LAWRENCE	16978	218	33.0	42.7	21.1	1.4	1.8	31702	34242	11	7	188	50.0	23.9	19.1	6.9	0.0	50000
68958	LOOMIS	20988	250	20.8	34.4	37.2	6.4	1.2	45603	47203	50	70	190	18.4	26.3	40.0	11.6	3.7	97143
68959	MINDEN	21307	1615	20.6	33.2	39.7	5.4	1.1	46950	47521	54	75	1201	11.9	29.6	45.7	12.0	0.7	100052
68960	NAPONEE	16239	120	38.3	40.0	18.3	2.5	0.8	31978	31114	11	7	98	58.2	20.4	13.3	6.1	2.0	39167
68961	NELSON	18818	378	27.0	45.2	24.1	3.4	0.3	38223	40493	27	36	301	49.8	24.6	16.9	7.3	1.3	50238
68964	OAK	17794	98	27.6	45.9	22.4	4.1	0.0	37950	41115	27	35	78	50.0	24.4	16.7	7.7	1.3	50000
68966	ORLEANS	18284	278	33.5	34.9	27.0	2.2	2.5	34377	34911	16	17	216	42.1	23.1	24.5	9.7	0.5	63000
68967	OXFORD	19254	494	27.9	36.0	31.0	3.2	1.8	37465	41293	25	32	378	43.1	29.1	21.2	3.4	3.2	56190
68969	RAGAN	17559	35	28.6	34.3	31.4	2.9	2.9	39059	43636	30	39	28	28.6	39.3	21.4	7.1	3.6	65000
68970	RED CLOUD	18462	673	33.3	40.3	23.3	2.4	0.7	33876	34192	15	15	507	47.7	31.2	16.8	3.7	0.6	52018
68971	REPUBLICAN CITY	20391	228	32.0	39.5	24.1	2.6	1.8	35000	35615	18	20	187	40.1	29.9	21.4	8.0	0.5	63462
68972	RIVERTON	15252	93	41.9	40.9	16.1	1.1	0.0	29032	30307	7	2	76	56.6	22.4	11.8	7.9	1.3	41667
68973	ROSELAND	21513	222	17.1	34.2	42.8	3.2	2.7	48830	50175	59	79	177	15.3	20.9	40.1	19.8	4.0	111500
68974	RUSKIN	17652	104	29.8	43.3	21.2	5.8	0.0	36806	38609	23	29	84	54.8	14.3	17.9	11.9	1.2	43333
68975	SARONVILLE	16883	79	25.3	43.0	25.3	6.3	0.0	41077	42021	36	52	60	21.7	26.7	43.3	8.3	0.0	93333
68976	SMITHFIELD	21705	105	21.9	38.1	31.4	5.7	2.9	41390	44204	37	54	80	21.3	28.8	30.0	13.8	6.3	90000
68977	STAMFORD	19380	156	26.9	35.9	32.1	3.2	1.9	40402	44607	34	47	124	33.1	33.1	22.6	7.3	4.0	65000
68978	SUPERIOR	19789	1080	36.7	39.6	19.8	1.9	2.0	32394	34058	12	9	841	49.1	25.2	23.2	2.5	0.0	51087
68979	SUTTON	20168	722	24.5	37.0	31.3	5.1	2.1	41109	43000	36	52	568	21.7	28.7	37.9	10.9	0.9	89565
68980	TRUMBULL	17166	144	26.4	35.4	31.3	4.9	2.1	39485	41441	31	42	113	36.3	26.5	30.1	6.2	0.9	65625
68981	UPLAND	19442	89	25.8	34.8	32.6	4.5	2.2	41755	46974	39	57	71	39.4	26.8	21.1	8.5	4.2	63000
68982	WILCOX	21150	214	22.4	35.0	36.4	4.2	1.9	43697	46702	44	64	162	21.6	24.1	37.7	13.0	3.7	97778
69001	MC COOK	20391	3729	28.5	34.0	31.0	5.1	1.3	40193	42131	33	46	2592	22.6	32.1	35.9	9.0	0.3	84896
69020	BARTLEY	15756	187	30.5	39.0	27.3	2.1	1.1	36325	38111	21	27	146	44.5	36.3	17.8	1.4	0.0	55333
69021	BENKELMAN	18681	640	37.2	31.6	26.1	3.6	1.6	32385	33454	12	9	479	47.4	24.4	17.7	6.3	4.2	52907
69022	CAMBRIDGE	21826	573	32.6	35.4	24.4	4.4	3.1	37439	38193	25	32	430	43.3	24.2	22.1	9.5	0.9	61111
69023	CHAMPION	18367	216	30.6	38.0	25.5	4.6	1.4	37643	38446	26	33	157	31.2	29.3	26.1	8.3	5.1	72273
69024	CULBERTSON	17914	488	33.2	33.4	27.3	4.7	1.4	35983	38331	21	25	395	40.5	39.0	15.4	4.3	0.8	57653
69025	CURTIS	16753	416	31.3	38.5	27.2	2.2	1.0	33913	36039	15	16	276	37.3	35.5	19.9	4.3	2.9	62500
69026	DANBURY	19104	93	32.3	34.4	29.0	3.2	1.1	40960	42326	36	51	73	46.6	30.1	20.5	2.7	0.0	55000
69027	ENDERS	18295	84	34.5	36.9	22.6	4.8	1.2	35000	38174	18	20	64	37.5	29.7	21.9	6.3	4.7	63333
69028	EUSTIS	21751	309	26.2	36.2	28.8	4.9	3.9	40504	41073	34	49	248	24.2	27.0	36.7	10.5	1.6	88125
69029	FARNAM	21862	112	19.6	40.2	33.0	4.5	2.7	41513	44302	38	55	78	20.5	20.5	32.1	19.2	7.7	110417
69030	HAIGLER	16966	146	34.2	34.9	24.7	4.8	1.4	33282	33764	14	12	99	49.5	23.2	23.2	2.0	2.0	50625
	NEBRASKA	24998		20.5	28.3	37.5	9.0	4.6	50953	53316				15.1	21.8	43.3	17.4	2.4	109174
	UNITED STATES	27277		20.9	24.4	35.3	11.7	7.6	54719	56938				9.3	13.1	31.6	32.6	13.5	162279

SPENDING POTENTIAL INDICES

ZIP CODE # POST OFFICE NAME	FINANCIAL SERVICES				THE HOME						ENTERTAINMENT						PERSONAL			
					Home Improvements		Furnishings													
	Auto Loan	Home Loan	Investments	Retirement Plans	Home Repair	Lawn & Garden	Computers & Hardware-Personal	Major Appliances	TV, Radio, Sound Equipment	Furniture	Dine out/Carry out	Sports Equipment	Fees & Tickets	Toys & Games	Travel	Cable TV	Apparel & Services	Auto Repairs	Health Insurance	Pets & Supplies
68852 LITCHFIELD	73	50	80	50	53	77	56	69	58	45	57	57	41	57	55	63	37	65	73	85
68853 LOUP CITY	64	46	66	45	48	67	50	62	55	44	54	48	40	54	49	61	36	58	67	74
68854 MARQUETTE	102	70	112	70	73	107	78	97	81	63	80	80	57	79	77	88	52	90	102	119
68855 MASON CITY	86	59	94	59	62	90	65	81	68	53	67	67	48	67	65	74	44	76	86	100
68856 MERNA	86	59	95	59	62	91	66	82	69	53	68	68	48	67	66	75	44	76	86	101
68858 MILLER	84	58	92	58	61	89	64	80	67	52	66	66	47	66	64	73	43	75	84	98
68859 NORTH LOUP	67	46	74	46	48	71	51	64	53	42	53	53	38	52	51	58	34	60	67	79
68860 OCONTO	79	54	87	54	57	83	60	75	63	49	62	62	44	61	60	68	40	70	79	92
68861 ODESSA	88	100	86	102	97	98	89	92	87	89	88	72	95	90	94	88	61	89	91	109
68862 ORD	70	50	74	49	52	74	55	68	59	47	58	53	42	58	54	65	38	63	73	81
68863 OVERTON	82	56	90	56	59	86	62	78	65	51	64	64	46	64	62	71	42	72	82	95
68864 PALMER	80	55	87	55	57	84	61	76	63	49	62	62	45	62	60	69	41	71	80	93
68865 PHILLIPS	101	70	111	69	73	107	77	96	80	63	79	79	57	79	77	88	51	90	101	118
68866 PLEASANTON	86	59	94	59	62	90	65	81	68	53	67	67	48	67	65	74	44	76	86	100
68869 RAVENNA	79	56	81	55	58	83	62	76	67	54	65	59	48	66	60	74	43	71	82	91
68870 RIVERDALE	87	90	86	93	89	95	83	89	83	81	83	70	85	84	87	84	57	85	89	106
68871 ROCKVILLE	72	50	80	50	52	76	55	69	58	45	57	57	41	56	55	63	37	64	73	85
68872 SAINT LIBORY	91	62	100	62	65	96	69	86	72	56	71	71	51	71	69	79	46	80	91	106
68873 SAINT PAUL	81	62	80	62	65	83	68	78	72	61	70	60	57	71	66	77	47	75	84	93
68874 SARGENT	62	44	63	43	46	65	48	59	53	42	51	46	38	52	47	58	34	55	64	71
68875 SCOTIA	69	47	76	47	50	73	53	65	55	43	54	54	39	54	52	60	35	61	69	81
68876 SHELTON	91	64	83	63	65	89	68	81	74	63	73	64	53	76	64	81	49	77	86	99
68878 SUMNER	84	58	93	58	61	89	65	80	67	52	66	66	47	66	64	73	43	75	85	99
68879 TAYLOR	64	44	70	44	46	67	49	61	51	40	50	50	36	50	49	55	33	57	64	75
68881 WESTERVILLE	88	60	96	60	63	93	67	83	70	54	69	69	49	68	67	76	45	78	88	103
68882 WOLBACH	73	50	80	50	52	77	56	69	58	45	57	57	41	57	55	63	37	65	73	85
68883 WOOD RIVER	95	65	104	65	68	100	73	90	75	59	75	75	53	74	72	82	48	84	95	111
68901 HASTINGS	81	80	73	81	78	85	82	81	84	79	83	62	81	84	80	86	57	82	88	97
68920 ALMA	72	53	85	52	57	76	56	70	59	48	58	55	44	57	58	63	38	65	72	85
68922 ARAPAHOE	74	53	75	52	55	77	58	71	64	51	62	54	46	63	56	70	41	67	78	84
68923 ATLANTA	93	64	103	64	67	99	71	89	74	58	73	73	52	73	71	81	48	83	94	109
68924 AXTELL	93	64	102	64	67	98	71	88	74	58	73	73	52	72	71	81	47	82	93	109
68925 AYR	96	66	106	66	69	102	74	91	76	60	76	76	54	75	73	83	49	85	97	112
68926 BEAVER CITY	72	51	73	50	53	75	56	69	62	49	60	53	44	61	55	68	40	65	75	82
68927 BERTRAND	91	62	99	62	65	96	69	86	72	56	71	71	51	71	69	78	46	80	91	106
68928 BLADEN	84	58	92	58	60	88	64	80	67	52	66	66	47	65	64	73	43	74	84	98
68929 BLOOMINGTON	69	47	75	47	50	73	53	65	55	43	54	54	39	54	52	60	35	61	69	80
68930 BLUE HILL	79	56	81	55	58	82	61	76	67	53	65	58	48	66	60	74	43	71	82	90
68932 CAMPBELL	73	50	80	50	52	77	56	69	58	45	57	57	41	57	55	63	37	64	73	85
68933 CLAY CENTER	90	64	93	62	67	92	67	84	73	61	72	64	53	73	66	80	47	78	88	101
68934 DEWEESE	84	58	93	58	61	89	65	80	67	52	66	66	47	66	64	73	43	75	85	99
68935 EDGAR	85	59	94	59	61	90	65	81	68	53	67	67	48	66	65	74	43	76	86	100
68936 EDISON	81	56	89	55	58	85	62	77	64	50	63	63	45	63	61	70	41	72	81	94
68937 ELWOOD	91	66	105	65	70	96	71	88	74	60	73	70	54	71	72	80	47	82	91	107
68938 FAIRFIELD	86	59	94	59	62	91	66	81	68	53	67	67	48	67	65	74	44	76	86	100
68939 FRANKLIN	70	50	74	49	52	74	55	68	59	47	57	53	42	58	53	65	38	63	73	81
68940 FUNK	94	64	103	64	67	99	71	89	74	58	74	73	52	73	71	81	48	83	94	109
68941 GLENVIL	88	61	97	61	63	93	67	84	70	55	69	69	49	69	67	76	45	78	88	103
68942 GUIDE ROCK	67	47	73	46	49	71	52	64	54	42	53	52	38	53	51	59	35	60	68	78
68943 HARDY	76	53	83	52	55	80	58	73	61	48	60	59	43	60	58	67	39	68	77	89
68944 HARVARD	83	57	92	57	60	88	64	79	66	52	66	65	47	65	63	72	43	74	84	97
68945 HEARTWELL	98	67	107	67	70	103	75	93	78	60	77	77	55	76	74	85	50	87	98	114
68946 HENDLEY	89	61	98	61	64	94	68	85	71	55	70	70	50	69	68	77	45	79	89	104
68947 HILDRETH	93	64	102	64	67	98	71	88	74	57	73	73	52	72	70	80	47	82	93	108
68948 HOLBROOK	80	55	88	55	58	84	61	76	64	50	63	63	45	62	61	69	41	71	80	93
68949 HOLDREGE	92	77	87	77	77	96	80	89	84	73	82	69	71	84	78	89	56	86	96	107
68950 HOLSTEIN	101	69	111	69	72	106	77	96	80	62	79	79	56	78	76	87	51	89	101	118
68952 INAVALE	66	45	72	45	47	69	50	63	53	41	52	51	37	52	50	58	34	58	66	77
68954 INLAND	84	58	92	58	60	89	64	80	67	52	66	66	47	65	64	73	43	74	84	98
68955 JUNIATA	85	74	75	72	73	82	72	79	75	71	74	59	65	77	69	78	50	76	80	95
68956 KENESAW	89	62	98	61	64	94	68	85	71	55	70	70	50	70	68	78	46	79	90	104
68957 LAWRENCE	72	49	79	49	52	76	55	68	57	44	56	56	40	56	54	62	36	63	72	84
68958 LOOMIS	94	65	102	65	68	99	72	89	75	59	74	73	53	73	72	82	48	83	94	109
68959 MINDEN	87	67	87	68	70	92	71	86	76	62	74	66	59	76	70	83	50	80	91	101
68960 NAPONEE	69	47	75	47	49	72	52	65	54	42	54	54	38	53	52	59	35	61	69	80
68961 NELSON	74	51	82	51	54	78	57	71	59	46	58	58	42	58	57	64	38	66	75	87
68964 OAK	74	51	81	51	53	78	57	70	59	46	58	58	41	58	56	64	38	66	74	87
68966 ORLEANS	71	55	89	55	60	75	56	71	59	52	58	53	48	56	60	63	38	66	71	83
68967 OXFORD	81	56	89	56	58	85	62	77	64	50	64	64	45	63	61	70	41	72	81	95
68969 RAGAN	82	56	90	56	59	86	62	77	65	51	64	64	46	64	62	71	42	72	82	95
68970 RED CLOUD	69	48	73	48	50	72	53	66	57	45	56	52	40	56	52	62	37	61	70	79
68971 REPUBLICAN CITY	74	53	84	52	56	78	57	71	59	48	59	57	44	58	58	64	38	66	74	86
68972 RIVERTON	65	45	72	45	47	69	50	62	52	40	51	51	36	51	50	56	33	58	65	76
68973 ROSELAND	97	67	106	66	70	102	74	92	77	60	76	76	54	75	73	84	49	86	97	113
68974 RUSKIN	76	52	84	52	55	80	58	72	61	47	60	60	43	59	58	66	39	68	76	89
68975 SARONVILLE	84	58	91	58	60	88	64	79	67	53	66	65	47	66	63	73	43	74	84	97
68976 SMITHFIELD	90	62	98	61	64	95	68	85	71	55	70	70	50	70	68	78	46	79	90	105
68977 STAMFORD	83	57	91	57	60	88	63	79	66	51	65	65	46	65	63	72	42	74	83	97
68978 SUPERIOR	70	50	70	49	52	73	55	68	61	48	59	51	43	59	53	67	39	63	73	80
68979 SUTTON	87	61	93	60	64	92	67	83	72	57	70	66	51	70	66	79	46	78	89	101
68980 TRUMBULL	85	58	93	58	61	89	65	80	67	52	67	67	47	66	64	73	43	75	85	99
68981 UPLAND	91	63	100	62	66	96	69	86	72	56	71	71	51	71	69	79	46	81	91	106
68982 WILCOX	93	64	102	63	67	98	71	88	73	57	73	73	52	72	70	80	47	82	93	108
69001 MC COOK	77	61	76	60	62	81	64	75	70	59	68	56	55	69	63	75	46	71	82	88
69020 BARTLEY	74	53	76	51	55	76	55	69	60	50	59	52	43	60	54	66	39	64	72	83
69021 BENKELMAN	71	50	75	49	52	75	55	68	59	47	58	54	42	58	54	65	38	64	73	82
69022 CAMBRIDGE	84	59	88	58	62	88	65	81	71	56	69	63	50	69	64	77	45	75	87	97
69023 CHAMPION	78	54	86	54	56	82	60	74	62	48	61	61	44	61	59	68	40	69	78	91
69024 CULBERTSON	77	55	81	53	57	80	58	73	63	51	62	57	45	62	57	69	40	67	76	88
69025 CURTIS	71	51	72	49	53	74	55	69	61	49	59	52	44	60	54	67	39	64	74	81
69026 DANBURY	80	55	88	55	58	85	61	76	64	50	63	63	45	62	61	69	41	71	80	94
69027 ENDERS	75	51	82	51	54	79	57	71	59	46	59	59	42	58	57	65	38	66	75	87
69028 EUSTIS	95	65	104	65	68	100	73	90	75	59	75	75	53	74	72	82	48	84	95	111
69029 FARNAM	93	64	102	64	67	98	71	88	74	58	73	73	52	73	71	81	47	83	93	109
69030 HAIGLER	78	53	85	53	56	82	59	74	62	48	61	61	43	61	59	67	40	69	78	91
NEBRASKA	95	85	88	86	84	94	89	91	90	85	90	72	83	91	86	92	62	91	94	109
UNITED STATES	100	100	100	100	100	100	100	100	100	100	100	100	100	100	100	100	100	100	100	100

69032-69367

ZIP CODE #	POST OFFICE NAME	COUNTY FIPS CODE	POPULATION 2000	POPULATION 2009	POPULATION 2014	2000-2009 ANNUAL RATE % Rate	2000-2009 ANNUAL RATE State Centile	HOUSEHOLDS 2000	HOUSEHOLDS 2009	HOUSEHOLDS 2014	HOUSEHOLDS % Annual Rate 2000-2009	HOUSEHOLDS 2009 Average HH Size	FAMILIES 2000	FAMILIES 2009	FAMILIES % Annual Rate 2000-2009
69032	HAYES CENTER	085	878	817	785	-0.8	30	346	328	316	-0.6	2.49	254	240	-0.6
69033	IMPERIAL	029	2431	2241	2141	-0.9	26	976	923	888	-0.6	2.36	679	639	-0.7
69034	INDIANOLA	145	1177	1104	1059	-0.7	34	467	444	427	-0.5	2.48	343	325	-0.6
69036	LEBANON	145	161	140	131	-1.5	6	70	62	58	-1.3	2.26	54	48	-1.3
69037	MAX	057	136	121	115	-1.3	10	59	53	51	-1.2	2.28	39	35	-1.2
69038	MAYWOOD	063	725	646	608	-1.2	13	266	240	227	-1.1	2.69	205	185	-1.1
69039	MOOREFIELD	063	315	284	268	-1.1	17	126	115	109	-1.0	2.38	91	83	-1.0
69040	PALISADE	087	689	626	593	-1.0	21	281	263	252	-0.7	2.38	202	188	-0.8
69041	PARKS	057	228	210	201	-0.9	26	83	77	74	-0.8	2.62	60	56	-0.7
69042	STOCKVILLE	063	113	100	94	-1.3	10	50	45	43	-1.1	2.22	38	34	-1.2
69043	STRATTON	087	665	597	562	-1.2	13	278	258	245	-0.8	2.31	198	183	-0.8
69044	TRENTON	087	739	670	638	-1.1	17	325	301	287	-0.8	2.03	194	178	-0.9
69045	WAUNETA	029	856	782	746	-1.0	21	366	344	330	-0.7	2.18	247	231	-0.7
69046	WILSONVILLE	065	229	205	198	-1.2	13	99	90	87	-1.0	2.28	72	65	-1.1
69101	NORTH PLATTE	111	28121	29118	29439	0.4	78	11570	12305	12545	0.7	2.32	7545	7986	0.6
69120	ARNOLD	041	1050	956	911	-1.0	21	467	431	412	-0.9	2.22	313	287	-0.9
69121	ARTHUR	005	434	403	392	-0.8	30	182	172	168	-0.6	2.34	136	128	-0.7
69122	BIG SPRINGS	049	685	641	618	-0.7	34	302	293	285	-0.3	2.19	207	200	-0.4
69123	BRADY	111	1023	1018	1007	-0.1	63	425	438	437	0.3	2.32	316	322	0.2
69125	BROADWATER	123	405	377	362	-0.8	30	166	158	152	-0.5	2.33	123	116	-0.6
69127	BRULE	101	752	710	684	-0.6	37	318	311	302	-0.2	2.28	224	218	-0.3
69128	BUSHNELL	105	379	343	326	-1.1	17	151	140	134	-0.8	2.45	108	100	-0.8
69129	CHAPPELL	049	1451	1394	1353	-0.4	49	624	616	603	-0.1	2.23	407	399	-0.2
69130	COZAD	047	5677	5470	5428	-0.4	49	2304	2207	2181	-0.5	2.44	1573	1497	-0.5
69131	DALTON	033	580	595	601	0.3	75	260	273	278	0.5	2.18	171	178	0.4
69132	DICKENS	111	120	126	130	0.5	81	44	48	50	0.9	2.63	33	36	0.9
69133	DIX	105	474	429	407	-1.1	17	183	170	162	-0.8	2.52	131	121	-0.9
69134	ELSIE	135	453	442	435	-0.3	54	170	170	168	0.0	2.60	130	129	-0.1
69138	GOTHENBURG	047	4225	4244	4262	0.0	66	1701	1700	1699	0.0	2.43	1182	1172	-0.1
69140	GRANT	135	1816	1760	1730	-0.3	54	748	744	738	-0.1	2.29	493	486	-0.2
69141	GURLEY	033	469	480	484	0.3	75	188	197	200	0.5	2.44	124	129	0.4
69142	HALSEY	171	137	118	110	-1.6	4	62	58	54	-0.7	2.03	41	38	-0.8
69143	HERSHEY	111	1731	1850	1913	0.7	84	660	727	760	1.1	2.53	510	557	1.0
69144	KEYSTONE	101	311	298	288	-0.5	42	137	136	132	-0.1	2.18	95	93	-0.2
69145	KIMBALL	105	3236	3037	2931	-0.7	34	1393	1342	1305	-0.4	2.22	896	858	-0.5
69146	LEMOYNE	101	238	228	220	-0.5	42	114	113	110	-0.1	2.02	79	78	-0.1
69147	LEWELLEN	069	821	774	755	-0.6	37	396	385	378	-0.3	1.97	260	251	-0.4
69148	LISCO	069	209	202	201	-0.4	49	93	93	93	0.0	2.17	66	65	-0.2
69149	LODGEPOLE	033	684	678	679	-0.1	63	290	294	295	0.1	2.30	202	203	0.1
69150	MADRID	135	523	508	500	-0.3	54	189	188	186	-0.1	2.70	144	143	-0.1
69151	MAXWELL	111	877	873	864	0.0	66	324	331	330	0.2	2.64	255	258	0.1
69152	MULLEN	091	783	749	728	-0.5	42	335	324	316	-0.4	2.23	220	212	-0.4
69153	OGALLALA	101	6234	5671	5397	-1.0	21	2566	2387	2288	-0.8	2.33	1721	1591	-0.8
69154	OSHKOSH	069	1446	1352	1325	-0.7	34	646	621	614	-0.4	2.11	413	394	-0.5
69155	PAXTON	101	1044	1019	1001	-0.3	54	412	412	407	0.0	2.47	305	303	-0.1
69156	POTTER	033	659	642	636	-0.3	54	259	257	256	-0.1	2.49	182	180	-0.1
69157	PURDUM	009	175	161	156	-0.9	26	68	64	62	-0.7	2.52	48	45	-0.7
69161	SENECA	171	120	103	96	-1.6	4	58	54	51	-0.8	1.91	39	36	-0.9
69162	SIDNEY	033	7473	7706	7806	0.3	75	3089	3235	3289	0.5	2.34	2017	2103	0.5
69163	STAPLETON	113	927	897	884	-0.4	49	371	376	375	0.1	2.39	274	276	0.1
69165	SUTHERLAND	111	1602	1738	1810	0.9	89	613	683	716	1.2	2.49	448	496	1.1
69166	THEDFORD	171	472	406	379	-1.6	4	205	190	180	-0.8	2.14	136	126	-0.8
69167	TRYON	117	533	513	508	-0.4	49	202	194	192	-0.4	2.64	158	151	-0.5
69168	VENANGO	135	367	348	339	-0.6	37	150	146	144	-0.3	2.38	114	110	-0.4
69169	WALLACE	111	582	610	628	0.5	81	232	251	261	0.9	2.43	176	188	0.7
69170	WELLFLEET	111	313	325	332	0.4	78	116	125	129	0.8	2.60	88	93	0.6
69201	VALENTINE	031	4267	4110	3987	-0.4	49	1748	1731	1693	-0.1	2.33	1154	1137	-0.2
69210	AINSWORTH	017	2499	2314	2214	-0.8	30	1105	1054	1018	-0.5	2.17	714	677	-0.6
69211	CODY	031	351	318	302	-1.1	17	144	135	130	-0.7	2.36	105	98	-0.7
69212	CROOKSTON	031	237	237	234	0.0	66	95	98	98	0.3	2.42	71	72	0.2
69214	JOHNSTOWN	017	455	419	400	-0.9	26	171	162	157	-0.6	2.57	114	107	-0.7
69216	KILGORE	031	228	206	195	-1.1	17	90	84	81	-0.7	2.45	65	60	-0.9
69217	LONG PINE	017	689	643	617	-0.7	34	300	289	279	-0.4	2.17	202	193	-0.5
69218	MERRIMAN	031	672	608	579	-1.1	17	266	250	240	-0.7	2.43	194	181	-0.7
69221	WOOD LAKE	031	191	175	167	-0.9	26	85	81	78	-0.5	2.16	64	61	-0.5
69301	ALLIANCE	013	10591	9673	9246	-1.0	21	4193	3943	3800	-0.7	2.41	2875	2691	-0.7
69331	ANGORA	123	105	97	92	-0.9	26	38	36	34	-0.6	2.64	29	27	-0.8
69333	ASHBY	075	152	139	135	-1.0	21	61	56	55	-0.9	2.48	46	43	-0.7
69334	BAYARD	123	2619	2536	2466	-0.3	54	1022	1008	986	-0.1	2.47	734	720	-0.2
69335	BINGHAM	161	200	176	166	-1.4	7	78	71	68	-1.0	2.48	55	50	-1.0
69336	BRIDGEPORT	123	2606	2426	2329	-0.8	30	1029	971	933	-0.6	2.45	700	656	-0.7
69337	CHADRON	045	6996	6633	6470	-0.6	37	2664	2580	2530	-0.3	2.19	1507	1448	-0.4
69339	CRAWFORD	045	1605	1511	1461	-0.7	34	671	645	630	-0.4	2.26	444	423	-0.5
69340	ELLSWORTH	161	218	189	176	-1.5	6	100	90	85	-1.1	2.10	70	63	-1.1
69341	GERING	157	10601	10554	10488	0.0	66	4263	4371	4381	0.3	2.38	2974	3028	0.2
69343	GORDON	161	2529	2411	2329	-0.5	42	1041	1019	992	-0.2	2.32	701	682	-0.3
69345	HARRISBURG	007	817	777	753	-0.5	42	310	304	298	-0.2	2.56	237	231	-0.3
69346	HARRISON	165	857	783	743	-1.0	21	370	346	331	-0.7	2.26	266	247	-0.8
69347	HAY SPRINGS	161	1557	1377	1288	-1.3	10	623	564	532	-1.1	2.34	430	388	-1.1
69348	HEMINGFORD	013	1727	1501	1405	-1.5	6	647	577	545	-1.2	2.53	469	415	-1.3
69350	HYANNIS	075	454	414	402	-1.0	21	184	168	164	-1.0	2.46	142	130	-0.9
69351	LAKESIDE	161	53	46	43	-1.5	6	22	20	19	-1.0	2.30	15	14	-0.7
69352	LYMAN	157	737	711	702	-0.4	49	274	270	268	-0.2	2.63	200	196	-0.2
69354	MARSLAND	045	106	102	100	-0.4	49	41	41	41	0.0	2.49	31	31	0.0
69356	MINATARE	157	2218	2155	2134	-0.3	54	869	865	862	0.0	2.49	662	656	-0.1
69357	MITCHELL	157	3929	3985	3983	0.2	73	1506	1547	1551	0.3	2.54	1100	1124	0.2
69358	MORRILL	157	2106	2077	2058	-0.1	63	860	867	864	0.1	2.40	585	586	0.0
69360	RUSHVILLE	161	1725	1510	1413	-1.4	7	711	645	608	-1.0	2.28	477	431	-1.1
69361	SCOTTSBLUFF	157	17551	17249	17088	-0.2	58	7179	7177	7144	0.0	2.34	4697	4671	-0.1
69366	WHITMAN	031	256	233	226	-1.0	21	91	84	82	-0.9	2.77	69	64	-0.8
69367	WHITNEY	045	269	266	263	-0.1	63	113	115	115	0.2	2.04	84	85	0.1
	NEBRASKA					0.6					0.8	2.46			0.7
	UNITED STATES					1.0					1.1	2.59			0.9

ZIP CODE		RACE (%)								2009 AGE DISTRIBUTION (%)										MEDIAN AGE		
#	POST OFFICE NAME	White		Black		Asian/Pacific		% Hispanic Origin													%	%
		2000	2009	2000	2009	2000	2009	2000	2009	0-4	5-9	10-14	15-19	20-24	25-44	45-64	65-84	85+	18+	2009	2009 Males	2009 Females
69032	HAYES CENTER	96.6	96.3	0.2	0.2	0.3	0.4	3.1	3.3	4.3	4.7	5.8	8.0	5.1	18.2	34.5	17.0	2.4	80.4	47.3	50.6	49.4
69033	IMPERIAL	98.1	97.2	0.1	0.1	0.2	0.3	4.3	6.3	6.1	6.5	7.4	6.6	4.4	21.6	29.2	14.1	4.1	75.5	43.0	49.0	51.0
69034	INDIANOLA	98.0	97.3	0.3	0.3	0.2	0.3	2.0	3.1	5.8	6.2	6.6	7.1	5.0	22.0	29.8	15.7	1.9	77.4	43.0	50.6	49.4
69036	LEBANON	99.4	99.3	0.0	0.0	0.0	0.0	0.6	0.7	5.7	6.4	6.4	6.4	5.7	18.6	30.7	18.6	1.4	77.9	45.4	48.6	51.4
69037	MAX	97.1	96.7	0.0	0.0	0.7	0.8	0.0	0.0	4.1	5.0	5.8	5.0	4.1	17.4	37.2	18.2	3.3	82.6	49.0	47.1	52.9
69038	MAYWOOD	98.9	98.5	0.0	0.0	0.1	0.2	0.7	1.1	7.0	7.0	7.0	7.1	4.8	22.4	29.1	13.6	2.0	73.8	40.4	50.2	49.8
69039	MOOREFIELD	98.1	97.5	0.3	0.4	0.3	0.4	0.9	1.4	4.9	5.6	6.0	6.7	4.2	21.5	30.3	18.3	2.5	80.3	45.8	53.5	46.5
69040	PALISADE	98.5	98.2	0.1	0.2	0.1	0.2	1.3	1.8	5.6	6.1	6.5	7.2	4.6	19.6	31.9	15.8	2.6	77.5	45.2	50.5	49.5
69041	PARKS	96.1	94.8	0.0	0.0	0.0	0.5	7.5	11.4	6.2	7.1	7.1	6.7	4.3	23.3	31.4	11.9	1.9	74.8	41.2	54.3	45.7
69042	STOCKVILLE	100.0	99.0	0.0	0.0	0.0	0.0	0.9	2.0	6.0	6.0	6.0	5.0	4.0	20.0	33.0	18.0	2.0	79.0	46.9	54.0	46.0
69043	STRATTON	98.3	97.8	0.0	0.0	0.2	0.3	0.8	1.2	4.0	4.9	5.7	6.2	4.4	18.4	34.7	18.6	3.2	81.6	49.1	51.9	48.1
69044	TRENTON	98.4	97.8	0.0	0.0	0.1	0.1	1.8	2.4	3.0	3.3	3.6	5.2	4.9	19.4	30.0	21.6	9.0	86.7	51.9	46.9	53.1
69045	WAUNETA	97.1	95.7	0.4	0.4	0.5	0.8	2.7	4.1	4.7	5.0	6.1	6.0	3.3	21.7	28.3	18.4	6.4	79.7	47.1	48.5	51.5
69046	WILSONVILLE	98.7	98.5	0.0	0.0	0.0	0.0	1.7	2.0	6.3	6.8	7.8	7.3	3.4	23.4	28.3	15.1	1.5	73.7	41.3	53.2	46.8
69101	NORTH PLATTE	94.1	92.0	0.6	0.7	0.4	0.7	6.0	8.8	6.7	6.5	6.6	7.0	6.2	24.7	27.3	12.3	2.6	75.9	38.5	49.3	50.7
69120	ARNOLD	98.9	98.6	0.0	0.0	0.0	0.0	1.1	1.7	5.8	6.0	6.3	6.5	4.6	21.2	30.3	15.9	3.5	78.0	44.7	51.5	48.5
69121	ARTHUR	96.3	96.0	0.0	0.0	0.9	1.0	1.4	1.5	5.5	6.2	6.0	6.0	4.2	24.8	27.5	17.9	2.0	78.9	43.2	47.9	52.1
69122	BIG SPRINGS	97.1	96.9	0.0	0.0	0.0	0.0	5.3	5.6	4.1	4.7	5.0	5.8	5.1	17.9	35.4	18.7	3.3	82.7	49.1	49.5	50.5
69123	BRADY	98.7	98.5	0.1	0.1	0.1	0.2	0.8	1.2	6.4	7.3	7.8	6.6	3.4	22.9	30.5	13.5	1.8	74.4	41.8	50.4	49.6
69125	BROADWATER	97.3	96.0	0.0	0.0	0.0	0.0	3.7	5.6	5.3	5.8	7.2	8.2	4.8	21.8	29.4	15.4	2.1	75.6	42.5	51.5	48.5
69127	BRULE	96.9	96.2	0.1	0.1	0.1	0.1	3.6	4.9	3.8	4.6	4.9	5.1	3.5	15.5	38.7	21.5	2.3	83.4	52.4	52.1	47.9
69128	BUSHNELL	98.2	97.1	0.0	0.0	0.0	0.3	4.0	5.8	5.2	5.8	6.1	6.7	4.4	20.7	32.7	16.3	2.0	78.7	45.6	50.4	49.6
69129	CHAPPELL	97.5	97.4	0.1	0.1	0.6	0.6	1.5	1.6	4.9	5.7	5.8	5.9	4.4	20.4	32.0	16.1	4.7	79.7	46.5	49.3	50.7
69130	COZAD	94.6	91.5	0.1	0.1	0.4	0.6	8.9	14.3	7.0	6.9	7.1	6.7	4.9	23.8	27.3	13.7	2.5	74.9	39.9	48.8	51.2
69131	DALTON	99.0	98.7	0.0	0.0	0.0	0.0	1.6	2.0	5.4	5.7	6.4	6.9	4.5	21.0	34.6	12.9	2.5	78.2	45.0	49.4	50.6
69132	DICKENS	97.5	97.6	0.0	0.0	0.0	0.0	2.5	4.0	5.6	7.1	7.1	7.1	4.8	21.4	32.5	11.9	2.4	75.4	43.0	50.8	49.2
69133	DIX	98.3	97.2	0.0	0.0	0.0	0.2	4.0	5.8	5.1	5.6	6.3	6.5	4.4	20.3	34.0	15.6	2.1	79.0	46.0	51.3	48.7
69134	ELSIE	97.1	96.2	0.0	0.0	0.4	0.5	3.5	5.2	6.8	7.2	7.5	7.5	5.0	24.9	26.9	12.2	2.0	74.0	37.8	51.8	48.2
69138	GOTHENBURG	97.4	95.8	0.4	0.4	0.2	0.3	3.7	6.4	7.7	8.0	7.5	6.5	4.7	22.4	25.9	13.5	3.8	72.7	39.2	47.5	52.5
69140	GRANT	98.2	97.7	0.0	0.0	0.2	0.2	1.7	2.5	4.9	5.6	6.3	6.6	4.4	20.5	30.5	15.8	5.4	78.6	46.1	49.1	50.9
69141	GURLEY	98.7	98.5	0.0	0.0	0.0	0.0	1.5	2.3	5.4	5.8	6.3	7.1	4.6	21.3	33.8	13.3	2.5	77.9	44.7	49.2	50.8
69142	HALSEY	100.0	100.0	0.0	0.0	0.0	0.0	0.7	0.8	5.1	6.8	6.8	5.1	3.4	22.0	33.9	14.4	2.5	78.0	45.6	49.2	50.8
69143	HERSHEY	95.9	94.2	0.2	0.3	0.6	0.8	4.2	6.1	5.5	5.8	6.4	6.9	4.5	23.2	33.8	12.1	1.8	77.9	43.2	49.9	50.1
69144	KEYSTONE	97.4	96.6	0.0	0.0	0.0	0.0	3.2	4.7	3.0	4.0	4.7	5.0	3.4	14.1	41.3	22.5	2.0	84.6	54.0	52.7	47.3
69145	KIMBALL	96.7	96.1	0.3	0.3	0.1	0.1	3.2	4.7	5.7	5.7	5.9	6.6	5.7	19.3	28.3	18.6	4.2	78.5	45.7	47.8	52.2
69146	LEMOYNE	97.5	96.5	0.0	0.0	0.0	0.0	3.4	4.8	3.1	3.9	4.4	4.8	3.5	14.0	40.8	22.8	2.6	85.1	53.9	51.8	48.2
69147	LEWELLEN	97.8	97.2	0.1	0.1	0.2	0.4	2.1	2.8	3.6	4.1	4.5	5.9	4.8	16.4	34.0	22.1	4.5	83.5	51.5	49.9	50.1
69148	LISCO	99.0	98.5	0.0	0.0	0.0	0.0	1.4	2.0	4.5	6.4	5.9	8.9	3.0	22.3	34.7	12.4	2.0	76.2	44.2	51.5	48.5
69149	LODGEPOLE	99.3	99.1	0.0	0.0	0.1	0.3	2.2	3.2	4.6	5.2	6.0	6.9	4.1	21.1	33.3	15.9	2.8	79.6	46.3	52.1	47.9
69150	MADRID	97.1	96.1	0.0	0.0	0.4	0.4	3.3	5.1	6.5	7.1	7.5	7.5	4.7	24.2	28.1	12.2	2.2	74.2	38.7	52.0	48.0
69151	MAXWELL	98.5	98.1	0.2	0.2	0.0	0.0	2.2	3.4	5.7	7.9	7.6	6.9	4.5	22.9	31.0	11.5	2.1	74.3	41.0	50.9	49.1
69152	MULLEN	98.7	98.7	0.0	0.0	0.1	0.1	1.0	1.1	4.5	5.1	5.6	6.5	5.1	17.2	32.2	17.1	6.7	80.5	48.6	47.5	52.5
69153	OGALLALA	96.6	95.6	0.0	0.1	0.2	0.3	4.7	6.7	6.4	6.3	6.2	6.5	6.5	22.2	27.6	15.5	2.9	77.2	41.6	48.3	51.7
69154	OSHKOSH	98.3	97.8	0.1	0.1	0.3	0.4	1.5	2.2	3.8	4.3	4.4	6.3	5.5	17.5	31.4	21.2	5.5	83.0	50.2	48.7	51.3
69155	PAXTON	97.0	96.1	0.3	0.3	0.1	0.2	2.8	4.0	6.8	7.2	7.4	6.6	4.3	22.0	30.4	13.4	2.0	74.6	41.7	50.1	49.9
69156	POTTER	98.0	97.7	0.2	0.2	0.0	0.0	2.1	3.3	6.7	7.3	7.6	6.7	4.4	21.5	31.6	12.1	2.0	74.1	40.5	52.3	47.7
69157	PURDUM	98.9	98.8	0.0	0.0	0.0	0.0	0.0	0.0	5.6	6.8	6.8	7.5	2.5	23.0	28.6	15.5	3.7	74.5	43.1	49.7	50.3
69161	SENECA	100.0	100.0	0.0	0.0	0.0	0.0	0.8	1.0	4.9	5.8	5.8	3.9	2.9	21.4	36.9	15.5	2.9	79.6	48.9	52.4	47.6
69162	SIDNEY	95.6	94.0	0.2	0.2	0.5	0.8	5.3	7.6	6.9	6.6	6.4	6.2	6.2	24.5	26.8	13.4	2.9	76.1	39.4	49.2	50.8
69163	STAPLETON	98.6	98.4	0.1	0.1	0.0	0.0	1.1	1.3	5.1	6.1	6.4	6.4	4.5	21.3	33.7	14.5	2.1	78.5	45.2	50.7	49.3
69165	SUTHERLAND	96.4	94.8	0.1	0.2	0.2	0.3	3.9	5.9	5.9	6.2	6.6	6.7	4.2	22.4	29.8	15.4	2.9	77.2	43.5	50.9	49.1
69166	THEDFORD	99.6	99.5	0.0	0.0	0.0	0.0	0.8	1.5	5.2	6.4	6.7	4.9	3.2	22.2	33.0	15.3	3.2	78.6	46.1	50.2	49.8
69167	TRYON	97.9	97.9	0.0	0.0	0.4	0.4	1.5	1.6	6.8	8.0	7.8	5.7	4.3	21.6	29.8	13.3	2.7	74.1	41.7	50.3	49.7
69168	VENANGO	97.0	96.0	0.0	0.0	0.0	0.0	2.7	3.7	4.9	6.9	8.3	8.0	3.4	20.7	33.6	12.1	2.0	73.9	42.9	53.7	46.3
69169	WALLACE	98.5	97.9	0.0	0.0	0.0	0.0	2.6	3.9	6.2	6.9	7.0	7.2	4.8	21.8	32.5	11.6	2.0	75.4	42.3	50.2	49.8
69170	WELLFLEET	98.7	97.8	0.0	0.0	0.0	0.0	2.2	3.4	6.2	6.8	7.1	7.1	4.9	21.5	32.6	11.7	2.2	75.4	42.6	49.8	50.2
69201	VALENTINE	94.0	92.9	0.0	0.0	0.5	0.8	0.9	1.2	6.3	6.3	6.5	6.5	5.6	22.9	27.4	15.0	3.5	76.5	41.5	48.4	51.6
69210	AINSWORTH	98.6	98.3	0.0	0.0	0.3	0.4	0.8	1.1	5.6	6.1	6.4	6.1	4.3	21.0	30.0	16.4	4.1	77.3	45.3	50.0	50.0
69211	CODY	94.0	92.5	0.3	0.3	0.3	0.6	1.4	1.9	5.7	6.0	6.3	7.2	4.7	21.4	30.2	16.4	2.2	77.4	43.9	50.6	49.4
69212	CROOKSTON	92.8	91.6	0.0	0.0	0.4	0.4	0.4	0.8	6.8	7.6	7.6	5.9	4.2	23.6	31.2	11.0	2.1	73.4	39.9	50.6	49.4
69214	JOHNSTOWN	98.5	98.3	0.0	0.0	0.2	0.2	0.7	1.0	6.2	6.4	6.9	6.4	4.3	22.0	29.4	15.3	3.1	75.9	43.2	51.1	48.9
69216	KILGORE	93.0	91.3	0.4	0.5	0.4	1.0	1.3	1.5	4.4	5.3	5.3	8.3	5.8	19.9	31.6	17.0	2.4	79.6	45.6	49.5	50.5
69217	LONG PINE	98.8	98.4	0.0	0.0	0.3	0.6	1.0	1.4	5.1	5.8	5.9	5.9	4.4	20.5	30.0	17.7	4.7	78.7	46.6	49.3	50.7
69218	MERRIMAN	94.9	93.9	0.1	0.2	0.3	0.5	1.2	1.5	5.8	6.4	6.7	7.4	4.6	22.5	29.4	15.3	1.8	76.5	42.3	51.5	48.5
69221	WOOD LAKE	95.8	95.4	0.0	0.0	0.0	0.0	1.6	2.3	7.4	7.4	8.0	5.7	2.9	26.9	25.7	14.3	1.7	73.1	39.5	53.7	46.3
69301	ALLIANCE	90.2	87.1	0.4	0.5	0.6	0.9	8.1	11.6	6.7	6.7	6.6	6.9	6.6	24.2	28.3	11.3	2.7	75.4	38.5	49.7	50.3
69331	ANGORA	96.2	94.8	0.0	0.0	0.0	0.0	4.8	7.2	5.2	6.2	8.2	7.2	5.2	22.7	30.9	12.4	2.1	75.3	42.2	52.6	47.4
69333	ASHBY	99.3	99.3	0.0	0.0	0.0	0.0	1.3	1.4	5.0	6.5	7.9	10.1	2.2	20.9	34.5	11.5	1.4	73.4	43.3	55.4	44.6
69334	BAYARD	93.9	91.2	0.0	0.0	0.3	0.4	10.2	14.9	5.8	6.1	6.9	6.8	5.4	22.2	29.3	14.6	3.0	76.7	42.6	50.2	49.8
69335	BINGHAM	97.5	96.6	0.0	0.0	0.0	0.0	1.5	1.1	5.7	7.4	7.4	6.8	4.0	22.2	31.3	13.6	1.7	75.0	42.3	52.3	47.7
69336	BRIDGEPORT	93.2	90.8	0.1	0.1	0.2	0.3	10.7	15.3	6.2	6.3	6.9	7.1	5.7	21.9	27.6	15.2	3.0	75.8	41.6	49.1	50.9
69337	CHADRON	93.1	91.4	0.9	1.0	0.4	0.7	2.5	3.7	4.9	4.5	4.7	13.7	17.4	19.7	21.2	11.2	2.8	81.8	29.2	49.3	50.7
69339	CRAWFORD	94.3	92.7	0.2	0.3	0.1	0.1	2.0	3.0	5.0	5.1	5.8	8.7	5.5	20.2	28.3	17.3	4.2	78.1	44.8	46.2	53.8
69340	ELLSWORTH	96.8	95.8	0.0	0.0	0.0	0.0	1.4	2.1	5.8	7.4	7.4	6.3	3.7	21.7	31.7	14.3	1.6	75.7	43.3	52.4	47.6
69341	GERING	90.8	87.2	0.1	0.1	0.3	0.5	14.5	20.9	6.5	6.3	6.1	6.3	5.9	23.6	28.3	14.0	3.1	77.3	40.9	47.5	52.5
69343	GORDON	86.2	84.0	0.0	0.0	0.3	0.4	1.2	1.6	6.0	6.3	6.7	7.1	5.2	21.5	27.5	15.2	4.4	75.9	42.5	48.4	51.6
69345	HARRISBURG	95.8	95.6	0.1	0.1	0.1	0.1	5.6	5.9	4.8	6.3	10.3	6.8	1.9	21.0	32.2	15.3	1.4	73.7	44.0	52.4	47.6
69346	HARRISON	98.5	98.3	0.0	0.0	0.1	0.1	0.9	1.0	4.2	5.2	5.7	5.7	4.3	19.3	35.4	18.1	1.9	81.5	48.1	52.1	47.9
69347	HAY SPRINGS	93.2	91.8	0.1	0.1	0.1	0.1	1.6	2.4	5.0	5.9	5.7	5.1	4.7	20.4	29.6	18.3	5.3	80.2	47.5	50.0	50.0
69348	HEMINGFORD	95.3	93.4	0.0	0.0	0.1	0.1	4.3	6.6	5.3	6.1	6.9	8.0	4.7	20.9	31.0	14.1	3.1	76.0	43.4	51.8	48.2
69350	HYANNIS	98.7	98.6	0.0	0.0	0.2	0.2	1.3	1.2	4.8	6.0	8.5	9.9	2.4	21.5	32.4	13.0	1.4	73.2	42.8	53.4	46.6
69351	LAKESIDE	96.2	95.7	0.0	0.0	0.0	0.0	1.9	0.0	6.5	8.7	8.7	6.5	4.3	21.7	26.1	17.4	0.0	69.6	40.0	50.0	50.0
69352	LYMAN	83.8	76.9	0.0	0.0	1.8	2.3	21.3	30.5	8.0	8.2	8.3	7.0	4.2	21.7	27.7	13.2	1.7	71.3	38.9	49.1	50.9
69354	MARSLAND	97.2	95.1	0.0	0.0	0.0	0.0	1.9	2.0	3.9	4.9	5.9	6.9	4.9	18.6	33.3	19.6	2.0	79.4	48.6	52.9	47.1
69356	MINATARE	90.8	86.7	0.5	0.6	0.1	0.2	11.6	17.5	7.2	6.9	6.9	6.6	5.8	24.8	28.5	11.9	1.4	75.0	38.7	49.7	50.3
69357	MITCHELL	91.2	87.2	0.1	0.1	0.9	1.3	13.4	20.0	5.9	6.3	6.6	7.3	5.4	23.8	28.3	13.7	2.6	76.5	40.5	48.4	51.6
69358	MORRILL	92.1	88.3	0.1	0.1	1.1	1.6	10.7	16.1	5.0	5.8	5.9	6.9	5.5	22.0	29.6	16.8	2.6	79.2	44.2	49.0	51.0
69360	RUSHVILLE	84.5	82.4	0.1	0.1	0.1	0.1	1.7	2.5	5.5	6.3	6.6	6.8	4.8	21.7	29.3	16.0	3.2	77.1	43.5	49.1	50.9
69361	SCOTTSBLUFF	84.1	79.9	0.4	0.4	0.7	1.0	20.8	27.4	6.9	6.5	6.2	6.7	6.9	23.6	25.9	14.0	3.2	76.3	38.6	47.7	52.3
69366	WHITMAN	98.4	98.3	0.0	0.0	0.4	0.4	1.2	1.3	5.6	6.0	8.6	9.9	2.6	21.9	31.8	12.4	1.3	73.4	41.9	54.1	45.9
69367	WHITNEY	93.7	92.1	2.2	2.3	0.4	0.8	2.2	3.0	4.1	4.5	4.9	14.7	5.3	19.9	28.6	15.8	2.3	77.4	41.3	54.1	45.9
	NEBRASKA	89.6	86.9	4.0	4.4	1.3	2.1	5.5	7.9	6.9	6.8	6.8	7.3	6.9	26.3	25.7	11.0	2.3	75.3	36.5	49.4	50.6
	UNITED STATES	75.1	72.0	12.3	12.7	3.8	4.6	12.5	15.7	6.8	6.7	6.6	7.1	6.9	27.0	26.0	10.9	1.9	75.7	36.9	49.2	50.8

#	POST OFFICE NAME	2009 Per Capita Income	2009 HH Income Base	2009 Household Income Distribution (%): Less than $25,000	$25,000 to $49,999	$50,000 to $99,999	$100,000 to $149,999	$150,000 or More	Median Household Income: 2009	2014	2009 National Centile	2009 State Centile	2009 Home Value Base	2009 Home Value Distribution (%): Less than $50,000	$50,000 to $89,999	$90,000 to $174,999	$175,000 to $399,999	$400,000 or More	2009 Median Home Value
69032	HAYES CENTER	15685	328	36.3	36.9	22.0	3.7	1.2	31286	31768	10	6	237	43.0	23.6	19.0	8.9	5.5	61364
69033	IMPERIAL	21638	923	26.2	34.7	30.2	5.9	3.0	41146	44096	36	53	710	23.1	34.4	34.8	6.9	0.8	81719
69034	INDIANOLA	17412	444	29.5	38.5	28.4	2.5	1.1	37698	40332	26	33	346	41.6	34.7	20.2	3.5	0.0	59063
69036	LEBANON	19832	62	32.3	35.5	25.8	4.8	1.6	40890	45000	36	51	49	44.9	30.6	20.4	4.1	0.0	58333
69037	MAX	16916	53	37.7	28.3	32.1	1.9	0.0	32333	33639	12	8	40	42.5	15.0	22.5	10.0	10.0	60000
69038	MAYWOOD	18212	240	23.3	41.3	30.0	2.9	2.5	40799	40389	35	50	173	26.6	28.9	28.9	12.1	3.5	78929
69039	MOOREFIELD	21558	115	26.1	39.1	25.2	5.2	4.3	40740	41646	35	50	88	28.4	26.1	28.4	13.6	3.4	82000
69040	PALISADE	17640	263	39.2	35.7	19.8	3.0	2.3	32186	32016	12	8	195	39.0	29.7	20.5	9.2	1.5	63750
69041	PARKS	16414	77	33.8	35.1	24.7	5.2	1.3	33784	33882	15	15	52	48.1	23.1	25.0	1.9	1.9	52500
69042	STOCKVILLE	21250	45	24.4	40.0	28.9	4.4	2.2	41703	40746	38	57	35	22.9	25.7	31.4	17.1	2.9	92500
69043	STRATTON	17908	258	35.3	35.3	23.3	4.3	1.9	32757	33005	13	10	200	35.0	28.5	25.0	7.0	4.5	70000
69044	TRENTON	17531	301	38.9	36.9	20.9	3.0	0.3	30759	30097	9	5	232	51.3	30.2	15.1	3.0	0.4	49143
69045	WAUNETA	19298	344	27.3	42.7	25.3	3.5	1.2	34240	37138	16	17	279	46.2	30.5	17.6	5.7	0.0	53500
69046	WILSONVILLE	21991	90	26.7	41.1	24.4	3.3	4.4	39195	40449	30	40	68	33.8	30.9	19.1	8.8	7.4	71667
69101	NORTH PLATTE	24192	12305	25.2	28.5	35.0	7.9	3.3	46841	50010	54	74	8344	13.6	21.8	44.9	17.9	1.9	112740
69120	ARNOLD	19848	431	32.9	35.3	27.8	2.8	1.2	33651	35000	15	14	317	37.9	30.6	17.4	6.3	7.9	65952
69121	ARTHUR	18468	172	34.3	37.2	21.5	3.5	3.5	32302	33982	12	8	109	41.3	22.0	23.9	11.0	1.8	67500
69122	BIG SPRINGS	21282	293	29.0	35.8	29.0	4.4	1.7	37344	39407	25	31	219	29.7	24.7	34.2	9.1	2.3	80500
69123	BRADY	19341	438	29.2	35.6	29.5	3.9	1.8	37582	41337	25	33	319	24.8	24.8	30.7	15.0	4.7	90938
69125	BROADWATER	17597	158	32.9	43.7	17.7	3.8	1.9	33400	33856	14	13	110	44.5	17.3	23.6	11.8	2.7	64000
69127	BRULE	21048	311	28.0	35.0	30.5	4.2	2.3	40504	41958	34	49	250	22.0	26.8	37.2	11.2	2.8	93000
69128	BUSHNELL	17209	140	36.4	35.7	22.1	3.6	2.1	33764	35000	15	14	114	43.9	24.6	18.4	11.4	1.8	56364
69129	CHAPPELL	20855	616	26.0	34.9	33.3	4.4	1.5	40801	43001	35	51	491	30.3	36.3	22.8	9.8	0.8	67981
69130	COZAD	21056	2207	26.4	32.7	33.8	3.8	3.4	42004	44879	39	58	1535	20.5	35.5	33.1	9.9	1.0	82438
69131	DALTON	22435	273	28.9	34.8	28.2	4.8	3.3	35656	38477	20	23	222	26.1	32.4	24.3	14.0	3.2	81364
69132	DICKENS	18175	48	27.1	33.3	31.3	8.3	0.0	43197	46127	43	63	36	16.7	36.1	41.7	5.6	0.0	86667
69133	DIX	16675	170	34.7	36.5	22.9	4.1	1.8	35000	35000	18	20	139	43.2	25.9	18.0	10.8	2.2	55938
69134	ELSIE	22232	170	21.2	32.9	33.5	8.8	3.5	46934	49002	54	75	125	46.4	20.0	18.4	10.4	4.8	54091
69138	GOTHENBURG	20627	1700	25.7	32.4	34.8	5.5	1.6	43972	46891	45	65	1276	15.8	32.4	43.5	7.2	1.0	92316
69140	GRANT	20381	744	30.9	32.4	30.2	5.0	1.5	39073	40224	30	39	570	22.5	32.6	38.8	5.3	0.9	83256
69141	GURLEY	19968	197	28.9	34.5	28.9	4.6	3.0	35861	38430	20	24	160	25.6	33.8	24.4	13.8	2.5	80625
69142	HALSEY	19534	58	36.2	34.5	24.1	5.2	0.0	32361	37370	12	9	43	48.8	20.9	20.9	9.3	0.0	51667
69143	HERSHEY	23048	727	19.4	29.4	41.0	7.2	3.0	50917	51759	63	83	593	10.6	17.0	42.3	24.8	5.2	123307
69144	KEYSTONE	21676	136	28.7	34.6	30.9	3.7	2.2	40000	41140	33	46	112	22.3	27.7	38.4	9.8	1.8	90000
69145	KIMBALL	21283	1342	30.6	35.3	27.8	4.4	1.9	36723	38255	23	29	1002	33.6	32.0	28.4	5.8	0.1	67746
69146	LEMOYNE	23559	113	28.3	35.4	30.1	3.5	2.7	40275	41994	34	47	93	24.7	25.8	35.5	11.8	2.2	89167
69147	LEWELLEN	21337	385	33.8	35.1	26.2	3.6	1.3	34062	35906	16	16	295	32.5	28.5	31.5	6.1	1.4	72500
69148	LISCO	18073	93	33.3	38.7	25.8	1.1	1.1	35269	35368	19	21	47	31.9	31.9	34.0	2.1	0.0	75000
69149	LODGEPOLE	19606	294	29.3	37.4	27.6	3.4	2.4	36567	37436	22	28	225	30.7	30.7	24.4	12.4	1.8	77813
69150	MADRID	20805	188	21.3	34.0	33.5	8.0	3.2	46047	49006	51	72	139	42.4	20.9	20.1	10.8	5.8	58077
69151	MAXWELL	19254	331	26.9	26.6	39.6	5.4	1.5	45824	48920	51	71	244	24.6	17.2	34.4	17.6	6.1	109375
69152	MULLEN	18912	324	34.0	42.3	19.8	2.2	1.9	33090	33703	13	11	243	41.2	29.2	21.8	2.1	5.8	60789
69153	OGALLALA	21666	2387	23.2	36.1	33.7	5.3	1.8	42245	44625	40	60	1689	18.5	37.2	36.5	6.1	1.7	83275
69154	OSHKOSH	18399	621	36.9	35.6	23.2	3.4	1.0	31209	32044	10	6	453	38.4	29.6	27.8	3.8	0.4	63194
69155	PAXTON	18507	412	29.1	36.9	29.6	3.4	1.0	37759	39155	26	33	297	32.7	33.3	22.9	6.7	4.4	73654
69156	POTTER	19264	257	29.6	31.1	33.1	3.5	2.7	37171	38898	24	30	177	32.2	33.3	20.3	11.9	2.3	70417
69157	PURDUM	13767	64	35.9	45.3	17.2	1.6	0.0	30000	30000	8	4	42	57.1	19.0	7.1	2.4	14.3	37500
69161	SENECA	20935	54	33.3	35.2	25.9	5.6	0.0	37370	33639	25	31	40	50.0	20.0	20.0	10.0	0.0	50000
69162	SIDNEY	22289	3235	23.3	34.2	34.4	5.6	2.6	44099	45281	46	65	2315	17.1	35.1	34.0	11.1	2.7	87659
69163	STAPLETON	19314	376	22.6	40.2	31.4	4.8	1.1	41408	42054	37	54	277	24.9	23.8	35.0	11.9	4.3	92333
69165	SUTHERLAND	20779	683	22.7	29.6	40.0	6.0	1.8	48143	50598	57	78	532	7.9	25.0	50.0	14.3	2.8	112766
69166	THEDFORD	18772	190	36.3	34.2	25.3	4.2	0.0	33211	34088	14	12	140	48.6	20.0	20.0	10.0	1.4	52222
69167	TRYON	14693	194	37.1	34.0	23.7	5.2	0.0	31029	32844	10	5	131	42.0	29.0	13.0	10.7	5.3	62083
69168	VENANGO	19441	146	24.0	37.7	34.2	3.4	0.7	39233	40765	30	40	112	33.0	26.8	27.7	8.9	3.6	71111
69169	WALLACE	22308	251	25.5	32.7	30.7	8.4	2.8	44478	47717	47	67	191	19.9	35.1	32.5	9.4	3.1	82692
69170	WELLFLEET	20182	125	26.4	32.0	32.0	8.0	1.6	43967	47347	45	64	94	18.1	36.2	31.9	10.6	3.2	84286
69201	VALENTINE	19527	1731	32.4	33.1	27.7	5.3	1.6	37206	39037	24	30	1117	21.7	30.3	34.2	10.7	3.2	88130
69210	AINSWORTH	18811	1054	35.6	38.2	21.9	2.9	1.3	33622	35422	15	14	783	36.7	31.7	24.6	5.9	1.1	64683
69211	CODY	17757	135	35.6	35.6	23.0	3.7	2.2	32086	33686	12	8	81	48.1	17.3	13.6	9.9	11.1	53000
69212	CROOKSTON	20055	98	27.6	32.7	31.6	7.1	1.0	41984	46541	39	58	72	30.6	23.6	33.3	12.5	0.0	82500
69214	JOHNSTOWN	15930	162	34.0	38.9	22.8	3.1	1.2	33490	34760	14	13	106	34.0	30.2	22.6	6.6	6.6	70000
69216	KILGORE	16634	84	36.9	34.5	23.8	4.8	0.0	31675	34634	11	7	58	53.4	17.2	13.8	6.9	8.6	47143
69217	LONG PINE	19104	289	34.9	39.4	21.5	2.4	1.7	35498	36925	19	22	223	40.4	29.1	24.2	5.8	0.4	59773
69218	MERRIMAN	17019	250	33.2	37.2	24.8	3.6	1.2	33067	34107	13	11	140	45.0	17.9	12.1	7.9	17.1	58750
69221	WOOD LAKE	20392	81	32.1	39.5	23.5	2.5	2.5	33025	33579	13	11	35	28.6	14.3	14.3	14.3	28.6	137500
69301	ALLIANCE	24497	3943	23.6	25.5	39.0	8.9	3.0	50926	51562	63	83	2752	19.9	32.1	38.9	8.2	0.8	87881
69331	ANGORA	16052	36	33.3	38.9	22.2	2.8	2.8	33153	37343	14	11	24	33.3	16.7	33.3	16.7	0.0	90000
69333	ASHBY	17202	56	26.8	39.3	30.4	1.8	1.8	40000	41722	33	46	36	50.0	25.0	19.4	2.8	2.8	50000
69334	BAYARD	17757	1008	31.7	30.3	33.2	3.8	1.0	39499	41860	31	42	737	30.0	32.2	28.0	8.1	1.8	73644
69335	BINGHAM	16705	71	29.6	39.4	26.8	4.2	0.0	38354	38886	28	36	46	39.1	23.9	21.7	10.9	4.3	63333
69336	BRIDGEPORT	16811	971	32.7	37.6	25.3	3.3	1.0	34821	35610	17	18	691	38.4	29.8	22.6	8.0	1.3	64831
69337	CHADRON	21282	2580	34.0	27.6	28.1	6.7	3.5	37487	39382	25	32	1508	27.2	31.5	31.4	8.8	1.1	82012
69339	CRAWFORD	18813	645	33.3	36.1	25.9	3.1	1.6	35165	36578	18	20	470	47.2	28.9	14.9	6.4	2.6	52955
69340	ELLSWORTH	19352	90	30.0	40.0	26.7	3.3	0.0	38184	38619	27	36	60	41.7	21.7	20.0	10.0	6.7	60000
69341	GERING	22386	4371	24.6	32.3	32.9	7.8	2.4	44645	47216	47	67	3102	13.9	29.4	44.9	11.2	0.6	97536
69343	GORDON	17463	1019	36.9	34.1	24.4	3.0	1.6	33329	34413	14	12	702	38.0	30.1	23.9	6.0	2.0	63878
69345	HARRISBURG	18772	304	27.3	33.2	32.9	3.6	3.0	37747	38837	26	33	196	20.4	32.1	28.6	18.9	0.0	87500
69346	HARRISON	18723	346	31.2	41.0	22.0	4.3	1.4	33793	35503	15	15	242	37.2	27.3	18.2	5.8	11.6	65789
69347	HAY SPRINGS	17641	564	33.9	35.8	25.7	3.5	1.1	36920	38474	23	30	417	41.7	27.3	22.3	5.8	2.9	59857
69348	HEMINGFORD	19991	577	27.2	29.5	36.9	4.0	2.4	43367	46789	43	63	436	26.8	34.4	25.5	10.1	3.2	74412
69350	HYANNIS	17478	168	27.4	38.7	29.8	2.4	1.8	40542	41393	34	49	116	52.6	22.4	19.8	4.3	0.9	46667
69351	LAKESIDE	20068	20	25.0	45.0	25.0	5.0	0.0	40000	47368	33	46	13	30.8	23.1	30.8	7.7	7.7	75000
69352	LYMAN	16284	270	36.3	35.2	21.5	5.2	1.9	35000	36894	18	20	192	44.8	18.8	21.4	11.5	3.6	61429
69354	MARSLAND	20163	41	24.4	39.0	29.3	2.4	4.9	39067	43648	30	39	30	26.7	23.3	16.7	20.0	13.3	90000
69356	MINATARE	18099	865	32.5	35.3	25.7	4.7	1.8	37511	40182	25	32	586	32.3	27.0	25.3	13.5	2.0	73721
69357	MITCHELL	20560	1547	26.7	33.4	31.2	5.6	3.2	41665	44218	38	56	1095	17.7	24.5	42.9	12.2	2.6	100852
69358	MORRILL	20107	867	29.5	36.0	28.6	3.7	2.2	36878	38495	23	29	598	21.7	34.8	29.8	10.9	2.8	82200
69360	RUSHVILLE	18342	645	32.9	37.4	24.8	3.9	1.1	34939	35782	17	18	466	39.9	30.0	23.4	4.7	1.9	63143
69361	SCOTTSBLUFF	22544	7177	27.9	32.0	30.7	5.8	3.6	40893	43990	36	51	4443	14.0	27.2	40.7	16.7	1.4	102783
69366	WHITMAN	15396	84	28.6	38.1	31.0	1.2	1.2	39192	40000	30	40	52	50.0	21.2	17.3	3.8	7.7	50000
69367	WHITNEY	21881	115	25.2	36.5	33.9	3.5	0.9	40972	44453	36	51	85	24.7	24.7	24.7	18.8	7.1	91250
	NEBRASKA	24998		20.5	28.3	37.5	9.0	4.6	50953	53316				15.1	21.8	43.3	17.4	2.4	109174
	UNITED STATES	27277		20.9	24.4	35.3	11.7	7.6	54719	56938				9.3	13.1	31.6	32.6	13.5	162279

ZIP CODE		FINANCIAL SERVICES				THE HOME						ENTERTAINMENT						PERSONAL			
						Home Improvements		Furnishings													
#	POST OFFICE NAME	Auto Loan	Home Loan	Invest-ments	Retire-ment Plans	Home Repair	Lawn & Garden	Comput-ers & Hard-ware-Personal	Major Appli-ances	TV, Radio, Sound Equip-ment	Furni-ture	Dine out/ Carry out	Sports Equip-ment	Fees & Tickets	Toys & Games	Travel	Cable TV	Apparel & Services	Auto Repairs	Health Insur-ance	Pets & Supplies
69032	HAYES CENTER	70	48	77	48	50	74	53	66	55	43	55	55	39	54	53	61	36	62	70	82
69033	IMPERIAL	92	65	98	64	67	96	69	87	74	60	73	69	53	73	69	81	48	81	91	106
69034	INDIANOLA	77	55	81	53	57	79	57	73	63	51	62	56	45	62	57	69	40	67	76	87
69036	LEBANON	80	55	88	55	58	85	61	76	64	50	63	63	45	62	61	69	41	71	80	94
69037	MAX	69	48	76	47	50	73	53	66	55	43	54	54	39	54	52	60	35	61	69	81
69038	MAYWOOD	88	60	96	60	63	92	67	83	70	54	69	69	49	68	67	76	45	78	88	102
69039	MOOREFIELD	92	64	99	64	67	97	71	88	75	59	74	71	53	73	70	82	48	82	94	107
69040	PALISADE	75	52	82	52	54	79	57	71	60	46	59	59	42	58	57	65	38	67	75	88
69041	PARKS	78	54	86	53	56	82	60	74	62	48	61	61	44	61	59	68	40	69	78	91
69042	STOCKVILLE	84	58	93	58	61	89	64	80	67	52	66	66	47	66	64	73	43	75	85	99
69043	STRATTON	74	51	81	51	53	78	57	70	59	46	58	58	41	58	56	64	38	66	74	87
69044	TRENTON	63	45	64	44	46	65	49	60	54	43	52	46	38	53	48	59	35	56	66	72
69045	WAUNETA	76	53	84	52	55	81	58	72	61	47	60	60	43	59	58	66	39	68	77	89
69046	WILSONVILLE	90	62	98	61	64	95	68	85	71	55	70	70	50	70	68	78	46	79	90	105
69101	NORTH PLATTE	83	79	73	79	77	84	80	81	82	77	81	62	77	83	78	85	56	81	86	97
69120	ARNOLD	79	54	86	54	57	83	60	75	63	49	62	62	44	61	60	68	40	70	79	92
69121	ARTHUR	77	53	85	53	56	82	59	73	61	48	61	61	43	60	59	67	39	69	78	90
69122	BIG SPRINGS	83	57	92	57	60	88	64	79	66	52	65	65	47	65	63	72	42	74	83	97
69123	BRADY	80	55	88	55	58	85	61	76	64	50	63	63	45	63	61	70	41	71	81	94
69125	BROADWATER	74	51	81	51	53	78	56	70	59	46	58	58	41	57	56	64	38	65	74	86
69127	BRULE	81	63	102	62	69	86	64	82	67	59	67	61	54	64	69	72	44	75	81	95
69128	BUSHNELL	75	52	83	52	54	80	58	72	60	47	59	59	42	59	57	65	38	67	76	88
69129	CHAPPELL	84	57	92	57	60	88	64	79	66	52	66	66	47	65	64	72	43	74	84	98
69130	COZAD	86	66	82	66	68	88	71	82	76	63	74	63	59	76	68	82	50	78	88	98
69131	DALTON	87	60	96	60	63	92	67	83	69	54	69	69	49	68	66	76	45	77	88	102
69132	DICKENS	85	59	94	59	61	90	65	81	68	53	67	67	48	66	65	74	43	76	86	100
69133	DIX	75	52	83	52	54	79	57	71	60	47	59	59	42	59	57	65	38	67	75	88
69134	ELSIE	103	71	114	71	74	109	79	98	82	64	81	81	58	81	79	90	53	92	104	121
69138	GOTHENBURG	85	65	85	65	66	89	69	81	74	62	72	63	57	73	67	80	48	77	87	98
69140	GRANT	82	58	87	57	60	86	64	79	69	54	67	62	49	67	63	75	44	74	85	95
69141	GURLEY	87	60	96	60	63	92	66	83	69	54	68	68	49	68	66	75	44	77	87	102
69142	HALSEY	71	49	78	49	51	75	54	67	56	44	56	56	40	55	54	62	36	63	71	83
69143	HERSHEY	94	80	98	82	83	100	80	95	83	72	82	72	71	83	82	89	55	88	97	111
69144	KEYSTONE	79	63	102	62	70	84	63	81	66	59	66	59	55	63	69	71	44	74	80	93
69145	KIMBALL	81	58	82	57	60	84	63	78	70	56	68	59	50	69	61	78	45	73	85	92
69146	LEMOYNE	79	63	102	62	70	84	64	81	66	60	66	59	55	63	69	71	44	74	80	94
69147	LEWELLEN	72	53	80	52	57	75	57	71	61	51	60	53	46	59	57	67	40	66	74	83
69148	LISCO	70	48	77	48	51	74	54	67	56	43	55	55	39	55	53	61	36	62	70	82
69149	LODGEPOLE	81	56	89	55	58	85	62	77	64	50	63	63	45	63	61	70	41	72	81	94
69150	MADRID	101	69	110	69	72	106	77	95	80	62	79	79	56	78	76	87	51	89	101	117
69151	MAXWELL	91	62	100	62	65	96	69	86	72	56	71	71	51	71	69	79	46	80	91	106
69152	MULLEN	76	53	84	52	55	81	58	73	61	47	60	60	43	60	58	66	39	68	77	89
69153	OGALLALA	81	67	77	67	67	83	71	78	74	65	73	60	62	74	69	79	49	76	84	93
69154	OSHKOSH	67	48	69	47	50	70	52	65	58	46	56	50	41	57	51	63	37	60	70	77
69155	PAXTON	82	57	90	56	59	86	62	78	65	51	64	64	46	64	62	71	42	73	82	95
69156	POTTER	86	59	94	59	62	91	66	82	68	53	68	68	48	67	65	75	44	76	86	100
69157	PURDUM	62	43	68	43	45	65	47	59	49	38	49	49	35	48	47	54	32	55	62	72
69161	SENECA	71	49	78	49	51	75	55	68	57	44	56	56	40	56	54	62	36	63	72	83
69162	SIDNEY	81	70	74	71	69	84	74	79	77	67	75	62	67	77	71	81	51	77	85	95
69163	STAPLETON	81	58	88	58	60	86	63	77	65	52	65	64	48	64	63	71	42	72	81	95
69165	SUTHERLAND	93	65	103	65	68	98	71	89	74	58	73	73	53	73	71	81	48	83	93	109
69166	THEDFORD	72	49	79	49	52	76	55	68	57	44	56	56	40	56	55	62	37	64	72	84
69167	TRYON	69	48	76	48	50	73	53	66	55	43	55	55	39	54	53	60	35	62	70	81
69168	VENANGO	83	57	91	57	60	87	63	79	66	51	65	65	46	65	63	72	42	73	83	97
69169	WALLACE	97	67	107	67	70	102	74	92	77	60	76	76	55	75	74	84	49	86	97	113
69170	WELLFLEET	94	65	103	64	68	99	72	89	75	58	74	74	52	73	71	81	48	83	94	110
69201	VALENTINE	77	57	78	57	59	80	62	74	67	55	65	57	50	66	61	72	43	70	80	89
69210	AINSWORTH	73	50	80	50	53	77	56	69	58	45	58	57	41	57	56	63	37	65	73	86
69211	CODY	75	51	82	51	54	79	57	71	59	46	59	59	42	58	57	65	38	66	75	87
69212	CROOKSTON	87	60	95	60	62	92	66	82	69	54	68	68	49	68	66	75	44	77	87	101
69214	JOHNSTOWN	73	50	80	50	53	77	56	70	58	45	58	58	41	57	56	63	37	65	73	86
69216	KILGORE	73	50	80	50	53	77	56	69	58	45	57	57	41	57	55	63	37	65	73	85
69217	LONG PINE	75	51	82	51	54	79	57	71	59	46	59	59	42	58	57	65	38	66	75	87
69218	MERRIMAN	74	51	81	51	53	78	57	70	59	46	58	58	41	58	56	64	38	66	74	86
69221	WOOD LAKE	79	54	87	54	57	83	60	75	63	49	62	62	44	61	60	68	40	70	79	92
69301	ALLIANCE	90	83	82	82	81	92	84	88	86	80	85	67	78	87	81	89	58	87	93	105
69331	ANGORA	77	53	84	53	55	81	59	73	61	47	60	60	43	60	58	66	39	68	77	90
69333	ASHBY	76	53	84	52	55	81	58	72	61	47	60	60	43	59	58	66	39	68	77	89
69334	BAYARD	78	55	81	54	57	81	59	74	64	52	63	57	46	63	58	70	41	68	78	89
69335	BINGHAM	74	51	81	51	53	78	57	70	59	46	58	58	41	58	56	64	38	66	74	86
69336	BRIDGEPORT	71	51	74	50	53	75	55	69	60	48	59	53	43	59	54	66	39	64	74	82
69337	CHADRON	77	56	62	59	56	67	80	68	76	67	76	57	63	76	65	77	52	74	73	84
69339	CRAWFORD	74	53	76	52	55	77	58	71	63	50	61	55	45	62	56	69	41	67	77	85
69340	ELLSWORTH	73	50	80	50	52	77	56	69	58	45	57	57	41	57	55	63	37	64	73	85
69341	GERING	78	74	76	73	74	82	74	78	77	72	77	58	72	77	74	81	53	77	84	92
69343	GORDON	71	50	76	49	52	75	55	68	59	46	58	54	42	58	54	65	38	64	73	83
69345	HARRISBURG	86	59	94	59	62	91	66	81	68	53	67	67	48	67	65	74	44	76	86	100
69346	HARRISON	76	52	83	52	55	80	58	72	60	47	60	59	42	59	58	66	39	67	76	89
69347	HAY SPRINGS	73	51	77	51	53	77	56	70	61	48	59	55	43	60	55	67	39	65	75	84
69348	HEMINGFORD	91	63	100	63	66	97	70	87	73	57	72	72	51	71	69	79	47	81	92	107
69350	HYANNIS	77	53	85	53	55	81	59	73	61	48	60	60	43	60	59	67	39	68	77	90
69351	LAKESIDE	83	57	91	57	59	87	63	78	66	51	65	65	46	64	63	72	42	73	83	96
69352	LYMAN	77	53	84	53	55	81	59	73	61	47	60	60	43	60	58	66	39	68	77	90
69354	MARSLAND	90	62	98	62	65	95	69	85	71	56	70	70	50	70	68	78	46	79	90	105
69356	MINATARE	76	55	70	56	56	76	64	70	66	55	65	57	50	66	59	71	43	69	76	86
69357	MITCHELL	86	68	84	68	68	91	72	83	76	64	75	65	61	76	71	82	50	79	90	100
69358	MORRILL	84	59	88	58	61	88	65	80	70	55	68	63	50	69	63	77	45	75	86	96
69360	RUSHVILLE	72	51	75	50	53	76	56	69	61	48	59	54	44	60	55	67	39	65	75	83
69361	SCOTTSBLUFF	78	70	70	71	70	78	76	76	78	72	77	57	71	78	72	81	53	77	82	91
69366	WHITMAN	76	53	84	52	55	81	58	72	61	47	60	60	43	59	58	66	39	68	77	89
69367	WHITNEY	85	58	93	58	61	89	65	80	67	52	66	66	47	66	64	73	43	75	85	99
	NEBRASKA	95	85	88	86	84	94	89	91	90	85	90	72	83	91	86	92	62	91	94	109
	UNITED STATES	100	100	100	100	100	100	100	100	100	100	100	100	100	100	100	100	100	100	100	100

ZIP CODE #	POST OFFICE NAME	COUNTY FIPS CODE	POPULATION 2000	POPULATION 2009	POPULATION 2014	2000-2009 ANNUAL RATE % Rate	2000-2009 ANNUAL RATE State Centile	HOUSEHOLDS 2000	HOUSEHOLDS 2009	HOUSEHOLDS 2014	HOUSEHOLDS % Annual Rate 2000-2009	HOUSEHOLDS 2009 Average HH Size	FAMILIES 2000	FAMILIES 2009	FAMILIES % Annual Rate 2000-2009
89001	ALAMO	017	947	1049	1096	1.1	42	344	390	412	1.4	2.69	255	287	1.3
89002	HENDERSON	003	18543	28422	34106	4.7	77	6306	9774	11712	4.9	2.91	5101	7826	4.7
89003	BEATTY	023	901	1382	1706	4.7	77	414	640	793	4.8	2.16	210	317	4.6
89005	BOULDER CITY	003	15070	15816	16662	0.5	25	6442	6894	7279	0.7	2.26	4318	4443	0.3
89008	CALIENTE	017	1343	1462	1527	0.9	36	502	565	598	1.3	2.26	301	335	1.2
89011	HENDERSON	003	10039	19748	25102	7.6	84	3738	7333	9349	7.6	2.68	2637	5052	7.3
89012	HENDERSON	003	15452	30462	38292	7.6	84	6655	13368	16819	7.8	2.28	4685	8912	7.2
89013	GOLDFIELD	009	355	356	357	0.0	8	174	180	183	0.4	1.95	93	94	0.1
89014	HENDERSON	003	35366	39103	42681	1.1	42	13720	15252	16556	1.2	2.56	9018	9620	0.7
89015	HENDERSON	003	35686	46267	52330	2.8	62	12782	16734	18940	3.0	2.73	9301	11866	2.7
89017	HIKO	017	149	165	173	1.1	42	48	54	57	1.3	3.06	36	40	1.1
89018	INDIAN SPRINGS	003	3484	4374	4851	2.5	58	700	1059	1260	4.6	2.46	461	673	4.2
89019	JEAN	003	3585	4687	5924	2.9	63	1052	1444	1882	3.5	2.83	654	764	1.7
89020	AMARGOSA VALLEY	023	1553	2529	3183	5.4	81	614	995	1252	5.4	2.54	384	611	5.1
89021	LOGANDALE	003	234	329	398	3.8	69	72	103	125	3.9	3.19	62	87	3.7
89027	MESQUITE	003	9059	12611	15066	3.6	67	3366	4831	5830	4.0	2.60	2475	3443	3.6
89029	LAUGHLIN	003	7133	7607	8142	0.7	29	3208	3508	3763	1.0	2.16	2007	2107	0.5
89030	NORTH LAS VEGAS	003	53650	59225	63264	1.1	42	13973	15004	15952	0.8	3.86	10992	11493	0.5
89031	NORTH LAS VEGAS	003	32031	64441	81477	7.9	85	10360	19673	24704	7.2	3.28	8424	15552	6.9
89032	NORTH LAS VEGAS	003	27233	40967	49219	4.5	75	8762	13291	15927	4.6	3.08	7049	10408	4.3
89040	OVERTON	003	9113	18839	23762	8.2	86	3037	6315	7934	8.2	2.98	2318	4614	7.7
89043	PIOCHE	017	1726	1912	2030	1.1	42	646	742	798	1.5	2.35	419	476	1.4
89044	HENDERSON	003	508	19720	27175	48.5	96	230	9002	12392	48.7	2.19	178	6787	48.2
89045	ROUND MOUNTAIN	023	1756	2766	3433	5.0	79	635	1021	1277	5.3	2.71	446	710	5.2
89046	SEARCHLIGHT	003	1094	1144	1339	0.5	25	607	607	736	0.0	1.35	232	215	-0.8
89047	SILVERPEAK	009	531	547	554	0.3	17	233	246	252	0.6	2.22	141	147	0.5
89048	PAHRUMP	023	14194	20862	25143	4.3	72	5948	8764	10603	4.3	2.38	4121	6033	4.2
89049	TONOPAH	023	3229	4828	5910	4.4	73	1339	2074	2566	4.8	2.25	815	1249	4.7
89052	HENDERSON	003	14739	39548	52879	11.3	89	6001	16376	21910	11.5	2.41	4195	11263	11.3
89054	SLOAN	003	169	231	318	3.4	66	74	95	131	2.7	2.43	55	67	2.2
89060	PAHRUMP	023	7500	9446	10747	2.5	58	3070	3941	4508	2.7	2.39	2139	2718	2.6
89061	PAHRUMP	023	2937	4953	6326	5.8	82	1135	2000	2563	6.3	2.48	846	1478	6.2
89074	HENDERSON	003	46759	51647	56105	1.1	42	17533	19687	21414	1.3	2.61	12479	13565	0.9
89081	NORTH LAS VEGAS	003	2676	22342	30184	25.8	94	947	7032	9459	24.2	3.18	676	4716	23.4
89084	NORTH LAS VEGAS	003	10	23312	32332	131.2	100	5	9240	12814	125.5	2.52	3	6164	128.1
89086	NORTH LAS VEGAS	003	8	9632	13359	115.3	99	5	3484	4832	102.9	2.76	3	2324	105.3
89101	LAS VEGAS	003	50438	57217	62701	1.4	49	15902	18090	20208	1.4	2.88	8495	8935	0.5
89102	LAS VEGAS	003	36229	38497	40582	0.7	29	14117	14807	15558	0.5	2.58	8035	8007	0.0
89103	LAS VEGAS	003	44496	49434	53075	1.1	42	19285	21558	23113	1.2	2.29	10670	11157	0.5
89104	LAS VEGAS	003	35501	38142	40407	0.8	32	13540	14355	15123	0.6	2.63	7865	8002	0.2
89106	LAS VEGAS	003	25964	30179	32851	1.6	52	8915	9896	10705	1.1	2.89	5551	5917	0.7
89107	LAS VEGAS	003	36774	37714	39360	0.3	17	13195	13496	14037	0.2	2.79	8672	8487	-0.2
89108	LAS VEGAS	003	68739	74269	79375	0.8	32	24893	26971	28738	0.9	2.74	16809	17481	0.4
89109	LAS VEGAS	003	8612	13010	15903	4.6	75	4256	6661	8353	5.0	1.95	1584	2183	3.5
89110	LAS VEGAS	003	64216	73792	80733	1.5	51	20213	23146	25276	1.5	3.17	15534	17389	1.2
89113	LAS VEGAS	003	8462	20048	26304	9.8	87	3577	8323	10843	9.6	2.41	2306	5115	9.0
89115	LAS VEGAS	003	51742	60634	67402	1.7	53	16569	19008	20921	1.5	3.15	12225	13726	1.3
89117	LAS VEGAS	003	50702	54816	59019	0.8	32	21046	23071	24804	1.0	2.37	13507	14127	0.5
89118	LAS VEGAS	003	18075	23386	26778	2.8	62	7858	9823	11100	2.4	2.37	4289	5306	2.3
89119	LAS VEGAS	003	45433	47788	50212	0.5	25	19712	20463	21414	0.4	2.31	9557	9294	-0.3
89120	LAS VEGAS	003	21762	23495	25097	0.8	32	8534	9410	10071	1.1	2.48	5544	5862	0.6
89121	LAS VEGAS	003	61090	64089	67578	0.5	25	25421	27056	28529	0.7	2.35	15172	15359	0.1
89122	LAS VEGAS	003	29464	45244	52262	4.7	77	12032	18624	21505	4.8	2.43	7639	11417	4.4
89123	LAS VEGAS	003	39925	59344	71053	4.4	73	15178	22806	27276	4.5	2.60	10543	15126	4.0
89124	LAS VEGAS	003	1492	10119	13546	23.0	93	614	4118	5521	22.8	2.45	412	2774	22.9
89128	LAS VEGAS	003	37047	37890	39560	0.2	12	14693	15215	15881	0.4	2.49	9845	9783	-0.1
89129	LAS VEGAS	003	32247	50797	60265	5.0	79	11406	18475	22017	5.4	2.74	8703	13610	5.0
89130	LAS VEGAS	003	24077	29178	32914	2.1	54	8907	10860	12212	2.2	2.67	6838	8145	1.9
89131	LAS VEGAS	003	11041	40842	55283	15.2	90	3508	13776	18643	15.9	2.96	2813	10896	15.8
89134	LAS VEGAS	003	25250	25791	26926	0.2	12	11584	12022	12558	0.4	2.14	8502	8537	0.0
89135	LAS VEGAS	003	3539	13629	18716	15.7	91	1490	5877	8055	16.0	2.32	1055	4014	15.5
89138	LAS VEGAS	003	0	8662	12019	0.0	8	0	3999	5541	0.0	2.17	0	2556	0.0
89139	LAS VEGAS	003	2325	28461	39104	31.1	95	827	10368	14287	31.4	2.74	625	8077	31.9
89141	LAS VEGAS	003	274	17157	23548	56.4	97	98	6253	8591	56.7	2.74	68	4162	56.0
89142	LAS VEGAS	003	22606	31381	36670	3.6	67	7263	9769	11290	3.3	3.21	5736	7650	3.2
89143	LAS VEGAS	003	2368	11213	15277	18.3	92	800	3716	5062	18.1	3.02	635	2856	17.7
89144	LAS VEGAS	003	11638	16539	19816	3.9	70	4589	6653	7974	4.1	2.49	3306	4603	3.6
89145	LAS VEGAS	003	23873	25832	27691	0.9	36	9133	10007	10722	1.0	2.58	6223	6632	0.7
89146	LAS VEGAS	003	17495	18090	18959	0.4	21	7017	7370	7727	0.5	2.41	4412	4423	0.0
89147	LAS VEGAS	003	39460	51190	58564	2.9	63	14985	19643	22459	3.0	2.60	10305	13021	2.6
89148	LAS VEGAS	003	1014	34099	46844	46.2	95	413	13290	18283	45.5	2.57	303	9417	45.0
89149	LAS VEGAS	003	11488	27448	35270	9.9	88	4251	10889	14010	10.7	2.51	3377	8800	10.9
89154	LAS VEGAS	003	1861	1883	1939	0.1	10	376	386	402	0.3	3.49	128	120	-0.7
89156	LAS VEGAS	003	23204	28413	31999	2.2	55	7945	9784	11007	2.3	2.84	5808	6925	1.9
89166	LAS VEGAS	003	137	5389	7323	48.7	97	20	876	1192	50.5	6.13	15	729	52.2
89169	LAS VEGAS	003	32310	33339	34833	0.3	17	14857	14768	15287	-0.1	2.24	6693	6359	-0.6
89178	LAS VEGAS	003	313	21663	29755	58.1	98	117	9340	12825	60.6	2.32	81	6280	60.1
89179	LAS VEGAS	003	5	1326	1820	82.8	99	2	492	676	81.3	2.70	1	327	87.0
89183	LAS VEGAS	003	7641	28632	37984	15.4	90	2846	10219	13522	14.8	2.80	1973	7372	15.3
89191	NELLIS AFB	003	3795	3488	3582	-0.9	1	694	686	706	-0.1	4.47	517	495	-0.5
89301	ELY	033	8587	8808	8929	0.3	17	3025	3198	3277	0.6	2.42	1978	2070	0.5
89310	AUSTIN	015	481	431	423	-1.2	1	230	211	210	-0.9	2.00	143	130	-1.0
89311	BAKER	033	228	233	235	0.2	12	114	119	123	0.5	1.96	73	76	0.4
89316	EUREKA	011	1110	1070	1091	-0.4	5	434	419	427	-0.4	2.53	282	269	-0.5
89317	LUND	033	366	374	378	0.2	12	143	152	155	0.7	2.12	110	115	0.5
89403	DAYTON	019	7803	13906	17527	6.4	82	2900	5168	6515	6.4	2.69	2173	3818	6.3
89404	DENIO	013	147	172	185	1.7	53	67	79	85	1.8	2.18	49	57	1.6
89405	EMPIRE	031	247	283	301	1.5	51	73	89	96	2.2	2.39	44	50	1.4
89406	FALLON	001	23898	25858	26900	0.9	36	8886	9623	10000	0.9	2.66	6445	6922	0.8
89408	FERNLEY	019	8690	20207	26643	9.6	86	3200	7437	9821	9.5	2.72	2404	5498	9.4
89409	GABBS	023	500	748	919	4.5	75	202	309	383	4.7	2.42	132	200	4.6
89410	GARDNERVILLE	005	7448	10466	11762	3.7	68	3055	4345	4901	3.9	2.38	2098	2994	3.9
89412	GERLACH	031	640	804	899	2.5	58	271	351	396	2.8	2.15	169	206	2.2
89413	GLENBROOK	005	5895	7482	8387	2.6	59	2628	3376	3801	2.7	2.22	1578	2003	2.6
89414	GOLCONDA	013	413	473	504	1.5	51	161	179	189	1.2	2.64	123	136	1.1
	NEVADA					3.5					3.5	2.63			3.4
	UNITED STATES					1.0					1.1	2.59			0.9

ZIP CODE #	POST OFFICE NAME	RACE (%) White 2000	White 2009	Black 2000	Black 2009	Asian/Pacific 2000	Asian/Pacific 2009	% Hispanic Origin 2000	% Hispanic Origin 2009	2009 AGE DISTRIBUTION (%) 0-4	5-9	10-14	15-19	20-24	25-44	45-64	65-84	85+	18+	MEDIAN AGE 2009	% 2009 Males	% 2009 Females
89001	ALAMO	93.0	92.1	0.1	0.1	0.2	0.3	3.9	5.3	6.7	6.2	9.2	10.8	3.3	18.7	30.2	13.9	1.0	70.7	41.4	51.1	48.9
89002	HENDERSON	89.9	86.5	1.9	2.8	1.9	2.1	8.7	14.1	7.4	7.4	7.6	7.1	5.0	27.6	27.7	9.5	0.8	73.2	37.5	49.1	50.9
89003	BEATTY	91.0	89.5	0.2	0.2	1.1	1.2	8.8	11.5	6.2	6.2	6.7	6.4	4.7	21.7	30.4	16.1	1.6	77.1	43.4	52.7	47.3
89005	BOULDER CITY	94.5	92.5	0.7	1.0	0.9	1.0	4.4	7.6	3.8	4.1	4.8	5.5	4.4	17.3	33.2	23.4	3.6	83.7	51.8	49.2	50.8
89008	CALIENTE	88.3	86.3	1.9	2.2	0.7	0.7	6.6	8.6	5.9	5.9	9.8	15.3	2.7	16.6	27.4	13.7	2.7	65.7	38.5	48.8	51.2
89011	HENDERSON	81.9	78.7	4.6	4.8	3.4	3.5	15.9	23.0	7.0	6.8	6.4	5.8	4.8	27.5	27.5	12.9	1.1	76.1	39.0	50.0	50.0
89012	HENDERSON	87.1	81.7	2.9	4.2	4.7	5.2	7.1	13.5	6.9	6.1	5.8	5.1	5.9	31.7	23.4	13.9	1.1	78.1	37.7	48.9	51.1
89013	GOLDFIELD	93.2	93.3	0.3	0.3	0.3	0.3	5.4	5.1	3.9	3.7	3.1	5.9	2.8	17.4	43.5	16.9	2.8	85.7	52.3	55.3	44.7
89014	HENDERSON	80.6	75.3	4.9	6.1	5.7	6.2	12.3	19.5	6.4	6.1	6.1	6.5	8.3	30.6	26.3	8.8	1.0	77.6	35.0	49.2	50.8
89015	HENDERSON	85.6	79.5	3.9	4.5	2.0	2.0	13.3	22.2	7.8	7.3	7.0	6.6	6.2	27.6	25.0	11.0	1.4	73.6	35.9	49.6	50.4
89017	HIKO	93.3	92.7	0.0	0.0	0.0	0.0	4.0	5.5	6.7	6.7	9.1	10.3	3.0	18.2	30.9	13.9	1.2	70.3	42.0	52.7	47.3
89018	INDIAN SPRINGS	73.0	67.3	19.9	21.8	2.0	2.0	11.4	19.8	3.9	4.2	4.2	6.4	10.0	37.7	25.9	7.2	0.6	84.5	36.6	71.0	29.0
89019	JEAN	82.0	73.8	6.7	9.7	3.0	3.6	10.6	17.6	2.5	3.1	3.2	3.6	3.5	25.5	40.7	16.6	1.3	89.0	49.6	60.5	39.5
89020	AMARGOSA VALLEY	78.7	74.3	0.1	0.1	0.8	0.9	25.2	32.0	8.4	6.5	6.3	7.8	6.1	21.3	32.2	10.5	0.9	73.7	39.5	51.4	48.6
89021	LOGANDALE	95.7	93.3	0.0	0.0	0.4	0.6	7.7	13.7	8.5	9.1	9.4	10.6	5.8	24.0	24.0	7.6	0.9	66.0	31.1	51.1	48.9
89027	MESQUITE	79.7	72.9	0.7	0.8	1.4	1.3	25.5	35.9	7.9	6.5	6.4	6.0	5.0	20.3	26.5	19.8	1.6	75.5	42.9	50.2	49.8
89029	LAUGHLIN	88.9	85.0	2.9	3.5	2.5	2.8	10.6	17.2	4.4	4.1	4.0	4.6	5.3	19.1	35.2	21.8	1.4	84.9	51.4	48.9	51.1
89030	NORTH LAS VEGAS	47.0	44.5	18.8	17.4	1.6	1.2	63.0	70.7	11.5	10.3	8.6	8.9	8.9	29.5	15.9	5.8	0.8	64.4	26.1	52.4	47.6
89031	NORTH LAS VEGAS	70.0	63.5	13.0	15.6	5.7	5.7	14.0	22.0	10.0	9.1	8.2	6.9	5.1	34.9	20.3	5.3	0.3	68.4	31.9	49.7	50.3
89032	NORTH LAS VEGAS	56.1	51.9	26.7	27.4	5.4	5.2	17.6	25.5	9.9	9.0	8.4	7.4	5.6	32.9	20.5	6.0	0.4	68.0	31.3	48.9	51.1
89040	OVERTON	85.0	74.0	0.5	0.5	1.0	1.2	14.8	30.7	7.9	7.5	7.1	7.3	6.5	23.7	25.6	13.1	1.3	73.0	36.5	50.3	49.7
89043	PIOCHE	93.0	91.8	2.7	3.0	0.2	0.3	5.2	6.9	5.9	6.2	6.4	6.9	3.8	21.9	30.4	16.3	2.4	76.7	44.2	53.8	46.2
89044	HENDERSON	91.3	88.4	1.6	2.1	3.3	3.9	5.1	9.0	3.0	3.2	3.6	3.3	2.1	14.2	37.8	29.7	3.2	88.3	57.7	48.0	52.0
89045	ROUND MOUNTAIN	84.1	82.5	0.1	0.1	0.2	0.3	8.0	10.4	8.4	7.6	7.0	7.9	8.7	26.6	25.3	7.7	0.6	72.3	31.7	51.1	48.9
89046	SEARCHLIGHT	68.4	60.3	13.6	16.4	5.2	5.4	14.4	21.3	0.8	1.3	0.8	1.5	3.3	29.7	44.3	17.2	1.0	96.2	51.1	69.4	30.6
89047	SILVERPEAK	72.7	73.3	0.0	0.0	0.2	0.2	14.3	14.1	4.8	5.1	5.7	6.4	4.8	22.9	32.0	16.8	1.6	80.6	45.3	55.6	44.4
89048	PAHRUMP	91.0	89.6	1.4	1.5	1.4	1.4	7.1	9.4	5.0	5.1	5.6	5.7	4.5	18.2	30.7	23.2	1.9	80.6	49.3	49.8	50.2
89049	TONOPAH	89.7	88.2	1.7	1.9	0.7	0.7	6.1	8.1	6.6	6.5	6.5	6.9	6.1	23.9	30.8	11.0	1.7	75.9	40.4	52.2	47.8
89052	HENDERSON	85.5	82.8	3.3	3.8	5.7	5.9	8.0	12.6	6.2	5.8	5.6	4.8	4.8	28.4	28.7	14.5	1.4	79.6	41.6	48.9	51.1
89054	SLOAN	92.3	89.2	1.2	1.7	2.4	2.6	6.0	11.3	3.5	4.3	4.8	4.8	2.6	17.7	37.7	22.5	2.2	84.4	52.5	48.9	51.1
89060	PAHRUMP	91.7	90.5	1.0	1.1	1.0	1.0	7.8	10.3	5.4	5.1	5.4	5.0	3.9	17.7	33.5	22.3	1.7	80.9	50.2	51.0	49.0
89061	PAHRUMP	89.3	87.7	1.8	1.9	1.3	1.3	9.4	12.2	5.2	5.1	5.3	5.5	4.5	16.0	31.8	24.8	1.8	81.0	51.2	50.5	49.5
89074	HENDERSON	83.9	79.6	3.7	4.8	5.9	6.5	9.2	14.9	6.2	6.2	6.4	6.4	5.8	28.7	28.8	10.4	1.2	77.2	38.6	48.8	51.2
89081	NORTH LAS VEGAS	66.5	72.7	17.4	11.8	6.9	1.0	14.3	23.7	6.8	6.9	7.5	7.7	5.0	24.1	27.7	12.5	1.8	74.0	39.4	51.3	48.7
89084	NORTH LAS VEGAS	80.0	75.0	10.0	10.3	0.0	0.0	10.0	24.0	6.1	6.7	7.6	7.9	4.4	22.4	29.0	13.8	2.1	74.6	41.4	51.2	48.8
89086	NORTH LAS VEGAS	77.8	75.0	11.1	10.3	0.0	0.0	0.0	24.0	6.1	6.7	7.6	7.9	4.4	22.4	29.0	13.8	2.1	74.6	41.4	51.2	48.8
89101	LAS VEGAS	53.2	48.9	12.0	12.0	4.0	3.4	53.4	62.3	9.2	7.6	6.3	7.0	8.7	32.8	20.4	7.2	0.8	73.1	31.1	58.0	42.0
89102	LAS VEGAS	64.0	59.1	7.5	7.7	6.0	5.5	38.6	48.8	8.1	6.8	5.6	6.2	8.4	28.2	21.9	13.0	2.0	76.0	34.4	51.6	48.4
89103	LAS VEGAS	69.8	63.0	6.5	7.9	9.2	9.4	22.7	32.3	6.6	5.3	4.6	5.4	8.5	30.0	25.5	12.3	1.7	80.6	37.1	50.5	49.5
89104	LAS VEGAS	68.5	63.0	6.3	6.9	7.6	6.9	33.5	46.0	7.0	6.3	6.0	6.1	6.2	26.0	25.8	14.8	2.0	77.1	39.2	51.6	48.4
89106	LAS VEGAS	35.0	32.2	44.9	44.7	3.2	2.7	29.3	36.0	9.2	8.1	6.9	8.1	8.9	27.1	22.0	8.6	1.1	71.2	30.6	51.7	48.3
89107	LAS VEGAS	73.4	66.5	6.5	7.5	4.2	4.1	25.2	36.2	7.4	6.9	6.7	7.2	6.6	27.4	24.0	11.9	1.9	74.6	36.1	49.9	50.1
89108	LAS VEGAS	68.2	61.6	12.4	14.1	4.6	4.4	21.8	31.2	8.2	7.4	6.7	7.2	8.0	29.5	23.0	8.8	1.2	73.5	32.7	49.7	50.3
89109	LAS VEGAS	71.0	60.0	7.4	9.2	7.7	10.9	32.3	40.7	5.2	4.4	3.9	4.2	6.3	26.4	28.1	17.8	3.7	84.1	44.7	53.7	46.3
89110	LAS VEGAS	61.1	56.1	11.3	11.8	6.4	5.9	36.0	46.1	9.3	8.7	7.9	8.1	7.6	28.8	21.5	7.3	0.7	69.0	30.1	50.1	49.9
89113	LAS VEGAS	78.5	71.3	4.0	5.7	9.7	11.2	10.0	17.9	6.5	5.1	4.6	4.9	9.4	33.8	25.7	9.1	0.9	81.2	34.6	49.4	50.6
89115	LAS VEGAS	55.8	50.1	20.6	21.6	3.6	3.2	34.1	44.5	11.6	9.9	7.9	8.1	10.1	30.2	17.3	4.6	0.4	65.9	26.2	51.1	48.9
89117	LAS VEGAS	78.0	72.5	5.9	7.4	9.0	10.2	9.1	14.5	6.1	5.7	5.7	5.6	6.2	29.5	28.1	11.9	1.2	79.0	39.1	49.0	51.0
89118	LAS VEGAS	72.1	69.2	6.5	7.2	10.2	9.4	14.5	20.5	6.0	5.1	5.0	5.4	8.8	31.7	27.6	9.4	0.9	80.8	36.5	50.9	49.1
89119	LAS VEGAS	65.9	60.2	8.3	9.1	7.1	6.6	32.3	43.4	7.2	6.1	5.1	6.2	9.4	32.6	23.1	9.4	1.1	78.5	33.5	53.0	47.0
89120	LAS VEGAS	80.3	75.3	4.4	5.4	5.1	5.4	15.8	23.6	5.5	5.3	5.5	5.7	5.5	28.8	28.1	14.0	1.7	80.4	40.4	49.5	50.5
89121	LAS VEGAS	78.1	72.6	6.2	7.4	4.3	4.3	19.4	28.8	5.9	5.4	5.0	5.6	6.5	24.9	27.3	17.0	2.4	80.4	42.3	49.1	50.9
89122	LAS VEGAS	74.5	64.2	7.9	9.2	3.9	5.9	21.0	31.7	6.8	6.3	6.0	6.0	5.8	25.5	26.5	15.5	1.7	77.3	40.3	49.4	50.6
89123	LAS VEGAS	79.0	73.6	3.8	4.8	8.7	9.5	12.5	20.2	7.2	6.8	6.6	5.9	5.3	31.9	25.6	9.8	0.9	75.7	37.0	49.5	50.5
89124	LAS VEGAS	89.4	77.1	1.8	4.5	2.6	9.5	4.6	11.7	6.0	6.0	6.3	5.9	5.1	27.2	31.1	11.1	1.2	78.1	40.9	48.8	51.2
89128	LAS VEGAS	77.5	72.0	7.9	10.0	7.0	7.5	9.7	15.4	7.1	6.6	6.3	6.7	7.0	29.6	26.1	9.7	0.9	75.9	36.4	49.0	51.0
89129	LAS VEGAS	80.4	75.7	7.1	8.2	5.6	6.6	9.2	14.9	8.9	8.5	8.0	6.4	4.6	32.0	24.0	7.0	0.6	70.5	34.8	48.8	51.2
89130	LAS VEGAS	83.3	77.8	6.4	8.5	3.6	4.0	9.5	15.7	7.5	7.3	7.2	6.2	4.3	27.5	25.9	12.8	1.3	74.0	39.1	48.9	51.1
89131	LAS VEGAS	82.4	78.0	6.3	8.0	3.4	3.2	11.0	16.0	9.7	9.0	8.2	6.5	4.2	34.6	22.1	5.3	0.4	69.2	33.5	49.6	50.4
89134	LAS VEGAS	89.7	87.0	2.6	3.5	4.9	5.7	3.7	6.3	3.9	4.2	4.3	3.7	2.0	14.1	21.3	41.9	4.4	84.9	62.3	46.5	53.5
89135	LAS VEGAS	78.9	73.5	4.0	5.2	10.5	11.7	8.1	13.6	6.4	6.2	6.4	6.0	5.3	28.5	29.7	10.3	1.2	77.4	39.5	48.5	51.5
89138	LAS VEGAS	0.0	94.9	0.0	0.0	0.0	0.0	0.0	0.1	5.7	5.5	5.5	5.1	4.5	27.3	32.4	11.9	2.0	80.2	42.7	48.6	51.4
89139	LAS VEGAS	91.3	87.0	1.5	2.3	1.6	2.1	6.8	10.8	5.1	6.0	7.1	6.9	3.6	21.8	36.4	11.8	1.2	77.4	44.6	49.5	50.5
89141	LAS VEGAS	92.4	89.6	1.5	1.7	1.5	1.4	7.6	13.2	4.6	5.1	6.0	6.0	3.7	20.5	36.6	15.9	1.7	80.6	47.3	50.1	49.9
89142	LAS VEGAS	66.0	60.9	9.2	10.4	11.6	11.6	21.8	29.7	8.8	7.9	7.4	7.4	6.9	31.8	22.3	6.9	0.6	71.3	31.8	48.7	51.3
89143	LAS VEGAS	81.9	77.3	5.6	7.2	4.3	4.7	10.5	16.3	10.0	8.9	8.0	6.4	5.0	34.9	21.1	5.3	0.5	69.1	32.2	49.5	50.5
89144	LAS VEGAS	81.2	77.2	4.4	5.7	8.1	8.6	6.8	11.1	8.2	7.6	7.1	5.3	4.0	33.7	25.1	8.4	0.5	73.6	37.0	48.6	51.4
89145	LAS VEGAS	79.3	73.8	6.6	8.1	4.9	5.5	11.8	18.0	6.4	6.5	6.6	6.8	5.8	28.7	27.3	11.0	1.0	76.4	38.0	49.4	50.6
89146	LAS VEGAS	76.6	70.7	6.5	8.0	6.6	6.8	14.1	21.8	5.5	4.8	4.9	5.6	7.1	27.3	28.9	14.2	1.6	81.7	40.9	49.5	50.5
89147	LAS VEGAS	70.3	64.6	4.6	5.7	15.0	15.8	12.9	19.5	6.5	6.0	5.8	5.9	6.5	31.4	27.2	9.8	1.0	78.2	37.1	49.0	51.0
89148	LAS VEGAS	72.4	66.5	3.9	5.0	13.6	14.5	11.1	17.6	6.3	6.2	6.3	6.1	5.6	28.4	29.8	10.0	1.2	77.5	39.2	48.2	51.8
89149	LAS VEGAS	88.7	83.9	4.3	6.5	2.7	3.1	6.3	10.9	5.3	6.1	7.2	7.0	3.5	21.7	35.6	12.4	1.2	76.5	44.5	49.3	50.7
89154	LAS VEGAS	65.3	59.1	10.2	12.1	12.4	12.5	16.5	24.6	3.1	3.2	1.6	20.7	17.7	19.7	17.9	13.4	2.7	90.5	27.5	51.8	48.2
89156	LAS VEGAS	72.1	65.6	10.3	12.2	4.6	4.6	17.7	26.3	8.3	7.2	6.8	6.7	7.0	31.9	23.3	8.1	0.7	73.7	33.3	48.8	51.2
89166	LAS VEGAS	86.9	82.6	5.1	7.1	2.2	3.2	6.6	11.1	5.5	6.3	7.5	7.3	3.5	22.4	35.5	10.9	1.1	75.5	43.5	49.2	50.8
89169	LAS VEGAS	64.0	58.7	9.9	10.4	6.5	6.0	36.0	47.9	7.4	5.8	4.6	6.0	9.8	30.6	23.8	10.6	1.4	79.1	34.5	54.3	45.7
89178	LAS VEGAS	90.7	82.8	1.6	3.2	2.6	5.8	7.7	13.3	5.4	5.6	6.1	6.0	4.4	24.0	33.6	13.4	1.5	79.2	44.0	49.4	50.6
89179	LAS VEGAS	100.0	89.5	0.0	1.7	0.0	1.4	0.0	13.0	4.6	5.1	6.0	6.0	3.7	20.4	36.6	15.9	1.7	80.5	47.4	50.1	49.9
89183	LAS VEGAS	76.3	70.4	3.8	4.6	11.2	11.9	13.8	22.5	9.1	8.1	7.4	6.3	5.5	35.2	21.9	6.0	0.5	71.3	33.1	49.3	50.7
89191	NELLIS AFB	67.9	61.0	14.9	18.1	5.8	5.9	12.4	18.8	12.5	9.8	6.0	6.2	18.9	36.0	9.1	1.3	0.0	69.4	24.1	56.6	43.4
89301	ELY	86.6	84.4	3.7	4.0	1.0	1.1	11.1	14.5	6.0	5.8	6.0	6.3	7.4	26.6	26.7	13.2	1.9	78.2	38.8	54.9	45.1
89310	AUSTIN	90.6	88.4	1.5	1.6	0.6	0.7	8.1	10.9	2.1	3.5	4.6	5.6	2.3	18.1	46.6	12.5	4.6	86.1	51.7	53.8	46.2
89311	BAKER	72.5	69.5	18.3	19.7	0.9	0.9	15.3	18.9	2.6	3.0	3.4	3.9	10.7	48.1	22.7	5.2	0.4	88.8	35.3	81.1	18.9
89316	EUREKA	88.9	88.6	0.5	0.5	0.9	0.9	9.6	9.7	6.0	6.0	6.3	7.3	6.6	22.8	31.6	12.2	1.2	76.8	41.7	49.4	50.6
89317	LUND	89.1	87.2	5.2	5.9	1.6	1.6	5.2	6.7	6.4	6.1	5.9	5.3	7.2	30.5	27.3	9.6	1.6	77.5	37.6	52.4	47.6
89403	DAYTON	90.7	87.9	0.4	0.5	1.0	1.0	10.1	14.5	6.7	6.9	7.2	7.2	5.4	25.1	29.4	11.2	0.9	74.4	39.1	50.1	49.9
89404	DENIO	85.0	82.6	0.7	0.6	0.7	0.6	20.4	26.2	7.0	7.0	8.1	7.6	4.7	25.6	29.7	9.9	0.6	73.3	38.8	50.0	50.0
89405	EMPIRE	82.6	78.1	0.0	0.0	0.4	0.4	37.7	49.1	4.6	5.3	4.9	6.0	6.0	28.3	27.6	13.4	3.9	82.3	40.5	59.0	41.0
89406	FALLON	84.2	82.2	1.6	1.7	2.9	3.2	8.7	11.4	8.3	7.4	7.3	7.1	6.6	25.5	25.3	11.0	1.5	72.7	35.7	50.0	50.0
89408	FERNLEY	90.2	88.0	0.4	0.6	0.9	0.9	8.8	11.6	7.2	7.4	7.7	7.3	5.2	26.3	28.4	9.5	1.0	73.1	37.6	50.0	50.0
89409	GABBS	73.6	72.9	0.0	0.0	1.0	1.1	6.6	8.4	5.6	6.8	8.8	6.6	4.1	19.9	35.2	11.8	1.2	73.5	43.3	51.1	48.9
89410	GARDNERVILLE	91.8	90.3	0.3	0.3	1.0	1.1	8.5	11.1	4.7	5.0	5.9	6.0	4.7	19.7	32.2	19.0	2.7	80.3	47.4	48.8	51.2
89412	GERLACH	88.8	85.3	0.0	0.0	0.3	0.2	18.3	25.5	5.1	5.2	5.7	5.7	6.0	26.7	32.3	11.3	1.9	80.6	41.4	54.2	45.8
89413	GLENBROOK	89.7	88.0	0.6	0.6	3.4	3.6	8.9	11.2	3.7	4.0	5.4	4.6	3.8	23.0	38.8	15.3	1.4	83.8	48.0	52.2	47.8
89414	GOLCONDA	86.4	83.1	0.2	0.2	0.5	0.6	19.7	25.2	8.9	8.9	8.9	8.0	6.1	26.2	26.4	6.1	0.4	68.3	32.4	53.3	46.7
	NEVADA	75.2	71.8	6.8	7.2	4.9	5.1	19.7	24.9	7.3	6.8	6.5	6.6	6.4	28.1	26.0	11.1	1.3	75.4	36.8	50.3	49.7
	UNITED STATES	75.1	72.0	12.3	12.7	3.8	4.6	12.5	15.7	6.8	6.7	6.6	7.1	6.9	27.0	26.0	10.9	1.9	75.7	36.9	49.2	50.8

#	ZIP CODE POST OFFICE NAME	2009 Per Capita Income	2009 HH Income Base	2009 HOUSEHOLD INCOME DISTRIBUTION (%) Less than $25,000	$25,000 to $49,999	$50,000 to $99,999	$100,000 to $149,999	$150,000 or More	MEDIAN HOUSEHOLD INCOME 2009	2014	2009 National Centile	2009 State Centile	2009 Home Value Base	2009 HOME VALUE DISTRIBUTION (%) Less than $50,000	$50,000 to $89,999	$90,000 to $174,999	$175,000 to $399,999	$400,000 or More	2009 Median Home Value
89001	ALAMO	18668	390	27.9	22.1	44.1	5.9	0.0	50000	47789	61	42	317	12.0	21.1	48.3	18.6	0.0	116042
89002	HENDERSON	29878	9774	7.8	13.9	49.7	20.9	7.8	77702	79440	91	89	8174	5.7	0.9	46.9	44.6	1.9	170797
89003	BEATTY	23964	640	31.7	17.7	39.8	10.3	0.5	50508	52220	62	45	363	15.7	24.2	53.4	1.9	4.7	105048
89005	BOULDER CITY	32840	6894	17.5	24.9	36.4	14.6	6.6	60744	63041	78	60	4889	13.8	4.6	31.3	43.4	7.0	175712
89008	CALIENTE	21315	565	34.9	26.4	30.4	6.4	1.9	35341	40161	19	9	391	23.0	29.2	41.2	6.1	0.5	87571
89011	HENDERSON	27322	7333	12.5	23.6	47.2	10.7	6.0	62135	64284	80	65	4695	4.9	4.7	66.1	18.6	5.7	139988
89012	HENDERSON	38437	13368	8.7	21.0	43.7	16.8	9.8	71880	73391	88	81	9322	0.9	0.4	27.1	67.8	3.7	202373
89013	GOLDFIELD	25612	180	28.9	27.8	31.7	11.7	0.0	40000	41817	33	14	120	26.7	31.7	40.0	1.7	0.0	79412
89014	HENDERSON	29796	15252	10.6	28.6	41.4	11.6	7.8	61753	63743	80	64	7584	0.9	2.0	48.3	46.0	2.8	173531
89015	HENDERSON	25153	16734	18.8	21.8	41.3	13.4	4.8	60765	62328	78	61	10929	5.6	9.7	59.3	24.2	1.3	139696
89017	HIKO	16560	54	29.6	24.1	38.9	7.4	0.0	46547	46892	53	31	44	9.1	20.5	52.3	18.2	0.0	117500
89018	INDIAN SPRINGS	26862	1059	13.4	29.4	46.0	8.5	2.7	58840	60552	76	58	570	24.4	11.1	40.0	20.4	4.2	112105
89019	JEAN	23145	1444	21.5	28.2	35.0	8.0	7.3	50213	51551	62	42	1011	9.9	13.3	51.4	21.8	3.7	128707
89020	AMARGOSA VALLEY	23310	995	28.0	29.1	29.3	8.3	5.1	45659	48341	50	27	659	17.3	19.9	52.7	4.4	5.8	106745
89021	LOGANDALE	23254	103	13.6	20.4	45.6	16.5	3.9	68213	70289	86	76	83	14.5	6.0	36.1	39.8	3.6	155357
89027	MESQUITE	24358	4831	17.1	35.4	35.9	7.1	4.6	48152	48976	58	36	2790	3.6	6.2	68.6	18.5	3.1	138142
89029	LAUGHLIN	25974	3508	20.2	34.9	35.5	5.9	3.4	45647	47252	50	27	1204	5.9	18.6	53.2	21.1	1.2	127885
89030	NORTH LAS VEGAS	12178	15004	31.5	36.9	26.4	3.2	2.0	34555	35598	17	8	6699	15.8	32.8	50.0	1.2	0.2	90750
89031	NORTH LAS VEGAS	25023	19673	5.7	13.1	56.7	19.7	4.8	76063	77203	90	85	16091	0.7	0.3	80.1	18.8	0.1	149342
89032	NORTH LAS VEGAS	23880	13291	11.4	20.6	49.2	14.5	4.3	66986	68963	85	75	9384	2.9	3.0	78.8	15.2	0.1	145882
89040	OVERTON	19912	6315	20.8	31.0	36.5	8.6	3.0	48679	49549	58	38	4121	16.9	11.7	46.7	22.8	1.9	122319
89043	PIOCHE	20392	742	37.9	17.7	36.8	5.5	2.2	41781	44108	39	20	569	21.3	10.5	52.0	12.8	3.3	112224
89044	HENDERSON	55044	9002	7.1	14.3	33.4	24.5	20.7	91394	93007	95	99	8336	1.5	8.8	54.1	31.7	4.0	150650
89045	ROUND MOUNTAIN	25218	1021	11.9	16.9	52.2	17.4	1.5	63020	63258	81	68	800	38.9	36.8	21.0	3.4	0.0	64310
89046	SEARCHLIGHT	34524	607	25.7	31.3	34.3	5.6	3.1	40327	42617	34	16	275	29.5	20.0	41.1	4.7	4.7	90441
89047	SILVERPEAK	22161	246	26.8	29.3	35.4	6.9	1.6	42386	44091	41	21	164	32.3	31.1	31.7	4.9	0.0	68947
89048	PAHRUMP	22860	8764	25.5	31.6	31.2	8.3	3.3	44366	47654	46	26	6831	5.6	10.8	51.6	29.9	2.1	145837
89049	TONOPAH	23834	2074	26.3	23.2	39.9	9.5	1.1	50357	52896	62	43	1260	19.6	31.3	44.0	5.0	0.0	89241
89052	HENDERSON	42290	16376	7.6	16.0	39.7	22.2	14.5	80782	82597	92	90	11771	1.5	5.1	42.2	47.3	3.9	177505
89054	SLOAN	39046	95	13.7	20.0	33.7	16.8	15.8	70974	73282	87	79	86	0.0	10.5	55.8	30.2	3.5	148214
89060	PAHRUMP	21721	3941	26.5	30.0	33.4	7.7	2.5	43098	47720	43	23	3228	3.6	13.5	54.3	25.7	2.9	142487
89061	PAHRUMP	22550	2000	19.0	33.4	37.0	8.1	2.7	48350	50780	57	34	1720	5.2	6.0	44.5	42.3	2.0	164918
89074	HENDERSON	36165	19687	9.3	18.6	41.3	18.1	12.6	75163	76787	89	84	13649	1.5	3.7	39.9	48.9	6.0	183798
89081	NORTH LAS VEGAS	16040	7032	1.5	49.9	46.3	2.0	0.3	49425	48552	60	40	5717	0.3	0.4	61.6	33.4	4.3	160557
89084	NORTH LAS VEGAS	19032	9240	0.0	54.2	45.8	0.0	0.0	48440	47853	58	37	7911	0.0	0.0	60.6	34.6	4.8	161715
89086	NORTH LAS VEGAS	17368	3484	0.0	54.2	45.8	0.0	0.0	48440	47855	58	37	2983	0.0	0.0	60.6	34.6	4.8	161702
89101	LAS VEGAS	13736	18090	48.2	31.1	16.8	2.7	1.2	25798	25226	4	1	3436	6.9	23.7	68.0	1.1	0.2	99694
89102	LAS VEGAS	19647	14807	32.5	31.9	26.6	5.5	3.5	36510	37641	22	10	4515	7.5	8.5	55.5	25.2	3.3	133536
89103	LAS VEGAS	22858	21558	22.5	35.7	33.0	6.5	2.3	43863	45559	45	24	7259	22.6	13.5	50.3	13.4	0.2	113711
89104	LAS VEGAS	19313	14355	31.7	27.8	32.1	6.0	2.4	41319	42935	37	18	7703	24.3	6.3	63.7	5.5	0.2	112958
89106	LAS VEGAS	15628	9896	38.3	30.1	25.3	5.1	1.2	33071	33875	13	5	3691	9.9	19.4	62.9	7.5	0.4	107344
89107	LAS VEGAS	21495	13496	22.1	30.1	36.6	7.3	3.8	47651	48835	56	33	7668	1.7	6.3	83.0	6.5	2.5	122125
89108	LAS VEGAS	22275	26971	18.6	29.8	38.9	9.5	3.2	51473	53034	65	47	12876	1.7	8.5	73.9	15.3	0.7	129440
89109	LAS VEGAS	21843	6661	38.7	36.7	19.8	2.6	2.3	29586	29260	7	3	945	1.0	14.7	34.1	38.3	12.0	175947
89110	LAS VEGAS	20255	23146	18.4	28.4	38.8	9.4	5.0	53411	56109	69	52	14262	14.0	11.8	54.7	17.4	2.0	120604
89113	LAS VEGAS	33825	8323	12.1	25.8	42.1	11.5	8.4	62168	63998	80	66	5311	1.2	6.9	45.9	35.5	10.4	168279
89115	LAS VEGAS	14577	19008	30.2	35.4	29.1	4.2	1.1	36749	38328	23	11	7339	29.2	12.6	55.1	2.8	0.3	99330
89117	LAS VEGAS	34134	23071	13.1	26.1	38.5	13.3	9.0	61672	63882	80	63	11470	2.2	1.4	30.3	54.4	11.7	204162
89118	LAS VEGAS	25748	9823	20.7	30.8	35.1	9.0	4.4	48792	50011	58	40	3192	0.0	8.0	52.9	32.2	6.9	152050
89119	LAS VEGAS	19159	20463	33.3	36.4	24.1	4.7	1.5	33805	34223	15	7	4407	5.4	20.4	58.7	14.8	0.7	128531
89120	LAS VEGAS	30896	9410	14.5	23.2	39.8	13.9	8.6	62667	64339	81	66	5893	0.5	10.7	54.7	27.8	6.4	148085
89121	LAS VEGAS	24558	27056	21.9	32.2	34.8	7.5	3.6	46670	47724	53	32	14354	20.0	8.4	59.9	10.7	1.0	119023
89122	LAS VEGAS	24143	18624	21.5	31.5	35.2	8.2	3.6	47001	48932	54	32	11424	20.2	19.4	47.7	10.9	1.8	104789
89123	LAS VEGAS	31160	22806	9.7	17.4	48.4	17.4	7.0	70824	73175	87	78	15726	4.4	3.2	41.8	49.1	1.6	176122
89124	LAS VEGAS	38848	4118	7.3	10.9	47.6	23.3	11.0	80459	81816	92	90	2766	0.9	6.7	47.3	35.5	9.7	166429
89128	LAS VEGAS	31798	15215	10.3	26.5	40.5	15.1	7.6	63355	65215	82	68	8846	0.9	9.5	49.6	36.7	3.4	160588
89129	LAS VEGAS	39284	18475	5.9	13.0	39.7	21.8	19.6	86474	89374	94	95	14256	1.3	0.2	46.9	46.8	4.8	177617
89130	LAS VEGAS	31495	10860	6.9	16.6	48.4	21.4	6.7	75279	76751	89	84	9188	0.0	0.1	56.2	42.6	1.1	168731
89131	LAS VEGAS	34349	13776	4.8	12.0	46.5	24.4	12.3	83865	84848	93	94	11938	0.9	0.3	42.7	48.5	7.5	183678
89134	LAS VEGAS	48261	12022	14.7	19.9	33.3	13.9	18.3	72159	74684	88	82	10614	0.5	0.3	25.2	61.2	12.9	215295
89135	LAS VEGAS	41580	5877	7.0	11.7	46.5	24.0	10.7	81467	82833	93	91	3882	0.1	6.1	55.7	34.0	4.1	156857
89138	LAS VEGAS	44153	3999	0.0	0.0	69.4	14.5	16.1	72670	74866	88	82	2443	0.0	0.0	0.0	0.0	100.0	684958
89139	LAS VEGAS	30159	10368	17.7	19.5	34.6	17.4	10.7	68537	71065	86	77	7814	0.2	7.0	56.5	32.9	3.5	153138
89141	LAS VEGAS	26200	6253	18.2	25.7	35.8	9.9	10.3	56285	58919	73	54	5579	2.2	10.7	55.3	28.6	3.2	144911
89142	LAS VEGAS	25131	9769	6.6	20.3	48.2	17.9	7.1	68905	71541	86	77	7221	1.2	11.5	66.0	20.1	1.2	140840
89143	LAS VEGAS	32981	3716	5.8	14.7	42.5	25.4	11.5	83349	84707	93	93	3291	0.7	0.2	35.2	54.5	9.5	193194
89144	LAS VEGAS	48192	6653	3.9	12.3	40.0	24.5	19.3	89776	92365	95	98	5145	0.0	0.3	36.3	51.4	12.1	194729
89145	LAS VEGAS	31723	10007	10.9	25.3	40.1	14.1	9.7	64661	67855	83	71	6544	1.3	5.3	70.7	18.8	3.9	138281
89146	LAS VEGAS	30165	7370	16.0	30.0	33.4	12.6	8.0	54132	55959	70	53	3517	1.5	5.5	41.8	42.3	8.9	179919
89147	LAS VEGAS	31019	19643	10.5	22.0	43.6	16.0	7.9	66117	68729	84	73	12315	4.1	4.4	54.5	35.0	2.0	156507
89148	LAS VEGAS	42049	13290	6.0	16.6	38.9	24.5	14.1	81935	84468	93	92	8093	0.0	6.5	56.5	33.0	4.0	154849
89149	LAS VEGAS	41894	10889	8.0	12.0	36.0	26.3	17.6	88192	90392	95	97	9035	1.1	0.5	26.0	61.6	10.8	227829
89154	LAS VEGAS	15245	386	44.3	36.3	16.1	2.6	0.8	26760	26485	4	2	0	0.0	0.0	0.0	0.0	0.0	0
89156	LAS VEGAS	22577	9784	13.4	28.8	46.1	9.2	2.5	57001	60058	74	55	6083	8.3	14.7	66.4	10.2	0.4	126707
89166	LAS VEGAS	17294	876	7.5	11.8	34.9	27.4	18.4	90626	92556	95	99	711	0.0	0.7	26.9	61.9	10.5	225645
89169	LAS VEGAS	19096	14768	35.6	37.1	21.4	4.1	1.9	31880	32383	11	5	2362	15.4	23.4	46.2	14.4	0.6	107683
89178	LAS VEGAS	35279	9340	13.6	19.8	40.5	15.8	10.4	67454	69666	85	75	7442	1.4	9.2	55.4	30.5	3.5	149099
89179	LAS VEGAS	26673	492	18.1	25.6	36.0	10.0	10.4	56491	58906	73	55	439	2.3	10.5	55.6	28.7	3.0	144692
89183	LAS VEGAS	31351	10219	7.8	13.5	49.4	20.1	9.3	76481	78547	90	87	6410	0.0	5.6	43.8	43.1	7.5	176282
89191	NELLIS AFB	13106	686	17.3	48.5	30.3	2.2	1.6	41377	42999	37	19	30	30.0	6.7	63.3	0.0	0.0	96667
89301	ELY	22238	3198	26.3	27.1	38.3	6.2	2.0	46433	48362	53	29	2403	13.3	33.2	45.2	6.5	1.8	94831
89310	AUSTIN	20935	211	30.8	30.8	34.1	4.3	0.0	43456	47406	44	23	159	32.1	26.4	39.6	1.9	0.0	62188
89311	BAKER	36621	119	26.1	22.7	42.0	0.8	8.4	50371	51396	62	44	93	5.4	30.1	28.0	19.4	17.2	131618
89316	EUREKA	21576	419	27.4	21.2	41.3	8.1	1.9	50773	52081	63	46	301	20.3	29.9	41.2	7.6	1.0	89848
89317	LUND	26987	152	7.9	43.4	38.8	6.6	3.3	48791	49115	58	39	133	3.8	18.8	68.4	9.0	0.0	107813
89403	DAYTON	21829	5168	14.1	32.2	45.5	5.3	2.9	51759	52802	65	49	3968	5.1	6.6	47.6	35.7	5.0	161859
89404	DENIO	31577	79	13.9	19.0	54.4	8.9	3.8	61017	58877	79	62	58	3.4	3.4	60.3	32.8	0.0	144231
89405	EMPIRE	17517	89	38.2	49.4	7.9	4.5	0.0	27558	27615	5	3	25	0.0	48.0	4.0	28.0	20.0	112500
89406	FALLON	22517	9623	19.6	29.6	39.3	7.8	3.7	50478	52344	62	45	6345	13.1	11.3	47.9	25.0	2.7	138322
89408	FERNLEY	21113	7437	18.1	28.3	43.6	8.1	1.9	51918	52711	66	51	5794	6.2	8.5	46.1	35.5	3.7	154462
89409	GABBS	16229	309	37.5	31.1	26.9	3.2	1.3	33217	36567	14	6	196	67.9	5.6	19.4	7.1	0.0	35000
89410	GARDNERVILLE	31675	4345	17.5	17.9	44.3	14.0	6.4	64075	63996	82	70	3173	8.8	5.9	22.3	50.4	12.6	215486
89412	GERLACH	19400	351	27.4	47.6	20.8	4.0	0.3	36064	37429	21	10	93	20.4	29.0	37.6	7.5	5.4	90556
89413	GLENBROOK	43866	3376	16.4	20.9	33.2	12.4	17.2	65074	64538	83	72	2166	8.7	7.2	6.0	25.6	52.5	421774
89414	GOLCONDA	23254	179	12.3	19.6	59.2	5.6	3.4	55499	55097	72	53	141	18.4	25.5	44.7	8.5	2.8	99444
	NEVADA	27428		16.9	25.3	38.5	12.4	6.9	58128	60817				6.3	7.5	45.8	34.1	6.2	157802
	UNITED STATES	27277		20.9	24.4	35.3	11.7	7.6	54719	56938				9.3	13.1	31.6	32.6	13.5	162279

ZIP CODE		FINANCIAL SERVICES				THE HOME						ENTERTAINMENT						PERSONAL			
						Home Improvements		Furnishings													
#	POST OFFICE NAME	Auto Loan	Home Loan	Invest-ments	Retire-ment Plans	Home Repair	Lawn & Garden	Comput-ers & Hard-ware-Personal	Major Appli-ances	TV, Radio, Sound Equip-ment	Furni-ture	Dine out/ Carry out	Sports Equip-ment	Fees & Tickets	Toys & Games	Travel	Cable TV	Apparel & Services	Auto Repairs	Health Insur-ance	Pets & Supplies
89001	ALAMO	81	74	66	72	72	76	70	74	72	73	73	54	66	75	67	74	49	72	74	88
89002	HENDERSON	125	141	123	139	135	125	124	126	119	131	121	98	131	125	127	115	85	120	116	145
89003	BEATTY	78	68	71	69	70	78	73	76	75	70	74	56	68	75	71	78	51	76	82	89
89005	BOULDER CITY	101	110	126	109	118	120	100	111	103	106	102	76	108	97	111	106	71	107	119	127
89008	CALIENTE	68	64	83	59	71	77	61	72	65	65	63	48	60	59	67	68	42	69	80	83
89011	HENDERSON	107	110	107	108	110	104	104	106	102	111	103	78	106	103	105	101	72	104	104	122
89012	HENDERSON	125	127	119	130	125	117	126	121	122	133	124	95	130	126	126	119	88	122	117	141
89013	GOLDFIELD	73	70	89	64	78	83	66	78	70	72	69	51	66	64	73	74	46	75	87	90
89014	HENDERSON	111	104	95	108	100	95	112	101	109	113	111	83	109	112	106	106	78	107	99	122
89015	HENDERSON	98	101	90	99	97	92	99	96	97	102	98	75	100	99	97	95	69	96	92	111
89017	HIKO	81	75	66	72	73	76	70	75	73	73	73	54	67	76	67	75	50	72	75	89
89018	INDIAN SPRINGS	97	91	79	88	87	87	91	89	91	95	91	69	87	95	86	90	63	90	86	106
89019	JEAN	100	86	126	83	95	109	85	104	89	85	87	73	78	83	92	94	58	98	108	120
89020	AMARGOSA VALLEY	91	85	77	81	82	85	85	86	86	87	85	64	80	88	80	86	59	86	86	101
89021	LOGANDALE	100	126	110	125	121	109	105	107	99	111	101	85	119	103	114	95	73	102	96	123
89027	MESQUITE	87	88	101	88	94	94	87	91	89	91	89	64	91	85	92	90	62	91	97	105
89029	LAUGHLIN	77	70	75	72	72	74	81	75	81	80	82	57	79	78	78	82	57	81	83	90
89030	NORTH LAS VEGAS	67	58	51	55	57	49	67	61	64	70	67	48	61	66	62	61	48	66	55	69
89031	NORTH LAS VEGAS	124	134	108	129	125	110	120	118	113	130	115	94	122	122	117	106	81	113	103	135
89032	NORTH LAS VEGAS	111	119	97	113	112	97	108	107	101	117	104	84	108	109	105	96	73	102	93	121
89040	OVERTON	91	86	94	83	88	92	82	90	84	85	83	65	80	83	84	86	57	87	91	105
89043	PIOCHE	73	63	92	60	70	79	62	76	65	62	64	53	57	60	67	69	42	71	79	87
89044	HENDERSON	165	174	237	173	201	206	157	185	166	178	163	116	172	149	181	173	112	177	206	210
89045	ROUND MOUNTAIN	106	100	85	95	95	95	98	98	99	102	99	74	93	103	92	99	68	98	95	116
89046	SEARCHLIGHT	77	73	94	68	81	88	70	82	74	75	72	54	69	68	76	78	48	79	92	94
89047	SILVERPEAK	88	63	90	61	66	89	65	82	72	60	70	62	52	71	64	79	47	75	86	98
89048	PAHRUMP	82	74	92	71	81	89	73	85	78	76	76	58	70	73	77	82	51	82	93	98
89049	TONOPAH	84	74	73	72	74	81	74	79	77	75	76	58	69	79	71	80	52	77	81	93
89052	HENDERSON	145	148	156	152	152	146	144	144	142	153	143	109	150	142	148	140	101	144	144	168
89054	SLOAN	145	132	196	130	148	165	125	154	132	129	130	105	122	122	140	139	87	144	161	176
89060	PAHRUMP	77	72	93	67	79	87	69	82	73	74	71	54	67	67	75	78	48	78	91	94
89061	PAHRUMP	82	78	100	72	87	93	74	88	79	80	77	57	74	72	81	83	52	84	98	100
89074	HENDERSON	132	146	138	148	144	131	136	133	129	142	131	105	144	133	139	125	94	131	123	154
89081	NORTH LAS VEGAS	89	63	93	64	65	90	71	83	73	60	72	69	54	72	69	78	47	79	87	102
89084	NORTH LAS VEGAS	86	59	94	59	62	91	66	81	68	53	67	67	48	67	65	74	44	76	86	100
89086	NORTH LAS VEGAS	86	59	94	59	62	91	66	81	68	53	67	67	48	67	65	74	44	76	86	100
89101	LAS VEGAS	48	37	36	38	36	36	52	43	52	50	54	35	46	50	46	52	38	51	47	52
89102	LAS VEGAS	69	57	57	60	57	57	74	63	74	71	76	51	68	72	67	74	53	72	68	76
89103	LAS VEGAS	77	62	59	65	60	62	77	67	78	75	78	54	70	78	69	77	55	75	71	82
89104	LAS VEGAS	68	68	68	67	68	68	72	70	72	72	73	52	71	70	71	73	51	72	75	82
89106	LAS VEGAS	61	51	48	52	49	51	62	55	64	60	65	43	58	64	56	65	45	61	59	67
89107	LAS VEGAS	82	85	80	84	84	81	86	82	84	87	85	64	88	85	86	84	60	85	83	96
89108	LAS VEGAS	88	81	73	81	77	74	89	81	88	90	89	65	85	90	83	86	63	86	80	96
89109	LAS VEGAS	54	46	51	49	47	50	61	53	63	58	63	41	57	58	57	65	44	61	64	65
89110	LAS VEGAS	94	90	81	88	88	80	94	89	90	98	92	69	91	93	90	87	65	91	82	102
89113	LAS VEGAS	122	109	104	115	106	102	120	108	117	123	119	88	115	121	112	113	84	114	105	130
89115	LAS VEGAS	70	55	47	55	52	49	68	58	66	69	69	48	60	70	59	64	48	66	55	70
89117	LAS VEGAS	113	115	114	119	115	107	118	111	113	121	115	89	120	115	118	110	82	114	106	130
89118	LAS VEGAS	91	72	69	78	70	69	92	77	90	91	91	65	84	91	82	87	64	87	78	95
89119	LAS VEGAS	63	48	46	52	47	47	66	54	66	64	67	45	59	65	57	64	47	63	57	67
89120	LAS VEGAS	104	111	109	113	111	104	110	106	107	112	108	82	114	107	112	105	77	108	104	125
89121	LAS VEGAS	80	76	75	77	76	78	82	78	83	82	84	60	81	82	80	84	58	82	84	93
89122	LAS VEGAS	84	83	84	82	84	84	83	84	83	85	83	62	82	82	83	84	58	84	86	98
89123	LAS VEGAS	114	124	112	123	120	109	117	113	112	121	114	90	122	116	118	109	81	113	106	131
89124	LAS VEGAS	128	145	144	147	146	136	136	135	131	139	132	104	145	131	143	128	94	133	130	157
89128	LAS VEGAS	114	113	104	115	109	102	116	108	112	120	113	87	116	115	112	108	80	111	102	127
89129	LAS VEGAS	157	177	153	178	170	148	156	154	146	170	149	126	167	156	158	137	107	146	133	175
89130	LAS VEGAS	117	135	128	133	134	121	119	121	114	127	116	93	129	118	125	111	82	116	113	138
89131	LAS VEGAS	150	171	141	168	162	140	147	147	137	162	140	119	157	149	149	128	100	138	125	166
89134	LAS VEGAS	129	157	184	148	177	171	136	157	139	156	137	100	161	128	162	143	95	148	177	171
89135	LAS VEGAS	131	146	140	148	144	136	137	134	133	140	135	105	146	134	143	131	96	134	131	158
89138	LAS VEGAS	119	150	175	152	165	129	142	141	125	153	125	112	156	120	159	114	93	136	118	157
89139	LAS VEGAS	111	133	141	136	137	129	114	123	110	121	111	91	128	109	128	109	79	116	117	141
89141	LAS VEGAS	120	96	155	94	105	127	96	122	101	90	99	89	83	95	104	107	66	113	121	141
89142	LAS VEGAS	118	124	107	122	119	106	118	113	112	124	114	91	120	118	116	107	81	112	103	131
89143	LAS VEGAS	152	165	133	158	154	134	146	145	137	158	140	115	148	148	143	129	98	137	125	164
89144	LAS VEGAS	169	190	172	196	185	164	172	168	163	185	166	138	186	172	176	154	120	162	149	193
89145	LAS VEGAS	113	122	114	124	119	113	117	113	114	120	115	89	123	116	119	112	82	114	110	132
89146	LAS VEGAS	99	98	99	101	99	93	106	97	103	107	104	78	107	103	104	101	74	103	96	115
89147	LAS VEGAS	113	118	111	120	116	109	117	111	113	118	115	88	120	116	117	111	81	113	108	131
89148	LAS VEGAS	146	163	157	166	161	152	154	150	149	157	151	117	163	150	160	146	107	150	147	177
89149	LAS VEGAS	139	171	175	176	176	162	146	154	140	156	142	115	167	140	164	138	102	146	146	176
89154	LAS VEGAS	41	30	37	35	32	37	49	40	53	44	53	31	44	46	44	57	37	49	56	52
89156	LAS VEGAS	94	94	83	93	89	86	92	90	90	95	91	71	91	94	90	88	64	90	86	105
89166	LAS VEGAS	139	172	177	177	177	163	147	155	141	157	142	115	167	140	165	138	102	147	147	178
89169	LAS VEGAS	64	44	42	48	42	44	64	52	64	62	66	44	55	65	54	63	46	62	54	65
89178	LAS VEGAS	126	115	152	115	121	132	112	129	114	109	114	96	107	111	120	117	78	122	126	150
89179	LAS VEGAS	120	96	155	94	105	127	96	122	101	90	99	89	83	95	104	107	66	113	121	141
89183	LAS VEGAS	128	141	123	138	135	119	128	125	121	136	123	100	133	128	128	115	87	121	111	143
89191	NELLIS AFB	86	45	33	52	40	38	81	56	76	75	80	56	61	91	58	70	56	71	50	68
89301	ELY	81	68	78	68	69	83	72	79	76	68	74	59	64	75	70	80	50	77	85	93
89310	AUSTIN	61	58	74	54	65	69	56	65	59	60	57	43	55	54	60	62	39	63	73	75
89311	BAKER	120	96	155	94	105	126	96	122	100	90	99	89	83	95	104	107	66	112	120	141
89316	EUREKA	87	80	71	78	78	82	76	80	79	79	79	58	72	82	72	81	54	78	81	95
89317	LUND	91	83	74	81	81	85	79	83	82	82	82	61	74	85	75	84	56	81	84	99
89403	DAYTON	94	86	79	83	85	89	81	87	85	84	85	63	77	88	78	87	58	84	87	104
89404	DENIO	96	108	93	111	105	106	96	100	95	97	95	78	103	97	102	95	67	96	99	118
89405	EMPIRE	60	43	49	42	43	57	45	52	50	44	49	40	36	52	41	54	33	49	55	63
89406	FALLON	90	84	78	85	82	86	85	85	85	84	86	66	82	88	83	86	59	85	86	101
89408	FERNLEY	85	88	76	88	85	87	81	84	81	82	81	64	82	83	81	81	56	81	83	99
89409	GABBS	66	48	67	47	50	69	52	64	58	47	56	48	42	57	50	64	37	60	70	76
89410	GARDNERVILLE	105	112	115	113	115	114	105	110	105	109	105	80	110	104	111	106	73	107	112	127
89412	GERLACH	73	52	60	51	52	69	54	63	60	53	59	49	44	63	49	66	40	60	67	77
89413	GLENBROOK	136	135	167	137	147	144	135	142	135	143	135	103	139	129	144	135	94	141	144	164
89414	GOLCONDA	99	91	80	88	89	93	85	91	89	89	89	66	81	92	81	91	60	88	91	108
	NEVADA	104	102	99	102	101	98	103	101	102	106	103	78	103	103	102	100	72	102	99	118
	UNITED STATES	100	100	100	100	100	100	100	100	100	100	100	100	100	100	100	100	100	100	100	100

ZIP CODE #	POST OFFICE NAME	COUNTY FIPS CODE	POPULATION 2000	POPULATION 2009	POPULATION 2014	2000-2009 ANNUAL RATE % Rate	2000-2009 ANNUAL RATE State Centile	HOUSEHOLDS 2000	HOUSEHOLDS 2009	HOUSEHOLDS 2014	HOUSEHOLDS % Annual Rate 2000-2009	HOUSEHOLDS 2009 Average HH Size	FAMILIES 2000	FAMILIES 2009	FAMILIES % Annual Rate 2000-2009
89415	HAWTHORNE	021	3954	3709	3597	-0.7	3	1743	1701	1672	-0.3	2.15	1102	1063	-0.4
89418	IMLAY	027	760	765	754	0.1	10	311	310	305	0.0	2.47	234	231	-0.1
89419	LOVELOCK	027	4922	4720	4580	-0.5	4	1335	1254	1200	-0.7	2.64	903	839	-0.8
89420	LUNING	021	287	267	259	-0.8	2	159	154	152	-0.3	1.73	86	82	-0.5
89423	MINDEN	005	8433	10760	12037	2.7	60	3254	4185	4699	2.8	2.56	2573	3308	2.8
89424	NIXON	031	479	545	611	1.4	49	153	179	201	1.7	3.04	107	121	1.3
89425	OROVADA	013	1087	1178	1233	0.9	36	378	412	432	0.9	2.81	267	287	0.8
89426	PARADISE VALLEY	013	301	328	344	0.9	36	117	127	134	0.9	2.51	83	89	0.8
89427	SCHURZ	021	830	831	824	0.0	8	295	309	310	0.5	2.50	192	199	0.4
89429	SILVER SPRINGS	019	6676	9422	11364	3.8	69	2530	3598	4344	3.9	2.58	1790	2497	3.7
89430	SMITH	019	351	547	700	4.9	78	126	201	258	5.2	2.70	93	144	4.8
89431	SPARKS	031	35979	37446	38356	0.4	21	13666	14256	14587	0.5	2.61	8448	8458	0.0
89433	SUN VALLEY	031	19503	20441	20807	0.5	25	6390	6673	6783	0.5	3.06	4784	4838	0.1
89434	SPARKS	031	21945	29076	31688	3.1	64	8222	10747	11669	2.9	2.68	5706	7357	2.8
89436	SPARKS	031	15645	30068	37114	7.3	83	5302	9776	12026	6.8	3.07	4390	7947	6.6
89440	VIRGINIA CITY	029	1221	1504	1745	2.3	56	556	683	798	2.2	2.20	378	457	2.1
89441	SPARKS	031	5954	6729	7916	1.3	47	1977	2319	2742	1.7	2.90	1684	1967	1.7
89442	WADSWORTH	031	953	1088	1219	1.4	49	355	418	470	1.8	2.60	249	282	1.4
89444	WELLINGTON	019	2646	3592	4216	3.4	66	1134	1539	1799	3.4	2.33	817	1102	3.3
89445	WINNEMUCCA	013	15169	16551	17292	0.9	36	5326	5801	6062	0.9	2.82	3859	4169	0.8
89447	YERINGTON	019	8094	9084	9856	1.3	47	3160	3584	3905	1.4	2.43	2150	2390	1.2
89451	INCLINE VILLAGE	031	9988	12723	14340	2.7	60	4192	5410	6110	2.8	2.33	2749	3396	2.3
89460	GARDNERVILLE	005	13723	15770	16761	1.5	51	5163	6039	6456	1.7	2.60	3910	4514	1.6
89501	RENO	031	2724	2982	3149	1.0	36	1539	1742	1846	1.3	1.58	392	408	0.4
89502	RENO	031	44858	47705	49071	0.7	29	18085	19100	19632	0.6	2.48	10128	10155	0.0
89503	RENO	031	25873	28516	30000	1.1	42	10804	12143	12858	1.3	2.24	5420	5736	0.6
89506	RENO	031	26408	38566	45292	4.2	71	9065	13575	16068	4.5	2.77	6784	9880	4.1
89508	RENO	031	6705	10889	13012	5.4	81	2390	3920	4691	5.5	2.78	1869	2962	5.1
89509	RENO	031	34121	35555	36461	0.4	21	15658	16503	16955	0.6	2.13	8592	8612	0.0
89510	RENO	031	1513	5958	7468	16.0	92	580	2095	2621	14.9	2.84	439	1621	15.2
89511	RENO	031	18413	24378	27598	3.1	64	7107	9387	10636	3.1	2.57	5170	6789	3.0
89512	RENO	031	24647	27444	28899	1.2	43	9023	10192	10768	1.3	2.59	5132	5479	0.7
89519	RENO	031	8110	8998	9598	1.1	42	3393	3820	4076	1.3	2.36	2416	2646	1.0
89521	RENO	031	10278	26009	32145	10.6	88	4119	10462	12903	10.6	2.49	2816	7130	10.6
89523	RENO	031	22042	31688	36525	4.0	71	8802	12511	14352	3.9	2.52	5528	7727	3.7
89701	CARSON CITY	510	26064	27151	27505	0.4	21	8961	9377	9508	0.5	2.58	6248	6475	0.4
89703	CARSON CITY	510	9800	10437	10672	0.7	29	4414	4712	4813	0.7	2.19	2723	2894	0.7
89704	WASHOE VALLEY	031	4115	4296	4414	0.5	25	1619	1725	1779	0.7	2.49	1189	1219	0.3
89705	CARSON CITY	005	4271	5236	5718	2.2	55	1622	2014	2206	2.4	2.60	1259	1553	2.3
89706	CARSON CITY	019	18931	21261	22656	1.3	47	7663	8413	8893	1.0	2.51	4943	5359	0.9
89801	ELKO	007	20215	21082	21648	0.5	25	7351	7665	7864	0.5	2.72	5163	5329	0.3
89815	SPRING CREEK	007	12635	14230	15028	1.3	47	4172	4694	4950	1.3	3.03	3451	3846	1.2
89820	BATTLE MOUNTAIN	015	5327	5101	5124	-0.5	4	1871	1813	1829	-0.3	2.77	1385	1331	-0.4
89821	CRESCENT VALLEY	011	527	522	533	-0.1	5	224	222	228	-0.1	2.35	152	150	-0.1
89822	CARLIN	007	2316	2376	2441	0.3	17	795	813	833	0.2	2.75	583	590	0.1
89823	DEETH	007	248	258	267	0.4	21	101	105	109	0.4	2.33	75	77	0.3
89825	JACKPOT	007	665	682	710	0.3	17	218	223	232	0.2	2.96	127	128	0.1
89831	MOUNTAIN CITY	007	1344	1386	1441	0.3	17	431	449	469	0.4	2.60	278	285	0.3
89833	RUBY VALLEY	007	64	68	71	0.7	29	29	31	33	0.7	1.97	19	21	1.1
89834	TUSCARORA	007	8	8	8	0.0	8	5	5	5	0.0	1.60	3	0	-100.0
89835	WELLS	007	7796	8808	9290	1.3	47	2536	2766	2906	0.9	3.13	1793	1935	0.8
	NEVADA					3.5					3.5	2.63			3.4
	UNITED STATES					1.0					1.1	2.59			0.9

ZIP CODE #	POST OFFICE NAME	RACE (%) White 2000	White 2009	Black 2000	Black 2009	Asian/Pacific 2000	Asian/Pacific 2009	% Hispanic Origin 2000	% Hispanic Origin 2009	2009 AGE DISTRIBUTION (%) 0-4	5-9	10-14	15-19	20-24	25-44	45-64	65-84	85+	18+	MEDIAN AGE 2009	% 2009 Males	% 2009 Females
89415	HAWTHORNE	85.3	83.9	5.6	6.1	1.1	1.2	8.5	11.0	4.9	5.4	5.5	5.9	5.2	19.6	30.8	19.7	3.0	80.4	47.5	49.3	50.7
89418	IMLAY	86.5	83.0	0.1	0.1	0.8	0.8	15.4	20.3	8.2	8.0	8.0	7.7	6.4	23.8	26.7	10.5	0.8	71.1	36.1	50.6	49.4
89419	LOVELOCK	75.1	71.1	7.2	7.7	0.8	0.9	20.3	25.6	5.6	5.8	5.6	6.3	8.6	35.4	22.9	8.3	1.4	79.4	35.4	65.4	34.6
89420	LUNING	93.7	94.0	1.0	1.1	0.0	0.0	3.1	4.1	2.2	2.2	2.6	3.7	3.7	14.6	36.7	31.5	2.6	90.3	58.2	51.3	48.7
89423	MINDEN	94.6	93.5	0.2	0.2	1.1	1.2	5.4	7.3	4.5	5.2	6.2	6.6	4.2	18.8	35.7	16.9	2.0	79.8	47.5	48.8	51.2
89424	NIXON	23.0	21.7	0.0	0.0	0.4	0.4	8.6	12.1	8.3	8.1	8.6	9.2	6.6	24.4	23.7	9.0	2.2	69.2	33.6	49.4	50.6
89425	OROVADA	58.0	56.5	0.2	0.2	0.3	0.3	17.5	22.3	6.5	7.5	8.5	8.1	4.5	23.3	30.0	10.7	1.1	72.2	39.0	52.7	47.3
89426	PARADISE VALLEY	79.1	75.9	0.3	0.3	0.3	0.3	24.5	30.8	6.1	7.9	9.5	7.6	3.4	22.9	32.3	9.8	0.6	71.0	39.8	54.3	45.7
89427	SCHURZ	12.8	14.3	2.0	2.5	0.2	0.2	10.0	12.5	7.8	7.6	8.5	14.2	7.3	20.7	23.2	9.1	1.4	65.1	28.5	52.9	47.1
89429	SILVER SPRINGS	91.3	89.5	0.9	1.1	0.7	0.6	4.7	7.0	5.4	5.7	6.4	7.0	5.3	22.6	31.7	14.6	1.3	78.1	43.4	49.3	50.7
89430	SMITH	85.5	80.3	0.3	0.2	0.3	0.4	21.9	30.5	3.7	5.1	6.8	6.4	2.7	20.1	37.5	16.3	1.5	79.5	48.0	50.8	49.2
89431	SPARKS	73.6	66.9	2.7	2.9	5.3	5.2	27.3	38.0	7.8	6.9	6.4	6.6	7.7	28.3	24.3	10.5	1.5	75.1	34.9	50.1	49.9
89433	SUN VALLEY	79.9	73.6	2.1	2.4	2.9	3.0	21.0	30.7	9.1	8.3	7.7	7.1	6.8	29.9	23.0	7.6	0.6	70.7	32.5	50.2	49.8
89434	SPARKS	82.3	78.8	2.3	2.5	6.5	7.1	11.3	15.5	6.2	6.3	6.6	7.0	6.4	26.9	29.4	9.6	1.6	76.6	38.3	48.6	51.4
89436	SPARKS	88.7	85.7	1.3	1.5	3.7	4.1	7.1	11.2	9.0	8.6	8.2	6.8	4.6	31.4	24.9	6.0	0.6	69.6	34.9	48.6	51.4
89440	VIRGINIA CITY	93.7	92.7	0.2	0.3	0.7	0.9	4.8	6.3	4.7	4.7	5.7	5.9	2.7	23.5	41.4	10.3	1.2	80.9	46.3	51.7	48.3
89441	SPARKS	87.2	85.2	0.6	0.7	1.1	1.3	5.5	8.6	7.7	8.0	8.4	8.2	5.4	25.2	30.2	6.6	0.4	70.8	36.7	49.7	50.3
89442	WADSWORTH	23.1	21.7	0.1	0.1	0.4	0.4	8.5	12.2	8.3	8.1	8.6	8.9	6.6	24.5	23.6	9.1	2.2	69.5	33.6	49.5	50.5
89444	WELLINGTON	90.3	87.3	0.5	0.5	0.9	0.8	11.9	17.6	3.2	4.5	5.8	5.1	3.1	16.8	37.1	22.4	2.0	83.0	51.9	51.1	48.9
89445	WINNEMUCCA	85.0	82.0	0.5	0.6	0.7	0.7	18.8	24.0	8.2	8.0	8.1	7.6	6.1	26.9	26.9	7.3	0.9	70.7	34.5	51.9	48.1
89447	YERINGTON	82.7	78.5	0.9	1.0	0.4	0.4	17.5	24.2	6.4	5.7	5.9	8.5	5.6	19.7	25.9	19.1	3.1	76.2	43.3	51.5	48.5
89451	INCLINE VILLAGE	91.0	87.9	0.5	0.6	1.7	1.9	12.1	17.3	4.6	4.6	5.1	5.5	5.6	24.6	34.5	14.4	1.2	82.6	45.0	51.5	48.5
89460	GARDNERVILLE	91.3	90.0	0.3	0.3	1.1	1.2	6.9	9.1	5.9	6.2	6.6	6.9	6.0	23.5	30.3	13.2	1.4	77.0	41.3	49.7	50.3
89501	RENO	74.6	69.7	4.6	5.4	11.9	12.7	13.1	19.4	2.5	2.5	2.0	5.7	8.3	26.2	34.9	15.9	1.9	91.2	46.5	61.5	38.5
89502	RENO	68.8	62.5	2.4	2.6	4.5	4.5	33.1	42.3	8.1	6.9	6.1	6.4	8.4	30.1	23.6	9.2	1.3	75.3	33.5	51.8	48.2
89503	RENO	82.5	77.9	1.7	2.0	7.1	7.7	10.0	15.7	4.9	4.6	4.6	7.5	9.9	28.6	26.6	11.4	1.8	82.9	37.3	52.0	48.0
89506	RENO	83.1	78.3	2.1	2.2	3.0	3.2	13.3	19.8	8.2	7.5	7.2	7.9	7.4	29.4	24.4	7.4	0.6	72.4	33.0	50.4	49.6
89508	RENO	93.2	90.9	0.8	1.2	1.0	1.2	4.4	6.9	6.7	6.8	7.3	7.3	5.6	25.9	32.4	7.4	0.5	74.6	39.0	50.5	49.5
89509	RENO	85.2	81.7	1.7	1.9	4.3	4.7	11.4	16.0	5.1	4.8	4.9	5.3	6.5	24.1	30.4	15.8	3.2	82.1	44.5	49.0	51.0
89510	RENO	80.4	80.8	0.8	0.8	0.9	1.0	4.8	7.2	7.6	7.7	7.8	7.5	5.0	26.6	28.8	8.1	0.8	72.2	37.0	50.1	49.9
89511	RENO	92.2	90.8	0.9	0.9	2.6	2.9	5.3	7.5	5.3	6.0	6.9	6.8	4.9	20.7	34.9	12.9	1.6	77.5	44.6	49.4	50.6
89512	RENO	64.3	59.8	5.8	5.8	8.7	8.1	32.0	41.0	8.3	6.9	6.2	7.5	9.4	27.3	21.9	10.9	1.7	74.9	32.7	51.7	48.3
89519	RENO	93.2	91.4	0.5	0.7	3.6	4.2	3.5	5.7	4.8	5.6	6.9	6.3	3.3	18.2	35.9	17.2	1.8	78.6	47.8	49.8	50.2
89521	RENO	91.1	85.4	1.0	2.1	2.9	5.1	5.7	10.3	7.5	7.1	7.0	6.2	5.5	29.3	28.1	8.3	0.9	74.4	37.2	49.4	50.6
89523	RENO	85.1	82.3	1.5	1.6	7.2	8.0	7.2	10.9	6.9	6.2	5.9	6.1	7.7	33.9	25.6	6.6	0.9	77.5	33.4	49.3	50.7
89701	CARSON CITY	83.4	80.9	3.0	3.3	2.0	2.1	16.1	20.4	6.4	5.7	5.6	6.4	7.5	28.6	26.7	11.5	1.5	78.5	37.7	54.2	45.8
89703	CARSON CITY	91.1	90.2	0.4	0.4	1.9	2.0	5.8	7.7	4.1	4.4	5.2	6.0	4.6	19.1	33.5	19.6	3.6	82.4	49.4	48.8	51.2
89704	WASHOE VALLEY	95.6	94.1	0.4	0.5	1.0	1.1	3.5	5.7	4.2	5.0	6.1	6.3	3.7	20.6	39.2	13.9	1.1	80.8	47.4	49.7	50.3
89705	CARSON CITY	91.0	88.8	0.4	0.4	0.9	1.0	9.1	12.4	6.1	6.6	7.3	6.8	4.5	22.1	31.2	14.0	1.4	75.8	42.6	48.8	51.2
89706	CARSON CITY	85.6	82.2	0.7	0.8	1.7	1.8	15.6	20.8	7.7	6.8	6.6	6.1	5.9	26.1	25.3	13.3	2.3	75.2	38.3	48.6	51.4
89801	ELKO	81.9	78.7	0.3	0.4	1.1	1.2	19.2	24.8	8.7	8.1	7.8	7.2	6.3	29.8	23.9	7.0	1.1	71.0	32.1	50.7	49.3
89815	SPRING CREEK	91.0	89.1	0.3	0.3	0.5	0.5	8.3	11.2	8.5	8.6	8.3	8.1	5.6	29.3	25.9	5.4	0.3	69.4	32.4	50.4	49.6
89820	BATTLE MOUNTAIN	83.9	80.4	0.1	0.1	0.4	0.4	19.4	24.8	8.1	8.2	7.9	8.4	6.9	25.4	27.0	7.4	0.8	70.2	33.2	50.6	49.4
89821	CRESCENT VALLEY	90.1	89.8	0.4	0.4	0.6	0.6	9.7	9.8	7.3	7.1	7.3	7.5	5.7	23.4	27.4	13.6	0.8	73.8	40.4	51.1	48.9
89822	CARLIN	90.2	87.9	1.8	2.0	0.6	0.7	8.4	11.9	7.8	7.6	7.3	6.6	6.5	29.1	25.8	8.6	0.7	73.3	35.3	53.8	46.2
89823	DEETH	89.1	87.2	0.4	0.4	0.4	0.4	13.7	18.6	7.4	7.8	7.4	7.8	6.2	27.9	26.7	7.8	1.2	72.5	34.4	53.9	46.1
89825	JACKPOT	67.9	62.6	0.0	0.0	0.3	0.3	44.3	53.5	8.5	7.9	7.0	7.5	8.7	30.5	23.9	5.7	0.3	72.1	30.3	50.6	49.4
89831	MOUNTAIN CITY	34.9	35.4	2.8	3.0	0.6	0.6	11.7	15.4	5.1	6.2	7.4	19.0	4.0	21.4	26.1	9.5	1.1	66.7	34.2	58.7	41.3
89833	RUBY VALLEY	83.9	79.4	3.2	4.4	0.0	0.0	12.9	17.6	5.9	5.9	5.9	5.9	7.4	32.4	27.9	8.8	0.0	79.4	35.8	57.4	42.6
89834	TUSCARORA	100.0	100.0	0.0	0.0	0.0	0.0	28.6	25.0	0.0	0.0	0.0	0.0	12.5	37.5	50.0	0.0	0.0	100.0	45.0	100.0	0.0
89835	WELLS	74.7	70.9	1.1	1.1	0.6	0.5	42.5	51.5	10.5	9.3	8.0	7.6	8.2	28.7	21.1	6.1	0.4	67.5	28.5	53.1	46.9
	NEVADA	75.2	71.8	6.8	7.2	4.9	5.1	19.7	24.9	7.3	6.8	6.5	6.6	6.4	28.1	26.0	11.1	1.3	75.4	36.8	50.3	49.7
	UNITED STATES	75.1	72.0	12.3	12.7	3.8	4.6	12.5	15.7	6.8	6.7	6.6	7.1	6.9	27.0	26.0	10.9	1.9	75.7	36.9	49.2	50.8

ZIP CODE #	POST OFFICE NAME	2009 Per Capita Income	2009 HH Income Base	2009 HOUSEHOLD INCOME DISTRIBUTION (%) Less than $25,000	$25,000 to $49,999	$50,000 to $99,999	$100,000 to $149,999	$150,000 or More	MEDIAN HOUSEHOLD INCOME 2009	2014	2009 National Centile	2009 State Centile	2009 Home Value Base	2009 HOME VALUE DISTRIBUTION (%) Less than $50,000	$50,000 to $89,999	$90,000 to $174,999	$175,000 to $399,999	$400,000 or More	2009 Median Home Value
89415	HAWTHORNE	23250	1701	28.2	28.2	35.4	7.2	0.9	44282	45731	46	25	1220	19.7	38.3	40.7	1.1	0.2	83618
89418	IMLAY	21496	310	27.1	21.6	42.9	6.5	1.9	50913	51677	63	47	237	15.2	28.3	43.5	10.5	2.5	102989
89419	LOVELOCK	22817	1254	23.4	27.0	40.4	7.3	1.9	49584	51002	60	41	824	22.5	22.9	46.8	7.4	0.4	96230
89420	LUNING	26610	154	31.2	32.5	27.9	5.8	2.6	40000	41668	33	14	117	22.2	33.3	41.0	3.4	0.0	85000
89423	MINDEN	34598	4185	9.2	11.3	50.6	20.7	8.3	76345	77748	90	86	3567	1.0	1.6	10.9	71.6	14.9	246780
89424	NIXON	15757	179	29.6	31.3	32.4	4.5	2.2	39720	41038	32	12	112	29.5	28.6	28.6	10.7	2.7	81000
89425	OROVADA	17069	412	37.1	17.2	39.3	5.1	1.2	41215	46081	37	18	302	25.2	21.2	28.8	23.5	1.3	99167
89426	PARADISE VALLEY	20727	127	32.3	15.7	44.1	7.1	0.8	51785	52114	65	50	86	10.5	24.4	34.9	29.1	1.2	118182
89427	SCHURZ	19187	309	35.6	24.9	30.4	7.8	1.3	37332	40000	25	12	237	12.2	38.8	45.6	1.7	1.7	88333
89429	SILVER SPRINGS	19435	3598	28.5	30.6	32.9	5.6	2.5	40847	45417	35	16	2915	5.8	26.8	54.4	12.8	0.2	105999
89430	SMITH	23423	201	26.4	24.4	36.8	5.5	7.0	48672	51255	58	38	125	3.2	5.6	8.8	43.2	39.2	291000
89431	SPARKS	20677	14256	21.1	33.1	38.1	6.0	1.8	46504	47556	53	30	6488	8.9	6.3	55.5	27.7	1.6	153817
89433	SUN VALLEY	19257	6673	14.0	31.7	45.6	7.0	1.8	53256	54073	68	51	5074	14.2	17.6	50.6	17.5	0.1	115864
89434	SPARKS	29812	10747	9.0	22.2	45.7	15.3	7.8	66801	69672	85	74	7058	2.1	4.2	25.7	62.7	5.3	203260
89436	SPARKS	34472	9776	3.5	9.0	46.5	24.7	16.3	88304	89605	95	97	8457	5.7	0.8	4.9	80.1	8.5	241608
89440	VIRGINIA CITY	29963	683	13.8	27.1	44.2	11.1	3.8	59372	62452	77	59	532	7.3	1.9	33.1	43.2	14.5	191016
89441	SPARKS	33780	2319	4.8	9.7	46.7	26.4	12.3	86512	86970	94	96	2104	0.5	2.7	11.5	72.8	12.5	260169
89442	WADSWORTH	18432	418	29.7	31.1	32.5	4.3	2.4	39766	40912	32	13	262	28.6	28.6	29.8	10.3	2.7	82083
89444	WELLINGTON	25030	1539	23.5	32.3	32.0	7.0	5.3	41947	48763	39	21	1184	8.7	14.4	33.5	25.8	17.5	149671
89445	WINNEMUCCA	23885	5801	15.6	19.9	48.2	12.2	4.2	59338	59521	77	58	4237	12.6	18.5	49.0	17.9	1.9	122286
89447	YERINGTON	22438	3584	27.4	34.6	28.9	4.5	4.5	41010	43678	36	17	2405	16.0	13.5	43.6	21.9	5.0	120167
89451	INCLINE VILLAGE	55318	5410	9.4	14.6	33.7	18.5	23.9	83068	87112	93	92	3465	1.5	2.9	5.5	20.1	69.9	634702
89460	GARDNERVILLE	31443	6039	11.1	24.5	40.4	14.6	9.4	64519	64273	83	71	4264	2.9	4.2	30.6	42.7	19.7	202994
89501	RENO	25137	1742	51.3	29.1	13.0	3.2	3.4	24016	23575	3	1	153	0.0	12.4	37.9	36.6	13.1	173611
89502	RENO	21785	19100	25.0	32.9	32.1	7.2	2.8	42923	45043	42	22	6775	14.9	16.1	30.4	32.8	5.8	143719
89503	RENO	25644	12143	24.5	27.2	36.5	8.6	3.2	48416	48639	58	35	5737	6.3	3.3	33.9	54.9	1.6	183521
89506	RENO	24261	13575	8.9	27.9	50.8	9.7	2.7	61034	62190	79	62	10030	14.7	11.9	39.7	32.8	0.9	145525
89508	RENO	28411	3920	7.9	19.5	48.1	20.7	3.8	71545	73493	88	80	3592	1.0	6.0	52.6	37.5	2.9	165605
89509	RENO	38326	16503	17.9	23.1	33.9	14.0	11.1	61699	63220	80	64	8313	3.1	2.1	12.4	56.6	25.8	276528
89510	RENO	29419	2095	4.5	14.7	58.1	17.7	5.0	76592	77907	90	88	1829	1.9	3.7	24.4	59.0	11.0	219639
89511	RENO	45070	9387	8.2	16.4	33.3	18.6	23.6	85486	88667	94	95	7211	4.4	5.0	6.2	39.1	45.2	369166
89512	RENO	17649	10192	35.1	32.6	25.4	5.2	1.7	34672	35829	17	8	3616	13.3	16.0	48.1	21.7	0.8	128571
89519	RENO	65186	3820	5.4	12.3	31.3	15.9	35.1	102948	107979	97	100	2903	0.0	0.0	2.5	36.5	60.9	450317
89521	RENO	35947	10462	8.4	17.8	42.7	21.0	10.1	76819	79180	90	88	7720	2.7	2.6	11.2	75.5	7.9	258421
89523	RENO	31422	12511	11.7	23.7	39.7	16.5	8.3	66734	70894	85	73	7135	7.0	2.2	7.2	74.6	8.9	242204
89701	CARSON CITY	25896	9377	16.4	26.3	40.8	12.1	4.4	57007	59244	74	56	5858	4.7	6.9	22.7	58.6	7.1	208715
89703	CARSON CITY	38424	4712	18.8	20.1	34.6	15.1	11.5	62984	63415	81	67	3290	5.6	2.4	8.7	47.8	35.6	317962
89704	WASHOE VALLEY	34457	1725	13.6	20.5	36.7	19.8	9.4	74585	76452	89	83	1478	6.8	3.5	23.7	48.2	17.7	212782
89705	CARSON CITY	31256	2014	9.7	15.4	54.3	13.2	7.4	70885	70612	87	79	1612	0.5	5.5	35.4	51.1	7.6	193194
89706	CARSON CITY	22761	8413	21.2	31.5	36.2	8.2	2.8	47783	51252	56	34	5212	17.0	10.8	29.3	38.0	4.9	156934
89801	ELKO	25913	7665	15.6	20.6	45.1	13.8	4.8	63383	63926	82	69	5067	15.6	11.5	42.6	28.2	2.1	139534
89815	SPRING CREEK	27344	4694	7.6	14.1	52.7	19.1	6.4	76225	76679	90	86	4017	5.3	15.2	49.7	27.2	2.6	144731
89820	BATTLE MOUNTAIN	21813	1813	17.5	22.2	48.4	10.5	1.3	59968	60244	77	60	1399	22.3	25.5	45.6	6.1	0.5	93144
89821	CRESCENT VALLEY	21717	222	33.8	19.8	36.5	7.2	2.7	45923	50388	51	29	174	26.4	31.6	29.9	8.6	3.4	78750
89822	CARLIN	22418	813	15.1	24.2	49.8	9.3	1.5	58193	58994	75	57	584	22.4	24.7	42.3	9.1	1.5	94722
89823	DEETH	25238	105	14.3	33.3	43.8	5.7	2.9	51598	53410	65	48	79	26.6	30.4	32.9	8.9	1.3	77000
89825	JACKPOT	15795	223	15.2	52.9	28.7	3.1	0.0	40253	42536	34	15	92	58.7	19.6	15.2	5.4	1.1	35000
89831	MOUNTAIN CITY	16659	449	43.0	31.4	19.6	5.6	0.4	30661	32418	9	4	267	43.4	29.6	15.7	9.0	2.2	62600
89833	RUBY VALLEY	27868	31	19.4	35.5	41.9	3.2	0.0	44271	48642	46	25	21	19.0	14.3	23.8	42.9	0.0	143750
89834	TUSCARORA	29481	5	0.0	40.0	60.0	0.0	0.0	51667	48333	65	49	0	0.0	0.0	0.0	0.0	0.0	0
89835	WELLS	17402	2766	20.2	34.9	36.8	6.3	1.8	45691	48374	50	28	1643	31.3	26.3	28.7	12.4	1.3	78750
	NEVADA	27428		16.9	25.3	38.5	12.4	6.9	58128	60817				6.3	7.5	45.8	34.1	6.2	157802
	UNITED STATES	27277		20.9	24.4	35.3	11.7	7.6	54719	56938				9.3	13.1	31.6	32.6	13.5	162279

#	POST OFFICE NAME	FINANCIAL SERVICES: Auto Loan	FINANCIAL SERVICES: Home Loan	FINANCIAL SERVICES: Invest-ments	FINANCIAL SERVICES: Retire-ment Plans	THE HOME: Home Improvements: Home Repair	THE HOME: Home Improvements: Lawn & Garden	THE HOME: Furnishings: Comput-ers & Hard-ware-Personal	THE HOME: Furnishings: Major Appli-ances	THE HOME: Furnishings: TV, Radio, Sound Equip-ment	THE HOME: Furnishings: Furni-ture	ENTERTAINMENT: Dine out/ Carry out	ENTERTAINMENT: Sports Equip-ment	ENTERTAINMENT: Fees & Tickets	ENTERTAINMENT: Toys & Games	ENTERTAINMENT: Travel	ENTERTAINMENT: Cable TV	PERSONAL: Apparel & Services	PERSONAL: Auto Repairs	PERSONAL: Health Insur-ance	PERSONAL: Pets & Supplies
89415	HAWTHORNE	74	68	82	65	71	84	66	77	71	65	70	54	63	68	69	77	47	74	86	89
89418	IMLAY	85	78	69	76	76	80	74	78	77	77	77	57	70	80	70	79	52	76	78	93
89419	LOVELOCK	84	77	70	75	75	79	76	78	78	77	77	58	71	80	72	79	53	77	79	93
89420	LUNING	68	65	82	59	72	77	61	73	65	66	63	47	61	59	67	69	43	70	81	83
89423	MINDEN	116	141	144	144	145	139	121	130	119	128	120	94	138	118	136	120	85	124	130	148
89424	NIXON	75	70	59	66	66	67	69	69	69	72	69	52	65	72	65	69	48	69	67	82
89425	OROVADA	78	60	78	60	61	81	64	74	68	58	67	59	54	67	63	74	45	72	80	91
89426	PARADISE VALLEY	92	64	99	64	67	96	70	87	73	58	72	71	53	72	70	80	47	81	91	107
89427	SCHURZ	65	66	52	68	61	69	66	63	67	63	66	51	67	68	64	68	46	65	71	78
89429	SILVER SPRINGS	85	68	79	66	69	83	67	79	72	66	72	58	58	73	65	77	48	74	81	94
89430	SMITH	105	84	136	83	92	111	84	107	88	79	87	78	73	84	91	94	58	99	106	124
89431	SPARKS	75	71	64	72	68	68	79	71	78	76	79	57	76	79	74	77	55	76	73	85
89433	SUN VALLEY	91	88	73	85	83	79	86	83	84	90	85	65	83	89	81	82	59	83	78	98
89434	SPARKS	110	121	113	122	119	111	114	112	110	118	112	87	121	113	117	108	80	111	107	130
89436	SPARKS	153	178	151	177	170	147	153	153	142	166	145	124	165	153	157	133	104	143	131	173
89440	VIRGINIA CITY	109	88	140	87	97	116	88	111	92	83	91	81	77	87	96	98	61	103	111	129
89441	SPARKS	139	163	141	160	157	138	141	142	132	150	135	112	152	139	146	126	96	135	125	161
89442	WADSWORTH	75	70	59	66	66	67	69	69	69	72	69	52	65	72	65	69	48	69	67	82
89444	WELLINGTON	91	80	114	76	88	100	78	95	82	79	80	66	73	76	85	87	54	90	100	109
89445	WINNEMUCCA	101	99	89	97	96	97	96	97	96	97	96	74	94	99	93	96	67	96	95	114
89447	YERINGTON	85	70	88	68	74	88	74	84	78	71	77	61	66	76	73	84	52	81	91	98
89451	INCLINE VILLAGE	163	197	235	201	217	183	187	189	171	200	172	144	206	164	209	163	126	184	173	211
89460	GARDNERVILLE	114	126	116	126	123	117	116	116	113	121	115	89	123	116	120	111	81	114	112	135
89501	RENO	49	36	41	41	37	42	58	46	61	51	60	37	50	54	50	63	42	56	60	59
89502	RENO	78	66	62	69	64	64	80	70	79	79	80	57	74	80	73	77	56	77	71	85
89503	RENO	78	73	70	75	71	75	85	76	84	80	84	60	81	82	79	84	59	81	82	91
89506	RENO	100	100	85	98	95	90	98	94	95	101	96	74	96	99	94	92	67	94	89	110
89508	RENO	118	127	110	124	122	113	113	115	109	120	110	89	116	115	113	106	77	110	106	133
89509	RENO	112	111	116	115	113	109	119	111	116	120	117	87	120	114	118	114	83	116	113	132
89510	RENO	122	136	121	133	131	119	120	122	114	129	116	94	126	120	123	110	82	116	110	139
89511	RENO	154	180	191	187	187	168	165	165	157	176	158	127	184	157	179	151	115	161	154	189
89512	RENO	64	51	50	53	50	51	66	57	66	64	67	46	59	66	59	66	47	64	61	70
89519	RENO	189	249	295	254	275	228	219	228	199	240	198	172	255	192	254	188	147	215	203	253
89521	RENO	131	137	125	136	132	124	129	127	124	135	126	100	131	129	129	120	88	125	119	148
89523	RENO	118	117	103	118	112	101	117	109	111	123	114	89	116	117	112	106	80	110	99	127
89701	CARSON CITY	91	94	89	95	92	92	94	91	93	94	94	70	96	94	94	93	66	93	94	108
89703	CARSON CITY	111	128	137	129	135	128	117	123	115	123	115	89	129	113	128	116	82	119	124	140
89704	WASHOE VALLEY	116	141	127	143	138	128	121	124	115	126	117	97	134	119	130	113	83	119	116	144
89705	CARSON CITY	105	130	121	131	127	127	111	116	111	114	112	87	127	112	123	112	79	113	119	135
89706	CARSON CITY	84	80	80	79	80	80	82	81	81	83	82	62	79	81	80	81	57	82	82	95
89801	ELKO	104	106	94	103	103	98	102	101	99	105	100	78	101	103	99	97	70	99	96	117
89815	SPRING CREEK	126	135	109	130	126	112	121	120	114	130	117	94	122	123	118	109	81	114	106	137
89820	BATTLE MOUNTAIN	94	91	77	87	86	85	86	87	86	90	87	65	83	90	82	86	59	85	84	102
89821	CRESCENT VALLEY	82	75	67	73	74	77	71	75	74	74	74	55	67	77	68	76	50	73	75	89
89822	CARLIN	97	89	79	86	87	91	84	89	87	88	87	65	80	91	80	90	59	86	89	106
89823	DEETH	97	83	88	81	82	94	81	90	84	79	84	69	72	86	79	87	56	86	91	108
89825	JACKPOT	72	65	61	62	62	67	65	67	65	66	66	51	59	68	61	66	45	66	66	80
89831	MOUNTAIN CITY	65	46	66	45	48	68	50	62	55	44	54	48	39	54	49	61	35	58	67	74
89833	RUBY VALLEY	88	81	72	79	79	83	77	81	80	80	80	59	73	83	73	82	54	79	81	96
89834	TUSCARORA	84	58	93	58	61	89	64	80	67	52	66	66	47	66	64	73	43	75	85	99
89835	WELLS	84	78	68	75	75	77	77	78	78	80	78	59	72	81	73	79	54	78	77	92
	NEVADA	104	102	99	102	101	98	103	101	102	106	103	78	103	103	102	100	72	102	99	118
	UNITED STATES	100	100	100	100	100	100	100	100	100	100	100	100	100	100	100	100	100	100	100	100

ZIP CODE #	POST OFFICE NAME	COUNTY FIPS CODE	POPULATION 2000	POPULATION 2009	POPULATION 2014	2000-2009 ANNUAL RATE % Rate	2000-2009 ANNUAL RATE State Centile	HOUSEHOLDS 2000	HOUSEHOLDS 2009	HOUSEHOLDS 2014	HOUSEHOLDS % Annual Rate 2000-2009	HOUSEHOLDS 2009 Average HH Size	FAMILIES 2000	FAMILIES 2009	FAMILIES % Annual Rate 2000-2009
03031	AMHERST	011	10807	11825	12223	1.0	54	3613	3950	4094	1.0	2.99	3086	3351	0.9
03032	AUBURN	015	4682	5067	5220	0.9	46	1580	1750	1816	1.1	2.89	1322	1453	1.0
03033	BROOKLINE	011	4181	4467	4550	0.7	34	1343	1418	1447	0.6	3.15	1147	1203	0.5
03034	CANDIA	015	4073	4491	4656	1.1	64	1410	1588	1659	1.3	2.83	1151	1285	1.2
03036	CHESTER	015	3814	4405	4615	1.6	89	1220	1431	1508	1.7	3.05	1013	1179	1.7
03037	DEERFIELD	015	3610	4197	4451	1.6	89	1206	1420	1511	1.8	2.94	968	1129	1.7
03038	DERRY	015	34181	35228	35154	0.3	11	12375	12886	12918	0.4	2.71	8824	9093	0.3
03042	EPPING	015	5571	5706	5732	0.3	11	2082	2178	2205	0.5	2.61	1502	1551	0.3
03043	FRANCESTOWN	011	1436	1667	1760	1.6	89	534	619	657	1.6	2.69	405	464	1.5
03044	FREMONT	015	3508	4340	4689	2.3	100	1164	1451	1578	2.4	2.96	982	1216	2.3
03045	GOFFSTOWN	011	12770	13085	13114	0.3	11	4362	4427	4448	0.2	2.74	3232	3243	0.0
03046	DUNBARTON	013	2332	2632	2748	1.3	74	842	952	997	1.3	2.76	676	758	1.2
03047	GREENFIELD	011	1657	1798	1854	0.9	46	563	611	635	0.9	2.69	406	435	0.7
03048	GREENVILLE	011	3324	3701	3853	1.2	71	1292	1434	1497	1.1	2.58	870	951	1.0
03049	HOLLIS	011	7030	8038	8445	1.5	85	2444	2793	2946	1.5	2.88	2027	2297	1.4
03051	HUDSON	011	23054	25238	26109	1.0	54	8095	8821	9147	0.9	2.84	6309	6829	0.9
03052	LITCHFIELD	011	7231	8435	8939	1.7	91	2295	2670	2836	1.6	3.16	1982	2291	1.6
03053	LONDONDERRY	015	23136	24891	25558	0.8	39	7595	8313	8596	1.0	2.99	6294	6830	0.9
03054	MERRIMACK	011	25135	26864	27455	0.7	34	8834	9488	9751	0.8	2.82	6985	7378	0.6
03055	MILFORD	011	13467	15096	15696	1.2	71	5172	5770	6015	1.2	2.59	3525	3905	1.1
03057	MONT VERNON	011	2114	2130	2115	0.1	7	724	728	724	0.1	2.89	601	601	0.0
03060	NASHUA	011	29539	30131	30176	0.2	10	12175	12338	12388	0.1	2.39	7072	7046	0.0
03062	NASHUA	011	26222	27789	28384	0.6	26	9989	10572	10842	0.6	2.59	6973	7324	0.5
03063	NASHUA	011	16175	16465	16463	0.2	10	6721	6817	6842	0.2	2.37	4280	4281	0.0
03064	NASHUA	011	14654	14718	14658	0.0	5	5725	5737	5737	0.0	2.55	3755	3710	-0.1
03070	NEW BOSTON	011	4143	4393	4481	0.6	26	1436	1520	1555	0.6	2.88	1163	1220	0.5
03071	NEW IPSWICH	011	4147	4764	4996	1.5	85	1316	1515	1596	1.5	3.13	1060	1208	1.4
03076	PELHAM	011	10914	12026	12447	1.1	64	3606	3970	4127	1.0	3.03	2983	3258	1.0
03077	RAYMOND	015	9487	10305	10671	0.9	46	3430	3818	3987	1.2	2.70	2519	2768	1.0
03079	SALEM	015	28083	29728	30198	0.6	26	10392	11211	11468	0.8	2.64	7594	8101	0.7
03082	LYNDEBOROUGH	011	1602	1733	1790	0.9	46	565	610	633	0.8	2.84	424	454	0.7
03084	TEMPLE	011	1274	1357	1377	0.7	34	429	456	465	0.7	2.94	341	360	0.6
03086	WILTON	011	3758	4179	4361	1.2	71	1421	1576	1649	1.1	2.65	1032	1130	1.0
03087	WINDHAM	015	10721	12762	13659	1.9	96	3574	4367	4714	2.2	2.90	3023	3668	2.1
03101	MANCHESTER	011	2629	2845	2892	0.9	46	1519	1591	1614	0.5	1.66	481	491	0.2
03102	MANCHESTER	011	30073	31940	32500	0.7	34	12766	13547	13839	0.6	2.25	7216	7470	0.4
03103	MANCHESTER	011	37204	38037	38182	0.2	10	14375	14582	14667	0.2	2.55	8947	8914	0.0
03104	MANCHESTER	011	31744	33473	34013	0.6	26	13221	13858	14127	0.5	2.31	7717	7951	0.3
03106	HOOKSETT	013	11672	13715	14536	1.8	95	4129	4889	5222	1.8	2.62	3017	3534	1.7
03109	MANCHESTER	011	9334	10003	10172	0.8	39	3575	3811	3883	0.7	2.58	2526	2658	0.6
03110	BEDFORD	011	18410	21092	22190	1.5	85	6302	7213	7614	1.5	2.86	5158	5857	1.4
03216	ANDOVER	013	2127	2384	2513	1.2	71	831	934	988	1.3	2.54	615	682	1.1
03217	ASHLAND	009	2524	2716	2795	0.8	39	1086	1183	1223	0.9	2.29	682	734	0.8
03218	BARNSTEAD	001	1036	1118	1170	0.8	39	373	413	437	1.1	2.71	288	315	1.0
03220	BELMONT	001	6880	7816	8163	1.4	81	2709	3174	3349	1.7	2.46	1914	2215	1.6
03221	BRADFORD	013	1512	2071	2315	3.5	100	587	807	903	3.5	2.54	423	574	3.4
03222	BRISTOL	009	4869	5630	5921	1.6	89	1946	2275	2406	1.7	2.46	1372	1584	1.6
03223	CAMPTON	009	2963	2761	2695	-0.8	1	1238	1166	1144	-0.6	2.37	824	765	-0.8
03224	CANTERBURY	013	1901	2263	2428	1.9	96	719	859	924	1.9	2.63	566	670	1.8
03225	CENTER BARNSTEAD	001	2838	3196	3297	1.3	74	1046	1216	1267	1.6	2.63	806	928	1.5
03226	CENTER HARBOR	001	763	842	863	1.1	64	320	364	378	1.4	2.30	227	256	1.3
03227	CENTER SANDWICH	003	984	1087	1135	1.1	64	435	491	517	1.3	2.21	302	337	1.2
03229	CONTOOCOOK	013	5527	5992	6137	0.9	46	2135	2321	2383	0.9	2.58	1583	1702	0.8
03230	DANBURY	013	1072	1221	1289	1.4	81	439	502	532	1.5	2.43	313	353	1.3
03234	EPSOM	013	3869	4223	4339	1.0	54	1434	1584	1641	1.1	2.59	1061	1158	1.0
03235	FRANKLIN	013	8564	9351	9635	1.0	54	3382	3698	3825	1.0	2.46	2242	2414	0.8
03237	GILMANTON	001	2103	2435	2576	1.6	89	815	975	1040	2.0	2.49	636	754	1.9
03240	GRAFTON	009	1100	1194	1233	0.9	46	440	483	502	1.0	2.47	303	330	0.9
03241	HEBRON	009	806	863	887	0.7	34	336	364	377	0.9	2.37	244	261	0.7
03242	HENNIKER	013	4459	5049	5306	1.4	81	1597	1808	1913	1.4	2.52	1028	1147	1.2
03243	HILL	013	1004	1185	1267	1.8	95	387	458	491	1.8	2.59	276	322	1.7
03244	HILLSBOROUGH	011	6981	8516	9126	2.2	99	2681	3267	3516	2.2	2.55	1859	2234	2.0
03245	HOLDERNESS	009	1193	1260	1285	0.6	26	465	497	508	0.7	2.51	330	350	0.6
03246	LACONIA	001	16299	16836	17007	0.4	13	6668	7103	7236	0.7	2.26	4141	4346	0.5
03249	GILFORD	001	7340	8097	8328	1.1	64	2994	3376	3501	1.3	2.40	2169	2419	1.2
03251	LINCOLN	009	1268	1326	1349	0.5	20	581	613	626	0.6	2.16	324	338	0.5
03253	MEREDITH	001	5883	6853	7248	1.7	91	2438	2912	3100	1.9	2.31	1687	1992	1.8
03254	MOULTONBOROUGH	003	4549	5222	5534	1.5	85	1912	2255	2405	1.8	2.30	1397	1633	1.7
03255	NEWBURY	013	2306	2611	2759	1.4	81	934	1061	1124	1.4	2.46	680	763	1.3
03256	NEW HAMPTON	001	2249	2552	2676	1.4	81	838	967	1021	1.6	2.63	620	709	1.5
03257	NEW LONDON	013	4221	4620	4757	1.0	54	1623	1771	1840	0.9	2.15	1089	1171	0.8
03258	CHICHESTER	013	2308	2353	2347	0.2	10	845	862	861	0.2	2.71	656	664	0.1
03259	NORTH SANDWICH	003	267	295	308	1.1	64	116	131	138	1.3	2.25	80	90	1.3
03261	NORTHWOOD	015	3766	4435	4699	1.8	95	1400	1675	1786	2.0	2.65	1043	1233	1.8
03262	NORTH WOODSTOCK	009	885	784	753	-1.3	0	387	339	326	-1.4	2.13	222	191	-1.6
03263	PITTSFIELD	013	4048	4455	4602	1.0	54	1538	1689	1750	1.0	2.63	1087	1180	0.9
03264	PLYMOUTH	009	6631	6898	6926	0.4	13	1975	2041	2060	0.4	2.49	1148	1171	0.2
03266	RUMNEY	009	1964	2170	2250	1.1	64	753	838	872	1.2	2.55	523	578	1.1
03268	SALISBURY	013	1075	1194	1255	1.1	64	406	452	475	1.2	2.64	305	336	1.1
03269	SANBORNTON	001	2587	3045	3246	1.8	95	974	1184	1274	2.1	2.57	753	907	2.0
03275	SUNCOOK	013	11780	12537	12766	0.7	34	4575	4862	4955	0.7	2.57	3139	3291	0.5
03276	TILTON	013	7802	8374	8567	0.8	39	2978	3233	3320	0.9	2.50	2026	2174	0.8
03278	WARNER	013	3430	3799	3952	1.1	64	1302	1444	1508	1.1	2.53	923	1011	1.0
03279	WARREN	009	873	878	875	0.1	7	355	361	362	0.2	2.43	228	229	0.0
03280	WASHINGTON	019	882	1006	1057	1.4	81	365	429	454	1.8	2.34	274	318	1.6
03281	WEARE	011	7787	8754	9131	1.3	74	2622	2939	3076	1.2	2.98	2122	2358	1.1
03282	WENTWORTH	009	801	862	890	0.8	39	311	338	350	0.9	2.55	221	238	0.8
03284	SPRINGFIELD	019	770	854	890	1.1	64	318	366	386	1.5	2.33	236	268	1.4
03285	THORNTON	009	2078	2246	2321	0.8	39	875	957	993	1.0	2.35	577	623	0.8
03287	WILMOT	013	1154	1308	1379	1.4	81	456	518	549	1.4	2.52	327	368	1.3
03290	NOTTINGHAM	015	3534	4034	4273	1.4	81	1256	1462	1557	1.7	2.76	988	1139	1.5
03291	WEST NOTTINGHAM	015	68	76	79	1.2	71	27	31	32	1.5	2.45	21	24	1.5
03301	CONCORD	013	31761	33819	34382	0.7	34	12718	13418	13672	0.6	2.26	7301	7605	0.4
03303	CONCORD	013	14204	15764	16387	1.1	64	5423	6025	6288	1.1	2.50	3720	4071	1.0
03304	BOW	013	6917	7843	8224	1.4	81	2236	2524	2646	1.3	3.11	1984	2229	1.3
	NEW HAMPSHIRE					0.9					0.9	2.51			0.8
	UNITED STATES					1.0					1.1	2.59			0.9

ZIP CODE # POST OFFICE NAME	RACE (%) White 2000	White 2009	Black 2000	Black 2009	Asian/Pacific 2000	Asian/Pacific 2009	% Hispanic Origin 2000	% Hispanic Origin 2009	2009 AGE DISTRIBUTION (%) 0-4	5-9	10-14	15-19	20-24	25-44	45-64	65-84	85+	18+	MEDIAN AGE 2009	% 2009 Males	% 2009 Females
03031 AMHERST	97.0	95.8	0.4	0.6	1.4	2.3	1.0	1.6	5.7	7.1	8.4	8.6	4.4	19.9	35.4	9.6	0.9	73.2	42.3	49.9	50.1
03032 AUBURN	98.3	97.8	0.2	0.3	0.4	0.7	0.9	1.4	6.6	7.4	7.9	7.4	4.2	25.6	32.7	7.3	0.9	73.4	39.4	51.2	48.8
03033 BROOKLINE	97.9	97.2	0.1	0.2	0.7	1.1	0.9	1.4	8.8	9.5	9.4	7.6	3.4	26.5	28.0	6.2	0.6	67.3	37.0	50.1	49.9
03034 CANDIA	98.2	97.5	0.4	0.6	0.6	1.0	0.9	1.2	6.2	7.0	7.7	7.1	3.9	25.4	34.0	8.0	0.7	74.6	40.8	50.2	49.8
03036 CHESTER	98.0	97.5	0.3	0.4	0.3	0.5	0.8	1.3	7.3	8.1	8.9	8.5	4.6	23.5	30.9	7.6	0.7	70.7	38.1	48.6	51.4
03037 DEERFIELD	98.5	98.3	0.2	0.2	0.1	0.3	0.3	0.5	6.7	7.5	8.1	7.6	4.6	24.4	32.4	7.8	1.0	72.8	39.7	48.0	52.0
03038 DERRY	96.1	94.8	0.9	1.1	1.1	1.8	1.9	2.8	7.0	7.0	7.2	7.8	6.9	28.2	28.2	6.8	1.0	73.8	35.8	49.4	50.6
03042 EPPING	97.1	96.5	0.3	0.4	0.4	0.7	0.8	1.1	6.7	7.0	7.1	7.1	5.5	27.0	29.6	8.9	1.1	74.9	38.3	49.2	50.8
03043 FRANCESTOWN	97.3	96.6	0.1	0.1	0.3	0.5	0.6	0.9	5.1	6.1	7.5	7.9	4.0	20.8	34.9	12.2	1.6	76.4	44.3	51.1	48.9
03044 FREMONT	98.1	97.6	0.1	0.1	0.3	0.6	0.8	1.2	7.9	8.7	8.9	7.2	3.6	26.0	29.1	7.5	1.2	69.7	38.1	48.6	51.4
03045 GOFFSTOWN	98.4	97.9	0.3	0.3	0.3	0.5	0.7	1.1	5.6	5.9	6.6	8.0	7.3	24.4	29.7	10.2	2.3	77.0	40.1	47.4	52.6
03046 DUNBARTON	98.4	97.9	0.1	0.1	0.5	0.9	0.3	0.5	7.0	7.9	8.7	7.5	3.6	22.8	33.2	8.7	0.6	71.5	41.0	50.0	50.0
03047 GREENFIELD	97.3	96.6	0.7	0.9	0.2	0.4	0.6	0.9	5.2	5.9	7.5	10.5	6.3	25.1	31.7	7.0	0.8	74.4	38.7	50.5	49.5
03048 GREENVILLE	97.9	97.3	0.2	0.3	0.6	0.9	0.8	1.2	6.5	6.6	6.8	7.4	5.9	24.9	31.4	9.3	1.2	75.6	39.5	50.7	49.3
03049 HOLLIS	96.6	95.1	0.4	0.5	1.7	2.8	0.9	1.4	6.0	8.1	8.8	7.5	3.2	20.5	35.9	8.9	1.0	72.1	42.6	50.2	49.8
03051 HUDSON	96.4	95.0	0.8	1.1	1.2	1.9	1.5	2.4	7.1	7.5	7.8	7.1	4.8	27.4	28.8	8.4	1.1	73.0	38.4	49.5	50.5
03052 LITCHFIELD	97.7	96.9	0.5	0.7	0.6	1.0	0.8	1.3	8.5	9.1	9.5	8.3	4.2	26.5	28.6	4.9	0.4	67.6	36.2	49.9	50.1
03053 LONDONDERRY	96.9	95.7	0.6	0.7	1.2	2.0	1.5	2.3	6.9	7.5	8.1	8.5	5.2	24.6	31.4	7.1	0.6	71.8	37.7	49.3	50.7
03054 MERRIMACK	96.6	95.1	0.7	1.0	1.5	2.6	1.1	1.7	6.5	7.2	7.6	7.5	4.8	26.3	30.5	8.7	0.8	74.0	39.2	49.6	50.4
03055 MILFORD	96.8	95.6	0.9	1.2	0.9	1.6	1.2	1.8	7.0	6.9	7.0	7.1	6.9	27.2	27.4	8.8	1.7	74.4	37.2	49.4	50.6
03057 MONT VERNON	98.6	98.2	0.1	0.2	0.2	0.4	0.6	0.8	5.9	8.5	8.5	7.2	2.5	27.0	31.0	8.5	1.0	72.0	40.3	51.2	48.8
03060 NASHUA	86.0	81.3	2.7	3.1	2.7	4.1	11.0	15.7	7.0	6.3	6.1	7.3	8.0	29.5	23.5	9.9	2.3	76.6	35.3	49.2	50.8
03062 NASHUA	90.1	85.8	1.5	1.8	6.1	9.6	2.4	3.6	6.0	6.2	6.5	6.5	5.2	26.1	29.9	11.8	1.9	77.0	40.8	49.6	50.4
03063 NASHUA	90.6	86.7	1.8	2.2	4.5	7.2	3.5	5.1	6.0	5.6	5.7	6.8	7.1	29.3	27.3	10.9	1.2	79.1	38.0	49.5	50.5
03064 NASHUA	92.7	90.0	1.7	2.1	1.8	2.9	6.5	9.2	6.7	6.4	6.7	6.6	6.4	27.6	27.6	10.5	1.6	76.1	38.1	49.3	50.7
03070 NEW BOSTON	98.0	97.4	0.4	0.5	0.4	0.6	0.6	1.0	6.9	7.6	8.4	7.9	4.3	24.4	32.9	7.0	0.5	71.8	39.6	50.2	49.8
03071 NEW IPSWICH	98.5	98.0	0.2	0.3	0.4	0.7	0.8	1.3	8.4	8.8	9.2	8.0	5.1	25.5	26.9	7.3	0.9	68.5	34.6	50.9	49.1
03076 PELHAM	97.3	96.3	0.4	0.6	1.0	1.8	1.0	1.5	6.9	7.7	8.0	7.2	4.2	26.4	29.9	8.7	1.0	72.8	39.0	49.3	50.7
03077 RAYMOND	97.8	97.4	0.5	0.7	0.2	0.4	0.8	1.2	6.9	7.1	7.0	6.8	6.4	28.2	29.3	7.6	0.8	74.8	36.8	49.3	50.7
03079 SALEM	95.0	93.2	0.6	0.7	2.3	3.7	2.0	2.8	6.1	6.4	6.8	6.9	5.4	24.8	30.3	11.7	1.6	76.2	41.1	49.7	50.3
03082 LYNDEBOROUGH	98.2	97.3	0.2	0.3	0.3	0.5	1.6	2.5	5.4	6.3	7.2	7.1	4.0	25.2	34.9	8.8	1.0	75.7	41.7	50.8	49.2
03084 TEMPLE	97.7	97.2	0.4	0.4	0.5	0.9	0.6	0.9	5.5	6.3	7.4	8.3	4.9	25.0	32.3	9.1	1.1	75.5	40.2	50.9	49.1
03086 WILTON	97.6	96.8	0.3	0.5	0.5	0.9	0.8	1.2	6.2	6.6	7.2	7.4	5.1	24.7	31.5	9.9	1.3	75.3	40.5	49.0	51.0
03087 WINDHAM	96.9	95.6	0.3	0.4	1.7	2.7	1.0	1.5	6.3	7.5	8.8	8.0	3.6	22.2	34.3	8.3	1.0	72.1	41.4	50.5	49.5
03101 MANCHESTER	78.2	72.9	5.2	5.9	3.4	5.2	16.0	21.9	6.2	5.8	5.1	6.8	9.3	32.1	24.9	8.2	1.7	80.0	34.8	54.7	45.3
03102 MANCHESTER	92.8	90.1	1.9	2.2	2.2	3.7	3.1	4.7	6.6	5.7	5.5	6.8	10.1	29.6	22.6	10.6	2.5	78.9	34.7	48.8	51.2
03103 MANCHESTER	90.5	87.2	2.4	2.8	2.6	4.1	6.9	10.1	7.3	6.6	6.3	7.5	7.9	29.1	24.2	9.4	1.7	75.6	34.9	49.9	50.1
03104 MANCHESTER	92.8	90.1	1.9	2.4	2.2	3.6	3.0	4.5	6.0	5.6	5.6	6.4	7.3	28.6	26.4	11.1	3.0	79.1	38.4	48.0	52.0
03106 HOOKSETT	96.4	95.1	0.7	0.8	1.7	2.7	1.4	2.1	5.9	6.3	6.6	9.4	8.7	23.8	28.7	9.3	1.2	77.0	37.6	49.4	50.6
03109 MANCHESTER	96.3	94.7	0.7	0.9	1.4	2.4	1.3	2.0	6.7	6.6	6.8	6.8	5.6	27.2	27.8	10.3	2.2	75.6	39.0	48.8	51.2
03110 BEDFORD	97.4	96.3	0.3	0.4	1.3	2.2	0.9	1.4	6.3	7.6	9.0	7.9	3.7	19.6	32.4	11.1	2.3	71.8	42.5	49.2	50.8
03216 ANDOVER	98.2	97.9	0.4	0.5	0.1	0.2	0.2	0.3	5.7	6.3	6.9	6.4	3.7	23.2	33.9	12.5	1.4	77.4	43.5	49.7	50.3
03217 ASHLAND	97.5	96.9	0.4	0.5	0.6	1.0	0.7	1.0	6.1	6.3	6.1	6.2	6.1	25.4	29.5	12.7	1.5	77.5	40.3	47.5	52.5
03218 BARNSTEAD	98.6	98.2	0.5	0.6	0.1	0.2	0.4	0.5	5.5	6.1	6.7	6.5	4.7	23.3	33.7	12.1	1.5	77.8	43.1	50.6	49.4
03220 BELMONT	97.5	97.0	0.1	0.2	0.5	0.9	1.0	1.4	5.3	6.1	6.8	6.6	5.1	26.5	31.8	10.4	1.2	77.5	41.1	49.3	50.7
03221 BRADFORD	97.4	96.9	0.3	0.3	0.1	0.2	1.1	1.5	5.2	6.0	7.8	7.2	4.7	23.9	32.6	11.6	1.1	76.3	42.2	50.1	49.9
03222 BRISTOL	96.8	95.8	0.2	0.2	1.0	1.7	0.7	1.1	5.7	5.4	5.9	6.3	5.6	24.1	31.9	13.1	1.9	79.1	42.8	49.4	50.6
03223 CAMPTON	97.9	97.4	0.1	0.1	0.8	1.3	0.4	0.6	5.4	5.6	6.2	6.2	5.7	24.7	33.3	11.6	1.3	79.1	42.2	49.7	50.3
03224 CANTERBURY	98.6	98.2	0.3	0.3	0.3	0.5	0.5	0.8	4.6	5.6	7.0	6.6	3.6	19.0	39.6	12.4	1.6	78.1	47.0	47.8	52.2
03225 CENTER BARNSTEAD	97.4	96.7	0.7	0.8	0.8	1.3	0.7	1.0	5.9	6.6	7.4	7.1	4.3	24.6	32.1	11.0	1.1	75.6	41.3	51.1	48.9
03226 CENTER HARBOR	98.7	98.2	0.0	0.0	0.8	1.3	0.9	1.4	3.9	4.3	5.1	5.5	3.8	19.4	39.7	16.7	1.7	82.8	49.7	50.6	49.4
03227 CENTER SANDWICH	97.9	97.5	0.6	0.7	0.3	0.5	0.5	0.6	3.7	4.1	5.1	5.7	4.1	15.5	41.0	17.9	2.9	83.6	52.0	47.7	52.3
03229 CONTOOCOOK	98.5	98.1	0.1	0.2	0.3	0.6	0.5	0.7	4.8	5.7	6.8	7.4	4.6	20.0	35.4	13.4	1.9	78.0	45.4	48.9	51.1
03230 DANBURY	99.5	99.5	0.2	0.2	0.0	0.0	0.5	0.7	4.2	4.8	5.6	6.6	4.6	22.9	36.0	13.9	1.4	81.3	45.7	49.6	50.4
03234 EPSOM	98.6	98.3	0.1	0.1	0.3	0.5	0.4	0.6	5.8	6.4	7.4	6.1	3.9	25.7	29.6	12.1	3.1	76.5	41.9	47.6	52.4
03235 FRANKLIN	97.1	96.4	0.4	0.5	0.5	0.9	1.2	1.8	7.0	6.1	6.1	6.2	7.1	25.1	26.3	13.0	3.0	76.9	38.8	48.3	51.7
03237 GILMANTON	98.6	98.4	0.1	0.1	0.1	0.2	0.3	0.4	4.8	5.5	6.5	6.6	4.0	23.7	36.3	11.3	1.3	79.1	44.3	50.6	49.4
03240 GRAFTON	98.5	98.0	0.2	0.2	0.3	0.5	0.5	0.7	5.8	6.4	6.7	5.9	5.4	24.8	33.8	10.2	1.0	77.6	42.0	51.3	48.7
03241 HEBRON	96.9	96.2	0.2	0.3	0.6	1.0	0.1	0.2	5.1	5.4	6.6	5.8	4.4	21.6	32.8	15.5	2.8	78.8	45.6	51.4	48.6
03242 HENNIKER	96.7	95.7	0.4	0.6	1.0	1.7	0.8	1.2	5.1	4.5	4.8	10.0	14.4	25.0	28.1	7.0	1.0	81.4	32.6	51.1	48.9
03243 HILL	99.0	98.6	0.1	0.1	0.5	0.8	0.2	0.3	4.6	7.6	7.5	7.5	3.9	27.2	31.1	8.7	1.9	75.1	40.9	51.0	49.0
03244 HILLSBOROUGH	97.7	97.0	0.2	0.3	0.7	1.1	0.7	1.1	6.0	6.3	7.1	7.2	5.6	25.2	30.3	10.8	1.5	75.9	40.0	49.5	50.5
03245 HOLDERNESS	97.9	97.5	0.4	0.6	0.3	0.6	0.4	0.6	4.8	6.0	6.2	7.6	4.8	21.2	36.3	11.4	1.6	77.5	44.6	49.2	50.8
03246 LACONIA	96.8	95.9	0.5	0.7	0.8	1.2	1.0	1.4	5.6	5.4	5.4	6.1	6.8	26.2	27.1	13.9	3.4	79.7	40.9	48.7	51.3
03249 GILFORD	98.3	97.9	0.2	0.2	0.5	0.8	0.6	0.9	4.8	5.4	6.2	6.2	4.1	18.8	35.7	16.8	2.0	79.6	47.6	47.9	52.1
03251 LINCOLN	97.2	96.5	0.0	0.0	1.1	1.8	0.8	1.1	4.6	5.0	5.4	4.3	5.2	23.3	34.6	15.3	2.3	82.4	46.3	51.1	48.9
03253 MEREDITH	97.9	97.3	0.2	0.2	0.6	1.1	0.5	0.8	4.7	5.5	6.2	6.0	3.8	22.2	34.7	14.1	2.8	79.5	45.9	49.9	50.1
03254 MOULTONBOROUGH	98.5	98.0	0.1	0.2	0.5	0.9	0.6	0.8	3.5	4.7	5.6	6.1	3.2	18.2	38.6	18.4	1.8	81.8	50.0	49.7	50.3
03255 NEWBURY	98.0	97.6	0.3	0.4	0.2	0.3	1.2	1.7	4.1	5.1	6.7	6.5	3.1	23.9	34.1	14.6	1.8	79.3	45.3	50.2	49.8
03256 NEW HAMPTON	97.5	97.1	0.3	0.3	0.3	0.5	0.6	0.9	5.3	6.1	7.0	7.6	3.9	25.0	32.8	10.9	1.6	76.4	41.8	49.3	50.7
03257 NEW LONDON	98.3	97.8	0.2	0.3	0.8	1.2	0.6	0.9	2.8	3.3	3.5	10.5	11.3	12.2	28.7	22.7	5.1	87.6	50.9	44.6	55.4
03258 CHICHESTER	98.1	97.9	0.2	0.3	0.2	0.3	0.6	0.9	5.8	6.5	7.2	7.2	4.0	25.0	33.5	9.7	1.1	75.9	41.9	50.9	49.1
03259 NORTH SANDWICH	97.8	97.6	0.7	0.7	0.4	0.3	0.4	0.7	3.7	4.4	5.1	5.8	4.1	15.6	41.0	17.6	2.7	83.4	51.8	48.1	51.9
03261 NORTHWOOD	97.6	96.7	0.3	0.4	0.8	1.3	0.6	0.8	5.9	6.5	7.1	6.9	4.4	26.4	32.4	9.6	0.9	76.1	40.8	50.1	49.9
03262 NORTH WOODSTOCK	97.2	97.1	0.1	0.1	0.2	0.3	0.6	0.8	5.4	5.6	5.9	6.5	4.5	26.9	28.8	14.4	2.0	79.3	41.8	48.5	51.5
03263 PITTSFIELD	97.5	97.1	0.4	0.4	0.1	0.2	1.1	1.7	7.0	6.8	6.7	7.0	7.1	27.0	27.7	9.6	1.1	75.1	36.6	48.3	51.7
03264 PLYMOUTH	96.8	95.9	0.4	0.5	0.8	1.3	1.4	2.0	3.9	3.7	4.0	17.6	25.4	16.8	19.1	8.2	1.4	85.8	24.1	50.3	49.7
03266 RUMNEY	97.7	97.1	0.4	0.4	0.5	0.8	0.5	0.8	4.7	6.8	7.9	5.7	3.5	22.1	34.4	12.7	2.2	76.5	44.5	51.4	48.6
03268 SALISBURY	97.9	97.2	0.7	0.8	0.4	0.7	0.7	1.0	5.4	6.3	6.8	6.4	3.7	24.1	34.2	12.0	1.2	77.4	43.2	52.0	48.0
03269 SANBORNTON	98.1	97.6	0.2	0.2	0.5	0.9	0.4	0.6	4.9	5.8	6.4	6.6	4.5	23.6	36.5	10.6	1.0	78.9	43.8	49.2	50.8
03275 SUNCOOK	97.8	97.3	0.4	0.5	0.4	0.6	0.7	1.1	6.5	6.4	6.6	7.1	6.7	26.2	29.8	9.3	1.3	76.1	38.7	49.6	50.4
03276 TILTON	97.5	97.0	0.1	0.1	0.5	0.9	0.9	1.4	5.7	6.0	6.3	7.2	6.5	26.3	30.0	10.3	1.6	77.5	39.7	49.7	50.3
03278 WARNER	98.2	97.8	0.1	0.1	0.3	0.5	0.8	1.1	4.9	5.8	7.2	7.4	4.4	24.6	31.9	11.3	2.4	77.6	42.5	49.5	50.5
03279 WARREN	96.1	95.4	0.1	0.1	0.8	1.4	0.1	0.1	5.2	5.2	5.7	6.2	5.2	26.2	30.9	13.7	1.7	80.2	42.7	49.9	50.1
03280 WASHINGTON	98.2	98.1	0.0	0.0	0.0	0.0	1.5	1.9	4.6	5.1	5.6	5.8	3.5	18.2	35.6	20.4	1.4	81.2	49.5	51.1	48.9
03281 WEARE	98.3	97.7	0.2	0.2	0.4	0.7	0.7	1.1	7.6	7.8	8.1	7.8	5.4	27.9	29.8	5.0	0.5	71.5	35.9	50.0	50.0
03282 WENTWORTH	97.6	97.1	0.4	0.5	0.2	0.5	0.4	0.7	2.9	5.6	9.7	7.7	3.9	26.1	29.7	12.6	1.7	75.9	41.9	51.2	48.8
03284 SPRINGFIELD	98.8	98.6	0.0	0.0	0.3	0.4	0.8	1.1	5.5	6.1	6.7	4.3	3.6	27.3	33.5	11.0	2.0	78.1	42.6	49.3	50.7
03285 THORNTON	97.7	97.1	0.2	0.3	0.4	0.6	0.8	1.2	4.3	5.2	7.2	6.6	5.3	28.4	29.9	12.1	0.9	78.9	40.7	49.8	50.2
03287 WILMOT	98.3	97.8	0.1	0.1	0.7	1.1	0.3	0.4	5.4	7.0	7.3	6.4	2.3	23.2	34.9	12.0	1.7	76.1	44.1	48.5	51.5
03290 NOTTINGHAM	98.4	97.9	0.2	0.2	0.6	1.0	0.7	1.1	6.1	6.9	7.6	7.3	4.4	23.7	34.5	8.8	0.8	74.9	41.7	50.1	49.9
03291 WEST NOTTINGHAM	100.0	98.7	0.0	0.0	0.0	1.3	0.0	1.3	6.6	7.9	7.9	7.9	3.9	25.0	32.9	7.9	0.0	71.1	41.1	47.4	52.6
03301 CONCORD	95.3	93.8	1.1	1.4	1.6	2.5	1.5	2.1	5.5	5.1	5.3	6.4	7.8	27.4	27.7	11.2	3.8	80.2	39.9	50.1	49.9
03303 CONCORD	97.0	96.0	0.6	0.7	0.9	1.6	1.1	1.7	6.4	6.3	6.2	6.6	6.7	29.4	26.6	9.6	2.2	77.2	37.4	49.4	50.6
03304 BOW	97.8	96.8	0.1	0.2	1.0	1.8	0.5	0.7	5.8	7.3	8.8	9.1	4.6	18.8	35.4	9.3	1.0	72.4	42.3	50.2	49.8
NEW HAMPSHIRE	96.0	94.8	0.7	0.9	1.3	2.1	1.7	2.4	5.9	6.1	6.5	7.4	6.6	25.3	29.3	10.9	1.9	77.1	39.8	49.2	50.8
UNITED STATES	75.1	72.0	12.3	12.7	3.8	4.6	12.5	15.7	6.8	6.7	6.6	7.1	6.9	27.0	26.0	10.9	1.9	75.7	36.9	49.2	50.8

C 03031-03304

ZIP CODE #	POST OFFICE NAME	2009 Per Capita Income	2009 HH Income Base	2009 HOUSEHOLD INCOME DISTRIBUTION (%) Less than $25,000	$25,000 to $49,999	$50,000 to $99,999	$100,000 to $149,999	$150,000 or More	MEDIAN HOUSEHOLD INCOME 2009	2014	2009 National Centile	2009 State Centile	2009 Home Value Base	2009 HOME VALUE DISTRIBUTION (%) Less than $50,000	$50,000 to $89,999	$90,000 to $174,999	$175,000 to $399,999	$400,000 or More	2009 Median Home Value
03031	AMHERST	48329	3950	4.3	7.8	27.8	23.8	36.2	122354	124109	99	99	3546	1.0	1.2	7.1	55.1	35.4	348036
03032	AUBURN	36846	1750	6.3	9.3	43.8	26.2	14.5	85703	90599	94	91	1590	0.0	0.4	20.3	64.8	14.6	239844
03033	BROOKLINE	36598	1418	4.4	7.9	35.1	34.8	17.8	103493	104254	97	97	1270	0.6	1.3	10.1	76.1	12.0	286914
03034	CANDIA	32133	1588	5.3	14.8	45.6	24.6	9.8	77534	81626	91	82	1440	2.7	0.8	19.9	68.8	7.8	228358
03036	CHESTER	32443	1431	8.2	12.2	34.6	32.6	12.4	89703	95603	95	93	1302	1.2	0.0	8.8	72.7	17.4	282667
03037	DEERFIELD	30731	1420	6.0	16.0	44.9	22.4	10.7	75915	80217	90	79	1255	0.7	0.8	19.1	68.4	11.0	237984
03038	DERRY	29451	12886	10.6	19.6	42.6	19.6	7.6	69440	74535	86	74	8485	3.3	3.7	25.3	65.6	2.2	206581
03042	EPPING	26493	2178	13.8	22.8	44.4	14.4	4.7	62886	65178	81	67	1678	7.8	5.0	27.8	54.0	5.4	193602
03043	FRANCESTOWN	37638	619	4.7	12.1	46.0	23.7	13.4	83889	85415	93	88	528	0.0	0.0	26.5	48.1	25.4	248256
03044	FREMONT	31739	1451	6.0	11.7	48.9	23.5	9.9	80058	83663	92	86	1269	0.3	2.0	15.4	76.8	5.4	247295
03045	GOFFSTOWN	29351	4427	11.1	17.6	42.2	21.3	7.7	73388	76275	89	77	3667	0.2	3.4	33.7	58.0	4.7	200619
03046	DUNBARTON	34823	952	7.1	10.2	49.6	20.3	12.8	80101	82283	92	86	844	0.7	1.3	18.1	69.4	10.4	244884
03047	GREENFIELD	24598	611	11.6	29.0	44.0	11.3	4.1	60659	62295	78	60	496	0.8	1.4	37.9	51.2	8.7	195417
03048	GREENVILLE	27139	1434	15.3	24.8	42.6	11.4	5.8	61578	64520	79	62	1102	16.2	10.6	33.3	35.3	4.5	144626
03049	HOLLIS	56393	2793	6.2	11.6	21.7	20.4	40.0	123370	128413	99	99	2514	0.6	2.3	6.3	33.4	57.3	439316
03051	HUDSON	33834	8821	6.4	13.8	43.9	23.7	12.2	81156	83117	92	87	6886	1.5	2.3	17.3	73.8	5.2	239696
03052	LITCHFIELD	32717	2670	3.7	9.1	41.9	31.6	13.6	92633	93040	96	94	2309	2.0	2.8	8.4	82.4	4.4	249309
03053	LONDONDERRY	36424	8313	6.2	10.3	39.2	27.9	16.3	90955	94865	95	93	7171	1.5	3.2	18.2	68.0	9.2	242129
03054	MERRIMACK	36550	9488	5.0	11.2	42.5	25.3	15.9	88282	89908	95	92	7974	1.6	2.0	25.5	63.1	7.8	222799
03055	MILFORD	30656	5770	10.7	19.9	44.9	16.6	7.9	68601	72166	86	73	3759	4.5	4.7	26.8	59.2	4.7	206152
03057	MONT VERNON	39966	728	3.3	10.4	40.0	27.2	19.1	93631	95056	96	94	652	3.4	2.8	11.0	60.0	22.9	300562
03060	NASHUA	26184	12338	23.4	25.0	34.8	12.1	4.7	52308	54677	67	37	5008	0.4	2.5	39.4	56.5	1.1	186095
03062	NASHUA	39335	10572	6.9	13.2	40.0	23.5	16.4	85780	87719	94	91	7749	5.4	5.6	17.3	59.9	11.8	222509
03063	NASHUA	36941	6817	9.5	16.6	41.7	22.5	9.6	76601	79022	90	80	4397	2.0	3.6	30.2	58.6	5.6	205287
03064	NASHUA	31009	5737	16.0	21.5	35.4	18.3	8.8	65281	68124	84	70	3494	0.6	0.6	20.0	69.1	9.7	224143
03070	NEW BOSTON	33998	1520	4.2	13.4	46.8	23.3	12.4	82480	83966	93	88	1299	0.9	2.2	18.3	61.0	17.5	241838
03071	NEW IPSWICH	23656	1515	10.6	23.7	50.2	10.2	5.3	65162	67592	83	70	1269	2.0	5.9	36.2	53.7	2.2	185582
03076	PELHAM	32911	3970	5.9	11.3	41.4	28.0	13.3	85528	87715	94	90	3356	0.2	0.6	7.9	78.6	12.8	290643
03077	RAYMOND	23207	3818	13.7	27.6	45.0	11.6	2.1	58971	60181	76	55	2981	6.4	9.3	37.6	46.1	0.6	168619
03079	SALEM	34953	11211	10.6	18.7	35.2	22.4	13.1	75139	79920	89	78	8783	3.5	4.1	10.5	67.5	14.4	259578
03082	LYNDEBOROUGH	30089	610	8.7	18.9	43.9	22.5	6.1	70991	74185	87	76	526	0.2	3.4	26.2	56.5	13.7	225909
03084	TEMPLE	29356	456	9.2	19.3	41.4	21.5	8.6	75887	77920	90	78	383	0.0	1.8	23.5	58.5	16.2	234191
03086	WILTON	31714	1576	14.1	21.4	38.8	15.2	10.6	67245	69839	85	73	1190	0.5	2.8	26.6	56.1	14.1	221542
03087	WINDHAM	55949	4367	4.0	5.3	23.5	25.0	42.2	134339	136115	99	100	4013	0.2	0.0	4.1	52.5	43.1	374469
03101	MANCHESTER	22315	1591	48.3	27.5	19.3	2.5	2.4	26129	26952	4	0	136	0.0	14.7	55.1	29.4	0.7	147917
03102	MANCHESTER	25862	13547	21.2	27.8	40.0	8.0	2.9	51058	53040	64	31	5458	1.3	2.3	55.0	40.5	0.9	163320
03103	MANCHESTER	22712	14582	22.8	27.7	38.4	8.4	2.7	49549	51099	60	25	7267	0.8	2.7	54.3	41.0	1.2	166766
03104	MANCHESTER	32206	13858	16.5	24.1	37.8	14.4	7.3	61911	63940	80	64	7066	0.3	0.9	29.4	63.1	6.3	211720
03106	HOOKSETT	31352	4889	9.0	16.2	45.1	19.7	10.0	76448	78401	90	80	3873	3.0	1.2	27.8	64.3	3.7	207039
03109	MANCHESTER	29705	3811	11.3	17.5	47.3	19.2	4.7	75038	76684	89	77	2923	1.5	3.4	42.5	50.3	2.4	178943
03110	BEDFORD	50083	7213	4.5	7.1	27.4	27.5	33.6	120042	122518	98	98	6162	0.1	0.6	4.5	56.5	38.2	359452
03216	ANDOVER	25071	934	14.8	26.3	47.1	8.1	3.6	57229	59775	74	51	772	1.3	5.7	46.4	40.5	6.1	168434
03217	ASHLAND	25673	1183	22.3	32.8	33.6	7.5	3.7	46276	47321	52	13	742	7.8	9.3	43.8	32.1	7.0	151989
03218	BARNSTEAD	23957	413	12.1	29.3	47.0	8.0	3.6	53620	54519	69	40	364	1.6	6.3	48.4	40.4	3.3	164352
03220	BELMONT	24428	3174	17.8	26.8	45.4	7.3	2.7	54835	56507	71	44	2487	9.2	16.2	44.0	27.9	2.7	138774
03221	BRADFORD	25577	807	15.1	24.8	47.5	8.2	4.5	58996	61391	76	55	639	1.6	5.0	36.5	49.3	7.7	188906
03222	BRISTOL	24994	2275	19.3	31.4	36.7	8.1	4.4	49342	50281	60	23	1679	4.5	8.1	46.5	35.4	5.5	157636
03223	CAMPTON	25923	1166	18.6	32.1	38.2	7.4	3.8	49311	50000	60	24	875	13.6	6.7	39.4	34.2	6.1	157038
03224	CANTERBURY	35795	859	6.6	12.3	49.2	19.4	12.3	76860	79315	91	81	762	0.1	1.4	24.9	61.4	12.1	222906
03225	CENTER BARNSTEAD	24732	1216	10.6	27.5	51.5	7.3	3.0	57258	58605	74	51	1060	0.8	4.5	56.1	36.4	2.1	155818
03226	CENTER HARBOR	31510	364	14.6	26.1	41.2	10.2	8.0	60347	64776	78	59	309	0.3	4.5	22.7	58.3	14.2	244712
03227	CENTER SANDWICH	28623	491	22.4	22.4	43.0	7.3	4.9	54961	57632	71	45	394	2.0	2.0	20.1	57.1	18.8	260000
03229	CONTOOCOOK	38520	2321	9.3	12.2	46.7	17.8	13.9	76670	79255	90	80	1979	0.2	3.5	26.3	56.7	13.3	229342
03230	DANBURY	21917	502	21.9	33.3	37.1	6.4	1.4	45167	47350	49	10	428	7.7	7.9	60.3	21.5	2.6	138587
03234	EPSOM	25813	1584	14.2	23.8	47.4	10.0	4.5	59936	62717	77	57	1279	10.5	6.3	36.0	44.0	3.1	170775
03235	FRANKLIN	20778	3698	28.5	27.2	36.9	5.4	1.9	43282	46176	43	7	2191	4.7	9.3	67.4	17.8	0.8	132670
03237	GILMANTON	28071	975	10.5	22.9	53.8	8.1	4.7	60916	62969	79	61	859	0.7	3.5	39.2	48.7	7.9	189714
03240	GRAFTON	20800	483	20.1	35.4	38.1	5.0	1.4	46817	47550	54	15	418	6.2	15.1	47.6	28.0	3.1	137879
03241	HEBRON	26233	364	19.5	31.6	34.9	11.0	3.0	49046	50591	59	22	308	3.2	10.4	40.6	34.4	11.4	165714
03242	HENNIKER	29950	1808	17.5	21.0	38.7	14.2	8.6	64110	67555	82	68	1246	6.4	2.2	38.5	48.0	4.9	181000
03243	HILL	24495	458	14.6	25.3	49.1	8.7	2.2	56713	59325	74	50	394	3.3	9.4	57.1	24.9	5.3	142727
03244	HILLSBOROUGH	25445	3267	17.6	24.2	43.8	10.1	4.3	60077	61391	77	58	2550	8.7	11.4	47.9	29.2	2.8	143938
03245	HOLDERNESS	29626	497	14.9	29.2	38.0	10.9	7.0	56472	58867	73	48	388	7.2	4.6	20.6	52.6	14.9	230508
03246	LACONIA	24637	7103	23.4	28.5	38.2	7.3	2.6	48024	49407	57	18	4172	0.5	4.7	56.9	32.7	5.3	154290
03249	GILFORD	36427	3376	12.6	24.9	39.0	14.2	9.2	61883	64458	80	63	2845	11.3	3.3	28.6	44.3	12.5	196791
03251	LINCOLN	23104	613	31.6	30.2	28.9	7.3	2.0	38886	41747	29	2	402	6.2	8.5	42.8	33.3	9.2	159375
03253	MEREDITH	30457	2912	16.9	31.5	34.7	9.2	7.8	51862	54348	66	33	2251	7.7	4.7	28.7	41.1	17.8	207155
03254	MOULTONBOROUGH	32428	2255	13.4	29.0	39.8	11.1	6.7	56542	59130	73	49	1946	0.7	1.3	24.3	44.5	29.2	260099
03255	NEWBURY	31083	1061	10.8	22.8	47.0	11.6	7.7	64102	67377	82	67	905	0.0	2.2	29.1	49.3	19.4	224320
03256	NEW HAMPTON	25286	967	15.1	23.4	48.3	9.6	3.6	56955	58866	74	50	823	2.9	5.1	37.2	47.4	7.4	185972
03257	NEW LONDON	46008	1771	10.6	18.6	31.7	15.6	23.5	78821	82819	92	84	1450	0.6	0.4	6.6	54.6	37.9	337722
03258	CHICHESTER	27533	862	8.7	23.7	50.7	10.7	6.3	66353	69260	84	71	749	2.4	3.2	35.6	55.3	3.5	191213
03259	NORTH SANDWICH	28125	131	22.1	22.9	44.3	6.9	3.8	54525	58078	70	43	105	2.9	2.9	20.0	56.2	18.1	256944
03261	NORTHWOOD	26712	1675	10.3	29.1	43.3	12.4	4.8	60378	61974	78	60	1416	2.8	7.6	34.6	50.6	4.4	181431
03262	NORTH WOODSTOCK	24904	339	24.5	30.1	36.9	5.9	2.7	45142	47358	49	10	238	7.1	7.6	53.4	26.5	5.5	148837
03263	PITTSFIELD	22014	1689	20.4	30.1	39.0	7.4	3.1	49345	50442	60	23	1065	4.9	7.2	52.8	31.5	3.7	149323
03264	PLYMOUTH	21754	2041	27.6	23.8	38.0	6.2	4.5	48730	49855	58	20	1256	12.7	8.3	41.4	32.2	5.5	150000
03266	RUMNEY	21952	838	23.0	30.9	37.4	6.2	2.5	46751	47913	53	14	675	2.4	8.1	47.0	34.5	8.0	160320
03268	SALISBURY	26298	452	11.9	21.0	52.2	11.5	3.3	63042	66649	81	67	408	1.7	2.7	45.6	44.6	5.4	175000
03269	SANBORNTON	27224	1184	12.1	26.9	46.8	9.6	4.6	57375	59471	74	52	1025	2.0	1.4	31.7	55.5	9.4	202179
03275	SUNCOOK	24822	4862	15.5	25.1	46.6	10.0	2.9	59527	62117	77	57	3407	13.5	4.4	42.3	38.9	0.9	162090
03276	TILTON	22616	3233	16.7	30.2	45.2	6.7	1.3	52402	53772	67	37	2147	8.5	10.0	51.2	26.7	3.7	143611
03278	WARNER	25233	1444	15.0	28.7	42.7	9.1	4.4	54900	57154	71	44	1129	3.7	5.0	35.8	45.8	9.7	187399
03279	WARREN	20441	361	23.8	38.8	29.9	4.4	3.0	41310	43378	37	4	289	9.3	19.0	52.2	18.3	1.0	117210
03280	WASHINGTON	25063	429	18.9	27.7	44.1	7.0	2.3	52731	53878	67	39	383	3.4	8.9	36.6	41.8	9.4	177679
03281	WEARE	29872	2939	6.5	12.5	50.4	21.2	9.5	78112	80149	91	83	2516	5.0	4.1	28.8	58.7	3.4	192308
03282	WENTWORTH	22409	338	18.3	28.1	45.0	6.8	1.8	52725	53728	67	38	285	2.8	7.4	46.7	42.8	0.4	163920
03284	SPRINGFIELD	27752	366	12.8	36.3	37.7	8.7	4.4	50694	51717	63	29	308	5.2	12.3	27.6	47.4	7.5	187097
03285	THORNTON	22874	957	22.9	32.4	36.5	6.3	2.0	46170	47460	52	13	701	3.4	8.1	39.4	43.9	5.1	173407
03287	WILMOT	31762	518	9.7	24.1	45.8	12.2	8.3	66154	70142	84	71	439	0.5	0.5	22.6	59.2	17.3	232639
03290	NOTTINGHAM	31651	1462	7.3	13.9	47.4	25.0	6.4	78515	81891	91	84	1307	0.8	1.4	21.3	65.8	10.7	223606
03291	WEST NOTTINGHAM	35179	31	3.2	16.1	54.8	22.6	3.2	77691	78757	91	83	28	0.0	0.0	25.0	71.4	3.6	212500
03301	CONCORD	28499	13418	19.7	24.7	39.4	10.4	5.8	55069	57307	71	45	6820	7.8	2.9	39.4	43.8	6.1	174754
03303	CONCORD	24153	6025	16.6	24.0	49.2	7.8	2.3	57674	59823	75	53	4047	8.4	8.5	47.6	33.7	1.9	153352
03304	BOW	40262	2524	6.1	5.4	36.1	23.6	28.8	104492	108635	97	97	2359	0.1	0.1	10.8	74.6	14.4	273513
	NEW HAMPSHIRE	30567		15.4	22.0	39.7	14.4	8.5	63279	65972				4.2	5.0	30.0	49.8	11.0	202897
	UNITED STATES	27277		20.9	24.4	35.3	11.7	7.6	54719	56938				9.3	13.1	31.6	32.6	13.5	162279

ZIP CODE		FINANCIAL SERVICES				THE HOME						ENTERTAINMENT						PERSONAL			
						Home Improvements		Furnishings													
#	POST OFFICE NAME	Auto Loan	Home Loan	Invest-ments	Retire-ment Plans	Home Repair	Lawn & Garden	Comput-ers & Hard-ware-Personal	Major Appli-ances	TV, Radio, Sound Equip-ment	Furni-ture	Dine out/ Carry out	Sports Equip-ment	Fees & Tickets	Toys & Games	Travel	Cable TV	Apparel & Services	Auto Repairs	Health Insur-ance	Pets & Supplies
03031	AMHERST	187	244	245	254	249	219	201	209	189	217	191	164	239	193	227	181	142	195	184	237
03032	AUBURN	145	176	153	177	170	159	151	154	144	156	146	122	167	149	161	140	104	147	143	179
03033	BROOKLINE	159	197	171	199	190	166	164	166	153	177	156	135	185	162	175	144	113	156	143	189
03034	CANDIA	124	151	131	152	145	135	128	131	122	133	124	104	143	127	138	119	89	125	121	152
03036	CHESTER	134	168	147	167	162	145	141	143	132	148	135	114	158	138	152	127	97	136	128	164
03037	DEERFIELD	124	149	130	150	144	135	128	131	122	132	124	104	141	127	137	120	88	125	122	152
03038	DERRY	114	121	107	122	116	108	116	111	111	120	113	89	120	115	116	108	80	112	104	131
03042	EPPING	103	105	92	102	101	98	98	99	98	102	99	75	98	101	97	98	69	97	96	116
03043	FRANCESTOWN	133	165	169	170	170	157	141	149	135	150	136	111	160	134	158	132	98	141	141	170
03044	FREMONT	127	160	140	160	154	138	134	136	126	141	128	108	151	131	145	121	92	129	122	156
03045	GOFFSTOWN	113	133	119	134	130	122	118	119	114	121	115	94	129	117	125	111	82	116	113	139
03046	DUNBARTON	129	163	144	163	158	141	136	139	128	143	130	110	154	133	148	123	94	132	124	159
03047	GREENFIELD	95	108	93	111	104	106	96	100	94	96	95	78	102	97	101	95	66	96	99	118
03048	GREENVILLE	98	108	96	106	104	99	100	99	97	103	98	77	104	101	102	96	70	98	95	116
03049	HOLLIS	209	273	282	286	282	247	225	235	211	244	214	183	269	215	255	202	159	219	207	266
03051	HUDSON	130	156	138	156	151	139	137	137	131	141	133	109	151	135	145	127	95	133	128	159
03052	LITCHFIELD	139	175	153	175	169	151	146	149	137	154	140	118	165	143	158	132	101	142	133	171
03053	LONDONDERRY	148	182	160	181	175	158	155	157	146	163	149	124	172	152	165	141	107	150	141	180
03054	MERRIMACK	138	169	153	169	165	149	147	147	139	152	141	117	163	143	157	135	102	142	135	170
03055	MILFORD	106	119	110	119	116	108	115	110	111	115	112	87	122	112	118	109	80	111	107	129
03057	MONT VERNON	153	190	193	195	194	179	161	171	155	172	157	127	184	154	181	152	112	162	161	195
03060	NASHUA	85	79	74	81	77	77	92	81	92	88	93	65	89	92	86	92	66	89	86	98
03062	NASHUA	142	153	147	157	152	141	148	143	142	153	144	113	156	144	152	137	103	144	135	167
03063	NASHUA	125	128	119	133	125	119	127	121	124	130	126	96	131	127	127	121	89	123	117	143
03064	NASHUA	107	115	109	116	114	110	114	109	112	113	113	85	118	112	115	111	80	111	110	129
03070	NEW BOSTON	132	166	146	166	160	144	139	141	131	146	133	113	157	136	150	126	96	134	127	162
03071	NEW IPSWICH	103	116	100	120	113	114	104	108	102	104	103	84	111	105	110	102	72	104	107	127
03076	PELHAM	134	169	148	168	163	146	141	144	133	148	135	114	159	138	152	127	97	136	128	165
03077	RAYMOND	96	94	82	91	91	91	88	91	89	91	90	67	86	92	86	90	62	89	89	107
03079	SALEM	119	146	142	142	146	134	130	131	126	131	127	100	144	127	140	125	91	129	128	150
03082	LYNDEBOROUGH	119	134	116	138	130	132	120	125	118	120	118	97	128	121	127	118	83	120	123	146
03084	TEMPLE	117	147	129	147	142	127	123	125	115	129	118	100	139	121	133	111	85	119	112	144
03086	WILTON	113	129	115	131	126	124	119	120	116	118	117	94	127	118	125	116	83	118	119	140
03087	WINDHAM	206	277	289	287	288	249	226	236	212	243	214	184	273	216	258	203	160	219	208	264
03101	MANCHESTER	50	37	38	40	36	40	56	45	57	51	58	36	49	54	48	59	41	54	54	57
03102	MANCHESTER	82	76	72	78	74	74	87	78	86	84	87	62	84	86	82	86	61	84	81	94
03103	MANCHESTER	78	79	72	80	76	75	84	77	84	81	85	61	85	84	82	84	60	82	80	92
03104	MANCHESTER	104	104	100	106	102	99	110	102	108	109	110	81	111	109	108	107	78	107	103	121
03106	HOOKSETT	112	133	123	133	130	120	121	119	116	123	118	94	132	119	128	114	84	118	114	138
03109	MANCHESTER	106	122	107	119	117	113	108	110	107	111	108	84	117	110	113	107	76	107	109	127
03110	BEDFORD	186	237	247	245	246	216	202	208	192	217	194	161	237	193	226	185	143	197	190	235
03216	ANDOVER	94	95	103	97	96	103	88	98	88	86	88	75	88	88	94	90	61	93	97	115
03217	ASHLAND	90	77	87	78	79	89	84	88	86	79	84	66	76	85	81	89	58	87	92	103
03218	BARNSTEAD	96	96	89	100	96	104	91	98	91	86	91	76	90	93	93	94	63	93	100	115
03220	BELMONT	93	90	80	89	88	91	84	88	86	86	86	66	82	89	82	87	59	85	88	105
03221	BRADFORD	108	87	139	86	96	115	87	110	91	82	90	81	76	87	94	97	60	102	109	128
03222	BRISTOL	90	87	98	86	89	96	86	94	87	81	87	71	83	86	89	90	60	90	95	109
03223	CAMPTON	96	81	104	82	86	99	85	96	88	81	87	71	76	86	86	92	59	92	99	112
03224	CANTERBURY	124	154	157	158	158	146	131	138	125	140	127	103	149	125	147	123	91	131	131	158
03225	CENTER BARNSTEAD	93	99	89	103	98	102	91	97	91	89	90	75	94	93	95	92	63	92	97	113
03226	CENTER HARBOR	120	97	156	96	107	128	97	123	102	92	100	89	85	96	105	108	67	113	122	142
03227	CENTER SANDWICH	106	85	137	83	93	112	85	108	89	79	88	79	73	84	92	94	58	99	106	125
03229	CONTOOCOOK	136	155	156	159	158	152	139	146	135	144	136	109	151	135	150	135	96	140	141	168
03230	DANBURY	82	76	75	79	77	88	74	84	76	67	75	63	69	78	74	81	51	77	86	97
03234	EPSOM	99	104	90	105	101	103	94	99	95	96	95	75	97	98	96	96	66	95	98	117
03235	FRANKLIN	71	68	66	68	67	72	74	72	75	69	75	55	71	75	71	78	52	74	77	85
03237	GILMANTON	99	108	101	111	106	109	98	104	97	97	97	80	102	98	103	97	67	99	103	122
03240	GRAFTON	81	74	69	74	74	81	72	78	74	70	73	58	67	76	70	77	50	74	79	92
03241	HEBRON	104	83	134	82	91	110	83	106	87	78	86	77	72	83	90	93	57	97	104	122
03242	HENNIKER	109	119	110	121	116	111	114	110	111	116	112	87	120	112	116	109	79	111	107	130
03243	HILL	88	99	86	102	96	98	89	92	87	89	88	72	95	90	94	88	61	89	92	109
03244	HILLSBOROUGH	93	101	88	101	97	96	93	94	91	94	92	73	96	93	95	91	64	92	92	110
03245	HOLDERNESS	124	100	160	98	109	131	100	126	104	94	103	92	87	99	108	111	69	117	125	147
03246	LACONIA	80	78	80	78	78	83	80	81	81	77	81	62	79	81	80	84	56	82	85	96
03249	GILFORD	122	132	154	132	137	143	118	133	120	122	120	95	126	116	131	123	83	126	136	153
03251	LINCOLN	79	66	88	66	71	82	69	79	71	65	70	58	62	69	70	75	47	76	81	92
03253	MEREDITH	114	95	135	94	102	119	97	115	101	91	99	85	86	97	101	106	67	109	117	134
03254	MOULTONBOROUGH	118	103	157	101	114	131	99	123	104	99	103	86	93	97	110	110	69	115	126	142
03255	NEWBURY	127	102	165	100	112	135	102	130	107	96	106	95	89	101	111	114	70	120	128	150
03256	NEW HAMPTON	95	102	98	105	101	105	93	99	92	92	92	77	96	93	98	93	64	95	98	117
03257	NEW LONDON	162	161	227	159	183	194	148	178	156	161	153	115	155	142	168	164	104	168	192	202
03258	CHICHESTER	104	118	101	121	114	115	105	109	103	105	104	85	112	106	111	103	73	105	108	128
03259	NORTH SANDWICH	106	85	137	83	93	112	85	108	89	79	87	79	73	84	92	94	58	99	106	125
03261	NORTHWOOD	98	111	96	114	108	109	99	103	97	100	98	81	106	100	105	97	69	99	102	121
03262	NORTH WOODSTOCK	86	73	93	73	77	89	76	86	78	72	77	63	68	76	77	82	52	82	89	100
03263	PITTSFIELD	81	86	79	84	84	82	82	82	82	82	82	63	84	83	83	82	58	82	82	96
03264	PLYMOUTH	91	73	81	75	75	84	90	85	89	81	88	67	77	88	80	91	61	89	90	102
03266	RUMNEY	94	75	121	74	83	99	75	96	79	71	78	70	65	75	82	84	52	88	94	111
03268	SALISBURY	97	109	94	112	106	107	97	101	96	98	96	79	104	98	103	96	67	97	100	119
03269	SANBORNTON	104	104	115	106	105	113	96	108	97	95	97	82	96	97	103	99	67	102	107	126
03275	SUNCOOK	87	95	86	94	93	89	91	89	89	91	90	70	95	91	93	89	64	90	88	105
03276	TILTON	85	82	81	81	81	85	81	84	82	80	82	63	78	83	80	83	56	82	84	99
03278	WARNER	101	92	120	92	96	109	88	104	90	85	90	78	83	88	95	94	61	97	103	121
03279	WARREN	89	64	91	62	66	90	65	83	72	61	71	62	52	72	65	80	47	76	86	99
03280	WASHINGTON	98	78	127	77	86	104	79	100	82	74	81	73	68	78	85	88	54	92	99	116
03281	WEARE	126	149	126	146	142	126	128	129	120	136	123	102	138	127	133	114	87	122	113	147
03282	WENTWORTH	95	76	123	75	84	101	76	97	80	72	79	71	66	76	83	85	52	90	96	112
03284	SPRINGFIELD	108	86	140	85	95	114	87	110	91	81	89	80	75	86	94	97	59	101	109	127
03285	THORNTON	90	72	116	71	79	95	72	91	75	67	74	67	62	71	78	80	49	84	90	106
03287	WILMOT	106	130	135	133	134	124	111	118	107	118	108	88	126	106	124	105	77	112	112	135
03290	NOTTINGHAM	118	147	129	147	142	128	124	126	116	130	119	100	139	121	133	112	85	120	113	145
03291	WEST NOTTINGHAM	116	146	128	146	141	126	122	124	115	128	117	99	138	120	132	110	84	118	111	143
03301	CONCORD	94	93	89	95	92	92	98	92	97	96	97	73	98	97	96	96	69	96	95	110
03303	CONCORD	88	88	79	89	85	82	89	85	87	90	88	67	89	89	87	86	62	87	83	100
03304	BOW	161	212	215	222	218	189	174	180	163	188	165	143	208	166	197	155	123	168	157	204
	NEW HAMPSHIRE	110	114	114	115	113	113	110	111	109	110	110	86	113	110	113	109	77	111	111	131
	UNITED STATES	100	100	100	100	100	100	100	100	100	100	100	100	100	100	100	100	100	100	100	100

ZIP CODE #	POST OFFICE NAME	COUNTY FIPS CODE	POPULATION 2000	POPULATION 2009	POPULATION 2014	2000-2009 ANNUAL RATE % Rate	2000-2009 ANNUAL RATE State Centile	HOUSEHOLDS 2000	HOUSEHOLDS 2009	HOUSEHOLDS 2014	HOUSEHOLDS % Annual Rate 2000-2009	HOUSEHOLDS 2009 Average HH Size	FAMILIES 2000	FAMILIES 2009	FAMILIES % Annual Rate 2000-2009
03307	LOUDON	013	4437	5141	5449	1.6	89	1605	1865	1982	1.6	2.76	1252	1439	1.5
03431	KEENE	005	24277	24504	24352	0.1	7	9708	9781	9765	0.1	2.23	5604	5553	-0.1
03440	ANTRIM	011	2513	2801	2927	1.2	71	959	1066	1118	1.2	2.62	645	706	1.0
03441	ASHUELOT	005	521	581	605	1.2	71	205	232	243	1.3	2.50	141	157	1.2
03442	BENNINGTON	011	1420	1578	1643	1.1	64	563	625	653	1.1	2.52	364	396	0.9
03443	CHESTERFIELD	005	668	705	716	0.6	26	256	273	279	0.7	2.58	188	198	0.6
03444	DUBLIN	005	1440	1503	1508	0.5	20	543	573	580	0.6	2.48	405	423	0.5
03445	SULLIVAN	005	740	776	777	0.5	20	277	295	298	0.7	2.63	196	206	0.5
03446	SWANZEY	005	6041	6573	6780	0.9	46	2292	2525	2618	1.1	2.60	1629	1771	0.9
03447	FITZWILLIAM	005	2130	2334	2397	1.0	54	835	929	961	1.2	2.51	585	642	1.0
03448	GILSUM	005	750	779	779	0.4	13	300	317	320	0.6	2.44	222	231	0.4
03449	HANCOCK	011	1716	1955	2058	1.4	81	695	790	834	1.4	2.47	487	546	1.2
03450	HARRISVILLE	005	1075	1149	1178	0.7	34	450	490	506	0.9	2.34	307	329	0.8
03451	HINSDALE	005	4139	4413	4517	0.7	34	1649	1776	1826	0.8	2.48	1108	1175	0.6
03452	JAFFREY	005	5507	6030	6218	1.0	54	2135	2356	2443	1.1	2.47	1475	1604	0.9
03455	MARLBOROUGH	005	2199	2231	2224	0.2	10	906	935	938	0.3	2.39	619	630	0.2
03456	MARLOW	005	793	835	854	0.6	26	311	333	342	0.7	2.51	235	249	0.6
03457	NELSON	005	592	618	618	0.5	20	239	253	255	0.6	2.44	168	176	0.5
03458	PETERBOROUGH	011	6243	6474	6536	0.4	13	2484	2565	2596	0.3	2.39	1642	1670	0.2
03461	RINDGE	005	5626	6779	7142	2.0	97	1550	1912	2053	2.3	2.84	1179	1437	2.2
03462	SPOFFORD	005	1578	1673	1714	0.6	26	618	664	684	0.8	2.52	451	479	0.7
03464	STODDARD	005	814	804	791	-0.1	4	346	348	344	0.1	2.31	232	229	-0.1
03465	TROY	005	1865	1986	2008	0.7	34	690	740	754	0.8	2.68	498	527	0.6
03466	WEST CHESTERFIELD	005	1306	1365	1375	0.5	20	494	523	530	0.6	2.61	367	384	0.5
03467	WESTMORELAND	005	1752	1918	1964	1.0	54	578	635	658	1.0	2.53	446	485	0.9
03470	WINCHESTER	005	4662	5177	5378	1.1	64	1708	1924	2011	1.3	2.63	1223	1357	1.1
03561	LITTLETON	009	6006	6506	6687	0.9	46	2574	2806	2894	0.9	2.30	1628	1755	0.8
03570	BERLIN	007	10382	9909	9623	-0.5	1	4573	4426	4335	-0.4	2.16	2914	2788	-0.5
03574	BETHLEHEM	009	2163	2304	2361	0.7	34	910	980	1007	0.8	2.32	580	619	0.7
03576	COLEBROOK	007	4123	4088	4008	-0.1	4	1702	1702	1686	0.0	2.25	1065	1051	-0.1
03579	ERROL	007	365	381	378	0.5	20	166	172	172	0.4	1.98	120	123	0.3
03580	FRANCONIA	009	1129	1195	1221	0.6	26	475	508	523	0.7	2.26	308	325	0.6
03581	GORHAM	007	3274	3155	3084	-0.4	2	1449	1444	1428	0.0	2.18	915	900	-0.2
03582	GROVETON	007	2610	2730	2722	0.5	20	1060	1141	1147	0.8	2.39	704	750	0.7
03583	JEFFERSON	007	953	932	917	-0.2	2	383	389	387	0.2	2.39	277	278	0.0
03584	LANCASTER	007	3630	3795	3771	0.5	20	1413	1490	1496	0.6	2.38	958	998	0.4
03585	LISBON	009	2542	2656	2695	0.5	20	1032	1091	1112	0.6	2.43	717	750	0.5
03586	SUGAR HILL	009	469	502	515	0.7	34	217	235	243	0.9	2.03	138	147	0.7
03588	MILAN	007	1658	1742	1741	0.5	20	668	722	729	0.8	2.36	487	522	0.8
03590	NORTH STRATFORD	007	982	1190	1244	2.1	98	415	519	548	2.4	2.29	268	333	2.4
03592	PITTSBURG	007	1173	1308	1328	1.2	71	511	590	605	1.6	2.21	356	406	1.4
03593	RANDOLPH	007	236	233	229	-0.1	4	105	107	106	0.2	2.13	73	73	0.0
03598	WHITEFIELD	007	3596	3593	3538	0.0	5	1467	1490	1483	0.2	2.33	993	999	0.1
03602	ALSTEAD	005	2677	2850	2914	0.7	34	1057	1148	1182	0.9	2.47	741	794	0.7
03603	CHARLESTOWN	019	4922	5454	5672	1.1	64	1988	2252	2363	1.4	2.40	1383	1544	1.2
03605	LEMPSTER	019	1272	1399	1457	1.0	54	496	566	595	1.4	2.47	356	402	1.3
03607	SOUTH ACWORTH	019	381	417	433	1.0	54	157	177	186	1.3	2.36	116	129	1.2
03608	WALPOLE	005	2625	2773	2800	0.6	26	1075	1145	1161	0.7	2.42	749	788	0.6
03609	NORTH WALPOLE	005	849	996	1049	1.7	91	366	435	462	1.9	2.29	234	274	1.7
03740	BATH	009	835	831	827	-0.1	4	327	329	329	0.1	2.53	234	234	0.0
03741	CANAAN	009	3619	3849	3932	0.7	34	1390	1494	1535	0.8	2.58	1008	1076	0.7
03743	CLAREMONT	019	14001	13973	13925	0.0	5	5925	6073	6103	0.3	2.24	3611	3642	0.1
03745	CORNISH	019	1577	1706	1762	0.9	46	610	684	715	1.2	2.49	441	487	1.1
03748	ENFIELD	009	4803	5327	5529	1.1	64	2043	2286	2383	1.2	2.32	1341	1485	1.1
03750	ETNA	009	1182	1248	1265	0.6	26	443	467	475	0.6	2.65	351	368	0.5
03752	GOSHEN	019	710	770	797	0.9	46	266	299	314	1.3	2.55	209	233	1.2
03753	GRANTHAM	019	2307	2727	2895	1.8	95	982	1202	1292	2.2	2.27	752	912	2.1
03755	HANOVER	009	9668	10272	10366	0.7	34	2388	2514	2561	0.6	2.43	1409	1468	0.4
03765	HAVERHILL	009	473	499	507	0.6	26	194	207	212	0.7	2.32	140	148	0.6
03766	LEBANON	009	8701	9292	9501	0.7	34	3811	4133	4257	0.9	2.19	2152	2285	0.7
03768	LYME	009	1746	1861	1908	0.7	34	708	760	782	0.8	2.43	495	526	0.7
03770	MERIDEN	019	198	219	228	1.1	64	75	85	89	1.4	2.58	60	67	1.2
03771	MONROE	009	759	822	848	0.9	46	310	340	353	1.0	2.42	227	247	0.9
03773	NEWPORT	019	7513	7888	7932	0.5	20	2964	3186	3232	0.8	2.40	2022	2143	0.6
03774	NORTH HAVERHILL	009	1710	1801	1831	0.6	26	652	694	709	0.7	2.45	428	451	0.6
03777	ORFORD	009	1024	1088	1112	0.7	34	440	473	486	0.8	2.30	293	311	0.6
03779	PIERMONT	009	774	822	840	0.7	34	323	347	356	0.8	2.36	217	230	0.6
03780	PIKE	009	472	496	504	0.5	20	168	178	182	0.6	2.68	121	127	0.5
03781	PLAINFIELD	019	2127	2337	2428	1.0	54	804	912	958	1.4	2.56	628	705	1.3
03782	SUNAPEE	019	3064	3442	3599	1.3	74	1298	1512	1600	1.7	2.28	882	1013	1.5
03784	WEST LEBANON	009	3801	4393	4638	1.6	89	1666	1944	2064	1.7	2.23	1010	1175	1.6
03785	WOODSVILLE	009	2123	2163	2178	0.2	10	855	884	896	0.4	2.27	526	538	0.2
03801	PORTSMOUTH	015	21569	22001	21903	0.2	10	10173	10595	10634	0.4	2.01	5073	5158	0.2
03809	ALTON	001	2830	3245	3427	1.5	85	1122	1321	1408	1.8	2.46	813	946	1.7
03810	ALTON BAY	001	1109	1278	1355	1.5	85	470	557	596	1.9	2.29	316	370	1.7
03811	ATKINSON	015	6248	7130	7542	1.4	81	2340	2726	2902	1.7	2.61	1796	2069	1.5
03812	BARTLETT	003	1675	1844	1918	1.0	54	740	835	877	1.3	2.18	473	527	1.2
03813	CENTER CONWAY	003	2837	3128	3263	1.1	64	1157	1307	1374	1.3	2.39	787	881	1.2
03814	CENTER OSSIPEE	003	2638	3073	3263	1.7	91	1094	1305	1397	1.9	2.31	739	872	1.8
03816	CENTER TUFTONBORO	003	1229	1384	1456	1.3	74	516	598	635	1.6	2.31	372	427	1.5
03817	CHOCORUA	003	449	492	508	1.0	54	209	235	245	1.3	2.09	134	149	1.2
03818	CONWAY	003	2450	2672	2773	0.9	46	1053	1176	1229	1.2	2.26	651	717	1.0
03819	DANVILLE	015	3940	4627	4973	1.8	95	1397	1664	1794	1.9	2.78	1099	1296	1.8
03820	DOVER	017	27163	30245	31387	1.2	71	11672	13052	13579	1.2	2.25	6576	7294	1.1
03823	MADBURY	017	1380	1586	1675	1.5	85	498	578	613	1.6	2.74	374	429	1.5
03824	DURHAM	017	12712	13604	13650	0.7	34	2912	3030	3059	0.4	2.78	1604	1657	0.4
03825	BARRINGTON	017	7624	8467	8810	1.1	64	2802	3151	3293	1.3	2.68	2114	2350	1.2
03826	EAST HAMPSTEAD	015	2237	2465	2581	1.1	64	864	975	1028	1.3	2.53	591	658	1.2
03827	EAST KINGSTON	015	2610	3075	3302	1.8	95	919	1106	1195	2.0	2.78	743	886	1.9
03830	EAST WAKEFIELD	003	1099	1257	1330	1.5	85	452	529	563	1.7	2.38	323	376	1.7
03833	EXETER	015	19076	21035	21759	1.1	64	7445	8282	8605	1.2	2.43	5010	5536	1.1
03835	FARMINGTON	017	5786	6921	7389	2.0	97	2142	2610	2803	2.2	2.64	1528	1838	2.0
03836	FREEDOM	003	1311	1390	1415	0.6	26	606	660	680	0.9	2.10	405	436	0.8
03837	GILMANTON IRON WORKS	001	1025	1269	1385	2.3	100	377	483	533	2.7	2.63	284	361	2.6
03838	GLEN	003	73	81	84	1.1	64	30	34	36	1.4	2.35	19	21	1.1
	NEW HAMPSHIRE					0.9					0.9	2.51			0.8
	UNITED STATES					1.0					1.1	2.59			0.9

ZIP CODE #	POST OFFICE NAME	RACE (%) White 2000	White 2009	Black 2000	Black 2009	Asian/Pacific 2000	Asian/Pacific 2009	% Hispanic Origin 2000	% Hispanic Origin 2009	2009 AGE DISTRIBUTION (%) 0-4	5-9	10-14	15-19	20-24	25-44	45-64	65-84	85+	18+	MEDIAN AGE 2009	% 2009 Males	% 2009 Females
03307	LOUDON	98.2	97.7	0.2	0.3	0.5	0.7	0.6	0.9	6.4	7.3	8.0	7.1	4.0	24.5	33.1	8.8	0.8	73.6	40.6	49.6	50.4
03431	KEENE	97.7	97.1	0.4	0.4	0.7	1.1	0.8	1.1	4.2	4.3	4.7	10.7	12.2	22.8	25.4	12.7	2.9	83.3	36.8	47.1	52.9
03440	ANTRIM	98.1	97.6	0.2	0.3	0.4	0.7	0.8	1.2	5.9	5.8	6.4	7.6	6.9	23.9	30.5	11.6	1.4	76.9	40.3	49.5	50.5
03441	ASHUELOT	97.9	97.4	0.4	0.5	0.0	0.2	0.6	0.7	5.9	5.7	6.0	6.7	6.0	25.3	29.4	13.3	1.7	78.3	41.2	50.1	49.9
03442	BENNINGTON	98.0	97.3	0.1	0.1	0.4	0.6	0.6	1.0	6.3	6.0	6.0	7.4	8.1	27.0	29.2	9.2	1.0	77.6	37.3	49.0	51.0
03443	CHESTERFIELD	97.9	97.6	0.3	0.3	0.1	0.3	0.7	0.7	4.8	5.5	6.5	7.1	4.8	22.3	34.9	13.0	1.0	78.9	44.3	51.5	48.5
03444	DUBLIN	97.2	96.3	0.3	0.4	1.0	1.5	1.2	1.7	4.3	5.1	6.3	6.9	5.1	19.6	35.5	15.4	1.9	79.6	46.7	50.1	49.9
03445	SULLIVAN	98.2	97.7	0.3	0.4	0.1	0.3	0.8	1.3	5.7	6.3	7.0	6.6	4.3	24.9	33.1	11.2	1.0	76.9	42.1	49.9	50.1
03446	SWANZEY	98.3	97.9	0.2	0.2	0.5	0.8	0.5	0.7	5.7	6.6	7.3	6.6	4.7	25.9	30.0	11.6	1.4	76.1	40.5	49.4	50.6
03447	FITZWILLIAM	97.5	97.0	0.4	0.5	0.4	0.6	0.8	1.1	4.9	5.7	6.6	7.2	4.5	23.3	35.4	11.2	1.2	78.2	43.5	50.5	49.5
03448	GILSUM	98.1	97.9	0.0	0.0	0.3	0.4	0.9	1.4	4.1	4.6	5.6	6.3	3.9	23.1	37.1	13.6	1.7	81.4	46.3	49.4	50.6
03449	HANCOCK	98.4	97.8	0.2	0.3	0.4	0.7	0.4	0.7	4.3	4.8	5.9	7.1	4.5	18.1	34.6	17.9	2.9	80.6	47.9	47.2	52.8
03450	HARRISVILLE	97.8	97.7	0.1	0.1	0.3	0.4	0.6	0.6	5.0	5.9	7.1	6.6	3.0	22.1	34.6	13.7	1.9	76.8	45.1	48.1	51.9
03451	HINSDALE	97.5	96.9	0.4	0.5	0.6	0.9	0.5	0.7	5.4	5.8	6.7	7.4	5.6	26.9	29.6	10.9	1.8	77.3	40.0	48.7	51.3
03452	JAFFREY	97.3	96.7	0.4	0.5	0.7	1.1	0.6	0.8	6.2	6.2	6.4	6.9	6.2	25.0	26.8	12.9	3.6	76.8	40.0	47.7	52.3
03455	MARLBOROUGH	98.5	98.2	0.2	0.2	0.3	0.5	0.6	0.9	4.9	5.1	5.7	6.4	5.2	25.0	31.9	13.5	2.3	80.3	43.5	48.5	51.5
03456	MARLOW	98.7	98.6	0.0	0.0	0.0	0.0	1.0	1.6	6.0	6.7	7.1	5.9	4.4	23.1	31.9	13.9	1.1	76.5	43.0	51.6	48.4
03457	NELSON	98.0	97.6	0.3	0.5	0.2	0.3	0.8	1.1	5.5	6.3	7.0	6.3	4.0	24.9	33.5	11.5	1.0	77.2	42.5	49.8	50.2
03458	PETERBOROUGH	97.0	95.8	0.6	0.8	1.3	2.1	0.8	1.3	5.4	5.6	6.9	7.1	4.6	21.0	28.9	16.0	4.5	77.4	44.6	45.8	54.2
03461	RINDGE	97.3	96.7	1.1	1.4	0.3	0.6	0.9	1.3	5.7	6.3	6.6	14.3	14.7	19.5	24.5	7.7	0.8	77.1	27.8	51.2	48.8
03462	SPOFFORD	97.7	97.3	0.3	0.3	0.1	0.2	0.6	1.1	4.8	5.0	5.7	7.1	5.6	24.2	34.0	12.3	1.4	80.2	43.3	49.9	50.1
03464	STODDARD	96.7	96.3	0.4	0.5	0.6	0.9	0.5	0.7	4.1	6.1	5.6	4.4	3.0	25.4	36.1	14.4	1.0	81.6	45.8	50.9	49.1
03465	TROY	98.6	98.1	0.1	0.1	0.2	0.3	1.4	2.1	5.8	6.1	6.5	6.8	5.3	27.1	30.7	10.2	1.4	77.4	40.4	48.2	51.8
03466	WEST CHESTERFIELD	97.9	97.7	0.2	0.2	0.2	0.4	0.4	0.6	4.7	5.5	6.6	7.3	4.8	19.9	36.0	14.2	1.0	78.8	45.6	51.6	48.4
03467	WESTMORELAND	97.8	96.9	0.3	0.4	0.8	1.4	0.9	1.4	3.4	4.1	5.0	6.2	4.7	20.3	34.1	17.3	5.1	84.0	48.6	48.8	51.2
03470	WINCHESTER	97.4	96.9	0.3	0.4	0.3	0.5	0.8	1.1	6.3	6.1	6.5	7.2	5.8	24.9	28.6	12.4	2.2	76.6	40.5	49.1	50.9
03561	LITTLETON	96.6	95.6	0.4	0.5	0.9	1.4	1.5	2.1	5.7	5.4	6.3	6.8	6.1	23.5	31.3	12.7	2.3	78.2	42.1	47.9	52.1
03570	BERLIN	98.3	98.2	0.2	0.2	0.4	0.4	0.7	0.7	5.1	5.0	5.1	5.9	6.2	22.9	28.6	17.1	4.2	81.2	44.9	48.8	51.2
03574	BETHLEHEM	96.9	96.5	0.1	0.2	0.3	0.5	0.8	1.2	5.5	4.6	6.3	6.6	5.6	25.2	34.1	10.7	1.5	79.3	42.6	50.8	49.2
03576	COLEBROOK	98.5	98.5	0.0	0.0	0.2	0.2	0.4	0.4	4.6	5.2	5.6	5.8	4.7	23.9	31.3	15.9	3.1	80.6	45.2	50.6	49.4
03579	ERROL	98.4	98.4	0.0	0.0	0.3	0.3	0.5	0.5	3.4	3.9	4.5	5.0	3.1	17.3	34.9	22.0	5.8	84.8	52.3	49.3	50.7
03580	FRANCONIA	97.9	97.2	0.1	0.1	0.9	1.4	0.3	0.4	3.4	3.9	4.4	5.6	3.8	18.1	38.3	18.2	4.3	84.5	51.3	48.8	51.2
03581	GORHAM	97.3	97.3	0.1	0.1	1.1	1.2	0.4	0.4	4.4	4.4	4.9	6.2	6.1	22.2	33.4	15.2	3.2	82.4	46.0	49.2	50.8
03582	GROVETON	98.0	97.9	0.0	0.0	0.3	0.4	0.5	0.5	5.2	5.2	5.6	6.7	6.2	23.6	30.5	14.9	2.0	80.0	43.1	49.1	50.9
03583	JEFFERSON	98.3	98.4	0.0	0.0	0.2	0.2	0.1	0.1	4.6	5.5	5.7	6.3	2.7	23.6	37.3	12.2	2.0	80.0	45.8	51.2	48.8
03584	LANCASTER	98.1	98.1	0.1	0.1	0.2	0.2	0.7	0.7	6.0	6.2	6.5	6.7	5.5	22.3	28.6	14.0	4.2	77.1	42.4	48.1	51.9
03585	LISBON	98.3	98.1	0.0	0.0	0.1	0.2	0.3	0.4	5.8	6.3	7.3	7.3	4.5	23.3	31.5	12.5	1.6	76.0	42.3	49.6	50.4
03586	SUGAR HILL	97.9	97.2	0.0	0.0	1.1	1.6	0.2	0.6	3.2	3.6	4.4	5.2	3.8	17.7	38.6	18.9	4.6	85.5	52.2	48.8	51.2
03588	MILAN	98.9	98.9	0.1	0.1	0.1	0.1	0.1	0.1	4.4	5.0	5.9	6.5	4.6	20.5	36.4	14.3	2.5	80.7	46.8	50.5	49.5
03590	NORTH STRATFORD	96.4	96.4	0.0	0.0	0.5	0.5	0.6	0.5	5.5	5.6	5.9	6.0	5.5	22.6	32.2	15.2	1.5	79.6	44.1	47.6	52.4
03592	PITTSBURG	97.6	97.6	0.1	0.1	0.0	0.0	0.9	0.8	4.3	4.6	4.7	4.2	3.6	19.6	37.6	20.0	1.4	83.4	50.4	52.1	47.9
03593	RANDOLPH	98.3	98.3	0.4	0.4	0.4	0.4	0.4	0.4	3.9	4.7	5.2	6.4	4.3	22.7	36.1	13.7	3.0	81.5	46.6	51.9	48.1
03598	WHITEFIELD	97.8	97.8	0.3	0.3	0.4	0.4	1.2	1.2	5.0	5.4	6.1	7.4	4.4	22.4	30.6	14.9	3.8	78.7	44.5	49.2	50.8
03602	ALSTEAD	98.5	98.1	0.2	0.2	0.4	0.6	0.4	0.6	5.3	6.0	6.8	6.8	4.4	22.6	34.5	12.0	1.5	77.6	43.6	51.3	48.7
03603	CHARLESTOWN	98.6	98.3	0.3	0.4	0.1	0.3	0.6	0.9	5.5	6.0	6.5	6.5	4.5	23.5	31.7	13.8	2.0	77.7	43.2	49.6	50.4
03605	LEMPSTER	97.0	96.8	0.2	0.2	0.2	0.4	0.4	0.6	5.0	5.7	6.9	6.9	4.1	21.6	35.5	12.5	1.8	78.1	44.9	50.4	49.6
03607	SOUTH ACWORTH	96.9	96.2	0.8	1.0	0.3	0.5	1.0	1.4	5.3	5.8	7.9	7.0	2.6	20.9	35.7	12.9	1.9	76.3	45.3	50.6	49.4
03608	WALPOLE	98.8	98.7	0.2	0.2	0.0	0.0	0.6	1.0	5.6	5.8	6.3	6.7	6.3	21.0	31.3	14.4	2.5	77.9	43.7	48.3	51.7
03609	NORTH WALPOLE	96.9	96.4	0.1	0.1	0.6	1.1	0.0	0.0	7.4	7.1	6.7	5.5	5.3	27.2	26.0	12.8	1.9	75.6	37.8	47.6	52.4
03740	BATH	98.2	98.2	0.1	0.1	0.0	0.0	0.4	0.5	4.3	5.5	5.8	8.1	3.9	20.9	35.5	13.8	2.2	78.5	45.8	49.6	50.4
03741	CANAAN	98.1	97.7	0.1	0.2	0.4	0.6	0.5	0.7	5.9	6.2	7.3	7.0	4.8	25.7	32.1	9.8	1.1	76.1	41.0	49.1	50.9
03743	CLAREMONT	97.8	97.2	0.3	0.4	0.6	1.0	0.5	0.7	6.1	5.6	5.6	6.1	6.9	24.9	28.0	13.7	3.0	79.0	41.1	48.7	51.3
03745	CORNISH	97.7	97.2	0.3	0.4	0.3	0.4	0.5	0.8	4.9	5.4	6.4	6.5	5.2	20.6	37.0	12.7	1.3	78.5	45.6	50.6	49.4
03748	ENFIELD	98.0	97.4	0.1	0.2	0.7	1.2	0.7	1.1	5.6	6.0	6.3	5.8	4.3	27.3	31.8	11.5	1.4	78.5	41.8	48.6	51.4
03750	ETNA	96.2	94.4	0.2	0.2	2.5	4.1	0.7	1.0	4.6	5.8	7.6	7.8	3.9	17.4	36.1	14.2	2.5	76.3	46.7	48.9	51.1
03752	GOSHEN	97.0	96.4	0.0	0.0	0.1	0.3	0.4	0.6	3.9	4.5	5.3	7.3	5.1	23.1	34.2	14.7	1.9	81.8	45.4	49.5	50.5
03753	GRANTHAM	98.3	97.8	0.2	0.3	0.4	0.7	0.6	0.8	4.5	5.1	5.9	5.6	3.3	19.8	31.8	21.7	2.3	80.9	48.5	47.4	52.6
03755	HANOVER	87.0	82.1	1.9	2.2	7.4	11.5	2.8	3.8	2.6	3.1	3.6	18.9	26.5	14.0	17.0	11.2	3.0	88.0	24.1	49.8	50.2
03765	HAVERHILL	98.9	98.6	0.2	0.2	0.4	0.6	0.6	1.0	5.0	6.4	8.4	7.8	4.0	23.2	31.1	12.4	1.6	74.1	41.8	50.3	49.7
03766	LEBANON	95.2	93.2	0.7	0.9	2.3	3.9	1.3	1.9	5.5	4.6	4.6	5.7	8.8	28.2	27.9	11.7	2.9	81.9	39.2	47.6	52.4
03768	LYME	98.5	98.0	0.4	0.5	0.5	0.9	0.4	0.6	5.1	5.6	6.7	6.8	5.1	19.7	33.7	15.3	2.0	78.0	45.6	49.0	51.0
03770	MERIDEN	97.5	96.8	0.0	0.5	0.5	0.9	0.0	0.5	4.6	5.5	7.3	7.8	4.1	21.9	37.9	10.0	0.9	77.2	44.3	49.3	50.7
03771	MONROE	97.9	97.8	0.1	0.1	0.1	0.2	0.1	0.1	3.5	4.5	7.4	6.8	3.0	23.7	34.5	15.2	1.2	80.2	45.5	50.5	49.5
03773	NEWPORT	98.1	97.7	0.1	0.2	0.3	0.5	0.6	0.8	5.9	6.0	6.3	7.2	5.8	25.0	28.4	12.7	2.7	77.0	40.7	49.9	50.1
03774	NORTH HAVERHILL	98.3	97.8	0.5	0.6	0.4	0.6	0.6	0.9	4.9	5.3	6.7	7.1	5.3	24.5	28.6	14.3	3.3	78.2	42.3	49.9	50.1
03777	ORFORD	97.6	97.0	0.1	0.2	0.5	0.8	1.0	1.4	5.6	6.2	6.3	5.0	3.1	23.2	35.9	13.1	1.7	78.8	45.4	50.5	49.5
03779	PIERMONT	97.7	97.1	0.1	0.1	0.5	0.9	0.9	1.3	5.5	6.1	6.4	5.2	3.2	23.2	35.8	13.0	1.6	78.5	45.2	50.6	49.4
03780	PIKE	98.7	98.4	0.2	0.2	0.4	0.6	0.6	1.0	5.0	6.3	8.5	7.9	4.0	23.2	31.0	12.5	1.6	74.2	41.8	50.4	49.6
03781	PLAINFIELD	98.1	97.6	0.3	0.3	0.4	0.7	0.4	0.6	4.9	6.2	7.3	6.9	3.9	22.3	36.5	10.8	1.1	77.2	44.1	51.1	48.9
03782	SUNAPEE	98.0	97.6	0.2	0.2	0.4	0.7	0.5	0.7	4.1	5.0	5.6	6.4	4.7	23.0	33.2	16.0	1.9	81.2	45.7	49.9	50.1
03784	WEST LEBANON	92.4	89.6	1.1	1.3	3.7	5.8	2.4	3.5	8.0	6.1	5.4	6.4	6.3	30.4	24.2	10.9	2.2	76.3	35.5	46.6	53.4
03785	WOODSVILLE	97.7	97.2	0.5	0.7	0.4	0.6	0.6	0.9	4.9	4.6	5.5	6.6	5.9	25.4	27.1	15.8	4.2	80.9	42.8	49.3	50.7
03801	PORTSMOUTH	93.6	91.5	2.1	2.6	2.4	3.9	1.4	2.0	4.7	4.2	4.3	4.8	7.0	30.8	27.8	13.2	3.3	84.0	41.3	49.1	50.9
03809	ALTON	98.9	98.7	0.1	0.1	0.2	0.4	0.5	0.7	5.7	5.8	6.8	6.5	3.7	22.2	34.5	13.3	1.4	77.4	44.5	50.4	49.6
03810	ALTON BAY	98.5	97.9	0.0	0.0	0.5	0.9	0.5	0.6	5.5	5.8	6.2	5.2	3.6	20.7	35.2	16.0	1.8	79.2	46.7	49.6	50.4
03811	ATKINSON	97.6	96.6	0.3	0.3	1.2	2.0	0.7	1.1	5.7	6.5	7.5	6.6	3.7	20.6	34.7	13.4	1.3	76.0	44.6	48.9	51.1
03812	BARTLETT	98.6	98.0	0.1	0.2	0.3	0.5	0.5	0.7	4.6	4.8	5.0	6.0	3.5	22.8	36.8	15.1	1.2	81.5	46.9	50.1	49.9
03813	CENTER CONWAY	98.0	97.5	0.1	0.1	0.7	1.2	0.3	0.4	5.6	6.4	6.8	6.2	4.9	24.8	32.2	11.9	1.3	77.0	42.0	49.2	50.8
03814	CENTER OSSIPEE	97.5	97.2	0.2	0.3	0.2	0.4	0.3	0.5	4.8	5.9	6.5	6.6	4.2	23.0	31.5	15.2	2.1	78.5	44.2	50.3	49.7
03816	CENTER TUFTONBORO	98.1	97.8	0.0	0.0	0.3	0.5	0.4	0.7	4.5	4.9	5.2	4.8	3.5	18.2	37.1	19.5	2.3	82.5	51.1	49.0	51.0
03817	CHOCORUA	98.0	97.6	0.0	0.2	0.2	0.6	0.4	0.6	5.9	6.3	6.5	5.7	4.5	25.8	30.7	12.4	2.2	77.4	42.3	51.0	49.0
03818	CONWAY	98.0	97.8	0.1	0.1	0.4	0.6	0.4	0.6	5.4	5.2	5.8	6.4	5.9	25.0	31.5	12.7	2.1	80.0	42.5	49.7	50.3
03819	DANVILLE	97.6	96.8	0.6	0.8	0.4	0.6	0.8	1.3	8.1	7.9	7.8	7.0	5.4	28.9	27.0	7.3	0.6	71.3	35.9	50.4	49.6
03820	DOVER	94.5	92.6	1.1	1.3	2.4	3.8	1.1	1.6	5.7	5.1	5.0	5.9	9.0	30.5	25.1	11.0	2.8	80.6	36.8	48.2	51.8
03823	MADBURY	96.4	95.5	0.4	0.5	1.3	2.1	0.5	0.7	5.3	4.9	5.3	8.2	8.8	26.1	31.0	9.2	1.1	79.8	38.2	49.3	50.7
03824	DURHAM	94.6	92.3	0.8	0.9	3.2	5.2	1.2	1.7	2.3	2.7	3.2	25.9	34.1	11.3	13.8	5.9	0.8	89.3	22.3	45.2	54.8
03825	BARRINGTON	98.1	97.6	0.2	0.3	0.5	0.8	0.9	1.3	6.1	7.2	7.5	6.5	4.6	27.8	31.8	7.9	0.7	74.8	39.5	50.7	49.3
03826	EAST HAMPSTEAD	97.9	97.2	0.2	0.2	0.8	1.3	0.6	1.0	6.3	6.2	6.3	6.5	6.6	25.1	33.1	9.2	0.7	77.2	40.0	48.8	51.2
03827	EAST KINGSTON	98.0	97.8	0.3	0.3	0.5	0.7	0.3	0.5	5.6	6.3	7.6	8.0	3.9	22.7	34.5	10.2	1.2	75.4	42.9	47.2	52.8
03830	EAST WAKEFIELD	98.2	98.1	0.1	0.1	0.3	0.4	0.5	0.6	5.6	6.3	6.2	5.5	4.0	20.4	34.5	16.2	1.4	78.4	46.3	50.4	49.6
03833	EXETER	97.2	96.3	0.5	0.6	0.9	1.5	0.9	1.3	5.7	6.1	6.5	6.6	5.5	23.2	30.5	12.3	3.7	77.5	42.8	48.1	51.9
03835	FARMINGTON	98.2	98.0	0.1	0.1	0.1	0.2	1.0	1.4	6.5	6.3	6.5	7.2	6.8	25.5	29.3	10.5	1.5	76.3	38.9	49.4	50.6
03836	FREEDOM	99.2	99.0	0.2	0.2	0.1	0.1	0.0	0.0	3.6	4.0	4.5	4.7	2.6	17.3	38.5	22.4	2.4	84.5	52.6	49.2	50.8
03837	GILMANTON IRON WORKS	98.6	98.5	0.1	0.2	0.1	0.2	0.4	0.6	5.2	6.1	7.6	7.3	3.7	24.3	32.9	10.9	1.3	76.4	42.3	50.1	49.9
03838	GLEN	100.0	100.0	0.0	0.0	0.0	0.0	0.0	0.0	4.9	4.9	4.9	4.9	2.5	22.2	38.3	16.0	1.2	80.2	47.5	50.6	49.4
	NEW HAMPSHIRE	96.0	94.8	0.7	0.9	1.3	2.1	1.7	2.4	5.9	6.1	6.5	7.4	6.6	25.3	29.3	10.9	1.9	77.1	39.8	49.2	50.8
	UNITED STATES	75.1	72.0	12.3	12.7	3.8	4.6	12.5	15.7	6.8	6.7	6.6	7.1	6.9	27.0	26.0	10.9	1.9	75.7	36.9	49.2	50.8

#	POST OFFICE NAME	2009 Per Capita Income	2009 HH Income Base	2009 HOUSEHOLD INCOME DISTRIBUTION (%) Less than $25,000	$25,000 to $49,999	$50,000 to $99,999	$100,000 to $149,999	$150,000 or More	MEDIAN HOUSEHOLD INCOME 2009	2014	2009 National Centile	2009 State Centile	2009 Home Value Base	2009 HOME VALUE DISTRIBUTION (%) Less than $50,000	$50,000 to $89,999	$90,000 to $174,999	$175,000 to $399,999	$400,000 or More	2009 Median Home Value
03307	LOUDON	26655	1865	10.6	20.2	55.3	10.6	3.3	64327	66745	83	69	1651	5.2	6.7	38.3	46.9	2.8	174686
03431	KEENE	25877	9781	24.0	27.2	36.7	7.5	4.6	48862	50334	59	21	5886	5.8	3.6	49.4	36.3	5.0	160968
03440	ANTRIM	23974	1066	22.6	20.6	42.7	11.6	2.4	60059	62073	77	58	803	2.0	6.8	55.3	30.3	5.6	150953
03441	ASHUELOT	21621	232	25.0	27.2	39.7	6.0	2.2	47380	49788	55	16	172	16.3	15.1	46.5	16.9	5.2	124074
03442	BENNINGTON	25507	625	14.9	20.8	51.5	11.0	1.8	62365	64194	80	65	440	3.6	4.3	57.7	30.7	3.6	152303
03443	CHESTERFIELD	27399	273	14.7	25.6	41.8	12.5	5.5	60471	62635	78	60	231	0.0	4.8	30.3	54.1	10.8	209884
03444	DUBLIN	36250	573	11.2	22.9	41.0	15.2	9.8	69377	74371	86	73	461	0.4	1.3	19.1	55.5	23.6	269932
03445	SULLIVAN	26873	295	18.3	26.1	41.7	8.8	5.1	55926	58157	73	47	238	1.7	8.0	43.7	40.3	6.3	168103
03446	SWANZEY	23827	2525	16.4	30.8	40.5	9.2	3.1	52523	54380	67	38	1920	6.4	9.5	39.5	40.6	4.1	164315
03447	FITZWILLIAM	26272	929	16.3	27.1	42.5	9.3	4.8	56027	58524	73	48	765	4.2	5.4	48.8	38.7	3.0	160164
03448	GILSUM	27493	317	14.2	23.7	50.5	7.3	4.4	58491	60293	76	54	274	2.9	5.8	40.9	46.7	3.6	175735
03449	HANCOCK	33745	790	10.4	24.8	37.5	20.0	7.3	66977	70460	85	72	640	1.4	1.9	17.3	55.0	24.4	276829
03450	HARRISVILLE	30567	490	13.7	24.3	48.4	8.4	5.3	57573	59648	75	52	394	0.8	4.1	28.9	53.0	13.2	210366
03451	HINSDALE	20075	1776	22.2	35.4	37.6	4.6	0.3	43998	45585	45	8	1308	14.7	9.8	53.9	20.3	1.4	134126
03452	JAFFREY	27582	2356	15.5	23.9	47.2	6.3	7.0	58527	61360	76	54	1606	4.7	5.5	44.4	36.5	8.8	168207
03455	MARLBOROUGH	25789	935	15.6	28.9	45.9	6.6	3.0	54164	55870	70	42	691	4.1	4.9	59.3	25.5	6.2	145982
03456	MARLOW	22285	333	14.1	32.1	48.0	4.8	0.9	52056	52635	66	34	277	5.1	8.7	54.5	31.4	0.4	144250
03457	NELSON	28211	253	19.0	26.9	40.7	8.3	5.1	54116	57557	70	41	206	1.9	7.3	43.2	40.3	7.3	170000
03458	PETERBOROUGH	32038	2565	13.2	21.1	39.8	16.8	9.0	65011	67684	83	69	1768	0.0	1.1	32.6	55.1	11.2	209471
03461	RINDGE	23663	1912	9.5	30.3	45.6	9.3	5.4	59151	61328	76	56	1586	4.9	3.5	39.0	47.5	5.1	179487
03462	SPOFFORD	29974	664	12.5	29.2	36.3	14.9	7.1	57781	59445	75	53	528	0.0	3.8	29.4	49.8	17.0	218229
03464	STODDARD	23244	348	22.1	31.3	37.1	7.5	2.0	46366	47477	52	13	299	1.7	3.3	43.1	41.8	10.0	179911
03465	TROY	19288	740	23.1	27.4	43.8	4.3	1.4	49509	50088	60	24	540	6.3	8.7	58.0	25.6	1.5	141187
03466	WEST CHESTERFIELD	28378	523	14.9	23.7	43.4	12.0	5.9	64210	67398	83	68	453	0.7	4.0	29.1	55.4	10.8	213172
03467	WESTMORELAND	32533	635	6.5	18.1	44.7	21.9	8.8	76362	78592	90	79	540	0.6	0.2	25.0	60.0	14.3	222963
03470	WINCHESTER	20790	1924	23.8	26.2	41.7	6.1	2.1	50000	50776	61	26	1459	8.0	7.1	52.4	27.6	4.9	142428
03561	LITTLETON	23194	2806	29.4	26.1	36.0	5.2	3.4	45086	47001	48	9	1819	7.0	13.6	40.6	32.8	6.0	153071
03570	BERLIN	19600	4426	35.8	29.0	30.8	3.6	0.9	36319	37482	21	1	2755	17.3	42.1	35.8	3.9	0.8	80892
03574	BETHLEHEM	25765	980	23.3	31.0	32.9	8.4	4.5	46148	47717	52	12	695	5.9	10.8	49.9	27.6	5.8	145446
03576	COLEBROOK	20909	1702	32.7	29.8	30.7	4.6	2.2	38764	40849	29	2	1222	14.8	21.3	40.5	21.4	2.0	112051
03579	ERROL	25862	172	27.9	29.7	34.3	3.5	4.7	40569	42368	35	3	145	11.0	19.3	44.8	19.3	5.5	125694
03580	FRANCONIA	26939	508	20.9	28.0	39.4	8.5	3.3	51105	52076	64	32	387	0.8	3.6	26.1	47.0	22.5	231048
03581	GORHAM	23345	1444	27.0	30.4	35.4	5.3	1.9	44494	46027	47	9	1062	15.2	23.1	42.6	19.0	0.2	109060
03582	GROVETON	17392	1141	34.7	33.0	29.0	2.5	0.9	36363	37667	22	1	852	22.1	30.2	38.0	8.8	0.9	87077
03583	JEFFERSON	23797	389	21.3	27.8	42.9	4.9	3.1	50589	50841	63	29	325	6.5	14.2	39.4	32.6	7.4	144167
03584	LANCASTER	22607	1490	24.0	26.8	36.7	9.9	2.6	48907	49849	59	21	1061	11.9	19.4	41.6	22.8	4.3	116127
03585	LISBON	21960	1091	20.9	33.8	38.7	4.6	2.0	46913	47545	54	15	832	2.8	15.0	49.0	28.2	4.9	141667
03586	SUGAR HILL	29730	235	21.3	28.5	37.9	8.5	3.8	50221	52554	62	27	176	0.0	2.3	23.9	48.9	25.0	243103
03588	MILAN	22786	722	20.1	31.7	41.7	4.6	1.9	48295	48889	57	19	641	9.4	18.7	49.1	21.5	1.2	122898
03590	NORTH STRATFORD	18857	519	31.8	33.3	31.8	2.7	0.4	38910	40540	29	3	389	21.9	26.5	37.3	13.9	0.5	92708
03592	PITTSBURG	22246	590	23.4	30.8	41.0	3.9	0.8	46807	47666	54	14	504	7.5	19.0	44.8	24.2	4.4	127857
03593	RANDOLPH	26586	107	16.8	31.8	41.1	7.5	2.8	50798	51776	63	30	87	2.3	6.9	39.1	46.0	5.7	180357
03598	WHITEFIELD	22401	1490	24.7	31.1	35.9	6.3	1.9	45289	46602	49	10	1152	12.1	18.5	42.2	24.0	3.3	125168
03602	ALSTEAD	24791	1148	17.9	30.9	40.9	6.8	3.5	50712	51336	63	30	922	6.0	7.9	47.4	32.3	6.4	148361
03603	CHARLESTOWN	22007	2252	22.5	33.3	37.9	5.1	1.2	45408	46475	49	11	1726	19.2	15.4	48.5	15.7	1.3	114007
03605	LEMPSTER	22279	566	19.8	33.6	41.0	2.7	3.0	47581	48060	56	16	490	6.5	13.7	49.2	28.0	2.7	144643
03607	SOUTH ACWORTH	23608	177	24.3	30.5	36.7	5.1	3.4	45682	47540	50	12	148	6.1	8.1	45.9	34.5	5.4	155263
03608	WALPOLE	29967	1145	17.6	24.1	40.8	10.8	6.6	57048	59744	74	50	861	1.3	2.4	29.4	46.9	20.0	214510
03609	NORTH WALPOLE	28279	435	18.4	26.7	42.5	7.6	4.8	54186	55455	70	42	273	3.7	10.6	70.0	13.6	2.2	126434
03740	BATH	23746	329	19.5	27.4	42.2	7.9	3.0	52041	52823	66	34	269	4.5	9.7	37.2	39.8	8.9	171983
03741	CANAAN	22377	1494	19.5	30.3	41.3	7.2	1.7	50162	50705	62	27	1236	5.9	10.1	42.5	38.0	3.5	158491
03743	CLAREMONT	23604	6073	27.9	30.0	34.4	5.4	2.3	43311	45143	43	7	3670	5.9	10.5	63.4	18.4	1.9	128622
03745	CORNISH	28058	684	17.5	18.7	48.0	9.6	6.1	61958	63867	80	64	588	1.9	5.1	36.2	46.3	10.5	195833
03748	ENFIELD	28115	2286	13.5	24.5	52.1	7.2	2.7	62169	63521	80	65	1676	5.4	4.9	41.8	45.3	2.6	170082
03750	ETNA	62427	467	0.6	11.3	21.8	20.1	46.0	138580	145169	99	100	400	0.0	0.0	1.5	44.0	54.5	428125
03752	GOSHEN	23468	299	22.1	27.4	40.8	7.0	2.7	50346	50728	62	27	264	1.5	10.2	46.2	38.6	3.4	162500
03753	GRANTHAM	38314	1202	7.4	18.1	47.5	17.7	9.2	70644	73787	87	75	1045	0.1	3.9	16.4	57.6	22.0	262576
03755	HANOVER	36508	2514	12.0	12.0	29.6	18.3	28.1	92482	95608	96	93	1583	0.0	0.6	3.5	43.1	52.8	415950
03765	HAVERHILL	22973	207	18.8	35.3	38.6	5.3	1.9	47692	48274	56	17	170	5.3	16.5	48.2	25.9	4.1	131731
03766	LEBANON	29252	4133	19.9	24.5	42.3	9.1	4.3	55571	56897	72	47	2225	5.9	7.0	30.1	53.1	3.9	188785
03768	LYME	43436	760	8.3	18.7	37.5	18.8	16.7	77618	80194	91	82	613	1.1	2.1	14.2	46.0	36.5	321429
03770	MERIDEN	32601	85	7.1	28.2	42.4	12.9	9.4	62519	64024	81	66	72	0.0	1.4	36.1	45.8	16.7	221429
03771	MONROE	24670	340	15.9	31.2	45.6	5.0	2.4	52000	52174	66	33	298	0.7	7.0	48.0	39.6	4.7	166827
03773	NEWPORT	22108	3186	22.8	30.2	38.6	6.5	1.9	47765	48395	56	17	2260	6.7	12.3	54.8	25.2	1.1	135132
03774	NORTH HAVERHILL	22049	694	20.7	31.4	39.6	5.8	2.4	48479	48839	58	20	505	8.3	13.5	51.7	23.4	3.2	132846
03777	ORFORD	27581	473	16.1	30.7	42.3	7.2	3.8	52749	53800	67	39	381	2.1	9.4	34.9	40.4	13.1	181888
03779	PIERMONT	26293	347	16.1	31.1	42.7	6.6	3.5	52268	53008	66	36	280	2.5	9.6	36.4	39.3	12.1	177632
03780	PIKE	20059	178	18.5	33.7	40.4	5.1	2.2	48689	48220	58	20	146	5.5	16.4	47.3	26.7	4.1	134091
03781	PLAINFIELD	30466	912	11.5	23.8	46.2	10.7	7.8	62771	65088	81	66	777	3.3	3.1	29.0	52.1	12.5	218043
03782	SUNAPEE	33259	1512	14.0	22.4	46.4	10.0	7.3	59068	60531	76	56	1139	3.0	3.9	27.1	45.1	20.9	228390
03784	WEST LEBANON	31806	1944	17.2	24.9	43.9	9.1	4.8	56681	58356	74	49	1016	1.5	4.1	27.6	63.7	3.1	199711
03785	WOODSVILLE	24052	884	22.3	28.6	40.2	6.3	2.6	49200	49843	59	23	596	9.9	11.2	53.2	22.7	3.0	135246
03801	PORTSMOUTH	37758	10595	18.2	20.9	35.0	17.2	8.6	61608	65906	80	63	5564	3.0	1.1	12.9	58.9	24.1	270975
03809	ALTON	28454	1321	20.1	26.7	40.2	8.7	4.3	52301	53708	66	36	1081	2.0	6.3	35.2	43.7	12.8	198480
03810	ALTON BAY	29197	557	21.0	23.5	41.8	9.9	3.8	53764	55055	69	40	429	0.9	2.3	31.5	47.1	18.2	220402
03811	ATKINSON	43303	2726	7.4	9.5	35.1	27.3	20.7	95485	100842	96	95	2395	0.5	0.0	3.0	72.0	24.4	330398
03812	BARTLETT	26783	835	22.6	26.6	39.6	7.4	3.7	50539	51532	62	28	633	1.3	3.9	35.1	40.8	19.0	207849
03813	CENTER CONWAY	23590	1307	20.9	31.1	36.8	7.3	3.8	48276	48905	57	19	1018	8.8	9.9	44.0	30.8	6.4	149128
03814	CENTER OSSIPEE	22360	1305	25.8	36.6	30.4	4.5	2.7	41863	43378	39	5	1047	16.8	12.4	41.9	22.1	6.8	137872
03816	CENTER TUFTONBORO	30369	598	14.4	27.6	43.5	8.9	5.7	55713	57402	72	47	517	3.3	3.1	22.4	51.1	20.1	249038
03817	CHOCORUA	25856	235	27.2	30.6	33.6	5.1	3.4	43637	46009	44	8	183	8.7	7.7	38.3	37.7	7.7	165341
03818	CONWAY	23643	1176	24.7	30.8	37.1	4.1	3.4	45326	46791	49	11	833	5.0	8.8	48.3	34.3	3.6	149938
03819	DANVILLE	33115	1664	4.9	9.8	50.5	26.4	8.4	80463	84639	92	87	1494	7.9	12.2	9.8	64.7	5.4	230945
03820	DOVER	30343	13052	16.9	24.2	43.0	10.4	5.5	59182	62878	76	57	6939	2.9	2.3	27.3	58.3	9.2	219852
03823	MADBURY	32167	578	12.6	17.6	42.9	18.2	8.7	70392	75058	87	74	430	5.1	4.2	14.0	56.7	20.0	276563
03824	DURHAM	26126	3030	24.6	16.3	29.2	12.9	17.0	65050	68961	83	70	1779	0.7	0.0	4.0	69.8	25.5	319908
03825	BARRINGTON	24869	3151	8.6	28.4	48.2	12.7	2.1	61633	64811	80	63	2642	8.6	5.6	24.0	57.4	4.4	209930
03826	EAST HAMPSTEAD	36674	975	9.9	16.0	36.5	26.4	11.2	79173	84295	92	85	715	0.4	1.0	15.5	67.8	15.2	263430
03827	EAST KINGSTON	38183	1106	6.4	11.2	40.6	25.3	16.5	84923	90568	94	90	997	2.3	0.4	8.6	58.5	30.2	319388
03830	EAST WAKEFIELD	26130	529	18.9	30.4	38.8	7.4	4.5	50466	51473	62	28	451	0.7	4.2	45.0	40.8	9.3	175266
03833	EXETER	34413	8282	14.4	18.3	39.1	18.1	10.1	67234	72258	85	72	6126	7.5	6.5	13.5	54.3	18.2	254093
03835	FARMINGTON	21224	2610	22.1	25.9	42.6	7.4	2.0	51503	52870	65	32	1840	8.8	10.7	55.8	20.8	4.0	129279
03836	FREEDOM	27834	660	20.8	31.1	37.4	5.9	4.8	48115	49613	57	18	581	2.4	3.3	23.9	54.6	15.8	229598
03837	GILMANTON IRON WORKS	26722	483	16.8	25.5	42.2	7.9	7.7	55314	57182	72	46	424	0.0	2.8	43.2	43.4	10.6	184043
03838	GLEN	25497	34	20.6	29.4	35.3	8.8	5.9	50000	50000	61	26	26	0.0	0.0	30.8	46.2	23.1	250000
	NEW HAMPSHIRE	30567		15.4	22.0	39.7	14.4	8.5	63279	65972				4.2	5.0	30.0	49.8	11.0	202897
	UNITED STATES	27277		20.9	24.4	35.3	11.7	7.6	54719	56938				9.3	13.1	31.6	32.6	13.5	162279

ZIP CODE #	POST OFFICE NAME	FINANCIAL SERVICES: Auto Loan	FINANCIAL SERVICES: Home Loan	FINANCIAL SERVICES: Investments	FINANCIAL SERVICES: Retirement Plans	THE HOME: Home Improvements: Home Repair	THE HOME: Home Improvements: Lawn & Garden	THE HOME: Furnishings: Computers & Hardware-Personal	THE HOME: Furnishings: Major Appliances	THE HOME: Furnishings: TV, Radio, Sound Equipment	THE HOME: Furnishings: Furniture	ENTERTAINMENT: Dine out/ Carry out	ENTERTAINMENT: Sports Equipment	ENTERTAINMENT: Fees & Tickets	ENTERTAINMENT: Toys & Games	ENTERTAINMENT: Travel	ENTERTAINMENT: Cable TV	PERSONAL: Apparel & Services	PERSONAL: Auto Repairs	PERSONAL: Health Insurance	PERSONAL: Pets & Supplies
03307	LOUDON	102	115	99	119	112	113	103	107	101	103	102	84	110	104	109	101	71	103	106	126
03431	KEENE	86	79	79	81	79	84	89	84	89	84	88	65	83	88	83	90	62	87	89	100
03440	ANTRIM	83	96	86	96	93	90	89	89	87	88	88	70	95	88	93	87	62	88	88	104
03441	ASHUELOT	88	71	85	70	73	89	74	84	79	71	77	63	65	78	72	84	52	81	89	99
03442	BENNINGTON	81	95	90	93	94	88	92	89	90	90	91	70	99	90	96	89	65	90	89	103
03443	CHESTERFIELD	99	111	96	114	108	109	99	103	98	99	98	81	106	100	105	98	69	99	102	121
03444	DUBLIN	122	151	155	156	155	143	129	136	123	138	125	101	147	123	144	121	89	129	129	156
03445	SULLIVAN	98	111	96	114	108	109	99	103	97	99	98	80	106	100	105	98	68	99	102	121
03446	SWANZEY	92	90	91	90	90	98	86	94	87	82	87	72	84	89	88	91	60	89	95	110
03447	FITZWILLIAM	95	100	90	103	99	104	92	99	92	89	92	76	94	94	96	94	64	94	99	116
03448	GILSUM	94	106	91	109	103	104	94	98	93	95	93	77	101	95	100	93	65	94	97	115
03449	HANCOCK	109	129	133	129	134	135	112	123	115	117	115	85	126	111	126	118	80	118	133	140
03450	HARRISVILLE	119	96	153	95	105	126	96	121	100	90	99	89	84	95	104	107	66	112	120	141
03451	HINSDALE	78	71	67	71	71	78	70	75	72	69	71	55	65	74	67	75	49	72	77	88
03452	JAFFREY	88	106	97	104	103	100	97	96	96	96	97	74	107	97	104	96	69	96	98	112
03455	MARLBOROUGH	94	85	86	87	87	98	86	94	89	81	87	70	80	89	85	93	60	90	98	110
03456	MARLOW	87	79	80	82	81	93	78	88	80	70	79	67	71	81	78	85	54	81	91	102
03457	NELSON	98	106	99	109	105	108	96	102	95	96	95	79	101	97	102	96	66	98	101	120
03458	PETERBOROUGH	105	119	114	120	118	111	112	110	109	114	110	86	120	110	117	107	78	110	107	129
03461	RINDGE	102	114	99	118	111	112	102	106	101	103	101	83	109	103	108	101	71	102	105	125
03462	SPOFFORD	104	116	106	119	114	112	107	108	104	108	105	84	114	106	112	103	74	106	106	127
03464	STODDARD	90	72	116	71	79	95	72	91	75	67	74	67	62	71	78	80	49	84	90	106
03465	TROY	81	74	70	75	75	83	72	79	74	69	74	59	67	77	71	78	50	75	81	93
03466	WEST CHESTERFIELD	103	116	100	120	113	114	104	108	102	104	103	84	111	105	110	102	72	104	107	127
03467	WESTMORELAND	119	148	151	152	152	140	126	133	121	134	122	99	143	120	141	118	87	126	126	152
03470	WINCHESTER	85	76	81	76	77	87	76	83	79	74	78	63	71	80	75	83	54	80	86	98
03561	LITTLETON	78	69	72	71	69	77	77	76	79	71	78	59	71	78	73	81	54	78	81	91
03570	BERLIN	63	55	60	54	55	66	59	63	63	54	62	46	54	62	57	67	42	62	70	74
03574	BETHLEHEM	95	80	104	80	85	98	83	95	86	79	85	70	74	84	84	90	57	91	98	111
03576	COLEBROOK	82	62	83	61	65	83	64	77	70	61	68	58	54	69	63	75	46	73	80	92
03579	ERROL	89	72	115	70	79	94	72	91	75	67	74	66	62	71	78	80	49	84	90	105
03580	FRANCONIA	103	83	133	81	91	109	83	105	87	78	86	77	72	82	90	92	57	97	104	122
03581	GORHAM	77	69	70	70	71	79	72	77	74	68	73	57	66	74	70	77	50	74	81	90
03582	GROVETON	73	52	70	51	53	73	55	68	62	51	60	51	44	62	53	68	40	63	72	81
03583	JEFFERSON	95	76	123	75	84	100	76	97	80	71	79	71	66	76	82	85	52	89	95	112
03584	LANCASTER	89	73	84	74	75	91	75	86	80	71	78	65	66	80	74	85	53	82	91	102
03585	LISBON	89	72	92	72	75	92	72	87	77	68	76	65	63	77	73	82	51	80	88	102
03586	SUGAR HILL	103	83	133	81	91	109	83	105	87	78	86	77	72	82	90	92	57	97	104	122
03588	MILAN	85	76	84	78	78	91	75	86	77	68	76	65	68	78	76	82	52	80	88	100
03590	NORTH STRATFORD	77	55	80	54	58	78	57	72	63	53	62	54	45	62	56	69	41	66	75	86
03592	PITTSBURG	82	66	106	65	72	87	66	84	69	62	68	61	57	65	71	73	45	77	82	97
03593	RANDOLPH	96	76	123	75	84	101	77	97	80	72	79	71	66	76	83	85	53	90	96	113
03598	WHITEFIELD	87	70	99	69	74	90	71	86	75	67	74	64	62	73	73	80	50	81	88	101
03602	ALSTEAD	92	90	85	93	90	99	86	94	87	80	86	72	83	89	87	90	59	88	96	110
03603	CHARLESTOWN	87	72	84	73	74	91	72	85	77	66	75	64	63	77	72	82	51	79	88	100
03605	LEMPSTER	87	77	87	79	80	93	76	88	79	69	77	66	69	79	77	83	52	81	90	102
03607	SOUTH ACWORTH	92	75	116	74	81	98	75	94	78	70	77	69	65	74	80	83	51	87	93	109
03608	WALPOLE	105	104	99	106	104	111	102	106	103	100	102	81	101	104	103	106	71	104	110	125
03609	NORTH WALPOLE	90	93	72	95	86	97	93	89	94	88	93	71	93	96	90	96	64	91	99	109
03740	BATH	100	80	129	79	88	106	80	102	84	75	83	74	69	80	87	89	55	94	101	118
03741	CANAAN	93	83	88	81	83	91	79	89	83	80	82	65	74	84	79	86	56	84	89	104
03743	CLAREMONT	77	71	68	72	70	79	76	76	78	71	77	57	71	78	72	82	53	77	83	90
03745	CORNISH	97	110	95	113	107	108	98	102	96	98	97	80	105	99	104	97	68	98	101	120
03748	ENFIELD	92	97	93	98	96	97	92	94	91	92	92	72	95	92	95	92	64	93	95	111
03750	ETNA	206	280	311	291	300	255	232	244	214	255	215	187	282	213	270	204	161	226	215	272
03752	GOSHEN	93	85	84	88	86	100	83	94	86	75	85	71	77	88	83	91	58	87	97	109
03753	GRANTHAM	116	132	138	133	138	142	116	129	120	121	120	90	129	116	130	124	83	123	139	147
03755	HANOVER	158	171	196	184	182	158	186	166	170	184	173	138	193	168	188	163	128	171	153	193
03765	HAVERHILL	90	72	116	71	79	95	72	92	76	68	75	67	63	72	78	80	50	85	91	106
03766	LEBANON	89	85	83	89	84	84	94	86	93	93	94	69	93	92	91	92	66	92	90	104
03768	LYME	131	171	206	174	189	156	153	159	137	166	137	121	175	132	176	129	102	149	139	175
03770	MERIDEN	117	132	113	136	128	129	118	122	116	118	116	96	126	119	124	116	81	118	121	144
03771	MONROE	99	80	129	78	87	105	80	101	83	75	82	74	69	79	86	89	55	93	100	117
03773	NEWPORT	78	75	69	77	74	83	76	79	77	71	76	61	73	79	74	80	53	77	83	93
03774	NORTH HAVERHILL	86	73	93	73	77	89	76	86	79	72	78	63	69	77	77	83	53	83	89	100
03777	ORFORD	106	85	137	84	93	112	85	108	89	80	88	79	74	84	92	94	58	99	106	125
03779	PIERMONT	104	83	134	82	91	110	83	106	87	78	86	77	72	83	90	93	57	97	104	122
03780	PIKE	90	72	116	71	79	95	73	92	76	68	75	67	63	72	78	81	50	85	91	107
03781	PLAINFIELD	109	122	105	126	119	120	109	114	108	110	108	89	117	110	116	108	76	109	113	134
03782	SUNAPEE	118	107	147	106	112	129	102	122	105	98	105	90	97	102	111	111	71	115	123	142
03784	WEST LEBANON	95	92	89	95	91	90	104	93	103	101	104	75	103	102	100	102	73	101	98	113
03785	WOODSVILLE	85	74	80	75	77	86	79	84	82	76	80	62	73	81	77	85	55	83	89	98
03801	PORTSMOUTH	104	105	105	109	105	100	113	103	109	111	111	83	114	109	112	108	79	109	104	123
03809	ALTON	110	99	131	99	104	118	95	113	97	91	97	84	89	95	102	101	65	105	111	131
03810	ALTON BAY	112	89	144	88	98	118	90	114	94	84	93	83	78	89	97	100	61	105	112	132
03811	ATKINSON	146	186	190	187	191	173	157	166	150	165	152	123	180	150	177	148	110	157	156	188
03812	BARTLETT	98	78	127	77	86	104	78	100	82	74	81	73	68	78	85	87	54	92	98	116
03813	CENTER CONWAY	88	80	105	79	84	95	76	91	79	75	78	67	72	76	82	82	53	85	91	105
03814	CENTER OSSIPEE	87	67	102	66	72	92	69	87	74	64	73	64	58	72	72	81	48	81	90	101
03816	CENTER TUFTONBORO	115	95	150	93	105	123	94	118	98	90	97	85	84	92	102	104	65	109	118	136
03817	CHOCORUA	90	72	116	71	79	95	72	92	75	68	75	67	63	72	78	80	50	85	91	106
03818	CONWAY	84	71	95	71	76	88	74	85	76	70	75	62	66	74	75	80	51	81	88	99
03819	DANVILLE	140	153	123	146	142	124	135	134	126	146	129	106	137	137	132	119	90	126	115	152
03820	DOVER	95	91	88	95	90	88	101	91	99	99	101	73	100	99	97	98	71	98	94	110
03823	MADBURY	121	130	125	133	129	122	127	122	123	129	124	96	132	124	129	121	88	123	119	144
03824	DURHAM	130	103	102	112	102	103	157	114	139	132	139	102	128	139	121	132	100	131	111	141
03825	BARRINGTON	96	105	91	106	102	101	94	97	92	96	93	75	98	95	97	92	65	94	95	114
03826	EAST HAMPSTEAD	126	141	134	143	139	131	132	130	128	136	130	101	140	130	137	126	92	129	126	152
03827	EAST KINGSTON	142	178	163	179	174	158	149	154	141	158	144	120	169	145	163	137	103	146	140	176
03830	EAST WAKEFIELD	104	83	134	82	91	110	83	105	87	78	86	77	72	82	90	93	57	97	104	122
03833	EXETER	120	127	124	129	127	128	120	124	119	121	120	95	124	120	124	120	84	121	124	145
03835	FARMINGTON	80	79	72	79	77	81	79	79	81	77	80	61	78	82	78	83	56	80	84	94
03836	FREEDOM	97	78	126	77	86	103	78	99	82	73	81	72	68	78	85	87	54	92	98	115
03837	GILMANTON IRON WORKS	112	98	135	98	104	119	95	114	98	91	97	85	88	95	102	102	65	107	113	133
03838	GLEN	101	81	130	79	89	107	81	103	84	76	83	75	70	80	87	90	55	95	101	119
	NEW HAMPSHIRE	110	114	114	115	113	113	110	111	109	110	110	86	113	110	113	109	77	111	111	131
	UNITED STATES	100	100	100	100	100	100	100	100	100	100	100	100	100	100	100	100	100	100	100	100

03839-03894

ZIP CODE #	POST OFFICE NAME	COUNTY FIPS CODE	POPULATION 2000	POPULATION 2009	POPULATION 2014	2000-2009 ANNUAL RATE % Rate	2000-2009 ANNUAL RATE State Centile	HOUSEHOLDS 2000	HOUSEHOLDS 2009	HOUSEHOLDS 2014	HOUSEHOLDS % Annual Rate 2000-2009	HOUSEHOLDS 2009 Average HH Size	FAMILIES 2000	FAMILIES 2009	FAMILIES % Annual Rate 2000-2009
03839	ROCHESTER	017	3294	3728	3906	1.3	74	1262	1449	1526	1.5	2.57	922	1046	1.4
03840	GREENLAND	015	3168	3318	3346	0.5	20	1192	1274	1292	0.7	2.59	883	932	0.6
03841	HAMPSTEAD	015	6224	6745	6965	0.9	46	2238	2472	2567	1.1	2.73	1735	1898	1.0
03842	HAMPTON	015	14822	16368	16919	1.1	64	6411	7227	7528	1.3	2.24	4005	4426	1.1
03844	HAMPTON FALLS	015	1880	2088	2191	1.1	64	704	801	846	1.4	2.61	546	615	1.3
03845	INTERVALE	003	1403	1545	1609	1.0	54	633	716	753	1.3	2.15	379	423	1.2
03846	JACKSON	003	835	932	975	1.2	71	377	431	455	1.5	2.15	240	271	1.3
03848	KINGSTON	015	5887	6399	6580	0.9	46	2137	2376	2461	1.2	2.69	1645	1811	1.0
03849	MADISON	003	1587	1747	1821	1.0	54	614	685	717	1.2	2.55	441	488	1.1
03851	MILTON	017	3261	3718	3918	1.4	81	1217	1407	1490	1.6	2.64	907	1036	1.4
03852	MILTON MILLS	017	525	609	644	1.6	89	195	230	245	1.8	2.65	143	166	1.6
03853	MIRROR LAKE	003	634	711	749	1.2	71	296	342	363	1.6	2.08	212	242	1.4
03854	NEW CASTLE	015	1010	1134	1189	1.3	74	443	498	524	1.3	2.25	314	347	1.1
03855	NEW DURHAM	017	2386	2902	3113	2.1	98	879	1100	1190	2.5	2.64	671	831	2.3
03856	NEWFIELDS	015	1560	1847	1971	1.8	95	521	618	661	1.9	2.99	435	509	1.7
03857	NEWMARKET	015	8018	9112	9587	1.4	81	3374	3872	4079	1.5	2.34	1946	2221	1.4
03858	NEWTON	015	4206	4689	4918	1.2	71	1483	1687	1783	1.4	2.78	1145	1290	1.3
03860	NORTH CONWAY	003	4136	4479	4633	0.9	46	1830	2023	2109	1.1	2.14	1036	1128	0.9
03861	LEE	017	4034	4678	4954	1.6	89	1415	1657	1762	1.7	2.81	1055	1222	1.6
03862	NORTH HAMPTON	015	4259	4479	4532	0.5	20	1671	1792	1825	0.8	2.50	1235	1308	0.6
03864	OSSIPEE	003	1723	1954	2052	1.4	81	643	748	795	1.6	2.45	459	529	1.5
03865	PLAISTOW	015	7747	7854	7785	0.1	7	2871	2978	2978	0.4	2.63	2149	2203	0.3
03867	ROCHESTER	017	20577	22115	22710	0.8	39	8361	9127	9429	1.0	2.39	5468	5860	0.8
03868	ROCHESTER	017	4884	5644	5947	1.6	89	1932	2270	2403	1.8	2.48	1361	1575	1.6
03869	ROLLINSFORD	017	2482	2765	2879	1.2	71	965	1093	1145	1.4	2.53	672	751	1.2
03870	RYE	015	4908	5589	5896	1.4	81	2067	2401	2554	1.6	2.29	1392	1592	1.5
03871	RYE BEACH	015	253	298	317	1.8	95	101	121	130	2.0	2.46	65	77	1.8
03872	SANBORNVILLE	003	3262	3574	3710	1.0	54	1279	1432	1498	1.2	2.50	931	1033	1.1
03873	SANDOWN	015	5138	6176	6633	2.0	97	1694	2078	2247	2.2	2.95	1381	1680	2.1
03874	SEABROOK	015	8049	8968	9347	1.2	71	3479	3904	4080	1.3	2.30	2190	2416	1.1
03875	SILVER LAKE	003	545	601	626	1.1	64	220	247	258	1.3	2.43	159	176	1.1
03878	SOMERSWORTH	017	11328	12234	12535	0.8	39	4620	5055	5202	1.0	2.41	3021	3254	0.8
03882	EFFINGHAM	003	1011	1147	1209	1.4	81	374	437	466	1.7	2.46	256	297	1.6
03883	SOUTH TAMWORTH	003	271	297	310	1.0	54	109	123	129	1.3	2.41	70	78	1.2
03884	STRAFFORD	017	3423	3668	3767	0.8	39	1222	1334	1379	1.0	2.74	975	1054	0.8
03885	STRATHAM	015	6396	7496	7987	1.7	91	2317	2730	2918	1.8	2.75	1753	2041	1.7
03886	TAMWORTH	003	1673	1836	1908	1.0	54	700	788	824	1.3	2.33	451	502	1.2
03887	UNION	017	1830	1923	1952	0.5	20	656	702	718	0.7	2.74	492	522	0.6
03890	WEST OSSIPEE	003	256	291	306	1.4	81	116	135	143	1.7	2.15	77	89	1.6
03894	WOLFEBORO	003	6359	7116	7456	1.2	71	2687	3049	3214	1.4	2.30	1808	2029	1.3
	NEW HAMPSHIRE					0.9					0.9	2.51			0.8
	UNITED STATES					1.0					1.1	2.59			0.9

ZIP CODE		RACE (%)								2009 AGE DISTRIBUTION (%)										MEDIAN AGE		
#	POST OFFICE NAME	White		Black		Asian/Pacific		% Hispanic Origin														
		2000	2009	2000	2009	2000	2009	2000	2009	0-4	5-9	10-14	15-19	20-24	25-44	45-64	65-84	85+	18+	2009	% 2009 Males	% 2009 Females
03839	ROCHESTER	97.8	97.0	0.5	0.6	0.7	1.2	0.7	1.0	7.1	7.3	7.1	6.4	5.4	30.1	27.9	7.7	0.9	74.4	37.1	51.2	48.8
03840	GREENLAND	97.8	96.8	0.3	0.3	1.3	2.1	0.7	1.1	6.4	7.1	7.8	7.4	4.2	22.2	31.8	11.8	1.3	73.4	42.0	47.7	52.3
03841	HAMPSTEAD	98.7	98.3	0.2	0.3	0.5	0.8	0.8	1.2	5.6	7.0	8.4	7.3	4.1	23.6	32.4	10.4	1.2	73.9	41.5	49.4	50.6
03842	HAMPTON	97.6	96.6	0.4	0.5	0.9	1.5	0.9	1.4	5.6	5.6	5.8	6.2	5.6	23.5	31.4	14.1	2.1	79.0	43.4	48.0	52.0
03844	HAMPTON FALLS	98.5	97.9	0.1	0.0	0.7	1.2	0.7	1.1	5.4	6.7	8.3	7.2	3.3	17.9	35.8	13.8	1.6	74.9	45.8	49.8	50.2
03845	INTERVALE	97.9	97.5	0.1	0.1	0.4	0.5	0.3	0.5	5.0	5.0	6.3	4.3	5.3	27.1	33.1	12.8	1.1	80.7	43.1	51.2	48.8
03846	JACKSON	98.4	98.3	0.2	0.2	0.5	0.8	0.1	0.2	4.2	4.5	5.3	5.6	3.3	18.1	38.0	19.3	1.7	82.1	49.7	48.8	51.2
03848	KINGSTON	97.9	97.3	0.3	0.3	0.5	0.8	0.8	1.2	5.7	6.7	7.7	6.5	4.0	26.7	33.1	8.3	1.3	75.8	40.9	49.2	50.8
03849	MADISON	97.8	97.4	0.1	0.1	0.2	0.3	0.6	1.0	4.2	6.0	8.1	7.1	3.0	26.3	33.3	10.4	1.7	77.0	42.4	51.2	48.8
03851	MILTON	97.9	97.6	0.2	0.2	0.2	0.3	0.3	0.5	5.9	6.3	6.8	7.4	5.5	25.3	31.4	10.6	0.9	76.5	40.4	49.6	50.4
03852	MILTON MILLS	97.1	96.6	0.2	0.3	0.8	1.1	0.8	1.1	4.9	5.6	6.4	6.9	4.9	22.8	33.7	13.6	1.1	78.7	44.0	49.4	50.6
03853	MIRROR LAKE	98.7	98.6	0.0	0.0	0.2	0.1	0.3	0.4	3.7	3.9	4.5	4.1	3.1	15.5	38.5	24.1	2.7	85.5	55.0	48.9	51.1
03854	NEW CASTLE	97.8	97.2	0.6	0.8	0.5	0.9	0.5	0.7	4.1	4.9	6.0	5.2	2.9	16.4	33.9	23.4	3.4	82.2	50.9	48.9	51.1
03855	NEW DURHAM	98.2	97.8	0.2	0.3	0.5	0.8	0.5	0.7	5.9	6.7	7.5	7.4	4.3	23.5	33.1	10.6	1.0	74.8	41.7	51.3	48.7
03856	NEWFIELDS	97.9	97.1	0.1	0.2	0.8	1.5	0.5	0.8	8.1	9.4	9.9	8.1	3.8	20.5	31.9	7.6	0.8	67.4	38.6	49.4	50.6
03857	NEWMARKET	94.2	91.9	0.6	0.8	3.0	5.0	1.7	2.4	6.2	5.6	5.3	5.7	8.1	36.3	24.6	7.0	1.3	79.3	34.0	50.2	49.8
03858	NEWTON	97.9	97.4	0.7	0.8	0.1	0.1	1.3	1.9	7.4	7.6	7.8	7.2	4.8	27.8	29.0	7.3	1.0	72.7	37.5	49.2	50.8
03860	NORTH CONWAY	96.8	96.0	0.4	0.5	0.9	1.5	0.5	0.7	5.1	5.1	5.5	5.4	6.3	26.1	29.0	13.7	3.7	80.8	42.5	48.4	51.6
03861	LEE	96.0	94.7	0.5	0.7	1.8	2.8	1.2	1.7	6.4	6.5	6.8	7.5	6.7	25.9	31.1	8.1	0.9	75.3	37.2	49.4	50.6
03862	NORTH HAMPTON	98.4	97.8	0.3	0.4	0.6	1.1	0.8	1.2	4.2	5.7	6.5	5.9	3.8	20.4	37.6	14.1	1.7	79.7	46.8	48.1	51.9
03864	OSSIPEE	98.6	98.3	0.1	0.1	0.2	0.4	0.3	0.5	4.6	6.4	7.1	6.9	3.8	22.2	31.0	14.6	3.5	77.6	44.4	49.9	50.1
03865	PLAISTOW	98.3	97.8	0.2	0.3	0.5	0.8	1.3	2.0	6.3	6.6	7.0	6.8	5.0	25.5	30.5	10.9	1.3	75.8	40.5	48.8	51.2
03867	ROCHESTER	97.0	96.0	0.5	0.6	1.0	1.7	0.9	1.4	6.6	6.6	6.4	6.2	5.9	26.6	27.5	11.7	2.3	76.4	38.9	48.4	51.6
03868	ROCHESTER	97.3	96.7	0.6	0.7	0.5	0.9	0.9	1.3	6.6	6.3	6.2	6.2	6.8	25.8	28.2	12.3	1.6	77.2	39.4	48.8	51.2
03869	ROLLINSFORD	97.7	97.0	0.7	0.9	0.6	0.9	0.6	0.9	6.5	6.7	6.9	6.7	5.3	27.2	28.2	11.1	1.4	75.8	38.9	49.9	50.1
03870	RYE	98.7	98.2	0.1	0.2	0.5	0.8	0.7	1.0	4.6	4.9	5.7	6.3	5.1	19.0	34.9	16.4	3.2	80.3	47.5	47.8	52.2
03871	RYE BEACH	99.2	99.3	0.0	0.0	0.4	0.3	0.0	0.0	3.7	6.0	6.7	3.7	2.0	17.8	33.9	22.1	4.0	80.5	50.7	48.0	52.0
03872	SANBORNVILLE	98.2	97.9	0.1	0.1	0.2	0.3	0.6	0.9	5.6	6.6	6.5	5.8	4.2	23.2	33.1	13.7	1.4	77.6	43.8	49.6	50.4
03873	SANDOWN	98.4	98.1	0.2	0.3	0.2	0.3	0.6	0.9	7.7	8.3	8.9	7.3	3.5	31.7	26.7	5.0	0.9	70.3	36.0	50.9	49.1
03874	SEABROOK	97.5	96.9	0.3	0.4	0.5	0.9	0.9	1.3	5.5	5.5	5.6	5.3	4.6	24.6	30.4	16.6	1.9	80.2	44.3	50.0	50.0
03875	SILVER LAKE	98.5	98.2	0.2	0.2	0.4	0.5	0.6	0.8	4.0	5.8	7.7	6.3	3.2	24.3	34.9	11.6	2.2	78.0	44.3	50.4	49.6
03878	SOMERSWORTH	96.2	95.1	0.6	0.7	1.0	1.6	1.6	2.3	7.5	6.7	6.5	6.8	7.5	28.3	25.3	9.8	1.4	75.2	35.8	48.6	51.4
03882	EFFINGHAM	98.4	97.8	0.4	0.5	0.2	0.4	0.4	0.7	4.4	6.0	8.3	8.4	3.9	25.6	30.3	11.7	1.3	75.6	40.9	51.8	48.2
03883	SOUTH TAMWORTH	98.5	98.3	0.4	0.3	0.0	0.3	1.1	1.3	5.4	6.7	6.7	5.4	4.4	26.3	30.0	13.1	2.0	77.1	42.1	49.2	50.8
03884	STRAFFORD	98.5	98.3	0.1	0.1	0.2	0.4	0.6	1.0	5.5	6.3	7.2	7.7	5.2	23.7	35.1	8.4	0.9	75.7	41.7	49.8	50.2
03885	STRATHAM	98.0	97.3	0.2	0.2	0.8	1.4	0.6	1.0	5.9	6.9	8.2	8.0	4.3	21.7	34.8	9.1	1.0	73.9	42.2	48.8	51.2
03886	TAMWORTH	98.3	98.0	0.2	0.3	0.2	0.3	0.8	1.1	5.7	6.5	6.6	5.5	4.5	26.4	29.9	12.8	2.0	77.5	41.9	50.4	49.6
03887	UNION	98.6	98.1	0.1	0.2	0.4	0.8	0.3	0.5	7.2	6.2	7.5	8.4	4.5	28.9	25.9	10.3	1.0	73.4	38.0	52.0	48.0
03890	WEST OSSIPEE	98.0	97.6	0.0	0.3	0.4	0.3	0.4	0.7	5.2	6.5	6.5	5.8	3.8	24.7	32.0	13.7	1.7	78.0	43.5	51.9	48.1
03894	WOLFEBORO	99.1	98.8	0.2	0.2	0.3	0.6	0.6	0.9	4.2	4.8	5.7	5.9	3.8	18.2	33.3	19.9	4.0	81.2	49.9	47.4	52.6
	NEW HAMPSHIRE	96.0	94.8	0.7	0.9	1.3	2.1	1.7	2.4	5.9	6.1	6.5	7.4	6.6	25.3	29.3	10.9	1.9	77.1	39.8	49.2	50.8
	UNITED STATES	75.1	72.0	12.3	12.7	3.8	4.6	12.5	15.7	6.8	6.7	6.6	7.1	6.9	27.0	26.0	10.9	1.9	75.7	36.9	49.2	50.8

03839-03894

ZIP CODE				2009 HOUSEHOLD INCOME DISTRIBUTION (%)					MEDIAN HOUSEHOLD INCOME					2009 HOME VALUE DISTRIBUTION (%)					
#	POST OFFICE NAME	2009 Per Capita Income	2009 HH Income Base	Less than $25,000	$25,000 to $49,999	$50,000 to $99,999	$100,000 to $149,999	$150,000 or More	2009	2014	2009 National Centile	2009 State Centile	2009 Home Value Base	Less than $50,000	$50,000 to $89,999	$90,000 to $174,999	$175,000 to $399,999	$400,000 or More	2009 Median Home Value
03839	ROCHESTER	24476	1449	14.3	28.1	47.1	8.7	1.8	54465	56678	70	43	997	11.3	5.0	44.2	35.9	3.5	157179
03840	GREENLAND	41355	1274	8.5	10.4	42.5	21.4	17.3	84295	88015	94	89	1039	1.2	0.0	6.4	51.8	40.7	354481
03841	HAMPSTEAD	39711	2472	7.0	12.5	32.0	29.6	19.0	96562	101812	96	96	2141	1.5	4.2	10.6	66.7	16.9	299775
03842	HAMPTON	39751	7227	13.1	18.2	36.1	20.4	12.2	71988	76747	88	76	4929	0.7	2.3	7.9	64.7	24.4	294785
03844	HAMPTON FALLS	48186	801	5.2	12.1	30.7	24.3	27.6	102891	106257	97	97	707	0.1	0.3	2.0	37.6	60.0	452222
03845	INTERVALE	27073	716	22.3	29.7	38.0	6.3	3.6	47899	49595	56	17	509	2.0	3.1	38.9	46.0	10.0	188147
03846	JACKSON	29676	431	21.1	25.8	38.7	7.9	6.5	52248	53811	66	35	340	1.8	4.1	21.8	45.3	27.1	269118
03848	KINGSTON	36341	2376	8.6	18.3	37.3	24.2	11.7	77672	82236	91	83	2031	0.4	1.6	15.3	71.3	11.4	248556
03849	MADISON	23913	685	18.4	28.5	42.9	6.9	3.4	52254	53149	66	35	555	0.9	5.8	40.2	45.6	7.6	180147
03851	MILTON	21492	1407	16.2	30.3	46.5	5.1	1.9	52337	54139	67	37	1107	12.2	7.9	46.0	32.1	1.9	143087
03852	MILTON MILLS	21185	230	10.4	40.9	40.4	5.7	2.6	49119	49870	59	22	188	2.1	4.3	51.1	39.9	2.7	165789
03853	MIRROR LAKE	38240	342	14.3	26.0	38.9	12.3	8.5	58186	60847	75	53	296	2.7	2.0	17.6	50.7	27.0	279268
03854	NEW CASTLE	74705	498	1.6	11.4	28.1	27.1	31.7	116500	121962	98	98	411	0.0	0.0	0.2	9.5	90.3	837924
03855	NEW DURHAM	25630	1100	12.3	25.3	50.8	9.0	2.6	61544	63474	79	62	958	1.4	6.4	38.6	45.5	8.1	187153
03856	NEWFIELDS	38502	618	5.7	10.7	37.1	30.3	16.3	94274	99618	96	95	545	0.0	0.0	7.7	54.5	37.8	336058
03857	NEWMARKET	29535	3872	17.3	22.2	40.7	14.8	5.0	61116	64046	79	61	2161	4.3	3.6	25.4	59.5	7.3	213835
03858	NEWTON	31576	1687	7.1	16.2	42.4	25.3	9.1	79841	83351	92	85	1414	0.6	2.1	9.5	83.9	3.9	243341
03860	NORTH CONWAY	26818	2023	27.2	30.6	30.7	6.6	4.8	43517	45581	44	7	1256	10.3	6.2	36.5	40.0	7.1	168874
03861	LEE	29215	1657	10.3	17.0	44.0	19.6	9.1	72566	75601	88	77	1246	8.6	1.8	7.5	65.6	16.5	268774
03862	NORTH HAMPTON	44149	1792	8.5	15.5	34.4	25.8	15.7	85694	89224	94	90	1547	2.6	8.0	10.6	42.7	36.1	322760
03864	OSSIPEE	21172	748	24.6	35.7	31.0	6.7	2.0	42152	44026	40	6	589	6.8	11.9	40.9	31.6	8.8	154228
03865	PLAISTOW	34049	2978	9.3	18.0	34.5	28.1	10.1	81080	85593	92	87	2353	0.0	0.9	14.0	71.9	13.2	247523
03867	ROCHESTER	23423	9127	22.2	27.9	41.3	6.1	2.5	49895	51458	61	25	5906	13.9	7.9	47.0	28.8	2.4	138899
03868	ROCHESTER	23118	2270	17.9	31.2	42.2	6.6	2.1	50702	52687	63	30	1690	16.5	14.9	51.1	17.1	0.5	116024
03869	ROLLINSFORD	28549	1093	16.4	24.0	45.7	9.3	4.6	60115	63114	77	59	760	1.3	0.4	27.2	58.3	12.8	217489
03870	RYE	49974	2401	12.1	15.0	30.6	19.4	22.9	84423	90083	94	89	1940	2.4	0.5	3.3	27.6	66.2	529540
03871	RYE BEACH	55754	121	6.6	17.4	46.3	8.3	21.5	77139	80335	91	81	91	0.0	0.0	2.2	17.6	80.2	732143
03872	SANBORNVILLE	26345	1432	20.5	27.0	40.4	7.2	4.9	52005	53304	66	33	1210	0.5	3.5	41.6	46.4	8.1	183710
03873	SANDOWN	33934	2078	7.1	9.6	42.1	28.2	13.0	87110	90732	94	92	1841	0.6	0.4	19.9	74.6	4.5	228323
03874	SEABROOK	27003	3904	20.1	24.4	41.2	10.8	3.5	54062	55073	70	41	2513	3.3	11.5	23.2	46.8	15.3	226821
03875	SILVER LAKE	25289	247	17.8	27.5	44.1	6.9	3.6	53336	54321	69	40	201	1.0	4.0	39.3	46.3	9.5	184914
03878	SOMERSWORTH	23984	5055	19.1	25.3	46.6	7.5	1.5	54286	56830	70	43	2879	12.5	7.6	46.3	33.2	0.5	150596
03882	EFFINGHAM	20562	437	25.2	35.2	31.6	6.2	1.8	43104	45196	43	6	354	3.4	13.6	48.6	30.5	4.0	149324
03883	SOUTH TAMWORTH	19398	123	31.7	30.9	30.9	4.9	1.6	40743	41793	35	3	92	7.6	6.5	50.0	29.3	6.5	145000
03884	STRAFFORD	29291	1334	7.1	16.1	53.7	17.8	5.2	70523	73753	87	75	1157	1.5	1.7	26.1	62.2	8.5	228069
03885	STRATHAM	45328	2730	5.0	11.3	31.9	28.1	23.7	102423	105732	97	96	2406	0.0	0.0	8.0	60.2	31.8	327197
03886	TAMWORTH	21433	788	29.8	31.3	31.1	5.3	2.4	41558	43190	38	4	599	8.0	7.2	44.7	33.4	6.7	153125
03887	UNION	21632	702	15.8	32.6	43.4	5.6	2.6	51007	52148	64	31	602	2.0	8.5	60.5	27.7	1.3	145227
03890	WEST OSSIPEE	25271	135	26.7	32.6	32.6	4.4	3.7	42043	44080	39	5	108	8.3	8.3	42.6	30.6	10.2	155769
03894	WOLFEBORO	32007	3049	18.4	25.8	38.6	8.9	8.4	55372	58131	72	46	2386	0.8	1.3	24.8	52.9	20.1	245122
	NEW HAMPSHIRE	30567		15.4	22.0	39.7	14.4	8.5	63279	65972				4.2	5.0	30.0	49.8	11.0	202897
	UNITED STATES	27277		20.9	24.4	35.3	11.7	7.6	54719	56938				9.3	13.1	31.6	32.6	13.5	162279

ZIP CODE		FINANCIAL SERVICES				THE HOME						ENTERTAINMENT						PERSONAL			
						Home Improvements		Furnishings													
#	POST OFFICE NAME	Auto Loan	Home Loan	Invest-ments	Retire-ment Plans	Home Repair	Lawn & Garden	Comput-ers & Hard-ware-Personal	Major Appli-ances	TV, Radio, Sound Equip-ment	Furni-ture	Dine out/ Carry out	Sports Equip-ment	Fees & Tickets	Toys & Games	Travel	Cable TV	Apparel & Services	Auto Repairs	Health Insur-ance	Pets & Supplies
03839	ROCHESTER	96	93	84	90	91	93	88	91	90	90	90	68	86	93	86	92	62	89	91	108
03840	GREENLAND	135	178	183	174	183	163	149	156	143	154	144	115	172	143	169	142	105	149	148	175
03841	HAMPSTEAD	143	177	177	181	180	165	151	158	144	160	146	119	171	145	168	141	105	150	148	181
03842	HAMPTON	119	132	132	132	133	126	128	124	125	128	126	95	135	125	132	124	90	126	125	145
03844	HAMPTON FALLS	165	205	210	211	210	194	174	184	167	186	169	137	198	166	195	164	121	174	174	211
03845	INTERVALE	95	78	118	78	85	99	79	96	82	75	81	71	70	78	84	86	54	90	95	112
03846	JACKSON	107	85	138	84	94	113	85	109	89	80	88	79	74	85	93	95	59	100	107	126
03848	KINGSTON	130	156	145	159	154	152	135	141	133	139	134	107	151	135	148	133	95	136	141	164
03849	MADISON	102	81	131	80	89	108	81	104	85	76	84	76	71	81	88	91	56	96	102	120
03851	MILTON	91	83	75	81	82	87	79	84	82	81	82	62	75	85	76	84	56	81	85	100
03852	MILTON MILLS	87	79	78	82	81	93	78	88	80	71	79	67	72	82	78	85	54	81	91	102
03853	MIRROR LAKE	122	110	165	109	124	138	105	129	110	107	109	89	102	102	117	117	73	121	134	148
03854	NEW CASTLE	202	283	343	290	316	263	238	254	217	265	215	188	291	209	286	206	162	235	227	278
03855	NEW DURHAM	94	105	91	108	102	103	95	98	93	95	94	77	101	96	100	94	66	95	98	116
03856	NEWFIELDS	155	194	170	194	187	168	163	166	153	171	156	132	184	160	176	147	112	158	148	190
03857	NEWMARKET	99	95	87	98	91	87	102	92	99	102	101	75	100	101	97	96	71	97	90	110
03858	NEWTON	123	145	124	143	138	127	125	126	119	132	121	99	136	125	131	115	86	121	116	145
03860	NORTH CONWAY	87	78	96	78	81	88	81	87	83	80	82	65	77	80	83	85	56	86	90	102
03861	LEE	111	130	120	131	127	117	117	116	112	121	114	91	127	115	123	109	81	114	110	135
03862	NORTH HAMPTON	158	167	215	169	180	180	151	173	149	155	148	128	158	144	170	150	104	161	165	197
03864	OSSIPEE	88	70	113	69	77	93	70	90	74	66	73	65	61	70	76	79	48	83	89	104
03865	PLAISTOW	120	142	130	143	139	131	126	127	122	130	124	99	139	125	135	121	88	124	123	148
03867	ROCHESTER	82	78	76	77	77	80	80	80	81	79	81	61	77	81	78	82	56	81	82	95
03868	ROCHESTER	88	79	75	78	79	84	82	83	83	82	83	62	76	85	78	85	57	83	86	98
03869	ROLLINSFORD	95	109	100	109	107	103	103	101	100	101	101	80	110	102	107	100	72	101	101	118
03870	RYE	154	177	217	179	193	169	167	175	153	176	154	134	178	148	186	147	111	167	157	197
03871	RYE BEACH	189	199	270	197	229	234	179	211	189	202	185	132	196	170	206	197	127	201	235	239
03872	SANBORNVILLE	104	92	120	93	97	111	90	106	92	85	91	79	83	90	95	97	62	99	106	124
03873	SANDOWN	135	170	149	170	164	147	142	145	134	150	137	115	161	140	154	129	98	138	129	166
03874	SEABROOK	90	89	98	86	92	96	85	92	88	87	87	67	85	86	89	91	60	90	97	107
03875	SILVER LAKE	103	82	133	81	90	108	82	104	86	77	85	76	71	82	89	92	56	96	103	121
03878	SOMERSWORTH	82	80	71	80	77	78	84	79	84	82	84	62	82	85	80	84	59	82	81	95
03882	EFFINGHAM	86	69	111	68	76	91	69	87	72	64	71	64	60	68	75	77	47	81	86	101
03883	SOUTH TAMWORTH	78	63	101	62	69	83	63	80	65	59	65	58	54	62	68	70	43	73	79	92
03884	STRAFFORD	110	131	114	133	126	121	113	117	109	116	110	92	124	113	121	107	78	112	110	136
03885	STRATHAM	165	206	197	209	206	188	174	181	165	185	168	139	198	168	192	161	121	172	167	208
03886	TAMWORTH	83	67	108	66	73	88	67	85	70	62	69	62	58	66	72	74	46	78	84	98
03887	UNION	92	84	83	87	85	98	82	93	85	75	83	70	76	87	82	90	57	86	96	108
03890	WEST OSSIPEE	91	73	117	71	80	96	73	92	76	68	75	67	63	72	79	81	50	85	91	107
03894	WOLFEBORO	116	101	146	100	111	126	99	120	104	98	102	85	93	98	107	110	69	113	123	139
	NEW HAMPSHIRE	110	114	114	115	113	113	110	111	109	110	110	86	113	110	113	109	77	111	111	131
	UNITED STATES	100	100	100	100	100	100	100	100	100	100	100	100	100	100	100	100	100	100	100	100

ZIP CODE #	POST OFFICE NAME	COUNTY FIPS CODE	POPULATION 2000	POPULATION 2009	POPULATION 2014	2000-2009 ANNUAL RATE % Rate	2000-2009 ANNUAL RATE State Centile	HOUSEHOLDS 2000	HOUSEHOLDS 2009	HOUSEHOLDS 2014	HOUSEHOLDS % Annual Rate 2000-2009	HOUSEHOLDS 2009 Average HH Size	FAMILIES 2000	FAMILIES 2009	FAMILIES % Annual Rate 2000-2009
07001	AVENEL	023	16702	17220	17300	0.3	50	4869	4941	4953	0.2	2.83	3550	3569	0.1
07002	BAYONNE	017	61908	60548	59712	-0.2	12	25568	24905	24521	-0.3	2.43	16040	15674	-0.2
07003	BLOOMFIELD	013	47928	46990	46018	-0.2	12	19040	18592	18191	-0.3	2.50	12123	11726	-0.4
07004	FAIRFIELD	013	7018	7825	7989	1.2	85	2284	2569	2629	1.3	3.01	1972	2210	1.2
07005	BOONTON	027	14964	15024	14991	0.0	28	5484	5514	5511	0.1	2.66	3904	3892	0.0
07006	CALDWELL	013	26328	25745	25234	-0.2	12	9425	9293	9117	-0.2	2.58	6806	6667	-0.2
07008	CARTERET	023	20725	21302	21468	0.3	50	7043	7179	7225	0.2	2.91	5216	5276	0.1
07009	CEDAR GROVE	013	12414	12710	12613	0.3	50	4449	4600	4571	0.4	2.55	3267	3364	0.3
07010	CLIFFSIDE PARK	003	22719	23297	23660	0.3	50	9810	10006	10146	0.2	2.32	5943	6010	0.1
07011	CLIFTON	031	37230	37923	37806	0.2	43	13123	12911	12787	-0.2	2.91	9096	8886	-0.3
07012	CLIFTON	031	10699	10557	10431	-0.1	19	4796	4680	4603	-0.3	2.25	2857	2760	-0.4
07013	CLIFTON	031	25515	26119	26131	0.3	50	10196	10323	10281	0.1	2.53	7021	7058	0.1
07014	CLIFTON	031	4713	5096	5164	0.8	73	1912	2038	2056	0.7	2.50	1237	1305	0.6
07016	CRANFORD	039	22668	22567	22436	0.0	28	8429	8307	8231	-0.2	2.65	6245	6120	-0.2
07017	EAST ORANGE	013	38653	38335	37714	-0.1	19	14292	14163	13916	-0.1	2.65	8807	8651	-0.2
07018	EAST ORANGE	013	30390	30193	29740	-0.1	19	11694	11669	11506	0.0	2.54	6994	6890	-0.2
07020	EDGEWATER	003	8230	9204	9548	1.2	85	4142	4649	4847	1.3	1.98	2136	2373	1.1
07021	ESSEX FELLS	013	2085	2011	1961	-0.4	4	704	678	661	-0.4	2.96	577	553	-0.5
07022	FAIRVIEW	003	13304	13850	13995	0.4	56	4884	4973	5009	0.2	2.78	3202	3235	0.1
07023	FANWOOD	039	7148	7267	7253	0.2	43	2569	2589	2576	0.1	2.78	2048	2056	0.0
07024	FORT LEE	003	35363	37130	37769	0.5	62	16507	17225	17510	0.5	2.15	9385	9707	0.4
07026	GARFIELD	003	29443	30626	31005	0.4	56	11135	11342	11440	0.2	2.69	7348	7432	0.1
07027	GARWOOD	039	4231	4257	4249	0.1	35	1763	1754	1744	-0.1	2.43	1151	1136	-0.1
07028	GLEN RIDGE	013	7962	7719	7536	-0.3	7	2755	2674	2611	-0.3	2.88	2144	2068	-0.4
07029	HARRISON	017	16902	16721	16786	-0.1	19	5928	5802	5806	-0.2	2.88	4262	4181	-0.2
07030	HOBOKEN	017	38590	43441	44337	1.3	87	19429	21964	22446	1.3	1.92	6847	7718	1.3
07031	NORTH ARLINGTON	003	15181	15326	15391	0.1	35	6392	6448	6474	0.1	2.37	4129	4136	0.0
07032	KEARNY	017	40412	39372	38829	-0.3	7	13514	13058	12831	-0.4	2.82	9790	9480	-0.3
07033	KENILWORTH	039	7672	7599	7528	-0.1	19	2862	2805	2769	-0.2	2.71	2121	2067	-0.3
07034	LAKE HIAWATHA	027	9156	9002	8946	-0.2	12	3655	3606	3587	-0.1	2.49	2363	2307	-0.3
07035	LINCOLN PARK	027	11079	11237	11230	0.2	43	4078	4142	4152	0.2	2.54	2754	2766	0.0
07036	LINDEN	039	40994	41464	41337	0.1	35	15774	15731	15622	0.0	2.62	10503	10398	-0.1
07039	LIVINGSTON	013	27290	27968	28000	0.3	50	9236	9554	9579	0.4	2.91	7881	8131	0.3
07040	MAPLEWOOD	013	24118	23522	22975	-0.3	7	8538	8274	8075	-0.3	2.82	6443	6202	-0.4
07041	MILLBURN	013	6737	6607	6461	-0.2	12	2697	2623	2563	-0.3	2.52	1876	1811	-0.4
07042	MONTCLAIR	013	26756	26438	25976	-0.1	19	10584	10444	10253	-0.1	2.48	6423	6276	-0.2
07043	MONTCLAIR	013	11746	11448	11191	-0.3	7	4209	4104	4012	-0.3	2.67	3113	3016	-0.3
07044	VERONA	013	14010	13499	13195	-0.4	4	5817	5649	5537	-0.3	2.38	3860	3714	-0.4
07045	MONTVILLE	027	10246	10712	10827	0.5	62	3698	3904	3965	0.6	2.71	2923	3056	0.5
07046	MOUNTAIN LAKES	027	4289	4355	4358	0.2	43	1343	1361	1362	0.1	3.19	1182	1192	0.1
07047	NORTH BERGEN	017	58432	57772	57085	-0.1	19	21352	20841	20542	-0.3	2.74	14323	13974	-0.3
07050	ORANGE	013	33544	33471	32927	0.0	28	11847	11687	11480	-0.1	2.82	7873	7691	-0.3
07052	WEST ORANGE	013	44869	45042	44754	0.0	28	16522	16520	16437	0.0	2.66	11712	11612	-0.1
07054	PARSIPPANY	027	27567	29074	29597	0.6	65	10838	11299	11463	0.5	2.55	7210	7565	0.5
07055	PASSAIC	031	67992	69655	69337	0.3	50	19525	19333	19112	-0.1	3.57	14483	14262	-0.2
07057	WALLINGTON	003	11583	11912	12019	0.3	50	4752	4821	4853	0.2	2.47	3043	3064	0.1
07058	PINE BROOK	027	5265	5272	5226	0.0	28	1901	1910	1897	0.1	2.74	1450	1446	0.0
07059	WARREN	035	14110	15955	16947	1.3	87	4581	5132	5444	1.2	3.08	3893	4336	1.2
07060	PLAINFIELD	039	43342	45131	45421	0.4	56	14012	14161	14195	0.1	3.12	9602	9607	0.0
07062	PLAINFIELD	039	13017	12918	12823	-0.1	19	4458	4371	4322	-0.2	2.94	3324	3241	-0.3
07063	PLAINFIELD	039	12415	12573	12574	0.1	35	3813	3825	3816	0.0	3.28	3018	3009	0.0
07064	PORT READING	023	4006	4103	4138	0.3	50	1400	1429	1440	0.2	2.87	1105	1116	0.1
07065	RAHWAY	039	26494	27240	27614	0.3	50	10027	10184	10287	0.2	2.66	6726	6785	0.1
07066	CLARK	039	14301	14250	14153	0.0	28	5491	5416	5361	-0.1	2.61	4046	3972	-0.2
07067	COLONIA	023	18031	17925	17836	-0.1	19	6263	6204	6172	-0.1	2.89	5139	5065	-0.2
07068	ROSELAND	013	5343	5783	5810	0.9	76	2156	2346	2360	0.9	2.47	1537	1658	0.8
07069	WATCHUNG	035	6210	7298	7777	1.8	93	2321	2702	2879	1.7	2.63	1802	2078	1.6
07070	RUTHERFORD	003	18110	18174	18215	0.0	28	7055	7084	7100	0.0	2.52	4672	4657	0.0
07071	LYNDHURST	003	19383	20158	20504	0.4	56	7877	8196	8346	0.4	2.45	5205	5381	0.4
07072	CARLSTADT	003	5900	5966	5986	0.1	35	2385	2412	2421	0.1	2.47	1587	1592	0.0
07073	EAST RUTHERFORD	003	8733	9183	9385	0.5	62	3652	3850	3939	0.6	2.34	2162	2261	0.5
07074	MOONACHIE	003	2745	2760	2758	0.1	35	1041	1044	1044	0.0	2.64	708	705	0.0
07075	WOOD RIDGE	003	7742	7769	7773	0.0	28	3073	3086	3091	0.0	2.51	2165	2160	0.0
07076	SCOTCH PLAINS	039	22753	23199	23172	0.2	43	8397	8469	8432	0.1	2.72	6299	6318	0.0
07077	SEWAREN	023	2587	2595	2589	0.0	28	952	950	946	0.0	2.73	716	711	-0.1
07078	SHORT HILLS	013	12885	12450	12136	-0.4	4	4268	4107	4000	-0.4	3.03	3689	3534	-0.5
07079	SOUTH ORANGE	013	16912	17155	17013	0.2	43	5509	5638	5593	0.3	2.68	3759	3801	0.1
07080	SOUTH PLAINFIELD	023	21804	23315	23817	0.7	68	7147	7602	7756	0.7	3.03	5854	6190	0.6
07081	SPRINGFIELD	039	14562	15220	15310	0.5	62	6116	6325	6340	0.4	2.40	4087	4195	0.3
07082	TOWACO	027	5022	5280	5377	0.5	62	1673	1768	1804	0.6	2.98	1404	1476	0.5
07083	UNION	039	51241	52279	52160	0.2	43	18252	18249	18122	0.0	2.79	13295	13217	-0.1
07086	WEEHAWKEN	017	13488	13014	12927	-0.4	4	5964	5788	5755	-0.3	2.25	3056	2973	-0.3
07087	UNION CITY	017	67088	66117	65345	-0.2	12	22872	22245	21904	-0.3	2.96	16067	15663	-0.3
07088	VAUXHALL	039	3330	3430	3434	0.3	50	1236	1261	1261	0.2	2.72	863	875	0.1
07090	WESTFIELD	039	29834	29478	29222	-0.1	19	10688	10448	10328	-0.2	2.80	8227	8004	-0.3
07092	MOUNTAINSIDE	039	6686	6646	6587	-0.1	19	2466	2426	2397	-0.2	2.63	1953	1913	-0.2
07093	WEST NEW YORK	017	56235	55878	55431	-0.1	19	21096	20834	20677	-0.1	2.68	13581	13395	-0.1
07094	SECAUCUS	017	15931	16030	15945	0.1	35	6214	6283	6256	0.1	2.40	3948	3999	0.1
07095	WOODBRIDGE	023	17218	17618	17735	0.2	43	6913	7025	7059	0.2	2.49	4643	4684	0.1
07102	NEWARK	013	10381	10540	10466	0.2	43	3975	4117	4099	0.4	1.98	1541	1582	0.3
07103	NEWARK	013	33124	34571	34483	0.5	62	10628	10957	10897	0.3	2.89	7025	7228	0.3
07104	NEWARK	013	51358	51188	50813	0.0	28	16445	16821	16706	0.2	2.91	11064	11243	0.2
07105	NEWARK	013	44532	45434	45118	0.2	43	15414	15723	15603	0.2	2.88	11316	11462	0.1
07106	NEWARK	013	33863	33469	32938	-0.1	19	11346	11260	11081	-0.1	2.97	8247	8133	-0.2
07107	NEWARK	013	36303	37193	36948	0.3	50	12087	12336	12253	0.2	2.98	8432	8558	0.2
07108	NEWARK	013	25439	24893	24530	-0.2	12	8701	8477	8339	-0.3	2.91	5924	5779	-0.3
07109	BELLEVILLE	013	35437	34824	34121	-0.2	12	13552	13321	13052	-0.2	2.60	8965	8728	-0.3
07110	NUTLEY	013	27548	27351	26895	-0.1	19	10957	11001	10842	0.0	2.48	7425	7359	-0.1
07111	IRVINGTON	013	60969	59870	58687	-0.2	12	22100	21621	21190	-0.2	2.76	14458	14021	-0.3
07112	NEWARK	013	26463	26752	26480	0.1	35	9385	9555	9472	0.2	2.79	6501	6576	0.1
07114	NEWARK	013	11894	12414	12429	0.5	62	3390	3558	3555	0.5	2.54	1938	2039	0.6
07201	ELIZABETH	039	27657	28514	28582	0.3	50	8301	8450	8436	0.2	3.11	6054	6122	0.1
07202	ELIZABETH	039	37062	38898	39124	0.5	62	13204	13534	13533	0.3	2.84	8881	9056	0.2
07203	ROSELLE	039	21172	21721	21714	0.3	50	7482	7498	7457	0.0	2.89	5196	5174	0.0
07204	ROSELLE PARK	039	13274	13245	13159	0.0	28	5123	5056	5003	-0.1	2.62	3406	3338	-0.2
	NEW JERSEY					0.5					0.5	2.69			0.5
	UNITED STATES					1.0					1.1	2.59			0.9

# ZIP CODE	POST OFFICE NAME	RACE (%) White 2000	White 2009	Black 2000	Black 2009	Asian/Pacific 2000	Asian/Pacific 2009	% Hispanic Origin 2000	% Hispanic Origin 2009	2009 AGE DISTRIBUTION (%) 0-4	5-9	10-14	15-19	20-24	25-44	45-64	65-84	85+	18+	MEDIAN AGE 2009	% 2009 Males	% 2009 Females
07001	AVENEL	53.9	46.2	19.9	20.1	18.4	23.6	9.9	14.2	6.2	5.6	5.2	5.1	6.4	38.6	24.5	7.3	1.1	79.8	36.3	57.5	42.5
07002	BAYONNE	78.6	72.0	5.5	5.7	4.2	6.1	17.8	26.7	6.0	5.6	5.7	6.4	6.9	27.8	26.9	12.1	2.6	78.8	39.0	47.7	52.3
07003	BLOOMFIELD	69.7	67.4	12.1	13.2	8.5	8.6	14.5	16.1	5.9	5.8	5.8	6.1	6.2	29.8	27.1	10.9	2.4	78.8	39.0	47.9	52.1
07004	FAIRFIELD	95.7	95.1	0.5	0.7	2.8	3.1	3.4	3.9	5.6	5.8	6.0	6.0	4.1	24.7	29.2	15.7	2.5	78.6	43.4	48.6	51.4
07005	BOONTON	86.3	80.5	2.8	3.4	7.1	10.8	4.9	8.0	6.3	6.5	6.9	6.2	4.9	25.3	29.7	11.8	2.3	76.4	41.4	49.8	50.2
07006	CALDWELL	89.1	88.1	5.1	5.7	4.2	4.4	3.1	3.6	5.8	6.2	6.8	6.6	5.6	24.4	28.0	13.3	3.3	77.3	41.5	48.9	51.1
07008	CARTERET	68.8	60.3	9.5	9.4	8.3	11.6	23.4	33.0	6.4	6.4	6.2	7.2	6.6	26.8	26.4	11.7	2.4	76.6	38.1	48.6	51.4
07009	CEDAR GROVE	90.1	89.3	3.0	3.2	5.4	5.7	3.2	3.7	5.3	5.5	6.0	5.4	3.6	23.1	28.6	17.0	5.5	79.7	45.7	46.8	53.2
07010	CLIFFSIDE PARK	77.6	69.9	1.8	2.0	12.2	17.2	18.4	24.9	4.9	4.7	4.6	5.0	5.5	29.3	28.2	14.9	2.9	82.8	42.5	48.5	51.5
07011	CLIFTON	66.1	53.2	4.5	5.4	4.5	5.5	32.4	48.6	6.7	6.2	6.1	6.9	7.3	29.5	25.0	9.3	3.0	76.9	36.0	48.2	51.8
07012	CLIFTON	84.4	75.0	2.2	3.4	8.9	13.4	7.8	15.2	5.5	5.4	5.4	4.8	4.3	25.3	28.8	16.0	4.4	80.7	44.4	48.3	51.7
07013	CLIFTON	86.0	76.3	1.3	2.1	7.4	11.5	8.6	17.1	5.4	5.5	5.7	5.4	5.0	25.2	29.4	14.6	3.7	80.1	43.5	47.9	52.1
07014	CLIFTON	78.8	66.5	2.5	3.7	10.2	14.1	14.8	27.5	6.2	6.2	6.3	5.6	4.5	27.8	28.2	12.5	2.7	77.8	40.9	47.9	52.1
07016	CRANFORD	93.5	90.3	2.8	3.7	2.2	3.4	3.9	7.1	6.1	6.4	6.9	6.1	4.8	22.9	29.2	13.8	3.8	76.8	43.0	47.7	52.3
07017	EAST ORANGE	4.5	4.0	88.3	88.8	0.6	0.5	5.3	5.4	7.8	7.9	7.5	7.3	6.7	27.0	23.9	10.3	1.6	72.3	34.4	44.9	55.1
07018	EAST ORANGE	3.3	3.0	90.7	91.0	0.4	0.4	4.0	4.1	7.9	7.9	7.6	7.5	7.1	26.8	22.8	10.6	1.7	72.0	33.9	44.9	55.1
07020	EDGEWATER	68.0	57.8	3.6	4.0	22.4	30.8	10.6	14.0	5.5	3.4	3.0	3.7	5.5	39.5	30.0	8.2	1.1	85.8	38.6	48.9	51.1
07021	ESSEX FELLS	96.9	96.6	0.5	0.5	1.1	1.1	1.2	1.4	8.4	9.7	9.6	5.9	2.6	18.3	30.8	12.7	1.9	68.5	42.3	49.4	50.6
07022	FAIRVIEW	72.5	65.7	1.7	1.8	5.1	6.7	36.8	47.3	6.7	6.3	5.7	5.8	7.0	33.5	23.1	9.9	2.0	78.0	35.4	51.7	48.3
07023	FANWOOD	88.3	83.2	5.1	6.6	4.4	6.9	3.7	6.6	7.4	8.0	8.7	6.4	3.8	22.2	29.4	11.3	2.7	71.6	41.6	48.1	51.9
07024	FORT LEE	62.7	53.2	1.7	1.8	31.5	40.1	7.8	10.3	5.1	4.7	4.6	4.6	4.7	26.1	29.0	17.6	3.5	82.8	45.1	46.7	53.3
07026	GARFIELD	82.3	76.0	3.0	3.4	2.7	4.0	19.9	28.1	6.4	5.8	5.7	6.6	7.5	31.0	25.2	9.7	2.1	78.2	36.3	49.3	50.7
07027	GARWOOD	95.9	93.2	0.4	0.5	1.4	2.2	5.0	9.0	5.7	5.7	5.7	5.9	6.1	28.5	28.4	11.3	2.8	79.4	40.9	48.8	51.2
07028	GLEN RIDGE	85.6	84.1	8.0	8.9	3.4	3.6	4.0	4.5	8.2	8.9	9.0	6.8	3.9	22.3	30.3	8.8	1.7	69.3	40.1	49.0	51.0
07029	HARRISON	66.3	58.7	1.1	1.1	10.6	13.0	38.4	50.0	6.8	6.3	5.7	6.0	7.9	33.6	24.1	8.4	1.2	77.7	34.6	51.1	48.9
07030	HOBOKEN	80.8	75.2	4.3	4.1	4.4	6.4	20.2	28.1	3.3	2.6	2.3	3.4	12.8	50.1	16.6	7.5	1.4	90.1	31.6	51.6	48.4
07031	NORTH ARLINGTON	89.6	84.8	0.5	0.5	5.6	8.5	10.6	15.9	4.8	4.6	4.7	5.3	5.8	29.0	28.1	14.3	3.4	82.8	42.2	47.9	52.1
07032	KEARNY	75.7	69.4	4.0	3.8	5.6	7.4	27.3	38.7	5.9	5.5	5.3	6.2	8.3	33.5	24.6	8.9	1.6	79.7	35.6	51.9	48.1
07033	KENILWORTH	91.2	87.1	2.4	3.0	3.0	4.4	8.7	14.7	5.8	5.9	6.0	6.2	5.1	27.2	28.3	12.6	2.9	78.5	41.3	48.7	51.3
07034	LAKE HIAWATHA	79.4	71.4	2.8	3.3	12.4	18.2	7.4	11.6	6.0	5.7	5.7	5.7	6.5	31.9	27.4	10.0	1.0	79.2	38.4	49.5	50.5
07035	LINCOLN PARK	90.1	85.1	1.7	2.1	5.3	8.3	5.7	9.8	5.3	5.4	5.7	5.5	4.9	25.9	30.5	13.7	3.1	80.0	43.3	48.0	52.0
07036	LINDEN	67.3	61.7	21.9	23.3	2.3	3.2	13.9	20.9	6.0	6.0	6.0	6.4	6.2	27.7	26.8	12.1	2.8	78.1	39.2	47.8	52.2
07039	LIVINGSTON	82.7	81.4	1.2	1.4	14.5	15.4	2.5	3.0	6.5	7.3	8.4	6.8	3.8	20.2	31.3	13.4	2.4	73.3	43.2	49.0	51.0
07040	MAPLEWOOD	58.8	56.2	32.6	34.9	2.9	3.0	5.2	5.7	7.1	7.8	8.5	7.0	5.3	23.1	29.6	9.2	2.4	72.0	39.5	48.2	51.8
07041	MILLBURN	89.2	88.3	1.2	1.4	7.8	8.2	2.9	3.3	6.9	7.6	8.7	6.8	4.3	22.9	31.1	9.4	2.3	72.2	41.0	48.8	51.2
07042	MONTCLAIR	48.0	45.4	43.1	45.5	3.0	3.0	5.7	6.1	6.0	6.2	6.7	6.7	6.9	27.1	28.3	9.7	2.6	76.8	38.9	46.6	53.4
07043	MONTCLAIR	87.2	85.0	5.9	7.1	3.8	4.2	4.0	4.8	6.6	7.7	9.0	7.9	5.1	20.7	31.9	9.5	1.7	72.2	40.8	48.1	51.9
07044	VERONA	92.9	92.2	1.7	1.9	3.4	3.6	3.4	3.9	6.0	6.4	7.2	6.0	4.0	21.5	30.0	14.8	4.1	76.6	44.4	47.6	52.4
07045	MONTVILLE	87.0	80.6	0.8	0.9	10.8	16.5	2.5	4.4	6.3	7.1	8.1	6.5	3.2	22.1	31.6	13.2	1.9	74.0	43.2	48.0	52.0
07046	MOUNTAIN LAKES	93.0	88.9	0.4	0.5	5.3	8.6	1.7	2.9	6.4	8.1	10.7	10.1	4.2	13.0	35.0	10.9	1.7	68.3	42.8	49.4	50.6
07047	NORTH BERGEN	67.3	63.7	2.7	2.5	6.5	7.3	57.3	67.9	6.5	6.1	5.7	6.3	7.6	29.5	24.6	11.3	2.4	78.0	36.8	48.1	51.9
07050	ORANGE	13.1	12.2	75.1	75.9	1.4	1.3	12.5	12.9	8.5	8.1	7.5	7.5	7.4	28.4	22.7	8.5	1.5	71.5	32.7	46.6	53.4
07052	WEST ORANGE	67.5	65.1	17.6	19.2	8.1	8.3	9.9	10.8	6.4	6.5	6.7	6.1	5.2	24.7	27.2	13.2	4.0	76.5	41.4	47.4	52.6
07054	PARSIPPANY	70.5	61.1	3.1	3.2	21.4	29.3	8.0	11.2	6.1	5.9	5.9	5.6	6.3	29.4	27.5	11.6	1.8	78.7	39.5	49.3	50.7
07055	PASSAIC	35.8	29.6	13.7	12.9	5.6	5.6	62.0	71.0	9.7	8.8	7.5	7.8	8.6	30.4	19.0	6.9	1.3	69.5	29.1	50.2	49.8
07057	WALLINGTON	87.6	83.3	2.7	3.0	5.0	7.1	6.7	10.0	5.3	5.1	5.0	5.4	6.3	31.3	28.2	11.0	2.4	81.4	39.5	48.7	51.3
07058	PINE BROOK	75.4	65.6	1.6	1.7	21.1	30.3	2.9	4.4	6.9	6.5	6.9	5.5	3.9	32.3	27.2	9.8	1.1	76.2	37.2	49.8	50.2
07059	WARREN	86.3	80.3	1.3	1.5	10.7	15.8	3.2	5.2	6.3	7.8	9.9	7.8	3.3	19.2	33.3	11.0	1.5	70.7	42.5	49.8	50.2
07060	PLAINFIELD	38.1	35.1	39.3	37.6	2.6	3.1	32.9	40.4	7.9	7.4	6.7	7.0	7.8	30.3	23.5	7.8	1.6	73.8	33.4	50.0	50.0
07062	PLAINFIELD	26.0	23.8	62.7	62.3	1.3	1.5	17.4	21.9	7.3	7.4	7.4	7.1	6.1	27.1	26.2	9.8	1.5	73.4	36.4	47.6	52.4
07063	PLAINFIELD	29.3	27.7	56.9	55.1	2.1	2.7	19.2	24.3	8.0	7.9	7.6	7.6	6.8	27.8	24.3	8.9	1.1	71.8	33.9	48.3	51.7
07064	PORT READING	86.3	79.6	4.3	5.3	4.9	8.1	8.0	13.1	6.3	6.4	6.3	6.3	5.4	28.3	26.3	12.9	1.8	77.1	39.7	48.9	51.1
07065	RAHWAY	60.2	53.2	27.1	29.6	3.6	4.8	13.9	20.1	6.3	6.2	6.3	6.7	6.3	27.4	27.3	11.3	2.3	77.2	38.9	48.1	51.9
07066	CLARK	95.6	92.9	0.3	0.4	2.8	4.4	3.7	6.6	5.3	5.6	6.1	6.0	4.6	23.2	29.4	15.9	3.8	79.3	44.4	47.7	52.3
07067	COLONIA	85.9	79.5	4.8	5.8	6.4	10.3	5.0	8.5	6.1	6.5	6.8	6.6	5.1	23.6	29.5	13.6	2.2	76.4	42.0	48.4	51.6
07068	ROSELAND	93.4	92.8	0.7	0.9	4.7	5.1	2.3	2.7	5.6	6.2	6.9	5.7	3.1	20.2	30.1	19.0	3.1	77.6	46.3	46.1	53.9
07069	WATCHUNG	84.8	78.7	3.2	3.7	9.7	14.2	3.0	4.9	5.7	6.2	7.3	6.2	3.2	21.6	31.4	15.8	2.7	76.8	44.9	48.7	51.3
07070	RUTHERFORD	82.0	75.0	2.7	3.1	11.4	16.6	8.6	12.4	5.3	5.2	5.6	6.2	6.1	27.9	29.6	11.8	2.4	80.3	41.2	48.1	51.9
07071	LYNDHURST	89.9	85.2	0.6	0.8	5.4	8.2	9.0	13.7	5.2	5.1	5.1	5.8	6.0	29.3	28.2	12.7	2.7	81.2	40.9	48.2	51.8
07072	CARLSTADT	88.9	83.4	1.4	1.7	6.2	9.7	8.0	12.2	5.3	5.0	5.1	5.4	6.2	29.9	28.7	12.3	2.1	81.4	40.7	48.6	51.4
07073	EAST RUTHERFORD	79.7	72.1	3.7	4.4	10.7	15.4	10.6	15.5	5.5	5.2	5.1	5.5	6.3	31.2	28.1	11.0	2.1	80.7	39.7	49.1	50.9
07074	MOONACHIE	85.6	79.3	0.9	1.2	6.7	10.0	12.6	18.6	4.8	5.2	5.4	5.8	6.0	25.4	31.1	14.3	2.1	81.1	43.2	48.9	51.1
07075	WOOD RIDGE	90.9	86.5	0.9	1.1	5.0	7.8	7.3	11.2	5.8	6.2	6.6	6.1	4.5	24.6	30.7	13.0	2.6	77.6	42.8	48.0	52.0
07076	SCOTCH PLAINS	79.0	72.5	11.2	13.2	7.2	10.6	3.9	6.5	7.2	7.6	8.0	6.2	4.1	23.9	29.0	11.6	2.3	73.1	40.9	48.1	51.9
07077	SEWAREN	87.7	82.5	4.5	5.4	4.1	6.4	9.5	15.6	5.7	5.9	6.0	6.3	5.7	27.5	29.1	11.9	2.0	78.5	40.7	48.1	51.9
07078	SHORT HILLS	88.8	88.0	1.0	1.2	8.7	9.3	1.6	1.8	8.1	9.6	11.3	8.0	2.7	17.3	31.1	10.2	1.7	65.6	40.9	49.3	50.7
07079	SOUTH ORANGE	60.1	57.3	31.6	33.9	3.9	4.0	4.9	5.4	5.4	6.1	6.8	11.1	10.4	22.4	25.9	9.6	2.4	77.8	35.2	48.2	51.8
07080	SOUTH PLAINFIELD	77.7	68.8	8.6	10.0	7.6	12.4	8.7	13.5	6.1	6.4	6.8	7.1	5.6	25.4	28.9	11.6	2.2	76.3	40.2	49.0	51.0
07081	SPRINGFIELD	89.3	84.5	4.1	5.1	4.7	7.4	4.2	7.2	5.9	6.1	6.4	5.6	4.2	23.1	29.6	15.4	3.7	78.0	44.2	47.6	52.4
07082	TOWACO	90.2	85.2	0.5	0.6	7.7	11.9	2.2	3.8	6.1	7.0	8.2	7.2	3.3	21.9	32.2	12.8	1.4	73.9	42.9	48.7	51.3
07083	UNION	71.8	64.5	15.3	17.3	8.1	11.2	9.4	14.8	5.6	5.7	5.9	7.2	6.6	25.6	27.7	12.5	3.2	78.9	40.5	47.3	52.7
07086	WEEHAWKEN	73.0	67.3	3.6	3.5	4.8	6.3	40.7	52.0	4.9	4.3	3.9	4.7	7.3	38.5	24.6	10.1	1.7	84.1	37.7	49.3	50.7
07087	UNION CITY	58.4	56.9	3.6	3.1	2.2	2.3	82.3	88.3	7.6	7.0	6.2	7.1	8.4	31.4	22.3	8.7	1.2	75.1	32.9	50.4	49.6
07088	VAUXHALL	9.9	8.0	82.9	83.8	1.7	2.0	4.6	5.9	6.5	6.2	6.9	6.9	6.2	26.6	26.5	11.9	2.3	76.1	38.1	45.4	54.6
07090	WESTFIELD	90.0	85.7	3.9	4.9	4.1	6.3	2.8	4.9	7.1	8.0	9.0	7.4	4.3	21.0	30.0	10.8	2.5	71.0	41.2	48.2	51.8
07092	MOUNTAINSIDE	95.0	92.3	1.0	1.3	2.9	4.6	3.0	5.4	5.8	6.6	7.5	5.6	2.8	18.0	29.7	18.8	5.1	76.2	47.2	47.4	52.6
07093	WEST NEW YORK	61.0	58.9	3.6	3.2	3.8	4.5	74.1	80.0	6.8	5.9	5.4	6.3	7.7	31.9	23.5	10.7	1.8	78.2	35.4	49.2	50.8
07094	SECAUCUS	78.5	70.9	4.5	4.6	11.8	17.2	12.3	18.7	5.1	5.0	5.3	5.8	4.9	29.0	28.5	13.7	2.6	80.9	41.8	49.7	50.3
07095	WOODBRIDGE	78.5	71.4	6.7	7.4	9.9	13.9	9.8	15.5	6.1	6.1	6.0	5.8	5.7	28.2	27.7	11.7	2.7	78.2	40.0	48.3	51.7
07102	NEWARK	17.7	16.7	62.8	64.0	2.1	2.1	24.7	24.4	5.0	4.4	3.8	7.4	11.7	31.5	22.1	12.2	1.9	84.0	35.2	54.3	45.7
07103	NEWARK	7.1	6.6	83.7	84.2	0.9	0.8	12.0	12.1	8.6	8.5	7.8	10.0	10.0	25.6	19.5	8.8	1.4	69.4	28.4	46.0	54.0
07104	NEWARK	39.2	37.7	23.9	24.1	1.7	1.6	63.2	65.1	8.4	7.5	6.6	8.1	9.5	29.8	20.5	8.2	1.5	73.1	30.9	49.8	50.2
07105	NEWARK	72.0	70.1	5.4	5.6	0.5	0.5	35.6	38.5	6.8	6.3	5.5	6.0	7.9	36.1	23.2	7.3	1.0	78.1	33.8	51.7	48.3
07106	NEWARK	9.5	8.6	81.2	82.3	2.9	2.7	6.6	6.8	8.3	8.2	7.7	8.2	7.7	28.7	22.4	7.9	0.9	70.8	31.5	45.7	54.3
07107	NEWARK	27.2	26.2	40.2	40.0	1.7	1.7	45.3	47.0	9.2	8.4	7.3	7.9	8.6	29.8	19.9	7.7	1.2	70.5	29.9	48.0	52.0
07108	NEWARK	2.3	2.1	92.0	92.2	0.1	0.1	7.2	7.1	8.9	9.1	8.3	9.0	8.0	25.5	20.9	9.1	1.2	68.2	29.7	43.7	56.3
07109	BELLEVILLE	69.5	67.5	5.4	5.9	11.3	11.5	23.7	25.8	6.0	5.7	5.6	6.3	7.1	30.5	26.3	10.4	2.1	79.0	37.9	48.6	51.4
07110	NUTLEY	87.8	86.7	1.9	2.1	7.2	7.6	6.8	7.8	5.4	5.5	5.9	6.3	5.9	26.7	29.6	12.2	2.6	79.4	41.4	47.7	52.3
07111	IRVINGTON	9.0	8.3	81.7	82.3	1.2	1.1	8.4	8.5	7.9	7.8	7.2	7.4	7.4	29.3	24.0	7.8	1.0	72.5	33.1	46.6	53.4
07112	NEWARK	1.2	1.2	94.4	94.5	0.5	0.4	3.7	3.8	8.6	8.4	7.9	7.9	7.2	27.1	22.8	9.2	0.9	70.2	32.4	44.2	55.8
07114	NEWARK	18.6	18.3	55.1	54.0	0.6	0.5	35.4	37.3	6.4	6.0	5.3	6.0	9.4	39.9	18.5	7.8	0.7	78.7	32.2	60.9	39.1
07201	ELIZABETH	44.2	42.5	33.5	31.6	1.2	1.3	44.2	52.9	7.7	6.9	6.4	7.6	8.9	32.1	21.9	7.6	1.0	74.6	32.2	52.0	48.0
07202	ELIZABETH	64.2	59.5	10.1	9.7	3.4	3.7	52.0	64.0	7.3	6.7	6.1	6.8	8.1	30.3	23.2	9.5	2.0	75.8	34.3	49.2	50.8
07203	ROSELLE	35.6	30.8	51.3	52.8	2.8	3.3	17.1	22.7	6.7	6.5	6.4	6.8	7.0	28.2	25.9	10.7	1.9	76.3	36.8	47.2	52.8
07204	ROSELLE PARK	80.9	74.0	2.4	2.9	9.1	11.9	16.3	25.2	5.9	5.8	5.8	6.2	6.4	30.1	27.9	10.0	1.9	78.8	38.5	49.0	51.0
	NEW JERSEY	72.6	68.2	13.6	14.0	5.7	7.9	13.3	16.9	6.6	6.6	6.7	6.8	6.2	26.4	27.0	11.5	2.2	76.0	38.7	48.7	51.3
	UNITED STATES	75.1	72.0	12.3	12.7	3.8	4.6	12.5	15.7	6.8	6.7	6.6	7.1	6.9	27.0	26.0	10.9	1.9	75.7	36.9	49.2	50.8

ZIP CODE #	POST OFFICE NAME	2009 Per Capita Income	2009 HH Income Base	2009 HOUSEHOLD INCOME DISTRIBUTION (%) Less than $25,000	$25,000 to $49,999	$50,000 to $99,999	$100,000 to $149,999	$150,000 or More	MEDIAN HOUSEHOLD INCOME 2009	2014	2009 National Centile	2009 State Centile	2009 Home Value Base	2009 HOME VALUE DISTRIBUTION (%) Less than $50,000	$50,000 to $89,999	$90,000 to $174,999	$175,000 to $399,999	$400,000 or More	2009 Median Home Value
07001	AVENEL	26649	4941	12.2	17.9	43.1	18.8	8.0	72194	75642	88	40	2751	5.2	5.2	7.1	77.2	5.3	262228
07002	BAYONNE	26227	24905	22.9	23.4	38.8	10.2	4.7	53682	58157	69	16	9889	0.5	0.6	3.3	70.4	25.1	320719
07003	BLOOMFIELD	31398	18592	14.3	18.5	45.1	14.1	8.1	69920	75635	87	37	9857	0.4	0.3	4.8	71.5	23.0	327814
07004	FAIRFIELD	39969	2569	6.2	11.4	32.3	23.8	26.3	100126	98547	97	76	2272	0.0	0.0	0.0	11.8	88.2	596974
07005	BOONTON	46722	5514	8.6	14.2	26.4	27.0	23.8	100910	105384	97	77	3943	0.3	0.2	1.6	36.7	61.2	454686
07006	CALDWELL	48371	9293	9.0	11.3	32.8	20.6	26.3	94790	89745	96	73	6778	0.0	0.1	0.6	18.4	80.8	583992
07008	CARTERET	24209	7179	18.7	20.3	40.3	15.3	5.3	60213	58343	78	23	4845	3.7	0.9	5.2	86.9	3.4	253352
07009	CEDAR GROVE	43703	4600	7.8	13.2	36.9	19.3	22.8	88476	87200	95	67	3521	0.2	0.0	1.4	22.3	76.1	483303
07010	CLIFFSIDE PARK	33871	10006	20.3	24.7	31.8	13.5	9.8	55646	53952	72	18	4751	0.1	0.4	0.7	42.0	56.8	430700
07011	CLIFTON	22534	12911	19.6	23.2	41.4	11.8	4.0	56572	60523	73	20	6311	0.1	0.2	1.6	81.3	16.8	313694
07012	CLIFTON	33747	4680	16.1	24.4	36.3	15.9	7.3	59765	62359	77	22	2645	0.0	0.1	0.0	69.9	29.9	353863
07013	CLIFTON	35726	10323	12.5	18.6	37.1	19.8	12.1	76923	78628	91	48	7467	0.1	0.1	1.0	57.5	41.3	374718
07014	CLIFTON	33454	2038	12.7	18.8	38.5	20.5	9.6	72405	75886	88	40	1441	0.1	0.3	1.2	78.9	19.5	325508
07016	CRANFORD	42583	8307	7.3	12.4	35.1	24.5	20.7	92902	99065	96	71	6649	0.0	0.2	1.3	30.6	67.9	467949
07017	EAST ORANGE	20472	14163	32.6	24.3	31.5	7.3	4.3	41600	48177	38	6	4156	0.8	2.2	13.2	78.7	5.1	242886
07018	EAST ORANGE	18069	11669	38.3	26.3	28.7	5.0	1.8	35430	39468	19	3	2766	0.9	2.8	16.6	74.8	4.9	235480
07020	EDGEWATER	63975	4649	10.7	10.9	28.7	28.7	21.0	99428	105005	97	75	2221	0.6	0.3	1.6	55.3	42.2	370361
07021	ESSEX FELLS	80280	678	1.9	4.9	21.8	11.9	59.4	201988	204523	100	100	616	0.0	0.0	0.0	2.1	97.9	1000001
07022	FAIRVIEW	22859	4973	23.9	24.3	35.3	12.7	3.8	51380	51925	65	13	1830	0.0	0.2	1.6	63.7	34.5	348644
07023	FANWOOD	45659	2589	4.9	9.3	33.8	23.4	28.5	104194	108903	97	79	2277	0.0	0.0	2.8	27.1	70.1	455187
07024	FORT LEE	47396	17225	16.2	17.7	29.5	19.9	16.6	77210	79811	91	49	9974	1.8	3.5	8.5	40.4	45.9	361746
07026	GARFIELD	24170	11342	20.5	24.1	38.9	12.7	3.8	54352	53811	70	16	4775	0.1	0.1	1.4	74.9	23.5	321018
07027	GARWOOD	33423	1754	12.7	22.2	34.8	22.7	7.6	69880	77827	87	37	1127	0.0	0.0	0.0	58.7	41.3	374741
07028	GLEN RIDGE	55637	2674	6.7	10.5	27.3	18.4	37.0	109347	109234	98	83	2157	0.1	0.0	4.5	23.7	71.7	532873
07029	HARRISON	22039	5802	22.6	23.7	39.4	9.3	4.9	53441	57630	69	15	1867	1.0	0.2	8.7	62.9	27.2	309640
07030	HOBOKEN	57128	21964	16.0	11.3	31.5	18.3	22.9	85295	86289	94	63	5164	0.0	0.3	0.7	34.9	64.2	480528
07031	NORTH ARLINGTON	30625	6448	16.4	21.5	38.5	18.6	5.0	65502	62070	84	31	3565	0.0	0.0	0.8	67.4	31.8	357034
07032	KEARNY	25196	13058	15.5	24.0	42.4	11.4	6.6	61180	66417	79	24	6121	0.3	0.2	4.2	73.5	21.9	311757
07033	KENILWORTH	31052	2805	9.6	19.8	43.0	19.9	7.7	77583	79826	91	50	2129	0.0	0.4	0.0	66.2	33.4	356358
07034	LAKE HIAWATHA	36707	3606	7.2	18.2	41.0	22.9	10.7	75588	76494	90	44	2186	0.2	0.4	4.5	76.7	18.2	320457
07035	LINCOLN PARK	40031	4142	7.8	12.3	37.2	28.2	14.6	87954	89531	95	66	3108	0.1	0.1	2.7	63.7	33.4	348300
07036	LINDEN	26560	15731	16.6	23.2	41.4	14.0	4.8	59066	57785	76	22	9017	0.8	0.7	6.6	78.4	13.4	277725
07039	LIVINGSTON	54016	9554	4.4	8.2	30.8	18.5	38.0	113461	112568	98	86	8483	0.6	0.5	0.3	12.4	86.2	626983
07040	MAPLEWOOD	44320	8274	8.5	11.9	36.2	17.5	25.8	89978	86599	95	69	6245	0.1	0.4	5.3	36.7	57.5	444852
07041	MILLBURN	58174	2623	5.5	10.8	35.1	19.2	29.5	98073	97438	96	75	1741	0.0	0.0	0.6	11.5	87.9	708333
07042	MONTCLAIR	44539	10444	14.9	16.2	34.6	15.3	19.1	76887	77893	91	48	4745	0.0	0.5	3.4	33.7	62.5	479637
07043	MONTCLAIR	71204	4104	5.0	8.4	18.9	19.7	48.0	143663	149605	100	97	3285	0.2	0.0	1.1	7.6	91.1	703500
07044	VERONA	49661	5649	13.1	12.5	34.5	15.8	24.1	84967	84919	94	62	4215	0.0	0.2	2.7	25.9	71.2	484322
07045	MONTVILLE	62876	3904	7.5	8.5	16.7	24.8	42.4	131783	140152	99	93	3607	0.2	1.9	2.5	16.9	78.5	616015
07046	MOUNTAIN LAKES	77332	1361	4.1	6.8	10.9	17.7	60.4	194558	204614	100	100	1259	0.5	0.2	0.1	4.7	94.5	845737
07047	NORTH BERGEN	23540	20841	22.4	24.5	38.2	9.2	5.6	52456	55951	67	14	7690	0.8	2.3	6.9	61.3	28.7	323469
07050	ORANGE	19798	11687	28.1	25.3	36.0	7.4	3.3	46591	51624	53	10	3156	1.6	1.3	22.1	64.9	10.2	249518
07052	WEST ORANGE	41205	16520	11.8	14.7	35.4	16.7	21.3	82899	83587	93	60	11341	0.5	0.3	2.2	42.7	54.2	421356
07054	PARSIPPANY	39531	11299	10.7	14.8	31.0	25.6	17.9	85868	86682	94	64	6227	0.4	0.3	1.6	35.5	62.3	449578
07055	PASSAIC	15327	19333	27.3	30.4	31.8	7.1	3.5	42190	46388	40	6	5387	0.1	0.6	8.5	74.4	16.4	280744
07057	WALLINGTON	29421	4821	17.1	25.7	36.3	16.1	4.9	57023	55338	74	20	2062	0.0	0.0	0.4	59.7	39.9	365455
07058	PINE BROOK	53311	1910	6.1	7.3	26.3	28.1	32.2	114488	128177	98	86	1129	0.2	0.4	0.8	9.4	89.2	641195
07059	WARREN	61839	5132	4.1	8.4	18.4	24.8	44.3	136016	142877	99	95	4604	0.0	0.3	0.8	6.5	92.3	809238
07060	PLAINFIELD	24008	14161	20.1	22.2	33.2	15.9	8.6	58976	55950	76	21	6461	0.1	0.9	10.9	70.4	17.7	287669
07062	PLAINFIELD	28834	4371	15.0	18.0	38.5	17.5	11.0	67151	69526	85	33	2840	0.3	0.7	11.4	76.2	11.4	243498
07063	PLAINFIELD	24187	3825	13.3	20.7	39.3	18.1	8.4	69366	71816	86	36	2571	0.2	0.3	12.6	81.6	5.3	251850
07064	PORT READING	31602	1429	8.5	15.6	46.1	19.0	10.7	79030	81543	92	53	1099	0.0	0.5	4.4	90.4	4.6	290253
07065	RAHWAY	28378	10184	17.1	18.8	41.7	15.7	6.7	66015	68742	84	31	6349	0.4	0.5	8.6	81.5	9.0	262693
07066	CLARK	37790	5416	7.7	16.7	37.9	24.3	13.3	83976	88948	93	61	4316	0.1	0.1	0.4	38.9	60.4	439805
07067	COLONIA	35594	6204	8.3	13.6	39.2	23.0	15.9	84845	90909	94	62	5379	0.2	0.1	1.5	69.2	28.9	352416
07068	ROSELAND	50392	2346	6.9	10.4	36.4	21.7	24.6	94245	90787	96	72	1822	0.0	0.0	3.1	9.3	87.6	614570
07069	WATCHUNG	69781	2702	5.5	8.6	23.9	19.5	42.5	128877	138628	99	91	2196	0.0	0.0	0.0	4.3	95.7	807487
07070	RUTHERFORD	39418	7084	11.2	15.6	34.3	24.7	14.2	82627	85836	93	59	4650	0.4	0.8	2.3	45.4	51.0	403678
07071	LYNDHURST	32400	8196	15.5	20.4	36.6	20.6	6.9	69614	73127	87	37	4984	0.1	0.2	0.8	65.0	33.8	355377
07072	CARLSTADT	34670	2412	14.8	20.1	36.2	20.1	8.7	74007	75952	89	41	1408	0.4	0.3	0.3	48.9	50.1	400522
07073	EAST RUTHERFORD	34269	3850	17.8	20.2	39.1	14.5	8.4	61783	59170	80	25	1716	0.3	0.0	0.3	62.9	36.4	360034
07074	MOONACHIE	31999	1044	13.1	25.5	34.0	17.0	10.3	62284	56167	80	26	804	22.8	3.5	0.9	47.3	25.6	292982
07075	WOOD RIDGE	38143	3086	9.7	13.5	40.1	23.1	13.5	80695	84281	92	56	2338	0.2	0.1	0.7	66.2	32.8	359271
07076	SCOTCH PLAINS	50857	8469	6.5	11.4	29.0	23.8	29.3	105159	109916	97	79	6450	0.0	0.4	3.1	24.2	72.4	537990
07077	SEWAREN	30398	950	16.9	18.1	34.4	19.5	11.1	75879	79026	90	46	748	0.0	0.7	5.2	82.5	11.6	283486
07078	SHORT HILLS	89059	4107	2.8	4.3	20.0	11.6	61.3	217022	220094	100	100	3560	0.0	0.3	0.9	2.1	96.7	1000001
07079	SOUTH ORANGE	50779	5638	11.6	11.5	30.1	16.1	30.7	94391	91516	96	72	3908	0.4	0.1	1.5	28.8	69.2	553447
07080	SOUTH PLAINFIELD	32137	7602	8.1	13.5	42.1	22.6	13.7	83918	89168	93	61	6522	0.2	0.0	1.4	77.9	20.4	318950
07081	SPRINGFIELD	46387	6325	10.0	12.1	33.5	26.0	18.4	90931	98703	95	69	4569	0.1	0.6	2.9	25.8	70.5	496355
07082	TOWACO	53978	1768	5.5	5.8	21.7	24.7	42.3	133611	141057	99	94	1624	0.2	0.7	0.8	17.8	80.5	598887
07083	UNION	31173	18249	12.7	17.7	39.1	19.7	10.7	78221	81365	91	51	13880	0.7	0.5	3.3	68.3	27.2	343081
07086	WEEHAWKEN	36418	5788	17.3	20.0	38.9	13.0	10.9	67723	75356	85	34	1841	0.0	0.3	7.0	29.3	63.3	458175
07087	UNION CITY	16511	22245	32.1	30.7	29.6	5.0	2.6	38686	43064	29	4	4088	0.4	2.2	8.3	69.3	19.8	297939
07088	VAUXHALL	24026	1261	18.9	25.1	41.4	10.8	3.9	55004	54478	71	17	786	1.9	0.5	18.8	70.2	8.5	223377
07090	WESTFIELD	58938	10448	6.8	10.2	23.4	20.1	39.4	125624	124619	99	90	8270	0.0	0.2	2.2	11.1	86.5	685161
07092	MOUNTAINSIDE	57729	2426	7.4	10.3	22.1	20.8	39.4	128450	129577	99	91	2187	0.0	0.0	0.0	5.1	94.9	686119
07093	WEST NEW YORK	22263	20834	29.4	26.1	31.6	7.0	6.0	44942	50072	48	8	4983	0.4	2.4	10.8	56.0	30.5	320107
07094	SECAUCUS	36504	6283	16.8	14.2	38.0	17.2	13.8	74778	76648	89	42	3735	0.2	0.0	1.7	47.7	50.4	401496
07095	WOODBRIDGE	33597	7025	14.8	15.9	40.7	19.0	9.6	75601	78002	90	45	4745	0.3	0.1	10.7	78.9	9.9	276552
07102	NEWARK	16006	4117	63.5	20.0	13.7	1.4	1.4	16975	18668	1	1	409	0.0	3.7	11.7	67.7	16.9	285377
07103	NEWARK	14021	10957	50.7	20.9	22.9	3.9	1.7	24436	28248	3	1	2469	3.9	4.9	36.1	53.0	2.1	187450
07104	NEWARK	16265	16821	39.4	23.6	28.7	5.8	2.5	35074	40343	18	3	3846	0.7	1.6	18.3	62.4	17.0	273630
07105	NEWARK	18816	15723	29.3	24.9	36.1	7.0	2.7	45493	51990	50	8	4224	1.2	0.6	5.9	47.5	44.8	375417
07106	NEWARK	17776	11260	30.3	26.0	33.9	7.4	2.4	41819	50340	39	6	3937	0.7	0.7	14.1	79.6	4.9	239454
07107	NEWARK	14746	12336	43.5	22.7	26.8	4.7	2.2	31565	35350	11	2	3040	0.9	1.8	19.3	67.3	10.7	258537
07108	NEWARK	13015	8477	51.0	21.3	23.1	3.2	1.3	24129	28383	3	1	1809	3.5	3.8	30.5	58.4	3.8	194668
07109	BELLEVILLE	26836	13321	16.0	21.8	45.9	11.6	4.7	61680	66669	80	25	6823	0.6	1.5	8.0	79.8	10.0	285064
07110	NUTLEY	33904	11001	14.3	16.1	43.1	16.1	10.5	75016	76872	89	42	7239	0.6	0.6	4.6	52.4	41.8	376707
07111	IRVINGTON	19815	21621	27.3	26.6	36.8	7.1	2.2	46254	51732	52	9	6642	0.7	0.9	14.5	80.0	3.9	240059
07112	NEWARK	17296	9555	33.8	28.8	29.9	5.2	2.3	36919	41486	23	3	2844	1.0	1.8	16.1	75.0	6.1	240320
07114	NEWARK	13903	3558	60.4	16.7	19.5	2.8	0.6	17761	20174	1	1	501	3.4	1.0	20.8	57.5	17.4	241295
07201	ELIZABETH	17642	8450	27.2	31.4	30.7	8.2	2.6	41876	44930	39	6	2641	0.1	1.4	10.6	71.3	16.6	259639
07202	ELIZABETH	19767	13534	26.8	27.1	34.7	8.5	2.9	45804	48149	51	9	4295	2.3	1.4	10.8	64.9	20.7	277070
07203	ROSELLE	25901	7498	15.3	21.4	39.8	17.0	6.5	64393	62560	83	29	4573	0.1	0.9	7.8	86.6	4.5	238008
07204	ROSELLE PARK	30166	5056	10.7	21.4	44.8	16.0	7.0	75033	76698	89	43	2997	0.0	0.0	7.2	78.5	14.3	292373
	NEW JERSEY	34433		15.4	18.6	34.9	16.8	14.2	72809	76895				1.0	1.6	9.9	50.1	37.4	336585
	UNITED STATES	27277		20.9	24.4	35.3	11.7	7.6	54719	56938				9.3	13.1	31.6	32.6	13.5	162279

ZIP CODE #	POST OFFICE NAME	FINANCIAL SERVICES: Auto Loan	Home Loan	Invest-ments	Retire-ment Plans	THE HOME: Home Improvements: Home Repair	Lawn & Garden	Furnishings: Comput-ers & Hard-ware-Personal	Major Appli-ances	TV, Radio, Sound Equip-ment	Furni-ture	ENTERTAINMENT: Dine out/ Carry out	Sports Equip-ment	Fees & Tickets	Toys & Games	Travel	Cable TV	PERSONAL: Apparel & Services	Auto Repairs	Health Insur-ance	Pets & Supplies
07001	AVENEL	109	120	115	119	119	108	117	111	113	117	115	88	123	116	119	111	83	113	106	128
07002	BAYONNE	72	87	92	85	89	82	89	82	90	80	92	61	96	88	92	95	68	87	87	95
07003	BLOOMFIELD	94	114	120	111	117	104	112	106	109	106	112	81	122	108	118	110	82	110	106	121
07004	FAIRFIELD	141	206	230	197	220	189	166	176	158	168	159	128	204	159	196	159	119	166	167	190
07005	BOONTON	145	199	220	194	211	184	174	176	169	170	171	130	205	167	197	172	128	172	172	195
07006	CALDWELL	155	206	232	204	221	194	181	186	174	186	174	137	212	170	206	174	129	180	182	207
07008	CARTERET	85	105	106	100	106	96	99	96	98	94	100	73	109	98	105	100	73	98	97	109
07009	CEDAR GROVE	137	188	211	183	201	177	160	167	155	163	156	121	191	152	185	157	115	161	166	184
07010	CLIFFSIDE PARK	93	105	117	104	110	102	110	104	111	103	114	77	117	106	114	115	83	109	111	120
07011	CLIFTON	77	92	94	88	93	82	93	87	92	86	94	66	100	90	96	93	70	91	86	98
07012	CLIFTON	91	112	119	109	116	108	105	104	105	102	106	76	117	103	114	108	77	105	110	118
07013	CLIFTON	105	141	152	135	148	132	124	126	123	121	124	92	144	121	139	126	91	124	128	140
07014	CLIFTON	100	127	131	123	129	117	116	114	115	111	117	85	131	115	125	118	86	115	115	130
07016	CRANFORD	137	184	200	179	194	170	159	163	153	160	154	121	186	152	180	153	113	158	159	181
07017	EAST ORANGE	64	64	66	67	63	64	76	66	81	67	82	50	77	77	72	87	60	74	75	82
07018	EAST ORANGE	53	52	53	54	51	52	65	55	70	56	70	41	64	65	60	74	52	62	63	68
07020	EDGEWATER	157	166	190	179	174	149	189	164	175	182	182	140	194	173	191	168	135	175	153	192
07021	ESSEX FELLS	281	400	489	416	448	375	325	350	304	363	301	261	416	299	391	291	233	321	309	381
07022	FAIRVIEW	75	86	87	83	87	78	91	83	89	84	92	64	95	88	92	91	68	88	84	95
07023	FANWOOD	148	216	242	208	232	199	175	185	167	177	167	135	215	168	207	168	125	175	176	201
07024	FORT LEE	127	144	158	146	152	135	147	141	141	148	142	109	155	135	155	139	103	144	141	161
07026	GARFIELD	76	89	91	86	90	80	93	85	92	85	95	65	98	90	94	94	70	90	85	97
07027	GARWOOD	91	121	128	115	124	111	111	108	112	102	115	79	127	111	121	118	86	110	112	122
07028	GLEN RIDGE	193	262	302	266	285	240	224	232	209	238	210	176	270	207	259	202	158	220	210	256
07029	HARRISON	80	79	75	78	78	66	95	82	89	90	94	68	92	89	90	86	69	90	75	93
07030	HOBOKEN	148	128	141	144	129	120	170	136	162	160	168	120	161	161	157	158	122	155	136	168
07031	NORTH ARLINGTON	83	105	111	100	108	100	100	97	102	91	103	71	111	100	107	107	76	100	103	110
07032	KEARNY	85	102	104	98	103	91	103	96	101	95	104	73	111	100	106	103	77	100	95	108
07033	KENILWORTH	99	137	142	128	141	122	116	119	113	113	114	87	136	114	131	115	85	116	115	131
07034	LAKE HIAWATHA	124	137	133	135	136	121	132	125	127	133	129	99	139	131	134	124	93	127	118	144
07035	LINCOLN PARK	134	160	162	158	162	147	149	145	145	146	147	111	163	147	158	146	107	146	142	166
07036	LINDEN	85	100	103	96	101	94	98	95	98	92	99	71	105	96	102	100	72	97	97	108
07039	LIVINGSTON	185	266	311	265	291	246	217	231	204	231	203	170	270	202	259	200	154	216	213	251
07040	MAPLEWOOD	152	201	217	199	211	186	174	178	168	177	169	133	204	167	196	168	125	172	172	199
07041	MILLBURN	174	234	271	235	255	211	207	211	192	216	193	160	243	188	236	186	145	202	191	233
07042	MONTCLAIR	137	155	170	160	161	146	160	148	156	156	158	117	172	153	166	155	116	154	148	173
07043	MONTCLAIR	237	317	382	329	352	291	278	286	254	302	254	219	333	249	322	241	193	269	252	315
07044	VERONA	140	185	208	182	198	177	163	169	159	166	159	123	191	154	186	160	117	164	170	187
07045	MONTVILLE	212	283	324	292	307	261	241	253	223	264	222	191	288	219	281	213	166	237	228	281
07046	MOUNTAIN LAKES	293	413	504	429	462	388	339	363	316	377	313	271	430	311	406	303	241	334	324	396
07047	NORTH BERGEN	78	83	83	82	84	73	95	83	92	87	95	66	95	90	92	92	70	90	82	96
07050	ORANGE	67	66	68	68	66	64	80	68	83	71	85	53	79	80	75	86	62	77	75	83
07052	WEST ORANGE	131	169	184	165	178	154	156	154	150	153	153	116	177	149	172	150	113	154	149	172
07054	PARSIPPANY	129	147	156	149	152	129	149	138	138	149	141	113	157	138	155	132	104	142	126	158
07055	PASSAIC	71	70	65	67	69	58	81	72	76	79	81	58	78	77	77	73	59	78	65	80
07057	WALLINGTON	85	100	103	97	102	92	102	94	103	93	105	72	110	102	105	106	78	100	97	108
07058	PINE BROOK	196	223	240	233	233	204	211	207	198	226	200	163	232	200	225	189	146	203	189	236
07059	WARREN	231	322	380	336	355	299	264	281	245	292	244	212	331	243	313	234	187	259	247	309
07060	PLAINFIELD	96	99	98	97	99	88	110	99	106	106	109	78	110	105	108	104	80	106	96	113
07062	PLAINFIELD	106	124	123	120	125	114	119	116	118	117	120	87	128	118	124	120	87	118	115	133
07063	PLAINFIELD	99	117	114	113	117	107	113	108	110	109	112	83	121	110	117	111	81	111	108	125
07064	PORT READING	113	146	148	140	149	132	127	129	122	127	124	97	144	124	140	122	90	126	124	145
07065	RAHWAY	95	113	111	109	113	105	107	105	105	104	106	80	116	105	113	106	77	106	105	120
07066	CLARK	116	159	171	152	166	148	135	140	133	133	134	102	160	132	154	136	99	136	141	155
07067	COLONIA	121	171	180	160	178	152	142	148	137	142	138	108	168	138	163	138	102	142	140	162
07068	ROSELAND	146	203	230	199	219	192	170	180	164	176	164	130	205	161	199	164	121	171	176	197
07069	WATCHUNG	225	308	368	316	341	280	264	275	241	288	240	210	319	237	309	229	183	257	241	301
07070	RUTHERFORD	117	153	166	149	160	140	140	138	137	135	139	104	160	136	154	139	103	138	136	155
07071	LYNDHURST	89	118	124	112	121	109	109	106	111	99	113	78	125	109	118	116	84	108	110	120
07072	CARLSTADT	95	125	132	119	128	116	118	113	120	105	122	83	133	118	126	127	91	116	118	128
07073	EAST RUTHERFORD	89	111	118	108	114	104	112	104	115	99	118	77	123	111	117	122	88	109	111	120
07074	MOONACHIE	113	134	130	126	135	122	119	121	116	121	117	90	129	119	126	117	84	119	116	138
07075	WOOD RIDGE	112	157	164	147	163	140	133	136	128	130	130	100	156	129	150	130	96	132	131	150
07076	SCOTCH PLAINS	167	225	254	223	241	204	195	200	183	202	184	151	230	182	223	179	138	192	184	220
07077	SEWAREN	100	134	135	126	137	119	116	117	111	114	112	88	132	112	128	111	82	115	113	131
07078	SHORT HILLS	318	453	556	474	508	426	367	394	344	408	341	296	474	342	440	330	266	361	346	429
07079	SOUTH ORANGE	181	228	259	232	244	210	210	207	198	216	200	161	241	196	233	192	149	204	193	233
07080	SOUTH PLAINFIELD	119	162	165	152	167	142	137	141	130	138	132	105	158	132	154	129	97	136	131	155
07081	SPRINGFIELD	132	174	195	171	186	162	156	158	149	157	150	117	179	146	176	149	111	155	155	176
07082	TOWACO	196	272	302	277	291	248	223	236	208	240	209	178	272	208	261	201	157	219	212	260
07083	UNION	104	140	147	132	145	127	122	124	119	119	120	91	141	119	136	121	89	121	121	137
07086	WEEHAWKEN	100	101	110	106	104	90	123	104	115	114	120	88	121	113	120	112	88	115	100	123
07087	UNION CITY	63	59	54	58	58	49	73	62	69	70	73	51	69	69	68	66	54	70	57	71
07088	VAUXHALL	74	88	92	86	89	83	90	83	94	80	96	62	98	91	92	100	71	88	90	98
07090	WESTFIELD	198	267	305	270	288	246	231	238	218	242	218	180	275	215	265	213	164	227	221	263
07092	MOUNTAINSIDE	185	262	310	264	289	242	217	232	201	237	200	171	266	196	260	194	150	215	211	253
07093	WEST NEW YORK	73	72	72	73	73	64	87	76	85	82	89	61	85	83	83	84	65	83	74	87
07094	SECAUCUS	108	135	145	132	141	126	126	125	124	124	125	93	141	121	138	126	92	125	126	141
07095	WOODBRIDGE	106	128	127	124	129	117	119	116	115	117	117	89	130	116	126	116	84	117	115	133
07102	NEWARK	37	28	31	31	28	31	45	35	47	40	48	28	39	42	38	50	34	43	45	45
07103	NEWARK	49	42	42	45	41	44	56	47	61	50	61	36	53	57	50	64	44	54	55	59
07104	NEWARK	61	55	50	54	53	46	70	59	68	66	71	48	65	67	64	66	53	67	55	68
07105	NEWARK	68	66	63	66	65	56	81	69	77	76	81	57	77	77	76	75	60	77	65	79
07106	NEWARK	63	64	65	66	63	61	75	65	78	67	79	51	76	75	71	81	58	72	70	79
07107	NEWARK	54	49	47	50	48	45	64	54	65	58	67	43	60	62	58	66	49	61	55	64
07108	NEWARK	48	40	40	43	39	42	53	44	58	48	58	34	51	56	47	62	42	52	52	57
07109	BELLEVILLE	83	98	99	95	99	88	100	93	98	93	100	71	106	97	102	99	74	97	92	105
07110	NUTLEY	99	130	136	124	134	119	117	116	115	112	117	86	133	115	128	118	86	116	116	130
07111	IRVINGTON	65	66	68	68	65	64	77	67	81	69	82	52	78	77	73	85	60	75	74	82
07112	NEWARK	57	56	57	58	54	56	68	58	73	59	74	44	68	69	63	78	54	65	66	72
07114	NEWARK	37	30	30	33	29	31	46	37	49	39	50	28	41	45	39	52	37	43	42	45
07201	ELIZABETH	69	66	62	66	65	57	81	70	79	76	82	57	78	78	75	77	61	77	66	80
07202	ELIZABETH	71	69	67	69	68	60	84	72	80	79	83	59	80	79	79	78	61	80	69	83
07203	ROSELLE	95	105	107	103	106	101	106	103	106	102	107	78	111	105	108	108	77	106	105	118
07204	ROSELLE PARK	91	120	127	114	124	109	110	108	108	104	110	80	125	108	120	111	82	109	107	121
	NEW JERSEY	119	138	141	137	141	129	132	129	129	132	131	98	143	128	139	129	95	130	128	148
	UNITED STATES	100	100	100	100	100	100	100	100	100	100	100	100	100	100	100	100	100	100	100	100

ZIP CODE #	POST OFFICE NAME	COUNTY FIPS CODE	POPULATION 2000	POPULATION 2009	POPULATION 2014	2000-2009 ANNUAL RATE % Rate	2000-2009 ANNUAL RATE State Centile	HOUSEHOLDS 2000	HOUSEHOLDS 2009	HOUSEHOLDS 2014	HOUSEHOLDS % Annual Rate 2000-2009	HOUSEHOLDS 2009 Average HH Size	FAMILIES 2000	FAMILIES 2009	FAMILIES % Annual Rate 2000-2009
07205	HILLSIDE	039	21841	22189	22149	0.2	43	7182	7182	7136	0.0	3.09	5589	5560	-0.1
07206	ELIZABETH	039	22887	25008	25436	1.0	80	6769	7292	7386	0.8	3.41	5320	5703	0.8
07208	ELIZABETH	039	32356	33318	33309	0.3	50	12027	12082	12017	0.0	2.74	7769	7736	0.0
07302	JERSEY CITY	017	31399	36230	37500	1.6	91	13932	16386	17038	1.8	2.18	6552	7581	1.6
07304	JERSEY CITY	017	41792	42398	42240	0.2	43	14235	14328	14248	0.1	2.92	9632	9724	0.1
07305	JERSEY CITY	017	58567	59806	59802	0.2	43	20190	20595	20577	0.2	2.87	14455	14765	0.2
07306	JERSEY CITY	017	55612	53576	52594	-0.4	4	20730	19793	19380	-0.5	2.63	12592	12024	-0.5
07307	JERSEY CITY	017	45571	45496	45078	0.0	28	15956	15653	15446	-0.2	2.89	10872	10689	-0.2
07310	JERSEY CITY	017	7048	8340	8687	1.8	93	3566	4180	4327	1.7	1.97	1514	1815	2.0
07401	ALLENDALE	003	6753	6823	6864	0.1	35	2102	2124	2139	0.1	3.07	1788	1802	0.1
07403	BLOOMINGDALE	031	7459	7494	7444	0.1	35	2771	2770	2744	0.0	2.66	2024	2010	-0.1
07405	BUTLER	027	16903	18594	19206	1.0	80	5994	6556	6759	1.0	2.83	4754	5210	1.0
07407	ELMWOOD PARK	003	18968	19420	19607	0.3	50	7104	7242	7308	0.2	2.68	5091	5158	0.1
07410	FAIR LAWN	003	31683	32119	32314	0.1	35	11820	11989	12080	0.2	2.67	8918	8980	0.1
07416	FRANKLIN	037	5752	5960	6090	0.4	56	2105	2205	2261	0.5	2.68	1469	1529	0.4
07417	FRANKLIN LAKES	003	10430	10971	11220	0.5	62	3328	3507	3592	0.6	3.13	2965	3115	0.5
07418	GLENWOOD	037	2351	2552	2642	0.9	76	728	807	840	1.1	3.16	629	694	1.1
07419	HAMBURG	037	6791	9395	10483	3.6	98	2601	3705	4172	3.9	2.53	1905	2694	3.8
07420	HASKELL	031	5046	6916	7490	3.5	98	1569	2222	2417	3.8	2.92	1237	1735	3.7
07421	HEWITT	031	7777	7993	8003	0.3	50	2726	2781	2772	0.2	2.87	2090	2120	0.2
07422	HIGHLAND LAKES	037	7003	7630	7892	0.9	76	2369	2638	2749	1.2	2.89	1910	2117	1.1
07423	HO HO KUS	003	4060	4079	4094	0.1	35	1433	1440	1446	0.1	2.82	1199	1202	0.0
07424	LITTLE FALLS	031	21588	23125	23666	0.7	68	8987	9132	9277	0.2	2.43	5829	5888	0.1
07430	MAHWAH	003	23225	24294	24523	0.5	62	8884	9153	9224	0.3	2.51	6082	6254	0.3
07432	MIDLAND PARK	003	6868	7309	7497	0.7	68	2586	2767	2843	0.7	2.63	1867	1985	0.7
07435	NEWFOUNDLAND	031	2543	2637	2668	0.4	56	923	951	959	0.3	2.73	718	736	0.3
07436	OAKLAND	003	12464	13020	13247	0.5	62	4255	4450	4531	0.5	2.87	3567	3707	0.4
07438	OAK RIDGE	027	11549	11900	11984	0.3	50	4043	4174	4206	0.3	2.84	3221	3303	0.3
07439	OGDENSBURG	037	2638	2616	2563	-0.1	19	881	892	879	0.1	2.93	705	710	0.1
07440	PEQUANNOCK	027	4610	4705	4780	0.2	43	1632	1683	1715	0.3	2.79	1281	1310	0.2
07442	POMPTON LAKES	031	10640	10944	10940	0.3	50	3949	4041	4028	0.2	2.71	2805	2851	0.2
07444	POMPTON PLAINS	027	9218	9992	10276	0.9	76	3373	3661	3768	0.9	2.73	2527	2724	0.8
07446	RAMSEY	003	15258	15404	15516	0.1	35	5797	5842	5889	0.1	2.62	4177	4185	0.0
07450	RIDGEWOOD	003	25049	24995	25020	0.0	28	8643	8601	8605	-0.1	2.88	6810	6752	-0.1
07452	GLEN ROCK	003	11457	11492	11507	0.0	28	3950	3946	3951	0.0	2.90	3299	3284	0.0
07456	RINGWOOD	031	12355	12326	12222	0.0	28	4096	4050	4001	-0.1	3.02	3436	3384	-0.2
07457	RIVERDALE	027	2498	3996	4622	5.2	99	919	1491	1736	5.4	2.66	672	1081	5.3
07458	SADDLE RIVER	003	10837	11610	11915	0.7	68	3601	3854	3955	0.7	2.98	3157	3374	0.7
07460	STOCKHOLM	037	3754	3864	3902	0.3	50	1312	1368	1388	0.5	2.82	1019	1065	0.5
07461	SUSSEX	037	19011	20684	21250	0.9	76	6335	6987	7201	1.1	2.96	5100	5614	1.0
07462	VERNON	037	7001	8238	8728	1.8	93	2664	3250	3485	2.2	2.53	1838	2186	1.9
07463	WALDWICK	003	9622	9650	9685	0.0	28	3428	3442	3455	0.0	2.80	2678	2675	0.0
07465	WANAQUE	031	5272	5933	6076	1.3	87	1891	2111	2154	1.2	2.81	1466	1632	1.2
07470	WAYNE	031	51438	50975	50473	-0.1	19	18406	18091	17839	-0.2	2.72	14108	13806	-0.2
07480	WEST MILFORD	031	15778	16629	16755	0.6	65	5476	5745	5770	0.5	2.85	4317	4491	0.4
07481	WYCKOFF	003	16537	16884	17023	0.2	43	5548	5665	5718	0.2	2.89	4637	4717	0.2
07501	PATERSON	031	32664	33280	33226	0.2	43	10133	10200	10148	0.1	3.14	6920	6895	0.0
07502	PATERSON	031	15371	15601	15489	0.2	43	4818	4728	4660	-0.2	3.29	3708	3620	-0.3
07503	PATERSON	031	19060	19039	18826	0.0	28	5890	5737	5639	-0.3	3.31	4350	4213	-0.3
07504	PATERSON	031	13092	12942	12805	-0.1	19	3724	3647	3594	-0.2	3.54	3017	2941	-0.3
07505	PATERSON	031	4732	4817	4821	0.2	43	920	926	919	0.1	2.92	517	518	0.0
07506	HAWTHORNE	031	18231	18677	18666	0.3	50	7264	7363	7324	0.1	2.53	4936	4966	0.1
07508	HALEDON	031	24576	25295	25288	0.3	50	7616	7707	7664	0.1	3.05	5744	5791	0.1
07512	TOTOWA	031	9889	10216	10233	0.4	56	3537	3615	3603	0.2	2.66	2643	2685	0.2
07513	PATERSON	031	13071	12966	12791	-0.1	19	3530	3402	3332	-0.4	3.81	2948	2829	-0.4
07514	PATERSON	031	18744	18419	18186	-0.2	12	6272	6103	6000	-0.3	2.98	4442	4291	-0.4
07522	PATERSON	031	19998	20791	20848	0.4	56	5856	5984	5965	0.2	3.45	4565	4655	0.2
07524	PATERSON	031	12579	12450	12313	-0.1	19	3599	3510	3453	-0.3	3.55	2909	2824	-0.3
07601	HACKENSACK	003	42796	44941	45716	0.5	62	18144	18865	19166	0.4	2.29	9604	9887	0.3
07603	BOGOTA	003	7838	7841	7861	0.0	28	2715	2709	2714	0.0	2.88	2007	1993	-0.1
07604	HASBROUCK HEIGHTS	003	11758	11765	11782	0.0	28	4599	4599	4608	0.0	2.55	3173	3153	-0.1
07605	LEONIA	003	8950	9092	9124	0.2	43	3290	3301	3309	0.0	2.75	2438	2433	0.0
07606	SOUTH HACKENSACK	003	2085	2309	2395	1.1	83	745	827	860	1.1	2.79	548	605	1.1
07607	MAYWOOD	003	9399	9458	9508	0.1	35	3662	3674	3690	0.0	2.57	2587	2579	0.0
07608	TETERBORO	003	32	33	33	0.3	50	12	12	12	0.0	2.75	8	8	0.0
07620	ALPINE	003	2127	2282	2356	0.8	73	687	737	761	0.8	3.09	604	647	0.7
07621	BERGENFIELD	003	26677	27791	28195	0.4	56	9168	9440	9565	0.3	2.94	6883	7037	0.2
07624	CLOSTER	003	8375	8396	8399	0.0	28	2786	2792	2795	0.0	2.98	2319	2316	0.0
07626	CRESSKILL	003	7801	8794	9210	1.3	87	2648	2991	3136	1.3	2.91	2178	2451	1.3
07627	DEMAREST	003	4873	4946	4997	0.2	43	1614	1639	1658	0.2	3.01	1399	1417	0.1
07628	DUMONT	003	17157	17200	17234	0.0	28	6196	6204	6214	0.0	2.77	4640	4623	0.0
07630	EMERSON	003	7456	7501	7535	0.1	35	2483	2501	2511	0.1	2.88	2052	2060	0.0
07631	ENGLEWOOD	003	26219	27540	28089	0.5	62	9275	9701	9888	0.5	2.81	6488	6732	0.4
07632	ENGLEWOOD CLIFFS	003	5170	5167	5183	0.0	28	1760	1759	1765	0.0	2.91	1516	1511	0.0
07640	HARRINGTON PARK	003	4760	4869	4925	0.2	43	1569	1607	1625	0.3	3.02	1349	1377	0.2
07641	HAWORTH	003	3394	3399	3406	0.0	28	1137	1139	1142	0.0	2.98	972	970	0.0
07642	HILLSDALE	003	9984	10048	10077	0.1	35	3469	3492	3503	0.1	2.86	2828	2836	0.0
07643	LITTLE FERRY	003	10849	11060	11104	0.2	43	4379	4394	4403	0.0	2.52	2796	2784	0.0
07644	LODI	003	24464	25271	25606	0.4	56	9679	9945	10071	0.3	2.53	6210	6332	0.2
07645	MONTVALE	003	7005	7380	7565	0.6	65	2498	2645	2712	0.6	2.78	1991	2099	0.6
07646	NEW MILFORD	003	16454	16451	16465	0.0	28	6364	6357	6363	0.0	2.55	4292	4263	-0.1
07647	NORTHVALE	003	4827	4840	4846	0.0	28	1639	1643	1645	0.0	2.84	1288	1286	0.0
07648	NORWOOD	003	5760	6106	6256	0.6	65	1863	1985	2038	0.7	2.96	1567	1664	0.7
07649	ORADELL	003	8084	8063	8072	0.0	28	2800	2794	2799	0.0	2.83	2306	2292	-0.1
07650	PALISADES PARK	003	16759	18353	18978	1.0	80	6116	6556	6754	0.8	2.80	4361	4645	0.7
07652	PARAMUS	003	25814	26749	27123	0.4	56	8108	8440	8577	0.4	2.99	6800	7046	0.4
07656	PARK RIDGE	003	8756	9086	9231	0.4	56	3180	3299	3349	0.4	2.67	2406	2492	0.4
07657	RIDGEFIELD	003	11119	11872	12186	0.7	68	4141	4366	4470	0.6	2.72	3043	3192	0.5
07660	RIDGEFIELD PARK	003	12910	13086	13134	0.1	35	5024	5077	5097	0.1	2.57	3251	3262	0.0
07661	RIVER EDGE	003	10786	10888	10922	0.1	35	4093	4109	4120	0.0	2.64	3050	3047	0.0
07662	ROCHELLE PARK	003	5523	5850	5994	0.6	65	2058	2189	2247	0.7	2.52	1392	1470	0.6
07663	SADDLE BROOK	003	12988	13397	13576	0.3	50	5004	5172	5250	0.4	2.57	3534	3626	0.3
07666	TEANECK	003	39497	40086	40318	0.2	43	13535	13663	13734	0.1	2.87	10154	10193	0.0
07670	TENAFLY	003	13654	13847	13944	0.2	43	4722	4761	4794	0.1	2.88	3824	3841	0.0
07675	WESTWOOD	003	26101	26767	27059	0.3	50	9595	9822	9923	0.3	2.69	7140	7295	0.2
	NEW JERSEY					0.5					0.5	2.69			0.5
	UNITED STATES					1.0					1.1	2.59			0.9

ZIP CODE		RACE (%)						% Hispanic Origin		2009 AGE DISTRIBUTION (%)										MEDIAN AGE		
#	POST OFFICE NAME	White		Black		Asian/Pacific															%	%
		2000	2009	2000	2009	2000	2009	2000	2009	0-4	5-9	10-14	15-19	20-24	25-44	45-64	65-84	85+	18+	2009	2009 Males	2009 Females
07205	HILLSIDE	40.1	35.3	46.4	47.5	3.5	4.4	14.6	20.5	6.5	6.3	6.5	7.1	6.5	27.8	26.9	10.9	1.6	76.4	37.6	47.0	53.0
07206	ELIZABETH	50.2	48.4	21.5	19.5	0.6	0.6	61.4	70.0	9.6	9.1	7.6	8.0	8.6	29.4	19.6	7.1	1.0	69.0	29.2	49.0	51.0
07208	ELIZABETH	59.5	55.9	19.0	18.4	3.5	4.0	43.0	53.5	7.5	7.0	6.5	6.9	7.6	30.7	23.9	8.4	1.5	75.0	34.2	49.1	50.9
07302	JERSEY CITY	45.5	41.0	18.3	16.3	15.4	17.8	29.9	37.6	5.7	4.8	4.1	4.8	9.0	40.4	22.0	7.8	1.4	82.6	34.3	51.2	48.8
07304	JERSEY CITY	20.5	19.0	46.8	42.4	11.9	14.0	25.7	32.2	7.9	7.5	7.0	8.1	8.5	29.4	22.4	8.0	1.2	72.8	31.8	47.5	52.5
07305	JERSEY CITY	23.2	20.5	51.5	48.5	12.1	15.0	17.5	22.6	7.7	7.3	6.9	7.7	7.5	28.4	23.4	9.5	1.6	73.6	33.9	45.7	54.3
07306	JERSEY CITY	37.0	31.7	16.0	13.6	23.0	27.1	29.2	36.1	6.8	6.2	5.7	7.1	8.3	31.8	23.1	9.4	1.7	77.5	34.8	50.7	49.3
07307	JERSEY CITY	47.4	40.5	6.4	5.6	14.5	16.9	45.0	54.2	7.4	6.8	6.2	7.3	9.0	31.9	22.3	7.8	1.3	75.3	32.5	49.2	50.8
07310	JERSEY CITY	42.0	32.5	10.7	9.7	38.7	46.5	11.5	15.7	6.3	2.4	1.9	2.6	12.6	56.8	14.6	2.7	0.2	87.9	29.9	52.8	47.2
07401	ALLENDALE	92.4	88.2	0.4	0.5	6.2	9.9	2.5	4.0	6.2	7.4	8.9	8.3	3.6	16.9	33.0	11.8	3.9	71.7	44.1	48.5	51.5
07403	BLOOMINGDALE	95.5	91.8	0.4	0.8	2.2	3.8	4.4	9.5	6.2	6.4	6.7	6.2	4.8	26.3	28.7	12.6	2.1	77.0	41.4	49.3	50.7
07405	BUTLER	95.3	92.7	0.6	0.8	2.5	4.1	3.6	5.9	6.4	7.4	8.4	7.3	4.1	22.7	31.5	10.8	1.4	73.1	41.2	49.8	50.2
07407	ELMWOOD PARK	82.5	76.3	2.2	2.4	7.8	11.0	13.4	19.1	5.9	5.6	5.6	6.2	6.3	28.5	27.3	12.0	2.6	79.2	39.6	47.9	52.1
07410	FAIR LAWN	91.5	87.1	0.7	0.9	4.9	7.9	5.5	8.5	5.2	5.6	6.2	6.5	4.8	22.7	31.4	14.1	3.5	78.9	44.3	47.5	52.5
07416	FRANKLIN	95.0	93.0	0.7	0.8	1.5	2.4	4.4	6.7	6.8	6.5	6.5	7.1	7.1	25.1	28.9	10.2	1.8	75.7	38.0	47.6	52.4
07417	FRANKLIN LAKES	91.4	86.7	0.9	1.2	6.3	10.2	2.7	4.3	6.3	7.6	9.5	7.9	3.2	18.9	32.3	13.0	1.3	71.1	42.9	49.5	50.5
07418	GLENWOOD	96.4	94.9	0.6	0.7	0.9	1.5	3.1	4.9	5.9	6.9	7.7	8.5	5.2	23.9	33.3	7.8	0.8	74.2	40.0	49.2	50.8
07419	HAMBURG	94.1	91.5	0.9	1.1	2.1	3.3	4.0	5.9	6.3	6.7	6.8	6.2	5.2	26.7	30.2	10.6	1.3	76.2	40.0	48.2	51.8
07420	HASKELL	88.8	79.8	1.9	3.5	3.8	6.3	6.5	13.2	6.2	6.4	6.6	6.4	5.1	25.1	27.9	12.7	3.6	76.7	41.1	48.5	51.5
07421	HEWITT	94.1	89.5	1.3	2.4	0.9	1.6	4.2	9.2	6.6	7.5	8.5	7.7	4.2	27.1	31.0	6.6	0.8	72.4	38.7	50.5	49.5
07422	HIGHLAND LAKES	96.6	95.2	0.8	0.9	0.4	0.7	3.8	5.8	6.2	6.9	7.7	8.3	5.1	25.5	32.7	6.7	0.9	74.0	39.0	49.4	50.6
07423	HO HO KUS	92.7	88.6	0.6	0.8	5.4	8.8	2.0	3.1	7.4	8.9	10.7	7.2	2.7	18.2	30.6	12.5	1.9	67.9	42.2	48.9	51.1
07424	LITTLE FALLS	89.3	80.2	1.9	4.4	4.0	6.6	7.7	15.7	5.4	5.3	5.3	6.0	6.2	29.3	27.4	12.8	2.3	81.0	40.4	48.4	51.6
07430	MAHWAH	87.8	82.7	2.2	2.6	6.4	9.8	4.3	6.4	6.3	6.8	7.4	8.1	6.6	22.8	29.2	11.5	1.3	75.6	40.4	47.8	52.2
07432	MIDLAND PARK	95.8	93.6	0.4	0.5	2.2	3.6	3.7	6.0	6.9	7.2	7.6	6.4	4.3	24.2	29.5	11.7	2.2	74.4	41.3	48.9	51.1
07435	NEWFOUNDLAND	94.7	91.1	1.6	2.5	1.2	2.1	3.3	6.7	7.1	7.7	8.5	6.8	3.8	25.4	29.5	10.0	1.1	72.1	40.1	51.5	48.5
07436	OAKLAND	94.8	91.8	0.8	1.0	2.7	4.5	3.9	6.2	7.1	7.8	8.4	6.4	3.9	22.2	30.1	12.2	2.1	72.6	41.9	49.0	51.0
07438	OAK RIDGE	96.4	94.4	0.7	1.0	1.2	2.0	2.9	5.3	7.2	7.9	8.4	7.1	4.1	24.6	30.2	9.4	1.0	71.8	39.8	49.3	50.7
07439	OGDENSBURG	97.5	96.4	0.2	0.2	0.7	1.1	4.2	6.5	6.8	7.1	7.4	7.9	6.3	25.5	29.0	8.9	1.2	73.9	37.9	50.3	49.7
07440	PEQUANNOCK	96.9	95.0	0.3	0.4	1.8	2.8	3.3	5.7	6.6	7.1	7.4	6.8	4.9	22.7	29.5	12.9	2.0	74.7	41.3	48.9	51.1
07442	POMPTON LAKES	93.0	87.5	1.2	2.1	3.0	5.1	5.7	12.0	6.6	6.7	6.9	6.6	5.4	26.6	27.9	11.3	2.0	75.8	39.8	47.9	52.1
07444	POMPTON PLAINS	96.5	94.5	0.3	0.4	2.0	3.2	2.8	4.8	6.4	6.6	7.3	7.0	5.1	22.6	30.3	12.6	2.2	75.0	41.8	47.9	52.1
07446	RAMSEY	91.6	87.0	0.8	1.0	5.8	9.4	3.0	4.7	6.8	7.1	7.7	6.8	4.1	24.0	31.0	11.0	1.6	73.7	41.2	48.4	51.6
07450	RIDGEWOOD	87.9	82.1	1.6	1.9	8.6	13.4	3.8	5.7	7.1	8.0	8.9	7.4	3.9	20.6	31.5	10.4	2.2	71.0	41.5	48.5	51.5
07452	GLEN ROCK	90.1	85.1	1.8	2.3	6.5	10.3	2.7	4.3	7.1	8.3	9.8	7.8	3.6	17.8	32.3	11.0	2.4	69.5	42.4	49.3	50.7
07456	RINGWOOD	93.9	89.3	1.6	2.9	1.2	2.1	4.2	9.3	6.8	7.5	8.4	7.0	3.7	24.7	30.7	10.0	1.1	72.6	40.6	50.0	50.0
07457	RIVERDALE	93.4	89.4	1.1	1.2	2.7	5.2	4.4	7.4	5.9	6.5	6.6	6.8	4.9	27.1	29.8	10.7	1.7	77.1	40.2	49.0	51.0
07458	SADDLE RIVER	90.9	86.0	0.9	1.1	6.5	10.6	2.3	3.7	6.4	7.9	10.0	7.8	3.0	16.6	32.7	13.6	2.0	70.5	43.9	48.8	51.2
07460	STOCKHOLM	97.0	95.7	0.6	0.7	0.7	1.1	2.5	4.0	6.9	7.6	8.0	7.5	5.0	23.5	31.6	8.8	1.1	72.6	39.7	50.0	50.0
07461	SUSSEX	96.9	95.7	0.7	0.9	0.8	1.3	2.8	4.4	6.5	7.0	7.7	8.2	5.4	24.7	30.7	8.8	1.1	73.7	38.5	49.2	50.8
07462	VERNON	96.2	94.6	0.9	1.1	0.8	1.3	4.4	6.7	6.5	6.6	6.8	7.2	6.3	30.3	28.2	7.5	0.6	75.4	36.3	51.1	48.9
07463	WALDWICK	92.7	88.7	0.6	0.8	4.5	7.2	5.3	8.3	7.1	7.4	8.1	7.0	4.3	23.7	28.5	11.7	2.2	72.8	40.9	49.0	51.0
07465	WANAQUE	92.4	86.1	1.2	2.0	3.5	5.9	4.3	9.6	6.6	6.9	7.2	6.5	4.6	27.4	30.3	9.4	1.2	75.3	39.5	47.0	53.0
07470	WAYNE	90.6	84.1	1.3	2.2	5.6	9.1	5.0	10.3	5.9	6.3	7.0	7.1	5.0	21.7	29.8	14.3	3.0	76.6	43.1	47.7	52.3
07480	WEST MILFORD	95.4	91.5	1.3	2.3	1.1	2.0	3.0	6.7	6.5	7.1	7.7	7.0	4.4	24.9	30.8	10.2	1.5	74.1	40.8	49.3	50.7
07481	WYCKOFF	94.5	91.4	0.5	0.6	3.7	6.1	2.3	3.7	6.4	7.7	9.4	7.7	3.5	17.4	31.9	12.7	3.3	71.3	43.6	48.3	51.7
07501	PATERSON	27.7	24.2	32.2	30.1	1.3	1.3	55.6	62.9	9.3	8.7	7.5	8.1	8.5	28.7	20.0	8.2	1.1	69.8	29.8	49.0	51.0
07502	PATERSON	48.8	40.4	17.2	18.1	5.2	5.0	46.7	59.1	8.3	7.6	7.1	7.1	7.7	29.4	22.8	8.3	1.7	72.9	32.9	48.3	51.7
07503	PATERSON	47.4	38.9	9.0	9.0	2.5	2.4	54.9	67.9	8.7	7.8	6.7	7.5	8.8	30.2	21.6	7.8	1.0	72.5	31.2	50.0	50.0
07504	PATERSON	14.8	13.6	58.9	56.1	0.8	0.7	32.8	38.8	7.3	7.0	6.6	8.0	8.2	29.5	24.5	8.1	0.7	74.2	32.9	46.7	53.3
07505	PATERSON	31.8	28.8	37.2	35.5	3.0	2.7	48.6	56.4	5.3	4.8	4.0	6.8	12.5	43.5	17.3	5.2	0.6	82.9	31.9	66.6	33.4
07506	HAWTHORNE	93.8	88.9	0.8	1.2	1.9	3.2	7.4	14.9	6.2	6.2	6.3	5.9	5.7	27.7	28.0	11.7	2.3	77.6	40.0	48.2	51.8
07508	HALEDON	78.1	69.0	7.0	9.1	3.4	4.5	18.6	29.0	6.6	6.3	6.3	8.3	9.0	26.1	23.6	11.2	2.6	76.6	35.7	47.3	52.7
07512	TOTOWA	93.4	88.1	1.1	1.8	2.3	3.8	6.4	13.1	4.7	4.9	5.5	5.5	4.6	26.4	28.6	16.0	3.6	81.5	43.9	47.3	52.7
07513	PATERSON	33.6	30.4	22.9	20.6	0.9	0.7	67.3	74.7	8.6	8.4	7.4	8.0	9.3	30.0	21.4	6.2	0.6	71.0	29.3	48.2	51.8
07514	PATERSON	20.9	17.4	51.6	50.1	0.7	0.7	34.9	41.8	8.0	7.5	7.1	7.7	7.9	28.2	22.2	9.3	1.9	72.7	32.6	45.6	54.4
07522	PATERSON	26.8	24.6	43.4	41.2	3.4	3.0	45.1	52.5	10.1	9.3	8.0	8.5	9.2	29.0	19.1	6.0	0.8	67.6	27.7	47.3	52.7
07524	PATERSON	26.3	22.5	27.1	24.8	0.4	0.3	63.6	71.1	9.3	8.6	7.8	8.9	8.8	29.5	20.2	6.3	0.7	69.1	29.1	49.6	50.4
07601	HACKENSACK	52.9	47.0	24.5	24.9	7.5	9.9	25.8	31.9	5.8	5.3	4.9	5.1	7.0	33.1	26.0	10.6	2.1	81.0	38.3	49.8	50.2
07603	BOGOTA	75.6	68.4	5.8	6.5	7.9	10.9	21.3	29.0	6.4	6.3	6.4	7.0	7.0	27.0	28.4	10.0	1.5	76.5	37.9	47.8	52.2
07604	HASBROUCK HEIGHTS	87.3	81.9	2.0	2.4	6.8	10.2	8.4	12.5	5.7	5.7	6.1	6.1	5.8	25.8	29.9	12.1	2.7	78.7	41.5	48.3	51.7
07605	LEONIA	65.7	55.7	2.3	2.4	26.1	34.5	12.7	16.6	5.4	5.8	6.4	6.7	5.2	23.4	32.2	12.7	2.2	78.1	43.1	48.3	51.7
07606	SOUTH HACKENSACK	82.0	75.6	2.5	2.7	5.9	8.7	16.1	22.1	6.2	5.6	5.5	5.9	6.3	30.7	24.8	12.9	2.0	79.2	38.4	49.5	50.5
07607	MAYWOOD	84.5	78.5	2.8	3.3	7.2	10.6	11.7	17.1	6.2	6.4	6.5	5.8	4.8	25.2	29.4	12.4	3.2	77.1	42.0	46.9	53.1
07608	TETERBORO	83.9	78.8	3.2	3.0	3.2	6.1	19.4	27.3	6.1	6.1	6.1	6.1	9.1	24.2	24.2	18.2	0.0	75.8	38.8	48.5	51.5
07620	ALPINE	77.5	67.5	1.5	1.8	19.0	28.1	2.5	3.6	4.9	5.8	7.9	7.4	3.2	19.4	33.4	16.3	1.7	76.3	45.8	50.6	49.4
07621	BERGENFIELD	63.3	53.9	6.8	7.1	20.3	26.9	16.8	21.7	6.5	6.6	6.9	6.9	5.6	26.0	28.1	11.2	2.1	75.7	39.3	48.1	51.9
07624	CLOSTER	75.3	65.1	0.9	1.1	21.5	31.0	4.1	5.8	6.0	6.7	7.8	7.7	4.8	20.0	32.8	12.3	2.0	74.3	43.1	49.3	50.7
07626	CRESSKILL	78.0	68.4	0.9	1.1	18.7	27.4	4.0	5.7	6.2	6.8	7.9	7.1	4.0	19.8	31.2	13.9	3.0	74.1	43.8	48.0	52.0
07627	DEMAREST	77.3	67.5	0.5	0.6	20.2	29.4	3.4	4.8	5.6	6.6	8.6	8.5	4.3	17.0	34.1	13.2	2.1	73.5	44.6	49.0	51.0
07628	DUMONT	83.8	76.5	1.5	1.8	10.9	16.4	8.4	12.2	6.5	6.7	7.0	6.8	5.4	24.8	28.2	12.3	2.3	75.5	40.7	48.4	51.6
07630	EMERSON	89.7	84.2	0.8	1.1	7.8	12.3	4.6	7.1	6.4	6.9	7.6	6.0	3.6	21.8	28.5	14.8	4.4	75.2	43.7	47.9	52.1
07631	ENGLEWOOD	42.6	38.5	38.9	38.9	5.3	7.0	21.7	26.2	6.8	6.8	6.9	6.5	5.7	26.5	27.1	11.8	2.0	75.6	39.0	47.2	52.8
07632	ENGLEWOOD CLIFFS	67.4	56.0	1.4	1.5	29.2	40.0	4.8	6.4	5.7	5.9	6.1	5.8	3.5	20.8	29.9	19.3	2.9	78.5	46.4	47.6	52.4
07640	HARRINGTON PARK	83.5	75.3	0.7	0.8	14.7	22.4	2.6	3.9	6.4	7.4	8.6	7.4	4.1	19.3	32.2	12.7	1.8	72.7	42.8	48.6	51.4
07641	HAWORTH	87.9	81.7	1.2	1.5	9.3	14.4	2.8	4.3	6.2	7.4	9.2	7.9	3.5	17.7	33.2	12.9	2.1	71.3	43.8	49.9	50.1
07642	HILLSDALE	92.4	88.3	0.9	1.1	5.1	8.3	4.2	6.7	6.8	7.4	8.0	6.7	4.0	21.6	30.5	12.8	2.2	73.2	42.4	48.6	51.4
07643	LITTLE FERRY	68.9	60.9	4.7	4.8	17.1	22.1	15.2	20.7	6.5	5.4	5.0	5.4	6.5	31.8	27.1	10.8	1.5	80.0	38.1	49.0	51.0
07644	LODI	78.1	71.2	3.6	4.0	8.8	11.9	18.1	25.3	6.5	6.1	5.8	5.9	6.4	30.4	26.0	10.7	2.3	78.1	38.0	47.7	52.3
07645	MONTVALE	92.8	88.7	0.4	0.6	5.4	8.6	3.1	4.9	6.4	6.8	7.9	6.8	4.0	21.4	30.9	14.3	1.6	74.4	43.0	48.9	51.1
07646	NEW MILFORD	78.6	70.2	2.6	3.0	14.8	21.4	8.1	11.5	6.1	6.3	6.5	5.8	4.8	25.8	28.3	13.0	3.4	77.5	41.8	48.5	51.5
07647	NORTHVALE	83.4	75.6	1.0	1.2	13.3	20.1	4.7	7.0	5.5	5.6	6.1	6.8	5.3	23.6	29.0	14.9	3.2	78.2	43.1	49.7	50.3
07648	NORWOOD	77.9	67.9	0.8	1.0	18.9	28.1	3.0	4.4	5.5	6.2	7.2	6.9	4.0	20.5	31.7	14.1	3.8	76.5	44.8	46.6	53.4
07649	ORADELL	90.0	84.5	0.5	0.6	8.1	12.9	3.2	4.9	6.0	6.7	7.6	6.6	3.9	20.6	31.3	14.5	2.9	75.3	44.2	48.3	51.7
07650	PALISADES PARK	48.5	38.6	1.3	1.3	41.1	49.9	16.1	18.9	6.5	6.0	5.5	5.2	5.4	32.7	25.7	11.4	1.6	79.0	38.5	49.5	50.5
07652	PARAMUS	79.2	70.0	1.1	1.3	17.2	25.3	4.9	7.1	5.2	5.5	6.3	6.6	4.7	21.0	29.0	17.4	4.3	78.5	45.4	48.3	51.7
07656	PARK RIDGE	93.5	90.0	0.9	1.1	3.9	6.3	5.3	8.1	6.3	6.9	7.6	6.2	3.7	21.7	29.9	14.4	3.3	75.0	43.5	48.6	51.4
07657	RIDGEFIELD	74.8	66.0	0.8	0.9	18.1	24.9	14.4	19.4	5.5	5.4	5.7	6.9	5.9	26.8	28.1	13.2	2.6	79.3	41.2	48.6	51.4
07660	RIDGEFIELD PARK	78.1	71.1	4.1	4.7	7.9	11.1	22.2	30.4	6.0	5.5	5.5	6.3	7.0	28.7	28.1	11.3	1.7	79.3	39.1	48.1	51.9
07661	RIVER EDGE	84.1	77.1	1.1	1.3	12.6	18.5	5.3	7.9	6.7	7.1	7.5	6.1	4.7	22.6	30.1	12.2	2.9	74.6	42.1	48.0	52.0
07662	ROCHELLE PARK	90.1	85.0	0.5	0.6	6.0	9.4	8.6	13.1	5.4	5.7	6.0	5.6	4.5	24.5	27.3	14.8	6.0	79.3	43.9	47.0	53.0
07663	SADDLE BROOK	90.7	86.3	1.4	1.7	4.8	7.4	6.3	9.8	5.7	5.8	6.0	5.7	5.3	26.6	28.6	13.2	3.1	78.9	41.8	47.6	52.4
07666	TEANECK	56.3	50.1	28.6	30.1	7.2	9.8	10.6	14.1	6.3	6.5	7.0	7.8	6.3	23.1	28.2	12.4	2.4	75.7	40.0	47.7	52.3
07670	TENAFLY	76.7	67.7	1.0	1.1	19.1	27.1	4.7	6.5	5.9	7.1	8.2	7.5	4.6	18.9	32.2	13.0	2.6	73.7	43.4	48.3	51.7
07675	WESTWOOD	87.9	82.4	2.8	3.2	7.3	11.5	4.3	6.6	6.3	6.8	7.7	6.4	4.2	22.0	30.9	12.8	2.7	74.9	42.8	48.2	51.8
	NEW JERSEY	72.6	68.2	13.6	14.0	5.7	7.9	13.3	16.9	6.6	6.6	6.7	6.8	6.2	26.4	27.0	11.5	2.2	76.0	38.7	48.7	51.3
	UNITED STATES	75.1	72.0	12.3	12.7	3.8	4.6	12.5	15.7	6.8	6.7	6.6	7.1	6.9	27.0	26.0	10.9	1.9	75.7	36.9	49.2	50.8

# ZIP CODE	POST OFFICE NAME	2009 Per Capita Income	2009 HH Income Base	2009 HOUSEHOLD INCOME DISTRIBUTION (%) Less than $25,000	$25,000 to $49,999	$50,000 to $99,999	$100,000 to $149,999	$150,000 or More	MEDIAN HOUSEHOLD INCOME 2009	2014	2009 National Centile	2009 State Centile	2009 Home Value Base	2009 HOME VALUE DISTRIBUTION (%) Less than $50,000	$50,000 to $89,999	$90,000 to $174,999	$175,000 to $399,999	$400,000 or More	2009 Median Home Value
07205	HILLSIDE	27939	7182	10.5	18.4	44.4	17.3	9.5	76943	79878	91	48	5085	0.0	0.3	10.1	80.1	9.5	251998
07206	ELIZABETH	14123	7292	36.3	26.8	27.6	6.8	2.6	37631	40400	26	4	2393	1.1	2.2	18.4	69.0	9.3	236800
07208	ELIZABETH	22410	12082	23.4	26.4	35.5	10.2	4.5	50147	50943	61	12	3684	0.6	0.7	7.0	72.1	19.7	296460
07302	JERSEY CITY	37974	16386	22.0	18.8	34.0	12.8	12.4	61924	68583	80	26	3730	1.3	2.4	7.7	46.5	42.0	352773
07304	JERSEY CITY	17584	14328	34.2	24.6	31.7	6.0	3.5	39402	45503	31	4	3963	1.5	2.9	19.8	69.1	6.8	230649
07305	JERSEY CITY	21471	20595	28.1	22.7	34.8	9.0	5.4	49031	53733	59	11	8441	1.3	1.2	14.4	71.6	11.5	261708
07306	JERSEY CITY	20637	19793	29.9	27.4	32.1	6.8	3.8	43408	48142	44	7	4341	0.9	2.4	16.1	70.0	10.7	251266
07307	JERSEY CITY	20703	15653	22.4	27.0	39.1	7.6	3.9	50539	55421	62	12	4849	0.5	1.2	9.3	75.9	13.2	274746
07310	JERSEY CITY	63810	4180	9.6	17.8	30.7	11.4	30.5	85928	88719	94	65	385	3.1	9.1	1.6	24.4	61.8	465000
07401	ALLENDALE	60697	2124	2.8	6.5	28.2	17.3	45.2	137182	141814	99	96	1873	0.1	0.4	0.1	6.0	93.5	804642
07403	BLOOMINGDALE	34681	2770	4.9	15.3	46.8	20.7	12.3	80962	82171	92	57	2003	0.0	0.0	1.5	73.7	24.8	333311
07405	BUTLER	50872	6556	8.1	12.4	25.8	22.2	31.4	105970	115614	97	80	5354	0.3	0.1	1.6	33.9	64.2	488565
07407	ELMWOOD PARK	28196	7242	16.4	21.3	37.5	18.7	6.2	66724	65838	85	32	4446	0.2	0.0	2.5	64.9	32.3	352909
07410	FAIR LAWN	41439	11989	10.1	14.0	30.0	26.7	19.1	92122	99943	95	70	9304	0.1	0.0	0.7	49.5	49.7	399147
07416	FRANKLIN	26563	2205	16.0	21.8	42.2	13.9	6.1	59062	56414	76	21	1593	7.4	2.1	14.6	67.5	8.4	223449
07417	FRANKLIN LAKES	67830	3507	5.7	5.3	17.2	15.3	56.5	177164	184405	100	99	3230	0.0	0.0	0.0	2.4	97.6	1000001
07418	GLENWOOD	34969	807	5.1	8.2	38.9	28.4	19.5	96124	104296	96	73	737	0.0	0.0	3.5	76.8	19.7	313035
07419	HAMBURG	37736	3705	8.0	16.8	38.0	23.9	13.3	80203	85898	92	55	2914	0.2	0.0	14.0	66.9	18.9	264299
07420	HASKELL	29039	2222	8.2	14.9	47.1	20.7	9.2	78907	81114	92	52	1841	0.0	0.0	0.8	85.0	14.2	280808
07421	HEWITT	33147	2781	7.6	13.0	43.7	22.6	13.2	81213	82202	93	58	2326	0.0	0.1	4.0	80.9	15.0	275452
07422	HIGHLAND LAKES	33276	2638	7.9	9.5	43.4	27.8	11.4	85490	90214	94	64	2406	0.0	0.4	10.1	77.1	12.4	264350
07423	HO HO KUS	76451	1440	4.4	8.6	13.1	19.2	54.6	170590	177450	100	99	1284	0.0	0.0	0.0	2.0	98.0	868421
07424	LITTLE FALLS	36697	9132	10.3	18.4	40.3	18.9	12.0	76783	78115	90	47	5732	0.3	0.1	2.1	52.0	45.5	384797
07430	MAHWAH	57195	9153	7.1	10.5	28.4	24.5	29.5	108661	113821	98	82	7603	0.4	0.5	1.2	32.5	65.4	542651
07432	MIDLAND PARK	43415	2767	6.9	13.3	29.3	32.7	17.9	100704	102787	97	76	2070	0.0	0.0	0.1	29.4	70.5	476951
07435	NEWFOUNDLAND	46585	951	3.6	9.5	34.5	25.9	26.6	104152	105994	97	78	761	0.0	0.0	0.8	44.4	54.8	422956
07436	OAKLAND	46152	4450	3.3	8.1	30.3	30.8	27.5	113271	115219	98	85	4035	0.0	0.0	0.3	32.9	66.8	470176
07438	OAK RIDGE	38581	4174	5.1	11.1	34.1	32.9	16.7	99284	101493	97	75	3694	0.3	0.6	4.0	58.4	36.7	354495
07439	OGDENSBURG	32701	892	10.2	14.9	39.6	23.0	12.3	79985	86221	92	54	743	2.8	0.3	6.7	86.0	4.2	267173
07440	PEQUANNOCK	38980	1683	10.5	11.5	34.0	26.3	17.6	88556	92774	95	67	1425	0.0	0.0	2.0	42.4	55.6	425238
07442	POMPTON LAKES	33614	4041	9.2	15.3	42.6	22.3	10.7	81005	82629	92	57	3006	0.0	0.2	4.9	67.7	27.2	326609
07444	POMPTON PLAINS	43087	3661	5.9	15.2	28.1	28.0	22.9	100956	104843	97	77	3257	0.0	0.6	2.9	34.4	62.2	454841
07446	RAMSEY	53882	5842	5.8	10.9	28.1	23.9	31.4	110148	112650	98	84	4818	0.0	0.4	1.7	23.7	74.1	572950
07450	RIDGEWOOD	61427	8601	7.3	7.6	21.5	19.0	44.5	136586	140601	99	95	6754	0.1	0.2	0.3	9.1	90.3	743340
07452	GLEN ROCK	59175	3946	4.0	8.8	21.1	23.5	42.6	135407	136896	99	95	3540	0.4	0.1	0.0	8.3	91.2	615565
07456	RINGWOOD	41457	4050	4.8	8.5	35.6	26.0	25.2	101999	102296	97	78	3652	0.0	0.0	0.4	58.3	41.3	373216
07457	RIVERDALE	42583	1491	8.4	13.2	30.6	28.1	19.7	94717	97505	96	72	1286	0.0	0.0	0.4	60.1	39.5	370524
07458	SADDLE RIVER	70657	3854	4.2	6.6	16.3	12.6	60.2	178868	182776	100	99	3556	0.0	0.2	0.4	1.8	97.6	1000001
07460	STOCKHOLM	34824	1368	10.3	14.5	37.8	25.5	11.8	82393	85812	93	59	1237	0.0	0.9	4.3	69.7	25.1	292100
07461	SUSSEX	31218	6987	9.9	17.7	36.8	23.5	12.3	77862	82649	91	50	5737	0.0	0.1	7.9	63.3	28.8	313416
07462	VERNON	33052	3250	10.6	17.7	43.4	21.9	6.4	73438	77015	89	41	2245	0.0	0.6	22.3	63.7	13.4	240691
07463	WALDWICK	40204	3442	7.1	11.3	33.6	30.2	17.8	96584	102055	96	74	2993	0.5	0.0	0.3	39.3	60.0	433020
07465	WANAQUE	38674	2111	6.6	12.4	40.1	23.6	17.3	88325	88391	95	67	1651	0.0	0.0	0.4	62.5	37.1	362478
07470	WAYNE	46068	18091	7.9	11.8	29.9	21.7	28.8	101245	97757	97	77	14286	0.2	0.6	1.4	22.5	75.3	541940
07480	WEST MILFORD	37466	5745	6.8	9.2	40.7	24.6	18.8	91221	90641	95	70	5053	0.4	0.0	2.7	67.9	29.0	315687
07481	WYCKOFF	60901	5665	4.7	9.3	21.1	20.0	44.9	136442	139863	99	95	5101	0.0	0.3	0.1	5.3	94.3	796995
07501	PATERSON	12958	10200	42.3	28.0	24.6	3.9	1.2	31060	33435	10	2	2082	0.8	2.5	14.2	76.7	5.8	258587
07502	PATERSON	20970	4728	18.9	25.8	35.9	12.6	6.8	54823	57035	71	17	2433	1.5	1.1	6.5	85.5	5.4	264826
07503	PATERSON	16336	5737	30.2	29.5	30.0	6.7	3.5	41746	45678	38	6	1988	0.7	0.3	9.7	81.9	7.5	268716
07504	PATERSON	19401	3647	20.4	23.8	37.4	12.1	6.3	55735	59195	72	18	1635	0.6	0.2	6.0	74.7	18.5	288447
07505	PATERSON	13551	926	53.5	31.0	13.2	1.5	0.9	22630	24580	2	1	53	5.7	0.0	5.7	39.6	49.1	395833
07506	HAWTHORNE	32852	7363	10.4	21.1	43.5	16.1	9.0	71074	75905	87	39	4749	0.1	0.0	0.3	53.1	46.5	388885
07508	HALEDON	28330	7707	13.2	19.0	40.1	15.3	12.4	72522	77242	88	40	4912	0.4	0.0	1.1	55.5	43.0	371285
07512	TOTOWA	32877	3615	12.7	20.0	37.5	17.9	11.8	77008	79029	91	48	2855	0.2	0.0	2.7	53.2	43.8	381441
07513	PATERSON	15804	3402	24.1	28.2	36.0	6.5	5.1	47436	50950	55	10	1203	0.4	0.2	3.9	83.0	12.5	284886
07514	PATERSON	18242	6103	27.0	28.9	34.5	6.5	3.1	43950	48622	45	7	2016	6.7	2.0	7.5	75.4	8.3	264442
07522	PATERSON	14458	5984	30.8	30.1	30.4	6.6	2.1	39945	45048	32	5	1731	1.2	1.7	18.6	73.8	4.6	251627
07524	PATERSON	14447	3510	29.9	29.3	31.7	6.9	2.2	40969	45578	36	5	958	0.2	0.0	6.5	84.7	8.7	278870
07601	HACKENSACK	33984	18865	17.0	21.5	36.4	16.9	8.1	61585	57442	79	25	6308	0.3	1.7	9.4	65.9	22.6	293630
07603	BOGOTA	31295	2709	10.1	21.3	33.7	23.9	11.0	78345	81651	91	51	1806	0.1	0.3	1.2	82.6	15.8	303443
07604	HASBROUCK HEIGHTS	38567	4599	11.7	14.5	35.7	25.6	12.5	83365	86099	93	60	3132	0.2	0.4	0.4	49.0	50.0	400000
07605	LEONIA	43548	3301	10.8	12.6	27.8	27.7	21.1	97433	101593	96	74	2175	0.3	0.4	1.1	25.6	72.5	527943
07606	SOUTH HACKENSACK	32515	827	8.5	25.5	35.1	20.1	10.9	75581	75607	90	44	461	0.0	0.0	0.0	49.0	51.0	406164
07607	MAYWOOD	35724	3674	11.6	15.8	36.5	25.2	10.9	81680	84530	93	58	2484	0.2	0.0	0.3	61.1	38.5	371053
07608	TETERBORO	27877	12	8.3	33.3	33.3	16.7	8.3	60000	54356	77	22	7	0.0	0.0	0.0	57.1	42.9	350000
07620	ALPINE	70771	737	7.3	5.6	17.2	10.7	59.2	180615	186946	100	99	645	0.0	0.5	0.0	3.7	95.8	1000001
07621	BERGENFIELD	32408	9440	9.8	17.2	35.7	24.8	12.4	81297	83471	93	58	6576	0.2	0.2	1.0	72.6	26.1	340991
07624	CLOSTER	47817	2792	5.1	9.4	31.1	20.6	34.0	110246	114065	98	84	2368	0.3	1.4	0.0	11.2	87.2	682927
07626	CRESSKILL	51302	2991	6.5	10.8	27.3	26.2	29.2	112890	116231	98	85	2603	0.5	0.8	0.4	16.9	81.4	559036
07627	DEMAREST	58516	1639	5.1	7.7	21.2	22.1	43.9	136347	138705	99	95	1463	0.3	0.2	0.2	6.8	92.5	703471
07628	DUMONT	33562	6204	11.7	15.0	35.8	25.6	11.8	82609	86336	93	59	4578	0.2	0.1	0.3	62.2	37.1	368704
07630	EMERSON	41230	2501	6.2	10.6	35.4	25.5	22.3	96511	101613	96	74	2247	0.0	0.3	0.2	23.9	75.5	493101
07631	ENGLEWOOD	41070	9701	16.0	17.3	28.5	17.8	20.5	76655	79712	90	47	5723	0.1	0.0	1.6	57.0	41.3	363058
07632	ENGLEWOOD CLIFFS	69484	1759	6.5	8.1	19.2	15.5	50.8	152115	160424	100	97	1574	0.0	0.4	0.5	2.5	96.6	929817
07640	HARRINGTON PARK	50389	1607	3.2	8.2	25.0	26.1	37.5	128220	129419	99	91	1469	0.3	0.2	0.6	7.5	91.4	655228
07641	HAWORTH	57482	1139	4.3	7.6	22.9	21.2	43.9	133633	132638	99	94	1043	0.3	0.7	0.0	5.4	93.7	718373
07642	HILLSDALE	45238	3492	6.9	9.4	27.7	27.1	28.9	109209	112288	98	83	3043	0.2	0.1	0.1	19.9	79.8	558597
07643	LITTLE FERRY	30256	4394	13.1	23.6	38.3	17.0	7.9	61720	57567	80	25	2090	0.2	0.0	4.2	60.5	35.1	352656
07644	LODI	27083	9945	18.4	25.5	36.1	15.0	4.8	55124	54472	71	18	4350	1.9	0.4	1.9	64.2	31.6	341891
07645	MONTVALE	55401	2645	4.8	8.5	24.4	26.0	36.4	126672	127156	99	90	2202	0.0	0.2	0.4	13.5	85.9	654289
07646	NEW MILFORD	38725	6357	10.7	15.2	36.0	23.1	14.9	80278	83677	92	55	3949	0.1	0.1	0.2	44.8	54.7	415439
07647	NORTHVALE	37929	1643	8.1	13.6	31.3	33.5	13.5	94121	102504	96	72	1324	0.0	0.3	0.1	31.6	68.0	470414
07648	NORWOOD	51213	1985	6.6	9.7	23.4	26.2	34.0	125206	124215	99	89	1653	0.0	0.5	0.9	12.3	86.3	662850
07649	ORADELL	50206	2794	5.9	9.6	24.8	24.3	35.4	125506	127593	99	89	2446	0.2	0.1	0.0	11.9	87.9	637052
07650	PALISADES PARK	28707	6556	17.2	23.4	30.9	19.5	9.0	61585	58347	79	25	2608	0.4	1.5	0.7	33.3	64.1	464841
07652	PARAMUS	38523	8440	6.9	11.4	31.4	28.6	21.6	100408	104479	97	76	7391	0.3	0.2	0.1	17.6	81.7	561439
07656	PARK RIDGE	50600	3299	5.8	11.0	27.4	26.6	29.3	111072	114675	98	84	2666	0.2	0.0	0.2	14.9	84.7	601547
07657	RIDGEFIELD	32034	4366	15.2	21.9	32.0	20.1	10.9	70100	71942	87	37	2459	0.2	0.1	0.6	38.1	61.0	448471
07660	RIDGEFIELD PARK	30458	5077	14.8	19.7	37.6	21.4	6.5	66833	65699	85	32	2767	1.1	0.3	2.5	73.8	22.3	325824
07661	RIVER EDGE	42997	4109	7.9	14.8	32.6	24.6	20.2	89879	93871	95	68	3004	0.1	0.0	0.8	25.9	73.2	470517
07662	ROCHELLE PARK	33174	2189	12.4	17.5	36.5	23.2	10.3	79385	83260	92	53	1638	0.4	0.1	0.1	68.4	31.0	359767
07663	SADDLE BROOK	36343	5172	11.5	13.7	36.8	27.0	10.9	82624	86057	93	59	3795	0.1	0.1	1.0	59.6	39.3	373067
07666	TEANECK	41852	13663	9.5	10.8	31.6	25.1	23.0	96358	102693	96	73	10402	0.0	0.2	0.7	54.0	45.1	384293
07670	TENAFLY	63346	4761	8.2	9.4	22.2	21.4	38.9	127457	128860	99	90	3776	0.3	0.3	0.3	10.7	88.4	758406
07675	WESTWOOD	49191	9822	8.2	11.6	28.6	23.9	27.7	102972	107972	97	78	7553	0.0	0.2	0.2	18.7	80.9	599762
	NEW JERSEY	34433		15.4	18.6	34.9	16.8	14.2	72809	76895				1.0	1.6	9.9	50.1	37.4	336585
	UNITED STATES	27277		20.9	24.4	35.3	11.7	7.6	54719	56938				9.3	13.1	31.6	32.6	13.5	162279

ZIP CODE #	POST OFFICE NAME	FINANCIAL SERVICES: Auto Loan	Home Loan	Invest-ments	Retire-ment Plans	THE HOME: Home Improvements: Home Repair	Lawn & Garden	Furnishings: Comput-ers & Hard-ware Personal	Major Appli-ances	TV, Radio, Sound Equip-ment	Furni-ture	ENTERTAINMENT: Dine out/ Carry out	Sports Equip-ment	Fees & Tickets	Toys & Games	Travel	Cable TV	PERSONAL: Apparel & Services	Auto Repairs	Health Insur-ance	Pets & Supplies
07205	HILLSIDE	104	131	132	125	133	117	122	119	118	118	121	90	134	118	130	120	89	120	116	134
07206	ELIZABETH	65	61	53	57	60	48	72	64	67	72	71	52	68	67	68	62	52	70	55	70
07208	ELIZABETH	74	79	78	78	79	69	90	80	87	84	90	63	90	86	88	86	67	86	76	91
07302	JERSEY CITY	107	95	103	104	96	87	128	103	121	118	125	90	119	118	118	117	91	117	101	125
07304	JERSEY CITY	61	61	61	62	60	57	74	63	76	66	78	50	73	73	69	78	57	70	66	76
07305	JERSEY CITY	73	78	81	79	78	75	87	77	90	78	92	59	90	87	85	95	67	84	84	93
07306	JERSEY CITY	64	64	66	66	64	60	79	67	80	70	82	53	78	76	75	82	60	75	72	80
07307	JERSEY CITY	74	76	73	75	75	64	89	77	85	83	89	63	87	84	85	82	66	84	72	88
07310	JERSEY CITY	176	130	133	149	124	125	195	146	191	179	198	132	172	191	165	188	142	176	154	188
07401	ALLENDALE	229	321	389	329	359	298	269	288	246	301	243	213	330	237	324	234	183	266	257	315
07403	BLOOMINGDALE	116	146	151	141	151	134	131	131	126	130	127	98	147	127	143	126	93	130	127	148
07405	BUTLER	176	235	249	237	245	214	200	205	191	206	193	156	237	192	225	188	144	196	189	229
07407	ELMWOOD PARK	84	110	116	105	113	101	104	100	105	95	108	74	117	103	112	110	80	103	104	113
07410	FAIR LAWN	130	181	199	174	192	167	152	159	147	153	148	116	182	146	176	148	109	153	155	174
07416	FRANKLIN	94	107	101	104	106	99	102	99	99	101	100	77	108	101	106	99	72	100	98	115
07417	FRANKLIN LAKES	251	356	436	371	399	334	290	312	270	324	268	233	371	267	349	259	207	286	275	340
07418	GLENWOOD	147	187	171	189	183	163	156	159	146	165	149	127	179	152	170	140	108	151	141	182
07419	HAMBURG	128	149	144	150	148	138	135	135	130	139	132	104	147	132	144	128	94	133	130	157
07420	HASKELL	104	145	149	135	150	128	121	125	116	120	117	92	141	117	137	116	86	121	119	137
07421	HEWITT	126	161	147	160	158	140	134	137	126	140	129	108	153	131	147	122	93	130	124	156
07422	HIGHLAND LAKES	126	163	148	160	159	141	136	139	128	141	130	108	155	133	148	124	94	132	125	158
07423	HO HO KUS	255	364	446	379	407	341	295	318	276	329	273	237	379	272	355	264	212	291	280	346
07424	LITTLE FALLS	105	136	148	132	143	123	128	124	124	122	127	94	144	122	140	126	94	125	122	140
07430	MAHWAH	190	238	258	241	251	214	212	215	198	226	199	166	242	198	235	190	147	206	194	240
07432	MIDLAND PARK	135	192	213	184	205	174	159	166	150	162	151	123	191	151	185	149	113	158	156	181
07435	NEWFOUNDLAND	156	218	235	217	229	198	177	186	167	184	169	140	215	169	206	164	126	175	171	205
07436	OAKLAND	161	225	243	222	237	205	185	193	176	190	177	145	223	178	214	174	132	183	181	213
07438	OAK RIDGE	142	186	174	181	184	162	154	158	146	160	148	123	177	150	170	142	108	151	144	179
07439	OGDENSBURG	114	161	167	149	167	142	133	138	127	132	128	101	157	129	152	128	95	133	131	151
07440	PEQUANNOCK	128	184	197	173	193	165	150	157	143	151	144	115	180	145	174	144	107	150	149	172
07442	POMPTON LAKES	108	143	149	136	148	132	126	128	123	123	125	94	145	123	140	126	91	126	128	142
07444	POMPTON PLAINS	144	192	205	187	201	177	163	168	156	165	158	125	191	158	185	156	116	162	161	187
07446	RAMSEY	180	224	245	227	237	205	201	202	189	211	190	155	229	189	223	183	140	196	187	228
07450	RIDGEWOOD	214	291	346	298	321	267	250	260	230	271	230	197	302	226	293	219	174	245	232	286
07452	GLEN ROCK	203	289	341	290	318	267	238	255	222	258	220	187	294	217	285	215	166	237	232	277
07456	RINGWOOD	158	213	216	213	218	191	175	182	165	183	167	140	208	169	198	161	123	171	165	203
07457	RIVERDALE	136	191	198	177	198	169	158	164	151	157	152	120	186	153	180	152	113	158	155	180
07458	SADDLE RIVER	250	358	440	375	401	337	288	310	270	321	268	232	374	269	346	259	209	283	272	337
07460	STOCKHOLM	125	166	159	160	166	145	138	142	130	141	133	108	159	134	153	128	97	135	130	159
07461	SUSSEX	121	152	139	151	149	134	131	132	124	135	126	104	147	127	141	121	91	127	122	151
07462	VERNON	120	124	109	125	118	110	123	115	117	126	119	93	124	122	120	113	84	117	108	136
07463	WALDWICK	131	187	206	179	199	171	154	161	149	154	150	118	187	149	180	151	112	155	155	176
07465	WANAQUE	134	178	174	171	179	157	152	154	146	151	149	116	174	149	167	146	109	149	145	173
07470	WAYNE	156	208	231	205	222	190	180	184	169	186	170	138	210	168	205	166	126	177	172	204
07480	WEST MILFORD	136	182	178	178	184	160	151	155	142	156	144	119	176	146	169	139	106	148	142	174
07481	WYCKOFF	213	302	364	310	336	282	248	266	230	273	228	197	311	226	297	222	175	245	238	289
07501	PATERSON	50	44	42	44	43	40	59	50	59	55	61	39	54	57	52	60	45	56	51	58
07502	PATERSON	86	94	92	91	95	80	102	92	96	97	100	73	103	96	101	93	74	97	85	103
07503	PATERSON	70	68	63	66	67	55	81	71	75	79	80	58	77	75	77	72	59	77	63	79
07504	PATERSON	82	89	89	88	88	81	99	87	99	90	102	68	101	97	96	101	75	95	89	103
07505	PATERSON	33	26	25	29	25	25	44	34	47	36	49	25	38	43	35	51	38	39	37	41
07506	HAWTHORNE	94	125	134	119	130	115	115	112	115	106	117	82	132	113	125	119	87	113	114	126
07508	HALEDON	105	133	140	128	138	119	126	122	121	121	124	92	140	121	135	122	92	123	117	136
07512	TOTOWA	107	143	149	136	148	135	123	127	122	120	123	92	143	122	138	126	90	124	129	142
07513	PATERSON	78	75	66	71	73	60	90	79	85	87	89	64	85	84	84	81	66	86	69	87
07514	PATERSON	66	68	69	69	68	64	78	69	78	72	81	54	79	76	76	80	59	76	73	82
07522	PATERSON	62	59	55	59	58	51	73	63	72	68	75	50	70	71	67	72	56	69	61	73
07524	PATERSON	66	64	57	61	63	52	76	67	72	74	76	54	72	71	71	69	56	73	60	74
07601	HACKENSACK	100	101	105	103	102	93	116	102	113	110	116	83	116	111	113	112	84	111	103	120
07603	BOGOTA	103	140	146	131	144	127	124	124	124	117	126	90	143	123	137	128	94	124	124	138
07604	HASBROUCK HEIGHTS	114	152	163	146	158	139	137	135	134	130	137	101	157	133	151	137	102	135	134	151
07605	LEONIA	143	193	219	190	209	173	171	175	157	179	157	132	197	153	196	152	117	168	161	192
07606	SOUTH HACKENSACK	101	132	139	125	135	122	125	120	127	112	130	88	141	125	134	134	97	123	125	135
07607	MAYWOOD	107	145	154	137	151	133	126	128	124	122	126	93	147	124	142	128	93	126	129	142
07608	TETERBORO	99	112	108	106	111	105	107	105	109	103	110	78	113	110	109	112	80	106	106	121
07620	ALPINE	258	369	454	387	414	348	297	320	279	331	276	240	386	277	358	268	216	293	281	348
07621	BERGENFIELD	112	150	159	143	156	134	133	133	128	130	131	100	153	129	148	129	97	132	128	148
07624	CLOSTER	170	238	277	237	260	217	201	211	186	213	186	157	241	183	237	180	139	198	192	230
07626	CRESSKILL	176	254	289	248	274	234	207	220	195	214	196	160	254	195	246	194	147	207	206	238
07627	DEMAREST	207	297	352	300	327	276	242	258	227	261	226	191	304	225	289	221	172	240	235	281
07628	DUMONT	107	150	159	141	156	136	128	130	125	124	127	95	151	125	145	128	94	128	128	144
07630	EMERSON	142	206	233	200	222	189	167	177	158	172	159	129	205	158	198	158	119	167	167	193
07631	ENGLEWOOD	137	168	183	167	175	153	164	156	160	159	163	120	182	157	175	161	121	160	153	178
07632	ENGLEWOOD CLIFFS	244	340	410	349	380	309	287	303	260	318	258	229	350	253	340	245	196	280	263	330
07640	HARRINGTON PARK	182	257	292	258	278	236	211	224	197	225	198	166	258	196	250	193	148	209	205	245
07641	HAWORTH	203	287	349	296	321	268	237	254	219	264	217	189	297	213	285	209	165	234	226	277
07642	HILLSDALE	152	217	248	213	235	200	179	189	169	185	170	138	219	168	212	168	127	179	178	206
07643	LITTLE FERRY	93	101	105	100	102	94	109	98	109	100	111	76	113	108	108	112	81	105	102	114
07644	LODI	79	97	101	93	99	89	96	91	96	87	98	68	105	95	100	100	73	94	93	103
07645	MONTVALE	185	250	290	250	273	231	216	225	202	229	202	168	256	197	251	197	150	214	209	248
07646	NEW MILFORD	118	153	169	150	161	138	142	138	133	139	136	107	160	133	156	132	101	138	131	154
07647	NORTHVALE	125	176	193	168	185	162	151	153	148	145	149	112	179	147	172	152	112	150	152	169
07648	NORWOOD	183	261	307	262	287	242	214	228	200	229	200	168	266	198	255	196	151	212	209	248
07649	ORADELL	169	237	278	238	260	219	200	211	187	214	186	155	243	182	237	183	140	198	195	231
07650	PALISADES PARK	94	115	127	114	123	98	119	112	109	117	111	87	125	104	126	106	83	113	101	125
07652	PARAMUS	139	199	224	193	214	182	164	173	155	168	156	126	199	155	193	155	117	164	163	188
07656	PARK RIDGE	161	226	252	222	241	208	190	197	182	193	183	145	229	181	220	182	137	189	187	217
07657	RIDGEFIELD	100	134	146	129	141	118	123	121	118	119	119	91	139	115	136	118	89	120	116	135
07660	RIDGEFIELD PARK	88	111	117	107	114	104	108	102	110	97	113	76	120	108	114	116	84	106	108	117
07661	RIVER EDGE	131	186	204	178	197	171	156	161	151	154	153	118	187	152	180	154	114	156	157	177
07662	ROCHELLE PARK	99	135	143	128	140	123	118	119	117	113	119	87	138	116	132	120	88	118	118	132
07663	SADDLE BROOK	111	149	157	141	154	133	132	131	126	128	128	98	150	127	146	127	95	130	126	146
07666	TEANECK	143	195	214	189	206	178	169	172	162	169	164	128	198	161	192	163	122	168	166	191
07670	TENAFLY	221	305	359	307	337	271	262	274	236	286	235	207	311	230	307	222	177	255	237	298
07675	WESTWOOD	158	213	244	213	230	198	186	191	176	192	177	143	221	174	213	174	132	184	181	211
	NEW JERSEY	119	138	141	137	141	129	132	129	129	132	131	98	143	128	139	129	95	130	128	148
	UNITED STATES	100	100	100	100	100	100	100	100	100	100	100	100	100	100	100	100	100	100	100	100

ZIP CODE #	POST OFFICE NAME	COUNTY FIPS CODE	POPULATION 2000	POPULATION 2009	POPULATION 2014	2000-2009 ANNUAL RATE % Rate	2000-2009 ANNUAL RATE State Centile	HOUSEHOLDS 2000	HOUSEHOLDS 2009	HOUSEHOLDS 2014	HOUSEHOLDS % Annual Rate 2000-2009	HOUSEHOLDS 2009 Average HH Size	FAMILIES 2000	FAMILIES 2009	FAMILIES % Annual Rate 2000-2009
07676	TOWNSHIP OF WASHINGT	003	8605	8967	9121	0.4	56	3080	3207	3261	0.4	2.79	2573	2670	0.4
07677	WOODCLIFF LAKE	003	5665	5782	5827	0.2	43	1796	1836	1853	0.2	3.08	1580	1610	0.2
07701	RED BANK	025	23597	23307	23138	-0.1	19	9820	9745	9689	-0.1	2.35	5776	5620	-0.3
07702	SHREWSBURY	025	3586	3960	4098	1.1	83	1205	1317	1360	1.0	2.99	1013	1098	0.9
07703	FORT MONMOUTH	025	491	534	561	0.9	76	61	81	89	3.1	3.43	58	77	3.1
07704	FAIR HAVEN	025	5981	6036	6009	0.1	35	2015	2016	2006	0.0	2.99	1669	1655	-0.1
07711	ALLENHURST	025	1872	1876	1879	0.0	28	726	734	738	0.1	2.56	514	515	0.0
07712	ASBURY PARK	025	38827	41282	42051	0.7	68	15503	16394	16725	0.6	2.49	9495	9976	0.5
07716	ATLANTIC HIGHLANDS	025	8986	8875	8796	-0.1	19	3651	3647	3627	0.0	2.38	2358	2315	-0.2
07717	AVON BY THE SEA	025	2244	2217	2194	-0.1	19	1043	1042	1034	0.0	2.12	535	521	-0.3
07718	BELFORD	025	6232	6349	6372	0.2	43	2131	2193	2208	0.3	2.89	1759	1804	0.3
07719	BELMAR	025	21880	22069	22082	0.1	35	8947	9059	9082	0.1	2.42	5503	5513	0.0
07720	BRADLEY BEACH	025	4793	4748	4702	-0.1	19	2297	2299	2286	0.0	2.07	1086	1056	-0.3
07721	CLIFFWOOD	025	2641	2891	2975	1.0	80	959	1054	1085	1.0	2.74	675	725	0.8
07722	COLTS NECK	025	10762	10483	10809	-0.3	7	3058	3371	3491	1.1	3.11	2746	3009	1.0
07723	DEAL	025	1517	1512	1502	0.0	28	571	574	573	0.1	2.62	374	370	-0.1
07724	EATONTOWN	025	23278	23279	23447	0.0	28	9283	9368	9446	0.1	2.44	5913	5880	-0.1
07726	ENGLISHTOWN	025	38863	42119	43520	0.9	76	12697	13953	14482	1.0	3.01	10536	11588	1.0
07727	FARMINGDALE	025	6019	6632	7193	1.1	83	2047	2263	2457	1.1	2.91	1529	1685	1.1
07728	FREEHOLD	025	50342	58598	61535	1.7	92	17660	20561	21621	1.7	2.77	13076	15124	1.6
07730	HAZLET	025	18085	17908	17782	-0.1	19	6124	6150	6137	0.0	2.88	4937	4906	-0.1
07731	HOWELL	025	37935	40370	41917	0.7	68	11856	12713	13230	0.8	3.17	9964	10589	0.7
07732	HIGHLANDS	025	4809	4635	4554	-0.4	4	2261	2203	2174	-0.3	2.09	1115	1058	-0.6
07733	HOLMDEL	025	15759	17523	18215	1.2	85	4934	5583	5836	1.3	3.06	4318	4839	1.2
07734	KEANSBURG	025	13923	13722	13593	-0.2	12	4949	4938	4912	0.0	2.74	3399	3335	-0.2
07735	KEYPORT	025	20792	20821	20719	0.0	28	7588	7669	7655	0.1	2.70	5180	5163	0.0
07737	LEONARDO	025	4421	5493	5480	2.4	95	1506	1531	1533	0.2	2.90	1205	1212	0.1
07738	LINCROFT	025	6220	6222	6203	0.0	28	2111	2132	2130	0.1	2.89	1709	1709	0.0
07739	LITTLE SILVER	025	6138	5955	5873	-0.3	7	2228	2188	2167	-0.2	2.72	1804	1755	-0.3
07740	LONG BRANCH	025	31594	32454	32638	0.3	50	12663	13068	13189	0.3	2.47	7304	7348	0.1
07746	MARLBORO	025	17758	20104	20986	1.4	88	5553	6288	6569	1.4	3.18	4948	5592	1.3
07747	MATAWAN	023	28878	30405	31075	0.6	65	10866	11446	11708	0.6	2.64	7926	8287	0.5
07748	MIDDLETOWN	025	27617	28962	29397	0.5	62	9311	9885	10083	0.6	2.93	7552	7928	0.5
07750	MONMOUTH BEACH	025	3590	3541	3518	-0.1	19	1632	1622	1617	-0.1	2.18	975	949	-0.3
07751	MORGANVILLE	025	16603	18294	18875	1.1	83	5167	5708	5900	1.1	3.18	4552	4994	1.0
07753	NEPTUNE	025	35447	36457	36804	0.3	50	13377	13953	14146	0.5	2.56	9170	9394	0.3
07755	OAKHURST	025	6743	6695	6635	-0.1	19	2340	2349	2338	0.0	2.85	1889	1877	-0.1
07756	OCEAN GROVE	025	4263	4094	4027	-0.4	4	2332	2278	2247	-0.3	1.65	787	744	-0.6
07757	OCEANPORT	025	5490	5470	5469	0.0	28	2032	2045	2053	0.1	2.67	1545	1535	-0.1
07758	PORT MONMOUTH	025	5209	5541	5652	0.7	68	1740	1871	1915	0.8	2.96	1376	1462	0.7
07760	RUMSON	025	10029	10042	9981	0.0	28	3839	3848	3831	0.0	2.60	2653	2629	-0.1
07762	SPRING LAKE	025	9532	9713	9762	0.2	43	4342	4455	4487	0.3	2.16	2549	2563	0.1
07764	WEST LONG BRANCH	025	8340	8157	8085	-0.2	12	2499	2497	2481	0.0	2.73	1890	1863	-0.2
07801	DOVER	027	24441	25833	26187	0.6	65	7586	7809	7895	0.3	3.26	5578	5707	0.2
07803	MINE HILL	027	3796	3736	3711	-0.2	12	1404	1388	1381	-0.1	2.69	1069	1048	-0.2
07821	ANDOVER	037	9880	10747	10935	0.9	76	3472	3835	3924	1.1	2.77	2749	3020	1.0
07822	AUGUSTA	037	853	904	935	0.6	65	274	298	310	0.9	2.84	229	247	0.8
07823	BELVIDERE	041	7147	8167	8504	1.5	89	2838	3322	3490	1.7	2.42	1934	2250	1.6
07825	BLAIRSTOWN	041	9080	9957	10344	1.0	80	3211	3597	3754	1.2	2.75	2547	2835	1.2
07826	BRANCHVILLE	037	5896	6324	6468	0.8	73	2114	2309	2370	1.0	2.66	1606	1744	0.9
07827	MONTAGUE	037	3747	4255	4461	1.4	88	1400	1619	1706	1.6	2.62	994	1140	1.5
07828	BUDD LAKE	027	12247	14329	15123	1.7	92	4761	5576	5890	1.7	2.56	3245	3817	1.8
07830	CALIFON	019	6557	7090	7289	0.8	73	2357	2562	2640	0.9	2.76	1923	2079	0.8
07832	COLUMBIA	041	4046	4508	4736	1.2	85	1413	1600	1686	1.4	2.79	1136	1279	1.3
07834	DENVILLE	027	17289	18486	18913	0.7	68	6552	7024	7197	0.8	2.59	4711	5011	0.7
07836	FLANDERS	027	12415	13341	13747	0.8	73	4445	4716	4841	0.6	2.82	3336	3584	0.8
07838	GREAT MEADOWS	041	2913	3322	3510	1.4	88	968	1123	1193	1.6	2.93	791	913	1.6
07840	HACKETTSTOWN	041	26309	28613	29451	0.9	76	10310	11368	11755	1.1	2.47	6896	7646	1.1
07843	HOPATCONG	037	12764	12998	12852	0.2	43	4581	4758	4737	0.4	2.73	3413	3522	0.3
07847	KENVIL	027	1476	1467	1488	-0.1	19	557	559	568	0.0	2.57	407	407	0.0
07848	LAFAYETTE	037	4723	5196	5435	1.0	80	1476	1652	1733	1.2	2.98	1195	1333	1.2
07849	LAKE HOPATCONG	027	7404	9136	9671	2.3	95	2763	3431	3639	2.4	2.66	2027	2493	2.3
07850	LANDING	027	6734	6596	6639	-0.2	12	2350	2308	2330	-0.2	2.86	1729	1682	-0.3
07851	LAYTON	037	518	557	563	0.8	73	188	204	207	0.9	2.73	137	147	0.8
07852	LEDGEWOOD	027	2651	3746	4038	3.8	99	1131	1546	1666	3.4	2.41	859	1162	3.3
07853	LONG VALLEY	027	13646	14522	14896	0.7	68	4383	4688	4822	0.7	3.06	3722	3952	0.7
07856	MOUNT ARLINGTON	027	3463	4582	4911	3.1	97	1490	1959	2104	3.0	2.33	987	1283	2.9
07857	NETCONG	027	3254	3256	3245	0.0	28	1375	1381	1377	0.0	2.35	891	910	0.2
07860	NEWTON	037	25183	26361	26626	0.5	62	9229	9780	9920	0.6	2.60	6655	7051	0.6
07863	OXFORD	041	3662	4048	4235	1.1	83	1308	1466	1541	1.2	2.68	953	1060	1.2
07865	PORT MURRAY	041	2665	2883	2953	0.9	76	925	1011	1038	1.0	2.78	745	809	0.9
07866	ROCKAWAY	027	22815	24454	24833	0.8	73	8225	8956	9143	0.9	2.73	6288	6725	0.7
07869	RANDOLPH	027	24491	25915	26476	0.6	65	8601	9073	9266	0.6	2.85	6749	7109	0.6
07871	SPARTA	037	18733	20086	20565	0.8	73	6464	6947	7118	0.8	2.89	5220	5618	0.8
07874	STANHOPE	037	8874	8925	8866	0.1	35	3088	3158	3157	0.2	2.82	2398	2439	0.2
07876	SUCCASUNNA	027	11150	11672	11885	0.5	62	3614	3803	3882	0.6	3.05	2969	3088	0.4
07882	WASHINGTON	041	14373	15742	16225	1.0	80	5335	5933	6145	1.2	2.64	3799	4180	1.0
07885	WHARTON	027	9900	10087	10550	0.2	43	3688	3747	3929	0.2	2.68	2528	2556	0.1
07901	SUMMIT	039	21894	21920	21766	0.0	28	8166	8055	7965	-0.1	2.72	5834	5716	-0.2
07920	BASKING RIDGE	035	24898	27353	28432	1.0	80	9418	10202	10581	0.9	2.60	6646	7160	0.8
07921	BEDMINSTER	035	7826	8081	8207	0.3	50	4047	4136	4187	0.2	1.95	1982	1982	0.0
07922	BERKELEY HEIGHTS	039	12466	12374	12275	-0.1	19	4149	4075	4028	-0.2	2.95	3436	3362	-0.2
07924	BERNARDSVILLE	035	7228	7587	7760	0.5	62	2677	2785	2844	0.4	2.72	2015	2074	0.3
07927	CEDAR KNOLLS	027	3574	4116	4324	1.5	89	1267	1471	1549	1.6	2.79	982	1134	1.6
07928	CHATHAM	027	18258	18171	18103	-0.1	19	6977	6927	6908	-0.1	2.60	5086	5009	-0.2
07930	CHESTER	027	8220	8849	9098	0.8	73	2695	2910	2997	0.8	2.97	2233	2406	0.8
07931	FAR HILLS	035	3981	4335	4529	0.9	76	1409	1522	1588	0.8	2.76	1079	1155	0.7
07932	FLORHAM PARK	027	8497	11624	12170	3.4	98	3049	3724	3947	2.2	2.64	2343	2801	1.9
07933	GILLETTE	027	3142	3077	3053	-0.2	12	1162	1143	1136	-0.2	2.68	915	894	-0.3
07934	GLADSTONE	035	1435	1593	1675	1.1	83	531	583	612	1.0	2.62	402	436	0.9
07935	GREEN VILLAGE	027	243	254	259	0.5	62	90	94	96	0.5	2.63	64	67	0.5
07936	EAST HANOVER	027	11712	11602	11562	-0.1	19	4017	3987	3984	-0.1	2.89	3335	3296	-0.1
07940	MADISON	027	16577	15519	15477	-0.7	2	5534	5508	5497	-0.1	2.53	3794	3731	-0.2
07945	MENDHAM	027	9449	9754	9812	0.3	50	3173	3255	3272	0.3	2.91	2574	2629	0.2
07946	MILLINGTON	027	3533	3479	3457	-0.2	12	1217	1202	1197	-0.1	2.89	962	944	-0.2
	NEW JERSEY					0.5					0.5	2.69			0.5
	UNITED STATES					1.0					1.1	2.59			0.9

ZIP CODE #	POST OFFICE NAME	RACE (%) White 2000	White 2009	Black 2000	Black 2009	Asian/Pacific 2000	Asian/Pacific 2009	% Hispanic Origin 2000	% Hispanic Origin 2009	2009 AGE DISTRIBUTION (%) 0-4	5-9	10-14	15-19	20-24	25-44	45-64	65-84	85+	18+	MEDIAN AGE 2009	% 2009 Males	% 2009 Females
07676	TOWNSHIP OF WASHINGT	92.0	87.7	1.0	1.3	5.6	9.1	3.3	5.2	6.4	7.0	7.6	5.9	3.3	21.5	29.9	16.5	2.1	75.1	44.1	47.7	52.3
07677	WOODCLIFF LAKE	93.8	90.3	0.9	1.1	4.5	7.3	2.3	3.7	6.1	7.7	9.9	8.4	3.3	16.2	33.5	12.2	2.7	70.4	43.9	48.0	52.0
07701	RED BANK	82.1	78.5	10.6	11.4	2.1	3.0	9.9	13.5	6.0	6.0	6.1	5.5	5.2	25.4	26.8	14.8	4.0	78.4	42.1	48.2	51.8
07702	SHREWSBURY	96.4	94.6	0.7	1.0	1.7	2.6	2.0	3.3	7.3	8.4	9.8	8.3	4.0	18.4	31.8	9.8	2.1	68.6	41.1	50.0	50.0
07703	FORT MONMOUTH	69.2	63.3	21.0	23.8	1.8	2.1	11.8	17.2	1.9	3.7	8.6	27.2	17.0	23.8	16.9	0.9	0.0	80.1	22.5	66.7	33.3
07704	FAIR HAVEN	93.8	91.2	4.2	5.7	1.0	1.5	1.4	2.2	8.3	9.0	9.6	7.6	3.4	21.7	29.8	9.1	1.6	67.6	39.2	48.5	51.5
07711	ALLENHURST	96.4	94.6	1.0	1.4	1.0	1.7	1.4	2.3	5.8	6.1	6.9	5.6	4.6	23.6	32.4	12.7	2.4	77.8	43.4	49.8	50.2
07712	ASBURY PARK	56.7	52.0	31.0	31.9	4.6	6.6	9.8	12.7	7.3	7.0	7.0	7.0	6.5	26.3	26.6	10.3	1.9	74.4	36.8	47.3	52.7
07716	ATLANTIC HIGHLANDS	91.6	88.0	4.5	6.0	1.8	2.7	3.3	5.4	5.5	5.9	6.3	5.8	4.9	23.8	31.6	13.5	2.7	78.6	43.6	48.4	51.6
07717	AVON BY THE SEA	97.1	95.5	0.5	0.8	0.9	1.4	2.4	4.0	5.2	5.0	5.3	4.8	4.7	25.2	28.9	17.5	3.4	81.5	44.9	50.5	49.5
07718	BELFORD	96.2	94.2	0.4	0.6	1.6	2.4	3.9	6.6	6.7	7.0	7.2	6.9	5.2	25.7	29.3	10.7	1.4	74.8	39.6	49.2	50.8
07719	BELMAR	94.1	91.6	2.0	2.6	1.3	2.0	3.8	6.1	6.0	6.1	6.5	6.5	6.0	25.3	30.3	11.3	2.1	77.4	41.0	49.1	50.9
07720	BRADLEY BEACH	88.1	83.5	3.9	4.9	1.5	2.1	12.8	19.2	5.5	5.1	4.8	5.1	5.8	31.4	29.5	10.9	1.9	81.7	40.3	49.7	50.3
07721	CLIFFWOOD	54.1	47.5	35.3	38.7	5.9	7.9	9.4	12.8	6.9	7.0	6.8	6.2	6.7	31.5	25.8	8.2	0.9	75.5	36.3	48.4	51.6
07722	COLTS NECK	90.1	91.1	4.3	1.3	3.6	5.5	3.2	3.8	7.5	8.4	9.1	7.6	3.3	20.2	31.0	11.6	1.3	70.0	41.3	49.2	50.8
07723	DEAL	94.6	91.9	1.0	1.5	0.4	0.7	4.0	6.7	5.4	4.8	5.0	5.6	5.2	21.9	25.7	21.7	4.6	81.3	46.6	47.4	52.6
07724	EATONTOWN	73.8	67.1	13.5	15.7	7.6	10.6	5.7	8.3	7.0	6.6	6.8	5.8	5.1	28.2	27.4	10.9	2.3	76.0	39.1	48.7	51.3
07726	ENGLISHTOWN	91.3	86.9	2.1	3.0	4.9	7.6	3.6	5.9	6.5	7.5	8.7	8.0	4.1	22.1	30.4	10.1	2.5	71.9	40.6	48.4	51.6
07727	FARMINGDALE	91.3	87.1	3.4	4.5	2.3	3.5	4.6	7.4	6.9	7.2	7.7	7.3	5.1	24.4	29.8	10.2	1.4	73.3	39.6	49.2	50.8
07728	FREEHOLD	84.4	80.0	7.0	7.9	4.4	6.5	10.0	13.3	6.6	7.0	7.4	6.6	4.5	25.3	28.3	12.0	2.4	74.8	40.4	49.3	50.7
07730	HAZLET	92.7	89.2	1.1	1.5	3.8	5.7	5.9	9.4	6.3	6.5	6.9	7.0	5.6	23.7	28.9	13.0	2.1	75.9	40.9	47.7	52.3
07731	HOWELL	89.6	85.1	3.7	4.9	3.6	5.4	5.6	9.0	8.0	8.0	8.3	7.8	4.9	27.4	28.3	6.6	0.8	70.5	35.9	49.2	50.8
07732	HIGHLANDS	94.9	92.5	1.6	2.3	1.0	1.6	4.1	6.7	4.8	4.7	4.8	5.3	5.7	30.0	31.6	11.4	1.6	82.5	41.8	50.3	49.7
07733	HOLMDEL	80.2	72.0	0.6	0.8	17.5	24.8	2.5	3.7	5.4	6.4	8.0	8.0	4.8	18.2	34.2	12.7	2.5	75.0	44.5	48.0	52.0
07734	KEANSBURG	93.8	91.0	1.9	2.5	1.3	2.0	7.4	11.9	6.9	6.6	6.5	7.1	7.1	27.0	26.7	10.5	1.7	75.8	36.5	49.0	51.0
07735	KEYPORT	87.5	83.0	6.2	7.7	1.9	2.7	9.5	14.7	6.2	6.4	6.5	6.7	6.2	27.5	28.4	10.3	1.9	76.8	38.9	49.2	50.8
07737	LEONARDO	97.0	87.2	0.7	6.2	0.9	3.1	3.7	7.7	5.2	5.6	6.1	9.7	9.9	25.9	27.5	9.0	1.1	80.1	36.0	51.2	48.8
07738	LINCROFT	93.1	89.5	0.8	1.1	4.5	7.0	2.5	4.1	6.1	7.1	8.0	7.5	4.5	19.4	32.0	13.1	2.4	73.6	43.3	48.9	51.1
07739	LITTLE SILVER	97.1	95.6	0.3	0.4	1.5	2.4	1.3	2.2	6.8	7.7	8.7	7.2	3.9	17.1	32.1	14.1	2.5	72.2	44.1	48.7	51.3
07740	LONG BRANCH	68.3	63.2	18.5	19.8	1.7	2.3	20.5	27.0	6.9	6.5	6.0	6.2	6.9	29.4	24.9	11.1	2.1	76.9	36.8	48.6	51.4
07746	MARLBORO	85.9	79.3	1.8	2.2	11.1	16.8	2.1	3.3	6.2	7.4	8.8	7.9	4.2	22.4	32.6	9.3	1.3	72.5	40.8	49.8	50.2
07747	MATAWAN	82.1	74.8	5.2	6.8	9.6	14.1	5.5	8.6	6.7	6.9	6.9	6.1	4.4	26.7	28.9	11.6	1.8	75.6	40.5	48.3	51.7
07748	MIDDLETOWN	94.5	91.7	0.9	1.2	3.3	5.0	3.4	5.6	6.5	7.0	7.7	7.1	5.1	23.3	31.0	10.8	1.5	74.3	40.5	49.0	51.0
07750	MONMOUTH BEACH	97.7	96.4	0.5	0.7	0.9	1.4	1.9	3.2	5.2	5.8	6.5	5.2	3.1	19.7	33.4	18.4	2.7	79.2	47.7	47.5	52.5
07751	MORGANVILLE	81.4	73.8	2.4	3.1	14.4	20.5	3.8	5.7	8.4	8.4	8.5	7.0	3.4	26.2	28.5	8.6	0.9	70.0	38.1	49.5	50.5
07753	NEPTUNE	59.4	53.8	33.7	37.3	2.1	2.8	5.9	8.0	6.6	6.5	6.3	6.7	6.5	25.7	27.3	11.9	2.4	76.6	39.0	47.4	52.6
07755	OAKHURST	95.1	92.6	0.8	1.2	2.4	3.7	2.1	3.6	6.7	6.8	7.4	7.4	5.4	22.8	29.0	12.5	2.1	74.4	40.6	48.8	51.2
07756	OCEAN GROVE	93.0	89.8	3.9	5.5	1.0	1.5	3.8	6.2	3.0	2.9	2.8	2.9	4.6	26.3	33.3	16.4	7.7	89.5	49.5	46.0	54.0
07757	OCEANPORT	97.6	96.5	0.6	0.8	0.7	1.1	1.5	2.4	5.6	6.1	7.2	6.9	4.9	18.9	33.0	14.9	2.4	76.7	45.2	47.5	52.5
07758	PORT MONMOUTH	95.7	93.4	1.1	1.7	1.1	1.7	5.9	9.8	6.7	6.8	7.2	7.4	5.3	25.9	29.0	9.9	1.7	74.6	38.7	48.7	51.3
07760	RUMSON	96.7	95.0	0.7	1.0	1.4	2.3	2.1	3.5	6.1	6.7	8.2	7.5	4.1	21.6	32.6	11.2	2.0	74.0	42.5	48.9	51.1
07762	SPRING LAKE	97.9	97.0	0.8	1.0	0.3	0.6	1.6	2.6	4.7	4.6	5.3	5.4	4.0	18.4	29.8	23.0	4.7	82.0	50.2	46.3	53.7
07764	WEST LONG BRANCH	94.1	91.6	2.3	3.0	1.3	2.0	3.1	5.0	5.1	5.4	5.9	15.3	12.0	17.9	24.7	11.5	2.3	79.6	33.6	47.1	52.9
07801	DOVER	71.1	66.9	7.0	6.5	3.6	4.5	48.6	58.8	7.0	6.9	6.7	6.7	6.2	30.9	24.7	8.9	1.8	75.4	36.3	50.7	49.3
07803	MINE HILL	90.4	86.3	3.4	4.2	2.6	4.0	8.8	14.5	7.6	8.1	8.2	6.7	4.0	24.1	28.7	11.0	1.6	71.8	40.4	48.6	51.4
07821	ANDOVER	95.7	93.8	1.0	1.3	1.2	1.9	3.3	5.1	7.2	7.3	7.6	6.9	4.1	25.8	30.8	8.8	1.4	73.7	39.9	50.2	49.8
07822	AUGUSTA	97.2	96.2	0.6	0.7	0.8	1.2	1.8	2.7	4.8	6.1	7.7	8.4	3.4	21.9	35.1	10.5	2.1	76.0	43.5	50.7	49.3
07823	BELVIDERE	97.2	96.0	0.8	1.0	0.5	0.9	2.2	3.5	5.8	6.0	6.6	6.6	5.3	23.6	29.5	14.0	2.7	77.5	42.6	48.6	51.4
07825	BLAIRSTOWN	97.9	96.9	0.4	0.5	0.5	0.9	2.1	3.3	5.6	6.4	7.3	7.0	4.2	21.9	33.7	12.2	1.8	76.1	43.5	49.6	50.4
07826	BRANCHVILLE	98.2	97.4	0.3	0.4	0.4	0.6	1.7	2.8	4.9	5.5	6.3	7.4	5.4	21.8	33.3	12.7	2.7	78.4	44.1	48.8	51.2
07827	MONTAGUE	95.5	93.9	1.7	2.0	0.6	1.1	3.1	4.8	6.6	6.8	7.1	7.4	5.6	25.1	29.1	11.1	1.3	74.8	39.6	51.0	49.0
07828	BUDD LAKE	86.4	80.1	3.8	4.7	5.6	8.8	7.4	12.5	7.7	7.3	6.9	6.5	7.4	29.3	26.2	7.7	0.9	74.1	35.4	49.2	50.8
07830	CALIFON	97.3	96.0	0.5	0.7	1.2	2.0	1.5	2.5	5.9	7.1	8.7	7.0	3.1	20.6	35.1	11.5	1.1	73.6	43.6	49.0	51.0
07832	COLUMBIA	97.8	96.8	0.4	0.5	0.6	1.0	1.8	3.0	6.1	6.9	7.8	7.2	3.9	22.7	32.1	11.6	1.7	74.2	42.0	50.1	49.9
07834	DENVILLE	91.3	87.0	1.2	1.6	5.8	9.0	2.9	4.8	6.5	6.9	7.5	6.0	3.8	23.1	30.0	12.4	3.7	75.1	42.9	48.3	51.7
07836	FLANDERS	87.6	82.9	3.7	4.3	6.2	9.2	4.2	6.8	8.5	9.3	9.7	7.1	4.0	26.3	27.6	6.9	0.6	67.6	36.9	50.4	49.6
07838	GREAT MEADOWS	97.3	95.9	0.5	0.6	0.8	1.3	2.5	4.0	6.8	7.7	8.6	8.2	4.4	23.5	32.2	7.5	1.1	71.3	39.4	49.6	50.4
07840	HACKETTSTOWN	92.4	87.7	1.7	3.7	2.5	3.9	5.6	8.5	6.4	6.4	6.5	6.5	5.7	28.1	28.3	10.2	1.8	77.0	38.9	48.3	51.7
07843	HOPATCONG	93.4	91.1	1.9	2.3	1.7	2.5	5.8	8.7	6.7	7.1	7.4	6.9	4.8	28.0	29.6	8.6	0.9	74.4	38.8	49.9	50.1
07847	KENVIL	91.8	87.9	2.2	2.7	3.0	4.8	8.4	13.8	6.1	6.5	6.8	7.0	5.1	26.6	28.5	10.8	2.6	76.0	40.4	48.5	51.5
07848	LAFAYETTE	95.6	93.9	1.3	1.5	1.8	2.8	2.6	4.1	5.8	6.4	7.4	7.8	4.4	21.5	32.6	11.6	2.5	75.1	42.9	48.4	51.6
07849	LAKE HOPATCONG	95.8	93.8	0.8	1.2	0.9	1.5	4.3	7.3	6.1	6.6	7.1	7.1	4.7	25.8	31.6	9.8	1.3	75.8	40.7	49.5	50.5
07850	LANDING	91.8	86.9	2.4	4.5	3.1	4.5	6.5	11.1	6.9	7.1	7.1	7.7	7.0	24.4	29.2	9.7	1.0	75.0	38.7	47.2	52.8
07851	LAYTON	97.9	96.8	0.4	0.5	0.6	0.9	1.4	2.0	5.4	5.9	6.5	7.9	5.7	21.4	33.2	12.0	2.0	77.0	42.9	50.6	49.4
07852	LEDGEWOOD	92.6	89.2	2.0	2.7	3.8	5.7	4.0	7.0	6.6	7.3	7.9	6.9	4.5	23.9	30.9	10.4	1.6	73.5	41.2	48.7	51.3
07853	LONG VALLEY	96.3	94.2	0.8	1.0	1.9	3.2	2.1	3.8	6.3	7.5	8.8	8.2	4.0	20.9	34.0	8.4	1.9	71.8	41.5	49.1	50.9
07856	MOUNT ARLINGTON	91.4	87.5	1.6	2.1	4.0	6.1	4.8	8.1	6.1	6.4	6.5	6.0	4.8	26.4	30.3	12.2	1.4	77.3	41.6	47.4	52.6
07857	NETCONG	92.5	84.5	2.2	6.1	2.2	4.0	7.9	12.5	5.6	5.5	5.2	5.5	6.3	34.4	25.7	10.0	1.8	80.6	36.9	50.4	49.6
07860	NEWTON	95.3	93.6	1.7	2.0	1.3	2.0	2.6	4.0	5.9	6.4	6.9	6.8	5.3	24.3	30.6	11.3	2.4	76.4	41.3	48.6	51.4
07863	OXFORD	96.5	95.0	1.1	1.4	0.6	1.0	2.9	4.7	6.2	6.9	7.6	7.4	4.0	24.1	30.5	11.0	2.4	74.6	41.7	48.4	51.6
07865	PORT MURRAY	89.7	87.5	7.7	8.8	0.7	1.1	2.4	3.5	5.5	6.5	7.4	7.4	4.6	22.5	32.8	11.1	2.4	75.9	42.6	48.4	51.6
07866	ROCKAWAY	89.4	84.3	2.0	2.5	5.9	8.9	6.1	10.0	6.9	7.3	7.8	6.8	4.7	25.7	29.8	9.8	1.3	73.6	40.0	49.3	50.7
07869	RANDOLPH	85.5	79.8	2.4	2.8	9.2	13.4	5.0	7.7	6.8	7.7	9.0	7.9	4.1	24.0	31.4	8.1	1.0	71.0	39.2	49.5	50.5
07871	SPARTA	96.6	95.1	0.3	0.4	1.4	2.2	2.5	3.9	7.2	8.1	9.0	7.8	3.8	22.0	31.8	9.0	1.3	70.8	40.4	49.4	50.6
07874	STANHOPE	93.7	91.4	1.5	1.8	1.9	2.8	4.5	6.7	6.7	7.1	7.5	6.9	4.5	27.2	31.2	8.1	0.8	74.4	39.1	48.0	52.0
07876	SUCCASUNNA	93.4	89.8	1.3	1.6	4.0	6.6	3.2	5.4	6.2	6.7	7.8	7.6	4.6	21.9	32.5	11.1	1.6	74.2	42.0	48.9	51.1
07882	WASHINGTON	93.8	91.5	2.8	3.4	1.2	1.9	3.1	4.9	6.4	6.8	7.2	7.5	5.9	25.1	29.9	9.7	1.6	74.7	39.3	49.2	50.8
07885	WHARTON	86.4	81.9	3.5	3.9	2.7	3.9	16.3	23.8	6.9	6.9	6.9	6.8	5.8	27.2	27.9	9.9	1.6	75.0	38.4	48.7	51.3
07901	SUMMIT	87.9	83.1	4.2	5.2	4.6	6.7	9.9	15.7	8.0	8.2	8.9	6.5	3.9	24.5	28.0	9.8	2.1	70.5	39.5	49.3	50.7
07920	BASKING RIDGE	89.5	84.3	1.4	1.7	7.6	11.8	2.6	4.4	6.8	8.1	9.6	7.5	3.8	19.3	32.1	11.0	1.9	70.1	42.2	49.3	50.7
07921	BEDMINSTER	90.0	85.6	1.8	2.2	6.5	9.7	3.8	6.4	5.2	5.2	5.4	4.6	5.8	28.0	32.8	11.7	1.3	81.1	43.0	46.2	53.8
07922	BERKELEY HEIGHTS	90.1	85.0	0.9	1.2	7.6	11.7	3.8	6.6	7.4	8.2	9.1	6.7	3.3	20.3	28.8	13.0	3.1	70.5	42.2	48.0	52.0
07924	BERNARDSVILLE	93.9	90.7	0.2	0.3	2.6	4.0	6.0	9.8	6.7	7.9	9.3	6.9	3.3	20.9	31.8	11.5	1.6	71.3	42.4	49.6	50.4
07927	CEDAR KNOLLS	90.0	84.6	1.1	1.4	7.4	11.6	3.8	6.4	5.7	6.0	6.5	5.7	4.8	25.1	31.0	13.2	2.2	78.1	42.9	49.9	50.1
07928	CHATHAM	94.7	91.6	0.3	0.4	3.9	6.4	2.3	3.9	7.8	8.6	9.7	6.7	3.6	20.8	29.7	10.9	2.2	69.2	41.2	48.1	51.9
07930	CHESTER	95.0	92.3	1.1	1.4	2.3	3.8	3.4	5.8	6.5	7.7	9.6	7.9	3.6	19.0	33.2	11.1	1.5	70.1	42.5	49.6	50.4
07931	FAR HILLS	92.8	89.5	1.7	2.2	4.2	6.5	3.3	5.6	6.4	7.6	8.9	6.9	3.1	20.3	32.6	12.4	1.8	72.4	43.1	48.7	51.3
07932	FLORHAM PARK	94.1	84.9	1.0	5.0	3.9	7.1	2.1	5.5	5.4	5.4	5.8	7.5	7.7	23.1	27.0	14.9	3.2	81.8	41.3	48.2	51.8
07933	GILLETTE	92.0	87.7	0.4	0.6	5.2	8.3	3.7	6.2	6.3	7.0	8.1	7.1	3.6	20.9	32.8	12.4	1.7	73.9	43.2	48.2	51.8
07934	GLADSTONE	95.3	93.3	2.2	2.9	1.2	1.8	3.6	6.3	6.3	7.2	8.1	7.5	4.8	20.7	32.0	11.4	2.0	73.1	42.0	48.7	51.3
07935	GREEN VILLAGE	95.1	92.1	0.4	0.4	3.3	5.5	2.1	3.1	6.3	6.7	7.5	6.3	3.9	19.3	31.1	15.0	3.9	74.8	45.0	48.4	51.6
07936	EAST HANOVER	87.2	80.5	0.6	0.9	10.9	16.8	2.7	4.5	5.9	6.3	7.0	6.0	3.8	23.7	29.9	15.5	2.0	77.0	43.3	48.5	51.5
07940	MADISON	89.7	84.8	3.0	4.1	4.0	6.6	6.0	9.8	5.8	5.9	6.4	10.2	10.1	23.8	25.0	10.6	2.3	78.4	36.4	48.2	51.8
07945	MENDHAM	96.2	94.1	0.7	1.0	2.0	3.4	2.1	3.7	6.2	7.7	9.6	8.7	3.3	16.2	32.9	12.9	2.5	70.4	43.8	48.8	51.2
07946	MILLINGTON	93.7	90.2	0.3	0.3	4.4	7.2	2.9	5.1	7.2	8.6	9.7	7.3	3.2	19.9	31.1	11.3	1.7	69.6	41.6	48.7	51.3
	NEW JERSEY	72.6	68.2	13.6	14.0	5.7	7.9	13.3	16.9	6.6	6.6	6.7	6.8	6.2	26.4	27.0	11.5	2.2	76.0	38.7	48.7	51.3
	UNITED STATES	75.1	72.0	12.3	12.7	3.8	4.6	12.5	15.7	6.8	6.7	6.6	7.1	6.9	27.0	26.0	10.9	1.9	75.7	36.9	49.2	50.8

ZIP CODE #	POST OFFICE NAME	2009 Per Capita Income	2009 HH Income Base	2009 Household Income Distribution (%) Less than $25,000	$25,000 to $49,999	$50,000 to $99,999	$100,000 to $149,999	$150,000 or More	Median Household Income 2009	2014	2009 National Centile	2009 State Centile	2009 Home Value Base	2009 Home Value Distribution (%) Less than $50,000	$50,000 to $89,999	$90,000 to $174,999	$175,000 to $399,999	$400,000 or More	2009 Median Home Value
07676	TOWNSHIP OF WASHINGT	49308	3207	4.2	11.8	29.3	25.6	29.2	108458	112562	98	82	2981	0.0	0.1	0.1	12.3	87.6	577940
07677	WOODCLIFF LAKE	64325	1836	4.1	9.5	18.8	14.9	52.7	158855	164058	100	98	1691	0.0	0.2	0.4	6.4	93.0	839026
07701	RED BANK	39338	9745	14.2	20.1	30.7	21.9	13.2	76959	79828	91	48	6611	0.1	0.3	5.8	47.2	46.6	383538
07702	SHREWSBURY	46760	1317	3.9	9.0	32.0	21.9	33.3	110028	112884	98	83	1221	0.0	0.0	0.0	26.5	73.5	543953
07703	FORT MONMOUTH	29223	81	0.0	0.0	13.6	61.7	24.7	133183	133450	99	94	20	0.0	0.0	0.0	25.0	75.0	450000
07704	FAIR HAVEN	53658	2016	6.0	9.9	24.9	19.1	40.1	124521	126112	99	88	1835	0.0	0.0	0.1	13.6	86.3	634804
07711	ALLENHURST	54710	734	6.5	8.7	24.9	31.6	28.2	115207	120239	98	86	596	0.0	0.0	0.8	23.0	76.2	555851
07712	ASBURY PARK	30636	16394	25.9	23.1	26.6	13.7	10.8	51124	51578	64	12	7368	0.1	0.8	7.9	44.8	46.4	384682
07716	ATLANTIC HIGHLANDS	47171	3647	10.0	14.1	32.3	25.7	17.9	87589	92759	95	66	2514	0.2	0.3	3.3	45.3	50.8	405222
07717	AVON BY THE SEA	52035	1042	10.1	20.3	31.7	19.4	18.5	78405	79368	91	51	627	0.0	0.0	0.8	18.2	81.0	651974
07718	BELFORD	35185	2193	7.5	13.3	43.2	21.1	14.9	83460	85091	93	61	1953	0.3	0.1	1.9	72.9	24.8	335752
07719	BELMAR	38930	9059	11.8	19.3	35.2	20.1	13.6	76190	79357	90	46	6336	0.6	0.2	3.2	48.3	47.6	389265
07720	BRADLEY BEACH	31758	2299	18.9	27.6	37.5	11.3	4.8	52199	51543	66	14	977	0.0	0.4	10.2	51.9	37.5	338442
07721	CLIFFWOOD	31525	1054	9.0	19.4	43.1	20.3	8.3	70203	72105	87	37	638	0.0	1.6	2.5	85.7	10.2	282961
07722	COLTS NECK	69774	3371	3.8	6.3	19.6	16.1	54.1	165685	174728	100	98	3108	0.0	0.3	1.7	4.9	93.1	829073
07723	DEAL	40551	574	20.9	18.3	23.5	20.2	17.1	75253	81420	89	44	374	0.0	0.0	0.3	11.5	88.2	897321
07724	EATONTOWN	37240	9368	11.5	19.8	35.5	20.0	13.2	75884	78172	90	46	5690	2.9	2.8	6.5	46.1	41.7	363174
07726	ENGLISHTOWN	45409	13953	9.5	10.7	24.9	23.3	31.5	110306	114345	98	84	12713	0.2	0.2	9.3	24.4	65.9	491833
07727	FARMINGDALE	32188	2263	11.1	18.8	36.1	21.1	12.8	77667	80566	91	50	1703	0.8	0.3	0.8	50.5	47.6	388310
07728	FREEHOLD	38542	20561	11.3	15.2	31.5	22.5	19.5	85963	92265	94	65	16646	0.7	0.6	8.6	42.7	47.3	385842
07730	HAZLET	33073	6150	10.7	15.1	36.8	26.1	11.2	82897	86601	93	60	5386	2.1	1.5	4.8	57.6	34.0	359550
07731	HOWELL	33402	12713	7.4	11.4	37.6	27.5	16.0	90623	97629	95	69	11163	0.7	1.9	4.6	59.5	33.3	349485
07732	HIGHLANDS	34473	2203	18.7	24.2	37.6	11.5	7.9	55749	53853	72	18	1230	2.4	1.6	17.0	64.0	15.0	266531
07733	HOLMDEL	59875	5583	7.1	8.8	16.6	19.5	48.1	144518	148689	100	97	5144	0.7	1.7	6.7	8.3	82.6	744515
07734	KEANSBURG	23396	4938	25.1	23.6	31.3	14.6	5.4	51360	51706	65	13	3016	1.1	2.1	18.0	72.1	6.8	231052
07735	KEYPORT	28601	7669	14.8	19.7	39.6	19.0	6.9	65913	63747	84	31	5279	0.2	0.5	7.3	84.4	7.7	269984
07737	LEONARDO	34544	1531	5.5	12.6	38.6	24.8	18.5	90246	95362	95	69	1333	0.7	0.0	4.3	55.7	39.3	359972
07738	LINCROFT	48212	2132	13.0	9.1	18.8	26.4	32.7	122194	124154	99	88	1801	0.0	0.3	0.0	14.4	85.3	598313
07739	LITTLE SILVER	58624	2188	2.5	7.6	28.5	27.1	34.4	124635	124360	99	88	2051	0.0	0.0	0.0	10.8	89.2	625153
07740	LONG BRANCH	25443	13068	26.2	25.5	31.6	11.2	5.4	48192	49575	57	11	5612	0.4	0.4	8.4	67.4	23.5	285525
07746	MARLBORO	51787	6288	5.2	8.1	22.2	21.0	43.5	134097	137233	99	94	5943	0.5	0.5	2.1	12.2	84.7	602171
07747	MATAWAN	41004	11446	8.9	12.8	33.7	25.4	19.1	91015	97319	95	70	8620	0.1	0.4	7.2	50.0	42.3	371931
07748	MIDDLETOWN	44928	9885	8.6	10.2	31.2	24.0	26.0	100008	105131	97	76	8116	0.0	0.2	1.5	34.5	63.8	474966
07750	MONMOUTH BEACH	65884	1622	6.6	8.4	26.9	29.0	29.1	110594	113127	98	84	1309	0.4	0.2	2.4	33.1	63.9	536204
07751	MORGANVILLE	52753	5708	6.3	6.6	22.5	21.6	43.0	132668	131168	99	93	5325	0.5	0.6	3.2	23.3	72.5	572705
07753	NEPTUNE	29711	13953	16.6	20.8	36.5	18.6	7.6	63511	58532	82	28	9592	0.4	0.6	6.5	78.0	14.5	284028
07755	OAKHURST	36002	2349	6.6	14.6	36.7	26.7	15.5	88599	93737	95	68	2064	0.0	0.2	0.4	49.3	50.0	400182
07756	OCEAN GROVE	33625	2278	28.4	30.3	28.9	7.3	5.1	40609	42682	35	5	987	0.0	0.0	10.6	58.2	31.2	309069
07757	OCEANPORT	42946	2045	7.9	11.1	38.1	21.8	21.0	89832	92262	95	68	1765	0.3	0.0	0.5	33.7	65.5	476184
07758	PORT MONMOUTH	33238	1871	11.6	18.0	38.7	19.7	12.0	77500	81208	91	49	1552	0.0	0.2	2.8	73.4	23.6	322538
07760	RUMSON	70928	3848	7.6	10.2	23.0	19.0	40.2	125215	123934	99	89	2995	0.0	0.0	2.3	19.4	78.3	723133
07762	SPRING LAKE	50828	4455	13.6	17.7	31.6	19.5	17.7	77076	82020	91	49	3050	0.4	0.2	0.5	23.3	75.6	615172
07764	WEST LONG BRANCH	36670	2497	10.8	15.0	32.0	21.4	20.8	86555	92466	94	65	2060	0.1	0.0	0.9	43.2	55.7	427442
07801	DOVER	26130	7809	14.2	19.0	33.7	21.3	11.8	72073	70470	88	40	4606	0.0	0.6	2.9	78.0	18.4	298082
07803	MINE HILL	35868	1388	9.1	16.3	35.9	24.1	14.6	81400	80591	93	58	1220	0.4	0.3	3.2	83.9	12.1	295257
07821	ANDOVER	43907	3835	6.0	10.6	31.6	26.3	25.6	102873	107070	97	78	3276	0.2	0.0	6.3	55.7	37.9	356000
07822	AUGUSTA	38398	298	8.1	7.7	28.2	36.9	19.1	110041	111940	98	84	264	0.0	0.0	5.7	42.0	52.3	407500
07823	BELVIDERE	31309	3322	17.0	18.4	41.4	15.1	8.1	68289	71961	86	35	2484	0.3	1.3	11.0	69.1	18.3	279600
07825	BLAIRSTOWN	36954	3597	8.8	13.3	38.2	25.2	14.4	85659	94282	94	64	3049	0.1	0.6	2.8	49.0	47.5	391474
07826	BRANCHVILLE	33571	2309	13.6	15.7	35.6	23.3	11.8	79570	82275	92	54	1947	0.2	0.3	5.9	57.5	36.2	344525
07827	MONTAGUE	27056	1619	18.7	21.5	39.7	15.2	4.9	61811	60703	80	26	1204	0.6	2.2	25.2	63.0	9.1	229025
07828	BUDD LAKE	33576	5576	9.5	18.9	40.1	22.0	9.5	71728	68676	88	39	2794	0.0	0.0	4.3	62.3	33.4	332263
07830	CALIFON	62192	2562	5.9	10.7	18.7	22.2	42.6	129610	138978	99	92	2253	0.3	0.0	0.6	26.1	73.0	571396
07832	COLUMBIA	33463	1600	8.6	12.8	41.9	25.5	11.2	83872	91204	93	61	1383	1.8	0.1	2.4	50.1	45.6	383773
07834	DENVILLE	51470	7024	7.0	11.7	27.7	26.4	27.1	105056	115086	97	79	5882	0.1	0.0	1.9	45.1	52.9	416168
07836	FLANDERS	46899	4716	3.0	9.4	31.9	29.7	26.0	106502	113200	97	80	3128	0.0	0.0	0.2	43.5	56.3	439558
07838	GREAT MEADOWS	32534	1123	6.6	11.4	46.2	24.0	11.8	84590	92228	94	62	992	0.0	1.2	4.5	56.7	37.6	361563
07840	HACKETTSTOWN	38845	11368	9.4	15.9	40.1	20.8	13.9	79285	83932	92	53	7576	0.1	0.1	4.7	62.9	32.2	335235
07843	HOPATCONG	34883	4758	8.6	14.5	40.1	25.1	11.7	82143	87768	93	59	4083	0.0	0.4	11.8	76.4	11.3	261536
07847	KENVIL	35369	559	12.5	18.2	31.8	22.4	15.0	74131	75000	89	42	444	1.8	0.0	1.8	77.5	18.9	293534
07848	LAFAYETTE	40039	1652	5.4	11.4	29.1	25.3	28.9	107043	111420	98	81	1386	0.5	0.1	7.9	35.1	56.3	449718
07849	LAKE HOPATCONG	37209	3431	8.9	12.6	39.6	25.2	13.6	82794	84064	93	60	2912	0.7	0.6	7.1	73.8	17.8	290089
07850	LANDING	31205	2308	10.6	18.7	34.9	24.8	11.0	76066	75692	90	46	1773	0.0	0.1	1.1	86.0	12.9	288653
07851	LAYTON	31002	204	12.7	18.1	42.6	16.2	10.3	75642	76949	90	45	178	0.6	1.1	10.7	65.7	21.9	283333
07852	LEDGEWOOD	50385	1546	6.5	13.3	28.3	27.7	24.2	102195	107563	97	78	1343	0.2	0.1	0.8	51.5	47.4	386852
07853	LONG VALLEY	52107	4688	5.7	8.2	16.7	28.6	40.8	132674	139458	99	93	4089	0.3	0.4	0.4	27.2	71.7	515388
07856	MOUNT ARLINGTON	41808	1959	9.3	14.0	34.4	30.8	11.6	84297	84287	94	62	1537	0.9	0.7	5.2	71.6	21.5	314047
07857	NETCONG	34349	1381	14.0	20.0	32.4	24.7	9.0	71233	72136	87	39	872	0.0	0.0	6.5	83.0	10.4	269406
07860	NEWTON	34874	9780	12.8	16.3	35.4	21.1	14.4	78974	83323	92	52	7317	0.4	0.8	6.6	62.0	30.3	305900
07863	OXFORD	30333	1466	11.7	14.8	44.9	21.9	6.8	77321	83243	91	49	1233	4.1	4.1	13.8	58.0	20.1	264623
07865	PORT MURRAY	39236	1011	5.8	12.6	35.0	25.6	21.0	93882	103009	96	71	866	0.1	0.8	7.0	47.6	44.5	378855
07866	ROCKAWAY	43873	8956	7.3	11.6	29.4	28.7	23.0	101982	107229	97	77	7242	0.2	0.2	3.0	58.4	38.3	368495
07869	RANDOLPH	63412	9073	3.8	8.4	22.2	21.7	43.8	130727	141479	99	92	6679	0.1	0.1	0.5	17.4	81.9	609643
07871	SPARTA	50219	6947	6.2	7.7	24.2	25.2	36.8	125222	125679	99	89	6195	0.1	0.0	1.7	36.3	61.8	469336
07874	STANHOPE	36574	3158	5.3	11.6	41.1	26.3	15.7	88222	95310	95	67	2759	0.0	0.4	9.8	71.4	18.4	290489
07876	SUCCASUNNA	42411	3803	6.5	9.7	26.4	29.8	27.6	109035	121008	98	83	3423	0.6	0.2	0.4	47.2	51.5	406197
07882	WASHINGTON	33683	5933	12.4	16.0	39.5	20.9	11.1	77939	83134	91	50	4078	1.0	0.6	9.0	65.9	23.5	281456
07885	WHARTON	33789	3747	12.0	18.0	29.6	28.8	11.6	79453	78101	92	53	2702	1.0	0.5	4.3	71.7	22.6	310507
07901	SUMMIT	68266	8055	8.9	9.4	21.5	20.7	39.5	125552	125439	99	89	5486	0.1	0.2	1.8	7.7	90.2	834010
07920	BASKING RIDGE	69516	10202	5.3	6.8	21.2	20.1	46.6	139107	147686	99	96	8667	0.0	0.2	1.2	16.4	82.2	686467
07921	BEDMINSTER	68874	4136	7.9	10.9	33.8	22.4	25.1	95279	99223	96	73	3269	0.2	1.1	8.2	38.1	52.4	412119
07922	BERKELEY HEIGHTS	55753	4075	5.4	7.0	24.9	18.3	44.4	131096	129368	99	92	3567	0.1	0.4	1.0	5.6	93.0	666411
07924	BERNARDSVILLE	74062	2785	4.3	10.0	21.7	16.3	47.7	139440	152397	99	96	2277	0.0	0.1	1.8	8.5	89.6	770944
07927	CEDAR KNOLLS	45059	1471	4.3	14.1	24.4	29.2	28.0	108473	119819	98	82	1289	0.4	0.4	1.5	34.9	62.8	473230
07928	CHATHAM	79022	6927	4.0	7.4	19.6	21.7	47.3	142212	149968	99	96	5583	0.0	0.4	0.7	13.8	85.2	686042
07930	CHESTER	64877	2910	5.1	8.2	17.3	17.8	51.6	154328	165114	100	97	2556	0.3	0.4	0.3	11.6	87.4	692509
07931	FAR HILLS	77875	1522	4.4	7.9	19.0	16.7	52.0	156577	163890	100	98	1243	0.2	0.3	3.3	6.8	89.3	809593
07932	FLORHAM PARK	54083	3724	6.0	12.8	17.9	27.3	36.1	123786	131912	99	88	3147	0.0	0.3	0.2	15.1	84.4	595166
07933	GILLETTE	62132	1143	7.3	12.6	19.2	23.0	37.9	119226	129218	98	88	1008	0.1	0.3	0.3	24.6	74.7	552147
07934	GLADSTONE	70692	583	4.8	7.0	23.2	23.7	41.3	129459	137799	99	92	440	0.2	0.0	0.7	5.5	93.6	805851
07935	GREEN VILLAGE	79786	94	5.3	11.7	19.1	19.1	44.7	134965	145396	99	94	68	0.0	0.0	0.0	4.4	95.6	875000
07936	EAST HANOVER	44634	3987	6.7	8.7	26.3	32.2	26.1	108922	118904	98	82	3638	0.0	0.6	2.5	17.7	79.2	582229
07940	MADISON	55855	5508	8.0	12.4	21.6	22.3	35.8	116505	128674	98	87	3668	0.0	0.0	0.1	9.6	90.3	661156
07945	MENDHAM	69993	3255	6.5	7.3	15.2	17.0	54.0	160243	165788	100	98	2849	0.0	0.2	0.8	7.3	91.8	788556
07946	MILLINGTON	59723	1202	6.2	9.8	18.4	23.9	41.8	129417	140029	99	92	1023	0.0	0.5	0.2	20.1	79.2	591776
	NEW JERSEY	34433		15.4	18.6	34.9	16.8	14.2	72609	76895				1.0	1.6	9.9	50.1	37.4	336585
	UNITED STATES	27277		20.9	24.4	35.3	11.7	7.6	54719	56938				9.3	13.1	31.6	32.6	13.5	162279

ZIP CODE #	POST OFFICE NAME	FINANCIAL SERVICES: Auto Loan	FINANCIAL SERVICES: Home Loan	FINANCIAL SERVICES: Invest-ments	FINANCIAL SERVICES: Retire-ment Plans	THE HOME: Home Improvements: Home Repair	THE HOME: Home Improvements: Lawn & Garden	THE HOME: Furnishings: Comput-ers & Hard-ware-Personal	THE HOME: Furnishings: Major Appli-ances	THE HOME: Furnishings: TV, Radio, Sound Equip-ment	THE HOME: Furnishings: Furni-ture	ENTERTAINMENT: Dine out/ Carry out	ENTERTAINMENT: Sports Equip-ment	ENTERTAINMENT: Fees & Tickets	ENTERTAINMENT: Toys & Games	ENTERTAINMENT: Travel	ENTERTAINMENT: Cable TV	PERSONAL: Apparel & Services	PERSONAL: Auto Repairs	PERSONAL: Health Insur-ance	PERSONAL: Pets & Supplies
07676	TOWNSHIP OF WASHINGT	162	232	268	229	253	214	190	202	179	200	178	148	233	177	227	176	134	190	188	220
07677	WOODCLIFF LAKE	238	338	413	351	378	316	276	297	257	308	254	221	351	252	332	245	196	272	263	323
07701	RED BANK	118	137	145	135	143	134	131	130	129	132	130	97	143	126	140	130	93	131	135	149
07702	SHREWSBURY	164	237	273	234	257	220	192	204	182	199	182	150	239	183	228	181	138	191	190	221
07703	FORT MONMOUTH	190	234	208	238	230	194	195	198	180	215	183	162	222	194	207	167	135	182	165	220
07704	FAIR HAVEN	190	271	313	274	295	251	220	234	207	235	207	174	275	207	261	203	157	218	213	256
07711	ALLENHURST	170	228	258	228	246	202	200	204	182	211	183	157	231	180	229	174	136	195	181	225
07712	ASBURY PARK	99	99	102	102	100	96	110	99	110	106	111	78	112	108	108	111	80	107	104	119
07716	ATLANTIC HIGHLANDS	143	179	186	176	185	161	162	162	153	165	154	125	181	153	177	150	113	159	152	183
07717	AVON BY THE SEA	138	173	203	176	191	149	165	163	144	177	145	130	180	139	184	132	107	157	137	181
07718	BELFORD	121	171	179	159	178	152	141	147	135	141	136	108	167	136	162	136	101	141	139	161
07719	BELMAR	118	146	151	143	150	133	134	133	128	135	130	102	149	128	145	127	95	132	127	151
07720	BRADLEY BEACH	85	90	89	90	90	85	95	88	93	92	94	70	97	92	95	93	67	93	90	104
07721	CLIFFWOOD	114	130	125	129	129	119	124	120	119	124	121	94	132	121	128	118	87	121	116	139
07722	COLTS NECK	269	366	415	380	397	333	301	318	279	336	278	244	372	281	351	264	212	292	277	349
07723	DEAL	137	158	192	158	175	161	148	157	144	159	143	112	162	135	166	144	102	153	160	177
07724	EATONTOWN	120	136	136	135	137	127	130	126	127	130	128	98	140	129	136	126	92	128	126	145
07726	ENGLISHTOWN	173	224	234	227	234	210	188	198	181	202	182	149	223	181	214	177	133	187	188	222
07727	FARMINGDALE	118	154	152	149	155	137	132	134	126	133	128	102	151	128	146	125	93	130	127	151
07728	FREEHOLD	137	171	176	170	177	160	150	155	146	156	147	116	172	145	166	145	107	150	152	174
07730	HAZLET	113	155	163	146	161	142	132	136	129	130	130	99	154	129	149	131	96	133	134	150
07731	HOWELL	144	173	158	171	170	151	151	152	143	157	145	119	166	149	160	138	104	146	138	173
07732	HIGHLANDS	96	100	96	102	99	95	105	97	102	103	104	77	107	102	104	102	73	102	99	116
07733	HOLMDEL	225	312	367	319	344	279	263	276	238	289	238	211	320	235	309	224	181	256	237	301
07734	KEANSBURG	81	92	90	90	91	87	91	87	91	87	91	67	96	90	94	92	66	90	90	102
07735	KEYPORT	97	118	116	114	119	111	108	109	106	108	107	81	119	105	117	107	77	108	111	123
07737	LEONARDO	134	188	198	179	196	168	154	161	147	156	149	119	184	149	178	147	110	154	151	177
07738	LINCROFT	172	222	242	226	235	213	192	200	187	203	187	149	226	182	218	186	137	192	198	225
07739	LITTLE SILVER	189	268	315	268	294	247	222	236	206	239	205	173	271	201	265	200	154	220	216	257
07740	LONG BRANCH	80	83	82	83	83	79	90	83	90	87	91	65	92	88	89	91	65	88	87	98
07746	MARLBORO	209	280	290	289	290	250	229	239	215	246	217	186	276	220	261	206	162	222	210	267
07747	MATAWAN	138	172	176	169	177	159	151	154	147	156	148	116	172	148	167	146	108	150	150	174
07748	MIDDLETOWN	161	216	232	212	227	195	184	189	174	190	175	142	216	175	209	171	130	181	176	210
07750	MONMOUTH BEACH	183	227	268	231	249	217	203	214	190	221	189	158	230	182	232	183	137	203	200	240
07751	MORGANVILLE	221	287	279	294	290	250	236	244	220	256	223	193	278	229	262	209	166	226	211	273
07753	NEPTUNE	100	113	110	111	113	107	108	105	107	106	108	81	116	108	112	108	77	107	107	122
07755	OAKHURST	123	171	180	162	178	155	141	148	136	143	137	109	168	137	162	137	101	142	142	162
07756	OCEAN GROVE	78	74	76	77	75	75	83	76	83	82	84	60	82	81	81	84	59	82	83	92
07757	OCEANPORT	136	183	207	180	197	176	157	165	153	162	152	119	187	149	182	154	112	159	166	182
07758	PORT MONMOUTH	120	160	163	152	164	146	136	141	132	137	133	104	157	132	153	133	97	136	138	157
07760	RUMSON	227	293	337	302	317	274	259	264	244	275	245	202	306	242	293	237	184	253	243	295
07762	SPRING LAKE	133	167	189	165	181	168	151	159	150	158	149	112	173	141	172	152	107	155	168	178
07764	WEST LONG BRANCH	131	183	195	174	191	165	153	159	146	154	147	117	181	147	176	146	109	153	151	175
07801	DOVER	110	130	126	120	134	104	127	122	114	130	118	96	131	115	132	107	87	122	104	132
07803	MINE HILL	115	162	168	150	168	143	134	139	128	133	129	102	158	130	153	129	96	134	132	152
07821	ANDOVER	160	203	191	203	202	181	172	176	163	180	166	137	196	168	188	159	120	167	162	200
07822	AUGUSTA	148	184	189	189	189	174	157	166	150	167	152	123	179	150	176	148	109	157	157	190
07823	BELVIDERE	96	116	114	114	117	112	105	107	105	106	106	80	117	103	114	107	75	106	112	123
07825	BLAIRSTOWN	133	168	166	168	170	155	142	149	136	148	138	112	162	137	158	134	99	141	140	169
07826	BRANCHVILLE	113	147	150	143	151	134	126	130	121	129	122	97	144	122	141	120	89	126	124	147
07827	MONTAGUE	93	109	100	108	107	103	101	100	98	99	99	78	108	100	106	98	70	99	99	117
07828	BUDD LAKE	123	121	108	123	116	112	126	116	122	127	124	94	125	125	121	119	87	122	114	139
07830	CALIFON	211	287	324	295	309	268	236	251	223	256	223	188	289	222	276	217	168	234	229	279
07832	COLUMBIA	127	153	141	156	151	142	132	136	126	137	128	106	146	129	143	124	91	130	128	158
07834	DENVILLE	159	222	245	215	236	205	185	194	178	189	179	142	222	177	214	178	133	185	187	212
07836	FLANDERS	177	209	210	215	212	188	188	186	178	197	181	147	211	184	201	172	133	181	169	213
07838	GREAT MEADOWS	129	161	142	161	156	141	135	138	128	142	130	109	152	133	146	123	93	132	125	159
07840	HACKETTSTOWN	129	148	144	151	148	137	138	135	133	141	135	106	149	135	145	130	97	134	130	158
07843	HOPATCONG	124	157	147	152	155	138	134	136	128	138	130	105	151	132	146	126	94	132	126	155
07847	KENVIL	110	154	160	143	160	136	128	133	122	127	123	97	150	124	146	123	91	128	125	145
07848	LAFAYETTE	163	196	195	200	199	183	172	177	165	181	167	135	192	166	188	162	120	171	168	204
07849	LAKE HOPATCONG	123	167	164	159	169	146	138	143	131	140	133	108	161	135	155	130	98	137	132	159
07850	LANDING	113	142	143	136	145	127	126	126	121	126	122	95	140	123	137	120	89	124	120	142
07851	LAYTON	101	142	147	132	147	126	117	122	112	117	113	90	138	114	134	113	84	117	115	134
07852	LEDGEWOOD	147	205	218	199	214	185	168	176	160	172	161	131	202	162	194	159	120	167	164	193
07853	LONG VALLEY	200	273	289	279	285	246	222	232	209	236	211	179	269	212	256	202	158	217	208	259
07856	MOUNT ARLINGTON	127	153	151	150	154	140	138	138	133	139	134	105	152	134	148	132	97	136	133	158
07857	NETCONG	102	123	118	119	122	112	115	112	112	113	113	87	125	113	122	111	82	113	111	129
07860	NEWTON	120	145	141	144	145	135	130	131	126	133	127	100	143	126	139	125	91	128	128	151
07863	OXFORD	110	132	121	133	130	127	114	119	112	117	113	91	127	114	124	112	80	115	117	138
07865	PORT MURRAY	141	185	185	185	188	166	154	160	146	161	148	122	180	149	173	142	108	152	146	180
07866	ROCKAWAY	151	193	196	192	197	174	167	169	160	171	163	130	192	163	184	158	120	164	158	191
07869	RANDOLPH	233	294	311	306	306	267	253	257	239	270	241	202	297	244	281	229	180	245	230	290
07871	SPARTA	185	242	246	248	249	218	202	209	191	216	192	162	238	194	227	184	142	196	189	235
07874	STANHOPE	138	168	155	168	165	149	146	147	139	151	141	115	163	143	157	136	102	143	136	169
07876	SUCCASUNNA	154	220	240	214	233	200	178	188	170	183	171	139	217	171	209	169	128	178	176	206
07882	WASHINGTON	117	136	128	137	135	127	126	125	122	127	124	97	137	124	133	121	89	124	123	145
07885	WHARTON	113	144	142	137	145	128	128	127	124	126	126	96	143	125	138	124	92	125	123	143
07901	SUMMIT	223	294	345	300	321	266	264	266	243	278	244	206	309	239	300	233	185	256	237	295
07920	BASKING RIDGE	235	296	329	308	315	274	258	264	244	278	245	203	305	246	289	235	183	252	239	297
07921	BEDMINSTER	194	188	183	198	186	170	198	181	189	205	192	148	199	196	192	181	137	187	169	214
07922	BERKELEY HEIGHTS	199	280	332	283	309	259	234	248	216	253	215	184	286	211	278	208	162	231	224	271
07924	BERNARDSVILLE	235	330	394	339	364	309	276	290	262	295	261	216	345	258	325	257	201	272	265	318
07927	CEDAR KNOLLS	146	214	239	205	229	196	172	183	164	174	165	133	212	166	204	165	124	173	174	198
07928	CHATHAM	251	336	401	345	373	303	295	304	267	321	266	234	349	261	342	251	201	286	263	334
07930	CHESTER	234	325	395	338	363	300	272	287	251	301	249	218	339	247	322	238	192	266	251	314
07931	FAR HILLS	262	367	446	379	410	341	306	327	282	341	279	244	380	274	367	268	213	301	289	357
07932	FLORHAM PARK	196	257	299	259	282	227	233	236	208	248	209	183	265	203	265	196	155	225	205	260
07933	GILLETTE	196	282	324	277	306	260	230	245	217	241	217	179	283	215	274	214	163	230	228	266
07934	GLADSTONE	233	308	366	315	342	275	277	284	247	302	246	218	319	238	319	230	184	268	245	313
07935	GREEN VILLAGE	261	345	412	354	383	309	309	317	277	337	276	245	359	268	357	258	207	299	273	349
07936	EAST HANOVER	158	213	235	211	226	196	180	187	170	188	171	140	214	170	207	168	127	179	175	208
07940	MADISON	187	231	271	239	252	206	222	216	201	233	203	172	248	196	246	189	152	212	190	243
07945	MENDHAM	248	349	420	362	388	325	288	308	266	321	264	230	360	260	345	254	201	283	273	337
07946	MILLINGTON	212	286	313	294	304	261	240	250	225	257	227	190	288	225	276	218	170	235	225	279
	NEW JERSEY	119	138	141	137	141	129	132	129	129	132	131	98	143	128	139	129	95	130	128	148
	UNITED STATES	100	100	100	100	100	100	100	100	100	100	100	100	100	100	100	100	100	100	100	100

POPULATION CHANGE

ZIP CODE #	POST OFFICE NAME	COUNTY FIPS CODE	POPULATION 2000	POPULATION 2009	POPULATION 2014	2000-2009 ANNUAL RATE % Rate	2000-2009 ANNUAL RATE State Centile	HOUSEHOLDS 2000	HOUSEHOLDS 2009	HOUSEHOLDS 2014	HOUSEHOLDS % Annual Rate 2000-2009	HOUSEHOLDS 2009 Average HH Size	FAMILIES 2000	FAMILIES 2009	FAMILIES % Annual Rate 2000-2009
07950	GREYSTONE PARK	027	17942	19191	19642	0.7	68	6662	7084	7237	0.7	2.59	4732	4947	0.5
07960	MORRISTOWN	027	42633	42899	42999	0.1	35	16155	16260	16320	0.1	2.53	10375	10328	0.0
07974	NEW PROVIDENCE	039	12156	12062	12018	-0.1	19	4494	4416	4384	-0.2	2.68	3391	3316	-0.2
07976	NEW VERNON	027	536	571	585	0.7	68	194	207	213	0.7	2.75	157	167	0.7
07980	STIRLING	027	2222	2166	2144	-0.3	7	799	782	776	-0.2	2.76	603	586	-0.3
07981	WHIPPANY	027	8384	8712	8804	0.4	56	3149	3287	3326	0.5	2.65	2358	2442	0.4
08002	CHERRY HILL	007	20806	21603	22091	0.4	56	8198	8667	8927	0.6	2.41	5483	5738	0.5
08003	CHERRY HILL	007	30734	30505	30396	-0.1	19	10740	10852	10864	0.1	2.76	8760	8796	0.0
08004	ATCO	007	12406	12581	12702	0.2	43	4309	4473	4549	0.4	2.77	3307	3405	0.3
08005	BARNEGAT	029	16881	23677	26596	3.7	99	6096	8690	9800	3.9	2.71	4617	6348	3.5
08007	BARRINGTON	007	5378	5226	5151	-0.3	7	2264	2245	2225	-0.1	2.33	1380	1352	-0.2
08008	BEACH HAVEN	029	8556	9156	9468	0.7	68	4158	4509	4678	0.9	2.03	2545	2709	0.7
08009	BERLIN	007	11710	13432	14220	1.5	89	4224	4933	5249	1.7	2.71	3146	3645	1.6
08010	BEVERLY	005	10592	11609	11966	1.0	80	4139	4686	4890	1.4	2.48	2818	3121	1.1
08012	BLACKWOOD	007	39098	40498	41089	0.4	56	14499	15319	15622	0.6	2.59	10227	10713	0.5
08014	BRIDGEPORT	015	629	716	764	1.4	88	239	276	298	1.6	2.57	164	188	1.5
08015	BROWNS MILLS	005	21068	22141	22481	0.5	62	7421	7959	8141	0.8	2.78	5546	5906	0.7
08016	BURLINGTON	005	30702	33341	34279	0.9	76	11216	12321	12717	1.0	2.62	7965	8677	0.9
08019	CHATSWORTH	005	607	633	634	0.5	62	185	198	200	0.7	2.98	144	152	0.6
08020	CLARKSBORO	015	2243	2742	3160	2.2	95	782	981	1139	2.5	2.73	606	751	2.3
08021	CLEMENTON	007	45816	46381	46447	0.1	35	18406	18901	19037	0.3	2.45	11636	11777	0.1
08022	COLUMBUS	005	6106	9497	10936	4.9	99	2389	3649	4192	4.7	2.60	1825	2822	4.8
08026	GIBBSBORO	007	2640	2577	2553	-0.3	7	902	899	895	0.0	2.84	730	724	-0.1
08027	GIBBSTOWN	015	4858	5062	5201	0.4	56	1860	1965	2028	0.6	2.57	1388	1453	0.5
08028	GLASSBORO	015	19762	20851	21920	0.6	65	6412	6803	7186	0.6	2.69	4204	4420	0.5
08029	GLENDORA	007	4934	4738	4661	-0.4	4	1956	1919	1900	-0.2	2.47	1304	1268	-0.3
08030	GLOUCESTER CITY	007	13757	13865	13862	0.1	35	5145	5255	5275	0.2	2.63	3423	3464	0.1
08031	BELLMAWR	007	11262	11065	10961	-0.2	12	4446	4455	4442	0.0	2.48	3136	3115	-0.1
08032	GRENLOCH	015	510	574	603	1.3	87	167	184	193	1.1	3.12	155	171	1.1
08033	HADDONFIELD	007	17414	16993	16785	-0.3	7	7288	7192	7132	-0.1	2.35	4841	4730	-0.3
08034	CHERRY HILL	007	18402	17836	17598	-0.3	7	7283	7204	7144	-0.1	2.44	5152	5052	-0.2
08035	HADDON HEIGHTS	007	7498	7262	7157	-0.3	7	3017	2978	2951	-0.1	2.43	2027	1982	-0.2
08036	HAINESPORT	005	4041	6173	7038	4.7	99	1450	2198	2504	4.6	2.80	1128	1698	4.5
08037	HAMMONTON	001	22437	24428	25091	0.9	76	7673	8547	8831	1.2	2.69	5624	6166	1.0
08041	JOBSTOWN	005	853	954	999	1.2	85	296	334	351	1.3	2.86	245	275	1.3
08043	VOORHEES	007	27919	30106	30899	0.8	73	10414	11302	11620	0.9	2.59	7005	7585	0.9
08045	LAWNSIDE	007	2662	2782	2826	0.5	62	1014	1080	1102	0.7	2.58	692	730	0.6
08046	WILLINGBORO	005	33169	33589	33432	0.1	35	10770	11121	11146	0.3	3.01	8818	9040	0.3
08048	LUMBERTON	005	9993	11440	12036	1.5	89	3829	4359	4592	1.4	2.59	2653	2989	1.3
08049	MAGNOLIA	007	5454	5452	5447	0.0	28	2084	2130	2143	0.2	2.55	1472	1489	0.1
08050	MANAHAWKIN	029	20952	25229	27167	2.0	94	8020	9835	10640	2.2	2.54	6088	7362	2.1
08051	MANTUA	015	10124	10765	11152	0.7	68	4179	4503	4687	0.8	2.39	2747	2928	0.7
08052	MAPLE SHADE	005	19101	19100	18981	0.0	28	8471	8561	8555	0.1	2.20	4726	4725	0.0
08053	MARLTON	005	42055	45928	47311	1.0	80	15639	17277	17878	1.1	2.65	11283	12437	1.1
08054	MOUNT LAUREL	005	40279	42572	43192	0.6	65	16587	17763	18127	0.7	2.38	11076	11714	0.6
08055	MEDFORD	005	26643	27509	27772	0.3	50	9538	9978	10120	0.5	2.73	7581	7888	0.4
08056	MICKLETON	015	2639	4320	5188	5.5	100	927	1518	1827	5.5	2.84	760	1243	5.5
08057	MOORESTOWN	005	19425	20215	20498	0.4	56	7106	7486	7630	0.6	2.65	5386	5658	0.5
08059	MOUNT EPHRAIM	007	5483	5646	5696	0.3	50	2210	2305	2334	0.5	2.44	1442	1489	0.3
08060	MOUNT HOLLY	005	24516	26273	26964	0.8	73	8725	9386	9657	0.8	2.74	6251	6708	0.8
08061	MOUNT ROYAL	015	528	1463	1769	11.6	100	188	549	677	12.3	2.49	144	415	12.1
08062	MULLICA HILL	015	11728	15737	17620	3.2	97	3916	5210	5834	3.1	2.99	3179	4206	3.1
08063	NATIONAL PARK	015	3317	3447	3533	0.4	56	1156	1218	1255	0.6	2.81	900	939	0.5
08065	PALMYRA	005	7077	7112	7068	0.1	35	2989	3074	3082	0.3	2.31	1844	1862	0.1
08066	PAULSBORO	015	7667	7706	7972	0.1	35	3115	3193	3339	0.3	2.40	2001	2029	0.2
08067	PEDRICKTOWN	033	1691	1672	1665	-0.1	19	614	609	607	-0.1	2.73	485	478	-0.2
08068	PEMBERTON	005	7067	7273	7399	0.3	50	2579	2752	2814	0.7	2.53	1735	1841	0.6
08069	PENNS GROVE	033	12867	13362	13608	0.4	56	5060	5274	5382	0.4	2.51	3361	3458	0.3
08070	PENNSVILLE	033	13003	13145	13124	0.1	35	5241	5308	5312	0.1	2.47	3663	3671	0.0
08071	PITMAN	015	9848	10013	10201	0.2	43	3675	3783	3872	0.3	2.56	2585	2631	0.2
08075	DELANCO	005	26344	28379	29056	0.8	73	9911	10846	11180	1.0	2.61	7119	7737	0.9
08077	RIVERTON	005	17304	18243	18880	0.6	65	6116	6567	6854	0.8	2.73	4878	5210	0.7
08078	RUNNEMEDE	007	8388	8126	8013	-0.3	7	3320	3282	3255	-0.1	2.47	2239	2192	-0.2
08079	SALEM	033	12143	11912	11819	-0.2	12	4862	4771	4744	-0.2	2.46	3297	3216	-0.3
08080	SEWELL	015	36904	40769	43030	1.1	83	11940	13440	14321	1.3	3.02	9906	11041	1.2
08081	SICKLERVILLE	007	43047	51193	54119	1.9	93	14088	16868	17887	2.0	3.03	11317	13517	1.9
08083	SOMERDALE	007	9733	9434	9443	-0.3	7	3704	3663	3690	-0.1	2.57	2677	2631	-0.2
08084	STRATFORD	007	7271	7083	6984	-0.3	7	2736	2723	2701	-0.1	2.55	1907	1876	-0.2
08085	SWEDESBORO	015	10797	16436	18756	4.6	99	3587	5488	6278	4.7	2.98	2891	4499	4.9
08086	THOROFARE	015	6426	8294	9007	2.8	96	2655	3544	3885	3.2	2.32	1674	2169	2.8
08087	LITTLE EGG HARBOR TW	029	20845	26053	28379	2.4	95	8165	10516	11546	2.8	2.46	5743	7374	2.7
08088	SHAMONG	005	24650	25324	25350	0.3	50	9251	9664	9745	0.5	2.59	7016	7258	0.4
08089	WATERFORD WORKS	007	4181	4255	4278	0.2	43	1402	1459	1476	0.4	2.82	1092	1128	0.4
08090	WENONAH	015	8390	8685	8899	0.4	56	2975	3127	3225	0.5	2.74	2357	2458	0.5
08091	WEST BERLIN	007	5274	5182	5530	-0.2	12	1887	1893	2046	0.0	2.73	1365	1358	-0.1
08092	WEST CREEK	029	2860	3514	3924	2.3	95	1022	1235	1377	2.1	2.85	726	865	1.9
08093	WESTVILLE	015	10015	10377	10603	0.4	56	3979	4153	4260	0.5	2.49	2498	2586	0.4
08094	WILLIAMSTOWN	015	32979	39725	43041	2.0	94	11869	14343	15585	2.1	2.75	8949	10736	2.0
08096	DEPTFORD	015	32109	35619	37403	1.1	83	12175	13750	14544	1.3	2.52	8413	9322	1.1
08097	WOODBURY HEIGHTS	015	3159	3221	3275	0.2	43	1087	1123	1148	0.4	2.85	868	889	0.3
08098	WOODSTOWN	033	8567	9893	10414	1.6	91	3012	3483	3673	1.6	2.69	2217	2561	1.6
08102	CAMDEN	007	9866	10020	10025	0.2	43	2557	2736	2772	0.7	2.90	1630	1674	0.3
08103	CAMDEN	007	15597	15016	14818	-0.4	4	4615	4516	4491	-0.2	2.91	3211	3099	-0.4
08104	CAMDEN	007	24571	25631	25917	0.5	62	8174	8529	8647	0.5	2.97	5815	6008	0.4
08105	CAMDEN	007	28192	27582	27227	-0.2	12	8365	8271	8194	-0.1	3.33	6403	6289	-0.2
08106	AUDUBON	007	10284	9981	9849	-0.3	7	4169	4097	4058	-0.2	2.43	2690	2615	-0.3
08107	HADDON TOWNSHIP	007	13480	13256	13120	-0.2	12	5593	5548	5511	-0.1	2.39	3235	3178	-0.2
08108	COLLINGSWOOD	007	17743	17411	17268	-0.2	12	7274	7263	7246	0.0	2.38	4536	4471	-0.2
08109	MERCHANTVILLE	007	22726	22700	22607	0.0	28	8437	8526	8520	0.1	2.59	5811	5833	0.0
08110	PENNSAUKEN	007	18554	18758	18713	0.1	35	5964	5992	5977	0.1	3.13	4623	4617	0.0
08201	ABSECON	001	9056	9847	10498	0.9	76	3318	3640	3892	1.0	2.66	2448	2646	0.8
08202	AVALON	009	2234	2173	2137	-0.3	7	1090	1097	1089	0.1	1.96	701	696	-0.1
08203	BRIGANTINE	001	12594	10983	10523	-1.5	0	5473	4805	4608	-1.4	2.29	3338	2876	-1.6
08204	CAPE MAY	009	19384	19322	19163	0.0	28	8032	8299	8304	0.4	2.25	5337	5430	0.2
08205	ABSECON	001	25798	29259	30272	1.4	88	8739	10162	10607	1.6	2.67	6250	7103	1.4
	NEW JERSEY					0.5					0.5	2.69			0.5
	UNITED STATES					1.0					1.1	2.59			0.9

#	POST OFFICE NAME	White 2000	White 2009	Black 2000	Black 2009	Asian/Pacific 2000	Asian/Pacific 2009	% Hispanic Origin 2000	% Hispanic Origin 2009	0-4	5-9	10-14	15-19	20-24	25-44	45-64	65-84	85+	18+	MEDIAN AGE 2009	% 2009 Males	% 2009 Females
07950	GREYSTONE PARK	83.8	76.5	2.8	4.0	11.1	16.1	4.1	6.8	6.0	6.3	6.8	5.6	4.6	26.7	30.2	12.0	1.8	77.5	41.8	49.9	50.1
07960	MORRISTOWN	79.8	75.5	10.1	10.7	3.7	5.4	13.7	18.9	6.0	6.3	6.6	5.9	5.4	27.1	27.8	12.3	2.6	77.5	40.6	49.3	50.7
07974	NEW PROVIDENCE	89.3	83.8	1.1	1.4	7.9	12.1	3.5	6.1	7.0	7.5	8.4	6.7	4.2	21.7	29.6	12.2	2.8	72.4	41.9	48.5	51.5
07976	NEW VERNON	97.2	96.1	0.2	0.2	0.7	1.2	2.4	4.2	5.1	6.1	7.5	6.7	3.2	16.3	32.6	19.8	2.8	76.4	48.4	49.0	51.0
07980	STIRLING	92.1	87.8	0.5	0.6	5.0	8.0	3.9	6.7	7.1	7.5	8.0	7.1	4.8	22.3	30.5	11.0	1.7	72.9	40.8	47.8	52.2
07981	WHIPPANY	88.2	82.2	1.1	1.4	9.2	14.3	3.6	6.0	6.5	6.7	7.3	5.9	3.6	24.4	29.1	14.3	2.4	75.6	42.7	48.0	52.0
08002	CHERRY HILL	83.8	75.7	5.4	7.3	7.9	12.2	3.5	6.6	5.1	5.2	5.6	5.7	4.7	22.4	28.5	17.2	5.6	80.3	45.8	46.8	53.2
08003	CHERRY HILL	83.3	75.2	4.2	5.6	11.2	17.3	1.8	3.3	5.5	6.3	7.3	7.1	4.1	20.6	31.6	15.1	2.5	76.1	44.4	48.0	52.0
08004	ATCO	86.9	81.4	10.0	13.6	0.9	1.4	2.4	4.7	6.6	6.8	6.9	6.7	5.6	27.8	29.6	8.6	1.4	75.4	38.5	49.5	50.5
08005	BARNEGAT	95.0	93.6	2.1	2.2	1.0	1.4	3.8	5.6	5.7	6.0	6.3	6.4	4.5	21.2	28.4	18.7	2.8	77.9	44.9	47.5	52.5
08007	BARRINGTON	91.6	87.0	4.4	6.3	1.3	2.1	2.7	5.5	5.7	5.6	5.8	5.8	5.1	27.9	26.3	14.3	3.4	79.3	41.2	47.6	52.4
08008	BEACH HAVEN	98.0	97.1	0.2	0.3	0.5	0.9	3.0	4.8	2.8	3.2	3.5	3.3	2.5	16.1	33.8	30.4	4.4	88.3	57.6	48.5	51.5
08009	BERLIN	87.0	81.8	8.5	11.0	1.6	2.6	3.3	6.3	6.6	6.6	6.7	6.6	5.5	28.4	27.0	10.9	1.6	75.9	38.5	49.6	50.4
08010	BEVERLY	67.2	60.3	23.3	27.0	2.7	3.6	6.1	8.6	6.0	6.0	6.2	6.6	5.6	26.3	28.8	12.7	1.7	77.7	40.1	48.1	51.9
08012	BLACKWOOD	86.4	81.0	8.4	10.8	2.6	4.1	3.0	5.1	6.0	5.9	6.0	6.4	6.5	28.0	27.7	11.6	1.9	78.1	38.9	48.3	51.7
08014	BRIDGEPORT	96.8	95.7	2.5	3.2	0.3	0.6	1.0	1.5	6.8	7.0	7.0	7.8	6.0	25.1	26.7	11.2	2.4	74.0	38.3	50.8	49.2
08015	BROWNS MILLS	69.7	61.7	19.2	23.2	3.4	4.7	8.1	12.0	6.6	6.8	7.0	7.4	6.3	27.5	27.9	9.7	0.9	75.0	36.7	48.5	51.5
08016	BURLINGTON	68.3	61.0	24.8	29.3	3.0	4.3	3.8	5.7	7.8	7.8	7.6	6.3	4.8	27.3	25.2	10.3	2.7	72.6	37.8	47.9	52.1
08019	CHATSWORTH	94.7	92.3	1.3	1.6	0.2	0.3	5.0	7.7	4.7	5.5	6.3	7.9	4.3	23.9	33.6	10.7	3.0	78.2	43.3	48.3	51.7
08020	CLARKSBORO	93.7	92.2	4.1	4.6	0.7	1.1	1.7	2.6	5.3	5.9	6.5	6.1	4.0	21.4	32.2	15.9	2.8	78.3	45.5	46.9	53.1
08021	CLEMENTON	73.3	65.0	19.6	24.4	2.6	3.6	4.9	8.2	6.7	6.3	6.3	6.5	7.4	30.0	26.2	9.2	1.3	76.8	36.1	48.3	51.7
08022	COLUMBUS	94.8	92.1	2.2	3.0	1.8	3.1	1.8	3.3	4.7	5.3	6.0	5.7	3.2	18.4	29.9	23.0	3.7	80.3	49.2	48.0	52.0
08026	GIBBSBORO	92.3	88.2	3.8	5.2	1.8	2.8	2.3	4.7	5.7	6.0	6.6	6.6	5.0	24.6	29.6	14.2	1.6	78.0	42.1	49.2	50.8
08027	GIBBSTOWN	94.5	92.8	3.3	4.1	0.7	1.1	1.5	2.4	5.9	6.0	6.1	5.6	4.9	25.1	29.2	14.7	2.6	78.5	42.5	48.8	51.2
08028	GLASSBORO	73.1	67.5	20.8	24.2	2.4	3.5	3.9	5.6	6.2	5.9	5.9	11.3	17.4	23.5	20.2	8.4	1.2	78.1	27.5	48.3	51.7
08029	GLENDORA	97.4	95.8	0.6	0.8	0.4	0.6	1.6	3.3	5.3	5.2	5.3	5.7	5.9	25.3	28.5	15.5	3.2	80.7	43.0	47.7	52.3
08030	GLOUCESTER CITY	96.0	93.4	1.3	1.8	0.8	1.3	2.4	4.7	6.7	6.5	6.4	6.9	6.9	26.7	26.7	11.4	1.8	76.3	37.1	48.8	51.2
08031	BELLMAWR	92.8	88.6	1.2	1.6	3.1	4.7	3.5	6.7	5.2	5.3	5.6	5.9	4.6	26.3	28.9	15.9	2.5	80.3	43.1	49.0	51.0
08032	GRENLOCH	89.8	85.5	3.5	4.2	5.7	8.9	1.2	1.7	9.6	10.1	10.1	7.1	3.3	30.3	24.6	4.2	0.7	64.8	34.5	49.5	50.5
08033	HADDONFIELD	95.6	93.0	1.5	2.1	1.5	2.4	1.7	3.4	5.5	5.9	7.0	6.6	5.3	21.0	31.2	14.1	3.3	77.3	44.1	47.5	52.5
08034	CHERRY HILL	87.7	81.5	3.9	5.3	6.2	9.7	2.7	5.2	5.4	5.5	6.2	6.1	5.0	22.4	29.1	16.9	3.4	78.8	44.6	47.9	52.1
08035	HADDON HEIGHTS	98.0	96.7	0.4	0.6	0.7	1.2	1.0	2.2	5.7	5.9	6.3	6.0	5.4	23.0	30.0	14.1	3.6	78.1	43.3	46.7	53.3
08036	HAINESPORT	94.1	90.9	2.7	3.7	1.7	3.1	2.1	3.6	7.0	7.9	8.5	7.1	3.9	23.7	30.9	9.9	1.3	71.6	40.2	48.5	51.5
08037	HAMMONTON	85.4	78.4	5.0	6.0	1.0	1.6	13.1	21.3	5.8	5.9	6.0	6.3	5.5	28.0	27.7	12.2	2.5	78.5	40.0	50.5	49.5
08041	JOBSTOWN	92.0	87.9	2.7	3.7	3.3	5.3	1.9	3.2	5.5	6.0	6.9	7.7	4.6	24.3	32.6	11.0	1.5	76.9	41.7	49.3	50.7
08043	VOORHEES	78.3	69.5	7.9	10.2	11.5	17.0	2.5	4.4	5.8	6.4	7.2	7.0	5.5	25.9	29.6	10.2	2.3	75.8	40.1	48.0	52.0
08045	LAWNSIDE	1.7	1.7	93.6	93.5	0.6	0.6	2.4	3.2	4.2	4.7	5.5	7.7	6.5	21.2	29.8	17.9	2.5	80.9	45.1	45.2	54.8
08046	WILLINGBORO	24.9	19.3	66.5	70.4	1.7	2.1	6.1	7.8	6.1	6.3	6.9	7.2	5.4	23.8	28.1	14.9	1.3	76.1	40.6	47.3	52.7
08048	LUMBERTON	78.1	71.7	13.9	16.9	3.5	5.0	5.2	7.8	8.0	8.1	8.2	6.9	5.2	27.9	26.0	7.8	1.7	71.0	35.9	47.9	52.1
08049	MAGNOLIA	78.7	70.3	16.1	21.2	1.3	1.9	3.9	7.3	6.8	6.8	6.9	6.7	5.4	27.9	26.5	11.4	1.6	75.4	38.5	48.7	51.3
08050	MANAHAWKIN	96.8	95.3	0.7	0.9	1.0	1.6	2.4	3.8	6.3	6.4	6.4	5.8	3.9	23.4	28.0	17.1	2.6	77.2	43.5	48.6	51.4
08051	MANTUA	93.8	91.7	3.4	4.1	1.3	2.0	1.4	2.1	7.4	7.3	6.9	5.6	4.8	28.9	26.8	11.0	1.4	75.0	38.4	47.6	52.4
08052	MAPLE SHADE	83.2	78.4	7.2	8.4	6.1	8.4	4.4	6.6	5.8	5.2	5.0	5.2	7.6	31.0	25.6	12.1	2.5	81.1	38.6	49.2	50.8
08053	MARLTON	91.2	87.0	3.1	4.2	4.1	6.5	2.0	3.2	6.9	7.2	7.4	6.8	4.8	27.7	28.6	9.3	1.3	73.9	38.6	48.4	51.6
08054	MOUNT LAUREL	87.1	81.8	6.9	9.1	3.8	5.9	2.2	3.6	5.6	5.9	6.4	6.1	5.0	24.5	29.5	14.8	2.1	78.1	42.8	47.3	52.7
08055	MEDFORD	97.0	95.3	0.7	1.0	1.3	2.2	1.1	1.9	5.9	6.7	7.5	6.8	4.0	21.7	32.4	12.6	2.3	75.4	43.2	48.3	51.7
08056	MICKLETON	95.9	95.0	2.2	2.4	0.6	0.9	1.1	1.5	5.7	6.5	7.4	7.6	4.6	23.1	33.4	10.4	1.3	75.1	41.6	49.2	50.8
08057	MOORESTOWN	89.3	84.6	5.7	7.4	3.2	5.4	1.7	2.8	6.1	6.8	8.0	7.7	4.7	19.0	31.1	13.1	3.4	73.9	43.3	47.3	52.7
08059	MOUNT EPHRAIM	97.1	95.0	0.6	0.9	0.8	1.3	2.1	4.3	5.8	5.9	6.0	6.0	5.0	25.7	29.5	13.0	3.2	78.6	42.1	48.1	51.9
08060	MOUNT HOLLY	72.2	65.6	18.7	21.8	2.9	4.3	6.9	9.9	6.7	6.9	7.1	7.3	6.4	26.7	28.3	9.3	1.4	74.7	37.6	49.0	51.0
08061	MOUNT ROYAL	93.2	91.0	4.4	5.5	0.6	1.0	1.9	2.9	6.1	6.5	6.8	6.0	4.0	24.1	27.9	14.3	4.4	76.3	42.6	46.5	53.5
08062	MULLICA HILL	94.8	93.1	3.1	3.8	0.6	1.0	2.1	3.1	7.8	8.6	9.0	7.3	4.3	26.3	28.1	7.6	1.1	69.6	37.4	49.7	50.3
08063	NATIONAL PARK	98.3	97.6	0.1	0.1	0.3	0.5	1.4	2.3	5.8	6.6	6.3	6.5	6.2	28.1	26.7	12.4	1.5	77.2	38.4	49.6	50.4
08065	PALMYRA	81.0	76.2	14.4	17.1	1.4	2.3	3.2	5.0	5.5	5.9	6.1	6.0	4.8	27.1	30.1	12.2	2.3	78.8	41.6	48.2	51.8
08066	PAULSBORO	68.5	64.4	27.0	29.6	0.6	0.9	4.0	5.6	7.3	7.4	7.3	7.3	6.4	27.0	24.5	10.9	1.8	73.5	35.8	47.4	52.6
08067	PEDRICKTOWN	86.8	81.8	9.6	12.8	0.2	0.2	4.2	6.8	5.1	5.6	6.5	6.9	4.7	24.3	32.7	12.4	1.8	78.2	42.6	49.9	50.1
08068	PEMBERTON	60.6	53.6	29.9	34.0	2.6	3.5	9.4	13.1	5.6	5.4	5.5	6.3	7.1	28.2	26.1	14.1	1.8	79.8	39.0	50.5	49.5
08069	PENNS GROVE	67.7	61.1	24.8	28.8	0.8	1.1	9.0	12.1	7.2	6.9	6.6	6.8	6.7	25.7	25.8	11.9	2.4	75.2	37.2	47.4	52.6
08070	PENNSVILLE	96.6	94.9	1.1	1.5	0.9	1.5	1.6	2.7	5.8	5.9	6.0	6.1	5.4	25.7	28.4	14.4	2.3	78.5	41.5	48.0	52.0
08071	PITMAN	97.0	95.8	1.0	1.2	0.6	1.0	1.5	2.3	5.7	6.1	6.4	6.7	5.6	25.0	27.9	13.3	3.3	77.5	41.0	46.3	53.7
08075	DELANCO	86.5	82.8	7.1	8.5	1.9	2.9	3.4	5.1	6.4	6.2	6.3	6.6	6.1	28.6	27.5	10.8	1.6	76.9	38.4	49.1	50.9
08077	RIVERTON	92.0	88.2	4.6	6.5	1.7	2.8	1.5	2.5	5.1	5.5	6.1	6.5	5.0	21.0	30.7	17.0	3.1	78.9	45.4	48.2	51.8
08078	RUNNEMEDE	92.0	87.9	3.6	4.9	1.5	2.4	3.5	6.8	5.8	5.8	5.8	5.9	5.9	27.5	28.0	12.9	2.4	79.1	40.6	48.3	51.7
08079	SALEM	64.0	60.2	32.0	34.7	0.3	0.5	3.1	4.2	7.1	7.1	7.2	7.2	5.5	23.0	27.1	13.4	2.4	74.1	39.4	47.3	52.7
08080	SEWELL	90.4	87.1	4.7	5.5	3.4	5.2	2.0	3.0	6.4	7.0	7.7	7.9	5.4	26.9	29.9	7.8	1.0	73.8	37.5	48.9	51.1
08081	SICKLERVILLE	68.4	60.8	26.2	30.9	2.2	3.2	3.4	6.1	8.6	8.6	8.4	7.6	5.6	29.3	25.5	5.9	0.6	69.6	33.4	48.7	51.3
08083	SOMERDALE	81.2	73.9	13.2	17.2	2.8	4.3	3.2	5.8	5.6	5.7	6.1	6.3	5.3	26.0	29.8	13.6	1.7	78.8	41.9	48.6	51.4
08084	STRATFORD	88.6	84.3	6.6	8.2	2.4	3.6	3.8	6.6	6.1	6.2	6.3	6.5	6.2	26.1	26.9	13.1	2.6	77.4	39.8	48.8	51.2
08085	SWEDESBORO	83.0	82.1	12.0	11.5	1.4	1.8	4.3	6.1	9.0	8.9	8.6	6.9	4.6	29.9	25.8	5.6	0.7	69.0	34.7	49.3	50.7
08086	THOROFARE	90.2	87.3	7.1	8.7	1.1	1.8	1.7	2.7	5.5	5.4	5.5	6.0	6.8	27.2	29.5	12.5	1.7	80.0	40.6	48.4	51.6
08087	LITTLE EGG HARBOR TW	96.5	94.9	0.7	0.9	0.6	0.9	3.2	5.0	5.6	5.6	5.8	6.3	5.4	22.9	28.4	17.2	2.7	79.1	43.8	48.4	51.6
08088	SHAMONG	96.7	94.8	1.5	2.2	0.7	1.2	1.4	2.5	4.9	5.6	6.5	6.6	3.9	21.3	31.4	16.4	3.3	79.1	45.7	48.8	51.2
08089	WATERFORD WORKS	73.7	68.5	22.0	24.7	0.7	1.2	3.1	5.7	4.8	5.2	5.8	6.4	4.9	25.8	32.8	12.6	1.6	79.9	43.0	49.7	50.3
08090	WENONAH	89.3	87.2	8.6	9.6	0.8	1.4	1.7	2.5	6.1	6.6	7.0	6.6	4.7	24.2	28.8	14.2	1.9	76.2	41.7	48.6	51.4
08091	WEST BERLIN	82.5	76.1	11.8	15.3	2.8	4.1	4.8	8.7	6.6	6.5	6.9	6.7	5.4	27.6	26.9	12.0	1.5	76.0	39.0	50.6	49.4
08092	WEST CREEK	98.0	97.1	0.3	0.4	0.8	1.3	1.7	2.7	5.5	5.6	6.1	7.0	5.4	22.8	31.0	14.6	2.0	78.5	43.2	49.2	50.8
08093	WESTVILLE	83.4	79.6	11.2	13.0	1.2	1.8	4.4	6.4	6.5	6.2	6.1	6.3	7.0	29.1	25.8	11.1	1.9	77.2	37.2	48.1	51.9
08094	WILLIAMSTOWN	84.6	79.7	11.1	14.2	1.2	1.8	3.3	4.8	6.5	6.8	7.0	6.7	5.0	26.8	27.8	11.8	1.6	75.5	39.2	48.5	51.5
08096	DEPTFORD	84.6	80.8	11.6	13.6	1.4	2.5	2.6	3.8	6.3	6.3	6.3	6.3	5.5	27.2	26.8	12.6	2.7	77.3	39.8	47.9	52.1
08097	WOODBURY HEIGHTS	90.6	88.8	7.2	8.0	0.9	1.5	1.3	2.0	5.9	6.2	6.6	6.9	5.0	24.9	29.6	13.0	1.8	76.7	41.5	48.1	51.9
08098	WOODSTOWN	85.0	81.5	12.4	14.7	0.8	1.2	2.4	3.6	5.2	6.0	6.4	7.1	5.5	24.7	29.9	12.4	2.9	77.8	41.5	49.6	50.4
08102	CAMDEN	19.6	18.0	48.6	44.2	1.1	1.4	53.2	60.2	7.6	7.4	6.3	8.0	11.4	31.4	18.6	8.0	1.3	74.8	29.8	55.0	45.0
08103	CAMDEN	11.7	11.2	69.9	65.9	0.4	0.5	26.1	32.2	7.9	7.9	7.4	9.1	9.8	28.6	19.4	8.6	1.4	71.7	30.1	49.8	50.2
08104	CAMDEN	16.4	14.2	64.3	60.4	1.1	1.1	23.2	31.1	10.3	10.0	9.1	9.1	7.9	25.7	19.5	7.5	0.9	64.9	27.4	45.7	54.3
08105	CAMDEN	18.8	17.7	37.7	31.7	4.6	4.4	54.0	63.2	10.5	9.4	8.2	9.1	9.8	27.8	19.0	5.7	0.5	66.4	26.6	48.4	51.6
08106	AUDUBON	97.5	95.8	0.5	0.8	0.8	1.4	1.4	2.9	5.5	5.5	5.9	6.5	6.4	26.1	29.4	12.1	2.7	79.1	41.1	48.0	52.0
08107	HADDON TOWNSHIP	79.5	72.6	9.5	11.2	5.0	6.7	7.7	12.9	6.0	5.7	5.7	6.3	7.3	27.5	26.5	12.1	3.0	78.9	38.9	48.4	51.6
08108	COLLINGSWOOD	93.0	88.8	2.7	3.8	1.8	2.9	3.4	6.6	5.8	5.7	6.0	6.1	6.2	27.1	28.4	11.6	3.0	78.6	40.3	47.8	52.2
08109	MERCHANTVILLE	75.6	66.4	14.6	18.0	3.2	4.7	8.0	14.1	6.0	6.0	6.3	6.7	5.8	24.6	27.6	13.9	3.2	77.7	41.2	47.4	52.6
08110	PENNSAUKEN	43.0	35.1	32.9	33.0	6.8	7.7	23.1	32.7	7.1	7.1	7.2	8.5	7.7	27.8	25.2	8.1	1.3	73.4	33.8	48.7	51.3
08201	ABSECON	73.5	64.5	14.5	17.0	7.1	11.6	5.9	8.6	6.3	6.5	6.7	6.7	5.2	25.0	28.8	12.5	2.4	76.2	40.6	48.3	51.7
08202	AVALON	98.1	97.3	0.6	0.8	0.6	1.0	0.6	1.2	2.5	2.6	3.1	3.8	2.6	12.4	34.7	33.8	4.5	89.1	60.8	50.1	49.9
08203	BRIGANTINE	83.2	76.1	3.9	4.8	5.8	8.7	9.4	14.3	5.3	5.3	5.6	6.0	5.6	23.2	30.0	17.0	2.1	80.2	44.3	48.9	51.1
08204	CAPE MAY	94.5	92.4	3.0	3.8	0.6	0.9	2.1	3.5	4.4	4.7	4.9	6.2	5.4	20.2	29.2	20.9	4.1	82.5	48.2	47.8	52.2
08205	ABSECON	75.6	67.4	10.2	12.1	8.9	13.2	6.3	9.5	6.3	6.1	6.4	9.4	11.0	25.6	26.1	8.3	0.9	76.9	33.7	47.7	52.3
	NEW JERSEY	72.6	68.2	13.6	14.0	5.7	7.9	13.3	16.9	6.6	6.6	6.7	6.8	6.2	26.4	27.0	11.5	2.2	76.0	38.7	48.7	51.3
	UNITED STATES	75.1	72.0	12.3	12.7	3.8	4.6	12.5	15.7	6.8	6.7	6.6	7.1	6.9	27.0	26.0	10.9	1.9	75.7	36.9	49.2	50.8

#	POST OFFICE NAME	2009 Per Capita Income	2009 HH Income Base	2009 HOUSEHOLD INCOME DISTRIBUTION (%) Less than $25,000	$25,000 to $49,999	$50,000 to $99,999	$100,000 to $149,999	$150,000 or More	MEDIAN HOUSEHOLD INCOME 2009	2014	2009 National Centile	2009 State Centile	2009 Home Value Base	2009 HOME VALUE DISTRIBUTION (%) Less than $50,000	$50,000 to $89,999	$90,000 to $174,999	$175,000 to $399,999	$400,000 or More	2009 Median Home Value
07950	GREYSTONE PARK	58006	7084	4.6	7.6	24.2	27.9	35.7	122541	132606	99	88	5624	0.1	0.8	5.5	21.7	71.9	504233
07960	MORRISTOWN	59699	16260	9.6	12.1	22.3	21.5	34.4	111833	126805	98	85	10610	0.2	0.3	3.0	22.6	73.9	578144
07974	NEW PROVIDENCE	56266	4416	4.7	10.0	27.9	22.3	35.0	115397	118230	98	86	3331	0.1	0.3	0.5	6.5	92.5	656366
07976	NEW VERNON	81959	207	3.4	8.7	22.2	15.0	50.7	151785	158188	100	97	187	0.0	0.0	0.0	0.0	100.0	1000001
07980	STIRLING	46314	782	6.0	17.1	26.2	22.8	27.9	100894	100983	97	76	600	0.2	0.2	1.2	35.0	63.5	472321
07981	WHIPPANY	51946	3287	4.5	12.2	28.7	25.6	29.0	106229	117480	97	80	2968	0.1	0.6	3.9	23.1	72.3	521166
08002	CHERRY HILL	31011	8667	16.1	21.8	39.6	16.2	6.3	64464	70670	83	29	6271	1.7	4.3	8.5	75.4	10.0	270440
08003	CHERRY HILL	49570	10852	7.9	9.6	29.5	21.9	31.1	105633	100191	97	80	9539	0.3	0.4	3.6	50.8	45.0	383839
08004	ATCO	28652	4473	12.6	16.4	46.8	17.4	6.9	75139	77547	89	43	3800	0.7	1.4	19.3	70.0	8.6	228391
08005	BARNEGAT	25876	8690	13.8	24.5	44.7	10.9	6.1	61362	65798	79	24	7794	3.8	1.9	14.1	67.2	13.1	249375
08007	BARRINGTON	27552	2245	16.7	28.2	40.2	12.7	2.2	54611	58243	71	17	1369	2.1	0.0	25.9	67.4	4.6	202024
08008	BEACH HAVEN	40837	4509	15.2	22.4	39.7	10.8	11.8	64120	75000	82	29	3633	0.2	0.0	0.8	10.7	88.3	706494
08009	BERLIN	29292	4933	12.4	17.4	46.6	17.3	6.3	72718	76910	88	41	3866	0.8	1.6	16.0	66.3	15.3	257703
08010	BEVERLY	28168	4686	14.9	23.8	41.1	16.0	4.2	60649	58269	78	23	3034	0.3	1.6	33.5	58.3	6.3	212859
08012	BLACKWOOD	29598	15319	11.4	21.9	43.4	16.8	6.5	68733	75532	86	35	10658	0.4	1.1	18.3	75.0	5.2	237179
08014	BRIDGEPORT	31915	276	19.2	32.2	30.4	5.8	12.3	48226	51854	57	11	204	4.9	0.5	27.9	64.2	2.5	196795
08015	BROWNS MILLS	24809	7959	13.7	23.1	43.6	16.3	3.2	61242	57764	79	24	6468	4.1	5.4	30.5	58.0	2.1	188585
08016	BURLINGTON	32104	12321	14.0	18.9	34.0	22.7	10.4	74438	79432	89	42	8959	0.4	2.5	19.8	58.9	18.3	271917
08019	CHATSWORTH	30202	198	7.6	17.2	35.4	34.8	5.1	85345	92656	94	63	169	0.6	2.4	16.0	58.6	22.5	289286
08020	CLARKSBORO	31621	981	10.7	20.6	34.5	23.5	10.7	77681	77631	91	50	880	0.1	1.4	9.9	73.6	15.0	306383
08021	CLEMENTON	24672	18901	20.1	28.0	39.3	9.3	3.2	51482	53799	65	13	10269	1.5	3.9	50.8	41.6	2.2	168931
08022	COLUMBUS	35741	3649	9.8	18.6	37.2	19.1	15.3	75141	79211	89	44	3437	0.3	0.0	4.1	53.7	41.9	367156
08026	GIBBSBORO	32486	899	9.1	17.0	45.2	17.0	11.7	77045	77995	91	48	803	1.2	1.6	14.6	66.9	15.7	236558
08027	GIBBSTOWN	29805	1965	12.3	23.2	40.0	18.7	5.9	67011	68094	85	33	1641	0.6	0.0	15.4	79.5	4.4	229434
08028	GLASSBORO	23952	6803	20.9	22.1	38.4	13.3	5.3	56847	56406	74	20	4187	0.5	0.6	20.3	75.4	3.2	224189
08029	GLENDORA	26466	1919	23.1	21.5	39.4	11.0	5.0	54951	58329	71	17	1468	0.0	1.2	36.0	60.1	2.6	196846
08030	GLOUCESTER CITY	21953	5255	22.8	27.3	38.2	9.5	2.3	49889	54546	61	12	3691	4.8	5.9	62.7	24.3	2.2	148688
08031	BELLMAWR	25736	4455	15.3	26.2	45.0	10.9	2.6	57596	61687	75	20	3230	1.7	1.5	40.1	55.8	0.9	181986
08032	GRENLOCH	47190	184	2.7	6.5	28.3	22.8	39.7	131186	136317	99	92	177	1.1	0.0	4.0	43.5	51.4	404630
08033	HADDONFIELD	46917	7192	12.0	17.5	31.2	17.6	21.7	82685	82503	93	60	5236	0.6	0.1	3.5	42.2	53.7	430203
08034	CHERRY HILL	39730	7204	9.6	17.1	39.6	20.5	13.2	80312	81581	92	55	5731	0.6	0.9	8.4	73.3	16.8	288248
08035	HADDON HEIGHTS	33550	2978	13.8	20.7	38.8	18.2	8.5	71583	75748	88	39	2285	0.0	0.0	5.5	75.6	18.9	298396
08036	HAINESPORT	35796	2198	8.6	13.8	38.4	25.1	14.2	85128	89883	94	63	1949	0.3	1.3	10.1	43.3	45.0	360041
08037	HAMMONTON	25692	8547	16.7	23.8	42.5	11.9	5.1	60270	64582	78	23	6340	0.3	0.6	15.7	61.6	21.9	266290
08041	JOBSTOWN	41471	334	6.9	10.8	36.2	22.5	23.7	94785	100897	96	73	296	0.0	0.0	1.7	40.5	57.8	434328
08043	VOORHEES	44102	11302	10.8	13.7	35.2	16.4	24.0	85540	84137	94	64	7526	0.6	1.4	10.9	38.3	48.7	391504
08045	LAWNSIDE	24549	1080	28.7	17.2	34.7	14.3	5.1	53996	56888	70	16	778	1.3	0.6	33.7	54.4	10.0	195290
08046	WILLINGBORO	28777	11121	7.3	15.4	44.1	26.5	6.8	79019	84745	92	52	10035	0.2	0.5	28.3	69.8	1.2	197978
08048	LUMBERTON	35569	4359	9.7	20.1	32.3	25.6	12.3	80219	86055	92	55	2840	0.8	0.0	19.5	40.9	38.8	328315
08049	MAGNOLIA	25978	2130	15.9	23.0	46.8	10.5	3.8	60225	65163	78	23	1614	1.1	0.0	46.0	49.4	3.5	178774
08050	MANAHAWKIN	32785	9835	10.8	17.9	47.3	14.9	9.1	74003	77162	89	41	8757	0.6	0.6	8.7	66.0	24.2	296312
08051	MANTUA	32077	4503	12.2	18.8	46.3	16.2	6.5	67626	72057	85	34	3635	1.2	4.5	34.5	51.3	8.6	193763
08052	MAPLE SHADE	30186	8561	14.3	27.9	40.9	12.6	4.2	55606	53240	72	18	4215	0.3	0.9	23.5	73.5	1.8	214947
08053	MARLTON	38373	17277	6.9	14.2	37.2	26.3	15.5	86436	94394	94	65	13245	0.1	0.6	10.0	62.4	26.9	324275
08054	MOUNT LAUREL	41917	17763	8.0	16.6	37.1	24.4	13.8	81122	85717	92	57	14504	0.3	0.2	19.5	52.0	28.1	303404
08055	MEDFORD	49364	9978	5.7	8.5	32.5	22.8	30.6	105792	111104	97	80	8495	0.0	0.1	3.7	38.4	57.8	438220
08056	MICKLETON	36728	1518	7.8	15.3	33.5	24.0	19.4	88598	89073	95	68	1403	0.0	0.4	7.1	66.2	26.4	334095
08057	MOORESTOWN	52419	7486	8.1	12.8	26.3	21.5	31.3	104805	110143	97	79	6007	0.1	0.2	4.5	28.7	66.5	590437
08059	MOUNT EPHRAIM	27042	2305	18.6	22.6	42.2	13.0	3.6	58139	63323	75	21	1863	2.2	0.3	43.6	53.8	0.0	178946
08060	MOUNT HOLLY	29795	9386	12.2	19.1	40.6	19.9	8.2	72034	76538	88	39	6905	1.4	1.5	17.9	67.1	12.1	248006
08061	MOUNT ROYAL	31035	549	8.7	24.6	35.3	25.7	5.6	70586	71056	87	38	511	0.0	0.0	12.9	71.6	15.5	306614
08062	MULLICA HILL	36383	5210	9.0	12.1	30.5	27.3	21.0	96396	89913	96	74	4483	2.2	1.0	4.8	50.6	41.4	364927
08063	NATIONAL PARK	23762	1218	15.8	20.8	49.8	10.5	3.1	62524	63776	81	27	1010	0.8	1.7	44.1	53.3	0.2	178500
08065	PALMYRA	30626	3074	11.5	23.2	44.1	18.2	3.0	63686	60353	82	28	2107	0.0	0.2	27.4	70.8	1.6	220236
08066	PAULSBORO	23443	3193	25.1	27.2	36.2	9.1	2.4	47751	51403	56	11	1755	2.2	3.9	64.4	25.9	3.5	153018
08067	PEDRICKTOWN	28248	609	14.1	14.4	49.3	15.4	6.7	75466	76988	90	44	514	0.0	3.3	32.9	52.3	11.5	213855
08068	PEMBERTON	28329	2752	16.3	23.8	40.4	14.1	5.5	59661	55623	77	22	1616	0.4	2.7	17.6	68.7	10.6	230787
08069	PENNS GROVE	21774	5274	27.1	26.6	36.1	7.9	2.4	45778	51215	51	8	3220	2.0	7.9	55.6	32.5	2.0	152998
08070	PENNSVILLE	27906	5308	14.9	21.2	49.3	10.6	4.1	63397	73020	82	28	3937	4.6	2.1	27.2	61.9	4.3	197959
08071	PITMAN	29099	3783	10.5	25.3	39.4	17.9	6.9	64344	66471	83	29	2784	0.0	0.5	16.6	75.3	7.6	240721
08075	DELANCO	30598	10846	12.5	20.1	40.3	19.5	7.5	69146	72423	86	36	7743	0.2	0.7	16.7	71.2	11.2	268344
08077	RIVERTON	36966	6567	6.9	16.4	34.7	28.7	13.3	86279	94052	94	65	5934	0.2	0.1	6.5	68.7	24.5	333112
08078	RUNNEMEDE	24962	3282	19.8	28.2	39.1	9.3	3.6	51753	54660	65	14	2275	0.7	1.5	35.7	60.0	2.0	186769
08079	SALEM	22862	4771	26.9	26.0	36.6	7.1	3.4	47004	51829	54	10	3017	4.8	10.3	36.1	40.5	8.3	172193
08080	SEWELL	33470	13440	6.5	13.3	41.1	22.8	16.4	85480	85471	94	64	11919	0.5	0.5	15.9	62.1	21.0	291534
08081	SICKLERVILLE	28890	16868	8.8	16.0	44.9	21.1	9.1	78807	80790	92	52	14394	1.1	2.3	24.0	62.7	9.9	232912
08083	SOMERDALE	30531	3663	13.5	21.2	41.7	14.8	8.8	68068	75447	86	34	2699	1.6	1.3	19.7	73.1	4.2	217787
08084	STRATFORD	28165	2723	12.7	22.2	46.6	13.0	5.4	64982	70471	83	30	1927	0.0	0.3	24.4	73.6	1.7	218869
08085	SWEDESBORO	38324	5488	7.1	11.4	32.5	24.0	25.0	98190	94255	96	75	4828	0.1	0.7	10.7	59.2	29.2	305467
08086	THOROFARE	30970	3544	12.2	25.8	41.4	15.7	5.0	62153	60022	80	26	2131	6.2	2.3	27.9	52.6	11.0	210580
08087	LITTLE EGG HARBOR TW	27777	10516	14.6	24.3	45.8	11.5	3.8	59857	64590	77	22	8244	1.5	1.9	25.5	63.2	7.9	211737
08088	SHAMONG	37097	9664	12.4	18.3	31.9	20.8	16.5	79409	84611	92	53	8825	3.4	3.9	17.0	45.5	30.3	308970
08089	WATERFORD WORKS	26948	1459	13.4	20.0	43.9	16.2	6.5	68834	75513	86	35	1286	6.0	4.7	18.3	63.5	7.6	223108
08090	WENONAH	30803	3127	10.0	16.5	45.4	19.8	8.3	76767	77701	90	47	2764	0.0	0.6	19.1	68.0	12.3	226718
08091	WEST BERLIN	28521	1893	12.7	21.7	42.9	16.4	6.3	71560	76601	88	39	1447	0.6	0.8	23.8	74.8	0.0	211463
08092	WEST CREEK	24054	1235	21.1	26.2	34.3	10.8	7.6	52587	56750	67	15	1028	4.2	5.5	15.6	51.7	23.1	262302
08093	WESTVILLE	24016	4153	20.1	27.8	39.7	10.4	2.0	51898	54058	66	14	2502	2.1	0.9	42.2	53.4	1.4	180571
08094	WILLIAMSTOWN	26620	14343	15.1	21.2	39.8	18.1	5.8	65397	67099	84	30	12000	4.5	2.3	19.1	65.9	8.2	220525
08096	DEPTFORD	28286	13750	18.4	19.7	39.7	16.6	5.7	63198	63866	81	27	10011	0.1	1.3	27.3	64.0	7.3	213545
08097	WOODBURY HEIGHTS	29122	1123	13.6	17.0	37.8	23.7	7.8	77121	77675	91	49	1009	0.0	0.6	11.0	82.8	5.6	248059
08098	WOODSTOWN	31007	3483	10.1	19.2	43.5	16.7	10.5	75749	78195	90	45	2626	0.6	2.6	14.9	55.8	26.2	296875
08102	CAMDEN	12168	2736	56.4	23.2	17.8	1.5	1.1	19552	22061	1	1	893	44.8	37.2	13.7	1.5	2.9	56200
08103	CAMDEN	13392	4516	44.0	30.6	21.6	2.4	1.4	28758	30560	6	2	2267	28.0	45.4	23.8	2.3	0.5	66438
08104	CAMDEN	12864	8529	43.3	30.2	23.0	2.3	1.2	30015	31610	8	2	4139	18.0	49.0	29.3	2.0	1.8	76355
08105	CAMDEN	11762	8271	41.1	30.6	24.4	3.2	0.9	31995	35120	11	2	3790	9.5	51.8	35.0	2.8	0.8	79504
08106	AUDUBON	29226	4097	16.1	22.9	45.6	10.9	4.5	61548	66284	79	24	2746	1.4	1.9	24.3	67.4	5.1	204644
08107	HADDON TOWNSHIP	25997	5548	21.2	27.5	38.4	9.1	3.8	51253	55701	64	13	3082	1.0	6.2	40.2	49.5	3.0	178533
08108	COLLINGSWOOD	31588	7263	12.5	22.7	45.4	12.8	6.7	64602	71770	83	30	5038	0.0	1.0	25.7	65.0	8.2	223107
08109	MERCHANTVILLE	27275	8526	16.9	22.4	41.6	13.9	5.1	61647	66854	80	25	6257	1.9	1.2	24.4	67.3	5.2	209069
08110	PENNSAUKEN	19873	5992	16.1	28.3	41.8	10.8	2.9	54819	56768	71	17	4769	1.1	4.1	63.2	30.6	0.9	159613
08201	ABSECON	28983	3640	8.4	25.1	45.7	13.4	7.5	65176	71746	83	30	2654	0.6	0.2	11.6	72.7	15.0	268974
08202	AVALON	60568	1097	9.4	21.8	37.3	10.9	20.6	76680	78534	90	47	926	0.0	0.0	0.3	5.3	94.4	965000
08203	BRIGANTINE	29517	4805	19.0	24.3	40.9	10.3	5.6	55774	58546	72	19	2982	0.4	1.0	6.8	59.6	32.3	332868
08204	CAPE MAY	29529	8299	17.9	28.4	39.6	8.3	5.8	53082	57094	68	15	6203	0.5	0.5	9.9	53.2	35.9	328238
08205	ABSECON	27327	10162	12.0	22.5	46.0	13.3	6.2	63518	67166	82	28	7174	1.0	2.2	20.8	56.1	20.0	275754
	NEW JERSEY	34433		15.4	18.6	34.9	16.8	14.2	72809	76895				1.0	1.6	9.9	50.1	37.4	336585
	UNITED STATES	27277		20.9	24.4	35.3	11.7	7.6	54719	56938				9.3	13.1	31.6	32.6	13.5	162279

ZIP CODE #	POST OFFICE NAME	FINANCIAL SERVICES: Auto Loan	FINANCIAL SERVICES: Home Loan	FINANCIAL SERVICES: Investments	FINANCIAL SERVICES: Retirement Plans	THE HOME: Home Improvements: Home Repair	THE HOME: Home Improvements: Lawn & Garden	THE HOME: Furnishings: Computers & Hardware-Personal	THE HOME: Furnishings: Major Appliances	THE HOME: Furnishings: TV, Radio, Sound Equipment	THE HOME: Furnishings: Furniture	ENTERTAINMENT: Dine out/Carry out	ENTERTAINMENT: Sports Equipment	ENTERTAINMENT: Fees & Tickets	ENTERTAINMENT: Toys & Games	ENTERTAINMENT: Travel	ENTERTAINMENT: Cable TV	PERSONAL: Apparel & Services	PERSONAL: Auto Repairs	PERSONAL: Health Insurance	PERSONAL: Pets & Supplies
07950	GREYSTONE PARK	197	245	264	247	257	223	219	220	207	228	209	169	250	209	242	202	154	214	204	247
07960	MORRISTOWN	189	235	268	241	252	215	223	218	208	229	211	170	251	205	245	201	157	215	201	245
07974	NEW PROVIDENCE	183	252	292	251	275	228	215	224	198	228	198	169	256	196	251	191	149	212	201	245
07976	NEW VERNON	269	377	456	387	421	350	316	339	289	353	286	250	387	278	380	275	216	312	302	370
07980	STIRLING	147	202	218	195	211	186	176	177	173	169	176	131	207	172	198	177	131	174	175	197
07981	WHIPPANY	160	233	261	224	250	214	188	199	180	191	181	145	231	181	223	181	135	189	190	216
08002	CHERRY HILL	98	113	112	112	114	114	103	107	105	106	106	78	114	103	112	108	74	106	116	124
08003	CHERRY HILL	172	227	244	230	239	210	192	200	182	204	183	151	227	181	219	178	135	190	187	224
08004	ATCO	104	124	113	123	121	115	112	112	109	113	111	87	123	111	120	109	79	111	111	130
08005	BARNEGAT	95	108	114	104	112	113	95	105	96	101	96	73	105	93	106	98	66	100	112	119
08007	BARRINGTON	80	92	91	92	93	94	87	88	90	87	90	65	96	87	94	93	63	89	100	103
08008	BEACH HAVEN	116	119	165	118	136	142	108	129	114	120	112	82	116	103	124	120	77	122	142	146
08009	BERLIN	106	124	111	123	120	113	112	112	109	115	111	87	122	112	118	108	79	110	108	129
08010	BEVERLY	90	106	99	104	104	101	98	98	97	97	98	74	107	97	104	98	69	98	100	113
08012	BLACKWOOD	105	114	105	115	111	107	110	106	108	111	109	83	115	109	112	107	77	108	107	125
08014	BRIDGEPORT	116	118	94	121	110	124	118	115	119	111	118	91	117	122	114	122	81	117	127	139
08015	BROWNS MILLS	97	104	93	102	100	99	98	97	97	100	98	74	101	99	99	96	68	97	98	114
08016	BURLINGTON	118	132	117	130	127	119	122	120	119	125	120	94	128	123	124	117	85	118	116	139
08019	CHATSWORTH	131	144	126	149	141	144	130	136	128	129	129	106	137	132	137	129	90	131	135	160
08020	CLARKSBORO	114	138	138	139	140	138	118	127	119	124	119	92	134	117	133	120	84	122	131	146
08021	CLEMENTON	85	82	75	83	79	78	88	81	87	87	88	64	86	88	84	86	62	86	82	97
08022	COLUMBUS	116	146	163	142	159	151	125	139	125	136	124	93	146	118	146	127	87	132	149	154
08026	GIBBSBORO	119	148	134	148	143	145	126	131	127	128	128	99	145	128	140	129	90	128	137	152
08027	GIBBSTOWN	99	119	109	118	116	118	104	109	106	105	107	81	118	107	114	109	75	107	116	126
08028	GLASSBORO	93	91	83	92	88	88	99	90	96	95	97	72	97	97	93	96	68	94	92	107
08029	GLENDORA	89	90	84	91	88	97	91	92	95	87	94	69	92	94	91	99	65	93	102	108
08030	GLOUCESTER CITY	80	81	73	81	78	85	81	81	84	77	83	62	82	84	80	87	58	82	89	96
08031	BELLMAWR	82	98	90	96	96	99	87	91	89	86	89	67	97	89	94	92	63	89	98	105
08032	GRENLOCH	205	253	227	261	249	211	209	213	193	233	197	175	240	207	224	178	145	195	176	238
08033	HADDONFIELD	140	168	182	170	177	166	152	157	150	159	150	116	173	146	168	151	108	154	161	179
08034	CHERRY HILL	121	151	160	149	157	146	134	138	133	136	134	101	154	131	150	135	96	136	142	156
08035	HADDON HEIGHTS	106	123	121	123	124	125	111	116	113	114	114	84	123	111	121	116	80	114	125	134
08036	HAINESPORT	133	167	147	166	160	150	140	144	135	146	137	112	159	139	153	132	98	138	136	166
08037	HAMMONTON	90	109	105	106	109	102	98	100	97	98	98	76	109	98	106	97	70	98	99	114
08041	JOBSTOWN	146	200	207	196	207	178	164	171	155	170	157	129	195	158	187	153	117	162	156	190
08043	VOORHEES	158	173	170	181	173	158	167	159	159	172	162	128	179	163	171	154	117	160	148	186
08045	LAWNSIDE	88	86	82	86	84	94	85	87	92	86	91	62	87	89	85	97	63	89	100	106
08046	WILLINGBORO	112	137	123	137	132	136	118	123	119	119	120	92	134	121	130	122	85	120	130	143
08048	LUMBERTON	132	143	128	145	139	125	134	130	128	142	130	104	141	133	134	122	93	127	119	149
08049	MAGNOLIA	84	101	93	99	98	94	93	92	92	92	93	71	102	93	99	92	66	93	93	107
08050	MANAHAWKIN	117	130	135	126	132	130	115	125	115	122	115	90	123	114	124	116	80	119	125	142
08051	MANTUA	105	118	110	115	116	110	108	109	106	112	107	84	115	108	113	105	76	107	108	126
08052	MAPLE SHADE	93	86	80	89	83	84	97	87	97	94	98	70	95	98	92	97	69	94	92	105
08053	MARLTON	138	160	148	162	157	144	145	143	139	151	141	113	157	143	152	135	101	140	135	166
08054	MOUNT LAUREL	135	148	147	150	150	142	142	140	138	147	140	107	151	138	148	137	99	140	141	163
08055	MEDFORD	176	218	224	224	224	202	189	194	181	200	183	149	217	182	209	177	133	186	182	221
08056	MICKLETON	139	172	162	173	171	158	146	152	140	154	142	116	165	142	160	137	101	144	143	174
08057	MOORESTOWN	170	228	256	229	245	215	194	203	186	204	186	151	232	184	224	184	139	193	193	225
08059	MOUNT EPHRAIM	86	101	94	99	99	103	89	94	92	89	93	69	99	92	97	96	65	92	103	109
08060	MOUNT HOLLY	109	125	115	124	122	117	116	114	115	116	116	88	125	116	120	115	83	114	114	133
08061	MOUNT ROYAL	102	127	115	127	123	125	108	113	109	111	110	85	124	110	120	111	78	110	118	131
08062	MULLICA HILL	152	177	171	180	176	163	154	160	147	163	149	125	169	151	165	143	107	151	146	183
08063	NATIONAL PARK	88	103	88	103	98	103	92	94	93	92	94	72	102	95	98	95	66	93	101	111
08065	PALMYRA	93	108	101	108	106	104	99	99	98	100	99	75	108	99	105	99	70	99	101	116
08066	PAULSBORO	81	75	64	77	69	80	80	76	83	77	82	60	78	84	75	85	57	80	85	94
08067	PEDRICKTOWN	99	123	110	123	118	121	105	109	106	106	107	82	121	107	116	108	75	107	116	127
08068	PEMBERTON	94	104	98	104	102	101	103	99	103	100	104	76	109	103	105	105	74	102	104	117
08069	PENNS GROVE	76	73	68	73	71	76	77	75	80	74	79	57	76	80	74	83	56	78	82	89
08070	PENNSVILLE	89	104	97	102	102	104	95	98	96	93	97	73	103	96	102	99	68	97	104	113
08071	PITMAN	95	115	112	113	115	112	104	106	104	104	105	79	116	103	113	106	75	105	112	122
08075	DELANCO	108	119	109	119	116	110	114	111	111	115	113	87	120	114	117	110	80	112	109	129
08077	RIVERTON	130	161	165	161	166	157	140	147	138	144	139	107	159	137	156	139	99	142	148	167
08078	RUNNEMEDE	81	90	85	89	88	91	85	87	87	83	87	65	91	87	89	90	61	87	93	101
08079	SALEM	80	77	74	77	76	85	77	80	82	76	81	59	77	82	77	87	56	80	89	95
08080	SEWELL	138	164	150	164	160	148	143	145	137	150	139	113	158	141	152	133	99	140	135	167
08081	SICKLERVILLE	128	140	120	138	134	122	126	126	120	134	123	98	131	126	127	116	86	121	115	145
08083	SOMERDALE	106	117	111	118	115	118	109	111	110	110	110	83	117	109	115	112	77	110	117	130
08084	STRATFORD	96	109	98	109	105	104	102	100	101	102	102	77	110	103	106	101	72	101	103	118
08085	SWEDESBORO	161	189	165	191	184	162	164	165	154	176	157	134	180	163	171	146	113	155	145	187
08086	THOROFARE	98	99	98	101	98	101	102	99	103	100	103	77	104	102	103	104	72	102	105	118
08087	LITTLE EGG HARBOR TW	95	99	106	98	102	106	94	101	96	95	96	73	98	94	100	98	66	98	106	116
08088	SHAMONG	125	154	164	152	162	153	131	143	130	142	130	101	151	126	150	130	92	136	145	161
08089	WATERFORD WORKS	100	120	108	120	116	120	104	108	107	106	108	80	118	107	113	110	75	107	117	127
08090	WENONAH	109	135	129	135	134	129	117	121	116	120	117	91	133	116	129	116	83	118	121	139
08091	WEST BERLIN	99	122	110	121	118	118	107	109	107	108	109	83	121	108	117	109	77	108	114	127
08092	WEST CREEK	106	94	101	96	97	111	95	106	98	88	97	79	87	99	95	104	66	100	110	124
08093	WESTVILLE	81	86	77	86	83	83	85	82	85	85	85	64	88	86	86	85	60	84	85	97
08094	WILLIAMSTOWN	98	114	107	113	112	109	102	105	101	105	102	80	112	102	109	101	72	103	105	121
08096	DEPTFORD	95	107	99	107	105	102	101	100	101	102	102	76	108	101	105	101	72	100	103	117
08097	WOODBURY HEIGHTS	107	132	118	132	127	130	113	118	114	115	116	88	130	116	125	117	81	115	124	137
08098	WOODSTOWN	114	131	127	133	132	127	120	123	117	121	118	94	129	118	128	117	84	120	122	143
08102	CAMDEN	39	34	34	34	33	35	43	38	47	39	47	27	40	44	38	51	34	43	45	46
08103	CAMDEN	45	49	50	46	49	49	50	47	55	45	55	33	53	54	49	60	40	51	55	57
08104	CAMDEN	49	47	46	46	46	48	52	47	58	48	57	34	52	56	48	62	41	52	55	58
08105	CAMDEN	53	46	40	45	43	45	56	49	59	53	59	38	52	58	49	60	43	55	52	59
08106	AUDUBON	94	105	102	104	104	107	98	102	100	96	100	77	105	100	104	102	70	100	107	118
08107	HADDON TOWNSHIP	82	84	79	85	82	86	88	83	89	85	89	64	90	88	87	91	63	87	92	100
08108	COLLINGSWOOD	98	110	106	110	109	107	106	104	106	106	106	80	114	105	111	106	75	106	109	122
08109	MERCHANTVILLE	93	107	100	106	105	104	99	100	99	99	100	75	107	99	105	101	71	100	104	116
08110	PENNSAUKEN	87	92	79	88	88	86	88	87	87	90	89	66	90	89	88	87	62	88	87	101
08201	ABSECON	103	114	110	115	113	108	110	107	108	111	109	83	117	108	114	107	78	109	107	125
08202	AVALON	164	173	232	172	198	203	156	183	164	176	161	115	171	148	180	171	111	175	203	207
08203	BRIGANTINE	91	96	97	98	97	95	95	93	95	97	95	71	100	93	98	95	67	95	97	110
08204	CAPE MAY	92	97	109	96	101	107	91	100	94	92	94	70	96	90	99	98	65	97	109	114
08205	ABSECON	108	108	97	110	104	98	109	102	105	112	107	82	110	109	106	102	76	105	97	121
	NEW JERSEY	119	138	141	137	141	129	132	129	129	132	131	98	143	128	139	129	95	130	128	148
	UNITED STATES	100	100	100	100	100	100	100	100	100	100	100	100	100	100	100	100	100	100	100	100

ZIP CODE			POPULATION			2000-2009 ANNUAL RATE		HOUSEHOLDS					FAMILIES		
#	POST OFFICE NAME	COUNTY FIPS CODE	2000	2009	2014	% Rate	State Centile	2000	2009	2014	% Annual Rate 2000-2009	2009 Average HH Size	2000	2009	% Annual Rate 2000-2009
08210	CAPE MAY COURT HOUSE	009	15440	16894	17068	1.0	80	5392	6126	6247	1.4	2.59	3966	4445	1.2
08215	EGG HARBOR CITY	001	12660	14641	15343	1.6	91	4668	5472	5747	1.7	2.64	3368	3895	1.6
08221	LINWOOD	001	7091	7322	7336	0.3	50	2617	2747	2762	0.5	2.61	1933	1999	0.4
08223	MARMORA	009	3991	3900	3828	-0.2	12	1478	1496	1482	0.1	2.60	1138	1139	0.0
08225	NORTHFIELD	001	7890	8482	8598	0.8	73	2897	3167	3224	1.0	2.61	2158	2331	0.8
08226	OCEAN CITY	009	15378	14040	13555	-1.0	1	7464	7129	6939	-0.5	1.93	4007	3765	-0.7
08230	OCEAN VIEW	009	6056	6557	6607	0.9	76	2039	2294	2335	1.3	2.83	1618	1802	1.2
08232	PLEASANTVILLE	001	18142	18774	18933	0.4	56	6066	6217	6261	0.3	2.94	4139	4175	0.1
08234	EGG HARBOR TOWNSHIP	001	29831	41147	45729	3.5	98	10834	14865	16513	3.5	2.77	7868	10861	3.5
08241	PORT REPUBLIC	001	1027	952	1056	-0.8	1	362	373	417	0.3	2.55	231	235	0.2
08242	RIO GRANDE	009	2906	2731	2913	-0.7	2	1208	1180	1268	-0.3	2.30	773	740	-0.5
08243	SEA ISLE CITY	009	2756	2702	2670	-0.2	12	1338	1380	1377	0.3	1.96	775	784	0.1
08244	SOMERS POINT	001	11665	11593	11391	-0.1	19	4952	4995	4924	0.1	2.28	2976	2941	-0.1
08247	STONE HARBOR	009	1204	1199	1196	0.0	28	632	651	655	0.3	1.80	356	361	0.2
08248	STRATHMERE	009	175	168	165	-0.4	4	93	93	92	0.0	1.81	55	54	-0.2
08251	VILLAS	009	9776	9524	9335	-0.3	7	4033	4002	3945	-0.1	2.38	2698	2642	-0.2
08260	WILDWOOD	009	15297	13686	13403	-1.2	1	6923	6472	6401	-0.7	2.10	4050	3724	-0.9
08270	WOODBINE	009	8336	8566	8541	0.3	50	2642	2794	2803	0.6	2.83	2049	2146	0.5
08302	BRIDGETON	011	45824	49312	50482	0.8	73	14037	14702	15098	0.5	2.88	10176	10588	0.4
08310	BUENA	001	1828	1977	2020	0.9	76	758	835	857	1.1	2.33	534	580	0.9
08311	CEDARVILLE	011	1845	2047	2148	1.1	83	628	696	734	1.1	2.86	479	526	1.0
08312	CLAYTON	015	6884	7930	8611	1.5	89	2375	2769	3024	1.7	2.85	1812	2095	1.6
08314	DELMONT	011	3723	2203	2220	-5.5	0	136	150	158	1.1	2.67	101	110	0.9
08317	DOROTHY	001	1283	1502	1600	1.7	92	410	490	524	1.9	3.04	324	381	1.8
08318	ELMER	033	12117	12954	13252	0.7	68	4198	4503	4620	0.8	2.83	3322	3535	0.7
08319	ESTELL MANOR	001	1100	1288	1371	1.7	92	383	458	489	2.0	2.79	302	356	1.8
08322	FRANKLINVILLE	015	9811	11368	12181	1.6	91	3300	3857	4149	1.7	2.94	2671	3111	1.7
08323	GREENWICH	011	689	806	860	1.7	92	259	303	324	1.7	2.65	195	227	1.7
08324	HEISLERVILLE	011	200	209	215	0.5	62	65	68	70	0.5	3.07	50	52	0.4
08326	LANDISVILLE	001	1312	1521	1608	1.6	91	467	552	588	1.8	2.72	340	396	1.7
08327	LEESBURG	011	393	410	422	0.5	62	144	150	155	0.4	2.73	110	114	0.4
08328	MALAGA	015	1485	1734	1869	1.7	92	511	603	653	1.8	2.86	393	461	1.7
08330	MAYS LANDING	001	21916	27425	29743	2.5	96	7723	9939	10854	2.8	2.65	5452	6811	2.4
08332	MILLVILLE	011	35935	40923	42860	1.4	88	13315	14220	14966	0.7	2.69	9453	10056	0.7
08340	MILMAY	001	869	949	974	1.0	80	315	349	359	1.1	2.68	237	260	1.0
08341	MINOTOLA	001	1504	1671	1747	1.1	83	604	682	716	1.3	2.45	374	412	1.1
08343	MONROEVILLE	033	4057	4505	4713	1.1	83	1382	1551	1633	1.3	2.85	1073	1195	1.2
08344	NEWFIELD	015	6316	6532	6896	0.4	56	2049	2307	2449	1.3	2.80	1612	1802	1.2
08345	NEWPORT	011	1010	1077	1117	0.7	68	433	461	479	0.7	2.34	284	297	0.5
08346	NEWTONVILLE	001	525	542	542	0.3	50	142	149	150	0.5	3.62	107	111	0.4
08349	PORT NORRIS	011	2507	2614	2683	0.5	62	869	905	932	0.4	2.88	639	658	0.3
08350	RICHLAND	001	490	517	521	0.6	65	168	181	183	0.8	2.81	126	135	0.7
08353	SHILOH	011	367	426	453	1.6	91	131	152	162	1.6	2.80	106	122	1.5
08360	VINELAND	011	40220	42071	42989	0.5	62	14495	15154	15529	0.5	2.72	10143	10506	0.4
08361	VINELAND	011	16547	18759	19761	1.4	88	5777	6561	6960	1.4	2.65	4278	4831	1.3
08401	ATLANTIC CITY	001	40517	41903	42455	0.4	56	15848	16256	16464	0.3	2.48	8708	8729	0.0
08402	MARGATE CITY	001	8193	7704	7534	-0.7	2	3984	3833	3773	-0.4	2.01	2303	2157	-0.7
08403	LONGPORT	001	1156	1170	1158	0.1	35	587	606	603	0.3	1.93	349	353	0.1
08406	VENTNOR CITY	001	12910	12659	12521	-0.2	12	5480	5389	5334	-0.2	2.35	3256	3135	-0.4
08501	ALLENTOWN	025	4714	6321	6984	3.2	97	1658	2223	2460	3.2	2.84	1321	1774	3.2
08502	BELLE MEAD	035	9382	12083	13288	2.8	96	2893	3695	4054	2.7	3.26	2495	3163	2.6
08505	BORDENTOWN	005	14164	16753	17651	1.8	93	5728	6817	7216	1.9	2.44	3926	4697	2.0
08510	MILLSTONE TOWNSHIP	025	3109	3687	3910	1.9	93	979	1164	1234	1.9	3.16	870	1029	1.8
08511	COOKSTOWN	005	1254	1306	1364	0.4	56	216	241	263	1.2	2.88	175	194	1.1
08512	CRANBURY	023	6482	7688	8262	1.9	93	2268	2640	2823	1.7	2.90	1722	1980	1.5
08514	CREAM RIDGE	025	3075	4018	4387	2.9	96	1098	1443	1580	3.0	2.77	910	1182	2.9
08515	CHESTERFIELD	005	1103	2024	2273	6.8	100	386	687	768	6.4	2.95	321	568	6.4
08518	FLORENCE	005	4846	4878	4874	0.1	35	1928	1977	1988	0.3	2.45	1269	1288	0.2
08520	HIGHTSTOWN	021	29382	32340	33421	1.0	80	11060	12080	12498	1.0	2.65	7679	8276	0.8
08525	HOPEWELL	021	4912	5211	5326	0.6	65	1855	1967	2014	0.6	2.58	1407	1490	0.6
08527	JACKSON	029	42459	55859	61358	3.0	97	14065	18665	20562	3.1	2.97	11173	14700	3.0
08528	KINGSTON	035	104	101	114	-0.3	7	46	46	52	0.0	2.13	33	33	0.0
08530	LAMBERTVILLE	019	7578	8458	8787	1.2	85	2980	3332	3464	1.2	2.41	1785	2014	1.3
08533	NEW EGYPT	029	6579	7440	7873	1.3	87	2220	2527	2677	1.4	2.94	1756	1978	1.3
08534	PENNINGTON	021	11267	12455	12934	1.1	83	4085	4541	4733	1.2	2.68	3259	3600	1.1
08535	PERRINEVILLE	025	2409	2596	2648	0.8	73	675	726	742	0.8	3.52	608	651	0.7
08536	PLAINSBORO	023	17773	19677	20224	1.1	83	7703	8194	8358	0.7	2.39	4435	4701	0.6
08540	PRINCETON	021	43356	48360	50597	1.2	85	14853	16920	17813	1.4	2.44	10185	11555	1.4
08542	PRINCETON	021	3909	3937	3923	0.1	35	1545	1535	1526	-0.1	2.36	765	748	-0.2
08544	PRINCETON	021	0	835	829	0.0	28	0	0	0	0.0	0.00	0	0	0.0
08550	PRINCETON JUNCTION	021	17584	20171	21262	1.5	89	5458	6214	6537	1.4	3.24	4806	5496	1.5
08551	RINGOES	019	5176	5681	5902	1.0	80	1756	1904	1971	0.9	2.97	1404	1507	0.8
08553	ROCKY HILL	035	662	697	713	0.6	65	284	297	303	0.5	2.35	190	196	0.3
08554	ROEBLING	005	3735	3802	3853	0.2	43	1427	1487	1518	0.4	2.56	1006	1035	0.3
08555	ROOSEVELT	025	426	469	487	1.0	80	153	170	177	1.1	2.76	117	128	1.0
08556	ROSEMONT	019	85	93	96	1.0	80	33	36	38	0.9	2.56	25	27	0.8
08558	SKILLMAN	035	5060	6370	7115	2.5	96	1696	2072	2310	2.2	3.04	1336	1617	2.1
08559	STOCKTON	019	4923	5318	5476	0.8	73	1835	1994	2060	0.9	2.66	1410	1521	0.8
08560	TITUSVILLE	021	3550	3900	4048	1.0	80	1325	1455	1512	1.0	2.63	1026	1118	0.9
08562	WRIGHTSTOWN	005	7124	7231	7269	0.2	43	2516	2582	2608	0.3	2.57	1907	1938	0.2
08608	TRENTON	021	1459	1464	1459	0.0	28	784	784	783	0.0	1.73	315	310	-0.2
08609	TRENTON	021	14590	14653	14651	0.0	28	4722	4722	4724	0.0	2.99	3124	3097	-0.1
08610	TRENTON	021	29162	29075	29142	0.0	28	11841	11803	11848	0.0	2.46	7784	7653	-0.2
08611	TRENTON	021	25382	25650	25577	0.1	35	8390	8264	8220	-0.2	2.82	5255	5113	-0.3
08618	EWING	021	41191	41948	42079	0.2	43	13587	13842	13911	0.2	2.63	8551	8633	0.1
08619	TRENTON	021	23159	23429	23494	0.1	35	9448	9572	9620	0.1	2.41	6186	6158	0.0
08620	TRENTON	021	15573	15719	16100	0.1	35	4467	4518	4653	0.1	2.75	3380	3355	-0.1
08628	EWING	021	8523	9137	9499	0.8	73	3429	3668	3815	0.7	2.34	2196	2328	0.6
08629	TRENTON	021	11187	11077	11014	-0.1	19	4045	3963	3938	-0.2	2.79	2824	2736	-0.3
08638	EWING	021	23607	24165	24343	0.3	50	8622	8717	8784	0.1	2.71	5871	5884	0.0
08640	FORT DIX	005	6834	6376	6296	-0.7	2	841	748	726	-1.3	3.01	711	640	-1.1
08641	TRENTON	005	5046	4934	4892	-0.2	12	1127	1125	1124	0.0	3.83	1105	1102	0.0
08648	TRENTON	021	27534	30549	31695	1.1	83	10227	11423	11902	1.2	2.47	6761	7477	1.1
08690	TRENTON	021	18349	19608	19985	0.7	68	6436	6919	7075	0.8	2.79	5143	5469	0.7
08691	TRENTON	021	11483	15146	16350	3.0	97	4424	5825	6310	3.0	2.59	3167	4172	3.0
	NEW JERSEY					0.5					0.5	2.69			0.5
	UNITED STATES					1.0					1.1	2.59			0.9

#	POST OFFICE NAME	White 2000	White 2009	Black 2000	Black 2009	Asian/Pacific 2000	Asian/Pacific 2009	% Hispanic Origin 2000	% Hispanic Origin 2009	0-4	5-9	10-14	15-19	20-24	25-44	45-64	65-84	85+	18+	MEDIAN AGE 2009	% 2009 Males	% 2009 Females
08210	CAPE MAY COURT HOUSE	87.2	83.0	9.5	12.0	1.4	2.2	1.6	2.8	5.9	6.5	6.9	6.6	4.7	22.9	28.5	14.5	3.5	76.4	42.6	48.3	51.7
08215	EGG HARBOR CITY	78.9	73.2	9.0	10.3	2.1	3.3	13.6	18.3	6.6	6.7	6.9	7.6	6.3	24.5	28.6	10.9	1.9	75.0	38.5	49.1	50.9
08221	LINWOOD	95.2	92.0	1.1	1.6	2.4	4.2	1.8	3.2	4.8	5.7	6.6	7.2	4.7	17.7	33.3	15.9	4.0	78.1	46.9	46.8	53.2
08223	MARMORA	97.8	96.9	0.7	0.9	0.7	1.1	1.2	2.1	5.5	6.1	7.2	7.6	4.4	21.7	33.1	12.2	2.2	75.8	43.3	48.0	52.0
08225	NORTHFIELD	91.6	86.6	2.6	3.7	2.6	4.4	4.3	7.4	5.2	5.8	6.6	7.5	4.9	21.4	30.7	14.5	3.3	77.2	44.0	47.5	52.5
08226	OCEAN CITY	93.6	91.9	4.3	5.1	0.6	0.9	2.0	3.2	3.3	3.8	3.9	4.2	4.6	20.6	32.2	22.8	4.6	86.3	51.5	46.7	53.3
08230	OCEAN VIEW	97.9	96.9	0.4	0.6	0.8	1.2	1.3	2.4	5.6	6.3	7.5	7.9	4.4	20.3	33.3	12.3	2.4	75.6	43.6	47.6	52.4
08232	PLEASANTVILLE	26.2	21.7	56.4	56.6	2.0	2.6	21.9	27.6	7.7	7.9	7.6	8.5	7.1	25.8	23.3	9.6	2.4	71.5	33.6	46.7	53.3
08234	EGG HARBOR TOWNSHIP	79.7	72.8	10.2	12.2	5.0	7.7	6.7	10.1	7.1	7.3	7.7	7.6	5.1	26.4	29.0	8.7	1.1	73.1	37.8	48.7	51.3
08241	PORT REPUBLIC	89.9	84.6	4.2	5.8	2.6	4.7	3.0	5.3	5.4	5.4	5.5	5.9	5.5	24.3	31.4	15.0	1.8	80.0	43.7	46.6	53.4
08242	RIO GRANDE	89.1	84.8	6.4	8.3	0.9	1.4	2.9	4.8	4.8	4.9	5.2	6.6	5.5	22.3	29.3	18.5	2.9	81.0	45.4	47.5	52.5
08243	SEA ISLE CITY	97.9	97.0	0.3	0.4	0.4	0.6	1.1	1.9	3.1	2.7	3.1	4.2	4.2	16.2	35.5	27.2	3.8	88.3	55.2	48.1	51.9
08244	SOMERS POINT	85.7	79.1	7.0	9.1	3.2	5.4	6.0	9.8	6.1	5.7	5.6	6.1	6.6	26.9	28.3	12.1	2.7	78.8	39.9	47.2	52.8
08247	STONE HARBOR	97.8	97.1	1.5	2.0	0.1	0.2	0.5	0.9	2.1	2.3	2.8	2.9	2.6	12.0	37.7	31.4	6.2	90.7	60.2	47.4	52.6
08248	STRATHMERE	97.7	96.4	0.0	0.0	1.1	1.8	1.7	3.0	2.4	1.2	1.2	2.4	2.4	16.1	32.1	38.1	4.2	94.6	61.2	52.4	47.6
08251	VILLAS	94.9	92.7	2.5	3.3	0.4	0.6	2.5	4.3	6.2	6.3	6.5	7.0	5.6	23.9	26.3	15.6	2.5	76.7	40.8	48.3	51.7
08260	WILDWOOD	86.9	84.7	6.5	6.2	0.6	0.8	8.1	11.5	5.1	4.7	4.8	5.1	5.9	21.2	28.1	21.3	3.9	82.3	47.3	47.5	52.5
08270	WOODBINE	82.2	79.3	11.6	12.1	0.3	0.5	8.4	11.7	7.2	6.6	7.0	7.0	5.2	27.4	29.6	8.9	1.1	75.0	38.4	53.1	46.9
08302	BRIDGETON	55.6	50.2	31.0	31.5	1.1	2.1	14.8	20.5	6.5	6.4	6.1	6.8	7.4	31.4	23.1	10.4	1.9	77.1	35.2	54.8	45.2
08310	BUENA	71.3	64.5	18.5	20.7	0.2	0.4	15.8	23.9	6.0	6.1	6.2	7.1	5.8	23.7	27.6	15.0	2.6	77.3	41.4	48.7	51.3
08311	CEDARVILLE	81.2	74.3	10.1	12.8	0.5	1.0	8.2	13.3	5.9	7.3	6.9	7.4	4.3	28.5	27.7	10.6	1.5	75.3	38.7	50.6	49.4
08312	CLAYTON	79.5	74.4	15.8	19.1	0.7	1.1	3.3	4.8	7.7	7.2	7.1	7.1	6.5	28.9	25.9	8.5	1.2	73.7	34.8	48.0	52.0
08314	DELMONT	28.4	54.8	59.1	27.6	0.4	7.4	15.5	14.1	1.8	2.0	1.7	17.5	25.1	36.3	11.3	3.4	0.8	93.5	25.8	61.5	38.5
08317	DOROTHY	94.0	91.1	3.9	5.7	0.2	0.5	1.6	2.9	5.8	6.3	7.2	7.8	4.9	22.3	30.5	13.3	1.9	75.6	42.1	47.9	52.1
08318	ELMER	89.9	86.2	6.6	8.7	0.6	0.9	3.0	4.8	5.5	5.9	6.4	6.9	5.4	25.9	31.3	11.0	1.7	77.9	40.8	49.4	50.6
08319	ESTELL MANOR	94.0	91.1	3.9	5.7	0.3	0.5	1.6	2.9	5.8	6.3	7.2	7.8	4.9	22.3	30.5	13.4	1.9	75.5	42.1	47.8	52.2
08322	FRANKLINVILLE	90.6	88.1	6.7	8.1	0.4	0.6	2.7	4.1	6.4	6.9	7.6	7.1	5.0	26.7	30.0	9.3	1.1	74.7	38.7	50.2	49.8
08323	GREENWICH	90.0	86.5	5.1	6.7	0.3	0.4	1.6	3.0	5.3	5.6	6.5	6.3	4.6	23.4	31.3	14.5	2.5	78.5	43.8	48.3	51.7
08324	HEISLERVILLE	96.0	94.3	1.0	1.4	0.0	0.0	1.5	2.9	6.2	6.7	7.2	7.2	4.3	24.9	28.7	13.4	1.4	74.6	40.8	49.8	50.2
08326	LANDISVILLE	74.4	66.0	8.0	9.3	0.5	0.6	29.2	41.9	6.8	6.8	6.4	7.3	6.4	28.7	25.3	10.4	1.8	75.7	35.8	50.8	49.2
08327	LEESBURG	95.4	93.7	1.3	1.7	0.0	0.0	1.5	2.4	6.1	6.6	7.1	7.1	4.1	24.6	29.5	13.4	1.5	75.9	41.3	50.7	49.3
08328	MALAGA	87.2	84.0	8.2	9.6	0.5	0.7	4.4	6.6	7.1	6.9	6.4	6.5	7.4	28.6	26.9	9.2	1.0	75.7	35.1	49.4	50.6
08330	MAYS LANDING	72.3	62.3	18.7	23.7	3.2	5.1	7.8	12.6	7.0	6.7	6.6	7.2	7.9	29.1	26.0	8.2	1.2	75.3	35.0	49.4	50.6
08332	MILLVILLE	78.2	71.3	13.9	16.6	0.7	1.6	9.5	14.8	6.7	6.3	6.3	8.0	8.4	26.9	25.3	10.3	1.7	76.4	35.6	48.6	51.4
08340	MILMAY	90.4	85.9	4.6	6.2	0.2	0.4	5.2	8.9	4.3	5.1	5.9	6.1	4.5	25.0	35.1	12.2	1.8	80.8	44.3	48.5	51.5
08341	MINOTOLA	79.3	70.9	7.4	9.2	0.5	0.7	18.6	28.6	6.5	6.1	6.0	6.5	7.4	27.6	24.9	12.3	2.8	77.4	37.6	48.5	51.5
08343	MONROEVILLE	92.6	89.8	4.0	5.1	0.2	0.3	3.2	5.1	5.5	6.0	6.7	7.1	4.8	23.8	32.2	11.9	2.0	77.1	42.3	50.0	50.0
08344	NEWFIELD	83.2	81.5	11.3	10.5	0.4	1.5	8.8	11.9	5.4	5.9	6.8	7.3	6.6	26.8	28.6	10.9	1.7	78.0	39.2	49.4	50.6
08345	NEWPORT	92.2	89.0	4.3	5.7	0.2	0.4	3.0	5.6	5.5	5.4	5.7	6.2	5.4	21.4	28.6	19.3	2.5	79.7	45.3	52.0	48.0
08346	NEWTONVILLE	50.8	41.3	39.5	45.2	0.2	0.4	12.8	18.3	6.1	6.6	7.2	9.2	6.6	22.7	28.4	11.4	1.7	73.6	38.8	48.2	51.8
08349	PORT NORRIS	71.6	65.1	23.9	28.5	0.2	0.3	3.7	6.1	5.9	6.4	6.8	7.5	5.8	23.4	28.4	13.7	2.1	76.1	40.8	48.4	51.6
08350	RICHLAND	69.8	62.9	22.7	25.9	0.2	0.4	9.6	14.7	5.2	5.6	6.4	7.4	5.6	23.4	32.1	12.6	1.7	77.9	42.3	48.0	52.0
08353	SHILOH	92.7	90.1	3.5	4.5	0.3	0.5	2.4	4.5	6.1	6.6	7.0	5.9	4.2	24.9	31.0	12.4	1.9	76.3	42.0	49.8	50.2
08360	VINELAND	62.3	57.4	14.9	14.5	0.9	1.2	36.9	46.2	6.7	6.7	6.6	7.2	6.8	26.4	25.3	11.8	2.4	75.6	37.2	48.8	51.2
08361	VINELAND	84.6	78.7	6.9	8.2	1.9	2.8	11.2	18.4	5.0	5.3	6.0	6.5	4.8	24.9	30.6	14.4	2.5	79.3	43.3	46.0	54.0
08401	ATLANTIC CITY	26.7	21.8	44.2	43.4	10.5	12.4	24.9	30.2	7.5	7.3	6.5	6.6	7.0	27.4	23.6	11.7	2.3	74.8	35.8	49.0	51.0
08402	MARGATE CITY	95.7	92.9	0.9	1.2	1.6	2.9	2.7	4.9	3.4	3.5	4.1	4.8	4.1	18.1	31.5	25.6	4.9	86.0	53.1	47.2	52.8
08403	LONGPORT	98.3	96.9	0.1	0.2	1.3	2.5	0.7	1.1	2.6	3.2	3.7	3.4	1.8	11.3	37.4	32.1	4.5	88.3	59.5	47.5	52.5
08406	VENTNOR CITY	77.1	67.6	2.9	3.5	7.5	10.9	17.1	25.1	5.4	5.0	5.3	5.5	6.3	25.0	27.5	16.7	3.3	81.0	43.1	48.2	51.8
08501	ALLENTOWN	92.7	89.9	3.6	4.2	1.1	1.7	2.6	4.7	7.0	7.7	8.0	7.0	4.2	23.6	32.6	8.8	1.1	72.5	40.6	49.7	50.3
08502	BELLE MEAD	81.2	73.6	2.2	2.6	14.5	20.9	2.1	3.5	8.4	10.7	10.3	6.9	2.9	27.3	27.2	5.7	0.6	65.3	36.8	49.9	50.1
08505	BORDENTOWN	87.0	81.3	7.7	10.1	2.5	4.3	2.7	4.6	6.3	6.4	6.6	6.0	5.0	28.4	29.7	10.2	1.5	77.2	39.9	48.6	51.4
08510	MILLSTONE TOWNSHIP	92.8	89.3	2.6	3.5	3.4	5.2	3.5	5.7	6.9	8.4	10.0	9.0	3.7	19.5	34.3	7.4	0.8	68.5	40.3	48.3	51.7
08511	COOKSTOWN	59.9	56.9	27.5	27.2	1.6	2.4	14.8	18.8	3.1	3.5	3.9	4.2	4.1	49.3	25.6	5.9	0.4	86.9	37.5	72.7	27.3
08512	CRANBURY	80.4	73.1	3.9	4.7	11.7	16.5	8.0	11.7	6.8	8.2	8.5	7.6	4.1	24.2	30.2	8.9	1.6	71.0	39.7	48.7	51.3
08514	CREAM RIDGE	95.1	92.9	1.6	2.0	1.2	1.8	3.6	5.9	6.2	7.2	8.0	7.2	3.8	22.7	33.5	10.1	1.2	73.6	42.0	49.7	50.3
08515	CHESTERFIELD	95.2	92.8	2.2	3.0	0.9	1.5	1.8	3.1	5.8	6.9	7.9	6.4	3.5	21.2	35.4	11.4	1.5	75.2	43.9	48.7	51.3
08518	FLORENCE	80.9	74.7	13.8	17.5	2.7	4.1	1.8	3.0	5.7	6.2	6.6	6.3	6.0	27.9	27.8	11.3	2.1	77.5	39.1	48.3	51.7
08520	HIGHTSTOWN	75.3	67.1	8.7	10.9	8.3	11.0	14.4	21.1	7.3	7.1	6.9	5.7	5.3	30.2	27.0	8.8	1.7	75.1	37.4	49.1	50.9
08525	HOPEWELL	93.3	90.1	3.1	4.2	1.5	2.4	1.9	3.4	5.1	5.7	6.7	6.9	5.2	20.9	35.3	12.6	1.7	77.7	44.7	50.5	49.5
08527	JACKSON	91.3	88.7	3.9	4.4	2.1	3.1	5.8	8.7	7.8	8.0	8.0	7.3	5.0	26.8	26.9	8.9	1.3	71.6	37.0	48.9	51.1
08528	KINGSTON	68.0	59.4	12.6	13.9	16.5	22.8	4.9	6.9	8.9	8.9	8.9	5.0	2.0	28.7	26.7	7.9	3.0	70.3	38.8	49.5	50.5
08530	LAMBERTVILLE	91.9	89.3	5.3	6.7	1.0	1.5	2.4	3.6	4.2	4.5	5.1	5.5	5.6	25.2	34.4	13.5	2.0	82.9	44.9	51.2	48.8
08533	NEW EGYPT	93.6	91.3	2.5	3.0	0.8	1.2	4.0	6.1	6.6	7.0	7.3	7.8	5.8	25.8	29.9	8.8	1.0	74.0	38.4	49.5	50.5
08534	PENNINGTON	89.4	84.5	4.3	5.9	4.5	6.7	2.4	4.2	7.3	7.3	7.4	6.5	3.7	23.9	31.3	11.2	1.5	73.6	41.0	49.5	50.5
08535	PERRINEVILLE	91.2	87.3	3.4	4.5	3.5	5.4	3.5	5.7	7.4	9.3	10.9	9.2	3.2	19.5	33.0	6.7	0.7	65.9	39.3	50.6	49.4
08536	PLAINSBORO	56.1	43.9	8.3	8.2	31.8	43.1	4.8	6.7	7.2	7.2	6.6	5.9	7.8	38.2	23.4	3.4	0.3	74.9	32.5	50.7	49.3
08540	PRINCETON	79.7	69.3	5.2	8.9	11.3	15.6	4.8	8.4	5.4	5.6	6.1	8.2	9.7	26.0	26.7	10.4	1.8	79.5	37.3	50.3	49.7
08542	PRINCETON	70.1	60.9	12.0	14.1	4.5	5.8	18.9	27.7	5.5	4.2	4.2	5.8	8.5	32.6	23.3	11.7	4.3	83.3	37.4	49.9	50.1
08544	PRINCETON	0.0	64.6	0.0	11.7	0.0	16.9	0.0	8.6	6.0	4.8	4.4	9.3	15.3	37.1	17.0	5.0	1.0	84.1	28.6	54.6	45.4
08550	PRINCETON JUNCTION	71.6	61.4	2.5	3.3	23.7	32.3	2.7	4.3	6.4	8.5	9.5	8.5	3.5	21.3	34.3	7.2	0.8	69.5	40.5	49.8	50.2
08551	RINGOES	95.3	93.1	1.0	1.3	2.1	3.3	2.0	3.2	6.1	7.3	8.5	7.2	3.2	22.7	33.5	9.9	1.5	72.9	42.1	49.7	50.3
08553	ROCKY HILL	95.2	93.0	1.4	1.7	1.1	1.7	3.9	6.9	5.2	5.2	6.2	6.0	4.7	20.9	34.3	14.8	2.7	79.9	46.0	48.5	51.5
08554	ROEBLING	90.7	87.2	6.0	7.7	1.5	2.2	2.5	4.1	6.7	6.4	6.7	7.4	6.5	26.9	27.7	9.8	1.8	75.7	37.9	47.4	52.6
08555	ROOSEVELT	89.0	84.4	2.6	3.4	2.1	3.4	4.5	7.2	4.7	5.8	7.2	8.1	4.1	19.8	37.1	11.1	2.1	77.2	45.2	48.0	52.0
08556	ROSEMONT	97.6	95.7	0.0	0.0	1.2	2.2	1.2	1.1	4.3	4.3	6.5	6.5	4.3	18.3	38.7	15.1	2.2	78.5	48.1	50.5	49.5
08558	SKILLMAN	88.4	83.1	2.0	2.4	8.1	12.1	2.3	3.9	7.4	9.0	10.3	7.9	2.9	21.6	31.5	8.6	0.9	67.3	40.4	49.5	50.5
08559	STOCKTON	97.8	96.7	0.4	0.5	0.9	1.5	1.2	1.9	5.1	6.3	6.8	6.4	4.2	21.6	36.8	11.5	1.4	77.7	44.8	49.7	50.3
08560	TITUSVILLE	94.4	91.8	2.5	3.3	1.7	2.6	1.6	2.8	5.2	5.7	6.5	6.4	4.8	20.5	33.7	14.8	2.3	78.6	45.5	49.4	50.6
08562	WRIGHTSTOWN	80.5	74.5	11.1	13.6	2.6	3.8	6.0	9.0	6.7	7.2	7.1	7.6	9.7	28.9	24.0	8.0	0.8	74.9	33.4	53.4	46.6
08608	TRENTON	24.5	22.4	57.4	56.0	1.2	1.3	29.6	35.4	6.6	6.2	5.3	6.7	7.4	25.7	29.0	12.0	1.2	77.7	39.0	51.6	48.4
08609	TRENTON	23.1	19.7	57.6	57.3	1.6	1.7	24.0	29.2	8.1	7.9	7.3	8.2	8.0	28.4	22.1	8.8	1.2	71.8	31.9	49.1	50.9
08610	TRENTON	82.4	76.0	10.7	13.6	1.9	2.7	7.6	12.3	5.8	5.9	6.0	6.0	5.4	27.3	28.0	13.0	2.7	78.7	40.9	48.0	52.0
08611	TRENTON	52.9	44.8	22.5	23.5	1.3	1.5	36.0	46.5	7.6	7.1	6.4	6.8	7.7	33.0	21.1	8.1	2.3	74.9	33.6	53.4	46.6
08618	EWING	31.0	27.2	62.2	64.4	1.3	1.7	6.6	8.5	6.7	6.7	6.4	11.0	10.8	24.9	22.3	9.5	1.7	75.9	31.7	46.6	53.4
08619	TRENTON	89.0	84.2	4.5	6.1	3.3	4.8	3.8	6.4	5.2	5.3	5.6	5.6	5.3	25.6	29.5	14.3	3.6	80.5	43.3	47.0	53.0
08620	TRENTON	76.0	72.8	16.4	17.1	1.8	2.7	6.8	9.4	4.8	5.1	5.4	6.8	16.8	25.9	24.4	9.4	1.3	81.1	31.4	59.8	40.2
08628	EWING	79.7	72.1	14.9	19.9	2.8	4.0	3.4	5.6	4.8	5.0	5.3	4.8	4.0	28.4	30.2	14.1	3.5	81.7	43.6	48.5	51.5
08629	TRENTON	56.7	49.0	28.2	30.6	1.4	1.8	18.8	26.1	7.1	7.1	6.8	7.3	7.1	29.2	25.0	8.6	1.7	74.6	35.3	49.2	50.8
08638	EWING	45.7	40.8	45.4	48.2	1.4	1.9	10.4	13.3	6.0	6.2	6.3	7.0	6.3	25.6	27.2	13.0	2.2	77.0	39.4	48.2	51.8
08640	FORT DIX	61.3	57.0	34.1	37.4	1.4	1.8	22.5	29.4	4.8	4.1	3.6	2.2	8.1	60.6	15.4	1.1	0.0	86.2	33.3	82.7	17.3
08641	TRENTON	68.5	59.6	19.3	23.6	2.9	4.1	8.7	12.9	15.2	11.5	9.1	6.3	17.1	39.1	1.6	0.1	0.0	61.3	22.3	54.4	45.6
08648	TRENTON	78.7	69.5	9.7	13.5	8.0	11.6	4.7	7.8	5.7	5.5	5.7	8.3	8.6	26.7	26.5	10.7	2.4	79.6	37.7	47.1	52.9
08690	TRENTON	93.6	90.3	1.2	1.8	3.5	5.3	2.3	4.1	5.2	5.8	6.5	6.8	5.0	23.3	31.8	13.2	2.4	78.2	43.2	47.7	52.3
08691	TRENTON	91.3	87.5	2.7	3.8	4.2	5.9	2.6	4.5	7.8	8.1	7.5	5.6	3.5	26.2	30.0	10.2	1.1	72.7	40.4	48.1	51.9
	NEW JERSEY	72.6	68.2	13.6	14.0	5.7	7.9	13.3	16.9	6.6	6.6	6.7	6.8	6.2	26.4	27.0	11.5	2.2	76.0	38.7	48.7	51.3
	UNITED STATES	75.1	72.0	12.3	12.7	3.8	4.6	12.5	15.7	6.8	6.7	6.6	7.1	6.9	27.0	26.0	10.9	1.9	75.7	36.9	49.2	50.8

ZIP CODE #	POST OFFICE NAME	2009 Per Capita Income	2009 HH Income Base	2009 HOUSEHOLD INCOME DISTRIBUTION (%) Less than $25,000	$25,000 to $49,999	$50,000 to $99,999	$100,000 to $149,999	$150,000 or More	MEDIAN HOUSEHOLD INCOME 2009	2014	2009 National Centile	2009 State Centile	2009 Home Value Base	2009 HOME VALUE DISTRIBUTION (%) Less than $50,000	$50,000 to $89,999	$90,000 to $174,999	$175,000 to $399,999	$400,000 or More	2009 Median Home Value
08210	CAPE MAY COURT HOUSE	26840	6126	16.6	21.3	46.0	10.7	5.5	63804	71109	82	28	5084	2.4	3.5	12.1	51.0	31.0	313417
08215	EGG HARBOR CITY	24579	5472	19.3	22.4	45.5	9.3	3.4	60524	67878	78	23	4117	1.1	1.8	19.6	56.5	20.9	241428
08221	LINWOOD	36646	2747	10.3	20.3	37.9	17.1	14.4	75736	77618	90	45	2359	0.0	0.0	1.4	49.4	49.2	396170
08223	MARMORA	34554	1496	7.6	29.9	33.7	16.8	12.0	70457	75450	87	38	1306	1.1	1.2	2.8	32.0	62.9	450448
08225	NORTHFIELD	31672	3167	11.2	18.3	46.4	15.5	8.6	75428	77038	90	44	2801	0.1	0.2	3.5	80.1	16.0	284401
08226	OCEAN CITY	42340	7129	16.2	25.8	34.5	11.3	12.2	56912	59401	74	20	4404	0.2	0.0	1.7	21.0	76.9	630111
08230	OCEAN VIEW	34540	2294	10.5	15.4	40.6	19.6	13.9	80689	81366	92	56	2035	0.6	1.1	6.6	36.0	55.7	426986
08232	PLEASANTVILLE	18500	6217	23.5	30.6	36.9	7.0	2.0	46415	50725	53	9	3569	1.0	1.3	39.5	57.3	1.0	183731
08234	EGG HARBOR TOWNSHIP	28767	14865	11.6	19.6	45.3	15.4	8.1	69492	75561	86	36	12476	6.5	5.7	12.4	51.9	23.5	273795
08241	PORT REPUBLIC	29022	373	11.5	24.7	47.7	11.3	4.8	65523	73269	84	31	280	0.7	4.3	14.6	53.2	27.1	315789
08242	RIO GRANDE	22245	1180	32.7	29.8	28.9	4.9	3.6	37366	43489	25	3	902	11.0	10.9	30.8	36.6	10.8	166304
08243	SEA ISLE CITY	40697	1380	17.6	25.7	30.8	13.0	12.9	59637	65319	77	22	1039	0.0	0.0	1.6	11.5	86.8	742500
08244	SOMERS POINT	28195	4995	14.7	31.5	41.4	8.8	3.6	54266	59230	70	16	2776	0.2	0.2	6.4	82.9	10.3	269551
08247	STONE HARBOR	54253	651	15.7	20.0	37.0	12.6	14.7	72594	76527	88	41	531	0.0	0.0	0.6	6.8	92.7	936655
08248	STRATHMERE	62068	93	0.0	9.7	35.5	38.7	16.1	107257	108371	98	81	79	0.0	0.0	0.0	1.3	98.7	805000
08251	VILLAS	23017	4002	24.3	33.1	35.2	5.0	2.3	45428	49372	50	8	3131	0.3	0.3	36.1	58.7	4.6	194012
08260	WILDWOOD	24329	6472	30.5	32.1	28.4	6.1	2.9	38328	43401	28	4	3831	0.0	1.7	12.5	51.6	34.2	329463
08270	WOODBINE	25357	2794	16.8	18.7	45.1	12.6	6.8	64793	68452	83	30	2189	0.5	1.1	13.6	56.4	28.5	316873
08302	BRIDGETON	19200	14702	28.0	25.5	35.4	8.0	3.1	46260	50442	52	9	9630	5.0	9.3	36.3	40.8	8.5	173766
08310	BUENA	24180	835	26.6	26.7	37.7	5.9	3.1	46943	51796	54	10	658	4.0	4.6	38.6	46.4	6.5	179798
08311	CEDARVILLE	21831	696	19.0	21.7	50.0	7.0	2.3	58566	59751	76	21	606	3.0	6.6	43.7	43.7	3.0	167857
08312	CLAYTON	27210	2769	11.4	23.1	38.2	20.2	7.0	69366	74002	86	36	2143	0.0	1.6	38.9	57.7	1.8	187813
08314	DELMONT	18788	150	20.7	34.7	27.3	11.3	6.0	45501	47642	50	8	125	8.0	20.8	43.2	26.4	1.6	126042
08317	DOROTHY	23046	490	13.3	23.3	46.7	12.7	4.1	67980	75376	86	34	449	1.3	3.1	19.6	62.1	13.8	254464
08318	ELMER	27069	4503	10.5	20.3	48.6	15.0	5.6	72274	76032	88	40	3810	8.7	5.2	19.7	52.9	13.4	225341
08319	ESTELL MANOR	25090	458	13.5	23.1	46.5	12.7	4.1	67553	75479	85	33	420	1.4	2.9	19.5	62.1	14.0	255128
08322	FRANKLINVILLE	26641	3857	11.9	17.4	43.9	21.4	5.4	75116	76790	89	43	3405	1.5	1.7	24.0	65.5	7.3	222128
08323	GREENWICH	26214	303	14.5	21.1	47.2	12.9	4.3	66452	72283	85	32	254	3.9	4.7	15.0	52.0	24.4	262000
08324	HEISLERVILLE	20323	68	17.6	30.9	36.8	8.8	5.9	51198	55435	64	12	57	3.5	14.0	54.4	24.6	3.5	137500
08326	LANDISVILLE	21161	552	28.1	25.0	36.8	5.6	4.5	47284	52508	55	10	359	0.0	0.3	32.9	63.5	3.3	197575
08327	LEESBURG	22951	150	17.3	30.0	38.0	9.3	5.3	52137	54434	66	14	127	5.5	14.2	52.0	22.8	5.5	136500
08328	MALAGA	24828	603	11.3	22.4	47.6	15.4	3.3	68371	73820	86	35	474	4.9	3.0	28.7	60.8	2.7	193605
08330	MAYS LANDING	26511	9939	11.5	24.1	49.7	10.3	4.5	62349	68741	80	26	6986	0.7	2.5	28.0	54.9	13.9	215814
08332	MILLVILLE	22141	14220	23.2	26.3	38.3	8.6	3.7	50478	53596	62	12	9676	5.4	12.8	42.1	34.0	5.8	155575
08340	MILMAY	24106	349	16.6	26.6	42.7	10.0	4.0	56082	59061	73	19	295	2.0	8.1	17.3	56.3	16.3	240517
08341	MINOTOLA	22110	682	33.6	23.9	30.8	7.9	3.8	42844	47471	42	7	386	0.0	0.3	23.3	72.5	3.9	230709
08343	MONROEVILLE	24743	1551	15.3	17.5	48.4	14.3	4.4	67084	73912	85	33	1348	6.4	5.6	17.7	53.9	16.5	236029
08344	NEWFIELD	25980	2307	14.3	22.1	42.3	16.0	5.4	66262	70189	84	32	1945	4.5	3.0	30.5	54.8	7.3	200636
08345	NEWPORT	22839	461	22.3	34.9	34.7	5.6	2.4	42734	48711	42	7	408	6.1	20.8	50.2	21.6	1.2	127206
08346	NEWTONVILLE	18337	149	14.1	33.6	41.6	6.0	4.7	53145	61145	68	15	121	0.8	0.8	37.2	56.2	5.0	191071
08349	PORT NORRIS	20438	905	21.7	26.4	40.8	7.5	3.6	51357	54397	65	13	753	5.2	13.5	57.8	20.1	3.5	133203
08350	RICHLAND	23144	181	14.9	30.9	41.4	8.3	4.4	54566	57392	71	16	149	1.3	6.0	20.8	62.4	9.4	213000
08353	SHILOH	29853	152	11.2	11.2	50.0	21.1	6.6	78505	78229	91	52	127	0.0	4.7	21.3	48.8	25.2	246429
08360	VINELAND	19967	15154	27.4	28.1	34.7	6.7	3.1	44764	49035	48	7	9269	6.9	5.0	43.1	41.4	3.6	168093
08361	VINELAND	29871	6561	13.4	22.7	41.7	13.2	9.1	67241	74897	85	33	5033	2.1	2.2	18.4	60.2	17.1	241212
08401	ATLANTIC CITY	18208	16256	39.1	30.2	23.2	4.9	2.6	32809	35048	13	3	4540	1.6	6.0	35.7	48.2	8.5	187710
08402	MARGATE CITY	39688	3833	19.4	24.9	35.0	11.2	9.5	56544	60684	73	19	2715	0.0	0.0	3.1	38.5	58.4	446811
08403	LONGPORT	60330	606	12.9	22.3	33.0	12.4	19.5	69411	74809	86	36	495	0.0	0.0	1.4	12.9	85.7	753233
08406	VENTNOR CITY	27416	5389	18.8	28.2	39.9	8.1	5.1	52834	57145	68	15	3154	0.3	0.1	10.6	59.2	29.9	295743
08501	ALLENTOWN	40347	2223	6.5	12.9	33.2	25.1	22.4	95483	102803	96	73	1837	0.9	0.5	2.0	37.5	59.1	453344
08502	BELLE MEAD	76886	3695	2.2	4.7	15.5	13.3	64.3	182574	189586	100	99	3085	0.1	0.7	0.1	5.2	93.9	732755
08505	BORDENTOWN	37339	6817	9.6	15.7	38.7	25.1	10.9	79867	88451	92	54	5227	0.8	0.1	9.5	68.6	21.1	283869
08510	MILLSTONE TOWNSHIP	48829	1164	6.7	5.6	21.8	33.2	32.7	125713	128383	99	90	1086	0.0	0.0	0.3	18.0	81.7	641967
08511	COOKSTOWN	24404	241	12.9	18.3	33.2	24.1	11.6	80919	82949	92	56	214	0.0	0.0	2.3	79.9	17.8	301429
08512	CRANBURY	52740	2640	7.5	11.3	28.6	18.7	34.0	108048	111853	98	81	1951	1.5	2.8	5.7	16.4	73.6	571008
08514	CREAM RIDGE	39846	1443	8.4	11.6	35.9	23.0	21.1	91288	95746	95	70	1244	1.9	0.6	2.1	29.7	65.6	472659
08515	CHESTERFIELD	44639	687	4.9	7.6	27.5	30.7	29.3	115521	116526	98	87	621	0.0	0.0	1.1	35.7	63.1	461278
08518	FLORENCE	29437	1977	13.2	24.2	41.2	16.3	5.1	63268	58534	81	27	1331	0.0	11.0	26.9	57.4	4.7	211771
08520	HIGHTSTOWN	35728	12080	9.2	13.2	45.0	18.7	13.8	80923	85162	92	57	7360	1.4	5.7	10.2	46.4	36.4	306431
08525	HOPEWELL	50214	1967	4.1	10.8	31.1	24.1	29.9	108866	116055	98	82	1578	0.0	0.0	0.4	15.4	84.2	612455
08527	JACKSON	31641	18665	9.0	13.8	43.6	19.5	14.0	81360	82299	93	58	16237	3.5	2.7	7.7	50.7	35.3	334049
08528	KINGSTON	77029	46	2.2	8.7	26.1	21.7	41.3	129222	135970	99	91	40	0.0	0.0	10.0	37.5	52.5	412500
08530	LAMBERTVILLE	43424	3332	13.8	14.0	29.7	24.8	17.8	83633	85747	93	61	2455	0.0	0.0	1.1	56.3	42.6	373772
08533	NEW EGYPT	28264	2527	8.6	18.1	47.4	17.9	8.0	77515	79186	91	50	2110	4.6	1.6	6.1	51.3	36.4	334624
08534	PENNINGTON	57979	4541	2.6	9.3	29.4	19.8	38.9	128135	127374	99	91	4050	0.2	1.1	3.4	10.4	84.8	619247
08535	PERRINEVILLE	46102	726	5.8	7.7	20.7	24.4	41.5	132442	133737	99	93	674	0.0	0.1	1.8	17.1	81.0	625536
08536	PLAINSBORO	47689	8194	5.9	12.6	39.9	20.5	21.1	88007	95031	95	67	3208	0.7	1.2	12.7	33.3	52.1	416190
08540	PRINCETON	59207	16920	8.1	10.6	26.2	17.1	38.0	114402	120903	98	86	11953	0.2	1.4	3.5	16.0	78.8	654523
08542	PRINCETON	44943	1535	13.0	14.7	32.2	20.5	19.6	85329	91535	94	63	662	0.0	3.8	2.7	18.7	74.8	620732
08544	PRINCETON	5969	0	0.0	0.0	0.0	0.0	0.0	0	0	0	0	0	0.0	0.0	0.0	0.0	0.0	0
08550	PRINCETON JUNCTION	65398	6214	3.7	5.7	15.3	15.4	59.9	172515	173573	100	99	5334	0.0	1.5	0.5	3.7	94.3	808817
08551	RINGOES	48424	1904	5.5	8.8	25.0	28.0	32.7	117608	127422	98	87	1631	0.2	0.2	1.5	34.2	63.9	460829
08553	ROCKY HILL	62318	297	7.7	8.8	30.0	20.9	32.7	106773	120567	98	80	234	0.0	0.0	0.0	20.9	79.1	561905
08554	ROEBLING	29954	1487	14.5	21.5	35.6	21.7	6.8	68301	75908	86	35	1189	0.8	1.3	46.1	44.2	7.7	178989
08555	ROOSEVELT	37874	170	9.4	6.5	37.6	30.6	15.9	94546	101799	96	72	145	0.0	0.0	4.8	80.7	14.5	273387
08556	ROSEMONT	53711	36	11.1	11.1	22.2	22.2	33.3	111111	111475	98	85	31	0.0	0.0	0.0	22.6	77.4	562500
08558	SKILLMAN	64711	2072	4.4	6.0	19.1	19.4	51.0	151683	153836	100	97	1774	0.3	0.0	0.7	16.1	82.9	640275
08559	STOCKTON	49655	1994	9.9	11.6	24.8	24.8	28.9	105179	108625	97	79	1657	0.1	0.7	0.7	31.9	66.6	475068
08560	TITUSVILLE	48492	1455	4.5	11.3	34.4	25.9	23.9	99759	104928	97	75	1277	0.0	0.0	0.0	18.4	81.6	543565
08562	WRIGHTSTOWN	28313	2582	14.6	24.2	34.8	21.0	5.5	62538	58784	81	27	1465	13.6	6.9	8.1	32.2	39.2	339189
08608	TRENTON	14490	784	70.4	18.9	9.6	0.6	0.5	14039	14100	1	0	60	0.0	20.0	30.0	36.7	13.3	175000
08609	TRENTON	16640	4722	33.5	27.3	31.0	6.1	2.1	39545	43031	31	5	1896	1.3	17.8	44.1	36.0	0.7	153510
08610	TRENTON	28615	11803	15.5	23.0	42.9	14.2	4.4	63395	64333	82	27	8210	0.6	2.4	14.8	73.0	9.2	249406
08611	TRENTON	18095	8264	30.4	29.4	31.8	6.2	2.2	40316	43577	34	5	3914	2.3	20.1	58.4	18.7	0.6	132253
08618	EWING	20644	13842	28.6	25.6	33.6	9.0	3.1	45347	47912	49	8	6726	2.0	9.4	27.5	53.1	8.0	207776
08619	TRENTON	33088	9572	13.7	18.0	44.2	16.4	7.7	75105	77697	89	43	6442	0.5	0.9	8.3	62.2	28.2	325569
08620	TRENTON	29745	4518	7.2	16.6	42.7	22.5	11.0	79977	84190	92	54	3493	0.0	0.0	2.8	65.3	31.9	351754
08628	EWING	38106	3668	9.2	16.3	44.3	17.9	12.3	80511	84606	92	55	2537	0.0	0.0	1.7	44.9	53.4	413528
08629	TRENTON	23125	3963	15.5	25.3	46.5	9.1	3.6	55898	55853	73	19	2692	1.0	3.3	41.8	51.4	2.5	179268
08638	EWING	23500	8717	21.9	23.9	38.9	11.3	4.0	53594	53803	69	16	5765	2.2	8.9	19.5	55.5	13.9	236150
08640	FORT DIX	18105	748	6.8	35.6	51.3	5.5	0.8	52378	52832	67	14	45	0.0	4.4	13.3	82.2	0.0	218056
08641	TRENTON	13364	1125	14.2	46.6	35.0	4.0	0.2	43232	43970	43	7	15	0.0	0.0	40.0	60.0	0.0	179688
08648	TRENTON	38182	11423	11.2	14.6	40.6	17.6	16.1	81389	85670	93	58	7564	0.1	1.1	9.0	43.1	46.7	381825
08690	TRENTON	36158	6919	5.1	11.3	44.7	24.8	14.0	87724	93348	95	66	6184	0.1	1.1	3.7	52.1	42.9	376606
08691	TRENTON	42631	5825	7.2	12.5	37.8	24.1	18.5	89901	96127	95	69	5104	3.1	4.3	3.8	35.9	52.9	427027
	NEW JERSEY	34433		15.4	18.6	34.9	16.8	14.2	72809	76895				1.0	1.6	9.9	50.1	37.4	336585
	UNITED STATES	27277		20.9	24.4	35.3	11.7	7.6	54719	56938				9.3	13.1	31.6	32.6	13.5	162279

#	POST OFFICE NAME	FINANCIAL SERVICES: Auto Loan	Home Loan	Investments	Retirement Plans	THE HOME: Home Improvements: Home Repair	Lawn & Garden	Furnishings: Computers & Hardware-Personal	Major Appliances	TV, Radio, Sound Equipment	Furniture	ENTERTAINMENT: Dine out/Carry out	Sports Equipment	Fees & Tickets	Toys & Games	Travel	Cable TV	PERSONAL: Apparel & Services	Auto Repairs	Health Insurance	Pets & Supplies
08210	CAPE MAY COURT HOUSE	97	110	110	110	111	111	97	105	98	100	98	77	106	97	106	99	69	101	107	121
08215	EGG HARBOR CITY	87	98	88	97	95	93	92	91	91	91	92	70	97	92	95	91	65	91	91	106
08221	LINWOOD	123	149	152	151	153	149	131	138	132	137	132	101	150	129	147	134	94	134	145	159
08223	MARMORA	117	147	151	149	151	138	125	132	120	132	121	98	143	119	140	118	87	125	125	150
08225	NORTHFIELD	105	135	128	133	134	129	114	119	113	116	115	89	132	114	128	115	82	116	121	136
08226	OCEAN CITY	114	114	136	114	123	128	113	120	116	118	115	83	116	109	119	120	80	120	133	139
08230	OCEAN VIEW	130	159	159	162	162	152	136	144	132	144	133	106	154	131	151	130	95	137	139	164
08232	PLEASANTVILLE	74	72	68	72	70	71	77	73	79	76	80	55	77	78	74	80	56	77	76	87
08234	EGG HARBOR TOWNSHIP	109	126	116	124	124	114	113	114	109	116	110	88	122	112	118	107	79	111	107	131
08241	PORT REPUBLIC	100	112	107	114	111	104	106	103	102	108	104	81	112	103	110	101	74	103	101	121
08242	RIO GRANDE	81	66	81	65	69	85	70	80	75	66	73	59	62	73	69	80	49	77	87	94
08243	SEA ISLE CITY	106	112	144	112	126	131	104	118	111	114	109	76	114	100	118	116	75	115	136	135
08244	SOMERS POINT	85	93	88	92	91	86	93	88	91	91	92	70	97	92	95	90	66	91	88	103
08247	STONE HARBOR	136	144	192	143	164	168	130	152	136	146	134	96	142	124	149	142	92	145	168	172
08248	STRATHMERE	154	162	220	161	187	191	146	172	154	165	151	108	160	138	169	161	104	164	192	195
08251	VILLAS	78	77	78	77	76	89	74	81	79	71	78	60	74	78	76	83	53	79	90	95
08260	WILDWOOD	68	66	72	66	69	74	70	71	74	69	73	51	71	70	71	78	51	73	83	83
08270	WOODBINE	103	112	106	112	110	108	104	107	102	105	102	83	108	103	108	101	72	104	103	124
08302	BRIDGETON	78	75	72	76	73	81	78	77	81	75	81	59	77	81	76	85	57	79	84	93
08310	BUENA	79	82	85	78	84	86	77	83	80	81	80	58	79	77	81	82	55	82	89	96
08311	CEDARVILLE	97	89	88	92	90	105	87	99	90	79	88	75	81	92	87	95	60	91	102	115
08312	CLAYTON	106	118	100	116	112	111	111	108	109	110	110	86	116	112	112	109	77	109	110	128
08314	DELMONT	108	82	101	81	82	110	84	101	92	78	90	77	70	94	81	100	60	94	105	121
08317	DOROTHY	90	112	100	111	107	110	95	99	96	96	97	74	109	97	105	98	68	97	105	115
08318	ELMER	110	119	107	119	116	118	108	113	107	108	108	86	112	110	111	109	75	108	112	132
08319	ESTELL MANOR	90	112	100	111	107	110	95	99	96	96	97	74	109	97	105	98	68	97	105	115
08322	FRANKLINVILLE	103	128	113	128	123	119	108	112	106	112	108	86	123	109	118	106	77	108	111	130
08323	GREENWICH	89	111	99	110	106	109	94	99	96	96	97	74	108	97	104	98	68	96	104	115
08324	HEISLERVILLE	97	88	87	92	90	104	87	98	90	79	88	74	80	91	87	95	60	91	101	114
08326	LANDISVILLE	78	86	78	81	84	75	84	81	80	85	82	62	85	81	84	78	58	82	77	92
08327	LEESBURG	97	88	88	92	90	104	87	99	90	79	88	75	80	92	87	95	60	91	102	114
08328	MALAGA	90	107	100	105	105	100	100	99	99	99	100	77	110	99	106	99	71	99	100	115
08330	MAYS LANDING	102	103	90	103	99	94	104	98	101	105	102	77	104	104	101	98	72	100	95	115
08332	MILLVILLE	85	85	78	85	83	87	85	85	87	83	87	65	84	88	84	89	61	86	89	101
08340	MILMAY	100	91	90	95	93	108	90	102	93	82	91	77	83	95	90	98	62	94	105	118
08341	MINOTOLA	68	80	75	78	79	74	78	74	75	75	76	59	83	76	81	75	55	76	74	86
08343	MONROEVILLE	107	103	105	105	103	117	97	109	100	93	100	83	95	102	100	105	68	102	112	128
08344	NEWFIELD	99	113	102	114	110	114	100	106	101	99	102	80	109	103	108	104	71	102	110	123
08345	NEWPORT	85	69	87	67	70	92	71	85	78	65	76	63	62	77	71	86	51	80	94	99
08346	NEWTONVILLE	91	95	87	96	91	102	88	92	95	92	95	64	94	92	90	100	65	93	105	112
08349	PORT NORRIS	84	84	81	85	83	94	79	86	84	78	84	61	81	83	81	89	57	84	95	102
08350	RICHLAND	96	93	89	95	92	105	89	97	94	86	93	71	88	93	90	99	63	93	105	115
08353	SHILOH	117	131	113	135	127	129	117	122	115	118	116	95	125	118	124	116	81	117	121	143
08360	VINELAND	77	74	68	73	72	75	77	76	79	76	79	58	75	79	75	80	55	78	79	89
08361	VINELAND	112	123	119	124	123	125	114	119	114	113	114	89	120	114	120	116	80	115	121	138
08401	ATLANTIC CITY	58	50	50	53	49	51	65	56	68	61	68	44	61	64	59	69	49	64	63	69
08402	MARGATE CITY	106	112	125	113	118	120	109	113	112	113	112	80	116	106	117	115	78	114	125	131
08403	LONGPORT	158	170	229	169	196	197	152	179	159	172	156	113	169	144	177	165	108	170	196	202
08406	VENTNOR CITY	79	86	90	87	88	86	90	86	92	86	93	64	95	88	92	95	67	90	93	101
08501	ALLENTOWN	149	190	189	193	194	171	160	165	152	169	154	128	186	155	178	147	113	156	150	187
08502	BELLE MEAD	342	430	405	446	432	365	355	364	329	396	333	296	415	349	386	305	248	333	304	405
08505	BORDENTOWN	121	144	132	144	141	130	130	129	125	133	127	102	143	128	137	122	91	126	123	149
08510	MILLSTONE TOWNSHIP	198	262	271	275	271	235	214	223	200	233	203	176	259	204	244	190	152	207	194	252
08511	COOKSTOWN	117	148	129	147	142	127	124	126	116	130	118	100	139	121	133	111	85	119	112	144
08512	CRANBURY	199	250	254	256	256	227	215	219	203	227	206	171	248	208	237	197	151	209	200	248
08514	CREAM RIDGE	145	184	180	187	186	167	155	161	147	164	149	124	178	149	172	142	108	152	147	183
08515	CHESTERFIELD	173	214	219	220	220	203	182	193	175	195	177	143	208	174	205	172	127	183	182	221
08518	FLORENCE	94	107	98	106	104	102	101	99	101	100	102	77	109	102	105	102	72	101	102	117
08520	HIGHTSTOWN	130	144	137	147	142	130	137	132	131	141	133	105	145	135	140	127	96	132	124	153
08525	HOPEWELL	162	214	251	219	235	193	189	196	170	207	170	149	219	165	219	160	127	184	171	216
08527	JACKSON	130	151	142	148	149	137	133	136	128	139	130	105	144	132	141	126	93	131	127	156
08528	KINGSTON	238	289	250	298	282	237	241	243	221	270	226	203	273	240	253	203	166	222	199	271
08530	LAMBERTVILLE	134	167	178	164	174	160	150	152	147	152	147	113	170	145	165	148	107	150	154	172
08533	NEW EGYPT	106	135	127	131	134	119	118	118	112	119	114	91	132	115	128	111	83	115	111	134
08534	PENNINGTON	206	264	264	269	271	233	221	229	208	243	209	179	259	214	246	197	155	213	204	254
08535	PERRINEVILLE	210	278	287	292	288	249	227	237	212	247	215	187	274	217	259	202	161	219	206	267
08536	PLAINSBORO	172	150	135	161	143	135	170	148	165	174	168	126	163	173	155	157	119	159	139	178
08540	PRINCETON	208	250	275	261	264	223	233	228	215	248	218	183	262	216	253	204	162	221	201	258
08542	PRINCETON	141	148	172	160	157	131	169	147	153	166	158	127	172	151	172	144	117	156	133	172
08544	PRINCETON	0	0	0	0	0	0	0	0	0	0	0	0	0	0	0	0	0	0	0	0
08550	PRINCETON JUNCTION	262	348	391	366	373	318	295	304	276	320	277	237	358	277	338	263	211	285	268	340
08551	RINGOES	186	241	248	250	248	221	200	210	189	215	191	161	236	191	226	182	141	196	189	238
08553	ROCKY HILL	182	229	268	233	252	197	218	215	190	233	191	172	238	184	243	175	142	208	181	239
08554	ROEBLING	96	117	111	114	116	106	109	107	105	107	107	83	119	107	115	105	77	107	104	122
08555	ROOSEVELT	137	170	174	175	175	161	145	153	139	155	140	114	165	138	163	136	101	145	145	175
08556	ROSEMONT	182	226	231	232	232	214	192	203	184	205	186	151	219	183	216	181	134	192	192	233
08558	SKILLMAN	254	335	346	352	347	301	274	286	256	299	259	226	331	262	312	244	195	265	248	322
08559	STOCKTON	168	214	221	216	220	201	183	191	177	190	179	142	211	176	205	176	130	183	183	217
08560	TITUSVILLE	150	219	246	211	235	201	177	188	168	180	169	137	217	169	210	169	127	178	178	204
08562	WRIGHTSTOWN	112	103	90	107	99	98	110	102	108	110	110	84	107	114	105	105	77	107	100	122
08608	TRENTON	31	23	25	25	23	25	35	29	37	33	38	23	31	34	31	39	26	35	36	36
08609	TRENTON	61	60	61	60	60	60	70	62	74	63	74	46	69	71	66	78	54	69	70	75
08610	TRENTON	91	105	98	104	104	102	99	98	98	97	99	75	107	99	104	99	70	99	101	114
08611	TRENTON	69	63	59	63	62	63	74	67	76	69	76	52	70	75	68	78	54	72	71	80
08618	EWING	70	72	70	72	71	72	77	71	81	73	82	54	79	80	75	85	59	77	79	86
08619	TRENTON	100	119	122	117	121	114	112	111	111	111	112	83	123	109	120	113	80	112	115	127
08620	TRENTON	115	141	138	140	141	131	127	128	123	128	124	98	141	123	137	122	89	126	125	147
08628	EWING	121	143	139	143	143	136	129	130	127	131	128	99	142	127	138	127	91	128	131	151
08629	TRENTON	82	93	87	90	91	87	91	87	92	87	93	66	96	91	92	94	66	90	90	102
08638	EWING	84	89	88	88	89	94	87	88	93	84	92	63	92	91	89	98	65	90	99	103
08640	FORT DIX	97	50	38	58	45	43	91	63	85	85	90	63	69	103	66	79	63	80	57	77
08641	TRENTON	86	45	33	52	40	38	81	56	76	75	80	56	61	91	58	70	56	71	50	68
08648	TRENTON	131	147	147	149	148	136	141	136	136	144	137	107	151	137	146	133	99	137	132	158
08690	TRENTON	130	162	163	160	165	151	142	145	137	145	139	109	160	138	156	136	100	141	141	165
08691	TRENTON	150	176	167	180	175	159	157	157	150	166	152	124	173	154	166	145	109	152	146	181
	NEW JERSEY	119	138	141	137	141	129	132	129	129	132	131	98	143	128	139	129	95	130	128	148
	UNITED STATES	100	100	100	100	100	100	100	100	100	100	100	100	100	100	100	100	100	100	100	100

ZIP CODE			POPULATION			2000-2009 ANNUAL RATE		HOUSEHOLDS					FAMILIES		
#	POST OFFICE NAME	COUNTY FIPS CODE	2000	2009	2014	% Rate	State Centile	2000	2009	2014	% Annual Rate 2000-2009	2009 Average HH Size	2000	2009	% Annual Rate 2000-2009
08701	LAKEWOOD	029	60622	72651	77100	2.0	94	20003	23477	24964	1.7	3.00	13446	15604	1.6
08721	BAYVILLE	029	17193	19261	20163	1.2	85	6170	7003	7355	1.4	2.71	4667	5262	1.3
08722	BEACHWOOD	029	10371	10820	10986	0.5	62	3474	3685	3760	0.6	2.93	2816	2967	0.6
08723	BRICK	029	31872	32429	32648	0.2	43	12470	12904	13042	0.4	2.50	8835	9028	0.2
08724	BRICK	029	42797	44398	45046	0.4	56	16365	17303	17648	0.6	2.53	11491	11958	0.4
08730	BRIELLE	025	4919	4752	4701	-0.4	4	1951	1903	1891	-0.3	2.50	1423	1367	-0.4
08731	FORKED RIVER	029	18445	22362	24107	2.1	94	6995	8536	9216	2.2	2.62	5301	6482	2.2
08732	ISLAND HEIGHTS	029	839	970	1037	1.6	91	342	403	432	1.8	2.41	242	281	1.6
08733	LAKEHURST	029	2971	2977	2983	0.0	28	951	972	981	0.2	2.88	732	739	0.1
08734	LANOKA HARBOR	029	6899	7675	8032	1.2	85	2340	2645	2777	1.3	2.90	1943	2185	1.3
08735	LAVALLETTE	029	4450	5030	5310	1.3	87	2182	2521	2678	1.6	1.94	1272	1443	1.4
08736	MANASQUAN	025	13146	13224	13201	0.1	35	5196	5265	5276	0.1	2.50	3614	3622	0.0
08738	MANTOLOKING	029	1353	1476	1535	0.9	76	663	736	769	1.1	2.00	447	488	1.0
08740	OCEAN GATE	029	2027	2271	2405	1.2	85	811	923	981	1.4	2.46	533	597	1.2
08741	PINE BEACH	029	2440	2710	2890	1.1	83	935	1059	1132	1.4	2.56	694	777	1.2
08742	POINT PLEASANT BEACH	029	26266	26541	26644	0.1	35	10610	10898	10985	0.3	2.40	7010	7103	0.1
08750	SEA GIRT	025	3807	3824	3810	0.0	28	1629	1651	1651	0.1	2.31	1074	1069	-0.1
08751	SEASIDE HEIGHTS	029	4915	4790	4796	-0.3	7	2342	2326	2338	-0.1	2.02	1153	1119	-0.3
08752	SEASIDE PARK	029	2927	2751	2752	-0.7	2	1468	1410	1419	-0.4	1.95	792	746	-0.6
08753	TOMS RIVER	029	64189	65972	66681	0.3	50	23346	24355	24716	0.5	2.68	17278	17838	0.3
08755	TOMS RIVER	029	23050	25554	26700	1.1	83	8691	9738	10204	1.2	2.51	6453	7143	1.1
08757	TOMS RIVER	029	33175	34974	35782	0.6	65	17124	18132	18544	0.6	1.91	10239	10737	0.5
08758	WARETOWN	029	5012	6849	7512	3.4	98	1885	2549	2794	3.3	2.67	1337	1801	3.3
08759	MANCHESTER TOWNSHIP	029	30475	32692	34153	0.8	73	17657	19049	19913	0.8	1.69	8571	9085	0.6
08801	ANNANDALE	019	9744	10574	10822	0.9	76	2519	2854	2952	1.4	3.01	1901	2148	1.3
08802	ASBURY	019	4052	4466	4636	1.1	83	1382	1534	1599	1.1	2.91	1155	1272	1.0
08804	BLOOMSBURY	019	2110	2307	2407	1.0	80	777	851	889	1.0	2.71	636	692	0.9
08805	BOUND BROOK	035	12016	12531	12703	0.5	62	4282	4348	4392	0.2	2.87	3007	3015	0.0
08807	BRIDGEWATER	035	36564	39096	40201	0.7	68	13293	14081	14485	0.6	2.72	9941	10414	0.5
08809	CLINTON	019	4817	5460	5771	1.4	88	2038	2268	2381	1.2	2.36	1256	1407	1.2
08810	DAYTON	023	6827	8210	8767	2.0	94	2209	2598	2758	1.8	3.16	1843	2165	1.8
08812	DUNELLEN	035	12145	13580	14176	1.2	85	4205	4678	4884	1.2	2.83	3099	3438	1.1
08816	EAST BRUNSWICK	023	45369	46773	47174	0.3	50	15914	16279	16401	0.2	2.86	12670	12853	0.2
08817	EDISON	023	45031	45182	45175	0.0	28	16233	16145	16079	-0.1	2.74	11677	11514	-0.2
08820	EDISON	023	37490	38470	38762	0.3	50	12771	13073	13171	0.3	2.93	10412	10586	0.2
08822	FLEMINGTON	019	28034	30886	31943	1.1	83	10176	11207	11602	1.0	2.72	7646	8366	1.0
08823	FRANKLIN PARK	035	6713	8021	8750	1.9	93	2812	3339	3635	1.9	2.38	1816	2124	1.7
08824	KENDALL PARK	023	12287	12634	12761	0.3	50	3976	4057	4086	0.2	3.11	3304	3360	0.2
08825	FRENCHTOWN	019	4898	5272	5433	0.8	73	1748	1884	1940	0.8	2.76	1269	1358	0.7
08826	GLEN GARDNER	019	5884	6316	6459	0.8	73	2080	2250	2306	0.9	2.68	1498	1611	0.8
08827	HAMPTON	019	4419	4606	4643	0.4	56	1479	1562	1583	0.6	2.68	1162	1220	0.5
08828	HELMETTA	023	1802	2121	2233	1.8	93	738	847	885	1.5	2.50	489	556	1.4
08829	HIGH BRIDGE	019	3751	3875	3908	0.4	56	1422	1478	1495	0.4	2.62	1047	1081	0.3
08830	ISELIN	023	16529	17570	17936	0.7	68	5946	6339	6484	0.7	2.77	4466	4701	0.6
08831	MONROE TOWNSHIP	023	34888	45871	51698	3.0	97	15005	18676	20569	2.4	2.39	10028	12821	2.7
08832	KEASBEY	023	3042	3019	2998	-0.1	19	1106	1079	1069	-0.3	2.80	765	739	-0.4
08833	LEBANON	019	8980	9914	10272	1.1	83	3165	3501	3641	1.1	2.80	2548	2800	1.0
08835	MANVILLE	035	10302	10540	10657	0.2	43	4098	4166	4211	0.2	2.53	2746	2752	0.0
08836	MARTINSVILLE	035	3968	4137	4226	0.5	62	1394	1440	1468	0.4	2.83	1220	1254	0.3
08837	EDISON	023	14969	15149	15574	0.1	35	6139	6170	6312	0.1	2.33	3788	3764	-0.1
08840	METUCHEN	023	15552	15786	15836	0.2	43	5886	5953	5969	0.1	2.65	4301	4313	0.0
08844	HILLSBOROUGH	035	37082	38510	39965	0.4	56	12798	13137	13586	0.3	2.91	9906	10117	0.2
08846	MIDDLESEX	023	13865	15185	15524	1.0	80	5105	5563	5683	0.9	2.72	3782	4095	0.9
08848	MILFORD	019	8143	8548	8657	0.5	62	2954	3113	3159	0.6	2.73	2355	2466	0.5
08850	MILLTOWN	023	8487	8466	8444	0.0	28	3129	3110	3098	-0.1	2.72	2386	2356	-0.1
08852	MONMOUTH JUNCTION	023	13930	15638	16739	1.3	87	5356	5891	6244	1.0	2.65	3646	4010	1.0
08853	NESHANIC STATION	035	5289	5510	5591	0.4	56	1762	1826	1854	0.4	3.02	1484	1527	0.3
08854	PISCATAWAY	023	50287	51156	51534	0.2	43	16373	16558	16662	0.1	2.87	12236	12316	0.1
08857	OLD BRIDGE	023	36197	40957	42611	1.3	87	12892	14346	14858	1.2	2.83	9607	10679	1.2
08859	PARLIN	023	21187	22763	23308	0.8	73	7756	8312	8517	0.8	2.74	5727	6043	0.6
08861	PERTH AMBOY	023	49815	50953	51197	0.2	43	15526	15531	15563	0.0	3.24	11416	11326	-0.1
08863	FORDS	023	13694	13725	13635	0.0	28	5186	5101	5058	-0.2	2.69	3621	3529	-0.3
08865	PHILLIPSBURG	041	28889	30873	31627	0.7	68	11278	12256	12607	0.9	2.49	7743	8341	0.8
08867	PITTSTOWN	019	4627	4959	5090	0.8	73	1583	1726	1781	0.9	2.53	1317	1426	0.9
08869	RARITAN	035	6338	6433	6473	0.2	43	2556	2574	2590	0.1	2.50	1671	1660	-0.1
08872	SAYREVILLE	023	18179	19524	20040	0.8	73	6624	7066	7243	0.7	2.75	4852	5138	0.6
08873	SOMERSET	035	41573	50956	55039	2.2	95	15554	18738	20218	2.0	2.67	10460	12680	2.1
08876	SOMERVILLE	035	22980	23489	23723	0.2	43	8643	8735	8815	0.1	2.61	5815	5801	0.0
08879	SOUTH AMBOY	023	21249	22207	22566	0.5	62	7983	8354	8499	0.5	2.64	5581	5786	0.4
08880	SOUTH BOUND BROOK	035	4513	5111	5389	1.4	88	1634	1805	1892	1.1	2.83	1110	1211	0.9
08882	SOUTH RIVER	023	15287	15647	15753	0.3	50	5592	5675	5700	0.2	2.74	3975	4002	0.1
08884	SPOTSWOOD	023	7903	8132	8196	0.3	50	3109	3201	3228	0.3	2.54	2173	2214	0.2
08886	STEWARTSVILLE	041	4967	6348	6927	2.7	96	1623	2074	2267	2.7	3.03	1369	1744	2.7
08887	THREE BRIDGES	019	835	834	824	0.0	28	453	455	450	0.0	1.81	197	192	-0.3
08889	WHITEHOUSE STATION	019	8968	9511	9770	0.6	65	3233	3442	3543	0.7	2.75	2529	2679	0.6
08901	NEW BRUNSWICK	023	48575	52319	53207	0.8	73	13058	13520	13732	0.4	3.40	7203	7344	0.2
08902	NORTH BRUNSWICK	023	36655	39757	40874	0.9	76	13767	14905	15345	0.9	2.59	9449	10157	0.8
08904	HIGHLAND PARK	023	14277	14250	14191	0.0	28	5990	5930	5890	-0.1	2.40	3480	3403	-0.2
	NEW JERSEY					0.5					0.5	2.69			0.5
	UNITED STATES					1.0					1.1	2.59			0.9

#	POST OFFICE NAME	RACE (%) White 2000	White 2009	Black 2000	Black 2009	Asian/Pacific 2000	Asian/Pacific 2009	% Hispanic Origin 2000	% Hispanic Origin 2009	2009 AGE DISTRIBUTION (%) 0-4	5-9	10-14	15-19	20-24	25-44	45-64	65-84	85+	18+	MEDIAN AGE 2009	% 2009 Males	% 2009 Females
08701	LAKEWOOD	78.8	74.6	12.0	13.0	1.4	2.0	14.8	20.1	11.9	8.6	6.8	6.1	7.4	22.0	17.8	15.7	3.8	69.0	31.8	48.1	51.9
08721	BAYVILLE	95.8	94.2	1.4	1.7	0.8	1.2	3.9	5.9	5.7	6.0	6.3	6.4	5.0	25.4	29.3	14.1	1.8	78.0	41.7	48.4	51.6
08722	BEACHWOOD	95.7	93.7	1.0	1.2	1.2	1.9	4.2	6.6	6.7	7.2	7.7	7.3	5.0	27.6	28.7	8.6	1.1	73.7	37.7	49.0	51.0
08723	BRICK	95.4	93.4	0.9	1.1	1.2	1.9	4.7	7.3	6.0	6.2	6.2	6.3	5.4	25.0	27.9	14.2	2.8	77.7	41.6	48.3	51.7
08724	BRICK	96.1	94.5	1.0	1.2	1.2	1.9	3.3	5.1	5.9	6.2	6.5	6.2	4.9	23.2	27.9	15.6	3.6	77.4	42.9	46.9	53.1
08730	BRIELLE	93.1	90.0	3.4	4.6	0.7	1.0	3.3	5.5	6.5	7.0	7.6	5.9	4.1	19.3	30.4	16.6	2.5	75.1	44.7	48.1	51.9
08731	FORKED RIVER	97.9	97.0	0.4	0.5	0.5	0.8	2.2	3.5	6.0	6.2	6.7	6.6	4.6	23.5	29.8	14.2	2.4	77.0	42.5	48.9	51.1
08732	ISLAND HEIGHTS	97.9	96.9	0.1	0.1	0.6	1.0	1.4	2.3	4.9	5.3	5.9	6.6	5.6	23.6	31.2	14.3	2.6	80.0	43.6	47.6	52.4
08733	LAKEHURST	81.5	77.3	9.9	10.8	2.9	4.1	8.1	11.9	8.7	7.7	6.5	6.4	7.6	33.8	21.4	6.9	0.9	73.4	31.9	53.7	46.3
08734	LANOKA HARBOR	97.8	96.8	0.2	0.3	0.6	1.0	2.0	3.3	6.2	6.5	6.9	7.4	5.6	24.7	30.4	11.0	1.2	75.8	39.8	48.8	51.2
08735	LAVALLETTE	98.4	97.7	0.2	0.2	0.3	0.5	1.6	2.4	2.6	2.8	3.0	2.8	2.0	13.8	34.1	32.6	6.2	89.9	60.1	47.6	52.4
08736	MANASQUAN	97.7	96.5	0.4	0.6	0.9	1.4	2.7	4.4	5.9	6.2	6.9	6.4	4.6	21.8	30.3	15.4	2.4	76.9	43.7	48.6	51.4
08738	MANTOLOKING	99.3	98.8	0.5	0.7	0.1	0.3	0.6	1.0	1.4	1.6	1.6	2.3	1.4	9.8	39.9	38.3	3.7	94.0	62.7	50.7	49.3
08740	OCEAN GATE	96.5	95.2	1.0	1.1	1.0	1.5	2.4	3.8	6.9	6.7	6.6	7.1	7.0	26.1	26.9	10.9	1.8	75.5	37.6	47.6	52.4
08741	PINE BEACH	98.2	97.3	0.3	0.4	0.7	1.1	2.5	4.1	5.4	5.9	6.4	6.8	5.0	23.3	31.5	13.5	2.3	78.1	43.0	48.9	51.1
08742	POINT PLEASANT BEACH	97.5	96.3	0.3	0.4	0.7	1.0	2.8	4.4	5.4	5.6	5.9	6.3	5.4	23.9	30.5	14.0	2.9	79.0	43.3	48.7	51.3
08750	SEA GIRT	98.7	98.0	0.2	0.3	0.6	1.0	1.2	2.1	5.3	5.8	6.7	5.9	3.6	16.4	30.8	20.7	4.8	78.4	48.6	48.0	52.0
08751	SEASIDE HEIGHTS	93.1	91.2	2.6	3.0	0.6	0.9	7.1	10.4	5.7	5.0	4.8	5.3	7.1	26.7	27.2	14.9	3.2	81.4	41.2	50.0	50.0
08752	SEASIDE PARK	97.8	96.8	0.3	0.4	0.6	0.9	2.1	3.2	4.1	3.7	3.5	3.3	3.5	20.4	33.2	23.8	4.4	86.4	52.6	49.1	50.9
08753	TOMS RIVER	94.2	91.8	1.4	1.7	2.1	3.3	4.7	7.2	5.8	5.9	6.2	6.4	5.4	25.8	29.2	13.1	2.2	78.1	41.1	48.6	51.4
08755	TOMS RIVER	91.3	87.7	2.8	3.3	3.8	6.0	4.3	6.6	5.1	5.3	5.8	6.0	4.5	20.3	27.4	21.9	3.8	79.9	47.0	47.0	53.0
08757	TOMS RIVER	93.0	91.0	4.6	5.3	0.6	1.1	3.1	4.9	2.7	2.8	2.7	2.9	2.4	11.3	18.0	44.1	13.2	90.1	69.3	43.4	56.6
08758	WARETOWN	97.4	96.6	0.7	0.8	0.4	0.6	3.0	4.5	6.1	6.1	6.5	6.9	5.9	25.8	28.5	12.2	2.0	77.0	40.4	49.4	50.6
08759	MANCHESTER TOWNSHIP	96.3	95.0	2.0	2.5	0.6	1.0	1.7	2.8	1.6	1.7	1.7	1.8	1.6	7.4	17.2	50.1	16.8	93.9	72.7	41.0	59.0
08801	ANNANDALE	81.1	77.4	12.5	13.7	2.2	3.4	5.7	7.8	4.9	6.1	7.2	6.8	10.5	25.6	29.9	8.3	0.8	77.7	37.8	52.6	47.4
08802	ASBURY	97.6	96.5	0.9	1.1	0.8	1.3	1.2	1.9	5.8	7.1	8.5	7.8	3.6	21.4	35.2	9.6	1.0	73.5	42.4	50.4	49.6
08804	BLOOMSBURY	97.3	96.1	0.8	1.0	0.7	1.0	1.8	2.8	8.0	8.5	8.8	6.9	3.6	22.8	30.8	9.2	1.3	70.0	39.9	48.6	51.4
08805	BOUND BROOK	84.0	79.7	2.3	2.4	3.3	4.2	30.3	39.6	6.8	6.6	6.4	5.9	6.3	31.5	24.8	9.8	1.9	76.7	36.8	51.5	48.5
08807	BRIDGEWATER	83.9	77.4	2.4	2.8	11.4	16.4	5.1	7.9	7.1	7.7	8.1	6.3	3.8	25.6	28.2	10.9	2.3	72.7	40.3	48.1	51.9
08809	CLINTON	92.8	90.0	2.0	2.4	3.1	4.7	3.4	5.2	5.9	6.1	6.8	6.2	4.9	27.3	32.6	9.0	1.1	76.9	40.8	48.5	51.5
08810	DAYTON	64.1	52.9	9.4	10.0	22.9	32.5	5.1	7.6	7.7	8.4	9.0	8.0	4.0	28.1	29.3	5.0	0.5	69.9	36.6	48.3	51.7
08812	DUNELLEN	84.7	78.3	3.9	4.2	5.5	8.8	10.5	16.1	6.6	6.8	7.0	6.6	4.9	25.7	28.9	11.1	2.4	75.3	40.5	48.9	51.1
08816	EAST BRUNSWICK	77.2	67.6	2.9	3.2	16.6	24.5	4.3	6.7	5.7	6.1	6.9	7.0	5.1	24.2	31.5	11.8	1.6	76.7	41.7	48.6	51.4
08817	EDISON	60.1	51.0	8.3	8.1	26.1	33.6	8.4	12.1	7.0	6.1	5.9	6.3	6.4	33.0	24.6	9.3	1.4	77.3	35.7	49.4	50.6
08820	EDISON	53.8	42.9	5.2	5.3	38.4	48.6	3.0	4.3	5.9	6.1	6.6	6.3	5.1	25.4	30.8	12.3	1.7	77.5	41.5	48.6	51.4
08822	FLEMINGTON	93.2	90.3	1.4	1.7	3.0	4.6	3.8	5.7	6.4	7.4	8.3	7.5	4.3	23.9	32.0	8.7	1.5	72.8	40.6	48.8	51.2
08823	FRANKLIN PARK	58.2	48.9	18.5	20.2	19.4	25.7	5.1	7.5	8.1	7.6	7.1	5.4	6.5	32.3	25.4	6.6	1.1	73.8	36.1	48.4	51.6
08824	KENDALL PARK	74.9	64.7	5.3	6.0	16.9	25.3	4.2	6.6	8.1	8.4	8.1	7.0	4.3	27.4	27.0	8.9	0.9	70.6	37.1	48.5	51.5
08825	FRENCHTOWN	97.0	95.6	0.6	0.9	0.9	1.5	2.0	3.2	6.1	6.7	7.4	6.8	4.7	22.6	33.2	10.6	1.9	75.5	42.4	49.7	50.3
08826	GLEN GARDNER	96.5	95.0	0.9	1.2	1.2	1.9	2.3	3.7	5.9	6.7	7.6	7.4	4.3	23.2	32.6	10.6	1.7	75.0	42.2	49.0	51.0
08827	HAMPTON	91.6	89.0	5.1	6.2	1.1	1.7	3.1	4.7	6.1	7.1	7.9	7.3	6.0	25.4	30.3	8.9	1.1	74.1	38.9	49.0	51.0
08828	HELMETTA	93.1	90.5	2.4	2.7	2.4	3.5	5.3	8.9	6.3	6.8	6.7	5.4	4.0	33.7	29.6	6.9	0.6	76.7	38.9	49.4	50.6
08829	HIGH BRIDGE	96.2	94.5	0.8	1.1	1.5	2.2	2.1	3.4	7.4	8.1	8.2	6.4	5.1	25.8	31.0	7.1	1.0	72.0	38.9	48.4	51.6
08830	ISELIN	64.4	52.2	6.0	6.6	25.4	35.7	5.4	7.9	6.2	5.7	5.7	5.8	6.0	30.3	27.3	11.1	1.8	78.9	38.5	49.0	51.0
08831	MONROE TOWNSHIP	91.5	85.9	3.9	6.0	2.4	4.4	3.7	6.6	4.8	5.2	5.6	5.8	2.9	18.1	24.2	26.5	6.9	80.6	50.7	46.8	53.2
08832	KEASBEY	44.4	37.6	19.1	17.4	9.3	11.5	36.8	46.0	8.7	8.3	7.6	5.9	7.1	34.7	20.7	6.2	0.8	71.7	31.8	48.9	51.1
08833	LEBANON	94.9	92.6	1.2	1.5	2.7	4.3	1.8	2.9	6.6	7.6	8.7	6.8	4.0	19.8	33.4	11.7	1.4	72.6	42.9	49.7	50.3
08835	MANVILLE	96.0	93.8	0.5	0.6	1.3	2.1	5.4	9.3	5.4	5.4	5.6	6.1	5.6	27.4	28.7	13.3	2.5	79.9	41.6	49.4	50.6
08836	MARTINSVILLE	92.0	87.9	0.8	1.1	6.1	9.5	1.9	3.2	6.1	7.8	10.0	8.0	3.0	17.6	34.1	11.6	1.8	70.3	43.4	49.6	50.4
08837	EDISON	72.3	63.3	7.0	7.6	15.7	22.1	8.4	13.0	5.7	5.2	5.2	5.1	6.0	29.1	26.1	14.0	3.7	80.9	41.1	48.7	51.3
08840	METUCHEN	81.3	73.9	5.5	6.4	9.9	15.0	4.7	7.6	6.1	6.4	7.0	6.3	4.5	24.4	30.3	12.7	2.3	76.5	42.2	47.9	52.1
08844	HILLSBOROUGH	86.1	80.6	3.7	4.5	7.3	10.8	4.7	7.6	7.1	7.6	8.2	7.4	5.3	25.9	30.2	7.3	1.0	72.2	37.8	49.5	50.5
08846	MIDDLESEX	86.9	78.3	3.6	5.5	4.4	7.9	9.0	14.8	6.5	6.7	6.8	6.4	5.3	26.7	28.5	11.2	2.0	76.0	40.1	48.8	51.2
08848	MILFORD	97.7	96.7	0.4	0.5	0.5	0.8	1.8	2.9	5.6	6.5	7.7	7.5	4.2	20.7	32.8	12.9	2.1	75.5	43.5	49.7	50.3
08850	MILLTOWN	93.3	89.2	0.9	1.2	3.6	6.0	3.5	6.2	5.5	5.8	6.4	6.8	5.1	23.8	30.7	13.6	2.3	78.1	42.6	49.0	51.0
08852	MONMOUTH JUNCTION	68.5	58.3	9.4	10.0	18.2	26.4	5.7	8.7	8.0	7.4	6.9	6.0	5.7	33.5	25.9	5.9	0.6	73.8	35.3	48.3	51.7
08853	NESHANIC STATION	90.6	86.4	2.0	2.6	6.1	9.3	2.3	3.9	7.4	8.5	9.6	7.4	2.9	24.6	31.1	7.7	0.8	69.7	39.6	50.4	49.6
08854	PISCATAWAY	48.8	39.7	20.2	20.4	24.9	32.2	7.9	11.0	6.0	5.9	5.9	9.4	8.6	28.6	25.2	9.4	1.1	78.5	35.6	49.6	50.4
08857	OLD BRIDGE	81.8	73.5	4.4	5.4	10.0	15.6	7.4	11.3	6.6	6.8	7.0	6.7	5.4	27.3	28.4	10.3	1.5	75.4	39.0	48.8	51.2
08859	PARLIN	73.8	66.4	7.4	8.1	13.6	18.5	8.8	13.5	6.7	6.7	6.7	6.7	5.5	28.2	27.8	10.2	1.5	75.8	38.6	49.0	51.0
08861	PERTH AMBOY	47.5	42.6	9.9	8.7	1.9	2.4	67.6	76.0	8.3	7.7	7.0	7.7	8.2	30.1	21.3	8.2	1.5	72.5	31.7	50.0	50.0
08863	FORDS	69.2	60.2	6.7	7.0	18.6	25.2	9.3	14.1	6.8	6.4	6.2	5.6	5.9	30.7	25.8	10.5	2.1	77.2	38.2	48.6	51.4
08865	PHILLIPSBURG	94.3	92.3	2.2	2.6	0.9	1.5	3.7	5.6	6.7	6.6	6.8	6.7	5.6	24.5	27.0	13.2	2.9	75.6	40.4	48.2	51.8
08867	PITTSTOWN	91.5	89.2	5.5	6.4	1.1	1.7	3.2	4.7	5.1	6.2	7.4	6.9	4.1	24.7	32.5	10.8	2.2	77.0	42.4	47.0	53.0
08869	RARITAN	87.7	82.4	0.9	1.1	8.3	12.0	8.4	13.3	7.2	7.2	6.9	5.8	5.0	29.0	26.0	10.7	2.2	74.9	38.5	47.9	52.1
08872	SAYREVILLE	71.1	64.7	12.4	12.6	11.8	16.1	7.8	11.9	7.1	6.9	6.8	6.2	6.0	29.6	26.6	9.2	1.7	75.5	37.3	49.2	50.8
08873	SOMERSET	53.8	49.8	28.0	27.1	11.4	14.8	8.8	12.0	6.5	6.3	6.3	5.9	5.8	28.4	27.7	10.8	2.2	77.0	39.4	47.9	52.1
08876	SOMERVILLE	80.3	75.5	7.8	8.2	6.7	9.3	10.4	14.9	7.2	7.5	7.5	6.3	5.2	27.5	27.3	10.1	1.6	73.9	38.5	49.7	50.3
08879	SOUTH AMBOY	87.1	82.2	4.1	4.7	4.3	6.4	6.8	11.5	6.0	6.0	6.2	6.6	6.2	28.0	28.3	10.9	1.9	77.9	39.3	49.4	50.6
08880	SOUTH BOUND BROOK	78.0	71.7	7.8	8.6	4.1	5.5	22.6	33.3	6.3	6.2	6.3	6.8	5.6	30.2	27.8	9.2	1.6	77.0	38.1	51.0	49.0
08882	SOUTH RIVER	83.5	76.7	6.1	7.2	3.6	5.8	9.7	15.8	6.6	6.6	6.4	6.3	5.5	29.2	26.4	10.6	2.3	76.5	38.4	49.8	50.2
08884	SPOTSWOOD	93.8	90.0	1.5	2.1	2.9	5.1	4.4	7.7	5.9	6.2	6.3	6.2	5.0	25.2	28.8	14.0	2.4	77.8	42.0	48.8	51.2
08886	STEWARTSVILLE	94.0	91.3	2.2	2.7	2.1	3.3	3.5	5.5	11.3	9.3	7.6	5.6	2.6	31.3	24.3	6.6	1.4	67.9	35.2	49.4	50.6
08887	THREE BRIDGES	92.0	87.8	0.5	0.6	6.3	9.7	3.4	5.2	5.2	4.6	4.7	5.0	7.9	31.9	30.0	9.4	1.4	81.9	39.8	47.4	52.6
08889	WHITEHOUSE STATION	95.3	93.1	0.7	0.9	2.2	3.5	2.0	3.2	6.8	7.1	7.6	6.4	3.5	23.5	32.1	11.5	1.4	74.1	42.2	49.1	50.9
08901	NEW BRUNSWICK	48.8	43.7	23.0	21.0	5.4	7.1	39.0	47.9	7.1	6.0	4.9	11.0	23.3	28.1	13.3	5.3	1.0	79.1	24.5	49.8	50.2
08902	NORTH BRUNSWICK	63.0	54.7	15.1	15.2	14.1	19.8	10.3	14.9	6.4	6.0	6.0	6.3	6.9	30.4	26.9	9.7	1.4	77.7	37.4	49.7	50.3
08904	HIGHLAND PARK	71.6	63.6	8.0	8.4	14.1	19.0	8.2	12.6	6.1	5.3	5.2	6.2	8.8	33.9	24.1	8.6	1.8	79.8	35.0	49.1	50.9
	NEW JERSEY	72.6	68.2	13.6	14.0	5.7	7.9	13.3	16.9	6.6	6.6	6.7	6.8	6.2	26.4	27.0	11.5	2.2	76.0	38.7	48.7	51.3
	UNITED STATES	75.1	72.0	12.3	12.7	3.8	4.6	12.5	15.7	6.8	6.7	6.6	7.1	6.9	27.0	26.0	10.9	1.9	75.7	36.9	49.2	50.8

08701-08904

ZIP CODE #	POST OFFICE NAME	2009 Per Capita Income	2009 HH Income Base	2009 HOUSEHOLD INCOME DISTRIBUTION (%) Less than $25,000	$25,000 to $49,999	$50,000 to $99,999	$100,000 to $149,999	$150,000 or More	MEDIAN HOUSEHOLD INCOME 2009	2014	2009 National Centile	2009 State Centile	2009 Home Value Base	2009 HOME VALUE DISTRIBUTION (%) Less than $50,000	$50,000 to $89,999	$90,000 to $174,999	$175,000 to $399,999	$400,000 or More	2009 Median Home Value
08701	LAKEWOOD	20859	23477	25.9	25.8	33.9	8.4	6.0	47704	53317	56	10	14862	0.7	4.1	26.1	47.5	21.7	256991
08721	BAYVILLE	27964	7003	13.0	20.3	46.3	13.3	7.2	67811	75559	85	34	5917	1.3	0.2	5.7	71.6	21.3	281260
08722	BEACHWOOD	28050	3685	6.6	16.4	54.3	15.1	7.6	75786	77543	90	45	3212	0.0	0.3	7.9	88.3	3.4	244973
08723	BRICK	30399	12904	12.4	21.9	46.0	12.4	7.3	65787	75144	84	31	10259	0.3	0.2	4.6	72.7	22.2	289725
08724	BRICK	30775	17303	13.3	21.0	44.4	12.8	8.4	67493	75638	85	33	14521	0.8	1.3	15.7	60.2	22.0	284855
08730	BRIELLE	46268	1903	10.3	12.4	34.1	19.9	23.3	88495	97037	95	67	1559	0.8	0.4	0.0	20.2	78.6	569575
08731	FORKED RIVER	30622	8536	10.6	19.7	46.1	15.6	7.9	73136	76947	88	41	7591	0.0	0.3	7.2	69.3	23.2	285109
08732	ISLAND HEIGHTS	38612	403	9.7	19.1	40.2	16.9	14.1	78429	79231	91	52	346	0.0	0.3	2.6	52.0	45.1	383168
08733	LAKEHURST	22851	972	14.2	25.9	48.0	7.3	4.5	57648	63513	75	20	614	3.4	6.7	34.0	48.7	7.2	183036
08734	LANOKA HARBOR	30507	2645	6.8	16.9	48.1	18.9	9.3	80907	81644	92	56	2374	0.0	0.0	4.4	63.3	32.3	317323
08735	LAVALLETTE	40129	2521	15.1	23.5	42.0	8.8	10.6	61399	74324	79	24	2049	0.3	0.4	1.2	18.7	79.3	636265
08736	MANASQUAN	47053	5265	7.6	13.6	30.6	25.7	22.4	96683	101662	96	74	4229	0.3	0.2	0.1	20.5	79.0	565036
08738	MANTOLOKING	67954	736	8.8	10.2	35.3	17.0	28.7	92719	89879	96	71	658	0.0	1.2	0.0	6.1	92.7	1000001
08740	OCEAN GATE	25655	923	19.0	24.5	44.6	7.3	4.7	55200	61191	72	18	640	0.0	0.0	21.6	67.2	11.3	219832
08741	PINE BEACH	33109	1059	9.4	20.3	41.7	17.6	11.0	76626	77932	90	47	928	0.8	0.6	3.3	62.2	33.1	335391
08742	POINT PLEASANT BEACH	35763	10898	12.2	17.7	43.5	13.9	12.6	75118	77584	89	43	8263	0.1	0.4	1.1	48.7	49.7	398789
08750	SEA GIRT	59904	1651	7.9	14.1	26.2	25.1	26.7	103266	107608	97	78	1353	0.1	0.1	0.7	13.0	86.1	824728
08751	SEASIDE HEIGHTS	24851	2326	34.4	27.0	28.7	7.4	2.5	38076	43367	27	4	1099	0.0	1.2	9.9	50.5	38.4	330328
08752	SEASIDE PARK	40183	1410	15.6	23.9	36.3	12.5	11.7	58460	59710	76	21	955	0.0	0.0	3.4	31.2	65.4	465848
08753	TOMS RIVER	31541	24355	13.2	18.5	42.6	14.4	11.2	75033	77590	89	43	19584	0.1	0.5	8.1	63.8	27.6	314619
08755	TOMS RIVER	32620	9738	14.3	19.5	42.8	12.4	11.0	68485	76015	86	35	8603	5.6	4.7	7.6	48.7	33.3	335158
08757	TOMS RIVER	25945	18132	25.3	36.9	32.5	3.4	1.8	40322	44793	34	5	16591	1.0	2.3	28.4	66.4	2.0	199616
08758	WARETOWN	28101	2549	13.9	20.9	48.5	9.4	7.3	61113	68841	79	24	2164	0.5	0.1	23.0	59.2	17.1	227778
08759	MANCHESTER TOWNSHIP	29241	19049	30.8	34.1	27.5	4.2	3.4	36199	39156	21	3	17393	8.9	19.5	33.9	32.7	5.1	143061
08801	ANNANDALE	47940	2854	3.6	5.3	21.2	29.2	40.7	132886	137625	99	93	2528	0.0	0.0	3.0	24.6	72.4	506826
08802	ASBURY	47177	1534	4.2	8.0	28.9	29.1	29.9	115458	122532	98	87	1388	0.5	0.0	2.7	33.4	63.4	458125
08804	BLOOMSBURY	43042	851	6.8	13.3	29.8	28.4	21.6	100073	101061	97	76	749	0.1	0.1	2.4	53.1	44.2	379384
08805	BOUND BROOK	31318	4348	13.0	23.2	33.9	16.7	13.0	64441	59761	83	29	2564	0.0	0.0	2.6	59.1	38.3	358759
08807	BRIDGEWATER	50611	14081	6.9	8.5	26.1	26.6	31.9	113366	126233	98	86	11584	0.1	0.6	4.5	27.0	67.8	504630
08809	CLINTON	50107	2268	7.2	14.3	29.3	23.7	25.4	97982	96643	96	75	1742	0.4	0.0	15.9	39.1	44.6	377934
08810	DAYTON	39772	2598	3.3	6.9	35.5	30.3	24.0	106899	112700	98	81	2146	0.5	0.1	3.9	60.7	34.8	338491
08812	DUNELLEN	39789	4678	9.1	14.8	35.7	21.9	18.5	84796	89533	94	62	3604	0.1	0.1	1.5	59.4	39.0	361284
08816	EAST BRUNSWICK	42393	16279	7.1	12.1	34.5	22.6	23.8	94004	101108	96	71	13182	0.7	0.7	6.7	44.4	47.5	387984
08817	EDISON	34357	16145	8.5	13.7	43.9	21.6	12.2	80818	85293	92	56	9332	1.9	1.8	3.4	78.5	14.3	291011
08820	EDISON	46548	13073	8.5	9.5	27.9	23.6	30.6	107991	112238	98	81	9949	0.4	0.6	0.6	36.1	62.3	454394
08822	FLEMINGTON	51759	11207	7.5	12.7	24.5	24.1	31.3	109027	114790	98	83	8927	0.1	0.2	1.8	37.3	60.7	457224
08823	FRANKLIN PARK	48270	3339	5.7	14.1	37.3	23.2	19.8	89341	90669	95	68	2302	0.3	0.4	9.9	54.5	34.9	316986
08824	KENDALL PARK	45348	4057	5.9	10.7	24.6	21.6	37.2	125682	124881	99	90	3474	1.9	0.2	1.8	50.1	45.9	387500
08825	FRENCHTOWN	38736	1884	12.7	17.1	27.2	24.7	18.2	85415	84807	94	63	1436	0.0	0.0	1.5	45.3	53.2	413855
08826	GLEN GARDNER	42506	2250	7.5	12.3	29.5	25.2	25.6	101016	101100	97	77	1825	0.0	0.4	10.7	37.3	51.6	407745
08827	HAMPTON	44671	1562	11.1	10.3	23.0	25.0	30.5	108171	113217	98	82	1290	0.5	0.2	2.1	37.6	59.7	452521
08828	HELMETTA	35503	847	6.8	11.9	51.1	22.1	8.0	81205	85001	93	57	731	0.0	0.1	24.1	61.7	14.1	224507
08829	HIGH BRIDGE	40168	1478	6.2	13.1	36.8	28.1	15.8	90875	94096	95	69	1225	0.0	0.0	7.8	72.8	19.3	300133
08830	ISELIN	35220	6339	9.5	14.5	40.5	22.4	13.1	81681	86997	93	59	4531	0.3	0.3	5.4	83.9	10.1	279757
08831	MONROE TOWNSHIP	40289	18676	11.4	18.6	35.1	18.3	16.6	78292	84000	91	51	16536	0.2	0.8	9.6	52.0	37.4	335325
08832	KEASBEY	25976	1079	18.4	19.6	43.3	12.9	5.8	63909	59476	82	29	355	0.3	1.7	13.0	83.7	1.4	245047
08833	LEBANON	63812	3501	3.7	6.5	20.4	24.8	44.7	138303	143643	99	96	3114	0.1	0.1	1.3	22.4	76.2	557297
08835	MANVILLE	29909	4166	13.0	23.1	37.6	19.5	6.8	65616	64566	84	31	2890	0.2	0.3	2.4	87.3	9.8	299293
08836	MARTINSVILLE	70312	1440	5.5	5.1	13.2	19.5	56.7	161432	164893	100	98	1352	0.0	0.3	0.5	6.5	92.7	731360
08837	EDISON	35038	6170	12.6	20.4	40.1	17.8	9.1	74539	76284	89	42	2958	0.8	6.1	6.9	62.7	23.5	308741
08840	METUCHEN	43850	5953	7.9	12.0	35.8	23.8	20.5	91099	98121	95	70	4708	0.2	0.0	2.6	60.3	36.8	357397
08844	HILLSBOROUGH	47168	13137	4.9	8.2	28.7	27.6	30.5	111556	124643	98	85	10713	0.1	0.1	3.6	30.9	65.3	479147
08846	MIDDLESEX	35568	5563	9.4	17.1	39.6	20.8	13.0	79601	84691	92	54	4163	0.3	0.3	2.1	76.8	20.4	306568
08848	MILFORD	40430	3113	8.3	12.9	32.7	26.8	19.3	92656	93043	96	71	2727	0.1	0.0	2.9	51.2	45.9	384418
08850	MILLTOWN	40190	3110	8.3	12.7	38.9	23.2	17.0	86953	92541	94	66	2589	0.0	0.0	2.6	61.6	35.8	357267
08852	MONMOUTH JUNCTION	43520	5891	5.9	9.2	40.5	23.6	20.8	92278	100906	95	71	3762	4.9	0.9	9.1	46.9	38.2	339702
08853	NESHANIC STATION	60550	1826	4.5	8.3	19.5	23.9	43.8	135506	140306	99	95	1522	0.0	0.0	0.2	9.7	90.1	631716
08854	PISCATAWAY	35101	16558	7.9	12.5	39.6	24.0	16.0	86450	92548	94	65	11220	0.2	0.4	4.4	69.6	25.4	321496
08857	OLD BRIDGE	34775	14346	8.5	14.8	38.0	23.6	15.1	84018	91087	94	61	9820	0.1	0.0	1.7	70.5	27.7	328846
08859	PARLIN	30656	8312	11.4	16.9	42.6	20.5	8.6	76538	78751	90	46	5130	0.5	0.2	2.8	79.3	17.2	285129
08861	PERTH AMBOY	18615	15531	24.9	25.9	35.0	10.1	4.1	49004	49881	59	11	6646	0.0	0.5	13.2	81.0	5.3	246128
08863	FORDS	35388	5101	10.4	16.3	38.4	20.8	14.1	79778	83975	92	54	3151	0.3	0.0	3.9	87.1	8.7	290789
08865	PHILLIPSBURG	26447	12256	22.8	20.3	40.1	12.1	4.7	56472	55499	73	19	8195	0.2	2.1	28.5	57.9	11.2	227298
08867	PITTSTOWN	55050	1726	5.7	8.7	19.5	28.2	37.9	127819	133885	99	90	1535	0.0	0.0	0.4	22.8	76.8	554873
08869	RARITAN	35076	2574	12.7	20.1	39.0	16.6	11.7	66202	64406	84	32	1619	0.0	0.3	1.0	50.1	48.6	395161
08872	SAYREVILLE	31372	7066	9.5	18.5	43.0	19.6	9.4	76138	78848	90	46	4422	0.3	0.2	2.5	75.6	21.5	289072
08873	SOMERSET	38732	18738	9.6	14.7	32.9	26.8	16.0	87475	90252	94	66	13579	0.4	0.2	3.5	60.4	35.6	349328
08876	SOMERVILLE	40779	8735	12.4	14.2	32.4	20.5	20.5	84970	87092	94	63	5804	0.7	0.6	1.4	42.9	54.3	423414
08879	SOUTH AMBOY	30237	8354	12.8	19.8	43.0	17.0	7.3	70211	75005	87	38	5288	0.2	0.3	9.6	78.7	11.1	268362
08880	SOUTH BOUND BROOK	26573	1805	15.1	22.6	38.0	17.1	7.1	63279	63535	81	27	1039	0.0	2.0	2.4	89.5	6.1	271024
08882	SOUTH RIVER	30336	5675	14.5	20.6	38.0	17.6	9.3	69694	75418	87	37	3903	0.6	0.2	8.0	76.5	14.7	278817
08884	SPOTSWOOD	32210	3201	17.2	16.7	36.1	20.9	9.1	70817	76000	87	38	2468	0.5	5.1	9.0	75.0	10.4	273746
08886	STEWARTSVILLE	44825	2074	6.6	10.5	24.3	26.6	32.2	115542	118467	98	87	1852	0.5	0.9	2.7	41.3	54.6	421662
08887	THREE BRIDGES	57958	455	14.1	20.0	25.1	25.1	15.8	80778	80699	92	56	321	0.0	0.0	22.7	65.4	11.8	200815
08889	WHITEHOUSE STATION	60624	3442	4.7	6.6	21.1	26.6	41.0	131557	137157	99	93	3064	0.3	0.1	2.4	28.5	68.7	496954
08901	NEW BRUNSWICK	18102	13520	26.4	26.8	31.8	10.1	5.0	46044	48302	51	9	3743	0.5	0.9	20.0	71.7	6.9	235404
08902	NORTH BRUNSWICK	36360	14905	10.7	15.8	41.0	19.2	13.3	78208	82077	91	51	9607	0.4	0.9	11.0	56.9	30.8	311322
08904	HIGHLAND PARK	37260	5930	14.1	21.0	35.5	16.5	12.8	70438	75907	87	38	2556	0.7	0.3	3.5	58.7	36.7	346105
	NEW JERSEY	34433		15.4	18.6	34.9	16.8	14.2	72809	76895				1.0	1.6	9.9	50.1	37.4	336585
	UNITED STATES	27277		20.9	24.4	35.3	11.7	7.6	54719	56938				9.3	13.1	31.6	32.6	13.5	162279

ZIP CODE #	POST OFFICE NAME	FINANCIAL SERVICES: Auto Loan	Home Loan	Invest-ments	Retire-ment Plans	THE HOME: Home Improvements: Home Repair	Lawn & Garden	Furnishings: Comput-ers & Hard-ware-Personal	Major Appli-ances	TV, Radio, Sound Equip-ment	Furni-ture	ENTERTAINMENT: Dine out/ Carry out	Sports Equip-ment	Fees & Tickets	Toys & Games	Travel	Cable TV	PERSONAL: Apparel & Services	Auto Repairs	Health Insur-ance	Pets & Supplies
08701	LAKEWOOD	82	88	93	84	93	91	87	90	88	91	88	62	92	84	93	89	61	90	98	101
08721	BAYVILLE	103	119	112	118	116	117	105	110	105	107	106	83	114	106	113	106	74	107	112	128
08722	BEACHWOOD	111	133	117	132	128	122	115	117	112	119	114	90	128	116	123	111	81	114	114	136
08723	BRICK	97	116	116	112	118	112	106	108	105	107	106	79	117	104	115	106	75	107	112	123
08724	BRICK	104	119	121	115	123	117	108	113	108	112	108	81	118	106	117	110	76	111	118	128
08730	BRIELLE	138	190	220	189	208	172	163	170	150	173	150	128	193	148	190	145	112	161	153	186
08731	FORKED RIVER	107	124	126	122	125	126	109	117	110	111	111	85	120	110	120	113	78	113	121	134
08732	ISLAND HEIGHTS	111	156	162	145	162	138	129	134	123	128	124	98	152	125	147	124	92	129	127	147
08733	LAKEHURST	97	91	98	91	91	92	96	95	95	93	96	75	93	96	95	95	67	97	93	111
08734	LANOKA HARBOR	115	142	127	141	137	132	123	125	121	125	122	97	139	123	134	120	87	122	124	145
08735	LAVALLETTE	109	114	155	113	132	135	103	121	109	116	107	76	113	98	119	114	73	116	135	137
08736	MANASQUAN	143	193	220	191	209	172	168	173	154	178	154	131	196	151	194	148	115	165	155	190
08738	MANTOLOKING	184	200	268	199	230	230	178	209	186	202	182	133	199	168	207	192	126	198	228	235
08740	OCEAN GATE	80	94	88	91	92	86	90	87	88	88	89	68	97	88	94	88	64	88	87	101
08741	PINE BEACH	104	141	142	133	144	126	118	122	113	117	114	91	136	115	133	114	84	118	117	136
08742	POINT PLEASANT BEACH	105	135	139	130	139	125	120	122	118	118	119	90	136	117	132	120	87	120	121	137
08750	SEA GIRT	165	227	266	228	249	212	193	204	181	207	180	150	232	175	227	176	134	192	191	224
08751	SEASIDE HEIGHTS	65	62	63	64	62	65	72	65	74	69	74	50	71	70	69	76	52	71	76	79
08752	SEASIDE PARK	104	114	149	112	128	129	103	118	108	112	107	75	114	98	118	113	74	113	130	133
08753	TOMS RIVER	110	132	132	129	134	125	118	122	116	121	117	91	131	116	129	116	83	119	121	138
08755	TOMS RIVER	112	125	144	118	134	134	113	126	115	118	114	87	122	110	126	119	80	121	134	142
08757	TOMS RIVER	61	72	87	64	84	86	64	77	68	73	66	44	75	60	78	73	45	73	96	83
08758	WARETOWN	94	121	114	117	119	113	103	107	102	104	103	80	119	103	115	103	74	104	108	121
08759	MANCHESTER TOWNSHIP	58	72	90	63	85	88	63	77	68	72	66	43	76	58	79	73	44	73	98	82
08801	ANNANDALE	213	272	280	283	281	247	231	237	217	247	220	185	270	220	258	209	162	224	213	270
08802	ASBURY	177	230	237	241	238	210	190	199	179	206	181	155	226	182	216	172	134	186	177	226
08804	BLOOMSBURY	147	195	197	193	200	175	162	168	154	169	156	128	190	157	183	151	115	159	155	188
08805	BOUND BROOK	109	130	132	126	132	115	129	122	124	124	127	94	139	124	134	123	94	125	116	137
08807	BRIDGEWATER	176	228	235	228	236	204	195	200	185	205	187	153	227	188	217	181	138	190	184	222
08809	CLINTON	153	189	204	193	199	171	172	172	159	180	160	135	193	158	189	152	118	166	155	194
08810	DAYTON	171	214	192	218	209	183	178	181	166	192	169	146	203	175	192	157	123	169	157	206
08812	DUNELLEN	138	186	198	178	195	165	161	164	152	163	153	124	186	152	182	149	113	159	153	182
08816	EAST BRUNSWICK	154	198	205	197	204	179	171	174	162	177	163	133	196	164	189	158	120	167	161	195
08817	EDISON	125	144	143	142	145	129	136	131	131	136	133	102	147	134	141	129	97	132	125	149
08820	EDISON	173	219	232	219	228	196	194	195	182	202	183	151	221	183	215	176	135	189	178	219
08822	FLEMINGTON	179	231	237	236	237	208	198	201	188	206	191	156	231	190	220	183	142	193	184	228
08823	FRANKLIN PARK	172	164	144	172	155	143	171	154	163	178	167	130	169	173	161	155	119	159	141	183
08824	KENDALL PARK	186	236	221	237	236	201	199	201	188	212	191	161	229	197	215	180	141	189	177	225
08825	FRENCHTOWN	138	176	176	176	179	160	151	154	144	156	146	118	173	146	167	141	106	148	144	174
08826	GLEN GARDNER	154	184	183	191	186	169	165	165	157	173	160	129	185	159	178	153	116	161	154	191
08827	HAMPTON	162	205	205	210	209	185	178	180	169	186	171	142	206	172	196	164	126	173	165	205
08828	HELMETTA	131	148	122	143	139	122	129	129	121	139	124	103	135	130	130	115	87	122	112	147
08829	HIGH BRIDGE	136	177	168	168	176	153	148	152	141	153	143	116	168	146	162	138	104	145	139	170
08830	ISELIN	127	151	149	146	152	133	139	136	133	140	135	105	151	137	147	132	98	136	128	154
08831	MONROE TOWNSHIP	119	152	172	144	168	161	130	147	131	143	130	96	154	122	155	135	91	139	163	161
08832	KEASBEY	98	97	89	98	94	85	108	95	103	105	106	79	106	105	103	100	77	102	90	111
08833	LEBANON	231	298	314	309	311	272	250	260	236	271	238	201	297	239	282	227	177	244	233	293
08835	MANVILLE	90	119	121	113	122	107	106	106	103	102	104	79	120	103	116	104	77	105	104	118
08836	MARTINSVILLE	242	339	401	355	374	316	275	294	257	305	256	222	350	257	327	246	198	269	258	322
08837	EDISON	109	120	120	119	120	112	120	113	117	118	119	88	126	118	122	118	85	117	115	132
08840	METUCHEN	138	191	207	183	201	175	160	167	154	162	155	122	190	154	184	155	115	161	162	184
08844	HILLSBOROUGH	186	220	215	225	221	195	196	194	186	207	188	155	219	192	208	178	138	188	176	221
08846	MIDDLESEX	118	157	159	150	161	140	136	138	130	135	132	103	156	132	150	131	97	134	131	153
08848	MILFORD	138	185	193	183	192	168	153	161	146	159	148	120	181	147	175	144	109	152	150	179
08850	MILLTOWN	130	182	193	172	190	164	151	157	145	151	146	116	179	146	174	146	108	151	150	173
08852	MONMOUTH JUNCTION	164	173	160	179	169	153	167	158	160	174	163	129	175	167	167	153	117	159	145	185
08853	NESHANIC STATION	234	309	320	324	320	276	254	264	237	276	239	208	305	241	289	225	180	245	229	298
08854	PISCATAWAY	135	159	162	157	163	139	152	146	142	153	144	115	163	143	160	137	105	146	134	165
08857	OLD BRIDGE	126	152	151	151	154	138	140	137	134	141	137	107	155	136	149	133	99	137	132	157
08859	PARLIN	102	128	130	124	130	115	118	116	115	116	117	88	131	115	127	115	86	116	112	131
08861	PERTH AMBOY	80	82	74	77	81	66	90	82	83	90	87	66	87	84	87	79	64	86	72	90
08863	FORDS	126	144	141	142	144	129	136	131	131	137	133	103	146	135	142	129	96	133	125	151
08865	PHILLIPSBURG	88	96	88	96	94	96	93	92	94	91	94	70	97	93	95	95	66	93	98	108
08867	PITTSTOWN	188	257	279	264	272	233	211	222	197	228	198	170	256	198	245	189	148	206	197	246
08869	RARITAN	110	135	131	128	135	118	124	121	120	121	123	92	136	123	130	121	90	121	116	136
08872	SAYREVILLE	113	134	130	131	134	121	123	121	118	123	120	93	133	121	129	117	87	120	116	138
08873	SOMERSET	140	155	152	156	155	142	149	143	145	150	147	112	159	147	154	143	106	145	139	167
08876	SOMERVILLE	138	163	166	165	166	148	154	149	148	155	150	117	169	148	163	145	110	149	142	171
08879	SOUTH AMBOY	101	123	121	118	124	111	113	111	110	111	112	85	124	111	121	110	81	112	109	127
08880	SOUTH BOUND BROOK	94	114	109	110	114	104	107	104	104	105	105	81	117	105	113	104	76	105	103	120
08882	SOUTH RIVER	102	131	129	124	132	117	118	117	113	116	115	89	131	115	128	113	84	116	113	132
08884	SPOTSWOOD	103	129	135	121	133	121	114	118	111	114	112	87	127	111	126	112	81	115	116	132
08886	STEWARTSVILLE	190	231	201	236	224	198	194	197	182	211	185	161	219	193	206	171	134	184	171	224
08887	THREE BRIDGES	159	141	126	149	133	125	158	138	152	160	156	117	150	160	145	146	110	148	130	167
08889	WHITEHOUSE STATION	211	284	294	288	295	253	232	242	218	249	220	188	279	224	264	210	164	226	215	269
08901	NEW BRUNSWICK	84	67	65	69	65	62	100	76	92	88	95	65	84	91	82	89	69	89	74	91
08902	NORTH BRUNSWICK	127	137	136	138	138	128	137	130	134	136	136	102	143	135	139	133	97	134	129	151
08904	HIGHLAND PARK	114	121	124	123	123	108	132	118	125	127	129	96	134	125	131	122	94	125	113	137
	NEW JERSEY	119	138	141	137	141	129	132	129	129	132	131	98	143	128	139	129	95	130	128	148
	UNITED STATES	100	100	100	100	100	100	100	100	100	100	100	100	100	100	100	100	100	100	100	100

ZIP CODE #	POST OFFICE NAME	COUNTY FIPS CODE	POPULATION 2000	POPULATION 2009	POPULATION 2014	2000-2009 ANNUAL RATE % Rate	2000-2009 ANNUAL RATE State Centile	HOUSEHOLDS 2000	HOUSEHOLDS 2009	HOUSEHOLDS 2014	HOUSEHOLDS % Annual Rate 2000-2009	HOUSEHOLDS 2009 Average HH Size	FAMILIES 2000	FAMILIES 2009	FAMILIES % Annual Rate 2000-2009
87001	ALGODONES	043	770	1341	1575	6.2	99	263	441	524	5.7	3.04	225	370	5.5
87002	BELEN	061	20460	21850	22514	0.7	51	7660	8383	8689	1.0	2.55	5528	5841	0.6
87004	BERNALILLO	043	10957	14602	16811	3.2	94	3304	4569	5307	3.6	3.19	2529	3367	3.1
87005	BLUEWATER	006	2086	2932	3055	3.7	96	740	872	934	1.8	2.55	542	615	1.4
87006	BOSQUE	053	463	544	576	1.8	81	175	209	224	1.9	2.57	130	150	1.6
87007	CASA BLANCA	006	3043	3306	3419	0.9	60	838	934	980	1.2	3.49	713	778	0.9
87008	CEDAR CREST	001	2725	3251	3599	1.9	82	1127	1425	1599	2.6	2.27	846	1012	2.0
87009	CEDARVALE	057	120	112	110	-0.7	6	51	49	48	-0.4	2.29	37	34	-0.9
87010	CERRILLOS	049	930	1090	1180	1.7	80	448	529	577	1.8	2.06	290	321	1.1
87012	COYOTE	039	20	20	19	0.0	20	9	9	9	0.0	1.89	7	7	0.0
87013	CUBA	043	4225	5929	7001	3.7	96	1240	1829	2186	4.3	3.24	967	1372	3.9
87014	CUBERO	006	7034	7752	8094	1.1	68	2025	2325	2467	1.5	3.21	1592	1773	1.2
87015	EDGEWOOD	049	12031	14147	15328	1.8	81	4212	5041	5492	2.0	2.81	3295	3795	1.5
87016	ESTANCIA	057	4366	4486	4494	0.3	33	1407	1461	1472	0.4	2.68	1051	1054	0.0
87017	GALLINA	039	934	929	915	-0.1	14	342	364	364	0.7	2.49	257	264	0.3
87018	COUNSELOR	043	619	895	1054	4.1	98	259	395	470	4.7	2.27	181	257	3.9
87020	GRANTS	006	11104	11419	11524	0.3	33	3827	4043	4137	0.6	2.61	2803	2855	0.2
87021	MILAN	006	2645	3077	3187	1.6	79	954	1081	1142	1.4	2.57	683	744	0.9
87023	JARALES	061	1337	1787	1981	3.2	94	436	591	655	3.3	3.02	338	446	3.0
87024	JEMEZ PUEBLO	043	2477	3427	4001	3.6	95	684	972	1147	3.9	3.51	567	792	3.7
87025	JEMEZ SPRINGS	043	1285	1769	2032	3.5	95	503	746	872	4.4	2.31	351	496	3.8
87026	LAGUNA	006	1819	2072	2259	1.4	75	470	565	624	2.0	3.66	381	442	1.6
87027	LA JARA	043	60	76	89	2.6	91	27	36	43	3.2	2.11	19	23	2.1
87028	LA JOYA	053	86	93	96	0.8	55	38	42	44	1.1	2.21	27	28	0.4
87029	LINDRITH	039	608	600	590	-0.1	14	201	211	211	0.5	2.52	150	153	0.2
87031	LOS LUNAS	061	36195	41826	44100	1.6	79	11721	13697	14545	1.7	2.93	9220	10434	1.3
87035	MORIARTY	057	7925	8285	8398	0.5	43	2844	3059	3121	0.8	2.71	2084	2160	0.4
87036	MOUNTAINAIR	057	1594	1486	1452	-0.8	5	641	617	608	-0.4	2.41	412	378	-0.9
87041	PENA BLANCA	043	1340	1918	2249	4.0	97	413	620	737	4.5	3.08	330	476	4.0
87042	PERALTA	061	3023	3130	3205	0.4	40	1050	1120	1153	0.7	2.79	823	853	0.4
87043	PLACITAS	043	3768	5010	5806	3.1	93	1619	2266	2659	3.7	2.21	1193	1600	3.2
87044	PONDEROSA	043	441	554	632	2.5	90	170	221	256	2.9	2.46	120	149	2.4
87045	PREWITT	031	1445	1502	1534	0.4	40	397	418	429	0.6	3.59	330	339	0.3
87046	REGINA	043	6	6	6	0.0	20	3	3	3	0.0	2.00	3	3	0.0
87047	SANDIA PARK	001	4203	5056	5603	2.0	84	1639	2078	2332	2.6	2.43	1234	1487	2.0
87048	CORRALES	043	7620	9610	10953	2.5	90	2930	3856	4442	3.0	2.49	2157	2723	2.6
87052	SANTO DOMINGO PUEBLO	043	3213	4461	5185	3.6	95	574	828	974	4.0	5.37	527	749	3.9
87053	SAN YSIDRO	043	907	982	1091	0.9	60	249	279	316	1.2	3.49	204	224	1.0
87056	STANLEY	049	1066	1240	1343	1.6	79	370	433	472	1.7	2.86	247	271	1.0
87059	TIJERAS	001	8480	10357	11391	2.2	85	3207	4102	4570	2.7	2.52	2441	2972	2.2
87060	TOME	061	184	178	175	-0.4	8	61	60	60	-0.2	2.82	48	46	-0.5
87062	VEGUITA	053	2055	2342	2453	1.4	75	678	791	838	1.7	2.92	504	566	1.3
87063	WILLARD	057	340	331	330	-0.3	9	139	139	139	0.0	2.38	95	91	-0.5
87068	BOSQUE FARMS	001	5346	5728	5975	0.7	51	1927	2155	2269	1.2	2.65	1508	1632	0.9
87083	COCHITI LAKE	043	394	447	491	1.4	75	205	245	273	1.9	1.82	125	137	1.0
87102	ALBUQUERQUE	001	21772	23527	24709	0.8	55	8146	9177	9784	1.3	2.35	4154	4350	0.5
87104	ALBUQUERQUE	001	11497	11939	12463	0.4	40	4822	5275	5578	1.0	2.21	2818	2840	0.1
87105	ALBUQUERQUE	001	54869	57489	60128	0.5	43	18148	19937	21118	1.0	2.87	13785	14390	0.5
87106	ALBUQUERQUE	001	23899	23561	23979	-0.2	10	11253	11544	11890	0.3	1.96	4834	4484	-0.8
87107	ALBUQUERQUE	001	30967	31926	33583	0.3	33	12455	13495	14403	0.9	2.33	7892	7914	0.0
87108	ALBUQUERQUE	001	38263	38529	39380	0.1	23	16768	17516	18178	0.5	2.14	8360	7840	-0.7
87109	ALBUQUERQUE	001	39223	41081	43120	0.5	43	17043	18891	20115	1.1	2.16	10242	10482	0.3
87110	ALBUQUERQUE	001	40168	40738	42019	0.2	28	18065	19147	20009	0.6	2.11	10240	9967	-0.3
87111	ALBUQUERQUE	001	54443	58020	61148	0.7	51	23772	26632	28392	1.2	2.15	14965	15679	0.5
87112	ALBUQUERQUE	001	43764	44481	46152	0.2	28	18389	19684	20689	0.7	2.25	11903	11842	-0.1
87113	ALBUQUERQUE	001	7337	14605	17700	7.7	100	2798	6097	7492	8.8	2.37	1880	3814	7.9
87114	ALBUQUERQUE	001	32257	57144	67524	6.4	99	12208	21781	25884	6.5	2.59	8607	14879	6.1
87116	ALBUQUERQUE	001	5193	5749	6134	1.1	68	1570	1843	1999	1.7	2.87	1316	1500	1.4
87120	ALBUQUERQUE	001	44244	56013	62237	2.6	91	16159	21306	23997	3.0	2.59	11861	14656	2.3
87121	ALBUQUERQUE	001	37805	64701	76509	6.0	98	11694	20788	24876	6.4	3.10	9342	15909	5.9
87122	ALBUQUERQUE	001	13090	17574	19921	3.2	94	4796	6620	7553	3.5	2.64	3819	5094	3.2
87123	ALBUQUERQUE	001	36094	38537	40598	0.7	51	15087	16844	17940	1.2	2.27	9591	9977	0.4
87124	RIO RANCHO	043	37497	48535	55155	2.8	91	13842	18541	21296	3.2	2.60	10047	12869	2.7
87131	ALBUQUERQUE	001	1943	1987	2000	0.2	28	340	357	371	0.5	1.18	29	25	-1.6
87144	RIO RANCHO	043	14942	29472	36191	7.6	100	5352	10621	13164	7.7	2.76	4211	8165	7.4
87301	GALLUP	031	39955	41071	41656	0.3	33	12266	12697	12924	0.4	3.17	9245	9281	0.0
87310	BRIMHALL	031	105	104	105	-0.1	14	41	41	42	0.0	2.54	31	30	-0.4
87312	CONTINENTAL DIVIDE	031	1106	1140	1158	0.3	33	292	306	312	0.5	3.73	236	240	0.2
87313	CROWNPOINT	031	7240	7490	7617	0.4	40	2019	2115	2163	0.5	3.54	1578	1599	0.1
87315	FENCE LAKE	006	164	178	185	0.9	60	73	83	88	1.4	2.13	51	56	1.0
87320	MEXICAN SPRINGS	031	1088	1147	1179	0.6	46	282	301	311	0.7	3.81	223	231	0.4
87321	RAMAH	031	589	597	601	0.1	23	191	196	199	0.3	3.05	148	148	0.0
87323	THOREAU	031	4557	4727	4814	0.4	40	1272	1336	1367	0.5	3.54	963	974	0.1
87325	TOHATCHI	031	7370	7648	7796	0.4	40	1987	2085	2135	0.5	3.67	1564	1591	0.2
87327	ZUNI	031	7748	7791	7849	0.1	23	1847	1882	1906	0.2	4.11	1637	1643	0.0
87328	NAVAJO	031	2929	2983	3023	0.2	28	709	734	749	0.4	4.06	587	592	0.1
87401	FARMINGTON	045	48079	53911	57355	1.2	69	16441	18517	19765	1.3	2.88	12163	13257	0.9
87402	FARMINGTON	045	8556	10599	11676	2.3	87	3069	3854	4274	2.5	2.75	2413	2948	2.2
87410	AZTEC	045	15038	16608	17607	1.1	68	5276	5889	6282	1.2	2.73	4002	4294	0.8
87412	BLANCO	045	931	1220	1364	3.0	93	363	475	536	2.9	2.56	270	339	2.5
87413	BLOOMFIELD	045	12599	14654	15876	1.6	79	4257	5040	5503	1.8	2.90	3341	3824	1.5
87415	FLORA VISTA	045	1964	2185	2320	1.2	69	706	800	858	1.4	2.68	554	607	1.0
87416	FRUITLAND	045	468	577	637	2.3	87	141	177	196	2.5	3.23	118	145	2.3
87417	KIRTLAND	045	6014	7478	8269	2.4	88	1763	2228	2480	2.6	3.35	1478	1821	2.3
87418	LA PLATA	045	660	744	791	1.3	72	228	259	277	1.4	2.87	177	194	1.0
87419	NAVAJO DAM	045	74	88	98	1.9	82	30	37	42	2.3	2.38	22	26	1.8
87420	SHIPROCK	045	18628	22857	25157	2.2	85	5191	6470	7171	2.4	3.53	4193	5071	2.1
87421	WATERFLOW	045	789	970	1070	2.3	87	246	307	341	2.4	3.14	198	240	2.1
87501	SANTA FE	049	15408	15673	15932	0.2	28	7675	7792	7951	0.2	1.97	3867	3633	-0.7
87505	SANTA FE	049	31862	33459	34355	0.5	43	13973	14637	15111	0.5	2.18	7590	7398	-0.3
87506	SANTA FE	049	11876	13162	13962	1.1	68	5123	5782	6184	1.3	2.27	3303	3529	0.7
87507	SANTA FE	049	36113	44414	48210	2.3	87	13023	15878	17282	2.2	2.78	8909	10310	1.6
87508	SANTA FE	049	14812	17851	19328	2.0	84	5576	6758	7391	2.1	2.49	3904	4481	1.5
87510	ABIQUIU	039	2594	2707	2699	0.5	43	932	1037	1049	1.2	2.60	652	696	0.7
87513	ARROYO HONDO	055	2215	2522	2651	1.4	75	952	1160	1236	2.2	2.17	565	654	1.6
	NEW MEXICO					1.3					1.6	2.56			1.2
	UNITED STATES					1.0					1.1	2.59			0.9

POPULATION COMPOSITION

ZIP CODE # POST OFFICE NAME	RACE (%) White 2000	White 2009	Black 2000	Black 2009	Asian/Pacific 2000	Asian/Pacific 2009	% Hispanic Origin 2000	% Hispanic Origin 2009	2009 AGE DISTRIBUTION (%) 0-4	5-9	10-14	15-19	20-24	25-44	45-64	65-84	85+	18+	MEDIAN AGE 2009	% 2009 Males	% 2009 Females
87001 ALGODONES	19.7	13.3	0.1	0.1	0.1	0.1	18.0	13.7	9.5	9.1	8.3	8.4	8.4	29.2	20.6	6.0	0.7	68.0	28.8	50.7	49.3
87002 BELEN	71.3	70.2	1.6	1.7	0.4	0.5	57.3	60.0	7.1	6.9	6.9	6.8	6.0	24.7	25.8	13.5	2.3	74.9	38.3	48.8	51.2
87004 BERNALILLO	45.5	43.4	0.6	0.8	0.2	0.4	54.6	51.0	8.8	8.6	8.0	8.3	7.5	28.0	22.4	7.5	1.0	69.7	30.8	49.1	50.9
87005 BLUEWATER	47.5	47.5	0.4	0.5	0.2	0.3	19.5	23.3	5.8	6.0	6.1	7.6	8.7	30.4	24.5	9.4	1.5	77.5	35.0	59.9	40.1
87006 BOSQUE	69.5	67.8	0.6	0.9	0.4	0.4	58.3	61.2	8.5	7.7	8.1	8.5	7.2	25.4	24.6	9.4	0.7	70.0	31.7	49.8	50.2
87007 CASA BLANCA	1.7	1.2	0.1	0.1	0.0	0.0	3.6	2.9	9.1	9.1	8.6	8.9	7.0	25.5	21.6	8.7	1.6	67.8	30.1	47.9	52.1
87008 CEDAR CREST	90.8	89.8	0.5	0.6	1.0	1.4	16.7	18.3	3.6	4.5	6.2	6.7	3.6	19.0	41.7	13.4	1.3	81.5	48.2	49.7	50.3
87009 CEDARVALE	69.2	67.0	0.0	0.0	0.0	0.0	56.7	60.7	5.4	5.4	6.3	5.4	5.4	18.8	33.9	17.0	2.7	80.4	47.2	51.8	48.2
87010 CERRILLOS	86.5	84.8	0.3	0.4	0.8	0.9	20.9	23.6	4.6	4.6	5.2	6.9	6.9	22.4	36.6	11.7	1.1	81.6	44.6	48.6	51.4
87012 COYOTE	73.7	75.0	0.0	0.0	0.0	0.0	57.9	55.0	0.0	5.0	5.0	10.0	0.0	20.0	40.0	10.0	10.0	85.0	50.0	60.0	40.0
87013 CUBA	15.5	12.8	0.1	0.1	0.1	0.1	20.2	18.5	8.2	10.7	10.3	9.9	7.6	21.4	23.0	8.0	0.9	64.3	27.6	49.4	50.6
87014 CUBERO	20.7	19.1	0.4	0.4	0.1	0.2	16.7	17.2	8.0	7.6	8.0	8.4	7.6	25.0	25.0	9.5	1.0	71.3	33.0	49.9	50.1
87015 EDGEWOOD	84.7	82.8	0.7	0.9	0.5	0.6	21.9	24.6	6.4	7.8	8.8	8.1	4.4	27.0	30.2	6.6	0.7	71.4	37.3	50.1	49.9
87016 ESTANCIA	74.4	72.8	4.0	4.3	0.5	0.5	43.6	46.9	6.1	6.3	6.6	7.0	6.5	27.8	27.9	10.7	1.1	76.7	37.7	56.4	43.6
87017 GALLINA	43.5	43.1	0.4	0.4	0.1	0.1	81.2	82.9	5.5	7.0	7.8	7.4	5.3	22.2	27.9	13.8	3.2	74.9	40.9	49.9	50.1
87018 COUNSELOR	59.9	55.3	0.3	0.3	0.3	0.2	59.3	58.5	5.3	5.0	6.6	6.7	3.5	20.6	36.1	14.4	1.9	78.4	46.4	49.8	50.2
87020 GRANTS	54.8	51.3	1.6	1.7	0.9	1.0	50.5	52.0	7.9	7.2	7.2	7.0	7.2	26.6	25.2	10.8	1.0	73.4	35.1	49.0	51.0
87021 MILAN	57.4	54.1	1.1	1.2	0.0	0.1	45.6	46.1	7.5	7.1	7.2	8.1	8.5	27.1	24.0	9.4	1.1	73.3	32.6	53.7	46.3
87023 JARALES	59.7	56.2	1.1	1.2	0.2	0.2	55.0	56.9	8.2	7.6	7.4	8.1	7.1	24.7	26.3	9.7	0.9	72.1	34.9	49.5	50.5
87024 JEMEZ PUEBLO	15.1	12.3	0.1	0.1	0.2	0.1	8.3	7.6	7.9	7.8	7.6	8.8	7.5	25.5	25.6	8.2	1.1	71.2	32.8	48.4	51.6
87025 JEMEZ SPRINGS	67.5	62.4	0.3	0.3	0.9	0.9	35.4	38.9	5.1	5.3	5.8	6.4	3.5	21.1	39.7	11.5	1.5	79.0	46.1	49.2	50.8
87026 LAGUNA	6.1	6.6	0.2	0.2	0.0	0.0	8.4	8.9	9.5	11.1	11.8	10.1	8.9	25.1	18.2	4.8	0.4	61.1	24.2	47.5	52.5
87027 LA JARA	67.8	63.2	0.0	0.0	0.0	0.0	55.9	55.3	3.9	5.3	6.6	6.6	2.6	18.4	39.5	15.8	1.3	77.6	48.6	51.3	48.7
87028 LA JOYA	74.4	72.0	1.2	1.1	0.0	0.0	52.3	53.8	5.4	6.5	6.5	7.5	5.4	22.6	31.2	12.9	2.2	76.3	42.1	48.4	51.6
87029 LINDRITH	68.8	67.7	0.0	0.0	0.0	0.0	56.9	59.7	4.2	4.7	5.2	6.3	4.7	21.2	29.8	17.2	6.8	82.5	47.7	49.0	51.0
87031 LOS LUNAS	63.7	62.5	1.2	1.4	0.5	0.6	57.5	60.2	8.4	7.8	7.4	7.7	7.5	28.5	24.5	7.3	0.8	71.7	32.7	51.7	48.3
87035 MORIARTY	74.3	72.2	0.8	0.9	0.4	0.5	33.2	36.1	7.3	7.6	8.7	7.8	5.9	25.3	28.1	8.4	0.8	71.2	35.6	50.0	50.0
87036 MOUNTAINAIR	65.9	63.9	1.3	1.3	0.4	0.4	48.2	51.7	7.1	7.3	7.3	7.1	5.8	21.3	26.4	15.3	2.4	73.8	39.3	48.0	52.0
87041 PENA BLANCA	11.8	9.0	0.4	0.4	0.1	0.1	36.8	32.1	8.3	8.9	8.8	8.9	7.6	24.8	21.5	9.7	1.6	68.9	30.2	48.2	51.8
87042 PERALTA	64.1	62.1	0.6	0.6	0.3	0.4	47.1	50.0	6.4	6.6	7.0	7.8	5.8	25.5	29.4	10.4	1.1	75.3	38.3	48.7	51.3
87043 PLACITAS	83.7	81.1	0.7	0.7	0.5	0.6	20.3	23.0	4.0	5.0	6.3	5.5	3.1	16.9	42.3	15.7	1.2	81.2	49.8	48.6	51.4
87044 PONDEROSA	58.6	53.6	0.2	0.2	0.5	0.5	41.4	44.8	6.3	5.8	6.1	7.0	4.3	21.7	37.0	10.3	1.4	76.0	44.2	51.4	48.6
87045 PREWITT	13.8	11.5	0.5	0.5	0.1	0.1	4.6	4.4	11.1	10.4	9.8	9.5	8.2	21.0	23.0	6.3	0.6	62.7	25.7	47.3	52.7
87046 REGINA	0.0	0.0	0.0	0.0	14.3	16.7	0.0	0.0	0.0	0.0	0.0	0.0	0.0	50.0	50.0	0.0	0.0	100.0	45.0	33.3	66.7
87047 SANDIA PARK	89.0	87.7	0.6	0.7	0.7	0.9	18.0	20.0	4.5	5.5	6.5	6.4	4.0	20.3	41.1	10.8	0.9	79.5	46.3	50.5	49.5
87048 CORRALES	85.5	83.0	0.7	0.7	0.9	1.0	26.1	29.5	4.7	5.5	6.6	7.0	4.2	20.5	37.1	13.2	1.2	78.9	45.8	47.8	52.2
87052 SANTO DOMINGO PUEBLO	2.4	1.9	0.0	0.0	0.0	0.0	5.2	4.4	9.3	10.4	10.4	10.0	8.3	25.1	19.8	6.1	0.5	64.0	25.9	51.1	48.9
87053 SAN YSIDRO	19.7	16.8	0.1	0.1	0.2	0.2	10.1	10.5	8.1	8.1	7.6	8.2	7.4	26.2	25.2	8.1	0.9	70.9	31.9	49.4	50.6
87056 STANLEY	83.8	81.9	0.3	0.3	0.6	0.7	25.2	28.2	4.7	5.1	5.6	6.8	5.8	23.9	37.2	10.2	0.9	80.4	43.8	49.0	51.0
87059 TIJERAS	85.4	84.6	0.4	0.4	0.6	0.9	23.5	25.3	5.7	6.5	7.6	7.1	4.5	21.7	37.5	8.7	0.7	75.7	43.0	50.7	49.3
87060 TOME	67.4	66.3	0.5	0.6	0.0	0.0	55.4	59.0	6.7	6.7	7.3	6.2	6.2	24.7	27.0	11.2	3.9	75.8	39.0	50.0	50.0
87062 VEGUITA	70.0	68.3	0.6	0.7	0.2	0.3	58.4	61.3	8.6	7.9	8.2	8.7	7.6	26.0	23.9	8.5	0.7	69.3	30.1	49.8	50.2
87063 WILLARD	65.6	64.0	0.6	0.6	0.3	0.3	56.8	60.1	7.6	7.3	6.9	6.0	5.1	19.3	29.0	16.3	2.4	74.3	43.2	53.8	46.2
87068 BOSQUE FARMS	61.7	59.7	0.6	0.6	0.2	0.2	27.7	29.6	5.9	6.4	6.8	7.1	5.6	22.6	32.0	12.2	1.3	76.6	41.7	48.8	51.2
87083 COCHITI LAKE	78.4	73.2	0.5	0.7	1.3	1.1	10.2	11.0	2.7	3.1	3.8	4.0	4.0	15.4	36.0	26.4	4.5	88.1	55.1	48.1	51.9
87102 ALBUQUERQUE	57.7	57.6	4.2	4.3	0.7	0.8	69.4	70.7	6.8	6.3	5.8	7.0	9.4	30.8	23.1	9.0	1.8	77.2	33.7	51.9	48.1
87104 ALBUQUERQUE	67.7	67.0	1.2	1.3	0.7	0.9	61.6	63.6	6.0	5.9	5.8	6.9	6.8	24.6	28.4	13.5	2.1	78.1	40.1	47.8	52.2
87105 ALBUQUERQUE	54.7	54.4	1.5	1.5	0.5	0.6	76.6	77.5	7.8	7.8	7.7	7.8	6.6	26.2	25.1	9.8	1.2	71.8	34.2	49.6	50.4
87106 ALBUQUERQUE	70.2	68.0	4.6	4.8	4.8	6.1	28.7	29.9	5.7	4.5	4.0	6.5	13.7	33.0	22.3	8.1	2.1	83.3	32.2	49.7	50.3
87107 ALBUQUERQUE	69.6	68.8	1.6	1.8	0.7	0.9	55.5	57.3	5.9	5.7	6.0	7.8	6.7	24.4	29.3	12.5	1.8	77.6	39.8	48.9	51.1
87108 ALBUQUERQUE	66.0	64.6	4.4	4.8	2.8	3.4	45.3	46.0	7.6	6.5	5.5	5.8	7.9	29.4	24.1	10.0	3.2	77.3	35.3	49.4	50.6
87109 ALBUQUERQUE	76.5	74.1	2.6	2.9	2.8	3.5	27.1	29.0	5.7	5.2	5.4	6.3	7.6	27.0	27.5	13.2	2.1	80.2	39.2	47.4	52.6
87110 ALBUQUERQUE	78.4	76.8	2.5	2.7	2.2	2.8	31.5	33.4	5.4	5.0	5.1	5.5	6.8	25.5	28.0	15.4	3.4	81.2	42.5	48.1	51.9
87111 ALBUQUERQUE	85.7	84.1	1.9	2.1	2.8	3.6	17.8	19.1	4.5	4.6	5.3	6.0	6.1	24.3	31.2	15.2	2.9	82.1	44.4	48.1	51.9
87112 ALBUQUERQUE	79.5	77.6	2.8	3.0	2.8	3.6	27.4	29.2	6.0	5.8	6.1	6.2	6.1	25.6	28.6	13.5	2.1	78.3	40.8	48.2	51.8
87113 ALBUQUERQUE	72.5	70.9	1.6	1.8	2.7	3.5	43.9	46.0	7.6	7.2	6.8	6.2	5.7	30.2	24.4	10.0	1.9	74.7	35.8	48.4	51.6
87114 ALBUQUERQUE	75.8	72.9	2.9	3.1	1.6	2.1	37.3	38.5	8.8	8.1	7.3	6.3	5.8	32.9	22.9	7.0	0.9	71.9	33.4	49.2	50.8
87116 ALBUQUERQUE	72.1	69.7	9.3	10.2	3.4	4.4	17.7	18.7	15.2	10.4	7.6	7.1	19.8	36.8	2.8	0.2	0.1	63.6	22.4	54.3	45.7
87120 ALBUQUERQUE	69.8	67.7	3.0	3.4	1.5	2.0	44.7	47.0	8.5	8.3	7.9	6.9	5.8	32.0	24.6	5.5	0.6	71.0	33.5	48.1	51.9
87121 ALBUQUERQUE	48.4	48.7	3.5	3.6	0.6	0.6	77.2	78.7	10.6	9.8	8.6	8.4	8.2	30.8	18.2	4.8	0.5	65.9	27.4	49.7	50.3
87122 ALBUQUERQUE	89.5	87.3	1.0	1.2	3.3	4.6	13.1	15.2	5.1	5.9	7.0	7.8	4.5	21.9	35.6	11.1	1.1	77.1	43.3	49.4	50.6
87123 ALBUQUERQUE	70.9	68.9	4.3	4.6	3.5	4.7	33.0	34.2	6.9	6.6	6.3	6.2	6.4	26.9	26.9	12.0	1.9	76.5	37.7	48.6	51.4
87124 RIO RANCHO	78.1	74.3	2.6	2.9	1.6	1.7	27.3	30.2	6.8	6.7	6.7	6.9	6.2	26.3	26.9	11.0	2.5	75.7	37.7	48.0	52.0
87131 ALBUQUERQUE	79.1	76.9	2.6	2.9	2.4	2.9	19.9	21.3	0.9	0.3	0.8	42.1	37.0	7.4	4.4	4.0	3.1	96.9	20.8	48.0	52.0
87144 RIO RANCHO	78.0	74.7	2.8	2.5	1.8	2.4	30.2	33.6	9.2	8.8	8.2	6.8	4.9	32.6	22.9	6.1	0.5	69.4	33.2	49.2	50.8
87301 GALLUP	25.4	23.0	0.7	0.7	0.8	1.0	21.3	21.0	9.3	8.8	8.3	9.1	8.6	25.8	22.0	7.2	0.9	67.9	28.6	48.5	51.5
87310 BRIMHALL	1.0	1.0	0.0	0.0	0.0	0.0	1.0	0.0	10.6	8.7	8.7	10.6	8.7	23.1	19.2	9.6	1.0	65.4	27.5	48.1	51.9
87312 CONTINENTAL DIVIDE	21.8	20.0	0.0	0.0	0.2	0.3	5.4	5.8	8.3	9.5	11.4	10.0	6.4	23.7	24.2	6.4	0.1	63.7	28.7	48.6	51.4
87313 CROWNPOINT	4.8	3.9	0.2	0.2	0.2	0.2	1.2	1.2	9.8	10.2	9.7	10.8	8.4	24.2	19.4	6.6	0.7	63.1	25.7	47.7	52.3
87315 FENCE LAKE	53.4	50.6	0.0	0.0	0.0	0.0	41.1	43.3	6.2	6.2	6.7	6.2	4.5	21.9	33.1	14.0	1.1	77.0	43.6	52.2	47.8
87320 MEXICAN SPRINGS	0.1	0.1	0.0	0.0	0.2	0.2	0.6	0.7	9.9	9.2	8.5	9.2	9.1	26.2	20.0	7.3	0.7	66.9	27.7	47.6	52.4
87321 RAMAH	58.1	52.9	0.0	0.0	0.7	0.8	5.9	6.4	7.2	7.7	7.5	8.9	7.4	26.1	24.6	8.7	1.8	72.2	32.0	51.9	48.1
87323 THOREAU	10.3	8.8	0.1	0.1	0.2	0.2	4.4	4.3	10.7	9.9	9.6	10.4	9.2	24.8	18.6	6.2	0.5	63.5	25.1	48.4	51.6
87325 TOHATCHI	1.8	1.5	0.1	0.1	0.1	0.1	1.3	1.3	9.8	9.4	10.1	10.6	8.4	24.3	20.3	6.1	0.9	63.8	26.2	48.9	51.1
87327 ZUNI	3.2	2.6	0.1	0.1	0.1	0.1	2.1	2.0	8.5	9.6	9.5	9.4	7.3	28.7	20.5	5.3	1.1	66.1	28.6	47.6	52.4
87328 NAVAJO	2.5	2.0	0.0	0.0	0.0	0.0	0.7	0.6	13.0	13.9	13.1	9.7	6.9	23.8	15.8	3.2	0.5	53.5	20.2	47.3	52.7
87401 FARMINGTON	55.8	51.6	0.7	0.8	0.4	0.5	16.1	16.5	8.7	8.1	7.8	8.1	7.6	25.9	23.9	8.5	1.3	70.4	31.4	49.3	50.7
87402 FARMINGTON	79.6	77.8	0.5	0.5	0.6	0.8	15.8	16.7	6.5	7.0	7.1	7.7	6.1	24.9	30.0	9.7	0.8	74.5	37.6	49.4	50.6
87410 AZTEC	80.9	78.0	0.3	0.3	0.2	0.3	17.9	19.9	7.5	7.2	7.0	7.6	7.2	27.8	25.7	9.0	1.2	73.7	34.0	50.8	49.2
87412 BLANCO	61.0	58.6	0.1	0.2	0.1	0.2	36.5	39.6	7.3	7.5	7.5	7.3	5.0	26.1	27.2	10.9	1.1	72.9	36.6	52.1	47.9
87413 BLOOMFIELD	63.3	59.7	0.2	0.3	0.3	0.3	28.7	30.6	8.3	7.9	8.0	8.2	6.8	26.0	25.2	8.5	1.1	70.5	33.2	49.5	50.5
87415 FLORA VISTA	84.2	81.9	0.3	0.3	0.3	0.3	16.1	17.9	5.9	6.1	6.6	7.4	5.9	25.0	30.1	11.3	1.6	76.5	39.6	50.3	49.7
87416 FRUITLAND	54.6	48.7	0.2	0.3	0.4	0.5	8.8	8.8	8.0	8.0	8.0	7.6	7.1	26.2	26.0	8.5	0.7	71.8	31.7	51.3	48.7
87417 KIRTLAND	42.9	37.6	0.2	0.3	0.3	0.3	9.5	9.4	9.1	8.6	9.2	10.4	7.9	25.5	23.2	5.6	0.6	66.4	28.4	49.7	50.3
87418 LA PLATA	81.4	78.0	0.5	0.5	0.3	0.5	10.3	11.4	7.7	8.1	8.1	7.0	5.8	25.8	29.8	7.1	0.7	71.8	35.1	54.0	46.0
87419 NAVAJO DAM	67.6	63.6	0.0	0.0	0.0	0.0	40.5	42.0	6.8	6.8	8.0	5.7	4.5	26.1	28.4	12.5	1.1	73.9	38.8	52.3	47.7
87420 SHIPROCK	1.7	1.3	0.1	0.1	0.1	0.1	1.0	0.9	8.9	9.1	9.4	10.1	8.2	24.9	21.2	7.3	1.0	66.4	27.9	48.9	51.1
87421 WATERFLOW	50.5	44.7	0.1	0.2	0.4	0.3	9.9	10.0	7.7	7.4	6.8	6.8	8.8	27.8	26.7	7.4	0.5	74.0	31.1	48.8	51.2
87501 SANTA FE	81.4	79.9	0.5	0.6	0.7	0.9	37.6	41.3	3.6	3.6	3.8	3.9	4.8	22.5	35.4	18.9	3.5	86.5	50.1	46.9	53.1
87505 SANTA FE	77.7	76.1	0.5	0.6	1.5	1.8	42.4	45.3	4.4	4.3	4.5	6.1	7.5	24.9	32.4	13.5	2.3	83.6	43.5	48.2	51.8
87506 SANTA FE	61.1	61.4	0.6	0.6	0.8	0.9	43.8	42.6	5.6	6.0	6.2	5.6	4.6	23.1	32.9	14.5	1.6	78.8	44.2	49.1	50.9
87507 SANTA FE	65.7	64.5	0.7	0.7	1.0	1.3	69.5	71.8	8.6	7.9	7.3	7.1	7.6	29.8	23.7	7.1	0.9	71.7	32.2	49.4	50.6
87508 SANTA FE	82.8	81.4	1.0	1.1	0.7	0.9	34.8	38.2	4.8	5.6	6.3	6.2	5.1	23.9	36.7	10.7	0.8	79.4	43.8	50.7	49.3
87510 ABIQUIU	48.1	47.5	0.2	0.1	0.2	0.2	79.5	81.2	6.6	6.7	6.9	7.3	6.6	27.1	28.4	9.4	1.0	75.2	36.5	48.5	51.5
87513 ARROYO HONDO	77.1	75.4	0.3	0.3	0.4	0.5	49.3	53.4	5.0	5.6	5.8	5.6	4.2	24.7	37.4	10.4	1.3	79.8	44.3	50.6	49.4
NEW MEXICO	66.8	65.0	1.9	2.0	1.1	1.4	42.1	44.2	7.3	7.1	7.0	7.5	7.2	26.0	25.9	10.5	1.6	74.2	35.5	49.3	50.7
UNITED STATES	75.1	72.0	12.3	12.7	3.8	4.6	12.5	15.7	6.8	6.7	6.6	7.1	6.9	27.0	26.0	10.9	1.9	75.7	36.9	49.2	50.8

ZIP CODE #	POST OFFICE NAME	2009 Per Capita Income	2009 HH Income Base	2009 HOUSEHOLD INCOME DISTRIBUTION (%) Less than $25,000	$25,000 to $49,999	$50,000 to $99,999	$100,000 to $149,999	$150,000 or More	MEDIAN HOUSEHOLD INCOME 2009	2014	2009 National Centile	2009 State Centile	2009 Home Value Base	2009 HOME VALUE DISTRIBUTION (%) Less than $50,000	$50,000 to $89,999	$90,000 to $174,999	$175,000 to $399,999	$400,000 or More	2009 Median Home Value
87001	ALGODONES	19539	441	25.2	31.1	28.8	10.2	4.8	43408	45395	44	77	412	21.1	10.0	22.1	26.5	20.4	154688
87002	BELEN	18832	8383	29.9	33.9	29.2	5.0	1.9	39029	41709	30	64	6699	9.8	13.4	46.0	27.2	3.6	136223
87004	BERNALILLO	16669	4569	26.1	28.6	34.8	8.8	1.8	45231	45865	49	80	3730	14.1	11.6	48.2	20.5	5.5	133696
87005	BLUEWATER	14982	872	38.5	34.9	22.0	4.4	0.2	31726	32881	11	32	700	28.3	20.0	30.4	14.6	6.7	95000
87006	BOSQUE	16191	209	36.4	34.0	24.9	4.8	0.0	32499	33427	12	36	176	23.9	17.0	27.3	29.0	2.8	115625
87007	CASA BLANCA	10994	934	39.3	30.1	27.9	2.5	0.2	33148	35000	14	40	748	25.1	21.9	40.2	9.1	3.6	94889
87008	CEDAR CREST	41165	1425	10.1	19.2	37.9	20.0	12.8	75591	75917	90	99	1230	5.9	4.2	11.8	55.5	22.5	280682
87009	CEDARVALE	13637	49	42.9	42.9	12.2	2.0	0.0	26620	27178	4	11	39	35.9	30.8	23.1	5.1	5.1	59167
87010	CERRILLOS	34276	529	19.3	20.2	38.2	17.2	5.1	62889	64814	81	94	432	1.2	9.3	20.8	48.8	19.9	248214
87012	COYOTE	14398	9	44.4	44.4	11.1	0.0	0.0	27247	32265	5	12	8	0.0	25.0	25.0	25.0	25.0	200000
87013	CUBA	8774	1829	59.5	22.6	15.7	1.1	1.1	19092	20063	1	2	1563	60.2	6.8	17.2	11.6	4.2	24719
87014	CUBERO	12111	2325	41.8	31.4	22.2	3.3	1.3	30476	32397	9	28	1969	34.5	21.6	27.4	11.1	5.4	74821
87015	EDGEWOOD	26340	5041	11.9	23.1	43.4	16.2	5.3	64020	65426	82	95	4525	3.5	6.9	33.8	47.0	8.9	191804
87016	ESTANCIA	16932	1461	36.6	32.4	25.1	3.1	2.9	33765	36911	15	42	1235	16.8	20.0	29.7	22.3	11.3	120799
87017	GALLINA	13865	364	48.9	26.1	22.3	1.9	0.8	25762	27569	4	10	324	27.2	18.8	36.1	13.0	4.9	98667
87018	COUNSELOR	17850	395	45.1	19.5	27.3	7.6	0.5	33132	35000	14	40	320	17.8	15.3	40.0	22.2	4.7	118421
87020	GRANTS	16450	4043	34.4	33.3	27.5	3.2	1.7	36116	38428	21	51	2846	16.8	24.4	45.5	11.9	1.3	101132
87021	MILAN	16317	1081	32.4	36.3	27.4	2.9	1.1	35633	37342	20	49	836	30.9	26.7	28.7	11.0	2.8	80000
87023	JARALES	16966	591	30.6	35.7	27.2	3.4	3.0	35432	39109	19	48	530	20.9	22.1	30.2	24.3	2.5	110294
87024	JEMEZ PUEBLO	14215	972	31.3	27.6	31.0	8.0	2.2	39533	40576	31	67	900	19.4	21.3	25.1	24.1	10.0	115323
87025	JEMEZ SPRINGS	29111	746	23.9	25.9	27.6	15.5	7.1	50349	51407	62	87	635	6.1	5.8	22.5	41.1	24.4	265909
87026	LAGUNA	8991	565	49.2	27.6	21.1	1.1	1.1	25397	26280	3	7	537	54.9	17.9	15.3	10.6	1.3	41167
87027	LA JARA	20098	36	50.0	13.9	27.8	8.3	0.0	27500	38642	5	13	30	20.0	16.7	36.7	23.3	3.3	115000
87028	LA JOYA	22998	42	33.3	31.0	31.0	2.4	2.4	38178	40000	27	61	36	19.4	19.4	33.3	19.4	8.3	112500
87029	LINDRITH	15960	211	40.3	33.2	21.8	3.3	1.4	32154	33208	12	33	182	16.5	22.5	29.7	22.5	8.8	117045
87031	LOS LUNAS	17573	13697	25.2	32.0	34.3	6.6	2.0	44075	46251	46	78	11437	8.2	13.7	40.7	33.0	4.3	146366
87035	MORIARTY	17430	3059	28.6	32.4	32.9	5.0	1.0	40336	42269	34	70	2525	15.5	15.0	46.7	20.5	2.3	123833
87036	MOUNTAINAIR	15596	617	45.2	34.8	16.4	1.6	1.9	27740	30322	5	15	466	23.2	29.0	25.5	16.5	5.8	86154
87041	PENA BLANCA	17156	620	30.6	26.8	30.6	9.4	2.6	38869	40424	29	64	495	13.1	16.6	42.2	23.6	4.4	131434
87042	PERALTA	19042	1120	19.4	35.4	37.5	5.4	2.3	45938	47685	51	81	947	3.5	8.6	38.9	39.3	9.8	172875
87043	PLACITAS	45202	2266	10.2	17.2	34.2	22.2	16.2	74042	82184	89	98	2034	1.6	2.7	5.3	29.5	60.9	421496
87044	PONDEROSA	28114	221	13.6	29.9	34.4	17.6	4.5	59613	61026	77	92	193	8.8	3.1	17.6	53.4	17.1	270313
87045	PREWITT	8471	418	59.1	26.6	9.8	2.6	1.9	20559	22177	2	3	374	61.0	18.4	13.4	5.3	1.9	33750
87046	REGINA	6250	3	100.0	0.0	0.0	0.0	0.0	12500	12500	1	1	3	0.0	100.0	0.0	0.0	0.0	82500
87047	SANDIA PARK	38364	2078	9.4	17.9	41.6	18.7	12.4	72451	71143	88	98	1833	2.8	3.3	19.4	49.1	25.4	255168
87048	CORRALES	43397	3856	10.4	17.5	31.2	21.3	19.6	81842	86741	93	99	3265	2.1	1.2	7.0	26.2	63.5	471906
87052	SANTO DOMINGO PUEBLO	7633	828	36.7	35.0	21.6	5.2	1.4	32527	33403	12	37	771	17.0	21.1	40.5	13.6	7.8	110534
87053	SAN YSIDRO	16114	279	25.8	27.6	34.4	9.7	2.5	45964	46619	51	81	262	7.6	15.3	46.6	21.4	9.2	136364
87056	STANLEY	24490	433	18.9	23.8	39.5	12.7	5.1	56255	59014	73	91	355	2.5	7.6	21.4	52.7	15.8	230660
87059	TIJERAS	32739	4102	12.2	19.1	43.0	16.8	8.9	70725	72610	87	97	3650	5.0	6.5	15.5	55.7	17.4	263569
87060	TOME	15638	60	38.3	30.0	25.0	3.3	3.3	35882	38623	20	50	51	17.6	7.8	31.4	35.3	7.8	145313
87062	VEGUITA	13947	791	37.9	32.4	24.9	4.6	0.3	32047	32466	11	33	663	25.9	17.0	25.0	28.1	3.9	112750
87063	WILLARD	13096	139	49.6	32.4	16.5	1.4	0.0	25136	26892	3	7	117	31.6	33.3	19.7	6.0	9.4	66500
87068	BOSQUE FARMS	21715	2155	18.7	33.5	38.7	6.1	3.1	47596	48724	56	84	1949	7.9	7.0	31.0	47.7	6.4	185920
87083	COCHITI LAKE	35358	245	12.2	35.5	35.5	13.1	3.7	54660	59377	71	90	220	0.0	0.0	19.1	79.5	1.4	210625
87102	ALBUQUERQUE	16121	9177	44.5	30.8	20.7	2.5	1.4	27705	28338	5	14	3785	4.6	16.9	53.7	21.0	3.8	126761
87104	ALBUQUERQUE	27012	5275	32.7	24.5	29.7	7.4	5.7	40935	42282	36	73	3172	7.6	5.3	28.6	45.0	13.6	197667
87105	ALBUQUERQUE	17238	19937	29.8	30.8	32.3	5.2	2.0	40356	41454	34	71	14422	7.1	9.7	50.0	30.1	3.2	146485
87106	ALBUQUERQUE	25279	11544	36.8	28.1	24.4	6.9	3.8	35465	36454	19	48	4378	4.8	2.6	25.9	58.1	8.5	214329
87107	ALBUQUERQUE	27191	13495	26.8	26.5	32.1	8.4	6.2	45893	47733	51	81	8555	6.5	3.5	35.1	39.0	16.0	187738
87108	ALBUQUERQUE	20738	17516	37.1	31.3	25.4	3.6	2.6	34158	35425	16	43	5999	4.3	3.4	42.5	45.4	4.4	174680
87109	ALBUQUERQUE	30027	18891	19.9	28.2	36.1	9.2	6.7	51621	53344	65	88	10916	9.3	4.5	15.0	68.2	3.0	221333
87110	ALBUQUERQUE	28014	19147	21.4	28.3	39.4	7.5	3.4	50203	52235	62	86	11600	1.3	2.0	33.8	59.5	3.5	192553
87111	ALBUQUERQUE	39914	26632	12.4	21.8	39.6	14.0	12.2	68368	69091	86	96	16398	0.3	0.3	9.4	72.6	17.4	262035
87112	ALBUQUERQUE	28658	19684	19.0	26.7	40.4	9.0	4.9	53763	56295	69	89	12331	1.2	0.9	34.0	58.7	5.2	190912
87113	ALBUQUERQUE	25869	6097	23.7	24.9	37.1	9.9	4.5	51035	53756	64	88	4708	10.1	10.5	33.2	41.1	5.1	162869
87114	ALBUQUERQUE	30809	21781	10.5	19.0	47.6	15.7	7.3	69242	70987	86	96	15818	3.1	1.9	16.4	70.4	8.1	235071
87116	ALBUQUERQUE	17203	1843	17.1	44.4	35.7	1.7	1.0	41372	42480	37	74	29	0.0	0.0	0.0	100.0	0.0	225000
87120	ALBUQUERQUE	30430	21306	9.0	18.3	49.9	16.5	6.2	71744	71979	88	97	16206	0.3	0.3	21.3	74.4	3.7	214930
87121	ALBUQUERQUE	17642	20788	19.3	33.2	40.8	4.8	1.9	47513	50144	55	84	16663	11.9	8.4	54.0	24.7	1.0	144195
87122	ALBUQUERQUE	55703	6620	3.8	7.9	27.5	23.0	37.8	127119	127800	99	100	5784	0.0	0.0	0.9	41.5	57.6	446838
87123	ALBUQUERQUE	26894	16844	23.7	28.1	34.4	9.0	4.8	47971	50839	57	84	10804	17.4	5.0	23.2	46.8	7.6	182878
87124	RIO RANCHO	27077	18541	12.4	24.7	43.9	15.1	3.8	61572	65775	79	94	14457	0.6	1.4	39.1	55.2	3.7	189096
87131	ALBUQUERQUE	16286	357	69.7	19.3	7.6	3.4	0.0	16471	16318	1	2	6	0.0	0.0	0.0	100.0	0.0	287500
87144	RIO RANCHO	29272	10621	5.9	15.5	55.5	17.1	6.0	72863	78085	88	98	9147	1.3	0.7	24.8	65.2	8.0	211192
87301	GALLUP	15094	12697	35.9	28.2	28.1	5.3	2.6	36742	37330	23	53	8979	30.6	13.3	32.5	19.9	3.7	109083
87310	BRIMHALL	13672	41	43.9	29.3	24.4	2.4	0.0	29049	28150	7	21	36	52.8	22.2	25.0	0.0	0.0	45000
87312	CONTINENTAL DIVIDE	11263	306	41.5	27.5	25.8	3.6	1.6	28637	29836	6	19	247	52.6	11.3	19.4	16.2	0.4	46750
87313	CROWNPOINT	8934	2115	50.7	28.9	19.0	1.2	0.2	24460	25270	3	5	1378	53.2	17.4	21.7	6.2	1.5	43889
87315	FENCE LAKE	17347	83	48.2	26.5	21.7	2.4	1.2	26714	37360	4	12	71	31.0	18.3	35.2	8.5	7.0	91667
87320	MEXICAN SPRINGS	8825	301	49.8	25.6	22.6	1.3	0.7	25096	25916	3	6	282	47.9	16.7	23.8	5.7	6.0	53158
87321	RAMAH	14047	196	37.2	25.5	32.7	2.0	2.6	40893	45387	36	72	164	32.9	10.4	32.9	23.8	0.0	105769
87323	THOREAU	9609	1336	48.5	27.5	21.5	1.9	0.5	25800	27012	4	10	1048	57.3	16.1	19.1	5.3	2.2	38250
87325	TOHATCHI	9861	2085	45.7	29.1	22.2	2.7	0.3	28293	29585	6	17	1712	49.2	20.7	23.6	6.0	0.5	51250
87327	ZUNI	8360	1882	48.8	30.5	17.5	2.0	1.3	25664	26611	4	9	1429	25.6	23.3	37.2	8.6	5.3	92013
87328	NAVAJO	7028	734	54.8	30.2	13.1	1.8	0.1	21552	23077	2	4	243	51.4	20.6	21.0	4.1	2.9	47941
87401	FARMINGTON	18634	18517	27.1	30.8	32.1	6.7	3.2	42402	44845	41	77	12926	18.0	13.7	35.3	28.5	4.5	138720
87402	FARMINGTON	27148	3854	14.2	20.0	46.7	13.2	5.9	64946	64644	83	95	3081	4.8	2.9	36.4	47.5	8.5	189959
87410	AZTEC	20028	5889	24.1	27.9	38.8	6.6	2.6	48005	49382	57	85	4733	12.7	14.4	37.7	28.2	6.8	144316
87412	BLANCO	23205	475	28.2	24.2	35.4	8.8	3.4	47475	48763	55	83	390	10.3	15.1	39.2	30.8	4.6	143519
87413	BLOOMFIELD	19055	5040	21.3	33.7	36.3	6.1	2.6	45506	47405	50	80	4055	15.5	16.9	36.4	28.6	2.6	127624
87415	FLORA VISTA	20471	800	27.1	26.5	36.3	8.5	1.6	45999	47491	51	82	652	8.6	11.7	28.7	36.0	15.0	179375
87416	FRUITLAND	18435	177	16.4	26.6	48.6	6.2	2.3	61095	61312	79	94	147	17.7	2.0	38.8	30.6	10.9	155469
87417	KIRTLAND	19097	2228	17.7	24.3	42.9	11.7	3.5	60121	59083	77	93	1821	12.4	14.3	50.7	20.4	2.1	126730
87418	LA PLATA	20680	259	19.3	29.3	42.1	5.8	3.5	50891	50604	63	88	218	11.9	16.5	24.8	40.4	6.4	167391
87419	NAVAJO DAM	26445	37	32.4	16.2	35.1	13.5	2.7	52234	47375	66	89	29	3.4	13.8	41.4	34.5	6.9	147500
87420	SHIPROCK	9716	6470	48.6	29.5	18.6	2.7	0.6	25879	27637	4	10	4817	49.1	20.7	18.6	9.1	2.5	51087
87421	WATERFLOW	17755	307	27.4	25.4	37.8	5.5	3.9	46624	48269	53	82	258	18.6	19.4	28.7	27.5	5.8	121250
87501	SANTA FE	41087	7792	21.4	23.2	30.6	14.0	10.9	56504	59950	73	91	4886	0.6	1.0	6.1	41.0	51.3	413248
87505	SANTA FE	36074	14637	18.1	23.8	32.5	16.1	9.5	59819	62441	77	93	8294	1.1	0.4	6.3	52.9	39.3	349718
87506	SANTA FE	37224	5782	20.9	22.9	28.4	16.6	11.2	59968	63099	77	93	4144	12.1	3.9	12.8	21.6	49.5	395274
87507	SANTA FE	22220	15878	21.5	28.6	33.8	11.5	4.5	49839	51366	61	86	10892	17.3	7.3	12.8	50.5	12.1	219663
87508	SANTA FE	36148	6758	12.0	16.0	38.6	21.4	12.1	76184	78460	90	99	5547	1.2	2.9	4.8	48.1	43.0	370122
87510	ABIQUIU	17928	1037	35.4	26.6	31.8	4.1	2.1	37445	40221	25	59	852	15.1	10.2	29.3	33.3	12.0	159848
87513	ARROYO HONDO	22812	1160	35.1	30.9	28.2	3.1	2.7	35000	35525	18	46	864	8.0	6.9	16.8	38.4	29.9	295192
	NEW MEXICO	22470		27.2	27.7	32.6	8.1	4.5	44681	46845				12.7	11.8	31.3	35.2	9.1	159744
	UNITED STATES	27277		20.9	24.4	35.3	11.7	7.6	54719	56938				9.3	13.1	31.6	32.6	13.5	162279

ZIP CODE		FINANCIAL SERVICES				THE HOME						ENTERTAINMENT						PERSONAL			
						Home Improvements		Furnishings													
#	POST OFFICE NAME	Auto Loan	Home Loan	Invest-ments	Retire-ment Plans	Home Repair	Lawn & Garden	Comput-ers & Hard-ware-Personal	Major Appli-ances	TV, Radio, Sound Equip-ment	Furni-ture	Dine out/ Carry out	Sports Equip-ment	Fees & Tickets	Toys & Games	Travel	Cable TV	Apparel & Services	Auto Repairs	Health Insur-ance	Pets & Supplies
87001	ALGODONES	89	88	80	78	87	75	87	87	82	93	84	65	82	84	85	78	59	87	77	97
87002	BELEN	75	67	69	65	67	76	66	72	70	66	69	53	62	70	65	73	47	70	77	85
87004	BERNALILLO	79	76	68	72	74	71	77	76	76	80	77	57	73	78	73	75	53	76	74	88
87005	BLUEWATER	68	49	67	47	50	68	50	63	56	48	55	48	40	57	49	62	37	58	65	75
87006	BOSQUE	66	60	55	57	58	61	59	61	60	61	60	46	55	62	56	61	41	60	60	72
87007	CASA BLANCA	61	48	47	48	44	57	52	53	57	51	57	41	47	58	47	61	39	55	59	67
87008	CEDAR CREST	123	153	156	157	157	145	130	138	125	139	126	102	148	124	146	122	90	130	130	157
87009	CEDARVALE	56	40	57	39	41	57	41	52	45	38	45	39	33	45	40	50	29	48	54	62
87010	CERRILLOS	96	107	104	108	107	99	101	99	97	104	98	77	107	98	105	95	70	99	96	116
87012	COYOTE	50	36	51	35	37	51	37	47	41	34	40	35	29	41	36	45	26	43	49	56
87013	CUBA	49	37	37	32	36	42	38	43	42	40	42	29	32	42	35	44	29	42	43	49
87014	CUBERO	68	49	65	47	48	67	51	61	57	49	56	47	41	58	48	62	37	58	64	75
87015	EDGEWOOD	112	119	100	115	113	104	106	108	102	113	104	83	108	109	105	99	73	103	98	124
87016	ESTANCIA	83	59	85	57	61	84	61	77	67	57	66	58	49	67	60	74	44	71	80	92
87017	GALLINA	63	42	62	40	43	63	45	56	51	42	50	44	34	52	42	57	33	53	59	69
87018	COUNSELOR	64	54	72	50	59	69	53	64	58	56	57	44	49	55	56	62	38	61	71	75
87020	GRANTS	68	57	59	56	56	66	61	64	64	58	63	49	54	64	57	67	43	64	68	77
87021	MILAN	68	60	57	58	58	63	60	63	61	61	61	47	55	63	57	63	42	62	62	74
87023	JARALES	86	70	79	67	70	82	71	79	74	70	74	60	62	76	68	78	50	76	80	94
87024	JEMEZ PUEBLO	84	67	66	59	67	70	67	76	72	71	72	49	58	72	63	75	50	74	74	84
87025	JEMEZ SPRINGS	112	91	144	89	100	119	91	115	95	87	94	83	80	90	98	102	63	106	115	133
87026	LAGUNA	54	44	34	37	42	41	44	47	47	49	48	30	39	48	40	49	33	47	45	52
87027	LA JARA	62	59	76	55	66	71	56	67	60	61	58	44	56	55	62	63	39	64	74	76
87028	LA JOYA	91	65	93	63	68	92	67	85	74	62	73	64	53	74	66	82	48	78	88	101
87029	LINDRITH	73	52	74	50	54	74	53	68	59	50	58	51	42	59	52	65	38	62	70	81
87031	LOS LUNAS	80	75	65	73	72	73	74	74	74	76	75	56	71	77	70	74	52	74	73	88
87035	MORIARTY	74	69	60	66	66	68	67	68	68	70	68	51	63	71	63	69	47	68	67	81
87036	MOUNTAINAIR	64	46	65	45	48	67	50	62	55	45	54	46	40	55	48	61	36	57	67	73
87041	PENA BLANCA	77	78	68	72	76	70	75	75	74	81	75	55	74	74	74	72	52	76	72	86
87042	PERALTA	83	79	70	77	77	81	74	78	76	77	76	57	72	79	72	78	52	76	78	93
87043	PLACITAS	128	163	173	167	171	154	140	148	132	149	132	111	161	131	159	129	96	139	138	167
87044	PONDEROSA	110	98	132	98	104	118	95	113	97	91	96	84	88	95	102	101	65	106	112	131
87045	PREWITT	56	37	54	35	37	55	40	50	46	38	44	38	30	46	37	51	30	47	52	61
87046	REGINA	0	0	0	0	0	0	0	0	0	0	0	0	0	0	0	0	0	0	0	0
87047	SANDIA PARK	129	148	145	152	148	144	130	138	127	133	127	106	142	128	141	126	90	131	132	159
87048	CORRALES	145	175	175	181	178	161	152	157	144	164	146	120	171	146	166	139	105	149	144	179
87052	SANTO DOMINGO PUEBLO	73	52	69	48	52	69	55	65	60	54	59	51	43	61	51	65	40	62	67	79
87053	SAN YSIDRO	87	81	89	74	83	79	80	86	78	83	79	64	74	78	81	77	55	84	79	97
87056	STANLEY	104	102	120	102	104	108	98	106	97	97	98	80	97	96	103	98	68	102	103	123
87059	TIJERAS	115	132	130	133	133	126	115	122	112	121	113	92	125	114	124	111	80	116	115	141
87060	TOME	71	65	58	63	64	67	61	65	64	64	64	47	58	66	59	66	43	63	65	77
87062	VEGUITA	63	59	50	56	56	57	58	58	59	61	59	44	55	61	55	59	41	58	57	69
87063	WILLARD	56	40	57	39	41	57	41	52	45	38	45	39	33	45	41	50	29	48	54	62
87068	BOSQUE FARMS	81	89	78	90	86	88	79	83	80	81	81	63	85	82	83	81	56	81	85	98
87083	COCHITI LAKE	85	96	91	94	96	105	85	94	91	84	91	66	94	89	93	97	63	91	107	107
87102	ALBUQUERQUE	57	46	41	45	45	47	56	51	57	54	57	38	49	57	49	58	40	55	53	60
87104	ALBUQUERQUE	84	80	81	80	81	84	85	85	88	83	87	63	82	86	83	90	61	86	90	99
87105	ALBUQUERQUE	75	71	60	65	69	66	70	71	70	74	71	51	66	72	67	70	50	71	69	81
87106	ALBUQUERQUE	72	61	58	63	59	61	78	65	75	72	76	54	69	75	67	74	53	72	67	80
87107	ALBUQUERQUE	93	87	87	87	88	90	91	91	91	91	91	69	88	91	89	92	64	92	93	106
87108	ALBUQUERQUE	63	52	50	54	51	52	65	57	66	64	67	46	60	65	59	65	47	64	61	69
87109	ALBUQUERQUE	93	86	86	89	86	87	93	88	93	94	94	68	92	93	91	93	66	93	91	105
87110	ALBUQUERQUE	80	81	78	82	80	84	83	81	85	82	85	61	85	84	84	87	59	84	90	96
87111	ALBUQUERQUE	116	126	127	129	127	121	123	120	120	126	121	93	130	119	128	119	86	122	121	141
87112	ALBUQUERQUE	87	91	86	93	90	92	91	89	92	90	92	68	94	91	92	93	64	91	95	106
87113	ALBUQUERQUE	98	89	89	85	86	93	87	93	88	87	88	72	80	91	84	90	60	89	92	109
87114	ALBUQUERQUE	119	122	107	121	116	108	116	113	112	122	114	90	117	118	114	108	80	112	105	132
87116	ALBUQUERQUE	88	46	34	53	41	39	83	57	78	77	82	57	63	93	60	71	57	73	52	70
87120	ALBUQUERQUE	117	123	105	122	117	107	115	112	110	122	112	89	118	116	114	106	79	110	102	130
87121	ALBUQUERQUE	82	78	66	71	75	65	81	77	77	86	79	59	76	79	76	73	56	79	68	86
87122	ALBUQUERQUE	197	250	250	257	257	218	208	216	193	232	195	171	243	199	231	181	144	199	186	241
87123	ALBUQUERQUE	89	85	84	84	85	84	88	86	87	90	88	66	86	88	86	87	61	88	87	102
87124	RIO RANCHO	101	107	96	105	104	100	100	100	99	104	100	75	102	101	100	98	69	99	100	117
87131	ALBUQUERQUE	30	22	27	26	23	28	37	29	39	33	39	23	32	34	32	42	27	36	41	38
87144	RIO RANCHO	123	133	108	128	125	110	118	118	111	128	114	93	120	120	116	106	80	111	103	134
87301	GALLUP	74	67	57	63	65	64	67	68	69	71	70	49	64	70	63	70	48	69	67	78
87310	BRIMHALL	65	42	62	40	42	63	45	57	52	43	51	44	34	53	42	58	34	53	60	70
87312	CONTINENTAL DIVIDE	69	59	47	52	56	57	57	61	61	62	62	40	51	63	52	63	42	61	60	69
87313	CROWNPOINT	51	42	32	38	39	41	43	44	47	46	47	30	39	47	39	48	32	45	45	51
87315	FENCE LAKE	62	44	63	42	45	63	45	57	50	42	49	43	36	50	44	56	33	53	60	69
87320	MEXICAN SPRINGS	57	45	34	38	43	43	45	49	49	51	50	30	39	50	41	51	35	49	47	53
87321	RAMAH	69	63	56	61	62	64	60	63	62	62	62	46	56	64	57	63	42	61	63	75
87323	THOREAU	55	48	38	43	45	45	47	49	49	51	50	34	43	51	43	50	34	49	48	56
87325	TOHATCHI	61	49	47	44	47	53	49	54	53	52	53	38	42	54	45	56	36	53	54	63
87327	ZUNI	61	42	57	40	41	60	45	54	51	43	50	42	35	52	42	56	33	52	57	67
87328	NAVAJO	48	39	30	33	37	37	39	41	42	43	42	26	34	42	35	43	29	42	40	46
87401	FARMINGTON	82	76	68	73	74	75	76	77	77	78	78	56	73	79	73	78	54	77	77	90
87402	FARMINGTON	107	115	104	114	112	107	106	107	104	110	105	82	110	107	108	102	74	105	102	125
87410	AZTEC	87	81	71	78	78	81	78	80	80	81	80	59	73	83	74	81	54	79	80	96
87412	BLANCO	97	84	95	81	86	94	81	92	85	82	85	67	74	86	81	89	57	88	92	108
87413	BLOOMFIELD	87	81	70	77	78	80	78	80	80	82	80	59	74	83	74	81	55	79	79	95
87415	FLORA VISTA	89	81	72	79	80	83	77	81	80	80	80	59	73	83	73	82	54	79	82	97
87416	FRUITLAND	96	88	78	85	86	90	83	88	86	86	86	64	79	90	79	88	59	85	88	104
87417	KIRTLAND	100	99	83	95	94	91	91	93	91	96	92	69	89	95	87	90	63	90	88	109
87418	LA PLATA	95	88	78	85	86	89	83	88	86	86	86	64	78	89	79	88	58	85	88	104
87419	NAVAJO DAM	104	87	118	85	92	106	85	102	89	83	88	75	76	87	89	94	59	96	101	119
87420	SHIPROCK	58	45	46	41	43	52	46	51	51	48	50	37	40	52	43	54	34	51	52	61
87421	WATERFLOW	88	82	71	79	79	81	79	81	81	82	81	60	75	84	75	82	55	80	80	96
87501	SANTA FE	108	119	133	120	126	119	115	117	113	120	113	87	123	109	124	113	80	117	119	135
87505	SANTA FE	107	114	120	117	117	107	117	112	112	119	114	88	122	110	121	109	81	115	109	130
87506	SANTA FE	123	122	138	123	126	127	119	125	118	121	118	95	120	118	123	119	83	121	122	145
87507	SANTA FE	91	87	80	85	85	81	90	86	88	93	89	67	87	90	87	86	63	89	83	101
87508	SANTA FE	127	148	151	149	152	139	131	137	125	140	127	102	143	125	142	123	90	131	128	156
87510	ABIQUIU	75	69	61	66	67	70	65	69	67	68	67	50	62	70	62	69	46	67	69	81
87513	ARROYO HONDO	84	65	103	64	71	88	66	84	70	62	69	62	56	67	70	75	46	77	84	98
	NEW MEXICO	88	81	80	79	80	83	82	84	83	83	83	63	78	84	80	84	58	84	84	98
	UNITED STATES	100	100	100	100	100	100	100	100	100	100	100	100	100	100	100	100	100	100	100	100

#	POST OFFICE NAME	COUNTY FIPS CODE	POPULATION 2000	POPULATION 2009	POPULATION 2014	2000-2009 ANNUAL RATE % Rate	2000-2009 ANNUAL RATE State Centile	HOUSEHOLDS 2000	HOUSEHOLDS 2009	HOUSEHOLDS 2014	HOUSEHOLDS % Annual Rate 2000-2009	HOUSEHOLDS 2009 Average HH Size	FAMILIES 2000	FAMILIES 2009	FAMILIES % Annual Rate 2000-2009
87514	ARROYO SECO	055	1028	1189	1255	1.6	79	483	596	638	2.3	1.99	280	328	1.7
87520	CHAMA	039	1353	1369	1355	0.1	23	532	575	578	0.8	2.32	361	373	0.4
87521	CHAMISAL	055	618	676	702	1.0	64	249	291	305	1.7	2.32	174	195	1.2
87522	CHIMAYO	039	5116	5233	5246	0.2	28	1968	2115	2144	0.8	2.47	1399	1439	0.3
87524	COSTILLA	055	547	626	657	1.5	76	212	258	275	2.1	2.43	121	139	1.5
87527	DIXON	039	1505	1550	1538	0.3	33	660	717	722	0.9	2.14	452	472	0.5
87528	DULCE	039	3198	3198	3158	0.0	20	992	1048	1047	0.6	3.03	739	755	0.2
87530	EL RITO	039	975	1015	1011	0.4	40	343	381	386	1.1	2.65	239	255	0.7
87531	EMBUDO	039	4892	5264	5259	0.8	55	1745	1953	1979	1.2	2.69	1270	1368	0.8
87532	ESPANOLA	039	17471	17015	16896	-0.3	9	6587	6607	6619	0.0	2.56	4686	4520	-0.4
87535	GLORIETA	049	952	1039	1085	0.9	60	355	387	407	0.9	2.55	238	246	0.4
87537	HERNANDEZ	039	1032	1122	1126	0.9	60	356	405	412	1.4	2.77	257	281	1.0
87539	LA MADERA	039	297	310	310	0.5	43	116	129	131	1.2	2.40	82	88	0.8
87540	LAMY	049	798	1098	1208	3.5	95	351	487	537	3.6	2.25	237	310	2.9
87544	LOS ALAMOS	043	18366	19539	19933	0.7	51	7508	8192	8408	0.9	2.37	5349	5619	0.5
87549	OJO CALIENTE	055	984	1152	1221	1.7	80	529	664	715	2.5	1.73	255	301	1.8
87552	PECOS	047	3946	4206	4371	0.7	51	1446	1643	1735	1.4	2.51	1023	1113	0.9
87553	PENASCO	055	1255	1356	1401	0.8	55	491	566	593	1.5	2.40	346	384	1.1
87556	QUESTA	055	3448	3868	4047	1.3	72	1448	1735	1839	2.0	2.23	927	1060	1.5
87557	RANCHOS DE TAOS	055	4226	4178	4215	-0.1	14	1712	1823	1870	0.7	2.27	1079	1090	0.1
87560	RIBERA	047	2201	2329	2412	0.6	46	817	916	962	1.2	2.53	594	640	0.8
87564	SAN CRISTOBAL	055	421	476	499	1.3	72	191	229	243	2.0	2.08	114	130	1.4
87565	SAN JOSE	047	1257	1373	1437	1.0	64	458	532	566	1.6	2.57	330	368	1.2
87566	SAN JUAN PUEBLO	039	5772	5963	5913	0.4	40	1911	2067	2078	0.9	2.83	1454	1520	0.5
87567	SANTA CRUZ	049	316	346	360	1.0	64	121	133	140	1.0	2.60	87	91	0.5
87571	TAOS	055	13624	14293	14545	0.5	43	5755	6342	6532	1.1	2.22	3452	3610	0.5
87573	TERERRO	047	118	123	128	0.4	40	57	64	67	1.3	1.81	39	42	0.8
87575	TIERRA AMARILLA	039	1952	1953	1929	0.0	20	776	830	832	0.7	2.27	543	556	0.3
87579	VADITO	055	1329	1434	1478	0.8	55	517	596	623	1.5	2.41	366	406	1.1
87580	VALDEZ	055	269	306	322	1.4	75	132	161	172	2.2	1.89	75	87	1.6
87581	VALLECITOS	039	598	627	627	0.5	43	256	287	291	1.2	2.18	180	193	0.8
87701	LAS VEGAS	047	21047	20202	20164	-0.4	8	7702	7759	7844	0.1	2.45	5085	4893	-0.4
87711	ANTON CHICO	019	245	250	248	0.2	28	87	93	93	0.7	2.59	60	61	0.2
87713	CHACON	033	238	244	247	0.3	33	85	92	95	0.9	2.65	59	62	0.5
87714	CIMARRON	007	2560	2886	3017	1.3	72	1093	1278	1353	1.7	2.25	764	858	1.3
87715	CLEVELAND	033	342	351	355	0.3	33	125	135	139	0.8	2.60	87	90	0.4
87718	EAGLE NEST	007	685	789	832	1.5	76	287	343	365	1.9	2.29	203	233	1.5
87722	GUADALUPITA	033	33	33	33	0.0	20	11	12	12	0.9	2.58	7	7	0.0
87724	LA LOMA	019	288	294	291	0.2	28	111	119	119	0.8	2.38	76	78	0.3
87728	MAXWELL	007	404	414	425	0.3	33	170	189	198	1.2	1.89	121	130	0.8
87729	MIAMI	007	72	74	76	0.3	33	33	37	38	1.2	1.73	23	25	0.9
87730	MILLS	021	34	34	35	0.0	20	15	16	16	0.7	2.13	9	10	1.1
87731	MONTEZUMA	047	60	61	62	0.2	28	20	21	22	0.5	2.67	14	14	0.0
87732	MORA	033	3456	3550	3585	0.3	33	1352	1463	1498	0.9	2.43	954	993	0.4
87733	MOSQUERO	021	233	235	236	0.1	23	110	117	119	0.7	2.01	69	69	0.0
87734	OCATE	033	383	382	383	0.0	20	154	161	164	0.5	2.25	101	101	0.0
87740	RATON	007	8443	8396	8460	-0.1	14	3506	3660	3734	0.5	2.26	2342	2335	0.0
87742	ROCIADA	047	824	910	949	1.1	68	325	374	396	1.5	2.43	239	263	1.0
87743	ROY	021	457	462	463	0.1	23	209	221	225	0.6	2.09	131	132	0.1
87745	SAPELLO	047	3	3	3	0.0	20	2	2	2	0.0	1.50	1	0	-100.0
87746	SOLANO	021	70	71	71	0.2	28	30	32	32	0.7	2.22	19	19	0.0
87747	SPRINGER	007	2018	2092	2147	0.4	40	729	800	832	1.0	2.46	522	550	0.6
87750	VALMORA	033	163	162	163	-0.1	14	61	64	65	0.5	2.41	40	40	0.0
87752	WAGON MOUND	033	565	563	565	0.0	20	229	240	245	0.5	2.23	150	150	0.0
87801	SOCORRO	053	11197	11154	11147	0.0	20	4344	4465	4511	0.3	2.36	2795	2731	-0.3
87820	ARAGON	003	191	196	198	0.3	33	82	90	92	1.0	2.17	53	56	0.6
87821	DATIL	003	630	685	710	0.9	60	276	319	335	1.6	2.15	186	206	1.1
87823	LEMITAR	053	600	644	666	0.8	55	234	261	273	1.2	2.47	162	172	0.6
87825	MAGDALENA	053	3257	3454	3558	0.6	46	1027	1131	1176	1.0	3.05	753	799	0.6
87827	PIE TOWN	003	639	695	720	0.9	60	289	334	350	1.6	2.08	195	216	1.1
87828	POLVADERA	053	26	28	29	0.8	55	13	15	15	1.6	1.87	9	10	1.1
87829	QUEMADO	003	327	356	368	0.9	60	133	154	161	1.6	2.31	90	99	1.0
87830	RESERVE	003	1295	1330	1339	0.3	33	585	643	658	1.0	2.06	376	395	0.5
87831	SAN ACACIA	053	612	658	680	0.8	55	234	261	273	1.2	2.52	162	173	0.7
87901	TRUTH OR CONSEQUENCE	051	10198	10070	9941	-0.1	14	4851	4891	4846	0.1	2.00	2791	2662	-0.5
87930	ARREY	051	864	882	877	0.2	28	270	282	282	0.5	3.13	176	175	-0.1
87931	CABALLO	051	1391	1415	1406	0.2	28	623	648	648	0.4	2.18	405	400	-0.1
87933	DERRY	051	166	177	178	0.7	51	57	62	63	0.9	2.84	39	41	0.5
87936	GARFIELD	013	562	707	791	2.5	90	174	220	247	2.6	3.21	146	179	2.2
87937	HATCH	013	3389	4285	4797	2.6	91	1038	1329	1497	2.7	3.22	803	988	2.3
87940	RINCON	013	619	817	923	3.0	93	187	248	282	3.1	3.29	159	206	2.8
87941	SALEM	013	1001	1262	1411	2.5	90	251	318	357	2.6	3.97	210	258	2.3
87942	WILLIAMSBURG	051	116	123	124	0.6	46	50	54	55	0.8	2.28	34	35	0.3
87943	WINSTON	051	163	166	165	0.2	28	75	78	78	0.4	2.13	49	48	-0.2
88001	LAS CRUCES	013	35293	37096	38965	0.5	43	13487	14976	15884	1.1	2.46	8314	8714	0.5
88002	WHITE SANDS MISSILE	013	1382	1043	985	-3.0	0	461	364	347	-2.5	2.85	371	283	-2.9
88003	LAS CRUCES	013	1628	2964	3032	6.7	99	8	38	48	18.3	2.55	6	33	20.2
88005	LAS CRUCES	013	26563	29493	31295	1.1	68	9881	11257	12075	1.4	2.51	6595	7139	0.9
88007	LAS CRUCES	013	21143	25120	27264	1.9	82	7465	9215	10141	2.3	2.58	5723	6771	1.8
88008	SANTA TERESA	013	3958	4936	5428	2.4	88	1320	1638	1805	2.4	2.98	1040	1249	2.0
88011	LAS CRUCES	013	17350	25303	29280	4.2	98	7221	10636	12356	4.3	2.34	4519	6384	3.8
88012	LAS CRUCES	013	15933	22336	25662	3.7	96	5319	7662	8876	4.0	2.91	4057	5615	3.6
88020	ANIMAS	023	640	551	526	-1.6	1	254	232	224	-1.0	2.38	176	154	-1.4
88021	ANTHONY	013	15701	19327	21474	2.3	87	4364	5521	6181	2.6	3.50	3764	4658	2.3
88022	ARENAS VALLEY	017	1054	1042	1040	-0.1	14	400	416	420	0.4	2.50	279	279	0.0
88023	BAYARD	017	3207	3189	3187	-0.1	14	1252	1313	1331	0.5	2.33	911	923	0.1
88025	BUCKHORN	017	1008	1045	1065	0.4	40	429	472	487	1.0	2.21	295	312	0.6
88026	SANTA CLARA	017	2219	2226	2226	0.0	20	803	846	858	0.6	2.62	570	578	0.2
88030	DEMING	029	25016	27807	29376	1.2	69	9397	10593	11211	1.3	2.60	6592	7144	0.9
88039	GLENWOOD	003	461	473	477	0.3	33	219	241	246	1.0	1.95	141	148	0.5
88041	HANOVER	017	379	396	403	0.5	43	169	186	191	1.0	2.13	118	125	0.6
88042	HILLSBORO	051	372	378	376	0.2	28	187	194	194	0.4	1.95	122	120	-0.2
88043	HURLEY	017	2195	2205	2204	0.0	20	767	806	816	0.5	2.64	552	559	0.1
88044	LA MESA	013	4009	4505	4884	1.3	72	1279	1501	1641	1.7	2.98	1024	1161	1.4
88045	LORDSBURG	023	5292	4917	4752	-0.8	5	1898	1835	1796	-0.4	2.63	1367	1273	-0.8
	NEW MEXICO					1.3					1.6	2.56			1.2
	UNITED STATES					1.0					1.1	2.59			0.9

ZIP CODE #	POST OFFICE NAME	RACE (%) White 2000	White 2009	Black 2000	Black 2009	Asian/Pacific 2000	Asian/Pacific 2009	% Hispanic Origin 2000	% Hispanic Origin 2009	2009 AGE DISTRIBUTION (%) 0-4	5-9	10-14	15-19	20-24	25-44	45-64	65-84	85+	18+	MEDIAN AGE 2009	% 2009 Males	% 2009 Females
87514	ARROYO SECO	80.9	79.1	0.2	0.2	0.4	0.5	44.0	48.4	4.7	5.4	5.6	5.4	3.9	24.9	39.2	9.7	1.3	80.7	45.1	51.1	48.9
87520	CHAMA	70.9	69.7	0.8	0.9	0.7	0.9	65.3	67.8	5.1	5.4	6.4	6.6	4.3	21.3	35.5	13.9	1.5	78.4	45.5	51.4	48.6
87521	CHAMISAL	51.7	50.9	0.3	0.3	0.5	0.4	80.1	81.8	5.2	5.5	6.1	6.8	5.2	21.6	33.7	14.1	1.9	79.3	44.8	50.7	49.3
87522	CHIMAYO	51.7	51.9	0.2	0.2	0.3	0.3	86.5	87.7	6.2	6.2	6.4	6.6	6.1	27.5	28.9	10.8	1.3	77.2	38.3	50.1	49.9
87524	COSTILLA	70.3	67.7	0.2	0.2	0.9	1.1	47.3	51.4	4.3	4.6	5.3	5.0	4.2	21.1	39.0	15.0	1.6	82.6	49.2	50.2	49.8
87527	DIXON	69.1	68.5	0.4	0.5	0.1	0.1	75.6	77.4	5.1	5.5	6.1	6.1	4.6	24.0	33.3	14.1	1.2	79.5	43.9	49.9	50.1
87528	DULCE	10.9	9.8	0.1	0.1	0.1	0.1	15.0	14.4	10.1	8.8	8.0	8.9	9.5	26.1	21.5	6.6	0.4	67.4	27.7	48.7	51.3
87530	EL RITO	48.4	47.8	0.2	0.2	0.1	0.2	78.5	80.2	6.6	6.6	6.8	7.2	6.6	26.9	29.0	9.4	1.0	75.3	36.5	48.4	51.6
87531	EMBUDO	58.8	58.8	0.3	0.3	0.1	0.1	86.1	87.3	8.1	7.7	7.2	7.4	8.2	27.6	24.7	8.2	0.9	72.6	32.8	49.8	50.2
87532	ESPANOLA	64.2	62.7	0.5	0.5	0.3	0.4	76.2	77.2	7.1	6.9	7.0	7.3	6.9	26.5	27.2	9.7	1.3	74.6	35.9	48.7	51.3
87535	GLORIETA	80.1	78.8	0.2	0.2	0.6	0.7	49.8	53.8	5.1	4.9	5.6	6.7	5.4	25.5	37.3	8.6	0.9	79.1	43.1	49.5	50.5
87537	HERNANDEZ	68.2	68.2	0.2	0.2	0.5	0.5	85.6	86.8	8.7	8.4	7.6	7.0	7.5	29.2	22.2	8.5	1.0	71.1	31.6	52.0	48.0
87539	LA MADERA	44.6	43.9	0.0	0.0	0.3	0.3	82.4	83.5	6.5	6.5	7.1	7.4	6.1	27.7	27.7	10.0	1.0	75.2	37.2	48.7	51.3
87540	LAMY	84.8	83.8	0.4	0.5	0.9	1.2	23.6	25.0	4.5	5.4	6.4	6.6	4.1	19.9	40.6	11.7	0.7	79.4	46.5	48.4	51.6
87544	LOS ALAMOS	90.2	88.5	0.4	0.4	3.8	4.9	11.8	13.2	5.4	5.9	6.8	6.8	4.9	21.4	33.7	13.2	1.8	77.6	44.2	49.6	50.4
87549	OJO CALIENTE	71.3	68.7	0.4	0.3	0.5	0.6	44.3	48.5	5.6	5.7	6.1	5.0	4.5	23.1	35.2	13.5	1.3	79.5	45.0	50.5	49.5
87552	PECOS	65.0	64.3	0.4	0.4	0.4	0.5	75.9	78.3	6.6	6.3	6.8	7.3	7.3	28.0	29.1	7.8	0.8	75.6	36.6	50.7	49.3
87553	PENASCO	28.3	27.7	0.2	0.2	0.2	0.2	82.4	82.4	5.7	5.8	6.3	7.5	5.5	22.5	30.7	14.0	2.0	77.6	42.6	49.6	50.4
87556	QUESTA	62.4	60.7	0.3	0.4	0.3	0.3	61.0	64.0	5.8	5.7	6.3	6.1	5.1	21.9	35.1	12.7	1.3	78.6	44.4	49.7	50.3
87557	RANCHOS DE TAOS	72.0	71.0	0.4	0.5	0.6	0.7	66.7	69.2	5.8	6.5	7.2	6.5	4.5	24.4	32.6	10.9	1.6	76.5	41.5	48.9	51.1
87560	RIBERA	43.0	42.2	0.7	0.8	0.2	0.2	83.1	84.8	6.4	7.2	7.1	7.7	5.4	24.3	29.4	11.2	1.4	74.3	38.9	50.6	49.4
87564	SAN CRISTOBAL	79.3	77.5	1.2	1.3	0.0	0.0	32.8	36.1	5.9	4.8	5.7	5.7	4.4	22.9	39.9	9.9	0.8	80.3	45.4	51.9	48.1
87565	SAN JOSE	59.6	58.8	0.7	0.8	0.6	0.7	74.5	76.8	6.6	6.6	7.2	7.6	5.8	25.6	29.8	10.0	0.9	74.8	38.4	49.2	50.8
87566	SAN JUAN PUEBLO	61.3	60.7	0.5	0.5	0.2	0.2	74.7	74.4	8.2	7.6	7.4	7.9	8.5	28.9	22.7	8.0	0.8	72.1	31.9	49.3	50.7
87567	SANTA CRUZ	58.9	58.4	0.6	0.6	0.6	0.6	76.9	79.5	6.1	6.1	6.6	6.9	5.8	27.5	30.1	10.1	0.9	76.9	38.5	50.0	50.0
87571	TAOS	63.0	61.3	0.3	0.3	0.6	0.7	53.5	55.6	5.7	5.6	6.3	6.4	5.5	24.8	31.9	12.0	1.8	78.1	41.7	48.4	51.6
87573	TERERRO	61.3	61.0	0.8	0.8	0.0	0.0	68.1	71.5	4.9	5.7	8.1	5.7	5.7	28.5	32.5	8.1	0.8	77.2	40.2	51.2	48.8
87575	TIERRA AMARILLA	65.8	64.9	0.7	0.8	0.9	1.1	68.2	70.4	5.0	5.5	6.8	7.0	4.0	22.1	34.4	13.4	1.7	77.8	44.6	51.5	48.5
87579	VADITO	35.8	35.4	0.4	0.3	0.4	0.3	84.6	85.9	6.6	6.7	7.1	7.4	4.7	21.6	30.5	13.8	1.6	75.0	41.8	49.5	50.5
87580	VALDEZ	81.9	80.4	0.4	0.3	0.4	0.3	43.3	48.0	4.6	4.9	5.9	5.6	4.6	25.8	37.9	9.8	1.0	80.7	44.2	51.0	49.0
87581	VALLECITOS	45.5	45.0	0.2	0.2	0.2	0.3	80.8	82.0	6.5	6.5	7.0	7.3	6.1	27.9	27.8	9.7	1.1	75.3	37.2	49.0	51.0
87701	LAS VEGAS	55.2	54.4	0.9	1.0	0.7	0.9	79.5	81.2	7.0	6.6	6.4	8.7	8.3	24.9	25.3	10.9	1.9	75.4	34.4	48.5	51.5
87711	ANTON CHICO	29.4	29.6	0.4	0.4	0.4	0.4	86.9	86.8	6.0	6.0	6.4	7.2	6.0	21.2	28.4	17.2	1.6	77.6	42.5	50.0	50.0
87713	CHACON	55.6	55.3	0.0	0.0	0.4	0.4	85.4	85.2	5.3	6.1	6.1	6.6	5.3	22.1	32.4	14.3	1.6	77.9	43.7	50.8	49.2
87714	CIMARRON	84.3	82.9	0.2	0.2	0.3	0.4	31.3	34.1	4.0	5.9	7.2	7.0	3.5	20.8	37.5	13.0	1.2	78.1	45.9	52.4	47.6
87715	CLEVELAND	54.1	53.6	0.0	0.0	0.3	0.3	87.4	86.9	6.0	6.3	6.3	6.3	5.4	22.5	32.2	13.1	2.0	77.5	42.7	49.6	50.4
87718	EAGLE NEST	88.0	86.4	0.1	0.3	0.4	0.6	15.9	18.5	3.9	6.1	6.1	5.6	2.5	20.3	42.3	12.4	0.8	80.2	47.7	52.6	47.4
87722	GUADALUPITA	61.8	60.6	0.0	0.0	0.0	0.0	67.6	69.7	6.1	6.1	6.1	9.1	6.1	24.2	27.3	15.2	0.0	72.7	38.8	48.5	51.5
87724	LA LOMA	29.2	29.6	0.3	0.3	0.7	0.7	87.2	87.1	5.8	6.1	6.1	7.5	6.1	21.1	29.3	16.7	1.4	77.6	42.5	50.3	49.7
87728	MAXWELL	86.1	84.8	1.7	1.9	0.5	0.5	42.3	47.1	3.6	5.1	6.3	19.3	2.4	19.3	30.4	12.1	1.4	72.2	40.2	58.7	41.3
87729	MIAMI	86.1	85.1	1.4	1.4	0.0	0.0	41.7	47.3	4.1	5.4	6.8	17.6	2.7	17.6	31.1	13.5	1.4	71.6	41.3	59.5	40.5
87730	MILLS	85.3	85.3	0.0	0.0	0.0	0.0	44.1	47.1	5.9	5.9	5.9	5.9	5.9	23.5	23.5	23.5	0.0	76.5	42.5	50.0	50.0
87731	MONTEZUMA	60.7	59.0	1.6	1.6	1.6	1.6	62.3	67.2	6.6	6.6	6.6	11.5	6.6	26.2	27.9	8.2	0.0	75.4	34.4	47.5	52.5
87732	MORA	58.5	58.1	0.1	0.1	0.1	0.1	85.2	84.7	6.7	6.9	6.8	6.3	5.5	21.9	30.0	14.2	1.6	75.7	41.6	50.0	50.0
87733	MOSQUERO	84.1	84.3	0.4	0.4	0.0	0.0	45.1	45.5	3.8	3.8	4.7	6.0	4.3	19.1	33.6	21.3	3.4	83.4	50.7	51.1	48.9
87734	OCATE	62.1	62.0	0.0	0.0	0.0	0.0	68.7	67.5	5.0	5.2	7.3	8.1	4.5	19.4	32.5	15.7	2.4	76.4	45.4	51.8	48.2
87740	RATON	79.8	78.6	0.2	0.2	0.4	0.4	52.3	56.4	6.1	6.1	6.2	6.8	5.6	21.8	29.5	14.9	3.0	77.5	42.8	48.9	51.1
87742	ROCIADA	59.3	57.6	0.1	0.1	0.2	0.3	64.3	67.7	5.3	6.8	6.9	5.9	4.3	20.9	36.7	12.0	1.2	76.8	44.9	50.8	49.2
87743	ROY	84.2	84.4	0.4	0.4	0.0	0.0	44.9	45.0	3.7	3.9	5.0	6.3	3.9	19.7	32.9	21.0	3.7	83.5	50.3	51.1	48.9
87745	SAPELLO	66.7	66.7	0.0	0.0	0.0	0.0	66.7	66.7	0.0	0.0	0.0	0.0	0.0	0.0	100.0	0.0	0.0	100.0	48.8	33.3	66.7
87746	SOLANO	85.5	84.5	0.0	0.0	0.0	0.0	44.9	45.1	2.8	4.2	5.6	5.6	2.8	18.3	33.8	22.5	4.2	81.7	52.1	49.3	50.7
87747	SPRINGER	81.9	81.0	0.6	0.7	0.1	0.2	59.9	64.2	5.4	6.0	6.4	12.0	4.3	20.7	26.6	15.8	2.8	73.7	41.2	52.7	47.3
87750	VALMORA	62.0	61.7	0.0	0.0	0.0	0.0	68.7	67.3	4.9	5.6	7.4	8.0	4.9	19.1	32.7	14.8	2.5	75.9	45.0	51.2	48.8
87752	WAGON MOUND	62.2	62.2	0.0	0.0	0.0	0.0	68.6	67.5	5.0	5.3	7.3	8.0	4.6	19.2	33.0	15.3	2.3	76.2	45.4	52.0	48.0
87801	SOCORRO	68.0	66.1	0.7	0.8	1.8	2.3	54.0	56.4	6.8	6.0	5.8	9.2	11.0	25.0	24.0	10.5	1.7	77.6	32.3	51.6	48.4
87820	ARAGON	88.0	87.2	0.5	0.5	0.5	0.5	23.6	25.5	4.6	4.6	5.6	5.1	2.6	16.3	40.3	18.4	2.6	81.6	51.3	51.5	48.5
87821	DATIL	87.3	86.1	0.2	0.1	1.1	1.3	13.5	15.0	2.9	3.6	4.4	5.5	3.8	15.6	40.7	21.8	1.6	85.7	53.4	50.8	49.2
87823	LEMITAR	74.3	72.5	0.8	0.8	0.2	0.2	48.5	51.9	5.6	5.7	6.8	7.1	5.0	22.0	32.9	13.5	1.2	77.2	43.1	50.3	49.7
87825	MAGDALENA	35.9	33.8	0.3	0.3	0.0	0.0	23.5	24.0	7.9	9.2	9.3	8.7	6.8	23.4	24.5	9.0	1.2	67.7	31.3	48.7	51.3
87827	PIE TOWN	87.3	85.9	0.2	0.1	1.1	1.3	13.6	15.1	2.9	3.6	4.3	5.5	3.9	15.7	40.6	22.0	1.6	85.9	53.4	50.5	49.5
87828	POLVADERA	76.0	75.0	0.0	0.0	0.0	0.0	56.0	53.6	7.1	7.1	7.1	7.1	7.1	28.6	28.6	7.1	0.0	71.4	35.0	50.0	50.0
87829	QUEMADO	87.2	85.7	0.3	0.3	0.9	1.4	13.4	15.2	2.8	3.7	4.5	5.6	3.9	15.7	40.4	21.9	1.4	85.7	53.1	50.8	49.2
87830	RESERVE	88.0	87.1	0.4	0.4	0.5	0.5	23.8	26.3	4.7	4.4	5.6	5.4	2.9	16.1	39.8	18.6	2.6	81.6	51.1	51.8	48.2
87831	SAN ACACIA	74.5	72.8	0.8	0.9	0.2	0.2	50.7	54.1	5.5	5.6	6.5	7.3	5.0	22.0	33.0	13.7	1.4	77.7	43.4	50.2	49.8
87901	TRUTH OR CONSEQUENCE	86.7	86.6	0.6	0.6	0.2	0.2	24.9	25.0	4.4	4.3	4.3	4.8	5.0	15.9	31.0	26.2	4.2	83.9	53.7	49.4	50.6
87930	ARREY	87.8	87.6	0.1	0.1	0.3	0.3	31.5	31.7	5.2	5.1	5.1	5.9	5.0	16.8	31.9	23.0	2.0	81.1	50.8	51.7	48.3
87931	CABALLO	87.6	87.6	0.1	0.1	0.4	0.4	32.5	32.9	5.4	5.2	5.4	6.1	5.2	17.0	31.8	22.0	1.9	80.3	49.9	51.7	48.3
87933	DERRY	90.3	90.4	0.0	0.0	0.0	0.0	18.8	19.2	3.4	3.4	3.4	4.5	4.0	11.9	33.9	33.3	2.3	86.4	58.6	49.7	50.3
87936	GARFIELD	42.1	41.0	0.4	0.4	0.2	0.1	82.9	84.7	10.3	9.3	8.6	10.0	9.8	22.8	19.8	8.2	1.1	65.5	26.2	50.5	49.5
87937	HATCH	45.8	44.6	0.2	0.2	0.1	0.1	80.0	82.5	10.4	9.6	8.8	9.4	8.6	23.0	20.0	9.0	1.1	65.5	27.1	48.7	51.3
87940	RINCON	51.8	50.7	0.2	0.2	0.0	0.0	81.1	83.4	10.5	9.5	8.7	9.8	8.8	23.5	19.6	8.6	1.0	65.4	26.7	49.4	50.6
87941	SALEM	42.0	41.0	0.3	0.3	0.2	0.2	82.5	84.6	10.3	9.4	8.6	9.8	9.4	23.1	19.9	8.3	1.1	65.7	26.5	50.2	49.8
87942	WILLIAMSBURG	90.4	90.2	0.0	0.0	0.0	0.0	20.0	20.3	3.3	3.3	3.3	4.9	4.1	12.2	34.1	31.7	3.3	87.0	58.1	50.4	49.6
87943	WINSTON	88.3	88.0	0.0	0.0	0.0	0.0	32.7	32.5	5.4	5.4	5.4	6.0	4.8	16.9	31.9	21.7	2.4	80.1	50.0	52.4	47.6
88001	LAS CRUCES	62.9	61.5	2.8	3.0	1.5	1.8	60.8	64.0	8.1	7.3	6.3	8.5	14.0	26.6	18.3	9.5	1.4	74.3	28.1	48.5	51.5
88002	WHITE SANDS MISSILE	72.0	68.4	11.3	12.8	3.7	4.6	17.5	19.5	12.8	9.4	9.6	6.8	7.2	35.9	16.5	1.7	0.1	64.3	27.3	52.3	47.7
88003	LAS CRUCES	77.7	69.0	4.3	4.7	1.9	2.6	36.2	39.4	2.5	1.2	0.8	46.6	33.4	11.9	2.8	0.6	0.1	94.6	19.9	45.4	54.6
88005	LAS CRUCES	72.2	70.7	1.5	1.6	0.6	0.7	53.9	57.5	6.9	6.3	6.3	7.0	8.2	26.3	25.8	11.7	1.5	76.3	36.0	50.0	50.0
88007	LAS CRUCES	71.9	70.4	1.1	1.3	0.4	0.5	54.1	57.6	6.7	6.4	6.5	7.3	7.0	26.6	27.2	10.9	1.4	76.0	36.7	50.9	49.1
88008	SANTA TERESA	79.9	78.2	1.0	1.1	0.5	0.6	65.4	70.7	9.0	8.6	8.8	7.5	5.0	27.9	23.7	8.5	0.9	68.6	32.9	48.4	51.6
88011	LAS CRUCES	78.9	76.3	1.7	1.9	2.1	2.6	33.6	37.2	5.7	5.7	5.7	6.9	8.4	23.9	27.6	13.4	2.8	79.2	39.6	48.1	51.9
88012	LAS CRUCES	65.3	64.3	1.7	2.0	0.5	0.6	59.4	62.7	8.7	8.0	7.5	7.9	8.2	27.5	23.8	7.7	0.7	71.1	31.1	49.7	50.3
88020	ANIMAS	93.0	92.2	0.0	0.0	0.0	0.0	22.8	25.8	7.4	7.4	7.4	7.4	5.4	20.7	30.5	12.3	1.3	73.0	40.1	52.6	47.4
88021	ANTHONY	62.4	62.2	0.3	0.4	0.3	0.3	90.6	92.2	10.1	10.0	9.2	9.2	8.0	25.6	19.8	7.4	0.7	65.1	27.2	48.7	51.3
88022	ARENAS VALLEY	75.8	75.3	0.4	0.4	0.1	0.1	48.0	48.6	8.4	7.7	7.1	7.4	7.6	26.5	25.0	9.4	1.0	72.2	33.1	49.2	50.8
88023	BAYARD	68.5	68.4	0.3	0.3	0.0	0.0	78.2	78.5	6.6	6.1	6.5	7.6	5.7	20.6	27.7	16.0	3.2	75.6	42.2	47.6	52.4
88025	BUCKHORN	95.8	95.9	0.6	0.6	0.0	0.0	8.7	9.0	4.6	5.3	5.6	5.5	5.7	17.5	35.7	17.9	2.2	81.1	48.9	52.1	47.9
88026	SANTA CLARA	64.9	64.6	0.4	0.4	0.0	0.0	78.9	79.3	9.1	8.8	8.6	7.5	5.8	22.7	23.9	12.1	1.6	68.5	33.8	48.1	51.9
88030	DEMING	74.3	73.3	0.9	1.0	0.3	0.4	57.7	60.8	7.9	7.8	7.4	7.5	5.7	21.2	24.4	15.7	2.3	72.1	37.9	48.4	51.6
88039	GLENWOOD	88.1	87.1	0.4	0.4	0.4	0.4	23.9	26.4	4.7	4.4	5.7	5.5	2.7	16.3	40.0	18.2	2.5	81.2	51.1	52.0	48.0
88041	HANOVER	82.5	82.3	0.3	0.3	0.3	0.3	39.7	40.2	5.6	5.8	6.1	6.1	5.6	18.7	32.3	17.4	2.5	78.5	46.4	50.3	49.7
88042	HILLSBORO	87.4	87.3	0.3	0.3	0.5	0.5	32.4	33.1	5.6	5.3	5.3	6.1	5.3	16.9	31.5	22.0	2.1	79.9	49.8	51.6	48.4
88043	HURLEY	74.2	74.0	0.2	0.2	0.0	0.0	56.2	56.6	6.5	6.4	6.7	6.8	4.9	21.6	26.1	17.8	3.3	76.0	42.6	48.8	51.2
88044	LA MESA	69.6	69.4	0.3	0.3	0.2	0.2	83.3	85.6	7.3	7.2	7.5	7.9	7.3	24.8	25.6	11.1	1.3	73.0	34.8	50.0	50.0
88045	LORDSBURG	82.7	81.9	0.5	0.5	0.4	0.4	60.1	63.1	8.1	7.7	7.5	8.2	6.5	23.2	25.0	11.7	2.0	71.5	35.0	49.6	50.4
	NEW MEXICO	66.8	65.0	1.9	2.0	1.1	1.4	42.1	44.2	7.3	7.1	7.0	7.5	7.2	26.0	25.9	10.5	1.6	74.2	35.5	49.3	50.7
	UNITED STATES	75.1	72.0	12.3	12.7	3.8	4.6	12.5	15.7	6.8	6.7	6.6	7.1	6.9	27.0	26.0	10.9	1.9	75.7	36.9	49.2	50.8

ZIP CODE #	POST OFFICE NAME	2009 Per Capita Income	2009 HH Income Base	2009 Household Income Distribution (%) Less than $25,000	$25,000 to $49,999	$50,000 to $99,999	$100,000 to $149,999	$150,000 or More	Median Household Income 2009	2014	2009 National Centile	2009 State Centile	2009 Home Value Base	2009 Home Value Distribution (%) Less than $50,000	$50,000 to $89,999	$90,000 to $174,999	$175,000 to $399,999	$400,000 or More	2009 Median Home Value
87514	ARROYO SECO	25479	596	32.4	33.7	28.0	3.2	2.7	35393	36067	19	47	451	7.8	7.3	15.5	34.6	34.8	317470
87520	CHAMA	19685	575	32.0	35.0	26.6	3.8	2.6	37132	40215	24	56	453	12.8	13.5	34.4	29.8	9.5	144773
87521	CHAMISAL	17067	291	39.2	29.6	27.1	3.8	0.3	36465	36807	22	52	262	19.5	10.7	30.5	30.5	8.8	144231
87522	CHIMAYO	18229	2115	36.2	30.1	26.0	5.1	2.6	35587	37371	19	49	1820	11.0	12.1	30.7	34.4	11.7	164799
87524	COSTILLA	15514	258	41.9	30.2	25.2	2.7	0.0	29733	31316	8	24	215	13.5	15.8	26.5	29.8	14.4	149342
87527	DIXON	18841	717	38.6	31.0	27.2	2.6	0.6	32170	34597	12	33	613	11.3	8.2	37.4	33.8	9.5	161526
87528	DULCE	14568	1048	36.7	28.1	29.3	4.6	1.2	33571	35263	15	41	726	33.2	26.7	25.9	12.4	1.8	75238
87530	EL RITO	18000	381	34.9	26.2	32.3	4.2	2.4	37865	41021	26	60	311	14.5	10.3	28.0	34.4	12.9	166500
87531	EMBUDO	19249	1953	26.3	33.9	30.0	7.6	2.2	39855	41627	32	67	1671	18.0	11.1	28.9	30.6	11.3	149508
87532	ESPANOLA	19465	6607	32.5	27.4	30.0	7.0	3.0	39403	41329	31	66	4954	18.3	7.5	25.1	36.3	12.7	171898
87535	GLORIETA	29182	387	20.2	24.5	32.6	15.0	7.8	57963	60216	75	91	323	6.8	11.5	16.7	45.2	19.8	226172
87537	HERNANDEZ	17983	405	26.2	36.5	30.9	4.0	2.5	38205	40000	27	62	348	25.3	13.8	24.7	23.3	12.9	143382
87539	LA MADERA	17428	129	38.8	27.9	28.7	3.1	1.6	35276	38299	19	47	109	20.2	11.0	30.3	30.3	8.3	138393
87540	LAMY	41780	487	12.3	17.2	38.2	19.1	13.1	70036	72542	87	96	415	1.2	4.1	10.1	47.0	37.6	338690
87544	LOS ALAMOS	50200	8192	6.6	10.2	30.1	28.7	24.4	104709	105273	97	100	6458	2.9	1.2	10.6	52.6	32.7	323140
87549	OJO CALIENTE	18871	664	52.7	29.4	16.6	0.6	0.8	22826	25428	2	4	572	25.3	12.6	25.7	26.4	10.0	125000
87552	PECOS	19549	1643	27.6	31.1	34.0	5.7	1.6	41685	43551	38	75	1299	15.6	8.7	33.3	36.0	6.4	154649
87553	PENASCO	14559	566	45.8	29.3	22.4	2.3	0.2	28261	29266	6	16	490	19.4	11.8	38.4	26.9	3.5	127119
87556	QUESTA	19355	1735	39.9	31.0	23.4	3.3	2.4	32324	32675	12	35	1383	14.0	10.1	29.2	34.9	11.8	163956
87557	RANCHOS DE TAOS	21472	1823	34.4	33.4	23.5	5.4	3.3	37031	37452	24	55	1400	6.4	5.1	21.7	43.7	23.0	238286
87560	RIBERA	15408	916	43.0	29.0	23.8	3.6	0.5	28191	29658	6	16	805	19.3	17.9	34.8	21.9	6.2	119066
87564	SAN CRISTOBAL	29014	229	33.2	27.9	26.2	5.7	7.0	41234	40869	37	74	163	2.5	4.9	20.2	46.6	25.8	253571
87565	SAN JOSE	16808	532	39.5	26.1	27.4	5.5	1.5	34471	36032	16	43	463	19.9	8.9	31.1	33.3	6.9	146944
87566	SAN JUAN PUEBLO	16270	2067	32.7	32.2	28.5	4.9	1.7	37209	38993	24	57	1667	14.5	15.5	34.0	31.9	4.1	137849
87567	SANTA CRUZ	23623	133	25.6	24.1	30.8	13.5	6.0	50270	52287	62	86	108	11.1	8.3	19.4	38.9	22.2	229167
87571	TAOS	20803	6342	38.6	29.6	24.9	3.8	3.1	32666	33347	13	38	4494	9.5	4.3	22.0	42.8	21.4	231514
87573	TERERRO	27491	64	23.4	35.9	32.8	6.3	1.6	40892	41904	36	72	51	7.8	7.8	39.2	33.3	11.8	162500
87575	TIERRA AMARILLA	19600	830	34.0	34.0	26.0	3.6	2.4	35684	39083	20	50	662	11.8	12.1	38.4	29.5	8.3	147778
87579	VADITO	15954	596	41.4	29.5	24.7	3.7	0.7	32719	33045	13	37	499	19.2	8.8	30.1	34.7	7.2	148904
87580	VALDEZ	29063	161	32.3	35.4	24.8	3.1	4.3	35220	36010	18	46	119	5.9	5.9	16.0	34.5	37.8	334091
87581	VALLECITOS	18993	287	39.4	27.2	28.2	3.5	1.7	35122	37344	18	46	243	19.3	11.1	31.7	29.2	8.6	138603
87701	LAS VEGAS	17354	7759	38.2	29.9	26.2	3.8	1.9	32920	34795	13	39	5294	16.5	13.4	47.1	19.3	3.6	129648
87711	ANTON CHICO	10783	93	57.0	29.0	11.8	2.2	0.0	20298	20694	1	2	81	40.7	23.5	21.0	4.9	9.9	62500
87713	CHACON	14650	92	39.1	31.5	23.9	5.4	0.0	31475	32850	11	31	77	22.1	13.0	33.8	24.7	6.5	133929
87714	CIMARRON	24492	1278	25.4	33.5	32.2	5.4	3.5	41884	44454	39	75	961	6.6	11.2	32.9	30.7	18.6	171991
87715	CLEVELAND	14312	135	37.8	34.1	23.7	3.7	0.7	31056	30869	10	30	109	24.8	11.9	30.3	23.9	9.2	129167
87718	EAGLE NEST	27507	343	21.0	29.4	37.9	7.3	4.4	49542	49888	60	85	252	3.6	5.2	23.4	41.7	26.2	258333
87722	GUADALUPITA	14712	12	50.0	8.3	41.7	0.0	0.0	25000	25000	3	6	9	0.0	55.6	44.4	0.0	0.0	67500
87724	LA LOMA	11651	119	56.3	29.4	11.8	2.5	0.0	20708	20872	2	3	103	39.8	24.3	21.4	4.9	9.7	63125
87728	MAXWELL	22790	189	30.7	31.2	32.3	4.2	1.6	39085	41252	30	65	147	13.6	16.3	32.7	21.1	16.3	137500
87729	MIAMI	24574	37	27.0	32.4	37.8	2.7	0.0	41146	42361	36	74	29	13.8	13.8	37.9	20.7	13.8	129167
87730	MILLS	16912	16	37.5	31.3	31.3	0.0	0.0	35000	30000	18	46	12	41.7	16.7	25.0	16.7	0.0	60000
87731	MONTEZUMA	17528	21	23.8	33.3	38.1	4.8	0.0	38596	40000	28	62	16	6.3	12.5	43.8	31.3	6.3	145000
87732	MORA	15046	1463	43.5	32.9	18.9	3.1	1.5	29021	30286	7	20	1226	18.3	15.7	34.4	23.1	8.6	132993
87733	MOSQUERO	20067	117	40.2	29.9	24.8	2.6	2.6	30959	31410	10	29	89	48.3	15.7	14.6	14.6	6.7	53000
87734	OCATE	17640	161	48.4	25.5	21.1	3.7	1.2	25616	26272	4	8	124	26.6	23.4	24.2	12.1	13.7	90000
87740	RATON	19737	3660	33.3	33.4	28.1	3.4	1.8	36321	37831	21	52	2626	11.5	21.3	44.5	17.8	4.8	115079
87742	ROCIADA	16136	374	44.4	27.8	24.6	2.4	0.8	28591	35202	6	19	294	12.2	19.4	25.2	23.8	19.4	141875
87743	ROY	19394	221	39.8	31.2	24.4	2.3	2.3	30792	31668	9	29	167	44.9	17.4	15.0	15.6	7.2	58500
87745	SAPELLO	0	0	0.0	0.0	0.0	0.0	0.0	0	0	0	0	0	0.0	0.0	0.0	0.0	0.0	0
87746	SOLANO	15035	32	43.8	31.3	25.0	0.0	0.0	28125	28125	6	16	24	41.7	16.7	16.7	20.8	4.2	70000
87747	SPRINGER	16974	800	32.5	34.5	28.4	3.4	1.3	34137	35628	16	42	579	14.9	32.6	34.4	12.3	5.9	96905
87750	VALMORA	16530	64	46.9	26.6	21.9	3.1	1.6	26228	26561	4	11	49	26.5	22.4	26.5	12.2	12.2	95000
87752	WAGON MOUND	17795	240	46.7	25.8	21.7	3.3	2.5	26391	27259	4	11	185	27.6	23.2	22.7	13.0	13.5	87857
87801	SOCORRO	18070	4465	42.5	25.1	24.2	6.1	2.1	30103	30896	8	26	2852	14.1	18.0	42.5	22.5	2.9	123205
87820	ARAGON	17453	90	41.1	31.1	23.3	3.3	1.1	30000	30737	8	26	72	13.9	16.7	34.7	23.6	11.1	139286
87821	DATIL	16574	319	45.8	30.1	20.7	3.4	0.0	28395	30417	6	18	260	21.5	10.8	29.2	24.6	13.8	140179
87823	LEMITAR	20008	261	36.0	28.4	29.5	3.1	3.1	36690	37744	23	53	221	17.2	17.2	34.4	21.7	9.5	121875
87825	MAGDALENA	11499	1131	48.4	26.7	21.2	2.8	0.9	25659	26371	4	9	906	28.8	20.8	29.0	15.1	6.3	90889
87827	PIE TOWN	17105	334	45.8	30.2	20.7	3.3	0.0	28339	30000	6	17	272	22.4	10.7	29.0	24.3	13.6	138393
87828	POLVADERA	26133	15	26.7	33.3	40.0	0.0	0.0	42343	42343	40	76	13	7.7	23.1	46.2	23.1	0.0	112500
87829	QUEMADO	15368	154	46.8	29.2	20.8	3.2	0.0	27592	29737	5	14	126	21.4	10.3	31.0	24.6	12.7	138333
87830	RESERVE	18353	643	42.1	30.5	22.7	3.4	1.2	29248	30000	7	21	515	13.4	15.7	36.3	22.7	11.8	140250
87831	SAN ACACIA	19764	261	35.2	29.1	29.5	3.1	3.1	37185	38139	24	56	222	17.1	18.0	34.7	21.2	9.0	119643
87901	TRUTH OR CONSEQUENCE	18918	4891	44.1	30.6	21.2	2.4	1.8	28616	29986	6	19	3569	17.5	28.0	35.9	16.2	2.5	97146
87930	ARREY	11805	282	39.0	38.7	18.4	2.8	1.1	30278	30926	9	27	234	18.8	17.9	43.2	18.4	1.7	122000
87931	CABALLO	16346	648	39.2	39.7	17.4	2.6	1.1	30114	30376	8	27	537	20.3	18.4	43.4	16.0	1.9	116886
87933	DERRY	17195	62	30.6	32.3	29.0	4.8	3.2	38625	39302	29	63	53	5.7	15.1	32.1	43.4	3.8	165625
87936	GARFIELD	11885	220	53.2	23.6	18.2	3.2	1.8	23245	24637	2	4	174	31.6	30.5	21.8	12.1	4.0	70000
87937	HATCH	12148	1329	48.5	30.2	15.6	3.6	2.0	25727	26757	4	9	884	42.6	16.2	29.3	9.5	2.4	64474
87940	RINCON	10852	248	49.2	35.5	11.3	2.8	1.2	25426	27700	4	7	196	60.2	12.8	14.8	9.2	3.1	41667
87941	SALEM	9624	318	52.5	23.9	18.6	3.1	1.9	23621	24753	3	5	252	32.5	28.6	21.8	12.3	4.8	72143
87942	WILLIAMSBURG	21132	54	33.3	35.2	24.1	5.6	1.9	35000	40756	18	46	46	4.3	17.4	37.0	37.0	4.3	150000
87943	WINSTON	16774	78	39.7	41.0	16.7	2.6	0.0	30000	30000	8	26	65	20.0	18.5	44.6	15.4	1.5	116071
88001	LAS CRUCES	16035	14976	44.4	26.8	24.7	2.6	1.5	29728	32448	8	24	7200	15.3	15.7	57.1	10.9	1.0	110101
88002	WHITE SANDS MISSILE	23209	364	5.5	37.6	48.4	5.8	2.7	59141	60446	76	92	15	0.0	0.0	40.0	0.0	60.0	416667
88003	LAS CRUCES	13668	38	71.1	21.1	5.3	2.6	0.0	15000	15000	1	1	0	0.0	0.0	0.0	0.0	0.0	0
88005	LAS CRUCES	21245	11257	29.0	26.4	34.6	7.0	3.0	43922	46122	45	78	7488	14.7	11.3	37.1	30.6	6.2	144623
88007	LAS CRUCES	22009	9215	25.7	27.0	36.7	7.0	3.6	46925	48359	54	83	7415	18.1	12.8	28.5	30.5	10.0	149010
88008	SANTA TERESA	25196	1638	13.5	26.4	38.7	13.9	7.6	64125	60910	82	95	1256	6.1	6.2	37.6	39.0	11.1	175658
88011	LAS CRUCES	28067	10636	22.9	22.9	38.2	9.8	6.3	54988	53708	71	90	6954	3.6	3.4	26.6	55.6	10.8	222078
88012	LAS CRUCES	17469	7662	23.4	33.1	38.0	4.4	1.1	44399	46248	47	78	6229	17.8	18.6	44.8	17.6	1.1	123633
88020	ANIMAS	19074	232	41.8	27.6	23.3	3.9	3.4	31376	31374	10	31	139	20.9	21.6	30.2	17.3	10.1	118056
88021	ANTHONY	10641	5521	42.9	32.5	20.6	3.2	0.9	29435	31062	7	22	4005	29.1	25.5	30.9	11.2	3.2	81285
88022	ARENAS VALLEY	20592	416	23.3	32.7	36.1	5.3	2.6	44799	46140	48	79	313	19.8	7.0	34.8	32.3	6.1	149643
88023	BAYARD	15169	1313	44.7	34.2	17.8	2.2	1.1	27573	29581	5	14	997	20.2	26.0	44.2	8.0	1.6	95000
88025	BUCKHORN	20796	472	33.3	33.3	24.8	7.4	1.3	36968	40651	23	54	388	8.2	14.9	32.2	34.8	9.8	159091
88026	SANTA CLARA	13247	846	44.6	32.7	20.1	2.0	0.6	27339	28914	5	13	605	16.4	25.6	46.4	10.2	1.3	99898
88030	DEMING	13569	10593	49.0	28.2	19.8	1.8	1.3	25493	27096	4	8	7934	23.6	25.7	38.5	10.3	1.8	91094
88039	GLENWOOD	19315	241	41.9	30.7	22.8	3.3	1.2	29337	30000	7	22	193	13.0	15.5	37.3	22.3	11.9	142763
88041	HANOVER	21629	186	33.9	30.6	31.2	2.2	2.2	37363	38978	25	59	155	12.3	20.6	36.1	20.6	10.3	141346
88042	HILLSBORO	18367	194	39.7	40.2	17.0	2.6	0.5	29715	30209	8	23	161	19.9	18.6	43.5	16.1	1.9	116912
88043	HURLEY	14673	806	35.0	39.5	22.5	2.2	0.9	33457	35066	14	41	645	13.6	29.6	41.6	11.0	4.2	96692
88044	LA MESA	13736	1501	44.0	31.6	18.3	3.9	2.1	30317	32426	9	27	1190	27.6	16.8	31.3	19.7	4.5	102614
88045	LORDSBURG	14692	1835	44.3	29.5	21.5	3.2	1.5	29477	30482	7	22	1266	28.5	31.7	33.7	5.4	0.7	78229
	NEW MEXICO	22470		27.2	27.7	32.6	8.1	4.5	44681	46845				12.7	11.8	31.3	35.2	9.1	159744
	UNITED STATES	27277		20.9	24.4	35.3	11.7	7.6	54719	56938				9.3	13.1	31.6	32.6	13.5	162279

ZIP CODE #	POST OFFICE NAME	FINANCIAL SERVICES: Auto Loan	FINANCIAL SERVICES: Home Loan	FINANCIAL SERVICES: Invest-ments	FINANCIAL SERVICES: Retire-ment Plans	THE HOME: Home Improvements: Home Repair	THE HOME: Home Improvements: Lawn & Garden	THE HOME: Furnishings: Comput-ers & Hard-ware-Personal	THE HOME: Furnishings: Major Appli-ances	THE HOME: Furnishings: TV, Radio, Sound Equip-ment	THE HOME: Furnishings: Furni-ture	ENTERTAINMENT: Dine out/ Carry out	ENTERTAINMENT: Sports Equip-ment	ENTERTAINMENT: Fees & Tickets	ENTERTAINMENT: Toys & Games	ENTERTAINMENT: Travel	ENTERTAINMENT: Cable TV	PERSONAL: Apparel & Services	PERSONAL: Auto Repairs	PERSONAL: Health Insur-ance	PERSONAL: Pets & Supplies
87514	ARROYO SECO	85	68	109	67	74	89	68	86	71	64	70	63	59	67	73	76	47	79	85	100
87520	CHAMA	77	61	99	60	67	81	61	78	64	57	63	57	53	61	66	68	42	72	77	90
87521	CHAMISAL	72	50	72	48	51	72	52	66	58	49	57	50	41	58	51	64	38	61	69	79
87522	CHIMAYO	73	65	57	61	63	66	62	67	65	65	65	47	57	67	59	67	45	65	66	78
87524	COSTILLA	64	50	77	48	53	67	50	64	53	47	53	47	42	52	53	58	35	59	64	74
87527	DIXON	72	52	74	50	54	73	53	68	59	49	58	51	42	59	53	65	38	62	70	80
87528	DULCE	69	63	60	60	61	64	62	64	63	64	63	48	58	65	60	64	43	64	64	76
87530	EL RITO	77	70	62	68	69	72	66	70	69	69	69	51	63	72	63	71	47	68	71	84
87531	EMBUDO	80	75	67	70	73	70	75	75	74	78	74	57	70	76	71	73	52	75	71	87
87532	ESPANOLA	77	71	65	68	69	73	71	73	72	71	72	55	66	74	67	74	49	72	74	86
87535	GLORIETA	123	110	114	107	110	119	105	116	109	107	109	85	98	112	103	113	74	111	116	137
87537	HERNANDEZ	76	73	63	68	71	66	73	72	70	77	71	54	68	73	69	69	50	72	67	82
87539	LA MADERA	67	62	55	60	60	63	58	62	60	61	60	45	55	63	56	62	41	60	62	73
87540	LAMY	135	143	168	145	149	150	130	144	128	133	129	107	136	126	142	129	90	136	139	166
87544	LOS ALAMOS	155	191	193	193	195	175	169	171	160	176	162	132	190	161	185	156	118	166	160	195
87549	OJO CALIENTE	58	42	60	41	43	59	43	55	48	40	47	41	34	47	43	52	31	50	57	65
87552	PECOS	79	70	75	68	70	75	69	75	70	70	70	56	64	72	68	72	48	73	74	88
87553	PENASCO	64	43	63	41	43	64	45	57	52	43	51	44	34	52	43	58	34	54	60	70
87556	QUESTA	77	55	83	53	57	78	57	72	63	53	62	54	46	62	57	69	41	67	74	86
87557	RANCHOS DE TAOS	81	67	94	66	71	83	66	80	69	64	68	58	59	67	69	73	46	75	79	93
87560	RIBERA	71	49	70	46	49	71	51	64	58	48	57	49	39	58	49	64	37	60	67	78
87564	SAN CRISTOBAL	102	80	127	78	87	107	80	102	85	75	84	75	69	81	86	91	56	94	102	119
87565	SAN JOSE	70	63	61	61	62	67	60	65	62	61	62	47	56	64	58	65	42	62	65	77
87566	SAN JUAN PUEBLO	71	68	58	63	65	63	66	66	66	70	66	50	63	69	63	65	46	66	64	78
87567	SANTA CRUZ	99	91	80	88	89	93	85	91	89	89	89	66	81	92	81	91	60	88	91	108
87571	TAOS	74	61	78	61	64	75	63	72	67	61	66	53	57	65	64	71	44	70	75	85
87573	TERERRO	85	68	110	67	75	90	68	87	71	64	71	63	59	68	74	76	47	80	86	100
87575	TIERRA AMARILLA	76	59	93	58	64	79	60	76	63	56	62	56	51	61	63	68	41	70	76	88
87579	VADITO	70	48	70	46	49	70	50	63	57	47	56	49	39	57	48	63	37	59	67	77
87580	VALDEZ	92	74	119	72	81	97	74	93	77	69	76	68	64	73	80	82	51	86	92	108
87581	VALLECITOS	67	61	55	59	60	63	58	61	60	60	60	45	54	62	55	62	41	59	62	73
87701	LAS VEGAS	66	58	54	55	57	60	61	62	63	61	63	45	56	63	57	65	43	62	64	72
87711	ANTON CHICO	51	33	49	31	33	50	36	45	41	34	40	35	27	42	33	46	27	42	47	55
87713	CHACON	69	50	71	48	52	70	51	65	57	47	56	49	41	56	50	62	37	60	68	77
87714	CIMARRON	94	73	113	71	78	98	73	93	78	69	77	69	62	75	77	84	51	86	94	109
87715	CLEVELAND	67	47	68	45	48	68	49	62	55	46	54	47	38	55	47	61	35	57	65	74
87718	EAGLE NEST	105	84	136	83	92	111	84	107	88	79	87	78	73	84	91	94	58	99	106	124
87722	GUADALUPITA	69	49	71	48	51	70	50	64	56	47	55	48	40	56	50	62	36	59	67	76
87724	LA LOMA	51	33	49	31	33	50	36	45	41	34	40	35	27	42	33	46	27	42	47	55
87728	MAXWELL	82	56	90	56	59	86	62	77	65	50	64	64	46	63	62	71	42	72	82	95
87729	MIAMI	81	56	89	55	58	85	62	77	64	50	63	63	45	63	61	70	41	72	81	94
87730	MILLS	64	44	71	44	46	68	49	61	51	40	50	50	36	50	49	56	33	57	64	75
87731	MONTEZUMA	76	66	81	63	67	75	65	74	67	64	66	55	59	66	66	69	45	71	73	87
87732	MORA	66	46	66	44	47	66	48	60	54	45	53	46	37	54	46	59	35	56	63	73
87733	MOSQUERO	72	50	79	49	52	76	55	68	57	45	57	57	40	56	55	62	37	64	72	84
87734	OCATE	72	51	74	50	53	73	53	67	59	49	57	50	42	58	52	64	38	62	70	80
87740	RATON	73	57	73	56	59	75	60	70	66	56	64	52	52	65	59	71	43	67	76	83
87742	ROCIADA	65	52	85	52	58	69	52	67	55	49	54	49	45	52	57	59	36	62	66	77
87743	ROY	73	50	80	50	52	77	55	69	58	45	57	57	41	56	55	63	37	64	73	85
87745	SAPELLO	0	0	0	0	0	0	0	0	0	0	0	0	0	0	0	0	0	0	0	0
87746	SOLANO	60	41	66	41	43	63	46	57	47	37	47	47	33	46	45	52	30	53	60	70
87747	SPRINGER	72	51	75	50	53	76	56	70	62	49	60	54	44	60	55	68	40	65	75	83
87750	VALMORA	71	51	73	50	53	73	52	67	58	49	57	50	42	58	52	64	38	61	70	79
87752	WAGON MOUND	72	51	73	50	53	73	53	67	58	49	57	50	42	58	52	64	38	61	70	80
87801	SOCORRO	68	55	56	55	54	60	63	61	64	60	63	48	55	65	57	65	44	63	63	74
87820	ARAGON	56	53	68	49	59	63	50	60	53	54	52	39	50	49	55	56	35	57	66	68
87821	DATIL	59	48	77	47	52	63	48	60	50	45	49	44	41	47	52	53	33	56	60	70
87823	LEMITAR	88	63	92	61	65	90	65	83	72	59	70	63	51	71	65	79	46	76	86	99
87825	MAGDALENA	62	45	56	42	46	58	47	56	51	45	51	41	38	51	45	55	34	54	58	66
87827	PIE TOWN	59	48	77	47	52	63	48	60	50	45	49	44	41	47	52	53	33	56	60	70
87828	POLVADERA	87	62	89	60	65	88	64	81	71	60	70	61	51	71	63	78	46	75	85	97
87829	QUEMADO	59	47	77	47	52	63	47	60	50	44	49	44	41	47	51	53	33	56	60	70
87830	RESERVE	55	53	68	49	59	63	50	59	53	54	52	39	50	49	55	56	35	57	66	68
87831	SAN ACACIA	89	63	92	62	66	91	66	83	72	60	71	63	52	72	65	80	47	77	87	99
87901	TRUTH OR CONSEQUENCE	55	52	64	48	57	62	51	59	55	54	53	39	50	50	54	58	36	57	66	67
87930	ARREY	54	52	66	48	57	62	49	58	52	53	51	38	49	48	54	55	34	56	65	66
87931	CABALLO	52	50	64	46	56	60	48	56	50	51	49	37	47	46	52	53	33	54	62	64
87933	DERRY	72	69	88	63	76	82	65	77	69	71	67	50	65	63	71	73	45	74	86	88
87936	GARFIELD	64	51	39	43	49	48	51	55	56	58	57	34	45	57	46	58	39	56	54	61
87937	HATCH	66	53	39	44	50	50	53	57	57	59	58	35	46	58	47	59	40	57	55	62
87940	RINCON	60	48	36	40	46	45	48	52	52	54	53	32	42	53	43	54	37	52	50	57
87941	SALEM	64	51	39	43	49	48	51	55	56	58	57	34	45	57	46	58	39	56	54	61
87942	WILLIAMSBURG	71	67	86	62	75	80	64	76	68	69	66	50	63	62	70	72	44	73	84	86
87943	WINSTON	52	50	64	46	56	60	48	56	50	51	49	37	47	46	52	53	33	54	62	64
88001	LAS CRUCES	59	49	44	49	47	49	61	53	59	57	59	42	52	59	52	59	41	57	54	63
88002	WHITE SANDS MISSILE	117	61	45	70	54	51	110	76	103	102	108	76	83	124	79	95	76	97	68	92
88003	LAS CRUCES	32	21	20	23	20	22	39	26	35	31	35	24	28	35	27	34	24	32	27	33
88005	LAS CRUCES	80	74	69	74	73	77	77	76	78	76	78	58	74	79	74	80	54	77	80	91
88007	LAS CRUCES	88	85	81	83	85	87	81	85	82	84	82	62	79	84	80	84	57	83	86	100
88008	SANTA TERESA	110	121	107	117	118	107	107	110	103	116	105	82	112	107	109	100	74	105	100	125
88011	LAS CRUCES	96	94	89	95	93	93	96	93	95	96	95	71	94	96	92	95	66	94	93	110
88012	LAS CRUCES	80	74	65	71	71	73	72	74	73	75	73	55	68	76	68	74	50	73	73	87
88020	ANIMAS	81	58	83	56	60	82	59	76	66	55	65	57	48	66	59	73	43	69	79	90
88021	ANTHONY	61	52	40	45	50	48	51	54	54	56	55	35	46	55	47	55	38	54	52	60
88022	ARENAS VALLEY	80	75	64	72	72	73	74	74	74	77	74	56	70	77	70	74	51	74	72	88
88023	BAYARD	59	47	53	44	47	57	47	55	51	47	51	39	41	52	45	55	35	52	57	64
88025	BUCKHORN	82	59	84	57	61	83	60	77	67	56	66	58	48	67	60	74	43	71	80	91
88026	SANTA CLARA	61	45	49	40	44	54	46	53	51	48	51	38	38	52	43	55	35	52	54	63
88030	DEMING	60	45	58	43	46	59	47	56	52	46	51	41	39	52	45	56	34	53	59	66
88039	GLENWOOD	55	53	67	49	59	63	50	59	53	54	52	39	50	49	55	56	35	57	66	68
88041	HANOVER	82	59	84	57	61	83	61	77	67	57	66	58	49	67	60	74	44	71	80	91
88042	HILLSBORO	52	50	64	46	56	60	48	56	50	52	49	37	47	46	52	53	33	54	63	64
88043	HURLEY	66	48	69	47	50	69	51	64	57	46	55	48	42	56	51	62	37	59	68	75
88044	LA MESA	68	57	46	51	55	55	56	60	60	61	60	39	50	61	51	61	41	59	59	67
88045	LORDSBURG	64	48	53	46	48	60	53	58	58	51	57	43	44	58	48	62	39	57	62	69
	NEW MEXICO	88	81	80	79	80	83	82	84	83	83	83	63	78	84	80	84	58	84	84	98
	UNITED STATES	100	100	100	100	100	100	100	100	100	100	100	100	100	100	100	100	100	100	100	100

ZIP CODE			POPULATION			2000-2009 ANNUAL RATE		HOUSEHOLDS					FAMILIES		
#	POST OFFICE NAME	COUNTY FIPS CODE	2000	2009	2014	% Rate	State Centile	2000	2009	2014	% Annual Rate 2000-2009	2009 Average HH Size	2000	2009	% Annual Rate 2000-2009
88047	MESILLA PARK	013	1578	2048	2209	2.9	92	512	682	742	3.1	3.00	424	551	2.9
88048	MESQUITE	013	3400	4102	4607	2.0	84	939	1160	1316	2.3	3.54	830	1004	2.1
88049	MIMBRES	017	1203	1260	1282	0.5	43	479	528	543	1.1	2.38	335	354	0.6
88061	SILVER CITY	017	19737	19647	19591	0.0	20	7847	8239	8330	0.5	2.33	5450	5499	0.1
88063	SUNLAND PARK	013	11986	15150	17095	2.6	91	2998	3959	4511	3.1	3.83	2692	3490	2.8
88072	VADO	013	3069	3809	4275	2.4	88	814	1045	1184	2.7	3.64	737	930	2.5
88081	CHAPARRAL	013	10172	12593	13786	2.3	87	2921	3730	4124	2.7	3.37	2438	3029	2.4
88101	CLOVIS	009	41494	42515	42873	0.3	33	15426	16334	16605	0.6	2.54	10888	11095	0.2
88103	CANNON AFB	009	547	433	407	-2.5	1	189	154	144	-2.2	2.40	143	113	-2.5
88112	BROADVIEW	009	88	98	101	1.2	69	38	44	46	1.6	2.23	28	31	1.1
88113	CAUSEY	041	93	102	106	1.0	64	33	37	38	1.2	2.76	26	28	0.8
88114	CROSSROADS	025	23	25	26	0.9	60	10	11	12	1.0	2.27	7	8	1.5
88116	ELIDA	041	484	518	534	0.7	51	201	219	226	0.9	2.37	156	165	0.6
88118	FLOYD	041	249	266	274	0.7	51	96	104	108	0.9	2.56	75	79	0.6
88119	FORT SUMNER	011	1917	1921	1930	0.0	20	792	812	820	0.3	2.28	518	506	-0.3
88120	GRADY	009	276	306	317	1.1	68	112	128	134	1.5	2.39	83	92	1.1
88121	HOUSE	037	147	156	158	0.6	46	66	73	75	1.1	2.00	48	51	0.7
88123	LINGO	041	49	54	56	1.1	68	16	18	19	1.3	3.00	13	13	0.0
88124	MELROSE	009	1167	1240	1261	0.7	51	477	522	537	1.0	2.34	332	347	0.5
88125	MILNESAND	041	18	20	21	1.1	68	5	6	6	2.0	3.33	4	4	0.0
88126	PEP	041	110	121	126	1.0	64	51	57	59	1.2	2.12	40	43	0.8
88130	PORTALES	041	16697	17884	18195	0.7	51	6132	6408	6532	0.5	2.57	4148	4152	0.0
88132	ROGERS	041	312	344	357	1.1	68	101	113	117	1.2	3.04	79	85	0.8
88133	SAINT VRAIN	009	27	27	26	0.0	20	10	10	10	0.0	2.60	8	8	0.0
88134	TAIBAN	011	117	115	114	-0.2	10	38	38	39	0.0	3.03	28	27	-0.4
88135	TEXICO	009	1528	1681	1736	1.0	64	547	620	647	1.4	2.71	412	451	1.0
88136	YESO	011	209	205	204	-0.2	10	94	95	96	0.1	2.16	71	69	-0.3
88201	ROSWELL	005	23540	24340	24647	0.4	40	9365	9885	10086	0.6	2.38	6493	6586	0.2
88203	ROSWELL	005	30001	30826	31134	0.3	33	10746	11130	11306	0.4	2.67	7593	7548	-0.1
88210	ARTESIA	015	16013	16688	16946	0.4	40	5913	6328	6478	0.7	2.63	4317	4453	0.3
88213	CAPROCK	025	25	27	29	0.8	55	11	13	13	1.8	2.08	8	9	1.3
88220	CARLSBAD	015	33198	32875	32838	-0.1	14	12635	12962	13066	0.3	2.48	9092	8989	-0.1
88230	DEXTER	005	5043	5471	5599	0.9	60	1530	1678	1727	1.0	3.17	1274	1362	0.7
88231	EUNICE	025	2892	3197	3333	1.1	68	1062	1212	1276	1.4	2.64	809	893	1.1
88232	HAGERMAN	005	1968	2160	2220	1.0	64	645	721	746	1.2	2.98	498	539	0.9
88240	HOBBS	025	31445	32686	33420	0.4	40	11109	11911	12297	0.8	2.63	8093	8364	0.4
88242	HOBBS	025	5214	5703	5936	1.0	64	1822	2068	2179	1.4	2.63	1495	1656	1.1
88250	HOPE	005	276	286	292	0.4	40	114	122	125	0.7	2.34	89	92	0.4
88252	JAL	025	2116	2317	2413	1.0	64	794	900	945	1.4	2.57	597	653	1.0
88253	LAKE ARTHUR	005	885	973	1003	1.0	64	278	311	323	1.2	3.13	224	244	0.9
88256	LOVING	015	2026	2193	2254	0.9	60	678	759	789	1.2	2.89	531	576	0.9
88260	LOVINGTON	025	12263	13094	13551	0.7	51	4297	4756	4971	1.1	2.70	3267	3499	0.7
88264	MALJAMAR	025	62	68	71	1.0	64	23	26	27	1.3	2.62	19	21	1.1
88265	MONUMENT	025	185	222	237	2.0	84	73	90	97	2.3	2.47	56	67	2.0
88267	TATUM	025	1284	1399	1453	0.9	60	497	565	593	1.4	2.48	362	396	1.0
88301	CARRIZOZO	027	1450	1667	1792	1.5	76	613	732	799	1.9	2.15	401	456	1.4
88310	ALAMOGORDO	035	41006	41544	41627	0.1	23	15762	16318	16494	0.4	2.50	11267	11222	0.0
88312	ALTO	027	1730	2507	2823	4.1	98	766	1159	1323	4.6	2.16	590	862	4.2
88314	BENT	035	288	329	345	1.4	75	109	129	137	1.8	2.55	78	89	1.4
88316	CAPITAN	027	2363	2864	3131	2.1	84	952	1196	1325	2.5	2.37	674	812	2.0
88317	CLOUDCROFT	035	3286	3718	3848	1.3	72	1440	1685	1761	1.7	2.21	1048	1168	1.2
88318	CORONA	027	417	472	502	1.3	72	166	196	212	1.8	2.41	114	129	1.3
88321	ENCINO	057	128	117	114	-1.0	1	59	55	54	-0.8	2.11	44	40	-1.0
88324	GLENCOE	027	197	212	238	0.8	55	81	90	102	1.1	2.36	62	66	0.7
88330	HOLLOMAN AIR FORCE B	035	2076	2574	2546	2.4	88	393	385	380	-0.2	3.12	380	371	-0.3
88336	HONDO	027	214	248	269	1.6	79	80	97	107	2.1	2.56	57	66	1.6
88337	LA LUZ	035	2342	2494	2549	0.7	51	958	1074	1110	1.2	2.32	702	757	0.8
88338	LINCOLN	027	51	59	64	1.6	79	26	32	35	2.3	1.84	18	21	1.7
88339	MAYHILL	035	509	581	625	1.4	75	221	260	283	1.8	2.23	155	174	1.3
88340	MESCALERO	035	3155	3142	3156	0.0	20	854	897	911	0.5	3.50	711	729	0.3
88341	NOGAL	027	561	659	713	1.8	81	232	284	312	2.2	2.23	170	201	1.8
88343	PICACHO	027	40	46	50	1.5	76	15	18	20	2.0	2.56	11	12	0.9
88344	PINON	005	67	66	66	-0.2	10	26	26	27	0.0	2.54	20	19	-0.6
88345	RUIDOSO	027	11328	12353	13005	0.9	60	4872	5502	5850	1.3	2.23	3249	3493	0.8
88346	RUIDOSO DOWNS	027	371	375	418	0.1	23	135	140	158	0.4	2.68	98	97	-0.1
88347	SACRAMENTO	035	114	128	139	1.3	72	51	58	64	1.4	2.21	36	38	0.6
88348	SAN PATRICIO	027	491	569	616	1.6	79	179	218	239	2.2	2.61	127	147	1.6
88351	TINNIE	027	198	230	249	1.6	79	85	103	114	2.1	2.22	60	70	1.7
88352	TULAROSA	035	5261	5559	5689	0.6	46	2028	2230	2303	1.0	2.49	1425	1504	0.6
88353	VAUGHN	019	616	592	574	-0.4	8	264	264	260	0.0	2.24	180	172	-0.5
88354	WEED	035	207	214	226	0.4	40	85	89	95	0.5	2.39	59	58	-0.2
88401	TUCUMCARI	037	7889	7314	7157	-0.8	5	3244	3119	3085	-0.4	2.29	2165	1990	-0.9
88410	AMISTAD	059	156	147	144	-0.6	7	58	56	56	-0.4	2.63	43	40	-0.8
88411	BARD	037	27	25	24	-0.8	5	13	13	13	0.0	1.92	9	9	0.0
88414	CAPULIN	059	59	55	54	-0.8	5	25	24	24	-0.4	2.29	18	17	-0.6
88415	CLAYTON	059	3145	3020	2979	-0.4	8	1317	1309	1302	-0.1	2.29	870	827	-0.5
88416	CONCHAS DAM	047	444	477	492	0.8	55	198	218	228	1.0	2.19	134	140	0.5
88417	CUERVO	019	68	73	73	0.8	55	31	33	33	0.7	1.73	23	24	0.5
88418	DES MOINES	059	292	275	269	-0.6	7	119	116	114	-0.3	2.37	88	82	-0.8
88419	FOLSOM	059	149	140	137	-0.7	6	64	62	61	-0.3	2.26	47	44	-0.7
88421	GARITA	047	84	90	93	0.7	51	40	44	46	1.0	2.05	27	28	0.4
88422	GLADSTONE	059	42	39	39	-0.8	5	19	18	18	-0.6	2.17	14	13	-0.8
88424	GRENVILLE	059	239	225	220	-0.7	6	103	100	99	-0.3	2.25	76	71	-0.7
88426	LOGAN	037	1207	1120	1093	-0.8	5	525	510	505	-0.3	2.20	371	346	-0.8
88427	MC ALISTER	037	142	147	148	0.4	40	55	59	60	0.8	2.36	40	42	0.5
88430	NARA VISA	037	123	114	111	-0.8	5	55	53	53	-0.4	2.15	39	36	-0.9
88431	NEWKIRK	019	23	25	25	0.9	60	10	11	11	1.0	1.73	7	8	1.5
88434	SAN JON	037	565	524	512	-0.8	5	223	217	214	-0.3	2.41	158	147	-0.8
88435	SANTA ROSA	019	3440	3461	3399	0.1	23	1152	1183	1173	0.3	2.46	799	788	-0.1
88436	SEDAN	059	111	104	102	-0.7	6	36	35	35	-0.3	2.97	26	25	-0.4
88439	TREMENTINA	047	142	153	157	0.8	55	69	76	79	1.1	2.01	47	49	0.5
	NEW MEXICO					1.3					1.6	2.56			1.2
	UNITED STATES					1.0					1.1	2.59			0.9

POPULATION COMPOSITION

ZIP CODE #	POST OFFICE NAME	RACE (%) White 2000	White 2009	Black 2000	Black 2009	Asian/Pacific 2000	Asian/Pacific 2009	% Hispanic Origin 2000	% Hispanic Origin 2009	2009 AGE DISTRIBUTION (%) 0-4	5-9	10-14	15-19	20-24	25-44	45-64	65-84	85+	18+	MEDIAN AGE 2009	% 2009 Males	% 2009 Females
88047	MESILLA PARK	68.5	66.3	0.6	0.6	0.5	0.6	70.8	76.4	9.2	8.7	8.2	8.7	7.7	26.4	23.1	7.4	0.7	68.7	29.7	49.4	50.6
88048	MESQUITE	57.7	57.6	0.4	0.5	0.2	0.2	90.8	92.1	9.9	9.5	8.9	9.4	8.3	25.9	20.7	6.8	0.7	66.0	27.6	49.1	50.9
88049	MIMBRES	82.2	81.9	0.2	0.2	0.6	0.6	40.1	41.0	5.6	5.8	6.1	6.0	5.6	18.7	32.1	17.6	2.5	78.8	46.4	50.7	49.3
88061	SILVER CITY	76.6	76.5	0.6	0.6	0.4	0.4	42.6	42.9	6.9	6.6	6.4	6.7	6.2	23.2	27.4	14.4	2.1	76.1	39.7	48.6	51.4
88063	SUNLAND PARK	69.2	69.5	0.5	0.5	0.1	0.1	97.5	97.8	10.0	9.8	9.3	9.5	7.9	26.1	19.4	7.3	0.7	65.0	27.3	48.4	51.6
88072	VADO	53.3	53.4	1.0	1.1	0.1	0.1	92.4	93.3	10.2	9.6	9.1	9.7	8.2	26.3	19.8	6.4	0.7	65.2	27.0	50.0	50.0
88081	CHAPARRAL	70.5	69.4	1.3	1.4	0.5	0.5	71.5	74.5	9.6	9.4	9.2	9.8	7.9	25.6	21.4	6.6	0.5	65.2	27.6	49.8	50.2
88101	CLOVIS	71.9	69.6	7.1	7.8	2.0	2.5	31.1	33.4	8.9	7.8	7.1	7.4	8.9	26.6	21.8	9.8	1.8	72.0	31.6	49.6	50.4
88103	CANNON AFB	69.0	64.2	12.1	14.1	5.9	7.6	12.5	13.6	14.1	8.5	5.1	9.0	30.9	31.4	0.9	0.0	0.0	70.0	22.1	57.3	42.7
88112	BROADVIEW	94.3	92.9	0.0	0.0	0.0	0.0	8.0	9.2	6.1	6.1	6.1	7.1	4.1	20.4	31.6	16.3	2.0	78.6	45.0	54.1	45.9
88113	CAUSEY	82.8	81.4	1.1	1.0	0.0	0.0	22.6	25.5	7.8	7.8	7.8	7.8	3.9	25.5	26.5	10.8	2.0	71.6	36.9	50.0	50.0
88114	CROSSROADS	72.7	72.0	0.0	0.0	0.0	0.0	31.8	32.0	8.0	8.0	8.0	8.0	4.0	32.0	32.0	0.0	0.0	68.0	33.8	52.0	48.0
88116	ELIDA	88.7	87.5	0.2	0.2	0.0	0.0	20.8	23.6	5.8	6.6	7.1	7.3	3.9	23.4	28.6	15.4	1.9	75.7	41.9	50.4	49.6
88118	FLOYD	88.8	87.6	0.0	0.0	0.0	0.0	21.3	24.1	5.6	6.4	7.1	7.1	3.8	24.1	28.6	15.4	1.9	76.3	41.8	49.6	50.4
88119	FORT SUMNER	83.8	83.8	0.1	0.1	0.1	0.1	37.6	37.8	5.4	5.9	6.8	5.9	3.8	19.5	26.0	21.1	5.5	78.2	46.9	48.2	51.8
88120	GRADY	93.8	93.1	0.0	0.0	0.0	0.0	8.0	9.2	5.6	6.2	6.5	6.9	4.6	21.6	30.1	16.3	2.3	77.5	44.0	53.6	46.4
88121	HOUSE	95.2	93.6	0.0	0.6	1.4	1.3	9.6	10.3	3.8	4.5	5.1	6.4	3.2	18.6	34.0	16.7	7.7	81.4	48.8	51.3	48.7
88123	LINGO	81.6	77.8	0.0	1.9	0.0	0.0	22.4	24.1	7.4	7.4	7.4	7.4	3.7	29.6	25.9	11.1	0.0	70.4	36.3	51.9	48.1
88124	MELROSE	92.8	91.6	0.4	0.5	0.6	0.8	10.7	12.4	5.6	6.2	6.6	6.8	5.4	22.1	28.6	15.6	3.0	76.9	42.3	49.8	50.2
88125	MILNESAND	83.3	85.0	0.0	0.0	0.0	0.0	22.2	25.0	10.0	10.0	10.0	10.0	0.0	35.0	25.0	0.0	0.0	60.0	32.5	50.0	50.0
88126	PEP	82.7	81.0	0.9	0.8	0.0	0.0	22.7	25.6	7.4	7.4	8.3	8.3	5.0	25.6	24.8	11.6	1.7	71.9	35.9	49.6	50.4
88130	PORTALES	73.2	71.1	1.7	1.9	0.7	0.9	34.2	36.9	7.5	6.9	6.6	10.9	10.9	25.4	20.4	9.5	1.8	74.4	29.4	48.9	51.1
88132	ROGERS	82.6	80.5	1.0	1.2	0.0	0.0	22.8	25.9	7.6	7.6	8.4	8.7	4.4	24.4	26.2	11.3	1.5	71.2	36.3	49.7	50.3
88133	SAINT VRAIN	96.2	92.6	0.0	0.0	0.0	0.0	7.7	7.4	3.7	7.4	7.4	7.4	7.4	25.9	37.0	3.7	0.0	74.1	38.8	51.9	48.1
88134	TAIBAN	84.6	84.3	0.0	0.0	0.9	0.9	23.9	23.5	6.1	7.0	6.1	4.3	4.3	22.6	31.3	16.5	1.7	76.5	44.7	53.9	46.1
88135	TEXICO	67.2	64.5	3.9	4.5	0.6	0.7	36.8	39.7	7.3	7.4	7.4	7.7	6.3	24.3	26.2	12.1	1.3	73.2	37.2	50.2	49.8
88136	YESO	85.2	84.9	0.0	0.0	1.0	1.0	20.0	20.5	6.8	6.8	6.8	4.9	3.9	22.4	30.7	16.6	1.0	76.1	43.7	54.1	45.9
88201	ROSWELL	82.1	80.7	1.1	1.2	0.8	1.0	29.8	32.1	5.8	5.9	6.2	7.8	5.8	21.1	28.5	15.4	3.4	77.6	42.5	48.7	51.3
88203	ROSWELL	65.6	63.6	3.0	3.3	0.5	0.6	51.3	54.6	8.1	7.8	7.5	8.3	7.4	25.1	22.9	10.7	2.1	71.5	32.7	49.3	50.7
88210	ARTESIA	74.0	72.4	1.2	1.3	0.3	0.3	42.3	45.4	7.8	7.4	7.4	8.0	6.2	23.4	26.3	11.5	1.9	72.5	36.5	49.1	50.9
88213	CAPROCK	72.0	70.4	0.0	0.0	0.0	0.0	32.0	33.3	7.4	7.4	7.4	7.4	7.4	29.6	29.6	3.7	0.0	70.4	33.8	48.1	51.9
88220	CARLSBAD	78.1	76.5	1.8	2.0	0.7	0.9	35.4	38.1	7.2	6.9	7.0	7.1	6.0	23.2	27.3	12.6	2.6	74.6	38.7	48.9	51.1
88230	DEXTER	64.2	62.2	0.8	0.8	0.1	0.2	57.3	60.8	7.6	7.4	8.0	8.9	6.9	26.2	24.8	9.2	0.9	71.1	33.3	51.7	48.3
88231	EUNICE	72.8	70.2	1.1	1.3	0.1	0.1	37.0	40.8	7.3	6.8	7.5	7.7	6.2	25.4	26.5	11.1	1.6	73.9	36.2	50.2	49.8
88232	HAGERMAN	68.6	66.9	0.3	0.3	0.5	0.6	60.2	63.9	8.5	10.2	9.2	9.6	4.6	22.9	22.8	11.1	1.2	65.4	32.3	50.0	50.0
88240	HOBBS	65.0	62.9	6.4	7.0	0.5	0.6	40.5	42.9	8.2	7.7	7.4	7.8	7.6	26.3	22.9	10.4	1.6	72.2	32.8	50.2	49.8
88242	HOBBS	83.3	81.0	1.1	1.2	0.6	0.8	20.9	23.7	6.8	7.1	7.9	8.5	6.3	27.3	27.4	7.9	0.7	72.9	35.7	51.8	48.2
88250	HOPE	78.3	76.6	0.7	0.7	0.0	0.0	32.9	36.7	6.6	6.6	7.3	7.3	6.3	24.8	30.8	9.4	0.7	74.8	37.9	51.4	48.6
88252	JAL	67.4	64.4	0.6	0.6	0.0	0.0	40.4	44.4	6.7	6.5	6.4	6.9	6.6	21.7	27.4	15.8	2.1	76.1	40.6	48.2	51.8
88253	LAKE ARTHUR	69.6	67.5	0.6	0.7	0.3	0.3	52.0	56.2	8.6	9.4	9.5	9.1	5.2	24.7	23.6	9.0	0.8	66.1	32.5	51.9	48.1
88256	LOVING	65.2	63.9	0.3	0.4	0.2	0.2	66.8	70.3	7.9	7.8	7.8	8.3	6.5	23.2	26.9	10.4	1.2	71.5	35.0	49.1	50.9
88260	LOVINGTON	63.9	61.3	2.5	2.8	0.4	0.5	46.8	50.2	8.1	7.6	7.5	8.5	6.9	24.2	24.3	11.1	1.7	71.4	33.9	49.5	50.5
88264	MALJAMAR	81.0	79.4	1.6	1.5	0.0	0.0	22.2	25.0	5.9	5.9	5.9	7.4	5.9	20.6	32.4	14.7	1.5	76.5	43.8	50.0	50.0
88265	MONUMENT	83.8	82.0	0.5	0.5	0.5	0.5	22.2	25.2	5.9	6.8	6.8	6.8	5.4	23.4	30.6	13.1	1.4	75.7	41.3	49.5	50.5
88267	TATUM	68.2	65.0	0.7	0.9	0.1	0.1	34.0	37.8	5.1	6.1	7.6	8.8	4.5	22.8	28.4	14.4	2.3	75.6	41.5	49.5	50.5
88301	CARRIZOZO	77.6	76.3	0.5	0.5	0.1	0.1	43.9	47.0	5.3	5.5	5.8	6.6	5.7	20.6	28.0	19.6	2.8	79.3	45.3	51.1	48.9
88310	ALAMOGORDO	76.4	73.9	5.0	5.5	1.6	2.1	31.0	33.2	7.7	7.0	6.7	7.0	7.3	26.8	24.4	11.5	1.6	74.3	35.5	49.7	50.3
88312	ALTO	88.8	87.8	0.0	0.0	0.1	0.1	16.7	18.4	3.7	4.2	4.7	4.7	3.6	17.1	39.1	21.6	1.4	84.5	52.5	49.2	50.8
88314	BENT	74.0	70.2	0.3	0.3	0.3	0.3	38.9	41.3	6.1	6.4	7.0	7.0	5.2	20.7	32.2	14.0	1.5	76.0	43.1	48.6	51.4
88316	CAPITAN	89.2	88.1	0.5	0.6	0.4	0.5	18.4	20.2	5.2	5.4	6.4	7.5	4.2	19.7	34.8	15.1	1.6	78.0	45.9	50.2	49.8
88317	CLOUDCROFT	93.4	92.5	0.2	0.2	0.4	0.4	14.6	15.6	4.0	4.6	5.1	5.5	4.2	16.1	38.4	20.8	1.3	82.8	51.1	49.8	50.2
88318	CORONA	80.8	79.4	0.0	0.0	0.2	0.2	30.2	32.6	5.3	6.4	7.0	6.4	3.8	19.3	32.8	17.2	1.9	77.5	46.4	50.4	49.6
88321	ENCINO	71.7	70.1	0.0	0.0	0.0	0.0	56.7	59.8	4.3	4.3	5.1	4.3	5.1	19.7	35.0	19.7	2.6	83.8	49.7	53.8	46.2
88324	GLENCOE	86.3	85.4	0.0	0.0	0.0	0.0	21.8	24.1	3.8	4.7	4.7	5.2	3.8	16.5	38.7	21.2	1.4	83.5	52.0	49.5	50.5
88330	HOLLOMAN AIR FORCE B	73.3	69.7	13.2	14.8	3.4	4.3	12.4	13.6	6.5	5.4	4.7	11.3	39.2	29.1	3.5	0.3	0.0	80.3	22.8	64.7	35.3
88336	HONDO	66.4	64.9	0.5	0.8	0.0	0.0	62.1	64.5	5.2	5.6	6.0	6.9	6.0	19.8	31.9	16.5	2.0	78.6	45.2	49.2	50.8
88337	LA LUZ	87.5	85.3	0.3	0.4	0.7	0.9	22.4	25.0	5.9	6.3	6.7	6.3	4.7	21.1	32.8	14.8	1.2	77.1	44.1	48.8	51.2
88338	LINCOLN	66.7	66.1	0.0	0.0	0.0	0.0	62.7	64.4	5.1	5.1	6.8	6.8	6.8	18.6	32.2	16.9	1.7	76.3	45.4	47.5	52.5
88339	MAYHILL	97.0	96.2	0.2	0.2	0.0	0.0	7.9	9.0	2.9	3.4	4.1	5.5	4.3	15.3	39.4	23.6	1.4	85.7	53.2	50.6	49.4
88340	MESCALERO	4.8	2.9	0.2	0.2	0.1	0.1	11.3	8.5	10.2	11.3	10.7	10.3	8.1	28.1	17.6	3.5	0.2	61.1	24.6	47.5	52.5
88341	NOGAL	87.4	86.6	0.4	0.3	0.0	0.0	22.8	24.6	4.9	4.6	6.4	9.7	3.3	20.6	35.2	13.5	1.8	77.7	45.3	53.0	47.0
88343	PICACHO	66.7	65.2	0.0	0.0	0.0	0.0	64.1	65.2	4.3	4.3	6.5	6.5	4.3	17.4	37.0	17.4	2.2	78.3	48.0	47.8	52.2
88344	PINON	80.9	78.8	0.0	0.0	0.0	0.0	29.4	33.3	6.1	6.1	6.1	7.6	6.1	24.2	28.8	15.2	0.0	75.8	40.0	51.5	48.5
88345	RUIDOSO	84.0	81.8	0.4	0.4	0.4	0.6	22.9	25.9	4.9	5.3	5.6	5.9	4.3	19.8	33.9	18.4	1.8	80.7	47.8	47.7	52.3
88346	RUIDOSO DOWNS	77.7	77.1	0.5	0.5	0.5	0.3	31.5	33.3	5.9	6.7	6.1	6.7	4.8	20.8	33.6	14.7	0.8	77.6	44.2	47.7	52.3
88347	SACRAMENTO	97.4	96.9	0.0	0.0	0.0	0.0	7.0	7.8	3.1	3.1	3.9	5.5	3.9	15.6	39.8	23.4	1.6	85.2	53.8	50.8	49.2
88348	SAN PATRICIO	66.2	65.2	0.6	0.7	0.0	0.0	61.9	64.9	5.4	5.6	6.0	7.0	6.0	19.9	32.0	16.2	1.9	78.6	45.1	50.1	49.9
88351	TINNIE	66.7	65.7	0.5	0.9	0.0	0.0	60.6	63.5	5.2	5.7	6.1	7.0	6.1	19.1	32.6	16.1	2.2	78.3	45.5	50.0	50.0
88352	TULAROSA	74.8	71.5	0.6	0.7	0.6	0.7	41.7	43.6	6.6	6.7	7.0	7.2	5.4	21.0	30.0	14.4	1.7	75.2	41.6	47.4	52.6
88353	VAUGHN	51.4	51.7	0.0	0.0	0.0	0.0	84.4	84.3	7.3	7.1	7.3	6.6	3.9	22.8	25.2	17.7	2.2	74.3	40.7	45.8	54.2
88354	WEED	96.1	94.4	0.0	0.0	0.0	0.0	8.7	9.8	2.8	3.7	4.2	6.1	3.7	15.0	39.7	23.4	1.4	84.6	53.8	51.4	48.6
88401	TUCUMCARI	79.6	78.2	1.0	1.1	1.1	1.4	43.6	46.8	5.9	5.9	5.9	7.2	5.8	21.7	28.7	15.9	3.0	77.7	43.0	48.6	51.4
88410	AMISTAD	87.7	86.4	0.0	0.0	0.6	0.7	18.1	20.4	6.1	7.5	7.5	6.8	4.1	21.1	31.3	14.3	1.4	74.8	42.2	49.7	50.3
88411	BARD	92.3	92.0	0.0	0.0	0.0	0.0	19.2	20.0	8.0	8.0	8.0	8.0	4.0	16.0	32.0	16.0	0.0	68.0	43.8	48.0	52.0
88414	CAPULIN	86.4	85.5	0.0	0.0	0.0	0.0	18.6	20.0	7.3	7.3	7.3	7.3	3.6	21.8	30.9	14.5	0.0	70.9	41.9	52.7	47.3
88415	CLAYTON	78.2	76.7	0.0	0.0	0.4	0.4	40.8	43.9	6.1	6.1	6.3	7.0	6.2	21.7	27.5	16.4	2.7	76.7	42.0	49.0	51.0
88416	CONCHAS DAM	70.5	68.6	0.0	0.0	0.2	0.4	50.0	53.7	5.0	5.9	5.7	5.0	2.1	19.3	35.8	17.4	3.8	80.3	49.5	51.6	48.4
88417	CUERVO	69.1	69.9	2.9	2.7	0.0	0.0	67.6	67.1	4.1	4.1	4.1	5.5	11.0	41.1	23.3	6.8	0.0	83.6	34.6	75.3	24.7
88418	DES MOINES	87.0	85.5	0.0	0.0	0.7	0.7	18.2	20.0	6.5	7.3	7.3	6.9	4.0	21.5	31.3	13.8	1.5	74.5	42.0	50.2	49.8
88419	FOLSOM	87.2	86.4	0.0	0.0	0.7	0.7	18.1	20.7	6.4	7.9	7.9	6.4	4.3	20.7	30.0	15.0	1.4	73.6	41.9	47.9	52.1
88421	GARITA	71.1	68.9	0.0	0.0	0.0	0.0	50.6	53.3	4.4	5.6	5.6	5.6	2.2	20.0	36.7	16.7	3.3	80.0	49.3	51.1	48.9
88422	GLADSTONE	88.1	87.2	0.0	0.0	0.0	0.0	19.0	20.5	5.1	7.7	7.7	5.1	5.1	20.5	30.8	17.9	0.0	74.4	43.8	46.2	53.8
88424	GRENVILLE	87.0	85.8	0.0	0.0	0.8	0.9	18.4	20.4	6.7	7.6	7.6	6.7	4.0	21.3	30.7	13.8	1.8	73.3	41.7	50.7	49.3
88426	LOGAN	90.1	88.7	0.2	0.3	0.1	0.1	19.9	23.0	4.6	5.5	6.4	6.8	3.5	18.6	31.0	21.5	2.1	78.6	47.9	49.6	50.4
88427	MC ALISTER	94.3	92.5	0.0	0.7	0.7	1.4	10.6	12.9	4.1	4.8	5.4	6.8	3.4	19.7	32.0	17.7	6.1	80.3	48.3	49.7	50.3
88430	NARA VISA	90.2	88.6	0.0	0.0	0.0	0.0	19.5	22.8	4.4	5.3	6.1	7.0	3.5	18.4	32.5	21.1	1.8	78.9	48.3	50.9	49.1
88431	NEWKIRK	69.6	68.0	4.3	4.0	0.0	0.0	69.6	68.0	4.0	4.0	4.0	4.0	16.0	48.0	20.0	0.0	0.0	88.0	32.5	88.0	12.0
88434	SAN JON	90.1	88.7	0.2	0.2	0.2	0.2	19.8	23.1	4.8	5.5	6.5	6.9	3.6	18.7	30.7	21.2	2.1	78.2	47.6	49.2	50.8
88435	SANTA ROSA	58.0	58.8	1.7	1.6	0.7	0.7	80.1	79.3	5.1	5.4	5.7	7.0	7.9	29.6	26.4	10.8	2.0	79.2	38.1	57.5	42.5
88436	SEDAN	86.6	85.6	0.0	0.0	0.9	1.0	17.9	21.2	6.7	7.7	7.7	6.7	3.8	21.2	29.8	14.4	1.9	72.1	41.7	50.0	50.0
88439	TREMENTINA	70.9	68.0	0.0	0.0	0.0	0.7	50.4	53.6	5.2	5.9	5.9	5.2	2.0	20.3	35.9	16.3	3.3	79.1	48.5	51.6	48.4
	NEW MEXICO	66.8	65.0	1.9	2.0	1.1	1.4	42.1	44.2	7.3	7.1	7.0	7.5	7.2	26.0	25.9	10.5	1.6	74.2	35.5	49.3	50.7
	UNITED STATES	75.1	72.0	12.3	12.7	3.8	4.6	12.5	15.7	6.8	6.7	6.6	7.1	6.9	27.0	26.0	10.9	1.9	75.7	36.9	49.2	50.8

#	POST OFFICE NAME	2009 Per Capita Income	2009 HH Income Base	2009 Household Income Distribution (%) Less than $25,000	$25,000 to $49,999	$50,000 to $99,999	$100,000 to $149,999	$150,000 or More	Median Household Income 2009	2014	2009 National Centile	2009 State Centile	2009 Home Value Base	2009 Home Value Distribution (%) Less than $50,000	$50,000 to $89,999	$90,000 to $174,999	$175,000 to $399,999	$400,000 or More	2009 Median Home Value
88047	MESILLA PARK	16718	682	35.2	30.1	24.6	4.8	5.3	35565	37081	19	48	527	36.8	11.2	20.7	23.7	7.6	97500
88048	MESQUITE	10249	1160	42.2	36.5	18.4	1.9	1.0	27813	29080	5	15	887	48.3	19.7	23.0	7.4	1.6	52981
88049	MIMBRES	19202	528	34.3	30.7	30.9	2.1	2.1	36915	38648	23	54	441	12.2	20.9	37.6	19.5	9.8	140357
88061	SILVER CITY	20688	8239	31.1	31.8	30.3	4.5	2.4	39302	40713	31	65	5996	11.1	8.6	41.1	33.4	5.8	148617
88063	SUNLAND PARK	7951	3959	52.0	30.9	15.2	1.7	0.2	24057	24884	3	5	2694	28.5	34.2	34.0	1.9	1.3	72095
88072	VADO	10276	1045	38.2	36.3	23.7	1.8	0.0	31582	34465	11	32	828	38.2	29.0	27.7	5.2	0.0	61125
88081	CHAPARRAL	10846	3730	44.4	32.3	20.0	2.0	1.2	28345	31280	6	17	2996	27.5	26.0	36.4	9.5	0.6	83576
88101	CLOVIS	18936	16334	32.1	32.2	28.6	4.3	2.8	37368	39737	25	59	9688	12.5	28.3	43.0	13.8	2.4	104578
88103	CANNON AFB	15771	154	38.3	37.7	20.1	2.6	1.3	30000	32537	8	26	2	50.0	50.0	0.0	0.0	0.0	55000
88112	BROADVIEW	21327	44	25.0	31.8	36.4	4.5	2.3	42370	45000	41	76	33	15.2	12.1	48.5	15.2	9.1	123214
88113	CAUSEY	19277	37	29.7	40.5	21.6	2.7	5.4	36290	37761	21	52	29	10.3	20.7	55.2	10.3	3.4	129688
88114	CROSSROADS	16300	11	36.4	36.4	27.3	0.0	0.0	32290	35000	12	35	8	37.5	25.0	37.5	0.0	0.0	60000
88116	ELIDA	19225	219	34.7	33.3	27.4	3.2	1.4	35385	37328	19	47	148	15.5	18.2	36.5	25.7	4.1	118421
88118	FLOYD	17805	104	36.5	32.7	26.9	2.9	1.0	34195	36711	16	43	70	17.1	18.6	37.1	25.7	1.4	113889
88119	FORT SUMNER	16476	812	43.6	30.2	22.2	3.4	0.6	29002	29838	7	20	649	29.6	25.3	30.4	13.3	1.5	81711
88120	GRADY	22619	128	26.6	32.0	32.8	4.7	3.9	39433	42370	31	66	96	13.5	13.5	46.9	15.6	10.4	123750
88121	HOUSE	23805	73	27.4	35.6	30.1	4.1	2.7	37331	39091	25	58	55	30.9	18.2	36.4	12.7	1.8	91250
88123	LINGO	12407	18	38.9	38.9	16.7	5.6	0.0	32265	36091	12	34	14	7.1	14.3	57.1	21.4	0.0	135000
88124	MELROSE	18031	522	34.3	35.1	27.0	2.7	1.0	34549	36260	17	44	397	28.2	35.5	25.7	7.8	2.8	73553
88125	MILNESAND	5125	6	66.7	33.3	0.0	0.0	0.0	10000	40000	0	1	5	0.0	0.0	100.0	0.0	0.0	120833
88126	PEP	25114	57	31.6	38.6	22.8	3.5	3.5	36091	36880	21	51	44	11.4	20.5	47.7	15.9	4.5	130000
88130	PORTALES	16544	6408	40.0	27.9	26.7	3.5	2.0	33162	35717	14	41	3968	20.1	29.1	36.7	12.9	1.1	91461
88132	ROGERS	17494	113	31.0	37.2	22.1	4.4	5.3	36107	37299	21	51	87	16.1	20.7	41.4	14.9	6.9	121591
88133	SAINT VRAIN	17178	10	20.0	40.0	40.0	0.0	0.0	45000	50000	48	80	8	25.0	12.5	37.5	25.0	0.0	125000
88134	TAIBAN	13199	38	34.2	36.8	26.3	2.6	0.0	32272	32244	12	34	25	24.0	8.0	24.0	24.0	20.0	156250
88135	TEXICO	15351	620	35.6	34.5	25.8	2.4	1.6	32955	35514	13	39	441	26.5	32.7	29.9	7.7	3.2	78939
88136	YESO	18905	95	31.6	38.9	26.3	2.1	1.1	32720	32670	13	37	60	23.3	8.3	23.3	21.7	23.3	162500
88201	ROSWELL	22278	9885	28.8	31.0	30.6	6.5	3.2	41123	42647	36	73	7379	18.0	16.7	34.2	26.5	4.7	129184
88203	ROSWELL	15126	11130	39.8	32.5	23.4	2.7	1.5	30340	32438	9	28	7435	20.9	35.8	36.2	5.7	1.4	81628
88210	ARTESIA	17099	6328	34.9	29.8	29.5	4.2	1.5	36788	38110	23	54	4599	17.9	25.1	39.6	16.0	1.4	98878
88213	CAPROCK	19429	13	30.8	38.5	23.1	7.7	0.0	37321	37321	25	58	10	30.0	30.0	40.0	0.0	0.0	65000
88220	CARLSBAD	21045	12962	30.1	29.5	32.0	5.6	2.9	40861	41487	36	72	9657	14.0	28.1	38.8	16.1	3.0	99980
88230	DEXTER	14704	1678	32.3	31.5	30.6	3.9	1.7	37911	39843	26	60	1276	27.4	31.0	28.9	8.8	4.0	78224
88231	EUNICE	17345	1212	31.8	32.8	30.7	3.5	1.2	37622	40652	26	60	942	35.1	34.9	25.8	3.5	0.6	64333
88232	HAGERMAN	13322	721	39.4	34.5	22.3	2.8	1.0	30552	32510	9	28	526	35.4	30.8	22.8	8.9	2.1	67949
88240	HOBBS	17550	11911	36.1	30.4	26.6	4.9	2.1	35585	37568	19	49	8059	25.6	29.0	35.2	9.7	0.5	81539
88242	HOBBS	21124	2068	19.5	26.8	44.0	8.6	1.1	52866	52037	68	89	1764	17.6	17.2	43.5	17.8	3.9	123611
88250	HOPE	26130	122	27.0	26.2	37.7	4.9	4.1	45000	45981	48	80	94	22.3	13.8	40.4	21.3	2.1	120000
88252	JAL	18201	900	31.3	35.7	26.9	3.9	2.2	37065	39445	24	55	724	52.8	27.8	15.6	2.3	1.5	47368
88253	LAKE ARTHUR	15330	311	29.9	33.8	30.9	3.5	1.9	39865	41483	32	68	244	32.4	28.3	26.2	9.8	3.3	73125
88256	LOVING	14921	759	39.1	29.8	26.9	2.5	1.7	32877	34675	13	38	617	31.3	28.7	25.9	12.2	1.9	73295
88260	LOVINGTON	16173	4756	35.0	33.3	26.4	3.8	1.5	34984	36790	18	44	3580	20.9	36.2	33.1	9.0	0.8	79901
88264	MALJAMAR	16397	26	15.4	53.8	26.9	3.8	0.0	37321	43624	25	58	21	9.5	19.0	42.9	28.6	0.0	152500
88265	MONUMENT	16044	90	38.9	31.1	30.0	0.0	0.0	31138	32339	10	30	71	40.8	14.1	26.8	18.3	0.0	79000
88267	TATUM	16552	565	34.9	33.3	28.0	3.2	0.7	33765	34840	15	42	437	40.0	30.7	21.3	4.8	3.2	59255
88301	CARRIZOZO	18255	732	40.6	33.3	22.5	2.5	1.1	31647	35258	11	32	564	25.7	26.8	35.5	10.1	2.0	85625
88310	ALAMOGORDO	19115	16318	27.1	34.2	32.3	4.8	1.6	40506	42605	34	71	10224	13.7	19.7	46.2	18.4	2.1	115996
88312	ALTO	32231	1159	11.9	32.5	37.4	12.9	5.3	54375	53767	70	90	1005	4.9	2.9	18.5	45.6	28.2	258607
88314	BENT	16847	129	33.3	38.0	22.5	5.4	0.8	37094	39289	24	56	105	19.0	21.9	37.1	18.1	3.8	108654
88316	CAPITAN	19300	1196	35.8	31.8	26.0	4.5	1.9	34520	36566	17	44	990	9.7	13.5	41.5	30.0	5.3	142248
88317	CLOUDCROFT	23284	1685	24.2	34.1	34.5	5.2	2.0	42184	44368	40	75	1431	6.8	12.5	39.0	35.6	6.0	153661
88318	CORONA	24361	196	30.6	29.1	33.2	4.1	3.1	40341	41524	34	70	148	17.6	25.0	49.3	4.1	4.1	107353
88321	ENCINO	15476	55	40.0	45.5	10.9	3.6	0.0	27136	27361	5	12	43	41.9	23.3	23.3	9.3	2.3	55833
88324	GLENCOE	28104	90	16.7	32.2	35.6	11.1	4.4	50824	50985	63	87	77	5.2	5.2	19.5	42.9	27.3	242500
88330	HOLLOMAN AIR FORCE B	15851	385	8.1	45.2	39.7	6.0	1.0	48143	49634	57	85	27	48.1	51.9	0.0	0.0	0.0	50714
88336	HONDO	16757	97	38.1	35.1	21.6	4.1	1.0	32747	35239	13	38	74	13.5	10.8	27.0	29.7	18.9	171429
88337	LA LUZ	20535	1074	26.0	34.4	34.1	4.5	1.1	39537	42154	31	67	902	12.9	15.0	36.0	32.0	4.1	139247
88338	LINCOLN	20339	32	37.5	37.5	21.9	3.1	0.0	32326	33622	12	36	25	12.0	8.0	32.0	28.0	20.0	171875
88339	MAYHILL	19318	260	33.8	33.5	28.5	3.1	1.2	39088	41625	30	65	224	8.0	13.8	50.9	22.3	4.9	151389
88340	MESCALERO	10256	897	43.6	31.7	21.5	2.3	0.9	28050	29653	6	15	522	29.1	39.3	22.0	5.9	3.6	71791
88341	NOGAL	22550	284	31.0	26.4	34.5	6.0	2.1	40322	40531	34	70	231	8.7	13.9	26.4	41.1	10.0	177604
88343	PICACHO	16940	18	38.9	33.3	22.2	5.6	0.0	30000	35000	8	26	14	0.0	14.3	21.4	35.7	28.6	250000
88344	PINON	35721	26	19.2	30.8	30.8	7.7	11.5	47500	42380	55	83	20	20.0	10.0	50.0	15.0	5.0	132143
88345	RUIDOSO	24723	5502	28.2	28.6	32.9	6.5	3.7	43031	43952	42	77	4094	6.2	10.6	41.7	30.9	10.6	158025
88346	RUIDOSO DOWNS	20725	140	22.1	35.0	32.9	7.1	2.9	44440	45000	47	79	107	8.4	13.1	37.4	25.2	15.9	151250
88347	SACRAMENTO	18663	58	34.5	36.2	27.6	1.7	0.0	38142	41258	27	61	50	10.0	16.0	52.0	18.0	4.0	142857
88348	SAN PATRICIO	16342	218	38.5	34.9	21.1	4.1	1.4	32522	35813	12	36	167	12.0	11.4	27.5	30.5	18.6	172917
88351	TINNIE	19389	103	39.8	34.0	21.4	3.9	1.0	31126	35485	10	30	79	13.9	10.1	25.3	31.6	19.0	177500
88352	TULAROSA	16464	2230	33.4	35.6	26.8	3.8	0.4	36596	39389	22	53	1787	16.8	27.0	38.4	14.5	3.2	99605
88353	VAUGHN	14616	264	50.0	27.7	20.1	1.5	0.8	25000	25289	3	6	212	40.6	34.0	19.8	1.4	4.2	57407
88354	WEED	17109	89	38.2	34.8	23.6	2.2	1.1	33034	38808	13	40	78	11.5	20.5	48.7	14.1	5.1	127273
88401	TUCUMCARI	17653	3119	43.8	29.0	22.5	3.0	1.7	28764	30011	6	20	2129	28.2	25.1	28.6	14.0	4.0	83500
88410	AMISTAD	18443	56	33.9	28.6	32.1	3.6	1.8	38198	38198	27	62	42	14.3	35.7	23.8	11.9	14.3	90000
88411	BARD	18635	13	38.5	38.5	23.1	0.0	0.0	32308	37321	12	35	11	18.2	27.3	54.5	0.0	0.0	95000
88414	CAPULIN	21247	24	33.3	29.2	29.2	4.2	4.2	40000	45000	33	69	18	5.6	33.3	27.8	16.7	16.7	112500
88415	CLAYTON	16996	1309	37.7	35.7	23.1	2.5	0.9	31530	31419	11	31	950	26.7	29.7	31.6	9.6	2.4	82278
88416	CONCHAS DAM	20564	218	28.4	35.8	29.8	4.1	1.8	38634	43447	29	63	168	20.8	23.2	29.8	19.0	7.1	103571
88417	CUERVO	23568	33	30.3	33.3	33.3	3.0	0.0	41140	41140	36	73	23	30.4	21.7	30.4	17.4	0.0	87500
88418	DES MOINES	20227	116	32.8	27.6	31.9	4.3	3.4	40000	38199	33	69	87	16.1	33.3	26.4	10.3	13.8	91000
88419	FOLSOM	21369	62	33.9	25.8	33.9	4.8	1.6	40000	41165	33	69	46	17.4	30.4	28.3	10.9	13.0	93333
88421	GARITA	22018	44	27.3	36.4	29.5	4.5	2.3	40000	43194	33	69	34	20.6	23.5	32.4	17.6	5.9	104167
88422	GLADSTONE	15833	18	44.4	27.8	27.8	0.0	0.0	30000	35000	8	26	13	15.4	30.8	30.8	7.7	15.4	95000
88424	GRENVILLE	21398	100	34.0	27.0	32.0	4.0	3.0	38905	39446	29	64	75	17.3	32.0	25.3	12.0	13.3	91250
88426	LOGAN	16798	510	40.6	32.7	23.7	2.5	0.4	29249	30845	7	21	411	29.0	27.5	33.8	6.1	3.6	81970
88427	MC ALISTER	20789	59	28.8	33.9	32.2	3.4	1.7	37311	41134	25	57	45	28.9	17.8	33.3	15.6	4.4	95000
88430	NARA VISA	17289	53	41.5	35.8	20.8	1.9	0.0	28554	32333	6	18	43	27.9	32.6	32.6	4.7	2.3	72500
88431	NEWKIRK	22461	11	36.4	36.4	27.3	0.0	0.0	37303	37303	24	57	8	25.0	12.5	37.5	25.0	0.0	112500
88434	SAN JON	15398	217	40.1	33.2	23.5	2.8	0.5	29611	30903	7	23	175	28.6	27.4	33.1	6.3	4.6	82500
88435	SANTA ROSA	14306	1183	42.4	34.6	20.6	1.6	0.8	29495	30295	7	23	834	22.5	23.7	37.9	13.9	1.9	95439
88436	SEDAN	16181	35	34.3	25.7	31.4	5.7	2.9	38632	36136	29	63	26	15.4	34.6	23.1	11.5	15.4	90000
88439	TREMENTINA	22342	76	27.6	34.2	32.9	3.9	1.3	40000	43370	33	69	59	22.0	22.0	30.5	18.6	6.8	104167
	NEW MEXICO	22470		27.2	27.7	32.6	8.1	4.5	44681	46845				12.7	11.8	31.3	35.2	9.1	159744
	UNITED STATES	27277		20.9	24.4	35.3	11.7	7.6	54719	56938				9.3	13.1	31.6	32.6	13.5	162279

ZIP CODE		FINANCIAL SERVICES				THE HOME						ENTERTAINMENT						PERSONAL			
						Home Improvements		Furnishings													
#	POST OFFICE NAME	Auto Loan	Home Loan	Investments	Retirement Plans	Home Repair	Lawn & Garden	Computers & Hardware-Personal	Major Appliances	TV, Radio, Sound Equipment	Furniture	Dine out/ Carry out	Sports Equipment	Fees & Tickets	Toys & Games	Travel	Cable TV	Apparel & Services	Auto Repairs	Health Insurance	Pets & Supplies
88047	MESILLA PARK	81	71	58	64	68	68	70	73	73	75	73	50	64	75	64	74	51	73	71	83
88048	MESQUITE	61	49	37	41	47	46	49	52	53	55	54	32	42	54	44	55	37	53	51	58
88049	MIMBRES	82	59	84	57	61	83	60	77	67	56	66	57	48	66	60	73	43	70	80	91
88061	SILVER CITY	74	67	72	66	69	75	67	73	70	67	69	53	64	69	67	73	47	71	76	85
88063	SUNLAND PARK	51	41	31	34	39	38	41	44	45	46	45	27	36	45	37	46	31	44	43	48
88072	VADO	63	50	38	42	48	47	50	54	55	56	55	33	44	56	45	57	39	55	53	59
88081	CHAPARRAL	59	51	40	45	48	48	50	52	53	55	54	35	45	54	46	54	37	53	51	60
88101	CLOVIS	72	65	58	65	63	67	70	67	71	68	71	52	65	73	65	72	49	69	70	80
88103	CANNON AFB	67	35	26	41	31	30	63	44	59	59	63	44	48	71	46	55	44	56	39	53
88112	BROADVIEW	85	58	93	58	61	90	65	81	67	53	67	67	48	66	65	74	43	75	85	99
88113	CAUSEY	95	65	104	65	68	100	73	90	75	59	75	75	53	74	72	82	48	84	95	111
88114	CROSSROADS	66	46	73	45	48	70	51	63	53	41	52	52	37	52	50	57	34	59	66	77
88116	ELIDA	81	56	89	56	59	86	62	77	65	51	64	63	46	63	62	71	42	72	81	95
88118	FLOYD	81	56	89	56	59	86	62	77	65	50	64	64	46	63	62	71	41	72	82	95
88119	FORT SUMNER	65	46	67	45	48	68	50	63	55	44	54	48	39	54	49	61	35	58	67	74
88120	GRADY	97	67	106	66	70	102	74	92	77	60	76	76	54	75	73	84	49	86	97	113
88121	HOUSE	87	60	96	60	63	92	67	83	69	54	69	69	49	68	66	76	45	77	88	102
88123	LINGO	67	46	73	46	48	70	51	63	53	41	52	52	37	52	51	58	34	59	67	78
88124	MELROSE	73	52	75	51	54	76	57	70	62	49	60	54	44	61	55	68	40	65	76	84
88125	MILNESAND	31	21	34	21	22	32	23	29	24	19	24	24	17	24	23	26	16	27	31	36
88126	PEP	95	66	105	65	69	101	73	90	76	59	75	75	53	74	72	83	49	84	96	111
88130	PORTALES	68	54	55	53	53	61	63	62	64	58	63	48	53	64	56	65	43	64	64	74
88132	ROGERS	95	66	105	65	69	100	73	90	76	59	75	75	53	74	72	83	49	84	95	111
88133	SAINT VRAIN	82	57	90	56	59	87	63	78	65	51	65	65	46	64	62	71	42	73	82	96
88134	TAIBAN	71	49	78	49	51	75	54	68	57	44	56	55	40	56	54	62	37	63	72	83
88135	TEXICO	76	53	74	50	52	74	55	68	61	52	60	53	43	62	52	67	40	64	70	82
88136	YESO	73	50	80	50	53	77	56	69	58	45	57	57	41	57	56	63	37	64	73	85
88201	ROSWELL	79	75	80	74	76	85	73	80	77	73	76	58	72	75	75	81	52	78	86	93
88203	ROSWELL	65	53	54	51	52	61	56	60	59	54	59	44	49	60	52	63	40	60	64	71
88210	ARTESIA	73	61	64	59	60	72	61	69	66	60	65	51	54	67	59	70	44	66	71	81
88213	CAPROCK	72	50	79	50	52	76	55	68	57	45	57	57	40	56	55	63	37	64	72	84
88220	CARLSBAD	80	73	71	71	72	79	74	77	76	73	75	57	69	77	71	79	52	76	81	91
88230	DEXTER	78	64	69	60	63	72	65	71	67	66	67	54	56	69	61	70	46	69	70	84
88231	EUNICE	82	57	74	55	58	80	61	73	68	57	67	56	48	70	57	75	44	69	78	89
88232	HAGERMAN	65	55	43	48	52	52	54	57	58	60	58	38	49	59	50	59	40	58	56	65
88240	HOBBS	72	63	55	60	61	65	65	67	68	66	67	48	60	68	61	69	47	67	68	77
88242	HOBBS	89	85	73	82	82	82	80	82	80	84	81	61	77	84	76	81	55	80	80	97
88250	HOPE	101	87	88	85	87	97	84	93	89	85	88	68	77	91	81	93	60	89	94	111
88252	JAL	83	58	83	56	59	84	62	77	69	57	68	59	48	69	59	77	45	72	82	92
88253	LAKE ARTHUR	75	70	60	67	67	68	68	69	69	71	69	52	65	72	64	70	48	69	68	82
88256	LOVING	80	52	77	49	52	79	56	70	65	53	63	55	42	66	52	72	42	66	74	87
88260	LOVINGTON	71	60	59	55	59	64	60	66	63	61	63	47	53	64	57	65	43	64	66	75
88264	MALJAMAR	77	55	79	53	57	78	56	72	62	52	61	54	45	62	56	69	41	66	75	85
88265	MONUMENT	71	51	73	49	53	72	52	66	58	48	57	50	42	57	51	63	37	61	69	79
88267	TATUM	73	51	78	51	54	76	55	69	59	48	58	54	42	58	54	65	38	64	72	83
88301	CARRIZOZO	68	48	69	47	50	71	53	66	59	47	57	50	42	58	51	65	38	61	71	77
88310	ALAMOGORDO	73	67	62	66	65	69	68	68	69	68	70	52	65	71	65	71	48	69	70	81
88312	ALTO	116	93	150	92	102	123	93	118	97	87	96	86	81	93	101	104	64	109	117	137
88314	BENT	77	55	79	53	57	78	56	72	63	52	61	54	45	62	56	69	41	66	75	85
88316	CAPITAN	80	59	88	58	63	82	60	77	66	56	65	57	50	65	62	72	43	71	79	91
88317	CLOUDCROFT	84	69	105	67	75	88	69	86	72	66	71	61	61	68	74	77	48	80	86	99
88318	CORONA	105	72	115	72	76	111	80	100	83	65	82	82	59	82	80	91	53	93	105	123
88321	ENCINO	58	42	60	40	43	59	43	54	47	40	47	41	34	47	42	52	31	50	57	65
88324	GLENCOE	111	88	140	86	96	117	88	112	93	83	92	82	76	89	95	100	61	103	112	130
88330	HOLLOMAN AIR FORCE B	93	49	36	56	43	41	88	61	83	82	87	61	67	99	63	76	61	77	55	74
88336	HONDO	77	55	79	53	57	78	56	72	62	52	61	54	45	62	56	69	40	66	74	85
88337	LA LUZ	81	65	83	63	67	81	64	77	69	62	68	57	56	68	64	73	45	72	78	91
88338	LINCOLN	67	48	69	46	50	68	49	63	55	46	54	47	39	54	49	60	35	57	65	74
88339	MAYHILL	72	58	93	57	63	76	58	73	60	54	60	53	50	57	62	64	40	68	72	85
88340	MESCALERO	53	45	37	47	40	49	50	46	54	50	53	36	48	55	45	56	37	50	52	59
88341	NOGAL	85	67	107	66	73	90	68	86	72	63	71	63	58	68	73	77	47	80	86	100
88343	PICACHO	77	55	79	54	57	78	57	72	63	53	62	54	45	63	56	69	41	66	75	86
88344	PINON	162	116	166	112	120	164	119	151	132	111	130	114	95	131	118	145	86	139	158	180
88345	RUIDOSO	90	76	107	74	81	93	75	90	78	73	77	65	68	75	79	82	52	85	89	105
88346	RUIDOSO DOWNS	89	78	89	75	79	86	78	85	79	78	79	64	71	80	77	81	54	83	84	100
88347	SACRAMENTO	69	55	89	54	60	73	55	70	58	52	57	51	48	55	60	61	38	65	69	81
88348	SAN PATRICIO	76	55	78	53	57	77	56	71	62	52	61	53	45	62	55	68	40	65	74	85
88351	TINNIE	77	55	80	54	58	78	57	72	63	53	62	54	46	62	56	69	41	66	75	86
88352	TULAROSA	72	52	74	50	54	74	54	68	60	50	59	51	43	59	53	66	39	63	72	81
88353	VAUGHN	55	40	56	39	41	58	44	54	49	39	47	40	35	48	42	54	31	50	59	63
88354	WEED	66	56	84	54	61	71	55	68	58	54	57	48	50	54	60	61	38	64	70	79
88401	TUCUMCARI	69	50	66	48	52	68	54	65	60	50	58	48	44	59	52	65	39	62	69	77
88410	AMISTAD	87	60	95	59	62	91	66	82	69	54	68	68	48	67	66	75	44	77	87	101
88411	BARD	53	50	64	46	56	60	48	56	51	52	49	37	47	46	52	53	33	54	63	64
88414	CAPULIN	87	60	96	60	63	92	67	83	69	54	68	68	49	68	66	75	44	77	87	102
88415	CLAYTON	66	48	67	46	49	69	52	64	58	46	56	49	41	57	50	63	37	60	70	76
88416	CONCHAS DAM	66	63	80	58	70	75	60	71	63	65	62	46	59	58	65	67	42	68	79	81
88417	CUERVO	71	51	72	49	52	72	52	66	58	48	57	50	41	57	51	63	37	61	69	78
88418	DES MOINES	86	59	94	59	62	90	65	81	68	53	67	67	48	67	65	74	44	76	86	100
88419	FOLSOM	86	59	95	59	62	91	66	82	69	53	68	68	48	67	66	75	44	76	87	101
88421	GARITA	66	63	80	58	70	75	60	71	63	65	62	46	59	58	66	67	42	68	79	81
88422	GLADSTONE	61	42	67	42	44	65	47	58	49	38	48	48	34	48	47	53	31	54	61	72
88424	GRENVILLE	86	59	95	59	62	91	66	82	68	53	68	68	48	67	65	75	44	76	86	101
88426	LOGAN	54	52	66	48	57	62	49	58	52	53	51	38	49	48	54	55	34	56	65	66
88427	MC ALISTER	89	61	98	61	64	94	68	85	71	55	70	70	50	69	68	77	45	79	89	104
88430	NARA VISA	54	52	66	48	58	62	50	58	52	54	51	38	49	48	54	55	34	56	65	67
88431	NEWKIRK	68	49	70	47	51	69	50	64	56	47	55	48	40	55	50	61	36	59	66	76
88434	SAN JON	55	52	67	48	58	62	50	59	52	53	51	39	49	48	54	55	34	56	65	67
88435	SANTA ROSA	62	43	62	41	44	63	46	57	52	42	50	44	36	52	44	57	33	54	61	69
88436	SEDAN	86	59	94	59	62	91	66	82	68	53	68	67	48	67	65	74	44	76	86	100
88439	TREMENTINA	66	63	80	58	70	75	60	71	63	65	62	46	59	58	65	67	41	68	79	81
	NEW MEXICO	88	81	80	79	80	83	82	84	83	83	83	63	78	84	80	84	58	84	84	98
	UNITED STATES	100	100	100	100	100	100	100	100	100	100	100	100	100	100	100	100	100	100	100	100

POPULATION CHANGE

ZIP CODE #	POST OFFICE NAME	COUNTY FIPS CODE	POPULATION 2000	POPULATION 2009	POPULATION 2014	2000-2009 ANNUAL RATE % Rate	2000-2009 ANNUAL RATE State Centile	HOUSEHOLDS 2000	HOUSEHOLDS 2009	HOUSEHOLDS 2014	HOUSEHOLDS % Annual Rate 2000-2009	HOUSEHOLDS 2009 Average HH Size	FAMILIES 2000	FAMILIES 2009	FAMILIES % Annual Rate 2000-2009
06390	FISHERS ISLAND	103	289	286	284	-0.1	30	138	137	136	-0.1	2.09	78	76	-0.3
10001	NEW YORK	061	18094	20860	21961	1.5	96	9464	10786	11390	1.4	1.74	2765	2978	0.8
10002	NEW YORK	061	84867	91368	94241	0.8	84	31512	32993	33937	0.5	2.73	18664	19090	0.2
10003	NEW YORK	061	53757	55905	56718	0.4	66	29562	29892	30276	0.1	1.65	7209	6996	-0.3
10004	NEW YORK	061	1445	1285	1249	-1.3	1	728	610	588	-1.9	1.91	261	215	-2.1
10005	NEW YORK	061	907	3224	4096	14.7	100	537	1919	2439	14.8	1.67	96	328	14.2
10006	NEW YORK	061	1441	2865	3416	7.7	100	808	1631	1946	7.9	1.70	202	394	7.5
10007	NEW YORK	061	5444	8043	8828	4.3	100	2259	3540	3900	5.0	1.98	1001	1503	4.5
10009	NEW YORK	061	58595	61764	63374	0.6	76	29144	30096	30773	0.3	2.03	11672	11713	0.0
10010	NEW YORK	061	26322	28609	29625	0.9	87	15497	16527	17080	0.7	1.66	4761	4889	0.3
10011	NEW YORK	061	45873	49368	51035	0.8	84	28132	29770	30730	0.6	1.59	6514	6609	0.2
10012	NEW YORK	061	26198	27677	28414	0.6	76	13810	14289	14627	0.4	1.80	4416	4424	0.0
10013	NEW YORK	061	25360	29120	30773	1.5	96	10603	12180	12922	1.5	2.21	5393	5962	1.1
10014	NEW YORK	061	32164	32772	33167	0.2	52	20220	20264	20453	0.0	1.58	4590	4432	-0.4
10016	NEW YORK	061	50273	53760	55256	0.7	80	30138	31458	32293	0.5	1.61	7555	7581	0.0
10017	NEW YORK	061	15593	16372	16736	0.5	71	10489	10875	11120	0.4	1.49	2582	2562	-0.1
10018	NEW YORK	061	4662	5490	5976	1.8	98	2142	2597	2858	2.1	1.89	630	726	1.5
10019	NEW YORK	061	38114	42891	45351	1.3	94	23389	25681	27018	1.0	1.65	6328	6849	0.9
10021	NEW YORK	061	51426	51557	51811	0.0	38	30856	30484	30593	-0.1	1.67	10677	10192	-0.5
10022	NEW YORK	061	32274	33516	34166	0.4	66	20875	21311	21675	0.2	1.57	6690	6588	-0.2
10023	NEW YORK	061	63138	68782	71497	0.9	87	38131	40625	42061	0.7	1.64	11784	12451	0.6
10024	NEW YORK	061	60936	61200	61577	0.0	38	33535	33179	33327	-0.1	1.81	12346	11816	-0.5
10025	NEW YORK	061	95103	97980	99502	0.3	59	46326	46955	47647	0.1	1.99	18986	18638	-0.2
10026	NEW YORK	061	30792	34489	36187	1.2	93	12263	13605	14289	1.1	2.46	6694	7215	0.8
10027	NEW YORK	061	59438	63582	65455	0.7	80	22778	24089	24861	0.6	2.31	11053	11348	0.3
10028	NEW YORK	061	50646	51215	51665	0.1	44	29650	29514	29700	0.0	1.72	10347	9954	-0.4
10029	NEW YORK	061	75914	81324	83966	0.7	80	28006	29497	30413	0.6	2.66	17045	17556	0.3
10030	NEW YORK	061	25003	28329	29902	1.4	95	10427	11665	12307	1.2	2.37	5519	5991	0.9
10031	NEW YORK	061	59893	62406	63698	0.4	66	20772	21215	21592	0.2	2.90	12556	12577	0.0
10032	NEW YORK	061	63490	65979	67126	0.4	66	20778	21088	21392	0.2	3.04	13259	13222	0.0
10033	NEW YORK	061	58611	60171	60929	0.3	59	19213	19314	19501	0.1	3.07	12713	12561	-0.1
10034	NEW YORK	061	42030	42848	43304	0.2	52	15346	15354	15476	0.0	2.79	9732	9556	-0.2
10035	NEW YORK	061	33381	37909	39684	1.4	95	11407	12842	13488	1.3	2.66	6773	7407	1.0
10036	NEW YORK	061	17205	22725	24185	3.1	99	10204	13110	13974	2.7	1.66	2213	2878	2.9
10037	NEW YORK	061	16383	17043	17398	0.4	66	8325	8510	8661	0.2	1.94	3688	3667	-0.1
10038	NEW YORK	061	15215	16608	17216	1.0	89	6373	6983	7289	1.0	2.11	2963	3045	0.3
10039	NEW YORK	061	22045	24065	24931	1.0	89	9017	9636	9974	0.7	2.47	5437	5667	0.4
10040	NEW YORK	061	46325	47439	47921	0.3	59	16115	16109	16229	0.0	2.88	10612	10424	-0.2
10044	NEW YORK	061	9520	11949	12974	2.5	99	3203	4134	4553	2.8	2.36	1739	2190	2.5
10065	NEW YORK	061	28331	29583	30248	0.5	71	17240	17686	18050	0.3	1.66	5804	5775	-0.1
10075	NEW YORK	061	20393	20735	20955	0.2	52	12202	12232	12347	0.0	1.68	3619	3490	-0.4
10128	NEW YORK	061	56342	58947	60418	0.5	71	30691	31687	32424	0.3	1.84	11667	11642	0.0
10280	NEW YORK	061	6432	7125	7886	1.1	91	3607	3918	4312	0.9	1.80	1477	1555	0.6
10301	STATEN ISLAND	085	40387	43276	44657	0.7	80	15056	16199	16778	0.8	2.50	9045	9533	0.6
10302	STATEN ISLAND	085	16317	18463	19478	1.3	94	5484	6178	6522	1.3	2.96	3882	4300	1.1
10303	STATEN ISLAND	085	21096	24209	25637	1.5	96	6616	7503	7939	1.4	3.19	5033	5632	1.2
10304	STATEN ISLAND	085	38356	43422	45713	1.4	95	12980	14699	15501	1.4	2.86	9245	10304	1.2
10305	STATEN ISLAND	085	38307	42757	44901	1.2	93	14080	15707	16521	1.2	2.65	9679	10633	1.0
10306	STATEN ISLAND	085	53544	57169	59077	0.7	80	19934	21478	22270	0.8	2.64	14417	15307	0.6
10307	STATEN ISLAND	085	11666	13763	14749	1.8	98	4044	4829	5193	1.9	2.84	3060	3605	1.8
10308	STATEN ISLAND	085	28535	30019	30834	0.5	71	10281	10931	11266	0.7	2.74	7995	8402	0.5
10309	STATEN ISLAND	085	27234	32247	34609	1.8	98	8840	10650	11501	2.0	2.92	7002	8328	1.9
10310	STATEN ISLAND	085	22389	23715	24395	0.6	76	7957	8464	8729	0.7	2.78	5586	5845	0.5
10312	STATEN ISLAND	085	58448	63793	66469	1.0	89	19898	21955	22956	1.1	2.90	15970	17411	0.9
10314	STATEN ISLAND	085	87449	93099	95981	0.7	80	31171	33482	34640	0.8	2.74	23137	24513	0.6
10451	BRONX	005	42101	44774	45800	0.7	80	15157	16078	16442	0.6	2.73	9771	10185	0.4
10452	BRONX	005	72934	77578	79513	0.7	80	23036	24403	24983	0.6	3.12	17049	17799	0.5
10453	BRONX	005	76252	77548	78230	0.2	52	23963	24374	24579	0.2	3.13	17762	17811	0.0
10454	BRONX	005	34962	36863	37686	0.6	76	11362	11997	12269	0.6	3.00	7774	8066	0.4
10455	BRONX	005	36719	37677	38220	0.3	59	11723	12035	12205	0.3	3.01	8374	8472	0.1
10456	BRONX	005	78490	82294	83983	0.5	71	25859	27139	27688	0.5	2.97	18173	18738	0.3
10457	BRONX	005	68383	70718	71723	0.4	66	21661	22365	22668	0.3	3.04	15552	15809	0.2
10458	BRONX	005	77461	80160	81127	0.4	66	25197	25735	25974	0.2	2.99	17219	17296	0.0
10459	BRONX	005	37887	41857	43470	1.1	91	12117	13292	13781	1.0	3.10	8776	9476	0.8
10460	BRONX	005	54433	57162	58326	0.5	71	18309	19185	19559	0.5	2.95	13133	13549	0.3
10461	BRONX	005	49406	50273	50654	0.2	52	20137	20418	20549	0.1	2.34	12089	12012	-0.1
10462	BRONX	005	71218	75360	76897	0.6	76	27930	28893	29354	0.4	2.59	17979	18243	0.2
10463	BRONX	005	69963	72222	73099	0.3	59	28818	29434	29727	0.2	2.37	17154	17148	0.0
10464	BRONX	005	4563	4578	4593	0.0	38	2065	2074	2079	0.0	2.20	1162	1140	-0.2
10465	BRONX	005	42515	44330	45126	0.5	71	16078	16802	17107	0.5	2.57	11152	11465	0.3
10466	BRONX	005	69840	73222	74642	0.5	71	24077	25144	25614	0.5	2.87	17231	17711	0.3
10467	BRONX	005	94583	97218	97939	0.3	59	34855	35148	35295	0.1	2.69	22575	22341	-0.1
10468	BRONX	005	73676	75106	75608	0.2	52	24304	24497	24594	0.1	2.98	17125	16983	-0.1
10469	BRONX	005	62448	64018	64793	0.3	59	21600	22116	22359	0.3	2.77	15320	15449	0.1
10470	BRONX	005	15342	15632	15761	0.2	52	6263	6333	6367	0.1	2.44	3757	3727	-0.1
10471	BRONX	005	23918	23848	23849	0.0	38	10009	9976	9967	0.0	2.08	5400	5251	-0.3
10472	BRONX	005	64863	65711	66169	0.1	44	21740	22005	22135	0.1	2.97	15862	15822	0.0
10473	BRONX	005	56170	57923	58739	0.3	59	19434	20045	20309	0.3	2.87	14188	14444	0.2
10474	BRONX	005	24145	25258	25636	0.5	71	3419	3713	3834	0.9	3.07	2493	2664	0.7
10475	BRONX	005	38150	38647	39157	0.1	44	16949	17158	17359	0.1	2.20	9942	9856	-0.1
10501	AMAWALK	119	1207	1351	1410	1.2	93	365	405	423	1.1	3.33	337	372	1.1
10502	ARDSLEY	119	5360	5755	5920	0.8	84	1768	1887	1941	0.7	3.02	1504	1591	0.6
10504	ARMONK	119	7167	7834	8103	1.0	89	2351	2553	2639	0.9	3.02	2039	2194	0.8
10505	BALDWIN PLACE	119	159	167	171	0.5	71	46	48	49	0.5	3.48	38	40	0.6
10506	BEDFORD	119	5190	5435	5549	0.5	71	1703	1768	1800	0.4	3.06	1468	1513	0.3
10507	BEDFORD HILLS	119	6051	6306	6368	0.4	66	1871	1908	1927	0.2	2.75	1293	1296	0.0
10509	BREWSTER	079	18459	19214	19295	0.4	66	6442	6724	6758	0.5	2.79	4789	4940	0.3
10510	BRIARCLIFF MANOR	119	9592	10183	10407	0.6	76	3104	3248	3315	0.5	2.86	2541	2640	0.4
10511	BUCHANAN	119	2465	2524	2552	0.3	59	921	935	944	0.2	2.69	682	684	0.0
10512	CARMEL	079	23416	24624	25234	0.5	71	8276	8768	9038	0.6	2.76	6283	6574	0.5
10514	CHAPPAQUA	119	12548	12806	12910	0.2	52	4045	4084	4106	0.1	3.09	3500	3507	0.0
10516	COLD SPRING	079	5208	5665	5828	0.9	87	2143	2344	2410	1.0	2.41	1413	1531	0.9
10518	CROSS RIVER	119	488	528	545	0.9	87	144	155	159	0.8	3.41	120	128	0.7
10520	CROTON ON HUDSON	119	12458	13141	13403	0.6	76	4957	5162	5257	0.4	2.44	3227	3315	0.3
10522	DOBBS FERRY	119	10562	10995	11150	0.4	66	3775	3862	3910	0.2	2.58	2556	2562	0.0
	NEW YORK					0.3					0.3	2.61			0.1
	UNITED STATES					1.0					1.1	2.59			0.9

#	POST OFFICE NAME	RACE (%) White 2000	White 2009	Black 2000	Black 2009	Asian/Pacific 2000	Asian/Pacific 2009	% Hispanic Origin 2000	% Hispanic Origin 2009	2009 AGE DISTRIBUTION (%) 0-4	5-9	10-14	15-19	20-24	25-44	45-64	65-84	85+	18+	MEDIAN AGE 2009	% 2009 Males	% 2009 Females
06390	FISHERS ISLAND	95.5	94.1	1.0	1.4	1.0	1.4	1.4	1.7	3.8	5.9	5.9	5.9	1.0	26.6	32.5	15.7	2.4	79.4	45.4	50.7	49.3
10001	NEW YORK	64.2	58.5	9.5	10.2	14.8	18.1	20.2	23.0	2.9	2.3	2.3	4.9	10.9	36.8	26.0	11.1	2.9	90.9	38.7	49.3	50.7
10002	NEW YORK	26.1	22.9	7.6	7.0	49.3	52.0	26.8	27.9	5.1	5.0	5.0	5.7	7.7	30.0	26.2	12.7	2.6	81.6	38.7	49.3	50.7
10003	NEW YORK	77.6	70.6	4.4	5.2	12.2	16.8	7.6	9.9	2.3	1.6	1.4	7.2	12.5	40.8	24.8	7.9	1.5	93.6	35.0	48.8	51.2
10004	NEW YORK	72.6	64.5	6.6	7.9	12.9	17.7	7.8	10.1	4.7	3.0	2.5	2.0	8.2	47.8	27.5	4.0	0.2	88.8	36.5	56.6	43.4
10005	NEW YORK	67.5	56.8	3.2	4.4	22.7	29.9	7.4	10.0	2.8	1.8	1.4	2.0	11.2	52.8	19.9	6.5	1.6	93.7	33.9	54.1	45.9
10006	NEW YORK	77.5	69.0	6.6	6.6	9.2	13.8	6.5	8.0	3.5	1.4	1.3	1.6	10.9	54.9	20.5	4.9	1.0	93.4	33.7	55.7	44.3
10007	NEW YORK	69.3	64.5	8.6	6.8	17.7	22.7	12.9	11.9	5.7	3.9	2.4	2.4	7.0	47.4	25.7	4.8	0.6	86.5	35.9	55.4	44.6
10009	NEW YORK	60.0	53.9	10.5	10.7	10.2	13.0	30.2	34.1	4.5	3.8	3.7	4.5	8.2	36.0	26.2	10.8	2.4	85.4	38.2	46.9	53.1
10010	NEW YORK	77.7	71.6	6.2	7.0	10.0	13.6	9.1	11.4	3.0	2.1	1.9	3.0	8.2	38.6	27.9	12.7	2.6	91.6	39.6	46.0	54.0
10011	NEW YORK	81.9	76.3	5.4	6.7	6.2	8.7	12.1	15.6	2.9	2.0	1.7	2.6	6.5	41.3	30.6	10.4	2.1	92.5	41.0	51.7	48.3
10012	NEW YORK	71.3	64.2	2.9	3.5	19.8	24.8	7.3	9.3	2.9	2.3	2.1	2.9	11.4	41.3	26.3	9.5	1.4	91.3	36.2	50.0	50.0
10013	NEW YORK	46.6	44.9	5.0	5.2	43.3	43.7	4.9	6.1	4.4	3.9	4.1	5.0	8.9	31.8	30.0	10.2	1.8	85.4	40.2	51.6	48.4
10014	NEW YORK	88.3	83.9	2.8	3.5	4.9	7.1	6.1	8.5	2.5	1.7	1.5	1.8	6.3	46.1	29.4	9.0	1.7	93.4	39.0	51.5	48.5
10016	NEW YORK	78.1	71.4	5.2	5.9	11.7	16.3	7.9	10.1	2.7	1.5	1.3	2.4	12.1	42.1	26.5	9.8	1.6	93.7	36.9	47.1	52.9
10017	NEW YORK	75.9	68.0	3.5	4.3	16.7	22.7	5.5	7.4	2.8	1.3	1.1	1.4	8.4	42.6	30.5	10.2	1.6	94.0	39.9	46.7	53.3
10018	NEW YORK	53.5	46.1	12.2	11.1	21.0	27.9	21.5	24.0	3.2	2.3	1.8	3.6	11.3	47.4	24.0	5.8	0.6	91.4	34.3	52.3	47.7
10019	NEW YORK	72.6	65.4	5.7	6.6	10.8	13.9	17.9	23.3	3.0	2.0	1.9	2.3	8.0	41.7	27.3	11.5	2.3	91.8	39.3	50.9	49.1
10021	NEW YORK	89.6	85.4	1.5	1.9	6.5	9.3	4.5	6.2	4.5	2.7	2.2	1.8	4.9	36.1	30.6	13.9	3.3	89.4	43.3	44.2	55.8
10022	NEW YORK	89.7	85.5	1.2	1.5	6.6	9.7	4.8	6.7	3.0	1.7	1.5	1.4	4.5	32.8	34.0	17.6	3.4	92.9	48.5	46.1	53.9
10023	NEW YORK	82.4	75.5	5.4	7.1	7.4	10.7	7.9	11.0	3.9	2.5	2.0	2.8	6.0	38.5	29.1	12.2	3.0	90.4	41.0	46.8	53.2
10024	NEW YORK	83.1	78.1	5.9	7.1	4.3	6.1	11.1	14.5	5.0	3.5	3.0	2.6	4.2	37.1	31.3	10.7	2.5	86.7	41.6	47.2	52.8
10025	NEW YORK	60.8	54.7	16.2	17.3	6.5	8.4	25.6	30.0	4.7	3.8	3.5	4.8	8.3	33.6	28.5	10.4	2.2	85.6	39.1	47.4	52.6
10026	NEW YORK	8.1	7.4	75.6	74.8	1.4	1.6	20.7	21.9	7.9	7.9	7.4	7.6	7.4	29.0	23.1	8.4	1.4	72.3	33.7	47.3	52.7
10027	NEW YORK	25.8	22.2	53.0	53.7	6.2	7.7	21.5	23.0	6.0	6.0	5.7	9.3	12.0	29.9	21.1	8.5	1.5	78.7	31.5	47.0	53.0
10028	NEW YORK	90.5	86.5	1.4	1.7	5.3	7.8	4.3	6.0	4.5	3.3	3.0	2.5	5.6	37.0	30.3	11.4	2.3	87.5	40.9	45.1	54.9
10029	NEW YORK	28.6	27.9	34.3	32.2	3.9	4.5	56.4	59.0	7.3	7.2	6.7	7.6	8.9	28.9	21.8	10.0	1.7	74.4	32.5	46.8	53.2
10030	NEW YORK	4.5	4.4	82.2	81.1	0.8	0.9	17.3	18.1	8.0	8.1	7.7	7.9	7.4	27.9	22.9	8.5	1.5	71.5	32.8	46.2	53.8
10031	NEW YORK	14.7	14.2	38.7	36.8	1.4	1.5	59.8	62.0	7.3	7.3	6.6	7.5	7.5	30.8	23.4	8.5	1.2	74.4	33.8	48.2	51.8
10032	NEW YORK	19.6	18.1	22.6	21.3	3.3	3.6	70.6	72.9	6.9	6.9	6.3	7.0	8.7	30.8	23.0	9.0	1.3	75.8	33.4	47.9	52.1
10033	NEW YORK	34.1	31.2	8.2	7.6	1.6	1.8	75.2	78.9	6.8	6.7	6.2	7.5	8.7	29.9	24.0	8.8	1.3	76.1	34.2	48.4	51.6
10034	NEW YORK	30.6	27.7	10.7	10.1	1.9	2.1	74.0	77.5	7.5	7.3	6.6	7.1	8.0	31.0	23.6	7.9	1.1	74.5	33.4	47.0	53.0
10035	NEW YORK	21.1	20.7	47.6	46.5	1.0	1.1	50.9	52.4	7.3	7.6	7.1	7.9	8.0	29.8	22.0	9.0	1.4	73.6	33.0	49.5	50.5
10036	NEW YORK	67.7	56.3	11.2	13.2	7.7	12.2	20.5	26.8	3.3	2.5	1.9	2.5	8.0	40.7	29.7	10.0	1.4	91.0	39.8	55.3	44.7
10037	NEW YORK	2.6	2.6	89.1	88.4	0.5	0.6	11.2	11.7	5.6	5.9	5.0	5.6	6.0	25.7	26.1	16.1	4.1	80.3	42.2	41.8	58.2
10038	NEW YORK	47.8	43.5	9.9	9.5	31.1	34.9	18.4	18.6	3.3	3.3	3.3	7.9	15.7	26.8	22.9	13.3	3.6	87.8	35.5	46.7	53.3
10039	NEW YORK	4.9	5.0	79.9	78.7	0.7	0.7	20.0	20.9	8.1	7.8	7.1	8.3	8.5	26.5	21.3	10.6	1.8	72.0	32.3	44.9	55.1
10040	NEW YORK	31.7	28.9	8.9	8.3	2.2	2.5	75.8	79.2	7.4	7.5	6.8	7.4	7.3	29.3	23.3	8.9	2.1	74.0	34.4	46.6	53.4
10044	NEW YORK	49.2	41.2	27.2	29.8	10.9	13.8	14.4	17.2	4.8	4.6	4.8	7.5	6.7	24.8	29.9	13.9	3.1	82.6	42.7	46.9	53.1
10065	NEW YORK	88.5	83.8	1.4	1.8	7.3	10.5	5.4	7.5	4.2	2.4	1.9	1.8	5.1	35.2	31.3	15.0	3.1	90.3	44.6	45.0	55.0
10075	NEW YORK	90.1	85.9	1.4	1.8	5.7	8.4	4.3	6.1	3.8	2.5	2.1	2.0	6.3	39.3	29.9	11.5	2.6	90.2	40.3	43.6	56.4
10128	NEW YORK	83.9	78.7	4.9	5.8	6.4	9.1	8.7	11.5	4.6	3.7	3.6	3.2	8.0	37.6	27.7	9.8	1.8	86.1	37.8	45.8	54.2
10280	NEW YORK	74.5	66.0	3.4	3.9	18.1	25.0	5.3	6.9	7.3	4.3	1.9	1.4	6.1	49.1	25.5	3.9	0.4	85.5	36.1	50.6	49.4
10301	STATEN ISLAND	58.4	53.6	23.0	24.6	6.8	8.5	17.7	19.6	6.6	6.2	6.0	7.4	8.1	28.2	25.2	10.1	2.1	77.3	36.1	48.3	51.7
10302	STATEN ISLAND	60.3	55.4	19.3	21.1	2.9	3.6	25.7	28.9	7.9	7.4	7.2	7.8	7.4	28.6	23.5	8.7	1.6	72.8	33.4	49.2	50.8
10303	STATEN ISLAND	41.1	37.2	35.9	37.0	4.5	5.4	27.8	29.9	8.9	8.8	8.2	8.7	8.0	27.4	22.0	6.9	1.1	68.7	29.9	47.4	52.6
10304	STATEN ISLAND	51.1	46.4	30.2	32.0	5.9	7.4	18.5	20.3	7.6	7.7	7.6	7.8	6.9	26.3	24.8	9.4	1.8	72.4	34.8	47.5	52.5
10305	STATEN ISLAND	82.5	78.3	3.8	4.2	6.3	8.5	13.8	16.5	6.4	5.9	5.9	6.7	7.2	28.3	26.4	11.1	2.1	77.8	37.7	48.7	51.3
10306	STATEN ISLAND	92.1	89.7	1.1	1.3	3.4	4.8	8.3	10.4	6.2	6.0	6.1	6.4	5.9	26.9	27.2	13.0	2.3	77.6	40.1	48.1	51.9
10307	STATEN ISLAND	95.3	93.7	0.7	0.8	2.2	3.1	5.3	6.8	7.9	7.7	7.7	6.9	5.7	28.7	26.6	7.6	1.1	72.1	35.8	49.6	50.4
10308	STATEN ISLAND	95.1	93.4	0.3	0.4	2.6	3.6	5.4	7.0	6.5	6.6	6.8	6.7	5.2	27.1	27.8	11.9	1.4	75.8	39.4	48.7	51.3
10309	STATEN ISLAND	91.0	88.0	2.6	3.3	3.8	5.1	6.3	8.1	6.8	6.6	6.8	7.0	6.3	29.5	27.4	8.5	1.0	75.2	37.1	50.4	49.6
10310	STATEN ISLAND	61.2	57.8	22.0	22.7	4.0	5.1	19.4	21.4	7.3	7.6	7.6	7.9	6.3	26.1	26.3	9.2	1.6	72.5	35.4	47.6	52.4
10312	STATEN ISLAND	93.2	90.6	0.7	0.9	3.9	5.5	5.7	7.4	6.2	6.3	6.6	6.6	5.2	28.8	28.6	10.4	1.2	76.8	38.8	48.6	51.4
10314	STATEN ISLAND	80.6	75.7	3.5	3.9	10.7	14.1	9.0	10.7	6.2	6.1	6.3	6.6	6.1	27.2	28.0	11.5	2.1	77.3	39.0	48.2	51.8
10451	BRONX	19.5	20.1	45.5	43.8	1.6	1.7	55.5	56.7	8.0	8.8	8.3	8.8	7.7	25.1	22.2	9.8	1.2	69.5	31.2	45.1	54.9
10452	BRONX	16.5	17.0	36.2	34.6	1.4	1.6	64.5	65.4	10.4	10.1	8.6	8.7	8.1	28.8	19.7	5.3	0.5	65.7	27.8	46.9	53.1
10453	BRONX	15.6	16.1	41.8	40.0	1.2	1.4	59.9	60.9	10.0	9.8	8.6	9.4	8.6	28.2	19.7	5.3	0.5	65.9	27.4	46.7	53.3
10454	BRONX	24.5	25.5	29.7	27.9	0.6	0.6	73.4	74.7	9.7	9.7	8.8	9.2	8.3	26.7	19.3	7.5	0.8	66.3	27.8	45.9	54.1
10455	BRONX	22.7	23.5	28.0	26.3	0.8	0.8	74.4	75.5	9.5	9.3	8.1	9.0	8.6	27.7	19.7	7.4	0.7	67.6	28.4	47.1	52.9
10456	BRONX	14.2	14.8	51.6	50.0	0.9	1.0	50.3	51.3	9.4	9.7	9.1	9.3	7.7	26.3	20.7	7.0	0.9	66.1	28.5	45.6	54.4
10457	BRONX	17.1	17.6	36.1	34.6	2.0	2.3	61.9	63.0	10.3	9.9	8.5	8.9	8.1	27.9	19.5	6.3	0.8	65.9	27.9	46.4	53.6
10458	BRONX	31.3	29.9	23.1	22.3	4.8	5.6	58.9	61.0	9.6	9.3	8.1	9.8	9.8	28.3	18.5	5.8	0.9	68.1	27.4	47.6	52.4
10459	BRONX	24.0	24.8	31.6	30.1	0.9	1.0	71.6	72.3	9.6	9.2	8.3	9.0	8.5	27.2	19.6	7.5	1.0	67.4	28.4	46.7	53.3
10460	BRONX	24.5	24.9	34.0	32.5	1.6	1.8	65.2	66.5	9.7	9.5	8.3	9.1	8.4	28.1	19.4	6.7	0.8	67.1	28.1	46.0	54.0
10461	BRONX	72.7	68.2	4.8	5.0	7.6	9.6	26.1	30.6	5.8	5.3	5.2	5.5	7.4	30.1	25.1	12.6	2.9	80.3	38.7	48.0	52.0
10462	BRONX	37.4	34.5	28.0	27.4	7.5	8.9	41.4	44.1	7.4	7.3	7.0	7.5	7.4	29.0	23.8	8.9	1.7	73.6	34.4	46.7	53.3
10463	BRONX	52.2	48.7	17.7	17.6	4.8	6.1	40.7	43.8	6.4	6.2	5.9	6.3	6.7	26.7	24.5	13.1	4.1	77.6	39.0	45.4	54.6
10464	BRONX	90.1	86.6	1.8	2.2	3.4	4.9	8.9	11.8	4.8	4.7	5.3	5.9	5.5	22.7	32.2	15.9	3.0	81.6	45.7	48.1	51.9
10465	BRONX	78.7	76.2	7.1	6.9	1.8	2.5	24.9	29.4	5.8	5.7	5.7	6.9	7.1	26.8	26.3	13.0	2.6	78.8	39.4	47.8	52.2
10466	BRONX	11.5	11.0	72.3	71.5	2.3	2.7	19.6	20.4	7.8	7.6	7.4	7.9	7.2	27.5	23.9	9.3	1.4	72.3	33.5	44.7	55.3
10467	BRONX	30.2	28.3	36.9	36.3	5.5	6.4	42.0	44.2	8.4	8.2	7.5	7.8	7.1	29.1	21.8	8.5	1.6	71.3	32.7	46.6	53.4
10468	BRONX	25.1	24.4	26.7	25.6	5.0	5.7	63.4	64.7	9.2	9.3	8.2	8.2	7.3	28.4	20.8	7.0	1.7	68.4	30.6	46.9	53.1
10469	BRONX	27.2	24.9	57.6	57.9	2.9	3.6	19.0	20.5	6.7	6.3	6.3	7.2	6.9	26.2	24.9	12.7	2.9	76.4	37.6	45.2	54.8
10470	BRONX	56.4	53.9	32.3	32.8	3.1	3.8	11.3	12.7	6.7	6.6	6.2	6.3	5.6	30.4	23.6	12.4	2.2	76.6	38.1	46.9	53.1
10471	BRONX	77.5	72.5	8.6	9.7	5.2	7.1	14.2	17.4	4.3	3.8	4.2	7.6	6.5	22.6	28.4	16.9	5.8	84.7	45.7	45.5	54.5
10472	BRONX	26.4	26.9	31.1	29.3	4.4	4.9	62.5	63.6	9.2	8.9	8.0	8.3	8.0	28.6	20.8	7.3	1.0	68.9	29.9	47.0	53.0
10473	BRONX	24.0	24.8	45.0	43.0	1.2	1.4	54.1	55.9	7.6	8.0	7.7	8.4	7.8	25.5	23.9	9.8	1.3	71.6	32.6	45.2	54.8
10474	BRONX	18.7	18.7	48.8	47.6	0.7	0.8	47.7	49.7	5.4	4.9	4.0	10.7	13.5	44.7	13.5	3.0	0.3	80.7	30.2	68.7	31.3
10475	BRONX	26.8	24.6	59.6	60.4	1.0	1.3	24.3	26.1	5.2	6.0	6.5	6.6	5.0	22.1	29.0	16.2	3.4	78.2	44.0	42.8	57.2
10501	AMAWALK	95.9	94.2	0.7	1.0	2.4	3.4	2.2	3.0	7.7	9.2	10.5	7.5	2.9	19.8	32.2	9.6	0.6	67.7	40.6	50.6	49.4
10502	ARDSLEY	83.9	78.3	2.1	2.6	11.8	16.2	4.0	5.1	5.2	6.2	7.8	7.8	3.9	18.5	34.5	13.9	2.1	75.1	45.3	48.6	51.4
10504	ARMONK	92.7	89.9	1.5	1.9	4.2	5.9	3.2	4.4	6.3	7.9	10.2	8.8	3.3	17.5	33.4	11.4	1.3	69.5	42.5	49.3	50.7
10505	BALDWIN PLACE	94.4	93.4	2.5	3.0	1.3	1.2	3.1	4.2	7.8	9.0	10.2	7.2	2.4	22.8	30.5	9.0	1.2	68.3	40.2	49.7	50.3
10506	BEDFORD	96.1	94.4	0.8	1.0	2.4	3.4	2.6	3.7	7.0	8.7	11.1	8.9	3.0	16.5	32.3	11.5	1.0	66.7	42.0	50.2	49.8
10507	BEDFORD HILLS	80.9	77.1	11.0	12.5	2.5	3.2	13.0	15.9	6.2	6.5	7.0	7.9	6.3	30.0	26.1	8.6	1.5	75.7	37.6	44.8	55.2
10509	BREWSTER	92.6	91.1	2.1	2.3	1.7	2.3	8.0	9.6	6.4	7.1	7.8	7.1	4.8	25.8	30.5	9.2	1.3	73.9	39.7	50.8	49.2
10510	BRIARCLIFF MANOR	90.4	86.9	1.8	2.4	5.5	7.7	3.8	5.0	6.2	7.6	9.4	9.4	6.3	16.1	30.6	11.5	2.9	71.4	41.5	47.3	52.7
10511	BUCHANAN	96.1	94.6	0.6	0.9	1.2	1.7	3.5	4.9	6.2	6.7	6.9	6.7	5.7	26.5	28.2	11.1	2.0	76.2	39.6	49.6	50.4
10512	CARMEL	94.1	92.6	1.4	1.7	1.1	1.5	6.2	7.6	6.4	6.9	7.4	7.3	5.1	24.6	30.5	10.2	1.6	74.8	40.5	49.2	50.8
10514	CHAPPAQUA	91.2	88.0	1.3	1.6	5.8	8.1	2.7	3.6	6.8	8.3	11.0	9.3	4.1	16.6	33.4	9.6	0.9	68.0	41.2	50.0	50.0
10516	COLD SPRING	95.8	94.5	0.7	0.8	1.0	1.4	3.4	4.4	5.8	6.0	6.8	6.8	5.0	21.6	33.0	12.9	2.1	77.1	43.6	48.9	51.1
10518	CROSS RIVER	94.3	91.5	1.2	1.7	2.9	4.0	3.5	4.9	6.8	8.5	11.2	9.1	3.2	17.2	35.4	7.8	0.8	67.6	41.5	49.4	50.6
10520	CROTON ON HUDSON	90.9	88.0	2.7	3.5	2.5	3.5	5.8	7.6	6.0	6.5	7.5	6.3	3.9	19.3	31.3	14.5	4.8	75.7	45.3	46.9	53.1
10522	DOBBS FERRY	80.6	75.3	7.4	9.0	7.7	10.1	7.0	8.8	4.9	5.8	8.1	8.9	5.9	21.0	29.9	12.0	3.5	76.0	41.5	49.3	50.7
	NEW YORK	67.9	64.8	15.9	16.5	5.6	6.9	15.1	16.7	6.5	6.4	6.4	7.1	7.0	27.0	26.3	11.2	2.1	76.6	37.5	48.4	51.6
	UNITED STATES	75.1	72.0	12.3	12.7	3.8	4.6	12.5	15.7	6.8	6.7	6.6	7.1	6.9	27.0	26.0	10.9	1.9	75.7	36.9	49.2	50.8

06390-10522

ZIP CODE #	POST OFFICE NAME	2009 Per Capita Income	2009 HH Income Base	2009 Household Income Distribution (%): Less than $25,000	$25,000 to $49,999	$50,000 to $99,999	$100,000 to $149,999	$150,000 or More	Median Household Income: 2009	2014	2009 National Centile	2009 State Centile	2009 Home Value Base	2009 Home Value Distribution (%): Less than $50,000	$50,000 to $89,999	$90,000 to $174,999	$175,000 to $399,999	$400,000 or More	2009 Median Home Value
06390	FISHERS ISLAND	39965	137	15.3	21.2	40.1	10.9	12.4	65374	69174	84	72	79	0.0	0.0	0.0	17.7	82.3	538194
10001	NEW YORK	51046	10786	20.5	20.5	26.6	17.4	14.9	66072	76215	84	73	2422	34.2	1.2	3.8	14.5	46.4	328333
10002	NEW YORK	17878	32993	40.4	25.7	22.9	7.7	3.3	32380	36674	12	5	4253	7.0	1.3	17.0	54.5	20.3	244231
10003	NEW YORK	72638	29892	12.6	13.0	28.7	22.3	23.4	91513	97256	95	89	7968	0.0	0.1	2.2	23.7	74.0	523958
10004	NEW YORK	80213	610	5.6	10.2	23.8	25.2	35.2	124072	128045	99	97	108	0.0	0.0	11.1	72.2	16.7	316279
10005	NEW YORK	88624	1919	9.2	6.4	27.6	22.9	33.9	111942	118877	98	96	577	0.0	0.0	5.0	82.3	12.7	288958
10006	NEW YORK	89000	1631	7.2	9.0	23.4	28.5	31.9	120528	125064	98	97	223	0.0	0.0	3.1	20.6	76.2	590116
10007	NEW YORK	92237	3540	7.3	9.7	19.5	17.9	45.6	138996	151566	99	99	1045	0.1	0.1	0.8	14.1	85.0	735021
10009	NEW YORK	38115	30096	24.9	19.1	29.2	17.1	9.7	59076	65801	76	62	2429	11.9	3.2	10.0	30.0	45.0	366529
10010	NEW YORK	76307	16527	10.8	11.4	30.4	25.8	21.6	95259	100559	96	90	3866	6.2	0.0	3.8	27.9	62.1	465960
10011	NEW YORK	81494	29770	12.1	11.5	28.9	23.7	23.8	94926	101067	96	89	9402	3.1	0.1	2.3	22.8	71.7	521798
10012	NEW YORK	63264	14289	15.7	14.5	25.3	24.1	20.4	88007	94319	95	88	2620	1.1	0.0	1.2	14.2	83.6	917458
10013	NEW YORK	52402	12180	23.5	18.6	22.0	14.8	21.1	60988	72385	79	66	3177	0.4	0.2	1.9	12.4	85.0	979013
10014	NEW YORK	90907	20264	9.2	11.8	27.9	23.9	27.4	102181	108019	97	92	4762	0.1	0.1	2.0	16.4	81.4	692708
10016	NEW YORK	81434	31458	12.9	11.7	26.8	22.0	26.7	97174	103830	96	90	7224	0.1	0.3	5.6	27.3	66.6	470423
10017	NEW YORK	94362	10875	9.9	10.0	28.0	26.6	25.6	103412	108091	97	93	2935	0.3	0.4	10.5	31.4	57.4	432556
10018	NEW YORK	54951	2597	17.3	16.2	28.6	20.5	17.4	77793	83159	91	83	563	0.9	0.0	2.0	28.8	68.4	467208
10019	NEW YORK	77220	25681	16.1	16.0	25.9	20.9	21.1	82948	87951	93	86	3763	0.2	0.9	6.4	17.4	75.2	566496
10021	NEW YORK	103323	30484	8.1	9.1	27.0	22.4	33.5	111234	118012	98	96	10510	0.1	0.0	1.6	15.4	82.9	721665
10022	NEW YORK	116176	21311	7.3	8.0	27.9	23.3	33.5	114654	122106	98	96	9250	0.5	0.0	1.8	17.0	80.7	653876
10023	NEW YORK	96484	40625	10.7	10.7	25.9	20.8	31.9	105953	113201	97	94	13707	0.3	0.1	1.0	16.3	82.4	664869
10024	NEW YORK	92373	33179	11.7	9.5	25.2	20.4	33.2	108437	117519	98	95	10204	1.1	0.2	1.2	11.1	86.2	758888
10025	NEW YORK	51602	46955	18.9	15.8	28.2	20.5	16.5	78167	82477	91	83	10389	2.3	0.3	3.1	20.1	74.2	551821
10026	NEW YORK	17855	13605	45.4	26.1	18.3	7.2	2.9	28103	30606	6	3	1151	4.4	1.4	12.2	41.2	40.8	339017
10027	NEW YORK	22033	24089	42.3	24.3	20.2	8.3	4.9	31705	35492	11	4	2197	3.7	2.2	22.7	37.0	34.5	251540
10028	NEW YORK	96957	29514	7.6	8.4	29.7	22.3	32.0	108844	115628	98	95	9413	0.3	0.0	1.6	14.0	84.0	747240
10029	NEW YORK	19170	29497	43.3	25.6	20.2	6.6	4.3	30471	33710	9	4	2008	7.8	4.4	6.4	12.3	69.2	545370
10030	NEW YORK	16300	11665	50.5	26.0	17.1	4.5	2.0	24530	26085	3	2	932	6.1	2.1	4.1	32.2	55.5	473913
10031	NEW YORK	15748	21215	40.7	27.6	21.8	7.7	2.2	31461	34900	10	4	1605	19.1	4.7	8.5	16.6	51.0	415421
10032	NEW YORK	16145	21088	38.6	26.9	23.9	8.1	2.4	34565	38497	17	5	1183	19.6	3.0	9.6	29.2	38.6	292026
10033	NEW YORK	19161	19314	32.0	26.4	26.5	11.5	3.7	41415	45215	37	18	1486	4.6	3.0	21.8	42.6	28.0	271805
10034	NEW YORK	18355	15354	33.2	27.9	27.0	9.6	2.3	39447	42920	31	13	1029	18.6	12.9	40.7	23.2	4.6	132275
10035	NEW YORK	13557	12842	55.8	22.2	15.2	5.0	1.8	20227	21691	1	1	764	10.3	3.7	16.2	32.9	36.9	331507
10036	NEW YORK	52922	13110	22.2	21.5	26.0	17.3	13.0	60194	70770	78	64	1159	0.6	1.0	11.8	22.0	64.5	466601
10037	NEW YORK	23292	8510	36.9	30.3	23.6	7.1	2.0	35987	38425	21	6	442	51.4	3.4	15.8	9.3	20.1	48182
10038	NEW YORK	36513	6983	32.1	18.8	21.1	14.8	13.2	48312	55665	57	41	1677	27.8	1.5	4.5	24.0	42.2	323988
10039	NEW YORK	14208	9636	52.1	25.9	16.9	3.3	1.8	23132	24776	2	2	561	41.9	4.8	17.1	6.8	29.4	100868
10040	NEW YORK	16877	16109	35.8	28.3	25.8	8.0	2.0	36993	40884	24	7	1182	21.9	5.4	18.4	35.3	19.0	193750
10044	NEW YORK	39020	4134	19.9	13.9	26.2	22.5	17.5	77042	84176	91	82	492	42.3	28.5	5.5	18.1	5.7	53800
10065	NEW YORK	103381	17686	8.4	8.6	28.8	22.7	31.4	107978	113990	98	94	5474	0.1	0.0	1.3	12.9	85.7	783230
10075	NEW YORK	99535	12232	8.3	9.0	30.4	22.0	30.3	103900	109136	97	93	3932	0.1	0.0	1.6	17.8	80.5	665809
10128	NEW YORK	81947	31687	11.2	11.4	25.9	22.1	29.4	103166	110014	97	93	8677	0.5	0.0	1.7	15.3	82.4	817524
10280	NEW YORK	109006	3918	6.6	8.0	22.2	19.1	44.2	138041	147179	99	99	734	0.0	0.0	0.1	18.4	81.5	496250
10301	STATEN ISLAND	31458	16199	18.6	21.1	31.9	18.1	10.3	62383	66392	80	68	7011	0.6	1.9	5.7	46.5	45.3	380951
10302	STATEN ISLAND	22986	6178	23.9	20.3	32.2	17.6	5.9	57280	62027	74	61	3378	0.4	0.2	5.1	76.8	17.5	301791
10303	STATEN ISLAND	21002	7503	22.7	22.8	33.0	15.7	5.8	55760	60869	72	58	3946	0.8	0.3	6.7	84.0	8.2	269334
10304	STATEN ISLAND	26112	14699	27.3	19.5	27.9	15.4	9.9	54104	59056	70	55	7147	0.5	0.1	5.7	53.6	40.2	355845
10305	STATEN ISLAND	28332	15707	21.2	19.6	32.8	18.8	7.6	62748	68089	81	69	9080	0.5	0.2	3.2	61.3	34.9	357232
10306	STATEN ISLAND	33277	21478	16.3	15.6	32.9	24.1	11.2	73186	78324	88	79	14105	0.1	0.2	2.5	47.0	50.2	400810
10307	STATEN ISLAND	36763	4829	8.9	11.2	36.1	28.4	15.4	87096	93366	94	87	3422	0.2	0.0	1.0	33.2	65.6	515750
10308	STATEN ISLAND	35044	10931	9.0	15.5	35.9	26.6	13.0	81839	87215	93	85	8128	0.2	0.0	1.3	48.4	49.9	399828
10309	STATEN ISLAND	34333	10650	9.8	12.7	34.3	28.1	15.1	87317	93146	94	87	7862	0.2	0.1	0.4	31.0	68.3	526075
10310	STATEN ISLAND	27278	8464	23.6	18.9	27.1	22.2	8.3	62565	68458	81	68	4645	0.2	0.2	2.7	65.2	31.7	346902
10312	STATEN ISLAND	35441	21955	9.0	10.6	35.1	30.4	14.8	90556	97091	95	88	16930	0.1	0.0	1.4	45.8	52.7	415945
10314	STATEN ISLAND	33184	33482	12.7	16.2	33.9	25.2	12.0	77586	82694	91	83	22220	0.4	0.2	3.2	55.0	41.2	372891
10451	BRONX	13358	16078	50.1	24.5	21.1	3.0	1.4	24919	26423	3	2	2234	32.3	11.3	13.7	33.9	8.8	125410
10452	BRONX	11591	24403	47.6	27.1	22.0	2.1	1.2	27043	29566	5	3	1026	16.2	8.0	8.7	51.0	16.2	283221
10453	BRONX	12147	24374	47.8	25.6	21.8	3.3	1.4	26879	29010	5	3	1480	4.3	1.4	3.6	62.9	27.8	333871
10454	BRONX	10741	11997	58.4	21.2	16.8	2.1	1.5	18887	20356	1	1	705	2.3	3.1	10.5	66.0	18.2	312984
10455	BRONX	12052	12035	49.9	27.8	17.9	2.5	1.9	25048	26498	3	2	980	3.8	1.1	8.8	62.9	23.5	332292
10456	BRONX	11765	27139	54.0	23.1	19.0	2.5	1.5	21718	23244	2	1	2030	3.1	4.9	11.9	59.6	20.5	279020
10457	BRONX	12289	22365	50.4	23.6	20.9	3.5	1.6	24622	26695	3	2	2026	4.1	0.1	7.9	61.9	26.0	338665
10458	BRONX	13022	25735	45.7	25.4	23.8	3.7	1.4	29308	31957	7	3	1674	2.4	2.1	7.3	66.6	21.6	307573
10459	BRONX	11660	13292	52.4	23.0	20.2	2.7	1.7	22855	24194	2	2	2110	4.7	0.5	11.4	61.1	22.4	306869
10460	BRONX	12507	19185	48.7	24.3	22.6	3.2	1.3	26245	28506	4	3	2468	2.0	5.2	7.0	51.1	34.7	354070
10461	BRONX	26159	20418	23.8	22.5	38.2	10.8	4.7	54291	60042	70	56	7309	0.4	0.4	3.2	53.7	42.3	382026
10462	BRONX	20703	28893	26.4	27.1	36.5	7.2	2.8	46495	50565	53	35	7315	6.2	13.2	21.1	34.0	25.5	303113
10463	BRONX	28424	29434	25.2	21.3	35.4	10.3	7.8	53881	59078	69	55	8536	11.0	6.1	19.6	40.9	22.4	257254
10464	BRONX	39868	2074	15.7	15.9	36.0	19.3	13.1	71221	73705	87	77	1224	0.2	0.0	0.4	26.9	72.5	504024
10465	BRONX	26941	16802	22.5	19.6	36.9	14.1	7.0	60730	63481	78	65	10131	0.1	0.2	2.4	57.9	39.4	374035
10466	BRONX	20871	25144	28.3	21.4	34.3	10.8	5.2	50265	54404	62	45	9710	0.1	0.1	2.2	63.2	34.4	365390
10467	BRONX	17649	35148	34.4	26.4	31.4	5.5	2.4	39962	43625	32	14	5219	5.9	3.5	6.9	49.2	34.6	354024
10468	BRONX	15183	24497	38.7	25.4	29.2	4.6	2.1	35483	40031	19	6	2620	16.6	16.9	19.5	29.4	17.5	156982
10469	BRONX	24229	22116	21.9	21.8	37.3	12.5	6.5	57110	61339	74	60	11525	0.1	0.2	0.8	59.8	39.1	374618
10470	BRONX	26272	6333	22.0	24.7	37.4	10.3	5.6	53737	59481	69	55	2374	0.7	1.0	1.7	51.9	44.7	386814
10471	BRONX	43998	9976	13.9	15.1	36.8	15.7	18.4	73515	76630	89	79	4448	0.3	2.2	14.9	40.1	42.4	350074
10472	BRONX	14212	22005	42.6	25.6	25.1	4.7	2.0	31618	34415	11	4	3881	1.8	0.5	1.5	52.9	43.2	382418
10473	BRONX	16719	20045	36.3	23.5	31.6	5.8	2.7	40002	43694	33	14	5279	0.6	0.4	2.5	67.5	29.0	351168
10474	BRONX	12911	3713	56.9	21.7	18.9	1.9	0.6	20656	21408	2	1	363	18.7	0.0	4.7	53.7	22.9	296622
10475	BRONX	28401	17158	19.0	22.1	45.2	10.3	3.5	59077	62159	76	62	7859	69.8	2.0	5.6	13.2	9.5	24805
10501	AMAWALK	50385	405	2.5	4.2	19.5	29.1	44.7	141209	148864	99	99	368	0.0	0.0	0.3	9.8	89.9	683929
10502	ARDSLEY	63556	1887	4.0	6.9	22.2	23.1	43.8	137770	145804	99	98	1649	0.0	0.1	0.2	5.8	93.9	704134
10504	ARMONK	72113	2553	2.5	6.6	19.5	21.4	49.9	149819	165767	100	99	2240	0.0	0.0	0.1	1.3	98.6	1000001
10505	BALDWIN PLACE	43106	48	4.2	2.1	29.2	22.9	41.7	132150	147050	99	98	43	0.0	0.0	0.0	39.5	60.5	456250
10506	BEDFORD	81369	1768	2.5	4.6	13.0	23.5	56.4	176949	195786	100	100	1545	0.0	0.1	0.0	2.6	97.3	1000001
10507	BEDFORD HILLS	46389	1908	10.2	14.8	28.7	19.5	26.8	92079	98760	95	89	1149	0.0	0.0	0.1	25.0	74.9	595000
10509	BREWSTER	39343	6724	8.4	12.8	30.4	29.1	19.3	95883	101999	96	90	5265	0.2	0.2	1.5	55.5	42.5	376844
10510	BRIARCLIFF MANOR	68829	3248	7.3	6.3	16.2	18.3	52.0	156408	170843	100	99	2735	0.0	0.1	0.9	6.5	92.5	871094
10511	BUCHANAN	36996	935	11.1	19.0	32.3	24.5	13.0	78102	81487	91	83	670	0.0	0.0	1.8	48.4	49.9	399550
10512	CARMEL	41853	8768	8.1	11.0	29.9	30.5	20.4	101078	105695	97	92	7150	0.0	0.1	4.1	61.5	34.3	343132
10514	CHAPPAQUA	78753	4084	3.4	5.4	13.8	18.3	59.1	199833	206554	100	100	3588	0.1	0.1	0.1	5.0	94.6	988761
10516	COLD SPRING	49432	2344	13.1	13.4	28.2	24.5	20.7	84081	94016	94	86	1732	1.8	1.0	2.2	45.5	49.5	398085
10518	CROSS RIVER	71796	155	1.9	2.6	12.9	27.1	55.5	175359	194212	100	100	139	0.0	0.0	0.0	7.2	92.8	845833
10520	CROTON ON HUDSON	50453	5162	11.3	12.8	27.4	22.0	26.5	96365	103067	96	90	3348	0.5	2.0	3.7	20.4	73.5	513196
10522	DOBBS FERRY	46122	3862	8.1	17.8	27.7	20.6	25.7	91300	99342	95	89	2284	0.0	0.1	1.0	17.1	81.8	612712
	NEW YORK	29893		21.9	21.3	32.7	14.0	9.9	58747	62337				3.4	5.7	23.0	38.7	29.1	269816
	UNITED STATES	27277		20.9	24.4	35.3	11.7	7.6	54719	56938				9.3	13.1	31.6	32.6	13.5	162279

ZIP CODE		FINANCIAL SERVICES				THE HOME						ENTERTAINMENT						PERSONAL			
						Home Improvements		Furnishings													
#	POST OFFICE NAME	Auto Loan	Home Loan	Invest-ments	Retire-ment Plans	Home Repair	Lawn & Garden	Comput-ers & Hard-ware-Personal	Major Appli-ances	TV, Radio, Sound Equip-ment	Furni-ture	Dine out/ Carry out	Sports Equip-ment	Fees & Tickets	Toys & Games	Travel	Cable TV	Apparel & Services	Auto Repairs	Health Insur-ance	Pets & Supplies
06390	FISHERS ISLAND	104	131	153	133	144	112	124	123	109	133	109	98	136	105	139	100	81	118	103	137
10001	NEW YORK	121	110	118	120	111	109	140	118	141	130	144	96	136	135	131	142	105	131	127	143
10002	NEW YORK	52	51	54	55	51	51	69	58	74	58	76	42	67	68	63	80	57	65	66	70
10003	NEW YORK	176	157	175	176	159	147	200	162	190	191	197	144	194	190	188	184	144	182	159	199
10004	NEW YORK	243	172	172	196	163	167	255	194	249	240	257	175	223	253	215	242	182	234	203	249
10005	NEW YORK	210	155	161	179	149	150	229	172	222	213	230	159	204	224	197	216	164	208	180	222
10006	NEW YORK	220	162	169	187	156	157	240	180	232	222	241	166	213	235	206	225	172	217	188	232
10007	NEW YORK	252	268	315	295	283	246	302	263	283	295	293	223	317	279	307	274	219	277	247	308
10009	NEW YORK	97	86	93	96	86	82	116	94	115	106	119	78	110	111	105	116	88	106	97	115
10010	NEW YORK	168	164	186	180	170	151	196	165	185	189	191	142	196	183	191	179	141	180	159	198
10011	NEW YORK	172	166	189	184	171	154	200	168	190	193	196	145	200	188	195	184	144	183	163	202
10012	NEW YORK	154	145	163	161	149	136	180	149	172	171	178	129	178	171	172	168	131	165	147	180
10013	NEW YORK	143	156	178	167	164	150	175	156	173	165	178	124	185	166	178	175	132	166	161	183
10014	NEW YORK	184	191	225	212	202	176	217	188	203	213	210	161	226	201	220	195	156	199	175	221
10016	NEW YORK	183	160	177	180	161	151	208	167	199	197	206	148	199	199	193	193	150	190	167	206
10017	NEW YORK	189	167	187	188	170	157	214	173	203	205	211	153	207	204	201	197	153	195	171	213
10018	NEW YORK	151	129	142	145	130	119	173	137	162	163	168	124	162	162	159	154	122	158	134	170
10019	NEW YORK	167	148	164	166	150	139	194	156	187	182	193	136	186	184	180	183	142	176	155	192
10021	NEW YORK	220	233	274	256	247	216	257	227	240	255	247	191	272	239	263	231	184	237	212	266
10022	NEW YORK	226	250	297	273	267	230	268	241	249	268	256	201	288	246	280	240	192	248	222	279
10023	NEW YORK	201	211	247	233	222	193	241	208	226	234	234	177	250	223	242	219	175	220	195	245
10024	NEW YORK	211	226	266	248	239	207	251	220	234	247	242	187	265	231	257	225	181	231	205	257
10025	NEW YORK	130	133	153	146	139	121	158	135	149	151	154	114	160	146	156	146	115	145	128	160
10026	NEW YORK	44	40	38	44	38	39	63	50	71	49	72	35	57	63	52	78	56	56	57	61
10027	NEW YORK	59	51	52	57	49	51	77	61	83	65	84	46	70	76	65	88	64	70	69	75
10028	NEW YORK	215	218	252	240	228	202	249	215	234	245	241	184	258	234	248	226	179	229	204	255
10029	NEW YORK	55	49	48	54	47	47	74	59	81	61	82	43	68	73	62	87	63	66	66	72
10030	NEW YORK	40	36	36	40	34	36	55	44	61	44	62	31	51	55	46	67	48	50	51	54
10031	NEW YORK	46	40	39	45	38	39	66	51	73	52	75	36	59	65	54	80	58	58	58	63
10032	NEW YORK	50	43	42	48	41	43	71	55	79	56	80	39	64	70	58	86	62	63	64	68
10033	NEW YORK	63	57	56	63	55	54	86	69	93	70	94	50	78	83	72	99	73	76	75	83
10034	NEW YORK	55	49	49	55	48	47	75	60	80	62	81	45	68	72	64	84	62	67	64	72
10035	NEW YORK	36	31	31	35	30	31	51	40	57	41	58	28	46	50	42	62	44	46	47	49
10036	NEW YORK	122	104	113	116	104	99	137	110	132	130	136	97	129	131	126	128	98	126	112	137
10037	NEW YORK	52	43	48	48	44	49	65	53	71	56	71	40	59	62	57	76	51	62	68	67
10038	NEW YORK	96	94	101	101	96	95	118	102	123	107	125	78	117	114	111	128	92	111	114	122
10039	NEW YORK	36	30	30	34	29	31	50	39	56	40	57	28	45	49	41	62	44	45	47	48
10040	NEW YORK	50	44	42	49	42	43	70	55	78	56	79	39	63	69	57	85	61	62	62	67
10044	NEW YORK	134	129	144	139	133	110	163	134	145	156	152	122	156	144	159	134	111	150	121	160
10065	NEW YORK	218	225	263	248	237	207	256	221	240	252	248	190	266	238	258	231	184	235	208	262
10075	NEW YORK	217	214	246	237	222	198	251	213	236	245	244	184	255	235	248	228	180	230	204	255
10128	NEW YORK	197	196	225	216	205	182	226	194	213	223	219	167	232	212	224	204	162	209	185	232
10280	NEW YORK	246	262	309	289	277	240	293	255	273	288	282	219	308	270	299	263	211	268	237	299
10301	STATEN ISLAND	97	106	113	107	108	99	117	105	116	108	119	81	121	113	117	119	88	112	108	123
10302	STATEN ISLAND	80	94	96	92	95	86	96	89	97	88	99	67	103	95	98	100	73	94	91	103
10303	STATEN ISLAND	79	88	90	88	88	83	95	85	97	85	99	65	100	94	94	101	73	92	90	101
10304	STATEN ISLAND	86	101	108	102	103	96	105	97	109	96	110	73	114	104	107	114	82	102	102	114
10305	STATEN ISLAND	87	107	112	103	109	100	106	100	107	96	109	74	116	105	111	112	81	104	105	114
10306	STATEN ISLAND	100	130	140	126	135	122	122	118	122	113	124	87	138	119	132	127	92	121	123	134
10307	STATEN ISLAND	130	167	170	163	171	147	147	147	141	149	143	113	167	143	160	140	106	143	138	164
10308	STATEN ISLAND	111	154	162	145	160	139	133	135	130	128	131	99	155	130	149	133	98	132	132	149
10309	STATEN ISLAND	124	164	170	157	169	146	143	144	138	142	140	108	164	139	158	138	103	140	138	160
10310	STATEN ISLAND	86	107	113	105	109	100	106	100	108	97	110	74	117	105	110	113	82	103	103	115
10312	STATEN ISLAND	126	168	172	162	173	150	144	146	138	144	140	110	166	139	160	137	103	141	138	163
10314	STATEN ISLAND	106	142	149	135	146	129	127	126	125	120	127	93	146	125	140	129	94	126	126	141
10451	BRONX	37	31	31	35	30	32	52	41	58	41	59	29	47	51	42	64	45	47	48	50
10452	BRONX	35	30	29	34	28	30	52	40	58	40	59	27	46	51	41	64	47	45	46	49
10453	BRONX	37	32	31	36	30	32	55	42	61	42	62	29	49	54	44	68	49	48	48	51
10454	BRONX	31	27	26	30	25	27	46	35	52	35	52	24	41	45	37	57	41	40	40	43
10455	BRONX	35	30	29	34	29	30	52	40	58	40	59	28	46	51	41	64	46	45	46	49
10456	BRONX	34	30	29	34	28	29	50	39	56	39	57	27	45	49	40	62	45	44	44	47
10457	BRONX	36	31	30	35	29	31	53	41	60	41	61	28	47	53	42	66	48	47	47	50
10458	BRONX	39	33	31	37	31	32	56	43	62	44	64	30	50	55	45	68	50	49	49	53
10459	BRONX	37	32	31	35	31	31	52	41	57	41	58	29	47	51	42	63	45	46	46	49
10460	BRONX	37	33	32	36	31	32	53	42	59	42	60	29	48	52	43	64	47	47	47	51
10461	BRONX	71	82	87	81	84	78	89	80	90	78	92	60	93	86	89	94	68	86	86	93
10462	BRONX	60	61	62	63	60	58	77	65	81	66	83	49	76	76	71	85	62	72	70	78
10463	BRONX	76	77	80	81	78	78	96	85	103	85	104	61	95	94	90	109	78	92	96	101
10464	BRONX	103	127	138	124	133	122	122	120	122	118	123	88	135	116	132	125	89	122	127	136
10465	BRONX	77	98	103	94	100	91	97	91	99	86	101	67	107	96	101	105	76	94	96	104
10466	BRONX	66	70	72	72	69	68	84	73	90	71	92	53	85	85	79	97	69	80	81	88
10467	BRONX	49	46	46	50	45	45	68	55	75	55	76	39	64	67	58	81	59	62	62	67
10468	BRONX	46	40	38	45	38	40	65	51	73	51	74	35	58	64	53	80	57	58	59	62
10469	BRONX	76	89	94	89	90	85	95	86	99	83	101	64	102	95	95	105	75	92	93	102
10470	BRONX	74	85	90	85	87	84	89	82	93	80	94	61	96	89	90	99	69	88	92	97
10471	BRONX	122	139	153	140	146	136	141	136	139	140	141	103	152	133	150	141	101	140	144	157
10472	BRONX	44	41	40	44	40	39	61	49	66	50	68	36	57	60	52	71	52	55	53	59
10473	BRONX	52	52	52	54	51	49	69	57	73	57	75	42	66	68	61	78	57	63	62	69
10474	BRONX	30	26	24	29	24	25	43	33	49	33	50	23	39	43	35	54	39	38	38	41
10475	BRONX	85	89	81	89	85	94	84	86	91	86	92	60	89	88	86	96	63	88	98	105
10501	AMAWALK	205	284	324	298	307	262	230	244	216	254	216	187	290	217	270	206	165	225	213	270
10502	ARDSLEY	235	321	376	331	353	293	272	286	249	300	247	217	328	243	320	235	186	266	252	315
10504	ARMONK	261	371	454	386	415	348	301	324	281	336	278	242	386	277	363	269	216	297	286	353
10505	BALDWIN PLACE	189	253	270	265	266	229	208	218	194	228	195	170	252	196	240	184	147	202	190	244
10506	BEDFORD	295	420	515	439	471	395	341	367	318	380	315	274	438	315	410	305	245	336	323	399
10507	BEDFORD HILLS	179	222	249	226	237	201	206	203	194	213	196	157	233	192	226	189	146	199	186	229
10509	BREWSTER	140	180	182	178	184	159	157	158	148	162	151	123	179	150	173	144	111	153	144	178
10510	BRIARCLIFF MANOR	252	349	422	361	389	325	293	310	272	323	270	233	363	266	347	260	206	288	276	340
10511	BUCHANAN	117	161	167	151	166	145	138	141	134	134	136	103	160	135	155	137	101	138	137	155
10512	CARMEL	143	193	199	186	199	173	162	168	155	164	157	125	190	157	183	155	116	161	157	186
10514	CHAPPAQUA	292	411	502	429	460	383	338	360	314	375	312	272	429	311	403	300	242	332	315	393
10516	COLD SPRING	136	191	208	182	201	175	164	167	160	158	162	122	194	160	186	164	121	163	165	184
10518	CROSS RIVER	288	412	506	432	462	388	331	357	311	370	308	268	431	310	399	299	241	326	314	388
10520	CROTON ON HUDSON	156	199	224	200	214	185	178	182	169	187	169	138	205	164	201	165	124	176	174	204
10522	DOBBS FERRY	153	199	229	200	215	179	182	182	168	188	169	140	208	165	205	162	126	177	165	202
	NEW YORK	100	106	110	108	107	104	112	106	113	106	114	81	115	110	112	116	83	110	110	124
	UNITED STATES	100	100	100	100	100	100	100	100	100	100	100	100	100	100	100	100	100	100	100	100

10523-10976

ZIP CODE #	POST OFFICE NAME	COUNTY FIPS CODE	POPULATION 2000	POPULATION 2009	POPULATION 2014	2000-2009 ANNUAL RATE % Rate	2000-2009 ANNUAL RATE State Centile	HOUSEHOLDS 2000	HOUSEHOLDS 2009	HOUSEHOLDS 2014	HOUSEHOLDS % Annual Rate 2000-2009	HOUSEHOLDS 2009 Average HH Size	FAMILIES 2000	FAMILIES 2009	FAMILIES % Annual Rate 2000-2009
10523	ELMSFORD	119	7967	8092	8107	0.2	52	2775	2760	2757	-0.1	2.93	2058	2015	-0.2
10524	GARRISON	079	4411	4652	4700	0.6	76	1514	1621	1647	0.7	2.75	1182	1249	0.6
10526	GOLDENS BRIDGE	119	1814	1955	2009	0.8	84	617	652	668	0.6	2.96	498	522	0.5
10527	GRANITE SPRINGS	119	1097	1231	1288	1.3	94	343	382	399	1.2	3.22	316	349	1.1
10528	HARRISON	119	11850	11965	12023	0.1	44	4385	4389	4404	0.0	2.72	3237	3192	-0.2
10530	HARTSDALE	119	12357	12348	12359	0.0	38	5611	5559	5551	-0.1	2.22	3550	3448	-0.3
10532	HAWTHORNE	119	5295	5358	5374	0.1	44	1659	1656	1658	0.0	3.00	1319	1300	-0.2
10533	IRVINGTON	119	7592	7661	7675	0.1	44	2824	2822	2823	0.0	2.68	2012	1978	-0.2
10535	JEFFERSON VALLEY	119	372	440	470	1.8	98	122	143	152	1.7	3.08	98	114	1.6
10536	KATONAH	119	12255	13024	13300	0.7	80	3673	3853	3934	0.5	3.09	3018	3143	0.4
10537	LAKE PEEKSKILL	079	1679	1989	2106	1.8	98	619	743	789	2.0	2.68	450	533	1.8
10538	LARCHMONT	119	16268	16334	16364	0.0	38	6029	5983	5981	-0.1	2.72	4468	4372	-0.2
10541	MAHOPAC	079	26571	27517	27660	0.4	66	8562	8965	9032	0.5	3.07	7102	7363	0.4
10543	MAMARONECK	119	20338	21051	21412	0.4	66	7705	7894	8031	0.3	2.62	5350	5373	0.0
10546	MILLWOOD	119	1013	1017	1024	0.0	38	363	361	361	-0.1	2.76	311	306	-0.2
10547	MOHEGAN LAKE	119	8359	8635	8789	0.4	66	2762	2812	2858	0.2	2.87	2132	2143	0.1
10548	MONTROSE	119	3696	3738	3747	0.1	44	1263	1258	1259	0.0	2.71	935	917	-0.2
10549	MOUNT KISCO	119	15548	16257	16524	0.5	71	5828	6016	6100	0.3	2.65	3986	4053	0.2
10550	MOUNT VERNON	119	37616	38502	38841	0.3	59	13689	13830	13920	0.1	2.75	9104	9025	-0.1
10552	MOUNT VERNON	119	19220	19427	19502	0.1	44	8245	8241	8258	0.0	2.32	4861	4759	-0.2
10553	MOUNT VERNON	119	11471	11708	11802	0.2	52	3759	3785	3808	0.1	3.07	2684	2660	-0.1
10560	NORTH SALEM	119	5194	5702	5910	1.0	89	1763	1925	1995	1.0	2.83	1381	1489	0.8
10562	OSSINING	119	31192	32453	32870	0.4	66	10676	10894	11012	0.2	2.66	7219	7233	0.0
10566	PEEKSKILL	119	22441	23954	24542	0.7	80	8696	9147	9349	0.5	2.59	5344	5509	0.3
10567	CORTLANDT MANOR	119	18308	19718	20302	0.8	84	5820	6214	6391	0.7	3.10	4873	5153	0.6
10570	PLEASANTVILLE	119	12806	13014	13164	0.2	52	4266	4272	4312	0.0	2.87	3236	3201	-0.1
10573	PORT CHESTER	119	36461	38433	39196	0.6	76	12650	13075	13318	0.4	2.91	8808	8991	0.2
10576	POUND RIDGE	119	4834	5108	5228	0.6	76	1735	1819	1858	0.5	2.79	1433	1487	0.4
10577	PURCHASE	119	3399	3782	3900	1.2	93	737	810	842	1.0	3.37	645	704	1.0
10578	PURDYS	119	790	854	882	0.8	84	274	294	303	0.8	2.88	233	248	0.7
10579	PUTNAM VALLEY	079	7860	8234	8315	0.5	71	2715	2877	2914	0.6	2.84	2143	2248	0.5
10580	RYE	119	17046	17467	17627	0.3	59	6173	6248	6294	0.1	2.79	4600	4592	0.0
10583	SCARSDALE	119	37796	38089	38279	0.1	44	13261	13229	13273	0.0	2.87	10568	10445	-0.1
10588	SHRUB OAK	119	1986	2132	2314	0.8	84	702	751	812	0.7	2.84	579	612	0.6
10589	SOMERS	119	7394	7871	8068	0.7	80	3382	3589	3684	0.6	2.12	2220	2314	0.4
10590	SOUTH SALEM	119	6848	7140	7260	0.5	71	2414	2495	2530	0.4	2.86	1933	1978	0.2
10591	TARRYTOWN	119	21510	22798	23192	0.6	76	8256	8570	8683	0.4	2.59	5358	5490	0.3
10594	THORNWOOD	119	5171	5234	5253	0.1	44	1633	1635	1641	0.0	3.04	1353	1342	-0.1
10595	VALHALLA	119	7742	8218	8338	0.6	76	2054	2139	2180	0.4	2.85	1538	1585	0.3
10597	WACCABUC	119	979	1058	1092	0.8	84	333	357	367	0.8	2.96	279	296	0.6
10598	YORKTOWN HEIGHTS	119	29044	29931	30366	0.3	59	10149	10343	10448	0.2	2.86	7948	8016	0.1
10601	WHITE PLAINS	119	9318	10643	11165	1.4	95	4274	4822	5051	1.3	2.09	1995	2184	1.0
10603	WHITE PLAINS	119	15792	16501	16727	0.5	71	6438	6610	6679	0.3	2.46	3943	3981	0.1
10604	WEST HARRISON	119	10460	10931	11121	0.5	71	3838	3949	4007	0.3	2.69	2622	2658	0.1
10605	WHITE PLAINS	119	18402	19152	19443	0.4	66	7320	7563	7676	0.4	2.51	4928	4990	0.1
10606	WHITE PLAINS	119	14993	16825	17501	1.3	94	5014	5373	5537	0.8	3.04	3359	3557	0.6
10607	WHITE PLAINS	119	7061	7234	7345	0.3	59	2316	2344	2374	0.1	3.05	1809	1809	0.0
10701	YONKERS	119	62435	63585	63841	0.2	52	22215	22253	22283	0.0	2.81	15047	14837	-0.2
10703	YONKERS	119	22723	21972	21783	-0.4	11	8342	7973	7888	-0.5	2.68	5645	5305	-0.7
10704	YONKERS	119	29187	29875	30178	0.3	59	11964	12124	12220	0.1	2.46	7658	7606	-0.1
10705	YONKERS	119	37150	38576	39009	0.4	66	12934	13138	13234	0.2	2.93	8942	8912	0.0
10706	HASTINGS ON HUDSON	119	8685	8932	8995	0.3	59	3474	3518	3542	0.1	2.51	2405	2388	-0.1
10707	TUCKAHOE	119	9670	10088	10268	0.5	71	3917	4042	4105	0.3	2.49	2627	2669	0.2
10708	BRONXVILLE	119	23454	23624	23681	0.1	44	10139	10072	10069	-0.1	2.25	5999	5831	-0.3
10709	EASTCHESTER	119	8433	8473	8495	0.1	44	3357	3345	3348	0.0	2.53	2329	2282	-0.2
10710	YONKERS	119	25772	26015	26095	0.1	44	10401	10390	10409	0.0	2.49	7077	6956	-0.2
10801	NEW ROCHELLE	119	36214	38671	39503	0.7	80	12718	13230	13458	0.4	2.87	8382	8585	0.3
10803	PELHAM	119	11970	12299	12424	0.3	59	4186	4262	4299	0.2	2.88	3219	3233	0.0
10804	NEW ROCHELLE	119	14195	14370	14428	0.1	44	4858	4866	4876	0.0	2.94	4010	3977	-0.1
10805	NEW ROCHELLE	119	18020	19003	19359	0.6	76	7336	7606	7737	0.4	2.30	4073	4115	0.1
10901	SUFFERN	087	22535	24061	24547	0.7	80	8389	8916	9096	0.7	2.65	5838	6138	0.5
10913	BLAUVELT	087	5180	5330	5382	0.3	59	1550	1597	1616	0.3	2.99	1256	1279	0.2
10916	CAMPBELL HALL	071	3960	4719	5068	1.9	98	1239	1483	1598	2.0	3.12	1034	1223	1.8
10917	CENTRAL VALLEY	071	1705	1883	1958	1.1	91	609	677	708	1.2	2.77	470	512	0.9
10918	CHESTER	071	11594	13127	13765	1.4	95	3728	4180	4394	1.2	2.94	2864	3177	1.1
10919	CIRCLEVILLE	071	689	779	822	1.3	94	241	274	290	1.4	2.84	183	204	1.2
10920	CONGERS	087	8715	8807	8844	0.1	44	2869	2921	2943	0.2	2.96	2335	2347	0.1
10921	FLORIDA	071	4951	5527	5781	1.2	93	1632	1846	1948	1.3	2.69	1196	1333	1.2
10923	GARNERVILLE	087	8041	8126	8152	0.1	44	2618	2653	2666	0.1	3.02	2012	2012	0.0
10924	GOSHEN	071	11943	13151	13665	1.0	89	3927	4362	4563	1.1	2.73	2837	3099	1.0
10925	GREENWOOD LAKE	071	5089	6099	6559	2.0	98	2032	2453	2652	2.1	2.49	1323	1554	1.8
10926	HARRIMAN	071	3316	3711	3971	1.2	93	1289	1450	1557	1.3	2.55	901	993	1.1
10927	HAVERSTRAW	087	10117	11094	11458	1.0	89	2816	3087	3197	1.0	3.43	2169	2351	0.9
10928	HIGHLAND FALLS	071	5366	5988	6263	1.2	93	2238	2504	2626	1.2	2.39	1388	1513	0.9
10930	HIGHLAND MILLS	071	7377	8854	9474	2.0	98	2399	2865	3073	1.9	3.08	2011	2371	1.8
10931	HILLBURN	087	881	869	861	-0.1	30	273	267	265	-0.2	3.25	222	215	-0.3
10940	MIDDLETOWN	071	42756	47877	49941	1.2	93	15428	17329	18151	1.3	2.70	10374	11474	1.1
10941	MIDDLETOWN	071	13136	14406	15253	1.0	89	4745	5198	5503	1.0	2.75	3448	3717	0.8
10950	MONROE	071	38511	46683	50238	2.1	98	10444	12556	13487	2.0	3.65	8746	10471	2.0
10952	MONSEY	087	30193	32337	33171	0.7	80	7404	7800	7991	0.6	4.06	6299	6595	0.5
10954	NANUET	087	22274	22707	22858	0.2	52	7975	8182	8268	0.3	2.70	5897	5951	0.1
10956	NEW CITY	087	30938	30973	30965	0.0	38	9874	9936	9962	0.1	3.04	8573	8552	0.0
10958	NEW HAMPTON	071	2706	3034	3191	1.2	93	939	1054	1115	1.3	2.84	754	832	1.1
10960	NYACK	087	14737	14637	14583	-0.1	30	6045	6018	6008	0.0	2.32	3392	3297	-0.3
10962	ORANGEBURG	087	5641	6332	6345	1.3	94	1792	1863	1868	0.4	2.84	1356	1398	0.3
10963	OTISVILLE	071	4260	4823	4975	1.4	95	784	897	953	1.5	2.89	586	658	1.3
10964	PALISADES	087	1453	1466	1469	0.1	44	560	569	573	0.2	2.57	375	373	-0.1
10965	PEARL RIVER	087	14470	14323	14300	-0.1	30	5277	5247	5249	-0.1	2.71	3983	3904	-0.2
10968	PIERMONT	087	2323	2523	2601	0.9	87	1070	1168	1209	1.0	2.16	606	644	0.7
10969	PINE ISLAND	071	1158	1394	1501	2.0	98	413	500	541	2.1	2.76	300	357	1.9
10970	POMONA	087	9966	10046	10086	0.1	44	3742	3779	3803	0.1	2.61	2646	2631	-0.1
10973	SLATE HILL	071	1867	2176	2316	1.7	97	629	737	789	1.7	2.94	516	596	1.6
10974	SLOATSBURG	087	3353	3342	3332	0.0	38	1129	1133	1132	0.0	2.88	897	890	-0.1
10975	SOUTHFIELDS	071	415	471	499	1.4	95	191	218	231	1.4	2.14	130	146	1.3
10976	SPARKILL	087	1477	1111	1123	-3.0	0	322	333	338	0.4	3.15	225	228	0.1
	NEW YORK					0.3					0.3	2.61			0.1
	UNITED STATES					1.0					1.1	2.59			0.9

ZIP CODE #	POST OFFICE NAME	RACE (%) White 2000	White 2009	Black 2000	Black 2009	Asian/Pacific 2000	Asian/Pacific 2009	% Hispanic Origin 2000	% Hispanic Origin 2009	2009 AGE DISTRIBUTION (%) 0-4	5-9	10-14	15-19	20-24	25-44	45-64	65-84	85+	18+	MEDIAN AGE 2009	% 2009 Males	% 2009 Females
10523	ELMSFORD	55.4	49.3	25.4	28.0	7.2	8.9	18.4	21.1	6.7	6.7	6.7	6.4	5.6	28.1	27.2	11.0	1.6	76.1	38.7	48.7	51.3
10524	GARRISON	95.3	94.2	1.7	1.9	1.3	1.8	4.3	5.2	5.7	6.6	7.6	6.6	3.5	20.4	34.7	13.5	1.4	75.4	44.7	48.1	51.9
10526	GOLDENS BRIDGE	95.3	93.5	1.7	2.2	2.3	3.3	2.5	3.6	5.9	8.6	9.8	7.9	3.0	22.6	32.4	8.8	1.0	69.7	40.6	49.5	50.5
10527	GRANITE SPRINGS	96.1	94.6	1.2	1.5	1.4	1.9	2.9	4.1	7.6	8.9	10.2	7.1	2.5	20.5	32.7	9.7	0.7	68.6	41.0	49.6	50.4
10528	HARRISON	89.2	85.4	0.6	0.8	7.6	10.3	5.5	7.2	6.7	6.7	7.4	7.1	5.2	23.7	29.2	11.8	2.2	74.7	40.6	47.8	52.2
10530	HARTSDALE	76.4	70.2	7.4	8.9	12.3	15.9	8.0	10.0	5.5	5.8	6.2	4.8	3.8	23.2	31.9	16.1	2.6	79.2	45.4	46.4	53.6
10532	HAWTHORNE	93.1	90.9	3.3	4.1	1.6	2.2	5.9	7.8	5.7	6.0	8.1	9.3	4.2	23.9	28.5	12.4	1.9	73.2	40.5	49.5	50.5
10533	IRVINGTON	86.4	81.9	2.5	3.0	7.9	10.7	4.4	5.7	7.0	7.9	10.0	6.9	3.7	21.7	30.0	10.9	1.9	70.4	40.8	48.5	51.5
10535	JEFFERSON VALLEY	90.6	87.5	2.1	2.5	4.6	6.4	5.9	8.0	6.4	6.8	7.7	7.0	5.0	22.3	32.0	11.4	1.4	75.0	41.6	48.4	51.6
10536	KATONAH	89.6	87.1	5.7	6.6	2.2	3.0	5.0	6.3	6.6	7.8	9.4	8.5	4.2	21.5	31.0	9.5	1.6	70.3	40.4	47.4	52.6
10537	LAKE PEEKSKILL	94.8	93.6	1.7	1.9	1.1	1.5	9.4	11.7	5.4	5.8	6.5	7.7	5.9	25.6	32.2	9.5	1.3	77.6	40.7	48.9	51.1
10538	LARCHMONT	92.9	90.4	1.5	2.0	3.1	4.3	4.8	6.4	7.6	8.2	9.4	7.3	3.7	21.5	29.6	10.7	2.1	69.8	40.7	48.4	51.6
10541	MAHOPAC	94.8	93.5	1.0	1.1	1.3	1.8	5.5	6.9	6.7	7.0	7.7	7.2	4.9	24.4	30.6	10.3	1.2	74.1	40.2	49.3	50.7
10543	MAMARONECK	85.1	81.3	3.9	4.7	3.8	5.0	16.3	20.1	6.0	6.1	6.5	6.6	5.5	26.1	28.4	11.8	2.9	77.0	40.7	48.3	51.7
10546	MILLWOOD	88.9	85.1	2.7	3.4	6.8	9.4	3.7	4.7	6.4	7.6	10.4	8.8	3.3	18.4	33.9	10.4	0.8	68.8	42.3	50.8	49.2
10547	MOHEGAN LAKE	84.7	80.5	6.6	8.1	2.7	3.7	10.6	13.5	6.9	7.2	7.6	9.2	5.2	24.1	28.7	9.2	1.8	72.5	38.5	49.4	50.6
10548	MONTROSE	89.7	86.4	4.2	5.4	2.8	3.9	6.0	7.9	5.9	6.4	6.9	6.8	4.8	21.9	32.4	13.0	1.9	76.7	43.2	51.3	48.7
10549	MOUNT KISCO	83.7	79.9	4.3	4.9	3.8	5.0	16.9	20.3	6.5	6.9	7.7	7.3	5.5	25.7	28.8	10.2	1.5	74.3	39.0	50.3	49.7
10550	MOUNT VERNON	18.5	16.1	68.4	69.6	1.9	2.2	11.9	12.7	7.8	7.6	7.2	7.4	7.2	27.2	24.4	9.6	1.6	72.8	34.3	45.4	54.6
10552	MOUNT VERNON	60.3	53.9	27.5	31.2	3.5	4.3	9.7	11.6	5.6	5.3	5.3	4.9	5.3	26.5	28.8	14.6	3.9	80.8	43.3	45.8	54.2
10553	MOUNT VERNON	8.9	7.5	84.4	85.2	0.8	0.9	6.4	6.6	7.0	6.7	6.7	7.9	7.7	26.3	25.3	10.8	1.6	74.9	35.5	45.1	54.9
10560	NORTH SALEM	95.4	93.4	0.8	1.0	1.0	1.4	3.6	5.1	6.6	7.5	8.5	6.6	3.3	20.2	31.1	12.3	3.9	72.9	43.5	47.8	52.2
10562	OSSINING	66.9	65.6	16.4	15.3	4.3	5.8	22.6	24.2	5.7	5.7	6.0	8.2	7.8	27.6	26.0	10.5	2.3	79.0	37.8	50.6	49.4
10566	PEEKSKILL	57.1	51.7	25.5	28.1	2.4	3.0	21.9	25.0	7.1	7.0	6.8	6.6	5.8	28.6	26.5	9.7	1.9	74.9	37.5	48.6	51.4
10567	CORTLANDT MANOR	86.5	82.5	6.1	7.7	2.9	4.0	8.1	10.4	7.0	7.8	8.6	8.3	4.7	21.3	30.9	9.8	1.5	71.2	40.1	49.3	50.7
10570	PLEASANTVILLE	90.8	87.6	2.2	2.8	3.9	5.5	5.7	7.5	6.6	7.3	9.0	9.1	5.7	20.1	30.6	10.1	1.6	71.8	40.1	49.9	50.1
10573	PORT CHESTER	68.1	65.0	5.6	5.8	2.6	3.4	36.6	39.8	7.0	6.9	6.8	6.2	5.8	29.7	25.1	10.0	2.4	75.5	37.0	50.1	49.9
10576	POUND RIDGE	95.5	93.8	1.2	1.6	1.7	2.4	2.4	3.3	6.3	7.9	10.1	7.0	2.7	17.8	34.0	12.9	1.3	70.8	44.0	48.8	51.2
10577	PURCHASE	87.7	82.2	4.1	6.6	4.3	5.7	5.5	7.6	6.3	6.3	6.0	16.5	14.0	18.3	21.5	9.4	1.6	79.0	26.5	47.5	52.5
10578	PURDYS	96.8	95.6	0.5	0.7	0.8	1.1	2.3	3.2	7.7	8.0	9.0	6.9	3.7	19.0	31.7	12.6	1.3	70.3	42.4	48.8	51.2
10579	PUTNAM VALLEY	94.3	93.1	1.7	1.9	0.8	1.1	5.6	7.0	6.6	7.1	7.8	6.6	4.4	24.9	31.8	9.7	1.1	74.2	40.8	49.5	50.5
10580	RYE	90.0	86.4	1.2	1.6	6.2	8.6	4.8	6.2	8.0	8.7	9.5	7.1	3.5	21.4	28.6	11.2	2.0	68.8	40.4	48.8	51.2
10583	SCARSDALE	84.6	79.5	1.9	2.4	11.6	15.6	3.1	4.0	6.6	7.7	9.4	7.7	3.5	17.9	31.7	13.2	2.3	71.2	43.2	48.2	51.8
10588	SHRUB OAK	92.0	89.2	2.8	3.7	1.9	2.6	8.1	10.7	6.8	7.6	8.1	7.3	5.1	22.9	31.4	9.7	1.1	72.9	40.4	48.4	51.6
10589	SOMERS	95.2	93.3	1.7	2.2	2.0	2.9	2.3	3.0	4.2	4.8	5.6	4.7	2.2	13.8	31.6	27.5	5.6	81.8	55.2	45.6	54.4
10590	SOUTH SALEM	95.1	93.2	1.1	1.4	2.0	2.8	2.3	3.1	6.6	7.8	9.3	8.0	4.4	17.0	35.9	10.2	0.8	70.9	42.9	49.3	50.7
10591	TARRYTOWN	73.0	68.5	6.4	7.1	5.0	6.4	28.1	32.0	6.9	6.6	6.5	6.5	6.8	29.3	25.4	10.1	1.8	76.3	37.4	47.9	52.1
10594	THORNWOOD	91.2	88.2	2.8	3.5	3.4	4.7	5.7	7.4	6.6	6.8	8.5	8.5	4.1	22.8	28.3	12.5	1.9	71.9	40.1	49.6	50.4
10595	VALHALLA	79.2	75.8	14.2	15.7	4.3	5.5	6.4	7.7	5.1	4.9	5.8	6.7	8.1	29.5	23.1	12.9	3.7	80.5	38.9	55.1	44.9
10597	WACCABUC	95.0	92.9	1.2	1.6	2.2	3.1	3.1	4.3	6.3	7.8	10.3	9.2	3.4	16.3	36.1	9.6	0.9	69.6	42.9	48.3	51.7
10598	YORKTOWN HEIGHTS	92.1	89.1	2.2	2.8	3.5	4.9	4.8	6.4	6.3	6.8	8.0	7.5	4.5	20.6	31.3	12.3	2.6	73.7	42.6	47.7	52.3
10601	WHITE PLAINS	48.0	44.2	27.5	27.8	5.1	6.2	29.4	32.7	5.7	5.4	5.1	5.2	7.5	31.1	24.0	12.4	3.6	80.8	38.6	46.3	53.7
10603	WHITE PLAINS	56.5	51.6	29.2	31.2	5.0	6.2	13.3	15.7	6.1	6.1	6.2	6.0	5.8	27.1	28.3	12.3	2.2	78.1	40.6	47.3	52.7
10604	WEST HARRISON	80.1	77.0	8.9	9.2	3.7	4.8	13.3	16.0	6.8	6.5	6.2	7.6	6.9	27.1	25.7	11.2	2.0	77.0	38.4	46.3	53.7
10605	WHITE PLAINS	78.8	74.0	9.4	11.1	4.1	5.4	12.6	15.3	5.9	6.2	6.7	5.8	4.4	23.0	30.5	14.8	2.5	77.4	43.6	47.5	52.5
10606	WHITE PLAINS	58.3	53.1	17.0	19.6	3.8	4.4	35.6	39.2	6.2	6.0	6.0	6.1	6.1	30.5	25.3	10.6	3.2	78.1	37.8	49.6	50.4
10607	WHITE PLAINS	50.2	44.7	32.1	34.5	8.2	10.0	13.1	14.6	5.7	6.0	6.5	5.8	4.6	25.0	29.6	14.7	2.1	78.2	42.7	48.4	51.6
10701	YONKERS	42.6	39.2	28.0	28.5	3.3	4.0	34.6	37.2	8.2	7.8	7.0	7.6	8.0	28.3	22.1	9.0	1.8	72.3	32.6	47.3	52.7
10703	YONKERS	63.2	59.5	17.5	18.0	4.0	5.2	22.4	25.1	6.6	6.2	6.0	6.4	6.9	26.1	24.4	13.9	3.5	77.5	38.7	46.9	53.1
10704	YONKERS	83.9	79.3	4.6	5.6	4.5	5.9	11.0	14.0	6.0	5.8	5.7	5.3	5.0	29.7	25.8	13.9	2.8	79.3	40.6	48.3	51.7
10705	YONKERS	46.0	42.0	16.7	17.2	5.7	6.6	44.8	48.1	8.5	7.9	7.1	7.8	8.1	29.4	21.2	8.6	1.4	71.8	31.7	48.2	51.8
10706	HASTINGS ON HUDSON	89.0	84.9	2.4	3.3	5.0	6.9	4.5	6.1	4.8	5.8	7.3	7.2	4.8	20.6	34.0	13.2	2.4	77.5	44.7	48.3	51.7
10707	TUCKAHOE	80.6	76.2	6.9	7.9	7.6	9.8	7.2	8.9	7.0	7.1	7.1	5.9	5.0	25.8	27.1	12.6	2.2	75.1	40.6	48.0	52.0
10708	BRONXVILLE	88.7	85.3	3.8	4.8	4.0	5.4	6.5	8.4	5.2	5.2	5.7	6.4	5.8	22.8	29.7	15.8	3.4	80.9	44.2	45.5	54.5
10709	EASTCHESTER	90.6	87.2	0.6	0.8	5.9	8.2	3.4	4.5	5.8	6.6	7.1	6.4	3.6	21.2	29.8	15.9	3.5	76.4	44.5	47.2	52.8
10710	YONKERS	73.4	68.0	10.5	11.7	9.8	12.4	10.9	13.4	5.3	5.4	5.7	5.3	4.2	24.3	28.1	17.7	3.9	80.2	44.8	46.7	53.3
10801	NEW ROCHELLE	56.2	52.7	27.8	29.0	3.0	3.5	28.2	31.4	7.1	6.7	6.3	7.4	7.6	28.4	23.6	10.8	2.2	75.9	35.3	48.4	51.6
10803	PELHAM	87.2	83.5	4.6	5.6	3.9	5.4	6.1	7.9	7.0	7.7	8.7	7.2	4.5	22.4	29.6	11.0	1.9	71.8	40.3	49.1	50.9
10804	NEW ROCHELLE	86.4	82.4	8.0	10.1	3.0	4.1	3.8	4.9	6.5	7.3	8.9	7.3	3.2	18.9	31.0	14.1	2.7	72.2	43.6	48.6	51.4
10805	NEW ROCHELLE	72.2	66.7	13.8	16.1	3.9	5.0	20.2	24.1	5.7	5.0	4.8	5.9	7.4	28.2	24.4	13.5	5.1	81.9	40.2	45.7	54.3
10901	SUFFERN	89.5	86.9	3.1	3.7	3.0	4.2	8.3	9.9	6.2	6.7	7.3	6.7	4.9	23.0	28.5	13.8	2.9	75.3	41.8	47.8	52.2
10913	BLAUVELT	88.4	83.9	1.7	2.6	7.1	9.7	5.6	7.1	6.5	6.6	7.5	9.5	7.2	20.8	25.0	14.2	2.7	75.3	39.4	47.3	52.7
10916	CAMPBELL HALL	94.0	92.0	1.9	2.3	1.4	1.9	4.6	6.2	6.4	6.9	7.6	7.8	5.3	22.1	31.8	10.3	1.8	74.0	40.5	48.7	51.3
10917	CENTRAL VALLEY	94.1	92.0	0.8	1.0	1.7	2.4	7.0	9.3	6.5	6.5	7.2	7.7	5.5	23.8	31.2	9.9	1.6	74.7	39.7	50.4	49.6
10918	CHESTER	87.8	85.1	6.6	7.6	2.4	3.2	9.7	12.2	6.8	7.3	7.6	6.5	4.1	28.0	30.5	8.4	1.0	74.2	40.1	53.0	47.0
10919	CIRCLEVILLE	92.6	90.0	2.5	3.1	1.6	2.3	3.5	4.6	6.2	6.9	7.2	6.5	4.9	24.9	30.8	10.9	1.7	75.6	40.4	50.3	49.7
10920	CONGERS	84.2	79.3	2.0	2.3	9.5	12.9	7.6	9.5	6.8	7.1	7.7	6.5	4.4	25.9	29.1	10.9	1.5	74.1	40.1	49.2	50.8
10921	FLORIDA	93.6	91.5	2.9	3.8	0.6	0.9	5.6	7.7	5.6	6.2	6.7	6.5	4.5	21.0	28.4	14.7	6.2	77.3	44.6	44.9	55.1
10923	GARNERVILLE	69.4	65.5	11.8	12.4	4.4	5.5	24.2	27.7	6.9	6.8	7.0	6.9	6.0	29.0	26.4	10.0	1.0	75.1	37.1	48.6	51.4
10924	GOSHEN	88.5	85.6	6.7	8.0	1.8	2.5	7.5	9.5	5.5	5.8	6.4	8.5	6.2	24.9	27.6	11.4	3.5	76.7	39.8	50.9	49.1
10925	GREENWOOD LAKE	95.2	93.6	1.0	1.2	1.0	1.4	5.5	7.5	6.1	6.5	6.8	6.3	5.8	27.0	30.2	9.9	1.4	76.3	39.9	50.6	49.4
10926	HARRIMAN	88.6	84.5	2.9	3.6	4.2	5.8	8.3	11.0	6.7	6.8	7.2	7.2	6.0	27.4	29.6	7.8	1.1	74.1	38.3	50.0	50.0
10927	HAVERSTRAW	46.0	42.4	12.1	12.4	1.2	1.4	59.3	63.7	7.6	7.5	7.1	8.2	8.4	28.3	21.5	9.0	2.4	73.0	32.2	48.7	51.3
10928	HIGHLAND FALLS	82.1	77.9	9.2	10.9	1.9	2.5	9.2	11.6	5.9	5.8	6.0	6.6	6.3	25.8	28.8	12.6	2.2	78.4	40.8	49.3	50.7
10930	HIGHLAND MILLS	90.7	88.1	3.2	3.7	2.0	2.7	7.7	10.3	7.8	8.3	8.5	7.3	4.5	25.0	29.4	8.3	0.9	70.5	37.5	48.8	51.2
10931	HILLBURN	49.0	41.9	11.1	12.3	5.0	6.2	5.6	6.1	7.8	8.2	8.1	7.1	6.0	24.6	26.1	10.1	2.0	71.7	36.0	45.5	54.5
10940	MIDDLETOWN	75.2	71.3	11.9	13.3	1.7	2.2	19.6	22.7	7.3	7.0	7.1	7.2	6.2	27.2	26.0	9.9	2.1	74.1	36.5	48.8	51.2
10941	MIDDLETOWN	81.1	76.9	9.1	10.7	2.9	3.8	12.6	15.6	6.5	6.9	7.1	7.1	6.3	28.0	28.0	9.0	1.1	74.9	37.2	49.1	50.9
10950	MONROE	94.0	92.1	1.7	2.1	1.4	1.9	5.6	7.3	12.0	10.0	8.4	9.6	7.8	23.4	21.6	6.4	0.8	64.0	26.6	51.4	48.6
10952	MONSEY	90.6	88.2	4.7	5.6	2.5	3.3	3.4	4.2	13.0	10.6	9.6	9.2	7.8	21.5	19.4	7.8	1.1	60.9	24.9	50.1	49.9
10954	NANUET	74.7	69.1	11.6	13.1	9.0	12.1	8.1	9.7	6.4	6.5	6.9	6.5	5.1	25.5	28.2	13.0	1.9	76.1	40.6	48.1	51.9
10956	NEW CITY	85.3	81.3	4.5	5.1	6.9	9.5	5.8	7.2	6.0	6.5	7.5	7.0	4.1	21.9	31.2	14.0	1.8	75.4	43.0	49.0	51.0
10958	NEW HAMPTON	91.9	89.2	2.7	3.4	1.8	2.5	6.7	8.9	6.2	6.4	6.9	7.8	6.1	24.3	30.3	10.7	1.5	75.4	40.1	49.3	50.7
10960	NYACK	70.4	65.3	19.3	21.7	4.0	5.3	7.5	8.8	5.0	4.9	5.2	7.0	7.9	26.4	29.2	12.5	1.9	81.6	40.7	48.0	52.0
10962	ORANGEBURG	75.1	69.7	6.9	8.1	14.6	18.1	7.0	8.5	5.0	5.2	6.3	7.2	5.7	23.6	29.0	15.5	2.4	80.2	43.0	51.0	49.0
10963	OTISVILLE	70.7	68.1	23.6	25.0	1.9	2.2	19.5	21.9	3.4	3.3	3.4	4.3	7.8	46.2	25.0	6.0	0.7	87.3	36.6	72.8	27.2
10964	PALISADES	87.0	82.5	0.8	1.0	9.7	13.4	5.2	6.6	6.4	7.1	8.3	7.0	3.8	19.6	30.5	13.3	4.0	73.3	43.6	47.3	52.7
10965	PEARL RIVER	94.9	93.0	0.6	0.7	3.1	4.5	3.6	4.7	6.6	6.6	7.2	7.1	4.8	23.9	27.7	14.0	2.0	74.8	41.2	48.0	52.0
10968	PIERMONT	78.3	73.1	4.8	5.5	8.1	10.5	11.8	14.2	4.5	4.6	5.2	5.4	4.3	27.2	34.1	13.2	1.5	82.4	44.2	50.6	49.4
10969	PINE ISLAND	95.9	94.5	1.0	1.2	0.7	1.0	5.3	7.1	6.1	6.9	7.7	8.2	5.7	22.0	32.4	9.6	1.4	73.5	40.4	49.4	50.6
10970	POMONA	78.4	73.0	9.3	11.0	5.7	7.7	11.1	13.5	6.2	6.5	6.7	5.5	4.4	26.6	30.0	12.5	1.5	77.0	41.4	48.1	51.9
10973	SLATE HILL	93.8	91.9	1.5	1.9	1.8	2.4	4.4	5.9	6.4	6.9	7.2	7.9	6.3	24.2	30.3	9.6	1.3	73.9	39.1	49.9	50.1
10974	SLOATSBURG	91.2	88.6	3.5	4.2	2.4	3.4	5.5	7.0	6.9	7.3	7.6	6.6	4.7	24.5	29.1	11.4	1.9	73.8	40.5	50.0	50.0
10975	SOUTHFIELDS	91.3	88.1	1.4	1.7	4.6	6.4	3.6	4.9	5.3	5.3	5.5	5.7	5.1	24.4	34.2	12.7	1.7	79.8	44.2	50.3	49.7
10976	SPARKILL	85.4	72.1	3.0	14.8	6.0	7.2	7.4	7.2	6.7	6.9	7.5	7.3	5.3	21.2	25.7	15.1	4.3	77.9	41.3	44.2	55.8
	NEW YORK	67.9	64.8	15.9	16.5	5.6	6.9	15.1	16.7	6.5	6.4	6.4	7.1	7.0	27.0	26.3	11.2	2.1	76.6	37.5	48.4	51.6
	UNITED STATES	75.1	72.0	12.3	12.7	3.8	4.6	12.5	15.7	6.8	6.7	6.6	7.1	6.9	27.0	26.0	10.9	1.9	75.7	36.9	49.2	50.8

ZIP CODE				2009 HOUSEHOLD INCOME DISTRIBUTION (%)					MEDIAN HOUSEHOLD INCOME					2009 HOME VALUE DISTRIBUTION (%)					
#	POST OFFICE NAME	2009 Per Capita Income	2009 HH Income Base	Less than $25,000	$25,000 to $49,999	$50,000 to $99,999	$100,000 to $149,999	$150,000 or More	2009	2014	2009 National Centile	2009 State Centile	2009 Home Value Base	Less than $50,000	$50,000 to $89,999	$90,000 to $174,999	$175,000 to $399,999	$400,000 or More	2009 Median Home Value
10523	ELMSFORD	39178	2760	8.5	15.4	31.2	24.7	20.2	90546	94761	95	88	1836	0.1	0.0	0.5	36.7	62.8	448057
10524	GARRISON	50239	1621	4.7	6.7	29.1	34.0	25.5	111080	117794	98	96	1374	0.9	0.4	0.6	43.3	54.9	436413
10526	GOLDENS BRIDGE	72222	652	4.6	4.6	12.9	27.3	50.6	151994	166255	100	99	551	0.0	0.0	0.0	16.5	83.5	783390
10527	GRANITE SPRINGS	52418	382	6.8	5.0	17.5	26.7	44.0	139513	147189	99	99	340	0.0	0.0	0.0	8.2	91.8	694231
10528	HARRISON	52713	4389	9.3	14.1	26.5	22.8	27.3	100222	107061	97	91	2717	0.0	0.1	1.8	7.1	91.0	864986
10530	HARTSDALE	60167	5559	8.0	11.8	28.4	24.6	27.2	103129	108383	97	92	4076	0.0	0.5	9.8	30.0	59.7	474763
10532	HAWTHORNE	38049	1656	3.9	12.8	29.3	29.8	24.2	106600	110656	98	94	1387	0.4	0.4	0.0	12.0	87.2	559313
10533	IRVINGTON	68476	2822	7.4	8.9	25.8	22.1	35.8	119822	126916	98	97	2011	0.0	0.0	1.8	18.2	80.1	716968
10535	JEFFERSON VALLEY	43259	143	7.0	14.0	22.4	28.0	28.7	110315	120635	98	95	111	0.0	0.0	0.0	30.6	69.4	467188
10536	KATONAH	60469	3853	4.3	7.4	18.6	26.0	43.8	134148	144041	99	98	3158	0.0	0.0	0.1	5.9	94.1	834726
10537	LAKE PEEKSKILL	36446	743	9.8	18.2	32.7	29.3	10.0	82545	87409	93	86	607	0.0	0.0	4.1	90.0	5.9	250744
10538	LARCHMONT	82271	5983	6.8	8.6	20.4	17.1	47.2	140967	153357	99	99	4391	0.0	0.2	3.3	7.6	88.9	961089
10541	MAHOPAC	39704	8965	6.0	10.1	29.2	31.6	23.2	106255	112838	97	94	7616	0.2	0.2	1.5	45.2	52.9	412550
10543	MAMARONECK	50438	7894	12.4	16.2	28.3	20.6	22.4	85203	89352	94	87	4744	0.1	0.3	3.9	18.0	77.6	629434
10546	MILLWOOD	75994	361	1.1	5.5	20.8	19.1	53.5	172344	200163	100	100	314	0.0	0.0	0.0	8.6	91.4	889241
10547	MOHEGAN LAKE	38442	2812	6.7	12.8	30.0	32.8	17.6	100584	102762	97	92	2148	0.3	0.1	1.7	53.3	44.5	385952
10548	MONTROSE	35002	1258	12.5	17.6	27.4	27.5	15.0	84398	89784	94	86	954	0.0	0.0	2.1	55.7	42.2	374126
10549	MOUNT KISCO	56583	6016	12.4	13.7	24.8	18.8	30.4	97456	104651	96	91	3929	0.5	1.0	9.3	12.5	76.7	630517
10550	MOUNT VERNON	20256	13830	29.4	27.3	28.3	11.3	3.7	43998	47192	45	27	3613	0.5	0.4	2.3	49.2	47.6	393037
10552	MOUNT VERNON	39581	8241	14.3	19.5	33.2	20.2	12.8	71685	76043	88	78	4409	3.0	10.0	12.8	13.9	60.3	467783
10553	MOUNT VERNON	25295	3785	21.1	20.9	31.7	18.7	7.6	59256	63959	76	62	1756	0.5	1.1	3.4	39.2	55.9	424582
10560	NORTH SALEM	55688	1925	4.3	10.5	20.1	26.6	38.5	129207	133752	99	98	1602	0.0	0.0	1.0	16.4	82.6	628544
10562	OSSINING	39497	10894	12.4	16.9	30.1	22.1	18.4	80748	84856	92	85	6570	0.0	1.3	3.1	37.5	58.0	432411
10566	PEEKSKILL	29230	9147	18.8	21.6	32.5	19.9	7.1	60086	65147	77	64	4393	0.1	1.2	6.9	75.9	16.0	307576
10567	CORTLANDT MANOR	41894	6214	4.5	10.1	29.7	29.0	26.8	108654	112675	98	95	5359	0.1	0.1	0.5	42.7	56.6	429600
10570	PLEASANTVILLE	57336	4272	5.3	11.3	21.9	21.0	40.5	128337	136063	99	98	3306	0.2	0.3	0.7	12.8	86.1	670475
10573	PORT CHESTER	36693	13075	16.0	18.2	29.8	19.1	16.8	72494	77408	88	79	7194	0.9	2.3	2.2	18.2	76.3	566593
10576	POUND RIDGE	84323	1819	3.1	3.8	13.7	23.3	56.1	172040	188251	100	100	1613	0.0	0.1	0.2	1.7	98.0	1000001
10577	PURCHASE	59887	810	3.6	4.1	9.5	21.9	61.0	186504	200460	100	100	701	0.0	0.0	0.0	2.0	98.0	1000001
10578	PURDYS	45981	294	1.0	6.1	36.4	29.9	26.5	110034	114300	98	95	265	0.0	0.0	0.0	18.5	81.5	547454
10579	PUTNAM VALLEY	44017	2877	6.3	8.1	32.0	29.0	24.6	106228	115930	97	94	2503	0.0	0.1	2.8	52.8	44.3	383545
10580	RYE	82883	6248	6.0	8.3	17.4	21.7	46.5	141388	152190	99	99	4548	0.3	0.2	0.9	8.0	90.7	1000001
10583	SCARSDALE	79030	13229	4.8	7.2	17.4	20.5	50.1	150292	163411	100	99	11071	0.1	0.1	3.9	11.4	84.4	896269
10588	SHRUB OAK	43945	751	6.9	6.3	27.8	41.1	17.8	111425	112978	98	96	619	0.0	0.0	0.2	45.4	54.4	413819
10589	SOMERS	59157	3589	6.8	12.3	29.3	23.8	27.9	102785	107791	97	92	3167	0.0	0.0	0.1	28.3	71.6	491745
10590	SOUTH SALEM	71898	2495	2.9	6.0	20.8	29.2	41.0	132302	138907	99	98	2168	0.0	0.1	0.7	16.0	83.2	725835
10591	TARRYTOWN	46442	8570	11.2	15.9	30.7	21.6	20.8	83997	88213	93	86	4097	0.0	0.1	3.2	18.3	78.4	572771
10594	THORNWOOD	45050	1635	5.6	11.6	27.0	27.5	28.3	108614	113921	98	95	1361	0.0	0.1	0.7	9.0	90.2	644027
10595	VALHALLA	36071	2139	8.7	8.9	34.4	22.7	25.3	96280	100548	96	90	1571	0.0	0.1	0.2	8.6	91.1	628597
10597	WACCABUC	79309	357	3.1	3.6	15.7	26.1	51.5	154506	167265	100	99	318	0.0	0.0	0.0	6.3	93.7	833333
10598	YORKTOWN HEIGHTS	43965	10343	8.4	12.5	24.3	26.9	27.8	108009	113797	98	95	8683	0.0	0.0	0.5	32.5	67.0	459688
10601	WHITE PLAINS	30253	4822	28.3	22.0	32.4	11.6	5.8	49653	53579	60	44	1495	3.1	5.6	22.6	52.0	16.7	217085
10603	WHITE PLAINS	40968	6610	12.5	17.7	30.8	24.4	14.6	80310	84386	92	85	3946	0.3	0.8	8.2	43.6	47.2	389736
10604	WEST HARRISON	42914	3949	13.8	17.0	27.3	22.6	19.3	83226	88488	93	86	2148	0.6	0.0	3.6	7.1	88.7	700000
10605	WHITE PLAINS	58048	7563	10.7	13.8	24.6	19.7	31.2	101612	106227	97	92	5252	0.3	1.6	8.6	12.4	77.0	670880
10606	WHITE PLAINS	33623	5373	15.1	19.4	30.0	20.2	15.3	73562	77489	89	79	2430	0.2	0.3	4.1	24.0	71.4	495588
10607	WHITE PLAINS	47682	2344	7.4	9.8	21.8	27.3	33.7	123321	127530	99	97	1936	0.2	0.2	0.4	24.9	74.4	507051
10701	YONKERS	21682	22253	31.9	23.4	26.9	12.8	5.0	43760	47684	45	26	6393	0.5	1.6	11.2	37.4	49.3	396695
10703	YONKERS	26338	7973	24.1	22.1	27.8	19.7	6.3	55972	62288	73	59	3815	0.9	2.0	8.8	47.1	41.3	369376
10704	YONKERS	35678	12124	14.4	19.4	32.9	24.8	8.5	72393	76336	88	79	6379	0.3	2.6	6.0	32.1	59.0	431543
10705	YONKERS	22784	13138	27.6	25.8	27.4	13.1	6.1	45404	50050	49	32	3896	2.0	2.4	10.1	36.9	48.6	394820
10706	HASTINGS ON HUDSON	64520	3518	7.6	10.3	25.6	22.7	33.9	112530	119205	98	96	2340	0.2	0.3	3.2	10.9	85.3	736280
10707	TUCKAHOE	45680	4042	12.7	12.4	28.8	29.8	16.3	91412	95184	95	89	2388	0.0	0.3	3.4	18.9	77.4	551026
10708	BRONXVILLE	63103	10072	11.5	13.5	25.5	22.6	26.9	98743	103673	97	91	6664	0.8	4.4	13.8	24.7	56.3	482970
10709	EASTCHESTER	53577	3345	10.0	15.3	28.2	22.2	24.4	93106	98720	96	89	2478	0.2	0.1	4.9	18.8	76.0	630895
10710	YONKERS	37795	10390	14.2	16.6	30.5	26.3	12.5	77182	80850	91	83	6683	0.3	2.2	10.1	27.0	60.4	440388
10801	NEW ROCHELLE	26917	13230	24.9	22.3	27.3	17.1	8.4	53607	59598	69	54	5314	0.5	1.3	6.4	27.2	64.7	459664
10803	PELHAM	62861	4262	7.0	11.1	22.7	21.9	37.2	122006	128493	99	97	3142	0.0	0.3	1.4	7.3	91.0	753012
10804	NEW ROCHELLE	69674	4866	3.6	5.9	17.1	22.2	51.3	152997	162615	100	99	4286	0.0	0.1	1.1	5.1	93.7	814619
10805	NEW ROCHELLE	36223	7606	18.3	18.2	33.8	19.9	9.7	65843	70789	84	73	2706	0.4	4.1	14.9	29.8	50.8	407167
10901	SUFFERN	46921	8916	12.3	11.3	26.5	26.2	23.7	99775	103925	97	91	6568	0.5	2.1	4.6	41.5	51.4	408420
10913	BLAUVELT	43648	1597	8.0	9.7	23.5	27.7	31.1	113771	119078	98	96	1384	0.1	0.1	0.0	24.9	74.9	501613
10916	CAMPBELL HALL	36643	1483	6.9	8.0	34.9	28.9	21.3	100276	102709	97	92	1273	0.0	0.2	0.9	66.9	32.0	341603
10917	CENTRAL VALLEY	38577	677	4.4	15.4	30.0	36.3	13.9	100191	101744	97	91	464	0.0	0.0	4.7	62.1	33.2	340458
10918	CHESTER	36449	4180	7.6	10.2	32.6	30.9	18.7	98948	101415	97	91	3182	0.4	0.2	13.9	58.2	27.4	307336
10919	CIRCLEVILLE	27806	274	6.6	8.8	65.3	16.4	2.9	70495	71773	87	76	211	0.0	0.5	28.0	58.3	13.3	236429
10920	CONGERS	40929	2921	6.0	9.6	31.1	28.2	25.0	105036	108633	97	93	2408	0.0	0.1	0.8	38.0	61.1	436463
10921	FLORIDA	30152	1846	15.3	16.2	35.0	22.1	11.4	71970	76006	88	78	1425	0.1	0.0	11.2	66.7	22.0	279457
10923	GARNERVILLE	28498	2653	12.6	17.8	33.2	26.8	9.6	72138	74366	88	78	1781	0.1	0.1	2.8	67.0	30.0	351298
10924	GOSHEN	34260	4362	11.2	16.7	33.6	23.2	15.3	78825	83079	92	84	3002	0.2	0.0	7.3	67.7	24.9	300396
10925	GREENWOOD LAKE	33597	2453	14.3	18.3	35.3	23.6	8.4	70730	75725	87	77	1729	0.0	0.6	27.6	60.0	11.9	211226
10926	HARRIMAN	35369	1450	9.3	15.6	40.8	23.4	10.8	77185	80655	91	83	923	3.4	1.2	23.8	55.8	15.8	253195
10927	HAVERSTRAW	19856	3087	24.2	19.5	31.2	18.4	6.7	56380	61333	73	59	1438	0.0	0.3	6.6	77.1	16.0	275273
10928	HIGHLAND FALLS	32855	2504	10.8	22.0	39.1	21.3	6.8	68540	72591	86	75	1459	5.8	2.1	10.5	69.4	12.2	239083
10930	HIGHLAND MILLS	37723	2865	4.6	7.4	33.0	35.4	19.6	105358	105925	97	94	2431	0.9	0.4	3.8	73.4	21.5	307172
10931	HILLBURN	26453	267	9.7	19.9	40.4	20.6	9.4	73110	76564	88	79	199	0.0	0.0	5.0	86.4	8.5	293627
10940	MIDDLETOWN	26129	17329	20.1	20.4	37.1	16.7	5.7	61633	64654	80	67	9717	0.6	1.3	35.1	59.1	3.7	193463
10941	MIDDLETOWN	29368	5198	9.9	16.4	45.6	21.4	6.8	71616	75267	88	78	3087	2.0	1.6	16.8	71.3	8.2	239309
10950	MONROE	23163	12556	19.4	14.9	30.4	23.8	11.4	71570	75056	88	78	8711	0.8	0.7	10.4	70.9	17.2	287920
10952	MONSEY	25754	7800	19.8	16.4	24.3	19.4	20.2	75117	80134	89	81	4828	0.1	0.1	1.4	32.9	65.6	476711
10954	NANUET	42079	8182	8.5	12.1	29.3	28.6	21.5	100197	102923	97	91	5975	0.4	0.2	2.7	46.3	50.4	401621
10956	NEW CITY	50148	9936	5.0	7.0	23.5	28.6	36.0	125056	128673	99	97	8609	0.1	0.1	0.2	24.9	74.7	520178
10958	NEW HAMPTON	30885	1054	12.0	18.0	33.9	26.8	9.3	78099	81799	91	83	872	0.9	0.7	7.2	74.3	16.9	265123
10960	NYACK	48223	6018	11.4	15.3	29.4	24.6	19.4	86326	91244	94	87	3320	0.0	0.0	2.7	35.0	62.3	476836
10962	ORANGEBURG	40345	1863	10.1	13.2	24.2	26.5	26.0	103787	108037	97	93	1498	0.2	0.3	1.5	24.9	73.2	496657
10963	OTISVILLE	21976	897	11.0	22.9	33.4	26.5	6.1	70826	74543	87	77	689	0.4	1.5	26.9	64.0	7.3	215351
10964	PALISADES	62808	569	22.1	8.6	17.2	20.2	31.8	105007	115794	97	93	430	0.0	0.0	0.0	26.3	73.7	632022
10965	PEARL RIVER	42814	5247	7.7	12.3	29.2	26.8	24.1	101130	104467	97	92	4019	0.0	0.0	0.4	37.9	61.6	445203
10968	PIERMONT	59045	1168	7.7	12.8	33.1	28.0	18.3	89448	95623	95	88	719	0.0	0.0	7.1	21.7	71.2	635949
10969	PINE ISLAND	33452	500	15.8	17.6	29.2	22.6	14.8	68687	74093	86	75	388	0.0	0.0	12.4	60.8	26.8	282609
10970	POMONA	41943	3779	9.4	14.9	31.4	25.1	19.2	88609	92971	95	88	2755	5.3	3.0	11.5	34.3	45.8	371517
10973	SLATE HILL	29586	737	12.2	18.3	31.6	28.4	9.5	77005	81260	91	82	595	2.0	0.3	7.2	72.1	18.3	285142
10974	SLOATSBURG	38355	1133	5.1	13.5	33.2	29.9	18.3	96381	99817	96	90	891	0.0	0.1	2.2	68.0	29.6	350137
10975	SOUTHFIELDS	50782	218	6.0	14.7	41.3	17.4	20.6	76981	82272	91	82	150	0.0	0.7	10.0	51.3	38.0	358140
10976	SPARKILL	38640	333	7.8	12.9	30.6	29.1	19.5	96953	101585	96	90	248	0.8	0.0	0.0	25.4	73.8	489394
	NEW YORK	29893		21.9	21.3	32.7	14.0	9.9	58747	62337				3.4	5.7	23.0	38.7	29.1	269816
	UNITED STATES	27277		20.9	24.4	35.3	11.7	7.6	54719	56938				9.3	13.1	31.6	32.6	13.5	162279

ZIP CODE #	POST OFFICE NAME	FINANCIAL SERVICES Auto Loan	Home Loan	Invest-ments	Retire-ment Plans	THE HOME Home Improvements Home Repair	Lawn & Garden	Furnishings Comput-ers & Hard-ware-Personal	Major Appli-ances	TV, Radio, Sound Equip-ment	Furni-ture	ENTERTAINMENT Dine out/ Carry out	Sports Equip-ment	Fees & Tickets	Toys & Games	Travel	Cable TV	PERSONAL Apparel & Services	Auto Repairs	Health Insur-ance	Pets & Supplies
10523	ELMSFORD	135	176	192	172	185	159	162	160	155	159	157	121	183	153	178	155	117	159	153	178
10524	GARRISON	180	238	252	241	249	216	199	209	186	215	187	158	235	186	228	179	137	196	189	234
10526	GOLDENS BRIDGE	255	363	444	377	406	340	296	318	275	330	273	237	377	271	356	263	211	291	281	346
10527	GRANITE SPRINGS	200	283	346	294	317	265	233	250	215	259	213	186	294	211	280	206	164	229	221	272
10528	HARRISON	172	220	254	224	238	198	206	202	191	211	193	158	234	187	228	184	145	198	183	226
10530	HARTSDALE	168	203	228	207	218	190	191	192	179	202	179	146	212	173	211	173	130	187	183	217
10532	HAWTHORNE	139	202	226	194	216	185	163	173	156	165	157	126	200	157	193	157	117	164	165	188
10533	IRVINGTON	224	299	358	309	331	276	260	270	240	284	239	206	313	235	302	229	182	254	240	298
10535	JEFFERSON VALLEY	155	226	253	217	242	207	182	193	174	184	175	140	224	175	216	175	131	183	184	209
10536	KATONAH	241	330	397	343	367	306	278	293	257	307	255	222	343	253	327	244	195	272	258	321
10537	LAKE PEEKSKILL	116	164	170	152	170	145	135	141	129	135	131	103	159	131	155	130	97	135	133	154
10538	LARCHMONT	271	366	440	378	407	332	318	329	289	347	288	253	382	283	369	272	219	308	284	361
10541	MAHOPAC	146	203	217	197	212	183	169	175	161	171	162	131	201	162	194	160	120	167	165	193
10543	MAMARONECK	156	201	224	200	214	183	189	185	181	187	184	140	214	177	207	181	138	184	176	207
10546	MILLWOOD	251	359	442	377	403	339	289	311	272	322	269	233	376	270	348	260	210	285	274	338
10547	MOHEGAN LAKE	145	185	187	182	188	168	161	163	155	163	157	124	183	156	177	154	115	158	155	184
10548	MONTROSE	119	168	174	156	174	149	139	144	133	138	134	106	163	134	158	134	99	139	137	158
10549	MOUNT KISCO	189	226	255	233	242	211	217	211	206	222	207	165	243	203	235	200	153	211	199	240
10550	MOUNT VERNON	64	67	69	69	67	64	79	69	82	69	85	52	80	79	76	87	63	76	74	82
10552	MOUNT VERNON	113	130	139	130	135	129	129	126	130	127	130	94	140	125	137	132	94	129	135	145
10553	MOUNT VERNON	90	102	108	103	103	98	109	98	113	97	115	74	116	109	109	119	84	106	107	118
10560	NORTH SALEM	194	271	321	275	299	248	228	241	210	249	208	180	278	205	270	201	158	224	215	263
10562	OSSINING	137	166	177	165	173	150	161	155	154	159	157	120	176	152	171	152	116	156	148	175
10566	PEEKSKILL	93	106	107	105	106	99	107	100	108	102	109	77	114	106	109	110	79	105	104	118
10567	CORTLANDT MANOR	158	221	239	214	233	199	183	191	173	188	174	142	219	174	211	171	130	181	178	210
10570	PLEASANTVILLE	204	280	331	284	308	257	241	251	223	258	223	188	290	218	281	216	168	236	226	276
10573	PORT CHESTER	126	155	168	154	162	140	152	145	147	147	151	111	168	145	162	147	112	148	140	163
10576	POUND RIDGE	279	398	489	417	446	375	321	346	301	358	298	259	417	300	386	289	233	316	303	376
10577	PURCHASE	306	437	538	458	490	412	352	379	330	392	327	284	457	329	424	317	256	347	333	412
10578	PURDYS	155	226	253	217	242	207	182	193	174	184	175	140	224	175	216	175	131	183	184	209
10579	PUTNAM VALLEY	153	212	223	208	221	191	174	182	165	179	166	136	208	167	200	163	123	172	168	201
10580	RYE	279	374	452	389	415	343	326	337	299	356	299	259	394	294	379	283	228	317	295	371
10583	SCARSDALE	271	369	440	381	408	352	311	330	296	338	294	245	385	290	365	289	223	309	307	363
10588	SHRUB OAK	149	211	227	204	222	190	172	180	163	175	165	134	208	165	200	163	123	171	169	198
10589	SOMERS	169	197	253	197	223	212	172	195	172	193	170	130	197	160	201	175	121	184	202	218
10590	SOUTH SALEM	248	337	405	346	375	307	293	306	264	323	263	231	348	255	344	249	198	286	268	336
10591	TARRYTOWN	147	175	196	178	186	156	179	167	167	177	170	133	192	162	189	162	126	171	155	190
10594	THORNWOOD	165	237	267	230	255	218	194	205	186	198	186	149	238	185	229	186	140	195	195	223
10595	VALHALLA	148	199	227	198	214	181	174	177	162	180	163	134	204	161	199	158	121	171	164	196
10597	WACCABUC	278	394	482	410	442	369	323	347	300	360	297	258	410	294	388	287	229	318	307	378
10598	YORKTOWN HEIGHTS	149	213	237	208	227	196	174	183	166	178	167	135	212	166	204	166	124	174	174	200
10601	WHITE PLAINS	82	77	77	80	76	77	94	82	96	87	97	64	91	92	88	98	70	91	90	99
10603	WHITE PLAINS	121	149	159	147	154	135	145	137	140	138	143	107	159	139	154	140	105	141	134	157
10604	WEST HARRISON	137	176	194	175	186	164	164	163	160	160	162	122	186	156	180	162	121	161	160	183
10605	WHITE PLAINS	179	225	254	228	241	210	207	206	197	214	197	157	237	193	229	193	147	202	195	233
10606	WHITE PLAINS	124	144	153	143	148	130	149	137	145	141	148	107	159	142	154	145	110	143	135	157
10607	WHITE PLAINS	172	233	264	230	251	215	204	209	195	208	196	155	240	191	234	194	146	202	200	231
10701	YONKERS	71	73	73	74	73	68	88	76	90	78	93	58	87	86	82	94	69	83	79	89
10703	YONKERS	81	94	100	93	96	91	99	92	102	91	104	68	105	97	101	107	76	97	101	107
10704	YONKERS	98	131	139	124	135	121	121	117	122	110	124	86	138	120	131	128	93	119	121	132
10705	YONKERS	77	84	85	83	84	75	96	85	97	86	99	65	98	93	93	99	75	91	86	98
10706	HASTINGS ON HUDSON	198	250	296	259	274	233	232	233	216	246	217	180	268	209	262	207	162	226	215	260
10707	TUCKAHOE	139	170	182	169	176	158	160	155	157	156	159	118	179	156	171	158	117	156	154	177
10708	BRONXVILLE	179	212	239	215	227	215	201	205	201	209	200	150	226	189	222	203	144	204	221	233
10709	EASTCHESTER	162	207	234	209	222	197	189	192	183	192	184	142	218	177	212	183	136	187	187	215
10710	YONKERS	111	144	156	139	151	140	128	131	129	126	130	94	148	125	143	134	94	130	140	147
10801	NEW ROCHELLE	91	104	108	102	106	97	110	102	111	101	113	77	116	107	111	114	84	107	105	117
10803	PELHAM	214	289	341	295	316	268	253	259	238	267	238	196	304	234	292	231	180	248	238	287
10804	NEW ROCHELLE	243	345	419	357	385	323	282	303	263	313	260	225	357	258	339	252	200	279	269	330
10805	NEW ROCHELLE	106	114	125	117	118	106	128	115	122	121	126	92	130	119	129	121	92	123	115	134
10901	SUFFERN	152	193	208	192	202	184	174	176	171	174	172	131	199	168	193	173	126	173	177	198
10913	BLAUVELT	165	235	265	228	253	214	194	204	183	199	184	150	235	183	228	182	137	194	191	222
10916	CAMPBELL HALL	148	194	187	189	195	171	162	167	154	167	156	128	186	158	180	151	114	160	154	188
10917	CENTRAL VALLEY	136	171	176	168	175	158	150	152	144	152	146	115	170	146	165	143	106	148	146	172
10918	CHESTER	145	182	175	182	182	162	157	159	149	164	151	124	178	153	171	144	110	152	146	181
10919	CIRCLEVILLE	99	129	141	121	135	120	109	117	105	108	106	85	124	106	124	107	77	111	111	129
10920	CONGERS	147	207	220	199	217	187	169	177	161	172	163	131	203	164	196	161	121	169	167	195
10921	FLORIDA	114	135	127	133	133	124	121	122	117	122	118	94	131	119	128	116	84	119	118	141
10923	GARNERVILLE	104	132	135	126	135	117	123	119	118	118	121	91	136	118	132	118	89	120	114	133
10924	GOSHEN	127	153	151	152	154	142	139	139	135	141	136	106	153	134	149	134	98	138	137	160
10925	GREENWOOD LAKE	106	127	117	125	124	119	117	116	116	116	117	90	129	117	125	116	84	116	118	135
10926	HARRIMAN	122	138	133	140	137	129	128	127	124	132	126	98	138	125	134	122	89	126	123	148
10927	HAVERSTRAW	90	96	87	89	96	76	103	95	94	103	98	76	101	94	102	88	72	99	81	103
10928	HIGHLAND FALLS	97	120	119	115	121	112	110	110	108	108	109	83	122	107	119	109	79	110	112	125
10930	HIGHLAND MILLS	154	195	180	193	193	170	164	168	155	172	158	131	187	161	179	150	114	159	151	190
10931	HILLBURN	103	145	150	134	150	128	119	124	114	119	115	91	141	116	136	115	85	120	117	136
10940	MIDDLETOWN	93	102	97	101	101	97	102	98	100	99	101	76	106	101	103	101	72	100	99	114
10941	MIDDLETOWN	110	126	116	124	123	114	116	114	111	117	113	89	124	115	120	110	81	113	109	132
10950	MONROE	110	129	123	126	128	114	121	118	116	122	119	92	131	117	127	114	86	118	111	134
10952	MONSEY	127	160	176	158	170	144	150	147	142	150	144	112	168	141	164	140	107	147	138	164
10954	NANUET	145	176	185	175	181	166	161	160	158	161	160	121	181	158	175	159	116	160	161	183
10956	NEW CITY	184	259	293	257	279	238	215	226	202	225	203	167	261	201	252	199	152	213	210	248
10958	NEW HAMPTON	106	148	152	138	153	131	123	127	117	123	118	94	144	119	139	118	87	122	120	140
10960	NYACK	143	168	189	172	178	148	171	160	156	172	159	130	182	153	182	147	117	163	145	182
10962	ORANGEBURG	156	199	224	200	214	191	178	184	172	187	171	136	206	165	202	170	125	178	183	206
10963	OTISVILLE	103	122	114	120	120	112	113	112	110	112	111	87	123	111	119	109	80	111	109	129
10964	PALISADES	191	272	318	271	298	251	224	239	209	240	208	175	275	205	268	204	156	223	219	260
10965	PEARL RIVER	134	189	207	182	199	174	160	164	156	156	157	120	191	155	183	159	118	159	161	181
10968	PIERMONT	164	197	215	200	209	175	187	184	170	197	171	146	202	167	203	160	125	180	163	209
10969	PINE ISLAND	113	156	162	150	162	139	129	134	122	131	124	100	152	124	147	121	92	128	124	148
10970	POMONA	145	171	176	174	175	156	159	156	149	165	151	123	174	150	170	144	110	154	145	180
10973	SLATE HILL	105	146	150	136	151	129	121	126	116	121	117	93	142	117	138	116	86	121	118	138
10974	SLOATSBURG	133	189	202	178	198	169	155	162	148	156	149	119	185	149	179	148	110	155	153	177
10975	SOUTHFIELDS	148	165	159	168	164	154	156	153	151	159	153	119	166	153	162	149	109	153	149	179
10976	SPARKILL	149	211	240	206	228	193	175	184	164	181	165	136	212	163	206	162	123	174	171	200
	NEW YORK	100	106	110	108	107	104	112	106	113	106	114	81	115	110	112	116	83	110	110	124
	UNITED STATES	100	100	100	100	100	100	100	100	100	100	100	100	100	100	100	100	100	100	100	100

ZIP CODE #	POST OFFICE NAME	COUNTY FIPS CODE	POPULATION 2000	POPULATION 2009	POPULATION 2014	2000-2009 ANNUAL RATE % Rate	2000-2009 ANNUAL RATE State Centile	HOUSEHOLDS 2000	HOUSEHOLDS 2009	HOUSEHOLDS 2014	HOUSEHOLDS % Annual Rate 2000-2009	HOUSEHOLDS 2009 Average HH Size	FAMILIES 2000	FAMILIES 2009	FAMILIES % Annual Rate 2000-2009
10977	SPRING VALLEY	087	50500	53516	54319	0.6	76	13909	14373	14557	0.4	3.62	11188	11443	0.2
10980	STONY POINT	087	12539	12889	13010	0.3	59	4256	4388	4439	0.3	2.91	3359	3423	0.2
10983	TAPPAN	087	5813	5886	5915	0.1	44	2051	2094	2113	0.2	2.76	1651	1664	0.1
10984	THIELLS	087	2951	2940	2931	0.0	38	924	926	927	0.0	3.09	791	785	-0.1
10985	THOMPSON RIDGE	071	38	39	39	0.3	59	9	9	9	0.0	4.33	7	7	0.0
10986	TOMKINS COVE	087	1772	2021	2117	1.4	95	596	685	720	1.5	2.95	463	526	1.4
10987	TUXEDO PARK	071	2972	3210	3322	0.8	84	1172	1270	1319	0.9	2.52	854	907	0.7
10989	VALLEY COTTAGE	087	9399	9285	9219	-0.1	30	3393	3369	3354	-0.1	2.66	2438	2379	-0.3
10990	WARWICK	071	18935	21514	22636	1.4	95	6394	7318	7737	1.5	2.80	4805	5409	1.3
10992	WASHINGTONVILLE	071	9674	10881	11393	1.3	94	3156	3588	3783	1.4	3.03	2483	2780	1.2
10993	WEST HAVERSTRAW	087	4556	4550	4537	0.0	38	1630	1624	1623	0.0	2.79	1124	1100	-0.2
10994	WEST NYACK	087	6929	6889	6898	-0.1	30	2211	2212	2220	0.0	3.10	1849	1830	-0.1
10996	WEST POINT	071	7126	7256	7266	0.2	52	993	1012	1016	0.2	3.59	936	950	0.2
10998	WESTTOWN	071	3447	4031	4304	1.7	97	1147	1344	1440	1.7	2.99	916	1056	1.5
11001	FLORAL PARK	059	26925	26452	26039	-0.2	21	9391	9186	9032	-0.2	2.87	7096	6854	-0.4
11003	ELMONT	059	40556	40695	40123	0.0	38	12355	12139	11924	-0.2	3.34	9794	9517	-0.3
11004	GLEN OAKS	081	12499	12631	12715	0.1	44	4778	4751	4756	-0.1	2.63	3257	3186	-0.2
11005	FLORAL PARK	081	2500	2499	2515	0.0	38	1599	1591	1592	-0.1	1.54	588	566	-0.4
11010	FRANKLIN SQUARE	059	23782	23259	22807	-0.2	21	8242	8042	7884	-0.3	2.89	6393	6165	-0.4
11020	GREAT NECK	059	5554	5460	5362	-0.2	21	1857	1815	1782	-0.2	2.82	1551	1506	-0.3
11021	GREAT NECK	059	17507	17421	17192	-0.1	30	7849	7793	7692	-0.1	2.21	4694	4560	-0.3
11023	GREAT NECK	059	8490	8424	8286	-0.1	30	3005	2949	2897	-0.2	2.84	2395	2325	-0.3
11024	GREAT NECK	059	7953	7969	7844	0.0	38	2299	2246	2202	-0.3	3.23	1887	1825	-0.4
11030	MANHASSET	059	17365	17263	17006	-0.1	30	5897	5859	5775	-0.1	2.86	4904	4829	-0.2
11040	NEW HYDE PARK	059	39969	39518	38910	-0.1	30	13781	13579	13367	-0.2	2.90	11032	10761	-0.3
11042	NEW HYDE PARK	059	513	524	516	0.2	52	0	0	0	0.0	0.00	0	0	0.0
11050	PORT WASHINGTON	059	28645	29315	29128	0.3	59	10484	10727	10658	0.2	2.71	7832	7907	0.1
11096	INWOOD	059	8075	8059	7947	0.0	38	2628	2575	2531	-0.2	3.13	1946	1881	-0.4
11101	LONG ISLAND CITY	081	24829	27030	27818	0.9	87	9100	9931	10217	0.9	2.61	5372	5589	0.4
11102	ASTORIA	081	36104	37490	38179	0.4	66	13516	13826	13995	0.2	2.70	7933	7957	0.0
11103	ASTORIA	081	44054	45058	45651	0.2	52	17577	17763	17895	0.1	2.54	9906	9791	-0.1
11104	SUNNYSIDE	081	29308	29802	30071	0.2	52	12265	12246	12272	0.0	2.43	6698	6532	-0.3
11105	ASTORIA	081	42161	43268	43936	0.3	59	17139	17500	17695	0.2	2.47	10296	10300	0.0
11106	ASTORIA	081	42594	44195	44908	0.4	66	17553	17890	18080	0.2	2.46	9677	9638	0.0
11109	LONG ISLAND CITY	081	842	956	1181	1.4	95	503	669	820	3.1	1.34	176	226	2.7
11201	BROOKLYN	047	47729	50931	52365	0.7	80	21543	22952	23622	0.7	1.96	8960	9286	0.4
11203	BROOKLYN	047	82239	83581	84409	0.2	52	27122	27569	27867	0.2	2.96	20089	20134	0.0
11204	BROOKLYN	047	73915	73338	73270	-0.1	30	25326	24860	24797	-0.2	2.95	18462	17882	-0.3
11205	BROOKLYN	047	38398	41531	42982	0.9	87	14333	15455	15978	0.8	2.51	7848	8311	0.6
11206	BROOKLYN	047	69913	80103	84568	1.5	96	22347	25198	26482	1.3	3.10	15799	17663	1.2
11207	BROOKLYN	047	88168	93941	96742	0.7	80	28454	30305	31198	0.7	3.04	21202	22329	0.6
11208	BROOKLYN	047	86129	91534	94141	0.7	80	25531	27179	27975	0.7	3.34	20216	21256	0.5
11209	BROOKLYN	047	70117	70805	71227	0.1	44	31650	31670	31812	0.0	2.23	16964	16601	-0.2
11210	BROOKLYN	047	73915	73659	73665	0.0	38	24488	24078	24028	-0.2	3.05	17833	17302	-0.3
11211	BROOKLYN	047	86283	97014	101420	1.3	94	28433	31812	33214	1.2	3.03	17871	19521	1.0
11212	BROOKLYN	047	85377	88915	90801	0.4	66	28581	29816	30462	0.5	2.90	20715	21340	0.3
11213	BROOKLYN	047	63234	63716	64220	0.1	44	21723	21927	22116	0.1	2.86	14663	14558	-0.1
11214	BROOKLYN	047	83492	84312	84787	0.1	44	31652	31615	31733	0.0	2.63	21709	21352	-0.2
11215	BROOKLYN	047	62532	65509	67029	0.5	71	27125	28327	28947	0.5	2.30	13448	13764	0.3
11216	BROOKLYN	047	54916	58861	60652	0.8	84	21526	22902	23566	0.7	2.53	12514	13078	0.5
11217	BROOKLYN	047	36203	36838	37280	0.2	52	16070	16375	16583	0.2	2.15	6975	6911	-0.1
11218	BROOKLYN	047	73338	74981	75504	0.2	52	25142	25131	25229	0.0	2.95	16620	16342	-0.2
11219	BROOKLYN	047	86486	88347	89026	0.2	52	26654	26624	26737	0.0	3.27	19386	19112	-0.2
11220	BROOKLYN	047	91538	95318	97033	0.4	66	28053	28801	29244	0.3	3.30	20915	21215	0.2
11221	BROOKLYN	047	76294	83056	86248	0.9	87	25374	27673	28762	0.9	2.94	17431	18717	0.8
11222	BROOKLYN	047	39297	41650	42830	0.6	76	15843	16772	17248	0.6	2.47	8738	9043	0.4
11223	BROOKLYN	047	79405	79653	79906	0.0	38	29239	28931	28953	-0.1	2.74	20481	19974	-0.3
11224	BROOKLYN	047	51547	51790	52103	0.1	44	20317	20335	20430	0.0	2.47	12881	12677	-0.2
11225	BROOKLYN	047	64331	64430	64842	0.0	38	23580	23663	23816	0.0	2.72	15909	15713	-0.1
11226	BROOKLYN	047	108997	109304	110115	0.0	38	36684	36816	37054	0.0	2.95	26103	25830	-0.1
11228	BROOKLYN	047	41291	41492	41678	0.1	44	16053	16073	16146	0.0	2.56	10933	10763	-0.2
11229	BROOKLYN	047	79430	79089	79079	0.0	38	30095	29518	29437	-0.2	2.67	20853	20140	-0.4
11230	BROOKLYN	047	81485	82358	82653	0.1	44	28594	28282	28280	-0.1	2.89	19284	18769	-0.3
11231	BROOKLYN	047	33020	34076	34767	0.3	59	14990	15496	15795	0.4	2.19	7719	7786	0.1
11232	BROOKLYN	047	28205	29503	29866	0.5	71	8589	8732	8830	0.2	3.14	6143	6151	0.0
11233	BROOKLYN	047	62694	67929	70384	0.9	87	22593	24460	25343	0.9	2.73	14978	15973	0.7
11234	BROOKLYN	047	84644	84689	85083	0.0	38	30378	30264	30366	0.0	2.80	22728	22355	-0.2
11235	BROOKLYN	047	76037	77459	78110	0.2	52	31440	31609	31830	0.1	2.40	19350	19056	-0.2
11236	BROOKLYN	047	96060	96875	96915	0.1	44	31644	30949	30835	-0.2	3.07	24128	23324	-0.4
11237	BROOKLYN	047	48336	51317	52693	0.6	76	13853	14613	14987	0.6	3.50	11125	11623	0.5
11238	BROOKLYN	047	46142	50334	52238	0.9	87	19819	21629	22456	0.9	2.28	9659	10310	0.7
11239	BROOKLYN	047	14188	14149	14362	0.0	38	5889	5885	5928	0.0	2.34	3485	3413	-0.2
11354	FLUSHING	081	57856	59037	59784	0.2	52	20811	21113	21299	0.2	2.71	14134	14104	0.0
11355	FLUSHING	081	80362	82815	84104	0.3	59	27636	28173	28468	0.2	2.91	19716	19805	0.0
11356	COLLEGE POINT	081	20384	21053	21417	0.3	59	7214	7388	7479	0.3	2.85	5325	5384	0.1
11357	WHITESTONE	081	39602	39681	39972	0.0	38	15395	15341	15380	0.0	2.56	10976	10792	-0.2
11358	FLUSHING	081	38334	38614	38931	0.1	44	14033	14035	14081	0.0	2.74	10131	9989	-0.2
11359	BAYSIDE	081	204	204	206	0.0	38	72	72	72	0.0	2.83	42	41	-0.3
11360	BAYSIDE	081	19815	19744	19863	0.0	38	9056	9001	9006	-0.1	2.18	5487	5347	-0.3
11361	BAYSIDE	081	28690	29086	29419	0.1	44	10903	11017	11100	0.1	2.59	7292	7243	-0.1
11362	LITTLE NECK	081	17466	17507	17624	0.0	38	7013	6997	7013	0.0	2.48	4896	4808	-0.2
11363	LITTLE NECK	081	6953	6994	7055	0.1	44	2664	2665	2675	0.0	2.62	1890	1863	-0.2
11364	OAKLAND GARDENS	081	33875	34128	34399	0.1	44	13203	13216	13262	0.0	2.58	9238	9113	-0.1
11365	FRESH MEADOWS	081	38484	38873	39205	0.1	44	14522	14528	14575	0.0	2.67	10367	10226	-0.1
11366	FRESH MEADOWS	081	13292	13401	13523	0.1	44	4517	4537	4560	0.0	2.91	3461	3434	-0.1
11367	FLUSHING	081	40446	41606	42272	0.3	59	15495	15771	15928	0.2	2.63	10573	10596	0.0
11368	CORONA	081	98611	100626	101534	0.2	52	27520	27419	27458	0.0	3.64	21078	20758	-0.2
11369	EAST ELMHURST	081	36710	38003	38529	0.4	66	11262	11362	11436	0.1	3.30	8400	8368	0.0
11370	EAST ELMHURST	081	30003	30143	30285	0.1	44	9893	9762	9748	-0.1	3.08	7397	7201	-0.3
11372	JACKSON HEIGHTS	081	70945	73831	74578	0.4	66	24780	24774	24843	0.0	2.98	15951	15654	-0.2
11373	ELMHURST	081	100239	103239	104310	0.3	59	30845	30901	31023	0.0	3.32	22313	22030	-0.1
11374	REGO PARK	081	43985	44745	45179	0.2	52	19476	19465	19519	0.0	2.29	11368	11116	-0.2
11375	FOREST HILLS	081	70405	71119	71725	0.1	44	33250	33336	33469	0.0	2.11	17899	17530	-0.2
11377	WOODSIDE	081	89643	92274	93604	0.3	59	32148	32547	32808	0.1	2.82	20695	20584	-0.1
11378	MASPETH	081	34287	35473	36108	0.4	66	13155	13507	13686	0.3	2.61	8970	9064	0.1
	NEW YORK					0.3					0.3	2.61			0.1
	UNITED STATES					1.0					1.1	2.59			0.9

ZIP CODE #	POST OFFICE NAME	RACE (%) White 2000	White 2009	Black 2000	Black 2009	Asian/Pacific 2000	Asian/Pacific 2009	% Hispanic Origin 2000	% Hispanic Origin 2009	2009 AGE DISTRIBUTION (%) 0-4	5-9	10-14	15-19	20-24	25-44	45-64	65-84	85+	18+	MEDIAN AGE 2009	% 2009 Males	% 2009 Females
10977	SPRING VALLEY	51.8	48.6	33.1	33.9	6.7	8.1	11.4	12.2	10.4	9.1	8.1	8.0	7.5	25.5	21.6	8.3	1.5	67.3	29.7	49.7	50.3
10980	STONY POINT	94.3	92.4	1.4	1.7	1.4	2.0	6.9	9.0	6.6	7.1	7.6	7.3	4.9	24.1	29.1	11.8	1.5	73.8	40.3	49.6	50.4
10983	TAPPAN	85.0	78.0	1.5	4.3	10.3	13.8	6.6	8.0	6.8	7.1	7.7	6.7	4.4	21.0	27.6	16.3	2.3	74.7	42.5	47.3	52.7
10984	THIELLS	85.9	82.3	5.5	6.5	3.9	5.4	13.3	16.7	5.9	6.0	6.4	6.6	5.3	26.6	30.4	11.9	0.9	77.4	40.6	50.5	49.5
10985	THOMPSON RIDGE	100.0	100.0	0.0	0.0	0.0	0.0	5.4	5.1	5.1	7.7	10.3	10.3	5.1	25.6	30.8	5.1	0.0	66.7	36.3	48.7	51.3
10986	TOMKINS COVE	94.2	92.1	0.9	1.1	0.9	1.3	6.2	8.4	6.8	6.8	7.4	6.8	4.6	25.3	30.3	10.7	1.3	74.8	40.5	47.6	52.4
10987	TUXEDO PARK	92.9	90.4	1.2	1.6	3.0	4.2	4.4	5.9	5.2	5.9	6.0	5.4	3.6	24.5	35.1	12.8	1.6	79.2	44.7	49.8	50.2
10989	VALLEY COTTAGE	80.7	75.2	5.7	6.7	9.2	12.5	6.7	8.3	5.5	5.7	6.4	5.8	4.2	24.6	30.8	13.6	3.4	78.5	43.6	47.9	52.1
10990	WARWICK	89.1	87.2	6.1	6.7	1.0	1.4	7.0	8.6	6.1	6.9	7.5	7.3	4.8	24.0	30.4	10.8	2.0	74.6	40.8	50.2	49.8
10992	WASHINGTONVILLE	89.4	86.1	4.7	5.9	1.4	1.9	9.5	12.4	7.0	7.5	8.3	8.1	5.5	23.9	30.4	8.1	1.2	72.0	37.9	49.8	50.2
10993	WEST HAVERSTRAW	69.3	64.7	9.5	10.5	2.5	3.2	31.8	36.9	7.2	6.6	6.7	6.2	5.7	25.1	24.7	15.0	2.7	75.4	39.0	47.4	52.6
10994	WEST NYACK	85.7	81.2	3.5	4.1	7.8	10.8	5.8	7.3	6.4	6.9	7.6	6.4	3.9	23.0	30.2	14.1	1.6	74.7	42.4	48.3	51.7
10996	WEST POINT	82.3	77.5	9.1	11.1	3.5	4.7	6.6	8.3	8.8	7.0	4.5	16.7	36.1	22.1	4.6	0.1	0.0	77.5	21.8	67.2	32.8
10998	WESTTOWN	95.9	94.4	1.4	1.8	0.7	1.0	4.7	6.3	6.5	6.9	7.4	7.8	5.8	24.6	30.8	9.0	1.2	74.1	39.0	48.8	51.2
11001	FLORAL PARK	82.6	78.5	4.4	4.9	8.4	11.1	7.5	9.3	6.2	6.3	6.9	6.5	5.1	24.5	29.6	12.2	2.8	76.5	41.3	48.2	51.8
11003	ELMONT	46.0	40.4	35.1	38.1	8.7	10.0	13.3	14.7	6.4	6.5	6.6	7.3	6.6	27.6	27.2	9.9	1.9	76.1	37.4	47.8	52.2
11004	GLEN OAKS	59.9	50.8	4.1	4.2	30.6	38.7	7.7	8.7	5.5	5.5	6.0	6.1	5.3	25.2	29.4	13.8	3.2	79.2	42.5	46.9	53.1
11005	FLORAL PARK	91.0	88.3	2.7	3.0	4.6	6.3	1.4	1.7	0.8	1.2	1.6	1.0	0.8	5.6	23.7	50.3	15.0	95.8	72.6	37.3	62.7
11010	FRANKLIN SQUARE	93.1	90.5	0.6	0.8	3.4	4.7	6.4	8.5	6.0	6.0	6.6	6.3	4.7	26.3	27.8	13.0	3.3	77.5	41.4	47.9	52.1
11020	GREAT NECK	71.1	65.4	11.9	12.8	13.0	17.2	5.9	6.7	4.7	5.5	6.9	7.3	4.3	18.5	29.7	17.9	5.3	78.2	46.8	46.7	53.3
11021	GREAT NECK	87.7	83.8	2.1	2.6	6.5	8.8	6.4	8.2	5.4	5.3	6.0	5.2	3.9	24.3	28.5	16.7	4.7	79.8	44.9	46.3	53.7
11023	GREAT NECK	89.2	85.4	1.4	1.9	5.1	7.0	5.1	6.6	6.6	6.9	7.6	6.9	4.6	20.5	29.8	14.4	2.7	74.6	42.7	49.1	50.9
11024	GREAT NECK	87.0	82.7	2.5	3.2	4.1	5.6	6.9	8.7	5.9	6.1	7.3	10.0	9.7	20.1	26.1	12.6	2.2	76.1	37.5	53.2	46.8
11030	MANHASSET	87.6	83.6	2.5	2.9	8.2	11.4	3.5	4.4	6.3	7.5	8.8	6.5	3.3	18.4	30.9	15.2	3.1	72.9	44.4	48.3	51.7
11040	NEW HYDE PARK	77.0	70.4	1.3	1.4	18.4	24.0	6.2	7.6	5.6	5.9	6.6	6.2	4.4	23.5	29.7	14.8	3.4	78.1	43.5	47.7	52.3
11042	NEW HYDE PARK	77.5	70.6	5.9	7.4	16.0	21.2	1.8	2.1	2.1	2.5	3.6	4.8	2.1	11.5	22.1	32.6	18.7	88.0	66.3	40.1	59.9
11050	PORT WASHINGTON	84.1	79.4	2.2	2.6	8.4	11.3	11.7	14.4	6.4	6.9	8.0	6.8	4.4	23.4	29.9	12.2	2.1	74.3	41.6	48.4	51.6
11096	INWOOD	53.0	47.5	26.7	29.2	2.1	2.6	25.6	29.0	7.3	7.1	7.3	7.8	6.3	27.1	23.6	11.2	2.1	73.5	35.8	46.8	53.2
11101	LONG ISLAND CITY	38.3	37.0	25.8	23.5	10.6	13.1	37.0	38.2	6.9	6.4	5.7	6.5	8.2	35.2	22.3	7.5	1.1	77.1	33.4	50.9	49.1
11102	ASTORIA	51.0	45.6	9.8	9.3	14.7	18.4	31.6	34.2	6.7	6.5	6.0	6.2	6.8	36.8	22.1	7.7	1.4	77.3	34.4	50.4	49.6
11103	ASTORIA	62.5	56.0	1.4	1.4	14.3	18.0	25.9	28.8	5.7	5.3	4.7	5.0	6.5	38.8	23.7	8.9	1.4	81.4	36.5	51.0	49.0
11104	SUNNYSIDE	57.1	50.6	1.9	1.9	24.1	29.3	30.2	32.3	5.5	5.3	4.9	5.1	5.9	35.3	26.2	10.1	1.7	81.3	38.5	50.7	49.3
11105	ASTORIA	69.9	63.8	1.9	1.9	10.6	13.7	20.4	23.2	5.5	5.1	4.6	4.9	6.6	36.2	24.2	11.0	1.9	82.0	37.3	49.8	50.2
11106	ASTORIA	52.3	46.6	7.9	7.7	17.4	21.4	29.7	32.1	6.0	5.6	5.0	5.4	6.9	35.6	23.1	10.1	2.2	80.2	36.5	50.2	49.8
11109	LONG ISLAND CITY	71.4	63.9	4.6	5.0	15.1	20.4	8.0	9.5	3.0	2.2	1.7	1.9	11.2	43.4	26.9	8.5	1.3	91.8	37.2	53.9	46.1
11201	BROOKLYN	62.6	57.6	20.7	21.8	6.8	8.9	14.4	16.5	4.7	3.6	3.2	4.1	8.2	38.2	25.8	10.0	2.2	86.5	37.1	50.8	49.2
11203	BROOKLYN	3.6	3.1	90.9	91.1	1.0	1.1	4.8	4.6	6.8	6.8	6.6	7.2	7.4	28.0	25.1	10.8	1.2	75.6	35.3	44.4	55.6
11204	BROOKLYN	74.4	67.3	0.3	0.4	19.1	24.8	7.8	9.3	7.6	6.6	6.1	7.2	8.1	27.5	23.3	11.5	2.1	75.4	34.4	49.6	50.4
11205	BROOKLYN	21.6	20.0	55.9	54.9	2.9	3.4	28.8	31.4	7.5	7.1	6.3	8.3	10.1	31.1	20.2	8.2	1.3	74.9	30.6	46.6	53.4
11206	BROOKLYN	24.5	25.0	35.8	33.9	3.5	3.8	54.0	55.0	9.4	8.8	8.0	8.7	8.9	27.6	19.9	7.7	0.9	68.5	28.6	47.0	53.0
11207	BROOKLYN	9.1	8.8	65.6	65.4	1.1	1.2	34.0	33.8	9.2	9.0	8.3	8.8	8.4	27.1	21.0	7.4	0.8	68.2	28.9	44.8	55.2
11208	BROOKLYN	14.9	14.2	43.6	44.0	5.5	6.0	45.1	44.6	9.1	8.6	7.9	8.9	9.4	28.1	20.8	6.5	0.7	69.0	28.5	47.1	52.9
11209	BROOKLYN	78.2	71.8	1.7	1.8	10.1	13.8	11.0	13.4	5.6	5.3	5.0	5.2	5.8	30.7	27.0	12.8	2.7	81.0	40.4	48.5	51.5
11210	BROOKLYN	36.0	33.0	54.4	55.8	3.6	4.5	7.3	7.8	7.9	7.7	7.5	7.8	7.1	26.3	24.9	9.4	1.4	72.2	33.7	46.3	53.7
11211	BROOKLYN	62.5	58.6	5.2	5.7	2.9	3.5	36.1	39.0	10.7	8.8	7.7	8.2	9.1	29.0	18.1	7.1	1.2	68.0	27.9	49.6	50.4
11212	BROOKLYN	3.6	3.5	85.7	85.4	0.7	0.7	13.8	13.6	8.9	9.2	8.9	9.2	7.9	25.9	21.4	7.7	0.9	67.2	29.1	43.6	56.4
11213	BROOKLYN	12.4	10.4	79.9	81.4	0.6	0.7	8.4	8.3	8.0	8.2	7.9	8.6	8.0	27.4	22.1	8.6	1.3	70.8	31.2	44.6	55.4
11214	BROOKLYN	71.7	63.4	0.7	0.8	21.1	27.9	8.5	10.2	5.7	5.2	4.9	5.8	7.1	29.1	25.6	13.8	3.0	80.9	39.3	48.6	51.4
11215	BROOKLYN	68.3	62.4	8.0	9.1	5.7	7.5	26.3	30.6	6.1	5.0	4.3	4.6	7.4	39.5	24.6	7.2	1.2	81.8	34.9	48.3	51.7
11216	BROOKLYN	2.0	1.8	89.6	89.3	1.2	1.3	7.6	7.5	7.8	7.9	7.5	7.9	7.2	28.3	23.8	8.3	1.3	72.0	33.4	45.5	54.5
11217	BROOKLYN	47.6	42.5	31.2	33.4	4.0	5.1	25.5	27.6	5.6	4.4	4.0	4.6	8.3	39.7	24.8	7.4	1.4	83.2	35.1	48.4	51.6
11218	BROOKLYN	56.0	49.5	12.5	13.5	14.5	17.9	19.2	21.4	8.0	7.0	6.5	7.1	8.0	28.8	23.4	9.2	1.9	74.2	33.4	49.6	50.4
11219	BROOKLYN	71.5	65.8	1.0	1.1	16.3	20.1	12.0	13.6	11.0	8.3	7.3	7.9	8.7	24.8	19.1	10.4	2.5	68.8	28.9	50.0	50.0
11220	BROOKLYN	36.1	32.2	3.1	3.1	29.1	32.3	46.1	47.2	8.1	7.3	6.5	7.3	8.4	31.6	21.9	7.8	1.2	73.8	31.9	50.2	49.8
11221	BROOKLYN	8.9	8.9	64.3	64.1	1.0	1.1	34.8	34.6	9.2	9.0	8.1	8.7	8.0	27.1	21.1	7.8	1.0	68.5	29.6	45.9	54.1
11222	BROOKLYN	80.3	75.7	1.5	1.7	3.9	5.2	19.5	23.5	5.2	4.8	4.5	5.3	6.7	34.2	27.2	10.6	1.5	82.6	38.1	50.7	49.3
11223	BROOKLYN	74.8	68.6	4.1	4.2	14.6	19.4	9.6	11.1	6.5	6.0	5.9	6.6	7.1	26.6	25.5	13.1	2.6	77.7	37.9	48.5	51.5
11224	BROOKLYN	55.6	53.1	29.0	29.8	3.8	4.4	17.9	19.1	6.0	6.2	6.1	6.8	6.6	21.8	25.0	17.1	4.4	77.5	41.6	45.2	54.8
11225	BROOKLYN	8.1	6.8	84.4	85.3	0.8	0.9	9.0	8.7	7.4	7.6	7.2	7.5	7.5	28.1	24.5	9.2	1.1	73.3	33.6	44.1	55.9
11226	BROOKLYN	6.5	5.8	79.8	79.7	2.7	3.1	14.0	13.7	8.0	8.1	7.4	7.7	7.5	28.7	24.1	7.6	0.8	71.9	32.4	44.8	55.2
11228	BROOKLYN	81.3	75.1	0.3	0.3	13.2	17.8	6.5	8.1	5.9	5.5	5.4	5.8	6.2	28.7	26.2	13.3	3.0	79.7	39.9	48.2	51.8
11229	BROOKLYN	75.2	69.0	4.7	5.1	14.9	19.4	6.8	8.1	5.6	5.5	5.8	6.2	6.4	25.3	27.8	14.1	3.3	79.4	41.2	47.7	52.3
11230	BROOKLYN	73.7	67.7	6.9	7.6	11.9	15.7	7.8	9.3	8.0	6.9	6.6	7.1	7.4	24.4	23.8	12.6	3.3	74.1	35.6	49.1	50.9
11231	BROOKLYN	62.5	58.6	17.8	18.2	3.0	4.1	25.3	28.2	6.3	5.4	4.7	5.4	7.5	37.4	22.8	8.8	1.6	80.2	34.8	47.0	53.0
11232	BROOKLYN	43.6	40.8	6.0	6.4	10.9	12.1	64.3	66.5	8.0	7.1	6.2	7.5	9.4	36.3	19.1	5.8	0.7	74.4	30.5	53.8	46.2
11233	BROOKLYN	3.6	3.5	87.4	87.3	0.5	0.6	12.6	12.3	8.9	8.9	8.3	8.7	8.0	26.2	21.5	8.3	1.3	68.6	30.2	43.8	56.2
11234	BROOKLYN	59.1	55.4	33.6	35.3	3.1	4.2	7.0	8.1	6.3	6.1	6.2	6.6	6.5	27.1	27.5	11.9	1.9	77.5	38.7	46.6	53.4
11235	BROOKLYN	76.4	71.0	2.4	2.8	12.9	16.5	9.7	11.1	4.7	4.4	4.3	5.1	6.5	25.4	28.0	17.2	4.5	83.6	44.7	48.0	52.0
11236	BROOKLYN	17.1	13.9	71.6	73.5	4.0	4.6	8.8	9.1	7.3	7.3	7.2	7.9	7.7	27.2	25.5	8.5	1.4	73.3	34.1	44.6	55.4
11237	BROOKLYN	26.7	26.2	10.7	10.3	5.7	6.5	79.0	79.3	10.2	9.0	7.6	9.1	10.3	31.3	16.9	5.0	0.5	67.9	26.9	50.5	49.5
11238	BROOKLYN	18.2	14.7	68.5	70.7	3.5	4.0	11.6	12.0	6.3	5.6	5.1	6.0	8.2	35.9	23.4	8.3	1.4	79.6	34.5	46.6	53.4
11239	BROOKLYN	37.9	31.8	44.9	48.3	4.0	5.1	18.4	19.9	4.6	5.8	6.6	7.4	6.2	21.0	27.7	17.5	3.2	78.4	43.7	42.6	57.4
11354	FLUSHING	40.3	34.2	4.6	4.2	43.5	49.9	19.5	19.6	5.5	5.3	5.1	5.4	5.9	28.6	27.1	13.3	3.7	80.9	41.0	47.7	52.3
11355	FLUSHING	27.5	22.5	5.0	4.5	54.0	59.6	19.7	19.3	5.8	5.4	5.2	5.9	6.7	30.9	27.4	10.8	1.9	80.1	38.5	49.4	50.6
11356	COLLEGE POINT	69.5	62.9	1.2	1.2	15.5	20.2	24.2	27.6	6.8	6.3	6.1	6.7	7.1	29.1	25.8	10.4	1.6	76.7	36.9	48.3	51.7
11357	WHITESTONE	82.4	76.4	0.4	0.5	12.9	17.8	7.9	9.8	5.3	5.1	5.1	5.2	5.4	26.0	27.7	16.4	3.8	81.4	43.6	47.7	52.3
11358	FLUSHING	64.8	56.9	1.0	1.0	25.8	32.7	14.3	16.0	5.6	5.5	5.5	5.7	5.7	29.7	28.0	12.2	2.2	80.0	40.3	48.4	51.6
11359	BAYSIDE	78.8	71.6	2.0	2.0	16.7	23.0	6.4	7.8	3.4	3.9	4.4	4.4	2.5	22.5	33.8	21.1	3.9	85.3	50.3	46.1	53.9
11360	BAYSIDE	78.4	71.1	1.3	1.4	17.4	24.0	5.8	7.1	4.2	4.1	4.6	4.3	3.5	21.9	30.9	22.1	4.5	84.4	49.8	45.8	54.2
11361	BAYSIDE	65.3	57.8	4.6	4.5	22.8	29.3	11.9	13.6	5.3	5.2	5.3	5.7	5.8	30.1	27.9	11.8	2.9	80.7	40.5	48.4	51.6
11362	LITTLE NECK	71.1	63.6	1.1	1.1	23.9	30.7	6.8	7.9	4.4	4.7	5.1	5.2	4.6	23.7	30.8	17.6	3.9	82.5	46.5	47.0	53.0
11363	LITTLE NECK	73.5	65.8	0.4	0.5	21.5	28.4	7.7	9.0	4.5	4.6	5.2	5.7	5.4	24.9	32.0	15.3	2.3	82.1	44.7	48.1	51.9
11364	OAKLAND GARDENS	59.6	50.9	1.9	2.0	33.4	41.4	7.8	8.7	4.9	4.9	5.1	5.7	5.7	25.6	30.7	14.3	3.2	81.7	43.7	47.5	52.5
11365	FRESH MEADOWS	53.6	45.8	9.1	9.3	29.4	36.0	11.8	13.0	6.1	6.1	6.1	6.2	5.9	27.5	28.0	11.5	2.7	77.9	39.9	47.8	52.2
11366	FRESH MEADOWS	50.4	42.4	9.4	8.9	32.5	40.3	11.1	11.8	5.4	5.4	5.5	6.1	5.8	27.0	28.5	13.3	3.0	80.1	41.1	48.0	52.0
11367	FLUSHING	59.9	53.6	11.6	11.8	15.6	19.5	15.7	17.5	7.1	6.4	6.2	6.3	7.0	28.2	24.9	11.6	2.3	76.5	36.6	47.6	52.4
11368	CORONA	36.0	35.2	17.3	16.4	10.3	11.7	64.3	65.2	8.3	7.6	6.6	7.1	8.3	34.5	20.6	6.1	0.9	73.4	31.1	51.3	48.7
11369	EAST ELMHURST	29.2	28.3	33.6	32.3	7.1	8.3	49.6	51.0	7.4	7.0	6.6	7.4	7.8	29.6	23.3	9.3	1.5	74.7	33.7	47.6	52.4
11370	EAST ELMHURST	52.3	47.7	1.5	1.4	20.1	23.5	40.0	41.6	6.8	6.4	6.0	6.5	7.1	31.5	24.7	9.8	1.4	77.0	35.8	49.8	50.2
11372	JACKSON HEIGHTS	50.0	46.8	2.8	2.6	17.4	20.4	56.2	57.7	6.2	5.8	5.4	5.9	6.6	32.9	25.1	10.5	1.7	79.1	36.9	50.6	49.4
11373	ELMHURST	31.6	28.5	2.1	1.8	39.7	43.8	45.2	44.1	6.4	6.0	5.5	6.0	6.8	35.1	24.6	8.6	1.0	78.6	35.6	51.6	48.4
11374	REGO PARK	65.5	57.8	2.5	2.6	23.7	29.9	13.1	14.9	4.8	4.6	4.4	5.0	6.4	29.8	28.3	13.8	3.0	83.3	41.6	47.6	52.4
11375	FOREST HILLS	71.3	63.9	2.7	2.8	19.8	25.8	10.3	12.0	4.6	4.2	4.1	4.2	5.6	28.9	29.0	15.4	3.8	84.5	43.8	46.9	53.1
11377	WOODSIDE	43.4	38.4	3.3	3.1	29.8	34.7	37.5	38.2	6.0	5.6	5.2	5.8	6.4	34.5	24.8	10.0	1.7	79.8	37.0	50.0	50.0
11378	MASPETH	81.7	77.1	0.8	0.8	6.2	8.3	19.3	23.3	6.2	5.8	5.6	6.0	6.5	30.0	26.0	11.3	2.6	78.8	38.4	48.1	51.9
	NEW YORK	67.9	64.8	15.9	16.5	5.6	6.9	15.1	16.7	6.5	6.4	6.4	7.1	7.0	27.0	26.3	11.2	2.1	76.6	37.5	48.4	51.6
	UNITED STATES	75.1	72.0	12.3	12.7	3.8	4.6	12.5	15.7	6.8	6.7	6.6	7.1	6.9	27.0	26.0	10.9	1.9	75.7	36.9	49.2	50.8

10977-11378

#	POST OFFICE NAME	2009 Per Capita Income	2009 HH Income Base	2009 Household Income Distribution (%): Less than $25,000	$25,000 to $49,999	$50,000 to $99,999	$100,000 to $149,999	$150,000 or More	Median Household Income: 2009	2014	2009 National Centile	2009 State Centile	2009 Home Value Base	2009 Home Value Distribution (%): Less than $50,000	$50,000 to $89,999	$90,000 to $174,999	$175,000 to $399,999	$400,000 or More	2009 Median Home Value
10977	SPRING VALLEY	24763	14373	18.0	17.1	31.6	19.4	13.9	71978	75665	88	78	8103	2.0	1.8	4.4	54.8	36.9	358487
10980	STONY POINT	38575	4388	9.4	13.0	27.9	30.1	19.6	99301	102265	97	91	3610	2.1	0.9	2.4	45.6	49.0	396957
10983	TAPPAN	44342	2094	5.1	8.5	31.2	32.1	23.2	107199	109600	98	94	1811	0.2	0.6	0.0	30.4	68.9	478326
10984	THIELLS	41021	926	7.2	4.0	30.8	29.7	28.3	113171	116181	98	96	788	0.0	0.0	1.9	44.7	53.4	411157
10985	THOMPSON RIDGE	20256	9	0.0	0.0	55.6	33.3	11.1	85912	85912	94	87	7	0.0	0.0	14.3	71.4	14.3	262500
10986	TOMKINS COVE	41857	685	7.0	10.8	27.2	33.6	21.5	105997	108581	97	94	559	0.2	0.0	2.5	29.2	68.2	529255
10987	TUXEDO PARK	48969	1270	7.2	13.9	31.8	23.1	23.9	92307	98567	95	89	938	0.2	0.3	4.1	31.1	64.3	521795
10989	VALLEY COTTAGE	45403	3369	4.8	10.2	32.3	30.4	22.4	103647	106159	97	93	2598	0.0	0.1	4.2	47.8	47.9	392319
10990	WARWICK	34882	7318	11.1	13.8	31.1	29.1	14.8	86482	91328	94	87	5660	0.1	0.1	7.5	63.2	29.1	307210
10992	WASHINGTONVILLE	32737	3588	7.9	14.3	33.8	30.3	13.6	85797	89200	94	87	2797	5.3	2.6	9.7	67.7	14.7	284164
10993	WEST HAVERSTRAW	24882	1624	24.2	18.9	30.5	20.8	5.5	62158	66776	80	68	1012	0.0	0.0	0.8	93.9	5.3	274468
10994	WEST NYACK	51433	2212	5.9	6.4	21.8	26.5	39.4	131300	135941	99	98	1902	0.1	0.1	0.7	25.3	73.9	520894
10996	WEST POINT	19996	1012	4.2	11.1	53.7	23.0	8.0	73999	76289	89	80	16	0.0	0.0	0.0	0.0	100.0	1000001
10998	WESTTOWN	27201	1344	9.2	21.1	40.2	22.8	6.8	69243	72517	86	76	1076	1.2	0.3	16.2	69.7	12.6	248673
11001	FLORAL PARK	39205	9186	9.5	12.8	28.8	28.1	20.8	96727	103052	96	90	7263	0.2	0.1	1.9	35.0	62.8	454698
11003	ELMONT	28624	12139	12.7	14.5	30.3	29.0	13.6	79277	85139	92	84	9499	0.2	0.0	0.7	70.6	28.5	357132
11004	GLEN OAKS	32592	4751	13.1	18.1	38.1	20.7	10.0	71941	74497	88	78	3193	0.3	1.3	19.3	25.8	53.3	415525
11005	FLORAL PARK	74543	1591	15.2	16.7	29.9	14.9	23.3	76102	81278	90	81	1232	0.0	0.2	3.0	24.4	72.4	599231
11010	FRANKLIN SQUARE	32671	8042	11.4	14.9	31.3	28.9	13.4	80096	85939	92	85	6668	0.2	0.1	0.2	45.8	53.8	412220
11020	GREAT NECK	58042	1815	6.7	9.5	18.8	22.5	42.6	130532	139817	99	98	1574	0.0	0.0	0.2	6.2	93.6	939286
11021	GREAT NECK	66514	7793	9.1	11.7	26.6	21.8	30.9	104513	113386	97	93	5322	0.4	0.1	6.7	26.5	66.3	685920
11023	GREAT NECK	61837	2949	8.9	9.8	18.5	21.8	41.0	124631	136646	99	97	2385	0.3	0.3	1.5	4.0	94.0	965968
11024	GREAT NECK	55040	2246	9.7	10.7	13.8	20.1	45.6	135188	147997	99	98	1857	0.1	0.0	1.5	5.4	92.9	1000001
11030	MANHASSET	73097	5859	5.5	5.8	14.3	21.2	53.1	159819	170200	100	99	5153	0.0	0.1	0.1	2.4	97.5	1000001
11040	NEW HYDE PARK	41584	13579	9.9	11.5	29.4	26.3	22.9	97249	104860	96	90	11863	0.2	0.2	1.3	21.6	76.6	508831
11042	NEW HYDE PARK	6500	0	0.0	0.0	0.0	0.0	0.0	0	0	0	0	0	0.0	0.0	0.0	0.0	0.0	0
11050	PORT WASHINGTON	59653	10727	9.1	11.2	22.4	20.0	37.3	114860	127363	98	96	7154	0.2	0.3	0.2	9.8	89.5	805859
11096	INWOOD	20478	2575	27.1	18.6	30.9	18.8	4.6	54092	56561	70	55	1271	0.0	0.0	3.2	71.4	25.4	339320
11101	LONG ISLAND CITY	20964	9931	35.5	23.9	27.7	7.5	5.4	40356	44163	34	15	1370	0.7	0.5	2.9	46.7	49.1	396757
11102	ASTORIA	22192	13826	27.2	26.1	33.9	7.8	5.0	46876	50099	54	36	2539	1.1	0.2	2.0	25.6	71.1	520067
11103	ASTORIA	23934	17763	23.0	23.7	41.6	7.9	3.8	53208	57542	68	54	3337	0.3	0.6	1.4	19.5	78.2	559938
11104	SUNNYSIDE	24455	12246	24.8	24.2	39.4	7.3	4.2	50853	54615	63	48	1892	3.0	5.3	17.6	24.9	49.2	394182
11105	ASTORIA	26338	17500	23.7	24.4	36.2	9.6	6.2	51988	56636	66	51	5481	0.2	0.7	0.7	23.3	75.1	525092
11106	ASTORIA	23444	17890	29.6	24.4	32.6	9.2	4.2	46198	49246	52	35	3341	0.4	0.9	22.5	22.2	54.0	425093
11109	LONG ISLAND CITY	106985	669	4.9	3.6	25.7	33.3	32.4	127547	129408	99	98	523	0.0	0.8	4.2	62.0	33.1	324359
11201	BROOKLYN	55551	22952	17.1	12.3	31.7	13.7	25.1	79227	83119	92	84	8832	5.0	1.1	6.1	31.3	56.4	503566
11203	BROOKLYN	20456	27569	24.7	24.7	36.8	9.2	4.6	50646	55583	63	47	11411	0.6	0.2	1.2	68.5	29.4	358255
11204	BROOKLYN	19146	24860	33.4	21.9	32.3	8.0	4.4	43453	48786	44	25	9187	1.2	1.2	0.8	19.5	77.3	556862
11205	BROOKLYN	20996	15455	37.3	23.0	27.6	6.9	5.2	39298	43323	31	13	3368	11.2	3.1	11.9	31.1	42.7	345833
11206	BROOKLYN	12137	25198	50.7	23.8	20.8	3.1	1.7	24330	25947	3	2	2820	11.5	0.3	4.0	46.6	37.5	356527
11207	BROOKLYN	14338	30305	42.0	24.7	26.3	4.7	2.2	31957	35398	11	4	8013	0.9	0.3	4.4	75.5	18.8	320984
11208	BROOKLYN	14150	27179	35.8	27.3	29.1	5.6	2.2	36907	41014	23	7	8193	1.1	0.1	2.7	74.8	21.4	334410
11209	BROOKLYN	33754	31670	21.3	20.8	37.1	11.6	9.2	60096	64086	77	64	9992	0.3	1.1	5.7	22.4	70.5	548972
11210	BROOKLYN	22769	24078	23.1	22.6	35.4	11.3	7.6	54741	60118	71	56	9700	0.2	1.1	3.9	36.9	57.9	447688
11211	BROOKLYN	14946	31812	40.8	24.6	27.1	5.1	2.5	32643	36340	13	5	4884	3.5	1.1	3.9	38.2	53.2	419797
11212	BROOKLYN	13731	29816	46.6	24.3	23.2	4.0	1.9	27307	29324	5	3	4884	3.1	0.6	2.2	66.6	27.5	329389
11213	BROOKLYN	16060	21927	37.7	27.4	27.9	4.7	2.4	35685	39087	20	6	4113	2.6	0.7	3.3	47.2	46.2	387319
11214	BROOKLYN	21530	31615	31.9	21.9	33.4	8.1	4.6	45605	50487	50	32	10246	1.5	1.2	3.4	20.1	73.9	534564
11215	BROOKLYN	43442	28327	14.9	15.9	35.6	15.6	18.0	75293	77580	90	81	9842	0.2	0.4	1.7	26.6	71.0	637257
11216	BROOKLYN	18389	22902	39.1	26.1	27.0	4.9	2.8	33788	37490	15	5	4509	0.5	0.7	4.7	56.6	37.5	361191
11217	BROOKLYN	41355	16375	19.4	14.6	36.8	13.9	15.4	70203	72959	87	76	4208	0.2	0.6	2.4	19.7	77.2	775754
11218	BROOKLYN	20454	25131	28.9	22.3	34.8	8.7	5.2	48450	52936	58	42	7330	0.8	1.8	8.2	30.8	58.5	444982
11219	BROOKLYN	15295	26624	38.2	24.3	27.1	6.4	3.9	35494	39870	19	6	7452	0.8	0.7	1.2	17.5	79.8	610165
11220	BROOKLYN	16303	28801	32.5	25.4	32.2	6.1	3.8	40947	46306	36	17	8114	5.6	1.6	2.8	30.3	59.7	442182
11221	BROOKLYN	14014	27673	44.1	25.6	23.9	4.4	1.9	29413	32336	7	3	6516	1.0	0.8	2.8	62.4	33.0	355444
11222	BROOKLYN	22633	16772	26.5	28.1	34.2	7.8	3.5	45793	49398	51	33	3684	0.5	0.8	1.0	39.5	58.2	442025
11223	BROOKLYN	20861	28931	34.1	21.3	31.9	7.6	5.1	43447	48531	44	25	10629	0.8	1.3	2.7	24.7	70.4	499427
11224	BROOKLYN	17722	20335	45.4	21.5	25.2	5.0	2.9	28788	32470	6	3	4793	32.6	1.5	4.1	38.8	23.0	261222
11225	BROOKLYN	19010	23663	31.7	29.3	30.4	5.2	3.4	39911	43860	32	14	3834	2.3	1.7	3.4	42.8	49.9	399630
11226	BROOKLYN	16625	36816	32.5	29.0	30.3	5.4	2.7	38824	43091	29	11	4596	0.3	1.0	5.3	49.3	44.0	382679
11228	BROOKLYN	28065	16073	21.6	21.6	36.8	12.3	7.7	58467	63048	76	62	8671	0.5	0.8	1.2	14.2	83.3	572874
11229	BROOKLYN	23996	29518	28.5	21.5	32.4	10.9	6.7	49899	55969	61	45	13370	1.3	3.3	6.5	34.3	54.6	422102
11230	BROOKLYN	20935	28282	32.1	22.1	31.3	8.6	6.0	45165	50258	49	31	9119	1.0	1.4	6.1	20.7	70.7	565481
11231	BROOKLYN	41314	15496	24.0	15.8	30.5	14.2	15.5	64536	67760	83	71	3896	0.2	0.3	2.3	18.7	78.5	736364
11232	BROOKLYN	15410	8732	32.5	27.8	32.1	5.5	2.1	39391	44405	31	13	2129	0.7	5.2	12.6	41.1	40.4	366254
11233	BROOKLYN	15324	24460	44.3	24.2	24.6	4.6	2.3	29871	32950	8	4	5452	1.3	0.8	5.7	57.8	34.4	354921
11234	BROOKLYN	28641	30264	17.0	18.3	38.7	17.0	9.0	67581	70970	85	74	20119	0.2	0.3	1.5	45.6	52.4	411219
11235	BROOKLYN	23653	31609	34.7	21.4	30.2	8.2	5.6	41872	47497	39	20	11333	3.0	3.7	12.3	32.1	48.9	393964
11236	BROOKLYN	21004	30949	22.1	22.8	38.5	11.6	5.0	56291	61019	73	59	15266	0.7	0.3	0.6	45.3	53.1	412289
11237	BROOKLYN	11931	14613	42.2	28.6	23.4	3.8	1.9	30802	33699	9	4	1751	1.8	0.3	1.2	65.6	31.0	354075
11238	BROOKLYN	31624	21629	22.4	21.3	35.7	13.0	7.6	56878	61049	74	60	5248	0.6	0.5	5.5	37.9	55.4	443379
11239	BROOKLYN	15781	5885	51.1	21.5	21.8	3.9	1.8	19622	22000	1	1	192	1.6	0.0	2.6	66.7	29.2	313043
11354	FLUSHING	22462	21113	25.5	24.5	35.6	9.2	5.2	50007	53534	61	45	7922	1.6	6.3	25.7	19.5	46.9	372000
11355	FLUSHING	21091	28173	24.0	25.7	36.0	9.6	4.8	50389	54818	62	46	9077	2.5	5.7	15.7	27.2	48.8	392900
11356	COLLEGE POINT	27755	7388	16.9	20.7	39.0	14.3	9.0	63260	66319	81	69	4010	0.4	0.4	0.6	38.6	60.0	441237
11357	WHITESTONE	33871	15341	12.9	18.9	39.5	17.4	11.4	70590	73651	87	77	10843	0.2	0.5	4.9	25.3	69.0	527351
11358	FLUSHING	30589	14035	14.6	19.3	37.4	17.6	11.1	69906	72805	87	76	8064	0.3	1.0	1.7	18.8	78.3	549526
11359	BAYSIDE	35023	72	9.7	18.1	37.5	22.2	12.5	73295	76900	88	79	45	0.0	0.0	8.9	46.7	44.4	358333
11360	BAYSIDE	44011	9001	12.7	16.7	36.2	20.2	14.2	76265	78667	90	82	6093	0.3	0.5	6.2	38.6	54.4	461250
11361	BAYSIDE	33837	11017	12.6	16.5	40.1	18.3	12.4	73810	75812	89	80	6048	0.3	0.6	3.8	25.0	70.3	514640
11362	LITTLE NECK	39269	6997	12.8	17.2	33.8	20.7	15.4	78432	81422	91	84	5449	0.3	1.1	15.2	26.0	57.4	486373
11363	LITTLE NECK	45808	2665	6.0	12.9	37.6	19.4	24.1	89665	92531	95	88	1849	0.1	0.4	1.5	16.9	81.1	703906
11364	OAKLAND GARDENS	35476	13216	11.1	17.8	39.5	18.8	12.8	74668	76608	89	81	8761	0.5	2.7	20.4	22.5	53.9	433023
11365	FRESH MEADOWS	31658	14528	12.2	19.4	39.7	19.2	9.6	70767	73327	87	77	6907	5.4	1.3	3.8	24.8	64.8	474293
11366	FRESH MEADOWS	36320	4537	9.9	16.2	33.8	17.2	22.9	80126	83904	92	85	3242	0.5	1.3	0.1	22.4	75.7	538583
11367	FLUSHING	26299	15771	21.7	22.3	37.7	11.1	7.2	56585	60579	73	59	6414	1.4	5.4	18.1	29.3	45.7	379308
11368	CORONA	15775	27419	25.6	27.0	36.0	7.8	3.6	47324	51227	55	38	6226	2.2	5.3	7.7	27.9	56.8	437500
11369	EAST ELMHURST	18462	11362	21.8	25.1	41.3	8.1	3.7	53246	57920	68	54	6020	0.8	3.5	9.5	48.4	37.7	363809
11370	EAST ELMHURST	22741	9762	16.6	25.1	40.6	11.0	6.8	58575	62082	76	62	4634	0.8	0.5	2.5	30.6	65.7	470446
11372	JACKSON HEIGHTS	20909	24774	21.5	25.8	40.0	8.2	4.5	52668	56904	67	52	6987	2.3	13.8	30.9	25.9	27.2	189347
11373	ELMHURST	18027	30901	24.1	26.3	37.1	8.2	4.3	49650	53214	60	44	8053	2.1	3.7	8.7	30.4	55.2	432017
11374	REGO PARK	29512	19465	24.2	21.3	37.3	10.7	6.6	55540	60592	72	58	7026	1.1	9.6	25.0	27.1	37.2	292057
11375	FOREST HILLS	41622	33336	17.2	17.5	36.0	16.6	12.8	68576	72046	86	75	13907	0.8	2.0	16.8	36.8	43.7	352579
11377	WOODSIDE	21148	32547	23.1	25.9	38.7	8.3	4.0	50878	54552	63	48	9627	5.8	3.8	12.8	28.4	49.2	396008
11378	MASPETH	25621	13507	19.6	23.8	40.6	10.7	5.3	57783	61710	75	61	6903	0.5	0.4	1.0	45.8	52.3	409727
	NEW YORK	29893		21.9	21.3	32.7	14.0	9.9	58747	62337				3.4	5.7	23.0	38.7	29.1	269816
	UNITED STATES	27277		20.9	24.4	35.3	11.7	7.6	54719	56938				9.3	13.1	31.6	32.6	13.5	162279

ZIP CODE		FINANCIAL SERVICES				THE HOME						ENTERTAINMENT						PERSONAL			
						Home Improvements		Furnishings													
#	POST OFFICE NAME	Auto Loan	Home Loan	Investments	Retirement Plans	Home Repair	Lawn & Garden	Computers & Hardware-Personal	Major Appliances	TV, Radio, Sound Equipment	Furniture	Dine out/ Carry out	Sports Equipment	Fees & Tickets	Toys & Games	Travel	Cable TV	Apparel & Services	Auto Repairs	Health Insurance	Pets & Supplies
10977	SPRING VALLEY	114	129	130	127	131	116	130	122	125	127	129	95	137	126	133	125	94	126	118	139
10980	STONY POINT	137	185	193	178	192	167	156	161	150	157	152	120	183	152	176	151	113	155	152	179
10983	TAPPAN	144	210	236	202	225	193	170	180	162	172	162	131	208	163	201	162	122	170	171	195
10984	THIELLS	152	217	233	205	228	195	178	186	170	178	171	136	213	172	206	171	127	178	177	203
10985	THOMPSON RIDGE	118	149	130	148	143	128	124	126	117	131	119	101	140	122	134	112	86	120	113	145
10986	TOMKINS COVE	144	209	233	201	223	192	169	179	161	171	162	130	207	163	200	162	121	170	170	194
10987	TUXEDO PARK	161	193	199	196	198	180	175	176	167	184	168	135	195	167	190	163	121	172	168	202
10989	VALLEY COTTAGE	149	201	216	195	210	185	171	176	165	171	166	130	201	166	194	166	123	170	170	195
10990	WARWICK	129	162	155	160	162	147	140	143	135	144	137	109	158	136	153	134	99	138	138	163
10992	WASHINGTONVILLE	136	158	148	158	156	146	140	142	135	145	137	109	152	138	148	133	97	138	135	165
10993	WEST HAVERSTRAW	79	108	113	101	111	98	96	95	95	90	97	70	111	95	106	99	72	95	96	106
10994	WEST NYACK	189	268	307	265	290	247	221	235	208	234	208	172	269	205	262	204	155	220	219	256
10996	WEST POINT	155	80	60	93	72	68	145	101	137	135	144	100	110	164	105	126	101	128	91	123
10998	WESTTOWN	109	129	115	129	125	118	115	116	111	116	113	91	126	114	122	110	80	113	111	135
11001	FLORAL PARK	131	185	202	176	195	169	155	161	150	154	151	117	185	149	179	152	112	155	156	176
11003	ELMONT	112	153	160	143	159	137	133	134	129	129	131	99	154	129	148	132	97	132	130	148
11004	GLEN OAKS	99	133	145	127	140	121	120	119	117	115	119	88	138	115	133	119	88	119	118	133
11005	FLORAL PARK	135	166	217	144	202	211	145	183	160	170	153	97	177	134	186	174	102	173	240	193
11010	FRANKLIN SQUARE	110	157	169	148	165	142	130	135	125	129	126	99	155	126	150	127	94	130	130	148
11020	GREAT NECK	201	284	338	290	313	265	235	249	222	253	221	185	295	219	278	217	170	232	226	272
11021	GREAT NECK	183	221	254	229	238	210	210	208	200	220	200	160	236	193	231	195	148	205	201	236
11023	GREAT NECK	213	288	346	297	321	261	251	261	227	276	226	199	299	221	293	213	171	244	226	286
11024	GREAT NECK	229	313	379	325	349	287	267	279	244	294	243	213	327	240	313	231	186	260	243	306
11030	MANHASSET	253	357	434	371	399	333	294	314	274	326	272	235	372	270	351	262	210	289	277	342
11040	NEW HYDE PARK	141	201	226	195	215	185	166	174	159	168	160	127	202	159	195	160	119	166	167	190
11042	NEW HYDE PARK	0	0	0	0	0	0	0	0	0	0	0	0	0	0	0	0	0	0	0	0
11050	PORT WASHINGTON	192	257	298	259	279	234	229	232	215	237	216	176	269	211	260	210	163	223	213	257
11096	INWOOD	75	87	91	86	89	82	90	83	91	83	92	63	96	88	92	94	68	88	87	97
11101	LONG ISLAND CITY	62	59	61	63	59	55	81	66	83	70	86	52	77	77	73	86	65	74	70	80
11102	ASTORIA	69	69	73	72	70	63	88	74	88	77	91	59	86	83	83	89	68	82	76	87
11103	ASTORIA	67	69	75	73	71	66	87	74	89	75	92	57	87	83	84	93	69	82	80	88
11104	SUNNYSIDE	64	67	72	70	69	65	84	72	88	71	91	54	85	82	81	93	68	80	80	86
11105	ASTORIA	72	79	85	81	81	74	93	81	94	81	97	62	95	90	91	98	73	88	86	95
11106	ASTORIA	64	65	69	68	66	62	83	70	85	72	88	54	82	80	79	89	66	78	76	84
11109	LONG ISLAND CITY	216	160	166	184	153	154	236	177	228	219	237	163	209	231	202	222	169	214	185	229
11201	BROOKLYN	147	149	169	163	155	141	175	151	169	168	174	125	178	164	172	167	129	162	150	180
11203	BROOKLYN	70	73	75	75	72	72	85	74	91	74	92	56	87	86	81	97	68	82	83	91
11204	BROOKLYN	61	65	70	68	67	63	79	69	83	68	86	51	81	78	77	88	64	76	76	82
11205	BROOKLYN	65	59	61	63	59	56	79	66	80	71	82	52	74	76	72	82	61	74	69	79
11206	BROOKLYN	42	36	35	39	35	34	54	44	58	46	60	33	49	54	46	61	45	50	46	52
11207	BROOKLYN	49	47	47	50	46	46	62	51	67	52	68	38	60	62	55	71	51	58	57	63
11208	BROOKLYN	56	54	53	56	53	49	68	58	70	61	72	45	66	67	63	71	54	64	59	69
11209	BROOKLYN	86	93	101	95	96	90	107	95	109	97	111	73	110	102	106	113	82	103	104	112
11210	BROOKLYN	79	87	92	89	88	83	98	87	101	87	104	65	102	97	96	107	77	94	94	104
11211	BROOKLYN	51	48	49	51	48	44	67	54	68	57	70	42	63	63	60	70	53	61	57	65
11212	BROOKLYN	44	41	41	44	40	41	56	46	62	47	63	34	54	57	49	67	47	52	53	57
11213	BROOKLYN	50	49	49	52	47	48	65	54	71	54	72	39	63	65	58	76	54	60	61	66
11214	BROOKLYN	61	65	70	68	66	64	80	69	84	68	87	52	81	78	77	89	64	76	78	82
11215	BROOKLYN	125	127	142	136	131	112	151	128	140	145	145	111	151	138	149	133	107	139	119	151
11216	BROOKLYN	54	55	57	57	54	54	65	56	70	56	71	42	66	66	61	75	52	63	63	70
11217	BROOKLYN	114	109	123	120	113	99	138	114	130	130	135	99	135	127	132	126	100	126	110	137
11218	BROOKLYN	67	70	75	73	72	67	86	74	89	75	92	56	87	83	83	93	68	82	81	88
11219	BROOKLYN	54	56	61	59	58	55	71	60	74	60	76	45	71	69	68	79	57	67	67	72
11220	BROOKLYN	62	63	64	64	64	57	78	67	78	69	81	52	77	75	74	80	60	74	69	78
11221	BROOKLYN	46	44	44	46	43	43	58	48	63	49	64	36	56	59	52	67	48	55	54	60
11222	BROOKLYN	63	65	69	68	66	61	80	69	82	70	85	53	80	77	77	85	63	76	73	81
11223	BROOKLYN	62	66	71	68	67	64	81	69	85	69	87	52	82	79	78	90	65	77	78	83
11224	BROOKLYN	49	48	51	51	49	50	61	54	66	54	67	39	60	60	58	71	49	59	63	64
11225	BROOKLYN	56	54	55	58	53	53	73	60	80	60	81	44	71	73	65	86	61	68	68	74
11226	BROOKLYN	51	48	48	52	46	47	70	56	77	56	78	40	66	70	60	84	60	63	64	69
11228	BROOKLYN	80	100	106	97	103	94	100	94	102	89	104	69	110	99	105	108	78	98	100	107
11229	BROOKLYN	70	81	87	82	83	77	90	81	93	80	95	60	95	87	90	97	71	87	87	95
11230	BROOKLYN	66	71	76	74	73	69	85	74	89	74	92	56	87	83	83	94	68	82	82	88
11231	BROOKLYN	109	107	119	117	110	97	136	113	130	126	135	95	133	126	129	128	101	124	109	135
11232	BROOKLYN	60	58	56	58	57	50	72	61	69	67	72	50	69	68	67	67	54	68	58	70
11233	BROOKLYN	48	45	46	48	44	45	59	49	64	50	65	37	57	60	53	69	49	56	56	61
11234	BROOKLYN	91	117	125	113	121	109	111	107	112	102	114	78	125	109	119	117	85	109	110	121
11235	BROOKLYN	64	69	75	71	72	69	80	72	83	72	85	53	82	77	80	87	62	78	81	85
11236	BROOKLYN	73	81	84	82	81	78	90	80	96	78	97	60	95	91	88	102	72	87	88	96
11237	BROOKLYN	56	45	40	45	43	38	62	51	61	60	65	42	55	61	55	58	47	60	47	59
11238	BROOKLYN	89	86	93	93	87	79	109	91	105	100	109	76	106	102	103	104	80	101	90	110
11239	BROOKLYN	36	31	30	35	29	31	53	41	60	41	61	28	47	53	42	66	48	47	47	50
11354	FLUSHING	69	77	83	79	80	75	86	79	88	79	90	59	90	83	87	92	66	84	86	92
11355	FLUSHING	68	76	82	78	79	70	88	78	89	79	91	60	90	83	88	91	68	84	81	91
11356	COLLEGE POINT	90	113	119	109	116	101	112	105	110	104	112	80	122	108	118	112	84	109	105	119
11357	WHITESTONE	101	131	141	126	137	122	121	120	120	116	121	88	137	117	133	123	89	120	122	135
11358	FLUSHING	98	126	139	123	134	109	122	118	114	119	115	90	133	110	132	112	86	117	109	131
11359	BAYSIDE	130	153	157	153	159	161	132	146	136	139	136	101	150	132	149	141	95	140	158	166
11360	BAYSIDE	118	139	150	138	146	145	130	135	134	132	133	95	145	126	143	139	94	135	153	154
11361	BAYSIDE	105	133	146	130	140	116	128	123	120	125	122	96	140	118	139	117	91	124	114	138
11362	LITTLE NECK	121	154	169	151	165	144	138	143	130	144	131	106	155	126	156	128	95	138	139	159
11363	LITTLE NECK	152	191	212	190	205	166	177	177	158	189	159	138	194	154	196	148	116	170	155	197
11364	OAKLAND GARDENS	111	140	155	137	150	124	133	132	122	137	123	101	145	117	146	118	90	130	124	147
11365	FRESH MEADOWS	99	130	142	125	138	112	122	119	114	120	116	91	135	111	134	112	86	118	110	132
11366	FRESH MEADOWS	126	171	190	165	183	147	154	155	140	156	142	118	174	138	174	135	105	149	138	169
11367	FLUSHING	78	89	95	90	91	83	98	89	100	89	102	67	103	95	98	103	76	94	92	103
11368	CORONA	70	70	68	70	69	61	84	73	82	78	86	58	82	80	80	82	63	80	71	84
11369	EAST ELMHURST	74	80	79	79	80	73	88	79	87	81	89	62	89	85	86	88	65	85	80	92
11370	EAST ELMHURST	79	91	95	90	93	83	99	90	100	89	103	68	104	96	100	104	77	96	93	103
11372	JACKSON HEIGHTS	70	72	75	74	73	70	88	77	92	77	94	57	88	86	85	96	70	84	85	91
11373	ELMHURST	65	68	73	71	69	66	85	72	89	72	92	55	85	83	81	94	68	80	80	86
11374	REGO PARK	75	82	88	84	84	78	96	85	98	85	101	64	98	92	95	102	75	92	91	100
11375	FOREST HILLS	110	118	125	121	122	113	128	118	125	124	127	92	131	120	129	125	91	124	122	138
11377	WOODSIDE	65	69	74	72	71	67	84	73	88	73	91	55	85	82	82	93	67	81	81	87
11378	MASPETH	75	95	99	91	97	87	93	88	94	84	97	65	103	92	98	99	72	91	91	100
	NEW YORK	100	106	110	108	107	104	112	106	113	106	114	81	115	110	112	116	83	110	110	124
	UNITED STATES	100	100	100	100	100	100	100	100	100	100	100	100	100	100	100	100	100	100	100	100

11379-11733

ZIP CODE #	POST OFFICE NAME	COUNTY FIPS CODE	POPULATION 2000	POPULATION 2009	POPULATION 2014	2000-2009 ANNUAL RATE % Rate	2000-2009 ANNUAL RATE State Centile	HOUSEHOLDS 2000	HOUSEHOLDS 2009	HOUSEHOLDS 2014	HOUSEHOLDS % Annual Rate 2000-2009	HOUSEHOLDS 2009 Average HH Size	FAMILIES 2000	FAMILIES 2009	FAMILIES % Annual Rate 2000-2009
11379	MIDDLE VILLAGE	081	34699	35305	35761	0.2	52	14125	14336	14462	0.2	2.43	9421	9400	0.0
11385	RIDGEWOOD	081	97196	102054	104033	0.5	71	34740	35468	35874	0.2	2.87	24683	24849	0.1
11411	CAMBRIA HEIGHTS	081	20422	20506	20668	0.0	38	6371	6385	6412	0.0	3.21	5199	5163	-0.1
11412	SAINT ALBANS	081	36855	37809	38423	0.3	59	11493	11763	11911	0.3	3.21	8761	8859	0.1
11413	SPRINGFIELD GARDENS	081	40240	40972	41526	0.2	52	12647	12856	12984	0.2	3.18	10032	10089	0.1
11414	HOWARD BEACH	081	28121	28256	28497	0.1	44	11312	11335	11379	0.0	2.48	7826	7724	-0.1
11415	KEW GARDENS	081	20340	20635	20768	0.2	52	8283	8219	8219	-0.1	2.41	4637	4500	-0.3
11416	OZONE PARK	081	23668	24403	24610	0.3	59	7339	7281	7288	-0.1	3.34	5757	5645	-0.2
11417	OZONE PARK	081	28607	29627	30013	0.4	66	9430	9494	9550	0.1	3.12	7162	7119	-0.1
11418	RICHMOND HILL	081	37165	37192	37227	0.0	38	11543	11263	11207	-0.3	3.27	8426	8097	-0.4
11419	SOUTH RICHMOND HILL	081	48867	49529	49878	0.1	44	13351	13256	13266	-0.1	3.73	11331	11166	-0.2
11420	SOUTH OZONE PARK	081	45727	46768	47378	0.2	52	13281	13447	13556	0.1	3.45	10814	10848	0.0
11421	WOODHAVEN	081	37664	39493	40211	0.5	71	12174	12372	12486	0.2	3.19	9090	9133	0.1
11422	ROSEDALE	081	30368	30090	30156	-0.1	30	9394	9237	9216	-0.2	3.25	7462	7262	-0.3
11423	HOLLIS	081	31727	31912	32154	0.1	44	9759	9771	9806	0.0	3.22	7562	7482	-0.1
11426	BELLEROSE	081	19106	19267	19419	0.1	44	6480	6474	6491	0.0	2.81	4721	4656	-0.1
11427	QUEENS VILLAGE	081	23336	23496	23680	0.1	44	7977	7963	7985	0.0	2.94	5963	5875	-0.2
11428	QUEENS VILLAGE	081	20383	20463	20540	0.0	38	5767	5699	5693	-0.1	3.59	4857	4759	-0.2
11429	QUEENS VILLAGE	081	27876	27860	28032	0.0	38	7890	7869	7888	0.0	3.52	6535	6461	-0.1
11430	JAMAICA	081	28	28	28	0.0	38	12	12	12	0.0	2.33	8	8	0.0
11432	JAMAICA	081	57275	58399	59154	0.2	52	18655	18901	19064	0.1	2.96	12905	12857	0.0
11433	JAMAICA	081	29257	31476	32554	0.8	84	9342	9990	10276	0.7	3.13	6731	7105	0.6
11434	JAMAICA	081	58363	59813	60728	0.3	59	19720	20140	20335	0.2	2.86	13587	13700	0.1
11435	JAMAICA	081	53543	54127	54582	0.1	44	17474	17476	17539	0.0	3.05	12298	12116	-0.2
11436	JAMAICA	081	19152	19580	19859	0.2	52	5792	5903	5965	0.2	3.32	4634	4674	0.1
11439	JAMAICA	081	797	775	774	-0.3	15	11	11	11	0.0	2.55	8	8	0.0
11501	MINEOLA	059	19603	19039	18640	-0.3	15	7597	7388	7234	-0.3	2.58	5048	4826	-0.5
11507	ALBERTSON	059	7176	6989	6843	-0.3	15	2383	2321	2274	-0.3	3.01	1980	1911	-0.4
11509	ATLANTIC BEACH	059	2911	2888	2847	-0.1	30	1086	1081	1068	0.0	2.65	813	798	-0.2
11510	BALDWIN	059	32442	31745	31145	-0.2	21	10900	10657	10452	-0.2	2.97	8588	8301	-0.4
11514	CARLE PLACE	059	5061	4930	4827	-0.3	15	1843	1802	1767	-0.2	2.73	1325	1278	-0.4
11516	CEDARHURST	059	6942	6844	6730	-0.2	21	2539	2495	2453	-0.2	2.74	1842	1785	-0.3
11518	EAST ROCKAWAY	059	11330	11095	10886	-0.2	21	4358	4268	4188	-0.2	2.58	3093	2986	-0.4
11520	FREEPORT	059	44135	44183	43519	0.0	38	13578	13345	13113	-0.2	3.26	9979	9671	-0.3
11530	GARDEN CITY	059	26542	26299	25876	-0.1	30	9141	9017	8880	-0.1	2.78	7243	7070	-0.3
11542	GLEN COVE	059	27426	27516	27222	0.0	38	9742	9769	9666	0.0	2.72	6877	6779	-0.2
11545	GLEN HEAD	059	12619	13823	13628	1.0	89	4288	4225	4157	-0.2	2.94	3546	3462	-0.3
11548	GREENVALE	059	2494	1226	1200	-7.4	0	452	440	431	-0.3	2.78	336	322	-0.5
11549	HEMPSTEAD	059	0	1751	1837	0.0	38	0	0	0	0.0	0.00	0	0	0.0
11550	HEMPSTEAD	059	59000	56011	55233	-0.6	4	15990	15671	15384	-0.2	3.47	11804	11405	-0.4
11552	WEST HEMPSTEAD	059	22799	22420	22000	-0.2	21	7236	7084	6949	-0.2	3.14	5875	5692	-0.3
11553	UNIONDALE	059	23500	25825	25625	1.0	89	6166	6077	5981	-0.2	3.83	4946	4816	-0.3
11554	EAST MEADOW	059	37549	37163	36572	-0.1	30	12218	12051	11860	-0.1	2.94	9676	9437	-0.3
11557	HEWLETT	059	8116	7900	7728	-0.3	15	2898	2818	2759	-0.3	2.80	2346	2262	-0.4
11558	ISLAND PARK	059	8553	8373	8220	-0.2	21	3011	2943	2888	-0.2	2.73	2262	2183	-0.4
11559	LAWRENCE	059	8114	8136	8027	0.0	38	2633	2590	2545	-0.2	3.14	2031	1972	-0.3
11560	LOCUST VALLEY	059	6734	6656	6571	-0.1	30	2378	2344	2311	-0.2	2.81	1800	1754	-0.3
11561	LONG BEACH	059	41091	40157	39378	-0.2	21	17255	16801	16461	-0.3	2.27	9677	9207	-0.5
11563	LYNBROOK	059	22974	22729	22358	-0.1	30	8448	8348	8215	-0.1	2.67	6017	5857	-0.3
11565	MALVERNE	059	9077	8864	8689	-0.3	15	3160	3095	3035	-0.2	2.85	2582	2505	-0.3
11566	MERRICK	059	35534	34797	34200	-0.2	21	11781	11571	11375	-0.2	3.00	10030	9768	-0.3
11568	OLD WESTBURY	059	4102	4222	4208	0.3	59	986	996	991	0.1	3.45	891	895	0.0
11570	ROCKVILLE CENTRE	059	28123	27520	27012	-0.2	21	10189	9952	9761	-0.3	2.73	7318	7066	-0.4
11572	OCEANSIDE	059	31297	30484	29881	-0.3	15	10756	10491	10283	-0.3	2.89	8735	8436	-0.4
11575	ROOSEVELT	059	15946	15774	15536	-0.1	30	4122	4071	4011	-0.1	3.85	3417	3341	-0.2
11576	ROSLYN	059	13539	14079	14059	0.4	66	4888	5107	5107	0.5	2.69	3866	3967	0.3
11577	ROSLYN HEIGHTS	059	10897	10556	10329	-0.3	15	3751	3624	3545	-0.4	2.90	3146	3014	-0.5
11579	SEA CLIFF	059	5066	4988	4904	-0.2	21	2013	1983	1949	-0.2	2.49	1356	1313	-0.3
11580	VALLEY STREAM	059	37984	37423	36767	-0.2	21	12654	12364	12132	-0.3	3.01	9760	9415	-0.4
11581	VALLEY STREAM	059	20333	20046	19716	-0.2	21	7137	7021	6906	-0.2	2.85	5722	5568	-0.3
11590	WESTBURY	059	42502	43766	43283	0.3	59	12440	12631	12511	0.2	3.39	9914	9968	0.1
11596	WILLISTON PARK	059	10469	10156	9945	-0.3	15	3656	3556	3485	-0.3	2.85	2869	2759	-0.4
11598	WOODMERE	059	13198	13023	12783	-0.1	30	4229	4129	4046	-0.3	3.06	3498	3384	-0.4
11691	FAR ROCKAWAY	081	56913	61238	63181	0.8	84	18552	19667	20163	0.6	2.96	12517	13107	0.5
11692	ARVERNE	081	14939	16474	17147	1.1	91	4586	5021	5208	1.0	3.04	3350	3636	0.9
11693	FAR ROCKAWAY	081	11179	12037	12447	0.8	84	4189	4455	4575	0.7	2.68	2767	2906	0.5
11694	ROCKAWAY PARK	081	19256	19854	20194	0.3	59	7838	8132	8272	0.4	2.26	4497	4561	0.2
11697	BREEZY POINT	081	4226	4213	4242	0.0	38	1796	1787	1790	-0.1	2.35	1167	1140	-0.3
11701	AMITYVILLE	103	25197	25918	25847	0.3	59	8320	8516	8492	0.3	2.96	5741	5782	0.1
11702	BABYLON	059	14969	14788	14505	-0.1	30	5417	5340	5241	-0.2	2.71	3910	3808	-0.3
11703	NORTH BABYLON	103	16555	16464	16281	-0.1	30	5723	5709	5653	0.0	2.88	4391	4333	-0.1
11704	WEST BABYLON	103	40199	40441	40038	0.1	44	13157	13253	13128	0.1	3.00	10094	10053	0.0
11705	BAYPORT	103	8659	8804	8773	0.2	52	3220	3313	3317	0.3	2.64	2303	2331	0.1
11706	BAY SHORE	103	60587	61239	60729	0.1	44	18710	18844	18699	0.1	3.20	14163	14080	-0.1
11709	BAYVILLE	059	7090	6958	6828	-0.2	21	2547	2505	2460	-0.2	2.74	1897	1841	-0.3
11710	BELLMORE	059	34680	33977	33365	-0.2	21	11629	11423	11222	-0.2	2.96	9505	9251	-0.3
11713	BELLPORT	103	9371	11197	11447	1.9	98	2788	3347	3446	2.0	3.17	2187	2659	2.1
11714	BETHPAGE	059	23090	22737	22343	-0.2	21	7990	7937	7817	-0.1	2.86	6265	6145	-0.2
11715	BLUE POINT	103	4407	4552	4538	0.4	66	1571	1627	1625	0.4	2.77	1178	1206	0.3
11716	BOHEMIA	103	10529	10980	10981	0.5	71	3535	3683	3689	0.4	2.88	2722	2803	0.3
11717	BRENTWOOD	103	51479	53447	52931	0.4	66	12040	12076	11930	0.0	4.33	10417	10383	0.0
11718	BRIGHTWATERS	103	3284	3273	3227	0.0	38	1133	1128	1112	0.0	2.89	907	896	-0.1
11719	BROOKHAVEN	103	3149	3383	3456	0.8	84	1069	1152	1182	0.8	2.51	823	878	0.7
11720	CENTEREACH	103	28087	29346	29405	0.5	71	8464	8876	8913	0.5	3.25	7219	7514	0.4
11721	CENTERPORT	103	5923	5926	5854	0.0	38	2205	2210	2186	0.0	2.66	1687	1672	-0.1
11722	CENTRAL ISLIP	103	31524	32373	32034	0.3	59	8499	8603	8510	0.1	3.68	6673	6685	0.0
11724	COLD SPRING HARBOR	103	2839	2837	2786	0.0	38	914	912	899	0.0	3.11	786	780	-0.1
11725	COMMACK	103	29796	29407	28986	-0.1	30	9567	9451	9322	-0.1	3.05	8290	8137	-0.2
11726	COPIAGUE	103	18729	19240	19218	0.3	59	5961	6038	6011	0.1	3.15	4285	4296	0.0
11727	CORAM	103	25376	27703	28230	1.0	89	9312	10099	10275	0.9	2.73	6803	7278	0.7
11729	DEER PARK	103	27865	27894	27657	0.0	38	9377	9373	9292	0.0	2.97	7307	7216	-0.1
11730	EAST ISLIP	103	16073	16202	16070	0.1	44	5229	5293	5257	0.1	3.02	4277	4288	0.0
11731	EAST NORTHPORT	103	30939	30470	30002	-0.2	21	10211	10064	9919	-0.2	2.98	8486	8296	-0.2
11732	EAST NORWICH	059	3039	3000	2955	-0.1	30	1061	1051	1037	-0.1	2.82	814	798	-0.2
11733	EAST SETAUKET	103	18850	19773	19752	0.5	71	6474	6792	6794	0.5	2.89	5015	5206	0.4
	NEW YORK					0.3					0.3	2.61			0.1
	UNITED STATES					1.0					1.1	2.59			0.9

#	POST OFFICE NAME	RACE (%) White 2000	White 2009	Black 2000	Black 2009	Asian/Pacific 2000	Asian/Pacific 2009	% Hispanic Origin 2000	% Hispanic Origin 2009	2009 AGE DISTRIBUTION (%) 0-4	5-9	10-14	15-19	20-24	25-44	45-64	65-84	85+	18+	MEDIAN AGE 2009	% 2009 Males	% 2009 Females
11379	MIDDLE VILLAGE	86.9	83.0	0.7	0.7	6.8	9.3	10.0	12.3	5.1	5.0	5.0	5.5	5.9	28.2	27.7	14.4	3.1	81.5	41.9	47.5	52.5
11385	RIDGEWOOD	65.3	61.0	2.1	2.0	6.3	7.9	37.9	42.3	7.4	6.8	6.3	7.2	8.0	31.1	23.1	8.7	1.4	75.3	33.4	49.2	50.8
11411	CAMBRIA HEIGHTS	3.0	2.6	91.7	91.3	0.5	0.6	4.0	4.0	6.0	6.0	6.1	6.7	5.8	27.1	26.8	14.0	1.5	77.8	39.6	45.0	55.0
11412	SAINT ALBANS	1.2	1.1	94.0	93.5	0.5	0.6	3.5	3.5	6.5	7.0	7.1	7.7	6.5	25.7	26.0	11.7	1.8	74.7	37.3	44.3	55.7
11413	SPRINGFIELD GARDENS	2.9	2.6	91.3	90.8	0.6	0.7	4.5	4.5	6.3	6.4	6.5	7.4	6.5	27.5	26.6	11.8	1.1	76.4	37.7	45.8	54.2
11414	HOWARD BEACH	92.5	90.3	1.0	1.2	2.9	4.0	9.8	12.4	4.8	4.8	5.0	5.2	4.6	25.3	27.4	19.4	3.5	82.2	45.2	46.9	53.1
11415	KEW GARDENS	65.5	59.3	7.5	7.6	13.1	17.0	20.7	23.4	6.8	5.7	5.2	5.7	7.8	32.8	24.3	9.7	2.0	79.1	36.0	49.4	50.6
11416	OZONE PARK	42.5	38.2	6.9	6.5	14.4	17.1	40.4	42.4	8.1	7.4	6.7	7.5	8.3	30.8	22.1	7.8	1.3	73.3	32.0	48.3	51.7
11417	OZONE PARK	52.6	47.2	4.2	4.0	13.9	16.9	28.0	30.5	7.5	6.9	6.4	7.2	7.1	30.5	24.3	8.7	1.4	74.9	34.5	49.0	51.0
11418	RICHMOND HILL	41.3	37.4	8.6	8.1	16.1	19.0	37.2	38.7	7.5	6.9	6.4	7.1	8.4	31.4	23.5	7.5	1.2	75.1	32.9	49.8	50.2
11419	SOUTH RICHMOND HILL	18.4	16.2	15.9	14.5	24.7	27.8	24.4	24.1	7.5	7.1	6.8	7.6	8.3	31.3	24.0	6.7	0.7	74.1	32.4	49.6	50.4
11420	SOUTH OZONE PARK	20.7	18.4	35.6	34.0	12.8	15.0	22.8	23.4	7.4	7.1	6.8	7.7	7.6	29.5	24.3	8.6	1.1	74.0	33.7	48.2	51.8
11421	WOODHAVEN	48.0	43.2	5.3	5.0	13.8	16.8	43.7	46.3	7.2	6.6	6.5	7.2	8.2	30.0	23.9	8.6	1.8	75.4	33.8	48.4	51.6
11422	ROSEDALE	12.8	11.1	75.5	75.4	2.5	3.1	8.8	9.3	6.9	6.6	6.8	7.7	7.4	28.1	26.7	8.7	1.1	74.9	35.3	45.7	54.3
11423	HOLLIS	17.7	15.6	45.0	43.7	16.5	19.1	15.7	15.8	6.7	6.7	6.6	6.8	6.5	27.9	25.9	10.9	1.9	75.7	36.7	46.5	53.5
11426	BELLEROSE	61.4	53.7	5.9	6.0	23.0	29.3	13.4	15.1	5.9	5.8	6.3	6.2	5.6	27.8	28.7	11.3	2.5	78.3	40.5	49.1	50.9
11427	QUEENS VILLAGE	36.2	31.7	23.8	22.7	21.1	25.7	17.5	18.2	6.2	6.2	6.2	6.5	6.0	26.3	27.6	12.1	2.8	77.4	39.6	46.6	53.4
11428	QUEENS VILLAGE	26.5	23.2	26.2	24.5	21.3	25.0	23.9	24.5	6.9	6.8	6.8	7.5	7.0	29.4	26.0	8.6	1.0	75.0	35.0	47.9	52.1
11429	QUEENS VILLAGE	5.5	5.1	84.1	83.1	1.5	1.9	8.7	9.0	6.8	6.8	7.0	7.9	6.9	27.3	25.3	10.7	1.3	74.6	35.7	45.3	54.7
11430	JAMAICA	71.4	64.3	3.6	3.6	0.0	0.0	0.0	0.0	14.3	3.6	0.0	3.6	7.1	28.6	35.7	7.1	0.0	78.6	37.5	50.0	50.0
11432	JAMAICA	27.1	23.8	22.8	21.4	24.9	28.9	25.2	25.6	6.7	6.4	5.9	6.5	6.9	30.0	25.4	10.0	2.1	77.3	36.5	48.0	52.0
11433	JAMAICA	2.8	2.7	86.4	85.5	1.9	2.3	8.4	8.4	7.8	7.6	7.6	8.2	7.9	26.2	23.4	10.0	1.5	72.0	32.9	45.1	54.9
11434	JAMAICA	2.6	2.4	91.3	90.8	0.7	0.9	5.3	5.3	6.9	7.2	7.3	7.7	6.4	25.2	25.8	11.8	1.8	74.0	37.3	44.6	55.4
11435	JAMAICA	26.8	24.2	33.2	32.1	14.4	17.2	29.4	30.0	7.3	6.9	6.5	6.9	7.2	31.1	23.9	8.8	1.2	75.1	34.3	48.7	51.3
11436	JAMAICA	1.7	1.6	89.6	88.6	1.2	1.5	6.6	6.7	7.5	7.5	7.5	8.3	7.8	26.2	24.2	9.7	1.4	72.5	33.5	45.3	54.7
11439	JAMAICA	53.5	46.1	18.8	19.4	21.7	27.7	8.6	9.5	0.5	1.2	1.7	44.5	21.3	10.2	12.5	6.3	1.8	94.6	20.5	48.4	51.6
11501	MINEOLA	86.6	82.5	1.0	1.3	4.5	6.1	12.9	16.1	5.9	6.0	6.0	5.3	5.1	29.3	27.8	12.2	2.4	78.8	40.5	48.3	51.7
11507	ALBERTSON	78.3	72.0	0.5	0.6	17.8	23.1	4.5	5.6	5.7	6.4	7.5	6.6	3.7	21.5	31.2	14.3	3.0	76.2	44.0	48.3	51.7
11509	ATLANTIC BEACH	97.3	96.2	0.4	0.6	0.8	1.2	2.8	3.8	5.4	5.8	6.3	5.3	3.7	20.3	33.7	16.9	2.5	79.2	47.0	48.8	51.2
11510	BALDWIN	72.0	66.6	17.7	20.5	3.6	4.7	10.1	12.3	6.5	6.7	7.1	6.9	5.3	24.7	29.4	11.5	1.8	75.4	40.3	47.7	52.3
11514	CARLE PLACE	90.0	86.6	1.9	2.5	5.4	7.3	7.6	9.8	5.6	5.8	6.3	6.2	4.9	26.9	30.1	11.4	2.7	78.3	41.3	47.8	52.2
11516	CEDARHURST	91.1	88.2	1.3	1.7	3.0	4.1	7.8	10.0	7.8	7.2	6.7	5.9	4.8	23.6	27.8	13.7	2.4	74.6	40.3	47.7	52.3
11518	EAST ROCKAWAY	95.8	94.2	0.5	0.7	1.6	2.2	5.6	7.4	6.1	6.4	6.8	6.6	5.1	24.4	30.1	12.1	2.4	76.4	41.6	47.8	52.2
11520	FREEPORT	42.6	38.3	33.0	35.0	1.4	1.7	33.3	35.8	6.9	6.9	6.9	7.4	6.8	28.2	25.7	9.5	1.7	74.8	36.0	48.2	51.8
11530	GARDEN CITY	93.9	91.1	1.5	2.1	3.3	4.6	3.3	4.6	6.3	7.1	8.1	8.5	5.0	19.4	28.8	14.1	2.7	74.3	41.7	48.2	51.8
11542	GLEN COVE	80.7	76.4	6.2	7.4	4.1	5.4	19.6	23.4	6.1	6.0	6.0	6.1	5.6	26.7	26.2	13.5	3.9	78.3	40.8	48.1	51.9
11545	GLEN HEAD	91.4	85.7	1.2	3.7	5.1	6.9	3.7	5.7	5.6	6.4	7.8	9.9	6.5	19.8	29.3	12.6	2.1	75.4	40.9	48.9	51.1
11548	GREENVALE	68.0	60.1	11.6	4.9	10.7	20.7	11.7	14.0	4.2	3.8	5.1	12.9	22.2	20.9	20.8	8.6	1.7	84.6	26.8	42.7	57.3
11549	HEMPSTEAD	0.0	62.6	0.0	23.4	0.0	5.3	0.0	14.4	6.0	4.9	3.3	22.5	24.3	28.2	7.4	2.5	0.9	85.0	22.7	55.6	44.4
11550	HEMPSTEAD	27.7	23.0	51.0	54.2	1.4	1.4	30.9	32.9	8.1	7.8	7.2	7.9	7.5	30.1	21.5	8.1	1.8	72.6	32.7	48.4	51.6
11552	WEST HEMPSTEAD	73.0	68.7	16.5	17.9	4.4	5.8	9.3	11.4	6.7	6.9	7.5	7.5	4.9	25.1	27.3	11.8	2.3	74.1	39.5	48.8	51.2
11553	UNIONDALE	26.7	26.0	56.0	56.1	2.2	2.6	22.6	22.5	6.4	6.5	6.4	10.2	9.1	27.4	22.9	9.2	1.8	76.7	33.6	49.1	50.9
11554	EAST MEADOW	85.3	80.9	4.3	5.3	6.7	9.1	7.0	8.8	5.9	6.0	6.6	6.8	5.3	26.2	27.9	12.8	2.5	77.4	40.7	49.8	50.2
11557	HEWLETT	91.5	88.6	0.9	1.2	4.7	6.4	6.2	7.9	5.5	6.1	7.4	7.4	4.9	19.8	32.0	14.4	2.4	76.2	44.2	48.1	51.9
11558	ISLAND PARK	91.1	88.4	0.9	1.0	1.5	2.0	13.6	17.4	5.8	5.8	6.1	5.7	4.8	26.6	29.5	13.4	2.1	78.6	42.0	48.0	52.0
11559	LAWRENCE	87.2	84.5	5.5	6.5	1.9	2.5	8.0	9.7	7.9	8.8	9.1	7.5	5.1	20.4	25.8	12.9	2.6	69.2	37.8	48.8	51.2
11560	LOCUST VALLEY	90.3	87.7	2.3	2.7	2.6	3.7	9.3	11.3	6.6	7.2	8.2	6.4	3.8	23.4	29.8	12.3	2.2	73.6	41.7	49.0	51.0
11561	LONG BEACH	85.9	83.1	5.4	6.2	2.2	2.9	11.5	14.0	4.8	4.6	4.9	5.7	5.9	27.2	29.8	13.2	4.0	82.3	43.1	48.3	51.7
11563	LYNBROOK	92.1	89.4	1.0	1.3	3.0	4.1	8.0	10.5	5.7	5.9	6.3	6.4	5.0	24.6	28.4	14.2	3.6	78.2	42.6	47.2	52.8
11565	MALVERNE	92.2	89.5	1.8	2.3	3.0	4.2	6.2	8.1	5.9	6.4	7.3	6.2	4.3	22.3	31.1	13.8	2.7	76.5	43.3	48.0	52.0
11566	MERRICK	94.6	92.6	0.7	1.0	2.6	3.6	3.7	5.0	6.3	7.0	8.1	7.2	4.2	21.8	31.4	12.0	1.9	73.9	42.2	48.3	51.7
11568	OLD WESTBURY	67.6	60.4	14.6	17.4	11.7	14.7	7.3	8.6	4.9	5.8	7.6	13.5	11.3	19.4	25.2	10.8	1.6	78.7	35.0	47.6	52.4
11570	ROCKVILLE CENTRE	83.2	80.7	11.0	12.0	1.4	2.0	7.7	9.5	6.2	6.7	7.7	6.9	4.9	21.8	29.9	12.8	3.0	74.9	42.0	47.0	53.0
11572	OCEANSIDE	94.9	93.1	0.5	0.7	1.8	2.6	6.1	8.0	5.7	6.1	7.0	6.9	4.7	22.6	30.7	14.0	2.3	76.8	43.0	48.1	51.9
11575	ROOSEVELT	8.3	7.4	78.9	79.7	0.6	0.6	15.9	15.8	8.0	8.2	7.9	8.1	6.6	27.4	23.7	9.3	0.8	70.7	33.3	46.5	53.5
11576	ROSLYN	85.4	80.6	1.3	1.8	10.6	13.8	3.2	4.3	5.3	6.1	7.7	6.6	3.4	18.5	34.1	15.4	3.0	76.5	46.4	48.5	51.5
11577	ROSLYN HEIGHTS	83.9	79.2	3.9	4.6	8.9	12.0	4.5	5.5	6.4	7.3	8.8	7.6	4.1	19.9	30.7	12.7	2.4	72.5	42.4	48.9	51.1
11579	SEA CLIFF	94.8	93.0	1.7	2.2	1.2	1.7	4.8	6.3	4.9	5.7	6.9	6.9	4.6	20.9	34.7	12.8	2.7	78.1	45.1	49.6	50.4
11580	VALLEY STREAM	68.9	63.0	14.9	17.2	8.2	10.2	13.1	15.5	6.1	6.3	6.7	6.9	5.2	26.1	28.1	11.8	2.9	76.6	40.3	47.3	52.7
11581	VALLEY STREAM	85.5	81.1	3.4	4.3	7.6	10.1	6.7	8.5	5.4	5.9	6.6	6.6	5.1	22.7	30.5	14.4	2.8	78.0	43.3	48.1	51.9
11590	WESTBURY	60.1	56.4	23.5	24.7	5.5	6.9	22.0	23.9	6.8	6.8	6.9	7.3	6.1	28.1	25.7	10.5	1.9	75.4	37.0	49.2	50.8
11596	WILLISTON PARK	89.2	85.5	0.4	0.5	8.4	11.2	3.8	5.0	6.2	6.6	7.4	6.7	4.1	23.8	29.5	13.0	2.7	75.6	42.0	47.7	52.3
11598	WOODMERE	93.2	90.7	1.6	2.2	3.0	4.2	4.1	5.3	7.1	7.6	8.4	7.4	4.4	20.3	28.2	13.7	2.8	72.1	41.1	48.7	51.3
11691	FAR ROCKAWAY	29.2	26.9	52.6	52.8	1.6	2.0	22.9	24.8	8.7	8.1	7.6	8.0	7.8	25.3	21.7	10.5	2.3	70.7	32.0	45.9	54.1
11692	ARVERNE	16.9	15.2	68.7	68.4	0.9	1.2	16.4	17.4	8.1	8.0	8.1	8.6	8.1	25.4	21.7	9.9	2.1	70.6	31.8	45.5	54.5
11693	FAR ROCKAWAY	57.8	53.6	30.2	32.0	2.0	2.7	15.3	17.8	7.3	8.4	8.4	8.2	6.4	24.4	25.5	9.8	1.5	70.6	35.0	45.9	54.1
11694	ROCKAWAY PARK	88.0	84.8	5.7	6.6	2.4	3.4	8.3	10.6	5.6	5.5	6.0	5.7	4.8	24.1	28.2	16.4	3.7	79.2	43.8	48.6	51.4
11697	BREEZY POINT	99.2	98.9	0.1	0.1	0.4	0.6	1.2	1.7	5.3	5.8	6.5	5.9	3.5	21.2	28.9	19.2	3.7	78.8	46.1	47.1	52.9
11701	AMITYVILLE	49.7	46.4	40.0	41.8	1.3	1.5	12.1	13.5	6.5	6.8	7.0	7.3	5.8	26.0	26.6	11.4	2.5	75.1	38.6	47.1	52.9
11702	BABYLON	92.9	90.8	2.4	3.0	1.6	2.2	5.0	6.5	6.4	6.6	7.1	6.8	5.3	24.7	30.4	10.9	2.0	75.6	41.1	48.4	51.6
11703	NORTH BABYLON	91.9	89.3	2.0	2.5	2.1	2.9	7.5	9.8	6.6	6.9	7.1	6.7	4.7	26.2	28.2	11.6	1.8	75.1	40.0	48.2	51.8
11704	WEST BABYLON	82.2	79.9	11.6	12.0	2.0	2.8	8.0	10.0	6.8	6.9	7.0	7.0	5.4	26.4	26.7	11.6	2.2	75.0	39.0	47.6	52.4
11705	BAYPORT	96.1	94.5	0.9	1.2	1.2	1.7	3.9	5.3	7.1	7.3	7.4	6.3	4.6	23.5	28.9	13.0	1.9	73.9	40.9	47.7	52.3
11706	BAY SHORE	67.2	63.3	13.8	15.0	2.2	2.7	28.3	31.7	7.1	7.1	7.1	7.8	6.8	27.3	25.5	10.0	1.3	74.1	36.0	49.4	50.6
11709	BAYVILLE	96.2	94.8	0.3	0.4	1.6	2.2	4.6	6.2	5.9	6.0	6.8	6.3	4.7	24.2	31.5	12.5	2.2	76.9	42.7	49.3	50.7
11710	BELLMORE	94.3	92.2	1.2	1.6	2.6	3.6	3.9	5.2	6.4	6.8	7.5	7.0	4.5	23.6	29.8	12.2	2.0	74.7	41.4	48.7	51.3
11713	BELLPORT	64.7	64.3	22.6	22.5	1.9	2.4	14.2	16.2	7.1	7.5	7.6	7.9	6.1	25.9	26.8	9.5	1.5	73.1	36.3	49.4	50.6
11714	BETHPAGE	94.8	92.7	0.3	0.5	2.5	3.6	5.0	6.6	6.2	6.4	6.8	6.3	4.6	24.8	27.4	14.7	2.7	76.5	41.9	48.0	52.0
11715	BLUE POINT	96.4	95.2	0.7	0.8	1.1	1.6	4.4	5.8	6.7	7.0	7.4	6.9	5.3	22.6	30.9	11.4	1.7	74.1	41.7	48.9	51.1
11716	BOHEMIA	94.2	92.3	1.1	1.3	2.4	3.4	4.8	6.2	5.9	6.3	6.5	6.4	5.0	26.9	27.8	12.2	2.9	77.1	40.5	49.8	50.2
11717	BRENTWOOD	48.3	44.9	18.3	18.9	2.1	2.4	53.0	56.9	8.1	8.1	7.8	8.5	7.6	29.2	21.7	7.8	1.1	70.8	31.8	50.2	49.8
11718	BRIGHTWATERS	94.2	92.5	2.1	2.6	1.5	2.0	4.6	6.0	7.3	7.9	9.0	6.8	3.8	22.8	30.8	10.0	1.6	71.2	40.9	48.2	51.8
11719	BROOKHAVEN	84.5	81.3	10.1	11.9	0.8	1.1	7.4	9.2	6.6	6.7	6.7	6.1	4.8	23.8	28.1	13.0	4.1	75.9	41.5	46.6	53.4
11720	CENTEREACH	91.9	89.0	1.9	2.4	3.3	4.8	6.9	9.0	6.8	7.0	7.2	7.3	5.4	27.0	27.7	9.7	2.0	74.4	38.1	49.4	50.6
11721	CENTERPORT	97.5	96.6	0.3	0.3	1.2	1.8	2.1	2.9	6.6	7.5	8.5	6.6	3.2	20.2	32.9	12.5	1.9	72.9	43.5	48.1	51.9
11722	CENTRAL ISLIP	47.9	43.7	27.4	28.8	2.9	3.4	36.2	39.6	7.8	7.6	7.4	8.7	8.0	28.5	23.3	7.9	0.8	72.2	32.1	49.4	50.6
11724	COLD SPRING HARBOR	96.9	95.7	0.2	0.3	1.5	2.2	1.8	2.4	6.2	7.9	10.4	8.6	3.5	17.7	33.8	10.5	1.5	69.9	42.5	48.9	51.1
11725	COMMACK	94.5	92.4	0.6	0.7	3.7	5.2	3.0	4.0	7.3	7.8	8.5	6.8	3.9	22.3	27.5	13.7	2.2	71.8	41.4	48.3	51.7
11726	COPIAGUE	68.9	65.1	15.4	15.9	1.8	2.3	22.5	27.2	6.7	6.6	6.6	6.8	6.2	27.8	26.1	10.9	2.3	76.0	37.7	48.8	51.2
11727	CORAM	79.3	74.4	10.9	12.9	3.5	4.6	10.4	13.2	7.6	7.4	7.2	6.3	5.1	30.0	25.8	9.5	1.2	73.9	36.9	48.5	51.5
11729	DEER PARK	83.4	79.3	9.1	10.9	2.9	3.9	7.6	9.5	6.8	7.0	7.1	7.0	5.2	25.8	26.3	13.1	1.7	74.8	39.6	48.7	51.3
11730	EAST ISLIP	96.5	95.2	0.5	0.6	1.3	1.9	3.6	4.9	6.8	7.2	7.8	8.0	5.4	22.9	29.4	10.6	1.8	73.0	40.1	49.1	50.9
11731	EAST NORTHPORT	93.5	91.2	1.0	1.3	3.8	5.3	3.4	4.5	7.2	7.5	8.0	6.7	4.2	22.9	28.6	12.9	2.0	72.9	41.2	49.4	50.6
11732	EAST NORWICH	94.1	91.9	1.2	1.7	3.3	4.5	3.2	4.3	5.9	6.5	7.1	5.8	3.8	23.2	31.1	14.2	2.5	76.6	43.7	47.8	52.2
11733	EAST SETAUKET	88.1	83.9	1.5	1.8	8.4	11.5	3.7	4.7	6.4	7.2	7.4	6.7	5.5	24.9	30.4	10.3	1.2	74.6	39.6	49.2	50.8
	NEW YORK	67.9	64.8	15.9	16.5	5.6	6.9	15.1	16.7	6.5	6.4	6.4	7.1	7.0	27.0	26.3	11.2	2.1	76.6	37.5	48.4	51.6
	UNITED STATES	75.1	72.0	12.3	12.7	3.8	4.6	12.5	15.7	6.8	6.7	6.6	7.1	6.9	27.0	26.0	10.9	1.9	75.7	36.9	49.2	50.8

ZIP CODE #	POST OFFICE NAME	2009 Per Capita Income	2009 HH Income Base	2009 Household Income Distribution (%) Less than $25,000	$25,000 to $49,999	$50,000 to $99,999	$100,000 to $149,999	$150,000 or More	Median Household Income 2009	2014	2009 National Centile	2009 State Centile	2009 Home Value Base	2009 Home Value Distribution (%) Less than $50,000	$50,000 to $89,999	$90,000 to $174,999	$175,000 to $399,999	$400,000 or More	2009 Median Home Value
11379	MIDDLE VILLAGE	30628	14336	18.4	19.4	39.5	14.9	7.7	63572	66722	82	70	8059	0.4	0.2	0.4	29.4	69.7	475524
11385	RIDGEWOOD	20116	35468	24.7	25.8	38.3	7.9	3.2	49358	52960	60	44	11392	0.7	0.2	1.1	48.6	49.4	398551
11411	CAMBRIA HEIGHTS	29007	6385	9.2	16.0	41.1	21.0	12.7	77510	79207	91	83	5116	0.2	0.1	0.4	80.5	18.8	347259
11412	SAINT ALBANS	23908	11763	17.9	20.5	38.7	14.8	8.2	63784	66826	82	70	8298	0.4	0.2	1.0	83.5	14.9	327515
11413	SPRINGFIELD GARDENS	26118	12856	10.3	18.7	43.7	17.6	9.7	70686	72831	87	77	9322	0.3	0.2	0.8	75.8	22.9	346167
11414	HOWARD BEACH	32242	11335	14.7	20.3	40.8	15.1	9.2	66970	69770	85	74	7779	0.1	1.7	15.5	19.6	63.1	542866
11415	KEW GARDENS	30418	8219	18.2	20.6	41.5	12.3	7.4	62070	64963	80	68	2278	0.0	2.1	13.4	34.7	49.8	398447
11416	OZONE PARK	18233	7281	23.7	23.5	40.3	8.5	4.0	52567	56235	67	52	3329	0.4	0.3	0.5	58.2	40.7	376097
11417	OZONE PARK	20710	9494	20.9	23.6	40.2	11.2	4.1	56922	61364	74	60	5330	0.4	0.1	0.4	66.0	33.1	362416
11418	RICHMOND HILL	19735	11263	21.0	24.4	40.8	8.8	5.0	54941	59916	71	57	4501	0.3	0.9	1.6	47.8	49.4	398291
11419	SOUTH RICHMOND HILL	17762	13256	19.4	24.9	40.6	9.5	5.6	56122	60649	73	59	7165	0.2	0.1	0.6	68.3	30.8	360509
11420	SOUTH OZONE PARK	20447	13447	17.0	23.1	41.4	12.6	5.9	61271	64206	79	66	8963	0.2	0.1	0.7	73.5	25.6	347293
11421	WOODHAVEN	20776	12372	20.1	22.2	41.1	11.9	4.6	59582	62571	77	63	6522	0.9	4.0	4.7	63.7	26.6	343551
11422	ROSEDALE	25628	9237	11.3	18.3	42.7	18.6	9.2	73972	75745	89	80	6350	0.3	0.8	1.4	68.1	29.4	360030
11423	HOLLIS	23761	9771	16.7	23.0	37.2	14.2	9.0	60967	63801	79	66	5833	1.0	7.1	4.7	52.4	34.8	353944
11426	BELLEROSE	29342	6474	12.2	17.3	40.9	20.2	9.4	71931	74928	88	78	4672	0.3	1.8	5.8	43.6	48.6	395981
11427	QUEENS VILLAGE	28125	7963	12.0	22.5	40.8	15.4	9.3	65524	67959	84	72	4790	0.3	2.6	10.8	42.6	43.7	380581
11428	QUEENS VILLAGE	22216	5699	10.9	21.4	42.5	16.7	8.5	68811	71125	86	75	3956	0.0	0.1	0.7	75.9	23.4	350794
11429	QUEENS VILLAGE	23171	7869	10.6	19.9	44.9	15.2	9.3	68870	71142	86	75	5403	0.1	0.1	0.5	81.3	18.1	341548
11430	JAMAICA	27143	12	0.0	0.0	100.0	0.0	0.0	63750	63750	82	70	9	0.0	0.0	0.0	100.0	0.0	262500
11432	JAMAICA	24849	18901	18.8	23.4	37.5	11.2	9.1	59180	62419	76	62	7264	0.9	2.9	5.5	33.3	57.5	447341
11433	JAMAICA	16977	9990	34.0	21.8	33.0	7.6	3.6	43014	46776	42	23	4885	0.9	0.3	2.6	79.3	16.9	313464
11434	JAMAICA	23732	20140	19.1	22.0	42.0	11.2	5.8	60053	62756	77	63	10475	3.3	1.3	3.6	77.3	14.5	309481
11435	JAMAICA	20482	17476	21.7	25.0	39.3	9.8	4.2	53105	56996	68	53	6329	0.7	3.1	11.5	57.0	27.7	323346
11436	JAMAICA	19414	5903	24.4	23.4	36.1	10.6	5.4	52547	58066	67	52	3951	0.7	0.2	2.3	86.6	10.3	291660
11439	JAMAICA	11385	11	0.0	0.0	63.6	18.2	18.2	79776	86037	92	84	9	0.0	0.0	0.0	33.3	66.7	437500
11501	MINEOLA	38594	7388	11.0	13.5	32.8	29.0	13.7	79961	85782	92	85	4717	0.0	0.1	5.3	32.9	61.7	443686
11507	ALBERTSON	48908	2321	7.0	10.6	24.5	23.8	34.1	112625	122614	98	96	2111	0.0	0.7	0.5	15.5	83.3	616724
11509	ATLANTIC BEACH	54944	1081	10.5	9.0	23.7	24.3	32.5	114858	127326	98	96	913	0.0	0.0	0.1	12.6	87.3	748574
11510	BALDWIN	39685	10657	8.6	11.5	28.4	28.5	23.0	101861	108133	97	92	9041	0.1	0.0	1.4	60.1	38.4	372186
11514	CARLE PLACE	41969	1802	13.0	9.8	27.4	33.8	16.0	99340	104913	97	91	1313	0.5	0.0	0.6	41.9	57.0	426734
11516	CEDARHURST	41292	2495	12.8	18.7	26.7	20.7	21.2	74973	82504	89	81	1697	0.0	0.5	1.7	22.5	75.3	585008
11518	EAST ROCKAWAY	40064	4268	11.5	15.6	31.1	26.3	15.5	74461	81775	89	80	3130	0.1	0.6	6.4	40.6	52.3	411973
11520	FREEPORT	26793	13345	14.3	18.0	31.1	25.1	11.6	69359	71439	86	76	8745	0.3	2.4	3.6	73.7	20.0	323860
11530	GARDEN CITY	62568	9017	6.4	7.0	20.4	24.8	41.5	129526	138136	99	98	8040	0.1	0.1	1.2	9.3	89.2	785576
11542	GLEN COVE	35436	9769	14.1	17.9	29.9	23.5	14.7	70926	72659	87	77	5901	0.1	0.2	3.1	29.0	67.6	488514
11545	GLEN HEAD	57257	4225	6.6	8.8	21.4	22.0	41.2	125412	136322	99	97	3688	0.0	0.0	0.1	6.4	93.5	871429
11548	GREENVALE	56895	440	8.6	12.5	28.0	23.2	27.7	101351	107307	97	92	343	0.0	0.0	0.0	16.6	83.4	695479
11549	HEMPSTEAD	10727	0	0.0	0.0	0.0	0.0	0.0	0	0	0	0	0	0.0	0.0	0.0	0.0	0.0	0
11550	HEMPSTEAD	21624	15671	21.3	20.9	28.8	20.2	8.8	60541	62856	78	65	7299	0.3	0.3	1.8	83.9	13.7	307747
11552	WEST HEMPSTEAD	35486	7084	8.1	12.1	30.4	30.6	18.9	98409	104102	96	91	6153	0.1	0.1	1.3	55.0	43.6	383989
11553	UNIONDALE	23194	6077	14.7	15.2	29.9	26.6	13.6	74678	78220	89	81	4795	0.1	0.0	1.6	89.7	8.6	309214
11554	EAST MEADOW	35791	12051	8.6	13.1	31.6	29.4	17.3	89809	99284	95	88	10433	0.1	0.0	0.7	58.3	40.8	377100
11557	HEWLETT	61065	2818	7.8	8.7	24.9	19.0	39.5	121591	132370	99	97	2391	0.0	0.2	2.3	20.9	76.5	646239
11558	ISLAND PARK	35516	2943	17.1	11.9	26.3	31.1	13.7	84965	93049	94	87	2133	0.5	0.1	0.2	50.5	48.7	396148
11559	LAWRENCE	51061	2590	15.5	13.7	19.5	14.0	37.3	103754	119652	97	93	1923	0.0	0.4	4.2	13.2	82.2	911149
11560	LOCUST VALLEY	61507	2344	9.0	13.2	22.7	17.2	37.8	110747	123535	98	95	1846	0.0	0.1	0.0	12.2	87.7	776654
11561	LONG BEACH	44690	16801	13.1	14.8	31.1	23.5	17.5	74452	79962	89	80	9883	0.1	0.1	3.9	43.1	52.8	417543
11563	LYNBROOK	36414	8348	13.2	15.0	28.4	29.2	14.2	79800	88850	92	84	6182	0.3	0.5	4.2	46.6	48.3	395266
11565	MALVERNE	43447	3095	7.6	6.6	26.5	34.6	24.7	109680	116598	98	95	2833	0.0	0.2	0.9	35.4	63.5	446655
11566	MERRICK	46553	11571	6.0	7.9	22.9	32.1	31.1	117048	126011	98	96	10601	0.1	0.0	0.5	31.1	68.3	483570
11568	OLD WESTBURY	60557	996	3.5	6.3	10.1	20.8	59.2	184099	198291	100	100	890	0.0	0.0	1.2	1.9	96.9	1000001
11570	ROCKVILLE CENTRE	51460	9952	11.2	10.5	22.4	25.3	30.6	108647	116887	98	95	7277	0.0	0.2	3.9	22.0	74.0	595694
11572	OCEANSIDE	41082	10491	8.8	12.0	25.8	29.0	24.5	104199	110992	97	93	9087	0.0	0.1	1.0	40.8	58.0	434983
11575	ROOSEVELT	22765	4071	13.2	18.9	30.6	26.5	10.8	71139	73349	87	77	3052	0.5	0.1	3.6	89.0	6.7	284186
11576	ROSLYN	76366	5107	4.7	6.8	18.1	18.3	52.1	156016	165540	100	99	4430	0.2	0.3	6.9	3.1	89.5	1000001
11577	ROSLYN HEIGHTS	58426	3624	6.4	8.6	18.5	24.0	42.5	129280	140317	99	98	3178	0.1	0.2	0.2	9.0	90.5	787132
11579	SEA CLIFF	57384	1983	8.8	10.7	26.4	21.5	32.5	108115	120955	98	95	1483	0.0	0.0	0.0	10.7	89.3	710595
11580	VALLEY STREAM	32790	12364	11.9	13.3	30.1	30.4	14.3	83873	91999	93	86	10059	0.3	0.4	0.9	61.2	37.2	371810
11581	VALLEY STREAM	40662	7021	8.4	15.8	26.3	27.5	22.0	98510	104295	96	91	5769	0.2	0.2	0.7	43.5	55.3	427148
11590	WESTBURY	32570	12631	8.9	12.7	29.0	29.9	19.6	98229	103124	96	91	9714	0.2	0.1	0.9	57.5	41.3	376131
11596	WILLISTON PARK	46131	3556	8.2	11.0	23.3	31.6	25.9	109625	118535	98	95	2916	0.1	0.1	0.0	19.1	80.7	546999
11598	WOODMERE	56125	4129	7.4	7.2	19.4	24.0	42.0	129081	137771	99	98	3559	0.1	0.2	1.2	11.9	86.6	713695
11691	FAR ROCKAWAY	16517	19667	37.5	24.5	28.8	6.1	3.2	37481	41820	25	8	4841	0.6	0.3	2.3	58.2	38.5	366455
11692	ARVERNE	16459	5021	35.6	25.9	27.3	8.1	3.1	38797	42563	29	11	1757	9.7	0.5	3.2	76.6	10.1	302978
11693	FAR ROCKAWAY	20981	4455	31.7	21.7	33.9	9.2	3.5	46675	49548	53	36	2000	30.2	1.5	4.0	50.3	14.1	256102
11694	ROCKAWAY PARK	34861	8132	21.8	18.5	33.0	13.9	12.8	64020	66675	82	71	3663	6.9	0.8	2.1	13.6	76.5	614896
11697	BREEZY POINT	40148	1787	13.9	18.9	34.0	20.4	12.8	75088	77461	89	81	1645	0.2	0.0	0.8	41.9	57.1	448340
11701	AMITYVILLE	29471	8516	14.1	18.5	35.0	19.9	12.5	70092	74677	87	76	5855	6.2	1.5	7.7	65.1	19.5	282239
11702	BABYLON	41789	5340	6.9	12.0	33.6	28.5	19.0	94155	100564	96	89	4045	0.1	0.0	2.1	54.3	43.5	377885
11703	NORTH BABYLON	32662	5709	8.3	14.9	36.7	28.8	11.2	81388	87202	93	85	4587	0.1	0.3	1.8	82.1	15.7	313559
11704	WEST BABYLON	29480	13253	11.9	15.1	34.4	28.5	10.2	78277	83688	91	84	9826	0.2	0.2	3.9	86.1	9.7	297010
11705	BAYPORT	43425	3313	12.6	11.3	24.2	29.4	22.5	102720	105912	97	92	2275	0.0	0.0	1.5	50.5	48.0	393750
11706	BAY SHORE	27883	18844	13.6	17.2	35.3	22.6	11.3	71250	75581	87	77	13332	0.4	0.3	5.0	80.6	13.7	274643
11709	BAYVILLE	47483	2505	8.1	13.9	28.9	27.3	21.8	97033	104599	96	90	1958	0.3	0.0	0.6	20.2	78.9	579017
11710	BELLMORE	40026	11423	7.4	10.1	30.5	29.1	22.9	102449	108283	97	92	9959	0.0	0.1	0.8	45.4	53.6	415814
11713	BELLPORT	30423	3347	9.9	12.6	35.9	28.7	12.8	83058	89090	93	86	2641	0.0	0.3	9.8	73.2	16.6	275201
11714	BETHPAGE	37732	7937	10.2	14.4	29.9	27.4	18.1	86190	96274	94	87	6834	0.2	0.1	1.2	55.4	43.2	381772
11715	BLUE POINT	38964	1627	8.7	8.4	36.8	29.7	16.5	92719	97255	96	89	1342	0.0	0.0	0.8	64.5	34.6	351756
11716	BOHEMIA	34141	3683	10.3	16.6	32.0	27.2	13.9	82124	87010	93	86	2880	1.0	5.9	3.9	64.1	25.0	332139
11717	BRENTWOOD	19202	12076	11.0	19.6	37.0	25.5	6.9	71277	75425	87	77	9494	0.2	0.2	5.4	92.4	1.8	254758
11718	BRIGHTWATERS	50634	1128	2.9	10.0	28.9	23.2	34.9	115901	122419	98	96	984	0.0	0.0	1.0	40.7	58.3	450307
11719	BROOKHAVEN	39698	1152	6.5	12.2	35.2	26.2	19.8	90788	99145	95	89	950	0.0	0.2	3.3	62.7	33.8	329358
11720	CENTEREACH	31662	8876	7.7	9.2	37.9	29.7	15.5	90540	96727	95	88	7651	0.1	0.0	2.4	82.7	14.9	291726
11721	CENTERPORT	59297	2210	3.2	6.0	23.4	29.3	38.1	127884	131200	99	98	1978	0.4	0.0	0.0	12.2	87.4	631031
11722	CENTRAL ISLIP	22896	8603	14.3	16.2	38.7	21.3	9.5	72137	76294	88	78	6535	0.2	0.1	11.7	84.3	3.8	244730
11724	COLD SPRING HARBOR	67063	912	3.5	4.4	20.6	20.8	50.7	153367	173137	100	99	828	0.0	0.0	1.1	2.8	96.1	1000001
11725	COMMACK	41031	9451	5.8	8.5	27.8	29.4	28.6	112175	116129	98	96	8545	0.1	0.0	0.4	31.8	67.6	466615
11726	COPIAGUE	26206	6038	15.2	20.7	34.8	18.9	10.4	67601	71833	85	74	4198	0.1	0.0	3.8	84.9	11.2	276484
11727	CORAM	33733	10099	10.5	12.9	35.9	29.8	10.8	81595	87160	93	85	6827	0.4	0.6	4.8	84.2	10.1	283514
11729	DEER PARK	31870	9373	10.4	14.2	35.9	27.7	11.8	78637	84378	91	84	7557	0.2	0.0	1.0	83.6	15.2	320989
11730	EAST ISLIP	36852	5293	7.4	10.7	31.8	33.9	16.2	100090	103434	97	91	4468	0.0	0.0	1.0	59.9	39.1	363985
11731	EAST NORTHPORT	41638	10064	5.6	8.6	30.6	30.1	25.1	108167	112155	98	95	8860	0.1	0.1	0.2	35.6	64.1	458143
11732	EAST NORWICH	52551	1051	7.4	8.0	21.0	26.0	37.6	126874	134892	99	97	867	0.5	0.0	0.0	13.7	85.8	630277
11733	EAST SETAUKET	53276	6792	8.0	9.0	24.0	21.7	37.4	120222	127232	98	97	5498	0.1	0.3	2.0	27.8	69.8	550542
	NEW YORK	29893		21.9	21.3	32.7	14.0	9.9	58747	62337				3.4	5.7	23.0	38.7	29.1	269816
	UNITED STATES	27277		20.9	24.4	35.3	11.7	7.6	54719	56938				9.3	13.1	31.6	32.6	13.5	162279

ZIP CODE		FINANCIAL SERVICES				THE HOME						ENTERTAINMENT						PERSONAL			
						Home Improvements		Furnishings													
#	POST OFFICE NAME	Auto Loan	Home Loan	Invest-ments	Retire-ment Plans	Home Repair	Lawn & Garden	Comput-ers & Hard-ware-Personal	Major Appli-ances	TV, Radio, Sound Equip-ment	Furni-ture	Dine out/ Carry out	Sports Equip-ment	Fees & Tickets	Toys & Games	Travel	Cable TV	Apparel & Services	Auto Repairs	Health Insur-ance	Pets & Supplies
11379	MIDDLE VILLAGE	83	106	113	102	109	99	103	98	105	92	108	72	115	103	110	111	80	101	103	112
11385	RIDGEWOOD	68	74	75	73	74	66	83	74	82	76	85	58	85	80	82	83	63	80	74	85
11411	CAMBRIA HEIGHTS	111	152	157	142	156	136	129	132	125	126	127	97	150	126	145	127	93	129	128	146
11412	SAINT ALBANS	99	105	101	106	102	108	104	102	111	102	112	73	110	107	105	117	79	106	115	124
11413	SPRINGFIELD GARDENS	100	124	126	120	126	117	114	113	116	109	117	82	128	114	122	120	85	114	117	130
11414	HOWARD BEACH	95	118	125	115	123	117	109	110	111	106	112	79	123	107	119	116	81	111	121	125
11415	KEW GARDENS	85	87	94	92	89	81	109	92	109	96	113	74	108	103	105	111	83	102	96	110
11416	OZONE PARK	75	80	77	78	80	67	91	80	85	85	89	64	90	85	88	83	66	86	74	90
11417	OZONE PARK	75	90	91	86	91	79	92	85	90	85	93	65	98	89	94	92	69	89	84	96
11418	RICHMOND HILL	77	80	81	80	81	71	94	82	92	86	96	65	94	90	91	93	71	90	81	95
11419	SOUTH RICHMOND HILL	82	90	87	86	91	75	98	89	92	94	96	70	98	91	97	90	71	93	81	99
11420	SOUTH OZONE PARK	85	106	106	99	109	90	102	98	96	99	99	74	109	95	107	96	73	98	91	108
11421	WOODHAVEN	80	88	88	86	89	78	96	87	93	90	96	68	98	92	95	93	71	92	85	99
11422	ROSEDALE	96	129	134	121	133	116	116	115	114	109	116	84	132	113	127	117	86	114	114	128
11423	HOLLIS	93	110	113	106	114	97	111	106	107	108	108	79	117	103	115	107	80	107	102	119
11426	BELLEROSE	99	132	142	127	138	122	117	117	115	113	116	87	136	114	130	118	86	117	117	131
11427	QUEENS VILLAGE	97	119	126	116	124	110	116	112	115	110	117	83	127	112	123	118	86	114	114	127
11428	QUEENS VILLAGE	97	128	129	117	132	108	114	114	106	114	109	85	126	106	124	105	80	111	104	124
11429	QUEENS VILLAGE	101	124	123	118	126	113	114	114	113	113	114	83	125	111	122	114	83	113	113	129
11430	JAMAICA	83	95	90	92	95	103	84	92	90	83	89	64	92	88	91	95	62	89	105	105
11432	JAMAICA	85	92	98	95	95	83	109	96	108	100	110	74	109	101	106	109	83	102	95	111
11433	JAMAICA	64	63	65	66	63	64	74	65	79	67	80	49	75	75	70	84	58	73	75	81
11434	JAMAICA	87	93	90	94	91	95	93	90	100	90	101	65	99	96	94	105	71	95	102	110
11435	JAMAICA	73	74	75	76	73	70	90	77	93	80	95	60	89	88	85	96	70	85	83	93
11436	JAMAICA	78	81	81	83	79	82	89	80	95	81	96	60	92	91	86	101	70	88	91	99
11439	JAMAICA	117	171	191	164	182	157	137	146	131	139	132	106	169	132	163	132	99	138	139	158
11501	MINEOLA	119	154	164	149	160	142	139	139	135	136	137	103	158	134	153	136	100	137	137	155
11507	ALBERTSON	172	249	288	246	271	230	202	215	191	212	191	158	251	190	241	188	144	201	200	234
11509	ATLANTIC BEACH	174	244	288	246	269	224	205	217	189	223	188	161	249	184	244	181	141	203	196	237
11510	BALDWIN	137	194	209	184	204	176	163	168	157	160	159	123	194	158	187	160	118	163	162	184
11514	CARLE PLACE	132	186	202	177	196	170	158	162	153	154	155	118	188	154	180	157	116	157	158	178
11516	CEDARHURST	134	182	203	178	195	164	160	162	150	162	151	122	185	148	182	148	112	157	151	179
11518	EAST ROCKAWAY	119	166	178	158	174	151	143	145	140	138	142	106	168	140	162	143	106	142	143	160
11520	FREEPORT	109	134	134	126	138	115	127	124	118	126	122	95	137	119	134	116	90	124	113	136
11530	GARDEN CITY	218	294	349	297	324	279	249	264	235	268	234	194	301	230	292	230	175	249	247	290
11542	GLEN COVE	113	146	158	142	153	135	136	134	135	130	137	99	155	132	149	139	102	135	135	150
11545	GLEN HEAD	213	308	357	306	335	285	249	265	236	262	236	195	311	236	297	233	179	248	245	288
11548	GREENVALE	179	246	277	243	262	229	216	218	214	212	216	161	259	211	244	218	164	214	214	243
11549	HEMPSTEAD	0	0	0	0	0	0	0	0	0	0	0	0	0	0	0	0	0	0	0	0
11550	HEMPSTEAD	89	98	99	97	99	89	108	98	109	100	111	74	111	105	106	112	83	104	99	113
11552	WEST HEMPSTEAD	132	189	204	179	199	170	154	162	147	155	148	118	186	149	180	148	110	155	154	176
11553	UNIONDALE	111	150	154	140	156	131	130	132	123	129	125	98	148	124	144	122	92	128	123	145
11554	EAST MEADOW	128	179	193	170	188	164	148	155	143	149	144	113	177	143	172	145	107	149	152	170
11557	HEWLETT	199	283	327	281	307	263	234	246	224	242	224	181	289	223	275	223	170	232	230	268
11558	ISLAND PARK	113	158	172	151	166	145	136	139	134	131	136	101	161	133	155	137	101	136	137	153
11559	LAWRENCE	192	253	297	260	277	231	226	230	210	240	211	176	267	206	257	202	160	220	205	254
11560	LOCUST VALLEY	205	282	333	287	310	260	243	252	227	258	227	189	294	223	282	221	172	238	229	277
11561	LONG BEACH	128	150	160	150	155	142	148	142	146	144	148	108	161	143	156	148	108	145	144	163
11563	LYNBROOK	114	153	165	147	161	144	135	137	133	131	135	99	157	131	151	137	99	135	140	153
11565	MALVERNE	145	210	233	201	224	192	170	180	163	172	164	131	208	164	201	164	122	171	171	195
11566	MERRICK	164	236	269	231	255	217	192	204	182	200	182	149	237	182	228	180	137	192	191	222
11568	OLD WESTBURY	288	412	506	432	462	388	331	357	311	370	308	268	431	310	399	299	241	326	314	388
11570	ROCKVILLE CENTRE	168	218	248	219	234	205	197	199	190	202	190	149	229	184	222	189	141	195	195	223
11572	OCEANSIDE	140	199	220	192	212	185	163	173	157	165	158	125	197	157	191	158	117	164	167	188
11575	ROOSEVELT	110	136	135	129	139	122	123	124	120	124	121	92	136	119	132	120	88	123	120	139
11576	ROSLYN	250	347	421	360	387	320	292	308	268	322	267	233	361	264	345	255	205	285	268	336
11577	ROSLYN HEIGHTS	200	280	331	284	308	258	235	247	220	252	220	185	289	217	277	214	167	232	224	270
11579	SEA CLIFF	176	232	276	237	257	207	209	214	186	228	185	165	240	179	241	173	139	202	184	236
11580	VALLEY STREAM	116	162	173	153	170	147	136	141	132	134	133	103	161	132	156	134	99	136	137	155
11581	VALLEY STREAM	137	189	208	182	201	175	160	167	154	162	155	121	190	153	184	155	115	160	162	183
11590	WESTBURY	136	178	187	169	187	156	158	159	149	159	151	120	179	150	175	146	112	156	147	174
11596	WILLISTON PARK	153	221	251	215	238	203	181	191	172	186	172	140	221	171	214	171	129	181	181	208
11598	WOODMERE	209	288	343	294	319	264	247	259	227	269	226	194	297	220	291	217	170	242	231	284
11691	FAR ROCKAWAY	55	52	54	55	51	52	70	58	75	60	76	43	67	68	63	80	56	66	68	71
11692	ARVERNE	56	54	55	57	53	54	71	60	77	59	78	44	69	72	64	84	59	67	68	73
11693	FAR ROCKAWAY	69	74	74	74	73	74	78	74	82	73	83	53	80	79	77	87	60	77	81	88
11694	ROCKAWAY PARK	95	116	128	116	122	111	114	111	115	109	116	82	126	110	123	118	85	113	116	126
11697	BREEZY POINT	116	154	163	149	161	148	129	138	127	132	127	98	151	126	148	129	92	132	139	153
11701	AMITYVILLE	112	136	137	130	138	129	122	125	121	122	122	91	135	121	132	124	88	123	126	142
11702	BABYLON	134	186	202	178	196	168	160	163	153	158	155	120	187	153	181	154	115	158	156	180
11703	NORTH BABYLON	113	156	161	146	161	139	131	135	125	130	127	100	153	127	148	126	93	131	128	149
11704	WEST BABYLON	107	145	150	136	150	131	124	127	120	123	121	94	143	120	139	121	89	124	123	141
11705	BAYPORT	139	180	192	175	189	174	157	163	156	159	156	118	182	152	177	159	113	159	169	182
11706	BAY SHORE	113	141	141	132	145	120	130	129	121	131	123	99	140	121	140	117	90	127	117	142
11709	BAYVILLE	157	216	246	212	233	193	186	192	171	193	172	145	218	170	215	166	128	183	174	210
11710	BELLMORE	140	200	218	190	212	181	164	172	156	166	157	126	197	157	191	157	117	164	163	187
11713	BELLPORT	129	160	156	154	161	145	138	142	134	142	135	107	155	136	151	133	98	138	135	160
11714	BETHPAGE	128	178	191	169	187	163	148	155	143	149	144	113	176	143	171	145	106	149	151	170
11715	BLUE POINT	128	183	197	173	193	165	150	157	143	150	144	115	180	144	174	144	107	150	149	171
11716	BOHEMIA	129	159	168	151	163	151	139	146	136	137	137	109	154	137	153	138	99	141	142	164
11717	BRENTWOOD	113	138	127	121	143	100	128	129	107	139	111	99	129	108	134	95	81	121	97	132
11718	BRIGHTWATERS	172	246	280	241	265	226	202	212	191	207	192	157	248	192	237	190	145	201	199	231
11719	BROOKHAVEN	132	185	190	172	190	163	153	159	146	153	147	117	179	148	174	146	109	153	149	174
11720	CENTEREACH	124	174	180	162	180	154	144	150	138	143	139	110	169	140	164	138	103	144	141	164
11721	CENTERPORT	187	267	310	264	291	247	219	233	205	232	205	171	269	203	262	202	154	219	216	254
11722	CENTRAL ISLIP	112	136	128	124	140	109	126	126	112	133	115	96	131	113	133	105	83	121	107	135
11724	COLD SPRING HARBOR	246	351	430	367	393	329	284	305	266	316	263	229	367	264	341	255	205	279	267	331
11725	COMMACK	149	215	237	208	229	196	174	184	165	178	166	135	213	167	205	165	124	174	173	200
11726	COPIAGUE	101	130	131	122	134	116	117	118	112	117	114	87	130	111	128	112	83	116	114	130
11727	CORAM	124	141	132	140	138	127	131	128	127	133	129	100	141	130	135	126	93	128	124	148
11729	DEER PARK	113	154	160	144	160	140	131	135	127	130	128	99	152	127	148	129	94	132	133	149
11730	EAST ISLIP	134	186	197	177	194	167	156	162	149	157	150	119	184	150	178	149	111	155	153	178
11731	EAST NORTHPORT	148	212	232	203	225	192	172	182	164	175	165	133	209	166	202	165	123	173	172	198
11732	EAST NORWICH	177	249	286	246	270	227	208	218	194	218	194	162	251	193	245	190	146	206	200	238
11733	EAST SETAUKET	189	256	284	260	274	233	216	224	201	229	203	171	259	202	249	195	152	211	202	248
	NEW YORK	100	106	110	108	107	104	112	106	113	106	114	81	115	110	112	116	83	110	110	124
	UNITED STATES	100	100	100	100	100	100	100	100	100	100	100	100	100	100	100	100	100	100	100	100

POPULATION CHANGE

ZIP CODE #	POST OFFICE NAME	COUNTY FIPS CODE	POPULATION 2000	POPULATION 2009	POPULATION 2014	2000-2009 ANNUAL RATE % Rate	2000-2009 ANNUAL RATE State Centile	HOUSEHOLDS 2000	HOUSEHOLDS 2009	HOUSEHOLDS 2014	HOUSEHOLDS % Annual Rate 2000-2009	HOUSEHOLDS 2009 Average HH Size	FAMILIES 2000	FAMILIES 2009	FAMILIES % Annual Rate 2000-2009
11735	FARMINGDALE	103	32165	31953	31516	-0.1	30	10808	10737	10598	-0.1	2.92	8263	8104	-0.2
11738	FARMINGVILLE	103	17463	18151	18169	0.4	66	5286	5509	5521	0.4	3.29	4510	4661	0.4
11740	GREENLAWN	103	10248	10242	10085	0.0	38	3631	3623	3567	0.0	2.74	2650	2613	-0.2
11741	HOLBROOK	103	28396	28732	28508	0.1	44	9263	9418	9363	0.2	3.04	7572	7611	0.1
11742	HOLTSVILLE	103	12075	13022	13262	0.8	84	4092	4405	4482	0.8	2.95	3182	3405	0.7
11743	HUNTINGTON	103	42045	41961	41459	0.0	38	14930	14894	14723	0.0	2.79	11431	11293	-0.1
11746	HUNTINGTON STATION	103	63042	62956	62181	0.0	38	20228	20047	19796	-0.1	3.11	16350	16078	-0.2
11747	MELVILLE	103	15723	18468	19180	1.8	98	5228	6100	6328	1.7	2.91	4235	4928	1.7
11749	ISLANDIA	103	3947	4053	4032	0.3	59	1391	1423	1416	0.2	2.85	984	993	0.1
11751	ISLIP	103	14875	14748	14543	-0.1	30	5065	5021	4958	-0.1	2.92	3920	3847	-0.2
11752	ISLIP TERRACE	103	9928	9763	9607	-0.2	21	3024	2982	2940	-0.2	3.27	2552	2498	-0.2
11753	JERICHO	059	11719	11593	11429	-0.1	30	4162	4124	4067	-0.1	2.77	3490	3429	-0.2
11754	KINGS PARK	103	18849	18622	18290	-0.1	30	6365	6347	6242	0.0	2.86	4851	4784	-0.2
11755	LAKE GROVE	103	11232	12056	12202	0.8	84	3709	3990	4045	0.8	3.00	2985	3182	0.7
11756	LEVITTOWN	059	43789	42956	42199	-0.2	21	14019	13779	13544	-0.2	3.12	11521	11219	-0.3
11757	LINDENHURST	103	46525	46540	45940	0.0	38	15240	15263	15084	0.0	3.03	11891	11785	-0.1
11758	MASSAPEQUA	059	55746	54468	53436	-0.3	15	18287	17917	17593	-0.2	3.03	15114	14662	-0.3
11762	MASSAPEQUA PARK	059	23781	23282	22858	-0.2	21	7808	7671	7539	-0.2	3.02	6675	6505	-0.3
11763	MEDFORD	103	24875	26451	26901	0.7	80	7581	8021	8152	0.6	3.26	6258	6548	0.5
11764	MILLER PLACE	103	11179	12988	13856	1.6	97	3567	4088	4351	1.5	3.16	2920	3342	1.5
11765	MILL NECK	059	471	485	486	0.3	59	162	166	166	0.3	2.92	126	127	0.1
11766	MOUNT SINAI	103	9068	11765	12406	2.9	99	2770	3634	3841	3.0	3.22	2317	3018	2.9
11767	NESCONSET	103	14005	14641	14688	0.5	71	4549	4751	4772	0.5	3.05	3759	3902	0.4
11768	NORTHPORT	103	21938	21751	21402	-0.1	30	7835	7777	7662	-0.1	2.74	6078	5975	-0.2
11769	OAKDALE	103	9773	10291	10327	0.6	76	3628	3849	3874	0.6	2.62	2610	2726	0.5
11770	OCEAN BEACH	103	176	157	149	-1.2	1	79	70	67	-1.3	2.21	49	42	-1.7
11771	OYSTER BAY	059	11147	10974	10798	-0.2	21	4268	4196	4127	-0.2	2.58	3010	2923	-0.3
11772	PATCHOGUE	103	41302	42031	41750	0.2	52	14737	14895	14785	0.1	2.77	10134	10109	0.0
11776	PORT JEFFERSON STATI	103	22262	23506	23727	0.6	76	7186	7602	7681	0.6	3.04	5607	5878	0.5
11777	PORT JEFFERSON	103	9047	9398	9400	0.4	66	3393	3518	3525	0.4	2.51	2317	2368	0.2
11778	ROCKY POINT	103	11419	12310	12501	0.8	84	3979	4259	4322	0.7	2.88	3016	3193	0.6
11779	RONKONKOMA	103	38428	38438	37908	0.0	38	12786	12804	12642	0.0	2.96	9888	9798	-0.1
11780	SAINT JAMES	103	14920	15154	14966	0.2	52	5142	5215	5151	0.2	2.81	3982	4006	0.1
11782	SAYVILLE	103	15710	16337	16393	0.4	66	5263	5502	5537	0.5	2.90	4093	4214	0.3
11783	SEAFORD	059	22094	21851	21498	-0.1	30	7335	7276	7165	-0.1	2.99	5966	5852	-0.2
11784	SELDEN	103	25466	26130	26078	0.3	59	8065	8295	8288	0.3	3.15	6417	6527	0.2
11786	SHOREHAM	103	6113	6781	6940	1.1	91	1956	2157	2208	1.1	3.14	1593	1734	0.9
11787	SMITHTOWN	103	34433	35097	34832	0.2	52	11437	11681	11603	0.2	2.91	9448	9566	0.1
11788	HAUPPAUGE	103	16388	16401	16182	0.0	38	5639	5667	5606	0.1	2.87	4476	4449	-0.1
11789	SOUND BEACH	103	7601	8245	8407	0.9	87	2651	2870	2925	0.9	2.86	2009	2150	0.7
11790	STONY BROOK	103	18036	18328	18157	0.2	52	4821	4842	4794	0.0	2.88	3807	3787	-0.1
11791	SYOSSET	059	24348	23794	23324	-0.2	21	8101	7933	7783	-0.2	2.97	6918	6725	-0.3
11792	WADING RIVER	103	7500	8286	8481	1.1	91	2591	2865	2932	1.1	2.82	2004	2192	1.0
11793	WANTAGH	059	32398	31707	31144	-0.2	21	10918	10716	10529	-0.2	2.95	8944	8693	-0.3
11794	STONY BROOK	103	2561	2735	2736	0.7	80	2	2	2	0.0	2.50	2	2	0.0
11795	WEST ISLIP	103	27063	26770	26389	-0.1	30	8338	8257	8148	-0.1	3.19	7135	7016	-0.2
11796	WEST SAYVILLE	103	3768	3722	3664	-0.1	30	1298	1283	1265	-0.1	2.83	983	961	-0.2
11797	WOODBURY	059	9120	9198	9110	0.1	44	2888	2889	2858	0.0	2.81	2333	2317	-0.1
11798	WYANDANCH	103	15041	15929	16051	0.6	76	3817	4001	4026	0.5	3.94	3194	3322	0.4
11801	HICKSVILLE	059	39329	38491	37760	-0.2	21	13055	12757	12514	-0.2	3.00	10294	9946	-0.4
11803	PLAINVIEW	059	27768	28176	27941	0.2	52	9219	9369	9293	0.2	2.96	7886	7959	0.1
11804	OLD BETHPAGE	059	5012	4921	4827	-0.2	21	1747	1709	1675	-0.2	2.81	1480	1436	-0.3
11901	RIVERHEAD	103	22194	25147	25871	1.4	95	8569	9680	9971	1.3	2.53	5666	6312	1.2
11933	CALVERTON	103	7238	8132	8383	1.3	94	2543	2889	2994	1.4	2.43	1693	1875	1.1
11934	CENTER MORICHES	103	6643	7264	7397	1.0	89	2291	2506	2557	1.0	2.85	1753	1901	0.9
11935	CUTCHOGUE	103	3972	4562	4728	1.5	96	1586	1831	1903	1.6	2.45	1117	1272	1.4
11937	EAST HAMPTON	103	14798	16862	17397	1.4	95	6026	6746	6937	1.2	2.49	3767	4146	1.0
11939	EAST MARION	103	781	832	838	0.7	80	344	369	373	0.8	2.25	230	243	0.6
11940	EAST MORICHES	103	4492	5843	6291	2.9	99	1490	1968	2123	3.1	2.90	1155	1497	2.8
11941	EASTPORT	103	3481	3811	3920	1.0	89	1316	1422	1463	0.8	2.63	949	1015	0.7
11942	EAST QUOGUE	103	5010	6338	6776	2.6	99	1983	2498	2671	2.5	2.53	1338	1660	2.4
11944	GREENPORT	103	3696	4570	4854	2.3	99	1512	1885	2011	2.4	2.33	899	1103	2.2
11946	HAMPTON BAYS	103	12648	13514	13542	0.7	80	5042	5301	5300	0.5	2.52	3197	3304	0.4
11948	LAUREL	103	729	762	764	0.5	71	292	306	307	0.5	2.47	220	228	0.4
11949	MANORVILLE	103	11657	13912	14652	1.9	98	4301	5020	5242	1.7	2.76	3072	3601	1.7
11950	MASTIC	103	14770	15752	15868	0.7	80	4201	4485	4524	0.7	3.49	3561	3762	0.6
11951	MASTIC BEACH	103	13227	14265	14491	0.8	84	4196	4528	4604	0.8	3.13	3204	3417	0.7
11952	MATTITUCK	103	4470	4811	4892	0.8	84	1748	1884	1917	0.8	2.54	1305	1392	0.7
11953	MIDDLE ISLAND	103	12231	13752	14149	1.3	94	4590	5128	5276	1.2	2.61	3203	3550	1.1
11954	MONTAUK	103	3849	4557	4762	1.8	98	1591	1865	1949	1.7	2.44	991	1141	1.5
11955	MORICHES	103	2409	2889	3045	2.0	98	1172	1402	1477	2.0	2.03	714	869	2.1
11957	ORIENT	103	697	702	688	0.1	44	322	325	318	0.1	2.16	202	201	-0.1
11958	PECONIC	103	688	816	857	1.9	98	278	331	347	1.9	2.46	200	233	1.7
11961	RIDGE	103	12211	13400	13659	1.0	89	5136	5562	5652	0.9	2.36	3266	3496	0.7
11963	SAG HARBOR	103	8297	9186	9421	1.1	91	3698	4100	4208	1.1	2.24	2208	2405	0.9
11964	SHELTER ISLAND	103	1183	1209	1172	0.2	52	508	520	505	0.3	2.33	335	337	0.1
11965	SHELTER ISLAND HEIGH	103	1045	1048	1036	0.0	38	488	487	481	0.0	2.15	321	316	-0.2
11967	SHIRLEY	103	24053	25836	26252	0.8	84	7061	7603	7736	0.8	3.39	5878	6277	0.7
11968	SOUTHAMPTON	103	12036	12902	13039	0.8	84	4738	5060	5117	0.7	2.42	2974	3121	0.5
11971	SOUTHOLD	103	5302	6301	6607	1.9	98	2254	2657	2782	1.8	2.36	1558	1809	1.6
11976	WATER MILL	103	2086	2419	2518	1.6	97	883	1032	1078	1.7	2.34	574	656	1.5
11977	WESTHAMPTON	103	2521	3119	3298	2.3	99	1002	1222	1288	2.2	2.49	714	860	2.0
11978	WESTHAMPTON BEACH	103	3858	4209	4288	0.9	87	1490	1623	1655	0.9	2.44	934	999	0.7
11980	YAPHANK	103	3849	4461	4771	1.6	97	1193	1370	1432	1.5	3.03	852	985	1.6
12007	ALCOVE	001	205	203	201	-0.1	30	71	72	71	0.2	2.82	54	54	0.0
12008	ALPLAUS	093	450	502	525	1.2	93	180	201	210	1.2	2.47	128	141	1.1
12009	ALTAMONT	001	7319	7530	7568	0.3	59	2767	2887	2920	0.5	2.54	1979	2022	0.2
12010	AMSTERDAM	057	29209	29008	28829	-0.1	30	12179	12304	12291	0.1	2.29	7673	7621	-0.1
12015	ATHENS	039	3358	3563	3631	0.6	76	1334	1446	1483	0.9	2.45	916	977	0.7
12017	AUSTERLITZ	021	317	311	306	-0.2	21	126	127	126	0.1	2.45	85	84	-0.1
12018	AVERILL PARK	083	7252	7523	7642	0.4	66	2714	2839	2894	0.5	2.65	2005	2060	0.3
12019	BALLSTON LAKE	091	13435	14446	14894	0.8	84	5027	5474	5679	0.9	2.63	3859	4118	0.7
12020	BALLSTON SPA	091	28008	31244	32728	1.2	93	10584	11979	12632	1.3	2.56	7577	8401	1.1
12022	BERLIN	083	901	881	875	-0.2	21	349	345	343	-0.1	2.55	242	234	-0.4
12023	BERNE	001	1921	1967	1974	0.3	59	743	778	787	0.5	2.53	551	566	0.3
	NEW YORK					0.3					0.3	2.61			0.1
	UNITED STATES					1.0					1.1	2.59			0.9

#	POST OFFICE NAME	RACE (%) White 2000	White 2009	Black 2000	Black 2009	Asian/Pacific 2000	Asian/Pacific 2009	% Hispanic Origin 2000	% Hispanic Origin 2009	2009 AGE DISTRIBUTION (%) 0-4	5-9	10-14	15-19	20-24	25-44	45-64	65-84	85+	18+	MEDIAN AGE 2009	% 2009 Males	% 2009 Females
11735	FARMINGDALE	87.4	84.2	3.9	4.5	3.6	4.8	8.9	11.2	6.6	6.9	7.1	7.2	5.5	26.0	27.4	11.3	2.1	75.1	39.5	49.3	50.7
11738	FARMINGVILLE	93.6	91.5	1.3	1.7	1.8	2.4	8.4	11.0	7.2	7.4	7.7	7.3	5.3	29.1	27.5	7.8	0.8	73.1	36.8	49.4	50.6
11740	GREENLAWN	89.9	87.1	5.0	6.0	2.6	3.6	4.5	5.7	6.3	6.7	7.4	7.0	4.6	20.4	28.8	14.4	4.4	75.0	43.4	46.7	53.3
11741	HOLBROOK	93.9	91.6	1.3	1.7	2.9	4.1	6.0	7.8	6.9	7.2	7.4	6.7	4.5	28.8	28.0	9.5	1.0	74.3	38.3	48.5	51.5
11742	HOLTSVILLE	94.8	93.0	1.0	1.3	1.4	2.0	7.2	9.6	7.5	7.7	7.8	6.8	4.7	28.1	27.5	9.1	0.9	72.6	37.8	48.7	51.3
11743	HUNTINGTON	87.8	85.1	6.5	7.4	2.4	3.3	5.1	6.4	6.5	6.9	7.8	6.5	4.0	22.9	31.2	12.2	2.0	74.5	42.2	48.7	51.3
11746	HUNTINGTON STATION	80.8	76.8	6.7	7.6	4.8	6.4	12.4	14.6	7.0	7.4	7.8	7.0	4.8	25.1	28.2	11.1	1.6	73.3	39.5	49.7	50.3
11747	MELVILLE	89.9	85.3	2.2	3.1	5.4	8.0	3.7	5.3	6.7	7.2	8.1	6.4	3.3	22.8	29.9	13.4	2.2	73.6	42.4	49.1	50.9
11749	ISLANDIA	66.4	61.1	16.3	17.8	8.0	10.0	21.2	24.4	7.4	7.1	6.8	6.2	5.8	29.6	26.8	9.5	0.8	74.9	37.6	48.6	51.4
11751	ISLIP	91.4	88.9	2.9	3.5	2.0	2.7	7.3	9.4	7.3	7.6	7.8	7.5	5.5	24.9	27.9	10.1	1.4	72.5	38.3	49.0	51.0
11752	ISLIP TERRACE	94.3	92.6	1.5	1.8	1.4	2.0	7.2	9.4	7.1	7.3	7.5	7.9	5.9	25.9	26.9	10.3	1.2	73.1	37.7	48.7	51.3
11753	JERICHO	87.0	82.6	1.3	1.7	10.2	13.8	2.5	3.2	5.8	6.7	7.9	6.9	3.9	19.0	32.6	15.3	1.9	75.0	44.9	48.5	51.5
11754	KINGS PARK	95.7	94.3	0.8	0.8	1.8	2.6	3.2	4.2	7.2	7.5	7.7	6.7	4.3	24.0	26.8	12.8	3.0	73.3	40.8	48.5	51.5
11755	LAKE GROVE	91.7	89.0	1.4	1.8	4.5	6.2	4.9	6.4	7.2	7.4	7.6	7.3	4.9	27.7	27.2	9.6	1.2	73.0	38.0	49.6	50.4
11756	LEVITTOWN	93.8	91.5	0.5	0.7	3.0	4.1	7.4	9.7	6.3	6.7	7.1	7.5	5.4	25.4	29.2	10.8	1.7	75.3	39.8	48.5	51.5
11757	LINDENHURST	93.0	90.8	1.6	1.9	1.5	2.1	7.9	10.3	6.7	7.0	7.2	7.1	5.5	27.2	27.9	9.9	1.5	74.6	38.4	49.1	50.9
11758	MASSAPEQUA	91.5	89.5	4.6	5.3	1.5	2.0	4.5	5.7	6.6	7.0	7.6	6.9	4.4	24.1	28.8	12.6	2.0	74.4	41.1	48.5	51.5
11762	MASSAPEQUA PARK	97.1	96.0	0.3	0.4	1.6	2.3	3.0	4.0	6.9	7.2	7.9	6.8	4.0	22.8	28.2	13.7	2.5	73.5	41.7	48.9	51.1
11763	MEDFORD	83.5	79.3	9.3	11.1	1.4	1.9	11.1	14.3	7.1	7.3	7.4	7.3	5.0	28.8	27.1	8.7	1.2	73.7	36.6	48.9	51.1
11764	MILLER PLACE	96.7	95.3	0.4	0.6	1.3	1.9	3.2	4.5	7.1	7.7	8.5	7.7	4.5	24.7	30.7	8.1	1.0	71.3	38.6	49.2	50.8
11765	MILL NECK	94.1	92.0	0.8	1.0	3.0	4.1	4.4	6.0	7.0	8.2	9.7	6.8	2.7	21.0	29.7	12.6	2.3	70.1	42.4	48.7	51.3
11766	MOUNT SINAI	94.5	92.6	1.5	1.6	2.0	3.0	4.2	5.7	6.9	7.5	8.4	8.2	4.9	25.7	29.9	7.2	1.3	71.8	37.6	49.1	50.9
11767	NESCONSET	94.3	92.2	1.0	1.2	3.0	4.2	4.1	5.3	7.3	7.6	8.1	6.9	3.9	27.3	27.9	9.8	1.3	72.6	39.3	48.9	51.1
11768	NORTHPORT	96.7	95.5	0.7	0.9	1.5	2.2	2.3	3.1	6.2	6.9	7.9	6.5	3.5	20.7	32.6	14.0	1.7	74.5	44.0	49.7	50.3
11769	OAKDALE	96.7	95.5	1.3	1.6	1.0	1.4	2.9	3.9	5.8	6.0	6.5	7.2	5.6	23.3	29.0	14.5	2.0	77.6	42.0	47.8	52.2
11770	OCEAN BEACH	96.6	95.5	0.0	0.0	2.3	3.2	2.3	3.2	3.2	3.2	4.5	7.6	5.7	19.7	38.2	15.3	2.5	84.7	47.6	52.2	47.8
11771	OYSTER BAY	90.5	87.5	2.6	3.3	3.2	4.5	8.6	10.8	5.9	6.3	7.1	6.4	4.8	22.7	31.2	13.1	2.5	76.5	42.9	48.4	51.6
11772	PATCHOGUE	85.7	82.2	4.7	5.6	1.6	2.1	14.0	17.5	6.7	6.7	6.6	6.6	5.9	27.9	27.1	10.3	2.2	75.9	38.2	49.1	50.9
11776	PORT JEFFERSON STATI	90.4	87.4	2.2	2.8	2.7	3.7	8.7	11.3	7.3	7.4	7.5	6.9	4.7	27.9	26.3	10.2	1.5	73.3	38.0	49.0	51.0
11777	PORT JEFFERSON	92.0	89.3	1.6	2.0	3.5	4.9	5.0	6.4	5.1	5.2	5.7	6.0	5.1	25.5	29.4	14.8	3.1	79.8	43.2	48.4	51.6
11778	ROCKY POINT	95.8	94.2	0.6	0.8	1.1	1.6	4.8	6.5	8.2	8.1	8.0	7.4	5.8	28.3	25.9	7.2	1.1	71.1	35.2	49.7	50.3
11779	RONKONKOMA	93.6	91.4	1.1	1.4	2.5	3.4	6.3	8.2	6.6	6.7	6.8	6.8	5.4	27.6	27.8	10.5	1.9	75.6	39.1	49.0	51.0
11780	SAINT JAMES	97.2	96.1	0.3	0.4	1.4	1.9	3.2	4.3	6.4	7.1	7.8	6.9	3.6	20.5	28.0	15.2	4.5	74.2	43.6	47.7	52.3
11782	SAYVILLE	96.0	94.4	0.7	0.8	1.9	2.9	2.8	3.8	6.6	6.9	7.5	7.3	4.9	23.8	29.5	11.0	2.5	74.1	40.7	48.2	51.8
11783	SEAFORD	97.0	95.7	0.3	0.4	1.6	2.3	3.5	4.7	6.6	6.9	7.5	6.7	4.5	24.2	29.5	12.0	2.1	74.7	41.2	48.5	51.5
11784	SELDEN	91.9	89.3	2.1	2.6	2.4	3.4	8.0	10.3	7.0	7.2	7.2	7.2	5.8	27.9	26.8	9.5	1.3	74.2	37.1	48.8	51.2
11786	SHOREHAM	95.9	94.4	0.9	1.2	1.6	2.2	3.3	4.5	6.1	6.2	6.8	7.0	4.2	19.3	30.1	16.7	3.5	76.2	45.1	48.6	51.4
11787	SMITHTOWN	96.1	94.6	0.6	0.8	2.0	2.8	3.4	4.5	7.1	7.4	8.0	6.6	3.9	22.8	27.8	13.5	2.8	73.0	41.6	48.2	51.8
11788	HAUPPAUGE	92.3	89.6	1.4	1.7	4.2	5.8	4.8	6.2	6.4	6.5	7.0	6.2	4.6	26.0	28.2	13.8	1.1	76.0	41.1	49.5	50.5
11789	SOUND BEACH	96.0	94.5	0.7	0.9	1.4	2.0	3.5	4.7	7.2	7.3	7.6	7.5	5.7	28.2	27.5	7.7	1.3	73.0	36.8	49.1	50.9
11790	STONY BROOK	78.4	73.8	4.9	5.5	13.5	17.0	4.2	4.9	5.0	5.3	6.0	14.5	15.4	18.9	22.6	10.5	1.7	79.8	29.7	50.1	49.9
11791	SYOSSET	85.6	80.6	0.7	0.9	12.1	16.4	2.8	3.6	6.0	6.8	8.5	7.4	3.8	20.5	31.7	13.2	2.1	73.7	43.1	49.0	51.0
11792	WADING RIVER	95.2	93.6	1.9	2.3	1.1	1.6	3.6	4.9	6.2	6.9	8.1	7.6	4.7	23.9	30.7	10.4	1.4	73.8	40.3	49.7	50.3
11793	WANTAGH	95.7	94.1	0.6	0.7	2.2	3.1	3.8	5.1	7.0	7.4	8.1	6.9	4.4	22.5	29.7	11.9	2.1	73.2	41.2	48.5	51.5
11794	STONY BROOK	34.9	28.1	17.6	18.1	37.7	43.1	10.8	11.4	0.3	0.1	0.1	39.5	53.8	5.5	0.4	0.3	0.0	98.9	20.9	49.7	50.3
11795	WEST ISLIP	97.0	95.9	0.4	0.4	1.1	1.6	3.4	4.5	6.9	7.3	7.9	7.9	5.0	22.7	28.6	11.5	2.2	72.9	40.3	48.9	51.1
11796	WEST SAYVILLE	97.5	96.6	0.5	0.7	1.0	1.4	2.4	3.2	6.4	7.0	7.3	7.5	5.4	24.1	29.8	10.8	1.7	74.3	40.2	48.3	51.7
11797	WOODBURY	90.9	87.2	1.0	1.5	7.0	9.8	1.4	1.9	4.8	5.8	7.4	7.2	3.0	19.4	30.3	15.5	6.5	76.7	46.4	47.2	52.8
11798	WYANDANCH	19.0	16.8	69.1	70.5	1.3	1.5	15.0	15.7	8.7	8.7	8.4	9.0	7.8	26.7	22.3	7.7	0.8	68.6	30.2	47.2	52.8
11801	HICKSVILLE	85.4	80.9	0.7	0.9	8.9	11.9	9.5	11.9	6.0	6.3	6.6	6.3	4.6	26.5	28.8	12.5	2.4	77.1	41.0	48.8	51.2
11803	PLAINVIEW	93.4	90.8	0.4	0.5	4.8	6.8	2.7	3.6	6.0	6.6	7.5	6.5	4.1	20.9	31.2	14.5	2.7	75.6	44.0	48.4	51.6
11804	OLD BETHPAGE	94.7	92.6	1.2	1.6	3.0	4.3	1.8	2.4	5.8	6.3	7.4	7.1	3.9	21.0	30.9	15.3	2.4	75.9	44.1	48.6	51.4
11901	RIVERHEAD	75.7	70.8	18.6	22.2	0.9	1.2	8.2	9.9	6.0	6.1	6.3	6.4	5.3	23.6	27.3	15.7	3.3	77.5	42.2	48.1	51.9
11933	CALVERTON	82.2	79.9	12.9	13.8	0.9	1.2	7.6	9.2	5.3	5.4	5.8	6.8	6.0	29.0	26.7	13.0	2.2	79.9	40.2	54.8	45.2
11934	CENTER MORICHES	90.3	87.7	5.0	5.9	1.0	1.4	6.6	8.8	7.2	7.4	7.3	6.4	5.6	26.2	27.7	10.3	1.9	73.9	38.5	49.1	50.9
11935	CUTCHOGUE	94.1	92.5	2.0	2.4	0.6	0.9	5.2	6.6	4.2	4.6	5.3	6.3	4.2	19.4	33.4	19.5	3.1	81.7	48.8	49.5	50.5
11937	EAST HAMPTON	88.9	85.5	3.4	4.4	1.3	1.8	12.9	16.7	5.0	5.3	5.6	5.8	4.8	22.5	33.6	15.1	2.3	80.3	45.6	49.6	50.4
11939	EAST MARION	95.4	94.0	0.9	1.2	0.9	1.2	2.9	3.7	4.2	4.4	5.3	5.5	3.0	16.8	34.5	21.8	4.4	82.6	51.6	51.1	48.9
11940	EAST MORICHES	94.3	91.7	1.6	2.1	1.6	2.5	5.9	8.7	6.4	6.6	7.0	7.3	5.6	24.5	29.6	10.7	2.2	74.7	40.0	49.3	50.7
11941	EASTPORT	94.2	92.3	1.7	2.2	1.5	2.0	5.7	7.5	5.6	6.2	7.0	7.2	4.2	23.6	31.6	12.2	2.5	78.3	42.8	49.7	50.3
11942	EAST QUOGUE	94.9	93.1	1.4	1.5	0.7	0.9	5.0	7.1	6.1	6.5	6.9	6.4	4.4	23.4	31.4	12.8	2.2	76.9	42.6	49.2	50.8
11944	GREENPORT	82.8	79.9	10.4	11.8	0.7	0.9	12.2	14.5	5.5	5.3	5.3	6.1	5.5	19.4	28.4	19.2	5.3	80.2	46.9	46.5	53.5
11946	HAMPTON BAYS	92.9	90.9	0.9	1.1	0.8	1.0	12.6	16.2	6.0	6.3	6.2	5.3	4.0	26.5	30.0	13.3	2.4	80.0	42.3	50.0	50.0
11948	LAUREL	97.0	96.2	1.2	1.6	0.0	0.0	2.3	3.1	5.2	5.5	6.2	7.9	5.2	22.6	30.6	14.0	2.8	78.7	43.0	50.4	49.6
11949	MANORVILLE	96.2	94.8	1.2	1.6	0.7	1.0	4.3	5.7	8.0	8.2	8.3	6.9	4.8	25.7	26.7	9.7	1.7	70.9	37.7	49.2	50.8
11950	MASTIC	84.8	81.2	6.0	7.3	1.2	1.7	12.5	15.9	8.0	7.9	7.8	8.2	6.6	29.9	25.1	5.6	0.6	71.2	32.3	49.8	50.2
11951	MASTIC BEACH	88.7	85.6	4.6	5.6	0.8	1.1	10.2	13.1	8.0	7.9	7.7	8.1	6.6	28.0	25.6	6.9	1.0	71.3	33.0	49.5	50.5
11952	MATTITUCK	96.7	95.6	1.2	1.5	0.5	0.7	2.4	3.2	5.4	5.9	6.5	6.4	4.8	20.7	31.7	15.7	3.0	78.1	45.2	48.6	51.4
11953	MIDDLE ISLAND	80.7	77.5	11.8	13.3	2.5	3.2	7.5	9.3	7.0	6.9	6.7	5.7	5.6	27.3	26.5	12.2	2.1	75.8	38.8	47.6	52.4
11954	MONTAUK	87.0	84.1	0.9	1.1	0.8	1.1	23.9	28.9	5.0	5.0	5.1	5.7	5.3	26.5	32.2	13.5	1.6	81.4	43.3	50.7	49.3
11955	MORICHES	94.0	93.1	1.9	2.0	1.9	2.4	4.2	4.9	3.7	3.4	3.2	3.1	4.3	25.7	28.3	25.5	2.8	87.5	50.2	49.6	50.4
11957	ORIENT	97.3	96.6	0.6	0.7	1.3	1.7	1.0	1.3	3.4	4.0	4.4	4.7	3.3	9.1	37.2	28.5	5.4	84.8	58.6	48.9	51.1
11958	PECONIC	92.9	90.4	1.5	1.8	1.0	1.5	4.7	6.1	4.3	4.9	5.4	5.8	3.9	19.0	36.4	18.0	2.3	81.7	49.0	51.6	48.4
11961	RIDGE	92.5	90.3	3.8	4.7	0.9	1.3	3.9	5.1	5.8	6.3	6.4	6.5	4.2	21.4	24.3	19.1	5.8	77.1	44.5	46.6	53.4
11963	SAG HARBOR	90.4	88.0	5.4	6.3	1.0	1.4	4.9	6.5	4.4	4.8	5.4	5.2	3.4	19.8	36.2	17.8	3.1	82.1	48.9	48.8	51.2
11964	SHELTER ISLAND	95.0	93.2	1.0	1.3	0.6	0.7	3.1	4.4	4.4	5.0	5.7	6.0	3.1	19.6	36.6	16.5	3.2	81.1	49.0	48.6	51.4
11965	SHELTER ISLAND HEIGH	97.8	96.9	0.4	0.5	0.4	0.7	1.5	1.9	2.6	3.1	4.0	4.4	2.1	11.0	39.1	28.4	5.3	87.7	58.3	47.7	52.3
11967	SHIRLEY	89.6	86.6	3.5	4.4	1.3	1.8	10.9	14.0	7.5	7.6	7.8	8.1	5.8	29.4	26.4	6.6	0.8	72.1	34.2	49.5	50.5
11968	SOUTHAMPTON	84.0	81.2	6.6	7.8	1.2	1.6	8.8	11.2	5.4	5.4	5.7	7.6	5.6	23.1	29.9	14.5	2.8	80.2	42.9	48.5	51.5
11971	SOUTHOLD	96.7	95.5	0.9	1.2	0.2	0.3	2.6	3.4	4.8	5.2	5.6	5.6	4.2	17.9	30.9	21.1	4.6	80.7	49.1	47.7	52.3
11976	WATER MILL	94.6	93.2	3.2	3.8	0.9	1.3	3.3	4.4	4.3	4.9	5.7	5.5	2.9	17.9	37.0	19.1	2.7	81.5	49.9	49.2	50.8
11977	WESTHAMPTON	95.4	94.3	1.7	1.9	1.0	1.4	3.6	4.6	6.0	6.2	6.8	6.2	4.5	23.5	31.7	12.4	2.7	78.8	43.1	49.8	50.2
11978	WESTHAMPTON BEACH	85.0	80.9	6.8	8.4	1.3	1.8	9.5	12.2	5.1	4.8	5.4	6.5	5.7	24.5	28.4	15.6	4.0	82.2	43.4	49.7	50.3
11980	YAPHANK	88.5	84.8	7.7	10.2	1.4	2.0	8.1	11.0	6.0	6.4	6.9	6.7	5.1	27.9	29.7	9.6	1.7	76.7	39.6	50.5	49.5
12007	ALCOVE	99.0	98.5	0.5	0.5	0.0	0.5	1.0	1.5	5.9	5.9	6.4	6.9	5.9	23.2	32.5	11.8	1.5	76.8	42.0	50.2	49.8
12008	ALPLAUS	97.3	96.2	0.2	0.4	2.0	2.8	1.1	1.6	5.4	5.6	6.6	7.6	5.2	22.3	29.5	15.5	2.4	76.9	43.3	50.2	49.8
12009	ALTAMONT	95.5	93.3	1.6	2.5	1.2	1.8	1.3	1.8	5.4	5.6	6.2	7.1	6.3	23.5	32.1	10.9	2.8	77.9	42.2	48.4	51.6
12010	AMSTERDAM	92.8	91.4	1.7	1.9	0.6	0.8	10.9	13.2	5.9	5.8	5.9	6.6	5.5	22.8	27.8	15.4	4.3	78.1	43.1	47.2	52.8
12015	ATHENS	89.5	84.6	6.0	8.1	0.8	2.0	3.8	5.2	5.1	5.6	5.3	7.5	7.5	23.3	30.6	13.2	1.9	80.8	41.9	49.2	50.8
12017	AUSTERLITZ	98.1	97.4	0.3	0.6	0.3	0.6	0.6	1.0	3.9	4.5	5.1	5.1	3.5	18.6	40.5	16.7	1.9	83.0	50.9	52.1	47.9
12018	AVERILL PARK	98.0	97.2	0.3	0.4	0.4	0.6	0.9	1.2	5.3	6.0	6.7	7.0	5.1	24.1	34.0	10.5	1.2	77.5	42.2	49.2	50.8
12019	BALLSTON LAKE	96.8	95.9	0.7	0.8	1.3	1.8	0.9	1.1	5.6	6.3	7.2	7.0	4.5	23.2	32.4	12.5	1.4	76.1	42.7	49.8	50.2
12020	BALLSTON SPA	96.6	95.6	1.0	1.2	0.6	0.9	1.7	2.1	7.5	7.4	7.4	6.7	5.6	27.7	27.1	9.0	1.6	73.4	37.1	49.0	51.0
12022	BERLIN	97.8	96.9	0.0	0.0	0.1	0.1	1.0	1.2	6.2	6.8	6.9	6.8	5.6	21.1	31.7	12.9	1.9	75.9	42.3	49.5	50.5
12023	BERNE	97.4	96.5	0.7	0.9	0.6	0.8	0.9	1.2	5.5	5.9	6.7	6.5	4.7	23.9	33.7	11.8	1.3	77.8	42.9	49.2	50.8
	NEW YORK	67.9	64.8	15.9	16.5	5.6	6.9	15.1	16.7	6.5	6.4	6.4	7.1	7.0	27.0	26.3	11.2	2.1	76.6	37.5	48.4	51.6
	UNITED STATES	75.1	72.0	12.3	12.7	3.8	4.6	12.5	15.7	6.8	6.7	6.6	7.1	6.9	27.0	26.0	10.9	1.9	75.7	36.9	49.2	50.8

ZIP CODE				2009 HOUSEHOLD INCOME DISTRIBUTION (%)					MEDIAN HOUSEHOLD INCOME					2009 HOME VALUE DISTRIBUTION (%)					
#	POST OFFICE NAME	2009 Per Capita Income	2009 HH Income Base	Less than $25,000	$25,000 to $49,999	$50,000 to $99,999	$100,000 to $149,999	$150,000 or More	2009	2014	2009 National Centile	2009 State Centile	2009 Home Value Base	Less than $50,000	$50,000 to $89,999	$90,000 to $174,999	$175,000 to $399,999	$400,000 or More	2009 Median Home Value
11735	FARMINGDALE	35005	10737	8.5	12.2	34.9	28.5	15.9	85155	92447	94	87	8393	0.2	0.4	2.6	60.3	36.6	368222
11738	FARMINGVILLE	33213	5509	4.5	9.9	39.2	28.3	18.2	92628	99077	96	89	4519	0.1	0.1	4.1	80.8	14.8	295412
11740	GREENLAWN	40837	3623	13.8	11.0	26.6	27.8	20.8	95835	103338	96	90	2831	0.1	0.0	1.0	33.7	65.3	495686
11741	HOLBROOK	36992	9418	6.4	8.7	35.5	31.7	17.7	98724	102636	96	91	7388	0.3	0.4	2.0	75.8	21.5	326415
11742	HOLTSVILLE	31679	4405	7.8	13.7	37.6	30.1	10.6	84614	89374	94	86	3495	0.0	0.7	11.5	74.8	12.9	292219
11743	HUNTINGTON	55652	14894	7.5	9.0	24.3	24.4	34.8	117703	122873	98	96	12513	0.1	0.0	1.3	24.5	74.2	610476
11746	HUNTINGTON STATION	42798	20047	7.2	11.9	27.6	25.7	27.6	104911	109102	97	93	16377	0.3	0.1	1.1	38.8	59.7	475514
11747	MELVILLE	55446	6100	5.6	9.0	23.1	24.3	38.1	125271	129720	99	97	5208	0.3	0.1	0.3	17.6	81.7	665970
11749	ISLANDIA	31290	1423	11.0	16.7	39.9	21.8	10.6	73083	76223	88	79	862	0.0	0.0	5.6	88.2	6.3	286207
11751	ISLIP	35561	5021	8.6	13.8	33.2	28.1	16.3	88723	95020	95	88	3770	1.0	0.4	1.8	67.2	29.6	331429
11752	ISLIP TERRACE	31314	2982	4.5	11.9	40.5	29.9	13.1	87112	92540	94	87	2620	0.2	0.1	1.4	84.7	13.7	317520
11753	JERICHO	65416	4124	6.4	5.5	18.1	25.0	44.9	136735	145828	99	98	3496	0.1	0.3	0.0	6.5	93.0	776930
11754	KINGS PARK	38683	6347	10.6	12.5	27.9	30.4	18.6	97450	102149	96	90	5017	0.1	0.0	2.2	45.1	52.6	411583
11755	LAKE GROVE	36520	3990	5.8	12.5	36.0	27.1	18.5	91611	97705	95	89	3129	0.0	0.0	1.7	65.8	32.5	346942
11756	LEVITTOWN	33041	13779	6.0	10.4	36.4	33.4	13.9	92860	100090	96	89	12125	0.0	0.0	0.6	78.8	20.5	342829
11757	LINDENHURST	30400	15263	10.5	15.0	36.0	27.2	11.3	79383	84492	92	84	11936	0.1	0.0	2.1	85.7	12.0	298393
11758	MASSAPEQUA	40130	17917	7.4	10.1	27.5	31.4	23.6	105815	112680	97	94	15721	0.2	0.1	0.3	39.0	60.4	443355
11762	MASSAPEQUA PARK	40597	7671	4.6	9.9	27.5	34.8	23.2	108661	115554	98	95	7190	0.1	0.0	0.2	40.8	58.8	429485
11763	MEDFORD	29917	8021	6.6	11.1	38.2	32.7	11.4	88692	93779	95	88	6921	0.1	0.0	6.9	85.0	7.8	261112
11764	MILLER PLACE	36971	4088	4.7	7.7	31.4	36.0	20.2	106849	108815	98	94	3666	0.1	0.6	1.9	59.6	37.9	362192
11765	MILL NECK	76760	166	8.4	9.6	12.0	18.1	51.8	156668	171707	100	99	136	0.0	0.0	0.0	5.1	94.9	1000001
11766	MOUNT SINAI	40165	3634	4.5	8.3	28.9	32.8	25.5	109520	112114	98	95	3268	0.1	0.1	1.6	49.1	49.1	397089
11767	NESCONSET	42082	4751	5.1	7.2	27.8	32.2	27.7	115507	118936	98	96	3979	0.0	0.1	1.4	41.9	56.6	425913
11768	NORTHPORT	56356	7777	5.1	8.5	25.0	24.5	36.8	126290	130293	99	97	6548	0.0	0.0	0.2	14.3	85.4	664118
11769	OAKDALE	40236	3849	13.1	11.4	30.0	24.0	21.6	89943	98393	95	88	3065	0.0	0.1	11.7	45.1	43.1	376725
11770	OCEAN BEACH	53059	70	8.6	15.7	34.3	18.6	22.9	77864	89620	91	83	56	0.0	0.0	0.0	16.1	83.9	636364
11771	OYSTER BAY	63297	4196	11.1	10.4	26.0	19.2	33.3	105335	116926	97	93	2946	0.0	0.2	3.1	13.4	83.3	799716
11772	PATCHOGUE	30470	14895	15.1	16.5	35.5	22.8	10.1	70998	75154	87	77	9553	0.3	0.7	6.8	82.5	9.8	266995
11776	PORT JEFFERSON STATI	32075	7602	8.1	13.0	37.0	27.7	14.2	85942	91050	94	87	6095	0.1	0.0	4.2	81.3	14.4	296146
11777	PORT JEFFERSON	48479	3518	9.2	12.2	29.9	21.7	27.0	96424	104424	96	90	2623	0.0	0.0	0.7	32.3	67.0	499443
11778	ROCKY POINT	31299	4259	10.9	16.8	38.0	24.3	10.1	76423	80166	90	82	3320	0.2	0.2	8.0	81.3	10.2	253576
11779	RONKONKOMA	31839	12804	11.1	12.9	35.8	27.8	12.4	82889	87681	93	86	9781	0.1	0.1	4.5	84.0	11.4	292866
11780	SAINT JAMES	46386	5215	8.6	10.5	27.2	27.1	26.7	106642	111534	98	94	4597	0.0	0.0	0.6	35.4	64.0	486608
11782	SAYVILLE	40072	5502	9.2	11.7	27.2	29.4	22.6	102596	106428	97	92	4579	0.2	0.2	1.1	55.6	43.0	378076
11783	SEAFORD	38711	7276	6.7	10.4	28.4	34.1	20.4	104561	110120	97	93	6479	0.1	0.0	0.8	41.7	57.5	426902
11784	SELDEN	28264	8295	9.3	14.6	39.3	27.5	9.3	76395	81056	90	82	6614	0.2	0.3	5.7	89.4	4.5	267409
11786	SHOREHAM	38444	2157	8.5	8.9	26.9	29.8	25.9	107507	110700	98	94	1987	0.1	0.3	6.6	52.1	41.0	369211
11787	SMITHTOWN	42999	11681	7.0	7.7	29.0	29.1	27.4	110149	114370	98	95	10053	0.0	0.1	1.0	31.1	67.8	476898
11788	HAUPPAUGE	41292	5667	4.8	9.8	30.9	32.2	22.3	106022	109218	97	94	4423	0.1	0.1	2.3	30.7	66.8	472211
11789	SOUND BEACH	28837	2870	10.2	19.4	38.3	24.4	7.7	73535	77231	89	79	2220	0.3	0.0	5.4	88.1	6.3	265067
11790	STONY BROOK	40055	4842	6.0	7.1	25.5	31.5	29.9	118019	121318	98	97	4308	0.3	0.0	0.8	37.4	61.5	447969
11791	SYOSSET	56984	7933	5.7	7.0	18.9	25.9	42.5	132598	141700	99	98	7214	0.2	0.3	0.1	8.7	90.7	666249
11792	WADING RIVER	35615	2865	10.1	12.3	33.5	26.4	17.8	87654	94013	95	88	2548	2.1	1.1	4.0	53.2	39.6	353263
11793	WANTAGH	41956	10716	6.1	10.4	27.6	32.3	23.5	106684	113783	98	94	9682	0.1	0.0	0.5	42.0	57.3	425681
11794	STONY BROOK	15204	2	0.0	0.0	100.0	0.0	0.0	87500	87500	94	88	2	0.0	0.0	0.0	0.0	100.0	500000
11795	WEST ISLIP	38522	8257	4.7	8.3	33.1	32.9	20.9	104491	107366	97	93	7529	0.0	0.0	1.0	53.8	45.2	385661
11796	WEST SAYVILLE	34667	1283	9.7	10.4	35.1	30.2	14.6	88665	95449	95	88	979	0.0	0.2	3.7	72.9	23.2	324569
11797	WOODBURY	69125	2889	6.2	5.0	14.2	21.1	53.6	161135	173268	100	100	2335	0.0	0.1	0.0	5.0	94.9	1000001
11798	WYANDANCH	21938	4001	15.8	23.1	29.3	18.9	12.9	64770	69678	83	71	2682	0.3	0.3	17.0	68.8	13.7	266189
11801	HICKSVILLE	34909	12757	8.5	12.9	32.9	28.9	16.8	88725	98278	95	88	10754	0.3	0.1	0.3	61.6	37.7	373525
11803	PLAINVIEW	48760	9369	6.7	7.9	20.7	29.0	35.7	122162	130728	99	97	8559	0.0	0.2	0.0	17.3	82.5	555618
11804	OLD BETHPAGE	49851	1709	9.0	8.8	21.5	23.8	37.0	119879	130245	98	97	1514	0.3	0.2	0.0	12.5	87.0	575611
11901	RIVERHEAD	27914	9680	20.0	26.7	31.3	15.1	7.0	54037	59110	70	55	6769	5.2	4.5	14.7	61.2	14.4	241290
11933	CALVERTON	34121	2889	16.2	21.7	31.2	22.7	8.2	64057	68636	82	71	2342	8.1	6.4	10.4	53.8	21.3	260771
11934	CENTER MORICHES	30753	2506	9.3	12.1	43.6	25.6	9.5	79456	82890	92	84	1985	0.0	0.1	4.0	77.1	18.8	291082
11935	CUTCHOGUE	44803	1831	15.7	13.8	30.7	21.9	17.9	78885	86586	92	84	1556	0.0	0.3	0.7	38.8	60.2	471946
11937	EAST HAMPTON	41863	6746	14.6	19.0	27.9	22.7	15.8	71554	79078	88	78	5273	0.3	0.7	3.1	25.6	70.4	591237
11939	EAST MARION	30115	369	20.9	25.7	38.2	11.7	3.5	53615	58274	69	54	301	0.0	0.0	3.0	54.2	42.9	378500
11940	EAST MORICHES	33592	1968	8.9	14.1	36.6	25.9	14.5	81416	85660	93	85	1634	0.4	0.6	3.3	71.1	24.7	310000
11941	EASTPORT	39371	1422	11.3	11.5	36.5	24.4	16.2	77707	83959	91	83	1140	1.1	0.1	3.6	52.4	42.9	362326
11942	EAST QUOGUE	39347	2498	12.4	12.4	35.2	27.9	12.0	79618	85894	92	84	2042	2.9	0.6	1.1	43.7	51.7	412456
11944	GREENPORT	28355	1885	25.3	26.6	29.7	12.3	6.1	47936	54430	56	40	1267	0.3	0.2	8.7	62.7	28.2	292532
11946	HAMPTON BAYS	33730	5301	16.1	19.9	34.1	21.0	8.9	64826	68120	83	72	3753	0.5	0.5	2.4	64.6	32.0	332819
11948	LAUREL	40898	306	12.1	17.3	31.0	26.1	13.4	77169	84185	91	82	260	0.0	0.0	3.1	50.8	46.2	386667
11949	MANORVILLE	38145	5020	8.5	13.7	32.0	31.2	14.6	90831	98764	95	89	3971	0.3	0.7	6.4	58.7	34.0	336286
11950	MASTIC	23082	4485	13.0	18.5	41.1	21.3	6.1	69393	72314	86	76	3552	1.5	0.3	26.3	70.6	1.4	201363
11951	MASTIC BEACH	23001	4528	17.3	19.9	41.7	15.9	5.2	63007	66373	81	69	3385	0.1	0.1	41.8	55.9	2.1	184154
11952	MATTITUCK	34502	1884	13.5	19.1	29.4	26.0	12.0	74541	81140	89	80	1595	0.0	0.2	0.3	55.4	44.2	381969
11953	MIDDLE ISLAND	30829	5128	11.0	21.7	37.5	21.0	8.8	68663	72923	86	75	3608	0.2	2.4	18.0	73.0	6.5	250124
11954	MONTAUK	30882	1865	21.2	23.3	30.2	16.8	8.4	56289	61639	73	59	1246	0.3	0.3	0.6	20.9	77.8	593324
11955	MORICHES	49633	1402	11.5	13.5	26.7	35.7	12.6	95858	101952	96	90	752	0.0	0.0	0.7	67.0	32.3	348846
11957	ORIENT	41906	325	15.7	25.2	32.3	13.2	13.5	63911	67145	82	70	271	0.0	0.0	0.7	25.8	73.4	583929
11958	PECONIC	29727	331	15.7	26.0	34.1	16.9	7.3	60571	63750	78	65	270	0.0	0.0	0.0	40.7	59.3	480645
11961	RIDGE	34543	5562	18.2	18.8	34.2	17.7	11.1	65506	69594	84	72	4701	0.4	0.4	16.1	71.9	11.2	253540
11963	SAG HARBOR	47959	4100	11.2	21.0	30.2	22.9	14.7	73816	78647	89	80	3264	0.1	0.1	1.4	21.3	77.1	683931
11964	SHELTER ISLAND	31750	520	14.8	26.3	32.5	18.5	7.9	57146	61257	74	61	411	0.0	0.0	0.7	34.3	65.0	505787
11965	SHELTER ISLAND HEIGH	52687	487	13.6	14.0	26.3	28.7	17.5	89290	100546	95	88	425	0.0	0.0	1.6	21.6	76.7	642992
11967	SHIRLEY	25452	7603	9.4	16.5	40.9	25.1	8.0	74991	78564	89	81	6238	0.1	0.0	17.8	78.5	3.6	220466
11968	SOUTHAMPTON	42325	5060	15.2	18.4	29.3	21.1	16.0	71395	77723	88	77	3891	1.0	0.1	1.2	23.8	74.0	635555
11971	SOUTHOLD	38113	2657	15.2	23.0	24.5	26.9	10.3	68195	77145	86	75	2194	0.0	0.0	1.0	47.1	51.9	411615
11976	WATER MILL	62259	1032	13.4	12.2	21.6	23.4	29.4	105447	112072	97	94	891	0.0	0.0	1.9	7.4	90.7	1000001
11977	WESTHAMPTON	48387	1222	9.5	16.0	22.4	29.8	22.3	103383	109099	97	93	948	0.2	0.2	4.9	26.8	67.9	598837
11978	WESTHAMPTON BEACH	41889	1623	15.8	18.7	26.2	23.0	16.3	74596	82366	89	80	1135	1.6	0.6	2.0	32.3	63.4	551798
11980	YAPHANK	31503	1370	5.8	9.9	37.7	34.4	12.2	93280	100056	96	89	1146	0.0	0.0	4.5	91.4	4.2	248560
12007	ALCOVE	31750	72	5.6	15.3	52.8	18.1	8.3	78739	78100	91	84	57	0.0	0.0	35.1	61.4	3.5	209615
12008	ALPLAUS	33851	201	4.5	19.4	47.3	23.4	5.5	76931	77147	91	82	167	0.0	1.2	21.0	76.0	1.8	219898
12009	ALTAMONT	33161	2887	10.8	22.2	40.1	16.8	10.1	69854	73218	87	76	1981	2.2	0.5	16.7	67.4	13.1	240292
12010	AMSTERDAM	21899	12304	30.0	28.7	32.4	6.6	2.3	40605	44065	35	16	7747	6.9	21.2	51.1	18.6	2.1	119011
12015	ATHENS	26112	1446	21.2	26.6	38.0	9.3	5.0	51748	53457	65	50	1067	8.0	8.0	48.1	31.3	4.7	146420
12017	AUSTERLITZ	34799	127	15.0	25.2	38.6	10.2	11.0	59541	57898	77	63	105	1.0	6.7	25.7	41.9	24.8	237500
12018	AVERILL PARK	30250	2839	12.3	20.9	42.8	16.5	7.6	68562	71255	86	75	2249	2.5	2.4	25.9	57.3	11.8	214924
12019	BALLSTON LAKE	37210	5474	5.2	15.7	39.7	26.3	13.1	83503	86064	93	86	4094	0.9	0.5	11.4	76.7	10.5	247617
12020	BALLSTON SPA	30764	11979	10.5	20.5	40.9	21.9	6.2	68445	72224	86	75	8906	6.3	2.5	28.7	56.6	5.9	196112
12022	BERLIN	21599	345	20.9	31.6	39.7	6.1	1.7	48088	50572	57	41	259	5.8	6.6	51.4	29.0	7.3	156510
12023	BERNE	26935	778	13.0	26.2	47.9	8.6	4.2	60082	61878	77	64	634	3.2	2.7	35.2	53.2	5.8	190489
	NEW YORK	29893		21.9	21.3	32.7	14.0	9.9	58747	62337				3.4	5.7	23.0	38.7	29.1	269816
	UNITED STATES	27277		20.9	24.4	35.3	11.7	7.6	54719	56938				9.3	13.1	31.6	32.6	13.5	162279

#	POST OFFICE NAME	FINANCIAL SERVICES				THE HOME						ENTERTAINMENT						PERSONAL			
						Home Improvements		Furnishings													
ZIP CODE		Auto Loan	Home Loan	Invest-ments	Retire-ment Plans	Home Repair	Lawn & Garden	Comput-ers & Hard-ware-Personal	Major Appli-ances	TV, Radio, Sound Equip-ment	Furni-ture	Dine out/ Carry out	Sports Equip-ment	Fees & Tickets	Toys & Games	Travel	Cable TV	Apparel & Services	Auto Repairs	Health Insur-ance	Pets & Supplies
11735	FARMINGDALE	124	168	175	158	175	150	144	147	138	143	140	109	167	139	162	139	103	143	140	162
11738	FARMINGVILLE	137	184	181	175	186	161	153	158	145	156	147	119	177	149	171	143	108	151	146	175
11740	GREENLAWN	135	183	199	176	193	173	156	163	153	158	153	118	184	150	179	155	112	158	165	180
11741	HOLBROOK	143	185	183	181	187	165	158	161	151	162	153	123	180	154	174	148	111	156	150	182
11742	HOLTSVILLE	120	152	147	148	152	136	132	133	126	134	128	102	148	128	143	124	92	130	126	151
11743	HUNTINGTON	190	256	291	256	277	232	220	228	204	233	205	172	260	202	254	197	153	216	206	251
11746	HUNTINGTON STATION	160	217	238	212	231	195	187	192	176	192	178	144	220	176	213	174	133	185	177	211
11747	MELVILLE	198	277	321	277	302	253	232	244	215	247	215	182	281	212	273	208	162	229	221	266
11749	ISLANDIA	114	132	130	129	133	118	128	123	122	127	125	96	136	123	133	120	91	125	116	140
11751	ISLIP	126	168	174	159	174	150	146	148	139	145	142	111	167	141	163	139	104	145	140	164
11752	ISLIP TERRACE	122	172	178	160	178	152	142	148	136	142	137	108	167	138	162	137	102	142	140	162
11753	JERICHO	218	300	358	307	332	278	256	268	237	278	236	201	312	232	302	227	179	252	241	294
11754	KINGS PARK	134	182	193	175	190	168	154	160	150	155	151	117	182	150	176	152	111	155	157	177
11755	LAKE GROVE	135	181	189	173	188	162	153	157	146	154	148	117	179	149	173	146	109	152	149	174
11756	LEVITTOWN	123	173	180	161	180	153	143	149	136	142	138	109	168	138	163	137	102	143	140	163
11757	LINDENHURST	110	153	158	142	158	135	129	133	123	128	125	98	150	124	146	124	92	128	126	146
11758	MASSAPEQUA	143	204	224	195	217	185	168	176	160	170	161	129	202	161	196	161	120	168	167	192
11762	MASSAPEQUA PARK	143	208	233	200	223	191	169	179	160	172	161	130	207	161	199	161	121	169	169	194
11763	MEDFORD	128	160	149	157	158	143	137	140	132	142	134	108	154	135	149	130	96	135	133	159
11764	MILLER PLACE	150	197	192	195	199	176	164	170	155	170	157	130	190	159	183	152	114	161	156	191
11765	MILL NECK	265	377	463	394	423	355	305	329	286	341	283	246	393	283	368	274	220	301	290	358
11766	MOUNT SINAI	166	217	215	217	220	193	181	187	171	190	174	144	212	176	203	167	128	177	169	210
11767	NESCONSET	157	218	232	215	229	197	178	187	169	185	171	140	215	171	206	167	127	176	172	206
11768	NORTHPORT	188	260	304	262	285	237	221	232	202	238	202	173	264	198	260	194	151	217	208	254
11769	OAKDALE	127	174	187	165	183	161	147	153	142	147	143	111	173	142	168	145	105	148	152	168
11770	OCEAN BEACH	148	186	217	189	204	160	177	175	154	189	155	139	193	149	197	142	115	168	146	194
11771	OYSTER BAY	196	261	296	262	280	242	230	234	220	236	220	175	271	216	261	217	165	226	221	261
11772	PATCHOGUE	104	130	131	124	132	117	120	118	117	117	118	89	133	116	129	117	86	119	116	133
11776	PORT JEFFERSON STATI	124	163	159	156	164	144	138	141	131	140	133	107	158	134	153	130	97	136	132	158
11777	PORT JEFFERSON	160	196	220	200	210	177	184	182	169	193	170	142	205	166	202	161	125	178	164	205
11778	ROCKY POINT	123	145	129	140	140	126	129	129	124	133	126	100	139	128	134	121	90	125	119	147
11779	RONKONKOMA	117	153	155	145	157	138	132	135	128	132	129	100	151	129	147	129	94	132	131	151
11780	SAINT JAMES	158	218	245	215	234	205	182	192	176	188	176	140	221	174	212	176	131	183	187	211
11782	SAYVILLE	139	199	216	189	210	179	163	171	155	165	156	125	196	156	190	155	116	163	161	186
11783	SEAFORD	136	196	214	186	208	178	160	168	152	161	154	123	193	154	187	153	114	160	160	183
11784	SELDEN	108	144	147	136	148	130	124	127	120	123	121	94	142	121	138	120	88	124	123	141
11786	SHOREHAM	149	197	211	189	209	191	164	179	160	176	160	125	195	156	192	161	115	169	182	197
11787	SMITHTOWN	150	214	237	207	228	197	175	185	168	178	168	135	213	168	206	168	125	176	177	202
11788	HAUPPAUGE	144	196	213	190	207	179	165	170	158	167	159	126	196	160	189	158	118	164	162	187
11789	SOUND BEACH	101	136	136	128	138	120	116	118	111	115	112	89	133	112	129	111	82	115	112	132
11790	STONY BROOK	161	231	263	226	250	213	189	200	179	196	180	147	232	179	224	178	134	189	188	218
11791	SYOSSET	201	287	337	287	315	265	235	251	220	252	219	185	291	217	281	214	166	233	228	272
11792	WADING RIVER	125	172	175	163	176	152	142	147	135	143	136	110	167	137	161	134	100	141	138	163
11793	WANTAGH	145	210	231	200	223	191	170	180	163	172	164	131	207	164	200	163	122	171	171	195
11794	STONY BROOK	102	148	166	143	159	136	120	127	114	121	115	93	147	115	142	115	86	120	121	138
11795	WEST ISLIP	147	209	225	198	220	187	172	180	163	174	164	132	205	164	199	163	122	172	169	196
11796	WEST SAYVILLE	118	167	174	155	173	148	138	144	132	137	133	105	163	134	158	133	98	138	136	157
11797	WOODBURY	254	359	439	373	403	337	295	316	273	329	271	236	373	268	354	261	208	290	280	345
11798	WYANDANCH	113	128	122	122	127	116	123	120	121	123	123	91	130	121	126	121	88	122	117	137
11801	HICKSVILLE	124	175	186	165	183	157	145	151	139	144	141	110	173	141	167	141	105	145	144	165
11803	PLAINVIEW	171	245	280	240	265	227	200	213	190	209	190	155	246	189	238	189	142	201	201	232
11804	OLD BETHPAGE	167	241	274	235	260	221	196	208	185	203	185	152	241	184	233	184	139	196	195	226
11901	RIVERHEAD	93	105	108	102	108	104	100	102	100	99	100	75	107	98	106	101	71	101	105	117
11933	CALVERTON	131	130	134	130	134	137	126	133	127	129	126	97	126	126	129	130	87	130	137	155
11934	CENTER MORICHES	108	145	147	135	150	126	125	128	118	125	119	95	142	119	139	116	88	123	118	140
11935	CUTCHOGUE	149	169	197	166	180	180	149	167	151	154	151	116	164	146	168	157	106	159	174	189
11937	EAST HAMPTON	142	158	195	155	170	160	146	159	141	149	141	119	155	136	163	140	100	152	150	180
11939	EAST MARION	110	89	143	88	98	117	89	112	93	84	92	81	78	88	96	99	61	104	111	130
11940	EAST MORICHES	119	161	164	151	165	144	138	141	132	137	134	105	159	134	154	133	98	137	135	156
11941	EASTPORT	132	171	172	171	174	158	146	151	140	153	141	115	169	140	164	137	102	145	144	171
11942	EAST QUOGUE	122	164	176	159	172	149	139	144	132	142	133	107	163	133	158	131	98	138	136	159
11944	GREENPORT	91	87	102	88	93	99	92	95	98	91	96	67	92	92	93	103	67	97	106	112
11946	HAMPTON BAYS	124	123	161	120	131	138	116	133	118	113	118	97	116	114	127	123	81	127	133	152
11948	LAUREL	122	170	178	158	176	152	141	147	135	141	136	107	165	136	161	136	100	141	140	161
11949	MANORVILLE	142	167	158	167	167	151	149	150	143	156	145	117	164	147	158	140	104	145	142	171
11950	MASTIC	120	127	106	123	120	110	116	116	112	123	114	88	117	117	114	109	80	112	106	134
11951	MASTIC BEACH	100	111	97	107	107	100	103	102	100	105	102	78	107	103	105	99	72	101	98	118
11952	MATTITUCK	110	141	146	136	147	137	120	128	119	123	119	91	138	117	136	121	86	123	130	143
11953	MIDDLE ISLAND	111	122	117	120	122	114	116	115	114	118	115	87	122	115	119	113	81	115	113	132
11954	MONTAUK	108	104	137	104	112	110	107	115	103	105	104	89	104	100	114	103	74	112	107	131
11955	MORICHES	135	137	168	141	149	140	146	143	141	150	143	108	149	134	154	138	101	147	145	166
11957	ORIENT	124	131	178	130	151	154	118	139	124	133	122	87	129	112	136	130	84	133	155	157
11958	PECONIC	122	98	158	96	107	129	98	124	102	92	101	91	85	97	106	109	67	115	123	144
11961	RIDGE	100	127	141	118	139	134	109	123	112	119	111	80	129	104	129	116	77	118	139	135
11963	SAG HARBOR	155	157	208	157	172	175	147	169	146	151	145	122	150	139	164	149	101	159	166	192
11964	SHELTER ISLAND	122	99	159	97	109	130	99	125	103	93	102	91	86	98	107	110	68	115	124	145
11965	SHELTER ISLAND HEIGH	159	163	225	161	187	194	148	176	156	165	153	112	159	141	170	163	105	167	194	199
11967	SHIRLEY	119	141	125	136	136	123	123	124	117	128	119	95	132	122	128	114	85	120	114	142
11968	SOUTHAMPTON	142	163	203	162	177	161	150	162	141	154	141	122	160	137	168	139	101	153	149	182
11971	SOUTHOLD	117	136	159	133	146	144	121	133	123	125	123	92	135	118	137	128	87	128	142	150
11976	WATER MILL	191	230	298	233	257	235	201	225	192	217	189	164	229	183	236	189	138	209	211	251
11977	WESTHAMPTON	151	197	229	201	216	177	177	181	159	192	159	139	203	155	202	150	118	172	159	201
11978	WESTHAMPTON BEACH	131	162	184	162	174	149	151	152	143	156	144	115	168	138	167	140	105	149	143	171
11980	YAPHANK	121	167	167	157	170	147	138	143	131	139	133	107	161	134	156	131	98	137	134	158
12007	ALCOVE	115	143	127	142	137	140	121	127	123	123	124	95	140	124	134	125	87	124	134	147
12008	ALPLAUS	108	134	120	133	129	132	114	119	115	116	117	89	131	117	126	118	82	116	126	139
12009	ALTAMONT	115	131	123	134	129	125	120	121	118	123	119	93	130	119	127	117	84	119	119	141
12010	AMSTERDAM	74	66	71	67	67	76	71	74	74	66	73	55	66	73	69	78	50	74	80	87
12015	ATHENS	100	89	110	88	91	107	87	101	91	83	90	76	81	90	90	96	61	96	104	119
12017	AUSTERLITZ	142	114	184	112	125	150	114	145	119	107	118	106	99	113	123	127	78	134	143	168
12018	AVERILL PARK	108	126	111	128	122	124	111	115	110	112	111	88	121	113	119	111	78	112	117	135
12019	BALLSTON LAKE	132	154	150	158	154	146	137	140	133	144	135	107	151	134	148	131	96	136	136	162
12020	BALLSTON SPA	114	121	109	120	117	111	114	113	111	118	112	88	117	114	114	108	79	111	108	131
12022	BERLIN	85	78	77	81	79	92	77	87	79	69	78	66	71	81	77	84	53	80	89	101
12023	BERNE	93	106	97	107	103	108	93	99	94	93	95	75	101	96	101	96	66	96	102	116
	NEW YORK	100	106	110	108	107	104	112	106	113	106	114	81	115	110	112	116	83	110	110	124
	UNITED STATES	100	100	100	100	100	100	100	100	100	100	100	100	100	100	100	100	100	100	100	100

ZIP CODE #	POST OFFICE NAME	COUNTY FIPS CODE	POPULATION 2000	POPULATION 2009	POPULATION 2014	2000-2009 ANNUAL RATE % Rate	2000-2009 ANNUAL RATE State Centile	HOUSEHOLDS 2000	HOUSEHOLDS 2009	HOUSEHOLDS 2014	HOUSEHOLDS % Annual Rate 2000-2009	HOUSEHOLDS 2009 Average HH Size	FAMILIES 2000	FAMILIES 2009	FAMILIES % Annual Rate 2000-2009
12024	BRAINARD	021	103	108	109	0.5	71	43	46	47	0.7	2.35	30	32	0.7
12025	BROADALBIN	035	5371	6049	6323	1.3	94	2101	2406	2527	1.5	2.51	1511	1700	1.3
12027	BURNT HILLS	091	3542	3783	3886	0.7	80	1306	1417	1467	0.9	2.66	1016	1083	0.7
12028	BUSKIRK	115	1583	1663	1692	0.5	71	573	614	631	0.7	2.63	428	451	0.6
12029	CANAAN	021	1395	1384	1375	-0.1	30	467	482	481	0.3	2.33	302	305	0.1
12031	CARLISLE	095	54	54	53	0.0	38	18	18	18	0.0	3.00	13	13	0.0
12032	CAROGA LAKE	041	652	658	655	0.1	44	295	305	306	0.4	2.16	195	197	0.1
12033	CASTLETON ON HUDSON	083	8149	8588	8699	0.6	76	3076	3258	3314	0.6	2.60	2274	2370	0.4
12035	CENTRAL BRIDGE	095	918	936	940	0.2	52	347	363	367	0.5	2.58	255	262	0.3
12036	CHARLOTTEVILLE	095	249	259	262	0.4	66	95	101	103	0.7	2.56	65	68	0.5
12037	CHATHAM	021	3981	4120	4137	0.4	66	1673	1773	1792	0.6	2.31	1095	1135	0.4
12041	CLARKSVILLE	001	293	302	305	0.3	59	112	118	120	0.6	2.56	82	84	0.3
12042	CLIMAX	039	236	234	230	-0.1	30	86	87	86	0.1	2.69	65	65	0.0
12043	COBLESKILL	095	7863	7815	7773	-0.1	30	2789	2830	2836	0.2	2.28	1696	1685	-0.1
12046	COEYMANS HOLLOW	001	632	623	616	-0.2	21	218	219	218	0.0	2.84	166	164	-0.1
12047	COHOES	001	18179	18680	18766	0.3	59	7935	8269	8349	0.4	2.22	4578	4634	0.1
12051	COXSACKIE	039	6672	6660	6620	0.0	38	1551	1591	1581	0.3	2.38	988	996	0.1
12052	CROPSEYVILLE	083	1551	1675	1726	0.8	84	591	644	666	0.9	2.60	441	472	0.7
12053	DELANSON	093	4568	4770	4873	0.5	71	1645	1724	1765	0.5	2.76	1279	1322	0.4
12054	DELMAR	001	15690	16991	17319	0.9	87	6263	6790	6926	0.9	2.46	4379	4663	0.7
12056	DUANESBURG	093	2215	2431	2530	1.0	89	846	928	968	1.0	2.62	637	687	0.8
12057	EAGLE BRIDGE	115	2153	2330	2407	0.9	87	793	880	917	1.1	2.62	584	637	0.9
12058	EARLTON	039	1516	1583	1611	0.5	71	589	626	642	0.7	2.53	411	429	0.5
12059	EAST BERNE	001	1953	2042	2068	0.5	71	733	784	799	0.7	2.60	548	575	0.5
12060	EAST CHATHAM	021	1382	1417	1410	0.3	59	565	594	594	0.5	2.26	372	384	0.3
12061	EAST GREENBUSH	083	8149	8826	9088	0.9	87	3085	3377	3495	1.0	2.53	2135	2293	0.8
12062	EAST NASSAU	083	1921	2013	2043	0.5	71	738	781	796	0.6	2.58	541	563	0.4
12064	EAST WORCESTER	077	435	438	432	0.1	44	174	179	178	0.3	2.45	116	117	0.1
12065	CLIFTON PARK	091	38757	42067	43238	0.9	87	15652	17185	17756	1.0	2.43	10556	11362	0.8
12066	ESPERANCE	057	2038	2015	2005	-0.1	30	751	758	760	0.1	2.66	558	556	0.0
12067	FEURA BUSH	001	1681	1676	1667	0.0	38	619	630	632	0.2	2.65	447	446	0.0
12068	FONDA	057	3726	3652	3607	-0.2	21	1420	1421	1412	0.0	2.55	1018	1002	-0.2
12070	FORT JOHNSON	057	1657	1614	1599	-0.3	15	654	659	659	0.1	2.23	458	454	-0.1
12071	FULTONHAM	095	211	215	217	0.2	52	96	101	102	0.6	1.80	67	69	0.3
12072	FULTONVILLE	057	2509	2483	2461	-0.1	30	914	925	923	0.1	2.52	665	663	0.0
12074	GALWAY	091	3113	3504	3696	1.3	94	1167	1338	1422	1.5	2.62	889	1001	1.3
12075	GHENT	021	3255	3461	3505	0.7	80	1168	1274	1299	0.9	2.61	852	914	0.8
12076	GILBOA	095	1379	1417	1426	0.3	59	570	599	607	0.5	2.35	408	422	0.4
12077	GLENMONT	001	5675	5906	6145	0.4	66	2078	2222	2326	0.7	2.57	1625	1703	0.5
12078	GLOVERSVILLE	035	23868	23754	23700	-0.1	30	9807	9950	9983	0.2	2.31	6233	6209	0.0
12083	GREENVILLE	039	3465	3423	3396	-0.1	30	1393	1401	1398	0.1	2.44	956	944	-0.1
12084	GUILDERLAND	001	4693	4930	4970	0.5	71	2363	2494	2531	0.6	1.86	1296	1326	0.2
12086	HAGAMAN	091	1322	1362	1371	0.3	59	525	552	561	0.5	2.46	378	391	0.4
12087	HANNACROIX	039	1360	1308	1289	-0.4	11	509	500	496	-0.2	2.57	378	367	-0.3
12090	HOOSICK FALLS	083	5987	6053	6084	0.1	44	2351	2391	2409	0.2	2.50	1618	1614	0.0
12092	HOWES CAVE	095	1412	1431	1439	0.1	44	554	577	585	0.4	2.48	394	405	0.3
12093	JEFFERSON	095	1672	1702	1706	0.2	52	679	710	719	0.5	2.36	482	495	0.3
12094	JOHNSONVILLE	083	2037	2165	2214	0.7	80	692	742	764	0.8	2.92	527	556	0.6
12095	JOHNSTOWN	035	12808	12740	12717	-0.1	30	4834	4924	4945	0.2	2.45	3134	3129	0.0
12106	KINDERHOOK	021	2576	2673	2673	0.4	66	1047	1117	1130	0.7	2.39	731	765	0.5
12108	LAKE PLEASANT	041	528	500	485	-0.6	4	225	220	216	-0.2	2.20	148	143	-0.4
12110	LATHAM	001	18587	18971	19003	0.2	52	7147	7386	7437	0.4	2.49	4955	5018	0.1
12115	MALDEN BRIDGE	021	83	88	89	0.6	76	41	45	45	1.0	1.96	29	31	0.7
12116	MARYLAND	077	1625	1608	1576	-0.1	30	677	685	678	0.1	2.35	455	450	-0.1
12117	MAYFIELD	035	3112	3382	3486	0.9	87	1216	1354	1406	1.2	2.49	865	946	1.0
12118	MECHANICVILLE	091	11817	13015	13505	1.0	89	4892	5438	5668	1.2	2.39	3198	3516	1.0
12120	MEDUSA	001	536	491	476	-0.9	2	211	197	192	-0.7	2.45	144	131	-1.0
12121	MELROSE	083	2023	2088	2110	0.3	59	718	749	761	0.5	2.79	592	610	0.3
12122	MIDDLEBURGH	095	4310	4416	4449	0.3	59	1748	1830	1859	0.5	2.40	1166	1199	0.3
12123	NASSAU	083	5407	5551	5615	0.3	59	2116	2192	2224	0.4	2.53	1508	1532	0.2
12125	NEW LEBANON	021	1397	1398	1360	0.0	38	551	565	554	0.3	2.36	365	367	0.1
12130	NIVERVILLE	021	838	848	833	0.1	44	319	332	328	0.4	2.54	232	237	0.2
12131	NORTH BLENHEIM	095	92	94	94	0.2	52	39	41	41	0.5	1.66	27	27	0.0
12134	NORTHVILLE	041	3759	3960	4037	0.6	76	1584	1707	1756	0.8	2.32	1094	1156	0.6
12136	OLD CHATHAM	021	890	888	880	0.0	38	377	384	383	0.2	2.30	255	255	0.0
12137	PATTERSONVILLE	093	1451	1604	1668	1.1	91	535	591	616	1.1	2.70	403	439	0.9
12138	PETERSBURG	083	3114	3237	3286	0.4	66	1164	1220	1245	0.5	2.65	844	869	0.3
12139	PISECO	041	218	209	203	-0.5	7	92	90	88	-0.2	2.32	65	62	-0.5
12140	POESTENKILL	083	1460	1548	1586	0.6	76	568	608	625	0.7	2.53	422	444	0.6
12143	RAVENA	001	6247	6154	6092	-0.2	21	2426	2426	2417	0.0	2.50	1663	1628	-0.2
12144	RENSSELAER	083	18075	19242	19757	0.7	80	7551	8151	8417	0.8	2.35	4805	5046	0.5
12147	RENSSELAERVILLE	001	580	555	544	-0.5	7	232	227	224	-0.2	2.39	156	149	-0.5
12148	REXFORD	091	3184	3932	4429	2.3	99	1231	1559	1773	2.6	2.52	936	1168	2.4
12149	RICHMONDVILLE	095	2350	2396	2411	0.2	52	937	980	994	0.5	2.44	657	675	0.3
12150	ROTTERDAM JUNCTION	093	850	941	981	1.1	91	341	377	394	1.1	2.50	211	227	0.8
12151	ROUND LAKE	091	528	533	535	0.1	44	229	235	238	0.3	2.27	151	152	0.1
12153	SAND LAKE	083	859	892	907	0.4	66	328	344	351	0.5	2.59	242	250	0.4
12154	SCHAGHTICOKE	083	2716	2726	2729	0.0	38	1004	1024	1032	0.2	2.66	776	779	0.0
12155	SCHENEVUS	077	2068	2045	2008	-0.1	30	835	843	834	0.1	2.39	573	567	-0.1
12156	SCHODACK LANDING	083	822	826	819	0.1	44	315	319	319	0.1	2.58	248	248	0.0
12157	SCHOHARIE	095	4071	4160	4190	0.2	52	1561	1631	1656	0.5	2.50	1094	1125	0.3
12158	SELKIRK	001	6230	6789	6833	0.9	87	2228	2422	2453	0.9	2.67	1621	1730	0.7
12159	SLINGERLANDS	001	8141	8159	8166	0.0	38	3259	3285	3297	0.1	2.46	1871	1827	-0.3
12160	SLOANSVILLE	095	1009	1016	1015	0.1	44	369	382	385	0.4	2.66	273	279	0.2
12164	SPECULATOR	041	348	329	320	-0.6	4	163	160	157	-0.2	1.99	108	104	-0.4
12165	SPENCERTOWN	021	166	175	176	0.6	76	72	78	79	0.9	2.24	51	54	0.6
12166	SPRAKERS	057	1563	1574	1564	0.1	44	575	591	591	0.3	2.66	430	436	0.1
12167	STAMFORD	025	2771	2924	2920	0.6	76	1086	1178	1189	0.9	2.34	723	770	0.7
12168	STEPHENTOWN	083	1883	1923	1941	0.2	52	755	778	788	0.3	2.47	543	549	0.1
12169	STEPHENTOWN	083	364	370	373	0.2	52	137	141	142	0.3	2.62	98	98	0.0
12170	STILLWATER	091	5287	5659	5832	0.7	80	1947	2117	2197	0.9	2.67	1447	1542	0.7
12173	STUYVESANT	021	2291	2261	2208	-0.1	30	877	890	877	0.2	2.54	660	659	0.0
12175	SUMMIT	095	896	928	939	0.4	66	260	278	284	0.7	3.02	178	187	0.5
12176	SURPRISE	039	122	112	108	-0.9	2	51	48	47	-0.7	2.33	36	34	-0.6
12180	TROY	083	52532	52237	52091	-0.1	30	20866	20810	20812	0.0	2.30	11844	11562	-0.3
	NEW YORK					0.3					0.3	2.61			0.1
	UNITED STATES					1.0					1.1	2.59			0.9

#	POST OFFICE NAME	RACE (%) White 2000	White 2009	Black 2000	Black 2009	Asian/Pacific 2000	Asian/Pacific 2009	% Hispanic Origin 2000	% Hispanic Origin 2009	2009 AGE DISTRIBUTION (%) 0-4	5-9	10-14	15-19	20-24	25-44	45-64	65-84	85+	18+	MEDIAN AGE 2009	% 2009 Males	% 2009 Females
12024	BRAINARD	97.1	95.4	1.0	0.9	1.0	1.9	1.0	1.9	3.7	4.6	5.6	5.6	3.7	15.7	40.7	18.5	1.9	82.4	52.0	49.1	50.9
12025	BROADALBIN	98.3	97.8	0.5	0.7	0.2	0.2	1.0	1.4	5.7	6.3	6.9	7.8	5.2	24.2	30.4	11.8	1.8	76.0	40.9	50.2	49.8
12027	BURNT HILLS	98.7	98.3	0.2	0.3	0.4	0.6	0.5	0.7	5.5	6.1	6.8	7.3	5.4	21.4	32.2	13.2	2.2	76.8	43.4	49.3	50.7
12028	BUSKIRK	97.9	97.1	0.6	0.8	0.3	0.3	0.9	1.3	6.6	7.0	7.5	7.2	4.9	23.8	29.4	11.1	2.6	74.0	40.3	49.3	50.7
12029	CANAAN	86.8	83.5	9.3	11.5	0.8	1.2	2.5	3.0	3.9	5.1	8.7	17.8	2.7	16.8	30.9	12.4	1.7	66.4	40.7	58.2	41.8
12031	CARLISLE	100.0	100.0	0.0	0.0	0.0	0.0	1.9	1.9	7.4	7.4	7.4	7.4	3.7	20.4	35.2	11.1	0.0	70.4	42.5	51.9	48.1
12032	CAROGA LAKE	98.9	98.5	0.0	0.0	0.5	0.8	0.3	0.3	4.9	4.9	6.4	6.1	3.0	22.2	34.2	16.4	2.0	79.6	46.5	53.5	46.5
12033	CASTLETON ON HUDSON	97.6	96.6	0.6	0.8	0.6	0.9	1.3	1.7	5.5	6.0	6.8	7.2	4.9	23.5	30.8	13.1	2.3	77.1	42.6	48.7	51.3
12035	CENTRAL BRIDGE	97.8	96.9	0.2	0.3	0.3	0.6	1.3	1.6	5.6	5.8	6.3	7.6	5.4	27.1	30.8	10.1	1.3	77.7	39.9	50.2	49.8
12036	CHARLOTTEVILLE	96.8	96.5	1.2	1.5	0.4	0.4	1.2	1.2	5.8	6.2	6.6	5.0	3.1	20.8	34.7	16.2	1.5	78.0	46.9	51.0	49.0
12037	CHATHAM	96.5	95.2	1.4	1.8	0.5	0.7	1.2	1.6	5.6	5.8	6.2	6.4	5.5	21.7	32.5	13.9	2.5	78.3	44.2	48.9	51.1
12041	CLARKSVILLE	98.0	97.4	0.0	0.0	0.7	0.7	0.7	1.3	6.0	6.3	7.3	6.6	4.3	21.2	31.8	14.9	1.7	76.2	43.8	51.3	48.7
12042	CLIMAX	97.5	96.6	0.4	0.9	0.0	0.0	0.8	1.3	5.6	5.6	6.0	6.4	4.7	25.2	31.2	13.7	1.7	78.6	42.9	49.6	50.4
12043	COBLESKILL	95.3	94.0	1.9	2.2	0.9	1.3	2.4	3.1	4.4	4.3	5.0	16.8	9.7	19.9	24.4	12.2	3.4	82.3	34.6	49.2	50.8
12046	COEYMANS HOLLOW	98.6	97.9	0.5	0.6	0.2	0.3	1.1	1.8	5.5	5.8	6.4	7.1	5.8	23.4	33.2	11.6	1.3	78.2	42.2	50.6	49.4
12047	COHOES	94.7	92.7	2.2	2.9	1.2	1.7	1.9	2.6	6.2	5.9	5.7	6.2	6.8	26.3	26.6	13.2	3.0	78.3	39.6	47.2	52.8
12051	COXSACKIE	69.2	65.8	22.6	23.8	0.7	1.9	12.4	13.7	3.9	4.0	3.7	15.9	21.8	24.9	17.2	7.4	1.2	85.8	25.5	63.6	36.4
12052	CROPSEYVILLE	98.2	97.4	0.1	0.2	0.2	0.4	0.5	0.5	5.9	6.4	6.8	6.3	4.8	25.1	31.9	11.6	1.2	77.0	41.7	50.6	49.4
12053	DELANSON	97.8	96.9	0.5	0.6	0.3	0.4	0.7	0.9	5.6	6.2	7.0	7.2	4.7	23.6	33.8	10.5	1.3	76.4	42.3	50.2	49.8
12054	DELMAR	96.3	94.9	1.2	1.5	1.4	2.0	1.4	1.8	5.6	6.2	7.1	6.9	4.9	20.2	32.7	13.2	3.3	76.4	44.4	47.7	52.3
12056	DUANESBURG	98.0	97.1	0.3	0.4	0.3	0.5	0.9	1.2	4.3	4.8	5.8	7.4	4.9	23.2	36.0	12.2	1.5	80.5	44.7	49.7	50.3
12057	EAGLE BRIDGE	97.1	96.1	1.0	1.3	0.5	0.7	0.9	1.2	5.1	5.5	6.1	6.8	4.8	23.8	32.5	13.8	1.6	78.7	43.4	49.6	50.4
12058	EARLTON	97.7	96.8	0.9	1.1	0.1	0.2	2.0	2.7	6.5	6.7	6.9	6.4	5.0	22.9	30.9	13.3	1.3	75.8	42.1	51.0	49.0
12059	EAST BERNE	98.0	97.1	0.4	0.6	0.4	0.6	0.7	1.0	5.2	5.7	6.6	6.9	5.1	23.1	34.3	11.8	1.4	78.4	43.3	48.9	51.1
12060	EAST CHATHAM	94.0	92.2	2.9	3.7	1.2	1.8	1.2	1.6	4.8	5.7	6.8	9.3	4.0	19.5	35.0	13.0	1.8	75.7	44.8	50.3	49.7
12061	EAST GREENBUSH	95.0	93.4	2.3	2.8	1.7	2.4	1.4	1.8	5.4	5.6	6.1	6.4	5.5	24.3	31.0	12.7	2.9	78.7	42.7	47.0	53.0
12062	EAST NASSAU	96.7	95.7	0.9	1.2	0.6	0.8	1.0	1.3	5.4	5.8	6.4	6.8	5.4	23.6	33.4	11.9	1.2	78.2	42.7	48.9	51.1
12064	EAST WORCESTER	97.0	95.7	0.7	0.9	0.2	0.5	0.9	0.9	5.3	5.9	6.2	6.2	4.6	21.9	32.6	15.3	2.1	78.5	45.0	49.8	50.2
12065	CLIFTON PARK	94.4	92.7	1.4	1.7	2.5	3.5	1.7	2.1	6.2	6.4	6.8	6.5	5.4	26.1	30.4	10.8	1.3	76.5	40.6	49.1	50.9
12066	ESPERANCE	98.0	97.3	0.5	0.6	0.3	0.4	1.0	1.3	6.1	6.5	6.9	6.8	4.7	24.7	31.5	11.4	1.4	76.1	41.3	50.9	49.1
12067	FEURA BUSH	97.7	96.9	0.5	0.7	0.6	0.8	1.3	1.8	6.0	6.5	7.0	6.5	4.8	22.6	32.5	12.8	1.4	76.3	42.5	50.2	49.8
12068	FONDA	97.3	96.5	0.5	0.5	0.7	1.0	1.5	1.9	6.1	6.0	6.1	6.6	5.7	25.0	29.4	13.0	2.1	77.5	41.3	47.8	52.2
12070	FORT JOHNSON	92.5	91.0	5.7	6.8	0.2	0.2	3.5	4.5	4.4	5.1	7.1	11.5	3.6	22.7	30.2	13.0	2.4	74.0	41.7	51.7	48.3
12071	FULTONHAM	89.6	87.9	8.1	9.3	0.0	0.0	5.2	6.5	4.7	4.7	5.6	6.0	7.9	27.4	28.4	13.5	1.9	81.4	39.6	56.7	43.3
12072	FULTONVILLE	95.7	94.7	1.9	2.2	0.8	1.2	2.2	2.9	5.1	5.6	6.3	7.3	5.6	26.3	30.1	11.9	1.8	78.4	40.6	52.0	48.0
12074	GALWAY	98.3	97.7	0.2	0.3	0.4	0.5	1.1	1.4	5.3	5.9	6.6	7.0	4.8	23.3	33.8	12.0	1.4	77.8	43.2	50.0	50.0
12075	GHENT	96.9	95.7	1.1	1.4	0.3	0.5	1.3	1.8	4.9	5.4	6.0	6.5	4.2	21.6	33.8	14.1	3.5	79.4	45.8	49.6	50.4
12076	GILBOA	96.3	95.3	0.9	1.1	0.3	0.4	2.1	2.8	4.9	4.8	5.8	5.3	3.5	21.5	35.1	17.4	1.9	81.2	47.8	48.8	51.2
12077	GLENMONT	93.3	90.8	3.3	4.5	1.9	2.7	2.1	2.8	7.1	7.4	7.8	9.1	4.9	22.4	30.7	9.4	1.2	71.3	39.0	48.9	51.1
12078	GLOVERSVILLE	95.5	94.2	2.0	2.2	0.6	1.1	1.7	2.1	6.2	6.0	5.9	6.5	5.9	25.1	27.3	13.6	3.4	77.7	40.8	48.7	51.3
12083	GREENVILLE	97.5	96.5	0.5	0.7	0.6	1.0	1.5	2.0	5.2	5.6	6.3	6.8	4.4	21.9	32.2	15.5	2.2	78.4	44.9	48.3	51.7
12084	GUILDERLAND	86.5	82.2	4.0	5.2	7.5	10.0	2.5	3.2	5.1	4.6	4.9	5.6	6.6	27.4	27.8	13.0	5.1	81.6	42.1	45.9	54.1
12086	HAGAMAN	98.3	97.4	0.2	0.2	0.5	0.7	1.4	2.1	5.4	5.8	6.3	6.5	4.8	22.6	31.4	14.8	2.4	78.4	44.0	49.3	50.7
12087	HANNACROIX	97.4	96.5	0.6	0.8	0.4	0.6	1.3	1.8	5.3	5.7	6.3	6.7	4.7	22.0	33.4	13.6	2.4	78.5	44.6	48.5	51.5
12090	HOOSICK FALLS	97.9	97.3	0.5	0.6	0.4	0.6	0.9	1.1	6.4	6.4	6.5	6.6	6.3	23.7	28.2	13.1	2.9	76.6	40.8	47.5	52.5
12092	HOWES CAVE	97.7	97.1	0.4	0.5	0.2	0.3	1.3	1.5	5.5	5.9	6.8	6.6	5.2	24.2	31.7	12.4	1.7	77.8	42.0	48.6	51.4
12093	JEFFERSON	96.0	95.2	2.2	2.5	0.1	0.1	1.9	2.3	5.5	5.0	6.5	6.0	4.3	21.3	34.8	14.6	2.1	79.0	45.8	51.2	48.8
12094	JOHNSONVILLE	97.7	97.1	0.6	0.8	0.2	0.3	0.5	0.7	7.5	7.5	7.3	7.0	5.9	27.2	27.9	8.8	0.9	73.4	36.7	50.1	49.9
12095	JOHNSTOWN	94.7	93.0	2.4	2.7	1.0	1.8	1.9	2.3	5.5	5.7	6.0	7.2	5.9	25.5	27.3	13.7	3.2	78.3	40.8	49.6	50.4
12106	KINDERHOOK	98.0	97.2	0.5	0.7	0.5	0.9	1.0	1.4	4.9	5.1	5.8	6.8	5.3	21.5	32.9	15.3	2.4	79.9	45.4	48.0	52.0
12108	LAKE PLEASANT	97.5	97.0	0.9	1.2	0.4	0.4	0.9	1.4	4.6	5.2	5.0	4.2	3.2	22.4	33.2	19.6	2.6	82.4	48.5	50.6	49.4
12110	LATHAM	91.0	87.4	2.6	3.0	4.6	6.3	1.8	2.9	4.9	5.2	5.7	6.5	6.6	25.4	30.0	13.3	2.5	80.5	41.9	47.5	52.5
12115	MALDEN BRIDGE	96.4	94.3	1.2	1.1	1.2	2.3	1.2	1.1	3.4	3.4	5.7	6.8	3.4	19.3	36.4	19.3	2.3	83.0	50.6	51.1	48.9
12116	MARYLAND	98.2	97.8	0.5	0.5	0.1	0.2	1.8	2.4	4.0	4.2	4.8	5.8	4.0	22.2	36.7	16.4	1.9	83.4	47.8	48.6	51.4
12117	MAYFIELD	98.6	98.1	0.4	0.5	0.0	0.1	0.9	1.2	4.8	6.6	7.0	7.5	5.4	23.6	31.9	11.3	1.9	76.7	41.4	50.4	49.6
12118	MECHANICVILLE	97.7	97.0	0.5	0.6	0.7	0.9	1.1	1.3	6.3	6.3	6.6	6.7	5.7	27.0	27.9	11.3	2.2	76.5	39.4	48.9	51.1
12120	MEDUSA	96.5	95.3	2.1	2.6	0.2	0.4	1.1	1.2	5.7	5.9	6.7	6.5	3.3	20.8	34.6	14.7	1.8	77.0	45.7	49.7	50.3
12121	MELROSE	98.4	97.8	0.4	0.5	0.6	0.9	0.7	0.9	5.5	5.9	6.8	7.1	5.0	23.4	32.1	12.9	1.2	77.5	42.5	49.1	50.9
12122	MIDDLEBURGH	97.7	97.1	0.4	0.5	0.2	0.2	1.7	2.1	5.6	5.7	6.0	6.3	5.3	24.0	30.9	14.2	2.2	78.8	42.9	48.8	51.2
12123	NASSAU	96.7	95.7	1.0	1.3	0.5	0.8	1.4	1.9	5.4	5.6	6.1	6.8	5.8	25.1	32.4	11.3	1.6	78.8	41.8	49.4	50.6
12125	NEW LEBANON	95.5	93.8	1.3	1.7	1.5	2.2	1.1	1.5	5.2	5.9	6.2	8.9	5.2	20.9	33.3	12.8	1.6	76.4	43.1	48.1	51.9
12130	NIVERVILLE	97.6	96.6	0.8	1.2	0.2	0.5	0.5	0.6	5.1	5.3	5.9	6.7	5.3	24.9	30.8	14.4	1.7	79.6	43.0	50.9	49.1
12131	NORTH BLENHEIM	81.3	78.7	15.4	17.0	0.0	0.0	9.9	11.7	3.2	3.2	4.3	5.3	16.0	31.9	23.4	10.6	2.1	85.1	35.6	67.0	33.0
12134	NORTHVILLE	98.4	97.9	0.2	0.3	0.3	0.4	1.0	1.3	5.2	5.5	5.5	6.0	4.3	21.4	34.3	15.8	1.9	80.1	46.2	50.5	49.5
12136	OLD CHATHAM	96.6	95.4	1.2	1.6	0.8	1.1	0.6	0.8	3.8	5.4	6.3	6.8	3.3	20.4	38.1	14.1	1.9	80.0	47.3	50.5	49.5
12137	PATTERSONVILLE	98.5	97.8	0.3	0.3	0.3	0.5	0.8	1.0	5.0	5.8	6.4	6.7	4.9	23.8	35.2	10.9	1.3	78.4	43.4	51.9	48.1
12138	PETERSBURG	98.3	97.7	0.1	0.2	0.5	0.8	0.6	0.8	6.1	6.5	6.9	6.8	5.0	23.9	30.9	12.5	1.4	76.0	41.7	50.1	49.9
12139	PISECO	99.1	99.0	0.0	0.0	0.0	0.0	0.5	0.5	3.3	4.3	3.8	3.8	3.8	19.6	37.8	21.5	1.9	85.6	52.6	51.7	48.3
12140	POESTENKILL	98.4	97.5	0.2	0.3	0.3	0.6	0.5	0.8	5.0	5.7	6.8	7.8	4.4	24.8	33.1	11.0	1.3	76.7	42.1	50.0	50.0
12143	RAVENA	93.9	91.9	2.4	3.2	0.5	0.7	3.5	4.6	6.9	6.7	6.5	6.6	7.0	27.0	26.3	11.1	1.9	75.6	37.2	48.6	51.4
12144	RENSSELAER	92.0	89.9	4.5	5.4	1.5	2.1	1.6	2.0	6.1	6.0	6.3	6.6	6.0	25.3	29.5	12.2	2.0	77.4	40.7	47.8	52.2
12147	RENSSELAERVILLE	94.8	93.2	2.2	2.9	0.0	0.0	1.6	2.0	4.9	4.7	7.2	7.6	3.2	21.4	36.9	12.6	1.4	77.3	45.4	53.5	46.5
12148	REXFORD	95.2	93.6	0.8	0.9	2.3	3.4	1.4	1.8	6.6	7.4	8.4	7.2	3.6	21.7	31.9	11.2	1.9	72.9	42.2	48.3	51.7
12149	RICHMONDVILLE	96.7	95.9	0.9	1.0	0.5	0.6	1.6	2.0	6.6	7.1	7.3	6.9	4.9	24.3	28.1	13.0	1.7	74.6	39.8	51.1	48.9
12150	ROTTERDAM JUNCTION	97.8	96.8	0.7	1.0	0.7	1.1	1.3	1.9	4.7	4.5	4.7	5.1	7.0	25.0	31.6	14.9	2.7	83.0	44.3	48.4	51.6
12151	ROUND LAKE	95.6	94.4	0.9	1.1	0.9	1.3	2.1	2.4	6.0	6.4	6.8	6.2	4.7	29.1	31.0	9.0	0.9	76.9	39.6	49.3	50.7
12153	SAND LAKE	98.5	98.1	0.0	0.0	0.3	0.6	1.0	1.3	5.4	5.6	6.3	6.7	5.4	22.5	34.2	12.7	1.2	78.4	43.7	48.7	51.3
12154	SCHAGHTICOKE	98.1	97.5	0.6	0.8	0.3	0.4	0.7	0.9	6.6	6.8	7.3	7.5	5.5	24.2	30.2	10.6	1.3	74.8	39.9	49.9	50.1
12155	SCHENEVUS	98.3	97.8	0.4	0.4	0.3	0.4	1.2	1.6	5.8	5.8	5.9	6.5	5.0	23.3	29.9	15.4	2.4	78.5	43.2	50.4	49.6
12156	SCHODACK LANDING	97.7	97.0	0.7	1.0	0.4	0.5	1.5	1.9	6.3	6.8	7.4	7.6	4.4	25.8	29.5	10.9	1.3	74.7	40.8	50.4	49.6
12157	SCHOHARIE	98.4	98.0	0.4	0.5	0.1	0.2	1.1	1.3	5.9	5.8	6.3	6.9	6.1	23.6	29.8	13.1	2.4	77.7	41.7	48.0	52.0
12158	SELKIRK	92.4	89.9	4.3	5.7	1.2	1.7	2.5	3.1	6.5	6.5	6.8	9.0	6.2	24.1	28.6	10.8	1.5	74.4	38.4	49.0	51.0
12159	SLINGERLANDS	91.5	88.0	2.3	3.5	4.8	6.5	1.8	2.5	5.3	5.6	6.3	6.4	5.6	24.0	31.4	11.7	3.6	78.5	42.7	47.4	52.6
12160	SLOANSVILLE	98.0	97.4	0.5	0.5	0.3	0.5	1.4	1.9	6.7	7.1	7.6	7.2	4.9	24.5	30.5	10.3	1.2	74.1	39.7	51.2	48.8
12164	SPECULATOR	97.4	96.7	1.1	1.2	0.3	0.6	1.1	1.2	4.9	5.2	5.2	4.3	3.3	22.8	33.1	18.8	2.4	81.8	47.7	51.1	48.9
12165	SPENCERTOWN	96.4	94.9	1.8	2.3	0.6	1.1	1.2	1.7	3.4	3.4	4.6	5.7	3.4	17.7	40.6	19.4	1.7	85.1	52.0	48.6	51.4
12166	SPRAKERS	98.1	97.5	0.5	0.6	0.3	0.4	1.1	1.5	5.3	5.7	6.5	7.2	5.4	23.4	33.2	11.8	1.4	78.0	42.4	50.8	49.2
12167	STAMFORD	96.8	96.0	0.8	0.9	0.6	0.8	2.5	3.2	5.2	5.1	6.1	5.7	4.7	20.8	29.8	17.8	4.8	79.6	46.7	48.1	51.9
12168	STEPHENTOWN	98.2	97.7	0.3	0.4	0.2	0.3	1.1	1.5	6.1	6.4	6.9	7.0	5.4	24.4	32.0	10.8	1.0	76.2	41.1	48.7	51.3
12169	STEPHENTOWN	98.4	97.3	0.3	0.5	0.0	0.5	1.1	1.4	5.9	6.5	6.8	6.8	5.1	24.6	32.7	10.8	0.8	76.2	41.4	49.7	50.3
12170	STILLWATER	98.0	97.4	0.5	0.5	0.5	0.7	0.7	1.0	6.5	6.7	6.9	7.0	5.6	26.4	29.6	9.9	1.4	75.6	39.1	50.4	49.6
12173	STUYVESANT	97.4	96.5	1.0	1.4	0.3	0.5	1.1	1.4	6.3	6.4	6.9	7.2	5.5	25.7	29.4	11.1	1.7	75.8	40.0	49.2	50.8
12175	SUMMIT	91.6	90.5	6.0	6.6	0.3	0.3	3.9	4.6	4.8	5.4	5.8	5.4	6.0	24.0	31.9	14.9	1.7	80.6	43.7	55.3	44.7
12176	SURPRISE	98.3	97.3	0.0	0.0	0.8	1.8	1.7	0.9	5.4	6.3	8.0	6.3	3.6	24.1	27.7	17.0	1.8	75.0	42.5	49.1	50.9
12180	TROY	82.7	78.6	9.7	11.8	3.4	4.4	3.6	4.6	6.1	5.7	5.5	8.5	10.4	26.5	23.2	11.4	2.7	79.4	35.0	49.6	50.4
	NEW YORK	67.9	64.8	15.9	16.5	5.6	6.9	15.1	16.7	6.5	6.4	6.4	7.1	7.0	27.0	26.3	11.2	2.1	76.6	37.5	48.4	51.6
	UNITED STATES	75.1	72.0	12.3	12.7	3.8	4.6	12.5	15.7	6.8	6.7	6.6	7.1	6.9	27.0	26.0	10.9	1.9	75.7	36.9	49.2	50.8

#	POST OFFICE NAME	2009 Per Capita Income	2009 HH Income Base	2009 Household Income Distribution (%): Less than \$25,000	\$25,000 to \$49,999	\$50,000 to \$99,999	\$100,000 to \$149,999	\$150,000 or More	Median Household Income: 2009	2014	2009 National Centile	2009 State Centile	2009 Home Value Base	2009 Home Value Distribution (%): Less than \$50,000	\$50,000 to \$89,999	\$90,000 to \$174,999	\$175,000 to \$399,999	\$400,000 or More	2009 Median Home Value
12024	BRAINARD	42970	46	8.7	13.0	50.0	17.4	10.9	76513	73658	90	82	37	0.0	2.7	21.6	54.1	21.6	246875
12025	BROADALBIN	23362	2406	17.8	30.1	42.0	6.6	3.5	51656	53332	65	50	1957	6.8	16.4	45.7	27.9	3.3	136329
12027	BURNT HILLS	31800	1417	8.1	19.3	36.1	30.3	6.2	77528	80683	91	83	1162	0.7	0.3	18.3	71.7	9.0	224320
12028	BUSKIRK	23877	614	17.1	25.9	45.4	7.7	3.9	54896	56841	71	57	480	4.2	4.4	33.3	47.5	10.6	193056
12029	CANAAN	33319	482	13.5	22.6	36.7	15.8	11.4	65519	66330	84	72	385	1.6	1.6	27.0	49.1	20.8	243750
12031	CARLISLE	16435	18	22.2	33.3	38.9	5.6	0.0	45000	45000	48	31	14	0.0	0.0	64.3	35.7	0.0	165000
12032	CAROGA LAKE	25485	305	23.9	29.8	37.7	5.6	3.0	46500	48197	53	35	265	9.4	31.3	38.1	17.0	4.2	104435
12033	CASTLETON ON HUDSON	32242	3258	8.4	17.7	44.1	21.7	8.1	73801	75617	89	80	2526	4.0	1.2	22.4	66.5	5.9	215532
12035	CENTRAL BRIDGE	22059	363	17.6	30.6	41.3	9.1	1.4	51399	51906	65	49	272	3.3	4.0	54.4	33.5	4.8	161207
12036	CHARLOTTEVILLE	19593	101	22.8	30.7	39.6	5.9	1.0	47348	48079	55	39	88	8.0	8.0	50.0	30.7	3.4	145588
12037	CHATHAM	30874	1773	18.0	27.7	38.8	8.7	6.7	55146	54934	71	57	1287	12.0	5.4	36.1	35.3	11.2	167891
12041	CLARKSVILLE	31668	118	11.0	27.1	40.7	12.7	8.5	61485	67361	79	67	93	0.0	1.1	35.5	47.3	16.1	199038
12042	CLIMAX	23878	87	16.1	18.4	50.6	12.6	2.3	60314	61297	78	64	72	2.8	5.6	55.6	30.6	5.6	155769
12043	COBLESKILL	22497	2830	28.6	27.1	33.1	8.1	3.2	44000	46762	45	27	1693	2.7	3.9	48.7	41.1	3.5	168784
12046	COEYMANS HOLLOW	31119	219	6.4	17.4	51.1	17.4	7.8	76686	77980	90	82	174	1.1	1.1	35.1	58.6	4.0	205556
12047	COHOES	24669	8269	27.9	27.4	34.3	6.6	3.7	44225	48086	46	28	4033	0.9	2.0	57.3	36.8	3.0	164442
12051	COXSACKIE	20526	1591	24.5	25.1	37.4	10.4	2.6	50352	51759	62	46	1041	5.8	6.4	54.1	30.5	3.3	152340
12052	CROPSEYVILLE	28751	644	11.5	22.7	46.6	13.5	5.7	65436	67869	84	72	550	2.0	4.4	38.4	50.0	5.3	185069
12053	DELANSON	27141	1724	10.6	21.0	46.0	16.9	5.5	66212	68100	84	73	1451	2.0	2.5	29.9	56.6	9.0	205733
12054	DELMAR	43335	6790	5.2	17.1	39.1	20.8	17.8	81442	84499	93	85	4988	0.2	0.0	7.5	78.8	13.5	266836
12056	DUANESBURG	28427	928	10.6	27.0	38.1	19.5	4.7	65703	68525	84	72	756	1.1	2.4	27.8	61.1	7.7	206597
12057	EAGLE BRIDGE	21428	880	22.8	34.8	30.9	8.3	3.2	44060	46545	46	27	715	4.3	4.9	37.6	43.8	9.4	181320
12058	EARLTON	21150	626	20.1	31.6	40.4	5.9	1.9	48354	49460	57	41	482	7.7	13.5	49.0	28.2	1.7	147222
12059	EAST BERNE	27823	784	14.5	23.2	45.9	11.0	5.4	62425	65850	81	68	633	5.1	2.4	30.0	56.4	6.2	197083
12060	EAST CHATHAM	32899	594	14.5	27.4	38.6	11.6	7.9	60487	60849	78	65	464	5.0	3.0	33.2	44.0	14.9	204054
12061	EAST GREENBUSH	33938	3377	6.0	23.3	41.1	19.4	10.2	71562	74089	88	78	2381	1.5	1.1	21.6	61.6	14.2	237354
12062	EAST NASSAU	26114	781	14.7	25.5	46.2	9.9	3.7	60198	62073	78	64	611	5.6	4.6	34.5	48.4	6.9	185156
12064	EAST WORCESTER	18427	179	31.3	33.0	29.6	4.5	1.7	36946	39195	23	7	145	11.0	12.4	55.9	17.2	3.4	126250
12065	CLIFTON PARK	38522	17185	7.8	18.4	38.4	22.2	13.0	75217	79130	89	81	11625	7.4	1.4	14.3	64.7	12.2	239480
12066	ESPERANCE	22072	758	16.0	29.7	43.8	8.8	1.7	54059	54496	70	55	627	7.8	9.3	46.9	32.1	4.0	150142
12067	FEURA BUSH	31182	630	13.5	21.6	40.8	15.2	8.9	66638	70094	85	73	488	3.9	1.0	26.6	48.4	20.1	220270
12068	FONDA	21735	1421	23.4	27.7	38.9	7.6	2.4	48753	49609	58	42	1097	11.4	18.2	46.9	22.4	1.0	123509
12070	FORT JOHNSON	28599	659	13.1	35.1	35.7	10.8	5.5	52244	53073	66	52	553	7.1	18.8	43.4	29.7	1.1	124617
12071	FULTONHAM	26286	101	26.7	32.7	30.7	5.9	4.0	43069	46128	43	23	88	5.7	6.8	45.5	36.4	5.7	161538
12072	FULTONVILLE	20878	925	19.9	32.3	41.3	4.4	2.1	47692	48656	56	40	738	17.6	20.1	44.9	16.4	1.1	108884
12074	GALWAY	27456	1338	13.8	22.1	46.9	13.5	3.7	62943	66296	81	69	1118	2.5	2.5	30.7	55.5	8.8	200463
12075	GHENT	27537	1274	16.2	27.2	40.5	8.6	7.5	60197	58879	78	64	985	3.0	6.1	40.6	42.2	8.0	175644
12076	GILBOA	21710	599	24.9	34.6	30.9	7.3	2.3	41921	44829	39	20	520	9.0	10.4	39.4	31.0	10.2	156148
12077	GLENMONT	41424	2222	6.0	11.7	41.0	23.7	17.6	86176	88729	94	87	1726	0.2	0.1	11.0	71.8	17.0	286957
12078	GLOVERSVILLE	21286	9950	30.3	29.2	32.2	6.1	2.3	39437	43310	31	13	6514	7.2	30.2	48.8	11.6	2.3	104865
12083	GREENVILLE	24980	1401	21.0	25.3	41.6	8.9	3.1	53621	56370	69	54	1081	1.1	5.3	43.6	45.5	4.5	175115
12084	GUILDERLAND	46117	2494	10.9	19.7	42.1	16.6	10.7	74219	76277	89	80	1177	0.1	0.2	17.7	57.9	24.2	302097
12086	HAGAMAN	25878	552	16.3	23.9	46.2	11.1	2.5	60909	62051	79	66	451	2.4	10.0	49.0	34.6	4.0	156866
12087	HANNACROIX	25350	500	10.4	26.2	50.0	11.4	2.0	61160	62577	79	66	412	2.2	7.5	42.5	45.1	2.7	170673
12090	HOOSICK FALLS	23357	2391	20.3	28.8	41.3	6.9	2.7	50655	53921	63	47	1641	2.2	3.9	53.7	35.1	5.1	163229
12092	HOWES CAVE	24152	577	17.9	35.2	34.8	9.2	2.9	47212	49112	55	38	434	7.1	4.6	48.6	30.9	8.8	161446
12093	JEFFERSON	23854	710	24.4	31.3	33.0	6.9	4.5	43764	46968	45	26	589	5.9	13.6	44.1	32.6	3.7	148289
12094	JOHNSONVILLE	21331	742	16.2	19.8	54.9	7.8	1.3	60548	62566	78	65	599	8.2	6.2	36.7	46.9	2.0	173253
12095	JOHNSTOWN	20844	4924	28.7	27.7	34.9	6.5	2.3	43731	46566	45	26	3251	5.3	26.1	50.3	16.8	1.4	115090
12106	KINDERHOOK	32071	1117	10.8	26.2	39.7	15.5	7.7	66641	66937	85	74	870	2.5	4.5	32.0	52.5	8.5	202857
12108	LAKE PLEASANT	22396	220	27.7	37.3	26.4	5.9	2.7	36563	38252	22	7	170	4.7	14.1	42.9	30.0	8.2	147500
12110	LATHAM	33676	7386	8.6	21.3	44.9	15.3	9.8	70682	72888	87	77	5222	1.0	0.2	18.0	73.0	7.9	222081
12115	MALDEN BRIDGE	54668	45	6.7	13.3	46.7	20.0	13.3	78022	79149	91	83	36	0.0	2.8	16.7	55.6	25.0	260000
12116	MARYLAND	21981	685	26.6	30.7	32.0	9.1	1.8	41828	43850	39	20	555	9.0	19.6	49.4	21.4	0.5	127522
12117	MAYFIELD	21463	1354	22.9	31.5	37.2	6.1	2.3	46369	48059	52	35	1073	5.6	26.1	40.1	22.9	5.3	124753
12118	MECHANICVILLE	25988	5438	17.6	27.8	38.9	12.2	3.5	54035	59008	70	55	3531	5.4	3.2	39.5	45.9	6.0	177999
12120	MEDUSA	23507	197	19.8	29.4	41.6	5.6	3.6	50922	57403	63	48	158	1.3	3.8	42.4	44.3	8.2	180263
12121	MELROSE	26067	749	14.7	16.2	48.1	18.4	2.7	73098	75238	88	79	648	0.6	1.5	30.1	59.1	8.6	201563
12122	MIDDLEBURGH	21825	1830	24.5	31.4	35.5	6.6	2.0	43912	46406	45	27	1409	6.4	7.3	50.3	31.4	4.6	156914
12123	NASSAU	28653	2192	12.1	26.3	43.7	12.5	5.4	62062	64721	80	68	1652	5.3	2.8	37.0	45.6	9.3	184375
12125	NEW LEBANON	26521	565	15.2	28.0	44.2	9.0	3.5	59293	58521	77	62	416	9.1	4.8	34.1	42.8	9.1	181452
12130	NIVERVILLE	29600	332	8.1	25.9	41.6	20.2	4.2	66490	66748	85	73	273	4.8	5.1	62.6	24.2	3.3	145034
12131	NORTH BLENHEIM	29068	41	22.0	34.1	34.1	4.9	4.9	45747	47948	51	33	36	0.0	5.6	50.0	38.9	5.6	166667
12134	NORTHVILLE	24014	1707	23.3	29.1	37.8	7.0	2.9	47831	50209	56	40	1333	4.8	10.3	45.4	32.7	6.8	150612
12136	OLD CHATHAM	39933	384	13.0	25.3	38.0	12.2	11.5	62974	62336	81	69	288	0.7	2.1	26.4	50.0	20.8	239623
12137	PATTERSONVILLE	27419	591	10.2	19.8	51.3	14.6	4.2	67343	68854	85	74	498	1.0	2.2	24.5	60.4	11.8	236517
12138	PETERSBURG	23802	1220	18.2	26.6	40.7	11.5	3.0	55960	60694	73	59	1000	4.5	7.7	42.3	39.9	5.6	168952
12139	PISECO	24919	90	25.6	33.3	32.2	6.7	2.2	43430	45000	44	24	79	7.6	11.4	46.8	30.4	3.8	142500
12140	POESTENKILL	28633	608	8.1	26.5	49.0	12.8	3.6	73601	75533	89	80	488	1.8	2.5	24.6	61.1	10.0	220513
12143	RAVENA	27742	2426	15.2	25.0	42.4	12.3	5.2	60927	64198	79	66	1580	7.0	2.2	45.6	42.5	2.8	170843
12144	RENSSELAER	28895	8151	16.4	27.9	38.1	13.2	4.4	56917	61318	74	60	5335	0.8	2.6	44.6	48.3	3.7	177837
12147	RENSSELAERVILLE	26659	227	21.1	25.1	41.0	7.5	5.3	54909	61018	71	57	181	1.7	1.7	35.4	50.3	11.0	197283
12148	REXFORD	43425	1559	7.9	11.7	29.9	34.5	16.0	100654	103198	97	92	1291	0.2	0.0	12.5	63.7	23.5	290568
12149	RICHMONDVILLE	21208	980	22.6	35.0	33.6	6.6	2.2	43804	46401	45	26	717	9.6	5.6	46.9	35.3	2.6	154405
12150	ROTTERDAM JUNCTION	25700	377	17.0	27.6	43.5	7.4	4.5	57611	62649	75	61	250	0.0	2.4	41.2	54.0	2.4	187121
12151	ROUND LAKE	30994	235	8.5	30.6	43.0	11.9	6.0	60805	63466	79	65	180	15.6	10.6	30.6	40.6	2.8	159211
12153	SAND LAKE	34174	344	10.5	17.4	39.0	20.6	12.5	73014	75506	88	79	287	4.9	3.1	31.0	49.5	11.5	192898
12154	SCHAGHTICOKE	25970	1024	16.7	23.8	41.7	13.4	4.4	60327	62970	78	64	811	3.3	1.6	27.0	58.1	10.0	206988
12155	SCHENEVUS	20826	843	27.3	32.6	32.3	6.0	1.8	40194	42251	33	15	651	10.9	21.8	48.8	16.0	2.5	116557
12156	SCHODACK LANDING	28416	319	8.2	24.5	46.7	16.3	4.4	63930	66531	82	71	260	1.5	2.3	28.5	64.2	3.5	216071
12157	SCHOHARIE	23618	1631	18.6	30.8	38.0	8.4	4.2	50510	51767	62	46	1231	6.4	4.7	40.5	41.8	6.6	173010
12158	SELKIRK	28569	2422	9.7	25.3	42.4	15.7	6.8	63997	67122	82	71	1775	5.9	0.8	34.2	54.1	5.0	188503
12159	SLINGERLANDS	39088	3285	11.8	23.1	34.9	15.8	14.9	68986	72744	86	75	1840	0.6	0.1	15.9	56.2	27.2	300475
12160	SLOANSVILLE	20752	382	16.5	31.2	44.5	6.8	1.0	51813	51830	66	51	314	5.7	9.2	52.2	29.6	3.2	151316
12164	SPECULATOR	24610	160	27.5	37.5	26.3	6.3	2.5	36883	38920	23	7	123	2.4	13.0	46.3	29.3	8.9	147500
12165	SPENCERTOWN	43617	78	12.8	21.8	37.2	12.8	15.4	65891	64270	84	73	62	0.0	0.0	24.2	54.8	21.0	242308
12166	SPRAKERS	19731	591	21.8	31.3	39.3	5.9	1.7	46795	47919	54	36	499	19.0	18.4	42.1	16.8	3.6	113393
12167	STAMFORD	22417	1178	28.3	30.1	31.8	6.4	3.4	42903	44705	42	22	841	7.0	16.1	45.9	28.2	2.9	135585
12168	STEPHENTOWN	22717	778	16.2	31.0	45.4	6.0	1.4	51636	53927	65	50	614	8.1	4.4	38.8	45.3	3.4	173276
12169	STEPHENTOWN	21711	141	14.9	30.5	47.5	6.4	0.7	52746	54421	67	53	111	9.9	3.6	37.8	45.0	3.6	173125
12170	STILLWATER	24622	2117	17.3	24.0	41.3	13.9	3.4	59654	63929	77	63	1645	7.7	3.7	36.5	45.1	7.1	178536
12173	STUYVESANT	26704	890	12.2	24.5	47.6	11.6	4.0	62815	63074	81	69	689	6.7	5.7	53.3	29.9	4.5	149424
12175	SUMMIT	16713	278	23.4	30.6	38.1	6.5	1.4	47096	47920	54	37	242	7.0	8.3	47.5	33.1	4.1	150781
12176	SURPRISE	24958	48	27.1	16.7	45.8	4.2	6.3	53709	55298	69	55	40	0.0	7.5	45.0	47.5	0.0	170000
12180	TROY	24232	20810	27.9	26.0	32.6	9.3	4.3	45111	49500	49	31	10107	2.0	4.7	41.9	46.3	5.1	177176
	NEW YORK	29893		21.9	21.3	32.7	14.0	9.9	58747	62337				3.4	5.7	23.0	38.7	29.1	269816
	UNITED STATES	27277		20.9	24.4	35.3	11.7	7.6	54719	56938				9.3	13.1	31.6	32.6	13.5	162279

ZIP CODE		FINANCIAL SERVICES				THE HOME						ENTERTAINMENT						PERSONAL			
						Home Improvements		Furnishings													
#	POST OFFICE NAME	Auto Loan	Home Loan	Investments	Retirement Plans	Home Repair	Lawn & Garden	Computers & Hardware-Personal	Major Appliances	TV, Radio, Sound Equipment	Furniture	Dine out/ Carry out	Sports Equipment	Fees & Tickets	Toys & Games	Travel	Cable TV	Apparel & Services	Auto Repairs	Health Insurance	Pets & Supplies
12024	BRAINARD	135	160	164	164	164	155	140	148	136	148	137	110	155	135	154	135	97	141	143	170
12025	BROADALBIN	88	84	83	86	85	94	82	90	84	77	83	67	78	85	83	87	57	85	92	104
12027	BURNT HILLS	113	133	120	134	129	129	117	121	116	119	118	92	130	118	127	117	83	118	123	141
12028	BUSKIRK	102	89	110	89	93	106	87	102	90	83	89	75	79	89	90	94	60	95	102	119
12029	CANAAN	134	121	181	119	136	152	115	142	121	118	119	97	112	112	129	128	80	133	148	163
12031	CARLISLE	76	70	69	72	71	82	69	77	71	62	69	59	63	72	68	75	47	71	80	90
12032	CAROGA LAKE	81	78	96	77	81	93	73	86	77	71	77	61	73	75	79	82	52	81	92	99
12033	CASTLETON ON HUDSON	110	133	126	134	132	128	117	121	115	120	116	91	131	116	128	115	82	117	121	140
12035	CENTRAL BRIDGE	90	83	76	82	82	88	79	86	82	79	82	63	74	85	77	85	56	82	87	101
12036	CHARLOTTEVILLE	84	67	107	66	73	89	67	85	70	63	70	62	58	67	72	75	46	79	84	99
12037	CHATHAM	105	100	120	99	104	111	99	109	100	95	100	82	97	99	104	104	69	105	109	126
12041	CLARKSVILLE	104	129	115	129	124	127	110	115	111	111	113	86	126	113	122	114	79	112	121	133
12042	CLIMAX	84	102	90	102	98	100	87	91	88	89	89	69	99	90	96	90	63	89	95	107
12043	COBLESKILL	78	73	75	74	74	81	78	78	79	74	79	58	74	78	75	82	54	79	86	92
12046	COEYMANS HOLLOW	114	141	125	141	135	139	120	125	122	122	123	94	138	123	133	124	86	123	132	146
12047	COHOES	74	72	68	73	70	74	79	74	81	74	80	57	78	79	76	83	56	78	81	88
12051	COXSACKIE	80	80	82	79	80	84	81	83	83	78	83	63	81	82	82	85	58	83	86	97
12052	CROPSEYVILLE	96	119	108	119	116	117	101	106	102	104	103	80	117	103	113	104	73	104	111	124
12053	DELANSON	104	119	105	120	115	115	105	109	103	106	104	85	113	106	111	103	73	105	108	127
12054	DELMAR	143	167	167	169	170	164	149	155	147	156	148	115	165	146	162	147	105	151	156	179
12056	DUANESBURG	99	118	104	119	114	116	102	107	102	103	103	81	114	104	111	104	72	104	110	125
12057	EAGLE BRIDGE	87	79	79	83	81	94	78	89	81	71	79	67	72	82	78	86	54	82	91	103
12058	EARLTON	85	77	84	76	78	85	74	82	76	74	76	61	69	77	74	79	51	78	82	97
12059	EAST BERNE	95	115	102	115	111	113	99	104	100	100	101	78	111	101	108	102	71	101	108	121
12060	EAST CHATHAM	123	103	156	102	113	132	103	126	107	99	106	91	92	102	110	114	71	118	128	146
12061	EAST GREENBUSH	117	131	124	134	129	126	123	122	121	125	122	94	132	122	129	120	86	122	123	144
12062	EAST NASSAU	95	102	92	102	100	104	93	97	95	94	95	73	97	96	96	97	66	95	101	114
12064	EAST WORCESTER	80	58	85	56	61	81	59	76	65	55	64	56	48	64	60	72	42	69	78	89
12065	CLIFTON PARK	131	142	135	145	141	134	134	132	130	138	132	103	141	132	138	128	93	132	128	155
12066	ESPERANCE	90	85	80	87	85	94	82	90	84	78	83	67	78	86	81	87	57	84	91	105
12067	FEURA BUSH	116	126	115	129	124	131	114	122	116	112	116	93	120	118	121	119	80	117	126	143
12068	FONDA	82	80	76	80	80	86	77	82	80	76	79	60	76	80	77	83	54	80	87	96
12070	FORT JOHNSON	92	101	95	102	99	107	91	98	93	89	93	74	96	94	97	97	65	94	103	114
12071	FULTONHAM	88	66	101	65	71	91	67	86	73	63	72	63	56	71	70	79	47	79	87	101
12072	FULTONVILLE	91	71	89	70	73	93	72	87	78	67	76	65	61	78	71	84	51	80	90	103
12074	GALWAY	100	112	99	113	109	111	99	104	100	101	100	78	107	102	105	101	70	101	105	122
12075	GHENT	107	109	116	111	110	116	101	111	101	100	101	85	103	102	108	103	70	106	110	130
12076	GILBOA	85	68	110	67	75	90	68	87	72	64	71	63	59	68	74	76	47	80	86	101
12077	GLENMONT	146	175	168	179	175	159	154	156	146	163	148	122	171	150	165	142	107	149	144	179
12078	GLOVERSVILLE	73	66	69	66	66	76	69	72	72	65	71	54	65	71	68	76	49	72	79	85
12083	GREENVILLE	94	87	117	86	91	104	82	98	85	79	84	72	79	82	89	89	57	92	99	114
12084	GUILDERLAND	127	127	119	131	124	119	129	121	126	132	128	97	131	129	127	124	90	125	119	144
12086	HAGAMAN	83	98	90	97	96	102	85	91	89	85	89	66	96	88	94	93	62	89	101	105
12087	HANNACROIX	89	103	92	104	100	102	91	95	90	91	91	73	99	92	98	91	64	92	96	111
12090	HOOSICK FALLS	87	79	75	82	79	89	84	86	85	77	84	66	78	86	80	89	58	85	91	102
12092	HOWES CAVE	96	83	101	84	87	101	82	96	85	77	84	71	74	85	84	90	57	89	97	112
12093	JEFFERSON	95	75	121	74	83	100	76	96	79	71	78	70	65	75	82	85	52	89	95	111
12094	JOHNSONVILLE	92	94	83	93	92	93	87	91	88	89	88	68	88	91	87	89	61	88	90	107
12095	JOHNSTOWN	75	70	67	72	69	78	73	74	76	69	75	57	70	76	71	79	51	75	81	89
12106	KINDERHOOK	100	118	116	118	119	118	105	110	106	108	106	80	116	104	115	107	75	108	115	127
12108	LAKE PLEASANT	83	66	107	65	73	88	67	85	70	62	69	62	58	66	72	74	46	78	83	98
12110	LATHAM	114	127	119	128	125	121	121	118	119	122	120	92	129	120	125	118	85	119	119	139
12115	MALDEN BRIDGE	141	174	178	179	179	165	148	157	142	158	144	117	169	141	166	140	103	148	148	180
12116	MARYLAND	89	68	103	66	72	92	68	87	74	64	72	64	57	71	71	80	48	80	88	102
12117	MAYFIELD	87	72	94	71	74	91	72	86	76	68	76	64	64	75	74	81	51	81	89	101
12118	MECHANICVILLE	87	90	81	90	87	92	87	88	89	86	89	66	89	90	87	91	62	88	93	104
12120	MEDUSA	97	77	125	76	85	102	77	98	81	73	80	72	67	77	84	86	53	91	97	114
12121	MELROSE	94	116	102	116	111	113	99	103	100	100	101	78	113	101	109	102	71	101	108	120
12122	MIDDLEBURGH	81	72	82	72	73	85	73	80	75	69	74	60	67	75	73	79	51	78	84	95
12123	NASSAU	96	112	99	112	108	109	101	102	101	101	102	79	110	102	107	102	71	101	106	120
12125	NEW LEBANON	101	85	114	85	90	105	88	102	91	83	90	75	79	88	90	96	61	97	104	118
12130	NIVERVILLE	97	120	107	119	115	118	102	107	103	104	105	80	117	105	113	106	74	104	112	124
12131	NORTH BLENHEIM	94	75	121	74	82	99	75	95	79	70	78	70	65	75	81	84	52	88	94	111
12134	NORTHVILLE	91	74	111	74	81	95	75	92	79	71	78	67	66	75	80	83	52	86	92	107
12136	OLD CHATHAM	144	131	185	131	141	156	125	150	127	122	126	110	119	122	137	132	86	139	146	173
12137	PATTERSONVILLE	105	114	101	117	112	115	104	109	103	103	103	84	109	105	109	104	72	105	109	128
12138	PETERSBURG	94	92	88	94	92	104	87	97	90	81	89	73	85	91	89	94	61	91	100	113
12139	PISECO	97	77	125	76	85	102	77	98	81	72	80	72	67	77	84	86	53	91	97	114
12140	POESTENKILL	99	114	100	117	111	112	101	105	100	102	101	81	110	102	108	101	70	101	106	123
12143	RAVENA	89	104	98	101	102	96	100	97	97	97	98	76	107	98	104	97	70	98	97	112
12144	RENSSELAER	91	98	90	98	96	97	97	94	97	94	97	73	100	97	98	98	68	96	99	111
12147	RENSSELAERVILLE	107	86	136	85	94	113	86	109	90	81	89	79	75	86	93	96	59	100	108	126
12148	REXFORD	144	175	179	179	180	169	151	160	147	160	148	118	171	146	169	146	106	152	156	183
12149	RICHMONDVILLE	83	71	75	71	70	85	71	79	75	67	74	61	64	77	69	80	50	76	84	95
12150	ROTTERDAM JUNCTION	96	85	88	86	87	97	91	95	93	87	92	70	84	93	88	97	63	94	101	111
12151	ROUND LAKE	109	106	96	103	104	106	98	103	100	102	100	76	96	103	96	102	69	100	103	122
12153	SAND LAKE	118	139	126	139	134	140	120	128	123	120	123	96	134	124	131	126	86	124	134	149
12154	SCHAGHTICOKE	94	105	98	106	103	104	97	100	96	95	96	78	102	97	102	96	68	98	100	117
12155	SCHENEVUS	82	66	89	65	69	85	68	81	72	64	71	60	59	70	69	77	47	76	83	95
12156	SCHODACK LANDING	100	116	103	119	113	114	102	106	101	103	102	82	111	103	110	101	71	103	106	125
12157	SCHOHARIE	90	83	81	84	84	92	83	89	86	80	85	66	78	87	82	89	58	86	93	105
12158	SELKIRK	107	116	116	116	115	116	109	112	109	108	109	86	114	109	114	110	77	110	113	131
12159	SLINGERLANDS	129	138	138	142	140	137	136	134	135	138	136	102	143	133	141	135	96	135	139	157
12160	SLOANSVILLE	87	79	75	80	79	89	77	85	79	73	78	63	71	81	75	83	53	80	87	99
12164	SPECULATOR	83	66	107	65	73	87	66	84	69	62	69	62	57	66	72	74	46	78	83	98
12165	SPENCERTOWN	163	131	211	129	144	173	131	166	137	123	135	121	113	130	142	146	90	153	164	193
12166	SPRAKERS	88	72	83	71	73	89	71	84	76	67	75	63	62	77	70	81	50	78	86	99
12167	STAMFORD	85	71	96	71	76	88	73	85	76	69	75	63	65	74	75	80	51	81	87	99
12168	STEPHENTOWN	90	83	73	80	81	85	78	83	81	81	81	60	74	84	75	83	55	80	83	98
12169	STEPHENTOWN	90	85	75	82	83	86	79	84	82	82	82	61	76	85	76	84	56	81	84	100
12170	STILLWATER	98	96	97	94	96	99	92	97	93	92	93	73	91	94	93	95	65	95	97	114
12173	STUYVESANT	89	105	94	105	102	100	95	96	94	94	95	74	104	95	101	94	67	95	97	112
12175	SUMMIT	85	68	110	67	75	90	68	86	71	64	70	63	59	68	74	76	47	80	85	100
12176	SURPRISE	96	78	124	77	86	102	78	98	81	73	80	72	68	78	84	87	54	91	97	114
12180	TROY	78	74	69	76	72	75	85	76	85	80	85	60	81	84	79	86	60	82	82	92
	NEW YORK	100	106	110	108	107	104	112	106	113	106	114	81	115	110	112	116	83	110	110	124
	UNITED STATES	100	100	100	100	100	100	100	100	100	100	100	100	100	100	100	100	100	100	100	100

POPULATION CHANGE

ZIP CODE #	POST OFFICE NAME	COUNTY FIPS CODE	POPULATION 2000	POPULATION 2009	POPULATION 2014	2000-2009 ANNUAL RATE % Rate	2000-2009 ANNUAL RATE State Centile	HOUSEHOLDS 2000	HOUSEHOLDS 2009	HOUSEHOLDS 2014	HOUSEHOLDS % Annual Rate 2000-2009	HOUSEHOLDS 2009 Average HH Size	FAMILIES 2000	FAMILIES 2009	FAMILIES % Annual Rate 2000-2009
12182	TROY	083	14149	14168	14166	0.0	38	5871	5910	5928	0.1	2.36	3672	3615	-0.2
12183	TROY	001	2278	2478	2547	0.9	87	1073	1191	1231	1.1	2.08	581	624	0.8
12184	VALATIE	021	7372	7756	7810	0.6	76	2783	3022	3070	0.9	2.47	1973	2105	0.7
12185	VALLEY FALLS	083	2259	2296	2309	0.2	52	809	832	841	0.3	2.76	616	623	0.1
12186	VOORHEESVILLE	001	6371	6668	6725	0.5	71	2477	2649	2692	0.7	2.51	1905	2006	0.6
12187	WARNERVILLE	095	696	689	689	-0.1	30	279	284	286	0.2	2.43	199	200	0.1
12188	WATERFORD	091	10815	11582	11952	0.7	80	4373	4759	4942	0.9	2.42	2849	3022	0.6
12189	WATERVLIET	001	16427	16787	16850	0.2	52	7581	7916	8037	0.5	2.01	4119	4179	0.2
12190	WELLS	041	737	705	687	-0.5	7	322	319	314	-0.1	2.14	205	200	-0.3
12192	WEST COXSACKIE	039	2104	2200	2218	0.5	71	803	860	874	0.7	2.50	582	614	0.6
12193	WESTERLO	001	2081	2234	2278	0.8	84	788	865	889	1.0	2.58	578	622	0.8
12194	WEST FULTON	095	161	164	165	0.2	52	68	71	73	0.5	1.68	46	48	0.5
12196	WEST SAND LAKE	083	3052	3373	3499	1.1	91	1131	1264	1318	1.2	2.63	855	938	1.0
12197	WORCESTER	077	2348	2379	2347	0.1	44	960	991	984	0.3	2.39	645	652	0.1
12198	WYNANTSKILL	083	7301	7706	7845	0.6	76	2791	2972	3035	0.7	2.56	2036	2132	0.5
12202	ALBANY	001	9830	9362	9145	-0.5	7	4457	4290	4217	-0.4	2.09	2075	1924	-0.8
12203	ALBANY	001	32195	33253	33142	0.4	66	11916	12132	12154	0.2	2.07	5701	5620	-0.2
12204	ALBANY	001	6561	6773	6812	0.3	59	3020	3124	3153	0.4	2.09	1620	1634	0.1
12205	ALBANY	001	26414	26262	26114	-0.1	30	11056	11181	11183	0.1	2.31	7167	7084	-0.1
12206	ALBANY	001	16147	15443	15118	-0.5	7	6855	6566	6446	-0.5	2.27	3423	3160	-0.9
12207	ALBANY	001	2018	1972	1939	-0.2	21	1214	1184	1168	-0.3	1.52	406	383	-0.6
12208	ALBANY	001	21053	20792	20589	-0.1	30	9383	9347	9300	0.0	2.10	4219	4077	-0.4
12209	ALBANY	001	10129	10028	9922	-0.1	30	4427	4432	4407	0.0	2.20	2517	2443	-0.3
12210	ALBANY	001	9841	9374	9165	-0.5	7	5030	4859	4779	-0.4	1.86	1688	1558	-0.9
12211	ALBANY	001	14567	15267	15328	0.5	71	4382	4631	4669	0.6	2.78	3154	3222	0.2
12302	SCHENECTADY	093	26932	28484	29214	0.6	76	10663	11257	11571	0.6	2.45	7466	7725	0.4
12303	SCHENECTADY	001	28144	29148	29558	0.4	66	11449	11881	12075	0.4	2.44	7756	7929	0.2
12304	SCHENECTADY	093	20844	21299	21527	0.2	52	8333	8500	8606	0.2	2.43	5177	5149	-0.1
12305	SCHENECTADY	093	5887	5237	5198	-1.3	1	2430	2327	2303	-0.5	1.59	608	552	-1.0
12306	SCHENECTADY	093	24691	25407	25797	0.3	59	10194	10458	10624	0.3	2.43	6857	6888	0.0
12307	SCHENECTADY	093	6843	6606	6536	-0.4	11	2695	2587	2563	-0.4	2.54	1459	1357	-0.8
12308	SCHENECTADY	093	13281	13747	13774	0.4	66	5811	5755	5767	-0.1	2.23	3138	3023	-0.4
12309	SCHENECTADY	093	28627	30154	30858	0.6	76	11241	11881	12195	0.6	2.47	8069	8368	0.4
12401	KINGSTON	111	34807	35337	35411	0.2	52	14485	14848	14946	0.3	2.31	8618	8655	0.0
12404	ACCORD	111	3857	3910	3910	0.1	44	1451	1488	1497	0.3	2.61	997	1004	0.1
12405	ACRA	039	496	619	658	2.4	99	205	258	276	2.5	2.39	139	172	2.3
12406	ARKVILLE	111	735	732	721	0.0	38	343	345	343	0.1	1.97	209	205	-0.2
12409	BEARSVILLE	111	1043	1121	1155	0.8	84	488	533	552	1.0	2.08	273	292	0.7
12410	BIG INDIAN	111	491	525	539	0.7	80	219	238	246	0.9	2.16	129	136	0.6
12411	BLOOMINGTON	111	375	400	410	0.7	80	145	157	162	0.9	2.51	97	103	0.7
12412	BOICEVILLE	111	497	515	521	0.4	66	205	216	219	0.6	2.38	141	146	0.4
12413	CAIRO	039	3018	3303	3389	1.0	89	1286	1422	1466	1.1	2.31	828	899	0.9
12414	CATSKILL	039	10995	11377	11450	0.4	66	4418	4668	4729	0.6	2.35	2823	2927	0.4
12416	CHICHESTER	111	232	242	247	0.5	71	118	125	128	0.6	1.85	57	58	0.2
12418	CORNWALLVILLE	039	524	587	615	1.2	93	204	233	245	1.4	2.47	143	160	1.2
12419	COTTEKILL	111	701	737	749	0.5	71	274	293	300	0.7	2.51	168	176	0.5
12421	DENVER	025	193	184	179	-0.5	7	86	85	83	-0.1	2.16	58	56	-0.4
12422	DURHAM	039	224	237	242	0.6	76	90	97	101	0.8	2.37	64	68	0.7
12423	EAST DURHAM	039	988	1231	1332	2.4	99	438	561	611	2.7	2.18	296	372	2.5
12424	EAST JEWETT	039	249	267	275	0.8	84	108	118	122	1.0	2.26	75	80	0.7
12427	ELKA PARK	039	890	923	931	0.4	66	239	254	257	0.7	2.72	152	158	0.4
12428	ELLENVILLE	111	8195	9446	9460	1.5	96	2502	2565	2582	0.3	2.81	1681	1693	0.1
12430	FLEISCHMANNS	025	1327	1291	1262	-0.3	15	568	558	548	-0.2	2.31	360	346	-0.4
12431	FREEHOLD	039	1482	1613	1659	0.9	87	561	617	638	1.0	2.61	394	426	0.8
12433	GLENFORD	111	663	648	642	-0.2	21	292	290	289	-0.1	2.20	199	194	-0.3
12435	GREENFIELD PARK	111	312	308	305	-0.1	30	122	120	119	-0.2	2.38	81	78	-0.4
12439	HENSONVILLE	039	232	246	251	0.6	76	104	113	116	0.9	2.18	67	72	0.8
12440	HIGH FALLS	111	1835	1906	1932	0.4	66	782	826	843	0.6	2.27	498	515	0.4
12442	HUNTER	039	427	457	470	0.7	80	183	199	206	0.9	2.30	120	128	0.7
12443	HURLEY	111	4254	4436	4509	0.5	71	1769	1876	1918	0.6	2.35	1198	1246	0.4
12444	JEWETT	039	408	440	453	0.8	84	160	176	182	1.0	2.50	111	120	0.8
12446	KERHONKSON	111	5073	5271	5340	0.4	66	1984	2085	2122	0.5	2.29	1329	1371	0.3
12448	LAKE HILL	111	44	46	47	0.5	71	19	20	21	0.6	2.25	10	11	1.0
12449	LAKE KATRINE	111	3538	3679	3718	0.4	66	1209	1278	1300	0.6	2.44	838	871	0.4
12450	LANESVILLE	039	794	846	869	0.7	80	374	402	415	0.8	2.10	210	221	0.6
12451	LEEDS	039	1483	1708	1791	1.5	96	597	701	741	1.8	2.44	402	464	1.6
12454	MAPLECREST	039	394	423	435	0.8	84	150	165	170	1.0	2.56	100	107	0.7
12455	MARGARETVILLE	025	2325	2298	2246	-0.1	30	918	916	900	0.0	2.30	557	544	-0.3
12456	MOUNT MARION	111	555	558	552	0.1	44	200	204	203	0.2	2.74	154	154	0.0
12457	MOUNT TREMPER	111	1101	1163	1191	0.6	76	490	527	543	0.8	2.16	273	286	0.5
12458	NAPANOCH	111	2247	2329	2356	0.4	66	909	958	975	0.6	2.39	631	654	0.4
12460	OAK HILL	039	453	470	479	0.4	66	159	168	172	0.6	2.73	112	117	0.5
12461	OLIVEBRIDGE	111	1694	1787	1815	0.6	76	687	737	756	0.8	2.39	452	476	0.6
12463	PALENVILLE	039	1471	1455	1426	-0.1	30	579	585	575	0.1	2.36	386	384	-0.1
12464	PHOENICIA	111	1213	1277	1300	0.6	76	558	595	609	0.7	2.11	318	331	0.4
12465	PINE HILL	111	360	383	392	0.7	80	169	183	189	0.9	2.03	98	104	0.6
12466	PORT EWEN	111	2815	2961	3010	0.5	71	1102	1178	1204	0.7	2.51	750	787	0.5
12468	PRATTSVILLE	039	1427	1390	1375	-0.3	15	572	565	562	-0.1	2.45	387	378	-0.3
12469	PRESTON HOLLOW	001	693	651	636	-0.7	3	306	294	290	-0.4	2.19	207	194	-0.7
12470	PURLING	039	547	532	526	-0.3	15	200	198	197	-0.1	2.66	135	131	-0.3
12472	ROSENDALE	111	1878	1976	2012	0.6	76	817	874	895	0.7	2.25	507	532	0.5
12473	ROUND TOP	039	580	628	648	0.9	87	230	254	263	1.1	2.42	155	168	0.9
12474	ROXBURY	025	2272	2165	2096	-0.5	7	979	962	942	-0.2	2.23	652	630	-0.4
12477	SAUGERTIES	111	20307	20285	20606	0.0	38	7686	8207	8382	0.7	2.46	5183	5434	0.5
12480	SHANDAKEN	039	488	504	506	0.3	59	205	213	214	0.4	2.36	126	128	0.2
12481	SHOKAN	111	1591	1614	1615	0.2	52	644	664	668	0.3	2.41	445	450	0.1
12482	SOUTH CAIRO	039	550	627	656	1.4	95	242	283	298	1.7	2.21	163	187	1.5
12484	STONE RIDGE	111	2827	2968	3007	0.5	71	1114	1187	1209	0.7	2.49	761	796	0.5
12485	TANNERSVILLE	039	898	952	974	0.6	76	404	434	445	0.8	2.07	249	262	0.6
12486	TILLSON	111	1593	1684	1727	0.6	76	595	640	659	0.8	2.63	394	416	0.6
12487	ULSTER PARK	111	3935	4157	4233	0.6	76	1442	1550	1590	0.8	2.44	943	994	0.6
12491	WEST HURLEY	111	1945	1956	1955	0.1	44	800	816	820	0.2	2.35	533	535	0.0
12492	WEST KILL	039	367	330	317	-1.1	1	168	154	149	-0.9	2.14	100	89	-1.3
12494	WEST SHOKAN	111	701	703	694	0.0	38	296	300	298	0.1	2.34	201	200	-0.1
12495	WILLOW	111	365	382	390	0.5	71	178	189	194	0.7	1.98	98	102	0.4
	NEW YORK					0.3					0.3	2.61			0.1
	UNITED STATES					1.0					1.1	2.59			0.9

ZIP CODE #	POST OFFICE NAME	RACE (%) White 2000	White 2009	Black 2000	Black 2009	Asian/Pacific 2000	Asian/Pacific 2009	% Hispanic Origin 2000	% Hispanic Origin 2009	2009 AGE DISTRIBUTION (%) 0-4	5-9	10-14	15-19	20-24	25-44	45-64	65-84	85+	18+	MEDIAN AGE 2009	% 2009 Males	% 2009 Females
12182	TROY	91.0	88.5	5.1	6.3	1.0	1.3	2.7	3.5	6.2	5.6	5.7	6.7	7.6	26.2	26.8	12.8	2.4	78.4	38.7	48.2	51.8
12183	TROY	96.9	95.7	1.3	1.9	0.4	0.5	0.7	1.0	6.3	6.1	5.7	5.6	6.1	30.2	25.8	11.9	2.1	78.5	38.3	49.3	50.7
12184	VALATIE	96.8	95.4	1.0	1.4	1.0	1.5	1.4	1.9	5.4	5.6	6.1	6.6	5.5	23.2	30.8	13.6	3.2	78.4	43.3	48.0	52.0
12185	VALLEY FALLS	97.8	97.1	0.5	0.6	0.3	0.4	0.9	1.2	6.8	7.2	7.7	7.4	5.1	25.3	29.2	10.0	1.2	73.6	38.5	50.2	49.8
12186	VOORHEESVILLE	97.9	91.0	0.5	5.6	0.6	0.9	0.7	2.2	4.7	5.4	6.6	6.7	4.1	20.8	35.2	14.5	1.8	79.0	45.9	48.7	51.3
12187	WARNERVILLE	98.4	98.0	0.3	0.4	0.4	0.6	1.3	1.7	5.8	6.7	7.0	6.1	3.9	23.2	30.6	14.8	1.9	76.6	43.2	51.5	48.5
12188	WATERFORD	97.0	96.1	0.7	0.8	1.1	1.5	1.0	1.3	6.0	6.0	5.9	6.2	6.0	28.6	28.3	11.1	1.9	78.3	39.4	48.3	51.7
12189	WATERVLIET	90.8	87.5	3.9	5.3	2.7	3.7	3.0	3.9	6.2	5.3	5.1	8.2	9.7	28.0	23.9	11.1	2.5	80.0	35.4	47.7	52.3
12190	WELLS	96.6	95.6	0.5	0.7	0.3	0.4	0.3	0.3	3.5	4.1	4.5	5.7	3.8	19.1	37.3	18.9	3.0	83.5	50.3	51.3	48.7
12192	WEST COXSACKIE	91.1	86.6	5.7	7.7	0.5	1.6	4.2	5.6	4.8	5.5	5.5	8.1	7.4	23.2	30.1	12.9	2.4	80.5	41.8	49.1	50.9
12193	WESTERLO	98.3	97.6	0.6	0.9	0.3	0.4	0.8	1.1	6.0	6.4	7.1	7.3	4.7	21.8	33.1	12.0	1.7	75.9	42.9	49.6	50.4
12194	WEST FULTON	80.7	78.0	15.5	17.7	0.0	0.0	9.3	11.6	3.7	3.0	4.3	6.1	11.0	32.9	25.6	11.6	1.8	86.0	37.1	62.8	37.2
12196	WEST SAND LAKE	98.6	98.1	0.3	0.4	0.5	0.8	0.8	1.1	5.4	6.0	7.0	7.4	4.5	21.6	33.4	12.5	2.1	76.9	43.6	47.9	52.1
12197	WORCESTER	97.8	97.3	0.5	0.5	0.3	0.4	1.0	1.3	5.4	5.7	6.3	6.9	5.3	21.9	31.4	14.7	2.3	78.1	43.8	48.8	51.2
12198	WYNANTSKILL	97.1	95.8	0.8	1.0	0.7	1.1	0.7	1.0	5.8	6.2	6.7	6.5	4.8	24.4	30.4	13.2	2.1	77.0	42.1	48.2	51.8
12202	ALBANY	36.3	30.7	53.8	58.3	1.4	1.7	9.3	9.7	8.3	7.7	7.0	7.3	8.8	29.4	21.8	7.6	2.0	72.6	31.7	46.0	54.0
12203	ALBANY	84.1	79.3	7.9	10.0	4.9	6.6	3.8	4.8	3.5	3.4	3.6	15.7	17.4	21.7	20.6	10.9	3.2	86.7	30.4	48.1	51.9
12204	ALBANY	68.8	62.4	23.4	27.7	4.1	5.2	3.7	4.3	6.0	5.3	5.7	6.2	6.5	25.2	27.6	14.0	3.6	79.1	41.5	46.9	53.1
12205	ALBANY	91.2	88.2	4.2	5.6	2.7	3.7	1.7	2.2	5.0	5.3	5.7	6.0	4.7	24.8	29.3	16.0	3.1	80.2	43.9	48.1	51.9
12206	ALBANY	45.3	39.6	45.1	49.0	3.0	3.7	6.4	7.0	7.5	7.2	7.0	7.7	9.8	27.2	21.6	10.1	2.0	73.7	32.2	49.1	50.9
12207	ALBANY	30.7	25.5	60.4	64.7	2.2	2.5	7.0	7.4	6.6	6.0	5.2	5.7	6.4	24.4	27.5	14.9	3.4	78.7	41.9	51.0	49.0
12208	ALBANY	80.8	76.2	11.4	13.7	3.5	4.7	3.7	4.4	4.4	4.0	4.1	6.1	12.4	29.6	23.6	12.2	3.6	84.4	36.8	47.6	52.4
12209	ALBANY	72.0	65.7	20.6	25.0	2.6	3.4	5.2	6.1	6.3	5.9	5.9	6.2	7.4	28.1	25.3	11.9	3.1	78.2	38.4	46.5	53.5
12210	ALBANY	42.0	37.4	48.5	51.5	2.6	3.2	7.1	7.7	7.0	5.9	5.0	5.4	13.4	33.9	20.9	6.8	1.6	79.0	30.6	50.6	49.4
12211	ALBANY	87.8	83.7	6.5	8.2	3.5	4.9	2.6	3.6	4.3	4.6	5.4	10.9	9.0	20.3	27.2	15.3	3.0	82.2	41.3	49.1	50.9
12302	SCHENECTADY	97.4	96.2	0.7	1.0	0.9	1.3	1.2	1.7	4.9	5.4	6.1	6.7	4.8	21.1	31.1	15.8	4.1	79.1	45.6	47.8	52.2
12303	SCHENECTADY	91.6	89.5	4.6	5.5	1.0	1.4	2.5	3.1	6.0	6.5	6.9	7.0	5.2	23.9	29.1	12.8	2.6	76.1	41.4	47.9	52.1
12304	SCHENECTADY	78.7	74.3	13.2	15.4	2.8	3.7	4.7	5.6	6.9	6.8	6.9	6.8	6.0	24.1	26.3	13.1	3.3	75.1	39.5	48.0	52.0
12305	SCHENECTADY	76.4	68.3	14.2	19.5	4.0	4.8	4.6	7.3	2.9	2.2	2.1	10.9	15.9	30.0	23.4	9.8	2.7	91.6	35.4	57.7	42.3
12306	SCHENECTADY	96.4	95.1	1.4	1.8	0.7	1.0	1.4	1.9	5.9	6.0	6.3	6.4	5.6	24.7	29.0	13.7	2.4	77.8	41.7	48.7	51.3
12307	SCHENECTADY	43.0	37.1	42.8	46.3	1.4	1.6	13.1	14.5	10.1	8.9	8.2	8.2	8.5	25.7	20.5	8.5	1.4	67.7	29.1	47.6	52.4
12308	SCHENECTADY	82.9	77.6	9.4	12.0	1.6	2.4	5.4	7.1	6.9	6.2	5.7	7.7	9.1	28.4	22.7	10.5	2.8	77.4	34.5	48.1	51.9
12309	SCHENECTADY	90.2	87.0	2.9	3.6	4.9	6.7	2.0	2.5	5.5	6.1	7.0	6.8	4.7	21.0	31.7	14.0	3.2	76.6	44.2	48.5	51.5
12401	KINGSTON	84.9	82.0	9.4	10.8	1.4	1.8	5.2	6.3	6.1	5.8	5.9	6.6	6.5	24.4	28.1	13.6	2.9	78.0	41.0	48.0	52.0
12404	ACCORD	93.8	92.1	2.1	2.5	0.7	1.0	4.1	5.1	5.7	6.6	7.0	7.2	5.0	24.2	33.1	9.9	1.3	76.0	41.2	50.4	49.6
12405	ACRA	97.8	96.9	0.2	0.3	0.2	0.3	2.6	3.4	5.0	5.3	5.7	6.1	4.7	21.2	33.6	16.3	2.1	80.1	46.2	48.9	51.1
12406	ARKVILLE	96.3	95.1	0.7	0.8	1.0	1.4	3.9	4.9	4.4	4.5	4.9	5.5	4.1	18.9	31.4	21.2	5.2	82.7	50.5	48.2	51.8
12409	BEARSVILLE	94.3	92.5	1.1	1.2	1.5	2.2	2.5	3.1	3.1	3.7	4.5	4.6	3.6	17.8	41.3	19.4	2.1	85.6	52.5	50.3	49.7
12410	BIG INDIAN	95.3	93.9	1.0	1.1	1.0	1.5	2.4	3.2	4.8	4.2	5.3	5.5	3.2	21.7	38.1	15.2	1.9	82.1	47.4	50.7	49.3
12411	BLOOMINGTON	96.3	95.3	1.1	1.3	0.5	0.8	1.3	1.5	7.0	6.5	6.5	7.0	6.8	24.8	28.0	11.5	2.0	75.0	38.8	49.5	50.5
12412	BOICEVILLE	96.8	96.1	0.4	0.4	1.0	1.4	2.6	3.3	4.9	5.4	6.0	6.6	4.3	21.6	36.7	12.4	2.1	79.2	45.7	50.1	49.9
12413	CAIRO	96.0	94.9	0.7	0.8	0.4	0.5	4.7	6.0	5.7	5.5	6.0	6.9	5.8	21.4	30.2	16.2	2.3	78.7	44.0	47.7	52.3
12414	CATSKILL	89.4	86.7	6.4	7.8	0.6	0.9	4.0	5.1	6.0	5.6	5.8	6.2	5.8	23.3	29.1	14.6	3.6	78.7	42.8	48.0	52.0
12416	CHICHESTER	95.3	93.8	0.9	0.8	0.4	0.8	3.0	4.1	2.9	3.3	4.1	5.0	3.7	23.1	40.1	15.3	2.5	86.4	50.2	50.0	50.0
12418	CORNWALLVILLE	98.5	98.0	0.0	0.0	0.4	0.5	1.1	1.5	4.8	5.1	5.5	6.0	4.4	20.6	34.9	16.9	1.9	80.9	47.4	49.9	50.1
12419	COTTEKILL	94.0	92.1	2.6	3.1	0.3	0.4	2.9	3.7	4.3	4.1	4.5	6.8	8.3	26.2	33.6	10.7	1.5	83.0	41.8	49.0	51.0
12421	DENVER	97.4	96.2	0.5	0.5	0.5	1.1	2.6	3.3	6.0	6.5	6.0	4.3	3.3	16.8	35.9	20.1	1.1	78.3	49.6	48.9	51.1
12422	DURHAM	98.7	98.3	0.0	0.0	0.4	0.4	0.9	1.3	4.6	5.1	5.1	5.9	4.2	20.7	36.3	16.0	2.1	81.0	48.1	48.9	51.1
12423	EAST DURHAM	98.2	97.6	0.1	0.2	0.5	0.7	1.5	2.1	4.8	5.2	5.6	5.7	4.0	20.1	35.8	17.0	1.9	80.7	47.8	50.2	49.8
12424	EAST JEWETT	98.0	97.4	0.0	0.0	0.8	1.1	2.8	4.1	3.7	5.6	7.9	4.5	2.2	21.0	37.8	15.0	2.2	80.5	48.1	51.3	48.7
12427	ELKA PARK	97.9	97.2	0.1	0.1	0.2	0.3	1.1	1.4	7.0	8.8	7.9	7.4	4.0	19.3	30.2	13.5	1.8	71.3	40.7	50.2	49.8
12428	ELLENVILLE	69.4	64.8	15.3	17.7	1.2	1.9	22.2	24.5	5.1	5.3	5.5	8.4	9.1	31.3	24.1	9.5	1.7	80.7	35.8	55.4	44.6
12430	FLEISCHMANNS	96.7	95.7	0.6	0.7	0.9	1.2	6.6	8.2	5.2	5.4	5.9	6.4	4.3	20.5	31.3	19.1	1.9	79.6	46.5	49.2	50.8
12431	FREEHOLD	96.8	95.7	0.3	0.4	1.0	1.5	2.1	2.9	5.8	6.3	6.7	6.2	3.9	20.6	34.0	14.6	1.8	77.2	45.2	48.5	51.5
12433	GLENFORD	95.5	93.8	1.1	1.4	1.2	1.9	2.9	3.7	3.1	3.5	4.5	5.1	3.7	17.9	37.7	22.1	2.5	85.5	52.5	48.5	51.5
12435	GREENFIELD PARK	81.1	77.3	9.0	10.4	0.6	0.6	11.5	14.3	4.9	6.2	5.5	5.8	5.5	26.6	31.8	12.3	1.3	79.9	42.0	51.0	49.0
12439	HENSONVILLE	97.9	97.6	0.4	0.4	0.0	0.4	1.7	2.4	4.1	4.5	5.3	6.1	4.1	18.7	35.8	19.5	2.0	82.1	49.5	48.4	51.6
12440	HIGH FALLS	95.6	94.5	1.6	1.9	0.3	0.4	3.3	4.1	4.6	5.4	5.5	4.9	4.4	24.1	36.8	12.9	1.5	81.4	45.7	49.1	50.9
12442	HUNTER	97.4	96.7	0.5	0.4	0.7	0.9	3.0	3.9	4.2	5.7	7.4	4.8	2.6	20.8	36.5	16.0	2.0	79.9	47.8	51.4	48.6
12443	HURLEY	94.5	92.9	2.0	2.4	1.8	2.5	2.0	2.5	4.4	4.8	5.7	6.3	4.5	19.8	33.9	17.9	2.6	81.0	47.5	48.0	52.0
12444	JEWETT	97.5	97.0	0.2	0.2	1.0	1.1	2.9	3.6	3.9	5.9	7.7	4.8	2.5	21.6	35.9	15.5	2.3	79.3	47.2	50.7	49.3
12446	KERHONKSON	87.8	86.5	6.3	6.3	0.8	1.3	8.3	9.6	5.7	5.4	6.0	7.5	7.5	28.0	27.6	10.4	1.7	79.1	38.2	53.7	46.3
12448	LAKE HILL	93.3	93.5	2.2	2.2	2.2	2.2	2.2	2.2	4.3	4.3	4.3	4.3	4.3	17.4	39.1	19.6	2.2	82.6	51.3	45.7	54.3
12449	LAKE KATRINE	92.8	90.7	3.1	3.7	2.0	2.8	1.7	2.2	5.1	5.2	5.7	6.3	5.2	22.8	28.8	15.4	5.5	80.0	44.8	46.2	53.8
12450	LANESVILLE	96.5	95.3	1.1	1.4	0.3	0.5	3.1	4.1	5.1	5.6	5.9	5.8	3.7	19.5	35.7	17.1	1.7	80.0	48.0	52.0	48.0
12451	LEEDS	96.8	95.6	0.9	1.3	0.3	0.4	3.0	4.2	5.3	5.6	6.1	6.2	4.3	22.0	33.7	14.8	1.9	79.0	45.2	49.3	50.7
12454	MAPLECREST	98.5	97.9	0.0	0.0	0.0	0.2	1.8	2.4	3.5	3.8	4.7	6.6	4.3	18.2	36.4	20.6	1.9	83.7	50.8	48.5	51.5
12455	MARGARETVILLE	94.1	92.6	0.6	0.7	0.6	0.7	6.1	7.7	3.9	4.6	5.4	5.5	4.1	17.6	31.3	21.1	6.3	82.3	51.0	47.6	52.4
12456	MOUNT MARION	95.5	94.6	4.0	4.8	0.0	0.0	0.7	1.1	6.3	6.6	6.6	5.9	5.0	23.5	31.0	13.6	1.4	77.2	42.2	47.1	52.9
12457	MOUNT TREMPER	95.0	93.5	1.2	1.4	1.0	1.4	2.5	3.2	3.8	3.5	4.6	5.8	4.5	20.6	39.9	15.5	2.0	84.6	48.9	49.4	50.6
12458	NAPANOCH	91.1	89.2	3.2	3.5	0.9	1.3	8.1	9.9	5.8	6.1	6.7	7.1	5.1	24.0	30.0	13.3	2.0	77.1	41.4	49.1	50.9
12460	OAK HILL	98.7	97.9	0.2	0.2	0.2	0.4	0.9	1.3	4.7	5.1	5.5	6.0	4.5	20.9	35.1	16.6	1.7	80.9	47.5	50.0	50.0
12461	OLIVEBRIDGE	96.4	95.4	0.5	0.7	1.2	1.7	2.1	2.7	4.7	6.8	6.7	4.9	3.4	22.0	36.7	12.1	2.7	78.2	45.7	49.9	50.1
12463	PALENVILLE	96.2	95.0	0.5	0.8	0.9	1.2	2.0	2.7	6.8	6.4	6.6	6.7	5.9	24.9	29.3	11.8	1.6	76.2	40.0	48.5	51.5
12464	PHOENICIA	95.0	93.5	1.2	1.3	1.1	1.6	3.0	3.8	4.5	4.3	5.5	6.1	3.4	20.9	39.1	14.3	2.0	82.0	47.8	50.2	49.8
12465	PINE HILL	95.3	93.2	0.6	0.8	1.4	2.1	3.1	3.9	4.2	4.4	5.0	5.0	3.1	21.7	35.5	18.8	2.3	82.8	49.0	50.9	49.1
12466	PORT EWEN	93.4	91.5	2.7	3.3	1.4	2.0	1.7	2.2	6.0	6.0	6.2	7.1	6.4	23.8	30.3	12.6	1.7	77.6	41.1	46.8	53.2
12468	PRATTSVILLE	98.1	97.6	0.1	0.1	0.4	0.5	1.8	2.4	5.8	6.8	6.7	5.8	3.8	22.2	31.1	15.5	2.3	76.8	44.2	48.1	51.9
12469	PRESTON HOLLOW	96.7	95.7	1.6	2.2	0.3	0.3	1.2	1.5	5.4	5.5	6.1	6.0	3.4	20.9	35.2	15.7	1.8	79.0	46.7	49.5	50.5
12470	PURLING	97.3	96.4	0.7	0.9	0.2	0.4	2.4	2.8	5.8	5.5	5.8	7.3	7.7	22.4	28.9	14.5	2.1	77.8	41.7	49.6	50.4
12472	ROSENDALE	95.7	94.5	1.9	2.3	0.4	0.6	2.5	3.2	5.8	5.6	6.0	6.6	7.3	26.7	29.4	11.0	1.6	78.5	39.4	49.1	50.9
12473	ROUND TOP	97.9	97.5	0.5	0.6	0.2	0.2	3.1	4.3	6.4	5.7	5.9	7.0	7.6	20.9	28.8	15.3	2.4	77.7	42.0	47.8	52.2
12474	ROXBURY	97.2	96.5	0.4	0.5	0.6	0.8	1.5	1.8	5.4	5.9	5.7	4.5	3.4	19.7	34.6	18.4	2.3	80.2	48.5	49.4	50.6
12477	SAUGERTIES	92.1	91.6	4.0	3.3	0.8	1.5	4.6	5.0	5.7	5.8	6.1	7.5	6.1	25.5	28.9	12.7	1.8	78.3	40.7	49.5	50.5
12480	SHANDAKEN	93.7	91.7	1.2	1.6	2.0	2.8	3.1	4.0	4.2	4.8	6.0	6.7	3.4	18.5	38.5	16.3	1.8	81.0	49.9	49.4	50.6
12481	SHOKAN	96.9	96.0	0.9	1.1	1.1	1.7	2.8	3.6	3.7	6.1	6.8	7.4	3.9	21.8	37.1	11.8	1.6	78.6	45.2	51.0	49.0
12482	SOUTH CAIRO	96.5	95.2	1.1	1.4	0.2	0.3	3.1	4.3	5.4	5.6	6.1	6.4	4.6	22.2	33.0	14.7	2.1	79.1	44.8	49.1	50.9
12484	STONE RIDGE	95.8	94.5	1.1	1.3	1.0	1.4	2.3	2.9	4.4	5.3	6.3	6.8	3.9	20.5	37.7	13.1	1.9	79.5	46.4	49.5	50.5
12485	TANNERSVILLE	96.3	94.9	0.6	0.7	0.1	0.3	2.2	2.8	4.8	5.5	5.7	6.0	3.8	20.8	35.6	16.0	1.9	80.3	47.3	51.3	48.7
12486	TILLSON	96.9	95.9	1.2	1.4	0.4	0.7	2.3	3.1	6.7	7.0	7.2	6.9	5.6	24.6	28.4	11.8	1.7	74.8	40.1	49.1	50.9
12487	ULSTER PARK	95.2	93.8	2.1	2.5	0.7	0.9	2.0	2.5	5.7	5.9	6.4	6.8	5.7	24.6	31.6	11.6	1.6	77.7	41.5	49.0	51.0
12491	WEST HURLEY	94.7	93.1	1.7	2.1	1.8	2.6	2.2	2.7	4.1	4.6	5.6	6.3	4.4	18.6	34.9	19.3	2.2	81.4	49.3	48.5	51.5
12492	WEST KILL	97.5	96.7	0.0	0.0	0.5	0.9	1.6	1.8	4.2	4.5	4.8	4.8	3.3	18.2	39.4	18.2	2.4	83.3	51.1	46.1	53.9
12494	WEST SHOKAN	96.7	95.9	0.3	0.3	0.6	0.9	2.7	3.7	5.7	6.1	6.0	4.8	2.4	23.9	36.7	11.7	2.7	78.5	45.5	49.6	50.4
12495	WILLOW	94.5	92.9	1.4	1.6	1.4	1.8	2.2	2.9	3.1	3.1	3.9	5.8	5.5	19.1	39.5	17.8	2.1	85.9	50.5	48.4	51.6
	NEW YORK	67.9	64.8	15.9	16.5	5.6	6.9	15.1	16.7	6.5	6.4	6.4	7.1	7.0	27.0	26.3	11.2	2.1	76.6	37.5	48.4	51.6
	UNITED STATES	75.1	72.0	12.3	12.7	3.8	4.6	12.5	15.7	6.8	6.7	6.6	7.1	6.9	27.0	26.0	10.9	1.9	75.7	36.9	49.2	50.8

12182-12495

#	POST OFFICE NAME	2009 Per Capita Income	2009 HH Income Base	2009 Household Income Distribution (%) Less than $25,000	$25,000 to $49,999	$50,000 to $99,999	$100,000 to $149,999	$150,000 or More	Median Household Income 2009	2014	2009 National Centile	2009 State Centile	2009 Home Value Base	2009 Home Value Distribution (%) Less than $50,000	$50,000 to $89,999	$90,000 to $174,999	$175,000 to $399,999	$400,000 or More	2009 Median Home Value
12182	TROY	23303	5910	24.8	29.7	34.7	8.1	2.7	45964	49178	51	33	3354	3.6	3.8	55.2	34.7	2.7	163035
12183	TROY	23172	1191	21.0	38.0	37.7	2.8	0.6	44066	46961	46	27	537	0.0	1.9	82.9	15.3	0.0	153998
12184	VALATIE	31733	3022	12.2	25.0	39.2	14.7	8.9	66989	67263	85	74	2236	3.8	3.0	34.3	50.4	8.5	197534
12185	VALLEY FALLS	24379	832	15.1	20.9	48.0	13.2	2.8	62527	64546	81	68	658	6.7	5.6	30.9	51.2	5.6	189803
12186	VOORHEESVILLE	39129	2649	5.9	18.8	41.9	21.0	12.5	78781	80334	91	84	2110	0.7	0.2	15.5	66.5	17.1	239823
12187	WARNERVILLE	23343	284	21.5	31.0	35.9	7.4	4.2	47535	49733	56	39	222	2.3	5.9	42.8	46.4	2.7	173387
12188	WATERFORD	29616	4759	11.7	26.7	41.9	14.6	5.0	62701	66548	81	69	3001	1.1	0.8	32.2	62.7	3.3	194294
12189	WATERVLIET	26236	7916	23.5	31.6	36.6	5.8	2.5	45367	48987	49	32	3599	0.7	1.3	51.0	44.5	2.4	171988
12190	WELLS	19971	319	33.5	33.5	26.6	5.6	0.6	33489	34707	14	5	254	5.9	21.3	46.5	23.6	2.8	121196
12192	WEST COXSACKIE	24884	860	14.2	29.1	44.0	10.1	2.7	55764	58743	72	58	690	5.5	7.7	48.8	35.9	2.0	153158
12193	WESTERLO	24294	865	17.8	23.1	50.8	6.0	2.3	57149	60335	74	61	695	1.7	3.0	38.4	49.1	7.8	186995
12194	WEST FULTON	29067	71	22.5	31.0	36.6	5.6	4.2	47346	49593	55	39	63	7.9	3.2	47.6	36.5	4.8	161250
12196	WEST SAND LAKE	33220	1264	17.9	12.6	40.7	17.2	11.6	69739	72409	87	76	985	0.2	0.8	26.7	60.5	11.8	237865
12197	WORCESTER	20021	991	29.4	31.6	32.2	5.0	1.8	38844	40690	29	11	771	10.9	14.1	56.8	15.8	2.3	123278
12198	WYNANTSKILL	29236	2972	11.0	22.4	42.8	18.6	5.1	72112	75353	88	78	2373	0.8	1.5	30.8	57.2	9.7	202056
12202	ALBANY	17044	4290	47.4	29.6	19.0	3.2	0.8	26434	27745	4	3	1110	2.7	15.0	63.5	15.3	3.4	135417
12203	ALBANY	28848	12132	21.2	23.8	36.8	11.6	6.5	56123	60924	73	59	6309	0.3	0.3	31.2	63.3	4.9	198847
12204	ALBANY	33322	3124	20.6	28.2	38.3	5.6	7.3	51090	54960	64	49	1284	0.8	6.3	43.5	28.3	21.1	174240
12205	ALBANY	30220	11181	14.4	22.2	46.0	12.6	4.8	63829	66426	82	70	7906	1.7	0.5	38.8	56.9	2.1	185474
12206	ALBANY	18680	6566	42.2	26.7	25.4	4.2	1.7	31217	34585	10	4	2081	2.3	10.7	53.6	31.2	2.2	154276
12207	ALBANY	17723	1184	64.8	20.7	11.3	1.7	1.5	16231	16938	1	1	148	0.0	7.4	66.2	25.0	1.4	151351
12208	ALBANY	29682	9347	22.2	27.2	35.1	9.7	5.7	50576	55043	63	47	4367	0.4	0.4	34.8	60.0	4.4	192603
12209	ALBANY	26369	4432	21.2	28.9	38.9	7.5	3.5	49945	53806	61	45	2532	0.5	0.6	56.5	40.8	1.7	168457
12210	ALBANY	23267	4859	40.3	31.2	20.7	4.2	3.6	32196	35317	12	4	952	1.9	5.5	37.6	45.7	9.3	185084
12211	ALBANY	34110	4631	10.7	18.1	36.0	18.2	16.9	77166	78988	91	82	3460	0.2	0.5	11.8	66.9	20.6	265750
12302	SCHENECTADY	31439	11257	11.1	22.4	43.0	16.5	7.0	66719	69477	85	74	8671	1.6	0.9	39.3	54.8	3.4	187731
12303	SCHENECTADY	28711	11881	17.8	24.4	40.5	10.5	6.7	57547	61218	75	61	8526	1.0	3.4	41.7	48.7	5.2	182638
12304	SCHENECTADY	22075	8500	26.4	28.0	37.8	5.6	2.2	45283	49099	49	31	4989	1.7	7.6	67.9	22.5	0.2	146307
12305	SCHENECTADY	21603	2327	48.4	27.6	17.8	4.0	2.2	26069	28038	4	2	387	4.7	8.3	49.9	31.8	5.4	158048
12306	SCHENECTADY	26440	10458	17.3	27.9	40.3	10.6	3.9	54889	59435	71	57	7506	0.4	2.0	50.1	44.5	3.1	172404
12307	SCHENECTADY	12045	2587	54.8	28.7	14.0	1.5	1.0	21753	22544	2	2	687	10.0	36.0	45.1	7.9	1.0	94583
12308	SCHENECTADY	22719	5755	28.4	30.9	32.0	5.9	2.7	42231	45659	40	21	2666	0.8	5.3	68.3	24.0	1.7	151213
12309	SCHENECTADY	39997	11881	9.0	15.9	38.2	21.5	15.3	81032	83000	92	85	9004	0.2	0.2	24.9	62.9	11.9	243255
12401	KINGSTON	25688	14848	26.2	26.3	34.4	8.4	4.7	47263	50934	55	38	8415	2.6	3.3	44.5	42.5	7.1	174546
12404	ACCORD	28228	1488	16.1	23.3	42.8	12.4	5.4	60192	61987	78	64	1163	2.8	3.9	25.0	56.1	12.2	219258
12405	ACRA	22613	258	25.2	30.2	32.9	9.3	2.3	44025	46746	45	27	197	4.1	10.2	55.3	26.9	3.6	142448
12406	ARKVILLE	25504	345	27.2	32.8	30.7	6.1	3.2	40715	43081	35	16	259	3.9	9.3	47.5	31.3	8.1	149709
12409	BEARSVILLE	42378	533	16.5	18.9	38.1	12.4	14.1	65218	68294	83	72	414	0.0	0.0	15.9	46.9	37.2	332911
12410	BIG INDIAN	26405	238	29.8	31.1	29.0	5.0	5.0	40939	43477	36	17	179	1.7	7.3	39.7	43.0	8.4	177841
12411	BLOOMINGTON	28704	157	25.5	14.6	45.2	6.4	8.3	62298	63974	80	68	125	9.6	1.6	44.0	38.4	6.4	169196
12412	BOICEVILLE	30264	216	14.8	19.9	49.5	9.3	6.5	63450	65349	82	70	169	0.0	1.2	27.8	58.0	13.0	209615
12413	CAIRO	23633	1422	27.0	28.4	34.5	6.6	3.4	43903	46744	45	27	963	2.6	10.4	56.8	28.2	2.0	146476
12414	CATSKILL	22551	4668	30.0	27.5	31.4	7.8	3.3	42444	45038	41	21	2977	4.3	11.5	51.7	28.1	4.4	142242
12416	CHICHESTER	33942	125	37.6	22.4	18.4	14.4	7.2	33600	36874	15	5	78	3.8	0.0	37.2	56.4	2.6	187500
12418	CORNWALLVILLE	22266	233	23.2	30.0	36.9	8.2	1.7	45771	48272	51	33	187	8.6	8.0	43.9	32.6	7.0	149519
12419	COTTEKILL	26113	293	15.4	27.0	43.7	9.9	4.1	60105	62740	77	64	192	3.6	1.0	28.1	56.8	10.4	229032
12421	DENVER	27841	85	28.2	30.6	24.7	10.6	5.9	39529	42999	31	13	70	2.9	5.7	47.1	34.3	10.0	163889
12422	DURHAM	24251	97	20.6	29.9	37.1	9.3	3.1	49323	51930	60	43	78	10.3	7.7	43.6	32.1	6.4	145000
12423	EAST DURHAM	23510	561	28.0	30.1	34.0	6.4	1.4	41598	44141	38	18	441	10.0	7.7	42.0	34.9	5.4	154167
12424	EAST JEWETT	28426	118	23.7	25.4	34.7	9.3	6.8	50847	52973	63	48	91	5.5	8.8	34.1	42.9	8.8	182500
12427	ELKA PARK	17606	254	26.4	28.7	36.6	6.7	1.6	43454	46151	44	25	192	0.0	3.1	58.3	35.9	2.6	149500
12428	ELLENVILLE	17756	2565	36.0	20.9	32.0	8.5	2.6	42227	46571	40	21	1378	6.0	4.7	42.7	41.4	5.2	170599
12430	FLEISCHMANNS	21313	558	29.9	36.0	25.4	4.7	3.9	38007	40000	27	9	432	2.1	13.0	48.8	29.4	6.7	142164
12431	FREEHOLD	22435	617	22.4	28.5	36.0	9.1	4.1	49184	49582	59	43	477	0.6	9.2	50.1	35.2	4.8	154526
12433	GLENFORD	37624	290	11.0	27.6	37.6	13.8	10.0	60809	63234	79	66	239	0.0	0.0	11.3	76.2	12.6	236397
12435	GREENFIELD PARK	23951	120	27.5	18.3	40.8	12.5	0.8	55876	56414	72	58	87	0.0	2.3	28.7	59.8	9.2	203571
12439	HENSONVILLE	27504	113	26.5	29.2	31.9	7.1	5.3	44649	48635	47	29	83	1.2	4.8	39.8	44.6	9.6	187500
12440	HIGH FALLS	29286	826	22.3	24.9	37.5	8.5	6.8	53584	60033	69	54	607	1.3	0.5	25.4	55.5	17.3	229360
12442	HUNTER	26869	199	26.6	25.1	33.7	8.0	6.5	47390	50000	55	39	146	3.4	8.9	36.3	43.8	7.5	182143
12443	HURLEY	32754	1876	11.8	24.9	40.5	14.5	8.3	63256	65388	81	69	1415	2.3	1.1	24.7	67.6	4.2	204420
12444	JEWETT	25217	176	23.9	26.7	35.2	8.0	6.3	48934	51868	59	43	136	5.1	8.8	36.0	42.6	7.4	175000
12446	KERHONKSON	24663	2085	20.8	25.8	42.2	8.1	3.2	52519	55927	67	52	1478	3.0	3.9	39.2	44.7	9.2	182632
12448	LAKE HILL	36844	20	0.0	35.0	40.0	15.0	10.0	75000	72612	89	81	16	0.0	0.0	12.5	43.8	43.8	350000
12449	LAKE KATRINE	26231	1278	11.3	28.0	44.7	10.6	5.5	60000	62653	77	63	894	7.0	4.5	40.3	44.0	4.3	172802
12450	LANESVILLE	25912	402	37.3	22.4	31.6	4.7	4.0	40588	43373	35	16	241	5.8	9.5	43.2	34.4	7.1	156019
12451	LEEDS	24054	701	28.8	23.8	33.5	9.4	4.4	46990	49123	54	37	552	5.8	14.7	48.0	28.6	2.9	151606
12454	MAPLECREST	23897	165	23.6	30.3	33.9	6.7	5.5	46283	48058	52	35	128	0.8	7.0	39.8	42.2	10.2	183333
12455	MARGARETVILLE	22214	916	26.9	27.9	34.4	8.6	2.2	42450	46177	41	22	698	4.3	10.2	48.6	29.8	7.2	145363
12456	MOUNT MARION	17650	204	12.7	50.0	33.3	3.4	0.5	44428	45869	47	28	172	0.0	2.3	85.5	5.2	7.0	141379
12457	MOUNT TREMPER	35321	527	20.3	29.2	27.7	12.3	10.4	50700	56615	63	47	399	1.5	3.8	25.6	42.1	27.1	238690
12458	NAPANOCH	22467	958	29.2	23.0	37.2	8.8	1.9	47994	51284	57	40	723	9.0	5.5	43.4	39.8	2.2	166016
12460	OAK HILL	20915	168	20.8	31.0	38.1	8.3	1.8	47741	50457	56	40	135	7.4	6.7	45.2	33.3	7.4	154167
12461	OLIVEBRIDGE	24741	737	20.6	27.0	38.0	11.4	3.0	51539	54199	65	50	579	1.4	1.6	27.6	58.0	11.4	220913
12463	PALENVILLE	27631	585	17.4	27.9	38.5	12.6	3.6	54269	55748	70	56	424	1.7	3.8	54.7	37.7	2.1	155455
12464	PHOENICIA	25948	595	31.1	29.9	27.7	7.2	4.0	38486	41885	28	10	424	3.5	6.1	43.2	43.6	3.5	170775
12465	PINE HILL	30297	183	25.7	30.1	30.6	7.7	6.0	43854	47619	45	26	137	1.5	5.1	36.5	43.1	13.9	191964
12466	PORT EWEN	28634	1178	17.6	22.8	38.8	12.6	8.3	59596	62800	77	63	888	1.9	5.9	38.0	51.6	2.7	180689
12468	PRATTSVILLE	20653	565	26.0	37.3	28.1	5.5	3.0	39308	41645	31	13	454	10.8	11.7	40.1	32.4	5.1	140678
12469	PRESTON HOLLOW	25366	294	21.4	30.6	39.1	6.1	2.7	47875	51892	56	40	240	3.8	6.3	42.5	39.6	7.9	171429
12470	PURLING	24270	198	18.2	29.3	47.5	2.5	2.5	53205	55890	68	54	136	0.0	2.2	72.8	25.0	0.0	152632
12472	ROSENDALE	30159	874	17.5	22.3	44.9	10.5	4.8	62007	64004	80	67	618	5.7	1.8	42.6	44.5	5.5	175000
12473	ROUND TOP	23208	254	15.0	29.1	44.9	9.4	1.6	54660	56307	71	56	197	1.0	7.6	59.9	31.0	0.5	147356
12474	ROXBURY	24572	962	27.7	30.9	27.4	11.1	2.9	38583	41646	28	11	757	4.6	14.1	43.7	28.9	8.6	139784
12477	SAUGERTIES	26662	8207	18.1	25.4	42.2	10.8	3.5	56564	60420	73	59	5740	2.0	1.8	37.4	53.5	5.3	189063
12480	SHANDAKEN	21659	213	23.9	33.8	34.3	5.6	2.3	41631	46547	38	19	158	5.1	5.7	48.7	36.1	4.4	164583
12481	SHOKAN	27831	664	16.9	22.4	45.2	11.0	4.5	61424	63312	79	67	509	1.0	1.4	25.1	60.9	11.6	206203
12482	SOUTH CAIRO	26891	283	29.0	23.0	34.3	9.2	4.6	47590	49692	56	40	222	5.4	14.0	50.5	27.5	2.7	152083
12484	STONE RIDGE	29538	1187	16.3	26.0	38.7	12.2	6.8	60227	63158	78	64	932	0.3	0.5	13.8	65.7	19.6	271429
12485	TANNERSVILLE	23217	434	27.4	30.9	34.1	5.8	1.8	42713	45471	42	22	291	1.4	2.1	47.4	45.0	4.1	173476
12486	TILLSON	25899	640	15.9	20.0	48.3	12.0	3.8	63323	65052	82	70	492	2.4	1.2	40.9	50.4	5.1	181888
12487	ULSTER PARK	27808	1550	13.2	19.7	51.5	9.9	5.7	64582	66156	83	71	1079	1.0	4.4	30.6	55.6	8.4	199918
12491	WEST HURLEY	34158	816	17.3	20.1	37.4	13.6	11.6	63705	65642	82	70	665	0.2	0.9	25.3	66.9	6.8	217248
12492	WEST KILL	25599	154	34.4	29.2	23.4	7.8	5.2	37068	41022	24	8	124	3.2	12.1	44.4	33.9	6.5	150000
12494	WEST SHOKAN	28310	300	9.7	26.3	48.3	11.7	4.0	60410	61951	78	65	244	2.0	0.4	28.3	52.0	17.2	227941
12495	WILLOW	48326	189	6.3	31.2	29.6	17.5	15.3	69106	72195	86	76	151	0.0	0.7	11.9	41.1	46.4	377083
	NEW YORK	29893		21.9	21.3	32.7	14.0	9.9	58747	62337				3.4	5.7	23.0	38.7	29.1	269816
	UNITED STATES	27277		20.9	24.4	35.3	11.7	7.6	54719	56938				9.3	13.1	31.6	32.6	13.5	162279

ZIP CODE #	POST OFFICE NAME	FINANCIAL SERVICES: Auto Loan	Home Loan	Investments	Retirement Plans	THE HOME: Home Improvements: Home Repair	Lawn & Garden	Furnishings: Computers & Hardware-Personal	Major Appliances	TV, Radio, Sound Equipment	Furniture	ENTERTAINMENT: Dine out/Carry out	Sports Equipment	Fees & Tickets	Toys & Games	Travel	Cable TV	PERSONAL: Apparel & Services	Auto Repairs	Health Insurance	Pets & Supplies
12182	TROY	76	73	67	74	71	77	80	75	81	75	81	58	77	81	76	83	56	79	83	90
12183	TROY	67	66	56	67	63	70	69	66	70	65	70	51	68	71	66	72	48	68	73	80
12184	VALATIE	107	123	116	124	121	118	112	113	110	114	111	87	122	111	119	110	79	112	113	132
12185	VALLEY FALLS	91	105	92	106	102	103	93	97	93	94	94	74	102	95	100	94	66	94	98	113
12186	VOORHEESVILLE	128	159	153	161	158	153	135	142	133	141	134	106	154	133	151	133	95	136	141	164
12187	WARNERVILLE	90	79	89	79	81	96	77	90	81	72	80	66	71	81	78	87	54	83	94	105
12188	WATERFORD	95	107	99	107	104	102	102	99	100	101	101	77	108	102	105	101	72	101	101	117
12189	WATERVLIET	76	68	65	70	67	70	79	72	79	75	79	57	74	79	73	80	55	77	77	87
12190	WELLS	72	58	93	57	63	76	58	73	60	54	60	53	50	57	62	64	40	68	72	85
12192	WEST COXSACKIE	91	93	93	93	92	100	86	94	88	85	88	71	88	89	90	91	61	90	97	110
12193	WESTERLO	94	91	88	94	91	103	87	97	89	80	88	73	84	91	88	94	61	90	100	112
12194	WEST FULTON	94	76	122	74	83	100	76	96	79	71	78	70	66	75	82	84	52	89	95	111
12196	WEST SAND LAKE	115	141	132	143	139	137	121	127	120	125	121	95	137	121	134	120	85	122	127	147
12197	WORCESTER	80	62	85	62	66	82	64	78	69	61	68	58	55	68	65	74	45	73	80	91
12198	WYNANTSKILL	98	118	106	117	114	117	103	107	104	103	105	81	115	105	112	106	74	105	113	125
12202	ALBANY	49	36	36	40	35	38	53	42	55	49	55	35	47	54	44	56	39	51	48	54
12203	ALBANY	93	92	89	94	91	93	101	92	99	97	100	72	99	98	97	100	70	97	98	110
12204	ALBANY	97	92	93	96	92	94	102	95	103	101	103	74	101	101	99	104	73	101	100	114
12205	ALBANY	90	107	99	107	105	107	96	99	98	96	98	73	107	97	104	100	69	98	106	115
12206	ALBANY	54	48	48	50	47	49	62	52	64	55	65	41	59	61	56	67	46	59	60	65
12207	ALBANY	34	25	28	28	25	30	39	31	42	35	42	25	35	38	34	45	29	38	41	41
12208	ALBANY	88	80	79	83	79	82	96	84	94	90	95	67	90	93	88	94	66	91	91	102
12209	ALBANY	79	79	73	80	77	80	84	79	85	81	85	61	84	85	82	86	60	83	85	95
12210	ALBANY	61	45	45	51	44	46	67	52	67	60	68	44	59	66	56	67	48	62	57	66
12211	ALBANY	132	158	167	161	164	156	144	148	143	149	143	109	162	139	159	144	103	145	151	170
12302	SCHENECTADY	104	118	117	118	119	122	107	113	109	109	109	82	117	107	116	112	76	110	120	130
12303	SCHENECTADY	94	103	97	104	102	104	98	99	99	97	99	74	103	99	101	101	70	98	104	116
12304	SCHENECTADY	72	73	68	73	71	77	75	73	79	73	78	55	76	77	74	82	55	76	83	88
12305	SCHENECTADY	51	39	42	43	39	43	59	46	58	53	59	38	51	55	50	59	41	55	55	59
12306	SCHENECTADY	87	93	84	94	91	96	90	90	92	87	91	68	93	92	91	94	63	91	98	106
12307	SCHENECTADY	40	32	29	34	30	34	44	36	47	40	47	29	40	45	38	49	33	43	43	46
12308	SCHENECTADY	72	65	60	67	63	67	76	68	76	71	76	55	72	76	70	77	54	74	74	83
12309	SCHENECTADY	130	157	159	158	161	151	140	145	136	145	137	108	157	135	154	136	98	140	143	166
12401	KINGSTON	81	80	78	81	79	82	86	81	87	82	87	63	85	85	84	89	61	85	88	97
12404	ACCORD	113	109	116	109	110	118	102	113	104	103	104	84	100	105	105	107	71	107	112	132
12405	ACRA	88	72	109	71	78	93	73	90	76	69	75	66	64	73	77	81	50	84	90	104
12406	ARKVILLE	82	69	99	68	74	87	70	83	73	67	72	61	63	70	74	78	49	79	86	97
12409	BEARSVILLE	129	133	169	134	142	142	123	139	120	125	120	104	125	117	136	121	84	130	131	159
12410	BIG INDIAN	96	77	124	75	84	101	77	98	80	72	79	71	67	76	83	86	53	90	96	113
12411	BLOOMINGTON	92	108	101	105	106	99	104	100	101	101	102	79	111	102	108	101	73	102	100	116
12412	BOICEVILLE	106	106	127	105	108	120	97	112	100	95	100	82	99	98	107	104	68	106	114	130
12413	CAIRO	86	72	93	72	77	88	75	86	78	72	77	63	68	76	76	82	52	82	89	100
12414	CATSKILL	82	71	82	71	72	85	74	81	78	70	77	60	68	77	73	82	52	79	86	95
12416	CHICHESTER	107	86	139	85	94	113	86	109	90	81	89	80	75	85	93	96	59	101	108	127
12418	CORNWALLVILLE	92	74	119	73	81	98	74	94	77	69	76	69	64	73	80	82	51	87	93	109
12419	COTTEKILL	89	96	92	97	94	91	94	90	92	95	93	71	98	92	95	91	66	92	90	107
12421	DENVER	101	80	130	79	88	106	81	102	84	75	83	75	70	80	87	90	55	94	101	119
12422	DURHAM	97	78	125	76	85	103	78	99	81	73	80	72	67	77	84	87	53	91	97	114
12423	EAST DURHAM	86	69	111	67	75	91	69	87	72	64	71	64	59	68	74	77	47	80	86	101
12424	EAST JEWETT	107	86	139	85	94	113	86	109	90	81	89	80	74	85	93	96	59	101	108	127
12427	ELKA PARK	83	67	108	66	73	88	67	85	70	63	69	62	58	66	72	74	46	78	84	98
12428	ELLENVILLE	75	64	70	65	64	72	74	73	77	68	76	57	68	76	69	80	54	75	77	87
12430	FLEISCHMANNS	79	66	91	65	70	82	67	79	70	64	69	58	60	68	70	74	46	75	81	92
12431	FREEHOLD	98	78	126	77	86	103	78	100	82	73	81	73	68	78	85	87	54	92	98	115
12433	GLENFORD	109	129	133	129	134	136	112	123	115	117	115	85	126	111	126	119	80	118	133	140
12435	GREENFIELD PARK	98	78	126	77	86	103	78	99	82	73	81	73	68	78	85	87	54	92	98	115
12439	HENSONVILLE	100	80	129	79	88	106	80	102	84	75	83	74	69	80	87	89	55	94	100	118
12440	HIGH FALLS	109	89	130	89	96	114	91	110	95	86	94	81	80	91	95	101	63	103	111	128
12442	HUNTER	103	82	133	81	90	109	82	105	86	77	85	77	71	82	89	92	57	97	103	121
12443	HURLEY	102	116	113	116	116	119	106	110	107	108	108	80	116	106	114	110	75	109	118	128
12444	JEWETT	105	84	136	83	92	111	84	107	88	79	87	78	73	84	91	94	58	99	106	124
12446	KERHONKSON	87	82	97	81	84	91	81	89	83	78	82	68	78	82	84	86	57	86	90	104
12448	LAKE HILL	105	132	154	134	145	113	125	124	110	134	110	99	137	106	140	100	82	119	104	138
12449	LAKE KATRINE	97	99	95	98	98	102	96	99	98	95	97	74	97	98	97	100	68	98	103	116
12450	LANESVILLE	91	73	118	72	80	96	73	93	76	68	75	68	63	72	79	81	50	85	91	107
12451	LEEDS	101	77	117	75	82	104	78	99	83	73	82	73	65	81	81	90	55	91	100	116
12454	MAPLECREST	102	82	132	81	90	108	82	104	86	77	85	76	71	81	89	91	56	96	103	121
12455	MARGARETVILLE	80	70	100	69	76	88	70	83	74	67	73	60	65	70	75	79	49	80	88	97
12456	MOUNT MARION	63	72	68	71	72	78	64	70	68	63	68	49	70	67	70	73	47	68	80	80
12457	MOUNT TREMPER	112	113	152	114	123	120	109	122	104	110	104	92	109	100	120	104	73	115	112	139
12458	NAPANOCH	83	76	85	75	75	90	73	82	77	70	77	62	70	77	75	82	52	79	87	97
12460	OAK HILL	96	77	124	75	84	101	77	98	80	72	79	71	66	76	83	86	53	90	96	113
12461	OLIVEBRIDGE	99	79	128	78	87	105	79	101	83	75	82	74	69	79	86	89	55	93	100	117
12463	PALENVILLE	91	97	103	95	97	97	94	97	93	90	94	75	96	93	98	94	66	96	96	112
12464	PHOENICIA	92	74	119	72	81	97	74	94	77	69	76	68	64	73	80	82	51	86	92	108
12465	PINE HILL	104	83	135	82	92	110	83	106	87	78	86	77	72	83	90	93	57	98	105	123
12466	PORT EWEN	93	108	101	107	106	104	101	101	100	99	101	77	109	101	107	101	72	101	104	117
12468	PRATTSVILLE	87	66	102	65	71	91	67	85	72	63	71	63	56	70	70	78	47	79	86	100
12469	PRESTON HOLLOW	93	74	120	73	82	98	74	95	78	70	77	69	65	74	81	83	51	87	93	110
12470	PURLING	97	85	89	87	88	98	92	96	94	88	93	70	85	93	88	98	63	95	102	112
12472	ROSENDALE	90	100	94	100	98	97	96	94	95	96	96	73	102	96	99	96	68	95	97	111
12473	ROUND TOP	85	75	78	76	77	86	80	84	82	77	81	62	74	82	77	86	56	83	90	98
12474	ROXBURY	92	74	119	72	81	97	74	93	77	69	76	68	64	73	80	82	51	86	92	108
12477	SAUGERTIES	88	97	93	96	95	98	91	93	92	89	92	70	96	92	95	94	65	93	99	109
12480	SHANDAKEN	85	68	110	67	75	90	68	87	72	64	71	63	59	68	74	76	47	80	86	101
12481	SHOKAN	104	95	129	94	100	115	90	108	94	87	93	80	87	91	99	98	63	102	109	126
12482	SOUTH CAIRO	101	78	119	77	84	105	79	100	85	74	83	73	67	82	83	91	55	92	101	117
12484	STONE RIDGE	104	114	132	116	118	118	101	112	100	104	100	83	108	98	112	100	70	106	108	129
12485	TANNERSVILLE	82	65	106	64	72	86	65	83	68	61	68	61	57	65	71	73	45	77	82	96
12486	TILLSON	87	104	96	103	102	99	95	95	94	94	95	73	105	95	102	95	68	95	97	110
12487	ULSTER PARK	95	108	99	109	105	107	98	100	99	99	99	76	106	99	104	100	70	99	104	118
12491	WEST HURLEY	111	122	125	123	126	133	110	122	113	111	112	86	117	111	120	117	78	115	130	139
12492	WEST KILL	91	73	118	72	80	97	73	93	77	69	76	68	64	73	79	82	50	86	92	108
12494	WEST SHOKAN	111	89	143	87	97	117	89	113	93	83	92	82	77	88	96	99	61	104	111	131
12495	WILLOW	121	152	178	155	167	131	145	143	127	155	127	114	158	122	161	116	94	138	120	159
	NEW YORK	100	106	110	108	107	104	112	106	113	106	114	81	115	110	112	116	83	110	110	124
	UNITED STATES	100	100	100	100	100	100	100	100	100	100	100	100	100	100	100	100	100	100	100	100

#	POST OFFICE NAME	COUNTY FIPS CODE	POPULATION 2000	POPULATION 2009	POPULATION 2014	2000-2009 ANNUAL RATE % Rate	2000-2009 ANNUAL RATE State Centile	HOUSEHOLDS 2000	HOUSEHOLDS 2009	HOUSEHOLDS 2014	HOUSEHOLDS % Annual Rate 2000-2009	HOUSEHOLDS 2009 Average HH Size	FAMILIES 2000	FAMILIES 2009	FAMILIES % Annual Rate 2000-2009
12496	WINDHAM	039	1453	1543	1567	0.7	80	640	694	709	0.9	2.22	407	433	0.7
12498	WOODSTOCK	111	4503	4694	4774	0.5	71	2098	2220	2269	0.6	2.10	1169	1208	0.4
12501	AMENIA	027	2515	2709	2759	0.8	84	982	1060	1080	0.8	2.52	665	703	0.6
12502	ANCRAM	021	855	921	934	0.8	84	368	406	414	1.1	2.25	261	283	0.9
12503	ANCRAMDALE	021	946	1076	1113	1.4	95	363	424	441	1.7	2.54	263	301	1.5
12507	BARRYTOWN	027	289	302	306	0.5	71	85	90	91	0.6	2.68	55	57	0.4
12508	BEACON	027	19535	20214	20370	0.4	66	6620	6878	6964	0.4	2.51	4286	4365	0.2
12513	CLAVERACK	021	730	702	684	-0.4	11	297	294	289	-0.1	2.18	206	200	-0.3
12514	CLINTON CORNERS	027	2768	3015	3084	0.9	87	1015	1106	1132	0.9	2.69	731	784	0.8
12515	CLINTONDALE	111	1180	1253	1283	0.7	80	439	474	487	0.8	2.64	276	291	0.6
12516	COPAKE	021	1715	1870	1912	0.9	87	651	736	759	1.3	2.41	438	487	1.2
12517	COPAKE FALLS	021	446	479	486	0.8	84	181	199	204	1.0	2.32	123	133	0.8
12518	CORNWALL	071	6081	6445	6584	0.6	76	2354	2490	2547	0.6	2.57	1663	1726	0.4
12520	CORNWALL ON HUDSON	071	3110	3279	3333	0.6	76	1188	1256	1282	0.6	2.60	816	844	0.4
12521	CRARYVILLE	021	1400	1424	1410	0.2	52	568	595	594	0.5	2.35	389	400	0.3
12522	DOVER PLAINS	027	5203	5502	5565	0.6	76	1993	2105	2130	0.6	2.58	1366	1418	0.4
12523	ELIZAVILLE	021	1876	1914	1897	0.2	52	756	794	794	0.5	2.34	518	534	0.3
12524	FISHKILL	027	13409	15356	16092	1.5	96	4933	5733	6064	1.6	2.40	3162	3634	1.5
12525	GARDINER	111	3030	3349	3478	1.1	91	1137	1274	1330	1.2	2.60	817	901	1.1
12526	GERMANTOWN	021	3607	3890	3948	0.8	84	1411	1549	1581	1.0	2.46	956	1031	0.8
12528	HIGHLAND	111	13309	14067	14329	0.6	76	4945	5306	5439	0.8	2.46	3289	3466	0.6
12529	HILLSDALE	021	2702	2792	2780	0.4	66	1051	1117	1123	0.7	2.47	713	744	0.5
12531	HOLMES	027	3263	3434	3472	0.6	76	1067	1129	1144	0.6	2.99	823	857	0.4
12533	HOPEWELL JUNCTION	027	22170	24850	26026	1.2	93	7264	8142	8536	1.2	3.05	6035	6694	1.1
12534	HUDSON	021	20447	19781	19320	-0.4	11	8150	8077	7939	-0.1	2.29	5060	4918	-0.3
12538	HYDE PARK	027	13379	13859	14175	0.4	66	5086	5283	5414	0.4	2.49	3504	3574	0.2
12540	LAGRANGEVILLE	027	6682	7092	7141	0.6	76	2210	2343	2361	0.6	2.95	1815	1905	0.5
12542	MARLBORO	111	5381	5854	6035	0.9	87	1970	2164	2241	1.0	2.70	1389	1503	0.9
12543	MAYBROOK	071	3118	3495	3677	1.2	93	1054	1182	1245	1.2	2.95	790	868	1.0
12545	MILLBROOK	027	4618	4762	4747	0.3	59	1730	1779	1770	0.3	2.54	1121	1129	0.1
12546	MILLERTON	027	2931	3305	3434	1.3	94	1108	1255	1309	1.4	2.53	753	838	1.2
12547	MILTON	111	2511	2855	2992	1.4	95	913	1053	1109	1.6	2.71	653	741	1.4
12548	MODENA	111	1424	1585	1653	1.2	93	517	585	613	1.3	2.70	375	419	1.2
12549	MONTGOMERY	071	8793	10130	10719	1.5	96	2992	3452	3661	1.6	2.89	2346	2671	1.4
12550	NEWBURGH	071	51969	56346	57899	0.9	87	17629	18958	19506	0.8	2.90	12580	13332	0.6
12553	NEW WINDSOR	071	22517	24830	26174	1.1	91	8383	9239	9719	1.1	2.66	6012	6527	0.9
12561	NEW PALTZ	111	17004	17861	18141	0.5	71	6003	6384	6529	0.7	2.38	3356	3489	0.4
12563	PATTERSON	079	8611	9344	9555	0.9	87	2661	2931	3013	1.1	2.85	2019	2197	0.9
12564	PAWLING	027	6294	7067	7290	1.3	94	2411	2703	2788	1.2	2.57	1670	1850	1.1
12566	PINE BUSH	111	9511	10436	10814	1.0	89	3418	3784	3942	1.1	2.65	2566	2797	0.9
12567	PINE PLAINS	027	2866	2947	2942	0.3	59	1119	1157	1158	0.4	2.54	788	801	0.2
12569	PLEASANT VALLEY	027	9201	10123	10530	1.0	89	3486	3839	4005	1.0	2.62	2548	2759	0.9
12570	POUGHQUAG	027	6186	7162	7478	1.6	97	1990	2319	2427	1.7	3.05	1628	1875	1.5
12571	RED HOOK	027	12382	10716	10877	-1.6	1	3470	3699	3764	0.7	2.77	2468	2589	0.5
12572	RHINEBECK	027	9669	10103	10197	0.5	71	3722	3905	3951	0.5	2.30	2314	2381	0.3
12575	ROCK TAVERN	071	2395	2676	2811	1.2	93	773	866	913	1.2	3.08	640	712	1.2
12577	SALISBURY MILLS	071	1538	1670	1706	0.9	87	493	534	548	0.9	3.12	405	433	0.7
12578	SALT POINT	027	1960	2172	2253	1.1	91	706	784	813	1.1	2.76	527	576	1.0
12580	STAATSBURG	027	4026	4238	4316	0.6	76	1511	1598	1630	0.6	2.60	1137	1183	0.4
12581	STANFORDVILLE	027	2336	2454	2456	0.5	71	936	986	989	0.6	2.45	652	674	0.4
12582	STORMVILLE	027	4530	7064	7180	4.9	100	1417	1513	1550	0.7	3.19	1214	1284	0.6
12583	TIVOLI	027	2296	2549	2588	1.1	91	870	936	949	0.8	2.14	549	582	0.6
12585	VERBANK	027	951	1008	1012	0.6	76	325	343	345	0.6	2.76	269	281	0.5
12586	WALDEN	071	11506	12999	13626	1.3	94	4082	4602	4839	1.3	2.80	3016	3342	1.1
12589	WALLKILL	111	14984	15848	16155	0.6	76	4338	4650	4777	0.8	2.92	3272	3457	0.6
12590	WAPPINGERS FALLS	027	34221	36286	36734	0.6	76	12398	13240	13431	0.7	2.71	8963	9336	0.4
12592	WASSAIC	027	1048	1155	1195	1.1	91	413	457	473	1.1	2.48	276	299	0.9
12594	WINGDALE	027	4081	4516	4679	1.1	91	1375	1521	1579	1.1	2.84	1012	1101	0.9
12601	POUGHKEEPSIE	027	43525	44939	45119	0.3	59	15566	15978	16031	0.3	2.53	9186	9222	0.0
12603	POUGHKEEPSIE	027	38299	40073	40511	0.5	71	14518	15140	15314	0.5	2.55	10249	10519	0.3
12604	POUGHKEEPSIE	027	1997	1980	1962	-0.1	30	48	46	46	-0.5	2.54	32	30	-0.7
12701	MONTICELLO	105	12559	12996	13200	0.4	66	4917	5177	5289	0.6	2.39	3035	3129	0.3
12719	BARRYVILLE	105	1013	1089	1115	0.8	84	377	415	429	1.0	2.46	257	278	0.9
12720	BETHEL	105	160	165	164	0.3	59	64	68	68	0.7	2.40	40	42	0.5
12721	BLOOMINGBURG	105	5962	6709	6983	1.3	94	2082	2379	2491	1.5	2.81	1573	1770	1.3
12723	CALLICOON	105	2060	2111	2126	0.3	59	713	751	763	0.6	2.33	487	504	0.4
12725	CLARYVILLE	111	319	338	344	0.6	76	128	138	142	0.8	2.39	79	84	0.7
12726	COCHECTON	105	1251	1274	1276	0.2	52	501	524	530	0.5	2.42	341	351	0.3
12729	CUDDEBACKVILLE	071	2563	2932	3112	1.5	96	934	1073	1143	1.5	2.73	697	787	1.3
12732	ELDRED	105	731	778	791	0.7	80	298	326	334	1.0	2.25	203	218	0.8
12733	FALLSBURG	105	881	926	927	0.5	71	216	236	241	1.0	3.13	133	141	0.6
12734	FERNDALE	105	1346	1455	1489	0.8	84	569	627	644	1.1	2.10	347	374	0.8
12736	FREMONT CENTER	105	152	147	145	-0.4	11	63	63	63	0.0	2.33	44	43	-0.2
12737	GLEN SPEY	105	1491	1656	1725	1.1	91	596	670	702	1.3	2.47	409	452	1.1
12738	GLEN WILD	105	207	221	227	0.7	80	79	86	90	0.9	2.53	53	56	0.6
12740	GRAHAMSVILLE	111	2278	2535	2643	1.2	93	885	997	1043	1.3	2.53	644	716	1.2
12741	HANKINS	105	307	298	294	-0.3	15	121	121	120	0.0	2.46	85	83	-0.3
12742	HARRIS	105	290	299	298	0.3	59	110	115	115	0.5	2.43	70	72	0.3
12743	HIGHLAND LAKE	105	345	364	364	0.6	76	142	153	155	0.8	2.37	97	103	0.7
12745	HORTONVILLE	105	122	130	134	0.7	80	44	48	50	0.9	2.38	30	32	0.7
12746	HUGUENOT	071	1039	1209	1316	1.7	97	369	435	475	1.8	2.78	264	306	1.6
12747	HURLEYVILLE	105	3241	3518	3620	0.9	87	1084	1210	1256	1.2	2.59	740	811	1.0
12748	JEFFERSONVILLE	105	2111	2206	2207	0.5	71	835	888	893	0.7	2.42	560	585	0.5
12750	KENOZA LAKE	105	77	81	81	0.5	71	33	35	36	0.6	2.31	23	25	0.9
12751	KIAMESHA LAKE	105	284	346	371	2.2	99	121	149	160	2.3	2.32	82	99	2.1
12752	LAKE HUNTINGTON	105	124	127	127	0.3	59	60	63	64	0.5	2.00	41	42	0.3
12754	LIBERTY	105	6652	6811	6827	0.3	59	2547	2662	2688	0.5	2.42	1548	1584	0.2
12758	LIVINGSTON MANOR	105	4591	4758	4774	0.4	66	1785	1895	1917	0.6	2.48	1225	1278	0.5
12759	LOCH SHELDRAKE	105	736	787	811	0.7	80	249	271	280	0.9	2.90	160	174	0.9
12760	LONG EDDY	025	601	580	568	-0.4	11	244	241	238	-0.1	2.41	173	169	-0.3
12762	MONGAUP VALLEY	105	235	254	263	0.8	84	101	112	117	1.1	2.08	66	72	0.9
12763	MOUNTAIN DALE	105	990	1073	1113	0.9	87	363	403	420	1.1	2.61	253	276	0.9
12764	NARROWSBURG	105	1747	1829	1834	0.5	71	715	766	773	0.7	2.28	458	481	0.5
12765	NEVERSINK	105	748	803	821	0.8	84	268	294	303	1.0	2.73	200	216	0.8
12766	NORTH BRANCH	105	632	684	704	0.9	87	245	269	278	1.0	2.53	163	176	0.8
	NEW YORK					0.3					0.3	2.61			0.1
	UNITED STATES					1.0					1.1	2.59			0.9

ZIP CODE #	POST OFFICE NAME	RACE (%) White 2000	White 2009	Black 2000	Black 2009	Asian/Pacific 2000	Asian/Pacific 2009	% Hispanic Origin 2000	% Hispanic Origin 2009	2009 AGE DISTRIBUTION (%) 0-4	5-9	10-14	15-19	20-24	25-44	45-64	65-84	85+	18+	MEDIAN AGE 2009	% 2009 Males	% 2009 Females
12496	WINDHAM	97.8	97.1	0.6	0.6	0.2	0.3	2.1	2.8	4.3	5.3	5.6	6.2	4.3	19.5	35.0	17.7	2.2	80.9	47.8	48.5	51.5
12498	WOODSTOCK	94.3	92.6	1.3	1.6	1.6	2.3	2.6	3.3	3.2	3.7	4.5	5.5	4.5	17.9	39.9	18.4	2.3	84.7	51.1	48.0	52.0
12501	AMENIA	92.6	90.5	2.9	3.7	0.5	0.7	3.6	4.7	6.0	5.9	6.2	7.1	6.1	24.9	28.9	13.0	1.8	77.3	40.7	49.6	50.4
12502	ANCRAM	97.9	97.2	0.7	1.0	0.2	0.3	0.9	1.3	4.0	5.2	6.3	5.9	3.3	22.7	35.1	15.3	2.3	80.6	46.6	51.4	48.6
12503	ANCRAMDALE	97.9	96.9	1.0	1.4	0.1	0.2	1.0	1.2	4.3	5.0	5.9	6.3	3.3	22.4	35.0	15.4	2.3	80.7	46.6	51.4	48.6
12507	BARRYTOWN	93.4	91.4	1.4	1.7	2.4	3.3	3.1	3.6	4.3	4.0	4.3	13.9	15.2	20.9	24.8	10.9	1.7	83.8	31.5	48.0	52.0
12508	BEACON	66.3	62.5	21.6	23.5	1.6	2.1	16.8	18.9	6.0	5.8	5.9	6.4	7.5	31.8	25.6	9.3	1.7	78.8	36.9	54.0	46.0
12513	CLAVERACK	90.4	87.5	7.5	9.5	0.4	0.7	4.0	5.0	4.1	4.6	5.1	12.3	4.8	20.8	28.3	17.2	2.7	77.9	43.7	52.4	47.6
12514	CLINTON CORNERS	94.8	93.1	2.1	2.7	1.0	1.6	2.5	3.3	4.7	5.7	6.9	6.8	3.7	21.4	35.8	13.3	1.7	78.0	45.4	50.5	49.5
12515	CLINTONDALE	91.1	88.7	4.1	4.9	1.0	1.4	6.0	7.7	6.1	6.5	6.3	6.1	5.6	25.0	28.6	14.1	1.8	77.3	41.1	48.3	51.7
12516	COPAKE	96.8	95.7	0.9	1.2	0.1	0.2	1.3	1.7	4.3	4.7	6.0	5.3	3.7	24.5	31.4	17.2	2.8	81.7	46.0	50.8	49.2
12517	COPAKE FALLS	96.4	95.4	0.7	1.0	0.2	0.2	2.2	2.9	4.2	5.0	6.7	5.6	4.2	24.4	31.7	15.9	2.3	80.6	44.9	51.1	48.9
12518	CORNWALL	94.3	92.3	1.2	1.6	1.4	1.9	5.5	7.4	6.6	6.8	7.4	7.1	5.2	23.2	30.3	11.4	2.0	74.2	41.0	47.4	52.6
12520	CORNWALL ON HUDSON	96.2	94.9	0.6	0.7	0.7	0.9	4.2	5.6	5.8	5.9	6.2	7.3	6.5	21.8	30.2	13.6	2.7	77.3	42.5	47.4	52.6
12521	CRARYVILLE	96.7	95.6	0.8	1.1	0.4	0.5	2.4	3.2	4.0	5.7	6.5	6.4	3.9	22.3	34.0	15.0	2.3	79.6	45.7	50.8	49.2
12522	DOVER PLAINS	94.1	92.3	2.1	2.6	0.9	1.3	4.4	5.7	6.2	6.4	6.3	7.1	6.1	24.1	29.7	12.4	1.7	76.6	40.7	50.3	49.7
12523	ELIZAVILLE	97.3	96.3	1.2	1.6	0.4	0.5	2.1	2.8	4.8	5.8	6.4	5.5	4.0	24.1	31.5	15.0	2.9	79.3	44.6	50.1	49.9
12524	FISHKILL	83.9	82.0	9.2	9.4	2.9	4.2	8.1	9.1	5.3	5.2	5.4	5.9	6.2	27.4	28.4	13.3	2.8	80.6	41.5	52.2	47.8
12525	GARDINER	93.2	91.3	2.2	2.7	0.9	1.2	6.6	8.6	6.2	6.2	6.7	7.4	5.9	25.4	31.7	9.3	1.3	75.6	40.3	50.2	49.8
12526	GERMANTOWN	96.8	95.7	1.3	1.7	0.4	0.6	1.7	2.4	5.0	6.1	6.6	6.9	4.6	23.1	31.1	13.9	2.9	77.9	43.7	49.1	50.9
12528	HIGHLAND	90.2	87.8	4.7	5.5	1.2	1.6	6.1	7.7	6.0	6.0	6.3	8.0	5.9	25.8	27.6	11.4	3.0	76.1	39.5	48.3	51.7
12529	HILLSDALE	96.9	95.8	0.7	0.9	0.4	0.5	2.3	3.1	4.9	5.8	6.7	6.2	4.8	21.0	33.6	14.8	2.3	78.8	45.4	50.3	49.7
12531	HOLMES	95.8	94.6	1.0	1.2	1.1	1.6	3.8	4.8	6.6	7.2	7.6	7.4	5.4	23.7	31.4	8.9	1.9	73.9	40.0	49.7	50.3
12533	HOPEWELL JUNCTION	91.8	89.1	2.5	3.1	3.0	4.2	4.7	6.0	7.3	8.1	8.6	7.8	4.6	24.1	29.6	8.9	1.0	70.9	38.3	49.7	50.3
12534	HUDSON	83.1	79.9	10.9	12.5	1.4	1.8	4.6	5.5	5.9	5.5	5.6	6.6	6.3	24.5	28.1	14.4	3.1	78.9	41.8	50.2	49.8
12538	HYDE PARK	91.6	89.1	3.9	4.8	1.5	2.0	3.3	4.1	5.8	5.8	6.3	8.2	7.1	23.8	27.8	12.9	2.4	77.6	39.7	49.2	50.8
12540	LAGRANGEVILLE	93.9	91.8	2.0	2.5	1.9	2.6	3.4	4.5	6.3	7.4	8.2	7.6	4.4	24.0	31.2	9.7	1.1	73.0	40.3	49.7	50.3
12542	MARLBORO	95.0	93.6	2.5	3.1	0.3	0.5	4.2	5.3	6.4	6.5	6.8	7.5	6.0	25.6	29.0	10.5	1.7	75.8	39.3	49.3	50.7
12543	MAYBROOK	82.8	78.7	8.9	10.8	1.2	1.6	12.7	16.1	7.7	7.5	7.4	7.9	7.8	28.0	26.6	6.1	1.1	72.2	32.7	48.2	51.8
12545	MILLBROOK	94.5	92.9	2.9	3.6	0.7	1.0	3.7	4.7	5.6	5.6	6.4	8.1	5.8	22.2	29.5	14.3	2.4	76.3	42.2	48.7	51.3
12546	MILLERTON	95.6	94.3	2.0	2.6	0.6	0.8	3.2	4.1	4.2	4.7	6.1	8.8	6.1	23.5	32.4	12.0	2.2	79.9	42.6	50.0	50.0
12547	MILTON	93.3	91.6	3.4	4.1	0.4	0.6	4.0	5.0	6.0	6.5	6.9	7.2	5.0	26.3	31.0	9.6	1.5	76.1	39.9	49.3	50.7
12548	MODENA	90.6	88.3	3.6	4.2	0.5	0.6	11.2	14.3	6.1	6.6	6.8	6.6	5.6	26.1	30.2	10.6	1.4	76.3	39.6	50.9	49.1
12549	MONTGOMERY	93.6	91.5	2.6	3.3	0.7	1.0	5.9	7.9	6.7	7.0	7.5	7.6	5.2	25.4	29.6	9.5	1.5	73.4	38.9	49.7	50.3
12550	NEWBURGH	61.4	57.8	21.6	22.9	1.5	1.9	24.2	27.1	8.5	7.7	7.2	8.3	7.9	25.9	23.3	9.7	1.7	71.9	32.9	48.3	51.7
12553	NEW WINDSOR	84.7	80.9	6.8	8.2	1.9	2.5	11.0	13.7	6.8	6.7	7.0	6.9	5.9	25.7	28.0	11.2	1.8	75.0	38.5	49.4	50.6
12561	NEW PALTZ	85.3	82.1	5.0	5.6	3.3	4.3	7.0	8.4	4.3	4.5	4.7	12.0	17.0	21.7	24.3	9.8	1.7	82.9	31.4	46.9	53.1
12563	PATTERSON	91.1	89.0	3.6	4.1	1.3	1.8	7.1	8.8	6.3	6.7	7.3	7.0	6.3	28.8	29.1	7.7	0.9	75.2	37.7	51.0	49.0
12564	PAWLING	93.5	92.1	1.9	2.2	1.4	1.9	5.3	6.4	5.5	5.9	6.6	7.1	5.2	22.7	30.9	13.7	2.4	77.3	43.0	49.1	50.9
12566	PINE BUSH	95.1	93.8	1.7	2.0	0.6	0.9	4.3	5.6	5.9	6.3	7.0	7.5	6.2	25.7	30.6	9.6	1.3	75.9	39.7	50.8	49.2
12567	PINE PLAINS	96.5	95.5	0.9	1.1	0.6	0.9	1.4	1.8	4.9	5.3	7.0	8.2	5.1	23.6	30.4	13.2	2.3	76.9	42.4	48.9	51.1
12569	PLEASANT VALLEY	94.9	93.3	2.1	2.6	1.0	1.4	2.9	3.8	6.2	6.5	7.0	6.8	5.3	24.4	31.3	11.1	1.4	76.0	41.1	49.1	50.9
12570	POUGHQUAG	94.4	92.5	2.0	2.5	1.7	2.4	4.9	6.5	7.1	7.9	8.3	7.9	4.9	23.8	30.6	8.5	1.0	71.5	38.8	50.1	49.9
12571	RED HOOK	84.6	85.6	9.1	6.8	1.6	3.0	6.5	6.0	4.9	5.1	5.7	10.0	9.3	23.9	28.2	11.4	1.4	79.7	37.9	51.7	48.3
12572	RHINEBECK	91.0	88.0	4.8	6.0	1.3	2.0	4.4	5.7	3.9	4.4	5.4	6.9	5.7	21.9	29.4	17.0	5.5	82.5	46.3	49.6	50.4
12575	ROCK TAVERN	92.7	90.3	3.0	3.9	0.8	1.2	5.8	7.8	6.7	7.2	7.9	7.8	5.0	24.9	30.8	8.7	1.0	72.9	38.5	50.4	49.6
12577	SALISBURY MILLS	92.1	89.3	2.9	3.8	1.4	2.0	7.3	9.8	7.0	7.8	8.4	8.2	5.1	23.7	30.2	8.4	1.1	71.6	38.0	49.2	50.8
12578	SALT POINT	95.8	94.4	1.5	1.9	0.7	1.0	2.1	2.8	5.8	6.7	7.6	6.9	4.1	23.0	33.6	11.0	1.3	75.3	42.5	49.8	50.2
12580	STAATSBURG	94.2	92.4	2.6	3.3	0.8	1.2	2.3	3.0	5.1	6.2	7.1	6.9	4.4	22.9	34.5	11.5	1.4	77.1	43.4	49.8	50.2
12581	STANFORDVILLE	93.1	90.5	3.0	3.8	1.1	1.8	3.3	4.4	4.3	5.1	6.3	6.9	4.2	23.5	34.4	13.6	1.6	80.0	44.8	51.5	48.5
12582	STORMVILLE	94.4	83.5	2.0	8.7	1.7	3.4	3.3	7.0	5.2	5.9	6.3	14.5	12.4	24.2	24.1	6.3	1.0	79.1	30.8	52.6	47.4
12583	TIVOLI	92.4	90.2	2.0	2.5	2.6	3.5	3.3	4.2	4.7	4.9	4.8	14.4	16.1	23.0	22.3	8.3	1.4	81.9	28.6	47.8	52.2
12585	VERBANK	94.2	92.0	2.3	2.9	1.2	1.7	3.6	4.9	6.3	6.9	7.6	7.6	4.6	23.8	31.7	10.1	1.2	73.9	40.8	49.7	50.3
12586	WALDEN	92.5	90.4	2.7	3.3	0.5	0.7	7.5	9.8	6.8	7.0	7.2	7.7	6.5	26.1	27.2	9.8	1.6	74.2	37.2	48.9	51.1
12589	WALLKILL	84.1	81.7	8.4	9.1	1.0	1.3	12.8	15.5	5.7	6.1	6.5	6.4	7.0	31.4	27.8	8.0	1.1	77.8	37.1	55.2	44.8
12590	WAPPINGERS FALLS	86.9	83.2	4.8	6.0	3.9	5.3	7.3	9.0	6.6	6.5	6.7	6.9	6.2	27.2	27.7	10.8	1.5	75.9	38.3	49.6	50.4
12592	WASSAIC	94.0	92.3	3.3	4.2	0.4	0.6	3.4	4.5	5.5	5.4	5.5	6.8	7.5	25.5	29.4	12.4	1.9	79.2	40.0	49.4	50.6
12594	WINGDALE	85.4	82.3	9.3	10.8	1.1	1.6	6.2	7.6	6.7	6.7	7.3	10.8	5.8	26.4	27.0	8.4	0.9	72.4	35.7	52.0	48.0
12601	POUGHKEEPSIE	63.8	58.8	25.9	28.6	2.7	3.5	8.6	10.1	6.8	6.2	5.9	10.0	11.7	25.1	22.2	9.9	2.1	77.2	31.7	48.5	51.5
12603	POUGHKEEPSIE	83.8	79.9	8.1	9.6	4.4	5.9	5.2	6.4	6.0	6.1	6.5	8.1	7.6	22.7	28.1	12.6	2.1	76.9	39.9	48.1	51.9
12604	POUGHKEEPSIE	78.5	72.8	7.1	8.3	9.1	12.0	5.5	6.6	4.0	3.0	2.8	30.0	28.5	13.9	11.9	4.9	0.9	88.2	21.8	44.4	55.6
12701	MONTICELLO	71.5	67.9	18.7	20.7	1.7	2.1	15.8	18.1	6.4	6.0	5.9	6.9	7.1	23.2	28.6	14.1	1.9	77.5	40.7	49.4	50.6
12719	BARRYVILLE	93.2	91.4	3.6	4.5	1.0	1.3	4.5	6.0	4.4	4.8	5.1	6.1	4.1	22.6	35.6	15.2	2.0	81.5	46.8	50.7	49.3
12720	BETHEL	94.3	92.7	1.9	2.4	0.0	0.0	8.8	10.9	4.8	5.5	6.1	6.1	3.6	20.6	35.8	15.8	1.8	78.8	47.1	52.7	47.3
12721	BLOOMINGBURG	94.6	93.1	1.8	2.3	0.8	1.1	5.4	7.2	6.7	7.2	7.4	7.5	5.9	26.0	28.8	9.4	1.1	73.8	37.7	49.7	50.3
12723	CALLICOON	85.6	83.4	11.2	12.7	1.0	1.2	7.0	8.5	4.1	4.4	5.0	18.1	7.9	17.7	26.9	14.1	1.8	75.0	38.6	51.1	48.9
12725	CLARYVILLE	95.3	94.1	0.6	0.9	1.3	1.5	2.2	2.7	4.4	5.0	5.9	5.0	3.0	22.5	35.5	16.6	2.1	81.7	47.4	50.3	49.7
12726	COCHECTON	96.0	94.7	1.3	1.6	0.6	0.9	2.4	3.1	4.3	4.9	5.4	6.4	3.3	22.6	36.0	15.3	1.7	81.0	46.8	50.6	49.4
12729	CUDDEBACKVILLE	94.9	93.4	2.2	2.8	0.4	0.5	4.6	6.1	6.0	6.4	7.0	7.3	5.1	24.4	31.1	11.5	1.2	76.1	40.9	50.1	49.9
12732	ELDRED	93.8	92.3	3.3	4.1	0.8	1.2	4.0	5.0	4.4	4.6	5.3	5.9	4.4	21.7	35.9	15.7	2.2	81.4	47.3	50.5	49.5
12733	FALLSBURG	81.0	77.2	13.3	15.7	1.0	1.3	10.0	12.2	9.5	8.6	6.8	9.6	12.6	20.2	22.6	8.6	1.4	70.3	27.4	53.6	46.4
12734	FERNDALE	85.3	82.3	6.7	7.8	1.5	1.9	12.8	15.8	5.1	4.9	5.2	6.1	6.7	24.1	30.0	15.1	2.8	80.6	43.4	50.4	49.6
12736	FREMONT CENTER	94.7	92.5	1.3	2.0	1.3	1.4	1.3	1.4	6.1	6.8	6.8	5.4	4.1	19.0	34.0	15.6	2.0	76.9	46.0	51.7	48.3
12737	GLEN SPEY	96.8	95.7	0.2	0.2	0.9	1.3	2.1	2.7	5.4	7.7	6.4	6.8	2.3	24.5	28.4	16.1	2.4	76.0	43.0	48.7	51.3
12738	GLEN WILD	89.9	87.8	3.4	4.1	1.9	2.3	7.2	9.0	5.0	5.9	6.3	7.7	4.5	23.1	32.1	14.5	0.9	77.4	43.4	50.2	49.8
12740	GRAHAMSVILLE	96.8	95.7	0.3	0.4	0.4	0.6	2.4	3.2	5.7	6.7	7.5	6.3	4.3	22.7	32.5	12.7	1.6	76.0	42.8	50.1	49.9
12741	HANKINS	95.1	93.3	1.6	2.0	1.0	1.3	1.3	1.3	6.0	6.7	6.0	5.4	3.7	19.8	34.2	16.4	1.7	77.5	46.5	51.0	49.0
12742	HARRIS	88.9	86.0	6.2	7.4	2.1	3.0	9.0	11.4	4.7	4.7	5.4	5.4	4.0	22.1	34.1	18.1	1.7	81.9	47.4	49.5	50.5
12743	HIGHLAND LAKE	97.1	96.2	1.2	1.4	0.6	0.8	1.2	1.4	4.9	5.2	6.0	5.8	3.8	19.2	36.0	16.8	2.2	79.1	48.2	49.7	50.3
12745	HORTONVILLE	88.5	87.7	8.2	9.2	0.8	0.8	6.6	6.9	3.8	3.8	6.2	15.4	7.7	19.2	26.9	14.6	2.3	76.2	40.0	50.8	49.2
12746	HUGUENOT	94.9	93.1	1.7	2.2	0.6	0.8	3.8	5.2	6.9	7.0	7.2	7.1	5.9	25.5	27.2	11.7	1.4	74.5	38.3	47.0	53.0
12747	HURLEYVILLE	83.5	79.7	8.1	9.7	1.2	1.6	11.3	14.1	6.9	6.8	6.0	7.6	8.8	24.4	27.1	11.2	1.3	75.8	36.9	48.9	51.1
12748	JEFFERSONVILLE	94.9	93.3	1.8	2.2	0.4	0.6	3.7	4.9	5.0	6.0	6.3	6.2	3.9	22.1	31.8	15.4	3.3	78.6	45.3	49.5	50.5
12750	KENOZA LAKE	96.1	91.4	2.6	3.7	0.0	1.2	2.6	3.7	4.9	6.2	7.4	6.2	3.7	23.5	33.3	13.6	1.2	77.8	43.5	53.1	46.9
12751	KIAMESHA LAKE	81.3	77.2	11.3	13.6	2.8	3.8	12.3	15.0	5.8	5.2	5.5	8.1	6.6	22.8	26.9	17.1	2.0	78.6	41.7	46.8	53.2
12752	LAKE HUNTINGTON	96.8	96.1	0.8	1.6	0.8	0.8	1.6	2.4	3.9	4.7	4.7	5.5	3.1	22.8	38.6	15.0	1.6	82.7	48.0	52.0	48.0
12754	LIBERTY	82.0	78.4	10.2	12.0	1.6	2.0	11.3	13.8	6.1	5.8	6.2	7.2	7.0	23.1	27.1	14.0	3.5	77.4	40.8	47.6	52.4
12758	LIVINGSTON MANOR	91.6	89.4	3.4	4.1	0.9	1.3	6.9	8.8	6.2	5.6	6.5	6.6	5.7	21.6	31.5	14.6	1.7	77.6	43.3	50.0	50.0
12759	LOCH SHELDRAKE	77.9	74.1	11.0	12.3	0.7	0.8	14.4	17.3	7.2	7.8	5.8	9.5	10.5	21.9	24.7	11.6	1.0	73.8	33.2	50.6	49.4
12760	LONG EDDY	96.2	94.8	1.2	1.6	0.8	1.2	1.2	1.4	5.7	5.9	6.2	6.4	5.0	21.0	31.6	16.4	1.9	78.1	44.9	51.2	48.8
12762	MONGAUP VALLEY	91.0	89.0	3.4	3.9	1.3	1.6	17.9	22.0	5.1	5.9	6.3	5.9	4.7	26.4	30.3	14.2	1.2	80.3	42.1	52.8	47.2
12763	MOUNTAIN DALE	85.7	82.6	6.5	7.7	0.6	0.9	13.8	17.1	5.4	6.7	7.0	9.7	6.0	22.6	30.2	11.6	0.8	74.3	39.5	52.8	47.2
12764	NARROWSBURG	90.4	88.0	5.8	7.2	0.9	1.1	3.3	4.2	5.1	5.4	5.7	5.5	3.8	20.1	33.8	18.0	2.5	79.9	47.9	51.1	48.9
12765	NEVERSINK	96.7	95.5	1.1	1.4	0.1	0.4	2.3	3.1	6.2	7.3	8.3	7.6	3.5	24.3	30.0	11.2	1.5	73.5	40.5	49.9	50.1
12766	NORTH BRANCH	94.9	93.6	0.6	0.7	0.8	1.0	4.9	6.4	5.4	5.8	6.1	5.8	3.4	20.9	34.8	15.4	2.3	78.8	46.4	49.4	50.6
	NEW YORK	67.9	64.8	15.9	16.5	5.6	6.9	15.1	16.7	6.5	6.4	6.4	7.1	7.0	27.0	26.3	11.2	2.1	76.6	37.5	48.4	51.6
	UNITED STATES	75.1	72.0	12.3	12.7	3.8	4.6	12.5	15.7	6.8	6.7	6.6	7.1	6.9	27.0	26.0	10.9	1.9	75.7	36.9	49.2	50.8

#	POST OFFICE NAME	2009 Per Capita Income	2009 HH Income Base	2009 Household Income Distribution (%): Less than $25,000	$25,000 to $49,999	$50,000 to $99,999	$100,000 to $149,999	$150,000 or More	Median Household Income: 2009	2014	2009 National Centile	2009 State Centile	2009 Home Value Base	2009 Home Value Distribution (%): Less than $50,000	$50,000 to $89,999	$90,000 to $174,999	$175,000 to $399,999	$400,000 or More	2009 Median Home Value
12496	WINDHAM	25644	694	28.7	28.1	30.5	8.2	4.5	43231	46115	43	24	489	3.3	6.1	39.9	43.8	7.0	176786
12498	WOODSTOCK	39288	2220	18.2	20.6	34.5	14.5	12.1	63726	66667	82	70	1620	0.5	0.1	10.6	63.2	25.6	291000
12501	AMENIA	29117	1060	10.9	29.1	40.8	14.6	4.5	61508	65975	79	67	706	1.3	1.7	14.6	67.3	15.2	234615
12502	ANCRAM	30289	406	17.0	26.8	42.4	7.4	6.4	55190	54870	71	57	318	3.8	8.8	31.4	41.8	14.2	194000
12503	ANCRAMDALE	26698	424	16.0	28.1	42.2	7.3	6.4	54478	53877	70	56	332	6.3	10.8	34.0	36.4	12.3	172059
12507	BARRYTOWN	26874	90	13.3	23.3	35.6	18.9	8.9	66417	70739	84	73	65	0.0	0.0	18.5	55.4	26.2	252778
12508	BEACON	27039	6878	15.8	22.6	38.0	17.8	5.7	64066	68019	82	71	3948	1.5	1.2	21.8	72.1	3.4	213693
12513	CLAVERACK	31553	294	16.0	21.8	46.9	8.8	6.5	61376	61678	79	67	235	5.5	3.8	45.1	38.3	7.2	166532
12514	CLINTON CORNERS	37441	1106	6.6	17.3	34.7	28.8	12.6	82300	87270	93	86	849	0.4	0.4	4.8	63.1	31.3	307849
12515	CLINTONDALE	22397	474	20.7	28.9	37.3	10.1	3.0	50378	53866	62	46	316	4.1	7.6	24.1	59.2	5.1	210909
12516	COPAKE	28180	736	15.9	33.4	38.6	6.4	5.7	50615	51548	63	47	554	0.0	3.6	52.9	34.1	9.4	163608
12517	COPAKE FALLS	28409	199	19.6	29.6	37.2	8.5	5.0	50797	51932	63	47	146	2.1	4.8	43.8	37.0	12.3	173611
12518	CORNWALL	37301	2490	11.5	17.8	30.4	26.9	13.3	76635	82810	90	82	1686	0.7	1.5	13.5	60.3	24.1	282550
12520	CORNWALL ON HUDSON	35152	1256	13.2	19.5	29.3	25.2	12.8	72222	78444	88	79	844	0.0	0.1	7.3	73.1	19.4	279358
12521	CRARYVILLE	28730	595	24.0	24.2	35.3	10.6	5.9	52325	53900	67	52	447	1.8	6.0	34.9	41.2	16.1	201042
12522	DOVER PLAINS	28601	2105	14.8	27.6	34.0	18.1	5.5	62568	65601	81	68	1526	12.3	9.5	14.4	52.9	10.8	216094
12523	ELIZAVILLE	24755	794	19.1	36.4	33.2	7.4	3.8	46694	48111	53	36	577	6.1	9.5	35.2	44.0	5.2	173185
12524	FISHKILL	33915	5733	11.9	19.0	34.8	24.3	10.1	72163	76621	88	79	4104	0.9	1.0	12.5	73.1	12.5	254212
12525	GARDINER	28379	1274	12.2	21.7	46.2	13.5	6.3	63133	64869	81	69	953	3.8	1.0	6.5	74.5	14.2	268048
12526	GERMANTOWN	27067	1549	20.1	27.7	36.5	10.8	5.0	52243	53485	66	51	1127	4.7	6.1	32.9	44.9	11.4	192625
12528	HIGHLAND	29614	5306	14.2	22.7	39.2	16.1	7.7	65148	67878	83	72	3458	1.5	1.5	20.2	67.4	9.4	231576
12529	HILLSDALE	27092	1117	20.7	29.8	34.1	9.8	5.6	49533	51107	60	44	802	1.0	5.1	35.4	41.8	16.7	205392
12531	HOLMES	33811	1129	5.8	8.8	47.3	23.7	14.4	81077	83909	92	85	924	0.1	0.0	5.1	65.6	29.2	327273
12533	HOPEWELL JUNCTION	36391	8142	7.1	9.9	33.9	28.8	20.3	97826	100741	96	91	6901	0.7	0.3	6.8	59.8	32.5	343197
12534	HUDSON	23199	8077	27.9	29.2	33.6	5.6	3.7	43930	46799	45	27	4705	8.2	9.5	52.7	25.0	4.6	138534
12538	HYDE PARK	29655	5283	13.0	23.1	39.4	17.9	6.6	65290	68246	84	72	3731	3.4	1.7	15.3	70.5	9.2	222411
12540	LAGRANGEVILLE	36065	2343	6.1	10.6	37.3	30.3	15.6	91858	94602	95	89	2004	0.1	0.3	2.5	63.4	33.6	341039
12542	MARLBORO	26652	2164	17.0	21.2	40.8	14.5	6.5	62657	64850	81	69	1454	0.6	0.8	8.3	77.7	12.7	268849
12543	MAYBROOK	26107	1182	10.7	20.8	39.8	24.7	4.1	69998	73870	87	76	715	0.4	0.7	47.3	50.3	1.3	178059
12545	MILLBROOK	35228	1779	12.3	23.8	30.4	21.4	12.2	68867	74164	86	75	1119	0.5	0.0	2.1	59.2	38.2	341372
12546	MILLERTON	25880	1255	17.5	29.5	37.5	11.4	4.2	54307	60599	70	56	861	3.0	1.5	24.2	54.6	16.7	226067
12547	MILTON	27280	1053	13.9	22.5	43.0	13.6	7.0	62430	64420	81	68	725	1.9	0.6	9.0	71.9	16.7	280396
12548	MODENA	23733	585	16.9	32.5	36.8	8.9	5.0	50541	54095	62	46	444	13.5	5.4	21.6	52.0	7.4	196875
12549	MONTGOMERY	29677	3452	7.0	18.8	39.6	25.6	9.0	76156	79515	90	82	2705	0.9	0.5	16.8	69.4	12.5	243030
12550	NEWBURGH	24191	18958	20.4	23.2	32.9	17.1	6.5	59634	63396	77	63	10581	0.9	2.4	25.5	61.8	9.4	218858
12553	NEW WINDSOR	29645	9239	11.0	23.6	36.9	20.8	7.8	66110	69520	84	73	6348	5.0	1.6	16.2	71.8	5.3	230175
12561	NEW PALTZ	26601	6384	25.2	20.8	34.4	12.0	7.6	54533	59099	70	56	3820	1.0	2.1	13.1	66.1	17.7	255396
12563	PATTERSON	34292	2931	6.7	11.0	38.3	28.0	16.1	86969	92144	94	87	2350	0.8	0.5	5.6	65.1	28.1	322323
12564	PAWLING	38491	2703	9.4	13.3	39.4	24.6	13.4	78520	82172	91	84	1942	0.6	0.1	6.6	61.2	31.6	315962
12566	PINE BUSH	27415	3784	14.5	21.1	40.9	17.3	6.2	65471	68340	84	72	2873	0.3	1.5	20.8	65.5	11.9	240620
12567	PINE PLAINS	28771	1157	17.9	29.2	34.1	11.9	6.8	53029	57722	68	53	817	0.9	1.8	30.1	49.2	18.0	216250
12569	PLEASANT VALLEY	32879	3839	10.6	20.3	35.7	22.4	11.0	71804	75831	88	78	2813	5.4	2.9	8.9	61.8	21.0	276156
12570	POUGHQUAG	35640	2319	2.9	8.1	38.6	37.2	13.2	100323	101001	97	92	1960	1.0	0.8	3.0	65.2	30.1	340184
12571	RED HOOK	27819	3699	14.7	23.4	34.0	18.6	9.2	64672	68675	83	71	2824	2.6	1.1	16.2	62.4	17.7	245372
12572	RHINEBECK	37244	3905	13.3	22.2	30.8	22.0	11.7	70673	75981	87	77	2739	1.2	0.4	6.9	62.5	29.0	296947
12575	ROCK TAVERN	28671	866	8.1	21.7	35.3	23.8	11.1	73884	77971	89	80	749	2.7	1.3	7.3	65.3	23.4	292257
12577	SALISBURY MILLS	34379	534	3.0	9.6	37.6	37.3	12.5	99521	100622	97	91	433	0.0	0.7	10.9	69.1	19.4	274760
12578	SALT POINT	35157	784	7.8	17.0	37.5	24.6	13.1	79979	83378	92	85	619	3.6	1.8	6.3	62.8	25.5	289286
12580	STAATSBURG	37652	1598	5.9	16.8	33.8	31.2	12.4	85213	89658	94	87	1297	1.1	0.5	10.1	67.9	20.4	247054
12581	STANFORDVILLE	39169	986	8.2	19.5	36.5	24.9	10.9	74116	78576	89	80	707	0.0	0.6	5.8	62.1	31.5	318944
12582	STORMVILLE	29759	1513	2.7	7.1	38.5	34.0	17.7	101968	102667	97	92	1313	0.4	0.0	2.2	59.6	37.8	366068
12583	TIVOLI	30177	936	19.8	21.8	36.5	14.9	7.1	61870	64271	80	67	568	2.3	1.8	19.4	64.3	12.3	237281
12585	VERBANK	37414	343	3.2	10.2	43.4	27.4	15.7	87066	89638	94	87	287	0.0	0.0	3.1	65.2	31.7	344149
12586	WALDEN	26047	4602	14.9	25.2	34.3	20.3	5.4	62589	66769	81	68	3254	3.5	1.0	26.7	61.6	7.1	210629
12589	WALLKILL	24602	4650	12.6	19.5	44.0	16.7	7.3	65866	67868	84	73	3460	2.7	1.2	10.4	72.1	13.7	264933
12590	WAPPINGERS FALLS	33068	13240	9.5	18.0	36.4	24.6	11.5	75040	79085	89	81	8836	1.9	1.4	9.4	76.5	10.8	267410
12592	WASSAIC	27773	457	12.5	37.0	33.3	12.0	5.3	50955	60554	63	48	306	3.6	3.3	17.3	66.0	9.8	225714
12594	WINGDALE	27760	1521	9.1	18.9	43.4	23.6	5.0	71923	74911	88	78	1145	5.2	1.8	13.6	72.4	6.9	242708
12601	POUGHKEEPSIE	22493	15978	29.8	24.9	27.9	12.7	4.6	44000	48076	45	27	7190	1.6	1.5	30.4	61.2	5.3	209283
12603	POUGHKEEPSIE	35803	15140	10.6	15.8	35.5	25.6	12.4	77479	81530	91	83	10946	0.6	0.8	11.6	74.9	12.1	248051
12604	POUGHKEEPSIE	10027	46	10.9	17.4	34.8	26.1	10.9	75000	77711	89	81	27	0.0	0.0	3.7	92.6	3.7	257500
12701	MONTICELLO	22508	5177	34.4	23.4	29.4	8.4	4.3	41660	45202	38	19	2636	5.3	13.1	52.8	25.8	3.0	137980
12719	BARRYVILLE	25670	415	23.6	25.3	38.8	8.0	4.3	50918	51942	63	48	334	0.3	6.0	41.3	49.1	3.3	179000
12720	BETHEL	37204	68	29.4	25.0	30.9	5.9	8.8	45000	46849	48	31	52	0.0	15.4	26.9	46.2	11.5	184091
12721	BLOOMINGBURG	24978	2379	15.9	22.9	39.0	17.1	5.1	63396	64771	82	70	1872	11.6	9.3	24.8	48.7	5.6	185340
12723	CALLICOON	23105	751	23.4	28.9	35.8	9.6	2.3	46971	49449	54	37	562	1.1	6.8	48.0	35.8	8.4	164815
12725	CLARYVILLE	25581	138	22.5	31.2	34.1	8.0	4.3	45768	48646	51	33	104	3.8	2.9	37.5	42.3	13.5	190000
12726	COCHECTON	24274	524	25.2	26.1	36.8	8.0	3.8	48439	50335	58	42	419	4.3	9.3	41.1	41.8	3.6	162500
12729	CUDDEBACKVILLE	23808	1073	17.5	20.1	46.4	13.2	2.7	62218	64625	80	68	826	5.2	4.0	37.8	49.2	3.9	178592
12732	ELDRED	28169	326	23.6	25.5	39.0	8.0	4.0	50841	51324	63	48	262	0.4	6.1	42.4	47.7	3.4	176875
12733	FALLSBURG	11996	236	53.0	25.4	19.9	0.4	1.3	23376	24290	2	2	96	8.3	15.6	56.3	19.8	0.0	129412
12734	FERNDALE	24470	627	29.7	28.9	30.8	7.2	3.5	40734	43788	35	16	399	9.8	12.8	40.1	33.3	4.0	144947
12736	FREMONT CENTER	22725	63	25.4	30.2	34.9	6.3	3.2	42981	44307	42	23	49	4.1	14.3	42.9	30.6	8.2	157813
12737	GLEN SPEY	23702	670	26.0	21.8	38.5	9.3	4.5	51344	52106	64	49	533	1.1	5.3	40.5	48.8	4.3	180288
12738	GLEN WILD	23084	86	25.6	27.9	31.4	9.3	5.8	46158	48437	52	34	60	5.0	6.7	41.7	38.3	8.3	166667
12740	GRAHAMSVILLE	25349	997	17.4	27.9	40.4	9.7	4.6	55294	56268	72	57	769	5.9	3.3	32.4	45.9	12.6	193822
12741	HANKINS	21530	121	25.6	30.6	35.5	5.8	2.5	42354	45000	40	21	93	3.2	12.9	41.9	34.4	7.5	162500
12742	HARRIS	25985	115	22.6	27.8	33.0	9.6	7.0	49651	50377	60	44	71	1.4	4.2	53.5	39.4	1.4	161458
12743	HIGHLAND LAKE	27925	153	21.6	26.8	39.2	8.5	3.9	51412	52168	65	49	124	0.8	6.5	45.2	43.5	4.0	170313
12745	HORTONVILLE	22981	48	25.0	25.0	37.5	12.5	0.0	50000	47334	61	45	35	0.0	2.9	45.7	40.0	11.4	178125
12746	HUGUENOT	20904	435	19.1	27.1	40.7	10.1	3.0	53393	58723	69	54	352	7.7	5.7	42.0	44.3	0.3	167803
12747	HURLEYVILLE	20242	1210	33.2	22.4	31.7	10.2	2.5	43045	45573	43	23	700	20.4	9.7	44.7	24.3	0.9	132828
12748	JEFFERSONVILLE	23985	888	28.2	27.5	31.0	7.8	5.6	44489	47267	47	29	675	2.2	7.9	48.3	35.0	6.7	151059
12750	KENOZA LAKE	23642	35	25.7	22.9	40.0	8.6	2.9	50637	52129	63	47	26	0.0	3.8	53.8	38.5	3.8	158333
12751	KIAMESHA LAKE	24791	149	24.2	26.2	35.6	11.4	2.7	49692	50971	60	44	93	0.0	36.6	37.6	24.7	1.1	114063
12752	LAKE HUNTINGTON	28522	63	23.8	25.4	39.7	7.9	3.2	50502	51830	62	46	50	4.0	10.0	42.0	42.0	2.0	160000
12754	LIBERTY	22635	2662	28.5	26.6	32.6	8.2	4.2	42995	46387	42	23	1507	8.5	8.0	57.3	24.8	1.3	137823
12758	LIVINGSTON MANOR	20616	1895	28.2	30.1	33.1	6.1	2.4	43293	45586	43	24	1351	3.1	12.1	53.0	29.9	1.9	144431
12759	LOCH SHELDRAKE	25012	271	29.5	19.2	34.3	9.6	7.4	50965	52242	63	48	152	28.3	6.6	32.9	29.6	2.6	138333
12760	LONG EDDY	20481	241	29.5	33.2	29.5	5.4	2.5	37851	40000	26	9	194	9.8	22.7	41.8	20.6	5.2	126786
12762	MONGAUP VALLEY	26053	112	33.9	20.5	33.0	8.0	4.5	41877	45578	39	20	80	3.8	16.3	30.0	42.5	7.5	175000
12763	MOUNTAIN DALE	21806	403	18.6	31.3	38.0	8.4	3.7	50097	50651	61	45	273	9.5	11.7	50.2	28.2	0.4	121607
12764	NARROWSBURG	23873	766	26.0	24.7	39.4	7.6	2.3	49129	50484	59	43	602	4.7	5.5	51.7	32.6	5.6	155056
12765	NEVERSINK	21920	294	20.7	27.6	40.5	9.9	1.4	56904	51701	74	60	237	5.5	7.2	46.4	32.5	8.4	148633
12766	NORTH BRANCH	23822	269	22.7	27.1	39.4	4.5	6.3	50152	51844	62	45	208	1.0	10.1	43.3	34.6	11.1	163750
	NEW YORK	29893		21.9	21.3	32.7	14.0	9.9	58747	62337				3.4	5.7	23.0	38.7	29.1	269816
	UNITED STATES	27277		20.9	24.4	35.3	11.7	7.6	54719	56938				9.3	13.1	31.6	32.6	13.5	162279

ZIP CODE #	POST OFFICE NAME	FINANCIAL SERVICES: Auto Loan	Home Loan	Invest-ments	Retire-ment Plans	THE HOME: Home Improvements: Home Repair	Lawn & Garden	Furnishings: Comput-ers & Hard-ware-Personal	Major Appli-ances	TV, Radio, Sound Equip-ment	Furni-ture	ENTERTAINMENT: Dine out/ Carry out	Sports Equip-ment	Fees & Tickets	Toys & Games	Travel	Cable TV	PERSONAL: Apparel & Services	Auto Repairs	Health Insur-ance	Pets & Supplies
12496	WINDHAM	95	76	123	75	84	101	76	97	80	71	79	71	66	76	83	85	52	89	96	112
12498	WOODSTOCK	114	123	135	124	128	129	114	122	115	118	115	88	121	111	123	117	80	118	126	141
12501	AMENIA	95	111	106	109	109	105	104	103	102	102	104	80	113	103	110	103	74	104	104	120
12502	ANCRAM	114	91	147	90	100	121	91	116	96	86	94	85	79	91	99	102	63	107	115	135
12503	ANCRAMDALE	113	90	146	89	99	119	91	115	95	85	94	84	78	90	98	101	62	106	114	133
12507	BARRYTOWN	106	119	119	120	121	121	110	114	111	113	111	83	119	108	117	113	78	112	120	132
12508	BEACON	95	105	101	103	104	97	105	99	102	102	104	78	109	103	106	102	74	102	99	115
12513	CLAVERACK	102	104	117	102	107	120	96	110	102	93	101	78	99	99	104	108	69	105	120	126
12514	CLINTON CORNERS	133	165	169	169	170	156	141	149	135	149	136	110	160	135	158	133	98	141	140	170
12515	CLINTONDALE	80	86	91	83	89	87	82	86	83	84	82	63	86	80	87	84	58	85	89	99
12516	COPAKE	116	93	150	91	102	123	93	118	97	87	96	86	81	92	101	104	64	109	117	137
12517	COPAKE FALLS	112	89	144	88	98	118	90	114	94	84	93	83	78	89	97	100	62	105	112	132
12518	CORNWALL	127	149	149	148	151	142	135	138	132	137	133	104	147	132	145	132	95	135	136	158
12520	CORNWALL ON HUDSON	110	149	155	139	154	136	126	131	123	126	124	95	147	123	143	125	91	127	130	145
12521	CRARYVILLE	110	92	140	91	100	117	92	113	95	86	94	83	82	91	99	101	63	105	112	131
12522	DOVER PLAINS	104	110	105	107	109	107	105	106	104	106	104	80	107	105	106	105	73	105	107	123
12523	ELIZAVILLE	99	77	121	76	84	104	78	99	83	73	82	73	66	80	82	89	54	91	99	115
12524	FISHKILL	111	129	130	128	131	123	121	120	120	122	121	91	132	118	129	120	86	121	123	139
12525	GARDINER	108	113	106	110	113	110	104	107	104	106	105	79	106	107	105	105	73	105	106	125
12526	GERMANTOWN	110	90	137	89	98	116	90	111	94	85	93	82	80	91	97	100	63	104	111	129
12528	HIGHLAND	98	115	110	114	114	106	107	106	104	108	105	82	116	105	113	103	75	106	104	123
12529	HILLSDALE	111	90	143	89	99	117	90	113	94	85	93	83	79	90	98	100	62	105	112	131
12531	HOLMES	129	172	166	166	173	151	143	147	135	147	137	113	165	139	159	133	100	140	135	165
12533	HOPEWELL JUNCTION	145	185	178	183	186	163	156	160	148	163	150	123	178	152	171	144	109	152	145	181
12534	HUDSON	77	72	81	71	73	81	76	79	79	72	78	59	73	76	76	82	54	79	85	93
12538	HYDE PARK	98	116	115	113	117	110	106	108	104	106	105	81	116	104	114	105	75	106	108	123
12540	LAGRANGEVILLE	142	180	171	180	179	161	151	157	144	159	146	120	172	147	167	140	105	149	144	178
12542	MARLBORO	89	112	109	109	113	104	101	101	99	98	100	77	112	100	109	100	73	100	100	115
12543	MAYBROOK	109	118	103	115	113	105	111	109	108	114	109	83	114	111	111	106	77	108	104	126
12545	MILLBROOK	113	142	146	136	145	133	128	129	127	123	128	96	143	127	139	130	93	128	129	146
12546	MILLERTON	107	90	136	89	98	113	90	110	93	85	92	81	81	89	97	98	62	103	109	127
12547	MILTON	97	120	112	118	119	112	103	107	100	103	101	82	115	102	113	101	72	103	104	122
12548	MODENA	101	94	90	90	94	99	88	96	92	93	92	68	85	94	87	95	62	93	98	113
12549	MONTGOMERY	114	139	126	138	136	126	122	123	117	124	119	96	135	120	130	115	85	120	117	142
12550	NEWBURGH	94	99	94	98	98	93	101	96	100	100	101	74	104	100	101	100	73	100	96	111
12553	NEW WINDSOR	107	118	113	117	117	112	112	111	110	113	112	85	118	112	116	110	79	111	110	129
12561	NEW PALTZ	94	92	90	93	91	90	105	92	98	97	99	74	99	98	96	97	70	97	92	109
12563	PATTERSON	136	170	161	167	169	151	147	149	140	151	142	115	165	144	159	137	103	144	138	170
12564	PAWLING	125	158	160	156	161	146	139	142	135	141	137	107	158	135	154	135	99	138	138	161
12566	PINE BUSH	99	117	106	117	115	111	104	106	101	104	102	82	113	103	111	101	73	103	104	123
12567	PINE PLAINS	116	100	144	98	107	123	99	119	102	94	102	88	90	99	106	108	69	112	118	138
12569	PLEASANT VALLEY	121	133	129	133	133	128	122	125	119	125	120	94	129	121	127	119	85	121	122	145
12570	POUGHQUAG	140	184	175	178	184	161	154	158	145	158	148	121	177	150	170	143	108	151	145	177
12571	RED HOOK	110	116	119	118	117	118	110	114	110	111	110	86	114	109	115	111	77	112	115	133
12572	RHINEBECK	123	135	137	137	137	136	128	130	128	131	128	97	136	125	135	129	90	129	136	152
12575	ROCK TAVERN	120	146	129	146	141	131	124	127	119	130	121	100	138	124	133	116	86	122	118	147
12577	SALISBURY MILLS	142	181	164	179	177	157	152	155	143	158	146	121	172	148	165	138	105	147	140	176
12578	SALT POINT	132	158	152	159	158	147	136	142	131	143	132	107	150	133	147	129	94	135	134	163
12580	STAATSBURG	128	162	161	163	164	153	137	144	133	143	134	107	157	133	154	132	96	138	139	164
12581	STANFORDVILLE	128	157	161	161	161	149	134	142	129	143	130	106	152	128	150	127	93	135	135	163
12582	STORMVILLE	154	197	183	200	194	172	163	167	153	174	156	133	188	159	179	147	114	158	148	191
12583	TIVOLI	105	102	109	103	102	106	104	105	104	102	104	81	102	103	104	105	72	105	106	124
12585	VERBANK	143	181	161	180	176	157	152	154	143	159	145	122	172	148	164	137	105	147	138	177
12586	WALDEN	97	113	109	109	113	106	103	104	101	101	102	79	110	103	108	102	73	103	103	120
12589	WALLKILL	103	119	110	116	117	111	107	109	105	107	106	83	115	107	113	105	75	107	107	126
12590	WAPPINGERS FALLS	120	137	131	136	136	124	129	125	124	130	126	98	138	127	134	123	91	125	120	144
12592	WASSAIC	88	103	98	101	102	95	99	96	97	97	98	75	107	97	104	96	70	97	95	111
12594	WINGDALE	110	126	110	124	121	112	114	114	110	117	111	90	121	114	118	107	79	111	107	131
12601	POUGHKEEPSIE	77	75	73	76	74	73	85	76	86	81	86	60	84	85	81	87	62	83	81	92
12603	POUGHKEEPSIE	116	143	147	139	146	134	131	130	128	130	129	98	146	127	142	129	93	130	130	148
12604	POUGHKEEPSIE	127	129	122	132	125	124	132	124	130	132	131	98	134	130	130	128	92	128	126	149
12701	MONTICELLO	80	67	81	68	69	81	76	79	80	71	79	59	69	77	74	85	54	81	87	94
12719	BARRYVILLE	108	87	140	85	95	114	87	110	91	81	90	80	75	86	94	97	59	102	109	127
12720	BETHEL	150	120	193	118	132	158	120	152	125	112	124	111	104	119	130	134	82	141	150	177
12721	BLOOMINGBURG	100	108	97	107	104	102	100	101	98	101	99	78	103	101	101	97	69	99	98	118
12723	CALLICOON	96	77	124	76	84	101	77	98	80	72	79	71	67	76	83	86	53	90	96	113
12725	CLARYVILLE	103	82	133	81	91	109	83	105	86	77	85	77	72	82	89	92	57	97	104	122
12726	COCHECTON	98	78	127	77	86	104	79	100	82	74	81	73	68	78	85	88	54	92	99	116
12729	CUDDEBACKVILLE	88	100	93	100	98	99	90	94	90	90	91	72	97	91	96	91	64	91	95	109
12732	ELDRED	109	87	140	86	96	115	87	111	91	82	90	81	75	87	94	97	60	102	109	128
12733	FALLSBURG	49	40	43	42	41	45	50	47	52	47	52	36	46	51	46	54	36	50	53	56
12734	FERNDALE	78	70	83	70	73	80	75	80	77	71	76	59	70	75	75	80	52	79	83	93
12736	FREMONT CENTER	88	71	114	70	78	94	71	90	74	66	73	66	61	70	77	79	49	83	89	104
12737	GLEN SPEY	98	78	126	77	86	103	78	99	82	73	81	73	68	78	85	87	54	92	98	115
12738	GLEN WILD	98	79	127	77	86	104	79	100	82	74	81	73	68	78	85	88	54	92	99	116
12740	GRAHAMSVILLE	104	88	113	89	93	110	88	105	91	81	90	78	78	90	91	97	61	97	106	122
12741	HANKINS	88	71	114	70	78	94	71	90	74	66	73	66	61	70	77	79	49	83	89	104
12742	HARRIS	108	87	140	85	95	115	87	110	91	81	90	81	75	86	94	97	60	102	109	128
12743	HIGHLAND LAKE	111	89	143	87	97	117	89	113	93	83	92	82	77	88	96	99	61	104	111	131
12745	HORTONVILLE	95	76	123	75	84	101	76	97	80	71	79	71	66	76	83	85	52	89	96	112
12746	HUGUENOT	93	86	76	83	84	88	81	86	84	84	84	62	77	87	77	86	57	83	86	102
12747	HURLEYVILLE	77	75	69	73	73	73	78	74	78	77	78	58	76	79	75	78	55	77	76	88
12748	JEFFERSONVILLE	98	78	126	77	86	103	78	99	82	73	81	73	68	78	85	87	54	92	98	115
12750	KENOZA LAKE	91	73	118	72	80	97	73	93	77	69	76	68	63	73	79	82	50	86	92	108
12751	KIAMESHA LAKE	86	76	79	77	78	87	82	85	84	78	82	63	75	83	79	87	56	84	91	100
12752	LAKE HUNTINGTON	96	77	124	75	84	101	77	97	80	72	79	71	66	76	83	86	53	90	96	113
12754	LIBERTY	78	74	74	75	74	77	80	78	81	77	80	60	78	80	78	82	56	80	82	92
12758	LIVINGSTON MANOR	81	68	91	67	71	83	70	81	74	66	73	60	63	72	71	78	49	77	83	94
12759	LOCH SHELDRAKE	112	95	83	93	90	93	112	99	108	107	108	79	97	112	96	107	75	105	99	120
12760	LONG EDDY	85	64	97	63	69	88	65	83	71	61	69	61	54	69	67	77	46	76	84	97
12762	MONGAUP VALLEY	94	75	121	74	82	99	75	95	79	70	78	70	65	75	81	84	52	88	94	111
12763	MOUNTAIN DALE	93	76	110	76	82	97	78	93	81	74	80	68	69	78	81	86	54	88	94	108
12764	NARROWSBURG	92	74	119	73	81	98	74	94	77	69	77	69	64	74	80	83	51	87	93	109
12765	NEVERSINK	91	87	102	88	89	98	82	94	83	80	83	71	80	83	88	86	57	88	93	110
12766	NORTH BRANCH	101	81	130	79	89	107	81	103	84	76	83	75	70	80	87	90	55	95	101	119
	NEW YORK	100	106	110	108	107	104	112	106	113	106	114	81	115	110	112	116	83	110	110	124
	UNITED STATES	100	100	100	100	100	100	100	100	100	100	100	100	100	100	100	100	100	100	100	100

POPULATION CHANGE

ZIP CODE #	POST OFFICE NAME	COUNTY FIPS CODE	POPULATION 2000	POPULATION 2009	POPULATION 2014	2000-2009 ANNUAL RATE % Rate	2000-2009 ANNUAL RATE State Centile	HOUSEHOLDS 2000	HOUSEHOLDS 2009	HOUSEHOLDS 2014	HOUSEHOLDS % Annual Rate 2000-2009	HOUSEHOLDS 2009 Average HH Size	FAMILIES 2000	FAMILIES 2009	FAMILIES % Annual Rate 2000-2009
12768	PARKSVILLE	105	1179	1216	1228	0.3	59	402	427	434	0.7	2.42	256	267	0.5
12770	POND EDDY	105	305	345	361	1.3	94	120	137	145	1.4	2.52	84	95	1.3
12771	PORT JERVIS	071	13844	15668	16431	1.3	94	5261	5953	6257	1.3	2.61	3498	3883	1.1
12775	ROCK HILL	105	1692	2094	2222	2.3	99	694	878	938	2.6	2.38	475	591	2.4
12776	ROSCOE	025	2567	2543	2521	-0.1	30	1037	1052	1051	0.2	2.32	682	679	0.0
12777	FORESTBURGH	105	705	759	785	0.8	84	281	311	324	1.1	2.42	191	207	0.9
12779	SOUTH FALLSBURG	105	1465	1539	1563	0.5	71	593	637	651	0.8	2.32	379	400	0.6
12780	SPARROW BUSH	071	2287	2727	2923	1.9	98	895	1069	1152	1.9	2.55	636	746	1.7
12783	SWAN LAKE	105	1920	1983	2006	0.3	59	652	693	707	0.7	2.58	434	452	0.4
12786	WHITE LAKE	105	640	682	698	0.7	80	243	265	273	0.9	2.41	157	168	0.7
12787	WHITE SULPHUR SPRING	105	18	20	21	1.1	91	5	6	6	2.0	3.33	3	3	0.0
12788	WOODBOURNE	105	2690	2750	2756	0.2	52	672	707	714	0.6	2.42	469	486	0.4
12789	WOODRIDGE	105	2465	2721	2827	1.1	91	678	808	862	1.9	2.38	413	481	1.7
12790	WURTSBORO	105	5472	5850	6028	0.7	80	2206	2414	2503	1.0	2.42	1490	1602	0.8
12791	YOUNGSVILLE	105	200	214	221	0.7	80	90	99	102	1.0	2.16	62	66	0.7
12792	YULAN	105	368	393	401	0.7	80	159	174	179	1.0	2.10	108	116	0.8
12801	GLENS FALLS	113	14177	14004	13886	-0.1	30	6203	6323	6340	0.2	2.17	3378	3337	-0.1
12803	SOUTH GLENS FALLS	091	7110	7397	7529	0.4	66	2948	3118	3195	0.6	2.37	1933	2005	0.4
12804	QUEENSBURY	113	23987	26084	26803	0.9	87	9333	10445	10835	1.2	2.46	6712	7402	1.1
12808	ADIRONDACK	113	244	258	262	0.6	76	118	129	133	1.0	2.00	82	88	0.8
12809	ARGYLE	115	3568	3806	3911	0.7	80	1277	1409	1465	1.1	2.61	969	1056	0.9
12810	ATHOL	113	626	686	714	1.0	89	243	275	289	1.3	2.48	174	193	1.1
12812	BLUE MOUNTAIN LAKE	041	244	236	230	-0.4	11	110	109	107	-0.1	2.13	69	67	-0.3
12814	BOLTON LANDING	113	1453	1566	1624	0.8	84	651	726	762	1.2	2.16	424	461	0.9
12815	BRANT LAKE	113	1110	1175	1196	0.6	76	468	513	527	1.0	2.29	326	349	0.7
12816	CAMBRIDGE	115	4296	4428	4476	0.3	59	1702	1803	1841	0.6	2.39	1178	1227	0.4
12817	CHESTERTOWN	113	2145	2407	2520	1.3	94	915	1056	1117	1.6	2.17	619	700	1.3
12819	CLEMONS	115	429	498	526	1.6	97	170	204	218	2.0	2.44	125	147	1.8
12821	COMSTOCK	115	1326	1370	1386	0.4	66	89	99	103	1.2	4.89	67	73	0.9
12822	CORINTH	091	5309	5785	5882	0.9	87	2095	2210	2265	0.6	2.54	1466	1515	0.4
12823	COSSAYUNA	115	243	256	262	0.6	76	91	99	102	0.9	2.59	70	75	0.7
12824	DIAMOND POINT	113	860	915	957	0.7	80	375	414	438	1.1	2.21	265	286	0.8
12827	FORT ANN	115	3778	3872	3915	0.3	59	1393	1484	1522	0.7	2.20	1059	1115	0.6
12828	FORT EDWARD	115	8389	8807	8991	0.5	71	3122	3368	3472	0.8	2.55	2261	2401	0.7
12831	GANSEVOORT	091	14417	17771	19205	2.3	99	4854	6255	6840	2.8	2.75	3696	4681	2.6
12832	GRANVILLE	115	6973	7240	7367	0.4	66	2627	2806	2883	0.7	2.48	1830	1925	0.5
12833	GREENFIELD CENTER	091	5014	5601	5890	1.2	93	1824	2078	2201	1.4	2.65	1357	1514	1.2
12834	GREENWICH	115	6451	6536	6581	0.1	44	2504	2613	2658	0.5	2.49	1780	1830	0.3
12835	HADLEY	091	2657	2992	3159	1.3	94	1043	1200	1277	1.5	2.48	756	851	1.3
12836	HAGUE	113	904	1246	1385	3.5	100	390	551	619	3.8	2.26	273	377	3.6
12837	HAMPTON	115	704	788	823	1.2	93	258	299	316	1.6	2.58	186	211	1.4
12838	HARTFORD	115	563	627	652	1.2	93	203	233	245	1.5	2.69	161	182	1.3
12839	HUDSON FALLS	115	11965	12534	12769	0.5	71	4815	5198	5349	0.8	2.37	3168	3371	0.7
12842	INDIAN LAKE	041	1227	1162	1126	-0.6	4	541	524	513	-0.3	2.18	356	339	-0.5
12843	JOHNSBURG	113	1227	1247	1251	0.2	52	479	503	510	0.5	2.41	333	342	0.3
12844	KATTSKILL BAY	115	295	298	300	0.1	44	140	146	149	0.5	2.03	105	108	0.3
12845	LAKE GEORGE	113	5157	5589	5868	0.9	87	2172	2412	2556	1.1	2.30	1468	1589	0.9
12846	LAKE LUZERNE	113	3219	3675	3881	1.4	95	1264	1477	1572	1.7	2.48	884	1011	1.5
12847	LONG LAKE	041	852	806	785	-0.6	4	387	378	371	-0.3	2.07	237	227	-0.5
12849	MIDDLE GRANVILLE	115	301	336	350	1.2	93	111	129	136	1.6	2.50	83	94	1.4
12850	MIDDLE GROVE	091	2376	2729	2895	1.5	96	867	1013	1083	1.7	2.69	652	747	1.5
12851	MINERVA	031	273	282	279	0.4	66	111	117	117	0.6	2.41	78	81	0.4
12852	NEWCOMB	031	481	437	417	-1.0	1	211	197	190	-0.7	2.19	141	130	-0.9
12853	NORTH CREEK	113	1847	1899	1913	0.3	59	760	800	815	0.6	2.06	502	517	0.3
12854	NORTH GRANVILLE	115	35	38	39	0.9	87	12	13	14	0.9	2.92	9	10	1.1
12855	NORTH HUDSON	031	243	240	236	-0.1	30	103	105	104	0.2	2.29	70	70	0.0
12857	OLMSTEDVILLE	031	620	634	627	0.2	52	246	257	256	0.5	2.40	172	177	0.3
12858	PARADOX	031	13	13	12	0.0	38	6	6	6	0.0	2.17	4	3	-3.1
12859	PORTER CORNERS	091	1539	1714	1799	1.2	93	572	651	688	1.4	2.55	438	488	1.2
12860	POTTERSVILLE	113	911	906	898	-0.1	30	166	168	168	0.1	4.06	119	118	-0.1
12861	PUTNAM STATION	115	574	665	702	1.6	97	217	260	277	2.0	2.56	160	187	1.7
12863	ROCK CITY FALLS	091	540	580	598	0.8	84	206	223	231	0.9	2.60	149	158	0.6
12865	SALEM	115	3467	3823	3965	1.1	91	1325	1504	1577	1.4	2.50	948	1060	1.2
12866	SARATOGA SPRINGS	091	34588	38101	39803	1.1	91	14016	15700	16519	1.2	2.27	8403	9350	1.2
12870	SCHROON LAKE	031	1696	1648	1612	-0.3	15	709	703	692	-0.1	2.30	455	444	-0.3
12871	SCHUYLERVILLE	091	4100	4238	4339	0.4	66	1597	1689	1740	0.6	2.50	1112	1157	0.4
12872	SEVERANCE	031	6	6	6	0.0	38	3	3	3	0.0	2.00	2	2	0.0
12873	SHUSHAN	115	790	886	926	1.2	93	333	387	409	1.6	2.27	217	247	1.4
12878	STONY CREEK	113	678	731	755	0.8	84	270	300	312	1.1	2.43	189	205	0.9
12883	TICONDEROGA	031	5214	5290	5225	0.2	52	2052	2126	2116	0.4	2.43	1371	1401	0.2
12885	WARRENSBURG	113	4658	4881	4975	0.5	71	1870	2017	2080	0.8	2.39	1287	1358	0.6
12886	WEVERTOWN	113	33	32	32	-0.3	15	15	15	15	0.0	2.13	11	11	0.0
12887	WHITEHALL	115	6819	6999	7072	0.3	59	2037	2150	2194	0.6	2.67	1408	1460	0.4
12901	PLATTSBURGH	019	32170	32630	32933	0.2	52	12743	13229	13471	0.4	2.24	7178	7331	0.2
12903	PLATTSBURGH	019	104	938	1127	26.8	100	57	477	582	25.8	1.97	23	237	28.7
12910	ALTONA	019	2439	2494	2478	0.2	52	635	634	631	0.0	2.76	465	456	-0.2
12911	KEESEVILLE	031	73	74	75	0.1	44	30	31	32	0.4	2.39	21	21	0.0
12912	AU SABLE FORKS	019	2107	2148	2145	0.2	52	832	865	872	0.4	2.48	583	597	0.3
12913	BLOOMINGDALE	031	1062	1046	1027	-0.2	21	429	432	428	0.1	2.42	279	276	-0.1
12914	BOMBAY	033	894	886	875	-0.1	30	347	355	354	0.2	2.50	238	239	0.0
12916	BRUSHTON	033	2277	2320	2327	0.2	52	897	943	956	0.5	2.45	620	640	0.3
12917	BURKE	033	1330	1423	1451	0.7	80	480	527	543	1.0	2.62	359	389	0.9
12918	CADYVILLE	019	2569	2709	2774	0.6	76	948	1023	1057	0.8	2.46	706	750	0.7
12919	CHAMPLAIN	019	2949	3144	3244	0.7	80	1206	1323	1380	1.0	2.36	813	872	0.8
12920	CHATEAUGAY	033	2568	2669	2648	0.4	66	941	959	960	0.2	2.39	635	635	0.0
12921	CHAZY	019	2501	2585	2629	0.4	66	937	994	1019	0.6	2.57	681	707	0.4
12922	CHILDWOLD	089	35	35	34	0.0	38	19	19	19	0.0	1.84	12	12	0.0
12923	CHURUBUSCO	019	717	783	813	1.0	89	265	296	310	1.2	2.65	197	216	1.0
12924	KEESEVILLE	019	221	230	235	0.4	66	82	88	91	0.8	2.61	57	60	0.6
12926	CONSTABLE	033	2113	2163	2178	0.3	59	790	832	846	0.6	2.59	584	606	0.4
12928	CROWN POINT	031	2113	2096	2060	-0.1	30	796	811	803	0.2	2.56	578	582	0.1
12930	DICKINSON CENTER	033	584	576	569	-0.1	30	236	239	238	0.1	2.41	175	175	0.0
12932	ELIZABETHTOWN	031	1504	1479	1456	-0.2	21	572	577	570	0.1	2.30	372	370	-0.1
12934	ELLENBURG CENTER	019	1387	1388	1390	0.0	38	463	473	478	0.2	2.86	319	320	0.0
12935	ELLENBURG DEPOT	019	1433	1503	1526	0.5	71	539	576	590	0.7	2.51	383	401	0.5
	NEW YORK					0.3					0.3	2.61			0.1
	UNITED STATES					1.0					1.1	2.59			0.9

ZIP CODE #	POST OFFICE NAME	RACE (%) White 2000	White 2009	Black 2000	Black 2009	Asian/Pacific 2000	Asian/Pacific 2009	% Hispanic Origin 2000	% Hispanic Origin 2009	2009 AGE DISTRIBUTION (%) 0-4	5-9	10-14	15-19	20-24	25-44	45-64	65-84	85+	18+	MEDIAN AGE 2009	% 2009 Males	% 2009 Females
12768	PARKSVILLE	87.1	84.5	8.6	10.2	0.9	1.2	10.1	12.5	4.6	4.9	6.3	5.8	5.4	29.0	29.1	12.5	2.3	80.2	41.4	52.9	47.1
12770	POND EDDY	96.4	95.7	0.3	0.3	1.3	1.7	1.3	1.7	5.8	7.8	6.1	6.4	2.6	23.2	31.6	14.5	2.0	75.7	43.5	49.9	50.1
12771	PORT JERVIS	91.7	89.2	3.4	4.1	0.7	1.1	6.3	8.2	7.3	7.0	7.1	7.0	6.6	25.6	26.3	11.0	2.1	74.1	36.9	48.6	51.4
12775	ROCK HILL	94.1	92.4	1.2	1.5	2.0	2.9	4.3	5.5	5.7	6.1	6.6	6.1	3.6	20.8	34.7	15.1	1.4	77.5	45.7	49.8	50.2
12776	ROSCOE	95.9	94.6	1.2	1.5	0.7	0.9	2.9	3.8	5.0	5.2	5.5	5.7	4.5	20.3	31.7	18.2	3.9	80.5	47.4	49.5	50.5
12777	FORESTBURGH	95.7	94.6	2.0	2.5	0.0	0.0	4.8	6.3	5.0	5.4	5.4	5.7	3.6	19.2	37.3	16.7	1.7	80.4	48.1	49.1	50.9
12779	SOUTH FALLSBURG	73.2	68.9	16.3	18.6	1.6	2.1	16.2	19.0	7.4	6.6	6.3	8.4	7.3	23.8	26.6	11.8	1.8	74.3	38.4	49.5	50.5
12780	SPARROW BUSH	97.2	96.0	0.7	1.0	0.7	1.1	2.6	3.5	6.2	6.5	6.7	6.7	5.5	24.4	31.4	11.3	1.3	76.5	40.5	50.7	49.3
12783	SWAN LAKE	87.2	84.8	6.4	7.4	0.9	1.2	12.3	15.3	4.7	4.9	5.4	5.7	4.8	23.4	35.0	14.5	1.6	81.4	45.6	52.7	47.3
12786	WHITE LAKE	91.7	89.9	3.0	3.5	0.9	1.2	15.0	19.1	5.4	5.6	6.0	5.9	4.4	24.9	32.0	14.2	1.6	79.8	43.5	51.8	48.2
12787	WHITE SULPHUR SPRING	94.4	95.0	5.6	5.0	0.0	0.0	5.6	5.0	0.0	0.0	0.0	5.0	0.0	35.0	45.0	15.0	0.0	95.0	50.0	40.0	60.0
12788	WOODBOURNE	70.4	68.5	22.3	23.2	0.9	1.1	13.8	15.1	4.0	4.3	5.1	4.6	4.7	40.4	28.2	8.0	0.8	83.7	38.7	68.2	31.8
12789	WOODRIDGE	66.7	64.1	21.6	22.0	1.7	2.4	18.7	21.0	4.4	4.2	4.4	5.4	5.7	36.4	26.8	11.4	1.2	83.6	39.4	63.3	36.7
12790	WURTSBORO	93.3	91.4	2.2	2.7	1.2	1.6	4.4	5.7	6.7	6.6	6.6	6.4	6.0	24.4	28.2	13.5	1.6	76.4	40.3	50.4	49.6
12791	YOUNGSVILLE	96.5	95.8	1.0	0.9	1.0	1.4	4.5	6.5	4.7	4.7	5.6	5.6	3.7	21.5	36.9	15.9	1.4	81.8	47.4	50.0	50.0
12792	YULAN	93.2	91.6	3.8	4.8	0.8	1.0	4.6	5.9	4.3	4.6	5.1	6.1	4.3	21.9	36.1	15.5	2.0	82.2	47.3	50.6	49.4
12801	GLENS FALLS	96.5	95.6	1.3	1.5	0.4	0.6	1.4	1.7	6.2	5.5	5.4	6.7	8.2	28.7	26.3	10.5	2.5	78.8	37.3	49.0	51.0
12803	SOUTH GLENS FALLS	98.6	98.2	0.5	0.6	0.2	0.3	0.6	0.8	5.9	6.1	6.1	6.3	5.6	25.4	28.1	14.5	2.2	77.8	41.8	47.6	52.4
12804	QUEENSBURY	97.5	96.8	0.6	0.7	0.7	1.0	1.1	1.4	5.6	5.9	6.5	6.9	4.9	23.0	30.5	14.0	2.8	77.6	43.2	47.9	52.1
12808	ADIRONDACK	99.6	98.1	0.0	0.4	0.0	0.4	0.4	0.4	2.7	3.1	3.5	5.0	4.3	19.0	39.9	20.5	1.9	87.2	52.0	48.4	51.6
12809	ARGYLE	98.8	98.3	0.3	0.4	0.0	0.1	1.0	1.3	5.1	5.8	6.9	6.8	4.3	25.1	30.3	13.0	2.8	77.8	42.3	48.9	51.1
12810	ATHOL	97.6	96.8	0.3	0.4	0.5	0.7	1.0	1.2	4.7	4.8	5.5	7.4	5.1	23.8	32.7	14.6	1.5	79.6	44.1	51.7	48.3
12812	BLUE MOUNTAIN LAKE	98.8	98.3	0.0	0.0	0.0	0.0	1.2	1.7	3.4	3.8	4.2	5.9	3.0	19.5	39.8	18.2	2.1	84.3	51.2	50.0	50.0
12814	BOLTON LANDING	98.0	97.4	0.7	0.8	0.3	0.4	0.6	0.9	3.6	4.2	4.7	5.2	3.3	18.1	39.7	19.2	2.2	84.5	51.0	50.8	49.2
12815	BRANT LAKE	98.6	98.2	0.2	0.3	0.2	0.3	0.5	0.6	2.8	3.2	3.7	5.1	4.6	19.1	38.6	20.8	2.0	87.2	51.7	49.8	50.2
12816	CAMBRIDGE	97.8	97.0	0.7	0.9	0.4	0.6	1.1	1.5	5.6	6.2	6.8	7.0	4.9	23.2	29.2	14.1	3.0	76.1	42.3	48.9	51.1
12817	CHESTERTOWN	98.6	98.3	0.1	0.1	0.4	0.6	0.5	0.6	5.1	5.4	5.5	7.4	5.3	19.5	33.0	16.8	2.0	80.7	46.1	50.4	49.6
12819	CLEMONS	99.8	99.2	0.0	0.2	0.0	0.2	0.7	1.0	5.4	5.8	6.6	6.8	4.8	22.1	31.5	15.1	1.8	77.7	43.9	51.8	48.2
12821	COMSTOCK	51.0	44.4	37.5	42.3	0.5	0.5	19.1	21.9	2.1	2.0	3.1	9.6	18.7	43.9	16.6	3.8	0.3	90.4	31.1	82.3	17.7
12822	CORINTH	98.2	96.8	0.3	0.9	0.3	0.5	0.8	1.3	5.9	5.9	6.1	7.1	6.6	24.8	28.7	12.8	2.1	79.5	40.6	49.6	50.4
12823	COSSAYUNA	98.4	98.0	0.4	0.4	0.4	0.4	0.4	0.8	4.7	5.5	6.3	7.0	4.7	21.5	35.5	12.9	2.0	78.9	45.2	48.8	51.2
12824	DIAMOND POINT	98.1	97.4	0.3	0.4	0.7	1.0	1.3	1.5	3.7	4.2	4.7	5.1	3.4	19.3	37.0	20.7	1.9	84.0	51.0	51.1	48.9
12827	FORT ANN	87.6	85.5	9.0	10.3	0.1	0.2	5.0	5.9	5.5	5.6	6.6	7.5	7.5	29.9	26.8	9.6	1.0	78.4	37.3	59.1	40.9
12828	FORT EDWARD	97.8	96.9	0.7	0.8	0.4	0.8	0.7	1.0	5.8	6.3	6.5	6.9	5.3	26.9	28.6	11.6	2.0	77.0	40.1	49.7	50.3
12831	GANSEVOORT	93.9	92.7	3.5	3.3	0.5	1.6	2.4	2.5	6.7	7.2	7.7	6.9	4.7	27.9	29.8	8.3	0.8	75.1	38.8	51.8	48.2
12832	GRANVILLE	97.8	97.0	0.5	0.7	0.3	0.4	0.8	1.1	6.3	6.5	6.9	7.0	5.1	24.1	27.5	13.4	3.2	75.8	41.0	49.7	50.3
12833	GREENFIELD CENTER	97.5	96.3	0.6	1.0	0.3	0.5	1.1	1.6	6.2	6.6	7.2	7.5	5.4	26.6	30.3	9.3	1.0	75.8	39.1	50.6	49.4
12834	GREENWICH	98.0	97.3	0.4	0.5	0.7	0.9	0.6	0.8	5.9	6.1	6.4	6.6	5.6	22.9	31.1	13.3	2.1	77.3	42.4	48.9	51.1
12835	HADLEY	98.1	97.5	0.6	0.8	0.2	0.2	0.3	0.4	5.5	5.6	5.8	5.9	4.7	24.6	31.7	14.6	1.6	79.2	43.5	50.3	49.7
12836	HAGUE	98.6	98.0	0.1	0.2	0.1	0.2	0.4	0.6	3.8	4.1	4.8	5.8	3.9	19.5	34.0	21.6	2.6	83.6	50.0	48.9	51.1
12837	HAMPTON	98.4	97.8	0.6	0.8	0.1	0.3	1.0	1.3	6.1	6.5	8.2	6.6	4.9	24.5	31.6	10.3	1.3	74.9	39.7	50.4	49.6
12838	HARTFORD	97.2	96.2	0.7	1.0	0.0	0.0	0.9	1.0	7.0	7.0	8.3	7.3	3.2	27.8	29.7	8.3	1.4	73.0	37.5	50.7	49.3
12839	HUDSON FALLS	98.1	97.5	0.4	0.6	0.2	0.3	0.6	0.9	6.2	5.8	5.9	6.6	6.9	26.7	27.4	12.5	2.0	78.0	39.4	48.2	51.8
12842	INDIAN LAKE	97.8	97.4	0.4	0.4	0.1	0.1	1.2	1.5	4.1	4.6	4.9	5.1	3.4	20.7	36.1	18.6	2.6	82.9	49.3	50.7	49.3
12843	JOHNSBURG	98.0	97.6	0.3	0.3	0.4	0.6	0.2	0.2	4.6	5.7	6.0	5.5	4.3	23.1	32.6	14.9	3.2	80.1	45.5	49.4	50.6
12844	KATTSKILL BAY	98.6	98.3	0.0	0.0	0.3	0.3	0.3	0.3	4.4	4.7	6.7	6.7	3.4	20.5	35.9	16.1	1.7	79.9	46.7	50.7	49.3
12845	LAKE GEORGE	97.8	97.2	0.4	0.5	0.6	0.9	0.8	1.1	4.2	4.7	5.3	5.7	4.3	21.0	35.6	16.9	2.3	81.9	48.0	50.0	50.0
12846	LAKE LUZERNE	97.8	97.1	0.2	0.3	0.3	0.4	1.0	1.3	5.4	5.9	7.4	6.9	4.6	26.1	29.9	12.4	1.4	76.8	40.8	49.6	50.4
12847	LONG LAKE	97.4	96.5	0.6	0.7	0.4	0.6	1.1	1.2	3.2	3.6	4.1	4.1	3.6	18.7	39.3	21.0	2.4	86.1	52.3	50.1	49.9
12849	MIDDLE GRANVILLE	98.3	97.6	0.3	0.6	0.3	0.3	0.7	1.2	6.0	6.5	7.1	6.5	5.1	22.9	31.0	12.8	2.1	76.2	42.1	50.9	49.1
12850	MIDDLE GROVE	97.7	97.1	0.6	0.8	0.4	0.5	1.4	1.8	6.1	6.6	7.5	7.4	5.2	27.0	30.7	8.6	0.9	75.2	38.9	50.7	49.3
12851	MINERVA	96.7	95.7	0.4	0.4	0.0	0.0	0.0	0.0	3.5	5.3	7.8	6.7	3.5	22.3	32.3	16.7	1.8	78.7	45.4	52.8	47.2
12852	NEWCOMB	95.2	93.8	0.0	0.0	0.0	0.0	0.4	0.5	4.1	4.1	4.3	4.6	4.1	13.7	32.7	29.7	2.5	83.8	55.9	47.4	52.6
12853	NORTH CREEK	97.9	97.4	0.2	0.2	0.4	0.6	1.0	1.2	4.5	4.6	4.9	11.0	6.8	20.5	29.4	15.0	3.2	82.4	43.1	48.1	51.9
12854	NORTH GRANVILLE	100.0	100.0	0.0	0.0	0.0	0.0	0.0	0.0	5.3	5.3	5.3	5.3	5.3	23.7	36.8	13.2	0.0	78.9	45.0	47.4	52.6
12855	NORTH HUDSON	94.7	93.3	0.0	0.0	0.4	0.4	0.0	0.0	5.0	5.0	8.3	6.3	5.0	19.2	32.9	15.8	2.5	77.5	45.4	51.3	48.7
12857	OLMSTEDVILLE	97.1	95.9	0.3	0.5	0.2	0.3	0.3	0.3	3.8	5.0	7.3	7.9	4.4	21.9	31.4	16.6	1.7	79.7	44.7	52.2	47.8
12858	PARADOX	100.0	100.0	0.0	0.0	0.0	0.0	0.0	0.0	0.0	0.0	0.0	0.0	0.0	23.1	76.9	0.0	0.0	100.0	51.9	53.8	46.2
12859	PORTER CORNERS	97.8	96.1	0.5	1.3	0.3	0.6	0.8	1.3	6.1	6.8	7.5	7.9	5.4	26.7	29.4	9.3	0.9	76.1	38.8	50.8	49.2
12860	POTTERSVILLE	96.6	95.7	0.3	0.3	0.9	1.1	1.6	2.1	4.2	4.2	4.5	19.3	11.9	17.0	25.3	12.5	1.1	83.6	33.3	48.9	51.1
12861	PUTNAM STATION	99.7	99.2	0.0	0.2	0.0	0.2	0.7	1.1	5.3	5.9	6.6	6.9	4.8	22.1	31.3	15.5	1.7	77.9	43.9	51.4	48.6
12863	ROCK CITY FALLS	95.2	94.1	0.7	0.9	0.6	0.7	2.6	3.1	7.9	7.6	7.1	7.1	7.8	29.7	25.0	7.4	0.5	73.3	33.1	50.0	50.0
12865	SALEM	97.8	97.0	0.8	1.0	0.2	0.3	0.7	1.0	5.2	5.4	6.0	7.4	5.3	23.8	30.7	14.3	1.7	78.7	42.9	50.3	49.7
12866	SARATOGA SPRINGS	94.5	92.0	2.6	3.9	0.9	1.4	1.7	2.5	5.4	5.5	5.7	7.6	8.4	25.8	27.4	11.6	2.6	79.8	38.8	48.7	51.3
12870	SCHROON LAKE	98.1	97.6	0.8	1.1	0.2	0.2	0.5	0.6	4.1	4.2	4.7	6.3	4.6	23.7	33.7	16.5	2.3	83.1	46.6	48.1	51.9
12871	SCHUYLERVILLE	97.7	97.3	1.0	1.1	0.2	0.2	1.1	1.3	6.6	6.6	6.6	6.3	5.9	26.9	28.5	10.9	1.7	76.3	39.2	49.6	50.4
12872	SEVERANCE	100.0	100.0	0.0	0.0	0.0	0.0	0.0	0.0	0.0	0.0	0.0	0.0	0.0	0.0	100.0	0.0	0.0	100.0	53.3	50.0	50.0
12873	SHUSHAN	98.2	97.6	0.9	1.2	0.5	0.7	0.9	1.2	3.7	4.6	6.0	6.7	4.2	20.1	36.5	15.3	2.9	80.9	47.3	51.7	48.3
12878	STONY CREEK	97.3	96.7	0.3	0.3	0.4	0.7	0.7	1.0	4.9	4.7	5.5	7.9	4.5	23.8	32.4	14.6	1.6	79.2	44.1	52.3	47.7
12883	TICONDEROGA	98.1	97.5	0.5	0.6	0.3	0.4	0.4	0.6	6.3	6.2	6.7	6.8	5.8	22.9	28.1	14.5	2.6	76.2	41.5	48.9	51.1
12885	WARRENSBURG	98.1	97.5	0.2	0.2	0.5	0.7	0.5	0.7	5.4	6.1	6.4	6.5	5.4	24.9	30.0	13.0	2.4	77.6	41.6	48.3	51.7
12886	WEVERTOWN	100.0	100.0	0.0	0.0	0.0	0.0	0.0	0.0	6.3	6.3	6.3	6.3	6.3	25.0	31.3	12.5	0.0	75.0	40.0	50.0	50.0
12887	WHITEHALL	85.3	82.9	10.4	11.9	0.3	0.4	6.1	7.2	5.3	5.1	5.5	7.6	9.3	29.9	25.1	10.9	1.3	80.4	36.5	58.5	41.5
12901	PLATTSBURGH	94.7	93.0	1.9	2.5	1.2	1.6	1.7	2.2	5.0	5.0	5.1	9.2	13.0	24.4	24.7	11.4	2.2	81.5	34.8	48.0	52.0
12903	PLATTSBURGH	92.4	91.8	5.7	4.7	0.0	0.5	1.9	2.6	6.1	5.9	6.2	5.3	5.2	24.0	29.0	15.1	3.2	78.5	43.0	47.7	52.3
12910	ALTONA	77.5	76.5	15.5	15.8	0.2	0.2	10.4	11.0	3.8	4.2	4.7	5.5	8.6	40.3	23.7	8.2	1.0	84.0	36.7	65.1	34.9
12911	KEESEVILLE	97.3	95.9	1.4	1.4	0.0	0.0	1.4	2.7	5.4	6.8	8.1	6.8	5.4	27.0	27.0	12.2	1.4	75.7	39.2	50.0	50.0
12912	AU SABLE FORKS	98.4	97.9	0.2	0.4	0.1	0.2	0.6	0.9	6.1	6.2	6.3	6.7	5.8	24.1	29.0	14.0	1.8	77.2	41.4	48.7	51.3
12913	BLOOMINGDALE	97.4	96.8	0.4	0.5	0.2	0.3	1.0	1.4	5.2	5.3	6.3	6.7	6.7	23.4	33.1	11.8	1.6	79.3	42.7	49.7	50.3
12914	BOMBAY	83.3	85.0	0.4	0.5	0.1	0.1	0.9	1.0	6.2	6.3	6.7	6.9	5.2	24.6	30.5	12.3	1.4	76.5	41.2	48.0	52.0
12916	BRUSHTON	97.2	97.3	0.4	0.3	0.3	0.3	0.8	0.9	5.3	6.0	6.3	6.9	5.1	25.2	31.0	12.2	1.8	77.9	41.7	49.7	50.3
12917	BURKE	96.3	96.3	1.1	1.3	0.1	0.1	1.4	1.5	6.6	7.1	7.4	7.2	4.4	25.3	28.8	11.7	1.5	73.9	39.9	52.8	47.2
12918	CADYVILLE	93.2	92.3	4.3	4.7	0.3	0.4	2.6	3.1	5.1	5.8	6.7	6.8	5.6	29.5	28.6	10.6	1.3	77.9	39.2	52.5	47.5
12919	CHAMPLAIN	97.9	97.0	0.4	0.6	0.4	0.6	0.8	1.2	5.6	5.8	6.2	7.3	5.6	24.6	29.6	13.4	2.0	78.1	41.8	48.8	51.2
12920	CHATEAUGAY	91.8	90.8	4.7	5.4	0.2	0.2	4.6	5.2	4.8	5.1	5.3	7.6	6.3	31.0	27.0	11.4	1.5	80.2	38.9	56.4	43.6
12921	CHAZY	97.7	96.8	0.4	0.5	0.4	0.5	0.7	1.0	6.3	6.7	6.8	7.0	5.6	25.6	28.9	11.7	1.4	75.6	39.7	49.2	50.8
12922	CHILDWOLD	100.0	100.0	0.0	0.0	0.0	0.0	0.0	0.0	2.9	5.7	5.7	5.7	2.9	20.0	40.0	17.1	0.0	80.0	50.6	51.4	48.6
12923	CHURUBUSCO	98.3	97.7	0.3	0.4	0.1	0.3	0.3	0.5	4.1	6.8	7.7	7.7	3.7	26.3	28.7	13.4	1.7	75.9	40.2	53.4	46.6
12924	KEESEVILLE	98.6	97.8	0.5	0.4	0.5	0.9	0.9	1.3	5.2	6.1	6.5	7.4	4.3	22.6	31.3	14.3	2.2	77.0	43.4	50.9	49.1
12926	CONSTABLE	97.3	97.5	0.3	0.3	0.1	0.1	0.4	0.4	5.5	7.6	8.5	7.6	3.9	28.2	27.0	10.8	0.9	73.8	38.0	51.0	49.0
12928	CROWN POINT	97.5	96.7	0.1	0.1	0.4	0.5	0.1	0.2	7.0	7.1	7.1	6.6	5.8	22.2	29.7	12.8	1.8	75.0	40.7	50.5	49.5
12930	DICKINSON CENTER	97.6	97.7	0.3	0.3	0.2	0.2	0.5	0.3	4.5	7.8	6.3	6.9	4.3	24.0	30.9	13.7	1.6	77.1	42.2	51.9	48.1
12932	ELIZABETHTOWN	97.9	97.2	0.5	0.7	0.5	0.6	0.3	0.5	4.7	5.8	6.2	6.2	4.9	19.3	30.8	16.0	6.2	78.5	46.9	49.8	50.2
12934	ELLENBURG CENTER	96.9	95.8	1.4	1.9	0.3	0.4	1.4	1.9	4.7	5.5	5.6	6.8	5.1	26.3	29.6	14.4	2.0	79.7	42.2	51.1	48.9
12935	ELLENBURG DEPOT	95.2	93.9	2.6	3.2	0.2	0.3	1.7	2.1	5.5	6.3	6.9	7.4	5.6	28.2	27.5	11.1	1.5	76.3	38.7	53.6	46.4
	NEW YORK	67.9	64.8	15.9	16.5	5.6	6.9	15.1	16.7	6.5	6.4	6.4	7.1	7.0	27.0	26.3	11.2	2.1	76.6	37.5	48.4	51.6
	UNITED STATES	75.1	72.0	12.3	12.7	3.8	4.6	12.5	15.7	6.8	6.7	6.6	7.1	6.9	27.0	26.0	10.9	1.9	75.7	36.9	49.2	50.8

#	POST OFFICE NAME (ZIP CODE)	2009 Per Capita Income	2009 HH Income Base	2009 HOUSEHOLD INCOME DISTRIBUTION (%)					MEDIAN HOUSEHOLD INCOME				2009 Home Value Base	2009 HOME VALUE DISTRIBUTION (%)					2009 Median Home Value
				Less than $25,000	$25,000 to $49,999	$50,000 to $99,999	$100,000 to $149,999	$150,000 or More	2009	2014	2009 National Centile	2009 State Centile		Less than $50,000	$50,000 to $89,999	$90,000 to $174,999	$175,000 to $399,999	$400,000 or More	
12768	PARKSVILLE	19210	427	34.0	30.7	26.0	6.6	2.8	39462	41800	31	13	308	5.8	7.8	51.3	30.8	4.2	152451
12770	POND EDDY	24962	137	20.4	24.1	40.1	10.2	5.1	53200	53726	68	54	113	0.0	7.1	38.1	51.3	3.5	183594
12771	PORT JERVIS	22819	5953	23.7	27.5	34.4	11.2	3.3	48280	53855	57	41	3501	2.1	4.1	48.6	41.1	4.1	170155
12775	ROCK HILL	29559	878	16.5	24.5	42.9	8.2	7.9	60058	59875	77	63	674	0.7	4.6	35.2	49.7	9.8	195779
12776	ROSCOE	21496	1052	26.9	32.3	33.7	4.8	2.2	41961	44101	39	20	816	5.8	16.5	47.2	23.5	7.0	133271
12777	FORESTBURGH	34207	311	15.4	21.5	44.4	10.3	8.4	63919	64958	82	71	251	0.8	4.4	22.3	56.2	16.3	219167
12779	SOUTH FALLSBURG	25634	637	29.2	25.1	30.5	10.4	4.9	44473	47295	47	29	331	2.1	8.5	56.8	28.4	4.2	151815
12780	SPARROW BUSH	23660	1069	21.3	23.2	41.2	9.2	5.1	54784	60036	71	57	842	11.6	4.5	34.9	45.8	3.1	173295
12783	SWAN LAKE	21987	693	25.4	34.6	27.4	8.7	3.9	41956	44004	39	20	514	4.7	13.8	36.0	39.7	5.8	164151
12786	WHITE LAKE	27152	265	32.5	21.9	32.1	6.8	6.8	43728	47172	45	26	192	2.6	16.1	28.6	44.3	8.3	180682
12787	WHITE SULPHUR SPRING	17013	6	33.3	33.3	0.0	33.3	0.0	40000	40000	33	14	4	0.0	0.0	50.0	50.0	0.0	175000
12788	WOODBOURNE	21903	707	24.6	30.0	30.1	10.5	4.8	44431	46977	47	28	542	8.7	12.4	45.2	26.9	6.8	137977
12789	WOODRIDGE	22024	808	27.1	24.4	32.4	11.8	4.3	46908	50482	54	37	445	5.2	15.5	58.9	17.8	2.7	130191
12790	WURTSBORO	25693	2414	18.6	28.9	40.0	7.7	4.8	51946	52630	66	51	1802	8.3	9.6	47.7	33.5	0.8	147712
12791	YOUNGSVILLE	26373	99	24.2	29.3	34.3	9.1	3.0	47346	48476	55	39	78	0.0	5.1	55.1	37.2	2.6	159615
12792	YULAN	29864	174	24.1	25.3	39.1	7.5	4.0	50522	51652	62	46	140	0.7	5.7	42.9	47.1	3.6	176190
12801	GLENS FALLS	22809	6323	29.4	31.6	32.2	4.3	2.4	39562	43051	31	13	3017	0.3	0.9	61.3	34.3	3.2	165097
12803	SOUTH GLENS FALLS	24050	3118	20.5	30.9	37.2	9.3	2.0	48530	51411	58	42	2253	2.8	2.5	59.8	33.7	1.2	160693
12804	QUEENSBURY	30127	10445	11.8	26.9	41.4	13.1	6.8	61239	63878	79	66	7749	1.8	2.1	26.0	56.9	13.3	226259
12808	ADIRONDACK	27814	129	24.8	31.0	35.7	4.7	3.9	45280	49082	49	31	110	3.6	4.5	37.3	34.5	20.0	188889
12809	ARGYLE	22026	1409	17.6	30.4	43.6	6.0	2.5	51317	52414	64	49	1173	2.5	5.1	42.5	43.6	6.3	174823
12810	ATHOL	19584	275	26.9	34.2	32.0	4.7	2.2	42079	45799	40	20	231	1.7	4.8	51.5	39.8	2.2	166591
12812	BLUE MOUNTAIN LAKE	22817	109	26.6	36.7	28.4	5.5	2.8	39100	39645	30	12	82	4.9	8.5	52.4	32.9	1.2	145313
12814	BOLTON LANDING	29502	726	18.3	25.9	43.1	9.1	3.6	54964	59690	71	57	555	0.4	1.1	16.8	52.4	29.4	281522
12815	BRANT LAKE	24241	513	25.0	30.8	35.5	4.7	4.1	45216	48562	49	31	436	3.9	4.8	36.0	35.1	20.2	190541
12816	CAMBRIDGE	24187	1803	21.5	26.9	39.0	9.3	3.3	51215	52218	64	49	1362	3.6	5.8	32.6	45.2	12.8	189651
12817	CHESTERTOWN	23780	1056	24.6	33.1	33.8	5.8	2.7	44508	47140	47	29	820	4.4	5.6	38.8	42.4	8.8	177604
12819	CLEMONS	23433	204	26.0	25.5	34.8	11.8	2.0	47397	49013	55	39	163	4.9	8.6	43.6	24.5	18.4	164732
12821	COMSTOCK	13883	99	20.2	31.3	39.4	6.1	3.0	48391	48469	58	42	75	0.0	6.7	54.7	36.0	2.7	163194
12822	CORINTH	20738	2210	24.5	31.2	33.8	8.0	2.4	44569	48060	47	29	1601	7.2	7.2	54.5	26.7	4.4	149360
12823	COSSAYUNA	22868	99	22.2	25.3	44.4	6.1	2.0	53205	50940	68	54	84	6.0	0.0	40.5	41.7	11.9	180357
12824	DIAMOND POINT	32250	414	18.8	22.7	41.8	9.9	6.8	58291	61418	76	61	321	0.9	1.6	13.4	47.0	37.1	305682
12827	FORT ANN	24917	1484	18.9	27.8	43.6	6.7	3.0	52557	53102	67	52	1199	2.3	5.6	38.6	42.5	11.0	182699
12828	FORT EDWARD	23704	3368	19.0	27.9	40.9	8.8	3.3	52640	54683	67	52	2524	4.3	3.5	50.8	38.3	3.1	164363
12831	GANSEVOORT	26366	6255	12.9	22.4	42.4	17.1	5.2	63521	66797	82	70	5120	7.8	4.2	24.8	57.0	6.2	197617
12832	GRANVILLE	20816	2806	26.4	29.3	34.9	7.5	1.9	44279	46835	46	28	2032	3.0	9.1	53.4	31.3	3.3	150923
12833	GREENFIELD CENTER	23464	2078	16.7	28.2	41.0	10.5	3.6	53799	57599	69	55	1695	10.9	4.2	29.1	48.1	7.7	186616
12834	GREENWICH	23766	2613	21.5	26.8	40.6	7.4	3.8	51445	52141	65	50	1945	3.6	1.5	34.9	49.9	10.0	193606
12835	HADLEY	22662	1200	21.7	32.3	36.2	6.8	3.1	46498	49579	53	35	961	5.4	5.2	46.4	37.4	5.6	164773
12836	HAGUE	27802	551	24.9	28.3	35.4	6.5	4.9	47284	50938	55	38	467	1.3	2.4	30.2	37.0	29.1	231250
12837	HAMPTON	20328	299	20.1	33.8	37.8	7.7	0.7	46076	47986	52	34	244	3.7	9.8	50.4	32.4	3.7	150714
12838	HARTFORD	21040	233	19.3	24.5	46.8	6.9	2.6	54462	54992	70	56	189	1.6	4.8	39.7	47.6	6.3	182813
12839	HUDSON FALLS	21783	5198	25.8	29.8	36.5	6.1	1.8	43675	46661	44	26	3395	3.3	2.8	62.2	30.8	0.9	157292
12842	INDIAN LAKE	22815	524	28.1	34.0	30.5	4.8	2.7	40130	41022	33	15	407	5.2	10.1	56.8	25.6	2.5	136912
12843	JOHNSBURG	19419	503	32.4	33.4	28.2	4.2	1.8	37639	40405	26	9	391	12.0	4.6	44.0	30.7	8.7	159280
12844	KATTSKILL BAY	33767	146	15.1	25.3	42.5	11.0	6.2	58523	60452	76	62	127	0.8	3.1	25.2	37.0	33.9	285417
12845	LAKE GEORGE	29282	2412	15.8	27.5	40.7	10.7	5.2	57169	61019	74	61	1763	2.7	1.5	22.3	47.3	26.3	259362
12846	LAKE LUZERNE	20246	1477	23.0	35.9	35.3	4.2	1.6	43759	46518	45	26	1180	6.3	6.1	42.6	39.5	5.5	169861
12847	LONG LAKE	25027	378	30.2	26.7	34.9	5.0	3.2	34867	39463	17	6	287	4.5	7.3	43.9	34.5	9.8	163214
12849	MIDDLE GRANVILLE	19726	129	23.3	33.3	35.7	7.8	0.0	45246	46978	49	31	107	2.8	11.2	56.1	28.0	1.9	143750
12850	MIDDLE GROVE	23462	1013	17.0	29.0	41.0	9.8	3.3	52857	56812	68	53	849	8.7	5.3	33.0	48.4	4.6	180269
12851	MINERVA	19887	117	30.8	30.8	31.6	6.0	0.9	38291	40741	28	10	98	13.3	18.4	46.9	20.4	1.0	126389
12852	NEWCOMB	20903	197	32.0	29.4	32.0	6.6	0.0	40475	42321	34	15	171	0.6	9.9	74.3	14.6	0.6	133413
12853	NORTH CREEK	22472	800	29.9	31.3	32.9	4.5	1.5	41201	44509	37	17	598	6.7	4.8	44.1	35.6	8.7	168145
12854	NORTH GRANVILLE	16382	13	23.1	38.5	30.8	7.7	0.0	42330	50000	40	21	11	0.0	0.0	72.7	27.3	0.0	154167
12855	NORTH HUDSON	19717	105	28.6	33.3	30.5	7.6	0.0	35569	38906	19	6	87	18.4	25.3	48.3	4.6	3.4	95000
12857	OLMSTEDVILLE	19945	257	29.6	31.1	31.5	6.2	1.6	39504	42081	31	13	212	12.7	16.0	47.6	22.2	1.4	130769
12858	PARADOX	12308	6	66.7	0.0	33.3	0.0	0.0	20000	15000	1	1	4	0.0	0.0	100.0	0.0	0.0	125000
12859	PORTER CORNERS	24923	651	19.4	20.9	46.2	10.1	3.4	57936	61454	75	61	549	5.5	4.7	39.7	41.5	8.6	175187
12860	POTTERSVILLE	13990	168	22.0	35.1	35.1	4.2	3.6	45000	47330	48	31	137	7.3	6.6	41.6	34.3	10.2	166477
12861	PUTNAM STATION	22307	260	26.2	26.2	34.6	11.2	1.9	46173	49414	52	34	208	5.8	9.1	42.3	24.5	18.3	163636
12863	ROCK CITY FALLS	22283	223	12.1	36.3	40.4	7.6	3.6	50872	53004	63	48	178	37.1	14.0	26.4	20.2	2.2	86667
12865	SALEM	22789	1504	17.9	31.3	40.8	7.0	3.0	50517	51169	62	46	1202	3.9	6.7	46.3	35.9	7.2	163736
12866	SARATOGA SPRINGS	33558	15700	16.7	21.5	35.6	18.1	8.1	63212	67166	81	69	9800	4.2	2.0	22.5	54.9	16.4	228541
12870	SCHROON LAKE	18999	703	37.0	28.9	27.9	4.6	1.7	35961	38986	20	6	490	3.1	9.4	54.9	27.6	5.1	145874
12871	SCHUYLERVILLE	25544	1689	18.1	25.4	42.0	10.2	4.2	57455	61285	75	61	1240	2.9	3.1	49.7	40.2	4.1	168173
12872	SEVERANCE	0	0	0.0	0.0	0.0	0.0	0.0	0	0	0	0	2	0.0	0.0	100.0	0.0	0.0	137500
12873	SHUSHAN	26370	387	24.0	30.7	31.8	9.6	3.9	44669	47618	47	30	313	1.9	8.6	37.7	39.0	12.8	178929
12878	STONY CREEK	19400	300	29.3	32.0	32.7	5.0	1.0	41608	44416	38	18	251	1.6	7.2	52.6	37.5	1.2	162716
12883	TICONDEROGA	20657	2126	26.4	28.8	36.8	6.3	1.6	43845	45899	45	26	1542	4.9	20.0	54.9	16.6	3.6	120761
12885	WARRENSBURG	19533	2017	31.3	31.8	30.3	5.1	1.6	39300	42636	31	13	1427	5.7	6.2	47.8	34.8	5.5	164146
12886	WEVERTOWN	17266	15	40.0	33.3	26.7	0.0	0.0	32320	32320	12	5	12	16.7	0.0	50.0	25.0	8.3	150000
12887	WHITEHALL	18918	2150	25.3	29.8	34.0	9.6	1.2	44394	47049	47	28	1522	3.5	10.7	60.6	21.4	3.7	139529
12901	PLATTSBURGH	23398	13229	29.8	25.4	33.6	8.0	3.2	43361	47165	43	24	7216	10.0	10.5	46.4	28.5	4.7	150103
12903	PLATTSBURGH	27089	477	35.0	11.7	44.2	5.0	4.0	52628	53338	67	52	335	0.9	0.0	56.1	35.5	7.5	163250
12910	ALTONA	17282	634	27.1	24.9	42.3	5.4	0.3	47637	50736	56	40	501	16.8	23.4	46.7	12.2	1.0	102827
12911	KEESEVILLE	23920	31	19.4	32.3	41.9	6.5	0.0	48639	52929	58	42	22	0.0	22.7	63.6	13.6	0.0	128571
12912	AU SABLE FORKS	20536	865	28.1	30.3	33.2	6.2	2.2	43115	45710	43	23	652	6.9	24.4	52.8	14.0	2.0	112500
12913	BLOOMINGDALE	24135	432	22.0	26.6	40.3	8.8	2.3	51576	53940	65	50	327	8.9	18.0	43.1	26.3	3.7	135459
12914	BOMBAY	16664	355	38.3	28.7	28.2	4.2	0.6	32494	34771	12	5	273	26.7	27.1	37.0	7.0	2.2	82500
12916	BRUSHTON	16866	943	37.4	29.6	27.5	5.0	0.5	31590	33783	11	4	691	20.8	33.9	37.5	6.8	1.0	83750
12917	BURKE	17968	527	25.2	35.1	33.8	4.4	1.5	41417	43660	37	18	423	11.3	30.7	42.1	13.7	2.1	101823
12918	CADYVILLE	24386	1023	15.3	22.7	50.5	10.4	1.1	60165	60661	78	64	809	6.7	15.5	52.4	25.0	0.5	133422
12919	CHAMPLAIN	23398	1323	27.5	25.3	36.1	8.2	2.9	46904	49876	54	36	971	10.3	19.6	51.6	16.8	1.8	116735
12920	CHATEAUGAY	18835	959	29.9	30.6	34.0	4.5	1.0	41173	44140	37	17	747	13.5	36.3	39.6	9.6	0.9	90283
12921	CHAZY	24220	994	21.3	23.0	42.6	9.7	3.4	57145	60064	74	60	767	5.9	12.4	50.2	28.0	3.5	144092
12922	CHILDWOLD	27256	19	21.1	31.6	42.1	5.3	0.0	47368	52140	55	39	16	6.3	37.5	37.5	18.8	0.0	100000
12923	CHURUBUSCO	15496	296	36.1	26.4	34.1	2.7	0.7	37366	41806	25	8	238	23.5	36.6	29.4	9.7	0.8	77895
12924	KEESEVILLE	16174	88	35.2	33.0	27.3	4.5	0.0	36518	39531	22	7	66	4.5	27.3	54.5	12.1	1.5	111364
12926	CONSTABLE	18167	832	29.4	32.9	30.9	5.4	1.3	37266	41183	24	8	669	16.7	29.9	45.7	6.6	1.0	94091
12928	CROWN POINT	19999	811	24.9	32.9	35.5	5.3	1.4	42524	44122	41	22	622	10.6	23.0	50.6	14.8	1.0	114693
12930	DICKINSON CENTER	19317	239	33.1	29.3	32.2	3.8	1.7	37931	40697	26	9	200	12.5	41.0	41.0	4.0	1.5	85882
12932	ELIZABETHTOWN	22460	577	26.3	31.5	34.1	4.7	3.3	43592	44664	44	25	411	7.5	16.3	50.9	22.1	3.2	123645
12934	ELLENBURG CENTER	16808	473	29.2	30.4	32.3	6.3	1.7	41061	43863	36	17	372	12.9	32.5	38.4	13.7	2.4	94857
12935	ELLENBURG DEPOT	19773	576	27.8	26.9	38.0	6.6	0.7	44771	48011	48	30	467	25.1	26.3	38.8	8.8	1.1	87833
	NEW YORK	29893		21.9	21.3	32.7	14.0	9.9	58747	62337				3.4	5.7	23.0	38.7	29.1	269816
	UNITED STATES	27277		20.9	24.4	35.3	11.7	7.6	54719	56938				9.3	13.1	31.6	32.6	13.5	162279

ZIP CODE		FINANCIAL SERVICES				THE HOME						ENTERTAINMENT						PERSONAL			
						Home Improvements		Furnishings													
#	POST OFFICE NAME	Auto Loan	Home Loan	Invest-ments	Retire-ment Plans	Home Repair	Lawn & Garden	Comput-ers & Hard-ware-Personal	Major Appli-ances	TV, Radio, Sound Equip-ment	Furni-ture	Dine out/ Carry out	Sports Equip-ment	Fees & Tickets	Toys & Games	Travel	Cable TV	Apparel & Services	Auto Repairs	Health Insur-ance	Pets & Supplies
12768	PARKSVILLE	77	63	94	62	68	81	65	78	68	61	67	57	57	65	68	73	45	74	79	91
12770	POND EDDY	105	84	136	83	92	111	84	107	88	79	87	78	73	83	91	94	58	99	105	124
12771	PORT JERVIS	82	84	78	83	82	83	86	83	86	82	86	64	86	86	84	87	61	84	85	98
12775	ROCK HILL	117	94	152	93	103	124	94	120	98	88	97	87	82	93	102	105	65	110	118	139
12776	ROSCOE	83	66	96	66	71	87	68	83	72	64	71	61	59	70	70	77	47	77	84	97
12777	FORESTBURGH	139	111	179	109	122	147	111	141	116	104	115	103	96	110	120	124	76	130	139	164
12779	SOUTH FALLSBURG	79	86	86	84	86	84	86	85	85	83	86	66	89	85	88	86	61	86	86	98
12780	SPARROW BUSH	95	89	80	86	87	91	84	89	87	87	87	65	80	90	81	89	59	86	89	105
12783	SWAN LAKE	96	78	119	77	85	101	79	97	82	74	81	71	69	79	84	88	54	91	97	113
12786	WHITE LAKE	112	90	145	89	99	119	90	114	94	84	93	84	78	89	98	100	62	106	113	133
12787	WHITE SULPHUR SPRING	95	76	122	75	83	100	76	96	79	71	78	70	66	75	82	85	52	89	95	112
12788	WOODBOURNE	99	86	115	86	91	104	85	100	88	81	87	75	78	85	90	92	59	94	101	117
12789	WOODRIDGE	89	78	86	79	81	91	83	88	86	79	84	65	76	84	81	89	57	87	94	103
12790	WURTSBORO	86	90	83	90	88	91	88	88	88	86	88	68	90	89	89	90	62	88	92	104
12791	YOUNGSVILLE	95	76	122	75	83	101	76	97	80	71	79	71	66	76	82	85	52	89	96	112
12792	YULAN	109	87	140	86	96	115	87	111	91	82	90	81	75	86	94	97	60	102	109	128
12801	GLENS FALLS	69	64	57	65	61	66	73	66	74	67	73	53	69	73	67	75	51	71	73	81
12803	SOUTH GLENS FALLS	79	79	78	80	79	86	79	82	82	76	81	61	79	81	80	85	56	81	89	96
12804	QUEENSBURY	102	112	108	112	113	115	102	108	104	105	104	78	109	103	108	107	73	105	114	125
12808	ADIRONDACK	93	74	120	73	82	98	74	94	78	70	77	69	64	74	81	83	51	87	93	109
12809	ARGYLE	91	81	91	83	84	98	80	93	83	73	81	70	73	83	82	88	55	86	95	108
12810	ATHOL	85	63	94	61	66	87	64	82	70	60	69	61	53	69	65	76	46	75	84	96
12812	BLUE MOUNTAIN LAKE	82	65	105	64	72	86	65	83	68	61	68	61	57	65	71	73	45	77	82	96
12814	BOLTON LANDING	106	85	137	84	93	112	85	108	89	80	88	79	74	84	92	95	58	100	107	125
12815	BRANT LAKE	93	74	120	73	81	98	74	94	78	70	77	69	64	74	80	83	51	87	93	109
12816	CAMBRIDGE	91	80	100	80	84	96	80	92	83	76	82	69	74	81	83	87	55	88	94	108
12817	CHESTERTOWN	87	70	110	69	76	91	71	88	74	66	73	64	61	70	76	78	48	82	88	102
12819	CLEMONS	89	81	80	84	82	95	80	90	82	72	81	68	73	84	79	87	55	83	93	104
12821	COMSTOCK	96	69	99	67	71	98	71	90	78	66	77	67	56	78	70	86	51	82	93	107
12822	CORINTH	86	70	81	70	71	88	73	83	77	67	76	62	63	78	71	83	51	79	88	98
12823	COSSAYUNA	92	83	83	87	85	98	82	93	85	74	83	70	76	86	82	90	57	86	96	108
12824	DIAMOND POINT	118	95	152	94	104	125	95	120	100	89	99	88	83	95	103	106	66	111	119	140
12827	FORT ANN	96	80	97	81	83	100	80	95	84	75	83	71	71	84	80	90	56	88	97	111
12828	FORT EDWARD	87	90	76	92	86	94	86	88	87	83	86	69	87	89	86	89	60	86	92	105
12831	GANSEVOORT	110	114	103	113	112	110	103	107	103	108	103	81	105	106	104	103	72	103	104	126
12832	GRANVILLE	84	70	79	72	72	88	71	83	76	65	74	63	63	76	70	81	50	77	87	97
12833	GREENFIELD CENTER	94	94	84	94	92	96	87	92	89	88	89	70	87	91	87	90	61	89	92	109
12834	GREENWICH	92	80	87	82	83	96	83	91	85	77	84	69	75	86	82	90	57	87	96	107
12835	HADLEY	92	79	95	77	82	91	77	89	80	76	80	65	70	80	78	84	54	84	88	104
12836	HAGUE	104	84	134	83	92	111	84	106	88	79	87	78	73	84	91	94	58	98	105	123
12837	HAMPTON	82	74	74	78	76	88	73	83	76	66	74	63	68	77	73	80	51	76	85	96
12838	HARTFORD	88	80	79	83	81	94	79	89	81	71	80	67	73	83	79	86	54	82	92	103
12839	HUDSON FALLS	76	69	64	71	68	77	74	74	76	68	75	57	70	77	70	79	52	75	81	89
12842	INDIAN LAKE	83	67	108	66	73	88	67	85	70	63	69	62	58	66	72	75	46	78	84	98
12843	JOHNSBURG	81	62	94	60	66	84	62	79	67	58	66	59	52	65	65	73	44	73	80	93
12844	KATTSKILL BAY	108	96	137	95	103	118	92	112	96	89	95	81	86	91	101	101	64	105	114	130
12845	LAKE GEORGE	104	94	122	93	100	113	92	107	95	89	94	77	87	92	97	100	64	101	110	124
12846	LAKE LUZERNE	86	66	103	65	71	90	67	85	71	62	70	63	56	69	70	77	47	78	85	99
12847	LONG LAKE	87	70	113	69	77	92	70	89	73	66	72	65	61	70	76	78	48	82	88	103
12849	MIDDLE GRANVILLE	77	70	70	73	72	83	69	78	71	63	70	59	64	73	69	76	48	72	81	91
12850	MIDDLE GROVE	96	95	83	95	93	95	88	92	90	91	90	70	88	93	88	91	62	90	92	109
12851	MINERVA	80	64	103	63	70	85	64	81	67	60	66	59	56	64	69	71	44	75	80	94
12852	NEWCOMB	67	64	82	59	71	77	61	72	65	66	63	47	61	59	67	69	42	69	80	83
12853	NORTH CREEK	81	65	105	64	71	86	65	82	68	61	67	60	56	64	70	72	45	76	81	95
12854	NORTH GRANVILLE	74	68	67	70	69	80	67	75	69	60	67	57	61	70	67	73	46	69	78	87
12855	NORTH HUDSON	80	58	83	56	60	82	59	75	66	55	64	56	47	65	59	72	43	69	78	89
12857	OLMSTEDVILLE	80	64	104	63	71	85	64	82	67	60	67	60	56	64	70	72	44	75	81	95
12858	PARADOX	44	36	57	35	39	47	36	45	37	33	37	33	31	35	39	40	24	42	45	52
12859	PORTER CORNERS	93	98	88	101	96	102	90	96	90	88	90	74	92	92	94	92	62	91	96	113
12860	POTTERSVILLE	92	73	118	72	81	97	73	93	77	69	76	68	64	73	80	82	50	86	92	108
12861	PUTNAM STATION	88	81	80	84	82	95	79	90	82	72	80	68	73	83	79	87	55	83	92	104
12863	ROCK CITY FALLS	90	85	72	80	80	81	83	83	84	87	84	63	79	87	78	84	58	83	81	98
12865	SALEM	89	80	89	81	82	97	78	90	82	72	81	67	72	82	79	88	55	84	95	105
12866	SARATOGA SPRINGS	110	111	108	113	110	108	114	109	112	114	113	85	114	112	113	112	80	112	110	129
12870	SCHROON LAKE	73	59	94	58	64	77	59	75	61	55	61	54	51	58	63	65	40	69	74	86
12871	SCHUYLERVILLE	95	92	89	93	92	97	90	96	91	88	90	73	87	92	90	93	62	92	96	111
12872	SEVERANCE	0	0	0	0	0	0	0	0	0	0	0	0	0	0	0	0	0	0	0	0
12873	SHUSHAN	100	80	129	79	88	106	80	102	84	75	83	74	70	80	87	89	55	94	101	118
12878	STONY CREEK	81	62	96	61	67	84	63	80	67	58	66	59	53	65	66	72	44	73	80	93
12883	TICONDEROGA	77	68	75	68	69	80	70	76	73	66	72	57	65	73	69	77	49	74	81	90
12885	WARRENSBURG	79	60	80	59	63	81	63	76	68	59	67	56	53	67	62	74	45	71	79	89
12886	WEVERTOWN	66	47	68	46	49	67	48	62	54	45	53	46	39	53	48	59	35	56	64	73
12887	WHITEHALL	81	72	68	74	71	83	74	79	77	68	75	61	68	78	71	81	51	76	84	93
12901	PLATTSBURGH	77	71	68	72	71	73	79	74	79	77	79	57	75	78	74	80	55	77	78	88
12903	PLATTSBURGH	73	69	74	69	71	78	74	76	78	71	76	54	72	75	73	82	53	77	85	88
12910	ALTONA	81	70	69	70	70	81	69	77	72	66	71	58	62	75	66	76	49	72	79	91
12911	KEESEVILLE	88	80	77	79	80	86	80	84	83	80	82	62	75	84	77	86	56	83	87	99
12912	AU SABLE FORKS	79	69	83	68	72	84	69	79	73	66	72	58	64	72	70	78	49	76	84	93
12913	BLOOMINGDALE	89	77	87	78	80	91	82	88	85	78	83	65	75	83	81	88	57	86	93	103
12914	BOMBAY	74	53	76	52	55	75	55	69	61	51	60	52	44	60	54	67	39	64	72	82
12916	BRUSHTON	74	53	76	51	55	75	54	69	60	51	59	52	43	60	54	66	39	63	72	82
12917	BURKE	85	58	92	58	61	89	64	80	67	53	67	66	48	66	64	74	43	75	84	98
12918	CADYVILLE	85	95	85	96	93	95	85	89	86	86	86	67	91	87	90	87	60	86	91	104
12919	CHAMPLAIN	89	74	80	74	73	91	76	85	81	71	79	65	68	82	73	86	54	81	91	101
12920	CHATEAUGAY	83	59	86	58	62	84	61	78	67	57	66	58	49	67	61	74	44	71	80	92
12921	CHAZY	90	91	87	92	91	96	88	93	88	83	88	71	87	90	90	91	61	89	94	108
12922	CHILDWOLD	84	67	108	66	74	89	67	85	70	63	69	62	58	67	73	75	46	79	84	99
12923	CHURUBUSCO	73	52	75	51	54	74	54	68	60	50	59	51	43	59	53	66	39	63	71	81
12924	KEESEVILLE	75	54	78	52	56	77	55	71	62	52	60	53	44	61	55	68	40	65	73	84
12926	CONSTABLE	84	60	86	58	63	85	62	79	69	58	67	59	49	68	61	76	45	72	82	94
12928	CROWN POINT	90	65	92	63	67	92	68	85	75	62	74	64	54	75	67	83	49	79	90	101
12930	DICKINSON CENTER	83	60	85	58	62	84	61	78	68	57	67	58	49	68	60	75	44	71	81	92
12932	ELIZABETHTOWN	82	72	81	72	74	87	73	81	77	70	76	60	68	77	73	82	52	79	88	95
12934	ELLENBURG CENTER	85	62	89	60	64	88	64	80	70	58	69	62	51	69	64	76	45	74	84	96
12935	ELLENBURG DEPOT	83	67	80	65	67	87	67	79	73	63	72	60	58	73	66	79	48	75	85	94
	NEW YORK	100	106	110	108	107	104	112	106	113	106	114	81	115	110	112	116	83	110	110	124
	UNITED STATES	100	100	100	100	100	100	100	100	100	100	100	100	100	100	100	100	100	100	100	100

POPULATION CHANGE

 12936-13118

#	POST OFFICE NAME	COUNTY FIPS CODE	POPULATION 2000	POPULATION 2009	POPULATION 2014	2000-2009 ANNUAL RATE % Rate	2000-2009 ANNUAL RATE State Centile	HOUSEHOLDS 2000	HOUSEHOLDS 2009	HOUSEHOLDS 2014	HOUSEHOLDS % Annual Rate 2000-2009	HOUSEHOLDS 2009 Average HH Size	FAMILIES 2000	FAMILIES 2009	FAMILIES % Annual Rate 2000-2009
12936	ESSEX	031	622	612	601	-0.2	21	265	268	264	0.1	2.28	177	176	-0.1
12937	FORT COVINGTON	033	1496	1448	1421	-0.4	11	574	572	567	0.0	2.53	431	424	-0.2
12941	JAY	031	1144	1121	1098	-0.2	21	457	457	451	0.0	2.43	324	321	-0.1
12942	KEENE	031	542	543	536	0.0	38	230	235	234	0.2	2.21	145	146	0.1
12943	KEENE VALLEY	031	521	521	515	0.0	38	213	218	216	0.3	2.29	134	135	0.1
12944	KEESEVILLE	031	4342	4407	4396	0.2	52	1707	1776	1787	0.4	2.46	1221	1252	0.3
12945	LAKE CLEAR	033	616	661	684	0.8	84	250	277	289	1.1	2.35	162	174	0.8
12946	LAKE PLACID	031	6431	6997	7080	0.9	87	2297	2614	2670	1.4	2.16	1293	1445	1.2
12950	LEWIS	031	622	626	617	0.1	44	249	257	256	0.3	2.44	179	182	0.2
12952	LYON MOUNTAIN	019	430	433	433	0.1	44	205	212	214	0.4	1.78	139	141	0.2
12953	MALONE	033	16373	15861	15773	-0.3	15	4629	4646	4645	0.0	2.35	2995	2952	-0.2
12955	LYON MOUNTAIN	019	298	285	280	-0.5	7	134	132	131	-0.2	2.13	91	88	-0.4
12956	MINEVILLE	031	2013	1970	1934	-0.2	21	716	720	711	0.1	2.35	484	481	-0.1
12957	MOIRA	033	1403	1383	1369	-0.2	21	547	556	555	0.2	2.47	383	383	0.0
12958	MOOERS	019	1791	1938	2006	0.9	87	671	738	769	1.0	2.63	495	536	0.9
12959	MOOERS FORKS	019	1354	1424	1448	0.5	71	493	527	540	0.7	2.70	371	390	0.5
12960	MORIAH	031	987	998	986	0.1	44	388	403	401	0.4	2.47	259	265	0.2
12961	MORIAH CENTER	031	180	176	172	-0.2	21	67	67	66	0.0	2.61	46	45	-0.2
12962	MORRISONVILLE	019	5622	5886	5975	0.5	71	2085	2246	2306	0.8	2.59	1560	1653	0.6
12964	NEW RUSSIA	031	160	158	155	-0.1	30	61	61	61	0.0	2.59	45	45	0.0
12965	NICHOLVILLE	089	428	412	404	-0.4	11	161	158	156	-0.2	2.61	119	115	-0.4
12966	NORTH BANGOR	033	2763	2879	2916	0.4	66	992	1067	1092	0.8	2.67	750	795	0.6
12967	NORTH LAWRENCE	089	1086	1071	1059	-0.2	21	404	406	404	0.1	2.64	301	298	-0.1
12969	OWLS HEAD	033	408	415	416	0.2	52	174	182	185	0.5	2.26	119	122	0.3
12970	PAUL SMITHS	033	817	788	783	-0.4	11	114	116	116	0.2	3.24	73	73	0.0
12972	PERU	019	5631	6208	6481	1.1	91	2063	2331	2457	1.3	2.63	1556	1733	1.2
12973	PIERCEFIELD	089	114	112	111	-0.2	21	49	49	49	0.0	2.29	31	31	0.0
12974	PORT HENRY	031	1592	1655	1652	0.4	66	683	729	732	0.7	2.25	438	462	0.6
12978	REDFORD	019	503	507	506	0.1	44	178	184	185	0.4	2.76	133	135	0.2
12979	ROUSES POINT	019	2408	2444	2466	0.2	52	1026	1067	1084	0.4	2.25	638	649	0.2
12980	SAINT REGIS FALLS	033	1562	1531	1523	-0.2	21	626	631	632	0.1	2.43	433	428	-0.1
12981	SARANAC	019	6245	6375	6409	0.2	52	1267	1337	1364	0.6	2.71	929	963	0.4
12983	SARANAC LAKE	033	7783	8124	8180	0.5	71	3182	3400	3446	0.7	2.14	1724	1800	0.5
12985	SCHUYLER FALLS	019	1293	1375	1414	0.7	80	465	508	528	1.0	2.70	350	377	0.8
12986	TUPPER LAKE	033	6322	6181	6108	-0.2	21	2514	2519	2504	0.0	2.32	1583	1554	-0.2
12987	UPPER JAY	031	142	140	137	-0.2	21	58	58	57	0.0	2.38	42	41	-0.3
12989	VERMONTVILLE	033	1903	1879	1873	-0.1	30	611	629	633	0.3	2.33	409	414	0.1
12992	WEST CHAZY	019	4674	4787	4822	0.3	59	1716	1806	1838	0.6	2.64	1300	1350	0.4
12993	WESTPORT	031	1742	1656	1605	-0.5	7	740	721	705	-0.3	2.27	483	465	-0.4
12996	WILLSBORO	031	1913	1837	1791	-0.4	11	808	798	784	-0.1	2.28	552	537	-0.3
12997	WILMINGTON	031	1286	1291	1272	0.0	38	521	530	524	0.2	2.44	346	347	0.0
13021	AUBURN	011	41705	40638	40100	-0.3	15	16314	16200	16068	-0.1	2.34	10269	10010	-0.3
13026	AURORA	011	1824	1748	1719	-0.5	7	611	597	589	-0.3	2.54	432	414	-0.5
13027	BALDWINSVILLE	067	29427	30311	30384	0.3	59	11575	12242	12364	0.6	2.46	8020	8324	0.4
13028	BERNHARDS BAY	075	1404	1375	1358	-0.2	21	520	522	519	0.0	2.63	383	378	-0.1
13029	BREWERTON	067	5181	5595	5675	0.8	84	1962	2165	2210	1.1	2.58	1438	1556	0.9
13030	BRIDGEPORT	053	4136	4193	4261	0.1	44	1617	1685	1730	0.4	2.49	1160	1188	0.3
13031	CAMILLUS	067	15312	15509	15511	0.1	44	6156	6411	6458	0.4	2.42	4365	4459	0.2
13032	CANASTOTA	053	12398	12779	12893	0.3	59	4866	5130	5216	0.6	2.48	3374	3492	0.4
13033	CATO	011	4058	4108	4094	0.1	44	1408	1447	1451	0.3	2.84	1107	1122	0.1
13034	CAYUGA	011	1978	2017	2013	0.2	52	750	778	782	0.4	2.59	564	576	0.2
13035	CAZENOVIA	053	7881	8468	8656	0.8	84	2855	3118	3216	1.0	2.52	2035	2196	0.8
13036	CENTRAL SQUARE	075	8512	8717	8737	0.3	59	3329	3492	3528	0.5	2.50	2322	2395	0.3
13037	CHITTENANGO	053	8383	8605	8693	0.3	59	3144	3298	3355	0.5	2.58	2301	2377	0.4
13039	CICERO	067	15164	17126	17556	1.3	94	5525	6420	6626	1.6	2.67	4153	4716	1.4
13040	CINCINNATUS	023	3057	3105	3089	0.2	52	1128	1177	1182	0.5	2.62	830	852	0.3
13041	CLAY	067	9631	10019	10073	0.4	66	3278	3502	3547	0.7	2.86	2656	2800	0.6
13042	CLEVELAND	065	2524	2580	2593	0.2	52	937	986	999	0.6	2.62	706	732	0.4
13044	CONSTANTIA	075	2600	2619	2609	0.1	44	952	983	989	0.3	2.66	706	719	0.2
13045	CORTLAND	023	28945	28713	28366	-0.1	30	10898	10941	10868	0.0	2.33	6251	6143	-0.2
13052	DE RUYTER	053	1818	1871	1883	0.3	59	685	728	742	0.7	2.43	501	522	0.4
13053	DRYDEN	109	4663	5130	5316	1.0	89	1755	1966	2055	1.2	2.54	1159	1268	1.0
13054	DURHAMVILLE	065	1644	1517	1469	-0.9	2	583	554	541	-0.6	2.74	435	407	-0.7
13057	EAST SYRACUSE	067	14978	14561	14374	-0.3	15	6325	6341	6314	0.0	2.28	3994	3913	-0.2
13060	ELBRIDGE	067	3073	3057	3049	-0.1	30	1218	1255	1263	0.3	2.43	894	903	0.1
13061	ERIEVILLE	053	1148	1263	1306	1.0	89	434	487	507	1.3	2.53	320	353	1.1
13063	FABIUS	067	2026	2226	2263	1.0	89	685	768	787	1.2	2.89	531	585	1.1
13066	FAYETTEVILLE	067	12407	12306	12216	-0.1	30	5002	5085	5087	0.2	2.39	3479	3460	-0.1
13068	FREEVILLE	109	5463	5701	5832	0.5	71	2114	2235	2300	0.6	2.49	1380	1430	0.4
13069	FULTON	075	25941	25450	25046	-0.2	21	10020	10015	9925	0.0	2.52	6818	6707	-0.2
13071	GENOA	011	1015	1008	997	-0.1	30	376	381	381	0.1	2.65	280	279	0.0
13072	GEORGETOWN	053	1131	1207	1229	0.7	80	305	329	337	0.8	3.22	219	232	0.6
13073	GROTON	109	5996	6359	6510	0.6	76	2224	2383	2457	0.7	2.61	1595	1678	0.5
13074	HANNIBAL	075	4894	4915	4841	0.0	38	1739	1780	1767	0.3	2.69	1299	1310	0.1
13076	HASTINGS	075	1808	1915	1946	0.6	76	631	684	700	0.9	2.80	483	516	0.7
13077	HOMER	023	6908	6796	6716	-0.2	21	2650	2672	2662	0.1	2.52	1907	1890	-0.1
13078	JAMESVILLE	067	8314	8900	9008	0.7	80	3033	3356	3429	1.1	2.50	2189	2357	0.8
13080	JORDAN	067	3621	3578	3549	-0.1	30	1353	1378	1379	0.2	2.59	996	997	0.0
13081	KING FERRY	011	1077	1165	1180	0.9	87	408	448	457	1.0	2.50	296	319	0.8
13082	KIRKVILLE	053	5134	5106	5076	-0.1	30	1947	1989	1994	0.2	2.55	1445	1451	0.0
13083	LACONA	075	1937	2043	2070	0.6	76	741	800	817	0.8	2.55	526	558	0.6
13084	LA FAYETTE	067	4486	4708	4741	0.5	71	1651	1789	1817	0.9	2.62	1240	1319	0.7
13088	LIVERPOOL	067	22418	21903	21666	-0.3	15	9815	9886	9859	0.1	2.20	5902	5774	-0.2
13090	LIVERPOOL	067	30463	30269	30053	-0.1	30	11337	11572	11569	0.2	2.61	8258	8305	0.1
13092	LOCKE	011	2873	2995	3013	0.5	71	1071	1137	1152	0.6	2.62	814	850	0.5
13101	MC GRAW	023	2409	2393	2364	-0.1	30	879	892	887	0.2	2.67	660	660	0.0
13103	MALLORY	075	456	465	467	0.2	52	154	161	162	0.5	2.89	121	125	0.4
13104	MANLIUS	067	14572	15305	15420	0.5	71	5511	5889	5967	0.7	2.59	4084	4298	0.6
13108	MARCELLUS	067	5886	5742	5675	-0.3	15	2216	2227	2220	0.1	2.58	1646	1624	-0.1
13110	MARIETTA	067	2186	2199	2190	0.1	44	827	859	864	0.4	2.56	626	638	0.2
13111	MARTVILLE	011	1839	1953	1962	0.7	80	626	678	687	0.9	2.88	479	511	0.7
13112	MEMPHIS	067	1784	1771	1761	-0.1	30	658	676	678	0.3	2.62	486	490	0.1
13114	MEXICO	075	6949	7228	7280	0.4	66	2556	2727	2772	0.7	2.65	1855	1947	0.5
13116	MINOA	067	3308	3220	3180	-0.3	15	1237	1245	1242	0.1	2.52	922	912	-0.1
13118	MORAVIA	011	6505	6590	6608	0.1	44	1890	2005	2028	0.6	2.59	1354	1407	0.4
	NEW YORK					0.3					0.3	2.61			0.1
	UNITED STATES					1.0					1.1	2.59			0.9

ZIP CODE #	POST OFFICE NAME	RACE (%) White 2000	White 2009	Black 2000	Black 2009	Asian/Pacific 2000	Asian/Pacific 2009	% Hispanic Origin 2000	% Hispanic Origin 2009	2009 AGE DISTRIBUTION (%) 0-4	5-9	10-14	15-19	20-24	25-44	45-64	65-84	85+	18+	MEDIAN AGE 2009	% 2009 Males	% 2009 Females
12936	ESSEX	99.7	99.7	0.0	0.0	0.0	0.0	0.2	0.2	3.3	4.2	6.4	6.9	3.8	20.3	34.3	17.6	3.3	80.7	48.4	51.1	48.9
12937	FORT COVINGTON	91.5	92.3	0.5	0.6	0.5	0.5	1.1	1.2	6.1	6.2	6.6	6.8	5.5	22.7	29.9	14.6	1.5	76.5	42.0	48.8	51.2
12941	JAY	98.4	98.0	0.3	0.4	0.3	0.4	0.5	0.8	5.7	6.4	7.2	5.5	3.7	23.8	33.1	13.0	1.5	77.0	43.5	49.6	50.4
12942	KEENE	98.3	98.0	0.2	0.2	0.6	0.7	0.4	0.6	4.1	3.7	7.7	6.8	3.3	19.2	35.7	14.9	4.6	80.1	47.9	46.4	53.6
12943	KEENE VALLEY	99.0	98.7	0.0	0.0	0.4	0.6	0.4	0.6	4.0	3.6	7.9	6.9	3.1	19.0	35.7	15.0	4.8	80.4	48.0	46.4	53.6
12944	KEESEVILLE	97.6	96.8	0.6	0.8	0.2	0.3	1.1	1.5	5.8	6.3	7.0	7.2	5.0	25.4	30.4	11.7	1.2	76.4	40.7	49.7	50.3
12945	LAKE CLEAR	97.4	97.3	0.3	0.5	1.0	1.1	0.6	0.6	5.1	5.9	6.7	6.8	4.5	24.5	33.7	10.4	2.3	77.8	42.8	49.3	50.7
12946	LAKE PLACID	87.0	85.6	8.9	9.4	1.1	1.5	5.9	6.7	4.4	4.4	4.7	4.9	6.6	34.7	26.1	11.6	2.7	83.3	39.1	57.6	42.4
12950	LEWIS	99.0	98.7	0.2	0.3	0.0	0.0	0.2	0.2	6.1	6.7	7.5	6.7	3.7	26.5	30.8	10.5	1.4	74.6	40.8	52.6	47.4
12952	LYON MOUNTAIN	87.9	84.5	7.7	9.7	0.5	0.7	3.9	5.5	4.2	4.8	4.6	4.8	5.8	27.9	29.8	15.9	2.1	83.6	43.6	55.9	44.1
12953	MALONE	75.7	74.3	16.9	18.1	0.6	0.6	10.2	10.9	3.8	3.8	4.0	5.0	8.8	37.9	23.6	10.7	2.4	85.4	37.4	62.8	37.2
12955	LYON MOUNTAIN	97.7	97.2	0.7	0.7	0.3	0.7	1.0	1.1	4.6	4.6	5.6	7.0	4.2	25.6	31.2	15.1	2.1	80.4	43.8	49.5	50.5
12956	MINEVILLE	90.8	88.6	6.1	7.4	0.4	0.6	5.7	7.3	4.6	4.9	5.4	5.5	9.5	30.2	26.6	11.5	1.9	81.5	37.5	57.1	42.9
12957	MOIRA	96.2	96.5	0.6	0.7	0.1	0.1	0.8	0.8	6.3	6.6	6.7	6.8	4.8	25.7	29.4	12.4	1.3	76.0	40.5	50.2	49.8
12958	MOOERS	98.7	98.2	0.2	0.3	0.1	0.2	0.9	1.2	5.9	5.9	6.2	6.8	6.0	26.9	29.2	12.0	1.2	77.9	40.2	50.4	49.6
12959	MOOERS FORKS	97.6	96.8	0.1	0.2	0.4	0.6	0.7	0.8	6.6	6.5	6.7	6.8	5.8	26.5	28.1	12.0	1.0	76.2	39.8	51.9	48.1
12960	MORIAH	97.6	96.9	0.3	0.4	0.7	0.9	1.0	1.5	5.6	5.9	6.2	6.7	5.0	23.7	30.3	14.1	2.4	77.9	42.5	50.3	49.7
12961	MORIAH CENTER	97.2	96.6	0.6	0.6	0.6	1.1	0.6	0.6	5.1	5.1	6.3	6.8	4.5	25.0	31.8	13.1	2.3	79.0	42.9	50.0	50.0
12962	MORRISONVILLE	97.2	96.3	1.2	1.6	0.3	0.4	1.1	1.5	5.8	6.5	7.1	7.4	5.5	26.2	29.6	10.5	1.3	75.4	39.5	50.2	49.8
12964	NEW RUSSIA	97.5	97.5	0.6	0.6	1.3	1.3	0.0	0.0	3.8	7.6	7.6	6.3	3.2	19.6	34.2	13.3	4.4	75.3	46.4	50.0	50.0
12965	NICHOLVILLE	98.4	98.1	0.0	0.0	0.0	0.0	0.5	0.7	5.6	6.8	7.0	7.5	5.3	25.7	30.1	10.7	1.2	75.7	40.0	51.0	49.0
12966	NORTH BANGOR	96.9	96.7	0.6	0.6	0.3	0.3	1.4	1.7	6.0	6.7	7.8	8.3	5.6	25.9	27.1	11.3	1.3	74.1	38.1	50.7	49.3
12967	NORTH LAWRENCE	98.5	98.2	0.0	0.0	0.1	0.1	0.9	1.2	6.4	7.3	7.2	7.3	5.5	24.8	28.9	11.6	1.0	74.4	39.2	49.3	50.7
12969	OWLS HEAD	98.3	98.6	0.0	0.0	0.0	0.0	0.5	0.5	3.6	5.8	5.5	7.2	3.1	23.4	34.9	14.9	1.4	80.2	45.8	52.5	47.5
12970	PAUL SMITHS	79.3	77.9	18.6	20.1	1.2	1.3	0.5	0.4	2.9	2.5	3.2	19.2	20.6	28.2	17.9	4.8	0.8	88.7	26.0	67.9	32.1
12972	PERU	97.5	96.6	0.8	1.1	0.6	0.8	0.9	1.3	5.6	6.1	6.8	7.2	5.4	25.3	30.1	12.0	1.4	76.6	40.6	48.4	51.6
12973	PIERCEFIELD	97.4	96.4	0.0	0.0	0.0	0.9	0.9	1.8	3.6	4.5	4.5	4.5	2.7	17.0	40.2	21.4	1.8	84.8	52.5	50.0	50.0
12974	PORT HENRY	97.8	97.1	0.3	0.3	0.6	0.8	1.8	2.5	6.3	6.3	6.5	6.2	5.4	22.6	28.0	16.1	2.6	76.7	42.4	49.2	50.8
12978	REDFORD	98.4	98.0	0.0	0.0	0.4	0.4	1.4	1.8	5.5	8.3	8.9	7.5	4.1	29.0	25.4	10.3	1.0	72.8	37.0	49.7	50.3
12979	ROUSES POINT	97.6	96.6	0.6	0.9	0.3	0.5	1.0	1.6	6.2	6.3	6.8	6.8	4.7	25.5	27.9	13.6	2.1	76.3	40.5	49.0	51.0
12980	SAINT REGIS FALLS	98.3	98.3	0.1	0.1	0.1	0.1	0.3	0.3	5.0	5.3	5.9	7.3	5.4	22.8	33.6	12.8	2.0	79.6	43.9	51.9	48.1
12981	SARANAC	67.9	64.2	23.6	25.8	0.7	0.8	11.9	13.6	3.4	4.1	4.5	5.0	8.7	45.6	21.5	6.3	0.9	84.9	35.2	70.6	29.4
12983	SARANAC LAKE	92.8	92.1	4.4	4.8	0.7	0.8	3.1	3.5	4.8	4.7	5.1	6.3	7.4	28.0	28.8	11.9	2.9	81.8	40.6	52.8	47.2
12985	SCHUYLER FALLS	98.3	97.6	0.2	0.4	0.3	0.4	0.9	1.2	5.5	7.6	8.8	7.4	4.1	28.9	27.6	9.5	0.7	73.3	38.4	50.3	49.7
12986	TUPPER LAKE	97.6	97.4	1.2	1.4	0.1	0.1	0.6	0.6	5.3	5.6	6.1	6.5	6.5	26.2	27.6	13.4	2.7	78.6	40.8	50.5	49.5
12987	UPPER JAY	99.3	98.6	0.0	0.7	0.0	0.0	0.7	0.7	5.7	6.4	7.1	6.4	3.6	24.3	32.9	12.1	1.4	76.4	42.7	50.0	50.0
12989	VERMONTVILLE	89.5	89.0	8.2	8.7	0.6	0.6	0.5	0.5	3.9	4.4	6.6	12.5	10.7	26.9	24.5	9.3	1.1	80.6	35.7	58.1	41.9
12992	WEST CHAZY	98.3	97.8	0.4	0.5	0.4	0.6	0.7	1.0	5.7	6.4	6.9	7.2	5.5	27.0	30.7	9.8	0.9	76.5	39.5	49.3	50.7
12993	WESTPORT	97.5	96.7	0.5	0.6	0.6	0.8	1.2	1.6	4.4	5.3	6.6	5.6	3.1	22.0	33.7	16.7	2.7	79.6	47.1	50.3	49.7
12996	WILLSBORO	98.4	98.0	0.3	0.4	0.0	0.0	0.5	0.6	4.2	5.0	6.2	5.4	4.1	23.2	31.6	17.5	2.8	81.3	46.1	50.4	49.6
12997	WILMINGTON	98.6	98.2	0.1	0.1	0.2	0.2	0.6	0.9	6.8	6.7	6.8	6.4	6.3	24.3	28.0	13.0	1.7	75.8	39.9	48.1	51.9
13021	AUBURN	91.6	90.0	5.4	6.3	0.6	0.7	2.2	2.6	6.1	5.8	6.0	6.4	6.4	26.0	26.8	13.2	3.3	78.1	40.3	50.1	49.9
13026	AURORA	96.3	95.2	0.6	0.9	1.2	1.5	1.3	1.7	4.6	5.0	6.2	13.3	9.4	20.6	27.6	11.6	1.8	80.4	37.9	43.6	56.4
13027	BALDWINSVILLE	96.5	95.2	0.9	1.3	0.9	1.4	0.8	1.2	6.4	6.8	7.1	6.7	5.5	24.5	30.0	11.5	1.6	75.4	40.6	48.5	51.5
13028	BERNHARDS BAY	98.2	98.0	0.3	0.3	0.1	0.1	0.5	0.6	5.9	6.5	7.2	7.3	6.0	25.9	30.6	9.7	0.9	75.0	39.2	51.6	48.4
13029	BREWERTON	97.6	96.7	0.7	0.9	0.3	0.4	0.9	1.4	7.5	7.4	6.8	7.4	5.0	27.4	26.6	10.6	1.2	73.6	37.6	48.8	51.2
13030	BRIDGEPORT	97.4	96.4	0.7	1.0	0.3	0.5	0.6	0.7	5.4	6.1	6.4	6.7	5.2	24.6	31.0	13.3	1.2	77.6	41.9	50.2	49.8
13031	CAMILLUS	96.5	95.2	0.9	1.2	1.2	1.7	0.8	1.2	5.7	6.0	6.4	6.5	5.3	21.9	29.9	15.8	2.5	77.9	43.7	47.9	52.1
13032	CANASTOTA	97.9	97.4	0.6	0.6	0.3	0.4	0.7	0.9	6.5	6.6	6.9	6.7	5.0	24.8	29.1	12.6	1.8	75.5	40.8	49.3	50.7
13033	CATO	97.2	96.3	0.4	0.6	0.2	0.2	0.7	1.0	6.5	6.6	7.2	7.5	5.6	25.2	31.1	9.2	1.0	75.0	39.3	50.2	49.8
13034	CAYUGA	98.3	97.7	0.3	0.4	0.2	0.1	0.9	1.2	6.0	6.6	7.1	7.1	5.1	24.0	29.3	13.1	1.7	75.7	40.6	49.9	50.1
13035	CAZENOVIA	97.5	96.9	0.9	1.0	0.5	0.6	1.3	1.6	5.4	6.0	6.7	10.2	7.5	19.0	30.5	12.7	1.9	77.3	41.1	47.7	52.3
13036	CENTRAL SQUARE	97.7	97.1	0.3	0.4	0.4	0.6	0.6	0.8	6.0	6.0	6.3	7.3	6.1	26.4	29.1	11.4	1.3	77.2	40.1	49.3	50.7
13037	CHITTENANGO	98.0	97.5	0.3	0.4	0.3	0.5	0.6	0.7	6.3	6.6	7.0	7.4	5.4	25.3	29.6	10.6	1.9	75.2	39.6	48.1	51.9
13039	CICERO	96.2	94.5	1.3	1.8	0.9	1.3	1.0	1.4	7.9	7.7	8.0	7.0	4.9	28.0	26.9	8.8	0.9	71.9	36.7	49.1	50.9
13040	CINCINNATUS	98.1	97.6	0.2	0.3	0.1	0.1	1.2	1.5	6.7	7.0	7.2	7.1	4.9	24.5	29.6	11.5	1.5	74.5	40.0	49.8	50.2
13041	CLAY	92.3	89.4	3.6	5.1	1.3	1.8	1.3	1.8	7.8	7.6	7.6	7.4	5.3	29.3	27.4	7.2	0.5	72.4	35.7	48.8	51.2
13042	CLEVELAND	97.7	96.9	0.4	0.5	0.4	0.5	0.8	1.0	5.9	6.3	6.9	7.4	5.6	25.3	30.7	10.7	1.1	75.9	40.3	50.7	49.3
13044	CONSTANTIA	98.2	97.7	0.2	0.3	0.2	0.2	0.2	0.2	5.5	7.4	8.4	5.6	4.8	27.8	29.6	9.6	1.1	74.3	39.4	51.7	48.3
13045	CORTLAND	96.2	94.2	1.2	2.0	0.6	1.0	1.5	2.1	5.5	5.2	5.4	11.3	13.5	23.3	22.7	10.6	2.5	80.2	32.4	48.0	52.0
13052	DE RUYTER	94.3	92.9	3.6	4.4	0.2	0.3	1.9	2.5	6.3	6.5	6.9	6.9	5.9	27.4	28.0	10.6	1.4	76.1	38.4	52.9	47.1
13053	DRYDEN	95.7	94.5	1.6	1.9	0.6	1.0	1.7	2.2	5.9	6.7	6.0	8.6	8.4	24.3	29.2	9.6	1.2	77.1	37.5	50.3	49.7
13054	DURHAMVILLE	97.7	97.0	0.4	0.5	0.2	0.3	0.5	0.7	5.7	5.9	6.4	6.9	5.3	24.1	31.0	13.2	1.5	77.7	42.3	50.2	49.8
13057	EAST SYRACUSE	95.0	93.1	1.3	1.8	1.5	2.3	1.0	1.4	5.3	5.4	5.8	6.4	5.8	23.0	30.6	15.2	2.5	79.4	43.8	47.6	52.4
13060	ELBRIDGE	97.6	96.6	0.5	0.7	0.4	0.6	1.1	1.5	6.4	6.6	7.0	7.1	5.3	23.7	30.3	12.2	1.6	75.5	41.1	49.5	50.5
13061	ERIEVILLE	97.7	97.1	0.7	0.8	0.1	0.2	1.3	1.7	5.5	6.2	6.8	8.4	6.2	22.0	33.7	10.1	1.1	77.1	41.6	50.8	49.2
13063	FABIUS	98.0	97.2	0.4	0.5	0.3	0.4	1.1	1.7	6.7	7.3	8.3	7.8	4.5	23.5	31.3	9.5	1.0	72.9	39.4	50.0	50.0
13066	FAYETTEVILLE	94.3	91.9	1.0	1.3	3.2	4.7	1.2	1.6	5.4	5.9	6.8	7.0	5.3	18.8	32.3	15.4	3.2	77.3	45.5	47.3	52.7
13068	FREEVILLE	95.6	94.3	1.2	1.4	1.1	1.6	1.2	1.5	6.3	6.4	7.1	8.1	5.8	27.7	28.3	9.2	1.1	74.8	37.1	49.6	50.4
13069	FULTON	97.4	96.8	0.6	0.6	0.3	0.4	1.4	1.7	7.1	6.8	6.8	7.0	6.3	26.0	27.0	11.0	1.9	74.9	37.5	49.1	50.9
13071	GENOA	97.2	96.1	0.7	1.0	0.4	0.5	2.2	3.1	5.7	5.9	6.2	7.0	5.8	25.2	31.2	11.8	1.4	78.2	41.2	51.7	48.3
13072	GEORGETOWN	88.8	86.6	7.9	9.3	0.2	0.2	4.0	5.0	6.0	6.0	6.4	6.4	7.0	29.6	25.9	11.2	1.4	77.5	37.7	55.1	44.9
13073	GROTON	97.1	96.1	0.9	1.0	0.4	0.6	0.9	1.1	5.6	6.1	6.9	7.7	6.3	23.7	30.1	11.6	1.9	76.2	40.4	49.7	50.3
13074	HANNIBAL	97.8	97.3	0.4	0.4	0.2	0.2	1.0	1.2	6.8	6.8	7.3	8.9	7.1	25.8	27.9	8.4	1.1	74.1	36.0	50.0	50.0
13076	HASTINGS	97.7	97.1	0.2	0.3	0.2	0.2	0.8	0.9	6.6	6.7	7.1	7.9	5.8	27.6	28.3	9.1	0.8	74.8	37.9	50.2	49.8
13077	HOMER	98.1	97.6	0.4	0.4	0.3	0.4	0.7	0.9	5.8	6.2	6.7	6.9	5.7	24.9	29.9	11.9	1.9	77.0	40.6	48.9	51.1
13078	JAMESVILLE	91.7	88.7	3.2	4.3	2.3	3.4	0.8	1.1	5.4	6.3	7.0	6.6	4.8	20.0	30.3	14.5	5.1	76.7	44.9	48.5	51.5
13080	JORDAN	98.0	97.1	0.3	0.4	0.5	0.7	0.9	1.3	6.0	6.3	6.7	7.1	5.7	24.3	30.9	11.4	1.6	76.4	40.9	49.7	50.3
13081	KING FERRY	96.6	95.5	0.3	0.3	0.5	0.5	2.2	3.1	4.5	6.9	8.3	9.1	5.5	21.5	29.3	12.9	2.1	74.9	40.9	49.3	50.7
13082	KIRKVILLE	98.2	97.6	0.2	0.3	0.3	0.5	0.4	0.5	5.5	6.0	6.4	6.4	5.2	23.9	31.6	13.6	1.5	78.0	42.8	49.3	50.7
13083	LACONA	98.3	98.0	0.1	0.1	0.1	0.1	0.8	1.0	5.9	6.9	7.0	6.9	4.9	24.1	30.7	12.2	1.5	75.8	41.1	50.3	49.7
13084	LA FAYETTE	95.9	94.4	0.5	0.7	0.7	1.1	0.4	0.7	5.4	6.1	6.9	7.4	5.2	21.8	33.7	11.9	1.7	77.0	43.1	50.0	50.0
13088	LIVERPOOL	92.6	89.7	2.7	3.6	2.6	3.9	1.5	2.0	5.4	5.3	5.5	5.8	6.4	27.1	27.6	14.1	2.7	80.2	41.1	47.5	52.5
13090	LIVERPOOL	91.0	87.7	4.2	5.6	2.4	3.4	1.4	1.9	7.2	7.4	7.3	6.8	6.3	28.4	27.2	8.5	0.8	73.6	35.9	48.3	51.7
13092	LOCKE	97.8	97.2	0.7	0.8	0.4	0.5	0.9	1.2	6.3	6.6	7.1	7.5	5.9	25.5	29.8	10.1	1.0	75.2	38.6	50.2	49.8
13101	MC GRAW	97.8	97.2	0.2	0.3	0.0	0.1	0.6	0.8	6.5	6.6	6.9	7.4	6.0	25.7	28.0	11.5	1.5	75.2	38.1	49.6	50.4
13103	MALLORY	97.2	96.6	0.2	0.2	0.2	0.2	0.4	0.4	6.7	6.7	7.1	8.0	6.2	27.5	29.2	8.2	0.4	74.6	37.3	52.3	47.7
13104	MANLIUS	94.1	91.6	0.9	1.3	3.5	5.1	1.1	1.5	6.0	6.9	8.1	8.0	4.7	18.7	33.4	12.3	1.9	73.6	43.2	48.8	51.2
13108	MARCELLUS	98.4	97.8	0.3	0.5	0.3	0.4	0.9	1.2	5.7	6.2	7.0	7.7	5.6	22.0	31.6	12.3	1.8	76.3	42.0	48.1	51.9
13110	MARIETTA	97.7	96.8	0.4	0.6	0.4	0.6	0.3	0.5	6.1	6.7	7.4	7.5	5.0	22.7	32.8	10.5	1.2	75.1	41.4	50.6	49.4
13111	MARTVILLE	98.2	97.6	0.1	0.2	0.2	0.3	0.5	0.7	6.7	6.6	6.9	7.7	7.0	26.1	28.6	9.5	0.9	75.2	37.4	51.6	48.4
13112	MEMPHIS	98.2	97.5	0.4	0.6	0.3	0.4	0.5	0.6	5.8	6.2	6.5	6.3	4.7	25.0	32.4	11.7	1.5	77.6	42.3	50.3	49.7
13114	MEXICO	98.1	97.6	0.2	0.2	0.3	0.4	0.8	1.0	6.4	6.6	7.0	7.4	6.1	26.3	29.8	9.3	1.0	75.1	38.2	49.6	50.4
13116	MINOA	96.6	95.2	0.5	0.7	1.3	1.9	0.5	0.7	5.1	5.2	5.8	7.1	5.7	22.8	31.6	13.4	3.3	79.1	43.6	46.7	53.3
13118	MORAVIA	82.1	79.8	13.4	14.8	0.4	0.5	6.4	7.4	4.7	4.9	5.1	6.0	7.9	33.9	26.0	9.9	1.5	81.3	37.6	60.0	40.0
	NEW YORK	67.9	64.8	15.9	16.5	5.6	6.9	15.1	16.7	6.5	6.4	6.4	7.1	7.0	27.0	26.3	11.2	2.1	76.6	37.5	48.4	51.6
	UNITED STATES	75.1	72.0	12.3	12.7	3.8	4.6	12.5	15.7	6.8	6.7	6.6	7.1	6.9	27.0	26.0	10.9	1.9	75.7	36.9	49.2	50.8

#	POST OFFICE NAME	2009 Per Capita Income	2009 HH Income Base	2009 HOUSEHOLD INCOME DISTRIBUTION (%) Less than $25,000	$25,000 to $49,999	$50,000 to $99,999	$100,000 to $149,999	$150,000 or More	MEDIAN HOUSEHOLD INCOME 2009	2014	2009 National Centile	2009 State Centile	2009 Home Value Base	2009 HOME VALUE DISTRIBUTION (%) Less than $50,000	$50,000 to $89,999	$90,000 to $174,999	$175,000 to $399,999	$400,000 or More	2009 Median Home Value
12936	ESSEX	22937	268	22.4	31.7	35.8	8.6	1.5	45984	47742	51	34	222	8.1	14.0	34.7	31.1	12.2	148438
12937	FORT COVINGTON	18399	572	30.8	32.2	30.8	4.9	1.4	36727	39897	23	7	451	20.6	34.8	36.4	6.2	2.0	83194
12941	JAY	21062	457	25.4	29.5	38.5	4.2	2.4	45757	46800	51	33	360	4.4	16.7	48.9	25.6	4.4	128431
12942	KEENE	22147	235	25.5	29.4	38.3	5.1	1.7	43327	46034	43	24	185	3.2	3.8	33.5	45.9	13.5	202885
12943	KEENE VALLEY	21400	218	25.7	29.4	39.0	5.0	0.9	43294	44403	43	24	171	1.2	3.5	33.9	48.0	13.5	208036
12944	KEESEVILLE	22445	1776	24.3	27.7	37.6	7.4	2.9	47481	49549	55	39	1359	10.4	19.4	51.8	15.8	2.6	119818
12945	LAKE CLEAR	23480	277	19.9	32.1	36.1	10.8	1.1	48961	49756	59	43	215	4.2	13.0	44.2	34.0	4.7	151442
12946	LAKE PLACID	23600	2614	24.3	28.4	37.2	7.0	3.0	47125	48289	54	37	1597	7.0	5.4	35.0	37.3	15.2	184463
12950	LEWIS	21100	257	23.3	34.6	34.6	5.4	1.9	43903	45573	45	27	208	13.5	16.8	41.8	25.0	2.9	121875
12952	LYON MOUNTAIN	29169	212	25.9	22.2	41.5	9.0	1.4	51711	53193	65	50	178	30.9	21.9	36.0	10.1	1.1	84444
12953	MALONE	18975	4646	31.3	32.4	28.9	4.2	3.1	34379	39083	16	5	3040	10.0	31.4	44.7	12.5	1.3	101646
12955	LYON MOUNTAIN	22537	132	28.8	31.8	31.1	6.8	1.5	40000	43969	33	14	104	11.5	30.8	40.4	14.4	2.9	98000
12956	MINEVILLE	21162	720	32.1	26.5	32.4	6.0	3.1	41706	44301	38	19	549	11.7	27.5	45.5	14.9	0.4	103360
12957	MOIRA	16350	556	35.4	34.4	25.5	4.3	0.4	31973	33535	11	4	419	22.4	34.8	35.8	6.4	0.5	77361
12958	MOOERS	19716	738	26.6	28.0	37.0	7.3	1.1	46470	48556	53	35	608	11.0	19.4	55.6	13.0	1.0	112417
12959	MOOERS FORKS	17410	527	32.4	26.0	35.5	5.3	0.8	43842	46313	45	26	436	19.5	25.9	42.2	12.2	0.2	95714
12960	MORIAH	21575	403	30.3	28.5	32.5	4.7	4.0	41317	43801	37	18	309	11.7	28.8	50.5	9.1	0.0	101815
12961	MORIAH CENTER	20352	67	31.3	28.4	31.3	4.5	4.5	40562	43636	35	16	52	11.5	26.9	51.9	9.6	0.0	104545
12962	MORRISONVILLE	24231	2246	18.1	22.2	45.0	12.0	2.7	59282	60549	77	62	1772	9.5	12.6	43.9	30.6	3.3	142885
12964	NEW RUSSIA	23270	61	21.3	27.9	41.0	6.6	3.3	51085	54650	64	49	46	0.0	13.0	60.9	23.9	2.2	136364
12965	NICHOLVILLE	16590	158	31.0	32.3	32.9	3.2	0.6	38712	41747	29	11	124	17.7	36.3	34.7	11.3	0.0	85000
12966	NORTH BANGOR	16657	1067	30.8	33.6	29.7	5.0	0.9	34593	38888	17	5	856	19.3	31.9	43.3	4.8	0.7	88077
12967	NORTH LAWRENCE	16542	406	30.3	32.5	34.2	2.5	0.5	38931	41909	30	12	316	15.2	31.6	42.1	10.4	0.6	93704
12969	OWLS HEAD	21288	182	23.1	34.1	37.4	3.3	2.2	42863	44746	42	22	155	14.8	28.4	38.7	16.8	1.3	101875
12970	PAUL SMITHS	16293	116	20.7	25.0	43.1	9.5	1.7	53091	54992	68	53	90	10.0	5.6	55.6	24.4	4.4	135000
12972	PERU	22751	2331	20.5	30.7	37.5	7.4	3.9	48303	52111	57	41	1812	9.2	12.9	45.0	30.4	2.5	142763
12973	PIERCEFIELD	21966	49	22.4	34.7	40.8	2.0	0.0	44082	49086	46	27	41	14.6	26.8	41.5	14.6	2.4	102083
12974	PORT HENRY	23476	729	29.6	27.8	34.0	5.6	2.9	41666	43505	38	19	544	10.3	27.9	53.1	8.6	0.0	103654
12978	REDFORD	18851	184	19.6	34.8	38.0	7.1	0.5	45916	48252	51	33	154	9.1	19.5	61.0	9.1	1.3	120455
12979	ROUSES POINT	24909	1067	25.6	24.7	38.7	8.2	2.8	49585	51944	60	44	641	5.0	16.5	59.6	16.7	2.2	126771
12980	SAINT REGIS FALLS	18876	631	33.8	27.9	31.1	6.7	0.6	38843	41725	29	11	488	23.2	30.7	28.1	14.1	3.9	82400
12981	SARANAC	19038	1337	19.9	24.5	44.3	9.9	1.5	55117	57152	71	57	1043	8.2	17.6	56.1	17.0	1.1	122599
12983	SARANAC LAKE	23401	3400	30.8	25.9	32.5	7.9	2.9	43159	45685	43	23	1915	3.9	13.5	48.3	27.7	6.6	145459
12985	SCHUYLER FALLS	21248	508	19.7	30.5	39.2	8.1	2.6	49728	52274	60	44	425	7.1	17.6	48.5	24.7	2.1	134964
12986	TUPPER LAKE	21710	2519	23.9	27.3	43.0	4.6	1.2	48588	51558	58	42	1723	3.2	16.9	58.9	18.6	2.4	131458
12987	UPPER JAY	22037	58	24.1	29.3	37.9	5.2	3.4	47348	46354	55	39	46	4.3	17.4	47.8	26.1	4.3	132143
12989	VERMONTVILLE	21788	629	21.6	25.0	44.7	7.5	1.3	52522	54820	67	52	519	9.8	12.5	45.9	26.8	5.0	141602
12992	WEST CHAZY	18935	1806	28.9	24.0	40.1	5.5	1.4	46200	50000	52	35	1479	13.7	15.7	48.7	19.9	2.0	128798
12993	WESTPORT	26080	721	21.9	29.4	37.0	6.5	5.1	48365	49280	57	41	544	3.7	14.3	42.8	28.5	10.7	146296
12996	WILLSBORO	22818	798	26.2	30.5	34.8	6.6	1.9	44417	45866	47	28	639	8.1	22.8	43.2	21.9	3.9	119318
12997	WILMINGTON	22510	530	27.0	28.5	35.1	5.7	3.8	45290	46592	49	31	386	5.7	16.1	42.0	31.3	4.9	140094
13021	AUBURN	23059	16200	26.8	26.3	36.0	7.9	3.1	45587	50255	50	32	10206	1.9	17.3	56.6	21.4	2.8	126781
13026	AURORA	23123	597	17.4	31.2	38.7	9.0	3.7	51564	55518	65	50	463	4.8	12.1	44.1	30.9	8.2	148438
13027	BALDWINSVILLE	31229	12242	15.2	20.8	40.3	14.9	8.8	64796	67780	83	71	8732	2.1	7.5	49.3	37.1	4.0	156238
13028	BERNHARDS BAY	19226	522	22.0	29.7	42.0	6.1	0.2	48083	51736	57	41	439	12.8	21.2	47.6	15.7	2.7	118527
13029	BREWERTON	27748	2165	14.0	21.7	47.9	12.5	3.8	66074	68691	84	73	1647	1.4	2.8	55.9	37.3	2.6	158676
13030	BRIDGEPORT	26372	1685	16.5	25.3	43.6	11.5	3.0	59873	62757	77	63	1345	1.6	14.8	49.2	32.0	2.3	147245
13031	CAMILLUS	30758	6411	13.0	23.2	43.5	14.0	6.3	64673	67432	83	71	4809	0.4	2.5	51.3	43.2	2.8	169188
13032	CANASTOTA	22925	5130	21.6	27.5	39.6	9.3	2.0	50767	54103	63	47	3795	4.8	11.2	53.3	27.9	2.7	140696
13033	CATO	20710	1447	18.7	26.0	46.2	6.9	2.2	54471	57396	70	56	1205	7.1	17.8	51.8	20.2	3.0	129110
13034	CAYUGA	22829	778	21.6	25.8	41.8	8.1	2.7	52176	54867	66	51	618	8.4	15.7	53.2	19.1	3.6	123551
13035	CAZENOVIA	34583	3118	13.5	20.8	37.2	15.2	13.3	67888	70363	86	75	2428	2.5	3.4	27.3	51.4	15.4	218112
13036	CENTRAL SQUARE	22661	3492	20.9	28.2	41.6	7.0	2.2	50686	53945	63	47	2662	8.7	13.0	54.7	22.2	1.5	136586
13037	CHITTENANGO	26655	3298	15.2	27.9	40.0	11.6	5.4	56400	60064	73	59	2512	6.2	10.1	48.4	33.0	2.4	146043
13039	CICERO	30280	6420	10.2	19.3	46.3	16.8	7.4	71875	73854	88	78	5103	0.6	3.2	53.1	42.4	0.6	165474
13040	CINCINNATUS	19399	1177	24.6	32.7	36.5	4.5	1.7	44317	46688	46	28	928	13.5	28.9	45.4	11.5	0.8	97978
13041	CLAY	27798	3502	8.1	16.0	53.6	16.7	5.6	72469	73886	88	79	3028	0.6	9.3	64.5	24.4	1.3	146059
13042	CLEVELAND	20624	986	21.0	28.9	41.1	8.3	0.7	50123	56289	61	45	821	9.5	16.8	44.1	28.3	1.3	135417
13044	CONSTANTIA	19534	983	20.4	28.4	45.3	5.8	0.1	50909	54470	63	48	804	16.7	11.1	42.9	25.7	3.6	135600
13045	CORTLAND	20358	10941	33.0	26.4	32.0	6.1	2.5	38514	43270	28	10	5977	3.5	12.8	64.8	17.3	1.5	123778
13052	DE RUYTER	20580	728	25.4	32.4	36.8	3.7	1.6	43852	46686	45	26	577	17.0	23.2	43.8	15.1	0.9	105147
13053	DRYDEN	24167	1966	19.2	25.5	41.7	9.8	3.8	56016	60587	73	59	1336	7.0	6.1	43.2	41.3	2.4	167683
13054	DURHAMVILLE	20402	554	16.1	28.5	49.5	4.5	1.4	55088	60063	71	57	451	7.1	10.4	54.5	25.5	2.4	139511
13057	EAST SYRACUSE	29700	6341	17.6	27.2	39.7	10.0	5.5	55633	60520	72	58	4593	1.3	8.5	63.6	26.0	0.7	141073
13060	ELBRIDGE	25510	1255	16.6	30.8	40.2	8.6	3.8	52370	56891	67	52	1022	18.6	7.2	38.6	33.1	2.4	145915
13061	ERIEVILLE	26403	487	12.9	27.3	43.1	12.9	3.7	60429	62608	78	65	403	3.5	8.2	41.9	42.9	3.5	168527
13063	FABIUS	24592	768	9.5	31.6	43.8	10.2	4.9	60936	63526	79	66	616	1.0	7.3	43.5	45.3	2.9	171014
13066	FAYETTEVILLE	47275	5085	8.3	17.5	35.0	17.6	21.5	80880	84555	92	85	3949	1.1	2.5	26.6	53.5	16.3	224572
13068	FREEVILLE	25437	2235	17.4	27.2	41.7	9.8	3.8	55769	60487	72	58	1507	9.0	6.9	40.3	39.9	3.8	166118
13069	FULTON	20914	10015	26.6	29.7	33.9	7.1	2.7	44492	47555	47	29	6787	10.1	22.3	51.1	15.4	1.1	114961
13071	GENOA	20405	381	19.9	29.4	45.1	4.2	1.3	50461	53271	62	46	301	7.6	24.9	52.2	13.3	2.0	113294
13072	GEORGETOWN	15301	329	24.9	35.0	35.3	3.6	1.2	42814	45092	42	22	264	19.7	23.5	41.7	14.4	0.8	101471
13073	GROTON	22932	2383	17.7	26.1	46.0	8.1	2.1	54692	58400	71	56	1742	5.9	10.2	57.3	24.4	2.1	141317
13074	HANNIBAL	20220	1780	25.0	32.8	31.6	7.8	2.9	44155	46972	46	28	1432	19.5	23.7	41.3	14.9	0.6	103774
13076	HASTINGS	19781	684	21.2	25.1	45.2	7.7	0.7	52468	55269	67	52	587	11.1	13.3	57.4	16.5	1.7	129876
13077	HOMER	25008	2672	19.2	27.2	39.0	10.7	3.9	53253	55358	68	54	2012	6.2	10.5	58.2	22.0	3.2	133412
13078	JAMESVILLE	39844	3356	9.6	19.2	35.5	18.2	17.5	78003	81029	91	83	2637	4.4	2.8	28.4	50.2	14.3	207315
13080	JORDAN	23645	1378	18.5	28.1	40.9	9.4	3.0	53193	57343	68	54	1082	9.7	12.3	53.1	24.1	0.7	134405
13081	KING FERRY	26241	448	15.8	27.2	42.0	9.8	5.1	56644	60410	74	59	359	5.3	12.8	41.2	33.1	7.5	149728
13082	KIRKVILLE	26006	1989	15.2	26.0	43.3	11.8	3.6	60654	62985	78	65	1714	11.8	14.8	44.7	26.9	1.8	137134
13083	LACONA	20019	800	27.1	29.0	33.6	8.6	1.6	44391	47710	47	28	620	14.7	20.5	42.6	20.3	1.9	118831
13084	LA FAYETTE	30221	1789	12.4	24.3	42.4	13.5	7.5	62949	66675	81	69	1448	2.2	8.8	39.2	43.0	6.8	174671
13088	LIVERPOOL	30103	9886	17.1	27.0	40.8	9.9	5.2	55766	60259	72	58	5904	1.1	3.2	68.8	25.2	1.7	144514
13090	LIVERPOOL	29878	11572	9.9	20.9	45.7	17.2	6.4	68250	70331	86	75	8096	3.2	3.1	55.7	37.0	1.0	158893
13092	LOCKE	20375	1137	20.3	32.9	39.9	5.4	1.5	46626	50000	53	36	928	16.6	16.4	50.6	15.0	1.4	116258
13101	MC GRAW	23078	892	18.4	29.8	41.8	6.5	3.5	51847	54298	66	51	684	7.5	25.0	55.6	10.8	1.2	108833
13103	MALLORY	19556	161	18.6	28.0	44.7	6.2	2.5	53014	57136	68	53	138	28.3	18.8	32.6	19.6	0.7	95714
13104	MANLIUS	43338	5889	9.7	15.9	35.6	17.6	21.2	80912	84049	92	85	4467	0.2	2.2	19.4	58.3	19.9	249102
13108	MARCELLUS	30919	2227	10.6	24.5	46.7	11.3	7.0	66449	68889	84	73	1706	0.1	4.1	41.0	50.5	4.3	181308
13110	MARIETTA	27759	859	9.2	29.5	46.8	10.4	4.2	60107	62350	77	64	700	1.9	6.9	47.0	39.4	4.9	165741
13111	MARTVILLE	16504	678	25.5	34.2	33.3	6.2	0.7	41636	44180	38	19	554	10.3	27.4	47.5	13.5	1.3	104126
13112	MEMPHIS	27403	676	14.9	24.1	45.7	8.6	6.7	60719	63427	78	65	557	9.5	7.9	44.2	35.2	3.2	151964
13114	MEXICO	20933	2727	22.3	27.4	40.8	8.0	1.5	50228	53551	62	45	2122	11.8	17.3	52.0	17.7	1.2	126144
13116	MINOA	26714	1245	10.9	29.3	46.2	9.3	4.3	61444	64987	79	67	940	0.0	6.8	80.0	13.2	0.0	136804
13118	MORAVIA	19980	2005	21.9	27.7	42.8	5.0	2.6	50305	52976	62	46	1585	10.7	17.9	49.7	18.0	3.7	121336
	NEW YORK	29893		21.9	21.3	32.7	14.0	9.9	58747	62337				3.4	5.7	23.0	38.7	29.1	269816
	UNITED STATES	27277		20.9	24.4	35.3	11.7	7.6	54719	56938				9.3	13.1	31.6	32.6	13.5	162279

#	POST OFFICE NAME	FINANCIAL SERVICES: Auto Loan	Home Loan	Invest-ments	Retire-ment Plans	THE HOME: Home Improvements: Home Repair	Lawn & Garden	Furnishings: Comput-ers & Hard-ware-Personal	Major Appli-ances	TV, Radio, Sound Equip-ment	Furni-ture	ENTERTAINMENT: Dine out/ Carry out	Sports Equip-ment	Fees & Tickets	Toys & Games	Travel	Cable TV	PERSONAL: Apparel & Services	Auto Repairs	Health Insur-ance	Pets & Supplies
12936	ESSEX	87	70	113	69	77	92	70	89	73	65	72	65	61	69	76	78	48	82	88	103
12937	FORT COVINGTON	83	60	85	58	62	84	61	78	68	57	67	58	49	67	60	75	44	71	81	92
12941	JAY	86	69	111	68	75	91	69	87	72	64	71	64	59	68	74	77	47	81	86	101
12942	KEENE	83	66	107	65	73	88	66	84	69	62	69	62	58	66	72	74	46	78	83	98
12943	KEENE VALLEY	83	66	107	65	73	87	66	84	69	62	68	61	57	66	72	74	46	78	83	98
12944	KEESEVILLE	89	75	87	75	76	90	76	86	80	73	79	64	69	80	75	84	53	82	89	102
12945	LAKE CLEAR	90	76	104	76	81	96	75	92	78	70	77	68	67	76	79	83	52	85	92	106
12946	LAKE PLACID	76	76	82	76	78	82	77	80	79	75	78	59	77	77	79	81	54	80	85	93
12950	LEWIS	92	66	94	64	68	93	67	86	75	63	74	64	54	74	67	82	49	79	89	102
12952	LYON MOUNTAIN	74	83	79	81	83	90	74	81	79	72	78	57	80	77	80	84	54	78	92	93
12953	MALONE	75	61	72	62	63	76	67	74	71	62	69	55	59	70	65	75	47	72	79	87
12955	LYON MOUNTAIN	85	62	87	60	65	87	63	80	70	59	69	60	52	70	63	77	46	74	84	95
12956	MINEVILLE	88	68	87	67	70	91	69	85	76	63	74	64	58	75	69	82	49	78	89	100
12957	MOIRA	72	52	74	50	54	73	53	68	59	49	58	51	42	58	52	65	38	62	70	80
12958	MOOERS	87	72	80	69	72	85	70	81	75	70	74	60	62	76	68	80	50	76	83	96
12959	MOOERS FORKS	84	61	73	60	62	81	63	75	70	61	68	57	51	72	59	76	46	70	78	90
12960	MORIAH	93	67	94	65	69	95	70	88	78	64	76	66	56	77	69	86	51	82	94	104
12961	MORIAH CENTER	95	68	98	66	71	97	70	89	78	65	76	67	56	77	69	86	50	82	93	106
12962	MORRISONVILLE	89	96	87	96	94	94	88	90	88	89	89	69	93	90	91	89	62	88	90	106
12964	NEW RUSSIA	80	90	86	88	90	98	80	88	85	79	85	62	87	84	87	91	58	85	100	101
12965	NICHOLVILLE	77	55	79	54	57	78	57	72	63	53	62	54	45	63	56	69	41	66	75	86
12966	NORTH BANGOR	79	57	78	55	59	80	59	73	65	55	64	55	47	65	57	72	42	68	77	88
12967	NORTH LAWRENCE	78	56	80	54	58	79	57	73	64	53	62	55	46	63	57	70	41	67	76	87
12969	OWLS HEAD	80	64	104	63	71	85	64	82	67	60	67	60	56	64	70	72	44	76	81	95
12970	PAUL SMITHS	93	75	120	73	82	99	75	95	78	70	77	69	65	74	81	83	51	88	94	110
12972	PERU	90	90	84	89	88	94	83	89	85	83	85	66	83	87	84	88	58	86	92	105
12973	PIERCEFIELD	84	67	108	66	74	89	67	85	70	63	69	62	58	67	73	75	46	79	84	99
12974	PORT HENRY	90	64	90	63	67	93	70	87	79	63	76	65	56	77	68	87	51	81	95	102
12978	REDFORD	80	73	73	76	75	86	72	82	75	65	73	62	67	76	72	79	50	75	84	95
12979	ROUSES POINT	81	81	72	83	79	85	80	81	81	77	80	63	80	82	79	83	55	81	86	96
12980	SAINT REGIS FALLS	82	59	85	57	61	83	60	77	67	56	65	57	48	66	60	73	43	70	79	91
12981	SARANAC	86	85	84	87	85	94	81	88	84	79	83	66	81	84	84	87	57	85	92	103
12983	SARANAC LAKE	77	66	73	68	68	75	75	75	76	70	76	57	68	75	71	79	52	76	80	89
12985	SCHUYLER FALLS	87	85	83	86	84	92	79	87	81	78	81	67	79	82	81	83	55	82	87	102
12986	TUPPER LAKE	77	69	81	70	72	81	71	78	73	69	72	57	66	72	72	77	49	76	82	91
12987	UPPER JAY	88	71	112	70	77	93	71	89	74	66	73	65	62	71	76	79	49	83	88	103
12989	VERMONTVILLE	91	73	115	72	80	96	74	92	77	69	76	68	64	73	79	82	51	86	92	107
12992	WEST CHAZY	80	70	70	71	71	82	69	77	72	66	71	58	63	74	67	76	49	73	79	91
12993	WESTPORT	100	79	123	78	86	105	79	100	84	74	83	74	68	80	85	90	55	93	100	117
12996	WILLSBORO	90	69	106	67	74	93	69	88	74	65	73	65	58	72	73	80	49	81	89	103
12997	WILMINGTON	83	72	80	73	75	85	77	82	80	74	78	61	71	79	75	83	53	81	87	96
13021	AUBURN	76	76	71	77	75	80	78	77	80	75	79	59	78	79	77	82	55	79	84	92
13026	AURORA	102	83	124	83	90	108	83	103	87	77	86	76	73	84	89	92	57	95	103	120
13027	BALDWINSVILLE	110	112	103	114	110	113	109	110	109	109	109	85	111	111	109	110	76	109	112	129
13028	BERNHARDS BAY	81	73	68	72	72	79	70	76	73	71	73	56	66	76	68	76	50	73	77	90
13029	BREWERTON	101	114	97	112	108	105	101	103	99	104	101	79	107	103	104	98	70	100	100	120
13030	BRIDGEPORT	90	98	85	99	94	102	91	94	93	88	93	72	96	94	94	95	64	92	101	111
13031	CAMILLUS	102	110	107	111	110	114	103	107	104	103	104	79	108	104	108	107	73	105	113	125
13032	CANASTOTA	85	79	79	80	79	91	79	86	82	73	81	65	75	83	78	87	55	82	92	101
13033	CATO	90	85	81	88	85	96	82	91	84	77	83	69	78	86	82	88	57	85	92	106
13034	CAYUGA	90	84	83	87	85	98	82	92	85	75	83	70	77	86	83	89	57	85	95	107
13035	CAZENOVIA	128	138	136	140	140	140	126	133	126	130	126	98	133	126	133	127	88	129	134	155
13036	CENTRAL SQUARE	87	79	76	79	79	86	79	84	82	79	81	62	74	83	77	85	55	82	87	99
13037	CHITTENANGO	102	104	95	104	101	105	97	102	97	97	98	77	97	100	98	99	67	98	102	119
13039	CICERO	114	128	110	127	122	116	115	115	111	120	113	90	122	116	117	109	79	112	110	133
13040	CINCINNATUS	86	68	81	68	70	87	69	81	74	65	73	61	59	75	67	80	49	76	84	96
13041	CLAY	118	126	107	123	120	113	114	115	110	120	112	88	116	116	113	108	78	111	107	133
13042	CLEVELAND	85	77	73	78	78	86	75	83	78	72	77	62	70	80	74	81	52	78	84	97
13044	CONSTANTIA	81	73	73	76	75	87	72	82	75	66	73	62	67	76	72	79	50	75	84	95
13045	CORTLAND	69	62	58	64	61	65	73	66	72	67	72	52	67	72	66	73	50	70	70	80
13052	DE RUYTER	83	69	74	70	70	85	70	80	74	65	73	60	62	75	68	79	49	75	83	94
13053	DRYDEN	89	84	80	87	83	87	89	86	89	87	89	67	86	89	86	90	62	89	90	103
13054	DURHAMVILLE	81	81	79	82	82	92	76	85	80	71	79	62	76	80	79	84	54	80	91	98
13057	EAST SYRACUSE	92	98	92	98	96	104	93	97	97	91	96	71	98	96	97	101	67	96	107	113
13060	ELBRIDGE	88	96	86	95	93	96	85	89	87	87	87	66	91	89	89	89	61	87	92	105
13061	ERIEVILLE	95	104	92	107	102	104	95	99	94	94	94	77	99	96	99	94	65	95	99	116
13063	FABIUS	99	112	97	115	109	110	100	104	98	100	99	81	107	100	106	98	69	100	103	122
13066	FAYETTEVILLE	148	178	185	181	184	173	158	164	154	167	155	122	178	152	175	153	111	159	163	188
13068	FREEVILLE	93	93	85	92	91	92	90	91	91	91	92	69	90	93	89	92	64	91	92	108
13069	FULTON	81	72	68	71	70	79	74	76	78	72	77	57	69	79	70	81	53	76	81	91
13071	GENOA	84	76	75	79	78	90	75	85	77	68	76	64	69	79	75	82	52	78	87	99
13072	GEORGETOWN	82	65	75	65	66	84	67	78	72	61	70	59	57	73	64	78	47	73	83	93
13073	GROTON	90	85	83	87	86	94	85	90	86	81	85	68	81	87	85	89	59	87	94	106
13074	HANNIBAL	97	72	81	71	72	93	74	85	81	72	80	66	61	85	68	88	54	81	90	104
13076	HASTINGS	89	82	72	79	80	83	77	82	80	80	80	59	73	83	73	82	54	79	82	97
13077	HOMER	90	93	84	94	91	96	88	91	90	87	89	69	90	91	89	92	62	89	95	108
13078	JAMESVILLE	135	160	161	162	164	158	143	149	141	148	141	112	159	140	156	141	100	144	151	171
13080	JORDAN	90	90	84	92	89	98	85	92	87	81	87	69	85	89	87	91	60	87	95	108
13081	KING FERRY	110	90	137	89	97	117	90	112	93	83	92	82	78	90	96	100	62	103	111	130
13082	KIRKVILLE	97	101	91	100	99	102	91	97	94	94	94	71	94	96	93	96	65	94	99	114
13083	LACONA	90	65	91	63	67	92	67	85	75	62	73	63	54	74	66	82	48	78	89	100
13084	LA FAYETTE	108	124	115	126	123	125	109	116	109	110	110	88	119	111	118	111	77	111	117	135
13088	LIVERPOOL	93	91	84	92	88	93	94	91	96	93	96	70	94	96	92	97	67	94	97	108
13090	LIVERPOOL	112	116	101	116	110	106	112	108	110	115	112	84	114	114	110	108	78	109	106	127
13092	LOCKE	88	76	74	75	75	85	74	81	78	73	77	61	67	81	70	82	52	77	83	97
13101	MC GRAW	89	91	77	91	87	94	86	88	88	85	88	67	87	90	86	91	61	87	94	105
13103	MALLORY	91	83	74	81	81	85	79	83	82	82	82	61	74	85	75	84	56	81	83	99
13104	MANLIUS	147	175	179	180	180	170	156	162	152	163	153	122	174	151	171	151	110	156	160	186
13108	MARCELLUS	107	123	112	123	120	124	110	115	111	110	111	86	120	112	117	113	78	112	120	134
13110	MARIETTA	104	106	98	109	105	114	99	107	100	94	99	82	99	102	102	103	69	101	109	125
13111	MARTVILLE	77	69	64	67	68	74	66	71	69	67	69	52	61	72	63	72	47	68	72	85
13112	MEMPHIS	101	111	99	111	108	112	99	105	100	99	101	79	105	102	104	102	70	101	107	123
13114	MEXICO	90	81	75	78	79	85	77	83	80	79	80	61	72	83	74	83	54	80	84	98
13116	MINOA	94	100	95	100	99	105	94	98	96	93	96	73	98	96	98	99	67	97	105	115
13118	MORAVIA	89	75	88	74	77	90	75	86	79	73	78	64	67	79	75	84	53	82	89	101
	NEW YORK	100	106	110	108	107	104	112	106	113	106	114	81	115	110	112	116	83	110	110	124
	UNITED STATES	100	100	100	100	100	100	100	100	100	100	100	100	100	100	100	100	100	100	100	100

ZIP CODE			POPULATION			2000-2009 ANNUAL RATE		HOUSEHOLDS					FAMILIES		
#	POST OFFICE NAME	COUNTY FIPS CODE	2000	2009	2014	% Rate	State Centile	2000	2009	2014	% Annual Rate 2000-2009	2009 Average HH Size	2000	2009	% Annual Rate 2000-2009
13120	NEDROW	067	3111	3324	3331	0.7	80	925	960	966	0.4	3.46	736	755	0.3
13122	NEW WOODSTOCK	053	1136	1240	1274	1.0	89	418	465	482	1.2	2.66	320	352	1.0
13124	NORTH PITCHER	017	130	133	134	0.2	52	46	49	49	0.7	2.61	35	36	0.3
13126	OSWEGO	075	36481	37089	36732	0.2	52	13266	13486	13441	0.2	2.43	8292	8267	0.0
13131	PARISH	075	4000	4077	4086	0.2	52	1409	1471	1485	0.5	2.77	1088	1122	0.3
13132	PENNELLVILLE	075	4339	4234	4182	-0.3	15	1569	1569	1561	0.0	2.70	1208	1192	-0.1
13135	PHOENIX	075	5994	5992	5960	0.0	38	2297	2353	2357	0.3	2.54	1635	1650	0.1
13136	PITCHER	017	592	613	620	0.4	66	205	219	223	0.7	2.69	153	160	0.5
13140	PORT BYRON	011	4918	4863	4807	-0.1	30	1793	1806	1799	0.1	2.69	1342	1329	-0.1
13141	PREBLE	023	826	869	871	0.6	76	308	334	338	0.9	2.60	223	237	0.7
13142	PULASKI	075	6695	6970	7029	0.4	66	2612	2777	2822	0.7	2.50	1793	1874	0.5
13143	RED CREEK	117	3374	3384	3359	0.0	38	1051	1088	1090	0.4	2.86	749	761	0.2
13144	RICHLAND	075	1203	1250	1256	0.4	66	397	418	424	0.6	2.78	296	307	0.4
13145	SANDY CREEK	075	1629	1684	1693	0.4	66	650	688	698	0.6	2.45	433	449	0.4
13146	SAVANNAH	117	2620	2561	2519	-0.2	21	932	934	926	0.0	2.65	697	688	-0.1
13147	SCIPIO CENTER	011	1320	1311	1299	-0.1	30	477	483	482	0.1	2.71	356	354	-0.1
13148	SENECA FALLS	099	10769	10681	10518	-0.1	30	4331	4285	4244	-0.1	2.36	2863	2785	-0.3
13152	SKANEATELES	067	8417	8657	8666	0.3	59	3290	3474	3506	0.6	2.49	2392	2479	0.4
13155	SOUTH OTSELIC	017	656	732	758	1.2	93	237	269	279	1.4	2.69	183	204	1.2
13156	STERLING	011	2372	2281	2240	-0.4	11	968	947	935	-0.2	2.40	682	654	-0.5
13158	TRUXTON	023	1476	1451	1433	-0.2	21	527	531	529	0.1	2.73	401	397	-0.1
13159	TULLY	067	5433	5658	5678	0.4	66	2042	2186	2214	0.7	2.57	1500	1576	0.5
13160	UNION SPRINGS	011	2013	1956	1926	-0.3	15	776	766	759	-0.1	2.55	554	538	-0.3
13164	WARNERS	067	1686	1922	1959	1.4	95	609	725	747	1.9	2.65	469	552	1.8
13165	WATERLOO	099	11067	11235	11110	0.2	52	4227	4268	4252	0.1	2.47	2915	2893	-0.1
13166	WEEDSPORT	011	6022	6063	6040	0.1	44	2201	2258	2264	0.3	2.65	1603	1617	0.1
13167	WEST MONROE	075	3615	3669	3672	0.2	52	1260	1311	1321	0.4	2.80	975	1002	0.3
13202	SYRACUSE	067	5490	5356	5280	-0.3	15	2393	2312	2275	-0.4	1.93	902	859	-0.5
13203	SYRACUSE	067	15850	15159	14865	-0.5	7	7428	7245	7150	-0.3	2.00	3237	3027	-0.7
13204	SYRACUSE	067	21260	20236	19831	-0.5	7	8745	8484	8364	-0.3	2.34	4714	4411	-0.7
13205	SYRACUSE	067	19923	18804	18366	-0.6	4	7809	7555	7437	-0.4	2.42	4653	4346	-0.7
13206	SYRACUSE	067	16566	15975	15731	-0.4	11	7812	7747	7690	-0.1	2.06	4009	3835	-0.5
13207	SYRACUSE	067	14825	14311	14088	-0.4	11	5565	5450	5391	-0.2	2.61	3770	3605	-0.5
13208	SYRACUSE	067	21123	20219	19826	-0.5	7	9036	8736	8603	-0.4	2.30	4961	4645	-0.7
13209	SYRACUSE	067	13470	13202	13067	-0.2	21	5549	5592	5580	0.1	2.36	3646	3581	-0.2
13210	SYRACUSE	067	25304	24710	24435	-0.3	15	9443	9384	9316	-0.1	2.13	3291	3180	-0.4
13211	SYRACUSE	067	6400	6304	6250	-0.2	21	2634	2664	2663	0.1	2.36	1677	1652	-0.2
13212	SYRACUSE	067	20550	19991	19755	-0.3	15	8428	8477	8449	0.1	2.35	5672	5576	-0.2
13214	SYRACUSE	067	8696	8443	8350	-0.3	15	3070	3059	3042	0.0	2.24	2020	1971	-0.3
13215	SYRACUSE	067	14648	15138	15185	0.4	66	5288	5545	5591	0.5	2.62	3785	3894	0.3
13219	SYRACUSE	067	15353	14810	14604	-0.4	11	6139	6107	6073	-0.1	2.37	4314	4199	-0.3
13224	SYRACUSE	067	9378	9068	8928	-0.4	11	3919	3873	3843	-0.1	2.30	2454	2366	-0.4
13244	SYRACUSE	067	2119	2115	2111	0.0	38	35	32	31	-1.0	3.53	4	4	0.0
13301	ALDER CREEK	065	54	51	50	-0.6	4	26	25	25	-0.4	1.88	17	16	-0.7
13302	ALTMAR	075	1657	1800	1841	0.9	87	569	632	652	1.1	2.81	428	468	1.0
13303	AVA	065	1320	1352	1359	0.3	59	496	522	529	0.6	2.59	376	389	0.4
13304	BARNEVELD	065	1816	1879	1892	0.4	66	700	746	758	0.7	2.51	514	538	0.5
13308	BLOSSVALE	065	4994	5137	5177	0.3	59	1960	2074	2107	0.6	2.46	1365	1415	0.4
13309	BOONVILLE	065	6267	6113	6029	-0.3	15	2397	2401	2389	0.0	2.48	1671	1644	-0.2
13310	BOUCKVILLE	053	595	617	621	0.4	66	249	260	264	0.5	1.97	180	184	0.2
13314	BROOKFIELD	053	71	72	73	0.2	52	26	27	28	0.4	2.67	20	21	0.5
13315	BURLINGTON FLATS	077	1259	1366	1372	0.9	87	459	507	512	1.1	2.67	348	378	0.9
13316	CAMDEN	065	6993	6946	6902	-0.1	30	2559	2618	2627	0.2	2.62	1857	1867	0.1
13317	CANAJOHARIE	057	3867	3741	3685	-0.4	11	1513	1491	1477	-0.2	2.48	1043	1010	-0.3
13318	CASSVILLE	065	1899	1987	2014	0.5	71	670	717	731	0.7	2.77	512	539	0.6
13319	CHADWICKS	065	743	782	792	0.6	76	299	324	331	0.9	2.40	217	231	0.7
13320	CHERRY VALLEY	077	1921	2029	2024	0.6	76	748	805	808	0.8	2.51	552	583	0.6
13322	CLAYVILLE	043	1234	1316	1336	0.7	80	449	493	506	1.0	2.67	338	364	0.8
13323	CLINTON	065	12205	12388	12448	0.2	52	4203	4435	4498	0.6	2.39	2781	2870	0.3
13324	COLD BROOK	043	1928	1902	1879	-0.1	30	744	752	749	0.1	2.53	532	527	-0.1
13325	CONSTABLEVILLE	049	969	949	931	-0.2	21	362	366	363	0.1	2.59	255	254	0.0
13326	COOPERSTOWN	077	5487	5440	5327	-0.1	30	2236	2224	2184	-0.1	2.27	1405	1365	-0.3
13327	CROGHAN	049	2069	2044	2008	-0.1	30	735	748	743	0.2	2.73	569	572	0.1
13328	DEANSBORO	065	1066	1136	1161	0.7	80	411	457	471	1.2	2.23	289	316	1.0
13329	DOLGEVILLE	035	3917	3928	3913	0.0	38	1569	1609	1614	0.3	2.42	1077	1085	0.1
13331	EAGLE BAY	043	720	618	584	-1.6	1	318	278	265	-1.4	2.16	202	172	-1.7
13332	EARLVILLE	053	2545	2498	2479	-0.2	21	953	952	951	0.0	2.60	687	673	-0.2
13333	EAST SPRINGFIELD	077	114	121	121	0.6	76	44	48	48	0.9	2.52	32	34	0.7
13334	EATON	053	1465	1465	1452	0.0	38	532	529	526	-0.1	2.07	368	358	-0.3
13335	EDMESTON	077	1618	1791	1802	1.1	91	573	646	656	1.3	2.64	421	467	1.1
13337	FLY CREEK	077	772	789	782	0.2	52	314	327	326	0.4	2.41	219	222	0.1
13338	FORESTPORT	043	1338	1355	1359	0.1	44	576	601	608	0.5	2.25	377	384	0.2
13339	FORT PLAIN	057	6464	6439	6409	0.0	38	2483	2516	2519	0.1	2.54	1725	1718	0.0
13340	FRANKFORT	043	8056	7929	7834	-0.2	21	3208	3234	3221	0.1	2.44	2264	2244	-0.1
13342	GARRATTSVILLE	077	103	111	111	0.8	84	46	51	51	1.1	2.18	34	36	0.6
13343	GLENFIELD	049	1941	1928	1894	-0.1	30	764	781	776	0.2	2.47	559	564	0.1
13345	GREIG	049	461	453	445	-0.2	21	187	189	188	0.1	2.39	134	134	0.0
13346	HAMILTON	053	5730	5958	5974	0.4	66	1589	1635	1654	0.3	2.26	957	983	0.3
13348	HARTWICK	077	1549	1597	1582	0.3	59	578	608	606	0.5	2.63	425	437	0.3
13350	HERKIMER	043	10196	10128	10044	-0.1	30	4202	4265	4254	0.2	2.26	2457	2433	-0.1
13353	HOFFMEISTER	041	151	145	141	-0.4	11	65	64	62	-0.2	2.27	46	44	-0.5
13354	HOLLAND PATENT	065	3458	3624	3667	0.5	71	1272	1374	1404	0.8	2.62	948	1006	0.6
13355	HUBBARDSVILLE	053	751	828	856	1.1	91	268	301	314	1.3	2.72	196	217	1.1
13357	ILION	043	11361	11060	10898	-0.3	15	4463	4437	4403	-0.1	2.46	2995	2925	-0.3
13360	INLET	041	404	394	388	-0.3	15	187	189	188	0.1	2.08	128	127	-0.1
13361	JORDANVILLE	043	782	822	824	0.5	71	286	308	312	0.8	2.62	214	227	0.6
13363	LEE CENTER	065	2339	2308	2280	-0.1	30	873	889	887	0.2	2.59	664	666	0.0
13365	LITTLE FALLS	043	9101	8709	8511	-0.5	7	3801	3699	3637	-0.3	2.31	2370	2272	-0.5
13367	LOWVILLE	049	8339	8495	8403	0.2	52	3167	3306	3299	0.5	2.50	2202	2266	0.3
13368	LYONS FALLS	049	1053	1014	992	-0.4	11	401	398	393	-0.1	2.54	282	276	-0.2
13402	MADISON	053	1488	1540	1559	0.4	66	591	627	641	0.6	2.43	407	423	0.4
13403	MARCY	065	8032	8106	8184	0.1	44	1445	1586	1629	1.0	2.64	1102	1191	0.8
13406	MIDDLEVILLE	043	283	296	297	0.5	71	104	112	113	0.8	2.58	80	84	0.5
13407	MOHAWK	043	5622	5519	5435	-0.2	21	2241	2248	2229	0.0	2.41	1516	1499	-0.1
13408	MORRISVILLE	053	3760	3729	3690	-0.1	30	938	924	918	-0.2	3.13	663	640	-0.4
	NEW YORK					0.3					0.3	2.61			0.1
	UNITED STATES					1.0					1.1	2.59			0.9

ZIP CODE #	POST OFFICE NAME	RACE (%) White 2000	White 2009	Black 2000	Black 2009	Asian/Pacific 2000	Asian/Pacific 2009	% Hispanic Origin 2000	% Hispanic Origin 2009	2009 AGE DISTRIBUTION (%) 0-4	5-9	10-14	15-19	20-24	25-44	45-64	65-84	85+	18+	MEDIAN AGE 2009	% 2009 Males	% 2009 Females
13120	NEDROW	67.5	62.5	3.3	4.3	0.3	0.4	0.8	1.1	11.1	9.5	9.3	8.7	6.7	23.9	22.5	7.2	1.1	64.7	28.3	50.9	49.1
13122	NEW WOODSTOCK	98.2	97.6	0.4	0.5	0.4	0.6	0.8	1.1	6.3	7.2	8.1	7.2	4.3	20.9	33.1	11.5	1.6	74.0	42.4	50.2	49.8
13124	NORTH PITCHER	96.9	95.5	3.1	3.0	0.0	0.0	1.6	2.3	6.8	6.8	6.8	6.8	6.8	27.1	27.8	9.8	1.5	75.2	37.5	54.9	45.1
13126	OSWEGO	95.7	94.6	1.1	1.3	0.8	1.2	2.3	2.8	5.2	5.1	5.4	10.5	13.9	22.4	24.6	10.6	2.4	80.6	33.5	48.2	51.8
13131	PARISH	98.7	98.3	0.3	0.3	0.1	0.1	0.5	0.7	6.8	6.8	7.0	7.7	6.3	26.6	28.5	9.4	0.9	74.7	37.1	49.3	50.7
13132	PENNELLVILLE	97.7	97.1	0.4	0.4	0.3	0.4	0.8	1.0	6.2	6.4	6.8	7.4	5.9	25.4	31.3	9.7	0.9	75.5	39.5	50.8	49.2
13135	PHOENIX	97.4	96.6	0.5	0.6	0.6	0.8	1.1	1.4	6.4	6.5	6.8	6.9	6.2	24.4	30.8	10.7	1.3	75.8	39.7	49.2	50.8
13136	PITCHER	96.1	95.4	2.7	3.1	0.2	0.2	2.0	2.4	6.2	6.2	6.7	6.9	5.7	26.8	29.7	10.6	1.3	76.5	39.1	54.0	46.0
13140	PORT BYRON	97.6	96.7	0.5	0.7	0.1	0.2	1.0	1.4	6.2	6.6	7.1	7.1	5.7	25.6	29.0	11.2	1.4	75.7	39.0	48.9	51.1
13141	PREBLE	98.5	98.2	0.2	0.2	0.2	0.3	0.4	0.6	5.9	6.6	7.4	6.8	4.7	23.7	32.3	11.4	1.3	76.1	41.2	51.4	48.6
13142	PULASKI	98.3	97.8	0.2	0.2	0.3	0.4	0.7	0.8	6.6	6.4	6.6	7.4	6.4	24.2	28.8	11.7	1.9	75.8	39.1	49.5	50.5
13143	RED CREEK	91.3	89.8	5.7	6.6	0.2	0.3	3.4	4.2	6.4	6.2	6.6	6.9	7.1	29.3	27.4	9.1	1.1	76.4	36.8	54.9	45.1
13144	RICHLAND	97.7	97.3	0.8	1.0	0.1	0.1	1.1	1.3	6.3	6.6	7.0	7.4	6.3	25.2	30.2	10.0	1.0	74.9	38.9	54.9	45.1
13145	SANDY CREEK	97.9	97.4	0.1	0.1	0.1	0.1	0.4	0.7	5.7	5.7	6.2	6.8	5.4	23.0	30.3	15.1	1.8	78.3	43.0	50.5	49.5
13146	SAVANNAH	94.0	92.7	3.3	3.9	0.2	0.3	2.0	2.5	6.8	6.8	7.3	7.1	6.1	26.5	27.6	10.4	1.4	74.7	37.6	51.3	48.7
13147	SCIPIO CENTER	97.7	97.0	0.2	0.2	0.5	0.7	1.4	2.0	5.2	6.8	7.9	7.8	5.3	25.8	29.1	10.9	1.3	75.1	39.6	50.1	49.9
13148	SENECA FALLS	96.1	95.2	0.8	0.8	1.3	1.9	1.3	1.4	5.5	5.4	5.7	6.1	8.4	26.3	27.4	12.9	2.2	79.4	39.5	49.9	50.1
13152	SKANEATELES	98.9	98.5	0.1	0.2	0.3	0.5	0.4	0.5	4.6	5.7	6.7	7.3	4.4	18.6	34.8	15.4	2.4	78.0	46.5	49.3	50.7
13155	SOUTH OTSELIC	97.6	97.1	0.9	1.0	0.2	0.1	2.4	2.9	7.8	7.8	7.9	7.4	6.3	24.7	26.4	10.7	1.1	71.9	35.1	51.2	48.8
13156	STERLING	98.2	97.9	0.1	0.1	0.0	0.0	0.5	0.7	5.5	5.8	6.3	6.7	4.3	22.8	32.0	15.0	1.6	78.3	44.1	50.1	49.9
13158	TRUXTON	97.5	96.8	0.3	0.3	0.2	0.3	0.9	1.2	6.8	7.2	7.6	8.1	5.0	25.8	28.9	9.4	1.2	73.5	37.9	50.5	49.5
13159	TULLY	97.1	95.9	0.5	0.7	0.5	0.8	0.9	1.3	6.4	7.0	8.1	7.5	5.2	23.3	31.3	10.1	1.1	73.5	40.1	49.8	50.2
13160	UNION SPRINGS	98.1	97.5	0.6	0.9	0.2	0.3	0.7	1.0	5.2	5.9	6.4	7.3	5.3	23.6	29.2	15.1	2.0	77.7	42.6	48.1	51.9
13164	WARNERS	98.3	97.6	0.4	0.5	0.2	0.2	0.7	1.0	6.1	6.5	6.9	6.4	4.9	24.9	30.7	11.9	1.8	76.6	41.2	50.5	49.5
13165	WATERLOO	97.3	96.8	0.8	0.8	0.4	0.6	1.5	1.8	5.5	5.8	6.1	6.6	5.8	25.0	28.4	13.7	3.0	78.4	41.5	48.8	51.2
13166	WEEDSPORT	97.7	96.7	0.4	0.6	0.4	0.6	0.7	1.0	6.4	6.6	6.7	6.9	6.4	25.0	29.6	10.9	1.5	76.0	39.3	49.1	50.9
13167	WEST MONROE	97.4	96.7	0.2	0.2	0.3	0.5	0.4	0.5	6.5	6.8	6.8	7.7	5.9	27.7	29.5	8.5	0.5	75.2	37.8	52.0	48.0
13202	SYRACUSE	28.3	23.0	59.5	63.6	5.0	5.6	9.6	10.1	10.3	7.3	6.3	7.5	10.0	33.6	18.5	5.8	0.8	72.5	29.1	52.9	47.1
13203	SYRACUSE	75.2	68.9	13.8	17.3	4.3	5.6	3.9	4.9	6.6	5.8	5.4	6.2	8.1	28.6	24.3	11.5	3.5	78.8	37.2	48.5	51.5
13204	SYRACUSE	63.5	58.4	21.8	24.6	0.7	0.9	13.1	14.6	9.7	8.6	7.4	7.1	8.2	27.3	20.8	9.0	1.8	70.0	30.6	47.6	52.4
13205	SYRACUSE	40.9	36.8	51.2	54.1	1.7	2.3	3.4	3.5	7.6	7.7	7.4	7.9	6.9	22.5	22.8	13.5	3.8	72.3	35.6	44.9	55.1
13206	SYRACUSE	88.1	84.4	6.9	8.9	1.2	1.7	2.4	3.1	6.2	5.7	5.4	5.6	7.0	28.5	27.0	12.1	2.5	79.3	39.5	47.8	52.2
13207	SYRACUSE	59.1	53.1	33.7	38.4	0.5	0.7	4.4	5.1	8.0	8.1	8.1	8.2	6.9	25.5	24.9	8.8	1.4	70.7	33.6	46.1	53.9
13208	SYRACUSE	81.5	76.2	6.9	8.9	5.6	7.5	3.1	3.9	7.8	7.1	6.4	6.8	7.3	27.1	23.8	11.0	2.8	74.5	35.9	47.8	52.2
13209	SYRACUSE	96.6	95.4	0.7	0.9	0.5	0.8	1.6	2.2	6.2	6.2	6.3	6.5	5.7	24.7	27.8	13.9	2.6	77.3	40.9	46.9	53.1
13210	SYRACUSE	64.4	57.3	22.8	26.8	7.4	9.4	4.4	5.1	4.4	4.1	3.6	14.5	30.1	22.0	13.1	6.3	2.1	85.5	23.9	48.1	51.9
13211	SYRACUSE	94.3	92.3	1.8	2.4	0.8	1.2	2.1	2.8	6.0	5.8	5.9	7.0	7.0	26.5	26.8	12.6	2.4	77.9	39.2	48.4	51.6
13212	SYRACUSE	95.1	93.1	1.7	2.4	1.1	1.6	0.9	1.3	6.0	5.9	6.2	6.4	5.5	24.8	27.4	15.0	2.7	77.9	41.7	47.6	52.4
13214	SYRACUSE	82.8	76.0	11.4	14.3	3.0	5.0	2.0	4.7	4.5	4.9	5.1	11.2	11.1	19.9	24.5	15.2	3.5	82.8	39.2	47.1	52.9
13215	SYRACUSE	95.4	93.7	1.5	2.0	1.3	1.9	1.1	1.5	5.5	6.0	7.0	7.4	5.4	20.2	30.5	13.9	4.0	76.8	43.8	48.4	51.6
13219	SYRACUSE	96.7	95.4	0.8	1.2	0.9	1.3	1.1	1.5	5.3	5.7	6.3	6.1	4.4	20.5	30.0	17.2	4.6	78.7	46.0	47.0	53.0
13224	SYRACUSE	55.8	49.9	37.0	41.2	2.8	3.8	3.1	3.5	6.3	5.8	6.3	8.1	7.3	22.4	27.8	13.6	2.5	77.0	40.0	46.2	53.8
13244	SYRACUSE	85.1	79.6	5.0	6.6	5.8	8.2	4.1	5.4	0.1	0.1	0.0	64.4	33.7	1.1	0.4	0.2	0.0	99.3	18.9	46.1	53.9
13301	ALDER CREEK	100.0	100.0	0.0	0.0	0.0	0.0	0.0	0.0	5.9	3.9	5.9	3.9	3.9	23.5	31.4	15.7	5.9	80.4	46.9	47.1	52.9
13302	ALTMAR	98.1	97.7	0.4	0.4	0.2	0.3	0.7	0.8	7.6	7.6	7.8	8.2	6.1	26.0	26.1	9.5	1.2	72.2	35.2	47.6	52.4
13303	AVA	97.7	96.8	0.5	0.6	0.4	0.6	0.6	0.8	5.8	6.4	7.0	8.3	4.7	25.7	28.4	11.9	1.8	75.2	39.8	51.4	48.6
13304	BARNEVELD	98.1	97.2	0.4	0.6	0.5	0.7	0.4	0.6	5.4	5.9	6.6	7.4	5.4	22.6	31.8	13.4	1.5	77.5	42.8	49.5	50.5
13308	BLOSSVALE	93.2	89.6	4.2	6.2	0.5	1.1	2.8	4.5	5.5	5.9	5.8	7.9	6.5	27.5	28.8	10.8	1.2	78.7	39.0	53.0	47.0
13309	BOONVILLE	99.1	98.8	0.2	0.2	0.1	0.2	0.2	0.3	5.7	5.8	6.6	7.0	5.8	25.3	27.6	13.4	2.9	77.1	40.7	49.7	50.3
13310	BOUCKVILLE	92.6	90.9	4.9	5.5	1.0	1.5	1.5	1.8	5.0	5.3	5.5	12.6	9.7	21.6	25.6	12.2	2.4	79.7	36.5	49.9	50.1
13314	BROOKFIELD	98.6	97.2	1.4	1.4	0.0	0.0	0.0	0.0	6.9	6.9	8.3	6.9	5.6	27.8	23.6	12.5	1.4	72.2	37.5	48.6	51.4
13315	BURLINGTON FLATS	97.1	96.4	0.6	0.6	0.3	0.4	1.5	1.8	5.6	5.9	6.5	6.7	4.8	24.6	30.8	13.2	1.8	77.6	42.1	51.0	49.0
13316	CAMDEN	98.1	97.4	0.4	0.5	0.4	0.6	0.7	1.0	6.1	6.3	6.6	7.1	5.9	25.3	29.6	11.5	1.6	78.3	40.0	50.6	49.4
13317	CANAJOHARIE	97.1	96.3	0.6	0.8	0.5	0.7	1.2	1.5	5.7	6.3	6.6	6.5	5.4	23.7	28.3	14.5	3.0	77.0	41.7	48.7	51.3
13318	CASSVILLE	97.6	96.6	0.6	0.9	0.6	0.9	0.9	1.2	7.2	7.3	8.4	7.9	5.4	26.8	27.9	8.4	0.7	71.9	36.7	51.1	48.9
13319	CHADWICKS	96.2	94.1	0.7	0.9	2.7	4.2	0.4	0.6	5.1	5.4	6.3	7.0	5.0	21.4	32.0	15.3	2.6	78.3	44.9	48.1	51.9
13320	CHERRY VALLEY	98.5	97.9	0.1	0.1	0.4	0.6	0.9	1.2	4.2	6.2	8.1	8.0	3.9	22.9	31.0	13.6	2.1	75.4	42.9	50.7	49.3
13322	CLAYVILLE	98.5	97.9	0.3	0.5	0.2	0.3	0.5	0.6	5.5	6.2	7.0	7.5	4.7	24.7	32.3	10.7	1.4	76.5	40.7	51.0	49.0
13323	CLINTON	96.6	95.4	1.1	1.4	1.1	1.6	1.2	1.7	3.8	4.3	5.1	10.8	10.6	19.6	28.2	14.3	3.3	82.9	41.4	48.2	51.8
13324	COLD BROOK	97.3	96.7	0.5	0.5	0.5	0.6	0.5	0.6	5.6	6.3	7.0	7.1	5.0	25.2	32.2	10.6	0.9	76.3	40.8	52.4	47.6
13325	CONSTABLEVILLE	99.4	99.2	0.0	0.0	0.1	0.2	0.1	0.2	6.2	6.5	7.0	6.5	5.3	24.4	29.4	13.3	1.4	75.6	40.7	48.9	51.1
13326	COOPERSTOWN	97.1	96.4	0.7	0.8	0.9	1.2	1.5	1.9	4.4	5.1	6.4	6.0	4.3	20.7	30.9	17.2	4.9	79.8	46.9	47.6	52.4
13327	CROGHAN	98.8	98.5	0.2	0.2	0.2	0.3	0.6	0.8	6.2	6.9	8.1	8.1	5.5	25.5	27.7	10.7	1.3	73.6	38.0	50.0	50.0
13328	DEANSBORO	97.5	96.4	0.8	1.1	0.7	1.0	0.9	1.3	4.8	4.9	5.3	10.5	11.6	24.0	26.1	11.2	1.5	81.1	35.2	49.8	50.2
13329	DOLGEVILLE	97.8	97.2	0.4	0.5	0.4	0.6	0.8	0.9	5.8	6.0	6.2	6.3	5.7	24.9	29.2	13.6	2.3	77.8	41.1	49.4	50.6
13331	EAGLE BAY	97.9	97.6	0.7	0.8	0.3	0.3	0.8	0.8	3.7	4.4	5.2	6.3	5.5	20.7	35.3	16.8	2.1	82.5	47.5	49.4	50.6
13332	EARLVILLE	98.2	97.6	0.7	0.8	0.3	0.4	1.1	1.4	6.0	6.6	7.1	7.4	5.3	24.0	30.2	12.0	1.3	75.6	40.7	49.2	50.8
13333	EAST SPRINGFIELD	99.1	98.3	0.0	0.0	0.0	0.8	0.9	0.8	5.0	5.8	8.3	8.3	3.3	24.0	29.8	13.2	2.5	73.6	42.3	50.4	49.6
13334	EATON	91.9	90.4	5.3	6.0	0.9	1.2	1.8	2.3	4.4	4.4	4.6	18.6	14.5	19.8	21.0	10.8	1.9	82.3	28.0	50.9	49.1
13335	EDMESTON	98.2	97.8	0.4	0.5	0.1	0.1	1.0	1.2	6.8	6.9	7.3	7.2	4.9	25.0	27.1	13.2	1.6	74.5	39.5	50.8	49.2
13337	FLY CREEK	98.2	97.8	0.8	0.9	0.3	0.4	0.9	1.1	4.3	5.7	6.2	6.5	4.4	18.8	36.8	15.2	2.2	79.5	47.1	50.1	49.9
13338	FORESTPORT	98.4	97.9	0.4	0.4	0.2	0.3	0.1	0.1	5.0	5.2	5.7	5.5	3.8	19.5	35.9	17.6	1.7	80.6	48.0	50.7	49.3
13339	FORT PLAIN	98.4	97.9	0.2	0.2	0.5	0.7	1.0	1.3	6.2	6.3	6.5	6.7	5.5	24.0	28.2	14.3	2.5	76.7	41.3	49.6	50.4
13340	FRANKFORT	97.9	97.2	0.4	0.5	0.2	0.3	0.9	1.1	5.6	5.7	6.1	6.8	5.4	24.5	29.5	13.7	2.7	78.3	42.2	47.7	52.3
13342	GARRATTSVILLE	98.0	95.5	1.0	0.9	0.0	0.9	1.0	1.8	5.4	5.4	7.2	8.1	3.6	23.4	34.2	10.8	1.8	77.5	43.1	49.5	50.5
13343	GLENFIELD	98.1	97.7	0.3	0.3	0.7	0.9	0.6	0.7	6.0	6.0	6.7	7.2	5.1	23.7	30.1	14.0	1.2	76.7	41.9	50.9	49.1
13345	GREIG	98.5	98.5	0.7	0.7	0.4	0.4	0.4	0.4	6.0	6.4	6.8	6.4	4.9	22.7	30.2	15.0	1.5	76.8	42.5	50.1	49.9
13346	HAMILTON	93.3	91.4	2.2	2.5	2.5	3.5	1.9	2.3	2.9	3.7	4.0	24.0	21.9	14.0	18.1	9.4	1.9	86.3	23.5	47.9	52.1
13348	HARTWICK	98.1	97.4	0.5	0.6	0.6	0.9	1.1	1.3	4.8	5.9	7.8	8.6	3.9	23.1	30.9	13.0	1.9	75.6	42.3	50.3	49.7
13350	HERKIMER	96.9	96.0	1.0	1.1	1.0	1.4	1.2	1.5	5.0	4.7	4.7	5.9	6.6	26.5	25.7	16.3	4.7	82.7	42.0	47.7	52.3
13353	HOFFMEISTER	98.7	98.6	0.0	0.0	0.0	0.0	0.7	0.7	3.4	4.1	4.1	3.4	4.1	20.0	37.2	21.4	2.1	85.5	52.3	50.3	49.7
13354	HOLLAND PATENT	97.7	96.8	0.5	0.6	0.4	0.7	0.5	0.7	5.9	6.7	7.6	7.5	4.7	23.6	30.7	11.9	1.4	74.8	41.0	50.3	49.7
13355	HUBBARDSVILLE	98.0	97.3	0.5	0.6	0.4	0.6	0.8	1.1	5.6	6.3	7.0	6.9	5.3	23.8	31.6	12.1	1.4	76.3	41.8	51.1	48.9
13357	ILION	97.7	97.0	0.6	0.7	0.2	0.3	1.3	1.7	6.7	6.4	6.5	6.9	6.5	25.1	27.1	12.0	2.7	76.0	38.3	47.3	52.7
13360	INLET	96.3	95.7	0.0	0.0	0.2	0.3	2.5	3.0	5.6	6.1	6.1	4.3	2.0	21.3	33.0	19.8	1.8	79.2	47.6	49.0	51.0
13361	JORDANVILLE	97.8	97.0	0.4	0.5	0.6	1.0	0.6	1.0	6.0	6.4	7.1	7.5	6.0	23.8	29.4	12.0	1.7	75.7	40.8	53.5	46.5
13363	LEE CENTER	97.8	96.9	0.6	0.8	0.3	0.4	0.6	0.9	6.1	6.1	6.6	8.1	6.2	26.4	28.6	10.5	1.4	76.0	39.0	50.0	50.0
13365	LITTLE FALLS	98.1	97.5	0.4	0.4	0.5	0.7	0.5	0.6	6.0	6.0	6.1	6.6	5.7	23.8	28.6	13.6	3.5	77.8	41.7	48.9	51.1
13367	LOWVILLE	97.7	97.2	0.6	0.6	0.5	0.6	0.8	0.9	6.2	6.0	6.2	7.1	6.4	23.7	28.0	13.4	3.2	77.2	40.9	48.7	51.3
13368	LYONS FALLS	98.9	98.7	0.5	0.5	0.0	0.0	0.2	0.3	6.2	6.8	6.9	6.4	5.1	23.0	30.5	13.4	1.7	75.9	41.1	51.2	48.8
13402	MADISON	97.7	96.9	0.3	0.4	0.9	1.2	0.8	1.0	6.4	6.9	6.9	6.0	4.4	24.8	30.0	13.2	1.4	75.9	41.2	49.8	50.2
13403	MARCY	65.3	64.4	24.5	23.6	0.6	2.1	15.5	15.5	2.5	2.8	3.3	10.8	15.3	36.5	20.8	7.0	1.1	89.3	33.4	66.1	33.9
13406	MIDDLEVILLE	98.6	98.3	0.4	0.3	0.0	0.0	0.4	0.3	5.4	6.1	6.8	6.4	5.1	25.3	31.1	12.2	1.7	77.7	41.4	50.7	49.3
13407	MOHAWK	98.6	98.2	0.5	0.5	0.2	0.2	1.2	1.4	5.4	5.6	6.0	6.4	6.0	24.3	30.0	13.8	2.4	79.3	42.1	50.3	49.7
13408	MORRISVILLE	92.4	90.8	4.9	5.7	0.8	1.1	1.6	2.0	4.7	4.6	4.8	17.2	13.4	20.4	22.7	10.4	1.9	81.7	29.6	50.7	49.3
	NEW YORK	67.9	64.8	15.9	16.5	5.6	6.9	15.1	16.7	6.5	6.4	6.4	7.1	7.0	27.0	26.3	11.2	2.1	76.6	37.5	48.4	51.6
	UNITED STATES	75.1	72.0	12.3	12.7	3.8	4.6	12.5	15.7	6.8	6.7	6.6	7.1	6.9	27.0	26.0	10.9	1.9	75.7	36.9	49.2	50.8

#	POST OFFICE NAME	2009 Per Capita Income	2009 HH Income Base	2009 Household Income Distribution (%): Less than $25,000	$25,000 to $49,999	$50,000 to $99,999	$100,000 to $149,999	$150,000 or More	Median Household Income: 2009	2014	2009 National Centile	2009 State Centile	2009 Home Value Base	2009 Home Value Distribution (%): Less than $50,000	$50,000 to $89,999	$90,000 to $174,999	$175,000 to $399,999	$400,000 or More	2009 Median Home Value
13120	NEDROW	23798	960	11.6	18.8	44.8	15.6	9.3	68830	71456	86	75	811	1.8	9.5	44.5	42.5	1.6	163125
13122	NEW WOODSTOCK	33971	465	10.5	19.8	40.6	18.1	11.0	68781	70575	86	75	377	6.6	6.4	32.9	43.8	10.3	186742
13124	NORTH PITCHER	18181	49	30.6	34.7	30.6	2.0	2.0	37289	37686	24	8	39	23.1	33.3	35.9	7.7	0.0	81667
13126	OSWEGO	21514	13486	29.7	25.5	32.7	9.0	3.1	44619	48261	47	29	8703	9.6	13.7	48.3	26.5	1.9	132543
13131	PARISH	19461	1471	20.1	31.3	40.2	7.7	0.6	48832	51646	59	42	1199	12.8	18.6	50.5	17.1	1.0	123071
13132	PENNELLVILLE	21215	1569	18.8	28.7	42.3	8.2	2.0	52091	55765	66	51	1336	16.6	13.3	44.2	24.3	1.5	133824
13135	PHOENIX	26155	2353	20.1	26.1	38.2	8.8	6.7	52932	56386	68	53	1689	7.8	12.7	47.0	28.9	3.7	138279
13136	PITCHER	17364	219	32.4	33.8	28.3	3.7	1.8	36955	38221	23	7	178	23.6	33.1	35.4	7.9	0.0	80000
13140	PORT BYRON	19193	1806	22.1	31.5	38.6	6.8	1.1	46059	49605	51	34	1459	12.9	25.8	48.3	12.3	0.8	106458
13141	PREBLE	24708	334	13.5	26.6	44.9	11.4	3.6	56884	58430	74	60	270	7.8	6.7	47.4	33.3	4.8	148000
13142	PULASKI	20457	2777	28.0	27.4	34.6	8.3	1.7	45395	48504	49	32	1882	8.6	18.8	54.9	16.4	1.3	126786
13143	RED CREEK	17226	1088	28.1	28.1	36.9	4.8	2.1	43272	47183	43	24	850	13.5	26.9	46.1	12.1	1.3	101897
13144	RICHLAND	17490	418	25.1	30.4	38.5	5.7	0.2	44806	48486	48	30	326	11.7	28.5	51.5	8.0	0.3	102128
13145	SANDY CREEK	21695	688	30.1	24.3	34.4	8.3	2.9	43466	48532	44	25	511	7.6	24.9	40.1	26.4	1.0	124745
13146	SAVANNAH	19993	934	24.8	27.6	40.5	5.7	1.4	47373	50980	55	39	760	17.8	31.2	42.0	8.2	0.9	91212
13147	SCIPIO CENTER	20469	483	19.5	27.5	44.5	7.0	1.4	52899	56904	68	53	397	9.6	17.4	47.4	20.7	5.0	126844
13148	SENECA FALLS	23564	4285	23.7	25.7	39.5	8.6	2.6	50665	54990	63	47	2878	4.7	18.8	56.9	18.1	1.5	121791
13152	SKANEATELES	35941	3474	11.7	20.8	39.4	14.9	13.2	69172	72843	86	76	2785	1.3	3.2	22.9	51.8	20.9	234808
13155	SOUTH OTSELIC	18061	269	27.5	35.3	31.6	3.3	2.2	38300	39107	28	10	214	22.4	27.1	41.6	8.9	0.0	90769
13156	STERLING	20804	947	22.6	33.9	35.4	7.6	0.5	43636	46865	44	25	744	11.2	25.0	42.7	17.1	4.0	109956
13158	TRUXTON	18522	531	24.7	29.6	39.9	4.1	1.7	46368	48913	52	35	415	16.1	21.9	47.7	13.5	0.7	104899
13159	TULLY	28452	2186	13.7	26.3	40.0	12.4	7.5	59626	62435	77	63	1665	5.5	5.7	40.5	41.3	7.0	170952
13160	UNION SPRINGS	26408	766	18.3	21.7	45.0	10.8	4.2	60548	62298	78	65	586	5.6	14.3	45.7	29.5	4.8	141209
13164	WARNERS	27464	725	11.0	23.0	44.3	16.8	4.8	66231	68672	84	73	598	0.3	6.5	64.2	27.6	1.3	149853
13165	WATERLOO	21195	4268	23.5	30.7	36.2	8.1	1.4	46135	49250	52	34	3116	8.7	26.5	50.1	13.8	0.9	110254
13166	WEEDSPORT	22065	2258	18.3	29.6	41.6	7.7	2.8	51559	54219	65	50	1775	19.6	12.2	48.6	18.2	1.4	118307
13167	WEST MONROE	19995	1311	18.3	28.9	44.5	6.1	2.2	52662	57447	67	52	1101	22.9	18.2	35.2	22.4	1.3	113985
13202	SYRACUSE	13622	2312	67.1	21.8	8.5	1.1	1.4	13316	13418	1	1	130	36.2	25.4	23.1	12.3	3.1	71000
13203	SYRACUSE	21579	7245	39.0	34.7	19.0	4.7	2.7	31486	33377	11	4	2269	6.3	18.5	48.8	24.2	2.1	120183
13204	SYRACUSE	15726	8484	46.7	29.3	20.1	2.9	1.0	26763	28257	4	3	3050	12.9	29.4	52.0	5.0	0.7	95909
13205	SYRACUSE	17192	7555	41.8	29.4	23.0	4.3	1.6	29443	31672	7	3	3531	5.7	30.0	60.2	3.8	0.2	99833
13206	SYRACUSE	24534	7747	30.8	27.9	33.5	5.6	2.2	41746	46058	38	19	4138	3.7	9.8	79.4	7.1	0.1	121056
13207	SYRACUSE	22654	5450	26.7	26.1	34.3	9.4	3.4	47339	50569	55	38	3433	2.9	21.2	63.9	11.5	0.4	113497
13208	SYRACUSE	18552	8736	35.9	33.3	25.4	4.1	1.4	32699	35658	13	5	4233	3.2	22.7	69.8	4.0	0.4	109321
13209	SYRACUSE	25651	5592	18.9	30.0	39.5	8.2	3.5	50989	55011	64	48	3918	2.8	6.3	70.2	19.5	1.2	134946
13210	SYRACUSE	17107	9384	52.0	22.8	18.6	4.6	2.0	23279	24583	2	2	2448	4.5	7.3	68.5	19.2	0.5	133926
13211	SYRACUSE	24703	2664	22.1	30.3	37.3	7.2	3.1	47501	52290	55	39	1872	1.1	17.3	80.4	1.1	0.1	105919
13212	SYRACUSE	26941	8477	17.3	26.8	43.5	8.7	3.7	55030	59120	71	57	6083	0.1	5.2	79.8	14.4	0.4	132675
13214	SYRACUSE	32688	3059	16.9	20.8	33.5	16.6	12.3	66921	70200	85	74	2179	0.5	1.1	38.4	58.5	1.6	185041
13215	SYRACUSE	32407	5545	11.8	19.2	41.2	16.5	11.3	70527	73178	87	76	4063	0.8	0.9	27.9	63.4	7.0	208705
13219	SYRACUSE	29556	6107	14.7	21.8	44.4	14.4	4.7	64345	67407	83	71	5126	0.7	1.7	64.3	32.8	0.6	153128
13224	SYRACUSE	33044	3873	24.2	18.1	34.9	12.6	10.1	56745	60485	74	60	2435	0.0	5.9	53.6	36.1	4.4	159849
13244	SYRACUSE	14855	32	71.9	28.1	0.0	0.0	0.0	10960	11498	0	0	2	0.0	100.0	0.0	0.0	0.0	65000
13301	ALDER CREEK	27160	25	32.0	28.0	32.0	4.0	4.0	37367	52187	25	8	18	5.6	22.2	55.6	16.7	0.0	118750
13302	ALTMAR	18030	632	25.0	32.4	36.1	4.7	1.7	43634	47464	44	25	524	18.5	30.9	41.6	7.6	1.3	90882
13303	AVA	22554	522	20.5	26.6	43.7	6.7	2.5	52164	55574	66	51	422	15.2	14.0	43.4	23.9	3.6	130385
13304	BARNEVELD	28506	746	11.3	24.4	49.3	9.8	5.2	62348	64314	80	68	611	10.3	7.9	38.3	38.8	4.7	162656
13308	BLOSSVALE	22218	2074	21.5	30.3	39.6	5.6	3.0	47454	51762	55	39	1644	15.6	18.4	44.3	19.7	2.1	124215
13309	BOONVILLE	20230	2401	24.9	29.4	39.1	5.2	1.4	45594	49163	50	32	1796	8.7	23.4	50.4	16.6	0.8	116980
13310	BOUCKVILLE	25946	260	25.8	38.5	26.5	5.4	3.8	41500	44233	38	18	200	15.5	21.5	41.0	21.0	1.0	121250
13314	BROOKFIELD	17295	27	29.6	37.0	29.6	3.7	0.0	38616	40000	28	11	23	34.8	21.7	30.4	13.0	0.0	77500
13315	BURLINGTON FLATS	18982	507	21.9	32.5	39.1	5.3	1.2	46464	47136	53	35	426	8.9	23.5	42.7	21.8	3.1	121094
13316	CAMDEN	20660	2618	23.8	26.3	42.7	5.2	2.1	49943	54127	61	45	1969	7.1	19.8	49.1	23.2	0.9	128587
13317	CANAJOHARIE	21458	1491	25.4	32.1	32.5	6.1	4.0	42294	45581	40	21	1013	6.9	30.6	46.3	13.0	3.2	105313
13318	CASSVILLE	18966	717	21.8	32.8	36.7	6.6	2.2	44516	50180	47	29	575	29.0	18.4	30.4	20.2	1.9	96042
13319	CHADWICKS	37867	324	9.9	22.5	37.7	17.6	12.3	67206	70640	85	74	261	5.7	3.1	36.4	49.8	5.0	182267
13320	CHERRY VALLEY	22019	805	22.9	30.3	38.0	5.6	3.2	46908	48136	54	37	662	7.1	15.1	44.7	27.9	5.1	139063
13322	CLAYVILLE	19246	493	22.1	32.0	38.5	6.7	0.6	45971	49449	51	34	393	5.1	12.5	44.8	34.6	3.1	152955
13323	CLINTON	27636	4435	16.7	22.9	41.5	12.2	6.7	60410	62628	78	65	3222	8.4	10.4	35.7	39.0	6.6	164650
13324	COLD BROOK	18801	752	29.3	33.1	29.8	6.4	1.5	38499	41530	28	10	627	18.3	20.7	38.6	19.3	3.0	113051
13325	CONSTABLEVILLE	18457	366	28.7	29.8	35.8	4.1	1.6	42222	43220	40	21	295	15.3	26.8	43.1	11.5	3.4	101716
13326	COOPERSTOWN	28329	2224	20.6	30.6	33.9	8.2	6.7	48877	49595	59	43	1562	4.3	7.9	33.1	38.1	16.6	195977
13327	CROGHAN	17576	748	28.1	31.6	34.2	4.7	1.5	41757	43326	39	19	613	9.5	24.6	49.1	14.4	2.4	109759
13328	DEANSBORO	26550	457	20.6	25.2	41.4	8.3	4.6	53682	58599	69	55	339	5.3	15.0	48.4	27.4	3.8	138826
13329	DOLGEVILLE	18318	1609	29.9	32.5	32.6	4.4	0.7	38786	42585	29	11	1153	12.5	36.9	39.4	10.1	1.1	90773
13331	EAGLE BAY	25031	278	23.7	33.5	32.0	5.8	5.0	43088	46896	43	23	211	2.4	5.7	27.0	43.6	21.3	217708
13332	EARLVILLE	19718	952	24.9	35.7	31.8	5.1	2.4	42753	45085	42	22	757	14.9	27.2	40.2	16.1	1.6	101122
13333	EAST SPRINGFIELD	21255	48	22.9	31.3	35.4	6.3	4.2	46540	50000	53	35	38	2.6	13.2	52.6	28.9	2.6	137500
13334	EATON	24268	529	21.9	33.6	34.6	7.4	2.5	46190	48179	52	35	385	14.8	16.1	43.6	24.7	0.8	131352
13335	EDMESTON	19575	646	26.3	30.8	33.7	6.7	2.5	44099	45094	46	28	512	12.9	25.0	44.5	15.0	2.5	110366
13337	FLY CREEK	32392	327	14.4	30.0	35.8	10.1	9.8	53979	56275	70	55	269	0.7	4.8	34.9	35.3	24.2	218939
13338	FORESTPORT	21993	601	24.0	34.4	35.9	4.7	1.0	42817	45942	42	22	511	12.9	27.6	32.7	24.3	2.5	121875
13339	FORT PLAIN	18588	2516	31.7	30.8	30.5	4.8	2.2	37295	39247	24	8	1798	16.5	32.1	39.3	10.6	1.6	91699
13340	FRANKFORT	21651	3234	22.7	26.8	43.0	6.1	1.5	50419	53784	62	46	2408	11.5	11.4	48.9	26.7	1.5	137396
13342	GARRATTSVILLE	23957	51	23.5	31.4	39.2	5.9	0.0	43657	44083	44	25	43	2.3	18.6	48.8	27.9	2.3	127500
13343	GLENFIELD	18955	781	27.0	35.9	30.6	5.0	1.5	39115	41044	30	12	634	10.9	28.4	44.0	15.1	1.6	105652
13345	GREIG	19261	189	28.6	32.3	34.4	4.2	0.5	39207	42360	30	12	159	13.2	26.4	40.3	17.6	2.5	106771
13346	HAMILTON	22935	1635	24.7	27.2	32.8	9.6	5.7	48273	52670	57	41	1143	7.3	13.6	33.2	41.4	4.5	165104
13348	HARTWICK	19621	608	25.8	32.1	34.4	5.3	2.5	41559	43153	38	18	495	7.7	14.9	46.9	25.5	5.1	129963
13350	HERKIMER	21315	4265	35.7	23.6	31.8	6.6	2.2	37761	42522	26	9	2493	6.1	20.6	51.1	20.2	1.9	126272
13353	HOFFMEISTER	25377	64	23.4	32.8	34.4	6.3	3.1	45000	45000	48	31	57	8.8	10.5	49.1	28.1	3.5	141346
13354	HOLLAND PATENT	26854	1374	10.8	26.3	48.7	8.4	5.8	60697	62859	78	65	1142	15.1	6.5	40.5	34.3	3.5	150699
13355	HUBBARDSVILLE	20694	301	23.3	31.2	34.9	7.0	3.7	46646	49533	53	36	247	17.4	19.0	30.8	29.1	3.6	126389
13357	ILION	19443	4437	31.3	23.5	39.2	4.8	1.1	45673	48809	50	33	2901	9.3	21.8	50.0	17.2	1.7	119092
13360	INLET	26236	189	25.4	42.3	21.2	3.7	7.4	38094	38680	27	9	149	7.4	4.0	32.9	36.2	19.5	200781
13361	JORDANVILLE	17839	308	26.0	35.7	33.4	3.6	1.3	39822	42916	32	14	252	15.9	21.0	38.5	21.4	3.2	112903
13363	LEE CENTER	20474	889	19.9	33.4	38.7	6.5	1.5	46130	50949	52	34	704	20.2	15.3	45.2	18.3	1.0	117105
13365	LITTLE FALLS	19328	3699	33.8	31.7	28.0	4.7	1.8	36061	38732	21	6	2430	14.0	26.7	39.2	17.7	2.3	105603
13367	LOWVILLE	19696	3306	29.9	26.8	35.9	5.8	1.6	43501	45034	44	25	2332	5.7	21.7	55.1	13.8	3.8	116339
13368	LYONS FALLS	18458	398	32.4	30.2	31.2	4.3	2.0	36901	39341	23	7	308	11.0	30.2	43.5	12.3	2.9	102830
13402	MADISON	19216	627	28.7	38.1	26.2	4.6	2.4	38647	41770	29	11	475	14.5	20.4	42.3	20.6	2.1	115927
13403	MARCY	20699	1586	11.7	26.2	48.8	9.7	3.6	60967	62868	79	66	1288	0.7	3.8	45.4	47.7	2.3	175117
13406	MIDDLEVILLE	21380	112	20.5	27.7	45.5	4.5	1.8	51719	56873	65	50	94	13.8	17.0	44.7	22.3	2.1	126563
13407	MOHAWK	20188	2248	27.3	31.0	35.2	5.0	1.6	43101	46579	43	23	1665	11.4	20.6	51.3	16.0	0.7	116163
13408	MORRISVILLE	17532	924	21.3	32.6	36.1	7.8	2.2	47196	49488	55	38	691	13.2	15.2	44.0	26.6	1.0	134102
	NEW YORK	29893		21.9	21.3	32.7	14.0	9.9	58747	62337				3.4	5.7	23.0	38.7	29.1	269816
	UNITED STATES	27277		20.9	24.4	35.3	11.7	7.6	54719	56938				9.3	13.1	31.6	32.6	13.5	162279

#	POST OFFICE NAME	FINANCIAL SERVICES: Auto Loan	FINANCIAL SERVICES: Home Loan	FINANCIAL SERVICES: Investments	FINANCIAL SERVICES: Retirement Plans	THE HOME: Home Improvements: Home Repair	THE HOME: Home Improvements: Lawn & Garden	THE HOME: Furnishings: Computers & Hardware-Personal	THE HOME: Furnishings: Major Appliances	THE HOME: Furnishings: TV, Radio, Sound Equipment	THE HOME: Furnishings: Furniture	ENTERTAINMENT: Dine out/Carry out	ENTERTAINMENT: Sports Equipment	ENTERTAINMENT: Fees & Tickets	ENTERTAINMENT: Toys & Games	ENTERTAINMENT: Travel	ENTERTAINMENT: Cable TV	PERSONAL: Apparel & Services	PERSONAL: Auto Repairs	PERSONAL: Health Insurance	PERSONAL: Pets & Supplies
13120	NEDROW	116	127	104	127	119	120	117	116	116	119	116	92	122	120	118	115	81	115	118	137
13122	NEW WOODSTOCK	126	142	141	146	144	143	126	135	124	128	124	102	135	124	136	124	87	127	132	156
13124	NORTH PITCHER	86	62	74	60	62	83	64	76	71	62	70	58	51	73	59	77	47	71	80	92
13126	OSWEGO	79	73	68	73	71	77	78	75	79	74	79	58	74	80	73	82	55	78	81	90
13131	PARISH	87	80	70	77	78	81	75	79	78	78	78	58	71	81	72	80	53	77	80	94
13132	PENNELLVILLE	92	84	75	82	82	86	80	84	83	83	83	61	75	86	76	85	56	82	85	100
13135	PHOENIX	99	96	86	96	93	100	94	96	96	93	95	73	92	98	91	98	66	95	99	114
13136	PITCHER	84	60	78	59	61	83	62	76	69	59	68	58	50	71	59	76	45	71	79	91
13140	PORT BYRON	83	70	76	70	71	84	71	80	75	68	74	60	63	76	69	80	50	76	83	94
13141	PREBLE	91	100	87	102	97	100	90	95	89	89	89	73	94	91	94	90	62	90	94	111
13142	PULASKI	79	67	70	67	67	78	71	76	75	67	74	56	64	75	68	80	51	75	82	90
13143	RED CREEK	86	67	74	65	67	83	67	77	73	66	72	59	57	76	63	79	49	73	80	93
13144	RICHLAND	86	66	73	64	65	82	67	76	73	66	72	58	56	75	62	78	48	72	79	92
13145	SANDY CREEK	90	65	91	63	67	94	70	87	79	63	76	65	56	77	68	87	51	81	95	103
13146	SAVANNAH	94	70	79	69	70	91	72	84	79	70	78	64	59	82	67	86	52	79	88	101
13147	SCIPIO CENTER	83	81	77	84	81	90	77	85	79	72	78	65	75	80	79	82	54	80	87	100
13148	SENECA FALLS	81	78	75	79	78	85	80	82	82	76	81	61	78	82	79	85	56	81	88	96
13152	SKANEATELES	119	139	144	140	143	143	121	132	122	126	122	95	136	120	136	124	86	126	136	151
13155	SOUTH OTSELIC	88	63	73	61	63	84	65	77	73	64	71	59	52	75	60	79	48	72	81	93
13156	STERLING	81	69	88	69	72	85	68	81	71	64	70	60	61	70	70	75	47	75	82	95
13158	TRUXTON	79	73	68	73	73	80	70	77	73	68	72	57	66	75	69	76	49	73	78	90
13159	TULLY	106	110	103	113	110	114	103	109	103	102	102	83	105	104	106	104	71	104	109	127
13160	UNION SPRINGS	92	103	99	104	101	108	92	99	94	90	94	74	99	95	99	97	65	95	103	115
13164	WARNERS	94	116	103	115	111	114	99	103	100	100	101	77	113	101	109	102	71	101	109	120
13165	WATERLOO	81	73	77	73	73	86	74	81	77	69	76	61	69	77	73	82	52	78	86	95
13166	WEEDSPORT	89	84	76	85	83	90	83	87	84	80	84	67	79	87	81	87	57	84	89	103
13167	WEST MONROE	89	82	74	80	81	86	78	84	81	79	80	61	73	84	75	83	55	80	84	99
13202	SYRACUSE	36	24	24	28	23	27	38	29	40	35	40	24	33	38	31	41	28	36	35	38
13203	SYRACUSE	57	49	48	52	48	53	64	55	66	58	66	43	59	63	57	68	46	62	64	68
13204	SYRACUSE	51	41	37	43	39	43	54	46	57	49	56	37	49	56	46	58	40	52	52	57
13205	SYRACUSE	59	49	45	52	47	54	59	54	63	56	62	42	55	62	53	66	43	59	62	67
13206	SYRACUSE	71	65	59	66	62	69	73	68	75	68	74	54	69	74	68	77	51	72	76	83
13207	SYRACUSE	84	79	67	81	74	82	84	79	87	82	87	62	83	88	79	89	60	83	86	97
13208	SYRACUSE	58	54	48	55	51	57	62	56	64	57	63	44	59	63	57	66	45	61	63	68
13209	SYRACUSE	83	86	79	86	84	91	84	86	87	82	86	64	86	86	85	90	60	86	94	101
13210	SYRACUSE	54	37	35	40	35	38	64	45	59	53	59	40	49	58	47	57	42	54	47	57
13211	SYRACUSE	81	82	69	83	78	86	83	81	85	79	84	63	83	86	81	87	58	83	90	97
13212	SYRACUSE	84	92	84	92	90	95	87	89	90	85	90	66	93	90	91	93	63	89	98	104
13214	SYRACUSE	106	121	126	122	125	123	114	116	114	115	114	85	124	111	122	116	81	116	123	134
13215	SYRACUSE	115	131	125	133	130	128	120	122	120	123	121	92	131	120	128	121	85	121	126	142
13219	SYRACUSE	93	108	104	108	109	113	95	103	99	97	98	74	106	97	104	102	69	99	111	118
13224	SYRACUSE	105	106	101	108	104	108	107	104	109	108	110	79	110	108	107	111	77	108	113	125
13244	SYRACUSE	23	10	10	12	9	11	32	16	26	22	26	17	19	25	17	23	18	23	16	22
13301	ALDER CREEK	90	65	92	64	68	94	71	88	79	63	76	65	57	77	69	87	51	82	95	103
13302	ALTMAR	88	69	72	67	68	83	69	78	75	69	74	59	59	78	64	80	50	74	81	94
13303	AVA	93	82	94	81	82	99	78	91	84	76	83	68	73	84	80	89	56	86	95	107
13304	BARNEVELD	94	113	101	114	109	112	97	102	99	98	100	77	110	100	107	101	70	100	107	119
13308	BLOSSVALE	84	77	76	77	78	88	76	83	79	74	78	61	71	80	75	83	53	79	88	97
13309	BOONVILLE	82	67	76	67	69	83	69	79	73	66	72	58	61	74	67	78	49	75	82	92
13310	BOUCKVILLE	98	71	103	69	74	100	73	93	80	68	79	69	59	79	73	88	52	85	96	110
13314	BROOKFIELD	82	59	85	57	61	84	61	77	67	56	66	58	48	67	60	74	44	71	80	92
13315	BURLINGTON FLATS	82	70	80	71	72	87	70	82	73	64	72	61	62	73	70	78	48	75	84	95
13316	CAMDEN	84	76	72	78	75	88	76	82	79	70	77	63	71	80	74	83	53	78	87	97
13317	CANAJOHARIE	83	72	76	73	71	88	74	82	78	68	76	63	67	78	72	83	52	78	88	97
13318	CASSVILLE	81	77	67	75	74	76	75	76	75	77	75	58	72	78	72	76	52	75	75	90
13319	CHADWICKS	118	143	138	142	143	146	123	132	125	127	126	95	140	124	137	129	88	128	141	152
13320	CHERRY VALLEY	92	74	118	73	81	98	74	94	78	69	77	69	64	74	80	83	51	87	93	109
13322	CLAYVILLE	79	72	72	75	74	85	71	81	74	65	72	61	66	75	71	78	49	74	83	94
13323	CLINTON	97	103	105	103	105	111	97	104	100	98	99	75	101	97	103	104	69	102	113	120
13324	COLD BROOK	81	63	81	62	65	84	64	78	69	59	68	59	53	69	63	75	45	72	81	92
13325	CONSTABLEVILLE	83	62	84	61	64	85	63	79	69	59	68	59	52	69	63	76	45	72	82	93
13326	COOPERSTOWN	102	91	118	91	96	107	91	104	94	89	93	77	86	91	95	98	64	99	105	121
13327	CROGHAN	75	68	67	70	69	80	67	76	69	60	68	57	61	70	67	73	46	70	78	88
13328	DEANSBORO	86	90	76	92	86	94	88	87	89	84	88	68	90	90	87	91	61	88	96	105
13329	DOLGEVILLE	77	55	75	54	57	78	59	72	66	54	64	54	47	65	57	72	43	68	78	86
13331	EAGLE BAY	91	73	118	72	80	96	73	93	76	68	75	68	63	73	79	81	50	86	92	107
13332	EARLVILLE	92	66	94	64	68	93	67	86	75	63	73	64	54	74	67	82	49	79	89	102
13333	EAST SPRINGFIELD	89	72	116	70	79	95	72	91	75	67	74	66	62	71	78	80	49	84	90	105
13334	EATON	92	73	89	73	76	93	77	88	82	73	81	65	67	82	75	88	54	84	93	104
13335	EDMESTON	88	69	87	69	72	92	70	85	76	64	74	64	59	76	70	82	50	78	88	100
13337	FLY CREEK	122	109	156	108	118	135	104	128	109	101	108	92	98	104	114	115	73	119	129	147
13338	FORESTPORT	83	66	105	65	72	87	66	84	69	62	69	61	58	66	71	74	46	77	83	97
13339	FORT PLAIN	82	59	82	58	61	84	63	78	70	57	68	59	50	69	61	76	45	72	83	93
13340	FRANKFORT	75	75	72	75	75	82	73	77	76	71	75	56	73	76	74	80	52	75	83	90
13342	GARRATTSVILLE	85	71	103	70	76	91	70	87	73	65	72	64	62	71	75	78	48	80	87	101
13343	GLENFIELD	83	59	86	58	62	85	62	78	68	56	67	60	49	67	61	74	44	72	82	94
13345	GREIG	82	59	84	57	61	83	60	77	67	56	66	58	48	67	60	74	43	70	80	91
13346	HAMILTON	97	77	104	77	81	97	88	94	91	81	90	71	76	87	85	95	61	93	100	112
13348	HARTWICK	89	67	96	66	71	92	68	86	74	64	73	64	57	73	69	81	48	79	88	101
13350	HERKIMER	72	62	67	62	63	74	68	72	72	63	70	53	62	71	65	77	48	71	80	84
13353	HOFFMEISTER	96	77	124	76	84	101	77	98	80	72	79	71	67	76	83	86	53	90	96	113
13354	HOLLAND PATENT	94	111	99	111	107	111	96	101	98	97	98	76	107	99	104	100	69	98	106	118
13355	HUBBARDSVILLE	97	74	114	72	79	101	75	95	80	70	79	70	63	78	78	87	52	88	96	112
13357	ILION	70	65	62	65	63	73	67	69	70	63	69	52	64	70	65	74	47	69	76	82
13360	INLET	91	73	118	72	80	96	73	93	76	68	75	68	63	73	79	81	50	86	92	107
13361	JORDANVILLE	83	60	81	59	62	83	63	76	68	59	67	59	50	69	61	75	45	71	80	92
13363	LEE CENTER	92	72	77	70	72	88	72	82	78	72	77	62	62	81	67	84	52	78	85	99
13365	LITTLE FALLS	70	58	63	58	58	71	62	67	66	58	65	51	55	66	59	71	44	66	73	80
13367	LOWVILLE	78	65	77	65	66	81	68	77	72	63	71	58	60	71	67	77	48	74	82	91
13368	LYONS FALLS	79	63	77	63	64	82	63	76	68	58	67	57	54	68	63	73	45	70	79	90
13402	MADISON	83	60	88	59	63	84	62	78	68	57	67	59	50	67	62	74	44	72	81	93
13403	MARCY	93	104	93	105	102	106	93	99	94	92	94	75	99	95	99	96	66	95	102	115
13406	MIDDLEVILLE	86	78	78	82	80	92	77	87	80	70	78	66	71	81	77	84	53	81	90	101
13407	MOHAWK	77	65	75	65	66	80	67	75	71	63	70	56	60	70	66	76	47	72	80	89
13408	MORRISVILLE	89	77	83	77	78	91	79	87	82	75	81	65	71	82	77	87	55	83	91	102
	NEW YORK	100	106	110	108	107	104	112	106	113	106	114	81	115	110	112	116	83	110	110	124
	UNITED STATES	100	100	100	100	100	100	100	100	100	100	100	100	100	100	100	100	100	100	100	100

#	POST OFFICE NAME	COUNTY FIPS CODE	POPULATION 2000	POPULATION 2009	POPULATION 2014	2000-2009 ANNUAL RATE % Rate	2000-2009 ANNUAL RATE State Centile	HOUSEHOLDS 2000	HOUSEHOLDS 2009	HOUSEHOLDS 2014	HOUSEHOLDS % Annual Rate 2000-2009	HOUSEHOLDS 2009 Average HH Size	FAMILIES 2000	FAMILIES 2009	FAMILIES % Annual Rate 2000-2009
13409	MUNNSVILLE	053	2299	2299	2293	0.0	38	825	845	848	0.3	2.64	629	634	0.1
13411	NEW BERLIN	017	3472	3632	3630	0.5	71	1307	1393	1401	0.7	2.54	913	958	0.5
13413	NEW HARTFORD	065	15969	16260	16256	0.2	52	6375	6662	6726	0.5	2.29	4216	4314	0.2
13415	NEW LISBON	077	95	103	103	0.9	87	39	43	44	1.1	2.40	28	31	1.1
13416	NEWPORT	043	2366	2438	2441	0.3	59	856	906	913	0.6	2.64	633	658	0.4
13417	NEW YORK MILLS	065	3074	3177	3202	0.4	66	1490	1574	1596	0.6	2.02	745	764	0.3
13418	NORTH BROOKFIELD	053	217	222	225	0.2	52	73	77	78	0.6	2.88	54	55	0.2
13420	OLD FORGE	043	1180	1048	1001	-1.3	1	523	476	460	-1.0	2.16	329	292	-1.3
13421	ONEIDA	053	13668	13174	12965	-0.4	11	5477	5363	5314	-0.2	2.38	3489	3338	-0.5
13424	ORISKANY	065	2791	2815	2824	0.1	44	894	938	949	0.5	2.53	656	678	0.4
13425	ORISKANY FALLS	065	2087	2069	2066	-0.1	30	801	823	829	0.3	2.51	574	577	0.1
13428	PALATINE BRIDGE	057	1858	1859	1848	0.0	38	702	709	708	0.1	2.56	503	501	0.0
13431	POLAND	043	1951	2008	2005	0.3	59	730	767	772	0.5	2.61	536	553	0.3
13433	PORT LEYDEN	049	1691	1654	1623	-0.2	21	624	628	622	0.1	2.61	453	449	-0.1
13437	REDFIELD	075	492	499	499	0.2	52	194	202	203	0.4	2.47	140	143	0.2
13438	REMSEN	065	4520	4675	4713	0.4	66	1733	1844	1874	0.7	2.53	1242	1297	0.5
13439	RICHFIELD SPRINGS	077	4073	4190	4156	0.3	59	1599	1674	1672	0.5	2.48	1112	1141	0.3
13440	ROME	065	44802	43695	43169	-0.3	15	17270	17321	17232	0.0	2.33	11153	10992	-0.2
13450	ROSEBOOM	077	193	199	197	0.3	59	74	76	76	0.3	2.32	54	55	0.2
13452	SAINT JOHNSVILLE	035	4685	4701	4698	0.0	38	1827	1875	1885	0.3	2.43	1244	1253	0.1
13454	SALISBURY CENTER	043	588	605	604	0.3	59	208	220	221	0.6	2.75	153	159	0.4
13456	SAUQUOIT	065	4311	4496	4544	0.5	71	1623	1741	1776	0.8	2.56	1204	1270	0.6
13459	SHARON SPRINGS	095	2108	2112	2092	0.0	38	782	802	801	0.3	2.56	566	571	0.1
13460	SHERBURNE	017	4340	4294	4257	-0.1	30	1725	1741	1738	0.1	2.46	1165	1153	-0.1
13461	SHERRILL	065	3143	3069	3014	-0.3	15	1263	1267	1255	0.0	2.41	880	865	-0.2
13464	SMYRNA	017	1564	1501	1478	-0.4	11	533	523	519	-0.2	2.85	392	379	-0.4
13468	SPRINGFIELD CENTER	077	534	553	548	0.4	66	211	223	223	0.6	2.48	148	154	0.4
13469	STITTVILLE	065	767	786	790	0.3	59	280	299	303	0.7	2.43	217	228	0.5
13470	STRATFORD	035	772	732	716	-0.6	4	280	272	268	-0.3	2.65	199	191	-0.4
13471	TABERG	065	3497	3548	3553	0.2	52	1228	1286	1300	0.5	2.72	918	945	0.3
13473	TURIN	049	919	886	865	-0.4	11	337	336	331	0.0	2.63	237	232	-0.2
13475	VAN HORNESVILLE	043	17	18	18	0.6	76	8	8	9	0.0	2.25	6	6	0.0
13476	VERNON	065	3178	3201	3203	0.1	44	1264	1317	1331	0.4	2.42	900	920	0.2
13477	VERNON CENTER	065	1179	1289	1324	1.0	89	428	484	502	1.3	2.65	304	337	1.1
13478	VERONA	065	3182	3014	2943	-0.6	4	1193	1167	1151	-0.2	2.58	914	879	-0.4
13480	WATERVILLE	065	3859	3854	3836	0.0	38	1391	1422	1426	0.2	2.65	1022	1028	0.1
13482	WEST BURLINGTON	077	61	66	67	0.9	87	21	23	24	1.0	2.87	16	18	1.3
13483	WESTDALE	065	239	240	240	0.0	38	90	93	94	0.4	2.58	68	69	0.2
13485	WEST EDMESTON	053	1637	1696	1708	0.4	66	586	622	632	0.6	2.73	443	463	0.5
13486	WESTERNVILLE	065	637	663	670	0.4	66	229	245	250	0.7	2.70	175	184	0.5
13488	WESTFORD	077	130	132	131	0.2	52	49	51	50	0.4	2.59	35	36	0.3
13489	WEST LEYDEN	049	564	562	554	0.0	38	197	203	202	0.3	2.77	142	144	0.2
13490	WESTMORELAND	065	1278	1299	1301	0.2	52	449	471	476	0.5	2.75	344	355	0.3
13491	WEST WINFIELD	077	3840	4021	4033	0.5	71	1426	1528	1544	0.7	2.63	1069	1126	0.6
13492	WHITESBORO	065	11737	11714	11661	0.0	38	4796	4913	4925	0.3	2.38	3298	3321	0.1
13493	WILLIAMSTOWN	075	2299	2322	2305	0.1	44	806	834	833	0.4	2.78	599	611	0.2
13494	WOODGATE	065	325	331	332	0.2	52	141	148	150	0.5	2.24	92	94	0.2
13495	YORKVILLE	065	2255	2162	2128	-0.5	7	966	951	942	-0.2	2.14	581	557	-0.5
13501	UTICA	065	36095	35204	34715	-0.3	15	14673	14490	14354	-0.1	2.31	8439	8126	-0.4
13502	UTICA	065	32854	31653	31154	-0.4	11	13752	13555	13419	-0.2	2.22	8195	7936	-0.3
13601	WATERTOWN	045	38190	38704	39289	0.1	44	15059	15643	16024	0.4	2.36	9504	9660	0.2
13602	FORT DRUM	045	6696	6948	7086	0.4	66	616	717	762	1.7	3.35	597	695	1.7
13603	WATERTOWN	045	5431	5905	6095	0.9	87	1639	1801	1869	1.0	3.28	1607	1763	1.0
13605	ADAMS	045	4761	5153	5351	0.9	87	1842	2031	2122	1.1	2.53	1300	1411	0.9
13606	ADAMS CENTER	045	2571	2685	2757	0.5	71	940	1002	1035	0.7	2.67	681	713	0.5
13607	ALEXANDRIA BAY	045	2054	2370	2511	1.6	97	895	1060	1132	1.8	2.19	587	680	1.6
13608	ANTWERP	045	1703	1961	2072	1.5	96	601	708	753	1.8	2.77	439	508	1.6
13611	BELLEVILLE	045	106	113	117	0.7	80	34	37	39	0.9	3.05	25	27	0.8
13612	BLACK RIVER	045	2724	2972	3090	0.9	87	1050	1175	1231	1.2	2.53	756	830	1.0
13613	BRASHER FALLS	089	2226	2374	2393	0.7	80	901	982	997	0.9	2.41	616	659	0.7
13614	BRIER HILL	089	469	501	506	0.7	80	199	218	222	1.0	2.29	139	149	0.8
13616	CALCIUM	045	2015	2175	2258	0.8	84	648	714	746	1.1	3.05	551	601	0.9
13617	CANTON	089	10818	10844	10772	0.0	38	3360	3409	3405	0.2	2.40	2153	2140	-0.1
13618	CAPE VINCENT	045	1706	1833	1902	0.8	84	735	811	846	1.1	2.22	510	552	0.9
13619	CARTHAGE	049	11569	11523	11596	0.0	38	4350	4439	4503	0.2	2.57	3112	3121	0.0
13620	CASTORLAND	049	2268	2215	2169	-0.3	15	794	800	792	0.1	2.76	609	606	-0.1
13621	CHASE MILLS	089	630	635	632	0.1	44	244	252	253	0.3	2.47	172	175	0.2
13622	CHAUMONT	045	2391	2665	2788	1.2	93	911	1043	1102	1.5	2.53	652	733	1.3
13624	CLAYTON	045	5998	6228	6382	0.4	66	1913	2056	2136	0.8	2.42	1346	1420	0.6
13625	COLTON	089	2208	2254	2250	0.2	52	898	937	942	0.5	2.40	620	635	0.3
13626	COPENHAGEN	049	2226	2221	2197	0.0	38	775	798	798	0.3	2.65	585	593	0.1
13630	DE KALB JUNCTION	089	1292	1335	1336	0.4	66	469	496	501	0.6	2.66	345	360	0.5
13633	DE PEYSTER	089	212	222	221	0.5	71	63	70	70	1.1	3.17	48	52	0.9
13634	DEXTER	045	3874	4234	4412	1.0	89	1439	1611	1691	1.2	2.62	1054	1160	1.0
13635	EDWARDS	089	1109	1110	1101	0.0	38	414	423	423	0.2	2.62	313	314	0.0
13636	ELLISBURG	045	318	340	352	0.7	80	104	114	119	1.0	2.98	79	85	0.8
13637	EVANS MILLS	045	4155	4306	4423	0.4	66	1434	1524	1580	0.7	2.81	1101	1151	0.5
13638	FELTS MILLS	045	274	308	323	1.3	94	105	121	128	1.5	2.55	76	86	1.3
13639	FINE	089	262	253	248	-0.4	11	92	91	90	-0.1	2.74	68	66	-0.3
13640	WELLESLEY ISLAND	045	323	363	381	1.3	94	158	182	193	1.5	1.94	100	113	1.3
13642	GOUVERNEUR	089	10226	10151	10051	-0.1	30	3528	3565	3555	0.1	2.53	2467	2453	-0.1
13646	HAMMOND	089	2511	2776	2822	1.1	91	1006	1132	1159	1.3	2.45	712	787	1.1
13648	HARRISVILLE	049	2259	2214	2179	-0.2	21	866	873	867	0.1	2.53	660	658	0.0
13650	HENDERSON	045	1375	1472	1523	0.7	80	573	629	656	1.0	2.33	415	448	0.8
13652	HERMON	089	1953	2068	2083	0.6	76	707	767	779	0.9	2.65	509	545	0.7
13654	HEUVELTON	089	2468	2386	2346	-0.4	11	832	823	816	-0.1	2.87	612	596	-0.3
13655	HOGANSBURG	033	2831	2983	3029	0.6	76	966	1045	1072	0.9	2.84	711	759	0.7
13656	LA FARGEVILLE	045	2420	2645	2758	1.0	89	845	946	995	1.2	2.79	649	715	1.1
13658	LISBON	089	2482	2482	2467	0.0	38	894	916	917	0.3	2.70	668	673	0.1
13659	LORRAINE	045	499	555	581	1.2	93	191	217	229	1.4	2.54	145	163	1.3
13660	MADRID	089	1934	2008	2010	0.4	66	671	712	720	0.6	2.69	490	511	0.5
13661	MANNSVILLE	045	1587	1723	1791	0.9	87	573	637	667	1.2	2.70	438	480	1.0
13662	MASSENA	089	16937	16460	16192	-0.3	15	7003	6920	6854	-0.1	2.32	4514	4371	-0.3
13665	NATURAL BRIDGE	049	745	715	700	-0.4	11	282	278	275	-0.2	2.57	212	206	-0.3
13666	NEWTON FALLS	089	274	262	257	-0.5	7	104	102	101	-0.2	2.56	71	68	-0.5
	NEW YORK					0.3					0.3	2.61			0.1
	UNITED STATES					1.0					1.1	2.59			0.9

ZIP CODE		RACE (%)						% Hispanic Origin		2009 AGE DISTRIBUTION (%)										MEDIAN AGE		
#	POST OFFICE NAME	White		Black		Asian/Pacific																
		2000	2009	2000	2009	2000	2009	2000	2009	0-4	5-9	10-14	15-19	20-24	25-44	45-64	65-84	85+	18+	2009	% 2009 Males	% 2009 Females
13409	MUNNSVILLE	95.7	94.6	1.0	1.2	0.4	0.6	0.9	1.2	7.7	8.1	7.9	7.4	5.5	25.0	26.3	10.8	1.3	72.0	37.0	50.5	49.5
13411	NEW BERLIN	98.3	97.9	0.3	0.3	0.2	0.3	1.0	1.2	6.1	6.4	6.8	6.6	5.1	22.8	28.2	14.9	2.9	76.5	42.1	48.3	51.7
13413	NEW HARTFORD	95.8	93.8	0.9	1.3	2.5	3.7	0.8	1.1	4.7	5.0	6.0	6.2	4.5	20.6	29.2	18.4	5.5	80.3	47.1	46.6	53.4
13415	NEW LISBON	97.9	97.1	1.1	1.0	0.0	1.0	1.1	1.9	5.8	5.8	6.8	6.8	3.9	22.3	35.0	11.7	1.9	76.7	44.1	46.6	53.4
13416	NEWPORT	98.5	98.1	0.3	0.4	0.0	0.0	0.5	0.6	5.3	5.8	6.3	7.3	5.6	24.7	31.6	11.7	1.7	80.0	41.4	49.6	50.4
13417	NEW YORK MILLS	98.1	97.3	0.4	0.5	0.4	0.6	1.1	1.5	5.2	4.8	4.8	4.9	5.8	26.4	25.9	16.5	5.8	82.4	43.6	45.8	54.2
13418	NORTH BROOKFIELD	98.6	98.2	0.5	0.5	0.5	0.9	0.0	0.0	6.8	5.9	8.1	8.1	5.9	25.7	28.8	9.0	1.8	74.3	37.3	50.9	49.1
13420	OLD FORGE	98.3	97.8	0.5	0.6	0.2	0.3	0.8	1.0	3.6	4.6	5.8	6.5	4.8	21.1	35.4	16.2	2.0	81.7	47.2	49.3	50.7
13421	ONEIDA	96.6	95.8	0.7	0.9	0.4	0.6	0.8	1.0	6.0	6.1	6.2	7.2	6.6	25.7	27.6	11.8	2.7	77.0	39.8	48.8	51.2
13424	ORISKANY	92.8	90.6	4.7	6.0	0.7	1.0	2.6	3.4	4.4	4.7	5.2	7.6	6.4	27.3	28.3	12.2	4.0	81.1	41.4	51.8	48.2
13425	ORISKANY FALLS	98.1	97.4	0.4	0.5	0.6	0.9	0.6	0.9	5.9	5.9	5.9	6.7	6.6	26.8	28.3	12.1	1.7	77.9	39.3	49.9	50.1
13428	PALATINE BRIDGE	97.8	97.1	0.6	0.8	0.5	0.8	0.5	0.6	6.3	6.5	6.6	6.3	5.4	23.1	28.7	13.6	3.4	76.5	41.6	49.2	50.8
13431	POLAND	98.5	98.1	0.2	0.3	0.4	0.5	0.6	0.8	5.6	6.1	6.5	7.1	5.1	24.0	30.5	13.3	1.8	79.2	42.0	49.7	50.3
13433	PORT LEYDEN	98.8	98.4	0.2	0.2	0.0	0.0	0.4	0.5	6.3	6.3	6.7	7.3	6.4	25.4	28.5	11.4	1.7	76.1	38.4	49.7	50.3
13437	REDFIELD	98.4	98.2	0.2	0.2	0.2	0.2	1.0	1.4	6.6	7.2	7.4	7.8	6.2	24.2	28.5	11.0	1.0	73.9	37.6	48.9	51.1
13438	REMSEN	98.3	97.5	0.4	0.6	0.4	0.7	0.3	0.4	5.8	6.0	6.2	6.7	6.2	24.9	31.0	11.9	1.4	77.7	40.9	49.6	50.4
13439	RICHFIELD SPRINGS	97.5	96.9	0.5	0.6	0.6	0.8	0.6	0.7	5.2	5.5	6.0	6.4	4.8	22.2	31.2	15.8	2.7	79.3	44.8	49.6	50.4
13440	ROME	90.5	88.4	5.7	6.3	0.8	1.5	3.6	4.2	5.8	5.6	5.8	8.1	7.5	24.6	26.0	13.6	2.9	78.8	39.3	49.5	50.5
13450	ROSEBOOM	96.9	95.5	1.0	1.5	1.0	1.0	1.0	1.5	5.0	5.5	6.5	6.5	4.0	22.6	29.1	15.6	5.0	77.9	44.8	49.7	50.3
13452	SAINT JOHNSVILLE	98.6	98.2	0.3	0.3	0.2	0.3	0.9	1.2	5.8	5.8	6.0	6.6	5.8	23.7	29.3	14.0	3.0	78.3	42.0	49.7	50.3
13454	SALISBURY CENTER	98.5	97.7	0.2	0.2	0.3	0.7	0.2	0.2	6.3	6.3	6.6	6.9	6.8	26.0	29.3	10.7	1.2	76.7	38.7	51.2	48.8
13456	SAUQUOIT	97.8	96.9	0.4	0.5	0.7	1.1	0.6	0.8	5.0	5.4	6.2	7.4	5.3	23.6	32.2	12.8	2.1	78.6	43.0	48.8	51.2
13459	SHARON SPRINGS	98.0	97.6	0.5	0.6	0.0	0.0	1.6	2.0	5.8	6.2	6.8	7.6	5.2	23.3	28.7	13.8	2.7	76.7	42.0	50.0	50.0
13460	SHERBURNE	98.7	98.4	0.2	0.2	0.1	0.2	0.8	0.9	6.1	6.4	6.8	7.0	5.6	23.6	29.4	13.2	1.9	76.1	40.9	48.6	51.4
13461	SHERRILL	98.0	97.3	0.2	0.3	0.6	0.9	0.8	1.1	6.1	6.1	6.7	7.1	6.0	21.2	30.5	13.2	3.1	76.3	42.5	47.4	52.6
13464	SMYRNA	98.5	98.1	0.3	0.3	0.1	0.1	0.5	0.7	7.0	7.0	7.2	7.4	5.5	25.6	28.0	10.9	1.3	73.8	38.5	50.1	49.9
13468	SPRINGFIELD CENTER	98.7	98.4	0.2	0.2	0.4	0.4	0.6	0.7	4.3	5.1	8.0	8.3	4.0	22.6	29.7	14.8	3.3	76.1	43.7	49.7	50.3
13469	STITTVILLE	79.0	64.0	14.1	22.5	0.5	2.0	9.7	16.9	3.8	4.2	5.6	10.4	8.7	33.8	25.1	7.6	0.8	82.7	35.6	60.2	39.8
13470	STRATFORD	97.4	96.7	0.9	1.1	0.1	0.1	1.3	1.6	4.9	5.5	7.5	7.0	5.2	26.0	30.9	12.3	0.8	77.3	41.8	53.0	47.0
13471	TABERG	97.1	95.9	1.9	2.6	0.1	0.1	0.8	1.2	6.3	6.3	6.8	8.9	6.3	27.0	28.1	9.2	1.0	74.8	37.8	52.4	47.6
13473	TURIN	99.0	98.6	0.1	0.1	0.0	0.1	0.2	0.2	6.4	6.8	7.1	6.7	5.1	23.8	29.7	12.9	1.6	75.1	40.4	50.9	49.1
13475	VAN HORNESVILLE	100.0	100.0	0.0	0.0	0.0	0.0	0.0	0.0	11.1	5.6	11.1	11.1	11.1	16.7	33.3	0.0	0.0	61.1	25.0	55.6	44.4
13476	VERNON	98.0	97.2	0.5	0.7	0.4	0.6	0.7	1.0	5.8	5.9	6.4	7.3	5.7	24.3	30.2	12.5	1.8	77.2	41.2	49.1	50.9
13477	VERNON CENTER	98.0	97.1	0.5	0.7	0.6	0.9	0.8	1.2	6.6	7.0	7.2	7.1	5.0	24.7	29.0	11.9	1.6	74.9	39.8	50.0	50.0
13478	VERONA	97.4	96.4	0.6	0.9	0.5	0.8	0.5	0.8	5.7	5.9	6.3	7.1	5.3	25.4	29.7	13.0	1.5	77.7	41.5	50.3	49.7
13480	WATERVILLE	98.3	97.6	0.4	0.6	0.4	0.5	0.6	0.9	6.7	6.7	7.8	7.4	6.5	23.7	26.3	12.4	2.4	73.9	38.6	49.2	50.8
13482	WEST BURLINGTON	98.3	97.0	0.0	0.0	0.0	0.0	1.7	1.5	6.1	6.1	7.6	7.6	6.1	25.8	25.8	13.6	1.5	74.2	38.8	51.5	48.5
13483	WESTDALE	98.7	98.3	0.4	0.4	0.4	0.4	0.4	0.4	7.1	7.5	7.5	7.1	6.7	23.8	29.6	10.0	0.8	75.4	38.0	52.1	47.9
13485	WEST EDMESTON	98.1	97.5	0.6	0.7	0.2	0.4	0.5	0.7	6.8	7.0	7.3	7.1	5.7	25.2	28.7	10.8	1.4	74.4	38.4	49.4	50.6
13486	WESTERNVILLE	97.8	97.1	0.5	0.6	0.3	0.6	0.6	0.8	5.9	6.6	7.2	8.1	4.4	25.9	28.1	12.1	1.7	74.8	39.7	51.6	48.4
13488	WESTFORD	98.5	98.5	0.0	0.0	0.8	0.8	1.5	1.5	4.5	5.3	6.8	7.6	4.5	22.7	33.3	13.6	1.5	78.0	43.9	51.5	48.5
13489	WEST LEYDEN	99.3	99.1	0.4	0.4	0.0	0.0	0.2	0.4	5.3	5.3	9.4	9.6	5.0	27.6	25.3	11.4	1.1	73.7	37.8	51.6	48.4
13490	WESTMORELAND	97.9	97.1	0.9	1.2	0.3	0.4	1.1	1.6	5.3	5.7	6.5	7.9	5.3	24.5	32.6	10.8	1.5	77.6	41.9	50.7	49.3
13491	WEST WINFIELD	98.5	98.1	0.3	0.3	0.3	0.5	0.6	0.7	6.4	7.1	7.1	7.2	4.9	24.8	28.7	12.1	1.7	74.7	39.6	50.2	49.8
13492	WHITESBORO	98.3	97.5	0.4	0.6	0.5	0.7	1.0	1.3	5.2	5.5	6.1	6.6	4.9	22.9	30.0	15.8	3.0	79.1	44.1	47.5	52.5
13493	WILLIAMSTOWN	97.5	96.9	0.7	0.9	0.1	0.2	0.9	1.1	6.8	6.8	7.4	8.3	6.5	25.5	28.1	9.6	0.9	73.9	36.9	49.5	50.5
13494	WOODGATE	98.5	97.9	0.3	0.6	0.3	0.3	0.0	0.0	4.8	5.1	5.4	5.4	3.6	19.0	36.9	18.1	1.5	81.0	48.6	51.1	48.9
13495	YORKVILLE	98.3	97.3	0.5	0.9	0.4	0.7	1.2	1.9	5.6	5.5	5.6	5.7	6.0	26.0	26.0	14.9	4.7	80.3	41.2	46.2	53.8
13501	UTICA	76.2	71.9	14.6	16.4	3.0	4.0	6.4	7.8	7.1	6.8	6.5	7.1	6.5	23.7	23.6	14.2	4.4	75.9	38.5	47.2	52.8
13502	UTICA	87.6	84.2	8.1	10.0	1.0	1.5	3.8	4.9	6.1	5.7	5.6	7.0	7.2	25.3	25.5	14.6	3.0	79.0	40.0	47.9	52.1
13601	WATERTOWN	89.8	87.5	5.0	5.8	1.1	1.5	3.5	4.4	7.3	6.4	6.0	6.4	7.7	27.6	24.8	11.1	2.7	76.4	36.2	49.5	50.5
13602	FORT DRUM	63.8	57.9	21.1	23.7	3.0	4.0	12.2	14.4	5.8	4.2	3.0	11.4	41.2	32.5	1.8	0.0	0.0	85.6	23.1	76.3	23.7
13603	WATERTOWN	64.7	59.3	18.2	20.2	3.2	4.1	14.6	17.0	20.5	10.9	5.9	4.9	17.2	38.6	1.8	0.1	0.1	60.3	22.3	49.8	50.2
13605	ADAMS	98.1	97.5	0.3	0.4	0.2	0.4	0.8	1.0	6.3	6.5	6.7	6.8	5.8	24.3	29.7	12.1	1.7	76.1	40.6	49.6	50.4
13606	ADAMS CENTER	97.8	97.0	0.6	0.7	0.4	0.6	0.7	1.0	6.7	6.7	6.9	7.3	6.4	24.6	29.3	10.5	1.5	74.9	38.9	49.7	50.3
13607	ALEXANDRIA BAY	98.6	98.1	0.3	0.4	0.0	0.1	0.8	1.0	4.3	4.6	4.9	5.4	4.7	20.6	34.1	17.8	3.6	82.8	48.4	49.2	50.8
13608	ANTWERP	97.8	97.1	0.5	0.6	0.3	0.5	1.1	1.4	6.1	7.6	7.7	7.4	6.4	25.7	28.7	9.3	1.1	73.8	36.8	50.8	49.2
13611	BELLEVILLE	99.0	99.1	0.0	0.0	0.0	0.0	1.9	1.8	5.3	8.0	8.8	8.0	4.4	24.8	24.8	14.2	1.8	72.6	38.6	49.6	50.4
13612	BLACK RIVER	93.4	91.3	2.4	3.0	1.7	2.4	1.7	2.3	5.7	6.5	6.7	7.3	5.8	27.5	28.7	10.3	1.4	76.4	39.0	49.5	50.5
13613	BRASHER FALLS	96.9	95.9	0.2	0.4	0.4	0.6	0.8	1.2	5.8	6.1	6.3	6.4	5.1	24.8	30.4	13.3	1.9	77.6	42.0	49.3	50.7
13614	BRIER HILL	97.7	97.4	0.2	0.2	0.0	0.0	0.2	0.4	5.6	6.8	5.6	5.6	3.6	23.6	34.9	13.2	1.2	77.4	44.5	49.7	50.3
13616	CALCIUM	82.3	78.0	10.5	12.6	1.3	1.9	6.7	8.6	11.4	9.8	7.6	6.0	8.9	29.6	20.8	5.5	0.5	67.5	28.3	49.9	50.1
13617	CANTON	94.9	91.8	2.5	4.5	0.7	1.3	1.3	2.0	4.2	4.2	4.8	15.5	16.2	19.9	22.7	10.4	2.1	84.4	30.0	50.1	49.9
13618	CAPE VINCENT	97.2	96.6	1.1	1.2	0.4	0.5	0.9	1.2	3.9	4.2	4.5	5.2	4.3	20.8	36.3	18.4	2.3	83.9	49.2	49.2	50.8
13619	CARTHAGE	93.3	91.5	2.7	3.2	1.0	1.4	2.4	3.0	7.3	7.1	7.1	7.0	6.7	26.3	25.9	10.6	2.0	74.3	36.5	48.9	51.1
13620	CASTORLAND	97.7	97.1	0.7	0.9	0.1	0.2	0.7	0.9	6.6	7.0	7.3	7.1	5.1	26.3	28.8	10.6	1.2	74.7	38.3	50.3	49.7
13621	CHASE MILLS	97.9	97.3	0.5	0.6	0.3	0.6	0.6	0.8	5.2	6.0	6.9	6.5	4.6	23.9	31.7	14.0	1.3	77.6	43.0	50.7	49.3
13622	CHAUMONT	97.3	96.4	1.0	1.2	0.1	0.2	0.8	1.1	4.5	6.0	6.5	8.3	5.0	23.3	31.0	13.5	1.8	77.9	42.8	50.2	49.8
13624	CLAYTON	82.6	80.2	12.6	13.9	0.3	0.4	8.1	9.6	4.7	4.6	5.3	5.7	6.7	34.1	25.8	11.4	1.8	81.7	38.7	59.0	41.0
13625	COLTON	98.6	98.3	0.1	0.1	0.3	0.4	0.7	1.1	5.1	5.5	5.7	6.0	4.7	22.8	33.6	15.4	1.3	79.7	45.1	50.9	49.1
13626	COPENHAGEN	94.1	92.8	3.0	3.5	0.3	0.4	2.7	3.4	6.9	6.8	6.9	6.9	6.0	29.7	26.7	9.1	0.9	75.1	36.4	53.8	46.2
13630	DE KALB JUNCTION	98.1	97.7	0.4	0.5	0.2	0.1	0.4	0.5	7.0	7.9	8.5	8.5	5.9	25.1	26.7	9.4	1.0	71.6	34.7	50.1	49.9
13633	DE PEYSTER	98.1	97.3	0.9	0.9	0.0	0.0	0.5	0.5	7.7	7.7	8.1	7.7	5.0	24.3	27.9	10.8	0.9	71.2	36.5	50.9	49.1
13634	DEXTER	97.9	97.3	0.3	0.4	0.3	0.4	0.6	0.7	5.9	6.1	6.4	7.4	5.9	25.0	30.5	11.4	1.4	76.9	40.5	48.5	51.5
13635	EDWARDS	98.1	97.6	0.5	0.6	0.1	0.1	0.8	0.9	5.9	7.6	9.0	7.7	4.1	26.2	26.6	12.1	1.0	72.4	37.8	49.1	50.9
13636	ELLISBURG	98.1	97.1	0.3	0.6	0.3	0.3	1.3	1.8	5.3	7.9	8.2	9.7	4.7	24.1	25.9	12.1	2.1	72.4	37.8	49.4	50.6
13637	EVANS MILLS	78.9	75.2	11.3	12.7	1.6	2.1	8.3	10.0	11.5	9.8	8.3	7.5	7.7	33.2	16.9	4.5	0.5	65.7	27.6	50.7	49.3
13638	FELTS MILLS	92.7	90.9	2.9	3.6	0.7	1.0	2.5	2.9	6.8	7.1	7.5	7.1	4.9	30.2	27.3	8.1	1.0	74.0	37.1	50.6	49.4
13639	FINE	97.3	96.8	0.0	0.0	0.8	0.8	0.0	0.0	5.5	6.3	5.9	5.1	4.3	22.9	30.4	17.4	2.0	79.4	44.8	47.0	53.0
13640	WELLESLEY ISLAND	98.8	98.6	0.3	0.3	0.0	0.0	0.6	0.6	3.3	3.9	4.4	4.7	4.1	19.0	35.3	21.2	4.1	84.8	51.4	48.2	51.8
13642	GOUVERNEUR	89.2	87.4	6.9	7.9	0.4	0.5	4.4	5.3	6.5	6.3	6.2	6.7	7.8	30.2	24.3	10.4	1.7	76.9	35.8	54.3	45.7
13646	HAMMOND	97.5	96.6	0.4	0.6	0.1	0.2	0.7	0.9	5.7	6.2	6.7	6.3	4.6	23.4	31.2	14.1	1.8	77.5	42.8	50.6	49.4
13648	HARRISVILLE	98.1	97.7	0.1	0.1	0.3	0.5	0.5	0.6	5.9	7.2	7.5	7.4	4.4	24.6	30.3	11.3	1.4	74.3	39.8	50.7	49.3
13650	HENDERSON	98.8	98.2	0.1	0.1	0.1	0.1	0.9	1.2	5.0	6.8	6.9	7.3	4.1	23.2	29.9	14.8	2.0	76.5	42.6	49.8	50.2
13652	HERMON	98.4	97.8	0.5	0.7	0.4	0.6	0.3	0.5	6.1	6.3	6.7	7.4	6.3	24.5	30.8	10.7	1.3	76.5	39.4	49.9	50.1
13654	HEUVELTON	98.1	97.4	0.4	0.6	0.2	0.3	0.3	0.4	7.3	7.4	7.7	7.4	5.2	24.1	28.7	10.8	1.4	72.8	38.1	49.3	50.7
13655	HOGANSBURG	6.0	6.1	0.0	0.0	0.0	0.0	0.7	0.8	8.3	7.9	7.6	8.7	9.2	26.7	22.9	7.6	0.9	70.6	30.2	50.3	49.7
13656	LA FARGEVILLE	96.1	94.9	1.1	1.4	0.5	0.7	1.3	1.7	7.3	7.6	7.4	7.4	5.4	27.4	27.6	8.8	1.1	73.0	36.4	50.7	49.3
13658	LISBON	98.2	97.7	0.2	0.2	0.2	0.2	0.7	1.0	6.3	6.8	7.0	6.8	4.7	25.2	31.1	10.7	1.3	75.5	40.3	50.1	49.9
13659	LORRAINE	98.8	98.2	0.2	0.4	0.0	0.0	0.6	0.9	7.4	7.6	7.6	7.4	6.1	24.7	28.6	9.4	1.3	72.6	37.4	52.6	47.4
13660	MADRID	97.6	96.5	1.1	1.6	0.3	0.6	0.7	1.0	5.4	7.0	7.8	6.8	4.2	26.2	30.1	11.0	1.5	75.0	39.8	50.4	49.6
13661	MANNSVILLE	97.5	96.7	0.6	0.7	0.5	0.8	1.1	1.4	7.0	7.7	7.7	8.2	5.9	24.8	27.7	9.7	1.3	72.5	36.9	48.8	51.2
13662	MASSENA	95.3	94.3	0.3	0.4	0.5	0.8	1.1	1.5	5.8	5.8	5.9	6.2	5.8	23.5	29.7	14.6	2.8	78.6	42.8	48.0	52.0
13665	NATURAL BRIDGE	96.1	95.1	0.4	0.6	0.5	0.7	1.1	1.3	6.6	7.6	8.4	7.8	3.8	26.4	28.3	10.5	0.7	72.6	38.1	50.3	49.7
13666	NEWTON FALLS	95.3	94.7	0.0	0.0	0.0	0.0	1.5	1.9	3.8	6.9	6.9	8.8	3.1	22.5	30.9	15.3	1.9	76.3	43.7	51.1	48.9
	NEW YORK	67.9	64.8	15.9	16.5	5.6	6.9	15.1	16.7	6.5	6.4	6.4	7.1	7.0	27.0	26.3	11.2	2.1	76.6	37.5	48.4	51.6
	UNITED STATES	75.1	72.0	12.3	12.7	3.8	4.6	12.5	15.7	6.8	6.7	6.6	7.1	6.9	27.0	26.0	10.9	1.9	75.7	36.9	49.2	50.8

#	POST OFFICE NAME	2009 Per Capita Income	2009 HH Income Base	2009 Household Income Distribution (%): Less than $25,000	$25,000 to $49,999	$50,000 to $99,999	$100,000 to $149,999	$150,000 or More	Median Household Income: 2009	2014	2009 National Centile	2009 State Centile	2009 Home Value Base	2009 Home Value Distribution (%): Less than $50,000	$50,000 to $89,999	$90,000 to $174,999	$175,000 to $399,999	$400,000 or More	2009 Median Home Value
13409	MUNNSVILLE	20084	845	24.9	29.9	38.5	4.9	1.9	45710	48807	50	33	655	11.3	20.8	46.3	20.2	1.5	123750
13411	NEW BERLIN	18772	1393	32.2	29.7	30.5	5.6	1.9	37205	38799	24	8	1057	17.1	26.9	43.5	11.4	1.0	99203
13413	NEW HARTFORD	32444	6662	17.1	23.0	38.2	11.8	9.8	61094	63711	79	66	4825	3.4	4.3	42.9	42.7	6.7	173669
13415	NEW LISBON	19345	43	27.9	32.6	32.6	7.0	0.0	39286	45000	31	12	36	8.3	22.2	41.7	25.0	2.8	120833
13416	NEWPORT	19461	906	24.2	29.7	39.2	5.6	1.3	46892	49790	54	36	744	11.2	18.8	43.1	24.2	2.7	133571
13417	NEW YORK MILLS	24062	1574	29.6	29.7	32.7	6.3	1.7	40048	43944	33	15	772	1.6	2.6	69.9	25.0	0.9	143817
13418	NORTH BROOKFIELD	14506	77	28.6	39.0	29.9	2.6	0.0	37740	40903	26	9	64	35.9	23.4	28.1	10.9	1.6	74000
13420	OLD FORGE	24845	476	23.3	33.0	34.0	5.3	4.4	44052	47900	46	27	353	1.7	4.5	27.5	49.0	17.3	215865
13421	ONEIDA	23641	5363	25.4	29.6	34.6	6.9	3.5	46036	48948	51	34	3345	4.2	13.8	52.7	27.7	1.7	137317
13424	ORISKANY	22234	938	19.5	23.7	45.7	9.0	2.1	56467	60592	73	59	713	3.8	8.0	53.9	32.3	2.1	148698
13425	ORISKANY FALLS	21930	823	21.5	30.7	39.7	5.1	2.9	47163	51402	55	38	626	8.6	19.8	49.8	19.6	2.1	123698
13428	PALATINE BRIDGE	20609	709	27.9	31.7	31.7	4.9	3.7	39254	42293	31	12	538	14.7	35.5	36.4	11.7	1.7	89773
13431	POLAND	21370	767	24.1	29.7	35.1	8.9	2.2	46729	49475	53	36	619	9.5	14.2	43.1	30.0	3.1	144716
13433	PORT LEYDEN	16774	628	31.1	34.4	29.6	3.7	1.3	37411	38876	25	8	486	23.7	33.1	35.0	7.2	1.0	80294
13437	REDFIELD	18476	202	25.7	36.1	33.2	5.0	0.0	40965	44012	36	17	159	18.9	27.0	42.8	10.7	0.6	95417
13438	REMSEN	22445	1844	19.1	31.1	40.7	6.6	2.5	49758	53996	60	44	1477	11.0	17.5	44.5	23.9	3.1	131460
13439	RICHFIELD SPRINGS	20540	1674	25.4	31.5	35.5	5.9	1.6	43488	45423	44	25	1293	8.2	18.9	49.4	19.5	3.9	122426
13440	ROME	23260	17321	25.1	26.6	38.0	7.0	3.2	47581	51893	56	40	10913	7.0	15.4	55.8	20.2	1.6	127364
13450	ROSEBOOM	25167	76	21.1	32.9	35.5	6.6	3.9	47336	48186	55	38	60	6.7	10.0	45.0	26.7	11.7	145000
13452	SAINT JOHNSVILLE	18759	1875	29.7	30.9	34.3	3.3	1.8	39593	42947	31	14	1419	17.5	32.6	38.9	9.3	1.7	89862
13454	SALISBURY CENTER	15852	220	29.5	33.2	33.6	2.7	0.9	39147	42364	30	12	185	11.4	28.1	47.6	12.4	0.5	103879
13456	SAUQUOIT	25484	1741	15.0	27.9	41.9	11.1	4.0	57713	61395	75	61	1379	8.8	6.6	40.0	41.1	3.5	164653
13459	SHARON SPRINGS	21031	802	23.1	30.9	39.2	4.6	2.2	45619	48385	50	32	631	5.4	10.8	51.3	26.5	6.0	151185
13460	SHERBURNE	20252	1741	31.4	27.3	33.6	4.8	2.9	39876	42179	32	14	1254	16.6	23.0	45.3	13.6	1.4	105618
13461	SHERRILL	27873	1267	15.5	22.1	46.4	12.2	3.9	62072	64235	80	68	958	0.0	0.7	54.4	43.3	1.6	169302
13464	SMYRNA	16857	523	27.0	35.6	31.4	3.8	2.3	40587	41553	35	16	417	22.1	30.7	36.0	10.3	1.0	86515
13468	SPRINGFIELD CENTER	20735	223	24.2	32.7	35.9	4.9	2.2	45390	46126	49	32	172	5.8	15.7	42.4	27.9	8.1	138750
13469	STITTVILLE	25603	299	11.4	30.4	46.2	9.7	2.3	56556	60082	73	59	250	5.2	8.4	54.4	29.2	2.8	146311
13470	STRATFORD	15627	272	35.3	30.9	30.5	2.2	1.1	35597	37575	20	6	227	22.5	25.6	40.1	11.9	0.0	94500
13471	TABERG	18237	1286	23.4	32.7	39.0	3.7	1.2	43798	48190	45	26	1026	28.4	18.0	36.7	16.6	0.3	97255
13473	TURIN	18094	336	31.5	29.5	32.4	4.2	2.4	38563	40532	28	11	257	10.5	30.0	45.9	10.5	3.1	103186
13475	VAN HORNESVILLE	14167	8	37.5	37.5	25.0	0.0	0.0	30000	32265	8	4	6	33.3	16.7	33.3	16.7	0.0	80000
13476	VERNON	23431	1317	20.7	27.9	42.1	7.2	2.1	51111	54849	64	49	995	10.6	8.7	49.6	27.7	3.3	143390
13477	VERNON CENTER	19570	484	24.4	29.8	39.0	5.0	1.9	45764	49809	51	33	360	16.9	10.0	42.8	25.6	4.7	136413
13478	VERONA	22605	1167	12.5	26.6	55.0	4.9	1.0	58703	60952	76	62	968	5.9	8.1	62.9	22.2	0.9	137275
13480	WATERVILLE	21484	1422	21.4	27.2	41.1	7.2	3.0	51124	55165	64	49	1013	8.2	11.3	52.0	27.1	1.4	137380
13482	WEST BURLINGTON	17792	23	21.7	34.8	39.1	4.3	0.0	46120	50000	52	34	19	5.3	21.1	47.4	26.3	0.0	129167
13483	WESTDALE	18905	93	26.9	28.0	40.9	2.2	2.2	44535	48914	47	29	75	17.3	22.7	42.7	16.0	1.3	106250
13485	WEST EDMESTON	17031	622	28.9	36.2	28.5	4.2	2.3	38582	41000	28	11	514	22.8	29.8	35.6	10.3	1.6	85938
13486	WESTERNVILLE	21320	245	21.6	25.7	43.7	6.5	2.4	51886	54851	66	51	199	13.1	15.6	43.2	24.1	4.0	131855
13488	WESTFORD	20301	51	23.5	33.3	35.3	5.9	2.0	43657	46543	44	25	44	6.8	18.2	50.0	22.7	2.3	130556
13489	WEST LEYDEN	17721	203	25.1	31.0	37.4	4.9	1.5	44694	45000	47	30	170	12.4	27.6	44.7	12.4	2.9	101515
13490	WESTMORELAND	22876	471	10.4	22.9	54.6	10.6	1.5	61918	63170	80	67	406	3.2	8.6	57.1	27.8	3.2	146814
13491	WEST WINFIELD	19485	1528	23.4	34.4	34.8	5.1	2.4	42193	45965	40	21	1212	15.1	19.0	42.7	21.0	2.1	120748
13492	WHITESBORO	27023	4913	17.6	24.9	41.2	11.6	4.7	58604	61447	76	62	3703	2.3	6.5	53.4	36.7	1.0	152589
13493	WILLIAMSTOWN	16837	834	24.9	35.6	34.2	4.8	0.5	41557	44947	38	18	674	19.3	30.4	38.7	11.1	0.4	90526
13494	WOODGATE	22114	148	24.3	34.5	35.8	4.7	0.7	42510	45568	41	22	126	12.7	28.6	33.3	23.8	1.6	119444
13495	YORKVILLE	23676	951	23.7	27.0	42.5	5.4	1.5	48806	53129	58	42	604	0.0	16.9	72.7	9.6	0.8	121894
13501	UTICA	19220	14490	41.9	26.9	23.5	4.8	2.9	30592	33300	9	4	6949	10.9	28.4	44.1	14.9	1.8	105880
13502	UTICA	21015	13555	32.9	27.2	32.9	5.1	1.9	39340	42810	31	13	8088	10.2	18.5	58.6	11.8	0.9	116877
13601	WATERTOWN	20832	15643	32.0	28.3	31.0	6.3	2.4	39714	43997	32	14	8109	6.7	22.4	51.2	17.7	2.0	118396
13602	FORT DRUM	16185	717	2.8	43.5	45.9	6.6	1.3	53092	57167	68	53	0	0.0	0.0	0.0	0.0	0.0	0
13603	WATERTOWN	14816	1801	16.0	45.6	34.8	2.4	1.2	41663	45418	38	19	13	30.8	46.2	0.0	23.1	0.0	78333
13605	ADAMS	21530	2031	23.2	31.5	34.9	7.3	3.1	46050	49110	51	34	1510	8.3	22.5	49.1	17.1	3.0	121279
13606	ADAMS CENTER	22843	1002	21.8	27.7	38.0	9.7	2.8	50464	54004	62	46	771	10.5	16.1	48.2	18.5	6.6	128650
13607	ALEXANDRIA BAY	24316	1060	29.1	24.8	34.2	8.4	3.6	46043	49660	51	34	771	8.4	17.3	45.8	20.1	8.4	130888
13608	ANTWERP	18778	708	26.4	29.2	36.7	5.6	2.0	45000	48078	48	31	535	14.8	30.5	41.3	12.7	0.7	99107
13611	BELLEVILLE	19450	37	29.7	27.0	29.7	8.1	5.4	42393	50651	41	21	27	11.1	25.9	48.1	7.4	7.4	107813
13612	BLACK RIVER	21953	1175	21.7	29.5	39.5	7.3	2.0	48886	51548	59	43	793	10.2	13.6	59.1	16.6	0.4	122952
13613	BRASHER FALLS	20005	982	32.6	30.5	27.7	7.2	1.9	38333	41348	28	10	738	19.6	27.9	44.0	8.1	0.3	93103
13614	BRIER HILL	24443	218	26.6	33.0	31.2	5.5	3.7	45000	46421	48	31	176	17.0	23.3	38.6	17.6	3.4	104167
13616	CALCIUM	16823	714	20.4	36.4	35.6	6.4	1.1	45000	47423	48	31	390	14.1	13.6	51.5	20.8	0.0	119079
13617	CANTON	21439	3409	23.5	27.2	37.2	9.7	2.4	49345	51406	60	43	2304	13.3	18.5	45.1	21.7	1.4	117007
13618	CAPE VINCENT	23524	811	24.5	30.0	36.6	6.2	2.7	45499	49107	50	32	639	7.2	18.8	42.6	26.4	5.0	132982
13619	CARTHAGE	18280	4439	32.6	26.8	33.7	5.1	1.8	40135	43739	33	15	2745	9.9	22.7	51.1	14.0	2.2	112636
13620	CASTORLAND	17258	800	26.6	30.9	37.3	4.0	1.3	44069	45000	46	27	615	6.5	21.0	55.9	14.3	2.3	116515
13621	CHASE MILLS	20954	252	25.8	28.2	36.9	6.7	2.4	46063	49141	52	34	201	11.9	30.3	34.8	20.9	2.0	106250
13622	CHAUMONT	21017	1043	23.0	30.5	38.4	5.9	2.2	46875	50217	54	36	820	6.8	18.4	49.1	22.8	2.8	127022
13624	CLAYTON	21046	2056	22.1	30.2	37.7	8.0	2.0	47569	51224	56	39	1516	6.4	14.9	49.4	22.4	6.9	133981
13625	COLTON	22471	937	21.8	29.3	40.2	7.0	1.6	48921	50713	59	43	771	13.2	20.9	41.5	20.8	3.6	125825
13626	COPENHAGEN	19243	798	25.1	26.7	41.0	6.0	1.3	48254	49759	57	41	608	8.4	21.9	48.0	18.3	3.5	115038
13630	DE KALB JUNCTION	17179	496	28.0	33.5	32.9	4.6	1.0	40698	44117	35	16	379	18.5	34.8	36.7	10.0	0.0	84792
13633	DE PEYSTER	14437	70	31.4	34.3	28.6	2.9	2.9	37833	40000	26	9	58	15.5	32.8	39.7	12.1	0.0	92500
13634	DEXTER	19499	1611	26.1	27.5	38.7	6.3	1.4	47044	49661	54	37	1215	5.7	16.0	55.7	20.7	1.8	125205
13635	EDWARDS	16067	423	35.0	33.3	27.4	3.1	1.2	37173	39747	24	8	321	26.8	35.2	34.3	2.8	0.9	76250
13636	ELLISBURG	19590	114	28.1	25.4	32.5	6.1	7.9	45924	50266	51	33	86	11.6	29.1	43.0	11.6	4.7	105000
13637	EVANS MILLS	17301	1524	20.9	37.3	35.7	4.9	1.3	42449	46224	41	21	706	5.8	20.4	54.4	19.4	0.0	119760
13638	FELTS MILLS	18715	121	23.1	36.4	34.7	5.0	0.8	42354	46844	40	21	82	12.2	19.5	62.2	6.1	0.0	110227
13639	FINE	17625	91	26.4	33.0	37.4	2.2	1.1	43379	46119	43	24	76	27.6	46.1	21.1	3.9	1.3	67500
13640	WELLESLEY ISLAND	28357	182	28.0	24.7	34.1	8.8	4.4	47097	50204	54	37	130	6.2	6.9	50.0	24.6	12.3	147727
13642	GOUVERNEUR	16988	3565	32.9	32.3	30.2	3.4	1.2	37309	40063	24	8	2393	13.8	35.0	41.1	9.3	0.8	91695
13646	HAMMOND	16975	1132	35.2	34.5	25.5	3.9	0.9	34916	36998	17	6	877	15.3	27.0	39.8	14.9	3.0	104076
13648	HARRISVILLE	18601	873	28.4	33.2	32.2	4.9	1.3	39580	41884	31	14	721	18.9	32.3	39.1	8.6	1.1	88396
13650	HENDERSON	23492	629	24.0	32.9	33.1	5.6	4.5	44581	47701	47	29	501	7.4	24.4	42.7	18.6	7.0	121948
13652	HERMON	17388	767	26.1	33.8	35.6	4.3	0.3	42430	45660	41	21	621	19.5	30.8	38.5	10.5	0.8	89595
13654	HEUVELTON	16188	823	30.9	33.0	30.1	4.3	1.7	38842	41722	29	11	631	14.9	28.5	45.3	10.9	0.3	99022
13655	HOGANSBURG	16887	1045	29.3	26.2	37.8	5.4	1.3	44333	46109	46	28	678	2.5	3.1	63.9	30.2	0.3	143208
13656	LA FARGEVILLE	17699	946	26.0	31.3	36.8	4.8	1.2	43318	46929	43	24	729	10.6	25.8	46.5	14.7	2.5	114803
13658	LISBON	18319	916	24.7	34.8	33.7	5.7	1.1	42830	45032	42	22	731	16.4	17.8	43.6	18.9	3.3	114478
13659	LORRAINE	20937	217	23.5	30.0	38.2	5.5	2.8	46979	49446	54	37	180	14.4	28.9	34.4	20.6	1.7	105952
13660	MADRID	17875	712	28.5	27.9	37.9	4.5	1.1	43780	46880	45	26	549	13.7	30.8	40.3	13.8	1.5	97625
13661	MANNSVILLE	20606	637	24.6	25.7	39.2	6.6	3.8	49584	52216	60	44	505	11.7	32.5	41.2	13.1	1.6	99516
13662	MASSENA	21925	6920	30.4	26.7	34.0	6.4	2.5	42106	45920	40	20	4565	6.1	17.2	56.8	17.7	2.2	123558
13665	NATURAL BRIDGE	17375	278	29.1	32.4	34.9	3.2	0.4	37901	39896	26	9	219	24.2	30.1	39.3	6.4	0.0	78846
13666	NEWTON FALLS	18302	102	31.4	31.4	32.4	4.9	0.0	41715	44646	38	19	80	31.3	33.8	22.5	8.8	3.8	68571
	NEW YORK	29893		21.9	21.3	32.7	14.0	9.9	58747	62337				3.4	5.7	23.0	38.7	29.1	269816
	UNITED STATES	27277		20.9	24.4	35.3	11.7	7.6	54719	56938				9.3	13.1	31.6	32.6	13.5	162279

ZIP CODE #	POST OFFICE NAME	FINANCIAL SERVICES: Auto Loan	Home Loan	Investments	Retirement Plans	THE HOME: Home Improvements: Home Repair	Lawn & Garden	Furnishings: Computers & Hardware Personal	Major Appliances	TV, Radio, Sound Equipment	Furniture	ENTERTAINMENT: Dine out/ Carry out	Sports Equipment	Fees & Tickets	Toys & Games	Travel	Cable TV	PERSONAL: Apparel & Services	Auto Repairs	Health Insurance	Pets & Supplies
13409	MUNNSVILLE	83	75	77	78	77	89	74	84	77	67	75	64	68	78	74	81	51	78	87	98
13411	NEW BERLIN	84	60	84	59	62	86	63	79	70	58	69	59	51	70	62	77	46	73	84	94
13413	NEW HARTFORD	104	112	119	112	115	121	104	112	108	106	107	81	111	104	112	112	74	109	122	129
13415	NEW LISBON	79	61	96	60	66	82	62	78	65	58	65	58	52	63	65	70	43	72	78	91
13416	NEWPORT	82	72	76	74	73	87	71	82	74	65	73	62	64	75	71	79	49	75	85	95
13417	NEW YORK MILLS	66	63	64	64	64	70	68	67	71	65	70	49	67	68	67	74	48	69	77	79
13418	NORTH BROOKFIELD	75	54	77	52	56	76	55	70	61	51	60	52	44	61	54	67	40	64	73	83
13420	OLD FORGE	90	72	116	71	79	95	72	92	76	68	75	67	63	72	78	81	50	85	91	106
13421	ONEIDA	81	75	73	77	75	83	81	81	83	75	82	61	77	83	77	87	57	82	88	96
13424	ORISKANY	78	91	84	90	90	95	79	86	83	79	83	62	88	83	87	87	58	83	95	99
13425	ORISKANY FALLS	81	78	69	80	75	86	78	80	79	73	79	62	75	81	76	82	54	79	86	96
13428	PALATINE BRIDGE	95	68	97	66	70	96	70	89	77	65	76	67	56	77	69	85	50	81	92	105
13431	POLAND	86	79	78	82	81	92	78	87	80	71	79	66	72	82	78	84	54	81	89	101
13433	PORT LEYDEN	78	56	74	55	57	77	58	71	64	55	63	54	47	65	55	71	42	66	74	85
13437	REDFIELD	81	60	69	59	60	78	62	72	68	59	66	55	50	70	57	74	45	68	76	87
13438	REMSEN	84	82	78	83	80	90	79	84	81	76	81	64	78	82	79	84	55	81	88	99
13439	RICHFIELD SPRINGS	86	66	95	64	69	90	68	85	74	62	72	63	57	72	69	80	48	78	88	99
13440	ROME	77	76	72	76	75	81	78	78	81	75	80	58	77	80	77	84	56	79	86	92
13450	ROSEBOOM	102	82	132	81	90	108	82	104	86	77	85	76	71	82	89	92	56	96	103	121
13452	SAINT JOHNSVILLE	80	57	75	56	59	80	61	74	68	57	66	56	49	69	58	75	44	69	80	88
13454	SALISBURY CENTER	79	56	65	55	56	75	59	68	65	57	64	53	47	68	53	71	43	65	72	83
13456	SAUQUOIT	88	102	93	103	100	103	90	95	91	90	91	71	99	92	97	93	64	92	99	110
13459	SHARON SPRINGS	90	73	87	74	75	94	74	88	79	67	77	66	64	79	73	85	52	81	91	103
13460	SHERBURNE	82	65	80	65	68	84	68	79	73	64	71	59	59	72	67	78	48	75	83	93
13461	SHERRILL	92	100	95	100	99	104	93	97	95	92	95	72	98	95	98	97	66	95	103	113
13464	SMYRNA	81	65	74	65	66	83	65	77	70	61	69	58	56	71	64	75	46	71	80	91
13468	SPRINGFIELD CENTER	86	69	111	68	75	91	69	87	72	64	71	64	60	68	74	77	47	81	86	101
13469	STITTVILLE	97	95	88	95	94	102	89	96	91	87	91	72	87	94	90	95	62	92	99	113
13470	STRATFORD	74	53	73	51	55	74	55	68	61	51	59	51	44	61	53	67	39	63	71	81
13471	TABERG	90	64	74	63	64	85	67	78	74	65	73	60	54	77	61	81	49	74	82	95
13473	TURIN	79	64	78	65	66	83	65	77	69	58	67	59	55	69	65	74	45	72	80	92
13475	VAN HORNESVILLE	58	41	47	40	41	55	43	50	48	42	47	38	34	50	39	52	31	47	53	61
13476	VERNON	86	79	79	82	81	90	80	86	82	75	80	65	75	82	79	85	55	82	90	101
13477	VERNON CENTER	80	73	73	76	75	86	72	82	74	65	73	62	67	76	72	79	50	75	84	95
13478	VERONA	87	84	82	86	85	96	80	90	83	74	82	67	77	84	82	88	56	84	95	104
13480	WATERVILLE	88	79	79	79	80	89	80	86	83	77	82	64	74	84	78	87	56	83	90	101
13482	WEST BURLINGTON	79	72	71	75	73	85	71	80	73	64	72	61	65	75	71	78	49	74	83	93
13483	WESTDALE	85	65	71	64	65	83	66	77	72	63	71	59	55	75	62	78	48	72	80	92
13485	WEST EDMESTON	83	59	85	58	62	84	61	78	68	57	66	58	49	67	60	74	44	71	81	92
13486	WESTERNVILLE	91	81	95	80	81	99	77	91	82	74	82	68	72	82	80	88	55	85	95	107
13488	WESTFORD	88	70	113	69	77	93	70	89	73	66	73	65	61	70	76	78	48	82	88	103
13489	WEST LEYDEN	76	69	69	72	71	82	68	77	70	62	69	58	63	72	68	75	47	71	79	90
13490	WESTMORELAND	89	98	85	101	95	98	88	93	87	88	88	72	93	89	93	88	61	89	92	109
13491	WEST WINFIELD	90	66	92	65	69	92	68	85	75	63	73	64	55	74	67	82	49	78	88	101
13492	WHITESBORO	86	94	89	94	93	99	88	92	91	87	91	67	94	90	92	95	63	91	101	107
13493	WILLIAMSTOWN	83	62	69	60	61	79	63	73	70	62	69	56	52	73	58	75	46	69	76	88
13494	WOODGATE	82	66	107	65	73	87	66	84	69	62	68	61	57	66	72	74	45	77	83	97
13495	YORKVILLE	70	75	64	75	71	79	72	72	75	69	74	55	75	74	73	77	51	73	82	86
13501	UTICA	61	55	54	56	54	61	63	60	67	59	66	45	60	65	59	70	46	64	69	72
13502	UTICA	64	63	58	63	61	67	66	64	69	63	69	49	66	68	64	72	48	67	72	77
13601	WATERTOWN	71	63	60	65	62	67	72	68	73	68	73	53	67	73	67	75	51	71	73	82
13602	FORT DRUM	103	54	40	62	48	46	97	67	91	90	96	67	74	110	70	84	67	86	61	82
13603	WATERTOWN	85	44	33	51	40	38	80	56	75	75	79	55	61	91	58	69	56	71	50	68
13605	ADAMS	86	75	83	75	77	86	76	83	78	74	78	61	70	78	75	82	53	80	86	98
13606	ADAMS CENTER	96	87	82	86	87	92	85	90	88	87	88	66	80	90	82	91	60	88	92	107
13607	ALEXANDRIA BAY	86	71	98	71	76	89	73	86	76	69	75	63	65	74	75	81	51	82	88	101
13608	ANTWERP	87	69	85	68	69	90	70	83	76	65	74	63	60	76	69	82	50	78	87	99
13611	BELLEVILLE	106	73	117	73	76	112	81	101	84	66	83	83	59	83	81	92	54	94	106	124
13612	BLACK RIVER	86	78	73	77	78	83	78	81	80	78	80	60	73	82	75	83	55	80	84	96
13613	BRASHER FALLS	84	61	85	59	63	86	64	80	71	59	69	60	52	70	63	78	46	74	84	95
13614	BRIER HILL	94	75	119	73	82	99	75	95	79	70	78	70	64	75	81	84	52	88	94	111
13616	CALCIUM	78	67	58	68	63	61	77	68	75	78	76	56	71	78	69	72	53	73	65	82
13617	CANTON	84	75	80	75	76	85	79	82	81	76	81	61	74	80	77	85	55	82	88	97
13618	CAPE VINCENT	88	70	113	69	77	93	70	89	73	66	73	65	61	70	76	78	48	82	88	103
13619	CARTHAGE	73	62	66	62	61	72	66	69	69	63	68	53	59	69	63	72	46	69	74	83
13620	CASTORLAND	75	67	67	69	68	78	66	74	68	61	68	56	61	70	66	72	46	69	76	87
13621	CHASE MILLS	84	70	79	72	72	88	71	82	75	66	74	62	63	76	70	80	50	77	86	97
13622	CHAUMONT	88	73	104	72	78	91	72	88	75	69	75	64	64	73	76	79	50	82	87	102
13624	CLAYTON	86	75	84	74	77	85	75	83	78	74	77	61	69	78	75	81	52	80	85	98
13625	COLTON	89	74	104	72	78	92	73	89	76	70	76	65	65	74	76	81	51	83	88	103
13626	COPENHAGEN	81	76	68	74	74	78	72	76	74	74	74	56	69	76	69	76	50	73	76	90
13630	DE KALB JUNCTION	80	58	82	57	61	82	61	76	66	56	65	58	49	66	60	72	43	70	79	90
13633	DE PEYSTER	82	57	88	56	59	85	62	77	65	52	65	62	46	64	61	72	42	72	81	94
13634	DEXTER	80	72	70	73	73	82	71	78	74	68	73	58	66	75	70	77	50	74	80	91
13635	EDWARDS	75	54	77	52	56	76	55	70	61	52	60	53	44	61	55	68	40	65	73	84
13636	ELLISBURG	102	75	107	74	77	106	80	97	83	69	83	78	62	83	79	90	54	91	101	118
13637	EVANS MILLS	76	67	58	67	64	64	71	67	71	72	71	53	66	74	65	70	49	69	66	81
13638	FELTS MILLS	76	70	62	68	69	72	66	70	69	69	69	51	63	72	63	71	47	68	70	83
13639	FINE	86	62	89	60	64	88	63	81	70	59	69	61	51	70	63	77	46	74	84	96
13640	WELLESLEY ISLAND	90	74	105	74	80	93	76	90	79	72	78	66	67	76	79	84	52	85	92	105
13642	GOUVERNEUR	68	56	60	56	55	66	61	64	64	57	63	49	54	65	57	68	43	64	68	77
13646	HAMMOND	73	54	79	52	56	75	55	70	60	51	59	52	45	59	55	66	39	64	72	82
13648	HARRISVILLE	81	62	81	61	64	84	63	77	68	58	67	58	52	68	62	74	45	71	81	92
13650	HENDERSON	93	72	116	71	78	98	74	93	77	67	76	70	61	74	78	83	50	86	94	110
13652	HERMON	81	59	82	58	62	82	61	76	67	57	66	57	50	67	60	73	44	70	79	90
13654	HEUVELTON	83	59	86	57	61	85	62	78	67	55	66	60	48	67	61	74	44	72	81	94
13655	HOGANSBURG	68	71	65	66	70	63	70	69	67	71	68	52	69	68	69	65	48	69	64	78
13656	LA FARGEVILLE	81	71	71	68	70	78	68	75	72	69	71	55	62	74	65	75	48	72	76	89
13658	LISBON	87	63	95	62	66	90	67	83	71	58	70	65	52	70	67	77	46	77	86	100
13659	LORRAINE	85	78	70	76	77	82	74	79	77	75	77	58	70	80	71	79	52	76	80	94
13660	MADRID	85	62	87	60	64	87	64	80	70	60	69	60	52	70	63	77	46	74	83	95
13661	MANNSVILLE	92	79	82	76	78	89	77	85	80	76	80	64	69	82	74	84	54	82	87	102
13662	MASSENA	76	69	71	70	69	80	72	76	74	67	73	57	67	74	70	78	50	74	82	90
13665	NATURAL BRIDGE	80	57	82	55	59	81	59	75	65	55	64	56	47	65	58	72	42	68	78	89
13666	NEWTON FALLS	79	58	82	56	60	83	62	77	69	56	67	57	50	68	61	76	44	72	83	90
	NEW YORK	100	106	110	108	107	104	112	106	113	106	114	81	115	110	112	116	83	110	110	124
	UNITED STATES	100	100	100	100	100	100	100	100	100	100	100	100	100	100	100	100	100	100	100	100

#	POST OFFICE NAME	COUNTY FIPS CODE	POPULATION 2000	POPULATION 2009	POPULATION 2014	2000-2009 ANNUAL RATE % Rate	2000-2009 ANNUAL RATE State Centile	HOUSEHOLDS 2000	HOUSEHOLDS 2009	HOUSEHOLDS 2014	HOUSEHOLDS % Annual Rate 2000-2009	HOUSEHOLDS 2009 Average HH Size	FAMILIES 2000	FAMILIES 2009	FAMILIES % Annual Rate 2000-2009
13667	NORFOLK	089	3459	3557	3555	0.3	59	1382	1452	1463	0.5	2.44	970	1002	0.4
13668	NORWOOD	089	3601	3489	3429	-0.3	15	1405	1395	1383	-0.1	2.47	993	971	-0.2
13669	OGDENSBURG	089	17687	17119	16832	-0.4	11	6100	5973	5901	-0.2	2.41	3976	3821	-0.4
13670	OSWEGATCHIE	089	487	472	464	-0.3	15	205	203	201	-0.1	2.24	144	140	-0.3
13672	PARISHVILLE	089	346	366	369	0.6	76	145	158	161	0.9	2.32	105	112	0.7
13673	PHILADELPHIA	045	2369	2690	2835	1.4	95	836	971	1031	1.6	2.77	639	733	1.5
13675	PLESSIS	045	86	102	109	1.9	98	35	43	46	2.3	2.37	27	32	1.9
13676	POTSDAM	089	15138	14835	14694	-0.2	21	5269	5307	5283	0.1	2.29	2974	2944	-0.1
13679	REDWOOD	045	1660	1911	2019	1.5	96	632	745	794	1.8	2.56	442	511	1.6
13680	RENSSELAER FALLS	089	1218	1234	1229	0.1	44	413	428	430	0.4	2.83	305	311	0.2
13681	RICHVILLE	089	806	827	825	0.3	59	295	310	312	0.5	2.65	218	226	0.4
13682	RODMAN	045	892	987	1029	1.1	91	303	339	355	1.2	2.67	242	267	1.1
13684	RUSSELL	089	1018	1058	1060	0.4	66	389	414	418	0.7	2.55	283	297	0.5
13685	SACKETS HARBOR	045	2126	2417	2540	1.4	95	943	1101	1170	1.7	2.19	597	681	1.4
13687	SOUTH COLTON	089	479	479	477	0.0	38	188	193	193	0.3	2.48	128	129	0.1
13690	STAR LAKE	089	866	826	809	-0.5	7	363	354	350	-0.3	2.30	238	227	-0.5
13691	THERESA	045	2735	3235	3452	1.8	98	964	1167	1256	2.1	2.77	714	850	1.9
13693	THREE MILE BAY	045	267	287	298	0.8	84	121	133	139	1.0	2.15	84	90	0.7
13694	WADDINGTON	089	1453	1448	1433	0.0	38	607	619	619	0.2	2.31	402	402	0.0
13695	WANAKENA	089	191	186	183	-0.3	15	74	73	73	-0.1	2.38	48	47	-0.2
13696	WEST STOCKHOLM	089	185	174	170	-0.7	3	75	72	71	-0.4	2.42	55	52	-0.6
13697	WINTHROP	089	2274	2358	2358	0.4	66	882	938	948	0.7	2.51	635	663	0.5
13699	POTSDAM	089	1370	1604	1601	1.7	97	53	51	50	-0.4	3.02	10	9	-1.1
13730	AFTON	017	2925	2998	3020	0.3	59	1168	1231	1251	0.6	2.43	822	851	0.4
13731	ANDES	025	1198	1147	1113	-0.5	7	532	525	515	-0.1	2.18	337	327	-0.3
13732	APALACHIN	107	8273	8002	7857	-0.4	11	2980	2950	2923	-0.1	2.71	2395	2343	-0.2
13733	BAINBRIDGE	017	5333	5454	5472	0.2	52	2093	2195	2221	0.5	2.48	1461	1504	0.3
13734	BARTON	107	2505	2607	2607	0.4	66	889	945	953	0.7	2.76	666	698	0.5
13736	BERKSHIRE	107	2498	2552	2554	0.2	52	925	970	978	0.5	2.63	681	703	0.3
13739	BLOOMVILLE	025	1102	1094	1073	-0.1	30	416	422	416	0.2	2.43	293	292	0.0
13740	BOVINA CENTER	025	568	553	539	-0.3	15	233	231	227	-0.1	2.39	162	160	-0.1
13743	CANDOR	107	4335	4360	4328	0.1	44	1656	1710	1712	0.3	2.55	1197	1216	0.2
13744	CASTLE CREEK	007	1417	1410	1401	-0.1	30	552	567	568	0.3	2.49	405	408	0.1
13746	CHENANGO FORKS	007	3000	2988	2968	0.0	38	1150	1176	1177	0.2	2.54	844	849	0.1
13748	CONKLIN	007	4030	3880	3814	-0.4	11	1519	1502	1488	-0.1	2.58	1129	1096	-0.3
13750	DAVENPORT	025	891	882	863	-0.1	30	350	357	353	0.2	2.47	241	243	0.1
13751	DAVENPORT CENTER	025	173	166	161	-0.4	11	66	65	64	-0.2	2.55	46	45	-0.2
13752	DELANCEY	025	889	822	788	-0.8	2	386	366	354	-0.6	2.21	252	235	-0.8
13753	DELHI	025	5259	5202	5091	-0.1	30	1718	1709	1678	-0.1	2.30	1107	1083	-0.2
13754	DEPOSIT	007	3422	3430	3390	0.0	38	1387	1437	1436	0.4	2.39	930	944	0.2
13755	DOWNSVILLE	025	1169	1152	1130	-0.2	21	490	492	487	0.0	2.30	324	320	-0.1
13756	EAST BRANCH	025	747	731	713	-0.2	21	288	289	284	0.0	2.53	199	196	-0.2
13757	EAST MEREDITH	025	1268	1330	1320	0.5	71	504	544	546	0.8	2.44	358	381	0.7
13760	ENDICOTT	007	44508	43069	42359	-0.4	11	18891	18706	18540	-0.1	2.27	12066	11734	-0.3
13775	FRANKLIN	025	1807	1727	1674	-0.5	7	708	694	678	-0.2	2.48	494	475	-0.4
13776	GILBERTSVILLE	077	437	466	465	0.7	80	194	211	212	0.9	2.20	136	145	0.7
13777	GLEN AUBREY	007	421	430	430	0.2	52	153	161	162	0.6	2.67	116	121	0.5
13778	GREENE	017	5646	5613	5557	-0.1	30	2242	2281	2277	0.2	2.45	1538	1536	0.0
13780	GUILFORD	017	931	991	1011	0.7	80	370	405	417	1.0	2.25	263	282	0.8
13782	HAMDEN	025	843	807	783	-0.5	7	364	359	351	-0.1	2.24	245	237	-0.4
13783	HANCOCK	025	2611	2541	2480	-0.3	15	1085	1091	1075	0.1	2.33	699	690	-0.1
13786	HARPERSFIELD	025	218	212	206	-0.3	15	80	80	79	0.0	2.63	60	59	-0.2
13787	HARPURSVILLE	007	3734	3733	3716	0.0	38	1332	1372	1378	0.3	2.72	994	1008	0.2
13788	HOBART	025	696	666	647	-0.5	7	276	271	264	-0.2	2.32	200	193	-0.4
13790	JOHNSON CITY	007	19042	18353	18027	-0.4	11	8321	8178	8088	-0.2	2.15	4563	4374	-0.5
13795	KIRKWOOD	007	3761	3652	3604	-0.3	15	1471	1471	1466	0.0	2.48	1063	1043	-0.2
13796	LAURENS	077	1198	1267	1267	0.6	76	473	512	515	0.9	2.47	343	364	0.6
13797	LISLE	007	2513	2585	2579	0.3	59	890	939	946	0.6	2.75	665	691	0.4
13801	MC DONOUGH	017	1267	1368	1402	0.8	84	498	552	572	1.1	2.46	360	393	1.0
13802	MAINE	007	692	692	689	0.0	38	262	269	270	0.3	2.57	201	203	0.1
13803	MARATHON	023	4080	4098	4063	0.0	38	1492	1538	1540	0.3	2.66	1111	1127	0.2
13804	MASONVILLE	025	324	309	301	-0.5	7	113	111	109	-0.2	2.66	85	83	-0.3
13806	MERIDALE	025	33	38	39	1.5	96	18	22	22	2.2	1.73	13	15	1.6
13807	MILFORD	077	1676	1708	1686	0.2	52	635	656	651	0.4	2.57	445	449	0.1
13808	MORRIS	077	1698	1801	1797	0.6	76	678	728	731	0.8	2.47	485	510	0.5
13809	MOUNT UPTON	017	1785	1897	1925	0.7	80	692	754	772	0.9	2.52	487	520	0.7
13810	MOUNT VISION	077	1272	1382	1387	0.9	87	495	550	557	1.1	2.51	354	385	0.9
13811	NEWARK VALLEY	107	4328	4300	4258	-0.1	30	1583	1618	1615	0.2	2.62	1195	1205	0.1
13812	NICHOLS	107	2379	2420	2408	0.2	52	891	932	935	0.5	2.60	664	686	0.4
13813	NINEVEH	007	733	719	711	-0.2	21	276	277	276	0.0	2.57	206	203	-0.2
13815	NORWICH	017	14306	14174	14062	-0.1	30	5844	5887	5881	0.1	2.29	3644	3611	-0.1
13820	ONEONTA	077	20975	21631	21304	0.3	59	7335	7403	7301	0.1	2.22	3974	3929	-0.1
13825	OTEGO	077	3683	3676	3614	0.0	38	1438	1461	1444	0.2	2.47	1021	1017	0.0
13826	OUAQUAGA	007	217	222	221	0.2	52	83	87	88	0.5	2.55	62	64	0.3
13827	OWEGO	107	11640	11204	10999	-0.4	11	4644	4586	4538	-0.1	2.41	3205	3117	-0.3
13830	OXFORD	017	5070	5207	5231	0.3	59	1841	1935	1959	0.5	2.57	1320	1364	0.4
13832	PLYMOUTH	017	397	416	421	0.5	71	136	146	149	0.8	2.85	101	107	0.6
13833	PORT CRANE	007	4648	4450	4380	-0.5	7	1751	1727	1713	-0.1	2.58	1283	1245	-0.3
13834	PORTLANDVILLE	077	141	141	139	0.0	38	60	61	61	0.2	2.31	38	38	0.0
13835	RICHFORD	107	1276	1324	1325	0.4	66	476	507	512	0.7	2.61	348	365	0.5
13838	SIDNEY	025	4421	4143	3988	-0.7	3	1887	1810	1757	-0.4	2.24	1157	1085	-0.7
13839	SIDNEY CENTER	025	1549	1494	1451	-0.4	11	599	595	584	-0.1	2.49	439	429	-0.2
13841	SMITHVILLE FLATS	017	389	402	405	0.4	66	138	146	149	0.6	2.72	105	110	0.5
13842	SOUTH KORTRIGHT	025	336	326	317	-0.3	15	82	81	79	-0.1	3.41	57	55	-0.4
13843	SOUTH NEW BERLIN	077	1937	2086	2106	0.8	84	738	809	824	1.0	2.57	539	580	0.8
13844	SOUTH PLYMOUTH	017	878	949	970	0.8	84	237	259	267	1.0	3.23	174	187	0.8
13846	TREADWELL	025	247	238	232	-0.4	11	104	104	102	0.0	2.29	75	74	-0.1
13849	UNADILLA	025	5235	5310	5244	0.2	52	2087	2165	2153	0.4	2.44	1477	1501	0.2
13850	VESTAL	007	26617	26793	26480	0.1	44	8547	8545	8497	0.0	2.38	5948	5834	-0.2
13856	WALTON	025	6515	6756	6707	0.4	66	2750	2942	2949	0.7	2.28	1819	1909	0.5
13859	WELLS BRIDGE	077	206	204	201	-0.1	30	83	84	83	0.1	2.43	59	58	-0.2
13861	WEST ONEONTA	077	673	663	649	-0.2	21	263	264	260	0.0	2.49	180	177	-0.2
13862	WHITNEY POINT	007	4598	4799	4809	0.5	71	1673	1801	1823	0.8	2.66	1229	1301	0.6
13863	WILLET	023	471	469	464	0.0	38	176	180	180	0.2	2.61	134	135	0.1
13864	WILLSEYVILLE	107	1144	1189	1211	0.4	66	469	501	515	0.7	2.37	320	336	0.5
	NEW YORK					0.3					0.3	2.61			0.1
	UNITED STATES					1.0					1.1	2.59			0.9

ZIP CODE #	POST OFFICE NAME	RACE (%) White 2000	White 2009	Black 2000	Black 2009	Asian/Pacific 2000	Asian/Pacific 2009	% Hispanic Origin 2000	% Hispanic Origin 2009	2009 AGE DISTRIBUTION (%) 0-4	5-9	10-14	15-19	20-24	25-44	45-64	65-84	85+	18+	MEDIAN AGE 2009	% 2009 Males	% 2009 Females
13667	NORFOLK	96.8	96.0	0.4	0.6	0.8	1.1	0.7	1.0	6.0	6.2	6.5	6.0	5.3	24.7	29.8	13.7	1.8	77.5	41.6	49.8	50.2
13668	NORWOOD	98.3	97.7	0.3	0.4	0.4	0.7	0.5	0.7	5.5	5.5	5.9	6.8	6.2	25.3	30.6	12.8	1.5	78.8	41.2	49.0	51.0
13669	OGDENSBURG	89.1	87.7	7.0	7.6	0.6	0.8	4.5	5.2	5.0	4.9	5.1	6.2	7.5	30.4	26.6	11.7	2.6	81.1	39.0	54.3	45.7
13670	OSWEGATCHIE	97.5	96.8	0.6	0.8	0.4	0.4	0.0	0.0	4.2	5.1	5.9	6.4	5.5	22.0	32.8	16.3	1.7	80.5	45.5	50.0	50.0
13672	PARISHVILLE	98.8	98.4	0.3	0.5	0.3	0.3	0.3	0.3	4.4	5.5	6.3	7.7	4.1	19.9	32.8	18.3	1.1	78.7	46.3	50.5	49.5
13673	PHILADELPHIA	89.8	87.0	4.5	5.4	1.2	1.7	3.8	4.9	9.3	7.9	7.3	7.9	9.5	29.1	20.7	7.1	1.1	70.9	29.2	48.8	51.2
13675	PLESSIS	98.8	97.1	1.2	1.0	0.0	0.0	1.2	1.0	7.8	6.9	6.9	6.9	3.9	29.4	28.4	8.8	1.0	73.5	37.5	51.0	49.0
13676	POTSDAM	94.7	92.9	1.4	1.7	2.3	3.1	1.2	1.9	4.6	4.8	5.1	13.3	19.3	20.3	21.5	9.2	1.9	82.4	27.5	49.3	50.7
13679	REDWOOD	98.3	97.6	0.5	0.7	0.1	0.1	1.0	1.3	5.7	6.8	6.8	6.7	5.5	25.0	30.4	11.4	1.7	76.5	40.3	50.2	49.8
13680	RENSSELAER FALLS	97.5	96.5	0.6	0.7	0.2	0.4	0.8	1.1	7.1	7.2	7.5	8.3	6.6	24.8	26.5	10.5	1.5	72.9	35.9	50.5	49.5
13681	RICHVILLE	98.1	97.6	0.5	0.7	0.2	0.4	0.4	0.5	6.8	7.6	8.1	7.9	5.4	24.3	28.1	10.6	1.2	72.3	36.9	50.7	49.3
13682	RODMAN	90.9	89.7	5.7	6.2	0.2	0.3	3.8	4.4	5.2	6.4	7.1	8.0	6.3	30.2	28.3	7.6	1.0	75.9	37.4	56.1	43.9
13684	RUSSELL	98.6	98.2	0.2	0.3	0.2	0.3	0.3	0.6	6.1	6.8	7.4	7.1	4.7	24.5	30.9	11.4	1.0	75.0	40.2	48.8	51.2
13685	SACKETS HARBOR	97.3	96.3	0.4	0.5	0.4	0.6	1.4	1.8	5.5	5.8	5.2	6.9	6.9	30.3	26.9	11.3	1.2	79.1	37.3	52.5	47.5
13687	SOUTH COLTON	99.2	99.0	0.0	0.0	0.0	0.0	0.8	1.3	4.8	4.8	5.2	5.6	3.8	20.7	34.2	19.2	1.7	81.0	47.9	51.8	48.2
13690	STAR LAKE	96.4	95.8	0.6	0.7	0.3	0.5	1.0	1.3	4.5	5.7	6.4	7.1	4.5	22.6	31.8	15.1	2.2	78.7	44.4	49.4	50.6
13691	THERESA	97.4	96.5	1.2	1.5	0.3	0.5	0.8	1.1	6.6	7.4	7.3	7.4	5.8	28.3	28.0	8.4	0.8	74.0	36.7	51.7	48.3
13693	THREE MILE BAY	98.1	97.6	0.4	0.3	0.4	0.7	0.4	0.7	4.2	4.2	4.5	5.2	4.2	19.5	36.9	19.2	2.1	83.3	49.9	48.8	51.2
13694	WADDINGTON	98.3	97.8	0.2	0.3	0.3	0.4	0.3	0.6	5.2	5.5	5.9	5.4	5.0	24.1	31.0	15.5	2.2	79.5	44.0	48.7	51.3
13695	WANAKENA	97.9	97.3	1.1	1.6	0.0	0.0	0.0	0.0	2.7	3.8	6.5	8.1	7.0	21.0	33.3	16.1	1.6	81.2	45.6	52.2	47.8
13696	WEST STOCKHOLM	97.8	97.1	0.5	0.6	0.0	0.0	0.5	0.6	5.2	5.7	6.3	8.0	5.2	25.3	31.6	11.5	1.1	77.6	40.8	46.6	53.4
13697	WINTHROP	97.9	97.2	0.3	0.4	0.2	0.3	0.5	0.8	6.3	6.6	6.7	7.1	5.6	25.9	28.8	11.5	1.4	76.1	39.1	50.2	49.8
13699	POTSDAM	91.1	88.2	2.9	3.7	3.4	4.8	1.5	2.0	0.3	0.1	0.1	46.0	50.3	2.4	0.7	0.1	0.0	98.1	20.4	72.6	27.4
13730	AFTON	98.7	98.4	0.2	0.2	0.1	0.1	1.0	1.2	4.8	6.1	7.0	7.7	5.2	23.4	30.5	13.5	1.8	77.0	42.1	50.6	49.4
13731	ANDES	96.7	96.0	0.5	0.6	0.6	0.7	2.0	2.4	4.0	5.2	4.5	4.4	4.3	18.6	36.4	20.2	2.4	83.6	51.3	51.6	48.4
13732	APALACHIN	96.9	96.0	0.6	0.7	0.9	1.3	1.1	1.4	6.0	6.5	7.2	7.5	6.0	22.1	31.5	12.1	1.0	75.5	41.0	49.5	50.5
13733	BAINBRIDGE	98.5	98.0	0.3	0.4	0.2	0.4	1.1	1.4	5.5	6.2	6.5	7.0	5.0	23.4	31.6	13.1	1.8	77.2	42.2	50.5	49.5
13734	BARTON	97.9	97.3	0.2	0.2	0.2	0.3	1.0	1.3	7.2	7.6	7.2	8.0	5.4	26.3	27.0	10.4	1.0	72.9	36.8	50.1	49.9
13736	BERKSHIRE	98.2	97.6	0.6	0.8	0.2	0.4	0.5	0.7	6.4	6.6	6.9	6.6	5.8	24.7	30.7	11.1	1.2	75.9	40.0	50.3	49.7
13739	BLOOMVILLE	92.6	91.6	4.6	5.1	0.4	0.5	2.8	3.5	5.8	5.9	7.2	10.0	4.1	21.7	28.0	15.4	1.9	73.1	41.4	51.9	48.1
13740	BOVINA CENTER	98.2	97.6	0.2	0.2	0.4	0.5	2.6	3.6	4.3	4.0	4.5	4.7	4.0	18.6	37.6	20.1	2.2	84.1	49.9	51.2	48.8
13743	CANDOR	97.3	96.6	0.8	0.9	0.2	0.3	1.0	1.4	6.9	6.8	7.1	7.5	5.7	25.0	28.2	11.4	1.5	74.5	38.4	49.3	50.7
13744	CASTLE CREEK	97.0	96.2	1.0	1.2	0.6	0.9	0.7	0.9	5.5	5.5	5.9	6.7	7.1	23.0	31.9	13.0	1.3	79.2	42.2	50.2	49.8
13746	CHENANGO FORKS	98.0	97.4	0.7	0.8	0.2	0.3	0.7	1.0	5.9	6.4	6.7	7.2	6.0	23.3	31.4	11.9	1.2	76.3	41.3	50.9	49.1
13748	CONKLIN	97.5	96.9	0.9	1.1	0.2	0.3	0.9	1.2	5.7	6.1	7.1	7.3	6.4	23.4	30.6	12.1	1.4	76.4	41.1	49.2	50.8
13750	DAVENPORT	98.1	97.6	0.6	0.7	0.1	0.1	1.0	1.2	5.9	6.2	6.7	6.2	4.5	23.0	31.3	14.5	1.6	77.3	43.0	50.6	49.4
13751	DAVENPORT CENTER	97.7	97.0	0.6	0.6	0.0	0.0	0.6	0.6	6.0	6.6	7.2	6.0	4.2	22.9	30.7	14.5	1.8	75.9	42.5	51.2	48.8
13752	DELANCEY	97.2	96.7	0.2	0.2	0.4	0.5	1.1	1.2	4.0	4.5	4.9	4.9	3.8	20.2	34.7	20.6	2.6	83.7	49.7	51.0	49.0
13753	DELHI	92.9	91.3	3.7	4.3	1.1	1.6	2.5	3.1	3.2	3.4	4.0	17.7	11.4	18.3	24.2	13.8	4.0	86.1	35.4	50.3	49.7
13754	DEPOSIT	97.6	96.9	0.8	1.0	0.4	0.6	1.9	2.4	6.4	6.4	6.5	6.6	5.6	21.9	29.0	15.5	2.2	76.7	42.1	48.6	51.4
13755	DOWNSVILLE	98.8	98.5	0.2	0.2	0.2	0.3	0.8	1.0	5.8	6.2	6.2	5.6	4.3	20.6	30.4	18.2	2.9	78.4	45.9	48.1	51.9
13756	EAST BRANCH	96.4	95.5	0.9	1.1	0.9	1.4	1.7	2.1	5.2	5.5	5.9	6.7	5.5	21.3	31.9	16.1	1.9	79.1	44.9	51.3	48.7
13757	EAST MEREDITH	98.3	97.7	0.3	0.4	0.2	0.3	1.2	1.4	5.0	6.4	7.3	7.1	4.8	23.6	31.4	12.7	1.7	76.8	42.2	50.6	49.4
13760	ENDICOTT	94.6	93.1	2.0	2.4	1.7	2.4	1.2	1.5	5.7	5.8	6.0	6.3	5.6	24.1	28.5	15.2	2.8	78.6	42.4	48.1	51.9
13775	FRANKLIN	98.3	97.9	0.7	0.8	0.2	0.3	0.7	0.9	5.4	5.4	5.6	6.1	6.3	22.6	31.6	14.7	2.3	79.6	44.0	50.6	49.4
13776	GILBERTSVILLE	97.3	96.8	0.7	0.9	0.2	0.2	1.1	1.3	4.3	4.9	6.2	6.9	4.1	22.3	36.7	12.4	2.1	79.6	45.6	49.1	50.9
13777	GLEN AUBREY	97.6	96.5	0.5	0.5	0.2	0.5	0.7	0.7	6.3	6.3	6.5	7.7	6.5	26.0	30.7	9.1	0.9	76.7	38.5	50.2	49.8
13778	GREENE	98.4	98.0	0.3	0.3	0.3	0.4	0.7	0.9	5.7	5.8	6.3	6.8	6.3	23.2	30.8	13.3	1.9	77.9	41.8	49.8	50.2
13780	GUILFORD	97.5	96.9	0.8	0.9	0.2	0.4	1.1	1.3	5.0	5.7	5.5	6.7	4.5	20.7	31.2	16.9	3.8	79.6	46.1	51.7	48.3
13782	HAMDEN	97.9	97.4	0.1	0.1	0.1	0.1	1.1	1.2	4.8	5.1	6.3	6.1	3.5	20.4	33.5	18.0	2.4	79.6	47.3	49.8	50.2
13783	HANCOCK	97.0	96.2	0.6	0.7	0.4	0.6	2.6	3.2	5.1	5.2	5.7	6.3	5.4	21.4	30.9	17.5	2.6	80.0	45.6	48.9	51.1
13786	HARPERSFIELD	97.7	97.2	0.9	0.9	0.0	0.0	2.3	2.8	5.2	5.7	7.5	4.7	4.2	20.8	34.4	16.0	1.4	78.3	46.0	48.6	51.4
13787	HARPURSVILLE	98.0	97.2	0.3	0.3	0.5	0.7	0.7	0.9	6.2	6.4	7.1	7.4	6.5	23.1	31.4	10.7	1.2	75.5	39.7	50.3	49.7
13788	HOBART	95.1	93.7	2.3	2.7	0.4	0.6	1.7	2.3	6.0	6.6	6.8	6.2	4.4	22.5	28.1	16.5	3.0	75.5	43.3	50.0	50.0
13790	JOHNSON CITY	90.0	87.3	2.7	3.0	4.5	6.0	2.0	2.7	5.7	5.4	5.2	5.8	7.1	25.9	25.8	13.8	5.2	80.3	40.9	47.0	53.0
13795	KIRKWOOD	97.6	96.9	0.8	0.9	0.5	0.6	0.6	0.7	5.9	6.0	6.3	6.8	5.4	23.3	29.5	15.1	1.6	77.7	42.4	50.0	50.0
13796	LAURENS	96.8	96.1	0.3	0.3	0.3	0.3	1.4	1.7	4.9	5.2	6.1	7.2	5.2	23.1	33.5	13.2	1.7	79.3	43.8	49.2	50.8
13797	LISLE	98.2	97.3	0.3	0.5	0.1	0.2	0.5	0.6	6.8	6.8	7.1	7.4	6.5	25.1	29.1	10.2	1.1	74.9	38.1	50.3	49.7
13801	MC DONOUGH	97.3	96.7	1.0	1.2	0.2	0.2	1.3	1.5	5.4	7.2	7.1	6.6	4.8	25.0	32.1	10.7	1.1	75.5	40.9	53.0	47.0
13802	MAINE	97.8	96.8	0.3	0.4	0.3	0.6	0.6	0.7	5.3	5.6	6.2	7.7	6.4	25.4	31.9	10.3	1.2	78.3	40.7	50.4	49.6
13803	MARATHON	98.3	97.9	0.5	0.6	0.1	0.1	0.4	0.6	7.0	7.0	7.1	7.8	6.2	25.0	28.0	10.6	1.2	74.1	37.4	50.0	50.0
13804	MASONVILLE	96.6	95.8	2.5	2.9	0.0	0.0	2.2	1.9	6.1	6.1	7.4	7.1	4.9	22.3	28.2	16.2	1.6	74.4	41.5	55.7	44.3
13806	MERIDALE	100.0	100.0	0.0	0.0	0.0	0.0	3.1	2.6	5.3	7.9	7.9	5.3	5.3	26.3	28.9	10.5	2.6	76.3	38.8	55.3	44.7
13807	MILFORD	97.4	96.7	0.5	0.6	0.8	1.1	1.6	2.0	5.0	6.0	7.3	7.8	4.2	23.7	31.4	13.1	1.6	76.1	42.3	48.8	51.2
13808	MORRIS	96.9	96.2	0.7	0.8	0.3	0.4	1.6	1.9	6.0	6.1	6.7	7.3	5.1	22.4	31.3	13.4	1.8	76.6	42.6	48.9	51.1
13809	MOUNT UPTON	96.7	95.9	1.0	1.1	0.2	0.3	1.0	1.2	5.5	5.8	6.3	6.4	5.5	23.4	32.4	13.0	1.6	78.3	42.6	50.9	49.1
13810	MOUNT VISION	97.3	96.7	0.6	0.7	0.4	0.6	1.5	1.8	5.6	5.4	7.2	7.8	4.4	23.4	31.1	13.2	2.0	76.8	42.5	49.1	50.9
13811	NEWARK VALLEY	98.0	97.5	0.5	0.6	0.3	0.5	0.7	0.9	6.4	6.7	7.0	7.3	5.8	24.6	30.5	10.3	1.4	75.5	39.0	50.7	49.3
13812	NICHOLS	99.1	98.8	0.4	0.5	0.2	0.3	0.8	1.0	6.4	6.5	6.7	6.7	5.5	22.5	30.6	13.4	1.6	76.3	41.7	50.1	49.9
13813	NINEVEH	97.8	97.2	0.8	1.0	0.0	0.0	0.7	0.8	5.8	6.7	9.2	7.6	4.9	24.5	29.2	11.0	1.1	72.7	38.3	51.2	48.8
13815	NORWICH	96.8	96.1	1.3	1.5	0.5	0.7	1.1	1.4	6.3	6.3	6.5	6.7	6.0	23.7	27.3	13.8	3.4	76.6	40.9	47.5	52.5
13820	ONEONTA	92.3	87.6	4.0	6.4	1.2	2.1	3.3	4.7	3.7	3.8	4.1	14.2	19.7	19.2	21.7	10.9	2.6	84.5	29.1	47.6	52.4
13825	OTEGO	97.5	96.9	1.0	1.1	0.4	0.5	1.2	1.5	5.1	5.4	6.0	7.1	5.9	22.8	32.0	13.6	2.1	78.6	43.4	48.3	51.7
13826	OUAQUAGA	98.6	97.7	0.0	0.0	0.5	0.5	1.4	1.8	5.4	7.2	7.7	8.1	5.0	24.8	29.3	10.4	2.3	73.9	40.7	50.9	49.1
13827	OWEGO	96.9	96.2	0.7	0.8	0.8	1.1	1.1	1.4	5.6	5.7	6.1	6.5	6.0	24.0	30.5	13.6	2.1	78.7	42.1	49.4	50.6
13830	OXFORD	97.6	97.1	0.8	0.9	0.3	0.4	1.1	1.3	5.5	5.8	6.3	6.8	5.4	21.9	30.0	15.4	2.9	78.2	43.6	50.7	49.3
13832	PLYMOUTH	98.2	98.1	0.0	0.0	0.3	0.2	1.5	1.9	8.7	8.2	8.2	7.5	6.3	24.0	26.2	10.1	1.0	70.7	34.8	50.7	49.3
13833	PORT CRANE	97.6	97.0	0.6	0.8	0.1	0.2	1.0	1.3	5.9	6.7	6.7	7.1	5.2	22.8	31.7	12.5	1.5	76.2	42.0	50.6	49.4
13834	PORTLANDVILLE	97.9	97.9	0.7	0.7	0.0	0.0	2.1	2.8	2.8	3.5	4.3	5.0	3.5	20.6	40.4	17.7	2.1	85.8	50.6	46.8	53.2
13835	RICHFORD	98.5	98.2	0.6	0.7	0.0	0.0	0.5	0.8	6.5	6.1	6.3	7.8	8.3	26.0	29.0	9.1	1.0	76.4	36.7	50.2	49.8
13838	SIDNEY	96.0	95.0	0.9	1.0	0.9	1.3	1.5	1.8	6.6	5.9	6.3	7.1	6.3	22.3	27.2	14.8	3.5	76.6	41.5	47.2	52.8
13839	SIDNEY CENTER	96.8	95.9	1.2	1.3	0.3	0.4	1.2	1.4	5.2	5.4	6.1	7.3	4.9	22.0	31.7	15.6	1.8	78.5	44.4	51.0	49.0
13841	SMITHVILLE FLATS	98.5	98.3	0.3	0.2	0.3	0.5	0.5	0.7	6.2	6.5	7.0	7.0	4.7	22.4	32.8	12.2	1.2	75.9	42.8	53.2	46.8
13842	SOUTH KORTRIGHT	83.3	80.7	11.6	12.9	0.9	1.2	4.8	5.8	5.2	5.2	8.3	17.2	3.1	18.7	26.4	14.7	1.2	65.6	38.8	56.7	43.3
13843	SOUTH NEW BERLIN	97.6	97.1	0.6	0.7	0.3	0.4	1.2	1.5	5.9	6.4	7.1	7.1	4.6	22.7	32.6	12.0	1.5	75.8	42.4	49.4	50.6
13844	SOUTH PLYMOUTH	91.0	89.9	7.1	7.8	0.1	0.2	4.9	5.7	5.7	5.9	6.4	6.4	6.4	28.5	28.7	10.9	1.2	77.7	39.0	56.6	43.4
13846	TREADWELL	98.8	98.3	0.4	0.8	0.4	0.4	0.8	0.8	5.0	5.9	5.9	5.0	3.8	22.3	34.0	16.0	2.1	80.3	46.5	49.6	50.4
13849	UNADILLA	97.2	96.4	0.9	1.1	0.2	0.4	1.3	1.7	6.1	6.1	6.5	7.3	5.6	23.8	29.2	13.5	1.9	76.7	41.0	50.0	50.0
13850	VESTAL	87.2	83.1	2.2	2.5	8.3	11.5	2.4	3.0	3.9	4.4	5.0	17.7	12.4	16.3	23.2	14.1	3.1	83.2	34.4	47.3	52.7
13856	WALTON	97.8	97.2	0.4	0.5	0.4	0.6	1.1	1.4	5.0	5.2	5.6	6.1	5.6	22.0	32.2	15.8	2.6	80.3	45.4	48.4	51.6
13859	WELLS BRIDGE	97.1	96.6	1.0	1.0	0.0	0.5	1.5	1.5	7.8	7.8	7.8	7.4	5.9	23.5	25.5	12.7	1.5	71.1	37.5	47.5	52.5
13861	WEST ONEONTA	97.3	96.8	0.6	0.6	0.1	0.2	1.3	1.8	4.1	4.7	5.6	5.7	4.1	20.2	33.5	18.7	3.5	81.4	48.6	49.2	50.8
13862	WHITNEY POINT	97.7	96.7	0.3	0.5	0.3	0.5	0.8	1.1	6.1	6.1	6.3	7.6	7.6	25.5	29.4	10.1	1.3	76.8	37.8	49.5	50.5
13863	WILLET	98.3	97.9	0.0	0.0	0.2	0.2	0.0	0.0	7.5	7.2	7.5	7.2	6.6	24.7	27.5	10.9	0.9	73.6	37.8	52.0	48.0
13864	WILLSEYVILLE	97.0	95.8	1.0	1.4	0.5	0.8	0.7	1.0	6.6	6.8	6.8	5.8	4.6	24.4	31.3	12.1	1.6	75.9	41.3	50.0	50.0
	NEW YORK	67.9	64.8	15.9	16.5	5.6	6.9	15.1	16.7	6.5	6.4	6.4	7.1	7.0	27.0	26.3	11.2	2.1	76.6	37.5	48.4	51.6
	UNITED STATES	75.1	72.0	12.3	12.7	3.8	4.6	12.5	15.7	6.8	6.7	6.6	7.1	6.9	27.0	26.0	10.9	1.9	75.7	36.9	49.2	50.8

13667-13864

#	POST OFFICE NAME	2009 Per Capita Income	2009 HH Income Base	2009 Household Income Distribution (%): Less than $25,000	$25,000 to $49,999	$50,000 to $99,999	$100,000 to $149,999	$150,000 or More	Median Household Income: 2009	2014	2009 National Centile	2009 State Centile	2009 Home Value Base	2009 Home Value Distribution (%): Less than $50,000	$50,000 to $89,999	$90,000 to $174,999	$175,000 to $399,999	$400,000 or More	2009 Median Home Value
13667	NORFOLK	20413	1452	30.6	27.5	34.2	6.5	1.2	41356	45332	37	18	1083	12.7	30.9	40.1	15.1	1.2	100257
13668	NORWOOD	21813	1395	22.4	26.2	43.5	6.5	1.4	50966	52565	63	48	1057	12.7	26.1	45.5	14.7	1.0	104105
13669	OGDENSBURG	20118	5973	30.8	28.7	31.5	6.3	2.6	40363	43688	34	15	3984	15.1	31.3	39.6	11.2	2.8	95652
13670	OSWEGATCHIE	19923	203	30.5	34.5	29.6	3.9	1.5	38845	41226	29	11	169	27.2	39.1	26.6	5.3	1.8	72188
13672	PARISHVILLE	23060	158	24.1	41.8	25.3	6.3	2.5	39703	41720	32	14	130	13.1	24.6	43.1	15.4	3.8	117308
13673	PHILADELPHIA	17974	971	29.0	27.1	36.9	5.4	1.6	42139	47484	40	20	505	10.9	25.3	52.5	11.1	0.2	108221
13675	PLESSIS	17741	43	37.2	32.6	25.6	4.7	0.0	34062	42372	16	5	34	17.6	29.4	44.1	8.8	0.0	95000
13676	POTSDAM	19990	5307	34.4	26.8	29.6	6.6	2.6	37865	40989	26	9	3073	10.0	20.2	44.6	23.1	2.1	125259
13679	REDWOOD	19194	745	30.1	28.6	32.8	7.1	1.5	41158	45799	37	17	549	12.0	30.1	43.5	12.8	1.6	103699
13680	RENSSELAER FALLS	16501	428	29.4	29.2	35.0	5.6	0.7	42136	45903	40	20	309	17.8	28.5	43.0	10.4	0.3	95476
13681	RICHVILLE	17349	310	27.7	33.9	33.2	3.5	1.6	40801	44084	35	16	245	17.6	33.5	38.0	10.6	0.4	88214
13682	RODMAN	19936	339	20.9	31.0	38.9	6.8	2.4	48166	50575	57	41	282	7.8	18.8	45.4	24.5	3.5	130000
13684	RUSSELL	17982	414	30.4	31.4	33.1	4.3	0.7	39418	43459	31	13	337	19.3	32.9	37.7	9.2	0.9	87000
13685	SACKETS HARBOR	26930	1101	21.6	24.0	44.7	7.1	2.6	53941	58103	70	55	662	10.9	13.7	50.9	21.6	2.9	133673
13687	SOUTH COLTON	22560	193	21.8	29.0	39.4	7.8	2.1	49252	50480	59	43	160	8.8	18.8	45.6	22.5	4.4	137963
13690	STAR LAKE	22632	354	30.5	24.3	35.3	8.2	1.7	45251	47719	49	31	270	26.3	33.3	29.3	9.6	1.5	73333
13691	THERESA	18282	1167	25.1	33.8	33.4	5.8	1.9	44621	46886	47	29	899	17.8	27.3	43.4	10.5	1.1	98558
13693	THREE MILE BAY	24449	133	24.8	30.8	35.3	6.8	2.3	44543	48977	47	29	104	7.7	19.2	43.3	26.0	3.8	130357
13694	WADDINGTON	25076	619	21.8	28.1	39.3	7.3	3.6	50072	52585	61	45	451	10.2	23.3	46.6	17.3	2.7	116952
13695	WANAKENA	17009	73	37.0	35.6	20.5	5.5	1.4	34432	37297	16	5	61	27.9	31.1	32.8	6.6	1.6	77000
13696	WEST STOCKHOLM	20044	72	30.6	26.4	36.1	5.6	1.4	39183	40765	30	12	58	8.6	36.2	39.7	13.8	1.7	96000
13697	WINTHROP	19079	938	29.3	31.4	32.4	5.7	1.2	38686	41512	29	11	720	13.3	28.9	41.9	14.7	1.1	102226
13699	POTSDAM	14497	51	68.6	23.5	7.8	0.0	0.0	11568	11740	1	1	0	0.0	0.0	0.0	0.0	0.0	0
13730	AFTON	20464	1231	25.4	33.7	33.8	5.6	1.5	42031	42959	39	20	979	9.7	24.7	50.7	13.1	1.8	112799
13731	ANDES	25286	525	26.9	32.8	29.5	6.7	4.2	42059	44088	39	20	433	6.2	12.2	40.0	33.3	8.3	154722
13732	APALACHIN	29143	2950	10.3	23.1	44.1	15.3	7.2	65258	67836	84	72	2509	6.7	3.3	44.8	42.4	2.9	166840
13733	BAINBRIDGE	20661	2195	24.2	30.3	38.1	5.3	2.1	46083	46843	52	34	1725	11.0	24.4	46.1	15.8	2.7	111823
13734	BARTON	19698	945	25.8	33.3	29.7	7.6	3.5	42947	45798	42	23	755	15.1	20.4	41.6	19.3	3.6	117370
13736	BERKSHIRE	20895	970	23.7	29.4	37.9	6.4	2.6	46932	50655	54	37	783	11.4	16.3	47.4	23.5	1.4	132801
13739	BLOOMVILLE	19650	422	25.6	34.4	34.1	4.3	1.7	42246	43639	40	21	345	13.9	18.8	43.8	19.4	4.1	116595
13740	BOVINA CENTER	24984	231	17.3	27.7	43.3	8.2	3.5	53452	54758	69	54	187	6.4	8.0	45.5	29.9	10.2	157212
13743	CANDOR	22164	1710	22.7	31.0	35.4	7.4	3.5	45922	49940	51	33	1333	13.3	17.2	46.9	21.7	1.0	128836
13744	CASTLE CREEK	24914	567	18.0	30.7	39.5	7.2	4.6	51279	56271	64	49	451	11.3	9.1	48.8	28.8	2.0	141869
13746	CHENANGO FORKS	22163	1176	21.9	29.6	37.3	8.8	2.3	48223	51187	57	41	972	16.2	17.3	39.9	24.4	2.3	128393
13748	CONKLIN	22413	1502	19.4	29.9	37.2	10.9	2.7	50599	54358	63	47	1254	14.9	14.2	53.8	17.1	0.0	129623
13750	DAVENPORT	20493	357	26.6	36.4	28.6	6.2	2.2	38901	40336	29	12	280	19.6	12.1	47.5	17.9	2.9	118367
13751	DAVENPORT CENTER	19906	65	27.7	36.9	27.7	6.2	1.5	38347	40000	28	10	51	15.7	11.8	54.9	15.7	2.0	119318
13752	DELANCEY	24894	366	20.8	32.2	38.8	5.5	2.7	47244	48580	55	38	284	9.5	12.7	43.0	28.2	6.7	136806
13753	DELHI	22521	1709	23.4	29.7	36.6	7.3	3.0	47238	48576	55	38	1241	7.5	12.3	47.0	29.5	3.7	142644
13754	DEPOSIT	21153	1437	30.4	29.9	31.1	5.3	3.3	40478	43351	34	16	1036	9.0	23.7	45.7	19.2	2.4	118121
13755	DOWNSVILLE	20015	492	29.7	31.1	32.9	5.1	1.2	40287	41364	34	15	383	11.0	25.1	46.2	13.8	3.9	106346
13756	EAST BRANCH	18195	289	30.1	34.9	29.1	4.8	1.0	36679	38023	23	7	241	12.9	27.0	42.7	11.6	5.8	108456
13757	EAST MEREDITH	22007	544	25.0	31.6	35.1	6.1	2.2	43794	45336	45	26	440	11.4	15.0	43.9	25.5	4.3	129825
13760	ENDICOTT	27228	18706	22.8	26.4	36.1	9.8	5.0	50795	54661	63	47	12198	2.3	6.4	56.8	30.9	3.6	151160
13775	FRANKLIN	22169	694	20.9	34.6	32.7	9.7	2.2	45524	46973	50	32	561	8.4	13.5	51.3	23.4	3.4	126637
13776	GILBERTSVILLE	25891	211	21.8	26.1	41.7	7.1	3.3	51830	52543	66	51	173	9.2	15.6	44.5	27.2	3.5	133173
13777	GLEN AUBREY	19562	161	19.3	35.4	39.8	5.0	0.6	46461	50000	53	35	137	16.1	18.2	46.7	18.2	0.7	126389
13778	GREENE	21773	2281	22.5	31.1	36.3	8.3	1.8	47155	48138	55	38	1708	10.0	19.5	44.2	24.0	2.3	126651
13780	GUILFORD	19051	405	26.2	37.5	32.8	3.0	0.5	37483	38912	25	8	342	11.1	32.2	42.4	13.5	0.9	101250
13782	HAMDEN	22534	359	25.3	32.0	34.8	6.1	1.7	42200	43571	40	21	284	12.3	14.4	45.1	23.2	4.9	128571
13783	HANCOCK	20762	1091	31.1	30.6	30.4	6.1	1.7	38034	39660	27	9	788	12.6	32.2	39.6	12.4	3.2	98913
13786	HARPERSFIELD	19584	80	28.8	31.3	35.0	3.8	1.3	38895	41748	29	12	66	6.1	25.8	42.4	24.2	1.5	120000
13787	HARPURSVILLE	19714	1372	21.7	31.7	39.5	5.1	2.0	47323	50000	55	38	1131	12.2	23.7	43.1	19.5	1.6	115856
13788	HOBART	23651	271	20.3	29.2	41.0	6.3	3.3	50292	51390	62	46	210	8.1	15.2	51.0	21.9	3.8	131250
13790	JOHNSON CITY	22534	8178	32.3	28.9	30.1	6.2	2.5	38296	42278	28	10	4539	3.7	16.2	62.0	16.9	1.1	126515
13795	KIRKWOOD	22897	1471	17.3	33.1	40.5	6.7	2.4	49602	53282	60	44	1053	9.4	9.4	56.8	22.9	1.5	136225
13796	LAURENS	21280	512	21.5	32.4	38.5	6.1	1.6	45598	47480	50	32	407	8.6	16.2	49.4	23.1	2.7	129107
13797	LISLE	17507	939	24.3	36.5	34.3	3.6	1.3	41527	44512	38	18	760	21.7	21.1	42.1	14.5	0.7	107099
13801	MC DONOUGH	18473	552	28.8	34.6	32.2	2.5	1.8	38691	39805	29	11	472	21.0	33.9	31.8	12.5	0.8	83030
13802	MAINE	21197	269	13.8	37.5	42.4	5.6	0.7	48985	51532	59	43	227	6.6	18.1	53.3	19.8	2.2	135938
13803	MARATHON	19392	1538	22.9	32.9	36.4	6.2	1.6	45238	47613	49	31	1153	12.4	24.3	48.4	13.4	1.6	104203
13804	MASONVILLE	16750	111	28.8	41.4	23.4	6.3	0.0	35485	37390	19	6	93	10.8	18.3	50.5	19.4	1.1	119853
13806	MERIDALE	31328	22	22.7	27.3	40.9	9.1	0.0	50000	60000	61	45	18	5.6	11.1	50.0	33.3	0.0	143750
13807	MILFORD	19351	656	27.0	33.7	30.9	5.8	2.6	40820	42593	35	17	507	10.3	18.7	47.5	16.6	6.9	121449
13808	MORRIS	20722	728	26.9	32.1	32.4	6.3	2.2	41042	42685	36	17	545	10.1	17.1	51.2	18.3	3.3	120686
13809	MOUNT UPTON	19197	754	24.3	36.6	33.6	3.7	1.9	40956	41795	36	17	623	14.9	25.7	45.1	13.3	1.0	102576
13810	MOUNT VISION	21135	550	23.6	31.8	35.8	5.8	2.9	44289	45838	46	28	441	9.1	15.6	46.3	26.5	2.5	128728
13811	NEWARK VALLEY	21528	1618	19.3	31.1	38.7	8.2	2.7	49548	52198	60	44	1324	11.0	11.3	51.6	24.1	2.0	137959
13812	NICHOLS	20400	932	20.0	35.9	35.2	6.8	2.1	46375	48372	52	35	729	8.5	16.2	61.6	11.9	1.8	130878
13813	NINEVEH	18826	277	27.1	34.7	31.8	4.7	1.8	42846	45166	42	22	225	21.8	17.8	41.8	16.9	1.8	107197
13815	NORWICH	21616	5887	31.3	29.7	29.6	6.8	2.6	38253	39532	27	10	3847	15.9	22.6	43.5	16.1	1.8	107359
13820	ONEONTA	20805	7403	33.5	27.7	29.4	6.6	2.9	37518	39511	25	9	4283	8.0	13.0	55.9	20.9	2.3	127811
13825	OTEGO	19556	1461	26.6	33.6	32.1	6.8	1.0	40366	42240	34	15	1140	13.6	12.5	51.8	20.6	1.4	126842
13826	OUAQUAGA	21388	87	25.3	32.2	31.0	6.9	4.6	41929	46571	39	20	70	17.1	20.0	42.9	20.0	0.0	118750
13827	OWEGO	23748	4586	22.1	28.7	36.5	10.1	2.6	49059	52874	59	43	3209	8.9	12.5	48.4	28.0	2.2	143019
13830	OXFORD	19771	1935	24.4	30.7	36.4	7.1	1.4	44965	46106	48	30	1532	11.9	26.6	45.3	14.9	1.2	108560
13832	PLYMOUTH	16419	146	27.4	37.0	30.1	3.4	2.1	37297	38183	24	8	120	29.2	26.7	34.2	9.2	0.8	81250
13833	PORT CRANE	22405	1727	18.8	31.8	38.7	8.5	2.3	49295	52743	60	43	1444	19.9	14.7	40.2	24.4	0.8	129199
13834	PORTLANDVILLE	22986	61	29.5	29.5	29.5	9.8	1.6	38342	48669	28	10	50	10.0	16.0	52.0	22.0	0.0	130000
13835	RICHFORD	19735	507	23.9	31.0	39.6	4.1	1.4	44925	49027	48	30	407	19.4	24.3	41.3	14.3	0.7	100255
13838	SIDNEY	19744	1810	31.0	35.3	27.8	4.3	1.6	36805	38226	23	7	1101	10.4	32.3	47.6	8.8	0.8	97035
13839	SIDNEY CENTER	20973	595	22.5	36.5	32.1	6.4	2.5	41060	43408	36	17	505	11.5	21.4	47.7	17.4	2.0	115522
13841	SMITHVILLE FLATS	16299	146	20.5	47.3	28.8	3.4	0.0	39559	41022	31	13	122	14.8	34.4	37.7	13.1	0.0	91429
13842	SOUTH KORTRIGHT	13625	81	27.2	34.6	33.3	3.7	1.2	40567	41373	35	16	69	11.6	20.3	43.5	21.7	2.9	116346
13843	SOUTH NEW BERLIN	21126	809	25.2	29.2	35.7	7.3	2.6	46046	46376	51	34	664	12.3	22.1	42.6	20.3	2.6	115227
13844	SOUTH PLYMOUTH	14918	259	29.3	33.2	32.0	3.5	1.9	38264	39322	27	10	210	24.8	24.3	40.5	10.0	0.5	91538
13846	TREADWELL	22140	104	22.1	28.8	42.3	4.8	1.9	48242	50000	57	41	84	3.6	15.5	47.6	27.4	6.0	137500
13849	UNADILLA	21182	2165	22.7	34.6	35.3	5.6	1.8	43173	44630	43	23	1771	16.0	19.7	48.5	14.3	1.5	111659
13850	VESTAL	29823	8545	16.1	21.3	37.3	15.8	9.4	65192	68136	83	72	6502	3.0	4.9	42.5	41.2	8.4	174181
13856	WALTON	21274	2942	30.4	29.6	32.5	5.3	2.1	38211	39807	27	10	2091	11.0	19.1	46.5	18.5	4.8	120190
13859	WELLS BRIDGE	20003	84	23.8	36.9	34.5	4.8	0.0	39284	40448	31	12	69	14.5	13.0	52.2	20.3	0.0	119531
13861	WEST ONEONTA	22515	264	20.1	30.7	37.1	10.2	1.9	49020	49545	59	43	220	9.1	17.3	43.6	27.3	2.7	130000
13862	WHITNEY POINT	20092	1801	22.3	30.9	39.0	6.3	1.6	46775	50843	53	36	1422	16.7	18.2	46.6	17.4	1.1	121098
13863	WILLET	18627	180	24.4	38.9	30.0	5.0	1.7	41681	45000	38	19	141	14.2	29.8	44.0	12.1	0.0	97083
13864	WILLSEYVILLE	25613	501	20.4	28.7	40.7	5.4	4.8	50575	53451	63	47	375	11.7	19.5	43.2	24.0	1.6	137716
	NEW YORK	29893		21.9	21.3	32.7	14.0	9.9	58747	62337				3.4	5.7	23.0	38.7	29.1	269816
	UNITED STATES	27277		20.9	24.4	35.3	11.7	7.6	54719	56938				9.3	13.1	31.6	32.6	13.5	162279

#	POST OFFICE NAME	FINANCIAL SERVICES: Auto Loan	FINANCIAL SERVICES: Home Loan	FINANCIAL SERVICES: Invest-ments	FINANCIAL SERVICES: Retire-ment Plans	THE HOME: Home Improvements: Home Repair	THE HOME: Home Improvements: Lawn & Garden	THE HOME: Furnishings: Comput-ers & Hard-ware Personal	THE HOME: Furnishings: Major Appli-ances	THE HOME: Furnishings: TV, Radio, Sound Equip-ment	THE HOME: Furnishings: Furni-ture	ENTERTAINMENT: Dine out/ Carry out	ENTERTAINMENT: Sports Equip-ment	ENTERTAINMENT: Fees & Tickets	ENTERTAINMENT: Toys & Games	ENTERTAINMENT: Travel	ENTERTAINMENT: Cable TV	PERSONAL: Apparel & Services	PERSONAL: Auto Repairs	PERSONAL: Health Insur-ance	PERSONAL: Pets & Supplies
13667	NORFOLK	85	65	79	65	67	86	67	80	73	62	71	61	56	74	65	79	48	75	84	95
13668	NORWOOD	85	71	81	71	73	86	75	83	79	71	77	61	67	78	73	83	52	80	88	97
13669	OGDENSBURG	77	66	72	66	66	78	71	75	74	66	73	57	64	73	68	78	50	74	81	89
13670	OSWEGATCHIE	74	60	81	57	64	79	59	73	65	59	63	52	53	62	62	70	42	68	78	85
13672	PARISHVILLE	93	69	105	68	74	96	71	90	77	66	75	67	58	75	72	83	50	83	92	106
13673	PHILADELPHIA	75	66	62	67	64	67	73	69	72	72	73	54	67	74	67	73	50	72	71	83
13675	PLESSIS	75	54	77	52	56	76	55	70	61	51	60	53	44	61	55	67	40	64	73	84
13676	POTSDAM	72	60	64	61	59	68	72	67	72	65	71	53	63	71	64	73	49	70	72	82
13679	REDWOOD	82	64	83	63	66	84	66	79	71	63	70	59	56	71	66	77	47	74	82	93
13680	RENSSELAER FALLS	77	60	77	60	62	79	64	74	68	59	67	57	54	67	63	72	45	71	78	88
13681	RICHVILLE	81	58	84	57	61	83	62	77	67	55	66	59	49	66	61	73	43	71	80	92
13682	RODMAN	82	79	75	82	79	88	76	83	77	71	76	63	73	79	77	80	52	78	85	97
13684	RUSSELL	81	59	85	57	62	83	60	77	67	56	65	57	49	66	60	73	43	70	79	91
13685	SACKETS HARBOR	92	78	96	79	82	94	82	91	85	78	84	67	74	83	82	89	57	88	95	107
13687	SOUTH COLTON	93	75	121	74	82	99	75	95	78	70	77	69	65	74	81	83	51	88	94	110
13690	STAR LAKE	75	74	82	71	76	87	69	80	75	68	74	56	70	72	74	80	50	76	89	92
13691	THERESA	85	70	77	68	70	83	69	78	73	68	73	58	61	75	67	77	49	74	80	93
13693	THREE MILE BAY	88	70	113	69	77	93	70	89	74	66	73	65	61	70	76	78	48	82	88	104
13694	WADDINGTON	89	76	84	77	79	90	82	87	85	78	83	65	74	84	79	89	57	86	93	103
13695	WANAKENA	60	57	73	53	64	68	55	64	58	59	56	42	54	53	60	61	38	62	72	74
13696	WEST STOCKHOLM	87	62	89	60	64	88	64	81	71	59	69	61	51	70	63	78	46	74	84	96
13697	WINTHROP	79	64	77	63	63	82	65	75	70	60	69	58	56	70	63	75	46	71	80	90
13699	POTSDAM	25	11	11	13	10	13	36	18	29	24	29	19	21	28	19	26	21	25	18	24
13730	AFTON	86	65	85	65	67	88	66	82	72	61	71	61	55	72	66	79	47	75	85	97
13731	ANDES	92	74	119	73	81	97	74	94	77	69	76	68	64	73	80	82	51	86	92	109
13732	APALACHIN	110	122	106	122	117	122	109	113	111	110	111	86	117	113	114	113	77	111	118	133
13733	BAINBRIDGE	88	68	85	67	70	89	69	83	75	64	73	63	58	75	68	81	49	77	86	99
13734	BARTON	95	72	89	70	73	94	73	87	80	70	78	65	61	81	70	86	52	81	90	104
13736	BERKSHIRE	86	78	76	79	78	88	77	84	79	73	78	64	71	81	75	83	53	80	86	99
13739	BLOOMVILLE	82	64	92	63	68	85	65	80	69	60	68	60	55	68	67	75	45	74	82	94
13740	BOVINA CENTER	100	80	129	79	88	105	80	102	84	75	83	74	69	79	87	89	55	94	100	118
13743	CANDOR	92	77	85	76	76	93	77	87	82	74	81	66	69	83	75	87	55	83	91	104
13744	CASTLE CREEK	92	90	84	89	89	94	86	91	89	87	88	67	85	90	86	91	61	89	94	106
13746	CHENANGO FORKS	84	83	80	81	83	87	78	83	80	80	80	60	77	81	78	82	55	81	86	97
13748	CONKLIN	83	85	74	85	82	87	81	83	83	81	82	63	82	84	81	85	57	82	87	98
13750	DAVENPORT	90	65	93	63	67	92	66	85	74	62	72	63	53	73	66	81	48	78	88	101
13751	DAVENPORT CENTER	91	65	93	63	67	92	67	85	74	62	73	64	53	74	66	81	48	78	88	101
13752	DELANCEY	92	74	119	73	81	98	74	94	77	69	76	69	64	74	80	83	51	87	93	109
13753	DELHI	89	75	92	76	79	91	79	88	82	76	81	65	72	80	79	86	55	85	92	103
13754	DEPOSIT	86	63	90	61	66	89	67	83	74	61	72	62	54	73	66	81	48	78	89	98
13755	DOWNSVILLE	78	59	88	58	63	82	62	77	67	56	65	57	51	65	63	73	43	72	80	90
13756	EAST BRANCH	82	59	85	57	61	83	60	77	67	56	66	58	48	66	60	74	43	70	80	91
13757	EAST MEREDITH	92	71	110	69	76	96	71	91	76	67	75	67	60	74	75	82	50	84	91	106
13760	ENDICOTT	86	87	83	88	86	92	87	88	89	85	89	66	88	89	87	92	62	88	94	103
13775	FRANKLIN	88	73	94	73	77	90	76	87	79	72	78	64	67	77	76	84	53	83	90	102
13776	GILBERTSVILLE	92	78	104	79	83	98	78	94	81	72	80	69	69	79	81	86	54	86	94	109
13777	GLEN AUBREY	84	77	68	75	75	79	73	77	75	76	75	56	69	79	69	77	51	75	77	92
13778	GREENE	83	72	76	73	74	85	75	81	77	71	76	60	68	78	73	81	52	78	85	95
13780	GUILFORD	77	56	81	55	59	78	58	72	63	54	62	54	47	62	58	69	41	67	75	86
13782	HAMDEN	84	67	109	66	74	89	67	86	71	63	70	63	58	67	73	75	46	79	85	99
13783	HANCOCK	83	60	85	58	62	86	64	80	71	58	69	60	51	70	62	78	46	74	85	94
13786	HARPERSFIELD	86	69	111	68	75	91	69	87	72	64	71	64	60	68	74	77	47	81	86	101
13787	HARPURSVILLE	93	71	80	71	72	91	73	84	79	70	78	64	61	81	68	85	52	79	88	101
13788	HOBART	88	78	85	80	81	93	78	89	80	71	79	67	71	81	78	85	54	82	91	103
13790	JOHNSON CITY	71	63	63	64	62	71	70	69	72	65	72	53	65	72	66	75	50	71	76	82
13795	KIRKWOOD	83	81	81	80	79	92	77	84	82	74	81	63	77	82	79	86	55	82	92	99
13796	LAURENS	83	72	78	74	74	87	73	83	76	67	75	62	66	76	72	81	51	77	86	97
13797	LISLE	84	64	77	62	65	82	65	76	71	63	70	57	55	72	62	76	47	72	79	92
13801	MC DONOUGH	81	58	83	56	60	82	60	76	66	56	65	57	48	66	59	73	43	70	79	90
13802	MAINE	87	80	72	78	79	84	76	82	79	77	78	60	71	81	73	81	53	78	82	96
13803	MARATHON	80	74	68	74	72	81	72	77	75	69	74	58	68	76	70	78	50	74	81	91
13804	MASONVILLE	80	57	82	55	59	81	59	75	65	55	64	56	47	65	58	72	42	68	78	89
13806	MERIDALE	90	72	117	71	79	95	72	92	76	68	75	67	63	72	78	81	50	85	91	106
13807	MILFORD	87	65	96	63	68	89	66	84	72	61	70	62	54	70	67	78	47	77	86	99
13808	MORRIS	90	66	91	65	69	92	68	85	74	63	73	64	56	74	67	81	48	78	88	100
13809	MOUNT UPTON	86	62	82	61	64	85	64	79	71	61	70	59	52	72	62	78	46	73	82	94
13810	MOUNT VISION	86	71	97	71	75	89	72	86	76	68	75	63	64	74	75	80	50	81	88	100
13811	NEWARK VALLEY	90	82	78	81	81	89	78	86	82	78	81	64	73	84	76	85	55	82	87	101
13812	NICHOLS	83	73	83	73	75	90	71	83	76	67	75	61	66	76	73	82	51	78	89	97
13813	NINEVEH	87	62	88	60	64	88	64	81	71	60	70	61	51	71	63	78	46	74	84	96
13815	NORWICH	77	65	70	66	65	76	71	74	74	66	73	56	64	73	67	78	50	73	79	88
13820	ONEONTA	75	61	67	62	62	70	75	70	74	68	74	55	65	73	67	76	51	73	75	84
13825	OTEGO	77	68	80	67	68	83	65	76	69	62	69	57	60	69	67	74	46	72	80	90
13826	OUAQUAGA	97	70	100	68	72	99	72	91	80	67	78	68	57	79	71	87	52	84	95	108
13827	OWEGO	86	79	79	79	78	89	80	85	83	76	82	64	75	84	78	88	57	83	90	100
13830	OXFORD	84	68	81	69	71	87	70	82	74	65	73	61	61	74	69	80	49	76	85	96
13832	PLYMOUTH	84	61	71	59	60	81	63	74	70	61	68	57	50	72	58	76	46	70	78	90
13833	PORT CRANE	86	85	82	83	84	92	78	86	82	79	82	63	78	83	80	86	56	83	91	101
13834	PORTLANDVILLE	89	71	115	70	78	94	71	90	74	67	73	66	62	71	77	79	49	83	89	105
13835	RICHFORD	84	73	68	70	71	77	72	76	75	74	75	57	66	78	68	77	51	75	76	91
13838	SIDNEY	63	59	58	59	58	65	63	63	65	59	64	47	60	64	60	68	45	64	70	74
13839	SIDNEY CENTER	92	68	100	66	71	94	69	88	76	64	74	65	56	74	70	82	49	81	90	104
13841	SMITHVILLE FLATS	79	57	81	55	59	80	58	74	65	54	64	56	47	64	58	71	42	68	77	88
13842	SOUTH KORTRIGHT	76	61	98	60	66	80	61	77	63	57	63	56	52	60	66	68	42	71	76	89
13843	SOUTH NEW BERLIN	91	74	94	73	76	94	73	88	78	70	77	66	64	78	74	84	52	82	90	104
13844	SOUTH PLYMOUTH	86	62	82	60	63	85	64	78	71	60	69	59	51	72	61	77	46	73	82	94
13846	TREADWELL	84	68	109	67	74	89	68	86	71	63	70	63	59	67	73	76	47	79	85	100
13849	UNADILLA	84	73	77	71	73	83	71	79	75	71	74	59	65	76	70	78	50	76	81	94
13850	VESTAL	110	119	118	121	121	124	114	117	115	113	115	86	120	113	119	118	81	116	125	136
13856	WALTON	79	61	87	60	65	81	66	78	71	61	69	58	56	68	66	76	46	74	82	92
13859	WELLS BRIDGE	78	72	63	69	70	73	68	72	70	70	70	52	64	73	64	72	48	69	72	85
13861	WEST ONEONTA	77	85	87	86	88	92	76	84	78	77	78	60	82	77	83	81	54	80	90	96
13862	WHITNEY POINT	80	78	65	77	74	80	75	76	77	75	77	58	74	80	73	79	53	76	81	92
13863	WILLET	86	63	72	62	63	83	66	76	72	64	71	58	54	75	60	78	48	72	80	92
13864	WILLSEYVILLE	101	83	102	82	84	105	81	97	87	78	86	74	72	87	82	93	58	91	100	115
	NEW YORK	100	106	110	108	107	104	112	106	113	106	114	81	115	110	112	116	83	110	110	124
	UNITED STATES	100	100	100	100	100	100	100	100	100	100	100	100	100	100	100	100	100	100	100	100

ZIP CODE #	POST OFFICE NAME	COUNTY FIPS CODE	POPULATION 2000	POPULATION 2009	POPULATION 2014	2000-2009 ANNUAL RATE % Rate	2000-2009 ANNUAL RATE State Centile	HOUSEHOLDS 2000	HOUSEHOLDS 2009	HOUSEHOLDS 2014	HOUSEHOLDS % Annual Rate 2000-2009	HOUSEHOLDS 2009 Average HH Size	FAMILIES 2000	FAMILIES 2009	FAMILIES % Annual Rate 2000-2009
13865	WINDSOR	007	6347	6431	6403	0.1	44	2326	2417	2426	0.4	2.66	1734	1772	0.2
13901	BINGHAMTON	007	19498	19058	18800	-0.2	21	8618	8624	8575	0.0	2.18	4892	4780	-0.3
13903	BINGHAMTON	007	19387	18551	18206	-0.5	7	7948	7790	7705	-0.2	2.38	5112	4918	-0.4
13904	BINGHAMTON	007	9343	9150	9023	-0.2	21	3684	3659	3631	-0.1	2.36	2355	2293	-0.3
13905	BINGHAMTON	007	27922	27271	26856	-0.3	15	11921	11759	11643	-0.1	2.18	5919	5666	-0.5
14001	AKRON	029	9245	9476	9405	0.3	59	3676	3850	3845	0.5	2.46	2588	2665	0.3
14004	ALDEN	029	12112	11974	11798	-0.1	30	3881	3916	3879	0.1	2.59	2950	2931	-0.1
14005	ALEXANDER	037	1897	1883	1860	-0.1	30	666	678	674	0.2	2.78	509	511	0.0
14006	ANGOLA	029	10900	10423	10124	-0.5	7	4193	4115	4032	-0.2	2.52	2956	2840	-0.4
14008	APPLETON	063	1560	1620	1624	0.4	66	527	554	558	0.5	2.90	407	420	0.3
14009	ARCADE	121	5648	5538	5433	-0.2	21	2213	2226	2202	0.1	2.49	1534	1519	-0.1
14011	ATTICA	121	8071	9577	9444	1.9	98	2234	2201	2166	-0.2	2.64	1632	1588	-0.3
14012	BARKER	063	2574	2579	2556	0.0	38	904	914	911	0.1	2.81	713	710	0.0
14013	BASOM	037	1803	1712	1660	-0.6	4	631	612	597	-0.3	2.80	452	431	-0.5
14020	BATAVIA	037	22820	21902	21356	-0.4	11	9028	8822	8648	-0.2	2.35	5703	5465	-0.5
14024	BLISS	121	1707	1664	1633	-0.3	15	602	603	597	0.0	2.76	460	456	-0.1
14025	BOSTON	029	2904	3093	3103	0.7	80	1086	1185	1198	0.9	2.61	823	883	0.8
14026	BOWMANSVILLE	029	859	876	872	0.2	52	341	352	351	0.3	2.34	278	283	0.2
14028	BURT	063	2037	1951	1909	-0.5	7	794	769	755	-0.3	2.53	556	527	-0.6
14030	CHAFFEE	029	1454	1475	1461	0.2	52	538	559	558	0.4	2.64	411	420	0.2
14031	CLARENCE	029	8989	9689	9713	0.8	84	3291	3550	3563	0.8	2.59	2356	2500	0.6
14032	CLARENCE CENTER	029	5315	6094	6201	1.5	96	1762	2059	2107	1.7	2.96	1469	1695	1.6
14033	COLDEN	029	2638	2679	2658	0.2	52	983	1025	1026	0.5	2.61	737	755	0.3
14034	COLLINS	029	6058	2188	2144	-10.4	0	813	814	802	0.0	2.62	598	587	-0.2
14036	CORFU	037	5476	5313	5179	-0.3	15	1987	1969	1935	-0.1	2.70	1479	1445	-0.3
14037	COWLESVILLE	121	1183	1173	1155	-0.1	30	415	423	420	0.2	2.77	333	336	0.1
14039	DALE	121	117	117	116	0.0	38	44	45	45	0.2	2.60	35	35	0.0
14040	DARIEN CENTER	037	2261	2220	2182	-0.2	21	788	793	787	0.1	2.79	633	629	-0.1
14041	DAYTON	009	50	52	52	0.4	66	17	18	18	0.6	2.89	13	13	0.0
14042	DELEVAN	009	5051	4976	4879	-0.2	21	1969	2002	1981	0.2	2.48	1354	1353	0.0
14043	DEPEW	029	27700	27252	26687	-0.2	21	11240	11368	11220	0.1	2.38	7755	7699	-0.1
14047	DERBY	029	6774	6777	6698	0.0	38	2482	2550	2542	0.3	2.63	1846	1864	0.1
14048	DUNKIRK	013	16082	15029	14608	-0.7	3	6522	6300	6157	-0.4	2.33	4039	3811	-0.6
14051	EAST AMHERST	029	18283	20098	20273	1.0	89	6213	6962	7070	1.2	2.88	5116	5660	1.1
14052	EAST AURORA	029	17489	17157	16820	-0.2	21	6624	6648	6564	0.0	2.52	4823	4754	-0.2
14054	EAST BETHANY	037	1453	1435	1417	-0.1	30	536	542	539	0.1	2.65	420	419	0.0
14055	EAST CONCORD	029	1500	1523	1511	0.2	52	523	544	544	0.4	2.79	402	411	0.2
14057	EDEN	029	8416	8308	8165	-0.1	30	2973	3003	2971	0.1	2.70	2323	2312	-0.1
14058	ELBA	037	2369	2275	2215	-0.4	11	827	808	791	-0.3	2.78	649	625	-0.4
14059	ELMA	029	9124	9315	9250	0.2	52	3402	3556	3557	0.5	2.61	2678	2757	0.3
14060	FARMERSVILLE STATION	003	586	577	568	-0.2	21	212	215	213	0.2	2.67	153	153	0.0
14062	FORESTVILLE	013	3293	3251	3202	-0.1	30	1254	1264	1252	0.1	2.56	926	917	-0.1
14063	FREDONIA	013	14553	14549	14362	0.0	38	5140	5181	5127	0.1	2.28	3036	2994	-0.2
14065	FREEDOM	009	1786	1786	1762	0.0	38	620	641	638	0.4	2.78	479	490	0.2
14066	GAINESVILLE	121	1622	1617	1597	0.0	38	586	601	598	0.3	2.69	457	464	0.2
14067	GASPORT	063	5615	5629	5600	0.0	38	2020	2053	2053	0.2	2.70	1540	1538	0.0
14068	GETZVILLE	029	6689	7198	7189	0.8	84	2224	2444	2458	1.0	2.83	1694	1821	0.8
14069	GLENWOOD	029	750	772	769	0.3	59	298	315	316	0.6	2.45	227	236	0.4
14070	GOWANDA	009	5547	9364	9242	5.8	100	2221	2213	2172	0.0	2.34	1401	1366	-0.3
14072	GRAND ISLAND	029	18621	19000	18827	0.2	52	6898	7191	7174	0.5	2.63	5219	5358	0.3
14075	HAMBURG	029	41661	41488	40842	0.0	38	16321	16640	16494	0.2	2.44	11350	11315	0.0
14080	HOLLAND	029	4634	4650	4607	0.0	38	1698	1750	1747	0.3	2.66	1269	1286	0.1
14081	IRVING	029	3675	3694	3650	0.1	44	1340	1372	1364	0.3	2.66	926	930	0.0
14082	JAVA CENTER	121	472	446	432	-0.6	4	175	170	166	-0.3	2.62	128	123	-0.4
14083	JAVA VILLAGE	121	206	196	191	-0.5	7	67	66	64	-0.2	2.97	49	47	-0.4
14085	LAKE VIEW	029	5692	6667	6825	1.7	97	1949	2318	2385	1.9	2.86	1561	1832	1.7
14086	LANCASTER	029	28157	29769	29731	0.6	76	10523	11261	11295	0.7	2.60	7430	7843	0.6
14091	LAWTONS	029	1211	1191	1172	-0.2	21	405	409	406	0.1	2.90	305	302	-0.1
14092	LEWISTON	063	11124	11082	10968	0.0	38	4476	4511	4489	0.1	2.39	3191	3157	-0.1
14094	LOCKPORT	063	50361	50080	49566	-0.1	30	20073	20161	20032	0.0	2.43	13277	13068	-0.2
14098	LYNDONVILLE	073	2959	3108	3102	0.5	71	1080	1155	1161	0.7	2.69	793	833	0.5
14101	MACHIAS	009	2024	2028	2000	0.0	38	717	740	736	0.3	2.60	516	522	0.1
14102	MARILLA	029	1673	1722	1713	0.3	59	563	596	598	0.6	2.89	471	492	0.5
14103	MEDINA	073	11599	10947	10629	-0.6	4	4392	4223	4116	-0.4	2.51	2994	2837	-0.6
14105	MIDDLEPORT	063	4345	4247	4183	-0.2	21	1621	1600	1582	-0.1	2.65	1202	1168	-0.3
14108	NEWFANE	063	5973	6031	5993	0.1	44	2175	2219	2214	0.2	2.63	1623	1625	0.0
14109	NIAGARA UNIVERSITY	063	1347	1469	1466	0.9	87	0	0	0	0.0	0.00	0	0	0.0
14111	NORTH COLLINS	029	2962	2967	2929	0.0	38	1129	1159	1152	0.3	2.55	814	821	0.1
14113	NORTH JAVA	121	685	652	634	-0.5	7	246	241	236	-0.2	2.71	184	178	-0.4
14120	NORTH TONAWANDA	063	43233	43830	43424	0.1	44	17226	17641	17561	0.3	2.47	11718	11832	0.1
14125	OAKFIELD	037	3680	3451	3334	-0.7	3	1321	1256	1219	-0.5	2.73	987	925	-0.7
14127	ORCHARD PARK	029	27962	28391	28055	0.2	52	10436	10869	10824	0.4	2.55	7744	7928	0.3
14129	PERRYSBURG	009	1642	1557	1503	-0.6	4	615	603	587	-0.2	2.51	443	428	-0.4
14131	RANSOMVILLE	063	5999	5981	5917	0.0	38	2155	2178	2169	0.1	2.67	1641	1629	-0.1
14132	SANBORN	063	5847	5725	5743	-0.2	21	2182	2168	2186	-0.1	2.63	1654	1612	-0.3
14134	SARDINIA	029	107	107	106	0.0	38	40	41	41	0.3	2.61	30	31	0.4
14136	SILVER CREEK	013	5375	5162	5033	-0.4	11	2112	2054	2009	-0.3	2.43	1460	1394	-0.5
14138	SOUTH DAYTON	009	2027	1949	1890	-0.4	11	735	725	710	-0.1	2.67	529	513	-0.3
14139	SOUTH WALES	029	2071	2054	2024	-0.1	30	807	822	816	0.2	2.50	606	606	0.0
14141	SPRINGVILLE	029	7914	7847	7742	-0.1	30	3033	3084	3060	0.2	2.47	2082	2076	0.0
14143	STAFFORD	037	1105	1068	1041	-0.4	11	418	414	407	-0.1	2.58	312	305	-0.2
14145	STRYKERSVILLE	121	1547	1543	1516	0.0	38	535	547	542	0.2	2.81	418	424	0.2
14150	TONAWANDA	029	44600	42575	41341	-0.5	7	18865	18491	18092	-0.2	2.30	12394	11860	-0.5
14167	VARYSBURG	121	1697	1686	1663	-0.1	30	625	637	633	0.2	2.65	471	474	0.1
14170	WEST FALLS	029	2335	2278	2226	-0.3	15	887	888	876	0.0	2.55	676	666	-0.2
14171	WEST VALLEY	009	2100	2138	2117	0.2	52	805	852	852	0.6	2.51	587	611	0.4
14172	WILSON	063	3354	3470	3465	0.4	66	1308	1374	1382	0.5	2.53	978	1008	0.3
14174	YOUNGSTOWN	063	5592	5536	5477	-0.1	30	2171	2183	2171	0.1	2.53	1581	1559	-0.2
14201	BUFFALO	029	13569	12599	12136	-0.8	2	6270	5838	5652	-0.8	2.02	2658	2360	-1.3
14202	BUFFALO	029	3856	3922	3882	0.2	52	1671	1707	1688	0.2	1.45	417	402	-0.4
14203	BUFFALO	029	1156	1359	1392	1.8	98	595	702	721	1.8	1.65	170	209	2.3
14204	BUFFALO	029	9685	8710	8312	-1.1	1	4520	4119	3949	-1.0	2.10	2349	2059	-1.4
14206	BUFFALO	029	23116	20821	19921	-1.1	1	10341	9525	9176	-0.9	2.18	5973	5360	-1.2
14207	BUFFALO	029	22838	21279	20500	-0.8	2	9769	9165	8855	-0.7	2.32	5567	5074	-1.0
14208	BUFFALO	029	13300	11851	11288	-1.2	1	5142	4573	4353	-1.3	2.30	2945	2542	-1.6
	NEW YORK					0.3					0.3	2.61			0.1
	UNITED STATES					1.0					1.1	2.59			0.9

ZIP CODE #	POST OFFICE NAME	RACE (%) White 2000	White 2009	Black 2000	Black 2009	Asian/Pacific 2000	Asian/Pacific 2009	% Hispanic Origin 2000	% Hispanic Origin 2009	2009 AGE DISTRIBUTION (%) 0-4	5-9	10-14	15-19	20-24	25-44	45-64	65-84	85+	18+	MEDIAN AGE 2009	% 2009 Males	% 2009 Females
13865	WINDSOR	98.0	97.3	0.6	0.7	0.3	0.4	0.8	1.1	6.4	6.8	7.3	7.9	6.0	22.8	30.3	11.1	1.4	74.5	40.3	50.1	49.9
13901	BINGHAMTON	90.5	88.5	5.0	5.7	1.5	1.9	2.1	2.5	5.7	5.6	6.1	6.4	7.1	22.6	28.4	15.3	3.0	78.8	42.4	48.9	51.1
13903	BINGHAMTON	88.2	85.7	6.2	7.1	1.9	2.5	2.6	3.1	6.6	6.6	6.7	6.8	5.8	24.7	28.2	12.5	2.1	75.8	39.3	48.0	52.0
13904	BINGHAMTON	90.5	88.6	4.4	4.8	0.9	1.2	3.0	3.6	6.2	6.1	6.1	6.3	5.8	23.7	28.6	13.6	3.7	77.8	41.9	48.5	51.5
13905	BINGHAMTON	86.1	83.0	6.4	7.3	3.7	5.0	3.4	4.0	5.0	4.6	4.7	5.7	13.0	24.4	24.6	13.9	4.1	82.6	38.4	48.4	51.6
14001	AKRON	98.1	97.2	0.4	0.7	0.1	0.2	0.5	0.8	5.8	6.2	6.2	6.5	5.0	25.0	29.5	13.7	2.2	77.8	41.9	49.3	50.7
14004	ALDEN	92.1	89.0	5.9	8.3	0.3	0.4	2.4	2.9	4.7	5.3	5.6	5.9	5.4	27.0	28.6	14.5	3.1	80.8	42.4	53.8	46.2
14005	ALEXANDER	98.5	98.1	0.3	0.4	0.3	0.4	0.4	0.6	7.3	7.8	8.4	7.1	4.7	25.3	28.4	9.8	1.2	72.2	37.6	49.9	50.1
14006	ANGOLA	97.4	96.1	0.4	0.8	0.1	0.2	1.1	1.7	5.8	5.9	6.4	7.0	6.0	24.1	30.3	12.7	1.8	77.7	41.4	48.3	51.7
14008	APPLETON	95.3	93.9	1.3	1.8	0.3	0.4	2.1	2.7	5.5	6.9	8.0	8.5	5.0	24.8	28.7	11.3	1.4	74.1	39.7	51.4	48.6
14009	ARCADE	98.8	98.3	0.2	0.2	0.3	0.5	0.7	1.1	5.8	6.0	6.4	7.2	5.6	25.4	29.9	11.8	1.8	77.3	40.6	49.6	50.4
14011	ATTICA	80.2	74.4	15.1	18.5	0.3	1.3	6.7	9.0	3.9	4.1	4.3	10.0	11.9	35.0	22.3	7.3	1.2	85.2	33.6	62.2	37.8
14012	BARKER	97.4	96.5	0.7	1.0	0.4	0.6	1.2	1.6	6.2	7.3	7.5	8.0	5.1	23.8	29.4	11.1	1.5	73.9	39.4	50.9	49.1
14013	BASOM	82.9	81.1	1.4	1.6	0.3	0.4	2.1	2.5	6.0	8.3	9.1	8.6	5.3	26.0	24.4	11.6	0.8	71.1	36.1	50.7	49.3
14020	BATAVIA	92.1	90.4	4.1	4.7	0.9	1.2	1.9	2.3	6.1	5.9	5.8	6.3	6.6	26.0	26.2	13.7	3.4	78.5	40.0	48.9	51.1
14024	BLISS	97.7	96.9	0.5	0.6	0.5	0.7	0.4	0.5	6.0	7.5	8.0	8.1	5.5	24.4	29.6	9.6	1.4	73.3	38.5	50.5	49.5
14025	BOSTON	99.0	98.4	0.2	0.5	0.1	0.2	0.8	1.3	5.8	6.3	7.0	6.9	4.6	24.6	31.8	11.6	1.3	76.4	41.5	50.6	49.4
14026	BOWMANSVILLE	97.4	95.8	1.0	1.9	0.6	0.8	0.7	1.1	5.6	6.1	6.7	7.2	5.4	20.4	31.2	12.8	4.7	77.1	44.0	48.1	51.9
14028	BURT	96.8	95.8	0.6	0.8	0.4	0.6	1.6	2.1	5.3	5.7	6.5	6.5	5.1	22.9	31.6	14.7	1.8	78.4	43.5	50.2	49.8
14030	CHAFFEE	97.5	96.0	0.3	0.6	0.3	0.5	0.6	0.9	6.2	6.8	7.4	6.9	5.5	24.5	30.2	11.4	1.2	75.3	40.2	50.3	49.7
14031	CLARENCE	97.7	96.3	0.5	0.9	0.9	1.4	0.7	1.0	4.8	5.5	6.5	7.1	4.1	19.1	32.0	16.3	4.6	78.4	46.6	47.4	52.6
14032	CLARENCE CENTER	97.6	95.8	0.6	1.3	0.6	1.0	1.0	1.5	6.8	7.8	8.7	8.1	4.2	22.0	31.3	9.9	1.2	71.3	40.3	50.1	49.9
14033	COLDEN	98.5	97.6	0.1	0.2	0.4	0.6	0.5	0.7	5.0	5.6	6.4	7.0	4.9	23.0	34.1	12.8	1.3	78.5	43.9	49.4	50.6
14034	COLLINS	59.8	40.0	30.0	44.4	0.3	2.4	15.3	18.0	3.1	3.1	3.3	10.1	10.5	42.7	20.8	5.6	0.7	89.0	34.1	70.7	29.3
14036	CORFU	98.2	97.7	0.3	0.4	0.1	0.2	0.5	0.7	6.0	6.2	6.6	7.5	6.1	24.6	29.6	11.9	1.4	76.7	40.5	49.2	50.8
14037	COWLESVILLE	99.1	98.6	0.0	0.0	0.3	0.3	0.2	0.3	5.1	5.4	6.0	6.1	4.3	26.0	33.2	12.8	1.3	79.8	43.3	50.8	49.2
14039	DALE	98.3	98.3	0.0	0.0	0.0	0.0	0.0	0.0	4.3	6.8	9.4	8.5	3.4	26.5	25.6	14.5	0.9	74.4	39.7	53.0	47.0
14040	DARIEN CENTER	99.0	98.6	0.1	0.1	0.0	0.0	0.3	0.4	5.4	5.9	6.7	7.9	5.2	24.7	30.2	12.8	1.1	76.9	41.3	52.4	47.6
14041	DAYTON	96.1	96.2	0.0	0.0	0.0	0.0	0.0	0.0	3.8	5.8	7.7	7.7	5.8	21.2	34.6	11.5	1.9	75.0	43.8	50.0	50.0
14042	DELEVAN	98.4	97.9	0.2	0.3	0.3	0.4	0.8	1.0	6.9	6.9	6.8	6.8	6.3	25.7	27.9	11.3	1.5	75.2	38.0	50.4	49.6
14043	DEPEW	97.6	96.1	0.8	1.6	0.5	0.7	0.8	1.2	5.7	5.7	5.9	5.9	5.0	26.1	28.2	15.2	2.3	78.9	42.1	48.4	51.6
14047	DERBY	98.3	97.4	0.3	0.5	0.3	0.5	1.3	2.0	5.6	6.0	6.8	7.4	5.5	24.6	31.6	10.8	1.7	76.8	41.2	48.5	51.5
14048	DUNKIRK	84.9	81.8	4.4	5.3	0.3	0.5	16.9	20.3	6.1	6.0	5.9	6.9	6.5	24.7	26.7	14.0	3.3	77.9	40.1	48.4	51.6
14051	EAST AMHERST	92.2	88.2	1.6	2.9	5.1	7.3	0.9	1.3	6.2	7.2	8.5	8.1	4.3	20.6	33.8	10.2	1.0	72.6	41.6	48.9	51.1
14052	EAST AURORA	98.9	98.1	0.2	0.3	0.3	0.5	0.6	0.9	5.3	6.0	6.8	6.8	4.8	21.1	31.5	14.7	2.9	77.2	44.3	48.4	51.6
14054	EAST BETHANY	97.0	96.2	0.8	1.0	0.2	0.3	0.4	0.4	5.6	6.1	6.3	6.4	4.8	25.7	31.4	12.6	1.1	78.3	41.5	52.1	47.9
14055	EAST CONCORD	98.1	96.8	0.4	0.8	0.3	0.4	0.8	1.2	5.6	6.6	7.6	6.4	5.0	23.8	32.1	11.7	1.2	76.0	41.6	50.3	49.7
14057	EDEN	98.3	97.3	0.4	0.8	0.2	0.3	1.0	1.6	5.3	6.3	7.2	7.4	4.6	23.6	30.5	12.9	2.3	76.3	42.3	49.7	50.3
14058	ELBA	93.4	92.0	1.6	1.9	0.1	0.1	5.0	6.2	6.2	6.9	7.3	7.5	5.1	24.5	29.9	11.4	1.3	74.9	39.6	50.9	49.1
14059	ELMA	99.1	98.5	0.1	0.1	0.3	0.4	0.6	0.9	4.8	5.8	6.6	6.8	4.3	20.4	33.2	16.2	2.0	78.2	45.8	49.2	50.8
14060	FARMERSVILLE STATION	98.5	97.9	0.2	0.2	0.2	0.3	1.0	1.2	6.9	7.1	7.3	6.9	5.9	23.1	28.8	12.7	1.4	74.5	39.3	49.6	50.4
14062	FORESTVILLE	97.4	96.2	0.3	0.7	0.2	0.3	1.5	1.9	5.4	5.9	6.5	6.3	4.7	24.4	31.6	13.7	1.5	78.1	42.9	50.6	49.4
14063	FREDONIA	95.0	93.6	2.3	2.7	0.8	1.2	2.5	3.3	3.9	3.8	4.0	15.0	16.3	22.8	21.8	10.2	2.2	84.9	30.0	47.3	52.7
14065	FREEDOM	98.4	98.0	0.2	0.2	0.2	0.3	0.9	1.2	7.0	7.2	7.4	7.2	5.8	24.7	29.7	10.0	0.9	73.9	37.9	50.8	49.2
14066	GAINESVILLE	97.9	97.1	0.4	0.6	0.6	0.8	0.6	0.8	5.3	7.8	9.1	9.0	4.6	25.2	29.1	8.6	1.2	71.3	37.8	51.1	48.9
14067	GASPORT	97.0	95.9	0.7	1.0	0.4	0.5	0.8	1.0	5.8	6.2	6.7	6.8	4.7	24.7	30.1	13.1	1.7	77.0	41.8	49.7	50.3
14068	GETZVILLE	91.4	86.7	2.0	3.6	5.0	7.3	1.1	1.5	5.4	6.3	7.3	7.7	4.5	21.2	32.8	11.0	3.9	75.7	43.3	47.1	52.9
14069	GLENWOOD	98.8	97.9	0.3	0.5	0.1	0.3	0.5	0.8	5.2	6.1	6.6	6.9	4.9	22.7	35.1	11.5	1.0	77.8	43.4	51.2	48.8
14070	GOWANDA	84.6	70.5	1.0	13.2	0.2	2.4	1.7	6.8	4.5	4.0	4.1	16.4	15.9	23.6	18.7	10.1	2.7	84.6	29.4	53.0	47.0
14072	GRAND ISLAND	95.8	93.1	1.7	3.0	1.2	1.8	1.1	1.6	5.6	6.2	7.1	7.4	4.6	22.6	32.8	12.3	1.5	76.2	42.6	49.1	50.9
14075	HAMBURG	98.2	97.1	0.4	0.8	0.4	0.6	1.2	1.8	5.5	5.9	6.5	6.5	5.0	23.2	30.1	14.2	3.1	77.9	43.2	47.5	52.5
14080	HOLLAND	98.3	97.3	0.4	0.8	0.3	0.5	0.4	0.7	5.9	7.0	7.4	7.1	4.4	26.4	30.2	10.5	1.1	75.2	40.0	50.2	49.8
14081	IRVING	65.2	61.3	0.8	1.2	0.1	0.1	1.7	2.3	7.1	6.6	6.7	7.1	6.5	24.8	26.9	12.3	2.1	75.0	38.4	47.1	52.9
14082	JAVA CENTER	99.2	98.9	0.2	0.2	0.0	0.0	0.4	0.7	6.7	7.0	7.2	6.5	4.9	26.7	28.9	10.8	1.3	75.1	39.1	49.8	50.2
14083	JAVA VILLAGE	99.5	99.5	0.0	0.0	0.0	0.0	0.5	0.5	6.1	7.1	7.1	6.1	5.1	27.0	30.1	10.2	1.0	75.5	40.8	52.0	48.0
14085	LAKE VIEW	99.2	98.5	0.1	0.2	0.2	0.3	1.0	1.5	6.7	7.2	7.7	7.5	5.3	24.0	29.9	10.5	1.2	73.7	39.7	49.9	50.1
14086	LANCASTER	98.1	96.7	0.8	1.6	0.4	0.6	0.7	1.0	6.3	6.5	6.8	6.5	5.2	25.3	29.1	11.9	2.3	76.1	40.7	48.2	51.8
14091	LAWTONS	70.4	68.9	1.3	2.4	0.2	0.3	1.5	2.2	7.6	6.9	7.1	7.6	5.5	26.5	26.4	11.0	1.4	73.9	37.7	49.6	50.4
14092	LEWISTON	95.4	94.4	1.0	1.3	0.7	1.0	0.8	1.0	4.6	5.1	6.0	6.6	4.7	20.6	31.0	17.8	3.6	80.4	46.5	47.4	52.6
14094	LOCKPORT	92.9	90.7	4.2	5.5	0.7	1.0	1.5	1.9	6.5	6.3	6.4	7.0	6.5	25.6	28.0	11.5	2.2	76.5	38.9	48.9	51.1
14098	LYNDONVILLE	97.0	96.0	0.9	1.1	0.3	0.4	1.1	1.5	6.0	6.5	6.9	7.1	5.9	22.6	31.9	11.4	1.7	76.3	40.8	50.7	49.3
14101	MACHIAS	98.1	97.3	0.2	0.3	0.1	0.2	0.9	1.2	5.3	5.8	6.5	7.2	4.4	22.6	30.3	14.0	3.9	77.7	43.7	49.6	50.4
14102	MARILLA	99.2	98.8	0.1	0.2	0.2	0.3	0.8	1.3	5.7	6.3	6.8	6.9	4.9	23.5	31.6	13.4	1.0	77.0	42.1	49.2	50.8
14103	MEDINA	90.7	88.7	5.8	6.8	0.4	0.6	2.8	3.5	6.9	6.7	6.5	7.7	6.8	23.9	26.4	12.2	2.9	75.1	38.0	48.3	51.7
14105	MIDDLEPORT	97.8	97.0	0.6	0.8	0.4	0.6	1.1	1.4	6.8	7.0	6.9	6.4	6.0	24.4	29.2	11.7	1.6	75.4	40.0	49.2	50.8
14108	NEWFANE	97.7	96.9	0.6	0.8	0.2	0.3	0.6	0.8	6.0	6.2	6.5	6.7	5.2	24.2	28.2	13.7	3.3	76.8	41.7	48.6	51.4
14109	NIAGARA UNIVERSITY	91.7	88.9	4.6	6.3	1.2	1.6	2.3	3.1	1.2	0.5	0.7	49.8	38.5	3.9	3.6	1.6	0.2	95.0	19.8	41.0	59.0
14111	NORTH COLLINS	91.4	89.3	0.5	0.8	0.7	0.9	2.5	3.4	5.5	6.2	6.9	7.4	5.2	25.3	28.8	13.0	1.7	76.7	41.0	49.0	51.0
14113	NORTH JAVA	98.4	97.7	0.3	0.5	0.1	0.2	0.3	0.3	7.1	7.4	7.5	6.7	5.1	26.7	27.0	11.2	1.4	73.8	38.0	49.5	50.5
14120	NORTH TONAWANDA	97.8	97.0	0.4	0.6	0.5	0.7	1.0	1.3	5.7	5.8	6.0	6.5	5.8	25.4	29.8	12.6	2.4	78.4	41.2	49.1	50.9
14125	OAKFIELD	96.8	96.1	1.1	1.2	0.2	0.3	1.2	1.4	6.0	6.4	6.7	7.8	6.1	26.5	28.0	10.9	1.5	75.9	38.3	48.8	51.2
14127	ORCHARD PARK	97.6	96.1	0.5	1.0	1.0	1.6	1.0	1.4	5.2	5.7	6.6	6.9	4.8	20.9	31.2	15.7	3.1	78.1	45.0	48.1	51.9
14129	PERRYSBURG	85.1	84.1	0.4	0.4	0.1	0.1	0.9	1.0	6.4	5.9	6.4	6.3	4.6	25.6	29.7	13.3	1.9	77.2	41.5	50.0	50.0
14131	RANSOMVILLE	97.5	96.7	0.5	0.7	0.2	0.2	0.8	1.0	5.4	5.9	6.6	6.7	5.1	24.0	30.8	13.7	1.8	78.0	42.4	49.7	50.3
14132	SANBORN	94.2	93.1	1.4	1.8	0.5	0.6	0.7	0.9	5.8	6.8	7.3	7.3	4.9	25.3	28.1	12.9	1.6	75.2	40.2	49.7	50.3
14134	SARDINIA	98.1	97.2	0.9	0.9	0.0	0.9	0.0	0.9	4.7	6.5	9.3	5.6	3.7	25.2	32.7	10.3	1.9	74.8	41.6	48.6	51.4
14136	SILVER CREEK	96.6	93.3	0.5	2.8	0.2	0.8	1.8	2.1	5.6	5.7	5.9	6.5	6.0	24.0	28.2	14.1	3.9	78.4	42.2	47.7	52.3
14138	SOUTH DAYTON	97.7	97.1	0.2	0.3	0.1	0.2	1.0	1.2	6.4	8.3	8.3	7.7	5.2	23.7	27.5	10.6	2.5	71.9	37.3	49.6	50.4
14139	SOUTH WALES	98.5	97.7	0.1	0.1	0.4	0.7	0.6	0.9	5.6	6.3	7.0	6.5	4.1	22.5	33.6	12.9	1.5	77.0	43.5	48.9	51.1
14141	SPRINGVILLE	98.3	97.3	0.5	1.0	0.3	0.4	1.2	1.9	6.0	5.9	6.2	6.7	6.2	23.2	29.6	13.2	3.0	77.5	42.0	48.8	51.2
14143	STAFFORD	97.3	96.4	1.2	1.5	0.4	0.5	0.3	0.3	4.6	5.0	5.8	6.8	4.5	25.7	31.4	14.2	2.1	80.4	43.4	49.9	50.1
14145	STRYKERSVILLE	99.8	99.7	0.1	0.1	0.1	0.1	0.1	0.2	7.5	7.9	8.1	6.8	4.2	27.3	26.9	9.7	1.5	72.6	37.0	51.8	48.2
14150	TONAWANDA	96.2	94.2	1.3	2.2	1.2	1.7	1.1	1.6	5.2	5.3	5.5	6.0	5.7	24.6	28.6	16.4	2.8	80.4	43.3	48.3	51.7
14167	VARYSBURG	99.1	98.9	0.1	0.1	0.2	0.3	0.4	0.6	5.3	6.3	7.1	7.8	4.7	25.1	31.7	10.9	1.1	76.2	41.0	50.4	49.6
14170	WEST FALLS	98.5	97.6	0.2	0.4	0.6	1.0	0.7	1.0	5.5	6.2	7.1	6.8	5.0	21.4	32.6	13.8	1.6	76.7	43.6	49.3	50.7
14171	WEST VALLEY	97.5	96.5	1.0	1.4	0.1	0.2	0.8	1.1	6.2	6.4	6.7	7.0	5.4	24.2	31.1	12.0	1.2	76.5	41.3	50.1	49.9
14172	WILSON	97.7	96.9	0.4	0.6	0.2	0.4	0.8	1.1	5.3	5.7	6.2	6.5	5.1	22.8	32.2	13.9	2.1	78.8	43.8	49.2	50.8
14174	YOUNGSTOWN	97.6	96.8	0.4	0.5	0.6	0.8	0.8	1.0	5.1	5.9	6.6	7.1	4.7	22.1	32.4	13.9	2.2	77.8	43.9	49.3	50.7
14201	BUFFALO	43.4	35.2	26.5	33.4	2.0	2.0	37.2	38.0	8.2	7.5	6.0	6.8	8.9	27.4	22.9	10.0	2.4	74.8	33.0	48.0	52.0
14202	BUFFALO	61.9	49.8	33.3	44.6	1.0	1.3	5.3	6.1	1.9	1.5	1.4	7.5	11.1	38.9	21.1	14.3	2.3	91.7	37.9	61.0	39.0
14203	BUFFALO	23.0	15.1	70.8	78.9	0.1	0.1	5.1	4.8	5.7	7.7	6.1	6.9	6.5	23.1	26.0	16.4	1.7	76.0	41.2	54.7	45.3
14204	BUFFALO	19.6	16.6	74.0	76.8	0.5	0.5	7.6	7.5	7.2	7.5	7.1	7.5	6.7	21.8	26.8	13.5	1.9	73.7	38.2	45.4	54.6
14206	BUFFALO	88.5	87.2	9.1	9.6	0.5	0.6	1.5	2.1	6.0	5.8	5.8	6.0	5.8	25.3	27.6	14.6	3.1	78.8	41.7	47.9	52.1
14207	BUFFALO	84.3	77.7	6.4	9.9	1.0	1.4	8.6	11.4	7.6	7.3	7.0	7.1	7.4	26.7	24.2	10.7	1.9	73.7	35.1	48.4	51.6
14208	BUFFALO	11.7	8.2	85.0	88.4	0.6	0.6	1.7	1.7	5.8	6.6	6.5	11.4	9.7	19.2	21.9	15.0	3.9	77.0	35.9	43.6	56.4
	NEW YORK	67.9	64.8	15.9	16.5	5.6	6.9	15.1	16.7	6.5	6.4	6.4	7.1	7.0	27.0	26.3	11.2	2.1	76.6	37.5	48.4	51.6
	UNITED STATES	75.1	72.0	12.3	12.7	3.8	4.6	12.5	15.7	6.8	6.7	6.6	7.1	6.9	27.0	26.0	10.9	1.9	75.7	36.9	49.2	50.8

#	POST OFFICE NAME	2009 Per Capita Income	2009 HH Income Base	2009 HOUSEHOLD INCOME DISTRIBUTION (%) Less than $25,000	$25,000 to $49,999	$50,000 to $99,999	$100,000 to $149,999	$150,000 or More	MEDIAN HOUSEHOLD INCOME 2009	2014	2009 National Centile	2009 State Centile	2009 Home Value Base	2009 HOME VALUE DISTRIBUTION (%) Less than $50,000	$50,000 to $89,999	$90,000 to $174,999	$175,000 to $399,999	$400,000 or More	2009 Median Home Value
13865	WINDSOR	20241	2417	19.5	31.8	40.5	5.9	2.3	48660	52112	58	42	1921	12.8	15.4	50.4	20.4	1.1	130304
13901	BINGHAMTON	24372	8624	34.9	22.6	30.7	8.1	3.8	41939	45063	39	20	4773	4.0	11.3	56.7	26.8	1.3	143563
13903	BINGHAMTON	25315	7790	25.3	25.1	36.7	8.0	4.9	49487	53114	60	44	5041	2.5	13.0	57.4	23.8	3.4	137827
13904	BINGHAMTON	21661	3659	27.5	29.9	34.5	5.4	2.7	43286	46835	43	24	2366	5.1	12.8	64.6	14.5	3.0	127971
13905	BINGHAMTON	22536	11759	36.3	26.5	27.9	6.0	3.3	36659	40616	23	7	5704	3.4	12.0	56.2	25.9	2.5	140459
14001	AKRON	23771	3850	17.5	29.6	43.8	7.5	1.6	52680	57151	67	52	2928	7.2	9.3	46.2	36.1	1.2	155213
14004	ALDEN	24449	3916	13.9	24.1	49.1	8.6	4.3	61439	63623	79	67	3161	5.9	5.1	44.3	43.1	1.6	168117
14005	ALEXANDER	22514	678	14.5	28.2	47.9	7.5	1.9	56739	60465	74	60	550	2.9	7.1	68.0	19.8	2.2	129960
14006	ANGOLA	23725	4115	18.3	31.1	36.9	10.4	3.3	50666	55453	63	47	3172	5.7	18.3	52.4	21.7	2.0	131864
14008	APPLETON	21449	554	15.9	27.1	45.8	8.3	2.9	56416	60301	73	59	454	3.7	12.1	58.8	24.0	1.3	136697
14009	ARCADE	21282	2226	21.4	31.9	37.7	8.1	0.9	47154	49347	55	38	1732	9.9	15.8	47.5	25.6	1.2	129118
14011	ATTICA	20373	2201	16.3	25.1	47.2	8.8	2.6	60010	61141	77	63	1646	2.6	10.6	63.4	21.9	1.5	133333
14012	BARKER	21137	914	19.4	28.6	39.2	10.7	2.2	51696	54853	65	50	708	5.5	14.7	59.6	18.8	1.4	132865
14013	BASOM	16819	612	26.1	33.2	35.1	5.4	0.2	42490	45401	41	22	500	16.6	20.8	45.2	16.4	1.0	108611
14020	BATAVIA	22712	8822	25.3	30.8	34.3	6.5	3.0	44777	48045	48	30	5582	6.0	9.5	64.0	19.7	0.9	126990
14024	BLISS	19663	603	20.6	36.0	36.0	5.3	2.2	45790	47826	51	33	494	8.3	32.0	46.6	12.1	1.0	101111
14025	BOSTON	25214	1185	12.7	30.4	43.0	9.5	4.4	56902	61159	74	60	931	1.0	3.1	44.4	46.9	4.6	177483
14026	BOWMANSVILLE	35647	352	10.8	15.3	42.6	22.7	8.5	77099	79585	91	82	304	1.6	3.6	22.4	71.1	1.3	217532
14028	BURT	25341	769	10.0	30.4	48.8	8.6	2.2	60712	62860	78	65	611	6.5	11.8	56.8	23.6	1.3	134896
14030	CHAFFEE	20793	559	19.3	32.2	39.4	7.5	1.6	48190	51598	57	41	458	5.9	8.7	55.0	28.4	2.0	151064
14031	CLARENCE	37620	3550	12.2	18.6	34.8	19.7	14.6	75506	78435	90	81	2818	12.3	2.4	16.0	53.7	15.5	223581
14032	CLARENCE CENTER	33998	2059	5.3	16.8	43.2	19.5	15.2	77843	80003	91	83	1764	0.0	0.8	17.7	64.3	17.1	242790
14033	COLDEN	27416	1025	13.1	26.7	44.1	10.3	5.8	61256	64738	79	66	846	4.4	4.1	36.9	46.2	8.4	182500
14034	COLLINS	21688	814	24.3	27.5	38.0	6.6	3.6	47013	52583	54	37	659	8.8	23.8	49.9	16.5	0.9	113209
14036	CORFU	22252	1969	12.7	31.6	45.9	7.8	2.1	54784	58779	71	57	1550	1.5	6.2	59.3	31.9	1.1	149177
14037	COWLESVILLE	23738	423	11.6	28.4	47.3	7.3	5.4	58861	60363	76	62	366	3.3	8.2	51.9	35.0	1.6	155556
14039	DALE	22500	45	17.8	26.7	46.7	8.9	0.0	54495	57071	70	56	40	2.5	17.5	65.0	12.5	2.5	117308
14040	DARIEN CENTER	23719	793	9.1	29.1	46.4	13.4	2.0	62379	63853	80	68	666	0.3	4.1	55.7	38.9	1.1	153797
14041	DAYTON	16833	18	33.3	27.8	33.3	5.6	0.0	40000	45000	33	14	15	0.0	26.7	46.7	26.7	0.0	115625
14042	DELEVAN	19403	2002	28.0	30.7	35.4	4.2	1.7	40641	43602	35	16	1506	19.3	18.3	50.6	10.8	1.1	107588
14043	DEPEW	27757	11368	15.7	25.6	43.6	11.3	3.9	60284	63299	78	64	8232	2.5	2.9	60.8	33.3	0.5	155805
14047	DERBY	27461	2550	12.6	20.2	47.5	15.1	4.6	66356	69095	84	73	2058	9.1	9.7	56.9	22.8	1.6	140632
14048	DUNKIRK	20482	6300	33.4	27.1	32.7	4.6	2.2	37899	41636	26	9	4023	11.1	33.2	45.8	8.9	1.1	97311
14051	EAST AMHERST	47868	6962	4.9	7.9	33.7	24.9	28.6	106911	110821	98	94	6192	0.0	0.6	14.2	66.4	18.8	281489
14052	EAST AURORA	29970	6648	13.0	23.3	40.8	16.2	6.7	65239	68018	83	72	5290	6.7	2.7	28.6	54.9	7.0	193329
14054	EAST BETHANY	23110	542	11.1	32.7	45.6	9.4	1.3	55069	58857	71	57	437	4.3	13.7	56.5	24.7	0.7	135441
14055	EAST CONCORD	21108	544	17.8	30.1	41.5	7.9	2.6	51701	55779	65	50	448	2.7	7.1	52.7	35.0	2.5	157716
14057	EDEN	28538	3003	10.6	22.6	45.8	13.6	7.3	67652	70298	85	74	2508	0.8	1.1	44.2	50.4	3.5	180865
14058	ELBA	23151	808	13.7	24.4	48.5	9.9	3.5	60075	62225	77	64	662	5.1	12.7	66.3	14.4	1.5	132532
14059	ELMA	33173	3556	10.2	18.6	43.3	17.3	10.6	70639	73134	87	77	3026	0.9	1.2	20.7	66.9	10.3	224570
14060	FARMERSVILLE STATION	17159	215	26.5	37.7	31.2	4.2	0.5	38275	40158	28	10	174	14.4	26.4	45.4	13.8	0.0	102679
14062	FORESTVILLE	20884	1264	21.0	29.3	42.0	6.1	1.7	49766	52625	60	44	1022	8.0	17.3	54.2	17.5	2.9	122821
14063	FREDONIA	23035	5181	24.4	27.3	36.4	8.7	3.2	48055	51946	57	40	3254	5.7	10.4	54.3	26.5	3.1	142548
14065	FREEDOM	17048	641	24.2	36.7	33.5	4.2	1.4	40171	42494	33	15	527	11.2	23.0	46.5	18.6	0.8	112656
14066	GAINESVILLE	18763	601	20.6	36.1	37.4	4.7	1.2	44936	47485	48	30	490	10.6	31.6	45.3	11.6	0.8	99268
14067	GASPORT	23129	2053	13.6	30.8	43.9	7.9	3.8	55867	60275	72	58	1690	2.4	9.3	60.7	27.2	0.4	141985
14068	GETZVILLE	34064	2444	15.1	11.3	33.7	20.9	19.1	84020	87118	94	86	1907	0.1	1.2	26.2	68.0	4.5	230371
14069	GLENWOOD	27884	315	14.0	31.1	42.5	6.0	6.3	54211	58861	70	55	262	3.8	6.5	43.1	42.4	4.2	169512
14070	GOWANDA	18083	2213	30.5	31.6	29.8	7.0	1.1	39982	42226	32	14	1548	9.2	32.4	48.3	9.8	0.2	98217
14072	GRAND ISLAND	33480	7191	9.2	21.2	36.7	21.9	11.0	74349	76770	89	80	5785	1.0	2.0	35.9	54.9	6.3	193541
14075	HAMBURG	29283	16640	14.0	23.0	42.5	15.0	5.6	63131	65966	81	69	12420	6.3	3.8	46.8	40.8	2.3	166060
14080	HOLLAND	23340	1750	16.6	26.4	44.3	10.6	2.0	57857	61184	75	61	1373	5.3	5.5	42.2	44.8	2.1	170817
14081	IRVING	20824	1372	24.1	30.0	35.9	8.0	2.1	47171	49215	55	38	1035	9.4	24.3	47.1	17.4	1.8	112301
14082	JAVA CENTER	24619	170	15.9	27.1	42.4	10.6	4.1	55495	56548	72	58	139	2.2	10.8	55.4	29.5	2.2	142672
14083	JAVA VILLAGE	21207	66	15.2	25.8	43.9	12.1	3.0	54814	54981	71	57	54	0.0	7.4	61.1	27.8	3.7	147727
14085	LAKE VIEW	30869	2318	6.7	11.9	52.8	22.5	6.1	76668	77348	90	82	2057	0.2	2.1	46.7	46.8	4.2	176342
14086	LANCASTER	28219	11261	14.3	19.8	43.8	16.3	5.8	66123	68903	84	73	8693	0.8	2.7	44.4	50.2	1.8	178101
14091	LAWTONS	20083	409	22.0	29.3	38.1	7.3	3.2	48523	51298	58	42	332	9.6	20.2	39.2	29.2	1.8	133125
14092	LEWISTON	33832	4511	14.3	22.6	36.8	16.2	10.2	67286	69998	85	74	3499	1.0	1.7	45.0	46.2	6.1	178639
14094	LOCKPORT	26303	20161	21.2	26.3	35.5	11.9	5.1	52697	57425	67	53	13785	7.8	14.7	47.2	28.5	1.9	139252
14098	LYNDONVILLE	19482	1155	20.7	29.2	42.4	6.9	0.8	50114	53318	61	45	945	10.2	28.4	46.9	13.2	1.4	103054
14101	MACHIAS	18615	740	30.9	28.9	30.0	8.6	1.5	40274	43908	34	15	584	11.8	19.5	46.2	20.4	2.1	113696
14102	MARILLA	26994	596	7.7	23.7	51.8	14.1	2.7	67162	68419	85	74	518	0.0	2.1	27.6	68.0	2.3	202083
14103	MEDINA	21304	4223	26.1	29.4	34.7	7.1	2.6	43133	46498	43	23	2915	11.6	34.7	44.0	8.9	0.9	94222
14105	MIDDLEPORT	22191	1600	16.2	31.4	42.9	6.8	2.7	52066	55897	66	51	1210	4.8	16.3	62.9	15.8	0.2	125685
14108	NEWFANE	23645	2219	16.1	30.5	40.2	8.6	4.6	53900	59854	69	55	1783	5.6	8.5	63.2	22.3	0.4	133806
14109	NIAGARA UNIVERSITY	13600	0	0.0	0.0	0.0	0.0	0.0	0	0	0	0	0	0.0	0.0	0.0	0.0	0.0	0
14111	NORTH COLLINS	24154	1159	18.3	25.6	44.3	8.7	3.0	54663	58802	71	56	908	3.6	12.3	59.9	22.5	1.7	135756
14113	NORTH JAVA	25014	241	14.9	24.1	45.2	11.2	4.6	61163	62072	79	66	196	1.5	6.1	57.7	33.2	1.5	147917
14120	NORTH TONAWANDA	25875	17641	19.6	25.7	39.3	11.4	4.1	55331	60160	72	58	12485	1.6	7.7	56.6	33.1	1.0	150475
14125	OAKFIELD	21057	1256	18.1	28.6	41.8	9.9	1.7	52604	56207	67	52	968	4.0	13.4	68.9	12.4	1.2	118080
14127	ORCHARD PARK	36472	10869	9.6	19.0	39.3	18.0	14.1	74993	77133	89	81	8257	0.5	1.3	28.2	57.9	12.0	219477
14129	PERRYSBURG	19802	603	24.5	33.8	33.8	6.3	1.5	42876	45352	42	22	476	10.7	25.6	47.5	15.8	0.4	111218
14131	RANSOMVILLE	25983	2178	14.8	23.6	44.9	11.1	5.6	61480	63614	79	67	1743	9.0	9.0	44.6	35.9	1.5	156420
14132	SANBORN	25400	2168	17.0	26.1	40.3	11.5	5.1	58402	61921	76	61	1701	2.1	3.5	48.4	44.8	1.3	170343
14134	SARDINIA	21668	41	22.0	29.3	41.5	7.3	0.0	48654	53313	58	42	33	0.0	6.1	54.5	36.4	3.0	157500
14136	SILVER CREEK	22301	2054	21.8	30.0	39.3	6.3	2.6	48376	52232	57	41	1544	10.6	14.0	58.5	14.2	2.7	120000
14138	SOUTH DAYTON	17498	725	27.0	34.3	32.6	4.8	1.2	39411	42833	31	13	570	14.0	29.6	43.9	10.5	1.9	97059
14139	SOUTH WALES	29642	822	12.8	24.1	42.0	15.2	6.0	64476	67278	83	71	679	12.1	2.1	27.8	48.0	10.0	192695
14141	SPRINGVILLE	23849	3084	20.1	28.5	40.7	7.2	3.6	51093	54420	64	49	2180	6.1	10.8	53.5	27.8	1.7	143100
14143	STAFFORD	27662	414	11.6	21.7	50.7	10.9	5.1	64651	67533	83	71	338	3.0	10.4	62.1	22.8	1.8	138333
14145	STRYKERSVILLE	22457	547	9.9	34.6	43.7	8.8	3.1	53465	54612	69	54	454	0.0	5.1	53.7	38.3	2.9	161842
14150	TONAWANDA	25708	18491	19.8	27.0	42.5	8.2	2.5	52737	56357	67	53	13220	0.9	6.9	76.0	16.1	0.2	138386
14167	VARYSBURG	21213	637	19.5	29.4	43.3	6.0	1.9	51291	53801	64	49	523	6.1	16.3	49.9	26.0	1.7	135648
14170	WEST FALLS	33169	888	9.3	21.7	41.4	18.0	9.5	72719	75438	88	79	735	1.2	2.3	33.3	53.9	9.3	194775
14171	WEST VALLEY	22396	852	19.7	30.5	41.3	6.2	2.2	49804	50582	61	44	700	5.7	12.4	54.0	25.0	2.9	135714
14172	WILSON	25984	1374	12.4	28.0	47.0	9.7	2.8	60215	62339	78	64	1132	7.5	9.9	51.5	30.0	1.1	148507
14174	YOUNGSTOWN	30537	2183	12.8	23.9	40.4	14.8	8.1	63754	66793	82	70	1706	4.3	6.6	42.1	43.0	3.9	170113
14201	BUFFALO	15623	5838	59.8	21.6	14.2	2.8	1.5	18418	19226	1	1	1052	14.0	30.8	39.4	15.0	0.8	95046
14202	BUFFALO	28548	1707	39.7	31.4	19.4	2.7	6.8	30671	32839	9	4	336	6.0	1.5	11.3	57.4	23.8	233333
14203	BUFFALO	13290	702	73.1	20.1	4.7	1.3	0.9	12700	12345	1	1	59	13.6	81.4	5.1	0.0	0.0	57963
14204	BUFFALO	15192	4119	57.8	23.2	14.5	2.6	1.9	19318	20370	1	1	1255	35.1	25.2	34.8	4.9	0.0	70068
14206	BUFFALO	19709	9525	35.1	30.8	29.2	4.0	1.0	35278	38814	19	6	5913	11.6	25.0	60.4	3.0	0.0	100903
14207	BUFFALO	16378	9165	41.6	31.6	22.9	3.1	0.8	29463	31393	7	4	4133	10.4	41.8	45.5	2.0	0.3	88315
14208	BUFFALO	16331	4573	45.7	30.3	19.4	3.2	1.4	27404	29106	5	3	2100	23.7	39.0	34.5	2.6	0.3	76649
	NEW YORK	29893		21.9	21.3	32.7	14.0	9.9	58747	62337				3.4	5.7	23.0	38.7	29.1	269816
	UNITED STATES	27277		20.9	24.4	35.3	11.7	7.6	54719	56938				9.3	13.1	31.6	32.6	13.5	162279

#	POST OFFICE NAME	FINANCIAL SERVICES: Auto Loan	Home Loan	Invest-ments	Retire-ment Plans	THE HOME: Home Improvements: Home Repair	Lawn & Garden	Furnishings: Comput-ers & Hard-ware-Personal	Major Appli-ances	TV, Radio, Sound Equip-ment	Furni-ture	ENTERTAINMENT: Dine out/ Carry out	Sports Equip-ment	Fees & Tickets	Toys & Games	Travel	Cable TV	PERSONAL: Apparel & Services	Auto Repairs	Health Insur-ance	Pets & Supplies
13865	WINDSOR	87	75	81	74	75	88	74	83	78	73	77	62	67	79	72	82	52	79	85	98
13901	BINGHAMTON	71	70	67	71	69	74	75	72	78	72	77	55	75	76	73	80	54	75	81	86
13903	BINGHAMTON	83	83	76	84	80	87	85	83	87	81	87	64	85	87	83	90	61	85	90	99
13904	BINGHAMTON	77	69	71	69	68	80	72	76	76	67	74	58	68	75	70	80	51	75	82	90
13905	BINGHAMTON	71	60	60	62	60	65	75	67	75	69	74	52	67	74	67	76	52	72	73	81
14001	AKRON	85	84	79	86	84	93	81	87	84	77	83	66	80	84	82	87	57	84	93	102
14004	ALDEN	90	105	92	106	101	105	92	96	93	92	94	73	102	95	99	95	66	94	101	113
14005	ALEXANDER	90	96	85	95	93	96	86	91	88	88	88	67	90	90	89	90	61	88	93	106
14006	ANGOLA	82	89	82	89	86	94	82	86	85	80	84	65	87	85	86	88	59	85	93	101
14008	APPLETON	91	92	88	94	92	102	86	95	88	81	87	71	86	90	89	92	60	89	98	110
14009	ARCADE	82	74	78	75	75	88	72	82	76	68	75	62	68	77	73	81	51	77	86	96
14011	ATTICA	86	93	83	93	91	93	87	89	87	86	88	68	91	89	90	89	61	87	92	105
14012	BARKER	92	84	83	87	86	99	83	93	85	75	84	71	76	87	83	90	57	86	96	108
14013	BASOM	77	63	71	64	64	80	64	74	68	58	66	57	56	69	62	73	45	69	77	88
14020	BATAVIA	78	72	69	73	71	80	77	77	80	72	79	59	73	79	74	83	54	78	84	92
14024	BLISS	87	75	82	77	76	93	75	87	78	67	76	67	66	79	75	83	52	80	90	102
14025	BOSTON	89	103	92	104	100	103	90	95	91	90	91	73	99	93	97	93	64	92	98	111
14026	BOWMANSVILLE	111	138	123	137	132	135	117	122	119	119	120	91	135	120	130	121	84	120	129	142
14028	BURT	84	98	91	97	97	103	86	92	90	85	90	66	96	89	94	94	63	90	103	106
14030	CHAFFEE	85	78	75	80	79	89	77	85	79	71	78	64	71	81	76	83	53	79	87	99
14031	CLARENCE	131	160	157	163	162	158	137	146	136	144	137	108	156	135	153	137	97	140	147	168
14032	CLARENCE CENTER	136	161	149	166	159	155	140	146	136	144	138	113	155	139	152	136	98	140	142	170
14033	COLDEN	96	113	99	115	109	111	99	103	98	100	99	79	109	101	107	99	70	100	105	121
14034	COLLINS	98	75	97	75	78	101	76	94	83	71	81	70	64	83	76	90	54	86	97	111
14036	CORFU	83	90	84	91	89	91	84	87	84	81	84	67	87	85	88	86	59	85	89	102
14037	COWLESVILLE	95	100	90	104	99	104	92	98	92	90	92	76	95	94	96	93	64	93	98	115
14039	DALE	91	83	82	86	84	97	81	92	84	74	82	70	75	86	81	89	56	85	95	107
14040	DARIEN CENTER	89	105	92	106	101	103	91	95	91	92	92	73	101	93	99	92	64	92	97	111
14041	DAYTON	75	69	68	71	70	81	68	76	70	61	69	58	62	71	68	74	47	71	79	89
14042	DELEVAN	80	65	70	64	65	78	66	75	71	64	69	56	58	72	63	75	47	71	77	88
14043	DEPEW	89	100	91	99	97	102	91	95	93	91	93	70	98	94	96	96	65	93	102	110
14047	DERBY	95	114	99	113	108	113	99	102	101	100	101	77	112	102	107	103	71	101	109	120
14048	DUNKIRK	69	63	60	64	62	70	68	67	70	64	70	52	65	70	65	73	48	69	73	81
14051	EAST AMHERST	181	229	225	236	231	207	193	199	182	206	185	156	224	186	214	176	135	188	179	227
14052	EAST AURORA	103	118	111	118	117	120	105	111	106	107	106	82	114	106	113	108	74	107	116	128
14054	EAST BETHANY	94	87	85	90	88	102	85	96	88	77	86	72	79	89	85	93	59	89	99	111
14055	EAST CONCORD	91	83	82	87	85	98	82	93	85	74	83	70	76	86	82	90	57	86	96	108
14057	EDEN	101	124	110	124	119	122	106	111	107	108	108	83	121	109	117	109	76	108	116	129
14058	ELBA	91	97	91	99	96	104	89	96	91	85	90	73	92	92	94	94	63	92	101	112
14059	ELMA	113	138	134	139	138	136	118	126	118	123	119	92	135	118	132	119	84	121	129	145
14060	FARMERSVILLE STATION	78	59	74	58	61	80	61	74	67	56	66	56	51	67	60	73	44	69	78	88
14062	FORESTVILLE	89	72	85	73	74	92	73	86	77	67	76	65	63	78	72	83	51	80	89	101
14063	FREDONIA	79	77	79	77	77	80	82	79	81	78	81	62	79	81	80	82	57	81	82	94
14065	FREEDOM	80	64	72	64	65	81	65	75	69	60	68	57	55	71	62	75	46	70	79	90
14066	GAINESVILLE	81	69	77	71	71	87	70	81	72	62	71	63	61	73	70	77	48	75	84	95
14067	GASPORT	89	94	88	96	93	101	86	94	88	82	88	71	89	89	91	92	61	89	98	109
14068	GETZVILLE	129	161	155	164	161	147	137	141	131	145	133	109	157	133	151	128	96	135	133	161
14069	GLENWOOD	102	100	94	104	100	111	95	105	97	89	96	80	92	99	97	101	66	98	107	122
14070	GOWANDA	71	61	64	61	61	71	66	69	70	62	69	52	60	69	63	74	47	69	75	82
14072	GRAND ISLAND	117	140	134	142	140	136	122	128	120	126	121	96	136	121	133	120	86	123	127	147
14075	HAMBURG	95	108	103	108	108	111	99	103	101	99	101	76	108	100	106	104	71	101	111	119
14080	HOLLAND	90	94	85	97	93	98	87	93	87	84	86	72	88	89	90	88	60	88	93	109
14081	IRVING	80	81	73	79	79	85	77	80	80	76	79	59	78	80	77	83	55	79	86	94
14082	JAVA CENTER	89	100	90	101	97	102	89	95	90	88	90	72	95	91	95	92	63	91	97	110
14083	JAVA VILLAGE	88	99	85	102	96	97	88	92	87	89	87	72	94	89	93	87	61	88	91	108
14085	LAKE VIEW	115	144	128	143	138	135	122	126	120	125	122	96	139	123	134	120	86	122	126	146
14086	LANCASTER	101	115	101	113	110	110	103	105	103	105	104	80	111	105	108	104	73	103	108	122
14091	LAWTONS	88	83	77	85	82	91	81	87	84	78	83	66	78	85	81	87	57	84	89	103
14092	LEWISTON	108	123	123	123	126	129	111	119	114	114	114	84	122	111	121	118	79	116	129	136
14094	LOCKPORT	90	90	81	91	87	91	92	89	93	89	93	69	92	94	90	95	65	91	95	106
14098	LYNDONVILLE	81	74	73	77	75	87	73	82	75	66	74	62	67	77	73	80	50	76	85	95
14101	MACHIAS	85	64	92	62	67	87	65	81	70	61	69	61	54	69	66	76	46	75	83	96
14102	MARILLA	109	122	105	126	119	120	109	114	107	110	108	89	117	110	115	108	76	109	112	134
14103	MEDINA	80	73	69	74	71	83	76	79	79	70	78	61	71	79	73	83	53	78	86	94
14105	MIDDLEPORT	87	84	75	86	82	93	83	87	85	77	84	68	80	87	82	88	57	84	93	104
14108	NEWFANE	88	93	85	94	91	100	87	92	89	83	89	69	89	90	90	93	61	89	100	108
14109	NIAGARA UNIVERSITY	0	0	0	0	0	0	0	0	0	0	0	0	0	0	0	0	0	0	0	0
14111	NORTH COLLINS	85	91	81	92	89	97	85	89	88	82	87	67	88	88	88	91	60	87	97	105
14113	NORTH JAVA	90	106	97	106	102	107	92	97	93	92	94	74	102	94	101	96	66	95	102	114
14120	NORTH TONAWANDA	87	93	82	94	90	96	90	90	91	87	91	69	93	92	91	93	63	90	97	106
14125	OAKFIELD	86	82	74	85	80	92	81	86	83	75	82	66	78	85	80	87	56	83	91	102
14127	ORCHARD PARK	125	146	142	147	146	146	129	136	130	132	130	101	143	129	140	132	92	132	140	157
14129	PERRYSBURG	81	69	76	70	70	84	69	79	72	64	71	60	61	73	68	77	48	74	82	93
14131	RANSOMVILLE	96	107	99	108	105	113	95	103	98	93	98	77	103	99	102	102	68	99	109	119
14132	SANBORN	90	103	93	103	101	105	91	96	93	91	94	71	100	94	98	96	65	94	102	112
14134	SARDINIA	88	80	79	83	81	94	79	89	81	71	80	67	73	83	79	86	54	82	92	103
14136	SILVER CREEK	82	77	79	77	78	88	75	83	79	73	78	60	72	79	76	83	53	79	89	96
14138	SOUTH DAYTON	81	61	81	61	63	84	63	77	68	57	67	59	52	68	62	74	44	71	80	92
14139	SOUTH WALES	99	116	106	117	114	116	101	107	102	103	102	80	113	102	111	104	72	104	111	125
14141	SPRINGVILLE	91	81	82	83	83	94	84	90	86	79	85	67	77	87	82	90	58	87	95	105
14143	STAFFORD	93	113	101	113	109	112	97	102	98	98	99	76	110	100	107	101	70	99	107	118
14145	STRYKERSVILLE	88	99	85	102	96	97	89	92	87	89	88	72	94	89	94	87	61	89	91	109
14150	TONAWANDA	80	83	77	83	82	90	81	83	85	79	84	61	84	84	83	89	59	84	93	98
14167	VARYSBURG	84	83	78	86	83	91	78	86	79	74	79	66	77	81	80	82	54	80	87	100
14170	WEST FALLS	109	137	125	138	133	132	115	120	115	119	117	91	134	117	129	116	83	117	123	139
14171	WEST VALLEY	89	81	78	81	81	90	78	86	81	75	80	64	73	83	77	84	54	81	88	101
14172	WILSON	88	100	93	100	98	105	88	96	92	87	92	70	97	92	96	96	64	92	104	110
14174	YOUNGSTOWN	104	119	112	120	118	124	105	113	107	105	107	83	115	108	114	111	75	109	119	131
14201	BUFFALO	43	32	30	35	31	35	47	38	49	42	49	31	41	48	39	51	35	45	44	48
14202	BUFFALO	67	63	66	65	64	68	74	67	76	71	77	51	73	72	72	79	53	74	80	81
14203	BUFFALO	26	19	21	21	19	23	30	24	33	27	33	19	27	29	26	35	23	30	33	32
14204	BUFFALO	45	33	32	36	32	39	44	39	49	42	48	30	40	47	38	52	33	45	49	50
14206	BUFFALO	61	56	52	57	55	63	60	60	64	57	63	45	58	63	57	67	43	62	68	72
14207	BUFFALO	54	44	40	46	42	49	55	49	58	50	57	39	50	57	48	60	40	54	56	61
14208	BUFFALO	56	45	43	46	43	53	51	50	58	52	56	36	48	56	47	61	38	54	59	63
	NEW YORK	100	106	110	108	107	104	112	106	113	106	114	81	115	110	112	116	83	110	110	124
	UNITED STATES	100	100	100	100	100	100	100	100	100	100	100	100	100	100	100	100	100	100	100	100

#	POST OFFICE NAME	COUNTY FIPS CODE	POPULATION 2000	POPULATION 2009	POPULATION 2014	2000-2009 ANNUAL RATE % Rate	2000-2009 ANNUAL RATE State Centile	HOUSEHOLDS 2000	HOUSEHOLDS 2009	HOUSEHOLDS 2014	HOUSEHOLDS % Annual Rate 2000-2009	HOUSEHOLDS 2009 Average HH Size	FAMILIES 2000	FAMILIES 2009	FAMILIES % Annual Rate 2000-2009
14209	BUFFALO	029	7849	7595	7417	-0.4	11	3853	3760	3680	-0.3	1.90	1482	1393	-0.7
14210	BUFFALO	029	16836	15666	15111	-0.8	2	6826	6492	6303	-0.5	2.41	4249	3943	-0.8
14211	BUFFALO	029	28898	24315	23041	-1.8	1	11532	9793	9308	-1.8	2.45	7122	5887	-2.0
14212	BUFFALO	029	16139	13447	12751	-2.0	0	7228	6077	5786	-1.9	2.21	3936	3228	-2.1
14213	BUFFALO	029	28573	25791	24731	-1.1	1	10526	9483	9074	-1.1	2.48	6008	5244	-1.5
14214	BUFFALO	029	22780	21598	20963	-0.6	4	8752	8387	8166	-0.5	2.31	4605	4261	-0.8
14215	BUFFALO	029	43924	40910	39451	-0.8	2	17197	16094	15558	-0.7	2.49	11015	10062	-1.0
14216	BUFFALO	029	23161	22157	21516	-0.5	7	10647	10419	10182	-0.2	2.11	5607	5302	-0.6
14217	BUFFALO	029	24384	23448	22806	-0.4	11	10557	10377	10160	-0.2	2.20	6210	5932	-0.5
14218	BUFFALO	029	20264	19334	18774	-0.5	7	8639	8441	8259	-0.3	2.26	5146	4893	-0.5
14219	BUFFALO	029	13044	12377	11988	-0.6	4	5388	5245	5118	-0.3	2.34	3451	3279	-0.6
14220	BUFFALO	029	26445	25036	24240	-0.6	4	10439	10117	9858	-0.3	2.40	6612	6248	-0.6
14221	BUFFALO	029	51494	50655	49648	-0.2	21	20609	20750	20485	0.1	2.36	13997	13808	-0.1
14222	BUFFALO	029	12797	12358	12041	-0.4	11	7044	6890	6738	-0.2	1.72	2222	2079	-0.7
14223	BUFFALO	029	24468	23394	22704	-0.5	7	10244	9995	9759	-0.3	2.31	6732	6413	-0.5
14224	BUFFALO	029	40512	40258	39595	-0.1	30	16058	16382	16232	0.2	2.42	11196	11213	0.0
14225	BUFFALO	029	35555	33628	32559	-0.6	4	15587	15057	14663	-0.4	2.22	9968	9392	-0.6
14226	BUFFALO	029	29690	28517	27716	-0.4	11	12702	12434	12151	-0.2	2.25	7989	7620	-0.5
14227	BUFFALO	029	23937	23436	22966	-0.2	21	10101	10152	10025	0.1	2.26	6598	6474	-0.2
14228	BUFFALO	029	18176	18794	18685	0.4	66	7509	7996	8014	0.7	2.29	4542	4702	0.4
14260	BUFFALO	029	4443	4568	4568	0.3	59	0	0	0	0.0	0.00	0	0	0.0
14301	NIAGARA FALLS	063	13982	12784	12356	-1.0	1	6346	5782	5592	-1.0	2.13	3324	2949	-1.3
14303	NIAGARA FALLS	063	7285	6373	6115	-1.4	1	3447	3039	2925	-1.4	2.07	1786	1525	-1.7
14304	NIAGARA FALLS	063	30482	29870	29431	-0.2	21	12699	12606	12483	-0.1	2.34	8324	8067	-0.3
14305	NIAGARA FALLS	063	18911	17801	17338	-0.7	3	7658	7282	7126	-0.5	2.41	5012	4666	-0.8
14410	ADAMS BASIN	055	157	155	153	-0.1	30	53	53	53	0.0	2.92	43	42	-0.3
14411	ALBION	073	14239	14882	14652	0.5	71	4735	4712	4642	-0.1	2.62	3242	3168	-0.2
14414	AVON	051	6463	6733	6714	0.4	66	2521	2672	2677	0.6	2.49	1711	1783	0.4
14415	BELLONA	123	110	116	117	0.6	76	42	45	45	0.7	2.58	32	33	0.3
14416	BERGEN	037	3854	3890	3858	0.1	44	1423	1468	1466	0.3	2.64	1040	1057	0.2
14418	BRANCHPORT	123	1391	1460	1476	0.5	71	552	584	592	0.6	2.49	397	414	0.5
14420	BROCKPORT	055	19734	20388	20234	0.4	66	6625	6754	6716	0.2	2.59	4320	4322	0.0
14422	BYRON	037	2660	2763	2758	0.4	66	945	1002	1007	0.6	2.76	716	748	0.5
14423	CALEDONIA	051	4966	4909	4819	-0.1	30	1829	1825	1798	0.0	2.68	1378	1354	-0.2
14424	CANANDAIGUA	069	24759	26516	27151	0.7	80	9857	10691	11012	0.9	2.40	6410	6862	0.7
14425	FARMINGTON	069	9422	9858	10033	0.5	71	3435	3710	3817	0.8	2.66	2557	2708	0.6
14427	CASTILE	121	2005	1991	1961	-0.1	30	778	794	789	0.2	2.47	562	565	0.1
14428	CHURCHVILLE	055	7464	8137	8169	0.9	87	2663	2927	2945	1.0	2.76	2024	2168	0.7
14432	CLIFTON SPRINGS	069	5972	6137	6173	0.3	59	2233	2340	2369	0.5	2.53	1542	1581	0.3
14433	CLYDE	117	4769	4567	4460	-0.5	7	1759	1722	1692	-0.2	2.64	1259	1213	-0.4
14435	CONESUS	051	2572	2618	2598	0.2	52	966	997	992	0.3	2.61	731	744	0.2
14437	DANSVILLE	051	12367	9850	9669	-2.4	0	3869	3845	3787	-0.1	2.54	2689	2632	-0.2
14441	DRESDEN	123	330	332	326	0.1	44	132	134	132	0.2	2.46	98	98	0.0
14445	EAST ROCHESTER	055	9014	8649	8463	-0.4	11	3475	3376	3311	-0.3	2.35	2095	1981	-0.6
14450	FAIRPORT	055	41063	42123	41911	0.3	59	15765	16359	16349	0.4	2.54	11529	11766	0.2
14454	GENESEO	051	10436	10658	10611	0.2	52	2839	2984	2980	0.5	2.49	1551	1608	0.4
14456	GENEVA	069	20493	20415	20390	0.0	38	7769	7860	7895	0.1	2.36	4856	4801	-0.1
14462	GROVELAND	051	597	620	616	0.4	66	211	223	223	0.6	2.78	151	157	0.4
14464	HAMLIN	055	7787	7606	7465	-0.3	15	2715	2684	2644	-0.1	2.81	2096	2038	-0.3
14466	HEMLOCK	069	1890	2016	2050	0.7	80	670	726	742	0.9	2.77	529	567	0.8
14467	HENRIETTA	055	8832	9269	9286	0.5	71	3300	3522	3540	0.7	2.62	2480	2593	0.5
14468	HILTON	055	16763	18394	18536	1.0	89	5824	6453	6529	1.1	2.82	4597	5038	1.0
14469	BLOOMFIELD	069	6180	6658	6846	0.8	84	2315	2555	2648	1.1	2.60	1727	1871	0.9
14470	HOLLEY	073	9060	7687	7590	-1.8	1	2892	2940	2921	0.2	2.61	2088	2089	0.0
14471	HONEOYE	069	2871	3177	3307	1.1	91	1186	1343	1411	1.4	2.36	819	906	1.1
14472	HONEOYE FALLS	055	8047	8181	8139	0.2	52	3022	3093	3083	0.3	2.60	2262	2274	0.1
14475	IONIA	069	214	221	222	0.3	59	78	83	84	0.7	2.66	61	63	0.3
14476	KENDALL	073	2367	2408	2387	0.2	52	820	849	848	0.4	2.84	665	681	0.3
14477	KENT	073	1912	1922	1902	0.1	44	678	694	689	0.3	2.77	519	523	0.1
14478	KEUKA PARK	123	1357	1325	1337	-0.3	15	317	336	341	0.6	2.84	221	229	0.4
14480	LAKEVILLE	051	413	445	448	0.8	84	180	197	199	1.0	2.24	127	137	0.8
14481	LEICESTER	051	3679	1894	1865	-6.9	0	700	706	698	0.1	2.65	529	526	-0.1
14482	LE ROY	037	9116	8790	8574	-0.4	11	3518	3469	3409	-0.2	2.47	2418	2344	-0.3
14485	LIMA	051	4471	4523	4488	0.1	44	1540	1588	1583	0.3	2.54	1095	1111	0.2
14486	LINWOOD	051	275	283	282	0.3	59	96	100	100	0.4	2.83	73	75	0.3
14487	LIVONIA	051	5862	6328	6377	0.8	84	2139	2340	2366	1.0	2.69	1580	1703	0.8
14489	LYONS	117	7650	7329	7157	-0.5	7	2858	2809	2763	-0.2	2.54	1913	1846	-0.4
14502	MACEDON	117	9384	9834	9839	0.5	71	3413	3654	3679	0.7	2.69	2615	2763	0.6
14504	MANCHESTER	069	1374	1439	1470	0.5	71	593	639	659	0.8	2.25	389	410	0.6
14505	MARION	117	5355	5383	5331	0.1	44	1884	1939	1933	0.3	2.77	1447	1469	0.2
14506	MENDON	055	1223	1278	1278	0.5	71	412	435	436	0.6	2.93	349	363	0.4
14507	MIDDLESEX	123	1375	1482	1511	0.8	84	512	556	570	0.9	2.61	375	401	0.7
14510	MOUNT MORRIS	051	5145	7248	7097	3.8	100	2005	1911	1854	-0.5	2.46	1297	1214	-0.7
14512	NAPLES	069	4584	4862	4962	0.6	76	1830	1986	2042	0.9	2.44	1272	1354	0.7
14513	NEWARK	117	14474	13908	13602	-0.4	11	5605	5510	5422	-0.2	2.41	3767	3634	-0.4
14514	NORTH CHILI	055	4945	5787	5913	1.7	97	1810	2099	2151	1.6	2.50	1291	1471	1.4
14516	NORTH ROSE	117	2514	2476	2438	-0.2	21	942	952	945	0.1	2.59	689	685	-0.1
14517	NUNDA	051	2682	2683	2648	0.0	38	1015	1032	1022	0.2	2.56	748	749	0.0
14519	ONTARIO	117	10835	11313	11320	0.5	71	4014	4294	4325	0.7	2.63	3023	3191	0.6
14521	OVID	099	3767	4745	4772	2.5	99	1127	1251	1266	1.1	2.61	745	816	1.0
14522	PALMYRA	117	9107	8941	8805	-0.2	21	3556	3560	3529	0.0	2.50	2472	2439	-0.1
14525	PAVILION	037	2955	2921	2881	-0.1	30	1034	1045	1038	0.1	2.80	808	805	0.0
14526	PENFIELD	055	19850	19834	19584	0.0	38	7358	7415	7354	0.1	2.61	5539	5486	-0.1
14527	PENN YAN	123	12748	13070	13005	0.3	59	4899	4947	4931	0.1	2.49	3278	3254	-0.1
14530	PERRY	121	5743	5498	5347	-0.5	7	2241	2199	2158	-0.2	2.48	1561	1509	-0.4
14532	PHELPS	069	4399	4459	4458	0.1	44	1707	1777	1793	0.4	2.50	1222	1246	0.2
14533	PIFFARD	051	2234	2292	2277	0.3	59	819	855	854	0.5	2.64	610	623	0.2
14534	PITTSFORD	055	30422	31505	31477	0.4	66	10956	11428	11448	0.5	2.70	8762	9058	0.4
14536	PORTAGEVILLE	121	698	699	690	0.0	38	264	272	271	0.3	2.57	196	200	0.2
14541	ROMULUS	099	2017	2105	2081	0.5	71	717	750	747	0.5	2.65	538	556	0.4
14543	RUSH	055	3024	3105	3085	0.3	59	1050	1078	1076	0.3	2.58	811	818	0.1
14544	RUSHVILLE	123	2051	2106	2110	0.3	59	760	789	792	0.4	2.63	564	576	0.2
14545	SCOTTSBURG	051	267	271	268	0.2	52	103	106	106	0.3	2.56	80	81	0.1
14546	SCOTTSVILLE	055	5323	5229	5168	-0.2	21	2104	2103	2089	0.0	2.47	1454	1418	-0.3
14548	SHORTSVILLE	069	4194	4271	4295	0.2	52	1584	1651	1673	0.4	2.57	1150	1177	0.3
	NEW YORK					0.3					0.3	2.61			0.1
	UNITED STATES					1.0					1.1	2.59			0.9

ZIP CODE #	POST OFFICE NAME	RACE (%) White 2000	White 2009	Black 2000	Black 2009	Asian/Pacific 2000	Asian/Pacific 2009	% Hispanic Origin 2000	% Hispanic Origin 2009	2009 AGE DISTRIBUTION (%) 0-4	5-9	10-14	15-19	20-24	25-44	45-64	65-84	85+	18+	MEDIAN AGE 2009	% 2009 Males	% 2009 Females
14209	BUFFALO	42.3	33.6	53.0	61.1	1.2	1.4	3.2	3.6	5.4	5.3	5.0	5.7	8.7	26.8	24.8	14.3	4.1	80.8	39.3	46.4	53.6
14210	BUFFALO	91.6	88.6	3.9	5.1	0.5	0.7	5.1	7.0	7.9	7.6	6.9	7.3	6.8	27.8	24.0	10.3	1.5	73.1	35.0	48.6	51.4
14211	BUFFALO	24.2	20.4	71.8	75.5	1.1	1.2	1.9	2.0	8.5	8.4	8.0	8.2	7.0	24.1	23.2	10.7	1.9	70.0	33.4	46.0	54.0
14212	BUFFALO	49.8	44.0	45.6	51.2	1.6	1.6	1.8	2.0	8.1	8.0	7.0	6.8	6.1	24.9	24.4	12.4	2.4	72.7	36.7	47.2	52.8
14213	BUFFALO	56.1	44.7	19.0	26.4	3.0	3.3	26.0	30.0	8.6	7.4	6.5	9.0	13.4	27.0	19.7	6.9	1.6	73.2	28.0	48.1	51.9
14214	BUFFALO	55.1	46.8	38.5	45.5	2.8	3.4	2.7	3.3	5.4	5.2	5.2	9.4	16.3	24.1	22.4	10.0	2.0	80.8	30.9	47.7	52.3
14215	BUFFALO	23.1	16.6	71.9	78.5	1.8	1.8	2.3	2.2	7.9	8.2	7.9	8.1	7.9	25.2	23.7	9.4	1.6	70.9	32.6	45.5	54.5
14216	BUFFALO	84.6	76.3	9.7	16.0	1.3	1.8	4.2	5.7	5.9	5.5	5.3	6.0	7.4	29.1	26.5	11.6	2.6	79.6	38.8	47.3	52.7
14217	BUFFALO	96.9	95.1	1.0	1.8	0.6	1.0	1.3	1.9	5.6	5.6	5.7	5.7	5.6	25.1	28.4	14.0	4.3	79.5	42.6	46.4	53.6
14218	BUFFALO	84.9	82.1	9.0	10.5	0.3	0.4	4.8	6.0	6.9	6.4	6.6	6.6	6.0	24.6	25.0	15.1	2.8	76.0	39.7	48.2	51.8
14219	BUFFALO	96.9	95.1	0.7	1.3	0.4	0.6	2.7	4.1	5.9	5.8	5.9	6.3	6.1	27.1	27.6	13.1	2.1	78.5	40.1	48.3	51.7
14220	BUFFALO	95.0	92.4	1.0	1.8	0.6	0.9	4.5	6.7	6.9	6.5	6.3	6.4	6.2	27.0	25.6	12.4	2.7	76.3	38.3	47.4	52.6
14221	BUFFALO	92.8	88.8	2.1	3.8	3.9	5.6	1.0	1.5	4.8	5.2	6.0	6.1	4.4	20.1	29.2	18.9	5.2	80.0	47.2	46.4	53.6
14222	BUFFALO	83.2	74.2	10.5	17.3	1.8	2.4	4.6	6.3	3.6	3.0	3.0	3.0	10.5	35.7	25.3	12.3	3.6	88.7	38.9	49.2	50.8
14223	BUFFALO	96.0	93.5	1.3	2.4	1.2	1.8	1.3	2.0	5.3	5.6	6.0	6.2	5.3	23.4	29.0	15.5	3.7	79.2	43.6	46.7	53.3
14224	BUFFALO	98.1	96.9	0.5	0.9	0.6	0.8	0.8	1.3	5.0	5.3	5.7	6.1	4.8	23.6	30.0	16.5	3.0	80.1	44.6	47.6	52.4
14225	BUFFALO	95.6	92.9	2.5	4.3	0.6	0.9	1.0	1.4	5.7	5.8	5.8	5.6	4.9	24.5	27.3	16.9	3.5	79.2	43.4	47.1	52.9
14226	BUFFALO	87.9	82.0	5.9	9.6	4.2	5.5	1.6	2.3	5.8	5.6	5.9	6.5	6.8	23.3	27.7	14.8	3.6	79.1	42.1	46.5	53.5
14227	BUFFALO	96.3	93.9	1.7	3.1	1.1	1.5	1.0	1.4	4.8	4.8	5.1	5.3	4.7	25.4	28.2	18.0	3.7	82.2	45.0	47.0	53.0
14228	BUFFALO	85.6	78.7	5.3	8.8	7.1	9.8	1.8	2.4	5.8	5.3	5.1	5.9	7.8	30.5	24.9	11.6	3.2	80.1	37.4	48.4	51.6
14260	BUFFALO	76.6	65.5	9.8	16.6	12.7	16.8	2.3	2.6	0.0	0.0	0.0	53.4	44.4	2.2	0.1	0.0	0.0	99.8	19.7	54.9	45.1
14301	NIAGARA FALLS	73.5	68.2	20.2	24.3	0.8	1.0	2.8	3.1	6.9	6.4	5.7	6.5	7.1	24.5	23.7	14.8	4.3	77.1	39.1	45.3	54.7
14303	NIAGARA FALLS	72.2	66.6	20.4	24.6	0.6	0.8	3.1	3.6	6.7	6.0	6.0	6.0	6.8	25.4	25.0	14.1	4.0	77.6	39.7	48.3	51.7
14304	NIAGARA FALLS	94.5	92.7	2.4	3.2	0.9	1.2	1.0	1.3	5.4	5.4	5.7	6.2	5.4	25.4	29.0	14.7	2.8	79.7	42.5	48.2	51.8
14305	NIAGARA FALLS	65.1	61.1	30.2	33.4	0.4	0.5	1.9	2.1	7.1	6.9	6.8	7.3	6.9	23.7	25.6	13.3	2.4	74.9	37.8	46.8	53.2
14410	ADAMS BASIN	96.8	95.5	1.3	1.9	0.6	1.3	1.3	1.9	5.8	7.1	7.1	6.5	4.5	25.8	32.3	9.7	1.3	76.1	41.0	51.0	49.0
14411	ALBION	83.8	78.8	10.9	12.6	0.4	2.4	6.0	7.6	5.6	5.5	5.6	13.0	11.0	25.6	22.3	9.3	2.2	81.0	32.1	51.7	48.3
14414	AVON	95.8	94.5	1.5	1.9	0.7	1.1	1.4	1.9	6.1	6.0	6.2	6.6	7.5	24.4	29.4	11.7	2.1	77.2	40.5	48.8	51.2
14415	BELLONA	100.0	100.0	0.0	0.0	0.0	0.0	0.0	0.0	7.8	7.8	8.6	7.8	4.3	21.6	29.3	11.2	1.7	70.7	38.8	52.6	47.4
14416	BERGEN	97.4	96.7	0.4	0.4	0.5	0.7	1.0	1.3	6.7	6.9	7.1	6.7	5.2	25.6	29.5	10.7	1.6	75.1	39.5	51.1	48.9
14418	BRANCHPORT	98.6	98.3	0.5	0.5	0.1	0.1	0.6	0.8	5.0	6.7	6.7	6.5	4.5	22.4	34.3	12.5	1.4	77.2	43.9	51.6	48.4
14420	BROCKPORT	93.1	89.9	3.2	4.7	1.0	1.4	2.8	4.1	4.9	5.1	5.5	12.1	16.4	23.1	22.6	8.4	1.9	80.7	29.5	48.6	51.4
14422	BYRON	95.9	94.8	0.4	0.5	0.4	0.5	3.5	4.5	6.4	6.8	7.1	7.1	5.4	25.7	30.9	9.6	0.9	75.3	39.2	49.9	50.1
14423	CALEDONIA	94.5	93.0	3.2	4.0	0.6	0.9	0.8	1.1	6.6	7.1	7.2	6.6	5.3	25.2	29.9	10.8	1.3	74.7	39.6	49.9	50.1
14424	CANANDAIGUA	96.8	95.7	1.0	1.4	0.6	0.9	1.0	1.4	5.6	5.8	6.3	6.8	5.7	24.2	29.6	13.3	2.8	78.2	41.9	48.9	51.1
14425	FARMINGTON	96.4	95.2	1.1	1.4	1.0	1.4	1.3	1.7	7.3	7.2	7.2	7.2	6.4	26.7	29.7	7.6	0.6	73.9	36.5	48.8	51.2
14427	CASTILE	98.4	97.7	0.5	0.7	0.3	0.5	0.5	0.7	5.3	6.1	7.0	7.1	6.4	24.7	29.1	12.5	1.9	76.9	40.7	50.4	49.6
14428	CHURCHVILLE	96.1	93.7	1.6	2.9	0.8	1.1	1.0	1.5	6.2	6.4	7.0	7.6	6.0	26.1	30.0	9.5	1.2	75.4	38.8	49.8	50.2
14432	CLIFTON SPRINGS	97.7	96.9	0.7	0.9	0.3	0.4	1.1	1.5	6.0	6.2	6.2	7.1	6.1	25.1	28.8	11.5	3.0	76.8	40.5	49.6	50.4
14433	CLYDE	94.3	93.0	3.2	3.8	0.1	0.2	1.4	1.7	7.0	7.0	7.1	7.2	6.2	25.1	27.4	11.2	1.8	74.4	37.8	49.3	50.7
14435	CONESUS	96.7	95.1	1.6	2.5	0.1	0.3	0.9	1.3	5.3	6.1	7.6	8.4	4.6	27.3	30.6	9.2	0.9	75.7	39.6	50.8	49.2
14437	DANSVILLE	89.2	94.6	7.4	2.0	0.5	0.8	4.1	2.0	6.1	6.4	6.5	7.1	5.6	24.3	29.0	13.0	2.0	76.6	40.8	49.7	50.3
14441	DRESDEN	97.3	97.0	0.0	0.0	0.0	0.0	3.3	3.9	6.0	6.0	7.2	6.6	4.5	22.6	27.7	17.2	2.1	76.5	42.2	52.7	47.3
14445	EAST ROCHESTER	95.6	94.1	1.5	2.0	1.0	1.3	2.2	3.2	5.8	5.5	5.5	9.1	8.9	26.4	25.7	11.0	2.0	79.4	36.7	47.4	52.6
14450	FAIRPORT	93.9	91.0	1.7	2.6	2.9	4.1	1.4	2.1	6.4	6.7	7.3	6.9	4.7	23.1	30.9	11.8	2.2	75.0	41.6	48.2	51.8
14454	GENESEO	92.8	90.1	2.7	3.6	2.5	3.6	2.6	3.4	3.2	3.1	3.4	21.0	26.7	17.1	16.7	7.2	1.7	88.0	23.6	44.1	55.9
14456	GENEVA	86.3	83.4	7.3	8.5	1.2	1.6	6.2	7.5	5.8	5.7	5.9	9.1	10.5	21.8	25.3	13.2	2.8	79.0	37.2	47.6	52.4
14462	GROVELAND	62.9	40.2	29.9	45.8	0.2	4.4	14.0	20.5	1.3	2.7	2.6	12.7	13.4	40.6	21.8	4.2	0.6	92.4	33.8	72.6	27.4
14464	HAMLIN	96.9	95.3	1.0	1.5	0.3	0.4	1.6	2.6	6.9	7.0	7.3	7.9	6.2	27.0	29.1	7.8	0.7	73.7	35.8	49.3	50.7
14466	HEMLOCK	97.9	97.3	0.4	0.4	0.3	0.5	0.8	1.0	5.8	7.2	7.7	7.6	5.0	24.7	32.9	8.2	0.9	73.9	40.3	50.6	49.4
14467	HENRIETTA	87.6	82.4	6.2	8.9	3.4	4.6	2.5	3.5	5.9	6.3	7.0	7.3	5.0	25.6	29.9	11.7	1.3	75.9	40.5	48.3	51.7
14468	HILTON	96.7	95.1	1.4	2.1	0.7	1.0	1.2	1.8	6.3	6.9	7.4	7.7	5.6	24.5	30.2	9.9	1.5	74.4	39.4	49.1	50.9
14469	BLOOMFIELD	98.5	98.0	0.4	0.5	0.2	0.4	0.9	1.2	6.3	6.6	7.2	6.9	4.3	25.0	31.3	11.0	1.3	75.4	41.2	49.9	50.1
14470	HOLLEY	88.4	85.6	9.6	8.0	0.3	2.3	4.6	6.6	5.9	6.2	6.6	11.9	8.2	27.8	24.3	8.2	0.9	78.2	33.8	47.2	52.8
14471	HONEOYE	98.5	98.0	0.2	0.2	0.4	0.6	0.8	1.0	4.8	5.6	5.7	6.8	4.2	24.9	34.8	11.7	1.4	79.5	43.7	51.0	49.0
14472	HONEOYE FALLS	97.4	96.2	0.9	1.3	0.8	1.2	1.0	1.5	5.3	6.1	7.4	8.0	4.8	20.6	34.0	11.3	2.5	75.5	43.5	49.0	51.0
14475	IONIA	99.1	98.6	0.0	0.0	0.0	0.5	0.9	1.4	5.4	6.3	6.3	6.8	4.1	24.0	32.6	13.1	1.4	76.9	43.2	51.1	48.9
14476	KENDALL	96.7	95.8	0.8	1.0	0.2	0.2	1.3	1.7	5.9	6.6	7.1	7.2	5.9	22.4	31.6	12.0	1.2	76.0	41.4	51.1	48.9
14477	KENT	94.8	93.4	2.6	3.0	0.2	0.4	1.6	2.1	5.4	6.8	8.0	8.5	3.8	25.3	31.7	9.4	1.1	74.5	39.8	51.5	48.5
14478	KEUKA PARK	98.2	97.7	0.8	0.9	0.3	0.5	0.7	0.8	3.9	4.2	4.2	18.7	15.9	15.6	22.0	13.7	1.7	84.2	28.7	43.2	56.8
14480	LAKEVILLE	97.8	96.9	0.5	0.7	0.5	0.7	0.7	1.3	6.1	6.5	7.4	7.6	4.7	23.6	30.6	11.5	2.0	74.4	41.1	49.4	50.6
14481	LEICESTER	74.5	96.6	20.1	1.6	0.1	0.1	9.9	1.5	6.1	6.4	6.8	6.4	5.6	26.3	28.8	12.2	1.3	76.6	40.2	51.4	48.6
14482	LE ROY	96.1	95.1	1.8	2.2	0.4	0.5	0.8	1.0	6.1	6.5	6.6	6.6	6.0	25.5	28.3	11.7	2.7	76.5	39.9	49.1	50.9
14485	LIMA	96.8	95.9	1.1	1.3	0.5	0.8	1.3	1.6	4.9	4.9	5.3	9.0	10.2	25.6	28.8	9.6	1.7	80.4	37.7	49.7	50.3
14486	LINWOOD	98.2	97.5	0.4	0.4	0.4	0.7	1.1	1.4	6.0	6.7	7.1	7.1	4.2	23.3	32.2	12.4	1.1	75.6	41.7	48.4	51.6
14487	LIVONIA	97.8	97.0	0.5	0.6	0.4	0.5	0.8	1.1	6.3	6.9	7.6	7.7	4.9	23.7	31.0	10.3	1.7	73.6	40.4	49.4	50.6
14489	LYONS	90.0	88.2	6.9	8.0	0.4	0.6	2.3	2.8	5.8	6.0	6.3	7.1	6.2	25.2	29.0	12.3	2.1	77.5	40.2	49.1	50.9
14502	MACEDON	97.1	96.2	0.8	0.9	0.8	1.1	1.4	1.9	7.9	8.3	8.3	6.9	5.0	26.5	28.0	8.4	0.7	71.2	37.3	49.7	50.3
14504	MANCHESTER	97.3	96.4	0.4	0.5	0.3	0.3	1.2	1.7	5.4	5.8	6.4	6.3	5.4	24.5	29.2	14.2	2.8	78.4	42.5	49.5	50.5
14505	MARION	97.7	97.0	0.9	1.1	0.3	0.4	1.4	1.8	6.5	6.6	7.1	7.9	5.9	25.2	29.7	9.7	1.3	74.6	38.9	48.7	51.3
14506	MENDON	97.3	96.1	0.4	0.5	1.8	2.5	0.8	1.3	5.6	7.2	9.0	8.4	4.1	17.6	36.5	10.9	0.9	72.4	43.8	50.2	49.8
14507	MIDDLESEX	98.6	98.2	0.2	0.3	0.1	0.3	0.7	0.8	5.3	7.8	7.7	7.4	4.5	22.5	31.8	12.0	1.0	74.4	41.6	50.8	49.2
14510	MOUNT MORRIS	93.7	79.6	2.3	12.3	0.6	2.6	4.7	8.3	4.2	4.4	4.7	14.5	14.2	25.4	20.4	9.1	3.0	84.6	31.3	52.9	47.1
14512	NAPLES	97.9	97.2	0.3	0.4	0.5	0.6	0.7	0.9	5.1	5.5	6.2	6.9	5.2	22.6	32.8	13.5	2.0	78.7	43.9	49.7	50.3
14513	NEWARK	91.2	89.3	4.0	4.6	0.5	0.7	5.7	6.9	6.3	6.1	6.1	6.9	6.8	24.3	27.6	12.6	3.2	77.0	40.1	48.3	51.7
14514	NORTH CHILI	94.1	91.2	3.0	4.5	1.2	1.7	1.9	2.6	5.4	5.4	5.8	11.2	8.4	23.3	25.3	12.5	2.7	78.8	37.7	47.2	52.8
14516	NORTH ROSE	95.9	94.8	1.7	2.0	0.2	0.3	1.5	1.9	5.4	5.5	6.0	7.0	5.5	23.6	31.6	13.7	1.7	78.6	42.8	49.1	50.9
14517	NUNDA	97.8	97.1	0.6	0.7	0.2	0.3	1.0	1.4	6.7	6.9	7.0	6.9	5.9	25.6	28.1	11.1	1.9	74.7	38.4	48.9	51.1
14519	ONTARIO	96.4	95.3	1.3	1.5	0.6	0.9	1.2	1.6	6.9	7.2	7.6	7.4	5.0	25.4	30.2	9.2	1.0	73.4	39.4	51.1	48.9
14521	OVID	81.8	80.6	13.1	13.3	0.3	0.5	6.3	7.3	4.6	4.6	4.8	6.4	10.6	35.4	22.5	9.2	1.7	81.8	34.7	61.8	38.2
14522	PALMYRA	97.5	96.8	0.4	0.5	0.4	0.6	0.9	1.1	6.1	6.4	6.7	6.7	5.6	25.7	30.3	10.9	1.5	76.6	40.3	49.8	50.2
14525	PAVILION	97.4	96.7	0.6	0.8	0.3	0.5	0.6	0.8	6.1	6.7	7.0	7.6	5.1	25.1	29.7	11.3	1.3	75.5	39.9	50.6	49.4
14526	PENFIELD	92.9	89.8	2.2	3.2	3.5	4.9	1.5	2.1	5.5	6.3	7.2	7.2	4.7	21.0	32.6	13.0	2.6	76.0	43.8	47.9	52.1
14527	PENN YAN	98.0	97.5	0.4	0.5	0.3	0.4	0.9	1.1	6.4	6.4	6.4	8.0	6.8	20.8	27.1	15.0	3.2	76.4	41.0	48.5	51.5
14530	PERRY	92.5	90.3	4.8	5.9	0.5	1.0	3.3	4.0	6.0	5.7	5.6	7.1	7.4	28.5	26.4	11.2	2.0	78.9	37.2	52.5	47.5
14532	PHELPS	98.2	97.6	0.3	0.3	0.2	0.2	1.3	1.7	6.0	6.4	6.8	7.1	6.0	25.6	29.6	11.0	1.5	76.2	39.5	48.9	51.1
14533	PIFFARD	97.4	96.6	1.1	1.4	0.5	0.8	0.8	1.1	5.8	6.5	6.8	6.7	4.8	24.3	32.3	11.6	1.3	76.4	41.7	50.5	49.5
14534	PITTSFORD	91.8	88.1	2.2	3.2	4.8	6.8	1.3	1.9	5.5	6.9	8.4	7.7	3.8	16.6	33.6	14.9	2.5	73.6	45.5	48.3	51.7
14536	PORTAGEVILLE	97.9	97.1	0.3	0.3	0.1	0.3	0.4	0.7	6.0	6.7	6.9	7.3	5.6	23.7	30.2	11.9	1.7	76.1	40.6	49.1	50.9
14541	ROMULUS	95.7	94.6	2.4	2.9	0.4	0.6	1.3	1.7	5.9	6.5	7.4	7.8	6.0	23.9	27.6	13.1	1.8	74.6	39.4	51.2	48.8
14543	RUSH	91.3	87.4	5.9	8.6	1.0	1.4	2.1	3.1	4.3	5.5	9.9	12.3	2.8	20.4	31.2	12.3	1.3	69.7	41.6	55.2	44.8
14544	RUSHVILLE	97.7	96.9	0.5	0.6	0.2	0.4	0.9	1.2	6.8	7.3	7.5	7.3	5.5	23.2	30.1	11.1	1.3	73.6	39.9	50.9	49.1
14545	SCOTTSBURG	96.3	95.2	0.7	0.7	0.7	1.1	0.4	0.7	4.4	5.2	6.3	7.0	4.8	21.4	34.7	14.8	1.5	79.3	45.5	50.6	49.4
14546	SCOTTSVILLE	92.1	88.6	4.6	6.6	1.0	1.4	2.3	3.3	6.0	6.3	6.8	6.9	6.3	27.3	27.9	11.1	1.4	76.5	38.5	48.1	51.9
14548	SHORTSVILLE	97.9	97.2	0.2	0.3	0.3	0.4	1.1	1.5	6.0	6.2	6.6	6.8	5.3	25.0	30.1	12.4	1.7	76.9	41.5	50.0	50.0
	NEW YORK	67.9	64.8	15.9	16.5	5.6	6.9	15.1	16.7	6.5	6.4	6.4	7.1	7.0	27.0	26.3	11.2	2.1	76.6	37.5	48.4	51.6
	UNITED STATES	75.1	72.0	12.3	12.7	3.8	4.6	12.5	15.7	6.8	6.7	6.6	7.1	6.9	27.0	26.0	10.9	1.9	75.7	36.9	49.2	50.8

#	POST OFFICE NAME	2009 Per Capita Income	2009 HH Income Base	2009 Household Income Distribution (%): Less than $25,000	$25,000 to $49,999	$50,000 to $99,999	$100,000 to $149,999	$150,000 or More	Median Household Income: 2009	2014	2009 National Centile	2009 State Centile	2009 Home Value Base	2009 Home Value Distribution (%): Less than $50,000	$50,000 to $89,999	$90,000 to $174,999	$175,000 to $399,999	$400,000 or More	2009 Median Home Value
14209	BUFFALO	23022	3760	46.9	28.9	16.2	4.0	4.0	26814	28420	4	3	1000	18.8	16.0	29.3	26.3	9.6	125943
14210	BUFFALO	17308	6492	35.7	31.8	28.0	3.9	0.6	33333	36502	14	5	3333	14.9	21.3	61.1	2.7	0.0	102305
14211	BUFFALO	13924	9793	49.2	29.1	19.1	1.8	0.8	25459	26447	4	2	4657	31.8	36.0	29.1	2.8	0.2	68378
14212	BUFFALO	14511	6077	50.8	28.0	18.8	1.9	0.6	24340	25346	3	2	2741	30.1	24.9	42.0	3.0	0.0	81086
14213	BUFFALO	13891	9483	50.8	26.4	19.9	2.1	0.8	24486	25273	3	2	3160	20.2	41.6	33.1	5.1	0.1	77980
14214	BUFFALO	22424	8387	34.3	25.1	28.6	7.6	4.4	40129	43548	33	15	3993	4.7	17.5	50.0	24.9	2.9	138243
14215	BUFFALO	17611	16094	36.7	29.8	27.4	4.6	1.5	33501	36627	14	5	8653	8.4	44.1	44.0	3.4	0.2	87964
14216	BUFFALO	25318	10419	28.5	29.1	32.6	6.6	3.3	42700	46156	41	22	5002	0.3	3.4	70.5	23.0	2.9	146767
14217	BUFFALO	27433	10377	20.7	26.3	41.4	8.0	3.7	53463	58934	69	54	6722	1.7	4.4	82.6	10.7	0.6	137947
14218	BUFFALO	21226	8441	32.9	28.0	32.7	4.4	2.0	39578	43595	31	13	4903	7.6	16.9	64.4	11.0	0.1	126058
14219	BUFFALO	25927	5245	18.3	27.8	42.8	7.7	3.4	53336	57132	69	54	3185	1.2	5.6	75.0	17.3	0.9	139194
14220	BUFFALO	22635	10117	23.6	29.8	36.9	7.5	2.2	46536	50190	53	35	6470	0.9	14.4	79.4	5.3	0.1	118728
14221	BUFFALO	40068	20750	10.8	17.4	38.6	18.5	14.7	76516	78779	90	82	15741	0.8	2.0	28.4	62.2	6.7	198643
14222	BUFFALO	35711	6890	29.8	26.0	28.9	8.3	6.9	43288	47701	43	24	2233	0.0	5.5	38.6	45.5	10.4	185755
14223	BUFFALO	27343	9995	18.1	25.6	43.1	9.8	3.4	56959	61196	74	60	7619	0.4	4.3	73.4	21.1	0.8	144642
14224	BUFFALO	27553	16382	14.6	23.2	46.4	12.3	3.5	62058	64490	80	67	12523	0.9	4.8	54.5	38.7	1.2	163618
14225	BUFFALO	24557	15057	21.9	31.6	39.0	5.4	2.1	46804	50235	54	36	10893	3.3	8.5	79.4	8.5	0.2	130027
14226	BUFFALO	33391	12434	18.9	21.9	38.7	11.8	8.7	60837	63677	79	66	8801	0.9	3.3	57.4	34.0	4.4	156913
14227	BUFFALO	27201	10152	17.5	25.9	44.7	9.0	2.8	55841	60117	72	58	6586	3.3	2.4	68.3	25.8	0.1	151938
14228	BUFFALO	29291	7996	18.6	25.0	37.1	13.4	5.9	56968	61623	74	60	4334	0.3	3.4	38.7	56.3	1.2	183624
14260	BUFFALO	15456	0	0.0	0.0	0.0	0.0	0.0	0	0	0	0	0	0.0	0.0	0.0	0.0	0.0	0
14301	NIAGARA FALLS	16190	5782	47.9	29.5	19.2	2.2	1.2	26163	27523	4	3	2450	14.0	46.4	37.8	1.8	0.0	80039
14303	NIAGARA FALLS	16780	3039	47.7	31.7	16.6	2.7	1.3	26033	27159	4	2	1449	11.9	51.9	34.2	2.1	0.0	79038
14304	NIAGARA FALLS	25299	12606	19.7	28.6	40.5	8.2	3.0	51883	56903	66	51	9231	11.0	13.7	54.8	19.2	1.3	121934
14305	NIAGARA FALLS	19951	7282	37.3	27.4	26.4	5.7	3.2	34619	37402	17	5	4363	12.1	31.3	46.8	9.6	0.2	95859
14410	ADAMS BASIN	26937	53	5.7	17.0	58.5	11.3	7.5	69969	74027	87	76	43	0.0	0.0	37.2	62.8	0.0	194643
14411	ALBION	19138	4712	26.4	28.5	36.1	7.2	1.8	43668	47698	44	25	3324	19.3	24.2	45.4	10.8	0.3	98594
14414	AVON	25518	2672	21.7	25.2	39.6	9.1	4.3	54011	59767	70	55	1970	19.9	3.2	43.3	29.5	4.1	149112
14415	BELLONA	19369	45	22.2	37.8	33.3	6.7	0.0	38173	39615	27	10	34	0.0	23.5	55.9	17.6	2.9	120833
14416	BERGEN	26200	1468	11.7	25.8	46.7	12.2	3.6	63689	65983	82	70	1170	2.1	8.0	64.7	24.4	0.8	142182
14418	BRANCHPORT	19570	584	27.6	29.6	35.3	6.0	1.5	41828	45000	39	20	488	11.1	23.8	41.4	20.3	3.5	116418
14420	BROCKPORT	24081	6754	17.9	23.4	43.2	11.7	3.9	61315	64089	79	67	4287	6.1	5.6	52.6	34.4	1.3	154598
14422	BYRON	24718	1002	14.3	24.0	47.5	9.9	4.4	61113	63290	79	66	834	5.9	10.2	61.6	20.5	1.8	138503
14423	CALEDONIA	24021	1825	15.5	29.0	40.8	11.7	3.1	56668	60705	74	59	1434	10.3	4.5	54.1	29.5	1.5	145913
14424	CANANDAIGUA	28071	10691	17.9	24.6	40.2	12.2	5.1	57414	61085	74	61	7121	5.9	5.8	38.7	42.3	7.2	174153
14425	FARMINGTON	25846	3710	11.7	22.7	49.1	13.8	2.7	63251	64838	81	69	2729	18.1	3.4	45.7	32.0	0.7	152332
14427	CASTILE	20978	794	22.3	34.4	35.8	5.8	1.8	45382	47677	49	32	590	7.1	23.1	55.9	10.3	3.6	112138
14428	CHURCHVILLE	28031	2927	10.4	19.0	49.6	15.1	6.0	70574	73145	87	77	2345	3.9	2.2	50.6	41.8	1.5	165713
14432	CLIFTON SPRINGS	22994	2340	21.1	25.6	43.2	8.1	2.1	52970	56672	68	53	1728	16.3	14.1	51.4	16.8	1.4	118980
14433	CLYDE	20184	1722	25.7	29.8	36.6	5.5	2.4	44349	48330	46	28	1304	11.6	34.6	45.0	8.1	0.8	93289
14435	CONESUS	26505	997	14.3	26.8	40.8	13.5	4.5	59674	62163	77	63	852	5.6	11.7	43.4	36.3	2.9	155508
14437	DANSVILLE	20916	3845	25.1	28.3	37.5	6.9	2.2	46791	49894	54	36	2763	7.8	25.1	53.3	13.1	0.8	108868
14441	DRESDEN	20946	134	23.9	32.8	37.3	3.7	2.2	43242	45000	43	24	106	11.3	17.0	43.4	24.5	3.8	115909
14445	EAST ROCHESTER	24720	3376	19.4	28.9	40.3	8.3	3.3	51658	55911	65	50	2092	2.5	9.8	70.2	16.8	0.6	131092
14450	FAIRPORT	41347	16359	7.4	15.9	37.1	22.1	17.6	84128	86831	94	86	12479	0.7	1.4	22.9	67.2	7.8	216382
14454	GENESEO	23463	2984	24.9	21.3	34.9	12.8	6.1	53963	58485	70	55	1714	0.7	2.5	43.7	46.7	6.4	179402
14456	GENEVA	22806	7860	25.2	27.7	36.4	8.0	2.7	46938	50479	54	37	4812	4.2	19.2	51.1	22.8	2.8	124146
14462	GROVELAND	22824	223	16.1	26.0	44.4	9.0	4.5	55501	58505	72	58	169	0.6	9.5	47.9	36.7	5.3	159659
14464	HAMLIN	22871	2684	14.7	27.1	45.7	9.7	2.7	60656	63988	78	65	2176	22.7	2.8	51.8	22.1	0.6	136349
14466	HEMLOCK	23620	726	12.8	24.1	48.3	12.4	2.3	62498	64151	81	68	636	6.1	6.8	46.4	40.3	0.5	161468
14467	HENRIETTA	30825	3522	8.0	21.6	45.0	19.2	6.3	71782	74003	88	78	2606	0.0	0.2	52.6	45.1	2.0	172510
14468	HILTON	26951	6453	7.8	20.8	51.4	14.7	5.3	68668	70704	86	75	5287	0.4	1.8	57.9	38.4	1.6	164159
14469	BLOOMFIELD	25969	2555	16.0	24.7	42.4	12.7	4.1	59315	61921	77	62	2080	13.6	7.8	38.8	35.4	4.3	157516
14470	HOLLEY	23717	2940	12.3	30.6	46.3	7.5	3.2	57136	60863	74	60	2330	17.9	17.8	44.5	19.5	0.4	113415
14471	HONEOYE	26909	1343	16.5	24.0	46.5	9.8	3.2	58942	61292	76	62	1057	7.5	14.5	38.9	36.6	2.6	156532
14472	HONEOYE FALLS	41483	3093	9.7	17.2	33.7	19.2	20.3	82013	85486	93	86	2455	2.5	2.5	21.0	56.9	17.1	244469
14475	IONIA	23046	83	16.9	30.1	37.3	13.3	2.4	52729	57143	67	53	71	22.5	16.9	26.8	29.6	4.2	117500
14476	KENDALL	25948	849	10.0	24.1	46.2	13.8	5.9	62850	65031	81	69	720	1.3	5.0	58.3	35.3	0.1	152371
14477	KENT	22028	694	14.7	28.7	45.8	8.2	2.6	57066	60836	74	60	584	5.5	11.1	61.5	21.4	0.5	130388
14478	KEUKA PARK	20371	336	16.1	29.8	40.2	11.0	3.0	57521	60181	75	61	274	2.9	5.5	40.5	41.6	9.5	178261
14480	LAKEVILLE	31136	197	13.2	16.2	55.8	11.2	3.6	67360	69217	85	74	151	6.0	6.0	51.0	36.4	0.7	156250
14481	LEICESTER	20629	706	19.3	32.4	40.4	6.8	1.1	48853	50913	59	42	566	15.0	15.0	49.6	19.1	1.2	117763
14482	LE ROY	24845	3469	14.7	31.3	41.5	10.0	2.5	54705	59749	71	56	2451	2.7	6.2	65.3	24.9	0.9	139664
14485	LIMA	25205	1588	14.9	23.6	43.8	14.7	3.1	61976	64128	80	67	1193	11.0	3.4	44.8	38.7	2.1	162993
14486	LINWOOD	20203	100	18.0	30.0	45.0	6.0	1.0	60000	61101	77	63	80	5.0	11.3	61.3	21.3	1.3	134615
14487	LIVONIA	25534	2340	13.2	18.8	53.1	11.7	3.1	65708	67282	84	72	1870	6.1	6.4	51.1	35.7	0.6	154085
14489	LYONS	23039	2809	20.9	26.4	42.3	7.8	2.7	52759	57094	67	53	2027	10.4	36.5	42.7	8.8	1.6	93094
14502	MACEDON	27492	3654	10.1	24.0	43.3	18.2	4.5	66693	69137	85	74	3004	6.9	3.0	44.3	44.3	1.5	169903
14504	MANCHESTER	24339	639	20.3	31.3	39.7	7.7	0.9	48505	51527	58	42	522	23.9	13.8	55.4	6.9	0.0	106473
14505	MARION	22942	1939	14.3	24.9	47.1	11.1	2.7	60816	62585	79	66	1599	8.0	4.4	61.0	25.3	1.3	140642
14506	MENDON	47350	435	3.4	9.7	38.9	17.9	30.1	97011	103055	96	90	391	0.0	1.3	11.8	58.6	28.4	306111
14507	MIDDLESEX	22932	556	18.5	29.5	39.2	9.5	3.2	51433	51616	65	50	476	5.5	18.1	50.4	22.9	3.2	123947
14510	MOUNT MORRIS	18837	1911	26.2	32.9	32.3	6.3	2.4	43386	46353	44	24	1286	12.8	21.6	52.6	10.6	2.3	105952
14512	NAPLES	23591	1986	21.2	28.6	39.9	7.3	3.0	50132	53104	61	45	1611	6.2	16.1	44.3	28.9	4.5	137434
14513	NEWARK	22906	5510	25.1	27.7	37.2	7.4	2.6	46757	50802	53	36	3628	10.9	17.9	56.4	13.3	1.5	113387
14514	NORTH CHILI	27502	2099	10.1	27.8	47.3	9.8	5.1	61795	64467	80	67	1447	0.0	0.1	56.3	43.2	0.4	168076
14516	NORTH ROSE	21466	952	20.4	28.3	41.8	7.7	1.9	51073	54261	64	49	771	8.8	25.0	46.7	17.0	2.5	111794
14517	NUNDA	21915	1032	18.5	30.4	41.4	8.0	1.6	50846	53900	63	48	774	13.2	29.3	46.8	10.3	0.4	96824
14519	ONTARIO	27651	4294	14.2	25.3	38.4	16.1	6.0	63294	66040	82	70	3523	11.9	2.1	42.8	41.8	1.4	167550
14521	OVID	19921	1251	20.8	32.8	36.0	6.9	3.6	45949	50298	51	33	893	7.1	25.9	42.6	19.7	4.8	118482
14522	PALMYRA	25111	3560	17.6	23.4	46.8	9.0	3.1	59401	61565	77	63	2598	10.7	7.2	56.0	24.7	1.4	138782
14525	PAVILION	22870	1045	10.5	30.4	46.6	10.4	2.0	58625	60995	76	62	857	4.7	13.5	60.6	19.7	1.5	131530
14526	PENFIELD	38231	7415	8.3	16.3	39.1	21.3	15.0	79722	82031	92	84	5979	0.2	0.3	33.2	60.2	6.0	196861
14527	PENN YAN	20898	4947	25.4	30.5	35.5	6.4	2.2	42917	44990	42	23	3582	6.8	16.5	48.5	22.0	6.2	127372
14530	PERRY	22488	2199	21.2	29.7	39.8	8.0	1.2	49069	51688	59	43	1530	3.2	30.7	54.3	10.1	1.6	106395
14532	PHELPS	26515	1777	14.3	26.4	44.9	11.2	3.3	59893	62440	77	63	1378	7.4	15.5	52.4	23.7	1.0	129207
14533	PIFFARD	22976	855	16.8	32.4	39.6	9.0	2.1	51273	58687	64	49	681	1.9	12.6	63.9	21.0	0.6	137177
14534	PITTSFORD	50599	11428	4.7	10.4	33.1	20.6	31.3	104575	110986	97	93	9817	0.8	1.3	11.5	65.4	21.0	280076
14536	PORTAGEVILLE	18708	272	26.1	37.9	29.8	4.8	1.5	42212	45063	40	21	215	12.6	27.4	47.0	12.1	0.9	101276
14541	ROMULUS	22315	750	19.1	30.5	37.2	9.2	4.0	50330	53515	62	46	615	9.6	17.1	35.8	32.2	5.4	141373
14543	RUSH	34324	1078	4.4	14.5	46.5	26.5	8.2	79867	80845	92	85	898	0.0	2.8	28.4	62.7	6.1	204186
14544	RUSHVILLE	23651	789	16.7	31.8	38.9	8.2	4.3	51175	52328	64	49	640	6.9	15.3	49.5	21.4	6.9	125278
14545	SCOTTSBURG	23085	106	17.9	28.3	43.4	7.5	2.8	53191	57695	68	53	94	7.4	20.2	53.2	19.1	0.0	120833
14546	SCOTTSVILLE	31049	2103	10.8	20.9	45.6	16.7	5.9	67672	70593	85	74	1381	3.3	7.0	56.3	32.2	1.2	152762
14548	SHORTSVILLE	24256	1651	15.9	27.3	44.6	9.9	2.2	55832	59614	72	58	1387	15.9	10.2	50.4	21.2	2.3	133893
	NEW YORK	29893		21.9	21.3	32.7	14.0	9.9	58747	62337				3.4	5.7	23.0	38.7	29.1	269816
	UNITED STATES	27277		20.9	24.4	35.3	11.7	7.6	54719	56938				9.3	13.1	31.6	32.6	13.5	162279

#	POST OFFICE NAME	FINANCIAL SERVICES: Auto Loan	Home Loan	Invest-ments	Retire-ment Plans	THE HOME: Home Improvements: Home Repair	Lawn & Garden	Furnishings: Comput-ers & Hard-ware-Personal	Major Appli-ances	TV, Radio, Sound Equip-ment	Furni-ture	ENTERTAINMENT: Dine out/ Carry out	Sports Equip-ment	Fees & Tickets	Toys & Games	Travel	Cable TV	PERSONAL: Apparel & Services	Auto Repairs	Health Insur-ance	Pets & Supplies
14209	BUFFALO	59	48	49	51	47	55	63	56	68	59	67	43	58	63	57	71	47	63	68	70
14210	BUFFALO	59	53	45	55	50	57	60	56	62	56	61	44	57	62	55	64	43	59	62	68
14211	BUFFALO	50	39	35	40	36	44	47	44	53	46	51	33	43	51	41	56	36	48	51	55
14212	BUFFALO	46	37	36	38	35	43	44	42	49	43	48	32	41	48	40	52	33	46	49	52
14213	BUFFALO	45	39	33	40	36	39	50	42	52	45	52	34	47	51	43	53	37	48	46	52
14214	BUFFALO	76	66	63	69	64	69	80	70	80	75	80	56	74	79	71	81	56	76	76	86
14215	BUFFALO	63	56	48	57	52	60	62	58	66	60	65	44	59	66	56	68	45	62	65	72
14216	BUFFALO	74	68	64	70	67	70	79	71	79	74	79	56	75	78	73	80	55	76	77	86
14217	BUFFALO	83	85	78	86	83	91	85	85	88	82	87	64	87	87	86	91	61	86	95	101
14218	BUFFALO	66	63	61	63	62	70	67	67	71	63	70	49	66	69	65	75	49	69	76	79
14219	BUFFALO	83	87	80	86	85	90	85	86	87	82	87	65	87	87	86	90	60	86	93	101
14220	BUFFALO	76	76	66	77	73	81	77	76	80	73	79	58	78	80	75	83	55	78	85	91
14221	BUFFALO	123	146	151	147	151	147	131	137	133	135	133	100	148	129	145	135	94	134	146	157
14222	BUFFALO	86	75	76	80	75	76	95	80	93	89	94	66	88	91	86	92	66	89	86	99
14223	BUFFALO	84	94	87	93	93	100	86	91	90	85	90	66	93	89	91	94	62	89	101	105
14224	BUFFALO	89	101	95	100	100	105	91	96	94	91	94	70	100	93	98	97	65	94	105	112
14225	BUFFALO	74	78	74	77	78	85	75	78	78	73	78	57	78	77	77	82	54	78	88	91
14226	BUFFALO	101	108	106	109	109	112	107	106	108	105	107	80	112	106	110	110	76	107	114	124
14227	BUFFALO	83	90	88	89	90	96	84	88	88	83	88	64	90	86	89	92	61	88	99	103
14228	BUFFALO	93	94	89	96	92	92	97	92	97	97	98	71	99	96	96	97	68	96	96	109
14260	BUFFALO	0	0	0	0	0	0	0	0	0	0	0	0	0	0	0	0	0	0	0	0
14301	NIAGARA FALLS	48	40	39	41	39	45	49	45	52	45	52	35	45	51	44	55	36	49	52	55
14303	NIAGARA FALLS	50	40	41	41	39	47	49	47	53	46	52	35	44	52	44	56	36	50	54	57
14304	NIAGARA FALLS	82	87	80	87	85	92	82	85	85	80	84	64	85	85	84	88	58	84	93	100
14305	NIAGARA FALLS	67	62	57	63	60	69	66	65	72	65	71	48	65	70	63	76	49	68	75	79
14410	ADAMS BASIN	110	124	106	127	120	121	110	115	109	111	109	90	118	111	117	109	76	110	114	135
14411	ALBION	78	68	65	70	67	78	74	75	77	69	75	57	68	77	69	81	52	76	82	90
14414	AVON	99	89	85	88	89	96	90	94	93	90	92	69	84	94	86	96	63	92	97	111
14415	BELLONA	89	61	98	61	64	94	68	85	71	55	70	70	50	70	68	77	45	79	90	104
14416	BERGEN	96	104	96	105	103	105	98	101	97	94	97	78	100	99	101	99	68	98	102	118
14418	BRANCHPORT	83	65	102	63	70	86	65	83	69	61	68	61	55	66	69	74	45	76	82	96
14420	BROCKPORT	93	94	84	95	91	91	97	91	94	95	95	71	96	96	93	94	66	93	93	108
14422	BYRON	101	102	93	103	100	108	95	102	96	93	96	77	94	99	96	99	66	97	104	120
14423	CALEDONIA	93	98	88	98	96	100	89	94	90	90	91	71	92	93	92	93	63	91	96	111
14424	CANANDAIGUA	95	97	98	98	97	100	96	97	97	94	97	75	98	96	98	98	68	97	100	115
14425	FARMINGTON	102	104	90	102	99	97	98	98	97	102	98	75	98	100	97	95	68	97	94	115
14427	CASTILE	76	75	77	75	76	86	71	80	74	66	73	59	70	74	74	79	50	75	85	92
14428	CHURCHVILLE	108	120	105	119	115	113	109	110	108	112	109	84	116	111	113	108	77	108	109	128
14432	CLIFTON SPRINGS	89	82	79	81	81	89	82	86	85	81	85	64	78	87	79	89	58	85	90	102
14433	CLYDE	83	73	68	74	71	84	75	79	78	70	77	61	68	80	71	82	52	77	85	95
14435	CONESUS	103	106	93	107	103	107	97	102	98	98	98	78	98	101	98	99	68	98	102	120
14437	DANSVILLE	81	73	71	74	72	83	75	79	77	70	76	61	70	78	72	81	52	77	84	94
14441	DRESDEN	92	66	94	64	68	93	68	86	75	63	74	65	54	75	67	83	49	79	89	102
14445	EAST ROCHESTER	83	82	71	84	78	85	86	82	87	82	87	64	85	88	83	89	60	85	90	99
14450	FAIRPORT	142	167	162	170	168	156	148	151	144	156	145	116	165	145	160	141	104	147	146	174
14454	GENESEO	95	87	80	91	85	88	103	90	98	94	99	74	94	99	92	98	69	96	93	109
14456	GENEVA	79	73	74	74	73	81	78	78	81	74	80	59	75	79	76	84	55	80	86	93
14462	GROVELAND	98	90	89	93	91	106	88	100	91	80	89	75	81	93	88	96	61	92	103	116
14464	HAMLIN	99	98	85	95	94	95	90	94	92	94	92	69	89	95	88	93	63	91	93	111
14466	HEMLOCK	95	100	99	102	99	104	91	99	91	90	91	76	94	92	97	92	63	94	98	116
14467	HENRIETTA	104	129	116	129	124	127	110	115	111	112	112	86	127	112	122	113	79	112	121	133
14468	HILTON	106	118	103	118	113	112	107	108	106	110	107	83	114	109	111	106	75	106	107	127
14469	BLOOMFIELD	100	101	92	103	100	107	94	101	95	91	95	77	94	98	96	98	65	96	103	119
14470	HOLLEY	91	90	74	90	85	93	88	87	90	86	89	68	87	92	85	92	61	88	94	106
14471	HONEOYE	101	89	109	90	93	108	87	103	90	81	89	77	80	89	91	95	60	95	103	119
14472	HONEOYE FALLS	145	174	173	180	177	162	153	156	146	160	148	122	172	149	166	143	107	150	146	180
14475	IONIA	95	87	86	90	88	102	85	96	88	77	86	73	79	90	85	93	59	89	99	112
14476	KENDALL	97	116	104	116	112	116	100	105	102	100	102	79	112	103	109	104	72	102	111	123
14477	KENT	94	86	85	90	88	101	85	95	88	77	86	72	78	89	85	93	59	88	99	111
14478	KEUKA PARK	98	86	117	85	93	106	86	101	89	84	88	72	80	85	91	94	60	96	105	117
14480	LAKEVILLE	90	112	99	111	107	110	95	99	96	96	97	74	109	97	105	98	68	97	105	115
14481	LEICESTER	90	75	79	76	76	92	75	86	80	70	78	66	66	82	73	86	53	80	90	102
14482	LE ROY	85	91	82	92	88	92	88	88	88	84	88	68	91	89	89	89	62	87	91	103
14485	LIMA	88	101	92	101	99	96	95	95	93	93	94	74	101	94	99	93	67	94	94	110
14486	LINWOOD	89	81	80	84	82	95	80	90	82	72	81	68	73	84	79	87	55	83	93	104
14487	LIVONIA	90	109	96	110	105	107	94	98	94	95	95	74	106	96	103	96	67	96	102	115
14489	LYONS	90	82	75	83	79	93	83	87	86	78	85	68	77	88	80	90	58	85	93	104
14502	MACEDON	105	114	100	113	111	110	104	106	103	106	104	82	108	106	107	103	73	104	105	125
14504	MANCHESTER	79	78	81	75	79	87	75	81	78	77	77	58	75	75	78	81	52	80	90	96
14505	MARION	93	96	83	97	92	98	89	92	90	89	90	71	91	92	90	91	62	90	94	110
14506	MENDON	180	232	238	241	239	213	193	202	182	208	184	155	227	184	218	176	135	189	183	230
14507	MIDDLESEX	101	81	122	79	87	105	81	101	85	77	84	74	70	82	85	90	56	93	100	117
14510	MOUNT MORRIS	78	67	62	68	65	76	73	73	75	67	74	57	66	77	67	79	51	74	79	88
14512	NAPLES	87	82	86	82	83	94	79	88	82	76	81	66	76	82	81	86	56	84	92	103
14513	NEWARK	84	75	69	76	73	83	80	79	83	76	82	61	74	84	75	86	56	81	86	96
14514	NORTH CHILI	101	103	100	104	103	110	100	104	102	98	101	77	101	102	102	105	70	103	111	122
14516	NORTH ROSE	92	75	91	76	78	95	76	89	80	71	79	67	66	81	75	86	53	83	92	105
14517	NUNDA	87	77	77	78	75	91	78	84	82	74	81	65	73	83	76	86	55	82	90	101
14519	ONTARIO	110	111	97	111	108	110	102	107	103	105	103	81	102	107	102	104	71	103	105	126
14521	OVID	92	77	93	77	78	95	79	89	83	74	81	67	70	82	78	87	55	86	94	106
14522	PALMYRA	92	90	81	92	88	97	89	92	90	84	90	71	86	92	88	94	62	90	97	109
14525	PAVILION	91	97	89	99	96	102	88	95	89	86	89	72	92	91	93	92	62	90	97	111
14526	PENFIELD	135	161	157	163	162	153	141	146	137	147	139	110	157	137	154	136	99	141	143	168
14527	PENN YAN	83	69	85	69	72	85	73	82	76	69	75	61	65	75	72	81	51	79	86	96
14530	PERRY	80	78	72	79	77	86	79	81	81	74	80	61	77	81	77	84	55	80	88	95
14532	PHELPS	95	98	82	100	93	101	94	95	95	91	94	74	95	97	94	96	65	94	100	113
14533	PIFFARD	95	86	85	89	88	101	85	96	88	77	86	73	78	89	85	93	59	88	99	111
14534	PITTSFORD	178	225	235	232	234	214	191	202	184	204	185	151	222	183	216	181	134	191	193	229
14536	PORTAGEVILLE	76	66	70	68	67	81	66	76	70	60	68	58	59	70	66	74	46	71	80	89
14541	ROMULUS	97	83	110	83	87	102	82	98	85	77	84	73	74	83	86	90	57	91	98	114
14543	RUSH	125	150	146	152	151	148	129	138	128	135	129	102	145	127	143	128	91	132	138	158
14544	RUSHVILLE	102	88	106	86	91	103	86	99	89	84	88	73	78	89	87	93	60	93	99	116
14545	SCOTTSBURG	91	83	82	87	85	98	82	93	85	74	83	70	76	86	82	90	57	86	96	108
14546	SCOTTSVILLE	104	116	103	115	111	111	108	107	108	109	109	82	116	110	112	108	77	108	109	125
14548	SHORTSVILLE	91	91	83	91	89	96	87	91	89	87	89	68	87	90	87	92	61	89	97	108
	NEW YORK	100	106	110	108	107	104	112	106	113	106	114	81	115	110	112	116	83	110	110	124
	UNITED STATES	100	100	100	100	100	100	100	100	100	100	100	100	100	100	100	100	100	100	100	100

ZIP CODE #	POST OFFICE NAME	COUNTY FIPS CODE	POPULATION 2000	POPULATION 2009	POPULATION 2014	2000-2009 ANNUAL RATE % Rate	2000-2009 ANNUAL RATE State Centile	HOUSEHOLDS 2000	HOUSEHOLDS 2009	HOUSEHOLDS 2014	HOUSEHOLDS % Annual Rate 2000-2009	HOUSEHOLDS 2009 Average HH Size	FAMILIES 2000	FAMILIES 2009	FAMILIES % Annual Rate 2000-2009
14550	SILVER SPRINGS	121	1705	1660	1625	-0.3	15	660	660	652	0.0	2.51	458	451	-0.2
14551	SODUS	117	5734	5519	5398	-0.4	11	2142	2110	2077	-0.2	2.57	1483	1435	-0.4
14555	SODUS POINT	117	1263	1221	1193	-0.4	11	533	530	524	-0.1	2.30	365	357	-0.2
14559	SPENCERPORT	055	16114	16645	16597	0.4	66	5852	6138	6153	0.5	2.69	4444	4575	0.3
14560	SPRINGWATER	069	2140	2102	2073	-0.2	21	828	830	825	0.0	2.52	590	581	-0.2
14561	STANLEY	069	2898	2922	2909	0.1	44	1004	1027	1027	0.2	2.82	781	787	0.1
14564	VICTOR	069	10141	12446	13458	2.2	99	3753	4750	5161	2.6	2.61	2798	3480	2.4
14568	WALWORTH	117	6079	5937	5831	-0.3	15	2043	2047	2025	0.0	2.90	1629	1612	-0.1
14569	WARSAW	121	6332	6252	6157	-0.1	30	2448	2483	2464	0.2	2.33	1610	1605	0.0
14571	WATERPORT	073	1266	1250	1234	-0.1	30	482	484	481	0.0	2.58	339	334	-0.2
14572	WAYLAND	101	5282	5204	5118	-0.2	21	2027	2017	1994	-0.1	2.55	1435	1404	-0.2
14580	WEBSTER	055	43503	48299	49015	1.1	91	16739	18815	19181	1.3	2.53	12106	13328	1.0
14586	WEST HENRIETTA	055	6678	7410	7478	1.1	91	2468	2737	2780	1.1	2.38	1560	1688	0.9
14589	WILLIAMSON	117	7820	7990	7950	0.2	52	2987	3132	3138	0.5	2.53	2215	2283	0.3
14590	WOLCOTT	117	5403	5365	5293	-0.1	30	2115	2154	2141	0.2	2.40	1461	1460	0.0
14591	WYOMING	121	1816	1800	1771	-0.1	30	636	643	638	0.1	2.79	498	498	0.0
14604	ROCHESTER	055	1339	1481	1480	1.1	91	938	1019	1024	0.9	1.21	129	133	0.3
14605	ROCHESTER	055	14537	13833	13466	-0.5	7	5023	4765	4652	-0.6	2.80	3360	3119	-0.8
14606	ROCHESTER	055	29407	28610	28013	-0.3	15	11329	11116	10931	-0.2	2.56	7494	7181	-0.5
14607	ROCHESTER	055	16571	16024	15641	-0.4	11	10018	9693	9490	-0.4	1.55	1990	1809	-1.0
14608	ROCHESTER	055	12997	12302	11934	-0.6	4	5520	5313	5187	-0.4	2.27	2842	2615	-0.9
14609	ROCHESTER	055	43809	41801	40705	-0.5	7	17740	17061	16681	-0.4	2.42	10986	10269	-0.7
14610	ROCHESTER	055	14607	14331	14079	-0.2	21	7057	6958	6853	-0.2	2.01	3428	3280	-0.5
14611	ROCHESTER	055	18853	17363	16689	-0.9	2	6871	6318	6083	-0.9	2.68	4314	3864	-1.2
14612	ROCHESTER	055	35673	35453	35057	-0.1	30	13993	14036	13923	0.0	2.49	9382	9256	-0.1
14613	ROCHESTER	055	15607	15178	14849	-0.3	15	5854	5627	5500	-0.4	2.66	3587	3353	-0.7
14614	ROCHESTER	055	920	1122	1126	2.2	99	2	3	3	4.5	2.67	0	0	0.0
14615	ROCHESTER	055	15455	15206	14965	-0.2	21	6777	6724	6637	-0.1	2.25	3898	3745	-0.4
14616	ROCHESTER	055	27600	27115	26660	-0.2	21	11311	11209	11059	-0.1	2.39	7567	7330	-0.3
14617	ROCHESTER	055	23732	22932	22455	-0.4	11	9885	9664	9499	-0.2	2.37	6681	6387	-0.5
14618	ROCHESTER	055	21718	21489	21072	-0.1	30	8844	8612	8458	-0.3	2.25	5535	5245	-0.6
14619	ROCHESTER	055	14697	14112	13754	-0.4	11	5364	5146	5025	-0.4	2.71	3573	3349	-0.7
14620	ROCHESTER	055	25178	25047	24592	-0.1	30	11104	10790	10585	-0.3	1.98	4538	4231	-0.8
14621	ROCHESTER	055	34863	32493	31374	-0.8	2	13042	12134	11739	-0.8	2.60	7968	7175	-1.1
14622	ROCHESTER	055	12013	11756	11554	-0.2	21	5234	5200	5135	-0.1	2.26	3327	3230	-0.3
14623	ROCHESTER	055	26673	27689	27420	0.4	66	8641	8640	8550	0.0	2.39	4756	4638	-0.3
14624	ROCHESTER	055	37833	37447	37024	-0.1	30	14197	14201	14096	0.0	2.60	10515	10325	-0.2
14625	ROCHESTER	055	11049	10596	10338	-0.5	7	4617	4441	4341	-0.4	2.37	3159	2997	-0.6
14626	ROCHESTER	055	28375	28923	28771	0.2	52	11042	11381	11364	0.3	2.50	7838	7939	0.1
14627	ROCHESTER	055	2423	2937	2937	2.1	98	11	11	11	0.0	3.00	5	5	0.0
14642	ROCHESTER	055	453	440	429	-0.3	15	291	279	273	-0.5	1.31	93	86	-0.8
14701	JAMESTOWN	013	42880	40830	39580	-0.5	7	17933	17217	16772	-0.4	2.30	11103	10463	-0.6
14706	ALLEGANY	009	7677	7744	7584	0.1	44	2476	2491	2453	0.1	2.51	1699	1680	-0.1
14708	ALMA	003	154	160	160	0.4	66	58	62	62	0.7	2.58	44	47	0.7
14709	ANGELICA	003	1572	1574	1558	0.0	38	626	644	643	0.3	2.44	434	440	0.1
14710	ASHVILLE	013	3954	4129	4112	0.5	71	1481	1576	1581	0.7	2.62	1129	1186	0.5
14711	BELFAST	003	1687	1756	1752	0.4	66	654	697	702	0.7	2.52	443	465	0.5
14712	BEMUS POINT	013	3458	3517	3478	0.2	52	1424	1469	1461	0.3	2.34	993	1005	0.1
14714	BLACK CREEK	003	493	525	526	0.7	80	162	177	179	1.0	2.97	118	127	0.8
14715	BOLIVAR	003	2988	2866	2798	-0.4	11	1131	1109	1090	-0.2	2.58	807	780	-0.4
14716	BROCTON	013	3413	3425	3386	0.0	38	848	847	835	0.0	2.71	587	576	-0.2
14717	CANEADEA	003	809	829	824	0.3	59	318	333	333	0.5	2.46	216	222	0.3
14718	CASSADAGA	013	2518	2504	2476	-0.1	30	864	875	869	0.1	2.79	613	610	-0.1
14719	CATTARAUGUS	009	3764	3783	3727	0.1	44	1387	1433	1425	0.4	2.64	987	1002	0.2
14721	CERES	003	19	18	18	-0.6	4	9	9	9	0.0	2.00	7	6	-1.7
14723	CHERRY CREEK	013	1347	1321	1296	-0.2	21	480	479	472	0.0	2.75	372	367	-0.1
14724	CLYMER	013	2495	2472	2431	-0.1	30	900	907	898	0.1	2.73	701	696	-0.1
14726	CONEWANGO VALLEY	009	2218	2220	2188	0.0	38	609	628	625	0.3	3.53	475	483	0.2
14727	CUBA	003	5344	5276	5183	-0.1	30	2080	2103	2083	0.1	2.47	1462	1454	-0.1
14728	DEWITTVILLE	013	1261	1255	1235	-0.1	30	486	494	489	0.2	2.39	336	335	0.0
14729	EAST OTTO	009	921	907	891	-0.2	21	347	356	354	0.3	2.55	250	252	0.1
14731	ELLICOTTVILLE	009	1721	1719	1697	0.0	38	776	806	802	0.4	2.12	472	480	0.2
14733	FALCONER	013	3977	3795	3689	-0.5	7	1683	1629	1592	-0.4	2.32	1105	1047	-0.6
14735	FILLMORE	003	2740	2726	2687	-0.1	30	1029	1048	1042	0.2	2.58	734	737	0.0
14736	FINDLEY LAKE	013	314	317	314	0.1	44	128	132	132	0.3	2.40	94	96	0.2
14737	FRANKLINVILLE	009	4311	4296	4221	0.0	38	1642	1681	1665	0.3	2.54	1180	1186	0.1
14738	FREWSBURG	009	3920	3827	3748	-0.3	15	1465	1463	1446	0.0	2.57	1105	1087	-0.2
14739	FRIENDSHIP	003	3015	2931	2870	-0.3	15	1156	1146	1130	-0.1	2.52	793	774	-0.3
14740	GERRY	013	1575	1634	1634	0.4	66	460	484	486	0.6	2.95	355	367	0.4
14741	GREAT VALLEY	009	2033	1994	1954	-0.2	21	775	790	783	0.2	2.50	544	545	0.0
14743	HINSDALE	009	2051	1943	1877	-0.6	4	787	775	756	-0.2	2.49	576	558	-0.3
14744	HOUGHTON	003	2278	2455	2445	0.8	84	480	504	505	0.5	2.81	326	336	0.3
14747	KENNEDY	013	2496	2493	2470	0.0	38	940	961	958	0.2	2.59	708	714	0.1
14748	KILL BUCK	009	648	625	609	-0.4	11	264	264	259	0.0	2.33	183	180	-0.2
14750	LAKEWOOD	013	4450	4367	4285	-0.2	21	1932	1940	1920	0.0	2.25	1254	1235	-0.2
14753	LIMESTONE	009	1340	1397	1387	0.5	71	523	568	570	0.9	2.41	360	381	0.6
14754	LITTLE GENESEE	003	1126	1096	1076	-0.3	15	428	428	423	0.0	2.56	324	319	-0.2
14755	LITTLE VALLEY	009	2952	2886	2819	-0.2	21	1097	1110	1094	0.1	2.49	778	773	-0.1
14757	MAYVILLE	013	3669	3633	3569	-0.1	30	1497	1512	1495	0.1	2.29	1019	1010	-0.1
14760	OLEAN	009	20349	18841	18190	-0.8	2	8355	8092	7874	-0.3	2.24	5123	4876	-0.5
14767	PANAMA	013	2078	2161	2157	0.4	66	708	749	752	0.6	2.89	568	593	0.5
14769	PORTLAND	013	1192	1120	1084	-0.7	3	453	434	422	-0.5	2.57	315	297	-0.6
14770	PORTVILLE	003	3117	3011	2942	-0.4	11	1175	1178	1162	0.0	2.56	858	846	-0.2
14772	RANDOLPH	009	4332	4172	4057	-0.4	11	1576	1569	1540	0.0	2.59	1131	1106	-0.2
14775	RIPLEY	013	2796	2713	2661	-0.3	15	1057	1047	1033	-0.1	2.59	762	742	-0.3
14777	RUSHFORD	003	375	357	348	-0.5	7	153	150	147	-0.2	2.38	104	100	-0.4
14779	SALAMANCA	009	7578	7205	6958	-0.5	7	3050	2966	2887	-0.3	2.38	1997	1904	-0.5
14781	SHERMAN	013	2174	2103	2054	-0.4	11	774	759	745	-0.2	2.77	565	544	-0.4
14782	SINCLAIRVILLE	013	2504	2503	2477	0.0	38	940	958	953	0.2	2.52	710	712	0.0
14784	STOCKTON	013	1049	1019	998	-0.3	15	356	353	348	-0.1	2.82	275	269	-0.2
14787	WESTFIELD	013	5486	5208	5041	-0.6	4	2187	2104	2049	-0.4	2.41	1504	1418	-0.6
14801	ADDISON	101	5361	5031	4888	-0.7	3	1995	1888	1841	-0.6	2.66	1429	1335	-0.7
14802	ALFRED	003	3698	4121	4126	1.2	93	438	476	482	0.9	3.77	208	221	0.7
14803	ALFRED STATION	003	1555	1639	1624	0.6	76	605	629	629	0.4	1.55	328	330	0.1
14804	ALMOND	003	1486	1430	1396	-0.4	11	581	571	562	-0.2	2.36	392	379	-0.4
	NEW YORK					0.3					0.3	2.61			0.1
	UNITED STATES					1.0					1.1	2.59			0.9

#	POST OFFICE NAME	RACE (%) White 2000	White 2009	Black 2000	Black 2009	Asian/Pacific 2000	Asian/Pacific 2009	% Hispanic Origin 2000	% Hispanic Origin 2009	2009 AGE DISTRIBUTION (%) 0-4	5-9	10-14	15-19	20-24	25-44	45-64	65-84	85+	18+	MEDIAN AGE 2009	% 2009 Males	% 2009 Females
14550	SILVER SPRINGS	98.1	97.6	0.2	0.2	0.4	0.4	1.1	1.3	5.3	5.4	6.0	6.9	5.0	25.8	31.1	12.5	2.0	79.2	42.1	49.6	50.4
14551	SODUS	85.8	83.0	10.0	11.5	0.6	0.7	2.9	3.5	6.4	6.3	6.5	7.0	6.2	24.6	28.4	12.4	2.2	76.4	40.0	48.4	51.6
14555	SODUS POINT	93.9	92.4	3.4	4.0	0.2	0.3	1.6	2.1	5.2	5.7	6.5	6.9	4.6	23.1	33.2	13.4	1.6	78.5	43.7	50.9	49.1
14559	SPENCERPORT	96.9	95.4	1.0	1.5	0.7	1.0	1.4	2.1	5.6	5.9	6.5	7.2	5.8	24.8	31.7	11.3	1.4	77.6	41.0	49.2	50.8
14560	SPRINGWATER	97.3	96.6	0.4	0.5	0.6	0.8	0.7	0.9	5.2	6.6	6.5	6.7	3.6	25.8	33.0	11.7	1.0	77.3	42.5	51.3	48.7
14561	STANLEY	98.2	97.7	0.5	0.6	0.2	0.2	1.2	1.5	5.9	6.7	7.5	7.7	5.3	22.6	30.8	11.7	1.7	74.9	41.2	49.7	50.3
14564	VICTOR	96.5	95.5	0.9	1.0	1.1	1.6	1.6	2.2	6.3	6.9	7.7	7.3	4.8	21.9	32.4	11.2	1.4	75.3	41.8	49.5	50.5
14568	WALWORTH	96.6	95.7	0.9	1.1	0.9	1.2	1.5	1.9	8.1	8.3	8.4	7.2	5.1	27.7	27.9	6.7	0.6	70.6	36.0	50.1	49.9
14569	WARSAW	96.1	95.1	1.5	1.7	0.9	1.3	1.2	1.4	5.7	5.7	5.9	6.7	6.6	25.7	27.3	12.3	4.2	78.8	40.3	48.6	51.4
14571	WATERPORT	94.6	93.2	3.2	4.1	0.1	0.2	1.1	1.4	5.9	6.1	6.6	7.0	5.3	23.9	32.7	11.1	1.4	77.0	41.4	52.8	47.2
14572	WAYLAND	97.2	96.6	0.8	0.9	0.5	0.6	0.8	1.0	5.6	6.7	7.2	7.9	4.9	24.8	29.5	12.0	1.5	74.9	40.5	50.0	50.0
14580	WEBSTER	94.9	92.5	1.7	2.6	2.0	2.8	1.6	2.3	5.9	6.6	6.9	6.8	4.6	23.3	30.5	13.0	2.4	76.0	42.3	48.3	51.7
14586	WEST HENRIETTA	84.1	77.6	7.6	10.7	5.5	7.3	3.1	4.3	5.9	5.7	6.3	11.5	15.9	26.9	21.2	5.8	0.8	78.3	28.6	53.5	46.5
14589	WILLIAMSON	93.3	91.6	4.0	4.8	0.4	0.6	1.8	2.3	5.8	5.8	6.3	7.5	6.4	23.6	30.0	12.7	1.8	77.0	41.2	49.2	50.8
14590	WOLCOTT	93.3	92.0	3.5	4.0	0.2	0.2	3.4	4.2	6.2	6.2	6.4	6.7	6.0	24.9	29.4	12.5	1.6	76.8	40.1	51.2	48.8
14591	WYOMING	95.7	94.6	2.1	2.5	0.1	0.3	1.3	1.5	5.2	6.6	7.9	8.1	4.9	26.9	27.8	11.1	1.5	75.1	38.9	52.3	47.7
14604	ROCHESTER	53.7	45.6	32.0	37.1	2.4	3.2	15.0	17.0	3.8	3.2	2.4	6.3	7.4	25.1	28.8	19.3	3.6	89.3	46.3	47.5	52.5
14605	ROCHESTER	16.7	14.9	59.4	60.0	0.9	1.1	32.3	33.0	10.7	10.6	8.6	9.8	9.6	25.6	18.3	6.2	0.5	64.6	25.4	45.7	54.3
14606	ROCHESTER	73.3	67.2	15.5	18.9	3.8	4.8	8.3	10.1	7.3	7.0	6.7	7.2	7.0	25.7	25.3	11.7	2.1	74.5	36.9	48.0	52.0
14607	ROCHESTER	79.7	73.4	13.3	17.4	2.4	3.2	4.3	5.7	3.0	2.0	2.0	3.1	14.7	45.1	19.8	6.9	3.3	91.7	32.5	52.5	47.5
14608	ROCHESTER	21.8	18.0	67.1	69.5	1.7	1.8	11.0	12.1	9.7	9.0	7.6	7.7	8.1	27.0	21.8	7.9	1.1	69.1	30.1	47.2	52.8
14609	ROCHESTER	63.2	57.8	27.4	30.9	0.9	1.1	10.3	12.1	7.6	7.4	7.0	7.0	6.6	26.4	25.2	10.1	2.7	73.8	36.7	46.9	53.1
14610	ROCHESTER	90.3	86.4	5.7	8.0	1.7	2.4	2.4	3.5	4.8	4.5	4.8	4.8	6.9	26.2	28.3	14.0	5.7	82.8	43.5	46.7	53.3
14611	ROCHESTER	23.7	19.0	68.7	72.4	1.4	1.6	7.1	7.7	9.2	9.0	8.4	8.7	8.0	25.6	22.4	7.7	1.0	68.1	29.9	46.8	53.2
14612	ROCHESTER	92.5	89.4	3.6	5.1	1.3	1.8	2.7	3.9	6.0	6.2	6.4	6.8	5.9	24.7	30.5	11.1	2.5	77.2	40.7	48.3	51.7
14613	ROCHESTER	56.5	47.5	30.2	36.3	2.0	2.3	11.8	14.3	9.5	8.5	8.0	8.4	8.9	27.9	21.6	6.0	1.1	68.8	29.2	48.7	51.3
14614	ROCHESTER	37.1	27.8	62.0	71.1	0.2	0.3	1.0	1.1	0.1	0.1	0.1	10.7	18.1	59.0	10.1	1.7	0.2	96.3	31.3	97.9	2.1
14615	ROCHESTER	80.0	74.0	11.8	15.1	2.2	2.9	7.2	9.5	6.9	6.4	5.9	6.4	7.4	28.5	25.8	10.8	2.0	76.9	37.1	48.5	51.5
14616	ROCHESTER	94.2	91.6	2.4	3.5	1.1	1.5	2.4	3.5	5.8	6.0	6.3	6.7	5.5	25.5	28.1	13.1	2.9	77.5	41.0	47.9	52.1
14617	ROCHESTER	94.9	92.6	2.2	3.2	1.0	1.5	2.1	3.1	4.9	5.2	6.0	6.4	5.1	21.0	31.7	15.5	4.1	79.6	45.9	47.1	52.9
14618	ROCHESTER	89.9	86.0	2.7	3.9	5.6	7.6	1.9	2.8	4.5	4.8	5.5	8.6	8.1	20.2	29.1	15.1	4.1	81.6	43.6	45.9	54.1
14619	ROCHESTER	25.8	18.9	69.2	75.6	0.8	0.9	2.8	3.0	7.7	7.7	7.8	8.4	7.7	25.9	25.6	7.9	1.3	71.5	33.0	45.8	54.2
14620	ROCHESTER	73.5	66.3	15.0	19.0	6.2	7.8	5.0	6.5	5.0	4.3	4.3	4.8	12.4	31.3	21.8	11.2	5.0	83.9	36.1	48.6	51.4
14621	ROCHESTER	32.5	27.7	44.0	46.4	2.3	2.4	26.4	28.8	9.2	8.7	8.1	8.3	8.1	24.4	21.2	8.8	3.3	69.0	30.3	46.2	53.8
14622	ROCHESTER	95.4	93.3	2.2	3.3	0.8	1.2	2.1	3.1	5.0	5.2	5.6	5.8	4.7	22.5	31.0	16.2	4.0	80.6	45.7	46.9	53.1
14623	ROCHESTER	80.3	73.4	7.3	10.0	8.9	11.6	3.4	4.7	4.1	3.9	3.8	14.3	20.2	25.6	17.3	8.6	2.1	85.6	27.3	55.0	45.0
14624	ROCHESTER	90.6	86.7	6.1	8.7	1.3	1.8	1.9	2.7	5.6	5.9	6.3	7.0	6.0	25.1	29.5	12.6	2.0	77.9	41.1	48.6	51.4
14625	ROCHESTER	94.6	92.2	1.6	2.4	2.5	3.5	1.5	2.2	5.1	5.7	6.6	6.6	4.5	19.5	33.3	16.1	2.6	78.1	46.2	48.4	51.6
14626	ROCHESTER	93.3	90.1	3.1	4.6	1.8	2.5	2.5	3.8	5.4	6.0	6.6	6.5	4.8	24.4	28.2	15.1	3.1	77.7	42.5	47.8	52.2
14627	ROCHESTER	73.1	64.8	4.8	6.5	17.3	22.2	5.0	6.8	0.1	0.1	0.0	60.4	36.9	2.3	0.1	0.0	0.0	99.3	19.1	57.5	42.5
14642	ROCHESTER	60.4	51.4	6.6	8.4	29.1	35.5	5.1	6.1	4.5	1.8	1.4	5.0	28.0	46.1	9.5	3.0	0.7	91.6	26.8	54.3	45.7
14701	JAMESTOWN	93.2	91.5	2.6	3.1	0.5	0.7	3.9	5.0	6.8	6.3	6.2	6.8	6.6	24.2	26.7	13.4	3.0	76.7	39.4	48.4	51.6
14706	ALLEGANY	96.4	92.3	0.8	3.4	1.1	1.5	0.9	2.5	3.9	4.1	4.6	15.6	14.6	19.4	24.8	11.2	1.9	84.2	32.0	47.4	52.6
14708	ALMA	98.7	98.1	0.0	0.0	0.7	0.6	0.0	0.0	5.6	6.3	6.3	6.3	4.4	21.9	33.8	14.4	1.3	78.1	44.5	50.0	50.0
14709	ANGELICA	98.0	97.4	0.3	0.3	0.1	0.2	0.4	0.4	6.4	6.4	6.9	6.5	5.1	22.9	30.4	13.7	1.7	76.2	41.6	50.4	49.6
14710	ASHVILLE	98.4	97.8	0.3	0.3	0.1	0.2	0.6	0.8	5.5	6.6	7.2	6.7	4.5	22.3	32.9	12.7	1.6	76.7	43.1	50.4	49.6
14711	BELFAST	98.3	97.9	0.1	0.1	0.2	0.3	0.8	1.0	6.5	6.4	7.0	8.7	6.2	23.1	28.2	12.4	1.7	74.8	38.8	50.5	49.5
14712	BEMUS POINT	98.4	98.0	0.2	0.3	0.2	0.3	0.9	1.2	4.5	4.9	5.5	6.3	4.6	18.3	34.3	18.2	3.4	81.1	48.7	49.2	50.8
14714	BLACK CREEK	98.6	98.3	0.2	0.2	0.0	0.0	0.6	0.8	6.1	6.5	7.0	8.4	5.5	21.3	30.7	12.8	1.7	75.0	41.6	49.5	50.5
14715	BOLIVAR	98.5	98.1	0.4	0.4	0.2	0.3	0.1	0.2	7.3	7.2	7.7	7.7	6.0	23.6	27.1	11.5	2.0	73.1	37.9	49.3	50.7
14716	BROCTON	77.1	73.1	16.8	19.3	0.0	0.0	11.5	14.2	4.0	4.0	4.2	9.5	14.1	33.0	20.9	9.0	1.2	83.8	31.8	62.7	37.3
14717	CANEADEA	98.4	97.9	0.1	0.1	0.2	0.4	1.0	1.2	6.3	6.2	6.8	8.4	6.8	22.1	28.2	13.5	1.8	75.9	39.5	50.1	49.9
14718	CASSADAGA	95.9	94.8	1.7	2.0	0.3	0.4	2.3	3.1	5.4	5.6	6.2	8.2	5.6	22.9	31.3	13.0	1.8	78.1	42.3	50.1	49.9
14719	CATTARAUGUS	98.6	98.1	0.2	0.2	0.1	0.1	0.9	1.2	7.1	7.2	7.2	7.7	5.9	24.0	27.8	11.6	1.4	73.5	38.2	50.4	49.6
14721	CERES	100.0	100.0	0.0	0.0	0.0	0.0	0.0	0.0	0.0	11.1	11.1	11.1	5.6	27.8	33.3	0.0	0.0	66.7	35.0	50.0	50.0
14723	CHERRY CREEK	97.3	96.3	0.1	0.2	0.3	0.4	1.8	2.4	5.8	7.6	9.2	9.2	4.5	25.7	26.8	10.3	0.9	71.4	37.4	50.6	49.4
14724	CLYMER	98.8	98.5	0.2	0.2	0.2	0.3	0.4	0.4	7.8	8.4	8.6	7.5	4.4	24.5	26.0	11.5	1.2	70.4	36.9	50.7	49.3
14726	CONEWANGO VALLEY	98.5	98.1	0.1	0.1	0.1	0.1	0.4	0.5	10.1	10.2	9.6	10.2	5.5	22.1	22.7	8.2	1.3	63.4	28.9	50.4	49.6
14727	CUBA	97.9	97.4	0.4	0.4	0.3	0.4	0.8	1.0	5.8	6.1	6.6	6.6	6.0	22.9	30.1	13.6	2.3	77.4	41.9	48.6	51.4
14728	DEWITTVILLE	96.2	95.1	1.7	2.1	0.2	0.3	1.0	1.4	4.7	4.9	5.2	6.3	5.7	21.8	30.9	18.2	2.4	81.4	46.0	51.2	48.8
14729	EAST OTTO	98.8	98.3	0.1	0.2	0.2	0.3	0.4	0.7	5.8	6.6	6.9	7.2	4.4	25.9	31.4	10.6	1.1	76.1	40.3	50.5	49.5
14731	ELLICOTTVILLE	97.7	97.1	0.2	0.2	0.2	0.3	1.1	1.5	4.2	4.7	5.4	5.3	3.8	20.1	38.3	16.5	1.6	82.3	49.0	49.6	50.4
14733	FALCONER	98.0	97.5	0.5	0.7	0.3	0.3	1.1	1.4	5.2	5.3	5.7	6.6	5.8	22.7	29.1	16.5	3.1	79.8	44.0	48.7	51.3
14735	FILLMORE	98.0	97.6	0.2	0.2	0.3	0.4	0.7	0.8	6.5	6.5	6.7	7.4	6.7	23.5	28.2	13.0	1.6	76.0	39.4	49.4	50.6
14736	FINDLEY LAKE	98.1	98.1	0.3	0.3	0.3	0.3	1.0	0.9	4.1	6.9	7.6	6.3	4.1	24.0	31.5	14.2	1.3	77.3	43.2	50.5	49.5
14737	FRANKLINVILLE	98.4	97.9	0.1	0.1	0.2	0.3	0.6	0.8	6.5	6.4	6.8	6.9	6.2	24.1	28.8	12.5	1.8	75.7	39.8	49.3	50.7
14738	FREWSBURG	98.0	97.7	0.2	0.2	0.2	0.2	0.5	0.6	5.3	5.5	6.0	7.0	5.6	21.4	30.8	15.5	2.8	78.6	44.3	48.6	51.4
14739	FRIENDSHIP	97.4	96.8	0.9	0.9	0.2	0.3	0.6	0.6	6.1	6.5	6.9	7.2	5.8	24.3	27.9	13.2	2.1	75.9	40.0	50.7	49.3
14740	GERRY	98.4	97.9	0.3	0.4	0.1	0.1	0.7	1.0	5.3	6.7	5.9	6.8	4.5	21.9	26.1	15.4	7.5	77.9	44.2	47.2	52.8
14741	GREAT VALLEY	96.7	95.8	0.6	0.8	0.4	0.7	0.7	1.0	5.1	5.7	5.9	6.4	4.9	22.3	33.6	14.5	1.6	79.0	44.8	51.6	48.4
14743	HINSDALE	97.4	96.6	0.5	0.7	0.3	0.5	0.7	0.9	5.1	5.7	6.6	6.6	5.1	22.8	33.0	13.8	1.2	78.1	43.4	50.3	49.7
14744	HOUGHTON	96.1	95.2	1.1	1.3	0.9	1.3	2.1	2.6	3.5	3.5	3.4	20.4	26.2	17.2	14.2	8.6	3.0	86.3	23.7	43.3	56.7
14747	KENNEDY	98.2	97.6	0.6	0.7	0.1	0.1	0.9	1.2	5.2	5.7	6.2	7.6	5.2	23.7	32.1	12.9	1.5	78.1	42.5	50.2	49.8
14748	KILL BUCK	89.4	87.4	0.9	1.1	1.1	1.4	0.8	1.0	4.3	5.0	6.1	8.0	5.3	23.7	30.1	16.6	1.0	78.9	43.2	52.0	48.0
14750	LAKEWOOD	97.9	97.3	0.6	0.7	0.6	0.8	0.7	0.9	4.8	5.1	5.9	6.4	4.5	20.7	32.2	17.4	3.0	80.3	46.6	48.2	51.8
14753	LIMESTONE	93.2	91.8	1.6	1.8	0.2	0.4	0.8	1.1	5.4	6.1	7.0	8.7	5.2	23.8	29.1	14.2	0.4	75.4	41.2	51.0	49.0
14754	LITTLE GENESEE	99.0	98.9	0.1	0.1	0.0	0.0	0.7	0.8	6.8	7.6	8.4	7.0	5.4	25.8	28.6	9.3	1.1	72.8	37.8	49.4	50.6
14755	LITTLE VALLEY	96.1	95.1	0.9	1.1	0.3	0.5	0.9	1.1	6.1	6.3	6.3	6.2	6.5	24.5	30.1	12.3	1.7	77.5	40.7	52.3	47.7
14757	MAYVILLE	96.5	95.5	1.4	1.7	0.5	0.6	1.1	1.6	4.7	4.8	5.1	6.5	6.0	22.0	31.1	17.6	2.2	81.4	45.6	51.1	48.9
14760	OLEAN	94.2	92.6	2.8	3.4	0.9	1.2	1.1	1.4	6.1	5.7	6.1	6.9	7.3	24.1	27.1	13.6	3.1	78.0	40.1	47.5	52.5
14767	PANAMA	98.7	98.2	0.2	0.3	0.1	0.1	0.5	0.6	7.4	7.7	7.8	7.4	5.2	24.7	27.4	11.1	1.2	72.5	37.7	50.2	49.8
14769	PORTLAND	97.2	96.3	0.3	0.4	0.0	0.0	1.8	2.3	6.3	6.4	6.6	7.1	5.6	24.1	29.5	12.4	1.9	76.3	40.6	49.8	50.2
14770	PORTVILLE	98.4	97.9	0.5	0.6	0.1	0.1	0.9	1.1	4.9	5.7	7.0	7.5	5.3	24.4	31.0	12.6	1.6	77.7	41.6	49.6	50.4
14772	RANDOLPH	97.2	96.5	0.6	0.8	0.2	0.3	0.6	0.6	6.7	6.7	7.6	8.0	5.2	22.7	28.3	13.0	1.8	73.6	39.9	50.3	49.7
14775	RIPLEY	98.1	97.5	0.2	0.2	0.1	0.2	1.4	1.9	5.9	6.3	6.7	7.2	5.1	25.3	28.9	12.7	1.8	76.7	39.6	51.3	48.7
14777	RUSHFORD	99.2	98.9	0.0	0.0	0.0	0.0	0.8	0.8	6.2	6.2	6.2	5.6	5.9	21.6	28.9	17.6	2.0	78.4	43.5	48.5	51.5
14779	SALAMANCA	81.4	79.0	0.6	0.7	0.3	0.4	1.8	2.2	7.6	6.8	7.0	7.1	6.3	23.6	26.1	13.0	2.5	73.9	38.2	48.5	51.5
14781	SHERMAN	98.1	97.5	0.2	0.2	0.5	0.6	0.6	0.8	6.5	7.4	7.7	6.9	4.7	23.5	29.9	11.9	1.7	74.2	39.8	49.7	50.3
14782	SINCLAIRVILLE	98.4	97.8	0.2	0.2	0.2	0.2	1.0	1.4	6.0	6.5	6.6	7.3	5.2	24.3	28.2	12.8	3.2	76.5	41.1	49.1	50.9
14784	STOCKTON	96.3	95.2	1.4	1.7	0.3	0.4	1.9	2.6	6.6	6.5	6.9	8.9	6.6	23.4	27.5	12.4	1.4	74.8	38.6	48.8	51.2
14787	WESTFIELD	97.0	96.1	0.3	0.3	0.5	0.7	2.5	3.4	5.7	5.7	6.0	6.6	6.1	22.1	29.9	14.4	3.5	78.4	43.2	48.4	51.6
14801	ADDISON	98.1	97.6	0.3	0.3	0.3	0.3	0.6	0.8	7.0	6.8	7.0	7.0	6.2	25.9	27.9	10.7	1.4	74.9	37.4	49.1	50.9
14802	ALFRED	91.9	90.0	3.4	3.7	2.5	3.4	2.2	2.7	1.6	1.9	2.4	31.8	36.7	9.0	11.2	4.6	0.8	92.2	21.7	57.2	42.8
14803	ALFRED STATION	93.8	91.9	2.3	2.7	2.1	2.9	1.7	2.1	2.7	2.9	3.4	24.8	28.7	12.6	16.4	7.2	1.1	88.5	22.8	54.2	45.8
14804	ALMOND	96.7	95.6	0.4	0.6	1.9	2.5	0.7	0.8	4.4	5.6	6.2	10.6	8.7	22.5	29.3	11.2	1.5	79.2	38.5	51.8	48.2
	NEW YORK	67.9	64.8	15.9	16.5	5.6	6.9	15.1	16.7	6.5	6.4	6.4	7.1	7.0	27.0	26.3	11.2	2.1	76.6	37.5	48.4	51.6
	UNITED STATES	75.1	72.0	12.3	12.7	3.8	4.6	12.5	15.7	6.8	6.7	6.6	7.1	6.9	27.0	26.0	10.9	1.9	75.7	36.9	49.2	50.8

14550-14804

ZIP CODE #	POST OFFICE NAME	2009 Per Capita Income	2009 HH Income Base	2009 HOUSEHOLD INCOME DISTRIBUTION (%) Less than $25,000	$25,000 to $49,999	$50,000 to $99,999	$100,000 to $149,999	$150,000 or More	MEDIAN HOUSEHOLD INCOME 2009	2014	2009 National Centile	2009 State Centile	2009 Home Value Base	2009 HOME VALUE DISTRIBUTION (%) Less than $50,000	$50,000 to $89,999	$90,000 to $174,999	$175,000 to $399,999	$400,000 or More	2009 Median Home Value
14550	SILVER SPRINGS	21058	660	19.4	31.2	41.5	7.3	0.6	49516	51538	60	44	508	13.4	31.5	44.9	9.3	1.0	96842
14551	SODUS	22721	2110	23.5	25.8	38.0	9.9	2.8	50812	55434	63	48	1585	11.1	22.5	51.8	13.1	1.5	109017
14555	SODUS POINT	24743	530	22.6	31.3	35.5	7.5	3.0	46937	49725	54	37	421	14.5	16.2	47.3	17.8	4.3	119464
14559	SPENCERPORT	29628	6138	8.4	20.8	46.1	18.1	6.6	70350	72551	87	76	4783	1.4	1.5	45.5	48.6	2.9	177127
14560	SPRINGWATER	23809	830	18.4	25.8	44.2	8.9	2.7	55886	60306	73	58	706	10.3	19.0	44.8	24.6	1.3	123673
14561	STANLEY	20715	1027	17.2	30.6	40.3	10.9	1.0	52094	55420	66	51	832	3.7	8.7	59.5	24.9	3.2	140461
14564	VICTOR	38124	4750	8.5	13.5	45.3	15.6	17.1	72714	74618	88	79	3887	1.2	5.1	33.3	40.4	20.0	199251
14568	WALWORTH	27550	2047	8.6	18.4	45.2	21.3	6.5	73574	75135	89	80	1764	8.1	1.6	47.1	42.1	1.0	167204
14569	WARSAW	21980	2483	26.9	25.5	40.1	5.7	1.8	48037	50299	57	40	1680	4.6	16.6	60.4	17.8	0.7	118897
14571	WATERPORT	21694	484	18.8	28.7	43.0	7.2	2.3	51803	55778	66	50	389	4.4	18.8	55.0	20.8	1.0	125605
14572	WAYLAND	21834	2017	20.9	25.3	45.2	6.9	1.7	52952	54282	68	53	1556	12.2	20.6	55.5	10.6	1.0	110693
14580	WEBSTER	34550	18815	9.4	18.8	41.6	19.0	11.1	75150	76563	89	81	13838	0.9	1.1	34.4	59.0	4.5	191442
14586	WEST HENRIETTA	28542	2737	14.1	21.1	42.9	18.2	3.8	66534	69131	85	73	1825	0.9	1.7	60.7	35.3	1.5	163412
14589	WILLIAMSON	27427	3132	16.8	20.8	44.8	12.8	4.9	64035	66510	82	71	2539	4.1	7.1	61.4	26.0	1.4	142567
14590	WOLCOTT	21823	2154	27.2	28.1	35.6	6.4	2.7	44021	48337	45	27	1652	15.6	25.7	43.8	13.6	1.4	101154
14591	WYOMING	20319	643	15.9	31.6	43.9	6.8	1.9	51824	53838	66	51	546	5.9	19.2	58.4	15.2	1.3	118561
14604	ROCHESTER	20338	1019	69.0	16.3	12.2	1.2	1.4	13147	13332	1	1	25	0.0	0.0	0.0	80.0	20.0	346429
14605	ROCHESTER	10576	4765	57.8	27.6	11.9	1.6	1.1	20207	21214	1	1	1110	25.0	47.8	24.1	2.3	0.7	66744
14606	ROCHESTER	21456	11116	25.4	27.6	37.1	7.5	2.4	46950	50744	54	37	6955	3.2	17.2	67.0	12.2	0.4	126825
14607	ROCHESTER	34315	9693	29.2	30.1	29.3	6.6	4.9	41761	45380	39	19	1569	0.0	7.6	39.6	47.0	5.7	182348
14608	ROCHESTER	15471	5313	51.5	27.8	16.7	2.6	1.4	23983	24781	3	2	1370	18.0	34.2	40.1	7.4	0.2	84918
14609	ROCHESTER	21852	17061	27.4	28.0	35.2	7.0	2.3	44628	48296	47	29	10563	2.0	20.8	69.0	7.8	0.4	112468
14610	ROCHESTER	42536	6958	16.9	26.0	34.5	11.1	11.4	59286	63362	77	62	3964	0.1	4.0	44.0	38.2	13.7	178330
14611	ROCHESTER	13845	6318	45.8	27.0	23.8	2.9	0.6	27335	29188	5	3	2726	9.3	53.3	34.8	2.5	0.0	78366
14612	ROCHESTER	28866	14036	16.9	21.4	41.3	14.3	6.1	62773	65303	81	69	9460	0.7	2.8	50.8	44.5	1.2	168883
14613	ROCHESTER	16642	5627	36.4	29.4	28.7	4.2	1.3	34914	38853	17	6	2386	3.1	43.5	47.6	5.7	0.1	91876
14614	ROCHESTER	14867	3	66.7	33.3	0.0	0.0	0.0	7500	7500	0	0	0	0.0	0.0	0.0	0.0	0.0	0
14615	ROCHESTER	24820	6724	23.3	34.3	33.0	6.8	2.6	43585	46878	44	25	3597	0.4	15.7	65.9	17.6	0.4	119560
14616	ROCHESTER	27343	11209	12.5	28.2	46.1	10.2	3.0	57886	61168	75	61	8433	0.7	3.6	77.1	18.3	0.2	135975
14617	ROCHESTER	32486	9664	11.8	22.3	45.0	14.4	6.6	66772	69543	85	74	7774	0.4	1.5	68.0	29.3	0.8	152759
14618	ROCHESTER	42267	8612	7.9	17.7	39.4	18.9	16.1	77459	79406	91	83	5983	0.0	1.3	30.4	57.5	10.9	200070
14619	ROCHESTER	20211	5146	23.0	30.0	37.4	7.8	1.8	46612	50790	53	35	3183	1.1	29.5	67.3	2.1	0.0	98295
14620	ROCHESTER	25497	10790	30.6	29.3	29.2	7.0	3.9	40371	43477	34	15	3966	1.2	17.5	58.1	22.3	0.9	129638
14621	ROCHESTER	14539	12134	45.6	28.5	21.7	2.9	1.3	27426	29174	5	3	4791	10.5	51.9	35.5	1.7	0.4	78768
14622	ROCHESTER	28608	5200	15.9	27.5	43.0	9.5	4.2	55490	59834	72	58	4130	0.8	5.3	74.0	18.5	1.4	137540
14623	ROCHESTER	23259	8640	17.5	26.1	44.4	9.2	2.8	55939	60323	73	58	4667	1.0	3.2	77.4	18.0	0.5	145971
14624	ROCHESTER	29677	14201	10.8	20.7	46.7	15.7	6.2	69143	71925	86	76	11406	1.0	3.1	61.7	33.7	0.5	157187
14625	ROCHESTER	40151	4441	9.7	19.2	37.5	19.6	14.1	76122	78374	90	81	3677	11.2	3.4	26.8	53.3	5.2	187891
14626	ROCHESTER	31540	11381	10.8	22.1	43.0	16.1	7.9	66215	69241	84	73	8443	0.3	0.9	52.7	44.2	1.8	170466
14627	ROCHESTER	15357	11	63.6	36.4	0.0	0.0	0.0	17207	17207	1	1	0	0.0	0.0	0.0	0.0	0.0	0
14642	ROCHESTER	30890	279	34.8	29.4	29.7	3.9	2.2	36064	38922	21	6	71	0.0	0.0	95.8	4.2	0.0	138281
14701	JAMESTOWN	20759	17217	34.1	27.1	31.4	5.1	2.3	37674	40639	26	9	10131	9.1	33.4	45.3	11.2	1.1	99106
14706	ALLEGANY	20638	2491	24.5	27.9	36.7	8.9	2.0	48037	49391	57	40	1970	15.8	16.0	42.6	23.3	2.3	128709
14708	ALMA	19094	62	22.6	37.1	32.3	6.5	1.6	41549	43633	38	18	52	15.4	26.9	50.0	7.7	0.0	100000
14709	ANGELICA	18437	644	28.1	38.5	28.7	3.3	1.4	37705	39113	26	9	506	17.4	33.6	43.5	5.1	0.4	88837
14710	ASHVILLE	22395	1576	19.6	29.4	40.3	7.2	3.5	50802	54604	63	48	1304	9.1	22.5	45.6	18.4	4.4	116049
14711	BELFAST	17727	697	33.1	31.3	30.3	4.2	1.1	36748	38301	23	7	524	19.1	33.0	42.2	4.2	1.5	87317
14712	BEMUS POINT	26026	1469	19.2	27.2	40.7	8.8	4.2	52690	55723	67	52	1175	11.2	10.0	38.9	29.1	10.8	144297
14714	BLACK CREEK	15854	177	28.8	34.5	31.6	5.1	0.0	39160	40558	30	12	146	14.4	31.5	43.2	11.0	0.0	95455
14715	BOLIVAR	17264	1109	31.7	29.2	33.8	4.2	1.0	39034	40157	30	12	827	24.3	38.2	33.1	4.1	0.2	75197
14716	BROCTON	15911	847	30.3	29.9	35.8	3.7	0.4	37315	39139	25	8	651	15.1	28.0	47.6	8.9	0.5	98125
14717	CANEADEA	18132	333	31.5	33.3	29.7	4.5	0.9	36872	38227	23	7	253	18.6	31.6	41.9	7.1	0.8	89722
14718	CASSADAGA	19982	875	18.7	30.7	42.5	6.2	1.8	50314	52677	62	46	726	10.5	22.9	46.4	18.5	1.8	112500
14719	CATTARAUGUS	18918	1433	24.4	33.3	35.5	5.3	1.5	43041	45541	43	23	1150	13.7	27.8	43.3	13.5	1.7	101225
14721	CERES	23194	9	22.2	33.3	44.4	0.0	0.0	47295	61559	55	38	8	12.5	37.5	37.5	12.5	0.0	95000
14723	CHERRY CREEK	17403	479	27.1	29.6	38.6	3.1	1.5	41161	46837	37	17	376	18.6	29.5	41.2	10.1	0.5	92188
14724	CLYMER	19023	907	21.9	34.4	36.9	4.3	2.4	45323	48038	49	32	719	12.1	24.8	47.0	14.5	1.7	108929
14726	CONEWANGO VALLEY	13953	628	29.9	32.0	31.4	4.3	2.4	38881	42148	29	12	512	19.1	27.0	43.9	9.0	1.0	94167
14727	CUBA	19695	2103	26.8	31.9	34.9	4.7	1.8	42786	44751	42	22	1624	15.4	30.7	41.6	11.5	0.9	95378
14728	DEWITTVILLE	23567	494	25.9	28.1	34.0	7.9	4.0	45415	49452	49	32	390	11.0	14.6	42.3	20.8	11.3	130500
14729	EAST OTTO	19635	356	22.2	36.5	34.8	5.3	1.1	41144	43852	36	17	293	8.2	21.8	48.8	18.4	2.7	119104
14731	ELLICOTTVILLE	28437	806	21.5	27.3	37.1	9.4	4.7	50992	52070	64	49	593	5.6	8.3	36.4	40.6	9.1	174235
14733	FALCONER	23680	1629	25.9	26.2	38.4	6.9	2.7	47880	51778	56	40	1090	8.3	27.4	53.5	10.1	0.7	101083
14735	FILLMORE	17952	1048	29.9	32.5	31.2	4.6	1.8	38563	39939	28	11	783	15.5	29.1	46.9	7.8	0.8	96071
14736	FINDLEY LAKE	23583	132	16.7	33.3	40.9	6.1	3.0	50000	52657	61	45	109	7.3	21.1	36.7	31.2	3.7	137500
14737	FRANKLINVILLE	19265	1681	26.9	29.7	36.0	6.3	1.1	44714	46334	47	30	1313	15.7	30.3	42.7	10.7	0.6	94565
14738	FREWSBURG	21816	1463	19.5	28.2	43.4	6.6	2.3	51879	54953	66	51	1159	4.5	21.1	55.2	17.9	1.3	121421
14739	FRIENDSHIP	17562	1146	32.8	32.9	28.9	4.3	1.1	37235	38746	24	8	856	21.6	36.1	36.3	5.4	0.6	80149
14740	GERRY	16324	484	28.7	29.1	36.4	4.5	1.2	42364	46541	41	21	405	17.8	24.0	44.9	12.6	0.7	103045
14741	GREAT VALLEY	20303	790	24.8	32.9	34.6	5.6	2.2	44066	46123	46	27	658	14.0	21.6	41.5	21.1	1.8	111408
14743	HINSDALE	19584	775	26.7	31.2	36.1	4.8	1.2	43545	45704	44	25	650	18.5	20.5	43.7	15.4	2.0	110052
14744	HOUGHTON	16638	504	27.0	25.2	40.5	6.3	1.0	47380	49592	55	39	311	6.8	15.4	54.0	22.5	1.3	131090
14747	KENNEDY	19215	961	25.6	33.6	34.7	4.8	1.4	41179	45570	37	17	786	22.9	28.5	38.7	9.4	0.5	88226
14748	KILL BUCK	19338	264	31.4	27.7	36.7	3.0	1.1	41265	44366	37	18	219	28.3	18.7	40.2	12.8	0.0	94063
14750	LAKEWOOD	31084	1940	17.9	27.6	37.2	9.1	8.2	54907	60395	71	57	1432	5.7	19.8	46.2	22.5	5.9	134810
14753	LIMESTONE	17971	568	33.8	29.2	31.9	4.0	1.1	36562	39226	22	7	440	25.2	35.2	32.0	7.0	0.5	77027
14754	LITTLE GENESEE	18577	428	25.5	29.9	40.0	4.7	0.0	45808	45819	51	33	357	23.8	34.2	32.2	9.5	0.3	81094
14755	LITTLE VALLEY	19532	1110	26.8	31.9	33.8	6.5	1.1	40445	44012	34	15	848	12.0	31.6	40.4	14.5	1.4	98182
14757	MAYVILLE	25439	1512	23.4	25.9	38.8	7.9	4.0	50549	54083	62	46	1165	9.5	18.3	38.5	22.2	11.5	129395
14760	OLEAN	22361	8092	29.6	29.3	32.6	6.4	2.2	40813	44939	35	16	5168	8.5	26.6	49.4	14.6	0.9	109724
14767	PANAMA	18062	749	25.1	33.0	34.2	5.2	2.5	41082	45893	36	17	616	12.5	27.3	46.9	11.2	2.1	104918
14769	PORTLAND	18642	434	27.0	29.7	36.6	6.0	0.7	41682	47369	38	19	321	12.1	36.1	41.4	10.3	0.0	92391
14770	PORTVILLE	20958	1178	22.8	31.8	37.1	5.7	2.5	45000	46889	48	31	948	15.5	26.3	46.3	11.3	0.6	100877
14772	RANDOLPH	19497	1569	25.2	31.9	35.8	5.5	1.6	43302	45893	43	24	1205	12.8	28.9	46.5	11.1	0.7	100055
14775	RIPLEY	19484	1047	24.5	35.1	33.4	6.0	1.0	39917	45326	32	14	805	15.8	35.0	38.4	8.3	2.5	89015
14777	RUSHFORD	18786	150	26.7	41.3	26.7	4.0	1.3	36461	37791	22	7	120	15.8	34.2	37.5	12.5	0.0	90000
14779	SALAMANCA	17566	2966	37.5	29.0	28.7	3.7	1.1	35151	37674	18	6	1902	19.3	40.2	30.2	9.5	0.8	80670
14781	SHERMAN	18030	759	24.6	32.9	35.2	5.4	1.8	43901	47251	45	27	560	11.3	32.7	38.0	16.4	1.6	97727
14782	SINCLAIRVILLE	19761	958	26.1	28.1	39.7	4.5	1.7	45763	49648	51	33	766	17.5	22.3	46.3	13.3	0.5	102759
14784	STOCKTON	18758	353	23.2	30.9	38.0	5.1	2.8	47155	49453	55	38	282	17.7	23.8	38.7	18.8	1.1	105500
14787	WESTFIELD	20943	2104	28.7	28.0	34.3	6.7	2.3	45092	48106	49	31	1469	7.2	24.5	47.5	18.2	2.6	119609
14801	ADDISON	18375	1888	29.7	30.1	32.6	5.2	2.3	41255	43432	37	18	1408	17.3	27.3	41.0	13.4	1.0	97075
14802	ALFRED	15062	476	35.1	22.9	27.5	9.7	4.8	40000	42774	33	14	260	7.3	13.5	42.7	36.5	0.0	153125
14803	ALFRED STATION	27817	629	31.5	24.5	30.7	9.1	4.3	43900	46157	45	26	386	9.6	18.7	44.0	27.7	0.0	135776
14804	ALMOND	25010	571	23.1	26.8	38.0	8.1	4.0	50078	51300	61	45	440	13.4	19.3	47.7	18.6	0.9	120902
	NEW YORK	29893		21.9	21.3	32.7	14.0	9.9	58747	62337				3.4	5.7	23.0	38.7	29.1	269816
	UNITED STATES	27277		20.9	24.4	35.3	11.7	7.6	54719	56938				9.3	13.1	31.6	32.6	13.5	162279

ZIP CODE #	POST OFFICE NAME	FINANCIAL SERVICES: Auto Loan	Home Loan	Invest-ments	Retire-ment Plans	THE HOME: Home Improvements: Home Repair	Lawn & Garden	Furnishings: Comput-ers & Hard-ware-Personal	Major Appli-ances	TV, Radio, Sound Equip-ment	Furni-ture	ENTERTAINMENT: Dine out/ Carry out	Sports Equip-ment	Fees & Tickets	Toys & Games	Travel	Cable TV	PERSONAL: Apparel & Services	Auto Repairs	Health Insur-ance	Pets & Supplies
14550	SILVER SPRINGS	78	75	70	77	73	84	74	78	76	69	75	61	71	77	74	79	51	76	84	93
14551	SODUS	87	83	73	86	80	92	83	86	85	77	84	67	80	87	81	88	57	84	92	102
14555	SODUS POINT	88	80	80	84	82	95	79	90	82	72	80	68	73	83	79	87	55	83	92	104
14559	SPENCERPORT	108	125	112	125	121	122	111	115	111	111	111	88	120	113	118	112	78	112	116	134
14560	SPRINGWATER	101	80	114	79	85	105	80	100	86	75	84	74	69	84	83	92	56	92	101	117
14561	STANLEY	92	82	89	85	84	98	81	92	83	74	82	70	74	84	82	88	56	86	95	108
14564	VICTOR	137	158	153	160	158	148	141	145	136	148	137	110	152	138	150	133	97	139	138	167
14568	WALWORTH	119	126	106	125	121	116	114	117	111	119	112	90	116	117	114	109	78	112	110	136
14569	WARSAW	78	72	67	74	71	80	75	76	76	69	75	59	70	77	72	79	52	76	81	91
14571	WATERPORT	83	80	71	82	78	89	79	83	81	73	80	64	76	82	78	84	55	80	89	99
14572	WAYLAND	86	78	82	79	77	91	77	85	80	72	79	65	72	81	77	84	54	82	90	101
14580	WEBSTER	121	134	128	136	134	131	124	127	122	127	123	96	132	123	130	122	86	124	126	147
14586	WEST HENRIETTA	98	108	102	110	106	101	104	100	100	105	102	78	109	102	106	99	72	101	99	118
14589	WILLIAMSON	98	103	89	103	97	108	97	99	99	94	99	77	100	101	98	102	69	98	107	119
14590	WOLCOTT	90	69	84	68	70	90	72	84	78	67	76	64	60	79	69	84	51	79	88	100
14591	WYOMING	87	81	79	84	82	94	79	89	81	72	80	67	74	83	79	86	55	82	91	103
14604	ROCHESTER	31	23	28	27	24	28	37	30	40	33	39	24	33	35	33	42	28	36	40	38
14605	ROCHESTER	42	28	25	31	26	32	42	34	46	40	45	27	36	45	34	48	32	41	40	44
14606	ROCHESTER	75	73	67	74	71	76	78	75	81	74	80	57	77	80	75	83	56	78	81	89
14607	ROCHESTER	77	57	59	65	56	57	85	65	83	78	85	58	74	82	72	81	60	78	70	83
14608	ROCHESTER	51	36	33	39	34	40	50	42	55	48	54	33	44	54	42	57	38	50	50	55
14609	ROCHESTER	74	69	61	71	66	74	76	71	79	72	78	55	73	78	71	81	54	75	80	87
14610	ROCHESTER	116	114	114	119	114	113	126	115	124	123	125	92	126	122	123	124	89	122	122	138
14611	ROCHESTER	53	42	37	44	39	46	53	46	57	50	56	36	48	57	45	60	39	52	54	59
14612	ROCHESTER	98	104	97	105	102	102	103	101	102	101	103	78	106	103	104	103	72	102	104	118
14613	ROCHESTER	63	51	44	54	48	54	65	56	68	60	67	45	59	67	56	69	47	63	62	70
14614	ROCHESTER	15	11	13	13	11	14	18	14	19	16	19	11	16	17	16	21	13	18	20	19
14615	ROCHESTER	78	72	63	74	68	75	81	74	83	76	83	59	78	83	75	84	58	80	82	90
14616	ROCHESTER	89	97	84	98	93	101	91	92	93	89	93	70	96	94	94	96	65	92	102	109
14617	ROCHESTER	100	116	112	116	116	120	104	110	107	105	107	79	115	105	113	111	75	108	120	127
14618	ROCHESTER	132	148	154	151	152	147	142	142	141	146	141	106	154	137	152	141	100	143	148	165
14619	ROCHESTER	79	72	60	74	67	77	77	73	81	76	81	57	75	82	72	84	56	77	82	91
14620	ROCHESTER	74	62	61	65	61	66	81	68	81	74	81	55	73	79	71	83	57	77	77	85
14621	ROCHESTER	52	42	39	44	40	46	54	47	58	50	57	37	49	55	47	60	40	53	56	59
14622	ROCHESTER	85	94	89	93	94	102	87	92	92	86	91	66	93	90	92	97	63	91	105	107
14623	ROCHESTER	89	78	72	81	75	77	93	81	91	89	92	65	86	92	84	91	64	88	84	98
14624	ROCHESTER	102	120	109	120	117	117	107	110	107	108	108	83	118	109	115	109	76	108	114	128
14625	ROCHESTER	128	148	152	148	152	147	132	140	131	138	131	101	145	129	144	132	93	135	141	160
14626	ROCHESTER	108	122	113	122	120	121	110	114	110	112	111	85	119	111	116	112	78	111	119	132
14627	ROCHESTER	31	13	13	16	12	15	43	21	34	29	35	23	25	33	23	31	25	30	21	29
14642	ROCHESTER	68	44	42	48	43	48	81	55	73	64	73	50	59	73	57	71	51	67	58	70
14701	JAMESTOWN	66	63	59	64	61	68	68	66	71	64	70	51	67	70	65	73	49	68	72	79
14706	ALLEGANY	83	78	79	77	78	85	77	81	79	76	79	61	74	80	76	82	54	79	84	96
14708	ALMA	85	65	99	63	69	88	65	83	70	61	69	61	55	68	68	76	46	76	84	97
14709	ANGELICA	80	58	82	56	60	82	59	75	66	55	64	56	48	65	59	72	43	69	78	89
14710	ASHVILLE	93	81	105	82	86	100	80	95	83	74	82	71	73	81	84	87	55	88	96	111
14711	BELFAST	79	56	80	55	58	80	59	74	65	54	64	56	47	65	58	72	42	68	78	88
14712	BEMUS POINT	98	85	113	84	90	107	82	100	87	79	86	73	76	85	87	93	58	93	103	116
14714	BLACK CREEK	84	60	86	58	62	85	62	79	69	57	67	59	49	68	61	75	44	72	82	93
14715	BOLIVAR	73	59	69	58	59	76	60	70	65	56	64	53	53	65	59	70	43	66	75	83
14716	BROCTON	76	55	77	53	57	78	58	72	64	53	63	54	47	64	57	71	42	67	77	85
14717	CANEADEA	77	56	79	54	58	80	59	74	66	54	64	55	47	65	58	72	42	68	79	87
14718	CASSADAGA	83	81	88	80	83	92	76	86	80	74	79	62	75	79	80	84	54	82	91	99
14719	CATTARAUGUS	80	68	76	68	67	84	68	78	72	63	71	60	61	73	67	77	48	74	82	93
14721	CERES	72	65	65	68	67	77	65	73	67	58	65	55	60	68	64	70	45	67	75	85
14723	CHERRY CREEK	83	62	83	61	65	85	64	79	69	59	68	59	53	69	63	76	45	72	82	93
14724	CLYMER	86	69	90	70	72	91	71	85	74	63	73	66	60	73	72	79	49	79	88	101
14726	CONEWANGO VALLEY	83	65	84	66	67	88	68	81	70	58	69	64	56	70	68	76	46	75	84	97
14727	CUBA	79	65	76	65	66	81	67	76	71	63	70	57	59	71	65	76	47	72	81	90
14728	DEWITTVILLE	94	78	102	77	83	101	76	92	82	75	81	66	69	80	79	89	54	86	98	108
14729	EAST OTTO	82	68	78	69	70	86	68	80	72	62	71	61	60	73	68	77	48	74	83	94
14731	ELLICOTTVILLE	101	80	128	79	88	107	81	102	85	75	84	75	69	81	87	91	56	94	102	119
14733	FALCONER	86	73	84	73	74	91	75	86	80	70	78	64	67	80	74	86	53	81	92	100
14735	FILLMORE	80	58	81	56	60	83	61	77	68	56	66	57	49	67	60	75	44	71	82	90
14736	FINDLEY LAKE	94	76	122	74	83	100	76	96	79	71	78	70	66	75	82	84	52	89	95	111
14737	FRANKLINVILLE	78	66	75	66	66	83	66	76	71	62	70	57	60	71	66	76	47	72	82	90
14738	FREWSBURG	82	81	82	81	82	94	76	86	81	72	79	63	75	80	79	86	54	81	93	99
14739	FRIENDSHIP	77	55	78	54	57	79	58	73	65	53	63	55	47	64	57	72	42	68	78	87
14740	GERRY	82	65	80	65	67	85	65	79	70	60	69	59	56	71	65	76	46	73	82	93
14741	GREAT VALLEY	88	67	91	65	69	91	68	84	74	63	72	63	56	73	68	80	48	77	87	100
14743	HINSDALE	83	65	80	65	67	85	66	79	71	61	70	59	56	71	65	76	47	73	82	93
14744	HOUGHTON	74	65	69	66	67	75	70	73	72	67	70	54	64	71	67	75	48	72	78	86
14747	KENNEDY	78	70	71	73	71	83	69	78	72	63	70	59	63	73	69	76	48	72	81	91
14748	KILL BUCK	75	60	70	61	61	78	61	72	66	56	64	55	53	67	60	71	43	67	75	85
14750	LAKEWOOD	101	100	116	99	104	117	93	107	98	93	97	77	95	96	100	104	67	102	115	124
14753	LIMESTONE	74	57	73	57	59	77	58	71	63	54	62	54	49	63	57	69	41	65	74	84
14754	LITTLE GENESEE	81	63	70	63	64	81	65	75	70	61	69	57	55	72	61	76	46	70	79	90
14755	LITTLE VALLEY	81	65	77	65	66	84	67	79	72	61	70	59	57	72	65	77	47	73	83	93
14757	MAYVILLE	92	82	97	82	85	100	80	92	85	78	84	67	76	83	82	90	57	87	99	108
14760	OLEAN	72	67	66	68	67	75	72	72	74	67	73	54	68	74	69	77	51	73	79	85
14767	PANAMA	84	71	80	74	73	89	72	83	75	64	73	65	63	75	72	80	49	77	87	98
14769	PORTLAND	82	59	83	57	61	85	64	79	71	57	69	59	51	70	62	78	46	73	85	93
14770	PORTVILLE	84	74	77	76	76	90	74	85	77	67	76	64	67	78	74	82	51	78	88	99
14772	RANDOLPH	82	69	84	68	70	88	67	81	73	63	72	60	60	73	68	79	48	75	86	95
14775	RIPLEY	81	67	77	69	69	86	69	81	73	62	71	61	61	74	68	79	48	75	85	94
14777	RUSHFORD	76	54	76	53	56	79	59	73	66	53	64	55	48	65	57	73	43	68	80	86
14779	SALAMANCA	66	52	54	52	51	64	60	61	63	55	61	47	51	63	54	67	42	62	67	74
14781	SHERMAN	85	64	92	65	67	90	68	83	71	58	70	66	55	70	69	76	46	77	86	100
14782	SINCLAIRVILLE	81	69	74	70	70	85	69	80	73	63	71	60	61	74	68	78	48	74	82	93
14784	STOCKTON	89	72	79	70	72	90	71	82	78	70	77	62	63	80	69	84	52	78	87	98
14787	WESTFIELD	81	67	77	67	69	84	70	79	74	65	73	59	62	74	68	79	49	76	85	93
14801	ADDISON	80	65	68	65	65	80	68	74	72	64	71	57	59	74	64	77	48	72	79	89
14802	ALFRED	82	61	60	64	60	67	90	72	84	76	84	60	71	84	71	84	58	81	76	89
14803	ALFRED STATION	84	66	69	69	67	75	87	78	85	77	84	62	73	84	74	86	58	83	82	94
14804	ALMOND	89	84	84	86	85	92	85	89	87	83	86	67	82	87	84	89	59	87	93	105
	NEW YORK	100	106	110	108	107	104	112	106	113	106	114	81	115	110	112	116	83	110	110	124
	UNITED STATES	100	100	100	100	100	100	100	100	100	100	100	100	100	100	100	100	100	100	100	100

POPULATION CHANGE

14805-14905

ZIP CODE #	POST OFFICE NAME	COUNTY FIPS CODE	POPULATION 2000	POPULATION 2009	POPULATION 2014	2000-2009 ANNUAL RATE % Rate	2000-2009 ANNUAL RATE State Centile	HOUSEHOLDS 2000	HOUSEHOLDS 2009	HOUSEHOLDS 2014	HOUSEHOLDS % Annual Rate 2000-2009	HOUSEHOLDS 2009 Average HH Size	FAMILIES 2000	FAMILIES 2009	FAMILIES % Annual Rate 2000-2009
14805	ALPINE	097	1297	1335	1334	0.3	59	506	534	537	0.6	2.50	359	372	0.4
14806	ANDOVER	003	2291	2152	2082	-0.7	3	874	836	816	-0.5	2.55	614	578	-0.7
14807	ARKPORT	101	2977	2916	2863	-0.2	21	1170	1155	1138	-0.1	2.52	843	822	-0.3
14808	ATLANTA	101	432	412	400	-0.5	7	159	153	150	-0.4	2.69	117	111	-0.6
14809	AVOCA	101	2619	2656	2637	0.2	52	964	988	985	0.3	2.65	683	687	0.1
14810	BATH	101	12418	12338	12178	-0.1	30	4956	4955	4908	0.0	2.35	3092	3025	-0.2
14812	BEAVER DAMS	097	3813	3859	3821	0.1	44	1264	1304	1299	0.3	2.79	979	996	0.2
14813	BELMONT	003	2494	2376	2310	-0.5	7	980	946	927	-0.4	2.25	654	620	-0.6
14814	BIG FLATS	015	1676	1640	1607	-0.2	21	653	657	649	0.1	2.50	512	506	-0.1
14815	BRADFORD	097	927	1040	1060	1.3	94	359	410	421	1.4	2.40	260	293	1.3
14816	BREESPORT	015	702	685	673	-0.3	15	246	248	245	0.1	2.73	185	183	-0.1
14817	BROOKTONDALE	109	1980	2160	2236	0.9	87	764	847	884	1.1	2.50	499	540	0.9
14818	BURDETT	097	1734	1792	1793	0.4	66	688	731	736	0.7	2.45	494	517	0.5
14819	CAMERON	101	681	674	663	-0.1	30	252	252	249	0.0	2.67	188	185	-0.2
14820	CAMERON MILLS	101	918	869	844	-0.6	4	300	286	279	-0.5	3.04	228	215	-0.6
14821	CAMPBELL	101	3450	3446	3415	0.0	38	1286	1298	1291	0.1	2.65	950	945	-0.1
14822	CANASERAGA	003	1170	1160	1142	-0.1	30	436	442	438	0.1	2.62	319	320	0.0
14823	CANISTEO	101	4039	4124	4092	0.2	52	1589	1631	1624	0.3	2.53	1108	1119	0.1
14824	CAYUTA	097	672	673	666	0.0	38	260	267	267	0.3	2.52	203	206	0.2
14825	CHEMUNG	015	832	827	814	-0.1	30	296	303	301	0.3	2.69	229	231	0.1
14826	COHOCTON	101	2277	2337	2327	0.3	59	848	880	880	0.4	2.64	610	623	0.2
14830	CORNING	101	19638	19083	18703	-0.3	15	8330	8149	8015	-0.2	2.32	5169	4975	-0.4
14836	DALTON	051	1048	1045	1030	0.0	38	388	393	389	0.1	2.66	294	293	0.0
14837	DUNDEE	123	5301	5318	5276	0.0	38	1899	1908	1896	0.1	2.68	1362	1349	-0.1
14838	ERIN	015	2043	2019	1992	-0.1	30	743	756	752	0.2	2.67	602	604	0.0
14839	GREENWOOD	101	810	778	763	-0.4	11	308	298	293	-0.4	2.61	225	215	-0.5
14840	HAMMONDSPORT	101	3357	3632	3675	0.9	87	1439	1573	1595	1.0	2.26	1014	1087	0.8
14841	HECTOR	097	874	923	928	0.6	76	353	383	387	0.9	2.40	242	258	0.7
14842	HIMROD	123	870	912	923	0.5	71	291	305	308	0.5	2.98	232	239	0.3
14843	HORNELL	101	13428	13356	13185	-0.1	30	5353	5359	5308	0.0	2.42	3406	3344	-0.2
14845	HORSEHEADS	015	20399	20491	20227	0.0	38	7958	8179	8132	0.3	2.43	5668	5739	0.1
14846	HUNT	051	835	833	821	0.0	38	303	307	305	0.1	2.71	230	230	0.0
14847	INTERLAKEN	099	2270	2304	2291	0.2	52	882	903	904	0.3	2.48	598	602	0.1
14850	ITHACA	109	63115	66994	68287	0.6	76	23525	24980	25688	0.7	2.19	10418	10749	0.3
14853	ITHACA	109	8	8	8	0.0	38	5	5	5	0.0	1.60	2	0	-100.0
14855	JASPER	101	920	941	937	0.2	52	290	300	300	0.4	3.14	233	238	0.2
14858	LINDLEY	101	1753	1615	1558	-0.9	2	627	584	566	-0.8	2.77	487	448	-0.9
14859	LOCKWOOD	107	1105	1135	1130	0.3	59	392	410	411	0.5	2.77	297	306	0.3
14860	LODI	099	1027	1085	1095	0.6	76	399	429	435	0.8	2.52	282	298	0.6
14861	LOWMAN	015	1292	1276	1256	-0.1	30	512	521	517	0.2	2.44	387	387	0.0
14864	MILLPORT	015	1396	1329	1287	-0.5	7	555	542	529	-0.3	2.37	402	385	-0.5
14865	MONTOUR FALLS	097	2680	2669	2638	0.0	38	1049	1067	1064	0.2	2.36	692	693	0.0
14867	NEWFIELD	109	5544	5609	5660	0.1	44	2234	2285	2319	0.2	2.45	1491	1492	0.0
14869	ODESSA	097	1377	1334	1313	-0.3	15	525	522	517	-0.1	2.53	369	361	-0.2
14870	PAINTED POST	101	9073	9129	9048	0.1	44	3732	3787	3768	0.2	2.36	2497	2487	0.0
14871	PINE CITY	015	5018	4790	4656	-0.5	7	1911	1871	1832	-0.2	2.55	1465	1411	-0.4
14872	PINE VALLEY	015	300	291	284	-0.3	15	125	124	122	-0.1	2.34	88	86	-0.2
14873	PRATTSBURGH	101	2602	2583	2553	-0.1	30	1004	1008	1001	0.0	2.56	702	693	-0.1
14874	PULTENEY	101	247	239	234	-0.4	11	101	99	97	-0.2	2.41	67	64	-0.5
14877	REXVILLE	101	494	556	567	1.3	94	175	198	202	1.3	2.81	130	145	1.2
14878	ROCK STREAM	097	813	812	802	0.0	38	316	321	319	0.2	2.45	240	241	0.0
14879	SAVONA	101	2057	2066	2049	0.0	38	791	804	800	0.2	2.56	567	566	0.0
14880	SCIO	003	1745	1744	1720	0.0	38	646	652	647	0.1	2.42	464	460	-0.1
14881	SLATERVILLE SPRINGS	109	242	249	253	0.3	59	116	122	125	0.5	2.03	77	79	0.3
14882	LANSING	109	3996	4258	4377	0.7	80	1499	1616	1673	0.8	2.49	1047	1105	0.6
14883	SPENCER	107	3734	4039	4102	0.9	87	1438	1595	1635	1.1	2.53	1015	1106	0.9
14884	SWAIN	003	374	385	383	0.3	59	153	162	162	0.6	2.38	102	106	0.4
14885	TROUPSBURG	101	769	817	821	0.7	80	278	299	302	0.8	2.73	212	225	0.6
14886	TRUMANSBURG	097	6573	6782	6867	0.3	59	2571	2701	2756	0.5	2.47	1768	1820	0.3
14889	VAN ETTEN	015	1449	1411	1376	-0.3	15	567	570	562	0.1	2.48	399	393	-0.2
14891	WATKINS GLEN	097	4557	4441	4362	-0.3	15	1855	1837	1815	-0.1	2.35	1227	1194	-0.3
14892	WAVERLY	107	8382	8222	8098	-0.2	21	3330	3325	3292	0.0	2.40	2203	2170	-0.2
14894	WELLSBURG	015	2520	2437	2389	-0.4	11	585	568	554	-0.3	2.62	410	389	-0.6
14895	WELLSVILLE	003	10224	9907	9672	-0.3	15	4166	4090	4016	-0.2	2.35	2671	2582	-0.4
14897	WHITESVILLE	003	875	864	847	-0.1	30	334	338	334	0.1	2.56	246	246	0.0
14898	WOODHULL	101	1456	1504	1499	0.4	66	486	508	509	0.5	2.96	365	376	0.3
14901	ELMIRA	015	16266	15530	15123	-0.5	7	6283	6082	5939	-0.4	2.26	3615	3428	-0.6
14903	ELMIRA	015	7754	7543	7371	-0.3	15	3299	3282	3231	-0.1	2.29	2084	2033	-0.3
14904	ELMIRA	015	16768	15934	15427	-0.6	4	6794	6589	6424	-0.3	2.40	4334	4103	-0.6
14905	ELMIRA	015	10918	10444	10194	-0.5	7	3896	3767	3681	-0.4	2.25	2403	2280	-0.6
	NEW YORK					0.3					0.3	2.61			0.1
	UNITED STATES					1.0					1.1	2.59			0.9

ZIP CODE #	POST OFFICE NAME	RACE (%) White 2000	White 2009	Black 2000	Black 2009	Asian/Pacific 2000	Asian/Pacific 2009	% Hispanic Origin 2000	% Hispanic Origin 2009	2009 AGE DISTRIBUTION (%) 0-4	5-9	10-14	15-19	20-24	25-44	45-64	65-84	85+	18+	MEDIAN AGE 2009	% 2009 Males	% 2009 Females
14805	ALPINE	97.2	97.2	0.5	0.5	0.2	0.1	1.2	1.2	6.5	6.8	7.1	7.1	4.6	26.2	29.3	11.0	1.3	74.9	39.5	50.5	49.5
14806	ANDOVER	98.1	97.5	0.2	0.2	0.3	0.4	1.1	1.4	7.1	7.0	6.6	6.9	7.2	23.9	27.6	12.1	1.7	75.5	36.7	49.3	50.7
14807	ARKPORT	98.0	97.4	0.3	0.3	0.3	0.4	1.0	1.2	5.5	7.1	7.3	7.3	5.2	22.5	29.4	13.6	2.2	75.2	41.7	49.2	50.8
14808	ATLANTA	98.1	97.8	0.2	0.2	0.2	0.2	0.0	0.0	6.3	6.8	6.6	6.8	6.1	23.8	31.1	11.4	1.2	76.0	40.4	50.0	50.0
14809	AVOCA	97.4	96.9	1.1	1.3	0.3	0.4	0.9	1.1	5.3	6.3	6.7	8.2	5.9	23.9	29.2	12.6	1.9	75.9	40.5	50.3	49.7
14810	BATH	96.0	95.0	1.8	2.1	0.8	1.0	0.8	0.9	5.3	5.2	5.6	6.2	5.9	22.5	28.9	17.0	3.3	79.9	44.4	50.3	49.7
14812	BEAVER DAMS	94.6	94.1	3.3	3.6	0.4	0.4	1.9	2.1	5.9	6.8	7.0	9.8	6.7	23.6	29.0	10.2	1.0	75.3	37.8	51.6	48.4
14813	BELMONT	96.8	96.0	1.4	1.7	0.4	0.5	0.8	1.0	5.6	5.7	5.9	10.9	9.8	22.3	25.3	12.4	2.1	78.7	36.6	52.7	47.3
14814	BIG FLATS	95.6	94.2	1.5	1.8	1.7	2.4	0.9	1.2	5.4	6.0	7.0	7.2	4.6	20.8	31.5	15.9	1.8	77.3	44.4	48.7	51.3
14815	BRADFORD	94.2	94.1	3.1	3.0	0.5	0.7	2.2	2.3	5.2	6.1	6.6	9.8	6.5	21.9	30.4	12.3	1.2	76.6	40.4	53.3	46.7
14816	BREESPORT	97.3	96.4	0.9	1.0	1.0	1.5	0.4	0.6	5.4	5.5	6.6	7.3	5.5	23.9	31.2	13.0	1.5	77.8	42.2	49.3	50.7
14817	BROOKTONDALE	93.1	91.4	3.5	4.1	0.8	1.1	2.2	2.8	5.6	5.8	6.3	9.0	6.4	24.8	30.8	10.1	1.3	76.1	39.2	50.0	50.0
14818	BURDETT	98.1	98.0	0.5	0.6	0.2	0.2	0.5	0.5	5.3	6.4	5.9	7.0	4.1	22.9	35.2	11.8	1.5	77.6	43.8	50.9	49.1
14819	CAMERON	98.2	97.8	0.1	0.1	0.1	0.3	0.3	0.4	4.7	8.2	9.2	7.6	4.0	27.0	29.2	9.1	1.0	73.1	37.6	52.4	47.6
14820	CAMERON MILLS	97.9	97.5	0.2	0.2	0.1	0.1	0.4	0.6	5.6	7.7	8.5	7.6	4.9	26.1	29.0	9.6	0.9	73.4	37.9	51.3	48.7
14821	CAMPBELL	98.3	98.0	0.4	0.4	0.3	0.3	0.5	0.6	6.6	6.6	6.8	7.1	5.7	24.9	28.8	12.3	1.1	75.5	39.8	49.5	50.5
14822	CANASERAGA	97.7	97.2	0.1	0.1	0.1	0.1	0.9	1.2	6.3	6.6	7.0	6.8	5.5	22.0	32.1	12.3	1.4	75.8	42.0	50.9	49.1
14823	CANISTEO	98.3	97.8	0.2	0.2	0.4	0.6	0.8	1.0	6.0	6.5	7.0	7.2	5.5	23.5	29.3	12.9	2.2	76.1	40.5	48.5	51.5
14824	CAYUTA	96.4	96.1	0.9	1.0	0.4	0.4	0.9	1.0	6.1	6.4	6.8	6.4	4.6	24.1	32.4	11.9	1.3	76.5	41.9	49.6	50.4
14825	CHEMUNG	97.6	96.7	0.5	0.7	0.2	0.2	0.8	1.2	7.0	7.3	7.4	7.1	6.2	24.8	27.7	11.4	1.2	73.4	38.2	50.2	49.8
14826	COHOCTON	97.4	96.7	0.6	0.7	0.3	0.4	0.3	0.3	6.0	6.2	6.6	7.5	5.8	24.5	29.8	12.1	1.5	76.5	40.7	49.6	50.4
14830	CORNING	94.8	93.6	2.4	2.8	1.3	1.8	0.7	0.9	6.2	6.0	6.1	6.6	6.4	25.3	28.1	12.8	2.6	77.7	40.3	48.0	52.0
14836	DALTON	97.3	96.7	0.3	0.3	0.3	0.4	0.6	0.8	6.5	6.9	7.5	6.6	5.0	24.0	30.8	11.3	1.4	75.0	40.4	50.9	49.1
14837	DUNDEE	97.3	96.8	1.0	1.1	0.3	0.5	1.0	1.2	7.1	7.1	7.7	9.3	5.0	20.7	27.2	13.9	2.0	71.9	39.4	49.6	50.4
14838	ERIN	98.5	98.0	0.2	0.2	0.4	0.5	0.4	0.5	6.1	6.5	7.5	7.9	4.4	27.3	29.7	9.7	0.9	75.1	39.1	51.6	48.4
14839	GREENWOOD	98.2	97.7	0.2	0.3	0.1	0.3	0.2	0.3	7.2	7.6	7.3	6.0	5.4	24.7	27.2	13.1	1.4	74.2	37.8	51.8	48.2
14840	HAMMONDSPORT	97.8	97.1	0.6	0.7	0.5	0.7	0.4	0.6	4.5	4.8	5.3	5.5	3.9	19.5	35.0	18.8	2.7	81.7	49.2	49.8	50.2
14841	HECTOR	98.2	98.2	0.9	0.9	0.5	0.4	1.3	1.4	5.4	6.1	6.9	5.5	3.6	23.0	34.6	12.7	2.3	77.4	44.7	50.4	49.6
14842	HIMROD	96.3	95.4	1.5	1.8	0.1	0.1	0.6	0.7	9.1	9.2	9.4	7.7	4.1	22.9	23.7	12.7	1.2	67.1	34.3	51.1	48.9
14843	HORNELL	96.5	95.7	1.7	2.0	0.6	0.9	1.1	1.3	6.8	6.1	6.2	6.6	7.2	24.3	26.0	13.7	3.0	76.8	38.9	48.1	51.9
14845	HORSEHEADS	96.1	94.1	1.2	1.5	1.6	2.2	0.7	1.5	5.3	5.6	6.1	6.5	5.5	21.5	30.7	15.5	3.2	79.4	44.6	47.4	52.6
14846	HUNT	98.0	97.4	0.1	0.1	0.1	0.2	0.4	0.5	7.6	7.6	7.9	7.0	5.5	24.6	28.5	10.1	1.3	72.5	38.0	50.4	49.6
14847	INTERLAKEN	97.2	96.7	0.7	0.7	0.2	0.2	1.4	1.5	4.9	5.4	5.9	6.3	5.8	21.2	33.1	14.9	2.4	79.1	45.3	49.3	50.7
14850	ITHACA	80.3	74.0	4.6	7.1	10.7	13.2	3.9	5.4	3.8	3.5	3.5	11.8	22.3	25.9	19.4	7.8	1.9	86.7	27.9	50.5	49.5
14853	ITHACA	87.5	87.5	0.0	0.0	12.5	12.5	0.0	0.0	0.0	0.0	0.0	37.5	62.5	0.0	0.0	0.0	0.0	100.0	21.0	75.0	25.0
14855	JASPER	98.3	97.7	0.3	0.4	0.7	1.0	0.2	0.3	7.7	7.2	7.5	8.3	7.4	26.9	24.5	9.4	1.1	72.5	32.9	50.5	49.5
14858	LINDLEY	98.2	97.6	0.5	0.6	0.2	0.2	0.6	0.8	6.6	6.7	7.7	7.9	5.0	26.2	29.3	9.5	1.1	74.1	37.9	50.0	50.0
14859	LOCKWOOD	97.9	97.2	0.2	0.3	0.6	0.9	0.7	0.8	6.9	7.1	7.8	8.1	5.7	25.0	28.5	9.7	1.1	73.0	37.2	50.6	49.4
14860	LODI	95.7	95.1	0.5	0.5	0.5	0.6	2.2	2.6	5.4	7.5	8.3	5.3	4.1	23.8	30.6	12.9	2.0	74.7	41.5	52.4	47.6
14861	LOWMAN	97.8	96.9	0.7	0.9	0.2	0.4	0.4	0.5	5.4	5.7	6.4	6.7	5.3	24.0	31.9	13.1	1.5	78.1	42.7	52.3	47.7
14864	MILLPORT	97.8	97.3	0.4	0.5	0.2	0.2	0.8	1.0	4.8	5.4	5.9	5.9	4.7	21.7	32.5	15.9	3.0	79.5	45.8	49.0	51.0
14865	MONTOUR FALLS	97.9	97.8	0.7	0.7	0.3	0.3	0.5	0.5	5.1	5.0	5.3	5.6	5.7	22.1	29.0	17.1	5.1	81.1	45.8	47.0	53.0
14867	NEWFIELD	95.7	94.4	1.2	1.4	0.5	0.7	1.2	1.6	6.4	6.3	6.8	7.5	5.6	26.4	30.0	9.8	1.2	75.8	39.0	48.7	51.3
14869	ODESSA	97.2	97.2	0.4	0.4	0.0	0.0	0.9	0.9	5.5	6.1	6.6	7.0	4.7	25.2	31.2	12.1	1.6	76.8	41.7	48.4	51.6
14870	PAINTED POST	93.4	91.1	2.0	2.4	3.5	5.2	1.1	1.4	6.5	6.2	6.5	6.2	4.8	22.6	29.3	14.6	3.3	76.9	43.0	48.1	51.9
14871	PINE CITY	98.5	98.1	0.6	0.7	0.3	0.4	0.5	0.6	4.8	5.2	6.1	7.0	4.8	21.5	32.7	15.8	2.1	79.6	45.4	49.1	50.9
14872	PINE VALLEY	98.0	97.3	0.3	0.3	0.3	0.3	0.7	0.7	6.5	6.5	6.9	6.2	5.2	24.4	30.9	12.0	1.4	75.9	41.1	52.6	47.4
14873	PRATTSBURGH	96.9	96.1	1.2	1.5	0.1	0.1	1.3	1.6	5.8	6.2	6.8	7.1	5.0	23.7	31.2	12.6	1.5	76.5	41.8	50.0	50.0
14874	PULTENEY	99.6	99.6	0.0	0.0	0.0	0.0	0.8	0.8	5.0	6.3	7.9	5.4	3.8	21.8	35.6	13.0	1.3	76.2	44.9	51.9	48.1
14877	REXVILLE	98.8	98.6	0.0	0.0	0.2	0.4	0.6	0.7	5.9	6.3	6.7	6.8	4.1	23.6	31.5	14.0	1.1	77.0	42.5	50.4	49.6
14878	ROCK STREAM	96.3	95.8	1.4	1.5	0.5	0.6	1.0	0.9	6.5	6.8	7.3	8.1	4.3	22.4	28.6	14.5	1.5	74.3	41.0	50.5	49.5
14879	SAVONA	98.2	97.8	0.4	0.4	0.3	0.4	0.5	0.5	6.3	6.5	6.5	7.0	5.9	25.3	29.3	11.9	1.3	76.1	39.6	49.9	50.1
14880	SCIO	97.0	96.2	0.7	0.8	0.6	0.7	0.5	0.6	5.4	5.9	6.1	7.6	5.8	22.0	27.6	15.3	4.3	78.2	42.9	49.2	50.8
14881	SLATERVILLE SPRINGS	93.8	91.6	2.5	2.8	1.2	2.0	1.2	1.6	5.2	5.2	6.0	8.0	5.2	22.9	34.5	11.6	1.2	78.7	43.2	47.4	52.6
14882	LANSING	91.9	89.8	4.8	5.5	0.8	1.2	2.1	2.5	4.8	6.0	7.9	11.6	4.4	23.1	29.8	11.2	1.1	72.0	40.1	50.3	49.7
14883	SPENCER	96.9	96.1	0.8	0.9	0.5	0.7	1.4	1.7	6.7	7.0	7.2	6.9	5.5	25.2	30.4	9.8	1.2	74.7	39.1	49.0	51.0
14884	SWAIN	96.0	95.3	0.8	0.8	0.3	0.3	1.1	1.3	5.5	6.0	6.5	5.7	4.4	21.6	33.0	15.6	1.8	78.4	45.3	51.9	48.1
14885	TROUPSBURG	97.9	97.7	0.1	0.1	0.5	0.6	1.3	1.6	8.2	8.2	8.1	7.1	4.4	24.8	26.7	11.3	1.2	71.0	36.6	48.0	52.0
14886	TRUMANSBURG	96.8	96.0	1.0	1.2	0.5	0.8	1.2	1.4	5.0	5.7	7.1	7.4	4.9	22.9	33.0	11.9	2.0	77.2	42.9	48.8	51.2
14889	VAN ETTEN	98.5	98.2	0.3	0.3	0.2	0.3	0.5	0.6	7.0	7.2	7.4	7.0	5.8	23.9	29.8	10.6	1.3	74.1	38.5	49.9	50.1
14891	WATKINS GLEN	97.1	97.0	0.9	0.9	0.6	0.6	1.0	1.1	6.1	6.0	6.2	6.3	5.9	22.7	29.0	15.0	2.7	77.8	42.5	48.4	51.6
14892	WAVERLY	98.0	97.5	0.4	0.5	0.4	0.6	1.0	1.3	6.3	6.5	6.6	6.5	5.3	24.7	27.5	13.4	3.2	76.3	40.6	48.3	51.7
14894	WELLSBURG	69.3	67.3	24.5	25.8	0.0	0.1	10.8	11.9	3.3	3.6	3.9	5.3	10.8	42.4	21.1	8.6	1.1	86.3	34.4	69.6	30.4
14895	WELLSVILLE	97.0	96.2	0.4	0.5	1.0	1.4	0.6	0.7	6.0	5.9	6.0	6.1	5.7	23.1	28.2	15.8	3.3	78.4	42.8	48.3	51.7
14897	WHITESVILLE	98.6	98.4	0.3	0.3	0.1	0.1	0.6	0.6	6.0	6.5	6.6	7.1	5.1	22.7	29.9	14.2	2.0	76.6	41.7	50.1	49.9
14898	WOODHULL	97.3	96.3	0.5	0.6	0.5	0.9	1.2	1.6	8.0	7.9	8.0	7.5	5.3	26.1	25.4	10.4	1.3	71.1	35.3	49.8	50.2
14901	ELMIRA	83.4	77.7	12.1	15.6	0.6	1.2	1.9	3.8	7.1	6.5	6.2	8.4	10.4	24.2	22.5	12.0	2.7	77.0	34.3	48.2	51.8
14903	ELMIRA	96.6	95.6	1.1	1.4	0.9	1.2	0.7	0.9	5.2	5.7	6.3	6.7	5.7	24.0	28.4	15.5	2.7	78.7	42.5	47.4	52.6
14904	ELMIRA	92.2	90.2	5.0	6.1	0.3	0.3	1.4	1.9	6.9	6.6	6.6	7.4	7.0	24.8	26.0	12.4	2.5	75.3	37.3	47.9	52.1
14905	ELMIRA	81.2	78.4	13.4	15.0	1.1	1.5	4.5	5.3	5.2	4.9	5.0	5.6	7.6	31.7	25.6	11.8	2.6	81.6	38.4	56.7	43.3
	NEW YORK	67.9	64.8	15.9	16.5	5.6	6.9	15.1	16.7	6.5	6.4	6.4	7.1	7.0	27.0	26.3	11.2	2.1	76.6	37.5	48.4	51.6
	UNITED STATES	75.1	72.0	12.3	12.7	3.8	4.6	12.5	15.7	6.8	6.7	6.6	7.1	6.9	27.0	26.0	10.9	1.9	75.7	36.9	49.2	50.8

C 14805-14905

#	POST OFFICE NAME	2009 Per Capita Income	2009 HH Income Base	2009 HOUSEHOLD INCOME DISTRIBUTION (%) Less than $25,000	$25,000 to $49,999	$50,000 to $99,999	$100,000 to $149,999	$150,000 or More	MEDIAN HOUSEHOLD INCOME 2009	2014	2009 National Centile	2009 State Centile	2009 Home Value Base	2009 HOME VALUE DISTRIBUTION (%) Less than $50,000	$50,000 to $89,999	$90,000 to $174,999	$175,000 to $399,999	$400,000 or More	2009 Median Home Value
14805	ALPINE	20329	534	20.2	37.8	35.8	4.7	1.5	44208	45046	46	28	432	17.8	20.8	46.1	13.7	1.6	107792
14806	ANDOVER	21357	836	25.4	31.0	34.6	6.1	3.0	45238	46192	49	31	628	17.2	35.2	37.4	10.0	0.2	87458
14807	ARKPORT	21187	1155	24.2	31.1	36.1	6.8	1.7	44751	46875	47	30	931	14.6	24.5	42.6	16.6	1.6	106031
14808	ATLANTA	17835	153	28.8	27.5	36.6	5.9	1.3	43398	46152	44	24	125	15.2	31.2	38.4	12.8	2.4	95000
14809	AVOCA	17388	988	26.6	34.7	34.4	2.7	1.5	39323	42119	31	13	760	11.6	33.8	43.3	10.1	1.2	95932
14810	BATH	21394	4955	28.6	28.9	34.3	5.5	2.7	43086	45703	43	23	3323	15.7	19.3	48.1	16.2	0.8	113781
14812	BEAVER DAMS	19526	1304	20.6	32.2	39.0	6.1	2.1	47063	48472	54	37	1094	15.4	28.3	41.4	13.5	1.3	101094
14813	BELMONT	20486	946	30.5	29.0	33.0	6.3	1.2	41221	42900	37	18	676	17.8	35.4	38.0	8.6	0.3	86557
14814	BIG FLATS	30298	657	7.5	24.0	47.5	14.2	6.8	63906	65112	82	70	542	4.1	7.9	47.4	38.2	2.4	162621
14815	BRADFORD	19434	410	26.3	33.7	34.1	5.1	0.7	42803	44253	42	22	344	14.0	26.2	47.4	11.3	1.2	101563
14816	BREESPORT	24319	248	14.5	24.2	43.5	15.3	2.4	61400	63540	79	67	200	12.5	12.0	48.0	25.0	2.5	136806
14817	BROOKTONDALE	26601	847	18.8	22.0	43.8	10.6	4.8	60371	64250	78	65	582	1.9	8.9	36.3	48.3	4.6	180247
14818	BURDETT	23135	731	20.5	33.4	36.3	7.0	2.9	47378	47135	55	39	599	5.8	20.9	42.2	26.7	4.3	134738
14819	CAMERON	18309	252	28.2	31.3	34.1	3.2	3.2	41687	43550	38	19	192	21.9	26.6	36.5	13.0	2.1	92308
14820	CAMERON MILLS	15775	286	28.0	31.8	35.3	3.5	1.4	41750	43863	38	19	227	20.3	22.9	39.2	15.9	1.8	99688
14821	CAMPBELL	21338	1298	21.5	29.4	38.1	8.8	2.2	49165	50570	59	43	1086	16.9	19.6	44.7	17.4	1.4	111465
14822	CANASERAGA	17813	442	28.1	34.4	31.4	5.0	1.1	39031	40000	30	12	346	12.4	36.1	42.5	7.5	1.4	92000
14823	CANISTEO	19622	1631	26.5	25.2	43.0	4.5	0.9	47864	49562	56	40	1237	12.2	35.2	44.9	7.5	0.2	93066
14824	CAYUTA	21526	267	19.5	34.8	39.3	3.0	3.4	46071	46938	52	34	219	15.5	26.0	44.3	13.2	0.9	104392
14825	CHEMUNG	17944	303	22.4	35.6	36.6	4.6	0.7	42932	45942	42	23	254	28.7	25.2	32.3	11.0	2.8	82308
14826	COHOCTON	19052	880	25.1	30.1	37.0	6.4	1.4	44464	46926	47	29	714	10.2	31.1	46.8	11.2	0.7	101799
14830	CORNING	27162	8149	23.7	27.2	34.4	8.7	6.0	48773	51200	58	42	5336	5.4	17.6	51.4	21.5	4.1	126138
14836	DALTON	19304	393	21.4	30.0	40.7	6.6	1.3	48587	51258	58	42	331	12.1	30.5	44.4	10.0	3.0	97424
14837	DUNDEE	17936	1908	29.5	33.2	30.6	5.1	1.6	37305	39713	24	8	1431	9.6	21.8	45.5	17.7	5.4	115739
14838	ERIN	21292	756	15.7	27.8	48.4	7.1	0.9	54449	57926	70	56	664	28.3	21.4	33.4	16.1	0.8	90541
14839	GREENWOOD	16736	298	31.9	33.2	28.9	5.0	1.0	37838	41250	26	9	234	24.8	26.5	31.6	15.4	1.7	87692
14840	HAMMONDSPORT	25601	1573	20.9	30.7	37.4	6.8	4.3	48211	50223	57	41	1279	8.0	18.2	43.2	25.2	5.4	133561
14841	HECTOR	27415	383	21.7	27.9	32.6	11.2	6.5	50621	51043	63	47	318	11.0	15.7	37.4	28.6	7.2	141071
14842	HIMROD	17803	305	19.3	33.8	38.7	6.2	2.0	46905	47468	54	36	262	19.8	19.5	21.8	18.3	20.6	114167
14843	HORNELL	20010	5359	32.9	28.3	31.1	5.6	2.1	40067	42613	33	15	3523	13.7	36.7	39.1	9.6	0.9	89550
14845	HORSEHEADS	26269	8179	18.1	25.6	41.3	10.5	4.6	56745	60759	74	60	6202	8.8	13.8	49.9	24.6	2.9	138218
14846	HUNT	17644	307	25.7	30.0	38.1	5.5	0.7	43553	47708	44	25	252	16.3	32.9	42.5	6.7	1.6	91000
14847	INTERLAKEN	23922	903	20.0	31.8	35.8	8.7	3.7	48323	51747	57	41	722	9.4	24.7	42.0	20.4	3.6	114407
14850	ITHACA	27145	24980	29.8	24.2	29.4	8.8	7.8	45059	49531	48	31	10698	3.4	2.1	29.8	51.6	13.0	215172
14853	ITHACA	39224	5	60.0	0.0	0.0	40.0	0.0	12000	85357	1	1	2	0.0	0.0	0.0	100.0	0.0	350000
14855	JASPER	15864	300	24.7	35.7	32.0	5.7	2.0	40953	44205	36	17	243	20.6	28.4	28.8	20.2	2.1	91786
14858	LINDLEY	18357	584	23.6	31.0	39.7	4.3	1.4	45454	47350	50	32	496	17.1	24.0	40.5	16.9	1.4	109127
14859	LOCKWOOD	18288	410	24.1	38.0	32.4	2.4	2.9	43500	46125	44	25	345	22.6	21.4	38.3	16.2	1.4	105978
14860	LODI	20814	429	20.0	33.3	39.4	6.1	1.2	46725	50373	53	36	360	15.0	25.0	34.2	21.7	4.2	108537
14861	LOWMAN	21056	521	23.2	32.1	39.3	4.2	1.2	44470	48699	47	29	439	33.9	21.2	29.6	13.2	2.1	77885
14864	MILLPORT	25204	542	24.9	24.2	39.3	6.6	5.0	50756	54053	63	47	445	13.7	16.2	37.1	29.9	3.1	145573
14865	MONTOUR FALLS	21489	1067	26.5	30.5	34.0	6.5	2.5	43881	45574	45	26	746	13.8	20.8	49.7	13.9	1.7	110688
14867	NEWFIELD	21545	2285	20.8	32.9	40.1	4.6	1.6	47451	49959	55	39	1645	13.9	8.3	55.2	20.6	2.1	142042
14869	ODESSA	20134	522	24.9	32.0	34.9	7.3	1.0	44287	45283	46	28	388	10.8	20.6	54.9	11.6	2.1	114286
14870	PAINTED POST	31133	3787	19.6	26.8	32.8	12.4	8.4	54375	56205	70	56	2699	9.2	10.6	49.4	21.9	8.9	139405
14871	PINE CITY	27175	1871	12.2	27.2	43.1	13.3	4.2	59910	61968	77	63	1609	5.0	19.4	56.2	18.5	0.8	132715
14872	PINE VALLEY	22229	124	26.6	31.5	33.1	5.6	3.2	43286	44522	43	24	102	33.3	14.7	29.4	20.6	2.0	100000
14873	PRATTSBURGH	18491	1008	27.6	33.1	34.3	3.8	1.2	40628	43192	35	16	810	14.3	29.3	41.7	12.5	2.2	101079
14874	PULTENEY	20684	99	23.2	30.3	41.4	3.0	2.0	45575	47777	50	32	84	11.9	16.7	39.3	25.0	7.1	130556
14877	REXVILLE	15654	198	30.8	29.3	34.8	5.1	0.0	41414	43168	37	18	156	17.9	25.0	32.1	19.2	5.8	100000
14878	ROCK STREAM	21822	321	21.8	34.6	35.8	5.6	2.2	44484	45091	47	29	264	11.7	23.1	44.3	17.8	3.0	114286
14879	SAVONA	19395	804	21.9	36.4	35.3	5.2	1.1	44096	45925	46	28	627	15.9	27.8	42.4	13.2	0.6	96583
14880	SCIO	18743	652	28.2	32.4	33.4	5.8	0.2	40607	42157	35	16	487	15.4	41.7	38.8	4.1	0.0	82959
14881	SLATERVILLE SPRINGS	31358	122	24.6	23.0	37.7	9.8	4.9	52153	56690	66	51	87	2.3	9.2	35.6	49.4	3.4	179808
14882	LANSING	30515	1616	12.8	21.6	44.4	14.5	6.7	65169	67145	83	72	1190	4.4	4.2	39.6	39.7	12.2	179074
14883	SPENCER	20826	1595	21.7	32.6	38.9	5.3	1.5	47034	49464	54	37	1240	11.6	11.7	51.6	23.1	1.9	137402
14884	SWAIN	18991	162	32.1	29.0	35.2	3.1	0.6	39086	40000	30	12	133	14.3	27.1	51.1	6.8	0.8	103241
14885	TROUPSBURG	16304	299	30.1	29.8	36.1	3.0	1.0	40529	42660	34	16	237	14.8	25.7	31.6	24.5	3.4	111029
14886	TRUMANSBURG	25407	2701	19.8	29.3	37.6	8.6	4.6	50966	55367	63	48	2000	8.6	9.9	38.4	39.1	4.2	164759
14889	VAN ETTEN	18436	570	28.4	31.4	36.0	3.7	0.5	39843	43559	32	14	432	27.3	22.9	35.6	11.1	3.0	89474
14891	WATKINS GLEN	21341	1837	29.1	30.0	32.6	5.2	3.2	41717	43230	38	19	1270	10.0	20.4	51.6	16.5	1.5	115900
14892	WAVERLY	19822	3325	26.7	33.9	33.0	5.5	0.8	42157	45453	40	20	2277	15.3	13.6	50.2	19.8	1.1	128357
14894	WELLSBURG	18492	568	22.7	30.3	40.5	4.8	1.8	44862	52149	48	30	476	46.0	16.8	27.1	9.5	0.6	54750
14895	WELLSVILLE	21361	4090	32.2	27.2	31.4	6.6	2.5	40165	42777	33	15	2759	15.9	33.3	40.2	9.4	1.2	91037
14897	WHITESVILLE	17567	338	27.5	33.7	35.5	2.7	0.6	40568	41965	35	16	269	20.4	43.1	28.3	8.2	0.0	78281
14898	WOODHULL	14946	508	30.9	32.1	32.3	3.3	1.4	38824	41416	29	11	412	20.1	25.5	35.7	17.5	1.2	96429
14901	ELMIRA	19261	6082	37.8	28.5	27.5	4.1	2.1	35240	37985	18	6	3026	20.7	41.4	31.0	5.0	1.9	78245
14903	ELMIRA	25283	3282	23.6	28.2	34.9	9.2	4.1	47629	51868	56	40	2134	8.9	28.1	40.0	19.4	3.7	106688
14904	ELMIRA	19256	6589	30.0	28.8	36.0	3.9	1.3	41348	44450	37	18	3996	16.6	59.1	22.7	1.6	0.0	69255
14905	ELMIRA	27493	3767	21.0	23.9	36.6	12.4	6.1	55179	60342	71	57	2497	2.2	14.9	51.5	26.6	4.9	142165
	NEW YORK	29893		21.9	21.3	32.7	14.0	9.9	58747	62337				3.4	5.7	23.0	38.7	29.1	269816
	UNITED STATES	27277		20.9	24.4	35.3	11.7	7.6	54719	56938				9.3	13.1	31.6	32.6	13.5	162279

ZIP CODE	FINANCIAL SERVICES				THE HOME						ENTERTAINMENT						PERSONAL			
					Home Improvements		Furnishings													
# POST OFFICE NAME	Auto Loan	Home Loan	Invest-ments	Retire-ment Plans	Home Repair	Lawn & Garden	Comput-ers & Hard-ware-Personal	Major Appli-ances	TV, Radio, Sound Equip-ment	Furni-ture	Dine out/ Carry out	Sports Equip-ment	Fees & Tickets	Toys & Games	Travel	Cable TV	Apparel & Services	Auto Repairs	Health Insur-ance	Pets & Supplies
14805 ALPINE	83	72	74	71	72	82	70	78	73	68	73	58	63	75	68	77	49	74	80	93
14806 ANDOVER	82	74	73	75	73	85	77	80	79	73	78	61	72	80	74	83	54	79	86	96
14807 ARKPORT	84	75	85	73	76	91	71	83	77	69	76	61	67	76	73	82	51	78	89	97
14808 ATLANTA	86	61	88	59	64	87	63	80	70	59	69	60	50	70	62	77	45	74	83	95
14809 AVOCA	82	59	84	57	61	84	61	77	67	56	66	58	49	67	60	74	44	71	80	91
14810 BATH	79	67	76	67	68	80	70	77	74	67	73	57	64	73	69	79	50	75	83	91
14812 BEAVER DAMS	90	76	84	77	77	94	75	88	79	70	78	66	67	81	75	85	53	81	90	103
14813 BELMONT	77	61	75	61	63	81	64	76	69	59	68	57	55	69	63	75	46	71	81	89
14814 BIG FLATS	101	116	113	117	117	122	102	111	105	104	105	80	113	104	112	108	73	106	118	128
14815 BRADFORD	83	62	86	60	64	83	63	78	69	60	67	58	52	69	62	75	45	72	80	92
14816 BREESPORT	97	97	93	97	97	100	94	98	95	94	94	74	93	96	94	96	65	96	99	114
14817 BROOKTONDALE	92	98	93	97	97	97	95	96	95	91	95	75	97	96	97	96	67	95	97	112
14818 BURDETT	92	77	108	77	83	98	77	94	80	72	79	69	68	78	81	85	53	86	93	109
14819 CAMERON	88	63	76	62	63	85	66	78	73	64	71	59	53	75	61	80	48	73	82	94
14820 CAMERON MILLS	87	62	71	60	62	82	65	75	72	63	70	58	52	75	59	78	47	71	79	91
14821 CAMPBELL	90	81	84	79	80	92	77	86	81	76	81	64	73	83	76	86	55	82	89	102
14822 CANASERAGA	83	60	85	58	62	85	61	78	68	57	67	58	50	68	61	75	44	71	81	93
14823 CANISTEO	77	68	74	67	68	82	67	76	72	64	71	57	63	72	67	77	48	73	82	90
14824 CAYUTA	91	74	92	73	75	94	73	87	78	69	77	66	63	78	73	84	52	81	90	104
14825 CHEMUNG	82	67	68	65	66	78	66	73	71	67	70	55	58	74	62	75	48	70	76	88
14826 COHOCTON	79	70	74	71	69	84	70	78	73	64	72	60	64	74	69	77	49	74	82	92
14830 CORNING	87	87	82	88	86	92	89	88	91	86	91	67	89	91	88	94	63	90	96	105
14836 DALTON	84	70	80	71	71	88	70	82	74	64	73	62	61	75	69	80	49	76	85	97
14837 DUNDEE	80	61	86	60	64	82	66	78	70	60	69	58	55	68	65	76	46	74	82	92
14838 ERIN	89	84	77	83	83	88	79	86	81	79	81	64	75	84	78	84	55	81	86	101
14839 GREENWOOD	78	56	77	54	58	78	58	72	64	54	63	54	46	64	56	70	42	67	75	86
14840 HAMMONDSPORT	98	78	123	76	85	103	78	99	82	73	81	72	67	78	84	87	54	91	98	115
14841 HECTOR	110	88	141	86	96	117	88	112	92	83	91	82	76	88	95	99	61	103	111	130
14842 HIMROD	85	73	80	76	75	91	74	85	76	65	75	65	65	77	73	81	51	78	88	100
14843 HORNELL	71	63	64	63	62	71	69	69	72	64	71	52	64	71	65	76	49	71	77	82
14845 HORSEHEADS	92	92	93	93	93	101	89	95	92	87	91	71	89	92	91	96	63	93	101	111
14846 HUNT	82	64	73	63	64	82	65	76	70	61	69	58	55	72	62	76	46	71	79	91
14847 INTERLAKEN	92	81	100	81	85	99	81	94	86	77	84	68	76	84	84	91	57	89	99	109
14850 ITHACA	93	77	75	81	75	77	105	83	98	94	99	71	91	97	87	95	70	93	85	102
14853 ITHACA	96	41	40	50	37	47	135	67	108	91	109	72	80	105	72	98	77	95	67	90
14855 JASPER	90	64	74	63	64	85	67	78	74	65	73	60	54	78	61	81	49	74	82	95
14858 LINDLEY	86	69	73	68	69	84	69	79	75	67	73	60	60	77	65	80	50	74	82	94
14859 LOCKWOOD	84	72	71	69	71	80	70	77	74	71	73	57	63	77	66	77	50	73	78	92
14860 LODI	90	69	105	67	74	94	70	89	75	65	74	65	58	73	72	81	49	81	90	104
14861 LOWMAN	90	67	86	66	68	91	69	84	75	64	74	63	56	76	67	82	49	78	88	100
14864 MILLPORT	94	84	86	87	86	100	84	95	87	77	86	71	77	88	84	92	58	88	98	110
14865 MONTOUR FALLS	75	70	70	70	70	78	72	74	75	68	74	56	69	74	71	78	51	74	81	88
14867 NEWFIELD	83	75	70	74	74	79	74	78	77	75	76	57	70	78	71	79	52	76	80	92
14869 ODESSA	79	72	71	75	73	84	71	80	73	65	72	60	66	75	71	77	49	74	82	93
14870 PAINTED POST	107	107	114	107	110	117	102	111	105	102	104	82	103	103	106	108	72	107	116	128
14871 PINE CITY	93	106	101	105	106	111	93	101	97	94	97	73	102	96	101	101	67	98	109	117
14872 PINE VALLEY	90	69	76	69	70	88	71	82	77	67	75	62	60	80	66	83	51	77	86	98
14873 PRATTSBURGH	84	61	90	59	64	85	62	79	68	58	67	59	51	68	63	75	45	73	82	94
14874 PULTENEY	83	67	108	66	73	88	67	85	70	63	69	62	58	66	72	74	46	78	84	98
14877 REXVILLE	79	54	85	54	57	82	60	74	63	50	62	60	44	62	59	69	40	69	78	91
14878 ROCK STREAM	94	70	107	69	75	97	72	91	77	67	76	67	59	75	74	84	50	84	93	107
14879 SAVONA	79	68	71	68	67	82	68	76	72	65	71	58	62	74	66	77	48	73	80	91
14880 SCIO	81	58	83	57	60	83	61	76	67	56	66	57	49	67	60	74	44	71	80	91
14881 SLATERVILLE SPRINGS	95	91	89	93	92	102	89	98	91	82	90	74	85	93	90	95	62	92	100	113
14882 LANSING	108	120	115	122	119	125	107	116	108	106	108	87	114	109	115	111	76	110	118	134
14883 SPENCER	84	78	69	76	76	80	73	78	76	76	76	57	70	79	71	78	52	75	78	92
14884 SWAIN	81	58	83	56	60	82	59	75	66	55	65	57	47	65	59	72	43	69	78	90
14885 TROUPSBURG	80	55	87	55	57	84	61	76	63	49	63	63	45	62	61	69	41	71	80	93
14886 TRUMANSBURG	95	90	90	91	91	97	88	94	90	87	90	70	85	91	88	93	62	91	96	111
14889 VAN ETTEN	78	61	67	61	61	77	62	72	67	59	66	55	53	69	59	72	45	67	75	86
14891 WATKINS GLEN	79	66	81	66	69	83	69	78	73	64	72	58	62	72	69	79	49	75	84	92
14892 WAVERLY	76	62	69	61	62	76	66	72	71	62	69	55	58	71	63	75	47	71	78	86
14894 WELLSBURG	86	73	79	70	72	86	72	82	77	70	76	60	65	78	70	82	51	78	86	97
14895 WELLSVILLE	78	66	78	66	68	82	69	78	74	65	72	57	63	72	68	79	49	75	84	91
14897 WHITESVILLE	80	57	82	56	60	82	59	75	65	55	64	56	47	65	58	72	42	69	78	89
14898 WOODHULL	80	57	70	55	57	77	60	70	66	56	64	55	47	68	55	71	43	67	74	86
14901 ELMIRA	65	53	52	55	52	61	65	60	67	59	66	48	58	66	58	70	46	64	68	74
14903 ELMIRA	81	80	77	81	79	87	82	82	84	78	83	62	81	83	80	87	58	83	90	97
14904 ELMIRA	66	59	58	60	57	68	65	65	68	60	67	50	61	67	61	72	47	67	73	78
14905 ELMIRA	93	97	92	97	96	103	94	97	98	92	97	71	97	97	96	102	67	97	107	113
NEW YORK	100	106	110	108	107	104	112	106	113	106	114	81	115	110	112	116	83	110	110	124
UNITED STATES	100	100	100	100	100	100	100	100	100	100	100	100	100	100	100	100	100	100	100	100

ZIP CODE #	POST OFFICE NAME	COUNTY FIPS CODE	POPULATION 2000	POPULATION 2009	POPULATION 2014	2000-2009 ANNUAL RATE % Rate	2000-2009 ANNUAL RATE State Centile	HOUSEHOLDS 2000	HOUSEHOLDS 2009	HOUSEHOLDS 2014	HOUSEHOLDS % Annual Rate 2000-2009	HOUSEHOLDS 2009 Average HH Size	FAMILIES 2000	FAMILIES 2009	FAMILIES % Annual Rate 2000-2009
27006	ADVANCE	059	10613	13621	15161	2.7	87	4231	5511	6156	2.9	2.46	3269	4157	2.6
27007	ARARAT	171	1946	2161	2246	1.1	56	733	815	848	1.2	2.65	589	640	0.9
27009	BELEWS CREEK	067	2455	2618	2739	0.7	40	966	1041	1092	0.8	2.51	756	792	0.5
27011	BOONVILLE	197	5149	5663	5872	1.0	53	2066	2299	2392	1.2	2.46	1534	1662	0.9
27012	CLEMMONS	067	21990	26627	29017	2.1	81	8310	10179	11130	2.2	2.58	6488	7727	1.9
27013	CLEVELAND	159	5896	6946	7505	1.8	76	2139	2532	2740	1.8	2.74	1631	1883	1.6
27016	DANBURY	169	1855	1888	1879	0.2	21	705	737	739	0.5	2.52	531	542	0.2
27017	DOBSON	171	8483	9041	9231	0.7	40	3186	3385	3459	0.7	2.62	2374	2452	0.4
27018	EAST BEND	197	7244	7493	7536	0.4	28	2893	3030	3051	0.5	2.47	2111	2151	0.2
27019	GERMANTON	169	4357	4597	4699	0.6	36	1730	1858	1908	0.8	2.45	1306	1366	0.5
27020	HAMPTONVILLE	197	6084	6711	6948	1.1	56	2357	2613	2707	1.1	2.56	1767	1908	0.8
27021	KING	169	15954	16213	16204	0.2	21	6231	6498	6545	0.5	2.45	4619	4687	0.2
27022	LAWSONVILLE	169	1615	1655	1653	0.3	24	653	686	692	0.5	2.40	493	506	0.3
27023	LEWISVILLE	067	9792	10779	11469	1.0	53	3798	4205	4481	1.1	2.56	2960	3196	0.8
27024	LOWGAP	171	2534	2810	2917	1.1	56	1005	1119	1165	1.2	2.46	756	818	0.9
27025	MADISON	157	10843	11344	11506	0.5	32	4251	4519	4609	0.7	2.47	3119	3225	0.4
27027	MAYODAN	157	4241	4229	4222	0.0	15	1897	1914	1918	0.1	2.21	1197	1164	-0.3
27028	MOCKSVILLE	059	23995	28064	30464	1.7	74	9424	11245	12264	1.9	2.48	6920	8028	1.6
27030	MOUNT AIRY	171	38343	38944	39157	0.2	21	15444	15672	15766	0.2	2.44	10996	10842	-0.2
27040	PFAFFTOWN	067	9905	11436	12295	1.6	72	3797	4434	4780	1.7	2.56	2996	3409	1.4
27041	PILOT MOUNTAIN	171	7098	7495	7623	0.6	36	2923	3094	3151	0.6	2.42	2137	2200	0.3
27042	PINE HALL	169	645	708	731	1.0	53	259	292	304	1.3	2.42	189	208	1.0
27043	PINNACLE	171	5462	5805	5908	0.7	40	2127	2275	2322	0.7	2.55	1623	1695	0.5
27045	RURAL HALL	067	7303	8014	8521	1.0	53	3056	3403	3629	1.2	2.35	2177	2337	0.8
27046	SANDY RIDGE	169	1951	2122	2188	0.9	48	779	868	901	1.2	2.44	576	625	0.9
27047	SILOAM	171	971	942	933	-0.3	8	377	366	362	-0.3	2.57	299	283	-0.6
27048	STONEVILLE	157	8544	8858	8976	0.4	28	3344	3509	3570	0.5	2.52	2514	2571	0.2
27050	TOBACCOVILLE	067	3797	4099	4290	0.8	44	1523	1669	1752	1.0	2.46	1155	1228	0.7
27051	WALKERTOWN	067	6734	7631	8173	1.4	66	2683	3078	3304	1.5	2.45	2015	2243	1.2
27052	WALNUT COVE	169	10702	11479	11796	0.8	44	4229	4641	4801	1.0	2.43	3065	3272	0.7
27053	WESTFIELD	169	2993	3072	3064	0.3	24	1179	1231	1235	0.5	2.48	882	899	0.2
27054	WOODLEAF	159	2476	2739	2879	1.1	56	916	1015	1067	1.1	2.70	700	754	0.8
27055	YADKINVILLE	197	13397	14016	14243	0.5	32	5245	5553	5663	0.6	2.45	3836	3949	0.3
27101	WINSTON SALEM	067	19683	20784	21481	0.6	36	8336	8758	9066	0.5	2.13	4134	4168	0.1
27103	WINSTON SALEM	067	26422	31164	33618	1.8	76	11871	14033	15140	1.8	2.19	6823	7714	1.3
27104	WINSTON SALEM	067	26792	28574	29907	0.7	40	12497	13483	14145	0.8	2.09	7250	7446	0.3
27105	WINSTON SALEM	067	40013	43094	45016	0.8	44	15198	16407	17188	0.8	2.57	10244	10636	0.4
27106	WINSTON SALEM	067	41997	46591	49173	1.1	56	16837	18687	19802	1.1	2.29	10339	10970	0.6
27107	WINSTON SALEM	057	38961	44638	47726	1.5	69	14828	17115	18376	1.6	2.57	10770	12021	1.2
27110	WINSTON SALEM	067	1138	1265	1293	1.2	60	0	0	0	0.0	0.00	0	0	0.0
27127	WINSTON SALEM	067	25434	32317	35614	2.6	86	10428	13317	14724	2.7	2.39	6926	8486	2.2
27203	ASHEBORO	151	20032	21289	21833	0.7	40	8123	8453	8644	0.4	2.44	5107	5131	0.1
27205	ASHEBORO	151	29996	32468	33757	0.9	48	11288	12250	12762	0.9	2.62	8676	9193	0.6
27207	BEAR CREEK	037	3332	3818	4124	1.5	69	1308	1529	1658	1.7	2.47	998	1144	1.5
27208	BENNETT	037	1874	2061	2172	1.0	53	746	828	874	1.1	2.49	561	608	0.9
27209	BISCOE	123	3907	3944	3944	0.1	18	1355	1379	1383	0.2	2.79	1005	995	-0.1
27212	BLANCH	033	2480	2713	2739	1.0	53	569	669	686	1.8	3.09	423	480	1.4
27214	BROWNS SUMMIT	081	6812	9000	9922	3.1	88	2551	3427	3791	3.2	2.61	1907	2437	2.7
27215	BURLINGTON	001	33436	38534	41288	1.5	69	14290	16576	17790	1.6	2.30	9150	10267	1.3
27217	BURLINGTON	001	34614	37381	39188	0.8	44	13177	14284	14995	0.9	2.56	9296	9790	0.6
27229	CANDOR	123	3389	3653	3736	0.8	44	1173	1257	1287	0.8	2.88	876	915	0.5
27231	CEDAR GROVE	135	1835	1876	1911	0.2	21	690	759	778	1.0	2.47	510	542	0.7
27233	CLIMAX	151	2935	3295	3492	1.3	63	1113	1262	1343	1.4	2.61	875	967	1.1
27235	COLFAX	081	2140	3049	3480	3.9	93	817	1343	1543	5.5	2.27	618	992	5.2
27239	DENTON	057	8780	9632	9999	1.0	53	3395	3762	3921	1.1	2.53	2575	2774	0.8
27242	EAGLE SPRINGS	125	2220	2430	2564	1.0	53	813	890	945	1.0	2.57	614	653	0.7
27243	EFLAND	135	3467	4094	4310	1.8	76	1368	1722	1821	2.5	2.38	1015	1236	2.2
27244	ELON	001	11870	13160	13912	1.1	56	3856	4401	4707	1.4	2.53	2653	2924	1.1
27248	FRANKLINVILLE	151	4236	4752	4998	1.3	63	1662	1872	1973	1.3	2.54	1265	1389	1.0
27249	GIBSONVILLE	081	10005	11745	12765	1.7	74	3879	4631	5047	1.9	2.52	2884	3308	1.5
27252	GOLDSTON	037	1915	2234	2429	1.7	74	787	936	1022	1.9	2.37	569	660	1.6
27253	GRAHAM	001	24911	28090	29945	1.3	63	10058	11404	12173	1.4	2.42	7006	7700	1.0
27258	HAW RIVER	001	5544	6139	6502	1.1	56	2284	2554	2712	1.2	2.38	1656	1802	0.9
27260	HIGH POINT	081	25527	26159	26756	0.3	24	9455	9730	9966	0.3	2.61	6325	6275	-0.1
27262	HIGH POINT	081	23058	23957	24598	0.4	28	9312	9735	10039	0.5	2.31	5916	5912	0.0
27263	HIGH POINT	151	18416	20491	21534	1.2	60	7529	8439	8882	1.2	2.41	5362	5805	0.9
27265	HIGH POINT	081	32328	43251	48356	3.2	89	13000	17463	19555	3.2	2.46	9171	12105	3.0
27278	HILLSBOROUGH	135	20292	22722	23827	1.2	60	7783	9320	9828	2.0	2.39	5642	6504	1.5
27281	JACKSON SPRINGS	125	3218	3680	3916	1.5	69	1011	1158	1240	1.5	3.13	778	869	1.2
27282	JAMESTOWN	081	13505	15489	16647	1.5	69	5232	6087	6571	1.6	2.54	3951	4480	1.4
27283	JULIAN	081	3216	3433	3617	0.7	40	1242	1353	1433	0.9	2.54	974	1033	0.6
27284	KERNERSVILLE	067	41491	51096	56120	2.3	83	16506	20533	22606	2.4	2.47	12115	14677	2.1
27288	EDEN	157	24814	24016	23690	-0.4	7	10232	9978	9883	-0.3	2.37	7063	6666	-0.6
27291	LEASBURG	033	1818	1835	1834	0.1	18	726	755	761	0.4	2.43	525	532	0.1
27292	LEXINGTON	057	39351	41154	41885	0.5	32	15478	16326	16672	0.6	2.46	10973	11257	0.3
27295	LEXINGTON	057	34606	37169	38274	0.8	44	13775	14963	15475	0.9	2.46	10156	10725	0.6
27298	LIBERTY	151	9594	10557	11084	1.0	53	3732	4119	4334	1.1	2.56	2750	2948	0.8
27299	LINWOOD	057	4577	4937	5098	0.8	44	1739	1898	1969	1.0	2.57	1299	1377	0.6
27301	MC LEANSVILLE	081	5914	7730	8467	2.9	88	2196	2970	3271	3.3	2.56	1688	2219	3.0
27302	MEBANE	001	20955	24816	26785	1.8	76	8148	9950	10777	2.2	2.48	5941	7026	1.8
27305	MILTON	033	1361	1350	1330	-0.1	13	491	500	496	0.2	2.68	371	368	-0.1
27306	MOUNT GILEAD	123	5806	6087	6216	0.5	32	2250	2433	2506	0.8	2.48	1665	1752	0.6
27310	OAK RIDGE	081	4306	5835	6584	3.3	90	1497	2046	2314	3.4	2.85	1240	1655	3.2
27311	PELHAM	033	3952	3916	3857	-0.1	13	1550	1573	1562	0.2	2.49	1141	1129	-0.1
27312	PITTSBORO	037	13068	16684	18764	2.7	87	5396	6995	7898	2.8	2.34	3729	4699	2.5
27313	PLEASANT GARDEN	081	6483	7281	7748	1.3	63	2447	2785	2971	1.4	2.60	1950	2167	1.1
27314	PROSPECT HILL	033	822	862	858	0.5	32	328	355	357	0.9	2.41	247	261	0.6
27315	PROVIDENCE	033	1745	1833	1826	0.5	32	732	790	793	0.8	2.32	532	559	0.5
27316	RAMSEUR	151	6927	7448	7685	0.8	44	2643	2825	2916	0.7	2.63	1941	2017	0.4
27317	RANDLEMAN	151	14482	16620	17637	1.5	69	5640	6505	6911	1.6	2.55	4178	4674	1.2
27320	REIDSVILLE	157	38124	38468	38552	0.1	18	15110	15459	15579	0.2	2.44	10762	10684	-0.1
27325	ROBBINS	125	6643	7403	7819	1.2	60	2531	2770	2923	1.0	2.67	1828	1940	0.6
27326	RUFFIN	157	3591	3734	3763	0.4	28	1428	1515	1538	0.6	2.45	1033	1066	0.3
27330	SANFORD	105	32465	38525	42072	1.9	77	12107	14367	15709	1.9	2.62	8667	9995	1.6
27332	SANFORD	105	22534	28835	32377	2.7	87	8463	10768	12064	2.6	2.68	6321	7841	2.4
	NORTH CAROLINA					1.7					1.8	2.46			1.5
	UNITED STATES					1.0					1.1	2.59			0.9

ZIP CODE #	POST OFFICE NAME	RACE (%) White 2000	White 2009	Black 2000	Black 2009	Asian/Pacific 2000	Asian/Pacific 2009	% Hispanic Origin 2000	% Hispanic Origin 2009	2009 AGE DISTRIBUTION (%) 0-4	5-9	10-14	15-19	20-24	25-44	45-64	65-84	85+	18+	MEDIAN AGE 2009	% 2009 Males	% 2009 Females
27006	ADVANCE	95.8	95.0	2.7	2.8	0.3	0.5	1.4	2.0	5.5	6.0	6.7	6.3	3.8	22.1	33.2	14.3	2.1	77.6	44.7	49.3	50.7
27007	ARARAT	94.8	92.2	0.7	0.7	0.2	0.2	5.7	8.9	6.7	6.8	7.0	6.5	5.0	30.0	27.0	9.9	1.0	75.4	37.6	51.1	48.9
27009	BELEWS CREEK	89.8	86.7	7.9	9.5	0.1	0.2	1.8	3.2	6.6	7.3	7.5	6.0	3.9	26.2	30.7	10.8	1.0	74.8	40.9	49.9	50.1
27011	BOONVILLE	92.7	90.5	3.7	3.9	0.2	0.3	5.0	7.4	6.3	6.5	6.9	6.6	4.9	26.2	28.4	12.7	1.6	76.3	40.5	49.6	50.4
27012	CLEMMONS	92.4	90.0	4.6	5.5	1.3	1.9	1.7	2.9	6.1	6.5	7.3	7.3	4.4	24.7	31.7	10.6	1.5	75.3	41.3	48.7	51.3
27013	CLEVELAND	80.6	77.5	16.3	18.0	0.5	0.7	2.6	4.0	7.3	7.3	7.4	7.3	5.6	27.4	27.0	9.6	1.1	73.4	36.8	49.9	50.1
27016	DANBURY	96.1	94.8	1.5	1.5	0.2	0.3	2.5	3.8	5.3	5.7	6.2	6.2	4.3	25.8	31.4	13.0	2.0	78.8	42.6	50.1	49.9
27017	DOBSON	85.9	80.6	2.1	2.0	0.1	0.1	15.6	21.7	7.0	7.0	7.1	6.3	5.1	28.5	26.3	11.5	1.3	75.2	37.8	51.9	48.1
27018	EAST BEND	94.5	92.8	2.4	2.6	0.3	0.4	4.3	6.2	6.2	6.5	6.8	6.5	5.1	25.8	30.4	11.4	1.3	76.4	40.6	50.0	50.0
27019	GERMANTON	94.5	93.0	3.8	4.4	0.2	0.3	1.2	2.0	5.8	6.1	6.5	6.3	4.9	25.2	30.7	13.0	1.4	77.6	42.0	49.5	50.5
27020	HAMPTONVILLE	93.8	90.7	1.1	1.2	0.2	0.2	8.7	12.8	6.9	6.9	7.2	6.7	5.1	27.2	26.9	11.8	1.4	74.9	38.5	51.1	48.9
27021	KING	97.2	96.5	1.2	1.3	0.3	0.5	1.5	2.2	6.3	6.5	6.8	6.5	5.0	26.7	29.4	11.2	1.7	76.3	40.0	49.3	50.7
27022	LAWSONVILLE	95.5	94.0	1.5	1.6	0.2	0.2	3.3	5.1	5.1	5.6	6.1	6.2	4.5	25.8	32.3	12.7	1.8	79.3	42.9	49.8	50.2
27023	LEWISVILLE	92.7	90.3	4.6	5.5	1.2	1.7	1.3	2.3	6.3	6.8	7.3	6.7	5.0	24.0	33.2	9.8	0.9	75.3	41.2	49.3	50.7
27024	LOWGAP	96.8	95.4	0.6	0.6	0.0	0.0	2.2	3.5	5.9	6.1	7.0	7.0	5.0	27.1	28.4	12.2	1.2	76.2	39.9	50.4	49.6
27025	MADISON	82.6	80.9	14.7	15.3	0.3	0.4	2.3	3.5	6.0	6.1	6.4	6.0	5.0	26.0	28.9	13.2	2.3	77.8	41.3	49.5	50.5
27027	MAYODAN	89.0	86.9	7.5	7.9	0.3	0.4	3.4	5.3	5.7	5.7	5.7	5.8	5.2	25.6	28.9	14.7	2.6	79.2	42.2	47.9	52.1
27028	MOCKSVILLE	88.1	86.0	8.6	9.0	0.3	0.5	4.4	6.5	6.5	6.6	6.8	6.4	5.2	26.8	28.0	12.1	1.6	76.2	39.5	49.8	50.2
27030	MOUNT AIRY	90.1	87.5	5.4	5.6	1.0	1.4	5.1	7.8	6.3	6.3	6.5	6.2	5.1	25.8	27.1	14.3	2.4	77.2	40.8	49.0	51.0
27040	PFAFFTOWN	90.1	87.4	7.8	9.6	0.5	0.8	1.2	2.0	5.2	6.0	7.0	6.6	3.9	21.4	34.3	13.7	1.8	77.6	44.9	48.8	51.2
27041	PILOT MOUNTAIN	93.5	91.7	3.6	3.9	0.3	0.4	2.6	4.2	6.1	6.1	6.4	6.3	5.4	26.1	29.2	12.6	1.8	77.6	40.8	49.1	50.9
27042	PINE HALL	86.2	84.7	11.8	12.0	0.2	0.1	1.7	2.8	6.2	6.5	6.6	5.8	4.9	28.5	29.1	10.9	1.4	77.3	39.7	48.3	51.7
27043	PINNACLE	94.8	93.6	3.0	3.2	0.1	0.1	2.2	3.3	6.2	6.4	6.7	6.5	4.9	26.7	30.1	11.4	1.2	76.7	40.4	49.9	50.1
27045	RURAL HALL	84.6	80.7	11.1	12.5	0.4	0.5	3.7	6.3	6.0	6.1	6.4	6.1	4.8	25.0	30.0	14.1	1.5	77.7	42.1	48.8	51.2
27046	SANDY RIDGE	95.8	94.5	1.6	1.6	0.6	0.7	2.9	4.3	5.0	5.2	5.8	6.4	4.9	28.1	30.1	12.9	1.6	80.1	41.3	49.2	50.8
27047	SILOAM	95.7	94.1	1.3	1.4	0.2	0.3	2.1	3.5	6.5	6.6	6.6	5.7	4.6	29.5	26.8	12.6	1.2	76.9	39.3	52.8	47.2
27048	STONEVILLE	82.0	79.1	13.0	13.4	0.2	0.3	6.3	9.1	6.0	6.3	6.8	6.6	4.7	26.1	29.7	12.5	1.4	76.9	40.7	49.6	50.4
27050	TOBACCOVILLE	91.6	89.5	6.8	8.1	0.2	0.3	1.6	2.4	6.4	6.6	7.0	6.5	5.2	25.6	30.8	10.7	1.1	76.0	40.3	49.3	50.7
27051	WALKERTOWN	83.3	79.8	14.1	16.4	0.3	0.4	1.6	2.8	6.4	6.7	6.9	6.1	4.6	26.3	29.2	12.3	1.5	76.1	40.7	48.9	51.1
27052	WALNUT COVE	86.5	85.3	11.7	12.1	0.2	0.3	1.4	2.2	6.4	6.6	6.8	6.1	4.8	26.1	29.0	12.3	1.9	76.4	40.8	49.2	50.8
27053	WESTFIELD	91.6	90.5	6.4	6.4	0.1	0.1	2.6	3.9	6.6	6.9	7.2	6.3	5.0	25.4	29.2	11.5	1.8	75.3	40.0	49.4	50.6
27054	WOODLEAF	76.0	71.6	19.2	20.9	0.2	0.3	5.5	8.4	7.1	7.1	7.3	7.0	5.7	26.9	27.1	10.6	1.2	74.1	37.4	50.1	49.9
27055	YADKINVILLE	92.2	89.8	3.2	3.3	0.1	0.2	8.1	11.6	6.5	6.7	6.9	6.2	4.4	26.0	27.6	13.3	2.5	76.1	40.8	49.9	50.1
27101	WINSTON SALEM	37.6	35.4	55.8	55.2	0.6	0.8	6.7	9.8	6.4	6.3	5.8	7.4	8.9	29.0	24.1	10.3	1.9	78.0	35.5	48.7	51.3
27103	WINSTON SALEM	75.5	70.3	16.4	18.0	2.2	2.8	7.3	11.0	6.3	5.8	5.4	5.2	6.5	29.2	25.2	13.5	2.9	79.3	39.3	46.7	53.3
27104	WINSTON SALEM	86.6	83.7	9.5	10.6	1.9	2.6	2.7	4.2	5.1	5.1	5.8	6.1	6.5	24.3	29.2	14.8	3.1	80.2	42.9	46.8	53.2
27105	WINSTON SALEM	31.0	28.6	61.9	61.9	0.3	0.4	10.4	13.4	7.2	7.3	7.0	7.2	6.9	25.7	24.9	11.6	2.3	74.0	36.2	47.4	52.6
27106	WINSTON SALEM	71.4	67.5	22.2	23.1	1.4	2.0	6.8	9.9	5.9	5.6	5.7	9.1	11.2	24.7	24.3	11.0	2.6	79.3	34.8	47.8	52.2
27107	WINSTON SALEM	61.8	60.0	31.1	29.7	0.3	0.4	10.0	13.5	7.0	7.1	7.0	6.8	6.2	27.4	26.6	10.7	1.2	74.8	37.1	48.5	51.5
27110	WINSTON SALEM	5.3	5.8	88.7	85.5	0.1	0.1	13.6	17.3	4.0	4.1	2.8	41.0	30.5	11.9	4.3	1.1	0.2	88.1	19.8	39.5	60.5
27127	WINSTON SALEM	67.0	62.8	25.8	26.5	1.2	1.7	7.6	11.3	7.4	7.2	6.9	6.8	6.2	28.8	25.1	10.0	1.5	74.4	36.4	48.0	52.0
27203	ASHEBORO	74.8	69.8	13.4	12.6	1.4	1.8	20.7	28.9	7.8	7.0	6.2	6.2	7.6	28.9	22.2	11.5	2.7	75.5	34.8	49.6	50.4
27205	ASHEBORO	92.0	89.2	2.9	3.2	0.6	0.8	5.8	8.6	6.4	6.6	6.9	6.5	5.0	26.3	28.9	11.8	1.6	76.0	40.1	49.6	50.4
27207	BEAR CREEK	81.3	78.6	16.4	17.5	0.1	0.2	2.9	5.1	5.6	5.8	6.5	6.7	5.0	24.9	31.2	12.8	1.6	78.0	41.8	49.8	50.2
27208	BENNETT	91.4	89.5	6.5	7.0	0.2	0.2	2.0	3.5	5.8	6.1	6.4	5.8	4.6	25.9	29.6	13.8	2.0	78.1	42.0	50.9	49.1
27209	BISCOE	68.5	61.7	15.8	14.8	0.8	0.9	23.7	33.6	7.7	7.3	8.1	6.9	6.0	27.7	23.8	10.1	2.4	72.4	34.8	49.2	50.8
27212	BLANCH	49.3	48.8	47.9	48.3	0.4	0.4	1.7	1.7	5.2	5.3	5.4	5.2	7.4	31.7	26.4	11.5	2.0	80.9	38.3	58.6	41.4
27214	BROWNS SUMMIT	72.7	65.7	23.8	28.8	0.3	0.4	3.1	5.3	7.1	6.9	6.9	6.6	6.0	29.6	26.1	9.7	1.0	75.2	36.4	50.1	49.9
27215	BURLINGTON	82.4	80.1	11.8	11.4	1.7	2.3	6.1	8.6	5.9	5.8	5.8	6.1	5.8	26.9	27.2	13.8	2.6	78.6	40.3	48.0	52.0
27217	BURLINGTON	57.5	54.1	34.1	33.8	0.8	1.0	10.2	14.4	6.8	6.7	6.7	6.4	5.7	26.5	26.3	12.5	2.3	75.8	39.0	48.6	51.4
27229	CANDOR	53.8	47.5	28.9	27.3	0.6	0.7	24.8	34.3	8.5	8.6	8.3	6.9	4.8	28.5	23.4	9.4	1.6	70.3	33.9	51.1	48.9
27231	CEDAR GROVE	68.5	65.0	25.8	26.5	0.2	0.3	5.0	7.6	5.5	5.8	6.8	6.2	4.8	26.5	31.4	11.4	1.4	78.2	41.4	49.3	50.7
27233	CLIMAX	94.9	93.2	2.6	2.9	0.2	0.3	1.5	2.5	5.9	6.3	6.7	6.6	5.2	24.8	31.4	12.1	1.1	76.9	41.7	49.1	50.9
27235	COLFAX	92.8	89.9	4.2	5.5	1.6	2.7	1.3	2.0	6.4	6.7	7.0	6.5	4.7	27.9	30.2	9.6	1.0	75.8	39.4	49.0	51.0
27239	DENTON	98.3	97.5	0.4	0.4	0.3	0.4	1.0	1.6	5.9	6.0	6.4	6.5	5.3	26.3	30.0	11.7	1.9	77.7	40.9	49.4	50.6
27242	EAGLE SPRINGS	63.6	59.2	30.1	31.3	0.2	0.3	7.0	10.8	6.8	7.2	9.2	10.7	5.3	24.2	25.8	9.4	1.4	68.4	34.7	50.1	49.9
27243	EFLAND	71.7	69.5	24.8	25.2	0.3	0.5	3.3	5.1	6.1	6.5	7.0	6.6	4.7	26.4	31.7	10.0	1.0	76.3	40.5	48.1	51.9
27244	ELON	85.6	83.8	12.1	13.0	0.8	1.1	1.7	2.4	4.4	4.8	5.3	15.9	14.7	19.1	24.5	9.9	1.6	82.0	31.6	47.2	52.8
27248	FRANKLINVILLE	93.9	91.4	2.1	2.3	0.2	0.2	4.0	6.4	6.9	7.0	7.1	6.6	5.6	26.3	28.9	10.5	1.1	74.9	38.8	49.9	50.1
27249	GIBSONVILLE	79.6	76.1	17.1	18.9	0.4	0.7	2.7	4.3	6.0	6.3	6.7	6.5	4.8	25.8	30.1	11.9	1.8	76.9	41.0	49.3	50.7
27252	GOLDSTON	78.2	75.5	20.2	21.8	0.1	0.2	1.4	2.5	4.7	5.1	5.9	6.0	4.4	23.6	34.2	14.2	2.0	80.8	45.2	49.5	50.5
27253	GRAHAM	79.5	76.1	15.0	15.5	0.6	0.8	8.4	12.6	6.9	6.8	6.6	6.2	5.8	28.5	26.2	11.4	1.7	75.9	37.9	48.8	51.2
27258	HAW RIVER	83.4	80.0	12.4	13.5	0.4	0.5	5.2	8.3	6.5	6.7	6.9	6.4	4.9	27.7	28.8	10.5	1.6	75.8	39.4	48.6	51.4
27260	HIGH POINT	28.4	25.4	62.5	62.0	3.7	5.0	6.4	8.8	8.4	8.1	7.4	7.5	7.0	26.6	23.0	9.9	2.0	71.4	33.6	47.2	52.8
27262	HIGH POINT	70.5	66.0	21.9	23.0	2.3	3.3	6.3	9.2	6.4	6.2	6.1	7.8	8.1	25.3	24.6	12.6	2.9	77.8	37.7	48.2	51.8
27263	HIGH POINT	88.2	84.3	6.1	7.4	2.7	4.0	2.4	3.9	6.3	6.3	6.5	6.2	5.4	27.6	27.4	12.7	1.6	77.2	39.6	49.7	50.3
27265	HIGH POINT	81.0	77.5	14.4	15.7	2.3	3.4	2.4	3.6	6.6	6.5	6.6	6.3	5.7	28.5	27.9	10.4	1.6	76.5	38.4	48.5	51.5
27278	HILLSBOROUGH	78.2	76.4	17.7	18.0	0.6	0.9	3.0	4.4	5.8	6.2	6.5	6.5	5.6	26.4	31.2	10.4	1.4	77.4	40.6	49.1	50.9
27281	JACKSON SPRINGS	65.9	62.2	23.7	23.0	0.3	0.4	14.4	19.6	6.8	7.0	7.4	7.4	4.8	24.4	26.8	13.3	2.0	73.9	39.0	50.5	49.5
27282	JAMESTOWN	81.2	76.2	12.2	14.1	4.3	6.4	2.0	3.1	7.5	7.4	7.4	6.5	5.0	30.1	26.9	8.4	0.8	73.5	36.9	48.6	51.4
27283	JULIAN	95.3	94.0	3.2	3.8	0.3	0.5	1.0	1.6	5.4	5.9	6.4	6.1	4.3	24.4	32.8	13.0	1.6	78.5	43.4	50.6	49.4
27284	KERNERSVILLE	88.3	84.6	7.1	8.3	1.0	1.5	4.1	6.4	6.5	6.6	6.7	6.5	5.4	27.1	29.2	10.8	1.2	76.2	39.5	49.3	50.7
27288	EDEN	78.0	75.9	19.8	20.8	0.3	0.5	2.2	3.2	5.9	6.0	6.0	5.9	5.5	25.2	28.3	14.7	2.7	78.5	41.8	47.4	52.6
27291	LEASBURG	74.7	74.0	23.6	24.1	0.1	0.1	1.5	1.7	5.0	5.3	5.9	6.9	5.0	24.2	32.2	13.7	1.9	79.4	43.5	49.2	50.8
27292	LEXINGTON	79.5	77.1	15.4	15.5	1.0	1.4	5.1	7.3	6.6	6.5	6.5	6.3	5.5	27.7	27.9	11.4	1.7	76.6	39.1	49.6	50.4
27295	LEXINGTON	91.6	89.4	4.2	4.8	1.6	2.2	2.2	3.3	6.2	6.3	6.6	6.3	4.6	26.8	29.1	12.5	1.6	77.0	40.8	49.4	50.6
27298	LIBERTY	84.2	81.5	10.9	11.2	0.2	0.3	5.9	8.7	6.0	6.5	7.1	6.7	5.1	26.3	29.0	11.5	1.7	76.0	40.0	50.3	49.7
27299	LINWOOD	96.2	94.8	1.6	1.9	0.5	0.7	1.2	2.1	6.2	6.3	6.8	7.1	5.3	29.1	28.3	9.8	1.1	75.9	38.6	50.5	49.5
27301	MC LEANSVILLE	79.6	75.6	16.9	19.4	0.5	0.8	2.6	3.9	6.4	6.6	6.9	6.5	5.0	27.7	29.2	10.7	1.0	76.0	39.6	50.4	49.6
27302	MEBANE	75.0	72.1	21.2	22.4	0.4	0.6	3.9	5.8	6.7	6.8	6.9	6.6	5.5	27.7	28.1	10.4	1.4	75.4	38.6	48.9	51.1
27305	MILTON	47.3	46.5	50.0	50.7	0.7	0.7	1.8	1.8	6.0	6.2	6.6	6.5	5.3	25.8	31.2	11.1	1.3	77.1	40.5	48.5	51.5
27306	MOUNT GILEAD	53.6	50.9	40.2	40.4	3.7	5.1	2.6	3.9	5.8	6.1	6.3	5.9	4.6	22.9	31.0	15.5	1.8	78.1	43.7	49.9	50.1
27310	OAK RIDGE	92.9	91.2	4.6	5.0	0.6	0.9	1.8	2.9	5.6	6.5	7.5	7.6	4.3	23.5	34.7	9.3	1.1	75.7	42.2	49.6	50.4
27311	PELHAM	71.8	71.3	26.4	26.7	0.1	0.1	1.8	2.1	5.1	5.4	5.8	6.2	5.3	25.6	31.5	13.5	1.6	79.9	42.6	49.6	50.4
27312	PITTSBORO	77.6	74.9	18.9	19.8	0.5	0.7	3.2	5.2	5.6	5.9	6.5	5.9	4.4	25.1	31.7	12.8	2.2	78.2	42.9	48.7	51.3
27313	PLEASANT GARDEN	90.9	88.9	6.8	7.7	0.2	0.2	1.3	2.2	5.8	6.3	6.7	6.4	4.5	24.2	32.4	12.1	1.6	77.1	42.5	48.8	51.2
27314	PROSPECT HILL	69.7	69.3	28.6	29.1	0.1	0.1	1.5	1.4	5.3	5.6	6.4	7.3	4.9	25.1	32.0	11.9	1.5	78.1	42.2	50.3	49.7
27315	PROVIDENCE	85.4	85.7	12.6	12.3	0.1	0.1	1.3	1.3	5.0	5.3	5.7	5.7	4.4	24.2	33.0	15.2	1.6	80.5	44.8	49.6	50.4
27316	RAMSEUR	81.0	76.9	12.1	12.6	0.4	0.6	8.6	12.9	7.1	7.0	7.1	6.7	5.3	27.5	26.4	11.2	1.7	74.8	37.9	50.5	49.5
27317	RANDLEMAN	92.0	89.3	4.0	4.4	0.3	0.4	5.6	8.9	7.2	7.1	7.1	6.4	5.6	27.8	27.4	10.2	1.1	74.6	37.8	49.6	50.4
27320	REIDSVILLE	70.1	68.2	26.5	27.0	0.4	0.5	3.0	4.4	5.9	6.1	6.4	6.4	5.3	25.6	29.3	12.9	2.1	77.5	41.1	48.7	51.3
27325	ROBBINS	78.2	71.0	7.7	7.5	0.3	0.4	18.5	26.6	7.3	7.3	7.2	6.5	5.5	27.9	24.8	11.7	1.8	74.2	37.0	50.5	49.5
27326	RUFFIN	75.6	73.7	21.7	22.6	0.1	0.1	3.2	4.6	5.6	5.9	6.2	5.8	4.8	26.1	30.5	13.2	1.8	78.8	42.0	50.3	49.7
27330	SANFORD	67.8	64.1	22.8	22.2	0.9	1.1	11.7	16.6	6.9	6.9	6.7	6.5	6.2	26.9	27.0	11.1	1.8	75.6	37.7	49.4	50.6
27332	SANFORD	72.6	68.1	18.2	18.3	0.7	1.0	9.7	14.3	7.6	7.2	6.9	6.8	6.0	28.7	24.7	11.0	1.2	74.2	36.0	49.5	50.5
	NORTH CAROLINA	72.1	69.8	21.6	21.5	1.5	2.1	4.7	6.9	6.6	6.5	6.5	6.8	6.9	27.7	26.5	10.9	1.6	76.5	37.4	49.3	50.7
	UNITED STATES	75.1	72.0	12.3	12.7	3.8	4.6	12.5	15.7	6.8	6.7	6.6	7.1	6.9	27.0	26.0	10.9	1.9	75.7	36.9	49.2	50.8

27006-27332

#	POST OFFICE NAME	2009 Per Capita Income	2009 HH Income Base	2009 HOUSEHOLD INCOME DISTRIBUTION (%) Less than $25,000	$25,000 to $49,999	$50,000 to $99,999	$100,000 to $149,999	$150,000 or More	MEDIAN HOUSEHOLD INCOME 2009	2014	2009 National Centile	2009 State Centile	2009 Home Value Base	2009 HOME VALUE DISTRIBUTION (%) Less than $50,000	$50,000 to $89,999	$90,000 to $174,999	$175,000 to $399,999	$400,000 or More	2009 Median Home Value
27006	ADVANCE	33483	5511	14.1	22.6	40.6	11.4	11.3	64890	64230	83	91	4895	11.9	8.9	32.7	36.5	10.0	163639
27007	ARARAT	18330	815	25.6	32.8	36.2	3.3	2.1	44156	45344	46	50	674	17.2	13.6	43.9	23.7	1.5	120127
27009	BELEWS CREEK	25026	1041	16.4	21.9	51.2	7.9	2.6	56079	57033	73	84	925	14.9	18.8	40.5	23.6	2.2	117083
27011	BOONVILLE	20766	2299	27.1	32.0	33.8	4.8	2.3	42241	45374	40	42	1821	19.8	23.3	43.0	12.6	1.3	99234
27012	CLEMMONS	35618	10179	8.0	16.4	44.7	17.8	13.0	76272	76237	90	96	8386	3.2	4.5	36.9	51.6	3.8	184859
27013	CLEVELAND	20144	2532	21.8	29.1	40.9	6.2	2.0	48911	50515	59	67	2084	15.7	14.2	34.7	29.8	5.5	136066
27016	DANBURY	19040	737	27.0	30.0	38.4	3.1	1.5	43185	47439	43	46	615	29.8	24.1	33.2	12.0	1.0	84535
27017	DOBSON	18824	3385	30.4	29.5	33.9	4.6	1.6	40859	41958	36	36	2591	19.2	18.1	35.0	25.3	2.3	121055
27018	EAST BEND	22082	3030	22.1	30.0	38.9	7.1	1.7	47536	48947	56	62	2544	25.3	18.2	39.0	16.2	1.4	100175
27019	GERMANTON	22153	1858	22.2	30.8	38.8	6.1	2.0	46771	49630	53	61	1556	18.8	17.7	41.6	21.0	0.9	111961
27020	HAMPTONVILLE	20514	2613	24.6	30.8	37.4	5.4	1.8	44984	46802	48	53	2143	22.7	23.9	38.5	13.4	1.4	95035
27021	KING	24361	6498	19.6	26.3	43.3	8.1	2.7	53267	53214	68	79	5203	14.0	18.1	52.6	14.1	1.2	110100
27022	LAWSONVILLE	20219	686	27.4	30.6	36.9	3.1	2.0	41949	46401	39	41	573	29.0	23.7	32.5	13.8	1.0	86026
27023	LEWISVILLE	33921	4205	8.9	18.9	46.3	15.6	10.3	71766	71329	88	93	3571	4.2	7.0	45.1	37.1	6.6	162158
27024	LOWGAP	17822	1119	29.9	36.5	29.0	3.2	1.4	37980	39314	27	24	932	17.9	25.0	39.7	15.3	2.0	103214
27025	MADISON	20372	4519	25.6	31.4	35.8	5.3	1.9	44327	47687	46	51	3555	20.6	24.8	43.2	10.9	0.6	95156
27027	MAYODAN	20124	1914	32.0	31.5	31.3	4.1	1.0	37128	40417	24	21	1331	25.2	38.4	31.0	5.3	0.1	78063
27028	MOCKSVILLE	22396	11245	24.1	30.9	36.0	6.1	2.9	45402	48858	49	56	8965	22.5	23.5	37.8	13.9	2.4	95203
27030	MOUNT AIRY	20108	15672	30.8	33.0	29.2	4.3	2.6	39668	40365	32	32	11695	14.5	20.9	41.3	20.0	3.2	113968
27040	PFAFFTOWN	31470	4434	10.3	15.6	53.0	13.9	7.3	71916	71631	88	93	3965	4.4	8.2	51.6	33.6	2.1	145492
27041	PILOT MOUNTAIN	22689	3094	25.2	28.8	36.9	5.9	3.2	46383	47330	52	59	2421	16.6	12.8	41.2	25.8	3.6	129513
27042	PINE HALL	17000	292	33.6	39.4	22.3	1.7	3.1	30886	33780	10	7	240	24.6	25.4	40.4	9.6	0.0	90000
27043	PINNACLE	21791	2275	21.8	28.4	40.9	7.4	1.5	49728	50284	60	69	1875	18.1	14.3	37.5	26.0	4.1	122111
27045	RURAL HALL	26260	3403	18.0	25.3	46.1	7.4	3.2	54777	56621	71	81	2677	8.7	19.7	57.4	13.2	1.0	113031
27046	SANDY RIDGE	21230	868	26.3	33.1	34.8	2.4	3.5	41413	45536	37	38	747	32.3	23.4	36.8	7.5	0.0	77500
27047	SILOAM	20020	366	27.9	31.1	33.6	5.2	2.2	41856	42426	39	40	305	19.7	9.8	45.2	25.2	0.0	120772
27048	STONEVILLE	20570	3509	23.2	30.7	38.8	5.4	1.8	46462	50112	53	60	2831	20.3	24.4	46.2	8.5	0.5	94918
27050	TOBACCOVILLE	24749	1669	15.9	24.8	51.3	5.9	2.0	56353	58028	73	85	1426	12.8	14.0	57.2	14.9	1.1	114193
27051	WALKERTOWN	23863	3078	19.0	25.0	47.1	7.1	1.8	55092	57609	71	82	2574	13.1	25.8	51.0	9.6	0.5	103372
27052	WALNUT COVE	20767	4641	24.1	29.9	40.3	4.7	1.1	45737	48934	50	57	3778	22.2	21.1	42.5	13.7	0.4	98203
27053	WESTFIELD	18734	1231	30.7	32.2	32.0	3.0	2.1	38646	42537	29	28	1017	25.1	25.7	37.6	10.6	1.1	89138
27054	WOODLEAF	19133	1015	22.6	29.9	41.8	4.7	1.1	47679	49153	56	62	808	18.1	13.4	40.5	21.0	7.1	126202
27055	YADKINVILLE	22050	5553	24.1	29.6	37.7	5.6	2.9	45428	47157	50	56	4460	19.5	21.1	43.5	14.7	1.3	103435
27101	WINSTON SALEM	19045	8758	42.4	27.4	23.9	4.3	2.1	29541	31486	7	4	3298	15.3	28.6	43.1	11.9	1.2	96454
27103	WINSTON SALEM	30230	14033	17.3	22.8	46.0	8.8	5.1	57539	60115	75	86	8604	7.1	14.1	59.2	19.2	0.4	121334
27104	WINSTON SALEM	47029	13483	12.6	22.2	35.0	12.7	17.5	66153	66751	84	91	8502	2.1	8.6	32.1	43.2	14.1	199640
27105	WINSTON SALEM	18609	16407	33.8	26.3	33.2	4.9	1.9	37900	41470	26	24	8862	14.3	38.5	41.3	5.4	0.5	87525
27106	WINSTON SALEM	33215	18687	19.6	22.0	36.4	11.5	10.6	57822	59780	75	86	10812	4.6	9.9	44.2	33.3	8.0	154616
27107	WINSTON SALEM	21637	17115	23.5	27.7	39.7	6.6	2.5	48247	51664	57	65	12081	14.3	21.9	40.6	21.6	1.6	115420
27110	WINSTON SALEM	9437	0	0.0	0.0	0.0	0.0	0.0	0	0	0	0	0	0.0	0.0	0.0	0.0	0.0	0
27127	WINSTON SALEM	25772	13317	18.9	23.9	46.0	7.6	3.6	55492	57884	72	83	9277	10.7	21.8	54.2	12.8	0.5	111012
27203	ASHEBORO	19602	8453	30.0	31.5	31.9	4.3	2.3	40133	43605	33	33	4455	16.3	28.5	47.8	7.0	0.4	95356
27205	ASHEBORO	22874	12250	19.1	30.4	39.8	6.5	4.0	50313	51931	62	71	10182	16.0	19.7	45.9	16.7	1.6	108624
27207	BEAR CREEK	20508	1529	27.1	26.4	40.4	4.0	2.2	46350	50878	52	59	1303	24.2	25.0	34.0	14.7	2.1	91117
27208	BENNETT	20218	828	27.7	26.7	39.0	5.2	1.4	43887	48665	45	49	720	16.8	22.9	46.3	14.0	0.0	105147
27209	BISCOE	17761	1379	29.4	34.4	30.6	3.6	2.0	38935	39706	30	29	1014	23.6	23.2	41.2	11.1	0.9	93708
27212	BLANCH	15910	669	31.2	25.6	34.1	6.6	2.5	43309	45000	43	47	537	12.8	22.0	42.6	21.2	1.3	111970
27214	BROWNS SUMMIT	22994	3427	18.3	29.1	42.4	6.8	3.4	51798	54750	66	76	2536	16.9	18.6	42.2	19.1	3.2	109382
27215	BURLINGTON	28879	16576	18.9	25.9	40.0	9.6	5.7	55057	56951	71	82	10641	9.7	14.2	47.6	26.0	2.5	124556
27217	BURLINGTON	18971	14284	28.9	28.9	36.5	4.5	1.3	41378	45939	37	38	9781	23.2	26.1	42.1	7.4	1.2	90662
27229	CANDOR	15575	1257	34.1	32.5	28.8	2.6	1.9	36741	38026	23	20	972	22.2	29.1	40.4	7.6	0.6	88267
27231	CEDAR GROVE	23696	759	27.7	15.0	44.1	10.0	3.2	54880	57390	71	82	603	15.6	16.7	36.2	25.2	6.3	119778
27233	CLIMAX	21719	1262	19.7	30.3	41.5	6.7	1.8	50000	52317	61	70	1087	14.4	21.7	47.7	13.8	2.3	108101
27235	COLFAX	37475	1343	9.7	20.8	42.3	17.3	10.0	72841	74885	88	94	1129	3.8	6.2	54.9	30.2	4.9	144652
27239	DENTON	19362	3762	26.6	30.4	37.2	4.3	1.5	43926	46845	45	50	3077	18.9	20.1	40.0	17.7	3.3	107786
27242	EAGLE SPRINGS	16662	890	35.5	36.3	25.1	1.5	1.7	33197	34477	14	11	683	27.5	13.5	36.7	17.1	5.1	103555
27243	EFLAND	24475	1722	21.3	24.6	43.4	8.1	2.6	52549	55035	67	77	1405	19.8	15.7	40.6	18.9	5.1	113441
27244	ELON	24259	4401	24.0	24.4	35.2	9.8	6.5	51280	53458	64	74	3346	16.1	14.4	43.5	22.7	3.3	116229
27248	FRANKLINVILLE	20328	1872	24.6	31.9	36.5	5.1	2.0	43706	48047	44	48	1561	22.5	26.3	40.7	9.4	1.0	91277
27249	GIBSONVILLE	26899	4631	17.6	24.7	42.8	9.7	5.2	57279	60479	74	86	3628	8.8	21.9	43.7	23.0	2.6	115602
27252	GOLDSTON	20983	936	28.0	27.8	37.9	4.6	1.7	43616	49307	44	48	781	30.0	26.1	32.9	9.7	1.3	80686
27253	GRAHAM	23959	11404	21.1	27.1	42.2	6.7	2.8	51317	53501	64	74	8057	19.4	17.0	47.5	14.0	2.1	105914
27258	HAW RIVER	22678	2554	21.5	30.2	41.4	4.8	2.1	48109	51372	57	64	2091	32.0	15.1	38.8	13.0	1.1	93805
27260	HIGH POINT	15515	9730	42.2	27.1	26.2	2.9	1.7	31350	33433	10	8	3797	23.4	49.9	25.2	1.2	0.3	71405
27262	HIGH POINT	26517	9735	23.2	28.4	37.0	5.8	5.7	47887	52147	56	64	5861	7.1	30.5	37.8	20.2	4.4	108838
27263	HIGH POINT	22523	8439	21.7	30.8	39.2	6.3	2.0	47503	50749	55	62	5823	12.2	29.2	48.0	10.0	0.7	100669
27265	HIGH POINT	34682	17463	10.8	20.0	44.6	13.9	10.7	69703	70004	87	93	12822	3.0	11.2	51.9	29.8	4.2	140877
27278	HILLSBOROUGH	29601	9320	18.7	21.0	43.8	10.8	5.7	58194	60742	75	87	7022	21.6	11.9	32.0	25.3	9.1	125927
27281	JACKSON SPRINGS	17791	1158	25.6	28.9	35.8	6.9	2.8	46574	47942	53	60	951	18.1	20.4	30.2	26.3	5.0	114302
27282	JAMESTOWN	42814	6087	8.2	13.7	38.3	20.3	19.5	85767	84906	94	98	4615	2.4	4.7	46.7	43.4	2.7	167113
27283	JULIAN	23390	1353	19.7	27.1	43.1	7.0	3.1	52812	56421	68	78	1165	8.0	15.2	53.6	20.4	2.7	120575
27284	KERNERSVILLE	30410	20533	12.9	20.9	46.7	12.6	6.8	64229	65436	83	90	15062	8.0	9.5	48.5	32.1	1.9	142034
27288	EDEN	19643	9978	35.0	28.5	29.7	4.6	2.3	37850	41266	26	24	6999	21.5	35.9	36.0	6.3	0.3	82108
27291	LEASBURG	23568	755	23.7	30.1	36.6	6.0	3.7	46949	47445	54	61	620	6.3	26.0	40.6	24.0	3.1	120161
27292	LEXINGTON	20715	16326	27.8	29.6	34.5	5.5	2.7	42402	45789	41	43	11181	10.6	17.9	41.4	26.3	3.9	132495
27295	LEXINGTON	22566	14963	22.2	28.6	40.2	6.9	2.1	49066	49964	59	67	11689	12.8	9.9	38.8	34.6	3.9	148976
27298	LIBERTY	21236	4119	22.5	27.7	43.0	4.9	1.8	49665	51908	60	69	3286	17.2	20.5	46.7	14.3	1.3	106442
27299	LINWOOD	19837	1898	19.4	35.4	40.1	3.9	1.2	46374	48201	52	59	1520	18.3	14.9	44.6	21.0	1.3	121811
27301	MC LEANSVILLE	23744	2970	18.0	25.3	46.9	6.4	3.3	54924	57963	71	82	2507	15.8	16.4	54.6	12.0	1.3	112734
27302	MEBANE	24018	9950	21.7	25.2	42.0	8.1	3.1	52266	54242	66	76	7569	19.8	15.5	44.1	18.7	1.9	109223
27305	MILTON	17867	500	29.8	22.4	43.8	3.8	0.2	46995	47972	54	61	382	16.8	27.0	48.2	8.1	0.0	97059
27306	MOUNT GILEAD	19778	2433	35.6	26.2	30.9	4.1	3.2	37558	38432	25	22	1954	23.0	20.8	37.5	12.9	5.9	98472
27310	OAK RIDGE	36415	2046	5.9	15.6	42.2	19.6	16.7	82141	82664	93	97	1804	2.1	6.7	35.1	47.4	8.8	192903
27311	PELHAM	20555	1573	26.0	29.5	38.3	4.9	1.3	44862	46148	48	53	1248	16.8	20.6	43.0	16.9	2.6	106385
27312	PITTSBORO	28824	6995	19.4	23.9	41.7	8.9	6.2	57538	59027	75	86	5547	13.2	11.4	36.1	33.4	6.0	149980
27313	PLEASANT GARDEN	25920	2785	14.9	23.0	46.9	11.7	3.4	59631	60376	77	88	2431	9.3	14.2	48.6	26.6	1.4	126717
27314	PROSPECT HILL	20234	355	24.5	32.4	38.6	2.5	2.0	42662	44861	41	44	281	10.7	18.5	52.0	18.5	0.4	115931
27315	PROVIDENCE	21641	790	26.8	26.8	40.6	4.4	1.3	45430	46427	50	56	640	11.1	22.0	45.8	19.2	1.9	111992
27316	RAMSEUR	18712	2825	28.0	28.7	37.7	3.9	1.8	44510	47894	47	52	2186	21.9	23.0	41.1	12.2	1.9	95459
27317	RANDLEMAN	20520	6505	23.6	32.2	37.2	5.0	2.0	44357	48411	46	51	4888	22.9	24.7	40.1	11.9	0.5	93561
27320	REIDSVILLE	21697	15459	27.4	30.0	33.6	6.1	2.9	42985	46647	42	45	11186	16.1	26.7	44.9	11.3	1.0	97818
27325	ROBBINS	17011	2770	33.0	29.0	33.0	3.8	1.2	38456	42378	28	27	2175	24.9	24.9	34.6	14.3	1.2	90417
27326	RUFFIN	19151	1515	26.3	31.6	36.4	5.3	0.4	42751	46172	42	44	1162	12.0	27.8	48.2	10.1	2.0	101716
27330	SANFORD	22480	14367	24.4	27.3	36.1	8.2	4.0	47997	50114	57	64	9835	8.3	12.6	41.5	31.2	6.4	149425
27332	SANFORD	22649	10768	20.3	27.0	41.2	8.5	3.0	52135	52803	66	76	8447	12.8	10.7	43.0	30.1	3.4	143750
	NORTH CAROLINA	25989		22.3	26.1	36.6	9.4	5.6	51418	53634				12.2	15.1	38.7	27.9	6.1	132724
	UNITED STATES	27277		20.9	24.4	35.3	11.7	7.6	54719	56938				9.3	13.1	31.6	32.6	13.5	162279

#	POST OFFICE NAME	FINANCIAL SERVICES				THE HOME						ENTERTAINMENT						PERSONAL			
						Home Improvements		Furnishings													
ZIP CODE		Auto Loan	Home Loan	Investments	Retirement Plans	Home Repair	Lawn & Garden	Computers & Hardware-Personal	Major Appliances	TV, Radio, Sound Equipment	Furniture	Dine out/ Carry out	Sports Equipment	Fees & Tickets	Toys & Games	Travel	Cable TV	Apparel & Services	Auto Repairs	Health Insurance	Pets & Supplies
27006	ADVANCE	122	124	126	126	127	132	114	125	115	117	114	93	116	116	119	117	79	117	125	144
27007	ARARAT	85	65	70	64	65	80	66	75	72	66	71	57	56	75	61	77	48	71	78	91
27009	BELEWS CREEK	98	91	86	93	91	100	88	96	90	84	89	72	83	92	87	93	61	90	97	112
27011	BOONVILLE	92	66	79	64	66	88	69	81	76	66	75	62	55	79	63	83	50	76	85	98
27012	CLEMMONS	129	147	138	148	145	136	131	134	127	137	128	103	141	130	137	124	91	129	126	154
27013	CLEVELAND	91	79	74	76	77	85	76	82	80	79	80	61	70	84	72	83	54	80	83	98
27016	DANBURY	86	62	83	60	63	86	64	79	71	60	70	60	51	72	61	78	46	73	82	94
27017	DOBSON	88	65	77	63	65	85	67	78	73	65	72	60	55	76	62	79	48	74	82	95
27018	EAST BEND	93	75	77	73	74	90	75	84	80	73	79	63	65	83	70	85	53	80	87	101
27019	GERMANTON	89	78	74	77	77	86	75	83	79	75	78	61	69	82	72	83	53	79	84	98
27020	HAMPTONVILLE	95	68	78	66	68	90	71	82	79	69	77	63	57	82	64	86	52	78	87	100
27021	KING	94	85	81	85	84	93	84	90	87	82	86	68	79	89	81	90	59	87	92	106
27022	LAWSONVILLE	87	63	83	61	64	86	65	79	72	61	70	60	52	73	62	79	47	74	83	95
27023	LEWISVILLE	119	134	122	138	132	129	123	124	120	124	121	97	131	122	129	119	85	121	122	146
27024	LOWGAP	79	57	66	56	57	75	59	69	66	58	65	53	48	69	54	72	43	65	73	84
27025	MADISON	85	67	73	66	67	83	69	78	75	67	73	59	59	77	65	80	50	75	82	93
27027	MAYODAN	73	55	61	55	55	71	62	67	67	57	65	51	51	68	56	72	44	66	73	81
27028	MOCKSVILLE	93	74	79	74	74	91	77	85	82	73	81	65	66	84	72	87	55	82	90	102
27030	MOUNT AIRY	82	65	73	64	65	81	67	76	73	65	72	57	58	74	64	78	48	73	81	91
27040	PFAFFTOWN	110	127	118	129	126	127	112	118	111	113	112	90	122	113	121	112	78	113	119	137
27041	PILOT MOUNTAIN	93	72	79	71	73	91	75	85	81	73	80	64	64	83	70	87	54	81	90	101
27042	PINE HALL	74	53	61	52	53	71	56	65	62	54	60	50	45	64	51	67	41	61	68	79
27043	PINNACLE	93	78	77	76	77	89	76	84	81	77	80	63	68	84	72	86	55	81	86	101
27045	RURAL HALL	91	87	82	89	87	96	87	91	89	82	88	69	84	90	86	92	60	89	97	107
27046	SANDY RIDGE	94	67	77	65	67	89	70	81	78	68	76	63	56	81	64	85	51	77	86	99
27047	SILOAM	93	67	77	65	66	88	69	81	77	68	76	62	56	80	63	84	51	77	85	98
27048	STONEVILLE	89	68	78	68	69	89	70	82	77	67	75	62	59	79	66	83	51	77	86	98
27050	TOBACCOVILLE	97	87	83	86	86	96	84	91	88	84	87	68	79	91	82	92	60	88	93	108
27051	WALKERTOWN	92	86	80	83	84	91	81	87	85	82	85	64	77	87	79	88	58	84	90	103
27052	WALNUT COVE	88	69	74	67	68	84	69	78	75	68	74	59	59	78	64	80	50	75	81	95
27053	WESTFIELD	83	61	69	59	60	79	63	73	69	61	68	56	51	72	57	75	46	69	77	88
27054	WOODLEAF	92	68	76	66	67	87	70	80	77	69	75	61	57	80	64	83	51	76	84	97
27055	YADKINVILLE	93	72	81	72	73	93	74	86	80	70	79	66	63	82	71	87	53	81	91	103
27101	WINSTON SALEM	61	48	46	50	46	53	60	54	63	57	63	42	54	62	53	65	44	60	61	67
27103	WINSTON SALEM	95	90	85	92	88	90	97	91	96	95	97	71	94	96	93	96	67	95	94	109
27104	WINSTON SALEM	135	137	141	143	140	134	143	135	140	145	141	105	147	139	144	138	100	140	136	159
27105	WINSTON SALEM	69	61	55	63	58	65	67	64	71	67	71	49	65	71	63	74	49	68	71	79
27106	WINSTON SALEM	112	106	103	110	105	103	118	107	115	116	116	85	115	116	112	113	82	114	108	128
27107	WINSTON SALEM	82	79	70	80	76	81	79	79	80	78	80	60	77	82	76	82	56	79	82	94
27110	WINSTON SALEM	0	0	0	0	0	0	0	0	0	0	0	0	0	0	0	0	0	0	0	0
27127	WINSTON SALEM	90	87	76	87	83	86	89	86	90	88	90	67	87	92	85	90	62	88	88	103
27203	ASHEBORO	74	60	59	61	59	70	69	68	73	64	71	53	61	73	62	76	49	70	74	83
27205	ASHEBORO	97	85	86	84	85	98	83	92	87	81	86	69	76	89	81	92	59	87	95	109
27207	BEAR CREEK	88	68	76	67	68	86	69	80	75	67	74	60	58	77	65	81	50	75	83	96
27208	BENNETT	90	65	84	63	66	89	67	82	74	64	73	62	54	75	64	81	48	76	86	98
27209	BISCOE	88	66	73	64	65	83	67	77	74	67	73	59	56	77	62	80	49	73	81	94
27212	BLANCH	92	65	90	63	67	92	68	84	76	64	74	64	54	76	65	83	49	78	88	101
27214	BROWNS SUMMIT	91	86	77	86	83	86	86	86	86	86	87	67	83	89	83	87	60	86	86	102
27215	BURLINGTON	95	94	89	96	93	97	94	95	95	93	95	72	94	96	94	97	66	95	99	112
27217	BURLINGTON	78	64	66	64	63	77	68	73	72	64	71	56	60	73	63	77	48	72	78	87
27229	CANDOR	81	57	70	56	57	78	60	71	67	58	66	55	48	70	55	73	44	67	75	87
27231	CEDAR GROVE	99	81	92	78	81	97	79	92	85	78	84	68	69	86	77	90	56	87	94	109
27233	CLIMAX	96	77	82	77	77	95	78	88	83	74	82	67	67	86	74	89	55	83	92	105
27235	COLFAX	129	133	118	132	129	126	122	128	118	124	119	99	121	124	122	117	83	119	120	146
27239	DENTON	89	64	73	62	63	84	66	77	73	64	72	59	53	77	60	80	48	73	81	94
27242	EAGLE SPRINGS	79	54	71	52	54	77	57	69	65	55	63	54	44	67	53	71	42	66	73	85
27243	EFLAND	94	83	82	81	82	91	80	88	84	81	84	65	74	87	77	88	57	84	89	104
27244	ELON	102	89	90	92	89	98	99	96	97	92	96	76	88	98	90	98	67	96	96	114
27248	FRANKLINVILLE	90	69	74	67	68	86	70	80	76	70	75	61	59	80	64	82	51	76	83	96
27249	GIBSONVILLE	100	100	92	102	98	107	95	100	96	93	96	77	95	99	96	99	66	97	103	119
27252	GOLDSTON	88	64	86	63	66	89	66	82	73	62	71	62	54	73	65	80	47	76	85	97
27253	GRAHAM	89	82	75	80	80	85	83	84	85	82	85	63	78	87	79	87	58	84	87	100
27258	HAW RIVER	90	76	75	74	75	85	75	82	79	76	78	60	67	82	71	83	53	79	84	97
27260	HIGH POINT	60	48	42	50	45	54	58	53	62	55	61	41	52	62	50	65	42	58	61	66
27262	HIGH POINT	88	85	79	86	83	88	91	87	92	87	91	67	88	91	87	94	64	90	94	104
27263	HIGH POINT	84	74	71	76	72	84	77	79	80	73	79	62	71	81	73	83	54	79	85	96
27265	HIGH POINT	122	127	115	129	124	119	123	120	120	126	121	95	126	124	123	118	85	120	117	141
27278	HILLSBOROUGH	108	103	100	103	101	108	100	105	102	100	102	80	97	104	99	104	70	103	106	124
27281	JACKSON SPRINGS	94	74	96	72	78	97	74	89	81	75	80	64	65	80	74	87	54	84	94	105
27282	JAMESTOWN	157	176	154	178	171	152	156	156	148	168	151	125	167	156	159	141	108	148	138	178
27283	JULIAN	93	84	84	87	85	99	82	93	85	75	84	70	76	87	82	90	57	86	96	108
27284	KERNERSVILLE	107	113	102	113	110	108	107	107	106	109	107	83	110	108	108	105	75	106	105	125
27288	EDEN	76	60	67	60	60	76	64	71	69	60	68	54	56	70	60	74	46	69	77	85
27291	LEASBURG	97	78	84	77	78	95	78	89	84	76	83	67	67	86	74	90	56	84	92	107
27292	LEXINGTON	82	69	68	69	68	80	72	76	76	69	75	58	64	78	67	80	51	75	81	91
27295	LEXINGTON	88	78	76	79	78	89	77	84	81	74	80	64	72	83	75	85	54	81	88	100
27298	LIBERTY	92	74	78	74	74	91	74	85	80	70	78	65	64	82	71	86	53	80	89	101
27299	LINWOOD	92	66	76	65	66	88	69	80	76	67	75	62	56	80	63	83	50	76	85	98
27301	MC LEANSVILLE	93	91	82	91	89	95	86	91	87	85	87	69	83	90	85	90	60	87	92	108
27302	MEBANE	90	86	79	85	84	89	84	87	86	84	86	66	82	88	82	87	59	85	88	103
27305	MILTON	87	62	74	60	61	83	64	76	72	62	70	58	51	74	59	78	47	72	80	92
27306	MOUNT GILEAD	87	63	90	61	65	88	65	81	72	62	70	61	52	72	64	79	47	75	84	97
27310	OAK RIDGE	138	172	163	175	171	157	145	151	138	153	140	117	165	141	160	134	101	143	139	173
27311	PELHAM	90	68	78	66	68	87	69	80	76	67	74	61	57	78	65	82	50	76	84	97
27312	PITTSBORO	99	101	98	102	102	104	95	100	96	97	96	74	97	97	97	98	66	97	102	117
27313	PLEASANT GARDEN	101	102	91	103	100	105	94	100	95	94	95	76	94	98	95	97	66	96	100	118
27314	PROSPECT HILL	83	66	71	66	66	83	67	77	72	63	71	59	57	74	63	78	48	72	80	92
27315	PROVIDENCE	88	67	85	65	68	87	67	81	73	64	72	61	56	74	65	79	48	76	84	97
27316	RAMSEUR	88	64	72	63	64	83	67	77	73	65	72	59	54	77	61	80	49	73	80	93
27317	RANDLEMAN	89	71	73	69	69	84	72	79	77	71	76	61	62	80	67	82	52	77	83	96
27320	REIDSVILLE	86	70	75	70	70	86	74	81	79	70	77	61	65	80	70	84	52	78	86	96
27325	ROBBINS	81	59	64	56	58	74	61	70	68	61	67	52	50	70	56	73	45	67	74	84
27326	RUFFIN	84	61	72	59	61	81	63	74	70	61	69	57	51	72	58	76	46	70	78	90
27330	SANFORD	87	83	75	83	81	86	84	84	86	83	86	64	81	87	81	88	59	85	87	100
27332	SANFORD	95	88	82	85	86	92	84	89	87	87	87	66	81	89	82	90	60	87	91	105
	NORTH CAROLINA	100	89	90	89	88	96	91	94	94	91	93	73	85	95	88	96	64	93	96	112
	UNITED STATES	100	100	100	100	100	100	100	100	100	100	100	100	100	100	100	100	100	100	100	100

ZIP CODE #	POST OFFICE NAME	COUNTY FIPS CODE	POPULATION 2000	POPULATION 2009	POPULATION 2014	2000-2009 ANNUAL RATE % Rate	2000-2009 ANNUAL RATE State Centile	HOUSEHOLDS 2000	HOUSEHOLDS 2009	HOUSEHOLDS 2014	HOUSEHOLDS % Annual Rate 2000-2009	HOUSEHOLDS 2009 Average HH Size	FAMILIES 2000	FAMILIES 2009	FAMILIES % Annual Rate 2000-2009
27341	SEAGROVE	151	5063	5539	5770	1.0	53	1983	2167	2260	1.0	2.56	1500	1599	0.7
27343	SEMORA	145	1936	2083	2135	0.8	44	762	845	874	1.1	2.44	555	596	0.8
27344	SILER CITY	037	16081	19002	20673	1.8	76	5862	6868	7465	1.7	2.74	4240	4854	1.5
27349	SNOW CAMP	001	5114	5850	6279	1.5	69	1952	2255	2423	1.6	2.59	1475	1661	1.3
27350	SOPHIA	151	6369	6782	7004	0.7	40	2427	2597	2686	0.7	2.61	1923	2010	0.5
27355	STALEY	151	1921	1992	2033	0.4	28	752	781	800	0.4	2.55	565	572	0.1
27356	STAR	123	3092	3123	3135	0.1	18	1251	1288	1300	0.3	2.41	877	876	0.0
27357	STOKESDALE	157	6532	7996	8670	2.2	82	2493	3091	3364	2.4	2.57	1903	2303	2.1
27358	SUMMERFIELD	081	9985	12589	13881	2.5	84	3634	4640	5128	2.7	2.71	2927	3657	2.4
27360	THOMASVILLE	057	42087	45059	46335	0.7	40	16795	18084	18637	0.8	2.46	12085	12619	0.5
27370	TRINITY	151	14713	15818	16374	0.8	44	5520	5953	6176	0.8	2.63	4357	4593	0.6
27371	TROY	123	8554	8449	8486	-0.1	13	3120	3194	3226	0.3	2.41	2244	2233	-0.1
27376	WEST END	125	7577	9116	10002	2.0	79	3107	3713	4072	1.9	2.44	2366	2747	1.6
27377	WHITSETT	081	3750	5974	6873	5.2	96	1539	2464	2841	5.2	2.42	1163	1805	4.9
27379	YANCEYVILLE	033	5092	5054	4944	-0.1	13	1962	1969	1937	0.0	2.26	1371	1333	-0.3
27401	GREENSBORO	081	18639	18772	19096	0.1	18	7447	7582	7782	0.2	2.17	3895	3712	-0.5
27403	GREENSBORO	081	19853	20176	20550	0.2	21	8407	8598	8791	0.2	2.23	4044	3887	-0.4
27405	GREENSBORO	081	39521	43729	46310	1.1	56	15994	17804	18893	1.2	2.42	10039	10680	0.7
27406	GREENSBORO	081	50328	54872	57743	0.9	48	19662	21776	23031	1.1	2.44	13639	14563	0.7
27407	GREENSBORO	081	41987	45319	47395	0.8	44	16759	18211	19094	0.9	2.46	10681	11038	0.4
27408	GREENSBORO	081	17021	17346	17877	0.2	21	7813	8094	8364	0.4	2.14	4810	4768	-0.1
27409	GREENSBORO	081	13036	16281	17939	2.4	83	6361	8144	9024	2.7	1.96	2974	3559	2.0
27410	GREENSBORO	081	45304	52588	56497	1.6	72	19410	22959	24813	1.8	2.24	12469	14004	1.3
27411	GREENSBORO	081	1207	1313	1323	0.9	48	0	0	0	0.0	0.00	0	0	0.0
27413	GREENSBORO	081	2913	3156	3156	0.9	48	12	12	12	0.0	3.58	2	2	0.0
27455	GREENSBORO	081	22605	26242	28409	1.6	72	9432	10995	11915	1.7	2.37	6067	6878	1.4
27501	ANGIER	085	13334	16875	19086	2.6	86	5001	6305	7153	2.5	2.62	3567	4362	2.2
27502	APEX	183	18150	29051	35698	5.2	96	6440	10534	13016	5.5	2.75	4950	7767	5.0
27503	BAHAMA	063	3350	3745	4107	1.2	60	1285	1471	1621	1.5	2.47	1017	1134	1.2
27504	BENSON	101	13539	16398	18592	2.1	81	5282	6264	7075	1.9	2.61	3722	4262	1.5
27505	BROADWAY	085	4608	5913	6692	2.7	87	1744	2225	2517	2.7	2.65	1303	1617	2.4
27507	BULLOCK	077	1770	1983	2091	1.2	60	665	769	819	1.6	2.58	503	566	1.3
27508	BUNN	069	1867	2215	2428	1.9	77	578	689	760	1.9	2.93	409	471	1.5
27509	BUTNER	077	9239	11368	11559	2.3	83	1748	1916	2006	1.0	2.50	1214	1287	0.6
27510	CARRBORO	135	13105	14042	14420	0.7	40	6242	6988	7209	1.2	1.99	2495	2591	0.4
27511	CARY	183	31419	34534	37902	1.0	53	12328	13721	15117	1.2	2.50	8389	8806	0.5
27513	CARY	183	36276	44062	51035	2.1	81	13804	16765	19388	2.1	2.62	9050	10353	1.5
27514	CHAPEL HILL	135	30153	29774	30624	-0.1	13	10745	10373	10798	-0.4	2.17	4936	5099	0.4
27516	CHAPEL HILL	135	32139	36590	38179	1.4	66	12082	14261	14951	1.8	2.39	6830	7745	1.4
27517	CHAPEL HILL	037	18281	24545	27380	3.2	89	8086	11400	12792	3.8	2.11	4840	6550	3.3
27518	CARY	183	15147	21016	25100	3.6	91	5107	7145	8552	3.7	2.93	4118	5580	3.3
27519	CARY	183	14407	30143	38494	8.3	99	4818	10209	13085	8.5	2.95	3999	8198	8.1
27520	CLAYTON	101	23391	35116	42445	4.5	94	8831	13166	15901	4.4	2.65	6619	9560	4.1
27521	COATS	085	5402	7076	8072	3.0	88	2082	2711	3093	2.9	2.59	1481	1866	2.5
27522	CREEDMOOR	077	7689	9732	10894	2.6	86	3089	3984	4490	2.8	2.42	2186	2725	2.4
27523	APEX	037	7364	9376	11620	2.6	86	2965	3794	4712	2.7	2.46	2227	2776	2.4
27524	FOUR OAKS	101	9681	12326	14150	2.6	86	3884	4900	5630	2.5	2.49	2699	3266	2.1
27525	FRANKLINTON	069	10382	13984	15867	3.3	90	3945	5374	6113	3.4	2.60	2859	3794	3.1
27526	FUQUAY VARINA	085	23855	37205	45516	4.9	95	8759	13861	17002	5.1	2.67	6653	10045	4.6
27527	CLAYTON	101	8485	17631	22452	8.2	99	2942	6052	7687	8.1	2.91	2374	4712	7.7
27529	GARNER	183	30493	42932	51299	3.8	92	11578	16256	19452	3.7	2.62	8538	11524	3.3
27530	GOLDSBORO	191	37866	38326	38394	0.1	18	14522	15009	15123	0.4	2.39	9772	9865	0.1
27531	GOLDSBORO	191	2192	1524	1433	-3.9	0	343	265	248	-2.8	4.95	327	252	-2.8
27534	GOLDSBORO	191	30582	31023	31420	0.2	21	11834	12520	12780	0.6	2.42	8530	8690	0.2
27536	HENDERSON	181	18165	17326	16875	-0.5	6	7121	6946	6806	-0.3	2.42	4672	4372	-0.7
27537	HENDERSON	181	22211	23684	23939	0.7	40	8124	8864	9023	0.9	2.64	6214	6599	0.7
27539	APEX	183	10510	18041	21976	6.0	97	3908	6793	8301	6.2	2.65	3120	5251	5.8
27540	HOLLY SPRINGS	183	12930	23519	29405	6.7	98	4690	8597	10777	6.8	2.73	3644	6438	6.3
27541	HURDLE MILLS	145	3327	3571	3665	0.8	44	1305	1463	1514	1.2	2.44	981	1066	0.9
27542	KENLY	101	8276	9573	10471	1.6	72	3285	3788	4144	1.6	2.53	2355	2608	1.1
27544	KITTRELL	181	2934	3259	3398	1.1	56	1143	1304	1371	1.4	2.50	901	999	1.1
27545	KNIGHTDALE	183	15769	21912	26033	3.6	91	5792	8136	9689	3.7	2.68	4323	5778	3.2
27546	LILLINGTON	085	16416	21293	23806	2.9	88	5594	7255	8202	2.9	2.62	3857	4836	2.5
27549	LOUISBURG	069	20449	24074	26299	1.8	76	7657	9158	10088	2.0	2.51	5435	6306	1.6
27551	MACON	185	2799	2827	2770	0.1	18	1129	1174	1162	0.4	2.28	800	806	0.1
27553	MANSON	185	2353	2506	2522	0.7	40	890	974	990	1.0	2.57	641	685	0.7
27557	MIDDLESEX	127	6865	7791	8350	1.4	66	2633	2995	3211	1.4	2.60	1922	2105	1.0
27559	MONCURE	037	1847	2331	2630	2.5	84	717	920	1042	2.7	2.52	510	642	2.5
27560	MORRISVILLE	183	6039	19190	24915	13.3	100	2935	8273	10711	11.9	2.32	1886	5751	12.8
27562	NEW HILL	183	1719	1822	2119	0.6	36	656	714	832	0.9	2.55	481	508	0.6
27563	NORLINA	185	3603	3616	3520	0.0	15	1238	1241	1218	0.0	2.46	848	824	-0.3
27565	OXFORD	077	23536	25751	27008	1.0	53	8808	9898	10469	1.3	2.54	6352	6942	1.0
27569	PRINCETON	101	6583	7922	8789	2.0	79	2602	3151	3510	2.1	2.47	1933	2259	1.7
27571	ROLESVILLE	183	1015	2648	3488	10.9	99	385	941	1238	10.1	2.81	305	702	9.4
27572	ROUGEMONT	145	6132	6898	7338	1.3	63	2295	2684	2872	1.7	2.55	1771	2015	1.4
27573	ROXBORO	145	10883	10744	10645	-0.1	13	4574	4614	4604	0.1	2.27	2940	2845	-0.4
27574	ROXBORO	145	13554	14443	14811	0.7	40	5179	5685	5881	1.0	2.52	3897	4154	0.7
27576	SELMA	101	16806	20196	22837	2.0	79	6487	7697	8705	1.9	2.62	4581	5208	1.4
27577	SMITHFIELD	101	18890	22841	25446	2.1	81	7261	8648	9637	1.9	2.49	4726	5414	1.5
27581	STEM	077	2287	2558	2704	1.2	60	864	979	1040	1.4	2.57	670	740	1.1
27583	TIMBERLAKE	145	5271	6392	6813	2.1	81	2021	2532	2726	2.5	2.52	1562	1902	2.2
27587	WAKE FOREST	183	30045	52191	65537	6.2	98	10917	19346	24307	6.4	2.69	8445	14440	6.0
27589	WARRENTON	185	9728	9593	9349	-0.2	10	3723	3774	3718	0.1	2.44	2626	2582	-0.2
27591	WENDELL	183	15287	19764	23123	2.8	87	5692	7433	8724	2.9	2.64	4194	5215	2.4
27592	WILLOW SPRING	183	8660	13281	16076	4.7	95	3231	4983	6044	4.8	2.66	2460	3628	4.3
27596	YOUNGSVILLE	069	9124	12384	14282	3.4	90	3451	4725	5461	3.5	2.62	2582	3436	3.1
27597	ZEBULON	183	17616	21205	23949	2.0	79	6647	8065	9133	2.1	2.61	4848	5623	1.6
27601	RALEIGH	183	9727	10056	10549	0.4	28	3359	3459	3672	0.3	2.42	1767	1641	-0.8
27603	RALEIGH	183	32351	42215	49187	2.9	88	13016	16947	19825	2.9	2.43	7848	9793	2.4
27604	RALEIGH	183	32249	39372	45261	2.2	82	13424	16514	19021	2.3	2.35	8275	9602	1.6
27605	RALEIGH	183	3933	4170	4523	0.6	36	2289	2470	2691	0.8	1.60	547	512	-0.7
27606	RALEIGH	183	40932	47612	53957	1.6	72	14251	17726	20471	2.4	2.32	6408	7296	1.4
27607	RALEIGH	183	18572	22135	24236	1.9	77	7274	8658	9740	1.9	2.09	3620	3904	0.8
27608	RALEIGH	183	9962	10515	11360	0.6	36	5007	5351	5811	0.7	1.91	2426	2363	-0.3
27609	RALEIGH	183	32711	36323	40090	1.1	56	14604	16438	18206	1.3	2.21	8396	8720	0.4
	NORTH CAROLINA					1.7					1.8	2.46			1.5
	UNITED STATES					1.0					1.1	2.59			0.9

#	POST OFFICE NAME	RACE (%) White 2000	White 2009	Black 2000	Black 2009	Asian/Pacific 2000	Asian/Pacific 2009	% Hispanic Origin 2000	% Hispanic Origin 2009	2009 AGE DISTRIBUTION (%) 0-4	5-9	10-14	15-19	20-24	25-44	45-64	65-84	85+	18+	MEDIAN AGE 2009	% 2009 Males	% 2009 Females
27341	SEAGROVE	91.8	90.0	5.9	6.6	0.2	0.3	2.0	3.1	6.5	6.6	6.8	6.3	5.2	26.7	28.6	12.0	1.3	76.3	39.5	50.1	49.9
27343	SEMORA	55.8	54.6	42.1	43.1	0.3	0.3	2.2	2.5	5.2	5.6	6.0	6.0	4.8	23.3	34.7	12.9	1.4	79.2	44.3	50.6	49.4
27344	SILER CITY	64.0	56.8	19.0	17.2	0.5	0.6	22.3	32.7	7.1	6.5	6.3	6.6	6.7	28.1	25.5	11.5	1.7	76.2	37.0	50.6	49.4
27349	SNOW CAMP	91.2	89.2	6.3	6.9	0.2	0.2	2.4	4.1	6.4	6.6	7.0	6.7	5.1	26.7	29.7	10.5	1.3	75.9	39.8	50.9	49.1
27350	SOPHIA	96.6	95.6	1.2	1.3	0.3	0.4	1.2	1.9	5.9	6.3	6.9	6.6	5.2	27.3	31.2	9.5	1.0	76.7	40.0	51.0	49.0
27355	STALEY	85.5	82.0	9.9	10.6	0.2	0.3	5.1	8.2	6.0	6.2	6.9	6.6	5.0	25.9	30.2	11.7	1.5	76.8	40.7	51.6	48.4
27356	STAR	92.1	89.4	3.6	3.7	0.4	0.5	5.2	8.2	6.6	6.8	6.8	6.0	5.1	28.2	27.4	11.5	1.6	76.3	38.2	50.1	49.9
27357	STOKESDALE	91.8	89.7	5.3	6.1	0.3	0.6	2.6	3.9	6.8	7.3	7.5	6.4	4.4	28.1	28.8	9.4	1.3	74.1	39.1	50.3	49.7
27358	SUMMERFIELD	92.8	90.5	4.4	5.3	0.6	0.9	1.7	2.8	6.0	6.8	7.5	7.1	4.2	25.8	32.1	9.5	0.9	75.1	40.5	49.5	50.5
27360	THOMASVILLE	84.2	81.6	11.9	12.3	0.5	0.8	3.8	6.0	6.9	6.7	6.7	6.3	5.3	27.0	26.9	12.2	2.0	75.9	39.1	48.4	51.6
27370	TRINITY	95.1	94.1	3.0	3.2	0.5	0.7	0.9	1.4	6.2	6.4	6.7	6.2	4.9	26.9	30.6	10.8	1.4	76.8	40.6	49.6	50.4
27371	TROY	74.9	71.9	19.3	19.6	1.8	2.5	4.5	6.9	6.2	6.3	6.5	6.0	5.4	28.7	26.2	12.6	1.9	77.1	38.5	53.0	47.0
27376	WEST END	81.7	80.5	15.9	16.3	0.3	0.4	1.4	2.1	4.6	4.8	5.4	5.5	3.9	19.3	31.3	22.4	2.8	81.6	49.5	48.6	51.4
27377	WHITSETT	88.1	86.3	9.4	10.8	0.2	0.3	1.3	1.8	6.2	6.5	6.7	6.3	5.0	26.2	29.6	12.2	1.3	76.7	40.5	50.1	49.9
27379	YANCEYVILLE	51.2	50.7	46.5	46.9	0.1	0.1	1.4	1.5	5.5	5.6	6.0	6.2	6.2	27.5	28.2	12.7	2.3	79.1	40.3	53.0	47.0
27401	GREENSBORO	23.1	21.4	71.9	71.8	1.1	1.4	3.7	5.2	5.8	5.5	5.4	12.9	11.7	24.9	21.6	10.1	2.1	79.7	31.6	46.9	53.1
27403	GREENSBORO	72.3	67.9	18.5	19.3	4.1	5.6	4.9	7.1	5.1	4.6	4.6	7.5	17.4	28.7	22.4	7.9	1.8	82.9	31.4	48.9	51.1
27405	GREENSBORO	42.4	39.5	50.5	50.7	2.1	2.7	5.4	7.7	7.3	6.8	6.5	6.9	8.0	28.7	23.7	10.3	1.8	75.3	34.5	48.0	52.0
27406	GREENSBORO	41.8	39.5	53.4	53.9	1.4	1.8	2.5	3.8	6.5	6.7	6.6	7.1	6.3	26.6	26.8	11.6	1.7	76.2	38.0	46.6	53.4
27407	GREENSBORO	63.0	57.7	25.1	25.9	5.8	7.9	6.8	9.4	7.2	6.5	6.1	6.0	7.7	32.9	23.2	9.0	1.5	76.7	34.4	49.2	50.8
27408	GREENSBORO	87.6	84.6	9.3	10.6	1.0	1.5	2.3	3.6	5.8	6.0	6.2	5.2	4.6	25.0	29.0	15.5	2.8	78.8	43.3	47.8	52.2
27409	GREENSBORO	70.6	65.8	22.0	24.1	2.9	3.9	5.3	7.3	5.3	4.7	4.6	5.4	11.2	37.7	22.0	7.3	1.9	82.4	33.2	49.5	50.5
27410	GREENSBORO	85.4	81.9	9.4	10.8	2.7	4.0	2.4	3.6	5.6	5.4	5.7	6.3	7.3	26.6	28.1	12.3	2.6	79.5	39.8	48.1	51.9
27411	GREENSBORO	0.7	0.5	97.4	97.0	0.1	0.2	1.2	1.5	0.3	0.2	0.4	59.3	33.7	3.4	1.8	0.7	0.2	98.7	19.1	48.4	51.6
27413	GREENSBORO	63.3	57.9	31.8	35.3	2.6	3.7	2.1	3.1	0.1	0.0	0.0	60.5	37.1	2.1	0.1	0.0	0.0	99.6	19.1	29.3	70.7
27455	GREENSBORO	77.8	74.0	18.7	21.0	1.4	2.0	2.3	3.3	6.7	6.6	6.6	6.1	5.6	28.9	28.1	9.9	1.4	76.4	38.4	47.9	52.1
27501	ANGIER	77.9	74.0	13.6	13.4	0.6	0.8	10.4	14.9	7.8	7.6	7.4	6.8	5.7	31.5	24.0	8.1	0.9	73.3	35.3	50.1	49.9
27502	APEX	80.9	76.9	12.0	12.4	3.3	5.1	3.8	6.1	9.6	9.1	8.6	6.3	3.9	35.4	22.3	4.4	0.5	68.5	34.5	49.9	50.1
27503	BAHAMA	83.9	80.3	13.4	15.8	0.7	1.0	1.9	3.2	4.6	5.5	6.6	6.5	3.7	22.3	35.6	13.1	2.0	78.9	45.4	49.7	50.3
27504	BENSON	81.9	78.2	11.9	12.4	0.3	0.4	6.3	9.9	7.6	7.4	7.1	6.2	5.0	29.8	25.7	10.0	1.3	74.3	37.0	49.5	50.5
27505	BROADWAY	79.5	76.4	15.1	15.7	0.2	0.3	6.8	9.8	7.1	7.1	7.0	6.6	5.9	28.0	27.1	10.1	1.2	74.8	37.3	50.3	49.7
27507	BULLOCK	54.2	50.7	43.3	45.4	0.2	0.2	2.9	4.1	6.4	6.5	6.9	6.8	5.5	25.2	28.9	12.4	1.4	76.0	40.0	48.6	51.4
27508	BUNN	53.6	50.2	41.8	43.4	0.4	0.5	5.8	8.1	6.6	6.5	6.5	7.1	7.9	30.8	26.0	7.6	1.0	76.2	34.7	53.5	46.5
27509	BUTNER	49.9	45.8	43.2	45.0	0.7	1.0	6.5	9.2	3.4	3.4	3.8	7.0	12.6	42.3	21.4	5.6	0.6	85.7	34.1	73.2	26.8
27510	CARRBORO	70.1	65.1	15.6	15.1	5.1	6.6	12.9	17.8	5.0	4.6	4.4	5.2	15.7	41.9	17.7	4.5	0.9	83.1	30.0	50.5	49.5
27511	CARY	83.0	78.8	7.1	7.3	4.7	6.3	7.4	10.6	5.6	5.6	5.8	6.3	6.3	29.8	28.8	10.3	1.4	79.0	38.4	49.7	50.3
27513	CARY	79.2	73.9	7.3	7.6	10.1	13.9	3.3	4.9	8.0	7.4	7.2	6.1	6.6	37.3	23.3	3.7	0.4	73.5	33.1	49.9	50.1
27514	CHAPEL HILL	79.1	75.1	10.1	9.1	7.3	10.7	3.1	5.0	3.4	3.4	4.0	17.1	22.3	20.9	19.7	7.8	1.3	83.2	24.9	44.8	55.2
27516	CHAPEL HILL	79.7	76.7	13.0	12.9	3.9	5.8	3.9	5.6	5.0	5.2	5.6	9.0	13.8	28.7	25.1	6.5	1.1	80.6	32.0	48.6	51.4
27517	CHAPEL HILL	82.8	79.3	8.9	9.6	5.0	6.2	3.9	6.2	4.8	4.6	4.9	4.9	6.9	27.6	28.0	15.3	2.9	82.6	42.2	47.4	52.6
27518	CARY	87.6	83.4	3.2	3.5	7.4	10.6	1.6	2.4	7.2	7.6	8.4	8.0	4.6	27.3	30.4	5.9	0.5	71.5	36.3	48.8	51.2
27519	CARY	84.3	80.1	5.2	6.3	8.2	10.1	2.5	4.0	10.3	10.4	9.4	6.5	2.9	33.6	23.1	3.6	0.3	65.6	34.0	49.9	50.1
27520	CLAYTON	78.9	75.0	15.3	16.3	0.6	0.7	6.4	9.8	8.6	7.9	7.3	6.1	5.2	33.7	23.6	6.9	0.7	73.1	34.3	49.5	50.5
27521	COATS	81.6	78.3	11.9	11.9	0.5	0.6	9.8	14.0	7.1	6.8	6.7	6.7	6.4	29.5	25.5	10.0	1.2	75.5	36.0	49.9	50.1
27522	CREEDMOOR	77.3	74.9	19.7	20.8	0.4	0.5	2.0	3.2	7.0	7.0	7.0	6.3	4.7	29.3	27.4	9.9	1.2	75.0	38.2	49.7	50.3
27523	APEX	85.2	80.9	7.8	8.2	4.3	6.9	2.8	4.4	9.1	9.2	8.5	5.9	2.9	33.3	23.6	5.9	1.5	69.1	36.4	49.4	50.6
27524	FOUR OAKS	83.1	78.3	9.5	10.4	0.2	0.3	10.2	15.4	7.0	7.1	7.1	6.2	5.2	28.5	26.9	10.5	1.4	75.5	37.7	50.5	49.5
27525	FRANKLINTON	61.4	60.2	33.3	32.2	0.4	0.5	5.2	7.4	7.5	7.4	7.3	6.4	5.2	29.2	26.9	9.0	1.0	73.9	36.7	50.0	50.0
27526	FUQUAY VARINA	79.7	76.0	15.7	16.8	0.5	0.8	5.5	8.8	7.8	7.7	7.6	6.8	5.1	30.1	25.8	8.0	1.1	72.7	36.2	49.4	50.6
27527	CLAYTON	79.5	75.4	13.9	13.6	0.5	0.7	7.1	12.1	9.3	8.7	8.0	6.2	4.7	34.0	22.8	5.7	0.5	70.1	33.4	50.7	49.3
27529	GARNER	70.6	66.7	24.4	26.2	0.8	1.0	4.5	6.8	7.5	7.3	7.2	6.4	5.4	30.8	26.0	8.3	1.0	74.4	36.4	49.0	51.0
27530	GOLDSBORO	53.0	52.5	43.7	42.9	0.7	1.0	2.4	3.5	6.9	6.8	6.5	6.3	6.0	27.2	26.4	12.2	1.6	76.1	38.0	48.9	51.1
27531	GOLDSBORO	68.8	64.4	22.4	23.5	2.1	2.9	6.3	8.8	14.6	9.8	7.4	5.9	19.7	39.1	3.2	0.3	0.0	65.9	23.1	56.0	44.0
27534	GOLDSBORO	65.9	62.1	27.8	29.1	2.0	2.8	4.1	5.9	6.6	6.3	6.3	6.4	7.2	27.6	26.7	11.6	1.3	77.2	37.2	49.4	50.6
27536	HENDERSON	39.0	38.4	56.8	55.4	0.7	0.9	5.5	7.8	7.2	7.1	6.8	7.1	6.7	24.3	24.5	13.2	2.9	74.6	37.5	46.1	53.9
27537	HENDERSON	55.2	51.9	41.7	43.5	0.2	0.3	4.1	5.9	6.6	6.6	6.9	7.9	6.4	27.5	27.1	9.9	1.0	75.1	36.8	49.3	50.7
27539	APEX	83.9	81.0	11.0	11.8	1.8	2.5	4.0	5.3	7.6	7.9	8.4	7.5	4.8	28.5	29.3	5.5	0.5	71.1	36.4	50.3	49.7
27540	HOLLY SPRINGS	76.6	74.4	18.9	19.3	1.1	1.4	3.2	4.9	9.3	9.1	8.6	6.5	4.2	33.4	23.7	4.8	0.5	68.8	34.8	49.8	50.2
27541	HURDLE MILLS	79.9	77.9	16.8	17.3	0.1	0.2	3.4	5.0	5.4	5.9	6.4	6.2	4.5	26.4	32.1	11.8	1.3	78.5	41.9	50.7	49.3
27542	KENLY	78.6	74.0	16.4	18.1	0.1	0.2	6.5	10.1	6.1	6.5	6.7	6.5	5.0	26.5	29.5	11.8	1.5	76.9	40.0	49.9	50.1
27544	KITTRELL	58.8	55.4	39.8	42.7	0.1	0.2	1.3	1.9	6.4	6.5	7.1	7.1	5.3	26.1	29.6	10.7	1.1	75.5	39.2	48.5	51.5
27545	KNIGHTDALE	66.7	61.0	26.1	27.7	1.1	1.5	6.9	11.1	8.3	7.9	7.7	6.7	5.2	33.9	23.9	5.8	0.7	71.8	34.1	49.3	50.7
27546	LILLINGTON	69.7	67.1	24.7	24.8	0.8	1.2	5.0	7.4	6.3	6.1	6.1	8.6	9.6	29.7	22.8	9.5	1.4	77.7	34.1	51.1	48.9
27549	LOUISBURG	61.3	58.6	35.3	36.6	0.3	0.4	4.1	5.9	6.0	6.2	6.6	7.4	6.0	25.9	28.1	11.7	2.0	77.3	39.5	48.9	51.1
27551	MACON	47.9	46.8	44.0	44.8	0.1	0.1	1.2	1.2	3.7	5.0	5.3	6.2	4.8	23.0	33.3	16.8	1.9	81.9	46.3	50.7	49.3
27553	MANSON	25.7	24.5	71.7	72.3	0.0	0.0	3.1	3.6	5.9	5.9	6.4	7.3	5.9	24.1	29.7	13.0	1.7	77.3	40.7	46.3	53.7
27557	MIDDLESEX	67.4	62.7	25.2	26.0	0.2	0.2	9.8	14.5	7.6	7.4	7.2	7.1	6.2	27.7	26.1	9.7	1.0	73.3	35.8	49.4	50.6
27559	MONCURE	70.0	66.5	25.2	26.8	0.5	0.6	2.9	4.8	5.8	6.0	6.6	6.4	4.8	25.6	32.6	10.7	1.5	77.6	41.8	50.4	49.6
27560	MORRISVILLE	81.4	76.5	7.8	8.5	7.8	10.9	2.8	4.5	8.4	7.5	7.1	6.5	7.2	33.6	24.5	4.9	0.4	73.2	33.0	50.0	50.0
27562	NEW HILL	83.1	79.5	12.3	13.5	1.0	1.4	4.2	7.0	8.2	8.2	7.8	5.8	4.1	29.4	26.9	8.4	1.1	71.9	37.5	50.5	49.5
27563	NORLINA	43.1	41.2	54.9	56.6	0.2	0.2	1.4	1.4	4.7	4.9	5.3	6.3	8.7	30.0	25.9	12.1	2.0	81.2	37.8	55.0	45.0
27565	OXFORD	53.9	50.7	42.0	43.1	0.3	0.4	4.2	6.3	6.0	6.4	7.0	7.0	5.1	24.5	28.9	13.1	2.0	76.2	40.8	48.4	51.6
27569	PRINCETON	85.8	82.7	11.3	12.7	0.2	0.2	3.3	5.2	6.5	6.6	6.7	6.3	5.1	27.9	28.2	11.3	1.4	76.4	38.7	49.6	50.4
27571	ROLESVILLE	78.4	66.9	18.2	28.0	0.6	1.1	2.9	4.6	7.3	7.2	7.4	7.5	5.4	28.9	27.6	8.0	0.8	73.5	36.3	50.2	49.8
27572	ROUGEMONT	83.4	80.6	13.8	15.2	0.3	0.5	2.2	3.6	5.5	6.0	6.7	6.4	4.3	25.8	33.2	10.8	1.3	77.6	42.0	49.7	50.3
27573	ROXBORO	54.4	51.3	41.7	43.3	0.2	0.3	2.9	4.4	6.5	6.3	6.3	6.1	6.0	25.1	26.6	14.2	2.9	77.2	40.2	46.0	54.0
27574	ROXBORO	70.9	68.3	26.4	28.0	0.1	0.2	1.5	2.4	5.7	6.1	6.5	6.2	4.7	25.5	31.0	12.7	1.7	77.7	41.8	49.6	50.4
27576	SELMA	68.3	64.8	22.6	21.9	0.2	0.2	12.4	17.4	7.2	7.0	7.1	6.6	5.5	28.2	26.3	10.6	1.4	74.7	37.1	49.7	50.3
27577	SMITHFIELD	71.7	69.1	22.2	21.7	0.5	0.8	8.3	12.2	6.4	6.2	6.2	6.3	6.1	27.5	26.2	12.9	2.3	78.1	38.9	49.8	50.2
27581	STEM	83.4	80.0	12.9	14.5	0.3	0.5	3.2	5.1	6.3	6.5	6.9	7.2	5.4	28.2	30.5	8.4	0.7	75.9	38.6	52.1	47.9
27583	TIMBERLAKE	81.9	80.2	15.6	16.2	0.2	0.3	1.3	2.0	6.6	6.9	7.2	6.6	4.6	27.7	30.2	9.3	1.0	75.2	39.4	49.7	50.3
27587	WAKE FOREST	83.7	81.0	12.3	13.1	1.3	1.7	2.7	4.5	8.3	8.1	8.0	6.9	5.1	30.7	26.0	6.1	0.7	71.1	34.6	49.5	50.5
27589	WARRENTON	30.5	29.2	61.4	62.1	0.1	0.1	1.7	1.8	6.3	6.4	6.5	6.7	5.7	23.2	28.1	14.1	2.9	76.5	41.3	48.1	51.9
27591	WENDELL	71.7	68.4	23.1	23.7	0.5	0.6	5.7	8.9	7.4	7.6	7.6	7.1	5.8	28.9	26.6	8.0	1.1	73.0	36.1	49.1	50.9
27592	WILLOW SPRING	86.5	82.4	8.4	9.3	0.4	0.5	5.2	8.6	8.4	8.1	7.8	6.5	4.8	33.3	24.7	6.0	0.5	71.7	34.9	50.3	49.7
27596	YOUNGSVILLE	83.4	80.5	12.5	13.4	0.5	0.6	4.4	6.5	8.2	8.1	7.8	6.1	4.5	30.8	26.6	7.1	0.7	72.0	36.1	49.8	50.2
27597	ZEBULON	70.3	67.0	24.7	25.3	0.4	0.6	6.5	9.9	7.1	7.1	7.3	6.8	5.3	27.9	27.9	9.3	1.2	74.2	37.6	49.7	50.3
27601	RALEIGH	14.3	14.3	80.5	78.4	0.5	0.6	5.7	8.0	8.1	7.4	6.2	10.3	12.5	25.6	19.6	8.7	1.6	74.2	28.6	47.1	52.9
27603	RALEIGH	69.8	65.6	22.1	22.6	1.6	2.1	7.8	11.5	6.9	6.5	6.2	6.3	8.8	32.4	24.7	7.4	0.8	77.0	34.2	51.5	48.5
27604	RALEIGH	57.6	53.5	32.1	31.9	4.0	5.4	7.2	10.4	7.5	6.8	6.2	6.3	7.4	33.6	23.7	7.6	0.9	76.0	35.1	48.8	51.2
27605	RALEIGH	88.8	86.2	7.4	8.5	1.4	2.0	1.7	2.7	2.4	1.8	1.6	2.8	11.2	45.1	23.4	9.5	2.3	92.9	35.7	51.2	48.8
27606	RALEIGH	73.9	69.0	14.5	14.3	5.9	8.1	6.8	10.1	4.6	4.1	4.0	9.4	22.9	29.5	18.9	5.8	0.7	84.0	27.3	54.5	45.5
27607	RALEIGH	82.3	77.3	9.1	10.9	5.0	6.8	3.9	5.5	4.2	3.8	3.9	10.7	15.0	29.3	22.0	9.0	2.2	84.9	32.6	49.1	50.9
27608	RALEIGH	91.4	89.4	5.8	6.2	0.9	1.2	2.4	3.9	5.5	4.9	5.1	4.4	5.7	31.9	27.1	11.5	4.0	81.8	40.2	46.1	53.9
27609	RALEIGH	76.9	72.3	14.9	15.6	2.5	3.4	9.0	13.0	5.8	5.2	5.0	5.3	8.1	31.3	25.4	12.2	1.7	81.1	37.4	49.0	51.0
	NORTH CAROLINA	72.1	69.8	21.6	21.5	1.5	2.1	4.7	6.9	6.6	6.5	6.5	6.8	6.9	27.7	26.5	10.9	1.6	76.5	37.4	49.3	50.7
	UNITED STATES	75.1	72.0	12.3	12.7	3.8	4.6	12.5	15.7	6.8	6.7	6.6	7.1	6.9	27.0	26.0	10.9	1.9	75.7	36.9	49.2	50.8

#	ZIP CODE POST OFFICE NAME	2009 Per Capita Income	2009 HH Income Base	2009 Household Income Distribution (%) Less than $25,000	$25,000 to $49,999	$50,000 to $99,999	$100,000 to $149,999	$150,000 or More	Median Household Income 2009	2014	2009 National Centile	2009 State Centile	2009 Home Value Base	2009 Home Value Distribution (%) Less than $50,000	$50,000 to $89,999	$90,000 to $174,999	$175,000 to $399,999	$400,000 or More	2009 Median Home Value
27341	SEAGROVE	19074	2167	26.3	29.4	38.9	4.3	1.1	45501	48720	50	56	1872	25.5	21.3	38.6	12.8	1.8	94688
27343	SEMORA	21921	845	30.7	30.1	31.4	5.2	2.7	40566	42745	35	35	693	12.4	21.2	43.6	20.1	2.7	106287
27344	SILER CITY	18847	6868	27.3	29.9	35.4	5.1	2.3	43613	47328	44	48	5037	24.1	24.2	36.5	12.1	3.1	92158
27349	SNOW CAMP	21159	2255	19.3	29.3	43.3	6.7	1.4	50894	52954	63	73	1987	21.2	19.9	42.1	13.8	2.9	99750
27350	SOPHIA	20787	2597	20.9	30.9	40.4	6.2	1.5	48171	50671	57	64	2216	22.2	18.1	46.6	12.0	1.1	102165
27355	STALEY	20163	781	23.2	26.0	46.5	3.3	1.0	50461	51717	62	71	650	18.9	26.0	43.1	8.6	3.4	97674
27356	STAR	19446	1288	31.3	29.9	33.9	3.4	1.6	39631	41335	32	31	1007	27.3	19.0	37.5	14.4	1.8	95597
27357	STOKESDALE	23941	3091	15.2	26.5	48.0	8.0	2.3	55178	56557	71	83	2540	18.0	11.5	54.8	13.6	2.0	114400
27358	SUMMERFIELD	33403	4640	13.6	17.5	38.3	17.8	12.8	75533	74825	90	95	3976	6.7	9.1	39.3	35.6	9.3	161579
27360	THOMASVILLE	21473	18084	25.5	29.5	37.0	5.8	2.3	44758	47358	48	52	12310	11.2	14.0	49.0	24.0	1.8	129504
27370	TRINITY	21908	5953	18.8	29.0	43.4	6.4	2.3	51689	52583	65	75	5005	16.4	16.4	51.7	14.0	1.4	110927
27371	TROY	20904	3194	32.0	26.8	33.3	5.1	2.9	41459	42958	38	38	2298	12.4	22.6	39.7	20.9	4.4	114150
27376	WEST END	28688	3713	14.7	27.0	44.7	7.6	6.0	58019	58891	75	87	3247	8.6	9.4	25.6	42.5	13.9	193818
27377	WHITSETT	25493	2464	19.3	27.8	41.1	7.0	4.9	52082	55388	66	76	2078	16.5	19.2	42.8	19.3	2.2	110014
27379	YANCEYVILLE	19509	1969	35.4	28.3	30.0	4.3	1.9	37164	39654	24	21	1417	14.8	23.6	45.0	15.6	0.9	107284
27401	GREENSBORO	19122	7582	36.2	32.9	25.1	3.7	2.1	32815	34539	13	10	2861	8.8	44.7	33.2	12.0	1.2	86979
27403	GREENSBORO	27696	8598	24.3	28.2	33.5	7.7	6.4	46432	51270	53	60	4371	3.2	30.9	39.4	23.9	2.6	112943
27405	GREENSBORO	21700	17804	26.7	31.6	33.8	5.0	2.8	41649	45633	38	39	9242	13.0	37.1	41.6	6.1	2.3	89958
27406	GREENSBORO	24003	21776	21.2	28.1	40.0	7.4	3.2	50523	54438	62	72	14216	11.1	22.7	52.3	13.3	0.6	105725
27407	GREENSBORO	29273	18211	15.4	25.0	43.5	9.5	6.7	59769	62252	77	88	9867	3.0	17.6	58.4	17.5	3.5	118607
27408	GREENSBORO	43348	8094	13.6	23.6	38.2	9.7	14.9	64360	66281	83	90	5796	0.3	11.4	48.3	26.9	13.0	146448
27409	GREENSBORO	32997	8144	13.2	33.2	40.6	8.1	4.9	52704	56287	67	77	3825	4.0	33.8	44.3	14.1	3.9	106665
27410	GREENSBORO	41804	22959	9.2	18.9	40.7	16.6	14.6	75882	75266	90	95	14790	0.8	3.6	47.8	42.6	5.3	170742
27411	GREENSBORO	12353	0	0.0	0.0	0.0	0.0	0.0	0	0	0	0	0	0.0	0.0	0.0	0.0	0.0	0
27413	GREENSBORO	13777	12	0.0	8.3	91.7	0.0	0.0	62143	62143	80	89	0	0.0	0.0	0.0	0.0	0.0	0
27455	GREENSBORO	35403	10995	11.7	21.3	43.9	13.0	10.2	67086	68182	85	92	7567	1.7	8.7	54.3	28.6	6.8	143872
27501	ANGIER	21686	6305	21.6	27.1	41.8	6.4	3.0	50966	51987	63	73	4554	13.3	10.3	41.0	31.1	4.4	149881
27502	APEX	39221	10534	6.5	11.2	35.8	29.2	17.4	93911	103514	96	99	8218	10.7	4.4	12.3	65.2	7.4	227370
27503	BAHAMA	39396	1471	8.8	15.7	44.2	15.0	16.3	75520	78147	90	95	1263	3.5	4.1	24.3	47.3	20.8	228791
27504	BENSON	20435	6264	26.1	29.4	36.5	5.8	2.2	44016	48501	45	50	4382	19.6	19.7	40.1	18.4	2.3	108543
27505	BROADWAY	20818	2225	21.8	32.7	38.1	5.7	1.8	45322	47444	49	55	1796	19.0	14.6	38.6	24.0	3.7	127594
27507	BULLOCK	18483	769	30.3	33.0	31.9	3.3	1.6	38732	41788	29	28	636	15.1	20.0	46.4	16.8	1.7	110047
27508	BUNN	17600	689	29.6	22.5	40.6	6.1	1.2	47463	50887	55	62	515	31.1	25.0	33.6	9.1	1.2	82500
27509	BUTNER	19097	1916	19.8	25.2	41.8	8.7	4.5	53698	53904	69	80	1314	25.0	11.5	38.3	25.1	0.2	128993
27510	CARRBORO	26820	6988	30.4	27.8	30.3	7.7	3.8	39716	43468	32	32	1943	3.6	13.5	40.1	40.6	2.2	163297
27511	CARY	38572	13721	8.0	18.4	37.5	22.5	13.5	79076	83457	92	96	9249	4.2	1.0	22.1	61.1	11.5	217832
27513	CARY	42132	16765	5.5	14.1	33.5	28.7	18.2	94421	103379	96	99	10024	0.7	1.9	15.1	67.7	14.6	242804
27514	CHAPEL HILL	35860	10373	24.8	19.5	28.1	9.3	18.3	56739	60401	74	85	5028	5.8	3.5	17.5	50.6	22.5	258333
27516	CHAPEL HILL	32720	14261	21.7	19.3	34.2	12.9	11.9	58902	62146	76	87	8581	8.4	6.9	30.5	43.9	10.3	189193
27517	CHAPEL HILL	48230	11400	12.9	16.9	39.2	16.3	14.7	75273	76199	89	95	7422	6.5	2.2	23.2	46.5	21.6	234340
27518	CARY	54916	7145	4.1	7.2	21.1	29.3	38.4	130238	132829	99	100	5759	0.3	0.7	4.5	54.3	40.1	369398
27519	CARY	49298	10209	4.9	8.5	24.1	28.0	34.6	125985	126950	99	100	8096	1.5	2.2	6.7	61.8	27.8	309512
27520	CLAYTON	27143	13166	14.1	20.0	48.5	12.3	5.1	65807	66212	84	91	10272	15.4	8.1	39.6	34.9	2.0	150129
27521	COATS	20250	2711	27.8	27.6	37.4	5.1	2.1	43154	46426	43	46	1853	16.6	13.1	43.2	22.7	4.5	132227
27522	CREEDMOOR	25774	3984	20.5	25.7	40.3	10.3	3.3	53899	54513	69	80	3019	13.3	10.1	35.8	35.1	5.6	156350
27523	APEX	46618	3794	5.8	10.0	34.8	29.0	20.4	98817	104414	97	99	2940	7.4	2.6	10.0	69.0	11.0	257228
27524	FOUR OAKS	20278	4900	29.2	27.2	36.7	5.3	1.6	42512	46557	41	43	3320	21.8	24.8	35.9	16.7	0.9	96230
27525	FRANKLINTON	22778	5374	23.1	24.0	41.3	8.5	3.1	52987	54917	68	79	4248	21.9	19.4	34.3	22.2	2.3	104096
27526	FUQUAY VARINA	27528	13861	14.5	23.6	40.0	16.0	5.8	62164	60937	80	89	10614	9.7	7.7	33.1	43.2	6.3	173958
27527	CLAYTON	28971	6052	8.5	17.0	50.3	16.1	8.1	76887	77304	91	96	5415	4.9	13.1	33.7	42.0	6.3	170637
27529	GARNER	28777	16256	11.4	22.1	42.4	18.9	5.2	67252	67833	85	92	12476	11.1	7.5	42.6	37.0	1.9	158053
27530	GOLDSBORO	20793	15009	31.2	28.7	31.0	6.1	3.0	39918	43453	32	33	9018	14.7	24.0	51.3	9.7	0.3	101234
27531	GOLDSBORO	10316	265	11.7	52.5	31.3	4.2	0.4	42187	44585	40	42	9	77.8	0.0	22.2	0.0	0.0	24375
27534	GOLDSBORO	25448	12520	19.3	29.2	39.7	7.8	4.0	51217	53444	64	74	7726	17.0	18.4	47.9	14.7	2.0	108520
27536	HENDERSON	18933	6946	42.3	26.5	23.5	4.3	3.4	30067	33113	8	5	3375	13.4	21.8	41.1	19.6	4.2	112056
27537	HENDERSON	19656	8864	26.2	30.7	35.2	5.7	2.2	43781	45930	45	49	6982	20.2	19.7	37.7	19.3	3.2	108360
27539	APEX	42664	6793	4.5	11.5	36.3	28.7	19.1	96086	104296	96	99	5805	10.1	3.7	16.7	55.1	14.4	231673
27540	HOLLY SPRINGS	37311	8597	8.5	14.3	37.9	24.6	14.7	83615	91047	93	97	7180	6.5	6.9	24.6	48.4	13.6	208611
27541	HURDLE MILLS	25301	1463	20.6	25.9	41.4	8.3	3.8	53208	54337	68	79	1193	9.6	16.8	45.9	23.1	4.7	126672
27542	KENLY	18058	3788	33.8	29.8	30.9	4.1	1.5	37693	40095	26	23	2622	23.0	25.9	33.7	16.2	1.2	91871
27544	KITTRELL	22392	1304	22.3	33.7	37.6	3.5	3.0	46344	47548	52	59	1035	19.2	25.2	40.8	12.4	2.4	100911
27545	KNIGHTDALE	28787	8136	9.7	22.8	43.2	19.4	5.0	68270	67708	86	92	6303	12.8	7.1	45.9	32.9	1.2	154763
27546	LILLINGTON	20116	7255	26.8	26.8	37.4	6.0	3.1	45993	48805	51	58	5143	13.4	13.8	37.0	30.4	5.4	141603
27549	LOUISBURG	19949	9158	28.2	28.4	36.3	5.5	1.7	43297	47091	43	46	6710	21.3	21.1	36.8	18.7	2.1	101149
27551	MACON	19857	1174	34.6	27.1	31.6	5.9	0.9	38638	40627	29	28	970	23.2	20.6	35.7	17.6	2.9	103935
27553	MANSON	16446	974	39.0	27.2	29.9	2.6	1.3	34860	37194	17	14	791	25.3	26.7	26.9	19.3	1.8	85694
27557	MIDDLESEX	18815	2995	30.5	30.4	32.4	4.1	2.7	40158	43862	33	33	2250	25.7	24.9	38.2	7.2	4.0	88879
27559	MONCURE	22417	920	19.9	30.5	42.9	3.9	2.7	49456	52264	60	68	763	27.9	23.5	31.7	15.1	1.8	87766
27560	MORRISVILLE	55409	8273	6.4	11.3	31.2	24.4	26.7	101890	108462	97	99	4643	3.0	2.2	10.5	45.1	39.2	342391
27562	NEW HILL	30218	714	13.2	21.1	43.3	14.7	7.7	68959	69268	86	93	598	16.4	13.7	25.4	37.6	6.9	151429
27563	NORLINA	16441	1241	40.4	28.8	26.5	2.3	2.0	32005	33416	11	9	850	30.9	23.9	32.8	11.8	0.6	82407
27565	OXFORD	21147	9898	29.2	24.8	37.2	6.0	2.9	44893	48736	48	53	7130	9.0	14.2	42.9	28.9	5.0	141343
27569	PRINCETON	20417	3151	25.5	32.9	34.1	5.6	1.8	43221	46225	43	46	2254	23.8	25.5	38.3	11.9	0.4	90732
27571	ROLESVILLE	25274	941	12.1	25.7	40.8	17.4	3.9	63554	61356	82	89	862	6.1	8.1	34.8	45.2	5.7	177532
27572	ROUGEMONT	27575	2684	17.1	22.5	43.4	11.2	5.7	60526	60697	78	88	2247	7.8	14.6	39.6	29.8	8.2	141288
27573	ROXBORO	20535	4614	34.4	28.5	31.2	4.3	1.7	36594	39631	22	19	2578	14.0	25.1	48.8	11.4	0.7	103213
27574	ROXBORO	21578	5685	22.1	30.2	40.6	5.1	2.0	47632	48878	56	62	4603	8.9	23.1	48.5	17.4	2.0	111367
27576	SELMA	17835	7697	31.4	30.9	31.9	4.4	1.4	39262	41776	31	30	4815	23.2	25.9	34.0	16.0	1.0	91413
27577	SMITHFIELD	20928	8648	30.3	28.8	32.6	5.2	3.1	42203	44985	40	42	5295	12.2	19.8	39.0	26.2	2.9	120150
27581	STEM	23684	979	18.8	21.8	49.8	8.2	1.4	57396	57788	74	86	814	3.3	18.2	39.7	35.4	3.4	158022
27583	TIMBERLAKE	23373	2532	20.3	25.7	44.5	6.9	2.6	52715	52462	67	78	2167	10.7	13.6	53.8	21.4	0.6	119225
27587	WAKE FOREST	33092	19346	10.8	19.3	37.0	22.6	10.3	75977	79785	90	95	15188	8.9	7.2	26.3	46.7	10.9	196610
27589	WARRENTON	15965	3774	39.8	34.0	22.4	2.1	1.6	30897	32390	10	7	2844	26.4	29.6	34.0	8.5	1.5	78405
27591	WENDELL	23688	7433	18.3	24.4	42.7	12.1	2.6	56683	56646	74	85	5853	16.9	12.5	43.6	24.5	2.5	124204
27592	WILLOW SPRING	26864	4983	11.2	21.7	49.1	14.0	4.0	64669	65753	83	90	4144	13.8	12.2	39.3	32.4	2.3	145936
27596	YOUNGSVILLE	26382	4725	11.6	24.3	49.5	10.4	4.2	62951	63810	81	89	4024	15.3	12.5	44.1	25.9	2.2	133742
27597	ZEBULON	22508	8065	23.8	26.9	36.7	9.7	2.9	49279	51274	59	68	5962	16.9	16.4	41.0	22.0	3.7	117927
27601	RALEIGH	14403	3459	54.4	24.5	15.8	2.9	2.5	21727	22572	2	1	778	12.1	21.7	32.0	27.8	6.4	120278
27603	RALEIGH	27864	16947	19.2	24.6	34.7	16.3	5.2	55795	55813	72	84	10513	21.0	7.0	31.2	37.6	3.2	155881
27604	RALEIGH	32123	16514	11.6	22.9	42.3	17.2	6.0	66717	67313	85	91	10290	8.5	2.3	38.9	47.5	2.9	175592
27605	RALEIGH	42324	2470	19.4	25.3	37.7	11.9	5.7	55215	55549	72	83	930	1.9	4.9	11.2	59.8	22.2	243722
27606	RALEIGH	27004	17726	21.9	27.8	29.9	13.4	7.0	50235	51849	62	70	6592	6.4	4.6	25.1	51.5	12.4	207430
27607	RALEIGH	36342	8658	14.6	23.2	30.5	20.6	11.2	66522	68984	85	91	4309	2.4	2.2	10.1	61.3	24.0	274442
27608	RALEIGH	51325	5351	13.8	21.0	31.0	18.4	15.8	67864	70024	85	92	3140	0.3	1.6	8.2	42.5	47.4	382708
27609	RALEIGH	37331	16438	11.6	25.4	35.9	18.5	8.5	65119	66636	83	91	8795	0.5	1.5	22.2	63.2	12.6	219404
	NORTH CAROLINA	25989		22.3	26.1	36.6	9.4	5.6	51418	53634				12.2	15.1	38.7	27.9	6.1	132724
	UNITED STATES	27277		20.9	24.4	35.3	11.7	7.6	54719	56938				9.3	13.1	31.6	32.6	13.5	162279

ZIP CODE #	POST OFFICE NAME	FINANCIAL SERVICES Auto Loan	Home Loan	Invest-ments	Retire-ment Plans	THE HOME: Home Improvements Home Repair	Lawn & Garden	Furnishings Comput-ers & Hard-ware-Personal	Major Appli-ances	TV, Radio, Sound Equip-ment	Furni-ture	ENTERTAINMENT Dine out/ Carry out	Sports Equip-ment	Fees & Tickets	Toys & Games	Travel	Cable TV	PERSONAL Apparel & Services	Auto Repairs	Health Insur-ance	Pets & Supplies
27341	SEAGROVE	88	63	73	61	63	84	66	76	73	64	71	59	53	76	60	79	48	72	81	93
27343	SEMORA	97	68	97	65	69	97	70	89	79	66	77	67	55	79	68	87	51	82	93	107
27344	SILER CITY	86	69	73	68	68	84	71	79	77	68	75	60	62	78	67	82	51	76	83	94
27349	SNOW CAMP	90	79	74	77	77	85	76	82	80	77	79	61	70	83	72	83	54	79	83	98
27350	SOPHIA	92	73	78	73	73	91	74	85	80	71	78	64	63	82	70	86	53	80	88	101
27355	STALEY	90	68	76	67	68	88	70	81	76	67	75	62	58	79	65	83	50	76	85	97
27356	STAR	85	61	70	59	61	80	63	74	70	62	69	56	51	73	58	76	46	70	78	90
27357	STOKESDALE	95	91	83	91	90	96	86	92	88	86	88	69	83	91	85	90	60	88	92	109
27358	SUMMERFIELD	130	144	130	147	142	136	127	133	124	133	125	103	136	129	133	122	88	126	125	154
27360	THOMASVILLE	81	73	69	73	71	82	74	78	78	71	77	59	69	79	71	81	53	77	82	93
27370	TRINITY	95	82	80	81	81	92	80	87	84	80	83	65	73	87	76	88	57	84	89	104
27371	TROY	88	68	80	68	69	88	71	82	77	67	75	62	60	78	68	83	51	77	86	98
27376	WEST END	108	99	120	97	106	117	93	108	100	100	98	74	92	96	98	105	67	103	115	126
27377	WHITSETT	95	89	83	90	89	97	87	93	88	83	88	71	82	91	86	91	60	89	94	109
27379	YANCEYVILLE	82	57	76	55	57	80	61	73	68	58	67	57	48	70	57	75	45	70	78	89
27401	GREENSBORO	61	50	46	53	47	54	63	54	65	60	65	43	57	64	55	68	45	61	62	69
27403	GREENSBORO	90	79	76	83	78	81	100	84	94	90	94	69	89	94	86	93	66	91	87	102
27405	GREENSBORO	78	67	60	69	64	70	77	70	78	74	78	56	71	79	69	79	54	75	75	86
27406	GREENSBORO	85	82	74	83	79	82	84	82	86	84	86	63	83	87	81	87	60	84	85	98
27407	GREENSBORO	107	99	88	100	95	92	106	98	104	107	106	78	102	107	99	102	74	102	96	117
27408	GREENSBORO	125	137	138	139	139	137	130	132	129	132	130	98	139	128	136	130	92	130	136	152
27409	GREENSBORO	101	78	70	84	74	73	99	82	97	99	99	70	89	101	85	93	69	93	81	102
27410	GREENSBORO	133	136	132	140	135	128	137	130	133	140	135	103	140	135	137	131	95	133	128	153
27411	GREENSBORO	0	0	0	0	0	0	0	0	0	0	0	0	0	0	0	0	0	0	0	0
27413	GREENSBORO	99	42	41	52	38	49	139	69	111	94	113	74	82	108	75	101	80	98	69	93
27455	GREENSBORO	119	125	114	127	121	115	122	117	118	124	119	93	125	121	121	115	84	118	113	138
27501	ANGIER	91	85	74	82	82	83	82	83	82	84	83	62	77	86	77	83	57	81	82	99
27502	APEX	159	181	151	179	172	149	157	156	146	172	149	127	167	158	158	136	106	146	133	177
27503	BAHAMA	133	159	151	163	159	153	138	145	134	143	135	110	154	135	151	133	96	138	140	168
27504	BENSON	87	75	78	73	74	83	74	81	77	74	77	61	67	79	71	80	52	78	82	96
27505	BROADWAY	92	77	76	75	75	88	77	84	81	76	80	64	68	84	72	85	54	81	86	100
27507	BULLOCK	87	61	74	59	61	83	64	75	71	62	70	58	51	74	58	78	47	71	79	92
27508	BUNN	91	70	81	66	68	86	72	81	78	71	77	63	60	80	67	83	52	79	83	99
27509	BUTNER	99	96	83	92	92	94	93	94	94	96	94	70	90	97	89	95	65	94	94	111
27510	CARRBORO	82	57	52	62	53	56	85	65	82	79	83	57	70	84	68	80	58	77	68	82
27511	CARY	135	143	134	147	140	132	139	134	135	143	137	106	145	138	140	131	97	135	129	157
27513	CARY	163	164	144	171	156	141	162	150	154	171	158	126	165	164	157	146	113	151	135	176
27514	CHAPEL HILL	129	118	123	127	119	111	144	120	134	137	137	102	137	135	132	130	99	130	115	144
27516	CHAPEL HILL	118	111	104	116	108	106	123	110	117	120	119	89	117	120	113	114	84	115	107	132
27517	CHAPEL HILL	141	145	156	151	150	141	149	143	144	154	145	111	154	142	152	141	103	145	141	167
27518	CARY	230	277	238	284	269	227	231	234	213	259	217	194	260	231	242	196	159	214	192	261
27519	CARY	207	251	216	258	244	205	208	211	192	234	195	176	236	208	219	176	144	192	172	235
27520	CLAYTON	110	114	96	109	108	102	103	105	101	110	102	81	103	107	101	99	71	101	98	121
27521	COATS	86	70	72	69	70	82	74	79	77	72	76	60	65	79	69	81	52	77	82	94
27522	CREEDMOOR	95	95	84	93	92	93	88	91	89	91	89	68	87	92	87	90	61	89	91	107
27523	APEX	161	193	172	196	189	167	162	167	154	179	156	133	182	162	172	145	113	155	147	188
27524	FOUR OAKS	88	67	76	65	67	85	69	79	75	67	74	60	58	77	64	81	50	75	83	95
27525	FRANKLINTON	98	85	86	81	82	92	83	90	86	84	85	69	74	89	78	88	58	86	89	106
27526	FUQUAY VARINA	105	114	100	112	111	105	105	106	103	108	104	82	108	107	106	101	73	103	101	123
27527	CLAYTON	128	138	112	132	129	115	123	122	116	132	119	97	125	125	121	111	83	116	108	139
27529	GARNER	111	116	100	114	111	106	108	108	106	113	108	83	110	111	107	105	75	106	103	125
27530	GOLDSBORO	76	68	62	68	65	73	71	71	75	70	74	53	67	76	66	78	51	72	77	86
27531	GOLDSBORO	85	44	33	51	40	38	80	55	75	74	79	55	61	90	58	69	56	71	50	67
27534	GOLDSBORO	94	87	81	87	85	88	89	88	90	89	90	68	85	92	85	90	62	89	89	105
27536	HENDERSON	68	58	58	58	57	67	64	64	69	62	68	47	59	68	60	73	47	66	73	78
27537	HENDERSON	86	73	72	70	71	81	72	78	76	73	75	59	65	79	68	79	51	76	79	94
27539	APEX	164	188	162	186	181	160	162	164	153	175	156	130	174	163	167	146	111	155	144	187
27540	HOLLY SPRINGS	152	169	142	166	161	143	147	148	139	160	141	118	155	149	148	132	100	139	129	169
27541	HURDLE MILLS	97	91	88	89	89	97	85	93	88	86	88	70	82	90	84	91	60	89	94	110
27542	KENLY	81	60	78	58	61	80	61	74	67	58	66	56	50	67	59	73	44	69	77	89
27544	KITTRELL	100	73	83	71	73	96	76	88	83	73	82	67	61	87	69	91	55	83	92	107
27545	KNIGHTDALE	119	124	102	119	116	108	111	113	108	119	110	87	111	115	108	105	76	108	103	130
27546	LILLINGTON	88	74	71	73	72	80	80	79	81	77	80	62	70	83	72	83	55	79	81	95
27549	LOUISBURG	88	68	81	65	68	86	68	80	74	67	73	60	58	76	65	80	49	76	83	96
27551	MACON	81	59	91	58	63	83	61	77	66	57	65	58	50	65	62	72	43	71	79	91
27553	MANSON	78	53	71	50	52	75	56	68	63	53	62	53	43	65	51	70	41	64	72	83
27557	MIDDLESEX	85	65	73	63	64	81	67	76	72	66	71	58	56	74	62	77	48	72	78	91
27559	MONCURE	95	78	81	78	78	93	78	87	83	76	82	66	69	86	74	88	55	83	90	104
27560	MORRISVILLE	191	187	164	196	178	161	189	173	180	199	184	146	190	191	181	170	131	176	156	204
27562	NEW HILL	120	120	102	115	115	111	109	113	109	116	110	85	108	115	106	108	76	108	107	131
27563	NORLINA	78	51	75	48	50	76	54	68	62	51	61	53	40	63	50	70	40	64	72	84
27565	OXFORD	87	73	77	73	73	87	74	82	79	72	78	61	67	80	71	84	53	79	87	98
27569	PRINCETON	85	70	73	68	69	82	69	78	74	69	73	58	61	76	66	78	49	74	80	93
27571	ROLESVILLE	112	110	94	106	105	103	101	104	101	107	102	79	99	106	98	100	70	100	99	122
27572	ROUGEMONT	104	108	98	109	106	108	98	104	99	101	99	78	101	102	100	100	69	100	103	122
27573	ROXBORO	73	59	63	59	59	72	66	69	70	61	69	52	57	70	61	75	47	69	76	83
27574	ROXBORO	91	75	80	74	75	91	75	85	79	72	78	64	65	82	72	85	53	80	88	101
27576	SELMA	78	61	66	60	60	75	64	71	69	62	68	54	55	70	59	74	46	69	75	85
27577	SMITHFIELD	83	71	74	70	71	81	74	79	78	72	77	58	67	78	70	82	52	77	84	93
27581	STEM	98	90	80	87	88	92	85	90	88	89	88	66	81	92	81	91	60	87	91	107
27583	TIMBERLAKE	95	86	77	84	85	89	82	87	85	85	85	63	77	89	78	88	58	84	87	104
27587	WAKE FOREST	133	144	120	140	136	124	129	129	123	137	125	102	132	131	128	118	88	123	116	148
27589	WARRENTON	73	48	71	45	48	72	51	64	59	48	57	50	38	59	48	65	38	60	68	79
27591	WENDELL	94	95	85	92	92	92	88	91	89	90	89	69	88	92	87	90	62	89	90	107
27592	WILLOW SPRING	111	114	95	110	108	100	103	104	100	110	101	81	103	107	100	97	70	100	95	120
27596	YOUNGSVILLE	109	107	91	103	103	100	98	101	98	104	99	77	96	103	95	97	68	97	96	118
27597	ZEBULON	95	83	82	81	82	92	81	88	85	82	85	66	75	88	78	89	58	85	89	105
27601	RALEIGH	49	38	37	41	37	44	49	44	54	47	53	33	45	52	43	57	37	50	54	55
27603	RALEIGH	102	93	83	94	89	88	103	93	99	101	100	75	95	102	93	98	70	97	92	111
27604	RALEIGH	110	106	93	106	100	96	112	102	109	113	111	83	109	113	106	106	78	107	100	122
27605	RALEIGH	101	75	76	85	72	73	109	83	105	101	109	75	96	107	93	102	77	99	86	106
27606	RALEIGH	100	76	72	82	74	76	111	84	103	97	103	74	92	104	88	100	73	97	86	105
27607	RALEIGH	119	116	117	121	117	112	132	117	124	127	125	95	127	124	124	121	89	123	115	139
27608	RALEIGH	130	146	157	149	152	135	146	140	137	150	138	111	155	135	153	132	100	141	132	162
27609	RALEIGH	117	107	103	111	105	104	120	108	119	120	120	87	117	120	114	118	85	117	112	130
	NORTH CAROLINA	100	89	90	89	88	96	91	94	94	91	93	73	85	95	88	96	64	93	96	112
	UNITED STATES	100	100	100	100	100	100	100	100	100	100	100	100	100	100	100	100	100	100	100	100

ZIP CODE #	POST OFFICE NAME	COUNTY FIPS CODE	POPULATION 2000	POPULATION 2009	POPULATION 2014	2000-2009 ANNUAL RATE % Rate	2000-2009 ANNUAL RATE State Centile	HOUSEHOLDS 2000	HOUSEHOLDS 2009	HOUSEHOLDS 2014	HOUSEHOLDS % Annual Rate 2000-2009	HOUSEHOLDS 2009 Average HH Size	FAMILIES 2000	FAMILIES 2009	FAMILIES % Annual Rate 2000-2009
27610	RALEIGH	183	42930	58190	67928	3.3	90	14757	20478	24074	3.6	2.70	10199	13473	3.1
27612	RALEIGH	183	27523	35688	41596	2.8	87	12562	16443	19200	3.0	2.15	6683	7909	1.8
27613	RALEIGH	183	33249	45600	54426	3.5	91	13487	18622	22214	3.5	2.45	8707	11132	2.7
27614	RALEIGH	183	11151	33379	43005	12.6	100	3732	12020	15568	13.5	2.77	3252	9361	12.1
27615	RALEIGH	183	39863	45204	50504	1.4	66	15633	17937	20077	1.5	2.50	10739	11629	0.9
27616	RALEIGH	183	21968	40278	50230	6.8	98	8031	14218	17653	6.4	2.83	5582	9701	6.2
27617	RALEIGH	183	3607	12327	16085	14.2	100	1287	5824	7716	17.7	2.12	1090	3184	12.3
27695	RALEIGH	183	4	8	9	7.8	99	1	3	4	12.6	1.67	0	1	0.0
27701	DURHAM	063	25316	25444	25715	0.1	18	9288	9162	9260	-0.1	2.49	4850	4527	-0.7
27703	DURHAM	063	31617	43808	49423	3.6	91	11674	16641	18901	3.9	2.63	8211	11369	3.6
27704	DURHAM	063	26753	30610	33262	1.5	69	10710	12432	13531	1.6	2.43	6932	7761	1.2
27705	DURHAM	063	41102	45225	48026	1.0	53	17242	19123	20378	1.1	2.15	8917	9400	0.6
27707	DURHAM	063	41582	45421	47914	1.0	53	16785	18496	19610	1.1	2.33	9814	10306	0.5
27709	DURHAM	063	29	105	132	14.9	100	11	32	40	12.2	3.25	5	17	14.1
27712	DURHAM	063	17376	20243	21968	1.7	74	6418	7658	8338	1.9	2.60	5122	5996	1.7
27713	DURHAM	063	31915	45960	52951	4.0	93	13673	19847	22852	4.1	2.29	8179	11208	3.5
27801	ROCKY MOUNT	065	23183	21152	20256	-1.0	2	8290	7631	7337	-0.9	2.73	6037	5434	-1.1
27803	ROCKY MOUNT	127	23397	23092	23078	-0.1	13	9025	9018	9043	0.0	2.54	6446	6260	-0.3
27804	ROCKY MOUNT	127	25698	28905	30096	1.3	63	10274	11762	12329	1.5	2.37	6850	7614	1.1
27805	AULANDER	015	2927	2882	2842	-0.2	10	1175	1205	1201	0.3	2.39	840	837	0.0
27806	AURORA	013	2747	2881	2895	0.5	32	1146	1240	1259	0.9	2.32	791	825	0.5
27807	BAILEY	127	5517	6425	6841	1.7	74	2058	2409	2569	1.7	2.67	1516	1723	1.4
27808	BATH	013	2188	2147	2098	-0.2	10	935	954	942	0.2	2.25	684	677	-0.1
27809	BATTLEBORO	127	4939	5384	5485	0.9	48	1769	1947	1996	1.0	2.60	1365	1465	0.8
27810	BELHAVEN	013	3939	3918	3924	-0.1	13	1644	1703	1725	0.4	2.28	1141	1142	0.0
27812	BETHEL	147	2742	3041	3276	1.1	56	1049	1209	1314	1.5	2.51	748	832	1.2
27814	BLOUNTS CREEK	013	1698	1866	1931	1.0	53	707	802	840	1.4	2.33	517	568	1.0
27816	CASTALIA	069	2506	2854	3053	1.4	66	954	1100	1181	1.6	2.58	698	782	1.2
27817	CHOCOWINITY	013	6152	6917	7192	1.3	63	2440	2838	2983	1.6	2.44	1826	2065	1.3
27818	COMO	091	1421	1400	1378	-0.2	10	567	581	577	0.3	2.38	409	407	-0.1
27820	CONWAY	131	3159	3069	2986	-0.3	8	1308	1317	1298	0.1	2.32	882	859	-0.3
27821	EDWARD	013	106	114	117	0.8	44	45	50	52	1.1	2.28	31	33	0.7
27822	ELM CITY	195	6697	7184	7444	0.8	44	2648	2882	2997	0.9	2.47	2010	2131	0.6
27823	ENFIELD	083	8805	8268	7960	-0.7	4	3119	3000	2910	-0.4	2.72	2261	2118	-0.7
27824	ENGELHARD	095	1708	1623	1565	-0.6	5	705	696	681	-0.1	2.33	450	428	-0.5
27826	FAIRFIELD	095	1161	1099	1066	-0.6	5	237	229	223	-0.4	3.62	165	154	-0.7
27828	FARMVILLE	147	8335	8391	8643	0.1	18	3239	3396	3532	0.5	2.45	2268	2290	0.1
27829	FOUNTAIN	147	1724	1951	2068	1.3	63	692	807	864	1.7	2.42	510	575	1.3
27830	FREMONT	191	4337	4442	4472	0.3	24	1703	1793	1819	0.6	2.45	1194	1214	0.2
27831	GARYSBURG	131	3610	3534	3454	-0.2	10	1419	1444	1427	0.2	2.43	990	977	-0.1
27832	GASTON	131	2987	2960	2902	-0.1	13	1228	1271	1261	0.4	2.33	853	856	0.0
27834	GREENVILLE	147	43390	49633	53713	1.5	69	16535	20275	22260	2.2	2.38	10419	12182	1.7
27837	GRIMESLAND	147	4629	5756	6323	2.4	83	1740	2214	2448	2.6	2.60	1290	1584	2.2
27839	HALIFAX	083	4197	4161	4099	-0.1	13	1287	1314	1298	0.2	2.31	889	879	-0.1
27840	HAMILTON	117	927	816	774	-1.4	1	344	315	302	-0.9	2.53	257	230	-1.2
27842	HENRICO	131	1325	1377	1363	0.4	28	651	709	711	0.9	1.94	465	491	0.6
27843	HOBGOOD	065	1857	1686	1604	-1.0	2	700	656	630	-0.7	2.57	520	475	-1.0
27844	HOLLISTER	083	2864	2821	2769	-0.2	10	1070	1096	1087	0.3	2.57	788	786	0.0
27845	JACKSON	131	1948	1887	1848	-0.3	8	756	763	752	0.1	2.05	503	490	-0.3
27846	JAMESVILLE	117	2796	2787	2749	0.0	15	1093	1119	1115	0.3	2.47	817	814	0.0
27847	KELFORD	015	364	342	332	-0.7	4	131	128	126	-0.3	2.66	85	80	-0.7
27849	LEWISTON WOODVILLE	015	1648	1571	1530	-0.5	6	592	581	572	-0.2	2.69	405	384	-0.6
27850	LITTLETON	083	6676	7042	7015	0.6	36	2916	3189	3209	1.0	2.21	2073	2204	0.7
27851	LUCAMA	195	4776	5341	5592	1.2	60	1841	2081	2186	1.3	2.56	1371	1504	1.0
27852	MACCLESFIELD	065	3387	3231	3134	-0.5	6	1352	1317	1284	-0.3	2.45	996	943	-0.6
27853	MARGARETTSVILLE	131	404	391	380	-0.4	7	144	142	140	-0.2	2.75	103	99	-0.4
27855	MURFREESBORO	091	5842	6163	6051	0.6	36	2304	2361	2343	0.3	2.43	1600	1591	-0.1
27856	NASHVILLE	127	14931	16785	17713	1.3	63	5392	6178	6570	1.5	2.56	4026	4481	1.2
27857	OAK CITY	117	1554	1423	1372	-0.9	2	628	598	581	-0.5	2.38	434	400	-0.9
27858	GREENVILLE	147	44143	51079	54785	1.6	72	17904	21153	22995	1.8	2.19	9148	10403	1.4
27860	PANTEGO	013	1957	2095	2152	0.7	40	763	850	883	1.2	2.42	556	598	0.8
27862	PENDLETON	131	1164	1135	1103	-0.3	8	452	454	447	0.0	2.49	321	313	-0.3
27863	PIKEVILLE	191	8528	9319	9566	1.0	53	3252	3660	3790	1.3	2.53	2452	2681	1.0
27864	PINETOPS	065	4031	3546	3361	-1.4	1	1511	1359	1295	-1.1	2.61	1110	975	-1.4
27865	PINETOWN	013	1944	2044	2068	0.5	32	751	822	840	1.0	2.46	550	583	0.6
27866	PLEASANT HILL	131	650	638	624	-0.2	10	232	238	235	0.3	2.53	165	164	-0.1
27869	RICH SQUARE	131	3005	2907	2837	-0.4	7	965	966	952	0.0	2.57	644	624	-0.3
27870	ROANOKE RAPIDS	083	28024	26875	26044	-0.5	6	11253	11084	10839	-0.2	2.40	7687	7338	-0.5
27871	ROBERSONVILLE	117	4950	4604	4478	-0.8	3	1921	1866	1832	-0.3	2.47	1333	1256	-0.6
27872	ROXOBEL	015	672	635	617	-0.6	5	288	282	277	-0.2	2.25	188	178	-0.6
27874	SCOTLAND NECK	083	5474	5202	5035	-0.5	6	2123	2089	2039	-0.2	2.42	1391	1322	-0.5
27875	SCRANTON	095	1195	1122	1085	-0.7	4	479	453	437	-0.6	1.76	335	308	-0.9
27876	SEABOARD	131	1518	1436	1390	-0.6	5	624	614	601	-0.2	2.34	411	391	-0.5
27880	SIMS	195	1949	2162	2266	1.1	56	732	825	866	1.3	2.61	547	597	1.0
27882	SPRING HOPE	127	6083	6780	7108	1.2	60	2361	2671	2813	1.3	2.54	1733	1904	1.0
27883	STANTONSBURG	195	2883	2968	3004	0.3	24	1134	1183	1203	0.5	2.51	823	832	0.1
27884	STOKES	147	1072	1203	1290	1.3	63	396	462	499	1.7	2.60	305	346	1.4
27885	SWANQUARTER	095	1100	1108	1099	0.1	18	433	454	456	0.5	2.24	292	296	0.1
27886	TARBORO	065	20183	19690	19135	-0.3	8	7553	7457	7276	-0.1	2.54	5402	5176	-0.5
27888	WALSTONBURG	079	3326	3717	3884	1.2	60	1206	1360	1426	1.3	2.73	915	1007	1.0
27889	WASHINGTON	013	25969	26503	26658	0.2	21	10479	11025	11192	0.6	2.36	7305	7468	0.2
27890	WELDON	083	2531	2399	2307	-0.6	5	962	931	902	-0.4	2.50	665	623	-0.7
27891	WHITAKERS	127	5338	5115	5024	-0.5	6	1932	1891	1869	-0.2	2.69	1422	1353	-0.5
27892	WILLIAMSTON	117	15506	14545	14004	-0.7	4	6096	5868	5695	-0.4	2.44	4397	4113	-0.7
27893	WILSON	195	41942	42182	42399	0.1	18	16145	16322	16432	0.1	2.49	10505	10249	-0.3
27896	WILSON	195	13885	17579	19086	2.6	86	5527	7131	7781	2.8	2.45	4114	5085	2.3
27897	WOODLAND	131	2290	2187	2119	-0.5	6	895	887	869	-0.1	2.45	604	579	-0.5
27909	ELIZABETH CITY	139	34897	41991	45804	2.0	79	12907	15910	17595	2.3	2.45	9094	10883	2.0
27910	AHOSKIE	091	12197	11963	11687	-0.2	10	4798	4815	4750	0.0	2.40	3332	3244	-0.3
27916	AYDLETT	053	441	503	534	1.4	66	173	199	211	1.5	2.53	128	143	1.2
27917	BARCO	053	980	1198	1338	2.2	82	340	444	501	2.9	2.56	243	309	2.6
27919	BELVIDERE	143	1339	1459	1542	0.9	48	541	612	655	1.3	2.38	399	439	1.0
27921	CAMDEN	029	3098	4935	5938	5.2	96	1196	1939	2350	5.4	2.55	918	1452	5.1
27922	COFIELD	091	677	582	550	-1.6	1	286	255	244	-1.2	2.28	199	172	-1.6
27923	COINJOCK	053	553	622	654	1.3	63	233	264	279	1.4	2.33	172	190	1.1
	NORTH CAROLINA					1.7					1.8	2.46			1.5
	UNITED STATES					1.0					1.1	2.59			0.9

#	POST OFFICE NAME	RACE (%) White 2000	White 2009	Black 2000	Black 2009	Asian/Pacific 2000	Asian/Pacific 2009	% Hispanic Origin 2000	% Hispanic Origin 2009	2009 AGE DISTRIBUTION (%) 0-4	5-9	10-14	15-19	20-24	25-44	45-64	65-84	85+	18+	MEDIAN AGE 2009	% 2009 Males	% 2009 Females
27610	RALEIGH	23.2	26.1	68.7	62.2	0.6	0.9	9.2	13.1	7.5	7.2	7.0	7.6	7.8	30.9	23.4	7.6	1.0	74.0	33.4	47.2	52.8
27612	RALEIGH	82.7	78.0	11.0	12.2	3.1	4.6	4.5	7.3	5.7	5.1	4.7	4.6	9.1	35.9	24.5	8.8	1.6	81.8	34.9	49.0	51.0
27613	RALEIGH	85.1	81.5	8.4	8.9	4.2	6.2	2.8	4.3	6.7	6.4	6.5	6.2	7.3	33.9	27.3	5.3	0.4	76.7	35.2	49.5	50.5
27614	RALEIGH	88.1	79.7	7.7	13.2	2.6	3.8	1.8	4.0	8.3	8.5	8.7	7.4	4.1	27.8	28.3	6.3	0.7	69.6	36.3	49.4	50.6
27615	RALEIGH	82.7	78.6	10.7	11.8	3.6	5.2	3.7	5.6	6.3	6.2	6.5	6.7	5.9	27.9	30.5	8.5	1.5	76.6	38.6	48.5	51.5
27616	RALEIGH	56.8	55.6	31.8	29.6	3.6	5.0	9.5	11.6	9.4	8.6	7.8	6.6	6.4	35.2	21.4	4.2	0.3	70.0	31.9	50.1	49.9
27617	RALEIGH	86.7	68.1	7.0	28.2	4.2	2.4	2.3	1.6	7.7	6.9	6.4	5.7	7.1	36.5	24.3	5.0	0.5	75.7	33.1	49.4	50.6
27695	RALEIGH	100.0	75.0	0.0	12.5	0.0	12.5	0.0	0.0	0.0	0.0	0.0	25.0	50.0	25.0	0.0	0.0	0.0	100.0	22.5	37.5	62.5
27701	DURHAM	28.1	25.9	59.6	56.0	1.5	2.0	14.4	20.7	7.4	6.5	5.8	12.8	10.5	29.3	19.5	6.5	1.5	76.7	28.8	51.1	48.9
27703	DURHAM	40.7	43.9	50.4	44.2	1.2	1.9	10.3	12.7	8.2	7.5	7.1	6.7	6.8	32.0	23.4	7.3	0.9	73.2	33.8	49.1	50.9
27704	DURHAM	40.9	36.7	52.1	53.1	1.1	1.4	6.7	10.2	7.1	7.0	6.7	6.5	6.8	29.0	24.8	10.1	1.9	75.2	35.9	46.5	53.5
27705	DURHAM	66.7	61.3	20.9	21.4	5.3	6.6	7.8	12.0	5.3	4.6	4.6	7.0	15.6	28.9	22.6	9.2	2.2	82.5	33.2	49.8	50.2
27707	DURHAM	43.1	41.8	47.5	44.9	2.9	3.8	8.7	12.5	6.3	5.8	5.7	7.4	10.7	30.1	23.6	8.8	1.6	78.7	33.9	48.1	51.9
27709	DURHAM	63.3	63.8	20.0	18.1	10.0	5.7	6.7	15.2	5.7	5.7	5.7	5.7	7.6	29.5	25.7	12.4	1.9	80.0	38.2	48.6	51.4
27712	DURHAM	81.2	77.6	15.0	17.3	2.0	2.8	1.3	2.1	4.9	5.7	6.7	6.7	3.9	22.4	34.4	13.2	2.1	78.2	44.8	48.5	51.5
27713	DURHAM	53.9	47.3	34.8	37.0	7.3	9.7	3.7	6.0	7.6	6.6	6.0	5.1	7.5	37.8	22.6	5.9	0.9	76.6	33.7	47.9	52.1
27801	ROCKY MOUNT	24.5	24.0	74.2	74.2	0.2	0.2	1.1	1.4	7.3	7.8	8.0	7.8	6.1	24.8	26.0	10.5	1.5	72.0	35.8	45.6	54.4
27803	ROCKY MOUNT	57.8	56.5	39.8	40.3	0.3	0.4	1.4	2.2	6.9	7.3	7.4	7.3	5.2	24.8	27.7	11.7	1.7	74.1	38.6	46.9	53.1
27804	ROCKY MOUNT	62.1	60.6	33.3	33.2	1.3	1.8	2.6	3.7	6.0	5.9	6.3	7.6	6.8	26.3	27.3	11.8	2.1	77.8	38.6	47.4	52.6
27805	AULANDER	48.9	46.4	49.6	51.5	0.1	0.2	1.1	1.6	5.4	5.5	6.0	6.9	5.7	23.1	30.8	14.5	2.2	79.7	42.8	47.3	52.7
27806	AURORA	48.9	46.5	49.7	51.6	0.0	0.0	1.2	1.7	5.2	5.4	5.9	7.0	5.5	20.7	31.0	16.7	2.6	79.2	45.2	48.4	51.6
27807	BAILEY	67.9	62.0	21.4	22.7	0.1	0.1	11.8	16.6	7.5	7.5	7.5	6.4	5.4	27.9	26.8	10.1	1.0	73.6	37.1	50.6	49.4
27808	BATH	85.4	83.7	13.1	14.0	0.0	0.0	1.3	2.1	4.0	4.3	4.8	5.7	4.0	21.0	33.2	21.1	1.9	83.4	49.0	49.0	51.0
27809	BATTLEBORO	47.1	46.8	50.5	49.9	0.2	0.3	1.8	2.5	6.1	6.7	7.0	7.3	5.5	28.2	28.4	9.7	1.1	75.9	38.1	44.8	55.2
27810	BELHAVEN	58.3	58.3	39.8	39.0	0.3	0.3	3.5	4.7	5.5	5.4	5.8	6.4	4.7	21.5	31.3	16.6	2.7	79.3	45.4	48.0	52.0
27812	BETHEL	47.5	44.8	49.9	51.6	0.2	0.3	2.7	3.7	6.3	6.6	6.9	7.0	5.4	23.4	29.6	12.8	2.0	75.7	40.2	48.1	51.9
27814	BLOUNTS CREEK	60.6	58.4	37.6	39.1	0.2	0.3	1.1	1.6	4.6	4.9	5.1	5.6	4.7	20.4	37.4	15.5	1.8	81.9	47.8	48.8	51.2
27816	CASTALIA	63.3	59.9	32.2	34.0	0.2	0.3	3.7	5.4	6.0	6.1	6.5	6.5	5.3	26.4	29.9	11.6	1.6	77.5	40.7	50.4	49.6
27817	CHOCOWINITY	73.8	71.2	24.2	26.0	0.1	0.2	2.5	3.7	5.9	6.1	6.1	6.4	5.1	24.3	33.4	11.7	1.1	78.0	42.0	49.6	50.4
27818	COMO	27.6	26.5	71.6	72.5	0.1	0.1	1.2	1.5	5.8	6.3	6.5	6.6	5.1	20.7	33.0	13.7	2.3	77.1	44.1	46.7	53.3
27820	CONWAY	58.0	56.3	40.9	42.4	0.4	0.5	0.4	0.4	5.9	6.3	6.7	6.6	5.0	22.2	30.4	14.6	2.4	77.0	43.0	47.1	52.9
27821	EDWARD	49.5	46.5	50.5	52.6	0.0	0.0	1.0	1.8	4.4	6.1	6.1	5.3	4.4	22.8	32.5	15.8	2.6	81.6	45.6	47.4	52.6
27822	ELM CITY	70.4	66.6	27.4	30.0	0.2	0.3	2.3	3.9	5.9	6.6	6.9	6.2	4.6	24.2	31.3	13.0	1.4	77.0	41.8	48.6	51.4
27823	ENFIELD	16.4	15.3	79.2	79.5	0.1	0.2	1.1	1.4	6.9	7.1	7.3	8.3	6.2	23.9	26.6	11.8	1.9	73.5	37.3	47.2	52.8
27824	ENGELHARD	53.9	52.6	43.9	44.4	0.2	0.2	3.3	4.6	5.1	5.5	6.0	8.1	5.3	21.3	31.7	14.4	2.6	78.2	43.9	47.3	52.7
27826	FAIRFIELD	60.0	58.7	37.5	38.0	0.4	0.5	2.0	2.5	4.0	4.3	4.7	5.7	8.6	32.9	25.8	11.9	1.9	83.1	38.4	61.6	38.4
27828	FARMVILLE	51.7	49.8	43.7	43.3	0.3	0.4	4.6	7.0	6.4	6.4	6.7	7.1	5.8	25.2	28.3	11.9	2.2	76.4	39.5	46.8	53.2
27829	FOUNTAIN	62.8	59.0	35.0	37.8	0.1	0.1	2.5	3.8	6.3	6.5	6.8	6.4	5.2	23.7	30.7	12.6	1.9	76.5	41.5	47.4	52.6
27830	FREMONT	69.2	65.8	27.0	28.5	0.4	0.5	3.2	5.1	6.2	6.3	6.5	6.9	5.6	24.4	28.8	13.6	1.7	76.3	40.9	47.8	52.2
27831	GARYSBURG	20.3	19.4	78.0	78.5	0.1	0.1	0.8	1.0	5.5	6.1	6.5	7.3	5.9	23.2	30.3	13.2	2.0	77.3	41.1	46.5	53.5
27832	GASTON	37.2	35.8	61.2	62.0	0.0	0.0	1.0	1.4	5.9	6.6	6.6	6.7	5.2	21.8	29.9	15.8	1.6	76.8	42.8	47.7	52.3
27834	GREENVILLE	42.8	40.8	52.4	52.6	1.0	1.3	3.9	5.6	7.6	6.9	6.5	7.4	10.0	29.4	22.7	8.0	1.5	75.6	31.9	47.2	52.8
27837	GRIMESLAND	69.4	64.7	24.9	26.0	0.2	0.2	6.2	10.2	6.9	6.8	6.8	6.6	6.4	29.5	27.0	9.1	0.9	75.4	36.1	50.7	49.3
27839	HALIFAX	29.0	27.3	69.1	70.1	0.2	0.3	1.4	1.9	3.9	4.0	4.4	5.2	8.6	35.2	25.8	11.4	1.5	84.5	37.8	61.3	38.7
27840	HAMILTON	40.2	37.4	58.7	60.9	0.1	0.2	2.4	2.9	4.5	5.6	7.7	8.6	3.9	19.5	33.3	14.6	2.2	79.5	45.1	45.8	54.2
27842	HENRICO	64.6	63.3	34.5	35.8	0.2	0.3	0.5	0.7	2.3	2.5	2.8	3.5	3.1	14.2	37.6	31.8	2.2	90.3	58.9	50.0	50.0
27843	HOBGOOD	39.7	37.2	58.9	60.7	0.2	0.2	1.6	2.3	5.8	6.0	6.2	6.8	5.6	25.0	30.4	12.7	1.7	78.0	41.2	48.5	51.5
27844	HOLLISTER	5.6	4.9	44.3	42.4	0.1	0.1	1.4	1.6	7.4	7.6	7.4	7.7	6.0	25.5	26.6	10.6	1.2	72.6	36.3	48.7	51.3
27845	JACKSON	35.6	34.2	63.3	64.3	0.1	0.1	0.5	0.6	4.7	4.9	5.1	5.8	7.2	28.2	26.7	14.4	3.0	82.0	40.7	54.3	45.7
27846	JAMESVILLE	66.8	64.4	30.0	31.1	0.0	0.0	2.8	4.1	5.7	5.9	6.6	7.1	5.0	24.2	30.2	13.5	1.7	77.1	41.7	48.7	51.3
27847	KELFORD	28.3	26.6	69.5	70.5	0.0	0.0	1.1	1.5	6.4	6.7	7.3	7.9	5.8	21.6	28.4	13.5	2.3	74.3	39.4	48.2	51.8
27849	LEWISTON WOODVILLE	18.2	16.9	80.8	81.9	0.1	0.1	0.9	1.1	6.3	6.6	6.9	7.6	6.1	23.6	30.0	11.2	1.7	77.0	39.3	47.7	52.3
27850	LITTLETON	54.5	53.6	42.0	42.3	0.2	0.3	0.8	1.1	4.3	4.5	5.0	5.1	3.8	18.2	34.2	22.7	2.2	82.9	51.7	48.1	51.9
27851	LUCAMA	80.0	74.4	16.6	19.7	0.3	0.4	3.8	6.9	6.3	6.3	6.5	6.6	5.5	26.1	29.5	11.6	1.4	76.8	39.7	49.1	50.9
27852	MACCLESFIELD	73.0	69.6	25.1	27.4	0.1	0.2	2.7	4.1	6.0	6.3	6.6	6.3	4.7	25.3	30.0	13.2	1.5	77.0	41.4	49.3	50.7
27853	MARGARETTSVILLE	48.8	46.8	49.0	50.6	0.0	0.0	0.7	1.0	6.6	6.9	7.4	7.9	5.6	19.9	30.7	12.8	2.0	73.9	40.4	46.3	53.7
27855	MURFREESBORO	36.7	37.4	60.8	58.9	0.3	0.5	2.3	3.4	6.0	6.5	6.3	7.2	7.3	24.7	27.1	12.5	2.3	77.3	38.4	47.8	52.2
27856	NASHVILLE	63.3	60.0	33.7	35.8	0.4	0.5	2.6	3.8	5.9	6.1	6.5	6.2	5.5	27.9	29.2	11.2	1.7	77.9	39.7	51.1	48.9
27857	OAK CITY	38.9	36.5	59.1	60.5	0.1	0.1	3.3	4.7	4.7	4.8	5.6	6.8	5.8	20.4	33.5	16.1	2.2	80.9	46.2	48.2	51.8
27858	GREENVILLE	80.7	77.3	14.9	16.5	1.8	2.6	2.2	3.4	4.8	4.8	4.7	11.4	20.4	24.2	20.7	7.8	1.1	82.6	27.4	48.0	52.0
27860	PANTEGO	68.4	66.7	29.2	29.5	0.1	0.0	3.5	5.4	5.4	5.8	6.1	6.0	4.6	23.7	31.0	14.7	2.7	78.8	43.8	49.1	50.9
27862	PENDLETON	52.9	50.6	44.5	45.8	0.3	0.4	1.4	2.2	6.0	6.2	6.7	7.5	5.3	21.7	30.6	13.8	2.3	76.4	42.2	48.7	51.3
27863	PIKEVILLE	83.2	80.7	13.6	14.7	0.8	1.1	2.5	3.8	7.9	7.7	7.6	6.8	5.5	28.5	26.1	9.1	0.9	72.4	36.5	50.5	49.5
27864	PINETOPS	58.5	56.4	40.1	41.5	0.0	0.0	2.0	2.9	6.2	6.7	7.0	7.3	5.0	24.6	31.0	10.9	1.2	75.5	40.1	48.3	51.7
27865	PINETOWN	88.0	86.2	10.6	11.6	0.2	0.2	2.7	4.1	5.4	5.7	6.0	5.7	4.5	23.3	31.0	16.0	2.3	79.3	44.6	48.6	51.4
27866	PLEASANT HILL	33.0	31.3	65.9	67.1	0.0	0.0	0.5	0.6	4.1	4.5	5.2	6.3	5.5	19.9	34.3	17.6	2.7	81.8	47.8	48.3	51.7
27869	RICH SQUARE	28.6	27.2	69.5	70.3	0.0	0.0	1.1	1.6	5.0	5.0	5.1	6.0	6.9	24.6	26.6	16.1	4.7	81.3	42.9	50.9	49.1
27870	ROANOKE RAPIDS	60.7	58.6	36.8	38.1	1.0	1.4	0.8	1.2	6.5	6.6	6.7	7.2	6.2	24.8	27.7	12.4	2.0	75.8	39.1	46.9	53.1
27871	ROBERSONVILLE	35.5	33.5	62.0	63.0	0.4	0.5	2.2	3.3	6.2	6.3	6.5	6.8	5.5	23.1	30.0	13.5	2.2	76.9	41.4	46.7	53.3
27872	ROXOBEL	27.3	25.5	70.7	72.1	0.0	0.0	0.9	1.3	6.3	6.6	7.2	7.7	5.8	22.5	29.3	12.4	2.0	75.7	39.4	47.7	52.3
27874	SCOTLAND NECK	28.0	27.4	70.3	70.3	0.1	0.1	1.6	2.2	6.1	6.2	6.7	7.8	5.7	21.8	27.2	15.5	3.0	76.0	41.7	46.8	53.2
27875	SCRANTON	58.8	57.2	39.0	39.7	0.3	0.4	1.6	2.3	3.7	3.9	4.5	5.3	9.2	34.8	25.0	11.7	1.9	84.1	38.0	64.3	35.7
27876	SEABOARD	32.4	30.8	66.5	67.8	0.2	0.3	0.4	0.4	7.1	7.5	7.6	7.0	5.6	19.3	30.1	13.3	2.5	73.5	40.5	45.6	54.4
27880	SIMS	76.5	68.4	16.0	17.9	0.1	0.0	10.6	18.5	6.1	6.4	6.8	6.7	5.1	26.4	29.8	11.4	1.4	77.2	39.7	50.3	49.7
27882	SPRING HOPE	61.9	58.3	34.1	35.7	0.1	0.2	4.8	7.1	6.2	6.4	6.8	6.5	4.9	25.7	29.9	12.2	1.5	76.6	40.5	48.7	51.3
27883	STANTONSBURG	62.6	57.1	33.6	36.4	0.1	0.1	5.1	8.5	6.0	6.2	6.3	6.0	5.8	25.2	30.4	12.5	1.6	77.6	41.0	49.7	50.3
27884	STOKES	68.7	64.9	28.9	31.3	0.1	0.1	3.2	4.7	6.1	6.3	6.7	6.3	5.7	25.1	30.8	11.9	1.2	77.0	40.8	50.7	49.3
27885	SWANQUARTER	60.9	59.5	36.2	36.6	0.7	1.0	2.3	3.1	4.4	4.9	5.0	5.0	6.3	22.4	31.5	15.9	4.7	82.4	46.3	46.6	53.4
27886	TARBORO	51.2	48.9	44.6	44.9	0.2	0.3	5.2	7.4	5.9	6.0	6.0	6.6	6.4	25.2	28.2	13.1	2.7	78.0	40.4	47.7	52.3
27888	WALSTONBURG	53.1	49.4	36.4	34.8	0.1	0.1	13.4	19.5	8.1	8.0	7.4	6.5	6.9	26.4	25.3	10.1	1.3	72.6	34.7	50.0	50.0
27889	WASHINGTON	67.0	64.8	29.9	30.5	0.3	0.5	3.8	5.6	6.4	6.5	6.4	6.1	5.4	24.9	28.4	13.8	2.1	77.0	40.6	47.4	52.6
27890	WELDON	28.2	26.5	70.4	71.7	0.2	0.2	0.6	0.7	6.9	7.4	7.3	7.6	5.1	21.2	25.1	15.9	3.5	73.3	40.5	45.8	54.2
27891	WHITAKERS	36.0	32.9	60.6	62.5	0.2	0.2	2.0	3.0	5.8	6.7	6.9	7.2	5.9	25.3	29.3	11.4	1.6	76.0	39.4	49.0	51.0
27892	WILLIAMSTON	56.9	55.1	41.2	42.3	0.3	0.5	1.8	2.6	6.4	6.6	6.8	6.7	5.2	24.1	28.4	13.6	2.2	75.9	40.7	46.2	53.8
27893	WILSON	41.3	38.7	52.6	52.5	0.4	0.5	8.2	11.7	7.3	7.2	6.9	7.4	6.8	25.9	25.1	11.6	1.9	74.6	36.2	47.6	52.4
27896	WILSON	83.5	78.7	13.2	16.5	1.0	1.3	2.0	3.1	5.7	6.1	6.6	6.3	4.6	24.6	31.4	13.0	1.6	77.4	42.4	48.2	51.8
27897	WOODLAND	43.7	41.8	54.8	56.2	0.0	0.0	0.8	1.1	7.4	7.3	7.4	7.3	5.6	21.0	26.4	15.1	2.4	73.2	40.3	46.4	53.6
27909	ELIZABETH CITY	56.9	55.1	40.0	40.9	0.9	1.3	1.2	1.7	6.3	6.1	6.2	7.5	8.2	25.2	26.2	12.1	2.2	77.4	37.7	48.9	51.1
27910	AHOSKIE	38.1	37.1	58.5	58.7	0.4	0.5	1.4	1.8	5.5	5.8	6.0	7.0	6.2	23.1	29.0	14.7	2.6	78.3	42.1	46.2	53.8
27916	AYDLETT	94.8	93.2	2.3	2.6	0.2	0.4	1.6	2.4	4.8	5.6	6.0	6.0	5.0	25.0	29.2	15.9	2.6	80.1	43.6	48.3	51.7
27917	BARCO	79.5	77.7	15.9	16.4	0.6	0.9	3.9	5.2	6.2	6.5	6.7	6.3	5.0	25.8	28.0	12.7	2.8	76.8	40.3	49.0	51.0
27919	BELVIDERE	75.7	74.1	23.2	24.5	0.4	0.5	0.4	0.5	5.1	5.4	5.8	5.8	4.9	24.0	31.8	14.7	2.6	80.3	44.3	48.8	51.2
27921	CAMDEN	79.4	78.7	19.2	19.5	0.1	0.2	0.7	1.0	5.7	6.2	7.2	6.7	4.4	25.2	30.7	12.6	1.3	76.7	41.8	49.0	51.0
27922	COFIELD	32.8	32.1	64.5	64.9	0.1	0.2	1.0	1.2	4.6	5.5	6.7	6.9	4.8	25.4	30.9	13.4	1.7	78.7	42.4	46.0	54.0
27923	COINJOCK	92.9	91.2	4.0	4.5	0.2	0.3	2.0	3.2	5.0	5.6	6.1	5.9	5.0	25.4	29.3	15.0	2.7	79.7	43.0	48.2	51.8
	NORTH CAROLINA	72.1	69.8	21.6	21.5	1.5	2.1	4.7	6.9	6.6	6.5	6.5	6.8	6.9	27.7	26.5	10.9	1.6	76.5	37.4	49.3	50.7
	UNITED STATES	75.1	72.0	12.3	12.7	3.8	4.6	12.5	15.7	6.8	6.7	6.6	7.1	6.9	27.0	26.0	10.9	1.9	75.7	36.9	49.2	50.8

ZIP CODE #	POST OFFICE NAME	2009 Per Capita Income	2009 HH Income Base	2009 Household Income Distribution (%): Less than $25,000	$25,000 to $49,999	$50,000 to $99,999	$100,000 to $149,999	$150,000 or More	Median Household Income: 2009	2014	2009 National Centile	2009 State Centile	2009 Home Value Base	2009 Home Value Distribution (%): Less than $50,000	$50,000 to $89,999	$90,000 to $174,999	$175,000 to $399,999	$400,000 or More	2009 Median Home Value
27610	RALEIGH	22233	20478	19.4	29.2	36.1	11.9	3.3	51116	52188	64	74	12645	12.8	11.2	46.4	28.1	1.5	134911
27612	RALEIGH	42258	16443	9.3	20.8	36.7	21.9	11.3	74326	77610	89	94	7898	1.4	0.9	13.3	64.0	20.5	265135
27613	RALEIGH	43712	18622	7.5	14.8	34.6	26.5	16.6	88169	99477	95	98	12478	0.9	0.7	11.5	69.8	17.1	249986
27614	RALEIGH	46433	12020	7.8	13.6	26.7	26.7	25.2	102720	107147	97	99	9881	1.3	1.1	21.1	48.8	27.6	276057
27615	RALEIGH	44715	17937	6.8	17.9	32.7	23.8	18.8	86690	96925	94	98	12159	1.2	1.3	12.6	60.2	24.8	279520
27616	RALEIGH	30457	14218	9.0	19.5	39.8	23.1	8.6	75424	79574	90	95	10450	16.1	4.5	32.0	42.6	4.8	170668
27617	RALEIGH	49941	5824	7.7	14.6	37.5	22.8	17.4	85987	91554	94	98	3729	0.4	0.3	3.4	57.3	38.6	346120
27695	RALEIGH	4394	0	0.0	0.0	0.0	0.0	0.0	0	108333	0	0	0	0.0	0.0	0.0	0.0	0.0	0
27701	DURHAM	17532	9162	41.0	30.2	21.7	3.9	3.1	30083	31410	8	5	2397	6.9	25.2	39.3	25.8	2.8	117535
27703	DURHAM	26693	16641	17.7	24.7	40.0	11.3	6.3	60836	64212	79	88	10346	6.3	10.8	47.7	32.2	2.9	145887
27704	DURHAM	22894	12432	23.0	27.4	41.1	5.9	2.5	49539	52061	60	68	6847	4.1	17.5	63.8	14.1	0.6	120722
27705	DURHAM	28920	19123	23.3	27.6	33.3	8.7	7.0	48836	51775	59	66	8864	7.2	6.1	40.1	39.6	7.0	166992
27707	DURHAM	32516	18496	20.7	24.8	33.9	9.6	10.9	55791	59080	72	84	9031	2.2	10.0	33.4	43.3	11.1	188314
27709	DURHAM	19287	32	18.8	31.3	37.5	9.4	3.1	50000	60000	61	70	11	0.0	9.1	63.6	27.3	0.0	131250
27712	DURHAM	36292	7658	6.9	13.7	47.3	18.4	13.7	80117	82169	92	97	6954	2.2	1.7	35.1	55.2	5.9	195704
27713	DURHAM	35774	19847	10.9	19.5	44.9	15.2	9.4	73661	76551	89	94	11568	1.9	5.0	38.1	52.9	2.1	186075
27801	ROCKY MOUNT	15940	7631	36.7	30.7	27.6	3.5	1.5	36055	38757	21	16	4291	18.6	38.2	40.4	2.5	0.2	85534
27803	ROCKY MOUNT	22094	9018	31.9	24.1	32.1	7.7	4.2	42146	46090	40	41	5664	19.2	20.2	44.2	14.8	1.6	103400
27804	ROCKY MOUNT	26928	11762	20.4	26.2	39.5	8.7	5.1	53182	54917	68	79	7244	16.5	16.8	48.0	15.8	2.9	110740
27805	AULANDER	16559	1205	43.2	26.8	25.6	3.7	0.7	30100	31486	8	6	899	25.6	33.7	36.0	4.7	0.0	81566
27806	AURORA	17106	1240	43.7	24.3	27.5	3.8	0.7	30723	33386	9	7	940	29.1	29.3	31.5	8.7	1.4	78611
27807	BAILEY	19398	2409	28.1	28.4	36.9	4.1	2.6	43328	47134	43	47	1848	28.3	24.8	39.1	6.9	0.9	85714
27808	BATH	26519	954	24.5	31.1	32.1	7.5	4.7	43618	45780	44	48	821	15.8	16.3	35.4	25.7	6.7	129790
27809	BATTLEBORO	20033	1947	30.7	25.1	35.6	5.4	3.2	42260	48187	40	42	1462	21.9	26.7	38.1	12.1	1.2	92800
27810	BELHAVEN	18462	1703	43.4	26.2	25.0	2.5	2.9	30556	32671	9	6	1256	26.8	22.1	29.9	18.3	2.9	92593
27812	BETHEL	17705	1209	38.2	26.9	29.6	3.7	1.6	36436	39880	22	18	829	21.8	35.0	34.7	8.3	0.1	84817
27814	BLOUNTS CREEK	21791	802	34.8	22.6	32.5	8.0	2.1	45000	46633	48	54	679	21.6	21.1	29.5	18.4	9.4	106039
27816	CASTALIA	17487	1100	35.6	27.4	31.1	4.4	1.5	36664	40181	23	19	871	41.9	20.8	26.9	9.2	1.3	64904
27817	CHOCOWINITY	22217	2838	27.3	30.5	31.8	6.7	3.7	41316	44890	37	38	2311	18.2	25.4	32.6	14.8	9.0	100776
27818	COMO	18787	581	33.6	26.0	36.5	3.1	0.9	37901	42832	26	24	458	38.2	30.3	25.3	6.1	0.0	70278
27820	CONWAY	19997	1317	38.5	27.4	26.1	5.2	2.8	33790	35652	15	13	1034	24.7	33.0	34.9	7.1	0.4	81023
27821	EDWARD	19396	50	38.0	24.0	32.0	6.0	0.0	45000	46633	48	54	41	22.0	19.5	43.9	14.6	0.0	101250
27822	ELM CITY	20756	2882	27.4	29.2	36.5	4.4	2.4	42963	43830	42	45	2282	15.2	18.6	49.4	15.1	1.7	111443
27823	ENFIELD	13912	3000	44.1	29.1	22.6	3.4	0.8	28790	31179	6	3	1937	31.0	27.6	35.4	5.5	0.5	75072
27824	ENGELHARD	16271	696	44.4	29.6	20.1	3.7	2.2	28513	32211	6	3	511	31.5	29.7	27.6	9.6	1.6	76778
27826	FAIRFIELD	11513	229	37.1	38.9	19.7	3.1	1.3	33340	35648	14	12	185	40.0	23.8	31.9	3.8	0.5	64091
27828	FARMVILLE	20590	3396	34.5	27.2	29.7	5.2	3.4	39877	42564	32	32	2148	18.6	26.8	45.5	7.8	1.3	94737
27829	FOUNTAIN	17423	807	41.1	25.5	28.7	2.7	1.9	32938	35274	13	11	558	28.3	32.4	32.6	5.6	1.1	77073
27830	FREMONT	19463	1793	32.4	30.3	30.4	4.9	2.0	38135	40385	27	25	1269	24.9	28.4	40.7	5.5	0.5	85430
27831	GARYSBURG	16391	1444	43.8	26.4	24.1	3.9	1.7	29369	31159	7	4	1073	30.7	31.3	32.7	4.9	0.4	75000
27832	GASTON	16846	1271	41.3	29.9	24.6	2.8	1.3	30723	31823	9	7	945	35.0	29.8	24.3	7.5	3.3	70461
27834	GREENVILLE	20461	20275	33.5	27.3	31.5	4.8	2.9	40268	42920	34	34	9873	20.2	26.3	42.6	8.9	2.0	94144
27837	GRIMESLAND	20708	2214	26.1	24.5	40.1	7.5	1.9	49115	51639	59	67	1786	23.6	27.0	36.8	11.4	1.1	89471
27839	HALIFAX	14972	1314	43.8	31.7	21.6	2.1	0.8	28755	30253	6	3	974	28.7	30.4	35.4	4.7	0.7	75200
27840	HAMILTON	16630	315	35.6	30.8	27.3	5.4	1.0	32996	33219	13	11	241	29.5	25.3	36.5	6.6	2.1	83235
27842	HENRICO	32102	709	20.9	27.5	38.4	8.9	4.4	51084	52704	64	73	635	12.6	14.0	23.3	36.2	13.9	175403
27843	HOBGOOD	16581	656	38.6	26.8	29.1	4.1	1.4	33092	34745	13	11	516	30.0	40.9	27.5	1.6	0.0	74462
27844	HOLLISTER	13741	1096	52.7	24.3	19.1	3.1	0.8	22906	24313	2	1	780	36.9	29.6	26.8	6.3	0.4	65522
27845	JACKSON	20715	763	38.9	25.4	27.9	5.4	2.4	34509	35766	17	14	597	21.3	32.7	35.7	10.1	0.3	84268
27846	JAMESVILLE	20076	1119	32.4	28.2	32.1	4.4	2.9	40330	42598	34	34	918	30.6	19.5	41.3	8.5	0.1	89825
27847	KELFORD	13363	128	46.1	34.4	17.2	0.8	1.6	26698	26897	4	2	96	35.4	35.4	22.9	5.2	1.0	62222
27849	LEWISTON WOODVILLE	13623	581	44.1	30.6	21.7	2.4	1.2	27742	28049	5	2	442	32.8	34.4	28.1	4.8	0.0	69231
27850	LITTLETON	24721	3189	28.9	28.8	31.1	6.8	4.4	42571	45944	41	43	2559	15.4	15.0	32.0	27.0	10.6	131445
27851	LUCAMA	19713	2081	26.6	30.5	36.5	4.8	1.6	43951	44150	45	50	1567	23.1	20.9	43.1	12.3	0.6	100411
27852	MACCLESFIELD	19700	1317	30.8	30.4	32.7	4.1	1.9	40603	42831	35	35	987	24.6	32.1	37.7	5.2	0.4	80500
27853	MARGARETTSVILLE	14033	142	40.8	35.2	21.1	1.4	1.4	30000	29548	8	5	115	25.2	35.7	31.3	7.8	0.0	70833
27855	MURFREESBORO	19058	2361	34.6	31.4	25.2	6.1	2.8	37358	39668	25	21	1718	32.0	24.7	32.4	10.0	0.9	77692
27856	NASHVILLE	21371	6178	26.8	26.5	36.6	6.1	4.0	45821	50072	51	57	4560	21.3	22.7	42.2	12.9	0.8	97787
27857	OAK CITY	16832	598	42.1	30.3	20.6	3.8	3.2	28825	30848	6	3	436	21.8	21.6	46.6	7.8	2.3	94462
27858	GREENVILLE	26115	21153	30.9	22.5	32.3	8.7	5.6	44755	49669	48	52	11006	9.3	12.6	50.1	24.4	3.6	125790
27860	PANTEGO	20202	850	32.9	29.5	30.2	4.2	3.1	37286	39168	24	21	707	28.3	24.0	31.3	15.4	1.0	85417
27862	PENDLETON	16350	454	44.9	25.3	24.2	3.7	1.8	30650	32951	9	6	373	24.4	35.4	30.0	9.9	0.3	75972
27863	PIKEVILLE	22423	3660	18.7	31.6	41.0	6.4	2.4	49749	51650	60	69	2944	21.2	19.5	50.7	7.8	0.7	99891
27864	PINETOPS	18850	1359	28.4	31.0	34.1	4.7	1.8	42099	45989	40	41	959	23.9	35.9	35.7	4.5	0.1	81262
27865	PINETOWN	20859	822	29.7	28.1	35.2	4.4	2.7	43157	45596	43	46	696	23.6	20.8	35.3	17.5	2.7	100000
27866	PLEASANT HILL	16268	238	37.0	33.2	22.7	6.7	0.4	35554	36338	19	16	195	25.1	32.8	35.4	6.7	0.0	79167
27869	RICH SQUARE	15707	966	40.0	28.6	25.6	5.1	0.8	31953	33125	11	9	722	24.5	40.3	28.1	6.0	1.1	75060
27870	ROANOKE RAPIDS	19245	11084	35.6	27.5	30.1	4.7	2.1	36912	39211	23	20	7370	18.7	23.7	43.8	12.7	1.1	98247
27871	ROBERSONVILLE	16339	1866	42.2	29.4	22.8	4.7	1.0	29456	30983	7	4	1272	24.4	31.1	38.4	5.5	0.6	84496
27872	ROXOBEL	16050	282	45.0	33.7	18.8	1.4	1.1	27172	27320	5	2	211	33.6	38.4	23.2	4.3	0.5	62955
27874	SCOTLAND NECK	16193	2089	47.1	30.2	17.0	3.4	2.4	26373	27872	4	2	1290	26.8	35.3	29.8	7.1	1.0	75692
27875	SCRANTON	19471	453	35.5	42.8	17.4	2.9	1.3	33162	35058	14	11	377	44.0	21.0	32.4	2.7	0.0	57759
27876	SEABOARD	18416	614	44.1	25.9	23.0	4.4	2.6	28423	29219	6	3	437	25.4	29.7	35.7	9.2	0.0	82241
27880	SIMS	19188	825	25.9	29.2	38.9	4.2	1.7	45250	44818	49	55	620	21.3	17.4	38.1	21.8	1.5	112829
27882	SPRING HOPE	19718	2671	30.1	29.5	33.1	5.2	2.1	41058	45067	36	37	1958	27.8	26.5	33.5	10.2	2.0	85170
27883	STANTONSBURG	17527	1183	31.4	32.5	30.9	4.0	1.2	37808	39195	26	23	889	15.2	23.3	51.2	10.1	0.2	103299
27884	STOKES	20363	462	28.8	26.2	37.2	5.2	2.6	43721	48531	45	49	381	22.0	36.2	35.7	5.2	0.8	83000
27885	SWANQUARTER	18615	454	33.0	27.5	35.0	4.2	0.2	38122	36714	27	25	357	17.6	36.7	34.7	10.9	0.0	85156
27886	TARBORO	20350	7457	28.8	27.8	35.0	5.3	3.1	43418	47303	44	47	5059	23.6	33.9	36.5	5.5	0.5	81710
27888	WALSTONBURG	17556	1360	28.4	32.0	32.9	5.1	1.6	42485	44754	41	43	998	33.2	16.2	45.3	3.2	2.1	90638
27889	WASHINGTON	20405	11025	32.2	29.0	30.6	6.1	2.1	40352	42537	34	34	7812	16.0	18.2	39.5	21.8	4.4	116486
27890	WELDON	16718	931	40.3	32.7	22.3	2.0	2.7	30550	32098	9	6	552	19.2	39.7	30.6	9.8	0.7	81404
27891	WHITAKERS	17503	1891	30.4	31.5	33.4	3.5	1.3	41185	43979	37	37	1446	34.2	30.5	29.9	4.6	0.8	70619
27892	WILLIAMSTON	18832	5868	33.5	29.5	30.5	4.8	1.8	37120	38554	24	21	4148	20.2	27.3	40.9	10.4	1.3	92804
27893	WILSON	17440	16322	39.4	28.3	26.6	3.6	2.0	33250	35685	14	12	8010	11.5	18.5	53.3	15.0	1.8	115006
27896	WILSON	32104	7131	13.8	20.0	45.7	12.7	7.9	63938	62065	82	90	5402	3.7	5.1	40.3	43.2	7.6	177440
27897	WOODLAND	17178	887	43.2	26.2	23.4	5.3	1.9	29663	31579	8	5	622	24.3	32.3	38.1	4.3	1.0	80238
27909	ELIZABETH CITY	18806	15910	33.8	28.2	30.9	4.9	2.2	38127	40458	27	25	10473	11.4	12.3	47.9	24.9	3.6	133838
27910	AHOSKIE	18863	4815	37.9	31.8	24.1	3.6	2.7	32250	34056	12	9	3206	19.7	30.9	38.2	10.1	1.0	89399
27916	AYDLETT	24318	199	14.6	29.6	43.7	6.5	5.5	53403	54880	69	79	158	13.3	9.5	16.5	50.6	10.1	204348
27917	BARCO	15089	444	30.6	43.2	24.3	1.8	0.0	37578	39109	25	23	301	38.2	24.3	24.3	13.3	0.0	69342
27919	BELVIDERE	17366	612	33.5	34.5	28.9	2.9	0.2	38262	40043	27	26	495	23.8	15.4	40.6	19.8	0.4	110980
27921	CAMDEN	22260	1939	21.5	31.0	35.5	10.0	2.0	47710	49188	56	63	1616	6.9	6.0	32.5	46.7	7.9	189231
27922	COFIELD	14976	255	47.5	32.9	16.9	2.0	0.8	25986	26266	4	2	195	35.4	32.3	28.7	3.6	0.0	68929
27923	COINJOCK	25515	264	14.4	31.8	42.8	6.1	4.9	52255	54038	66	76	206	18.0	9.2	15.0	47.6	10.2	197222
	NORTH CAROLINA	25989		22.3	26.1	36.6	9.4	5.6	51418	53634				12.2	15.1	38.7	27.9	6.1	132724
	UNITED STATES	27277		20.9	24.4	35.3	11.7	7.6	54719	56938				9.3	13.1	31.6	32.6	13.5	162279

ZIP CODE #	POST OFFICE NAME	FINANCIAL SERVICES: Auto Loan	Home Loan	Invest-ments	Retire-ment Plans	THE HOME: Home Improvements: Home Repair	Lawn & Garden	Furnishings: Comput-ers & Hard-ware-Personal	Major Appli-ances	TV, Radio, Sound Equip-ment	Furni-ture	ENTERTAINMENT: Dine out/ Carry out	Sports Equip-ment	Fees & Tickets	Toys & Games	Travel	Cable TV	PERSONAL: Apparel & Services	Auto Repairs	Health Insur-ance	Pets & Supplies
27610	RALEIGH	91	86	75	85	82	82	88	84	88	90	89	65	85	90	83	88	62	86	85	101
27612	RALEIGH	132	129	120	134	125	118	134	123	129	137	131	100	134	133	130	125	93	128	118	147
27613	RALEIGH	158	152	136	159	145	134	157	143	151	163	154	120	157	159	150	144	110	148	132	170
27614	RALEIGH	181	218	196	222	214	184	184	186	171	202	174	151	206	182	194	160	127	173	158	210
27615	RALEIGH	156	168	162	174	167	154	161	156	155	167	158	124	170	159	165	150	113	156	147	182
27616	RALEIGH	131	130	109	131	123	110	127	120	121	135	123	98	127	129	121	114	87	119	106	139
27617	RALEIGH	157	152	133	159	144	132	156	142	149	163	152	120	155	158	148	141	108	145	128	168
27695	RALEIGH	0	0	0	0	0	0	0	0	0	0	0	0	0	0	0	0	0	0	0	0
27701	DURHAM	64	48	45	52	45	50	66	54	69	62	68	44	58	68	56	70	48	64	61	69
27703	DURHAM	104	99	85	99	93	93	102	96	101	103	102	77	99	105	95	100	71	98	95	115
27704	DURHAM	82	74	69	75	72	77	80	77	82	78	82	60	76	83	76	83	57	80	81	93
27705	DURHAM	96	82	78	86	80	81	98	86	96	95	97	69	91	97	89	95	68	93	88	104
27707	DURHAM	111	100	98	105	99	100	113	103	114	113	114	81	110	113	107	113	80	110	107	124
27709	DURHAM	96	77	76	81	77	83	92	86	93	89	93	68	82	94	83	94	64	91	90	104
27712	DURHAM	126	155	145	157	153	146	132	138	129	138	130	105	149	130	145	127	93	132	134	159
27713	DURHAM	122	114	100	120	108	103	122	109	118	125	120	92	119	123	114	113	85	115	104	131
27801	ROCKY MOUNT	66	56	52	57	54	64	60	60	65	60	64	45	56	65	55	69	44	62	67	75
27803	ROCKY MOUNT	84	78	77	78	76	86	77	81	81	77	81	61	75	82	76	85	56	80	85	97
27804	ROCKY MOUNT	94	91	84	92	89	90	93	91	93	93	94	70	91	94	90	93	65	92	92	108
27805	AULANDER	71	48	70	46	48	71	52	65	59	48	57	50	40	59	49	66	38	61	69	78
27806	AURORA	72	48	70	46	49	72	52	65	59	48	58	50	40	60	49	66	38	61	69	79
27807	BAILEY	92	68	75	66	67	87	70	80	77	69	76	62	58	80	64	83	51	77	84	97
27808	BATH	106	77	112	75	81	108	79	100	86	73	85	75	64	85	79	95	56	92	103	118
27809	BATTLEBORO	86	74	80	74	73	88	72	82	77	71	76	63	66	79	71	81	52	78	84	98
27810	BELHAVEN	73	52	70	51	53	73	55	67	63	53	61	50	45	62	53	69	41	64	73	81
27812	BETHEL	81	56	78	53	56	80	58	73	66	55	65	56	45	67	55	73	43	68	76	88
27814	BLOUNTS CREEK	87	66	94	63	69	91	66	83	74	65	72	61	56	72	67	81	48	77	88	98
27816	CASTALIA	81	58	76	56	58	79	60	73	67	58	66	56	48	68	57	73	44	68	76	88
27817	CHOCOWINITY	91	73	88	71	75	91	73	85	79	73	77	62	64	79	71	84	52	80	89	101
27818	COMO	83	54	80	51	54	82	58	73	67	55	65	57	43	68	54	75	43	69	77	90
27820	CONWAY	85	58	80	56	59	83	61	76	69	58	68	58	48	70	58	76	45	71	79	92
27821	EDWARD	79	57	81	55	59	80	58	74	64	54	63	55	46	64	57	71	42	68	77	88
27822	ELM CITY	88	69	80	68	69	88	70	81	75	66	74	62	59	77	67	81	50	76	85	97
27823	ENFIELD	66	45	61	44	45	65	49	59	57	48	55	45	39	57	46	63	37	57	65	73
27824	ENGELHARD	71	46	68	43	46	69	49	62	57	47	55	48	37	58	46	63	37	58	66	76
27826	FAIRFIELD	73	47	70	45	47	71	51	64	58	48	57	50	38	59	47	65	38	60	67	78
27828	FARMVILLE	85	65	75	64	64	83	69	78	75	66	74	59	58	76	64	81	50	75	83	94
27829	FOUNTAIN	77	52	72	50	52	76	55	68	63	53	61	53	42	64	51	70	41	64	72	83
27830	FREMONT	84	62	78	59	62	83	64	77	71	61	69	58	52	72	60	77	46	72	81	92
27831	GARYSBURG	74	48	71	46	48	73	52	65	60	49	58	51	39	61	48	67	39	61	69	80
27832	GASTON	66	48	61	46	48	65	51	60	59	51	57	44	43	58	48	65	38	59	66	73
27834	GREENVILLE	78	60	56	61	57	63	72	66	74	71	74	53	63	76	63	74	51	71	68	81
27837	GRIMESLAND	91	76	76	73	74	86	74	82	79	75	78	61	66	82	70	83	53	78	83	98
27839	HALIFAX	65	43	62	41	43	64	46	58	54	44	52	45	35	54	43	60	35	55	61	71
27840	HAMILTON	79	51	76	48	51	77	55	69	63	52	62	54	41	64	51	71	41	65	73	85
27842	HENRICO	91	87	112	81	97	104	83	98	88	90	86	64	83	80	91	93	58	94	109	112
27843	HOBGOOD	78	54	69	51	53	75	56	68	64	54	62	53	44	66	52	70	42	64	72	83
27844	HOLLISTER	66	43	63	40	43	65	46	58	53	44	52	45	34	54	43	59	34	54	61	71
27845	JACKSON	81	56	80	53	56	82	59	75	68	55	66	57	46	68	57	75	44	70	80	90
27846	JAMESVILLE	89	62	82	60	63	88	66	80	74	62	72	61	52	76	62	82	48	75	85	97
27847	KELFORD	66	43	64	41	43	65	46	58	53	44	52	45	35	54	43	60	35	55	62	72
27849	LEWISTON WOODVILLE	68	44	66	42	44	67	48	60	55	45	54	47	36	56	44	61	35	56	63	74
27850	LITTLETON	90	71	103	69	76	97	71	88	79	71	77	63	63	76	74	85	52	83	94	104
27851	LUCAMA	90	65	77	63	65	87	68	80	75	65	74	61	55	78	63	82	49	75	85	96
27852	MACCLESFIELD	86	60	84	58	61	87	64	79	72	59	70	60	50	72	61	79	46	74	84	95
27853	MARGARETTSVILLE	72	47	69	44	47	70	50	63	58	48	56	49	38	59	47	65	37	59	67	78
27855	MURFREESBORO	78	61	70	59	61	76	65	72	70	63	69	54	56	71	61	75	47	70	76	86
27856	NASHVILLE	89	78	84	77	77	92	76	85	81	74	80	65	70	82	75	86	54	82	89	102
27857	OAK CITY	75	49	72	46	48	73	52	65	60	49	59	51	39	61	48	67	39	62	69	81
27858	GREENVILLE	89	74	68	78	71	73	97	78	90	88	91	66	83	91	80	87	64	86	78	96
27860	PANTEGO	88	63	90	61	65	89	65	82	72	60	70	62	52	71	64	79	46	75	85	98
27862	PENDLETON	76	50	73	47	50	74	53	67	61	50	59	52	40	62	50	68	39	63	70	82
27863	PIKEVILLE	91	84	74	81	81	85	80	84	82	83	82	62	75	86	76	84	56	81	83	99
27864	PINETOPS	87	64	81	61	64	85	65	78	73	64	71	59	54	74	62	79	48	74	81	95
27865	PINETOWN	92	66	95	64	69	93	68	86	75	63	73	64	54	74	67	82	49	79	89	102
27866	PLEASANT HILL	77	50	74	47	50	76	54	68	62	51	61	53	40	63	50	69	40	64	72	83
27869	RICH SQUARE	75	50	73	48	50	74	54	67	62	50	60	52	41	62	51	68	40	63	72	82
27870	ROANOKE RAPIDS	76	59	70	58	59	76	63	71	69	60	67	54	54	69	59	74	45	69	76	85
27871	ROBERSONVILLE	74	50	70	47	49	72	53	65	60	50	59	51	40	61	49	67	39	62	69	80
27872	ROXOBEL	67	44	65	41	44	66	47	59	54	45	53	46	35	55	44	60	35	56	62	73
27874	SCOTLAND NECK	68	48	62	47	48	67	52	61	59	50	57	46	42	59	49	65	38	59	67	75
27875	SCRANTON	71	47	69	44	46	70	50	63	57	47	56	49	37	58	46	64	37	59	66	77
27876	SEABOARD	80	52	77	49	52	79	56	70	64	53	63	55	42	66	52	72	42	66	74	87
27880	SIMS	85	67	73	67	68	85	68	79	74	65	72	60	58	76	65	79	49	74	82	94
27882	SPRING HOPE	90	64	83	62	64	88	66	80	74	64	73	61	53	76	62	81	48	75	84	97
27883	STANTONSBURG	80	56	70	54	55	77	59	70	66	57	64	54	46	68	54	72	43	66	74	85
27884	STOKES	96	69	79	67	68	91	71	83	79	70	78	64	57	83	65	86	52	79	88	101
27885	SWANQUARTER	77	54	78	52	56	77	56	71	62	52	61	54	44	62	55	69	40	65	74	85
27886	TARBORO	83	68	74	67	67	83	72	78	77	69	76	59	64	78	68	82	52	77	84	94
27888	WALSTONBURG	82	65	69	62	63	77	66	73	71	66	70	56	56	73	61	75	47	71	75	88
27889	WASHINGTON	75	66	69	65	66	74	67	71	71	67	70	53	63	71	65	74	48	70	75	85
27890	WELDON	67	52	57	52	50	65	57	61	63	55	62	46	50	63	52	68	42	62	68	75
27891	WHITAKERS	86	59	78	57	59	83	62	75	70	60	69	58	49	72	58	77	46	71	79	92
27892	WILLIAMSTON	77	61	70	60	61	77	62	72	68	60	66	54	53	68	60	73	45	68	76	86
27893	WILSON	67	54	55	55	53	64	61	61	66	59	64	47	55	65	56	69	44	63	68	75
27896	WILSON	113	117	116	118	118	119	111	115	110	113	111	86	113	111	114	112	77	112	115	134
27897	WOODLAND	78	51	75	48	51	77	55	69	63	52	61	54	41	64	51	70	41	65	73	85
27909	ELIZABETH CITY	75	62	64	62	62	72	65	69	69	64	68	52	59	70	61	73	47	69	74	83
27910	AHOSKIE	75	57	69	56	57	75	61	69	68	59	67	52	52	68	58	74	45	68	76	84
27916	AYDLETT	103	82	130	80	89	109	82	104	86	77	85	76	70	83	88	93	57	96	104	121
27917	BARCO	69	50	71	48	51	70	51	65	56	47	55	49	41	56	50	62	37	59	67	77
27919	BELVIDERE	74	53	76	51	55	75	54	69	60	51	59	52	43	60	54	66	39	63	72	82
27921	CAMDEN	92	78	103	78	82	95	77	92	80	74	79	67	69	79	80	85	53	86	92	107
27922	COFIELD	64	41	61	39	41	62	44	56	51	42	50	44	33	52	41	57	33	53	59	69
27923	COINJOCK	101	79	126	78	86	106	80	101	84	75	83	74	68	81	85	90	55	93	101	118
	NORTH CAROLINA	100	89	90	89	88	96	91	94	94	91	93	73	85	95	88	96	64	93	96	112
	UNITED STATES	100	100	100	100	100	100	100	100	100	100	100	100	100	100	100	100	100	100	100	100

ZIP CODE #	POST OFFICE NAME	COUNTY FIPS CODE	POPULATION 2000	POPULATION 2009	POPULATION 2014	2000-2009 ANNUAL RATE % Rate	2000-2009 ANNUAL RATE State Centile	HOUSEHOLDS 2000	HOUSEHOLDS 2009	HOUSEHOLDS 2014	HOUSEHOLDS % Annual Rate 2000-2009	HOUSEHOLDS 2009 Average HH Size	FAMILIES 2000	FAMILIES 2009	FAMILIES % Annual Rate 2000-2009
27924	COLERAIN	015	3449	3363	3306	-0.3	8	1369	1394	1387	0.2	2.41	977	965	-0.1
27925	COLUMBIA	177	3917	4001	3946	0.2	21	1438	1469	1464	0.2	2.32	989	978	-0.1
27926	CORAPEAKE	073	1748	2161	2347	2.3	83	646	815	892	2.5	2.65	494	610	2.3
27927	COROLLA	053	648	1117	1367	6.1	97	314	554	680	6.3	2.02	205	349	5.9
27928	CRESWELL	187	2108	2066	2006	-0.2	10	828	840	825	0.2	2.45	623	616	-0.1
27929	CURRITUCK	053	716	793	866	1.1	56	276	309	339	1.2	2.53	221	241	0.9
27932	EDENTON	041	12351	12677	13019	0.3	24	4729	5149	5330	0.9	2.41	3386	3582	0.6
27935	EURE	073	1531	1685	1788	1.0	53	599	673	719	1.3	2.49	445	488	1.0
27937	GATES	073	3171	3746	4076	1.8	76	1163	1398	1529	2.0	2.68	893	1048	1.7
27938	GATESVILLE	073	1457	1647	1762	1.3	63	472	550	594	1.7	2.72	344	388	1.3
27939	GRANDY	053	1613	2350	2719	4.2	93	681	1024	1192	4.5	2.29	491	718	4.2
27941	HARBINGER	053	766	1246	1491	5.4	96	302	502	603	5.6	2.48	222	360	5.4
27942	HARRELLSVILLE	091	1228	1228	1209	0.0	15	497	515	513	0.4	2.38	351	352	0.0
27944	HERTFORD	143	10284	11632	12379	1.3	63	4205	4920	5293	1.7	2.34	3052	3475	1.4
27946	HOBBSVILLE	073	920	1043	1121	1.4	66	376	439	476	1.7	2.38	275	312	1.4
27947	JARVISBURG	053	771	1087	1271	3.8	92	297	422	496	3.9	2.58	217	300	3.6
27948	KILL DEVIL HILLS	055	9295	11195	11904	2.0	79	3988	4913	5265	2.3	2.27	2446	2901	1.9
27949	KITTY HAWK	055	6003	6592	6680	1.0	53	2565	2852	2900	1.2	2.31	1865	2022	0.9
27950	KNOTTS ISLAND	053	1825	2200	2354	2.0	79	688	837	899	2.1	2.63	518	614	1.9
27953	MANNS HARBOR	055	877	969	1047	1.1	56	329	368	400	1.2	2.63	250	273	1.0
27954	MANTEO	055	5197	6238	6674	2.0	79	2107	2574	2766	2.2	2.40	1465	1740	1.9
27956	MAPLE	053	201	244	273	2.1	81	57	84	95	4.3	2.75	41	58	3.8
27957	MERRY HILL	015	1132	1113	1095	-0.2	10	465	479	478	0.3	2.32	332	332	0.0
27958	MOYOCK	053	7168	10208	11672	3.9	93	2546	3668	4207	4.0	2.78	2023	2870	3.9
27959	NAGS HEAD	055	6763	8189	8762	2.1	81	2956	3663	3943	2.3	2.20	1893	2267	2.0
27960	OCRACOKE	095	769	675	638	-1.4	1	370	339	325	-0.9	1.99	219	192	-1.4
27962	PLYMOUTH	187	7793	7118	6777	-1.0	2	3068	2899	2790	-0.6	2.40	2206	2024	-0.9
27964	POINT HARBOR	053	376	581	698	4.8	95	161	253	305	5.0	2.30	117	179	4.7
27965	POPLAR BRANCH	053	615	847	970	3.5	91	240	330	379	3.5	2.57	174	233	3.2
27966	POWELLS POINT	053	785	1263	1520	5.3	96	296	483	583	5.4	2.61	214	340	5.1
27970	ROPER	187	3947	3887	3791	-0.2	10	1531	1573	1553	0.3	2.47	1117	1117	0.0
27973	SHAWBORO	053	1132	1574	1815	3.6	91	454	651	756	4.0	2.41	337	469	3.6
27974	SHILOH	029	1094	1381	1587	2.6	86	415	535	618	2.8	2.57	317	398	2.5
27976	SOUTH MILLS	029	2293	3227	3757	3.8	92	895	1304	1532	4.2	2.47	670	954	3.9
27978	STUMPY POINT	055	305	454	490	4.4	94	131	199	216	4.6	2.28	99	147	4.4
27979	SUNBURY	073	1711	1949	2103	1.4	66	656	769	837	1.7	2.53	491	560	1.4
27980	TYNER	041	1898	1979	2041	0.5	32	739	794	825	0.8	2.49	540	566	0.5
27981	WANCHESE	055	1527	1853	2003	2.1	81	614	762	829	2.4	2.43	433	522	2.0
27983	WINDSOR	015	9467	9160	8982	-0.4	7	3697	3733	3707	0.1	2.41	2587	2536	-0.2
27986	WINTON	091	1440	2667	2644	6.9	99	577	595	592	0.3	2.28	393	392	0.0
28001	ALBEMARLE	167	27549	27988	27987	0.2	21	10931	11122	11138	0.2	2.41	7580	7474	-0.2
28006	ALEXIS	071	741	770	827	0.4	28	291	308	333	0.6	2.50	230	238	0.4
28012	BELMONT	071	18705	20591	21643	1.0	53	7339	8172	8624	1.2	2.45	5191	5608	0.8
28016	BESSEMER CITY	071	13100	13940	14456	0.7	40	5055	5435	5657	0.8	2.56	3746	3920	0.5
28018	BOSTIC	161	4832	5010	4994	0.4	28	1915	2038	2047	0.7	2.43	1401	1446	0.3
28020	CASAR	045	2442	2730	2822	1.2	60	993	1116	1156	1.3	2.44	739	806	0.9
28021	CHERRYVILLE	071	12513	13221	13641	0.6	36	4954	5284	5471	0.7	2.45	3614	3750	0.4
28023	CHINA GROVE	159	13336	14372	14959	0.8	44	5102	5519	5752	0.9	2.59	3871	4074	0.6
28025	CONCORD	025	40967	49364	55002	2.0	79	15546	18959	21177	2.2	2.56	11159	13131	1.8
28027	CONCORD	025	38716	55027	64615	3.9	93	14370	20803	24501	4.1	2.62	10854	15304	3.8
28031	CORNELIUS	119	14160	24477	29858	6.1	97	5966	10540	12876	6.3	2.32	3966	6562	5.6
28032	CRAMERTON	071	2427	2921	3143	2.0	79	997	1220	1321	2.2	2.38	654	775	1.9
28033	CROUSE	109	2657	3272	3573	2.3	83	990	1220	1336	2.3	2.68	784	944	2.0
28034	DALLAS	071	15219	16982	17902	1.2	60	5900	6670	7071	1.3	2.50	4393	4836	1.0
28036	DAVIDSON	119	9705	12471	14120	2.7	87	3059	4131	4771	3.3	2.56	2307	2952	2.7
28037	DENVER	109	12397	16732	18919	3.3	90	4827	6638	7541	3.5	2.51	3749	5025	3.2
28040	ELLENBORO	161	7495	7831	7816	0.5	32	3044	3255	3271	0.7	2.39	2209	2290	0.4
28043	FOREST CITY	161	21295	20629	20170	-0.3	8	8629	8545	8409	-0.1	2.35	6004	5773	-0.4
28052	GASTONIA	071	36297	36182	36450	0.0	15	13518	13547	13691	0.0	2.63	9748	9499	-0.3
28054	GASTONIA	071	33152	35944	37364	0.9	48	13771	15002	15659	0.9	2.32	8899	9361	0.5
28056	GASTONIA	071	28488	32076	33920	1.3	63	10534	11930	12661	1.4	2.68	8288	9174	1.1
28071	GOLD HILL	159	2612	2975	3176	1.4	66	977	1126	1206	1.5	2.61	749	840	1.2
28073	GROVER	045	4774	5038	5120	0.6	36	1802	1910	1943	0.6	2.64	1344	1383	0.3
28075	HARRISBURG	025	8203	14024	17397	6.0	97	2847	4968	6179	6.2	2.81	2395	4064	5.9
28078	HUNTERSVILLE	119	27698	46603	57536	5.8	96	10221	17579	21844	6.0	2.62	7668	12745	5.6
28079	INDIAN TRAIL	179	15500	28010	36641	6.6	98	5575	10210	13393	6.8	2.74	4523	7973	6.3
28080	IRON STATION	109	6153	7637	8391	2.4	83	2242	2831	3126	2.6	2.70	1761	2167	2.3
28081	KANNAPOLIS	025	23039	24568	26000	0.7	40	8984	9699	10287	0.8	2.51	6396	6630	0.4
28083	KANNAPOLIS	025	20184	23105	25195	1.5	69	8270	9551	10426	1.6	2.39	5543	6111	1.1
28086	KINGS MOUNTAIN	045	26592	27385	27642	0.3	24	10077	10411	10527	0.4	2.60	7580	7629	0.1
28088	LANDIS	159	2910	2983	3045	0.3	24	1169	1196	1221	0.2	2.49	819	809	-0.1
28090	LAWNDALE	045	8610	9235	9464	0.8	44	3283	3546	3644	0.8	2.57	2479	2604	0.5
28091	LILESVILLE	007	2972	2745	2657	-0.9	2	1171	1108	1079	-0.6	2.48	843	776	-0.9
28092	LINCOLNTON	109	34470	38445	41112	1.2	60	12965	14635	15696	1.3	2.57	9573	10518	1.0
28097	LOCUST	167	4080	4441	4610	0.9	48	1540	1710	1782	1.1	2.60	1192	1290	0.9
28098	LOWELL	071	2927	3519	3777	2.0	79	1201	1457	1572	2.1	2.42	843	989	1.7
28103	MARSHVILLE	179	9308	11934	14234	2.7	87	3435	4433	5303	2.8	2.66	2624	3255	2.4
28104	MATTHEWS	179	15976	26883	34487	5.8	96	5561	9507	12207	6.0	2.83	4647	7695	5.6
28105	MATTHEWS	119	30189	38719	44399	2.7	87	10994	14467	16670	3.0	2.65	8154	10449	2.7
28107	MIDLAND	025	5642	6832	7786	2.1	81	2102	2609	2986	2.4	2.62	1646	1964	1.9
28110	MONROE	179	35683	53216	66075	4.4	94	12508	18834	23507	4.5	2.80	9717	14216	4.2
28112	MONROE	179	22982	29091	34118	2.6	86	8104	10249	12084	2.6	2.76	6096	7408	2.1
28114	MOORESBORO	045	7040	7302	7339	0.4	28	2810	2949	2974	0.5	2.47	2053	2091	0.2
28115	MOORESVILLE	097	24316	32671	37812	3.2	89	9329	12602	14636	3.3	2.56	6740	8844	3.0
28117	MOORESVILLE	097	19321	32709	39787	5.9	97	7407	12517	15227	5.8	2.61	5795	9495	5.5
28119	MORVEN	007	3539	3341	3252	-0.6	5	1230	1175	1149	-0.5	2.84	932	871	-0.7
28120	MOUNT HOLLY	071	15757	18233	19517	1.6	72	6279	7352	7903	1.7	2.46	4529	5147	1.4
28124	MOUNT PLEASANT	025	6307	7295	8046	1.6	72	2276	2697	2994	1.9	2.63	1818	2085	1.5
28125	MOUNT ULLA	159	2053	2427	2632	1.8	76	781	929	1009	1.9	2.60	592	684	1.6
28127	NEW LONDON	167	7048	7907	8201	1.3	63	2448	2840	2982	1.6	2.63	1877	2118	1.3
28128	NORWOOD	167	7465	7774	7860	0.4	28	2960	3140	3191	0.6	2.47	2180	2245	0.3
28129	OAKBORO	167	5182	5876	6151	1.4	66	2043	2357	2476	1.6	2.49	1568	1764	1.3
28133	PEACHLAND	007	2950	2740	2650	-0.8	3	1111	1002	972	-1.1	2.44	841	741	-1.4
28134	PINEVILLE	119	7314	9244	11212	2.6	86	2778	3617	4396	2.9	2.45	1802	2204	2.2
28135	POLKTON	007	6008	6260	6102	0.4	28	1871	1763	1717	-0.6	2.63	1361	1250	-0.9
	NORTH CAROLINA					1.7					1.8	2.46			1.5
	UNITED STATES					1.0					1.1	2.59			0.9

#	ZIP CODE POST OFFICE NAME	RACE (%) White 2000	White 2009	Black 2000	Black 2009	Asian/Pacific 2000	Asian/Pacific 2009	% Hispanic Origin 2000	% Hispanic Origin 2009	2009 AGE DISTRIBUTION (%) 0-4	5-9	10-14	15-19	20-24	25-44	45-64	65-84	85+	18+	MEDIAN AGE 2009	% 2009 Males	% 2009 Females
27924	COLERAIN	45.3	43.4	53.3	54.7	0.0	0.0	1.3	1.7	6.5	6.8	6.9	6.3	5.0	22.6	28.6	15.2	2.1	75.9	41.8	47.9	52.1
27925	COLUMBIA	55.8	55.4	40.1	40.6	0.7	0.7	3.6	3.6	4.7	5.0	5.2	5.7	7.3	29.3	28.0	12.6	2.2	81.6	40.1	55.2	44.8
27926	CORAPEAKE	69.6	67.9	27.4	28.6	0.5	0.6	1.7	2.0	6.2	6.4	6.7	7.4	6.0	24.1	30.1	11.8	1.4	76.2	40.4	49.3	50.7
27927	COROLLA	97.4	96.6	1.2	1.3	0.3	0.4	0.6	1.0	3.0	2.3	3.0	3.0	3.0	16.8	55.9	13.1	0.1	89.5	54.2	51.5	48.5
27928	CRESWELL	62.3	59.0	32.4	33.0	0.4	0.5	4.1	6.4	5.5	5.8	6.2	6.4	4.9	25.0	28.9	15.4	1.8	78.6	42.2	49.9	50.1
27929	CURRITUCK	94.6	92.7	3.1	4.0	0.4	0.5	1.8	2.8	5.3	5.9	6.7	6.2	4.4	23.0	33.3	13.7	1.5	77.8	44.0	51.1	48.9
27932	EDENTON	58.8	56.6	39.3	40.5	0.3	0.4	1.5	2.5	5.7	5.9	6.4	7.5	6.1	20.5	28.7	16.2	3.1	77.8	43.3	47.0	53.0
27935	EURE	76.8	75.4	21.9	23.0	0.3	0.5	0.5	0.7	5.7	6.1	6.8	7.0	4.9	23.9	30.6	13.2	1.8	77.0	41.8	49.2	50.8
27937	GATES	52.8	51.6	45.6	46.4	0.1	0.2	0.6	0.7	6.2	6.6	7.3	7.3	5.4	24.5	29.2	12.0	1.5	75.4	40.0	49.1	50.9
27938	GATESVILLE	48.1	46.3	50.6	52.0	0.1	0.2	0.3	0.4	5.7	6.2	6.4	6.7	5.8	24.0	27.4	14.4	3.4	77.7	41.5	51.1	48.9
27939	GRANDY	88.9	88.3	8.0	7.7	0.6	0.9	0.6	1.0	5.5	6.0	6.6	5.7	4.6	24.7	30.4	14.8	1.7	78.2	42.8	49.3	50.7
27941	HARBINGER	94.2	93.4	4.7	5.0	0.1	0.2	0.8	1.1	5.1	5.5	5.9	5.4	4.1	22.2	35.5	14.4	1.8	80.0	45.9	49.8	50.2
27942	HARRELLSVILLE	41.5	40.0	57.8	59.2	0.1	0.1	0.7	0.9	5.0	5.0	5.1	6.0	5.7	22.6	33.1	15.4	2.1	81.1	45.3	45.7	54.3
27944	HERTFORD	70.4	69.0	28.4	29.4	0.2	0.3	0.6	0.9	5.3	5.3	5.5	5.8	5.5	21.3	30.2	18.7	2.5	80.2	45.9	48.0	52.0
27946	HOBBSVILLE	57.8	55.9	41.2	42.7	0.3	0.5	0.9	1.2	4.6	6.2	6.9	7.0	4.1	25.5	29.2	14.1	2.3	77.8	42.1	48.7	51.3
27947	JARVISBURG	89.8	89.2	8.0	7.9	0.3	0.5	0.8	1.1	5.5	6.0	6.4	5.7	4.5	24.4	32.3	13.6	1.6	78.4	43.2	49.0	51.0
27948	KILL DEVIL HILLS	96.6	95.4	0.6	0.6	0.6	0.9	2.6	3.8	5.5	6.0	6.4	5.2	5.2	31.1	29.0	10.7	0.9	78.7	39.4	50.6	49.4
27949	KITTY HAWK	98.1	97.6	0.4	0.5	0.3	0.4	1.2	1.6	4.5	4.9	5.7	4.6	2.1	19.4	37.3	20.3	1.2	81.9	49.9	50.3	49.7
27950	KNOTTS ISLAND	98.7	98.3	0.1	0.0	0.4	0.6	1.0	1.5	5.4	5.7	6.3	7.0	5.6	26.3	32.5	10.3	0.9	78.4	40.8	51.1	48.9
27953	MANNS HARBOR	95.1	92.7	0.6	0.6	0.0	0.0	5.1	7.6	6.6	7.0	7.1	5.7	4.3	24.8	30.7	12.5	1.3	75.6	41.5	49.6	50.4
27954	MANTEO	82.9	80.8	12.7	13.0	0.2	0.2	3.7	5.4	5.6	5.6	6.2	6.2	5.3	26.1	32.0	11.7	1.4	78.8	41.5	50.3	49.7
27956	MAPLE	79.6	77.5	15.9	16.4	0.5	1.2	4.0	4.9	6.1	6.6	6.6	6.6	4.9	25.4	27.9	13.1	2.9	76.6	40.6	49.2	50.8
27957	MERRY HILL	51.6	49.4	47.6	49.5	0.0	0.0	0.6	0.8	4.8	5.0	6.3	6.1	5.1	22.1	33.5	15.0	2.1	80.1	45.4	48.2	51.8
27958	MOYOCK	90.1	89.2	7.7	7.8	0.5	0.7	1.5	2.1	6.8	6.9	7.0	7.1	6.1	25.6	29.8	9.7	0.9	74.8	38.4	50.2	49.8
27959	NAGS HEAD	97.5	96.8	0.6	0.6	0.6	0.8	1.0	1.5	4.1	4.5	5.4	5.2	4.1	25.1	35.1	14.6	1.8	82.5	45.8	50.1	49.9
27960	OCRACOKE	96.1	95.3	1.7	1.8	0.3	0.3	2.0	2.8	3.9	4.3	4.3	2.7	1.6	24.3	39.7	17.5	1.8	85.8	50.8	51.0	49.0
27962	PLYMOUTH	44.7	43.3	53.0	53.3	0.5	0.7	2.0	2.8	7.0	6.8	6.9	6.6	5.7	21.6	28.6	14.0	2.9	75.0	41.2	46.4	53.6
27964	POINT HARBOR	89.4	88.5	9.0	9.3	0.0	0.2	1.1	1.7	6.2	6.5	6.7	6.2	5.0	26.2	31.3	10.7	1.2	76.6	40.5	48.5	51.5
27965	POPLAR BRANCH	88.1	87.2	8.8	8.7	0.5	0.8	0.7	0.9	5.5	6.1	6.7	5.8	4.6	25.3	30.0	14.3	1.7	77.7	42.2	49.1	50.9
27966	POWELLS POINT	87.4	86.2	10.7	11.2	0.1	0.1	1.4	2.1	6.7	7.0	7.0	6.5	5.3	28.0	29.0	9.4	1.0	75.2	38.0	47.8	52.2
27970	ROPER	48.4	45.8	49.4	50.9	0.2	0.2	1.9	2.9	5.7	6.1	6.5	6.4	5.1	23.4	30.8	14.1	1.8	77.8	42.4	48.8	51.2
27973	SHAWBORO	82.0	80.0	16.0	17.3	0.4	0.4	1.5	2.2	6.4	6.4	6.5	6.4	5.5	24.5	29.6	13.1	1.6	76.9	41.0	49.9	50.1
27974	SHILOH	87.4	85.4	8.3	8.3	2.6	4.1	0.5	0.7	6.9	7.2	7.2	5.8	4.6	25.9	26.9	13.8	1.7	75.2	40.0	49.3	50.7
27976	SOUTH MILLS	78.5	77.3	19.2	19.7	0.4	0.6	0.7	0.8	5.1	5.7	6.1	6.6	5.0	25.6	32.0	12.4	1.5	79.1	42.5	49.6	50.4
27978	STUMPY POINT	94.8	92.5	0.7	0.7	0.0	0.0	4.9	7.7	6.6	7.0	7.0	5.5	4.2	25.1	30.0	13.0	1.5	75.6	41.5	49.1	50.9
27979	SUNBURY	54.5	52.9	43.8	44.8	0.3	0.5	0.7	0.9	6.0	6.1	6.5	7.4	6.0	23.4	29.6	13.2	1.9	76.9	41.3	47.8	52.2
27980	TYNER	69.5	67.3	28.4	29.8	0.5	0.8	1.5	2.1	5.7	6.0	6.5	6.8	4.6	22.6	30.5	14.9	2.4	77.6	43.2	49.6	50.4
27981	WANCHESE	98.1	97.6	0.3	0.3	0.1	0.2	1.8	2.6	5.1	5.3	5.6	5.6	5.3	30.4	31.2	10.1	1.4	80.7	40.9	51.6	48.4
27983	WINDSOR	34.1	33.1	64.5	65.1	0.2	0.3	0.9	1.2	6.3	6.5	6.6	6.7	5.6	22.6	29.3	14.1	2.4	77.2	41.6	47.2	52.8
27986	WINTON	29.5	28.9	65.8	65.7	0.6	0.9	1.5	1.9	3.3	3.7	3.7	6.4	11.3	43.3	21.3	6.3	0.7	85.2	34.5	70.2	29.8
28001	ALBEMARLE	81.0	78.7	14.0	14.3	3.0	4.3	1.4	2.1	6.7	6.6	6.6	6.6	5.7	25.8	25.9	13.2	2.8	76.0	39.3	48.9	51.1
28006	ALEXIS	90.1	89.0	8.1	8.6	0.1	0.3	0.8	1.3	5.5	6.6	7.4	7.5	4.4	27.5	30.8	9.4	0.9	75.7	39.1	51.0	49.0
28012	BELMONT	89.1	86.6	6.2	6.8	2.2	3.2	2.4	3.6	6.0	6.2	6.4	7.0	6.3	26.4	28.8	11.0	1.7	77.8	39.5	49.0	51.0
28016	BESSEMER CITY	88.7	86.7	8.9	9.9	0.4	0.5	2.5	3.7	7.2	6.9	7.0	6.5	6.1	29.2	26.0	10.2	1.0	75.0	36.5	49.2	50.8
28018	BOSTIC	96.6	95.8	2.2	2.5	0.4	0.5	0.7	1.1	5.7	5.8	6.4	6.8	5.2	26.2	28.4	13.4	2.1	77.8	40.9	49.7	50.3
28020	CASAR	97.6	96.9	1.2	1.3	0.0	0.0	1.9	2.7	5.2	5.5	6.0	6.2	4.4	27.1	30.4	13.3	1.8	79.4	42.3	50.5	49.5
28021	CHERRYVILLE	88.9	87.0	9.3	10.3	0.5	0.7	2.0	2.9	6.1	6.2	6.5	6.2	4.7	25.5	28.4	13.8	2.5	77.2	41.4	49.3	50.7
28023	CHINA GROVE	90.7	88.1	5.2	5.8	0.8	1.1	4.6	6.8	6.6	6.5	6.5	6.4	5.4	27.2	28.4	11.3	1.6	76.4	39.0	49.5	50.5
28025	CONCORD	80.6	78.9	14.3	13.5	0.7	0.9	6.6	9.7	7.1	6.9	6.7	6.5	6.2	28.6	25.8	10.6	1.7	75.5	37.2	49.3	50.7
28027	CONCORD	85.2	82.1	9.8	10.7	1.4	1.9	5.4	7.8	7.8	7.5	7.3	6.8	5.4	30.3	25.5	8.3	1.1	73.1	35.5	49.4	50.6
28031	CORNELIUS	92.6	88.1	4.7	7.4	1.3	1.9	2.5	5.0	7.0	6.8	6.8	5.7	5.3	30.9	28.7	8.2	0.8	76.0	37.9	50.0	50.0
28032	CRAMERTON	93.8	92.2	3.4	4.0	0.8	1.2	0.9	1.4	6.2	6.3	6.0	6.5	6.1	28.6	26.9	11.7	1.7	77.6	37.8	48.3	51.7
28033	CROUSE	94.7	92.5	2.4	2.7	0.6	0.9	5.0	8.0	6.8	7.0	7.1	6.9	5.3	28.6	28.2	9.3	0.9	74.8	38.1	50.2	49.8
28034	DALLAS	89.3	88.2	9.2	9.6	0.3	0.4	1.6	2.3	6.4	6.6	6.7	6.5	5.3	28.3	27.4	11.5	1.2	76.2	38.6	50.0	50.0
28036	DAVIDSON	89.2	86.6	7.6	8.6	1.4	1.9	2.0	3.4	6.2	6.4	6.0	10.4	11.2	23.3	25.5	9.0	1.9	78.1	35.3	49.7	50.3
28037	DENVER	95.0	93.9	3.5	3.9	0.3	0.5	1.2	1.9	5.8	6.2	6.9	6.6	4.1	26.0	31.8	11.4	1.1	76.9	41.6	50.1	49.9
28040	ELLENBORO	93.9	93.2	4.5	4.8	0.2	0.3	1.1	1.5	6.5	6.5	6.8	6.8	4.9	27.0	27.5	12.2	1.8	76.0	39.4	49.1	50.9
28043	FOREST CITY	80.5	79.0	16.8	17.3	0.5	0.7	3.0	4.1	6.6	6.5	6.7	6.4	5.2	25.8	26.2	13.8	2.7	76.2	39.7	47.3	52.7
28052	GASTONIA	64.5	62.6	32.6	33.3	0.4	0.6	4.8	6.4	7.6	7.2	7.0	7.0	6.4	26.8	25.1	11.3	1.7	74.0	36.5	48.0	52.0
28054	GASTONIA	79.1	76.1	16.2	17.3	1.5	2.1	5.2	7.3	6.3	5.8	5.6	5.9	6.8	27.8	25.5	13.6	2.8	79.0	39.1	47.3	52.7
28056	GASTONIA	89.8	87.5	7.0	7.8	1.1	1.6	2.0	3.1	6.4	6.5	6.8	6.8	5.4	26.6	30.3	10.2	1.0	76.3	39.5	48.8	51.2
28071	GOLD HILL	96.8	95.9	1.4	1.5	0.3	0.5	1.0	1.5	6.0	5.9	7.0	7.2	6.1	26.9	30.1	9.7	1.1	76.8	39.0	51.7	48.3
28073	GROVER	83.2	81.1	14.7	16.1	0.4	0.6	1.3	1.7	8.1	8.2	8.2	6.8	5.1	29.0	25.0	8.7	0.9	71.3	35.6	49.9	50.1
28075	HARRISBURG	92.0	90.7	5.6	6.1	1.1	1.4	1.1	1.8	6.3	7.0	7.8	7.8	4.4	25.2	31.8	8.8	0.9	73.9	40.0	49.6	50.4
28078	HUNTERSVILLE	88.1	84.0	7.9	9.8	1.4	2.0	3.8	6.2	8.9	8.7	8.3	6.3	4.7	31.8	24.5	5.9	1.0	70.1	35.2	49.3	50.7
28079	INDIAN TRAIL	91.7	88.2	4.7	6.1	1.0	1.3	2.2	5.1	9.3	8.7	8.1	6.4	4.6	33.0	22.8	6.6	0.5	69.9	33.8	49.4	50.6
28080	IRON STATION	88.5	86.3	9.2	10.3	0.3	0.4	2.0	3.1	6.2	7.0	7.5	7.1	4.5	28.3	29.1	9.4	0.9	74.7	38.3	50.3	49.7
28081	KANNAPOLIS	82.9	78.8	11.7	12.6	1.0	1.4	5.5	8.9	7.2	7.0	6.8	6.3	5.5	28.2	25.6	11.4	1.9	75.1	37.8	49.4	50.6
28083	KANNAPOLIS	76.8	71.5	18.4	21.1	0.7	1.0	5.6	8.5	6.6	6.4	6.3	6.1	5.4	27.2	26.0	13.4	2.7	77.1	39.4	48.8	51.2
28086	KINGS MOUNTAIN	80.7	78.5	16.2	17.3	1.5	2.1	1.4	2.0	6.8	6.9	7.1	7.0	5.1	26.3	27.6	11.6	1.7	74.9	38.9	48.9	51.1
28088	LANDIS	88.1	84.9	6.6	7.1	1.0	1.4	7.7	11.2	6.7	6.6	6.5	6.3	5.3	27.2	25.8	13.6	2.1	76.6	38.7	49.8	50.2
28090	LAWNDALE	84.3	82.6	14.2	15.1	0.1	0.2	2.0	2.9	6.8	6.7	6.9	6.5	5.2	26.3	27.6	12.4	1.5	75.5	39.5	49.0	51.0
28091	LILESVILLE	46.0	44.0	52.7	54.5	0.3	0.5	0.7	0.8	6.1	6.4	6.7	7.2	5.7	23.9	30.5	11.4	2.1	76.4	40.7	47.9	52.1
28092	LINCOLNTON	87.9	85.4	7.6	7.8	0.3	0.4	8.8	12.9	6.3	6.3	6.5	6.5	5.4	27.6	27.6	11.9	1.8	76.8	39.3	49.6	50.4
28097	LOCUST	96.5	95.6	1.2	1.1	0.3	0.5	2.0	2.9	6.4	6.8	7.2	6.8	4.4	26.6	28.9	11.6	1.3	75.4	40.1	50.8	49.2
28098	LOWELL	92.1	91.6	5.4	5.2	0.8	1.1	1.9	2.6	7.0	6.7	6.5	6.3	6.0	27.5	25.8	12.4	1.9	75.9	37.9	47.9	52.1
28103	MARSHVILLE	78.6	71.6	19.6	25.4	0.2	0.2	1.8	3.6	6.5	6.9	7.0	6.9	5.3	26.1	27.9	11.4	2.0	75.3	39.0	49.4	50.6
28104	MATTHEWS	92.2	88.5	4.6	6.3	0.9	1.1	2.0	4.2	7.3	7.7	8.2	7.4	4.6	26.9	29.5	7.8	0.7	72.1	37.6	50.0	50.0
28105	MATTHEWS	86.1	81.7	8.4	9.9	2.8	4.0	3.4	5.7	7.1	7.1	7.4	7.1	5.8	28.2	28.4	7.4	1.4	74.1	36.8	48.7	51.3
28107	MIDLAND	93.2	91.6	4.8	5.5	0.2	0.3	1.7	2.9	5.8	6.9	7.1	6.6	4.9	26.2	30.2	11.2	1.2	76.1	40.3	50.4	49.6
28110	MONROE	78.5	76.4	14.2	12.9	0.6	0.8	11.0	15.1	8.5	8.2	7.7	6.8	5.7	31.2	23.0	7.9	1.1	71.5	34.1	50.3	49.7
28112	MONROE	77.1	72.8	17.4	18.3	0.3	0.4	9.8	15.1	7.2	7.2	7.2	6.7	5.5	27.4	25.9	11.2	1.8	74.3	37.7	50.3	49.7
28114	MOORESBORO	92.1	91.0	6.6	7.2	0.3	0.5	1.4	1.8	6.4	6.5	6.7	6.7	5.1	26.4	27.7	12.9	1.7	76.3	40.1	50.1	49.9
28115	MOORESVILLE	84.6	82.0	12.2	13.4	1.0	1.4	2.2	3.4	7.1	7.1	6.9	6.8	5.9	28.1	26.4	10.0	1.7	74.7	36.9	49.2	50.8
28117	MOORESVILLE	93.9	92.2	3.7	4.2	1.1	1.7	1.1	1.8	7.0	7.5	7.9	6.8	3.7	26.3	30.1	9.8	0.9	73.2	40.0	50.4	49.6
28119	MORVEN	29.9	28.4	69.0	70.3	0.0	0.0	0.6	0.7	8.5	8.2	8.2	8.1	5.7	24.5	26.4	9.3	1.1	70.0	35.2	46.4	53.6
28120	MOUNT HOLLY	88.7	86.5	8.1	9.1	1.6	2.1	1.4	2.3	6.0	6.1	6.3	6.3	5.2	27.4	28.8	12.1	1.8	77.8	40.3	49.2	50.8
28124	MOUNT PLEASANT	93.6	92.0	4.8	5.6	0.5	0.8	0.7	1.3	6.1	6.5	6.9	6.4	4.6	27.4	29.9	11.0	1.4	76.5	40.3	51.3	48.7
28125	MOUNT ULLA	88.8	86.1	7.9	8.9	0.2	0.2	3.3	5.1	7.4	7.4	7.4	6.6	5.4	27.3	27.0	10.1	1.4	73.6	37.3	50.9	49.1
28127	NEW LONDON	81.0	79.8	16.7	17.0	1.0	1.4	0.7	1.1	5.0	5.3	5.9	6.4	4.9	26.5	31.1	13.4	1.5	79.9	42.4	52.4	47.6
28128	NORWOOD	80.7	77.9	14.8	15.4	1.3	1.9	3.2	5.0	5.5	5.6	6.1	6.6	5.0	25.7	30.1	13.7	1.6	78.7	41.8	50.2	49.8
28129	OAKBORO	92.5	91.3	5.6	5.6	0.1	0.2	2.0	3.4	6.2	6.3	6.3	5.6	4.8	27.4	28.7	13.0	1.7	77.8	40.4	50.5	49.5
28133	PEACHLAND	76.2	72.9	20.0	22.3	1.9	2.5	1.3	1.7	5.9	6.1	6.4	6.2	6.3	30.8	26.3	10.4	1.6	77.8	37.5	54.9	45.1
28134	PINEVILLE	75.0	67.8	16.1	18.2	2.8	3.9	7.7	12.7	8.4	7.6	6.6	6.0	8.2	35.0	19.0	7.4	1.8	73.6	31.9	48.3	51.7
28135	POLKTON	54.4	52.4	43.6	45.0	0.5	0.6	1.0	1.4	5.1	5.1	5.2	5.0	7.7	36.9	24.2	9.3	1.4	81.6	36.8	62.0	38.0
	NORTH CAROLINA	72.1	69.8	21.6	21.5	1.5	2.1	4.7	6.9	6.6	6.5	6.5	6.8	6.9	27.7	26.5	10.9	1.6	76.5	37.4	49.3	50.7
	UNITED STATES	75.1	72.0	12.3	12.7	3.8	4.6	12.5	15.7	6.8	6.7	6.6	7.1	6.9	27.0	26.0	10.9	1.9	75.7	36.9	49.2	50.8

ZIP CODE #	POST OFFICE NAME	2009 Per Capita Income	2009 HH Income Base	2009 HOUSEHOLD INCOME DISTRIBUTION (%) Less than $25,000	$25,000 to $49,999	$50,000 to $99,999	$100,000 to $149,999	$150,000 or More	MEDIAN HOUSEHOLD INCOME 2009	2014	2009 National Centile	2009 State Centile	2009 Home Value Base	2009 HOME VALUE DISTRIBUTION (%) Less than $50,000	$50,000 to $89,999	$90,000 to $174,999	$175,000 to $399,999	$400,000 or More	2009 Median Home Value
27924	COLERAIN	17146	1394	41.3	32.1	21.3	3.7	1.6	29135	29633	7	4	1061	25.2	29.2	38.1	6.3	1.2	85694
27925	COLUMBIA	17201	1469	40.4	30.4	24.3	3.2	1.8	30329	30293	9	6	1098	28.8	29.6	31.2	8.7	1.6	77708
27926	CORAPEAKE	19283	815	25.4	33.3	35.8	3.4	2.1	44554	44939	47	52	656	21.0	13.9	47.0	15.7	2.4	115777
27927	COROLLA	62161	554	18.4	6.3	44.9	11.2	19.1	72427	71749	88	94	470	0.0	0.0	3.4	41.9	54.7	439286
27928	CRESWELL	19445	840	34.5	30.1	28.7	3.6	3.1	36656	37419	23	19	645	23.3	27.0	36.3	10.9	2.6	89674
27929	CURRITUCK	24862	309	15.9	25.2	43.7	12.9	2.3	58351	60479	76	87	262	7.3	13.7	11.8	49.2	17.9	255172
27932	EDENTON	19350	5149	31.4	30.9	31.1	5.5	1.1	39268	41240	31	30	3609	14.4	20.7	38.0	21.9	5.0	116075
27935	EURE	20449	673	27.8	26.4	37.6	7.0	1.2	44028	44492	45	50	537	11.7	28.1	39.9	16.8	3.5	104853
27937	GATES	17620	1398	36.1	24.8	32.6	3.9	2.6	40067	42173	33	33	1147	22.4	22.9	42.4	11.2	1.1	97230
27938	GATESVILLE	18567	550	26.5	28.0	37.1	6.7	1.6	45174	44639	49	54	451	22.0	14.6	40.8	21.1	1.6	114583
27939	GRANDY	20469	1024	31.1	30.7	31.3	5.5	1.5	38039	41108	27	25	777	4.6	27.0	36.4	29.5	2.4	120568
27941	HARBINGER	21994	502	20.5	36.3	35.3	5.4	2.6	45126	48703	49	54	419	3.6	11.0	19.8	56.1	9.5	207422
27942	HARRELLSVILLE	16315	515	42.5	35.1	19.0	2.3	1.0	28089	29030	6	2	404	28.0	41.3	27.7	3.0	0.0	71714
27944	HERTFORD	19849	4920	33.9	30.4	28.6	5.7	1.4	37529	38844	25	22	3842	14.5	18.2	39.6	20.5	7.2	118935
27946	HOBBSVILLE	21623	439	27.8	26.4	36.0	9.1	0.7	44791	45000	48	53	372	18.5	17.5	39.8	23.9	0.3	110268
27947	JARVISBURG	19926	422	24.6	33.9	33.9	5.7	1.9	43022	46728	42	45	334	3.6	15.9	28.7	45.2	6.6	178659
27948	KILL DEVIL HILLS	28064	4913	15.2	30.3	42.9	7.5	4.1	53423	54483	69	80	3460	3.2	3.8	42.2	45.1	5.6	176501
27949	KITTY HAWK	38847	2852	10.2	21.0	45.7	13.1	9.9	68261	66907	86	92	2420	1.3	1.2	10.5	57.9	29.0	298913
27950	KNOTTS ISLAND	21782	837	24.7	26.6	38.6	7.9	2.2	48040	53726	57	64	672	15.6	10.3	32.3	36.8	5.1	142727
27953	MANNS HARBOR	16897	368	34.2	30.2	32.3	3.3	0.0	40664	43237	35	35	282	27.3	5.0	29.4	38.3	0.0	142708
27954	MANTEO	24325	2574	26.0	26.3	37.6	5.4	4.7	46726	51183	53	60	1806	8.4	5.6	31.3	40.3	14.5	188281
27956	MAPLE	14068	84	31.0	42.9	25.0	1.2	0.0	37268	39052	24	21	57	38.6	24.6	24.6	12.3	0.0	69286
27957	MERRY HILL	20897	479	27.1	31.1	33.8	5.2	2.7	42622	46797	41	44	379	23.0	31.4	33.2	8.7	3.7	86071
27958	MOYOCK	22262	3668	17.6	23.8	48.4	8.0	2.3	56834	59413	74	85	3180	15.3	13.7	22.9	42.9	5.3	169076
27959	NAGS HEAD	30314	3663	16.9	26.6	42.1	9.0	5.4	54840	55803	71	81	2773	4.7	2.4	29.2	48.9	14.8	212849
27960	OCRACOKE	23781	339	17.4	44.2	33.0	5.3	0.0	42234	46372	40	42	267	0.0	5.2	18.4	66.3	10.1	265203
27962	PLYMOUTH	18105	2899	40.9	26.5	25.0	5.2	2.3	32201	33144	12	9	2005	21.8	25.4	44.0	8.0	0.7	93447
27964	POINT HARBOR	23664	253	20.6	34.8	37.2	4.7	2.8	45451	50246	50	56	195	3.6	7.7	34.9	47.7	6.2	181250
27965	POPLAR BRANCH	18346	330	30.3	31.5	30.9	6.1	1.2	38559	41606	28	27	250	3.6	25.2	36.4	32.4	2.4	125000
27966	POWELLS POINT	20739	483	20.5	34.0	38.3	4.6	2.7	45638	50526	50	57	357	3.6	6.2	42.6	42.9	4.8	172377
27970	ROPER	19077	1573	31.5	33.8	28.1	4.1	2.6	38203	38799	27	26	1252	18.0	25.6	44.6	10.1	1.8	96279
27973	SHAWBORO	22326	651	24.4	26.7	39.6	7.8	1.4	48516	52013	58	66	519	11.4	16.4	29.9	38.3	4.0	153989
27974	SHILOH	20692	535	25.8	27.9	35.1	8.6	2.6	46287	48337	52	59	426	13.4	13.8	35.4	31.9	5.4	148077
27976	SOUTH MILLS	22247	1304	23.1	29.4	37.3	7.4	2.8	47720	49239	56	63	1098	6.1	6.8	34.2	50.0	2.9	182273
27978	STUMPY POINT	19502	199	34.7	30.2	31.7	3.5	0.0	40607	42968	35	35	152	27.6	5.3	30.3	36.8	0.0	138462
27979	SUNBURY	18670	769	31.9	28.5	32.6	5.3	1.7	40563	41854	35	34	630	25.7	14.0	34.8	23.0	2.5	112162
27980	TYNER	19394	794	32.2	30.2	32.2	3.5	1.8	39542	41259	31	31	648	19.6	18.1	41.2	20.5	0.6	108036
27981	WANCHESE	22106	762	16.8	34.0	41.5	6.7	1.0	48489	51586	58	66	581	11.7	16.2	38.0	34.1	0.0	145833
27983	WINDSOR	18231	3733	40.3	29.3	23.7	4.1	2.6	30893	31882	10	7	2752	24.2	28.9	37.7	8.9	0.3	86217
27986	WINTON	14699	595	48.7	29.2	18.2	2.5	1.3	25656	26895	4	1	398	27.9	34.2	28.1	9.0	0.8	77143
28001	ALBEMARLE	21061	11122	30.0	28.7	33.7	5.3	2.3	41898	44270	39	40	7822	9.9	17.8	45.6	24.0	2.8	126092
28006	ALEXIS	22497	308	17.9	32.1	41.9	7.1	1.0	50000	52682	61	70	265	12.8	15.5	44.2	25.3	2.3	127244
28012	BELMONT	26275	8172	17.8	26.4	41.9	9.9	4.0	55559	58017	72	84	5979	11.2	17.0	48.3	20.3	3.3	123651
28016	BESSEMER CITY	20286	5435	23.6	31.0	38.4	5.7	1.4	45544	50324	50	57	3889	15.1	26.3	49.2	9.1	0.3	99240
28018	BOSTIC	18089	2038	31.5	32.8	31.8	3.0	0.9	37682	39355	26	23	1661	17.9	19.4	43.9	16.5	2.3	108431
28020	CASAR	19764	1116	29.7	30.0	33.6	4.7	2.0	39746	41771	32	32	931	16.6	22.4	38.8	21.3	0.9	107319
28021	CHERRYVILLE	22387	5284	24.0	30.4	36.1	6.4	3.0	45094	48343	49	54	4147	12.1	23.7	43.4	17.6	3.2	109691
28023	CHINA GROVE	21106	5519	22.6	30.1	38.4	6.5	2.3	47548	48860	56	62	4434	9.5	13.0	48.5	25.8	3.3	132579
28025	CONCORD	25263	18959	18.3	27.5	40.7	8.5	4.9	53532	56851	69	80	13282	13.3	16.5	43.2	23.4	3.6	123623
28027	CONCORD	30527	20803	11.2	21.1	44.3	14.6	8.7	69005	74357	86	93	15973	13.0	10.5	35.3	35.6	5.6	152807
28031	CORNELIUS	50110	10540	7.8	15.9	34.9	20.0	21.3	84579	85672	94	98	7776	0.4	5.2	23.0	40.8	30.5	251615
28032	CRAMERTON	26294	1220	20.2	27.6	39.9	7.5	4.8	51516	53951	65	75	768	9.8	38.3	39.6	7.8	4.6	92273
28033	CROUSE	20001	1220	19.9	29.8	44.0	5.3	0.9	50162	51475	62	70	988	12.7	15.6	46.8	21.8	3.2	131286
28034	DALLAS	22195	6670	21.8	29.1	40.4	6.7	1.9	49031	52356	59	67	4713	14.3	25.8	47.1	12.4	0.4	102609
28036	DAVIDSON	39841	4131	12.0	18.1	30.2	16.9	22.9	79487	82720	92	96	3332	4.6	5.9	18.6	37.6	33.3	293798
28037	DENVER	31027	6638	11.7	23.0	43.6	13.7	8.1	63498	61846	82	89	5639	6.6	4.3	22.9	43.3	22.9	233084
28040	ELLENBORO	18314	3255	32.0	32.8	31.0	3.4	0.8	38299	39689	28	26	2546	22.2	21.2	41.2	14.4	1.1	100369
28043	FOREST CITY	19788	8545	33.3	30.8	29.4	4.3	2.2	36854	38592	23	20	5731	15.2	26.3	39.7	17.4	1.3	105438
28052	GASTONIA	18097	13547	32.7	27.4	33.6	4.6	1.8	39950	44137	32	33	8234	13.2	33.4	46.9	6.3	0.2	93357
28054	GASTONIA	26749	15002	22.9	25.9	37.4	8.4	5.4	51138	54492	64	74	8272	5.5	24.4	51.6	16.9	1.6	116836
28056	GASTONIA	28655	11930	14.5	21.9	43.2	13.1	7.3	64289	65305	83	90	9529	9.0	13.5	47.2	27.0	3.4	132001
28071	GOLD HILL	21087	1126	20.2	32.6	39.4	5.1	2.7	46689	49396	53	60	941	13.3	14.9	39.2	29.3	3.3	124921
28073	GROVER	18282	1910	25.2	33.7	36.6	3.7	0.8	42924	43570	42	45	1422	19.2	23.2	46.2	10.7	0.7	101051
28075	HARRISBURG	32818	4968	5.7	13.8	51.5	18.0	10.9	79611	80973	92	97	4607	3.6	3.9	35.0	52.2	5.2	191922
28078	HUNTERSVILLE	40078	17579	8.2	13.8	34.1	26.2	17.7	88387	90807	95	98	13549	3.8	4.8	21.3	61.9	8.2	222426
28079	INDIAN TRAIL	30166	10210	7.8	13.5	55.4	16.7	6.6	75457	76788	90	95	8897	5.7	5.2	34.0	49.7	5.3	185564
28080	IRON STATION	20336	2831	18.8	32.4	40.9	6.1	1.9	49025	50820	59	67	2403	9.0	15.7	42.6	30.8	1.8	136810
28081	KANNAPOLIS	21637	9699	24.0	30.8	36.3	6.1	2.8	45558	47913	50	57	6628	10.7	20.1	47.3	20.2	1.7	114807
28083	KANNAPOLIS	21630	9551	26.2	30.2	36.4	4.9	2.3	44222	47103	46	51	6254	8.3	24.3	52.1	14.1	1.2	108819
28086	KINGS MOUNTAIN	20617	10411	26.5	27.8	37.2	6.5	2.0	45687	46375	50	57	7827	14.9	16.1	45.0	21.1	2.9	122628
28088	LANDIS	20439	1196	24.8	29.7	37.8	6.9	0.8	46285	48087	52	59	900	10.6	15.0	50.7	23.1	0.7	128529
28090	LAWNDALE	17701	3546	29.0	33.5	32.3	4.1	1.1	40192	41843	33	34	2832	21.9	21.2	38.6	16.9	1.4	100649
28091	LILESVILLE	18408	1108	36.4	24.7	32.7	5.3	0.9	36323	39496	21	17	874	27.5	33.2	34.7	4.0	0.7	82377
28092	LINCOLNTON	20083	14635	24.0	30.0	39.0	5.2	1.9	46358	49541	52	59	10619	10.4	14.8	43.5	28.7	2.6	135773
28097	LOCUST	21411	1710	19.6	29.2	42.9	6.2	2.1	50824	49483	63	73	1426	8.7	11.9	45.4	31.5	2.5	140625
28098	LOWELL	21619	1457	22.2	32.9	39.1	5.1	0.8	46195	49057	52	58	885	12.8	42.1	41.8	3.3	0.0	87331
28103	MARSHVILLE	20120	4433	23.4	27.8	41.8	5.1	1.8	48682	50443	58	66	3489	18.2	21.6	32.7	24.4	3.2	110334
28104	MATTHEWS	33615	9507	8.1	14.8	44.9	17.7	14.5	78832	80147	92	96	8420	3.4	4.8	27.5	46.1	18.2	219472
28105	MATTHEWS	37478	14467	7.0	12.5	44.3	22.0	14.3	81656	83592	93	97	10499	2.1	1.5	27.6	60.0	8.7	214460
28107	MIDLAND	25404	2609	14.5	25.2	45.8	10.9	3.6	58968	62312	76	87	2141	12.1	12.6	39.5	30.4	5.4	131281
28110	MONROE	24202	18834	15.0	23.8	47.3	9.7	4.1	61846	64818	80	88	13494	10.5	11.1	35.2	38.5	4.7	161124
28112	MONROE	21499	10249	20.2	27.1	43.3	6.2	3.2	53142	55902	68	79	7372	10.1	13.4	38.7	34.8	3.0	152321
28114	MOORESBORO	19985	2949	32.9	28.7	32.5	3.4	2.5	37999	40479	27	24	2389	20.7	23.8	41.1	11.6	2.8	97645
28115	MOORESVILLE	23017	12602	20.0	29.5	40.2	7.4	3.0	50465	52324	62	72	8908	7.1	6.0	37.9	42.9	6.1	173032
28117	MOORESVILLE	38756	12517	8.5	13.2	46.3	17.8	14.2	78706	79069	91	96	10708	1.0	1.9	11.0	45.7	40.3	350048
28119	MORVEN	14631	1175	38.1	30.9	26.9	2.9	1.2	32624	33877	13	10	903	40.0	33.9	23.0	2.8	0.3	60449
28120	MOUNT HOLLY	24867	7352	19.7	23.7	45.8	8.4	2.4	55668	58207	72	84	5409	9.9	19.9	49.1	20.2	0.9	116754
28124	MOUNT PLEASANT	24239	2697	15.1	26.0	45.9	10.4	2.6	57811	60576	75	86	2207	14.0	13.8	37.4	28.9	5.9	123534
28125	MOUNT ULLA	21579	929	18.4	28.6	44.7	6.9	1.4	52309	52491	67	77	796	12.9	10.1	31.4	37.4	8.2	162319
28127	NEW LONDON	23249	2840	24.9	27.9	35.7	6.0	5.5	47702	48010	56	63	2395	10.6	15.2	42.5	26.3	5.4	132971
28128	NORWOOD	20977	3140	25.8	29.4	37.5	5.3	2.1	45646	46730	50	57	2518	12.5	21.0	39.1	20.1	7.2	115743
28129	OAKBORO	22731	2357	21.8	27.4	42.0	6.4	2.4	50552	50114	62	72	1921	8.0	11.5	49.8	28.0	2.8	137127
28133	PEACHLAND	21499	1002	24.2	27.8	40.9	4.4	2.7	47836	50993	56	63	838	20.9	27.0	37.6	11.5	3.1	94091
28134	PINEVILLE	30096	3617	12.0	23.4	41.2	16.5	6.9	63984	67099	82	90	1844	3.1	6.2	43.8	39.3	7.5	169423
28135	POLKTON	16970	1763	32.6	29.4	32.3	3.3	2.4	38941	41552	30	29	1436	25.0	32.9	32.5	7.7	1.9	81102
	NORTH CAROLINA	25989		22.3	26.1	36.6	9.4	5.6	51418	53634				12.2	15.1	38.7	27.9	6.1	132724
	UNITED STATES	27277		20.9	24.4	35.3	11.7	7.6	54719	56938				9.3	13.1	31.6	32.6	13.5	162279

ZIP CODE #	POST OFFICE NAME	FINANCIAL SERVICES Auto Loan	Home Loan	Invest-ments	Retire-ment Plans	THE HOME Home Improvements Home Repair	Lawn & Garden	Furnishings Comput-ers & Hard-ware-Personal	Major Appli-ances	TV, Radio, Sound Equip-ment	Furni-ture	ENTERTAINMENT Dine out/ Carry out	Sports Equip-ment	Fees & Tickets	Toys & Games	Travel	Cable TV	PERSONAL Apparel & Services	Auto Repairs	Health Insur-ance	Pets & Supplies
27924	COLERAIN	77	50	74	47	50	75	54	68	62	51	60	53	40	63	50	69	40	64	71	83
27925	COLUMBIA	76	51	74	48	51	75	54	68	62	51	60	53	41	62	51	69	40	64	72	83
27926	CORAPEAKE	86	71	79	68	71	84	69	80	74	69	74	59	61	76	67	79	49	75	82	95
27927	COROLLA	172	181	246	180	209	214	163	193	172	185	169	120	179	155	188	180	116	184	214	218
27928	CRESWELL	87	60	83	58	61	86	63	78	71	59	69	60	49	72	60	78	46	73	82	94
27929	CURRITUCK	94	95	92	97	94	101	87	95	88	86	88	74	88	90	91	90	61	90	95	112
27932	EDENTON	76	59	76	58	61	77	64	73	69	60	67	54	55	68	62	74	46	70	78	86
27935	EURE	92	65	93	62	67	93	67	85	75	63	73	64	53	75	65	83	48	78	89	102
27937	GATES	84	61	77	58	61	81	63	75	70	62	69	57	51	72	59	76	46	71	78	91
27938	GATESVILLE	93	66	92	64	68	93	68	86	76	64	74	65	54	76	67	83	49	79	89	102
27939	GRANDY	84	60	86	58	62	85	62	78	68	57	67	59	49	68	61	75	44	72	82	93
27941	HARBINGER	90	75	107	73	80	93	74	90	77	71	76	66	65	75	77	81	51	84	89	105
27942	HARRELLSVILLE	72	47	70	44	47	71	50	64	58	48	57	50	38	59	47	65	38	60	67	78
27944	HERTFORD	74	62	77	59	65	77	63	73	67	63	66	52	56	65	63	72	44	70	79	86
27946	HOBBSVILLE	92	66	91	64	68	92	68	85	75	64	74	64	54	75	66	83	49	78	89	101
27947	JARVISBURG	88	69	94	67	72	89	69	84	74	66	73	62	59	73	70	79	48	78	85	99
27948	KILL DEVIL HILLS	99	87	120	86	93	105	87	102	90	83	89	76	81	87	92	94	61	97	102	118
27949	KITTY HAWK	136	125	184	124	141	156	118	145	124	123	122	98	117	115	133	131	83	136	152	166
27950	KNOTTS ISLAND	89	86	75	84	84	87	80	84	82	82	82	62	78	85	78	84	56	81	84	100
27953	MANNS HARBOR	79	57	82	55	59	81	58	74	65	54	64	56	47	64	58	71	42	68	77	88
27954	MANTEO	95	84	89	82	85	92	81	90	84	82	84	65	75	86	80	87	57	86	90	106
27956	MAPLE	69	50	71	48	51	70	51	65	56	47	55	49	41	56	50	62	37	59	67	77
27957	MERRY HILL	89	60	88	58	62	88	63	80	72	60	70	61	49	72	61	79	46	75	84	97
27958	MOYOCK	97	92	81	90	89	93	87	91	89	89	89	67	83	92	84	91	61	88	91	108
27959	NAGS HEAD	109	92	138	91	99	115	91	111	94	86	93	82	81	90	98	99	62	104	110	129
27960	OCRACOKE	79	63	102	62	69	84	63	80	66	59	65	59	55	63	69	71	43	74	79	93
27962	PLYMOUTH	72	55	64	54	54	71	59	66	65	56	64	50	51	65	55	70	43	65	72	80
27964	POINT HARBOR	88	78	82	76	79	85	75	83	78	76	78	60	70	79	74	81	53	79	83	98
27965	POPLAR BRANCH	84	60	86	58	63	85	62	79	69	58	67	59	49	68	61	75	44	72	82	94
27966	POWELLS POINT	87	80	71	77	78	82	75	80	78	79	78	58	71	81	72	80	53	77	80	95
27970	ROPER	86	59	80	57	60	84	62	76	70	59	68	59	49	71	58	77	46	72	80	93
27973	SHAWBORO	85	76	76	77	76	87	75	83	77	70	76	63	69	79	74	81	52	78	85	98
27974	SHILOH	91	70	90	70	73	94	71	87	77	66	76	66	60	77	71	84	51	80	91	103
27976	SOUTH MILLS	86	78	76	80	79	90	77	85	79	72	78	64	71	81	76	83	53	80	87	100
27978	STUMPY POINT	79	57	82	55	59	81	58	74	65	54	64	56	47	64	58	71	42	68	77	88
27979	SUNBURY	84	63	72	61	62	80	64	74	70	63	69	56	53	72	59	76	46	70	77	90
27980	TYNER	88	60	88	58	62	88	63	80	71	59	70	61	49	72	61	79	46	74	84	96
27981	WANCHESE	86	79	70	77	77	81	75	79	78	78	78	58	71	81	71	80	53	77	79	94
27983	WINDSOR	80	54	77	52	55	79	58	72	66	55	64	55	45	66	55	73	43	68	76	87
27986	WINTON	66	43	64	41	43	65	46	58	53	44	52	45	35	54	43	60	35	55	62	72
28001	ALBEMARLE	81	68	71	69	68	82	71	78	76	67	74	59	64	77	68	81	51	75	83	92
28006	ALEXIS	93	77	80	78	77	94	77	88	82	73	81	67	68	85	74	88	55	82	91	104
28012	BELMONT	93	95	84	96	92	97	92	93	93	90	93	73	92	95	92	94	64	92	97	111
28016	BESSEMER CITY	85	70	69	70	68	82	72	77	77	70	76	59	64	79	67	81	52	76	82	94
28018	BOSTIC	80	57	66	55	57	76	59	69	66	58	65	53	48	69	54	72	43	65	73	84
28020	CASAR	82	65	70	65	65	82	66	76	71	62	70	58	56	73	63	77	47	71	79	91
28021	CHERRYVILLE	93	74	82	73	73	92	75	86	81	72	80	65	65	83	72	87	54	82	91	103
28023	CHINA GROVE	90	76	77	74	75	88	75	83	80	74	79	62	68	82	72	85	54	80	87	99
28025	CONCORD	97	91	83	91	89	93	93	93	94	92	94	71	89	96	89	96	65	93	95	110
28027	CONCORD	121	122	103	120	116	113	116	116	114	119	114	91	114	119	112	112	79	113	110	135
28031	CORNELIUS	166	178	167	181	174	157	168	162	160	177	163	130	177	167	169	154	117	160	148	188
28032	CRAMERTON	90	86	74	88	82	91	90	87	92	86	91	69	87	93	86	94	63	90	94	105
28033	CROUSE	90	75	74	73	74	85	74	81	78	75	78	60	66	82	69	83	53	78	83	97
28034	DALLAS	89	76	75	76	75	89	77	84	82	74	81	64	70	84	74	87	55	81	89	100
28036	DAVIDSON	164	174	160	177	171	161	162	162	158	171	160	127	169	163	164	154	113	158	152	188
28037	DENVER	115	120	110	120	119	119	109	114	109	113	109	85	112	112	111	110	76	110	113	134
28040	ELLENBORO	79	57	66	55	56	75	59	69	65	57	64	53	47	68	54	71	43	65	73	84
28043	FOREST CITY	78	61	67	60	60	76	64	71	70	61	68	55	55	71	60	75	46	69	76	86
28052	GASTONIA	73	62	58	63	60	70	67	68	71	65	70	51	61	72	62	75	48	69	74	82
28054	GASTONIA	91	83	79	84	81	88	90	87	92	87	92	68	86	92	85	94	64	90	94	104
28056	GASTONIA	114	115	106	114	112	115	108	112	108	110	109	86	108	112	108	110	76	109	110	132
28071	GOLD HILL	97	74	80	72	73	92	75	85	82	74	81	65	63	85	69	88	54	81	89	103
28073	GROVER	87	63	72	61	62	82	65	75	72	64	71	58	53	75	59	78	48	72	79	92
28075	HARRISBURG	127	153	133	153	147	137	131	134	125	136	127	106	144	130	140	121	90	128	124	155
28078	HUNTERSVILLE	153	170	146	170	163	145	153	150	145	164	147	122	162	154	154	137	105	145	133	172
28079	INDIAN TRAIL	125	137	111	132	128	113	121	120	114	130	116	95	124	122	119	108	81	114	105	137
28080	IRON STATION	93	76	77	74	75	89	75	84	81	75	80	63	66	84	70	85	54	80	86	100
28081	KANNAPOLIS	84	74	70	75	72	83	77	80	80	73	79	62	71	82	73	83	54	79	84	95
28083	KANNAPOLIS	79	69	68	69	68	80	73	76	77	68	75	58	66	77	69	81	52	76	83	91
28086	KINGS MOUNTAIN	88	73	74	73	72	86	74	81	79	73	78	61	66	81	70	84	53	78	85	97
28088	LANDIS	74	73	62	75	69	79	72	73	73	67	73	58	71	75	71	76	50	72	79	88
28090	LAWNDALE	82	59	70	57	58	79	61	72	68	59	67	55	49	71	56	75	45	68	76	88
28091	LILESVILLE	85	55	82	52	55	83	59	75	68	56	67	58	44	69	55	76	44	70	79	92
28092	LINCOLNTON	87	70	74	69	69	85	72	80	77	69	75	60	62	79	67	82	51	76	83	95
28097	LOCUST	87	79	77	81	80	92	77	87	80	71	79	65	71	82	77	84	54	81	89	101
28098	LOWELL	76	70	58	72	66	77	75	72	77	70	76	57	71	79	70	80	52	75	81	88
28103	MARSHVILLE	90	73	78	73	73	90	73	84	79	70	77	63	64	81	70	84	52	79	87	100
28104	MATTHEWS	137	155	137	154	150	138	135	138	130	144	131	108	144	136	139	125	93	131	125	159
28105	MATTHEWS	142	154	140	158	150	137	144	140	137	151	140	112	152	143	146	132	100	138	128	163
28107	MIDLAND	103	97	96	97	96	106	92	101	94	91	94	77	88	97	92	98	64	96	102	119
28110	MONROE	102	102	88	100	98	95	98	98	96	101	97	76	96	100	95	95	68	96	93	114
28112	MONROE	88	87	80	88	86	92	85	89	85	81	85	68	82	87	84	88	59	86	90	104
28114	MOORESBORO	90	63	78	61	63	86	66	78	74	64	72	61	52	76	60	81	48	74	83	96
28115	MOORESVILLE	91	84	77	83	82	87	84	86	86	84	85	66	80	88	80	88	59	85	87	102
28117	MOORESVILLE	141	167	154	169	165	148	144	147	136	155	138	115	158	141	153	130	99	139	132	168
28119	MORVEN	77	51	73	48	51	75	54	68	62	52	61	53	41	63	50	69	40	64	71	83
28120	MOUNT HOLLY	91	87	78	88	84	94	86	89	89	83	88	68	83	91	84	92	60	88	95	106
28124	MOUNT PLEASANT	99	94	88	96	94	103	90	98	92	86	91	74	86	94	90	95	63	92	100	115
28125	MOUNT ULLA	91	82	74	79	80	86	78	83	81	81	81	61	73	85	74	84	55	81	84	99
28127	NEW LONDON	100	88	101	88	90	105	86	99	89	81	88	74	78	90	87	94	60	93	100	116
28128	NORWOOD	89	68	80	67	69	89	70	83	76	66	75	63	59	78	67	83	50	77	87	99
28129	OAKBORO	87	82	77	82	82	91	78	86	81	76	80	63	75	83	78	85	55	81	89	100
28133	PEACHLAND	98	71	81	70	71	94	74	86	82	72	80	66	60	85	68	89	54	81	90	104
28134	PINEVILLE	117	104	86	104	96	90	113	101	109	117	111	83	105	115	102	104	77	106	94	120
28135	POLKTON	87	60	79	57	59	84	63	76	71	60	70	59	49	73	58	79	46	72	81	94
	NORTH CAROLINA	100	89	90	89	88	96	91	94	94	91	93	73	85	95	88	96	64	93	96	112
	UNITED STATES	100	100	100	100	100	100	100	100	100	100	100	100	100	100	100	100	100	100	100	100

POPULATION CHANGE

28137-28384

#	POST OFFICE NAME	COUNTY FIPS CODE	POPULATION 2000	POPULATION 2009	POPULATION 2014	2000-2009 ANNUAL RATE % Rate	2000-2009 ANNUAL RATE State Centile	HOUSEHOLDS 2000	HOUSEHOLDS 2009	HOUSEHOLDS 2014	HOUSEHOLDS % Annual Rate 2000-2009	HOUSEHOLDS 2009 Average HH Size	FAMILIES 2000	FAMILIES 2009	FAMILIES % Annual Rate 2000-2009
28137	RICHFIELD	167	3159	3325	3376	0.6	36	1097	1158	1183	0.6	2.51	801	820	0.3
28138	ROCKWELL	159	9977	11371	12115	1.4	66	3757	4330	4627	1.5	2.59	2870	3217	1.2
28139	RUTHERFORDTON	161	17712	17726	17525	0.0	15	6823	6944	6902	0.2	2.46	4985	4935	-0.1
28144	SALISBURY	159	26154	26397	26685	0.1	18	10072	10210	10342	0.1	2.36	6307	6168	-0.2
28146	SALISBURY	159	25136	27285	28481	0.9	48	9940	10928	11442	1.0	2.46	7291	7764	0.7
28147	SALISBURY	159	21900	24449	25713	1.2	60	7971	8987	9479	1.3	2.58	5799	6327	0.9
28150	SHELBY	045	28713	28800	28794	0.0	15	11243	11287	11299	0.0	2.47	7852	7676	-0.2
28152	SHELBY	045	23545	23985	24047	0.2	21	8948	9160	9209	0.3	2.50	6517	6474	-0.1
28159	SPENCER	159	3185	3055	3022	-0.4	7	1244	1186	1171	-0.5	2.47	792	724	-1.0
28160	SPINDALE	161	3529	3176	3030	-1.1	1	1441	1314	1258	-1.0	2.25	928	812	-1.4
28163	STANFIELD	167	4727	4777	4780	0.1	18	1731	1781	1790	0.3	2.68	1321	1324	0.0
28164	STANLEY	071	11723	13676	14817	1.7	74	4400	5190	5649	1.8	2.62	3392	3894	1.5
28166	TROUTMAN	097	6323	8159	9329	2.8	87	2497	3251	3732	2.9	2.51	1857	2338	2.5
28167	UNION MILLS	161	2245	2441	2461	0.9	48	867	969	986	1.2	2.48	644	698	0.9
28168	VALE	109	9405	10755	11511	1.5	69	3576	4127	4431	1.6	2.60	2731	3065	1.3
28170	WADESBORO	007	9936	10444	10417	0.5	32	3871	4097	4117	0.6	2.42	2729	2806	0.3
28173	WAXHAW	179	17815	41813	55920	9.7	99	6076	13981	18639	9.4	2.99	5121	11714	9.4
28174	WINGATE	179	6429	10263	12791	5.2	96	2134	3472	4446	5.4	2.64	1564	2442	4.9
28202	CHARLOTTE	119	5027	8800	10703	6.2	98	2445	4473	5567	6.7	1.69	686	1114	5.4
28203	CHARLOTTE	119	10018	11540	12729	1.5	69	4695	5741	6448	2.2	1.96	2118	2267	0.7
28204	CHARLOTTE	119	5242	5503	5778	0.5	32	2484	2620	2754	0.6	1.87	831	833	0.0
28205	CHARLOTTE	119	46669	50775	54590	0.9	48	19394	21162	22767	0.9	2.35	10515	10654	0.1
28206	CHARLOTTE	119	12508	13264	14108	0.6	36	4347	4712	5046	0.9	2.71	2852	2910	0.2
28207	CHARLOTTE	119	7598	7846	8239	0.3	24	3490	3678	3897	0.6	1.99	1947	1913	-0.2
28208	CHARLOTTE	119	35966	37772	40054	0.5	32	13116	13998	14906	0.7	2.66	8769	8826	0.1
28209	CHARLOTTE	119	20028	20947	22228	0.5	32	10226	10959	11691	0.8	1.90	4513	4414	-0.2
28210	CHARLOTTE	119	41168	43139	45847	0.5	32	18634	20030	21397	0.8	2.14	10084	10060	0.0
28211	CHARLOTTE	119	27207	29503	31835	0.9	48	11795	13254	14419	1.3	2.18	7156	7506	0.5
28212	CHARLOTTE	119	35367	39671	43289	1.2	60	14878	16918	18556	1.4	2.33	8277	8721	0.6
28213	CHARLOTTE	119	25891	38888	45407	4.5	94	9542	14483	17015	4.6	2.67	5982	8762	4.2
28214	CHARLOTTE	119	20334	29415	34466	4.1	93	7734	11554	13636	4.4	2.55	5746	8278	4.0
28215	CHARLOTTE	119	41367	52495	59690	2.6	86	14956	19420	22182	2.9	2.68	10654	13322	2.4
28216	CHARLOTTE	119	29762	42659	50253	4.0	93	10982	16439	19593	4.5	2.48	7786	11239	4.0
28217	CHARLOTTE	119	19524	26053	30140	3.2	89	7077	9693	11279	3.5	2.69	4727	6111	2.8
28226	CHARLOTTE	119	34889	38663	42120	1.1	56	14182	16235	17785	1.5	2.36	9678	10558	0.9
28227	CHARLOTTE	119	40481	47953	53464	1.8	76	15482	18861	21128	2.2	2.53	11051	12953	1.7
28262	CHARLOTTE	119	21483	37529	45210	6.2	98	7117	13581	16749	7.2	2.50	3852	7326	7.2
28269	CHARLOTTE	119	42430	71648	88164	5.8	96	16142	28023	34673	6.1	2.54	10836	18226	5.8
28270	CHARLOTTE	119	26998	31255	34815	1.6	72	10177	12059	13471	1.9	2.59	7670	8853	1.6
28273	CHARLOTTE	119	18391	27469	32782	4.4	94	7042	10722	12845	4.6	2.55	4766	6894	4.1
28274	CHARLOTTE	119	401	418	436	0.4	28	14	15	16	0.7	2.53	8	8	0.0
28277	CHARLOTTE	119	33815	62766	76731	6.9	99	12805	23945	29356	7.0	2.62	9451	17316	6.8
28278	CHARLOTTE	119	6572	13118	16481	7.8	99	2615	5350	6759	8.0	2.45	1980	3937	7.7
28301	FAYETTEVILLE	051	18167	16658	16329	-0.9	2	6810	6687	6616	-0.2	2.16	4146	3875	-0.7
28303	FAYETTEVILLE	051	31597	29595	29178	-0.7	4	12766	12733	12708	0.0	2.32	8620	8267	-0.5
28304	FAYETTEVILLE	051	36514	36051	36281	-0.1	13	13725	14352	14604	0.5	2.49	10002	10156	0.2
28305	FAYETTEVILLE	051	6476	6016	5850	-0.8	3	3117	3053	3008	-0.2	1.96	1690	1561	-0.9
28306	FAYETTEVILLE	051	31787	36544	38424	1.5	69	11857	14215	15078	2.0	2.55	8787	10323	1.8
28307	FORT BRAGG	051	13263	12307	12132	-0.8	3	3229	3209	3170	-0.1	2.20	3135	3104	-0.1
28308	POPE A F B	051	2583	2451	2448	-0.6	5	501	513	518	0.3	3.39	488	498	0.2
28310	FORT BRAGG	093	16209	15064	14861	-0.8	3	1194	1194	1181	0.0	2.55	1167	1162	0.0
28311	FAYETTEVILLE	051	33073	34282	35042	0.4	28	12488	13709	14184	1.0	2.45	8935	9504	0.7
28312	FAYETTEVILLE	051	16817	16590	16585	-0.1	13	6442	6714	6798	0.4	2.44	4738	4771	0.1
28314	FAYETTEVILLE	051	47916	53005	55093	1.1	56	17250	19940	20924	1.6	2.66	12726	14340	1.3
28315	ABERDEEN	125	9292	11536	12733	2.4	83	3751	4734	5275	2.5	2.33	2628	3193	2.1
28318	AUTRYVILLE	163	4319	4840	5100	1.2	60	1692	1939	2053	1.5	2.50	1258	1403	1.2
28320	BLADENBORO	017	8335	8280	8177	-0.1	13	3537	3659	3658	0.4	2.24	2446	2450	0.0
28323	BUNNLEVEL	085	2332	2761	3039	1.8	76	849	995	1093	1.7	2.77	634	722	1.4
28326	CAMERON	085	10490	13515	15187	2.8	87	3772	4841	5433	2.7	2.79	2871	3593	2.5
28327	CARTHAGE	125	13621	15991	17310	1.7	74	5308	6177	6703	1.7	2.54	3960	4477	1.3
28328	CLINTON	163	25494	27038	27810	0.6	36	9481	10167	10485	0.8	2.55	6697	6971	0.4
28333	DUDLEY	191	11727	12120	12210	0.4	28	4169	4382	4441	0.5	2.76	3102	3173	0.2
28334	DUNN	163	23726	26518	28310	1.2	60	9261	10312	11032	1.2	2.52	6471	6978	0.8
28337	ELIZABETHTOWN	017	10580	10887	10788	0.3	24	4154	4376	4371	0.6	2.37	2786	2842	0.2
28338	ELLERBE	153	4459	4809	4897	0.8	44	1770	1941	1988	1.0	2.47	1247	1326	0.7
28339	ERWIN	085	6688	7878	8557	1.8	76	2682	3121	3391	1.7	2.47	1844	2077	1.3
28340	FAIRMONT	155	11504	11565	11624	0.1	18	4215	4259	4293	0.1	2.68	3064	3011	-0.2
28341	FAISON	163	4180	4529	4719	0.9	48	1530	1675	1753	1.0	2.67	1097	1166	0.7
28343	GIBSON	165	1691	1843	1853	0.9	48	613	685	696	1.2	2.66	444	483	0.9
28344	GODWIN	163	3312	3600	3743	0.9	48	1088	1217	1272	1.2	2.90	839	914	0.9
28345	HAMLET	153	12530	12581	12530	0.0	15	4893	5001	5007	0.2	2.47	3431	3404	-0.1
28347	HOFFMAN	153	2369	2643	2692	1.2	60	468	526	543	1.3	3.70	352	385	1.0
28348	HOPE MILLS	051	24055	27239	28485	1.4	66	8556	10252	10875	2.0	2.64	6507	7553	1.6
28349	KENANSVILLE	061	3447	3857	4064	1.2	60	1148	1319	1406	1.5	2.66	818	914	1.2
28351	LAUREL HILL	165	5576	5960	5976	0.7	40	2105	2323	2352	1.1	2.56	1524	1637	0.8
28352	LAURINBURG	165	25135	25545	25061	0.2	21	9379	9412	9303	0.0	2.50	6736	6567	-0.3
28356	LINDEN	051	4244	4663	4915	1.0	53	1588	1818	1928	1.5	2.56	1221	1351	1.1
28357	LUMBER BRIDGE	155	3061	3498	3728	1.5	69	1034	1204	1291	1.7	2.90	791	897	1.4
28358	LUMBERTON	155	36635	37334	37605	0.2	21	13599	13824	13978	0.2	2.56	9529	9401	-0.1
28360	LUMBERTON	155	12965	14077	14525	0.9	48	4425	4837	5015	1.0	2.84	3349	3556	0.7
28363	MARSTON	153	535	565	568	0.6	36	221	237	240	0.8	1.97	171	178	0.4
28364	MAXTON	155	13871	14774	15171	0.7	40	4793	5137	5294	0.8	2.87	3676	3847	0.5
28365	MOUNT OLIVE	061	15267	15759	16026	0.3	24	5753	6009	6123	0.5	2.54	4006	4063	0.2
28366	NEWTON GROVE	163	4556	4826	5002	0.6	36	1668	1780	1850	0.7	2.67	1191	1231	0.4
28369	ORRUM	155	2374	2514	2581	0.6	36	914	976	1006	0.7	2.57	676	701	0.4
28371	PARKTON	155	4935	6078	6466	2.3	83	1662	2041	2181	2.2	2.95	1309	1567	2.0
28372	PEMBROKE	155	11477	12464	12843	0.9	48	3869	4203	4353	0.9	2.73	2865	3029	0.6
28373	PINEBLUFF	125	1863	1975	2055	0.6	36	725	758	788	0.5	2.60	524	532	0.2
28374	PINEHURST	125	10498	13293	14681	2.6	86	4928	6174	6831	2.5	2.10	3649	4444	2.2
28376	RAEFORD	093	25513	35663	41530	3.7	91	8583	12281	14401	3.9	2.85	6586	9219	3.7
28377	RED SPRINGS	093	11599	13035	13794	1.3	63	3866	4334	4595	1.2	2.97	2915	3187	1.0
28379	ROCKINGHAM	153	26127	25740	25401	-0.2	10	10314	10340	10271	0.0	2.40	7225	7030	-0.3
28382	ROSEBORO	163	6455	6949	7213	0.8	44	2497	2749	2869	1.0	2.52	1857	1990	0.8
28383	ROWLAND	155	7863	8486	8772	0.8	44	2807	3053	3168	0.9	2.77	2097	2217	0.6
28384	SAINT PAULS	155	10394	11056	11433	0.7	40	3706	3960	4105	0.7	2.76	2736	2845	0.4
	NORTH CAROLINA					1.7					1.8	2.46			1.5
	UNITED STATES					1.0					1.1	2.59			0.9

#	POST OFFICE NAME	RACE (%) White 2000	White 2009	Black 2000	Black 2009	Asian/Pacific 2000	Asian/Pacific 2009	% Hispanic Origin 2000	% Hispanic Origin 2009	2009 AGE DISTRIBUTION (%) 0-4	5-9	10-14	15-19	20-24	25-44	45-64	65-84	85+	18+	MEDIAN AGE 2009	% 2009 Males	% 2009 Females
28137	RICHFIELD	91.7	90.0	5.3	5.7	1.2	1.8	1.1	1.9	6.3	6.1	6.8	10.9	10.7	23.7	25.0	9.5	1.1	77.4	33.6	50.7	49.3
28138	ROCKWELL	96.5	95.4	1.4	1.6	0.4	0.5	1.3	2.1	6.4	6.6	7.1	6.9	5.1	27.2	29.0	10.0	1.5	75.5	38.9	50.0	50.0
28139	RUTHERFORDTON	89.6	88.3	8.7	9.5	0.3	0.4	1.4	2.0	5.9	6.0	6.4	6.6	5.3	25.3	28.5	13.4	2.6	77.5	41.2	48.9	51.1
28144	SALISBURY	53.8	51.8	41.6	42.0	1.3	1.8	3.8	5.2	6.3	6.0	6.0	7.7	8.4	23.1	24.9	14.6	3.1	78.1	38.7	48.0	52.0
28146	SALISBURY	89.8	87.9	7.4	8.1	0.7	1.0	2.8	4.0	6.4	6.6	6.7	6.1	5.1	26.4	28.0	12.4	2.2	76.4	40.0	49.2	50.8
28147	SALISBURY	79.8	75.5	14.2	15.5	1.2	1.7	5.7	8.7	6.7	6.4	6.5	6.3	6.8	29.3	26.6	9.8	1.5	76.5	37.1	51.6	48.4
28150	SHELBY	67.0	66.0	31.3	31.6	0.4	0.5	1.4	2.0	6.0	6.1	6.4	6.8	5.7	24.2	27.8	14.2	2.8	77.3	41.2	47.9	52.1
28152	SHELBY	77.4	75.2	20.2	21.3	0.6	0.8	1.6	2.4	6.5	6.7	6.8	7.9	7.3	26.0	26.2	11.2	1.5	76.2	36.9	48.4	51.6
28159	SPENCER	71.0	66.4	23.0	24.6	0.5	0.8	6.4	9.6	6.3	6.2	6.2	5.9	6.0	26.4	26.9	12.5	3.6	77.7	39.9	49.2	50.8
28160	SPINDALE	72.2	69.6	25.9	28.0	0.5	0.7	0.9	1.3	5.4	5.5	5.8	5.8	6.0	26.8	27.5	14.5	2.8	79.9	41.3	50.6	49.4
28163	STANFIELD	96.6	95.5	0.8	0.8	0.1	0.2	7.2	9.6	6.5	6.7	6.9	6.9	5.1	27.6	28.6	10.5	1.1	75.5	39.0	51.5	48.5
28164	STANLEY	90.9	89.5	7.5	8.2	0.4	0.6	0.9	1.5	6.6	6.9	7.0	6.6	5.0	27.5	28.4	10.7	1.2	75.4	38.8	49.8	50.2
28166	TROUTMAN	86.4	84.2	12.2	13.8	0.3	0.5	0.7	1.2	6.2	6.4	6.6	6.6	4.9	27.5	29.1	11.3	1.3	76.7	39.9	49.6	50.4
28167	UNION MILLS	90.7	89.0	7.9	9.0	0.1	0.2	1.1	1.7	5.7	5.9	6.4	6.8	5.3	25.1	31.0	12.3	1.5	77.6	41.4	49.9	50.1
28168	VALE	94.0	92.6	3.5	3.8	0.7	1.1	2.1	3.1	6.2	6.3	6.7	6.7	5.1	27.8	29.6	10.4	1.2	76.6	39.5	50.6	49.4
28170	WADESBORO	47.3	46.6	51.1	51.2	0.6	0.8	0.8	1.0	6.1	6.3	6.3	6.6	5.4	23.6	26.6	15.3	3.8	77.3	41.7	45.7	54.3
28173	WAXHAW	90.2	88.1	7.6	8.5	0.6	1.0	1.6	3.2	8.4	8.7	8.8	7.3	4.3	26.9	28.0	6.8	0.7	69.3	36.1	49.5	50.5
28174	WINGATE	68.4	60.5	27.5	32.2	0.3	0.4	5.6	10.4	7.2	6.6	5.8	10.6	13.7	25.3	22.0	7.6	1.0	76.4	28.9	50.4	49.6
28202	CHARLOTTE	41.3	31.9	55.2	63.9	1.2	1.4	1.6	1.9	5.1	4.3	3.6	4.4	11.1	38.8	21.3	9.7	1.6	84.7	34.4	54.5	45.5
28203	CHARLOTTE	55.3	55.6	42.4	40.9	0.7	1.1	1.5	2.5	6.2	5.2	4.9	5.1	7.2	35.2	24.6	9.7	1.9	80.4	35.7	47.5	52.5
28204	CHARLOTTE	60.6	53.4	36.3	42.3	1.0	1.2	1.5	2.5	5.8	4.7	4.2	6.0	9.1	39.1	20.8	7.9	2.4	82.7	33.0	48.0	52.0
28205	CHARLOTTE	46.0	39.3	40.1	40.2	3.8	4.5	12.6	19.4	7.4	6.4	5.9	6.3	8.9	33.3	21.9	8.0	2.0	76.7	33.3	49.9	50.1
28206	CHARLOTTE	11.9	11.1	78.7	75.1	1.7	2.1	12.3	17.2	8.5	8.3	7.7	8.2	9.2	28.5	21.9	6.7	1.0	70.8	30.0	49.1	50.9
28207	CHARLOTTE	95.8	94.2	2.9	3.8	0.5	0.8	0.8	1.4	6.0	6.4	7.2	6.9	6.1	22.9	28.1	13.3	3.1	76.8	41.5	46.3	53.7
28208	CHARLOTTE	21.2	17.9	71.3	72.0	2.6	3.2	5.6	8.0	7.9	8.2	7.8	7.9	7.6	27.7	23.9	8.0	1.1	71.3	32.4	47.8	52.2
28209	CHARLOTTE	81.3	74.7	9.3	10.5	2.6	3.4	9.5	15.2	5.3	4.5	4.1	4.4	7.5	35.5	25.3	10.8	2.8	83.7	38.2	48.3	51.7
28210	CHARLOTTE	79.2	73.1	10.9	12.0	3.9	5.2	8.5	13.4	5.7	5.2	5.3	5.4	7.4	31.9	26.1	10.7	2.2	80.4	37.8	49.0	51.0
28211	CHARLOTTE	84.3	80.6	11.2	12.6	2.4	3.4	2.8	4.6	5.9	5.8	5.9	5.0	5.6	28.0	27.4	13.5	2.9	79.0	40.8	47.6	52.4
28212	CHARLOTTE	48.8	42.2	39.0	40.7	4.3	5.2	12.5	17.9	7.6	6.2	5.5	6.2	11.4	36.0	19.6	6.3	1.2	77.3	30.5	49.1	50.9
28213	CHARLOTTE	34.9	37.3	47.2	41.5	3.9	5.4	16.0	17.8	7.4	6.8	6.6	7.2	10.6	33.2	22.0	5.8	0.5	75.4	30.5	51.7	48.3
28214	CHARLOTTE	71.5	67.6	21.8	23.6	4.0	4.6	2.6	4.5	6.8	7.0	7.2	6.7	5.2	27.6	28.2	10.2	1.1	74.8	38.3	49.2	50.8
28215	CHARLOTTE	44.5	41.2	44.8	44.4	3.3	3.9	9.2	12.5	7.9	7.5	7.2	7.0	7.1	32.0	23.7	6.8	0.8	73.1	33.7	49.3	50.7
28216	CHARLOTTE	36.6	41.9	59.2	52.2	1.5	2.2	3.3	4.4	7.0	7.0	7.0	8.3	6.7	27.9	24.9	9.9	1.3	74.9	36.0	48.2	51.8
28217	CHARLOTTE	29.9	28.8	56.6	52.2	2.9	4.0	17.9	23.5	7.5	6.6	5.9	7.3	11.6	31.5	21.7	7.3	0.7	76.0	30.2	50.4	49.6
28226	CHARLOTTE	89.0	84.7	5.3	6.6	3.5	5.1	2.9	4.9	5.9	6.2	6.8	6.4	5.5	26.8	29.8	10.6	1.9	76.8	39.9	48.0	52.0
28227	CHARLOTTE	73.9	69.3	19.9	21.6	2.3	3.1	5.3	8.1	6.8	6.9	7.0	6.6	6.0	29.3	27.6	8.9	1.0	75.4	37.1	48.7	51.3
28262	CHARLOTTE	63.4	57.2	26.4	28.9	6.2	8.5	4.3	6.3	6.5	5.3	4.6	10.4	19.2	33.5	16.5	3.5	0.5	80.8	26.7	50.8	49.2
28269	CHARLOTTE	63.7	59.5	28.4	29.4	4.7	6.0	3.5	5.7	9.0	8.0	7.1	5.9	6.7	36.3	21.6	4.8	0.5	72.1	32.4	49.5	50.5
28270	CHARLOTTE	89.8	86.5	5.3	6.2	2.9	4.3	2.6	4.1	7.3	7.9	8.2	6.9	4.6	27.6	29.7	7.1	0.7	72.2	37.7	48.4	51.6
28273	CHARLOTTE	61.5	55.7	28.6	30.1	5.7	7.4	5.5	8.7	8.4	7.7	7.3	6.2	6.3	35.8	23.2	4.4	0.5	72.7	33.8	48.5	51.5
28274	CHARLOTTE	94.8	92.8	3.0	3.8	1.0	1.4	1.2	2.2	5.5	5.0	5.5	13.9	13.9	20.3	23.2	10.8	1.9	80.9	31.8	42.1	57.9
28277	CHARLOTTE	89.7	85.0	4.2	5.7	4.3	6.1	2.7	4.9	8.1	8.3	8.2	6.5	4.0	31.7	27.2	5.5	0.5	71.1	36.6	49.3	50.7
28278	CHARLOTTE	86.5	81.8	9.1	10.8	2.1	3.8	2.1	3.5	7.2	7.2	7.1	5.7	4.2	29.2	29.4	9.1	0.8	74.9	39.3	50.4	49.6
28301	FAYETTEVILLE	17.5	16.5	79.0	78.9	0.7	1.0	1.9	2.6	7.1	6.2	5.6	9.8	9.8	20.8	23.0	14.7	2.9	77.3	36.1	45.5	54.5
28303	FAYETTEVILLE	51.8	48.6	36.9	36.2	3.8	5.1	7.1	9.7	7.6	7.0	6.7	6.4	7.1	30.1	23.9	10.1	1.1	74.9	34.2	48.8	51.2
28304	FAYETTEVILLE	58.8	54.6	31.0	31.5	2.4	3.3	7.0	9.9	8.0	7.3	6.9	6.9	7.4	30.7	23.1	8.8	0.9	73.7	33.4	47.8	52.2
28305	FAYETTEVILLE	70.8	68.8	24.7	25.1	0.8	1.2	2.8	4.0	5.2	5.2	5.3	5.6	5.9	24.5	28.8	16.1	3.5	80.9	43.8	47.0	53.0
28306	FAYETTEVILLE	65.3	62.6	25.6	25.5	1.4	2.0	4.6	6.8	8.1	7.7	7.4	7.1	6.3	29.4	25.2	8.1	0.7	72.2	34.4	48.6	51.4
28307	FORT BRAGG	57.5	51.8	25.8	25.1	2.8	3.6	15.6	21.9	12.1	8.4	4.6	8.9	32.9	31.4	1.6	0.1	0.0	73.5	22.4	67.4	32.6
28308	POPE A F B	76.9	72.6	14.1	14.6	2.9	4.1	6.2	9.1	12.8	10.3	6.7	6.6	17.6	44.3	1.6	0.1	0.0	68.0	23.9	61.2	38.8
28310	FORT BRAGG	58.1	52.3	25.2	24.5	2.7	3.5	15.8	22.1	12.1	8.4	4.6	9.0	33.2	31.4	1.3	0.1	0.0	73.6	22.4	67.7	32.3
28311	FAYETTEVILLE	53.3	51.5	38.8	37.8	1.9	2.7	5.9	8.2	8.0	7.5	6.9	7.5	9.0	31.2	22.5	6.8	0.6	73.4	31.2	49.0	51.0
28312	FAYETTEVILLE	64.6	61.6	28.7	30.0	0.6	0.8	2.6	3.9	6.2	6.2	6.5	6.4	5.6	25.5	30.0	11.9	1.6	77.2	40.5	48.8	51.2
28314	FAYETTEVILLE	44.7	40.8	43.2	43.0	3.4	4.4	8.9	12.3	8.8	7.7	7.0	7.2	9.0	33.4	21.0	5.4	0.4	72.1	30.0	49.2	50.8
28315	ABERDEEN	70.6	68.2	23.7	24.2	0.7	1.1	3.5	5.5	5.8	5.8	6.0	6.1	6.2	25.2	27.5	15.1	2.3	78.7	41.3	50.2	49.8
28318	AUTRYVILLE	85.5	82.8	8.8	8.9	0.3	0.4	6.3	9.3	6.9	7.0	7.2	6.5	4.7	28.6	27.3	10.9	1.0	74.9	37.8	50.1	49.9
28320	BLADENBORO	76.8	75.1	21.1	22.1	0.1	0.1	1.4	2.0	6.1	6.4	6.6	5.7	4.4	25.3	29.6	14.1	1.7	77.4	41.6	49.0	51.0
28323	BUNNLEVEL	55.8	52.0	37.8	39.8	0.8	1.0	3.8	5.3	8.4	7.9	7.4	7.5	6.9	31.1	22.8	7.3	0.8	71.8	32.8	50.2	49.8
28326	CAMERON	73.3	69.4	20.4	21.5	0.6	0.9	4.9	7.4	8.9	8.1	7.7	7.4	7.0	30.8	22.3	7.1	0.6	70.8	32.1	50.0	50.0
28327	CARTHAGE	85.4	83.7	11.8	12.2	0.3	0.4	2.2	3.5	6.1	6.0	6.3	6.6	5.3	24.0	27.5	15.4	2.7	77.6	41.8	48.5	51.5
28328	CLINTON	54.3	50.6	34.5	33.6	0.5	0.7	10.5	15.5	7.2	7.0	6.9	6.3	5.7	27.0	25.5	12.3	2.3	75.2	37.8	49.4	50.6
28333	DUDLEY	46.7	41.8	43.1	43.3	0.6	0.8	10.6	15.5	7.5	7.3	7.1	7.4	7.6	28.7	25.5	8.3	0.7	73.5	33.2	49.3	50.7
28334	DUNN	70.3	67.6	24.0	24.4	0.4	0.6	4.8	7.1	6.9	6.8	6.8	6.5	5.6	26.1	26.8	12.4	1.9	75.4	38.6	48.5	51.5
28337	ELIZABETHTOWN	54.2	52.3	41.6	41.6	0.2	0.3	4.4	6.6	6.3	6.6	7.0	6.8	5.6	23.6	27.7	13.8	2.6	76.0	40.2	48.7	51.3
28338	ELLERBE	64.7	62.7	30.8	30.9	0.6	0.7	7.7	10.5	6.3	6.3	6.7	7.3	5.4	25.0	28.5	12.6	1.9	76.3	40.1	49.9	50.1
28339	ERWIN	73.9	71.0	22.5	23.8	0.2	0.3	3.5	5.1	6.0	6.4	6.4	7.0	5.7	25.2	27.3	13.8	2.2	77.0	40.2	48.4	51.6
28340	FAIRMONT	30.6	28.1	38.0	37.6	0.2	0.2	1.8	2.6	7.1	7.8	7.4	7.1	6.2	24.4	27.5	11.0	1.4	73.1	36.9	47.7	52.3
28341	FAISON	47.5	42.0	32.8	30.1	0.2	0.2	23.8	32.6	7.0	7.2	6.7	7.2	7.2	27.9	25.0	10.3	1.5	74.4	35.4	50.9	49.1
28343	GIBSON	49.0	45.6	40.2	42.2	0.1	0.2	1.0	1.5	7.5	7.1	7.2	8.0	6.8	25.9	26.7	9.7	1.1	73.1	35.5	48.3	51.7
28344	GODWIN	71.8	66.9	18.2	18.4	0.5	0.7	11.1	16.5	6.9	6.9	7.3	6.8	5.3	29.1	26.1	10.1	1.4	74.5	36.8	51.1	48.9
28345	HAMLET	60.3	58.7	34.9	35.5	0.4	0.5	1.2	1.7	6.9	6.7	7.0	7.4	5.6	24.0	27.2	12.9	2.2	74.8	38.9	48.3	51.7
28347	HOFFMAN	53.4	51.3	41.9	42.4	0.8	1.0	3.9	5.4	5.4	5.4	5.6	14.8	17.7	23.8	19.0	7.4	0.9	78.8	25.7	61.3	38.7
28348	HOPE MILLS	70.5	67.4	20.6	21.1	0.9	1.3	5.1	7.4	7.9	7.7	7.5	7.6	6.4	29.9	25.1	7.2	0.7	72.2	34.3	48.5	51.5
28349	KENANSVILLE	54.0	51.0	41.0	41.2	0.2	0.3	5.5	8.6	5.9	5.8	6.0	6.4	7.2	26.8	27.1	12.3	2.7	78.6	39.2	50.2	49.8
28351	LAUREL HILL	62.9	59.5	25.5	27.3	0.2	0.3	1.1	1.6	7.3	7.1	7.1	7.3	6.8	26.7	27.9	8.9	0.9	74.0	36.0	48.4	51.6
28352	LAURINBURG	50.8	49.2	38.8	38.8	0.7	0.9	1.2	1.6	6.8	6.7	6.7	8.4	7.7	24.2	25.6	11.5	2.3	75.2	36.4	47.1	52.9
28356	LINDEN	67.7	64.0	28.0	30.2	0.6	0.8	2.5	3.6	7.0	7.3	7.4	7.0	5.6	27.6	28.3	9.1	0.7	73.7	37.5	49.6	50.4
28357	LUMBER BRIDGE	44.1	41.5	36.2	36.1	0.3	0.4	3.9	5.2	7.8	7.7	8.1	7.4	7.3	27.2	25.9	7.9	0.7	73.2	33.9	50.0	50.0
28358	LUMBERTON	49.9	48.0	29.4	28.6	0.7	0.9	3.9	5.2	7.5	7.1	6.8	6.9	7.0	26.9	25.1	10.9	1.9	74.4	36.2	48.2	51.8
28360	LUMBERTON	25.3	23.6	11.1	10.8	0.2	0.2	7.7	9.8	7.9	7.6	7.4	7.6	7.4	30.1	23.8	7.5	0.6	72.4	32.7	51.8	48.2
28363	MARSTON	62.6	60.0	31.6	32.6	1.1	1.4	3.0	4.4	6.2	6.2	6.5	11.9	12.9	24.6	22.7	8.1	0.9	76.6	29.6	58.1	41.9
28364	MAXTON	11.0	9.6	24.3	23.2	0.3	0.4	1.2	1.6	8.5	8.5	8.1	8.1	7.1	27.3	24.3	7.3	0.8	69.8	31.5	47.9	52.1
28365	MOUNT OLIVE	64.1	59.9	25.8	24.8	0.2	0.3	13.0	18.9	6.5	6.3	6.6	7.5	7.4	26.1	25.8	11.8	2.0	76.5	37.0	49.6	50.4
28366	NEWTON GROVE	71.5	66.7	17.9	17.7	0.1	0.1	15.5	21.5	6.6	6.9	6.6	6.4	6.1	28.3	26.0	11.4	1.8	76.6	37.2	50.6	49.4
28369	ORRUM	61.5	58.2	22.3	23.1	0.2	0.3	2.7	3.9	5.9	6.8	6.5	6.4	6.3	25.6	30.0	11.8	0.8	76.7	39.5	49.5	50.5
28371	PARKTON	61.2	57.3	27.9	28.6	0.7	1.0	5.8	8.4	9.3	8.4	7.6	7.3	7.8	30.5	22.5	6.0	0.6	71.3	30.8	49.7	50.3
28372	PEMBROKE	9.9	9.1	5.0	5.0	0.4	0.5	1.6	2.2	8.1	7.3	7.1	9.8	9.6	25.6	22.3	9.0	1.3	73.7	31.1	48.9	51.1
28373	PINEBLUFF	69.7	66.1	25.6	26.9	0.6	0.9	3.1	5.1	7.6	7.5	7.4	7.3	6.2	28.4	25.8	8.9	0.9	72.9	35.8	49.5	50.5
28374	PINEHURST	90.4	88.9	7.9	8.6	0.7	1.0	1.1	1.6	3.4	3.6	3.9	3.5	2.4	14.0	29.9	34.0	5.5	87.5	59.5	46.8	53.2
28376	RAEFORD	47.3	44.5	39.9	39.3	1.1	1.4	7.9	11.0	9.4	8.3	7.6	7.3	7.3	31.0	21.2	7.0	0.9	70.3	31.7	50.2	49.8
28377	RED SPRINGS	23.4	20.9	34.1	31.2	0.4	0.5	8.2	11.1	9.2	7.9	7.4	7.9	7.8	27.1	22.7	8.6	1.3	70.7	31.2	48.7	51.3
28379	ROCKINGHAM	68.3	66.6	27.1	27.5	0.9	1.1	2.7	3.8	6.7	6.8	6.7	7.0	6.6	25.6	26.0	12.6	1.9	75.7	37.8	49.0	51.0
28382	ROSEBORO	64.5	61.4	29.9	30.6	0.4	0.5	5.2	7.7	6.7	7.1	7.1	6.3	5.1	26.4	28.1	11.8	1.4	75.3	38.7	49.8	50.2
28383	ROWLAND	12.7	11.4	27.6	27.1	0.1	0.1	1.1	1.4	7.5	7.6	7.7	7.3	6.6	26.4	26.2	9.5	1.2	72.5	35.1	47.8	52.2
28384	SAINT PAULS	50.6	46.4	28.8	28.6	0.4	0.5	10.6	14.8	7.7	7.5	7.3	6.8	6.3	28.3	25.7	9.4	1.1	74.2	35.0	50.5	49.5
	NORTH CAROLINA	72.1	69.8	21.6	21.5	1.5	2.1	4.7	6.9	6.6	6.5	6.5	6.8	6.9	27.7	26.5	10.9	1.6	76.5	37.4	49.3	50.7
	UNITED STATES	75.1	72.0	12.3	12.7	3.8	4.6	12.5	15.7	6.8	6.7	6.6	7.1	6.9	27.0	26.0	10.9	1.9	75.7	36.9	49.2	50.8

ZIP CODE				2009 HOUSEHOLD INCOME DISTRIBUTION (%)					MEDIAN HOUSEHOLD INCOME					2009 HOME VALUE DISTRIBUTION (%)					
# POST OFFICE NAME	2009 Per Capita Income	2009 HH Income Base	Less than $25,000	$25,000 to $49,999	$50,000 to $99,999	$100,000 to $149,999	$150,000 or More	2009	2014	2009 National Centile	2009 State Centile	2009 Home Value Base	Less than $50,000	$50,000 to $89,999	$90,000 to $174,999	$175,000 to $399,999	$400,000 or More	2009 Median Home Value	
28137 RICHFIELD	19471	1158	22.4	37.1	32.6	4.8	3.0	43743	45422	45	49	928	15.1	13.8	38.5	26.9	5.7	126823	
28138 ROCKWELL	21023	4330	19.5	30.9	42.2	5.4	2.0	49510	50662	60	68	3477	10.2	13.4	44.6	29.0	2.8	136113	
28139 RUTHERFORDTON	20909	6944	27.1	30.3	34.3	5.6	2.7	43470	45707	44	48	5392	15.9	18.6	38.1	23.6	3.8	120369	
28144 SALISBURY	22145	10210	32.5	25.8	31.4	6.2	4.0	41067	45232	36	37	5819	4.9	15.1	43.9	28.6	7.6	139920	
28146 SALISBURY	22597	10928	21.7	27.7	41.5	7.1	2.1	50408	51077	62	71	8510	9.4	11.1	40.9	34.6	3.9	145915	
28147 SALISBURY	22393	8987	20.1	29.4	39.7	7.9	2.9	50397	51158	62	71	6592	13.8	10.2	38.1	35.0	2.9	146809	
28150 SHELBY	22025	11287	30.4	28.2	32.1	4.9	4.4	41028	42596	36	36	7740	11.9	15.1	45.1	23.0	4.9	124250	
28152 SHELBY	20730	9160	25.0	28.9	38.7	5.5	2.0	45966	45950	51	58	6498	11.3	16.0	51.4	20.6	0.8	120399	
28159 SPENCER	22951	1186	25.3	24.7	42.3	4.1	3.5	50000	51367	61	70	758	3.2	17.8	58.3	17.4	3.3	119974	
28160 SPINDALE	17068	1314	42.9	31.1	20.9	3.4	1.7	30242	31816	8	6	826	15.4	32.8	41.3	10.0	0.5	92727	
28163 STANFIELD	21908	1781	23.4	27.1	40.3	5.5	3.8	49460	49147	60	68	1459	12.5	9.5	38.4	35.0	4.7	149457	
28164 STANLEY	23479	5190	15.0	30.3	43.9	8.2	2.5	54179	56627	70	81	4188	11.9	15.1	44.8	27.1	1.2	124425	
28166 TROUTMAN	25050	3251	16.5	27.3	45.8	7.6	2.8	54384	54765	70	81	2705	5.0	8.6	38.8	37.6	10.1	169401	
28167 UNION MILLS	16965	969	31.8	34.7	29.8	3.6	0.1	36718	37451	23	20	832	13.2	26.4	39.2	18.5	2.6	107718	
28168 VALE	20290	4127	21.9	29.9	42.4	4.0	1.9	48333	50862	57	65	3420	15.4	18.9	40.6	22.2	2.8	120335	
28170 WADESBORO	18906	4097	34.5	32.4	26.8	3.8	2.5	34582	36350	17	14	2860	20.5	34.0	37.4	7.7	0.4	85994	
28173 WAXHAW	34312	13981	8.7	16.7	39.7	17.7	17.2	80417	82509	92	97	12756	3.3	6.6	20.7	44.8	24.6	260604	
28174 WINGATE	19946	3472	25.1	26.2	41.8	5.0	2.0	48732	50989	58	66	2369	16.0	18.1	42.1	23.0	0.8	119115	
28202 CHARLOTTE	34782	4473	37.2	18.0	25.4	11.7	7.6	42361	45451	41	43	1484	0.3	5.6	31.4	42.9	19.7	216092	
28203 CHARLOTTE	40061	5741	29.3	19.8	24.8	13.0	13.2	51525	54926	65	75	2346	1.5	10.5	13.0	45.2	29.8	267179	
28204 CHARLOTTE	31721	2620	29.5	24.0	26.7	13.5	6.3	45367	47379	49	55	773	1.8	6.3	22.8	53.9	15.1	225303	
28205 CHARLOTTE	22311	21162	23.6	34.8	33.2	5.8	2.6	42590	44947	41	44	7992	3.4	20.2	56.7	17.8	1.9	116607	
28206 CHARLOTTE	14628	4712	35.5	39.9	20.9	2.7	0.9	32040	32822	11	9	1285	15.2	49.0	34.4	1.2	0.2	82981	
28207 CHARLOTTE	79527	3678	9.6	12.0	21.4	21.6	35.3	114185	117538	98	100	2593	0.8	1.8	6.5	20.7	70.2	634834	
28208 CHARLOTTE	16371	13998	32.4	35.6	26.7	4.3	1.0	35410	36281	19	16	5632	11.1	39.0	48.1	1.6	0.3	89978	
28209 CHARLOTTE	40225	10959	16.1	24.6	38.6	12.4	8.3	59924	61445	77	88	5403	0.6	4.2	37.2	41.6	16.3	197841	
28210 CHARLOTTE	41507	20030	11.3	24.1	38.8	14.4	11.4	65626	68793	84	91	11041	1.0	3.5	31.7	46.7	17.2	208158	
28211 CHARLOTTE	49086	13254	11.8	18.4	31.4	20.6	17.8	79060	82595	92	96	7675	0.4	1.8	15.4	52.2	30.1	295258	
28212 CHARLOTTE	23904	16918	16.9	34.9	39.8	6.4	2.0	48396	50308	58	65	6176	1.3	10.0	75.4	13.0	0.3	130037	
28213 CHARLOTTE	25866	14483	16.1	23.8	42.0	13.4	4.8	61266	64359	79	88	8282	5.6	11.7	46.9	35.0	0.8	149979	
28214 CHARLOTTE	28502	11554	11.0	25.2	45.0	14.4	4.4	63903	66691	82	89	9880	7.9	12.3	50.2	25.8	3.8	141292	
28215 CHARLOTTE	26431	19420	13.0	24.6	43.4	13.8	5.2	62238	64284	80	89	13253	4.8	11.1	55.9	25.8	2.5	138201	
28216 CHARLOTTE	27220	16439	18.1	24.0	38.2	14.6	5.1	59254	62629	76	88	12130	4.7	15.4	48.5	25.8	5.6	137322	
28217 CHARLOTTE	22802	9693	18.0	30.7	39.8	8.6	2.9	51067	53429	64	73	4346	3.0	31.4	54.1	11.0	0.5	104293	
28226 CHARLOTTE	51034	16235	6.6	16.5	35.7	19.6	21.6	83931	86479	93	97	11523	0.7	2.5	21.4	51.3	24.1	241328	
28227 CHARLOTTE	29465	18861	9.8	22.8	45.8	16.3	5.3	65633	69065	84	91	14281	5.1	5.7	58.2	28.2	2.8	144804	
28262 CHARLOTTE	32163	13581	9.8	19.7	42.9	18.8	8.7	70758	75366	87	93	7105	2.9	3.5	30.6	57.4	5.5	198126	
28269 CHARLOTTE	37004	28023	10.5	16.7	37.8	21.1	13.9	78097	81156	91	96	19382	1.9	6.4	29.8	58.0	3.9	200928	
28270 CHARLOTTE	49476	12059	4.9	12.8	32.2	23.8	26.3	100200	100959	97	99	9102	1.4	1.7	14.3	57.7	24.9	281725	
28273 CHARLOTTE	32631	10722	7.1	15.4	50.1	21.2	6.1	73911	77655	89	94	7514	2.8	4.1	46.2	45.4	1.5	170824	
28274 CHARLOTTE	8971	15	0.0	0.0	20.0	40.0	40.0	130219	125000	99	100	11	0.0	0.0	0.0	27.3	72.7	687500	
28277 CHARLOTTE	52592	23945	4.5	9.2	29.9	28.2	28.2	110135	111471	98	99	18439	1.3	0.8	15.4	60.3	22.3	249066	
28278 CHARLOTTE	43538	5350	7.4	12.7	38.5	25.7	15.6	87103	88803	94	98	4851	3.2	5.3	17.1	56.9	17.5	227919	
28301 FAYETTEVILLE	16041	6687	52.4	24.6	18.5	2.8	1.7	23145	24319	2	1	3067	10.8	33.1	52.2	3.6	0.2	95485	
28303 FAYETTEVILLE	28057	12733	17.7	28.8	40.2	7.3	6.0	52152	53899	66	76	7201	4.9	11.6	63.6	15.9	4.0	122309	
28304 FAYETTEVILLE	25244	14352	15.1	28.2	45.2	7.5	3.8	54863	56195	71	81	8992	3.4	17.5	66.2	12.6	0.2	112558	
28305 FAYETTEVILLE	35815	3053	27.2	26.5	27.5	9.8	9.0	44664	49687	47	52	1687	3.0	12.1	44.3	32.7	7.9	145123	
28306 FAYETTEVILLE	24477	14215	21.8	23.6	40.9	9.7	3.9	53591	55856	69	80	10354	16.4	19.5	47.4	16.2	0.4	108466	
28307 FORT BRAGG	18410	3209	17.2	45.6	33.9	2.3	1.0	40672	43182	35	35	73	8.2	8.2	82.2	1.4	0.0	111638	
28308 POPE A F B	14603	513	6.4	61.8	28.5	1.2	2.1	41114	42852	36	37	7	0.0	71.4	28.6	0.0	0.0	82500	
28310 FORT BRAGG	9790	1194	16.8	45.9	34.0	2.3	1.0	40747	43269	35	36	19	10.5	0.0	89.5	0.0	0.0	113750	
28311 FAYETTEVILLE	25931	13709	18.8	26.0	40.5	9.8	4.9	54094	56332	70	80	7596	5.2	12.8	59.0	22.0	1.0	122587	
28312 FAYETTEVILLE	22302	6714	27.9	28.3	35.4	5.0	3.4	43790	47771	45	49	5128	20.1	21.1	44.5	13.4	1.0	102611	
28314 FAYETTEVILLE	23837	19940	14.1	27.1	48.0	7.9	3.0	56137	57666	73	84	11391	5.0	11.7	75.3	7.3	0.7	118709	
28315 ABERDEEN	25615	4734	24.4	27.9	35.8	7.1	4.8	47410	50495	55	61	3263	11.0	12.2	39.2	28.5	9.1	142430	
28318 AUTRYVILLE	18834	1939	31.4	30.1	32.2	4.4	1.9	40886	42384	36	36	1593	25.2	23.2	40.5	9.3	1.8	92500	
28320 BLADENBORO	18894	3659	38.3	28.7	27.4	3.9	1.7	34106	35050	16	13	2771	20.2	30.5	39.6	9.4	0.2	89089	
28323 BUNNLEVEL	19117	995	24.3	28.6	40.0	4.8	2.2	46681	48993	53	60	725	22.1	16.7	43.3	17.2	0.7	116614	
28326 CAMERON	20819	4841	19.4	29.6	40.9	7.4	2.7	50836	51787	63	73	3747	18.3	14.5	42.3	22.6	2.2	122451	
28327 CARTHAGE	23185	6177	23.2	25.9	40.1	7.9	2.9	50719	52480	63	72	5040	12.0	12.9	31.5	36.4	7.2	150758	
28328 CLINTON	19358	10167	33.9	26.8	31.5	4.7	3.1	39519	40842	31	31	6971	13.5	18.9	44.8	20.2	2.6	116830	
28333 DUDLEY	18116	4382	23.2	37.1	34.3	3.9	1.6	41941	45284	39	41	3216	34.6	34.4	27.9	2.7	0.4	65836	
28334 DUNN	19388	10312	34.7	26.6	30.9	4.3	3.5	38556	40930	28	27	6973	13.7	14.9	44.9	23.0	3.5	125036	
28337 ELIZABETHTOWN	19049	4376	38.0	26.6	28.0	4.5	3.0	33600	35724	15	13	3191	25.1	24.8	34.9	12.8	2.3	90096	
28338 ELLERBE	16189	1941	41.5	28.1	25.7	3.0	1.7	31074	33162	10	7	1487	27.3	29.1	33.6	8.6	1.3	78650	
28339 ERWIN	19235	3121	34.9	25.6	32.6	4.4	2.5	38854	42575	29	28	2266	14.5	17.7	49.8	16.2	1.8	112557	
28340 FAIRMONT	14623	4259	41.2	30.2	24.3	3.0	1.3	31272	34109	10	8	3087	25.8	29.4	35.1	9.5	0.2	81089	
28341 FAISON	16645	1675	35.9	28.3	29.4	4.3	2.0	34106	35428	16	13	1174	24.4	19.4	40.5	15.1	0.7	100921	
28343 GIBSON	17474	685	36.8	25.8	32.1	3.5	1.8	35062	36872	18	15	497	32.4	33.4	26.0	6.8	1.4	73889	
28344 GODWIN	15881	1217	26.1	35.0	34.3	3.7	0.8	41377	42626	37	38	989	17.7	21.3	46.1	13.4	1.4	107410	
28345 HAMLET	17743	5001	35.1	29.9	29.0	4.6	1.3	36518	38205	22	18	3565	24.8	36.3	32.3	5.6	1.0	78632	
28347 HOFFMAN	14580	526	29.1	27.9	34.2	5.5	3.2	42884	46682	42	44	415	23.9	19.8	31.8	22.2	2.4	100977	
28348 HOPE MILLS	21089	10252	21.6	26.2	44.5	6.0	1.6	51427	53272	65	74	7430	12.6	19.0	58.4	9.8	0.2	108057	
28349 KENANSVILLE	19868	1319	27.4	30.1	33.6	5.6	3.3	43061	46276	43	45	1062	20.1	18.4	41.1	17.6	2.8	111620	
28351 LAUREL HILL	17330	2323	33.6	29.7	31.8	3.2	1.7	36083	38053	21	17	1772	28.9	32.7	29.5	8.5	0.5	78475	
28352 LAURINBURG	20290	9412	33.1	25.7	32.0	5.8	3.4	39349	41420	31	31	6155	14.9	25.7	40.7	17.0	1.7	102543	
28356 LINDEN	24086	1818	22.9	26.7	37.2	8.5	4.7	50335	52258	62	71	1528	18.0	19.2	42.6	19.8	0.4	110417	
28357 LUMBER BRIDGE	15517	1204	33.4	29.4	33.0	3.0	1.2	38761	42619	29	28	1001	26.6	23.6	40.7	8.2	1.0	89783	
28358 LUMBERTON	18090	13824	35.3	27.7	29.5	5.1	2.2	37403	40722	25	22	9264	22.6	23.0	39.6	11.8	3.0	100446	
28360 LUMBERTON	16268	4837	32.2	31.4	28.8	5.7	1.9	39065	41860	30	30	3585	23.8	25.2	38.4	11.1	1.5	91420	
28363 MARSTON	26681	237	26.6	30.4	32.5	6.3	4.2	43370	46402	43	47	194	17.5	21.1	34.5	25.3	1.5	108333	
28364 MAXTON	13921	5137	40.9	30.5	24.3	2.6	1.6	32239	35403	12	9	3945	29.2	31.2	33.0	6.6	0.1	77445	
28365 MOUNT OLIVE	18131	6009	33.4	30.8	29.3	4.2	2.2	37711	39921	26	23	4198	26.0	21.9	39.7	11.8	0.5	92105	
28366 NEWTON GROVE	19349	1780	27.9	29.0	35.2	5.2	2.8	43563	45252	44	48	1290	18.1	18.1	44.4	17.9	1.4	110911	
28369 ORRUM	17475	976	33.5	30.3	30.7	3.8	1.6	36232	39442	21	17	774	28.6	24.3	33.9	13.2	0.1	85849	
28371 PARKTON	19735	2041	21.9	24.0	43.9	8.3	2.0	52932	54499	68	78	1658	12.3	22.1	54.9	9.7	1.0	110509	
28372 PEMBROKE	15597	4203	37.0	30.6	26.6	4.4	1.4	34716	37307	17	14	3046	25.4	23.3	35.9	13.7	1.6	91832	
28373 PINEBLUFF	20413	758	25.1	31.0	35.9	5.8	2.2	45000	48418	48	54	571	21.5	12.6	46.2	16.8	2.8	112976	
28374 PINEHURST	45009	6174	9.1	18.3	45.9	14.0	12.7	72939	72694	88	94	5389	2.2	2.0	14.7	53.3	27.7	281625	
28376 RAEFORD	18706	12281	24.5	30.6	36.0	6.2	2.6	45234	48725	49	55	8989	19.1	23.3	46.0	10.9	0.7	102255	
28377 RED SPRINGS	15342	4334	36.5	30.3	26.4	4.4	2.4	34929	37406	17	14	3314	27.6	28.2	33.4	9.8	1.0	82280	
28379 ROCKINGHAM	18768	10340	35.4	28.6	29.4	4.7	1.8	36555	39194	22	19	7268	23.3	28.6	36.8	10.5	0.8	87125	
28382 ROSEBORO	18232	2749	33.1	32.8	28.3	4.0	1.8	38205	39377	27	26	2138	17.5	24.4	44.9	12.1	1.0	100528	
28383 ROWLAND	14766	3053	41.5	27.4	26.5	3.5	1.2	32556	36412	13	10	2370	33.8	27.2	34.2	4.4	0.4	69437	
28384 SAINT PAULS	14828	3960	39.2	28.6	27.7	3.6	0.9	33029	36022	13	11	2915	22.0	24.4	43.5	9.7	0.4	95960	
NORTH CAROLINA	25989		22.3	26.1	36.6	9.4	5.6	51418	53634				12.2	15.1	38.7	27.9	6.1	132724	
UNITED STATES	27277		20.9	24.4	35.3	11.7	7.6	54719	56938				9.3	13.1	31.6	32.6	13.5	162279	

#	POST OFFICE NAME	FINANCIAL SERVICES: Auto Loan	FINANCIAL SERVICES: Home Loan	FINANCIAL SERVICES: Invest-ments	FINANCIAL SERVICES: Retire-ment Plans	THE HOME: Home Improvements: Home Repair	THE HOME: Home Improvements: Lawn & Garden	THE HOME: Furnishings: Comput-ers & Hard-ware-Personal	THE HOME: Furnishings: Major Appli-ances	THE HOME: Furnishings: TV, Radio, Sound Equip-ment	THE HOME: Furnishings: Furni-ture	ENTERTAINMENT: Dine out/ Carry out	ENTERTAINMENT: Sports Equip-ment	ENTERTAINMENT: Fees & Tickets	ENTERTAINMENT: Toys & Games	ENTERTAINMENT: Travel	ENTERTAINMENT: Cable TV	PERSONAL: Apparel & Services	PERSONAL: Auto Repairs	PERSONAL: Health Insur-ance	PERSONAL: Pets & Supplies
28137	RICHFIELD	84	72	73	71	72	82	70	78	74	70	73	58	64	76	68	78	50	74	80	93
28138	ROCKWELL	89	77	76	77	77	88	76	84	80	74	79	63	68	82	72	84	53	79	86	99
28139	RUTHERFORDTON	88	69	76	68	70	86	71	80	77	69	75	60	61	79	67	82	51	77	84	96
28144	SALISBURY	77	69	66	71	68	77	76	75	80	73	79	56	73	79	72	84	55	77	83	90
28146	SALISBURY	88	79	77	78	78	87	78	83	81	77	80	62	72	83	75	85	55	81	86	99
28147	SALISBURY	93	82	74	81	80	86	84	85	86	83	86	64	77	89	78	88	59	85	87	102
28150	SHELBY	87	72	77	72	72	88	75	82	81	73	80	61	67	82	72	87	54	80	89	98
28152	SHELBY	85	72	73	71	70	85	72	79	77	70	76	60	65	79	69	82	52	77	84	95
28159	SPENCER	84	80	73	81	76	90	81	83	84	76	82	65	78	84	79	87	56	83	91	100
28160	SPINDALE	70	48	68	45	48	70	51	64	58	47	56	49	40	58	48	64	37	60	68	77
28163	STANFIELD	97	81	83	82	81	98	81	92	86	76	84	69	71	88	78	91	57	86	95	109
28164	STANLEY	96	89	80	88	86	95	86	91	89	86	89	68	82	92	83	93	61	88	94	108
28166	TROUTMAN	96	92	83	93	90	98	88	94	90	86	89	72	85	93	87	92	61	90	95	110
28167	UNION MILLS	76	55	63	53	54	72	57	66	63	55	62	51	46	66	52	69	42	63	70	81
28168	VALE	93	70	77	69	70	89	72	82	78	70	77	63	60	81	66	85	52	78	86	99
28170	WADESBORO	79	56	73	55	57	78	62	72	70	58	68	55	51	69	58	76	45	70	79	87
28173	WAXHAW	148	167	146	171	163	151	146	150	139	155	141	120	157	147	151	134	101	140	135	171
28174	WINGATE	86	76	69	76	75	82	77	80	80	76	79	60	71	83	72	83	54	79	83	96
28202	CHARLOTTE	90	69	70	77	66	69	97	77	97	91	99	67	87	96	84	96	70	91	84	98
28203	CHARLOTTE	108	93	96	102	92	94	117	99	118	112	119	82	111	115	107	118	85	111	107	123
28204	CHARLOTTE	85	69	73	76	68	67	96	76	94	89	96	66	88	92	86	93	69	89	81	96
28205	CHARLOTTE	77	64	57	67	61	65	78	68	79	75	79	55	72	80	69	79	55	75	72	84
28206	CHARLOTTE	58	43	39	45	40	47	57	49	61	55	61	39	51	60	48	63	42	57	56	62
28207	CHARLOTTE	207	259	307	270	285	235	243	241	220	259	221	189	276	215	272	207	165	233	213	269
28208	CHARLOTTE	65	54	46	55	49	57	62	56	66	61	65	44	58	66	55	68	45	62	63	71
28209	CHARLOTTE	108	96	91	101	94	95	113	99	112	110	113	81	108	112	105	111	79	109	105	122
28210	CHARLOTTE	126	119	116	123	117	115	129	119	128	130	129	94	128	128	125	126	91	126	121	142
28211	CHARLOTTE	142	154	165	161	159	144	158	148	150	161	152	118	166	148	163	146	110	152	143	174
28212	CHARLOTTE	85	64	57	68	60	61	85	69	83	83	85	59	74	86	72	81	59	80	71	86
28213	CHARLOTTE	102	95	83	96	90	89	103	93	100	102	102	75	97	103	94	98	71	98	92	112
28214	CHARLOTTE	108	112	97	110	106	107	102	105	102	105	103	80	104	106	102	102	71	102	104	123
28215	CHARLOTTE	104	103	89	102	98	94	103	98	101	105	102	78	102	105	99	99	72	100	95	116
28216	CHARLOTTE	99	103	88	102	98	98	97	97	98	100	99	74	100	100	96	98	68	96	98	114
28217	CHARLOTTE	92	76	67	79	72	74	91	79	90	90	91	64	83	92	81	89	63	87	81	97
28226	CHARLOTTE	167	184	178	189	183	168	173	169	167	182	169	133	185	170	178	161	121	167	159	196
28227	CHARLOTTE	110	112	98	112	108	102	108	105	105	112	106	82	108	109	106	102	74	105	100	124
28262	CHARLOTTE	129	111	97	116	104	99	134	110	125	130	127	96	121	130	115	118	90	120	103	134
28269	CHARLOTTE	139	141	122	146	134	124	138	129	132	144	134	107	141	140	133	126	96	129	118	152
28270	CHARLOTTE	180	197	182	205	194	176	184	178	176	194	178	144	197	183	188	168	128	176	163	207
28273	CHARLOTTE	128	123	102	122	114	105	124	115	118	130	121	93	119	126	115	113	84	116	105	135
28274	CHARLOTTE	210	264	308	269	290	227	251	248	219	269	220	198	275	212	280	201	163	239	208	276
28277	CHARLOTTE	195	226	205	232	222	193	197	197	185	215	188	160	218	196	205	173	137	186	170	223
28278	CHARLOTTE	152	172	154	170	167	153	153	154	146	162	148	120	162	152	157	141	104	148	142	177
28301	FAYETTEVILLE	51	41	39	43	40	47	49	46	54	48	53	34	46	52	44	57	37	50	54	57
28303	FAYETTEVILLE	94	91	82	92	88	88	94	90	93	95	94	69	92	95	91	93	65	92	91	106
28304	FAYETTEVILLE	93	90	76	90	85	85	92	87	91	92	91	69	89	94	87	90	63	89	88	104
28305	FAYETTEVILLE	96	93	93	95	94	100	98	96	102	97	101	71	99	99	98	105	70	100	108	115
28306	FAYETTEVILLE	96	92	81	90	88	90	89	90	90	91	90	69	86	93	85	91	62	89	89	107
28307	FORT BRAGG	84	44	33	51	40	38	80	55	75	74	79	55	61	90	58	69	55	70	50	67
28308	POPE A F B	89	46	35	54	41	39	84	58	79	78	83	58	64	95	60	72	58	74	52	71
28310	FORT BRAGG	85	44	33	51	40	38	80	55	75	74	79	55	61	90	58	69	56	71	50	68
28311	FAYETTEVILLE	98	85	74	86	80	81	94	86	94	95	95	69	87	97	85	93	66	91	86	104
28312	FAYETTEVILLE	91	75	81	73	74	88	75	84	80	74	79	63	66	82	72	84	53	81	86	100
28314	FAYETTEVILLE	96	88	74	88	82	80	93	86	92	95	93	68	88	96	85	89	64	89	83	102
28315	ABERDEEN	92	85	84	85	86	92	85	89	88	86	87	65	82	88	83	91	60	88	93	105
28318	AUTRYVILLE	85	61	70	59	61	81	63	74	70	62	69	57	51	73	58	77	46	70	78	90
28320	BLADENBORO	75	55	69	53	55	74	56	67	63	54	62	52	46	64	53	69	41	64	72	82
28323	BUNNLEVEL	85	76	68	72	73	77	76	77	77	78	77	59	70	80	71	78	53	77	76	92
28326	CAMERON	92	85	75	81	81	84	83	84	84	86	84	64	77	88	78	84	58	83	83	100
28327	CARTHAGE	92	85	89	83	86	94	81	89	85	83	84	64	78	85	81	89	58	86	93	105
28328	CLINTON	84	65	74	63	65	82	68	77	74	66	73	57	58	75	64	80	49	74	82	92
28333	DUDLEY	79	72	65	69	69	74	71	73	73	73	72	55	66	75	67	74	50	72	73	87
28334	DUNN	82	65	73	64	65	80	67	76	72	65	71	57	58	73	64	78	48	73	80	90
28337	ELIZABETHTOWN	79	58	76	57	59	79	61	72	68	59	66	54	51	68	58	74	44	69	77	87
28338	ELLERBE	74	49	71	46	49	72	52	65	60	50	58	51	39	61	49	66	39	61	69	80
28339	ERWIN	83	60	75	59	61	82	65	76	71	61	70	58	52	72	60	78	47	72	81	91
28340	FAIRMONT	68	50	59	48	49	65	52	60	59	51	57	46	44	59	49	64	39	58	65	74
28341	FAISON	82	56	74	53	55	79	59	72	67	56	65	55	45	69	54	74	43	68	76	88
28343	GIBSON	80	63	71	59	61	76	64	72	69	64	68	55	54	71	60	73	46	69	73	87
28344	GODWIN	81	61	70	59	61	78	62	72	68	61	67	55	52	71	58	74	45	68	76	87
28345	HAMLET	72	56	62	55	56	71	59	66	66	58	64	49	51	66	55	71	43	65	73	80
28347	HOFFMAN	87	81	71	78	78	81	78	80	79	81	80	59	73	83	74	81	54	79	80	95
28348	HOPE MILLS	87	84	72	81	80	81	79	81	80	83	80	60	76	83	76	80	55	79	79	96
28349	KENANSVILLE	91	74	78	71	72	86	75	83	80	74	79	63	66	82	71	84	54	80	86	99
28351	LAUREL HILL	77	60	64	57	58	72	61	68	66	61	65	52	52	68	56	70	44	65	70	82
28352	LAURINBURG	80	70	69	69	68	78	72	75	77	72	76	56	67	77	69	80	52	75	80	90
28356	LINDEN	106	86	87	83	83	98	86	94	90	86	90	73	74	95	79	95	61	90	95	113
28357	LUMBER BRIDGE	77	61	68	58	60	73	61	69	66	61	65	52	52	68	57	70	44	67	71	84
28358	LUMBERTON	74	62	64	61	61	71	65	68	69	64	68	52	59	70	61	72	47	68	72	82
28360	LUMBERTON	76	66	63	63	63	71	65	69	67	66	67	53	59	70	61	70	46	67	69	82
28363	MARSTON	94	84	77	81	82	89	80	86	84	83	84	63	74	87	76	87	57	83	87	102
28364	MAXTON	68	50	60	49	49	66	54	61	60	53	58	47	45	61	49	65	39	59	65	74
28365	MOUNT OLIVE	81	60	70	58	60	79	62	72	69	60	68	55	52	71	58	75	46	69	78	87
28366	NEWTON GROVE	90	70	82	67	70	88	70	82	76	68	75	62	59	78	67	82	50	77	85	98
28369	ORRUM	80	57	79	55	58	80	59	73	66	56	65	56	47	66	57	72	43	68	76	88
28371	PARKTON	91	88	74	84	83	81	84	84	83	89	84	65	81	88	80	82	58	83	80	99
28372	PEMBROKE	73	55	62	54	54	70	59	65	64	57	63	50	49	66	54	69	43	64	69	79
28373	PINEBLUFF	85	78	68	75	76	78	75	78	77	78	77	57	70	80	71	78	52	76	77	92
28374	PINEHURST	130	141	176	141	157	161	126	145	132	139	130	94	140	122	144	138	90	139	161	165
28376	RAEFORD	85	78	73	74	75	79	76	79	77	78	77	60	71	80	72	78	53	77	78	93
28377	RED SPRINGS	75	61	65	58	59	71	63	68	67	63	66	52	55	68	59	71	45	67	71	82
28379	ROCKINGHAM	75	59	66	58	58	74	62	68	67	59	66	52	54	68	58	73	45	67	74	83
28382	ROSEBORO	83	59	77	57	60	81	61	74	68	59	67	57	49	69	58	74	44	69	78	90
28383	ROWLAND	73	52	67	50	52	70	55	65	61	53	60	50	44	62	51	66	40	62	67	79
28384	SAINT PAULS	70	54	60	52	53	67	56	63	61	55	60	48	47	63	52	65	40	61	65	76
	NORTH CAROLINA	100	89	90	89	88	96	91	94	94	91	93	73	85	95	88	96	64	93	96	112
	UNITED STATES	100	100	100	100	100	100	100	100	100	100	100	100	100	100	100	100	100	100	100	100

ZIP CODE #	POST OFFICE NAME	COUNTY FIPS CODE	POPULATION 2000	POPULATION 2009	POPULATION 2014	2000-2009 ANNUAL RATE % Rate	2000-2009 ANNUAL RATE State Centile	HOUSEHOLDS 2000	HOUSEHOLDS 2009	HOUSEHOLDS 2014	HOUSEHOLDS % Annual Rate 2000-2009	HOUSEHOLDS 2009 Average HH Size	FAMILIES 2000	FAMILIES 2009	FAMILIES % Annual Rate 2000-2009
28385	SALEMBURG	163	2868	3192	3357	1.2	60	1078	1217	1283	1.3	2.61	789	867	1.0
28386	SHANNON	155	5329	6357	6822	1.9	77	1714	2054	2211	2.0	3.09	1302	1518	1.7
28387	SOUTHERN PINES	125	13076	14180	14877	0.9	48	5674	6113	6427	0.8	2.25	3560	3726	0.5
28390	SPRING LAKE	085	19834	19557	19935	-0.2	10	7541	7587	7741	0.1	2.58	5225	5084	-0.3
28391	STEDMAN	051	4875	5409	5620	1.1	56	1879	2201	2315	1.7	2.46	1433	1625	1.4
28392	TAR HEEL	017	1692	1818	1842	0.8	44	674	755	775	1.2	2.40	488	530	0.9
28393	TURKEY	163	1951	2145	2240	1.0	53	719	800	839	1.2	2.68	531	573	0.8
28394	VASS	125	4561	5073	5370	1.2	60	1812	1999	2121	1.1	2.50	1284	1368	0.7
28395	WADE	051	2096	2102	2118	0.0	15	838	892	910	0.7	2.28	613	629	0.3
28396	WAGRAM	165	3147	3197	3169	0.2	21	1140	1195	1196	0.5	2.67	841	860	0.2
28398	WARSAW	061	6719	6745	6811	0.0	15	2571	2610	2644	0.2	2.50	1805	1781	-0.1
28399	WHITE OAK	017	1833	1930	1934	0.6	36	690	748	759	0.9	2.58	504	531	0.6
28401	WILMINGTON	129	21724	23634	24972	0.9	48	9617	10797	11565	1.3	2.08	4844	5033	0.4
28403	WILMINGTON	129	30288	33889	36177	1.2	60	13893	16175	17573	1.7	1.93	6103	6485	0.7
28405	WILMINGTON	129	23913	28514	31285	1.9	77	9957	12488	13913	2.5	2.25	6693	7962	1.9
28409	WILMINGTON	129	26333	31280	34138	1.9	77	10030	12283	13579	2.2	2.55	7818	9234	1.8
28411	WILMINGTON	129	19434	30895	36866	5.1	95	7825	13114	15866	5.7	2.35	5718	9151	5.2
28412	WILMINGTON	129	23646	32597	37386	3.5	91	10219	14594	16913	3.9	2.21	6413	8912	3.6
28420	ASH	019	3793	5252	6376	3.6	91	1439	2054	2518	3.9	2.54	1076	1497	3.6
28421	ATKINSON	141	1376	1724	1947	2.5	84	574	741	842	2.8	2.33	397	499	2.5
28422	BOLIVIA	019	4605	6447	7840	3.7	91	1757	2562	3167	4.2	2.48	1331	1895	3.9
28423	BOLTON	047	2291	2369	2381	0.4	28	848	909	924	0.8	2.58	629	655	0.4
28425	BURGAW	141	9798	12319	13907	2.5	84	3450	4493	5152	2.9	2.51	2500	3171	2.6
28428	CAROLINA BEACH	129	5189	5476	5753	0.6	36	2534	2791	2964	1.0	1.94	1430	1466	0.3
28429	CASTLE HAYNE	129	7342	7873	8339	0.8	44	2773	3094	3320	1.2	2.51	2061	2204	0.7
28430	CERRO GORDO	047	1975	1990	1985	0.1	18	761	791	797	0.4	2.51	550	554	0.1
28431	CHADBOURN	047	6024	5925	5858	-0.2	10	2393	2424	2419	0.1	2.43	1648	1613	-0.2
28432	CLARENDON	047	2445	2419	2396	-0.1	13	970	994	995	0.3	2.43	718	715	0.0
28433	CLARKTON	017	4993	5012	4927	0.0	15	1948	2020	2006	0.4	2.45	1363	1371	0.1
28434	COUNCIL	017	1570	1533	1488	-0.3	8	640	652	640	0.2	2.34	448	442	-0.1
28435	CURRIE	141	2187	2762	3170	2.6	86	866	1115	1287	2.8	2.45	625	784	2.5
28436	DELCO	047	1789	1879	1905	0.5	32	688	751	769	1.0	2.50	529	564	0.7
28438	EVERGREEN	047	2180	2087	2045	-0.5	6	850	843	835	-0.1	2.47	626	604	-0.4
28439	FAIR BLUFF	047	1954	1873	1837	-0.5	6	806	800	793	-0.1	2.31	531	508	-0.5
28441	GARLAND	163	3110	3395	3514	1.0	53	1127	1256	1307	1.2	2.63	831	900	0.9
28442	HALLSBORO	047	1796	1706	1668	-0.6	5	745	734	726	-0.2	2.29	505	480	-0.5
28443	HAMPSTEAD	141	10397	15387	18306	4.3	94	4357	6582	7878	4.6	2.34	3259	4789	4.2
28444	HARRELLS	163	1927	2043	2096	0.6	36	725	781	805	0.8	2.58	518	542	0.5
28445	HOLLY RIDGE	133	4693	5621	6182	2.0	79	2005	2503	2793	2.4	2.23	1351	1612	1.9
28447	IVANHOE	141	1246	1370	1440	1.0	53	447	502	530	1.3	2.68	327	358	1.0
28448	KELLY	017	985	1044	1052	0.6	36	436	477	485	1.0	2.18	290	306	0.6
28449	KURE BEACH	129	1458	1657	1800	1.4	66	704	840	924	1.9	1.97	444	497	1.2
28450	LAKE WACCAMAW	047	2323	2413	2431	0.4	28	866	930	947	0.8	2.35	602	625	0.4
28451	LELAND	019	15894	24917	30643	5.0	95	5978	9727	12104	5.4	2.56	4399	6970	5.1
28452	LONGWOOD	019	547	636	807	1.6	72	200	230	295	1.5	2.75	157	174	1.1
28453	MAGNOLIA	061	3709	4332	4630	1.7	74	1272	1470	1567	1.6	2.85	923	1037	1.3
28454	MAPLE HILL	141	2358	2504	2631	0.7	40	869	955	1011	1.0	2.61	634	677	0.7
28455	NAKINA	047	1727	1685	1664	-0.3	8	690	697	695	0.1	2.42	501	490	-0.2
28456	RIEGELWOOD	047	3550	3900	4024	1.0	53	1349	1541	1604	1.4	2.53	1023	1140	1.2
28457	ROCKY POINT	141	7922	10028	11280	2.6	86	2986	3792	4270	2.6	2.64	2204	2737	2.4
28458	ROSE HILL	061	5646	6260	6591	1.1	56	2115	2358	2486	1.2	2.65	1530	1657	0.9
28460	SNEADS FERRY	133	5226	6644	7185	2.6	86	2268	3045	3341	3.2	2.18	1559	2038	2.9
28461	SOUTHPORT	019	9056	15387	19362	5.9	97	3955	6966	8848	6.3	2.20	2807	4797	6.0
28462	SUPPLY	019	10330	14251	17079	3.5	91	4448	6334	7667	3.9	2.24	3183	4398	3.6
28463	TABOR CITY	047	7594	7520	7456	-0.1	13	2897	2931	2926	0.1	2.53	2040	2004	-0.2
28464	TEACHEY	061	1639	1910	2049	1.7	74	626	741	798	1.8	2.56	450	517	1.5
28465	OAK ISLAND	019	6755	8297	9539	2.2	82	3180	4037	4686	2.6	2.05	2189	2691	2.3
28466	WALLACE	061	8464	9221	9648	0.9	48	3292	3647	3835	1.1	2.49	2311	2484	0.8
28467	CALABASH	019	5206	7644	9192	4.2	93	2513	3765	4574	4.5	2.03	1812	2637	4.1
28468	SUNSET BEACH	019	2637	5058	6594	7.3	99	1264	2482	3267	7.6	2.04	935	1788	7.3
28469	OCEAN ISLE BEACH	019	4361	6533	8042	4.5	94	1952	3025	3757	4.8	2.16	1385	2083	4.5
28470	SHALLOTTE	019	6880	9307	10957	3.3	90	2650	3732	4463	3.8	2.41	1925	2633	3.4
28472	WHITEVILLE	047	19754	19737	19620	0.0	15	7677	7895	7920	0.3	2.38	5316	5303	0.0
28478	WILLARD	141	4369	4887	5278	1.2	60	1693	1927	2095	1.4	2.48	1236	1372	1.1
28479	WINNABOW	019	2853	5198	6609	6.7	98	1034	2018	2604	7.5	2.52	776	1467	7.1
28480	WRIGHTSVILLE BEACH	129	2564	2723	2865	0.7	40	1258	1382	1471	1.0	1.95	580	583	0.1
28501	KINSTON	107	21163	19316	18513	-1.0	2	8829	8305	8022	-0.7	2.26	5491	4965	-1.1
28504	KINSTON	107	21856	20749	20141	-0.6	5	8599	8423	8234	-0.2	2.37	6079	5762	-0.6
28508	ALBERTSON	061	2090	2562	2794	2.2	82	693	841	913	2.1	3.04	516	609	1.8
28510	ARAPAHOE	137	1384	1601	1675	1.6	72	597	712	751	1.9	2.24	432	500	1.6
28511	ATLANTIC	031	817	840	833	0.3	24	362	379	378	0.5	1.91	246	248	0.1
28512	ATLANTIC BEACH	031	3684	3739	3795	0.2	21	1915	2028	2083	0.6	1.84	1172	1168	0.0
28513	AYDEN	147	8505	9254	9789	0.9	48	3421	3906	4177	1.4	2.35	2333	2562	1.0
28515	BAYBORO	137	3007	3042	3008	0.1	18	1007	1036	1031	0.3	2.52	700	698	0.0
28516	BEAUFORT	031	11002	12077	12456	1.0	53	4720	5348	5566	1.4	2.24	3227	3531	1.0
28518	BEULAVILLE	061	6815	7504	7887	1.0	53	2653	2969	3135	1.2	2.50	1949	2123	0.9
28520	CEDAR ISLAND	031	328	359	376	1.0	53	137	155	164	1.3	2.32	99	108	0.9
28521	CHINQUAPIN	061	1434	1469	1503	0.3	24	591	619	635	0.5	2.37	437	446	0.2
28523	COVE CITY	049	2475	2718	2843	1.0	53	963	1097	1161	1.4	2.48	724	804	1.1
28525	DEEP RUN	107	2919	3144	3151	0.8	44	1094	1191	1199	0.9	2.64	837	886	0.6
28526	DOVER	049	2222	2334	2398	0.5	32	901	983	1022	0.9	2.37	664	706	0.7
28527	ERNUL	049	772	804	831	0.4	28	297	328	343	1.1	2.12	221	238	0.8
28528	GLOUCESTER	031	449	509	536	1.4	66	190	223	238	1.7	2.28	141	161	1.4
28529	GRANTSBORO	137	2192	2297	2295	0.5	32	844	900	906	0.7	2.30	610	633	0.4
28530	GRIFTON	107	6763	7452	7873	1.1	56	2625	2968	3158	1.3	2.49	1908	2088	1.0
28531	HARKERS ISLAND	031	1525	1663	1731	0.9	48	661	748	788	1.3	2.21	498	548	1.0
28532	HAVELOCK	049	27456	27557	28032	0.0	15	8318	8881	9184	0.7	2.72	6677	6870	0.3
28537	HOBUCKEN	137	217	182	171	-1.9	0	99	86	81	-1.5	2.12	68	57	-1.9
28538	HOOKERTON	079	2491	2695	2769	0.9	48	895	990	1024	1.1	2.72	668	721	0.8
28539	HUBERT	133	13543	14647	14900	0.9	48	4486	4879	5010	0.9	2.70	3427	3652	0.7
28540	JACKSONVILLE	133	46805	48749	49248	0.4	28	15979	16992	17341	0.7	2.60	11675	12189	0.5
28543	TARAWA TERRACE	133	6401	5586	5278	-1.5	1	1908	1548	1451	-2.2	2.72	1865	1510	-2.3
28544	MIDWAY PARK	133	6213	5762	5633	-0.8	3	2290	2202	2170	-0.4	2.61	1799	1694	-0.6
28546	JACKSONVILLE	133	32489	36917	38813	1.4	66	11747	13722	14491	1.7	2.66	8988	10285	1.5
28547	CAMP LEJEUNE	133	19201	23351	23236	2.1	81	1432	1412	1395	-0.2	4.00	1418	1397	-0.2
	NORTH CAROLINA					1.7					1.8	2.46			1.5
	UNITED STATES					1.0					1.1	2.59			0.9

ZIP CODE		RACE (%)						% Hispanic Origin		2009 AGE DISTRIBUTION (%)										MEDIAN AGE		
#	POST OFFICE NAME	White		Black		Asian/Pacific															% 2009	% 2009
		2000	2009	2000	2009	2000	2009	2000	2009	0-4	5-9	10-14	15-19	20-24	25-44	45-64	65-84	85+	18+	2009	Males	Females
28385	SALEMBURG	67.0	64.1	27.0	27.4	0.3	0.4	6.9	10.1	6.8	7.0	7.2	6.2	4.6	26.0	27.6	12.9	1.7	75.1	39.4	49.2	50.8
28386	SHANNON	24.0	23.0	14.7	13.4	0.2	0.3	15.5	19.4	9.7	8.7	7.8	7.5	8.0	30.0	21.6	6.2	0.6	69.3	29.6	50.6	49.4
28387	SOUTHERN PINES	73.2	71.9	23.9	24.1	0.7	1.0	2.1	3.2	5.3	5.2	5.3	5.6	5.4	20.9	27.1	19.5	5.8	80.8	46.7	45.4	54.6
28390	SPRING LAKE	50.9	48.7	36.9	35.4	2.7	3.4	9.1	12.3	10.4	8.7	7.4	7.2	9.4	32.2	18.6	5.7	0.4	69.3	28.6	50.6	49.4
28391	STEDMAN	81.5	78.7	13.5	14.7	0.4	0.6	2.1	3.3	6.2	6.2	6.4	6.2	5.5	26.9	30.6	10.9	1.0	77.4	39.9	49.9	50.1
28392	TAR HEEL	53.8	52.0	42.3	42.7	0.2	0.3	3.5	5.0	5.8	5.8	6.2	6.8	5.1	28.5	29.7	10.8	1.3	78.1	39.7	47.3	52.7
28393	TURKEY	52.7	48.2	37.7	37.2	0.6	0.8	8.1	12.7	7.1	7.1	7.2	7.2	6.0	26.1	26.2	11.4	1.7	74.3	37.8	50.5	49.5
28394	VASS	83.6	81.0	11.3	11.9	0.4	0.6	4.0	6.2	6.5	6.5	6.5	5.7	4.9	26.4	27.5	13.3	2.6	77.1	40.6	50.2	49.8
28395	WADE	72.0	69.1	24.2	25.9	0.5	0.8	1.7	2.6	5.5	5.9	6.6	6.3	4.3	24.9	30.4	14.1	2.0	77.8	42.5	49.0	51.0
28396	WAGRAM	39.1	36.1	46.4	48.0	0.2	0.3	1.3	1.6	7.5	7.6	7.9	7.4	5.1	25.7	26.7	11.1	1.0	72.3	36.3	49.3	50.7
28398	WARSAW	39.9	36.6	48.8	46.5	0.5	0.6	12.9	18.9	7.9	7.8	7.8	6.8	5.4	26.2	24.6	11.8	1.9	72.3	36.3	48.2	51.8
28399	WHITE OAK	64.5	61.9	29.0	29.2	0.1	0.2	9.7	13.0	7.4	6.2	6.4	6.7	6.9	26.1	29.5	9.9	1.0	76.4	37.3	50.8	49.2
28401	WILMINGTON	44.9	41.3	51.4	53.6	0.4	0.5	3.0	4.3	6.6	6.1	5.4	6.0	7.6	28.7	24.9	11.9	2.8	78.6	37.3	46.9	53.1
28403	WILMINGTON	82.8	79.8	13.3	14.5	1.2	1.7	3.0	4.4	4.7	4.0	3.8	10.5	16.9	27.2	19.7	10.7	2.6	85.3	30.1	47.6	52.4
28405	WILMINGTON	75.8	73.1	21.4	22.9	0.8	1.1	1.6	2.3	5.7	5.7	5.9	6.2	7.6	26.8	26.8	13.7	1.5	79.0	39.1	48.4	51.6
28409	WILMINGTON	91.9	90.2	5.5	6.2	1.1	1.6	1.1	1.6	5.3	6.0	6.9	6.7	4.1	23.3	33.5	12.9	1.3	77.6	43.6	48.9	51.1
28411	WILMINGTON	88.6	85.8	9.2	11.1	0.7	1.1	1.3	1.9	6.3	6.4	6.5	5.5	3.6	29.9	28.9	11.8	1.3	77.4	40.0	49.1	50.9
28412	WILMINGTON	88.7	86.8	7.5	8.2	1.3	1.7	2.6	3.7	6.1	5.9	5.8	5.5	5.6	31.0	25.9	12.3	1.9	79.0	38.3	47.8	52.2
28420	ASH	73.1	69.3	22.0	23.2	0.5	0.6	6.8	10.3	7.2	7.0	6.8	6.6	5.8	27.3	26.5	11.6	1.3	74.9	37.4	49.4	50.6
28421	ATKINSON	56.1	52.1	40.4	42.9	0.3	0.3	2.3	3.6	5.6	5.8	6.3	6.1	4.7	24.7	30.7	14.2	1.7	78.4	42.4	50.0	50.0
28422	BOLIVIA	71.9	71.3	25.4	25.1	0.3	0.4	0.9	1.2	5.3	5.1	5.1	5.8	6.0	22.1	30.2	19.1	1.3	80.8	45.4	49.1	50.9
28423	BOLTON	38.8	37.5	35.7	35.8	0.1	0.1	1.3	1.6	6.9	6.9	7.3	6.8	5.6	25.7	27.3	11.9	1.4	74.5	37.8	47.2	52.8
28425	BURGAW	59.6	55.3	36.4	38.6	0.1	0.2	4.4	6.7	6.1	6.3	6.4	6.1	5.8	27.5	27.4	12.3	2.2	77.3	39.4	50.2	49.8
28428	CAROLINA BEACH	97.1	96.2	1.1	1.4	0.4	0.6	0.8	1.1	3.4	3.2	3.9	4.3	4.3	23.8	39.8	15.9	1.5	87.3	48.8	50.5	49.5
28429	CASTLE HAYNE	71.0	67.3	26.2	29.1	0.2	0.3	1.8	2.6	6.2	6.4	6.7	6.5	5.6	27.8	30.2	9.7	1.0	76.6	39.0	49.7	50.3
28430	CERRO GORDO	76.3	75.3	19.9	20.3	0.4	0.4	3.1	3.9	6.6	6.8	6.8	6.5	4.7	25.7	28.7	12.6	1.5	75.7	39.4	48.3	51.7
28431	CHADBOURN	55.8	55.3	40.5	40.7	0.3	0.3	1.5	1.9	7.1	7.2	6.8	7.3	6.0	23.5	27.6	12.9	1.7	74.2	38.5	48.1	51.9
28432	CLARENDON	91.0	90.5	6.3	6.4	0.2	0.2	2.0	2.5	6.5	6.9	6.6	6.9	5.3	26.5	28.3	11.5	1.5	75.7	38.5	48.6	51.4
28433	CLARKTON	47.2	45.5	47.6	48.2	0.1	0.1	3.0	4.1	6.8	6.9	7.1	6.8	5.3	24.0	29.1	12.4	1.6	74.9	39.7	48.4	51.6
28434	COUNCIL	30.8	29.0	60.7	61.0	0.0	0.0	2.6	3.3	5.9	6.3	6.7	7.0	5.0	22.7	30.3	14.6	1.7	76.7	42.1	47.6	52.4
28435	CURRIE	63.2	58.4	30.2	32.0	0.3	0.4	4.8	7.5	6.0	6.3	6.6	7.2	5.7	25.2	30.3	11.7	1.1	76.6	40.2	49.4	50.6
28436	DELCO	60.9	60.2	30.3	30.7	0.1	0.1	1.7	2.0	6.6	6.7	7.2	6.7	5.4	25.8	28.6	12.0	1.1	75.4	38.4	48.7	51.3
28438	EVERGREEN	66.3	65.4	30.6	31.0	0.1	0.1	2.2	2.7	5.8	6.0	6.1	6.1	5.4	25.1	31.5	12.4	1.4	78.2	41.5	48.3	51.7
28439	FAIR BLUFF	53.5	52.7	43.8	44.2	0.0	0.0	1.8	2.2	6.3	6.5	6.6	6.3	5.3	23.2	29.8	13.7	2.3	76.7	41.8	46.6	53.4
28441	GARLAND	48.5	44.3	41.2	40.1	0.1	0.1	11.2	16.8	7.2	8.0	7.5	7.1	5.1	26.6	25.5	11.6	1.5	73.0	36.5	49.5	50.5
28442	HALLSBORO	58.8	58.1	34.6	34.9	0.3	0.4	1.4	1.6	6.0	6.0	6.3	6.7	5.5	25.4	29.7	12.6	1.9	77.5	40.8	48.2	51.8
28443	HAMPSTEAD	89.6	88.1	8.5	9.3	0.2	0.3	1.4	2.1	4.5	4.8	5.1	5.0	3.6	19.2	34.7	21.3	1.8	82.5	50.0	49.8	50.2
28444	HARRELLS	36.9	33.7	54.8	54.0	0.5	0.6	9.0	13.2	6.5	7.0	7.0	6.9	5.2	24.9	29.0	12.0	1.6	75.5	39.1	49.3	50.7
28445	HOLLY RIDGE	93.0	92.2	3.9	3.8	0.7	1.0	1.7	2.5	5.5	5.4	5.5	5.2	4.8	25.4	31.5	15.1	1.4	80.1	43.6	49.5	50.5
28447	IVANHOE	40.5	36.9	52.8	53.4	0.2	0.3	7.1	10.3	6.0	6.8	7.2	6.9	5.4	24.3	29.9	12.0	1.5	75.5	39.7	49.6	50.4
28448	KELLY	60.2	57.7	36.6	37.6	0.2	0.2	3.0	4.6	5.2	5.8	6.2	5.0	3.6	23.9	31.9	16.2	2.1	79.9	45.1	48.5	51.5
28449	KURE BEACH	97.9	97.3	0.3	0.5	0.3	0.5	0.8	1.1	2.8	3.3	3.8	3.6	2.2	19.2	42.8	20.8	1.5	87.9	53.8	48.9	51.1
28450	LAKE WACCAMAW	61.9	61.0	19.5	19.7	0.1	0.1	1.3	1.5	5.5	5.7	6.6	6.3	3.6	22.3	28.9	16.9	4.1	78.0	44.9	46.8	53.2
28451	LELAND	70.8	69.5	23.7	23.5	0.4	0.5	4.5	6.0	7.7	7.4	7.1	6.8	6.1	29.5	25.7	8.9	0.8	73.6	35.4	49.9	50.1
28452	LONGWOOD	57.8	57.1	39.7	38.5	0.4	0.3	5.3	7.7	5.8	5.8	6.1	6.6	5.3	24.4	28.5	16.0	1.4	78.3	42.1	49.2	50.8
28453	MAGNOLIA	40.4	35.1	38.9	35.2	0.2	0.2	23.0	32.6	8.1	8.0	7.8	6.6	5.7	28.9	24.1	9.6	1.2	72.0	34.4	51.0	49.0
28454	MAPLE HILL	62.4	58.4	34.6	37.5	0.4	0.5	2.0	2.9	7.3	7.0	6.7	6.7	7.6	25.8	26.8	10.7	1.4	74.8	35.6	50.3	49.7
28455	NAKINA	89.2	88.4	7.1	7.1	0.0	0.0	6.1	7.6	6.6	6.5	6.2	5.6	6.4	27.2	27.5	12.8	1.3	77.3	38.8	49.8	50.2
28456	RIEGELWOOD	36.3	36.2	53.9	52.8	0.0	0.1	3.9	4.8	6.5	6.8	7.0	6.6	5.3	25.1	28.9	12.4	1.4	75.4	39.1	47.7	52.3
28457	ROCKY POINT	73.0	68.6	20.9	22.2	0.2	0.3	6.9	10.1	6.9	6.7	6.7	6.9	6.6	27.8	28.0	9.6	0.8	75.4	37.2	50.6	49.4
28458	ROSE HILL	45.9	41.3	40.5	38.4	0.3	0.4	16.7	24.1	7.5	7.5	7.4	6.5	5.3	26.7	26.4	11.1	1.7	73.6	37.1	49.4	50.6
28460	SNEADS FERRY	92.3	90.7	4.4	4.8	0.8	1.2	1.6	2.3	5.0	5.1	5.3	4.9	4.3	26.1	31.8	16.2	1.1	81.5	44.3	50.7	49.3
28461	SOUTHPORT	85.9	85.3	11.9	11.8	0.5	0.8	0.9	1.3	4.7	4.9	5.3	5.4	4.4	21.0	32.7	19.6	2.1	81.8	48.1	48.5	51.5
28462	SUPPLY	86.9	86.0	10.7	10.6	0.1	0.2	1.6	2.4	4.9	5.2	5.5	5.2	3.9	20.5	32.4	20.9	1.6	81.3	48.3	49.4	50.6
28463	TABOR CITY	64.5	63.2	32.2	32.7	0.1	0.1	3.3	4.3	7.2	7.5	7.4	7.1	5.3	24.7	26.5	12.8	1.6	73.4	37.6	47.7	52.3
28464	TEACHEY	44.6	41.5	47.7	46.5	0.1	0.2	11.5	16.9	7.1	7.1	7.2	6.2	5.3	24.9	27.2	13.1	1.9	74.7	39.0	46.9	53.1
28465	OAK ISLAND	98.1	97.5	0.4	0.4	0.2	0.2	0.8	1.1	3.1	3.5	3.9	3.5	2.6	17.5	38.3	25.9	1.7	87.3	55.4	48.7	51.3
28466	WALLACE	62.6	59.0	28.2	27.7	0.2	0.3	11.0	15.5	7.0	7.0	6.9	6.2	5.0	25.8	26.9	13.2	2.0	75.2	39.1	48.6	51.4
28467	CALABASH	87.7	83.5	10.2	13.1	0.3	0.4	2.4	4.2	3.3	3.4	3.6	3.8	3.1	14.4	28.5	36.7	3.3	87.4	60.1	48.2	51.8
28468	SUNSET BEACH	93.1	91.8	4.4	4.6	0.3	0.5	2.2	3.3	2.6	2.9	3.2	2.9	2.4	13.0	35.1	35.2	2.7	89.5	60.1	49.0	51.0
28469	OCEAN ISLE BEACH	91.7	89.8	5.2	5.5	0.2	0.3	2.7	4.3	3.9	4.1	4.3	4.0	3.3	18.0	33.4	27.4	1.6	85.2	54.0	48.7	51.3
28470	SHALLOTTE	82.5	80.6	13.6	13.6	0.4	0.5	3.8	6.1	5.6	5.8	6.1	7.8	5.4	22.1	29.3	16.1	1.8	78.8	42.9	49.1	50.9
28472	WHITEVILLE	65.0	64.2	30.6	30.9	0.4	0.4	2.0	2.5	6.3	6.1	6.2	6.3	6.0	25.8	28.1	13.3	1.9	77.4	40.1	48.9	51.1
28478	WILLARD	64.2	60.8	31.9	33.4	0.1	0.1	4.6	6.9	6.1	6.4	6.6	6.3	5.8	26.9	28.5	12.0	1.4	76.9	39.2	50.9	49.1
28479	WINNABOW	80.3	76.8	16.0	18.2	0.2	0.3	1.9	3.0	6.5	6.5	6.8	7.0	5.5	26.9	28.2	10.8	1.8	76.2	38.9	49.3	50.7
28480	WRIGHTSVILLE BEACH	98.1	97.5	0.3	0.4	0.6	0.8	0.6	1.0	2.9	2.4	2.6	3.3	13.5	29.5	29.7	14.4	1.6	90.6	41.1	55.5	44.5
28501	KINSTON	33.0	32.5	65.1	64.9	0.3	0.4	1.5	2.1	6.5	6.4	6.5	6.9	5.9	21.9	27.9	14.9	3.0	76.2	41.5	45.7	54.3
28504	KINSTON	70.9	67.5	25.9	28.0	0.6	0.9	3.2	4.4	5.6	5.7	6.1	6.6	5.6	24.8	29.8	14.2	1.4	78.3	41.6	49.1	50.9
28508	ALBERTSON	65.1	54.8	6.8	5.9	0.4	0.6	36.0	47.9	9.5	8.6	7.4	6.5	7.4	32.3	20.1	7.4	0.8	70.6	31.1	54.4	45.6
28510	ARAPAHOE	78.2	77.0	19.7	19.9	0.4	0.6	2.5	3.5	4.2	4.5	5.1	5.7	3.9	19.9	34.4	20.4	2.1	82.7	49.5	49.5	50.5
28511	ATLANTIC	98.0	97.5	0.2	0.2	0.1	0.1	0.9	1.2	4.5	4.6	4.9	4.5	3.8	19.2	28.2	21.7	8.6	82.7	51.0	50.6	49.4
28512	ATLANTIC BEACH	98.5	98.0	0.4	0.4	0.5	0.8	0.8	1.1	1.8	2.1	2.4	2.6	2.0	16.9	38.5	30.9	2.8	92.2	58.4	50.1	49.9
28513	AYDEN	61.0	59.2	35.4	35.3	0.2	0.3	3.7	5.7	6.3	6.3	6.4	6.6	6.0	25.3	28.1	12.8	2.2	76.9	40.0	48.0	52.0
28515	BAYBORO	51.4	49.8	46.2	47.0	0.3	0.5	1.5	2.1	4.8	5.2	5.4	6.1	6.3	27.3	28.7	13.5	2.7	81.8	41.3	54.1	45.9
28516	BEAUFORT	83.6	82.5	14.1	14.3	0.3	0.4	1.9	2.6	4.9	5.3	5.5	5.8	4.6	23.7	33.3	15.2	1.7	80.8	45.1	49.0	51.0
28518	BEULAVILLE	75.9	71.6	17.4	17.7	0.1	0.2	7.1	11.2	6.5	6.7	6.7	6.8	5.1	26.6	28.1	12.0	1.4	75.7	38.9	49.6	50.4
28520	CEDAR ISLAND	98.8	98.9	0.6	0.6	0.3	0.3	0.0	0.3	4.7	5.0	5.8	5.3	3.1	23.4	32.9	17.3	2.5	81.1	46.5	49.6	50.4
28521	CHINQUAPIN	80.8	79.0	16.8	17.4	0.1	0.1	2.8	4.3	5.9	6.1	6.5	6.1	4.4	25.6	28.6	15.1	1.7	77.2	42.1	51.1	48.9
28523	COVE CITY	62.5	60.0	35.2	36.5	0.2	0.3	1.8	2.9	5.3	5.7	6.1	6.7	5.0	23.6	32.3	13.6	1.6	78.8	43.1	48.8	51.2
28525	DEEP RUN	83.6	78.4	9.7	10.8	0.1	0.2	8.1	12.6	7.5	7.3	7.3	7.0	5.9	27.4	26.4	9.8	1.2	73.6	36.7	49.9	50.1
28526	DOVER	59.8	57.5	38.1	39.2	0.2	0.3	3.2	4.9	4.8	5.2	5.6	6.3	4.6	23.9	32.3	15.8	1.7	80.6	44.8	48.4	51.6
28527	ERNUL	79.5	78.6	18.0	18.0	0.3	0.5	2.1	3.0	5.1	5.3	5.6	5.5	6.6	32.0	29.0	10.1	0.9	80.6	38.9	58.0	42.0
28528	GLOUCESTER	99.1	98.8	0.0	0.0	0.2	0.4	0.2	0.2	4.1	4.5	6.1	5.9	3.9	23.0	36.3	13.8	2.4	81.7	46.3	48.7	51.3
28529	GRANTSBORO	78.1	77.1	19.3	19.6	0.5	0.7	1.1	1.6	4.8	5.2	5.5	5.3	5.2	27.1	29.3	15.2	2.4	81.8	42.9	54.2	45.8
28530	GRIFTON	64.5	60.4	32.7	35.4	0.2	0.3	3.1	4.7	6.2	6.6	7.0	6.6	5.4	24.2	30.1	12.5	1.4	75.8	40.8	50.1	49.9
28531	HARKERS ISLAND	98.6	98.1	0.0	0.0	0.2	0.3	0.1	0.2	3.2	3.6	4.0	4.1	2.9	19.2	38.4	22.2	2.3	86.4	52.7	49.1	50.9
28532	HAVELOCK	68.0	63.3	22.2	23.1	2.4	3.3	7.8	11.0	10.0	6.8	5.6	7.2	18.8	28.6	17.0	5.5	0.6	74.5	25.8	55.0	45.0
28537	HOBUCKEN	98.6	98.4	0.5	0.5	0.0	0.0	0.9	1.1	4.4	4.9	5.5	5.5	3.8	21.4	31.3	19.8	3.3	80.8	48.1	46.2	53.8
28538	HOOKERTON	51.6	48.5	41.3	40.4	0.1	0.1	7.3	11.2	7.5	7.8	7.6	6.4	5.1	24.7	28.2	11.3	1.4	73.1	38.0	48.5	51.5
28539	HUBERT	84.4	81.1	7.9	8.0	1.6	2.2	5.0	7.6	8.5	7.2	7.1	9.6	15.5	29.7	16.4	5.5	0.4	72.8	26.1	54.9	45.1
28540	JACKSONVILLE	69.3	66.0	21.9	22.0	1.9	2.5	6.4	9.0	8.8	7.0	6.0	9.4	14.6	28.3	18.5	6.5	0.8	74.4	27.2	52.9	47.1
28543	TARAWA TERRACE	60.5	54.2	21.1	20.6	1.6	2.1	17.0	23.5	22.2	6.0	1.2	16.3	33.7	20.1	0.5	0.0	0.0	70.1	20.6	60.6	39.4
28544	MIDWAY PARK	63.1	58.1	23.8	23.9	1.9	2.6	10.5	14.9	16.0	5.6	3.8	6.2	29.2	25.7	10.4	2.8	0.3	72.2	23.1	49.9	50.1
28546	JACKSONVILLE	64.2	60.4	25.1	24.9	3.0	4.1	7.6	10.6	9.4	7.5	6.6	6.9	10.5	31.4	20.2	6.8	0.7	72.4	29.5	48.6	51.4
28547	CAMP LEJEUNE	69.8	64.5	17.3	17.1	1.8	2.4	11.6	17.2	3.8	4.0	3.3	14.3	54.8	18.7	1.1	0.0	0.0	87.5	22.2	85.9	14.1
	NORTH CAROLINA	72.1	69.8	21.6	21.5	1.5	2.1	4.7	6.9	6.6	6.5	6.5	6.8	6.9	27.7	26.5	10.9	1.6	76.5	37.4	49.3	50.7
	UNITED STATES	75.1	72.0	12.3	12.7	3.8	4.6	12.5	15.7	6.8	6.7	6.6	7.1	6.9	27.0	26.0	10.9	1.9	75.7	36.9	49.2	50.8

ZIP CODE #	POST OFFICE NAME	2009 Per Capita Income	2009 HH Income Base	2009 Household Income Distribution (%) Less than $25,000	$25,000 to $49,999	$50,000 to $99,999	$100,000 to $149,999	$150,000 or More	Median Household Income 2009	2014	2009 National Centile	2009 State Centile	2009 Home Value Base	2009 Home Value Distribution (%) Less than $50,000	$50,000 to $89,999	$90,000 to $174,999	$175,000 to $399,999	$400,000 or More	2009 Median Home Value
28385	SALEMBURG	19298	1217	30.2	28.5	32.3	6.2	2.8	40906	42586	36	36	929	17.5	20.3	44.5	15.3	2.4	104605
28386	SHANNON	15259	2054	35.6	27.8	29.6	4.7	2.3	38392	42122	28	27	1517	33.6	32.9	26.2	6.3	1.1	64533
28387	SOUTHERN PINES	31184	6113	20.8	25.3	37.1	8.7	8.1	54121	55539	70	80	4062	6.5	6.8	28.4	42.7	15.6	198264
28390	SPRING LAKE	17991	7587	28.7	34.4	31.6	4.1	1.3	39311	42435	31	30	3565	23.2	18.2	47.6	10.7	0.4	100185
28391	STEDMAN	23019	2201	22.6	25.3	43.6	6.7	1.9	51483	53248	65	75	1798	20.0	27.2	43.3	8.8	0.6	93497
28392	TAR HEEL	19040	755	26.5	32.6	36.4	3.4	1.1	41482	46281	38	39	620	29.8	26.1	37.6	5.6	0.8	80513
28393	TURKEY	15281	800	37.3	29.6	29.3	2.1	1.8	33471	35837	14	12	626	19.0	24.6	45.7	9.7	1.0	96154
28394	VASS	23557	1999	20.4	32.2	35.8	6.5	5.1	47637	50610	56	62	1531	15.5	15.0	34.7	26.5	8.2	131250
28395	WADE	21489	892	29.8	31.6	31.5	4.1	2.9	38914	41842	29	29	722	20.8	18.8	47.1	12.9	0.4	102713
28396	WAGRAM	18999	1195	28.8	21.6	42.3	5.8	1.6	49291	48965	60	68	970	20.5	24.9	30.3	23.0	1.2	98000
28398	WARSAW	16923	2610	38.5	30.7	25.0	4.1	1.7	33381	33992	14	12	1808	19.7	20.0	47.7	11.1	1.4	105878
28399	WHITE OAK	14429	748	38.1	34.1	25.8	1.6	0.4	31365	33590	10	8	615	31.9	30.4	34.0	3.4	0.3	71146
28401	WILMINGTON	17451	10797	46.0	29.0	21.6	2.1	1.3	27175	28428	5	2	4197	14.6	23.0	40.9	15.8	5.6	103191
28403	WILMINGTON	28197	16175	32.3	26.1	30.3	5.5	5.8	38428	42671	28	27	6754	4.0	4.8	31.3	43.4	16.4	202879
28405	WILMINGTON	30943	12488	18.3	24.3	42.2	8.5	6.7	56563	58357	73	85	9006	10.9	7.0	34.2	35.7	12.2	171977
28409	WILMINGTON	33651	12283	11.5	17.6	47.1	14.6	9.2	71639	71002	88	93	10595	7.0	3.8	18.6	53.8	16.8	229171
28411	WILMINGTON	34161	13114	10.4	19.5	48.6	13.8	7.7	68872	68800	86	92	10825	4.7	3.4	27.1	51.3	13.4	207507
28412	WILMINGTON	28763	14594	17.2	25.5	45.3	7.5	4.5	55436	56931	72	83	9719	9.8	3.9	29.6	49.6	7.1	188869
28420	ASH	19334	2054	36.1	25.2	30.8	4.7	3.2	36147	38808	21	17	1620	20.9	26.2	26.7	21.9	4.4	94476
28421	ATKINSON	21099	741	35.9	25.1	30.4	6.1	2.6	38423	41912	28	27	621	18.0	31.1	38.3	11.9	0.6	92391
28422	BOLIVIA	25819	2562	19.2	26.7	40.2	8.5	5.3	52894	54790	68	78	2182	18.7	15.4	28.6	20.3	17.0	117490
28423	BOLTON	16948	909	35.1	30.1	31.0	2.3	1.4	37418	39055	25	22	766	22.8	21.5	39.3	16.2	0.1	97414
28425	BURGAW	17701	4493	34.7	27.8	31.9	3.9	1.6	37696	41154	26	23	3417	17.7	20.5	43.0	17.0	1.8	112403
28428	CAROLINA BEACH	30708	2791	21.9	32.2	35.4	5.2	5.3	45984	50102	51	58	1847	5.7	2.9	22.2	55.9	13.3	225000
28429	CASTLE HAYNE	22365	3094	19.2	30.4	42.8	5.3	2.4	50254	52313	62	71	2500	19.3	9.9	40.8	27.4	2.6	131081
28430	CERRO GORDO	17558	791	43.0	25.7	24.3	3.9	3.2	29655	30748	8	5	627	22.6	28.9	35.6	12.3	0.6	87286
28431	CHADBOURN	15667	2424	43.6	28.1	24.1	3.2	1.0	28924	29778	7	4	1760	24.9	27.2	36.3	10.5	1.1	85488
28432	CLARENDON	16345	994	34.4	35.0	27.2	2.8	0.6	32747	33776	13	10	787	17.4	16.5	41.7	22.4	2.0	111322
28433	CLARKTON	15011	2020	44.7	29.2	23.1	1.8	1.2	28328	30420	6	3	1609	21.9	30.8	36.9	8.7	1.6	87166
28434	COUNCIL	17307	652	37.3	31.3	26.8	3.8	0.8	32312	33378	12	10	567	19.0	24.2	46.6	9.0	1.2	98750
28435	CURRIE	18330	1115	41.5	22.8	28.9	4.9	1.9	35047	38882	18	15	932	23.3	15.0	43.6	15.5	2.7	110085
28436	DELCO	17416	751	33.6	31.2	31.7	1.9	1.7	37493	40365	25	22	628	17.2	25.3	37.1	20.4	0.0	103916
28438	EVERGREEN	17436	843	41.2	31.6	20.4	4.4	2.5	30062	31022	8	5	670	32.5	24.8	32.5	9.9	0.3	80577
28439	FAIR BLUFF	14788	800	49.1	27.3	20.4	2.5	0.8	25459	26393	4	1	597	37.9	26.3	27.3	8.5	0.0	67870
28441	GARLAND	17238	1256	35.3	30.7	28.3	2.9	2.9	35088	37559	18	15	958	29.4	16.8	46.2	5.0	2.5	94444
28442	HALLSBORO	18502	734	37.2	26.8	30.9	4.4	0.7	36992	38629	24	20	572	28.0	19.4	40.2	11.4	1.0	93261
28443	HAMPSTEAD	28601	6582	19.1	24.7	42.7	8.4	5.1	55387	54810	72	83	5688	14.0	10.2	29.6	34.8	11.3	164678
28444	HARRELLS	15246	781	42.6	27.5	25.4	3.3	1.2	31227	33712	10	8	613	25.4	24.8	42.9	5.4	1.5	89516
28445	HOLLY RIDGE	26410	2503	22.4	28.5	38.3	6.7	4.2	49125	50985	59	67	1822	14.4	10.5	33.5	26.2	15.5	151970
28447	IVANHOE	14195	502	42.4	28.9	24.3	3.4	1.0	31367	33336	10	8	412	25.2	31.6	36.2	6.1	1.0	78235
28448	KELLY	23049	477	35.2	29.4	27.9	4.4	3.1	33480	36432	14	12	416	21.6	19.7	41.6	15.6	1.4	101974
28449	KURE BEACH	29769	840	24.8	26.5	37.7	6.4	4.5	47933	51015	56	64	584	0.0	7.0	18.8	59.2	14.9	250481
28450	LAKE WACCAMAW	22410	930	31.0	24.1	35.9	5.6	3.4	43029	47444	42	45	729	13.0	15.0	36.8	30.7	4.5	122957
28451	LELAND	21324	9727	24.5	29.0	37.8	5.8	2.9	46976	50150	54	61	7715	16.5	17.2	37.7	25.4	3.2	123354
28452	LONGWOOD	18580	230	36.1	25.7	29.1	4.3	4.8	36536	40207	22	18	191	22.5	28.8	16.2	21.5	11.0	88958
28453	MAGNOLIA	14103	1470	38.8	31.5	26.8	1.8	1.1	33244	34470	14	12	1046	21.8	19.3	43.1	13.5	2.3	108526
28454	MAPLE HILL	17222	955	35.2	29.8	30.6	2.1	2.3	38116	41247	27	25	736	25.7	22.4	41.7	8.4	1.8	94375
28455	NAKINA	18081	697	36.0	25.3	35.4	2.9	0.4	41797	46204	39	40	570	26.0	30.4	30.2	13.5	0.0	75238
28456	RIEGELWOOD	18163	1541	32.3	29.0	32.9	3.6	2.2	39331	42948	31	30	1294	19.0	23.6	42.5	14.3	0.5	98636
28457	ROCKY POINT	19451	3792	28.0	27.2	36.4	6.6	1.8	44275	46503	46	51	3097	17.0	13.0	48.1	19.5	2.4	124062
28458	ROSE HILL	17167	2358	37.3	29.1	27.4	3.3	3.0	34959	35993	17	15	1741	20.6	20.3	44.1	13.4	1.7	103941
28460	SNEADS FERRY	24919	3045	22.5	34.5	32.9	8.0	2.0	43961	47373	45	50	2236	17.2	9.8	36.3	30.9	5.8	146628
28461	SOUTHPORT	29049	6966	22.4	27.8	36.1	7.7	6.0	49682	52194	60	69	5713	12.3	11.7	26.4	33.1	16.5	173539
28462	SUPPLY	23514	6334	30.7	28.0	32.2	5.5	3.6	41640	45705	38	39	5185	15.0	23.5	30.6	21.8	9.0	110793
28463	TABOR CITY	15480	2931	43.8	28.8	23.3	2.8	1.4	28203	29287	6	3	2157	25.8	29.8	32.2	11.5	0.6	82591
28464	TEACHEY	18042	741	31.2	37.2	25.2	3.9	2.4	34474	34865	16	14	568	23.9	12.3	46.5	14.4	2.8	109706
28465	OAK ISLAND	30936	4037	17.0	28.6	42.4	8.4	3.7	53636	54332	69	80	3122	3.5	7.8	37.0	40.9	10.8	178863
28466	WALLACE	18324	3647	36.3	29.3	27.8	4.1	2.5	36070	37192	21	17	2721	15.7	15.9	46.6	20.0	1.8	116393
28467	CALABASH	28360	3765	20.6	33.7	36.7	5.4	3.7	46235	49560	52	59	3275	7.3	10.1	33.6	42.2	6.8	173056
28468	SUNSET BEACH	36745	2482	18.8	24.5	38.7	9.7	8.3	58004	59034	75	87	2224	2.3	11.5	30.6	38.4	17.2	192265
28469	OCEAN ISLE BEACH	31962	3025	21.7	27.6	32.4	10.2	8.1	50704	52967	63	72	2470	9.2	15.3	22.3	34.4	18.7	189179
28470	SHALLOTTE	21301	3732	30.0	28.9	31.6	6.1	3.3	41720	45684	38	40	2959	14.8	22.0	31.5	27.4	4.3	122246
28472	WHITEVILLE	19008	7895	37.8	28.3	27.2	4.1	2.6	33501	34171	14	12	5800	20.3	22.3	38.8	17.0	1.6	101960
28478	WILLARD	17790	1927	33.8	31.7	29.4	3.7	1.5	37367	39900	25	22	1580	19.6	26.0	44.1	9.4	0.9	97667
28479	WINNABOW	19162	2018	27.4	29.6	37.7	4.0	1.4	43859	47888	45	49	1752	17.8	11.2	36.2	30.9	3.9	143364
28480	WRIGHTSVILLE BEACH	47631	1382	10.0	25.5	39.7	12.7	12.2	72092	74339	88	94	774	0.0	0.0	3.6	13.4	82.9	701271
28501	KINSTON	17900	8305	44.7	27.7	22.9	2.5	2.1	28844	31564	6	4	4478	17.1	32.9	37.3	10.9	1.8	90000
28504	KINSTON	24456	8423	22.2	29.2	37.3	7.7	3.6	48384	49764	58	65	6152	16.4	18.0	45.1	18.8	1.8	116713
28508	ALBERTSON	15439	841	27.9	32.0	34.5	4.5	1.1	41807	43586	39	40	632	38.8	19.0	30.1	11.9	0.3	67436
28510	ARAPAHOE	23536	712	28.7	26.5	36.2	6.5	2.1	42783	44457	42	44	598	15.7	13.2	36.3	29.1	5.7	132792
28511	ATLANTIC	22777	379	36.1	33.0	22.7	4.7	3.4	35362	37636	19	16	323	21.1	16.1	41.5	18.0	3.4	118750
28512	ATLANTIC BEACH	38588	2028	16.6	27.8	38.5	10.2	7.0	54923	55685	71	82	1531	2.9	5.5	13.3	49.1	29.3	290077
28513	AYDEN	19688	3906	35.8	24.0	34.2	4.0	1.9	39686	42293	32	32	2545	17.7	28.9	44.9	8.1	0.4	94014
28515	BAYBORO	15630	1036	39.1	29.3	26.6	4.4	0.5	34184	36315	16	13	811	23.7	29.3	34.6	11.1	1.2	85625
28516	BEAUFORT	24344	5348	27.7	29.2	34.0	5.4	3.6	43103	46774	43	46	3978	15.3	14.1	31.0	28.9	10.8	138835
28518	BEULAVILLE	19231	2969	33.4	31.9	29.2	3.6	2.0	37559	38832	25	22	2399	27.6	16.0	42.0	13.5	0.8	98722
28520	CEDAR ISLAND	25947	155	19.4	22.6	44.5	11.0	2.6	57472	60000	75	86	139	13.7	20.9	41.0	20.1	4.3	122917
28521	CHINQUAPIN	20259	619	33.4	28.8	31.3	4.2	2.3	38346	39377	28	27	544	10.1	23.7	42.6	22.6	0.9	112500
28523	COVE CITY	17981	1097	32.4	30.3	32.1	4.3	1.0	37232	39746	24	21	912	20.4	24.6	41.9	12.3	0.9	100157
28525	DEEP RUN	19099	1191	31.0	24.3	40.1	2.8	1.8	42920	46019	42	45	924	28.4	22.2	42.7	6.7	0.0	89219
28526	DOVER	16364	983	42.5	25.5	28.7	2.5	0.7	30051	32449	8	5	790	26.8	28.1	33.3	8.9	2.9	79524
28527	ERNUL	22024	328	22.9	32.0	40.5	3.7	0.9	45000	46719	48	54	270	18.9	16.3	48.9	11.5	4.4	112791
28528	GLOUCESTER	24807	223	22.0	31.8	40.4	4.0	1.8	46048	49026	51	58	194	17.5	7.2	22.2	34.5	18.6	185714
28529	GRANTSBORO	19963	900	28.1	29.0	37.7	4.6	0.7	41964	44248	39	41	743	28.7	17.0	40.6	12.7	1.1	95508
28530	GRIFTON	18328	2968	29.0	33.7	32.7	3.5	1.1	41321	43635	37	38	2275	22.4	24.5	43.5	8.5	1.1	92871
28531	HARKERS ISLAND	24572	748	29.3	29.1	33.6	3.3	4.7	40356	45000	34	34	648	9.9	8.5	41.0	34.1	6.5	148058
28532	HAVELOCK	18645	8881	20.7	34.0	37.7	5.7	1.9	45230	48041	49	55	4522	12.2	7.5	57.6	19.9	2.7	132304
28537	HOBUCKEN	17860	86	43.0	26.7	27.9	2.3	0.0	31544	28639	11	8	70	41.4	37.1	15.7	2.9	2.9	60000
28538	HOOKERTON	15470	990	34.9	30.9	30.8	2.5	0.8	36665	38106	23	19	751	20.9	32.1	41.3	5.3	0.4	85673
28539	HUBERT	19854	4879	17.6	34.1	41.6	4.6	2.1	48260	51049	57	65	3544	19.5	15.7	51.0	11.2	2.5	109886
28540	JACKSONVILLE	19970	16992	22.4	33.3	35.7	6.1	2.5	44406	48250	47	51	9605	12.9	16.4	54.8	14.6	1.3	115061
28543	TARAWA TERRACE	13391	1548	26.6	56.7	15.9	0.5	0.5	32057	33277	12	9	102	69.6	11.8	8.8	9.8	0.0	39333
28544	MIDWAY PARK	17310	2202	25.1	43.7	25.7	4.1	1.5	36718	40000	23	20	811	28.1	23.3	37.1	11.2	0.2	88357
28546	JACKSONVILLE	21981	13722	17.7	31.1	41.3	6.9	2.9	50743	52715	63	72	7817	6.8	14.0	62.4	15.7	1.0	121095
28547	CAMP LEJEUNE	14253	1412	6.0	30.9	52.5	8.3	2.3	55086	56599	71	82	8	0.0	0.0	100.0	0.0	0.0	137500
	NORTH CAROLINA	25989		22.3	26.1	36.6	9.4	5.6	51418	53634				12.2	15.1	38.7	27.9	6.1	132724
	UNITED STATES	27277		20.9	24.4	35.3	11.7	7.6	54719	56938				9.3	13.1	31.6	32.6	13.5	162279

ZIP CODE #	POST OFFICE NAME	FINANCIAL SERVICES: Auto Loan	Home Loan	Investments	Retirement Plans	THE HOME: Home Improvements: Home Repair	Lawn & Garden	Furnishings: Computers & Hardware Personal	Major Appliances	TV, Radio, Sound Equipment	Furniture	ENTERTAINMENT: Dine out/ Carry out	Sports Equipment	Fees & Tickets	Toys & Games	Travel	Cable TV	PERSONAL: Apparel & Services	Auto Repairs	Health Insurance	Pets & Supplies
28385	SALEMBURG	88	63	87	62	65	90	67	83	74	62	72	62	54	74	65	82	48	77	88	98
28386	SHANNON	74	68	60	65	65	67	68	68	68	70	68	52	63	71	63	69	47	68	67	81
28387	SOUTHERN PINES	97	94	99	96	97	103	98	99	103	99	102	72	99	99	99	107	71	102	111	117
28390	SPRING LAKE	70	60	52	60	57	58	68	62	68	68	69	49	62	70	61	68	48	67	63	75
28391	STEDMAN	95	79	79	77	78	90	78	86	83	79	82	64	69	86	73	87	56	82	88	103
28392	TAR HEEL	82	59	73	57	59	80	61	73	68	59	66	56	49	70	57	74	44	69	77	88
28393	TURKEY	75	51	69	49	51	73	54	66	61	52	60	51	42	63	50	68	40	62	70	81
28394	VASS	97	83	88	80	83	95	81	91	86	81	85	67	73	87	79	90	57	87	94	108
28395	WADE	87	66	85	64	67	87	66	81	72	63	71	60	55	72	65	78	47	75	83	96
28396	WAGRAM	85	70	78	68	70	83	69	79	74	68	73	59	61	75	67	78	49	75	81	94
28398	WARSAW	75	53	68	51	53	73	57	67	64	54	62	52	46	65	53	69	42	64	71	81
28399	WHITE OAK	69	45	67	43	45	68	48	61	56	46	54	47	36	57	45	62	36	57	64	75
28401	WILMINGTON	52	42	42	44	41	47	53	48	55	50	55	37	48	54	47	58	38	53	55	59
28403	WILMINGTON	81	67	66	70	66	69	90	73	86	80	86	61	78	85	76	85	60	82	78	90
28405	WILMINGTON	102	100	99	99	99	101	101	100	100	101	100	75	99	100	98	101	70	100	101	118
28409	WILMINGTON	118	136	132	138	137	132	119	126	117	125	117	94	130	118	129	117	83	120	123	145
28411	WILMINGTON	116	128	121	126	127	120	113	118	110	121	111	89	119	113	118	109	78	113	113	136
28412	WILMINGTON	90	92	84	94	90	90	91	89	90	92	91	69	93	92	91	90	64	90	90	105
28420	ASH	81	69	70	66	68	76	68	74	71	69	71	56	61	74	65	74	48	72	75	89
28421	ATKINSON	88	63	85	61	65	88	65	81	72	61	71	61	52	73	63	79	47	75	84	96
28422	BOLIVIA	99	92	101	89	95	101	88	96	92	94	91	68	86	91	90	95	62	94	101	113
28423	BOLTON	79	56	67	55	56	76	59	69	66	57	64	53	47	68	54	72	43	65	73	84
28425	BURGAW	78	60	67	59	60	75	62	70	67	61	66	53	52	69	58	72	44	67	73	84
28428	CAROLINA BEACH	97	80	113	79	86	101	82	97	85	77	84	71	73	82	85	90	56	92	99	113
28429	CASTLE HAYNE	90	84	74	81	81	84	79	83	81	82	81	61	75	84	75	83	55	80	82	98
28430	CERRO GORDO	81	54	80	51	55	80	57	72	66	54	64	56	44	66	54	73	42	68	76	88
28431	CHADBOURN	67	46	63	44	46	67	50	60	57	47	55	46	39	57	47	63	37	58	66	74
28432	CLARENDON	71	51	68	50	52	71	53	65	59	50	57	49	42	59	51	64	38	60	68	78
28433	CLARKTON	67	45	66	43	46	67	48	60	55	45	53	47	37	55	46	61	35	57	64	73
28434	COUNCIL	74	50	73	48	51	74	53	67	60	50	59	51	41	61	50	67	39	62	70	81
28435	CURRIE	83	56	77	53	55	81	59	73	67	56	66	57	45	69	55	75	44	69	77	89
28436	DELCO	79	56	65	55	56	75	59	68	65	57	64	52	47	68	53	71	43	65	72	83
28438	EVERGREEN	80	52	77	49	52	79	56	71	65	53	63	55	42	66	52	72	42	66	75	87
28439	FAIR BLUFF	63	42	62	39	42	62	44	56	51	42	50	44	34	52	42	57	33	53	59	69
28441	GARLAND	85	56	81	52	55	83	59	74	68	57	67	58	45	70	55	76	44	70	79	91
28442	HALLSBORO	76	55	74	52	55	74	56	68	63	54	62	52	45	64	54	68	41	65	71	83
28443	HAMPSTEAD	102	94	130	92	103	113	89	106	93	92	92	73	88	88	98	97	62	100	110	122
28444	HARRELLS	73	48	69	46	48	71	51	64	59	49	58	50	39	60	48	66	38	60	68	79
28445	HOLLY RIDGE	95	83	104	81	86	96	81	93	84	81	83	68	74	83	83	87	56	89	93	109
28447	IVANHOE	70	47	66	45	47	68	50	62	57	47	55	48	38	58	47	63	37	58	65	76
28448	KELLY	90	66	80	64	66	87	68	80	75	66	73	61	55	77	63	81	49	75	84	97
28449	KURE BEACH	98	78	127	77	86	104	78	100	82	74	81	73	68	78	85	88	54	92	98	116
28450	LAKE WACCAMAW	94	72	104	71	76	96	73	90	79	70	78	67	62	78	75	85	52	84	91	107
28451	LELAND	86	81	70	78	78	79	77	79	78	81	79	59	74	82	74	79	54	78	77	94
28452	LONGWOOD	90	67	89	65	68	89	68	84	74	65	73	63	56	75	67	81	49	78	86	99
28453	MAGNOLIA	73	52	62	50	51	70	54	63	60	52	59	49	43	62	49	66	39	60	67	77
28454	MAPLE HILL	77	60	69	57	58	73	61	69	66	61	66	53	52	68	57	70	44	67	71	84
28455	NAKINA	75	59	62	57	58	70	60	67	64	60	64	51	52	67	56	68	43	64	68	80
28456	RIEGELWOOD	81	60	71	59	60	79	62	73	68	59	67	56	51	70	58	74	45	68	76	88
28457	ROCKY POINT	82	74	69	71	71	76	73	75	74	75	74	57	68	77	69	75	51	74	75	90
28458	ROSE HILL	83	57	76	55	57	81	60	73	68	58	66	56	47	69	56	75	44	69	77	89
28460	SNEADS FERRY	89	73	104	72	79	95	72	89	77	71	76	63	65	74	76	83	51	83	92	104
28461	SOUTHPORT	98	88	105	87	94	104	87	98	91	89	90	69	83	89	89	96	61	94	105	114
28462	SUPPLY	87	70	98	68	76	93	70	86	75	69	74	61	62	72	72	81	49	80	91	100
28463	TABOR CITY	72	48	69	46	49	71	51	64	58	48	57	49	39	59	48	65	38	60	68	78
28464	TEACHEY	85	57	80	54	57	83	61	75	69	58	67	58	46	70	56	77	45	71	79	92
28465	OAK ISLAND	101	86	132	85	96	111	85	105	89	83	87	74	78	83	93	94	58	98	107	121
28466	WALLACE	79	59	69	58	59	77	62	71	68	60	67	54	52	69	58	73	45	68	76	86
28467	CALABASH	84	80	104	73	89	99	76	91	81	81	79	59	75	74	84	87	53	87	103	104
28468	SUNSET BEACH	106	107	141	102	121	127	98	116	104	109	102	74	103	94	111	110	69	111	130	132
28469	OCEAN ISLE BEACH	103	97	130	94	107	115	92	109	96	97	95	74	91	90	101	101	64	103	115	125
28470	SHALLOTTE	86	70	89	68	73	89	69	83	75	68	74	61	62	74	70	80	50	78	87	98
28472	WHITEVILLE	77	58	74	57	59	77	62	72	68	59	66	54	52	68	59	73	45	69	76	86
28478	WILLARD	80	57	71	55	57	78	59	71	66	57	65	54	47	68	55	72	43	67	75	86
28479	WINNABOW	79	70	65	68	68	74	67	72	71	69	70	53	62	74	64	73	48	70	73	86
28480	WRIGHTSVILLE BEACH	119	131	160	139	143	127	135	130	127	139	129	101	144	123	144	124	95	131	124	149
28501	KINSTON	62	49	53	50	49	60	55	57	61	54	60	42	50	59	52	65	41	59	66	70
28504	KINSTON	93	82	84	80	82	92	82	89	86	81	85	66	75	87	79	89	58	86	92	105
28508	ALBERTSON	75	68	60	64	64	68	67	68	68	69	68	52	62	71	63	69	47	68	67	81
28510	ARAPAHOE	89	70	106	68	75	94	70	88	75	66	74	65	60	72	73	81	49	82	90	103
28511	ATLANTIC	83	59	85	57	61	84	61	77	67	56	66	58	49	67	60	74	44	71	80	92
28512	ATLANTIC BEACH	111	98	148	96	109	124	94	117	99	95	97	81	89	92	104	105	65	109	120	134
28513	AYDEN	71	62	63	61	61	71	64	68	68	63	67	50	59	68	61	72	46	67	73	81
28515	BAYBORO	75	49	72	46	49	73	52	66	60	50	59	51	39	61	49	67	39	62	70	81
28516	BEAUFORT	92	71	96	70	74	94	74	88	79	69	78	66	62	78	73	85	52	83	92	104
28518	BEULAVILLE	87	61	83	59	62	86	64	79	71	60	70	60	50	72	61	78	46	73	83	95
28520	CEDAR ISLAND	107	74	118	74	77	113	82	102	85	67	84	84	60	84	82	93	55	95	108	126
28521	CHINQUAPIN	86	62	80	60	63	85	64	78	71	61	69	59	51	72	61	78	46	72	81	94
28523	COVE CITY	79	57	77	55	58	79	59	72	65	56	64	55	47	66	57	72	43	68	75	87
28525	DEEP RUN	84	72	68	69	70	79	70	75	73	71	73	56	63	77	65	77	50	73	77	90
28526	DOVER	72	48	70	45	48	71	51	64	58	48	57	49	38	59	48	64	37	60	67	78
28527	ERNUL	83	69	76	66	68	80	67	77	72	67	71	57	60	73	65	76	48	73	78	91
28528	GLOUCESTER	94	76	122	74	83	100	76	96	79	71	78	70	66	75	82	84	52	89	95	111
28529	GRANTSBORO	85	60	89	58	63	86	62	79	69	58	68	60	50	69	62	76	45	73	82	94
28530	GRIFTON	82	59	78	56	59	81	60	74	67	58	66	56	48	68	58	74	44	69	78	89
28531	HARKERS ISLAND	91	73	117	72	80	96	73	93	76	68	75	68	63	72	79	81	50	85	91	107
28532	HAVELOCK	84	68	60	69	65	67	78	72	77	77	79	58	70	83	69	76	54	76	70	86
28537	HOBUCKEN	68	46	74	46	49	71	52	64	54	42	53	53	38	53	51	59	34	60	68	79
28538	HOOKERTON	78	52	72	50	52	75	55	68	63	53	62	53	42	64	51	70	41	64	72	83
28539	HUBERT	87	84	77	81	81	81	79	82	78	82	79	62	76	82	77	78	54	79	78	96
28540	JACKSONVILLE	81	73	63	72	69	70	78	73	78	78	79	58	73	81	72	78	55	77	73	88
28543	TARAWA TERRACE	63	33	25	38	29	28	60	41	56	55	59	41	45	67	43	52	41	53	37	50
28544	MIDWAY PARK	76	51	41	54	47	46	71	57	68	69	71	51	59	78	57	65	49	66	53	68
28546	JACKSONVILLE	90	80	66	80	75	74	87	79	85	87	87	64	81	90	79	84	60	83	78	95
28547	CAMP LEJEUNE	112	58	43	67	52	49	105	73	99	98	104	73	80	119	76	91	73	93	66	89
	NORTH CAROLINA	100	89	90	89	88	96	91	94	94	91	93	73	85	95	88	96	64	93	96	112
	UNITED STATES	100	100	100	100	100	100	100	100	100	100	100	100	100	100	100	100	100	100	100	100

NORTH CAROLINA POPULATION CHANGE

 28551-28704

ZIP CODE #	POST OFFICE NAME	COUNTY FIPS CODE	POPULATION 2000	POPULATION 2009	POPULATION 2014	2000-2009 ANNUAL RATE % Rate	2000-2009 ANNUAL RATE State Centile	HOUSEHOLDS 2000	HOUSEHOLDS 2009	HOUSEHOLDS 2014	HOUSEHOLDS % Annual Rate 2000-2009	HOUSEHOLDS 2009 Average HH Size	FAMILIES 2000	FAMILIES 2009	FAMILIES % Annual Rate 2000-2009
28551	LA GRANGE	107	11781	12099	12082	0.3	24	4551	4818	4845	0.6	2.47	3256	3338	0.3
28552	LOWLAND	137	318	267	250	-1.9	0	143	123	117	-1.6	2.17	98	82	-1.9
28553	MARSHALLBERG	031	477	540	570	1.4	66	208	244	261	1.7	2.21	155	176	1.4
28555	MAYSVILLE	103	4594	4662	4701	0.2	21	1741	1834	1866	0.6	2.54	1290	1331	0.3
28556	MERRITT	137	1119	1147	1136	0.3	24	466	490	490	0.5	2.34	342	350	0.3
28557	MOREHEAD CITY	031	13155	13642	13809	0.4	28	5806	6160	6279	0.6	2.17	3705	3827	0.4
28560	NEW BERN	049	26267	26908	27714	0.3	24	10879	11557	12014	0.7	2.29	7393	7650	0.4
28562	NEW BERN	049	27365	32243	34379	1.8	76	11511	14006	15061	2.1	2.28	8125	9674	1.9
28570	NEWPORT	031	18459	20553	21337	1.2	60	7032	8036	8426	1.5	2.48	5218	5784	1.1
28571	ORIENTAL	137	2480	2509	2453	0.1	18	1164	1206	1190	0.4	2.08	829	836	0.1
28572	PINK HILL	061	5301	5966	6181	1.3	63	1975	2265	2360	1.5	2.59	1462	1628	1.2
28573	POLLOCKSVILLE	103	2393	2532	2560	0.6	36	922	1013	1036	1.0	2.42	660	707	0.7
28574	RICHLANDS	133	9012	9822	10250	0.9	48	3450	3901	4098	1.3	2.51	2561	2827	1.1
28577	SEALEVEL	031	461	474	470	0.3	24	127	133	133	0.5	3.07	86	87	0.1
28578	SEVEN SPRINGS	191	4436	5071	5256	1.5	69	1537	1744	1806	1.4	2.91	1103	1215	1.1
28579	SMYRNA	031	699	780	827	1.2	60	298	344	369	1.6	2.27	218	244	1.2
28580	SNOW HILL	079	11770	13218	13531	1.3	63	4125	4539	4688	1.0	2.51	2998	3210	0.7
28581	STACY	031	206	225	236	1.0	53	97	110	116	1.4	2.05	70	77	1.0
28582	STELLA	133	1052	1114	1147	0.6	36	420	456	475	0.9	2.44	309	325	0.5
28584	SWANSBORO	031	7765	8650	8954	1.2	60	3375	3860	4028	1.5	2.24	2377	2642	1.1
28585	TRENTON	103	5272	5175	5115	-0.2	10	2083	2112	2108	0.1	2.44	1530	1511	-0.1
28586	VANCEBORO	049	6826	7245	7495	0.6	36	2474	2748	2879	1.1	2.48	1817	1966	0.9
28587	VANDEMERE	137	388	374	368	-0.4	7	159	157	155	-0.1	2.38	112	108	-0.4
28590	WINTERVILLE	147	14364	21221	24520	4.3	94	5720	8792	10238	4.8	2.41	3875	5710	4.3
28594	EMERALD ISLE	031	3489	4203	4512	2.0	79	1645	2022	2186	2.3	2.08	1089	1289	1.8
28601	HICKORY	035	47818	51847	53987	0.9	48	19354	20954	21839	0.9	2.42	12851	13425	0.5
28602	HICKORY	035	27339	29413	30437	0.8	44	10696	11516	11932	0.8	2.54	7492	7849	0.5
28604	BANNER ELK	189	5840	6586	6792	1.3	63	2358	2689	2807	1.4	2.25	1555	1709	1.0
28605	BLOWING ROCK	189	3508	3856	3953	1.0	53	1584	1785	1845	1.3	2.09	920	988	0.8
28606	BOOMER	193	1863	1958	1979	0.5	32	736	780	791	0.6	2.51	556	574	0.3
28607	BOONE	189	26703	27975	28165	0.5	32	9747	10524	10706	0.8	2.14	4863	4994	0.3
28608	BOONE	189	2	2	2	0.0	15	1	1	1	0.0	2.00	0	1	0.0
28609	CATAWBA	035	5489	6150	6528	1.2	60	2130	2402	2554	1.3	2.56	1620	1777	1.0
28610	CLAREMONT	035	8729	10047	10752	1.5	69	3319	3845	4129	1.6	2.57	2459	2762	1.3
28611	COLLETTSVILLE	027	1028	1195	1258	1.6	72	415	492	521	1.9	2.43	320	370	1.6
28612	CONNELLYS SPRINGS	023	13434	13547	13463	0.1	18	5141	5206	5182	0.1	2.58	3822	3766	-0.2
28613	CONOVER	035	20007	23145	24735	1.6	72	7494	8703	9325	1.6	2.63	5524	6232	1.3
28615	CRESTON	009	2092	2049	2022	-0.2	10	874	889	887	0.2	2.30	650	644	-0.1
28617	CRUMPLER	009	2213	2381	2445	0.8	44	910	1016	1056	1.2	2.33	677	736	0.9
28618	DEEP GAP	189	1762	1857	1886	0.6	36	721	780	798	0.9	2.34	521	547	0.5
28621	ELKIN	171	10559	10737	10792	0.2	21	4255	4302	4325	0.1	2.41	2966	2907	-0.2
28622	ELK PARK	011	2495	2555	2547	0.3	24	1027	1074	1082	0.5	2.26	742	757	0.2
28623	ENNICE	005	1672	1668	1657	0.0	15	670	686	687	0.3	2.41	490	488	0.0
28624	FERGUSON	193	1705	1733	1741	0.2	21	713	731	737	0.3	2.30	524	522	0.0
28625	STATESVILLE	097	30485	37710	42451	2.3	83	11613	14586	16503	2.5	2.55	8763	10657	2.1
28626	FLEETWOOD	009	1685	1792	1824	0.7	40	706	778	802	1.1	2.30	521	558	0.7
28627	GLADE VALLEY	005	1548	1644	1682	0.7	40	687	754	779	1.0	2.18	496	529	0.7
28630	GRANITE FALLS	027	17861	19013	19386	0.7	40	7001	7526	7705	0.8	2.50	5185	5432	0.5
28631	GRASSY CREEK	009	528	600	633	1.4	66	229	270	289	1.8	2.22	162	186	1.5
28634	HARMONY	097	5117	5937	6527	1.6	72	1935	2273	2509	1.8	2.58	1444	1644	1.4
28635	HAYS	193	3643	3884	3951	0.7	40	1416	1521	1557	0.8	2.55	1077	1128	0.5
28636	HIDDENITE	003	4774	5409	5626	1.4	66	1849	2144	2243	1.6	2.52	1386	1565	1.3
28637	HILDEBRAN	023	1475	1572	1586	0.7	40	608	652	660	0.8	2.38	420	436	0.4
28638	HUDSON	027	10437	10795	10875	0.4	28	4158	4371	4429	0.5	2.45	3051	3113	0.2
28640	JEFFERSON	009	3892	4467	4721	1.5	69	1628	1953	2093	2.0	2.19	1115	1295	1.6
28642	JONESVILLE	197	5267	5272	5241	0.0	15	2257	2289	2282	0.2	2.30	1576	1550	-0.2
28643	LANSING	009	3501	3859	4007	1.1	56	1500	1720	1808	1.5	2.22	1065	1185	1.2
28644	LAUREL SPRINGS	005	1695	1724	1735	0.2	21	738	772	785	0.5	2.21	515	522	0.1
28645	LENOIR	027	46457	47826	48333	0.3	24	18576	19393	19697	0.5	2.42	13341	13540	0.2
28649	MC GRADY	193	993	1064	1090	0.7	40	409	441	455	0.8	2.40	309	324	0.5
28650	MAIDEN	035	11190	12972	13817	1.6	72	4344	5066	5410	1.7	2.55	3314	3765	1.4
28651	MILLERS CREEK	193	6259	6742	6932	0.8	44	2558	2773	2860	0.9	2.43	1888	1991	0.6
28654	MORAVIAN FALLS	193	3260	3428	3482	0.5	32	1317	1396	1423	0.6	2.43	963	992	0.3
28655	MORGANTON	023	56658	57132	56745	0.1	18	21562	21718	21569	0.1	2.48	15072	14744	-0.2
28657	NEWLAND	011	11349	11645	11562	0.3	24	4729	4890	4902	0.4	2.16	3332	3345	0.0
28658	NEWTON	035	23989	26706	28318	1.2	60	9211	10272	10904	1.2	2.56	6646	7196	0.9
28659	NORTH WILKESBORO	193	21194	21405	21402	0.1	18	8632	8765	8797	0.2	2.40	6084	6002	-0.1
28660	OLIN	097	1597	1864	2066	1.7	74	631	748	834	1.9	2.48	478	550	1.5
28663	PINEY CREEK	005	557	630	661	1.3	63	237	277	294	1.7	2.26	170	194	1.4
28665	PURLEAR	193	2021	2266	2361	1.2	60	824	932	974	1.3	2.40	616	679	1.1
28668	ROARING GAP	005	30	31	31	0.4	28	15	16	16	0.7	1.94	10	11	1.0
28669	ROARING RIVER	193	2742	2833	2845	0.4	28	1084	1129	1139	0.4	2.51	792	802	0.1
28670	RONDA	193	3045	3131	3141	0.3	24	1215	1256	1264	0.4	2.49	922	928	0.1
28672	SCOTTVILLE	009	10	10	10	0.0	15	3	3	3	0.0	3.33	2	2	0.0
28673	SHERRILLS FORD	035	4248	5749	6499	3.3	90	1766	2401	2718	3.4	2.39	1292	1705	3.0
28675	SPARTA	005	5938	6265	6388	0.6	36	2589	2808	2890	0.9	2.16	1727	1813	0.5
28676	STATE ROAD	171	3548	3720	3792	0.5	32	1470	1542	1573	0.5	2.40	1082	1103	0.2
28677	STATESVILLE	097	31938	36968	40652	1.6	72	12621	14750	16287	1.7	2.46	8580	9689	1.3
28678	STONY POINT	097	4757	5562	6016	1.7	74	1828	2165	2351	1.8	2.57	1398	1614	1.6
28679	SUGAR GROVE	189	1453	1509	1547	0.4	28	596	638	659	0.7	2.36	437	455	0.4
28681	TAYLORSVILLE	003	23160	25748	26434	1.2	60	9071	9943	10292	1.0	2.47	6665	7113	0.7
28682	TERRELL	035	779	1099	1233	3.8	92	342	486	547	3.9	2.26	240	330	3.5
28683	THURMOND	171	1675	1827	1887	0.9	48	683	747	773	1.0	2.45	514	548	0.7
28684	TODD	009	1609	1878	1957	1.7	74	646	787	829	2.2	2.38	489	583	1.9
28685	TRAPHILL	193	1856	1918	1941	0.4	28	755	786	798	0.4	2.44	562	569	0.1
28689	UNION GROVE	097	1753	2093	2326	1.9	77	675	819	913	2.1	2.55	509	600	1.8
28690	VALDESE	023	9278	9100	8975	-0.2	10	3920	3859	3808	-0.2	2.33	2629	2498	-0.6
28692	VILAS	189	3885	4172	4255	0.8	44	1609	1780	1832	1.1	2.33	1079	1150	0.7
28693	WARRENSVILLE	009	1517	1626	1668	0.8	44	662	737	766	1.2	2.20	482	522	0.9
28694	WEST JEFFERSON	009	7220	7676	7847	0.7	40	3162	3468	3584	1.0	2.20	2206	2349	0.7
28697	WILKESBORO	193	11849	12031	12020	0.2	21	4845	4955	4967	0.2	2.34	3415	3391	-0.1
28698	ZIONVILLE	189	1926	1981	1989	0.3	24	816	870	883	0.7	2.28	584	602	0.3
28701	ALEXANDER	021	3312	3855	4130	1.7	74	1294	1549	1676	2.0	2.48	974	1133	1.6
28702	ALMOND	075	580	584	579	0.1	18	260	274	275	0.6	2.13	190	194	0.2
28704	ARDEN	021	14697	17827	19338	2.1	81	5948	7337	8008	2.3	2.40	4106	4889	1.9
	NORTH CAROLINA					1.7					1.8	2.46			1.5
	UNITED STATES					1.0					1.1	2.59			0.9

ZIP CODE #	POST OFFICE NAME	RACE (%) White 2000	White 2009	Black 2000	Black 2009	Asian/Pacific 2000	Asian/Pacific 2009	% Hispanic Origin 2000	% Hispanic Origin 2009	2009 AGE DISTRIBUTION (%) 0-4	5-9	10-14	15-19	20-24	25-44	45-64	65-84	85+	18+	MEDIAN AGE 2009	% 2009 Males	% 2009 Females
28551	LA GRANGE	61.1	57.4	34.7	36.3	0.4	0.5	4.9	7.1	6.8	6.9	7.1	6.9	6.1	26.8	27.8	10.4	1.1	74.7	37.3	49.3	50.7
28552	LOWLAND	99.1	98.5	0.0	0.0	0.0	0.0	0.6	1.1	4.9	5.2	6.0	5.6	3.4	21.0	31.8	19.5	2.6	80.5	47.6	47.2	52.8
28553	MARSHALLBERG	99.2	98.9	0.0	0.0	0.2	0.4	0.2	0.2	4.1	4.4	5.9	5.9	4.1	22.8	36.5	13.9	2.4	81.9	46.5	49.1	50.9
28555	MAYSVILLE	67.3	65.4	28.8	29.0	0.5	0.8	2.6	3.9	6.8	6.9	7.0	6.9	5.1	25.8	29.1	11.1	1.2	75.0	38.9	49.9	50.1
28556	MERRITT	79.4	77.7	18.1	19.0	0.5	0.7	1.3	1.8	3.8	4.1	4.4	4.6	4.4	17.6	35.0	24.3	1.7	84.7	52.3	48.5	51.5
28557	MOREHEAD CITY	86.7	85.1	9.9	10.3	0.8	1.0	1.7	2.5	4.9	5.3	5.9	5.9	4.6	23.2	31.2	16.3	2.7	80.1	45.1	47.5	52.5
28560	NEW BERN	72.7	71.3	24.2	24.0	0.5	0.8	2.7	4.3	6.2	6.2	6.2	6.2	5.3	24.0	28.3	15.4	2.2	77.9	41.8	48.5	51.5
28562	NEW BERN	72.2	70.8	25.0	25.0	0.6	1.0	1.8	2.9	5.5	5.7	6.1	6.3	4.9	21.7	30.0	17.6	2.3	79.6	44.9	47.3	52.7
28570	NEWPORT	90.5	88.8	6.0	6.4	0.8	1.2	2.4	3.4	5.7	6.0	6.2	6.3	5.4	26.1	30.6	12.3	1.4	78.0	41.1	50.1	49.9
28571	ORIENTAL	78.4	76.6	19.5	20.6	0.3	0.4	1.3	2.0	2.7	2.9	3.5	3.8	3.1	13.3	36.8	30.9	3.0	88.4	58.0	48.1	51.9
28572	PINK HILL	81.2	75.7	10.3	10.9	0.2	0.3	10.9	16.4	7.1	7.1	7.2	6.4	5.2	28.7	25.2	11.4	1.7	75.3	37.2	51.6	48.4
28573	POLLOCKSVILLE	58.1	57.3	39.9	39.9	0.2	0.3	2.0	2.8	5.2	5.5	6.2	6.6	5.1	20.2	32.1	16.4	2.7	78.7	45.8	47.8	52.2
28574	RICHLANDS	84.0	81.7	11.4	11.4	0.4	0.5	4.2	6.4	7.0	6.9	6.8	6.3	5.8	28.4	27.3	10.4	1.1	75.4	37.1	49.3	50.7
28577	SEALEVEL	98.0	97.7	0.2	0.2	0.0	0.2	0.9	1.3	4.4	4.9	4.9	4.4	3.8	19.2	28.3	21.5	8.6	82.9	50.9	50.6	49.4
28578	SEVEN SPRINGS	68.5	58.9	8.3	8.0	0.2	0.3	26.9	37.5	8.2	7.1	6.3	7.5	9.6	29.4	22.6	8.1	1.1	74.0	31.6	52.3	47.7
28579	SMYRNA	98.9	98.6	0.1	0.1	0.1	0.3	0.4	0.5	4.7	5.1	6.2	5.9	4.0	23.8	34.4	14.0	1.9	80.1	45.1	49.2	50.8
28580	SNOW HILL	52.1	49.3	42.7	42.8	0.1	0.1	5.7	8.7	5.7	5.9	6.1	5.8	6.6	30.6	26.3	10.9	2.1	78.7	37.7	55.1	44.9
28581	STACY	99.0	98.7	0.5	0.4	0.0	0.4	0.0	0.0	4.9	4.9	5.8	5.3	3.1	22.7	34.2	16.9	2.2	80.9	46.8	50.2	49.8
28582	STELLA	93.6	92.5	3.4	3.7	0.7	1.0	2.0	3.0	5.5	6.1	6.3	6.5	4.6	25.6	31.4	12.7	1.3	78.0	42.0	49.7	50.3
28584	SWANSBORO	93.3	91.4	3.5	4.1	0.7	1.0	2.1	3.1	5.5	5.9	6.1	5.6	4.4	24.2	30.2	16.3	1.8	78.9	43.8	48.8	51.2
28585	TRENTON	66.3	63.9	29.9	30.5	0.1	0.2	3.2	4.9	6.1	6.2	6.7	6.6	5.5	24.0	30.1	12.9	1.8	76.5	41.3	48.8	51.2
28586	VANCEBORO	68.5	65.9	28.6	29.8	0.1	0.2	2.9	4.5	6.3	6.5	6.8	6.4	5.9	28.6	27.8	10.5	1.2	76.3	37.9	52.4	47.6
28587	VANDEMERE	34.3	32.9	64.2	64.7	0.5	0.5	1.3	1.9	4.8	5.1	5.9	6.7	6.1	20.3	33.2	15.8	2.1	79.9	45.7	46.8	53.2
28590	WINTERVILLE	69.9	68.0	26.3	26.9	1.3	1.7	2.2	3.4	7.4	6.9	7.0	9.5	8.9	30.4	22.4	6.4	1.0	75.3	31.3	47.4	52.6
28594	EMERALD ISLE	96.7	95.7	0.8	0.9	0.7	1.0	1.6	2.3	3.2	3.3	3.1	3.4	3.4	19.7	41.1	21.6	1.2	88.1	53.3	51.5	48.5
28601	HICKORY	87.9	84.3	4.9	5.2	2.9	4.0	6.8	9.9	6.4	6.3	6.3	6.8	6.3	27.8	26.4	11.9	1.9	77.5	38.2	49.2	50.8
28602	HICKORY	77.6	76.0	15.3	14.3	3.7	5.1	4.7	6.4	6.7	6.7	6.7	6.8	5.7	27.4	27.6	11.0	1.4	75.7	38.4	49.7	50.3
28604	BANNER ELK	97.0	96.2	1.0	1.0	0.3	0.5	1.1	1.6	4.7	4.8	5.2	8.2	7.4	23.5	30.7	13.5	1.8	82.0	42.0	50.0	50.0
28605	BLOWING ROCK	97.5	96.9	0.7	0.7	0.5	0.7	0.7	1.0	3.5	3.7	4.0	4.6	5.3	24.5	34.2	17.1	3.0	86.1	48.0	48.7	51.3
28606	BOOMER	85.8	83.7	12.6	13.8	0.2	0.2	1.6	2.4	6.4	6.3	6.5	6.2	5.2	26.3	29.3	12.5	1.4	77.0	40.3	50.3	49.7
28607	BOONE	95.5	91.0	2.3	5.2	0.9	1.2	1.7	2.9	3.8	3.7	3.9	10.9	20.9	22.4	23.5	9.4	1.5	84.6	30.1	49.8	50.2
28608	BOONE	100.0	100.0	0.0	0.0	0.0	0.0	0.0	0.0	0.0	0.0	0.0	50.0	50.0	0.0	0.0	0.0	0.0	100.0	20.0	0.0	100.0
28609	CATAWBA	90.1	88.1	7.8	8.9	0.7	1.0	1.9	2.9	6.0	6.2	6.7	6.6	5.1	27.2	30.3	10.5	1.3	76.9	40.2	51.0	49.0
28610	CLAREMONT	90.7	88.0	5.3	6.0	2.2	3.2	2.3	3.5	5.9	6.1	6.6	6.5	5.0	27.5	29.5	10.7	2.1	77.6	39.9	50.5	49.5
28611	COLLETTSVILLE	97.0	96.1	1.6	1.8	0.3	0.4	0.9	1.4	5.7	5.9	6.1	5.8	4.7	24.0	31.5	15.0	1.4	78.7	43.8	52.1	47.9
28612	CONNELLYS SPRINGS	93.8	91.6	1.0	1.0	3.7	5.2	1.0	1.5	6.2	6.3	6.7	6.8	5.4	27.3	28.3	11.5	1.5	76.5	39.7	50.0	50.0
28613	CONOVER	85.7	81.7	6.0	6.4	4.7	6.7	6.1	8.8	6.8	6.8	6.9	6.4	4.9	28.7	26.7	11.4	1.5	76.4	38.1	49.1	50.9
28615	CRESTON	98.6	98.0	0.1	0.1	0.3	0.4	1.2	1.9	5.5	5.7	5.8	5.0	4.1	24.4	31.6	15.8	2.1	79.9	44.6	50.3	49.7
28617	CRUMPLER	95.6	94.1	1.5	1.5	0.2	0.3	3.1	4.7	5.0	5.4	5.6	4.6	4.2	24.5	33.7	14.9	1.9	80.9	45.3	50.9	49.1
28618	DEEP GAP	96.9	96.2	0.8	0.9	0.5	0.8	1.1	1.5	4.8	5.1	5.5	5.6	5.2	29.0	32.4	11.2	1.2	81.1	41.3	52.0	48.0
28621	ELKIN	90.8	88.0	3.3	3.2	0.2	0.3	7.9	11.3	5.9	5.8	6.0	6.1	5.0	25.1	27.2	15.2	3.8	78.5	42.3	47.9	52.1
28622	ELK PARK	97.2	96.2	0.5	0.5	0.1	0.2	2.2	3.3	5.0	5.5	6.0	8.1	6.3	25.7	28.7	12.9	1.8	79.6	40.2	51.1	48.9
28623	ENNICE	95.0	92.9	1.0	1.0	0.1	0.1	5.8	8.6	6.2	6.5	7.0	5.5	4.1	25.9	28.7	14.4	1.6	77.0	41.4	49.7	50.3
28624	FERGUSON	94.8	94.2	4.3	4.7	0.0	0.0	0.6	0.9	5.4	5.7	5.9	4.5	3.9	24.2	32.8	15.9	1.7	80.3	45.3	51.4	48.6
28625	STATESVILLE	84.4	79.5	10.8	12.9	1.8	2.7	3.6	5.9	6.5	6.6	6.8	6.5	5.1	26.7	28.0	12.0	1.8	76.2	39.5	49.3	50.7
28626	FLEETWOOD	97.7	97.3	1.3	1.3	0.1	0.1	1.8	2.6	5.2	5.6	6.1	5.6	4.0	26.3	31.0	14.2	2.0	79.7	43.2	51.0	49.0
28627	GLADE VALLEY	95.8	94.3	1.6	1.6	0.2	0.3	3.1	4.7	4.6	4.9	5.1	4.6	3.2	22.6	32.3	20.4	2.3	82.5	48.5	50.1	49.9
28630	GRANITE FALLS	96.1	94.6	1.0	1.1	0.4	0.5	2.9	4.4	6.6	6.7	6.9	6.3	4.8	28.5	27.7	11.0	1.4	75.9	39.0	49.8	50.2
28631	GRASSY CREEK	94.9	92.7	0.8	0.7	0.0	0.0	4.2	6.5	4.8	5.2	5.8	5.5	3.7	22.2	32.5	18.3	2.0	80.7	46.9	52.5	47.5
28634	HARMONY	85.4	81.2	10.9	12.5	0.3	0.4	4.7	7.7	6.8	6.9	7.2	7.0	5.0	26.9	27.4	11.1	1.7	75.1	38.4	49.6	50.4
28635	HAYS	98.3	97.5	0.3	0.3	0.1	0.2	1.3	2.1	6.5	6.6	6.9	6.5	5.1	27.3	28.3	11.6	1.2	75.9	39.3	49.8	50.2
28636	HIDDENITE	93.4	91.3	2.9	3.2	0.3	0.4	4.1	6.0	7.1	7.2	7.3	6.0	4.9	28.5	27.1	10.6	1.3	74.6	38.1	50.8	49.2
28637	HILDEBRAN	93.5	91.1	0.9	1.0	3.7	5.3	0.9	1.5	6.2	6.0	6.0	6.0	5.1	26.2	29.1	13.2	2.1	78.0	41.2	48.7	51.3
28638	HUDSON	97.0	95.8	0.7	0.8	0.4	0.6	2.3	3.6	6.3	6.5	6.6	5.7	4.6	28.5	28.0	12.4	1.4	77.1	39.8	49.5	50.5
28640	JEFFERSON	95.9	94.4	1.1	1.1	0.4	0.5	3.3	4.8	5.1	5.3	5.6	5.3	4.1	24.0	30.2	16.7	3.8	80.9	45.4	48.7	51.3
28642	JONESVILLE	88.8	87.0	8.4	8.8	0.1	0.2	3.7	5.3	6.2	6.2	6.4	6.3	5.4	24.8	27.8	15.0	2.0	77.3	41.2	47.3	52.7
28643	LANSING	97.9	97.0	0.2	0.2	0.3	0.4	1.5	2.4	4.7	5.1	5.4	5.3	4.0	23.4	33.0	16.5	2.6	81.6	46.3	49.8	50.2
28644	LAUREL SPRINGS	97.4	96.3	0.5	0.5	0.1	0.1	3.0	4.3	4.7	5.3	5.5	5.0	3.7	24.8	31.5	17.3	2.1	81.3	45.6	51.5	48.5
28645	LENOIR	88.6	86.8	8.5	8.8	0.4	0.6	2.5	3.7	6.1	6.2	6.4	6.1	5.1	26.0	28.5	13.5	2.0	77.5	40.8	49.5	50.5
28649	MC GRADY	98.7	98.0	0.1	0.1	0.0	0.0	1.3	2.1	6.7	6.7	7.0	6.3	5.0	28.4	28.3	10.6	1.1	75.8	38.7	48.5	51.5
28650	MAIDEN	90.3	88.5	6.3	6.3	1.0	1.4	3.6	5.4	6.3	6.4	6.6	6.4	5.2	28.9	28.2	10.8	1.2	76.7	38.9	50.2	49.8
28651	MILLERS CREEK	97.3	95.8	0.1	0.1	0.1	0.2	2.7	4.3	6.1	6.0	6.6	5.7	4.4	28.3	30.1	11.5	1.3	77.7	40.3	49.5	50.5
28654	MORAVIAN FALLS	92.4	90.1	4.3	4.8	0.6	0.9	3.1	4.8	6.0	6.4	6.6	5.7	4.0	26.7	29.8	12.9	2.0	77.2	41.0	49.4	50.6
28655	MORGANTON	81.7	78.1	9.9	10.0	3.8	5.2	4.8	7.2	6.1	6.1	6.3	7.7	6.1	26.2	27.3	12.4	1.9	77.4	39.1	50.9	49.1
28657	NEWLAND	95.2	93.9	2.5	2.6	0.2	0.3	2.5	3.7	4.7	5.0	5.5	5.5	5.3	27.6	28.8	15.2	2.3	81.3	42.5	53.0	47.0
28658	NEWTON	83.4	79.5	9.2	9.7	3.0	4.2	6.1	9.0	6.4	6.4	6.7	6.5	5.2	27.9	27.9	11.2	1.7	76.9	39.0	50.1	49.9
28659	NORTH WILKESBORO	90.1	88.0	6.1	6.2	0.4	0.6	5.1	7.4	6.1	6.2	6.3	6.0	4.8	26.7	28.3	13.7	2.0	77.8	40.8	49.8	50.2
28660	OLIN	89.9	86.9	6.6	7.2	0.4	0.5	4.2	7.0	6.2	6.3	6.7	6.4	4.9	27.2	29.9	10.9	1.6	76.9	39.7	51.1	48.9
28663	PINEY CREEK	97.7	96.7	0.4	0.3	0.0	0.0	3.4	5.1	4.4	4.8	5.2	5.4	3.2	23.0	34.0	17.9	2.1	82.4	47.6	49.8	50.2
28665	PURLEAR	98.3	97.8	0.6	0.6	0.1	0.2	0.8	1.3	5.6	5.8	6.0	5.3	4.5	26.2	31.6	13.5	1.5	79.3	42.7	50.0	50.0
28668	ROARING GAP	100.0	96.8	0.0	0.0	0.0	0.0	3.4	3.2	3.2	3.2	3.2	6.5	3.2	25.8	32.3	22.6	0.0	83.9	48.8	58.1	41.9
28669	ROARING RIVER	91.0	89.3	6.6	7.1	0.1	0.1	3.1	4.8	5.9	5.9	6.3	6.5	5.2	28.2	28.7	12.0	1.3	78.0	39.9	49.9	50.1
28670	RONDA	95.6	94.3	2.4	2.5	0.1	0.1	2.6	4.1	6.1	6.2	6.5	6.1	4.8	26.9	28.6	13.2	1.5	77.3	40.4	50.1	49.9
28672	SCOTTVILLE	100.0	100.0	0.0	0.0	0.0	0.0	0.0	0.0	0.0	0.0	0.0	0.0	0.0	40.0	50.0	10.0	0.0	100.0	50.0	60.0	40.0
28673	SHERRILLS FORD	92.6	91.6	6.0	6.6	0.1	0.2	1.0	1.4	5.3	5.8	6.3	5.9	3.9	24.0	34.1	13.3	1.3	78.9	44.2	50.5	49.5
28675	SPARTA	95.6	94.0	1.4	1.4	0.3	0.4	5.5	7.7	5.0	5.4	5.6	5.4	3.9	24.1	29.6	18.1	3.0	80.7	45.5	49.4	50.6
28676	STATE ROAD	94.8	93.2	2.1	2.0	0.2	0.3	4.0	5.9	5.3	5.6	6.0	5.7	4.3	24.4	30.6	15.9	2.3	79.7	44.1	49.3	50.7
28677	STATESVILLE	68.7	66.1	25.3	25.4	1.5	2.0	5.8	8.4	7.0	6.8	6.8	6.7	6.0	27.2	25.4	12.1	2.0	75.1	37.5	48.4	51.6
28678	STONY POINT	90.0	87.4	6.1	6.7	1.5	2.1	2.6	4.1	7.0	7.1	7.3	6.6	5.2	27.4	27.7	10.4	1.3	74.5	38.0	50.5	49.5
28679	SUGAR GROVE	98.2	97.7	0.5	0.5	0.1	0.1	1.3	2.0	5.1	5.4	5.6	5.8	5.5	24.9	33.1	13.1	1.5	80.3	43.5	50.2	49.8
28681	TAYLORSVILLE	91.1	89.6	5.4	5.5	1.2	1.5	2.4	3.6	6.3	6.5	6.6	6.1	5.2	28.1	27.7	12.0	1.5	76.8	39.4	51.5	48.5
28682	TERRELL	98.3	97.5	0.4	0.5	0.1	0.3	0.4	0.7	3.5	4.0	4.5	3.8	3.0	20.1	40.3	19.7	1.2	85.7	51.6	51.0	49.0
28683	THURMOND	97.6	96.5	0.4	0.4	0.1	0.1	1.7	2.8	5.6	5.9	6.4	6.2	5.1	26.2	29.6	13.5	1.5	78.3	41.4	51.5	48.5
28684	TODD	98.6	98.5	0.4	0.4	0.1	0.2	1.2	1.5	5.3	5.6	6.1	5.8	4.0	24.9	32.6	14.0	1.7	79.3	43.8	51.0	49.0
28685	TRAPHILL	98.0	97.3	1.0	1.1	0.0	0.0	1.0	1.7	7.5	7.2	7.1	5.8	5.3	25.8	27.2	12.7	1.5	74.7	39.4	49.2	50.8
28689	UNION GROVE	95.3	92.3	1.3	1.5	0.2	0.2	3.6	6.5	5.9	6.1	6.5	6.5	4.9	26.0	31.0	11.6	1.6	77.5	41.0	51.0	49.0
28690	VALDESE	92.6	89.9	1.2	1.3	3.9	5.5	2.2	3.5	6.1	6.2	6.3	6.1	4.9	24.7	28.2	15.1	2.5	77.6	42.2	48.3	51.7
28692	VILAS	98.3	97.8	0.4	0.5	0.2	0.3	1.4	2.0	5.2	5.6	5.5	5.5	6.1	28.0	30.1	12.4	1.5	80.3	40.8	50.2	49.8
28693	WARRENSVILLE	98.0	97.2	0.3	0.4	0.4	0.6	1.8	2.8	5.4	5.7	6.0	5.0	3.9	25.3	31.5	15.3	1.8	79.7	44.0	50.2	49.8
28694	WEST JEFFERSON	97.0	95.8	0.6	0.6	0.2	0.3	3.0	4.2	5.4	5.5	5.8	5.3	4.3	24.2	30.7	16.6	2.3	80.2	44.7	49.2	50.8
28697	WILKESBORO	90.4	88.1	5.7	6.0	0.9	1.3	4.7	6.9	6.0	6.2	6.4	5.5	4.4	26.0	29.1	14.0	2.3	77.8	41.9	49.0	51.0
28698	ZIONVILLE	99.3	99.1	0.1	0.1	0.1	0.2	0.8	1.1	5.9	6.2	6.4	6.1	4.2	26.4	30.4	12.8	1.7	77.9	41.7	50.8	49.2
28701	ALEXANDER	96.6	95.4	0.3	0.4	0.4	0.5	2.7	3.9	6.1	7.3	7.2	6.7	4.3	28.0	28.5	10.5	1.3	75.0	38.9	49.6	50.4
28702	ALMOND	96.7	96.1	0.2	0.2	0.5	0.7	0.5	0.7	3.9	4.5	5.0	5.1	3.6	20.7	36.0	18.8	2.4	83.2	49.7	49.8	50.2
28704	ARDEN	90.6	89.2	6.2	6.4	0.9	1.3	2.1	2.9	5.7	6.1	6.5	6.5	5.2	26.3	29.8	11.7	2.0	78.0	40.8	47.9	52.1
	NORTH CAROLINA	72.1	69.8	21.6	21.5	1.5	2.1	4.7	6.9	6.6	6.5	6.5	6.8	6.9	27.7	26.5	10.9	1.6	76.5	37.4	49.3	50.7
	UNITED STATES	75.1	72.0	12.3	12.7	3.8	4.6	12.5	15.7	6.8	6.7	6.6	7.1	6.9	27.0	26.0	10.9	1.9	75.7	36.9	49.2	50.8

ZIP CODE				2009 HOUSEHOLD INCOME DISTRIBUTION (%)					MEDIAN HOUSEHOLD INCOME					2009 HOME VALUE DISTRIBUTION (%)					
#	POST OFFICE NAME	2009 Per Capita Income	2009 HH Income Base	Less than $25,000	$25,000 to $49,999	$50,000 to $99,999	$100,000 to $149,999	$150,000 or More	2009	2014	2009 National Centile	2009 State Centile	2009 Home Value Base	Less than $50,000	$50,000 to $89,999	$90,000 to $174,999	$175,000 to $399,999	$400,000 or More	2009 Median Home Value
28551	LA GRANGE	20699	4818	27.4	29.3	35.6	5.7	2.1	43384	46187	44	47	3626	27.3	19.0	38.8	12.8	2.1	94605
28552	LOWLAND	17545	123	44.7	26.0	27.6	1.6	0.0	29592	28647	7	4	100	39.0	38.0	15.0	5.0	3.0	64000
28553	MARSHALLBERG	25598	244	21.7	31.6	41.0	4.1	1.6	46555	49232	53	60	213	18.3	7.5	22.1	34.7	17.4	182500
28555	MAYSVILLE	18303	1834	32.9	35.1	25.2	5.1	1.7	38084	40132	27	25	1413	21.9	30.9	36.0	9.8	1.4	84527
28556	MERRITT	26887	490	23.7	26.5	38.0	6.7	5.1	49795	50329	61	69	428	13.1	25.0	30.6	20.6	10.7	114865
28557	MOREHEAD CITY	27357	6160	26.5	23.5	37.9	7.5	4.6	50000	51840	61	70	4261	7.4	6.3	34.6	42.4	9.4	178401
28560	NEW BERN	22712	11557	28.6	27.6	35.8	5.0	3.0	42166	45348	40	42	7522	10.6	15.8	40.9	27.5	5.2	131613
28562	NEW BERN	28603	14006	19.2	25.6	41.6	8.7	4.9	55151	54094	71	83	10395	8.4	8.5	34.6	40.6	7.8	170184
28570	NEWPORT	23121	8036	21.3	28.1	40.7	7.4	2.4	50402	51414	62	71	6360	15.8	13.2	37.3	27.5	6.1	132903
28571	ORIENTAL	32816	1206	22.1	26.4	36.2	8.5	6.8	51622	51725	65	75	1003	10.7	14.3	22.6	37.2	15.3	187250
28572	PINK HILL	18205	2265	30.5	34.0	30.4	1.7	3.4	39091	41405	30	30	1756	35.6	15.0	38.9	10.0	0.6	88571
28573	POLLOCKSVILLE	21883	1013	30.2	28.5	33.1	4.6	3.6	42264	46521	40	42	804	15.8	18.0	39.2	23.3	3.7	116387
28574	RICHLANDS	18272	3901	33.2	30.5	30.2	4.8	1.3	38647	41682	29	28	2991	20.8	19.3	46.6	12.4	0.9	104282
28577	SEALEVEL	14887	133	36.1	33.8	22.6	4.5	3.0	35196	36786	18	15	114	21.9	15.8	41.2	17.5	3.5	117308
28578	SEVEN SPRINGS	18182	1744	26.0	30.7	35.1	5.3	2.8	43540	46688	44	48	1242	35.3	17.9	35.3	11.0	0.5	80000
28579	SMYRNA	23578	344	23.5	32.0	37.8	5.2	1.5	43448	47744	44	47	294	19.7	11.9	29.9	26.9	11.6	136765
28580	SNOW HILL	17608	4539	34.0	28.8	31.9	3.9	1.5	38097	40018	27	25	3369	19.2	32.1	42.1	6.5	0.2	88878
28581	STACY	29312	110	19.1	22.7	45.5	10.9	1.8	57889	60417	75	86	99	14.1	18.2	43.4	21.2	3.0	126705
28582	STELLA	21756	456	26.3	30.3	34.2	7.0	2.2	45143	47867	49	54	360	16.7	17.5	34.4	25.3	6.1	125000
28584	SWANSBORO	25924	3860	25.7	26.3	37.0	7.0	4.0	47871	50374	56	64	2897	12.4	10.5	34.7	33.4	9.0	151642
28585	TRENTON	18515	2112	33.4	33.6	28.6	2.8	1.6	36472	37403	22	18	1734	23.7	22.8	41.9	9.2	2.4	95648
28586	VANCEBORO	17078	2748	30.9	34.4	31.0	2.9	0.9	38217	41471	27	26	2167	23.3	22.6	42.2	10.9	1.1	96581
28587	VANDEMERE	17065	157	38.2	31.2	26.8	3.2	0.6	32517	34777	12	10	127	19.7	36.2	33.9	7.9	2.4	77500
28590	WINTERVILLE	26393	8792	19.4	27.5	39.1	9.8	4.1	52859	54770	68	78	6464	14.0	18.9	46.9	19.4	0.7	112104
28594	EMERALD ISLE	38847	2022	12.6	20.3	44.3	14.9	8.0	69342	69806	86	93	1613	4.2	3.6	11.2	54.6	26.4	284833
28601	HICKORY	28219	20954	18.6	27.6	38.7	8.6	6.6	53403	55032	69	79	13633	8.3	12.8	47.8	25.8	5.4	132493
28602	HICKORY	21346	11516	23.5	30.0	38.6	5.3	2.6	45941	50261	51	58	7965	13.3	23.1	48.6	13.4	1.5	104916
28604	BANNER ELK	21815	2689	28.7	31.0	32.4	5.4	2.5	41110	42522	36	37	2001	10.6	9.5	31.6	35.3	12.9	169522
28605	BLOWING ROCK	33570	1785	21.4	24.9	37.9	8.7	7.1	54191	53687	70	81	1239	4.8	2.9	20.1	44.9	27.4	262660
28606	BOOMER	18997	780	35.3	30.0	29.6	3.1	2.1	38244	40603	27	26	656	18.9	19.1	34.3	24.5	3.2	112216
28607	BOONE	21322	10524	33.8	28.1	29.0	6.6	2.5	38238	39661	27	26	5638	7.1	6.3	28.6	46.7	11.3	197283
28608	BOONE	0	0	0.0	0.0	0.0	0.0	0.0	0	0	0	0	0	0.0	0.0	0.0	0.0	0.0	0
28609	CATAWBA	21571	2402	22.0	26.9	43.3	4.7	3.2	50673	52617	63	72	2018	17.0	20.9	47.6	13.4	1.1	103670
28610	CLAREMONT	22998	3845	16.8	30.4	43.1	6.7	3.0	52444	54843	67	77	3174	16.2	21.2	45.7	14.6	2.2	105663
28611	COLLETTSVILLE	18853	492	29.1	32.3	33.1	4.1	1.4	39208	42809	30	30	420	25.2	29.8	33.1	11.0	1.0	83438
28612	CONNELLYS SPRINGS	18922	5206	24.2	31.8	39.1	3.8	1.0	44739	46565	47	52	4179	24.1	24.6	43.3	7.1	0.7	91598
28613	CONOVER	21795	8703	17.8	30.6	43.4	5.2	2.9	51242	53673	64	74	6826	14.5	15.3	56.2	12.8	1.3	112013
28615	CRESTON	18180	889	41.2	31.4	23.1	2.6	1.8	30310	35189	9	6	770	25.6	18.1	33.5	19.4	3.5	107500
28617	CRUMPLER	19452	1016	30.1	32.9	31.4	4.2	1.4	38958	40856	30	29	840	16.3	10.1	40.6	25.8	7.1	138112
28618	DEEP GAP	21184	780	21.9	32.8	38.6	6.0	0.6	44024	44630	45	50	605	13.2	9.1	25.8	43.1	8.8	179957
28621	ELKIN	21644	4302	30.3	27.5	33.6	5.4	3.3	42770	44626	42	44	3218	13.8	18.8	40.8	24.7	1.9	120049
28622	ELK PARK	16869	1074	38.2	32.2	26.4	2.9	0.4	32695	34131	13	10	872	22.5	22.7	32.2	18.2	4.4	101923
28623	ENNICE	18816	686	39.1	29.2	24.8	2.8	4.2	34858	35636	17	14	577	17.5	10.1	41.9	17.2	13.3	116574
28624	FERGUSON	20122	731	31.9	33.2	27.9	4.2	2.7	38592	40513	28	28	612	26.8	13.1	29.7	25.2	5.2	119231
28625	STATESVILLE	23812	14586	19.6	27.1	43.6	6.4	3.3	52714	53789	67	78	11203	7.3	7.4	43.0	37.4	4.9	160742
28626	FLEETWOOD	21753	778	31.2	32.6	29.3	4.0	2.8	38157	39037	27	25	655	8.5	13.3	42.4	32.1	3.7	143445
28627	GLADE VALLEY	24161	754	32.2	34.6	26.3	3.7	3.2	36452	35578	22	18	633	10.9	14.1	35.4	27.8	11.8	137061
28630	GRANITE FALLS	21437	7526	22.7	28.7	40.7	6.2	1.6	48550	49614	58	66	5735	14.3	23.0	47.5	14.0	1.2	107294
28631	GRASSY CREEK	19536	270	38.5	26.3	29.3	3.7	2.2	37896	42167	26	24	235	17.9	8.9	39.1	24.7	9.4	142500
28634	HARMONY	18501	2273	25.9	33.7	35.5	4.0	0.9	41282	45305	37	37	1847	15.3	17.2	44.6	19.3	3.6	125392
28635	HAYS	17509	1521	30.4	34.1	33.3	1.3	0.9	39919	41472	32	33	1276	19.9	17.4	45.1	14.3	3.3	107254
28636	HIDDENITE	19898	2144	24.1	33.1	37.1	4.7	1.0	44486	46853	47	51	1748	25.9	25.6	36.7	11.3	0.5	87840
28637	HILDEBRAN	20757	652	25.5	30.8	38.8	3.5	1.4	44236	46217	46	51	451	17.1	25.7	51.0	5.8	0.4	97558
28638	HUDSON	20621	4371	23.2	32.4	38.7	4.4	1.3	45409	46924	49	56	3165	16.9	20.7	51.5	10.3	0.6	102967
28640	JEFFERSON	19874	1953	37.6	28.2	28.8	3.7	1.7	35381	36971	19	16	1480	10.2	11.6	41.1	30.3	6.9	148799
28642	JONESVILLE	21382	2289	34.3	27.0	31.8	4.7	2.2	37630	41283	26	23	1656	17.3	35.3	40.2	6.6	0.5	87934
28643	LANSING	18849	1720	37.2	33.3	25.5	2.7	1.3	34376	36104	16	13	1448	13.8	16.7	39.4	24.4	5.7	124872
28644	LAUREL SPRINGS	22527	772	33.0	32.1	27.8	1.9	5.1	36456	38463	22	18	653	6.9	14.1	45.2	30.9	2.9	135954
28645	LENOIR	20061	19393	28.5	31.5	33.3	4.7	2.0	41461	43882	38	38	14388	17.8	27.2	44.4	9.6	0.9	95100
28649	MC GRADY	17598	441	26.8	37.4	34.5	0.9	0.5	41882	43188	39	40	374	20.9	20.1	42.8	8.8	7.5	107456
28650	MAIDEN	22308	5066	19.1	28.2	44.5	5.8	2.5	51709	53279	65	75	4166	12.9	19.0	49.7	17.1	1.2	113263
28651	MILLERS CREEK	22078	2773	21.8	35.3	35.9	3.8	3.2	45245	46287	49	55	2206	16.5	13.1	36.4	28.7	5.1	132430
28654	MORAVIAN FALLS	23811	1396	22.3	32.4	37.0	4.5	3.7	46143	47537	52	58	1067	19.2	15.7	32.5	26.2	6.4	127319
28655	MORGANTON	21214	21718	24.6	30.5	37.2	4.8	2.9	44849	46819	48	53	15746	18.0	22.9	47.0	11.0	1.0	99538
28657	NEWLAND	20288	4890	33.0	31.0	30.8	3.4	1.8	38002	38883	27	24	4042	18.5	19.5	38.0	19.8	4.2	110039
28658	NEWTON	22122	10272	21.1	29.6	40.2	6.4	2.7	49093	52384	59	67	7539	10.5	20.5	50.9	16.9	1.2	110477
28659	NORTH WILKESBORO	19293	8765	30.9	32.3	31.3	3.8	1.7	38951	40595	30	29	6383	14.5	18.2	44.0	21.3	2.1	119212
28660	OLIN	21616	748	19.8	31.4	42.9	4.7	1.2	48752	51150	58	66	599	11.2	13.2	42.7	28.4	4.5	139844
28663	PINEY CREEK	22845	277	28.5	30.3	35.0	2.5	3.6	42350	45918	40	43	233	12.4	13.7	45.5	22.7	5.6	126389
28665	PURLEAR	21264	932	26.5	34.3	32.1	4.8	2.3	42580	44320	41	43	780	16.3	19.5	33.6	24.0	6.7	123750
28668	ROARING GAP	25161	16	25.0	31.3	37.5	6.3	0.0	42500	42500	41	43	13	0.0	7.7	38.5	38.5	15.4	187500
28669	ROARING RIVER	20139	1129	29.7	33.5	31.5	3.3	2.0	38876	40384	29	29	912	25.5	18.2	37.6	15.7	3.0	102174
28670	RONDA	19506	1256	28.8	31.5	32.7	5.3	1.6	41471	43171	38	39	1018	16.9	17.5	42.9	18.5	4.2	114489
28672	SCOTTVILLE	0	0	0.0	0.0	0.0	0.0	0.0	0	52500	0	0	0	0.0	0.0	0.0	0.0	0.0	0
28673	SHERRILLS FORD	27733	2401	18.1	24.2	42.6	10.2	4.9	56876	58383	74	85	2004	11.8	8.4	36.1	34.7	8.9	153103
28675	SPARTA	21142	2808	34.9	30.6	27.8	4.1	2.5	36191	37781	21	17	2090	9.7	17.4	43.4	22.0	7.6	125484
28676	STATE ROAD	21499	1542	30.4	26.7	35.2	4.7	3.0	43881	45714	45	49	1258	16.2	13.1	42.1	23.8	4.7	118852
28677	STATESVILLE	20926	14750	27.5	30.8	34.4	4.9	2.4	41501	45397	38	39	9643	9.2	12.0	44.7	30.4	3.7	141963
28678	STONY POINT	20607	2165	20.5	32.0	42.4	3.8	1.3	47724	50138	56	63	1718	16.4	19.2	40.9	20.0	3.6	118222
28679	SUGAR GROVE	21036	638	29.8	28.2	35.3	4.2	2.5	41943	43827	39	41	519	11.8	14.8	34.5	32.2	6.7	142880
28681	TAYLORSVILLE	21480	9943	22.9	30.3	39.5	5.2	2.1	46825	49006	54	61	7942	19.1	23.5	41.4	14.4	1.6	99672
28682	TERRELL	39417	486	16.0	17.1	38.5	16.3	12.1	67337	67445	85	92	396	5.1	7.8	21.7	45.2	20.2	231159
28683	THURMOND	19734	747	29.2	26.9	41.0	2.3	0.7	45402	46481	49	56	654	19.0	7.0	47.6	24.8	1.7	119660
28684	TODD	19985	787	29.9	33.4	30.6	3.4	2.7	39827	41375	32	32	660	10.9	14.2	37.1	32.3	5.5	140625
28685	TRAPHILL	18173	786	30.4	34.2	33.1	1.3	1.0	39797	41205	32	32	662	21.0	16.0	43.4	16.6	3.0	102885
28689	UNION GROVE	19604	819	23.8	33.1	38.6	3.1	1.5	43242	46935	43	46	675	18.7	15.3	36.3	26.2	3.6	126042
28690	VALDESE	22044	3859	27.6	31.2	33.2	5.4	2.6	41932	44668	39	41	2770	16.1	26.8	47.7	8.8	0.7	98571
28692	VILAS	20655	1780	29.6	29.3	35.7	3.7	1.8	41467	43695	38	39	1331	12.8	12.3	33.2	33.4	8.3	145592
28693	WARRENSVILLE	21211	737	38.4	33.5	23.1	3.0	2.0	31137	33265	10	7	613	18.9	16.3	38.0	20.6	6.2	121747
28694	WEST JEFFERSON	20495	3468	35.3	30.1	29.2	3.4	2.0	36268	38777	21	17	2644	10.3	13.0	41.3	29.0	6.5	142584
28697	WILKESBORO	24727	4955	27.1	24.7	36.4	6.9	5.0	47730	49240	56	63	3711	12.5	9.8	34.0	37.1	6.5	152773
28698	ZIONVILLE	20886	870	30.8	30.9	33.0	3.1	2.2	39612	41629	32	31	687	13.1	15.6	35.4	28.2	7.7	138345
28701	ALEXANDER	19563	1549	24.7	31.8	38.9	3.2	1.4	43900	47647	45	49	1292	27.2	14.9	28.2	27.9	1.9	112500
28702	ALMOND	20467	274	35.4	31.4	25.9	4.0	3.3	33215	33234	14	12	244	8.2	16.8	46.3	28.3	0.4	118860
28704	ARDEN	26678	7337	18.0	28.3	39.6	9.2	4.9	52944	54467	68	78	5425	17.4	8.8	30.5	35.4	7.9	160376
	NORTH CAROLINA	25989		22.3	26.1	36.6	9.4	5.6	51418	53634				12.2	15.1	38.7	27.9	6.1	132724
	UNITED STATES	27277		20.9	24.4	35.3	11.7	7.6	54719	56938				9.3	13.1	31.6	32.6	13.5	162279

#	POST OFFICE NAME	FINANCIAL SERVICES				THE HOME						ENTERTAINMENT						PERSONAL			
						Home Improvements		Furnishings													
ZIP CODE		Auto Loan	Home Loan	Invest-ments	Retire-ment Plans	Home Repair	Lawn & Garden	Comput-ers & Hard-ware-Personal	Major Appli-ances	TV, Radio, Sound Equip-ment	Furni-ture	Dine out/ Carry out	Sports Equip-ment	Fees & Tickets	Toys & Games	Travel	Cable TV	Apparel & Services	Auto Repairs	Health Insur-ance	Pets & Supplies
28551	LA GRANGE	87	70	75	68	69	83	71	78	75	71	75	60	62	78	66	80	51	75	80	94
28552	LOWLAND	68	47	75	47	49	72	52	65	54	42	53	53	38	53	52	59	35	60	68	80
28553	MARSHALLBERG	94	76	122	74	83	100	76	96	79	71	78	70	66	75	82	84	52	89	95	111
28555	MAYSVILLE	80	63	70	61	62	76	63	72	68	63	67	54	55	70	59	73	45	68	74	86
28556	MERRITT	101	85	114	80	92	109	83	102	90	85	88	71	76	85	87	97	59	96	110	118
28557	MOREHEAD CITY	89	84	93	83	87	94	82	90	85	82	85	64	80	84	84	89	58	87	95	105
28560	NEW BERN	79	72	75	71	72	80	72	77	76	73	75	56	69	75	71	79	51	76	82	91
28562	NEW BERN	95	94	99	93	96	102	90	97	93	91	92	69	90	92	92	97	64	94	103	113
28570	NEWPORT	92	82	89	80	82	92	80	88	83	80	83	65	74	84	79	87	56	85	90	105
28571	ORIENTAL	98	97	131	95	109	117	89	106	95	98	93	69	93	87	100	100	63	101	117	121
28572	PINK HILL	85	62	70	60	61	80	64	74	71	63	69	57	52	73	58	77	47	70	78	90
28573	POLLOCKSVILLE	95	69	95	67	71	96	71	88	78	67	77	67	57	79	69	86	51	81	91	105
28574	RICHLANDS	78	63	68	61	62	75	63	71	67	62	67	53	54	69	59	72	45	68	74	85
28577	SEALEVEL	83	59	85	57	61	84	61	77	67	56	66	58	49	67	60	74	44	71	80	92
28578	SEVEN SPRINGS	88	74	71	71	71	81	74	78	77	75	77	60	66	81	69	80	52	77	79	94
28579	SMYRNA	92	70	103	69	74	95	72	89	76	66	75	67	59	75	73	82	50	83	90	106
28580	SNOW HILL	83	58	74	55	58	80	61	73	68	58	67	56	48	70	56	75	45	69	78	89
28581	STACY	107	74	118	74	77	113	82	102	85	66	84	84	60	84	81	93	55	95	107	125
28582	STELLA	87	74	93	73	77	87	72	85	75	71	75	62	66	75	74	79	50	80	84	99
28584	SWANSBORO	92	81	100	78	85	95	79	92	83	79	82	66	73	81	81	87	55	87	94	107
28585	TRENTON	81	58	74	57	59	80	60	73	67	58	66	55	48	68	57	73	44	68	76	88
28586	VANCEBORO	77	55	66	54	56	74	58	68	64	56	63	52	46	66	53	70	42	64	71	82
28587	VANDEMERE	76	49	73	46	49	74	53	66	61	50	59	52	39	62	49	68	39	63	70	82
28590	WINTERVILLE	96	89	75	90	83	82	93	86	92	94	93	69	89	96	86	90	65	89	85	104
28594	EMERALD ISLE	120	113	165	112	128	140	106	129	112	112	110	86	107	103	120	118	74	121	137	148
28601	HICKORY	102	96	94	97	95	100	98	98	99	97	99	77	95	101	96	101	69	99	100	117
28602	HICKORY	84	73	70	73	71	81	76	79	80	73	79	61	70	81	71	83	54	78	83	95
28604	BANNER ELK	85	67	107	66	73	90	68	86	71	63	70	63	58	68	72	76	47	79	85	100
28605	BLOWING ROCK	117	95	143	95	103	121	97	117	101	92	100	87	86	97	102	106	67	110	117	137
28606	BOOMER	86	62	71	60	62	81	64	75	71	63	70	57	52	74	59	77	47	71	79	91
28607	BOONE	76	56	60	58	56	63	81	67	76	69	76	56	64	76	65	76	53	74	69	82
28608	BOONE	0	0	0	0	0	0	0	0	0	0	0	0	0	0	0	0	0	0	0	0
28609	CATAWBA	96	73	81	73	74	94	75	87	82	72	80	66	63	85	70	88	54	81	91	104
28610	CLAREMONT	100	82	84	81	82	98	82	92	87	80	86	69	71	91	77	93	58	87	95	110
28611	COLLETTSVILLE	83	59	70	58	59	79	62	72	68	60	67	55	49	71	56	75	45	68	76	88
28612	CONNELLYS SPRINGS	87	64	73	63	64	83	66	77	73	64	71	59	54	75	61	79	48	72	81	93
28613	CONOVER	94	79	81	78	79	93	79	88	84	77	83	66	71	86	76	89	56	84	92	105
28615	CRESTON	75	54	69	53	55	73	56	67	62	54	61	51	45	63	53	68	41	63	71	81
28617	CRUMPLER	81	58	83	56	60	82	60	76	66	55	65	57	48	66	59	73	43	69	79	90
28618	DEEP GAP	81	73	69	71	72	77	69	75	72	71	72	54	65	74	67	74	49	72	75	89
28621	ELKIN	87	68	80	66	69	88	72	82	78	67	76	62	61	79	68	85	52	79	88	98
28622	ELK PARK	69	49	71	47	50	70	50	64	56	47	55	48	40	56	50	62	36	59	66	76
28623	ENNICE	82	58	78	57	60	81	60	74	67	57	66	56	48	68	58	73	44	69	78	89
28624	FERGUSON	84	60	76	58	61	82	62	75	69	60	68	57	50	71	59	76	45	70	79	91
28625	STATESVILLE	96	87	85	86	86	96	85	91	88	84	88	69	79	91	82	92	60	88	94	108
28626	FLEETWOOD	83	67	77	68	69	86	68	80	73	63	71	61	59	74	67	78	48	74	83	95
28627	GLADE VALLEY	91	69	105	67	74	94	70	89	75	65	74	66	58	73	72	81	49	82	90	104
28630	GRANITE FALLS	91	73	76	72	72	89	74	82	79	72	78	63	64	82	69	84	53	79	86	99
28631	GRASSY CREEK	78	56	80	54	58	79	57	73	63	53	62	55	46	63	56	70	41	67	75	86
28634	HARMONY	86	62	71	60	62	82	65	75	72	63	70	58	52	75	59	78	47	71	79	91
28635	HAYS	81	58	67	56	58	77	60	70	67	59	65	54	48	70	55	73	44	66	74	85
28636	HIDDENITE	91	65	76	63	65	86	68	79	75	65	73	61	54	78	62	82	49	75	83	96
28637	HILDEBRAN	88	65	73	64	65	85	67	78	74	65	72	60	55	77	62	80	49	73	82	94
28638	HUDSON	87	67	74	66	67	85	69	79	75	66	73	60	58	77	64	81	50	75	83	95
28640	JEFFERSON	78	56	76	54	58	79	58	72	65	54	63	55	47	65	56	71	42	67	76	86
28642	JONESVILLE	83	62	70	61	62	80	68	75	74	64	72	57	55	75	61	80	49	73	81	91
28643	LANSING	75	54	77	52	56	76	55	70	61	51	60	53	44	61	55	67	40	64	73	83
28644	LAUREL SPRINGS	88	65	89	64	68	88	67	82	73	63	72	62	55	73	66	79	48	76	84	98
28645	LENOIR	82	63	70	63	63	80	67	75	73	64	71	57	57	74	62	78	48	72	80	90
28649	MC GRADY	76	55	63	53	55	73	57	66	63	56	62	51	46	66	52	69	42	63	70	81
28650	MAIDEN	95	79	78	78	78	92	78	86	83	78	82	65	70	86	74	88	56	83	89	103
28651	MILLERS CREEK	93	71	79	71	71	91	73	84	79	69	78	65	61	82	68	86	52	79	88	101
28654	MORAVIAN FALLS	97	79	84	79	80	97	80	91	85	75	83	69	69	88	76	91	57	85	94	108
28655	MORGANTON	88	72	77	71	72	86	74	82	79	72	78	62	65	81	70	84	53	79	86	98
28657	NEWLAND	80	58	83	57	61	81	60	75	66	56	65	56	49	65	59	72	43	69	78	89
28658	NEWTON	92	78	79	78	78	90	79	86	83	77	82	65	71	85	75	87	56	83	89	102
28659	NORTH WILKESBORO	78	60	68	59	60	77	64	72	69	60	68	55	54	71	59	75	46	69	77	86
28660	OLIN	91	73	77	72	73	89	73	83	79	71	78	63	63	82	69	84	53	79	87	100
28663	PINEY CREEK	90	66	106	65	70	95	70	88	73	60	72	69	55	71	72	79	47	82	91	106
28665	PURLEAR	92	66	81	64	67	89	69	82	76	66	75	62	55	78	64	83	50	77	86	99
28668	ROARING GAP	81	65	105	64	71	86	65	83	68	61	67	60	56	65	71	73	45	76	82	96
28669	ROARING RIVER	91	65	75	64	65	87	68	79	76	66	74	61	55	79	62	82	50	75	84	96
28670	RONDA	86	64	72	62	63	83	66	76	72	64	71	58	54	75	60	79	48	72	80	92
28672	SCOTTVILLE	0	0	0	0	0	0	0	0	0	0	0	0	0	0	0	0	0	0	0	0
28673	SHERRILLS FORD	104	96	107	96	97	109	91	103	94	89	93	78	87	95	94	97	64	97	103	121
28675	SPARTA	80	58	83	56	60	83	61	77	68	56	66	58	49	67	60	74	44	71	81	91
28676	STATE ROAD	88	68	79	67	69	87	70	81	76	66	75	62	59	78	67	83	50	77	86	97
28677	STATESVILLE	80	69	66	69	68	77	73	75	76	71	75	57	67	77	68	79	52	75	79	90
28678	STONY POINT	93	69	78	68	69	90	72	83	79	69	77	64	59	82	66	85	52	78	87	100
28679	SUGAR GROVE	88	64	94	62	67	90	65	83	72	61	71	62	53	71	66	79	47	76	86	99
28681	TAYLORSVILLE	94	72	80	70	72	90	73	84	80	72	79	64	62	83	68	85	53	80	87	101
28682	TERRELL	149	119	192	117	131	157	119	151	125	112	123	111	103	118	129	133	82	140	149	175
28683	THURMOND	87	63	72	61	62	83	65	76	72	63	71	58	52	75	59	79	48	72	80	92
28684	TODD	82	64	87	62	66	83	64	78	68	61	68	58	54	68	64	74	45	72	80	92
28685	TRAPHILL	80	57	66	56	57	76	60	70	66	58	65	53	48	69	54	72	44	66	73	85
28689	UNION GROVE	87	66	73	66	66	85	68	79	74	65	73	60	57	77	63	80	49	74	82	94
28690	VALDESE	89	66	84	64	67	90	69	83	76	64	74	63	56	77	66	83	50	78	89	99
28692	VILAS	82	63	84	62	65	83	65	78	70	61	69	59	55	69	64	75	46	73	80	92
28693	WARRENSVILLE	84	60	81	58	62	83	62	77	69	58	67	58	50	69	60	75	45	71	80	92
28694	WEST JEFFERSON	78	57	76	56	59	78	61	73	66	56	65	55	50	66	59	72	43	68	77	87
28697	WILKESBORO	92	83	86	84	84	95	81	90	85	78	84	68	76	86	81	89	57	85	93	106
28698	ZIONVILLE	85	61	86	59	63	86	62	79	69	58	68	60	50	69	62	76	45	73	82	94
28701	ALEXANDER	82	67	74	65	67	80	66	76	71	66	70	56	58	72	64	75	47	72	77	90
28702	ALMOND	78	56	81	54	58	79	57	73	63	53	62	55	46	63	57	70	41	67	76	87
28704	ARDEN	95	97	87	95	94	95	91	93	91	93	92	70	91	94	90	92	64	91	92	109
	NORTH CAROLINA	100	89	90	89	88	96	91	94	94	91	93	73	85	95	88	96	64	93	96	112
	UNITED STATES	100	100	100	100	100	100	100	100	100	100	100	100	100	100	100	100	100	100	100	100

POPULATION CHANGE

28705-28909

#	POST OFFICE NAME	COUNTY FIPS CODE	POPULATION 2000	POPULATION 2009	POPULATION 2014	2000-2009 ANNUAL RATE % Rate	2000-2009 ANNUAL RATE State Centile	HOUSEHOLDS 2000	HOUSEHOLDS 2009	HOUSEHOLDS 2014	HOUSEHOLDS % Annual Rate 2000-2009	HOUSEHOLDS 2009 Average HH Size	FAMILIES 2000	FAMILIES 2009	FAMILIES % Annual Rate 2000-2009
28705	BAKERSVILLE	121	6661	7043	7111	0.6	36	2790	3028	3083	0.9	2.31	2081	2198	0.6
28708	BALSAM GROVE	175	568	599	604	0.6	36	221	240	244	0.9	2.50	162	170	0.5
28709	BARNARDSVILLE	021	2245	2684	2920	1.9	77	887	1075	1176	2.1	2.49	658	773	1.8
28711	BLACK MOUNTAIN	021	11931	13786	14747	1.6	72	5033	5995	6490	1.9	2.16	3210	3653	1.4
28712	BREVARD	175	16783	17375	17619	0.4	28	7093	7603	7794	0.8	2.15	4800	4984	0.4
28713	BRYSON CITY	173	8647	9348	9668	0.8	44	3641	4040	4210	1.1	2.26	2523	2714	0.8
28714	BURNSVILLE	199	16185	17132	17592	0.6	36	6838	7450	7722	0.9	2.28	4890	5177	0.6
28715	CANDLER	021	20550	24913	27162	2.1	81	8249	10238	11250	2.4	2.41	5979	7162	2.0
28716	CANTON	087	16185	16960	17233	0.5	32	6749	7213	7376	0.7	2.32	4785	4962	0.4
28717	CASHIERS	099	1434	1610	1746	1.3	63	665	772	846	1.6	2.09	464	522	1.3
28718	CEDAR MOUNTAIN	175	294	315	326	0.7	40	126	140	146	1.1	2.24	92	99	0.8
28719	CHEROKEE	173	5373	5849	6058	0.9	48	1809	2036	2132	1.3	2.78	1338	1467	1.0
28721	CLYDE	087	8660	9938	10483	1.5	69	3590	4237	4509	1.8	2.33	2559	2925	1.5
28722	COLUMBUS	149	6855	7197	7289	0.5	32	2980	3197	3256	0.8	2.22	2026	2098	0.4
28723	CULLOWHEE	099	8199	9870	10315	2.0	79	2600	3143	3388	2.1	2.13	1458	1691	1.6
28726	EAST FLAT ROCK	089	3141	3145	3177	0.0	15	1271	1267	1280	0.0	2.46	879	844	-0.4
28729	ETOWAH	089	2326	2610	2892	1.3	63	1060	1252	1397	1.8	2.08	798	915	1.5
28730	FAIRVIEW	021	8017	8875	9421	1.1	56	2998	3388	3622	1.3	2.60	2313	2538	1.0
28731	FLAT ROCK	089	6229	7198	7782	1.6	72	2627	3068	3325	1.7	2.33	1920	2171	1.3
28732	FLETCHER	089	11966	15252	17082	2.7	87	4781	6164	6947	2.8	2.45	3532	4377	2.3
28733	FONTANA DAM	075	41	44	45	0.8	44	18	20	21	1.1	2.20	13	15	1.6
28734	FRANKLIN	113	23957	26746	28324	1.2	60	10224	11632	12376	1.4	2.26	7113	7861	1.1
28735	GERTON	089	169	248	287	4.2	93	74	116	135	5.0	2.14	54	81	4.5
28736	GLENVILLE	099	770	803	849	0.5	32	356	384	411	0.8	2.09	236	245	0.4
28739	HENDERSONVILLE	089	18168	20963	22563	1.6	72	8051	9464	10243	1.8	2.18	5543	6332	1.4
28740	GREEN MOUNTAIN	199	1717	1934	2027	1.3	63	686	801	846	1.7	2.39	523	594	1.4
28741	HIGHLANDS	113	2815	3661	4069	2.9	88	1280	1716	1922	3.2	2.09	835	1080	2.8
28742	HORSE SHOE	089	2156	2849	3190	3.1	88	848	1149	1292	3.3	2.48	653	861	3.0
28743	HOT SPRINGS	115	2832	2882	2888	0.2	21	1238	1304	1322	0.6	2.19	836	853	0.2
28745	LAKE JUNALUSKA	087	472	517	536	1.0	53	254	284	296	1.2	1.82	162	176	0.9
28746	LAKE LURE	161	2256	2940	3064	2.9	88	1022	1369	1440	3.2	2.14	725	939	2.8
28747	LAKE TOXAWAY	175	1999	2170	2231	0.9	48	836	939	975	1.3	2.31	587	637	0.9
28748	LEICESTER	021	10940	12698	13689	1.6	72	4239	5054	5494	1.9	2.49	3192	3685	1.6
28751	MAGGIE VALLEY	087	2901	3373	3556	1.6	72	1382	1643	1746	1.9	2.04	932	1069	1.5
28752	MARION	111	28576	30483	31270	0.7	40	11289	12319	12734	0.9	2.38	8013	8497	0.6
28753	MARSHALL	115	9489	10320	10680	0.9	48	3975	4477	4681	1.3	2.26	2782	3037	1.0
28754	MARS HILL	115	7392	7747	7854	0.5	32	2835	3044	3116	0.8	2.32	2014	2101	0.5
28756	MILL SPRING	149	3919	4521	4748	1.6	72	1543	1828	1934	1.8	2.47	1114	1279	1.5
28759	MILLS RIVER	089	3999	5664	6411	3.8	92	1617	2454	2797	4.6	2.31	1248	1846	4.3
28761	NEBO	111	6986	6952	6912	-0.1	13	2653	2712	2722	0.2	2.46	2001	1993	0.0
28762	OLD FORT	111	7166	7849	8157	1.0	53	2884	3249	3405	1.3	2.42	2110	2316	1.0
28763	OTTO	113	1652	2060	2245	2.4	83	708	894	979	2.6	2.30	520	637	2.2
28766	PENROSE	175	863	982	1036	1.4	66	355	417	444	1.8	2.35	276	316	1.5
28768	PISGAH FOREST	175	6796	7270	7450	0.7	40	2856	3169	3287	1.1	2.29	2141	2314	0.8
28771	ROBBINSVILLE	075	7404	7616	7655	0.3	24	3090	3329	3392	0.8	2.25	2217	2320	0.5
28772	ROSMAN	175	1637	1720	1746	0.5	32	654	710	728	0.9	2.42	484	510	0.6
28773	SALUDA	149	2747	3036	3165	1.1	56	1132	1278	1340	1.3	2.33	790	868	1.0
28774	SAPPHIRE	175	798	1311	1454	5.5	96	371	629	705	5.9	2.08	256	420	5.5
28775	SCALY MOUNTAIN	113	521	598	642	1.5	69	230	267	288	1.6	2.24	158	178	1.3
28777	SPRUCE PINE	121	9631	9765	9636	0.1	18	3519	3556	3532	0.1	2.45	2481	2433	-0.2
28778	SWANNANOA	021	8358	9706	10426	1.6	72	3234	3879	4214	2.0	2.38	2226	2565	1.5
28779	SYLVA	099	14121	16100	17000	1.4	66	6149	7216	7704	1.7	2.18	3960	4486	1.4
28781	TOPTON	113	842	880	908	0.5	32	373	400	416	0.8	2.20	274	287	0.5
28782	TRYON	149	5205	5305	5294	0.2	21	2422	2487	2490	0.3	2.06	1545	1527	-0.1
28783	TUCKASEGEE	099	1372	1430	1452	0.4	28	578	623	640	0.8	2.30	410	431	0.5
28785	WAYNESVILLE	087	6464	7467	7845	1.6	72	2725	3260	3460	2.0	2.26	1998	2317	1.6
28786	WAYNESVILLE	087	19325	19543	19634	0.1	18	8386	8736	8852	0.4	2.18	5597	5636	0.1
28787	WEAVERVILLE	021	17128	19904	21412	1.6	72	6851	8192	8888	2.0	2.40	5039	5829	1.6
28789	WHITTIER	099	5774	6536	6920	1.3	63	2346	2753	2945	1.7	2.37	1702	1937	1.4
28790	ZIRCONIA	089	2830	3488	3871	2.3	83	1102	1391	1554	2.5	2.51	842	1033	2.2
28791	HENDERSONVILLE	089	13279	14224	14881	0.7	40	5790	6318	6648	0.9	2.18	4022	4236	0.6
28792	HENDERSONVILLE	089	26790	31607	34240	1.8	76	10863	13055	14232	2.0	2.35	7415	8629	1.7
28801	ASHEVILLE	021	13268	13774	14150	0.4	28	5995	6366	6608	0.7	1.89	2462	2446	-0.1
28803	ASHEVILLE	021	24340	27846	29751	1.5	69	10709	12382	13285	1.6	2.21	6620	7356	1.1
28804	ASHEVILLE	021	18427	19720	20584	0.7	40	7621	8353	8796	1.0	2.20	4717	4959	0.5
28805	ASHEVILLE	021	17196	18770	19744	1.0	53	7626	8500	9009	1.2	2.12	4449	4744	0.7
28806	ASHEVILLE	021	33281	36239	38122	0.9	48	14107	15681	16606	1.2	2.28	8925	9500	0.7
28901	ANDREWS	039	4855	5668	6119	1.7	74	2143	2610	2852	2.2	2.14	1446	1704	1.8
28902	BRASSTOWN	043	1099	1228	1336	1.2	60	473	554	612	1.7	2.21	335	381	1.4
28904	HAYESVILLE	043	7198	8800	9707	2.2	82	3178	4057	4536	2.7	2.14	2258	2800	2.4
28905	MARBLE	039	3334	3824	4081	1.5	69	1352	1607	1734	1.9	2.35	985	1136	1.6
28906	MURPHY	039	15927	18045	19084	1.4	66	6768	7958	8518	1.8	2.25	4888	5595	1.5
28909	WARNE	043	660	832	891	2.5	84	269	355	386	3.0	2.34	188	241	2.7
	NORTH CAROLINA					1.7					1.8	2.46			1.5
	UNITED STATES					1.0					1.1	2.59			0.9

ZIP CODE		RACE (%)						% Hispanic Origin		2009 AGE DISTRIBUTION (%)										MEDIAN AGE		
#	POST OFFICE NAME	White		Black		Asian/Pacific																
		2000	2009	2000	2009	2000	2009	2000	2009	0-4	5-9	10-14	15-19	20-24	25-44	45-64	65-84	85+	18+	2009	% 2009 Males	% 2009 Females
28705	BAKERSVILLE	98.5	98.0	0.1	0.1	0.2	0.2	1.5	2.1	5.3	5.6	5.8	5.2	4.4	24.0	30.7	16.8	2.3	80.0	44.8	50.2	49.8
28708	BALSAM GROVE	98.8	98.3	0.0	0.0	0.2	0.2	0.5	0.5	6.3	6.5	6.5	6.0	5.8	25.9	29.0	12.4	1.5	76.6	40.2	48.9	51.1
28709	BARNARDSVILLE	98.7	98.0	0.0	0.0	0.2	0.3	0.8	1.3	5.5	5.6	6.0	6.3	5.6	27.2	30.1	12.3	1.4	78.8	40.5	51.4	48.6
28711	BLACK MOUNTAIN	92.2	90.5	5.1	5.8	0.7	1.0	1.1	1.7	4.6	4.6	5.4	7.4	5.7	22.7	29.7	16.3	3.6	80.9	44.7	47.8	52.2
28712	BREVARD	91.8	90.6	5.6	5.8	0.6	0.8	1.1	1.5	4.6	4.6	4.8	6.6	5.6	19.6	28.0	21.9	4.3	82.4	48.3	47.3	52.7
28713	BRYSON CITY	87.3	84.4	0.9	1.1	0.2	0.3	1.1	1.7	5.1	5.6	5.8	5.7	3.8	23.3	31.4	16.6	2.8	79.8	45.5	48.9	51.1
28714	BURNSVILLE	97.9	97.4	0.6	0.6	0.1	0.2	2.9	3.9	5.3	5.5	5.9	5.7	4.3	24.0	30.7	16.1	2.6	79.7	44.5	49.3	50.7
28715	CANDLER	97.3	96.3	0.5	0.6	0.4	0.5	1.5	2.3	6.2	6.4	6.6	6.1	5.2	26.6	28.5	12.5	1.9	77.0	40.2	48.6	51.4
28716	CANTON	96.8	96.1	1.5	1.6	0.1	0.2	1.7	2.5	5.5	5.8	6.0	6.0	4.5	24.8	29.1	15.5	2.8	78.9	43.3	49.1	50.9
28717	CASHIERS	98.3	97.5	0.1	0.1	0.1	0.2	1.4	2.0	3.3	3.5	4.0	3.7	2.2	16.5	37.3	27.1	2.2	86.8	56.2	49.8	50.2
28718	CEDAR MOUNTAIN	97.3	96.2	0.0	0.0	1.0	1.6	0.7	1.3	4.1	4.8	5.1	4.4	2.9	21.9	35.2	19.4	2.2	82.9	49.3	47.9	52.1
28719	CHEROKEE	22.0	17.4	2.6	2.4	0.2	0.3	2.3	2.8	7.5	8.2	8.2	10.0	7.1	25.1	25.2	7.6	1.0	70.5	32.7	49.6	50.4
28721	CLYDE	96.9	95.9	0.9	1.0	0.4	0.6	1.4	2.1	6.1	6.2	6.2	5.6	4.8	25.6	29.3	14.2	1.9	78.1	41.8	48.9	51.1
28722	COLUMBUS	93.4	92.3	4.6	5.0	0.4	0.5	3.1	4.2	4.7	5.0	5.2	4.8	4.2	20.7	29.9	19.2	6.2	81.8	48.7	47.9	52.1
28723	CULLOWHEE	93.0	91.2	3.7	3.9	0.8	1.1	1.8	2.7	3.3	2.8	3.1	20.1	26.9	15.1	19.6	7.9	1.2	88.6	23.9	49.7	50.3
28726	EAST FLAT ROCK	86.4	81.0	2.6	2.8	0.4	0.6	16.0	22.5	6.7	6.6	6.1	6.6	6.9	26.7	25.9	12.8	1.7	76.8	37.7	49.7	50.3
28729	ETOWAH	97.2	96.6	1.4	1.6	0.6	0.8	0.7	1.0	4.0	4.1	4.2	4.4	4.0	17.7	32.7	26.0	3.0	85.0	53.3	48.4	51.6
28730	FAIRVIEW	97.5	96.6	0.4	0.5	0.5	0.7	1.0	1.5	5.6	6.1	6.9	6.9	4.7	24.2	32.8	11.1	1.7	77.0	42.1	48.8	51.2
28731	FLAT ROCK	96.0	94.4	1.2	1.3	0.4	0.5	4.7	6.9	5.8	5.6	5.8	5.1	4.2	21.7	29.9	19.7	2.2	79.8	46.3	49.3	50.7
28732	FLETCHER	93.2	91.5	3.7	4.2	0.8	1.2	1.9	2.8	6.6	6.8	7.0	6.1	4.3	27.2	29.1	11.3	1.6	75.7	40.1	49.3	50.7
28733	FONTANA DAM	100.0	97.7	0.0	0.0	0.0	0.0	0.0	0.0	4.5	4.5	4.5	4.5	4.5	22.7	34.1	18.2	2.3	81.8	48.3	50.0	50.0
28734	FRANKLIN	96.8	96.1	1.5	1.6	0.5	0.7	1.4	1.9	5.0	5.2	5.5	5.9	4.2	20.6	31.5	19.1	2.9	80.4	47.4	48.4	51.6
28735	GERTON	96.4	94.4	0.6	0.8	0.0	0.4	4.2	5.6	6.9	6.5	6.9	4.4	4.4	24.6	30.2	14.5	1.6	76.2	42.4	50.4	49.6
28736	GLENVILLE	96.8	95.3	0.1	0.1	0.1	0.1	4.0	5.7	4.6	4.6	5.2	5.1	4.1	22.0	34.7	18.2	1.4	82.3	48.0	50.3	49.7
28739	HENDERSONVILLE	93.6	92.2	3.2	3.2	0.6	0.8	3.9	5.5	4.6	4.8	5.1	5.0	4.2	20.0	30.5	22.0	3.7	82.5	49.5	48.3	51.7
28740	GREEN MOUNTAIN	98.7	98.1	0.1	0.1	0.1	0.1	0.9	1.7	5.4	5.8	6.4	6.4	4.2	23.8	30.3	15.3	2.4	78.4	43.6	49.9	50.1
28741	HIGHLANDS	98.8	98.1	0.0	0.0	0.1	0.1	2.4	3.3	3.6	4.1	4.4	4.6	3.1	17.3	36.5	22.5	3.9	85.2	53.3	48.1	51.9
28742	HORSE SHOE	98.1	97.4	0.7	0.9	0.2	0.4	1.2	1.7	5.1	5.5	6.0	5.8	4.0	21.8	32.2	17.7	2.0	79.8	46.1	49.3	50.7
28743	HOT SPRINGS	98.1	97.5	0.1	0.1	0.3	0.3	0.8	1.2	5.4	5.8	6.1	5.3	4.5	22.2	32.4	16.2	2.0	79.3	45.4	49.6	50.4
28745	LAKE JUNALUSKA	99.4	98.8	0.0	0.0	0.0	0.2	1.3	1.7	3.1	2.9	3.5	3.1	1.9	13.9	29.0	36.8	5.8	88.8	61.2	46.4	53.6
28746	LAKE LURE	88.3	86.6	10.2	11.3	0.1	0.2	0.9	1.3	4.1	4.5	4.9	4.3	3.2	19.9	34.3	22.8	2.1	83.7	50.8	50.8	49.2
28747	LAKE TOXAWAY	98.8	98.4	0.1	0.1	0.3	0.4	0.6	0.7	5.3	6.2	6.2	6.1	4.2	21.2	33.5	15.9	1.4	78.5	45.5	49.4	50.6
28748	LEICESTER	96.3	95.0	0.9	1.0	0.4	0.5	2.0	3.1	6.6	6.8	7.0	6.4	4.8	28.2	28.0	10.9	1.3	75.6	38.8	49.8	50.2
28751	MAGGIE VALLEY	97.5	97.1	0.4	0.4	0.3	0.4	0.2	0.3	3.0	3.5	4.2	4.3	2.5	17.9	37.6	24.9	2.2	86.7	54.0	48.0	52.0
28752	MARION	91.6	89.8	4.5	4.7	0.8	1.0	3.6	5.2	6.0	6.0	6.2	5.9	5.4	27.5	27.5	13.4	2.0	78.2	40.1	50.3	49.7
28753	MARSHALL	98.3	97.7	0.3	0.3	0.2	0.3	1.5	2.1	5.6	5.9	6.3	6.3	4.8	24.7	29.5	14.4	2.4	78.5	42.4	49.6	50.4
28754	MARS HILL	96.7	96.0	1.8	1.9	0.3	0.4	1.3	1.9	5.3	5.6	5.8	9.6	8.0	22.5	27.3	13.5	2.4	79.8	40.0	49.6	50.4
28756	MILL SPRING	93.3	92.5	4.6	4.7	0.3	0.4	3.8	5.2	6.3	6.4	6.9	6.8	5.2	27.2	28.5	11.6	1.2	76.2	39.1	49.6	50.4
28759	MILLS RIVER	98.2	97.3	0.6	0.8	0.3	0.4	1.5	2.3	5.9	6.4	6.9	6.4	4.3	23.6	30.8	13.9	1.8	76.7	42.7	49.7	50.3
28761	NEBO	92.9	91.2	3.4	3.7	2.0	2.6	1.2	1.9	5.9	6.1	6.5	6.2	5.1	26.8	28.9	12.5	1.9	77.7	40.6	50.1	49.9
28762	OLD FORT	93.3	92.3	3.9	3.8	0.4	0.5	1.7	2.5	6.2	6.3	6.5	5.8	5.0	25.7	29.2	13.8	1.5	77.6	41.1	49.7	50.3
28763	OTTO	98.2	97.6	0.3	0.3	0.2	0.4	1.5	2.3	4.6	5.1	5.4	4.8	3.3	20.5	36.2	18.0	2.1	81.8	48.7	50.0	50.0
28766	PENROSE	98.1	97.5	0.5	0.6	0.1	0.2	0.8	1.1	4.8	5.2	5.8	5.6	3.6	21.2	35.3	17.0	1.5	80.8	47.5	50.4	49.6
28768	PISGAH FOREST	94.2	93.3	4.2	4.6	0.1	0.2	1.3	1.9	4.3	4.7	5.1	5.0	4.1	20.9	33.5	20.4	2.0	82.7	49.1	49.8	50.2
28771	ROBBINSVILLE	91.5	90.3	0.2	0.2	0.1	0.2	0.8	1.0	5.9	6.2	6.4	5.7	4.3	23.7	28.9	16.6	2.4	78.0	43.5	49.5	50.5
28772	ROSMAN	98.4	97.9	0.3	0.3	0.1	0.2	0.5	0.7	6.1	6.3	6.5	6.3	5.0	24.7	28.9	14.6	1.6	77.2	41.7	49.5	50.5
28773	SALUDA	96.9	95.9	1.2	1.1	0.2	0.2	2.8	4.2	4.9	5.3	5.6	4.7	3.1	19.7	35.3	18.6	2.7	81.1	49.5	48.8	51.2
28774	SAPPHIRE	98.0	97.1	0.1	0.2	0.1	0.2	1.3	2.4	4.8	5.3	5.6	4.7	3.1	20.6	34.4	20.1	1.4	81.2	49.5	49.9	50.1
28775	SCALY MOUNTAIN	99.4	99.0	0.0	0.0	0.0	0.2	2.9	3.8	4.2	4.5	4.7	5.7	3.3	19.9	36.5	18.7	2.5	84.1	49.7	49.8	50.2
28777	SPRUCE PINE	94.3	92.7	3.1	3.4	0.2	0.2	2.7	4.1	4.4	4.6	5.2	5.7	5.6	28.8	28.3	15.0	2.3	82.1	42.2	53.6	46.4
28778	SWANNANOA	93.1	91.5	3.8	4.2	0.6	0.8	3.7	5.2	5.3	5.4	5.7	7.2	6.0	24.7	29.3	13.7	2.7	79.5	42.0	48.1	51.9
28779	SYLVA	94.5	93.0	1.5	1.5	0.6	0.8	1.3	1.8	5.1	5.1	5.3	5.4	6.6	24.6	29.7	15.7	2.5	81.3	43.4	48.4	51.6
28781	TOPTON	98.8	98.6	0.4	0.3	0.0	0.0	1.4	1.9	4.2	4.2	4.1	4.0	4.2	19.9	31.6	25.5	2.4	85.1	52.9	48.4	51.6
28782	TRYON	88.4	87.5	10.0	10.3	0.2	0.2	2.5	3.4	4.1	4.5	4.8	4.5	3.3	17.2	32.7	23.1	5.7	83.5	53.2	46.5	53.5
28783	TUCKASEGEE	96.9	95.5	0.4	0.4	0.1	0.1	2.3	3.4	5.9	6.1	6.5	5.5	5.0	24.8	31.7	13.1	1.5	78.1	42.3	50.3	49.7
28785	WAYNESVILLE	97.9	97.5	0.3	0.3	0.4	0.5	0.9	1.3	4.9	5.3	5.6	5.3	3.4	22.2	33.0	18.4	1.8	80.9	47.0	49.5	50.5
28786	WAYNESVILLE	96.3	95.5	1.7	1.8	0.2	0.3	1.5	2.2	4.9	5.0	5.3	5.4	4.5	22.5	30.7	18.6	3.1	81.2	46.6	48.0	52.0
28787	WEAVERVILLE	96.8	95.6	0.7	0.8	0.4	0.6	1.9	2.9	5.7	6.1	6.5	6.2	4.8	25.6	30.3	12.9	1.8	77.8	41.7	49.1	50.9
28789	WHITTIER	59.3	54.7	0.3	0.3	0.2	0.3	2.3	3.0	6.0	6.3	6.6	6.9	4.9	25.6	30.1	12.2	1.4	76.9	40.5	49.0	51.0
28790	ZIRCONIA	97.0	95.2	0.2	0.2	0.0	0.0	2.9	4.7	6.0	6.3	6.6	5.9	4.5	25.6	30.9	12.7	1.5	77.4	41.5	50.7	49.3
28791	HENDERSONVILLE	94.2	86.7	3.1	9.4	0.8	1.0	3.1	4.5	3.7	3.8	4.1	4.4	4.1	17.4	30.1	26.7	5.7	85.9	54.4	47.2	52.8
28792	HENDERSONVILLE	88.4	84.5	4.4	4.3	0.8	1.1	9.5	14.3	6.2	6.2	6.3	5.8	5.0	25.1	26.8	15.0	3.7	77.7	41.8	48.5	51.5
28801	ASHEVILLE	52.3	49.1	44.0	46.1	0.5	0.7	2.4	3.4	4.9	4.6	4.2	7.2	10.4	30.1	25.1	11.2	2.3	83.0	37.1	48.7	51.3
28803	ASHEVILLE	83.7	81.0	11.8	12.6	1.2	1.7	3.4	4.9	5.4	5.5	5.7	5.7	5.6	24.2	28.9	15.3	3.6	79.7	43.3	47.8	52.2
28804	ASHEVILLE	93.4	91.7	3.7	4.1	0.6	0.9	2.5	3.8	4.2	4.3	4.7	6.3	6.7	23.2	30.2	17.3	3.1	83.7	45.4	48.0	52.0
28805	ASHEVILLE	90.9	89.1	5.9	6.5	0.9	1.3	2.1	3.1	4.2	4.4	4.7	5.8	7.1	24.6	30.3	16.0	2.9	83.3	44.4	46.8	53.2
28806	ASHEVILLE	86.2	83.2	8.0	8.6	0.9	1.3	5.9	8.5	6.4	6.2	6.0	5.9	5.9	28.4	26.2	12.7	2.2	77.7	38.9	48.1	51.9
28901	ANDREWS	95.1	94.0	1.8	2.0	0.1	0.1	1.3	2.0	5.3	5.6	6.0	5.7	4.0	23.0	30.0	17.2	3.1	79.4	45.3	49.4	50.6
28902	BRASSTOWN	98.0	97.6	0.6	0.7	0.1	0.1	0.6	0.9	4.2	4.6	4.9	4.6	3.4	21.3	36.2	18.8	1.8	83.5	49.6	48.0	52.0
28904	HAYESVILLE	98.0	97.7	0.8	0.9	0.2	0.2	0.8	1.1	4.0	4.4	4.8	4.8	3.4	20.3	35.0	20.1	3.2	83.8	50.7	49.5	50.5
28905	MARBLE	95.1	94.0	1.1	1.2	0.3	0.4	1.9	2.8	5.9	6.2	6.5	5.7	4.5	23.7	29.3	15.4	2.8	77.8	43.0	49.7	50.3
28906	MURPHY	94.6	93.6	1.7	1.7	0.4	0.5	1.1	1.5	5.1	5.4	5.7	5.3	4.0	22.0	31.0	19.0	2.5	80.3	46.8	49.0	51.0
28909	WARNE	97.9	97.2	0.8	0.7	0.2	0.2	1.7	2.3	3.6	4.0	4.4	5.0	3.2	21.0	37.6	18.8	2.3	85.1	50.3	48.8	51.2
	NORTH CAROLINA	72.1	69.8	21.6	21.5	1.5	2.1	4.7	6.9	6.6	6.5	6.5	6.8	6.9	27.7	26.5	10.9	1.6	76.5	37.4	49.3	50.7
	UNITED STATES	75.1	72.0	12.3	12.7	3.8	4.6	12.5	15.7	6.8	6.7	6.6	7.1	6.9	27.0	26.0	10.9	1.9	75.7	36.9	49.2	50.8

ZIP CODE #	POST OFFICE NAME	2009 Per Capita Income	2009 HH Income Base	2009 HOUSEHOLD INCOME DISTRIBUTION (%) Less than $25,000	$25,000 to $49,999	$50,000 to $99,999	$100,000 to $149,999	$150,000 or More	MEDIAN HOUSEHOLD INCOME 2009	2014	2009 National Centile	2009 State Centile	2009 Home Value Base	2009 HOME VALUE DISTRIBUTION (%) Less than $50,000	$50,000 to $89,999	$90,000 to $174,999	$175,000 to $399,999	$400,000 or More	2009 Median Home Value
28705	BAKERSVILLE	18261	3028	34.4	33.9	27.1	3.4	1.2	35000	35701	18	15	2526	19.8	23.6	40.6	14.6	1.5	101821
28708	BALSAM GROVE	19187	240	34.6	28.8	30.0	4.6	2.1	35215	37183	18	16	187	27.3	11.2	40.1	19.3	2.1	105804
28709	BARNARDSVILLE	17646	1075	31.0	35.1	28.9	3.9	1.1	36567	40079	22	19	839	21.1	26.1	32.4	17.2	3.2	94700
28711	BLACK MOUNTAIN	24658	5995	22.6	31.2	37.4	6.1	2.7	46905	49895	54	61	4354	15.0	15.5	34.7	28.9	5.9	132492
28712	BREVARD	25794	7603	22.6	27.2	40.4	6.7	3.2	50202	52125	62	70	5743	9.8	12.3	32.0	38.9	7.0	163781
28713	BRYSON CITY	19452	4040	33.0	33.0	28.8	3.5	1.7	36793	38126	23	20	3106	16.7	16.8	37.6	22.0	6.9	122392
28714	BURNSVILLE	19368	7450	33.1	32.5	29.4	3.3	1.6	36063	37601	21	16	5913	14.5	17.8	36.5	28.0	3.1	125772
28715	CANDLER	22753	10238	21.5	30.8	39.5	5.8	2.4	47731	50982	56	63	8199	22.8	12.1	35.9	26.4	2.8	121807
28716	CANTON	20912	7213	29.9	31.4	32.9	3.9	1.8	40657	42774	35	35	5718	14.9	22.6	44.7	15.9	1.8	108526
28717	CASHIERS	38327	772	13.6	28.6	39.1	9.5	9.2	56922	57363	74	85	640	7.5	8.4	11.1	27.0	45.9	354386
28718	CEDAR MOUNTAIN	23559	140	17.9	34.3	43.6	3.6	0.7	47996	50649	57	64	116	4.3	6.9	50.0	34.5	4.3	160227
28719	CHEROKEE	15007	2036	40.0	27.6	26.7	3.6	2.1	31179	34063	10	7	1610	18.3	23.7	38.7	14.8	4.5	103348
28721	CLYDE	22662	4237	26.1	28.7	37.8	5.5	1.9	45538	46583	50	57	3224	18.0	15.1	36.1	27.3	3.5	127446
28722	COLUMBUS	26435	3197	22.1	26.3	40.6	7.5	3.6	51434	51315	65	75	2525	10.4	12.5	33.7	33.1	10.3	148397
28723	CULLOWHEE	20863	3143	31.9	27.0	31.9	5.4	3.8	39598	40833	32	31	1901	9.8	9.0	30.4	40.2	10.6	177549
28726	EAST FLAT ROCK	17222	1267	33.0	36.1	27.2	2.8	1.0	36088	38255	21	17	853	30.4	22.0	33.6	10.4	3.5	86985
28729	ETOWAH	30498	1252	18.5	26.8	40.6	10.7	3.4	54326	56028	70	81	1106	12.8	8.2	37.2	38.2	3.6	153125
28730	FAIRVIEW	24078	3388	17.4	29.7	40.2	8.9	3.9	52533	53853	67	77	2834	13.8	12.6	25.7	35.9	12.1	168642
28731	FLAT ROCK	28916	3068	18.5	31.4	35.2	8.9	6.0	50099	51845	61	70	2538	16.8	16.4	23.5	24.9	18.4	146732
28732	FLETCHER	26504	6164	17.8	26.4	41.3	10.0	4.5	55330	56042	72	83	5054	17.5	10.3	26.4	38.6	7.2	163747
28733	FONTANA DAM	18295	20	40.0	25.0	30.0	5.0	0.0	35000	32344	18	15	18	27.8	27.8	27.8	16.7	0.0	80000
28734	FRANKLIN	20930	11632	31.9	32.4	29.1	4.7	2.0	38957	40678	30	29	9322	7.2	11.7	43.4	32.7	5.1	144876
28735	GERTON	26031	116	28.4	31.0	31.0	5.2	4.3	40000	44543	33	33	93	9.7	20.4	24.7	43.0	2.2	146875
28736	GLENVILLE	27973	384	24.5	27.1	39.6	3.9	4.9	48310	49640	57	65	299	8.4	5.7	25.8	30.4	29.8	229000
28739	HENDERSONVILLE	30777	9464	19.5	28.6	38.1	7.8	6.0	51718	53849	65	76	7385	6.1	10.9	26.9	42.6	13.6	196027
28740	GREEN MOUNTAIN	18917	801	30.1	40.2	25.5	2.4	1.9	37434	38091	25	22	697	13.5	19.1	39.7	25.1	2.6	117134
28741	HIGHLANDS	33395	1716	20.7	29.7	34.7	7.2	7.7	49441	51296	60	68	1428	1.6	1.4	15.8	38.4	42.8	346632
28742	HORSE SHOE	26948	1149	13.7	25.7	46.9	10.2	3.6	58814	58238	76	87	997	11.5	6.2	28.8	46.2	7.2	187684
28743	HOT SPRINGS	17717	1304	42.9	30.3	21.7	3.5	1.6	29488	31939	7	4	1014	25.8	29.5	18.6	17.9	8.2	81692
28745	LAKE JUNALUSKA	38929	284	15.1	23.9	40.8	14.1	6.0	64116	64069	82	90	223	4.5	4.9	18.4	51.1	21.1	259167
28746	LAKE LURE	23670	1369	29.1	30.5	31.6	6.0	2.8	41564	43215	38	39	1155	8.4	11.1	27.3	37.2	16.0	185776
28747	LAKE TOXAWAY	28503	939	22.6	29.4	35.5	6.5	6.1	47511	51499	55	62	789	13.2	9.4	34.0	20.5	22.9	146307
28748	LEICESTER	20281	5054	24.1	31.6	38.8	3.9	1.6	44979	48663	48	53	4222	26.1	21.0	27.7	20.9	4.2	99098
28751	MAGGIE VALLEY	24782	1643	25.0	30.8	38.0	5.2	1.0	45201	46260	49	55	1335	10.2	9.1	43.2	30.2	7.3	152726
28752	MARION	19964	12319	28.7	34.2	30.7	4.3	2.1	40141	41746	33	33	9246	19.1	21.2	42.0	15.6	2.1	106863
28753	MARSHALL	19514	4477	34.9	30.6	28.9	4.3	1.3	36851	38188	23	20	3471	24.3	21.2	31.0	19.5	3.9	98988
28754	MARS HILL	21175	3044	27.1	29.6	36.2	4.8	2.3	43454	45811	44	47	2291	17.5	17.9	37.2	23.2	4.3	126188
28756	MILL SPRING	18395	1828	25.7	37.4	32.8	3.2	1.0	39205	42618	30	30	1424	16.1	23.2	30.1	23.0	7.6	116340
28759	MILLS RIVER	26878	2454	16.7	26.0	44.7	10.1	2.4	55625	55707	72	84	2112	11.7	8.6	33.3	41.7	4.7	165564
28761	NEBO	19447	2712	29.4	28.9	35.7	4.1	1.9	41903	45356	39	40	2266	18.9	22.2	39.3	16.5	3.0	104489
28762	OLD FORT	20445	3249	24.9	34.8	34.7	3.8	1.8	42118	44435	40	41	2584	16.4	21.7	45.7	14.9	1.4	107100
28763	OTTO	20175	894	23.9	37.1	34.3	3.4	1.2	41234	43294	37	37	746	8.3	15.4	40.5	33.6	2.1	138636
28766	PENROSE	24187	417	19.4	28.3	43.4	7.7	1.2	51513	52889	65	75	364	10.2	12.6	23.9	44.2	9.1	184677
28768	PISGAH FOREST	26696	3169	20.6	25.7	40.1	9.9	3.7	52741	54398	67	78	2681	9.1	11.2	29.9	41.4	8.4	174219
28771	ROBBINSVILLE	17286	3329	41.3	29.1	25.2	3.3	1.1	31869	32994	11	9	2718	22.7	24.5	34.7	15.7	2.5	95571
28772	ROSMAN	20078	710	29.0	29.3	35.8	4.5	1.4	39540	45000	31	31	557	21.0	14.4	32.7	25.9	6.1	120117
28773	SALUDA	25735	1278	18.5	30.7	41.2	6.3	3.3	50572	51278	63	72	1067	7.5	14.4	38.6	32.2	7.2	148750
28774	SAPPHIRE	30491	629	21.1	26.4	39.0	7.9	5.6	52569	53981	67	77	518	6.6	9.3	24.1	27.4	32.6	224390
28775	SCALY MOUNTAIN	23932	267	22.5	29.2	42.7	4.1	1.5	48277	50000	57	65	222	4.1	6.3	35.6	37.8	16.2	187500
28777	SPRUCE PINE	19046	3556	29.9	30.3	33.5	3.7	2.6	40753	43072	35	36	2758	16.6	21.4	40.6	20.0	1.4	109647
28778	SWANNANOA	21824	3879	27.0	28.1	36.5	6.3	2.1	44437	48376	47	51	2885	21.0	17.3	39.7	20.1	2.0	110229
28779	SYLVA	23151	7216	29.1	29.5	33.0	5.5	2.9	40767	41552	35	36	5116	10.8	13.6	35.6	33.9	6.1	150571
28781	TOPTON	18688	400	39.0	34.0	23.3	1.8	2.0	31685	33472	11	8	346	12.1	10.7	39.6	34.1	3.5	140741
28782	TRYON	30199	2487	20.5	30.5	35.9	7.5	5.5	48895	49918	59	67	1908	5.8	7.8	31.4	43.6	11.4	188559
28783	TUCKASEGEE	18314	623	34.0	34.7	28.6	1.3	1.4	34070	36098	16	13	505	21.6	17.2	30.3	23.8	7.1	113542
28785	WAYNESVILLE	23378	3260	24.7	30.3	37.2	5.3	2.5	44919	46090	48	53	2704	22.5	10.8	27.8	32.6	6.3	141516
28786	WAYNESVILLE	23100	8736	29.3	30.0	33.3	4.9	2.5	40634	42991	35	35	6379	16.0	18.0	35.7	25.1	5.2	121686
28787	WEAVERVILLE	23691	8192	20.3	29.7	41.2	5.9	2.9	49957	51905	61	69	6496	16.2	10.8	30.5	34.8	7.7	156996
28789	WHITTIER	20175	2753	30.4	31.0	32.7	3.9	2.0	40269	40831	34	34	2199	13.8	19.8	40.0	19.8	6.6	118831
28790	ZIRCONIA	24578	1391	22.9	33.0	33.8	6.3	4.0	44574	47929	47	52	1156	23.5	9.5	36.2	26.8	4.0	121821
28791	HENDERSONVILLE	29816	6318	17.0	27.9	42.1	7.8	5.2	55119	56405	71	82	5056	5.9	8.7	28.7	50.0	6.7	189304
28792	HENDERSONVILLE	21356	13055	27.8	32.1	33.2	4.5	2.4	40866	44499	36	36	9566	22.1	15.0	34.1	25.1	3.8	118284
28801	ASHEVILLE	19747	6366	48.9	23.5	21.0	4.3	2.3	25690	27147	4	1	2123	7.3	20.3	38.8	26.4	7.3	142580
28803	ASHEVILLE	33833	12382	19.3	25.8	37.4	8.5	9.0	55437	56736	72	83	8008	7.9	14.7	27.0	35.9	14.5	176165
28804	ASHEVILLE	31551	8353	19.4	28.3	33.6	10.4	8.3	52668	54777	67	77	6022	9.0	10.2	19.7	45.6	15.5	217711
28805	ASHEVILLE	28295	8500	20.0	29.0	38.9	7.6	4.5	51016	53105	64	73	5425	8.0	10.3	40.8	35.9	4.9	160069
28806	ASHEVILLE	21378	15681	27.0	31.3	36.5	3.6	1.6	43139	46719	43	46	10452	21.1	19.6	43.3	15.4	0.7	106047
28901	ANDREWS	20416	2610	36.2	33.8	26.2	2.1	1.7	32979	33618	13	11	1997	19.6	16.7	45.0	16.4	2.2	112500
28902	BRASSTOWN	23213	554	30.1	30.5	32.1	4.9	2.3	41407	42933	37	38	477	5.0	21.6	42.8	25.8	4.8	134954
28904	HAYESVILLE	22491	4057	32.1	31.0	28.8	5.6	2.5	38763	40940	29	28	3391	6.4	11.5	37.1	31.5	13.4	162644
28905	MARBLE	17795	1607	33.8	33.0	29.9	2.6	0.7	36506	38382	22	18	1294	12.4	17.6	40.6	26.5	2.9	120109
28906	MURPHY	19603	7958	35.1	30.9	27.8	4.4	1.9	34485	35685	16	14	6652	12.9	15.4	39.8	28.0	3.9	132512
28909	WARNE	19442	355	32.4	36.1	25.4	4.2	2.0	36547	37828	22	19	305	4.3	16.7	43.6	29.5	5.9	144167
	NORTH CAROLINA	25989		22.3	26.1	36.6	9.4	5.6	51418	53634				12.2	15.1	38.7	27.9	6.1	132724
	UNITED STATES	27277		20.9	24.4	35.3	11.7	7.6	54719	56938				9.3	13.1	31.6	32.6	13.5	162279

ZIP CODE		FINANCIAL SERVICES				THE HOME						ENTERTAINMENT						PERSONAL			
						Home Improvements		Furnishings													
#	POST OFFICE NAME	Auto Loan	Home Loan	Invest-ments	Retire-ment Plans	Home Repair	Lawn & Garden	Comput-ers & Hard-ware-Personal	Major Appli-ances	TV, Radio, Sound Equip-ment	Furni-ture	Dine out/ Carry out	Sports Equip-ment	Fees & Tickets	Toys & Games	Travel	Cable TV	Apparel & Services	Auto Repairs	Health Insur-ance	Pets & Supplies
28705	BAKERSVILLE	75	54	72	52	55	75	56	69	62	53	61	52	45	63	54	68	40	64	73	83
28708	BALSAM GROVE	86	62	71	60	62	82	65	75	72	63	70	58	52	75	59	78	47	71	79	91
28709	BARNARDSVILLE	78	58	69	56	58	76	59	70	65	57	64	53	48	67	56	71	43	66	73	84
28711	BLACK MOUNTAIN	87	73	94	72	77	90	75	87	79	72	77	63	67	76	76	83	52	83	91	101
28712	BREVARD	89	75	96	74	80	95	77	89	82	75	81	64	71	79	78	88	55	85	96	104
28713	BRYSON CITY	77	57	83	56	60	79	59	74	64	55	63	55	48	63	59	70	42	68	76	87
28714	BURNSVILLE	78	57	77	55	58	79	59	73	65	55	64	55	47	65	57	71	42	67	76	87
28715	CANDLER	85	80	74	78	78	85	76	81	79	77	79	60	73	81	75	82	54	79	84	96
28716	CANTON	82	64	79	63	66	83	66	78	71	61	70	58	56	71	64	77	47	73	82	92
28717	CASHIERS	118	113	162	111	128	138	105	127	110	112	109	84	107	101	119	116	74	120	136	145
28718	CEDAR MOUNTAIN	88	71	114	70	78	93	71	90	74	66	73	66	61	70	77	79	49	83	89	104
28719	CHEROKEE	74	54	70	52	54	73	55	67	62	54	61	51	45	63	53	67	40	63	70	81
28721	CLYDE	87	72	83	71	74	86	72	82	76	71	76	61	64	77	71	81	51	78	85	97
28722	COLUMBUS	88	80	97	79	85	96	79	89	84	80	83	63	77	80	82	89	56	86	99	104
28723	CULLOWHEE	79	63	78	65	65	73	78	74	76	70	76	59	67	75	71	77	52	77	75	89
28726	EAST FLAT ROCK	77	54	71	52	55	75	56	68	63	54	62	52	45	64	53	69	41	64	72	83
28729	ETOWAH	93	89	113	82	99	106	85	100	90	91	87	66	84	82	92	95	59	96	111	114
28730	FAIRVIEW	95	95	86	95	93	97	87	93	88	89	89	70	87	91	88	90	61	89	92	110
28731	FLAT ROCK	107	94	118	91	100	115	90	106	96	93	95	74	85	94	93	102	64	100	113	124
28732	FLETCHER	101	99	92	97	96	99	92	97	92	94	92	74	90	96	91	93	64	93	94	114
28733	FONTANA DAM	72	51	74	50	53	73	53	67	59	49	58	50	42	58	52	65	38	62	70	80
28734	FRANKLIN	77	64	89	62	68	81	64	77	68	62	67	56	57	65	67	72	45	73	79	90
28735	GERTON	94	74	117	72	80	99	74	94	78	69	77	69	64	75	79	84	51	87	94	110
28736	GLENVILLE	98	78	126	77	86	103	78	99	82	73	81	73	68	78	85	87	54	92	98	115
28739	HENDERSONVILLE	102	93	113	92	98	109	92	104	97	92	95	73	88	93	95	101	65	100	110	120
28740	GREEN MOUNTAIN	80	59	72	58	60	79	61	73	67	58	66	55	50	68	58	73	44	68	76	87
28741	HIGHLANDS	114	96	150	95	106	124	94	118	99	91	97	84	85	93	103	105	65	109	119	136
28742	HORSE SHOE	100	96	99	98	99	109	92	103	95	89	93	76	89	94	95	99	64	97	107	120
28743	HOT SPRINGS	71	49	68	47	49	70	51	64	58	48	56	49	40	58	48	64	37	59	67	77
28745	LAKE JUNALUSKA	97	103	139	102	118	121	92	109	97	104	96	68	101	87	107	102	66	104	121	123
28746	LAKE LURE	85	68	106	66	74	89	68	86	71	64	71	63	58	69	72	76	47	79	85	100
28747	LAKE TOXAWAY	108	89	119	87	96	114	88	105	94	89	93	75	80	92	90	101	63	99	111	123
28748	LEICESTER	85	71	69	69	70	80	70	76	74	71	73	57	62	77	65	78	50	73	78	91
28751	MAGGIE VALLEY	85	68	109	67	74	90	68	86	71	64	70	63	59	67	73	76	47	80	85	100
28752	MARION	84	61	74	59	61	82	65	76	72	61	70	58	52	73	60	78	47	72	81	92
28753	MARSHALL	78	57	74	56	58	77	59	72	65	56	64	54	48	66	57	71	43	67	75	86
28754	MARS HILL	83	68	78	68	70	84	70	79	74	66	73	59	61	74	68	79	49	75	83	94
28756	MILL SPRING	81	60	68	58	59	77	61	71	68	60	67	54	50	71	56	74	45	67	75	86
28759	MILLS RIVER	95	89	86	92	90	102	86	96	89	80	87	73	81	91	86	93	60	90	99	112
28761	NEBO	87	63	74	61	63	83	65	76	72	63	71	58	52	75	60	79	47	72	80	93
28762	OLD FORT	88	63	77	61	64	86	66	79	74	63	72	60	53	76	61	80	48	74	83	95
28763	OTTO	78	62	100	61	68	82	62	79	65	58	64	58	54	62	67	69	43	73	78	91
28766	PENROSE	95	76	123	75	84	100	76	97	80	71	79	71	66	76	82	85	52	89	95	112
28768	PISGAH FOREST	100	83	108	82	88	106	81	97	88	82	86	70	74	86	84	94	58	92	103	114
28771	ROBBINSVILLE	71	49	69	48	51	70	51	64	57	48	56	49	40	58	49	63	37	60	67	77
28772	ROSMAN	87	63	82	61	64	86	65	79	72	62	70	60	52	73	62	78	47	74	82	95
28773	SALUDA	100	81	129	80	89	107	81	102	85	77	84	74	71	80	88	90	56	94	102	118
28774	SAPPHIRE	104	85	136	84	94	112	85	107	89	81	88	77	75	84	92	94	58	99	107	124
28775	SCALY MOUNTAIN	89	72	116	70	79	95	72	91	75	67	74	66	62	71	78	80	49	84	90	105
28777	SPRUCE PINE	86	62	82	60	63	86	64	79	71	60	70	60	51	72	61	78	46	73	83	94
28778	SWANNANOA	87	72	81	69	72	86	72	82	77	71	76	61	64	78	70	81	51	79	85	97
28779	SYLVA	81	67	82	67	69	82	71	79	74	67	73	59	63	72	70	78	49	76	82	93
28781	TOPTON	60	57	74	53	64	69	55	65	58	59	56	42	54	53	60	61	38	62	72	74
28782	TRYON	96	88	120	86	97	109	84	100	89	87	87	68	82	83	91	95	59	95	109	115
28783	TUCKASEGEE	73	55	83	54	58	75	56	71	60	52	59	52	46	59	57	65	39	65	72	83
28785	WAYNESVILLE	90	70	107	69	76	94	70	89	75	67	74	65	61	72	74	81	49	82	90	104
28786	WAYNESVILLE	84	65	91	64	69	87	68	82	74	63	72	61	58	72	69	80	48	78	87	97
28787	WEAVERVILLE	89	82	80	81	82	89	79	86	82	79	82	64	75	84	78	85	56	82	88	101
28789	WHITTIER	84	62	88	60	64	86	63	79	69	59	68	59	51	69	63	76	45	73	82	94
28790	ZIRCONIA	110	80	108	77	82	109	82	101	90	77	89	76	66	91	80	99	59	94	105	121
28791	HENDERSONVILLE	92	92	112	89	101	110	88	101	93	91	91	67	91	87	96	99	62	97	115	114
28792	HENDERSONVILLE	84	66	79	65	67	84	69	79	74	66	73	59	59	75	66	80	49	75	83	94
28801	ASHEVILLE	54	42	43	45	42	46	59	49	59	54	59	39	51	57	50	61	41	56	56	61
28803	ASHEVILLE	105	106	105	107	108	113	105	107	108	105	107	80	107	106	107	111	74	107	116	126
28804	ASHEVILLE	100	101	108	102	105	110	101	104	103	101	102	75	103	99	104	106	71	104	113	121
28805	ASHEVILLE	92	81	89	82	84	92	86	90	89	84	88	67	80	87	85	92	60	90	95	106
28806	ASHEVILLE	74	65	63	65	64	71	70	70	72	68	71	53	65	73	66	74	49	71	74	83
28901	ANDREWS	78	55	78	53	57	79	58	73	65	54	63	55	46	64	56	71	42	67	76	87
28902	BRASSTOWN	86	69	111	68	75	91	69	87	72	64	71	64	60	68	74	77	47	81	86	101
28904	HAYESVILLE	79	64	99	63	70	85	64	81	68	61	67	58	57	65	69	73	45	75	82	94
28905	MARBLE	75	54	72	52	55	75	55	69	62	52	60	52	44	62	53	68	40	64	72	82
28906	MURPHY	75	57	83	55	61	78	59	73	64	55	63	54	49	62	60	69	42	68	76	86
28909	WARNE	76	61	98	60	67	80	61	77	64	57	63	56	53	60	66	68	42	71	76	90
	NORTH CAROLINA	100	89	90	89	88	96	91	94	94	91	93	73	85	95	88	96	64	93	96	112
	UNITED STATES	100	100	100	100	100	100	100	100	100	100	100	100	100	100	100	100	100	100	100	100

POPULATION CHANGE

ZIP CODE #	POST OFFICE NAME	COUNTY FIPS CODE	POPULATION 2000	POPULATION 2009	POPULATION 2014	2000-2009 ANNUAL RATE % Rate	2000-2009 ANNUAL RATE State Centile	HOUSEHOLDS 2000	HOUSEHOLDS 2009	HOUSEHOLDS 2014	HOUSEHOLDS % Annual Rate 2000-2009	HOUSEHOLDS 2009 Average HH Size	FAMILIES 2000	FAMILIES 2009	FAMILIES % Annual Rate 2000-2009
58004	AMENIA	017	279	318	344	1.4	98	106	133	147	2.5	2.37	80	95	1.9
58005	ARGUSVILLE	017	463	509	545	1.0	97	183	221	241	2.1	2.30	143	161	1.3
58006	ARTHUR	017	506	488	490	-0.4	66	164	169	173	0.3	2.70	112	105	-0.7
58007	AYR	017	142	142	144	0.0	82	62	66	69	0.7	2.09	45	44	-0.2
58008	BARNEY	077	301	294	288	-0.3	71	104	107	106	0.3	2.75	78	77	-0.1
58009	BLANCHARD	097	90	84	81	-0.7	50	36	35	34	-0.3	2.40	27	26	-0.4
58011	BUFFALO	017	429	461	484	0.8	95	176	203	218	1.6	2.27	126	135	0.7
58012	CASSELTON	017	2038	2288	2484	1.3	98	777	934	1033	2.0	2.45	558	616	1.1
58013	CAYUGA	081	205	186	180	-1.0	24	82	79	77	-0.4	2.35	58	54	-0.8
58015	CHRISTINE	077	362	396	396	1.0	97	131	149	151	1.4	2.66	104	113	0.9
58016	CLIFFORD	097	108	101	97	-0.7	50	46	45	44	-0.2	2.24	35	33	-0.6
58017	COGSWELL	081	478	489	485	0.2	88	198	214	215	0.8	2.29	146	151	0.4
58018	COLFAX	077	380	375	369	-0.1	77	137	142	141	0.4	2.63	102	102	0.0
58021	DAVENPORT	017	450	459	473	0.2	88	158	173	182	1.0	2.65	125	128	0.3
58027	ENDERLIN	073	1458	1457	1443	0.0	82	604	632	632	0.5	2.22	385	380	-0.1
58029	ERIE	017	163	157	158	-0.4	66	62	64	65	0.3	2.30	43	40	-0.8
58030	FAIRMOUNT	077	748	741	730	-0.1	77	303	319	319	0.6	2.32	209	210	0.1
58031	FINGAL	017	502	468	457	-0.8	39	195	193	191	-0.1	2.42	148	138	-0.8
58032	FORMAN	081	755	717	698	-0.6	55	311	310	305	0.0	2.22	202	192	-0.5
58033	FORT RANSOM	073	479	471	462	-0.2	74	194	200	199	0.3	2.36	149	149	0.0
58035	GALESBURG	097	377	355	344	-0.6	55	146	144	141	-0.1	2.44	109	104	-0.5
58036	GARDNER	017	348	377	401	0.9	96	135	161	174	1.9	2.34	101	112	1.1
58038	GRANDIN	017	252	272	289	0.8	95	99	117	127	1.8	2.32	74	81	1.0
58040	GWINNER	081	909	907	896	0.0	82	374	396	396	0.6	2.29	264	267	0.1
58041	HANKINSON	077	1767	1659	1628	-0.7	50	698	716	710	0.3	2.22	444	430	-0.3
58042	HARWOOD	017	1305	1489	1638	1.4	98	428	531	596	2.4	2.80	373	443	1.9
58043	HAVANA	081	232	214	207	-0.9	32	95	93	91	-0.2	2.30	66	61	-0.8
58045	HILLSBORO	097	2401	2392	2336	0.0	82	984	1026	1011	0.5	2.27	655	647	-0.1
58046	HOPE	091	679	641	630	-0.6	55	273	266	262	-0.3	2.41	189	176	-0.8
58047	HORACE	017	2683	3689	4138	3.5	99	893	1330	1525	4.4	2.77	772	1136	4.3
58048	HUNTER	017	476	457	458	-0.4	66	200	204	209	0.2	2.09	136	127	-0.7
58049	KATHRYN	003	282	269	261	-0.5	60	115	115	112	0.0	2.34	89	86	-0.4
58051	KINDRED	017	1337	1476	1567	1.1	97	487	575	624	1.8	2.57	366	404	1.1
58052	LEONARD	017	664	657	664	-0.1	77	281	297	306	0.6	2.21	218	216	-0.1
58053	LIDGERWOOD	077	1348	1339	1308	-0.1	77	581	589	582	0.1	2.22	381	366	-0.4
58054	LISBON	073	3377	3396	3362	0.1	85	1355	1436	1433	0.6	2.22	882	887	0.1
58056	LUVERNE	091	240	229	226	-0.5	60	94	94	93	0.0	2.44	65	63	-0.3
58057	MCLEOD	073	137	135	133	-0.2	74	56	57	57	0.2	2.37	42	42	0.0
58058	MANTADOR	077	149	144	141	-0.4	66	64	66	65	0.3	2.18	41	39	-0.5
58059	MAPLETON	017	987	1051	1141	0.7	94	338	397	440	1.8	2.65	274	304	1.1
58060	MILNOR	081	1457	1405	1375	-0.4	66	553	557	551	0.1	2.52	384	370	-0.4
58061	MOORETON	077	418	407	400	-0.3	71	169	175	174	0.4	2.31	117	115	-0.2
58062	NOME	003	213	200	192	-0.7	50	85	83	81	-0.3	2.41	64	60	-0.7
58063	ORISKA	003	370	365	359	-0.1	77	134	140	139	0.5	2.61	105	106	0.1
58064	PAGE	017	515	527	541	0.2	88	209	228	240	0.9	2.31	157	160	0.2
58067	RUTLAND	081	316	295	286	-0.7	50	132	130	127	-0.2	2.27	93	88	-0.6
58068	SHELDON	073	372	368	361	-0.1	77	143	146	145	0.2	2.52	104	103	-0.1
58069	STIRUM	081	141	151	152	0.7	94	62	71	72	1.5	2.13	47	52	1.1
58071	TOWER CITY	017	412	438	457	0.7	94	168	192	204	1.5	2.28	122	130	0.7
58072	VALLEY CITY	003	8329	7890	7628	-0.6	55	3535	3512	3423	-0.1	2.08	2104	1971	-0.7
58075	WAHPETON	077	10003	9198	8944	-0.9	32	3946	3905	3836	-0.1	2.21	2390	2230	-0.7
58076	WAHPETON	077	487	390	389	-2.4	1	5	5	5	0.0	2.60	2	2	0.0
58077	WALCOTT	077	667	710	708	0.7	94	247	274	277	1.1	2.59	194	207	0.7
58078	WEST FARGO	017	15880	21985	24718	3.6	100	6070	8767	9948	4.1	2.51	4201	5721	3.4
58079	WHEATLAND	017	543	635	677	1.7	99	203	259	281	2.7	2.45	156	186	1.9
58081	WYNDMERE	077	985	965	943	-0.2	74	375	384	380	0.3	2.51	265	258	-0.3
58102	FARGO	017	31907	31896	32413	0.0	82	13190	14073	14617	0.7	2.01	6674	6392	-0.5
58103	FARGO	017	46792	47807	49579	0.2	88	21502	23813	25216	1.1	1.97	11092	10790	-0.3
58104	FARGO	017	14654	23809	27661	5.4	100	5434	9821	11640	6.6	2.40	3888	6787	6.2
58201	GRAND FORKS	035	32568	32033	31276	-0.2	74	13797	14270	14107	0.4	2.19	8027	7901	-0.2
58203	GRAND FORKS	035	18668	20374	20121	0.9	96	6553	6921	6894	0.6	2.21	3566	3530	-0.1
58204	GRAND FORKS AFB	035	1384	1139	1064	-2.1	2	233	177	164	-2.9	5.25	224	169	-3.0
58205	GRAND FORKS AFB	035	3444	2835	2647	-2.1	2	1045	794	736	-2.9	2.91	1005	759	-3.0
58210	ADAMS	099	429	384	366	-1.2	14	174	166	160	-0.5	2.31	123	112	-1.0
58212	ANETA	063	569	535	519	-0.7	50	229	229	225	0.0	2.23	147	140	-0.5
58214	ARVILLA	035	426	396	384	-0.8	39	171	171	168	0.0	2.32	117	112	-0.5
58216	BATHGATE	067	165	150	144	-1.0	24	70	67	65	-0.5	2.24	49	45	-0.9
58218	BUXTON	097	738	699	673	-0.6	55	278	275	267	-0.1	2.54	213	203	-0.5
58219	CALEDONIA	097	132	123	119	-0.8	39	47	47	45	0.0	2.62	37	35	-0.6
58220	CAVALIER	067	2705	2682	2653	-0.1	77	1110	1173	1175	0.6	2.22	727	731	0.1
58222	CRYSTAL	067	361	336	327	-0.8	39	147	146	144	-0.1	2.13	98	93	-0.6
58223	CUMMINGS	097	251	237	228	-0.6	55	102	101	98	-0.1	2.35	77	73	-0.6
58224	DAHLEN	063	62	58	56	-0.7	50	27	27	26	0.0	2.15	19	18	-0.6
58225	DRAYTON	067	1167	1053	1010	-1.1	19	512	491	478	-0.5	2.14	328	299	-1.0
58227	EDINBURG	099	581	524	502	-1.1	19	262	252	244	-0.4	2.04	180	165	-0.9
58228	EMERADO	035	1058	1054	1039	0.0	82	434	461	460	0.7	2.29	320	325	0.2
58229	FAIRDALE	099	149	133	127	-1.2	14	67	64	61	-0.5	2.08	47	42	-1.2
58230	FINLEY	091	1297	1228	1210	-0.6	55	532	521	515	-0.2	2.36	370	347	-0.7
58231	FORDVILLE	099	563	517	498	-0.9	32	218	215	210	-0.1	2.40	149	140	-0.7
58233	FOREST RIVER	099	350	344	340	-0.2	74	131	140	140	0.7	2.46	90	92	0.2
58235	GILBY	035	418	390	378	-0.7	50	163	161	157	-0.1	2.42	123	117	-0.5
58237	GRAFTON	099	5963	5461	5258	-0.9	32	2338	2259	2201	-0.4	2.29	1515	1393	-0.9
58238	HAMILTON	067	205	186	178	-1.0	24	86	83	80	-0.4	2.24	60	55	-0.9
58239	HANNAH	019	73	59	54	-2.3	1	38	33	31	-1.5	1.79	26	22	-1.8
58240	HATTON	097	1087	1092	1069	0.0	82	422	437	432	0.4	2.34	295	292	-0.1
58241	HENSEL	067	168	161	159	-0.5	60	75	78	77	0.4	2.04	58	58	0.0
58243	HOOPLE	099	623	551	527	-1.3	9	273	261	253	-0.5	2.10	185	169	-1.0
58244	INKSTER	035	372	347	336	-0.7	50	147	145	142	-0.1	2.39	111	105	-0.6
58249	LANGDON	019	3000	2630	2451	-1.4	7	1264	1173	1105	-0.8	2.16	823	726	-1.3
58250	LANKIN	099	351	316	301	-1.1	19	150	144	140	-0.4	2.19	110	102	-0.8
58251	LARIMORE	035	2166	2064	2004	-0.5	60	855	854	839	0.0	2.35	591	564	-0.5
58254	MCVILLE	063	743	694	670	-0.7	50	330	325	318	-0.2	1.97	183	168	-0.9
58255	MAIDA	019	78	64	59	-2.1	2	30	27	25	-1.1	2.37	23	20	-1.5
58256	MANVEL	035	1000	1066	1064	0.7	94	351	397	402	1.3	2.69	264	287	0.9
58257	MAYVILLE	097	2209	2231	2171	0.1	85	846	841	820	-0.1	2.13	486	455	-0.7
	NORTH DAKOTA					0.2					0.8	2.27			0.2
	UNITED STATES					1.0					1.1	2.59			0.9

ZIP CODE #	POST OFFICE NAME	RACE (%) White 2000	White 2009	Black 2000	Black 2009	Asian/Pacific 2000	Asian/Pacific 2009	% Hispanic Origin 2000	% Hispanic Origin 2009	2009 AGE DISTRIBUTION (%) 0-4	5-9	10-14	15-19	20-24	25-44	45-64	65-84	85+	18+	MEDIAN AGE 2009	% 2009 Males	% 2009 Females
58004	AMENIA	97.8	96.5	0.0	0.3	0.4	0.9	1.1	1.3	5.7	6.0	6.9	7.2	4.4	20.8	32.7	14.2	2.2	76.7	44.3	54.1	45.9
58005	ARGUSVILLE	99.6	99.4	0.0	0.0	0.0	0.0	0.6	1.2	5.5	6.1	6.7	6.9	4.7	22.6	34.4	11.8	1.4	77.2	43.3	51.1	48.9
58006	ARTHUR	97.6	96.7	0.0	0.0	0.0	0.2	2.0	3.3	5.9	5.9	7.0	8.0	4.1	19.7	26.6	17.2	5.5	74.8	44.6	50.0	50.0
58007	AYR	98.6	98.6	0.0	0.0	0.0	0.0	1.4	2.1	5.6	6.3	7.0	7.7	3.5	20.4	28.9	16.9	3.5	75.4	44.5	50.7	49.3
58008	BARNEY	99.0	99.0	0.0	0.0	0.0	0.0	0.3	0.0	5.4	7.1	9.5	8.8	3.7	22.4	26.5	13.6	2.7	72.1	40.8	52.4	47.6
58009	BLANCHARD	100.0	98.8	0.0	0.0	0.0	0.0	0.0	0.0	6.0	6.0	6.0	7.1	3.6	21.4	34.5	13.1	2.4	78.6	45.0	57.1	42.9
58011	BUFFALO	99.1	98.9	0.0	0.0	0.0	0.0	0.5	0.7	5.2	5.9	6.5	6.9	4.1	21.0	32.8	15.2	2.4	78.1	45.2	51.4	48.6
58012	CASSELTON	98.2	97.5	0.1	0.2	0.2	0.3	0.5	0.8	8.3	7.8	8.0	7.7	5.9	24.3	26.1	9.8	1.8	71.0	36.4	52.1	47.9
58013	CAYUGA	98.5	98.4	0.0	0.0	0.0	0.0	0.0	0.0	4.3	5.9	5.9	7.0	4.3	21.5	33.3	15.6	2.2	80.1	45.7	55.4	44.6
58015	CHRISTINE	99.7	98.7	0.0	0.3	0.0	0.3	0.6	0.8	7.6	7.1	9.1	8.1	3.0	26.3	27.0	9.6	2.3	70.2	39.0	52.0	48.0
58016	CLIFFORD	100.0	99.0	0.0	0.0	0.0	0.0	0.0	0.0	5.0	6.9	6.9	7.9	5.0	22.8	31.7	11.9	2.0	76.2	42.2	54.5	45.5
58017	COGSWELL	98.1	97.5	0.0	0.0	0.2	0.2	1.0	1.6	6.1	6.7	7.4	7.4	3.7	21.7	30.9	13.9	2.2	75.1	42.8	53.2	46.8
58018	COLFAX	98.7	98.1	0.3	0.3	0.0	0.3	0.3	0.3	6.9	7.7	8.3	7.2	4.3	22.4	28.8	12.5	1.9	72.0	40.6	52.3	47.7
58021	DAVENPORT	99.1	98.3	0.0	0.0	0.7	1.1	0.4	0.9	5.9	6.5	7.2	7.4	4.4	22.9	32.9	10.7	2.2	75.8	42.0	51.4	48.6
58027	ENDERLIN	96.9	96.8	0.3	0.3	0.3	0.3	1.8	1.9	5.8	6.1	6.2	6.1	4.7	20.2	29.5	16.6	4.7	77.8	45.5	50.9	49.1
58029	ERIE	97.5	97.5	0.0	0.0	0.0	0.0	1.8	3.2	5.7	6.4	6.4	7.6	4.5	19.7	27.4	17.2	5.1	75.2	44.8	51.0	49.0
58030	FAIRMOUNT	96.9	96.0	0.0	0.0	0.0	0.0	1.9	2.7	5.7	6.6	7.2	7.2	4.3	22.7	32.3	12.4	1.8	76.1	42.5	50.9	49.1
58031	FINGAL	99.0	98.7	0.0	0.0	0.0	0.0	0.6	0.9	6.4	7.3	7.7	6.2	4.3	19.2	32.9	13.2	2.8	74.6	44.1	53.0	47.0
58032	FORMAN	97.9	97.4	0.1	0.1	0.0	0.0	1.1	1.7	5.2	5.3	6.6	6.0	4.0	20.1	31.7	17.2	4.0	79.6	46.9	52.4	47.6
58033	FORT RANSOM	97.9	97.9	0.2	0.2	0.4	0.4	0.8	0.8	6.4	7.0	7.2	6.2	4.2	22.9	29.9	14.4	1.7	75.4	42.1	52.4	47.6
58035	GALESBURG	98.7	98.0	0.0	0.0	0.0	0.3	0.5	1.1	5.9	6.5	6.8	7.6	4.5	21.4	31.3	14.1	2.0	75.8	43.2	54.1	45.9
58036	GARDNER	100.0	99.5	0.0	0.0	0.0	0.0	0.9	1.3	5.0	5.8	6.1	6.6	4.8	22.5	34.0	13.3	1.9	78.5	44.3	50.7	49.3
58038	GRANDIN	100.0	99.6	0.0	0.0	0.0	0.0	0.8	1.1	5.1	5.9	5.9	6.3	4.8	21.7	34.6	14.0	1.8	78.7	45.2	51.5	48.5
58040	GWINNER	98.8	98.6	0.0	0.0	0.0	0.0	0.7	1.0	6.4	6.4	7.2	7.8	5.0	26.5	28.0	11.0	1.8	75.1	38.6	52.3	47.7
58041	HANKINSON	97.2	96.7	0.0	0.0	0.2	0.3	1.0	1.4	5.4	6.0	6.3	6.1	4.9	20.4	28.7	16.0	6.1	78.1	45.6	49.6	50.4
58042	HARWOOD	98.9	98.4	0.0	0.1	0.0	0.0	0.8	1.3	6.9	7.6	8.3	8.1	5.2	24.2	32.2	7.1	0.5	72.2	38.2	50.6	49.4
58043	HAVANA	97.4	97.2	0.0	0.0	0.0	0.0	0.0	0.0	3.3	4.7	6.5	7.9	3.7	22.0	30.4	18.2	3.3	80.4	46.1	55.1	44.9
58045	HILLSBORO	95.6	94.1	0.1	0.1	0.0	0.0	4.3	6.4	6.5	6.9	7.7	6.7	4.4	21.4	28.7	13.6	4.1	74.2	42.2	50.9	49.1
58046	HOPE	98.7	98.4	0.1	0.2	0.1	0.2	0.3	0.5	6.2	7.2	7.3	7.2	5.0	19.5	30.9	14.8	1.9	74.9	43.0	51.5	48.5
58047	HORACE	99.1	98.8	0.0	0.0	0.1	0.3	0.3	0.6	7.6	8.1	8.4	8.2	5.3	24.8	30.1	6.8	0.7	70.7	36.6	49.6	50.4
58048	HUNTER	97.7	96.7	0.0	0.0	0.0	0.2	2.1	3.5	5.9	6.1	6.8	7.9	4.4	19.3	26.7	17.3	5.7	74.6	44.8	50.1	49.9
58049	KATHRYN	98.9	98.9	0.0	0.0	0.0	0.0	0.4	0.4	5.6	6.7	6.7	6.7	4.5	20.1	33.5	14.1	2.2	76.6	44.8	52.0	48.0
58051	KINDRED	98.9	98.4	0.1	0.2	0.1	0.2	0.7	1.1	7.5	7.5	8.0	7.6	5.5	24.3	28.5	9.6	1.6	72.2	38.1	50.2	49.8
58052	LEONARD	98.8	98.2	0.2	0.2	0.5	0.8	0.5	0.9	6.5	7.0	7.3	7.0	4.1	21.9	32.1	11.9	2.1	74.9	42.2	51.9	48.1
58053	LIDGERWOOD	97.7	96.7	0.0	0.1	0.2	0.3	0.4	0.7	5.4	6.0	5.8	6.1	5.5	19.6	30.3	17.6	3.9	79.6	46.0	53.5	46.5
58054	LISBON	98.4	98.4	0.1	0.1	0.2	0.2	0.6	0.5	5.5	5.7	5.9	6.1	4.8	22.5	28.8	16.2	4.5	78.7	44.6	52.1	47.9
58056	LUVERNE	99.2	99.1	0.0	0.0	0.0	0.0	0.4	0.4	6.1	6.6	7.0	7.0	4.8	20.1	31.4	15.3	1.7	75.1	43.8	51.5	48.5
58057	MCLEOD	98.5	98.5	0.0	0.0	0.0	0.0	0.0	0.0	6.7	8.1	8.9	8.1	3.7	21.5	28.1	13.3	1.5	71.1	39.7	51.9	48.1
58058	MANTADOR	97.3	96.5	0.0	0.0	0.0	0.0	0.7	0.7	6.3	6.3	6.3	6.3	4.9	22.2	31.3	13.2	3.5	77.8	43.5	52.1	47.9
58059	MAPLETON	98.6	97.6	0.1	0.2	0.2	0.4	1.4	2.5	6.9	7.2	7.7	8.3	5.8	26.9	29.0	7.2	0.9	73.0	35.7	49.9	50.1
58060	MILNOR	98.1	97.7	0.1	0.1	0.0	0.0	0.8	1.1	6.3	6.8	7.1	7.5	4.4	21.6	29.8	14.2	2.3	75.1	42.2	52.5	47.5
58061	MOORETON	98.1	97.5	0.2	0.2	0.0	0.2	0.5	0.7	5.9	6.6	7.6	7.1	4.2	23.3	30.7	12.3	2.2	74.9	42.0	53.3	46.7
58062	NOME	98.6	98.5	0.0	0.0	0.0	0.0	0.5	0.5	6.5	7.0	7.5	6.0	4.5	21.0	30.5	14.0	3.0	75.0	42.7	52.0	48.0
58063	ORISKA	97.8	97.3	0.0	0.0	0.0	0.3	0.5	0.8	5.5	6.8	8.2	7.7	4.4	20.5	34.8	10.7	1.4	74.0	42.9	53.7	46.3
58064	PAGE	99.2	99.1	0.0	0.0	0.0	0.0	1.2	1.9	5.7	6.1	6.6	7.0	3.8	20.3	31.7	16.3	2.5	77.4	45.3	51.2	48.8
58067	RUTLAND	98.4	98.3	0.0	0.0	0.0	0.0	0.0	0.0	4.1	4.4	6.1	8.5	4.4	20.7	31.9	16.9	3.1	80.3	46.3	54.6	45.4
58068	SHELDON	98.1	98.1	0.5	0.5	0.0	0.0	0.0	0.0	7.9	7.9	7.9	8.7	4.6	21.7	26.1	13.6	1.6	71.5	38.4	50.5	49.5
58069	STIRUM	98.6	97.4	0.0	0.0	0.0	0.0	1.4	2.6	7.3	7.9	7.9	6.6	4.0	23.2	29.8	11.9	1.3	72.8	40.2	53.0	47.0
58071	TOWER CITY	98.8	98.9	0.0	0.0	0.0	0.0	0.2	0.7	5.0	5.9	6.6	7.1	4.1	20.5	34.0	14.6	2.1	78.3	45.4	52.1	47.9
58072	VALLEY CITY	97.6	96.9	0.6	0.7	0.2	0.4	0.7	1.1	5.0	4.5	5.1	8.3	8.6	21.3	26.4	15.7	5.1	81.8	42.5	48.5	51.5
58075	WAHPETON	96.2	95.0	0.4	0.5	0.4	0.7	0.7	1.1	6.4	5.9	5.8	10.2	11.3	23.9	23.9	10.4	2.2	77.9	33.5	51.8	48.2
58076	WAHPETON	91.6	88.7	3.3	4.4	0.2	0.5	0.8	1.0	0.5	0.5	1.5	42.1	29.5	6.2	4.6	6.4	8.7	97.2	20.9	66.2	33.8
58077	WALCOTT	99.2	98.7	0.2	0.3	0.0	0.1	0.5	0.7	7.6	7.2	9.0	7.9	3.5	25.4	27.3	10.0	2.1	70.3	38.9	51.7	48.3
58078	WEST FARGO	96.4	95.3	0.5	0.5	0.4	0.8	1.4	2.1	8.1	7.3	6.7	6.6	7.5	33.3	23.6	6.2	0.7	74.0	32.4	49.3	50.7
58079	WHEATLAND	98.5	97.8	0.0	0.2	0.4	0.6	0.7	1.1	5.8	6.6	7.1	6.6	4.3	20.5	33.9	13.5	1.7	76.2	44.4	54.6	45.4
58081	WYNDMERE	98.5	97.8	0.0	0.0	0.1	0.3	0.7	1.0	6.2	7.0	7.9	7.5	4.7	22.1	28.9	13.5	2.3	74.1	41.2	52.2	47.8
58102	FARGO	93.7	90.8	0.7	1.0	2.3	3.9	1.4	2.1	4.9	4.5	4.7	11.2	16.5	25.7	21.8	8.8	1.8	82.7	30.1	52.3	47.7
58103	FARGO	94.0	91.6	1.3	1.7	1.3	2.2	1.4	2.1	6.6	5.4	4.8	5.6	12.8	33.3	21.2	8.4	1.9	80.4	31.5	49.2	50.8
58104	FARGO	96.7	95.8	0.5	0.5	1.3	2.0	0.8	1.4	8.6	8.2	7.9	7.1	6.4	32.1	23.3	5.2	1.3	70.9	32.3	48.9	51.1
58201	GRAND FORKS	94.9	93.1	0.7	0.9	0.8	1.4	1.5	2.4	6.0	5.6	5.6	6.5	10.2	29.6	24.2	10.0	2.3	79.1	34.1	50.2	49.8
58203	GRAND FORKS	90.8	88.0	1.1	1.5	1.3	2.1	2.5	3.7	5.4	4.6	4.1	17.0	23.1	24.7	14.9	5.1	1.2	83.3	24.1	51.9	48.1
58204	GRAND FORKS AFB	80.9	75.3	8.4	10.5	2.7	4.1	6.0	9.0	13.5	10.7	8.3	9.6	21.3	34.9	1.7	0.0	0.0	63.7	21.9	56.4	43.6
58205	GRAND FORKS AFB	80.9	75.4	8.4	10.5	2.7	4.1	6.0	9.0	13.5	10.7	8.2	9.6	21.0	35.0	1.8	0.1	0.0	63.6	21.9	56.1	43.9
58210	ADAMS	97.0	96.1	0.2	0.3	0.0	0.0	2.1	3.6	4.9	5.7	6.0	5.7	3.9	19.5	33.3	16.9	3.9	79.7	47.4	51.8	48.2
58212	ANETA	98.6	97.8	0.2	0.4	0.4	0.6	0.2	0.4	4.7	5.4	5.6	6.2	4.1	17.8	32.1	18.9	5.2	79.6	49.1	52.0	48.0
58214	ARVILLA	96.0	94.4	1.6	2.3	0.2	0.5	1.9	3.5	4.3	4.5	4.8	5.6	7.3	27.8	31.8	12.6	1.3	83.1	41.7	55.8	44.2
58216	BATHGATE	97.6	97.3	0.0	0.0	0.0	0.0	3.0	4.7	4.7	5.3	5.3	6.0	4.7	24.0	32.0	14.7	3.3	81.3	45.0	53.3	46.7
58218	BUXTON	98.4	97.9	0.0	0.0	0.1	0.1	2.0	3.0	6.7	7.6	7.7	6.7	3.7	24.2	28.9	12.6	1.9	73.8	41.1	50.5	49.5
58219	CALEDONIA	97.0	95.1	0.0	0.0	0.0	0.0	3.8	6.5	5.7	6.5	8.1	8.9	3.3	21.1	32.5	13.0	0.8	72.4	42.8	53.7	46.3
58220	CAVALIER	95.6	94.0	0.3	0.4	0.4	0.7	2.8	4.5	5.2	5.2	5.7	6.3	6.3	21.4	30.8	14.8	4.3	80.1	44.9	49.3	50.7
58222	CRYSTAL	96.4	95.2	0.3	0.3	0.0	0.3	1.1	1.8	5.1	6.0	6.3	7.1	4.8	19.9	31.5	14.3	5.1	78.3	45.6	51.8	48.2
58223	CUMMINGS	98.4	97.5	0.0	0.0	0.0	0.4	1.6	2.5	6.3	7.6	7.6	6.8	3.8	24.5	29.5	12.2	1.7	73.4	41.3	50.2	49.8
58224	DAHLEN	98.4	98.3	0.0	0.0	0.0	0.0	0.0	0.0	5.2	5.2	5.2	6.9	3.4	17.2	34.5	19.0	3.4	77.6	47.9	56.9	43.1
58225	DRAYTON	97.3	96.6	0.0	0.0	0.0	0.0	3.6	5.5	5.2	5.3	5.7	6.4	6.1	23.5	30.8	14.2	2.9	79.8	43.3	51.4	48.6
58227	EDINBURG	96.4	95.4	0.3	0.4	0.2	0.2	2.1	3.2	4.8	5.5	6.1	6.3	4.2	19.8	32.1	16.8	4.4	79.6	47.1	51.0	49.0
58228	EMERADO	92.1	89.4	1.4	1.9	0.9	1.4	2.6	4.1	5.2	5.6	6.6	7.5	5.5	27.6	31.7	9.5	0.8	78.0	39.8	52.5	47.5
58229	FAIRDALE	97.3	96.2	0.0	0.0	0.0	0.0	2.0	3.8	4.5	5.3	6.0	6.0	4.5	21.1	30.8	18.0	3.8	80.5	46.6	50.4	49.6
58230	FINLEY	97.9	97.5	0.0	0.0	0.0	0.0	0.2	0.2	5.4	6.1	6.6	6.6	4.5	20.2	30.5	17.3	2.9	77.8	45.4	51.1	48.9
58231	FORDVILLE	97.3	96.3	0.2	0.4	0.2	0.4	0.9	1.5	5.6	6.2	6.4	6.0	4.3	20.5	31.7	17.0	2.3	77.9	45.6	51.8	48.2
58233	FOREST RIVER	98.6	97.7	0.0	0.0	0.3	0.3	4.0	6.7	6.4	7.0	7.0	6.4	4.7	21.5	31.1	14.0	2.0	75.3	42.6	52.0	48.0
58235	GILBY	97.6	96.2	0.2	0.5	0.7	1.3	1.0	1.8	5.4	6.2	6.2	5.6	5.1	24.9	31.8	13.3	1.5	79.0	42.8	51.0	49.0
58237	GRAFTON	93.0	90.4	0.4	0.6	0.4	0.5	8.4	12.6	5.8	6.0	6.6	6.5	5.5	23.4	28.7	13.9	3.6	77.2	41.8	49.2	50.8
58238	HAMILTON	96.6	95.7	0.0	0.0	0.0	0.0	6.8	10.2	4.8	5.9	5.9	6.5	4.8	23.1	30.6	15.6	2.7	79.0	44.1	52.2	47.8
58239	HANNAH	98.6	98.3	0.0	0.0	0.0	0.0	0.0	0.0	5.1	5.1	6.8	5.1	3.4	16.9	37.3	18.6	1.7	78.0	50.6	61.0	39.0
58240	HATTON	96.9	96.0	0.1	0.1	0.5	0.7	2.6	3.8	6.0	6.1	6.5	6.5	5.2	20.2	26.8	16.4	6.1	76.7	44.5	48.4	51.6
58241	HENSEL	97.0	96.3	0.0	0.0	0.6	0.6	1.2	1.2	4.3	5.6	5.6	6.8	5.6	21.7	36.0	12.4	1.9	80.1	45.2	52.2	47.8
58243	HOOPLE	97.6	96.6	0.2	0.2	0.2	0.2	3.4	5.4	5.4	6.2	6.5	6.2	4.4	22.0	33.8	13.1	2.5	77.9	44.5	51.4	48.6
58244	INKSTER	97.6	96.3	0.3	0.6	0.8	1.2	1.1	1.7	5.2	6.1	6.1	5.8	4.9	25.1	31.7	13.5	1.7	79.3	43.1	50.4	49.6
58249	LANGDON	98.4	98.1	0.1	0.2	0.1	0.2	0.7	1.0	4.2	4.6	5.2	7.0	4.7	17.4	32.1	19.1	5.7	81.3	49.3	49.2	50.8
58250	LANKIN	97.7	96.8	0.3	0.3	0.0	0.0	1.7	2.2	6.0	6.6	6.6	5.4	4.7	19.9	30.7	17.1	2.8	77.8	45.3	51.9	48.1
58251	LARIMORE	96.4	95.2	0.6	0.9	0.6	0.9	0.9	1.6	5.9	5.8	5.9	6.3	6.3	21.5	30.2	14.4	3.7	78.0	43.8	49.3	50.7
58254	MCVILLE	99.7	99.6	0.0	0.0	0.1	0.1	0.0	0.0	4.0	4.2	4.6	5.8	5.3	18.4	29.1	19.3	9.2	82.4	51.5	48.8	51.2
58255	MAIDA	98.7	98.4	0.0	0.0	0.0	0.0	0.0	0.0	4.7	6.3	6.3	9.4	1.6	20.3	35.9	12.5	3.1	73.4	45.8	51.6	48.4
58256	MANVEL	97.3	96.2	0.9	1.1	0.0	0.1	1.2	2.1	5.4	7.9	7.5	7.9	5.3	26.5	29.3	9.1	1.1	73.7	38.7	52.7	47.3
58257	MAYVILLE	97.7	96.8	0.2	0.3	0.3	0.4	0.6	0.9	4.4	4.4	4.5	11.5	11.5	21.9	21.2	13.8	6.8	83.1	35.3	48.5	51.5
	NORTH DAKOTA	92.4	90.8	0.6	0.7	0.6	1.0	1.2	1.8	6.3	6.1	6.2	7.7	8.3	25.2	26.0	11.6	2.7	77.3	36.9	50.0	50.0
	UNITED STATES	75.1	72.0	12.3	12.7	3.8	4.6	12.5	15.7	6.8	6.7	6.6	7.1	6.9	27.0	26.0	10.9	1.9	75.7	36.9	49.2	50.8

#	POST OFFICE NAME	2009 Per Capita Income	2009 HH Income Base	2009 Household Income Distribution (%): Less than $25,000	$25,000 to $49,999	$50,000 to $99,999	$100,000 to $149,999	$150,000 or More	Median Household Income: 2009	2014	2009 National Centile	2009 State Centile	2009 Home Value Base	2009 Home Value Distribution (%): Less than $50,000	$50,000 to $89,999	$90,000 to $174,999	$175,000 to $399,999	$400,000 or More	2009 Median Home Value
58004	AMENIA	24603	133	21.8	24.8	45.9	4.5	3.0	52579	55311	67	91	108	20.4	18.5	34.3	23.1	3.7	116667
58005	ARGUSVILLE	26801	221	13.1	24.4	51.6	8.1	2.7	59782	60234	77	96	196	19.4	20.9	37.2	20.9	1.5	112500
58006	ARTHUR	19027	169	24.3	26.0	44.4	3.6	1.8	49462	50692	60	84	128	39.1	28.1	21.9	8.6	2.3	66364
58007	AYR	22131	66	25.8	30.3	40.9	1.5	1.5	42351	46174	40	65	52	42.3	25.0	25.0	7.7	0.0	65000
58008	BARNEY	22120	107	19.6	30.8	40.2	5.6	3.7	49541	50665	60	85	96	17.7	20.8	45.8	13.5	2.1	110714
58009	BLANCHARD	23810	35	5.7	34.3	51.4	8.6	0.0	53589	53070	69	94	30	33.3	13.3	33.3	20.0	0.0	100000
58011	BUFFALO	21422	203	22.7	36.0	36.5	3.0	2.0	42802	43541	42	66	168	33.9	17.9	39.3	8.3	0.6	87692
58012	CASSELTON	23958	934	21.0	24.6	46.3	5.9	2.2	53210	55072	68	93	672	9.4	24.7	44.8	20.8	0.3	123750
58013	CAYUGA	23451	79	25.3	32.9	32.9	6.3	2.5	41920	43041	39	63	70	38.6	21.4	28.6	10.0	1.4	72500
58015	CHRISTINE	25582	149	13.4	24.2	47.7	10.1	4.7	61741	61468	80	98	135	14.1	15.6	40.7	28.1	1.5	141406
58016	CLIFFORD	28321	45	11.1	33.3	44.4	8.9	2.2	52199	52925	66	90	38	34.2	13.2	34.2	18.4	0.0	100000
58017	COGSWELL	22965	214	23.4	34.1	36.4	4.7	1.4	43823	45416	45	69	178	40.4	21.9	28.1	8.4	1.1	66667
58018	COLFAX	21806	142	18.3	28.9	44.4	6.3	2.1	52126	52860	66	90	123	20.3	15.4	36.6	26.0	1.6	124038
58021	DAVENPORT	22618	173	15.0	30.1	45.7	6.4	2.9	53179	54416	68	93	144	22.9	18.8	39.6	17.4	1.4	108333
58027	ENDERLIN	23882	632	28.2	30.5	32.4	4.9	4.0	42853	45473	42	67	477	36.1	25.2	29.1	9.0	0.6	69848
58029	ERIE	22125	64	23.4	26.6	43.8	4.7	1.6	50000	50387	61	87	49	42.9	26.5	20.4	10.2	0.0	63750
58030	FAIRMOUNT	22527	319	23.8	31.0	37.3	7.2	0.6	47059	47440	54	79	260	30.0	22.7	30.8	12.3	4.2	85333
58031	FINGAL	20922	193	24.9	32.1	37.3	3.6	2.1	45157	46340	49	72	173	45.7	20.2	22.5	9.8	1.7	56818
58032	FORMAN	24932	310	28.1	25.2	36.5	7.4	2.9	46929	47340	54	77	231	25.5	21.6	37.2	13.4	2.2	98125
58033	FORT RANSOM	22961	200	21.5	28.0	42.0	6.5	2.0	50269	49849	62	87	174	15.5	20.1	41.4	22.4	0.6	115323
58035	GALESBURG	25272	144	11.1	32.6	45.1	9.0	2.1	52719	52640	67	92	121	34.7	14.9	33.9	15.7	0.8	91250
58036	GARDNER	23697	161	16.1	28.6	49.7	4.3	1.2	52998	54018	68	92	140	25.7	25.7	30.7	16.4	1.4	88333
58038	GRANDIN	23901	117	17.1	28.2	48.7	4.3	1.7	52543	54132	67	91	101	27.7	25.7	28.7	15.8	2.0	86111
58040	GWINNER	24374	396	17.2	29.5	46.0	5.3	2.0	51485	50811	65	88	302	21.2	22.5	40.4	15.2	0.7	104605
58041	HANKINSON	20203	716	31.1	28.9	34.2	4.7	1.0	41058	44291	36	56	588	27.6	30.4	31.0	10.4	0.7	78627
58042	HARWOOD	27121	531	5.5	16.9	59.3	14.9	3.4	68162	68368	86	99	513	3.3	10.5	51.7	33.3	1.2	154297
58043	HAVANA	21004	93	29.0	34.4	29.0	5.4	2.2	40314	42631	34	53	79	46.8	24.1	20.3	6.3	2.5	54167
58045	HILLSBORO	23282	1026	22.5	30.2	37.8	8.3	1.2	46776	48494	53	77	754	18.7	22.5	46.6	12.1	0.1	106352
58046	HOPE	22195	266	21.8	33.1	35.7	6.4	3.0	45605	47213	50	74	209	40.2	27.3	23.0	8.6	1.0	61786
58047	HORACE	31881	1330	5.0	16.5	56.2	13.9	8.4	71333	72466	88	100	1244	5.0	4.6	39.4	45.7	5.3	177686
58048	HUNTER	24415	204	25.5	26.5	42.2	3.9	2.0	47037	50801	54	78	154	39.0	28.6	22.1	8.4	1.9	66923
58049	KATHRYN	23426	115	23.5	27.0	40.9	6.1	2.6	49604	50000	60	85	103	32.0	19.4	28.2	18.4	1.9	87000
58051	KINDRED	25343	575	15.3	20.7	54.8	6.3	3.0	60702	61228	78	98	469	17.9	17.7	39.4	22.6	2.3	120602
58052	LEONARD	25386	297	18.5	31.6	42.1	5.7	2.0	49853	50931	61	86	250	28.8	17.6	34.8	17.2	1.6	98182
58053	LIDGERWOOD	19043	589	31.4	38.0	26.0	3.2	1.4	35215	37210	18	27	498	45.2	25.1	23.1	5.2	1.4	56316
58054	LISBON	22355	1436	25.5	28.3	40.3	4.0	1.9	46961	47868	54	78	1054	12.8	22.3	48.9	15.3	0.8	112908
58056	LUVERNE	22828	94	23.4	28.7	38.3	7.4	2.1	47872	49538	56	82	76	39.5	23.7	22.4	13.2	1.3	65000
58057	MCLEOD	24260	57	21.1	31.6	36.8	7.0	3.5	47980	48351	57	82	50	22.0	16.0	40.0	18.0	4.0	110000
58058	MANTADOR	21894	66	28.8	28.8	34.8	6.1	1.5	42351	41735	40	65	56	33.9	23.2	28.6	14.3	0.0	75000
58059	MAPLETON	23858	397	12.8	28.2	49.4	7.1	2.5	56489	57817	73	95	351	12.8	13.7	53.3	19.4	0.9	118833
58060	MILNOR	21745	557	23.5	32.3	33.9	6.8	3.4	45436	46527	50	73	457	30.4	22.8	30.4	14.4	2.0	84423
58061	MOORETON	25683	175	17.7	24.0	48.0	7.4	2.9	55227	56277	72	94	154	18.8	20.8	38.3	22.1	0.0	108750
58062	NOME	20747	83	26.5	28.9	38.6	4.8	1.2	46134	47762	52	75	75	42.7	21.3	24.0	10.7	1.3	60833
58063	ORISKA	21140	140	25.7	22.9	41.4	8.6	1.4	50672	51441	63	88	125	17.6	19.2	41.6	21.6	0.0	113971
58064	PAGE	22989	228	24.6	32.9	36.8	2.2	3.5	42164	44628	40	63	184	41.3	22.8	27.2	8.7	0.0	67857
58067	RUTLAND	21914	130	27.7	33.1	32.3	5.4	1.5	41838	43830	39	62	110	43.6	24.5	22.7	6.4	2.7	58750
58068	SHELDON	21452	146	23.3	32.9	32.9	8.2	2.7	46125	46975	52	75	124	30.6	13.7	27.4	20.2	8.1	104167
58069	STIRUM	25801	71	19.7	32.4	40.8	5.6	1.4	47381	47853	55	80	59	37.3	18.6	33.9	10.2	0.0	75000
58071	TOWER CITY	21813	192	22.9	34.9	37.0	3.1	2.1	43180	45000	43	68	160	31.3	18.1	40.6	9.4	0.6	90769
58072	VALLEY CITY	22073	3512	33.0	28.1	32.1	4.2	2.7	38996	41164	30	49	2328	19.2	23.9	42.7	13.6	0.6	98798
58075	WAHPETON	23817	3905	24.8	26.1	40.3	6.2	2.5	49201	50388	59	84	2286	13.2	17.7	47.7	20.6	0.8	118325
58076	WAHPETON	8572	5	40.0	40.0	20.0	0.0	0.0	42176	42176	40	64	2	0.0	50.0	50.0	0.0	0.0	97500
58077	WALCOTT	25104	274	14.6	25.9	46.7	9.1	3.6	60000	59064	77	97	245	15.9	15.5	38.8	27.8	2.0	135985
58078	WEST FARGO	27882	8767	13.4	21.6	50.4	9.7	4.8	62072	63459	80	99	5897	10.2	10.9	46.1	31.3	1.6	149014
58079	WHEATLAND	23338	259	21.2	26.6	44.4	4.6	3.1	51593	53018	65	89	218	24.8	17.4	33.9	21.1	2.8	109091
58081	WYNDMERE	22041	384	17.2	29.2	47.7	4.4	1.6	51721	51897	65	89	315	23.5	24.1	40.6	11.1	0.6	93409
58102	FARGO	24874	14073	30.0	26.6	33.9	5.6	3.9	41371	42913	37	58	7043	8.9	14.7	48.5	25.7	2.2	135177
58103	FARGO	27305	23813	23.7	30.3	37.7	5.6	2.8	44729	46889	47	71	9984	8.4	14.0	48.7	28.0	0.9	136945
58104	FARGO	38990	9821	10.4	15.5	43.8	18.0	12.4	75178	76371	89	100	6557	1.0	2.1	27.6	59.6	9.7	221183
58201	GRAND FORKS	28966	14270	20.6	26.2	39.2	8.7	5.3	52935	54189	68	92	7743	6.0	9.3	46.9	34.8	3.0	149356
58203	GRAND FORKS	18516	6921	28.3	33.1	33.0	4.2	1.3	40434	42222	34	54	3241	16.3	22.3	50.9	10.3	0.1	106227
58204	GRAND FORKS AFB	9935	177	10.7	41.2	45.2	2.8	0.0	48283	50237	57	83	3	66.7	33.3	0.0	0.0	0.0	45000
58205	GRAND FORKS AFB	16528	794	11.0	40.9	44.8	2.8	0.5	48407	50265	58	83	13	46.2	46.2	0.0	7.7	0.0	62500
58210	ADAMS	19595	166	28.3	34.3	31.9	4.2	1.2	38177	40905	27	43	142	49.3	21.8	21.8	5.6	1.4	51429
58212	ANETA	18424	229	31.4	36.2	28.8	2.6	0.9	38713	40415	29	46	188	49.5	23.4	20.2	4.3	2.7	50625
58214	ARVILLA	25807	171	19.9	24.0	49.7	4.7	1.8	55353	55089	72	94	128	28.9	23.4	37.5	10.2	0.0	87273
58216	BATHGATE	27103	67	20.9	29.9	35.8	11.9	1.5	49098	49311	59	83	60	30.0	38.3	26.7	3.3	1.7	67000
58218	BUXTON	22518	275	17.1	27.3	46.5	7.3	1.8	52522	52309	67	91	238	12.6	25.6	50.8	9.7	1.3	106383
58219	CALEDONIA	23354	47	12.8	34.0	36.2	17.0	0.0	52593	51060	67	91	41	12.2	19.5	48.8	19.5	0.0	128125
58220	CAVALIER	23944	1173	24.4	29.0	38.1	5.0	3.5	47002	47458	54	78	891	19.9	16.9	43.7	17.8	1.7	109182
58222	CRYSTAL	20793	146	27.4	35.6	31.5	3.4	2.1	40000	41608	33	52	121	34.7	29.8	28.9	5.8	0.8	70625
58223	CUMMINGS	23787	101	16.8	28.7	44.6	7.9	2.0	51644	51673	65	89	88	13.6	26.1	50.0	8.0	2.3	103947
58224	DAHLEN	21282	27	29.6	33.3	33.3	3.7	0.0	38616	40000	28	45	23	34.8	26.1	34.8	4.3	0.0	75000
58225	DRAYTON	23752	491	24.2	29.1	40.1	4.7	1.8	47110	48488	54	79	363	20.1	33.1	40.8	6.1	0.0	86290
58227	EDINBURG	21854	252	28.6	34.5	31.3	4.8	0.8	38471	41063	28	44	212	47.6	23.6	23.1	5.2	0.5	53571
58228	EMERADO	24762	461	19.1	26.5	47.5	5.6	1.3	53045	53579	68	93	360	20.3	16.1	39.4	23.1	1.1	117949
58229	FAIRDALE	21364	64	28.1	34.4	31.3	4.7	1.6	37825	41730	26	41	54	55.6	18.5	20.4	5.6	0.0	42500
58230	FINLEY	22954	521	23.2	34.4	33.8	5.2	3.5	44338	45882	46	70	407	34.2	25.3	32.9	6.9	0.7	73750
58231	FORDVILLE	20276	215	31.6	29.3	33.5	4.2	1.4	38938	41990	30	48	190	38.4	31.1	24.2	5.3	1.1	60526
58233	FOREST RIVER	20347	140	26.4	31.4	35.7	3.6	2.9	42355	45000	40	65	123	35.0	28.5	26.0	8.9	1.6	72083
58235	GILBY	19115	161	22.4	42.9	31.1	3.7	0.0	38922	41572	30	48	135	31.9	37.8	20.0	7.4	3.0	64333
58237	GRAFTON	22454	2259	25.4	30.5	35.9	4.8	3.4	45496	46979	50	74	1591	15.7	28.5	39.7	14.7	1.5	99947
58238	HAMILTON	27095	83	22.9	30.1	32.5	9.6	4.8	46758	50654	53	76	72	33.3	33.3	26.4	5.6	1.4	66250
58239	HANNAH	23020	33	33.3	33.3	27.3	6.1	0.0	38629	38625	29	46	29	82.8	3.4	10.3	3.4	0.0	13500
58240	HATTON	20009	437	28.1	31.1	33.9	5.5	1.4	41949	44198	39	63	329	12.8	35.0	45.3	6.7	0.3	92885
58241	HENSEL	26531	78	23.1	24.4	43.6	6.4	2.6	51874	50356	66	89	70	20.0	17.1	40.0	21.4	1.4	107143
58243	HOOPLE	25802	261	24.5	35.2	32.2	5.0	3.1	43302	45094	43	68	217	31.3	26.3	30.9	8.8	2.8	74500
58244	INKSTER	19375	145	22.1	43.4	31.0	3.4	0.0	38833	41910	29	47	121	32.2	38.0	19.8	7.4	2.5	63929
58249	LANGDON	19816	1173	30.3	35.7	28.9	4.3	0.8	37742	38904	26	41	936	31.6	28.8	35.8	3.1	0.6	75634
58250	LANKIN	21855	144	27.8	34.7	31.3	3.5	2.8	38492	41365	28	45	128	38.3	26.6	24.2	7.8	3.1	65556
58251	LARIMORE	21455	854	21.1	35.1	38.5	4.1	1.2	44719	46982	47	71	663	24.3	33.0	34.2	8.1	0.3	81491
58254	MCVILLE	22300	325	38.2	32.3	23.4	3.4	2.8	33984	34785	15	20	256	43.0	26.6	29.7	0.4	0.4	56429
58255	MAIDA	22094	27	14.8	44.4	29.6	11.1	0.0	41127	41122	36	57	24	45.8	37.5	16.7	0.0	0.0	55000
58256	MANVEL	24096	397	12.3	29.0	50.9	5.0	2.8	57491	57499	75	96	358	15.1	29.9	37.2	17.9	0.0	95806
58257	MAYVILLE	22116	841	28.4	26.9	35.2	5.9	3.6	45239	46854	49	72	506	15.2	28.9	45.3	10.1	0.6	96522
	NORTH DAKOTA	23967		25.3	28.6	36.2	6.6	3.3	45981	48456				20.2	18.2	39.7	19.8	2.2	112133
	UNITED STATES	27277		20.9	24.4	35.3	11.7	7.6	54719	56938				9.3	13.1	31.6	32.6	13.5	162279

ZIP CODE #	POST OFFICE NAME	FINANCIAL SERVICES: Auto Loan	Home Loan	Investments	Retirement Plans	THE HOME: Home Improvements: Home Repair	Lawn & Garden	Furnishings: Computers & Hardware-Personal	Major Appliances	TV, Radio, Sound Equipment	Furniture	ENTERTAINMENT: Dine out/Carry out	Sports Equipment	Fees & Tickets	Toys & Games	Travel	Cable TV	PERSONAL: Apparel & Services	Auto Repairs	Health Insurance	Pets & Supplies
58004	AMENIA	105	72	115	72	75	111	80	99	83	65	82	82	59	82	80	91	53	93	105	122
58005	ARGUSVILLE	94	90	90	92	91	101	86	96	87	80	86	74	82	89	87	91	59	89	97	112
58006	ARTHUR	95	65	104	65	68	100	73	90	75	59	75	75	53	74	72	82	48	84	95	111
58007	AYR	84	58	92	58	61	89	64	80	67	52	66	66	47	66	64	73	43	75	84	98
58008	BARNEY	109	75	119	75	78	115	83	103	86	67	85	85	61	85	83	94	55	96	109	127
58009	BLANCHARD	102	70	112	70	74	108	78	97	81	63	80	80	57	80	78	89	52	91	102	119
58011	BUFFALO	87	60	96	60	63	92	66	83	69	54	68	68	49	68	66	75	44	77	87	102
58012	CASSELTON	92	81	81	80	82	90	82	87	85	81	84	65	76	86	79	88	57	85	91	103
58013	CAYUGA	99	68	108	68	71	104	75	94	78	61	78	77	55	77	75	86	50	88	99	115
58015	CHRISTINE	122	84	134	83	88	128	93	115	97	75	95	95	68	95	92	105	62	108	122	142
58016	CLIFFORD	114	78	125	78	82	120	87	108	90	70	89	89	64	89	86	98	58	101	114	133
58017	COGSWELL	94	65	103	64	68	99	72	89	75	58	74	74	52	73	71	81	48	83	94	110
58018	COLFAX	103	71	113	71	74	109	79	98	82	64	81	81	58	80	78	89	52	91	103	120
58021	DAVENPORT	105	75	115	76	78	112	82	101	85	68	84	83	62	84	82	92	55	94	106	124
58027	ENDERLIN	93	66	96	65	69	98	73	90	79	63	77	69	57	78	71	87	51	84	97	107
58029	ERIE	94	65	104	65	68	100	72	90	75	58	74	74	53	74	72	82	48	84	95	110
58030	FAIRMOUNT	94	64	103	64	67	99	71	89	74	58	73	73	52	73	71	81	48	83	94	109
58031	FINGAL	91	62	100	62	65	96	69	86	72	56	71	71	51	71	69	79	46	80	91	106
58032	FORMAN	102	70	112	70	73	107	78	96	81	63	80	80	57	79	77	88	52	90	102	119
58033	FORT RANSOM	97	67	106	66	70	102	74	92	77	60	76	76	54	75	73	84	49	86	97	113
58035	GALESBURG	111	76	122	76	80	117	85	105	88	69	87	87	62	87	84	96	57	98	111	130
58036	GARDNER	86	78	78	81	80	92	77	87	80	70	78	66	71	81	77	84	53	81	90	101
58038	GRANDIN	87	78	79	81	80	93	77	88	80	69	78	67	70	81	77	84	53	81	90	102
58040	GWINNER	92	79	82	77	78	89	77	85	80	76	80	64	69	82	74	84	54	82	87	102
58041	HANKINSON	80	56	84	55	58	84	61	76	66	52	64	60	47	65	60	72	42	71	82	92
58042	HARWOOD	106	125	108	125	120	112	108	110	103	112	105	86	117	107	114	100	74	105	101	127
58043	HAVANA	86	59	95	59	62	91	66	82	69	53	68	68	48	67	66	75	44	77	87	101
58045	HILLSBORO	87	70	91	68	72	94	72	86	78	64	76	65	62	76	72	85	51	81	94	102
58046	HOPE	96	66	105	66	69	101	73	91	76	59	75	75	53	75	73	83	49	85	96	112
58047	HORACE	127	143	122	141	136	128	126	128	121	131	123	99	132	126	129	118	86	123	119	149
58048	HUNTER	95	66	105	65	69	101	73	90	76	59	75	75	53	74	72	83	49	84	96	111
58049	KATHRYN	98	67	108	67	71	103	75	93	78	61	77	77	55	76	74	85	50	87	98	114
58051	KINDRED	97	92	89	94	88	104	92	96	93	85	92	77	88	94	91	96	63	94	102	116
58052	LEONARD	100	69	110	69	72	106	77	95	80	62	79	79	56	78	76	87	51	89	101	117
58053	LIDGERWOOD	74	52	77	51	54	77	57	71	62	49	61	55	44	61	56	69	40	66	77	85
58054	LISBON	88	63	91	61	65	92	69	85	76	60	73	65	54	74	67	83	49	79	92	101
58056	LUVERNE	99	68	109	68	72	105	76	94	79	62	78	78	56	77	76	86	51	88	100	116
58057	MCLEOD	103	71	113	71	74	108	78	98	82	64	81	81	57	80	78	89	52	91	103	120
58058	MANTADOR	85	59	94	59	62	90	65	81	68	53	67	67	48	67	65	74	44	76	86	100
58059	MAPLETON	102	93	96	90	90	97	89	96	89	88	89	75	82	91	87	90	61	92	93	114
58060	MILNOR	98	67	108	67	71	104	75	93	78	61	77	77	55	76	75	85	50	87	98	115
58061	MOORETON	107	73	117	73	77	112	81	101	85	66	84	84	60	83	81	92	54	94	107	125
58062	NOME	89	61	98	61	64	94	68	85	71	55	70	70	50	70	68	77	46	79	90	104
58063	ORISKA	99	68	108	68	71	104	75	94	78	61	77	77	55	77	75	85	50	87	99	115
58064	PAGE	95	65	104	65	68	100	73	90	75	59	75	75	53	74	72	82	48	84	95	111
58067	RUTLAND	89	61	98	61	64	94	68	84	71	55	70	70	50	69	68	77	45	79	89	104
58068	SHELDON	97	67	106	66	70	102	74	92	77	60	76	76	54	75	73	84	49	86	97	113
58069	STIRUM	98	67	108	67	71	104	75	93	78	61	77	77	55	76	75	85	50	87	98	115
58071	TOWER CITY	89	61	98	61	64	94	68	84	71	55	70	70	50	69	68	77	45	79	89	104
58072	VALLEY CITY	74	61	70	60	61	75	67	71	71	61	69	54	59	69	64	75	47	71	79	85
58075	WAHPETON	84	71	69	72	68	75	81	76	80	76	80	62	72	82	74	80	55	80	79	93
58076	WAHPETON	54	44	49	44	45	52	55	53	58	50	57	39	48	56	50	62	39	56	62	63
58077	WALCOTT	116	80	128	80	84	123	89	110	92	72	91	91	65	91	88	101	59	103	117	136
58078	WEST FARGO	106	104	86	103	98	92	103	98	99	106	101	78	100	105	97	96	70	98	92	115
58079	WHEATLAND	102	71	112	70	74	108	78	97	81	64	80	80	58	80	78	89	52	91	102	119
58081	WYNDMERE	99	68	109	68	71	105	76	94	79	61	78	78	55	77	75	86	50	88	99	116
58102	FARGO	75	66	63	69	65	68	83	70	80	76	80	57	75	79	73	80	56	77	75	86
58103	FARGO	81	65	59	68	62	64	83	69	81	79	82	58	74	82	71	80	57	78	72	86
58104	FARGO	140	148	125	148	140	124	138	132	130	147	133	108	142	139	135	123	94	129	116	153
58201	GRAND FORKS	92	84	78	87	81	83	94	86	94	92	94	69	91	94	89	93	66	92	90	104
58203	GRAND FORKS	72	53	47	56	50	55	79	60	74	68	74	52	64	74	61	72	52	69	63	75
58204	GRAND FORKS AFB	93	48	36	56	43	41	87	61	82	81	87	60	66	99	63	76	61	77	55	74
58205	GRAND FORKS AFB	93	48	36	56	43	41	87	61	82	81	87	60	66	99	63	76	61	77	55	74
58210	ADAMS	81	56	89	56	58	86	62	77	64	50	64	64	45	63	62	70	41	72	81	95
58212	ANETA	75	52	83	52	54	79	57	71	60	47	59	59	42	59	57	65	38	67	75	88
58214	ARVILLA	90	79	82	80	81	90	85	88	87	81	86	65	78	86	82	91	59	88	95	103
58216	BATHGATE	109	75	119	74	78	115	83	103	86	67	85	85	61	85	82	94	55	96	109	127
58218	BUXTON	102	70	112	70	74	108	78	97	81	63	80	80	57	80	78	89	52	91	103	120
58219	CALEDONIA	109	75	120	75	79	115	83	104	87	68	86	86	61	85	83	95	56	97	110	128
58220	CAVALIER	86	71	86	71	73	90	74	85	78	68	77	65	65	78	73	83	52	81	90	101
58222	CRYSTAL	82	57	90	57	60	87	63	78	66	51	65	65	47	64	63	72	42	73	83	96
58223	CUMMINGS	100	69	110	69	72	105	76	95	79	62	78	78	56	78	76	86	51	88	100	117
58224	DAHLEN	82	56	90	56	59	86	62	78	65	51	64	64	46	64	62	71	42	72	82	95
58225	DRAYTON	87	62	89	61	65	91	68	84	75	60	73	64	54	73	66	82	48	79	91	100
58227	EDINBURG	81	55	89	55	58	85	62	77	64	50	63	63	45	63	61	70	41	71	81	94
58228	EMERADO	89	81	77	80	80	87	79	84	82	79	81	63	74	83	77	84	55	82	86	100
58229	FAIRDALE	79	55	87	54	57	84	61	75	63	49	62	62	44	62	60	69	40	70	80	93
58230	FINLEY	97	67	106	66	70	102	74	92	77	60	76	76	54	75	74	84	49	86	97	113
58231	FORDVILLE	87	60	96	60	63	92	67	83	69	54	68	68	49	68	66	76	44	77	87	102
58233	FOREST RIVER	89	62	98	61	65	94	68	85	71	56	70	70	50	70	68	78	46	79	89	104
58235	GILBY	83	57	91	57	60	87	63	79	66	51	65	65	46	64	63	72	42	73	83	97
58237	GRAFTON	86	68	85	67	69	90	73	84	77	66	76	64	61	77	71	83	51	80	91	100
58238	HAMILTON	109	75	119	75	78	115	83	103	86	67	85	85	61	85	83	94	55	96	109	127
58239	HANNAH	74	51	81	51	53	78	56	70	58	46	58	58	41	57	56	64	38	65	74	86
58240	HATTON	83	59	85	58	62	87	65	80	71	57	69	61	51	70	63	78	46	75	87	95
58241	HENSEL	81	81	81	83	80	88	76	82	76	73	76	65	76	77	79	77	52	78	83	98
58243	HOOPLE	97	67	107	67	70	103	74	92	77	60	76	76	54	76	74	84	50	86	98	114
58244	INKSTER	83	57	91	57	60	87	63	79	66	51	65	65	46	65	63	72	42	73	83	97
58249	LANGDON	76	54	81	53	56	80	59	73	63	50	62	58	45	62	58	69	41	68	78	88
58250	LANKIN	86	59	94	59	62	90	66	81	68	53	67	67	48	67	65	74	44	76	86	100
58251	LARIMORE	87	63	90	62	65	91	69	84	75	60	73	65	54	74	67	82	48	79	91	100
58254	MCVILLE	79	56	81	55	58	83	62	76	68	54	66	58	48	67	60	75	44	71	83	90
58255	MAIDA	94	64	103	64	67	99	72	89	74	58	74	73	52	73	71	81	48	83	94	109
58256	MANVEL	97	95	89	98	95	105	90	99	92	85	91	76	88	94	92	95	62	93	101	116
58257	MAYVILLE	88	67	87	67	70	91	73	86	79	66	77	65	61	78	71	85	52	81	93	101
	NORTH DAKOTA	87	73	80	73	72	84	80	82	81	74	81	65	71	81	75	84	55	82	85	99
	UNITED STATES	100	100	100	100	100	100	100	100	100	100	100	100	100	100	100	100	100	100	100	100

ZIP CODE #	POST OFFICE NAME	COUNTY FIPS CODE	POPULATION 2000	POPULATION 2009	POPULATION 2014	2000-2009 ANNUAL RATE % Rate	2000-2009 ANNUAL RATE State Centile	HOUSEHOLDS 2000	HOUSEHOLDS 2009	HOUSEHOLDS 2014	HOUSEHOLDS % Annual Rate 2000-2009	HOUSEHOLDS 2009 Average HH Size	FAMILIES 2000	FAMILIES 2009	FAMILIES % Annual Rate 2000-2009
58258	MEKINOCK	035	322	323	318	0.0	82	119	126	125	0.6	2.56	92	94	0.2
58259	MICHIGAN	063	479	448	433	-0.7	50	222	219	214	-0.1	1.95	140	131	-0.7
58260	MILTON	019	183	154	142	-1.8	4	78	69	65	-1.3	2.13	56	48	-1.7
58261	MINTO	099	1282	1198	1158	-0.7	50	524	518	507	-0.1	2.31	363	343	-0.6
58262	MOUNTAIN	067	177	165	160	-0.8	39	64	64	63	0.0	2.38	43	40	-0.8
58265	NECHE	067	632	583	563	-0.9	32	236	231	226	-0.2	2.52	169	159	-0.7
58266	NIAGARA	035	268	251	244	-0.7	50	107	107	106	0.0	2.34	81	79	-0.3
58267	NORTHWOOD	035	1422	1382	1347	-0.3	71	581	586	576	0.1	2.16	383	366	-0.5
58269	OSNABROCK	019	516	433	401	-1.9	4	206	183	171	-1.3	2.27	147	126	-1.7
58270	PARK RIVER	099	2063	2069	2046	0.0	82	857	914	916	0.7	2.15	539	544	0.1
58271	PEMBINA	067	797	746	722	-0.7	50	320	314	308	-0.2	2.38	227	214	-0.6
58272	PETERSBURG	063	346	324	313	-0.7	50	144	142	139	-0.2	2.27	99	93	-0.7
58273	PISEK	099	261	242	234	-0.8	39	109	109	107	0.0	2.22	71	67	-0.6
58274	PORTLAND	097	935	867	831	-0.8	39	379	367	354	-0.3	2.34	254	234	-0.9
58275	REYNOLDS	035	872	871	852	0.0	82	306	320	317	0.5	2.72	252	256	0.2
58276	SAINT THOMAS	067	685	620	595	-1.1	19	271	261	255	-0.4	2.37	192	177	-0.9
58277	SHARON	091	153	145	143	-0.6	55	72	71	70	-0.2	2.04	48	45	-0.7
58278	THOMPSON	035	1697	1850	1926	0.9	96	571	639	673	1.2	2.90	466	505	0.9
58281	WALES	019	84	68	63	-2.3	1	39	34	32	-1.5	2.00	26	22	-1.8
58282	WALHALLA	067	1528	1425	1384	-0.8	39	641	637	626	-0.1	2.16	419	395	-0.6
58301	DEVILS LAKE	071	9977	9232	8909	-0.8	39	4120	4003	3897	-0.3	2.21	2579	2375	-0.9
58311	ALSEN	019	148	123	113	-2.0	3	56	49	46	-1.4	2.51	40	34	-1.7
58316	BELCOURT	079	6312	6476	6515	0.3	88	1929	2059	2086	0.7	3.12	1487	1532	0.3
58317	BISBEE	095	337	318	311	-0.6	55	142	143	142	0.1	2.22	96	93	-0.3
58318	BOTTINEAU	009	3954	3662	3530	-0.8	39	1612	1589	1548	-0.2	2.16	1032	969	-0.7
58321	BROCKET	071	145	138	134	-0.5	60	64	64	63	0.0	2.16	48	46	-0.5
58323	CALVIN	019	58	47	43	-2.2	2	24	21	20	-1.4	2.24	16	14	-1.4
58324	CANDO	095	1578	1485	1438	-0.7	50	692	688	674	-0.1	2.06	421	396	-0.7
58325	CHURCHS FERRY	071	187	172	165	-0.9	32	77	74	72	-0.4	2.32	59	55	-0.8
58327	CRARY	071	442	428	419	-0.3	71	165	168	167	0.2	2.55	128	125	-0.3
58329	DUNSEITH	079	3138	3135	3142	0.0	82	994	1046	1057	0.6	2.95	768	781	0.2
58330	EDMORE	071	463	402	382	-1.5	6	194	178	170	-0.9	2.12	126	108	-1.7
58331	EGELAND	095	197	167	156	-1.8	4	76	69	65	-1.0	2.42	55	48	-1.5
58332	ESMOND	005	387	357	349	-0.9	32	173	169	166	-0.3	2.10	120	112	-0.7
58338	HAMPDEN	071	131	114	108	-1.5	6	59	54	52	-1.0	2.04	40	34	-1.7
58339	HANSBORO	095	60	57	56	-0.6	55	22	22	22	0.0	2.59	15	15	0.0
58341	HARVEY	103	2941	2643	2504	-1.1	19	1301	1240	1188	-0.5	2.04	820	742	-1.1
58343	KNOX	005	84	78	77	-0.8	39	32	31	31	-0.3	2.52	25	23	-0.9
58344	LAKOTA	063	1096	1026	993	-0.7	50	473	468	458	-0.1	2.07	298	279	-0.7
58345	LAWTON	071	224	199	190	-1.3	9	99	93	90	-0.7	2.05	68	60	-1.3
58346	LEEDS	005	753	731	725	-0.3	71	319	323	322	0.1	2.26	212	204	-0.4
58348	MADDOCK	005	1039	995	989	-0.5	60	448	457	458	0.2	2.09	279	269	-0.4
58351	MINNEWAUKAN	005	532	519	516	-0.3	71	243	247	247	0.2	2.10	168	163	-0.3
58352	MUNICH	019	519	431	394	-2.0	3	207	183	169	-1.3	2.36	148	125	-1.8
58353	MYLO	079	264	259	256	-0.2	74	100	104	104	0.4	2.49	77	77	0.0
58356	NEW ROCKFORD	027	1976	1778	1691	-1.1	19	844	800	768	-0.6	2.16	531	477	-1.2
58357	OBERON	005	592	627	638	0.6	91	183	200	205	1.0	3.14	133	139	0.5
58361	PEKIN	063	177	160	153	-1.1	19	83	79	77	-0.5	2.00	51	46	-1.1
58362	PENN	071	139	129	125	-0.8	39	49	48	47	-0.2	2.69	39	37	-0.6
58363	PERTH	095	112	107	104	-0.5	60	40	41	40	0.3	2.61	27	26	-0.4
58365	ROCKLAKE	095	409	358	339	-1.4	7	170	158	152	-0.8	2.27	121	108	-1.2
58366	ROLETTE	079	950	929	923	-0.2	74	393	405	406	0.3	2.18	254	247	-0.3
58367	ROLLA	079	1786	1797	1796	0.1	85	734	768	775	0.5	2.32	463	459	-0.1
58368	RUGBY	069	4127	3684	3479	-1.2	14	1738	1633	1558	-0.7	2.17	1117	997	-1.2
58369	SAINT JOHN	079	1294	1314	1325	0.2	88	433	464	473	0.8	2.83	335	347	0.4
58370	SAINT MICHAEL	005	3043	3116	3145	0.3	88	748	791	802	0.6	3.93	626	644	0.3
58372	SARLES	095	123	102	94	-2.0	3	56	50	46	-1.2	2.04	39	33	-1.8
58374	SHEYENNE	027	679	643	623	-0.6	55	276	271	263	-0.2	2.27	182	170	-0.7
58377	STARKWEATHER	071	413	379	364	-0.9	32	158	153	148	-0.3	2.46	118	109	-0.9
58380	TOLNA	063	470	430	413	-1.0	24	211	203	198	-0.4	2.12	138	126	-1.0
58381	WARWICK	005	258	262	263	0.2	88	89	92	92	0.4	2.85	67	67	0.0
58382	WEBSTER	071	161	147	141	-1.0	24	64	62	60	-0.3	2.37	49	45	-0.9
58384	WILLOW CITY	009	668	599	567	-1.2	14	281	269	258	-0.5	2.23	197	179	-1.0
58385	WOLFORD	069	223	196	185	-1.4	7	87	83	79	-0.5	2.36	58	52	-1.2
58386	YORK	005	153	145	142	-0.6	55	66	66	65	0.0	2.20	45	43	-0.5
58401	JAMESTOWN	093	17387	16412	15793	-0.6	55	7381	7314	7110	-0.1	2.08	4504	4216	-0.7
58405	JAMESTOWN	093	740	782	770	0.6	91	54	54	52	0.0	4.43	26	24	-0.9
58413	ASHLEY	051	1414	1302	1269	-0.9	32	637	617	608	-0.3	2.03	409	376	-0.9
58415	BERLIN	045	179	173	168	-0.4	66	67	68	67	0.2	2.54	52	52	0.0
58416	BINFORD	039	400	380	374	-0.6	55	174	177	177	0.2	2.15	131	128	-0.3
58418	BOWDON	103	414	374	353	-1.1	19	184	175	167	-0.5	2.14	123	111	-1.1
58420	BUCHANAN	093	298	278	267	-0.7	50	111	111	108	0.0	2.50	88	85	-0.4
58421	CARRINGTON	031	3129	2888	2772	-0.9	32	1273	1238	1201	-0.3	2.26	833	769	-0.9
58422	CATHAY	103	270	247	234	-1.0	24	103	99	95	-0.4	2.49	81	75	-0.8
58423	CHASELEY	103	74	68	64	-0.9	32	36	34	33	-0.6	2.00	26	24	-0.9
58424	CLEVELAND	093	371	349	337	-0.7	50	157	157	154	0.0	2.22	109	104	-0.5
58425	COOPERSTOWN	039	1735	1623	1593	-0.7	50	747	748	743	0.0	2.09	465	440	-0.6
58426	COURTENAY	093	258	232	220	-1.1	19	99	96	92	-0.3	2.42	76	71	-0.7
58428	DAWSON	043	283	274	268	-0.3	71	116	122	122	0.5	2.25	85	86	0.1
58429	DAZEY	003	347	306	289	-1.4	7	140	131	125	-0.7	2.34	101	90	-1.2
58430	DENHOFF	083	145	138	134	-0.5	60	55	56	55	0.2	2.46	42	40	-0.5
58431	DICKEY	045	166	160	156	-0.4	66	72	74	72	0.3	2.16	56	55	-0.2
58433	EDGELEY	045	1308	1245	1209	-0.5	60	534	538	529	0.1	2.26	338	323	-0.5
58436	ELLENDALE	021	2247	2090	1994	-0.8	39	854	812	777	-0.5	2.18	543	490	-1.1
58438	FESSENDEN	103	849	737	689	-1.5	6	368	337	319	-0.9	2.18	244	211	-1.6
58439	FORBES	021	214	206	202	-0.4	66	91	93	92	0.2	2.22	65	64	-0.2
58440	FREDONIA	047	235	222	218	-0.6	55	97	99	98	0.2	2.24	73	71	-0.3
58441	FULLERTON	021	330	300	284	-1.0	24	125	121	116	-0.4	2.48	99	93	-0.7
58442	GACKLE	047	574	519	500	-1.1	19	266	257	251	-0.4	1.89	171	157	-0.9
58443	GLENFIELD	031	352	337	330	-0.5	60	144	147	146	0.2	2.29	108	105	-0.3
58444	GOODRICH	083	274	277	275	0.1	85	126	135	137	0.7	2.05	93	96	0.3
58445	GRACE CITY	031	139	132	129	-0.6	55	57	58	57	0.2	2.28	42	41	-0.3
58448	HANNAFORD	039	372	350	343	-0.7	50	161	164	163	0.2	2.13	115	111	-0.4
58451	HURDSFIELD	103	252	232	220	-0.9	32	98	94	91	-0.4	2.47	77	71	-0.9
58454	JUD	045	384	359	347	-0.7	50	171	171	167	0.0	2.09	117	111	-0.6
	NORTH DAKOTA					0.2					0.8	2.27			0.2
	UNITED STATES					1.0					1.1	2.59			0.9

ZIP CODE #	POST OFFICE NAME	RACE (%) White 2000	White 2009	Black 2000	Black 2009	Asian/Pacific 2000	Asian/Pacific 2009	% Hispanic Origin 2000	% Hispanic Origin 2009	2009 AGE DISTRIBUTION (%) 0-4	5-9	10-14	15-19	20-24	25-44	45-64	65-84	85+	18+	MEDIAN AGE 2009	% 2009 Males	% 2009 Females
58258	MEKINOCK	97.2	96.3	0.9	1.2	0.0	0.3	0.6	1.2	6.2	6.5	7.4	7.7	5.3	25.4	30.7	9.6	1.2	74.9	39.7	50.8	49.2
58259	MICHIGAN	97.9	97.5	0.2	0.2	0.4	0.7	0.2	0.4	4.5	5.4	5.4	6.5	4.0	17.9	31.0	20.3	5.1	79.7	49.3	51.8	48.2
58260	MILTON	96.7	95.5	0.0	0.0	0.0	0.6	1.1	1.3	3.9	4.5	5.2	5.2	4.5	16.9	36.4	18.2	5.2	81.8	49.7	54.5	45.5
58261	MINTO	95.8	93.8	0.0	0.1	0.1	0.2	6.3	9.8	6.5	6.9	7.3	6.8	5.0	22.3	31.2	11.9	2.0	74.9	41.3	52.2	47.8
58262	MOUNTAIN	96.0	94.5	0.6	0.6	0.0	0.0	1.1	1.8	4.8	6.1	6.1	7.3	5.5	19.4	31.5	13.9	5.5	78.2	45.7	51.5	48.5
58265	NECHE	97.2	96.7	0.2	0.2	0.2	0.2	2.4	3.8	4.6	5.3	5.8	5.8	4.5	23.2	32.9	15.3	2.6	80.4	45.5	52.0	48.0
58266	NIAGARA	97.4	96.0	0.0	0.0	0.4	0.8	0.4	0.4	5.6	6.4	6.4	5.2	3.6	21.1	33.9	15.5	2.4	78.1	46.2	53.4	46.6
58267	NORTHWOOD	98.7	98.3	0.3	0.4	0.1	0.3	0.6	1.1	4.4	4.8	5.4	6.4	4.6	18.5	30.3	18.4	7.3	80.8	49.2	48.2	51.8
58269	OSNABROCK	96.1	95.2	0.2	0.2	0.2	0.5	1.2	1.8	4.2	4.6	5.3	5.5	4.6	17.1	34.2	19.4	5.1	81.5	50.4	52.0	48.0
58270	PARK RIVER	95.9	94.5	0.4	0.4	0.0	0.1	2.2	3.4	5.4	5.6	5.7	5.6	5.3	19.9	28.1	18.3	6.1	79.7	46.8	48.0	52.0
58271	PEMBINA	96.9	95.7	0.1	0.1	0.4	0.5	1.9	2.8	5.1	6.2	9.7	7.6	2.9	26.0	28.6	12.5	1.5	73.1	39.8	50.4	49.6
58272	PETERSBURG	97.4	96.9	0.3	0.3	0.3	0.3	0.6	0.9	4.9	5.2	5.6	6.8	4.3	18.2	32.1	19.4	3.4	79.6	47.4	53.1	46.9
58273	PISEK	97.3	96.3	0.4	0.4	0.0	0.0	1.1	1.7	5.4	6.2	6.6	6.2	3.7	18.2	31.8	19.0	2.9	77.7	47.0	52.1	47.9
58274	PORTLAND	99.3	99.0	0.0	0.0	0.1	0.1	0.7	1.3	6.3	6.6	6.6	6.8	5.4	20.3	28.5	16.4	3.1	76.6	43.3	51.4	48.6
58275	REYNOLDS	98.6	98.0	0.2	0.3	0.1	0.2	1.4	2.2	6.0	6.4	9.8	9.0	2.9	24.8	27.3	12.5	1.4	72.0	39.5	51.5	48.5
58276	SAINT THOMAS	95.0	93.1	0.0	0.0	0.0	0.0	12.0	18.5	5.3	5.8	6.3	6.6	4.4	20.8	32.6	16.5	1.8	78.4	45.5	53.5	46.5
58277	SHARON	98.0	97.9	0.0	0.0	0.0	0.0	0.0	0.0	4.8	4.8	6.2	6.2	4.1	20.7	29.7	20.0	3.4	80.0	47.3	51.0	49.0
58278	THOMPSON	98.0	97.2	0.3	0.4	0.5	0.8	0.8	1.1	6.0	6.9	9.9	10.2	3.2	26.5	28.2	8.5	0.6	70.8	37.0	53.3	46.7
58281	WALES	98.8	98.5	0.0	0.0	0.0	0.0	0.0	0.0	4.4	5.9	5.9	4.4	2.9	19.1	35.3	19.1	2.9	80.9	49.2	52.9	47.1
58282	WALHALLA	92.1	90.5	0.0	0.0	0.0	0.0	0.7	0.9	5.2	5.6	5.8	6.0	4.7	18.8	32.0	17.1	4.8	79.4	47.6	48.7	51.3
58301	DEVILS LAKE	91.2	88.6	0.2	0.3	0.3	0.4	0.5	0.8	6.1	6.0	6.2	7.8	6.8	23.2	26.8	13.0	4.0	77.0	40.2	49.2	50.8
58311	ALSEN	98.6	98.4	0.0	0.0	0.0	0.0	0.7	0.8	5.7	6.5	7.3	8.1	5.7	17.9	30.9	15.4	2.4	75.6	43.9	48.8	51.2
58316	BELCOURT	5.1	3.5	0.1	0.1	0.0	0.0	1.0	0.8	10.8	9.8	8.7	9.5	9.0	25.3	19.5	6.9	0.6	64.9	26.3	48.8	51.2
58317	BISBEE	97.0	96.2	0.0	0.0	0.0	0.0	0.3	0.3	5.3	6.0	5.7	5.7	5.3	19.8	33.6	15.7	2.8	79.2	46.1	50.3	49.7
58318	BOTTINEAU	96.4	95.4	0.3	0.3	0.3	0.4	0.7	0.9	4.0	4.7	5.4	9.1	5.7	19.6	32.3	14.9	4.5	81.7	46.0	50.2	49.8
58321	BROCKET	97.9	97.1	0.0	0.0	0.0	0.0	0.7	0.7	5.8	5.8	6.5	7.2	3.6	21.7	31.2	16.7	1.4	76.8	44.4	52.9	47.1
58323	CALVIN	98.3	97.9	0.0	0.0	0.0	0.0	0.0	0.0	4.3	4.3	6.4	6.4	4.3	19.1	34.0	21.3	0.0	78.7	48.1	55.3	44.7
58324	CANDO	97.5	96.7	0.1	0.1	0.1	0.3	0.1	0.3	4.6	5.3	5.9	6.3	4.3	17.3	33.3	16.2	6.9	79.4	48.6	48.3	51.7
58325	CHURCHS FERRY	97.9	97.7	0.0	0.0	0.5	0.6	1.1	1.2	4.7	6.4	7.0	7.0	4.7	19.2	32.6	16.3	2.3	77.3	45.7	50.6	49.4
58327	CRARY	97.3	96.5	0.0	0.0	0.2	0.2	0.2	0.2	6.1	5.4	7.2	7.7	3.3	22.9	30.4	15.4	1.6	75.9	43.2	54.4	45.6
58329	DUNSEITH	18.5	12.9	0.1	0.1	0.0	0.0	0.9	0.9	9.9	10.4	10.6	10.2	6.6	23.7	20.7	6.7	1.2	62.3	26.9	48.6	51.4
58330	EDMORE	97.2	96.5	0.4	0.5	0.6	1.0	0.4	0.7	3.5	4.5	5.0	5.5	3.7	16.2	32.6	22.6	6.5	83.1	52.4	51.0	49.0
58331	EGELAND	98.0	97.0	0.0	0.0	0.0	0.0	0.0	0.0	5.4	6.0	6.0	4.8	5.4	19.2	33.5	17.4	2.4	79.0	47.0	49.1	50.9
58332	ESMOND	98.2	98.0	0.0	0.0	0.0	0.0	0.5	0.6	4.8	5.9	6.7	6.4	4.2	17.9	31.4	19.3	3.4	78.4	47.9	54.1	45.9
58338	HAMPDEN	98.5	97.4	0.0	0.0	0.0	0.9	0.8	0.9	4.4	4.4	6.1	7.0	4.4	15.8	31.6	21.1	5.3	79.8	50.0	50.0	50.0
58339	HANSBORO	98.3	96.5	0.0	0.0	0.0	0.0	0.0	0.0	5.3	5.3	5.3	5.3	5.3	17.5	36.8	15.8	3.5	80.7	47.5	54.4	45.6
58341	HARVEY	99.2	98.9	0.1	0.1	0.2	0.3	0.4	0.6	4.8	4.9	5.6	6.1	4.6	18.7	28.7	20.4	6.2	80.4	48.5	49.7	50.3
58343	KNOX	97.6	97.4	0.0	0.0	0.0	0.0	1.2	1.3	6.4	6.4	7.7	9.0	3.8	20.5	25.6	17.9	2.6	71.8	42.5	55.1	44.9
58344	LAKOTA	98.1	97.5	0.0	0.0	0.4	0.6	0.2	0.3	3.5	3.7	4.3	6.1	5.8	16.7	31.7	21.1	7.1	83.8	51.5	46.9	53.1
58345	LAWTON	97.3	96.0	0.4	0.5	0.4	1.0	0.9	1.5	4.5	5.0	5.5	6.0	4.0	18.1	31.7	20.1	5.0	80.4	49.2	51.8	48.2
58346	LEEDS	97.9	97.4	0.4	0.4	0.0	0.0	0.1	0.1	6.0	6.7	6.8	6.7	4.5	18.9	30.6	17.2	2.5	76.2	45.2	50.5	49.5
58348	MADDOCK	98.7	98.5	0.0	0.0	0.1	0.1	0.4	0.4	4.1	4.4	5.0	6.6	5.5	17.4	30.1	20.3	6.5	81.8	49.6	50.4	49.6
58351	MINNEWAUKAN	85.2	82.5	0.0	0.0	0.0	0.0	1.3	1.3	5.4	5.8	6.2	6.9	4.8	20.2	32.4	16.0	2.3	78.6	45.4	53.0	47.0
58352	MUNICH	98.3	97.7	0.2	0.2	0.0	0.0	0.4	0.7	5.8	6.3	7.0	8.4	5.1	17.4	31.3	16.5	2.3	75.6	45.1	49.7	50.3
58353	MYLO	92.4	89.2	0.0	0.0	0.0	0.4	0.0	0.0	5.4	7.3	8.5	6.2	1.9	22.8	32.8	12.7	2.3	74.9	43.6	52.1	47.9
58356	NEW ROCKFORD	96.6	95.7	0.1	0.1	0.2	0.2	0.6	1.0	4.6	5.0	5.6	6.9	5.1	19.2	30.3	17.9	5.4	80.6	47.3	47.9	52.1
58357	OBERON	41.2	38.3	0.3	0.3	0.0	0.0	2.0	1.9	11.6	9.9	8.0	7.7	8.9	24.2	19.8	8.8	1.1	66.0	27.0	49.6	50.4
58361	PEKIN	99.4	99.4	0.0	0.0	0.6	0.6	0.0	0.0	3.8	4.4	4.4	6.3	4.4	18.8	32.5	21.3	4.4	83.1	50.3	51.3	48.7
58362	PENN	99.3	97.7	0.0	0.0	0.0	0.8	0.0	0.0	4.7	6.2	7.0	7.8	3.1	23.3	34.9	12.4	0.8	76.7	43.8	52.7	47.3
58363	PERTH	96.4	96.3	0.0	0.0	0.0	0.0	0.9	0.0	4.7	6.5	5.6	5.6	5.6	19.6	33.6	15.9	2.8	81.3	46.3	50.5	49.5
58365	ROCKLAKE	97.5	96.6	0.0	0.0	0.0	0.0	0.0	0.0	5.3	6.1	5.6	5.0	5.3	18.4	34.6	16.8	2.8	80.2	47.1	48.9	51.1
58366	ROLETTE	78.3	70.9	0.1	0.1	0.0	0.1	0.1	0.0	6.9	7.1	6.9	6.0	4.7	19.9	27.4	16.1	4.8	75.3	43.7	49.5	50.5
58367	ROLLA	70.1	60.9	0.1	0.1	0.4	0.6	0.5	0.7	6.2	6.2	6.7	7.3	7.2	21.7	27.3	14.4	2.8	75.8	39.9	46.1	53.9
58368	RUGBY	98.4	98.0	0.1	0.1	0.3	0.4	0.6	0.8	5.3	5.5	5.7	6.1	5.6	20.3	27.9	17.8	5.8	79.6	45.9	49.5	50.5
58369	SAINT JOHN	29.9	21.3	0.0	0.0	0.0	0.0	0.9	1.0	8.8	7.9	7.1	8.4	10.0	26.1	24.4	6.7	0.7	71.3	28.5	52.5	47.5
58370	SAINT MICHAEL	11.2	9.1	0.0	0.0	0.0	0.0	0.8	0.8	13.4	11.5	11.2	10.5	8.5	24.1	16.0	4.4	0.4	57.3	22.0	49.7	50.3
58372	SARLES	98.4	98.0	0.0	0.0	0.0	0.0	0.0	0.0	5.9	5.9	5.9	5.9	3.9	16.7	34.3	19.6	2.0	78.4	48.3	52.0	48.0
58374	SHEYENNE	80.0	76.8	0.0	0.0	0.1	0.3	0.7	0.8	6.5	7.0	6.8	6.7	5.8	19.8	27.4	14.8	5.3	75.4	42.4	49.6	50.4
58377	STARKWEATHER	97.8	97.4	0.0	0.0	0.5	0.8	0.7	1.3	5.0	6.1	6.6	6.6	4.5	18.7	33.2	16.4	2.9	77.8	46.4	49.6	50.4
58380	TOLNA	97.9	97.7	0.0	0.0	0.4	0.5	0.2	0.2	4.7	5.1	5.6	6.5	4.2	18.4	32.8	20.2	2.6	80.5	48.3	52.6	47.4
58381	WARWICK	46.1	41.6	0.0	0.0	0.0	0.0	0.0	0.0	11.1	10.3	9.5	9.2	6.9	21.4	22.5	8.0	1.1	63.0	27.7	52.7	47.3
58382	WEBSTER	98.1	97.3	0.0	0.0	0.6	0.7	0.6	1.4	5.4	6.1	6.8	6.8	4.1	19.7	32.7	15.6	2.7	77.6	45.6	50.3	49.7
58384	WILLOW CITY	92.8	91.3	0.3	0.3	0.0	0.0	0.3	0.2	4.7	5.0	5.7	7.0	4.7	21.0	32.1	17.2	2.7	80.5	46.2	52.9	47.1
58385	WOLFORD	98.2	97.4	0.4	0.5	0.0	0.5	0.9	1.0	6.6	6.6	7.1	5.1	3.6	23.5	30.1	15.3	2.0	76.5	43.3	52.0	48.0
58386	YORK	98.7	98.6	0.0	0.0	0.0	0.0	0.7	0.0	5.5	6.9	6.9	6.9	4.1	19.3	31.0	16.6	2.8	76.6	45.2	53.1	46.9
58401	JAMESTOWN	97.3	96.4	0.3	0.3	0.4	0.7	1.1	1.7	5.5	5.4	6.0	6.8	7.0	23.1	28.0	14.5	3.7	79.0	42.2	48.9	51.1
58405	JAMESTOWN	95.8	94.4	1.2	1.5	1.1	1.7	0.8	1.5	2.9	0.8	1.3	31.6	44.5	8.6	7.4	2.4	0.5	93.7	21.5	47.4	52.6
58413	ASHLEY	98.7	98.5	0.0	0.0	0.6	0.7	0.6	0.9	3.8	3.8	4.5	5.0	2.8	14.2	27.2	30.3	8.4	85.1	57.3	47.8	52.2
58415	BERLIN	98.9	98.8	0.0	0.0	0.6	0.6	0.0	0.6	6.9	6.9	6.9	7.5	4.0	27.2	26.6	12.1	1.7	74.0	37.7	54.3	45.7
58416	BINFORD	99.8	99.7	0.0	0.0	0.3	0.3	0.0	0.0	4.5	5.0	5.5	5.3	4.5	18.2	36.3	17.1	3.7	81.8	49.7	51.3	48.7
58418	BOWDON	99.5	99.5	0.2	0.3	0.0	0.0	0.2	0.3	5.1	5.1	6.1	7.2	4.0	18.4	31.0	19.3	3.7	78.9	47.3	51.6	48.4
58420	BUCHANAN	99.3	98.2	0.0	0.4	0.0	0.4	0.3	0.7	3.6	6.5	8.6	7.9	3.6	23.4	33.5	10.8	2.2	75.5	43.1	55.0	45.0
58421	CARRINGTON	99.0	98.7	0.1	0.2	0.0	0.0	0.2	0.3	5.8	6.0	6.1	7.2	5.7	20.9	28.1	16.1	4.2	77.3	43.6	49.3	50.7
58422	CATHAY	99.6	99.6	0.0	0.0	0.0	0.0	0.0	0.4	4.9	5.7	6.9	6.9	3.6	19.8	32.4	17.0	2.8	78.1	46.2	52.2	47.8
58423	CHASELEY	100.0	100.0	0.0	0.0	0.0	0.0	0.0	0.0	5.9	5.9	5.9	5.9	4.4	19.1	30.9	19.1	2.9	76.5	47.0	51.5	48.5
58424	CLEVELAND	99.5	99.4	0.0	0.0	0.0	0.0	0.3	0.6	4.9	5.7	6.6	7.2	4.0	20.1	31.5	16.9	3.2	78.2	45.9	50.1	49.9
58425	COOPERSTOWN	99.1	98.7	0.0	0.0	0.2	0.3	0.6	1.0	4.9	5.6	6.0	6.1	4.4	19.0	30.5	17.1	6.3	79.5	47.8	50.0	50.0
58426	COURTENAY	99.6	99.6	0.0	0.0	0.0	0.0	0.0	0.0	4.7	5.6	6.0	6.9	4.7	18.5	37.1	14.2	2.2	78.4	46.9	53.0	47.0
58428	DAWSON	99.3	99.3	0.4	0.4	0.0	0.0	0.7	1.1	5.5	6.2	6.6	6.9	4.0	19.0	33.2	16.1	2.6	77.7	46.0	53.6	46.4
58429	DAZEY	99.4	99.3	0.0	0.0	0.0	0.0	0.0	0.0	5.9	6.5	6.9	6.9	4.6	20.9	32.4	13.7	2.3	76.5	43.7	51.0	49.0
58430	DENHOFF	100.0	99.3	0.0	0.0	0.0	0.0	0.0	0.0	2.9	5.1	5.8	6.5	3.6	18.1	34.1	21.0	2.9	81.9	50.0	52.2	47.8
58431	DICKEY	98.8	98.8	0.0	0.0	0.6	0.6	0.0	0.6	6.9	7.5	7.5	6.9	3.8	26.9	26.9	12.5	1.3	73.8	37.9	55.0	45.0
58433	EDGELEY	99.3	99.1	0.0	0.0	0.1	0.2	0.6	0.9	4.7	5.1	5.3	6.3	5.5	18.6	30.4	19.1	5.0	80.6	47.9	50.1	49.9
58436	ELLENDALE	97.8	97.0	0.1	0.1	0.2	0.3	0.8	1.3	4.5	4.9	5.0	10.2	10.0	20.4	23.6	15.3	6.0	81.0	39.4	48.8	51.2
58438	FESSENDEN	98.1	97.4	0.5	0.5	0.7	1.2	0.1	0.1	5.0	5.7	6.0	6.5	4.5	16.7	33.2	18.9	3.5	78.7	48.1	51.3	48.7
58439	FORBES	99.1	99.0	0.0	0.0	0.0	0.0	0.5	0.5	5.3	5.8	6.3	6.3	3.9	18.4	30.6	20.9	2.4	78.2	47.5	51.9	48.1
58440	FREDONIA	99.6	99.1	0.0	0.0	0.0	0.0	0.4	0.5	6.3	7.2	7.2	5.9	4.5	16.7	32.0	18.5	1.8	75.2	46.0	51.8	48.2
58441	FULLERTON	97.9	97.3	0.0	0.0	0.6	1.0	0.9	1.3	6.0	6.3	6.7	7.3	4.7	22.3	29.0	15.7	2.0	76.3	42.4	53.3	46.7
58442	GACKLE	99.5	99.2	0.0	0.0	0.0	0.0	1.0	1.7	3.5	4.2	4.4	4.4	2.7	17.0	32.9	22.4	8.5	85.0	53.6	49.9	50.1
58443	GLENFIELD	99.4	99.1	0.0	0.0	0.0	0.0	0.3	0.3	5.0	5.6	6.2	7.4	4.7	20.5	31.2	16.9	2.4	78.0	45.3	52.8	47.2
58444	GOODRICH	98.9	98.9	0.4	0.4	0.0	0.0	0.4	0.4	3.2	4.0	4.7	6.5	4.7	17.7	32.5	22.7	4.0	83.8	50.8	50.9	49.1
58445	GRACE CITY	99.3	99.2	0.0	0.0	0.0	0.0	0.7	0.0	5.3	6.1	6.8	6.8	4.5	21.2	28.8	18.2	2.3	77.3	44.4	50.8	49.2
58448	HANNAFORD	99.7	99.7	0.0	0.0	0.0	0.0	0.0	0.3	4.9	5.4	6.0	5.4	4.6	18.6	35.1	16.3	3.7	80.0	48.1	53.4	46.6
58451	HURDSFIELD	99.6	99.6	0.0	0.0	0.0	0.0	0.0	0.4	5.2	6.0	6.0	6.0	4.7	18.5	34.1	16.8	2.6	78.4	46.7	51.3	48.7
58454	JUD	99.0	98.6	0.0	0.0	0.3	0.3	0.3	0.6	3.6	3.9	4.5	6.7	4.5	18.7	33.4	20.9	3.9	83.3	50.1	51.8	48.2
	NORTH DAKOTA	92.4	90.8	0.6	0.7	0.6	1.0	1.2	1.8	6.3	6.1	6.2	7.7	8.3	25.2	26.0	11.6	2.7	77.3	36.9	50.0	50.0
	UNITED STATES	75.1	72.0	12.3	12.7	3.8	4.6	12.5	15.7	6.8	6.7	6.6	7.1	6.9	27.0	26.0	10.9	1.9	75.7	36.9	49.2	50.8

ZIP CODE #	POST OFFICE NAME	2009 Per Capita Income	2009 HH Income Base	2009 Household Income Distribution (%): Less than $25,000	$25,000 to $49,999	$50,000 to $99,999	$100,000 to $149,999	$150,000 or More	Median Household Income: 2009	2014	2009 National Centile	2009 State Centile	2009 Home Value Base	2009 Home Value Distribution (%): Less than $50,000	$50,000 to $89,999	$90,000 to $174,999	$175,000 to $399,999	$400,000 or More	2009 Median Home Value
58258	MEKINOCK	23466	126	17.5	24.6	49.2	6.3	2.4	60000	60780	77	97	109	16.5	29.4	33.9	20.2	0.0	93750
58259	MICHIGAN	20780	219	32.4	36.1	27.9	3.7	0.0	38008	40294	27	42	179	50.8	24.6	20.1	2.8	1.7	48846
58260	MILTON	23715	69	18.8	39.1	33.3	5.8	2.9	44440	44438	47	70	58	56.9	25.9	15.5	1.7	0.0	43333
58261	MINTO	21572	518	26.8	31.1	36.1	4.1	1.9	44142	45904	46	70	426	25.1	27.0	36.2	10.6	1.2	87750
58262	MOUNTAIN	18444	64	26.6	34.4	34.4	3.1	1.6	40892	42729	36	56	53	39.6	28.3	28.3	3.8	0.0	59167
58265	NECHE	23334	231	20.8	32.5	32.9	10.8	3.0	46983	47335	54	78	207	32.4	31.9	27.1	7.2	1.4	68269
58266	NIAGARA	22780	107	15.9	39.3	41.1	3.7	0.0	47070	48000	54	79	90	24.4	35.6	25.6	14.4	0.0	76000
58267	NORTHWOOD	23114	586	22.5	31.7	38.7	4.8	2.2	45337	48294	49	73	463	23.8	32.6	33.9	9.1	0.6	84636
58269	OSNABROCK	22269	183	18.0	38.3	35.0	5.5	3.3	45185	45134	49	72	154	54.5	26.0	16.9	2.6	0.0	45882
58270	PARK RIVER	20743	914	28.1	35.3	32.5	3.0	1.1	39201	41857	30	49	715	22.9	30.8	39.2	6.0	1.1	85000
58271	PEMBINA	26399	314	13.1	26.1	49.0	9.9	1.9	56407	54397	73	95	257	12.8	28.0	45.1	13.2	0.8	100765
58272	PETERSBURG	20133	142	29.6	33.1	30.3	7.0	0.0	39378	40850	31	49	118	34.7	25.4	31.4	5.9	2.5	73333
58273	PISEK	22340	109	34.9	25.7	33.9	3.7	1.8	38634	43070	29	46	98	38.8	31.6	25.5	4.1	0.0	59167
58274	PORTLAND	22406	367	25.3	28.6	38.7	4.4	3.0	45894	47247	51	74	286	23.4	22.7	39.5	14.0	0.3	97857
58275	REYNOLDS	23081	320	12.5	25.6	52.8	5.9	3.1	59688	58437	77	96	289	11.1	19.7	46.0	21.8	1.4	123397
58276	SAINT THOMAS	25946	261	23.8	28.0	33.7	8.8	5.7	47839	49141	56	81	220	29.5	28.2	31.8	10.0	0.5	78889
58277	SHARON	26584	71	25.4	31.0	33.8	5.6	4.2	45446	45739	50	73	55	36.4	23.6	32.7	5.5	1.8	73750
58278	THOMPSON	25869	639	5.5	21.1	57.4	10.0	5.9	66569	66392	85	99	549	3.1	12.0	43.7	37.0	4.2	159844
58281	WALES	20499	34	32.4	32.4	29.4	5.9	0.0	40000	37339	33	52	30	83.3	3.3	10.0	3.3	0.0	13000
58282	WALHALLA	21895	637	26.4	37.4	30.0	4.9	1.4	40427	42335	34	53	481	26.0	32.0	32.4	8.7	0.8	82300
58301	DEVILS LAKE	24381	4003	26.2	27.3	37.6	5.8	3.1	46627	48150	53	76	2503	19.9	23.6	42.3	13.6	0.6	98282
58311	ALSEN	18316	49	36.7	30.6	26.5	4.1	2.0	37340	38185	25	38	41	48.8	22.0	24.4	4.9	0.0	55000
58316	BELCOURT	12381	2059	45.8	25.4	23.7	3.3	1.8	28539	31137	6	4	1289	26.4	22.7	38.9	11.6	0.4	92130
58317	BISBEE	22449	143	23.8	41.3	28.0	4.2	2.8	41200	42664	37	57	116	48.3	24.1	17.2	6.9	3.4	52857
58318	BOTTINEAU	20688	1589	33.8	31.6	27.1	5.9	1.7	36153	36766	21	33	1228	23.8	28.3	35.1	11.6	1.1	87524
58321	BROCKET	26073	64	23.4	29.7	37.5	6.3	3.1	47356	46363	55	80	57	35.1	14.0	33.3	14.0	3.5	91250
58323	CALVIN	18251	21	38.1	28.6	33.3	0.0	0.0	37357	35000	25	38	18	83.3	5.6	11.1	0.0	0.0	15000
58324	CANDO	25580	688	32.8	27.8	30.2	4.5	4.7	41229	43464	37	57	492	28.5	27.0	38.4	5.3	0.8	85000
58325	CHURCHS FERRY	22567	74	21.6	33.8	36.5	6.8	1.4	45000	46854	48	71	60	41.7	25.0	20.0	13.3	0.0	62500
58327	CRARY	23943	168	22.6	31.0	32.7	9.5	4.2	47345	48113	55	80	150	32.7	9.3	33.3	19.3	5.3	100000
58329	DUNSEITH	12224	1046	40.3	29.6	27.9	2.0	0.1	32012	33432	11	12	726	31.4	26.9	31.5	9.1	1.1	78478
58330	EDMORE	20370	178	34.8	30.3	28.1	5.1	1.7	36373	40000	22	33	140	57.1	23.6	10.7	5.7	2.9	36429
58331	EGELAND	18020	69	30.4	39.1	26.1	1.4	2.9	35932	38013	20	30	55	56.4	32.7	9.1	1.8	0.0	45625
58332	ESMOND	22373	169	32.0	34.3	26.6	5.3	1.8	38105	37847	27	43	146	43.2	23.3	22.6	8.9	2.1	60000
58338	HAMPDEN	22234	54	33.3	29.6	29.6	5.6	1.9	38196	40000	27	43	43	55.8	23.3	16.3	4.7	0.0	38750
58339	HANSBORO	17018	22	22.7	45.5	27.3	4.5	0.0	40000	40000	33	52	18	55.6	22.2	22.2	0.0	0.0	40000
58341	HARVEY	23829	1240	32.7	29.1	30.7	4.6	2.8	40900	42394	36	56	924	32.4	28.1	27.4	10.4	1.7	77031
58343	KNOX	19361	31	29.0	22.6	41.9	6.5	0.0	47394	50419	55	81	27	44.4	18.5	14.8	22.2	0.0	57500
58344	LAKOTA	20179	468	33.8	33.5	26.7	4.3	1.7	34847	36409	17	24	363	31.4	27.0	35.0	6.1	0.6	80469
58345	LAWTON	22588	93	30.1	33.3	29.0	5.4	2.2	38625	41703	29	46	77	50.6	22.1	16.9	6.5	3.9	48333
58346	LEEDS	21948	323	31.9	26.6	34.1	5.0	2.5	41489	42918	38	59	263	32.3	21.7	30.4	15.2	0.4	81923
58348	MADDOCK	19439	457	37.9	35.0	21.7	4.2	1.3	34305	34493	16	21	359	43.5	28.1	20.6	4.5	3.3	57833
58351	MINNEWAUKAN	21002	247	27.5	34.4	33.6	4.5	0.0	37331	37927	25	37	190	38.9	28.9	22.6	8.4	1.1	63846
58352	MUNICH	19166	183	33.3	32.8	27.3	3.8	2.7	38750	39780	29	47	153	52.3	20.3	24.8	2.6	0.0	46818
58353	MYLO	17491	104	27.9	39.4	28.8	2.9	1.0	36118	36708	21	32	86	25.6	19.8	40.7	14.0	0.0	100000
58356	NEW ROCKFORD	21336	800	35.8	30.8	25.9	3.9	3.8	34276	34580	16	21	600	43.0	30.0	20.8	4.0	2.2	58235
58357	OBERON	13985	200	31.0	27.0	38.0	3.5	0.5	37639	38244	26	40	130	43.8	23.8	27.7	2.3	2.3	57273
58361	PEKIN	20861	79	36.7	36.7	22.8	3.8	0.0	35943	37740	20	30	66	37.9	22.7	28.8	7.6	3.0	70000
58362	PENN	21200	48	16.7	29.2	47.9	6.3	0.0	52024	52937	66	90	42	19.0	28.6	31.0	19.0	2.4	93333
58363	PERTH	18795	41	22.0	43.9	29.3	4.9	0.0	41693	42301	38	61	34	52.9	23.5	17.6	5.9	0.0	40000
58365	ROCKLAKE	19915	158	28.5	39.2	27.2	2.5	2.5	37465	40000	25	39	126	54.0	31.0	11.9	3.2	0.0	46875
58366	ROLETTE	19564	405	30.9	36.5	25.9	4.7	2.0	37241	38523	24	36	281	27.8	27.8	36.3	7.5	0.7	85303
58367	ROLLA	20952	768	32.9	27.0	33.6	4.4	2.1	41151	42516	37	57	524	21.0	26.9	41.8	9.7	0.6	93793
58368	RUGBY	19741	1633	33.8	36.3	24.1	4.0	1.8	35097	36913	18	26	1191	26.4	24.4	41.0	6.9	1.3	88542
58369	SAINT JOHN	17831	464	31.7	25.6	34.1	6.3	2.4	43317	45454	43	68	396	27.0	22.0	37.1	11.9	2.0	92857
58370	SAINT MICHAEL	10094	791	45.1	23.4	26.9	2.9	1.6	28981	31071	7	6	411	38.9	18.5	30.9	8.5	3.2	74333
58372	SARLES	20351	50	32.0	38.0	24.0	4.0	2.0	37317	38604	25	37	42	73.8	14.3	9.5	2.4	0.0	22500
58374	SHEYENNE	19826	271	38.4	29.2	25.1	4.1	3.3	33712	35138	15	19	203	44.3	26.1	21.2	5.4	3.0	58214
58377	STARKWEATHER	21368	153	22.2	35.3	33.3	6.5	2.6	44056	45000	46	69	119	42.0	27.7	21.0	9.2	0.0	61875
58380	TOLNA	19804	203	34.5	36.5	23.6	4.4	1.0	37163	38429	24	36	170	38.2	22.4	28.2	7.6	3.5	68571
58381	WARWICK	12738	92	48.9	19.6	29.3	2.2	0.0	26127	30000	4	1	67	46.3	16.4	25.4	9.0	3.0	61667
58382	WEBSTER	22465	62	19.4	35.5	37.1	6.5	1.6	46142	45893	52	75	50	38.0	30.0	22.0	10.0	0.0	65000
58384	WILLOW CITY	16772	269	34.2	40.9	22.3	2.2	0.4	32316	32907	12	14	216	54.6	26.9	13.0	3.7	1.9	40909
58385	WOLFORD	14537	83	39.8	42.2	15.7	2.4	0.0	29111	29741	7	7	60	55.0	23.3	15.0	3.3	3.3	38750
58386	YORK	21015	66	31.8	28.8	33.3	6.1	0.0	40000	40561	33	52	53	39.6	22.6	24.5	13.2	0.0	68333
58401	JAMESTOWN	22980	7314	28.1	29.1	35.6	5.0	2.2	42999	45065	42	67	4699	14.5	23.4	48.6	12.5	1.0	105241
58405	JAMESTOWN	9283	54	42.6	24.1	25.9	7.4	0.0	35000	32500	18	26	15	0.0	13.3	86.7	0.0	0.0	114583
58413	ASHLEY	16989	617	47.6	31.0	17.3	2.8	1.3	26681	27829	4	2	514	53.9	25.3	14.8	4.7	1.4	46000
58415	BERLIN	15231	68	38.2	30.9	26.5	4.4	0.0	31924	33224	11	12	58	34.5	15.5	34.5	10.3	5.2	90000
58416	BINFORD	21670	177	31.6	33.3	27.1	6.2	1.7	34851	36891	17	24	148	47.3	18.9	18.9	9.5	5.4	53333
58418	BOWDON	19601	175	36.6	36.0	22.3	3.4	1.7	33389	35785	14	18	143	55.9	23.8	14.7	2.8	2.8	40556
58420	BUCHANAN	28548	111	18.9	25.2	40.5	8.1	7.2	56870	57113	74	95	100	20.0	19.0	40.0	18.0	3.0	112500
58421	CARRINGTON	21477	1238	30.0	29.6	33.0	5.4	1.9	40238	41659	33	52	907	22.7	24.8	39.5	11.5	1.5	94500
58422	CATHAY	17703	99	35.4	34.3	23.2	4.0	3.0	35958	38945	20	31	85	42.4	25.9	15.3	12.9	3.5	60833
58423	CHASELEY	17868	34	41.2	35.3	20.6	2.9	0.0	31485	33333	11	10	28	50.0	25.0	14.3	7.1	3.6	50000
58424	CLEVELAND	23473	157	33.8	29.9	28.7	3.8	3.8	38259	41277	27	43	138	39.1	26.1	26.1	6.5	2.2	68750
58425	COOPERSTOWN	21722	748	32.2	32.6	28.3	4.1	2.7	36227	37399	21	33	565	27.4	26.7	34.5	10.1	1.2	80962
58426	COURTENAY	23354	96	26.0	24.0	37.5	8.3	4.2	50000	48757	61	87	84	39.3	14.3	32.1	11.9	2.4	76667
58428	DAWSON	16231	122	45.9	32.0	17.2	4.1	0.8	28417	29419	6	4	104	42.3	22.1	24.0	7.7	3.8	62000
58429	DAZEY	20329	131	24.4	36.6	33.6	3.8	1.5	40245	41790	33	53	107	49.5	26.2	18.7	5.6	0.0	50500
58430	DENHOFF	15471	56	42.9	35.7	19.6	1.8	0.0	28852	32336	6	5	49	51.0	14.3	16.3	14.3	4.1	49000
58431	DICKEY	20882	74	36.5	29.7	25.7	6.8	1.4	33394	34269	14	18	63	36.5	17.5	27.0	11.1	7.9	77500
58433	EDGELEY	21021	538	32.7	32.2	28.4	3.9	2.8	35540	36506	19	28	429	30.8	31.7	29.4	6.3	1.9	76613
58436	ELLENDALE	16960	812	40.4	32.9	21.9	3.6	1.2	31382	33402	10	10	569	40.4	30.8	22.8	4.6	1.4	61531
58438	FESSENDEN	21644	337	32.6	33.5	29.4	3.3	1.2	40233	41474	33	52	261	46.7	30.7	18.0	4.2	0.4	52656
58439	FORBES	22689	93	31.2	29.0	31.2	4.3	4.3	40371	43908	34	53	80	38.8	16.3	27.5	11.3	6.3	80000
58440	FREDONIA	22115	99	35.4	30.3	24.2	7.1	3.0	36133	38190	21	32	87	47.1	18.4	18.4	10.3	5.7	55000
58441	FULLERTON	20943	121	25.6	35.5	33.1	4.1	1.7	41590	41827	38	60	96	30.2	24.0	37.5	6.3	2.1	86923
58442	GACKLE	21023	257	41.6	34.6	17.1	3.9	2.7	30389	31174	9	8	222	41.4	32.0	18.0	6.3	2.3	59048
58443	GLENFIELD	21119	147	25.9	36.1	32.0	5.4	0.7	38986	39118	30	48	122	42.6	24.6	17.2	13.1	2.5	56429
58444	GOODRICH	18369	135	41.5	35.6	19.3	3.0	0.7	28960	29830	7	5	117	57.3	6.8	13.7	16.2	6.0	42273
58445	GRACE CITY	20531	58	27.6	36.2	31.0	5.2	0.0	38875	38213	29	47	47	46.8	27.7	12.8	10.6	2.1	52143
58448	HANNAFORD	20641	164	29.3	37.2	29.3	2.4	1.8	37846	40201	26	41	139	37.4	21.6	27.3	9.4	4.3	65000
58451	HURDSFIELD	16904	94	39.4	37.2	18.1	4.3	1.1	32564	35268	13	15	79	39.2	31.6	13.9	11.4	3.8	62143
58454	JUD	20418	171	40.9	33.3	18.7	4.1	2.9	29815	32307	8	8	144	47.2	26.4	16.7	5.6	4.2	53636
	NORTH DAKOTA	23967		25.3	28.6	36.2	6.6	3.3	45981	48456				20.2	18.2	39.7	19.8	2.2	112133
	UNITED STATES	27277		20.9	24.4	35.3	11.7	7.6	54719	56938				9.3	13.1	31.6	32.6	13.5	162279

ZIP CODE #	POST OFFICE NAME	FINANCIAL SERVICES: Auto Loan	Home Loan	Invest-ments	Retire-ment Plans	THE HOME: Home Improvements: Home Repair	Lawn & Garden	Furnishings: Comput-ers & Hard-ware-Personal	Major Appli-ances	TV, Radio, Sound Equip-ment	Furni-ture	ENTERTAINMENT: Dine out/ Carry out	Sports Equip-ment	Fees & Tickets	Toys & Games	Travel	Cable TV	PERSONAL: Apparel & Services	Auto Repairs	Health Insur-ance	Pets & Supplies
58258	MEKINOCK	85	93	81	95	91	92	84	88	83	84	84	68	89	85	88	84	58	85	88	103
58259	MICHIGAN	74	51	82	51	54	78	57	71	59	46	58	58	42	58	56	64	38	66	75	87
58260	MILTON	93	64	102	64	67	98	71	88	74	58	73	73	52	73	71	81	47	83	93	109
58261	MINTO	88	64	91	63	66	90	66	83	72	61	71	63	53	72	65	79	47	76	86	99
58262	MOUNTAIN	82	56	90	56	59	86	62	78	65	51	64	64	46	64	62	71	42	73	82	96
58265	NECHE	105	72	116	72	76	111	80	100	84	65	83	83	59	82	80	91	54	93	106	123
58266	NIAGARA	95	66	105	65	69	101	73	91	76	59	75	75	53	74	73	83	49	85	96	111
58267	NORTHWOOD	91	64	94	63	67	95	71	87	77	61	75	68	55	76	69	85	49	82	94	104
58269	OSNABROCK	93	64	102	64	67	98	71	88	74	57	73	73	52	72	70	80	47	82	93	108
58270	PARK RIVER	78	56	80	55	58	82	61	76	68	54	66	57	49	66	59	75	44	71	82	90
58271	PEMBINA	99	87	92	90	89	106	87	99	90	78	88	76	78	91	87	95	60	92	103	116
58272	PETERSBURG	82	56	90	56	59	86	63	78	65	51	64	64	46	64	62	71	42	73	82	96
58273	PISEK	89	61	97	61	64	94	68	84	70	55	70	70	50	69	67	77	45	79	89	104
58274	PORTLAND	90	64	92	63	67	94	70	87	77	62	75	67	56	76	69	85	50	81	94	103
58275	REYNOLDS	100	87	100	89	89	108	87	100	89	78	88	78	78	89	88	94	59	93	103	118
58276	SAINT THOMAS	110	76	121	76	79	116	84	105	88	68	87	86	62	86	84	95	56	98	110	129
58277	SHARON	97	67	107	67	70	102	74	92	77	60	76	76	54	76	74	84	49	86	97	113
58278	THOMPSON	104	117	107	121	116	116	105	110	103	105	103	85	112	105	111	103	72	105	108	129
58281	WALES	73	50	81	50	53	77	56	70	58	45	58	58	41	57	56	64	37	65	74	86
58282	WALHALLA	83	59	85	58	61	87	65	80	71	56	69	62	51	69	63	78	45	75	86	95
58301	DEVILS LAKE	83	72	77	73	73	82	78	81	81	74	80	61	71	80	75	84	55	81	86	96
58311	ALSEN	82	57	90	56	59	87	63	78	65	51	65	65	46	64	62	71	42	73	82	96
58316	BELCOURT	59	48	45	49	46	53	55	53	58	53	57	40	49	58	49	60	40	56	57	65
58317	BISBEE	89	61	98	61	64	94	68	85	71	55	70	70	50	70	68	77	45	79	89	104
58318	BOTTINEAU	79	58	85	56	61	83	62	77	67	55	66	58	50	66	62	74	43	72	82	91
58321	BROCKET	101	69	110	69	72	106	77	95	80	62	79	79	56	78	76	87	51	89	101	117
58323	CALVIN	73	50	80	50	53	77	56	69	58	45	57	57	41	57	55	63	37	65	73	85
58324	CANDO	97	67	107	67	70	103	74	92	77	60	76	76	54	76	74	84	49	86	97	113
58325	CHURCHS FERRY	94	65	103	64	68	99	72	89	75	58	74	74	52	73	71	81	48	83	94	110
58327	CRARY	108	75	119	74	78	114	83	103	86	67	85	85	61	84	82	94	55	96	109	127
58329	DUNSEITH	59	46	51	46	44	57	49	53	54	47	53	41	44	54	46	57	36	53	58	66
58330	EDMORE	80	55	88	55	58	84	61	76	64	50	63	63	45	62	61	69	41	71	80	93
58331	EGELAND	78	54	86	54	56	82	60	74	62	48	61	61	44	61	59	68	40	69	78	91
58332	ESMOND	84	58	92	58	61	88	64	80	67	52	66	65	47	66	64	73	43	75	85	98
58338	HAMPDEN	83	57	91	57	59	87	63	78	66	51	65	65	46	64	63	72	42	73	83	97
58339	HANSBORO	79	54	87	54	57	83	60	75	63	49	62	62	44	61	60	68	40	70	79	92
58341	HARVEY	86	61	88	60	63	90	67	83	73	58	71	64	52	72	65	80	47	77	89	98
58343	KNOX	87	60	96	60	63	92	67	83	69	54	68	68	49	68	66	75	44	77	87	102
58344	LAKOTA	74	53	76	52	55	77	58	71	63	50	61	55	45	62	56	70	41	67	77	85
58345	LAWTON	85	59	93	58	61	90	65	81	68	53	67	67	48	66	65	74	43	75	85	99
58346	LEEDS	89	61	98	61	64	94	68	84	71	55	70	70	50	69	67	77	45	79	89	104
58348	MADDOCK	72	51	75	50	53	75	56	69	61	48	59	54	43	60	54	67	39	64	74	82
58351	MINNEWAUKAN	78	55	83	55	57	81	61	73	63	51	62	60	46	62	60	68	41	69	77	90
58352	MUNICH	81	56	89	55	58	85	62	77	64	50	63	63	45	63	61	70	41	72	81	94
58353	MYLO	78	54	86	53	56	82	59	74	62	48	61	61	44	61	59	67	40	69	78	91
58356	NEW ROCKFORD	80	57	82	56	59	84	62	77	69	55	67	59	49	68	61	76	44	72	84	91
58357	OBERON	73	60	68	58	59	71	62	68	63	58	63	54	53	64	59	65	42	66	69	82
58361	PEKIN	74	52	81	51	54	78	57	71	60	47	59	58	42	59	57	66	39	66	75	87
58362	PENN	102	70	112	70	73	108	78	97	81	63	80	80	57	79	77	88	52	90	102	119
58363	PERTH	88	60	96	60	63	93	67	83	70	54	69	69	49	68	67	76	45	78	88	102
58365	ROCKLAKE	81	56	89	55	58	85	62	77	64	50	63	63	45	63	61	70	41	72	81	94
58366	ROLETTE	75	53	77	52	56	79	59	73	64	51	62	56	46	63	57	71	41	68	78	86
58367	ROLLA	79	62	77	61	64	81	67	77	72	61	70	58	57	71	65	77	47	73	83	90
58368	RUGBY	72	56	72	56	58	74	61	69	63	54	62	54	51	63	59	68	42	67	74	83
58369	SAINT JOHN	79	74	62	70	70	70	73	72	73	76	73	55	69	76	68	73	50	73	71	86
58370	SAINT MICHAEL	61	50	45	49	47	52	57	53	60	57	59	41	51	61	50	61	41	57	56	66
58372	SARLES	74	51	82	51	53	78	57	70	59	46	58	58	42	58	56	64	38	66	74	87
58374	SHEYENNE	78	58	77	56	59	80	62	74	67	56	66	57	50	67	60	73	44	70	79	88
58377	STARKWEATHER	94	65	104	65	68	100	72	90	75	58	74	74	53	73	72	82	48	84	95	110
58380	TOLNA	74	51	81	51	53	78	57	70	59	46	58	58	42	58	56	64	38	66	74	87
58381	WARWICK	66	45	65	43	45	66	48	59	54	44	53	47	36	54	45	59	35	56	62	73
58382	WEBSTER	95	66	105	65	69	101	73	90	76	59	75	75	53	74	72	83	49	84	95	111
58384	WILLOW CITY	67	46	73	46	48	70	51	63	53	41	52	52	37	52	51	58	34	59	67	78
58385	WOLFORD	61	42	67	42	44	65	47	58	49	38	48	48	34	48	47	53	31	54	62	72
58386	YORK	83	57	91	57	59	87	63	78	66	51	65	65	46	64	63	72	42	73	83	96
58401	JAMESTOWN	77	64	71	65	65	77	70	74	73	66	72	56	63	73	67	77	49	74	80	88
58405	JAMESTOWN	62	40	38	44	39	43	74	50	66	58	66	46	54	66	52	64	47	61	53	64
58413	ASHLEY	60	43	62	42	45	63	47	58	51	41	50	45	37	50	46	56	33	54	63	69
58415	BERLIN	69	48	76	48	50	73	53	66	55	43	54	54	39	54	53	60	35	61	69	81
58416	BINFORD	83	57	91	57	60	88	64	79	66	51	65	65	47	65	63	72	42	74	83	97
58418	BOWDON	75	52	82	51	54	79	57	71	60	46	59	59	42	58	57	65	38	66	75	88
58420	BUCHANAN	128	88	140	88	92	135	98	121	102	79	100	100	72	100	97	111	65	113	128	149
58421	CARRINGTON	85	60	87	59	63	89	66	82	73	58	70	63	52	71	64	80	47	76	89	97
58422	CATHAY	79	54	87	54	57	83	60	75	63	49	62	62	44	62	60	68	40	70	79	92
58423	CHASELEY	64	44	70	44	46	67	49	61	51	40	50	50	36	50	49	55	33	57	64	75
58424	CLEVELAND	93	64	102	64	67	98	71	89	74	58	73	73	52	73	71	81	48	83	94	109
58425	COOPERSTOWN	81	57	86	56	59	85	63	78	67	53	66	62	48	66	62	74	43	73	83	94
58426	COURTENAY	101	69	111	69	73	106	77	96	80	62	79	79	56	79	77	87	51	89	101	118
58428	DAWSON	65	45	72	45	47	69	50	62	52	40	51	51	36	51	50	56	33	58	65	76
58429	DAZEY	85	58	93	58	61	90	65	81	67	53	67	67	47	66	65	74	43	75	85	99
58430	DENHOFF	68	47	75	47	49	72	52	65	54	42	54	53	38	53	52	59	35	60	68	80
58431	DICKEY	81	56	89	55	58	85	62	77	64	50	63	63	45	63	61	70	41	72	81	94
58433	EDGELEY	83	59	87	58	61	87	65	80	70	55	68	63	50	69	63	77	45	75	86	96
58436	ELLENDALE	69	49	71	48	51	72	53	66	59	47	57	51	42	58	52	64	38	62	72	79
58438	FESSENDEN	84	58	93	58	61	89	64	80	67	52	66	66	47	66	64	73	43	75	85	99
58439	FORBES	90	62	99	62	65	95	69	85	71	56	71	71	50	70	68	78	46	80	90	105
58440	FREDONIA	89	61	97	61	64	94	68	84	70	55	70	70	50	69	67	77	45	79	89	104
58441	FULLERTON	93	64	102	64	67	98	71	88	74	57	73	73	52	72	71	80	47	82	93	108
58442	GACKLE	74	51	81	51	53	78	56	70	59	46	58	58	41	57	56	64	38	65	74	86
58443	GLENFIELD	87	60	95	59	62	91	66	82	69	54	68	68	48	67	66	75	44	77	87	101
58444	GOODRICH	67	46	74	46	49	71	51	64	54	42	53	53	38	53	51	58	34	60	68	79
58445	GRACE CITY	84	57	92	57	60	88	64	79	66	52	66	66	47	65	63	72	43	74	84	98
58448	HANNAFORD	79	54	86	54	57	83	60	75	63	49	62	62	44	61	60	68	40	70	79	92
58451	HURDSFIELD	75	51	82	51	54	79	57	71	59	46	59	59	42	58	57	65	38	66	75	87
58454	JUD	77	53	84	53	55	81	58	73	61	47	60	60	43	60	58	66	39	68	77	89
	NORTH DAKOTA	87	73	80	73	72	84	80	82	81	74	81	65	71	81	75	84	55	82	85	99
	UNITED STATES	100	100	100	100	100	100	100	100	100	100	100	100	100	100	100	100	100	100	100	100

58455-58647

ZIP CODE #	POST OFFICE NAME	COUNTY FIPS CODE	POPULATION 2000	POPULATION 2009	POPULATION 2014	2000-2009 ANNUAL RATE % Rate	2000-2009 ANNUAL RATE State Centile	HOUSEHOLDS 2000	HOUSEHOLDS 2009	HOUSEHOLDS 2014	HOUSEHOLDS % Annual Rate 2000-2009	HOUSEHOLDS 2009 Average HH Size	FAMILIES 2000	FAMILIES 2009	FAMILIES % Annual Rate 2000-2009
58455	KENSAL	093	360	325	310	-1.1	19	141	137	132	-0.3	2.37	108	101	-0.7
58456	KULM	045	634	589	567	-0.8	39	294	288	281	-0.2	2.05	198	185	-0.7
58458	LAMOURE	045	1457	1393	1353	-0.5	60	553	563	554	0.2	2.40	367	355	-0.4
58460	LEHR	047	295	282	278	-0.5	60	144	147	147	0.2	1.92	108	106	-0.2
58461	LITCHVILLE	003	534	496	477	-0.8	39	230	227	220	-0.1	2.19	170	161	-0.6
58463	MCCLUSKY	083	784	661	622	-1.8	4	350	311	296	-1.3	2.06	224	188	-1.9
58464	MCHENRY	027	257	242	235	-0.6	55	105	105	103	0.0	2.30	79	76	-0.4
58466	MARION	045	397	371	358	-0.7	50	168	168	164	0.0	2.20	118	113	-0.5
58467	MEDINA	093	665	628	607	-0.6	55	281	283	278	0.1	2.22	192	183	-0.5
58472	MONTPELIER	093	480	471	459	-0.2	74	184	193	191	0.5	2.44	135	136	0.1
58474	OAKES	021	2794	2621	2503	-0.7	50	1136	1107	1066	-0.3	2.27	738	683	-0.8
58475	PETTIBONE	043	205	184	178	-1.2	14	89	88	86	-0.1	2.09	67	63	-0.7
58476	PINGREE	093	309	273	257	-1.3	9	124	117	112	-0.6	2.33	93	84	-1.1
58477	REGAN	015	167	181	192	0.9	96	72	83	89	1.5	2.18	52	56	0.8
58478	ROBINSON	043	232	200	191	-1.6	5	108	102	99	-0.6	1.96	74	67	-1.1
58479	ROGERS	003	258	232	220	-1.1	19	95	90	87	-0.6	2.58	70	64	-1.0
58480	SANBORN	003	377	348	331	-0.9	32	144	140	136	-0.3	2.49	111	104	-0.7
58481	SPIRITWOOD	003	266	253	244	-0.5	60	110	110	108	0.0	2.30	85	82	-0.4
58482	STEELE	043	1101	1035	1008	-0.7	50	465	470	464	0.1	2.11	290	278	-0.5
58483	STREETER	093	356	332	318	-0.8	39	158	156	152	-0.1	2.12	110	104	-0.6
58484	SUTTON	039	90	86	84	-0.5	60	35	36	36	0.3	2.39	27	26	-0.4
58486	SYKESTON	103	362	326	307	-1.1	19	147	140	134	-0.5	2.33	98	89	-1.0
58487	TAPPEN	043	537	517	506	-0.4	66	204	214	213	0.5	2.42	150	151	0.1
58488	TUTTLE	043	326	283	271	-1.5	6	152	145	141	-0.5	1.95	105	96	-1.0
58490	VERONA	045	311	291	283	-0.7	50	120	121	119	0.1	2.40	90	88	-0.2
58492	WIMBLEDON	003	535	480	456	-1.2	14	206	195	187	-0.6	2.46	151	137	-1.0
58494	WING	015	368	389	408	0.6	91	167	189	201	1.3	2.06	119	126	0.6
58495	WISHEK	051	1525	1469	1452	-0.4	66	610	616	616	0.1	2.19	402	384	-0.5
58496	WOODWORTH	093	257	229	216	-1.2	14	111	106	101	-0.5	2.16	84	77	-0.9
58497	YPSILANTI	093	357	370	366	0.4	89	135	149	149	1.1	2.48	103	109	0.6
58501	BISMARCK	015	27188	28577	29367	0.5	91	11843	12801	13387	0.8	2.10	6977	6958	0.0
58503	BISMARCK	015	16570	22843	25689	3.5	99	6287	9011	10279	4.0	2.53	4703	6421	3.4
58504	BISMARCK	015	22652	24494	25862	0.8	95	8381	9687	10386	1.6	2.39	5638	6195	1.0
58520	ALMONT	059	286	300	305	0.5	91	104	114	118	1.0	2.46	80	85	0.7
58521	BALDWIN	015	405	478	530	1.8	99	159	201	226	2.6	2.38	126	152	2.0
58523	BEULAH	057	4245	4041	3900	-0.5	60	1617	1626	1589	0.1	2.44	1160	1119	-0.4
58524	BRADDOCK	029	161	154	152	-0.5	60	67	68	68	0.2	2.19	46	45	-0.2
58529	CARSON	037	863	788	756	-1.0	24	335	327	318	-0.3	2.32	240	225	-0.7
58530	CENTER	065	1438	1321	1284	-0.9	32	571	573	564	0.0	2.30	422	408	-0.4
58531	COLEHARBOR	055	337	327	320	-0.3	71	137	144	143	0.5	2.27	108	111	0.3
58532	DRISCOLL	015	263	298	316	1.4	98	105	126	137	2.0	2.36	78	90	1.6
58533	ELGIN	037	1032	1039	1021	0.1	85	464	490	486	0.6	1.96	279	279	0.0
58535	FLASHER	059	644	642	647	0.0	82	256	274	281	0.7	2.34	185	189	0.2
58538	FORT YATES	085	2301	2449	2512	0.7	94	598	653	675	1.0	3.59	474	502	0.6
58540	GARRISON	055	2067	1891	1812	-1.0	24	883	858	830	-0.3	2.10	585	544	-0.8
58541	GOLDEN VALLEY	057	183	171	165	-0.7	50	91	90	87	-0.1	1.90	64	60	-0.7
58542	HAGUE	029	327	299	288	-1.0	24	125	124	121	-0.1	2.41	99	95	-0.4
58544	HAZELTON	029	467	436	424	-0.7	50	214	213	210	-0.1	1.96	146	139	-0.5
58545	HAZEN	057	3645	3500	3394	-0.4	66	1376	1413	1389	0.3	2.45	1046	1036	-0.1
58549	KINTYRE	047	245	229	223	-0.7	50	87	87	86	0.0	2.56	61	59	-0.4
58552	LINTON	029	2135	1955	1882	-0.9	32	917	891	869	-0.3	2.16	615	570	-0.8
58554	MANDAN	059	20268	21635	22350	0.7	94	7864	8931	9345	1.4	2.38	5550	6040	0.9
58558	MENOKEN	015	591	632	660	0.7	94	205	232	247	1.3	2.72	164	178	0.9
58559	MERCER	055	221	222	219	0.0	82	108	118	117	1.0	1.88	75	77	0.3
58560	MOFFIT	015	186	203	213	0.9	96	71	82	87	1.6	2.45	54	59	1.0
58561	NAPOLEON	047	1211	1120	1081	-0.8	39	496	487	476	-0.2	2.23	338	316	-0.7
58562	NEW LEIPZIG	037	586	498	466	-1.7	5	255	231	219	-1.1	2.15	180	156	-1.5
58563	NEW SALEM	059	2104	2187	2239	0.4	89	811	897	936	1.1	2.40	570	600	0.6
58564	RALEIGH	037	78	70	66	-1.2	14	32	30	28	-0.7	2.10	24	21	-1.4
58565	RIVERDALE	055	273	249	237	-1.0	24	108	106	102	-0.2	2.35	82	78	-0.5
58566	SAINT ANTHONY	059	207	209	213	0.1	85	76	82	85	0.8	2.55	58	61	0.5
58568	SELFRIDGE	085	545	557	568	0.2	88	196	209	214	0.7	2.67	149	154	0.4
58569	SHIELDS	037	112	100	95	-1.2	14	47	44	42	-0.7	2.05	35	31	-1.3
58570	SOLEN	085	1452	1546	1585	0.7	94	380	418	432	1.0	3.67	306	327	0.7
58571	STANTON	057	572	506	483	-1.3	9	251	241	233	-0.4	2.07	172	157	-1.0
58572	STERLING	015	410	454	480	1.1	97	162	190	204	1.7	2.38	127	141	1.1
58573	STRASBURG	029	1087	1006	975	-0.8	39	399	397	389	-0.1	2.47	291	278	-0.5
58575	TURTLE LAKE	055	921	846	810	-0.9	32	428	423	411	-0.1	1.98	274	255	-0.8
58576	UNDERWOOD	055	1065	948	898	-1.3	9	421	400	383	-0.6	2.24	302	275	-1.0
58577	WASHBURN	055	1819	1710	1647	-0.7	50	721	726	709	0.1	2.35	529	511	-0.4
58579	WILTON	015	1376	1386	1399	0.1	85	530	570	584	0.8	2.41	387	395	0.2
58580	ZAP	057	231	211	201	-1.0	24	101	97	94	-0.4	2.18	78	73	-0.7
58581	ZEELAND	051	307	298	295	-0.3	71	136	141	141	0.4	2.11	101	101	0.0
58601	DICKINSON	089	19126	19387	19460	0.1	85	7584	8150	8294	0.8	2.27	4893	4993	0.2
58620	AMIDON	087	549	516	502	-0.7	50	215	218	215	0.1	2.37	153	149	-0.3
58621	BEACH	033	1367	1244	1183	-1.0	24	565	537	514	-0.5	2.12	365	330	-1.1
58622	BELFIELD	089	1432	1401	1393	-0.2	74	558	582	587	0.5	2.41	384	381	-0.1
58623	BOWMAN	011	2222	2125	2055	-0.5	60	926	937	918	0.1	2.17	584	561	-0.4
58625	DODGE	025	163	160	156	-0.2	74	65	68	68	0.5	2.35	43	43	0.0
58626	DUNN CENTER	025	226	209	202	-0.8	39	101	100	97	-0.1	2.08	78	75	-0.4
58627	FAIRFIELD	007	378	337	320	-1.2	14	151	149	143	-0.1	2.26	106	99	-0.7
58630	GLADSTONE	089	550	570	577	0.4	89	211	236	243	1.2	2.42	165	178	0.8
58631	GLEN ULLIN	059	1218	1274	1313	0.5	91	490	543	571	1.1	2.15	317	332	0.5
58632	GOLVA	033	269	245	231	-1.0	24	103	99	95	-0.4	2.47	75	69	-0.9
58634	GRASSY BUTTE	053	218	211	210	-0.4	66	91	94	95	0.4	2.24	71	71	0.0
58636	HALLIDAY	025	802	776	754	-0.4	66	315	325	320	0.3	2.38	217	214	-0.2
58638	HEBRON	059	991	1038	1070	0.5	91	430	472	495	1.0	2.19	285	296	0.4
58639	HETTINGER	001	2191	2038	1973	-0.8	39	943	936	917	-0.1	2.09	602	567	-0.6
58640	KILLDEER	025	1523	1419	1365	-0.8	39	581	572	557	-0.2	2.40	408	384	-0.7
58641	LEFOR	089	105	107	108	0.2	88	42	46	47	1.0	2.28	33	34	0.3
58642	MANNING	025	437	402	387	-0.9	32	157	155	151	-0.1	2.59	121	115	-0.5
58643	MARMARTH	087	218	205	200	-0.7	50	98	100	98	0.2	2.05	70	68	-0.3
58645	MEDORA	007	279	249	236	-1.2	14	128	126	121	-0.2	1.98	90	84	-0.7
58646	MOTT	041	1469	1468	1416	0.0	82	603	600	584	-0.1	2.18	407	385	-0.6
58647	NEW ENGLAND	041	977	878	837	-1.1	19	429	413	398	-0.4	2.11	281	257	-1.0
	NORTH DAKOTA					0.2					0.8	2.27			0.2
	UNITED STATES					1.0					1.1	2.59			0.9

#	POST OFFICE NAME	White 2000	White 2009	Black 2000	Black 2009	Asian/Pacific 2000	Asian/Pacific 2009	% Hispanic Origin 2000	% Hispanic Origin 2009	0-4	5-9	10-14	15-19	20-24	25-44	45-64	65-84	85+	18+	Median Age 2009	% 2009 Males	% 2009 Females
58455	KENSAL	99.4	99.1	0.3	0.3	0.0	0.0	0.0	0.0	4.6	5.8	6.2	6.8	5.2	18.8	35.4	15.1	2.2	79.1	46.4	52.9	47.1
58456	KULM	99.1	99.0	0.2	0.2	0.0	0.0	1.1	1.9	4.2	4.8	5.6	5.9	4.1	19.5	31.1	21.1	3.7	82.0	49.0	52.0	48.0
58458	LAMOURE	99.2	99.1	0.0	0.0	0.1	0.1	0.5	0.7	6.0	6.2	6.0	6.5	6.3	20.2	28.8	15.6	4.3	77.0	43.5	49.0	51.0
58460	LEHR	99.7	99.6	0.0	0.0	0.0	0.0	0.3	0.4	6.0	6.7	6.7	5.7	4.6	17.0	31.6	19.1	2.5	76.2	46.7	51.8	48.2
58461	LITCHVILLE	99.3	99.0	0.0	0.0	0.2	0.2	0.2	0.2	4.8	5.4	6.0	7.1	4.4	18.8	34.7	16.1	2.6	79.4	46.8	51.0	49.0
58463	MCCLUSKY	99.4	99.2	0.1	0.2	0.0	0.0	0.4	0.3	3.5	4.2	5.1	5.6	3.3	17.4	31.9	23.8	5.1	83.1	52.5	49.2	50.8
58464	MCHENRY	98.8	98.3	0.0	0.0	0.4	0.8	0.4	0.4	5.8	6.6	6.6	7.0	4.5	20.2	29.3	17.4	2.5	76.0	44.3	51.7	48.3
58466	MARION	99.0	98.9	0.0	0.0	0.3	0.3	0.3	0.3	3.8	4.3	5.1	7.0	4.3	19.1	33.7	19.4	3.2	82.2	48.6	51.2	48.8
58467	MEDINA	99.2	99.2	0.2	0.2	0.2	0.2	0.3	0.6	4.8	5.7	6.5	7.0	3.8	19.9	31.4	17.7	3.2	78.5	46.3	50.2	49.8
58472	MONTPELIER	99.2	98.9	0.0	0.0	0.0	0.2	0.4	0.4	4.5	4.9	6.8	7.6	3.6	23.1	32.3	15.1	2.1	78.8	44.7	52.2	47.8
58474	OAKES	97.7	96.6	0.1	0.1	0.8	1.3	1.9	3.1	6.4	6.8	7.0	6.4	4.1	22.2	26.9	15.3	4.8	75.5	42.6	50.5	49.5
58475	PETTIBONE	100.0	99.5	0.0	0.0	0.0	0.5	0.5	1.1	3.3	3.8	4.3	5.4	5.4	19.0	35.3	20.7	2.7	85.3	49.7	52.2	47.8
58476	PINGREE	98.7	98.5	0.3	0.4	0.3	0.4	0.6	1.1	5.1	5.9	6.6	6.2	4.0	22.7	33.0	14.7	1.8	78.4	44.6	54.6	45.4
58477	REGAN	97.6	97.8	0.0	0.0	0.6	0.6	0.6	0.0	5.5	6.6	6.6	6.1	3.9	22.1	30.9	16.0	2.2	77.3	44.3	52.5	47.5
58478	ROBINSON	99.6	99.5	0.0	0.0	0.0	0.0	1.3	2.5	2.5	3.0	4.0	4.5	4.5	18.0	37.0	22.5	4.0	88.0	52.9	52.5	47.5
58479	ROGERS	99.2	99.1	0.0	0.0	0.0	0.0	0.0	0.0	6.0	6.9	6.9	6.0	4.3	22.0	32.3	13.8	1.7	75.9	43.5	51.3	48.7
58480	SANBORN	98.4	97.7	0.3	0.3	0.0	0.3	0.0	0.0	6.6	7.5	7.2	5.5	4.0	22.1	31.9	13.5	1.7	75.3	43.1	52.3	47.7
58481	SPIRITWOOD	98.5	98.4	0.0	0.0	0.4	0.4	0.0	0.0	5.1	6.7	7.9	7.9	3.6	22.5	32.4	12.3	1.6	74.3	42.8	53.0	47.0
58482	STEELE	99.5	99.3	0.3	0.3	0.0	0.1	0.2	0.3	6.7	6.8	6.4	4.9	4.8	19.2	27.0	18.2	6.1	77.0	45.8	49.2	50.8
58483	STREETER	98.9	98.8	0.0	0.0	0.0	0.0	0.3	0.6	4.5	5.1	5.7	6.9	4.8	17.5	33.7	17.8	3.9	80.4	47.9	51.8	48.2
58484	SUTTON	100.0	100.0	0.0	0.0	0.0	0.0	0.0	0.0	4.7	4.7	4.7	4.7	4.7	18.6	37.2	17.4	3.5	81.4	50.6	47.7	52.3
58486	SYKESTON	99.4	99.4	0.3	0.3	0.0	0.0	0.3	0.3	4.6	5.2	5.8	7.1	4.0	18.4	32.2	19.0	3.7	79.8	47.9	52.1	47.9
58487	TAPPEN	99.6	99.2	0.2	0.4	0.0	0.2	0.6	1.0	5.6	6.0	6.6	6.8	4.1	19.0	33.7	16.1	2.3	77.8	46.1	53.4	46.6
58488	TUTTLE	99.7	99.3	0.0	0.0	0.0	0.4	1.2	2.1	2.5	3.2	3.5	4.9	4.2	17.7	37.5	22.6	3.9	88.0	52.7	52.3	47.7
58490	VERONA	99.7	99.3	0.0	0.0	0.0	0.0	0.3	0.3	4.5	5.2	5.5	6.2	4.5	18.9	34.4	18.6	2.4	81.4	47.7	52.6	47.4
58492	WIMBLEDON	99.3	99.2	0.2	0.2	0.0	0.0	0.2	0.2	5.6	6.5	6.9	6.9	4.4	20.8	32.7	14.0	2.3	76.7	44.2	51.3	48.7
58494	WING	98.1	97.7	0.0	0.0	0.3	0.3	0.5	0.5	5.9	6.4	6.9	5.9	3.9	22.4	30.6	15.7	2.3	76.9	43.9	51.7	48.3
58495	WISHEK	99.0	98.8	0.0	0.0	0.1	0.1	1.2	1.8	4.9	5.1	5.1	5.4	4.8	17.4	25.4	22.9	9.1	81.5	50.3	46.6	53.4
58496	WOODWORTH	99.2	98.7	0.0	0.4	0.0	0.0	0.4	0.9	4.8	6.1	6.6	6.1	3.9	22.7	33.6	14.0	2.2	78.6	44.9	54.6	45.4
58497	YPSILANTI	99.2	98.9	0.0	0.0	0.0	0.0	0.3	0.5	5.1	5.4	8.6	8.6	2.7	25.1	31.6	11.4	1.4	75.4	41.8	52.4	47.6
58501	BISMARCK	95.5	93.7	0.3	0.4	0.4	0.7	0.7	1.1	5.3	5.1	5.2	6.9	8.0	25.6	26.4	13.6	3.9	80.7	40.1	48.2	51.8
58503	BISMARCK	96.4	95.3	0.2	0.2	0.6	0.9	0.6	0.9	7.6	7.5	7.3	7.0	5.6	27.5	27.2	9.3	1.0	73.2	36.1	48.3	51.7
58504	BISMARCK	93.1	91.1	0.3	0.4	0.3	0.5	0.8	1.1	6.2	6.1	6.1	8.1	8.2	29.0	27.3	7.8	1.2	77.5	34.6	49.6	50.4
58520	ALMONT	98.3	98.3	0.0	0.0	0.3	0.3	0.0	0.0	6.3	6.7	7.0	7.7	4.3	19.7	27.7	15.3	5.3	74.3	43.9	50.3	49.7
58521	BALDWIN	97.8	96.9	0.0	0.0	1.0	1.9	0.2	0.4	5.9	6.3	6.5	6.7	3.8	23.6	31.8	14.0	1.5	77.0	43.2	52.7	47.3
58523	BEULAH	95.0	93.6	0.0	0.0	0.8	1.3	0.5	0.8	4.7	5.3	5.7	7.9	7.4	19.8	34.0	12.1	3.1	79.5	44.3	50.2	49.8
58524	BRADDOCK	98.8	98.7	0.0	0.0	0.6	0.6	1.9	1.9	5.2	5.8	6.5	7.1	3.9	16.2	29.9	20.1	5.2	76.6	48.1	50.0	50.0
58529	CARSON	96.4	95.4	0.0	0.0	0.1	0.1	0.7	1.0	4.7	5.5	7.1	8.5	3.9	20.4	30.7	16.5	2.7	76.4	44.9	53.0	47.0
58530	CENTER	96.9	96.4	0.2	0.2	0.0	0.0	0.5	0.7	4.5	5.5	5.8	6.5	4.5	21.3	36.9	13.1	1.9	79.4	46.1	51.9	48.1
58531	COLEHARBOR	98.5	97.6	0.0	0.0	0.0	0.3	0.0	0.0	4.6	5.2	5.8	5.8	4.3	19.0	34.6	19.0	1.8	80.7	48.4	51.7	48.3
58532	DRISCOLL	98.9	98.7	0.0	0.0	0.0	0.3	0.0	0.0	5.7	6.4	7.0	7.4	4.0	20.8	30.5	16.1	2.0	75.8	43.9	51.3	48.7
58533	ELGIN	96.8	95.6	0.0	0.0	0.8	1.3	0.7	1.0	3.9	4.4	5.0	5.5	4.4	16.3	27.9	23.2	9.3	82.5	53.1	48.3	51.7
58535	FLASHER	98.3	97.7	0.0	0.0	0.2	0.2	0.5	0.8	5.6	6.9	6.9	7.5	4.5	22.0	30.1	14.5	2.2	76.0	42.7	54.2	45.8
58538	FORT YATES	5.4	4.0	0.0	0.0	0.0	0.0	1.7	1.6	11.8	11.4	9.6	9.3	8.4	27.3	17.2	4.8	0.2	61.9	24.7	50.4	49.6
58540	GARRISON	94.1	91.3	0.0	0.0	0.2	0.3	0.9	1.2	4.3	4.5	5.0	5.4	4.6	18.7	29.5	21.4	6.6	82.5	50.4	46.3	53.7
58541	GOLDEN VALLEY	98.4	98.2	0.0	0.0	0.0	0.0	0.0	0.0	2.3	7.0	6.4	6.4	2.3	21.1	35.1	18.1	1.2	79.5	47.0	52.6	47.4
58542	HAGUE	99.7	99.3	0.0	0.0	0.0	0.3	0.3	0.7	7.4	8.0	8.0	6.7	4.7	19.7	27.8	15.7	2.0	72.6	41.6	51.5	48.5
58544	HAZELTON	98.9	98.6	0.0	0.0	0.4	0.7	1.9	2.5	5.3	5.7	6.2	6.9	3.9	16.1	29.8	20.4	5.7	77.5	48.5	50.7	49.3
58545	HAZEN	97.1	96.2	0.1	0.1	0.4	0.7	0.3	0.5	5.1	5.7	6.5	8.7	5.7	19.8	34.3	11.8	2.3	76.7	43.8	49.9	50.1
58549	KINTYRE	99.2	99.1	0.0	0.0	0.4	0.4	1.2	1.7	5.7	6.6	6.6	6.6	3.9	16.2	31.0	19.7	3.9	76.0	47.3	51.1	48.9
58552	LINTON	99.1	98.8	0.0	0.1	0.4	0.6	0.9	1.4	5.4	5.6	5.9	6.9	5.1	17.8	27.9	20.7	4.7	78.0	47.2	49.0	51.0
58554	MANDAN	95.3	94.0	0.2	0.2	0.3	0.5	0.7	1.1	6.6	6.6	6.7	7.2	6.4	25.7	28.3	10.5	1.8	75.4	37.9	49.8	50.2
58558	MENOKEN	99.0	98.7	0.2	0.2	0.0	0.2	0.3	0.6	4.9	5.7	6.5	6.6	4.3	22.0	35.6	13.1	1.3	78.6	45.0	53.2	46.8
58559	MERCER	99.5	98.6	0.0	0.0	0.0	0.5	0.5	0.9	4.5	5.4	6.3	6.8	4.1	19.8	36.5	14.9	1.8	78.8	46.9	52.3	47.7
58560	MOFFIT	99.5	99.0	0.0	0.0	0.0	0.0	0.5	0.5	5.4	6.4	6.4	6.9	4.4	21.2	31.5	15.8	2.0	76.4	44.4	52.2	47.8
58561	NAPOLEON	99.0	98.8	0.1	0.1	0.2	0.3	0.6	0.9	5.7	6.2	6.5	4.9	3.4	16.0	27.7	25.4	4.2	77.9	50.7	49.0	51.0
58562	NEW LEIPZIG	99.0	98.4	0.0	0.0	0.2	0.2	0.2	0.4	3.8	4.6	5.0	6.4	4.8	16.9	34.7	19.7	4.0	82.3	50.2	51.2	48.8
58563	NEW SALEM	98.0	97.4	0.0	0.0	0.2	0.3	0.2	0.3	5.8	6.4	6.8	7.4	4.8	19.4	28.9	16.8	3.9	75.9	44.6	49.3	50.7
58564	RALEIGH	93.6	91.4	0.0	0.0	0.0	0.0	1.3	1.4	2.9	5.7	8.6	12.9	4.3	18.6	28.6	15.7	2.9	71.4	42.5	57.1	42.9
58565	RIVERDALE	97.4	95.6	0.0	0.0	0.4	0.4	0.0	0.4	4.4	5.6	6.0	6.4	4.4	17.3	34.1	20.1	1.6	79.9	49.0	49.8	50.2
58566	SAINT ANTHONY	99.0	99.0	0.0	0.0	0.0	0.0	0.5	0.5	5.7	7.2	7.2	8.6	4.8	22.0	29.2	13.4	1.9	74.2	41.4	54.1	45.9
58568	SELFRIDGE	52.1	43.8	0.0	0.0	0.2	0.2	1.1	1.3	8.6	8.6	7.5	9.5	6.1	22.3	26.8	10.1	0.5	68.4	33.4	52.8	47.2
58569	SHIELDS	93.8	92.0	0.0	0.0	0.0	0.0	0.9	1.0	4.0	4.0	9.0	13.0	4.0	17.0	31.0	16.0	2.0	72.0	44.0	58.0	42.0
58570	SOLEN	29.0	25.2	0.0	0.0	0.1	0.1	1.5	1.5	10.0	9.8	9.5	10.9	7.5	23.8	20.8	7.0	0.7	63.3	26.5	48.3	51.7
58571	STANTON	96.7	95.7	0.0	0.0	0.7	1.2	0.2	0.2	3.4	5.3	7.9	5.7	3.0	22.3	35.2	15.6	1.6	79.2	46.2	52.8	47.2
58572	STERLING	99.0	98.7	0.0	0.0	0.2	0.2	0.2	0.2	5.3	5.9	6.6	6.8	4.4	21.6	33.5	14.3	1.5	77.5	44.5	52.4	47.6
58573	STRASBURG	99.2	98.9	0.0	0.0	0.4	0.5	1.3	1.7	6.1	6.8	7.0	6.9	4.2	17.6	29.6	18.1	3.9	75.3	45.9	51.4	48.6
58575	TURTLE LAKE	99.1	98.5	0.0	0.0	0.1	0.2	0.0	0.0	4.1	4.6	5.0	5.2	4.5	18.1	32.4	19.9	6.3	83.0	51.0	51.3	48.7
58576	UNDERWOOD	97.3	95.3	0.0	0.0	0.0	0.1	0.2	0.3	4.0	4.9	5.4	5.4	3.7	19.4	35.5	16.7	5.1	82.2	50.3	49.2	50.8
58577	WASHBURN	98.8	98.0	0.0	0.0	0.1	0.1	0.4	0.7	4.7	4.8	7.7	8.3	4.1	21.9	33.7	13.2	1.6	76.8	44.1	50.9	49.1
58579	WILTON	98.4	97.5	0.1	0.1	0.2	0.5	0.5	0.7	5.4	6.0	6.3	5.9	4.3	21.8	33.3	14.9	2.2	78.4	45.2	50.6	49.4
58580	ZAP	97.8	97.2	0.0	0.0	0.0	0.0	0.0	0.5	5.2	5.7	6.6	8.5	2.4	23.2	34.1	11.8	2.4	75.8	43.9	55.0	45.0
58581	ZEELAND	99.3	99.3	0.0	0.0	0.0	0.0	0.3	0.0	5.4	6.0	6.4	5.7	4.7	17.8	32.2	18.8	3.0	78.2	47.3	51.7	48.3
58601	DICKINSON	97.3	96.5	0.2	0.3	0.3	0.4	1.1	1.7	5.9	6.0	6.0	8.8	7.9	24.7	25.5	12.2	2.8	77.6	36.8	49.2	50.8
58620	AMIDON	99.6	99.6	0.0	0.0	0.0	0.0	0.2	0.2	4.3	5.4	5.8	5.8	4.1	19.6	36.4	16.5	2.1	80.8	48.0	53.3	46.7
58621	BEACH	97.4	96.8	0.0	0.0	0.1	0.2	1.4	1.7	5.4	5.9	7.3	10.6	4.4	18.3	27.0	15.4	5.6	72.9	42.9	46.7	53.3
58622	BELFIELD	98.0	97.6	0.2	0.2	0.3	0.6	1.0	1.5	5.8	6.4	7.6	8.3	4.9	22.8	29.1	12.8	2.5	74.1	41.1	52.5	47.5
58623	BOWMAN	99.0	98.8	0.0	0.0	0.0	0.0	0.7	1.1	4.8	5.2	5.7	6.4	4.8	19.9	31.2	17.0	5.0	80.0	47.0	48.5	51.5
58625	DODGE	96.9	93.8	0.0	0.0	0.0	0.0	1.2	1.9	4.4	5.0	6.3	6.3	4.4	19.4	33.1	17.5	3.8	80.6	48.2	50.6	49.4
58626	DUNN CENTER	97.3	94.7	0.0	0.0	0.0	0.0	0.4	0.5	4.3	5.3	5.7	6.2	4.3	18.7	34.9	18.2	2.4	80.9	48.4	52.6	47.4
58627	FAIRFIELD	99.2	99.1	0.0	0.0	0.0	0.0	0.3	0.3	3.6	5.0	7.7	8.6	2.7	22.6	32.6	14.5	2.7	76.9	44.9	53.4	46.6
58630	GLADSTONE	98.5	97.5	0.0	0.0	0.0	0.2	1.5	2.5	5.3	6.0	6.3	7.2	5.3	22.5	33.2	13.0	1.4	78.1	43.2	51.6	48.4
58631	GLEN ULLIN	99.0	98.7	0.0	0.0	0.2	0.3	0.0	0.0	4.6	4.6	5.5	7.1	3.0	17.6	24.4	25.4	7.9	80.2	50.6	48.5	51.5
58632	GOLVA	98.9	98.8	0.0	0.0	0.0	0.0	0.0	0.0	6.1	6.9	7.3	6.9	4.1	20.8	30.6	14.7	2.4	75.1	43.4	51.4	48.6
58634	GRASSY BUTTE	99.5	99.5	0.0	0.0	0.0	0.0	0.0	0.0	3.8	4.7	6.2	7.6	4.7	17.1	38.4	15.6	1.9	80.6	48.9	52.1	47.9
58636	HALLIDAY	69.1	65.7	0.0	0.0	0.1	0.1	1.0	1.2	6.4	7.0	6.7	7.1	5.0	20.0	30.4	14.6	2.8	75.5	43.3	52.3	47.7
58638	HEBRON	96.1	94.5	0.1	0.1	0.7	1.3	1.0	1.5	5.6	6.3	6.6	7.3	5.2	17.3	28.9	18.9	3.9	76.0	46.0	47.9	52.1
58639	HETTINGER	98.4	98.1	0.6	0.7	0.2	0.2	0.3	0.3	4.5	4.9	5.5	6.1	5.3	17.3	32.3	18.4	5.5	81.1	49.1	47.4	52.6
58640	KILLDEER	86.6	82.0	0.0	0.0	0.1	0.2	0.7	1.0	5.9	6.4	6.7	7.1	4.9	20.0	31.1	14.0	3.9	75.8	44.2	50.3	49.7
58641	LEFOR	100.0	99.1	0.0	0.0	0.0	0.9	1.0	0.9	5.6	7.5	7.5	7.5	3.7	23.4	29.9	13.1	1.9	73.8	41.1	50.5	49.5
58642	MANNING	98.4	97.3	0.0	0.0	0.0	0.0	0.7	1.2	5.0	6.2	6.7	7.0	4.2	21.1	33.1	14.9	1.7	77.6	44.8	53.7	46.3
58643	MARMARTH	100.0	100.0	0.0	0.0	0.0	0.0	0.0	0.0	3.9	4.9	5.9	5.9	4.4	20.5	36.1	16.6	2.0	81.5	47.6	53.2	46.8
58645	MEDORA	98.9	98.8	0.0	0.0	0.0	0.0	0.4	0.4	3.2	5.2	7.2	8.8	2.8	22.9	32.5	14.9	2.4	77.9	44.9	53.4	46.6
58646	MOTT	99.3	99.3	0.3	0.3	0.1	0.1	0.1	0.1	4.4	4.9	5.7	5.9	4.0	14.7	29.5	20.6	10.3	81.0	51.9	49.4	50.6
58647	NEW ENGLAND	98.6	98.1	0.0	0.0	0.2	0.3	0.4	0.6	4.7	4.2	5.4	6.0	3.6	19.1	35.0	18.7	3.3	81.7	49.5	50.3	49.7
	NORTH DAKOTA	92.4	90.8	0.6	0.7	0.6	1.0	1.2	1.8	6.3	6.1	6.2	7.7	8.3	25.2	26.0	11.6	2.7	77.3	36.9	50.0	50.0
	UNITED STATES	75.1	72.0	12.3	12.7	3.8	4.6	12.5	15.7	6.8	6.7	6.6	7.1	6.9	27.0	26.0	10.9	1.9	75.7	36.9	49.2	50.8

ZIP CODE				2009 HOUSEHOLD INCOME DISTRIBUTION (%)					MEDIAN HOUSEHOLD INCOME					2009 HOME VALUE DISTRIBUTION (%)					
#	POST OFFICE NAME	2009 Per Capita Income	2009 HH Income Base	Less than $25,000	$25,000 to $49,999	$50,000 to $99,999	$100,000 to $149,999	$150,000 or More	2009	2014	2009 National Centile	2009 State Centile	2009 Home Value Base	Less than $50,000	$50,000 to $89,999	$90,000 to $174,999	$175,000 to $399,999	$400,000 or More	2009 Median Home Value
58455	KENSAL	23474	137	25.5	27.0	35.0	8.0	4.4	47370	47321	55	80	120	36.7	15.8	31.7	12.5	3.3	85000
58456	KULM	23804	288	31.9	31.3	30.2	3.1	3.5	35846	38140	20	29	237	45.6	23.6	21.5	7.2	2.1	55526
58458	LAMOURE	20667	563	29.0	30.9	31.1	6.0	3.0	38518	39159	28	45	426	29.3	30.8	30.0	8.0	1.9	76774
58460	LEHR	24566	147	34.7	32.0	23.8	6.1	3.4	34759	37039	17	23	128	50.8	18.0	18.0	9.4	3.9	48889
58461	LITCHVILLE	22346	227	30.8	29.1	33.5	4.4	2.2	40479	41414	34	54	199	37.7	19.1	30.7	8.5	4.0	73889
58463	MCCLUSKY	17823	311	43.7	32.8	18.6	3.5	1.3	29588	30000	7	8	249	59.0	19.3	10.8	8.4	2.4	41346
58464	MCHENRY	20396	105	27.6	37.1	27.6	5.7	1.9	37873	37909	26	42	87	46.0	23.0	13.8	12.6	4.6	53889
58466	MARION	19363	168	38.7	32.1	23.2	4.2	1.8	32315	34558	12	14	143	42.0	24.5	23.1	6.3	4.2	60556
58467	MEDINA	21780	283	35.3	30.0	27.6	3.9	3.2	36715	40165	23	35	248	42.3	25.8	25.8	4.8	1.2	64286
58472	MONTPELIER	20672	193	25.9	36.8	30.6	4.1	2.6	41676	43354	38	61	169	33.7	24.9	27.8	11.2	2.4	75909
58474	OAKES	21187	1107	31.9	34.5	26.3	4.5	2.8	37449	38022	25	39	795	24.9	26.4	40.0	8.4	0.3	88433
58475	PETTIBONE	17880	88	44.3	27.3	25.0	3.4	0.0	29053	31136	7	6	76	36.8	11.8	30.3	11.8	9.2	92500
58476	PINGREE	29973	117	20.5	31.6	30.8	8.5	8.5	47790	46730	56	81	95	30.5	18.9	28.4	12.6	9.5	90833
58477	REGAN	20599	83	36.1	27.7	31.3	2.4	2.4	34436	37993	16	22	70	45.7	21.4	20.0	11.4	1.4	55000
58478	ROBINSON	20586	102	46.1	26.5	24.5	2.9	0.0	28164	28928	6	4	83	45.8	14.5	16.9	15.7	7.2	58750
58479	ROGERS	19289	90	22.2	37.8	34.4	4.4	1.1	40748	41929	35	55	73	38.4	27.4	27.4	6.8	0.0	62500
58480	SANBORN	21010	140	20.0	37.1	37.1	5.0	0.7	42843	43892	42	67	116	28.4	26.7	36.2	8.6	0.0	80000
58481	SPIRITWOOD	24386	110	19.1	30.0	44.5	4.5	1.8	50574	50925	63	88	95	23.2	18.9	47.4	10.5	0.0	106944
58482	STEELE	20318	470	35.5	33.8	24.3	4.3	2.1	34804	35905	17	24	365	26.8	21.1	40.5	9.9	1.6	93571
58483	STREETER	26046	156	38.5	29.5	23.7	3.2	5.1	37986	41181	27	42	136	47.1	22.8	19.1	7.4	3.7	54000
58484	SUTTON	19521	36	33.3	30.6	27.8	8.3	0.0	35000	33571	18	26	30	53.3	20.0	13.3	6.7	6.7	47500
58486	SYKESTON	18419	140	37.1	35.7	22.1	3.6	1.4	32821	35395	13	16	114	57.0	22.8	14.9	2.6	2.6	39000
58487	TAPPEN	15240	214	45.8	32.2	17.3	4.2	0.5	28609	29487	6	5	183	42.1	20.8	24.6	8.2	4.4	64375
58488	TUTTLE	20731	145	44.8	26.9	24.1	2.8	1.4	29057	29755	7	6	120	42.5	15.0	18.3	15.0	9.2	64286
58490	VERONA	22854	121	25.6	24.8	43.8	5.0	0.8	49457	50653	60	84	109	21.1	18.3	42.2	11.0	7.3	107237
58492	WIMBLEDON	19997	195	24.1	35.9	33.3	4.6	2.1	40866	42340	36	55	160	43.8	25.0	24.4	5.6	1.3	56667
58494	WING	21044	189	38.6	27.5	29.1	2.6	2.1	31883	34167	11	11	156	50.6	22.4	17.3	7.7	1.9	49231
58495	WISHEK	21639	616	32.5	37.0	23.7	2.8	4.1	36513	37979	22	34	496	35.7	27.4	30.4	5.6	0.8	69118
58496	WOODWORTH	32784	106	20.8	31.1	30.2	8.5	9.4	47880	48073	56	82	88	27.3	19.3	31.8	13.6	8.0	96000
58497	YPSILANTI	21750	149	17.4	37.6	37.6	4.0	3.4	46945	47136	54	77	133	28.6	23.3	33.8	12.8	1.5	87222
58501	BISMARCK	26379	12801	23.1	27.7	39.4	7.0	2.8	49141	51726	59	84	7273	4.0	7.4	65.9	21.9	0.9	143579
58503	BISMARCK	30515	9011	12.4	22.4	41.9	16.1	7.2	65586	67201	84	99	7074	14.2	7.5	24.4	49.3	4.6	184274
58504	BISMARCK	27006	9687	17.8	23.3	44.5	10.2	4.3	60020	60834	77	97	7035	24.5	6.4	35.7	29.8	3.6	138086
58520	ALMONT	19576	114	27.2	37.7	28.9	4.4	1.8	40000	42056	33	52	95	47.4	20.0	17.9	10.5	4.2	54167
58521	BALDWIN	25518	201	21.9	21.4	45.3	8.5	3.0	60100	60194	77	97	184	16.8	12.5	31.5	35.9	3.3	148529
58523	BEULAH	22427	1626	25.3	21.2	43.6	8.4	1.5	53323	53177	69	94	1322	18.0	23.5	47.3	10.2	1.0	101107
58524	BRADDOCK	18214	68	38.2	30.9	25.0	4.4	1.5	33877	36134	15	20	57	47.4	19.3	21.1	8.8	3.5	55000
58529	CARSON	15895	327	47.4	29.7	19.0	2.4	1.5	26746	27300	4	2	264	45.5	20.1	18.9	9.8	5.7	56667
58530	CENTER	22617	573	23.2	28.4	40.7	6.8	0.9	47907	48179	56	82	487	19.9	24.4	41.3	13.3	1.0	97432
58531	COLEHARBOR	22448	144	25.0	29.2	41.0	4.2	0.7	46854	47321	54	77	131	20.6	23.7	38.9	13.7	3.1	102083
58532	DRISCOLL	18932	126	31.7	33.3	31.7	3.2	0.0	36515	38090	22	34	104	48.1	19.2	22.1	8.7	1.9	53333
58533	ELGIN	18709	490	45.7	31.8	19.0	2.2	1.2	27161	28047	5	2	375	48.3	24.8	19.5	5.6	1.9	52321
58535	FLASHER	20781	274	34.7	28.5	29.6	4.7	2.6	41530	43494	38	60	232	39.7	18.1	22.0	11.6	8.6	66364
58538	FORT YATES	10808	653	39.4	30.6	26.6	2.6	0.8	32260	34247	12	13	239	32.2	13.0	40.6	11.7	2.5	107738
58540	GARRISON	20030	858	33.6	32.3	29.8	2.9	1.4	37288	39491	24	36	697	27.4	27.7	34.4	9.5	1.0	81744
58541	GOLDEN VALLEY	21619	90	41.1	24.4	30.0	3.3	1.1	34064	35446	16	20	80	43.8	20.0	25.0	7.5	3.8	60000
58542	HAGUE	19904	124	39.5	33.9	17.7	4.8	4.0	30877	30213	9	9	110	34.5	18.2	17.3	19.1	10.9	84000
58544	HAZELTON	20104	213	39.4	29.6	25.4	4.2	1.4	33235	35000	14	17	181	45.9	18.8	22.1	9.4	3.9	57500
58545	HAZEN	25379	1413	21.5	18.5	47.7	8.9	3.3	57180	57285	74	95	1215	14.2	23.5	49.2	11.8	1.3	105093
58549	KINTYRE	17471	87	37.9	28.7	26.4	5.7	1.1	35366	37849	19	27	75	46.7	18.7	21.3	9.3	4.0	56250
58552	LINTON	18555	891	39.7	30.8	23.9	4.2	1.5	32022	32562	11	12	715	37.2	24.5	28.8	6.6	2.9	69468
58554	MANDAN	24750	8931	20.9	25.8	43.0	6.8	3.5	52849	54429	68	92	6602	19.8	17.7	41.5	18.2	2.7	114708
58558	MENOKEN	22606	232	15.1	26.3	50.4	4.7	3.4	60126	60420	77	98	215	22.8	13.5	34.4	24.2	5.1	122500
58559	MERCER	25538	118	29.7	28.8	35.6	4.2	1.7	43449	43299	44	69	101	26.7	25.7	25.7	17.8	4.0	83750
58560	MOFFIT	20460	82	24.4	29.3	41.5	3.7	1.2	46156	45572	52	75	71	35.2	19.7	28.2	14.1	2.8	77500
58561	NAPOLEON	21940	487	36.1	29.2	27.1	3.7	3.9	35921	37541	20	30	411	43.1	30.7	17.5	7.1	1.7	59500
58562	NEW LEIPZIG	18572	231	37.7	35.1	22.5	3.5	1.3	33527	35203	14	19	191	50.3	20.9	17.3	7.9	3.7	49688
58563	NEW SALEM	20276	897	30.2	33.4	29.7	3.8	2.9	39577	41028	31	50	745	39.9	25.4	21.5	11.4	1.9	66146
58564	RALEIGH	17237	30	50.0	20.0	26.7	0.0	3.3	25000	30000	3	1	26	38.5	19.2	19.2	15.4	7.7	70000
58565	RIVERDALE	21978	106	22.6	27.4	42.5	6.6	0.9	50000	49210	61	87	96	14.6	36.5	40.6	8.3	0.0	88333
58566	SAINT ANTHONY	19622	82	29.3	36.6	25.6	4.9	3.7	41283	43051	37	58	71	39.4	15.5	23.9	15.5	5.6	68333
58568	SELFRIDGE	13248	209	42.6	37.8	16.7	1.4	1.4	28315	28653	6	4	134	41.8	14.9	28.4	8.2	6.7	70000
58569	SHIELDS	18170	44	50.0	20.5	25.0	0.0	4.5	25000	32344	3	1	38	34.2	15.8	23.7	13.2	13.2	90000
58570	SOLEN	9950	418	45.2	28.7	23.2	2.2	0.7	27558	28536	5	3	264	36.0	20.8	26.9	11.0	5.3	72500
58571	STANTON	26139	241	23.7	24.9	43.6	6.6	1.2	50951	51579	63	88	220	31.4	38.2	20.9	9.5	0.0	64615
58572	STERLING	23028	190	21.1	28.9	44.2	3.7	2.1	50000	51624	61	87	168	31.0	16.7	29.8	18.5	4.2	96667
58573	STRASBURG	17359	397	39.3	31.5	22.2	4.3	2.8	32142	32765	12	13	343	41.4	18.7	19.5	13.4	7.0	67941
58575	TURTLE LAKE	21309	423	34.3	32.4	28.6	3.3	1.4	35816	37987	20	29	347	34.9	37.5	19.9	6.3	1.4	58898
58576	UNDERWOOD	22331	400	26.5	27.0	38.3	6.5	1.8	45575	46663	50	74	341	29.3	34.3	33.4	2.3	0.6	73276
58577	WASHBURN	22767	726	25.6	26.4	39.0	7.2	1.8	47733	48144	56	81	590	19.0	21.9	43.1	15.1	1.0	107031
58579	WILTON	19780	570	28.8	29.8	36.0	4.4	1.1	41725	42576	38	61	482	24.3	23.2	38.4	11.6	2.5	94138
58580	ZAP	24225	97	33.0	23.7	37.1	3.1	3.1	42362	43196	41	65	84	40.5	22.6	26.2	7.1	3.6	61429
58581	ZEELAND	20541	141	37.6	31.9	23.4	4.3	2.8	32289	34153	12	13	122	53.3	19.7	15.6	9.0	2.5	46364
58601	DICKINSON	22400	8150	27.8	28.8	35.0	5.7	2.7	44181	46246	46	70	5532	7.8	14.7	58.5	17.2	1.8	125686
58620	AMIDON	18644	218	41.7	28.9	24.8	0.9	3.7	29415	30509	7	7	188	49.5	18.1	25.5	6.4	0.5	50833
58621	BEACH	18707	537	33.0	35.4	27.2	4.3	0.2	35664	36350	20	29	419	34.6	35.8	24.8	3.8	1.0	66282
58622	BELFIELD	17069	582	35.6	34.5	26.1	3.4	0.3	34435	36754	16	22	475	33.5	28.6	29.9	6.7	1.3	73387
58623	BOWMAN	22566	937	29.0	34.7	29.5	4.2	2.7	39395	40447	31	49	736	22.0	26.1	41.8	9.4	0.7	92222
58625	DODGE	19346	68	42.6	30.9	20.6	4.4	1.5	30882	33148	10	9	57	45.6	22.8	22.8	5.3	3.5	58333
58626	DUNN CENTER	18630	100	34.0	39.0	24.0	3.0	0.0	35978	36231	21	31	80	35.0	21.3	30.0	11.3	2.5	80000
58627	FAIRFIELD	21871	149	32.2	29.5	30.9	4.7	2.7	39688	40852	32	50	116	37.9	13.8	31.0	10.3	6.9	86000
58630	GLADSTONE	20698	236	22.5	30.5	43.2	3.8	0.0	46401	48955	53	76	209	18.7	10.5	47.8	18.2	4.8	133190
58631	GLEN ULLIN	19355	543	32.8	36.6	26.3	2.9	1.3	34860	36935	17	25	451	58.1	25.1	11.3	4.4	1.1	43364
58632	GOLVA	19050	99	31.3	33.3	29.3	4.0	2.0	38375	41384	28	44	79	41.8	21.5	29.1	6.3	1.3	61250
58634	GRASSY BUTTE	23853	94	23.4	37.2	29.8	7.4	2.1	42586	43282	41	66	86	29.1	16.3	47.7	5.8	1.2	104167
58636	HALLIDAY	18012	325	41.5	30.8	21.5	3.7	2.5	30955	32767	10	9	250	40.4	23.2	27.6	5.6	3.2	66429
58638	HEBRON	16912	472	43.0	32.8	21.2	2.1	0.8	28773	29938	6	5	398	69.1	18.3	9.8	2.5	0.3	32083
58639	HETTINGER	22143	936	36.4	34.4	21.9	4.2	3.1	34221	35231	16	20	664	33.9	27.1	31.2	6.2	1.7	74048
58640	KILLDEER	20240	572	34.3	27.6	31.1	3.7	3.3	39478	40375	31	50	447	26.2	30.0	32.4	8.9	2.5	80517
58641	LEFOR	19042	46	32.6	28.3	34.8	2.2	2.2	37362	41156	25	39	40	25.0	20.0	30.0	20.0	5.0	96667
58642	MANNING	19241	155	26.5	35.5	31.0	4.5	2.6	41571	42795	38	60	136	27.9	15.4	30.9	16.9	8.8	115000
58643	MARMARTH	21390	100	39.0	29.0	25.0	2.0	5.0	31281	30000	10	9	87	47.1	18.4	26.4	6.9	1.1	54167
58645	MEDORA	25078	126	31.7	27.8	34.1	4.0	2.4	41313	41653	37	58	98	39.8	14.3	28.6	11.2	6.1	80000
58646	MOTT	19221	600	36.2	33.5	23.2	4.3	2.8	34860	35739	17	25	510	46.3	30.2	17.8	5.5	0.2	53016
58647	NEW ENGLAND	20800	413	32.2	34.6	27.6	5.1	0.5	37502	38319	25	39	339	33.9	27.7	31.3	6.8	0.3	68036
	NORTH DAKOTA	23967		25.3	28.6	36.2	6.6	3.3	45981	48456				20.2	18.2	39.7	19.8	2.2	112133
	UNITED STATES	27277		20.9	24.4	35.3	11.7	7.6	54719	56938				9.3	13.1	31.6	32.6	13.5	162279

ZIP CODE		FINANCIAL SERVICES				THE HOME						ENTERTAINMENT						PERSONAL			
#	POST OFFICE NAME					Home Improvements		Furnishings													
		Auto Loan	Home Loan	Investments	Retirement Plans	Home Repair	Lawn & Garden	Computers & Hardware-Personal	Major Appliances	TV, Radio, Sound Equipment	Furniture	Dine out/ Carry out	Sports Equipment	Fees & Tickets	Toys & Games	Travel	Cable TV	Apparel & Services	Auto Repairs	Health Insurance	Pets & Supplies
58455	KENSAL	100	68	109	68	72	105	76	94	79	62	78	78	56	78	76	86	51	88	100	116
58456	KULM	87	60	96	60	63	92	66	83	69	54	68	68	49	68	66	75	44	77	87	102
58458	LAMOURE	86	61	88	60	64	90	67	83	74	59	72	63	53	73	65	82	48	78	90	98
58460	LEHR	84	58	93	58	61	89	64	80	67	52	66	66	47	66	64	73	43	75	84	98
58461	LITCHVILLE	87	60	96	60	63	92	67	83	69	54	69	69	49	68	66	76	44	77	88	102
58463	MCCLUSKY	67	46	73	46	48	70	51	63	53	41	52	52	37	52	51	58	34	59	67	78
58464	MCHENRY	84	58	92	58	61	89	64	80	67	52	66	66	47	65	64	73	43	74	84	98
58466	MARION	76	53	84	52	55	81	58	72	61	47	60	60	43	59	58	66	39	68	77	89
58467	MEDINA	86	59	95	59	62	91	66	82	69	53	68	68	48	67	66	75	44	77	87	101
58472	MONTPELIER	90	62	99	62	65	95	69	86	72	56	71	71	50	70	69	78	46	80	90	105
58474	OAKES	87	61	92	60	64	90	66	83	71	57	70	65	51	70	65	78	46	77	88	99
58475	PETTIBONE	67	46	73	46	48	71	51	63	53	41	53	52	37	52	51	58	34	59	67	78
58476	PINGREE	125	86	137	86	90	132	96	119	99	77	98	98	70	97	95	108	64	111	125	146
58477	REGAN	80	55	88	55	58	85	61	76	64	50	63	63	45	63	61	70	41	71	81	94
58478	ROBINSON	72	50	79	50	52	76	55	69	57	45	57	57	40	56	55	63	37	64	72	84
58479	ROGERS	89	61	98	61	64	94	68	84	71	55	70	70	50	69	68	77	45	79	89	104
58480	SANBORN	93	64	103	64	67	99	71	89	74	58	73	73	52	73	71	81	48	83	94	109
58481	SPIRITWOOD	100	69	110	69	72	106	77	95	80	62	79	79	56	78	76	87	51	89	101	117
58482	STEELE	75	54	77	52	56	79	59	73	64	51	62	56	46	63	57	71	41	68	79	86
58483	STREETER	99	68	109	68	71	104	76	94	79	61	78	78	55	77	75	86	50	88	99	116
58484	SUTTON	83	57	92	57	60	88	64	79	66	52	65	65	47	65	63	72	42	74	84	97
58486	SYKESTON	77	53	84	53	55	81	59	73	61	47	60	60	43	60	58	66	39	68	77	90
58487	TAPPEN	66	45	72	45	47	69	50	62	52	41	52	52	37	51	50	57	34	58	66	77
58488	TUTTLE	72	50	79	50	52	76	55	69	57	45	57	57	40	56	55	63	37	64	73	85
58490	VERONA	98	68	108	67	71	104	75	93	78	61	77	77	55	77	75	85	50	87	99	115
58492	WIMBLEDON	88	61	97	60	63	93	67	84	70	54	69	69	49	69	67	76	45	78	88	103
58494	WING	77	53	85	53	56	82	59	74	62	48	61	61	43	60	59	67	39	69	78	90
58495	WISHEK	85	61	87	59	63	89	66	82	73	58	71	63	52	72	65	81	47	77	89	97
58496	WOODWORTH	127	87	139	87	91	134	97	120	101	78	99	99	71	99	96	110	65	112	127	148
58497	YPSILANTI	97	66	106	66	70	102	74	92	77	60	76	76	54	75	73	84	49	86	97	113
58501	BISMARCK	81	76	72	78	74	78	83	78	84	80	84	61	80	83	79	85	58	82	84	94
58503	BISMARCK	112	117	108	116	115	111	110	111	108	114	109	85	112	111	111	107	76	109	107	130
58504	BISMARCK	97	97	85	96	93	91	97	93	95	98	96	73	95	98	93	94	67	94	92	110
58520	ALMONT	89	62	98	61	64	94	68	85	71	55	70	70	50	70	68	77	46	79	90	104
58521	BALDWIN	104	81	109	80	82	106	84	99	85	75	85	81	68	86	84	90	56	93	100	120
58523	BEULAH	90	78	83	76	77	87	77	85	79	75	79	65	69	81	74	82	53	81	85	101
58524	BRADDOCK	72	50	80	50	52	76	55	69	58	45	57	57	41	56	55	63	37	64	73	85
58529	CARSON	67	46	74	46	48	71	51	64	53	42	53	53	38	52	51	58	34	59	67	78
58530	CENTER	93	65	99	64	68	96	70	88	75	61	74	69	54	74	69	82	48	81	92	106
58531	COLEHARBOR	91	63	100	63	66	96	70	86	72	57	72	71	51	71	69	79	46	81	91	106
58532	DRISCOLL	80	55	88	55	57	84	61	76	63	49	63	63	45	62	61	69	41	71	80	93
58533	ELGIN	65	47	67	46	48	68	51	63	56	44	54	48	40	55	50	62	36	59	68	75
58535	FLASHER	87	60	96	60	63	92	66	83	69	54	68	68	49	68	66	75	44	77	87	102
58538	FORT YATES	59	50	42	52	46	54	54	51	58	54	57	40	52	59	49	60	39	55	57	65
58540	GARRISON	74	53	77	52	55	78	58	72	63	50	61	55	45	62	56	70	41	67	77	85
58541	GOLDEN VALLEY	73	51	81	50	53	78	56	70	58	45	58	58	41	57	56	64	37	65	74	86
58542	HAGUE	86	59	94	59	62	91	66	81	68	53	67	67	48	67	65	74	44	76	86	100
58544	HAZELTON	72	50	79	50	52	76	55	68	57	45	57	57	40	56	55	63	37	64	72	84
58545	HAZEN	101	85	98	84	85	101	87	97	90	82	89	75	76	90	85	94	60	93	100	116
58549	KINTYRE	81	56	89	56	58	86	62	77	64	50	64	64	45	63	62	70	41	72	81	95
58552	LINTON	69	49	72	48	51	73	54	67	59	47	57	52	42	58	53	65	38	62	72	80
58554	MANDAN	90	84	79	83	82	89	84	87	86	83	85	66	80	87	81	88	59	86	90	103
58558	MENOKEN	89	94	89	96	92	98	86	92	85	84	85	73	88	87	90	87	59	88	92	109
58559	MERCER	86	59	94	59	62	91	66	81	68	53	68	67	48	67	65	75	44	76	86	100
58560	MOFFIT	84	67	89	68	69	90	69	82	71	61	71	67	58	71	70	75	47	77	85	99
58561	NAPOLEON	89	61	98	61	64	94	68	84	71	55	70	70	50	69	68	77	45	79	89	104
58562	NEW LEIPZIG	72	49	79	49	52	76	55	68	57	44	56	56	40	56	54	62	36	63	72	84
58563	NEW SALEM	84	61	88	60	63	88	66	81	71	57	69	64	52	70	65	78	46	76	87	97
58564	RALEIGH	68	47	75	47	49	72	52	65	54	42	53	53	38	53	52	59	35	60	68	80
58565	RIVERDALE	92	64	101	63	66	97	71	88	73	57	73	72	52	72	70	80	47	82	93	108
58566	SAINT ANTHONY	89	62	98	61	64	94	68	85	71	55	70	70	50	70	68	77	46	79	90	104
58568	SELFRIDGE	63	44	69	44	46	66	48	60	50	39	50	49	36	49	48	55	32	56	63	73
58569	SHIELDS	70	48	77	48	50	74	54	67	56	43	55	55	39	55	53	61	36	62	70	82
58570	SOLEN	58	46	48	47	44	56	50	52	54	48	53	41	45	54	47	57	36	53	57	65
58571	STANTON	98	70	101	68	72	99	72	91	79	66	78	69	57	79	71	87	52	84	95	109
58572	STERLING	87	77	91	78	77	94	76	87	77	69	77	70	69	77	78	81	52	82	89	105
58573	STRASBURG	78	53	85	53	56	82	59	74	62	48	61	61	43	61	59	67	40	69	78	91
58575	TURTLE LAKE	73	52	75	51	54	76	57	70	62	49	60	54	44	61	55	68	40	66	76	84
58576	UNDERWOOD	92	66	96	64	68	94	68	87	75	62	74	66	54	74	68	82	49	80	90	104
58577	WASHBURN	84	75	84	77	76	91	74	84	76	67	75	66	67	76	75	80	51	79	87	100
58579	WILTON	80	63	80	65	65	85	66	78	68	57	67	62	55	68	66	73	45	73	82	94
58580	ZAP	94	65	103	65	68	99	72	89	75	58	74	74	53	73	72	82	48	84	94	110
58581	ZEELAND	78	53	85	53	56	82	59	74	62	48	61	61	43	60	59	67	40	69	78	91
58601	DICKINSON	78	69	70	70	68	75	75	75	76	71	76	58	69	76	71	78	52	76	79	89
58620	AMIDON	79	54	87	54	57	83	60	75	63	49	62	62	44	61	60	68	40	70	79	92
58621	BEACH	72	51	76	50	53	76	56	69	60	47	59	55	43	59	55	66	39	65	74	84
58622	BELFIELD	71	50	73	49	52	74	55	68	60	48	58	52	43	59	54	66	39	63	74	81
58623	BOWMAN	88	62	94	61	64	93	68	84	73	57	71	67	52	71	67	80	47	79	90	102
58625	DODGE	81	56	89	56	59	86	62	77	65	50	64	64	46	63	62	71	41	72	82	95
58626	DUNN CENTER	69	48	76	48	50	73	53	66	55	43	55	55	39	54	53	60	35	62	70	81
58627	FAIRFIELD	88	61	97	61	64	93	68	84	70	55	69	69	49	69	67	77	45	78	89	103
58630	GLADSTONE	80	69	76	71	70	86	69	80	72	61	70	62	61	72	69	76	48	74	83	94
58631	GLEN ULLIN	75	53	77	52	55	78	58	72	64	51	62	55	46	63	57	70	41	67	78	86
58632	GOLVA	84	58	93	58	61	89	64	80	67	52	66	66	47	66	64	73	43	75	85	98
58634	GRASSY BUTTE	96	66	105	66	69	101	73	91	76	59	75	75	54	75	73	83	49	85	96	112
58636	HALLIDAY	74	53	75	54	54	76	59	69	62	50	61	56	46	61	57	67	40	66	74	85
58638	HEBRON	63	45	64	44	47	66	49	61	55	44	53	46	39	54	48	60	35	57	66	72
58639	HETTINGER	82	58	85	57	60	86	64	79	69	55	67	61	49	68	62	76	45	73	85	94
58640	KILLDEER	87	61	93	61	63	91	68	82	71	56	70	68	51	69	67	77	46	77	87	101
58641	LEFOR	79	54	86	54	57	83	60	75	62	49	62	62	44	61	60	68	40	70	79	92
58642	MANNING	89	61	98	61	64	94	68	85	71	55	70	70	50	70	68	77	45	79	89	104
58643	MARMARTH	78	54	86	54	56	83	60	74	62	49	62	62	44	61	60	68	40	69	79	92
58645	MEDORA	89	61	97	61	64	94	68	84	70	55	70	70	50	69	67	77	45	79	89	104
58646	MOTT	80	55	87	55	57	84	61	76	63	49	63	63	45	62	61	69	41	71	80	93
58647	NEW ENGLAND	79	54	86	54	57	83	60	75	63	49	62	62	44	61	60	68	40	70	79	92
	NORTH DAKOTA	87	73	80	73	72	84	80	82	81	74	81	65	71	81	75	84	55	82	85	99
	UNITED STATES	100	100	100	100	100	100	100	100	100	100	100	100	100	100	100	100	100	100	100	100

ZIP CODE #	POST OFFICE NAME	COUNTY FIPS CODE	POPULATION 2000	POPULATION 2009	POPULATION 2014	2000-2009 ANNUAL RATE % Rate	2000-2009 ANNUAL RATE State Centile	HOUSEHOLDS 2000	HOUSEHOLDS 2009	HOUSEHOLDS 2014	HOUSEHOLDS % Annual Rate 2000-2009	HOUSEHOLDS 2009 Average HH Size	FAMILIES 2000	FAMILIES 2009	FAMILIES % Annual Rate 2000-2009
58649	REEDER	001	364	352	345	-0.4	66	165	172	170	0.5	2.05	113	111	-0.2
58650	REGENT	041	321	284	269	-1.3	9	138	132	126	-0.5	2.15	107	98	-0.9
58651	RHAME	011	424	386	368	-1.0	24	184	179	174	-0.3	2.16	128	119	-0.8
58652	RICHARDTON	089	1161	1162	1165	0.0	82	435	459	467	0.6	2.40	307	310	0.1
58653	SCRANTON	011	596	535	506	-1.2	14	248	237	228	-0.5	2.26	179	164	-0.9
58654	SENTINEL BUTTE	033	286	259	245	-1.1	19	92	89	85	-0.4	2.82	66	61	-0.8
58655	SOUTH HEART	089	503	510	511	0.1	85	171	185	188	0.9	2.76	137	143	0.5
58656	TAYLOR	089	357	354	353	-0.1	77	144	152	154	0.6	2.26	110	112	0.2
58701	MINOT	101	24446	24268	23800	-0.1	77	10648	11110	11010	0.5	2.15	6401	6368	-0.1
58703	MINOT	101	17962	17682	17299	-0.2	74	7111	7313	7220	0.3	2.31	4661	4597	-0.1
58704	MINOT AFB	101	3825	2982	2767	-2.7	1	1067	833	771	-2.6	3.12	982	758	-2.8
58705	MINOT AFB	101	3235	2522	2341	-2.7	1	884	690	639	-2.6	3.19	813	628	-2.8
58707	MINOT	101	442	432	425	-0.2	74	21	21	20	0.0	2.57	10	9	-1.1
58710	ANAMOOSE	049	573	518	495	-1.1	19	243	235	227	-0.4	2.20	166	152	-0.9
58711	ANTLER	009	232	213	203	-0.9	32	102	100	97	-0.2	2.13	72	68	-0.6
58712	BALFOUR	049	138	124	119	-1.1	19	57	55	53	-0.4	2.24	41	39	-0.5
58713	BANTRY	049	293	284	277	-0.3	71	121	126	125	0.4	2.25	83	83	0.0
58716	BENEDICT	055	143	144	143	0.1	85	56	61	62	0.9	2.36	45	48	0.7
58718	BERTHOLD	101	947	913	887	-0.4	66	358	363	357	0.2	2.50	270	263	-0.3
58721	BOWBELLS	013	575	537	517	-0.7	50	247	243	238	-0.2	2.21	171	161	-0.6
58722	BURLINGTON	101	1810	1822	1794	0.1	85	631	669	666	0.6	2.72	505	520	0.3
58723	BUTTE	055	276	246	233	-1.2	14	133	127	122	-0.5	1.94	94	85	-1.1
58725	CARPIO	101	332	341	337	0.3	88	137	149	149	0.9	2.29	99	103	0.4
58727	COLUMBUS	013	333	303	292	-1.0	24	163	159	155	-0.3	1.91	112	105	-0.7
58730	CROSBY	023	1367	1286	1249	-0.7	50	602	602	592	0.0	2.01	366	346	-0.6
58731	DEERING	049	312	311	306	0.0	82	98	105	104	0.7	2.91	66	67	0.2
58733	DES LACS	101	430	435	429	0.1	85	151	161	161	0.7	2.70	122	126	0.3
58734	DONNYBROOK	101	308	314	311	0.2	88	127	137	137	0.8	2.29	91	95	0.5
58735	DOUGLAS	055	302	280	268	-0.8	39	117	115	111	-0.2	2.43	82	76	-0.8
58736	DRAKE	049	572	518	495	-1.1	19	252	244	237	-0.3	2.12	169	155	-0.9
58737	FLAXTON	013	155	139	133	-1.2	14	78	75	73	-0.4	1.85	52	47	-1.1
58740	GLENBURN	075	1430	1313	1268	-0.9	32	529	521	510	-0.2	2.36	413	386	-0.7
58741	GRANVILLE	049	670	667	654	0.0	82	257	274	273	0.7	2.40	185	188	0.2
58744	KARLSRUHE	049	254	228	219	-1.2	14	103	100	97	-0.3	2.27	75	70	-0.7
58746	KENMARE	101	1696	1588	1530	-0.7	50	699	682	662	-0.3	2.22	456	423	-0.8
58748	KRAMER	009	176	158	148	-1.2	14	79	75	72	-0.6	2.11	54	49	-1.0
58750	LANSFORD	009	510	471	449	-0.9	32	203	201	194	-0.1	2.34	145	136	-0.7
58752	LIGNITE	013	256	233	224	-1.0	24	119	116	113	-0.3	2.01	82	76	-0.8
58755	MCGREGOR	105	99	91	89	-0.9	32	49	48	48	-0.2	1.88	33	31	-0.7
58756	MAKOTI	101	265	247	239	-0.8	39	125	122	119	-0.3	2.02	91	85	-0.7
58757	MANDAREE	053	1207	1297	1322	0.8	95	300	331	341	1.1	3.92	262	283	0.8
58758	MARTIN	083	286	253	239	-1.3	9	118	111	107	-0.7	2.28	92	84	-1.0
58759	MAX	055	610	570	551	-0.7	50	254	254	248	0.0	2.24	190	182	-0.5
58760	MAXBASS	009	284	261	248	-0.9	32	123	121	117	-0.2	2.16	87	82	-0.6
58761	MOHALL	075	1236	1088	1021	-1.4	7	511	478	453	-0.7	2.16	334	295	-1.3
58762	NEWBURG	009	215	198	188	-0.9	32	102	101	97	-0.1	1.96	72	68	-0.6
58763	NEW TOWN	061	2248	2285	2284	0.2	88	783	831	840	0.6	2.68	544	552	0.2
58765	NOONAN	023	277	260	252	-0.7	50	132	132	129	0.0	1.86	82	77	-0.7
58768	NORWICH	049	353	348	340	-0.2	74	126	131	130	0.4	2.63	96	97	0.1
58769	PALERMO	061	231	212	207	-0.9	32	97	96	95	-0.1	2.21	71	67	-0.6
58770	PARSHALL	061	1275	1263	1252	-0.1	77	459	471	472	0.3	2.58	329	324	-0.2
58771	PLAZA	061	437	402	390	-0.9	32	190	187	183	-0.2	2.15	139	131	-0.6
58772	PORTAL	013	186	167	160	-1.2	14	86	83	81	-0.4	2.01	57	53	-0.8
58773	POWERS LAKE	013	697	653	636	-0.7	50	300	301	298	0.0	2.17	194	185	-0.5
58775	ROSEGLEN	055	593	568	550	-0.5	60	182	182	179	0.0	3.12	146	142	-0.3
58776	ROSS	061	158	150	149	-0.6	55	68	69	70	0.2	2.17	50	49	-0.2
58778	RUSO	055	159	148	142	-0.8	39	67	67	65	0.0	2.21	48	46	-0.5
58779	RYDER	055	503	471	452	-0.7	50	200	197	191	-0.2	2.39	144	136	-0.6
58781	SAWYER	101	773	745	725	-0.4	66	301	303	297	0.1	2.46	239	233	-0.3
58782	SHERWOOD	075	443	409	388	-0.9	32	187	186	179	-0.1	2.20	127	120	-0.6
58783	SOURIS	009	431	387	365	-1.2	14	191	183	175	-0.5	2.11	132	120	-1.0
58784	STANLEY	061	1896	1836	1826	-0.3	71	817	847	852	0.4	2.10	514	506	-0.2
58785	SURREY	101	1042	1003	975	-0.4	66	349	353	347	0.1	2.84	299	296	-0.1
58787	TOLLEY	075	173	160	152	-0.8	39	81	81	78	0.0	1.98	55	52	-0.6
58788	TOWNER	049	1165	1066	1025	-1.0	24	522	517	504	-0.1	2.06	323	303	-0.7
58789	UPHAM	049	305	298	291	-0.3	71	144	152	151	0.6	1.96	97	98	0.1
58790	VELVA	049	1515	1440	1389	-0.5	60	608	607	593	0.0	2.29	408	388	-0.5
58792	VOLTAIRE	049	321	304	294	-0.6	55	132	134	131	0.2	2.27	102	101	-0.1
58793	WESTHOPE	009	752	667	633	-1.3	9	311	299	287	-0.4	2.10	192	174	-1.1
58794	WHITE EARTH	061	157	152	152	-0.3	71	60	62	63	0.4	2.45	44	44	0.0
58795	WILDROSE	105	262	241	234	-0.9	32	120	118	116	-0.2	2.03	83	78	-0.7
58801	WILLISTON	105	16253	16216	16423	0.0	82	6564	6972	7159	0.7	2.26	4220	4257	0.1
58830	ALAMO	105	181	167	163	-0.9	32	80	79	78	-0.1	2.09	55	51	-0.8
58831	ALEXANDER	053	455	442	439	-0.3	71	191	198	200	0.4	2.23	137	136	-0.1
58833	AMBROSE	023	215	197	188	-0.9	32	95	92	89	-0.3	2.12	69	64	-0.8
58835	ARNEGARD	053	162	157	155	-0.3	71	72	74	74	0.3	2.12	53	52	-0.2
58838	CARTWRIGHT	053	788	763	762	-0.3	71	324	335	339	0.4	2.28	231	229	-0.1
58843	EPPING	105	311	302	304	-0.3	71	132	138	141	0.5	2.19	98	99	0.1
58844	FORTUNA	023	205	187	177	-1.0	24	87	84	80	-0.4	2.23	65	61	-0.7
58845	GRENORA	023	439	409	401	-0.8	39	195	194	194	-0.1	2.11	139	132	-0.6
58847	KEENE	053	272	262	261	-0.4	66	122	125	127	0.3	2.10	92	91	-0.1
58849	RAY	105	778	751	758	-0.4	66	332	343	351	0.4	2.19	225	221	-0.2
58852	TIOGA	105	1592	1532	1546	-0.4	66	679	707	725	0.4	2.11	451	447	-0.1
58853	TRENTON	105	29	30	31	0.4	89	11	12	13	0.9	2.50	9	9	0.0
58854	WATFORD CITY	053	2635	2550	2534	-0.4	66	1051	1084	1091	0.3	2.30	702	687	-0.2
58856	ZAHL	105	82	77	76	-0.7	50	39	39	39	0.0	1.95	27	26	-0.4
	NORTH DAKOTA					0.2					0.8	2.27			0.2
	UNITED STATES					1.0					1.1	2.59			0.9

#	POST OFFICE NAME	RACE (%) White 2000	White 2009	Black 2000	Black 2009	Asian/Pacific 2000	Asian/Pacific 2009	% Hispanic Origin 2000	% Hispanic Origin 2009	2009 AGE DISTRIBUTION (%) 0-4	5-9	10-14	15-19	20-24	25-44	45-64	65-84	85+	18+	MEDIAN AGE 2009	% 2009 Males	% 2009 Females
58649	REEDER	99.2	99.1	0.0	0.0	0.3	0.3	0.0	0.0	4.5	5.1	5.4	6.0	4.8	18.8	32.7	19.9	2.8	81.3	48.2	52.8	47.2
58650	REGENT	98.8	98.2	0.0	0.0	0.0	0.0	0.6	0.7	3.9	4.2	4.9	6.7	5.6	19.4	34.2	18.7	2.5	83.1	48.4	53.5	46.5
58651	RHAME	98.1	97.9	0.2	0.3	0.2	0.3	1.2	1.8	4.7	5.4	5.7	6.5	4.7	24.6	34.2	11.9	2.3	80.3	43.9	49.0	51.0
58652	RICHARDTON	98.9	98.5	0.1	0.1	0.1	0.2	0.6	1.0	4.8	5.3	5.7	5.9	4.3	20.8	31.9	17.3	4.0	79.7	47.1	50.6	49.4
58653	SCRANTON	99.2	99.1	0.0	0.0	0.0	0.0	0.3	0.4	4.9	5.4	5.8	6.2	4.5	19.4	33.6	17.2	3.0	80.0	47.5	48.6	51.4
58654	SENTINEL BUTTE	98.3	98.1	0.0	0.0	0.0	0.0	0.3	0.4	5.8	6.6	7.3	8.1	3.9	19.7	31.3	14.7	2.7	74.1	44.0	51.7	48.3
58655	SOUTH HEART	99.2	99.0	0.2	0.4	0.0	0.0	0.0	0.0	5.9	6.3	10.2	10.0	3.1	24.1	27.8	10.6	2.0	70.8	39.2	52.9	47.1
58656	TAYLOR	99.2	98.9	0.0	0.0	0.0	0.0	0.3	0.6	5.6	6.2	6.2	5.6	4.5	19.8	32.8	16.4	2.8	78.0	46.3	48.6	51.4
58701	MINOT	94.2	92.2	1.0	1.4	0.6	1.1	1.2	2.1	6.6	6.2	5.9	6.1	7.1	26.7	25.3	12.8	3.3	77.7	37.9	48.9	51.1
58703	MINOT	93.2	90.9	1.4	2.0	0.6	1.1	1.5	2.4	6.6	6.1	6.2	7.7	7.9	28.5	24.7	10.2	2.2	76.9	34.5	49.3	50.7
58704	MINOT AFB	79.1	72.3	10.2	13.1	3.0	4.9	6.2	9.6	14.0	11.0	7.2	9.6	21.0	35.3	1.8	0.1	0.0	64.1	22.0	55.5	44.5
58705	MINOT AFB	79.1	72.3	10.2	13.1	3.0	4.8	6.2	9.5	14.0	11.0	7.2	9.6	21.3	35.3	1.6	0.0	0.0	64.2	21.9	55.6	44.4
58707	MINOT	90.0	86.3	2.5	3.5	0.7	1.4	3.2	5.1	3.5	3.7	3.7	28.0	29.4	21.5	7.9	1.9	0.5	85.9	21.9	46.1	53.9
58710	ANAMOOSE	99.7	99.6	0.0	0.0	0.0	0.0	0.3	0.6	3.5	4.1	4.8	6.2	5.6	18.7	31.1	22.0	4.1	83.6	49.3	51.7	48.3
58711	ANTLER	99.1	98.6	0.0	0.5	0.0	0.0	0.4	0.5	5.2	5.6	6.1	6.6	4.7	20.2	34.7	14.6	2.3	78.9	45.9	52.6	47.4
58712	BALFOUR	100.0	100.0	0.0	0.0	0.0	0.0	0.7	0.8	6.5	7.3	6.5	5.6	4.0	20.2	31.5	16.9	1.6	75.0	45.0	53.2	46.8
58713	BANTRY	98.3	98.2	0.0	0.0	0.0	0.0	0.3	0.4	4.9	5.3	5.6	5.6	4.6	23.9	32.7	15.1	2.1	80.3	45.0	53.9	46.1
58716	BENEDICT	100.0	99.3	0.0	0.0	0.0	0.0	0.0	0.0	5.6	5.6	5.6	5.6	4.2	20.8	32.6	18.1	2.1	79.9	46.7	52.1	47.9
58718	BERTHOLD	98.1	97.2	0.3	0.5	0.2	0.4	1.0	1.4	7.0	7.6	7.7	7.0	4.1	23.1	28.6	12.9	2.1	73.1	40.6	52.8	47.2
58721	BOWBELLS	99.3	99.1	0.0	0.0	0.2	0.2	0.2	0.4	4.7	5.2	6.0	7.3	4.1	18.4	33.5	17.7	3.2	79.7	47.4	50.5	49.5
58722	BURLINGTON	97.4	96.8	0.3	0.4	0.2	0.3	0.9	1.4	7.3	7.6	7.8	7.9	6.3	25.7	28.8	7.8	0.8	72.3	36.1	50.4	49.6
58723	BUTTE	100.0	100.0	0.0	0.0	0.0	0.0	0.4	0.4	3.7	4.9	5.7	5.7	4.1	19.5	35.0	18.7	2.8	81.7	49.2	52.4	47.6
58725	CARPIO	97.9	97.1	0.3	0.3	0.3	0.6	1.5	2.3	5.9	6.7	6.7	6.7	3.5	21.1	31.1	15.5	2.6	76.2	44.5	53.1	46.9
58727	COLUMBUS	99.4	99.3	0.3	0.3	0.3	0.3	0.3	0.7	3.6	4.0	4.6	5.3	3.0	17.5	37.6	20.5	4.0	84.5	52.2	52.1	47.9
58730	CROSBY	98.8	98.4	0.0	0.0	0.7	0.7	0.7	1.2	3.7	3.8	4.2	5.4	5.5	16.1	30.9	22.5	7.8	84.6	52.3	49.1	50.9
58731	DEERING	97.1	95.8	0.0	0.3	0.3	0.3	0.6	1.6	5.5	5.8	6.4	7.4	4.8	24.8	30.5	12.9	1.9	77.2	41.2	54.3	45.7
58733	DES LACS	97.9	97.0	0.2	0.5	0.2	0.2	0.9	1.4	6.9	7.4	8.0	7.8	5.5	25.5	30.1	8.0	0.7	72.9	37.8	51.3	48.7
58734	DONNYBROOK	97.7	97.1	0.3	0.3	0.3	0.3	1.3	1.9	5.7	6.7	7.0	6.7	3.8	20.7	31.2	15.3	2.9	76.1	44.5	51.6	48.4
58735	DOUGLAS	97.7	96.1	0.0	0.0	0.3	0.7	1.0	1.4	5.0	5.7	6.4	6.1	4.3	19.3	34.3	16.4	2.5	78.6	47.0	51.4	48.6
58736	DRAKE	99.7	99.6	0.0	0.0	0.0	0.0	0.3	0.6	3.5	4.1	4.8	6.0	5.6	18.7	31.1	22.0	4.2	83.8	49.3	51.7	48.3
58737	FLAXTON	99.4	99.3	0.6	0.7	0.0	0.0	0.6	0.7	2.9	2.9	2.9	5.8	3.6	15.8	36.7	27.3	2.2	88.5	54.0	50.4	49.6
58740	GLENBURN	89.3	87.1	4.2	4.6	2.0	3.0	3.6	5.1	7.7	7.0	6.7	9.2	9.9	28.9	21.2	8.6	0.7	72.9	30.7	54.3	45.7
58741	GRANVILLE	97.2	96.7	0.3	0.3	0.0	0.0	0.1	0.3	6.0	6.6	6.7	6.3	4.5	22.6	30.7	13.6	2.8	76.5	42.5	54.1	45.9
58744	KARLSRUHE	100.0	100.0	0.0	0.0	0.0	0.0	0.8	0.9	6.6	7.5	7.0	5.3	3.9	20.2	30.7	16.7	2.2	74.6	44.7	53.1	46.9
58746	KENMARE	98.5	97.9	0.0	0.0	0.2	0.3	0.1	0.3	4.7	5.4	5.7	6.2	4.2	18.8	30.5	18.1	6.5	80.4	48.3	49.2	50.8
58748	KRAMER	99.4	99.4	0.0	0.0	0.0	0.0	0.6	0.6	5.1	5.7	6.3	6.3	4.4	20.3	31.6	17.7	2.5	78.5	46.0	52.5	47.5
58750	LANSFORD	98.6	98.3	0.2	0.2	0.2	0.4	0.4	0.4	5.1	5.5	5.9	6.6	4.5	21.2	34.4	14.6	2.1	79.6	45.6	52.4	47.6
58752	LIGNITE	99.6	99.6	0.4	0.4	0.0	0.0	0.4	0.4	3.0	3.9	4.3	5.2	3.0	17.6	37.8	21.5	3.9	85.4	52.9	51.1	48.9
58755	MCGREGOR	99.0	98.9	0.0	0.0	1.0	1.1	0.0	0.0	4.4	4.4	5.5	5.5	4.4	18.7	33.0	19.8	4.4	81.3	49.6	52.7	47.3
58756	MAKOTI	85.3	85.8	0.0	0.0	0.8	0.8	0.8	1.2	5.3	6.1	6.5	6.5	3.2	20.2	34.4	15.8	2.0	77.3	46.5	49.4	50.6
58757	MANDAREE	4.6	3.9	0.0	0.0	0.0	0.0	2.0	1.9	12.8	13.0	11.9	9.7	7.4	23.3	15.7	5.7	0.5	56.4	21.7	48.0	52.0
58758	MARTIN	99.3	99.2	0.0	0.0	0.0	0.0	0.4	0.4	3.6	5.9	7.9	6.7	2.4	18.2	34.4	19.8	1.2	77.5	48.1	53.4	46.6
58759	MAX	97.7	96.5	0.0	0.0	0.3	0.5	0.7	0.9	5.1	5.6	6.3	6.7	4.2	19.3	34.0	16.1	2.6	78.8	46.7	52.1	47.9
58760	MAXBASS	98.9	98.9	0.4	0.4	0.0	0.0	0.4	0.4	5.0	5.4	6.1	6.5	4.6	20.7	34.9	14.6	2.3	79.3	45.9	52.5	47.5
58761	MOHALL	98.5	98.1	0.1	0.1	0.2	0.3	0.2	0.3	4.6	4.8	5.1	5.8	5.0	18.5	30.6	18.4	7.3	81.6	49.0	49.1	50.9
58762	NEWBURG	99.1	98.5	0.0	0.5	0.0	0.0	0.5	0.5	5.1	5.6	6.1	6.1	4.0	20.7	35.9	14.1	2.5	79.3	46.1	54.5	45.5
58763	NEW TOWN	32.8	23.8	0.1	0.1	0.3	0.4	1.9	1.9	8.3	8.3	8.2	9.1	7.1	23.5	24.2	9.4	1.9	69.9	31.2	47.7	52.3
58765	NOONAN	98.6	98.1	0.0	0.0	0.7	0.8	0.7	1.2	3.5	3.8	4.2	5.4	5.4	15.8	32.3	22.3	7.3	84.6	52.4	49.6	50.4
58768	NORWICH	97.5	96.8	0.3	0.3	0.3	0.6	0.6	0.6	6.6	6.9	7.5	8.0	4.6	23.9	28.7	12.1	1.7	73.3	39.3	52.6	47.4
58769	PALERMO	97.8	96.2	0.0	0.0	0.4	0.9	0.0	0.0	4.2	4.7	5.7	4.7	4.7	17.9	37.3	18.4	2.4	82.1	50.5	53.8	46.2
58770	PARSHALL	47.2	36.7	0.2	0.2	0.0	0.0	2.6	3.0	8.6	8.7	8.5	7.4	5.2	22.2	23.6	12.1	3.6	68.5	35.6	49.4	50.6
58771	PLAZA	94.7	93.0	0.0	0.0	0.5	0.7	0.2	0.0	4.7	5.5	5.7	5.2	4.5	19.9	35.6	16.7	2.2	80.6	48.0	53.0	47.0
58772	PORTAL	99.5	99.4	0.5	0.6	0.0	0.0	0.5	0.6	2.4	3.6	3.6	6.0	3.6	15.6	37.1	25.7	2.4	86.8	53.8	51.5	48.5
58773	POWERS LAKE	98.7	98.6	0.0	0.0	0.1	0.2	0.4	0.5	5.1	5.5	6.0	6.4	3.8	18.7	33.4	17.0	4.1	79.2	47.3	49.2	50.8
58775	ROSEGLEN	32.5	23.2	0.0	0.0	0.3	0.4	6.2	6.2	7.7	8.1	9.3	9.5	4.9	22.2	26.6	10.6	1.1	68.7	33.5	48.8	51.2
58776	ROSS	98.7	97.3	0.0	0.0	0.0	0.7	0.6	0.7	4.7	6.0	6.0	6.0	4.7	18.7	36.7	14.7	2.7	79.3	47.7	52.0	48.0
58778	RUSO	100.0	100.0	0.0	0.0	0.0	0.0	0.0	0.0	3.4	4.7	4.7	5.4	4.1	20.3	35.8	18.2	3.4	84.5	50.0	51.4	48.6
58779	RYDER	83.9	80.3	0.0	0.0	0.4	0.4	1.8	2.3	5.7	6.6	7.9	7.0	3.8	20.4	32.9	13.8	1.9	74.9	43.9	51.2	48.8
58781	SAWYER	98.6	97.9	0.1	0.3	0.5	0.9	0.6	1.1	7.0	7.5	8.2	8.7	3.4	24.7	29.1	10.5	0.9	71.0	38.6	51.4	48.6
58782	SHERWOOD	98.4	98.0	0.2	0.2	0.0	0.0	0.0	0.0	4.6	5.6	5.9	6.1	3.9	19.1	33.7	18.1	2.9	80.0	47.7	50.6	49.4
58783	SOURIS	98.8	98.7	0.0	0.0	0.2	0.3	0.5	0.8	5.2	5.7	5.7	6.2	4.4	19.9	33.1	17.6	2.3	79.6	46.6	52.7	47.3
58784	STANLEY	98.7	97.9	0.0	0.0	0.3	0.5	0.5	0.8	5.3	5.3	5.5	5.9	5.4	19.4	29.2	17.7	6.3	80.0	47.5	49.5	50.5
58785	SURREY	97.1	95.8	0.0	0.0	0.3	0.5	1.4	2.5	7.3	7.5	7.5	8.3	7.1	26.5	26.3	8.8	0.8	72.7	34.6	49.2	50.8
58787	TOLLEY	98.3	97.5	0.6	0.6	0.0	0.0	0.0	0.0	4.4	5.6	5.6	5.6	4.4	18.8	34.4	18.1	3.1	81.3	48.2	50.6	49.4
58788	TOWNER	98.7	98.5	0.2	0.2	0.0	0.0	0.6	1.0	4.4	4.9	5.3	4.9	4.3	21.2	32.2	19.6	3.3	82.6	48.4	51.0	49.0
58789	UPHAM	98.0	97.7	0.0	0.0	0.0	0.0	0.7	1.0	5.4	6.0	6.4	6.4	4.4	24.5	30.5	14.1	2.3	78.5	42.6	52.7	47.3
58790	VELVA	99.1	98.8	0.1	0.1	0.1	0.2	0.3	0.6	5.2	5.5	5.8	6.8	5.9	20.6	28.3	16.5	5.3	78.7	45.1	47.8	52.2
58792	VOLTAIRE	98.4	98.0	0.0	0.0	0.3	0.3	0.0	0.0	4.9	5.9	5.9	4.9	5.3	21.1	32.9	17.1	2.0	80.3	46.3	50.7	49.3
58793	WESTHOPE	98.5	98.2	0.0	0.0	0.0	0.0	0.0	0.0	3.3	3.4	4.0	6.3	5.5	17.7	34.2	19.0	6.4	85.3	50.8	48.7	51.3
58794	WHITE EARTH	98.1	96.7	0.0	0.0	0.0	0.0	0.6	0.7	5.3	5.9	6.6	5.9	4.6	19.7	34.9	14.5	2.6	78.3	46.3	49.3	50.7
58795	WILDROSE	99.2	98.8	0.0	0.0	0.4	0.8	0.0	0.0	4.1	4.1	5.0	6.2	4.1	17.8	34.0	20.7	3.7	82.2	50.1	53.1	46.9
58801	WILLISTON	91.9	90.0	0.1	0.2	0.2	0.3	1.1	1.7	6.1	6.2	6.6	8.1	6.4	22.8	28.1	12.7	2.9	76.0	40.3	48.8	51.2
58830	ALAMO	98.9	98.8	0.0	0.0	0.6	0.6	0.0	0.0	3.6	4.8	4.8	6.0	3.6	17.4	36.5	19.8	3.6	82.0	49.6	53.9	46.1
58831	ALEXANDER	96.0	95.7	0.0	0.0	0.2	0.2	1.5	1.6	4.3	5.0	5.4	6.1	4.8	18.1	37.8	16.1	2.5	81.4	48.7	51.6	48.4
58833	AMBROSE	100.0	100.0	0.0	0.0	0.0	0.0	0.5	0.5	3.0	3.6	4.1	6.6	4.6	15.2	37.1	21.3	4.6	85.8	51.6	53.8	46.2
58835	ARNEGARD	97.5	96.8	0.0	0.0	0.0	0.0	0.0	0.0	5.1	5.7	6.4	7.6	5.1	16.6	36.3	14.6	2.5	77.7	47.0	50.3	49.7
58838	CARTWRIGHT	97.3	97.1	0.1	0.1	0.1	0.1	1.1	1.2	4.3	5.8	7.1	7.1	3.8	20.2	33.4	15.7	2.6	77.6	46.1	52.7	47.3
58843	EPPING	96.5	95.4	0.0	0.0	0.0	0.3	0.6	1.0	3.6	5.3	6.0	7.3	4.0	19.9	37.1	15.2	1.7	80.1	47.2	53.0	47.0
58844	FORTUNA	100.0	100.0	0.0	0.0	0.0	0.0	0.5	0.5	3.2	3.7	4.3	7.0	4.3	15.5	36.4	21.9	3.7	85.0	51.6	53.5	46.5
58845	GRENORA	98.2	97.8	0.0	0.0	0.0	0.0	0.2	0.2	3.9	4.2	4.9	5.9	4.2	17.1	37.7	18.8	3.4	83.6	50.1	53.8	46.2
58847	KEENE	97.4	96.9	0.0	0.0	0.0	0.0	0.0	0.0	5.0	6.1	7.3	8.4	2.3	19.5	34.4	14.9	2.3	75.2	45.9	51.5	48.5
58849	RAY	98.7	98.5	0.0	0.0	0.1	0.1	0.5	0.9	4.0	4.4	4.8	5.6	5.6	17.3	35.8	19.7	2.8	83.5	50.4	50.5	49.5
58852	TIOGA	97.7	97.2	0.1	0.1	0.1	0.1	0.3	0.3	4.4	4.6	5.0	5.9	5.6	18.0	32.2	19.5	4.8	81.8	49.1	47.9	52.1
58853	TRENTON	65.5	56.7	0.0	0.0	0.0	0.0	0.0	0.0	6.7	6.7	10.0	6.7	6.7	26.7	33.3	3.3	0.0	70.0	35.0	50.0	50.0
58854	WATFORD CITY	96.4	95.9	0.1	0.1	0.1	0.1	0.6	0.7	4.8	5.3	5.8	6.9	6.0	17.9	33.8	15.3	4.1	79.2	47.1	48.8	51.2
58856	ZAHL	97.6	97.4	0.0	0.0	0.0	0.0	0.0	0.0	3.9	5.2	5.2	5.2	3.9	18.2	39.0	16.9	2.6	80.5	48.6	57.1	42.9
	NORTH DAKOTA	92.4	90.8	0.6	0.7	0.6	1.0	1.2	1.8	6.3	6.1	6.2	7.7	8.3	25.2	26.0	11.6	2.7	77.3	36.9	50.0	50.0
	UNITED STATES	75.1	72.0	12.3	12.7	3.8	4.6	12.5	15.7	6.8	6.7	6.6	7.1	6.9	27.0	26.0	10.9	1.9	75.7	36.9	49.2	50.8

ZIP CODE #	POST OFFICE NAME	2009 Per Capita Income	2009 HH Income Base	2009 HOUSEHOLD INCOME DISTRIBUTION (%) Less than $25,000	$25,000 to $49,999	$50,000 to $99,999	$100,000 to $149,999	$150,000 or More	MEDIAN HOUSEHOLD INCOME 2009	2014	2009 National Centile	2009 State Centile	2009 Home Value Base	2009 HOME VALUE DISTRIBUTION (%) Less than $50,000	$50,000 to $89,999	$90,000 to $174,999	$175,000 to $399,999	$400,000 or More	2009 Median Home Value
58649	REEDER	25646	172	31.4	37.2	25.6	2.3	3.5	38264	39617	27	44	134	50.0	23.1	20.1	4.5	2.2	50000
58650	REGENT	20887	132	37.1	31.1	27.3	2.3	2.3	35000	36306	18	26	111	38.7	25.2	25.2	9.9	0.9	68750
58651	RHAME	21037	179	33.0	32.4	29.6	2.8	2.2	38340	39091	28	44	140	32.1	23.6	28.6	12.1	3.6	82000
58652	RICHARDTON	18508	459	30.1	35.1	29.4	3.9	1.5	38838	40657	29	47	389	31.9	29.8	28.8	8.2	1.3	74200
58653	SCRANTON	20698	237	29.5	34.2	30.8	3.0	2.5	40987	42653	36	56	202	40.1	29.2	19.8	8.4	2.5	58333
58654	SENTINEL BUTTE	16342	89	30.3	32.6	30.3	4.5	2.2	40449	40568	34	54	71	40.8	22.5	28.2	7.0	1.4	63750
58655	SOUTH HEART	17831	185	22.2	40.0	31.9	5.9	0.0	41805	43613	39	62	169	18.3	21.3	43.8	14.8	1.8	111979
58656	TAYLOR	20029	152	27.6	38.2	28.3	3.3	2.6	37739	40000	26	40	125	32.0	20.8	24.8	19.2	3.2	85000
58701	MINOT	24978	11110	26.8	30.6	33.6	5.5	3.5	43441	45672	44	68	7126	17.5	14.9	44.2	21.2	2.2	115754
58703	MINOT	24363	7313	21.9	28.4	39.4	7.2	3.0	49593	51120	60	85	4805	5.1	17.3	57.3	19.5	0.7	121635
58704	MINOT AFB	14879	833	16.3	46.9	31.2	4.3	1.2	42375	44002	41	66	7	0.0	0.0	71.4	28.6	0.0	143750
58705	MINOT AFB	14600	690	16.2	47.1	31.0	4.5	1.2	42324	44107	40	64	6	0.0	0.0	66.7	33.3	0.0	150000
58707	MINOT	6168	21	38.1	28.6	28.6	4.8	0.0	32225	32279	12	13	8	0.0	37.5	62.5	0.0	0.0	100000
58710	ANAMOOSE	17390	235	38.7	32.3	24.7	3.8	0.4	32660	34467	13	15	200	50.0	23.5	17.0	7.0	2.5	50000
58711	ANTLER	22969	100	26.0	37.0	31.0	4.0	2.0	41713	42336	38	61	83	38.6	28.9	24.1	6.0	2.4	64167
58712	BALFOUR	18207	55	45.5	25.5	21.8	5.5	1.8	27931	27928	6	3	48	41.7	16.7	22.9	12.5	6.3	63333
58713	BANTRY	18554	126	35.7	34.1	26.2	3.2	0.8	33872	35318	15	19	107	39.3	18.7	28.0	12.1	1.9	75000
58716	BENEDICT	21507	61	26.2	31.1	37.7	3.3	1.6	45440	47313	50	73	56	21.4	14.3	42.9	17.9	3.6	112500
58718	BERTHOLD	18928	363	29.5	37.2	27.8	3.3	2.2	36673	40683	23	35	316	32.9	20.9	36.4	9.2	0.6	82000
58721	BOWBELLS	19498	243	32.1	36.6	27.2	2.9	1.2	35388	37475	19	27	206	37.4	27.7	22.8	8.7	3.4	70000
58722	BURLINGTON	19970	669	15.5	34.4	44.8	3.9	1.3	50049	49756	61	87	588	12.4	20.6	48.6	15.8	2.6	110124
58723	BUTTE	20732	127	40.2	33.9	22.0	3.1	0.8	32296	34368	12	14	109	38.5	17.4	22.9	15.6	5.5	76250
58725	CARPIO	20418	149	34.9	32.2	28.9	2.7	1.3	34759	37040	17	23	125	41.6	20.8	27.2	9.6	0.8	64375
58727	COLUMBUS	17506	159	50.9	24.5	22.6	1.9	0.0	24437	26413	3	0	137	57.7	11.7	28.5	2.2	0.0	39583
58730	CROSBY	20389	602	37.9	31.2	24.9	4.8	1.2	35130	36096	18	27	489	44.8	29.4	21.9	2.9	1.0	57083
58731	DEERING	13748	105	39.0	29.5	26.7	3.8	1.0	32320	34288	12	15	90	37.8	22.2	27.8	10.0	2.2	70000
58733	DES LACS	20458	161	16.8	33.5	44.1	3.7	1.9	49782	50465	61	85	142	12.7	21.1	44.4	17.6	4.2	111538
58734	DONNYBROOK	19462	137	36.5	33.6	25.5	2.9	1.5	33369	35277	14	17	116	44.0	19.0	30.2	6.9	0.0	60000
58735	DOUGLAS	17544	115	30.4	35.7	29.6	3.5	0.9	37341	40242	25	38	96	35.4	22.9	30.2	11.5	0.0	70000
58736	DRAKE	18047	244	39.3	30.7	25.8	3.7	0.4	32322	34169	12	15	206	51.9	21.8	16.5	6.8	2.9	47647
58737	FLAXTON	18902	75	46.7	32.0	18.7	2.7	0.0	29073	32969	7	6	65	67.7	15.4	9.2	3.1	4.6	24167
58740	GLENBURN	19834	521	22.3	37.6	35.5	3.1	1.5	43038	43893	43	67	305	26.2	23.6	40.3	9.2	0.7	90263
58741	GRANVILLE	18090	274	35.4	31.0	27.4	5.1	1.1	34372	35172	16	21	229	30.1	24.0	31.4	10.0	4.4	81364
58744	KARLSRUHE	18001	100	48.0	25.0	20.0	4.0	3.0	26268	28788	4	2	87	42.5	14.9	23.0	11.5	8.0	63000
58746	KENMARE	19042	682	32.4	35.9	26.5	4.1	1.0	36183	38407	21	33	550	36.0	24.7	29.6	9.1	0.5	70000
58748	KRAMER	19445	75	40.0	37.3	20.0	2.7	0.0	29627	30525	7	8	62	43.5	21.0	19.4	12.9	3.2	63333
58750	LANSFORD	20719	201	25.9	36.3	32.3	4.0	1.5	42172	41983	40	64	166	38.0	29.5	22.3	8.4	1.8	65000
58752	LIGNITE	16752	116	50.9	25.0	22.4	1.7	0.0	24497	27527	3	1	100	58.0	13.0	27.0	2.0	0.0	38750
58755	MCGREGOR	21973	48	41.7	29.2	25.0	4.2	0.0	31514	35000	11	10	41	51.2	19.5	17.1	12.2	0.0	47500
58756	MAKOTI	21526	122	28.7	37.7	29.5	3.3	0.8	37335	37647	25	37	103	34.0	23.3	29.1	11.7	1.9	76429
58757	MANDAREE	10962	331	32.3	30.8	33.5	3.0	0.3	35524	36245	19	28	127	35.4	22.0	29.9	12.6	0.0	76875
58758	MARTIN	17683	111	36.9	35.1	23.4	3.6	0.9	34595	35371	17	22	99	33.3	26.3	23.2	12.1	5.1	76429
58759	MAX	20420	254	28.0	34.6	32.7	3.1	1.6	40493	42061	34	55	222	27.0	22.1	31.5	17.6	1.8	91818
58760	MAXBASS	22604	121	25.6	37.2	30.6	5.0	1.7	42075	43299	40	63	101	39.6	29.7	19.8	7.9	3.0	62143
58761	MOHALL	20350	478	31.8	35.8	26.6	4.2	1.7	35949	37086	20	30	360	38.9	28.6	23.9	8.1	0.6	64074
58762	NEWBURG	24633	101	26.7	36.6	30.7	4.0	2.0	41416	42336	37	59	84	39.3	28.6	22.6	7.1	2.4	63333
58763	NEW TOWN	16544	831	31.3	34.3	29.1	4.1	1.2	37867	37969	26	42	530	29.8	28.3	35.5	5.8	0.6	80000
58765	NOONAN	22090	132	38.6	30.3	25.8	4.5	0.8	35000	36784	18	26	107	44.9	28.0	22.4	3.7	0.9	57857
58768	NORWICH	18234	131	29.0	30.5	35.1	4.6	0.8	42360	46007	41	65	113	20.4	23.0	42.5	10.6	3.5	100694
58769	PALERMO	18653	96	35.4	34.4	25.0	4.2	1.0	33443	33576	14	18	82	41.5	15.9	28.0	13.4	1.2	70000
58770	PARSHALL	15651	471	39.5	32.9	23.1	3.0	1.5	31797	31994	11	11	307	23.8	27.4	34.9	11.4	2.6	87308
58771	PLAZA	18989	187	35.8	34.2	25.7	3.2	1.1	32908	34514	13	16	161	38.5	14.9	31.1	14.3	1.2	78125
58772	PORTAL	17258	83	45.8	31.3	19.3	3.6	0.0	29296	29429	7	7	72	66.7	13.9	12.5	2.8	4.2	26667
58773	POWERS LAKE	17863	301	39.2	32.6	24.9	3.0	0.3	32108	33976	12	12	243	36.6	25.1	34.6	2.1	1.6	71071
58775	ROSEGLEN	11056	182	47.8	33.5	15.9	2.7	0.0	27698	30747	5	3	112	23.2	23.2	43.8	7.1	2.7	98000
58776	ROSS	22370	69	34.8	36.2	21.7	2.9	4.3	34629	35000	17	23	60	30.0	20.0	33.3	11.7	5.0	90000
58778	RUSO	19662	67	37.3	32.8	26.9	3.0	0.0	35558	39434	19	28	58	36.2	13.8	27.6	17.2	5.2	90000
58779	RYDER	17403	197	33.0	36.5	25.4	4.6	0.5	36727	38849	23	35	156	34.6	23.1	31.4	9.6	1.3	74444
58781	SAWYER	21142	303	25.4	30.0	37.3	5.6	1.7	44815	46979	48	71	268	14.6	19.8	44.8	18.3	2.6	117105
58782	SHERWOOD	20026	186	30.1	39.8	25.8	2.2	2.2	36505	36793	22	34	160	36.9	23.1	26.9	13.1	0.0	67778
58783	SOURIS	19432	183	36.6	36.6	21.9	3.3	1.6	31713	32533	11	11	151	43.7	17.9	21.2	13.9	3.3	65833
58784	STANLEY	19185	847	37.4	35.7	22.2	3.3	1.4	31680	31518	11	11	670	34.8	26.0	32.5	5.5	1.2	70811
58785	SURREY	22629	353	8.8	22.4	61.5	5.4	2.0	61075	60882	79	98	325	5.8	18.8	69.5	5.8	0.0	109375
58787	TOLLEY	22080	81	33.3	38.3	24.7	2.5	1.2	34634	37321	17	23	70	37.1	22.9	25.7	14.3	0.0	67500
58788	TOWNER	21405	517	36.4	31.9	27.9	1.5	2.3	34604	35935	17	22	394	43.4	25.6	22.6	6.6	1.8	60870
58789	UPHAM	21035	152	36.8	31.6	27.6	3.3	0.7	33486	35278	14	18	130	37.7	23.8	25.4	10.8	2.3	70000
58790	VELVA	19541	607	30.3	37.1	25.7	4.8	2.1	37612	38165	26	40	472	19.5	26.7	33.7	18.2	1.9	97826
58792	VOLTAIRE	23337	134	30.6	30.6	28.4	7.5	3.0	40441	40746	34	54	115	20.0	24.3	28.7	20.9	6.1	98125
58793	WESTHOPE	19576	299	35.8	39.5	21.4	2.7	0.7	32987	33692	13	16	253	53.8	30.4	14.2	1.6	0.0	45000
58794	WHITE EARTH	17137	62	35.5	40.3	21.0	1.6	1.6	33375	33767	14	17	53	35.8	22.6	30.2	9.4	1.9	68750
58795	WILDROSE	20659	118	39.8	28.0	28.8	3.4	0.0	33189	35914	14	16	100	54.0	18.0	17.0	11.0	0.0	42000
58801	WILLISTON	22369	6972	29.7	30.7	31.3	5.3	3.0	41283	42957	37	58	4781	16.6	23.8	46.2	12.6	0.8	103753
58830	ALAMO	19977	79	38.0	26.6	32.9	2.5	0.0	35562	36551	19	29	67	55.2	17.9	14.9	11.9	0.0	41250
58831	ALEXANDER	19740	198	33.8	32.8	27.3	4.0	2.0	36768	37689	23	36	162	23.5	20.4	43.8	8.0	4.3	97692
58833	AMBROSE	21152	92	31.5	29.3	33.7	4.3	1.1	41530	41381	38	60	76	48.7	21.1	25.0	5.3	0.0	53333
58835	ARNEGARD	20940	74	25.7	39.2	31.1	4.1	0.0	37315	37315	25	37	65	32.3	29.2	24.6	13.8	0.0	79167
58838	CARTWRIGHT	18620	335	33.4	34.9	26.6	4.2	0.9	36139	37347	21	32	278	28.4	21.2	37.1	9.4	4.0	90526
58843	EPPING	23440	138	25.4	34.1	33.3	4.3	2.9	41659	42113	38	60	127	25.2	19.7	37.8	13.4	3.9	99286
58844	FORTUNA	20424	84	31.0	28.6	33.3	4.8	2.4	41859	43646	39	62	70	50.0	18.6	25.7	5.7	0.0	50000
58845	GRENORA	22358	194	30.4	32.0	30.9	4.1	2.6	40000	41637	33	52	158	46.2	22.8	22.8	8.2	0.0	58571
58847	KEENE	23317	125	36.0	26.4	32.8	1.6	3.2	33600	35374	15	19	106	33.0	17.9	29.2	17.0	2.8	88571
58849	RAY	19538	343	32.7	30.0	34.7	2.0	0.6	37650	40289	26	40	301	35.9	29.2	31.6	2.7	0.7	69773
58852	TIOGA	20954	707	30.8	36.8	27.2	3.4	1.8	36030	38064	21	31	583	31.6	29.8	31.0	6.2	1.4	74512
58853	TRENTON	15167	12	33.3	41.7	25.0	0.0	0.0	35000	37321	18	26	9	0.0	33.3	55.6	11.1	0.0	106250
58854	WATFORD CITY	20744	1084	31.5	34.7	25.9	4.4	3.5	36717	37372	23	35	847	30.2	23.7	36.4	8.5	1.2	84322
58856	ZAHL	23131	39	35.9	30.8	28.2	5.1	0.0	36141	39065	21	32	32	50.0	21.9	15.6	12.5	0.0	50000
	NORTH DAKOTA	23967		25.3	28.6	36.2	6.6	3.3	45981	48456				20.2	18.2	39.7	19.8	2.2	112133
	UNITED STATES	27277		20.9	24.4	35.3	11.7	7.6	54719	56938				9.3	13.1	31.6	32.6	13.5	162279

ZIP CODE		FINANCIAL SERVICES				THE HOME						ENTERTAINMENT						PERSONAL			
						Home Improvements		Furnishings													
#	POST OFFICE NAME	Auto Loan	Home Loan	Invest-ments	Retire-ment Plans	Home Repair	Lawn & Garden	Comput-ers & Hard-ware-Personal	Major Appli-ances	TV, Radio, Sound Equip-ment	Furni-ture	Dine out/ Carry out	Sports Equip-ment	Fees & Tickets	Toys & Games	Travel	Cable TV	Apparel & Services	Auto Repairs	Health Insur-ance	Pets & Supplies
58649	REEDER	94	65	103	64	68	99	72	89	75	58	74	74	52	73	71	81	48	83	94	110
58650	REGENT	80	55	88	55	58	85	61	76	64	50	63	63	45	63	61	70	41	71	81	94
58651	RHAME	81	56	89	56	58	86	62	77	64	50	64	64	45	63	62	70	41	72	81	95
58652	RICHARDTON	82	56	90	56	59	86	62	78	65	51	64	64	46	64	62	71	42	72	82	95
58653	SCRANTON	84	57	92	57	60	88	64	79	66	52	66	66	47	65	63	72	43	74	84	98
58654	SENTINEL BUTTE	83	57	92	57	60	88	64	79	66	52	66	65	47	65	63	72	43	74	84	97
58655	SOUTH HEART	88	60	97	60	63	93	67	83	70	54	69	69	49	68	67	76	45	78	88	103
58656	TAYLOR	81	57	88	57	60	86	63	78	65	51	65	64	47	64	63	71	42	72	82	95
58701	MINOT	77	72	69	73	71	76	77	75	79	75	79	57	74	78	74	81	54	78	81	90
58703	MINOT	84	78	71	80	76	80	85	80	84	81	84	63	80	85	79	85	58	83	84	96
58704	MINOT AFB	86	45	33	52	40	38	81	56	76	75	80	56	62	92	59	70	56	72	51	68
58705	MINOT AFB	86	45	33	52	40	38	81	56	76	75	80	56	62	92	59	70	56	72	51	68
58707	MINOT	56	36	34	39	35	39	66	45	59	52	59	41	48	59	46	58	42	55	47	57
58710	ANAMOOSE	66	47	68	46	49	69	51	64	56	44	54	49	40	55	50	62	36	59	69	76
58711	ANTLER	88	60	96	60	63	92	67	83	69	54	69	69	49	68	66	76	45	78	88	102
58712	BALFOUR	73	50	80	50	53	77	56	69	58	45	57	57	41	57	56	63	37	65	73	85
58713	BANTRY	75	51	82	51	54	79	57	71	59	46	59	59	42	58	57	65	38	66	75	87
58716	BENEDICT	91	62	100	62	65	96	69	86	72	56	71	71	51	71	69	79	46	80	91	106
58718	BERTHOLD	85	58	93	58	61	89	65	80	67	53	67	66	48	66	64	73	43	75	85	99
58721	BOWBELLS	77	53	85	53	55	81	59	73	61	48	61	60	43	60	59	67	39	68	77	90
58722	BURLINGTON	86	81	73	79	79	83	76	80	78	78	78	59	73	81	73	80	53	78	81	96
58723	BUTTE	72	49	79	49	52	76	55	68	57	44	56	56	40	56	55	62	37	64	72	84
58725	CARPIO	84	57	92	57	60	88	64	79	66	52	66	66	47	65	63	72	43	74	84	98
58727	COLUMBUS	60	41	66	41	43	63	46	57	47	37	47	47	33	46	45	52	30	53	60	70
58730	CROSBY	72	52	73	50	54	75	56	70	63	50	61	53	45	61	55	69	40	65	76	82
58731	DEERING	72	50	79	49	52	76	55	68	57	45	57	56	40	56	55	62	37	64	72	84
58733	DES LACS	86	82	75	81	80	85	77	82	79	78	79	61	75	81	76	81	54	79	82	97
58734	DONNYBROOK	80	55	88	55	57	84	61	76	63	49	63	63	45	62	61	69	41	71	80	93
58735	DOUGLAS	76	53	84	52	55	81	58	72	61	47	60	60	43	59	58	66	39	68	77	89
58736	DRAKE	66	47	68	46	49	69	51	63	56	45	54	49	40	55	50	62	36	59	69	75
58737	FLAXTON	63	43	69	43	45	66	48	59	50	39	49	49	35	49	48	54	32	56	63	73
58740	GLENBURN	86	56	80	58	57	79	70	76	70	59	71	65	52	73	64	74	47	75	78	93
58741	GRANVILLE	78	54	86	54	56	83	60	74	62	48	61	61	44	61	59	68	40	69	78	91
58744	KARLSRUHE	73	50	80	50	53	77	56	69	58	45	57	57	41	57	56	63	37	65	73	85
58746	KENMARE	75	53	79	52	55	79	58	72	63	50	61	57	45	62	57	69	40	67	78	87
58748	KRAMER	73	50	80	50	53	77	56	70	58	45	58	57	41	57	56	63	37	65	73	86
58750	LANSFORD	87	60	95	60	63	92	66	82	69	54	68	68	49	68	66	75	44	77	87	101
58752	LIGNITE	60	41	66	41	43	63	46	57	48	37	47	47	34	47	46	52	31	53	60	70
58755	MCGREGOR	74	51	81	51	53	78	57	70	59	46	58	58	41	58	56	64	38	66	74	87
58756	MAKOTI	78	54	86	53	56	82	60	74	62	48	61	61	44	61	59	68	40	69	78	91
58757	MANDAREE	65	58	49	58	54	59	61	58	63	62	63	45	58	65	56	65	43	61	61	72
58758	MARTIN	72	50	79	49	52	76	55	68	57	45	57	57	40	56	55	62	37	64	72	84
58759	MAX	82	56	90	56	59	86	63	78	65	51	64	64	46	64	62	71	42	73	82	96
58760	MAXBASS	87	60	96	60	63	92	67	83	69	54	68	68	49	68	66	76	44	77	87	102
58761	MOHALL	78	55	81	54	57	82	61	75	66	52	64	58	47	65	59	73	42	70	81	89
58762	NEWBURG	86	59	95	59	62	91	66	82	69	53	68	68	48	67	66	75	44	77	87	101
58763	NEW TOWN	69	58	53	59	53	65	62	61	67	61	66	48	58	67	57	69	45	64	67	77
58765	NOONAN	73	52	74	51	54	76	57	70	63	50	61	53	45	61	55	69	40	66	76	83
58768	NORWICH	84	62	90	62	64	88	66	80	68	56	68	65	52	68	66	73	44	75	83	98
58769	PALERMO	74	51	81	51	53	78	56	70	59	46	58	58	41	57	56	64	38	65	74	86
58770	PARSHALL	70	50	72	49	52	73	55	68	60	48	58	52	43	59	53	66	39	63	73	80
58771	PLAZA	73	50	80	50	53	77	56	69	58	45	57	57	41	57	55	63	37	65	73	85
58772	PORTAL	62	43	68	43	45	66	47	59	49	38	49	49	35	48	47	54	32	55	62	73
58773	POWERS LAKE	69	48	76	48	50	73	53	66	55	43	54	54	39	54	53	60	35	61	69	81
58775	ROSEGLEN	62	44	64	43	46	63	46	58	50	41	49	44	36	50	45	55	32	53	60	69
58776	ROSS	87	60	95	60	63	92	66	83	69	54	68	68	49	68	66	75	44	77	87	102
58778	RUSO	78	53	85	53	56	82	59	74	62	48	61	61	43	60	59	67	40	69	78	91
58779	RYDER	74	51	81	51	54	78	57	70	59	47	59	58	42	58	56	65	38	66	74	86
58781	SAWYER	93	64	102	64	67	98	71	88	74	58	73	73	52	72	71	81	47	82	93	109
58782	SHERWOOD	79	54	86	54	57	83	60	75	63	49	62	62	44	61	60	68	40	70	79	92
58783	SOURIS	73	51	81	51	53	77	56	70	58	46	58	57	41	57	56	64	37	65	74	86
58784	STANLEY	70	50	72	49	52	73	55	68	60	48	58	52	43	59	53	66	39	63	73	80
58785	SURREY	98	101	83	98	95	89	92	93	90	98	92	70	92	94	89	87	63	90	85	108
58787	TOLLEY	78	54	86	54	56	82	60	74	62	48	61	61	44	61	59	68	40	69	78	91
58788	TOWNER	76	54	79	53	56	80	59	73	64	51	63	57	46	63	58	71	41	68	79	88
58789	UPHAM	74	51	81	51	53	78	56	70	59	46	58	58	41	57	56	64	38	65	74	86
58790	VELVA	78	56	79	54	58	81	61	75	67	53	65	57	48	66	59	74	43	70	82	89
58792	VOLTAIRE	95	65	104	65	68	100	72	90	75	59	74	74	53	74	72	82	48	84	95	111
58793	WESTHOPE	73	52	75	51	54	76	57	70	62	50	61	54	45	61	55	69	40	66	76	83
58794	WHITE EARTH	75	52	82	52	54	79	57	71	60	46	59	59	42	59	57	65	38	67	75	88
58795	WILDROSE	75	52	83	52	54	79	57	71	60	46	59	59	42	59	57	65	38	67	75	88
58801	WILLISTON	80	66	72	66	66	78	73	76	75	68	74	59	64	75	69	78	51	76	80	91
58830	ALAMO	75	52	83	52	54	79	57	71	60	47	59	59	42	59	57	65	38	67	75	88
58831	ALEXANDER	79	54	87	54	57	83	60	75	63	49	62	62	44	61	60	68	40	70	79	92
58833	AMBROSE	80	55	87	55	58	84	61	76	64	50	63	62	46	63	61	70	41	71	81	93
58835	ARNEGARD	79	55	87	55	57	84	61	75	63	49	62	62	44	62	60	69	40	70	80	93
58838	CARTWRIGHT	76	52	83	52	55	80	58	72	60	47	60	60	42	59	58	66	39	67	76	89
58843	EPPING	92	63	101	63	66	97	70	87	73	57	72	72	51	71	70	79	47	81	92	107
58844	FORTUNA	81	56	89	56	59	86	62	77	65	50	64	64	45	63	62	70	41	72	82	95
58845	GRENORA	84	58	93	58	61	89	64	80	67	52	66	66	47	66	64	73	43	75	85	98
58847	KEENE	87	60	96	60	63	92	67	83	69	54	69	69	49	68	66	76	45	77	88	102
58849	RAY	73	52	75	51	54	77	57	71	63	50	61	54	45	62	56	69	40	66	77	84
58852	TIOGA	77	55	78	54	57	80	60	74	66	52	64	57	47	65	58	73	42	69	80	88
58853	TRENTON	68	47	74	47	49	72	52	64	54	42	53	53	38	53	52	59	35	60	68	79
58854	WATFORD CITY	83	59	86	58	61	87	65	80	70	56	69	62	50	69	63	77	45	75	86	96
58856	ZAHL	82	56	90	56	59	86	62	77	65	50	64	64	46	64	62	71	42	72	82	95
	NORTH DAKOTA	87	73	80	73	72	84	80	82	81	74	81	65	71	81	75	84	55	82	85	99
	UNITED STATES	100	100	100	100	100	100	100	100	100	100	100	100	100	100	100	100	100	100	100	100

ZIP CODE #	POST OFFICE NAME	COUNTY FIPS CODE	POPULATION 2000	POPULATION 2009	POPULATION 2014	2000-2009 ANNUAL RATE % Rate	2000-2009 ANNUAL RATE State Centile	HOUSEHOLDS 2000	HOUSEHOLDS 2009	HOUSEHOLDS 2014	HOUSEHOLDS % Annual Rate 2000-2009	HOUSEHOLDS 2009 Average HH Size	FAMILIES 2000	FAMILIES 2009	FAMILIES % Annual Rate 2000-2009
43001	ALEXANDRIA	089	1766	2114	2216	2.0	97	626	752	793	2.0	2.78	514	606	1.8
43002	AMLIN	049	17	19	23	1.2	91	6	7	9	1.7	2.71	4	4	0.0
43003	ASHLEY	117	3030	3602	3986	1.9	96	1107	1357	1512	2.2	2.65	834	991	1.9
43004	BLACKLICK	049	8564	18152	21475	8.5	100	3484	7375	8771	8.4	2.46	2403	4815	7.8
43006	BRINKHAVEN	075	583	652	680	1.2	91	214	243	254	1.4	2.68	156	172	1.1
43008	BUCKEYE LAKE	089	1184	1296	1332	1.0	87	472	527	545	1.2	2.46	301	323	0.8
43009	CABLE	021	1764	1883	1926	0.7	79	606	664	685	1.0	2.83	508	549	0.8
43011	CENTERBURG	083	5832	6787	7248	1.7	95	2003	2366	2537	1.8	2.80	1612	1868	1.6
43013	CROTON	089	1335	1484	1544	1.2	91	472	535	561	1.4	2.77	394	439	1.2
43014	DANVILLE	083	3373	3780	3968	1.2	91	1161	1311	1378	1.3	2.87	872	961	1.1
43015	DELAWARE	041	35807	49439	57476	3.5	99	13439	19144	22443	3.9	2.48	9463	13157	3.6
43016	DUBLIN	049	19725	27575	30315	3.7	99	8151	11542	12763	3.8	2.38	4995	6882	3.5
43017	DUBLIN	049	34154	36765	38066	0.8	82	12616	13667	14177	0.9	2.67	9175	9740	0.6
43019	FREDERICKTOWN	083	8852	9484	9787	0.7	79	3211	3485	3604	0.9	2.71	2465	2620	0.7
43021	GALENA	041	5892	9504	11541	5.3	100	2077	3374	4110	5.4	2.82	1780	2860	5.3
43022	GAMBIER	083	3553	3963	4054	1.2	91	852	943	983	1.1	2.50	590	632	0.7
43023	GRANVILLE	089	11515	12717	13153	1.1	89	3564	4002	4177	1.3	2.68	2778	3048	1.0
43025	HEBRON	089	6502	7223	7556	1.1	89	2624	2971	3127	1.4	2.43	1829	2001	1.0
43026	HILLIARD	049	48052	55417	58253	1.6	95	18030	20901	22053	1.6	2.64	12895	14423	1.2
43028	HOWARD	083	5548	7169	7859	2.8	98	2123	2793	3075	3.0	2.56	1681	2168	2.8
43029	IRWIN	097	540	618	653	1.5	94	131	156	166	1.9	3.80	103	120	1.7
43031	JOHNSTOWN	089	9764	11299	11965	1.6	95	3637	4277	4556	1.8	2.63	2833	3244	1.5
43035	LEWIS CENTER	041	11044	20933	26286	7.2	100	4226	7880	9902	7.0	2.66	3061	5703	7.0
43037	MARTINSBURG	083	108	114	117	0.6	75	34	36	37	0.6	3.17	28	29	0.4
43040	MARYSVILLE	159	25731	31634	34478	2.3	97	8905	11223	12325	2.5	2.62	6574	8131	2.3
43044	MECHANICSBURG	021	5346	5430	5432	0.2	56	2012	2092	2109	0.4	2.58	1554	1581	0.2
43045	MILFORD CENTER	159	1566	1821	1942	1.6	95	571	679	729	1.9	2.68	463	538	1.6
43046	MILLERSPORT	045	3285	3733	3961	1.4	93	1360	1578	1686	1.6	2.36	952	1064	1.2
43050	MOUNT VERNON	083	27197	29228	30135	0.8	82	10523	11534	11952	1.0	2.38	7073	7508	0.6
43054	NEW ALBANY	049	8081	17840	21171	8.9	100	2839	6669	8013	9.7	2.66	2246	5111	9.3
43055	NEWARK	089	58172	59933	60435	0.3	61	23709	24833	25190	0.5	2.38	15637	15810	0.1
43056	HEATH	089	15634	17398	18077	1.2	91	6037	6858	7183	1.4	2.51	4457	4907	1.0
43060	NORTH LEWISBURG	021	2517	2782	2881	1.1	89	927	1050	1095	1.4	2.64	704	781	1.1
43061	OSTRANDER	041	3203	3845	4235	2.0	97	1160	1428	1584	2.3	2.67	941	1127	2.0
43062	PATASKALA	089	19958	25305	27567	2.6	98	7255	9349	10246	2.8	2.70	5803	7322	2.5
43064	PLAIN CITY	097	10366	11659	12415	1.3	92	3755	4338	4654	1.6	2.67	2906	3288	1.3
43065	POWELL	041	24976	36341	42325	4.1	99	8547	12651	14813	4.3	2.87	6913	9927	4.0
43066	RADNOR	041	1075	1317	1476	2.2	97	395	499	563	2.6	2.64	336	416	2.3
43067	RAYMOND	159	1597	1825	1996	1.5	94	544	632	695	1.6	2.89	446	505	1.4
43068	REYNOLDSBURG	089	46196	52190	54351	1.3	92	18594	21223	22179	1.4	2.45	12588	13926	1.1
43071	SAINT LOUISVILLE	089	2252	2247	2241	0.0	45	789	801	804	0.2	2.80	640	637	-0.1
43072	SAINT PARIS	021	5795	6061	6146	0.5	71	2217	2375	2427	0.7	2.55	1685	1763	0.5
43074	SUNBURY	041	8879	11970	13686	3.3	98	3165	4394	5065	3.6	2.71	2598	3526	3.4
43076	THORNVILLE	127	8079	8829	9152	1.0	87	3081	3454	3610	1.2	2.55	2323	2535	0.9
43078	URBANA	021	21358	21511	21497	0.1	51	8468	8755	8824	0.4	2.38	5840	5876	0.1
43080	UTICA	089	5345	5792	5967	0.9	85	1946	2141	2215	1.0	2.67	1477	1584	0.8
43081	WESTERVILLE	049	51275	55018	56424	0.8	82	19806	21535	22195	0.9	2.49	13629	14313	0.5
43082	WESTERVILLE	041	17910	31215	38627	6.2	100	5984	10524	13049	6.3	2.95	5101	8872	6.2
43084	WOODSTOCK	021	853	880	891	0.3	61	269	283	289	0.5	2.92	218	225	0.3
43085	COLUMBUS	049	23566	23215	23044	-0.2	32	9646	9700	9698	0.1	2.36	6473	6237	-0.4
43102	AMANDA	045	3509	4068	4323	1.6	95	1253	1480	1584	1.8	2.75	1028	1189	1.6
43103	ASHVILLE	129	9875	11145	11784	1.3	92	3675	4266	4550	1.6	2.61	2790	3154	1.3
43105	BALTIMORE	045	8111	9096	9571	1.2	91	2983	3409	3611	1.5	2.66	2334	2610	1.2
43106	BLOOMINGBURG	047	1646	1811	1859	1.0	87	583	660	685	1.4	2.72	446	495	1.1
43107	BREMEN	045	2857	2997	3065	0.5	71	1043	1116	1150	0.7	2.68	820	855	0.5
43110	CANAL WINCHESTER	045	18772	28897	32822	4.8	99	7042	11275	12941	5.2	2.55	5133	7716	4.5
43112	CARROLL	045	4185	4884	5278	1.7	95	1460	1740	1892	1.9	2.79	1187	1383	1.7
43113	CIRCLEVILLE	129	23476	23645	24020	0.1	51	9019	9379	9588	0.4	2.46	6539	6634	0.2
43115	CLARKSBURG	141	1402	1429	1439	0.2	56	506	523	529	0.4	2.69	398	402	0.1
43116	COMMERCIAL POINT	129	256	300	348	1.7	95	91	110	128	2.1	2.73	74	87	1.8
43119	GALLOWAY	049	22648	26225	27586	1.6	95	8282	9769	10340	1.8	2.68	6098	6957	1.4
43123	GROVE CITY	049	46100	54767	58120	1.9	96	17137	20717	22091	2.1	2.63	13002	15525	1.9
43125	GROVEPORT	049	9446	10764	11364	1.4	93	3827	4522	4830	1.8	2.38	2627	2941	1.2
43128	JEFFERSONVILLE	047	2353	2231	2175	-0.6	14	899	879	863	-0.2	2.53	665	635	-0.5
43130	LANCASTER	045	54799	59837	62335	1.0	87	21336	23731	24884	1.2	2.43	14906	16125	0.9
43135	LAURELVILLE	073	5158	5347	5450	0.4	66	1947	2072	2129	0.7	2.57	1455	1514	0.4
43137	LOCKBOURNE	049	2050	2202	2314	0.8	82	776	853	906	1.0	2.58	613	656	0.7
43138	LOGAN	073	18035	18612	18839	0.3	61	7110	7526	7680	0.6	2.43	5028	5189	0.3
43140	LONDON	097	22269	23462	23939	0.6	75	6994	7663	7919	1.0	2.51	5047	5390	0.7
43143	MOUNT STERLING	097	5362	5447	5483	0.2	56	2041	2112	2138	0.4	2.58	1524	1546	0.2
43145	NEW HOLLAND	129	1813	1808	1817	0.0	45	697	715	724	0.3	2.51	524	523	0.0
43146	ORIENT	129	13470	13590	14377	0.1	51	2786	3504	3827	2.5	2.70	2295	2826	2.3
43147	PICKERINGTON	045	28474	37216	41687	2.9	98	9547	12674	14303	3.1	2.92	7914	10309	2.9
43148	PLEASANTVILLE	045	2156	2490	2653	1.6	95	780	922	992	1.8	2.68	611	703	1.5
43149	ROCKBRIDGE	073	2528	2524	2517	0.0	45	955	982	988	0.3	2.57	746	753	0.1
43150	RUSHVILLE	045	1850	1933	1969	0.5	71	656	701	720	0.7	2.70	528	552	0.5
43152	SOUTH BLOOMINGVILLE	073	1129	1142	1147	0.1	51	443	461	467	0.4	2.45	338	345	0.2
43153	SOUTH SOLON	097	1164	1237	1267	0.7	79	431	469	484	0.9	2.64	343	367	0.7
43154	STOUTSVILLE	045	3132	3725	4040	1.9	96	1091	1332	1456	2.2	2.80	910	1087	1.9
43155	SUGAR GROVE	045	1964	2165	2263	1.1	89	739	832	876	1.3	2.60	583	640	1.0
43160	WASHINGTON COURT HOU	047	22009	22291	22243	0.1	51	8670	9023	9079	0.4	2.40	6017	6097	0.1
43162	WEST JEFFERSON	097	7091	7121	7141	0.0	45	2655	2751	2784	0.4	2.55	2003	2033	0.2
43164	WILLIAMSPORT	129	2299	2304	2321	0.0	45	815	834	847	0.2	2.74	656	657	0.0
43201	COLUMBUS	049	32773	32431	32265	-0.1	39	14809	14896	14915	0.1	2.12	3428	3165	-0.9
43202	COLUMBUS	049	20141	19671	19452	-0.3	27	10093	10056	10012	0.0	1.96	3499	3193	-1.0
43203	COLUMBUS	049	10508	10163	9991	-0.4	21	4741	4597	4538	-0.3	2.14	2147	1942	-1.1
43204	COLUMBUS	049	40591	39468	39049	-0.3	27	16582	16618	16618	0.0	2.35	10133	9569	-0.6
43205	COLUMBUS	049	14376	12752	12206	-1.3	2	5818	5270	5077	-1.1	2.34	3126	2679	-1.7
43206	COLUMBUS	049	24966	23283	22713	-0.8	9	10742	10353	10203	-0.4	2.23	5626	5061	-1.1
43207	COLUMBUS	049	44184	43477	43200	-0.2	32	17012	17162	17186	0.1	2.51	11756	11463	-0.3
43209	COLUMBUS	049	29785	29090	28783	-0.3	27	12349	12212	12144	-0.1	2.27	7382	6937	-0.7
43210	COLUMBUS	049	10014	10387	10462	0.4	66	615	715	750	1.6	2.42	363	398	1.0
43211	COLUMBUS	049	24974	22902	22184	-0.9	7	9206	8653	8443	-0.7	2.64	6340	5720	-1.1
43212	COLUMBUS	049	17769	17796	17802	0.0	45	9518	9854	9972	0.4	1.79	3653	3447	-0.6
43213	COLUMBUS	049	29435	29216	29128	-0.1	39	13127	13363	13442	0.2	2.17	7607	7281	-0.5
	OHIO					0.2					0.4	2.44			0.1
	UNITED STATES					1.0					1.1	2.59			0.9

# POST OFFICE NAME	RACE (%) White 2000	White 2009	Black 2000	Black 2009	Asian/Pacific 2000	Asian/Pacific 2009	% Hispanic Origin 2000	% Hispanic Origin 2009	2009 AGE DISTRIBUTION (%) 0-4	5-9	10-14	15-19	20-24	25-44	45-64	65-84	85+	18+	MEDIAN AGE 2009	% 2009 Males	% 2009 Females
43001 ALEXANDRIA	98.2	95.0	0.4	3.1	0.3	0.5	0.3	0.6	5.7	6.3	6.7	6.4	4.0	26.0	32.1	11.4	1.4	77.3	41.6	53.5	46.5
43002 AMLIN	76.5	68.4	5.9	5.3	17.6	26.3	0.0	0.0	10.5	10.5	10.5	5.3	10.5	42.1	10.5	0.0	0.0	68.4	26.3	47.4	52.6
43003 ASHLEY	97.6	97.1	0.8	0.9	0.2	0.3	0.6	0.8	6.7	6.7	7.0	7.4	5.7	26.1	28.2	10.9	1.3	74.7	38.2	49.5	50.5
43004 BLACKLICK	81.4	78.4	13.9	15.3	2.0	3.1	1.6	1.9	9.5	8.9	8.1	6.0	5.2	34.2	21.9	5.7	0.6	69.7	33.1	48.6	51.4
43006 BRINKHAVEN	99.0	98.8	0.2	0.2	0.0	0.0	0.7	0.9	7.2	7.4	7.5	7.1	5.7	24.7	27.6	11.5	1.4	73.5	37.8	50.9	49.1
43008 BUCKEYE LAKE	97.3	96.8	0.7	0.7	0.0	0.0	0.5	0.6	5.0	5.2	5.6	7.2	5.6	24.2	30.4	15.1	1.7	79.9	42.9	49.1	50.9
43009 CABLE	98.0	97.5	0.9	1.0	0.1	0.3	0.5	0.6	6.4	7.8	7.7	7.1	4.6	25.3	30.7	9.2	1.2	73.5	38.7	50.2	49.8
43011 CENTERBURG	98.3	98.0	0.4	0.4	0.1	0.2	0.5	0.6	6.6	7.2	7.7	7.5	4.5	25.7	28.9	10.4	1.5	73.6	39.3	50.5	49.5
43013 CROTON	98.1	97.8	0.3	0.3	0.2	0.3	0.5	0.7	7.4	7.9	8.2	7.1	4.0	27.4	27.6	9.5	0.9	72.0	37.9	52.2	47.8
43014 DANVILLE	98.7	98.4	0.2	0.2	0.1	0.2	0.5	0.7	7.9	8.3	8.1	7.2	5.1	24.5	26.3	11.0	1.6	71.3	36.3	50.5	49.5
43015 DELAWARE	94.1	93.1	3.1	3.3	0.8	1.3	1.0	1.2	7.3	7.2	7.1	7.3	6.8	27.6	25.8	9.4	1.5	74.5	36.3	48.7	51.3
43016 DUBLIN	85.3	78.8	2.4	3.1	9.9	15.5	2.1	2.7	8.0	7.0	7.1	5.9	6.1	35.4	24.0	5.6	1.1	74.3	34.2	50.2	49.8
43017 DUBLIN	88.9	84.5	2.4	3.0	6.9	10.4	1.8	2.3	7.2	7.7	8.3	8.0	4.8	28.6	28.4	5.9	1.1	71.5	36.0	49.9	50.1
43019 FREDERICKTOWN	98.4	98.1	0.2	0.2	0.1	0.2	0.5	0.6	6.7	7.1	7.2	7.0	5.2	25.5	28.6	11.3	1.4	74.7	38.7	50.6	49.4
43021 GALENA	97.1	96.1	0.9	1.2	0.6	1.0	0.7	0.9	6.8	7.8	8.7	7.8	3.8	22.4	33.0	8.8	0.8	71.6	40.8	49.7	50.3
43022 GAMBIER	96.3	94.1	1.4	2.8	0.8	1.2	1.1	1.5	3.4	3.6	4.3	22.6	23.0	15.3	19.5	7.4	1.0	85.2	23.5	48.1	51.9
43023 GRANVILLE	95.7	88.6	1.1	7.7	1.4	1.7	1.0	1.3	4.6	5.4	6.2	9.4	9.9	24.1	28.7	10.2	1.4	80.9	38.2	52.9	47.1
43025 HEBRON	97.5	96.9	0.5	0.6	0.4	0.6	0.7	0.9	7.4	7.4	7.3	6.5	5.3	24.9	28.4	11.7	1.2	73.8	38.6	48.6	51.4
43026 HILLIARD	91.3	87.3	2.5	3.4	3.6	5.9	2.1	2.9	9.4	8.6	7.9	6.8	6.8	34.5	20.4	4.9	0.7	69.8	31.7	49.5	50.5
43028 HOWARD	98.4	97.9	0.4	0.5	0.3	0.5	0.6	0.8	6.3	6.7	7.2	6.9	4.3	24.3	28.9	14.1	1.2	75.3	41.2	50.4	49.6
43029 IRWIN	98.3	97.9	0.4	0.5	0.4	0.5	0.6	0.6	7.1	7.8	7.9	8.9	6.1	26.4	26.2	8.6	1.0	72.5	35.4	50.5	49.5
43031 JOHNSTOWN	98.0	97.5	0.3	0.3	0.3	0.5	0.3	0.5	6.4	6.9	7.2	6.5	4.6	24.5	31.0	11.3	1.5	75.3	40.8	49.8	50.2
43035 LEWIS CENTER	90.5	88.2	4.2	4.6	3.0	4.4	1.6	1.9	10.4	9.5	8.6	6.1	5.7	34.6	21.0	3.7	0.4	67.5	31.0	49.7	50.3
43037 MARTINSBURG	99.1	99.1	0.0	0.0	0.0	0.0	0.0	0.0	6.1	6.1	7.9	7.9	5.3	25.4	28.9	10.5	1.8	74.6	39.4	49.1	50.9
43040 MARYSVILLE	93.7	92.5	4.0	4.5	0.7	1.2	0.9	1.1	8.0	7.7	7.5	6.9	6.0	31.2	23.8	7.6	1.3	72.6	35.0	47.0	53.0
43044 MECHANICSBURG	97.4	96.7	1.0	1.3	0.3	0.6	0.7	0.9	6.8	6.9	7.1	6.9	5.3	26.2	28.0	11.6	1.3	74.8	38.9	50.4	49.6
43045 MILFORD CENTER	98.0	97.5	0.3	0.3	0.3	0.4	0.3	0.3	6.8	7.2	7.4	6.6	4.7	26.6	30.0	9.4	1.2	74.5	38.8	50.2	49.8
43046 MILLERSPORT	98.4	98.1	0.2	0.2	0.1	0.2	0.6	0.7	5.8	6.3	6.5	5.5	4.2	22.8	33.0	14.2	1.6	77.9	44.2	49.0	51.0
43050 MOUNT VERNON	97.1	95.3	0.9	2.3	0.5	0.7	0.8	1.0	5.9	5.8	6.1	7.5	7.9	23.0	27.3	13.7	2.8	79.5	40.1	47.7	52.3
43054 NEW ALBANY	92.4	88.6	3.1	4.2	3.1	5.3	0.8	1.1	7.8	8.6	9.2	7.1	3.0	25.0	30.1	8.1	1.0	69.3	38.9	48.9	51.1
43055 NEWARK	95.0	94.0	2.6	2.9	0.6	0.9	0.8	1.0	7.0	6.7	6.5	6.4	6.1	25.7	26.8	12.4	2.3	75.9	38.4	48.3	51.7
43056 HEATH	96.7	95.9	1.4	1.6	0.5	0.8	0.7	0.9	6.1	6.3	6.6	6.5	5.6	25.4	28.8	13.0	1.7	77.0	40.6	48.8	51.2
43060 NORTH LEWISBURG	97.7	97.0	0.7	0.9	0.1	0.1	0.6	0.8	8.0	8.2	8.1	7.9	5.0	29.6	24.9	7.5	1.0	70.8	34.8	50.8	49.2
43061 OSTRANDER	97.7	97.3	1.0	1.1	0.2	0.3	0.5	0.7	5.4	6.4	7.4	8.0	4.1	25.2	33.3	9.1	1.1	75.3	41.6	50.6	49.4
43062 PATASKALA	96.2	95.3	1.8	2.0	0.5	0.8	0.8	1.0	7.4	7.6	7.7	6.5	4.7	26.8	28.5	9.9	0.9	73.2	38.2	49.7	50.3
43064 PLAIN CITY	97.4	96.8	1.1	1.2	0.3	0.5	0.8	1.0	6.6	7.1	7.5	7.5	5.5	25.4	29.3	9.9	1.0	74.2	38.3	50.0	50.0
43065 POWELL	92.5	90.7	2.0	2.2	4.0	5.4	1.2	1.5	8.5	9.0	8.9	7.5	3.9	27.7	28.2	5.7	0.5	68.6	36.4	49.8	50.2
43066 RADNOR	98.1	97.6	0.8	1.0	0.2	0.3	0.4	0.5	5.2	6.1	7.1	7.4	4.5	22.0	36.1	10.6	1.0	77.0	43.5	50.9	49.1
43067 RAYMOND	97.7	97.0	0.5	0.5	0.9	1.3	0.6	0.8	7.7	8.1	8.3	6.9	4.6	26.8	29.0	7.7	1.0	71.5	37.4	51.3	48.7
43068 REYNOLDSBURG	83.3	79.1	11.8	14.3	1.9	3.1	1.9	2.4	7.7	7.2	7.0	6.5	6.1	30.2	25.2	9.0	1.1	74.5	35.5	48.1	51.9
43071 SAINT LOUISVILLE	98.3	97.9	0.4	0.4	0.1	0.1	0.5	0.7	6.5	6.7	7.2	7.3	5.2	24.0	30.4	11.9	1.0	75.2	40.4	51.4	48.6
43072 SAINT PARIS	98.4	98.0	0.2	0.3	0.2	0.3	0.4	0.6	6.3	6.7	7.2	7.1	4.5	26.1	29.2	11.5	1.4	75.3	39.8	49.3	50.7
43074 SUNBURY	98.2	97.7	0.3	0.4	0.3	0.6	0.6	0.8	5.8	6.3	6.9	7.7	4.8	24.5	32.8	9.9	1.3	75.9	41.3	49.6	50.4
43076 THORNVILLE	97.9	97.6	0.2	0.3	0.1	0.2	0.3	0.4	5.4	5.9	6.8	6.8	3.9	24.2	32.1	13.6	1.3	77.4	43.1	50.7	49.3
43078 URBANA	93.9	92.8	3.7	4.3	0.3	0.5	0.9	1.1	6.5	6.5	6.6	6.8	6.0	24.7	27.9	12.6	2.4	76.3	39.9	48.6	51.4
43080 UTICA	98.4	98.1	0.2	0.3	0.1	0.2	0.6	0.8	6.2	6.5	6.9	7.6	5.5	24.8	28.9	12.1	1.6	75.7	39.8	49.6	50.4
43081 WESTERVILLE	91.1	87.7	4.5	5.9	2.4	4.0	1.3	1.7	6.4	6.3	6.5	7.3	7.0	28.2	27.9	9.0	1.4	76.7	36.9	48.2	51.8
43082 WESTERVILLE	93.3	91.3	3.0	3.6	2.1	3.2	1.0	1.4	8.1	8.9	9.3	7.5	3.6	27.1	28.3	6.3	0.8	68.6	36.8	49.2	50.8
43084 WOODSTOCK	97.5	97.0	0.8	1.0	0.0	0.0	0.1	0.1	6.1	7.0	7.3	7.3	4.8	24.2	29.1	11.8	2.4	75.1	39.9	50.6	49.4
43085 COLUMBUS	90.8	86.8	3.3	4.4	3.7	6.1	1.4	1.9	5.7	5.6	6.5	6.2	5.9	25.9	29.3	12.7	2.2	78.3	40.8	47.6	52.4
43102 AMANDA	98.5	98.3	0.2	0.2	0.1	0.1	0.5	0.7	6.8	7.2	7.7	7.2	4.5	26.4	28.6	10.3	1.2	73.6	38.7	50.5	49.5
43103 ASHVILLE	97.8	97.2	0.2	0.4	0.2	0.3	0.8	1.0	7.0	7.0	7.0	7.2	6.2	26.8	28.1	9.9	0.9	74.7	37.2	50.1	49.9
43105 BALTIMORE	98.3	97.9	0.3	0.3	0.2	0.3	0.7	0.9	6.1	6.4	6.9	6.8	5.0	24.7	30.4	12.2	1.6	76.3	41.1	49.9	50.1
43106 BLOOMINGBURG	95.3	94.3	2.7	3.1	0.1	0.2	2.2	2.8	7.7	7.6	7.5	6.6	5.9	27.7	27.1	9.0	1.1	73.3	36.1	50.2	49.8
43107 BREMEN	98.0	97.6	0.1	0.1	0.1	0.2	0.5	0.7	6.3	6.6	7.0	7.1	5.3	24.3	30.2	11.7	1.4	75.6	40.2	50.5	49.5
43110 CANAL WINCHESTER	87.2	81.6	9.1	13.2	0.9	1.4	1.4	2.0	8.6	7.9	7.6	6.8	6.2	30.9	23.4	7.6	1.2	72.8	33.6	48.1	51.9
43112 CARROLL	98.1	97.6	0.2	0.3	0.4	0.6	0.5	0.6	5.6	6.1	7.6	7.2	4.1	23.7	32.9	11.2	1.6	76.6	42.2	50.3	49.7
43113 CIRCLEVILLE	96.5	94.5	1.8	3.3	0.4	0.6	0.7	0.9	6.6	6.6	6.7	7.2	5.7	24.6	27.0	13.6	2.0	75.4	39.5	49.0	51.0
43115 CLARKSBURG	96.5	95.8	2.0	2.4	0.1	0.1	0.1	0.1	7.3	7.8	8.3	7.3	4.9	24.3	28.6	10.3	1.3	72.1	37.0	50.9	49.1
43116 COMMERCIAL POINT	98.8	98.3	0.0	0.0	0.0	0.3	0.4	0.7	6.0	6.3	7.0	7.3	4.3	25.3	32.7	10.0	1.0	76.0	41.5	51.0	49.0
43119 GALLOWAY	90.2	86.6	5.0	6.4	1.5	2.7	2.8	3.9	9.6	8.7	7.8	6.9	7.2	32.8	21.6	5.0	0.4	69.6	30.8	48.9	51.1
43123 GROVE CITY	94.4	93.0	2.9	3.3	1.0	1.6	1.1	1.4	7.4	7.3	7.5	6.8	5.1	28.0	26.9	9.9	1.2	73.6	37.3	48.8	51.2
43125 GROVEPORT	91.8	89.2	4.8	6.2	1.0	1.7	1.6	2.2	6.2	6.0	5.8	6.0	6.7	27.9	27.3	12.3	1.9	78.3	38.8	48.6	51.4
43128 JEFFERSONVILLE	93.7	92.8	3.9	4.3	0.1	0.2	0.4	0.6	6.9	7.0	7.2	6.8	5.4	25.8	27.6	11.7	1.5	74.6	38.1	50.2	49.8
43130 LANCASTER	96.1	95.6	2.1	2.1	0.4	0.7	0.7	0.9	6.7	6.4	6.4	6.2	6.4	26.2	26.7	12.8	2.2	76.8	38.8	50.2	49.8
43135 LAURELVILLE	98.3	97.8	0.4	0.6	0.1	0.1	0.4	0.6	6.5	6.8	7.1	7.0	5.1	25.6	29.1	11.8	1.0	75.1	39.2	50.4	49.6
43137 LOCKBOURNE	97.3	96.3	0.9	1.2	0.3	0.6	0.5	0.7	7.0	7.3	7.2	7.2	5.7	26.7	28.3	9.7	0.9	74.0	37.5	51.4	48.6
43138 LOGAN	97.9	97.5	0.5	0.6	0.1	0.1	0.5	0.7	6.7	6.7	6.7	6.5	5.5	25.0	27.6	13.0	2.2	75.8	39.5	48.7	51.3
43140 LONDON	86.9	84.5	10.7	11.8	0.6	1.3	0.7	1.1	5.7	5.5	5.6	7.8	8.7	29.6	25.1	10.2	1.9	79.7	36.8	55.2	44.8
43143 MOUNT STERLING	97.8	97.2	0.4	0.6	0.2	0.4	1.1	1.4	6.9	7.3	7.1	6.6	5.4	26.4	27.9	11.0	1.4	74.7	37.7	48.5	51.5
43145 NEW HOLLAND	97.4	96.6	0.5	0.8	0.1	0.1	1.0	1.3	5.8	6.1	6.6	6.9	4.6	25.6	30.6	12.1	1.7	77.2	41.3	50.2	49.8
43146 ORIENT	77.0	75.7	21.7	22.8	0.2	0.3	0.5	0.5	4.3	4.7	5.1	6.1	8.6	35.9	26.3	8.4	0.7	82.8	37.5	65.0	35.0
43147 PICKERINGTON	91.5	90.3	5.2	5.4	1.7	2.4	1.2	1.4	7.8	8.1	8.4	7.9	4.6	28.4	28.2	6.0	0.6	70.9	35.7	49.8	50.2
43148 PLEASANTVILLE	98.7	98.4	0.1	0.1	0.2	0.4	0.5	0.6	6.3	6.5	6.9	7.2	5.2	24.9	29.3	12.0	1.8	75.7	40.3	49.3	50.7
43149 ROCKBRIDGE	98.3	97.9	0.2	0.2	0.2	0.3	0.3	0.4	6.3	6.5	7.1	6.3	4.0	25.4	33.3	10.3	0.8	76.3	41.2	50.7	49.3
43150 RUSHVILLE	98.4	98.2	0.2	0.3	0.1	0.1	0.4	0.5	5.8	6.4	6.9	7.3	4.5	25.2	31.0	11.1	1.8	76.2	41.2	49.4	50.6
43152 SOUTH BLOOMINGVILLE	98.4	98.2	0.2	0.2	0.0	0.1	0.3	0.4	6.8	6.8	7.1	6.7	5.6	26.4	28.7	10.7	1.1	75.2	38.2	51.0	49.0
43153 SOUTH SOLON	98.1	97.6	1.0	1.3	0.3	0.4	0.4	0.5	6.1	6.4	6.6	6.8	5.1	25.1	30.6	11.8	1.5	76.7	40.9	50.4	49.6
43154 STOUTSVILLE	98.9	98.6	0.2	0.2	0.1	0.1	0.4	0.5	6.3	6.7	7.5	7.5	4.8	26.3	30.0	9.8	1.1	74.8	39.0	50.1	49.9
43155 SUGAR GROVE	98.8	98.7	0.1	0.1	0.1	0.1	0.4	0.6	5.6	7.0	8.1	7.0	4.6	24.7	30.3	11.1	1.6	74.6	40.0	50.1	49.9
43160 WASHINGTON COURT HOU	95.6	94.6	2.0	2.3	0.6	0.9	1.3	1.6	6.5	6.5	6.5	6.4	5.7	25.5	27.2	13.3	2.3	76.4	39.6	49.3	50.7
43162 WEST JEFFERSON	97.8	97.1	0.9	1.2	0.3	0.5	0.6	0.8	6.5	6.4	6.5	6.9	5.6	25.6	28.4	12.1	1.9	76.2	39.7	49.4	50.6
43164 WILLIAMSPORT	98.0	97.0	0.8	1.6	0.1	0.2	0.7	0.9	5.9	6.6	7.1	7.3	5.0	25.9	31.1	9.9	1.2	75.7	40.3	49.7	50.3
43201 COLUMBUS	69.7	63.7	20.9	23.4	5.4	8.2	2.7	3.4	3.9	3.0	2.6	8.3	45.5	24.5	9.4	2.5	0.4	89.0	23.5	55.5	44.5
43202 COLUMBUS	80.8	75.1	4.3	5.2	10.5	14.7	2.6	3.2	5.0	3.5	2.9	4.6	23.0	39.1	16.0	5.1	0.9	86.9	28.3	52.4	47.6
43203 COLUMBUS	9.7	7.5	84.7	86.7	0.8	1.0	1.2	1.2	8.2	8.5	7.9	8.8	6.8	22.5	22.5	12.4	2.4	70.4	33.5	44.9	55.1
43204 COLUMBUS	83.3	78.3	9.9	12.1	3.0	5.0	2.2	2.9	7.5	7.1	6.7	7.1	7.8	28.7	24.5	9.3	1.4	74.6	34.4	49.0	51.0
43205 COLUMBUS	15.2	12.1	80.7	83.6	0.5	0.7	1.4	1.5	8.1	8.2	7.5	8.2	7.8	26.0	24.1	8.8	1.1	71.0	32.7	48.5	51.5
43206 COLUMBUS	49.3	46.2	46.2	48.4	1.2	1.7	1.7	2.0	6.7	6.5	6.2	6.5	8.1	31.1	25.1	8.7	1.1	76.6	34.0	49.3	50.7
43207 COLUMBUS	71.6	68.0	24.0	26.5	1.2	1.8	1.4	1.8	7.3	7.1	6.8	7.1	6.7	26.1	25.1	12.4	1.3	74.5	36.7	48.2	51.8
43209 COLUMBUS	68.8	64.3	26.1	29.6	1.1	1.7	2.5	2.8	6.3	6.0	6.1	8.2	8.5	24.3	26.2	11.7	2.6	77.8	37.3	47.2	52.8
43210 COLUMBUS	73.2	65.1	10.3	12.6	11.8	16.9	2.4	3.0	1.6	0.9	0.3	59.3	24.1	10.9	1.9	0.9	0.2	96.7	19.0	50.4	49.6
43211 COLUMBUS	29.3	25.1	65.8	69.5	0.6	0.9	1.5	1.8	8.4	8.7	8.5	8.9	7.6	25.2	23.0	8.7	1.0	68.8	30.8	46.2	53.8
43212 COLUMBUS	93.0	89.8	2.1	3.0	2.7	4.3	1.7	2.4	4.4	3.4	3.3	4.1	12.8	38.4	23.0	8.2	2.4	86.7	33.9	48.4	51.6
43213 COLUMBUS	69.2	62.9	24.0	28.3	2.5	3.9	3.2	3.9	7.0	6.0	5.7	6.4	8.2	28.3	25.4	11.5	1.6	77.7	35.9	48.3	51.7
OHIO	85.0	83.1	11.5	12.2	1.2	1.9	1.9	2.4	6.6	6.5	6.6	7.1	6.7	25.9	26.9	11.7	2.1	76.2	38.2	48.7	51.3
UNITED STATES	75.1	72.0	12.3	12.7	3.8	4.6	12.5	15.7	6.8	6.7	6.6	7.1	6.9	27.0	26.0	10.9	1.9	75.7	36.9	49.2	50.8

43001-43213

ZIP CODE #	POST OFFICE NAME	2009 Per Capita Income	2009 HH Income Base	2009 Household Income Distribution (%): Less than $25,000	$25,000 to $49,999	$50,000 to $99,999	$100,000 to $149,999	$150,000 or More	Median Household Income: 2009	2014	2009 National Centile	2009 State Centile	2009 Home Value Base	2009 Home Value Distribution (%): Less than $50,000	$50,000 to $89,999	$90,000 to $174,999	$175,000 to $399,999	$400,000 or More	2009 Median Home Value
43001	ALEXANDRIA	29055	752	5.2	24.1	42.8	20.6	7.3	71406	71478	88	91	669	1.0	4.0	40.7	45.4	8.8	188702
43002	AMLIN	34342	7	0.0	0.0	57.1	42.9	0.0	85714	94125	94	98	4	0.0	0.0	0.0	100.0	0.0	200000
43003	ASHLEY	23990	1357	15.4	25.1	46.6	10.1	2.7	56171	57458	73	71	1068	13.1	11.0	51.4	21.2	3.3	129710
43004	BLACKLICK	37327	7375	11.5	20.8	37.9	16.6	13.3	70088	72620	87	90	5373	0.3	22.2	39.1	27.8	10.7	155434
43006	BRINKHAVEN	18244	243	26.7	32.9	35.0	3.7	1.6	41923	45000	39	25	197	24.4	26.9	28.4	15.7	4.6	88077
43008	BUCKEYE LAKE	19415	527	31.5	31.7	30.6	3.6	2.7	36564	39900	22	13	325	33.5	35.1	22.8	6.8	1.8	70595
43009	CABLE	23470	664	8.1	26.5	52.4	9.8	3.2	61838	61539	80	80	589	8.5	9.0	61.6	16.0	4.9	126322
43011	CENTERBURG	24227	2366	14.5	23.4	44.5	13.8	3.9	60628	60660	78	78	1971	5.8	12.7	48.4	30.1	2.9	142357
43013	CROTON	25392	535	11.8	19.6	53.3	13.6	1.7	66837	69674	85	88	438	6.4	14.2	36.5	41.3	1.6	161864
43014	DANVILLE	15712	1311	30.0	33.0	31.4	4.3	1.4	37943	40532	27	16	997	11.3	30.5	41.9	13.7	2.5	102748
43015	DELAWARE	32215	19144	14.2	20.3	37.1	20.5	7.9	67056	68866	85	88	12936	6.7	7.0	30.7	44.8	10.7	192093
43016	DUBLIN	41606	11542	7.6	15.7	41.8	20.1	14.8	78629	79327	91	96	6593	4.1	2.0	27.4	60.2	6.4	202421
43017	DUBLIN	49227	13667	6.7	12.2	30.8	21.6	28.7	100441	102278	97	99	9468	1.2	3.0	23.0	49.2	23.5	256380
43019	FREDERICKTOWN	22071	3485	19.5	26.7	42.1	8.5	3.3	52631	52824	67	60	2864	9.5	21.8	50.2	16.5	2.1	115705
43021	GALENA	44356	3374	6.4	12.2	30.3	28.3	22.9	101531	105049	97	99	3089	1.3	2.7	13.9	47.4	34.7	334423
43022	GAMBIER	21348	943	19.1	23.0	40.7	12.5	4.7	58444	56993	76	76	695	4.2	17.7	42.4	32.8	2.9	136234
43023	GRANVILLE	34508	4002	8.1	16.3	35.0	24.1	16.5	83487	83504	93	97	3360	2.1	2.3	28.6	51.6	15.4	219204
43025	HEBRON	25402	2971	23.0	29.0	34.3	8.8	4.9	47549	51618	56	40	2204	28.6	16.9	28.9	21.3	4.3	99901
43026	HILLIARD	34886	20901	7.5	14.4	45.6	21.4	11.1	79508	79516	92	96	14749	1.0	9.1	51.9	36.1	1.9	155382
43028	HOWARD	26208	2793	10.8	27.0	47.7	10.5	4.1	60209	60095	78	77	2439	2.7	13.7	60.6	19.5	3.5	129696
43029	IRWIN	19063	156	12.8	23.1	44.2	15.4	4.5	63762	63788	82	84	112	8.9	12.5	46.4	30.4	1.8	140789
43031	JOHNSTOWN	28084	4277	13.4	20.0	48.2	13.7	4.7	65545	67844	84	87	3417	4.7	11.4	43.9	37.1	2.9	154238
43035	LEWIS CENTER	44720	7880	5.3	13.4	30.7	28.8	21.8	100630	103444	97	99	5802	5.1	1.3	7.3	54.3	31.9	328071
43037	MARTINSBURG	19350	36	13.9	27.8	52.8	5.6	0.0	57113	57017	74	73	31	3.2	16.1	48.4	32.3	0.0	134375
43040	MARYSVILLE	27126	11223	13.7	19.3	45.7	15.6	5.7	67221	72064	85	88	8294	10.0	6.3	40.8	39.7	3.2	161794
43044	MECHANICSBURG	23754	2092	21.0	20.7	45.0	10.3	3.0	55792	55803	72	69	1655	11.9	19.9	50.8	15.8	1.6	117634
43045	MILFORD CENTER	29798	679	10.6	21.9	39.0	20.9	7.5	70773	72850	87	91	559	8.1	22.0	38.8	26.1	5.0	125906
43046	MILLERSPORT	27260	1578	18.6	26.6	41.2	11.1	2.5	55237	58764	72	67	1219	4.2	13.5	39.6	36.6	6.1	149439
43050	MOUNT VERNON	22059	11534	27.9	29.5	32.8	6.6	3.2	43332	46510	43	29	7945	10.7	22.9	46.3	18.9	1.2	113297
43054	NEW ALBANY	54793	6669	6.1	10.5	28.2	22.2	33.0	110231	110964	98	99	5284	0.0	0.9	19.3	49.9	29.9	272241
43055	NEWARK	23174	24833	24.8	29.1	35.7	7.2	3.2	45711	50323	50	35	15795	10.0	27.1	49.6	11.8	1.5	105417
43056	HEATH	25303	6858	17.7	28.6	41.1	9.0	3.5	53081	56017	68	61	5216	12.8	13.4	54.6	17.3	2.0	119903
43060	NORTH LEWISBURG	24048	1050	15.4	23.4	48.8	9.0	3.4	60475	60640	78	78	810	12.7	21.2	54.3	9.0	2.7	107093
43061	OSTRANDER	30729	1428	8.7	19.9	44.5	20.8	6.2	70869	69701	87	91	1253	1.8	18.6	23.9	43.3	12.4	199155
43062	PATASKALA	29842	9349	10.5	19.3	44.5	19.1	6.6	73586	75264	89	93	7879	7.5	8.8	45.7	34.8	3.3	155541
43064	PLAIN CITY	28520	4338	12.3	22.2	44.6	14.3	6.6	63847	65590	82	84	3369	16.2	5.5	35.9	36.6	5.8	159594
43065	POWELL	49603	12651	3.5	9.1	30.2	27.5	29.6	111491	113121	98	100	10959	2.2	2.6	18.8	42.3	34.1	313501
43066	RADNOR	34724	499	9.2	13.0	51.9	20.0	5.8	75814	74429	90	94	431	1.6	15.8	31.1	36.7	14.8	182386
43067	RAYMOND	25141	632	10.8	11.1	60.0	14.4	3.8	68918	71220	86	89	567	9.5	9.0	43.2	36.3	1.9	145772
43068	REYNOLDSBURG	29971	21223	11.2	22.9	46.0	14.6	5.3	64740	66270	83	85	13556	4.7	6.2	64.0	24.5	0.5	137216
43071	SAINT LOUISVILLE	19604	801	17.6	32.8	43.7	4.1	1.7	49682	52580	60	48	701	13.7	14.7	57.5	11.3	2.9	116031
43072	SAINT PARIS	22305	2375	19.3	29.1	43.5	5.6	2.4	51103	51405	64	54	1913	9.9	21.8	47.9	18.2	2.2	113699
43074	SUNBURY	32760	4394	8.9	16.2	40.5	26.8	7.5	80874	82573	92	96	3639	7.7	7.6	28.6	42.0	14.1	201654
43076	THORNVILLE	25643	3454	14.6	26.0	45.3	10.3	3.8	58142	59706	75	75	2933	9.1	16.7	45.1	25.5	3.5	128142
43078	URBANA	24666	8755	20.8	26.2	40.3	10.0	2.7	52206	52811	66	58	6274	11.2	20.3	49.0	18.2	1.2	114916
43080	UTICA	21871	2141	21.0	26.5	41.9	8.3	2.3	51824	53758	66	57	1673	15.6	21.2	39.8	21.2	2.2	109935
43081	WESTERVILLE	34949	21535	9.1	19.1	42.2	18.5	11.1	75631	75562	90	94	14130	0.9	6.9	50.0	38.9	3.3	160267
43082	WESTERVILLE	54407	10524	4.3	8.5	20.9	29.9	36.5	127178	128222	99	100	9743	3.0	0.7	10.4	55.1	30.8	324280
43084	WOODSTOCK	22072	283	13.1	21.9	57.2	6.0	1.8	56740	55004	74	72	236	8.9	21.6	49.6	16.5	3.4	116463
43085	COLUMBUS	39428	9700	8.9	17.4	41.8	18.8	13.1	77485	76804	91	95	7278	0.9	10.9	39.6	45.0	3.7	172520
43102	AMANDA	20623	1480	15.9	33.5	42.7	6.4	1.6	50481	51568	62	51	1202	6.4	14.8	45.2	27.6	6.0	125600
43103	ASHVILLE	24004	4266	17.4	24.5	45.1	10.3	2.7	57217	60543	74	74	3241	26.3	10.4	36.1	25.2	1.9	124963
43105	BALTIMORE	26915	3409	14.8	21.9	44.5	14.5	4.2	63396	67290	82	83	2709	2.1	10.1	44.1	39.3	4.4	162005
43106	BLOOMINGBURG	17624	660	24.5	33.3	36.5	4.8	0.8	43587	46897	44	30	465	17.0	35.5	38.3	6.2	3.0	87700
43107	BREMEN	20383	1116	18.6	31.6	43.5	5.0	1.2	49621	52139	60	47	913	3.4	17.6	57.8	20.6	0.5	122710
43110	CANAL WINCHESTER	28518	11275	12.7	21.5	45.4	14.6	5.8	63683	64499	82	83	7359	0.5	3.6	61.7	30.6	3.6	152766
43112	CARROLL	28985	1740	6.6	21.3	51.0	14.3	6.9	72841	76286	88	92	1530	5.9	6.4	39.5	42.9	5.3	171698
43113	CIRCLEVILLE	23878	9379	23.6	24.9	37.5	10.6	3.4	51161	54124	64	54	6406	13.4	15.3	46.3	23.2	1.8	122621
43115	CLARKSBURG	19636	523	26.2	23.9	40.5	7.3	2.1	49849	50947	61	49	402	16.2	35.1	38.3	9.0	1.5	88718
43116	COMMERCIAL POINT	27841	110	10.0	20.0	50.9	12.7	6.4	72401	71338	88	92	98	14.3	9.2	36.7	35.7	4.1	154167
43119	GALLOWAY	28843	9769	9.9	24.4	44.2	14.4	7.1	65498	66458	84	87	6556	1.3	8.9	64.7	23.8	1.3	133104
43123	GROVE CITY	30497	20717	10.0	18.7	47.0	16.8	7.6	70491	73210	87	91	16006	4.6	6.9	60.8	25.9	1.7	137651
43125	GROVEPORT	26428	4522	16.5	26.1	44.3	10.8	2.2	56013	58450	73	70	3061	7.3	11.9	63.8	16.7	0.3	120487
43128	JEFFERSONVILLE	20294	879	25.0	25.8	42.7	5.5	1.0	48850	50769	59	45	590	9.2	33.1	48.8	6.4	2.5	97302
43130	LANCASTER	23187	23731	21.2	31.6	37.1	7.0	3.1	46745	49433	53	38	16334	9.5	16.3	48.2	23.2	2.8	122853
43135	LAURELVILLE	20102	2072	25.1	30.1	36.5	6.4	1.9	44038	46066	45	31	1633	15.7	25.7	42.3	15.1	1.2	101720
43137	LOCKBOURNE	27852	853	10.9	24.5	45.3	14.5	4.8	61668	63420	80	80	669	25.0	9.9	42.3	21.4	1.5	124228
43138	LOGAN	20450	7526	28.8	29.4	33.9	5.6	2.3	41535	43461	38	24	5465	19.5	28.1	40.9	10.2	1.2	92942
43140	LONDON	23880	7663	19.5	24.2	39.4	12.9	4.0	55647	58784	72	69	5416	11.3	13.6	48.1	23.8	3.1	127106
43143	MOUNT STERLING	23680	2112	15.7	29.2	44.1	8.3	2.7	54017	56720	70	64	1473	13.5	19.2	45.4	18.7	3.1	114268
43145	NEW HOLLAND	21891	715	19.6	31.0	40.1	7.4	1.8	49318	51468	60	46	550	20.5	26.7	38.5	10.4	3.8	94545
43146	ORIENT	23473	3504	11.8	22.8	45.0	14.3	6.1	64747	66191	83	85	3048	17.0	9.4	40.5	30.7	2.5	140234
43147	PICKERINGTON	37255	12674	3.8	11.5	38.8	27.6	18.3	93754	93498	96	98	10721	0.4	0.6	38.6	57.5	2.9	194572
43148	PLEASANTVILLE	21618	922	20.9	31.2	37.4	7.8	2.6	47496	49647	55	40	738	5.6	19.8	37.0	33.6	4.1	140726
43149	ROCKBRIDGE	20508	982	22.3	33.3	37.6	4.4	2.4	46163	46742	52	36	837	13.1	17.4	53.4	14.3	1.7	113519
43150	RUSHVILLE	22812	701	14.1	30.0	46.1	7.7	2.1	55464	57340	72	68	599	5.7	17.5	48.6	26.0	2.2	132375
43152	SOUTH BLOOMINGVILLE	20443	461	23.4	32.1	37.5	5.6	1.3	43108	44728	43	28	374	24.1	24.3	36.9	12.6	2.1	92727
43153	SOUTH SOLON	22214	469	13.4	31.6	46.3	7.0	1.7	52518	54345	67	60	337	19.3	22.8	40.7	16.6	0.6	103472
43154	STOUTSVILLE	22246	1332	14.9	28.3	46.2	7.5	3.0	56695	58922	74	72	1116	7.0	12.5	45.4	29.2	5.9	136905
43155	SUGAR GROVE	21397	832	21.2	30.2	40.4	5.9	2.4	48590	49909	58	44	684	10.1	15.4	50.7	20.6	3.2	116038
43160	WASHINGTON COURT HOU	22767	9023	23.7	31.3	36.1	5.6	3.4	44473	48084	47	32	5864	8.7	25.9	53.1	11.4	1.0	105789
43162	WEST JEFFERSON	27879	2751	14.7	26.4	42.6	10.9	5.5	59560	61766	77	77	2175	13.4	12.6	55.8	14.9	3.3	116963
43164	WILLIAMSPORT	20798	834	20.1	28.3	41.2	8.9	1.4	51527	54978	65	56	622	10.0	20.6	42.4	22.2	4.8	120253
43201	COLUMBUS	16256	14896	52.4	27.2	16.0	2.7	1.7	23306	24085	2	3	2093	11.9	27.4	36.4	22.6	1.7	111241
43202	COLUMBUS	25008	10056	31.0	29.8	30.2	6.8	2.2	39413	41489	31	19	3027	2.3	14.2	68.2	14.7	0.6	124025
43203	COLUMBUS	14470	4597	57.5	23.6	15.2	2.2	1.5	19680	20483	1	1	1208	22.2	41.8	27.5	7.9	0.6	75847
43204	COLUMBUS	23243	16618	22.9	29.5	38.9	6.1	2.6	46613	51370	53	38	9631	7.7	40.3	47.8	3.5	0.7	91690
43205	COLUMBUS	18079	5270	47.9	24.2	20.5	4.0	3.4	26248	27597	4	3	1879	11.7	41.2	31.6	12.3	3.2	87038
43206	COLUMBUS	25227	10353	25.9	31.6	31.9	6.1	4.5	42071	46208	39	26	5059	12.5	45.8	24.5	14.3	3.0	81211
43207	COLUMBUS	20192	17162	27.6	27.7	37.5	5.5	1.6	43356	48976	43	29	11450	12.1	46.5	39.1	2.0	0.2	84004
43209	COLUMBUS	32602	12212	22.9	22.5	33.4	11.6	9.5	54613	58114	71	66	6657	2.3	11.0	45.1	32.0	9.6	156763
43210	COLUMBUS	14873	715	41.3	25.0	29.1	3.6	1.0	30274	31508	9	5	127	0.0	0.0	85.8	14.2	0.0	148897
43211	COLUMBUS	14972	8653	38.5	35.0	22.9	2.6	1.1	31182	32528	10	6	4819	23.4	69.0	6.7	0.7	0.2	63966
43212	COLUMBUS	37252	9854	18.8	30.3	34.0	9.6	7.3	50713	53425	63	52	3517	0.4	7.8	44.1	40.9	6.9	169633
43213	COLUMBUS	25842	13363	23.5	32.8	33.5	6.4	3.7	43408	47511	44	29	5804	6.2	38.4	38.9	15.2	1.3	96349
	OHIO	26577		21.4	25.9	36.7	10.4	5.7	52400	54553				10.3	22.0	45.6	19.3	2.8	114865
	UNITED STATES	27277		20.9	24.4	35.3	11.7	7.6	54719	56938				9.3	13.1	31.6	32.6	13.5	162279

ZIP CODE #	POST OFFICE NAME	FINANCIAL SERVICES: Auto Loan	FINANCIAL SERVICES: Home Loan	FINANCIAL SERVICES: Invest-ments	FINANCIAL SERVICES: Retire-ment Plans	THE HOME: Home Improvements: Home Repair	THE HOME: Home Improvements: Lawn & Garden	THE HOME: Furnishings: Comput-ers & Hard-ware-Personal	THE HOME: Furnishings: Major Appli-ances	THE HOME: Furnishings: TV, Radio, Sound Equip-ment	THE HOME: Furnishings: Furni-ture	ENTERTAINMENT: Dine out/ Carry out	ENTERTAINMENT: Sports Equip-ment	ENTERTAINMENT: Fees & Tickets	ENTERTAINMENT: Toys & Games	ENTERTAINMENT: Travel	ENTERTAINMENT: Cable TV	PERSONAL: Apparel & Services	PERSONAL: Auto Repairs	PERSONAL: Health Insur-ance	PERSONAL: Pets & Supplies
43001	ALEXANDRIA	111	129	117	133	127	125	114	119	111	116	112	91	123	113	122	111	79	114	116	139
43002	AMLIN	141	123	109	131	116	110	139	121	134	141	138	103	132	142	127	129	97	130	115	147
43003	ASHLEY	93	91	79	93	87	99	90	92	91	85	91	72	88	93	88	94	62	91	98	110
43004	BLACKLICK	136	140	122	139	134	120	135	129	128	143	130	103	136	135	131	122	92	128	116	149
43006	BRINKHAVEN	85	65	72	65	65	83	67	77	72	63	71	59	56	75	62	78	48	72	81	92
43008	BUCKEYE LAKE	80	58	77	57	60	82	64	77	71	58	69	58	52	70	61	78	46	73	84	90
43009	CABLE	98	99	91	103	99	106	93	101	93	89	93	77	93	96	95	96	64	95	102	118
43011	CENTERBURG	99	106	94	106	103	106	95	100	96	96	96	76	99	98	99	97	67	96	101	118
43013	CROTON	98	110	95	114	107	108	99	103	97	99	98	80	105	100	104	97	68	99	102	121
43014	DANVILLE	74	62	70	63	63	77	62	72	65	56	64	55	54	66	61	70	43	67	75	85
43015	DELAWARE	116	124	117	124	122	118	116	117	114	119	114	91	120	116	119	113	81	114	114	136
43016	DUBLIN	144	146	132	152	141	129	145	135	138	151	141	111	148	145	142	132	101	137	124	159
43017	DUBLIN	183	207	196	216	205	183	189	185	179	202	182	150	207	186	196	170	132	180	165	213
43019	FREDERICKTOWN	92	85	82	87	85	97	83	91	86	79	85	69	78	88	82	91	58	86	95	107
43021	GALENA	168	208	202	215	210	188	175	182	165	190	167	142	200	170	192	159	122	170	163	207
43022	GAMBIER	95	93	89	95	92	97	92	94	93	91	93	73	91	94	92	94	64	92	96	111
43023	GRANVILLE	138	160	160	164	163	154	144	150	139	149	140	114	157	139	156	137	99	143	144	172
43025	HEBRON	94	89	84	88	86	94	87	91	89	86	88	69	83	91	85	91	60	89	93	108
43026	HILLIARD	137	134	116	137	127	118	136	125	130	141	133	103	135	137	129	125	94	128	116	148
43028	HOWARD	97	102	93	104	100	106	93	99	94	92	94	76	96	96	97	96	65	95	101	116
43029	IRWIN	102	115	99	118	111	113	103	107	101	103	101	83	109	103	108	101	71	103	105	125
43031	JOHNSTOWN	103	112	99	115	109	113	104	107	103	103	103	83	109	105	108	104	72	104	109	126
43035	LEWIS CENTER	171	185	164	193	180	159	172	166	162	184	165	138	183	172	173	153	119	161	145	191
43037	MARTINSBURG	88	93	84	96	92	97	86	91	86	83	85	71	88	88	89	87	59	87	92	107
43040	MARYSVILLE	106	114	99	112	109	106	105	106	103	107	104	83	108	107	106	102	73	103	102	123
43044	MECHANICSBURG	89	90	78	92	87	96	87	90	88	82	87	70	86	89	87	90	60	87	95	107
43045	MILFORD CENTER	112	125	108	129	121	123	112	117	110	112	111	91	119	113	118	111	77	112	116	137
43046	MILLERSPORT	97	92	102	94	95	107	88	101	91	83	90	75	85	91	92	96	61	94	104	117
43050	MOUNT VERNON	79	72	73	73	72	82	75	79	78	71	77	60	70	78	73	82	53	78	85	93
43054	NEW ALBANY	194	246	247	254	252	220	204	213	192	225	194	167	240	198	228	182	143	197	187	239
43055	NEWARK	80	75	71	76	74	82	78	79	81	74	80	60	75	81	76	84	55	79	86	94
43056	HEATH	93	92	89	92	90	99	89	94	91	86	90	72	88	92	90	94	63	91	98	110
43060	NORTH LEWISBURG	99	95	84	94	93	97	89	94	91	91	91	70	86	94	87	93	62	90	94	111
43061	OSTRANDER	114	130	114	134	127	127	115	120	113	116	114	94	124	116	123	113	80	115	118	141
43062	PATASKALA	113	127	112	127	123	119	114	116	111	116	112	91	121	115	119	110	79	113	112	135
43064	PLAIN CITY	109	116	106	117	114	115	107	111	107	107	107	85	111	109	110	108	75	108	110	130
43065	POWELL	198	235	216	239	231	203	203	204	190	220	194	163	226	200	214	180	141	193	178	232
43066	RADNOR	128	144	124	148	140	141	128	134	126	129	127	104	137	130	136	127	89	128	132	157
43067	RAYMOND	102	114	98	117	110	111	102	106	100	103	101	83	108	103	107	100	70	102	104	124
43068	REYNOLDSBURG	107	109	96	109	105	101	106	103	104	108	105	81	107	107	104	102	73	103	101	121
43071	SAINT LOUISVILLE	88	76	78	79	78	92	76	86	79	70	78	65	69	81	75	85	53	80	89	101
43072	SAINT PARIS	87	81	79	84	82	94	79	89	81	72	80	67	74	83	79	86	55	82	91	103
43074	SUNBURY	122	142	128	145	139	136	125	129	122	128	123	100	136	124	133	121	87	124	126	151
43076	THORNVILLE	103	94	106	94	95	108	90	103	93	87	92	77	84	93	92	97	62	96	103	120
43078	URBANA	88	83	78	85	81	91	84	86	86	80	85	67	81	87	82	89	59	85	91	103
43080	UTICA	89	85	78	86	83	93	82	88	84	78	83	67	79	86	81	88	57	84	92	104
43081	WESTERVILLE	123	132	123	135	129	121	127	122	122	131	124	97	133	126	128	119	88	122	117	143
43082	WESTERVILLE	226	272	246	280	268	232	229	233	214	253	217	190	259	227	243	199	159	215	197	262
43084	WOODSTOCK	102	93	92	97	95	109	92	103	94	83	93	78	85	96	91	100	63	95	106	120
43085	COLUMBUS	128	142	140	144	142	135	132	132	129	138	131	101	142	130	139	128	93	131	130	153
43102	AMANDA	86	82	78	85	83	92	79	87	80	74	80	66	76	82	80	84	55	81	89	101
43103	ASHVILLE	93	91	79	91	88	92	89	90	90	89	90	69	87	93	87	91	62	89	92	107
43105	BALTIMORE	101	108	98	110	106	111	100	105	100	99	100	80	104	102	104	102	70	101	107	123
43106	BLOOMINGBURG	83	64	70	63	64	82	65	75	71	62	70	58	55	74	61	77	47	71	79	91
43107	BREMEN	85	77	76	80	79	91	76	86	78	69	77	65	70	80	76	83	53	79	88	100
43110	CANAL WINCHESTER	104	105	95	106	102	98	106	101	103	108	104	79	106	106	104	101	73	103	98	118
43112	CARROLL	115	126	123	129	127	127	113	121	111	115	112	91	119	113	120	112	78	114	118	140
43113	CIRCLEVILLE	87	83	78	85	82	91	84	87	86	81	84	66	81	86	82	88	58	85	91	102
43115	CLARKSBURG	95	70	79	68	69	91	72	83	79	70	78	64	59	82	66	86	52	79	87	101
43116	COMMERCIAL POINT	106	119	103	123	116	117	106	111	105	107	105	86	114	107	112	105	74	106	109	130
43119	GALLOWAY	116	111	95	112	105	99	114	106	110	117	112	86	111	115	108	106	78	109	100	125
43123	GROVE CITY	114	124	111	123	120	115	114	115	112	118	113	89	119	115	116	110	79	112	111	133
43125	GROVEPORT	88	92	82	92	89	88	89	87	89	91	90	67	91	90	89	89	63	88	89	103
43128	JEFFERSONVILLE	75	73	63	75	70	80	73	75	74	68	73	58	71	76	71	77	50	73	81	89
43130	LANCASTER	82	80	75	81	79	85	80	82	82	78	82	62	79	83	79	85	57	82	87	97
43135	LAURELVILLE	89	70	80	69	70	88	70	82	76	67	74	62	60	77	67	81	50	77	85	98
43137	LOCKBOURNE	107	107	97	106	104	108	102	106	102	102	102	81	100	105	101	103	71	103	105	124
43138	LOGAN	79	66	69	67	66	80	69	76	74	65	72	57	62	75	66	78	49	73	81	90
43140	LONDON	91	94	85	94	91	96	92	92	93	90	93	71	93	94	92	95	65	92	96	109
43143	MOUNT STERLING	86	91	78	92	87	94	86	88	87	83	86	68	88	88	87	89	60	86	93	104
43145	NEW HOLLAND	93	73	92	73	75	97	74	90	80	68	78	68	63	80	73	86	52	83	93	106
43146	ORIENT	104	115	101	116	112	114	103	107	103	104	103	82	109	106	108	104	72	104	108	126
43147	PICKERINGTON	156	184	156	181	175	154	157	158	147	169	150	127	170	156	163	139	107	149	137	180
43148	PLEASANTVILLE	88	83	86	84	82	95	80	89	82	76	82	68	77	83	81	86	56	84	92	105
43149	ROCKBRIDGE	82	74	74	77	76	87	73	83	76	67	74	62	67	77	73	80	51	76	85	96
43150	RUSHVILLE	92	92	86	95	92	100	87	95	88	82	87	73	86	90	89	91	60	89	96	110
43152	SOUTH BLOOMINGVILLE	86	69	71	67	68	82	69	77	74	68	73	58	59	77	64	79	49	73	80	93
43153	SOUTH SOLON	90	83	81	86	84	97	82	91	84	74	83	69	76	86	82	89	56	85	94	106
43154	STOUTSVILLE	95	89	86	93	90	102	87	97	89	80	87	73	82	91	87	93	60	90	99	112
43155	SUGAR GROVE	86	79	77	82	80	92	77	87	80	71	79	66	72	82	77	84	54	81	90	101
43160	WASHINGTON COURT HOU	84	74	72	76	74	87	78	82	81	72	79	63	71	82	74	85	54	80	88	97
43162	WEST JEFFERSON	98	108	94	110	104	109	101	102	101	98	101	79	106	102	104	102	70	101	106	121
43164	WILLIAMSPORT	85	84	79	86	84	93	80	87	81	75	80	67	77	83	81	84	55	82	90	102
43201	COLUMBUS	52	29	28	34	27	32	64	39	56	50	57	38	45	56	42	54	40	51	41	52
43202	COLUMBUS	72	52	50	56	50	54	83	60	76	70	76	53	66	76	63	73	54	71	62	76
43203	COLUMBUS	43	33	32	35	32	37	44	38	48	41	47	30	40	46	38	50	33	44	46	48
43204	COLUMBUS	79	71	64	73	68	74	79	73	81	76	81	58	75	82	73	82	56	78	80	89
43205	COLUMBUS	60	49	46	52	47	53	60	54	65	58	64	42	56	64	54	67	45	60	61	68
43206	COLUMBUS	81	71	64	74	67	74	81	73	84	79	84	58	77	84	74	85	58	80	81	92
43207	COLUMBUS	74	69	65	69	67	73	71	71	74	70	74	53	69	74	68	76	51	72	76	85
43209	COLUMBUS	105	101	99	106	101	101	110	102	109	109	110	80	110	109	106	109	78	107	106	122
43210	COLUMBUS	62	38	36	42	36	40	73	48	66	59	66	45	53	66	50	63	47	61	50	62
43211	COLUMBUS	59	49	41	51	45	54	55	51	60	54	59	40	52	60	49	62	41	56	59	65
43212	COLUMBUS	94	83	83	89	82	80	102	86	97	98	99	72	95	98	93	95	70	95	87	105
43213	COLUMBUS	81	70	64	73	67	72	82	74	83	79	83	59	77	83	75	84	58	80	79	90
	OHIO	94	92	87	93	90	96	93	93	94	91	94	72	92	95	91	96	66	93	98	110
	UNITED STATES	100	100	100	100	100	100	100	100	100	100	100	100	100	100	100	100	100	100	100	100

#	POST OFFICE NAME	COUNTY FIPS CODE	POPULATION 2000	POPULATION 2009	POPULATION 2014	2000-2009 ANNUAL RATE % Rate	2000-2009 ANNUAL RATE State Centile	HOUSEHOLDS 2000	HOUSEHOLDS 2009	HOUSEHOLDS 2014	HOUSEHOLDS % Annual Rate 2000-2009	HOUSEHOLDS 2009 Average HH Size	FAMILIES 2000	FAMILIES 2009	FAMILIES % Annual Rate 2000-2009
43214	COLUMBUS	049	25544	24692	24337	-0.4	21	12384	12224	12127	-0.1	1.96	6156	5719	-0.8
43215	COLUMBUS	049	10134	11096	11470	1.0	87	5816	6590	6896	1.4	1.49	1102	1107	0.0
43217	COLUMBUS	049	2510	2425	2388	-0.4	21	782	776	771	-0.1	3.13	583	559	-0.5
43219	COLUMBUS	049	20463	25054	26753	2.2	97	7972	9871	10582	2.3	2.47	5192	6384	2.3
43220	COLUMBUS	049	24187	23504	23196	-0.3	27	11706	11622	11553	-0.1	2.01	6073	5724	-0.6
43221	COLUMBUS	049	29583	31345	31932	0.6	75	12226	12994	13256	0.7	2.40	8006	8223	0.3
43222	COLUMBUS	049	6193	5371	5118	-1.5	1	2145	1899	1821	-1.3	2.69	1235	1054	-1.7
43223	COLUMBUS	049	26914	25855	25449	-0.4	21	9948	9673	9571	-0.3	2.52	6419	5998	-0.7
43224	COLUMBUS	049	39882	38573	38012	-0.4	21	16848	16518	16364	-0.2	2.33	10037	9339	-0.8
43227	COLUMBUS	049	22986	22174	21839	-0.4	21	9734	9567	9483	-0.2	2.32	6021	5628	-0.7
43228	COLUMBUS	049	45482	49731	51543	1.0	87	18842	20940	21851	1.1	2.36	11607	12292	0.6
43229	COLUMBUS	049	47054	46156	45725	-0.2	32	20993	20917	20832	0.0	2.19	11520	10869	-0.6
43230	COLUMBUS	049	48829	51965	53035	0.7	79	19114	20973	21622	1.0	2.46	13001	13752	0.6
43231	COLUMBUS	049	16792	17449	17742	0.4	66	7102	7413	7538	0.5	2.31	4216	4235	0.0
43232	COLUMBUS	049	40568	40839	40934	0.1	51	17124	17515	17639	0.2	2.32	10091	9891	-0.2
43235	COLUMBUS	049	37784	38092	38181	0.1	51	16478	16947	17095	0.3	2.23	9524	9245	-0.3
43240	COLUMBUS	041	1188	2670	3459	9.1	100	637	1379	1801	8.7	1.94	332	676	8.0
43302	MARION	101	54635	54302	53588	-0.1	39	20262	20357	20194	0.1	2.42	13896	13586	-0.2
43310	BELLE CENTER	065	2943	3096	3141	0.5	71	1142	1239	1269	0.9	2.49	854	905	0.6
43311	BELLEFONTAINE	091	19144	19631	19805	0.3	61	7446	7821	7945	0.5	2.48	5157	5264	0.2
43314	CALEDONIA	101	3004	3081	3070	0.3	61	1146	1199	1204	0.5	2.54	865	883	0.2
43315	CARDINGTON	117	6506	7182	7514	1.1	89	2407	2745	2899	1.4	2.60	1803	2010	1.2
43316	CAREY	175	6168	6049	5931	-0.2	32	2338	2376	2352	0.2	2.50	1662	1641	-0.1
43318	DE GRAFF	091	3618	3795	3867	0.5	71	1304	1395	1429	0.7	2.72	1001	1047	0.5
43319	EAST LIBERTY	091	947	1029	1062	0.9	85	353	393	408	1.2	2.62	285	312	1.0
43320	EDISON	117	1438	1567	1635	0.9	85	535	600	630	1.2	2.60	392	428	1.0
43321	FULTON	117	306	361	386	1.8	96	109	133	144	2.2	2.65	87	104	1.9
43323	HARPSTER	175	781	801	794	0.3	61	294	312	312	0.6	2.57	235	244	0.4
43324	HUNTSVILLE	091	2783	3017	3110	0.9	85	1118	1242	1290	1.1	2.40	825	897	0.9
43326	KENTON	065	13951	13409	13061	-0.4	21	5497	5379	5271	-0.2	2.43	3757	3579	-0.5
43331	LAKEVIEW	091	5265	5239	5217	-0.1	39	2328	2370	2379	0.2	2.20	1510	1487	-0.2
43332	LA RUE	101	2181	2172	2145	0.0	45	804	812	806	0.1	2.67	610	602	-0.1
43333	LEWISTOWN	091	1242	1212	1197	-0.3	27	513	511	508	0.0	2.29	354	343	-0.3
43334	MARENGO	117	5546	6270	6616	1.3	92	1992	2325	2478	1.7	2.68	1587	1819	1.5
43335	MARTEL	101	104	111	112	0.7	79	43	47	48	1.0	2.36	33	35	0.6
43337	MORRAL	101	1113	1066	1042	-0.5	17	408	401	395	-0.2	2.66	326	314	-0.4
43338	MOUNT GILEAD	117	8766	9610	10023	1.0	87	3318	3726	3920	1.3	2.51	2469	2718	1.0
43340	MOUNT VICTORY	065	1527	1625	1637	0.7	79	551	601	609	0.9	2.70	420	447	0.7
43341	NEW BLOOMINGTON	101	1261	1312	1311	0.4	66	432	456	458	0.6	2.88	346	357	0.3
43342	PROSPECT	101	3345	3346	3328	0.0	45	1234	1256	1256	0.2	2.66	976	973	0.0
43343	QUINCY	091	1515	1613	1651	0.7	79	553	604	624	1.0	2.67	436	466	0.7
43344	RICHWOOD	159	5381	5889	6115	1.0	87	1976	2181	2270	1.1	2.70	1503	1614	0.8
43345	RIDGEWAY	091	1049	1105	1114	0.6	75	332	357	362	0.8	3.10	281	298	0.6
43346	ROUNDHEAD	065	161	175	176	0.9	85	63	70	71	1.1	2.50	50	55	1.0
43347	RUSHSYLVANIA	091	1543	1611	1636	0.5	71	549	586	598	0.7	2.75	439	459	0.5
43348	RUSSELLS POINT	091	1885	1895	1901	0.1	51	805	830	840	0.3	2.28	494	492	0.0
43351	UPPER SANDUSKY	175	10260	10059	9836	-0.2	32	4053	4073	4015	0.1	2.39	2726	2665	-0.2
43356	WALDO	101	982	1026	1030	0.5	71	379	404	409	0.7	2.54	300	314	0.5
43357	WEST LIBERTY	091	4346	4596	4690	0.6	75	1546	1672	1718	0.9	2.59	1160	1226	0.6
43358	WEST MANSFIELD	159	2283	2505	2600	1.0	87	838	939	980	1.2	2.67	663	726	1.0
43359	WHARTON	175	857	829	810	-0.4	21	313	310	305	-0.1	2.67	253	246	-0.3
43360	ZANESFIELD	091	1565	1706	1759	0.9	85	606	675	700	1.2	2.53	467	508	0.9
43402	BOWLING GREEN	173	36250	38250	38963	0.6	75	12593	13861	14328	1.0	2.25	6330	6723	0.7
43403	BOWLING GREEN	173	125	130	131	0.4	66	48	54	57	1.3	2.41	4	4	0.0
43406	BRADNER	173	1943	2057	2114	0.6	75	727	801	832	1.1	2.56	536	574	0.7
43407	BURGOON	143	610	641	649	0.5	71	205	222	227	0.9	2.89	176	188	0.7
43410	CLYDE	143	9678	9597	9545	-0.1	39	3652	3752	3769	0.3	2.53	2688	2694	0.0
43412	CURTICE	095	4456	4569	4595	0.3	61	1599	1692	1719	0.6	2.66	1278	1325	0.4
43413	CYGNET	173	1776	1872	1903	0.6	75	642	702	723	1.0	2.67	514	551	0.8
43416	ELMORE	123	2902	3187	3295	1.0	87	1136	1275	1332	1.3	2.50	873	960	1.0
43420	FREMONT	143	32098	31047	30560	-0.4	21	12592	12561	12483	0.0	2.42	8668	8412	-0.3
43430	GENOA	123	4878	4725	4672	-0.3	27	1842	1850	1848	0.0	2.50	1361	1332	-0.2
43431	GIBSONBURG	143	4494	4814	4903	0.7	79	1666	1835	1888	1.1	2.57	1226	1316	0.8
43432	GRAYTOWN	123	1288	1377	1413	0.7	79	449	493	512	1.0	2.79	366	396	0.9
43435	HELENA	143	1588	1688	1717	0.7	79	573	632	651	1.1	2.64	461	499	0.9
43436	ISLE SAINT GEORGE	123	32	34	35	0.7	79	13	15	15	1.6	2.27	8	9	1.3
43438	KELLEYS ISLAND	043	367	384	381	0.5	71	183	197	198	0.8	1.93	113	117	0.4
43440	LAKESIDE MARBLEHEAD	123	4319	4446	4506	0.3	61	1954	2080	2132	0.7	2.11	1314	1356	0.3
43442	LINDSEY	143	1194	1209	1209	0.1	51	448	469	474	0.5	2.55	349	358	0.3
43443	LUCKEY	173	1702	1804	1844	0.6	75	615	671	695	0.9	2.56	448	473	0.6
43445	MARTIN	123	1757	1852	1888	0.6	75	563	612	630	0.9	2.91	460	492	0.7
43447	MILLBURY	173	3602	3782	3896	0.5	71	1352	1469	1529	0.9	2.57	1066	1134	0.7
43449	OAK HARBOR	123	8665	8811	8891	0.2	56	3294	3460	3526	0.5	2.50	2417	2476	0.3
43450	PEMBERVILLE	173	3616	3882	3976	0.8	82	1348	1498	1552	1.1	2.56	1017	1100	0.9
43451	PORTAGE	173	1161	1228	1256	0.6	75	425	467	484	1.0	2.42	330	354	0.8
43452	PORT CLINTON	123	14114	14077	14098	0.0	45	6046	6249	6325	0.4	2.22	4044	4061	0.0
43456	PUT IN BAY	123	731	787	810	0.8	82	342	383	400	1.2	2.05	217	235	0.9
43457	RISINGSUN	173	1805	1841	1850	0.2	56	649	690	701	0.7	2.67	508	527	0.4
43460	ROSSFORD	173	6332	6300	6247	-0.1	39	2555	2605	2607	0.2	2.41	1755	1733	-0.1
43462	RUDOLPH	173	1250	1317	1352	0.6	75	460	506	527	1.0	2.56	353	378	0.7
43464	VICKERY	143	1631	1629	1620	0.0	45	598	620	623	0.4	2.60	430	435	0.1
43465	WALBRIDGE	173	4354	4453	4456	0.2	56	1932	2052	2072	0.7	2.17	1269	1311	0.4
43466	WAYNE	173	2095	2182	2217	0.4	66	766	831	853	0.9	2.63	585	619	0.6
43469	WOODVILLE	143	3151	3201	3211	0.2	56	1177	1235	1252	0.5	2.54	873	892	0.2
43501	ALVORDTON	171	1018	991	976	-0.3	27	363	365	363	0.1	2.64	276	271	-0.2
43502	ARCHBOLD	051	7093	7120	7026	0.0	45	2653	2729	2713	0.3	2.57	1943	1953	0.1
43504	BERKEY	095	916	1062	1084	1.6	95	325	387	397	1.9	2.74	260	303	1.7
43506	BRYAN	171	15044	14938	14755	-0.1	39	6148	6287	6263	0.2	2.34	4154	4131	-0.1
43511	CUSTAR	173	1291	1345	1369	0.4	66	452	491	504	0.9	2.74	352	374	0.7
43512	DEFIANCE	039	29351	28559	28151	-0.3	27	11386	11501	11463	0.1	2.44	8178	8053	-0.2
43515	DELTA	051	8139	8194	8198	0.1	51	2978	3092	3123	0.4	2.64	2315	2359	0.2
43516	DESHLER	069	3039	2982	2938	-0.2	32	1126	1140	1133	0.1	2.58	844	836	-0.1
43517	EDGERTON	171	3774	3835	3812	0.2	56	1406	1459	1461	0.4	2.58	1057	1074	0.2
43518	EDON	171	2929	2947	2922	0.1	51	1079	1114	1113	0.3	2.65	822	830	0.1
43521	FAYETTE	051	2924	3067	3111	0.5	71	1104	1181	1207	0.7	2.60	803	838	0.5
	OHIO					0.2					0.4	2.44			0.1
	UNITED STATES					1.0					1.1	2.59			0.9

POPULATION COMPOSITION

#	POST OFFICE NAME	RACE (%) White 2000	White 2009	Black 2000	Black 2009	Asian/Pacific 2000	Asian/Pacific 2009	% Hispanic Origin 2000	% Hispanic Origin 2009	2009 AGE DISTRIBUTION (%) 0-4	5-9	10-14	15-19	20-24	25-44	45-64	65-84	85+	18+	MEDIAN AGE 2009	% 2009 Males	% 2009 Females
43214	COLUMBUS	92.3	89.4	2.9	3.7	2.8	4.5	1.2	1.6	4.8	4.6	4.8	4.2	8.8	25.7	28.6	13.5	5.1	83.5	43.2	46.8	53.2
43215	COLUMBUS	69.2	62.1	24.5	29.9	2.3	3.5	2.7	3.4	3.7	2.4	1.8	4.3	14.4	38.8	20.0	10.8	3.8	90.9	34.4	54.3	45.7
43217	COLUMBUS	80.4	74.9	15.0	19.3	0.8	1.2	1.5	2.0	11.0	13.4	9.9	9.5	10.1	31.4	13.3	1.2	0.1	61.8	23.1	51.7	48.3
43219	COLUMBUS	18.2	13.5	77.3	81.3	0.6	1.0	1.5	1.5	8.4	8.4	7.8	8.4	7.1	22.0	23.0	12.3	2.7	70.7	34.0	43.9	56.1
43220	COLUMBUS	88.6	83.5	2.0	2.5	7.4	11.6	1.7	2.3	4.0	3.9	4.4	4.9	10.5	27.5	27.2	15.0	2.6	84.7	40.2	48.5	51.5
43221	COLUMBUS	93.6	90.3	1.1	1.6	3.8	6.1	1.1	1.6	6.1	6.4	7.0	6.6	5.5	25.0	29.5	11.3	2.6	76.3	40.8	48.1	51.9
43222	COLUMBUS	80.9	75.5	12.6	16.1	1.9	2.9	1.8	2.4	9.0	7.3	6.5	8.2	9.4	29.2	22.4	7.2	0.9	72.6	31.0	51.4	48.6
43223	COLUMBUS	77.5	73.0	16.1	19.2	1.6	2.5	1.5	1.9	7.5	7.3	6.9	7.2	6.9	28.1	24.6	10.1	1.5	74.2	35.3	48.2	51.8
43224	COLUMBUS	60.3	54.3	31.1	35.4	2.2	3.3	2.7	3.3	7.9	7.2	6.5	6.8	8.0	28.1	24.1	9.6	1.8	74.3	34.2	48.2	51.8
43227	COLUMBUS	42.6	36.2	50.3	55.4	2.5	3.5	2.3	2.6	6.6	6.5	6.4	7.0	6.9	25.5	26.9	12.5	1.7	76.2	38.3	46.9	53.1
43228	COLUMBUS	82.7	78.5	9.1	11.0	1.8	3.0	7.8	8.5	9.2	7.5	6.5	6.0	8.4	32.7	21.1	7.5	1.0	73.4	31.4	49.0	51.0
43229	COLUMBUS	66.4	59.7	24.5	28.9	3.0	4.4	4.6	5.6	7.3	6.3	5.6	6.0	8.8	32.9	21.9	9.9	1.3	77.5	33.5	48.2	51.8
43230	COLUMBUS	84.5	79.6	9.9	12.3	3.1	5.1	1.4	1.9	7.1	7.0	7.0	6.8	6.1	29.8	27.2	8.0	1.1	74.6	36.1	48.3	51.7
43231	COLUMBUS	73.2	65.7	19.8	24.9	2.7	4.4	2.4	3.0	8.0	7.3	6.6	6.1	7.9	31.9	21.9	7.9	2.4	74.6	33.4	47.9	52.1
43232	COLUMBUS	59.0	51.6	34.3	40.2	1.9	2.8	2.5	3.0	7.9	6.9	6.4	6.6	8.0	31.9	22.9	8.4	1.0	75.0	32.8	48.0	52.0
43235	COLUMBUS	87.1	81.6	3.0	3.9	7.0	11.0	2.3	3.0	5.7	5.2	5.2	5.7	7.9	33.4	25.7	9.4	1.8	80.5	36.1	48.8	51.2
43240	COLUMBUS	89.5	86.4	3.7	4.0	4.6	7.0	1.4	1.8	6.9	5.5	4.8	4.6	8.9	41.5	21.3	5.9	0.7	80.4	32.8	49.9	50.1
43302	MARION	90.7	89.1	6.9	7.8	0.6	1.0	1.2	1.6	6.1	5.9	5.9	6.6	7.2	27.8	26.3	11.9	2.2	78.4	38.2	51.9	48.1
43310	BELLE CENTER	98.5	98.2	0.3	0.3	0.1	0.2	0.8	1.1	6.6	6.7	6.8	6.4	4.8	25.0	28.1	14.1	1.5	75.8	40.4	50.6	49.4
43311	BELLEFONTAINE	93.1	91.7	3.7	4.2	0.8	1.2	0.9	1.1	7.8	7.0	6.7	6.9	6.6	25.6	26.4	11.2	1.7	74.2	36.8	48.9	51.1
43314	CALEDONIA	98.8	98.5	0.4	0.4	0.1	0.1	0.6	0.8	5.4	5.8	6.3	6.8	4.9	25.5	31.4	12.5	1.4	78.1	41.8	50.9	49.1
43315	CARDINGTON	98.4	98.1	0.2	0.2	0.1	0.2	0.5	0.6	6.6	6.8	7.1	7.1	5.3	26.9	28.4	10.5	1.3	75.0	38.2	49.5	50.5
43316	CAREY	97.0	95.8	0.1	0.2	1.1	1.9	1.3	1.7	7.3	7.2	7.2	6.5	5.9	27.2	25.5	11.2	2.0	74.3	36.5	49.7	50.3
43318	DE GRAFF	98.9	98.6	0.4	0.5	0.1	0.2	0.7	1.0	7.0	7.4	7.7	7.5	5.2	25.9	27.9	10.1	1.4	73.3	36.9	50.6	49.4
43319	EAST LIBERTY	98.0	97.6	0.5	0.6	0.1	0.2	0.5	0.7	6.8	7.4	8.0	7.5	4.5	25.9	29.9	9.0	1.0	73.1	38.8	50.3	49.7
43320	EDISON	98.7	98.5	0.2	0.3	0.1	0.3	0.4	0.4	5.4	5.6	6.2	7.4	5.3	24.3	30.3	13.2	2.2	78.2	41.4	48.9	51.1
43321	FULTON	99.3	98.9	0.0	0.3	0.0	0.3	0.7	0.8	7.8	7.5	7.5	6.9	5.5	28.5	26.3	9.1	0.8	72.9	36.7	51.0	49.0
43323	HARPSTER	99.0	98.6	0.1	0.2	0.0	0.0	0.6	1.0	5.2	5.9	6.5	6.9	4.9	24.0	32.5	12.9	1.4	78.2	42.9	49.9	50.1
43324	HUNTSVILLE	98.2	97.7	0.4	0.5	0.1	0.2	0.7	0.9	5.6	6.1	6.4	5.8	3.9	23.2	31.9	15.2	1.9	78.3	44.2	49.9	50.1
43326	KENTON	97.6	97.1	0.7	0.8	0.3	0.5	1.0	1.3	6.8	6.6	6.7	6.7	6.0	25.3	26.5	12.5	2.9	75.8	38.7	48.5	51.5
43331	LAKEVIEW	97.7	97.2	0.2	0.2	0.3	0.5	0.7	1.0	5.4	5.6	5.5	5.6	4.4	22.4	31.3	17.8	2.0	80.1	45.8	50.3	49.7
43332	LA RUE	98.8	98.6	0.2	0.2	0.0	0.1	0.5	0.6	6.4	6.6	6.7	7.0	5.9	24.4	29.1	12.2	1.7	75.6	40.2	50.2	49.8
43333	LEWISTOWN	98.7	98.5	0.2	0.2	0.2	0.3	0.8	1.2	7.1	6.9	6.8	7.1	5.6	24.6	27.1	12.2	2.6	74.8	38.8	48.5	51.5
43334	MARENGO	98.4	98.0	0.2	0.2	0.1	0.2	0.6	0.8	6.2	6.6	6.9	6.7	5.2	26.9	30.0	10.4	1.0	75.8	39.5	50.9	49.1
43335	MARTEL	99.0	99.1	0.0	0.0	0.0	0.0	1.0	0.9	4.5	6.3	6.3	6.3	4.5	25.2	34.2	11.7	0.9	78.4	42.8	55.0	45.0
43337	MORRAL	98.7	98.6	0.3	0.3	0.0	0.0	0.7	0.8	4.6	5.0	5.6	7.0	5.3	23.5	33.0	14.3	1.6	80.6	44.2	49.6	50.4
43338	MOUNT GILEAD	98.1	97.7	0.5	0.6	0.2	0.4	0.7	0.9	6.2	6.6	6.8	6.8	5.2	24.8	28.5	12.8	2.2	76.3	40.3	49.6	50.4
43340	MOUNT VICTORY	97.7	97.2	0.7	0.7	0.1	0.2	0.7	1.0	7.6	7.7	7.9	7.0	5.2	25.4	26.6	11.1	1.5	72.4	36.8	50.0	50.0
43341	NEW BLOOMINGTON	98.0	97.6	0.2	0.2	0.2	0.3	1.2	1.4	6.3	6.3	6.7	8.1	7.5	25.3	29.8	9.1	1.0	75.9	38.1	48.7	51.3
43342	PROSPECT	99.0	98.8	0.2	0.2	0.1	0.1	0.4	0.5	5.8	6.3	6.8	7.1	5.1	24.4	31.1	11.9	1.4	76.6	41.2	50.0	50.0
43343	QUINCY	98.9	98.6	0.2	0.2	0.1	0.2	0.5	0.7	6.6	6.9	7.6	7.6	4.9	25.6	29.4	9.9	1.4	74.1	38.5	50.1	49.9
43344	RICHWOOD	98.3	98.0	0.4	0.4	0.1	0.1	0.5	0.6	7.6	7.7	7.9	7.5	5.3	26.7	25.3	10.5	1.6	72.0	36.5	49.4	50.6
43345	RIDGEWAY	98.4	98.1	0.7	0.7	0.0	0.0	0.7	0.9	7.1	8.2	8.6	8.5	5.7	25.9	25.9	8.6	1.4	70.2	35.7	50.0	50.0
43346	ROUNDHEAD	98.8	98.3	0.6	0.6	0.0	0.6	0.0	0.0	6.9	8.0	8.0	6.9	4.0	24.6	26.9	13.1	1.7	72.6	39.8	50.9	49.1
43347	RUSHSYLVANIA	98.2	97.6	0.3	0.4	0.3	0.5	0.5	0.6	6.6	7.1	7.6	7.8	5.2	26.3	27.9	10.1	1.4	73.7	37.4	49.6	50.4
43348	RUSSELLS POINT	98.1	97.7	0.2	0.2	0.2	0.4	1.0	1.4	6.1	5.8	5.6	5.4	4.5	22.4	29.9	18.3	2.0	79.3	45.2	48.4	51.6
43351	UPPER SANDUSKY	97.8	97.2	0.2	0.2	0.4	0.6	2.0	2.7	6.3	6.2	6.1	6.3	5.6	24.9	27.3	14.0	3.2	77.2	40.9	48.3	51.7
43356	WALDO	99.1	98.7	0.1	0.1	0.4	0.5	0.5	0.7	4.7	5.7	6.1	6.8	5.3	21.6	34.0	14.0	1.8	79.3	44.9	48.2	51.8
43357	WEST LIBERTY	98.3	97.9	0.4	0.5	0.2	0.3	0.3	0.4	5.8	6.1	6.7	6.6	5.2	23.9	28.6	12.7	4.3	76.9	41.8	47.8	52.2
43358	WEST MANSFIELD	98.2	97.7	0.4	0.5	0.1	0.2	0.6	0.7	6.5	7.3	8.1	7.7	4.6	27.8	26.9	9.6	1.6	72.9	37.6	50.0	50.0
43359	WHARTON	98.7	98.4	0.0	0.0	0.2	0.2	0.5	0.5	6.5	7.2	7.8	7.8	5.1	25.0	28.7	10.3	1.6	73.5	37.8	53.8	46.2
43360	ZANESFIELD	98.7	98.4	0.3	0.4	0.1	0.1	0.3	0.4	6.6	7.0	7.6	7.2	4.6	27.0	29.2	9.7	1.1	74.3	38.6	51.6	48.4
43402	BOWLING GREEN	92.6	90.7	2.4	2.7	1.6	2.5	3.6	4.6	4.1	3.8	3.7	15.4	25.2	20.9	18.1	7.4	1.4	85.7	24.6	47.7	52.3
43403	BOWLING GREEN	91.2	89.2	5.6	6.2	0.8	0.8	2.4	3.1	0.0	0.0	0.0	59.2	40.8	0.0	0.0	0.0	0.0	100.0	19.2	40.8	59.2
43406	BRADNER	98.4	97.9	0.1	0.0	0.2	0.2	2.6	3.5	6.7	6.6	6.7	7.0	6.3	26.9	27.5	11.1	1.3	75.6	37.2	50.1	49.9
43407	BURGOON	95.9	94.7	1.0	1.2	0.7	1.1	3.4	4.7	4.8	5.1	6.1	8.4	5.6	25.0	30.4	13.3	1.2	78.8	42.1	48.7	51.3
43410	CLYDE	96.4	95.4	0.1	0.2	0.3	0.5	4.4	5.8	6.5	6.5	6.6	6.8	5.9	26.8	27.8	11.5	1.7	76.2	38.7	49.5	50.5
43412	CURTICE	96.7	95.5	0.1	0.2	0.2	0.3	3.9	5.2	5.4	6.3	6.8	7.2	4.8	24.9	32.7	10.8	1.1	76.8	41.4	51.0	49.0
43413	CYGNET	97.5	97.0	0.2	0.3	0.2	0.2	2.6	3.4	6.7	7.0	7.2	7.4	4.9	24.6	30.0	11.1	1.1	74.4	39.8	50.1	49.9
43416	ELMORE	97.3	96.7	0.1	0.1	0.1	0.2	3.9	5.1	6.2	6.6	7.0	6.8	5.1	23.5	30.1	12.8	1.9	75.8	41.1	49.1	50.9
43420	FREMONT	88.1	85.8	5.0	5.7	0.4	0.6	9.2	11.6	6.7	6.6	6.4	6.5	6.1	25.1	27.2	12.8	2.6	76.3	39.0	48.8	51.2
43430	GENOA	95.2	93.8	0.2	0.3	0.3	0.6	6.0	8.0	5.5	5.8	6.4	7.0	5.2	24.7	29.9	12.8	2.7	77.7	41.7	50.0	50.0
43431	GIBSONBURG	94.5	93.0	0.2	0.3	0.2	0.3	7.8	10.3	6.5	6.6	6.8	7.0	5.7	25.1	27.3	12.5	2.6	75.6	39.6	49.6	50.4
43432	GRAYTOWN	97.1	96.2	0.1	0.1	0.2	0.4	3.3	4.3	6.0	6.5	6.9	6.5	5.1	23.8	32.0	11.7	1.5	76.3	41.5	50.6	49.4
43435	HELENA	98.2	97.7	0.3	0.4	0.1	0.1	3.7	5.0	5.5	6.1	6.6	6.6	4.7	24.5	31.6	12.4	1.8	77.4	42.3	50.8	49.2
43436	ISLE SAINT GEORGE	100.0	100.0	0.0	0.0	0.0	0.0	0.0	0.0	5.9	5.9	5.9	5.9	2.9	26.5	29.4	17.6	0.0	79.4	43.3	52.9	47.1
43438	KELLEYS ISLAND	99.5	99.5	0.3	0.3	0.0	0.0	0.3	0.3	3.1	3.6	4.4	4.2	2.6	13.8	41.4	24.7	2.1	84.6	56.0	50.3	49.7
43440	LAKESIDE MARBLEHEAD	97.7	97.1	0.5	0.5	0.2	0.3	1.6	2.2	3.9	4.1	4.6	4.8	3.1	19.6	36.4	20.5	2.9	84.4	51.1	49.5	50.5
43442	LINDSEY	94.0	92.2	0.1	0.1	0.1	0.2	9.0	12.0	6.5	7.0	7.3	6.9	4.4	23.9	29.8	12.3	1.8	74.5	40.4	50.4	49.6
43443	LUCKEY	97.1	96.3	0.2	0.2	0.1	0.2	2.4	3.0	6.4	6.7	6.9	7.4	5.3	21.9	26.1	13.4	5.9	74.6	41.5	47.3	52.7
43445	MARTIN	95.6	94.3	0.2	0.2	0.3	0.5	5.2	6.9	5.5	6.1	6.6	6.7	4.6	25.4	32.0	11.6	1.4	77.3	41.6	50.3	49.7
43447	MILLBURY	98.1	97.6	0.1	0.1	0.2	0.4	2.4	3.2	5.3	5.7	6.3	6.8	4.8	24.9	32.0	12.7	1.5	78.6	42.3	49.0	51.0
43449	OAK HARBOR	98.1	97.5	0.2	0.2	0.4	0.6	2.2	3.0	5.4	6.0	6.2	6.9	5.1	24.5	31.3	12.0	2.4	77.9	42.0	49.3	50.7
43450	PEMBERVILLE	97.2	96.5	0.2	0.2	0.1	0.2	3.2	4.3	5.9	6.5	6.9	7.5	5.1	23.1	30.8	11.8	2.3	75.6	41.2	48.5	51.5
43451	PORTAGE	95.6	94.6	0.7	0.7	0.3	0.3	4.3	5.5	5.5	6.1	6.6	8.7	5.0	25.1	30.3	10.1	2.6	75.3	39.7	50.7	49.3
43452	PORT CLINTON	95.2	94.1	1.5	1.7	0.3	0.5	5.0	6.4	5.0	4.9	5.3	5.9	4.8	22.1	32.2	17.4	2.5	81.1	46.4	49.2	50.8
43456	PUT IN BAY	98.8	98.5	0.3	0.4	0.0	0.0	0.5	0.6	3.7	5.2	5.0	4.3	2.8	23.0	37.5	17.0	1.5	83.2	48.6	49.9	50.1
43457	RISINGSUN	98.0	97.5	0.1	0.1	0.1	0.2	2.0	2.7	6.4	6.3	6.7	6.7	5.9	26.6	28.8	11.6	1.0	76.5	38.9	48.9	51.1
43460	ROSSFORD	96.2	95.1	1.2	1.4	0.9	1.4	1.7	2.2	5.9	6.3	6.3	7.0	5.7	25.8	28.4	12.2	2.3	77.1	39.7	48.7	51.3
43462	RUDOLPH	95.1	93.8	0.1	0.1	0.2	0.3	6.1	7.8	6.6	7.0	7.3	7.2	5.9	24.5	32.4	8.0	1.1	74.4	39.0	51.3	48.7
43464	VICKERY	95.5	94.4	1.5	1.8	0.1	0.2	3.5	4.6	6.2	6.9	7.2	5.9	4.4	25.8	30.9	11.4	1.4	75.8	40.3	50.2	49.8
43465	WALBRIDGE	97.5	97.0	0.3	0.3	0.2	0.3	2.9	3.8	5.3	5.5	5.6	5.7	4.7	23.4	30.5	17.4	2.0	80.0	44.8	48.2	51.8
43466	WAYNE	96.8	96.0	0.1	0.2	0.3	0.5	2.8	3.6	5.9	6.3	6.8	7.1	4.6	27.0	30.5	10.4	1.3	76.5	40.1	49.9	50.1
43469	WOODVILLE	96.7	95.7	0.2	0.2	0.1	0.2	4.5	6.1	6.3	6.7	7.1	6.9	5.0	23.6	28.5	12.9	3.0	75.3	40.7	48.8	51.2
43501	ALVORDTON	97.2	96.8	0.4	0.4	0.0	0.0	2.3	2.9	5.7	6.0	6.5	7.3	5.3	25.2	30.3	12.5	1.3	77.1	40.8	51.9	48.1
43502	ARCHBOLD	93.4	91.9	0.3	0.3	0.6	0.9	9.5	12.0	6.8	6.8	7.3	6.8	5.7	23.5	26.4	13.0	3.7	74.9	39.5	48.8	51.2
43504	BERKEY	98.9	98.4	0.3	0.5	0.1	0.2	0.4	0.7	5.3	5.7	6.7	7.3	5.4	22.9	33.5	12.1	1.1	77.8	42.5	49.2	50.8
43506	BRYAN	96.6	95.6	0.3	0.4	0.7	1.1	3.2	4.1	6.0	6.2	6.3	6.4	6.1	25.0	28.9	12.8	2.5	77.6	40.6	49.2	50.8
43511	CUSTAR	96.0	94.9	0.1	0.1	0.2	0.4	5.3	6.9	5.9	6.2	6.5	7.3	5.2	25.3	30.2	12.0	1.5	77.1	40.7	49.8	50.2
43512	DEFIANCE	90.8	88.6	2.3	2.6	0.5	0.8	9.0	11.5	6.9	6.7	6.7	6.9	6.2	25.4	27.9	11.5	1.8	75.8	37.9	49.5	50.5
43515	DELTA	96.5	95.6	0.1	0.1	0.3	0.4	4.1	5.4	7.1	7.4	7.7	7.0	4.7	26.5	28.3	10.0	1.2	73.1	37.8	49.4	50.6
43516	DESHLER	95.1	94.7	0.1	0.1	0.6	0.6	5.6	5.9	6.5	6.8	7.3	7.4	4.9	25.7	26.7	12.0	2.7	74.5	38.7	50.7	49.3
43517	EDGERTON	97.9	97.3	0.1	0.1	0.2	0.3	1.5	2.0	7.3	7.8	7.8	7.1	4.9	25.7	25.9	11.1	2.5	72.7	37.7	49.4	50.6
43518	EDON	99.0	98.7	0.0	0.0	0.2	0.3	0.5	0.6	6.1	6.9	7.3	7.5	5.1	24.9	29.0	11.7	1.5	75.1	39.3	49.7	50.3
43521	FAYETTE	95.6	94.4	0.2	0.2	0.4	0.6	6.5	8.4	8.4	8.4	8.0	6.7	5.4	26.0	25.3	10.3	1.5	71.0	35.4	50.4	49.6
	OHIO	85.0	83.1	11.5	12.2	1.2	1.9	1.9	2.4	6.6	6.5	6.6	7.1	6.7	25.9	26.9	11.7	2.1	76.2	38.2	48.7	51.3
	UNITED STATES	75.1	72.0	12.3	12.7	3.8	4.6	12.5	15.7	6.8	6.7	6.6	7.1	6.9	27.0	26.0	10.9	1.9	75.7	36.9	49.2	50.8

ZIP CODE #	POST OFFICE NAME	2009 Per Capita Income	2009 HH Income Base	2009 HOUSEHOLD INCOME DISTRIBUTION (%) Less than $25,000	$25,000 to $49,999	$50,000 to $99,999	$100,000 to $149,999	$150,000 or More	MEDIAN HOUSEHOLD INCOME 2009	2014	2009 National Centile	2009 State Centile	2009 Home Value Base	2009 HOME VALUE DISTRIBUTION (%) Less than $50,000	$50,000 to $89,999	$90,000 to $174,999	$175,000 to $399,999	$400,000 or More	2009 Median Home Value
43214	COLUMBUS	35135	12224	17.6	22.9	40.3	13.2	6.0	59454	61860	77	77	7754	1.1	4.4	59.0	34.4	1.0	152832
43215	COLUMBUS	27701	6590	44.6	24.4	22.9	5.1	3.0	29583	31048	7	5	1037	6.5	11.8	36.2	39.4	6.2	164844
43217	COLUMBUS	17343	776	15.2	30.8	49.7	3.7	0.5	51443	53196	65	55	89	15.7	55.1	0.0	29.2	0.0	60263
43219	COLUMBUS	17679	9871	38.0	29.5	25.9	4.3	2.2	34224	36202	16	8	5373	15.9	50.2	27.3	6.0	0.6	78064
43220	COLUMBUS	42586	11622	13.8	23.0	37.3	13.5	12.3	63420	64657	82	83	6678	1.8	7.5	32.0	45.5	13.2	201645
43221	COLUMBUS	42124	12994	7.9	15.5	40.2	20.5	15.9	81680	81828	93	97	9668	0.4	3.2	40.0	47.6	8.8	189981
43222	COLUMBUS	11972	1899	48.8	29.6	19.5	1.4	0.6	25527	26165	4	3	553	48.5	46.7	4.7	0.2	0.0	50825
43223	COLUMBUS	18383	9673	29.6	30.6	34.3	4.1	1.3	39211	42205	30	19	5670	14.7	52.9	30.9	1.2	0.3	76397
43224	COLUMBUS	20096	16518	27.8	34.1	33.0	3.7	1.4	39375	41962	31	19	9136	7.5	51.2	40.3	0.8	0.2	85257
43227	COLUMBUS	22484	9567	22.3	33.6	35.9	6.4	1.8	43304	48201	43	29	5798	2.7	48.7	47.2	1.1	0.3	89360
43228	COLUMBUS	24076	20940	20.9	28.1	40.4	8.2	2.3	50660	53946	63	52	10460	4.4	20.7	64.2	10.7	0.1	114268
43229	COLUMBUS	25464	20917	18.6	33.2	39.1	7.0	2.1	47882	51575	56	42	8681	2.1	8.5	86.4	2.9	0.1	119206
43230	COLUMBUS	37561	20973	8.2	16.6	44.0	19.0	12.2	77689	78165	91	95	14567	0.2	4.1	58.8	33.6	3.3	153739
43231	COLUMBUS	27927	7413	13.3	27.1	45.7	10.3	3.6	56744	60142	74	72	3985	2.2	16.8	71.3	9.7	0.0	123461
43232	COLUMBUS	23330	17515	20.7	31.2	39.9	6.7	1.5	47722	51591	56	41	8192	3.8	29.1	63.4	3.6	0.1	98453
43235	COLUMBUS	39458	16947	10.1	19.9	43.4	14.4	12.2	70381	69952	87	90	9647	0.8	5.8	43.8	45.1	4.5	174342
43240	COLUMBUS	49833	1379	8.0	24.6	34.7	21.0	11.7	70575	72461	87	91	973	0.0	0.0	19.6	57.0	23.3	250607
43302	MARION	22020	20357	23.2	30.3	36.6	7.4	2.4	46869	49414	54	39	14153	12.6	34.7	42.1	9.6	0.9	92625
43310	BELLE CENTER	24426	1239	18.8	21.5	47.8	8.7	3.2	57007	57397	74	73	1057	11.2	29.0	44.6	12.4	2.8	100998
43311	BELLEFONTAINE	24092	7821	20.9	27.2	39.4	8.7	3.8	51624	53098	65	56	5240	9.5	25.4	49.6	14.3	1.2	107408
43314	CALEDONIA	22665	1199	13.8	32.4	45.7	6.6	1.6	52488	53001	67	60	1006	21.3	22.3	45.1	9.5	1.8	96633
43315	CARDINGTON	21298	2745	21.3	28.3	42.2	6.6	1.6	50378	53274	62	51	2146	9.6	19.2	53.1	16.1	2.0	117898
43316	CAREY	20741	2376	23.1	30.2	39.9	5.6	1.3	44365	49385	46	32	1772	16.1	28.7	48.6	6.4	0.2	95444
43318	DE GRAFF	22524	1395	18.1	29.7	39.6	8.8	3.8	51760	52821	65	57	1129	12.2	29.3	42.8	14.9	0.8	99009
43319	EAST LIBERTY	29499	393	8.9	16.8	54.5	15.5	4.3	69345	68928	86	90	344	4.9	13.4	52.3	25.3	4.1	137500
43320	EDISON	20185	600	25.0	29.2	38.2	5.5	2.2	45631	50229	50	35	450	7.1	16.4	57.6	15.8	3.1	125595
43321	FULTON	23351	133	15.0	31.6	42.1	10.5	0.8	52393	53933	67	59	108	18.5	29.6	38.9	12.0	0.9	93333
43323	HARPSTER	22844	312	11.2	34.3	44.6	7.4	2.6	53007	53546	68	61	270	15.2	28.1	41.1	13.3	2.2	99474
43324	HUNTSVILLE	25422	1242	17.8	23.2	45.9	10.3	2.8	55984	55802	73	70	1050	10.2	22.0	43.9	20.3	3.6	113372
43326	KENTON	20693	5379	28.5	29.3	33.9	6.2	2.1	41898	43743	39	25	3807	16.0	38.3	37.7	7.2	0.7	85948
43331	LAKEVIEW	21884	2370	30.6	30.3	30.7	6.8	1.6	40157	42796	33	21	1835	30.8	31.0	26.5	9.3	2.3	71496
43332	LA RUE	21459	812	24.1	25.7	38.3	10.0	1.8	50095	51411	61	49	650	15.5	37.4	37.1	9.1	0.9	86935
43333	LEWISTOWN	21451	511	27.4	31.1	32.1	7.2	2.2	41716	45823	38	25	363	11.3	40.2	40.5	8.0	0.0	88103
43334	MARENGO	22581	2325	15.2	27.4	46.3	9.7	1.5	55622	57354	72	69	1993	6.0	21.4	49.3	22.3	1.0	128057
43335	MARTEL	25179	47	14.9	29.8	53.2	2.1	0.0	55833	54460	72	69	41	7.3	39.0	43.9	4.9	4.9	93750
43337	MORRAL	24312	401	14.2	27.9	46.1	7.2	4.5	55055	54447	71	66	355	14.4	23.1	51.8	8.5	2.3	103159
43338	MOUNT GILEAD	22999	3726	19.6	33.5	36.0	7.1	3.8	47091	50731	54	39	2927	11.3	17.5	46.4	23.5	1.3	126183
43340	MOUNT VICTORY	20380	601	23.3	26.3	40.1	8.2	2.2	50293	50584	62	50	502	17.1	28.5	42.8	11.6	0.0	94889
43341	NEW BLOOMINGTON	21849	456	14.3	30.3	43.4	9.9	2.2	53490	53901	69	62	406	25.9	32.3	35.2	6.7	0.0	80833
43342	PROSPECT	23912	1256	13.6	26.3	48.1	9.2	2.8	57629	57501	75	74	1049	4.2	19.7	56.5	19.1	0.5	114890
43343	QUINCY	20784	604	21.4	29.0	40.6	6.8	2.3	49634	51277	60	47	486	13.0	31.7	40.3	14.6	0.4	96500
43344	RICHWOOD	23010	2181	17.7	27.1	42.8	10.1	2.2	54490	56572	70	65	1713	14.7	23.0	41.2	20.3	0.9	109931
43345	RIDGEWAY	18949	357	15.1	28.9	48.5	5.9	1.7	54237	53345	70	64	311	11.3	30.2	45.0	13.2	0.3	99464
43346	ROUNDHEAD	19817	70	18.6	31.4	48.6	1.4	0.0	50000	50315	61	49	60	21.7	21.7	48.3	5.0	3.3	96667
43347	RUSHSYLVANIA	20248	586	18.9	28.7	43.2	8.4	0.9	51644	52344	65	56	512	10.2	35.0	35.2	18.9	0.8	95952
43348	RUSSELLS POINT	22200	830	29.9	26.0	34.0	7.6	2.5	42354	47311	40	26	599	23.0	32.9	26.4	12.7	5.0	80658
43351	UPPER SANDUSKY	22362	4073	18.3	32.0	41.9	6.3	1.5	49357	51184	60	47	2814	10.8	29.5	48.5	9.7	1.5	100619
43356	WALDO	29190	404	13.1	24.5	37.9	17.3	7.2	65044	65254	83	86	353	2.0	14.7	56.7	24.6	2.0	129873
43357	WEST LIBERTY	25216	1672	13.4	25.2	46.8	11.5	3.0	61389	60879	79	79	1342	5.2	15.5	60.4	17.4	1.5	123841
43358	WEST MANSFIELD	22290	939	15.0	26.4	49.5	8.4	0.6	56977	56917	74	73	792	10.0	25.5	49.1	14.9	0.5	107962
43359	WHARTON	19970	310	15.5	32.9	44.8	6.8	0.0	51079	51444	64	54	261	14.6	25.3	47.1	12.6	0.4	103269
43360	ZANESFIELD	27708	675	12.7	23.3	48.6	10.8	4.6	62063	61374	80	80	574	22.3	14.3	40.1	19.7	3.7	112791
43402	BOWLING GREEN	22368	13861	28.7	27.4	31.8	9.0	3.1	42566	46924	41	27	7003	13.5	9.9	49.8	25.2	1.6	130939
43403	BOWLING GREEN	8469	54	72.2	25.9	1.9	0.0	0.0	17520	18836	1	1	1	0.0	0.0	100.0	0.0	0.0	162500
43406	BRADNER	22300	801	17.1	32.3	40.6	7.7	2.2	50446	53971	62	51	611	27.0	35.8	31.6	5.4	0.2	76746
43407	BURGOON	26296	222	6.3	14.4	65.3	10.8	3.2	75724	76299	90	94	201	5.0	18.9	59.7	15.9	0.5	121071
43410	CLYDE	22924	3752	18.9	30.7	37.8	10.8	1.8	50283	51766	62	50	2915	12.5	23.0	54.3	9.4	0.8	104300
43412	CURTICE	25854	1692	17.3	21.6	40.0	16.6	4.4	62687	63014	81	82	1436	4.3	26.0	49.0	20.3	0.3	116421
43413	CYGNET	20375	702	13.8	34.2	47.3	4.1	0.6	51027	53669	64	53	614	24.8	32.9	31.1	9.9	1.3	78571
43416	ELMORE	24372	1275	19.5	24.1	45.2	8.7	2.6	55495	58358	72	69	1024	6.3	16.7	51.6	25.3	0.2	121825
43420	FREMONT	24434	12561	22.4	28.8	37.5	7.6	3.7	48775	51111	58	45	8906	9.5	27.4	48.4	13.6	1.1	104240
43430	GENOA	26016	1850	14.9	25.6	44.1	11.7	3.8	58149	60643	75	75	1548	9.8	22.1	58.8	9.2	0.1	106178
43431	GIBSONBURG	23343	1835	18.9	26.2	42.9	9.3	2.7	54228	54228	70	64	1430	7.5	23.1	54.6	14.5	0.2	110282
43432	GRAYTOWN	24287	493	9.3	24.9	50.3	13.6	1.8	65654	66802	84	87	435	9.2	13.1	57.9	18.4	1.4	119932
43435	HELENA	24102	632	16.6	24.8	46.5	7.9	4.1	57477	56142	75	74	541	7.6	18.7	56.7	16.1	0.9	121481
43436	ISLE SAINT GEORGE	27353	15	0.0	33.3	60.0	6.7	0.0	57921	54272	75	75	12	0.0	0.0	25.0	58.3	16.7	233333
43438	KELLEYS ISLAND	26545	197	32.0	27.9	27.9	8.1	4.1	43329	46420	43	29	159	3.8	5.0	46.5	31.4	13.2	162500
43440	LAKESIDE MARBLEHEAD	32202	2080	16.8	29.8	38.1	9.5	5.8	53376	57509	69	62	1712	13.4	15.2	43.9	23.5	4.0	120186
43442	LINDSEY	25263	469	12.4	32.2	43.3	9.0	3.2	53871	54219	69	63	392	5.6	17.1	56.9	19.4	1.0	122590
43443	LUCKEY	24827	671	15.5	21.3	46.8	13.9	2.5	60318	61875	78	78	513	9.9	15.2	56.5	17.7	0.6	116230
43445	MARTIN	24986	612	11.6	18.6	42.2	24.8	2.8	70411	70786	87	90	544	2.8	14.2	60.5	22.2	0.4	124669
43447	MILLBURY	26667	1469	12.3	22.6	47.6	14.7	2.9	62065	64326	80	81	1261	11.7	18.9	54.6	14.1	0.8	114482
43449	OAK HARBOR	27419	3460	15.1	23.7	46.0	10.3	5.0	58979	60847	76	77	2810	10.1	19.1	52.1	17.5	1.2	113420
43450	PEMBERVILLE	27547	1498	10.8	22.3	49.1	14.5	3.3	66237	66704	84	87	1199	4.8	12.3	57.7	24.1	1.0	127279
43451	PORTAGE	25025	467	15.6	26.6	45.2	10.1	2.6	55669	58403	72	69	387	26.9	19.6	35.1	17.8	0.5	97105
43452	PORT CLINTON	26165	6249	21.5	29.0	35.9	10.0	3.6	49302	52878	60	46	4726	10.4	21.7	47.7	17.3	3.0	113854
43456	PUT IN BAY	35060	383	12.5	23.5	46.0	12.3	5.7	58854	60982	76	76	300	1.3	2.3	17.3	61.3	17.7	252703
43457	RISINGSUN	23385	690	14.6	26.8	46.7	8.8	3.0	55391	56626	72	68	571	23.8	29.1	38.0	8.9	0.2	85769
43460	ROSSFORD	30735	2605	15.3	26.7	39.7	12.7	5.6	56972	59864	74	72	1963	4.3	17.2	60.0	13.3	5.1	121366
43462	RUDOLPH	23615	506	17.2	27.1	46.6	5.3	3.8	53783	56337	69	63	430	40.0	22.8	26.5	10.5	0.2	68696
43464	VICKERY	22699	620	14.8	34.0	41.9	6.6	2.6	50760	52433	63	52	474	13.3	29.7	42.0	12.9	2.1	97500
43465	WALBRIDGE	24707	2052	24.3	28.9	37.8	7.5	1.5	46176	50985	52	37	1624	41.0	19.4	35.0	4.3	0.3	74216
43466	WAYNE	20655	831	18.9	30.3	44.4	5.5	0.8	50545	54047	62	51	692	29.3	30.5	31.2	8.5	0.4	76508
43469	WOODVILLE	26241	1235	15.5	23.3	46.2	11.7	3.2	60904	61326	79	79	977	3.2	12.7	58.1	25.4	0.6	134128
43501	ALVORDTON	19682	365	20.0	31.2	43.0	3.8	1.9	48834	50796	59	45	290	23.4	29.0	36.2	10.0	1.4	86111
43502	ARCHBOLD	25481	2729	14.0	26.3	45.1	10.9	3.7	55911	57867	73	70	2088	11.0	16.4	52.3	19.8	0.6	116509
43504	BERKEY	31315	387	12.7	16.5	42.4	17.1	11.4	76707	77621	90	94	340	4.7	13.2	56.2	22.4	3.5	118085
43506	BRYAN	25501	6287	18.5	30.2	39.7	8.5	3.1	50874	52192	63	53	4595	11.1	24.9	51.2	12.0	0.8	106404
43511	CUSTAR	20532	491	19.3	33.0	38.5	7.1	2.0	48171	51046	57	42	424	24.8	26.4	39.6	8.5	0.7	88333
43512	DEFIANCE	25494	11501	17.5	23.8	45.2	10.7	2.8	56182	56091	73	71	8893	13.8	23.6	48.9	12.9	0.8	105632
43515	DELTA	23554	3092	15.0	28.8	43.5	10.1	2.7	55437	59211	72	68	2567	15.3	13.6	51.4	18.7	1.0	117346
43516	DESHLER	21844	1140	19.2	31.0	39.9	7.9	2.0	49827	51581	61	48	960	21.3	31.1	39.8	7.5	0.3	87356
43517	EDGERTON	22560	1459	17.5	28.6	43.9	8.0	2.0	52667	53433	67	60	1192	13.7	25.8	48.7	10.6	1.3	100204
43518	EDON	20667	1114	18.9	26.8	46.8	6.1	1.4	52094	52799	66	58	935	13.9	30.8	43.2	11.6	0.5	95690
43521	FAYETTE	20259	1181	21.3	36.5	34.9	5.8	1.5	43372	47245	43	29	853	17.4	35.8	34.1	11.5	1.3	83977
	OHIO	26577		21.4	25.9	36.7	10.4	5.7	52400	54553				10.3	22.0	45.6	19.3	2.8	114865
	UNITED STATES	27277		20.9	24.4	35.3	11.7	7.6	54719	56938				9.3	13.1	31.6	32.6	13.5	162279

ZIP CODE #	POST OFFICE NAME	FINANCIAL SERVICES: Auto Loan	Home Loan	Invest-ments	Retire-ment Plans	THE HOME: Home Improvements: Home Repair	Lawn & Garden	Furnishings: Comput-ers & Hard-ware-Personal	Major Appli-ances	TV, Radio, Sound Equip-ment	Furni-ture	ENTERTAINMENT: Dine out/ Carry out	Sports Equip-ment	Fees & Tickets	Toys & Games	Travel	Cable TV	PERSONAL: Apparel & Services	Auto Repairs	Health Insur-ance	Pets & Supplies
43214	COLUMBUS	96	96	94	98	96	97	102	95	100	100	101	74	102	99	100	100	71	99	100	113
43215	COLUMBUS	60	45	46	51	44	46	66	51	66	61	67	45	59	65	57	66	48	61	57	66
43217	COLUMBUS	83	53	50	58	50	51	83	64	82	80	85	56	69	84	67	79	59	79	65	81
43219	COLUMBUS	62	53	48	55	50	58	61	57	66	60	65	42	58	65	55	69	45	62	65	71
43220	COLUMBUS	121	113	116	119	115	110	127	114	123	127	124	91	125	123	122	120	88	122	114	136
43221	COLUMBUS	134	157	158	159	160	148	143	145	138	150	139	110	157	138	153	136	100	141	140	166
43222	COLUMBUS	44	35	32	37	33	37	47	39	49	42	48	32	42	48	40	50	34	45	45	49
43223	COLUMBUS	69	61	54	62	58	66	67	65	70	64	69	50	62	70	61	72	47	67	71	79
43224	COLUMBUS	67	58	53	60	56	62	68	62	70	64	69	49	63	70	62	71	48	67	68	76
43227	COLUMBUS	73	69	62	70	66	73	74	71	76	71	76	54	72	76	70	79	53	74	79	85
43228	COLUMBUS	84	73	66	75	70	71	84	76	84	83	84	61	78	86	76	83	59	81	77	91
43229	COLUMBUS	83	69	62	72	66	67	83	72	83	81	84	59	76	84	74	81	58	80	75	88
43230	COLUMBUS	132	137	124	140	133	124	134	127	130	139	132	102	138	134	133	126	93	129	121	150
43231	COLUMBUS	98	89	78	91	85	81	96	87	94	98	95	70	91	97	89	91	66	92	85	105
43232	COLUMBUS	80	69	60	71	65	67	80	71	80	78	80	57	74	81	72	79	56	77	74	86
43235	COLUMBUS	126	122	118	128	120	114	129	118	125	132	127	96	129	128	125	122	90	124	115	141
43240	COLUMBUS	146	128	113	135	120	114	144	125	139	146	143	106	136	147	131	133	100	135	119	152
43302	MARION	79	76	68	77	73	82	78	78	80	74	79	60	76	81	75	83	55	79	85	93
43310	BELLE CENTER	91	87	89	89	86	98	85	92	87	80	86	71	82	87	86	90	59	89	96	109
43311	BELLEFONTAINE	86	83	74	84	80	87	86	84	87	81	86	66	83	88	83	90	60	86	90	101
43314	CALEDONIA	96	79	83	79	79	97	79	91	85	74	83	69	69	87	76	91	56	85	94	108
43315	CARDINGTON	85	79	73	80	78	88	78	83	80	74	79	63	73	82	76	84	54	80	87	99
43316	CAREY	80	73	69	74	71	84	72	77	76	69	75	59	69	77	71	80	51	75	83	92
43318	DE GRAFF	92	88	82	91	87	99	86	93	88	79	86	72	82	89	86	92	59	88	97	109
43319	EAST LIBERTY	108	121	104	125	118	119	108	113	106	109	107	88	115	109	114	107	75	108	111	132
43320	EDISON	84	71	79	72	72	89	72	84	76	65	74	63	63	77	71	82	50	78	88	98
43321	FULTON	113	81	93	79	81	107	84	98	93	82	92	75	68	97	77	102	62	93	103	119
43323	HARPSTER	91	83	82	86	84	98	82	92	84	74	83	70	75	86	81	89	56	85	95	107
43324	HUNTSVILLE	97	86	101	88	89	103	84	98	87	78	86	74	77	87	87	92	58	91	100	114
43326	KENTON	76	68	64	69	66	78	72	74	75	66	73	57	66	75	68	78	50	73	80	88
43331	LAKEVIEW	79	64	82	62	68	82	65	77	70	64	68	56	57	68	65	75	46	73	82	90
43332	LA RUE	95	75	88	75	77	98	78	92	84	71	82	69	66	85	75	91	55	86	97	108
43333	LEWISTOWN	77	66	63	69	66	78	71	75	73	64	71	57	63	75	66	77	49	72	79	88
43334	MARENGO	96	87	83	88	87	97	84	93	87	82	87	69	78	90	82	91	59	87	94	109
43335	MARTEL	92	84	83	87	86	99	83	93	85	75	84	71	76	87	83	90	57	86	96	109
43337	MORRAL	99	92	90	95	93	107	90	101	92	82	91	76	84	94	90	98	62	93	104	117
43338	MOUNT GILEAD	92	80	84	82	81	98	80	91	85	73	83	69	72	86	79	90	56	85	96	107
43340	MOUNT VICTORY	94	74	80	74	74	93	75	86	81	71	80	66	64	84	71	88	54	81	90	104
43341	NEW BLOOMINGTON	111	82	93	81	82	107	85	99	93	82	92	76	70	97	78	102	62	93	104	119
43342	PROSPECT	95	93	88	97	94	103	89	97	90	83	89	74	87	92	91	94	61	91	99	113
43343	QUINCY	86	78	78	82	80	92	77	87	80	70	78	66	71	81	77	84	53	80	90	101
43344	RICHWOOD	90	90	77	93	86	97	88	90	89	83	88	71	87	91	87	92	61	88	96	108
43345	RIDGEWAY	91	83	82	86	84	98	82	92	84	74	83	70	75	86	81	89	56	85	95	107
43346	ROUNDHEAD	77	70	69	73	71	82	69	78	71	62	70	59	64	72	69	75	48	72	80	90
43347	RUSHSYLVANIA	86	79	78	82	80	92	77	87	80	70	78	66	72	81	78	84	54	81	90	101
43348	RUSSELLS POINT	83	64	87	64	67	84	69	81	74	64	72	60	59	72	68	79	49	77	85	95
43351	UPPER SANDUSKY	80	75	70	76	73	84	76	79	79	71	77	61	72	79	74	82	53	78	86	94
43356	WALDO	98	117	106	117	113	117	101	106	102	102	103	80	113	104	110	104	72	103	111	124
43357	WEST LIBERTY	98	98	92	101	98	105	94	100	95	91	94	77	93	96	96	97	65	96	102	117
43358	WEST MANSFIELD	90	86	82	89	87	97	83	92	85	77	83	70	79	86	84	89	57	86	94	107
43359	WHARTON	83	75	75	78	77	89	74	84	77	67	75	63	68	78	74	81	51	77	86	97
43360	ZANESFIELD	107	106	93	105	103	106	98	103	99	100	100	77	97	103	97	101	68	99	103	122
43402	BOWLING GREEN	79	65	62	69	64	66	87	70	81	78	82	59	75	82	73	80	58	78	72	86
43403	BOWLING GREEN	31	13	13	16	12	15	44	22	35	30	36	23	26	34	24	32	25	31	22	29
43406	BRADNER	81	83	68	85	78	87	81	81	82	77	82	64	81	84	80	84	56	81	88	98
43407	BURGOON	97	121	108	120	116	119	103	107	104	104	105	80	118	106	114	106	74	105	113	125
43410	CLYDE	88	82	75	84	80	92	82	86	84	77	83	67	77	86	80	88	57	84	91	103
43412	CURTICE	101	104	95	108	103	110	97	104	97	93	97	80	98	99	100	100	67	98	105	122
43413	CYGNET	84	77	76	80	78	90	76	85	78	69	77	64	70	80	75	82	52	79	88	99
43416	ELMORE	89	89	85	92	89	100	84	93	86	79	85	70	83	88	87	90	59	87	96	108
43420	FREMONT	88	82	78	83	81	91	84	86	87	80	86	66	81	87	82	90	59	86	93	103
43430	GENOA	91	100	88	101	96	103	91	95	92	89	92	73	96	94	95	95	64	92	100	112
43431	GIBSONBURG	87	88	82	89	87	97	83	90	86	79	85	67	84	87	85	91	59	86	97	105
43432	GRAYTOWN	100	100	93	104	100	109	95	103	96	89	95	79	93	98	97	99	65	97	105	120
43435	HELENA	97	92	89	95	93	105	89	99	91	82	90	75	84	93	90	96	62	92	102	116
43436	ISLE SAINT GEORGE	103	83	134	81	91	109	83	105	87	78	86	77	72	82	90	92	57	97	104	122
43438	KELLEYS ISLAND	86	69	111	68	76	91	69	88	72	65	71	64	60	68	75	77	47	81	86	101
43440	LAKESIDE MARBLEHEAD	114	91	147	90	100	121	91	116	96	86	94	85	79	91	99	102	63	107	115	135
43442	LINDSEY	99	92	90	96	94	107	90	101	93	82	91	77	84	94	90	98	62	94	104	117
43443	LUCKEY	88	98	90	97	97	104	87	94	92	87	91	68	94	91	93	96	63	91	104	109
43445	MARTIN	104	115	100	118	112	115	103	109	102	103	103	85	109	105	109	103	72	104	108	128
43447	MILLBURY	95	106	96	106	103	108	94	100	96	95	96	75	101	97	100	98	67	97	104	117
43449	OAK HARBOR	104	100	103	102	100	113	96	106	98	90	97	81	93	98	98	102	66	100	109	124
43450	PEMBERVILLE	96	111	98	113	108	110	98	102	98	98	99	78	107	100	105	99	69	99	105	120
43451	PORTAGE	95	93	85	95	92	99	88	94	89	86	89	71	86	92	88	92	61	90	95	111
43452	PORT CLINTON	88	79	98	79	82	94	80	90	84	76	83	66	76	81	83	88	56	87	94	105
43456	PUT IN BAY	120	96	155	95	106	127	96	122	101	90	100	89	83	96	104	107	66	113	121	142
43457	RISINGSUN	92	89	79	92	87	99	88	93	90	81	89	72	84	92	87	94	61	89	99	110
43460	ROSSFORD	99	111	102	112	108	111	103	104	104	103	105	79	111	105	108	106	73	104	110	122
43462	RUDOLPH	97	90	80	87	88	93	85	90	88	87	88	66	80	91	81	90	60	87	91	107
43464	VICKERY	96	82	84	84	83	99	82	93	86	75	84	71	73	88	80	92	57	87	97	109
43465	WALBRIDGE	80	76	79	75	78	86	74	81	76	74	75	58	72	75	75	80	51	78	87	95
43466	WAYNE	84	77	75	80	78	90	76	85	78	69	76	64	70	79	75	82	52	79	87	99
43469	WOODVILLE	90	104	94	105	102	106	92	98	94	92	94	73	100	94	99	96	65	94	103	113
43501	ALVORDTON	81	74	73	77	75	87	73	82	75	66	74	62	67	77	73	80	50	76	85	96
43502	ARCHBOLD	99	96	90	97	95	102	92	98	94	90	93	74	90	96	92	97	64	95	100	115
43504	BERKEY	120	135	116	139	131	132	120	125	118	121	119	98	128	122	127	119	83	120	124	147
43506	BRYAN	92	82	81	83	81	93	85	88	87	80	86	68	79	89	81	91	59	87	93	105
43511	CUSTAR	87	79	78	83	81	93	78	88	81	71	79	67	72	82	78	85	54	81	91	103
43512	DEFIANCE	94	87	82	88	86	97	88	92	91	84	90	71	84	92	86	94	62	90	97	109
43515	DELTA	93	92	83	94	91	98	87	93	88	85	88	71	86	91	88	91	61	89	95	110
43516	DESHLER	93	78	81	79	78	95	78	89	82	72	81	68	69	85	75	88	55	83	92	105
43517	EDGERTON	90	85	80	87	85	94	82	90	84	78	83	68	77	86	81	87	57	84	92	105
43518	EDON	86	76	77	79	78	91	76	86	79	69	77	65	69	81	75	84	53	79	89	100
43521	FAYETTE	81	70	65	72	69	81	75	77	78	69	76	60	67	79	70	82	52	76	83	92
	OHIO	94	92	87	93	90	96	93	93	94	91	94	72	92	95	91	96	66	93	98	110
	UNITED STATES	100	100	100	100	100	100	100	100	100	100	100	100	100	100	100	100	100	100	100	100

POPULATION CHANGE

ZIP CODE #	POST OFFICE NAME	COUNTY FIPS CODE	POPULATION 2000	POPULATION 2009	POPULATION 2014	2000-2009 ANNUAL RATE % Rate	2000-2009 ANNUAL RATE State Centile	HOUSEHOLDS 2000	HOUSEHOLDS 2009	HOUSEHOLDS 2014	HOUSEHOLDS % Annual Rate 2000-2009	HOUSEHOLDS 2009 Average HH Size	FAMILIES 2000	FAMILIES 2009	FAMILIES % Annual Rate 2000-2009
43522	GRAND RAPIDS	173	3684	3733	3726	0.1	51	1379	1443	1453	0.5	2.56	1036	1052	0.2
43524	HAMLER	069	1422	1420	1397	0.0	45	512	527	524	0.3	2.69	398	401	0.1
43525	HASKINS	173	608	613	667	0.1	51	230	246	270	0.7	2.49	172	180	0.5
43526	HICKSVILLE	039	6162	6147	6077	0.0	45	2331	2382	2375	0.2	2.56	1663	1660	0.0
43527	HOLGATE	069	2421	2455	2431	0.2	56	874	919	918	0.5	2.64	648	664	0.3
43528	HOLLAND	095	13885	15503	15718	1.2	91	5196	5920	6045	1.4	2.55	3775	4160	1.1
43532	LIBERTY CENTER	069	4110	4293	4282	0.5	71	1419	1524	1532	0.8	2.69	1083	1136	0.5
43533	LYONS	051	1525	1679	1729	1.0	87	562	636	662	1.3	2.63	424	470	1.1
43534	MC CLURE	069	1811	1840	1819	0.2	56	662	692	691	0.5	2.66	498	508	0.2
43535	MALINTA	069	782	804	800	0.3	61	308	328	330	0.7	2.45	237	246	0.4
43536	MARK CENTER	039	460	481	486	0.5	71	156	169	173	0.9	2.85	126	134	0.7
43537	MAUMEE	095	24818	26747	26726	0.8	82	9998	10846	10903	0.9	2.40	6717	7183	0.7
43540	METAMORA	051	1270	1462	1529	1.5	94	465	547	576	1.8	2.67	358	412	1.5
43542	MONCLOVA	095	2294	2895	3051	2.5	98	779	1003	1064	2.8	2.83	647	819	2.6
43543	MONTPELIER	171	8132	8036	7926	-0.1	39	3171	3214	3195	0.1	2.48	2255	2234	-0.1
43545	NAPOLEON	069	14727	14502	14241	-0.2	32	5698	5753	5693	0.1	2.47	4006	3945	-0.2
43548	NEW BAVARIA	069	740	730	719	-0.1	39	282	289	287	0.3	2.53	213	213	0.0
43549	NEY	039	1380	1407	1409	0.2	56	513	544	553	0.6	2.59	401	415	0.4
43551	PERRYSBURG	173	33616	37555	39003	1.2	91	12915	14829	15535	1.5	2.51	9072	10148	1.2
43554	PIONEER	171	2744	2760	2733	0.1	51	1066	1107	1107	0.4	2.49	775	784	0.1
43556	SHERWOOD	039	1990	2071	2089	0.4	66	727	783	799	0.8	2.64	572	604	0.6
43557	STRYKER	171	3378	3354	3315	-0.1	39	1037	1057	1052	0.2	2.61	789	787	0.0
43558	SWANTON	051	13766	13700	13587	-0.1	39	4971	5104	5108	0.3	2.64	3860	3880	0.1
43560	SYLVANIA	095	28328	31735	32190	1.2	91	10398	11668	11858	1.3	2.69	7710	8505	1.1
43566	WATERVILLE	095	6562	7029	7137	0.7	79	2361	2608	2674	1.1	2.62	1847	1994	0.8
43567	WAUSEON	051	12985	13211	13208	0.2	56	4786	4985	5023	0.4	2.63	3559	3625	0.2
43569	WESTON	173	2914	2975	2998	0.2	56	1097	1168	1190	0.7	2.55	807	835	0.4
43570	WEST UNITY	171	3454	3554	3547	0.3	61	1298	1377	1386	0.6	2.53	925	955	0.3
43571	WHITEHOUSE	095	5768	6409	6475	1.1	89	2031	2319	2365	1.4	2.71	1579	1759	1.2
43604	TOLEDO	095	10949	10162	9774	-0.8	9	4855	4495	4335	-0.8	2.05	2139	1849	-1.6
43605	TOLEDO	095	31788	28859	27616	-1.0	5	11751	10839	10427	-0.9	2.59	7702	6850	-1.3
43606	TOLEDO	095	28805	28050	27295	-0.3	27	11340	10968	10698	-0.4	2.21	6193	5703	-0.9
43607	TOLEDO	095	25305	23103	22147	-1.0	5	10401	9750	9428	-0.7	2.35	6098	5450	-1.2
43608	TOLEDO	095	19200	17372	16619	-1.1	4	7050	6439	6188	-1.0	2.68	4714	4156	-1.4
43609	TOLEDO	095	27402	25061	24028	-1.0	5	10333	9612	9274	-0.8	2.59	6523	5834	-1.2
43610	TOLEDO	095	6847	5888	5565	-1.6	1	2425	2126	2024	-1.4	2.71	1626	1378	-1.8
43611	TOLEDO	095	21153	20158	19555	-0.5	17	8415	8202	8018	-0.3	2.44	5757	5439	-0.6
43612	TOLEDO	095	31629	30004	29051	-0.6	14	13022	12575	12260	-0.4	2.37	8149	7568	-0.8
43613	TOLEDO	095	34310	32716	31755	-0.5	17	14640	14246	13919	-0.3	2.29	9026	8432	-0.7
43614	TOLEDO	095	30348	29625	28816	-0.3	27	13759	13626	13345	-0.1	2.11	7830	7433	-0.6
43615	TOLEDO	095	40075	40356	39808	0.1	51	17746	18254	18145	0.3	2.19	10563	10367	-0.2
43616	OREGON	095	16592	16516	16226	0.0	45	6690	6747	6667	0.1	2.39	4548	4451	-0.2
43617	TOLEDO	095	7768	7759	7657	0.0	45	2831	2898	2880	0.3	2.68	2265	2227	-0.2
43618	OREGON	095	3264	3261	3212	0.0	45	1193	1221	1212	0.3	2.65	933	933	0.0
43619	NORTHWOOD	173	7796	7735	7700	-0.1	39	2886	2968	2987	0.3	2.59	2150	2151	0.0
43620	TOLEDO	095	7166	6643	6390	-0.8	9	3113	2903	2801	-0.8	2.14	1494	1333	-1.2
43623	TOLEDO	095	20219	19685	19222	-0.3	27	8722	8643	8492	-0.1	2.27	5524	5293	-0.5
43701	SOUTH ZANESVILLE	119	55813	55850	55849	0.0	45	22210	22302	22353	0.0	2.45	15102	14745	-0.3
43713	BARNESVILLE	013	7167	7052	6970	-0.2	32	2847	2848	2833	0.0	2.42	1959	1898	-0.3
43716	BEALLSVILLE	111	2033	2046	2028	0.1	51	783	814	816	0.4	2.51	582	592	0.2
43718	BELMONT	013	3408	3418	3402	0.0	45	1296	1332	1337	0.3	2.50	982	986	0.0
43719	BETHESDA	013	2495	2449	2420	-0.2	32	1004	1009	1005	0.1	2.40	731	716	-0.2
43720	BLUE ROCK	119	1387	1477	1511	0.7	79	522	559	574	0.7	2.64	402	420	0.5
43723	BYESVILLE	059	5061	5041	4989	0.0	45	2007	2053	2050	0.2	2.46	1397	1387	-0.1
43724	CALDWELL	121	8733	8702	8617	0.0	45	2640	2670	2658	0.1	2.40	1825	1793	-0.2
43725	CAMBRIDGE	059	21272	20710	20407	-0.3	27	8698	8621	8528	-0.1	2.35	5780	5560	-0.4
43727	CHANDLERSVILLE	119	1347	1431	1463	0.7	79	501	535	550	0.7	2.67	392	409	0.5
43728	CHESTERHILL	115	1298	1353	1351	0.4	66	496	538	544	0.9	2.51	370	392	0.6
43730	CORNING	127	2730	2890	2966	0.6	75	1018	1099	1134	0.8	2.63	774	817	0.6
43731	CROOKSVILLE	127	5043	5006	4979	-0.1	39	1920	1940	1940	0.1	2.58	1424	1409	-0.1
43732	CUMBERLAND	059	1803	1813	1802	0.1	51	674	693	693	0.3	2.62	532	536	0.1
43734	DUNCAN FALLS	119	1044	1051	1053	0.1	51	426	430	432	0.1	2.44	312	306	-0.2
43739	GLENFORD	127	2040	2212	2286	0.9	85	703	778	809	1.1	2.84	566	615	0.9
43746	HOPEWELL	119	1138	1171	1181	0.3	61	400	412	416	0.3	2.84	322	325	0.1
43747	JERUSALEM	111	1195	1231	1228	0.3	61	451	480	484	0.7	2.56	347	362	0.5
43748	JUNCTION CITY	127	2753	2951	3033	0.8	82	939	1022	1053	0.9	2.89	738	787	0.7
43749	KIMBOLTON	059	2445	2549	2554	0.5	71	925	991	1000	0.7	2.55	701	732	0.5
43754	LEWISVILLE	111	1531	1349	1281	-1.4	2	577	523	502	-1.1	2.52	426	377	-1.3
43755	LORE CITY	059	1872	2015	2035	0.8	82	731	808	822	1.1	2.49	555	598	0.8
43756	MC CONNELSVILLE	115	5407	5172	5048	-0.5	17	2213	2194	2167	-0.1	2.28	1490	1434	-0.4
43758	MALTA	115	3471	3535	3508	0.2	56	1333	1414	1421	0.6	2.49	978	1012	0.4
43760	MOUNT PERRY	127	1912	2064	2123	0.8	82	654	716	740	1.0	2.88	526	565	0.8
43762	NEW CONCORD	119	5277	5301	5308	0.0	45	1620	1641	1647	0.1	2.53	1131	1113	-0.2
43764	NEW LEXINGTON	127	8315	8387	8423	0.1	51	3081	3170	3200	0.3	2.59	2229	2243	0.1
43766	NEW STRAITSVILLE	127	1659	1702	1716	0.3	61	644	674	684	0.5	2.53	457	467	0.2
43767	NORWICH	119	1476	1592	1636	0.8	82	516	560	577	0.9	2.83	417	442	0.6
43771	PHILO	119	1686	1810	1856	0.8	82	614	663	682	0.8	2.73	469	494	0.6
43772	PLEASANT CITY	121	1835	1846	1835	0.1	51	700	720	720	0.3	2.56	523	524	0.0
43773	QUAKER CITY	059	3123	3442	3494	1.1	89	1094	1213	1235	1.1	2.83	839	910	0.9
43777	ROSEVILLE	119	5004	4951	4928	-0.1	39	1840	1833	1831	0.0	2.70	1386	1349	-0.3
43778	SALESVILLE	059	1344	1494	1523	1.2	91	432	488	499	1.3	3.04	335	370	1.1
43779	SARAHSVILLE	121	949	953	947	0.0	45	333	341	340	0.3	2.79	268	270	0.1
43780	SENECAVILLE	121	2864	2926	2915	0.2	56	1137	1188	1192	0.5	2.46	818	831	0.2
43782	SHAWNEE	127	952	956	958	0.0	45	330	336	337	0.2	2.85	256	254	-0.1
43783	SOMERSET	127	4268	4531	4643	0.6	75	1540	1673	1726	0.9	2.65	1132	1198	0.6
43787	STOCKPORT	115	2569	2572	2541	0.0	45	1011	1049	1049	0.4	2.45	727	734	0.1
43788	SUMMERFIELD	121	938	923	911	-0.2	32	313	313	311	0.0	2.95	250	246	-0.2
43793	WOODSFIELD	111	5122	4761	4591	-0.8	9	2058	1971	1918	-0.5	2.36	1457	1361	-0.7
43802	ADAMSVILLE	119	1202	1296	1331	0.8	82	391	424	436	0.9	3.06	311	330	0.6
43804	BALTIC	075	2803	2898	2941	0.4	66	766	792	802	0.4	3.56	633	645	0.2
43811	CONESVILLE	031	799	764	745	-0.5	17	318	314	309	-0.1	2.42	243	234	-0.4
43812	COSHOCTON	031	20056	19154	18648	-0.5	17	8327	8126	7960	-0.3	2.32	5557	5262	-0.6
43821	DRESDEN	119	4288	4567	4667	0.7	79	1642	1758	1800	0.7	2.58	1192	1243	0.5
43822	FRAZEYSBURG	119	4220	4461	4553	0.6	75	1602	1712	1752	0.7	2.59	1203	1256	0.5
43824	FRESNO	031	4078	4238	4229	0.4	66	1286	1361	1365	0.6	3.11	1060	1100	0.4
	OHIO					0.2					0.4	2.44			0.1
	UNITED STATES					1.0					1.1	2.59			0.9

ZIP CODE #	POST OFFICE NAME	RACE (%) White 2000	White 2009	Black 2000	Black 2009	Asian/Pacific 2000	Asian/Pacific 2009	% Hispanic Origin 2000	% Hispanic Origin 2009	2009 AGE DISTRIBUTION (%) 0-4	5-9	10-14	15-19	20-24	25-44	45-64	65-84	85+	18+	MEDIAN AGE 2009	% 2009 Males	% 2009 Females
43522	GRAND RAPIDS	97.8	97.2	0.2	0.3	0.3	0.5	2.0	2.7	6.1	6.8	7.3	7.4	4.6	24.8	32.4	9.5	1.1	75.1	40.4	50.0	50.0
43524	HAMLER	93.4	93.1	0.4	0.4	0.1	0.1	10.4	10.8	7.0	7.4	8.2	8.0	5.1	24.9	26.3	11.3	1.8	72.4	37.6	50.3	49.7
43525	HASKINS	97.0	96.1	0.0	0.0	0.8	1.3	3.0	3.8	6.7	7.3	7.7	6.4	3.9	27.1	31.0	9.0	1.0	74.4	39.4	51.7	48.3
43526	HICKSVILLE	97.5	96.8	0.1	0.1	0.1	0.2	2.7	3.7	7.6	7.8	7.9	7.1	4.7	26.2	25.3	11.2	2.2	72.2	36.9	48.8	51.2
43527	HOLGATE	94.4	94.2	0.2	0.2	0.2	0.2	11.4	11.8	7.5	7.5	7.2	6.8	5.5	25.9	26.7	10.4	2.4	73.4	37.3	50.2	49.8
43528	HOLLAND	87.7	82.6	7.5	10.7	1.9	3.1	2.7	3.6	6.5	6.7	6.8	6.6	5.5	27.0	28.4	10.6	2.1	76.0	39.1	48.4	51.6
43532	LIBERTY CENTER	95.7	95.6	1.6	1.7	0.3	0.3	2.6	2.6	6.6	7.1	7.7	9.6	4.9	24.6	28.2	10.0	1.4	72.0	37.4	50.9	49.1
43533	LYONS	95.7	94.3	0.1	0.1	0.9	1.5	4.3	5.6	6.5	6.7	7.2	7.6	5.2	26.4	27.3	11.5	1.6	74.8	39.2	49.6	50.4
43534	MC CLURE	97.5	97.5	0.0	0.0	0.1	0.1	3.5	3.6	6.4	7.1	7.0	6.3	5.2	25.7	29.6	11.5	1.5	75.8	39.6	52.0	48.0
43535	MALINTA	96.5	96.4	0.0	0.1	0.3	0.2	5.5	5.6	5.6	6.2	8.0	8.0	4.1	23.5	31.0	11.8	1.9	75.6	40.9	50.5	49.5
43536	MARK CENTER	98.3	97.7	0.0	0.0	0.0	0.0	2.2	2.9	7.3	7.9	8.1	7.1	5.0	24.1	28.5	11.0	1.0	72.1	37.9	51.8	48.2
43537	MAUMEE	94.2	89.0	2.4	6.4	1.4	2.2	2.0	2.7	5.3	5.5	5.9	6.5	5.9	25.9	30.0	12.5	2.6	79.4	41.3	47.7	52.3
43540	METAMORA	98.2	97.7	0.2	0.3	0.2	0.3	2.1	2.9	6.4	6.8	7.6	7.0	5.5	23.3	31.8	9.8	1.8	74.8	40.5	50.9	49.1
43542	MONCLOVA	96.5	95.1	0.8	1.1	0.8	1.3	1.4	2.0	6.6	7.3	7.8	7.4	4.6	23.6	30.4	10.3	2.0	73.6	40.3	49.3	50.7
43543	MONTPELIER	97.1	96.3	0.2	0.2	0.9	1.3	1.6	2.1	7.2	6.9	6.9	7.0	5.9	25.7	26.0	12.2	2.2	74.6	37.5	49.5	50.5
43545	NAPOLEON	95.0	94.8	0.6	0.6	0.5	0.5	5.2	5.3	6.6	6.7	7.0	6.9	5.5	25.4	27.1	12.2	2.6	75.4	38.7	48.7	51.3
43548	NEW BAVARIA	98.5	98.5	0.4	0.4	0.1	0.1	1.9	1.9	5.8	5.9	6.3	6.4	4.7	25.2	30.4	12.9	2.5	77.8	42.1	51.1	48.9
43549	NEY	98.4	97.9	0.1	0.2	0.0	0.0	1.2	1.6	6.0	6.8	7.0	6.5	4.8	23.9	31.1	12.7	1.1	76.2	41.0	50.6	49.4
43551	PERRYSBURG	94.9	93.2	1.2	1.3	1.4	2.3	3.0	3.9	6.9	7.1	7.3	7.0	5.5	26.4	28.3	9.6	1.9	74.2	37.9	49.0	51.0
43554	PIONEER	97.6	97.0	0.2	0.2	0.1	0.1	2.2	2.9	6.0	6.6	6.9	6.8	4.4	27.5	28.8	11.4	1.7	76.3	39.2	50.7	49.3
43556	SHERWOOD	97.5	97.0	0.5	0.5	0.1	0.1	2.1	2.8	6.4	6.7	6.6	6.3	6.2	25.7	28.3	12.6	1.3	76.5	39.4	49.6	50.4
43557	STRYKER	90.1	88.5	5.7	6.4	0.1	0.2	6.0	7.6	5.6	5.8	5.8	7.8	7.8	30.9	24.5	10.2	1.7	78.2	36.1	54.7	45.3
43558	SWANTON	96.2	95.0	1.5	2.1	0.1	0.2	2.1	2.9	5.7	6.2	7.0	6.9	5.0	25.3	30.8	11.3	1.8	76.5	40.7	50.0	50.0
43560	SYLVANIA	94.4	91.4	1.4	2.1	2.4	4.1	1.8	2.6	6.2	6.6	7.2	7.8	5.7	23.0	30.5	10.9	2.2	75.1	40.3	48.0	52.0
43566	WATERVILLE	98.0	97.1	0.2	0.3	0.4	0.7	1.2	1.7	6.1	6.6	7.2	7.7	5.0	21.7	31.8	11.5	2.4	75.1	42.0	47.7	52.3
43567	WAUSEON	94.6	93.1	0.4	0.4	0.7	1.1	7.6	9.8	7.5	7.8	7.7	7.1	5.2	26.1	26.7	10.1	1.9	72.6	36.6	49.0	51.0
43569	WESTON	95.3	94.3	0.2	0.2	0.1	0.3	6.5	8.2	6.9	6.9	6.8	7.0	5.6	28.8	28.4	8.7	1.0	75.2	36.8	50.9	49.1
43570	WEST UNITY	97.3	96.5	0.3	0.4	0.2	0.3	2.7	3.5	6.8	6.6	7.2	7.9	6.1	26.0	26.5	10.1	2.6	74.0	37.3	49.9	50.1
43571	WHITEHOUSE	97.7	96.7	0.7	0.9	0.5	0.7	1.5	2.1	5.6	6.4	7.1	7.1	4.8	23.0	33.7	10.7	1.6	76.2	41.9	49.2	50.8
43604	TOLEDO	33.7	27.8	57.7	63.0	0.4	0.5	7.9	8.8	9.3	8.5	7.1	7.7	9.2	26.0	21.3	9.3	1.6	70.7	30.5	49.6	50.4
43605	TOLEDO	81.2	76.2	8.9	11.3	0.4	0.6	12.7	16.6	9.7	8.3	7.3	7.3	8.0	27.9	21.3	8.4	1.7	70.5	31.0	48.4	51.6
43606	TOLEDO	65.7	61.8	28.9	31.1	2.4	3.7	2.0	2.6	5.3	5.3	5.4	13.2	11.3	22.3	22.3	11.0	3.9	80.4	33.3	47.1	52.9
43607	TOLEDO	21.5	18.1	73.9	76.9	1.1	1.4	1.6	1.8	6.0	6.2	6.5	7.9	10.6	24.3	24.1	12.2	2.2	76.7	35.0	46.8	53.2
43608	TOLEDO	43.2	35.9	47.6	54.2	0.3	0.4	9.8	10.9	8.6	8.8	8.5	9.0	7.2	25.7	22.5	8.1	1.6	68.6	30.5	47.1	52.9
43609	TOLEDO	75.5	69.6	13.3	16.7	1.1	1.6	12.7	15.7	9.1	8.3	7.4	7.8	9.7	29.1	20.8	6.8	0.9	70.6	29.6	49.5	50.5
43610	TOLEDO	17.2	12.7	78.2	82.8	0.3	0.3	2.8	2.9	7.4	8.6	8.5	8.8	7.6	27.1	23.5	7.7	0.9	69.9	31.3	47.1	52.9
43611	TOLEDO	87.1	83.9	8.5	10.6	0.3	0.5	4.9	6.4	7.1	7.1	7.0	6.8	5.8	25.9	26.6	11.8	1.9	74.6	37.4	48.5	51.5
43612	TOLEDO	89.9	86.2	5.5	7.8	0.6	0.9	4.4	6.0	7.6	7.1	6.7	6.8	7.0	29.5	24.2	9.4	1.6	74.5	35.2	49.4	50.6
43613	TOLEDO	92.3	89.4	3.9	5.5	0.6	1.0	2.8	3.9	7.0	6.4	6.1	6.4	6.8	28.4	25.8	11.2	2.0	76.7	37.4	48.6	51.4
43614	TOLEDO	87.3	82.7	7.8	10.7	2.0	3.0	3.1	4.1	5.8	5.5	5.5	5.5	6.2	27.0	25.6	15.0	3.8	80.1	40.6	47.2	52.8
43615	TOLEDO	76.2	70.0	18.0	22.5	2.1	3.1	3.1	4.0	6.5	6.1	6.0	6.0	7.6	29.0	25.2	11.5	2.1	78.0	36.5	48.2	51.8
43616	OREGON	94.5	92.5	1.1	1.5	0.8	1.2	5.0	6.9	5.7	5.7	5.9	6.2	5.7	24.2	28.2	15.2	3.1	78.9	42.3	47.7	52.3
43617	TOLEDO	91.7	88.0	1.9	2.6	4.0	6.3	2.3	3.1	5.9	6.9	8.1	7.6	4.4	20.2	34.3	11.2	1.3	74.3	42.7	48.9	51.1
43618	OREGON	97.9	97.1	0.2	0.3	0.3	0.6	2.3	3.2	5.5	6.2	6.7	6.6	4.9	23.0	33.1	12.5	1.6	77.4	42.9	50.3	49.7
43619	NORTHWOOD	94.9	93.6	0.9	1.0	0.8	1.2	4.1	5.3	7.0	6.5	7.0	6.5	5.8	26.3	29.4	10.1	1.3	75.4	38.2	49.0	51.0
43620	TOLEDO	22.4	17.1	73.2	78.2	0.4	0.4	3.1	3.3	7.4	6.4	5.9	7.2	8.7	25.1	24.3	12.5	2.6	76.0	35.9	47.1	52.9
43623	TOLEDO	93.2	90.4	3.0	4.2	1.5	2.3	2.1	2.9	5.1	5.1	5.6	5.9	6.3	23.6	29.3	16.2	2.9	80.6	43.7	47.5	52.5
43701	SOUTH ZANESVILLE	91.8	90.5	5.7	6.6	0.3	0.4	0.6	0.7	6.8	6.5	6.4	6.6	5.8	25.2	26.5	13.5	2.7	76.3	39.5	47.6	52.4
43713	BARNESVILLE	98.4	98.0	0.6	0.6	0.3	0.4	0.2	0.3	6.1	6.2	6.3	6.4	5.6	23.8	28.1	14.4	3.2	77.4	41.6	47.2	52.8
43716	BEALLSVILLE	98.2	97.8	0.1	0.1	0.4	0.6	0.3	0.4	5.0	5.5	5.7	6.3	5.2	24.6	32.3	13.9	1.6	80.1	43.2	50.3	49.7
43718	BELMONT	97.1	96.4	1.4	1.7	0.3	0.5	0.6	0.9	5.8	6.1	6.3	6.3	5.5	25.2	31.1	11.9	1.7	77.9	41.2	51.2	48.8
43719	BETHESDA	98.6	98.3	0.3	0.4	0.2	0.2	0.4	0.5	5.4	5.7	5.8	6.9	5.7	25.3	30.6	12.7	2.0	78.8	41.6	48.8	51.2
43720	BLUE ROCK	98.3	98.0	0.5	0.6	0.1	0.2	0.2	0.3	5.8	6.8	6.9	7.5	5.0	25.1	29.9	12.0	1.1	75.8	40.0	51.5	48.5
43723	BYESVILLE	98.1	97.5	0.3	0.4	0.2	0.3	0.8	1.1	8.0	7.1	7.2	7.0	6.6	26.2	25.7	10.8	1.4	73.4	35.4	48.0	52.0
43724	CALDWELL	88.6	86.8	10.6	12.3	0.1	0.2	0.4	0.5	4.2	4.5	4.6	5.8	11.5	33.0	23.3	10.9	2.2	83.9	36.1	61.7	38.3
43725	CAMBRIDGE	94.6	93.5	2.5	2.9	0.4	0.7	0.7	0.9	6.5	6.4	6.4	6.5	6.2	24.2	27.5	13.8	2.5	76.8	40.3	48.3	51.7
43727	CHANDLERSVILLE	98.4	98.1	0.3	0.3	0.1	0.3	0.1	0.2	5.4	6.6	7.0	7.5	4.4	25.9	30.5	11.4	1.3	76.0	40.6	50.6	49.4
43728	CHESTERHILL	75.1	74.8	16.1	16.6	0.0	0.0	0.4	0.4	6.7	6.8	6.9	6.7	5.9	24.4	28.2	12.9	1.4	75.4	39.2	49.1	50.9
43730	CORNING	98.4	98.0	0.4	0.5	0.1	0.1	0.1	0.2	6.6	6.8	6.9	6.7	5.6	27.8	27.7	10.5	1.4	75.6	38.1	50.4	49.6
43731	CROOKSVILLE	98.6	98.4	0.2	0.3	0.0	0.1	0.4	0.5	7.4	7.6	7.4	7.1	5.3	26.6	26.4	10.7	1.4	73.2	37.0	49.2	50.8
43732	CUMBERLAND	98.4	98.0	0.3	0.4	0.1	0.2	0.3	0.4	5.7	6.2	6.7	7.4	5.5	23.6	30.4	13.1	1.4	76.8	41.5	51.7	48.3
43734	DUNCAN FALLS	98.8	98.4	0.2	0.3	0.1	0.1	0.1	0.1	6.1	6.8	7.0	6.9	4.9	23.7	29.5	12.7	2.4	75.5	40.6	50.6	49.4
43739	GLENFORD	98.2	97.8	0.4	0.5	0.1	0.2	0.5	0.6	7.2	7.4	7.5	7.2	5.1	27.2	27.9	9.6	0.9	73.3	37.6	50.8	49.2
43746	HOPEWELL	96.1	95.3	1.3	1.6	0.0	0.0	0.2	0.2	7.2	7.3	7.6	7.5	5.3	25.6	28.4	10.2	0.9	73.3	37.9	48.8	51.2
43747	JERUSALEM	98.2	97.8	0.5	0.6	0.3	0.3	0.1	0.1	5.2	5.4	5.9	6.1	5.1	23.2	32.9	14.5	1.6	79.6	44.3	49.6	50.4
43748	JUNCTION CITY	98.9	98.6	0.1	0.1	0.1	0.1	0.7	0.9	8.0	7.9	8.3	8.2	5.5	25.7	26.7	8.5	1.2	70.8	34.9	51.7	48.3
43749	KIMBOLTON	97.8	97.3	0.4	0.5	0.1	0.2	0.2	0.3	6.0	6.6	6.9	6.2	4.5	22.8	30.2	15.2	1.6	76.5	42.5	51.5	48.5
43754	LEWISVILLE	98.6	98.2	0.1	0.1	0.1	0.1	0.7	0.8	5.7	6.4	7.6	7.1	5.1	21.7	28.8	14.3	3.2	75.5	42.1	49.4	50.6
43755	LORE CITY	97.8	97.2	0.5	0.6	0.3	0.5	0.6	0.8	5.9	6.4	7.0	7.3	5.0	23.2	30.5	13.3	1.5	75.8	41.8	48.6	51.4
43756	MC CONNELSVILLE	95.6	95.4	1.9	2.0	0.1	0.1	0.3	0.3	6.0	6.4	6.5	6.2	5.1	22.9	28.2	15.5	3.2	77.1	42.7	48.4	51.6
43758	MALTA	94.4	94.4	3.0	3.1	0.1	0.1	0.4	0.4	5.9	5.8	6.4	7.4	5.6	23.5	29.1	14.5	1.8	77.1	41.6	49.3	50.7
43760	MOUNT PERRY	98.1	97.7	0.6	0.8	0.1	0.1	0.4	0.5	7.1	7.4	7.5	7.1	5.1	26.1	28.7	10.2	1.0	73.6	38.1	51.0	49.0
43762	NEW CONCORD	97.4	96.6	0.9	1.1	0.9	1.4	0.6	0.7	4.6	4.8	5.0	14.3	15.2	22.2	21.8	9.8	2.2	81.7	30.0	48.8	51.2
43764	NEW LEXINGTON	98.8	98.6	0.2	0.3	0.2	0.3	0.4	0.5	7.5	7.2	7.2	7.1	6.0	26.5	25.4	11.1	1.9	73.7	36.5	49.6	50.4
43766	NEW STRAITSVILLE	98.2	97.8	0.3	0.4	0.1	0.1	1.3	1.7	7.1	7.2	7.3	7.3	5.8	25.1	28.0	10.5	1.6	73.9	37.5	49.4	50.6
43767	NORWICH	99.1	98.7	0.3	0.4	0.1	0.3	0.1	0.3	5.6	6.3	8.0	7.4	5.1	26.4	28.8	11.4	0.9	74.9	39.5	51.0	49.0
43771	PHILO	97.9	97.2	0.7	0.8	0.4	0.7	0.1	0.2	6.7	6.7	6.8	7.2	6.9	25.5	27.3	11.5	1.3	75.4	38.5	49.3	50.7
43772	PLEASANT CITY	98.9	98.5	0.3	0.4	0.0	0.1	0.5	0.6	5.9	6.1	6.4	6.6	5.5	22.9	30.6	14.4	1.7	77.7	42.5	49.0	51.0
43773	QUAKER CITY	98.2	97.9	0.6	0.7	0.1	0.2	0.3	0.4	8.2	8.3	8.3	7.6	5.3	24.0	25.1	11.7	1.6	70.3	35.6	49.1	50.9
43777	ROSEVILLE	98.3	97.9	0.5	0.6	0.0	0.1	0.6	0.7	8.1	8.0	7.7	7.4	5.8	26.5	25.3	10.1	1.3	71.7	35.2	49.6	50.4
43778	SALESVILLE	98.4	98.1	0.4	0.5	0.3	0.5	0.7	1.0	6.6	6.8	7.3	8.1	5.6	23.4	28.6	12.0	1.6	73.7	39.8	50.0	50.0
43779	SARAHSVILLE	99.2	98.7	0.2	0.3	0.0	0.1	0.6	0.8	6.5	6.8	7.2	7.5	5.6	24.8	28.9	11.8	1.0	74.8	38.6	49.7	50.3
43780	SENECAVILLE	98.3	98.0	0.5	0.6	0.1	0.1	0.4	0.6	6.2	6.6	7.2	6.5	4.5	23.1	31.0	13.2	1.6	75.8	42.1	48.9	51.1
43782	SHAWNEE	99.3	99.2	0.0	0.0	0.3	0.4	0.3	0.4	6.3	8.1	7.8	8.8	6.1	28.7	25.9	7.0	1.4	72.2	33.9	49.5	50.5
43783	SOMERSET	98.8	98.6	0.1	0.1	0.1	0.2	0.5	0.7	7.0	7.2	7.3	6.8	4.9	23.9	28.1	12.4	2.3	74.3	40.1	49.0	51.0
43787	STOCKPORT	94.2	93.9	3.2	3.4	0.1	0.1	0.6	0.6	6.5	7.0	6.8	6.5	5.3	24.3	28.9	13.1	1.6	75.7	40.3	50.2	49.8
43788	SUMMERFIELD	99.1	99.1	0.1	0.1	0.0	0.0	0.6	0.9	8.3	8.1	8.7	7.9	6.5	25.0	24.6	9.5	1.3	69.9	33.8	50.4	49.6
43793	WOODSFIELD	98.7	98.5	0.2	0.2	0.2	0.3	0.6	0.7	5.8	6.0	6.3	6.1	4.9	22.7	28.7	16.4	3.2	78.2	43.6	48.1	51.9
43802	ADAMSVILLE	98.8	98.6	0.3	0.4	0.1	0.2	0.2	0.2	7.2	6.9	7.5	8.1	6.3	26.2	26.2	10.6	1.0	73.4	36.9	51.2	48.8
43804	BALTIC	99.1	99.0	0.3	0.3	0.1	0.1	0.5	0.6	11.0	9.9	10.4	9.8	7.6	22.6	18.2	8.4	2.2	62.5	26.1	49.9	50.1
43811	CONESVILLE	99.0	98.8	0.1	0.1	0.0	0.0	0.4	0.5	5.9	6.3	6.7	6.9	4.8	26.4	28.9	12.8	1.2	77.4	39.6	49.5	50.5
43812	COSHOCTON	96.5	93.5	1.6	4.1	0.5	0.9	0.6	0.8	6.2	6.3	6.4	6.4	5.6	23.8	28.1	14.6	2.6	77.6	41.3	48.1	51.9
43821	DRESDEN	98.6	98.2	0.4	0.5	0.1	0.2	0.3	0.5	6.4	6.6	6.9	7.2	5.4	25.5	28.7	11.9	1.4	75.7	39.2	49.2	50.8
43822	FRAZEYSBURG	97.9	97.4	0.7	0.9	0.2	0.3	0.4	0.5	6.8	6.9	7.0	7.0	5.5	27.7	28.5	9.4	1.2	74.9	37.5	49.9	50.1
43824	FRESNO	98.9	98.6	0.3	0.4	0.3	0.4	0.6	0.9	8.8	8.6	8.5	8.1	5.9	25.3	24.4	9.5	1.0	69.1	33.4	50.3	49.7
	OHIO	85.0	83.1	11.5	12.2	1.2	1.9	1.9	2.4	6.6	6.5	6.6	7.1	6.7	25.9	26.9	11.7	2.1	76.2	38.2	48.7	51.3
	UNITED STATES	75.1	72.0	12.3	12.7	3.8	4.6	12.5	15.7	6.8	6.7	6.6	7.1	6.9	27.0	26.0	10.9	1.9	75.7	36.9	49.2	50.8

INCOME

ZIP CODE #	POST OFFICE NAME	2009 Per Capita Income	2009 HH Income Base	2009 Household Income Distribution (%) Less than $25,000	$25,000 to $49,999	$50,000 to $99,999	$100,000 to $149,999	$150,000 or More	Median Household Income 2009	2014	2009 National Centile	2009 State Centile	2009 Home Value Base	2009 Home Value Distribution (%) Less than $50,000	$50,000 to $89,999	$90,000 to $174,999	$175,000 to $399,999	$400,000 or More	2009 Median Home Value
43522	GRAND RAPIDS	28534	1443	11.5	22.5	48.4	12.1	5.5	63929	64613	82	84	1238	17.0	16.1	41.4	24.5	1.1	116337
43524	HAMLER	20982	527	17.8	29.0	45.2	6.8	1.1	51808	52465	66	57	446	13.7	33.4	42.8	9.9	0.2	92955
43525	HASKINS	31510	246	11.4	20.7	42.7	19.5	5.7	69594	71194	87	90	201	20.9	12.9	31.8	28.4	6.0	127344
43526	HICKSVILLE	22604	2382	17.9	29.0	43.5	6.7	2.9	51567	52317	65	56	1904	13.7	26.9	48.5	10.1	0.7	99421
43527	HOLGATE	22148	919	19.7	29.2	39.6	9.4	2.2	51057	52644	64	53	762	14.3	42.4	37.5	5.0	0.8	84516
43528	HOLLAND	34689	5920	15.3	23.6	33.1	14.8	13.1	63982	62808	82	84	4479	12.7	19.2	33.6	27.6	6.9	121668
43532	LIBERTY CENTER	21245	1524	19.2	27.8	43.6	7.4	2.0	51951	52749	66	57	1307	12.5	22.6	50.2	14.1	0.7	105495
43533	LYONS	20095	636	21.2	30.2	42.0	5.3	1.3	49037	51601	59	46	523	17.2	22.8	47.0	11.9	1.1	104207
43534	MC CLURE	21937	692	14.7	30.3	45.7	7.8	1.4	53179	53650	68	61	590	18.3	27.8	43.9	8.5	1.5	95750
43535	MALINTA	22895	328	21.6	23.2	46.6	7.3	1.2	52435	52969	67	59	284	8.5	30.6	52.1	8.5	0.4	101471
43536	MARK CENTER	20914	169	24.3	25.4	37.9	8.9	3.6	50259	51307	62	50	145	5.5	26.2	48.3	20.0	0.0	107955
43537	MAUMEE	33346	10846	12.1	25.0	39.5	14.9	8.5	64322	64410	83	84	7742	2.7	14.8	56.5	23.3	2.7	127442
43540	METAMORA	21512	547	18.1	26.9	44.1	9.3	1.6	52664	54904	67	60	446	6.3	13.7	58.7	20.2	1.1	120872
43542	MONCLOVA	34421	1003	6.7	16.0	42.0	19.6	15.8	79913	80413	92	96	912	9.6	11.5	43.6	29.9	5.3	141071
43543	MONTPELIER	20756	3214	20.4	32.1	41.2	5.2	1.1	46391	50484	52	37	2455	14.9	33.1	44.8	6.9	0.3	92185
43545	NAPOLEON	24041	5753	18.3	28.4	41.8	8.6	3.0	52006	53076	66	57	4333	12.8	21.3	51.7	12.9	1.3	107882
43548	NEW BAVARIA	22635	289	17.3	32.9	38.4	9.3	2.1	49772	51983	60	48	256	17.6	34.0	43.4	5.1	0.0	89000
43549	NEY	22320	544	10.8	29.6	54.8	4.0	0.7	55079	54332	71	67	477	15.5	26.8	49.3	8.2	0.2	100412
43551	PERRYSBURG	34704	14829	12.4	21.3	37.5	17.6	11.2	68987	70352	86	89	11067	15.0	7.1	40.3	33.1	4.4	150523
43554	PIONEER	21675	1107	21.0	26.7	46.3	4.2	1.7	51187	52081	64	54	865	12.6	29.9	46.0	10.3	1.2	99485
43556	SHERWOOD	21394	783	18.4	27.7	44.8	8.6	0.5	52594	52985	67	60	681	16.4	32.5	39.1	11.6	0.4	91154
43557	STRYKER	20285	1057	15.8	29.9	47.6	5.5	1.2	52767	53308	67	61	880	12.2	33.2	44.9	9.2	0.6	94184
43558	SWANTON	25673	5104	14.2	24.7	42.1	15.0	4.0	60074	61586	77	77	4372	16.1	14.1	48.8	20.3	0.8	118782
43560	SYLVANIA	35680	11668	12.1	18.7	36.5	18.0	14.6	75366	75394	90	93	9235	2.6	12.3	50.1	31.3	3.7	147229
43566	WATERVILLE	31723	2608	7.6	19.7	43.6	20.6	8.5	76123	76355	90	94	2233	0.6	8.0	61.5	28.8	1.1	147328
43567	WAUSEON	22015	4985	16.4	30.6	43.6	7.6	1.8	52041	55203	66	57	3855	11.8	19.8	50.8	16.7	0.9	113516
43569	WESTON	24689	1168	15.0	28.8	41.3	12.4	2.6	54936	57895	71	66	967	35.9	26.9	26.5	10.4	0.3	72654
43570	WEST UNITY	21336	1377	20.1	29.5	42.8	6.0	1.6	50235	51910	62	50	1033	14.2	27.6	48.0	9.6	0.6	98802
43571	WHITEHOUSE	31010	2319	11.8	20.1	37.8	21.9	8.4	73225	74251	88	92	1911	5.9	12.1	48.5	30.4	3.2	135261
43604	TOLEDO	13228	4495	66.5	19.7	10.1	2.5	1.1	14900	15849	1	1	776	74.9	14.6	7.6	1.9	1.0	33600
43605	TOLEDO	16119	10839	36.7	31.5	26.9	4.0	0.8	34367	36663	16	9	6102	55.2	41.6	2.9	0.2	0.0	47679
43606	TOLEDO	27123	10968	28.1	25.0	29.9	11.3	5.7	44766	49154	48	33	6109	13.2	21.1	49.6	13.9	2.1	110950
43607	TOLEDO	17287	9750	42.2	27.4	24.3	4.9	1.2	30481	32678	9	6	5462	46.4	39.7	12.5	1.2	0.1	52636
43608	TOLEDO	14501	6439	41.7	31.6	22.6	3.3	0.9	30173	32014	8	5	3895	59.3	37.8	2.6	0.2	0.0	45255
43609	TOLEDO	17186	9612	35.0	30.3	28.4	5.4	0.9	35481	37590	19	11	5246	42.7	50.8	6.0	0.5	0.1	55392
43610	TOLEDO	15645	2126	39.6	28.5	25.2	5.4	1.3	31734	33782	11	7	1129	42.8	39.1	16.7	1.3	0.0	55821
43611	TOLEDO	23967	8202	23.1	27.7	36.5	9.5	3.2	49018	51371	59	46	6015	17.3	38.5	41.8	2.2	0.2	84256
43612	TOLEDO	23439	12575	20.3	28.2	42.7	7.7	1.1	51068	52338	64	54	8547	14.6	64.3	20.6	0.4	0.1	73134
43613	TOLEDO	25658	14246	20.5	29.1	39.0	9.0	2.4	50300	51983	62	51	10025	8.9	41.7	48.0	1.3	0.1	89507
43614	TOLEDO	29259	13626	21.1	27.4	36.3	11.4	3.8	51238	52637	64	54	8070	2.5	21.0	68.9	7.2	0.3	112337
43615	TOLEDO	28584	18254	24.4	26.1	35.4	8.6	5.5	49408	51430	60	47	10933	17.0	29.8	42.5	8.6	2.1	93201
43616	OREGON	27014	6747	18.7	26.3	37.1	13.9	3.9	55447	56029	72	68	4776	4.6	21.5	59.5	14.1	0.4	115339
43617	TOLEDO	38654	2898	10.9	20.4	30.5	16.5	21.7	78247	77903	91	95	2661	12.0	8.9	35.5	41.6	2.0	162891
43618	OREGON	27975	1221	13.3	21.7	43.4	15.5	6.1	65320	64527	84	86	1096	3.6	26.5	50.9	18.1	1.0	113617
43619	NORTHWOOD	26174	2968	17.8	20.5	46.6	9.9	5.2	62846	65078	81	82	2406	17.0	20.4	48.0	12.6	2.0	108087
43620	TOLEDO	17584	2903	52.4	20.2	21.3	4.2	2.0	22901	25277	2	2	762	22.4	37.7	32.0	7.7	0.1	79178
43623	TOLEDO	31684	8643	20.6	25.6	35.3	10.8	7.6	53994	54988	70	64	5940	4.0	30.8	48.1	14.8	2.2	105446
43701	SOUTH ZANESVILLE	21413	22302	29.5	28.4	33.8	5.4	3.0	41408	44657	37	24	15426	19.5	29.0	40.6	10.0	1.0	92147
43713	BARNESVILLE	18040	2848	38.5	27.0	28.8	4.2	1.5	34373	37979	16	9	2144	26.4	37.1	30.6	5.3	0.7	74236
43716	BEALLSVILLE	18197	814	34.3	28.1	31.9	4.8	0.9	36917	39377	23	14	673	29.1	37.6	29.3	4.0	0.0	73712
43718	BELMONT	20858	1332	24.9	30.3	36.9	5.7	2.3	44236	48132	46	32	1090	24.7	26.6	36.5	9.8	2.4	87846
43719	BETHESDA	19336	1009	29.1	34.6	30.4	4.0	1.9	37064	39268	24	14	773	22.8	33.9	37.0	5.7	0.6	82077
43720	BLUE ROCK	19361	559	22.0	34.0	35.2	6.6	2.1	43965	46388	45	31	475	20.6	28.2	39.2	12.0	0.0	91146
43723	BYESVILLE	17584	2053	33.4	36.9	24.8	3.8	1.0	36526	38471	22	13	1378	27.3	45.0	24.2	3.6	0.0	67610
43724	CALDWELL	18185	2670	30.8	32.1	31.4	4.0	1.6	39435	41121	31	20	1998	25.8	33.7	34.0	5.8	0.7	78276
43725	CAMBRIDGE	20036	8621	34.0	29.5	29.2	5.3	2.0	36802	39325	23	13	5758	19.4	38.5	33.3	7.6	1.3	82335
43727	CHANDLERSVILLE	20243	535	15.9	33.5	43.4	6.7	0.6	50340	50326	62	51	466	13.3	24.9	47.0	14.4	0.4	102308
43728	CHESTERHILL	17362	538	32.3	31.8	29.2	5.6	1.1	36756	38908	23	13	441	35.1	32.2	29.3	3.2	0.2	67400
43730	CORNING	17912	1099	28.4	32.8	32.5	4.6	1.6	39970	42469	32	21	936	34.6	32.8	28.8	3.7	0.0	66092
43731	CROOKSVILLE	17939	1940	29.3	32.7	32.5	3.8	1.7	38703	41417	29	18	1545	26.1	44.1	24.5	5.1	0.3	69972
43732	CUMBERLAND	20630	693	21.8	36.7	34.2	5.3	2.0	43819	47669	45	30	582	24.6	29.2	40.4	5.3	0.5	85849
43734	DUNCAN FALLS	21134	430	22.6	38.6	29.3	7.2	2.3	41160	43076	37	23	359	10.0	25.3	45.4	19.2	0.0	118611
43739	GLENFORD	23448	778	15.2	27.6	45.6	6.0	5.5	55180	55053	71	67	659	13.4	22.2	40.1	20.8	3.6	114919
43746	HOPEWELL	21022	412	13.1	26.5	52.9	5.1	2.4	55149	53154	71	67	346	16.5	20.2	35.5	27.2	0.6	112500
43747	JERUSALEM	18314	480	32.3	29.4	31.3	6.5	0.6	40000	41831	33	21	417	26.1	33.1	34.5	5.5	0.7	80128
43748	JUNCTION CITY	18643	1022	23.3	32.6	38.1	4.6	1.5	44418	45710	47	32	815	24.5	29.8	36.6	8.6	0.5	85920
43749	KIMBOLTON	18341	991	29.2	32.7	32.0	4.8	1.3	38515	42058	28	18	841	20.2	24.1	43.4	10.7	1.5	97661
43754	LEWISVILLE	16713	523	30.4	38.2	28.3	2.5	0.6	34814	36585	17	9	426	26.1	37.1	27.0	9.4	0.5	77234
43755	LORE CITY	18773	808	29.7	32.7	31.8	4.3	1.5	39443	42303	31	20	670	20.3	33.0	37.6	8.8	0.3	87067
43756	MC CONNELSVILLE	19308	2194	35.1	29.9	29.2	4.6	1.3	37197	38557	24	15	1539	18.6	32.5	41.7	6.7	0.5	88813
43758	MALTA	16349	1414	37.0	31.4	27.7	3.3	0.7	34338	35588	16	9	1122	25.8	38.0	27.8	7.4	1.1	74505
43760	MOUNT PERRY	20015	716	18.3	35.2	38.3	4.7	3.5	45769	47336	51	35	612	18.1	22.4	38.7	17.5	3.3	102368
43762	NEW CONCORD	19961	1641	28.1	25.5	36.7	7.4	2.3	46142	48406	52	36	1211	10.6	27.7	46.1	14.5	1.2	103466
43764	NEW LEXINGTON	17803	3170	29.4	30.9	34.7	3.5	1.5	40126	42993	33	21	2306	22.3	37.3	34.9	4.6	1.0	80558
43766	NEW STRAITSVILLE	16790	674	32.2	35.0	28.5	3.6	0.7	35074	37009	18	10	542	53.5	25.6	18.3	2.6	0.0	47324
43767	NORWICH	19980	560	16.8	31.8	45.4	4.3	1.8	50996	51022	64	53	487	13.6	20.5	42.1	22.4	1.4	108059
43771	PHILO	19439	663	25.8	30.2	37.1	4.4	2.6	43090	45828	43	28	568	26.1	36.3	31.7	6.0	0.0	79167
43772	PLEASANT CITY	17143	720	30.3	36.0	29.4	4.2	0.1	38140	39899	27	17	614	28.8	42.2	24.9	3.7	0.3	65055
43773	QUAKER CITY	15759	1213	30.8	34.0	30.8	3.1	1.2	37241	39503	24	15	1011	29.8	28.8	28.9	11.9	0.7	78879
43777	ROSEVILLE	16605	1833	32.7	32.2	29.9	3.4	1.7	36750	39334	23	13	1413	30.4	40.1	24.1	4.8	0.6	67599
43778	SALESVILLE	15290	488	27.9	34.4	32.2	4.5	1.0	40743	44117	35	23	412	24.3	32.8	32.8	10.2	0.0	81944
43779	SARAHSVILLE	18140	341	24.0	31.1	38.1	6.2	0.6	45929	48123	51	36	294	34.7	29.3	28.9	6.5	0.7	65882
43780	SENECAVILLE	18868	1188	34.6	30.1	27.3	5.6	2.4	36721	38619	23	13	990	27.1	32.9	26.8	12.5	0.7	74194
43782	SHAWNEE	16366	336	25.3	36.0	34.2	4.2	0.3	40823	42522	35	23	286	46.5	33.2	19.2	1.0	0.0	52778
43783	SOMERSET	19127	1673	24.3	32.9	35.3	6.2	1.3	42543	45026	41	27	1324	12.1	21.8	47.5	16.5	2.1	112226
43787	STOCKPORT	16877	1049	36.1	33.0	27.0	2.4	1.5	32281	33123	12	8	858	37.1	26.5	28.6	7.5	0.5	70000
43788	SUMMERFIELD	15727	313	26.5	34.5	36.4	1.6	1.0	39471	41779	31	20	261	44.4	31.8	16.1	7.7	0.0	54677
43793	WOODSFIELD	18721	1971	34.9	31.4	28.1	4.1	1.6	35063	37216	18	10	1466	27.4	38.5	29.4	4.4	0.3	72406
43802	ADAMSVILLE	18394	424	20.8	29.2	40.3	8.0	1.7	50000	50262	61	49	365	22.7	26.6	39.5	11.2	0.0	91190
43804	BALTIC	13510	792	22.5	36.9	36.2	3.4	1.0	42583	45387	41	27	612	11.1	20.6	45.4	19.4	3.4	114583
43811	CONESVILLE	21084	314	26.1	32.2	33.4	6.7	1.6	42183	46071	40	26	264	32.6	29.2	32.6	5.7	0.0	80313
43812	COSHOCTON	21344	8126	28.0	30.7	33.3	6.3	1.8	40628	44269	35	22	5652	21.5	31.2	37.7	8.9	0.6	86616
43821	DRESDEN	22836	1758	21.2	27.0	41.5	7.7	2.7	51239	50762	64	54	1386	15.9	26.0	47.0	9.6	1.4	98682
43822	FRAZEYSBURG	22295	1712	17.0	28.9	45.7	6.3	2.2	52308	52428	67	59	1368	17.7	21.9	43.0	15.8	1.6	104063
43824	FRESNO	17107	1361	24.1	30.6	34.9	8.9	1.5	45799	48040	51	35	1147	13.1	26.2	35.4	21.8	3.6	109215
	OHIO	26577		21.4	25.9	36.7	10.4	5.7	52400	54553				10.3	22.0	45.6	19.3	2.8	114865
	UNITED STATES	27277		20.9	24.4	35.3	11.7	7.6	54719	56938				9.3	13.1	31.6	32.6	13.5	162279

ZIP CODE		FINANCIAL SERVICES				THE HOME						ENTERTAINMENT						PERSONAL			
						Home Improvements		Furnishings													
#	POST OFFICE NAME	Auto Loan	Home Loan	Invest-ments	Retire-ment Plans	Home Repair	Lawn & Garden	Comput-ers & Hard-ware-Personal	Major Appli-ances	TV, Radio, Sound Equip-ment	Furni-ture	Dine out/ Carry out	Sports Equip-ment	Fees & Tickets	Toys & Games	Travel	Cable TV	Apparel & Services	Auto Repairs	Health Insur-ance	Pets & Supplies
43522	GRAND RAPIDS	107	113	99	115	110	112	103	107	103	105	103	82	106	106	105	104	72	104	106	127
43524	HAMLER	88	80	79	83	81	94	79	89	81	71	80	67	73	83	79	86	54	82	92	103
43525	HASKINS	109	123	106	127	120	121	110	114	108	110	109	89	117	111	116	108	76	110	113	135
43526	HICKSVILLE	90	82	79	84	81	95	81	88	84	75	82	68	75	86	79	88	56	84	92	105
43527	HOLGATE	86	84	73	86	81	92	83	86	85	77	84	67	81	86	82	88	57	84	92	102
43528	HOLLAND	128	136	128	138	134	131	127	129	125	131	126	100	132	128	130	124	89	126	125	150
43532	LIBERTY CENTER	89	82	81	86	84	96	81	91	83	74	82	69	75	85	81	88	56	84	93	105
43533	LYONS	82	75	74	78	76	88	74	83	76	67	75	63	68	77	74	80	51	77	86	97
43534	MC CLURE	89	84	81	87	85	96	81	90	83	75	82	69	77	85	82	87	56	84	93	105
43535	MALINTA	87	79	78	82	81	93	78	88	81	71	79	67	72	82	78	85	54	81	91	102
43536	MARK CENTER	92	84	83	87	86	99	83	94	85	75	84	71	76	87	83	90	57	86	96	109
43537	MAUMEE	109	122	116	124	121	118	114	114	113	116	114	87	123	113	120	112	80	114	115	134
43540	METAMORA	89	81	80	84	83	96	80	90	83	72	81	68	74	84	80	87	55	83	93	105
43542	MONCLOVA	138	160	145	160	156	147	139	144	134	144	136	111	150	139	146	132	96	137	134	166
43543	MONTPELIER	77	71	66	73	70	80	73	76	75	68	74	58	69	76	70	79	51	74	82	90
43545	NAPOLEON	90	85	82	86	84	94	84	89	86	80	85	68	80	87	83	89	59	86	93	105
43548	NEW BAVARIA	88	81	80	84	83	95	79	89	82	72	80	68	74	83	80	87	55	83	92	104
43549	NEY	89	81	81	85	83	96	80	91	83	73	81	69	74	84	80	88	56	84	93	105
43551	PERRYSBURG	123	132	121	133	129	125	124	123	122	128	123	96	130	125	126	120	87	122	121	144
43554	PIONEER	84	76	75	79	78	90	75	85	78	68	76	64	69	79	75	82	52	78	87	99
43556	SHERWOOD	94	77	81	78	78	95	78	89	83	73	81	68	68	85	75	89	55	83	93	105
43557	STRYKER	84	80	74	83	79	90	79	85	81	73	80	65	75	83	78	85	55	81	89	100
43558	SWANTON	98	104	93	105	101	107	95	101	96	94	96	77	98	98	99	98	66	97	102	118
43560	SYLVANIA	128	149	142	152	149	142	135	136	132	139	133	105	149	133	144	131	95	134	136	158
43566	WATERVILLE	112	136	124	137	133	127	118	120	114	122	116	93	132	117	128	113	83	117	117	139
43567	WAUSEON	88	84	76	85	83	88	82	86	83	80	83	65	78	86	80	85	57	83	87	101
43569	WESTON	96	93	81	92	90	96	88	92	90	88	90	69	86	93	86	93	62	89	94	109
43570	WEST UNITY	89	74	75	74	73	90	75	83	80	71	78	64	66	82	71	85	53	79	88	100
43571	WHITEHOUSE	119	134	116	137	130	130	119	124	117	120	118	97	127	120	126	117	82	119	121	145
43604	TOLEDO	36	25	26	28	25	30	38	31	42	35	41	25	33	39	32	44	29	38	40	41
43605	TOLEDO	62	51	44	52	48	57	61	56	64	56	62	44	54	64	53	67	43	60	63	69
43606	TOLEDO	89	84	82	87	83	87	96	86	94	91	94	68	91	93	88	95	66	92	92	104
43607	TOLEDO	60	49	48	50	48	57	58	55	62	55	60	41	52	60	52	65	42	59	63	68
43608	TOLEDO	58	49	43	50	45	54	54	52	58	53	58	40	51	58	49	61	40	55	59	65
43609	TOLEDO	63	56	47	57	52	59	66	58	67	60	67	47	61	67	58	69	47	63	65	72
43610	TOLEDO	62	55	46	57	51	60	59	56	63	59	63	43	57	63	54	66	43	60	64	71
43611	TOLEDO	81	82	70	83	78	86	83	81	85	79	84	63	83	86	81	88	59	83	89	97
43612	TOLEDO	80	75	64	77	71	80	80	76	82	76	81	60	77	83	75	84	56	79	84	93
43613	TOLEDO	82	82	71	83	78	86	83	81	85	80	85	63	83	86	81	88	59	83	90	97
43614	TOLEDO	86	84	80	86	83	86	89	85	90	88	91	65	90	89	88	91	63	89	92	101
43615	TOLEDO	91	85	78	87	83	86	91	86	91	90	91	67	88	92	86	91	63	90	89	103
43616	OREGON	90	93	87	94	91	96	91	92	93	90	93	69	94	93	92	95	65	92	98	108
43617	TOLEDO	145	164	159	167	165	160	143	152	141	149	142	115	156	144	153	141	101	144	146	175
43618	OREGON	108	112	103	116	112	118	104	112	104	101	104	86	106	106	108	107	72	106	113	130
43619	NORTHWOOD	98	99	84	100	94	99	97	96	97	95	97	75	97	99	96	98	67	96	99	114
43620	TOLEDO	53	41	39	44	40	45	55	47	58	51	58	37	49	56	48	61	40	54	55	60
43623	TOLEDO	96	101	97	102	100	105	100	100	103	99	102	75	104	100	102	106	71	102	110	118
43701	SOUTH ZANESVILLE	79	70	69	71	69	80	74	76	77	70	76	58	69	78	71	81	52	76	83	91
43713	BARNESVILLE	74	55	72	54	56	77	59	71	65	53	63	53	48	64	56	71	42	67	77	84
43716	BEALLSVILLE	81	59	79	57	61	81	60	75	67	57	66	56	49	67	59	73	44	69	78	89
43718	BELMONT	89	70	86	68	71	90	71	85	77	67	75	63	60	77	69	83	50	79	88	100
43719	BETHESDA	78	59	76	58	61	81	62	76	69	56	66	57	52	68	61	75	44	70	81	89
43720	BLUE ROCK	89	67	82	66	68	89	69	82	75	65	74	62	57	77	66	82	49	77	86	98
43723	BYESVILLE	69	56	57	55	55	66	61	64	64	58	63	49	53	65	56	67	43	64	68	76
43724	CALDWELL	79	62	73	61	63	81	63	75	69	58	67	57	54	69	61	74	45	70	79	89
43725	CAMBRIDGE	72	62	63	62	62	72	66	69	70	63	69	52	60	70	63	74	47	69	75	83
43727	CHANDLERSVILLE	87	75	82	77	77	92	74	86	78	68	76	65	67	79	74	83	52	79	88	101
43728	CHESTERHILL	79	56	69	55	57	76	58	70	65	56	64	53	47	67	54	71	43	65	73	84
43730	CORNING	84	62	70	60	61	80	64	74	70	62	69	57	52	73	59	76	46	70	78	89
43731	CROOKSVILLE	82	60	72	59	60	80	62	74	69	59	67	56	51	70	58	75	45	69	78	89
43732	CUMBERLAND	87	75	79	77	76	91	74	86	78	68	76	65	66	79	73	83	52	79	88	100
43734	DUNCAN FALLS	72	76	73	75	76	85	69	77	73	67	73	56	72	73	73	78	50	73	85	89
43739	GLENFORD	100	101	89	101	99	102	93	98	94	94	94	74	93	97	94	96	65	94	98	116
43746	HOPEWELL	90	87	82	91	88	97	83	91	85	78	84	70	81	87	85	88	58	86	93	107
43747	JERUSALEM	84	60	83	58	62	84	62	77	69	58	67	58	50	69	60	75	45	71	81	92
43748	JUNCTION CITY	96	70	80	69	70	92	73	84	80	71	79	65	59	84	67	87	53	80	89	102
43749	KIMBOLTON	84	60	86	58	62	85	61	78	68	57	67	59	49	68	61	75	44	72	81	93
43754	LEWISVILLE	74	53	75	51	55	76	56	70	62	51	60	52	45	61	55	68	40	65	74	83
43755	LORE CITY	84	60	86	58	62	85	61	78	68	57	67	59	49	68	61	75	44	72	81	93
43756	MC CONNELSVILLE	74	57	73	57	59	77	60	72	65	54	63	54	50	65	58	71	42	67	76	85
43758	MALTA	70	51	68	50	52	70	55	66	60	50	59	49	44	60	52	66	39	62	70	78
43760	MOUNT PERRY	89	85	78	85	84	90	80	87	82	79	82	65	77	85	79	85	56	83	88	102
43762	NEW CONCORD	85	73	76	74	75	86	76	82	79	73	78	61	69	80	73	83	53	80	87	97
43764	NEW LEXINGTON	73	62	60	62	60	72	65	68	68	61	67	53	58	70	60	72	46	67	73	82
43766	NEW STRAITSVILLE	78	53	72	50	52	76	56	68	63	53	62	53	43	65	52	70	41	64	72	84
43767	NORWICH	90	79	80	81	80	94	78	89	82	72	80	67	71	83	77	87	55	82	92	104
43771	PHILO	96	69	79	67	68	91	72	83	79	70	78	64	57	83	65	87	52	79	88	101
43772	PLEASANT CITY	76	55	76	53	56	78	58	72	65	53	63	54	47	64	57	71	42	67	78	85
43773	QUAKER CITY	79	57	73	55	58	78	59	72	66	56	65	55	48	67	56	72	43	67	76	86
43777	ROSEVILLE	77	58	63	57	57	74	62	69	67	59	66	53	51	69	56	72	44	66	73	83
43778	SALESVILLE	83	60	78	58	61	82	62	76	68	59	67	57	49	70	59	75	45	70	79	91
43779	SARAHSVILLE	91	65	87	63	67	90	67	83	74	63	73	63	54	75	65	82	49	77	87	99
43780	SENECAVILLE	83	59	85	58	62	84	61	78	68	57	67	58	49	67	60	74	44	71	81	92
43782	SHAWNEE	84	60	69	59	60	80	63	73	70	61	68	56	50	73	57	76	46	69	77	89
43783	SOMERSET	81	69	76	70	70	85	70	80	74	65	72	60	63	74	69	79	49	75	84	94
43787	STOCKPORT	71	53	69	53	55	73	55	68	60	51	59	51	46	61	54	66	39	62	71	80
43788	SUMMERFIELD	84	60	73	58	60	81	62	74	69	60	68	56	50	71	58	75	45	69	78	89
43793	WOODSFIELD	75	58	72	56	59	77	59	71	65	56	64	53	50	65	58	71	43	66	76	84
43802	ADAMSVILLE	99	74	83	73	74	96	76	88	83	73	82	68	63	87	70	91	55	83	93	107
43804	BALTIC	86	61	80	60	62	85	65	77	70	59	69	61	51	72	61	77	46	73	82	95
43811	CONESVILLE	87	68	74	68	69	87	70	80	75	66	74	61	59	78	66	81	50	75	84	96
43812	COSHOCTON	75	67	67	67	66	78	69	73	73	65	72	55	65	73	67	77	49	72	80	87
43821	DRESDEN	93	82	83	83	82	97	82	91	86	76	84	69	75	87	80	91	57	86	96	107
43822	FRAZEYSBURG	94	83	79	81	82	91	80	88	84	80	83	65	73	87	77	88	57	84	89	104
43824	FRESNO	88	72	76	74	73	90	73	84	78	68	76	64	64	80	70	83	52	78	87	99
	OHIO	94	92	87	93	90	96	93	93	94	91	94	72	92	95	91	96	66	93	98	110
	UNITED STATES	100	100	100	100	100	100	100	100	100	100	100	100	100	100	100	100	100	100	100	100

ZIP CODE #	POST OFFICE NAME	COUNTY FIPS CODE	POPULATION 2000	POPULATION 2009	POPULATION 2014	2000-2009 ANNUAL RATE % Rate	2000-2009 ANNUAL RATE State Centile	HOUSEHOLDS 2000	HOUSEHOLDS 2009	HOUSEHOLDS 2014	HOUSEHOLDS % Annual Rate 2000-2009	HOUSEHOLDS 2009 Average HH Size	FAMILIES 2000	FAMILIES 2009	FAMILIES % Annual Rate 2000-2009
43830	NASHPORT	119	5144	5575	5744	0.9	85	1860	2031	2100	1.0	2.74	1481	1581	0.7
43832	NEWCOMERSTOWN	157	7560	7541	7503	0.0	45	2973	2984	2976	0.0	2.50	2106	2061	-0.2
43837	PORT WASHINGTON	157	1897	1932	1937	0.2	56	701	718	723	0.3	2.69	555	558	0.1
43840	STONE CREEK	157	1165	1211	1226	0.4	66	427	448	455	0.5	2.65	340	350	0.3
43843	WALHONDING	031	923	1025	1060	1.1	89	349	394	408	1.3	2.58	270	298	1.1
43844	WARSAW	031	3948	4105	4095	0.4	66	1459	1561	1570	0.7	2.62	1103	1149	0.4
43845	WEST LAFAYETTE	031	4567	4410	4315	-0.4	21	1797	1780	1751	-0.1	2.41	1290	1239	-0.4
43901	ADENA	081	2340	2337	2305	0.0	45	945	973	971	0.3	2.37	676	677	0.0
43902	ALLEDONIA	013	281	274	270	-0.3	27	111	111	111	0.0	2.47	79	77	-0.3
43903	AMSTERDAM	019	2172	2110	2054	-0.3	27	891	890	875	0.0	2.37	643	627	-0.3
43906	BELLAIRE	013	10157	9573	9355	-0.6	14	4187	4020	3955	-0.4	2.36	2839	2650	-0.7
43907	CADIZ	067	5865	5615	5502	-0.5	17	2401	2366	2340	-0.2	2.32	1652	1584	-0.5
43908	BERGHOLZ	081	1746	1692	1643	-0.3	27	673	672	660	0.0	2.48	487	474	-0.3
43910	BLOOMINGDALE	081	3406	3290	3202	-0.4	21	1330	1335	1314	0.0	2.46	1023	1004	-0.2
43912	BRIDGEPORT	013	7323	7006	6875	-0.5	17	3244	3185	3150	-0.2	2.16	2053	1948	-0.6
43913	BRILLIANT	081	1246	1150	1098	-0.9	7	541	519	501	-0.4	2.22	360	333	-0.8
43915	CLARINGTON	111	2040	2059	2037	0.1	51	828	865	865	0.5	2.38	613	626	0.2
43917	DILLONVALE	081	4303	4109	3966	-0.5	17	1746	1709	1665	-0.2	2.36	1248	1189	-0.5
43920	EAST LIVERPOOL	029	25653	24531	23949	-0.5	17	10330	9966	9766	-0.4	2.43	7103	6669	-0.7
43930	HAMMONDSVILLE	081	1084	1102	1090	0.2	56	403	419	419	0.4	2.63	303	308	0.2
43932	IRONDALE	081	796	793	776	0.0	45	310	319	315	0.3	2.49	234	235	0.0
43933	JACOBSBURG	013	1987	1994	1982	0.0	45	767	791	794	0.3	2.52	599	605	0.1
43935	MARTINS FERRY	013	9351	8601	8355	-0.9	7	4042	3784	3695	-0.7	2.25	2577	2348	-1.0
43938	MINGO JUNCTION	081	6518	5993	5709	-0.9	7	2696	2562	2467	-0.5	2.34	1887	1741	-0.9
43942	POWHATAN POINT	013	2685	2529	2472	-0.6	14	1147	1111	1096	-0.3	2.28	803	754	-0.7
43943	RAYLAND	081	4456	4203	4048	-0.6	14	1806	1763	1715	-0.3	2.38	1317	1252	-0.5
43944	RICHMOND	081	2642	2607	2556	-0.1	39	1052	1079	1068	0.3	2.42	804	804	0.0
43945	SALINEVILLE	029	3352	3316	3267	-0.1	39	1279	1287	1275	0.1	2.56	934	915	-0.2
43946	SARDIS	111	2183	2041	1973	-0.7	11	899	874	854	-0.3	2.34	655	620	-0.6
43947	SHADYSIDE	013	5192	4934	4833	-0.5	17	2254	2178	2145	-0.4	2.21	1463	1370	-0.7
43950	SAINT CLAIRSVILLE	013	15638	16018	15985	0.3	61	5599	5812	5846	0.4	2.29	3886	3921	0.1
43952	STEUBENVILLE	081	20591	18521	17634	-1.1	4	8438	7748	7414	-0.9	2.17	5041	4456	-1.3
43953	STEUBENVILLE	081	11763	11126	10702	-0.6	14	5019	4913	4773	-0.2	2.20	3485	3310	-0.6
43963	TILTONSVILLE	081	1296	1250	1214	-0.4	21	596	589	578	-0.1	2.12	390	372	-0.5
43964	TORONTO	081	11167	10428	9970	-0.7	11	4592	4433	4280	-0.4	2.35	3197	3001	-0.7
43968	WELLSVILLE	029	7702	7362	7186	-0.5	17	3092	2986	2925	-0.4	2.46	2198	2068	-0.7
43971	YORKVILLE	081	1306	1164	1109	-1.2	3	567	516	494	-1.0	2.21	361	317	-1.4
43973	FREEPORT	067	1966	2112	2147	0.8	82	759	842	864	1.1	2.51	552	596	0.8
43976	HOPEDALE	067	1555	1545	1533	-0.1	39	600	612	614	0.2	2.46	453	452	0.0
43977	FLUSHING	013	2575	2784	2815	0.8	82	1041	1155	1177	1.1	2.41	742	800	0.8
43983	PIEDMONT	013	502	545	553	0.9	85	210	234	239	1.2	2.33	155	168	0.9
43986	JEWETT	067	2152	2164	2155	0.1	51	806	832	837	0.3	2.54	590	594	0.1
43988	SCIO	067	2476	2433	2408	-0.2	32	1060	1080	1080	0.2	2.25	735	728	-0.1
44001	AMHERST	093	20467	21131	21445	0.3	61	7632	8012	8186	0.5	2.61	5825	5959	0.2
44003	ANDOVER	007	4363	4663	4676	0.7	79	1578	1716	1733	0.9	2.57	1149	1218	0.6
44004	ASHTABULA	007	35882	34831	34067	-0.3	27	14534	14428	14213	-0.1	2.38	9753	9387	-0.4
44010	AUSTINBURG	007	1829	1771	1733	-0.3	27	686	683	674	0.0	2.53	528	515	-0.3
44011	AVON	093	11446	17882	20647	4.9	99	4088	6577	7682	5.3	2.67	3144	4931	5.0
44012	AVON LAKE	093	18145	22227	24029	2.2	97	6711	8375	9125	2.4	2.65	5134	6181	2.0
44017	BEREA	035	19052	18441	17938	-0.4	21	7199	7052	6867	-0.2	2.31	4484	4252	-0.6
44021	BURTON	055	7726	8204	8450	0.7	79	2589	2810	2918	0.9	2.89	2005	2134	0.7
44022	CHAGRIN FALLS	035	17076	16768	16378	-0.2	32	6608	6563	6435	-0.1	2.54	5000	4873	-0.3
44023	CHAGRIN FALLS	055	14741	16957	17785	1.5	94	5145	6045	6392	1.8	2.80	4212	4876	1.6
44024	CHARDON	055	22452	23469	23867	0.5	71	8111	8650	8857	0.7	2.65	6171	6449	0.5
44026	CHESTERLAND	055	11860	11848	11774	0.0	45	4290	4401	4410	0.3	2.67	3482	3514	0.1
44028	COLUMBIA STATION	093	8492	8938	9143	0.6	75	2938	3171	3276	0.8	2.70	2408	2548	0.6
44030	CONNEAUT	007	16192	15797	15470	-0.3	27	6405	6398	6314	0.0	2.44	4485	4369	-0.3
44032	DORSET	007	1700	1721	1705	0.1	51	593	617	617	0.4	2.79	455	463	0.2
44035	ELYRIA	093	64911	65465	65836	0.1	51	25902	26705	27054	0.3	2.42	17460	17485	0.0
44039	NORTH RIDGEVILLE	093	22461	28053	30608	2.4	98	8405	10726	11786	2.7	2.60	6472	8127	2.5
44040	GATES MILLS	035	3345	3346	3268	0.0	45	1239	1259	1237	0.2	2.64	997	993	0.0
44041	GENEVA	007	15014	14723	14437	-0.2	32	5812	5827	5757	0.0	2.43	3932	3827	-0.3
44044	GRAFTON	093	15578	16341	16817	0.5	71	4157	4484	4687	0.8	2.87	3417	3612	0.6
44046	HUNTSBURG	055	1691	1870	1956	1.1	89	488	545	572	1.2	3.38	417	459	1.0
44047	JEFFERSON	007	9632	9679	9568	0.1	51	3504	3615	3604	0.3	2.60	2655	2675	0.1
44048	KINGSVILLE	007	2554	2647	2634	0.4	66	880	926	928	0.6	2.69	689	709	0.3
44050	LAGRANGE	093	6060	6782	7149	1.2	91	2039	2329	2476	1.4	2.91	1710	1918	1.2
44052	LORAIN	093	33700	33414	33489	-0.1	39	13045	13189	13321	0.1	2.51	8773	8534	-0.3
44053	LORAIN	093	16727	17923	18466	0.7	79	7068	7720	8012	1.0	2.28	4565	4798	0.5
44054	SHEFFIELD LAKE	093	12271	13192	13636	0.8	82	4550	4965	5170	0.9	2.66	3408	3616	0.6
44055	LORAIN	093	22624	22144	22021	-0.2	32	8044	8017	8029	0.0	2.74	5843	5641	-0.4
44056	MACEDONIA	153	9269	11255	11925	2.1	97	3290	4105	4388	2.4	2.74	2663	3211	2.0
44057	MADISON	085	19213	20330	20842	0.6	75	7067	7689	7953	0.9	2.59	5269	5583	0.6
44060	MENTOR	085	63512	64141	64560	0.1	51	24015	24887	25267	0.4	2.55	17862	18093	0.1
44062	MIDDLEFIELD	055	13698	15022	15506	1.0	87	3792	4245	4422	1.2	3.49	2961	3245	1.0
44064	MONTVILLE	055	1932	2010	2033	0.4	66	688	735	750	0.7	2.71	564	592	0.5
44065	NEWBURY	055	4539	4774	4894	0.5	71	1641	1771	1828	0.8	2.66	1262	1335	0.6
44067	NORTHFIELD	153	17945	19538	20044	0.9	85	7245	8136	8424	1.3	2.36	5096	5543	0.9
44070	NORTH OLMSTED	035	34066	32242	31012	-0.6	14	13485	13065	12655	-0.3	2.45	9355	8820	-0.6
44072	NOVELTY	055	4400	4417	4401	0.0	45	1649	1700	1707	0.3	2.59	1344	1361	0.1
44074	OBERLIN	093	12236	12517	12636	0.2	56	4176	4340	4415	0.4	2.41	2585	2597	0.1
44076	ORWELL	007	4395	4774	4808	0.9	85	1565	1724	1746	1.1	2.74	1168	1256	0.8
44077	PAINESVILLE	085	50769	54762	56443	0.8	82	19343	21295	22115	1.0	2.53	13622	14703	0.8
44081	PERRY	085	6519	7259	7575	1.2	91	2242	2540	2667	1.4	2.84	1784	1980	1.1
44082	PIERPONT	007	1487	1533	1525	0.3	61	503	526	526	0.5	2.91	392	401	0.2
44084	ROCK CREEK	007	3639	3822	3823	0.5	71	1302	1410	1423	0.9	2.69	1009	1069	0.6
44085	ROME	007	2931	3212	3241	1.0	87	1048	1176	1196	1.3	2.70	803	881	1.0
44086	THOMPSON	055	2627	2786	2882	0.6	75	936	1020	1063	0.9	2.73	726	775	0.7
44087	TWINSBURG	153	18612	20584	21146	1.1	89	7217	8085	8361	1.2	2.53	5173	5619	0.9
44089	VERMILION	043	15959	16485	16591	0.4	66	6173	6555	6651	0.7	2.49	4587	4742	0.4
44090	WELLINGTON	093	10800	12008	12580	1.2	91	3878	4405	4653	1.4	2.69	2963	3277	1.1
44092	WICKLIFFE	085	17550	17414	17408	-0.1	39	7560	7676	7729	0.2	2.23	4862	4761	-0.2
44093	WILLIAMSFIELD	007	1478	1496	1480	0.1	51	530	550	548	0.4	2.72	403	408	0.1
44094	WILLOUGHBY	085	34240	35448	35982	0.4	66	14899	15794	16170	0.6	2.21	9191	9391	0.2
44095	EASTLAKE	085	35556	35331	35311	-0.1	39	14531	14839	14972	0.2	2.38	9934	9837	-0.1
	OHIO					0.2					0.4	2.44			0.1
	UNITED STATES					1.0					1.1	2.59			0.9

ZIP CODE #	POST OFFICE NAME	RACE (%) White 2000	White 2009	Black 2000	Black 2009	Asian/Pacific 2000	Asian/Pacific 2009	% Hispanic Origin 2000	% Hispanic Origin 2009	2009 AGE DISTRIBUTION (%) 0-4	5-9	10-14	15-19	20-24	25-44	45-64	65-84	85+	18+	MEDIAN AGE 2009	% 2009 Males	% 2009 Females
43830	NASHPORT	97.8	97.2	1.0	1.3	0.1	0.2	0.8	1.0	7.6	7.3	7.4	7.0	5.3	26.6	28.8	9.1	1.0	73.4	37.3	50.1	49.9
43832	NEWCOMERSTOWN	97.2	96.7	1.5	1.7	0.1	0.1	0.5	0.6	6.6	6.7	6.7	6.6	5.8	23.7	28.6	12.9	2.4	76.0	40.1	49.3	50.7
43837	PORT WASHINGTON	98.7	98.5	0.2	0.2	0.0	0.0	0.5	0.7	6.3	6.6	7.0	6.6	4.8	25.1	30.0	12.5	1.1	76.0	40.7	50.0	50.0
43840	STONE CREEK	99.5	99.3	0.1	0.1	0.0	0.1	0.5	0.7	6.1	6.8	7.3	6.6	4.1	24.7	29.9	12.0	2.6	75.6	41.0	49.0	51.0
43843	WALHONDING	98.3	97.9	0.5	0.7	0.1	0.2	0.4	0.4	6.4	6.5	6.9	7.6	6.0	26.1	29.5	9.9	1.1	75.4	38.1	51.6	48.4
43844	WARSAW	97.8	97.4	0.9	1.1	0.1	0.1	0.5	0.6	6.3	6.5	6.6	6.7	5.7	25.8	29.5	11.4	1.5	76.4	40.0	50.7	49.3
43845	WEST LAFAYETTE	98.4	98.0	0.2	0.2	0.0	0.1	0.6	0.8	6.0	6.1	6.2	6.3	5.3	25.0	28.5	14.4	2.2	78.0	41.3	48.5	51.5
43901	ADENA	98.5	98.0	0.6	0.8	0.3	0.4	0.2	0.3	4.8	5.0	5.3	5.5	4.9	22.6	32.4	16.3	3.2	81.6	46.2	49.1	50.9
43902	ALLEDONIA	96.1	94.9	0.4	0.4	1.4	2.2	0.7	0.7	5.1	5.1	5.8	6.2	4.7	23.4	34.3	13.9	1.5	79.9	44.7	51.1	48.9
43903	AMSTERDAM	99.0	98.9	0.1	0.1	0.1	0.1	0.4	0.4	6.3	6.4	6.7	6.4	5.0	23.7	29.8	13.6	2.0	76.6	41.7	49.8	50.2
43906	BELLAIRE	95.5	94.9	3.2	3.4	0.2	0.2	0.2	0.3	5.1	5.5	5.8	6.2	5.6	22.9	30.2	15.6	3.1	79.8	44.1	47.6	52.4
43907	CADIZ	92.2	90.8	5.5	6.4	0.3	0.3	0.3	0.4	5.5	5.7	6.0	5.8	4.8	22.6	30.0	16.1	3.5	79.1	44.6	47.6	52.4
43908	BERGHOLZ	98.7	98.3	0.2	0.4	0.3	0.5	0.1	0.2	5.5	5.7	6.0	6.1	5.2	25.2	30.7	13.7	1.8	79.2	42.3	49.9	50.1
43910	BLOOMINGDALE	97.8	97.2	1.1	1.4	0.3	0.5	0.4	0.4	4.4	5.3	5.7	6.4	4.3	23.7	34.7	13.7	1.8	80.4	45.1	49.9	50.1
43912	BRIDGEPORT	95.2	94.6	3.6	4.0	0.1	0.2	0.4	0.5	4.8	5.0	5.3	5.8	5.0	22.9	29.5	17.8	3.8	81.2	45.8	46.5	53.5
43913	BRILLIANT	98.6	98.3	0.2	0.3	0.0	0.0	0.2	0.2	5.1	5.5	5.6	5.5	4.9	25.0	28.7	17.1	2.6	80.5	43.8	47.1	52.9
43915	CLARINGTON	99.0	98.8	0.4	0.4	0.0	0.0	0.2	0.3	4.7	5.6	6.1	6.6	4.6	24.5	30.3	15.1	2.4	79.3	43.5	49.5	50.5
43917	DILLONVALE	96.4	95.7	2.2	2.7	0.1	0.1	0.2	0.3	5.0	5.2	5.6	5.9	4.8	22.3	30.7	17.0	3.5	80.6	45.8	48.7	51.3
43920	EAST LIVERPOOL	95.3	94.4	2.8	3.2	0.3	0.5	0.6	0.8	6.3	6.3	6.3	6.5	5.9	23.6	27.9	14.7	2.6	77.2	41.0	47.6	52.4
43930	HAMMONDSVILLE	96.8	95.9	2.1	2.7	0.1	0.1	0.7	1.1	5.3	5.6	5.8	6.2	5.4	24.9	30.9	14.4	1.6	79.6	43.0	50.7	49.3
43932	IRONDALE	97.6	96.8	1.3	1.5	0.1	0.3	0.4	0.6	5.4	5.8	6.3	6.3	4.9	24.2	31.1	14.2	1.6	78.7	42.9	50.6	49.4
43933	JACOBSBURG	99.2	99.0	0.1	0.1	0.1	0.2	0.4	0.5	5.3	6.1	6.3	5.6	4.5	24.5	33.6	12.6	1.7	79.0	43.1	49.9	50.1
43935	MARTINS FERRY	94.1	93.4	4.2	4.7	0.1	0.2	0.6	0.8	5.3	5.1	5.3	5.9	5.5	22.4	30.6	16.5	3.4	80.7	45.3	47.0	53.0
43938	MINGO JUNCTION	96.0	95.0	2.4	3.1	0.1	0.1	0.6	0.8	5.1	5.1	5.6	6.1	5.4	22.6	30.2	17.1	2.7	80.5	45.0	47.6	52.4
43942	POWHATAN POINT	98.4	98.1	0.4	0.5	0.0	0.0	0.1	0.2	5.5	5.8	6.1	5.5	4.4	24.3	30.1	15.9	2.5	79.4	43.7	48.9	51.1
43943	RAYLAND	97.5	97.0	1.3	1.6	0.0	0.1	0.3	0.4	4.2	4.6	5.1	6.2	4.7	23.2	32.9	16.5	2.5	82.4	46.2	48.9	51.1
43944	RICHMOND	98.4	97.9	0.5	0.6	0.5	0.7	0.4	0.5	4.8	5.3	5.8	5.9	4.3	22.5	33.8	15.8	1.8	80.3	45.8	49.8	50.2
43945	SALINEVILLE	98.4	98.2	0.7	0.8	0.0	0.0	0.7	0.8	6.3	6.5	7.2	7.5	5.3	25.6	27.9	12.2	1.4	75.1	39.2	50.2	49.8
43946	SARDIS	98.8	98.7	0.5	0.5	0.0	0.0	0.2	0.3	4.8	5.1	5.3	5.5	4.6	23.0	31.7	17.8	2.0	81.3	46.0	48.6	51.4
43947	SHADYSIDE	99.4	99.3	0.1	0.1	0.0	0.1	0.2	0.2	4.5	5.0	5.4	5.9	4.8	22.5	30.2	17.2	4.5	81.4	46.3	46.8	53.2
43950	SAINT CLAIRSVILLE	89.0	87.0	9.1	10.4	0.9	1.4	0.5	0.6	3.7	4.1	4.6	5.6	7.7	27.3	28.9	15.0	3.1	84.0	42.8	55.3	44.7
43952	STEUBENVILLE	81.2	75.5	15.8	20.7	0.5	1.0	1.1	1.3	5.0	5.0	5.1	6.9	7.8	23.8	26.9	16.0	3.6	81.4	42.1	48.5	51.5
43953	STEUBENVILLE	94.6	93.0	3.6	4.5	0.7	1.2	0.6	0.8	4.7	4.8	5.2	5.4	4.7	21.3	31.4	18.8	3.7	82.1	47.8	48.0	52.0
43963	TILTONSVILLE	98.8	98.5	0.2	0.2	0.1	0.1	0.2	0.4	4.6	4.7	5.2	5.6	4.6	23.0	30.2	17.5	4.6	82.2	46.8	45.0	55.0
43964	TORONTO	97.8	97.2	0.9	1.1	0.2	0.4	0.5	0.7	5.6	5.9	6.0	5.9	5.2	24.0	30.8	14.6	2.0	78.9	42.9	48.1	51.9
43968	WELLSVILLE	93.8	92.7	4.3	5.1	0.1	0.2	0.5	0.6	6.4	6.6	6.4	6.2	5.6	24.5	29.2	13.4	1.8	76.7	40.3	48.7	51.3
43971	YORKVILLE	98.1	97.6	1.1	1.4	0.1	0.2	0.4	0.5	4.6	4.6	5.0	5.8	5.8	24.3	28.8	16.5	4.5	82.0	44.8	48.7	51.3
43973	FREEPORT	98.1	97.8	0.3	0.3	0.1	0.0	0.5	0.7	5.9	6.3	7.1	7.2	4.7	23.4	29.5	14.4	1.5	76.4	41.5	48.9	51.1
43976	HOPEDALE	98.9	98.6	0.5	0.7	0.0	0.0	0.2	0.3	5.0	5.4	5.9	6.3	4.7	22.5	31.1	16.2	2.9	79.5	45.2	49.3	50.7
43977	FLUSHING	98.0	97.6	0.8	0.9	0.1	0.1	0.4	0.5	4.9	5.4	5.8	5.8	4.6	24.7	32.0	14.6	2.0	80.2	44.0	50.3	49.7
43983	PIEDMONT	98.0	97.6	0.6	0.7	0.0	0.0	0.4	0.6	5.3	5.7	6.1	5.5	4.4	23.3	32.3	15.8	1.7	79.6	44.8	50.3	49.7
43986	JEWETT	98.7	98.4	0.6	0.7	0.0	0.0	0.4	0.5	6.1	6.1	6.8	7.2	5.3	23.3	28.3	14.1	2.8	76.1	41.6	50.0	50.0
43988	SCIO	99.4	99.2	0.1	0.2	0.0	0.0	0.6	0.7	5.3	5.9	6.2	5.6	4.2	22.4	32.5	15.5	2.5	79.1	45.3	49.4	50.6
44001	AMHERST	96.5	95.0	0.7	1.0	0.6	0.9	3.1	4.9	5.6	6.4	7.0	7.0	4.6	23.8	30.5	12.9	2.1	76.4	41.9	48.7	51.3
44003	ANDOVER	96.9	96.2	2.0	2.4	0.1	0.2	0.5	0.7	5.9	6.0	6.3	6.6	5.3	24.6	29.5	13.9	1.9	77.5	41.7	49.6	50.4
44004	ASHTABULA	89.4	87.5	6.5	7.4	0.5	0.7	3.7	4.8	6.8	6.5	6.5	6.5	6.0	24.4	27.0	13.8	2.6	76.3	39.7	47.7	52.3
44010	AUSTINBURG	97.9	97.3	0.5	0.6	0.4	0.6	0.5	0.8	5.7	6.2	6.4	6.1	4.7	23.7	32.6	12.7	2.0	77.8	43.2	49.9	50.1
44011	AVON	97.0	95.7	0.7	1.0	1.0	1.6	1.3	2.0	7.4	8.2	8.8	6.9	3.5	23.0	29.9	10.5	1.8	70.7	40.5	48.3	51.7
44012	AVON LAKE	97.3	96.0	0.5	0.7	1.0	1.6	1.2	2.0	6.8	7.8	7.9	7.0	4.0	23.9	30.0	11.0	1.6	72.9	40.7	48.8	51.2
44017	BEREA	91.5	87.1	5.1	8.2	0.9	1.5	1.6	2.2	4.9	4.9	5.6	9.5	11.1	22.5	26.1	12.7	2.8	81.0	38.3	47.4	52.6
44021	BURTON	97.8	97.3	0.7	0.8	0.3	0.4	0.8	1.0	6.9	7.4	8.1	7.9	5.2	24.0	28.3	10.4	1.8	72.5	38.0	50.0	50.0
44022	CHAGRIN FALLS	94.2	91.4	3.2	4.8	1.7	2.8	0.7	1.0	5.2	6.5	7.8	7.1	4.3	17.4	34.2	15.0	2.5	75.6	45.9	48.8	51.2
44023	CHAGRIN FALLS	95.0	94.4	3.3	3.4	0.5	0.8	0.6	0.8	6.0	7.2	8.4	7.7	4.0	19.2	34.7	11.4	1.3	73.2	43.2	49.1	50.9
44024	CHARDON	98.0	97.4	0.7	0.8	0.4	0.7	0.4	0.6	5.8	6.5	7.1	6.7	4.5	22.7	32.0	12.5	2.2	76.4	42.7	49.0	51.0
44026	CHESTERLAND	98.1	97.5	0.6	0.8	0.6	0.9	0.8	1.0	4.7	5.5	6.7	7.3	3.8	20.2	33.6	16.2	2.1	78.0	46.0	49.3	50.7
44028	COLUMBIA STATION	96.3	95.1	2.2	2.7	0.4	0.6	1.3	1.9	5.0	6.2	6.8	6.4	4.8	26.1	32.2	11.0	1.5	77.9	41.7	52.4	47.6
44030	CONNEAUT	96.7	95.9	1.0	1.2	0.5	0.7	1.0	1.4	6.3	6.3	6.4	6.9	5.8	24.6	28.0	13.1	2.5	76.8	40.4	48.8	51.2
44032	DORSET	97.5	96.8	1.4	1.6	0.2	0.3	0.2	0.3	6.7	6.8	7.1	7.1	5.8	24.9	28.6	11.9	1.2	75.1	39.2	49.9	50.1
44035	ELYRIA	83.2	79.5	12.5	15.0	0.6	0.9	2.7	3.9	7.3	6.9	6.6	6.5	6.0	26.6	26.4	11.7	2.0	75.2	37.7	48.4	51.6
44039	NORTH RIDGEVILLE	96.4	94.9	0.9	1.1	0.9	1.5	2.0	3.0	6.2	6.5	6.8	6.3	4.7	25.6	30.2	12.3	1.5	76.7	41.2	49.1	50.9
44040	GATES MILLS	94.7	91.7	0.7	1.2	3.3	5.5	1.3	1.8	4.2	5.0	6.2	6.4	4.2	16.9	35.1	19.2	2.9	80.1	49.4	48.9	51.1
44041	GENEVA	95.9	94.9	0.9	1.1	0.3	0.4	3.9	5.1	6.0	6.0	5.9	6.2	6.4	25.6	28.5	13.3	2.2	78.4	40.7	48.9	51.1
44044	GRAFTON	85.5	81.9	12.8	15.8	0.3	0.5	1.5	2.1	4.5	5.2	5.6	6.0	6.6	32.8	28.8	9.4	1.0	81.3	38.9	60.4	39.6
44046	HUNTSBURG	97.9	97.5	1.2	1.5	0.1	0.1	0.4	0.5	9.8	10.0	9.9	8.0	4.2	24.8	24.3	7.5	1.5	65.1	32.8	49.0	51.0
44047	JEFFERSON	96.5	95.7	2.1	2.5	0.2	0.3	0.7	0.9	5.9	6.3	6.7	7.0	5.7	24.9	29.4	11.8	2.6	77.0	40.5	49.2	50.8
44048	KINGSVILLE	98.1	97.7	0.7	0.9	0.2	0.2	0.5	0.6	5.3	5.6	6.0	6.5	4.8	21.1	31.0	16.0	3.8	79.0	45.4	48.2	51.8
44050	LAGRANGE	98.4	97.7	0.2	0.3	0.2	0.3	0.9	1.4	7.0	7.4	7.7	7.5	4.9	25.7	30.2	8.7	0.9	73.2	38.1	49.8	50.2
44052	LORAIN	69.2	63.5	18.8	21.2	0.3	0.4	16.7	22.0	8.4	7.8	7.1	7.4	7.0	25.9	23.8	10.5	2.0	72.2	34.2	47.4	52.6
44053	LORAIN	82.7	76.9	9.0	11.5	0.7	1.0	10.5	15.0	6.6	6.3	6.2	6.0	5.3	26.1	25.7	14.9	2.8	77.3	39.8	47.0	53.0
44054	SHEFFIELD LAKE	95.3	93.1	1.7	2.5	0.4	0.7	3.7	6.0	6.6	6.8	6.9	6.6	5.4	26.5	29.6	10.6	1.1	75.7	38.8	48.4	51.6
44055	LORAIN	63.4	58.1	15.4	16.3	0.2	0.3	33.8	41.0	8.4	7.9	7.7	8.2	7.5	26.0	22.4	10.4	1.6	71.1	32.5	47.9	52.1
44056	MACEDONIA	90.1	84.8	6.9	10.8	1.8	2.9	0.7	1.0	6.1	6.6	7.4	6.9	4.0	25.2	32.4	10.5	0.9	75.4	41.4	49.4	50.6
44057	MADISON	98.1	97.6	0.4	0.4	0.3	0.5	1.1	1.6	6.4	6.6	6.9	6.9	5.1	26.6	28.8	11.2	1.5	75.5	39.7	49.6	50.4
44060	MENTOR	97.3	96.2	0.7	0.8	1.1	1.9	0.8	1.0	5.7	6.3	6.9	6.7	4.8	24.4	30.9	12.4	2.0	76.7	41.9	48.3	51.7
44062	MIDDLEFIELD	98.3	97.9	0.8	1.0	0.1	0.2	0.4	0.6	11.1	10.9	10.1	9.1	6.8	24.0	18.9	7.6	1.6	62.3	26.6	49.2	50.8
44064	MONTVILLE	97.8	97.1	1.1	1.3	0.5	0.8	0.3	0.3	6.6	7.0	7.5	6.7	4.0	25.9	30.4	10.4	1.6	74.7	40.8	51.7	48.3
44065	NEWBURY	97.6	96.9	1.0	1.3	0.4	0.8	0.6	0.7	6.4	7.2	7.8	6.6	4.0	21.8	31.3	12.7	2.1	74.3	42.4	48.8	51.2
44067	NORTHFIELD	95.0	92.7	2.6	3.8	1.2	2.0	0.8	1.1	6.2	6.4	6.4	5.6	3.7	27.1	28.8	14.0	1.8	77.5	42.1	48.4	51.6
44070	NORTH OLMSTED	94.0	90.8	1.0	1.7	2.8	4.6	1.7	2.4	5.4	5.5	6.0	6.5	5.5	24.2	29.9	14.6	2.3	79.1	42.7	48.4	51.6
44072	NOVELTY	96.9	95.8	1.2	1.4	1.0	1.6	1.0	1.2	4.6	5.6	6.7	6.2	3.6	17.6	35.1	18.5	2.2	79.2	48.7	48.5	51.5
44074	OBERLIN	78.7	73.4	13.9	17.0	2.5	3.6	2.7	3.7	4.0	4.2	4.5	12.9	15.6	19.8	24.1	11.9	3.0	84.2	33.3	46.2	53.8
44076	ORWELL	95.9	94.7	2.1	2.6	0.2	0.3	0.9	1.4	8.2	8.2	8.3	7.6	5.4	26.1	24.8	10.0	1.5	70.6	34.5	49.8	50.2
44077	PAINESVILLE	90.3	88.9	5.1	5.4	0.5	0.9	5.0	6.0	7.1	6.9	6.8	6.5	5.5	26.2	28.2	11.0	1.7	75.2	38.6	49.2	50.8
44081	PERRY	98.4	97.9	0.4	0.4	0.3	0.4	0.9	1.2	5.1	6.5	7.7	8.2	4.8	24.2	31.9	10.3	1.2	75.1	40.8	50.1	49.9
44082	PIERPONT	98.3	97.8	0.5	0.6	0.3	0.5	1.1	1.5	7.7	7.4	7.9	7.8	6.4	23.7	26.4	11.0	1.6	72.1	36.8	49.8	50.2
44084	ROCK CREEK	97.0	96.3	1.5	1.8	0.3	0.4	0.7	0.9	6.0	6.3	7.8	6.5	4.1	26.9	30.6	10.7	1.1	75.7	40.5	50.1	49.9
44085	ROME	97.5	97.0	1.4	1.6	0.1	0.2	0.5	0.7	6.8	7.0	7.3	6.7	4.8	26.8	28.3	10.8	1.5	74.7	39.2	51.1	48.9
44086	THOMPSON	98.4	98.0	0.5	0.6	0.2	0.3	0.5	0.6	6.3	6.7	7.4	6.9	3.9	26.8	30.1	10.6	1.2	75.2	40.4	50.9	49.1
44087	TWINSBURG	82.5	77.5	13.3	16.4	2.7	4.4	1.0	1.3	7.8	8.0	7.3	6.6	4.4	27.8	26.5	10.1	1.6	72.7	38.1	47.8	52.2
44089	VERMILION	98.3	97.7	0.2	0.2	0.2	0.3	1.6	2.4	5.7	5.8	6.2	6.4	5.3	23.9	31.1	13.7	1.9	78.3	42.5	48.9	51.1
44090	WELLINGTON	97.8	97.0	0.9	1.2	0.2	0.4	0.9	1.5	6.4	6.7	7.0	7.1	5.1	25.4	29.3	11.2	1.8	75.4	39.7	49.8	50.2
44092	WICKLIFFE	92.5	90.3	4.5	5.3	1.9	3.1	0.6	0.8	5.0	5.0	5.2	5.9	5.7	24.5	27.8	17.5	3.3	81.3	44.0	48.3	51.7
44093	WILLIAMSFIELD	97.4	96.9	1.5	1.7	0.0	0.0	0.1	0.1	7.2	7.0	7.2	7.2	5.9	25.4	26.8	12.0	1.4	74.3	38.1	51.8	48.2
44094	WILLOUGHBY	96.6	95.3	1.2	1.5	1.1	1.9	0.7	0.9	5.4	5.2	5.5	5.7	5.6	24.5	28.6	15.8	3.8	80.3	43.6	46.9	53.1
44095	EASTLAKE	97.7	96.8	0.6	0.7	0.8	1.3	0.7	1.0	5.5	5.6	5.9	6.1	5.2	25.9	28.9	14.7	2.2	79.2	42.2	48.3	51.7
	OHIO	85.0	83.1	11.5	12.2	1.2	1.9	1.9	2.4	6.6	6.5	6.6	7.1	6.7	25.9	26.9	11.7	2.1	76.2	38.2	48.7	51.3
	UNITED STATES	75.1	72.0	12.3	12.7	3.8	4.6	12.5	15.7	6.8	6.7	6.6	7.1	6.9	27.0	26.0	10.9	1.9	75.7	36.9	49.2	50.8

INCOME

#	POST OFFICE NAME	2009 Per Capita Income	2009 HH Income Base	2009 Household Income Distribution (%): Less than $25,000	$25,000 to $49,999	$50,000 to $99,999	$100,000 to $149,999	$150,000 or More	Median Household Income: 2009	2014	2009 National Centile	2009 State Centile	2009 Home Value Base	2009 Home Value Distribution (%): Less than $50,000	$50,000 to $89,999	$90,000 to $174,999	$175,000 to $399,999	$400,000 or More	2009 Median Home Value
43830	NASHPORT	25758	2031	15.4	23.6	44.7	10.9	5.3	58052	56826	75	75	1605	8.9	14.1	51.5	22.2	3.2	124732
43832	NEWCOMERSTOWN	18823	2984	31.2	31.2	31.4	4.4	1.8	40527	44470	34	22	2241	25.9	38.2	28.1	7.3	0.4	74080
43837	PORT WASHINGTON	17427	718	22.7	39.0	32.7	4.2	1.4	42012	45226	39	26	586	22.9	31.4	32.1	12.8	0.9	84186
43840	STONE CREEK	17828	448	20.8	39.3	35.0	4.0	0.9	44758	46985	48	33	368	11.1	28.0	39.9	18.2	2.7	106349
43843	WALHONDING	20941	394	21.3	29.4	42.4	4.8	2.0	49220	50544	59	46	328	21.6	25.9	34.1	15.2	3.0	95333
43844	WARSAW	19736	1561	21.9	33.0	39.1	4.4	1.7	45354	47457	49	34	1291	27.2	25.9	36.5	9.4	1.0	85235
43845	WEST LAFAYETTE	20484	1780	23.2	34.0	35.8	6.4	0.6	43653	46301	44	30	1426	25.4	39.3	31.6	3.7	0.0	79295
43901	ADENA	20994	973	29.0	33.7	28.4	6.9	2.1	37841	40514	26	16	814	38.0	36.0	21.6	4.2	0.2	60921
43902	ALLEDONIA	17370	111	36.9	29.7	27.0	6.3	0.0	36937	40454	23	14	96	32.3	24.0	39.6	4.2	0.0	8[illegible]429
43903	AMSTERDAM	18675	890	32.9	30.2	32.5	3.4	1.0	38656	41520	29	18	721	38.0	27.7	28.2	5.8	0.3	65566
43906	BELLAIRE	17104	4020	41.5	30.4	23.8	2.9	1.4	29254	31238	7	5	2747	25.2	40.2	29.6	4.5	0.5	73188
43907	CADIZ	21607	2366	33.1	29.2	29.2	5.6	2.9	36712	38516	23	13	1718	23.5	43.0	28.9	4.1	0.5	74468
43908	BERGHOLZ	19527	672	26.3	34.2	33.5	4.2	1.8	39698	43517	32	20	559	34.9	30.9	29.9	4.3	0.0	66742
43910	BLOOMINGDALE	21176	1335	23.2	30.3	39.8	5.1	1.6	46886	49944	54	39	1173	19.6	35.3	36.1	8.9	0.2	85248
43912	BRIDGEPORT	20516	3185	36.7	30.7	26.4	4.8	1.4	35307	37380	19	10	2325	31.7	41.2	24.3	2.8	0.0	67391
43913	BRILLIANT	17964	519	34.9	32.2	30.4	2.3	0.2	34069	36152	16	8	349	35.8	48.1	15.5	0.6	0.0	60091
43915	CLARINGTON	19311	865	32.9	27.5	34.5	4.5	0.6	39467	42234	31	20	721	32.3	34.8	30.2	2.1	0.6	66266
43917	DILLONVALE	20400	1709	32.5	31.0	27.6	6.8	2.1	37030	39502	24	14	1437	40.9	34.6	20.5	3.5	0.5	57373
43920	EAST LIVERPOOL	18446	9966	35.0	30.8	27.3	5.0	1.9	34852	37449	17	10	6970	31.1	32.8	29.6	6.1	0.5	71180
43930	HAMMONDSVILLE	19543	419	27.0	33.2	32.5	5.7	1.7	41050	44868	36	23	359	36.8	25.3	27.3	10.6	0.0	72037
43932	IRONDALE	20838	319	25.7	30.7	36.4	6.3	0.9	44561	47427	47	32	274	38.7	25.2	28.5	7.3	0.4	67727
43933	JACOBSBURG	18653	791	26.7	36.3	30.8	5.4	0.8	40982	43837	36	23	699	19.7	40.6	31.8	6.9	1.0	76736
43935	MARTINS FERRY	19408	3784	40.4	28.0	25.6	4.3	1.7	30996	32877	10	6	2527	23.9	48.0	24.1	4.0	0.0	68750
43938	MINGO JUNCTION	19251	2562	34.7	29.7	30.0	3.7	1.9	35498	37755	19	11	1925	28.3	44.1	25.2	2.4	0.0	66578
43942	POWHATAN POINT	19772	1111	34.7	30.4	27.5	6.0	1.4	35644	38058	20	11	849	25.1	42.6	29.3	2.8	0.1	74158
43943	RAYLAND	20070	1763	30.5	30.2	32.6	5.3	1.5	38963	42516	30	19	1495	31.7	41.3	23.6	3.1	0.2	67630
43944	RICHMOND	19594	1079	27.2	31.2	35.2	5.4	1.0	42756	46619	42	28	941	17.1	35.6	37.7	9.5	0.1	87548
43945	SALINEVILLE	18897	1287	28.1	35.5	29.3	5.3	1.8	38170	40208	27	17	1019	34.7	31.7	26.0	7.5	0.1	66835
43946	SARDIS	21494	874	25.9	33.5	34.1	4.7	1.8	42888	45955	42	28	726	26.0	28.4	39.5	5.9	0.1	84182
43947	SHADYSIDE	20365	2178	32.5	32.0	29.8	4.4	1.4	39207	42827	30	19	1612	17.6	42.2	36.7	3.5	0.0	82476
43950	SAINT CLAIRSVILLE	22828	5812	25.2	29.7	35.0	6.8	3.1	45000	48528	48	33	4462	12.8	21.2	46.1	18.0	1.8	114001
43952	STEUBENVILLE	20067	7748	40.2	27.0	25.2	5.2	2.4	32041	34815	11	7	4712	22.4	40.3	32.2	4.7	0.4	75597
43953	STEUBENVILLE	25260	4913	23.4	30.7	34.8	7.6	3.6	44991	49129	48	33	3620	11.9	34.1	45.6	7.0	1.4	93712
43963	TILTONSVILLE	19928	589	35.5	32.9	26.3	3.6	1.7	35398	37157	19	11	405	27.4	52.6	19.8	0.0	0.2	68188
43964	TORONTO	19376	4433	31.6	29.6	33.3	5.0	0.5	40093	44531	33	21	3421	29.2	34.3	32.2	3.9	0.3	74167
43968	WELLSVILLE	18384	2986	31.3	32.9	29.4	5.3	1.1	38407	41383	28	17	2225	33.5	37.3	24.9	4.2	0.0	67326
43971	YORKVILLE	19695	516	34.3	30.2	30.6	3.5	1.4	36588	38364	22	13	331	24.5	56.2	17.2	2.1	0.0	67329
43973	FREEPORT	18941	842	34.6	32.3	25.1	5.7	2.4	36315	37689	21	12	680	24.9	34.1	33.2	7.6	0.1	78030
43976	HOPEDALE	22324	612	27.5	30.4	34.3	5.1	2.8	43218	46544	43	28	503	21.3	45.9	27.2	4.6	1.0	75081
43977	FLUSHING	19355	1155	32.5	34.5	26.3	4.4	2.3	35851	37776	20	12	937	28.3	39.1	26.7	3.5	2.5	68659
43983	PIEDMONT	20136	234	32.5	32.1	29.1	4.7	1.7	37473	40187	25	15	199	29.1	32.2	31.2	6.0	1.5	71923
43986	JEWETT	17759	832	29.9	33.4	31.3	4.1	1.3	38147	39505	27	17	643	27.8	42.5	23.8	4.8	1.1	67722
43988	SCIO	22172	1080	30.1	35.6	27.8	4.0	2.5	38416	39043	28	17	850	22.0	41.9	29.2	6.0	0.9	76860
44001	AMHERST	29150	8012	12.9	22.2	43.7	14.9	6.3	65286	66280	84	86	6901	13.3	6.9	52.5	26.0	1.2	139928
44003	ANDOVER	19450	1716	30.0	26.3	35.5	6.0	2.2	39787	44087	32	20	1340	19.3	33.4	37.3	9.4	0.5	86864
44004	ASHTABULA	21074	14428	29.7	28.5	33.0	6.4	2.4	40596	44339	35	22	9819	15.7	35.6	39.8	8.2	0.7	88680
44010	AUSTINBURG	24252	683	13.6	26.8	49.9	6.6	3.1	54555	54580	71	65	574	8.7	14.1	50.9	24.0	2.3	131566
44011	AVON	34948	6577	8.0	18.4	38.3	22.9	12.3	78460	79361	91	95	5713	1.3	2.5	42.7	49.6	4.0	183863
44012	AVON LAKE	41500	8375	9.5	15.7	38.0	18.0	18.8	80078	79647	92	96	7113	0.6	6.5	39.3	45.1	8.5	184[illegible]22
44017	BEREA	27014	7052	16.6	27.3	39.8	10.6	5.6	55132	56450	71	67	4943	0.5	12.6	79.8	6.7	0.4	117322
44021	BURTON	27186	2810	14.2	22.1	40.5	15.7	7.5	67415	70098	85	88	2256	6.5	14.7	42.8	31.4	4.6	150619
44022	CHAGRIN FALLS	60548	6563	8.3	13.1	26.7	17.4	34.5	104398	108929	97	99	5745	0.5	2.4	17.5	52.7	26.9	271500
44023	CHAGRIN FALLS	48966	6045	6.9	12.8	27.4	25.0	27.9	105251	111184	97	99	5564	1.1	2.4	23.1	58.6	14.8	233875
44024	CHARDON	32480	8650	11.0	21.1	38.5	18.8	10.6	71586	75838	88	92	7262	11.9	3.5	34.4	44.8	5.4	175634
44026	CHESTERLAND	38187	4401	5.9	15.3	40.3	23.1	15.3	83443	92852	93	97	4089	4.5	2.0	37.1	46.7	9.7	187619
44028	COLUMBIA STATION	29897	3171	8.2	21.2	44.0	19.4	7.3	68875	68801	86	89	2834	0.7	6.7	49.0	39.4	4.3	163526
44030	CONNEAUT	20000	6398	27.5	30.7	34.7	5.8	1.2	42094	45927	40	26	4687	15.8	35.3	39.3	8.9	0.7	88756
44032	DORSET	19099	617	15.6	39.1	37.6	7.0	0.8	45737	48467	50	35	514	9.3	24.3	50.8	11.9	3.7	109036
44035	ELYRIA	24652	26705	20.9	28.8	38.3	8.4	3.6	50184	53081	62	50	17752	10.2	21.3	57.7	10.1	0.6	108123
44039	NORTH RIDGEVILLE	29271	10726	9.9	21.1	46.2	17.6	5.1	69142	69371	86	90	9471	4.5	6.1	68.1	20.6	0.7	138451
44040	GATES MILLS	66623	1259	3.7	13.2	22.9	18.9	41.3	125644	127453	99	100	1157	0.3	0.0	12.5	40.7	46.4	374848
44041	GENEVA	22555	5827	22.9	29.5	38.0	6.3	3.3	46766	50116	53	38	4163	15.2	19.7	47.5	16.6	1.0	109868
44044	GRAFTON	24556	4484	10.5	20.8	44.4	18.6	5.7	69654	70147	87	90	3954	1.7	8.6	57.2	29.9	2.7	149469
44046	HUNTSBURG	23621	545	11.7	21.3	41.8	20.9	4.2	70396	75952	87	90	483	2.9	6.4	54.0	31.1	5.6	155804
44047	JEFFERSON	22220	3615	19.8	29.4	39.3	8.8	2.7	50548	51574	62	51	2776	8.9	18.9	52.9	17.8	1.5	120231
44048	KINGSVILLE	21363	926	19.5	31.6	37.5	7.8	3.6	48562	50349	58	44	772	9.7	17.1	57.6	15.3	0.3	116813
44050	LAGRANGE	25541	2329	10.4	20.3	48.2	17.3	3.8	67450	69140	85	88	2009	2.1	11.7	56.2	28.7	1.3	146071
44052	LORAIN	19633	13189	32.0	28.8	31.2	5.6	2.4	39948	42733	32	21	7654	9.8	39.5	46.3	4.0	0.4	90461
44053	LORAIN	26093	7720	22.4	27.2	36.1	10.4	3.9	50323	53411	62	51	4632	5.6	9.7	68.6	15.4	0.7	123858
44054	SHEFFIELD LAKE	26970	4965	11.8	22.7	47.2	13.3	5.0	63199	64997	81	82	4010	1.7	15.2	65.1	16.8	1.2	119222
44055	LORAIN	17409	8017	31.2	29.8	32.6	4.9	1.5	39528	42024	31	20	4880	12.5	51.6	34.3	1.4	0.2	80935
44056	MACEDONIA	34756	4105	7.7	14.3	41.8	24.1	12.0	81230	81366	93	97	3832	1.4	2.3	59.1	35.8	1.4	160551
44057	MADISON	25163	7689	14.0	25.2	47.5	10.3	3.1	58781	61174	76	76	6308	14.5	12.6	56.0	16.0	0.8	118330
44060	MENTOR	31814	24887	9.1	20.6	44.7	17.3	8.3	70521	75144	87	91	20955	2.9	4.9	54.1	36.3	1.7	157655
44062	MIDDLEFIELD	17015	4245	19.5	32.5	35.8	8.8	3.4	48190	50401	57	42	3119	8.5	11.5	58.7	19.4	1.9	126210
44064	MONTVILLE	29050	735	8.7	20.5	52.0	13.3	5.4	75207	77187	89	93	658	5.6	7.3	59.9	22.2	5.0	146196
44065	NEWBURY	34086	1771	8.6	22.0	40.0	18.5	10.9	73506	76465	89	92	1490	6.7	10.0	37.4	39.9	5.9	166927
44067	NORTHFIELD	37067	8136	9.3	18.3	41.3	18.9	12.1	75209	74877	89	93	6926	0.4	8.6	53.3	36.8	0.9	152856
44070	NORTH OLMSTED	29995	13065	12.4	21.9	44.9	14.9	5.9	63509	63660	82	83	10224	2.1	9.0	72.9	15.9	0.1	139272
44072	NOVELTY	58273	1700	5.6	17.1	31.2	15.6	30.5	90220	103225	95	98	1561	0.1	2.2	29.0	44.4	24.3	231883
44074	OBERLIN	25306	4340	22.3	22.2	38.2	12.4	4.9	55469	59558	72	68	2715	2.1	12.3	52.9	30.6	2.2	147077
44076	ORWELL	19230	1724	24.7	27.7	39.5	5.9	2.3	46060	50158	51	36	1314	16.1	16.8	48.5	16.2	2.4	112639
44077	PAINESVILLE	28175	21295	16.3	23.6	40.7	13.5	5.8	60426	63430	78	78	15733	4.1	14.6	50.1	28.6	2.6	141046
44081	PERRY	26976	2540	12.6	19.6	46.5	15.7	5.6	69698	74793	87	90	2228	6.6	4.7	53.0	34.6	1.1	158676
44082	PIERPONT	18050	526	19.8	33.3	40.1	5.1	1.7	43915	50096	45	31	442	17.2	26.0	44.8	11.5	0.5	95660
44084	ROCK CREEK	24150	1410	16.7	24.9	43.1	11.3	4.0	57295	57342	74	74	1237	4.6	13.1	53.1	28.2	1.0	140728
44085	ROME	23387	1176	17.4	25.5	42.5	11.0	3.6	55656	56338	72	69	982	4.6	13.7	58.1	21.4	2.1	124249
44086	THOMPSON	25818	1020	10.1	28.3	46.2	13.8	1.6	62483	62434	81	81	927	21.1	12.2	42.7	22.1	1.8	126997
44087	TWINSBURG	35491	8085	12.9	15.9	36.8	22.5	12.0	76892	75650	91	95	6145	0.7	6.3	47.6	44.4	1.0	166955
44089	VERMILION	28672	6555	13.4	24.8	43.3	13.7	4.9	62283	63473	80	81	5131	6.6	14.5	54.3	22.7	1.8	124655
44090	WELLINGTON	25653	4405	14.8	23.6	44.7	13.0	3.9	59032	60970	76	77	3427	4.6	8.4	55.7	29.2	2.2	144052
44092	WICKLIFFE	28445	7676	16.9	28.3	41.0	10.0	3.9	54746	57867	71	66	5638	2.9	8.7	67.6	18.9	1.9	134467
44093	WILLIAMSFIELD	16699	550	31.3	24.4	40.0	4.0	0.4	43945	47658	45	31	446	15.2	31.8	46.9	6.1	0.0	94333
44094	WILLOUGHBY	32112	15794	15.2	26.5	40.4	11.2	6.7	57002	59546	74	73	10017	6.5	5.7	48.5	33.5	5.8	157850
44095	EASTLAKE	26847	14839	15.4	27.7	44.3	9.5	3.1	56069	58941	73	70	11829	2.3	10.0	78.6	8.8	0.2	123102
	OHIO	26577		21.4	25.9	36.7	10.4	5.7	52400	54553				10.3	22.0	45.6	19.3	2.8	114865
	UNITED STATES	27277		20.9	24.4	35.3	11.7	7.6	54719	56938				9.3	13.1	31.6	32.6	13.5	162279

ZIP CODE		FINANCIAL SERVICES				THE HOME						ENTERTAINMENT						PERSONAL			
						Home Improvements		Furnishings													
#	POST OFFICE NAME	Auto Loan	Home Loan	Invest-ments	Retire-ment Plans	Home Repair	Lawn & Garden	Comput-ers & Hard-ware-Personal	Major Appli-ances	TV, Radio, Sound Equip-ment	Furni-ture	Dine out/ Carry out	Sports Equip-ment	Fees & Tickets	Toys & Games	Travel	Cable TV	Apparel & Services	Auto Repairs	Health Insur-ance	Pets & Supplies
43830	NASHPORT	103	106	96	106	104	108	99	104	100	98	100	79	100	102	100	102	69	100	104	122
43832	NEWCOMERSTOWN	78	60	71	60	61	79	65	74	70	59	68	56	54	70	61	76	46	71	79	88
43837	PORT WASHINGTON	77	64	71	65	65	80	64	75	68	59	67	57	56	69	63	73	45	69	77	88
43840	STONE CREEK	76	66	70	67	67	80	65	75	68	59	67	57	59	69	65	73	45	69	78	88
43843	WALHONDING	92	75	76	73	74	87	74	82	80	75	79	62	65	83	69	84	53	79	85	99
43844	WARSAW	87	70	74	70	70	86	71	81	76	68	75	61	61	78	67	81	50	76	84	96
43845	WEST LAFAYETTE	77	68	70	70	68	82	69	77	72	63	71	59	63	73	68	76	48	73	82	90
43901	ADENA	83	63	85	61	65	88	66	81	73	60	71	60	55	72	65	81	48	76	88	95
43902	ALLEDONIA	77	55	79	53	57	78	56	72	62	52	61	54	45	62	56	69	41	66	75	85
43903	AMSTERDAM	77	56	77	55	58	79	59	73	65	54	63	55	48	64	58	71	42	67	77	86
43906	BELLAIRE	61	52	56	52	52	64	54	60	60	52	58	44	50	59	53	65	40	59	67	71
43907	CADIZ	87	63	88	61	65	90	67	83	74	60	72	62	54	73	65	82	48	77	89	98
43908	BERGHOLZ	87	63	81	61	64	86	65	79	72	62	70	60	52	73	62	79	47	74	83	95
43910	BLOOMINGDALE	79	73	80	73	74	88	70	81	75	66	74	60	67	74	72	80	50	76	87	94
43912	BRIDGEPORT	72	55	72	54	57	76	60	71	66	54	64	53	50	65	58	72	43	67	78	83
43913	BRILLIANT	67	48	67	47	50	70	53	65	59	47	57	49	42	58	51	65	38	61	71	77
43915	CLARINGTON	71	64	74	62	65	79	61	71	66	58	65	52	58	65	63	72	44	67	78	84
43917	DILLONVALE	79	61	80	60	63	84	64	78	71	59	69	57	55	70	64	78	46	73	86	91
43920	EAST LIVERPOOL	69	58	61	58	58	71	62	67	67	58	65	50	56	66	59	71	44	66	74	79
43930	HAMMONDSVILLE	91	66	93	64	68	93	68	86	75	63	74	64	55	75	67	82	49	79	89	102
43932	IRONDALE	93	66	95	64	69	94	68	86	75	63	74	65	54	75	67	83	49	79	90	103
43933	JACOBSBURG	82	62	80	60	64	83	63	77	68	59	67	57	52	69	61	74	45	71	79	91
43935	MARTINS FERRY	67	54	66	54	55	71	59	66	65	54	63	49	52	63	58	70	43	65	75	78
43938	MINGO JUNCTION	71	57	71	56	59	75	60	70	66	55	64	52	53	65	59	72	44	67	78	82
43942	POWHATAN POINT	77	57	72	55	58	78	60	72	67	56	65	54	49	67	57	73	43	68	78	86
43943	RAYLAND	77	63	80	62	65	83	63	76	69	59	68	56	56	68	64	76	46	71	83	90
43944	RICHMOND	79	63	79	63	65	83	63	77	68	59	67	57	55	68	63	74	45	71	80	90
43945	SALINEVILLE	87	62	79	60	63	85	65	78	72	62	70	60	52	74	61	79	47	73	82	94
43946	SARDIS	78	70	79	68	71	85	66	78	72	64	71	57	63	72	68	78	48	73	85	91
43947	SHADYSIDE	67	63	69	62	64	76	61	70	65	57	64	51	59	64	62	70	44	66	77	81
43950	SAINT CLAIRSVILLE	81	80	84	79	81	92	76	85	80	73	79	61	76	79	79	85	54	81	92	98
43952	STEUBENVILLE	64	57	59	58	57	68	61	63	66	58	65	46	58	64	59	71	45	64	73	76
43953	STEUBENVILLE	80	81	86	79	81	93	75	84	80	73	79	61	76	79	79	85	54	81	93	98
43963	TILTONSVILLE	71	51	72	50	53	75	56	69	63	50	60	52	45	62	54	69	40	65	76	81
43964	TORONTO	71	61	67	61	61	75	62	70	66	58	65	52	57	66	61	71	44	67	75	82
43968	WELLSVILLE	72	58	62	59	59	72	63	69	67	58	65	52	55	67	59	72	45	67	74	82
43971	YORKVILLE	73	54	73	52	56	77	58	71	65	52	62	53	48	63	57	71	42	67	78	83
43973	FREEPORT	83	60	85	58	62	85	63	79	70	57	68	59	50	69	61	77	45	73	84	93
43976	HOPEDALE	90	72	87	72	74	95	75	89	81	67	79	67	64	81	74	88	53	83	95	104
43977	FLUSHING	82	59	84	57	61	84	61	78	68	57	67	58	49	68	60	75	44	71	82	92
43983	PIEDMONT	84	60	86	58	62	85	62	78	68	57	67	59	49	68	61	75	44	72	81	93
43986	JEWETT	78	58	71	57	59	79	61	73	67	57	65	55	50	68	58	73	44	68	77	86
43988	SCIO	86	63	87	62	66	89	66	82	73	60	71	62	54	72	65	80	47	76	87	97
44001	AMHERST	103	120	106	121	117	118	106	110	105	107	106	84	116	107	113	107	74	107	112	128
44003	ANDOVER	91	66	79	64	66	88	68	81	75	66	74	62	55	78	63	82	50	76	85	98
44004	ASHTABULA	72	67	64	68	66	75	71	71	74	67	73	54	68	73	68	77	50	72	79	85
44010	AUSTINBURG	94	89	86	93	90	102	86	96	88	80	87	73	82	90	87	93	60	89	99	112
44011	AVON	124	155	147	157	154	143	131	137	126	138	128	104	149	128	145	124	91	130	129	157
44012	AVON LAKE	146	175	166	180	174	162	154	156	149	162	151	122	174	152	166	145	109	150	148	179
44017	BEREA	89	96	91	96	94	97	93	93	94	91	94	70	97	93	95	96	66	94	99	109
44021	BURTON	109	121	111	123	120	118	111	115	109	111	110	89	118	111	117	109	77	111	113	133
44022	CHAGRIN FALLS	190	252	291	258	275	231	219	228	201	237	200	173	257	196	253	191	149	214	203	252
44023	CHAGRIN FALLS	180	227	230	234	232	210	191	200	181	204	183	153	221	183	214	176	134	188	183	228
44024	CHARDON	119	137	129	138	136	132	122	127	119	126	120	96	132	121	130	119	85	122	124	147
44026	CHESTERLAND	135	167	171	172	172	158	142	151	136	152	138	112	162	136	160	134	99	142	142	172
44028	COLUMBIA STATION	115	130	117	134	128	128	116	121	113	117	114	94	124	116	123	114	80	116	119	142
44030	CONNEAUT	74	68	67	68	67	79	68	73	71	64	70	55	64	72	67	75	48	71	79	87
44032	DORSET	87	73	76	75	74	89	73	84	77	68	76	64	65	79	71	83	52	78	87	99
44035	ELYRIA	82	86	77	86	83	87	84	84	86	83	86	64	86	86	84	87	60	85	89	99
44039	NORTH RIDGEVILLE	103	119	105	120	115	116	106	108	106	107	107	83	116	108	113	106	75	106	111	127
44040	GATES MILLS	215	290	340	297	319	279	242	262	230	266	228	191	296	224	286	225	170	243	245	288
44041	GENEVA	84	76	75	76	74	85	78	82	81	74	80	63	73	82	75	84	55	81	86	97
44044	GRAFTON	108	122	109	124	119	122	109	114	108	108	109	88	117	111	115	110	76	110	115	134
44046	HUNTSBURG	112	127	110	130	123	122	113	117	110	114	111	91	121	113	119	110	78	112	114	137
44047	JEFFERSON	88	82	81	84	83	94	81	89	84	76	83	67	77	85	81	88	57	84	93	104
44048	KINGSVILLE	87	84	83	85	85	97	80	90	84	75	83	67	78	85	82	89	57	84	96	104
44050	LAGRANGE	109	114	100	114	111	114	104	109	104	106	105	82	107	108	106	106	73	105	108	128
44052	LORAIN	68	66	58	67	62	69	70	67	73	66	72	51	69	73	67	75	50	70	75	81
44053	LORAIN	78	88	82	86	86	84	85	83	84	83	85	64	90	84	88	85	60	84	85	97
44054	SHEFFIELD LAKE	98	109	97	109	106	106	100	102	100	100	101	78	106	102	104	101	70	100	104	119
44055	LORAIN	67	64	55	64	61	65	69	65	70	66	70	51	66	70	65	71	49	68	70	78
44056	MACEDONIA	129	153	137	155	149	146	133	138	130	136	131	106	147	133	143	129	93	132	135	161
44057	MADISON	94	101	90	100	98	99	92	95	92	94	93	72	96	94	95	93	64	93	95	112
44060	MENTOR	109	127	119	128	126	122	114	117	112	117	113	89	125	113	122	112	80	114	116	135
44062	MIDDLEFIELD	88	85	79	83	84	86	85	87	85	84	85	67	81	86	83	85	59	86	87	101
44064	MONTVILLE	110	124	107	128	120	122	111	115	109	111	110	90	118	112	117	109	77	111	114	136
44065	NEWBURY	122	145	141	149	146	140	127	132	124	133	125	100	141	124	139	123	88	127	130	154
44067	NORTHFIELD	121	139	125	139	135	129	125	126	122	130	123	98	135	125	130	120	87	122	122	146
44070	NORTH OLMSTED	96	112	105	112	110	109	102	103	102	103	103	78	113	102	109	103	73	103	106	120
44072	NOVELTY	182	252	300	258	279	234	212	226	194	235	193	167	257	188	253	185	144	209	203	248
44074	OBERLIN	90	93	89	95	93	96	94	92	94	92	94	70	96	93	94	96	66	93	98	108
44076	ORWELL	87	72	75	72	72	86	73	81	77	70	76	61	64	79	70	82	52	77	85	97
44077	PAINESVILLE	101	104	95	106	102	103	102	101	102	101	102	79	104	103	102	102	71	101	103	120
44081	PERRY	108	121	105	123	117	118	107	112	106	109	107	86	115	109	113	107	75	108	110	131
44082	PIERPONT	95	68	78	66	68	90	71	82	79	69	77	63	57	82	64	86	52	78	87	100
44084	ROCK CREEK	94	98	89	102	97	103	91	98	91	88	91	75	92	93	94	93	63	92	98	114
44085	ROME	93	95	86	96	93	98	89	94	89	88	89	71	89	91	90	91	62	90	95	110
44086	THOMPSON	105	108	94	108	105	108	98	103	99	100	99	78	100	102	100	100	69	100	103	122
44087	TWINSBURG	121	140	128	142	137	129	127	126	124	131	125	99	139	127	134	121	89	124	122	147
44089	VERMILION	102	106	103	107	105	111	100	105	101	98	101	80	103	102	104	103	70	102	109	123
44090	WELLINGTON	97	105	95	107	103	105	98	101	97	96	97	78	101	99	101	98	68	98	101	118
44092	WICKLIFFE	85	91	86	90	90	97	87	90	91	85	91	66	92	89	91	95	63	90	102	105
44093	WILLIAMSFIELD	75	62	65	63	63	76	62	71	66	58	65	54	55	68	60	71	44	66	74	84
44094	WILLOUGHBY	94	102	100	103	102	101	100	99	101	101	101	74	106	99	104	102	71	101	106	115
44095	EASTLAKE	86	95	87	95	93	99	88	91	90	86	90	68	94	90	92	93	63	90	99	107
	OHIO	94	92	87	93	90	96	93	93	94	91	94	72	92	95	91	96	66	93	98	110
	UNITED STATES	100	100	100	100	100	100	100	100	100	100	100	100	100	100	100	100	100	100	100	100

ZIP CODE #	POST OFFICE NAME	COUNTY FIPS CODE	POPULATION 2000	POPULATION 2009	POPULATION 2014	2000-2009 ANNUAL RATE % Rate	2000-2009 ANNUAL RATE State Centile	HOUSEHOLDS 2000	HOUSEHOLDS 2009	HOUSEHOLDS 2014	HOUSEHOLDS % Annual Rate 2000-2009	HOUSEHOLDS 2009 Average HH Size	FAMILIES 2000	FAMILIES 2009	FAMILIES % Annual Rate 2000-2009
44099	WINDSOR	007	1959	2171	2207	1.1	89	555	618	631	1.2	3.40	428	466	0.9
44102	CLEVELAND	035	52039	46771	44294	-1.1	4	20379	18440	17499	-1.1	2.49	11381	9925	-1.5
44103	CLEVELAND	035	25506	22173	20910	-1.5	1	9637	8465	8007	-1.4	2.50	5604	4674	-1.9
44104	CLEVELAND	035	28570	25087	23759	-1.4	2	10656	9457	8985	-1.3	2.61	6835	5879	-1.6
44105	CLEVELAND	035	54202	47047	44156	-1.5	1	20447	17967	16933	-1.4	2.61	13545	11551	-1.7
44106	CLEVELAND	035	32271	29009	27644	-1.1	4	13614	12406	11825	-1.0	2.05	5849	5008	-1.7
44107	LAKEWOOD	035	56644	52435	50032	-0.8	9	26709	25252	24235	-0.6	2.05	12564	11339	-1.1
44108	CLEVELAND	035	36746	32654	30859	-1.3	2	13656	12361	11747	-1.1	2.62	9107	7983	-1.4
44109	CLEVELAND	035	45876	41910	39808	-1.0	5	18406	17050	16274	-0.8	2.45	10946	9741	-1.3
44110	CLEVELAND	035	26765	23996	22681	-1.2	3	11297	10134	9594	-1.2	2.33	6298	5399	-1.7
44111	CLEVELAND	035	42737	39194	37292	-0.9	7	18059	16800	16056	-0.8	2.32	10625	9501	-1.2
44112	CLEVELAND	035	33149	28167	26426	-1.7	1	13236	11439	10776	-1.6	2.41	8060	6693	-2.0
44113	CLEVELAND	035	19844	19387	18905	-0.3	27	7445	7469	7333	0.0	2.16	3351	3124	-0.8
44114	CLEVELAND	035	3984	4324	4320	0.9	85	2080	2400	2430	1.6	1.63	637	634	-0.1
44115	CLEVELAND	035	8215	8043	7788	-0.2	32	3099	3063	2962	-0.1	2.12	1660	1481	-1.2
44116	ROCKY RIVER	035	20758	19387	18561	-0.7	11	9719	9251	8903	-0.5	2.07	5448	4973	-1.0
44117	EUCLID	035	12081	11222	10722	-0.8	9	5887	5488	5249	-0.8	1.98	2920	2611	-1.2
44118	CLEVELAND	035	44933	41458	39579	-0.9	7	17555	16487	15815	-0.7	2.40	10892	9883	-1.0
44119	CLEVELAND	035	13339	12472	11955	-0.7	11	6051	5689	5468	-0.7	2.14	3260	2933	-1.1
44120	CLEVELAND	035	47823	42367	39993	-1.3	2	20286	18227	17281	-1.2	2.30	12107	10468	-1.6
44121	CLEVELAND	035	34964	32162	30639	-0.9	7	14392	13495	12925	-0.7	2.36	9448	8578	-1.0
44122	BEACHWOOD	035	34672	32805	31536	-0.6	14	14136	13533	13039	-0.5	2.25	9072	8417	-0.8
44123	EUCLID	035	18478	17179	16424	-0.8	9	8572	8068	7747	-0.7	2.12	4795	4306	-1.2
44124	CLEVELAND	035	40820	38505	36953	-0.6	14	18660	17947	17331	-0.4	2.11	11314	10527	-0.8
44125	CLEVELAND	035	29964	27742	26486	-0.8	9	12263	11560	11090	-0.6	2.37	8113	7410	-1.0
44126	CLEVELAND	035	17656	16476	15757	-0.7	11	7896	7510	7223	-0.5	2.19	4732	4339	-0.9
44127	CLEVELAND	035	9182	7686	7185	-1.9	0	3314	2720	2535	-2.1	2.78	2109	1670	-2.5
44128	CLEVELAND	035	32517	29981	28607	-0.9	7	13325	12573	12076	-0.6	2.35	8716	7950	-1.0
44129	CLEVELAND	035	30085	28393	27243	-0.6	14	12399	11893	11469	-0.4	2.34	7972	7393	-0.8
44130	CLEVELAND	035	52752	50525	48756	-0.5	17	23005	22483	21829	-0.2	2.21	14453	13621	-0.6
44131	INDEPENDENCE	035	20742	19952	19343	-0.4	21	8052	7919	7726	-0.2	2.51	6216	5979	-0.4
44132	EUCLID	035	15241	14183	13548	-0.8	9	6856	6496	6241	-0.6	2.18	3986	3624	-1.0
44133	NORTH ROYALTON	035	28672	29383	29105	0.3	61	11255	11805	11783	0.5	2.46	7700	7810	0.2
44134	CLEVELAND	035	40301	38086	36591	-0.6	14	16442	15835	15294	-0.4	2.36	11072	10358	-0.7
44135	CLEVELAND	035	28592	26528	25365	-0.8	9	11878	11208	10770	-0.6	2.32	7202	6555	-1.0
44136	STRONGSVILLE	035	25210	24922	24409	-0.1	39	9312	9385	9237	0.1	2.63	6933	6884	-0.1
44137	MAPLE HEIGHTS	035	27105	24835	23637	-0.9	7	11084	10319	9862	-0.8	2.38	7259	6538	-1.1
44138	OLMSTED FALLS	035	18450	20484	20715	1.1	89	7475	8400	8527	1.3	2.42	5100	5581	1.0
44139	SOLON	035	22301	22596	22173	0.1	51	7772	7963	7847	0.3	2.84	6289	6324	0.1
44140	BAY VILLAGE	035	16087	15037	14395	-0.7	11	6239	5972	5755	-0.5	2.49	4683	4381	-0.7
44141	BRECKSVILLE	035	13704	13280	12897	-0.3	27	5158	5107	4986	-0.1	2.49	3852	3729	-0.4
44142	BROOK PARK	035	21158	19498	18626	-0.9	7	8173	7713	7415	-0.6	2.52	5975	5510	-0.9
44143	CLEVELAND	035	23573	23202	22642	-0.2	32	9610	9496	9271	-0.1	2.42	6586	6386	-0.3
44144	CLEVELAND	035	21828	20428	19536	-0.7	11	9997	9522	9159	-0.5	2.14	5893	5402	-0.9
44145	WESTLAKE	035	31721	31444	30858	-0.1	39	12823	12973	12789	0.1	2.33	8189	8048	-0.2
44146	BEDFORD	035	30748	28949	27793	-0.6	14	13518	12965	12508	-0.5	2.20	8012	7415	-0.8
44147	BROADVIEW HEIGHTS	035	15916	16912	16880	0.7	79	6392	6874	6882	0.8	2.44	4361	4561	0.5
44149	STRONGSVILLE	035	18648	19259	19066	0.3	61	6897	7230	7182	0.5	2.66	5456	5622	0.3
44201	ATWATER	133	6995	7195	7307	0.3	61	2473	2624	2691	0.6	2.74	2019	2098	0.4
44202	AURORA	133	16573	18469	19156	1.2	91	6200	7107	7441	1.5	2.55	4741	5289	1.2
44203	BARBERTON	153	41989	41516	41134	-0.1	39	16897	17042	16990	0.1	2.41	11587	11331	-0.2
44212	BRUNSWICK	103	38094	43112	45496	1.3	92	13536	15729	16744	1.6	2.72	10559	11969	1.4
44214	BURBANK	169	1819	1941	2003	0.7	79	638	702	729	1.0	2.75	516	557	0.8
44215	CHIPPEWA LAKE	103	2090	2691	2914	2.8	98	812	1065	1163	3.0	2.51	563	726	2.8
44216	CLINTON	153	9701	10209	10347	0.6	75	3489	3757	3832	0.8	2.72	2836	2989	0.6
44217	CRESTON	169	4111	4365	4451	0.7	79	1527	1651	1695	0.8	2.63	1194	1262	0.6
44221	CUYAHOGA FALLS	153	30846	31206	31100	0.1	51	13688	14176	14224	0.4	2.19	8208	8158	-0.1
44223	CUYAHOGA FALLS	153	17483	17766	17799	0.2	56	7533	7748	7797	0.3	2.27	4764	4715	-0.1
44224	STOW	153	36329	38176	38774	0.5	71	14112	15076	15411	0.7	2.49	10005	10344	0.4
44230	DOYLESTOWN	169	8323	8399	8409	0.1	51	3148	3261	3289	0.4	2.53	2325	2346	0.1
44231	GARRETTSVILLE	133	7796	7966	8038	0.2	56	2873	3028	3085	0.6	2.62	2126	2178	0.3
44233	HINCKLEY	103	6777	7770	8280	1.5	94	2341	2760	2967	1.8	2.82	1990	2312	1.6
44234	HIRAM	133	4170	4399	4470	0.6	75	1290	1386	1428	0.8	2.69	995	1046	0.5
44235	HOMERVILLE	103	1570	1727	1795	1.0	87	431	488	512	1.4	3.54	371	414	1.2
44236	HUDSON	153	24239	25344	25571	0.5	71	7993	8467	8587	0.6	2.95	6818	7077	0.4
44240	KENT	133	35511	36430	36736	0.3	61	14772	15437	15682	0.5	2.24	8289	8417	0.2
44241	STREETSBORO	133	13125	15720	16692	2.0	97	5166	6430	6912	2.4	2.43	3629	4345	2.0
44243	KENT	133	5277	5636	5615	0.7	79	4	4	4	0.0	2.50	1	1	0.0
44253	LITCHFIELD	103	3350	3835	4070	1.5	94	1070	1260	1351	1.8	3.04	919	1067	1.6
44254	LODI	103	5231	5322	5405	0.2	56	2031	2113	2161	0.4	2.51	1416	1441	0.2
44255	MANTUA	133	7470	7552	7579	0.1	51	2716	2833	2876	0.5	2.60	2060	2094	0.2
44256	MEDINA	103	51434	63018	68319	2.2	97	18637	23186	25293	2.4	2.69	14306	17528	2.2
44260	MOGADORE	133	13801	13506	13381	-0.2	32	5139	5186	5184	0.1	2.60	3997	3936	-0.2
44262	MUNROE FALLS	153	5312	5358	5329	0.1	51	1954	2017	2023	0.3	2.59	1530	1541	0.1
44264	PENINSULA	153	2306	2384	2382	0.4	66	928	1018	1024	1.0	2.32	629	672	0.7
44266	RAVENNA	133	33813	34425	34563	0.2	56	13236	13791	13964	0.4	2.45	9203	9329	0.1
44270	RITTMAN	169	8569	8677	8720	0.1	51	3224	3349	3390	0.4	2.55	2370	2401	0.1
44272	ROOTSTOWN	133	4150	4878	5155	1.8	96	1503	1836	1962	2.2	2.65	1196	1423	1.9
44273	SEVILLE	103	7557	8213	8649	0.9	85	2695	3007	3191	1.2	2.70	2174	2377	1.0
44275	SPENCER	103	3119	3525	3707	1.3	92	1075	1251	1328	1.7	2.82	877	1002	1.5
44276	STERLING	169	2126	2187	2204	0.3	61	730	775	789	0.6	2.77	574	597	0.4
44278	TALLMADGE	153	17088	17930	18156	0.5	71	6508	6969	7099	0.7	2.53	4868	5063	0.4
44280	VALLEY CITY	103	4490	5304	5708	1.8	96	1505	1837	2000	2.2	2.78	1285	1544	2.0
44281	WADSWORTH	103	26109	29833	31540	1.5	94	9940	11571	12317	1.7	2.56	7358	8361	1.4
44286	RICHFIELD	153	5433	5998	6185	1.1	89	1912	2117	2201	1.1	2.73	1532	1663	0.9
44287	WEST SALEM	169	7465	8266	8627	1.1	89	2564	2914	3062	1.4	2.84	2015	2239	1.1
44288	WINDHAM	133	4626	4241	4118	-0.9	7	1609	1535	1508	-0.5	2.76	1250	1164	-0.8
44301	AKRON	153	17277	16032	15519	-0.8	9	6977	6571	6397	-0.6	2.41	4469	4042	-1.1
44302	AKRON	153	6567	6031	5815	-0.9	7	3150	2926	2832	-0.8	2.02	1338	1172	-1.4
44303	AKRON	153	7942	7586	7425	-0.5	17	3617	3491	3430	-0.4	2.11	1896	1739	-0.9
44304	AKRON	153	7779	6986	6705	-1.2	3	2872	2485	2362	-1.6	2.07	968	777	-2.3
44305	AKRON	153	24141	22842	22276	-0.6	14	9711	9345	9162	-0.4	2.42	6364	5900	-0.8
44306	AKRON	153	25288	23466	22785	-0.8	9	10014	9416	9188	-0.7	2.47	6502	5892	-1.1
44307	AKRON	153	9463	8455	8098	-1.2	3	3965	3614	3485	-1.0	2.26	2422	2113	-1.5
44308	AKRON	153	789	723	697	-0.9	7	515	449	426	-1.5	1.11	33	26	-2.5
	OHIO					0.2					0.4	2.44			0.1
	UNITED STATES					1.0					1.1	2.59			0.9

POPULATION COMPOSITION

ZIP CODE #	POST OFFICE NAME	RACE (%) White 2000	White 2009	Black 2000	Black 2009	Asian/Pacific 2000	Asian/Pacific 2009	% Hispanic Origin 2000	% Hispanic Origin 2009	2009 AGE DISTRIBUTION (%) 0-4	5-9	10-14	15-19	20-24	25-44	45-64	65-84	85+	18+	MEDIAN AGE 2009	% 2009 Males	% 2009 Females
44099	WINDSOR	94.8	93.8	2.5	3.0	0.1	0.1	0.7	0.9	9.4	9.7	9.7	7.8	4.5	23.5	24.0	9.2	2.2	66.2	34.1	49.8	50.2
44102	CLEVELAND	67.4	57.9	14.4	20.0	2.2	3.0	20.8	25.1	8.8	7.8	7.1	7.5	8.4	29.3	21.7	7.9	1.5	71.8	31.2	49.7	50.3
44103	CLEVELAND	14.6	10.7	79.3	82.7	1.5	2.0	4.3	4.4	8.0	8.1	7.8	8.1	7.0	23.7	23.5	11.7	2.2	70.9	34.4	47.7	52.3
44104	CLEVELAND	2.0	1.2	96.5	97.5	0.1	0.1	0.6	0.6	11.0	11.0	9.1	8.9	7.3	22.4	20.0	8.8	1.5	63.3	27.1	43.8	56.2
44105	CLEVELAND	36.1	31.9	61.4	65.3	0.2	0.2	1.9	2.2	7.9	8.1	7.9	8.1	6.7	25.0	24.5	10.3	1.3	71.1	34.5	46.9	53.1
44106	CLEVELAND	36.6	31.7	56.2	58.9	5.1	7.1	1.4	1.7	5.6	5.1	4.8	9.3	13.0	27.4	19.9	11.7	3.0	80.9	31.7	48.8	51.2
44107	LAKEWOOD	93.1	89.8	2.0	3.3	1.4	2.3	2.2	3.1	5.8	5.2	5.0	5.7	8.3	33.1	24.8	9.6	2.4	80.8	36.5	48.7	51.3
44108	CLEVELAND	3.7	3.3	95.0	95.6	0.1	0.1	0.6	0.6	7.8	8.4	8.2	8.3	6.3	22.7	23.6	12.6	2.1	70.4	35.1	45.0	55.0
44109	CLEVELAND	78.1	72.1	7.0	9.8	1.1	1.6	19.6	23.4	8.2	7.6	7.0	7.2	7.2	28.6	23.9	8.7	1.5	72.7	34.1	49.3	50.7
44110	CLEVELAND	23.7	16.7	73.7	80.8	0.1	0.2	1.0	1.0	8.0	8.4	7.7	7.7	6.6	25.3	23.8	10.5	1.8	70.9	34.4	45.6	54.4
44111	CLEVELAND	83.5	77.2	7.4	10.9	1.9	2.9	8.5	11.1	7.4	7.1	6.8	6.4	6.1	28.4	26.5	9.6	1.7	74.8	37.4	48.9	51.1
44112	CLEVELAND	5.2	3.5	92.8	94.7	0.2	0.3	0.8	0.8	7.1	7.6	7.3	8.0	6.9	23.3	26.0	11.9	2.0	73.1	36.2	44.2	55.8
44113	CLEVELAND	55.7	46.1	28.5	36.4	0.9	1.1	21.3	23.6	7.2	6.2	5.2	6.4	9.6	34.3	22.3	7.6	1.2	78.1	33.5	55.1	44.9
44114	CLEVELAND	37.3	28.1	34.0	43.2	22.8	22.9	7.1	6.6	5.7	3.7	2.9	3.7	8.2	30.9	28.5	14.4	2.0	86.0	41.4	53.3	46.7
44115	CLEVELAND	11.1	10.5	85.1	85.9	1.7	1.8	1.3	1.3	12.7	10.4	7.6	9.0	11.9	29.3	14.0	4.3	0.7	64.8	24.3	43.8	56.2
44116	ROCKY RIVER	96.8	95.1	0.4	0.7	1.3	2.3	1.2	1.7	5.2	5.2	5.8	5.8	5.0	20.3	28.6	18.6	5.5	80.0	46.8	45.5	54.5
44117	EUCLID	45.9	35.4	51.6	62.0	0.7	0.8	1.0	1.1	4.6	4.6	4.8	5.8	5.9	19.8	28.7	20.9	4.9	82.5	48.2	43.8	56.2
44118	CLEVELAND	58.5	49.7	36.7	44.7	1.9	2.6	1.5	1.8	6.6	6.5	6.4	8.3	8.7	25.9	25.3	10.4	1.8	76.7	35.9	47.2	52.8
44119	CLEVELAND	80.3	71.5	16.7	24.6	0.8	1.2	1.4	1.8	6.4	6.3	6.2	6.1	5.7	25.8	27.2	11.5	4.8	77.3	40.9	47.5	52.5
44120	CLEVELAND	19.9	16.6	76.0	78.9	1.8	2.4	1.1	1.1	7.1	7.3	7.1	7.1	6.6	24.9	25.7	11.9	2.3	74.1	37.3	44.7	55.3
44121	CLEVELAND	63.1	53.8	33.0	41.4	1.6	2.2	1.2	1.4	6.2	6.5	6.9	6.8	5.5	25.4	29.0	11.3	2.4	76.2	40.2	46.3	53.7
44122	BEACHWOOD	63.8	56.6	31.5	37.3	2.7	3.9	0.9	1.1	4.3	4.8	5.8	7.1	4.9	18.4	29.2	18.8	6.7	80.4	48.3	46.0	54.0
44123	EUCLID	77.0	68.0	20.0	28.3	1.0	1.5	1.1	1.4	6.8	6.6	6.4	6.1	6.4	27.6	26.7	10.7	2.8	76.5	38.6	47.5	52.5
44124	CLEVELAND	93.2	89.3	2.8	4.6	3.0	4.9	0.9	1.3	4.6	5.0	5.5	5.2	4.5	22.2	27.7	19.7	5.6	81.6	47.1	46.0	54.0
44125	CLEVELAND	90.7	87.4	6.8	9.1	1.0	1.7	1.3	1.8	6.1	6.2	6.3	6.3	5.3	25.8	27.2	13.4	3.4	77.4	41.0	47.8	52.2
44126	CLEVELAND	95.9	93.8	0.7	1.1	1.6	2.7	1.5	2.2	5.6	5.8	6.1	5.8	5.1	23.4	29.6	15.2	3.5	78.9	43.9	47.4	52.6
44127	CLEVELAND	53.4	41.0	39.3	51.0	0.4	0.5	7.0	7.9	9.7	10.1	8.0	7.9	7.7	26.4	20.3	8.6	1.3	67.3	29.4	48.2	51.8
44128	CLEVELAND	3.8	2.4	93.8	95.5	0.5	0.6	0.8	0.7	6.2	6.7	6.9	7.5	5.9	22.1	26.6	15.8	2.3	75.7	40.8	44.0	56.0
44129	CLEVELAND	96.2	94.2	0.9	1.6	1.2	2.0	1.8	2.5	6.1	6.1	6.2	6.1	5.4	26.8	26.4	13.2	3.7	77.7	40.6	47.8	52.2
44130	CLEVELAND	94.3	91.2	1.6	2.7	2.2	3.6	1.5	2.2	5.1	4.9	5.1	5.3	5.3	24.6	27.3	18.4	4.0	81.7	44.8	47.0	53.0
44131	INDEPENDENCE	97.3	95.6	0.3	0.6	1.7	2.9	0.8	1.2	4.3	4.7	5.6	6.1	3.7	19.7	31.2	20.6	4.0	81.3	48.7	47.7	52.3
44132	EUCLID	62.4	55.6	34.1	40.4	1.0	1.5	1.1	1.3	6.7	6.7	6.6	6.2	5.6	27.4	26.4	11.9	2.5	76.2	39.0	46.4	53.6
44133	NORTH ROYALTON	96.2	93.7	0.7	1.5	2.0	3.3	1.0	1.3	5.2	5.4	5.9	6.6	5.8	27.1	30.8	11.4	1.9	79.3	40.5	48.7	51.3
44134	CLEVELAND	96.2	94.1	0.5	0.9	1.8	2.9	1.4	2.0	5.7	5.7	6.0	6.1	5.3	24.7	27.3	15.3	3.8	78.7	42.6	48.0	52.0
44135	CLEVELAND	76.7	70.2	16.3	20.6	2.2	3.3	5.7	7.3	7.4	7.3	6.8	6.1	5.2	26.3	25.8	12.5	2.5	74.6	39.0	48.3	51.7
44136	STRONGSVILLE	93.6	89.9	1.5	2.5	3.5	5.7	1.3	1.9	5.4	6.0	6.9	7.3	5.2	22.9	32.4	11.9	2.0	76.9	42.2	48.6	51.4
44137	MAPLE HEIGHTS	52.8	42.4	43.2	52.9	1.8	2.4	1.2	1.4	6.3	6.4	6.6	6.9	5.9	25.7	27.4	12.0	2.7	76.4	39.7	47.2	52.8
44138	OLMSTED FALLS	96.4	94.2	1.2	2.2	1.1	1.7	1.5	2.2	5.7	5.9	6.3	6.3	4.9	24.7	30.5	13.5	2.4	78.2	42.5	47.9	52.1
44139	SOLON	88.0	81.0	6.1	9.8	4.8	7.7	0.7	0.9	5.5	6.7	8.2	8.5	4.5	20.1	34.3	10.7	1.5	74.1	42.6	48.9	51.1
44140	BAY VILLAGE	98.0	97.0	0.3	0.5	0.7	1.2	1.0	1.4	5.7	6.2	7.2	6.9	3.8	21.0	33.2	13.4	2.5	76.1	44.4	47.8	52.2
44141	BRECKSVILLE	94.9	91.8	1.9	3.0	2.6	4.3	1.0	1.4	4.2	5.3	6.7	6.8	3.7	16.9	36.3	17.2	3.0	79.4	48.6	50.3	49.7
44142	BROOK PARK	94.5	91.8	2.0	3.0	1.3	2.1	2.0	2.8	5.1	5.4	5.8	6.4	4.9	24.9	28.0	17.5	2.1	79.7	43.3	48.5	51.5
44143	CLEVELAND	79.7	72.1	14.3	19.3	4.4	6.8	1.1	1.3	4.9	5.3	6.2	6.4	5.4	21.9	31.0	15.6	3.3	79.6	44.9	47.9	52.1
44144	CLEVELAND	91.8	87.9	1.8	2.9	1.7	2.8	5.7	8.0	6.0	5.9	5.8	5.3	4.9	27.3	27.0	14.5	3.2	79.0	41.7	48.6	51.4
44145	WESTLAKE	92.9	88.9	0.9	1.7	4.2	6.9	1.3	1.8	4.8	5.3	6.2	6.3	4.5	22.4	31.3	14.7	4.4	79.5	45.3	47.4	52.6
44146	BEDFORD	56.8	47.3	39.6	48.6	1.2	1.6	1.3	1.5	5.1	5.1	5.3	5.8	6.2	25.1	29.1	15.2	3.1	81.0	43.0	46.9	53.1
44147	BROADVIEW HEIGHTS	95.0	91.5	0.8	1.6	3.0	5.3	0.9	1.3	5.8	6.1	6.6	6.6	4.9	24.2	30.2	13.0	2.5	77.4	42.1	47.7	52.3
44149	STRONGSVILLE	94.9	91.7	0.9	1.8	2.8	4.8	1.2	1.7	6.5	7.1	7.2	6.3	3.4	23.2	31.1	13.5	1.6	74.9	42.6	48.3	51.7
44201	ATWATER	98.5	98.1	0.3	0.4	0.1	0.2	0.7	0.9	6.1	6.6	7.1	6.9	4.7	24.8	31.3	11.2	1.3	75.9	41.1	50.5	49.5
44202	AURORA	95.6	94.1	2.2	2.8	1.1	1.9	0.6	0.8	6.6	7.1	7.6	6.7	4.1	24.1	29.2	12.2	2.4	74.4	41.1	48.5	51.5
44203	BARBERTON	94.2	92.4	3.9	5.1	0.4	0.6	0.6	0.7	6.7	6.3	6.3	6.3	5.6	24.7	27.8	13.8	2.6	76.8	40.7	48.1	51.9
44212	BRUNSWICK	97.2	96.2	0.7	0.8	0.9	1.4	1.4	1.8	7.1	7.2	7.2	7.0	5.4	28.8	27.4	9.0	1.0	74.1	36.9	49.0	51.0
44214	BURBANK	99.1	98.9	0.2	0.3	0.2	0.3	0.8	1.0	6.1	6.7	7.5	7.5	4.4	26.2	29.9	10.8	0.9	74.9	39.7	52.1	47.9
44215	CHIPPEWA LAKE	98.6	98.1	0.2	0.4	0.2	0.3	0.7	0.9	5.6	5.8	6.0	6.4	6.2	27.9	30.7	10.2	1.3	78.6	39.9	51.1	48.9
44216	CLINTON	97.7	96.7	0.5	0.7	0.8	1.3	0.5	0.7	5.6	6.2	6.9	6.9	4.6	23.6	32.8	12.3	1.3	76.9	42.4	49.9	50.1
44217	CRESTON	98.5	98.1	0.4	0.5	0.1	0.3	0.4	0.5	6.7	6.9	7.3	7.0	4.9	26.7	27.8	11.5	1.2	74.7	39.3	50.0	50.0
44221	CUYAHOGA FALLS	96.3	94.4	1.3	2.0	1.1	1.9	0.7	1.0	6.1	5.9	5.8	5.7	6.5	30.3	25.7	11.8	2.2	78.8	38.2	48.1	51.9
44223	CUYAHOGA FALLS	95.7	93.3	2.5	3.9	0.8	1.4	0.5	0.6	6.6	6.6	6.4	5.1	4.5	25.1	27.6	14.8	3.2	77.1	42.0	46.9	53.1
44224	STOW	95.1	92.6	1.6	2.4	1.9	3.2	0.9	1.2	6.3	6.4	6.7	6.5	5.7	26.4	28.4	11.3	2.3	76.5	39.4	48.4	51.6
44230	DOYLESTOWN	98.5	98.0	0.4	0.5	0.2	0.4	0.3	0.5	5.7	6.0	6.4	6.5	4.9	24.7	30.8	12.7	2.1	77.5	42.0	49.5	50.5
44231	GARRETTSVILLE	98.4	98.0	0.5	0.6	0.1	0.2	0.4	0.6	6.6	6.8	7.2	7.5	5.9	25.1	28.9	10.8	1.3	74.8	38.5	49.2	50.8
44233	HINCKLEY	98.3	97.6	0.1	0.1	0.8	1.3	0.7	1.0	5.0	5.9	7.0	6.8	4.1	19.8	36.8	13.4	1.4	77.9	45.8	50.2	49.8
44234	HIRAM	96.7	96.0	1.7	1.9	0.4	0.7	0.8	1.0	4.8	5.5	6.1	12.9	11.9	21.5	27.3	8.8	1.1	79.3	34.8	50.2	49.8
44235	HOMERVILLE	97.6	97.1	1.1	1.3	0.0	0.0	1.1	1.4	9.2	9.2	9.3	8.6	4.7	26.4	24.6	7.2	0.8	66.8	32.3	50.4	49.6
44236	HUDSON	94.4	90.8	1.8	3.3	2.8	4.5	0.8	1.1	5.9	7.6	9.1	9.3	4.2	18.7	34.3	9.2	1.7	70.7	41.8	49.4	50.6
44240	KENT	89.5	87.3	6.3	7.1	1.9	2.9	0.9	1.2	5.9	5.6	5.4	8.5	16.0	27.1	22.1	8.4	1.2	79.8	30.0	48.5	51.5
44241	STREETSBORO	95.6	94.1	1.8	2.2	1.3	2.2	0.7	1.0	6.8	6.6	6.3	6.3	6.5	30.8	26.0	9.6	1.1	76.6	36.5	49.3	50.7
44243	KENT	84.6	81.4	11.1	12.7	1.9	3.0	1.7	2.3	0.2	0.1	0.1	46.8	43.3	4.3	1.6	3.1	0.5	99.3	20.3	39.2	60.8
44253	LITCHFIELD	97.9	97.3	0.7	0.9	0.4	0.7	0.4	0.6	5.2	7.5	8.8	9.2	4.9	25.3	31.0	7.6	0.6	72.2	38.4	52.3	47.7
44254	LODI	98.5	98.2	0.1	0.2	0.2	0.3	0.6	0.8	6.3	6.4	6.8	6.7	6.1	25.2	29.2	11.6	1.7	76.3	39.8	48.9	51.1
44255	MANTUA	98.2	97.8	0.6	0.7	0.1	0.2	0.7	1.0	5.7	6.2	6.8	7.4	5.3	25.8	31.3	10.3	1.2	76.7	40.1	50.4	49.6
44256	MEDINA	96.2	95.3	1.6	1.8	0.7	1.2	0.9	1.2	7.4	7.5	7.6	6.8	4.9	26.6	28.2	9.5	1.5	73.1	38.0	48.8	51.2
44260	MOGADORE	98.8	98.5	0.2	0.3	0.2	0.3	0.3	0.4	5.4	5.9	6.4	6.6	4.7	24.5	32.0	13.1	1.5	78.2	42.6	49.7	50.3
44262	MUNROE FALLS	97.1	95.6	0.9	1.3	1.2	2.1	0.7	1.0	4.5	6.4	6.8	6.7	3.7	22.7	33.0	14.1	2.2	77.7	44.5	48.1	51.9
44264	PENINSULA	96.3	94.8	0.8	1.1	1.1	1.8	0.7	1.0	5.0	5.4	6.1	6.4	4.7	23.8	34.4	12.6	1.7	79.2	44.1	50.5	49.5
44266	RAVENNA	94.7	93.8	3.2	3.6	0.3	0.4	0.7	0.9	6.6	6.6	6.8	6.3	5.6	27.1	27.9	11.2	1.8	76.0	38.8	49.3	50.7
44270	RITTMAN	98.3	97.9	0.2	0.2	0.3	0.5	0.7	0.9	6.6	6.7	6.7	6.8	5.6	26.5	27.2	12.0	2.0	75.8	38.7	49.3	50.7
44272	ROOTSTOWN	98.1	97.5	0.3	0.3	0.4	0.6	0.5	0.6	5.7	6.1	6.6	6.7	4.6	24.7	31.5	12.4	1.5	77.2	41.9	50.0	50.0
44273	SEVILLE	98.7	98.4	0.3	0.4	0.3	0.4	0.6	0.7	6.1	6.8	7.3	6.7	4.0	24.4	31.1	11.9	1.5	75.5	41.6	49.2	50.8
44275	SPENCER	98.9	98.6	0.3	0.4	0.1	0.2	0.9	1.1	7.2	7.9	8.3	7.4	4.2	24.9	29.8	9.4	1.0	72.0	38.5	50.2	49.8
44276	STERLING	98.9	98.5	0.1	0.2	0.2	0.4	0.8	1.1	5.5	5.8	6.4	7.6	5.3	24.8	29.7	12.2	2.7	77.4	41.0	50.0	50.0
44278	TALLMADGE	95.7	93.6	2.2	3.2	0.9	1.5	0.6	0.8	5.4	5.6	6.4	6.9	4.8	22.1	29.9	16.4	2.4	78.1	44.1	48.1	51.9
44280	VALLEY CITY	97.4	96.9	1.3	1.5	0.3	0.4	1.0	1.4	4.9	5.7	6.6	6.6	4.0	22.2	34.7	13.0	2.3	78.4	45.1	50.0	50.0
44281	WADSWORTH	98.0	97.4	0.4	0.4	0.6	1.0	0.6	0.8	6.6	6.8	7.2	6.7	5.0	23.9	28.8	12.7	2.4	75.2	40.7	48.8	51.2
44286	RICHFIELD	97.6	96.4	0.6	0.9	0.9	1.5	0.4	0.5	4.6	5.6	6.8	6.8	3.6	17.9	34.9	16.5	3.3	78.5	47.6	48.4	51.6
44287	WEST SALEM	98.3	97.8	0.3	0.4	0.3	0.4	0.7	0.9	7.3	7.5	7.8	7.6	5.7	24.7	27.9	10.5	1.0	72.6	37.4	51.6	48.4
44288	WINDHAM	95.0	94.5	3.2	3.5	0.1	0.1	0.5	0.6	8.4	8.7	8.7	8.1	6.4	26.3	24.5	8.0	0.8	69.2	32.7	49.3	50.7
44301	AKRON	77.9	73.2	17.9	21.4	1.6	2.5	1.1	1.3	7.6	7.6	7.1	6.9	6.1	27.8	25.0	10.0	2.0	73.5	36.3	48.3	51.7
44302	AKRON	57.4	49.2	37.6	44.9	1.5	2.2	1.8	2.0	6.4	6.1	5.9	6.0	8.1	31.0	24.9	9.3	2.2	78.1	36.2	48.2	51.8
44303	AKRON	79.4	74.7	16.6	20.1	1.6	2.5	1.2	1.4	5.5	5.3	5.6	5.7	6.3	25.9	29.5	12.5	3.8	80.1	42.0	48.6	51.4
44304	AKRON	60.6	51.9	30.4	36.2	5.1	7.5	2.2	2.5	4.5	3.5	2.8	17.5	28.8	24.0	13.0	4.6	1.3	86.7	23.8	55.3	44.7
44305	AKRON	81.4	76.3	15.4	19.7	0.5	0.9	1.0	1.2	7.5	7.1	6.9	7.0	6.6	28.5	25.2	9.7	1.6	74.2	35.9	48.2	51.8
44306	AKRON	58.3	51.8	35.9	41.3	1.9	2.7	1.4	1.6	9.4	8.6	7.2	7.4	7.8	26.3	22.3	9.4	1.6	70.5	32.0	46.8	53.2
44307	AKRON	12.3	9.2	83.9	87.0	0.7	0.9	1.0	1.1	8.9	8.7	7.6	8.3	8.1	23.4	23.1	10.3	1.7	69.9	31.8	45.5	54.5
44308	AKRON	60.9	51.7	33.7	41.9	1.0	1.7	0.9	1.0	1.5	0.4	0.4	9.8	9.4	27.8	37.6	11.2	1.8	97.4	45.2	61.7	38.3
	OHIO	85.0	83.1	11.5	12.2	1.2	1.9	1.9	2.4	6.6	6.5	6.6	7.1	6.7	25.9	26.9	11.7	2.1	76.2	38.2	48.7	51.3
	UNITED STATES	75.1	72.0	12.3	12.7	3.8	4.6	12.5	15.7	6.8	6.7	6.6	7.1	6.9	27.0	26.0	10.9	1.9	75.7	36.9	49.2	50.8

ZIP CODE #	POST OFFICE NAME	2009 Per Capita Income	2009 HH Income Base	2009 Household Income Distribution (%): Less than $25,000	$25,000 to $49,999	$50,000 to $99,999	$100,000 to $149,999	$150,000 or More	Median Household Income: 2009	2014	2009 National Centile	2009 State Centile	2009 Home Value Base	2009 Home Value Distribution (%): Less than $50,000	$50,000 to $89,999	$90,000 to $174,999	$175,000 to $399,999	$400,000 or More	2009 Median Home Value
44099	WINDSOR	16372	618	24.1	23.6	44.5	6.0	1.8	51173	51658	64	54	510	3.5	14.9	56.3	21.2	4.1	122746
44102	CLEVELAND	16737	18440	39.7	31.8	23.4	3.4	1.7	31531	33567	11	7	7258	29.6	53.8	12.5	3.2	0.9	62573
44103	CLEVELAND	12057	8465	57.4	25.0	14.8	1.9	0.8	20964	21718	2	2	2707	44.9	42.0	8.5	4.4	0.1	54117
44104	CLEVELAND	10414	9457	61.2	24.0	12.6	1.7	0.5	18360	19250	1	1	2754	39.4	52.9	6.4	1.3	0.0	56584
44105	CLEVELAND	16031	17967	39.1	30.3	25.6	3.5	1.4	31963	34455	11	7	10083	28.8	64.6	5.4	1.1	0.1	61443
44106	CLEVELAND	21785	12406	47.5	23.0	19.7	4.6	5.2	26686	28285	4	3	3486	19.2	32.3	21.5	21.3	5.7	87389
44107	LAKEWOOD	30166	25252	20.2	28.6	37.6	8.8	4.7	50860	53018	63	53	11301	3.8	17.0	65.9	11.1	2.2	116949
44108	CLEVELAND	15245	12361	46.5	29.6	18.4	3.0	2.5	27104	28476	5	4	6119	27.9	54.8	11.3	4.3	1.7	64566
44109	CLEVELAND	18786	17050	32.5	30.6	30.9	4.6	1.4	37715	40901	26	16	9393	14.1	54.0	30.7	1.0	0.2	79605
44110	CLEVELAND	16033	10134	45.3	29.4	21.2	3.2	0.9	27855	29440	5	4	4188	23.2	67.8	7.7	1.0	0.3	64411
44111	CLEVELAND	24288	16800	21.7	30.3	38.6	6.7	2.7	47722	51277	56	41	11117	4.4	51.6	41.5	2.3	0.3	86224
44112	CLEVELAND	16424	11439	46.0	27.8	20.5	3.7	1.9	27323	28750	5	4	5040	12.4	66.0	18.7	2.7	0.2	71424
44113	CLEVELAND	19228	7469	45.5	24.5	23.2	4.0	2.8	28306	30574	6	4	2063	33.3	31.1	21.9	13.0	0.8	66853
44114	CLEVELAND	21841	2400	53.5	23.2	17.0	3.5	2.8	22273	22842	2	2	284	59.2	34.9	4.9	1.1	0.0	46119
44115	CLEVELAND	11771	3063	74.8	12.3	9.8	2.0	1.1	10639	11056	0	0	162	16.0	21.6	59.3	0.6	2.5	102813
44116	ROCKY RIVER	40142	9251	15.0	23.9	38.3	11.9	10.9	60976	61680	79	79	6493	1.9	10.6	37.2	44.7	5.6	175496
44117	EUCLID	22532	5488	39.0	25.5	27.2	6.8	1.4	34593	38116	17	9	2516	4.3	27.9	66.0	1.8	0.0	102256
44118	CLEVELAND	32305	16487	18.1	19.9	37.8	14.5	9.6	62569	63170	81	81	10726	2.2	16.3	63.4	15.7	2.3	122542
44119	CLEVELAND	25343	5689	23.7	28.9	37.8	7.1	2.5	46860	50737	54	39	3770	3.6	55.7	39.0	1.6	0.2	85686
44120	CLEVELAND	25280	18227	34.0	29.2	23.6	6.6	6.5	36972	40079	24	14	8442	13.3	41.7	26.3	14.1	4.5	84896
44121	CLEVELAND	27783	13495	18.1	23.5	42.7	11.1	4.6	57748	58706	75	75	10356	1.2	27.1	67.6	4.2	0.0	102785
44122	BEACHWOOD	43472	13533	15.7	21.1	30.8	13.9	18.5	67232	68192	85	88	9077	2.0	17.4	27.7	43.2	9.8	183929
44123	EUCLID	25345	8068	22.3	30.9	38.7	6.1	2.0	46796	50292	54	38	5067	5.3	50.4	42.1	2.2	0.1	87615
44124	CLEVELAND	37266	17947	18.0	25.9	35.7	10.1	10.4	56203	57685	73	71	12280	1.0	6.7	60.9	24.7	6.8	140579
44125	CLEVELAND	24559	11560	21.5	26.9	41.3	7.6	2.7	51395	53577	65	55	9169	1.0	46.7	47.2	5.0	0.0	91100
44126	CLEVELAND	31686	7510	16.9	25.3	40.1	12.8	4.9	60423	61031	78	78	5384	0.9	6.0	74.2	18.1	0.8	134008
44127	CLEVELAND	12830	2720	46.4	33.5	17.3	1.5	1.3	26551	27483	4	3	1231	62.8	33.3	2.8	0.6	0.6	43000
44128	CLEVELAND	22066	12573	25.9	32.4	33.2	6.1	2.4	42684	46605	41	27	7638	8.5	70.9	20.0	0.5	0.0	75662
44129	CLEVELAND	25575	11893	19.1	27.3	41.2	9.5	2.9	52588	54309	67	60	8632	0.5	12.6	82.9	3.9	0.1	110550
44130	CLEVELAND	27228	22483	18.7	28.9	39.6	9.3	3.5	52066	54082	66	57	14669	1.1	10.3	75.4	13.1	0.0	124848
44131	INDEPENDENCE	30198	7919	14.8	21.3	39.9	17.3	6.6	64659	64860	83	85	7401	0.4	1.3	59.0	37.0	2.4	164080
44132	EUCLID	24183	6496	21.4	35.3	34.5	6.4	2.3	43747	47635	45	30	3721	5.2	43.5	48.6	2.7	0.0	90652
44133	NORTH ROYALTON	31994	11805	11.6	21.7	43.2	16.3	7.2	66169	65390	84	87	8676	0.4	11.1	42.1	44.0	2.3	169225
44134	CLEVELAND	26126	15835	17.9	26.0	43.9	9.1	3.1	54976	56250	71	66	12971	0.7	14.4	80.1	4.7	0.0	111627
44135	CLEVELAND	23651	11208	23.8	27.9	39.5	6.8	2.0	48078	51078	57	42	8035	8.6	53.3	37.7	0.3	0.0	82469
44136	STRONGSVILLE	36751	9385	10.0	16.6	37.7	20.9	14.8	79248	79467	92	96	7122	0.5	0.8	51.3	46.7	0.7	171996
44137	MAPLE HEIGHTS	23973	10319	19.0	28.8	43.2	7.1	1.9	51494	53277	65	55	8260	3.0	62.3	34.4	0.2	0.0	84777
44138	OLMSTED FALLS	30158	8400	12.3	21.6	46.0	14.6	5.5	62829	63436	81	82	6820	12.7	11.8	51.2	23.9	0.5	136780
44139	SOLON	45358	7963	8.0	14.7	32.3	19.6	25.4	90565	91382	95	98	6812	1.1	1.2	27.5	59.6	10.5	216520
44140	BAY VILLAGE	43140	5972	9.2	15.2	37.6	21.8	16.3	81429	81778	93	97	5394	0.4	2.8	50.1	41.9	4.8	169268
44141	BRECKSVILLE	46243	5107	8.2	16.0	34.9	19.4	21.6	85708	86396	94	98	4422	0.5	3.2	28.3	61.1	6.9	210148
44142	BROOK PARK	25355	7713	14.4	26.8	45.9	10.2	2.7	57446	58275	75	74	6351	0.6	12.2	86.2	1.1	0.0	111654
44143	CLEVELAND	35704	9496	12.9	24.4	35.6	14.7	12.5	64383	65577	83	85	7073	0.8	3.8	49.3	42.1	3.9	167891
44144	CLEVELAND	25109	9522	22.7	31.8	36.5	7.0	2.0	45461	49473	50	34	6223	3.0	34.6	60.9	1.3	0.2	96815
44145	WESTLAKE	44775	12973	9.7	16.8	40.4	15.5	17.6	75306	75510	90	93	9577	1.1	6.4	39.1	44.5	8.9	185168
44146	BEDFORD	25902	12965	21.9	30.3	36.9	7.6	3.3	47941	50898	56	42	7936	6.2	28.1	56.9	8.6	0.2	102287
44147	BROADVIEW HEIGHTS	34317	6874	11.2	22.4	40.4	15.9	10.2	65286	65024	84	86	5163	0.4	5.5	46.1	41.9	6.1	172153
44149	STRONGSVILLE	38790	7230	6.7	13.4	44.4	18.8	16.6	79899	80910	92	96	6417	0.0	1.6	53.4	44.4	0.6	168920
44201	ATWATER	24097	2624	12.3	26.9	47.9	11.0	1.9	59433	61449	77	77	2268	14.3	11.9	50.6	22.6	0.6	131522
44202	AURORA	42611	7107	8.6	14.1	38.9	17.2	21.2	82785	83066	93	97	5777	2.6	4.8	33.5	51.2	8.0	196208
44203	BARBERTON	23168	17042	23.6	29.9	36.7	6.9	2.9	46224	50495	52	37	12261	9.6	38.6	46.4	5.1	0.3	91506
44212	BRUNSWICK	29103	15729	9.7	19.1	48.0	16.0	7.2	74412	76984	89	93	12677	1.5	4.1	54.1	39.6	0.8	163204
44214	BURBANK	22358	702	14.2	26.9	47.9	8.3	2.7	56163	55688	73	71	592	6.3	12.8	47.6	29.4	3.9	142568
44215	CHIPPEWA LAKE	26581	1065	13.8	25.5	44.3	11.6	4.7	57690	57954	75	75	839	2.5	21.7	56.4	18.2	1.2	120074
44216	CLINTON	28041	3757	11.6	21.3	46.6	15.3	5.2	67533	68745	85	88	3306	1.5	17.0	64.7	15.4	1.5	119555
44217	CRESTON	21382	1651	16.4	30.3	45.0	7.0	1.3	52106	52812	66	58	1320	17.7	12.6	51.7	16.3	1.7	118382
44221	CUYAHOGA FALLS	26518	14176	20.5	26.9	42.6	7.8	2.2	51712	54528	65	57	8438	1.5	25.8	70.8	1.9	0.1	101357
44223	CUYAHOGA FALLS	30994	7748	17.7	23.8	39.3	13.6	5.6	58887	61533	76	76	5644	1.8	10.6	65.1	19.4	3.0	120785
44224	STOW	32976	15076	12.1	18.2	43.2	17.3	9.2	71423	71502	88	91	10617	1.5	9.0	60.7	27.6	1.2	141656
44230	DOYLESTOWN	26613	3261	13.7	26.2	42.7	13.1	4.3	60849	61160	79	79	2666	18.9	8.1	46.0	25.5	1.5	133967
44231	GARRETTSVILLE	23450	3028	17.6	26.1	42.3	12.0	2.0	55342	58195	72	68	2437	18.2	14.4	46.2	19.9	1.2	124149
44233	HINCKLEY	38033	2760	6.0	11.8	41.0	24.5	16.7	88484	98115	95	98	2581	0.8	0.4	21.2	62.7	14.9	248742
44234	HIRAM	25334	1386	13.0	20.8	45.7	15.4	5.2	66492	67174	85	87	1154	12.0	13.9	39.8	32.5	1.9	144048
44235	HOMERVILLE	18004	488	23.4	20.3	36.5	17.6	2.3	5666[illegible]	57944	74	72	417	14.1	12.2	29.3	41.5	2.9	151500
44236	HUDSON	50949	8467	5.5	8.3	27.4	22.3	36.4	124384	123822	99	100	7438	1.6	2.8	19.8	64.3	11.5	232457
44240	KENT	24739	15437	29.2	27.1	30.2	9.2	4.4	42633	46974	41	27	7834	6.4	12.2	58.4	21.6	1.4	130309
44241	STREETSBORO	28027	6430	12.9	23.6	48.1	12.1	3.3	61528	63103	79	80	4531	17.2	8.4	56.2	16.7	1.5	124671
44243	KENT	11559	4	75.0	25.0	0.0	0.0	0.0	10000	17500	0	0	0	0.0	0.0	0.0	0.0	0.0	0
44253	LITCHFIELD	26435	1260	7.7	19.4	51.3	14.4	7.3	75282	77853	89	93	1172	1.3	4.9	39.3	52.0	2.6	182048
44254	LODI	23532	2113	20.2	29.7	38.8	8.8	2.4	50067	51719	61	49	1578	14.3	12.2	44.7	27.9	1.0	131031
44255	MANTUA	26336	2833	11.5	23.6	49.3	12.2	3.4	64208	66239	83	84	2338	14.0	7.0	49.1	28.1	1.8	144437
44256	MEDINA	32917	23186	9.7	18.5	41.3	19.4	11.2	76275	81135	90	94	18209	2.0	2.8	37.4	51.8	6.0	188479
44260	MOGADORE	26100	5186	13.8	24.5	45.4	13.2	3.1	62087	63254	80	81	4364	7.2	13.2	59.8	18.0	1.9	125646
44262	MUNROE FALLS	34780	2017	6.2	19.7	43.5	17.0	13.6	75733	75984	90	94	1698	0.8	2.5	73.1	23.0	0.6	135043
44264	PENINSULA	36702	1018	12.2	24.1	36.9	15.9	10.9	70764	72213	87	91	843	23.5	6.4	30.6	29.2	10.3	146324
44266	RAVENNA	23739	13791	19.4	27.4	41.9	8.7	2.6	52153	54959	66	58	10099	23.9	17.8	44.6	13.1	0.8	101598
44270	RITTMAN	22491	3349	20.2	27.8	41.4	8.5	2.1	51272	52512	64	55	2397	5.5	18.6	60.4	15.0	0.6	116865
44272	ROOTSTOWN	25789	1836	11.9	24.1	48.0	12.7	3.3	59628	61598	77	77	1492	4.7	9.2	58.2	26.1	1.7	143154
44273	SEVILLE	29592	3007	9.7	20.0	48.4	14.6	7.4	67892	69101	86	89	2565	3.2	7.9	41.8	43.0	4.1	168750
44275	SPENCER	24521	1251	10.6	24.0	50.9	11.7	2.8	64360	65536	83	84	1066	4.0	10.7	42.7	40.2	2.4	159924
44276	STERLING	20952	775	16.9	24.5	50.5	6.7	1.4	55087	54867	71	67	629	5.9	11.1	62.3	19.4	1.3	136759
44278	TALLMADGE	27134	6969	15.5	24.4	41.6	13.6	4.9	60477	62688	78	78	5403	2.4	9.4	66.8	21.1	0.3	133711
44280	VALLEY CITY	32769	1837	9.0	19.0	40.4	19.8	11.8	77676	81952	91	95	1648	2.2	2.9	31.7	55.3	7.9	205849
44281	WADSWORTH	30963	11571	12.7	21.4	43.8	13.8	8.2	67328	71206	85	88	9009	2.2	7.6	46.5	39.2	4.5	163951
44286	RICHFIELD	40788	2117	8.1	16.4	34.3	22.0	19.2	86271	86456	94	98	1905	0.0	4.0	39.3	40.1	16.6	194522
44287	WEST SALEM	19778	2914	16.9	30.8	43.3	7.3	1.6	51255	52003	64	55	2483	12.9	14.5	52.0	18.7	1.9	124847
44288	WINDHAM	17861	1535	25.5	30.5	36.9	5.5	1.6	44044	48903	46	31	1025	24.1	31.4	37.0	6.7	0.8	83353
44301	AKRON	21628	6571	25.5	30.2	35.9	6.8	1.6	43990	48496	45	31	4497	11.8	53.5	34.2	0.2	0.2	82031
44302	AKRON	21794	2926	38.9	26.9	27.4	4.9	1.9	32536	34675	12	8	1027	15.2	44.6	37.6	2.4	0.2	82923
44303	AKRON	33703	3491	22.3	27.9	28.4	12.2	9.2	49777	53215	61	48	2082	4.9	17.2	50.3	22.9	4.6	123068
44304	AKRON	14868	2485	57.0	25.4	13.8	2.5	1.4	19716	20373	1	2	428	54.2	35.3	8.2	0.2	2.1	46667
44305	AKRON	21544	9345	21.5	31.8	41.1	4.5	1.1	46574	50963	53	38	6374	11.3	64.9	23.5	0.2	0.1	75577
44306	AKRON	16060	9416	38.2	31.6	27.1	2.4	0.8	32139	33745	12	8	5152	26.8	59.4	12.7	1.0	0.0	64184
44307	AKRON	13316	3614	55.2	26.8	16.1	1.5	0.3	22078	22782	2	2	1436	48.4	45.3	5.9	0.4	0.0	50983
44308	AKRON	20815	449	75.7	14.0	6.9	0.9	2.4	11318	11712	1	0	5	0.0	0.0	100.0	0.0	0.0	104167
	OHIO	26577		21.4	25.9	36.7	10.4	5.7	52400	54553				10.3	22.0	45.6	19.3	2.8	114865
	UNITED STATES	27277		20.9	24.4	35.3	11.7	7.6	54719	56938				9.3	13.1	31.6	32.6	13.5	162279

ZIP CODE #	POST OFFICE NAME	FINANCIAL SERVICES Auto Loan	Home Loan	Invest-ments	Retire-ment Plans	THE HOME Home Improvements Home Repair	Lawn & Garden	Furnishings Comput-ers & Hard-ware-Personal	Major Appli-ances	TV, Radio, Sound Equip-ment	Furni-ture	ENTERTAINMENT Dine out/ Carry out	Sports Equip-ment	Fees & Tickets	Toys & Games	Travel	Cable TV	PERSONAL Apparel & Services	Auto Repairs	Health Insur-ance	Pets & Supplies
44099	WINDSOR	85	80	78	83	81	92	78	87	80	71	79	66	73	81	78	84	54	81	89	101
44102	CLEVELAND	56	47	43	49	45	49	61	52	63	56	63	42	56	62	53	65	45	59	58	65
44103	CLEVELAND	42	32	30	34	31	37	42	37	46	40	45	28	38	44	36	49	32	42	45	47
44104	CLEVELAND	39	30	27	31	28	34	37	34	42	37	41	25	34	41	32	45	29	38	41	43
44105	CLEVELAND	61	53	46	54	49	58	58	56	63	57	62	42	55	62	53	66	43	59	64	69
44106	CLEVELAND	65	51	52	55	50	55	70	58	71	65	71	47	63	69	60	72	50	66	65	73
44107	LAKEWOOD	84	81	78	84	80	78	91	81	90	88	91	66	90	89	87	89	64	88	85	98
44108	CLEVELAND	57	49	46	50	47	55	54	52	60	55	59	38	53	59	50	64	41	56	61	65
44109	CLEVELAND	64	58	51	59	55	61	67	61	69	62	68	48	63	68	61	71	48	65	67	74
44110	CLEVELAND	52	44	40	46	41	48	53	47	57	50	56	37	50	55	47	59	39	53	55	59
44111	CLEVELAND	78	77	66	78	73	79	81	76	82	77	82	60	80	83	78	84	57	80	83	92
44112	CLEVELAND	57	47	43	50	45	53	55	51	60	54	59	39	52	58	50	63	41	56	60	64
44113	CLEVELAND	59	47	44	50	45	48	64	52	66	59	67	43	59	65	55	68	47	61	59	66
44114	CLEVELAND	45	35	38	39	35	41	53	43	57	47	56	34	48	51	46	60	40	52	56	55
44115	CLEVELAND	32	22	21	25	21	25	34	27	37	31	37	22	29	35	28	39	26	33	34	36
44116	ROCKY RIVER	107	121	125	122	125	125	114	118	117	117	117	85	125	112	123	120	82	117	129	136
44117	EUCLID	57	54	55	57	54	59	63	58	66	60	66	45	62	62	61	69	46	64	70	71
44118	CLEVELAND	107	112	108	114	111	110	113	108	112	113	113	84	118	112	114	112	80	112	112	128
44119	CLEVELAND	76	73	63	75	70	76	79	74	80	74	80	58	77	80	75	82	55	78	82	90
44120	CLEVELAND	82	74	71	77	72	79	82	77	86	82	86	59	81	85	77	89	60	82	85	95
44121	CLEVELAND	90	97	88	97	94	98	91	92	93	92	93	69	97	93	94	95	65	92	99	109
44122	BEACHWOOD	129	152	166	155	160	154	141	145	141	147	141	105	159	135	155	143	101	143	153	166
44123	EUCLID	75	73	62	74	69	75	78	73	78	74	78	58	76	79	74	80	54	76	79	88
44124	CLEVELAND	101	118	120	118	121	122	107	112	110	109	110	81	120	107	118	114	78	111	123	129
44125	CLEVELAND	79	85	76	85	83	90	80	82	83	78	83	62	85	83	83	87	57	82	92	97
44126	CLEVELAND	90	102	100	102	102	104	95	98	97	96	97	71	104	95	102	100	68	97	106	113
44127	CLEVELAND	50	42	36	43	39	45	51	45	54	48	54	36	47	54	44	57	38	50	52	57
44128	CLEVELAND	73	72	65	72	68	76	71	71	76	72	76	51	73	74	70	79	52	73	80	87
44129	CLEVELAND	80	88	79	88	85	92	83	84	86	81	86	63	88	85	86	89	59	85	95	100
44130	CLEVELAND	80	86	84	86	86	90	84	84	86	83	86	62	89	84	87	89	60	85	94	99
44131	INDEPENDENCE	99	118	119	118	121	122	102	111	104	107	104	78	115	101	114	107	73	107	119	127
44132	EUCLID	73	71	64	72	68	76	73	71	77	72	76	55	74	76	72	79	53	74	80	86
44133	NORTH ROYALTON	108	122	111	123	118	112	112	110	109	115	111	87	121	112	117	107	79	110	107	129
44134	CLEVELAND	83	91	83	91	89	95	85	88	88	84	88	65	91	88	89	91	61	87	97	103
44135	CLEVELAND	76	77	67	78	73	81	77	76	80	75	80	58	78	80	76	83	55	78	85	91
44136	STRONGSVILLE	131	148	144	152	148	139	137	136	133	142	135	105	149	134	144	131	96	135	132	158
44137	MAPLE HEIGHTS	79	82	71	83	78	87	80	80	83	77	82	60	82	82	80	85	57	81	90	96
44138	OLMSTED FALLS	103	113	109	112	113	109	103	107	101	107	102	81	109	102	108	101	71	103	105	123
44139	SOLON	166	214	216	220	219	196	179	186	169	191	171	144	210	172	201	164	126	175	170	211
44140	BAY VILLAGE	139	176	177	178	179	168	149	157	145	157	146	117	173	144	168	144	105	150	154	179
44141	BRECKSVILLE	152	192	205	196	202	186	163	175	158	176	158	128	189	155	186	156	114	165	169	197
44142	BROOK PARK	82	98	90	97	96	99	86	91	89	86	89	67	97	89	94	92	63	89	99	105
44143	CLEVELAND	116	128	128	131	130	127	121	122	120	125	121	91	131	119	128	121	86	122	125	141
44144	CLEVELAND	73	76	68	76	74	81	75	75	78	72	77	56	77	77	75	81	53	76	85	89
44145	WESTLAKE	142	167	169	170	170	158	150	152	145	156	147	115	166	146	162	144	105	149	148	175
44146	BEDFORD	79	76	74	77	75	81	81	79	83	78	83	60	80	82	79	86	58	82	87	94
44147	BROADVIEW HEIGHTS	112	129	126	131	129	123	118	119	115	122	117	91	129	116	126	114	83	117	117	138
44149	STRONGSVILLE	138	168	163	171	169	158	143	151	138	153	140	114	162	140	158	136	100	142	144	171
44201	ATWATER	100	97	92	99	96	107	92	100	94	87	93	77	89	96	93	97	64	95	102	118
44202	AURORA	151	180	169	184	179	160	155	159	148	168	150	125	173	153	166	141	108	150	143	181
44203	BARBERTON	78	79	74	79	77	85	77	80	81	74	80	60	79	80	78	84	56	79	87	94
44212	BRUNSWICK	112	122	106	123	117	112	114	112	110	117	112	88	119	114	115	108	79	111	107	131
44214	BURBANK	94	88	86	92	89	101	86	96	88	79	87	73	81	90	86	92	59	89	98	112
44215	CHIPPEWA LAKE	93	98	79	100	92	101	95	93	96	91	95	74	97	98	94	97	66	94	101	113
44216	CLINTON	106	118	107	121	116	120	106	112	105	105	106	86	113	108	112	107	74	107	113	131
44217	CRESTON	86	81	75	83	81	90	79	86	81	74	80	65	75	83	78	84	55	81	88	101
44221	CUYAHOGA FALLS	78	79	72	81	77	81	83	78	84	80	84	61	84	83	82	85	59	82	86	94
44223	CUYAHOGA FALLS	93	104	100	105	103	105	98	99	99	98	99	74	106	98	103	101	70	99	106	115
44224	STOW	112	126	118	128	124	118	117	116	114	120	116	90	126	116	122	113	82	115	114	135
44230	DOYLESTOWN	98	101	101	101	100	107	93	101	95	92	95	77	96	96	98	98	66	97	102	118
44231	GARRETTSVILLE	97	85	87	85	85	98	85	93	89	82	88	71	78	91	83	94	60	89	97	111
44233	HINCKLEY	143	173	171	178	176	165	149	157	144	157	145	118	167	144	165	142	103	149	150	181
44234	HIRAM	107	113	99	114	110	112	103	107	103	105	103	82	106	106	105	103	72	103	106	126
44235	HOMERVILLE	89	100	86	103	97	98	89	93	88	90	88	73	95	90	94	88	62	89	92	109
44236	HUDSON	201	253	251	263	257	229	212	220	200	229	203	172	246	205	236	192	149	206	197	250
44240	KENT	82	70	65	73	68	70	89	74	84	81	85	62	79	85	76	83	59	81	76	91
44241	STREETSBORO	100	97	85	98	92	91	99	94	97	100	99	75	97	101	95	96	69	96	92	112
44243	KENT	19	8	8	10	7	9	27	13	21	18	22	14	16	21	14	20	15	19	13	18
44253	LITCHFIELD	112	127	109	130	123	123	113	117	111	113	111	92	121	114	119	110	78	113	115	138
44254	LODI	86	86	77	87	84	88	84	85	84	83	84	66	83	86	83	85	58	84	88	101
44255	MANTUA	100	106	93	107	103	105	97	101	97	98	97	77	100	99	100	98	68	98	100	119
44256	MEDINA	124	139	127	140	136	126	127	127	122	132	124	99	135	126	131	119	88	124	119	147
44260	MOGADORE	92	106	95	107	103	106	93	98	94	94	94	74	102	96	100	96	66	95	101	114
44262	MUNROE FALLS	119	148	145	151	149	142	126	133	123	132	124	99	144	123	141	122	89	127	130	153
44264	PENINSULA	119	134	128	135	134	128	120	124	118	126	118	94	129	119	127	116	84	120	120	144
44266	RAVENNA	88	82	76	82	80	88	82	85	85	80	84	65	79	87	79	88	58	84	89	101
44270	RITTMAN	83	82	73	83	79	89	81	83	83	77	82	64	80	84	80	86	57	82	90	99
44272	ROOTSTOWN	94	106	95	107	103	108	94	100	95	93	95	76	101	97	100	97	66	96	103	116
44273	SEVILLE	114	124	116	128	124	127	112	120	111	111	111	92	117	113	119	113	78	113	119	140
44275	SPENCER	96	108	93	112	105	106	97	101	95	97	96	79	103	98	102	95	67	97	100	118
44276	STERLING	88	84	81	86	85	96	81	90	83	75	82	68	77	85	82	88	56	84	94	105
44278	TALLMADGE	93	104	101	104	105	107	95	100	96	95	96	74	102	96	102	99	67	97	105	116
44280	VALLEY CITY	126	149	142	153	149	144	130	136	126	134	127	104	143	127	141	125	90	130	132	158
44281	WADSWORTH	108	122	113	123	120	119	111	113	110	113	111	87	120	111	117	110	78	111	115	132
44286	RICHFIELD	150	183	188	187	189	178	157	168	153	167	154	122	178	151	176	152	110	159	164	191
44287	WEST SALEM	88	79	77	81	78	92	78	86	81	72	80	66	72	83	77	85	54	81	90	101
44288	WINDHAM	80	65	62	65	62	75	68	71	73	67	72	54	61	75	62	78	49	71	76	87
44301	AKRON	73	72	60	73	67	76	74	71	77	70	76	55	73	77	71	79	53	74	80	87
44302	AKRON	60	52	49	54	50	54	65	56	66	60	66	45	60	64	58	68	46	63	65	70
44303	AKRON	95	98	101	101	100	99	103	98	103	102	103	75	106	101	104	104	73	102	104	116
44304	AKRON	46	29	27	32	27	32	55	37	50	43	50	33	40	49	38	49	35	46	40	47
44305	AKRON	73	72	57	74	67	75	75	71	76	71	76	57	74	78	71	78	53	74	79	87
44306	AKRON	59	49	43	50	46	54	57	53	60	54	59	42	52	60	50	63	41	57	60	66
44307	AKRON	43	33	30	35	31	38	42	38	46	41	45	29	38	45	36	49	31	42	46	48
44308	AKRON	31	23	28	26	24	28	38	30	41	34	40	24	33	35	33	43	28	37	42	39
	OHIO	94	92	87	93	90	96	93	93	94	91	94	72	92	95	91	96	66	93	98	110
	UNITED STATES	100	100	100	100	100	100	100	100	100	100	100	100	100	100	100	100	100	100	100	100

ZIP CODE #	POST OFFICE NAME	COUNTY FIPS CODE	POPULATION 2000	POPULATION 2009	POPULATION 2014	2000-2009 ANNUAL RATE % Rate	2000-2009 ANNUAL RATE State Centile	HOUSEHOLDS 2000	HOUSEHOLDS 2009	HOUSEHOLDS 2014	HOUSEHOLDS % Annual Rate 2000-2009	HOUSEHOLDS 2009 Average HH Size	FAMILIES 2000	FAMILIES 2009	FAMILIES % Annual Rate 2000-2009
44310	AKRON	153	23984	22645	22087	-0.6	14	10242	9848	9666	-0.4	2.26	5835	5342	-0.9
44311	AKRON	153	10458	9440	9046	-1.1	4	3376	3047	2924	-1.1	2.78	1836	1569	-1.7
44312	AKRON	153	32362	31960	31640	-0.1	39	13464	13554	13503	0.1	2.35	9008	8754	-0.3
44313	AKRON	153	24614	25088	25060	0.2	56	11357	11694	11733	0.3	2.11	6477	6365	-0.2
44314	AKRON	153	20331	19054	18532	-0.7	11	8377	8006	7833	-0.5	2.38	5325	4889	-0.9
44319	AKRON	153	21929	22561	22652	0.3	61	9028	9495	9599	0.5	2.34	6207	6297	0.2
44320	AKRON	153	22879	21599	21059	-0.6	14	9261	8941	8780	-0.4	2.40	6129	5706	-0.8
44321	AKRON	153	11834	13975	14689	1.8	96	4290	5080	5347	1.8	2.68	3132	3623	1.6
44333	AKRON	153	18188	19103	19309	0.5	71	6993	7462	7586	0.7	2.46	5142	5325	0.4
44401	BERLIN CENTER	099	2606	2562	2537	-0.2	32	959	977	978	0.2	2.62	773	771	0.0
44402	BRISTOLVILLE	155	3480	3453	3402	-0.1	39	1247	1272	1266	0.2	2.71	993	992	0.0
44403	BROOKFIELD	155	4559	4402	4309	-0.4	21	1873	1875	1852	0.0	2.32	1347	1311	-0.3
44404	BURGHILL	155	1707	1640	1592	-0.4	21	659	657	644	0.0	2.49	511	497	-0.3
44405	CAMPBELL	099	9428	9051	8858	-0.4	21	3717	3638	3586	-0.2	2.49	2596	2457	-0.6
44406	CANFIELD	099	21086	21982	22035	0.5	71	8118	8671	8758	0.7	2.53	6042	6289	0.4
44408	COLUMBIANA	029	9999	10124	10057	0.1	51	4049	4153	4142	0.3	2.39	2847	2844	0.0
44410	CORTLAND	155	17225	16982	16664	-0.2	32	6851	6972	6909	0.2	2.42	4981	4929	-0.1
44411	DEERFIELD	133	2706	2631	2590	-0.3	27	983	981	977	0.0	2.68	767	747	-0.3
44412	DIAMOND	133	2707	2769	2785	0.2	56	969	1029	1047	0.7	2.69	808	842	0.4
44413	EAST PALESTINE	029	7786	7545	7388	-0.3	27	3043	2984	2935	-0.2	2.52	2215	2119	-0.5
44417	FARMDALE	155	2054	2006	1967	-0.3	27	736	740	732	0.1	2.71	589	579	-0.2
44418	FOWLER	155	1437	1437	1425	0.0	45	529	546	546	0.3	2.55	418	423	0.1
44420	GIRARD	155	17103	15865	15246	-0.8	9	7024	6697	6492	-0.5	2.37	4766	4402	-0.9
44423	HANOVERTON	029	2849	3134	3174	1.0	87	1096	1222	1245	1.2	2.56	821	894	0.9
44425	HUBBARD	155	15539	14796	14357	-0.5	17	6223	6108	5978	-0.2	2.42	4368	4158	-0.5
44427	KENSINGTON	029	1797	1918	1928	0.7	79	631	689	697	1.0	2.76	494	528	0.7
44428	KINSMAN	155	3437	3334	3269	-0.3	27	1270	1274	1262	0.0	2.58	964	944	-0.2
44429	LAKE MILTON	099	3083	3196	3197	0.4	66	1217	1307	1320	0.8	2.42	850	882	0.4
44430	LEAVITTSBURG	155	5789	5487	5336	-0.6	14	1628	1585	1545	-0.3	2.66	1216	1155	-0.6
44431	LEETONIA	029	4721	4681	4613	-0.1	39	1717	1723	1706	0.0	2.72	1307	1281	-0.2
44432	LISBON	029	13879	14082	13977	0.2	56	4285	4351	4327	0.2	2.69	3105	3078	-0.1
44436	LOWELLVILLE	099	4168	4066	4014	-0.3	27	1597	1603	1596	0.0	2.54	1163	1136	-0.3
44437	MC DONALD	155	4784	4611	4487	-0.4	21	1788	1783	1753	0.0	2.58	1384	1348	-0.3
44438	MASURY	155	5417	4887	4671	-1.1	4	2198	2050	1974	-0.8	2.30	1458	1315	-1.1
44440	MINERAL RIDGE	155	3980	3976	3928	0.0	45	1405	1452	1445	0.4	2.54	1033	1043	0.1
44441	NEGLEY	029	1786	1785	1770	0.0	45	678	687	684	0.1	2.60	515	511	-0.1
44442	NEW MIDDLETOWN	099	3448	3695	3751	0.8	82	1407	1564	1602	1.2	2.36	1020	1103	0.8
44443	NEW SPRINGFIELD	099	1720	1778	1781	0.4	66	658	703	711	0.7	2.53	492	512	0.4
44444	NEWTON FALLS	155	10779	10440	10212	-0.3	27	4263	4260	4204	0.0	2.43	3016	2937	-0.3
44445	NEW WATERFORD	029	3332	3436	3421	0.3	61	1255	1309	1312	0.5	2.32	954	972	0.2
44446	NILES	155	23250	21546	20719	-0.8	9	9760	9309	9032	-0.5	2.28	6141	5644	-0.9
44449	NORTH BENTON	099	1079	1071	1063	-0.1	39	425	431	432	0.2	2.48	318	314	-0.1
44450	NORTH BLOOMFIELD	155	2543	2675	2669	0.5	71	870	939	945	0.8	2.84	676	713	0.6
44451	NORTH JACKSON	099	3457	3543	3532	0.3	61	1274	1351	1363	0.6	2.60	995	1030	0.4
44452	NORTH LIMA	099	2087	2219	2235	0.7	79	718	790	804	1.0	2.67	554	595	0.8
44454	PETERSBURG	099	1386	1472	1480	0.7	79	460	501	508	0.9	2.91	373	398	0.7
44455	ROGERS	029	1594	1630	1626	0.2	56	574	595	596	0.4	2.48	445	450	0.1
44460	SALEM	029	27111	26192	25667	-0.4	21	10752	10525	10367	-0.2	2.45	7626	7280	-0.5
44470	SOUTHINGTON	155	3812	3746	3671	-0.2	32	1407	1428	1414	0.2	2.62	1115	1108	-0.1
44471	STRUTHERS	099	11960	11516	11284	-0.4	21	4776	4708	4651	-0.2	2.43	3312	3157	-0.5
44473	VIENNA	155	3633	3529	3442	-0.3	27	1494	1499	1477	0.0	2.35	1062	1034	-0.3
44481	WARREN	155	11429	11075	10810	-0.3	27	4505	4496	4426	0.0	2.45	3329	3258	-0.2
44483	WARREN	155	28960	26722	25741	-0.9	7	11891	11252	10924	-0.6	2.30	7583	6956	-0.9
44484	WARREN	155	24111	23106	22475	-0.5	17	9637	9540	9367	-0.1	2.38	6786	6548	-0.4
44485	WARREN	155	19662	17930	17132	-1.0	5	8046	7520	7247	-0.7	2.36	5292	4783	-1.1
44490	WASHINGTONVILLE	029	749	753	746	0.1	51	288	295	294	0.3	2.55	222	222	0.0
44491	WEST FARMINGTON	155	2727	2891	2905	0.6	75	918	994	1006	0.9	2.91	760	808	0.7
44502	YOUNGSTOWN	099	12970	11446	10960	-1.3	2	4937	4424	4256	-1.2	2.37	2966	2551	-1.6
44503	YOUNGSTOWN	099	555	542	537	-0.3	27	416	401	394	-0.4	1.35	26	22	-1.8
44504	YOUNGSTOWN	099	4935	4397	4248	-1.2	3	1890	1673	1614	-1.3	2.16	990	840	-1.8
44505	YOUNGSTOWN	099	22734	20816	20087	-0.9	7	8558	7921	7669	-0.8	2.31	5399	4815	-1.2
44506	YOUNGSTOWN	099	3685	3018	2829	-2.1	0	1412	1194	1132	-1.8	2.53	930	755	-2.2
44507	YOUNGSTOWN	099	8893	7534	7133	-1.8	0	3223	2701	2563	-1.9	2.75	2050	1653	-2.3
44509	YOUNGSTOWN	099	13187	11979	11554	-1.0	5	5433	5064	4924	-0.8	2.30	3507	3146	-1.2
44510	YOUNGSTOWN	099	2795	2254	2131	-2.3	0	1144	939	893	-2.1	2.33	692	545	-2.5
44511	YOUNGSTOWN	099	23811	21562	20817	-1.1	4	9872	9233	9003	-0.7	2.32	6606	5963	-1.1
44512	YOUNGSTOWN	099	36388	35057	34394	-0.4	21	15673	15505	15334	-0.1	2.23	9887	9403	-0.5
44514	YOUNGSTOWN	099	22702	22945	22778	0.1	51	8968	9307	9313	0.4	2.42	6565	6649	0.1
44515	YOUNGSTOWN	099	27787	27166	26748	-0.2	32	11613	11644	11558	0.0	2.28	7606	7412	-0.3
44555	YOUNGSTOWN	099	181	164	161	-1.1	4	1	1	1	0.0	3.00	0	0	0.0
44601	ALLIANCE	151	37189	36330	35973	-0.3	27	14092	13976	13911	-0.1	2.45	9620	9249	-0.4
44606	APPLE CREEK	169	7387	7988	8232	0.8	82	2055	2258	2343	1.0	3.44	1694	1833	0.9
44608	BEACH CITY	151	3029	3153	3202	0.4	66	1115	1182	1205	0.6	2.60	834	861	0.3
44609	BELOIT	099	3944	3933	3899	0.0	45	1531	1557	1552	0.2	2.51	1149	1139	-0.1
44611	BIG PRAIRIE	075	2056	2188	2261	0.7	79	671	731	761	0.9	2.99	520	554	0.7
44612	BOLIVAR	157	5094	5476	5596	0.8	82	1958	2116	2172	0.8	2.58	1493	1578	0.6
44613	BREWSTER	151	2223	2224	2216	0.0	45	815	830	831	0.2	2.61	621	615	-0.1
44614	CANAL FULTON	151	11216	12346	12750	1.0	87	3972	4480	4665	1.3	2.69	3139	3458	1.1
44615	CARROLLTON	019	11097	10940	10760	-0.2	32	4331	4377	4338	0.1	2.45	3088	3046	-0.1
44618	DALTON	169	7005	7412	7564	0.6	75	2279	2474	2548	0.9	2.95	1849	1966	0.7
44620	DELLROY	019	1723	1892	1910	1.0	87	645	731	746	1.4	2.59	494	547	1.1
44621	DENNISON	157	4857	4923	4943	0.1	51	1833	1875	1888	0.2	2.61	1351	1348	0.0
44622	DOVER	157	18321	18633	18734	0.2	56	7260	7428	7488	0.2	2.45	5135	5118	0.0
44624	DUNDEE	075	5036	5465	5659	0.9	85	1413	1556	1618	1.0	3.45	1213	1316	0.9
44625	EAST ROCHESTER	029	1272	1281	1271	0.1	51	434	445	444	0.3	2.87	349	351	0.1
44626	EAST SPARTA	151	3166	3376	3452	0.7	79	1202	1311	1351	0.9	2.58	936	996	0.7
44627	FREDERICKSBURG	075	5322	5968	6261	1.2	91	1224	1405	1484	1.5	4.24	1049	1186	1.3
44628	GLENMONT	075	1196	1358	1435	1.4	93	459	531	565	1.6	2.56	338	380	1.3
44629	GNADENHUTTEN	157	2979	3036	3047	0.2	56	1169	1200	1210	0.3	2.53	867	869	0.0
44632	HARTVILLE	151	9686	10492	10778	0.9	85	3399	3767	3900	1.1	2.76	2719	2943	0.9
44633	HOLMESVILLE	075	2372	2576	2687	0.9	85	661	733	770	1.1	3.40	558	609	0.9
44634	HOMEWORTH	029	2342	2342	2320	0.0	45	828	841	839	0.2	2.73	658	654	-0.1
44637	KILLBUCK	075	2291	2525	2644	1.1	89	911	1025	1079	1.3	2.46	655	717	1.0
44638	LAKEVILLE	075	1581	1686	1741	0.7	79	571	622	646	0.9	2.71	439	468	0.7
44641	LOUISVILLE	151	20057	20675	20877	0.3	61	7256	7626	7757	0.5	2.63	5511	5643	0.3
	OHIO					0.2					0.4	2.44			0.1
	UNITED STATES					1.0					1.1	2.59			0.9

#	POST OFFICE NAME	RACE (%) White 2000	White 2009	Black 2000	Black 2009	Asian/Pacific 2000	Asian/Pacific 2009	% Hispanic Origin 2000	% Hispanic Origin 2009	2009 AGE DISTRIBUTION (%) 0-4	5-9	10-14	15-19	20-24	25-44	45-64	65-84	85+	18+	MEDIAN AGE 2009	% 2009 Males	% 2009 Females
44310	AKRON	72.8	67.0	22.7	27.3	1.4	2.1	1.3	1.5	7.2	6.8	6.4	6.4	6.5	28.0	25.3	11.1	2.3	75.8	36.9	48.3	51.7
44311	AKRON	53.2	44.2	36.7	43.5	5.6	7.6	1.9	2.1	7.1	6.5	5.6	10.4	18.8	26.5	17.2	6.7	1.1	76.9	25.8	50.9	49.1
44312	AKRON	96.8	95.5	1.3	1.9	0.6	1.0	0.6	0.8	5.9	5.9	6.0	5.9	5.2	26.5	28.7	13.7	2.3	78.6	41.3	48.3	51.7
44313	AKRON	80.5	74.5	15.8	20.5	1.8	2.7	1.1	1.4	5.8	5.6	5.5	5.0	5.6	26.4	27.2	14.9	3.9	79.8	42.0	47.2	52.8
44314	AKRON	91.7	88.7	5.4	7.5	0.6	1.0	0.8	1.0	7.3	7.1	6.8	6.5	6.3	28.4	25.6	10.4	1.7	74.9	36.3	49.4	50.6
44319	AKRON	97.8	96.8	0.7	1.0	0.5	0.8	0.5	0.7	5.2	5.4	5.9	5.6	4.7	23.9	31.0	15.5	2.7	80.0	44.5	48.9	51.1
44320	AKRON	21.6	18.1	75.3	78.6	0.6	0.9	0.8	0.8	6.1	6.8	7.2	8.0	6.5	24.2	27.0	12.4	1.8	74.9	38.5	45.4	54.6
44321	AKRON	87.6	83.0	7.4	9.5	3.2	5.4	1.0	1.5	6.3	6.6	6.7	6.6	4.7	24.9	29.5	11.6	3.1	76.0	41.1	48.6	51.4
44333	AKRON	92.6	89.1	3.5	4.9	2.6	4.3	1.0	1.3	4.9	5.4	6.4	6.3	3.9	19.3	32.3	17.1	4.5	79.2	47.4	47.6	52.4
44401	BERLIN CENTER	98.8	98.1	0.1	0.2	0.0	0.1	0.6	1.0	4.7	5.2	6.0	6.6	4.3	25.0	33.9	13.0	1.2	79.9	43.7	51.9	48.1
44402	BRISTOLVILLE	98.6	98.2	0.4	0.6	0.2	0.3	0.3	0.5	5.8	6.3	7.2	6.7	4.6	25.1	31.9	11.4	1.1	76.6	41.3	50.8	49.2
44403	BROOKFIELD	98.1	97.5	0.9	1.1	0.3	0.4	0.7	0.9	4.6	5.0	5.6	6.1	4.5	22.1	31.9	17.2	3.0	81.0	46.4	48.6	51.4
44404	BURGHILL	98.9	98.7	0.2	0.3	0.1	0.1	0.4	0.5	5.9	7.0	7.3	6.5	4.1	23.7	30.1	13.8	1.6	75.5	42.3	50.2	49.8
44405	CAMPBELL	77.2	68.6	16.7	23.2	0.2	0.3	11.0	14.7	6.8	6.7	6.2	6.1	5.7	23.2	25.4	16.9	3.0	76.7	41.0	46.5	53.5
44406	CANFIELD	96.6	94.5	1.2	2.0	1.2	2.1	1.0	1.6	5.1	5.6	6.4	6.6	4.7	22.8	33.0	13.8	2.0	78.7	44.1	48.6	51.4
44408	COLUMBIANA	98.6	98.2	0.3	0.4	0.3	0.4	0.5	0.7	5.4	5.5	6.0	6.4	5.4	22.9	29.6	15.9	2.9	79.2	43.8	48.5	51.5
44410	CORTLAND	97.8	97.0	0.9	1.1	0.4	0.7	0.6	0.9	5.2	5.7	6.2	6.4	5.1	23.3	32.8	13.4	1.9	79.0	43.6	48.3	51.7
44411	DEERFIELD	98.2	97.8	0.6	0.8	0.1	0.2	0.3	0.4	6.8	6.8	7.1	6.8	5.3	27.8	27.7	10.5	1.1	75.0	38.0	50.6	49.4
44412	DIAMOND	98.2	97.8	1.1	1.2	0.0	0.1	0.5	0.7	5.3	5.9	6.5	6.7	4.6	25.4	33.0	11.6	1.1	78.1	42.3	51.0	49.0
44413	EAST PALESTINE	98.7	98.3	0.4	0.4	0.1	0.2	0.6	0.8	5.8	5.9	6.2	6.6	5.8	25.7	29.6	12.4	2.0	77.9	40.7	49.7	50.3
44417	FARMDALE	98.4	98.0	0.6	0.7	0.2	0.3	0.5	0.7	6.0	6.6	6.8	6.4	4.9	23.9	31.6	12.4	1.3	76.6	41.4	49.1	50.9
44418	FOWLER	98.7	98.3	0.5	0.7	0.1	0.2	0.3	0.5	5.0	5.6	6.4	6.4	4.1	21.5	33.2	15.2	2.6	78.9	45.6	49.1	50.9
44420	GIRARD	94.7	93.1	3.2	4.1	0.6	1.0	0.8	1.1	5.6	5.8	6.1	6.2	5.3	24.3	29.6	14.7	2.5	78.8	42.5	48.2	51.8
44423	HANOVERTON	98.9	98.5	0.2	0.3	0.1	0.2	0.5	0.6	6.0	6.3	6.6	6.3	5.6	24.6	30.1	13.0	1.5	77.2	41.3	50.0	50.0
44425	HUBBARD	96.4	95.4	2.4	2.9	0.3	0.5	0.7	0.9	5.0	5.3	5.8	6.4	5.4	23.7	30.8	15.2	2.4	80.0	43.8	48.4	51.6
44427	KENSINGTON	98.4	98.2	0.3	0.4	0.0	0.0	0.6	0.7	6.8	7.4	8.0	6.5	5.2	25.9	28.0	10.9	1.3	73.4	38.2	49.1	50.9
44428	KINSMAN	98.5	98.1	0.7	1.0	0.3	0.5	0.3	0.4	6.1	6.6	6.7	6.3	4.6	24.1	30.9	13.1	1.6	76.7	41.6	49.0	51.0
44429	LAKE MILTON	98.1	97.0	0.4	0.6	0.3	0.5	0.6	1.0	5.7	6.0	6.1	5.8	4.9	27.3	30.4	12.7	1.1	78.7	40.7	49.4	50.6
44430	LEAVITTSBURG	81.1	77.7	17.6	20.8	0.1	0.2	0.6	0.8	3.9	4.5	4.8	6.6	9.3	34.4	26.0	9.4	1.1	82.9	36.8	61.5	38.5
44431	LEETONIA	98.9	98.6	0.3	0.3	0.1	0.2	0.6	0.7	6.2	6.6	7.0	6.8	5.1	25.1	29.4	12.2	1.6	76.1	40.3	50.6	49.4
44432	LISBON	91.4	90.2	7.0	7.8	0.3	0.5	4.5	5.7	4.6	4.8	5.3	6.0	5.9	32.8	28.7	10.6	1.4	81.6	39.1	57.5	42.5
44436	LOWELLVILLE	96.4	94.4	2.0	3.3	0.1	0.1	2.0	3.0	4.8	5.0	5.5	6.4	5.1	23.3	31.6	15.7	2.6	80.8	44.9	49.4	50.6
44437	MC DONALD	97.2	96.4	1.4	1.9	0.1	0.2	1.1	1.5	5.6	5.9	6.5	7.1	5.2	25.5	30.2	12.2	1.9	77.7	40.9	48.2	51.8
44438	MASURY	92.3	90.2	6.0	7.6	0.3	0.5	0.7	0.8	5.7	5.9	5.9	6.1	5.2	24.3	28.7	14.4	3.7	78.7	42.5	48.2	51.8
44440	MINERAL RIDGE	97.1	95.7	1.6	2.5	0.1	0.2	1.1	1.6	5.0	5.5	6.1	6.2	4.1	24.6	29.9	14.2	4.5	79.6	44.0	47.7	52.3
44441	NEGLEY	98.2	97.8	0.3	0.3	0.2	0.3	0.8	1.1	5.5	6.4	7.0	7.2	5.4	25.2	31.1	11.1	1.2	76.6	39.9	51.8	48.2
44442	NEW MIDDLETOWN	99.2	98.9	0.0	0.1	0.1	0.1	0.9	1.4	4.4	4.6	5.1	6.4	5.2	23.0	31.3	17.5	2.5	82.0	45.8	46.1	53.9
44443	NEW SPRINGFIELD	99.0	98.3	0.0	0.0	0.2	0.3	0.9	1.5	5.5	5.7	5.9	5.7	5.1	25.7	30.6	14.0	1.9	79.4	42.5	47.8	52.2
44444	NEWTON FALLS	98.0	97.5	0.8	1.0	0.1	0.2	0.6	0.8	5.8	5.8	6.1	6.5	5.3	26.2	28.9	13.2	2.2	78.3	41.0	48.8	51.2
44445	NEW WATERFORD	93.4	92.4	5.3	5.8	0.2	0.3	3.7	4.6	5.2	5.7	6.2	6.0	5.1	30.1	29.8	10.7	1.3	79.1	39.8	56.2	43.8
44446	NILES	96.1	94.9	2.2	2.8	0.4	0.6	0.9	1.1	5.6	5.5	5.6	6.0	6.0	26.1	27.5	14.6	3.1	79.6	41.4	47.7	52.3
44449	NORTH BENTON	98.3	97.5	0.3	0.4	0.0	0.0	0.9	1.5	6.3	5.8	6.8	6.7	4.6	25.3	29.7	13.9	0.8	77.1	41.4	52.2	47.8
44450	NORTH BLOOMFIELD	96.7	95.5	2.0	2.7	0.1	0.1	0.7	1.2	8.5	8.5	8.3	7.5	5.4	25.2	25.4	9.9	1.3	70.0	34.7	50.3	49.7
44451	NORTH JACKSON	98.5	97.6	0.4	0.7	0.1	0.2	0.9	1.4	4.8	5.1	5.9	6.4	4.5	24.9	33.9	13.2	1.5	80.3	43.9	51.5	48.5
44452	NORTH LIMA	98.7	97.8	0.3	0.6	0.3	0.6	0.4	0.7	5.1	5.5	6.3	6.4	4.5	21.1	31.5	16.0	3.7	79.0	45.7	48.1	51.9
44454	PETERSBURG	97.7	96.7	0.1	0.1	0.0	0.0	1.3	2.0	7.3	7.3	7.3	6.5	5.9	26.5	28.1	9.9	1.2	73.6	37.4	47.8	52.2
44455	ROGERS	93.9	92.9	4.3	4.8	0.3	0.5	3.5	4.4	4.7	5.5	6.0	6.5	5.8	29.5	30.7	10.4	1.0	79.9	39.4	56.3	43.7
44460	SALEM	98.6	98.1	0.3	0.4	0.3	0.5	0.5	0.7	5.8	6.0	6.2	6.2	5.4	24.6	29.1	13.9	2.8	78.3	41.9	48.0	52.0
44470	SOUTHINGTON	97.9	97.3	1.2	1.6	0.1	0.2	0.8	1.0	5.6	5.9	6.4	6.0	4.1	26.4	31.0	13.2	1.3	78.3	42.2	51.1	48.9
44471	STRUTHERS	96.7	94.9	1.8	2.8	0.2	0.3	2.0	3.1	5.9	5.8	5.7	6.6	6.1	25.1	26.5	15.4	2.9	78.6	41.0	47.4	52.6
44473	VIENNA	98.7	98.4	0.6	0.8	0.1	0.2	0.6	0.9	5.0	5.4	5.8	5.9	4.6	22.7	31.9	16.4	2.3	80.2	45.4	50.3	49.7
44481	WARREN	95.4	94.4	3.4	4.1	0.2	0.4	0.5	0.7	5.2	5.8	6.5	6.4	4.7	24.0	32.3	13.5	1.5	78.5	43.1	49.9	50.1
44483	WARREN	86.3	84.4	11.6	12.9	0.3	0.5	1.0	1.3	6.9	6.4	6.1	6.1	5.8	24.3	26.2	14.9	3.3	77.0	40.8	47.3	52.7
44484	WARREN	86.7	84.4	10.4	11.5	1.4	2.2	1.0	1.3	5.8	5.6	5.9	6.5	5.6	22.7	29.7	15.6	2.6	78.6	43.4	47.7	52.3
44485	WARREN	62.0	56.7	35.1	39.9	0.4	0.6	0.8	0.9	7.8	7.1	6.9	7.0	6.6	24.0	25.4	13.2	2.1	74.0	37.2	47.2	52.8
44490	WASHINGTONVILLE	98.3	97.7	0.4	0.5	0.0	0.1	0.9	1.3	6.2	6.8	7.2	6.6	4.4	25.0	29.9	12.6	1.3	75.6	40.4	50.1	49.9
44491	WEST FARMINGTON	98.5	98.1	0.5	0.7	0.1	0.1	0.6	0.9	9.8	9.8	9.5	7.6	5.0	26.5	23.2	7.6	1.0	66.1	32.0	50.7	49.3
44502	YOUNGSTOWN	62.9	53.7	31.8	39.7	0.4	0.6	4.9	6.4	6.5	6.2	6.4	8.8	7.9	23.7	23.9	14.0	2.6	76.2	37.2	49.4	50.6
44503	YOUNGSTOWN	40.3	27.7	57.4	69.9	0.2	0.2	1.8	2.0	0.7	0.7	0.6	2.4	10.5	31.7	30.3	20.1	3.0	97.6	47.1	64.6	35.4
44504	YOUNGSTOWN	43.6	31.6	51.8	63.3	0.9	1.2	2.1	2.3	4.8	5.0	5.2	10.5	11.2	19.0	22.5	14.6	7.1	80.9	38.7	45.3	54.7
44505	YOUNGSTOWN	41.5	35.0	53.0	59.0	0.8	1.2	4.0	4.2	6.0	6.3	6.1	6.6	6.6	26.4	25.5	13.8	2.6	77.8	38.6	51.4	48.6
44506	YOUNGSTOWN	27.2	20.3	52.7	58.3	0.2	0.3	30.5	31.3	7.5	7.8	7.7	7.8	6.6	21.8	25.7	13.2	2.0	72.8	37.2	47.3	52.7
44507	YOUNGSTOWN	30.5	21.2	62.8	71.8	0.6	0.7	6.4	6.8	9.4	9.5	8.6	9.4	7.5	24.2	21.4	8.5	1.4	66.8	29.2	45.6	54.4
44509	YOUNGSTOWN	89.3	83.8	7.3	11.4	0.3	0.4	3.3	4.9	7.7	6.7	6.2	5.6	5.8	25.4	24.7	14.0	3.8	75.8	39.2	46.8	53.2
44510	YOUNGSTOWN	17.5	10.9	76.1	82.7	0.2	0.2	5.0	5.2	8.7	8.2	7.1	7.8	6.8	21.1	25.5	12.7	2.1	71.6	36.0	45.1	54.9
44511	YOUNGSTOWN	67.0	65.9	30.9	31.4	0.3	0.5	2.0	2.6	6.0	6.3	6.4	6.5	5.0	22.5	27.3	16.8	3.2	77.2	42.8	46.1	53.9
44512	YOUNGSTOWN	94.1	90.5	3.5	5.8	0.9	1.5	1.9	2.8	4.9	5.1	5.4	5.6	5.0	25.0	30.3	14.8	3.9	81.1	44.2	47.2	52.8
44514	YOUNGSTOWN	98.1	97.0	0.7	1.1	0.4	0.7	1.3	2.0	4.7	5.5	6.3	6.5	4.3	21.1	31.7	16.5	3.4	79.4	46.0	47.6	52.4
44515	YOUNGSTOWN	92.8	88.9	4.9	7.8	0.6	0.9	1.8	2.6	5.8	5.8	6.0	5.7	5.3	26.0	28.4	14.2	2.8	78.9	41.6	48.0	52.0
44555	YOUNGSTOWN	61.5	48.2	34.6	47.6	1.1	1.2	3.3	4.3	1.8	2.4	1.8	39.0	22.0	11.0	11.6	9.1	1.2	93.3	21.1	47.6	52.4
44601	ALLIANCE	89.5	87.2	7.9	9.4	0.7	1.0	0.9	1.2	6.2	6.0	6.1	8.2	7.6	23.6	26.0	13.5	2.8	77.8	38.5	47.7	52.3
44606	APPLE CREEK	98.3	97.8	0.4	0.5	0.4	0.6	0.9	1.2	11.7	10.8	9.3	8.5	7.6	25.0	19.4	7.1	0.7	63.0	26.6	50.3	49.7
44608	BEACH CITY	98.8	98.4	0.2	0.3	0.3	0.5	0.5	0.7	6.3	6.5	6.8	6.8	5.4	24.6	28.3	13.2	2.2	76.2	40.8	50.2	49.8
44609	BELOIT	98.8	98.2	0.2	0.3	0.2	0.2	0.3	0.5	4.9	5.4	6.0	6.9	4.6	23.5	32.1	14.2	2.4	79.4	44.0	48.9	51.1
44611	BIG PRAIRIE	98.3	98.0	0.6	0.7	0.3	0.4	0.8	1.0	8.6	8.7	8.7	7.7	4.9	24.6	26.1	9.6	1.0	69.1	35.1	49.6	50.4
44612	BOLIVAR	98.3	97.8	0.5	0.6	0.3	0.5	0.5	0.7	6.4	6.3	6.8	6.6	4.9	25.0	32.7	10.2	1.2	76.3	41.1	49.9	50.1
44613	BREWSTER	98.6	98.0	0.0	0.1	0.1	0.3	1.3	1.7	6.2	6.9	6.7	6.6	4.5	25.8	28.1	12.7	2.6	75.9	40.6	49.6	50.4
44614	CANAL FULTON	97.9	97.1	0.6	0.9	0.4	0.6	0.7	0.9	6.4	6.6	6.9	7.0	5.5	25.2	29.8	10.7	2.0	75.8	39.9	48.2	51.8
44615	CARROLLTON	98.6	98.5	0.3	0.3	0.1	0.1	0.5	0.5	5.8	6.1	6.4	6.3	5.0	24.6	29.7	13.8	2.3	77.8	41.9	49.0	51.0
44618	DALTON	98.3	97.8	0.3	0.4	0.4	0.6	0.7	0.9	7.5	7.7	7.8	7.4	5.5	25.1	26.9	10.3	1.9	72.3	36.3	49.0	51.0
44620	DELLROY	98.5	98.6	0.1	0.2	0.1	0.1	0.6	0.6	5.5	6.3	6.5	6.2	4.2	23.3	33.1	13.6	1.3	77.9	43.5	50.2	49.8
44621	DENNISON	97.0	95.9	1.5	2.2	0.2	0.3	0.7	0.8	6.9	6.6	7.0	6.8	5.8	25.5	27.4	12.0	1.8	75.3	38.3	50.2	49.8
44622	DOVER	97.6	97.1	1.0	1.1	0.4	0.6	0.6	0.8	5.7	5.9	6.1	6.1	5.6	23.5	29.7	14.3	3.2	78.5	42.8	48.4	51.6
44624	DUNDEE	99.2	99.0	0.2	0.3	0.1	0.1	0.3	0.4	11.5	10.4	9.3	9.0	8.3	25.2	17.7	7.1	1.5	63.5	26.0	51.2	48.8
44625	EAST ROCHESTER	98.8	98.7	0.2	0.2	0.0	0.0	0.5	0.5	7.2	7.6	8.1	6.6	4.9	25.5	28.4	10.5	1.1	72.8	37.8	50.4	49.6
44626	EAST SPARTA	98.2	97.8	0.8	1.0	0.0	0.0	0.3	0.3	4.9	5.8	6.2	6.5	5.0	23.2	32.8	14.1	1.5	79.1	43.9	50.2	49.8
44627	FREDERICKSBURG	99.2	99.1	0.2	0.2	0.0	0.1	0.6	0.7	12.7	11.3	10.0	9.5	8.5	24.4	16.8	6.0	0.8	60.2	23.8	50.9	49.1
44628	GLENMONT	99.3	99.2	0.2	0.2	0.1	0.1	0.7	0.9	7.4	7.5	7.8	7.3	5.2	24.7	28.0	10.9	1.2	72.8	37.7	50.9	49.1
44629	GNADENHUTTEN	99.0	98.8	0.1	0.1	0.1	0.1	0.3	0.3	6.8	6.9	6.8	6.1	4.9	26.1	27.9	12.9	1.6	75.8	39.2	49.7	50.3
44632	HARTVILLE	98.0	97.3	0.5	0.6	0.3	0.6	1.0	1.3	6.2	6.9	7.5	7.3	4.8	25.7	30.1	9.8	1.6	74.8	39.3	50.2	49.8
44633	HOLMESVILLE	99.0	98.8	0.2	0.3	0.0	0.0	1.0	1.2	10.4	9.7	9.4	8.0	6.2	26.2	20.7	8.0	1.4	65.6	29.9	50.7	49.3
44634	HOMEWORTH	99.0	98.6	0.2	0.2	0.3	0.5	0.3	0.4	5.8	6.1	6.7	6.8	4.9	23.8	30.9	13.0	2.0	77.1	42.2	49.4	50.6
44637	KILLBUCK	99.1	99.0	0.0	0.1	0.0	0.0	0.6	0.7	7.0	7.2	7.1	6.3	5.4	25.6	27.2	12.8	1.4	74.9	38.7	49.5	50.5
44638	LAKEVILLE	98.8	98.6	0.4	0.5	0.3	0.2	1.1	1.3	8.3	8.7	8.8	7.3	4.9	25.2	26.2	9.5	1.1	69.5	35.0	50.6	49.4
44641	LOUISVILLE	96.0	95.1	2.5	3.1	0.2	0.3	0.6	0.8	6.5	6.7	6.9	7.0	5.6	24.2	27.9	12.9	2.4	75.7	39.9	48.5	51.5
	OHIO	85.0	83.1	11.5	12.2	1.2	1.9	1.9	2.4	6.6	6.5	6.6	7.1	6.7	25.9	26.9	11.7	2.1	76.2	38.2	48.7	51.3
	UNITED STATES	75.1	72.0	12.3	12.7	3.8	4.6	12.5	15.7	6.8	6.7	6.6	7.1	6.9	27.0	26.0	10.9	1.9	75.7	36.9	49.2	50.8

#	POST OFFICE NAME	2009 Per Capita Income	2009 HH Income Base	2009 Household Income Distribution (%): Less than $25,000	$25,000 to $49,999	$50,000 to $99,999	$100,000 to $149,999	$150,000 or More	Median Household Income: 2009	2014	2009 National Centile	2009 State Centile	2009 Home Value Base	2009 Home Value Distribution (%): Less than $50,000	$50,000 to $89,999	$90,000 to $174,999	$175,000 to $399,999	$400,000 or More	2009 Median Home Value
44310	AKRON	20500	9848	31.7	30.2	32.4	4.4	1.3	38121	40793	27	16	5537	14.3	61.2	23.3	1.2	0.1	75295
44311	AKRON	12575	3047	51.3	26.8	18.8	2.1	0.9	24211	25288	3	3	978	46.1	39.1	13.5	1.3	0.0	52484
44312	AKRON	23651	13554	21.2	30.6	38.8	7.1	2.2	48002	51825	57	42	10318	11.6	35.2	47.0	5.6	0.5	92058
44313	AKRON	34217	11694	17.2	25.7	38.3	11.5	7.3	56976	60389	74	72	7313	1.9	12.8	61.6	20.1	3.6	128160
44314	AKRON	20502	8006	25.1	36.3	33.6	3.5	1.5	41232	43757	37	24	5354	16.8	70.0	13.0	0.2	0.1	69016
44319	AKRON	29188	9495	14.4	27.8	41.3	11.0	5.5	57107	60343	74	73	7600	5.2	20.0	59.1	14.3	1.4	113997
44320	AKRON	20652	8941	31.5	29.7	30.1	6.4	2.3	38582	41442	28	18	5701	16.2	52.1	29.2	1.8	0.6	76048
44321	AKRON	36060	5080	9.8	19.8	39.4	14.1	16.9	73340	74244	89	92	3871	0.5	8.8	46.9	39.2	4.7	163430
44333	AKRON	48795	7462	8.0	17.2	29.7	20.9	24.3	90340	91188	95	98	5853	0.3	1.1	33.6	48.7	16.2	210492
44401	BERLIN CENTER	27553	977	10.0	17.8	56.7	12.1	3.4	65334	65644	84	86	849	6.4	17.8	52.3	23.1	0.5	126413
44402	BRISTOLVILLE	21918	1272	14.7	24.8	50.6	9.4	0.5	57125	56265	74	73	1075	8.4	17.5	62.4	11.1	0.7	114459
44403	BROOKFIELD	25515	1875	23.2	24.6	37.8	10.3	4.1	51544	52680	65	56	1623	27.3	17.6	41.5	11.2	2.5	97455
44404	BURGHILL	22093	657	20.1	25.7	48.4	4.6	1.2	53705	54203	69	63	555	5.2	27.0	51.9	14.8	1.1	101550
44405	CAMPBELL	19323	3638	35.1	27.4	31.5	3.8	2.3	36161	39471	21	12	2691	33.7	44.3	20.3	1.5	0.1	63714
44406	CANFIELD	33154	8671	12.5	23.0	37.5	16.8	10.2	64712	64143	83	85	6903	1.1	12.3	52.3	30.3	4.0	136686
44408	COLUMBIANA	23159	4153	23.2	28.6	37.6	7.3	3.3	47958	50667	56	42	3098	8.3	20.8	51.3	19.1	0.6	116568
44410	CORTLAND	27752	6972	16.4	24.8	40.2	13.3	5.3	59555	58218	77	77	5609	5.4	17.7	57.1	19.3	0.6	119590
44411	DEERFIELD	23582	981	12.7	26.5	49.3	10.3	1.1	60299	61627	78	78	838	32.8	19.5	35.1	10.9	1.8	84571
44412	DIAMOND	25866	1029	10.4	25.9	45.8	14.6	3.4	63537	65077	82	83	907	10.0	16.9	48.4	22.9	1.8	132878
44413	EAST PALESTINE	19779	2984	24.7	34.0	33.6	6.3	1.3	43618	46829	44	30	2352	13.7	37.8	38.2	10.0	0.3	88571
44417	FARMDALE	21343	740	19.9	25.5	44.9	8.5	1.2	53609	53822	69	63	635	4.4	28.7	48.5	16.4	2.0	113206
44418	FOWLER	23547	546	17.8	24.5	44.9	11.2	1.6	57129	57516	74	73	475	5.9	26.1	45.7	20.6	1.7	115032
44420	GIRARD	24023	6697	27.8	27.2	32.9	7.6	4.5	45126	47934	49	34	4887	13.6	38.4	39.7	7.7	0.7	88705
44423	HANOVERTON	20039	1222	18.7	37.7	36.3	6.1	1.1	45000	47961	48	33	997	19.6	23.6	45.4	11.2	0.2	97366
44425	HUBBARD	23278	6108	24.4	29.7	35.0	7.7	3.2	45481	49139	50	35	4781	12.5	34.3	44.0	8.8	0.3	92547
44427	KENSINGTON	19471	689	27.4	29.8	35.3	5.4	2.2	43863	46370	45	31	565	15.9	31.7	35.8	16.3	0.4	93000
44428	KINSMAN	20236	1274	23.3	29.0	40.9	5.7	1.2	47706	50211	56	41	1049	11.9	29.8	45.0	11.4	1.8	100271
44429	LAKE MILTON	23117	1307	22.5	26.3	38.6	10.9	1.8	50957	52357	63	53	1014	10.9	34.9	36.2	16.0	2.0	95185
44430	LEAVITTSBURG	18850	1585	21.3	31.9	38.5	5.0	3.3	47119	50072	54	40	1301	29.1	38.7	29.1	2.8	0.2	71617
44431	LEETONIA	19649	1723	21.2	31.5	39.1	6.8	1.5	47075	50375	54	39	1433	13.5	33.5	39.4	11.9	1.6	94722
44432	LISBON	18194	4351	26.2	32.0	34.1	5.7	1.9	42643	46629	41	27	3317	18.2	31.5	42.3	7.1	0.9	90389
44436	LOWELLVILLE	21700	1603	24.3	28.3	36.2	9.2	2.0	46309	50211	52	37	1387	18.5	36.8	35.3	8.9	0.5	84966
44437	MC DONALD	23817	1783	19.1	24.7	43.3	9.9	2.9	56221	56571	73	71	1530	7.5	37.1	47.6	7.6	0.2	97119
44438	MASURY	22507	2050	29.5	28.0	34.7	5.7	2.1	40577	46027	35	22	1437	26.3	37.9	31.5	4.2	0.1	72600
44440	MINERAL RIDGE	23495	1452	15.8	27.8	41.8	12.7	1.9	55131	55571	71	67	1183	17.2	22.1	52.9	7.6	0.2	101314
44441	NEGLEY	22003	687	21.4	31.1	38.6	4.7	4.2	47621	50490	56	41	585	19.7	25.8	40.2	12.1	2.2	96463
44442	NEW MIDDLETOWN	24816	1564	22.2	30.4	35.7	7.8	3.9	46486	50155	53	38	1248	13.9	21.3	58.5	4.8	1.5	103298
44443	NEW SPRINGFIELD	23689	703	26.7	26.0	37.1	4.8	5.3	47301	50035	55	40	601	24.3	24.1	40.6	10.6	0.3	93519
44444	NEWTON FALLS	22608	4260	22.8	27.8	38.9	8.7	1.8	49375	51057	60	47	3021	10.6	29.9	49.6	9.1	0.9	100142
44445	NEW WATERFORD	22380	1309	22.0	31.3	38.6	5.8	2.3	46811	50216	54	39	1059	19.9	20.3	50.4	8.2	1.1	104530
44446	NILES	23770	9309	27.0	29.4	33.6	6.9	3.2	43590	47288	44	30	6037	15.4	37.1	40.9	6.2	0.4	87844
44449	NORTH BENTON	22345	431	19.5	28.8	42.9	7.4	1.4	51090	52042	64	54	368	17.1	27.2	39.4	15.8	0.5	102000
44450	NORTH BLOOMFIELD	18832	939	20.9	31.7	39.0	6.6	1.8	47674	49892	56	41	739	10.4	22.9	51.4	14.2	1.1	106774
44451	NORTH JACKSON	23274	1351	14.2	31.9	42.4	9.9	1.6	53499	54112	69	62	1125	4.5	24.3	47.9	22.6	0.7	119892
44452	NORTH LIMA	24810	790	17.6	25.8	40.0	11.1	5.4	54110	54970	70	64	677	7.4	18.2	52.1	20.4	1.9	118388
44454	PETERSBURG	22736	501	18.8	25.1	37.7	13.2	5.2	52536	52844	67	60	420	29.8	24.8	31.4	11.7	2.4	84242
44455	ROGERS	22083	595	21.0	29.7	40.3	5.5	3.4	49329	50972	60	46	503	22.7	26.4	36.6	12.7	1.6	91800
44460	SALEM	22407	10525	25.9	28.1	35.4	7.9	2.7	44934	49284	48	33	7920	11.0	30.2	44.5	12.7	1.6	99915
44470	SOUTHINGTON	25074	1428	15.1	23.8	45.1	12.7	3.4	60701	60045	78	79	1288	14.1	19.9	51.8	13.9	0.3	110283
44471	STRUTHERS	19826	4708	28.8	32.2	32.1	5.1	1.8	39134	42335	30	19	3585	25.2	56.9	15.8	2.1	0.0	66284
44473	VIENNA	26377	1499	18.9	25.4	41.2	11.3	3.2	56063	56350	73	70	1304	21.7	19.1	45.6	12.3	1.3	104270
44481	WARREN	26302	4496	17.9	24.9	42.5	10.2	4.5	56257	56408	73	71	3689	17.6	18.4	51.2	12.6	0.2	109398
44483	WARREN	23055	11252	27.2	28.5	34.7	6.9	2.7	43578	47854	44	30	7491	13.9	39.6	40.0	6.1	0.4	87059
44484	WARREN	28038	9540	20.3	23.6	37.9	13.4	4.9	55639	56187	72	69	7223	10.8	24.3	48.6	14.3	2.0	106443
44485	WARREN	19675	7520	34.3	31.4	26.9	5.3	2.1	36401	38629	22	12	4527	31.5	49.1	18.1	1.3	0.0	66325
44490	WASHINGTONVILLE	19392	295	24.1	33.2	38.0	3.7	1.0	44631	48109	47	32	233	16.3	44.2	33.5	5.2	0.9	81250
44491	WEST FARMINGTON	23133	994	13.6	24.1	46.1	13.2	3.0	61308	61509	79	79	874	4.0	15.7	60.3	19.1	0.9	122937
44502	YOUNGSTOWN	14761	4424	46.8	31.0	19.2	2.1	0.9	27202	28057	5	4	3085	72.9	24.6	1.9	0.3	0.3	39836
44503	YOUNGSTOWN	7953	401	93.3	5.7	1.0	0.0	0.0	8605	8717	0	0	9	44.4	0.0	55.6	0.0	0.0	95000
44504	YOUNGSTOWN	19687	1673	42.1	25.0	24.2	5.7	2.9	31694	33622	11	7	869	36.2	48.6	14.3	0.9	0.0	56988
44505	YOUNGSTOWN	19507	7921	41.2	26.4	24.0	4.5	3.8	31454	34129	10	6	4742	43.1	25.3	24.4	6.8	0.4	59235
44506	YOUNGSTOWN	11582	1194	59.7	25.6	12.1	1.8	0.8	19154	19951	1	1	762	92.7	4.3	3.0	0.0	0.0	18978
44507	YOUNGSTOWN	11509	2701	53.6	25.2	18.8	2.0	0.3	22574	23893	2	2	1362	85.8	12.3	1.8	0.0	0.0	32904
44509	YOUNGSTOWN	18654	5064	33.4	33.4	28.3	3.8	1.1	36264	38498	21	12	3648	44.5	49.1	6.2	0.1	0.1	52997
44510	YOUNGSTOWN	11546	939	69.9	15.3	12.9	1.2	0.7	15360	16272	1	1	476	89.3	9.5	1.3	0.0	0.0	21809
44511	YOUNGSTOWN	21815	9233	30.3	28.6	30.7	7.8	2.5	40295	45091	34	21	6817	21.9	38.4	36.5	3.2	0.1	80977
44512	YOUNGSTOWN	27923	15505	21.6	25.7	39.3	8.9	4.4	52209	53236	66	58	10756	5.0	30.6	52.1	11.5	0.8	106831
44514	YOUNGSTOWN	27520	9307	17.4	25.8	40.2	10.8	5.8	55960	56333	73	70	7917	6.7	23.4	52.0	16.7	1.2	112500
44515	YOUNGSTOWN	24098	11644	24.0	26.5	38.7	8.8	1.9	49344	51313	60	47	7661	6.1	40.9	47.0	5.9	0.2	92628
44555	YOUNGSTOWN	8502	0	0.0	0.0	0.0	0.0	0.0	0	0	0	0	0	0.0	0.0	0.0	0.0	0.0	0
44601	ALLIANCE	20736	13976	27.8	30.8	32.7	6.3	2.3	41617	45830	38	25	9583	18.7	34.3	37.8	8.0	1.1	86602
44606	APPLE CREEK	16131	2258	19.7	31.6	39.5	7.1	2.0	48372	50845	57	43	1756	10.6	12.7	47.6	26.1	3.0	131808
44608	BEACH CITY	21614	1182	15.2	35.0	42.7	5.0	2.0	49762	51588	60	48	949	15.4	41.1	31.2	10.1	2.2	82765
44609	BELOIT	21523	1557	21.6	29.5	42.1	5.1	1.8	48766	50921	58	44	1280	17.9	29.0	42.0	10.5	0.6	94167
44611	BIG PRAIRIE	16470	731	21.9	37.3	35.2	4.5	1.1	42242	45220	40	26	611	17.0	25.0	39.0	15.9	3.1	101520
44612	BOLIVAR	25299	2116	15.2	27.8	40.1	13.2	3.6	56557	55984	73	72	1612	5.0	10.2	52.2	31.5	1.2	144170
44613	BREWSTER	20035	830	21.9	36.6	35.3	3.7	2.4	43134	46741	43	28	673	13.1	35.4	45.0	6.4	0.1	91071
44614	CANAL FULTON	27152	4480	11.6	20.7	50.4	13.6	3.7	66076	66527	84	87	3464	1.4	11.6	71.8	14.2	1.0	123415
44615	CARROLLTON	19306	4377	28.4	30.8	34.7	4.6	1.5	41654	44228	38	25	3380	14.4	29.8	43.9	10.9	1.0	97076
44618	DALTON	21217	2474	13.9	31.4	42.5	8.4	3.7	53495	54683	69	62	2036	16.6	12.4	44.8	24.3	2.0	130839
44620	DELLROY	19911	731	22.7	34.1	35.6	6.0	1.6	44696	45936	47	32	627	16.4	21.5	44.5	16.1	1.4	106351
44621	DENNISON	17633	1875	27.9	36.6	29.1	5.3	1.1	38681	41420	29	18	1395	22.2	39.2	32.2	5.9	0.4	75315
44622	DOVER	23283	7428	21.9	28.9	38.9	6.9	3.4	49025	51087	59	46	5618	6.9	16.9	56.6	18.5	1.0	120166
44624	DUNDEE	16864	1556	19.0	32.1	38.2	6.9	3.8	48901	50330	59	45	1242	10.4	11.4	43.2	28.2	6.8	140000
44625	EAST ROCHESTER	19161	445	19.1	33.3	40.7	5.2	1.8	46805	50000	54	38	370	10.8	31.4	43.5	13.8	0.5	99667
44626	EAST SPARTA	20174	1311	21.3	32.3	40.2	5.0	1.3	46213	50246	52	37	1118	13.2	29.7	44.2	12.5	0.4	96124
44627	FREDERICKSBURG	14503	1405	18.6	33.5	35.4	8.2	4.3	47652	50157	56	41	1129	8.7	11.9	43.8	29.3	6.4	144238
44628	GLENMONT	19437	531	23.9	35.6	34.3	5.5	0.8	42325	45133	40	26	429	17.5	28.9	32.9	16.6	4.2	96200
44629	GNADENHUTTEN	19311	1200	23.7	36.3	34.7	3.6	1.8	40729	43892	35	23	981	17.1	32.6	43.2	6.6	0.4	90269
44632	HARTVILLE	27805	3767	10.6	21.5	47.5	15.0	5.3	70568	71266	87	91	2932	2.2	10.1	60.5	24.9	2.4	144120
44633	HOLMESVILLE	18922	733	18.7	35.1	36.7	4.6	4.9	45518	47482	50	35	580	7.8	21.6	40.7	24.3	5.7	130072
44634	HOMEWORTH	20960	841	18.1	27.9	45.5	6.5	1.9	52401	53165	67	59	716	8.1	21.8	49.0	19.6	1.5	122706
44637	KILLBUCK	20315	1025	23.8	32.8	36.9	5.5	1.1	43884	46176	45	31	750	19.6	33.1	35.3	10.9	1.1	87368
44638	LAKEVILLE	19362	622	21.5	32.2	39.2	5.3	1.8	45954	47803	51	36	495	16.0	20.2	39.2	20.4	4.2	114375
44641	LOUISVILLE	24726	7626	15.3	29.2	43.3	8.0	4.2	54498	55972	70	65	5688	3.8	19.0	60.5	15.6	1.1	118557
	OHIO	26577		21.4	25.9	36.7	10.4	5.7	52400	54553				10.3	22.0	45.6	19.3	2.8	114865
	UNITED STATES	27277		20.9	24.4	35.3	11.7	7.6	54719	56938				9.3	13.1	31.6	32.6	13.5	162279

ZIP CODE		FINANCIAL SERVICES				THE HOME						ENTERTAINMENT						PERSONAL			
						Home Improvements		Furnishings													
#	POST OFFICE NAME	Auto Loan	Home Loan	Invest-ments	Retire-ment Plans	Home Repair	Lawn & Garden	Comput-ers & Hard-ware-Personal	Major Appli-ances	TV, Radio, Sound Equip-ment	Furni-ture	Dine out/ Carry out	Sports Equip-ment	Fees & Tickets	Toys & Games	Travel	Cable TV	Apparel & Services	Auto Repairs	Health Insur-ance	Pets & Supplies
44310	AKRON	66	60	53	61	57	65	67	63	69	63	68	49	63	69	62	72	47	66	71	77
44311	AKRON	49	36	34	39	34	40	54	42	54	47	53	35	45	52	43	55	37	49	49	54
44312	AKRON	78	79	74	79	77	86	77	80	80	74	79	61	78	80	78	83	55	79	88	95
44313	AKRON	101	100	96	102	98	99	104	99	104	104	105	76	105	104	103	104	73	103	104	117
44314	AKRON	71	65	54	66	61	71	71	67	72	66	71	53	66	74	65	75	49	70	75	82
44319	AKRON	93	103	98	103	102	107	94	99	96	94	96	73	102	96	100	99	67	97	106	115
44320	AKRON	70	66	61	68	63	71	68	67	73	69	72	50	69	71	66	75	50	70	75	82
44321	AKRON	137	149	136	152	145	136	140	136	136	146	138	108	149	140	143	132	98	136	131	159
44333	AKRON	160	193	203	197	201	185	172	178	166	183	167	133	194	164	190	164	120	171	174	202
44401	BERLIN CENTER	101	113	98	116	110	112	101	106	100	101	100	83	107	102	107	100	70	101	105	124
44402	BRISTOLVILLE	92	84	83	88	86	99	83	93	85	75	84	71	77	87	83	90	57	86	96	108
44403	BROOKFIELD	97	80	102	78	82	104	79	96	86	75	84	70	70	85	80	93	57	89	102	112
44404	BURGHILL	85	78	77	81	79	91	77	86	79	70	78	65	71	80	77	83	53	80	89	100
44405	CAMPBELL	69	63	64	62	62	74	65	69	71	62	70	50	63	70	64	76	48	69	79	82
44406	CANFIELD	115	128	126	131	129	129	117	123	116	119	116	92	125	116	124	117	81	118	123	142
44408	COLUMBIANA	81	79	76	81	79	87	78	83	80	74	79	62	76	80	78	83	54	80	87	97
44410	CORTLAND	96	99	97	101	100	105	94	100	95	92	94	75	95	95	97	97	66	96	103	116
44411	DEERFIELD	101	93	83	90	91	95	88	93	91	92	91	68	83	95	84	94	62	90	93	111
44412	DIAMOND	99	107	95	110	105	109	97	103	97	96	97	80	101	99	102	98	67	98	103	121
44413	EAST PALESTINE	76	70	67	70	69	79	69	74	72	66	72	56	65	74	68	76	49	72	79	88
44417	FARMDALE	90	81	81	84	83	96	80	91	83	73	82	69	74	85	80	88	56	84	94	106
44418	FOWLER	90	90	84	93	89	97	85	92	86	81	85	71	84	88	87	89	59	87	93	108
44420	GIRARD	81	81	78	81	80	90	78	83	82	75	81	62	78	82	79	86	56	81	91	98
44423	HANOVERTON	89	68	84	67	69	90	69	83	75	64	74	63	57	76	67	82	49	77	87	99
44425	HUBBARD	81	79	81	79	79	90	77	83	81	74	80	62	76	80	79	85	55	81	91	98
44427	KENSINGTON	86	75	77	77	76	90	74	85	78	68	76	64	67	80	73	83	52	78	88	99
44428	KINSMAN	82	74	75	74	74	87	72	81	76	67	75	61	67	77	71	81	51	76	86	95
44429	LAKE MILTON	82	80	69	82	77	88	79	82	81	74	80	64	77	83	78	84	55	80	88	98
44430	LEAVITTSBURG	83	74	75	74	73	88	74	81	78	70	77	61	69	79	72	83	52	78	88	96
44431	LEETONIA	83	75	75	77	75	88	74	83	77	68	76	63	68	78	73	81	51	78	86	97
44432	LISBON	86	68	79	67	68	87	69	81	75	65	73	61	59	76	67	80	49	76	85	96
44436	LOWELLVILLE	83	77	83	77	78	92	75	86	79	70	78	63	71	79	76	84	53	80	91	99
44437	MC DONALD	84	93	82	94	90	97	85	89	87	83	86	67	90	88	89	89	60	87	95	104
44438	MASURY	83	67	75	67	67	85	72	80	78	66	75	61	62	78	68	84	51	78	88	95
44440	MINERAL RIDGE	93	89	91	90	88	101	84	93	87	82	87	71	82	89	86	91	60	89	96	110
44441	NEGLEY	96	79	80	78	79	93	78	87	84	78	83	66	69	87	74	89	56	83	90	105
44442	NEW MIDDLETOWN	77	87	83	86	87	95	77	85	83	77	82	60	85	81	84	88	57	82	97	97
44443	NEW SPRINGFIELD	100	81	102	79	82	104	80	96	86	76	85	72	70	86	80	93	57	89	100	114
44444	NEWTON FALLS	81	78	74	78	76	87	76	81	80	73	79	62	75	80	76	83	54	79	87	96
44445	NEW WATERFORD	87	76	80	77	77	91	75	86	78	69	77	64	68	80	74	83	52	79	88	100
44446	NILES	80	73	71	74	72	82	77	79	80	73	78	60	73	79	74	83	54	79	86	93
44449	NORTH BENTON	84	80	77	81	81	90	76	85	80	73	79	63	74	81	77	84	54	80	88	98
44450	NORTH BLOOMFIELD	83	76	74	78	77	86	75	83	76	70	76	63	70	78	75	80	52	78	84	96
44451	NORTH JACKSON	90	90	84	93	90	98	85	92	86	80	85	71	83	88	87	89	59	87	94	108
44452	NORTH LIMA	99	101	97	103	99	108	94	101	95	92	94	78	95	96	97	97	65	97	103	119
44454	PETERSBURG	107	98	87	95	96	100	92	98	96	96	96	71	88	100	88	99	65	95	98	116
44455	ROGERS	97	77	84	75	77	95	77	88	83	75	82	67	66	86	73	89	55	83	92	106
44460	SALEM	80	77	72	79	76	86	77	81	80	73	79	61	75	80	76	83	54	79	87	95
44470	SOUTHINGTON	101	95	93	97	95	107	91	100	94	87	93	76	87	96	91	98	64	94	103	118
44471	STRUTHERS	68	68	60	68	65	74	67	68	70	64	69	51	67	71	66	74	48	69	77	81
44473	VIENNA	94	89	99	87	89	105	83	95	88	80	88	71	81	88	87	94	60	90	102	112
44481	WARREN	98	91	94	92	91	106	88	98	93	84	92	74	85	93	89	98	63	93	103	115
44483	WARREN	75	73	68	73	71	80	75	75	79	72	77	56	74	78	73	82	54	77	84	89
44484	WARREN	95	95	94	95	94	102	93	97	96	92	96	72	94	96	94	100	66	96	104	114
44485	WARREN	67	61	55	62	59	69	65	64	69	62	68	49	62	69	61	73	47	66	74	78
44490	WASHINGTONVILLE	81	67	78	68	69	85	67	80	71	62	70	60	59	72	67	77	47	73	82	93
44491	WEST FARMINGTON	96	104	90	104	101	99	95	98	93	97	94	76	98	96	98	92	66	95	95	114
44502	YOUNGSTOWN	55	42	44	43	41	53	49	50	53	46	52	38	42	53	44	57	35	52	57	61
44503	YOUNGSTOWN	13	9	11	11	10	12	15	12	17	14	16	10	14	14	14	18	11	15	17	16
44504	YOUNGSTOWN	63	55	53	56	53	61	65	59	68	62	67	45	60	66	58	70	46	64	69	73
44505	YOUNGSTOWN	65	60	58	61	59	68	63	64	69	63	68	46	62	67	61	73	47	66	74	77
44506	YOUNGSTOWN	44	34	33	34	33	42	38	39	45	40	43	27	36	43	35	49	30	42	48	49
44507	YOUNGSTOWN	47	36	32	37	34	42	43	40	49	43	48	30	40	48	38	52	33	45	48	51
44509	YOUNGSTOWN	66	55	55	55	53	66	61	62	64	56	63	48	54	65	56	68	43	63	69	75
44510	YOUNGSTOWN	40	30	29	31	29	37	36	35	41	36	40	25	32	40	31	45	27	38	42	44
44511	YOUNGSTOWN	70	70	66	70	69	77	69	71	74	68	73	52	70	73	69	78	50	72	81	85
44512	YOUNGSTOWN	84	92	88	93	92	96	86	89	88	86	88	66	92	87	91	91	61	88	96	104
44514	YOUNGSTOWN	90	101	100	101	102	107	91	98	94	91	94	71	99	93	98	97	65	95	105	113
44515	YOUNGSTOWN	77	78	75	78	76	83	77	78	79	75	79	59	78	79	78	82	55	79	85	93
44555	YOUNGSTOWN	0	0	0	0	0	0	0	0	0	0	0	0	0	0	0	0	0	0	0	0
44601	ALLIANCE	74	70	67	71	69	78	72	74	76	69	74	56	70	75	70	79	51	74	82	88
44606	APPLE CREEK	85	78	74	75	78	80	80	84	78	78	79	65	73	80	78	78	55	81	80	95
44608	BEACH CITY	92	77	78	78	77	93	78	87	83	74	81	67	70	85	75	88	55	82	91	104
44609	BELOIT	85	74	79	76	76	91	75	86	78	67	76	65	67	79	74	83	52	79	89	100
44611	BIG PRAIRIE	77	69	69	72	71	82	69	77	71	62	70	59	63	72	68	75	47	72	80	90
44612	BOLIVAR	93	96	86	98	94	97	92	94	92	92	93	72	94	94	93	93	64	92	95	110
44613	BREWSTER	82	74	74	77	75	88	73	83	76	66	74	63	67	77	73	80	51	77	85	96
44614	CANAL FULTON	97	115	103	115	111	111	103	105	102	103	103	81	113	103	110	103	73	103	107	122
44615	CARROLLTON	76	64	73	65	65	81	65	75	69	59	68	57	57	69	64	74	46	70	79	88
44618	DALTON	97	92	86	93	91	99	88	95	90	86	89	71	84	93	87	93	61	90	96	112
44620	DELLROY	82	71	81	73	74	87	71	83	74	65	73	62	64	74	72	79	49	76	85	96
44621	DENNISON	77	59	69	59	60	77	63	72	68	58	66	55	53	69	60	74	45	69	77	86
44622	DOVER	82	83	78	84	82	90	80	84	82	77	82	63	81	83	81	86	56	82	90	98
44624	DUNDEE	89	81	74	77	80	79	84	87	82	84	83	67	77	84	81	80	59	85	80	97
44625	EAST ROCHESTER	85	78	77	81	79	91	76	86	79	69	77	65	71	80	76	83	53	80	89	100
44626	EAST SPARTA	79	74	73	76	75	86	72	80	74	66	73	60	68	75	72	79	50	75	84	93
44627	FREDERICKSBURG	97	82	92	79	82	91	88	94	85	83	87	77	76	86	86	86	60	93	90	109
44628	GLENMONT	84	67	72	67	67	84	68	78	73	64	72	60	58	75	64	79	48	73	82	93
44629	GNADENHUTTEN	77	67	70	68	66	81	67	75	71	63	70	58	61	72	66	75	47	71	79	89
44632	HARTVILLE	105	121	106	123	117	116	108	111	106	109	107	87	117	109	115	106	75	108	109	130
44633	HOLMESVILLE	112	87	95	86	87	110	88	102	96	84	94	78	74	99	83	103	63	96	107	122
44634	HOMEWORTH	89	81	80	85	83	96	80	90	83	72	81	68	74	84	80	87	55	83	93	105
44637	KILLBUCK	86	67	73	67	67	85	68	78	74	65	72	60	58	76	64	80	49	74	82	94
44638	LAKEVILLE	81	76	72	78	76	84	73	80	75	70	74	60	70	77	73	78	51	75	81	94
44641	LOUISVILLE	91	98	90	99	96	102	92	95	93	88	93	73	96	94	95	95	65	93	99	112
	OHIO	94	92	87	93	90	96	93	93	94	91	94	72	92	95	91	96	66	93	98	110
	UNITED STATES	100	100	100	100	100	100	100	100	100	100	100	100	100	100	100	100	100	100	100	100

ZIP CODE #	POST OFFICE NAME	COUNTY FIPS CODE	POPULATION 2000	POPULATION 2009	POPULATION 2014	2000-2009 ANNUAL RATE % Rate	2000-2009 ANNUAL RATE State Centile	HOUSEHOLDS 2000	HOUSEHOLDS 2009	HOUSEHOLDS 2014	HOUSEHOLDS % Annual Rate 2000-2009	HOUSEHOLDS 2009 Average HH Size	FAMILIES 2000	FAMILIES 2009	FAMILIES % Annual Rate 2000-2009
44643	MAGNOLIA	019	3241	3425	3462	0.6	75	1272	1368	1393	0.8	2.50	965	1015	0.5
44644	MALVERN	019	5076	4931	4838	-0.3	27	1994	2010	1992	0.1	2.45	1477	1452	-0.2
44645	MARSHALLVILLE	169	2408	2649	2750	1.0	87	836	948	992	1.4	2.79	675	750	1.1
44646	MASSILLON	151	45699	47021	47424	0.3	61	17948	18761	19029	0.5	2.44	12502	12730	0.2
44647	MASSILLON	151	18206	18719	18925	0.3	61	7217	7556	7676	0.5	2.47	5167	5264	0.2
44651	MECHANICSTOWN	019	720	726	718	0.1	51	255	264	264	0.4	2.73	199	202	0.2
44654	MILLERSBURG	075	18789	19851	20454	0.6	75	5505	5899	6099	0.8	3.27	4436	4682	0.6
44656	MINERAL CITY	157	3405	3470	3477	0.2	56	1310	1347	1357	0.3	2.58	974	978	0.0
44657	MINERVA	019	10576	10409	10302	-0.2	32	4024	4043	4028	0.1	2.55	2988	2926	-0.2
44662	NAVARRE	151	9640	10052	10194	0.5	71	3673	3936	4027	0.8	2.51	2668	2766	0.4
44663	NEW PHILADELPHIA	157	26296	26162	26078	-0.1	39	10844	10835	10825	0.0	2.38	7262	7061	-0.3
44666	NORTH LAWRENCE	151	2784	3019	3105	0.9	85	985	1093	1131	1.1	2.76	797	865	0.9
44667	ORRVILLE	169	13678	13640	13627	0.0	45	5002	5086	5114	0.2	2.65	3738	3714	-0.1
44669	PARIS	151	1406	1468	1494	0.5	71	513	548	561	0.7	2.65	403	420	0.4
44672	SEBRING	099	5340	4991	4849	-0.7	11	2262	2169	2125	-0.5	2.20	1382	1269	-0.9
44675	SHERRODSVILLE	019	1747	1837	1842	0.5	71	728	789	798	0.9	2.33	527	555	0.6
44676	SHREVE	169	4502	4834	5000	0.8	82	1656	1830	1907	1.1	2.64	1258	1357	0.8
44677	SMITHVILLE	169	2489	2534	2554	0.2	56	940	985	1001	0.5	2.56	739	757	0.3
44680	STRASBURG	157	3643	3864	3925	0.6	75	1448	1538	1566	0.7	2.48	1047	1082	0.4
44681	SUGARCREEK	157	7168	7534	7700	0.5	71	2143	2275	2330	0.6	3.25	1725	1799	0.5
44683	UHRICHSVILLE	157	8711	8604	8540	-0.1	39	3365	3349	3334	-0.1	2.55	2347	2269	-0.4
44685	UNIONTOWN	153	24641	27646	28698	1.3	92	9025	10237	10656	1.4	2.70	7047	7814	1.1
44688	WAYNESBURG	151	3225	3332	3361	0.4	66	1219	1287	1309	0.6	2.59	900	923	0.3
44689	WILMOT	075	289	307	316	0.7	79	90	96	99	0.7	3.20	73	77	0.6
44691	WOOSTER	169	42765	44501	45113	0.4	66	16524	17529	17893	0.6	2.39	11091	11449	0.3
44695	BOWERSTON	019	1678	1636	1612	-0.3	27	635	643	640	0.1	2.48	467	461	-0.1
44699	TIPPECANOE	067	1118	1188	1210	0.7	79	427	470	483	1.0	2.53	309	331	0.7
44702	CANTON	151	1042	965	941	-0.8	9	465	423	409	-1.0	1.61	119	100	-1.9
44703	CANTON	151	10856	9439	9021	-1.5	1	4357	3808	3649	-1.4	2.38	2433	2025	-2.0
44704	CANTON	151	5108	4613	4450	-1.1	4	2014	1851	1795	-0.9	2.41	1237	1092	-1.3
44705	CANTON	151	20812	19471	18998	-0.7	11	7888	7512	7372	-0.5	2.56	5520	5091	-0.9
44706	CANTON	151	18876	18445	18300	-0.2	32	7260	7232	7218	0.0	2.54	5221	5061	-0.3
44707	CANTON	151	10102	9684	9530	-0.5	17	4077	3977	3932	-0.3	2.43	2674	2521	-0.6
44708	CANTON	151	25982	25610	25443	-0.2	32	11324	11380	11378	0.1	2.23	7147	6900	-0.4
44709	CANTON	151	19324	19281	19251	0.0	45	8190	8286	8311	0.1	2.15	4770	4633	-0.3
44710	CANTON	151	9865	9564	9463	-0.3	27	4268	4226	4208	-0.1	2.25	2665	2525	-0.6
44714	CANTON	151	8890	8834	8814	-0.1	39	3873	3917	3931	0.1	2.23	2447	2391	-0.2
44718	CANTON	151	12343	12429	12438	0.1	51	5126	5258	5294	0.3	2.34	3409	3380	-0.1
44720	CANTON	151	36847	37889	38273	0.3	61	14715	15369	15600	0.5	2.41	10239	10395	0.2
44721	CANTON	151	12148	12781	13012	0.6	75	4525	4860	4981	0.8	2.62	3569	3748	0.5
44730	CANTON	151	6516	6393	6336	-0.2	32	2506	2512	2509	0.0	2.54	1921	1878	-0.2
44802	ALVADA	063	1205	1258	1264	0.5	71	422	459	467	0.9	2.74	341	363	0.7
44804	ARCADIA	063	1157	1167	1176	0.1	51	420	442	451	0.6	2.64	326	334	0.3
44805	ASHLAND	005	32822	33832	34376	0.3	61	12430	13052	13375	0.5	2.42	8576	8743	0.2
44807	ATTICA	147	2330	2431	2422	0.5	71	892	967	974	0.9	2.51	671	709	0.6
44811	BELLEVUE	147	13373	13098	12909	-0.2	32	5162	5203	5175	0.1	2.51	3716	3651	-0.2
44813	BELLVILLE	139	7427	7809	7843	0.5	71	2792	3033	3071	0.9	2.56	2128	2251	0.6
44814	BERLIN HEIGHTS	043	2821	2922	2903	0.4	66	1005	1074	1078	0.7	2.72	839	882	0.5
44817	BLOOMDALE	173	1428	1507	1536	0.6	75	512	555	572	0.9	2.72	394	417	0.6
44818	BLOOMVILLE	033	3045	2978	2914	-0.2	32	1102	1109	1096	0.1	2.66	865	854	-0.1
44820	BUCYRUS	033	19304	18382	17786	-0.5	17	7825	7668	7480	-0.2	2.35	5390	5138	-0.5
44822	BUTLER	139	3229	3576	3663	1.1	89	1122	1264	1300	1.3	2.82	897	990	1.1
44824	CASTALIA	043	4111	4009	3930	-0.3	27	1514	1526	1511	0.1	2.63	1225	1211	-0.1
44826	COLLINS	077	1758	1855	1882	0.6	75	619	675	691	0.9	2.74	506	541	0.7
44827	CRESTLINE	033	7206	6856	6612	-0.5	17	2859	2788	2711	-0.3	2.44	1999	1898	-0.6
44830	FOSTORIA	147	20116	18955	18381	-0.6	14	7904	7697	7541	-0.3	2.43	5409	5103	-0.6
44833	GALION	117	18383	17617	17177	-0.5	17	7515	7395	7264	-0.2	2.36	5244	5042	-0.4
44836	GREEN SPRINGS	147	2774	2808	2785	0.1	51	981	1031	1032	0.5	2.65	751	772	0.3
44837	GREENWICH	077	4351	4497	4489	0.4	66	1521	1609	1620	0.6	2.79	1176	1217	0.4
44839	HURON	043	12431	12383	12170	0.0	45	5071	5175	5128	0.2	2.34	3588	3564	-0.1
44840	JEROMESVILLE	005	3090	3368	3498	0.9	85	1140	1276	1337	1.2	2.63	888	970	1.0
44841	KANSAS	147	1174	1132	1104	-0.4	21	431	431	425	0.0	2.63	336	329	-0.2
44842	LOUDONVILLE	005	6059	6222	6316	0.3	61	2275	2366	2414	0.4	2.56	1590	1607	0.1
44843	LUCAS	139	2106	2280	2297	0.9	85	770	871	886	1.3	2.61	636	705	1.1
44844	MC CUTCHENVILLE	175	799	788	773	-0.1	39	295	300	297	0.2	2.52	233	232	0.0
44846	MILAN	043	3599	3622	3583	0.1	51	1274	1303	1296	0.2	2.73	995	994	0.0
44847	MONROEVILLE	077	3827	3887	3892	0.2	56	1353	1420	1435	0.5	2.73	1082	1114	0.3
44849	NEVADA	175	2428	2523	2509	0.4	66	933	1004	1010	0.8	2.51	709	746	0.6
44851	NEW LONDON	077	5094	5206	5217	0.2	56	1874	1972	1993	0.6	2.62	1385	1424	0.3
44853	NEW RIEGEL	147	1683	1693	1670	0.1	51	583	608	607	0.5	2.76	450	459	0.2
44854	NEW WASHINGTON	033	1829	1828	1805	0.0	45	681	707	706	0.4	2.52	509	516	0.1
44855	NORTH FAIRFIELD	077	1247	1345	1377	0.8	82	436	485	501	1.2	2.73	351	383	0.9
44857	NORWALK	077	23114	23529	23586	0.2	56	8898	9270	9357	0.4	2.50	6224	6317	0.2
44859	NOVA	005	1712	1835	1901	0.8	82	618	684	714	1.1	2.68	512	556	0.9
44864	PERRYSVILLE	005	2994	3175	3243	0.6	75	1169	1277	1320	1.0	2.37	890	948	0.7
44865	PLYMOUTH	077	3657	3664	3618	0.0	45	1346	1386	1380	0.3	2.64	1056	1063	0.1
44866	POLK	005	1873	2122	2235	1.4	93	631	735	780	1.7	2.88	513	585	1.4
44867	REPUBLIC	147	2499	2484	2433	-0.1	39	882	905	897	0.3	2.73	707	712	0.1
44870	SANDUSKY	043	43418	42003	40964	-0.4	21	17754	17659	17375	-0.1	2.29	11282	10857	-0.4
44875	SHELBY	139	15044	14747	14476	-0.2	32	5860	5924	5861	0.1	2.41	4095	4001	-0.3
44878	SHILOH	139	3318	3464	3457	0.5	71	1019	1086	1092	0.7	3.19	846	884	0.5
44880	SULLIVAN	005	2357	2934	3176	2.4	98	757	970	1058	2.7	3.02	630	791	2.5
44882	SYCAMORE	175	2945	3004	2974	0.2	56	1135	1197	1198	0.6	2.51	832	856	0.3
44883	TIFFIN	147	30414	29455	28650	-0.3	27	11845	11778	11552	-0.1	2.37	8037	7765	-0.4
44887	TIRO	033	1109	1083	1056	-0.3	27	402	406	399	0.1	2.64	322	319	-0.1
44889	WAKEMAN	077	6399	6620	6672	0.4	66	2321	2472	2514	0.7	2.68	1841	1920	0.5
44890	WILLARD	077	11865	11755	11632	-0.1	39	4349	4402	4387	0.1	2.64	3217	3187	-0.1
44902	MANSFIELD	139	6961	6179	5860	-1.3	2	2726	2475	2363	-1.0	2.38	1610	1403	-1.5
44903	MANSFIELD	139	29707	26587	25991	-1.2	3	10555	10521	10358	0.0	2.46	7411	7243	-0.2
44904	MANSFIELD	139	13475	14394	14504	0.7	79	5244	5792	5882	1.1	2.48	3957	4258	0.8
44905	MANSFIELD	139	15057	16727	16386	1.1	89	5185	5096	4999	-0.2	2.38	3652	3473	-0.5
44906	MANSFIELD	139	17944	17417	17036	-0.3	27	7567	7602	7504	0.0	2.26	5046	4916	-0.3
44907	MANSFIELD	139	14506	13822	13453	-0.5	17	6635	6546	6428	-0.1	2.07	3965	3741	-0.6
45001	ADDYSTON	061	965	973	975	0.1	51	342	349	351	0.2	2.79	249	245	-0.2
45002	CLEVES	061	12508	14541	15067	1.6	95	4392	5170	5385	1.8	2.78	3367	3909	1.6
	OHIO					0.2					0.4	2.44			0.1
	UNITED STATES					1.0					1.1	2.59			0.9

#	POST OFFICE NAME	RACE (%) White 2000	White 2009	Black 2000	Black 2009	Asian/Pacific 2000	Asian/Pacific 2009	% Hispanic Origin 2000	% Hispanic Origin 2009	2009 AGE DISTRIBUTION (%) 0-4	5-9	10-14	15-19	20-24	25-44	45-64	65-84	85+	18+	MEDIAN AGE 2009	% 2009 Males	% 2009 Females
44643	MAGNOLIA	97.6	97.0	1.1	1.4	0.1	0.1	1.0	1.2	5.8	6.0	6.6	7.0	5.3	23.8	30.1	13.5	1.9	77.3	41.8	49.6	50.4
44644	MALVERN	96.4	96.3	1.9	2.0	0.2	0.2	0.6	0.6	6.4	6.6	6.8	6.0	5.1	24.9	30.1	12.6	1.4	76.5	40.6	49.4	50.6
44645	MARSHALLVILLE	98.5	98.1	0.1	0.1	0.2	0.3	0.6	0.9	6.2	6.8	7.6	7.8	4.8	25.3	30.5	9.9	1.2	74.5	39.4	50.5	49.5
44646	MASSILLON	90.6	88.3	7.1	8.7	0.5	0.9	0.9	1.2	6.4	6.4	6.6	6.8	5.6	24.9	27.9	12.9	2.4	76.2	40.0	48.6	51.4
44647	MASSILLON	96.6	95.8	1.7	2.2	0.2	0.3	0.8	1.0	5.5	5.8	6.1	6.6	5.3	24.3	30.2	14.4	1.9	78.5	42.4	49.3	50.7
44651	MECHANICSTOWN	98.5	98.5	0.4	0.4	0.0	0.0	1.0	1.0	6.5	7.2	8.0	7.3	5.4	26.0	28.0	10.6	1.1	73.7	37.7	52.1	47.9
44654	MILLERSBURG	98.9	98.7	0.4	0.5	0.1	0.1	0.8	1.0	10.5	9.8	9.0	8.1	6.6	25.7	20.0	8.8	1.5	65.6	29.2	50.3	49.7
44656	MINERAL CITY	98.5	98.2	0.2	0.3	0.2	0.3	0.7	0.9	6.3	6.4	6.9	6.9	5.4	24.8	30.0	12.1	1.3	76.3	40.9	50.1	49.9
44657	MINERVA	98.5	98.2	0.2	0.3	0.2	0.3	0.5	0.6	6.1	6.4	6.8	6.6	5.0	25.1	28.5	13.5	2.0	76.7	40.6	49.2	50.8
44662	NAVARRE	98.5	98.1	0.4	0.5	0.2	0.4	0.5	0.7	5.8	6.0	6.3	6.2	4.7	23.5	29.6	15.2	2.8	78.0	43.1	48.8	51.2
44663	NEW PHILADELPHIA	97.6	95.8	0.7	2.0	0.4	0.7	1.0	1.3	6.1	6.2	6.4	6.2	5.1	25.8	28.3	13.6	2.3	77.8	40.7	48.6	51.4
44666	NORTH LAWRENCE	98.5	98.1	0.4	0.6	0.2	0.3	0.8	1.1	6.6	7.4	7.7	6.5	4.3	24.9	30.4	10.8	1.4	74.2	40.2	50.2	49.8
44667	ORRVILLE	93.2	91.4	4.1	4.8	1.0	1.7	1.1	1.5	7.2	7.2	7.4	7.0	6.0	25.7	26.9	10.6	1.9	73.6	36.9	49.5	50.5
44669	PARIS	97.8	97.1	1.1	1.3	0.3	0.5	0.3	0.4	5.2	6.2	6.5	6.1	4.4	23.2	32.0	14.5	1.8	78.2	43.8	50.2	49.8
44672	SEBRING	98.3	97.4	0.5	0.9	0.2	0.4	0.8	1.2	5.4	5.0	5.3	5.9	5.5	22.0	23.3	17.9	9.7	80.8	45.7	45.3	54.7
44675	SHERRODSVILLE	99.0	98.9	0.2	0.2	0.2	0.2	0.1	0.2	4.9	5.9	5.9	5.4	3.8	22.9	34.3	15.4	1.6	80.1	45.9	50.2	49.8
44676	SHREVE	98.8	98.5	0.3	0.4	0.1	0.2	0.4	0.5	7.6	7.8	8.1	7.4	5.1	24.9	27.8	10.1	1.2	71.9	36.8	50.6	49.4
44677	SMITHVILLE	98.6	98.1	0.2	0.3	0.5	0.8	0.4	0.5	6.9	7.0	7.1	7.5	6.2	25.8	27.1	11.0	1.3	73.9	36.9	49.7	50.3
44680	STRASBURG	98.6	98.1	0.1	0.1	0.4	0.6	1.3	1.6	7.0	6.9	7.1	6.5	5.3	25.5	27.1	12.3	2.2	74.8	39.2	49.1	50.9
44681	SUGARCREEK	99.2	99.0	0.1	0.1	0.2	0.3	0.4	0.6	9.6	9.1	8.7	8.0	6.4	24.4	21.6	9.9	2.5	67.7	31.4	49.7	50.3
44683	UHRICHSVILLE	97.8	97.3	0.9	1.0	0.1	0.2	0.6	0.8	7.4	6.9	6.8	6.6	6.7	25.2	25.5	12.5	2.3	74.9	37.5	48.8	51.2
44685	UNIONTOWN	97.7	96.6	0.7	1.0	0.7	1.2	0.7	1.0	6.2	6.6	7.2	7.2	4.9	23.9	31.0	11.5	1.3	75.4	40.8	49.1	50.9
44688	WAYNESBURG	95.4	94.1	3.5	4.5	0.2	0.3	1.1	1.4	6.6	6.5	6.9	7.0	5.0	24.4	29.0	12.5	2.1	75.6	40.6	49.6	50.4
44689	WILMOT	99.3	98.7	0.3	0.3	0.0	0.3	0.3	0.7	11.4	10.1	8.5	8.8	8.5	25.4	18.6	7.8	1.0	64.2	26.7	51.5	48.5
44691	WOOSTER	95.0	93.8	2.4	2.8	1.1	1.8	0.8	1.0	5.9	6.0	6.2	8.2	7.7	23.9	27.3	12.3	2.4	77.8	38.5	48.9	51.1
44695	BOWERSTON	99.0	98.9	0.2	0.2	0.1	0.1	0.2	0.3	5.7	6.2	6.5	5.9	4.3	22.1	31.5	14.7	3.1	77.6	44.4	49.6	50.4
44699	TIPPECANOE	98.9	98.7	0.0	0.0	0.0	0.0	0.4	0.5	5.4	5.8	6.5	6.3	4.6	23.1	31.5	15.1	1.7	78.5	43.6	50.0	50.0
44702	CANTON	60.9	54.3	33.9	39.8	0.6	0.7	1.4	1.7	3.8	3.5	3.1	4.2	6.6	23.3	27.7	20.9	6.7	86.6	48.5	49.1	50.9
44703	CANTON	77.5	73.0	16.2	19.5	0.2	0.4	2.1	2.7	8.2	7.2	6.5	7.1	8.2	30.1	23.9	7.5	1.3	73.8	33.1	49.4	50.6
44704	CANTON	33.1	29.0	61.3	65.3	0.2	0.2	1.4	1.6	7.9	7.8	7.4	7.6	6.1	21.1	25.5	14.1	2.4	71.8	38.0	46.5	53.5
44705	CANTON	71.7	67.0	23.8	27.9	0.4	0.5	1.0	1.3	7.4	7.0	7.0	7.5	6.7	24.3	26.6	11.8	1.7	74.0	37.3	47.7	52.3
44706	CANTON	91.9	89.9	5.6	7.1	0.2	0.3	0.9	1.2	6.2	6.4	6.6	7.0	5.6	25.3	28.8	12.3	1.5	76.3	39.7	49.6	50.4
44707	CANTON	64.5	60.7	31.6	35.1	0.2	0.2	1.0	1.1	9.4	7.6	6.8	7.6	7.0	22.7	25.4	11.8	1.7	71.9	35.1	46.9	53.1
44708	CANTON	93.8	91.9	3.3	4.2	0.9	1.6	1.1	1.4	5.6	5.8	6.0	5.8	4.7	23.2	28.8	16.1	4.0	78.9	44.2	47.0	53.0
44709	CANTON	91.4	88.9	5.6	7.2	0.7	1.1	1.0	1.3	5.6	5.3	5.3	7.1	7.9	24.8	25.3	14.1	4.6	80.7	40.1	45.8	54.2
44710	CANTON	91.9	89.7	5.9	7.6	0.3	0.4	0.7	0.9	7.2	7.2	6.7	5.9	5.6	26.2	25.2	13.3	2.8	75.3	38.6	46.5	53.5
44714	CANTON	80.0	76.8	17.2	19.9	0.3	0.5	0.9	1.2	5.8	5.6	5.7	6.1	6.1	24.3	28.5	14.9	3.0	79.1	42.3	47.0	53.0
44718	CANTON	94.6	92.4	2.2	2.9	2.1	3.5	1.1	1.4	4.9	5.4	6.2	6.1	4.8	23.8	31.0	15.0	2.8	79.7	44.1	48.5	51.5
44720	CANTON	96.6	95.2	1.1	1.5	1.2	1.9	0.9	1.2	5.4	5.6	6.1	6.9	5.7	23.6	29.8	14.0	2.8	79.0	42.5	48.1	51.9
44721	CANTON	95.5	94.0	2.5	3.2	0.5	0.8	1.0	1.4	5.9	6.5	7.1	6.8	4.5	23.3	31.5	12.7	1.5	76.1	42.1	49.1	50.9
44730	CANTON	93.1	91.2	4.9	6.2	0.3	0.5	0.6	0.8	5.0	5.5	6.1	6.6	4.7	25.0	30.9	14.7	1.5	79.4	42.9	50.2	49.8
44802	ALVADA	98.6	98.1	0.2	0.2	0.5	0.7	1.7	2.2	6.8	7.2	7.6	7.4	4.6	25.4	29.0	10.7	1.4	73.8	39.0	52.5	47.5
44804	ARCADIA	97.5	96.7	0.5	0.6	0.3	0.4	1.9	2.6	6.8	7.1	7.4	7.6	5.0	23.6	31.2	10.0	1.4	74.1	39.6	51.4	48.6
44805	ASHLAND	97.1	96.1	0.9	1.0	0.8	1.3	0.7	0.9	6.3	6.0	6.2	8.3	8.2	23.9	25.9	12.4	2.8	77.6	37.6	48.4	51.6
44807	ATTICA	98.8	98.6	0.0	0.0	0.0	0.1	0.9	1.1	6.4	6.9	6.9	6.7	4.4	26.2	27.6	13.1	1.8	75.6	39.6	50.2	49.8
44811	BELLEVUE	98.2	97.7	0.2	0.2	0.2	0.3	2.1	2.8	6.5	6.6	6.7	7.0	5.9	26.2	27.7	11.7	1.9	76.0	38.5	49.7	50.3
44813	BELLVILLE	98.8	98.4	0.2	0.3	0.3	0.4	0.6	0.8	6.3	6.7	7.0	6.9	5.1	23.6	29.8	12.8	1.8	75.7	40.9	48.9	51.1
44814	BERLIN HEIGHTS	98.3	97.8	0.4	0.4	0.1	0.1	1.8	2.5	5.5	6.2	7.1	7.0	4.3	23.8	33.7	11.2	1.2	76.7	42.3	51.4	48.6
44817	BLOOMDALE	97.6	97.0	0.2	0.3	0.2	0.3	2.2	2.9	7.0	7.4	7.6	7.5	4.6	26.3	28.1	10.2	1.2	73.1	38.1	50.5	49.5
44818	BLOOMVILLE	98.4	98.0	0.2	0.3	0.1	0.2	1.8	2.5	7.2	7.3	7.3	7.1	5.2	26.0	26.3	11.8	1.9	73.6	37.7	50.0	50.0
44820	BUCYRUS	97.8	97.1	0.7	0.8	0.4	0.7	0.8	1.1	6.5	6.5	6.4	6.2	5.7	24.9	27.8	13.6	2.5	77.0	40.2	48.8	51.2
44822	BUTLER	98.9	98.6	0.2	0.3	0.2	0.3	0.4	0.5	6.5	6.8	7.3	7.3	5.2	25.1	29.7	10.9	1.3	74.9	39.6	51.0	49.0
44824	CASTALIA	97.8	97.3	0.4	0.4	0.0	0.0	2.1	2.8	5.1	5.5	6.1	6.6	4.7	24.8	32.2	13.6	1.4	79.1	43.1	49.3	50.7
44826	COLLINS	98.4	98.0	0.3	0.4	0.1	0.2	1.1	1.5	6.3	6.8	7.7	6.8	4.5	25.6	30.1	10.9	1.3	74.9	40.1	50.6	49.4
44827	CRESTLINE	97.0	96.4	1.5	1.7	0.3	0.5	0.7	0.8	6.8	6.8	6.5	6.6	6.3	25.5	26.8	12.7	1.9	75.9	38.4	49.4	50.6
44830	FOSTORIA	90.0	88.0	4.2	4.8	0.4	0.6	6.9	8.9	6.8	6.7	6.7	7.0	6.3	25.4	26.6	12.1	2.4	75.5	37.8	48.9	51.1
44833	GALION	98.4	98.0	0.2	0.2	0.3	0.4	0.8	1.0	6.4	6.1	6.1	6.3	5.8	24.7	28.1	14.3	2.2	77.5	40.9	47.5	52.5
44836	GREEN SPRINGS	96.5	95.4	0.3	0.4	0.3	0.5	4.2	5.5	6.2	6.5	6.5	7.2	5.7	26.6	27.8	11.5	2.0	76.5	39.2	51.4	48.6
44837	GREENWICH	98.4	98.0	0.1	0.2	0.1	0.2	0.8	1.1	8.9	8.7	8.5	7.8	5.8	26.8	23.7	8.9	1.0	69.1	33.3	49.7	50.3
44839	HURON	97.4	96.5	0.8	1.0	0.6	0.9	1.6	2.1	5.7	5.8	6.5	6.6	4.8	22.6	30.3	15.2	2.6	77.7	43.7	48.3	51.7
44840	JEROMESVILLE	98.4	97.8	0.3	0.3	0.6	1.0	0.6	0.7	6.3	6.6	6.9	6.7	4.7	25.0	30.1	12.2	1.4	75.9	41.1	51.8	48.2
44841	KANSAS	96.3	95.2	0.3	0.4	0.3	0.4	4.3	5.7	5.7	6.0	6.5	7.1	5.5	26.7	29.6	11.7	1.2	77.5	40.1	49.7	50.3
44842	LOUDONVILLE	98.8	98.5	0.4	0.5	0.1	0.2	0.6	0.8	6.5	6.7	7.0	7.6	5.8	24.5	27.7	11.8	2.3	75.0	38.9	50.8	49.2
44843	LUCAS	98.0	97.3	1.1	1.4	0.1	0.3	0.4	0.5	5.1	5.6	6.3	6.8	4.7	24.0	32.3	13.7	1.4	78.8	43.1	50.4	49.6
44844	MC CUTCHENVILLE	99.2	98.5	0.0	0.1	0.0	0.1	1.3	1.6	5.3	6.7	7.4	7.9	5.1	23.9	28.4	12.1	3.3	75.5	40.8	49.5	50.5
44846	MILAN	98.0	97.4	0.4	0.4	0.2	0.4	1.3	1.8	6.0	6.5	6.9	7.1	4.9	23.7	30.0	13.2	1.7	76.0	41.4	49.0	51.0
44847	MONROEVILLE	98.3	97.8	0.2	0.2	0.2	0.3	1.2	1.6	6.5	6.8	7.1	6.8	5.2	26.1	29.5	10.7	1.2	75.3	38.8	50.6	49.4
44849	NEVADA	98.6	98.1	0.2	0.2	0.2	0.3	0.7	0.9	6.0	6.5	6.8	7.1	4.6	25.8	29.3	12.3	1.6	76.3	40.7	51.3	48.7
44851	NEW LONDON	97.1	96.6	1.5	1.6	0.3	0.4	0.7	1.0	6.7	6.8	7.1	7.1	5.6	26.1	27.8	10.9	1.8	75.1	38.0	49.7	50.3
44853	NEW RIEGEL	98.2	97.6	0.6	0.8	0.1	0.2	1.0	1.3	6.0	6.4	7.0	8.4	5.3	23.6	29.2	12.5	1.7	74.7	40.6	50.9	49.1
44854	NEW WASHINGTON	99.3	99.0	0.0	0.0	0.3	0.4	0.4	0.6	6.0	6.1	6.4	6.8	5.6	24.6	28.4	13.0	3.2	77.4	41.2	49.7	50.3
44855	NORTH FAIRFIELD	97.0	96.2	0.2	0.1	0.2	0.3	3.3	4.4	9.0	9.4	8.5	6.2	4.7	27.1	24.5	9.7	1.0	69.3	35.4	50.8	49.2
44857	NORWALK	95.4	94.2	1.5	1.8	0.3	0.5	3.2	4.2	7.4	7.1	7.1	7.2	6.5	26.1	25.5	11.0	2.1	73.9	36.4	48.6	51.4
44859	NOVA	98.9	98.7	0.1	0.1	0.0	0.1	0.4	0.5	5.8	6.4	6.8	6.8	4.6	25.2	30.4	12.7	1.3	76.8	41.3	51.7	48.3
44864	PERRYSVILLE	97.1	96.5	1.9	2.3	0.2	0.3	0.5	0.6	6.0	6.3	6.7	9.9	4.6	22.1	30.2	12.6	1.7	74.7	40.3	51.5	48.5
44865	PLYMOUTH	98.2	97.8	0.1	0.1	0.1	0.1	1.4	1.8	7.2	7.1	7.5	7.6	5.5	25.8	26.4	11.7	1.2	73.6	37.4	49.1	50.9
44866	POLK	98.3	97.7	0.3	0.3	0.2	0.3	0.9	1.2	7.8	8.0	8.0	7.0	5.0	25.1	27.3	10.8	1.0	71.9	36.8	50.6	49.4
44867	REPUBLIC	99.2	99.0	0.0	0.0	0.0	0.1	1.3	1.8	6.0	6.5	6.8	7.2	5.3	25.8	30.2	10.7	1.3	76.1	39.4	51.2	48.8
44870	SANDUSKY	80.8	77.8	15.5	17.7	0.5	0.7	2.5	3.1	6.3	6.1	6.2	6.6	6.1	23.7	27.6	14.6	2.8	77.3	40.9	48.6	51.4
44875	SHELBY	97.6	96.8	0.8	1.1	0.3	0.5	1.0	1.4	6.6	6.4	6.4	7.8	5.7	24.1	26.5	13.8	2.7	75.4	39.5	49.8	50.2
44878	SHILOH	98.1	97.6	0.7	0.9	0.1	0.1	0.5	0.7	8.7	8.6	8.6	8.2	5.8	25.1	24.9	9.2	0.9	69.0	32.6	49.8	50.2
44880	SULLIVAN	98.4	98.1	0.9	1.1	0.0	0.1	0.7	0.9	7.8	8.1	8.2	7.1	4.7	25.7	26.9	10.6	0.9	71.4	36.7	49.9	50.1
44882	SYCAMORE	99.4	99.2	0.0	0.0	0.0	0.1	0.5	0.7	6.3	6.5	6.7	6.8	5.7	25.4	28.5	12.5	1.7	76.4	39.2	49.3	50.7
44883	TIFFIN	96.7	95.7	1.0	1.2	0.5	0.9	2.0	2.8	5.8	6.0	6.1	8.1	7.5	24.2	27.8	12.3	2.2	78.0	38.7	49.5	50.5
44887	TIRO	98.8	98.5	0.0	0.0	0.2	0.3	0.8	1.1	6.1	6.5	7.0	6.9	4.8	24.0	29.9	12.7	2.1	76.1	40.9	51.1	48.9
44889	WAKEMAN	98.6	98.1	0.2	0.3	0.1	0.2	1.3	1.9	6.2	6.8	7.1	6.6	4.6	25.3	31.6	10.7	1.2	75.8	40.7	51.1	48.9
44890	WILLARD	93.2	91.8	0.9	1.0	0.3	0.5	8.4	10.7	7.9	7.6	7.3	7.2	6.4	25.4	25.4	11.1	1.7	73.0	35.8	48.4	51.6
44902	MANSFIELD	59.9	53.9	35.4	40.9	0.4	0.6	1.4	1.7	8.1	7.6	6.9	8.0	9.3	28.9	21.0	8.7	1.7	72.9	31.2	51.9	48.1
44903	MANSFIELD	79.4	80.2	17.7	16.4	0.4	0.7	1.0	1.2	6.6	6.5	6.5	6.9	6.1	24.9	28.7	12.4	1.6	76.2	39.5	49.4	50.6
44904	MANSFIELD	96.2	94.8	1.9	2.5	0.8	1.3	0.6	0.9	5.7	6.1	6.5	6.8	5.8	22.7	30.8	13.7	1.8	77.5	42.3	48.3	51.7
44905	MANSFIELD	86.3	79.6	11.5	17.3	0.4	0.8	0.9	1.2	4.7	4.8	5.0	6.1	8.7	33.0	24.8	11.3	1.7	82.7	37.4	59.3	40.7
44906	MANSFIELD	89.5	87.2	7.3	8.6	1.0	1.6	1.1	1.4	6.3	6.4	6.4	6.3	5.4	23.8	28.3	14.7	2.4	77.0	41.3	48.3	51.7
44907	MANSFIELD	91.1	88.7	6.3	8.0	0.7	1.1	1.1	1.4	6.4	6.3	6.2	5.9	5.4	24.1	25.7	16.2	3.9	77.6	41.7	46.5	53.5
45001	ADDYSTON	94.0	91.7	3.5	5.2	0.1	0.2	1.0	1.4	7.7	7.6	7.0	7.3	7.6	27.2	25.1	9.4	1.1	73.2	33.8	50.1	49.9
45002	CLEVES	98.3	97.7	0.5	0.8	0.2	0.4	0.6	0.8	7.4	7.4	7.3	7.3	5.8	27.0	26.0	10.2	1.5	73.3	36.3	49.9	50.1
	OHIO	85.0	83.1	11.5	12.2	1.2	1.9	1.9	2.4	6.6	6.5	6.6	7.1	6.7	25.9	26.9	11.7	2.1	76.2	38.2	48.7	51.3
	UNITED STATES	75.1	72.0	12.3	12.7	3.8	4.6	12.5	15.7	6.8	6.7	6.6	7.1	6.9	27.0	26.0	10.9	1.9	75.7	36.9	49.2	50.8

ZIP CODE #	POST OFFICE NAME	2009 Per Capita Income	2009 HH Income Base	2009 HOUSEHOLD INCOME DISTRIBUTION (%) Less than $25,000	$25,000 to $49,999	$50,000 to $99,999	$100,000 to $149,999	$150,000 or More	MEDIAN HOUSEHOLD INCOME 2009	2014	2009 National Centile	2009 State Centile	2009 Home Value Base	2009 HOME VALUE DISTRIBUTION (%) Less than $50,000	$50,000 to $89,999	$90,000 to $174,999	$175,000 to $399,999	$400,000 or More	2009 Median Home Value
44643	MAGNOLIA	21178	1368	22.1	33.6	36.2	5.7	2.4	45112	47617	49	33	1143	21.3	25.0	42.8	10.1	0.7	95061
44644	MALVERN	23836	2010	24.2	27.2	37.9	7.2	3.5	48281	48178	57	43	1591	21.1	21.4	41.2	15.0	1.3	102460
44645	MARSHALLVILLE	21733	948	14.8	25.0	50.6	7.6	2.0	56091	55976	73	70	749	10.7	13.1	49.8	24.4	2.0	124741
44646	MASSILLON	26933	18761	19.5	26.1	38.9	9.8	5.8	53397	54943	69	62	12993	7.0	24.0	52.2	15.2	1.6	112368
44647	MASSILLON	23115	7556	19.9	32.5	38.8	6.7	2.1	46988	50760	54	39	6177	14.9	36.7	40.7	6.7	0.9	88378
44651	MECHANICSTOWN	19866	264	31.1	29.2	31.8	4.2	3.8	40245	42322	33	21	222	14.4	25.2	45.5	14.4	0.5	101786
44654	MILLERSBURG	18270	5899	20.5	33.5	35.3	6.1	4.6	46449	47890	53	37	4333	10.4	17.1	43.4	23.7	5.4	130123
44656	MINERAL CITY	21409	1347	18.7	37.0	35.9	6.5	2.0	45301	47543	49	34	1115	24.2	21.1	43.7	10.0	1.1	98898
44657	MINERVA	20110	4043	23.1	34.6	35.3	4.8	2.2	43089	45720	43	28	3090	13.8	33.6	41.2	10.7	0.8	92618
44662	NAVARRE	21315	3936	21.0	35.2	34.6	6.6	2.7	43713	47965	44	30	3256	19.0	23.9	46.9	9.3	0.9	97030
44663	NEW PHILADELPHIA	21648	10835	25.6	33.0	33.2	5.9	2.2	42428	45641	41	27	7729	15.1	25.2	47.6	10.8	1.2	102007
44666	NORTH LAWRENCE	25488	1093	15.3	24.8	43.4	12.4	4.1	56824	57098	74	72	950	9.4	25.8	38.3	24.3	2.2	118644
44667	ORRVILLE	21591	5086	17.9	31.5	39.5	8.5	2.7	50355	51641	62	51	3457	12.7	12.8	55.3	18.3	0.9	123141
44669	PARIS	21880	548	17.9	25.7	49.1	5.7	1.6	53795	54441	69	63	466	14.4	17.2	47.2	19.5	1.7	113636
44672	SEBRING	21128	2169	30.3	28.4	35.4	4.4	1.5	39516	43609	31	20	1235	21.2	50.4	24.9	3.4	0.0	72627
44675	SHERRODSVILLE	23717	789	22.1	37.4	31.3	6.6	2.7	41172	43513	37	24	668	18.6	33.1	34.4	13.0	0.9	88103
44676	SHREVE	20394	1830	23.4	26.4	42.4	6.1	1.6	50101	51240	61	49	1416	14.3	20.1	48.7	14.5	2.5	110740
44677	SMITHVILLE	23592	985	13.9	29.8	45.7	8.4	2.1	53922	54236	70	63	727	6.7	9.1	60.4	21.9	1.9	136696
44680	STRASBURG	22133	1538	23.1	29.0	38.2	7.7	2.0	48074	50240	57	42	1105	9.6	26.4	45.0	17.2	1.8	111419
44681	SUGARCREEK	16657	2275	20.8	34.6	37.7	4.5	2.4	45239	47671	49	34	1730	4.9	16.8	53.1	21.7	3.4	124680
44683	UHRICHSVILLE	16731	3349	31.2	36.7	27.7	3.2	1.2	36807	39143	23	14	2397	21.3	44.6	30.8	3.0	0.3	73169
44685	UNIONTOWN	30903	10237	11.4	18.7	43.6	18.4	8.0	72656	72322	88	92	8514	2.7	8.8	62.2	25.4	0.9	141534
44688	WAYNESBURG	18919	1287	28.7	30.7	33.3	6.2	1.1	41464	45371	38	24	978	19.1	33.6	39.3	7.5	0.5	87429
44689	WILMOT	18753	96	17.7	35.4	35.4	7.3	4.2	46875	48072	54	39	73	12.3	26.0	38.4	17.8	5.5	111250
44691	WOOSTER	25091	17529	21.3	26.9	39.0	8.6	4.2	51169	52505	64	54	11903	12.3	13.1	50.1	22.0	2.5	128557
44695	BOWERSTON	19902	643	25.5	32.7	36.2	3.3	2.3	42335	45000	40	26	534	24.5	36.1	29.6	9.4	0.4	76444
44699	TIPPECANOE	18193	470	31.7	34.7	27.2	4.7	1.7	37111	38541	24	14	383	20.6	36.6	35.8	7.0	0.0	82143
44702	CANTON	14092	423	74.5	18.4	6.6	0.0	0.5	12199	12804	1	1	44	47.7	47.7	4.5	0.0	0.0	51000
44703	CANTON	18681	3808	34.1	33.6	26.6	3.5	2.2	35454	37465	19	11	1730	25.5	50.0	21.4	2.7	0.3	71577
44704	CANTON	14433	1851	46.9	33.7	14.7	3.0	1.7	26690	27592	4	4	1026	47.7	37.6	13.6	1.1	0.0	51890
44705	CANTON	19221	7512	29.7	32.6	30.0	5.5	2.1	37878	40499	26	16	5377	26.9	44.0	23.2	5.7	0.2	66359
44706	CANTON	19483	7232	24.3	33.1	37.3	4.5	0.9	42525	46843	41	27	5529	19.9	35.0	41.0	3.8	0.3	84376
44707	CANTON	15229	3977	45.4	26.2	24.7	2.9	0.7	29020	30705	7	5	2385	26.0	39.3	30.2	4.3	0.1	72833
44708	CANTON	29718	11380	19.6	30.0	36.1	8.6	5.7	50284	52462	62	50	7954	4.6	26.2	53.2	12.7	3.2	109986
44709	CANTON	27271	8286	22.4	28.5	36.7	7.8	4.6	48957	51568	59	45	5256	3.3	32.1	52.1	11.7	0.8	101889
44710	CANTON	21011	4226	30.8	32.0	30.5	5.4	1.3	37896	41037	26	16	2987	11.6	58.0	28.5	1.9	0.0	76694
44714	CANTON	27622	3917	21.1	33.5	32.3	8.5	4.5	46634	49300	53	38	2710	10.9	41.6	35.7	11.3	0.5	87818
44718	CANTON	39458	5258	15.3	20.4	32.4	17.4	14.5	68134	67194	86	89	3521	0.0	3.3	45.6	45.4	5.8	177538
44720	CANTON	32161	15369	13.2	24.2	39.9	14.7	8.0	61875	62425	80	80	11158	2.1	6.8	60.3	28.8	1.9	146205
44721	CANTON	30163	4860	7.9	21.0	50.1	15.2	5.7	68380	68716	86	89	4019	1.8	4.1	70.2	22.0	1.9	140067
44730	CANTON	20901	2512	21.7	32.9	37.6	5.5	2.3	45829	49458	51	36	2030	13.5	31.1	46.7	8.2	0.4	94431
44802	ALVADA	21555	459	16.3	25.7	48.6	7.4	2.0	54606	54186	71	65	386	10.1	22.0	49.0	16.8	2.1	118657
44804	ARCADIA	25281	442	19.7	20.6	43.0	11.8	5.0	58150	58053	75	75	382	13.4	24.3	44.8	15.4	2.1	108667
44805	ASHLAND	22497	13052	23.9	28.3	36.8	8.1	2.9	47586	50569	56	40	9274	10.4	20.9	50.0	17.1	1.6	117087
44807	ATTICA	20609	967	21.3	30.3	43.1	4.7	0.6	48397	50665	58	43	773	11.9	29.4	47.5	10.6	0.6	96618
44811	BELLEVUE	25250	5203	16.0	28.3	42.7	9.5	3.6	54539	55439	70	65	3903	7.2	21.0	57.3	13.8	0.7	111166
44813	BELLVILLE	20926	3033	22.5	30.8	37.5	6.7	2.5	46909	49535	54	39	2477	14.7	20.0	48.4	16.4	0.6	107724
44814	BERLIN HEIGHTS	26825	1074	10.2	23.0	50.6	11.6	4.6	63754	64435	82	84	936	3.5	16.5	60.1	18.5	1.4	124601
44817	BLOOMDALE	19637	555	15.5	34.2	44.1	5.0	1.1	50132	52329	61	50	467	24.8	35.8	34.9	4.3	0.2	79022
44818	BLOOMVILLE	20311	1109	16.6	30.7	46.4	5.2	1.1	51587	52189	65	56	911	15.4	31.9	41.1	9.9	1.8	92552
44820	BUCYRUS	22547	7668	24.3	30.4	35.9	7.2	2.3	45159	48053	49	34	5398	13.4	30.8	46.9	8.2	0.6	96653
44822	BUTLER	19518	1264	22.5	27.8	41.4	6.1	2.3	49726	50888	60	48	1069	12.9	21.0	45.1	19.1	1.9	113530
44824	CASTALIA	27293	1526	13.2	20.9	48.1	13.2	4.5	68060	68186	86	89	1303	6.1	15.7	58.5	19.0	0.8	124571
44826	COLLINS	22579	675	18.1	26.8	44.3	8.3	2.5	54100	54906	70	64	571	7.0	9.6	59.9	21.0	2.5	135181
44827	CRESTLINE	22507	2788	23.6	29.1	37.4	7.7	2.3	46460	49043	53	37	2111	18.0	36.6	38.9	6.2	0.2	86444
44830	FOSTORIA	20674	7697	26.5	31.4	34.2	6.0	1.9	41978	46025	39	25	5716	27.1	35.6	31.9	5.2	0.2	74720
44833	GALION	22073	7395	26.8	28.2	36.9	5.9	2.2	44486	47815	47	32	5336	12.8	35.3	42.9	8.3	0.7	92232
44836	GREEN SPRINGS	21569	1031	20.1	29.5	40.2	9.0	1.3	50318	51761	62	51	825	10.7	25.1	54.4	8.8	1.0	104236
44837	GREENWICH	18990	1609	22.7	29.1	41.7	5.5	1.1	47624	50603	56	41	1282	21.6	22.2	41.3	12.9	2.0	98333
44839	HURON	33342	5175	13.5	22.1	40.9	14.7	8.8	64218	65083	83	84	3973	6.7	9.5	50.1	30.8	2.9	141610
44840	JEROMESVILLE	22050	1276	15.8	28.1	46.2	8.4	1.6	53720	54674	69	63	1048	8.8	14.5	53.1	20.4	3.2	132039
44841	KANSAS	20934	431	14.8	31.8	47.1	5.3	0.9	52371	53323	67	59	367	17.4	30.2	46.0	6.0	0.3	91977
44842	LOUDONVILLE	21227	2366	19.6	31.5	39.3	7.7	1.8	48863	51073	59	45	1725	14.3	27.4	38.7	16.6	3.1	100511
44843	LUCAS	26882	871	14.1	21.1	47.1	13.4	4.2	63308	63282	82	83	753	1.7	20.8	57.5	18.6	1.3	120353
44844	MC CUTCHENVILLE	21435	300	19.3	25.0	48.7	6.7	0.3	54489	54682	70	65	256	10.9	24.6	52.7	10.5	1.2	107456
44846	MILAN	27201	1303	11.5	25.7	45.6	10.4	6.8	63696	65006	82	84	1041	8.5	13.6	50.1	26.2	1.5	126260
44847	MONROEVILLE	23402	1420	14.2	27.2	47.2	8.3	3.1	57141	58027	74	73	1115	3.5	14.4	58.3	21.7	2.1	124952
44849	NEVADA	21395	1004	19.4	32.6	40.2	5.7	2.1	46777	50250	53	38	826	17.2	26.8	38.1	15.5	2.4	97576
44851	NEW LONDON	21440	1972	19.2	30.7	38.6	9.7	1.8	50065	51564	61	49	1500	12.6	23.1	44.5	17.6	2.2	109737
44853	NEW RIEGEL	21105	608	19.1	27.1	44.6	7.1	2.1	52323	53233	67	59	524	6.1	26.0	51.5	14.7	1.7	111598
44854	NEW WASHINGTON	21594	707	16.4	28.7	47.9	5.8	1.1	52277	52646	66	59	592	13.0	33.1	44.9	7.6	1.4	94694
44855	NORTH FAIRFIELD	19477	485	15.5	31.5	48.0	4.5	0.4	51509	51913	65	56	412	12.9	25.7	50.2	10.0	1.2	105128
44857	NORWALK	24545	9270	19.8	27.5	40.0	8.9	3.8	52119	53419	66	58	6280	12.8	13.7	52.0	20.1	1.5	120369
44859	NOVA	20942	684	15.6	32.2	45.5	5.3	1.5	51250	52633	64	54	602	6.3	10.8	51.0	28.4	3.5	135484
44864	PERRYSVILLE	22057	1277	22.7	30.9	37.4	7.0	1.9	46099	49665	52	36	1010	12.9	30.3	34.1	21.1	1.7	100919
44865	PLYMOUTH	20987	1386	19.5	31.7	38.6	8.8	1.4	48982	50760	59	45	1033	18.2	28.6	42.0	10.3	1.0	94188
44866	POLK	18894	735	18.6	31.6	41.4	6.4	2.0	49846	51111	61	48	637	9.7	19.9	47.1	19.6	3.6	127900
44867	REPUBLIC	21212	905	18.3	30.8	42.0	7.1	1.8	50595	52067	63	52	755	12.3	25.7	51.8	9.5	0.7	101349
44870	SANDUSKY	24802	17659	24.5	29.2	34.3	8.4	3.7	45526	50127	50	35	11408	12.9	35.8	39.7	9.8	1.8	91407
44875	SHELBY	22477	5924	22.1	29.3	39.9	6.4	2.4	48506	50702	58	44	4216	9.7	34.6	45.9	8.9	0.9	95831
44878	SHILOH	17202	1086	20.5	32.3	38.8	5.8	2.6	47610	49652	56	41	883	21.2	31.8	30.9	12.8	3.3	87120
44880	SULLIVAN	19287	970	21.6	24.5	43.0	8.5	2.4	52156	53035	66	58	857	7.8	10.9	52.7	24.9	3.7	138897
44882	SYCAMORE	21670	1197	19.7	30.1	42.9	5.8	1.5	50116	51295	61	50	984	17.8	32.6	39.6	8.1	1.8	89540
44883	TIFFIN	22515	11778	21.6	30.5	39.2	6.5	2.3	47814	50617	56	41	8536	11.8	30.0	46.3	11.3	0.7	98032
44887	TIRO	21117	406	16.3	32.3	43.3	6.2	2.0	50859	51197	63	52	345	18.6	25.2	44.3	9.9	2.0	99773
44889	WAKEMAN	25032	2472	12.9	22.8	50.8	11.4	2.0	63193	63608	81	82	2111	12.0	8.0	50.8	27.8	1.4	138275
44890	WILLARD	20187	4402	24.0	30.0	36.6	7.7	1.6	45467	48942	50	35	3039	13.0	23.6	50.2	12.5	0.7	106671
44902	MANSFIELD	16268	2475	42.7	32.2	19.5	4.2	1.4	30325	31591	9	5	1170	48.5	46.2	3.8	1.1	0.3	51076
44903	MANSFIELD	22972	10521	24.8	26.5	36.5	8.9	3.3	48379	51165	57	43	7453	14.7	25.7	45.2	13.5	0.9	102746
44904	MANSFIELD	28760	5792	15.8	25.4	39.4	13.2	6.3	58860	59279	76	76	4418	5.4	11.7	60.4	21.5	1.1	128009
44905	MANSFIELD	19469	5096	23.8	31.6	37.6	5.7	1.3	44896	48365	48	33	3868	20.5	39.8	37.6	2.0	0.2	81881
44906	MANSFIELD	25927	7602	24.8	28.5	34.6	7.1	5.0	45414	49939	49	34	5353	17.1	31.6	39.2	11.1	0.9	92119
44907	MANSFIELD	27221	6546	25.5	30.7	32.6	7.0	4.3	43477	47368	44	29	4059	9.4	31.1	49.4	9.2	0.9	99987
45001	ADDYSTON	20579	349	23.8	30.7	35.2	6.9	3.4	44895	50280	48	33	198	24.7	35.4	25.8	11.6	2.5	78182
45002	CLEVES	26558	5170	13.1	23.8	43.8	13.1	6.2	60668	62477	78	79	3995	17.2	14.1	45.4	21.6	1.6	117507
	OHIO	26577		21.4	25.9	36.7	10.4	5.7	52400	54553				10.3	22.0	45.6	19.3	2.8	114865
	UNITED STATES	27277		20.9	24.4	35.3	11.7	7.6	54719	56938				9.3	13.1	31.6	32.6	13.5	162279

ZIP CODE		FINANCIAL SERVICES				THE HOME						ENTERTAINMENT						PERSONAL			
						Home Improvements		Furnishings													
#	POST OFFICE NAME	Auto Loan	Home Loan	Investments	Retirement Plans	Home Repair	Lawn & Garden	Computers & Hardware-Personal	Major Appliances	TV, Radio, Sound Equipment	Furniture	Dine out/ Carry out	Sports Equipment	Fees & Tickets	Toys & Games	Travel	Cable TV	Apparel & Services	Auto Repairs	Health Insurance	Pets & Supplies
44643	MAGNOLIA	83	74	77	73	74	89	71	81	77	69	76	60	67	78	71	83	52	77	88	96
44644	MALVERN	93	81	78	81	80	92	81	87	85	80	84	66	74	88	77	89	58	84	90	104
44645	MARSHALLVILLE	90	89	84	92	89	98	85	93	86	80	85	71	82	88	86	89	58	87	94	108
44646	MASSILLON	92	96	87	96	93	98	94	93	95	92	95	71	96	95	94	97	66	94	99	110
44647	MASSILLON	84	81	78	82	80	92	79	85	82	75	81	64	77	83	79	87	56	82	92	100
44651	MECHANICSTOWN	91	73	78	74	74	92	74	85	79	70	78	65	64	82	71	85	53	80	89	101
44654	MILLERSBURG	95	83	84	80	82	90	85	91	85	82	86	71	76	87	82	87	59	88	90	106
44656	MINERAL CITY	94	74	80	74	74	93	76	86	81	72	80	66	64	84	71	87	54	81	90	103
44657	MINERVA	79	72	72	73	73	85	71	79	74	66	73	60	66	75	70	79	50	74	84	93
44662	NAVARRE	81	77	77	77	77	89	73	81	77	70	76	60	71	78	74	82	52	77	88	95
44663	NEW PHILADELPHIA	77	71	70	72	71	81	72	76	75	68	74	58	69	76	71	79	51	75	82	90
44666	NORTH LAWRENCE	100	108	97	111	106	110	98	104	98	97	98	80	102	100	103	100	68	99	105	122
44667	ORRVILLE	84	82	74	83	80	87	81	83	83	78	82	64	80	84	80	85	57	82	86	99
44669	PARIS	90	82	81	85	84	97	81	91	83	73	82	69	75	85	81	88	56	84	94	106
44672	SEBRING	65	62	61	63	62	70	66	66	69	62	68	50	64	67	64	72	47	67	76	79
44675	SHERRODSVILLE	95	73	103	72	76	98	74	92	79	68	78	68	62	78	75	86	52	84	94	108
44676	SHREVE	87	75	77	76	75	90	74	84	78	69	77	64	66	80	72	83	52	79	87	99
44677	SMITHVILLE	84	89	84	90	89	90	86	88	85	82	85	68	88	86	88	86	60	86	88	102
44680	STRASBURG	81	76	73	78	76	85	78	81	80	74	78	62	74	80	76	82	54	80	86	96
44681	SUGARCREEK	84	76	75	75	76	83	77	83	77	73	77	64	70	78	75	79	53	79	82	96
44683	UHRICHSVILLE	68	55	55	55	53	66	60	63	64	56	62	49	52	65	55	68	42	63	69	76
44685	UNIONTOWN	115	131	118	132	128	126	117	121	115	119	116	93	126	117	123	115	81	117	119	140
44688	WAYNESBURG	78	67	77	66	67	83	66	76	71	62	70	57	60	71	66	76	47	72	82	90
44689	WILMOT	97	79	78	74	78	83	85	89	85	86	87	70	74	88	79	86	61	89	84	102
44691	WOOSTER	89	85	81	87	85	92	87	89	89	83	88	68	84	89	85	92	61	88	94	105
44695	BOWERSTON	89	63	91	61	66	90	65	83	72	61	71	62	52	72	64	80	47	76	86	99
44699	TIPPECANOE	81	58	82	56	60	83	61	76	67	56	66	57	48	67	60	74	44	70	81	91
44702	CANTON	27	20	24	23	21	25	32	26	34	29	34	20	28	30	28	37	24	32	36	34
44703	CANTON	62	54	47	56	51	55	67	57	68	60	67	47	62	68	58	69	48	64	63	71
44704	CANTON	51	44	42	45	43	51	46	48	52	47	51	34	45	50	44	56	35	50	56	59
44705	CANTON	73	65	60	65	63	74	70	70	73	66	72	53	65	73	65	77	49	71	78	84
44706	CANTON	74	66	65	68	66	77	69	73	73	64	71	55	64	73	67	77	49	72	79	87
44707	CANTON	55	44	42	46	43	52	51	50	56	49	55	38	46	55	46	60	38	53	58	62
44708	CANTON	90	95	92	96	96	102	91	95	95	90	94	69	95	93	94	99	65	94	105	111
44709	CANTON	82	83	78	85	82	86	86	83	88	84	87	64	87	86	85	89	61	86	91	99
44710	CANTON	69	62	55	63	60	69	68	66	70	63	69	51	63	71	63	74	48	68	74	80
44714	CANTON	88	84	79	85	83	92	88	88	90	84	89	66	85	90	85	94	61	89	97	104
44718	CANTON	121	138	142	143	142	136	129	130	128	134	128	99	143	126	138	127	92	129	132	151
44720	CANTON	107	118	113	119	118	117	110	112	109	111	109	85	117	109	115	110	77	110	114	131
44721	CANTON	106	124	112	126	122	124	108	114	109	110	110	86	120	110	118	111	77	111	118	133
44730	CANTON	82	75	74	78	76	88	74	83	76	67	75	63	68	78	74	81	51	77	86	97
44802	ALVADA	91	83	82	87	85	98	82	93	85	74	83	70	76	86	82	90	57	86	96	108
44804	ARCADIA	99	98	92	102	98	108	93	102	94	88	93	78	91	96	95	98	64	96	104	119
44805	ASHLAND	82	77	73	79	76	85	79	81	81	75	80	62	75	82	77	84	55	80	86	96
44807	ATTICA	80	73	72	76	75	86	72	81	74	65	73	62	67	76	72	79	50	75	84	94
44811	BELLEVUE	89	93	81	94	89	98	89	92	90	85	90	71	90	92	90	93	62	90	98	109
44813	BELLVILLE	83	76	75	78	77	89	74	84	77	68	76	63	69	79	74	81	52	78	86	98
44814	BERLIN HEIGHTS	102	114	101	117	111	113	102	107	101	102	101	83	108	103	108	101	71	103	106	126
44817	BLOOMDALE	83	75	74	78	76	88	74	83	77	68	75	63	68	78	74	81	51	77	86	97
44818	BLOOMVILLE	81	77	70	80	76	86	76	81	78	70	77	63	73	79	75	81	53	78	86	96
44820	BUCYRUS	81	72	69	74	71	83	75	78	78	70	77	60	70	79	72	82	53	77	84	93
44822	BUTLER	84	79	77	82	80	91	77	86	79	70	78	65	72	80	77	83	53	80	88	100
44824	CASTALIA	96	113	100	115	109	112	99	103	99	99	100	79	109	101	107	100	70	100	106	120
44826	COLLINS	93	90	86	93	91	101	86	95	88	80	87	73	83	90	88	92	60	89	97	111
44827	CRESTLINE	82	77	69	77	74	85	78	79	81	74	79	61	74	82	74	84	55	79	86	95
44830	FOSTORIA	79	66	66	67	65	79	71	75	75	65	73	58	63	75	66	79	50	74	81	90
44833	GALION	76	72	67	73	71	80	74	76	76	69	75	57	71	76	72	79	52	75	82	90
44836	GREEN SPRINGS	87	82	75	85	81	93	81	87	83	74	82	67	77	85	80	87	56	83	92	103
44837	GREENWICH	92	70	78	70	71	90	72	83	78	69	77	64	60	81	67	85	52	78	87	100
44839	HURON	109	119	114	120	118	121	110	114	110	110	110	86	116	110	116	112	77	112	118	134
44840	JEROMESVILLE	87	85	80	88	85	94	81	89	82	76	81	68	79	84	83	85	56	83	90	104
44841	KANSAS	84	78	77	81	79	91	76	86	79	70	77	65	72	80	77	83	53	79	89	100
44842	LOUDONVILLE	85	76	74	76	74	86	77	81	80	73	79	63	71	81	74	83	54	79	85	97
44843	LUCAS	97	109	97	111	106	111	97	103	97	96	98	78	104	99	103	99	68	99	105	120
44844	MC CUTCHENVILLE	88	76	78	78	77	92	76	86	79	69	78	65	68	81	74	84	53	80	89	101
44846	MILAN	103	117	102	118	113	116	104	108	104	104	104	83	112	106	110	105	73	105	110	127
44847	MONROEVILLE	95	94	88	98	94	103	89	98	90	84	90	75	88	92	91	94	62	92	99	114
44849	NEVADA	89	73	77	75	74	90	74	84	78	69	77	64	65	81	71	84	52	79	88	100
44851	NEW LONDON	86	80	76	81	78	91	78	84	81	74	80	64	74	83	77	86	55	81	90	100
44853	NEW RIEGEL	90	82	82	86	84	97	81	92	84	73	82	69	75	85	81	89	56	85	95	107
44854	NEW WASHINGTON	82	78	71	81	76	88	77	82	79	71	78	63	74	81	76	82	53	79	87	97
44855	NORTH FAIRFIELD	83	75	75	79	77	89	74	84	77	67	75	64	69	78	74	81	51	77	87	98
44857	NORWALK	88	86	78	87	84	91	88	88	89	84	88	68	86	90	85	92	61	88	93	104
44859	NOVA	87	79	78	83	81	93	78	88	81	71	79	67	72	82	78	85	54	81	91	102
44864	PERRYSVILLE	84	72	81	73	73	90	73	84	77	66	75	64	65	77	72	82	51	78	88	98
44865	PLYMOUTH	96	74	82	73	74	94	75	87	82	72	80	67	63	85	71	89	54	82	91	105
44866	POLK	84	77	76	80	78	91	76	86	78	68	77	65	70	80	76	83	52	79	88	99
44867	REPUBLIC	88	84	80	87	84	95	81	90	83	75	82	68	77	84	82	86	56	84	92	105
44870	SANDUSKY	80	79	73	80	77	85	81	80	84	78	83	61	81	84	79	87	58	82	88	96
44875	SHELBY	79	77	71	78	75	85	77	79	79	73	78	60	75	80	76	83	54	79	87	94
44878	SHILOH	96	72	90	71	72	96	75	88	80	68	79	70	60	81	72	86	52	83	92	107
44880	SULLIVAN	90	83	81	86	84	96	81	91	83	74	82	69	76	85	82	88	56	84	94	106
44882	SYCAMORE	86	75	73	76	74	88	75	82	79	71	78	63	69	81	73	84	53	79	87	98
44883	TIFFIN	81	76	73	77	75	85	76	80	79	72	78	61	73	79	75	82	53	79	86	95
44887	TIRO	87	79	78	82	80	93	78	88	80	70	79	66	72	82	78	85	54	81	91	102
44889	WAKEMAN	99	102	90	103	100	104	94	99	94	94	94	76	95	97	95	96	65	95	99	117
44890	WILLARD	78	72	69	74	71	80	76	77	78	70	77	60	71	78	73	82	54	77	82	92
44902	MANSFIELD	55	46	41	47	43	51	57	51	59	52	58	40	51	59	49	62	41	56	58	63
44903	MANSFIELD	80	81	72	82	78	84	80	80	82	78	82	61	81	83	79	84	57	81	85	96
44904	MANSFIELD	97	106	103	108	106	108	99	103	100	99	100	78	105	100	104	101	70	101	106	120
44905	MANSFIELD	78	70	70	70	69	81	70	75	74	67	73	58	66	75	69	78	50	74	81	90
44906	MANSFIELD	87	81	84	81	80	92	82	86	85	78	84	66	79	85	81	89	58	85	92	102
44907	MANSFIELD	80	76	73	77	76	83	80	80	83	77	82	60	78	82	78	86	57	81	88	95
45001	ADDYSTON	85	75	63	77	71	84	83	80	86	77	84	63	76	87	75	89	58	83	89	97
45002	CLEVES	109	112	98	111	107	109	105	106	105	107	105	83	106	108	105	105	73	104	105	125
	OHIO	94	92	87	93	90	96	93	93	94	91	94	72	92	95	91	96	66	93	98	110
	UNITED STATES	100	100	100	100	100	100	100	100	100	100	100	100	100	100	100	100	100	100	100	100

POPULATION CHANGE

45003-45242

ZIP CODE #	POST OFFICE NAME	COUNTY FIPS CODE	POPULATION 2000	POPULATION 2009	POPULATION 2014	2000-2009 ANNUAL RATE % Rate	2000-2009 ANNUAL RATE State Centile	HOUSEHOLDS 2000	HOUSEHOLDS 2009	HOUSEHOLDS 2014	HOUSEHOLDS % Annual Rate 2000-2009	HOUSEHOLDS 2009 Average HH Size	FAMILIES 2000	FAMILIES 2009	FAMILIES % Annual Rate 2000-2009
45003	COLLEGE CORNER	135	948	928	917	-0.2	32	404	410	409	0.2	2.26	295	291	-0.1
45005	FRANKLIN	165	27817	31935	34419	1.5	94	10737	12414	13427	1.6	2.56	7995	8999	1.3
45011	HAMILTON	017	55730	67421	72366	2.1	97	19479	23736	25554	2.2	2.78	14732	17790	2.1
45013	HAMILTON	017	49691	53468	55405	0.8	82	19333	21235	22144	1.0	2.50	14079	14922	0.6
45014	FAIRFIELD	017	43452	44769	45675	0.3	61	17469	18405	18900	0.6	2.40	11765	11890	0.1
45015	HAMILTON	017	12444	12355	12531	-0.1	39	5092	5128	5227	0.1	2.40	3366	3244	-0.4
45030	HARRISON	061	15579	16389	16575	0.5	71	5726	6110	6217	0.7	2.68	4293	4439	0.4
45034	KINGS MILLS	165	915	1123	1243	2.2	97	348	430	479	2.3	2.61	288	348	2.1
45036	LEBANON	165	30891	39599	44460	2.7	98	9528	12753	14547	3.2	2.68	7172	9416	3.0
45039	MAINEVILLE	165	14227	22225	26396	4.9	99	5427	8509	10127	5.0	2.61	4115	6417	4.9
45040	MASON	165	34030	50051	58439	4.3	99	11783	17495	20509	4.4	2.84	9204	13300	4.1
45042	MIDDLETOWN	017	28134	28537	28892	0.2	56	11299	11667	11874	0.3	2.43	8076	8079	0.0
45044	MIDDLETOWN	017	45173	51678	54610	1.5	94	17342	19822	20946	1.5	2.58	12052	13615	1.3
45050	MONROE	017	5247	7243	8307	3.5	99	2070	2982	3445	4.0	2.39	1549	2143	3.6
45052	NORTH BEND	061	3776	3892	3939	0.3	61	1313	1372	1397	0.5	2.83	1060	1076	0.2
45053	OKEANA	017	3061	3460	3654	1.3	92	1034	1195	1270	1.6	2.90	886	1003	1.3
45054	OREGONIA	165	1591	1912	2150	2.0	97	584	712	809	2.2	2.60	479	571	1.9
45056	OXFORD	017	27265	28084	28630	0.3	61	7833	8372	8629	0.7	2.48	3637	3767	0.4
45064	SOMERVILLE	017	2218	2325	2388	0.5	71	753	809	837	0.8	2.83	632	665	0.6
45065	SOUTH LEBANON	165	3294	3945	4409	2.0	97	1280	1552	1745	2.1	2.54	909	1057	1.6
45066	SPRINGBORO	165	16457	22947	26546	3.7	99	5666	7858	9077	3.6	2.92	4808	6618	3.5
45067	TRENTON	017	10516	12316	13130	1.7	95	3792	4514	4832	1.9	2.73	2986	3464	1.6
45068	WAYNESVILLE	165	9030	11347	12680	2.5	98	3283	4177	4692	2.6	2.69	2609	3236	2.4
45069	WEST CHESTER	017	43007	48146	50359	1.2	91	14965	17289	18262	1.6	2.78	12156	13465	1.1
45101	ABERDEEN	015	2502	2827	2946	1.3	92	1029	1197	1257	1.6	2.35	686	776	1.3
45102	AMELIA	025	18569	21346	22890	1.5	94	6826	8089	8759	1.9	2.64	5176	5967	1.5
45103	BATAVIA	025	27490	32305	34476	1.8	96	9904	11906	12817	2.0	2.65	7354	8656	1.8
45106	BETHEL	025	11860	12592	13008	0.6	75	4235	4594	4783	0.9	2.74	3315	3528	0.7
45107	BLANCHESTER	027	8708	9673	10109	1.1	89	3207	3656	3845	1.4	2.61	2430	2715	1.2
45111	CAMP DENNISON	061	420	393	387	-0.7	11	173	166	165	-0.4	2.37	121	112	-0.8
45113	CLARKSVILLE	027	3486	4453	4869	2.7	98	1239	1620	1785	2.9	2.75	1008	1297	2.8
45118	FAYETTEVILLE	015	3701	3939	4039	0.7	79	1315	1438	1487	1.0	2.74	1046	1123	0.8
45120	FELICITY	025	3456	3893	4119	1.3	92	1202	1393	1489	1.6	2.79	907	1027	1.4
45121	GEORGETOWN	015	8466	8918	8995	0.6	75	3260	3528	3590	0.9	2.48	2350	2475	0.6
45122	GOSHEN	025	11411	11926	12169	0.5	71	4003	4293	4419	0.8	2.77	3220	3384	0.5
45123	GREENFIELD	071	7785	7976	8074	0.3	61	3003	3142	3201	0.5	2.49	2097	2133	0.2
45130	HAMERSVILLE	015	3866	3978	3976	0.3	61	1356	1427	1434	0.6	2.79	1092	1130	0.4
45133	HILLSBORO	071	22997	24205	24804	0.6	75	8891	9538	9824	0.8	2.51	6478	6795	0.5
45135	LEESBURG	071	4332	4772	4954	1.1	89	1590	1792	1876	1.3	2.66	1201	1320	1.0
45140	LOVELAND	025	44896	53097	57307	1.8	96	15982	19195	20840	2.0	2.76	12487	14593	1.7
45142	LYNCHBURG	071	4396	4760	4939	0.9	85	1575	1745	1821	1.1	2.72	1221	1323	0.9
45144	MANCHESTER	001	4433	4407	4390	-0.1	39	1820	1875	1887	0.3	2.34	1264	1269	0.0
45146	MARTINSVILLE	027	1308	1444	1507	1.1	89	476	539	566	1.4	2.68	390	432	1.1
45148	MIDLAND	027	1520	1636	1697	0.8	82	532	591	618	1.1	2.77	426	463	0.9
45150	MILFORD	025	30629	35120	36996	1.5	94	11776	13790	14641	1.7	2.52	8436	9705	1.5
45152	MORROW	165	7469	10477	12031	3.7	99	2706	3825	4409	3.8	2.72	2129	2956	3.6
45153	MOSCOW	025	1976	2194	2315	1.1	89	691	790	841	1.5	2.78	550	615	1.2
45154	MOUNT ORAB	015	8064	9241	9652	1.5	94	2867	3353	3525	1.7	2.74	2222	2548	1.5
45157	NEW RICHMOND	025	9616	10014	10253	0.4	66	3285	3524	3646	0.8	2.84	2612	2747	0.5
45159	NEW VIENNA	027	3174	3609	3805	1.4	93	1161	1352	1434	1.7	2.67	867	982	1.4
45160	OWENSVILLE	025	462	493	507	0.7	79	226	245	253	0.9	2.01	151	159	0.6
45162	PLEASANT PLAIN	165	2467	2802	3003	1.4	93	860	992	1070	1.6	2.82	721	816	1.3
45167	RIPLEY	015	3745	3697	3669	-0.1	39	1436	1439	1437	0.0	2.52	1001	979	-0.2
45168	RUSSELLVILLE	015	1470	1585	1639	0.8	82	564	624	650	1.1	2.49	442	481	0.9
45169	SABINA	027	5088	5135	5162	0.1	51	1925	1987	2010	0.3	2.56	1438	1446	0.1
45171	SARDINIA	015	5561	6101	6329	1.0	87	2060	2319	2423	1.3	2.62	1620	1794	1.1
45174	TERRACE PARK	061	2273	2301	2309	0.1	51	760	765	769	0.1	3.01	646	639	-0.1
45176	WILLIAMSBURG	025	8404	9226	9656	1.0	87	2983	3364	3556	1.3	2.71	2310	2551	1.1
45177	WILMINGTON	027	20983	22369	23009	0.7	79	8205	8947	9264	0.9	2.42	5609	5975	0.7
45202	CINCINNATI	061	15225	14376	14220	-0.6	14	7470	7084	7047	-0.6	1.68	2216	1906	-1.6
45203	CINCINNATI	061	3276	3262	3257	0.0	45	1417	1402	1405	-0.1	1.87	556	521	-0.7
45204	CINCINNATI	061	7213	6594	6443	-1.0	5	2692	2475	2429	-0.9	2.44	1564	1370	-1.4
45205	CINCINNATI	061	23752	20614	19908	-1.5	1	9327	8208	7974	-1.4	2.47	5413	4529	-1.9
45206	CINCINNATI	061	12642	11703	11489	-0.8	9	6397	6024	5952	-0.6	1.84	2395	2088	-1.5
45207	CINCINNATI	061	8955	7865	7647	-1.4	2	2787	2411	2345	-1.6	2.71	1753	1448	-2.0
45208	CINCINNATI	061	19928	19148	18985	-0.4	21	10100	9897	9877	-0.2	1.89	4406	4055	-0.9
45209	CINCINNATI	061	9543	9041	8941	-0.6	14	5412	5248	5223	-0.3	1.71	1958	1765	-1.1
45211	CINCINNATI	061	39067	37364	36946	-0.5	17	17052	16574	16503	-0.3	2.21	9648	8987	-0.8
45212	CINCINNATI	061	24651	22635	22182	-0.9	7	10810	10128	9989	-0.7	2.21	5899	5242	-1.3
45213	CINCINNATI	061	12901	12026	11821	-0.8	9	5766	5482	5426	-0.5	2.16	3325	3012	-1.1
45214	CINCINNATI	061	10919	9202	8876	-1.8	0	4700	4006	3883	-1.7	2.21	2260	1810	-2.4
45215	CINCINNATI	061	31482	30293	30030	-0.4	21	13136	12833	12799	-0.3	2.32	8121	7600	-0.7
45216	CINCINNATI	061	10002	9578	9488	-0.5	17	4343	4244	4233	-0.2	2.24	2483	2307	-0.8
45217	CINCINNATI	061	7432	6982	6885	-0.7	11	3091	2954	2927	-0.5	2.33	1827	1665	-1.0
45218	CINCINNATI	061	4338	4083	4020	-0.7	11	1725	1658	1644	-0.4	2.41	1197	1110	-0.8
45219	CINCINNATI	061	17889	16587	16283	-0.8	9	7359	6776	6666	-0.9	2.02	2332	1965	-1.8
45220	CINCINNATI	061	15454	14590	14394	-0.6	14	7872	7504	7435	-0.5	1.81	2662	2356	-1.3
45223	CINCINNATI	061	14724	13150	12783	-1.2	3	6127	5584	5466	-1.0	2.35	3435	2973	-1.5
45224	CINCINNATI	061	22593	21947	21801	-0.3	27	9526	9396	9390	-0.1	2.27	5826	5499	-0.6
45225	CINCINNATI	061	12458	10644	10287	-1.7	1	4834	4180	4062	-1.6	2.44	2980	2488	-1.9
45226	CINCINNATI	061	5383	5098	5032	-0.6	14	2462	2380	2367	-0.4	2.14	1301	1194	-0.9
45227	CINCINNATI	061	19196	18771	18707	-0.2	32	8176	8104	8113	-0.1	2.30	4887	4629	-0.6
45228	CINCINNATI	061	473	506	514	0.7	79	189	200	203	0.6	2.53	146	150	0.3
45229	CINCINNATI	061	16110	14460	14088	-1.2	3	6961	6313	6180	-1.1	2.15	3505	3001	-1.7
45230	CINCINNATI	061	27898	27305	27230	-0.2	32	11812	11780	11815	0.0	2.29	7487	7172	-0.5
45231	CINCINNATI	061	42931	41977	41758	-0.2	32	16482	16433	16463	0.0	2.53	11805	11423	-0.4
45232	CINCINNATI	061	7458	7077	6995	-0.6	14	2803	2722	2711	-0.3	2.60	1770	1647	-0.8
45233	CINCINNATI	061	15952	16096	16118	0.1	51	5243	5319	5355	0.2	2.91	4134	4101	-0.1
45236	CINCINNATI	061	24799	23834	23624	-0.4	21	11321	11066	11041	-0.2	2.11	6657	6207	-0.8
45237	CINCINNATI	061	23587	21878	21477	-0.8	9	10489	9822	9685	-0.7	2.19	6003	5366	-1.2
45238	CINCINNATI	061	45849	44611	44376	-0.3	27	18859	18723	18755	-0.1	2.36	12091	11556	-0.5
45239	CINCINNATI	061	28989	28354	28243	-0.2	32	12108	12044	12068	-0.1	2.33	7761	7396	-0.5
45240	CINCINNATI	061	28650	28071	27966	-0.2	32	10621	10643	10682	0.0	2.63	7819	7603	-0.3
45241	CINCINNATI	061	25084	24751	24707	-0.1	39	10059	10074	10119	0.0	2.41	7002	6777	-0.4
45242	CINCINNATI	061	22183	22079	22066	-0.1	39	8391	8510	8564	0.2	2.55	6070	5980	-0.2
	OHIO					0.2					0.4	2.44			0.1
	UNITED STATES					1.0					1.1	2.59			0.9

#	POST OFFICE NAME	RACE (%) White 2000	White 2009	Black 2000	Black 2009	Asian/Pacific 2000	Asian/Pacific 2009	% Hispanic Origin 2000	% Hispanic Origin 2009	2009 AGE DISTRIBUTION (%) 0-4	5-9	10-14	15-19	20-24	25-44	45-64	65-84	85+	18+	MEDIAN AGE 2009	% 2009 Males	% 2009 Females
45003	COLLEGE CORNER	98.3	98.0	0.5	0.6	0.2	0.3	0.2	0.3	5.0	5.5	6.1	6.0	4.1	24.8	32.0	15.1	1.4	79.6	44.0	50.2	49.8
45005	FRANKLIN	97.7	97.0	0.8	1.2	0.4	0.6	0.6	0.8	6.7	6.6	6.5	6.4	5.9	27.6	26.9	12.1	1.2	76.3	38.2	48.9	51.1
45011	HAMILTON	87.6	86.5	8.4	8.4	1.1	1.9	2.7	3.0	8.9	8.4	7.8	7.1	5.9	29.6	24.1	7.2	1.0	70.4	33.2	49.6	50.4
45013	HAMILTON	96.3	95.2	1.7	2.1	0.5	0.8	0.8	1.1	6.3	6.2	6.3	6.3	5.7	25.3	28.2	13.5	2.2	77.3	40.4	48.3	51.7
45014	FAIRFIELD	90.3	87.3	5.8	7.1	2.2	3.5	1.5	1.9	6.2	5.8	5.8	6.1	7.1	30.3	26.4	10.7	1.6	78.6	36.6	48.4	51.6
45015	HAMILTON	93.4	91.8	4.5	5.3	0.4	0.6	1.6	2.1	7.4	7.0	6.6	6.3	6.4	28.8	25.0	10.6	1.9	75.2	36.3	47.8	52.2
45030	HARRISON	98.2	97.3	0.1	0.2	0.3	0.5	0.6	0.8	6.3	6.4	6.6	7.1	6.2	27.4	28.7	10.1	1.1	76.4	37.4	49.3	50.7
45034	KINGS MILLS	98.0	97.2	0.1	0.2	1.0	1.6	0.9	1.2	7.4	7.1	6.9	6.4	5.8	30.4	27.7	7.7	0.6	74.6	35.8	48.7	51.3
45036	LEBANON	88.7	88.3	9.0	8.6	0.6	1.0	1.1	1.3	7.1	7.2	7.0	6.9	7.5	30.3	23.3	8.7	2.1	74.8	34.9	53.2	46.8
45039	MAINEVILLE	96.3	95.7	0.9	1.0	1.6	2.0	1.3	1.6	7.8	7.5	7.3	6.4	5.6	30.4	26.1	7.9	0.8	73.3	36.0	48.8	51.2
45040	MASON	93.3	90.9	2.2	2.7	3.1	4.7	1.1	1.3	9.9	9.2	8.7	6.9	4.3	30.2	23.5	6.3	1.1	67.6	33.8	48.7	51.3
45042	MIDDLETOWN	96.4	94.2	1.9	3.7	0.3	0.6	0.5	0.6	5.8	5.9	6.2	6.4	5.5	24.1	30.0	13.9	2.2	78.2	42.2	48.7	51.3
45044	MIDDLETOWN	85.6	84.3	11.7	12.3	0.6	1.1	1.1	1.4	8.3	7.9	7.4	6.8	5.7	28.1	24.5	9.6	1.7	72.6	35.2	48.6	51.4
45050	MONROE	96.9	95.6	1.0	1.4	0.7	1.3	0.8	1.1	7.5	7.0	6.4	5.5	4.4	27.7	24.7	12.9	3.9	76.3	39.1	48.1	51.9
45052	NORTH BEND	97.6	96.4	0.8	1.3	0.2	0.4	0.6	1.0	6.4	6.8	7.3	8.2	6.2	22.7	30.7	10.4	1.2	74.3	38.8	49.4	50.6
45053	OKEANA	98.8	98.5	0.1	0.2	0.1	0.2	0.3	0.5	5.3	5.8	6.5	7.2	5.2	24.9	33.9	10.2	1.0	77.9	41.6	50.8	49.2
45054	OREGONIA	95.1	94.2	3.4	4.0	0.2	0.3	0.8	1.2	6.4	6.9	7.3	6.6	5.4	27.0	30.4	9.3	0.8	75.3	38.9	51.5	48.5
45056	OXFORD	92.5	90.2	3.6	4.4	2.0	3.2	1.3	1.6	2.7	2.7	2.9	19.6	36.4	13.6	14.9	6.0	1.1	89.6	23.0	47.2	52.8
45064	SOMERVILLE	98.5	98.2	0.3	0.4	0.3	0.4	0.4	0.6	5.8	6.5	7.1	6.6	4.4	24.7	32.0	11.0	1.7	76.3	41.8	50.2	49.8
45065	SOUTH LEBANON	98.5	98.0	0.4	0.6	0.2	0.3	0.9	1.2	7.8	7.8	7.8	6.8	5.3	27.7	26.7	9.1	1.1	72.4	35.9	49.8	50.2
45066	SPRINGBORO	96.6	95.4	0.8	1.0	1.4	2.2	0.9	1.2	8.5	9.2	9.6	7.5	4.0	25.0	28.4	7.1	0.6	67.8	36.5	49.9	50.1
45067	TRENTON	98.2	97.7	0.5	0.7	0.2	0.4	0.8	1.1	7.9	7.9	7.4	6.6	5.8	29.7	24.3	9.4	1.0	72.6	34.7	49.2	50.8
45068	WAYNESVILLE	98.1	97.6	0.3	0.4	0.3	0.4	0.9	1.2	6.2	6.9	7.5	6.9	4.5	24.0	31.4	11.3	1.4	75.1	41.2	49.1	50.9
45069	WEST CHESTER	89.0	84.5	4.1	5.2	4.9	7.7	1.8	2.4	7.4	7.9	8.1	7.2	4.9	28.0	28.1	7.7	0.7	72.0	36.7	49.6	50.4
45101	ABERDEEN	97.3	96.8	1.2	1.4	0.1	0.2	1.1	1.3	7.2	7.0	6.8	6.7	6.5	26.6	27.0	11.1	1.3	75.0	37.0	47.5	52.5
45102	AMELIA	97.4	96.6	0.6	0.7	0.4	0.7	0.9	1.3	8.9	8.1	7.5	6.6	6.2	31.1	23.6	7.0	0.8	71.4	33.1	48.7	51.3
45103	BATAVIA	96.7	95.7	1.1	1.2	0.8	1.4	0.9	1.1	8.3	7.5	7.2	7.0	6.7	28.5	25.5	8.2	1.2	72.7	34.7	49.1	50.9
45106	BETHEL	98.7	98.4	0.2	0.3	0.2	0.3	0.6	0.8	7.0	6.9	7.0	7.3	6.1	26.4	28.0	10.2	1.2	74.6	37.5	49.6	50.4
45107	BLANCHESTER	98.6	98.3	0.2	0.3	0.3	0.4	0.4	0.6	7.2	7.2	7.2	6.7	5.5	25.8	27.4	11.3	1.9	74.4	38.1	49.0	51.0
45111	CAMP DENNISON	77.3	69.5	18.6	25.4	0.0	0.0	1.7	2.5	2.5	3.6	4.6	6.9	5.1	24.2	38.9	12.0	2.3	85.0	46.7	51.7	48.3
45113	CLARKSVILLE	98.3	98.0	0.2	0.2	0.3	0.4	0.6	0.7	6.6	6.9	7.3	6.8	4.7	26.4	30.6	9.8	0.8	74.9	39.9	49.8	50.2
45118	FAYETTEVILLE	99.0	98.8	0.2	0.3	0.1	0.1	0.2	0.3	7.4	7.5	7.6	7.2	5.5	26.5	27.8	9.7	0.8	73.1	37.2	50.0	50.0
45120	FELICITY	98.1	97.7	0.5	0.7	0.1	0.2	0.6	0.8	7.5	7.6	7.5	7.1	5.9	26.7	27.3	9.5	1.0	73.0	36.3	49.6	50.4
45121	GEORGETOWN	97.8	97.3	1.2	1.3	0.3	0.4	0.3	0.4	6.7	6.8	6.9	7.0	5.4	26.4	27.0	11.5	2.2	75.4	38.4	48.0	52.0
45122	GOSHEN	98.2	97.9	0.5	0.6	0.2	0.3	0.5	0.7	6.8	7.1	7.3	7.3	5.2	26.7	28.5	10.3	0.8	74.2	38.1	49.6	50.4
45123	GREENFIELD	97.0	96.4	1.5	1.8	0.2	0.3	0.6	0.9	7.2	7.3	7.1	6.5	5.5	25.6	26.6	12.1	2.0	74.5	37.7	48.3	51.7
45130	HAMERSVILLE	99.0	98.8	0.2	0.3	0.1	0.2	0.5	0.7	6.8	6.8	7.0	7.3	5.6	27.1	27.9	10.5	0.9	74.8	38.1	49.5	50.5
45133	HILLSBORO	96.1	95.3	2.0	2.3	0.5	0.8	0.6	0.7	7.0	6.8	6.9	6.8	5.5	25.1	26.6	13.2	2.3	75.2	39.1	48.8	51.2
45135	LEESBURG	98.5	98.1	0.5	0.6	0.1	0.1	0.3	0.3	6.8	7.0	7.0	6.6	5.6	28.2	27.5	10.1	1.1	75.0	36.9	50.1	49.9
45140	LOVELAND	95.6	93.7	1.3	1.7	1.6	2.7	1.1	1.6	8.0	8.1	8.0	7.0	4.5	27.3	27.9	8.0	1.2	71.3	37.0	49.5	50.5
45142	LYNCHBURG	98.5	98.1	0.2	0.2	0.2	0.3	0.3	0.4	8.3	8.2	8.1	7.1	5.2	27.1	24.7	10.1	1.2	71.0	36.1	49.9	50.1
45144	MANCHESTER	97.5	97.2	0.2	0.2	0.1	0.2	0.6	0.7	5.9	6.1	6.3	6.5	5.2	25.6	29.9	12.7	1.9	77.7	41.1	49.6	50.4
45146	MARTINSVILLE	97.7	97.2	0.3	0.4	0.3	0.5	0.4	0.5	7.5	7.9	7.8	7.1	4.8	25.7	27.8	10.5	0.9	72.3	37.9	51.3	48.7
45148	MIDLAND	98.4	98.0	0.2	0.2	0.1	0.1	0.6	0.7	6.8	7.2	7.5	7.2	4.5	27.0	28.7	10.2	1.0	74.1	38.8	51.0	49.0
45150	MILFORD	96.5	95.7	1.6	1.8	0.6	1.0	0.9	1.2	6.7	6.9	7.1	6.6	5.2	25.6	28.2	11.2	2.3	75.1	39.3	47.9	52.1
45152	MORROW	98.9	98.5	0.2	0.3	0.3	0.5	1.0	1.2	6.4	6.7	7.0	6.5	4.5	26.0	30.4	11.1	1.3	75.8	40.6	49.2	50.8
45153	MOSCOW	97.9	97.5	0.4	0.5	0.2	0.4	0.5	0.7	6.7	6.7	6.9	7.5	6.8	26.6	28.6	9.4	0.8	75.2	37.0	49.4	50.6
45154	MOUNT ORAB	98.8	98.5	0.4	0.5	0.1	0.2	0.4	0.6	8.0	7.8	7.6	6.7	5.9	28.6	25.3	9.3	1.0	72.6	35.5	49.3	50.7
45157	NEW RICHMOND	97.6	97.2	0.9	1.1	0.1	0.2	0.8	1.0	6.7	6.8	6.9	7.4	6.6	26.4	29.3	9.0	1.0	75.0	36.9	49.8	50.2
45159	NEW VIENNA	97.7	97.2	0.3	0.4	0.3	0.4	0.6	0.7	7.9	7.7	7.6	7.6	6.1	26.7	26.4	9.0	1.1	72.2	35.6	48.1	51.9
45160	OWENSVILLE	97.2	96.6	0.6	0.6	0.2	0.4	2.2	2.6	8.9	6.9	6.7	6.9	6.7	23.5	25.4	12.6	2.4	73.0	37.8	47.3	52.7
45162	PLEASANT PLAIN	98.7	98.6	0.3	0.3	0.3	0.2	0.5	0.6	5.6	6.1	6.7	7.2	5.3	25.2	32.4	10.5	0.9	77.1	40.9	50.2	49.8
45167	RIPLEY	94.5	93.6	3.9	4.5	0.1	0.2	0.5	0.7	6.5	6.2	6.4	6.3	5.5	23.7	27.8	15.1	2.5	77.1	41.4	48.0	52.0
45168	RUSSELLVILLE	98.2	97.9	0.5	0.6	0.1	0.1	0.3	0.4	6.4	6.5	6.8	6.6	4.5	25.0	29.1	12.7	2.3	76.1	41.1	49.4	50.6
45169	SABINA	98.1	97.7	0.4	0.5	0.3	0.4	0.9	1.1	6.8	7.0	7.1	6.8	5.5	27.6	27.1	10.7	1.5	75.0	37.5	49.7	50.3
45171	SARDINIA	98.4	98.0	0.8	1.1	0.1	0.1	0.4	0.5	6.7	7.0	7.2	7.0	5.3	25.7	27.8	12.1	1.3	74.9	38.8	50.2	49.8
45174	TERRACE PARK	98.9	98.3	0.2	0.3	0.6	1.0	0.8	1.0	6.4	8.5	10.8	9.1	3.6	18.6	30.0	11.4	1.6	68.0	40.7	49.6	50.4
45176	WILLIAMSBURG	98.5	98.2	0.3	0.3	0.1	0.2	0.5	0.7	6.6	6.9	6.9	7.2	5.5	27.4	29.1	9.5	1.0	75.0	38.1	49.8	50.2
45177	WILMINGTON	93.9	92.8	4.0	4.6	0.5	0.8	0.7	0.9	6.9	6.4	6.3	7.7	7.5	25.5	27.2	10.8	1.8	76.9	37.3	49.2	50.8
45202	CINCINNATI	42.0	38.1	54.1	57.4	1.0	1.6	2.0	2.2	5.8	5.1	3.7	5.2	10.5	37.5	23.5	7.5	1.2	83.0	34.0	56.0	44.0
45203	CINCINNATI	17.7	13.2	79.9	84.4	0.6	0.8	1.0	1.0	7.5	6.2	4.9	9.5	11.1	32.3	20.7	6.8	1.1	77.0	30.3	53.6	46.4
45204	CINCINNATI	83.5	77.7	11.4	15.7	1.1	1.7	2.7	3.4	8.4	7.6	6.8	9.2	10.5	27.2	20.2	8.3	1.7	73.4	29.6	49.3	50.7
45205	CINCINNATI	78.0	71.5	18.0	23.4	1.1	1.8	1.2	1.5	9.0	7.8	7.1	7.6	8.9	28.6	21.4	8.2	1.3	71.6	30.9	48.7	51.3
45206	CINCINNATI	29.2	24.2	68.1	72.7	0.6	0.9	1.0	1.1	6.3	5.7	5.0	5.9	8.0	28.6	24.0	13.3	3.3	79.5	37.5	46.5	53.5
45207	CINCINNATI	18.7	18.3	78.7	78.9	0.5	0.9	0.7	0.8	6.0	6.9	6.8	17.3	13.4	20.2	17.7	9.7	1.9	75.7	24.8	44.1	55.9
45208	CINCINNATI	91.0	87.6	5.7	7.4	1.8	3.0	1.3	1.7	5.7	4.5	4.4	3.4	7.7	33.8	24.7	11.6	4.2	83.1	38.2	45.9	54.1
45209	CINCINNATI	86.7	81.8	8.8	12.1	1.5	2.4	2.3	2.9	5.0	4.0	3.8	3.9	9.7	38.8	23.0	9.5	2.3	85.0	35.7	47.8	52.2
45211	CINCINNATI	73.0	69.1	23.7	26.8	1.2	1.8	0.9	1.2	7.6	7.0	6.4	6.5	8.0	28.4	23.5	9.9	2.6	75.0	35.0	47.2	52.8
45212	CINCINNATI	87.9	84.4	8.5	10.8	0.9	1.5	1.8	2.4	6.4	5.7	5.4	6.0	8.9	30.7	24.8	10.3	1.8	79.1	35.7	48.9	51.1
45213	CINCINNATI	43.8	36.9	53.0	59.5	0.5	0.8	1.1	1.2	6.2	6.2	6.1	6.0	6.0	25.8	27.6	13.2	2.9	77.8	40.5	45.5	54.5
45214	CINCINNATI	30.2	25.4	65.6	69.8	1.0	1.3	2.1	2.2	8.5	7.4	6.5	8.5	11.0	26.3	21.5	9.0	1.3	72.7	29.6	48.8	51.2
45215	CINCINNATI	69.8	66.2	26.7	29.1	1.5	2.4	1.1	1.4	6.1	6.2	6.4	6.8	6.4	24.9	27.5	12.6	3.0	77.1	40.1	47.4	52.6
45216	CINCINNATI	80.2	74.9	16.9	21.3	0.6	1.0	1.2	1.6	7.6	7.3	6.8	6.2	6.3	26.9	26.1	10.9	1.9	74.5	37.2	49.6	50.4
45217	CINCINNATI	68.2	64.3	29.6	32.9	0.7	1.1	0.6	0.8	6.3	6.2	6.7	6.8	6.9	25.7	26.4	12.7	2.4	76.7	38.2	48.1	51.9
45218	CINCINNATI	94.6	92.3	2.9	4.2	0.4	0.6	1.2	1.6	7.1	6.7	6.5	6.4	7.4	26.3	23.8	13.4	2.5	75.5	37.0	47.7	52.3
45219	CINCINNATI	49.4	42.5	42.6	46.9	4.5	6.7	1.5	1.7	3.9	3.8	3.8	17.7	28.3	24.3	12.6	4.8	0.8	85.0	23.7	53.4	46.6
45220	CINCINNATI	60.5	53.4	28.7	31.6	8.0	12.0	1.9	2.3	3.9	3.1	3.1	5.9	18.8	33.3	18.9	10.1	2.8	87.7	30.7	49.7	50.3
45223	CINCINNATI	44.5	36.5	51.5	59.0	0.9	1.2	1.3	1.4	8.9	7.5	6.8	7.9	10.7	28.1	22.2	7.0	1.0	72.2	29.5	47.4	52.6
45224	CINCINNATI	50.9	43.0	46.4	53.8	0.7	1.0	0.7	0.8	6.1	6.0	6.4	6.6	6.0	22.5	27.0	14.6	4.8	77.3	42.1	44.6	55.4
45225	CINCINNATI	21.7	18.5	75.3	78.1	0.7	1.0	1.1	1.1	14.3	10.7	8.6	9.1	12.3	24.3	14.9	5.2	0.6	61.7	23.0	45.3	54.7
45226	CINCINNATI	92.4	89.8	5.7	7.7	0.6	1.0	0.9	1.3	7.0	5.8	5.3	5.1	8.4	34.4	24.4	8.3	1.2	78.6	35.2	48.6	51.4
45227	CINCINNATI	60.6	55.1	36.1	40.9	0.9	1.4	0.9	1.1	6.3	6.1	6.3	7.0	7.9	26.7	26.3	10.9	2.5	77.0	37.3	46.6	53.4
45228	CINCINNATI	98.9	98.2	0.0	0.2	0.4	0.6	1.5	2.2	5.9	8.9	8.9	5.9	3.2	24.7	33.6	7.5	1.4	72.1	41.1	52.2	47.8
45229	CINCINNATI	15.6	12.3	81.9	85.1	0.6	0.8	0.9	1.0	6.9	6.7	6.3	8.6	9.9	22.9	24.6	11.7	2.4	75.4	35.0	45.0	55.0
45230	CINCINNATI	95.5	93.2	2.0	2.9	1.3	2.2	1.0	1.3	6.5	6.6	6.9	6.1	5.6	25.7	28.4	11.6	2.8	76.3	40.3	48.1	51.9
45231	CINCINNATI	70.3	63.6	26.7	32.6	0.9	1.4	0.9	1.2	6.6	6.6	6.8	7.3	6.4	25.0	26.6	12.6	2.2	75.5	38.6	47.2	52.8
45232	CINCINNATI	24.5	18.3	72.5	78.5	0.7	0.9	1.3	1.4	15.3	11.7	9.1	8.8	9.5	22.0	15.3	7.2	1.0	58.6	22.6	41.8	58.2
45233	CINCINNATI	97.2	96.2	1.5	1.9	0.5	0.9	0.4	0.6	6.2	6.8	7.8	8.3	5.8	21.9	28.1	12.2	2.8	74.2	39.9	48.3	51.7
45236	CINCINNATI	83.9	79.9	12.3	14.6	2.2	3.6	1.2	1.5	5.5	5.4	5.5	5.5	5.6	24.7	27.3	15.8	4.7	80.1	43.5	46.3	53.7
45237	CINCINNATI	25.9	21.5	71.0	75.1	0.7	1.0	0.8	0.8	6.0	6.2	6.2	6.7	6.8	23.3	28.8	13.7	2.2	77.3	40.7	45.1	54.9
45238	CINCINNATI	92.1	89.0	5.1	6.9	1.6	2.6	0.6	0.8	7.0	6.6	6.7	6.6	6.5	27.5	24.7	11.9	2.5	75.7	37.2	48.1	51.9
45239	CINCINNATI	84.4	79.2	12.5	16.8	0.9	1.5	1.2	1.6	7.3	6.9	6.6	6.5	6.3	27.7	23.9	12.2	2.6	75.2	37.0	47.9	52.1
45240	CINCINNATI	45.9	37.5	48.0	55.4	3.0	4.0	1.4	1.5	6.9	6.8	7.0	7.3	6.5	27.8	26.2	10.5	1.0	74.8	36.2	47.5	52.5
45241	CINCINNATI	90.2	86.0	4.3	5.8	3.7	6.0	1.2	1.6	5.5	5.9	6.5	6.3	5.2	22.4	30.9	14.6	2.8	78.2	43.7	48.4	51.6
45242	CINCINNATI	90.2	85.5	3.3	4.5	5.1	8.3	1.0	1.2	5.1	5.9	6.9	7.2	5.4	20.7	31.6	14.2	2.8	77.3	43.9	47.5	52.5
	OHIO	85.0	83.1	11.5	12.2	1.2	1.9	1.9	2.4	6.6	6.5	6.6	7.1	6.7	25.9	26.9	11.7	2.1	76.2	38.2	48.7	51.3
	UNITED STATES	75.1	72.0	12.3	12.7	3.8	4.6	12.5	15.7	6.8	6.7	6.6	7.1	6.9	27.0	26.0	10.9	1.9	75.7	36.9	49.2	50.8

#	POST OFFICE NAME	2009 Per Capita Income	2009 HH Income Base	2009 HOUSEHOLD INCOME DISTRIBUTION (%) Less than $25,000	$25,000 to $49,999	$50,000 to $99,999	$100,000 to $149,999	$150,000 or More	MEDIAN HOUSEHOLD INCOME 2009	2014	2009 National Centile	2009 State Centile	2009 Home Value Base	2009 HOME VALUE DISTRIBUTION (%) Less than $50,000	$50,000 to $89,999	$90,000 to $174,999	$175,000 to $399,999	$400,000 or More	2009 Median Home Value
45003	COLLEGE CORNER	27567	410	14.4	35.6	36.3	10.2	3.4	50000	52589	61	49	311	15.1	23.2	33.4	23.2	5.1	112847
45005	FRANKLIN	24633	12414	18.3	26.1	40.5	12.4	2.7	54431	54248	70	65	8752	3.2	10.3	59.3	25.5	1.7	147682
45011	HAMILTON	27972	23736	16.5	21.6	36.2	15.7	10.0	64686	69068	83	85	17577	14.6	17.8	32.0	32.7	3.0	142075
45013	HAMILTON	26232	21235	16.8	25.7	43.3	10.3	3.9	56916	59587	74	72	15493	7.1	18.7	50.2	21.5	2.5	121001
45014	FAIRFIELD	29941	18405	10.9	24.5	46.5	13.4	4.8	62845	65752	81	82	11766	4.8	13.3	58.5	22.0	1.3	134022
45015	HAMILTON	23492	5128	20.6	29.8	39.7	7.6	2.4	49622	51133	60	47	3586	9.3	35.6	48.5	5.9	0.7	93421
45030	HARRISON	24962	6110	15.3	25.0	44.3	11.4	4.1	57773	59762	75	75	4843	18.6	11.4	54.9	14.2	0.9	116792
45034	KINGS MILLS	42958	430	7.9	16.3	37.9	17.0	20.9	78368	80831	91	95	373	1.6	4.3	22.5	46.1	25.5	264881
45036	LEBANON	28612	12753	12.5	20.0	40.1	18.5	9.0	68303	70873	86	89	8720	2.3	2.9	33.4	49.4	11.9	203408
45039	MAINEVILLE	38840	8509	5.2	13.6	42.2	25.8	13.2	84419	93836	94	97	6903	1.8	1.3	32.6	55.7	8.6	199252
45040	MASON	40412	17495	6.9	12.1	33.4	27.4	20.2	95645	104429	96	99	14681	3.9	0.5	29.7	52.3	13.5	218335
45042	MIDDLETOWN	27807	11667	18.2	24.4	40.3	12.6	4.5	57249	60000	74	74	8907	8.8	17.4	45.4	25.5	2.8	123800
45044	MIDDLETOWN	24793	19822	21.4	25.9	36.4	11.0	5.3	52641	55668	67	60	12420	8.8	23.0	43.9	21.7	2.6	117804
45050	MONROE	33512	2982	6.1	19.4	51.9	15.8	6.7	74502	76959	89	93	2222	2.3	3.2	76.6	17.5	0.5	138569
45052	NORTH BEND	28655	1372	11.9	22.5	40.0	16.8	8.7	70227	70523	87	90	1155	8.7	21.8	29.5	35.4	4.5	150318
45053	OKEANA	28539	1195	7.4	14.9	54.4	15.3	7.9	75789	77675	90	94	1087	5.7	8.0	27.3	53.3	5.7	200700
45054	OREGONIA	30139	712	13.3	15.2	48.2	17.8	5.5	73579	75761	89	93	604	11.8	5.5	26.2	42.2	14.4	194231
45056	OXFORD	20762	8372	35.1	21.4	28.0	10.8	4.7	41203	44546	37	24	3884	6.6	6.4	45.3	38.3	3.4	155136
45064	SOMERVILLE	24856	809	10.8	23.1	50.2	13.5	2.5	67150	71713	85	88	690	6.7	13.6	42.2	33.6	3.9	145652
45065	SOUTH LEBANON	21473	1552	23.3	30.0	37.0	8.0	1.7	45821	50038	51	35	1123	22.1	12.5	42.0	20.2	3.2	111095
45066	SPRINGBORO	42449	7858	5.8	12.0	33.5	23.4	25.3	97519	106018	96	99	7028	0.6	1.1	24.3	56.5	17.6	256189
45067	TRENTON	25113	4514	12.5	22.3	49.7	12.8	2.8	64446	67747	83	85	3377	4.1	9.1	74.6	11.2	1.1	123116
45068	WAYNESVILLE	29691	4177	10.6	21.5	44.1	16.3	7.6	68964	72096	86	89	3352	9.2	6.8	32.7	42.3	8.9	178435
45069	WEST CHESTER	38866	17289	5.5	13.8	37.8	24.4	18.5	89314	90228	95	98	14258	2.9	7.9	35.8	49.2	4.1	181782
45101	ABERDEEN	20733	1197	30.2	30.8	31.2	5.7	2.2	39892	41910	32	21	825	41.7	16.1	34.3	6.8	1.1	71667
45102	AMELIA	26526	8089	16.6	22.6	42.1	13.8	4.9	62744	66270	81	82	5752	16.8	7.6	50.0	24.5	1.0	139215
45103	BATAVIA	26847	11906	15.3	22.2	43.0	14.1	5.4	63014	65906	81	82	8596	8.0	11.6	48.7	29.1	2.6	140843
45106	BETHEL	22112	4594	20.1	27.4	40.5	8.8	3.3	51852	53336	66	57	3576	16.2	17.2	47.1	16.9	2.5	114081
45107	BLANCHESTER	23820	3656	19.1	26.7	42.0	8.7	3.4	53480	54261	69	62	2787	7.8	17.8	51.6	18.9	3.9	118418
45111	CAMP DENNISON	34465	166	21.1	22.3	29.5	18.7	8.4	75415	76095	90	94	125	12.8	28.0	43.2	11.2	4.8	97667
45113	CLARKSVILLE	24315	1620	14.4	22.9	47.8	11.8	3.1	60766	59932	78	79	1381	10.0	13.3	42.7	28.2	5.9	138979
45118	FAYETTEVILLE	26783	1438	9.5	27.7	45.9	12.0	4.9	60275	59858	78	78	1278	8.5	12.8	52.6	24.4	1.6	129389
45120	FELICITY	17474	1393	31.0	27.4	34.3	6.2	1.1	41314	44625	37	24	964	31.1	23.1	33.0	9.9	2.9	83881
45121	GEORGETOWN	21225	3528	27.6	30.4	33.0	5.6	3.3	41758	45067	39	25	2603	14.3	22.8	46.9	14.8	1.2	106669
45122	GOSHEN	23063	4293	16.1	27.1	45.1	8.0	3.6	56348	58260	73	71	3596	23.4	14.2	42.7	17.4	2.4	109572
45123	GREENFIELD	19687	3142	28.8	29.6	35.1	4.6	1.9	42552	44151	41	27	2141	16.0	37.5	34.7	9.6	2.2	85995
45130	HAMERSVILLE	24017	1427	20.3	27.3	39.5	6.9	6.0	51728	53226	65	57	1191	17.0	20.2	45.5	15.4	2.0	106434
45133	HILLSBORO	20210	9538	28.5	30.7	32.0	6.4	2.4	41226	43277	37	24	7183	16.5	24.2	43.3	14.5	1.6	102936
45135	LEESBURG	20486	1792	19.8	29.1	43.6	6.0	1.5	50704	50203	63	52	1397	12.5	26.3	44.9	14.7	1.6	105773
45140	LOVELAND	39020	19195	7.7	16.2	36.7	20.4	19.0	83652	86208	93	97	15424	8.6	5.3	35.5	41.0	9.6	176829
45142	LYNCHBURG	20051	1745	20.7	31.1	39.5	6.7	2.0	48422	48134	58	43	1365	10.4	23.7	53.3	9.9	2.7	109420
45144	MANCHESTER	18505	1875	35.8	31.3	26.1	5.1	1.6	34829	36691	17	9	1369	29.2	30.9	32.9	6.0	0.9	77150
45146	MARTINSVILLE	22721	539	17.8	23.2	48.8	7.4	2.8	55659	55933	72	69	441	13.4	17.5	44.7	22.7	1.8	117880
45148	MIDLAND	20506	591	22.0	22.8	45.5	8.0	1.7	53235	53967	68	61	470	16.4	19.4	42.6	21.1	0.6	111685
45150	MILFORD	30849	13790	14.4	21.9	39.3	15.8	8.6	65259	69691	84	86	10367	8.0	8.0	46.6	34.3	3.2	150143
45152	MORROW	29958	3825	11.0	19.8	43.7	18.1	7.3	73003	76640	88	92	3164	7.0	3.8	33.3	42.6	13.3	189577
45153	MOSCOW	22824	790	23.0	27.2	37.1	7.8	4.8	49704	52019	60	48	626	33.5	18.2	31.9	12.6	3.7	85000
45154	MOUNT ORAB	21518	3353	19.4	25.5	44.6	7.7	2.8	53362	54314	69	62	2631	16.5	19.7	49.0	12.7	2.1	106606
45157	NEW RICHMOND	26212	3524	15.7	24.4	40.2	12.9	6.8	61697	65728	80	80	2833	21.7	12.7	34.0	26.5	5.1	124711
45159	NEW VIENNA	19297	1352	23.3	30.8	38.8	6.1	1.0	45985	48555	51	36	1009	16.7	26.3	41.4	13.3	2.4	99662
45160	OWENSVILLE	29164	245	27.3	22.4	35.9	11.4	2.9	50199	51764	62	50	143	3.5	8.4	56.6	25.9	5.6	146875
45162	PLEASANT PLAIN	25651	992	12.5	20.2	50.6	12.3	4.4	65876	67825	84	87	864	11.3	13.9	40.9	29.2	4.7	139750
45167	RIPLEY	18963	1439	28.8	31.4	32.2	6.0	1.6	40456	42688	34	22	1068	24.4	28.1	37.7	8.3	1.4	86786
45168	RUSSELLVILLE	19612	624	24.0	31.7	36.7	6.9	0.6	41596	46119	38	25	508	19.3	27.6	39.2	11.0	3.0	93810
45169	SABINA	22346	1987	19.1	32.4	38.2	8.2	2.2	48550	50836	58	44	1404	15.4	29.6	43.2	10.4	1.4	95600
45171	SARDINIA	20796	2319	21.8	29.8	39.5	7.1	1.8	47428	49832	55	40	1929	12.6	22.0	48.5	15.7	1.1	112460
45174	TERRACE PARK	51475	765	6.0	8.9	24.1	25.9	35.2	123127	124213	99	100	706	0.0	0.0	19.5	50.7	29.7	302055
45176	WILLIAMSBURG	23052	3364	15.2	26.8	46.0	9.4	2.6	56084	57394	73	70	2645	11.3	17.9	49.0	18.2	3.6	118852
45177	WILMINGTON	24678	8947	21.6	26.6	38.2	10.6	3.0	51509	53024	65	56	5735	8.0	13.9	53.6	22.0	2.5	128347
45202	CINCINNATI	26338	7084	48.0	22.0	19.4	5.6	5.0	26538	28565	4	3	936	8.0	21.6	31.1	27.0	12.3	145357
45203	CINCINNATI	17062	1402	62.3	18.0	12.9	4.7	2.1	15874	16866	1	1	135	0.0	0.0	80.0	20.0	0.0	144947
45204	CINCINNATI	17648	2475	33.5	33.5	26.9	4.6	1.4	34878	37765	17	10	967	32.2	48.2	16.0	3.4	0.2	61415
45205	CINCINNATI	17835	8208	36.2	29.5	28.4	4.5	1.4	35018	37503	18	10	3451	14.4	58.9	25.4	1.3	0.1	76101
45206	CINCINNATI	27298	6024	44.2	26.1	18.6	5.6	5.5	28924	30341	7	5	1531	11.4	28.9	38.5	12.8	8.4	102836
45207	CINCINNATI	14974	2411	43.9	26.9	23.3	3.6	2.2	28724	30317	6	4	1183	16.1	58.3	23.1	1.9	0.7	73634
45208	CINCINNATI	54166	9897	13.2	20.6	33.8	13.0	19.4	70888	72178	87	91	5483	2.5	6.4	33.4	41.5	16.2	200388
45209	CINCINNATI	36919	5248	23.8	27.8	31.8	11.0	5.5	48219	51795	57	43	2229	2.1	14.9	66.2	16.1	0.7	128374
45211	CINCINNATI	24810	16574	25.2	31.9	32.4	7.5	3.0	42876	46939	42	28	8625	2.6	21.2	69.4	6.5	0.3	109355
45212	CINCINNATI	23703	10128	26.9	33.0	30.8	7.0	2.3	41098	44757	36	23	4972	3.0	32.1	60.9	3.9	0.2	102536
45213	CINCINNATI	30554	5482	22.1	30.2	31.0	10.5	6.2	46882	51357	54	39	3216	2.2	16.5	65.3	14.0	1.9	120637
45214	CINCINNATI	14054	4006	57.3	24.4	15.2	1.9	1.2	19196	20227	1	1	838	35.2	38.4	23.4	2.0	1.0	62946
45215	CINCINNATI	31319	12833	22.7	25.9	30.8	10.8	9.8	51432	54770	65	55	7062	5.8	24.7	46.5	18.4	4.7	118304
45216	CINCINNATI	21876	4244	29.6	32.0	31.7	4.9	1.8	39094	42033	30	19	2265	8.7	48.2	40.5	2.4	0.2	85972
45217	CINCINNATI	24982	2954	25.4	28.2	34.2	8.1	4.2	46316	50383	52	37	1675	9.6	18.1	61.9	8.8	1.6	107423
45218	CINCINNATI	30612	1658	12.9	28.3	39.9	12.1	6.8	57356	59237	74	74	1143	1.5	16.7	79.1	2.7	0.0	115151
45219	CINCINNATI	16904	6776	47.5	30.1	18.1	3.0	1.3	26099	27076	4	3	1288	11.6	41.0	40.3	7.1	0.1	88479
45220	CINCINNATI	27557	7504	42.0	25.9	19.4	6.8	5.8	31007	33045	10	6	1925	5.1	20.3	35.2	33.4	6.1	148921
45223	CINCINNATI	19161	5584	35.2	32.3	25.9	4.2	2.3	34617	36814	17	9	2208	16.8	41.7	36.2	4.7	0.6	84211
45224	CINCINNATI	27077	9396	24.0	26.6	35.8	9.2	4.4	49145	52502	59	46	5828	3.4	21.0	64.5	10.4	0.6	113123
45225	CINCINNATI	10569	4180	63.1	25.5	9.0	1.9	0.5	15560	16621	1	1	864	34.4	51.4	13.3	0.2	0.7	61985
45226	CINCINNATI	39386	2380	18.4	26.4	31.9	10.4	12.8	55274	57791	72	68	1387	8.8	12.3	41.3	23.9	13.7	151939
45227	CINCINNATI	29658	8104	22.0	28.9	33.6	8.4	7.1	48977	52305	59	45	4879	4.4	36.0	38.8	14.2	6.7	100455
45228	CINCINNATI	76516	200	7.5	11.5	16.5	15.5	49.0	143842	145349	100	100	166	2.4	25.3	18.7	16.3	37.3	222727
45229	CINCINNATI	20363	6313	46.6	25.2	18.8	5.5	4.0	27324	28969	5	4	1841	3.6	24.0	53.1	16.7	2.7	116372
45230	CINCINNATI	35935	11780	15.9	22.0	37.3	14.2	10.7	62455	63455	81	81	8339	0.5	8.0	68.2	19.8	3.4	134159
45231	CINCINNATI	27334	16433	15.5	24.1	43.2	11.6	5.6	58375	60215	76	76	11896	2.9	25.7	61.8	8.8	0.7	108455
45232	CINCINNATI	12743	2722	54.9	23.4	17.3	2.9	1.4	21480	22855	2	2	624	14.4	47.8	35.1	2.7	0.0	82000
45233	CINCINNATI	33016	5319	11.1	17.0	37.5	19.6	14.7	76838	76802	90	95	4366	2.0	8.7	46.9	37.4	5.0	163111
45236	CINCINNATI	32183	11066	17.3	28.3	37.7	10.3	6.4	53395	55670	69	62	7341	1.7	13.9	67.1	15.2	2.0	119534
45237	CINCINNATI	24730	9822	31.7	28.5	29.0	6.4	4.3	38915	42440	29	19	4549	3.9	31.1	52.5	9.7	2.7	103099
45238	CINCINNATI	27791	18723	17.1	27.4	40.8	10.4	4.3	54142	56333	70	64	12216	0.9	14.8	75.4	8.4	0.5	116743
45239	CINCINNATI	27046	12044	18.2	28.1	40.8	9.3	3.6	52759	55006	67	61	7982	3.2	21.3	70.3	5.0	0.2	111059
45240	CINCINNATI	27692	10643	11.5	24.4	45.9	12.8	5.3	63672	65249	82	83	7158	0.8	17.4	73.2	8.2	0.4	117698
45241	CINCINNATI	41048	10074	10.5	19.7	34.1	19.0	16.7	76515	77824	90	94	7670	7.4	2.8	41.6	41.6	6.6	170833
45242	CINCINNATI	43871	8510	9.4	15.5	35.5	19.8	19.7	83334	83312	93	97	6640	1.2	5.8	42.6	43.1	7.4	176127
	OHIO	26577		21.4	25.9	36.7	10.4	5.7	52400	54553				10.3	22.0	45.6	19.3	2.8	114865
	UNITED STATES	27277		20.9	24.4	35.3	11.7	7.6	54719	56938				9.3	13.1	31.6	32.6	13.5	162279

ZIP CODE #	POST OFFICE NAME	FINANCIAL SERVICES: Auto Loan	Home Loan	Invest-ments	Retire-ment Plans	THE HOME: Home Improvements: Home Repair	Lawn & Garden	Furnishings: Comput-ers & Hard-ware-Personal	Major Appli-ances	TV, Radio, Sound Equip-ment	Furni-ture	ENTERTAINMENT: Dine out/ Carry out	Sports Equip-ment	Fees & Tickets	Toys & Games	Travel	Cable TV	PERSONAL: Apparel & Services	Auto Repairs	Health Insur-ance	Pets & Supplies
45003	COLLEGE CORNER	93	90	90	93	93	103	86	96	88	81	87	71	84	89	89	93	60	90	101	111
45005	FRANKLIN	88	91	80	92	87	92	90	88	90	87	90	69	91	92	89	92	63	89	93	105
45011	HAMILTON	117	116	99	116	110	107	114	110	112	117	112	88	113	117	108	110	79	110	106	129
45013	HAMILTON	90	96	87	96	94	98	92	93	93	90	93	71	96	94	94	96	65	93	99	110
45014	FAIRFIELD	104	102	93	104	99	97	104	99	103	106	104	78	104	106	101	101	73	102	98	117
45015	HAMILTON	81	78	68	79	75	81	81	78	82	78	82	61	79	83	77	84	57	80	85	93
45030	HARRISON	96	100	91	99	97	99	94	97	94	94	95	75	96	97	95	96	66	95	97	114
45034	KINGS MILLS	167	187	153	180	175	154	163	163	153	176	157	130	170	165	163	145	110	154	141	185
45036	LEBANON	120	126	112	126	123	117	119	118	115	123	116	93	122	119	119	113	82	116	113	137
45039	MAINEVILLE	149	160	137	158	152	139	147	144	140	155	143	114	151	148	146	135	100	140	131	167
45040	MASON	165	188	165	192	182	159	166	164	156	180	159	134	180	166	170	146	115	156	142	187
45042	MIDDLETOWN	94	98	90	99	96	102	95	97	97	93	96	73	97	96	96	99	67	96	104	114
45044	MIDDLETOWN	92	90	79	91	87	90	92	89	93	91	92	70	91	94	89	93	65	91	92	106
45050	MONROE	114	130	115	127	126	119	113	117	111	120	112	88	122	115	119	109	79	112	114	134
45052	NORTH BEND	119	123	112	124	120	125	114	119	114	113	114	93	116	118	116	115	79	115	118	140
45053	OKEANA	113	134	117	136	130	124	116	120	112	119	113	94	127	116	124	110	80	115	113	139
45054	OREGONIA	114	125	110	127	122	121	112	118	110	113	111	92	117	114	117	110	77	112	113	137
45056	OXFORD	83	64	61	69	62	66	98	72	87	82	88	63	79	87	75	84	62	83	73	90
45064	SOMERVILLE	100	110	96	113	107	110	99	104	98	98	98	81	104	101	104	99	69	100	104	122
45065	SOUTH LEBANON	94	74	78	71	72	89	75	83	81	74	80	64	64	84	69	86	54	80	87	101
45066	SPRINGBORO	170	206	185	210	202	180	175	178	166	189	168	143	197	174	187	158	122	168	158	203
45067	TRENTON	97	102	88	102	98	97	98	96	96	99	97	75	100	99	98	96	68	96	96	114
45068	WAYNESVILLE	111	126	111	129	123	124	112	117	111	112	111	90	121	113	119	111	78	112	117	137
45069	WEST CHESTER	152	171	158	176	168	151	155	153	147	165	149	123	167	153	160	140	108	148	137	176
45101	ABERDEEN	80	68	65	65	66	74	69	72	71	70	71	55	61	74	64	74	48	71	73	87
45102	AMELIA	103	105	90	103	100	96	101	99	99	104	100	78	101	103	99	97	70	98	95	116
45103	BATAVIA	108	104	91	105	100	99	104	102	102	106	103	80	101	106	100	101	72	102	98	120
45106	BETHEL	93	85	80	86	84	93	85	90	88	82	87	68	80	90	82	91	59	87	93	106
45107	BLANCHESTER	93	90	82	91	88	97	88	92	90	85	89	70	85	91	87	93	61	90	96	109
45111	CAMP DENNISON	105	130	116	129	125	128	110	115	112	112	113	86	127	113	123	114	80	113	122	134
45113	CLARKSVILLE	100	101	90	101	99	103	93	99	94	94	94	75	93	97	94	96	65	95	99	117
45118	FAYETTEVILLE	115	109	96	107	106	111	102	108	105	106	105	79	98	109	99	108	72	104	108	128
45120	FELICITY	83	67	72	65	66	79	66	75	71	67	71	56	58	74	63	76	48	72	77	90
45121	GEORGETOWN	84	72	74	72	72	85	73	80	77	70	76	60	66	78	70	81	52	77	85	95
45122	GOSHEN	97	93	87	95	93	101	90	97	91	86	90	74	86	94	89	94	62	92	98	114
45123	GREENFIELD	77	65	68	67	65	80	69	75	72	63	71	58	61	73	66	77	48	72	81	89
45130	HAMERSVILLE	112	94	98	92	93	109	91	103	97	91	96	77	82	100	88	103	65	98	105	123
45133	HILLSBORO	83	67	75	67	68	83	70	79	74	66	73	59	61	75	67	80	50	75	83	93
45135	LEESBURG	93	73	79	73	73	92	74	85	80	70	79	65	63	83	70	86	53	80	89	102
45140	LOVELAND	152	168	155	172	165	154	153	153	148	161	149	122	164	153	158	144	107	148	144	177
45142	LYNCHBURG	83	79	72	80	78	86	76	82	78	73	78	62	73	80	75	82	53	78	85	97
45144	MANCHESTER	79	54	75	52	55	78	57	71	64	54	63	54	44	65	54	71	42	66	74	86
45146	MARTINSVILLE	92	91	82	92	89	95	85	91	86	84	86	69	83	89	85	89	59	87	92	107
45148	MIDLAND	86	83	78	85	83	91	79	87	81	75	80	66	76	83	80	84	55	81	88	101
45150	MILFORD	108	120	110	120	117	113	110	111	108	113	109	85	117	110	114	108	77	109	109	129
45152	MORROW	116	127	113	129	124	124	115	119	113	116	114	93	120	117	119	113	79	115	118	139
45153	MOSCOW	108	87	90	85	86	103	87	97	93	87	92	73	75	97	81	99	62	93	100	117
45154	MOUNT ORAB	93	87	76	84	84	88	83	86	85	85	85	64	79	89	79	87	58	84	87	103
45157	NEW RICHMOND	111	111	99	109	108	110	105	108	105	108	106	82	104	109	104	106	73	106	107	127
45159	NEW VIENNA	80	74	68	73	73	78	73	77	74	72	74	58	68	77	70	76	51	74	77	91
45160	OWENSVILLE	86	81	80	83	82	89	83	86	84	80	83	65	79	84	82	87	57	85	91	101
45162	PLEASANT PLAIN	105	112	97	114	109	111	101	106	101	102	101	82	105	104	105	102	70	102	106	125
45167	RIPLEY	79	61	76	60	62	82	65	76	71	59	69	58	55	70	63	77	46	72	83	90
45168	RUSSELLVILLE	82	66	79	66	68	85	66	80	71	61	70	60	57	71	66	77	47	73	82	94
45169	SABINA	95	78	81	78	77	95	79	88	84	76	83	68	69	87	75	90	56	84	92	106
45171	SARDINIA	89	75	77	76	76	90	75	85	79	71	78	64	67	82	73	84	53	80	88	100
45174	TERRACE PARK	191	260	292	270	280	238	216	228	199	238	199	174	262	198	252	189	150	211	201	253
45176	WILLIAMSBURG	95	92	83	93	90	98	88	93	90	86	89	71	86	92	87	92	61	90	96	110
45177	WILMINGTON	88	85	78	86	83	89	86	86	87	83	87	67	84	88	84	89	60	86	90	102
45202	CINCINNATI	67	48	49	55	47	51	72	57	74	67	75	48	63	72	61	75	53	68	65	73
45203	CINCINNATI	44	31	31	35	30	36	47	38	52	44	51	30	42	48	40	54	36	47	49	50
45204	CINCINNATI	60	51	44	53	48	53	65	55	66	59	66	45	59	66	56	68	47	62	61	69
45205	CINCINNATI	62	52	46	54	49	55	65	56	67	60	66	45	59	67	57	68	47	63	63	70
45206	CINCINNATI	69	55	57	60	55	60	75	63	78	70	78	50	69	75	67	80	55	73	74	79
45207	CINCINNATI	58	50	46	51	47	55	56	53	62	56	61	39	54	60	51	65	42	58	62	66
45208	CINCINNATI	138	139	146	147	141	134	151	138	147	150	149	111	154	145	150	145	107	145	140	164
45209	CINCINNATI	92	78	73	82	75	77	94	81	93	92	94	67	88	94	85	92	66	90	85	100
45211	CINCINNATI	79	70	62	72	67	72	81	73	82	77	82	58	76	82	74	82	57	79	79	89
45212	CINCINNATI	74	68	60	70	65	70	78	70	78	72	77	56	74	78	71	79	54	75	76	86
45213	CINCINNATI	90	91	87	92	90	93	94	91	96	92	95	69	96	94	93	98	67	94	99	108
45214	CINCINNATI	44	32	29	34	30	35	45	37	48	42	48	30	40	47	38	50	33	44	44	48
45215	CINCINNATI	100	101	96	103	99	103	104	100	105	103	105	77	106	104	103	107	74	103	107	119
45216	CINCINNATI	70	63	55	65	60	68	71	66	73	66	72	52	67	73	65	75	50	70	74	81
45217	CINCINNATI	80	79	71	80	76	82	83	79	86	78	85	62	83	85	80	88	60	83	87	96
45218	CINCINNATI	105	102	90	103	98	103	108	101	108	104	108	79	106	110	103	110	76	106	108	121
45219	CINCINNATI	52	33	31	37	31	36	61	41	56	49	56	37	45	56	43	55	40	51	45	53
45220	CINCINNATI	72	56	58	62	56	59	81	64	78	72	79	55	70	77	68	78	56	74	69	80
45223	CINCINNATI	66	52	46	55	49	54	67	57	68	63	68	46	60	69	57	69	47	64	63	72
45224	CINCINNATI	83	88	83	88	86	92	85	86	89	85	89	63	90	87	87	92	62	87	97	102
45225	CINCINNATI	37	25	22	28	23	29	37	30	40	35	39	24	32	40	30	42	28	36	35	39
45226	CINCINNATI	123	113	104	116	109	113	123	114	123	120	123	92	118	125	115	123	86	119	117	138
45227	CINCINNATI	94	92	85	95	89	93	98	92	99	96	99	72	98	98	95	100	69	97	99	111
45228	CINCINNATI	248	328	339	345	340	294	268	279	251	292	254	220	324	256	305	238	190	259	243	315
45229	CINCINNATI	60	49	48	52	48	53	64	55	68	59	68	43	59	65	57	71	48	63	64	69
45230	CINCINNATI	111	119	115	122	118	117	117	114	117	117	118	88	123	116	120	117	83	116	118	135
45231	CINCINNATI	95	99	90	100	96	101	98	96	99	96	99	73	100	99	98	101	69	98	103	115
45232	CINCINNATI	48	34	29	37	31	38	48	39	52	45	51	32	42	52	39	54	36	47	46	52
45233	CINCINNATI	132	153	145	155	152	148	136	141	135	141	136	106	150	136	146	135	96	136	141	163
45236	CINCINNATI	92	97	92	98	97	103	95	96	98	93	97	71	99	96	97	101	68	97	107	113
45237	CINCINNATI	77	69	66	71	67	75	76	73	81	74	80	55	73	79	72	84	55	78	83	89
45238	CINCINNATI	91	91	82	93	88	92	94	90	95	91	95	70	95	95	92	96	66	93	96	107
45239	CINCINNATI	89	88	79	89	85	91	90	88	91	87	91	68	90	92	88	93	63	90	95	105
45240	CINCINNATI	104	108	94	107	103	103	103	101	103	106	104	78	106	106	103	103	72	102	103	120
45241	CINCINNATI	131	153	152	156	155	146	140	141	137	144	138	108	155	137	150	136	99	139	140	163
45242	CINCINNATI	149	176	178	180	180	170	157	162	154	165	155	122	176	153	171	152	111	157	159	186
	OHIO	94	92	87	93	90	96	93	93	94	91	94	72	92	95	91	96	66	93	98	110
	UNITED STATES	100	100	100	100	100	100	100	100	100	100	100	100	100	100	100	100	100	100	100	100

ZIP CODE			POPULATION			2000-2009 ANNUAL RATE		HOUSEHOLDS					FAMILIES		
#	POST OFFICE NAME	COUNTY FIPS CODE	2000	2009	2014	% Rate	State Centile	2000	2009	2014	% Annual Rate 2000-2009	2009 Average HH Size	2000	2009	% Annual Rate 2000-2009
45243	CINCINNATI	061	16075	15597	15499	-0.3	27	5987	5874	5866	-0.2	2.60	4513	4300	-0.5
45244	CINCINNATI	061	25447	26588	27292	0.5	71	9073	9714	10045	0.7	2.74	7180	7487	0.5
45245	CINCINNATI	025	16029	17695	18424	1.1	89	6685	7539	7905	1.3	2.34	4368	4764	0.9
45246	CINCINNATI	061	14259	14015	13974	-0.2	32	6122	6127	6147	0.0	2.24	3787	3634	-0.4
45247	CINCINNATI	061	19669	21613	22123	1.0	87	7293	8217	8464	1.3	2.63	5580	6109	1.0
45248	CINCINNATI	061	24069	25214	25566	0.5	71	9192	9738	9920	0.6	2.58	6827	7011	0.3
45249	CINCINNATI	061	12166	13304	13615	1.0	87	4401	4849	5000	1.1	2.74	3358	3622	0.8
45251	CINCINNATI	061	23716	23057	22918	-0.3	27	8537	8459	8468	-0.1	2.71	6499	6268	-0.4
45252	CINCINNATI	061	5190	5206	5223	0.0	45	1993	2050	2070	0.3	2.54	1493	1490	0.0
45255	CINCINNATI	061	22881	22676	22813	-0.1	39	8964	9107	9238	0.2	2.48	6385	6267	-0.2
45302	ANNA	149	3899	4170	4295	0.7	79	1313	1454	1513	1.1	2.87	1053	1143	0.9
45303	ANSONIA	037	2179	2142	2107	-0.2	32	821	835	831	0.2	2.57	637	634	-0.1
45304	ARCANUM	037	7706	7571	7442	-0.2	32	2883	2918	2896	0.1	2.59	2280	2261	-0.1
45305	BELLBROOK	057	9757	10201	10429	0.5	71	3598	3894	4019	0.9	2.59	2840	3017	0.7
45306	BOTKINS	149	2490	2612	2674	0.5	71	871	947	978	0.9	2.76	681	725	0.7
45308	BRADFORD	037	4897	4845	4795	-0.1	39	1765	1798	1795	0.2	2.69	1383	1379	0.0
45309	BROOKVILLE	113	12002	12099	11958	0.1	51	4716	4886	4868	0.4	2.44	3458	3487	0.1
45311	CAMDEN	135	7529	7335	7203	-0.3	27	2799	2828	2808	0.1	2.59	2173	2144	-0.1
45312	CASSTOWN	109	1742	1849	1904	0.6	75	639	689	713	0.8	2.68	510	540	0.6
45314	CEDARVILLE	057	5526	5855	5857	0.6	75	1250	1293	1309	0.4	2.66	902	908	0.1
45315	CLAYTON	113	4087	4149	4111	0.2	56	1475	1533	1532	0.4	2.69	1173	1189	0.1
45317	CONOVER	109	1074	1147	1177	0.7	79	386	421	436	0.9	2.72	314	336	0.7
45318	COVINGTON	109	5550	5423	5392	-0.2	32	2092	2072	2073	-0.1	2.57	1593	1544	-0.3
45320	EATON	135	15318	15509	15369	0.1	51	5878	6096	6088	0.4	2.48	4331	4405	0.2
45321	ELDORADO	135	1172	1111	1081	-0.6	14	434	427	420	-0.2	2.60	332	319	-0.4
45322	ENGLEWOOD	113	20041	20587	20438	0.3	61	7967	8387	8387	0.6	2.44	5768	5914	0.3
45323	ENON	023	5444	5275	5152	-0.3	27	2217	2189	2153	-0.1	2.37	1629	1563	-0.4
45324	FAIRBORN	057	38980	40843	41469	0.5	71	15735	17256	17805	1.0	2.20	9213	9734	0.6
45325	FARMERSVILLE	113	2517	2475	2428	-0.2	32	917	918	906	0.0	2.69	758	745	-0.2
45326	FLETCHER	109	1144	1194	1220	0.5	71	418	443	456	0.6	2.70	338	351	0.4
45327	GERMANTOWN	113	8234	8462	8433	0.3	61	3136	3308	3321	0.6	2.55	2447	2523	0.3
45331	GREENVILLE	037	23513	23218	22855	-0.1	39	9540	9687	9617	0.2	2.32	6494	6429	-0.1
45332	HOLLANSBURG	037	595	593	585	0.0	45	227	234	233	0.3	2.53	185	187	0.1
45333	HOUSTON	149	1448	1530	1560	0.6	75	494	537	554	0.9	2.85	409	438	0.7
45334	JACKSON CENTER	149	2118	2182	2207	0.3	61	824	878	896	0.7	2.48	641	666	0.4
45335	JAMESTOWN	057	7245	7335	7384	0.1	51	2600	2746	2798	0.6	2.64	2078	2151	0.4
45337	LAURA	109	1707	1750	1763	0.3	61	623	648	657	0.4	2.70	495	505	0.2
45338	LEWISBURG	135	5999	6248	6232	0.4	66	2218	2389	2407	0.8	2.62	1721	1815	0.6
45339	LUDLOW FALLS	109	1623	1637	1652	0.1	51	606	618	627	0.2	2.65	485	486	0.0
45340	MAPLEWOOD	149	825	863	879	0.5	71	293	316	325	0.8	2.73	241	255	0.6
45341	MEDWAY	023	3995	3863	3780	-0.4	21	1679	1651	1625	-0.2	2.32	1153	1100	-0.5
45342	MIAMISBURG	113	31848	34842	34909	1.0	87	13109	14685	14812	1.2	2.34	8742	9421	0.8
45344	NEW CARLISLE	023	17811	17483	17229	-0.2	32	6555	6522	6459	-0.1	2.66	5028	4884	-0.3
45345	NEW LEBANON	113	6719	6420	6222	-0.5	17	2512	2446	2385	-0.3	2.58	1918	1821	-0.6
45346	NEW MADISON	037	2311	2296	2269	-0.1	39	859	881	879	0.3	2.61	680	682	0.0
45347	NEW PARIS	135	4177	3975	3877	-0.5	17	1607	1583	1558	-0.2	2.47	1176	1130	-0.4
45348	NEW WESTON	037	1351	1329	1311	-0.2	32	430	440	438	0.2	3.02	345	346	0.0
45356	PIQUA	109	25378	25233	25320	-0.1	39	10024	10125	10222	0.1	2.44	7000	6893	-0.2
45359	PLEASANT HILL	109	1874	1954	1995	0.5	71	690	728	746	0.6	2.68	563	583	0.4
45362	ROSSBURG	037	1195	1181	1166	-0.1	39	430	442	441	0.3	2.67	340	343	0.1
45363	RUSSIA	149	1595	1870	1977	1.7	95	515	625	668	2.1	2.99	425	507	1.9
45365	SIDNEY	149	30509	30599	30593	0.0	45	11521	11917	12033	0.4	2.51	8234	8296	0.1
45368	SOUTH CHARLESTON	023	4861	4960	4936	0.2	56	1831	1881	1877	0.3	2.62	1415	1422	0.1
45369	SOUTH VIENNA	023	3686	3848	3849	0.5	71	1356	1439	1447	0.6	2.67	1093	1135	0.4
45370	SPRING VALLEY	057	2322	2445	2497	0.6	75	875	948	977	0.9	2.58	683	728	0.7
45371	TIPP CITY	109	17393	18163	18472	0.5	71	6717	7092	7246	0.6	2.55	5005	5184	0.4
45373	TROY	109	32059	34292	35246	0.7	79	12592	13633	14081	0.9	2.46	8906	9388	0.6
45377	VANDALIA	113	14670	14335	14000	-0.2	32	6274	6260	6149	0.0	2.26	4144	4007	-0.4
45380	VERSAILLES	037	5247	5182	5110	-0.1	39	1903	1924	1911	0.1	2.65	1391	1370	-0.2
45381	WEST ALEXANDRIA	135	5838	5670	5558	-0.3	27	2180	2185	2164	0.0	2.59	1712	1682	-0.2
45382	WEST MANCHESTER	135	1172	1195	1187	0.2	56	433	460	462	0.7	2.60	330	343	0.4
45383	WEST MILTON	109	7048	6908	6855	-0.2	32	2823	2796	2792	-0.1	2.47	2073	2005	-0.4
45385	XENIA	057	36025	37913	38592	0.6	75	13413	14570	14986	0.9	2.47	9787	10395	0.7
45387	YELLOW SPRINGS	057	5767	5951	5999	0.3	61	2334	2475	2526	0.6	2.19	1459	1494	0.3
45388	YORKSHIRE	037	1054	1065	1058	0.1	51	358	376	378	0.5	2.83	288	297	0.3
45390	UNION CITY	037	3841	3722	3649	-0.3	27	1458	1456	1440	0.0	2.49	1062	1033	-0.3
45402	DAYTON	113	13789	12387	11871	-1.2	3	5618	5211	5038	-0.8	2.15	2714	2318	-1.7
45403	DAYTON	113	16852	15423	14785	-1.0	5	6913	6465	6237	-0.7	2.36	3960	3544	-1.2
45404	DAYTON	113	12420	11226	10797	-1.1	4	4943	4577	4436	-0.8	2.44	3177	2849	-1.2
45405	DAYTON	113	23559	20876	19911	-1.3	2	10531	9441	9034	-1.2	2.17	5474	4652	-1.7
45406	DAYTON	113	27246	24676	23613	-1.1	4	11223	10341	9949	-0.9	2.34	6778	6040	-1.2
45408	DAYTON	113	10731	9390	8887	-1.4	2	4275	3820	3639	-1.2	2.43	2743	2360	-1.6
45409	DAYTON	113	9937	9580	9379	-0.4	21	3156	3042	2969	-0.4	2.24	1569	1457	-0.8
45410	DAYTON	113	17823	15820	15049	-1.3	2	7839	7123	6821	-1.0	2.19	4125	3579	-1.5
45414	DAYTON	113	21850	21392	20948	-0.2	32	8959	8958	8835	0.0	2.38	6259	6085	-0.3
45415	DAYTON	113	12423	11984	11673	-0.4	21	5201	5153	5062	-0.1	2.27	3404	3259	-0.5
45416	DAYTON	113	6643	6383	6224	-0.4	21	2474	2437	2388	-0.2	2.41	1681	1600	-0.5
45417	DAYTON	113	11118	9732	9245	-1.4	2	4537	4063	3883	-1.2	2.31	2757	2373	-1.6
45418	DAYTON	113	7084	6730	6534	-0.6	14	2294	2213	2152	-0.4	2.46	1583	1479	-0.7
45419	DAYTON	113	17095	16541	16068	-0.4	21	7791	7588	7403	-0.3	2.17	4424	4157	-0.7
45420	DAYTON	113	25308	24361	23674	-0.4	21	11732	11539	11289	-0.2	2.09	6456	6091	-0.6
45424	DAYTON	113	49232	48889	47994	-0.1	39	18481	18788	18581	0.2	2.59	13824	13728	-0.1
45426	DAYTON	113	16646	15945	15508	-0.5	17	7143	7002	6862	-0.2	2.25	4540	4283	-0.6
45427	DAYTON	113	11816	11383	11054	-0.4	21	4493	4400	4301	-0.2	2.51	3113	2961	-0.5
45429	DAYTON	113	26553	25406	24649	-0.5	17	11981	11692	11414	-0.3	2.15	7374	6940	-0.7
45430	DAYTON	057	6867	7691	8001	1.2	91	2520	2960	3125	1.8	2.52	1997	2280	1.4
45431	DAYTON	057	23564	24656	25032	0.5	71	9172	9909	10175	0.8	2.49	6474	6840	0.6
45432	DAYTON	057	16054	15300	15045	-0.5	17	6564	6458	6407	-0.2	2.35	4581	4396	-0.4
45433	DAYTON	057	2833	2583	2483	-1.0	5	782	707	681	-1.1	3.20	776	701	-1.1
45434	DAYTON	057	9828	10994	11294	1.2	91	3516	4024	4167	1.5	2.67	2916	3306	1.4
45439	DAYTON	113	10762	9966	9565	-0.8	9	4667	4415	4271	-0.6	2.22	2909	2651	-1.0
45440	DAYTON	057	19987	20276	20327	0.2	56	8271	8582	8657	0.4	2.33	5629	5681	0.1
45449	DAYTON	113	19521	18379	17758	-0.6	14	8576	8276	8049	-0.4	2.18	5308	4949	-0.8
45458	DAYTON	113	25329	27922	28439	1.1	89	10223	11387	11666	1.2	2.44	7067	7631	0.8
45459	DAYTON	113	26957	26484	25932	-0.2	32	11505	11558	11395	0.0	2.21	7721	7518	-0.3
	OHIO					0.2					0.4	2.44			0.1
	UNITED STATES					1.0					1.1	2.59			0.9

ZIP CODE #	POST OFFICE NAME	RACE (%) White 2000	White 2009	Black 2000	Black 2009	Asian/Pacific 2000	Asian/Pacific 2009	% Hispanic Origin 2000	% Hispanic Origin 2009	2009 AGE DISTRIBUTION (%) 0-4	5-9	10-14	15-19	20-24	25-44	45-64	65-84	85+	18+	MEDIAN AGE 2009	% 2009 Males	% 2009 Females
45243	CINCINNATI	91.8	88.2	3.9	5.2	3.1	5.1	0.8	1.0	5.3	6.1	7.4	7.4	4.7	17.8	32.4	15.3	3.5	76.3	45.7	47.6	52.4
45244	CINCINNATI	96.8	95.2	0.8	1.3	1.1	1.9	1.0	1.4	7.0	7.5	8.1	7.7	5.0	24.6	30.0	9.3	0.8	72.6	38.4	49.2	50.8
45245	CINCINNATI	96.6	95.5	0.9	1.0	1.3	2.0	0.9	1.2	6.9	6.3	5.8	5.8	6.7	30.6	26.4	10.2	1.3	77.6	36.6	48.9	51.1
45246	CINCINNATI	70.2	62.4	22.8	28.6	3.2	4.7	4.0	4.7	6.1	5.7	5.6	5.4	6.0	25.1	25.6	15.8	4.7	79.3	41.8	46.4	53.6
45247	CINCINNATI	97.4	96.0	1.1	1.7	0.8	1.3	0.4	0.6	6.1	6.4	7.0	6.7	4.9	24.8	29.0	13.6	1.6	76.2	41.0	49.0	51.0
45248	CINCINNATI	98.4	97.7	0.4	0.6	0.4	0.7	0.5	0.7	5.7	6.3	7.1	7.3	5.1	23.7	27.9	14.5	2.4	76.2	41.4	48.2	51.8
45249	CINCINNATI	86.2	80.1	4.8	6.7	6.4	10.3	2.0	2.4	5.6	7.0	8.2	8.4	5.8	24.6	31.8	7.8	0.8	73.7	38.4	49.3	50.7
45251	CINCINNATI	86.2	81.1	10.4	14.4	1.1	1.8	1.3	1.6	7.1	7.1	7.0	7.1	6.0	27.3	26.3	10.5	1.6	74.5	36.6	48.5	51.5
45252	CINCINNATI	95.8	93.5	2.3	3.4	1.1	1.9	0.8	1.1	5.3	5.6	6.2	6.2	4.9	24.5	31.7	14.0	1.4	79.0	43.2	49.8	50.2
45255	CINCINNATI	95.8	93.7	0.9	1.3	2.0	3.4	1.1	1.6	6.5	6.3	6.8	7.0	5.9	24.1	29.0	12.1	2.3	76.0	40.2	47.6	52.4
45302	ANNA	98.4	97.7	0.2	0.2	0.6	1.1	0.4	0.6	7.7	8.5	8.2	8.1	4.9	26.8	25.9	8.7	1.2	70.3	35.0	50.6	49.4
45303	ANSONIA	98.9	98.6	0.0	0.0	0.0	0.1	1.0	1.3	6.3	6.6	7.0	7.4	5.8	26.3	28.5	10.7	1.4	75.5	38.6	48.9	51.1
45304	ARCANUM	98.4	98.1	0.2	0.3	0.2	0.3	0.4	0.5	6.5	6.6	6.9	6.8	5.1	26.1	28.4	11.9	1.7	75.8	39.5	50.1	49.9
45305	BELLBROOK	95.6	94.5	1.8	2.0	1.4	2.1	1.2	1.5	6.4	7.0	7.7	7.2	5.0	23.0	31.8	10.4	1.5	74.3	40.7	48.5	51.5
45306	BOTKINS	99.3	99.0	0.2	0.2	0.1	0.2	0.4	0.6	7.5	7.8	8.0	7.7	5.2	25.9	27.0	9.4	1.4	71.7	36.9	50.0	50.0
45308	BRADFORD	98.3	97.9	0.2	0.3	0.3	0.4	0.4	0.6	7.4	7.3	7.4	7.3	5.8	26.6	25.9	10.8	1.4	73.4	36.9	49.8	50.2
45309	BROOKVILLE	98.5	97.9	0.3	0.4	0.4	0.6	0.5	0.7	5.6	5.8	6.1	6.4	5.3	23.5	29.6	14.6	2.9	78.5	42.9	48.5	51.5
45311	CAMDEN	98.7	98.5	0.3	0.3	0.2	0.2	0.5	0.6	6.1	6.5	6.8	6.5	4.9	26.6	29.9	11.6	1.1	76.5	40.1	50.6	49.4
45312	CASSTOWN	99.1	99.0	0.1	0.1	0.2	0.2	0.5	0.6	4.8	5.2	5.9	6.8	5.1	23.9	32.9	14.1	1.1	79.8	43.7	50.5	49.5
45314	CEDARVILLE	95.2	94.1	2.3	2.6	0.7	1.1	0.7	0.9	3.3	3.5	3.7	23.6	27.2	16.1	15.8	6.1	0.7	87.0	22.9	47.0	53.0
45315	CLAYTON	91.3	87.1	6.0	9.1	1.1	1.7	0.6	0.8	5.4	6.0	6.8	7.6	5.0	21.7	32.9	12.8	1.8	77.0	43.1	49.5	50.5
45317	CONOVER	98.5	98.1	0.1	0.2	0.2	0.3	0.5	0.5	5.9	6.4	6.6	6.4	4.5	25.9	30.8	12.0	1.5	77.1	41.1	51.7	48.3
45318	COVINGTON	98.7	98.4	0.3	0.3	0.2	0.3	0.5	0.7	6.1	6.2	6.5	6.7	5.4	25.7	27.8	13.3	2.3	77.2	40.2	50.1	49.9
45320	EATON	98.3	97.7	0.5	0.5	0.4	0.6	0.4	0.5	6.6	6.7	6.8	6.4	5.3	25.9	27.4	12.6	2.4	75.9	39.5	49.6	50.4
45321	ELDORADO	97.6	97.0	0.8	0.9	0.0	0.0	0.9	1.3	7.4	8.0	8.1	6.8	4.4	24.8	28.4	10.7	1.5	72.0	37.9	49.6	50.4
45322	ENGLEWOOD	93.0	89.8	4.4	6.6	0.9	1.5	0.9	1.3	6.5	6.5	6.8	6.6	5.4	25.2	28.5	12.5	2.1	76.2	40.1	48.0	52.0
45323	ENON	97.0	96.0	0.7	1.0	0.6	1.0	1.0	1.4	5.5	5.7	6.1	5.8	4.5	24.1	30.1	16.0	2.2	79.1	43.8	48.1	51.9
45324	FAIRBORN	87.3	83.9	6.9	8.1	2.9	4.6	1.7	2.1	5.5	5.0	4.8	11.1	14.0	26.3	21.5	10.4	1.5	81.7	30.6	48.4	51.6
45325	FARMERSVILLE	97.6	96.6	1.5	2.2	0.2	0.4	0.4	0.6	5.9	6.3	7.0	6.9	4.6	24.9	31.5	11.6	1.3	76.4	41.6	49.2	50.8
45326	FLETCHER	98.3	98.1	0.4	0.5	0.1	0.1	0.3	0.4	6.3	7.0	7.1	6.7	4.5	25.6	30.0	11.6	1.3	75.5	39.9	49.9	50.1
45327	GERMANTOWN	97.3	96.4	1.8	2.4	0.2	0.4	0.6	0.8	5.6	6.1	6.6	6.8	4.9	24.3	31.6	12.3	1.7	77.4	42.1	49.6	50.4
45331	GREENVILLE	97.7	97.1	0.5	0.6	0.4	0.6	1.0	1.3	6.1	6.0	6.2	6.2	5.5	23.8	27.7	14.7	3.8	77.8	42.0	47.9	52.1
45332	HOLLANSBURG	98.1	97.8	0.7	0.7	0.0	0.2	0.3	0.3	6.6	6.9	7.3	6.6	4.2	26.5	28.7	12.0	1.3	75.0	39.8	52.3	47.7
45333	HOUSTON	98.3	97.8	0.4	0.5	0.1	0.2	0.3	0.5	7.3	7.6	7.8	7.3	4.7	26.5	28.5	9.4	1.0	72.9	37.9	51.4	48.6
45334	JACKSON CENTER	98.9	98.7	0.3	0.4	0.1	0.1	0.4	0.6	7.7	8.0	8.1	7.1	4.3	26.0	27.2	9.9	1.6	71.6	37.5	50.4	49.6
45335	JAMESTOWN	96.6	95.8	1.6	1.9	0.4	0.6	0.6	0.9	6.2	6.8	7.5	6.7	5.0	26.3	28.8	11.1	1.7	75.3	39.4	49.7	50.3
45337	LAURA	98.5	98.2	0.1	0.1	0.1	0.2	0.8	1.1	6.1	6.6	7.2	7.2	5.1	24.3	31.4	10.9	1.3	75.5	40.5	50.1	49.9
45338	LEWISBURG	98.6	98.3	0.1	0.1	0.4	0.6	0.6	0.8	6.2	6.6	6.9	7.1	5.0	25.0	29.9	12.0	1.4	76.0	40.6	49.8	50.2
45339	LUDLOW FALLS	99.2	99.0	0.1	0.1	0.1	0.1	0.4	0.5	5.8	6.2	6.5	6.0	4.8	22.6	31.5	15.0	1.7	77.7	43.7	50.9	49.1
45340	MAPLEWOOD	99.3	99.0	0.1	0.1	0.1	0.2	0.4	0.5	6.4	7.0	7.5	7.5	4.4	24.2	30.8	10.5	1.6	74.4	40.2	49.7	50.3
45341	MEDWAY	94.9	93.5	0.6	0.9	0.3	0.5	4.0	5.1	5.6	5.6	5.7	5.6	5.1	22.4	28.7	18.9	2.3	79.7	44.9	48.8	51.2
45342	MIAMISBURG	93.4	89.8	2.9	4.6	2.0	3.4	1.0	1.4	7.4	6.7	6.4	5.9	6.7	29.6	25.1	10.5	1.8	76.0	36.2	48.7	51.3
45344	NEW CARLISLE	96.7	95.6	0.3	0.4	0.3	0.5	2.1	2.8	6.3	6.4	6.7	6.9	5.7	26.0	28.4	12.1	1.6	76.3	39.2	49.2	50.8
45345	NEW LEBANON	94.8	93.1	3.9	5.2	0.1	0.2	0.6	0.8	6.6	6.8	6.9	6.7	5.1	23.8	28.7	13.2	2.3	75.5	40.7	48.9	51.1
45346	NEW MADISON	98.0	97.6	0.5	0.5	0.1	0.2	0.2	0.3	6.5	6.8	6.9	6.4	4.9	25.4	29.5	11.9	1.6	75.8	40.1	51.2	48.8
45347	NEW PARIS	98.7	98.4	0.4	0.4	0.2	0.3	0.2	0.2	5.9	6.0	6.1	6.1	5.6	24.6	29.6	14.3	1.8	78.4	41.5	50.1	49.9
45348	NEW WESTON	99.1	99.0	0.1	0.1	0.1	0.1	0.7	0.8	7.0	8.4	8.5	8.0	5.5	25.1	24.0	12.0	1.7	71.0	35.8	51.8	48.2
45356	PIQUA	94.9	94.0	2.9	3.3	0.4	0.6	0.7	0.9	6.8	6.3	6.3	6.7	6.8	25.8	26.7	12.2	2.4	76.4	38.3	48.7	51.3
45359	PLEASANT HILL	98.9	98.6	0.2	0.3	0.3	0.4	0.5	0.6	6.1	6.7	7.1	6.6	5.1	24.8	29.9	12.2	1.5	76.0	40.6	50.6	49.4
45362	ROSSBURG	98.7	98.6	0.1	0.1	0.1	0.1	0.8	1.1	7.6	8.5	8.3	7.2	5.1	25.9	25.1	10.8	1.5	71.0	35.8	50.7	49.3
45363	RUSSIA	99.2	98.9	0.1	0.1	0.1	0.2	0.5	0.7	9.8	10.1	9.7	7.5	4.2	27.5	21.8	8.2	1.2	65.6	32.7	50.3	49.7
45365	SIDNEY	94.4	92.7	2.2	2.6	1.5	2.4	1.0	1.3	7.3	7.1	7.1	7.1	5.9	26.0	26.3	10.8	2.4	74.0	37.4	49.4	50.6
45368	SOUTH CHARLESTON	97.0	96.1	1.4	1.9	0.3	0.5	0.3	0.4	6.6	6.9	7.2	6.7	5.0	25.7	29.1	11.5	1.5	75.2	39.0	49.4	50.6
45369	SOUTH VIENNA	97.4	96.3	0.7	1.0	0.2	0.3	0.7	1.1	6.7	7.2	7.5	6.6	4.2	26.5	29.8	10.3	1.0	74.4	39.3	49.6	50.4
45370	SPRING VALLEY	97.7	97.1	0.6	0.7	0.3	0.5	0.5	0.7	5.8	6.7	7.2	6.4	4.1	24.1	32.7	11.6	1.3	76.2	42.2	49.4	50.6
45371	TIPP CITY	98.0	97.4	0.2	0.2	0.6	0.9	0.9	1.2	6.1	6.3	6.7	6.7	5.0	24.0	30.5	12.9	1.8	76.7	41.6	49.1	50.9
45373	TROY	93.0	91.3	3.5	4.0	1.7	2.7	0.8	1.0	6.6	6.6	6.7	6.8	6.0	26.0	27.7	11.6	1.9	75.8	38.7	49.2	50.8
45377	VANDALIA	96.4	94.6	1.0	1.7	1.1	1.8	0.9	1.2	5.8	5.7	6.2	6.1	5.7	25.5	29.3	13.7	1.8	78.5	41.4	49.0	51.0
45380	VERSAILLES	99.4	99.2	0.0	0.0	0.1	0.2	0.2	0.2	7.5	7.7	7.9	7.5	5.0	25.3	24.9	11.8	2.5	72.1	37.8	49.6	50.4
45381	WEST ALEXANDRIA	98.6	98.3	0.2	0.3	0.2	0.4	0.2	0.3	5.9	6.3	6.7	6.9	4.9	25.5	30.3	12.1	1.5	76.5	40.9	50.7	49.3
45382	WEST MANCHESTER	98.8	98.6	0.0	0.0	0.1	0.2	0.7	0.9	6.1	6.5	6.9	6.4	4.7	26.7	30.0	11.1	1.5	76.5	40.2	50.4	49.6
45383	WEST MILTON	98.6	98.3	0.2	0.2	0.2	0.4	0.5	0.7	6.0	6.0	6.3	7.0	6.3	24.3	28.8	13.7	1.7	77.5	40.8	48.8	51.2
45385	XENIA	83.7	81.6	13.3	14.6	0.5	1.0	1.0	1.2	6.6	6.4	6.5	8.1	7.4	24.5	26.5	12.1	1.9	76.5	37.4	48.5	51.5
45387	YELLOW SPRINGS	82.5	79.4	10.8	12.4	1.2	1.8	1.5	1.8	4.0	4.5	4.9	8.4	8.4	20.4	31.2	15.4	2.8	82.8	44.6	45.3	54.7
45388	YORKSHIRE	98.7	98.3	0.2	0.2	0.4	0.6	0.5	0.6	8.7	8.6	8.4	7.7	5.7	25.2	22.1	12.0	1.6	69.5	34.6	51.3	48.7
45390	UNION CITY	96.5	95.6	0.9	1.0	0.3	0.5	3.0	4.0	8.2	7.9	7.4	6.4	5.7	25.1	24.9	12.5	1.8	72.7	36.8	49.5	50.5
45402	DAYTON	16.8	14.3	80.5	83.1	0.3	0.4	1.1	1.2	6.2	6.3	5.6	7.5	7.7	26.7	25.8	12.4	1.8	77.7	37.4	49.6	50.4
45403	DAYTON	90.5	86.7	4.9	7.4	1.0	1.5	2.2	2.9	7.6	7.2	6.4	6.4	7.3	29.9	25.2	8.8	1.3	75.1	34.6	50.9	49.1
45404	DAYTON	82.4	79.1	14.1	16.4	0.6	1.0	1.5	1.9	9.5	8.1	6.8	6.7	7.2	26.3	24.3	10.1	1.2	71.7	33.3	48.7	51.3
45405	DAYTON	47.0	37.8	48.5	57.6	0.5	0.7	1.7	1.7	7.1	6.5	6.1	7.0	8.4	27.9	25.9	9.5	1.7	76.3	35.5	48.2	51.8
45406	DAYTON	18.0	12.5	78.7	84.4	0.3	0.4	1.0	1.0	7.0	7.1	7.1	8.1	7.3	24.4	26.8	10.7	1.5	73.9	36.1	46.3	53.7
45408	DAYTON	1.8	1.2	96.2	97.0	0.2	0.2	0.9	0.9	8.8	9.1	8.6	8.8	6.9	21.4	22.5	11.6	2.3	67.9	32.2	43.7	56.3
45409	DAYTON	93.9	91.3	3.1	4.5	0.9	1.4	1.9	2.5	3.7	3.7	3.7	7.9	36.5	17.2	17.9	7.6	1.8	86.8	24.3	49.9	50.1
45410	DAYTON	91.5	88.2	3.9	5.9	1.1	1.6	2.4	3.1	7.3	7.0	6.4	5.7	6.1	31.1	25.1	9.6	1.6	75.8	36.2	50.7	49.3
45414	DAYTON	87.9	83.7	9.4	12.8	0.8	1.2	0.9	1.1	7.3	6.0	5.8	6.5	6.5	22.8	29.3	14.1	1.7	77.3	40.9	47.6	52.4
45415	DAYTON	81.0	73.5	15.9	22.4	1.6	2.3	1.1	1.3	4.8	5.1	5.8	5.8	4.9	21.4	32.3	16.4	3.4	80.6	46.4	47.4	52.6
45416	DAYTON	38.5	28.7	58.8	68.6	0.2	0.3	0.7	0.7	5.5	6.2	6.2	6.8	4.9	21.9	26.2	17.2	5.3	78.0	43.9	43.0	57.0
45417	DAYTON	3.8	3.1	94.2	95.2	0.1	0.1	0.8	0.8	6.9	7.1	6.8	7.7	6.5	21.5	25.3	15.4	2.7	74.6	39.7	46.7	53.3
45418	DAYTON	41.2	34.9	57.1	63.3	0.4	0.5	0.7	0.8	5.3	5.5	5.6	6.6	11.3	27.7	23.2	13.1	1.7	80.1	35.5	55.4	44.6
45419	DAYTON	95.7	93.8	1.6	2.4	1.1	1.8	1.2	1.6	6.1	6.0	6.3	6.6	7.9	25.4	27.9	11.2	2.6	77.6	39.1	47.5	52.5
45420	DAYTON	95.7	93.8	1.7	2.7	0.9	1.4	1.2	1.6	6.1	6.1	5.8	5.2	5.7	29.1	26.4	12.8	2.8	78.9	39.7	48.0	52.0
45424	DAYTON	84.9	78.6	9.7	14.2	2.3	3.5	1.7	2.2	7.0	6.9	6.9	6.9	6.1	28.0	26.9	10.4	0.9	75.0	36.7	48.6	51.4
45426	DAYTON	32.9	24.8	63.9	72.2	0.3	0.4	0.9	0.9	6.1	5.9	6.1	6.6	6.8	24.1	27.9	13.5	3.0	77.7	40.2	45.8	54.2
45427	DAYTON	39.8	32.6	57.5	64.7	0.2	0.2	0.8	0.8	7.7	7.4	7.0	9.6	7.7	21.5	25.0	12.7	1.4	72.2	34.8	46.4	53.6
45429	DAYTON	95.5	93.4	1.1	1.7	1.9	2.9	1.0	1.4	5.3	5.3	5.7	5.7	5.6	22.2	28.6	17.3	4.4	80.2	45.2	47.5	52.5
45430	DAYTON	95.0	93.1	0.9	1.1	2.4	3.7	1.1	1.4	5.0	6.2	7.0	6.6	3.5	20.9	34.8	13.9	2.1	77.4	45.4	49.5	50.5
45431	DAYTON	88.3	84.5	5.4	6.7	3.4	5.5	2.3	2.7	7.3	7.0	6.9	6.4	7.8	27.3	24.9	11.2	1.3	75.0	35.4	49.0	51.0
45432	DAYTON	93.9	91.6	2.3	3.2	1.9	2.9	1.2	1.6	5.2	5.7	6.1	6.0	5.0	24.5	30.3	15.1	2.1	79.3	43.3	49.2	50.8
45433	DAYTON	80.1	76.4	12.6	14.4	2.2	3.3	3.4	4.2	13.7	12.3	8.9	8.4	9.1	39.1	8.1	0.4	0.0	60.7	23.7	53.5	46.5
45434	DAYTON	94.1	91.6	1.2	1.5	3.3	5.2	1.0	1.3	4.9	5.5	7.0	7.6	4.2	20.5	35.2	12.7	2.4	77.6	45.1	48.5	51.5
45439	DAYTON	91.0	86.8	4.1	6.2	2.5	3.9	1.4	1.8	7.3	7.0	6.8	6.0	6.0	29.4	23.8	11.5	2.3	75.3	37.1	48.7	51.3
45440	DAYTON	93.6	91.0	2.5	3.4	2.3	3.6	1.1	1.4	5.3	5.3	5.7	6.5	6.6	23.6	28.8	15.4	2.8	79.7	42.7	48.5	51.5
45449	DAYTON	91.9	88.3	4.6	6.9	1.6	2.5	1.3	1.7	6.6	6.1	5.9	5.4	6.3	28.2	26.0	13.6	2.0	78.2	39.0	48.1	51.9
45458	DAYTON	90.6	86.6	3.6	5.3	4.1	6.2	1.3	1.6	6.3	6.6	7.3	6.9	4.7	25.0	30.9	10.8	1.6	75.4	40.6	47.8	52.2
45459	DAYTON	93.3	90.0	2.4	3.7	2.9	4.6	1.2	1.6	4.9	5.1	5.7	5.4	4.3	21.1	29.5	19.5	4.5	80.8	47.4	47.0	53.0
	OHIO	85.0	83.1	11.5	12.2	1.2	1.9	1.9	2.4	6.6	6.5	6.6	7.1	6.7	25.9	26.9	11.7	2.1	76.2	38.2	48.7	51.3
	UNITED STATES	75.1	72.0	12.3	12.7	3.8	4.6	12.5	15.7	6.8	6.7	6.6	7.1	6.9	27.0	26.0	10.9	1.9	75.7	36.9	49.2	50.8

ZIP CODE #	POST OFFICE NAME	2009 Per Capita Income	2009 HH Income Base	2009 HOUSEHOLD INCOME DISTRIBUTION (%) Less than $25,000	$25,000 to $49,999	$50,000 to $99,999	$100,000 to $149,999	$150,000 or More	MEDIAN HOUSEHOLD INCOME 2009	2014	2009 National Centile	2009 State Centile	2009 Home Value Base	2009 HOME VALUE DISTRIBUTION (%) Less than $50,000	$50,000 to $89,999	$90,000 to $174,999	$175,000 to $399,999	$400,000 or More	2009 Median Home Value
45243	CINCINNATI	49515	5874	10.4	15.8	29.7	17.0	27.1	86961	88011	94	98	5059	3.1	5.0	33.4	29.8	28.6	207538
45244	CINCINNATI	40049	9714	11.0	19.1	31.4	18.1	20.4	79154	81097	92	96	7667	0.7	6.4	47.3	39.8	5.7	165652
45245	CINCINNATI	30612	7539	13.7	25.0	43.7	11.3	6.3	61933	64778	80	80	4556	1.7	8.7	59.1	25.1	5.4	145579
45246	CINCINNATI	32169	6127	17.1	25.2	36.8	14.0	7.0	56504	58345	73	71	3583	1.7	11.4	70.2	12.1	4.5	120319
45247	CINCINNATI	35378	8217	9.4	19.5	39.2	18.5	13.4	74217	75193	89	93	6762	1.5	11.6	50.4	33.4	3.1	155425
45248	CINCINNATI	32264	9738	10.8	21.4	43.2	15.8	8.7	67066	68570	85	88	8274	1.9	9.3	64.5	21.8	2.6	133637
45249	CINCINNATI	50142	4849	6.8	12.0	31.7	20.3	29.2	98910	100556	97	99	3608	2.8	4.7	31.0	44.8	16.7	223210
45251	CINCINNATI	27090	8459	11.3	21.9	48.6	13.1	5.1	64922	65418	83	86	6804	2.8	27.5	61.1	8.3	0.3	108635
45252	CINCINNATI	37129	2050	9.5	17.7	37.1	25.2	10.5	77863	77552	91	95	1899	1.4	7.0	53.9	33.6	4.1	148859
45255	CINCINNATI	35789	9107	11.5	18.4	41.5	17.1	11.5	71739	74464	88	92	6510	0.9	6.1	56.8	29.8	6.4	157785
45302	ANNA	23736	1454	11.9	23.1	49.6	12.1	3.3	60772	58961	78	79	1218	3.8	15.0	56.2	23.8	1.1	125781
45303	ANSONIA	23129	835	20.0	28.3	41.3	6.9	3.5	51048	52190	64	53	646	14.4	31.0	42.7	10.4	1.5	95263
45304	ARCANUM	24828	2918	15.9	27.7	42.7	10.1	3.6	54539	54986	70	65	2330	3.2	15.5	59.0	20.6	1.7	127166
45305	BELLBROOK	36018	3894	10.1	18.1	36.4	23.2	12.1	79933	82884	92	96	3107	0.6	2.1	50.5	40.1	6.8	169805
45306	BOTKINS	23272	947	13.3	25.7	48.0	10.5	2.5	58720	57176	76	76	789	5.7	15.2	55.4	22.2	1.5	123673
45308	BRADFORD	20927	1798	16.2	31.6	43.8	6.8	1.6	51259	52878	64	55	1439	11.0	28.1	41.3	18.5	1.2	103648
45309	BROOKVILLE	26543	4886	17.3	26.6	40.3	12.2	3.7	55489	57811	72	68	3697	5.8	16.6	59.0	17.8	0.8	117160
45311	CAMDEN	21778	2828	18.6	31.4	40.4	7.9	1.8	50028	52531	61	49	2311	16.5	18.9	46.9	16.4	1.4	109015
45312	CASSTOWN	26176	689	11.5	22.8	50.8	11.5	3.5	64740	66259	83	85	587	3.2	13.1	48.7	31.7	3.2	140813
45314	CEDARVILLE	19897	1293	16.9	26.7	42.6	10.5	3.3	55670	57524	72	69	863	5.9	11.8	52.4	28.2	1.7	139015
45315	CLAYTON	32667	1533	8.6	16.7	45.1	20.3	9.3	77773	78322	91	95	1299	1.5	4.5	71.3	21.2	1.5	139793
45317	CONOVER	20884	421	14.7	36.1	41.6	5.5	2.1	49231	51192	59	46	341	12.6	23.5	44.3	17.0	2.6	113578
45318	COVINGTON	23972	2072	15.1	30.1	44.3	7.5	3.0	53138	55831	68	61	1618	6.8	15.5	59.6	16.6	1.5	116562
45320	EATON	23910	6096	17.1	28.2	44.0	8.4	2.2	54371	56489	70	64	4632	4.3	20.5	59.1	14.8	1.3	113222
45321	ELDORADO	19297	427	22.7	33.0	36.8	7.3	0.2	46692	48799	53	38	343	10.8	35.3	42.6	11.4	0.0	94355
45322	ENGLEWOOD	29296	8387	12.7	23.9	45.4	13.4	4.7	62099	63534	80	81	6519	1.4	13.8	75.9	8.5	0.4	114612
45323	ENON	30179	2189	9.9	26.8	44.1	14.5	4.7	63347	64190	82	83	1682	2.1	10.9	73.2	13.7	0.1	121101
45324	FAIRBORN	25278	17256	26.1	27.1	34.2	8.7	3.8	46456	48941	53	37	9090	6.2	26.3	54.0	12.5	0.9	107525
45325	FARMERSVILLE	27021	918	12.1	28.1	38.3	16.0	5.4	62540	64395	81	81	773	1.3	20.8	53.4	22.4	2.1	123084
45326	FLETCHER	23780	443	15.1	29.3	44.9	6.8	3.8	55096	57967	71	67	377	8.0	24.7	48.5	17.0	1.9	114674
45327	GERMANTOWN	28207	3308	12.5	26.8	43.3	11.9	5.5	62464	63901	81	81	2625	1.4	16.6	61.7	18.8	1.4	118019
45331	GREENVILLE	23403	9687	25.8	29.1	35.3	7.1	2.7	45404	48816	49	34	7053	9.2	24.3	52.5	12.6	1.4	110012
45332	HOLLANSBURG	21478	234	20.9	35.5	35.0	6.0	2.6	44749	48333	47	33	193	25.4	25.4	32.1	17.1	0.0	88125
45333	HOUSTON	22259	537	12.7	24.2	52.9	8.6	1.7	59265	58220	76	77	462	5.4	10.6	56.1	24.2	3.7	133333
45334	JACKSON CENTER	22974	878	20.5	23.1	47.8	6.6	1.9	53590	53650	69	62	693	11.5	19.5	51.1	16.0	1.9	113121
45335	JAMESTOWN	24214	2746	17.5	22.4	48.3	8.1	3.8	57989	59682	75	75	2211	5.7	18.3	58.6	14.9	2.4	114779
45337	LAURA	22991	648	11.4	30.7	47.7	8.3	1.9	54776	57147	71	66	554	4.9	21.5	54.2	18.6	0.9	118243
45338	LEWISBURG	22270	2389	17.7	30.0	40.9	9.8	1.5	52174	54734	66	58	1923	5.0	20.5	54.6	18.3	1.6	116155
45339	LUDLOW FALLS	23513	618	14.6	27.8	45.8	9.1	2.8	56153	59148	73	70	530	5.7	9.8	56.6	25.8	2.1	135000
45340	MAPLEWOOD	23879	316	15.2	21.5	50.9	9.5	2.8	60728	59400	78	79	281	9.6	15.3	52.0	21.7	1.4	120833
45341	MEDWAY	24999	1651	22.7	29.0	37.6	6.8	3.9	48707	52137	58	44	1426	35.7	30.6	28.4	5.3	0.0	75839
45342	MIAMISBURG	29164	14685	14.4	27.1	41.5	12.1	4.9	58477	60158	76	76	9505	7.7	17.6	58.1	15.7	0.9	119680
45344	NEW CARLISLE	24235	6522	15.1	26.7	43.3	10.8	4.0	55357	57241	72	68	5228	7.0	30.4	45.7	16.4	0.5	103083
45345	NEW LEBANON	23758	2446	16.8	29.8	45.0	5.4	3.0	52994	55637	68	61	1952	4.6	30.3	57.7	6.7	0.7	97623
45346	NEW MADISON	19755	881	24.2	28.4	40.4	5.4	1.6	46766	50528	53	38	728	10.2	29.1	45.3	14.1	1.2	102737
45347	NEW PARIS	21595	1583	21.1	33.5	37.7	6.7	1.0	46482	49199	53	37	1196	20.7	29.4	39.0	10.1	0.7	89750
45348	NEW WESTON	19018	440	22.5	28.0	41.8	5.7	2.0	49397	51414	60	47	368	11.1	20.4	48.9	12.8	6.8	114527
45356	PIQUA	23490	10125	23.5	28.2	37.7	7.4	3.2	48069	51744	57	42	6805	6.3	30.0	49.0	13.4	1.3	102145
45359	PLEASANT HILL	23866	728	11.5	26.4	52.7	7.3	2.1	59347	61608	77	77	591	1.7	10.7	66.5	18.8	2.4	130280
45362	ROSSBURG	20565	442	22.9	28.5	41.2	6.1	1.4	48229	50968	57	43	359	16.2	20.1	45.1	13.9	4.7	113377
45363	RUSSIA	25260	625	11.0	18.1	50.9	15.4	4.6	67853	67164	85	89	500	3.0	10.2	49.0	31.2	6.6	144872
45365	SIDNEY	24379	11917	19.4	27.0	40.7	8.9	4.0	52340	53111	67	59	8225	11.0	17.9	53.2	16.5	1.4	113933
45368	SOUTH CHARLESTON	24461	1881	16.6	26.3	44.1	10.3	2.7	57437	59349	75	74	1414	15.3	20.3	52.3	11.2	0.8	107931
45369	SOUTH VIENNA	26252	1439	12.4	22.0	49.5	12.8	3.4	62273	63389	80	81	1209	18.8	14.4	48.4	17.4	1.1	115234
45370	SPRING VALLEY	35972	948	11.6	23.1	32.3	17.1	15.9	72994	78042	88	92	835	15.9	9.7	29.8	35.8	8.7	149745
45371	TIPP CITY	31032	7092	12.5	22.3	43.2	14.0	8.0	65364	67436	84	86	5346	3.3	6.7	54.8	32.6	2.5	148449
45373	TROY	28424	13633	17.3	25.1	39.4	11.9	6.3	56993	59640	74	73	9330	2.5	12.8	58.4	24.0	2.3	126898
45377	VANDALIA	29527	6260	14.7	28.1	40.7	11.3	5.1	55838	57781	72	69	4141	0.5	14.2	65.5	18.4	1.4	122450
45380	VERSAILLES	22477	1924	20.1	25.8	42.6	8.8	2.7	53059	53873	68	61	1489	5.2	15.8	57.6	19.9	1.4	125475
45381	WEST ALEXANDRIA	22906	2185	17.3	31.1	39.9	9.2	2.6	51383	53913	65	55	1758	5.4	17.1	61.5	15.5	0.5	117022
45382	WEST MANCHESTER	21082	460	20.2	35.9	35.2	7.8	0.9	43828	47162	45	30	360	5.3	25.6	53.6	13.6	1.9	109593
45383	WEST MILTON	25567	2796	16.3	29.1	41.8	9.1	3.6	54330	57738	70	64	2050	5.7	12.5	62.8	17.6	1.4	118455
45385	XENIA	25829	14570	19.9	26.1	38.9	9.9	5.1	53884	56833	69	63	10621	4.7	27.3	46.3	19.3	2.4	109234
45387	YELLOW SPRINGS	35100	2475	15.1	22.4	36.3	15.5	10.7	64550	67966	83	85	1701	2.0	7.9	45.3	41.2	3.6	166682
45388	YORKSHIRE	20194	376	17.8	30.6	44.7	5.3	1.6	50926	51893	63	53	320	3.4	9.1	60.3	17.8	9.4	132000
45390	UNION CITY	20012	1456	29.5	30.6	34.5	3.2	2.2	40487	44908	34	22	1039	20.9	37.8	32.5	7.5	1.3	79279
45402	DAYTON	15971	5211	56.8	23.0	15.6	2.9	1.7	20561	21124	2	2	1877	38.1	41.3	16.3	3.7	0.5	58011
45403	DAYTON	18048	6465	35.3	32.7	26.9	3.8	1.3	34391	36562	16	9	3348	23.3	62.4	14.0	0.4	0.0	65735
45404	DAYTON	17136	4577	39.2	31.3	25.5	3.1	1.0	31724	33741	11	7	2370	24.9	55.5	18.9	0.6	0.0	64779
45405	DAYTON	20794	9441	32.2	33.6	28.1	4.3	1.8	36131	38211	21	12	4320	13.5	61.4	23.1	2.0	0.0	72441
45406	DAYTON	20501	10341	33.6	29.6	27.5	7.0	2.3	37465	40028	25	15	5734	17.8	52.5	28.0	1.6	0.1	71436
45408	DAYTON	13314	3820	54.0	25.2	17.1	2.5	1.2	22480	23673	2	2	1780	39.7	49.7	10.1	0.6	0.0	56536
45409	DAYTON	27943	3042	23.1	24.2	30.9	11.6	10.2	53245	56208	68	62	1775	1.0	13.0	57.8	24.1	4.1	124132
45410	DAYTON	20649	7123	34.4	28.0	32.1	4.6	0.9	37958	40870	27	16	3800	14.8	57.8	26.3	1.1	0.0	77627
45414	DAYTON	27370	8958	23.5	27.6	33.4	9.8	5.6	48598	52182	58	44	6036	13.5	26.6	42.1	16.0	1.8	104798
45415	DAYTON	32721	5153	14.6	22.6	42.0	12.8	8.0	63179	64170	81	82	3800	1.5	13.8	68.0	16.3	0.3	122289
45416	DAYTON	21499	2437	23.8	33.2	32.5	8.3	2.2	43922	47657	45	31	1791	12.5	58.6	28.2	0.7	0.0	71439
45417	DAYTON	15502	4063	48.8	30.7	17.2	2.0	1.3	25596	26610	4	3	2387	46.5	47.7	5.1	0.4	0.2	51813
45418	DAYTON	20746	2213	29.1	27.2	33.5	6.6	3.7	42880	47279	42	28	1593	13.9	41.9	37.7	5.9	0.6	85209
45419	DAYTON	39544	7588	17.1	22.6	35.0	12.8	12.5	61994	63344	80	80	5012	1.6	10.6	53.8	27.5	6.5	138058
45420	DAYTON	25806	11539	22.4	29.6	40.2	6.0	1.8	47935	51264	56	42	7430	2.5	49.2	47.6	0.7	0.1	89136
45424	DAYTON	27650	18788	11.8	23.3	46.6	13.1	5.1	63157	64355	81	82	13803	4.2	21.7	66.1	7.7	0.3	108042
45426	DAYTON	24396	7002	25.1	28.9	34.7	8.5	2.8	45308	50170	49	34	3949	5.1	34.5	56.8	3.4	0.2	97528
45427	DAYTON	15988	4400	41.6	30.9	21.5	4.4	1.7	29442	30664	7	5	2765	34.9	39.3	22.7	2.9	0.1	63095
45429	DAYTON	36471	11692	12.7	25.4	40.6	12.9	8.3	61792	63143	80	80	8131	0.7	8.4	69.1	19.3	2.6	129791
45430	DAYTON	36511	2960	6.3	16.7	42.0	23.5	11.5	81478	82962	93	97	2599	0.7	3.0	65.0	30.5	0.8	155360
45431	DAYTON	28707	9909	15.5	24.4	40.9	12.6	6.7	60339	63817	78	78	5762	5.6	23.8	46.3	22.7	1.6	115436
45432	DAYTON	29828	6458	15.2	25.7	39.4	13.3	6.5	58878	61273	76	76	5132	1.6	26.7	56.0	15.1	0.7	113151
45433	DAYTON	22463	707	3.4	23.5	58.8	9.8	4.5	63442	64608	82	83	12	0.0	8.3	75.0	16.7	0.0	158333
45434	DAYTON	41249	4024	5.8	10.2	37.8	27.9	18.3	94385	96081	96	99	3624	0.5	3.2	49.0	41.8	5.5	171423
45439	DAYTON	29385	4415	19.4	33.6	36.1	5.4	5.4	47154	50773	55	40	2818	16.0	34.9	43.2	3.0	2.8	89463
45440	DAYTON	34135	8582	12.0	24.7	38.3	15.5	9.6	65239	67370	83	86	5791	0.9	5.6	61.8	27.4	4.2	154196
45449	DAYTON	28416	8276	16.4	29.2	40.7	9.5	4.1	53600	55925	69	63	5167	7.2	23.1	64.2	5.2	0.2	106974
45458	DAYTON	41103	11387	11.0	17.2	35.4	19.5	16.9	79611	79766	92	96	7968	0.7	8.2	41.6	43.6	5.9	174037
45459	DAYTON	40577	11558	9.4	20.7	39.2	17.9	12.9	73100	73167	88	92	8606	0.7	8.7	49.5	37.6	3.5	161026
	OHIO	26577		21.4	25.9	36.7	10.4	5.7	52400	54553				10.3	22.0	45.6	19.3	2.8	114865
	UNITED STATES	27277		20.9	24.4	35.3	11.7	7.6	54719	56938				9.3	13.1	31.6	32.6	13.5	162279

#	POST OFFICE NAME	FINANCIAL SERVICES: Auto Loan	Home Loan	Invest-ments	Retire-ment Plans	THE HOME: Home Improvements: Home Repair	Lawn & Garden	Furnishings: Computers & Hardware-Personal	Major Appli-ances	TV, Radio, Sound Equip-ment	Furni-ture	ENTERTAINMENT: Dine out/ Carry out	Sports Equip-ment	Fees & Tickets	Toys & Games	Travel	Cable TV	PERSONAL: Apparel & Services	Auto Repairs	Health Insur-ance	Pets & Supplies
45243	CINCINNATI	164	210	227	214	221	205	178	190	174	190	174	140	212	172	204	173	127	180	186	214
45244	CINCINNATI	150	172	159	175	169	155	156	154	149	163	152	122	170	154	163	145	109	151	144	179
45245	CINCINNATI	102	102	93	104	99	96	104	98	102	104	103	78	104	104	102	100	72	101	97	117
45246	CINCINNATI	98	100	99	102	101	104	102	101	104	102	104	75	105	102	104	106	73	103	110	118
45247	CINCINNATI	126	144	137	145	143	140	129	133	128	133	129	101	141	129	138	128	91	130	134	155
45248	CINCINNATI	111	127	121	129	127	128	115	120	116	116	116	89	125	115	123	118	81	117	125	139
45249	CINCINNATI	188	214	204	222	212	194	196	192	187	204	190	154	214	192	205	181	137	188	178	223
45251	CINCINNATI	104	111	96	110	106	107	104	104	104	105	104	79	107	106	104	104	73	103	106	123
45252	CINCINNATI	126	147	142	149	146	139	132	134	129	137	130	102	145	130	142	127	93	131	131	156
45255	CINCINNATI	120	135	128	137	133	125	126	124	123	130	124	96	135	124	131	121	88	123	121	144
45302	ANNA	101	101	94	104	100	110	95	104	96	90	95	79	94	98	97	99	66	97	105	121
45303	ANSONIA	102	79	87	79	79	101	81	93	88	77	86	71	68	91	76	94	58	87	97	112
45304	ARCANUM	93	95	87	97	94	103	89	96	91	85	91	73	89	93	92	95	62	92	101	113
45305	BELLBROOK	124	150	149	154	152	140	131	134	126	138	128	103	148	127	143	123	92	129	127	154
45306	BOTKINS	97	93	89	97	94	105	89	99	91	83	90	76	86	93	91	95	62	92	101	115
45308	BRADFORD	83	80	71	83	78	89	79	83	81	73	80	65	77	83	78	84	55	81	89	99
45309	BROOKVILLE	90	97	89	98	95	101	90	94	92	90	92	71	95	92	94	94	63	93	100	111
45311	CAMDEN	89	80	80	81	80	93	78	87	81	73	80	67	72	83	77	86	55	82	90	103
45312	CASSTOWN	100	108	96	111	106	110	98	104	98	96	98	81	102	100	103	99	68	99	104	122
45314	CEDARVILLE	89	89	80	93	87	90	94	88	90	89	91	71	91	92	90	90	63	90	89	105
45315	CLAYTON	119	138	124	140	135	138	121	128	122	123	122	97	133	123	131	123	86	123	131	149
45317	CONOVER	88	80	79	84	82	95	79	89	82	72	80	68	73	83	79	86	55	83	92	104
45318	COVINGTON	92	88	80	91	87	98	87	92	89	81	88	71	84	91	86	93	60	89	98	109
45320	EATON	85	87	78	89	85	93	84	87	85	81	85	67	85	86	85	88	59	85	92	103
45321	ELDORADO	78	71	70	74	72	84	70	79	72	63	71	60	64	73	70	76	48	73	81	92
45322	ENGLEWOOD	100	108	99	108	106	108	100	103	101	101	101	77	104	102	103	102	70	101	106	120
45323	ENON	95	111	103	112	109	113	98	103	100	99	100	77	109	100	106	103	70	101	110	120
45324	FAIRBORN	82	72	66	75	69	74	89	75	85	81	86	62	80	85	77	85	60	82	80	92
45325	FARMERSVILLE	102	114	99	117	111	113	102	106	101	102	101	83	108	103	108	101	71	102	106	125
45326	FLETCHER	99	90	90	94	92	107	89	101	92	81	90	76	82	94	89	97	62	93	104	117
45327	GERMANTOWN	102	109	100	111	107	115	99	107	101	96	101	81	103	102	104	104	70	102	111	125
45331	GREENVILLE	81	75	74	76	75	86	77	82	80	71	78	62	72	80	75	84	54	79	88	96
45332	HOLLANSBURG	84	77	76	80	78	91	76	86	78	68	77	65	70	80	76	83	52	79	88	99
45333	HOUSTON	95	93	88	96	93	103	88	97	90	83	89	74	86	92	90	93	61	91	99	113
45334	JACKSON CENTER	87	82	79	85	83	94	79	89	81	73	80	67	75	83	80	86	55	82	91	103
45335	JAMESTOWN	92	96	88	98	94	102	89	96	91	86	90	73	91	92	92	93	62	91	99	112
45337	LAURA	94	90	86	93	90	102	87	96	88	80	87	73	82	90	87	93	60	89	98	112
45338	LEWISBURG	89	83	81	86	84	96	81	91	83	74	82	69	76	85	81	88	56	84	93	106
45339	LUDLOW FALLS	95	90	86	93	91	102	87	97	89	80	87	73	82	91	88	93	60	90	99	112
45340	MAPLEWOOD	96	97	90	100	96	105	91	99	92	87	91	76	90	94	93	95	63	93	100	116
45341	MEDWAY	80	85	82	83	85	93	79	85	83	79	82	61	83	81	83	87	56	83	95	99
45342	MIAMISBURG	99	95	88	98	93	95	99	95	99	97	99	75	97	101	96	99	69	97	97	113
45344	NEW CARLISLE	92	96	82	97	92	99	91	93	92	89	92	72	93	94	91	94	63	91	97	110
45345	NEW LEBANON	91	88	81	91	87	99	86	93	88	80	87	71	83	90	86	93	60	88	98	109
45346	NEW MADISON	80	73	72	76	74	86	72	81	74	65	73	61	66	75	72	78	50	75	83	94
45347	NEW PARIS	83	72	76	73	72	88	74	82	78	68	76	63	67	78	72	83	52	79	89	97
45348	NEW WESTON	97	75	100	76	77	103	79	95	82	67	81	76	64	82	79	88	53	88	99	114
45356	PIQUA	83	80	70	82	77	85	83	81	84	78	83	63	80	86	79	86	58	82	87	97
45359	PLEASANT HILL	96	94	89	97	94	104	89	98	91	84	90	75	87	93	91	94	62	92	100	114
45362	ROSSBURG	88	75	84	78	77	94	76	88	79	67	77	68	67	80	76	84	52	81	91	104
45363	RUSSIA	107	117	103	120	114	118	106	111	105	105	105	87	111	107	111	106	73	106	111	131
45365	SIDNEY	89	88	79	89	86	94	87	89	89	83	88	68	86	90	86	92	61	88	95	106
45368	SOUTH CHARLESTON	97	93	85	94	92	101	90	96	92	86	91	72	86	94	89	95	63	92	99	113
45369	SOUTH VIENNA	102	106	95	109	105	110	98	105	98	96	98	80	99	101	101	100	68	100	105	123
45370	SPRING VALLEY	131	148	145	151	150	141	129	135	126	137	127	102	141	129	137	124	91	128	127	156
45371	TIPP CITY	108	120	115	120	119	118	111	114	110	112	111	86	118	111	116	111	78	111	115	132
45373	TROY	98	103	94	105	101	102	101	99	100	100	100	77	104	101	101	100	70	99	102	117
45377	VANDALIA	92	96	90	97	94	97	96	94	96	94	96	72	98	96	96	97	67	95	98	111
45380	VERSAILLES	91	85	81	88	85	98	84	92	86	76	85	70	78	88	83	91	58	87	96	108
45381	WEST ALEXANDRIA	91	85	83	88	86	98	83	92	85	76	84	70	78	86	83	89	57	86	95	107
45382	WEST MANCHESTER	83	79	76	82	80	90	76	85	78	70	77	65	72	80	77	82	53	79	87	99
45383	WEST MILTON	95	88	84	89	87	99	89	93	91	85	90	71	84	93	87	95	62	91	99	111
45385	XENIA	93	95	85	96	92	95	92	92	93	92	93	71	93	94	92	94	65	92	95	109
45387	YELLOW SPRINGS	110	120	117	121	120	119	114	115	114	116	114	86	121	113	119	114	80	114	118	134
45388	YORKSHIRE	89	80	81	83	82	96	80	90	82	72	81	69	73	83	79	87	55	83	93	105
45390	UNION CITY	78	65	63	66	64	78	72	74	75	65	73	57	62	76	66	79	50	73	80	89
45402	DAYTON	49	38	37	40	37	44	48	44	53	47	52	33	44	50	43	56	36	49	53	55
45403	DAYTON	61	53	45	54	50	56	63	56	64	57	63	45	58	65	55	66	44	61	62	69
45404	DAYTON	63	52	47	53	50	60	60	58	64	56	62	45	53	64	53	67	43	61	65	71
45405	DAYTON	65	55	49	57	52	58	66	59	68	62	68	47	61	68	59	70	47	65	65	73
45406	DAYTON	68	61	54	63	57	66	67	63	72	66	71	48	65	71	62	75	49	68	72	79
45408	DAYTON	47	37	34	38	35	43	44	42	50	44	49	30	41	48	39	53	34	46	50	53
45409	DAYTON	102	98	97	101	98	99	113	100	109	107	109	80	109	107	105	108	77	106	105	119
45410	DAYTON	64	58	50	59	55	62	66	60	68	61	67	48	62	67	60	70	46	65	68	74
45414	DAYTON	90	92	88	93	91	95	92	92	93	90	93	70	93	93	92	95	65	93	97	109
45415	DAYTON	98	111	112	113	113	113	103	106	104	105	105	78	113	102	111	107	74	105	114	123
45416	DAYTON	75	74	64	75	70	79	73	73	78	73	77	54	75	77	72	81	53	75	83	89
45417	DAYTON	53	42	41	43	41	51	47	48	55	49	53	34	45	53	43	59	36	51	58	60
45418	DAYTON	76	76	70	76	74	84	74	77	79	73	79	55	75	78	74	84	54	77	88	92
45419	DAYTON	118	119	119	123	121	119	128	119	123	123	123	94	127	123	124	122	87	122	120	140
45420	DAYTON	75	73	62	75	69	77	77	73	79	73	79	58	76	79	74	81	54	77	83	89
45424	DAYTON	101	108	92	108	103	103	102	101	101	103	102	78	105	104	102	101	71	100	101	119
45426	DAYTON	78	74	71	75	73	78	78	77	80	76	79	58	76	79	76	82	55	79	84	91
45427	DAYTON	60	50	46	51	48	58	56	55	61	54	59	41	51	60	51	65	41	58	63	68
45429	DAYTON	106	114	115	114	117	121	109	113	111	110	111	82	115	109	115	114	77	112	124	131
45430	DAYTON	123	151	153	155	154	146	129	137	126	137	127	101	147	125	145	125	90	130	133	157
45431	DAYTON	103	98	93	101	96	100	103	99	103	101	103	78	101	105	99	103	72	101	102	117
45432	DAYTON	95	104	99	105	103	106	97	100	99	98	99	74	104	99	102	101	70	99	105	116
45433	DAYTON	132	69	52	80	62	59	125	86	117	116	123	86	95	141	90	108	87	110	78	105
45434	DAYTON	149	181	178	186	183	169	155	162	150	166	151	123	176	151	171	146	109	154	153	185
45439	DAYTON	98	86	79	88	84	95	95	92	97	89	96	72	88	98	88	100	66	95	100	111
45440	DAYTON	109	115	113	118	115	115	113	111	112	114	113	85	119	112	116	113	80	113	115	130
45449	DAYTON	90	85	78	87	82	87	89	85	90	88	91	66	88	91	87	91	63	89	90	102
45458	DAYTON	134	159	156	163	159	146	142	142	136	149	138	111	158	138	152	132	99	138	134	165
45459	DAYTON	122	137	139	140	140	135	129	130	127	133	127	98	139	125	137	126	90	129	132	151
	OHIO	94	92	87	93	90	96	93	93	94	91	94	72	92	95	91	96	66	93	98	110
	UNITED STATES	100	100	100	100	100	100	100	100	100	100	100	100	100	100	100	100	100	100	100	100

45469-45784

ZIP CODE			POPULATION			2000-2009 ANNUAL RATE		HOUSEHOLDS					FAMILIES		
#	POST OFFICE NAME	COUNTY FIPS CODE	2000	2009	2014	% Rate	State Centile	2000	2009	2014	% Annual Rate 2000-2009	2009 Average HH Size	2000	2009	% Annual Rate 2000-2009
45469	DAYTON	113	4050	4007	3990	-0.1	39	125	115	111	-0.9	3.08	17	14	-2.1
45502	SPRINGFIELD	023	17541	18162	18093	0.4	66	6683	7010	7016	0.5	2.56	5177	5336	0.3
45503	SPRINGFIELD	023	32357	31229	30542	-0.4	21	13441	13153	12930	-0.2	2.31	8794	8289	-0.6
45504	SPRINGFIELD	023	19621	18693	18246	-0.5	17	7160	6858	6701	-0.5	2.47	4746	4420	-0.8
45505	SPRINGFIELD	023	21864	20375	19710	-0.8	9	9039	8553	8315	-0.6	2.36	5837	5341	-1.0
45506	SPRINGFIELD	023	16165	15125	14656	-0.7	11	6228	5901	5743	-0.6	2.50	4164	3825	-0.9
45601	CHILLICOTHE	141	55495	57346	58077	0.4	66	20474	21237	21623	0.4	2.43	14103	14245	0.1
45612	BAINBRIDGE	141	5228	5536	5662	0.6	75	1891	2030	2086	0.8	2.71	1438	1509	0.5
45613	BEAVER	131	3646	3800	3816	0.4	66	1331	1435	1456	0.8	2.63	1016	1070	0.6
45614	BIDWELL	053	4542	4633	4654	0.2	56	1682	1787	1815	0.7	2.53	1237	1280	0.4
45616	BLUE CREEK	001	1792	1868	1892	0.5	71	700	758	776	0.9	2.46	509	536	0.6
45619	CHESAPEAKE	087	8407	8415	8338	0.0	45	3375	3492	3497	0.4	2.40	2425	2444	0.1
45620	CHESHIRE	053	1249	1211	1191	-0.3	27	501	501	498	0.0	2.42	369	359	-0.3
45622	CREOLA	163	490	482	477	-0.2	32	190	192	192	0.1	2.51	144	143	-0.1
45623	CROWN CITY	053	3656	3702	3703	0.1	51	1405	1481	1499	0.6	2.50	1088	1120	0.3
45628	FRANKFORT	141	4293	4546	4661	0.6	75	1618	1734	1787	0.8	2.58	1206	1259	0.5
45629	FRANKLIN FURNACE	145	3541	3567	3527	0.1	51	1261	1321	1319	0.5	2.54	985	1006	0.2
45631	GALLIPOLIS	053	15868	15235	14971	-0.4	21	6393	6321	6261	-0.1	2.32	4314	4147	-0.4
45634	HAMDEN	163	2062	2213	2279	0.8	82	762	841	873	1.1	2.58	571	615	0.8
45638	IRONTON	087	21402	20643	20215	-0.4	21	8788	8773	8683	0.0	2.30	5968	5798	-0.3
45640	JACKSON	079	14803	15484	15702	0.5	71	5800	6214	6345	0.7	2.46	4128	4318	0.5
45644	KINGSTON	141	3642	3845	3943	0.6	75	1357	1450	1495	0.7	2.62	1034	1079	0.5
45645	KITTS HILL	087	2929	3042	3062	0.4	66	1064	1141	1162	0.8	2.67	851	896	0.6
45646	LATHAM	131	353	384	392	0.9	85	133	148	153	1.2	2.59	102	112	1.0
45647	LONDONDERRY	163	1938	2051	2096	0.6	75	741	800	823	0.8	2.56	558	587	0.5
45648	LUCASVILLE	145	13002	12907	12714	-0.1	39	4300	4430	4398	0.3	2.54	3284	3290	0.0
45650	LYNX	001	72	72	71	0.0	45	30	31	31	0.4	2.32	21	22	0.5
45651	MC ARTHUR	163	5966	6098	6137	0.2	56	2268	2368	2400	0.5	2.54	1606	1636	0.2
45652	MC DERMOTT	145	3208	3189	3145	-0.1	39	1178	1218	1213	0.4	2.55	898	903	0.1
45653	MINFORD	145	3831	3682	3584	-0.4	21	1398	1389	1365	-0.1	2.62	1083	1048	-0.4
45654	NEW PLYMOUTH	163	955	949	942	-0.1	39	355	362	362	0.2	2.62	269	269	0.0
45656	OAK HILL	079	6349	6712	6834	0.6	75	2477	2688	2761	0.9	2.46	1836	1945	0.6
45657	OTWAY	145	2483	2541	2522	0.2	56	934	988	992	0.6	2.57	700	720	0.3
45658	PATRIOT	053	2437	2505	2506	0.3	61	834	869	876	0.4	2.88	656	668	0.2
45659	PEDRO	087	3417	3416	3401	0.0	45	1220	1265	1274	0.4	2.70	949	964	0.2
45660	PEEBLES	001	8375	8837	8993	0.6	75	3042	3292	3378	0.9	2.65	2284	2416	0.6
45661	PIKETON	131	7305	7582	7596	0.4	66	2617	2790	2817	0.7	2.65	1958	2034	0.4
45662	PORTSMOUTH	145	30816	28419	27288	-0.9	7	13191	12476	12063	-0.6	2.19	7994	7296	-1.0
45663	WEST PORTSMOUTH	145	7065	6627	6383	-0.7	11	2762	2672	2596	-0.4	2.48	2066	1944	-0.7
45669	PROCTORVILLE	087	10005	10048	9982	0.0	45	3993	4165	4187	0.5	2.41	3003	3056	0.2
45671	RARDEN	145	455	471	468	0.4	66	184	198	199	0.8	2.38	131	136	0.4
45672	RAY	163	1903	2007	2043	0.6	75	729	789	810	0.9	2.54	553	585	0.6
45673	RICHMOND DALE	141	394	392	390	-0.1	39	165	167	167	0.1	2.35	124	122	-0.2
45675	ROCK CAMP	087	230	224	219	-0.3	27	82	83	83	0.1	2.70	66	66	0.0
45678	SCOTTOWN	087	1048	1082	1086	0.3	61	409	437	444	0.7	2.48	315	329	0.5
45679	SEAMAN	001	2649	2714	2740	0.3	61	995	1049	1070	0.6	2.57	731	753	0.3
45680	SOUTH POINT	087	12704	12919	12939	0.2	56	4987	5280	5350	0.6	2.41	3629	3747	0.3
45681	SOUTH SALEM	141	1351	1535	1613	1.4	93	494	568	601	1.5	2.66	392	441	1.3
45682	SOUTH WEBSTER	145	2466	2459	2422	0.0	45	924	955	951	0.4	2.57	695	699	0.1
45684	STOUT	145	1560	1625	1624	0.4	66	595	640	646	0.8	2.54	430	449	0.5
45685	THURMAN	079	1471	1492	1500	0.2	56	575	602	610	0.5	2.15	415	423	0.2
45686	VINTON	053	3227	3364	3410	0.5	71	1207	1306	1337	0.9	2.56	914	966	0.6
45688	WATERLOO	087	450	473	478	0.5	71	177	193	198	0.9	2.45	126	134	0.7
45690	WAVERLY	131	14090	14079	13932	0.0	45	5542	5663	5639	0.2	2.45	3961	3951	0.0
45692	WELLSTON	079	9832	9676	9589	-0.2	32	3732	3751	3740	0.1	2.54	2689	2634	-0.2
45693	WEST UNION	001	8648	8586	8557	-0.1	39	3368	3459	3482	0.3	2.43	2411	2418	0.0
45694	WHEELERSBURG	145	11800	11508	11251	-0.3	27	4528	4555	4497	0.1	2.47	3390	3318	-0.2
45695	WILKESVILLE	163	801	837	856	0.5	71	330	356	367	0.8	2.34	245	258	0.6
45696	WILLOW WOOD	087	1546	1597	1604	0.4	66	571	610	621	0.7	2.62	437	457	0.5
45697	WINCHESTER	001	4866	5165	5270	0.6	75	1779	1934	1990	0.9	2.66	1379	1468	0.7
45701	ATHENS	009	31713	32076	31912	0.1	51	10474	10767	10783	0.3	2.27	4773	4717	-0.1
45710	ALBANY	105	4532	4663	4675	0.3	61	1795	1912	1935	0.7	2.42	1279	1324	0.4
45711	AMESVILLE	009	1215	1198	1184	-0.2	32	489	499	499	0.2	2.40	351	347	-0.1
45714	BELPRE	167	9674	9384	9216	-0.3	27	4210	4193	4150	0.0	2.24	2832	2738	-0.4
45715	BEVERLY	115	2502	2412	2366	-0.4	21	1012	1008	998	0.0	2.35	695	672	-0.4
45723	COOLVILLE	009	3806	3655	3594	-0.4	21	1493	1487	1476	0.0	2.42	1109	1074	-0.3
45724	CUTLER	167	2661	2612	2573	-0.2	32	996	1011	1006	0.2	2.57	775	768	-0.1
45727	DEXTER CITY	121	582	572	564	-0.2	32	214	216	215	0.1	2.64	157	155	-0.1
45729	FLEMING	167	1191	1195	1184	0.0	45	444	457	456	0.3	2.61	354	358	0.1
45732	GLOUSTER	009	6439	6459	6421	0.0	45	2539	2631	2642	0.4	2.43	1756	1764	0.0
45734	GRAYSVILLE	111	791	737	712	-0.8	9	325	313	306	-0.4	2.35	250	236	-0.6
45735	GUYSVILLE	009	1611	1579	1561	-0.2	32	622	631	631	0.2	2.50	460	453	-0.2
45741	LANGSVILLE	105	1119	1109	1097	-0.1	39	416	428	428	0.3	2.59	316	317	0.0
45742	LITTLE HOCKING	167	2884	2770	2715	-0.4	21	1064	1054	1041	-0.1	2.63	861	837	-0.3
45743	LONG BOTTOM	105	1503	1596	1606	0.7	79	577	635	645	1.0	2.48	438	469	0.7
45744	LOWELL	167	2633	2508	2445	-0.5	17	1024	1004	989	-0.2	2.50	749	714	-0.5
45745	LOWER SALEM	121	1308	1224	1192	-0.7	11	506	489	481	-0.4	2.48	370	349	-0.6
45746	MACKSBURG	167	439	427	420	-0.3	27	171	171	169	0.0	2.50	115	111	-0.4
45750	MARIETTA	167	28574	27980	27515	-0.2	32	11391	11376	11259	0.0	2.31	7604	7393	-0.3
45760	MIDDLEPORT	105	3926	3687	3585	-0.7	11	1659	1593	1560	-0.4	2.27	1067	995	-0.8
45761	MILLFIELD	009	2806	2766	2735	-0.2	32	1091	1105	1102	0.1	2.50	743	728	-0.2
45764	NELSONVILLE	009	9829	9666	9563	-0.2	32	3655	3677	3667	0.1	2.33	2183	2112	-0.4
45766	NEW MARSHFIELD	009	1638	1704	1708	0.4	66	662	711	719	0.8	2.36	458	476	0.4
45767	NEW MATAMORAS	167	2864	2706	2627	-0.6	14	1153	1123	1102	-0.3	2.41	837	793	-0.6
45768	NEWPORT	167	1767	1754	1733	-0.1	39	686	701	699	0.2	2.50	538	538	0.0
45769	POMEROY	105	6227	5962	5846	-0.5	17	2500	2476	2451	-0.1	2.35	1768	1707	-0.4
45770	PORTLAND	105	732	782	785	0.7	79	284	312	317	1.0	2.50	209	223	0.7
45771	RACINE	105	4072	4072	4038	0.0	45	1636	1698	1702	0.4	2.40	1173	1183	0.1
45772	REEDSVILLE	105	1930	1977	1975	0.3	61	768	814	822	0.6	2.42	564	582	0.3
45773	RENO	167	494	486	479	-0.2	32	189	191	190	0.1	2.54	149	147	-0.1
45775	RUTLAND	105	1455	1465	1456	0.1	51	547	568	570	0.4	2.58	417	422	0.1
45776	SHADE	105	748	776	778	0.4	66	306	330	334	0.8	2.35	221	231	0.5
45778	STEWART	009	1007	971	954	-0.4	21	374	372	369	-0.1	2.61	274	264	-0.4
45780	THE PLAINS	009	2936	2916	2895	-0.1	39	1225	1240	1238	0.1	2.19	716	699	-0.3
45784	VINCENT	167	2769	2737	2699	-0.1	39	1039	1060	1056	0.2	2.58	834	834	0.0
	OHIO					0.2					0.4	2.44			0.1
	UNITED STATES					1.0					1.1	2.59			0.9

ZIP CODE #	POST OFFICE NAME	RACE (%) White 2000	White 2009	Black 2000	Black 2009	Asian/Pacific 2000	Asian/Pacific 2009	% Hispanic Origin 2000	% Hispanic Origin 2009	2009 AGE DISTRIBUTION (%) 0-4	5-9	10-14	15-19	20-24	25-44	45-64	65-84	85+	18+	MEDIAN AGE 2009	% 2009 Males	% 2009 Females
45469	DAYTON	92.8	89.3	4.3	6.6	1.0	1.5	2.4	3.2	0.1	0.0	0.0	49.4	48.5	1.0	0.8	0.0	0.0	99.4	20.0	48.0	52.0
45502	SPRINGFIELD	96.1	94.9	2.1	2.8	0.4	0.6	0.6	0.8	5.2	5.7	6.3	6.7	5.0	23.5	32.2	13.6	1.8	78.7	43.3	49.3	50.7
45503	SPRINGFIELD	91.2	88.8	5.8	7.2	1.1	1.8	0.9	1.1	6.8	6.1	6.1	6.4	6.0	23.9	25.7	15.2	3.8	77.1	40.8	46.8	53.2
45504	SPRINGFIELD	93.3	91.3	3.7	4.8	0.8	1.3	1.0	1.2	5.6	5.4	5.6	9.6	10.9	21.6	25.4	13.0	2.9	79.9	37.5	47.9	52.1
45505	SPRINGFIELD	82.0	78.8	14.7	17.3	0.2	0.3	1.2	1.4	7.8	7.4	6.9	6.6	6.2	25.8	25.5	12.0	1.6	73.8	36.9	47.4	52.6
45506	SPRINGFIELD	55.9	51.7	40.3	44.2	0.2	0.3	1.1	1.2	6.8	6.8	6.9	7.5	6.5	23.7	26.6	12.7	2.6	74.9	38.3	47.7	52.3
45601	CHILLICOTHE	90.1	88.4	7.7	8.7	0.5	0.7	0.6	0.8	5.9	5.8	5.9	6.0	6.6	29.0	27.4	11.6	1.8	78.8	39.1	53.0	47.0
45612	BAINBRIDGE	98.3	98.0	0.5	0.6	0.1	0.1	0.6	0.7	6.9	7.1	7.2	7.4	6.0	26.4	27.2	10.6	1.3	74.2	37.1	50.3	49.7
45613	BEAVER	93.6	92.8	2.8	3.1	0.1	0.1	0.6	0.7	7.4	7.3	7.3	6.8	6.1	27.0	26.8	10.6	1.0	73.9	36.6	50.3	49.7
45614	BIDWELL	93.4	92.1	4.5	5.2	0.4	0.6	0.6	0.8	6.1	6.3	6.6	6.3	5.9	24.0	30.3	12.2	2.1	77.0	40.9	48.5	51.5
45616	BLUE CREEK	96.9	96.4	0.1	0.1	0.3	0.5	0.7	0.9	6.5	6.8	6.9	6.3	4.9	25.6	29.2	12.4	1.3	76.1	39.6	49.6	50.4
45619	CHESAPEAKE	98.0	97.5	0.9	1.1	0.2	0.4	0.5	0.7	6.1	6.3	6.3	6.0	5.2	26.9	28.5	13.2	1.5	77.6	40.4	49.0	51.0
45620	CHESHIRE	97.6	97.3	0.8	0.9	0.1	0.1	0.4	0.5	6.4	6.9	7.1	6.2	5.0	23.9	30.6	12.6	1.3	75.8	40.7	49.4	50.6
45622	CREOLA	98.8	98.5	0.2	0.2	0.0	0.0	0.2	0.4	6.4	6.4	6.6	7.1	6.8	25.3	29.0	11.2	1.0	76.8	38.4	51.2	48.8
45623	CROWN CITY	98.4	97.9	0.4	0.5	0.1	0.1	1.1	1.4	7.2	7.1	7.3	6.8	5.4	27.0	26.6	11.6	1.1	74.3	37.6	50.8	49.2
45628	FRANKFORT	93.6	92.5	4.3	5.0	0.1	0.2	0.4	0.5	6.0	6.4	6.7	6.7	5.5	25.7	29.4	11.7	1.8	76.5	40.0	50.1	49.9
45629	FRANKLIN FURNACE	95.6	94.6	2.6	3.3	0.1	0.1	0.5	0.7	5.9	6.0	7.0	10.8	4.7	23.7	28.8	11.8	1.3	73.5	38.3	51.7	48.3
45631	GALLIPOLIS	94.4	93.3	3.4	3.9	0.5	0.8	0.6	0.8	5.8	5.7	5.9	6.6	6.1	24.4	28.9	14.3	2.2	78.9	41.4	48.0	52.0
45634	HAMDEN	97.5	97.2	0.6	0.7	0.0	0.1	0.9	1.1	7.2	7.3	7.4	6.4	4.7	26.3	26.3	12.3	2.0	74.1	38.2	48.7	51.3
45638	IRONTON	95.7	95.0	3.0	3.5	0.2	0.3	0.5	0.7	5.8	5.9	6.1	6.4	5.4	24.7	27.6	15.3	2.6	78.2	41.7	47.4	52.6
45640	JACKSON	98.0	97.6	0.6	0.7	0.2	0.3	0.7	0.9	6.2	6.3	6.5	6.4	6.0	26.0	27.8	12.8	2.1	77.0	39.6	48.1	51.9
45644	KINGSTON	98.1	97.6	0.6	0.8	0.2	0.3	0.4	0.5	6.3	6.7	7.0	6.7	4.7	25.7	29.5	11.7	1.8	76.0	40.6	49.3	50.7
45645	KITTS HILL	98.9	98.6	0.1	0.1	0.1	0.2	0.6	1.0	6.7	6.6	6.6	6.8	5.8	28.5	27.5	10.6	0.9	76.0	37.7	49.7	50.3
45646	LATHAM	98.3	97.7	0.3	0.5	0.0	0.3	1.1	1.6	7.8	7.8	7.0	6.8	5.5	26.8	26.3	10.9	1.0	72.9	37.2	50.0	50.0
45647	LONDONDERRY	98.4	98.1	0.5	0.5	0.2	0.2	0.5	0.6	7.6	7.7	7.8	6.7	5.3	25.8	27.5	10.7	1.0	72.7	37.1	50.6	49.4
45648	LUCASVILLE	90.6	89.2	7.2	8.1	0.2	0.3	0.6	0.8	5.7	5.9	6.3	6.3	6.5	31.8	25.2	10.9	1.3	78.2	36.7	55.0	45.0
45650	LYNX	97.2	97.2	0.0	0.0	0.0	0.0	1.4	0.0	5.6	5.6	5.6	5.6	5.6	26.4	30.6	13.9	1.4	79.2	42.0	51.4	48.6
45651	MC ARTHUR	98.1	97.7	0.3	0.4	0.1	0.2	0.4	0.5	7.4	7.3	7.5	7.4	6.1	25.8	26.1	11.0	1.4	73.4	36.4	49.4	50.6
45652	MC DERMOTT	98.1	97.8	0.2	0.3	0.1	0.1	0.3	0.5	6.3	5.6	6.6	6.8	5.7	25.6	28.7	12.8	1.9	77.0	40.4	50.2	49.8
45653	MINFORD	98.7	98.4	0.0	0.0	0.1	0.1	0.5	0.6	6.2	6.6	6.7	6.3	5.0	26.6	29.1	11.8	1.7	76.5	39.9	50.5	49.5
45654	NEW PLYMOUTH	98.3	98.0	0.1	0.1	0.0	0.0	0.2	0.2	7.0	7.2	7.3	6.4	5.1	26.4	28.2	11.7	0.7	74.4	38.3	50.9	49.1
45656	OAK HILL	98.1	97.7	0.4	0.4	0.3	0.4	0.3	0.4	6.2	6.6	6.7	6.5	5.3	26.4	28.4	12.1	1.8	76.5	39.6	48.7	51.3
45657	OTWAY	96.9	96.3	0.0	0.0	0.2	0.2	0.7	0.9	6.5	6.7	6.9	7.0	5.3	28.1	27.1	11.2	1.3	75.6	37.9	50.4	49.6
45658	PATRIOT	97.8	97.3	0.6	0.7	0.1	0.2	0.5	0.5	7.8	7.7	7.8	7.5	6.0	26.1	25.7	10.5	1.0	72.1	35.1	50.9	49.1
45659	PEDRO	98.2	97.7	0.8	0.9	0.0	0.0	0.3	0.4	6.7	7.3	7.2	7.5	6.6	26.8	27.5	9.7	0.8	74.4	35.8	49.5	50.5
45660	PEEBLES	97.6	97.3	0.2	0.2	0.1	0.2	0.8	1.0	6.8	6.8	6.9	7.3	5.8	26.5	26.7	11.7	1.4	74.7	37.8	49.7	50.3
45661	PIKETON	97.6	97.1	0.5	0.6	0.2	0.3	0.5	0.6	7.0	7.0	7.0	6.8	5.7	27.2	26.5	11.2	1.6	74.9	37.3	48.6	51.4
45662	PORTSMOUTH	93.5	92.2	3.4	4.0	0.5	0.8	0.7	1.0	6.4	6.2	5.9	6.2	6.5	24.7	25.3	15.5	3.4	78.2	40.2	46.4	53.6
45663	WEST PORTSMOUTH	97.4	96.9	0.1	0.1	0.1	0.1	0.3	0.4	7.0	6.4	6.3	6.5	6.6	26.5	26.9	12.6	1.4	76.2	38.3	48.3	51.7
45669	PROCTORVILLE	98.1	97.6	0.5	0.6	0.4	0.7	0.5	0.7	5.4	5.6	5.9	6.4	5.0	25.2	30.0	14.8	1.8	79.3	42.6	49.0	51.0
45671	RARDEN	96.5	95.3	0.0	0.2	0.0	0.2	1.3	1.7	7.2	7.2	7.4	7.4	6.2	29.9	24.2	9.3	1.1	73.2	35.3	51.4	48.6
45672	RAY	97.0	96.5	1.1	1.2	0.2	0.3	0.6	0.8	6.6	6.6	7.0	6.9	6.3	27.2	28.2	10.3	1.0	75.6	38.0	51.7	48.3
45673	RICHMOND DALE	97.0	96.7	1.5	1.8	0.3	0.3	0.8	0.5	6.1	6.1	6.9	6.4	5.1	26.8	29.8	11.5	1.3	76.8	39.8	51.3	48.7
45675	ROCK CAMP	99.1	99.1	0.0	0.0	0.4	0.4	0.4	0.4	5.8	5.8	6.3	7.1	6.3	27.7	29.9	10.3	0.9	78.1	39.0	50.9	49.1
45678	SCOTTOWN	99.0	98.8	0.2	0.2	0.1	0.1	0.6	0.8	7.3	7.4	7.3	6.5	5.1	27.4	27.6	10.5	0.9	74.2	37.8	51.0	49.0
45679	SEAMAN	98.2	97.9	0.2	0.2	0.1	0.2	0.7	0.8	7.0	6.9	6.9	7.2	5.8	25.9	26.1	12.6	1.7	74.8	37.6	47.6	52.4
45680	SOUTH POINT	94.0	92.9	4.0	4.7	0.1	0.2	0.7	0.9	6.7	6.6	6.5	6.1	5.3	25.9	26.8	14.1	2.1	76.6	39.7	47.5	52.5
45681	SOUTH SALEM	97.8	97.4	1.2	1.4	0.1	0.1	1.1	1.6	5.7	6.1	6.4	8.4	5.1	26.6	29.8	10.8	1.0	76.2	39.3	51.3	48.7
45682	SOUTH WEBSTER	98.5	98.2	0.4	0.4	0.2	0.2	0.4	0.5	6.2	6.5	7.1	7.8	6.0	26.6	27.3	11.2	1.2	75.4	37.1	49.9	50.1
45684	STOUT	98.3	98.0	0.0	0.0	0.2	0.2	0.6	0.8	6.3	6.6	6.5	5.8	5.2	24.4	31.3	12.6	1.2	77.0	41.2	49.7	50.3
45685	THURMAN	95.7	94.8	1.6	1.9	0.7	1.1	0.5	0.7	6.6	6.3	6.1	10.7	12.1	24.4	22.4	10.1	1.3	77.5	31.1	49.1	50.9
45686	VINTON	97.0	96.5	1.1	1.3	0.1	0.1	0.5	0.6	6.3	6.7	6.9	6.4	5.6	26.1	29.5	11.2	1.2	76.1	39.2	50.4	49.6
45688	WATERLOO	98.0	97.7	0.9	1.1	0.0	0.0	0.9	1.3	6.3	6.3	6.1	6.1	6.1	25.6	30.0	11.6	1.7	77.8	40.6	48.2	51.8
45690	WAVERLY	97.0	96.4	0.8	0.9	0.3	0.5	0.5	0.7	6.9	6.9	6.7	6.5	5.9	25.7	25.6	12.8	3.1	75.6	38.4	48.2	51.8
45692	WELLSTON	97.8	97.4	0.5	0.5	0.2	0.3	0.7	0.9	7.2	6.9	7.1	6.8	6.1	26.4	26.3	11.2	2.0	74.7	37.0	48.2	51.8
45693	WEST UNION	97.7	97.3	0.3	0.3	0.2	0.3	0.6	0.8	6.4	6.5	6.6	6.4	5.3	26.1	27.4	13.1	2.3	76.6	39.8	48.0	52.0
45694	WHEELERSBURG	98.1	97.6	0.2	0.3	0.2	0.3	0.5	0.6	6.4	6.5	6.6	6.2	5.3	25.7	27.5	13.6	2.2	76.7	40.0	47.5	52.5
45695	WILKESVILLE	98.3	98.1	0.2	0.2	0.1	0.1	0.2	0.2	6.2	6.3	6.6	6.3	5.6	27.2	28.6	12.2	1.0	77.2	39.2	51.0	49.0
45696	WILLOW WOOD	99.2	99.1	0.1	0.1	0.1	0.3	0.5	0.7	7.4	7.5	7.1	6.6	5.1	25.9	28.2	11.0	1.1	74.0	38.7	50.3	49.7
45697	WINCHESTER	98.7	98.4	0.3	0.4	0.1	0.2	0.5	0.6	6.8	6.8	7.1	7.5	5.8	27.1	26.7	11.0	1.3	74.7	37.4	49.6	50.4
45701	ATHENS	91.1	88.3	3.1	3.5	3.4	5.4	1.3	1.7	3.4	2.9	2.9	17.5	32.1	19.0	15.3	6.1	0.8	88.9	23.6	47.9	52.1
45710	ALBANY	97.9	97.5	0.6	0.7	0.2	0.3	0.8	1.0	6.0	6.2	6.5	6.4	5.4	27.5	29.5	10.9	1.6	77.5	39.6	50.3	49.7
45711	AMESVILLE	87.2	85.6	7.7	8.5	0.1	0.1	0.7	0.8	5.8	7.0	6.5	6.8	5.3	27.5	29.7	10.1	1.2	76.0	38.7	49.2	50.8
45714	BELPRE	96.4	95.7	1.7	2.0	0.4	0.6	0.5	0.6	6.0	6.1	6.2	5.6	4.9	25.0	29.1	15.0	2.1	78.2	42.0	47.6	52.4
45715	BEVERLY	98.6	98.4	0.6	0.7	0.0	0.1	0.4	0.5	5.7	6.0	6.3	6.0	4.6	23.6	28.5	16.2	3.1	78.1	43.3	48.8	51.2
45723	COOLVILLE	98.4	98.1	0.5	0.5	0.1	0.2	0.4	0.4	4.8	5.9	6.8	6.8	4.7	24.8	30.6	13.5	2.2	78.1	42.4	50.6	49.4
45724	CUTLER	92.1	90.8	4.4	5.1	0.3	0.4	0.3	0.3	6.2	6.5	6.9	6.8	5.0	25.6	30.0	11.3	1.6	76.2	40.1	52.2	47.8
45727	DEXTER CITY	99.7	99.7	0.0	0.0	0.0	0.0	0.5	0.5	5.9	6.8	6.8	6.6	6.1	25.7	29.0	11.7	1.2	76.4	39.3	50.7	49.3
45729	FLEMING	98.2	97.7	0.3	0.4	0.1	0.2	0.4	0.6	6.4	6.9	7.4	6.4	4.5	24.4	31.6	11.1	1.2	75.2	40.8	50.4	49.6
45732	GLOUSTER	96.9	96.3	1.1	1.3	0.1	0.1	0.5	0.7	6.9	7.0	7.1	7.2	5.6	25.4	27.8	11.3	1.6	74.4	38.4	49.5	50.5
45734	GRAYSVILLE	99.4	99.2	0.0	0.0	0.0	0.0	0.6	0.8	5.2	5.6	6.1	6.1	4.7	23.9	31.8	14.8	1.9	79.5	43.8	51.6	48.4
45735	GUYSVILLE	95.8	95.0	1.4	1.5	0.4	0.7	0.6	0.7	6.2	6.7	7.4	7.2	5.3	25.8	29.8	10.3	1.4	75.0	38.6	50.7	49.3
45741	LANGSVILLE	97.9	97.7	0.3	0.3	0.1	0.1	1.0	1.2	6.0	6.1	6.1	5.9	5.0	25.5	31.7	12.5	1.3	78.3	41.8	49.2	50.8
45742	LITTLE HOCKING	96.8	96.2	1.4	1.6	0.3	0.4	0.6	0.8	5.3	5.8	6.4	6.4	4.7	24.9	32.4	13.0	1.1	78.5	42.7	50.1	49.9
45743	LONG BOTTOM	97.5	97.0	0.1	0.1	0.0	0.0	2.0	2.6	5.9	6.1	6.5	6.5	5.3	26.9	29.4	12.2	1.3	77.9	40.7	50.6	49.4
45744	LOWELL	98.8	98.4	0.3	0.3	0.5	0.7	0.5	0.7	6.3	6.5	6.9	6.8	4.4	24.4	28.6	14.5	1.6	75.9	41.4	49.8	50.2
45745	LOWER SALEM	98.8	98.6	0.1	0.1	0.1	0.1	0.4	0.5	5.6	6.0	6.3	6.3	5.0	25.0	31.0	12.7	2.0	78.2	42.0	50.9	49.1
45746	MACKSBURG	98.6	98.6	0.0	0.0	0.2	0.2	0.5	0.7	5.2	5.9	6.1	7.5	5.6	25.1	30.4	12.9	1.4	78.0	41.4	54.1	45.9
45750	MARIETTA	97.4	96.6	0.6	0.7	0.8	1.2	0.6	0.8	5.2	5.2	5.5	7.4	7.5	22.7	28.8	14.8	3.0	80.4	42.2	47.7	52.3
45760	MIDDLEPORT	96.5	95.9	1.7	2.0	0.1	0.2	0.7	0.9	6.1	6.1	6.0	6.2	5.6	23.9	27.9	15.4	2.8	78.0	42.0	47.3	52.7
45761	MILLFIELD	95.5	94.2	1.2	1.3	1.2	2.0	0.7	0.9	6.4	6.2	6.4	6.8	6.4	28.7	27.8	10.0	1.2	76.9	37.3	49.5	50.5
45764	NELSONVILLE	95.3	94.4	2.8	3.3	0.3	0.5	0.8	1.1	5.6	5.3	5.1	10.1	10.9	26.1	24.5	10.9	1.6	80.4	34.0	54.3	45.7
45766	NEW MARSHFIELD	98.2	97.9	0.2	0.2	0.1	0.2	0.2	0.2	6.9	7.0	6.9	6.3	5.0	29.2	28.0	9.7	1.0	75.8	36.9	49.3	50.7
45767	NEW MATAMORAS	99.0	98.9	0.2	0.2	0.1	0.1	0.3	0.4	5.8	5.8	5.9	6.0	5.2	24.2	28.5	16.7	1.9	78.9	42.8	48.7	51.3
45768	NEWPORT	99.8	99.7	0.1	0.1	0.0	0.1	0.3	0.5	5.9	6.2	6.4	6.1	4.4	26.6	30.1	12.9	1.4	77.8	41.4	49.1	50.9
45769	POMEROY	97.5	97.1	0.8	0.9	0.1	0.2	0.4	0.5	5.7	5.4	5.5	6.1	6.0	24.5	30.6	13.5	2.9	79.8	42.7	47.7	52.3
45770	PORTLAND	97.3	96.4	0.7	0.9	0.3	0.4	0.4	0.5	3.8	6.4	9.5	6.3	5.0	25.8	30.6	10.9	1.8	76.5	40.9	50.9	49.1
45771	RACINE	98.4	98.1	0.6	0.6	0.1	0.2	0.2	0.2	5.7	5.9	6.4	6.0	4.6	25.1	29.8	14.6	1.9	78.3	42.4	49.7	50.3
45772	REEDSVILLE	98.5	97.9	0.1	0.1	0.0	0.0	1.0	1.3	5.1	5.9	6.6	6.7	5.3	24.3	30.7	13.3	2.2	78.1	41.9	49.2	50.8
45773	RENO	98.8	98.6	0.2	0.2	0.2	0.4	0.4	0.4	6.0	6.4	6.8	6.0	4.3	25.9	30.7	12.8	1.2	77.2	41.9	49.6	50.4
45775	RUTLAND	98.4	98.2	0.2	0.2	0.1	0.2	0.8	1.0	6.0	6.1	6.3	6.3	5.5	24.6	31.9	11.7	1.6	77.8	41.7	49.6	50.4
45776	SHADE	97.9	97.4	0.7	0.8	0.1	0.3	0.5	0.6	6.3	6.3	6.2	6.3	6.8	27.2	29.4	9.9	1.5	77.3	38.6	50.4	49.6
45778	STEWART	89.4	88.0	6.0	6.7	0.2	0.3	0.7	0.8	5.9	6.8	7.2	7.2	5.7	27.1	29.2	10.0	0.9	75.3	38.0	49.5	50.5
45780	THE PLAINS	94.0	92.6	2.5	2.8	1.1	1.9	0.8	1.1	6.7	6.0	5.7	6.2	7.0	27.3	22.4	13.9	4.8	78.2	37.9	45.1	54.9
45784	VINCENT	96.7	96.1	1.6	1.8	0.2	0.4	0.5	0.7	5.9	6.7	7.3	6.6	4.3	23.7	33.1	11.4	0.9	76.0	42.0	50.9	49.1
	OHIO	85.0	83.1	11.5	12.2	1.2	1.9	1.9	2.4	6.6	6.5	6.6	7.1	6.7	25.9	26.9	11.7	2.1	76.2	38.2	48.7	51.3
	UNITED STATES	75.1	72.0	12.3	12.7	3.8	4.6	12.5	15.7	6.8	6.7	6.6	7.1	6.9	27.0	26.0	10.9	1.9	75.7	36.9	49.2	50.8

ZIP CODE				2009 HOUSEHOLD INCOME DISTRIBUTION (%)					MEDIAN HOUSEHOLD INCOME					2009 HOME VALUE DISTRIBUTION (%)					
#	POST OFFICE NAME	2009 Per Capita Income	2009 HH Income Base	Less than $25,000	$25,000 to $49,999	$50,000 to $99,999	$100,000 to $149,999	$150,000 or More	2009	2014	2009 National Centile	2009 State Centile	2009 Home Value Base	Less than $50,000	$50,000 to $89,999	$90,000 to $174,999	$175,000 to $399,999	$400,000 or More	2009 Median Home Value
45469	DAYTON	13957	115	53.9	37.4	4.3	1.7	2.6	21591	21884	2	2	16	0.0	31.3	37.5	31.3	0.0	100000
45502	SPRINGFIELD	29208	7010	11.6	23.4	45.2	13.4	6.4	66742	68280	85	87	5981	12.9	9.9	54.3	21.9	1.0	129444
45503	SPRINGFIELD	25892	13153	21.2	27.8	38.3	8.7	3.9	50687	53182	63	52	8836	7.4	31.2	53.8	6.7	1.0	99931
45504	SPRINGFIELD	25150	6858	20.6	26.5	36.9	10.3	5.7	52401	55324	67	59	4708	12.2	23.1	48.5	14.4	1.7	107438
45505	SPRINGFIELD	19936	8553	31.3	30.9	31.0	4.9	2.0	37300	40443	24	15	4960	18.0	54.7	22.9	4.2	0.2	73201
45506	SPRINGFIELD	20258	5901	31.5	27.1	31.1	8.1	2.3	40601	44111	35	22	3612	18.2	48.8	27.1	5.2	0.6	75082
45601	CHILLICOTHE	21928	21237	26.5	26.5	36.2	7.5	3.3	46141	49104	52	36	15085	20.5	23.8	42.0	12.8	0.9	98400
45612	BAINBRIDGE	17747	2030	32.1	31.4	28.7	5.7	2.1	38330	40761	28	17	1570	34.0	25.8	30.8	7.9	1.5	73030
45613	BEAVER	19115	1435	29.0	27.5	36.4	5.8	1.4	42007	45186	39	25	1095	34.0	23.7	34.1	7.7	0.5	75804
45614	BIDWELL	19008	1787	37.0	26.7	27.0	7.2	2.1	36562	37665	22	13	1375	28.1	26.0	37.5	7.7	0.6	84250
45616	BLUE CREEK	16068	758	43.1	28.9	22.6	3.3	2.1	31258	32868	10	6	588	38.8	33.8	22.1	4.9	0.3	62745
45619	CHESAPEAKE	19579	3492	31.2	32.2	29.4	5.6	1.7	37940	39441	26	16	2616	18.2	29.1	43.3	8.5	0.8	93125
45620	CHESHIRE	20359	501	27.5	30.3	35.1	6.0	1.0	43474	45765	44	29	398	26.6	31.7	39.4	2.3	0.0	81538
45622	CREOLA	16902	192	33.3	37.0	22.4	5.2	2.1	33873	35000	15	8	160	24.4	31.3	36.3	7.5	0.6	85263
45623	CROWN CITY	16924	1481	34.3	37.1	23.8	3.6	1.1	31832	32786	11	7	1193	32.6	30.3	30.4	5.9	0.8	73235
45628	FRANKFORT	21522	1734	23.9	28.3	38.2	7.1	2.5	47689	48821	56	41	1333	14.7	26.6	46.2	11.5	1.0	101974
45629	FRANKLIN FURNACE	18946	1321	30.2	34.7	27.3	4.9	2.9	37409	39374	25	15	1054	16.0	41.0	35.0	6.5	1.4	81868
45631	GALLIPOLIS	21375	6321	32.6	28.8	28.6	7.5	2.6	39205	40223	30	19	4422	25.3	28.4	35.7	9.5	1.1	85219
45634	HAMDEN	16741	841	31.6	35.7	28.1	3.6	1.1	35477	36231	19	11	642	24.1	44.4	29.1	2.3	0.0	76301
45638	IRONTON	18589	8773	40.4	26.8	26.3	4.9	1.7	32756	34094	13	8	6113	18.6	41.9	34.3	5.1	0.2	81057
45640	JACKSON	19026	6214	32.3	28.9	31.9	5.1	1.8	38348	40431	28	17	4500	18.1	34.4	36.5	9.7	1.2	87505
45644	KINGSTON	24181	1450	18.3	25.0	42.0	10.6	4.1	55473	55543	72	68	1193	12.7	16.5	45.1	24.2	1.5	123573
45645	KITTS HILL	17300	1141	34.0	26.8	30.9	6.9	1.3	38749	41300	29	18	937	25.6	31.5	36.7	6.2	0.0	77989
45646	LATHAM	13932	148	43.2	31.8	21.6	3.4	0.0	30665	31695	9	6	113	51.3	26.5	17.7	4.4	0.0	49063
45647	LONDONDERRY	19110	800	24.6	30.0	38.4	6.0	1.0	43368	48104	43	29	660	30.5	27.7	36.8	4.2	0.8	71724
45648	LUCASVILLE	17350	4430	35.8	29.3	27.7	5.7	1.4	35725	38336	20	11	3498	27.6	32.1	31.3	8.4	0.6	77663
45650	LYNX	14694	31	48.4	32.3	16.1	3.2	0.0	26108	28601	4	3	24	50.0	37.5	12.5	0.0	0.0	50000
45651	MC ARTHUR	17593	2368	34.0	32.3	26.9	4.5	2.3	35428	36496	19	11	1723	23.3	36.0	33.5	6.9	0.3	79971
45652	MC DERMOTT	19743	1218	36.0	32.4	24.1	4.5	3.0	34821	36677	17	9	988	31.3	37.9	25.1	4.5	1.3	69510
45653	MINFORD	18823	1389	29.0	28.9	34.0	6.8	1.3	42613	46088	41	27	1150	18.8	32.0	38.8	9.3	1.1	89182
45654	NEW PLYMOUTH	17055	362	28.2	33.4	34.5	2.2	1.7	39072	40717	30	19	291	34.0	26.8	31.6	5.8	1.7	71471
45656	OAK HILL	17343	2688	36.8	31.4	26.3	3.6	1.9	35027	36860	18	10	2080	30.2	36.3	23.8	9.0	0.6	69313
45657	OTWAY	18443	988	33.3	29.4	28.8	4.9	3.6	38806	41483	29	18	787	28.6	41.4	24.7	5.2	0.1	66807
45658	PATRIOT	16329	869	33.4	31.8	26.5	6.1	2.3	36890	37371	23	14	720	29.3	25.4	39.9	4.7	0.7	83200
45659	PEDRO	13809	1265	42.8	28.5	24.8	3.6	0.2	31381	32933	10	6	1032	36.2	32.9	27.2	3.2	0.4	67647
45660	PEEBLES	16374	3292	38.5	29.3	25.8	5.3	1.2	34037	36069	16	8	2467	30.6	29.9	30.6	7.6	1.3	76532
45661	PIKETON	18552	2790	34.3	27.4	30.3	5.5	2.5	38088	39553	27	16	2022	29.9	26.0	33.9	8.9	1.3	79123
45662	PORTSMOUTH	19718	12476	42.4	26.9	24.1	3.8	2.8	30960	32982	10	6	7219	26.7	42.0	26.0	5.0	0.3	69564
45663	WEST PORTSMOUTH	17304	2672	35.3	31.4	26.6	5.5	1.2	35000	37011	18	10	2044	39.4	39.9	16.1	4.2	0.3	58504
45669	PROCTORVILLE	21459	4165	28.0	30.5	33.1	5.3	3.1	41469	44385	38	24	3370	15.5	20.4	48.0	14.8	1.2	109797
45671	RARDEN	18138	198	34.8	31.3	28.3	4.5	1.0	35747	37550	20	11	147	32.7	37.4	25.2	4.8	0.0	65313
45672	RAY	19350	789	27.1	30.7	35.4	5.3	1.5	41747	45306	38	25	650	30.2	28.8	32.2	8.8	0.2	72826
45673	RICHMOND DALE	23676	167	25.1	30.5	31.7	7.2	5.4	44087	47872	46	32	130	26.2	29.2	30.0	14.6	0.0	85000
45675	ROCK CAMP	18970	83	31.3	24.1	34.9	6.0	3.6	43373	49104	43	29	67	22.4	41.8	32.8	3.0	0.0	76429
45678	SCOTTOWN	18243	437	37.8	25.4	29.7	5.5	1.6	37235	39693	24	15	358	28.8	21.5	36.9	11.2	1.7	89000
45679	SEAMAN	17706	1049	32.5	29.0	33.5	3.8	1.2	38340	40958	28	17	792	14.8	33.2	39.6	9.8	2.5	92078
45680	SOUTH POINT	18240	5280	34.8	29.5	30.0	3.8	1.8	36085	37877	21	12	3741	15.0	36.4	42.2	5.7	0.7	88380
45681	SOUTH SALEM	19578	568	23.4	29.9	40.3	4.6	1.8	46113	48429	52	36	476	20.0	28.2	39.3	11.8	0.8	95294
45682	SOUTH WEBSTER	16418	955	33.4	31.0	31.2	3.8	0.6	37619	41611	26	15	730	29.7	36.4	26.4	7.1	0.3	71429
45684	STOUT	17298	640	39.7	33.4	19.1	4.8	3.0	32578	33656	13	8	522	36.4	32.4	20.9	9.2	1.1	65581
45685	THURMAN	20470	602	37.0	27.4	26.6	7.5	1.5	36069	37273	21	12	421	29.5	26.8	30.6	10.7	2.4	78542
45686	VINTON	17666	1306	36.5	30.2	25.9	6.0	1.4	36425	37117	22	12	1098	39.0	31.1	24.1	5.7	0.0	64068
45688	WATERLOO	13090	193	46.6	32.6	18.1	2.6	0.0	28085	30950	6	4	144	40.3	11.8	29.9	18.1	0.0	75000
45690	WAVERLY	21001	5663	29.9	27.7	31.7	8.3	2.3	42209	45041	40	26	3740	19.3	28.7	40.4	11.1	0.6	92261
45692	WELLSTON	16886	3751	33.3	31.7	29.8	4.7	0.5	38185	39503	27	17	2656	28.2	37.8	27.6	6.1	0.3	69623
45693	WEST UNION	18947	3459	33.1	31.0	28.2	5.6	2.1	37078	38533	24	14	2496	18.8	36.1	34.7	10.0	0.4	85000
45694	WHEELERSBURG	20591	4555	28.9	30.0	33.0	5.5	2.6	41147	44887	36	23	3375	17.1	33.2	39.6	9.2	0.9	89777
45695	WILKESVILLE	19001	356	29.5	36.8	27.5	5.3	0.8	37135	37649	24	15	298	26.8	37.2	28.2	7.7	0.0	77500
45696	WILLOW WOOD	15168	610	39.8	30.7	24.6	4.4	0.5	35261	36257	19	10	499	35.5	22.0	30.1	12.2	0.2	69605
45697	WINCHESTER	20303	1934	24.5	28.9	38.2	6.0	2.4	45328	49086	49	34	1525	15.5	26.5	42.8	13.0	2.2	96943
45701	ATHENS	19799	10767	43.1	22.2	22.9	7.3	4.5	31924	34305	11	7	5201	17.7	20.4	43.2	17.1	1.6	107317
45710	ALBANY	21136	1912	27.9	27.0	35.7	6.9	2.5	43985	48497	45	31	1493	22.3	28.3	36.1	11.3	1.9	89152
45711	AMESVILLE	19718	499	28.3	34.1	31.5	5.2	1.0	39616	41456	32	20	393	24.4	35.1	23.9	12.7	3.8	75147
45714	BELPRE	23332	4193	28.1	31.3	30.1	7.9	2.5	40806	44315	35	23	2963	15.7	32.1	42.2	9.4	0.6	92509
45715	BEVERLY	22375	1008	30.0	30.0	29.6	8.5	2.0	40860	43999	36	23	767	17.3	33.1	42.0	6.8	0.8	89407
45723	COOLVILLE	21279	1487	27.6	34.1	29.8	4.8	3.8	40701	43261	35	23	1259	31.8	38.9	25.8	2.8	0.7	67659
45724	CUTLER	18844	1011	27.0	30.8	36.0	4.6	1.6	40488	44166	34	22	873	24.9	24.2	35.9	14.1	1.0	91214
45727	DEXTER CITY	16960	216	29.2	33.8	32.4	3.7	0.9	38816	40684	29	18	180	35.0	30.6	27.8	6.1	0.6	70000
45729	FLEMING	23083	457	20.6	20.1	48.4	7.7	3.3	54307	55530	70	64	402	16.4	22.4	30.6	28.4	2.2	120139
45732	GLOUSTER	16088	2631	40.1	30.3	25.6	3.1	0.8	31972	33919	11	7	1994	48.8	32.9	17.0	1.1	0.2	51319
45734	GRAYSVILLE	18445	313	27.2	35.5	34.5	2.9	0.0	40420	42481	34	22	263	39.5	29.7	25.9	4.2	0.8	59821
45735	GUYSVILLE	20213	631	33.9	28.7	29.2	5.2	3.0	39472	42205	31	20	530	25.3	31.9	32.5	8.3	2.1	78108
45741	LANGSVILLE	15522	428	41.6	26.9	25.7	5.4	0.5	30183	31728	8	5	358	32.7	32.4	31.0	3.6	0.3	76154
45742	LITTLE HOCKING	23274	1054	16.5	28.6	42.5	10.0	2.5	54735	55456	71	66	909	18.4	32.2	37.5	10.9	1.0	88942
45743	LONG BOTTOM	17474	635	32.4	33.1	29.3	3.3	1.9	35261	36733	19	10	531	25.0	37.7	31.8	5.5	0.0	69167
45744	LOWELL	20974	1004	27.1	30.3	36.2	4.0	2.5	43850	47302	45	30	843	29.3	29.2	29.9	10.3	1.3	80069
45745	LOWER SALEM	17714	489	28.0	36.4	31.9	3.3	0.4	38542	41212	28	18	408	31.1	26.7	37.3	4.9	0.0	74839
45746	MACKSBURG	15520	171	34.5	35.7	28.1	1.8	0.0	34457	36787	16	9	141	52.5	19.9	25.5	2.1	0.0	48971
45750	MARIETTA	22928	11376	28.3	30.5	30.9	7.1	3.3	41198	45237	37	24	8089	17.2	28.5	42.1	11.0	1.1	94702
45760	MIDDLEPORT	15584	1593	45.3	28.3	22.4	3.6	0.4	27252	28680	5	4	1083	41.5	38.7	19.1	0.7	0.0	58114
45761	MILLFIELD	17758	1105	35.0	30.2	28.7	4.6	1.4	35623	37927	20	11	794	39.8	31.6	21.7	5.7	1.3	60267
45764	NELSONVILLE	16190	3677	42.1	29.5	23.8	3.6	1.0	29833	31616	8	5	2255	38.4	34.1	24.4	2.5	0.5	62630
45766	NEW MARSHFIELD	22295	711	20.8	26.7	45.1	6.0	1.3	51358	52374	65	55	555	39.1	22.5	31.7	6.5	0.2	65000
45767	NEW MATAMORAS	19332	1123	34.4	33.9	24.7	4.6	2.4	36037	38029	21	12	836	36.2	36.6	23.2	3.2	0.7	65714
45768	NEWPORT	20527	701	23.5	32.1	36.9	5.0	2.4	44165	48260	46	32	575	23.3	35.1	36.2	4.3	1.0	81491
45769	POMEROY	17634	2476	36.5	33.0	25.3	4.0	1.3	33336	34461	14	8	1922	33.7	32.5	28.4	5.4	0.1	69684
45770	PORTLAND	16100	312	33.3	35.9	28.8	1.0	1.0	33193	34554	14	8	249	41.4	25.7	26.9	6.0	0.0	68500
45771	RACINE	19190	1698	32.9	30.9	30.4	4.4	1.5	37245	39403	24	15	1358	28.9	30.9	34.5	5.4	0.4	78544
45772	REEDSVILLE	18966	814	31.6	32.4	29.7	3.7	2.6	37838	40000	26	16	698	36.5	28.2	32.2	2.1	0.9	68367
45773	RENO	21741	191	25.7	32.5	31.4	7.3	3.1	43124	46206	43	28	163	22.1	30.1	38.0	8.0	1.8	87667
45775	RUTLAND	15146	568	39.8	31.0	24.6	3.5	1.1	31426	32698	10	6	469	38.8	34.1	24.7	2.3	0.0	63293
45776	SHADE	19224	330	37.3	26.7	29.7	4.2	2.1	36607	38488	22	13	265	35.5	21.5	33.6	9.1	0.4	77188
45778	STEWART	19007	372	35.5	28.2	29.0	4.6	2.7	37433	39648	25	15	295	27.5	33.6	23.7	12.5	2.7	72500
45780	THE PLAINS	21199	1240	35.2	24.7	32.4	5.8	1.9	38271	43048	27	17	672	25.9	24.7	42.1	7.0	0.3	89111
45784	VINCENT	23493	1060	16.3	29.0	40.8	11.7	2.2	54435	55365	70	65	934	14.2	20.3	43.5	21.1	0.9	115972
	OHIO	26577		21.4	25.9	36.7	10.4	5.7	52400	54553				10.3	22.0	45.6	19.3	2.8	114865
	UNITED STATES	27277		20.9	24.4	35.3	11.7	7.6	54719	56938				9.3	13.1	31.6	32.6	13.5	162279

ZIP CODE #	POST OFFICE NAME	FINANCIAL SERVICES: Auto Loan	FINANCIAL SERVICES: Home Loan	FINANCIAL SERVICES: Invest-ments	FINANCIAL SERVICES: Retire-ment Plans	THE HOME: Home Improvements: Home Repair	THE HOME: Home Improvements: Lawn & Garden	THE HOME: Furnishings: Comput-ers & Hard-ware-Personal	THE HOME: Furnishings: Major Appli-ances	THE HOME: Furnishings: TV, Radio, Sound Equip-ment	THE HOME: Furnishings: Furni-ture	ENTERTAINMENT: Dine out/ Carry out	ENTERTAINMENT: Sports Equip-ment	ENTERTAINMENT: Fees & Tickets	ENTERTAINMENT: Toys & Games	ENTERTAINMENT: Travel	ENTERTAINMENT: Cable TV	PERSONAL: Apparel & Services	PERSONAL: Auto Repairs	PERSONAL: Health Insur-ance	PERSONAL: Pets & Supplies
45469	DAYTON	42	18	18	22	16	21	59	29	47	40	48	32	35	46	32	43	34	42	29	40
45502	SPRINGFIELD	102	116	106	117	113	116	104	108	104	104	105	82	112	106	110	106	73	105	112	127
45503	SPRINGFIELD	83	83	78	84	82	90	84	85	88	81	87	64	85	87	84	91	60	86	95	100
45504	SPRINGFIELD	90	90	85	90	89	95	94	91	94	89	93	69	92	93	91	96	65	93	98	108
45505	SPRINGFIELD	68	61	57	62	59	68	67	66	70	62	69	51	63	70	63	73	48	68	73	79
45506	SPRINGFIELD	71	69	61	70	66	73	71	69	75	70	74	52	71	74	69	77	51	72	77	84
45601	CHILLICOTHE	85	76	74	75	75	84	78	81	81	76	80	61	72	82	74	84	55	80	86	96
45612	BAINBRIDGE	84	62	70	60	61	80	66	74	72	63	70	57	54	74	60	78	47	71	79	90
45613	BEAVER	91	65	75	63	65	86	68	79	75	66	74	61	54	78	62	82	50	75	83	96
45614	BIDWELL	85	62	83	60	64	85	64	79	71	61	70	59	53	71	63	77	46	73	82	94
45616	BLUE CREEK	72	50	67	47	50	70	52	64	59	50	58	49	40	60	49	65	38	60	67	78
45619	CHESAPEAKE	78	61	74	60	62	79	64	75	69	59	68	56	54	69	62	74	45	70	79	88
45620	CHESHIRE	88	63	90	61	65	89	65	82	72	60	71	62	51	72	64	79	47	75	85	98
45622	CREOLA	76	55	63	54	55	72	57	66	63	56	62	51	46	66	52	69	42	63	70	81
45623	CROWN CITY	77	54	66	52	54	74	57	67	63	55	62	52	45	66	52	69	41	63	71	82
45628	FRANKFORT	87	81	77	79	80	89	76	83	81	76	80	61	73	82	75	85	55	80	88	99
45629	FRANKLIN FURNACE	86	64	85	62	65	87	65	80	71	61	70	60	53	72	63	78	47	74	83	95
45631	GALLIPOLIS	79	66	73	65	67	80	69	76	74	66	72	56	62	73	66	78	49	74	82	90
45634	HAMDEN	78	56	71	54	56	76	58	70	64	55	63	53	46	65	54	70	42	65	73	84
45638	IRONTON	69	55	67	54	55	72	58	66	63	54	62	50	50	63	56	69	42	64	73	79
45640	JACKSON	76	62	68	61	62	76	64	71	69	62	68	54	57	70	61	74	46	69	76	85
45644	KINGSTON	95	93	84	95	91	100	89	94	91	86	90	72	87	93	89	94	62	91	97	112
45645	KITTS HILL	83	59	70	58	59	80	62	73	69	60	68	56	49	72	56	75	45	69	77	89
45646	LATHAM	67	44	63	42	44	65	47	59	54	45	53	46	36	55	44	60	35	55	62	72
45647	LONDONDERRY	88	63	77	61	64	85	66	78	73	63	71	60	53	75	61	80	48	73	82	94
45648	LUCASVILLE	78	59	75	57	59	79	60	72	66	57	65	55	50	67	58	72	44	68	75	87
45650	LYNX	63	41	61	39	41	62	44	56	51	42	50	44	33	52	41	57	33	52	59	69
45651	MC ARTHUR	78	57	63	56	57	74	61	69	67	59	66	53	50	70	55	73	44	66	73	84
45652	MC DERMOTT	89	67	85	64	67	87	68	81	74	66	73	61	56	75	65	80	49	76	84	98
45653	MINFORD	84	67	80	66	68	85	67	79	72	63	71	59	58	72	66	77	47	74	82	94
45654	NEW PLYMOUTH	80	58	66	57	58	76	60	70	67	59	65	54	49	70	55	73	44	66	74	85
45656	OAK HILL	77	54	73	52	54	76	56	70	63	53	62	53	44	64	53	70	41	65	73	84
45657	OTWAY	85	61	80	59	62	84	63	77	70	60	69	59	50	71	60	77	46	72	81	93
45658	PATRIOT	84	62	69	60	62	79	64	73	70	63	69	56	52	73	58	76	46	70	77	89
45659	PEDRO	69	46	65	43	46	67	49	61	56	46	54	47	37	57	45	62	36	57	64	74
45660	PEEBLES	78	55	70	53	55	76	58	69	65	55	63	53	46	67	54	71	42	65	74	84
45661	PIKETON	88	64	76	62	63	85	66	78	74	64	72	60	53	76	61	80	48	74	82	95
45662	PORTSMOUTH	64	55	59	55	55	65	61	63	65	57	63	47	56	63	58	69	44	64	70	75
45663	WEST PORTSMOUTH	72	55	67	54	55	72	58	68	63	55	62	51	49	64	55	68	42	64	72	80
45669	PROCTORVILLE	82	70	80	69	71	87	69	81	75	66	74	60	63	75	69	81	50	76	87	95
45671	RARDEN	78	56	64	54	56	74	58	68	65	57	63	52	47	67	53	70	42	64	71	82
45672	RAY	89	64	73	62	63	84	66	77	74	65	72	59	53	77	60	80	48	73	81	94
45673	RICHMOND DALE	100	72	83	70	72	95	75	87	83	73	81	67	60	87	68	91	55	83	92	106
45675	ROCK CAMP	92	66	76	64	66	88	69	80	77	67	75	62	55	80	63	83	50	76	85	98
45678	SCOTTOWN	81	58	77	56	59	80	60	74	66	57	65	56	48	67	57	73	43	68	77	88
45679	SEAMAN	77	59	71	59	60	79	62	73	67	57	65	55	52	68	59	73	44	68	78	86
45680	SOUTH POINT	70	58	65	57	59	71	60	67	65	58	63	50	54	65	58	69	43	65	72	79
45681	SOUTH SALEM	88	71	75	71	71	88	72	82	77	67	75	63	62	79	68	82	51	77	86	98
45682	SOUTH WEBSTER	75	55	68	53	56	73	57	68	62	55	61	51	46	64	53	68	41	63	71	81
45684	STOUT	78	56	78	54	57	79	58	72	64	54	63	55	46	65	56	71	42	67	76	87
45685	THURMAN	77	60	67	60	61	75	63	71	68	61	67	53	54	69	59	73	45	68	75	84
45686	VINTON	83	57	74	55	57	80	60	73	68	58	66	56	47	70	56	74	44	68	76	88
45688	WATERLOO	60	39	57	37	39	58	42	52	48	40	47	41	31	49	39	54	31	49	55	64
45690	WAVERLY	81	71	74	69	71	83	71	77	75	70	74	57	66	76	69	80	50	75	84	92
45692	WELLSTON	73	55	63	53	55	71	59	66	64	56	63	50	48	66	54	70	42	64	71	80
45693	WEST UNION	82	58	78	57	60	82	61	75	68	57	67	57	49	69	59	75	44	70	80	90
45694	WHEELERSBURG	80	70	74	70	71	83	71	78	74	67	73	59	65	74	70	78	50	75	83	92
45695	WILKESVILLE	80	58	66	56	57	76	60	70	67	58	65	54	48	69	55	73	44	66	74	85
45696	WILLOW WOOD	73	49	71	47	50	72	52	65	59	49	58	50	40	59	50	65	38	61	69	79
45697	WINCHESTER	93	73	78	72	72	91	74	84	80	71	78	64	62	83	69	86	53	80	88	101
45701	ATHENS	73	56	53	58	54	58	82	63	75	70	76	54	66	75	64	73	53	71	64	78
45710	ALBANY	83	71	74	69	71	81	71	78	75	70	74	58	64	76	68	78	50	75	80	93
45711	AMESVILLE	80	66	73	64	66	78	64	74	69	64	68	54	57	70	62	73	46	70	75	88
45714	BELPRE	77	74	73	74	73	82	72	77	75	70	74	58	71	75	73	78	51	75	82	91
45715	BEVERLY	90	68	90	67	70	93	71	87	77	64	75	65	58	77	69	85	50	80	92	102
45723	COOLVILLE	92	66	95	64	69	94	68	86	75	63	74	65	54	75	67	83	49	79	90	103
45724	CUTLER	83	65	71	65	65	82	66	76	72	63	70	58	56	74	62	77	47	71	80	91
45727	DEXTER CITY	81	57	74	56	58	79	60	72	66	57	65	55	47	68	56	73	43	68	76	87
45729	FLEMING	89	90	83	93	90	96	84	91	85	81	84	70	84	87	87	87	58	86	92	106
45732	GLOUSTER	70	48	66	46	49	69	52	63	58	49	57	49	41	59	49	64	38	60	67	77
45734	GRAYSVILLE	77	56	80	54	58	79	57	73	63	53	62	54	46	63	56	70	41	67	76	86
45735	GUYSVILLE	89	66	89	64	68	89	67	83	74	63	72	62	55	74	66	80	48	77	86	99
45741	LANGSVILLE	73	50	73	48	51	73	52	66	59	49	58	51	41	60	51	66	38	62	70	80
45742	LITTLE HOCKING	95	89	94	89	88	101	83	94	87	81	86	72	80	88	85	91	59	89	96	111
45743	LONG BOTTOM	78	56	73	54	57	77	58	71	64	55	63	53	46	65	55	70	42	66	74	85
45744	LOWELL	85	70	80	70	71	90	71	84	76	64	74	63	62	76	70	82	50	78	89	98
45745	LOWER SALEM	76	58	72	57	59	77	59	71	64	55	63	54	49	65	57	70	42	66	74	85
45746	MACKSBURG	71	47	69	45	48	70	50	63	58	48	56	49	38	59	47	64	37	59	67	78
45750	MARIETTA	79	73	74	73	74	82	76	79	79	72	78	59	72	78	74	83	53	78	86	93
45760	MIDDLEPORT	62	43	60	41	44	62	47	57	53	43	51	43	37	53	44	58	34	54	62	68
45761	MILLFIELD	71	60	58	59	59	68	63	65	66	61	65	49	56	67	58	69	44	65	68	79
45764	NELSONVILLE	61	46	52	46	46	57	56	56	58	50	57	44	46	58	49	61	39	57	60	68
45766	NEW MARSHFIELD	85	77	71	75	76	81	73	79	77	76	76	57	69	79	70	79	52	76	79	93
45767	NEW MATAMORAS	80	58	80	56	60	83	62	77	69	56	67	57	49	68	60	76	44	71	82	90
45768	NEWPORT	83	71	75	72	72	87	71	81	74	65	73	62	63	76	69	80	50	75	84	95
45769	POMEROY	69	53	64	52	53	68	57	65	62	53	60	49	48	62	54	66	41	62	69	77
45770	PORTLAND	72	52	74	50	54	73	53	67	59	49	58	51	42	58	52	65	38	62	70	80
45771	RACINE	81	58	83	57	61	83	61	77	67	56	66	57	48	67	60	74	44	70	80	91
45772	REEDSVILLE	82	59	83	57	61	83	60	76	67	57	66	57	48	67	59	74	44	70	79	91
45773	RENO	92	75	80	76	76	93	76	87	81	71	79	66	66	83	73	87	54	81	90	103
45775	RUTLAND	71	49	71	46	49	71	51	65	58	48	57	49	39	58	49	64	37	60	68	78
45776	SHADE	74	63	67	60	62	71	62	69	65	62	65	52	56	67	60	68	44	66	69	82
45778	STEWART	84	68	78	66	69	82	67	78	72	66	71	58	59	73	65	77	48	73	80	93
45780	THE PLAINS	70	61	58	62	60	67	69	66	70	65	69	51	63	70	64	72	48	69	72	80
45784	VINCENT	88	91	83	94	90	96	85	91	85	82	85	70	86	87	88	87	59	86	92	107
	OHIO	94	92	87	93	90	96	93	93	94	91	94	72	92	95	91	96	66	93	98	110
	UNITED STATES	100	100	100	100	100	100	100	100	100	100	100	100	100	100	100	100	100	100	100	100

POPULATION CHANGE

45786-45898

ZIP CODE			POPULATION			2000-2009 ANNUAL RATE		HOUSEHOLDS					FAMILIES		
#	POST OFFICE NAME	COUNTY FIPS CODE	2000	2009	2014	% Rate	State Centile	2000	2009	2014	% Annual Rate 2000-2009	2009 Average HH Size	2000	2009	% Annual Rate 2000-2009
45786	WATERFORD	167	3602	3553	3502	-0.1	39	1316	1344	1340	0.2	2.64	1012	1010	0.0
45788	WHIPPLE	167	1093	1056	1037	-0.4	21	433	431	428	-0.1	2.41	322	313	-0.3
45789	WINGETT RUN	167	377	368	362	-0.3	27	99	99	98	0.0	3.49	78	77	-0.1
45801	LIMA	003	26785	24846	24414	-0.8	9	9133	8885	8771	-0.3	2.48	6148	5835	-0.6
45804	LIMA	003	16760	15666	15253	-0.7	11	6758	6483	6365	-0.4	2.39	4286	3948	-0.9
45805	LIMA	003	23662	23620	23540	0.0	45	9654	9898	9925	0.3	2.32	6354	6305	-0.1
45806	LIMA	003	11317	11360	11304	0.0	45	4304	4432	4442	0.3	2.53	3251	3276	0.1
45807	LIMA	003	11905	12346	12409	0.4	66	4472	4744	4802	0.6	2.59	3366	3489	0.4
45808	BEAVERDAM	003	355	369	371	0.4	66	139	150	152	0.8	2.36	111	117	0.6
45810	ADA	065	7889	8123	8032	0.3	61	2658	2708	2687	0.2	2.31	1493	1462	-0.2
45812	ALGER	065	2417	2398	2362	-0.1	39	951	971	964	0.2	2.47	700	695	-0.1
45813	ANTWERP	125	3528	3386	3298	-0.4	21	1398	1403	1386	0.0	2.41	1005	985	-0.2
45814	ARLINGTON	063	2629	2928	3068	1.2	91	960	1122	1192	1.7	2.56	728	828	1.4
45817	BLUFFTON	003	6628	6444	6426	-0.3	27	2249	2283	2284	0.2	2.55	1612	1597	-0.1
45821	CECIL	125	1475	1489	1470	0.1	51	545	575	574	0.6	2.58	418	432	0.4
45822	CELINA	107	19499	19795	19919	0.2	56	7592	7970	8100	0.5	2.46	5362	5483	0.2
45827	CLOVERDALE	137	2813	2855	2853	0.2	56	919	967	978	0.6	2.92	731	754	0.3
45828	COLDWATER	107	6240	6220	6198	0.0	45	2164	2228	2241	0.3	2.74	1650	1662	0.1
45830	COLUMBUS GROVE	137	6390	6418	6384	0.0	45	2301	2389	2400	0.4	2.68	1782	1814	0.2
45831	CONTINENTAL	137	3325	3410	3432	0.3	61	1228	1306	1330	0.7	2.60	928	967	0.4
45832	CONVOY	161	2804	2796	2773	0.0	45	1022	1048	1051	0.3	2.64	812	816	0.1
45833	DELPHOS	003	11123	10875	10770	-0.2	32	4165	4192	4187	0.1	2.58	3037	2977	-0.2
45835	DOLA	065	362	372	370	0.3	61	153	160	160	0.5	2.33	119	122	0.3
45836	DUNKIRK	065	1756	1672	1625	-0.5	17	638	617	602	-0.4	2.70	497	470	-0.6
45840	FINDLAY	063	52035	56185	58003	0.8	82	20690	23125	24125	1.2	2.35	13678	14884	0.9
45841	JENERA	063	1103	1111	1126	0.1	51	405	429	440	0.6	2.59	313	323	0.3
45843	FOREST	065	3592	3544	3505	-0.1	39	1387	1415	1411	0.2	2.50	1033	1030	0.0
45844	FORT JENNINGS	137	4263	4194	4153	-0.2	32	1527	1567	1572	0.3	2.68	1200	1209	0.1
45845	FORT LORAMIE	149	3012	3246	3342	0.8	82	1018	1129	1174	1.1	2.88	789	854	0.9
45846	FORT RECOVERY	107	4348	4327	4288	-0.1	39	1430	1474	1477	0.3	2.93	1127	1140	0.1
45849	GROVER HILL	125	1283	1237	1206	-0.4	21	475	476	470	0.0	2.60	368	361	-0.2
45850	HARROD	003	3660	3749	3751	0.3	61	1323	1386	1396	0.5	2.70	1067	1095	0.3
45851	HAVILAND	125	666	659	644	-0.1	39	217	221	219	0.2	2.98	176	177	0.1
45856	LEIPSIC	137	5322	5189	5124	-0.3	27	1821	1839	1835	0.1	2.75	1372	1357	-0.1
45858	MC COMB	063	3110	3344	3461	0.8	82	1113	1240	1297	1.2	2.70	889	969	0.9
45860	MARIA STEIN	107	2151	2238	2270	0.4	66	641	688	706	0.8	3.17	549	582	0.6
45862	MENDON	107	1495	1612	1656	0.8	82	563	622	644	1.1	2.59	437	472	0.8
45863	MIDDLE POINT	161	1321	1333	1330	0.1	51	474	498	501	0.5	2.66	371	381	0.3
45865	MINSTER	011	4618	4774	4822	0.4	66	1658	1764	1798	0.7	2.65	1264	1316	0.4
45867	MOUNT BLANCHARD	063	1141	1188	1216	0.4	66	422	459	475	0.9	2.59	320	340	0.7
45868	MOUNT CORY	063	695	728	746	0.5	71	246	271	281	1.1	2.69	203	219	0.8
45869	NEW BREMEN	011	4174	4307	4332	0.3	61	1475	1559	1580	0.6	2.76	1140	1181	0.4
45871	NEW KNOXVILLE	011	2186	2249	2272	0.3	61	672	709	723	0.6	2.86	516	534	0.4
45872	NORTH BALTIMORE	173	4053	4054	4035	0.0	45	1533	1582	1592	0.3	2.51	1093	1094	0.0
45873	OAKWOOD	125	2906	2766	2684	-0.5	17	1111	1101	1081	-0.1	2.51	837	811	-0.3
45874	OHIO CITY	161	2626	2733	2744	0.4	66	1000	1074	1089	0.8	2.54	748	782	0.5
45875	OTTAWA	137	11255	11375	11381	0.1	51	3939	4130	4179	0.5	2.71	2930	3007	0.3
45877	PANDORA	137	2157	2211	2225	0.3	61	773	817	832	0.6	2.62	612	635	0.4
45879	PAULDING	125	6513	6300	6134	-0.4	21	2522	2524	2484	0.0	2.47	1800	1759	-0.2
45880	PAYNE	125	2555	2497	2435	-0.2	32	986	1005	994	0.2	2.43	716	711	-0.1
45881	RAWSON	063	1294	1355	1389	0.5	71	462	508	527	1.0	2.67	375	402	0.8
45882	ROCKFORD	107	3159	3194	3187	0.1	51	1136	1182	1190	0.4	2.57	873	890	0.2
45883	SAINT HENRY	107	3928	4160	4251	0.6	75	1195	1309	1352	1.0	3.18	1002	1081	0.8
45885	SAINT MARYS	011	13429	13452	13432	0.0	45	5177	5340	5379	0.3	2.47	3690	3712	0.1
45886	SCOTT	161	554	549	541	-0.1	39	197	201	201	0.2	2.73	160	160	0.0
45887	SPENCERVILLE	003	4876	4840	4809	-0.1	39	1801	1837	1841	0.2	2.59	1401	1396	0.0
45889	VAN BUREN	063	1212	1234	1257	0.2	56	418	448	461	0.8	2.75	347	364	0.5
45890	VANLUE	063	627	655	671	0.5	71	235	257	266	1.0	2.55	189	203	0.8
45891	VAN WERT	161	15687	14997	14734	-0.5	17	6350	6255	6202	-0.2	2.33	4389	4206	-0.5
45894	VENEDOCIA	161	749	764	765	0.2	56	280	297	300	0.6	2.57	223	232	0.4
45895	WAPAKONETA	011	18305	18510	18567	0.1	51	6905	7209	7300	0.5	2.50	5083	5186	0.2
45896	WAYNESFIELD	011	2247	2270	2265	0.1	51	805	838	845	0.4	2.71	611	621	0.2
45898	WILLSHIRE	161	1282	1266	1251	-0.1	39	475	480	479	0.1	2.64	335	328	-0.2
	OHIO					0.2					0.4	2.44			0.1
	UNITED STATES					1.0					1.1	2.59			0.9

ZIP CODE #	POST OFFICE NAME	RACE (%) White 2000	White 2009	Black 2000	Black 2009	Asian/Pacific 2000	Asian/Pacific 2009	% Hispanic Origin 2000	% Hispanic Origin 2009	2009 AGE DISTRIBUTION (%) 0-4	5-9	10-14	15-19	20-24	25-44	45-64	65-84	85+	18+	MEDIAN AGE 2009	% 2009 Males	% 2009 Females
45786	WATERFORD	98.9	98.7	0.2	0.2	0.1	0.2	0.5	0.6	7.0	7.0	7.3	6.9	4.9	24.9	28.6	12.2	1.2	74.5	39.8	50.9	49.1
45788	WHIPPLE	98.1	97.6	0.1	0.1	0.5	0.7	0.4	0.5	5.3	5.8	6.3	6.5	4.5	24.8	31.7	12.8	2.3	78.5	42.8	49.8	50.2
45789	WINGETT RUN	98.7	98.6	0.3	0.3	0.0	0.0	0.3	0.3	5.4	5.7	6.3	6.8	5.4	24.7	27.7	13.9	4.1	78.8	41.9	49.5	50.5
45801	LIMA	79.1	76.1	17.1	19.3	0.5	0.8	1.9	2.4	7.2	6.7	6.4	6.9	7.3	29.6	24.7	9.6	1.5	76.1	35.3	53.6	46.4
45804	LIMA	65.9	62.1	30.2	33.5	0.4	0.7	1.9	2.3	7.9	7.4	6.9	7.4	6.9	24.6	24.0	12.4	2.4	73.7	35.5	47.3	52.7
45805	LIMA	83.7	79.7	12.8	15.7	1.1	1.7	1.3	1.7	6.3	6.1	6.2	7.7	6.3	23.2	27.2	14.1	2.8	77.3	40.0	48.7	51.3
45806	LIMA	95.9	94.6	2.1	2.7	0.5	0.8	1.2	1.6	6.1	6.4	6.7	6.8	5.1	23.8	29.5	13.3	2.3	76.6	41.3	49.2	50.8
45807	LIMA	96.2	94.9	2.0	2.6	0.5	0.8	1.1	1.6	5.7	6.0	6.6	6.9	5.3	24.1	31.2	12.4	1.9	77.3	41.4	49.3	50.7
45808	BEAVERDAM	98.3	97.6	0.3	0.5	0.0	0.3	0.8	1.4	6.2	6.5	6.8	6.8	4.6	23.6	29.8	12.2	3.5	76.4	41.7	49.6	50.4
45810	ADA	96.2	95.1	1.2	1.4	1.1	1.7	0.6	0.8	4.3	4.1	4.1	16.4	23.9	19.7	18.1	8.3	1.1	84.8	24.4	49.5	50.5
45812	ALGER	99.0	98.7	0.1	0.2	0.0	0.1	0.3	0.3	6.8	6.8	7.0	6.8	5.7	27.0	26.3	12.3	1.3	75.2	37.9	48.2	51.8
45813	ANTWERP	97.7	97.3	0.5	0.6	0.1	0.1	1.8	2.3	6.3	6.7	6.8	6.7	5.0	25.9	28.8	12.2	1.4	75.9	39.8	49.4	50.6
45814	ARLINGTON	99.0	98.7	0.2	0.2	0.1	0.1	0.6	0.8	6.2	6.8	7.0	6.6	5.1	24.9	29.5	10.5	3.2	75.6	40.1	49.4	50.6
45817	BLUFFTON	98.2	97.6	0.6	0.7	0.4	0.6	0.9	1.2	5.7	6.3	6.8	9.1	9.0	22.4	25.1	11.8	3.7	76.8	37.9	47.0	53.0
45821	CECIL	96.3	95.2	0.5	0.7	0.1	0.1	2.6	3.4	7.1	7.4	7.5	7.1	4.8	26.7	28.1	10.5	0.7	73.2	38.1	49.7	50.3
45822	CELINA	97.7	97.0	0.1	0.2	0.5	0.9	1.6	2.1	6.6	6.7	6.8	6.9	5.8	24.7	27.7	12.6	2.0	75.6	38.8	49.8	50.2
45827	CLOVERDALE	98.8	98.5	0.2	0.2	0.0	0.1	1.0	1.4	7.2	7.3	7.5	8.1	6.1	25.9	27.8	8.7	1.5	73.0	36.0	49.8	50.2
45828	COLDWATER	98.9	98.6	0.1	0.1	0.1	0.2	1.0	1.3	8.1	8.4	8.3	7.7	5.4	23.6	25.4	10.7	2.4	70.2	36.1	50.1	49.9
45830	COLUMBUS GROVE	98.2	97.6	0.2	0.2	0.2	0.3	1.9	2.6	7.8	8.0	8.1	7.0	5.0	25.5	26.5	10.5	1.6	71.7	36.7	50.7	49.3
45831	CONTINENTAL	98.2	97.7	0.1	0.1	0.1	0.2	1.9	2.6	6.6	6.7	7.0	7.1	6.0	26.7	27.8	10.5	1.8	75.4	37.5	49.1	50.9
45832	CONVOY	97.8	97.4	0.1	0.1	0.2	0.3	1.3	1.8	6.5	7.2	7.7	7.5	4.8	25.4	27.6	11.3	2.1	73.8	38.6	50.6	49.4
45833	DELPHOS	98.8	98.4	0.2	0.3	0.1	0.2	0.7	1.0	6.9	6.9	6.9	6.9	5.9	25.6	26.8	11.9	2.2	75.1	37.8	50.6	49.4
45835	DOLA	98.3	97.8	0.0	0.0	0.3	0.5	0.3	0.5	6.5	7.0	7.0	7.0	4.6	24.5	29.0	12.9	1.6	75.5	40.2	52.4	47.6
45836	DUNKIRK	97.9	97.5	0.2	0.2	0.2	0.4	0.5	0.6	6.6	6.8	7.4	7.7	5.1	26.0	28.1	10.9	1.4	74.8	37.6	51.4	48.6
45840	FINDLAY	94.3	92.5	1.3	1.4	1.6	2.6	3.5	4.4	6.8	6.5	6.4	7.4	6.9	26.2	25.9	11.6	2.4	76.4	37.1	48.0	52.0
45841	JENERA	98.8	98.5	0.4	0.5	0.1	0.2	1.0	1.4	5.8	6.5	6.8	6.2	5.0	25.0	32.0	10.5	2.3	77.3	41.1	50.1	49.9
45843	FOREST	98.7	98.4	0.3	0.4	0.1	0.1	0.8	1.0	7.2	7.3	7.4	6.7	5.2	25.9	27.6	11.3	1.4	73.7	38.3	49.9	50.1
45844	FORT JENNINGS	99.1	98.8	0.1	0.1	0.2	0.3	0.6	0.8	7.3	7.5	7.7	7.9	5.6	24.8	28.2	9.7	1.4	72.3	37.1	50.6	49.4
45845	FORT LORAMIE	99.4	99.2	0.1	0.1	0.1	0.1	0.2	0.3	9.0	9.2	9.0	6.8	4.1	27.7	23.8	9.3	1.2	68.4	35.3	49.3	50.7
45846	FORT RECOVERY	99.1	98.9	0.0	0.0	0.3	0.4	0.3	0.5	8.2	8.3	8.3	8.2	5.4	25.7	24.6	9.7	1.5	70.0	34.2	51.2	48.8
45849	GROVER HILL	97.3	96.5	0.6	0.8	0.1	0.2	1.2	1.7	7.2	7.3	7.0	6.8	6.1	25.5	28.8	9.5	1.7	74.4	37.2	49.0	51.0
45850	HARROD	98.3	97.8	0.2	0.2	0.1	0.2	0.9	1.2	6.8	7.2	7.3	6.5	4.9	25.9	28.9	11.4	1.2	74.7	39.0	49.4	50.6
45851	HAVILAND	96.8	96.1	1.2	1.5	0.2	0.3	1.1	1.4	6.2	6.8	7.1	7.4	5.8	27.0	28.1	10.0	1.5	75.3	36.5	51.9	48.1
45856	LEIPSIC	88.1	85.0	0.2	0.2	0.2	0.3	14.8	18.8	7.9	8.1	8.0	7.8	4.8	24.3	24.2	12.0	2.9	71.1	36.8	48.9	51.1
45858	MC COMB	97.1	96.3	0.2	0.2	0.4	0.5	2.6	3.6	7.7	7.8	8.1	7.8	5.4	25.7	27.2	9.0	1.3	71.4	36.9	49.9	50.1
45860	MARIA STEIN	99.8	99.8	0.0	0.0	0.0	0.0	0.1	0.1	9.5	9.6	9.7	9.5	5.1	25.0	21.0	8.8	1.9	64.8	31.5	52.1	47.9
45862	MENDON	98.9	98.7	0.0	0.0	0.2	0.3	0.8	1.1	7.0	7.2	7.4	6.9	5.5	25.5	28.0	10.8	1.6	74.1	38.1	50.2	49.8
45863	MIDDLE POINT	98.2	97.7	0.5	0.5	0.1	0.2	1.1	1.4	6.7	7.1	7.6	7.1	4.7	24.5	29.7	11.1	1.6	74.0	39.3	50.3	49.7
45865	MINSTER	99.4	99.2	0.0	0.0	0.1	0.1	0.2	0.2	7.3	7.5	8.0	8.1	5.1	23.6	26.2	11.6	2.6	72.1	38.1	49.7	50.3
45867	MOUNT BLANCHARD	98.8	98.5	0.2	0.2	0.0	0.0	0.7	1.1	7.0	7.8	8.2	7.3	4.6	23.5	29.1	10.8	1.6	72.1	39.2	50.2	49.8
45868	MOUNT CORY	98.0	97.7	0.4	0.4	0.0	0.0	1.4	1.9	5.5	6.0	6.5	7.3	5.5	24.6	31.9	11.5	1.2	77.5	41.1	49.9	50.1
45869	NEW BREMEN	98.5	98.1	0.0	0.0	0.4	0.6	0.4	0.5	7.5	7.6	8.0	8.2	5.7	26.0	26.3	9.2	1.5	71.8	36.4	50.3	49.7
45871	NEW KNOXVILLE	98.0	97.6	0.6	0.7	0.3	0.4	1.0	1.4	7.1	7.4	7.2	6.2	6.0	28.0	27.8	8.8	1.5	74.4	37.4	48.6	51.4
45872	NORTH BALTIMORE	96.7	95.7	0.0	0.0	0.4	0.6	3.5	4.6	7.2	7.1	7.0	7.6	6.4	27.0	23.7	11.7	2.3	74.0	35.5	48.6	51.4
45873	OAKWOOD	97.4	96.8	0.3	0.4	0.2	0.3	1.8	2.3	6.6	6.6	7.0	7.0	5.6	25.8	28.2	11.9	1.3	75.5	38.7	49.1	50.9
45874	OHIO CITY	98.5	98.0	0.2	0.3	0.1	0.1	1.1	1.6	7.4	7.8	7.6	6.3	4.8	25.2	27.5	11.8	1.6	73.3	38.2	50.3	49.7
45875	OTTAWA	96.6	95.6	0.2	0.2	0.2	0.4	4.1	5.4	7.3	7.6	7.7	7.3	5.1	25.6	26.8	10.7	2.1	72.9	37.5	49.8	50.2
45877	PANDORA	97.7	97.0	0.3	0.4	0.1	0.2	1.7	2.2	6.9	7.4	7.6	6.9	4.8	24.2	25.9	12.9	3.3	73.9	38.9	49.0	51.0
45879	PAULDING	93.0	91.4	1.9	2.1	0.2	0.4	5.1	6.5	6.7	6.8	6.8	6.7	5.6	26.3	27.7	11.5	1.9	75.5	37.9	49.0	51.0
45880	PAYNE	97.1	96.4	0.5	0.5	0.2	0.3	2.6	3.4	6.2	6.3	6.3	6.2	5.2	25.3	27.4	14.0	3.2	77.6	41.1	47.6	52.4
45881	RAWSON	98.3	97.8	0.2	0.2	0.1	0.1	1.5	1.8	6.0	6.5	6.6	6.7	5.2	25.6	30.7	11.4	1.3	76.7	40.4	49.7	50.3
45882	ROCKFORD	99.0	98.8	0.1	0.1	0.0	0.1	0.9	1.1	6.1	6.4	6.7	6.5	5.0	23.4	27.9	14.1	3.9	76.6	41.6	48.8	51.2
45883	SAINT HENRY	99.3	99.0	0.1	0.0	0.0	0.0	0.9	1.1	9.5	9.6	9.5	8.8	5.6	24.7	22.4	8.6	1.3	65.7	31.3	52.2	47.8
45885	SAINT MARYS	97.7	96.9	0.3	0.3	0.8	1.3	0.5	0.7	6.5	6.5	6.7	6.9	5.6	25.1	27.6	12.4	2.7	75.9	39.6	49.6	50.4
45886	SCOTT	97.7	97.3	0.7	0.9	0.2	0.2	1.3	1.5	5.8	6.0	6.9	7.8	5.3	25.7	30.6	10.4	1.5	76.5	39.3	51.0	49.0
45887	SPENCERVILLE	98.2	97.7	0.4	0.5	0.2	0.3	0.5	0.7	6.1	6.4	6.8	7.4	5.6	24.6	28.4	12.3	2.3	76.1	39.8	50.0	50.0
45889	VAN BUREN	98.2	97.6	0.2	0.2	0.3	0.5	1.7	2.2	5.4	6.1	7.0	7.9	5.1	22.4	35.0	10.1	0.9	76.6	42.1	49.7	50.3
45890	VANLUE	98.2	97.9	0.2	0.2	0.0	0.0	1.0	1.4	5.2	7.6	8.7	6.7	4.4	25.2	30.5	9.9	1.7	73.1	39.3	49.6	50.4
45891	VAN WERT	96.5	95.6	1.2	1.4	0.3	0.5	2.1	2.7	6.1	6.1	6.5	7.0	5.3	24.7	27.4	13.8	3.0	76.9	40.4	48.4	51.6
45894	VENEDOCIA	98.9	98.7	0.1	0.1	0.1	0.1	0.4	0.5	5.4	5.8	6.3	7.3	5.4	24.1	31.5	12.3	2.0	77.9	41.9	50.4	49.6
45895	WAPAKONETA	98.3	97.8	0.2	0.3	0.3	0.5	0.8	1.0	6.8	6.8	6.9	6.5	5.2	26.2	27.5	11.5	2.6	75.5	38.9	49.4	50.6
45896	WAYNESFIELD	98.3	98.0	0.1	0.1	0.0	0.0	0.8	1.1	7.6	7.6	7.6	7.3	5.6	25.3	26.4	11.1	1.5	72.8	37.1	49.4	50.6
45898	WILLSHIRE	98.9	98.7	0.1	0.1	0.1	0.2	0.6	0.8	7.7	7.3	7.1	6.6	6.7	26.5	25.4	11.0	1.7	74.0	36.8	50.2	49.8
	OHIO	85.0	83.1	11.5	12.2	1.2	1.9	1.9	2.4	6.6	6.5	6.6	7.1	6.7	25.9	26.9	11.7	2.1	76.2	38.2	48.7	51.3
	UNITED STATES	75.1	72.0	12.3	12.7	3.8	4.6	12.5	15.7	6.8	6.7	6.6	7.1	6.9	27.0	26.0	10.9	1.9	75.7	36.9	49.2	50.8

ZIP CODE #	POST OFFICE NAME	2009 Per Capita Income	2009 HH Income Base	2009 HOUSEHOLD INCOME DISTRIBUTION (%) Less than $25,000	$25,000 to $49,999	$50,000 to $99,999	$100,000 to $149,999	$150,000 or More	MEDIAN HOUSEHOLD INCOME 2009	2014	2009 National Centile	2009 State Centile	2009 Home Value Base	2009 HOME VALUE DISTRIBUTION (%) Less than $50,000	$50,000 to $89,999	$90,000 to $174,999	$175,000 to $399,999	$400,000 or More	2009 Median Home Value
45786	WATERFORD	18984	1344	22.8	32.2	38.7	5.7	0.7	43971	48807	45	31	1127	19.7	28.4	41.2	9.7	1.1	92048
45788	WHIPPLE	20715	431	26.7	31.1	36.4	3.5	2.3	42348	46187	40	26	354	22.3	31.9	37.3	7.9	0.6	82105
45789	WINGETT RUN	12612	99	32.3	30.3	34.3	2.0	1.0	38590	39422	28	18	82	41.5	28.0	23.2	6.1	1.2	63333
45801	LIMA	18664	8885	31.3	28.4	33.3	5.4	1.7	40270	44091	34	21	5620	20.9	42.0	30.5	6.2	0.4	75043
45804	LIMA	17427	6483	39.9	29.9	24.6	4.0	1.6	32000	33794	11	7	3958	47.9	30.2	17.2	4.2	0.5	51967
45805	LIMA	26420	9898	22.4	27.8	35.9	8.3	5.6	49731	51506	60	48	6846	8.4	36.1	40.4	13.5	1.7	96397
45806	LIMA	25314	4432	16.7	24.2	43.3	12.6	3.2	57361	57013	74	74	3705	11.4	23.2	53.8	10.6	1.0	106409
45807	LIMA	24766	4744	16.0	24.8	43.8	12.4	3.0	58295	58167	76	76	3814	4.6	20.6	57.8	16.1	0.8	117253
45808	BEAVERDAM	20495	150	20.7	30.7	44.0	4.0	0.7	47401	51310	55	40	127	22.0	26.0	40.2	11.8	0.0	93125
45810	ADA	18749	2708	33.9	30.1	28.8	5.8	1.5	37001	39549	24	14	1637	21.7	26.2	44.4	7.3	0.4	92197
45812	ALGER	19323	971	29.0	32.2	32.9	4.5	1.3	40312	42123	34	22	755	28.6	29.7	36.3	5.2	0.3	79182
45813	ANTWERP	22693	1403	21.4	32.5	37.8	6.5	1.8	47558	47731	56	40	1132	15.5	32.3	42.7	8.7	0.8	92500
45814	ARLINGTON	22800	1122	19.2	25.8	46.2	7.5	1.3	55095	55201	71	67	912	6.5	22.8	50.9	19.0	0.9	114689
45817	BLUFFTON	24202	2283	20.4	21.6	43.6	10.7	3.7	56209	56454	73	71	1779	9.4	17.2	53.7	18.0	1.7	124054
45821	CECIL	23472	575	15.3	32.3	40.9	9.2	2.3	51689	51282	65	56	523	24.3	22.8	45.1	7.1	0.8	93974
45822	CELINA	23557	7970	20.8	28.9	39.4	7.6	3.3	50219	51817	62	50	6014	12.4	19.6	48.7	17.2	2.0	111163
45827	CLOVERDALE	21255	967	16.5	27.0	42.9	10.8	2.8	55015	55263	71	66	860	16.4	21.5	47.2	14.5	0.3	107914
45828	COLDWATER	23105	2228	15.1	25.4	47.4	7.9	4.1	55848	55706	72	70	1824	6.3	22.1	50.5	20.1	1.0	116168
45830	COLUMBUS GROVE	23197	2389	16.3	24.2	47.2	9.6	2.7	57385	57408	74	74	2008	12.3	19.4	52.8	14.6	0.8	112675
45831	CONTINENTAL	21569	1306	20.9	26.3	44.2	7.4	1.3	52159	52548	66	58	1098	23.1	25.2	40.1	11.2	0.4	92093
45832	CONVOY	22780	1048	15.3	33.7	42.6	5.6	2.9	50805	49928	63	52	935	13.7	30.3	47.3	8.3	0.4	95280
45833	DELPHOS	21213	4192	21.6	30.1	39.6	6.8	2.0	48350	50232	57	43	3355	14.3	35.7	40.3	8.9	0.8	90017
45835	DOLA	24977	160	17.5	34.4	38.8	8.1	1.3	48211	48170	57	43	141	11.3	28.4	48.9	9.9	1.4	101953
45836	DUNKIRK	21291	617	20.3	24.8	45.7	8.1	1.1	53397	52575	69	62	509	20.0	32.8	41.7	5.3	0.2	85857
45840	FINDLAY	28114	23125	18.2	26.2	38.8	11.6	5.2	55170	55954	71	67	15904	10.7	15.8	48.4	22.7	2.5	124180
45841	JENERA	21292	429	19.1	31.7	41.3	6.8	1.2	49407	50844	60	47	369	12.2	20.3	44.7	19.0	3.8	116314
45843	FOREST	22346	1415	21.8	28.3	39.2	8.2	2.4	49723	50473	60	48	1168	15.8	35.0	41.4	7.3	0.5	89196
45844	FORT JENNINGS	23163	1567	16.7	24.4	47.9	8.9	2.1	57067	56049	74	73	1380	7.4	20.8	52.5	18.3	0.9	119291
45845	FORT LORAMIE	25343	1129	9.7	22.8	48.5	14.0	5.0	63552	64032	82	83	950	5.1	8.7	50.9	32.7	2.5	145861
45846	FORT RECOVERY	20434	1474	17.8	27.1	43.6	8.6	3.0	53232	53482	68	61	1255	11.6	19.4	46.9	18.4	3.6	115759
45849	GROVER HILL	20808	476	20.4	32.4	39.5	6.3	1.5	48597	49034	58	44	417	27.3	32.1	34.1	6.0	0.5	76250
45850	HARROD	21337	1386	16.9	29.1	44.9	6.9	2.2	52390	52881	67	59	1187	10.9	23.6	50.0	13.6	2.0	109054
45851	HAVILAND	19933	221	14.9	38.9	34.8	7.7	3.6	48478	48382	58	44	192	20.3	33.9	39.6	6.3	0.0	83846
45856	LEIPSIC	19890	1839	21.9	27.1	42.5	6.9	1.6	50627	51679	63	52	1499	18.9	27.0	42.3	11.3	0.6	95482
45858	MC COMB	22234	1240	13.8	30.9	46.9	6.5	1.9	53791	54011	69	63	1015	10.8	23.3	49.8	15.7	0.4	107287
45860	MARIA STEIN	21892	688	9.7	17.0	57.8	12.9	2.5	65779	65627	84	87	599	5.5	12.7	43.9	34.1	3.8	152344
45862	MENDON	21219	622	17.5	33.3	39.5	9.2	0.5	49173	50761	59	46	514	28.4	29.0	33.1	8.6	1.0	80500
45863	MIDDLE POINT	19476	498	15.1	36.9	42.8	5.0	0.2	48260	49161	57	43	444	17.8	41.4	34.9	5.2	0.7	81800
45865	MINSTER	28750	1764	14.2	21.2	40.0	17.4	7.2	64724	63545	83	85	1473	5.0	11.3	53.2	28.2	2.3	144404
45867	MOUNT BLANCHARD	23635	459	14.8	27.7	49.2	6.3	2.0	56784	55700	74	72	381	9.4	21.3	50.4	16.8	2.1	108112
45868	MOUNT CORY	21648	271	12.5	25.1	56.1	5.5	0.7	54917	54395	71	66	239	10.0	22.6	50.6	16.3	0.4	113315
45869	NEW BREMEN	25873	1559	11.0	26.5	45.7	11.9	4.9	64602	64146	83	85	1247	0.8	12.3	60.0	24.5	2.5	131931
45871	NEW KNOXVILLE	23022	709	13.4	24.7	46.3	10.7	4.9	61647	61988	80	80	571	3.2	23.6	56.7	14.2	2.3	116159
45872	NORTH BALTIMORE	22549	1582	21.0	27.9	41.2	7.6	2.2	50719	53824	63	52	1187	32.8	37.4	26.8	2.8	0.3	71259
45873	OAKWOOD	21732	1101	21.3	30.3	40.2	5.9	2.2	48984	49011	59	45	945	22.0	36.3	36.2	5.2	0.3	79261
45874	OHIO CITY	21379	1074	16.3	35.1	42.5	4.4	1.8	48887	49229	59	45	936	24.0	37.1	32.2	6.7	0.0	76381
45875	OTTAWA	24295	4130	17.9	24.4	42.8	10.6	4.2	57833	57901	75	75	3335	8.3	20.6	48.9	21.2	0.9	119771
45877	PANDORA	22011	817	14.8	28.4	47.7	7.3	1.7	54386	54189	70	65	702	7.3	22.1	56.0	14.7	0.0	112579
45879	PAULDING	22664	2524	18.2	33.1	39.9	6.5	2.2	49166	49103	59	46	2026	16.0	38.9	40.2	4.7	0.1	85194
45880	PAYNE	23111	1005	19.1	32.1	39.1	7.6	2.1	49359	48929	60	47	818	15.4	39.5	39.0	5.9	0.2	85652
45881	RAWSON	22812	508	12.8	26.6	52.6	6.7	1.4	56497	55517	73	71	438	11.9	24.4	42.5	19.4	1.8	110870
45882	ROCKFORD	21080	1182	19.0	31.0	41.4	7.6	0.9	49905	51162	61	49	993	13.1	30.2	48.7	5.2	2.7	97151
45883	SAINT HENRY	21935	1309	11.8	24.8	49.6	10.5	3.4	60379	59332	78	78	1108	3.4	10.0	61.9	22.3	2.3	130964
45885	SAINT MARYS	24109	5340	18.8	27.8	41.6	9.4	2.4	52175	53045	66	58	3971	8.6	27.0	49.6	12.7	2.1	105920
45886	SCOTT	21901	201	15.9	32.3	41.3	7.5	3.0	51330	50405	64	55	175	12.6	26.9	49.1	10.3	1.1	100329
45887	SPENCERVILLE	21706	1837	20.3	28.2	42.7	6.6	2.3	50972	52054	63	53	1538	12.1	34.0	38.9	13.3	1.8	94878
45889	VAN BUREN	25584	448	10.9	21.4	51.8	12.9	2.9	65137	65073	83	86	401	11.0	13.2	48.1	24.7	3.0	128125
45890	VANLUE	22613	257	24.9	26.1	42.0	4.3	2.7	48663	50523	58	44	217	4.6	24.0	54.4	16.6	0.5	114541
45891	VAN WERT	23625	6255	20.2	33.0	37.3	7.2	2.3	47124	48792	54	40	4785	13.2	35.4	43.2	7.5	0.7	91514
45894	VENEDOCIA	22569	297	18.9	28.3	44.1	6.4	2.4	51567	50372	65	56	259	16.6	22.4	46.3	12.4	2.3	105278
45895	WAPAKONETA	25731	7209	16.9	26.4	42.8	10.0	3.9	54818	55219	71	66	5590	8.9	27.4	47.9	14.3	1.6	107113
45896	WAYNESFIELD	21088	838	20.6	27.8	42.1	7.3	2.1	50999	51704	64	53	709	13.1	32.2	44.1	10.0	0.6	94786
45898	WILLSHIRE	20943	480	17.3	28.5	46.7	6.9	0.6	52602	53541	67	60	404	26.5	36.9	33.4	2.7	0.5	78000
	OHIO	26577		21.4	25.9	36.7	10.4	5.7	52400	54553				10.3	22.0	45.6	19.3	2.8	114865
	UNITED STATES	27277		20.9	24.4	35.3	11.7	7.6	54719	56938				9.3	13.1	31.6	32.6	13.5	162279

ZIP CODE #	POST OFFICE NAME	FINANCIAL SERVICES: Auto Loan	Home Loan	Investments	Retirement Plans	THE HOME: Home Improvements: Home Repair	Lawn & Garden	Furnishings: Computers & Hardware-Personal	Major Appliances	TV, Radio, Sound Equipment	Furniture	ENTERTAINMENT: Dine out/Carry out	Sports Equipment	Fees & Tickets	Toys & Games	Travel	Cable TV	PERSONAL: Apparel & Services	Auto Repairs	Health Insurance	Pets & Supplies
45786	WATERFORD	84	67	82	68	69	87	68	81	73	62	71	61	58	73	67	78	48	75	84	96
45788	WHIPPLE	81	69	72	70	70	84	69	79	73	63	71	60	61	74	67	78	48	73	82	93
45789	WINGETT RUN	79	56	68	55	57	76	58	69	65	56	64	53	47	67	54	71	43	65	73	84
45801	LIMA	68	63	56	64	61	69	68	66	70	63	69	51	64	71	64	73	48	68	73	80
45804	LIMA	62	52	52	53	50	61	58	58	62	55	61	44	53	62	53	66	42	60	66	71
45805	LIMA	89	86	86	86	87	95	86	90	90	84	88	67	85	89	87	93	61	89	98	106
45806	LIMA	94	94	87	96	93	101	90	95	91	87	91	73	89	93	91	94	63	92	99	112
45807	LIMA	89	96	89	97	95	100	89	94	90	87	90	71	93	91	93	93	63	91	98	109
45808	BEAVERDAM	76	69	68	72	70	81	68	77	70	62	69	58	63	72	68	74	47	71	79	89
45810	ADA	70	55	54	57	54	62	73	64	70	63	69	52	60	70	61	71	48	68	67	77
45812	ALGER	85	62	71	61	62	82	65	75	71	62	70	57	53	74	59	77	47	71	79	91
45813	ANTWERP	85	77	76	80	79	91	76	86	79	69	77	65	70	80	76	83	53	79	89	100
45814	ARLINGTON	89	84	82	88	85	96	82	91	84	75	82	69	77	85	82	88	57	85	93	106
45817	BLUFFTON	91	95	92	97	96	102	89	95	90	87	90	71	91	91	93	93	62	92	100	111
45821	CECIL	104	81	88	81	82	103	83	95	89	78	88	73	70	92	78	96	59	89	100	114
45822	CELINA	85	82	77	83	81	89	82	85	84	78	83	65	80	85	81	87	57	83	90	100
45827	CLOVERDALE	100	88	89	89	87	102	86	95	90	83	89	73	79	93	84	95	61	90	98	114
45828	COLDWATER	93	94	84	97	92	101	90	95	91	85	90	74	89	92	91	93	62	91	98	112
45830	COLUMBUS GROVE	91	92	86	95	92	101	86	95	88	82	87	72	86	90	89	91	60	89	97	110
45831	CONTINENTAL	93	77	81	78	77	94	77	87	82	73	81	67	68	84	74	87	55	82	90	104
45832	CONVOY	94	85	84	89	87	100	84	95	87	76	85	72	78	88	84	92	58	88	98	110
45833	DELPHOS	84	76	75	77	75	89	76	83	79	71	78	63	71	81	74	84	53	79	89	98
45835	DOLA	90	82	81	85	83	97	81	91	83	73	82	69	74	85	80	88	56	84	94	106
45836	DUNKIRK	100	77	84	76	77	98	78	90	85	75	83	69	66	88	73	92	56	85	95	108
45840	FINDLAY	95	95	87	97	93	96	96	94	96	94	96	73	96	97	95	97	67	95	98	112
45841	JENERA	84	79	76	82	80	90	77	86	79	71	77	65	73	80	77	82	53	79	88	100
45843	FOREST	95	75	81	75	75	95	76	88	82	72	81	67	65	85	72	89	55	82	92	105
45844	FORT JENNINGS	95	88	86	92	90	103	86	97	89	79	87	73	80	90	87	93	60	90	100	113
45845	FORT LORAMIE	102	114	98	118	111	112	102	106	100	102	101	83	109	103	108	101	71	102	105	125
45846	FORT RECOVERY	93	85	85	88	86	100	83	94	86	76	84	72	77	87	84	90	58	87	96	110
45849	GROVER HILL	96	71	80	70	71	92	73	85	80	71	79	65	60	84	68	87	53	80	89	103
45850	HARROD	89	81	81	85	83	96	80	91	83	73	81	69	74	84	80	88	55	84	93	105
45851	HAVILAND	96	82	84	84	83	100	82	93	86	76	85	71	73	88	80	92	58	87	97	110
45856	LEIPSIC	83	78	73	81	78	89	77	84	79	71	78	64	73	81	77	83	53	79	88	98
45858	MC COMB	97	83	85	85	84	100	83	93	87	78	86	71	74	89	80	92	58	87	96	110
45860	MARIA STEIN	98	110	95	113	107	108	98	102	97	98	97	80	105	99	104	97	68	98	101	120
45862	MENDON	93	74	80	74	74	93	75	86	81	71	79	66	64	83	71	87	54	81	90	103
45863	MIDDLE POINT	80	73	72	76	75	86	72	82	74	65	73	62	67	76	72	79	50	75	84	95
45865	MINSTER	106	119	107	121	116	122	106	113	107	105	107	86	114	109	113	109	75	108	116	131
45867	MOUNT BLANCHARD	95	86	85	90	88	102	85	96	88	77	86	73	79	89	85	93	59	89	99	112
45868	MOUNT CORY	90	82	81	85	84	97	81	91	83	73	82	69	75	85	81	88	56	84	94	106
45869	NEW BREMEN	103	106	94	109	103	112	100	105	101	96	100	82	101	103	102	104	69	101	109	125
45871	NEW KNOXVILLE	97	101	83	104	96	104	97	97	98	93	97	77	99	100	97	99	67	97	104	117
45872	NORTH BALTIMORE	83	82	68	82	77	85	81	81	82	79	82	63	79	84	78	84	56	81	86	97
45873	OAKWOOD	95	72	80	72	72	93	74	86	81	71	79	66	62	84	69	87	53	81	90	103
45874	OHIO CITY	91	74	78	75	75	92	75	85	80	70	78	65	65	82	71	85	53	80	89	101
45875	OTTAWA	99	96	90	100	96	107	93	101	94	86	93	77	90	96	94	98	64	95	104	118
45877	PANDORA	90	82	81	86	84	97	81	91	84	73	82	69	75	85	81	88	56	84	94	106
45879	PAULDING	85	79	72	81	77	89	79	83	81	74	80	65	74	83	77	85	55	81	89	99
45880	PAYNE	91	76	88	76	77	96	77	90	82	71	80	68	68	82	76	88	54	84	95	105
45881	RAWSON	93	87	85	90	88	100	85	95	87	78	86	72	79	89	85	91	59	88	97	110
45882	ROCKFORD	90	76	78	77	76	92	76	86	80	70	78	66	67	82	74	85	53	80	90	102
45883	SAINT HENRY	103	104	96	107	103	112	97	106	98	93	97	81	97	100	100	101	67	99	107	123
45885	SAINT MARYS	85	88	82	89	86	95	83	88	85	81	85	66	85	86	85	88	58	86	94	103
45886	SCOTT	93	85	83	88	86	99	83	94	86	75	84	71	77	87	83	91	58	87	97	109
45887	SPENCERVILLE	84	81	75	84	80	91	79	85	81	73	80	66	76	83	79	84	55	81	89	100
45889	VAN BUREN	98	111	95	114	107	109	99	103	97	99	98	80	105	100	104	97	68	99	102	121
45890	VANLUE	89	81	80	85	83	96	80	91	83	72	81	69	74	84	80	88	55	84	93	105
45891	VAN WERT	83	77	73	79	76	87	78	81	81	74	80	62	75	81	76	84	55	80	88	97
45894	VENEDOCIA	90	82	81	85	84	97	81	91	83	73	82	69	74	85	81	88	56	84	94	106
45895	WAPAKONETA	93	96	84	98	93	101	91	95	92	88	92	72	92	94	92	95	64	92	100	112
45896	WAYNESFIELD	85	81	73	84	79	91	80	85	82	74	81	66	77	84	79	86	56	82	90	101
45898	WILLSHIRE	83	78	68	79	74	86	78	80	80	74	79	63	75	82	75	83	54	79	87	96
	OHIO	94	92	87	93	90	96	93	93	94	91	94	72	92	95	91	96	66	93	98	110
	UNITED STATES	100	100	100	100	100	100	100	100	100	100	100	100	100	100	100	100	100	100	100	100

ZIP CODE			POPULATION			2000-2009 ANNUAL RATE		HOUSEHOLDS					FAMILIES		
#	POST OFFICE NAME	COUNTY FIPS CODE	2000	2009	2014	% Rate	State Centile	2000	2009	2014	% Annual Rate 2000-2009	2009 Average HH Size	2000	2009	% Annual Rate 2000-2009
73002	ALEX	051	1099	1238	1318	1.3	89	410	474	509	1.6	2.61	328	370	1.3
73003	EDMOND	109	17189	21455	23347	2.4	95	6462	8075	8806	2.4	2.65	4713	5854	2.4
73004	AMBER	051	2722	2905	3250	0.7	75	942	1041	1172	1.1	2.79	775	836	0.8
73005	ANADARKO	015	10431	10322	10193	-0.1	38	3653	3618	3577	-0.1	2.70	2634	2551	-0.3
73006	APACHE	015	3667	3552	3490	-0.3	27	1384	1373	1356	-0.1	2.58	1036	1005	-0.3
73007	ARCADIA	109	1638	2184	2406	3.2	98	659	911	1013	3.6	2.33	486	660	3.4
73008	BETHANY	109	21299	21067	21103	-0.1	38	8580	8615	8682	0.0	2.29	5570	5364	-0.4
73009	BINGER	015	1862	1840	1819	-0.1	38	707	705	698	0.0	2.55	539	527	-0.2
73010	BLANCHARD	087	7206	10939	12477	4.6	99	2650	4059	4654	4.7	2.69	2090	3154	4.5
73011	BRADLEY	051	1036	1174	1253	1.4	90	403	465	499	1.6	2.52	303	339	1.2
73012	EDMOND	109	13422	23974	28235	6.5	100	4472	8007	9447	6.5	2.99	3864	6847	6.4
73013	EDMOND	109	32169	41732	46082	2.9	96	11832	15757	17571	3.1	2.54	8721	11104	2.6
73014	CALUMET	017	2354	2753	3046	1.7	92	899	1065	1185	1.8	2.58	684	783	1.5
73015	CARNEGIE	015	3643	3791	3805	0.4	64	1420	1500	1510	0.6	2.49	991	1021	0.3
73016	CASHION	073	588	659	691	1.2	86	229	260	274	1.4	2.53	173	192	1.1
73017	CEMENT	015	1525	1496	1477	-0.2	33	602	598	592	-0.1	2.49	426	414	-0.3
73018	CHICKASHA	051	19816	20798	21314	0.5	68	7926	8460	8728	0.7	2.36	5291	5447	0.3
73020	CHOCTAW	109	18225	21250	22720	1.7	92	6707	7970	8572	1.9	2.65	5399	6274	1.6
73021	COLONY	149	257	248	244	-0.4	22	108	106	105	-0.2	2.34	83	80	-0.4
73024	CORN	149	1177	1220	1235	0.4	64	422	444	452	0.6	2.54	304	312	0.3
73025	EDMOND	083	6542	9116	10315	3.7	98	2185	3116	3547	3.9	2.92	1889	2647	3.7
73026	NORMAN	027	10756	12146	12974	1.3	89	3903	4581	4948	1.7	2.65	3188	3619	1.4
73027	COYLE	083	2663	2311	2380	-1.5	2	594	642	675	0.8	2.39	379	392	0.4
73028	CRESCENT	083	3209	3556	3771	1.1	84	1308	1493	1597	1.4	2.37	915	1004	1.0
73029	CYRIL	015	1544	1563	1552	0.1	49	578	592	591	0.3	2.56	422	423	0.0
73030	DAVIS	099	4382	4701	4807	0.8	78	1741	1888	1935	0.9	2.46	1246	1319	0.6
73034	EDMOND	109	31068	36787	39562	1.8	93	11666	13991	15123	2.0	2.52	8153	9659	1.8
73036	EL RENO	017	18728	19180	19911	0.3	60	6663	7020	7347	0.6	2.49	4586	4644	0.1
73038	FORT COBB	015	1827	1778	1756	-0.3	27	707	697	689	-0.2	2.55	526	508	-0.4
73040	GEARY	011	1820	1840	1843	0.1	49	695	711	713	0.2	2.48	473	472	0.0
73041	GOTEBO	075	415	370	350	-1.2	4	181	166	158	-0.9	2.23	131	117	-1.2
73042	GRACEMONT	015	886	863	852	-0.3	27	347	346	343	0.0	2.49	250	244	-0.3
73043	GREENFIELD	011	185	176	170	-0.5	15	74	72	70	-0.3	2.44	53	50	-0.6
73044	GUTHRIE	083	18538	19713	20754	0.7	75	7028	7739	8196	1.0	2.48	4928	5283	0.8
73045	HARRAH	109	9581	10068	10323	0.5	68	3441	3692	3812	0.8	2.69	2736	2877	0.5
73047	HINTON	015	3070	3255	3293	0.6	73	916	963	980	0.5	2.56	666	684	0.3
73048	HYDRO	015	2181	2234	2227	0.3	60	836	871	872	0.4	2.51	599	609	0.2
73049	JONES	109	4914	5357	5634	0.9	80	1800	2009	2129	1.2	2.59	1361	1478	0.9
73051	LEXINGTON	027	8824	9843	10311	1.2	86	2334	2670	2874	1.5	2.61	1805	1986	1.0
73052	LINDSAY	049	5408	5637	5754	0.4	64	2199	2343	2404	0.7	2.38	1563	1619	0.4
73053	LOOKEBA	015	704	678	665	-0.4	22	257	251	246	-0.3	2.65	200	191	-0.5
73054	LUTHER	109	4244	4808	5116	1.4	90	1477	1715	1841	1.6	2.73	1146	1290	1.3
73055	MARLOW	137	8405	9591	10062	1.4	90	3347	3880	4092	1.6	2.44	2477	2804	1.3
73056	MARSHALL	083	403	423	440	0.5	68	169	182	191	0.8	2.32	132	139	0.6
73057	MAYSVILLE	049	2409	2392	2397	-0.1	38	953	950	952	0.0	2.48	690	674	-0.3
73058	MERIDIAN	083	213	228	240	0.7	75	94	102	108	0.9	2.23	68	72	0.6
73059	MINCO	051	2425	2505	2561	0.4	64	935	976	1002	0.5	2.57	697	705	0.1
73061	MORRISON	103	1302	1447	1466	1.1	84	499	571	583	1.5	2.53	373	417	1.2
73062	MOUNTAIN VIEW	075	1451	1280	1208	-1.3	3	606	548	520	-1.1	2.30	406	357	-1.4
73063	MULHALL	083	498	509	523	0.2	55	188	195	202	0.4	2.61	144	146	0.1
73064	MUSTANG	017	15617	19021	21216	2.2	95	5563	6980	7854	2.5	2.71	4516	5488	2.1
73065	NEWCASTLE	087	5396	6427	7174	1.9	94	1978	2409	2703	2.2	2.67	1642	1968	2.0
73067	NINNEKAH	051	1563	1716	1806	1.0	82	597	674	715	1.3	2.55	463	507	1.0
73068	NOBLE	027	10520	12132	12998	1.6	91	3788	4428	4787	1.7	2.70	2928	3295	1.3
73069	NORMAN	027	22174	23178	23886	0.5	68	9971	10531	10907	0.6	2.09	5006	5063	0.1
73071	NORMAN	027	27764	32604	35356	1.8	93	11518	13848	15126	2.0	2.30	6695	7756	1.6
73072	NORMAN	027	37995	42974	45536	1.3	89	14493	16746	17991	1.6	2.28	8548	9371	1.0
73073	ORLANDO	083	364	372	382	0.2	55	133	138	143	0.4	2.70	102	103	0.1
73074	PAOLI	049	1048	1040	1038	-0.1	38	402	405	406	0.1	2.57	309	306	-0.1
73075	PAULS VALLEY	049	9012	9145	9202	0.2	55	3534	3596	3623	0.2	2.44	2417	2398	-0.1
73077	PERRY	103	7296	6913	6721	-0.6	13	3028	2914	2846	-0.4	2.33	2100	1968	-0.7
73078	PIEDMONT	017	4961	6822	7917	3.5	98	1658	2306	2700	3.6	2.96	1446	1978	3.4
73079	POCASSET	051	922	907	905	-0.2	33	346	347	348	0.0	2.61	276	269	-0.3
73080	PURCELL	087	9530	10902	11751	1.5	91	3598	4163	4503	1.6	2.58	2669	3008	1.3
73082	RUSH SPRINGS	051	3740	4189	4437	1.2	86	1460	1668	1778	1.5	2.51	1096	1215	1.1
73084	SPENCER	109	6549	6852	7061	0.5	68	2501	2674	2773	0.7	2.53	1709	1758	0.3
73086	SULPHUR	099	8035	7870	7781	-0.2	33	3185	3161	3137	-0.1	2.40	2282	2212	-0.3
73089	TUTTLE	051	10575	12750	13820	2.0	94	3748	4647	5084	2.4	2.74	3118	3795	2.1
73090	UNION CITY	017	655	728	782	1.1	84	217	250	271	1.5	2.71	164	182	1.1
73092	VERDEN	051	823	928	988	1.3	89	308	353	378	1.5	2.63	233	260	1.2
73093	WASHINGTON	087	2171	2403	2623	1.1	84	779	870	953	1.2	2.76	631	695	1.0
73095	WAYNE	087	1589	1739	1863	1.0	82	591	654	703	1.1	2.66	445	481	0.8
73096	WEATHERFORD	039	11914	12336	12481	0.4	64	4706	4977	5074	0.6	2.31	2758	2829	0.3
73098	WYNNEWOOD	049	3749	3717	3718	-0.1	38	1524	1529	1532	0.0	2.38	1027	1004	-0.2
73099	YUKON	017	41603	54264	61502	2.9	96	15174	20145	22957	3.1	2.68	12000	15645	2.9
73102	OKLAHOMA CITY	109	1632	2344	2473	4.0	98	767	1236	1414	5.3	1.90	134	227	5.9
73103	OKLAHOMA CITY	109	4345	4390	4440	0.1	49	2254	2335	2383	0.4	1.85	876	843	-0.4
73104	OKLAHOMA CITY	109	1841	2487	2557	3.3	98	725	1025	1063	3.8	2.37	412	515	2.4
73105	OKLAHOMA CITY	109	4899	5423	5702	1.1	84	2145	2452	2604	1.5	2.13	1297	1419	1.0
73106	OKLAHOMA CITY	109	15677	15795	16028	0.1	49	5025	5070	5143	0.1	2.65	2637	2496	-0.6
73107	OKLAHOMA CITY	109	24883	24897	25060	0.0	43	11010	11044	11140	0.0	2.23	5867	5570	-0.6
73108	OKLAHOMA CITY	109	15255	15715	15899	0.3	60	5269	5374	5451	0.2	2.87	3504	3431	-0.2
73109	OKLAHOMA CITY	109	19642	20138	20398	0.3	60	7722	7813	7920	0.1	2.52	4517	4356	-0.4
73110	OKLAHOMA CITY	109	34464	35139	35790	0.2	55	14730	15274	15636	0.4	2.27	9123	9066	-0.1
73111	OKLAHOMA CITY	109	12687	12344	12310	-0.3	27	5188	5145	5170	-0.1	2.28	3195	3032	-0.6
73112	OKLAHOMA CITY	109	29674	29968	30276	0.1	49	14751	15099	15334	0.3	1.95	7226	6969	-0.4
73114	OKLAHOMA CITY	109	17253	17617	17927	0.2	55	6759	7034	7203	0.4	2.50	4253	4219	-0.1
73115	OKLAHOMA CITY	109	21977	22135	22448	0.1	49	8991	9234	9420	0.3	2.39	6117	6053	-0.1
73116	OKLAHOMA CITY	109	9453	9448	9492	0.0	43	4429	4506	4555	0.2	2.05	2559	2478	-0.3
73117	OKLAHOMA CITY	109	5118	5204	5293	0.2	55	2256	2350	2411	0.4	2.14	1199	1182	-0.2
73118	OKLAHOMA CITY	109	14222	14484	14699	0.2	55	6625	6812	6937	0.3	2.08	3267	3165	-0.3
73119	OKLAHOMA CITY	109	27307	27479	27642	0.1	49	10312	10354	10437	0.0	2.62	6698	6457	-0.4
73120	OKLAHOMA CITY	109	34865	35318	35784	0.1	49	17174	17728	18084	0.3	1.97	9088	8853	-0.3
73121	OKLAHOMA CITY	109	3105	3264	3354	0.5	68	1224	1315	1360	0.8	2.42	862	895	0.4
73122	OKLAHOMA CITY	109	13442	14104	14480	0.5	68	5877	6242	6431	0.7	2.25	3635	3693	0.2
	OKLAHOMA					0.7					0.8	2.46			0.6
	UNITED STATES					1.0					1.1	2.59			0.9

ZIP CODE #	POST OFFICE NAME	RACE (%) White 2000	White 2009	Black 2000	Black 2009	Asian/Pacific 2000	Asian/Pacific 2009	% Hispanic Origin 2000	% Hispanic Origin 2009	2009 AGE DISTRIBUTION (%) 0-4	5-9	10-14	15-19	20-24	25-44	45-64	65-84	85+	18+	MEDIAN AGE 2009	% 2009 Males	% 2009 Females
73002	ALEX	88.6	86.6	0.3	0.3	0.1	0.1	2.3	3.5	6.6	6.9	6.9	6.1	4.8	23.4	30.0	13.7	1.4	75.8	41.1	51.3	48.7
73003	EDMOND	85.3	81.8	5.7	6.4	2.0	2.9	3.5	5.3	9.3	8.5	7.9	7.1	6.9	32.4	22.0	5.3	0.7	69.9	31.2	47.9	52.1
73004	AMBER	89.6	87.1	0.1	0.2	0.5	0.7	2.7	4.0	7.8	7.8	7.8	7.4	5.9	27.4	26.2	9.1	0.7	72.1	35.3	50.2	49.8
73005	ANADARKO	47.2	46.9	4.3	4.3	0.3	0.3	7.6	7.7	7.6	7.8	8.9	10.1	6.4	22.2	24.1	10.9	1.9	68.7	32.8	48.1	51.9
73006	APACHE	66.6	65.9	0.4	0.4	0.2	0.3	3.7	4.0	6.7	7.2	7.5	7.2	5.3	23.8	28.8	11.7	1.8	73.8	38.5	49.2	50.8
73007	ARCADIA	80.0	77.9	11.6	11.5	0.3	0.5	2.1	3.3	5.3	5.7	6.4	7.7	4.8	22.3	34.2	12.1	1.4	76.9	43.5	51.4	48.6
73008	BETHANY	85.5	81.6	4.6	5.1	1.5	2.1	5.8	9.0	6.1	5.8	5.8	7.6	8.6	23.8	24.7	14.8	2.8	78.7	38.4	47.7	52.3
73009	BINGER	78.8	78.8	2.1	2.1	0.1	0.1	5.3	5.3	6.1	6.0	6.3	7.6	5.0	24.6	28.8	13.5	2.2	76.8	41.1	51.6	48.4
73010	BLANCHARD	89.7	87.4	0.2	0.2	0.2	0.2	2.9	4.2	7.2	7.3	7.2	6.8	5.8	26.5	27.5	10.7	1.0	74.0	37.3	49.6	50.4
73011	BRADLEY	89.7	87.9	0.1	0.1	0.1	0.3	2.1	3.2	7.4	7.6	7.4	6.6	5.5	23.3	26.1	14.1	2.0	73.5	38.4	51.6	48.4
73012	EDMOND	88.2	84.8	4.7	5.6	2.1	3.3	2.3	3.9	9.8	9.6	9.0	7.1	4.0	30.5	24.9	4.6	0.4	66.9	33.9	49.1	50.9
73013	EDMOND	86.8	82.2	5.6	6.7	2.6	4.3	2.3	4.2	6.5	6.7	7.0	7.8	7.9	25.3	27.1	9.5	2.2	75.4	36.7	48.0	52.0
73014	CALUMET	84.6	81.2	0.6	0.7	0.1	0.1	3.7	5.6	6.7	7.2	7.4	6.9	5.2	24.5	29.1	11.9	1.0	74.4	38.9	50.1	49.9
73015	CARNEGIE	66.2	65.8	0.8	0.8	0.1	0.1	7.8	8.1	6.3	6.4	6.6	6.7	5.6	22.2	26.6	16.3	3.4	76.4	41.6	49.5	50.5
73016	CASHION	94.2	93.2	0.0	0.0	0.2	0.2	2.4	3.5	6.2	6.4	7.0	7.9	6.8	24.6	30.2	9.4	1.5	75.6	38.9	48.9	51.1
73017	CEMENT	86.9	86.8	1.4	1.3	0.2	0.2	1.6	1.6	6.0	6.5	6.9	6.6	5.1	23.1	28.5	15.2	2.1	76.5	41.6	47.3	52.7
73018	CHICKASHA	83.0	79.9	6.8	7.8	0.6	0.9	3.5	4.9	6.7	6.4	6.2	7.0	6.9	24.8	25.9	13.2	2.9	76.8	38.1	47.5	52.5
73020	CHOCTAW	87.3	84.1	2.9	3.2	0.7	1.0	2.7	4.4	5.7	6.1	6.5	6.6	5.1	25.4	31.7	11.9	1.1	77.7	41.1	49.7	50.3
73021	COLONY	90.2	88.3	0.4	0.4	0.0	0.0	3.1	4.4	5.2	5.6	5.2	4.8	3.6	23.0	33.5	16.5	2.4	80.6	46.3	50.0	50.0
73024	CORN	92.5	90.9	0.8	0.8	0.0	0.0	4.2	6.1	6.5	6.9	7.0	6.3	4.4	20.7	26.5	14.3	7.4	75.4	43.7	48.4	51.6
73025	EDMOND	93.4	91.0	1.5	2.3	0.7	0.9	1.9	3.0	5.8	6.8	7.9	7.7	4.3	21.8	34.4	10.5	0.7	74.4	42.0	50.1	49.9
73026	NORMAN	88.3	85.7	1.2	1.5	0.6	1.0	2.1	3.1	5.6	6.1	6.4	6.3	5.2	24.9	33.4	11.4	0.7	78.1	41.8	50.1	49.9
73027	COYLE	32.2	33.1	62.6	61.0	0.1	0.2	1.7	2.2	3.5	4.3	4.3	17.8	25.6	15.8	18.6	8.7	1.3	85.0	23.9	49.3	50.7
73028	CRESCENT	90.6	86.7	2.9	5.1	0.1	0.1	1.7	2.6	6.1	6.3	6.4	6.2	5.0	22.9	27.7	16.6	2.8	77.4	42.7	49.6	50.4
73029	CYRIL	83.0	83.0	0.2	0.2	0.3	0.3	2.7	2.7	7.3	7.3	7.5	6.8	5.4	23.4	23.9	14.8	3.5	73.5	38.6	45.9	54.1
73030	DAVIS	80.4	78.4	3.7	3.9	0.3	0.4	1.3	1.8	6.9	6.8	6.6	6.4	5.1	23.5	26.6	15.3	2.7	75.6	40.8	49.3	50.7
73034	EDMOND	84.8	81.1	3.7	4.1	4.9	6.5	2.9	4.4	6.2	6.0	6.6	8.5	8.8	26.6	27.6	8.3	1.5	77.2	34.8	49.5	50.5
73036	EL RENO	78.7	75.0	6.9	8.0	0.6	0.7	7.2	10.2	6.6	6.4	6.3	6.6	6.6	28.8	25.7	11.3	1.8	76.8	36.6	53.1	46.9
73038	FORT COBB	70.2	70.0	1.4	1.5	0.1	0.1	3.7	3.8	5.5	6.5	6.3	8.1	4.8	22.8	27.0	16.5	2.5	76.5	41.4	49.4	50.6
73040	GEARY	75.6	73.8	3.2	2.9	0.1	0.1	4.7	6.3	6.8	6.5	6.6	7.0	5.8	22.5	24.6	15.7	4.6	75.6	41.1	48.1	51.9
73041	GOTEBO	74.0	71.1	0.5	0.5	0.2	0.3	3.4	4.1	4.1	4.6	4.9	5.7	4.1	20.8	34.3	18.4	3.2	83.0	48.5	51.6	48.4
73042	GRACEMONT	78.9	78.8	0.1	0.1	0.1	0.1	5.5	5.7	6.1	6.5	6.7	6.5	4.5	24.8	29.7	13.4	1.7	76.6	40.6	52.0	48.0
73043	GREENFIELD	88.6	88.1	1.6	1.1	0.0	0.0	0.5	0.6	4.0	4.5	5.1	6.3	6.3	21.0	36.9	14.2	1.7	82.4	47.3	52.3	47.7
73044	GUTHRIE	82.1	77.5	9.7	12.4	0.5	0.6	3.3	4.5	6.3	6.3	6.4	7.1	6.4	24.6	28.5	12.3	2.2	76.8	39.2	49.0	51.0
73045	HARRAH	87.9	85.0	0.6	0.8	0.4	0.6	2.4	3.8	6.6	6.7	6.8	6.9	6.0	26.0	28.7	10.6	1.7	75.6	38.3	49.2	50.8
73047	HINTON	78.5	78.1	9.4	9.5	0.2	0.2	6.6	6.8	5.3	5.4	5.5	5.6	7.6	32.4	24.8	11.2	2.3	80.7	37.5	60.3	39.7
73048	HYDRO	89.1	88.8	0.2	0.2	0.2	0.2	7.0	7.3	6.6	6.5	6.4	7.2	5.6	24.3	27.9	12.7	2.7	76.2	39.5	49.9	50.1
73049	JONES	82.2	78.9	8.9	9.8	0.3	0.4	2.5	4.1	6.3	6.5	6.5	6.1	5.3	24.3	31.2	12.2	1.6	76.9	41.2	49.8	50.2
73051	LEXINGTON	78.1	75.5	8.2	8.2	0.2	0.4	4.4	6.2	4.9	4.9	4.9	5.8	7.9	35.5	26.2	8.6	1.4	82.0	37.8	63.5	36.5
73052	LINDSAY	90.3	88.4	0.1	0.1	0.2	0.2	1.3	1.9	6.5	6.4	6.3	6.2	5.3	23.5	26.3	16.1	3.4	77.0	41.4	48.0	52.0
73053	LOOKEBA	79.8	79.6	1.0	1.0	0.1	0.1	12.6	12.8	5.9	6.0	6.3	6.9	4.7	24.0	28.8	15.3	1.9	77.3	41.9	51.2	48.8
73054	LUTHER	85.0	81.5	4.0	4.6	0.4	0.5	2.0	3.1	6.0	6.2	6.9	7.5	5.6	24.2	30.7	11.0	1.8	76.0	40.0	49.8	50.2
73055	MARLOW	91.3	89.6	0.1	0.1	0.2	0.3	1.8	2.6	6.1	6.4	6.5	6.2	5.1	22.8	29.4	14.6	3.0	77.1	42.6	49.2	50.8
73056	MARSHALL	93.1	90.3	1.5	2.8	0.0	0.0	2.0	3.3	5.9	6.4	6.4	6.1	4.5	23.9	30.0	14.4	2.4	77.5	42.5	52.2	47.8
73057	MAYSVILLE	87.3	85.1	0.2	0.3	0.1	0.2	2.1	3.0	7.0	7.1	6.9	6.6	5.1	23.4	26.0	15.2	2.8	74.9	40.0	49.3	50.7
73058	MERIDIAN	84.5	78.9	5.2	8.3	0.5	0.4	2.3	3.1	5.3	5.3	6.1	6.6	6.1	24.6	33.8	11.4	0.9	78.9	42.2	52.2	47.8
73059	MINCO	92.3	90.3	0.1	0.2	0.2	0.3	3.4	5.0	6.8	6.7	7.0	7.3	6.0	24.9	25.9	13.1	2.2	75.0	38.5	49.6	50.4
73061	MORRISON	88.4	86.0	0.2	0.2	0.4	0.5	2.5	3.6	6.8	7.0	7.3	6.9	5.7	27.9	27.9	9.5	1.0	74.6	37.1	49.8	50.2
73062	MOUNTAIN VIEW	79.6	76.7	0.3	0.4	0.1	0.2	2.9	3.7	5.5	5.4	5.6	6.2	5.4	20.9	28.4	18.1	4.5	79.9	45.8	47.5	52.5
73063	MULHALL	92.2	90.2	0.0	0.0	0.8	1.0	1.2	2.0	7.1	7.1	6.9	6.7	4.9	25.5	26.1	13.8	2.0	75.4	39.4	52.1	47.9
73064	MUSTANG	91.9	89.8	0.6	0.8	0.7	0.8	2.8	4.3	6.9	7.2	7.7	7.5	5.7	27.4	26.9	9.4	1.2	73.4	36.3	48.8	51.2
73065	NEWCASTLE	89.9	87.5	0.2	0.2	0.2	0.3	2.4	3.4	5.6	6.0	6.3	6.7	5.2	25.7	32.1	11.6	0.8	78.0	41.0	50.1	49.9
73067	NINNEKAH	89.6	87.3	0.5	0.6	0.0	0.0	2.4	3.6	6.0	6.3	6.5	5.9	5.2	23.8	31.6	13.3	1.3	77.6	42.0	50.8	49.2
73068	NOBLE	88.7	86.2	0.4	0.4	0.3	0.5	2.7	3.9	7.4	7.2	6.9	6.9	6.6	27.5	26.9	9.4	1.1	73.9	36.0	49.6	50.4
73069	NORMAN	83.6	80.3	3.2	3.4	2.9	4.0	4.9	6.6	5.5	4.8	4.7	7.1	14.9	28.2	22.2	10.3	2.3	81.6	32.6	50.4	49.6
73071	NORMAN	79.7	76.3	6.2	6.4	2.6	3.6	4.2	5.8	7.4	6.2	5.6	6.5	13.2	32.0	20.8	7.1	1.0	77.2	30.2	49.8	50.2
73072	NORMAN	82.4	78.3	4.2	4.4	5.2	7.4	3.6	5.0	5.5	4.8	4.6	12.0	17.6	26.4	20.5	7.5	1.3	82.4	28.2	50.2	49.8
73073	ORLANDO	92.3	90.3	0.0	0.0	0.5	1.1	1.4	1.9	7.0	7.3	6.7	6.7	5.1	25.0	26.6	13.7	1.9	74.5	39.4	51.3	48.7
73074	PAOLI	85.7	82.8	0.3	0.3	0.1	0.2	4.2	6.1	6.7	7.0	6.6	6.4	5.3	25.8	28.5	11.8	1.8	75.9	38.8	49.7	50.3
73075	PAULS VALLEY	81.3	78.4	3.7	4.0	0.5	0.8	6.7	9.5	6.6	6.2	6.2	6.4	5.7	24.9	26.3	14.3	3.3	77.0	40.4	48.1	51.9
73077	PERRY	91.0	89.4	2.3	2.5	0.4	0.7	1.5	2.0	6.4	6.7	6.7	6.1	5.0	24.9	27.5	14.0	2.8	76.6	40.7	49.5	50.5
73078	PIEDMONT	93.2	91.3	0.5	0.6	0.4	0.4	2.3	3.5	6.7	7.2	8.6	7.9	4.2	26.1	30.5	8.1	0.8	72.4	38.7	50.2	49.8
73079	POCASSET	92.2	90.5	0.2	0.2	0.2	0.3	2.6	3.6	6.5	6.9	6.6	5.8	5.7	23.4	31.6	12.0	1.3	76.4	41.0	51.2	48.8
73080	PURCELL	83.9	80.3	1.3	1.5	0.3	0.4	8.0	11.6	7.1	7.2	6.9	6.7	5.8	26.4	25.7	12.2	2.0	74.7	37.7	49.4	50.6
73082	RUSH SPRINGS	89.3	87.1	0.1	0.1	0.1	0.2	2.6	3.8	6.2	6.9	6.9	6.6	5.5	24.1	27.9	14.1	1.9	76.1	40.6	51.1	48.9
73084	SPENCER	31.3	27.7	61.7	63.8	0.4	0.5	2.3	3.3	6.2	6.6	7.2	8.0	6.4	20.9	28.7	14.1	1.9	74.8	40.0	49.0	51.0
73086	SULPHUR	81.0	78.3	0.9	1.0	0.4	0.5	4.1	5.9	6.4	6.5	6.3	5.3	4.6	23.4	28.3	16.3	3.0	77.5	42.8	49.8	50.2
73089	TUTTLE	91.4	89.7	0.1	0.1	0.2	0.3	2.1	3.0	6.8	7.0	7.2	6.7	5.6	25.4	29.9	10.3	0.9	74.8	38.8	49.4	50.6
73090	UNION CITY	89.3	86.3	2.4	3.2	0.5	0.5	1.5	2.3	6.5	6.6	6.0	7.1	7.0	26.2	29.4	10.0	1.1	75.7	36.3	51.4	48.6
73092	VERDEN	90.2	88.4	0.4	0.5	0.1	0.2	2.4	3.6	7.7	7.7	8.1	7.5	5.5	22.3	27.3	11.7	2.3	71.9	38.5	46.0	54.0
73093	WASHINGTON	88.5	85.6	0.3	0.3	0.5	0.7	4.5	6.5	6.1	6.5	7.1	7.1	5.0	26.3	30.1	10.7	1.0	75.6	39.3	50.2	49.8
73095	WAYNE	87.4	84.9	0.1	0.1	0.1	0.2	5.1	7.2	6.7	7.5	6.8	5.9	4.8	24.6	29.2	12.8	1.8	75.4	39.4	48.6	51.4
73096	WEATHERFORD	87.2	87.0	1.7	1.8	1.3	1.3	4.2	4.3	5.5	4.8	4.7	11.3	19.5	24.1	20.2	8.2	1.7	81.5	27.5	49.3	50.7
73098	WYNNEWOOD	81.7	79.4	6.9	7.6	0.1	0.2	2.4	3.5	5.8	5.8	6.0	6.3	5.4	23.3	27.4	16.7	3.2	78.3	42.8	48.2	51.8
73099	YUKON	88.4	85.1	1.0	1.2	4.4	5.8	3.0	4.3	6.8	6.9	7.0	7.0	5.8	27.2	28.9	9.2	1.1	75.0	37.4	48.5	51.5
73102	OKLAHOMA CITY	55.1	48.4	30.1	34.4	1.8	2.2	6.1	9.5	1.3	1.4	1.4	5.1	11.8	40.9	27.6	9.0	1.6	94.3	38.8	74.9	25.1
73103	OKLAHOMA CITY	63.6	57.4	20.7	22.2	5.8	7.7	5.4	8.1	5.7	4.9	4.8	5.6	9.6	33.8	27.2	7.0	1.3	81.3	35.1	50.5	49.5
73104	OKLAHOMA CITY	11.4	13.8	82.0	77.4	2.2	2.9	1.4	3.7	9.4	9.3	8.0	7.3	8.3	25.7	22.4	8.3	1.3	68.7	29.3	45.6	54.4
73105	OKLAHOMA CITY	13.8	11.5	80.8	82.0	0.9	1.1	1.4	2.0	6.3	5.9	5.8	6.8	7.1	22.9	27.4	15.4	2.4	78.1	40.9	45.8	54.2
73106	OKLAHOMA CITY	51.4	45.1	15.9	16.0	9.4	11.2	23.2	29.9	6.9	5.8	5.1	8.2	12.7	33.0	21.5	5.9	1.0	78.7	30.6	53.8	46.2
73107	OKLAHOMA CITY	71.3	64.5	8.0	8.5	4.3	5.8	14.8	21.4	7.7	7.0	6.4	5.9	6.5	30.1	24.8	9.2	2.4	75.4	36.1	49.9	50.1
73108	OKLAHOMA CITY	58.6	52.9	7.2	6.5	0.5	0.6	43.1	54.7	11.4	9.7	8.0	7.8	7.9	29.0	18.9	6.3	1.0	66.2	28.1	52.1	47.9
73109	OKLAHOMA CITY	61.9	54.3	5.3	5.3	1.1	1.4	31.9	41.5	8.7	8.1	7.3	6.7	6.6	26.9	21.7	11.6	2.3	71.7	34.0	48.9	51.1
73110	OKLAHOMA CITY	68.7	63.5	19.7	21.5	1.8	2.5	4.4	6.6	7.7	6.8	6.2	6.5	8.1	28.3	22.7	11.4	2.3	75.5	34.1	47.9	52.1
73111	OKLAHOMA CITY	6.5	5.8	89.4	89.4	0.2	0.2	1.9	2.6	6.2	6.2	6.1	7.4	6.5	21.8	26.3	16.7	2.8	76.9	41.3	44.0	56.0
73112	OKLAHOMA CITY	77.6	71.9	8.1	9.0	4.7	6.5	6.6	10.0	5.9	5.5	5.1	4.8	6.2	29.7	26.1	13.6	3.2	80.8	39.8	47.6	52.4
73114	OKLAHOMA CITY	33.4	29.7	55.5	56.3	1.8	2.4	6.7	9.6	9.3	8.9	7.9	7.8	9.8	28.4	20.7	6.5	0.9	69.2	28.5	47.4	52.6
73115	OKLAHOMA CITY	74.1	69.5	14.0	15.1	1.7	2.4	4.9	7.6	7.6	6.9	6.4	6.8	7.1	26.8	24.2	12.5	1.7	75.1	35.8	47.9	52.1
73116	OKLAHOMA CITY	87.0	83.3	3.5	3.9	3.8	5.4	2.9	4.6	5.2	5.2	5.7	5.3	5.3	23.7	29.1	15.9	4.5	80.6	44.6	46.8	53.2
73117	OKLAHOMA CITY	10.6	9.9	84.6	84.4	0.2	0.3	2.1	2.8	7.4	6.4	6.3	7.5	6.0	19.8	26.2	16.5	3.8	75.2	42.0	44.7	55.3
73118	OKLAHOMA CITY	69.1	63.1	14.0	15.2	6.2	8.0	6.3	9.4	6.7	5.9	5.5	5.4	7.0	31.1	26.4	9.6	2.3	78.5	37.2	49.9	50.1
73119	OKLAHOMA CITY	66.5	59.0	5.8	5.9	1.1	1.5	26.2	36.0	9.3	8.3	7.5	7.2	7.1	27.3	21.2	10.0	2.0	70.5	32.0	49.0	51.0
73120	OKLAHOMA CITY	76.3	71.7	15.2	17.0	2.4	3.5	3.3	5.0	5.9	5.1	4.9	4.9	9.0	29.0	23.6	14.4	3.2	81.7	37.6	46.8	53.2
73121	OKLAHOMA CITY	22.9	19.9	71.2	72.9	0.7	0.8	1.2	1.7	4.9	5.3	6.0	6.6	4.9	19.5	30.3	19.6	2.9	79.7	47.0	47.4	52.6
73122	OKLAHOMA CITY	81.6	76.7	7.9	9.1	1.6	2.2	7.5	11.6	6.9	6.4	6.1	6.2	6.9	27.5	24.8	13.2	2.2	77.1	37.0	48.2	51.8
	OKLAHOMA	76.2	73.0	7.6	7.8	1.4	2.0	5.2	7.0	6.9	6.6	6.5	7.1	7.2	26.2	25.9	11.6	2.0	75.9	36.8	49.3	50.7
	UNITED STATES	75.1	72.0	12.3	12.7	3.8	4.6	12.5	15.7	6.8	6.7	6.6	7.1	6.9	27.0	26.0	10.9	1.9	75.7	36.9	49.2	50.8

#	POST OFFICE NAME	2009 Per Capita Income	2009 HH Income Base	2009 Household Income Distribution (%): Less than $25,000	$25,000 to $49,999	$50,000 to $99,999	$100,000 to $149,999	$150,000 or More	Median Household Income: 2009	2014	2009 National Centile	2009 State Centile	2009 Home Value Base	2009 Home Value Distribution (%): Less than $50,000	$50,000 to $89,999	$90,000 to $174,999	$175,000 to $399,999	$400,000 or More	2009 Median Home Value
73002	ALEX	16435	474	33.1	35.2	26.8	4.0	0.8	35999	37521	21	44	390	38.5	24.1	25.6	11.0	0.8	68750
73003	EDMOND	28339	8075	15.9	23.4	40.6	12.2	7.9	61022	60774	79	96	5626	4.8	14.1	60.3	16.2	4.5	126164
73004	AMBER	19450	1041	20.7	28.9	42.1	6.2	2.1	50267	50851	62	89	866	23.7	26.6	30.8	17.6	1.4	89706
73005	ANADARKO	15946	3618	36.5	31.5	27.2	3.4	1.3	34175	35920	16	32	2470	36.0	29.1	29.6	4.5	0.8	65426
73006	APACHE	16434	1373	32.3	35.8	27.1	4.4	0.4	34614	36336	17	34	1029	28.6	36.9	27.6	6.5	0.4	74489
73007	ARCADIA	30497	911	18.6	22.3	39.4	14.5	5.3	58909	57683	76	94	783	17.0	17.5	31.7	28.7	5.1	136068
73008	BETHANY	23052	8615	21.8	34.5	35.8	5.6	2.4	44929	46798	48	80	5209	8.9	36.1	46.7	7.3	0.9	93832
73009	BINGER	16130	705	34.9	33.6	27.2	3.8	0.4	35543	37352	19	41	567	39.7	27.3	26.1	6.7	0.2	64271
73010	BLANCHARD	21679	4059	22.4	27.7	38.5	8.5	2.9	49823	51463	61	89	3398	17.7	21.0	38.8	19.3	3.2	108052
73011	BRADLEY	16406	465	33.5	36.3	24.7	4.5	0.9	34661	35535	17	34	356	51.7	24.2	17.4	5.9	0.8	48421
73012	EDMOND	37543	8007	3.7	8.1	47.2	24.9	16.3	90442	91925	95	99	7265	1.3	2.3	54.9	36.4	5.1	163736
73013	EDMOND	34540	15757	11.2	20.2	40.2	16.3	12.2	71538	70732	88	98	11735	1.2	8.8	46.4	36.9	6.6	158944
73014	CALUMET	20406	1065	25.3	31.6	35.7	4.6	2.8	43761	44384	45	77	849	35.3	21.4	28.0	13.3	1.9	79872
73015	CARNEGIE	16652	1500	40.4	31.0	23.6	3.1	1.9	30627	31949	9	15	1088	40.3	29.7	24.4	5.2	0.4	63846
73016	CASHION	21308	260	25.4	27.3	40.8	5.0	1.5	47672	49033	56	86	206	21.8	23.3	42.7	12.1	0.0	97692
73017	CEMENT	16843	598	36.5	30.9	27.8	3.8	1.0	33619	34516	15	29	455	47.7	24.2	23.5	4.0	0.7	55000
73018	CHICKASHA	19726	8460	34.2	31.5	27.5	4.1	2.8	35828	37872	20	43	5526	30.4	33.0	27.7	8.1	0.8	72506
73020	CHOCTAW	25818	7970	13.4	27.1	42.7	12.9	3.8	60778	60186	79	95	6742	13.8	22.5	46.0	16.8	1.0	109729
73021	COLONY	19821	106	31.1	29.2	33.0	3.8	2.8	39079	41390	30	62	82	28.0	26.8	31.7	13.4	0.0	85000
73024	CORN	16803	444	30.9	37.2	27.7	2.9	1.4	36186	37771	21	46	335	34.9	31.3	19.7	13.7	0.3	67903
73025	EDMOND	45616	3116	7.8	13.9	32.7	16.1	29.5	90908	92047	95	100	2833	5.6	8.6	15.1	43.2	27.5	245327
73026	NORMAN	27351	4581	14.4	23.6	43.8	12.0	6.2	61808	63676	80	96	4048	11.5	18.2	38.2	28.3	3.8	131408
73027	COYLE	16687	642	38.8	30.2	25.9	2.8	2.3	34356	35917	16	33	408	42.4	20.6	25.0	11.5	0.5	62333
73028	CRESCENT	18963	1493	31.3	37.4	25.6	3.9	1.8	36400	39898	22	48	1159	34.3	28.1	27.8	9.3	0.4	71838
73029	CYRIL	17143	592	33.1	31.9	29.7	3.5	1.7	37203	39355	24	52	455	27.7	29.5	38.7	4.0	0.2	78393
73030	DAVIS	18489	1888	35.5	29.3	28.2	5.1	1.8	36440	37800	22	48	1417	28.7	34.2	28.0	8.0	1.1	75560
73034	EDMOND	33691	13991	19.1	20.1	31.3	15.4	14.2	64754	64527	83	97	9611	6.1	9.4	26.2	51.7	6.6	192374
73036	EL RENO	19649	7020	28.7	30.8	32.5	5.6	2.4	40839	42153	35	70	4676	23.6	32.2	32.1	11.4	0.7	83764
73038	FORT COBB	16352	697	38.5	31.4	23.2	5.3	1.6	30568	31655	9	15	553	37.8	30.4	27.7	3.1	1.1	63229
73040	GEARY	16472	711	33.2	34.0	29.4	2.3	1.1	33905	34564	15	31	526	44.3	27.9	23.8	3.2	0.8	58571
73041	GOTEBO	19265	166	31.3	33.7	31.9	1.8	1.2	38640	41125	29	61	134	41.8	29.9	19.4	8.2	0.7	60667
73042	GRACEMONT	17407	346	35.5	33.8	26.9	2.0	1.7	35776	38344	20	43	266	28.9	38.7	24.8	6.8	0.8	69355
73043	GREENFIELD	18066	72	33.3	31.9	27.8	5.6	1.4	35000	34340	18	36	57	47.4	14.0	31.6	7.0	0.0	55000
73044	GUTHRIE	21821	7739	26.9	27.6	36.2	6.2	3.0	45354	47938	49	82	5785	19.1	27.9	36.6	15.1	1.2	94648
73045	HARRAH	22306	3692	17.5	29.0	43.7	7.5	2.4	52702	53550	67	92	3037	17.1	27.0	41.1	14.4	0.4	97067
73047	HINTON	16964	963	31.4	34.5	28.7	3.1	2.4	36365	38561	22	47	748	25.5	29.0	35.0	9.5	0.9	82917
73048	HYDRO	16171	871	33.1	35.8	28.1	2.0	1.0	35880	37336	20	44	618	35.9	26.5	25.9	9.1	2.6	67111
73049	JONES	23995	2009	21.3	29.5	36.1	7.9	5.3	49140	50972	59	88	1609	23.1	28.4	29.8	14.0	4.7	88024
73051	LEXINGTON	17885	2670	25.2	33.3	34.9	4.0	2.7	41610	43448	38	72	2058	33.6	26.0	28.6	11.2	0.6	76210
73052	LINDSAY	19111	2343	33.2	30.2	31.8	2.9	1.8	36618	38732	22	50	1762	35.8	34.2	22.6	7.0	0.3	62968
73053	LOOKEBA	15840	251	37.8	37.5	19.9	2.0	2.8	30145	32333	8	13	201	40.8	24.9	28.4	5.0	1.0	62692
73054	LUTHER	20062	1715	20.5	31.3	40.3	5.9	2.0	48567	50170	58	87	1469	32.0	25.6	28.3	12.0	2.1	78301
73055	MARLOW	17712	3880	35.3	32.3	27.2	3.4	1.8	35063	36603	18	37	3044	21.6	33.4	34.4	9.9	0.7	81784
73056	MARSHALL	18059	182	33.0	33.5	27.5	4.9	1.1	34239	37371	16	32	145	42.1	15.2	24.1	15.2	3.4	73000
73057	MAYSVILLE	17173	950	37.2	32.9	25.1	3.4	1.5	33960	35737	15	31	729	36.5	31.6	26.2	5.3	0.4	64747
73058	MERIDIAN	23310	102	29.4	27.5	34.3	5.9	2.9	45555	47318	50	83	86	37.2	20.9	27.9	14.0	0.0	76000
73059	MINCO	20370	976	27.7	31.6	33.7	4.7	2.4	39917	42467	32	66	767	31.8	30.0	28.2	9.1	0.9	73700
73061	MORRISON	20069	571	25.4	33.1	33.3	7.0	1.2	42955	44226	42	75	457	22.8	37.2	30.6	9.4	0.0	80319
73062	MOUNTAIN VIEW	19785	548	42.7	29.6	22.4	2.2	3.1	30427	31405	9	14	422	54.5	30.6	11.1	3.1	0.7	46122
73063	MULHALL	17154	195	26.2	38.5	29.7	5.1	0.5	39830	42018	32	66	158	35.4	24.1	25.9	13.3	1.3	75000
73064	MUSTANG	26117	6980	13.1	23.6	46.8	11.6	4.9	63260	66689	81	96	5325	2.7	18.4	53.2	23.6	2.2	124788
73065	NEWCASTLE	26197	2409	10.0	31.4	39.6	14.5	4.5	59641	59307	77	95	2064	4.0	13.9	51.6	27.0	3.5	134860
73067	NINNEKAH	19208	674	32.0	31.5	30.0	4.5	2.1	39031	41201	30	62	541	29.4	27.5	30.9	10.5	1.7	82188
73068	NOBLE	19443	4428	22.2	32.7	38.4	4.8	1.8	44962	46414	48	80	3336	23.2	32.3	32.8	11.1	0.6	83668
73069	NORMAN	24230	10531	32.0	27.7	30.2	6.6	3.5	39835	42191	32	66	5164	5.8	25.9	44.3	22.3	1.6	114489
73071	NORMAN	22862	13848	27.9	29.5	32.3	6.9	3.5	43201	44699	43	76	7074	6.7	21.0	57.9	12.8	1.5	114818
73072	NORMAN	31060	16746	24.9	18.6	33.1	13.5	10.0	58650	60816	76	94	9210	3.5	5.0	38.8	45.2	7.6	180270
73073	ORLANDO	16612	138	26.1	38.4	30.4	5.1	0.0	40000	41709	33	68	112	36.6	25.0	25.9	12.5	0.0	71667
73074	PAOLI	19464	405	25.7	33.1	35.1	4.2	2.0	44709	46368	47	79	315	28.3	37.8	26.3	7.3	0.3	74630
73075	PAULS VALLEY	19522	3596	35.0	28.8	28.7	4.7	2.8	35841	37699	20	43	2449	24.2	34.5	28.3	11.6	1.4	80252
73077	PERRY	22983	2914	26.1	32.6	30.6	7.6	3.0	43141	44874	43	76	2156	27.6	31.3	30.1	10.7	0.2	77751
73078	PIEDMONT	26887	2306	7.2	23.3	46.0	17.2	6.3	69120	75419	86	97	2086	4.3	9.9	45.9	35.9	4.0	153306
73079	POCASSET	19617	347	23.3	34.0	34.6	6.3	1.7	43572	44662	44	77	287	24.4	25.8	37.6	8.7	3.5	89800
73080	PURCELL	20416	4163	26.3	32.3	33.8	4.8	2.8	43674	45395	44	77	3081	21.8	30.3	28.6	15.9	3.3	87481
73082	RUSH SPRINGS	16006	1668	39.3	31.2	24.7	3.5	1.3	31491	32749	11	19	1316	37.1	29.9	20.8	11.4	0.8	66563
73084	SPENCER	18235	2674	34.5	29.0	30.3	4.9	1.3	36283	40472	21	46	2013	33.0	41.3	21.9	3.4	0.4	65761
73086	SULPHUR	19849	3161	29.0	34.0	30.6	4.7	1.6	38265	39637	27	59	2311	28.6	28.3	31.9	10.0	1.2	78210
73089	TUTTLE	23211	4647	14.3	24.7	47.4	10.7	2.8	59941	59123	77	95	3973	9.5	14.7	51.5	23.0	1.4	127666
73090	UNION CITY	18162	250	26.8	32.4	32.4	6.4	2.0	40000	40932	33	68	199	27.1	26.1	33.2	12.1	1.5	85938
73092	VERDEN	17021	353	36.8	34.3	22.1	3.7	3.1	32215	33103	12	22	261	39.5	34.9	18.0	5.0	2.7	57051
73093	WASHINGTON	28545	870	16.3	22.8	39.3	13.4	8.2	60502	60587	78	95	761	20.5	11.0	27.2	30.0	11.3	143822
73095	WAYNE	16873	654	33.3	33.0	28.1	4.1	1.4	36476	38596	22	49	492	31.1	32.3	23.2	10.8	2.6	68723
73096	WEATHERFORD	21395	4977	33.6	29.2	27.1	7.0	3.1	37062	38918	24	52	2795	14.3	16.9	49.4	17.9	1.4	115649
73098	WYNNEWOOD	18949	1529	33.5	33.6	25.8	4.9	2.2	36419	38175	22	48	1133	29.7	33.5	26.1	9.5	1.1	73235
73099	YUKON	27632	20145	11.3	22.6	46.8	13.4	5.9	65029	71219	83	97	16335	3.7	11.5	59.7	23.4	1.7	132970
73102	OKLAHOMA CITY	15847	1236	55.3	24.7	17.6	2.2	0.2	20125	21942	1	1	105	45.7	17.1	23.8	13.3	0.0	59000
73103	OKLAHOMA CITY	28341	2335	39.2	27.8	23.2	4.2	5.6	32030	33894	11	22	703	17.4	16.8	30.7	26.9	8.3	133272
73104	OKLAHOMA CITY	9049	1025	74.4	14.6	8.6	2.0	0.4	11598	11786	1	1	206	29.1	36.9	18.0	16.0	0.0	72105
73105	OKLAHOMA CITY	20238	2452	41.3	26.2	26.0	4.0	2.5	31143	32442	10	17	1457	25.1	26.2	35.3	13.1	0.3	88419
73106	OKLAHOMA CITY	15236	5070	44.7	27.8	22.4	2.5	2.7	27960	28988	6	7	1869	37.8	31.0	21.2	7.3	2.6	65510
73107	OKLAHOMA CITY	19504	11044	32.6	34.2	28.6	3.4	1.2	36570	39270	22	49	6252	26.9	48.3	22.3	2.5	0.0	67906
73108	OKLAHOMA CITY	11973	5374	46.8	34.1	16.2	2.0	0.9	26523	27208	4	4	2158	75.5	21.3	3.2	0.0	0.0	37151
73109	OKLAHOMA CITY	14351	7813	42.5	34.6	20.4	1.7	0.7	28837	29736	6	8	3858	42.0	46.6	10.6	0.8	0.1	55066
73110	OKLAHOMA CITY	20991	15274	25.6	36.5	32.5	4.1	1.4	40842	43114	35	70	7965	16.8	46.7	32.9	3.3	0.3	77692
73111	OKLAHOMA CITY	16087	5145	46.0	32.1	18.2	1.6	2.1	26761	27342	4	5	3153	36.9	39.7	20.4	2.6	0.4	62316
73112	OKLAHOMA CITY	26553	15099	25.2	34.1	32.9	5.0	2.8	41483	43954	38	72	7960	8.9	37.1	43.0	10.1	0.9	93759
73114	OKLAHOMA CITY	18111	7034	31.8	35.9	26.6	3.9	1.7	36814	39825	23	51	3019	30.1	49.4	15.5	4.2	0.8	65729
73115	OKLAHOMA CITY	20165	9234	25.3	36.5	33.2	3.3	1.7	41498	43308	38	72	5691	19.3	56.4	22.2	2.0	0.0	69655
73116	OKLAHOMA CITY	43762	4506	14.1	25.3	35.2	11.2	14.1	60663	59514	78	95	3176	3.2	15.2	35.1	29.0	17.5	163976
73117	OKLAHOMA CITY	12791	2350	60.1	24.2	13.1	2.2	0.4	17683	18183	1	1	1140	56.7	32.4	9.9	1.1	0.0	45309
73118	OKLAHOMA CITY	27010	6812	26.7	30.9	31.6	6.1	4.7	44057	45861	46	78	3801	14.5	31.0	31.8	18.2	4.5	95485
73119	OKLAHOMA CITY	15226	10354	35.4	36.7	25.2	1.8	0.9	33328	34945	14	28	5509	45.7	48.2	6.0	0.1	0.0	52409
73120	OKLAHOMA CITY	34900	17728	18.4	31.8	33.7	8.9	7.1	49793	51068	61	88	9564	2.7	21.8	41.5	28.7	5.4	128021
73121	OKLAHOMA CITY	25909	1315	24.6	25.6	35.3	8.4	6.2	49794	51341	61	88	1090	15.7	28.3	30.0	21.0	5.0	104279
73122	OKLAHOMA CITY	24072	6242	22.6	34.1	34.6	5.5	3.2	44560	46514	47	79	3454	6.3	37.4	47.8	8.4	0.2	96366
	OKLAHOMA	22515		27.2	29.2	32.3	7.2	4.0	43746	45901				20.4	25.6	36.1	15.4	2.4	96076
	UNITED STATES	27277		20.9	24.4	35.3	11.7	7.6	54719	56938				9.3	13.1	31.6	32.6	13.5	162279

ZIP CODE #	POST OFFICE NAME	FINANCIAL SERVICES: Auto Loan	FINANCIAL SERVICES: Home Loan	FINANCIAL SERVICES: Invest-ments	FINANCIAL SERVICES: Retire-ment Plans	THE HOME: Home Improvements: Home Repair	THE HOME: Home Improvements: Lawn & Garden	THE HOME: Furnishings: Comput-ers & Hard-ware-Personal	THE HOME: Furnishings: Major Appli-ances	THE HOME: Furnishings: TV, Radio, Sound Equip-ment	THE HOME: Furnishings: Furni-ture	ENTERTAINMENT: Dine out/Carry out	ENTERTAINMENT: Sports Equip-ment	ENTERTAINMENT: Fees & Tickets	ENTERTAINMENT: Toys & Games	ENTERTAINMENT: Travel	ENTERTAINMENT: Cable TV	PERSONAL: Apparel & Services	PERSONAL: Auto Repairs	PERSONAL: Health Insur-ance	PERSONAL: Pets & Supplies
73002	ALEX	77	55	79	53	57	78	56	72	63	52	61	54	45	62	56	69	41	66	75	85
73003	EDMOND	113	111	94	110	105	96	111	104	106	116	108	84	108	112	105	102	76	105	96	122
73004	AMBER	90	78	74	75	76	85	75	81	79	76	79	60	68	82	71	82	53	78	83	97
73005	ANADARKO	67	56	57	56	55	67	60	63	65	57	63	48	54	65	56	69	43	63	70	76
73006	APACHE	73	54	69	53	55	73	57	68	63	53	61	51	47	63	55	68	41	64	72	81
73007	ARCADIA	111	107	115	106	108	115	100	111	101	100	101	83	97	102	103	104	69	105	110	130
73008	BETHANY	77	72	70	73	72	78	77	76	79	74	79	58	75	79	75	82	54	78	83	90
73009	BINGER	74	53	76	51	55	75	54	69	60	50	59	52	43	59	54	66	39	64	72	82
73010	BLANCHARD	92	85	76	83	83	89	81	86	84	83	84	63	77	87	78	87	57	83	88	102
73011	BRADLEY	72	52	73	50	54	74	55	69	61	50	59	51	44	60	53	67	39	63	73	81
73012	EDMOND	160	190	165	192	184	159	161	162	150	177	153	132	178	160	168	140	111	151	138	183
73013	EDMOND	127	135	124	137	132	124	130	126	125	134	127	99	134	129	130	122	90	125	121	147
73014	CALUMET	88	71	92	71	74	90	72	85	75	67	74	65	62	75	73	80	50	80	87	101
73015	CARNEGIE	72	51	74	50	53	74	55	69	61	49	59	52	44	60	54	67	39	64	74	82
73016	CASHION	87	80	71	77	78	81	75	80	78	78	78	58	71	81	72	80	53	77	80	95
73017	CEMENT	73	52	74	51	54	75	55	69	62	50	60	52	44	61	54	68	40	64	74	82
73018	CHICKASHA	74	60	65	59	60	74	65	70	70	61	68	52	57	70	61	75	47	69	77	84
73020	CHOCTAW	102	102	96	103	101	107	95	102	97	95	97	77	95	99	97	99	67	98	103	120
73021	COLONY	83	57	91	57	60	88	63	79	66	51	65	65	46	65	63	72	42	73	83	97
73024	CORN	78	53	85	53	56	82	59	74	62	48	61	61	43	61	59	67	40	69	78	91
73025	EDMOND	175	218	218	227	224	206	185	194	177	195	178	151	215	180	206	173	130	182	179	221
73026	NORMAN	109	111	101	110	109	109	101	107	102	105	102	80	102	105	102	103	71	102	104	125
73027	COYLE	72	51	61	52	51	64	67	64	67	58	66	52	52	67	56	69	45	66	67	78
73028	CRESCENT	78	56	79	54	58	80	59	74	66	54	64	56	48	65	58	73	43	69	79	88
73029	CYRIL	75	54	76	53	56	78	59	73	65	53	63	54	47	64	57	72	42	68	79	86
73030	DAVIS	77	57	75	56	58	78	61	73	67	56	66	55	50	67	59	74	44	69	79	87
73034	EDMOND	124	126	116	132	124	118	129	120	123	129	124	98	130	127	125	119	89	121	114	142
73036	EL RENO	77	68	66	68	67	78	71	74	74	67	73	56	65	75	67	78	50	73	80	88
73038	FORT COBB	73	52	76	51	54	76	56	69	61	49	59	54	43	60	55	67	39	65	74	83
73040	GEARY	70	51	71	50	53	73	55	68	61	49	59	51	44	60	54	66	39	63	73	80
73041	GOTEBO	77	53	84	53	55	81	59	73	61	48	60	60	43	60	58	67	39	68	77	90
73042	GRACEMONT	77	55	79	54	58	79	57	72	63	53	62	54	46	63	56	69	41	66	75	86
73043	GREENFIELD	79	56	81	55	59	80	58	74	64	54	63	55	46	64	57	71	42	68	77	88
73044	GUTHRIE	84	76	75	76	75	84	76	81	79	74	78	61	71	80	74	83	54	79	85	96
73045	HARRAH	100	86	84	84	85	95	83	91	88	85	87	67	76	91	79	92	59	87	92	109
73047	HINTON	82	60	86	58	62	84	61	78	68	57	66	58	50	67	61	74	44	72	81	92
73048	HYDRO	69	50	65	50	51	69	57	64	60	49	59	52	45	60	54	64	39	62	69	78
73049	JONES	100	87	98	86	88	103	86	98	91	83	89	73	78	91	85	96	61	92	101	115
73051	LEXINGTON	87	71	80	68	70	84	71	81	75	70	75	60	62	77	68	79	50	77	82	96
73052	LINDSAY	76	56	76	55	58	78	62	73	67	55	66	55	50	66	59	74	44	69	79	87
73053	LOOKEBA	75	52	82	52	54	79	57	71	60	47	59	59	42	59	57	65	38	67	75	88
73054	LUTHER	93	77	81	75	77	89	75	85	80	76	80	63	67	83	72	85	54	81	86	101
73055	MARLOW	75	54	77	53	56	78	57	72	63	52	62	54	46	63	56	70	41	67	77	85
73056	MARSHALL	75	54	77	52	56	76	55	70	61	51	60	53	44	61	55	67	40	64	73	84
73057	MAYSVILLE	74	53	75	51	55	76	57	71	63	51	61	53	45	62	55	69	41	66	76	83
73058	MERIDIAN	87	73	77	71	73	84	71	80	75	71	75	59	64	77	68	79	50	76	81	95
73059	MINCO	90	64	94	63	66	95	70	87	76	60	74	68	54	75	69	84	49	81	94	104
73061	MORRISON	82	75	67	72	73	77	71	75	73	73	73	55	67	76	67	76	50	73	75	89
73062	MOUNTAIN VIEW	78	56	81	55	58	82	61	76	67	53	65	58	48	66	60	74	43	71	82	90
73063	MULHALL	80	57	82	55	59	81	59	75	65	55	64	56	47	65	58	72	42	69	78	89
73064	MUSTANG	104	107	90	107	102	98	102	100	100	105	101	78	102	104	100	98	70	99	96	118
73065	NEWCASTLE	107	105	92	104	103	106	97	103	99	100	100	76	96	103	96	101	68	99	102	122
73067	NINNEKAH	87	63	90	61	65	89	64	82	71	60	70	61	51	71	64	78	46	75	85	97
73068	NOBLE	83	77	67	75	74	77	75	76	76	77	76	57	71	79	70	78	52	75	77	91
73069	NORMAN	75	64	61	66	63	67	80	69	78	73	77	56	71	77	70	78	54	75	73	84
73071	NORMAN	80	68	59	70	65	64	82	70	78	78	79	58	73	81	70	77	55	76	69	85
73072	NORMAN	109	98	91	102	95	93	121	100	111	112	113	84	109	113	104	107	80	108	97	120
73073	ORLANDO	80	57	82	55	59	81	59	75	65	55	64	56	47	65	58	72	42	69	78	89
73074	PAOLI	85	64	83	62	65	87	67	81	73	62	72	60	55	73	65	80	48	76	86	95
73075	PAULS VALLEY	79	61	72	60	62	79	66	75	72	62	70	56	56	72	62	77	47	72	80	89
73077	PERRY	89	69	81	69	70	89	75	84	79	68	78	64	63	80	71	85	52	81	90	100
73078	PIEDMONT	112	124	107	127	121	122	111	116	110	112	111	90	118	113	117	110	77	112	115	137
73079	POCASSET	80	72	72	75	74	85	71	81	74	65	72	61	66	75	71	78	49	74	83	94
73080	PURCELL	86	70	76	69	70	84	73	81	78	70	76	60	64	79	69	83	52	78	85	96
73082	RUSH SPRINGS	70	50	71	49	52	72	53	67	59	48	57	50	42	58	52	65	38	61	71	79
73084	SPENCER	72	59	65	59	59	74	62	68	69	61	67	50	57	68	59	74	46	68	77	83
73086	SULPHUR	82	61	87	60	64	85	65	79	70	59	69	60	53	69	64	77	46	74	84	94
73089	TUTTLE	94	95	84	95	93	97	89	93	90	90	90	70	89	93	89	92	62	90	94	110
73090	UNION CITY	90	64	92	62	67	91	66	84	73	61	72	63	53	73	65	81	47	77	87	100
73092	VERDEN	80	57	82	55	59	81	59	75	65	55	64	56	47	65	58	72	42	69	78	89
73093	WASHINGTON	116	121	105	121	117	120	110	115	111	112	111	88	112	114	112	112	77	111	115	136
73095	WAYNE	80	57	82	56	60	81	59	75	65	55	64	56	47	65	58	72	42	69	78	89
73096	WEATHERFORD	73	63	62	66	63	67	78	69	75	70	75	55	69	75	69	76	53	73	72	83
73098	WYNNEWOOD	78	56	79	54	58	81	60	75	67	54	65	56	48	66	58	74	43	69	81	88
73099	YUKON	107	115	98	114	110	108	105	106	104	108	105	82	109	107	106	103	73	104	104	125
73102	OKLAHOMA CITY	36	27	32	31	28	32	43	35	46	38	46	27	38	40	38	49	32	43	48	45
73103	OKLAHOMA CITY	73	61	63	65	61	59	79	66	77	77	79	55	73	76	72	76	56	75	68	81
73104	OKLAHOMA CITY	30	23	21	25	22	25	30	26	33	29	32	21	28	32	26	34	22	30	30	33
73105	OKLAHOMA CITY	63	55	53	56	54	62	60	59	65	60	64	43	58	64	57	69	44	62	68	72
73106	OKLAHOMA CITY	57	47	43	49	45	48	63	51	63	56	63	42	56	62	53	64	45	59	56	64
73107	OKLAHOMA CITY	64	54	50	56	52	59	64	59	65	59	64	47	58	66	57	67	45	63	65	72
73108	OKLAHOMA CITY	53	41	34	39	39	41	49	46	51	49	52	33	43	52	42	52	36	50	47	54
73109	OKLAHOMA CITY	55	44	43	43	43	51	51	51	55	48	54	38	44	54	46	58	37	53	56	61
73110	OKLAHOMA CITY	69	61	55	62	59	65	69	65	71	66	70	51	65	71	64	73	49	69	71	78
73111	OKLAHOMA CITY	53	46	45	47	45	54	49	50	56	51	54	35	48	53	47	60	37	53	60	62
73112	OKLAHOMA CITY	74	66	63	68	65	71	75	70	77	72	77	55	71	76	70	79	53	75	78	85
73114	OKLAHOMA CITY	68	54	45	57	49	57	66	58	68	64	68	47	60	70	57	70	47	65	64	73
73115	OKLAHOMA CITY	70	64	57	65	61	69	69	67	71	65	70	52	65	72	65	73	48	69	74	81
73116	OKLAHOMA CITY	125	127	134	131	131	131	129	127	128	130	128	96	133	127	131	129	91	129	132	149
73117	OKLAHOMA CITY	39	31	30	32	30	37	37	36	42	37	41	26	34	40	33	45	28	39	44	45
73118	OKLAHOMA CITY	81	73	70	75	72	76	83	76	83	79	83	60	79	83	77	84	58	81	82	93
73119	OKLAHOMA CITY	62	49	45	48	47	55	57	56	60	54	59	42	49	61	50	63	41	58	61	67
73120	OKLAHOMA CITY	100	88	85	92	87	89	101	92	101	99	101	73	97	101	95	100	71	99	96	111
73121	OKLAHOMA CITY	87	91	88	91	91	98	85	90	91	87	90	64	91	89	89	95	62	90	101	106
73122	OKLAHOMA CITY	76	72	66	74	70	76	78	74	79	75	79	58	76	79	74	81	55	77	81	89
	OKLAHOMA	87	75	78	75	74	84	79	82	82	77	81	63	73	83	75	85	56	82	86	98
	UNITED STATES	100	100	100	100	100	100	100	100	100	100	100	100	100	100	100	100	100	100	100	100

73127-73620

ZIP CODE #	POST OFFICE NAME	COUNTY FIPS CODE	POPULATION 2000	POPULATION 2009	POPULATION 2014	2000-2009 ANNUAL RATE % Rate	2000-2009 ANNUAL RATE State Centile	HOUSEHOLDS 2000	HOUSEHOLDS 2009	HOUSEHOLDS 2014	HOUSEHOLDS % Annual Rate 2000-2009	HOUSEHOLDS 2009 Average HH Size	FAMILIES 2000	FAMILIES 2009	FAMILIES % Annual Rate 2000-2009
73127	OKLAHOMA CITY	109	25434	25661	26012	0.1	49	10197	10343	10519	0.2	2.44	6555	6370	-0.3
73128	OKLAHOMA CITY	109	2230	3755	4250	5.8	100	930	1481	1669	5.2	2.53	653	1084	5.6
73129	OKLAHOMA CITY	109	19380	19339	19464	0.0	43	7065	7100	7171	0.1	2.71	4729	4571	-0.4
73130	OKLAHOMA CITY	109	17808	18672	19245	0.5	68	6685	7157	7422	0.7	2.61	5097	5315	0.5
73131	OKLAHOMA CITY	109	2300	2618	2783	1.4	90	894	1042	1115	1.7	2.40	672	759	1.3
73132	OKLAHOMA CITY	109	24933	27112	28239	0.9	80	10214	11274	11803	1.1	2.40	6743	7155	0.6
73134	OKLAHOMA CITY	109	2094	3046	3532	4.1	99	896	1415	1655	5.1	2.04	478	656	3.5
73135	OKLAHOMA CITY	109	15112	17371	18495	1.5	91	5457	6343	6771	1.6	2.74	4136	4672	1.3
73139	OKLAHOMA CITY	109	15940	15939	16097	0.0	43	7154	7335	7464	0.3	2.15	4332	4237	-0.2
73141	OKLAHOMA CITY	109	2760	3007	3151	0.9	80	1150	1280	1350	1.2	2.35	780	832	0.7
73142	OKLAHOMA CITY	109	8100	9906	10686	2.2	95	3687	4471	4818	2.1	2.20	2166	2526	1.7
73145	OKLAHOMA CITY	109	3050	3170	3260	0.4	64	724	772	802	0.7	3.46	695	737	0.6
73149	OKLAHOMA CITY	109	5815	5579	5529	-0.4	22	2323	2257	2249	-0.3	2.47	1483	1376	-0.8
73150	OKLAHOMA CITY	109	4544	4688	4928	0.3	60	1696	1780	1880	0.5	2.63	1382	1421	0.3
73151	OKLAHOMA CITY	109	956	1254	1388	3.0	97	332	449	501	3.3	2.79	281	373	3.1
73159	OKLAHOMA CITY	109	31144	33013	33978	0.6	73	12128	13066	13581	0.8	2.36	8318	8608	0.4
73160	OKLAHOMA CITY	027	40822	50017	54933	2.2	95	14828	19106	21258	2.8	2.60	11439	14259	2.4
73162	OKLAHOMA CITY	109	25729	28356	29745	1.1	84	10177	11416	12034	1.2	2.47	7192	7805	0.9
73165	OKLAHOMA CITY	027	4773	6093	6712	2.7	96	1672	2224	2479	3.1	2.73	1393	1797	2.8
73169	OKLAHOMA CITY	109	1670	2249	2522	3.3	98	592	822	931	3.6	2.69	477	646	3.3
73170	OKLAHOMA CITY	027	21881	31668	36546	4.1	99	7799	11466	13369	4.3	2.73	6435	9211	4.0
73173	OKLAHOMA CITY	027	554	690	780	2.4	95	213	275	314	2.8	2.51	167	208	2.4
73179	OKLAHOMA CITY	109	1655	2442	2740	4.3	99	616	907	1023	4.3	2.62	442	652	4.3
73401	ARDMORE	019	32711	34401	35191	0.5	68	12964	13851	14239	0.7	2.42	8933	9302	0.4
73430	BURNEYVILLE	085	971	993	1003	0.2	55	417	436	442	0.5	2.28	321	329	0.3
73432	COLEMAN	069	1164	1142	1134	-0.2	33	458	456	454	0.0	2.50	336	328	-0.3
73433	ELMORE CITY	049	2520	2574	2601	0.2	55	1046	1083	1096	0.4	2.38	751	759	0.1
73434	FOSTER	049	625	596	588	-0.5	15	242	235	232	-0.3	2.54	183	174	-0.5
73437	GRAHAM	019	655	681	693	0.4	64	250	265	271	0.6	2.57	194	201	0.4
73438	HEALDTON	019	3086	3036	3034	-0.2	33	1247	1241	1244	-0.1	2.38	865	836	-0.4
73439	KINGSTON	095	5194	5753	6123	1.1	84	2247	2519	2689	1.2	2.27	1628	1783	1.0
73440	LEBANON	095	109	128	138	1.8	93	49	58	63	1.8	2.21	36	41	1.4
73441	LEON	085	888	904	906	0.2	55	354	368	371	0.4	2.46	273	279	0.2
73442	LOCO	137	326	319	317	-0.2	33	135	135	134	0.0	2.25	102	100	-0.2
73443	LONE GROVE	019	3603	4023	4220	1.2	86	1312	1492	1572	1.4	2.69	1032	1150	1.2
73444	HENNEPIN	019	655	679	692	0.4	64	263	273	278	0.4	2.49	193	196	0.2
73446	MADILL	095	7882	9235	9952	1.7	92	3076	3639	3932	1.8	2.47	2137	2468	1.6
73447	MANNSVILLE	069	1092	1084	1074	-0.1	38	402	395	391	-0.2	2.74	303	292	-0.4
73448	MARIETTA	085	5069	5386	5506	0.7	75	1947	2080	2130	0.7	2.54	1412	1475	0.5
73449	MEAD	013	2266	2415	2490	0.7	75	963	1048	1086	0.9	2.30	700	739	0.6
73450	MILBURN	069	604	679	697	1.3	89	222	253	260	1.4	2.68	166	186	1.2
73453	OVERBROOK	085	447	472	484	0.6	73	174	188	193	0.8	2.50	133	141	0.6
73456	RINGLING	067	2108	1993	1934	-0.6	13	846	801	778	-0.6	2.44	590	546	-0.8
73458	SPRINGER	019	1152	1253	1300	0.9	80	465	512	534	1.0	2.37	350	376	0.8
73459	THACKERVILLE	085	1456	1529	1566	0.5	68	550	591	608	0.8	2.59	417	438	0.5
73460	TISHOMINGO	069	5161	5212	5204	0.1	49	2003	2053	2056	0.3	2.42	1363	1362	0.0
73461	WAPANUCKA	069	780	755	746	-0.4	22	316	310	306	-0.2	2.44	231	221	-0.5
73463	WILSON	019	3123	3290	3373	0.6	73	1226	1308	1346	0.7	2.47	872	906	0.4
73481	RATLIFF CITY	019	776	790	800	0.2	55	316	329	334	0.4	2.40	243	246	0.1
73488	TUSSY	019	60	61	61	0.2	55	25	26	26	0.4	2.35	19	19	0.0
73501	LAWTON	031	18578	17776	17484	-0.5	15	6613	6567	6500	-0.1	2.35	4286	4124	-0.4
73503	FORT SILL	031	7994	8366	8478	0.5	68	1429	1638	1701	1.5	2.42	1382	1578	1.4
73505	LAWTON	031	46479	46948	46888	0.1	49	17379	18275	18428	0.5	2.52	12706	12993	0.2
73507	LAWTON	031	25803	25737	25617	0.0	43	8623	8741	8722	0.1	2.67	5964	5920	-0.1
73521	ALTUS	065	19940	18633	17868	-0.7	10	7615	7185	6898	-0.6	2.54	5278	4874	-0.9
73523	ALTUS AFB	065	2537	2067	1931	-2.2	1	659	544	505	-2.1	3.35	647	533	-2.1
73526	BLAIR	065	1110	951	889	-1.7	2	448	391	367	-1.5	2.43	327	278	-1.7
73527	CACHE	031	4370	4621	4786	0.6	73	1516	1663	1742	1.0	2.77	1257	1348	0.8
73528	CHATTANOOGA	031	494	457	445	-0.8	9	194	186	182	-0.5	2.46	136	124	-1.0
73529	COMANCHE	137	5072	5003	4986	-0.1	38	1992	1997	2000	0.0	2.48	1492	1462	-0.2
73530	DAVIDSON	141	622	517	475	-2.0	1	245	210	194	-1.7	2.46	170	141	-2.0
73531	DEVOL	033	287	282	280	-0.2	33	117	116	116	-0.1	2.43	89	87	-0.2
73532	DUKE	065	694	617	581	-1.3	3	268	240	226	-1.2	2.57	187	164	-1.4
73533	DUNCAN	137	29146	28736	28660	-0.2	33	11895	11892	11906	0.0	2.38	8449	8246	-0.3
73537	ELDORADO	065	704	626	590	-1.3	3	306	274	259	-1.2	2.28	212	186	-1.4
73538	ELGIN	031	3172	3531	3640	1.2	86	1207	1393	1447	1.6	2.53	917	1026	1.2
73539	ELMER	065	456	380	352	-2.0	1	178	151	141	-1.8	2.52	139	117	-1.8
73540	FAXON	031	353	334	327	-0.6	13	136	134	132	-0.2	2.49	102	96	-0.7
73541	FLETCHER	031	3889	3861	3820	-0.1	38	1462	1500	1499	0.3	2.57	1143	1149	0.1
73542	FREDERICK	141	5685	5123	4818	-1.1	5	2165	1977	1865	-1.0	2.44	1475	1312	-1.3
73543	GERONIMO	031	1442	1528	1552	0.6	73	514	566	581	1.0	2.70	402	429	0.7
73544	GOULD	057	508	451	431	-1.3	3	192	171	163	-1.2	2.64	142	124	-1.5
73546	GRANDFIELD	141	1320	1348	1345	0.2	55	518	536	537	0.4	2.47	376	380	0.1
73547	GRANITE	055	2248	2298	2295	0.2	55	611	610	610	0.0	2.48	403	392	-0.3
73548	HASTINGS	067	209	202	199	-0.4	22	94	91	90	-0.4	2.22	72	69	-0.5
73549	HEADRICK	065	2200	1987	1881	-1.1	5	824	758	722	-0.9	2.62	653	591	-1.1
73550	HOLLIS	057	2711	2555	2478	-0.6	13	1039	976	944	-0.7	2.46	695	635	-1.0
73551	HOLLISTER	141	106	92	87	-1.5	2	40	34	32	-1.7	2.09	29	25	-1.6
73552	INDIAHOMA	031	1165	1118	1095	-0.4	22	443	440	436	-0.1	2.54	349	337	-0.4
73553	LOVELAND	141	277	283	282	0.2	55	107	111	111	0.4	2.50	78	78	0.0
73554	MANGUM	055	3570	3420	3366	-0.5	15	1511	1435	1410	-0.6	2.28	961	885	-0.9
73559	MOUNTAIN PARK	075	523	463	436	-1.3	3	230	209	199	-1.0	2.22	152	135	-1.3
73560	OLUSTEE	065	810	710	666	-1.4	2	295	261	245	-1.3	2.72	225	195	-1.5
73562	RANDLETT	033	966	963	962	0.0	43	361	366	366	0.1	2.63	274	272	-0.1
73564	ROOSEVELT	075	601	532	501	-1.3	3	275	250	238	-1.0	2.13	182	161	-1.3
73565	RYAN	067	1282	1202	1166	-0.7	10	526	500	485	-0.5	2.30	356	330	-0.8
73566	SNYDER	075	1710	1604	1537	-0.7	10	689	657	632	-0.5	2.37	454	421	-0.8
73568	TEMPLE	033	1442	1400	1387	-0.3	27	612	602	600	-0.2	2.26	391	373	-0.5
73569	TERRAL	067	465	428	413	-0.9	8	210	196	190	-0.7	2.18	129	117	-1.0
73570	TIPTON	141	1258	1062	980	-1.8	1	512	440	408	-1.6	2.28	354	296	-1.9
73571	VINSON	057	64	57	54	-1.2	4	35	31	30	-1.3	1.84	26	23	-1.3
73572	WALTERS	033	3919	3925	3920	0.0	43	1524	1545	1547	0.1	2.45	1086	1074	-0.1
73573	WAURIKA	067	2754	2651	2602	-0.4	22	1040	1005	985	-0.4	2.39	717	675	-0.7
73601	CLINTON	039	9797	9590	9502	-0.2	33	3711	3694	3682	0.0	2.50	2569	2497	-0.3
73620	ARAPAHO	039	950	919	910	-0.4	22	347	343	341	-0.1	2.55	271	264	-0.3
	OKLAHOMA					0.7					0.8	2.46			0.6
	UNITED STATES					1.0					1.1	2.59			0.9

ZIP CODE #	POST OFFICE NAME	RACE (%) White 2000	White 2009	Black 2000	Black 2009	Asian/Pacific 2000	Asian/Pacific 2009	% Hispanic Origin 2000	% Hispanic Origin 2009	2009 AGE DISTRIBUTION (%) 0-4	5-9	10-14	15-19	20-24	25-44	45-64	65-84	85+	18+	MEDIAN AGE 2009	% 2009 Males	% 2009 Females
73127	OKLAHOMA CITY	65.0	59.2	16.0	16.5	5.4	7.1	9.7	14.0	9.2	7.5	6.3	7.2	9.8	27.7	21.5	9.3	1.3	72.9	30.5	48.4	51.6
73128	OKLAHOMA CITY	86.4	81.7	1.4	1.4	4.9	8.1	3.4	5.0	6.0	6.4	6.7	6.2	4.9	25.1	31.9	11.7	1.1	77.1	41.2	49.0	51.0
73129	OKLAHOMA CITY	60.8	53.7	12.3	12.6	1.0	1.3	25.1	33.9	9.8	9.1	8.0	7.7	7.4	27.6	21.3	8.1	1.0	68.4	30.0	50.2	49.8
73130	OKLAHOMA CITY	72.2	67.5	17.5	19.1	1.9	2.8	3.6	5.6	6.5	6.5	7.0	7.2	6.2	25.7	28.6	11.3	1.1	75.6	37.9	48.6	51.4
73131	OKLAHOMA CITY	83.1	79.1	9.7	11.1	1.4	2.2	2.6	4.1	4.7	5.6	6.5	5.6	3.9	23.1	35.6	13.4	1.5	79.6	45.3	51.3	48.7
73132	OKLAHOMA CITY	74.0	69.2	13.8	14.6	3.9	5.6	5.7	8.3	7.7	7.1	6.6	6.5	7.4	29.7	24.2	9.9	1.0	74.7	34.0	47.9	52.1
73134	OKLAHOMA CITY	81.3	75.9	8.9	10.5	3.8	5.5	3.2	5.1	5.7	4.3	3.9	5.3	11.1	32.9	22.9	9.5	4.3	82.8	34.4	48.3	51.7
73135	OKLAHOMA CITY	54.5	49.7	29.3	29.5	6.6	9.0	5.2	7.5	8.1	7.7	7.3	7.5	7.3	29.4	25.3	6.9	0.5	72.4	32.3	48.7	51.3
73139	OKLAHOMA CITY	76.9	71.3	5.4	5.9	3.5	4.8	10.9	15.6	6.6	5.6	5.0	5.2	8.1	30.5	23.5	13.4	2.0	80.0	35.3	48.8	51.2
73141	OKLAHOMA CITY	56.4	51.5	34.5	37.0	0.7	1.0	3.6	5.2	8.2	8.1	7.2	6.9	6.9	24.9	25.6	10.7	1.5	72.2	34.5	49.0	51.0
73142	OKLAHOMA CITY	80.8	74.8	9.5	11.4	3.7	5.5	3.5	5.4	7.6	6.2	5.3	5.3	9.3	37.6	21.1	6.5	1.0	77.8	31.5	47.5	52.5
73145	OKLAHOMA CITY	68.3	61.7	18.5	20.4	3.0	4.1	8.6	12.8	14.7	12.0	7.7	9.4	17.6	35.1	3.0	0.5	0.0	62.6	21.8	55.3	44.7
73149	OKLAHOMA CITY	73.3	66.3	6.2	6.8	2.9	4.1	12.3	17.9	8.2	7.6	6.8	6.8	7.2	31.5	22.4	8.5	1.0	73.3	32.7	50.6	49.4
73150	OKLAHOMA CITY	84.6	80.7	4.1	4.5	2.4	3.5	3.2	5.1	5.5	6.0	6.8	6.7	4.7	22.4	33.4	13.6	0.9	77.5	43.5	50.3	49.7
73151	OKLAHOMA CITY	85.0	81.1	8.2	9.6	1.5	2.2	1.0	1.6	5.9	7.3	8.7	8.4	3.5	18.3	35.6	11.6	0.7	72.7	43.7	49.4	50.6
73159	OKLAHOMA CITY	77.2	71.2	6.9	7.9	4.4	6.3	6.5	9.5	6.7	6.0	5.7	5.9	7.2	31.1	24.1	11.6	1.5	78.1	35.8	50.4	49.6
73160	OKLAHOMA CITY	84.8	81.3	2.9	3.2	1.7	2.7	5.0	6.9	7.8	7.4	7.0	6.9	6.4	30.8	24.5	8.4	0.8	73.5	34.0	48.4	51.6
73162	OKLAHOMA CITY	83.2	78.2	6.5	7.6	4.6	6.9	2.5	3.9	5.5	5.7	6.3	6.8	5.9	26.3	31.2	10.4	1.9	78.1	40.3	47.8	52.2
73165	OKLAHOMA CITY	88.0	85.1	1.3	1.5	0.7	1.2	3.2	4.7	6.2	6.4	6.7	6.8	5.3	26.1	31.3	10.5	0.7	76.5	39.7	50.9	49.1
73169	OKLAHOMA CITY	91.6	89.0	0.5	0.7	0.5	0.8	3.7	5.7	7.2	7.4	7.6	7.5	5.0	27.2	27.4	9.7	0.8	72.4	36.5	51.2	48.8
73170	OKLAHOMA CITY	85.6	81.7	2.4	2.8	4.1	5.9	3.6	5.2	7.0	6.9	6.9	6.8	5.9	29.5	28.2	8.0	0.7	75.1	35.8	48.3	51.7
73173	OKLAHOMA CITY	92.6	90.3	0.5	0.7	0.4	0.7	1.8	2.9	3.5	5.9	5.9	8.7	3.9	23.3	34.8	13.2	0.7	79.0	44.3	52.5	47.5
73179	OKLAHOMA CITY	85.8	81.6	2.7	2.7	4.2	6.4	4.4	6.5	6.1	6.4	6.7	6.1	5.0	29.1	30.6	9.6	0.5	76.8	39.1	52.0	48.0
73401	ARDMORE	75.2	72.2	9.4	9.9	0.8	1.2	3.2	4.4	6.7	6.7	6.8	6.4	5.6	23.8	27.4	13.9	2.7	75.9	40.1	47.9	52.1
73430	BURNEYVILLE	87.2	84.8	0.8	0.8	0.5	0.7	3.4	4.9	4.5	4.7	5.2	5.3	3.9	21.3	31.0	21.2	2.6	82.2	48.5	50.9	49.1
73432	COLEMAN	79.1	78.7	1.1	1.1	0.1	0.1	2.8	3.0	6.2	6.5	6.7	6.2	4.5	24.6	28.9	14.7	1.7	76.6	40.9	52.9	47.1
73433	ELMORE CITY	89.6	87.6	1.8	2.0	0.2	0.3	1.2	1.7	6.3	6.4	6.7	6.6	4.4	23.3	29.5	14.1	2.7	76.5	42.2	50.4	49.6
73434	FOSTER	89.9	87.9	2.2	2.5	0.2	0.2	1.4	2.3	5.2	5.5	6.0	7.7	4.5	21.5	33.9	13.1	2.5	78.2	44.6	50.8	49.2
73437	GRAHAM	86.6	84.1	0.6	0.7	0.2	0.1	2.4	3.5	5.3	5.7	6.0	7.2	5.0	22.3	32.0	14.8	1.6	78.4	43.8	48.6	51.4
73438	HEALDTON	87.1	84.8	0.8	0.9	0.2	0.3	1.7	2.6	6.3	6.3	5.7	5.7	5.7	23.2	29.2	14.9	3.0	78.4	42.5	47.9	52.1
73439	KINGSTON	86.6	84.3	0.1	0.1	0.2	0.3	2.5	3.6	4.6	4.7	4.7	4.8	4.4	18.3	32.0	24.4	2.2	83.1	51.4	49.7	50.3
73440	LEBANON	82.6	79.7	0.0	0.0	0.0	0.0	0.9	1.6	6.3	6.3	6.3	6.3	3.9	21.1	29.7	18.8	1.6	76.6	45.0	50.8	49.2
73441	LEON	86.3	83.7	0.3	0.4	0.2	0.3	4.4	6.3	5.0	5.2	5.5	5.5	4.9	21.9	29.5	20.0	2.4	80.8	46.4	51.2	48.8
73442	LOCO	87.1	85.6	0.0	0.0	0.0	0.0	0.9	1.3	5.0	5.3	5.6	5.6	5.3	19.7	31.7	16.9	4.7	80.9	46.9	49.2	50.8
73443	LONE GROVE	84.8	81.6	2.0	2.4	0.2	0.2	1.4	2.1	8.2	8.2	8.1	7.4	6.6	26.5	25.2	8.9	0.8	71.0	33.6	50.1	49.9
73444	HENNEPIN	62.8	58.5	25.7	27.8	0.0	0.0	1.7	2.4	5.9	6.0	6.2	6.8	5.7	22.8	29.6	15.0	1.9	77.8	42.2	51.0	49.0
73446	MADILL	72.3	67.4	3.0	3.0	0.2	0.3	12.8	17.0	7.1	7.1	7.1	6.6	5.1	23.7	26.1	14.4	2.8	74.8	39.6	49.1	50.9
73447	MANNSVILLE	84.1	83.9	0.1	0.1	0.1	0.1	0.3	0.3	8.0	8.0	8.2	7.4	4.8	25.1	26.5	10.5	1.5	71.0	37.2	49.6	50.4
73448	MARIETTA	81.3	78.0	3.4	3.6	0.3	0.3	9.8	13.7	6.4	6.5	6.8	7.1	5.6	23.9	27.3	13.6	2.8	75.6	39.7	48.6	51.4
73449	MEAD	84.4	82.3	0.1	0.1	0.2	0.3	1.7	2.3	4.6	5.6	5.7	6.0	4.6	22.1	32.7	17.5	1.1	80.5	45.9	49.9	50.1
73450	MILBURN	81.8	81.7	0.2	0.1	0.2	0.1	2.5	2.5	5.4	5.6	6.2	6.9	5.3	22.4	31.2	15.2	1.8	78.4	43.5	49.0	51.0
73453	OVERBROOK	85.7	83.3	0.7	0.8	0.0	0.2	2.7	3.8	5.3	5.7	6.4	7.2	5.1	21.2	31.6	16.1	1.5	78.0	44.3	48.7	51.3
73456	RINGLING	84.9	81.1	0.0	0.0	0.2	0.4	3.6	5.1	7.4	7.2	7.0	6.6	4.6	23.7	25.0	15.6	2.9	73.9	40.2	47.0	53.0
73458	SPRINGER	76.1	72.6	10.4	11.6	0.2	0.2	3.0	4.3	5.0	5.2	5.8	6.4	5.3	25.4	31.0	14.1	1.8	80.0	42.7	51.2	48.8
73459	THACKERVILLE	90.2	88.2	0.3	0.3	0.3	0.4	2.6	3.8	7.1	7.2	7.5	6.5	6.1	24.6	27.9	12.0	1.2	74.2	37.8	52.5	47.5
73460	TISHOMINGO	73.4	73.3	2.8	2.9	0.4	0.4	3.1	3.1	6.3	6.7	6.1	7.9	6.7	22.3	26.7	14.4	2.9	77.0	39.6	48.0	52.0
73461	WAPANUCKA	78.5	78.3	1.3	1.2	0.1	0.1	3.1	3.0	6.4	6.5	6.8	6.4	4.5	24.6	28.3	14.8	1.7	76.3	40.5	52.6	47.4
73463	WILSON	89.7	87.7	0.4	0.5	0.2	0.3	1.5	2.2	6.6	6.5	7.0	6.7	5.1	22.2	28.2	15.6	2.0	75.4	41.5	48.7	51.3
73481	RATLIFF CITY	84.9	81.6	0.4	0.4	0.1	0.1	1.8	2.7	5.6	5.9	6.2	6.7	4.9	19.7	31.6	17.1	2.2	78.1	45.5	49.4	50.6
73488	TUSSY	83.6	82.0	0.0	0.0	0.0	0.0	1.6	1.6	4.9	4.9	6.6	6.6	4.9	18.0	32.8	19.7	1.6	77.0	47.1	49.2	50.8
73501	LAWTON	58.4	54.5	25.9	26.9	1.9	2.6	8.3	11.1	6.9	6.5	6.1	6.9	8.5	31.8	23.0	8.7	1.6	76.4	34.1	54.4	45.6
73503	FORT SILL	58.3	53.5	26.6	27.2	2.8	3.7	13.3	17.7	8.8	7.3	4.2	16.4	28.5	32.7	2.0	0.1	0.0	76.9	22.3	70.3	29.7
73505	LAWTON	62.6	58.4	22.2	22.7	3.4	4.6	8.4	11.2	8.9	7.8	7.1	7.3	7.9	28.5	21.4	9.7	1.4	71.9	31.5	48.1	51.9
73507	LAWTON	67.6	63.6	16.6	17.3	2.3	3.3	9.3	12.5	8.1	7.7	6.7	8.8	10.1	28.2	21.3	7.8	1.3	73.4	29.9	52.6	47.4
73521	ALTUS	72.3	67.3	10.0	10.0	1.4	1.9	18.2	23.9	7.8	7.5	6.9	7.1	6.9	26.1	24.7	10.8	2.1	73.4	34.9	49.6	50.4
73523	ALTUS AFB	79.5	74.6	10.3	11.3	2.5	3.4	7.8	11.3	16.6	11.1	7.5	6.6	17.0	38.9	2.2	0.1	0.0	62.1	22.4	54.8	45.2
73526	BLAIR	87.2	82.1	0.2	0.2	0.6	0.8	9.1	13.4	6.8	6.5	6.6	7.4	5.5	25.6	26.5	13.1	2.0	75.6	38.0	47.1	52.9
73527	CACHE	75.5	72.3	2.8	3.2	1.0	1.4	5.1	7.2	7.4	7.6	7.6	7.5	6.3	24.8	28.6	9.4	0.8	72.6	36.2	49.8	50.2
73528	CHATTANOOGA	82.4	79.0	0.6	0.7	0.8	1.1	9.7	14.0	6.6	7.9	7.2	7.2	5.3	24.9	26.5	12.3	2.2	73.3	37.1	48.8	51.2
73529	COMANCHE	88.2	86.3	0.1	0.1	0.2	0.3	1.7	2.5	6.2	6.5	6.6	6.0	4.6	22.0	28.5	17.2	2.4	77.0	43.3	50.1	49.9
73530	DAVIDSON	81.1	75.4	1.0	1.0	0.0	0.0	24.4	33.1	7.5	7.4	7.0	7.0	5.4	21.7	25.3	16.4	2.3	73.9	40.9	50.3	49.7
73531	DEVOL	89.5	89.4	1.4	1.4	0.0	0.0	7.3	7.1	5.0	5.0	6.4	7.8	3.9	27.7	29.4	13.1	1.8	78.7	42.1	57.1	42.9
73532	DUKE	87.0	81.8	0.1	0.2	0.4	0.6	12.3	17.3	7.1	7.3	6.8	5.8	5.7	24.1	24.8	15.6	2.8	75.0	39.1	49.4	50.6
73533	DUNCAN	87.5	85.2	3.2	3.6	0.4	0.6	5.0	7.3	6.2	6.2	6.5	6.4	5.5	22.7	28.3	15.3	3.0	77.2	42.0	48.2	51.8
73537	ELDORADO	87.8	82.7	0.1	0.2	0.4	0.6	11.4	16.1	7.0	7.3	6.9	5.8	5.6	24.4	24.4	15.8	2.7	75.6	39.0	49.5	50.5
73538	ELGIN	80.8	78.4	0.6	0.6	0.5	0.7	4.4	6.3	7.0	7.0	7.0	7.1	5.9	24.7	27.8	12.2	1.4	74.7	38.4	49.4	50.6
73539	ELMER	87.9	83.4	0.7	0.8	0.9	1.1	10.1	15.3	5.3	6.3	6.8	6.3	3.9	24.2	31.1	14.5	1.6	77.6	42.7	55.8	44.2
73540	FAXON	83.9	80.5	1.4	1.5	0.6	0.9	4.2	6.0	6.3	6.3	6.9	7.2	4.8	22.5	30.8	13.5	1.8	75.7	41.9	50.6	49.4
73541	FLETCHER	91.3	89.7	0.2	0.2	0.3	0.5	2.3	3.3	6.8	6.7	6.9	7.0	6.1	24.4	28.0	12.3	1.8	75.2	38.8	48.9	51.1
73542	FREDERICK	71.0	66.0	10.5	10.3	0.5	0.6	19.4	25.7	6.8	6.7	6.7	7.9	5.5	23.0	24.8	14.6	4.0	74.5	39.6	50.0	50.0
73543	GERONIMO	77.0	73.4	1.5	1.8	1.2	1.8	6.1	8.4	8.0	8.2	7.9	6.9	5.8	26.6	25.5	10.1	1.0	71.5	35.9	51.1	48.9
73544	GOULD	86.6	82.0	1.4	1.6	0.4	0.4	12.2	17.3	5.3	6.0	6.0	6.0	4.0	23.3	31.3	15.3	2.9	79.2	44.6	53.2	46.8
73546	GRANDFIELD	77.9	72.6	6.7	7.1	0.2	0.2	14.7	20.5	6.3	6.4	6.5	5.9	5.0	23.3	27.1	16.3	3.1	76.9	42.3	48.9	51.1
73547	GRANITE	76.2	75.5	12.1	12.8	0.4	0.4	6.8	7.0	3.3	3.4	3.6	5.2	9.4	37.9	23.1	12.2	2.1	86.9	38.0	66.7	33.3
73548	HASTINGS	92.4	90.6	0.5	0.5	0.0	0.0	4.8	6.9	5.9	6.9	6.4	4.5	3.0	19.8	26.7	23.3	3.5	78.2	48.2	45.0	55.0
73549	HEADRICK	91.0	88.1	1.0	1.1	0.6	0.9	5.5	8.0	6.2	6.4	6.6	6.4	5.5	25.4	30.6	11.4	1.3	76.7	40.2	50.3	49.7
73550	HOLLIS	69.7	63.4	11.6	12.5	0.2	0.2	25.0	32.6	6.7	6.7	6.6	6.5	5.7	23.4	24.8	14.6	5.0	75.7	40.0	48.7	51.3
73551	HOLLISTER	85.7	81.5	6.7	7.6	0.0	0.0	5.7	8.7	3.3	4.3	5.4	13.0	4.3	23.9	32.6	10.9	2.2	75.0	42.1	66.3	33.7
73552	INDIAHOMA	71.3	68.6	1.1	1.2	0.3	0.5	6.1	8.1	7.3	7.6	7.5	6.4	5.0	22.9	27.7	13.8	1.7	73.4	39.2	51.3	48.7
73553	LOVELAND	78.0	72.4	6.5	7.1	0.4	0.4	14.8	20.5	6.0	6.4	6.7	5.7	4.9	23.7	26.9	16.6	3.2	77.0	42.5	49.5	50.5
73554	MANGUM	85.8	85.0	5.9	6.5	0.1	0.1	7.8	8.0	6.4	6.3	6.2	5.9	5.1	23.1	25.7	16.6	4.6	77.3	42.3	48.4	51.6
73559	MOUNTAIN PARK	92.5	90.1	1.2	1.3	0.0	0.0	5.4	7.6	4.1	4.8	5.0	5.0	4.5	22.2	33.7	17.5	3.2	82.9	47.4	53.3	46.7
73560	OLUSTEE	78.6	72.4	0.5	0.4	0.5	0.6	22.6	30.8	7.9	7.9	8.0	7.5	5.5	24.1	26.5	11.0	1.7	71.3	36.2	50.6	49.4
73562	RANDLETT	93.1	92.9	0.5	0.5	0.2	0.2	6.5	6.7	6.1	6.2	5.9	7.9	5.5	27.6	26.6	12.4	1.8	76.8	39.1	52.3	47.7
73564	ROOSEVELT	92.2	90.0	1.2	1.3	0.0	0.0	5.5	7.5	4.1	4.9	4.9	5.1	4.3	22.2	33.6	17.7	3.2	83.3	47.6	53.4	46.6
73565	RYAN	89.0	85.5	0.5	0.5	0.2	0.2	10.3	14.6	6.2	6.3	6.3	5.4	5.5	21.1	27.8	16.5	4.9	77.8	44.2	47.5	52.5
73566	SNYDER	85.3	82.4	6.6	7.0	0.1	0.1	9.4	12.7	6.5	6.4	6.4	7.2	5.6	22.1	27.1	15.6	3.1	76.1	41.1	47.7	52.3
73568	TEMPLE	78.7	78.4	9.3	9.4	0.2	0.2	6.7	7.0	6.4	6.4	6.7	6.6	5.0	23.8	24.5	16.1	4.5	76.6	40.9	49.6	50.4
73569	TERRAL	89.1	86.0	0.0	0.0	0.0	0.0	14.8	20.8	7.0	6.5	6.1	4.0	6.5	18.2	27.6	21.3	2.8	78.3	46.3	46.3	53.7
73570	TIPTON	79.7	74.9	9.6	10.4	0.3	0.5	11.2	16.1	5.6	6.7	7.2	7.1	6.3	20.3	26.1	17.4	3.3	75.7	41.7	48.2	51.8
73571	VINSON	87.5	82.5	1.6	1.8	0.0	0.0	12.5	17.5	5.3	5.3	5.3	5.3	3.5	26.3	31.6	14.0	3.5	78.9	44.4	54.4	45.6
73572	WALTERS	84.5	84.3	1.2	1.2	0.1	0.1	3.6	3.6	7.0	7.0	6.9	6.3	4.9	23.8	26.6	14.6	2.8	75.1	40.7	50.6	49.4
73573	WAURIKA	87.3	84.3	1.5	1.5	2.6	3.6	7.0	9.6	5.6	5.8	6.1	6.6	5.3	26.5	25.4	14.9	3.7	78.2	40.5	51.4	48.6
73601	CLINTON	70.9	70.3	5.4	5.4	0.7	0.7	17.3	17.8	7.7	7.0	6.7	6.7	6.5	24.2	24.3	13.9	3.2	74.5	37.6	49.1	50.9
73620	ARAPAHO	86.8	86.5	1.4	1.4	1.4	1.3	6.1	6.6	5.4	5.7	6.0	7.3	5.4	23.8	31.3	13.3	1.7	78.1	42.3	50.1	49.9
	OKLAHOMA	76.2	73.0	7.6	7.8	1.4	2.0	5.2	7.0	6.9	6.6	6.5	7.1	7.2	26.2	25.9	11.6	2.0	75.9	36.8	49.3	50.7
	UNITED STATES	75.1	72.0	12.3	12.7	3.8	4.6	12.5	15.7	6.8	6.7	6.6	7.1	6.9	27.0	26.0	10.9	1.9	75.7	36.9	49.2	50.8

ZIP CODE #	POST OFFICE NAME	2009 Per Capita Income	2009 HH Income Base	2009 HOUSEHOLD INCOME DISTRIBUTION (%) Less than $25,000	$25,000 to $49,999	$50,000 to $99,999	$100,000 to $149,999	$150,000 or More	MEDIAN HOUSEHOLD INCOME 2009	2014	2009 National Centile	2009 State Centile	2009 Home Value Base	2009 HOME VALUE DISTRIBUTION (%) Less than $50,000	$50,000 to $89,999	$90,000 to $174,999	$175,000 to $399,999	$400,000 or More	2009 Median Home Value
73127	OKLAHOMA CITY	19268	10343	32.4	33.2	27.7	4.1	2.6	37284	40271	24	53	4607	16.2	33.1	41.7	7.8	1.2	90786
73128	OKLAHOMA CITY	26538	1481	16.5	26.5	40.2	12.1	4.7	56553	58948	73	94	1313	27.9	17.1	34.6	20.0	0.5	100476
73129	OKLAHOMA CITY	13595	7100	42.2	36.1	18.9	1.9	0.8	28973	29916	7	9	3716	70.5	26.2	2.7	0.4	0.2	38833
73130	OKLAHOMA CITY	23790	7157	18.3	25.7	43.3	10.1	2.7	54557	55008	71	93	5530	14.8	29.4	45.5	9.7	0.5	99814
73131	OKLAHOMA CITY	43659	1042	8.0	19.1	41.5	15.5	15.9	76791	77041	90	99	905	3.9	9.6	40.6	35.0	10.9	163149
73132	OKLAHOMA CITY	25971	11274	17.1	29.7	40.7	9.4	3.0	52664	53782	67	92	6085	1.1	10.0	66.8	21.5	0.7	129194
73134	OKLAHOMA CITY	33713	1415	18.0	28.8	33.3	12.3	7.6	52419	53096	67	91	721	1.2	21.8	30.1	40.1	6.8	165466
73135	OKLAHOMA CITY	21932	6343	19.5	30.0	38.8	7.6	4.1	50375	52047	62	89	4196	9.1	25.8	56.1	8.8	0.2	110635
73139	OKLAHOMA CITY	24827	7335	25.1	33.6	31.8	6.5	3.0	42629	44154	41	75	3308	2.0	26.7	51.1	19.6	0.5	113822
73141	OKLAHOMA CITY	18691	1280	33.1	33.8	26.9	5.2	1.0	36981	40255	24	51	790	35.9	43.9	17.2	1.9	1.0	64146
73142	OKLAHOMA CITY	32205	4471	13.9	33.5	36.5	9.4	6.7	52443	52734	67	91	2236	0.0	2.7	58.3	28.1	10.9	153866
73145	OKLAHOMA CITY	13878	772	13.6	45.5	37.4	2.5	1.0	44232	45751	46	78	45	55.6	22.2	11.1	11.1	0.0	46875
73149	OKLAHOMA CITY	17937	2257	28.7	37.4	30.2	2.7	1.1	38326	41021	28	59	1151	52.5	29.4	17.0	0.1	1.0	48219
73150	OKLAHOMA CITY	33319	1780	11.5	16.7	40.4	21.9	9.6	76455	76802	90	99	1510	19.5	12.3	25.9	38.9	3.4	150214
73151	OKLAHOMA CITY	45924	449	14.0	10.9	22.3	21.2	31.6	105622	105954	97	100	419	4.5	2.9	14.6	43.9	34.1	332143
73159	OKLAHOMA CITY	21791	13066	23.8	31.3	37.0	6.1	1.8	45819	47633	51	83	8582	3.3	41.4	50.8	4.0	0.5	93849
73160	OKLAHOMA CITY	24842	19106	13.5	26.5	47.5	9.4	3.2	57561	60422	75	94	13944	6.9	30.9	53.2	8.3	0.7	98965
73162	OKLAHOMA CITY	33490	11416	10.8	21.5	40.9	18.5	8.4	69922	69368	87	98	8149	0.6	4.9	56.7	34.5	3.3	156250
73165	OKLAHOMA CITY	27012	2224	9.8	22.2	48.3	14.4	5.2	63669	64928	82	96	1926	8.5	14.9	43.9	31.3	1.4	137726
73169	OKLAHOMA CITY	23737	822	20.1	20.3	47.6	7.5	4.5	55277	54980	72	93	700	19.9	23.6	29.9	24.1	2.6	97797
73170	OKLAHOMA CITY	35118	11466	6.2	14.2	47.5	18.8	13.4	80425	81475	92	99	9804	2.4	4.7	46.1	41.8	4.9	168207
73173	OKLAHOMA CITY	28849	275	12.0	21.5	50.5	11.6	4.4	75204	75934	89	99	231	4.8	4.3	28.1	58.9	3.9	202717
73179	OKLAHOMA CITY	25319	907	13.3	27.2	46.0	8.6	4.9	57646	57525	75	94	753	23.2	21.1	38.5	16.5	0.7	97328
73401	ARDMORE	20480	13851	32.1	29.0	30.5	5.9	2.5	38501	40906	28	60	9486	21.3	25.4	34.9	16.0	2.4	96282
73430	BURNEYVILLE	22316	436	28.9	29.4	34.2	5.0	2.5	42620	44573	41	74	381	25.7	21.8	33.3	17.6	1.6	95938
73432	COLEMAN	16225	456	40.1	32.2	22.4	3.5	1.8	30280	30996	9	14	382	40.6	27.7	22.8	7.6	1.3	60000
73433	ELMORE CITY	17216	1083	37.1	33.8	24.7	3.0	1.5	32662	33642	13	25	845	30.4	33.6	25.4	9.5	1.1	72016
73434	FOSTER	15721	235	36.2	32.3	28.5	1.7	1.3	32793	34643	13	25	197	31.5	22.3	30.5	13.2	2.5	83182
73437	GRAHAM	16006	265	31.3	39.2	25.7	3.4	0.4	37909	40203	26	57	213	36.6	20.2	32.4	8.5	2.3	71667
73438	HEALDTON	15608	1241	42.1	31.9	21.5	3.3	1.1	30739	31942	9	15	895	51.5	28.5	16.8	3.2	0.0	48929
73439	KINGSTON	19653	2519	35.6	32.9	25.1	4.1	2.4	35277	36682	19	38	2110	24.3	26.3	35.3	11.9	2.2	88762
73440	LEBANON	19950	58	37.9	34.5	22.4	5.2	0.0	32318	32959	12	23	50	20.0	28.0	34.0	16.0	2.0	92500
73441	LEON	17888	368	38.9	28.3	27.4	3.8	1.6	33744	36328	15	30	326	31.9	22.7	31.0	13.5	0.9	80000
73442	LOCO	17342	135	36.3	32.6	28.1	3.0	0.0	36092	37305	21	45	115	37.4	22.6	29.6	8.7	1.7	66429
73443	LONE GROVE	17626	1492	29.8	27.7	36.1	5.3	1.1	40000	42780	33	68	1136	21.1	33.5	32.5	12.5	0.4	82535
73444	HENNEPIN	17030	273	43.6	27.5	22.3	4.8	1.8	29545	30935	7	11	222	42.8	22.5	22.1	9.9	2.7	61818
73446	MADILL	17133	3639	38.9	33.1	22.8	3.5	1.8	31667	32748	11	20	2738	25.5	32.5	31.4	8.8	1.7	77640
73447	MANNSVILLE	16391	395	35.4	28.1	28.1	6.6	1.8	36499	39803	22	49	304	36.8	40.5	18.1	3.6	1.0	58889
73448	MARIETTA	19591	2080	30.1	30.7	31.3	5.6	2.3	39909	41826	32	66	1602	23.7	33.2	29.3	11.0	2.8	77891
73449	MEAD	18678	1048	36.2	31.3	27.4	4.1	1.0	35870	38233	20	43	852	34.5	21.2	35.0	9.2	0.1	78036
73450	MILBURN	12192	253	42.7	41.5	13.4	2.0	0.4	28074	28280	6	7	212	46.2	28.8	12.7	7.1	5.2	53478
73453	OVERBROOK	21203	188	28.7	26.1	36.7	5.9	2.7	46142	46970	52	84	163	21.5	26.4	35.0	14.1	3.1	93500
73456	RINGLING	15902	801	46.3	27.1	20.8	4.2	1.5	27588	28599	5	5	600	52.0	25.8	13.5	5.3	3.3	48065
73458	SPRINGER	19006	512	36.3	26.6	30.3	4.7	2.1	37432	40349	25	54	409	32.5	29.8	23.2	13.0	1.5	76935
73459	THACKERVILLE	21396	591	24.9	31.5	34.3	5.8	3.6	44270	45501	46	78	493	26.6	29.2	28.8	12.6	2.8	82083
73460	TISHOMINGO	17254	2053	43.4	30.6	20.2	3.5	2.2	29116	29721	7	10	1356	31.1	30.3	30.6	7.8	0.1	70494
73461	WAPANUCKA	16467	310	41.3	32.3	21.3	3.5	1.6	29412	30000	7	11	258	42.6	27.1	22.1	7.0	1.2	57917
73463	WILSON	16206	1308	36.2	36.2	22.9	3.4	1.5	32362	33512	12	24	1064	39.9	24.1	27.9	5.7	2.3	64259
73481	RATLIFF CITY	17921	329	38.9	31.3	26.1	1.2	2.4	33410	34385	14	29	275	49.8	21.8	20.4	6.5	1.5	50217
73488	TUSSY	14098	26	46.2	26.9	26.9	0.0	0.0	30000	30000	8	12	22	54.5	22.7	18.2	4.5	0.0	46667
73501	LAWTON	17919	6567	38.8	29.0	25.6	4.8	1.8	33176	34828	14	27	3474	19.0	31.7	41.5	6.7	1.1	89228
73503	FORT SILL	18246	1638	8.5	43.9	37.7	7.5	2.4	48577	49910	58	87	23	0.0	17.4	30.4	52.2	0.0	176786
73505	LAWTON	21996	18275	22.8	31.5	35.6	7.1	2.9	46624	48455	53	85	10951	5.9	28.8	51.0	12.9	1.4	106782
73507	LAWTON	20126	8741	26.7	29.6	31.9	7.7	4.0	43582	46633	44	77	5414	12.4	32.2	37.1	17.4	0.9	97481
73521	ALTUS	20413	7185	30.7	28.9	31.1	6.4	2.9	39146	41609	30	63	4274	23.9	29.5	35.7	9.1	1.8	85290
73523	ALTUS AFB	16423	544	9.7	44.9	36.6	7.5	1.3	46310	47348	52	84	11	0.0	72.7	27.3	0.0	0.0	65833
73526	BLAIR	17543	391	31.5	33.8	30.7	3.3	0.8	39394	41652	31	64	266	35.0	35.7	25.6	3.4	0.4	64444
73527	CACHE	21416	1663	22.4	25.7	39.5	10.0	2.4	51643	52514	65	91	1352	14.6	23.0	34.2	26.8	1.3	115876
73528	CHATTANOOGA	17839	186	32.3	31.7	30.1	5.4	0.5	36014	39220	21	44	145	31.0	34.5	28.3	6.2	0.0	75000
73529	COMANCHE	17693	1997	35.6	33.2	26.5	3.3	1.4	35443	37079	19	39	1615	36.5	31.4	24.6	6.4	1.1	63179
73530	DAVIDSON	17308	210	37.1	30.0	27.1	3.8	1.9	36682	38789	23	50	159	57.9	20.1	15.1	4.4	2.5	43750
73531	DEVOL	20076	116	28.4	25.9	37.9	5.2	2.6	45000	46169	48	81	93	36.6	20.4	33.3	8.6	1.1	77000
73532	DUKE	17293	240	35.0	33.8	25.4	3.3	2.5	34247	36205	16	32	180	43.9	32.8	20.0	2.8	0.6	56875
73533	DUNCAN	21738	11892	30.3	30.4	29.8	6.4	3.1	40124	42085	33	68	8664	22.8	28.0	35.8	11.7	1.7	88708
73537	ELDORADO	19613	274	34.7	33.9	25.2	3.3	2.9	34552	36124	17	34	206	43.7	32.5	20.4	2.4	1.0	57222
73538	ELGIN	20822	1393	24.6	29.0	38.1	6.7	1.6	46918	49175	54	86	1083	24.4	28.1	33.5	12.7	1.3	87323
73539	ELMER	21490	151	26.5	29.8	37.7	2.6	3.3	44690	46807	47	79	121	33.1	33.9	21.5	7.4	4.1	64643
73540	FAXON	23394	134	24.6	32.8	32.1	5.2	5.2	45000	45000	48	81	108	26.9	17.6	43.5	11.1	0.9	103261
73541	FLETCHER	19896	1500	26.5	31.8	33.1	6.2	2.5	44763	46315	48	79	1207	23.6	26.5	35.5	11.7	2.7	89813
73542	FREDERICK	17446	1977	42.9	29.7	20.4	4.2	2.8	30168	30629	8	13	1523	58.2	20.4	16.9	3.2	1.2	39614
73543	GERONIMO	17411	566	29.5	34.8	30.7	3.2	1.8	40000	41624	33	68	460	22.6	36.5	37.0	3.9	0.0	82881
73544	GOULD	20743	171	32.7	32.2	27.5	4.1	3.5	38336	40433	28	59	141	56.7	22.0	12.1	9.2	0.0	46200
73546	GRANDFIELD	17309	536	42.0	33.8	19.0	3.5	1.7	29392	29945	7	11	418	44.0	27.8	20.6	5.3	2.4	57353
73547	GRANITE	15926	610	34.3	34.4	24.8	4.9	1.6	35476	37544	19	40	464	48.9	26.9	19.6	4.3	0.2	51786
73548	HASTINGS	16033	91	44.0	31.9	20.9	3.3	0.0	28242	27912	6	8	78	43.6	30.8	20.5	5.1	0.0	56250
73549	HEADRICK	21128	758	21.1	33.5	35.4	6.2	3.8	46877	47582	54	85	642	24.9	23.7	35.0	15.4	0.9	91915
73550	HOLLIS	14625	976	50.1	25.4	20.3	2.7	1.5	24935	25478	3	3	733	60.8	18.7	17.7	2.7	0.0	41359
73551	HOLLISTER	20419	34	32.4	38.2	20.6	5.9	2.9	36496	35000	22	49	26	50.0	26.9	23.1	0.0	0.0	50000
73552	INDIAHOMA	19452	440	31.4	28.6	31.4	7.0	1.6	41095	43863	36	71	373	30.3	23.1	28.7	17.2	0.8	84318
73553	LOVELAND	17034	111	41.4	33.3	18.9	3.6	2.7	29705	30312	8	12	87	41.4	27.6	25.3	4.6	1.1	61250
73554	MANGUM	17018	1435	43.1	31.1	20.5	3.7	1.6	30199	31574	8	14	1058	54.8	25.1	15.6	3.7	0.8	46890
73559	MOUNTAIN PARK	16249	209	42.6	34.4	19.6	2.4	1.0	30125	29827	8	13	164	52.4	29.3	12.8	4.3	1.2	47500
73560	OLUSTEE	14891	261	37.2	32.6	26.4	1.9	1.9	33316	35225	14	28	189	37.0	38.1	22.8	2.1	0.0	61190
73562	RANDLETT	17272	366	30.3	32.5	32.5	3.3	1.4	38722	40765	29	61	298	44.0	27.2	24.8	3.7	0.3	60000
73564	ROOSEVELT	16908	250	43.6	34.0	19.2	2.4	0.8	29361	29707	7	11	196	52.6	29.1	12.8	4.1	1.5	47368
73565	RYAN	16065	500	42.8	29.6	23.6	3.4	0.6	28954	30070	7	9	369	56.4	22.0	16.0	4.3	1.4	42656
73566	SNYDER	17589	657	40.8	27.5	25.4	3.8	2.4	30832	31259	9	16	463	45.8	30.0	17.3	6.7	0.2	53900
73568	TEMPLE	16943	602	47.7	26.2	19.3	4.5	2.3	26039	26577	4	4	449	53.5	25.6	15.6	4.7	0.7	45441
73569	TERRAL	14097	196	53.1	30.1	13.3	3.1	0.5	22896	23100	2	2	157	59.2	17.2	15.3	5.1	3.2	41944
73570	TIPTON	19577	440	37.3	28.9	28.2	3.6	2.0	33274	34325	14	28	323	48.6	31.3	14.6	5.6	0.0	51607
73571	VINSON	26886	31	29.0	32.3	32.3	3.2	3.2	41136	37333	36	71	25	60.0	20.0	12.0	8.0	0.0	45000
73572	WALTERS	19185	1545	34.8	28.1	29.1	6.4	1.7	37177	39073	24	52	1161	22.7	35.2	33.0	9.0	0.1	80054
73573	WAURIKA	16177	1005	42.0	30.0	24.1	2.4	1.5	31424	32242	10	19	714	45.2	31.0	17.1	6.7	0.0	54359
73601	CLINTON	17801	3694	33.5	34.1	27.6	3.0	1.9	34949	36192	17	35	2412	28.9	24.8	35.6	9.2	1.5	82623
73620	ARAPAHO	18932	343	24.8	36.2	31.2	5.8	2.0	42059	43442	39	73	271	44.6	31.0	18.8	4.4	1.1	55370
	OKLAHOMA	22515		27.2	29.2	32.3	7.2	4.0	43746	45901				20.4	25.6	36.1	15.4	2.4	96076
	UNITED STATES	27277		20.9	24.4	35.3	11.7	7.6	54719	56938				9.3	13.1	31.6	32.6	13.5	162279

ZIP CODE #	POST OFFICE NAME	FINANCIAL SERVICES: Auto Loan	Home Loan	Investments	Retirement Plans	THE HOME: Home Improvements: Home Repair	Lawn & Garden	Furnishings: Computers & Hardware-Personal	Major Appliances	TV, Radio, Sound Equipment	Furniture	ENTERTAINMENT: Dine out/Carry out	Sports Equipment	Fees & Tickets	Toys & Games	Travel	Cable TV	PERSONAL: Apparel & Services	Auto Repairs	Health Insurance	Pets & Supplies
73127	OKLAHOMA CITY	70	57	53	59	55	57	70	62	70	68	71	50	63	71	62	70	49	68	64	75
73128	OKLAHOMA CITY	104	97	97	96	96	106	93	102	96	92	95	77	89	98	93	99	65	97	103	120
73129	OKLAHOMA CITY	58	46	41	45	44	51	53	51	56	51	55	39	46	56	46	58	38	54	55	62
73130	OKLAHOMA CITY	87	92	78	92	87	91	87	87	88	87	89	67	90	90	87	89	61	87	91	103
73131	OKLAHOMA CITY	142	173	174	176	177	169	148	158	146	156	147	116	168	145	165	146	105	150	156	181
73132	OKLAHOMA CITY	92	85	77	86	82	81	91	85	90	92	91	67	87	92	85	88	63	89	84	101
73134	OKLAHOMA CITY	102	88	83	93	85	84	106	91	104	103	106	75	99	105	97	102	74	101	94	112
73135	OKLAHOMA CITY	91	86	72	84	81	79	87	83	86	90	87	65	83	89	81	85	60	85	81	99
73139	OKLAHOMA CITY	79	66	65	68	64	69	78	72	79	75	79	57	71	79	71	80	55	77	77	87
73141	OKLAHOMA CITY	69	57	54	57	54	65	62	63	65	59	64	49	55	66	57	68	44	64	68	76
73142	OKLAHOMA CITY	107	95	84	100	89	85	106	93	102	108	105	78	101	108	97	98	74	99	88	112
73145	OKLAHOMA CITY	85	44	33	51	40	38	80	55	75	75	79	55	61	91	58	69	56	71	50	68
73149	OKLAHOMA CITY	68	57	50	58	55	60	65	61	66	63	65	48	58	68	58	67	45	64	64	74
73150	OKLAHOMA CITY	122	139	132	141	139	133	123	128	120	129	121	97	133	122	131	118	85	123	123	149
73151	OKLAHOMA CITY	164	217	224	228	225	195	178	185	166	193	168	146	214	170	202	158	126	172	161	209
73159	OKLAHOMA CITY	79	71	64	71	68	72	76	73	77	75	77	57	71	78	71	77	53	76	76	87
73160	OKLAHOMA CITY	97	98	82	96	92	89	93	92	92	96	93	71	92	96	90	90	64	91	89	108
73162	OKLAHOMA CITY	114	127	119	128	125	117	118	117	114	123	116	90	125	116	122	112	82	115	113	136
73165	OKLAHOMA CITY	107	115	99	116	111	111	104	108	103	106	104	83	108	106	107	103	72	104	105	126
73169	OKLAHOMA CITY	101	95	86	93	94	98	89	95	92	93	92	69	86	95	87	95	63	92	96	112
73170	OKLAHOMA CITY	142	157	133	153	149	136	139	140	133	149	135	108	145	140	140	128	95	133	127	160
73173	OKLAHOMA CITY	95	111	115	111	116	117	97	107	99	102	99	74	109	96	109	103	69	102	115	121
73179	OKLAHOMA CITY	104	100	88	99	98	102	94	99	96	96	96	73	91	99	92	98	66	96	99	117
73401	ARDMORE	78	66	70	66	66	79	69	75	73	66	72	56	63	73	66	78	49	73	81	89
73430	BURNEYVILLE	91	65	93	63	67	92	67	85	74	62	73	64	53	74	66	81	48	78	88	101
73432	COLEMAN	73	52	74	50	54	74	53	68	59	50	58	51	43	59	53	65	38	62	71	81
73433	ELMORE CITY	71	51	74	50	53	74	55	68	60	48	58	52	43	59	54	66	38	63	73	81
73434	FOSTER	71	51	73	49	53	72	52	67	58	49	57	50	42	58	52	64	38	61	69	79
73437	GRAHAM	73	53	75	51	55	75	54	69	60	50	59	52	43	60	53	66	39	63	71	82
73438	HEALDTON	63	46	59	45	47	63	51	59	56	46	54	45	41	55	48	60	36	56	64	70
73439	KINGSTON	70	60	79	56	65	76	59	72	64	61	62	49	55	60	62	69	42	68	79	83
73440	LEBANON	79	56	81	55	58	80	58	74	64	54	63	55	46	64	57	71	42	67	77	87
73441	LEON	78	56	81	54	58	80	58	73	64	54	63	55	46	64	57	70	42	67	76	87
73442	LOCO	71	51	72	49	52	72	52	66	58	48	57	50	42	57	51	63	37	61	69	79
73443	LONE GROVE	79	67	64	64	65	73	66	71	69	67	69	53	59	72	62	72	47	69	72	85
73444	HENNEPIN	78	52	78	50	52	78	56	70	62	51	61	55	42	63	53	69	40	66	74	86
73446	MADILL	74	54	71	52	55	74	57	69	63	53	61	52	46	63	55	69	41	65	73	82
73447	MANNSVILLE	81	58	67	57	58	77	61	71	67	59	66	54	49	70	55	73	44	67	74	86
73448	MARIETTA	85	64	79	63	65	86	68	80	74	63	72	61	56	75	65	81	48	75	85	95
73449	MEAD	69	58	78	55	63	74	57	69	61	58	60	48	52	58	60	66	40	65	75	81
73450	MILBURN	58	42	60	41	43	59	43	55	48	40	47	41	34	47	43	52	31	50	57	65
73453	OVERBROOK	92	70	92	69	72	94	71	87	77	65	76	66	59	77	70	84	50	80	91	103
73456	RINGLING	67	48	70	47	49	70	52	65	57	45	55	50	40	56	51	62	36	60	70	77
73458	SPRINGER	81	58	83	56	60	83	60	76	66	56	65	57	48	66	59	73	43	70	79	90
73459	THACKERVILLE	100	72	82	70	71	95	75	87	83	73	81	67	60	86	68	90	55	82	92	106
73460	TISHOMINGO	70	51	68	50	53	71	56	66	63	52	61	49	47	62	54	69	41	64	73	79
73461	WAPANUCKA	72	51	74	50	53	73	53	67	58	49	57	50	42	58	52	64	38	61	70	80
73463	WILSON	72	50	72	48	52	73	53	67	59	49	58	50	42	59	51	65	38	62	70	80
73481	RATLIFF CITY	77	55	79	53	57	78	56	72	63	53	62	54	45	62	56	69	41	66	75	85
73488	TUSSY	59	42	61	41	44	60	43	55	48	40	47	41	35	48	43	53	31	51	57	66
73501	LAWTON	66	54	50	56	52	57	63	59	65	61	65	46	57	66	56	67	45	63	63	72
73503	FORT SILL	102	53	40	61	47	45	96	66	90	89	95	66	73	108	69	83	66	84	60	81
73505	LAWTON	82	76	67	77	73	75	81	76	81	80	81	60	78	83	76	81	57	79	78	91
73507	LAWTON	83	75	68	75	72	78	81	78	82	77	81	61	75	83	74	84	56	80	82	94
73521	ALTUS	80	67	67	68	66	76	75	74	77	71	76	57	67	78	69	80	52	76	80	89
73523	ALTUS AFB	99	52	39	60	46	44	93	65	88	87	92	64	71	105	67	81	65	82	58	79
73526	BLAIR	72	52	72	51	54	75	57	70	63	51	61	52	45	62	55	70	41	65	76	82
73527	CACHE	95	87	79	85	86	91	83	89	86	84	85	65	78	89	79	88	58	85	89	105
73528	CHATTANOOGA	78	56	80	54	58	79	58	73	64	54	63	55	46	63	57	70	41	67	76	87
73529	COMANCHE	77	55	79	54	58	79	58	73	65	53	63	55	46	64	57	71	42	67	77	87
73530	DAVIDSON	72	52	72	50	54	75	57	70	63	51	61	52	45	62	55	70	41	65	76	82
73531	DEVOL	87	60	96	60	63	92	67	83	69	54	69	68	49	68	66	76	44	77	87	102
73532	DUKE	76	55	77	53	57	79	59	73	66	53	64	55	47	65	57	72	42	68	79	86
73533	DUNCAN	81	69	78	68	70	85	71	80	76	67	74	59	64	76	70	81	51	77	86	94
73537	ELDORADO	76	55	77	53	57	79	59	74	66	53	64	55	48	65	58	73	43	69	80	87
73538	ELGIN	82	74	73	74	72	85	73	79	76	70	75	61	69	77	72	80	51	76	84	94
73539	ELMER	97	67	106	66	70	102	74	92	77	60	76	76	54	75	73	84	49	86	97	113
73540	FAXON	104	75	107	72	77	106	77	97	85	71	83	73	61	84	76	93	55	89	101	116
73541	FLETCHER	85	68	78	66	69	84	69	80	75	67	74	59	60	76	67	80	50	76	84	95
73542	FREDERICK	74	53	74	52	54	76	59	70	64	51	62	55	46	63	56	70	41	67	76	85
73543	GERONIMO	84	61	71	60	61	81	63	74	70	61	68	57	51	72	59	76	46	70	78	90
73544	GOULD	98	67	107	67	70	103	75	93	78	61	77	77	55	76	74	85	50	87	98	114
73546	GRANDFIELD	77	55	79	53	57	78	56	72	63	52	61	54	45	62	56	69	41	66	75	85
73547	GRANITE	74	53	77	52	55	78	58	72	63	50	61	55	45	62	57	69	41	67	77	86
73548	HASTINGS	64	46	65	44	47	65	47	59	52	43	51	45	37	52	46	57	34	55	62	71
73549	HEADRICK	91	79	79	77	78	87	77	84	80	77	80	62	70	82	74	83	54	81	85	100
73550	HOLLIS	61	44	62	43	46	64	48	60	54	43	52	45	38	53	47	59	34	56	65	70
73551	HOLLISTER	84	58	92	58	61	89	64	80	67	52	66	66	47	66	64	73	43	75	84	98
73552	INDIAHOMA	86	64	87	63	66	88	65	82	72	61	71	61	54	72	65	79	47	75	85	97
73553	LOVELAND	77	55	79	53	57	78	56	72	62	52	61	54	45	62	56	69	40	66	74	85
73554	MANGUM	67	48	69	47	50	70	52	65	57	46	56	50	41	56	51	63	37	60	70	77
73559	MOUNTAIN PARK	64	44	71	44	46	68	49	61	51	40	51	51	36	50	49	56	33	57	65	75
73560	OLUSTEE	72	52	74	50	54	73	53	68	59	49	58	51	43	59	53	65	38	62	70	80
73562	RANDLETT	82	58	74	57	59	80	61	73	67	57	66	57	48	69	57	73	44	69	77	89
73564	ROOSEVELT	64	44	71	44	46	68	49	61	51	40	51	50	36	50	49	56	33	57	65	75
73565	RYAN	64	46	65	45	47	66	50	62	55	44	53	46	39	54	48	61	35	57	66	73
73566	SNYDER	71	51	72	50	53	74	56	69	62	50	60	52	45	61	54	68	40	64	75	81
73568	TEMPLE	65	47	65	46	49	68	51	63	57	46	55	47	41	56	50	63	37	59	69	74
73569	TERRAL	52	37	52	36	39	54	41	51	46	36	44	38	33	45	40	50	29	47	55	59
73570	TIPTON	77	55	77	54	57	80	60	75	67	54	65	56	48	66	58	74	43	70	81	87
73571	VINSON	88	61	97	61	64	93	68	84	70	55	69	69	49	69	67	77	45	78	89	103
73572	WALTERS	82	59	85	57	61	86	63	79	70	56	68	60	50	68	62	77	45	73	85	94
73573	WAURIKA	69	49	70	48	51	71	52	65	58	47	56	49	41	57	51	64	37	61	70	78
73601	CLINTON	68	59	58	59	58	69	64	66	67	59	65	50	57	67	59	70	45	66	72	78
73620	ARAPAHO	88	63	90	61	65	89	64	82	71	60	70	61	52	71	64	79	46	75	85	97
	OKLAHOMA	87	75	78	75	74	84	79	82	82	77	81	63	73	83	75	85	56	82	86	98
	UNITED STATES	100	100	100	100	100	100	100	100	100	100	100	100	100	100	100	100	100	100	100	100

POPULATION CHANGE

ZIP CODE #	POST OFFICE NAME	COUNTY FIPS CODE	POPULATION 2000	POPULATION 2009	POPULATION 2014	2000-2009 ANNUAL RATE % Rate	2000-2009 ANNUAL RATE State Centile	HOUSEHOLDS 2000	HOUSEHOLDS 2009	HOUSEHOLDS 2014	HOUSEHOLDS % Annual Rate 2000-2009	HOUSEHOLDS 2009 Average HH Size	FAMILIES 2000	FAMILIES 2009	FAMILIES % Annual Rate 2000-2009
73622	BESSIE	149	214	239	249	1.2	86	97	111	116	1.5	2.15	69	76	1.1
73624	BURNS FLAT	149	18	19	20	0.6	73	7	8	8	1.5	2.38	5	6	2.0
73625	BUTLER	039	1119	1095	1084	-0.2	33	441	441	440	0.0	2.45	331	324	-0.2
73626	CANUTE	149	1183	1181	1190	0.0	43	473	481	486	0.2	2.46	337	334	-0.1
73627	CARTER	009	555	586	611	0.6	73	230	249	262	0.9	2.35	159	167	0.5
73628	CHEYENNE	129	1428	1408	1404	-0.2	33	612	629	635	0.3	2.18	390	389	0.0
73632	CORDELL	149	4072	3956	3913	-0.3	27	1649	1608	1593	-0.3	2.37	1144	1087	-0.6
73638	CRAWFORD	129	144	140	141	-0.3	27	55	56	57	0.2	2.50	41	41	0.0
73639	CUSTER CITY	039	654	625	615	-0.5	15	281	275	272	-0.2	2.27	198	190	-0.4
73641	DILL CITY	149	1038	1083	1103	0.5	68	420	444	454	0.6	2.44	314	325	0.4
73642	DURHAM	129	123	120	120	-0.3	27	60	61	62	0.2	1.97	45	44	-0.2
73644	ELK CITY	009	12575	13637	14188	0.9	80	4918	5451	5709	1.1	2.46	3421	3697	0.8
73645	ERICK	009	1467	1589	1666	0.9	80	620	674	708	0.9	2.33	412	435	0.6
73646	FAY	043	110	106	103	-0.4	22	52	51	50	-0.2	2.08	38	37	-0.3
73647	FOSS	149	2267	2441	2512	0.8	78	815	895	926	1.0	2.73	622	668	0.8
73650	HAMMON	129	700	682	671	-0.3	27	271	273	272	0.1	2.50	195	193	-0.1
73651	HOBART	075	4436	4341	4231	-0.2	33	1749	1729	1688	-0.1	2.37	1166	1123	-0.4
73654	LEEDEY	129	769	738	720	-0.4	22	307	301	296	-0.2	2.34	213	203	-0.5
73655	LONE WOLF	075	1112	1139	1131	0.3	60	488	514	515	0.6	2.18	333	341	0.3
73658	OAKWOOD	043	262	252	246	-0.4	22	112	111	109	-0.1	2.27	82	80	-0.3
73659	PUTNAM	043	105	101	99	-0.4	22	47	46	45	-0.2	2.15	34	32	-0.7
73660	REYDON	129	408	398	399	-0.3	27	177	180	182	0.2	2.21	131	130	-0.1
73661	ROCKY	149	249	240	237	-0.4	22	110	107	106	-0.3	2.24	82	79	-0.4
73662	SAYRE	009	5186	3772	3838	-3.4	0	1580	1651	1694	0.5	2.20	1009	1022	0.1
73663	SEILING	043	1613	1562	1526	-0.3	27	648	644	634	-0.1	2.39	441	428	-0.3
73664	SENTINEL	149	1012	976	964	-0.4	22	395	386	382	-0.2	2.53	296	282	-0.5
73666	SWEETWATER	129	326	331	336	0.2	55	137	143	147	0.5	2.31	99	101	0.2
73667	TALOGA	043	681	654	639	-0.4	22	280	274	268	-0.2	2.32	200	191	-0.5
73668	TEXOLA	009	106	114	119	0.8	78	38	42	43	1.1	2.71	27	28	0.4
73669	THOMAS	039	1708	1654	1633	-0.3	27	650	634	628	-0.3	2.51	454	432	-0.5
73673	WILLOW	055	313	319	319	0.2	55	148	142	142	-0.4	1.66	100	94	-0.7
73701	ENID	047	23205	23002	22916	-0.1	38	9123	9056	9026	-0.1	2.44	5868	5656	-0.4
73703	ENID	047	26237	26897	27158	0.3	60	10795	11211	11359	0.4	2.33	7504	7599	0.1
73705	ENID	047	220	218	216	-0.1	38	0	0	0	0.0	0.00	0	0	0.0
73716	ALINE	003	408	366	349	-1.2	4	185	168	161	-1.0	2.14	124	110	-1.3
73717	ALVA	151	6747	6267	6055	-0.8	9	2651	2529	2441	-0.5	2.16	1584	1465	-0.8
73718	AMES	093	508	494	485	-0.3	27	215	215	213	0.0	2.30	159	155	-0.3
73719	AMORITA	003	148	133	127	-1.1	5	70	64	61	-1.0	2.08	51	46	-1.1
73720	BISON	047	197	179	174	-1.0	7	86	80	78	-0.8	2.24	66	61	-0.8
73722	BURLINGTON	003	482	439	421	-1.0	7	192	177	170	-0.9	2.48	138	125	-1.1
73724	CANTON	011	1142	1097	1062	-0.4	22	470	460	448	-0.2	2.38	314	300	-0.5
73726	CARMEN	003	552	499	476	-1.1	5	222	203	194	-1.0	2.41	148	132	-1.2
73727	CARRIER	047	529	521	519	-0.2	33	193	194	194	0.1	2.69	151	148	-0.2
73728	CHEROKEE	003	1993	1959	1915	-0.2	33	861	854	837	-0.1	2.26	577	557	-0.4
73729	CLEO SPRINGS	093	550	537	528	-0.3	27	224	226	224	0.1	2.38	169	167	-0.1
73730	COVINGTON	047	939	892	876	-0.6	13	374	362	358	-0.4	2.46	281	267	-0.6
73731	DACOMA	151	306	259	240	-1.8	1	132	114	107	-1.6	2.27	90	76	-1.8
73733	DOUGLAS	047	213	202	199	-0.6	13	94	91	90	-0.4	2.22	71	67	-0.6
73734	DOVER	073	585	638	665	0.9	80	216	240	251	1.1	2.66	171	186	0.9
73735	DRUMMOND	047	791	764	756	-0.4	22	295	290	289	-0.2	2.63	236	228	-0.4
73736	FAIRMONT	047	651	708	731	0.9	80	255	282	292	1.1	2.51	198	214	0.8
73737	FAIRVIEW	093	3785	3641	3539	-0.4	22	1539	1515	1483	-0.2	2.32	1064	1020	-0.5
73738	GARBER	047	1145	1106	1092	-0.4	22	481	473	470	-0.2	2.34	334	318	-0.5
73739	GOLTRY	003	385	349	333	-1.1	5	170	156	149	-0.9	2.19	113	101	-1.2
73741	HELENA	003	1717	1650	1624	-0.4	22	291	270	259	-0.8	2.41	201	183	-1.0
73742	HENNESSEY	073	4138	4333	4435	0.5	68	1511	1598	1642	0.6	2.64	1155	1198	0.4
73744	HITCHCOCK	011	242	232	225	-0.5	15	91	88	86	-0.4	2.64	67	64	-0.5
73747	ISABELLA	093	353	340	330	-0.4	22	136	134	131	-0.2	2.54	105	101	-0.4
73749	JET	003	464	456	450	-0.2	33	226	225	223	0.0	2.02	141	137	-0.3
73750	KINGFISHER	073	6663	6971	7154	0.5	68	2540	2686	2763	0.6	2.54	1834	1897	0.4
73753	KREMLIN	047	481	479	479	0.0	43	187	189	189	0.1	2.53	148	147	-0.1
73754	LAHOMA	047	1188	1195	1197	0.1	49	469	481	485	0.3	2.46	351	351	0.0
73755	LONGDALE	011	686	662	641	-0.4	22	284	279	272	-0.2	2.37	193	184	-0.5
73756	LOYAL	073	136	144	148	0.6	73	56	60	62	0.7	2.40	45	48	0.7
73757	LUCIEN	103	109	107	106	-0.2	33	48	49	48	0.2	2.18	37	37	0.0
73758	MANCHESTER	053	200	182	173	-1.0	7	85	77	73	-1.1	2.23	57	50	-1.4
73759	MEDFORD	053	1842	1752	1683	-0.5	15	748	711	681	-0.5	2.38	509	471	-0.8
73760	MENO	093	518	512	505	-0.1	38	203	204	201	0.1	2.51	158	156	-0.1
73761	NASH	053	537	479	452	-1.2	4	219	196	185	-1.2	2.44	159	139	-1.4
73762	OKARCHE	073	2043	2153	2219	0.6	73	791	847	878	0.7	2.54	579	604	0.5
73763	OKEENE	011	1644	1526	1471	-0.8	9	666	625	602	-0.7	2.34	455	416	-1.0
73764	OMEGA	073	45	48	49	0.7	75	16	17	18	0.7	2.82	13	14	0.8
73766	POND CREEK	053	1065	970	921	-1.0	7	429	392	372	-1.0	2.47	312	279	-1.2
73768	RINGWOOD	093	1327	1311	1292	-0.1	38	511	514	509	0.1	2.55	396	391	-0.1
73770	SOUTHARD	011	9	9	8	0.0	43	3	3	3	0.0	3.00	2	2	0.0
73771	WAKITA	053	572	521	495	-1.0	7	235	214	203	-1.0	2.29	158	140	-1.3
73772	WATONGA	011	6139	7078	6989	1.6	91	1843	1826	1795	-0.1	2.54	1286	1243	-0.4
73773	WAUKOMIS	047	1597	1526	1500	-0.5	15	649	633	626	-0.3	2.41	459	436	-0.6
73801	WOODWARD	153	13734	14526	14847	0.6	73	5510	5905	6081	0.8	2.38	3828	4001	0.5
73832	ARNETT	045	1232	1143	1106	-0.8	9	531	505	494	-0.5	2.24	365	338	-0.8
73834	BUFFALO	059	1729	1589	1512	-0.9	8	714	669	641	-0.7	2.31	509	466	-0.9
73835	CAMARGO	043	139	133	129	-0.5	15	68	67	66	-0.2	1.99	47	45	-0.5
73838	CHESTER	093	462	442	427	-0.5	15	199	196	191	-0.2	2.26	142	136	-0.5
73840	FARGO	045	653	613	598	-0.7	10	262	255	251	-0.3	2.40	203	194	-0.5
73841	FORT SUPPLY	153	1211	1417	1422	1.7	92	257	261	264	0.2	2.90	201	201	0.0
73842	FREEDOM	151	497	429	400	-1.6	2	212	187	175	-1.3	2.29	147	126	-1.7
73843	GAGE	045	536	549	550	0.3	60	240	256	258	0.7	2.14	163	168	0.3
73844	GATE	007	302	287	279	-0.5	15	126	120	116	-0.5	2.39	95	89	-0.7
73848	LAVERNE	007	1932	1779	1706	-0.9	8	828	776	747	-0.7	2.29	560	511	-1.0
73851	MAY	059	72	65	62	-1.1	5	32	30	28	-0.7	2.17	23	21	-1.0
73852	MOORELAND	153	2111	2234	2307	0.6	73	815	861	892	0.6	2.51	602	623	0.4
73853	MUTUAL	153	230	236	245	0.3	60	101	106	111	0.5	2.23	81	83	0.3
73855	ROSSTON	059	222	201	191	-1.1	5	90	83	80	-0.9	2.42	65	59	-1.0
73857	SHARON	153	1200	1261	1299	0.5	68	458	490	508	0.7	2.57	367	386	0.5
73858	SHATTUCK	045	1654	1691	1688	0.2	55	736	776	782	0.6	2.12	489	503	0.3
	OKLAHOMA					0.7					0.8	2.46			0.6
	UNITED STATES					1.0					1.1	2.59			0.9

ZIP CODE #	POST OFFICE NAME	RACE (%) White 2000	White 2009	Black 2000	Black 2009	Asian/Pacific 2000	Asian/Pacific 2009	% Hispanic Origin 2000	% Hispanic Origin 2009	2009 AGE DISTRIBUTION (%) 0-4	5-9	10-14	15-19	20-24	25-44	45-64	65-84	85+	18+	MEDIAN AGE 2009	% 2009 Males	% 2009 Females
73622	BESSIE	91.6	89.5	0.0	0.0	0.5	0.4	4.2	6.3	5.9	6.7	6.7	5.9	5.0	23.0	31.8	13.0	2.1	76.6	42.5	52.7	47.3
73624	BURNS FLAT	88.9	84.2	0.0	0.0	0.0	0.0	5.6	10.5	10.5	10.5	10.5	10.5	10.5	31.6	15.8	0.0	0.0	57.9	23.8	47.4	52.6
73625	BUTLER	86.5	86.2	0.4	0.5	0.1	0.1	6.0	6.3	4.9	5.4	5.9	6.4	3.6	22.9	32.1	16.7	2.1	79.2	45.5	49.7	50.3
73626	CANUTE	91.4	89.2	0.5	0.5	0.5	0.5	4.7	6.7	5.8	6.3	6.3	5.3	4.1	24.2	31.8	14.1	2.2	78.4	43.1	49.6	50.4
73627	CARTER	91.4	88.4	0.0	0.0	0.2	0.2	8.1	11.8	4.6	5.6	5.3	9.2	7.2	22.5	29.5	12.8	3.2	78.5	40.9	52.2	47.8
73628	CHEYENNE	96.6	96.6	0.4	0.4	0.1	0.1	2.1	2.1	6.0	6.5	6.3	5.3	4.3	21.4	29.5	17.1	3.6	77.8	45.1	51.0	49.0
73632	CORDELL	94.8	93.7	0.2	0.2	0.1	0.2	2.6	3.6	6.0	6.0	6.1	6.4	4.8	22.9	26.5	17.1	4.3	78.0	43.3	47.5	52.5
73638	CRAWFORD	95.8	95.7	0.0	0.0	0.0	0.0	1.4	2.1	4.3	5.0	5.7	5.7	4.3	20.7	32.9	18.6	2.9	81.4	47.5	51.4	48.6
73639	CUSTER CITY	93.7	93.6	0.2	0.2	0.0	0.0	2.3	2.4	5.9	6.4	6.7	6.2	4.2	22.6	29.8	15.5	2.7	76.8	43.3	48.5	51.5
73641	DILL CITY	92.2	90.7	0.0	0.0	0.0	0.0	5.5	7.7	5.9	6.0	6.3	6.4	5.6	23.4	26.5	16.8	3.1	77.9	42.4	50.4	49.6
73642	DURHAM	95.2	95.0	0.0	0.0	0.0	0.0	1.6	1.7	4.2	5.0	5.0	5.8	4.2	20.0	35.8	17.5	2.5	82.5	47.5	47.5	52.5
73644	ELK CITY	89.5	85.0	2.7	5.2	0.5	0.7	5.6	7.9	7.2	6.9	6.8	7.1	6.0	25.9	26.8	11.1	2.2	74.6	37.2	48.8	51.2
73645	ERICK	92.5	89.4	0.5	1.2	0.3	0.6	4.2	6.4	6.7	6.8	6.9	6.4	4.9	21.2	27.1	15.9	4.0	75.3	42.1	47.4	52.6
73646	FAY	91.0	89.6	0.0	0.0	0.0	0.0	1.8	1.9	5.7	5.7	6.6	6.6	2.8	22.6	30.2	17.0	2.8	78.3	45.0	50.0	50.0
73647	FOSS	89.2	87.1	1.0	1.1	0.9	0.9	5.7	8.1	8.0	7.4	9.4	8.3	6.1	25.0	25.8	9.0	0.9	69.8	34.4	49.2	50.8
73650	HAMMON	79.7	79.2	0.3	0.3	0.1	0.1	4.3	4.4	5.1	7.2	6.2	10.7	3.8	24.2	29.0	11.3	2.5	74.0	40.3	50.6	49.4
73651	HOBART	80.9	77.7	7.5	7.9	0.7	1.0	8.3	11.0	6.6	6.3	6.2	6.6	6.4	22.6	26.1	15.4	3.9	76.7	41.4	49.7	50.3
73654	LEEDEY	93.5	92.5	0.1	0.1	0.0	0.0	1.8	2.3	4.9	5.7	6.0	6.8	3.5	21.1	29.0	17.6	5.4	78.7	46.5	49.7	50.3
73655	LONE WOLF	91.8	89.7	1.0	1.1	0.0	0.0	3.8	5.2	4.7	5.5	5.7	6.0	4.2	21.2	32.4	18.0	2.3	80.1	46.7	52.1	47.9
73658	OAKWOOD	91.6	90.1	0.0	0.0	0.0	0.0	1.9	2.4	5.6	6.0	6.7	6.3	3.2	23.0	29.0	17.5	2.8	77.4	44.4	51.2	48.8
73659	PUTNAM	95.2	92.1	0.0	1.0	0.0	0.0	4.8	5.9	2.0	5.9	6.9	8.9	3.0	24.8	31.7	12.9	4.0	78.2	44.1	50.5	49.5
73660	REYDON	95.6	95.5	0.2	0.3	0.0	0.0	1.7	1.8	4.5	5.3	5.3	5.8	4.3	20.9	32.9	18.1	3.0	81.2	47.3	49.5	50.5
73661	ROCKY	91.2	88.8	0.0	0.0	0.0	0.0	8.0	11.7	5.8	6.3	6.7	6.3	4.2	23.3	29.2	15.4	2.9	77.1	43.0	50.4	49.6
73662	SAYRE	79.0	81.0	14.5	11.7	0.3	0.2	5.2	6.7	5.8	5.4	5.8	5.9	5.9	23.5	28.8	16.0	2.9	79.8	43.0	49.8	50.2
73663	SEILING	85.9	84.3	0.1	0.1	0.1	0.1	2.5	3.6	6.2	6.4	6.3	6.4	5.2	21.7	27.8	16.1	3.8	77.1	42.7	49.9	50.1
73664	SENTINEL	91.2	88.8	0.1	0.1	0.0	0.0	8.0	11.5	5.6	6.1	6.7	6.5	4.5	23.6	28.6	15.5	3.0	77.6	42.7	49.4	50.6
73666	SWEETWATER	94.2	91.8	0.6	1.5	0.3	0.6	2.8	3.6	6.0	6.3	6.6	5.1	3.3	20.5	30.2	18.7	3.0	77.6	46.4	51.4	48.6
73667	TALOGA	94.7	93.6	0.4	0.6	0.0	0.0	4.1	5.8	3.1	5.5	7.0	8.3	3.1	23.1	31.7	13.6	4.7	78.3	45.0	50.6	49.4
73668	TEXOLA	90.6	86.8	1.9	3.5	0.9	0.9	3.8	4.4	6.1	7.0	7.0	5.3	3.5	21.9	29.8	16.7	2.6	76.3	44.3	52.6	47.4
73669	THOMAS	90.5	90.3	0.1	0.1	0.0	0.0	1.8	1.8	6.0	6.2	6.3	6.7	5.5	21.6	27.1	16.1	4.4	76.8	42.9	47.2	52.8
73673	WILLOW	71.9	70.2	15.3	16.6	0.6	0.6	6.7	7.5	2.2	2.8	2.8	4.7	10.0	41.1	23.2	11.0	2.2	90.0	37.9	71.5	28.5
73701	ENID	84.5	81.1	5.1	5.4	1.2	1.6	6.9	9.8	7.6	7.3	6.7	6.7	6.3	26.9	24.6	11.4	2.5	74.3	35.8	49.3	50.7
73703	ENID	90.5	88.1	2.4	2.6	1.8	2.5	2.5	3.6	6.2	6.1	6.1	5.8	5.6	24.7	27.6	15.0	3.0	78.1	41.3	48.2	51.8
73705	ENID	79.1	74.3	7.7	7.8	2.3	3.2	6.8	9.6	17.9	10.1	5.5	4.6	24.3	37.2	0.5	0.0	0.0	65.1	22.5	59.2	40.8
73716	ALINE	95.6	94.5	0.2	0.3	0.2	0.3	1.2	1.6	5.5	6.0	6.0	5.5	4.4	21.6	29.0	18.6	3.6	78.4	45.6	51.1	48.9
73717	ALVA	92.9	91.2	2.9	3.2	0.7	1.0	1.9	2.8	4.7	4.4	4.5	7.8	11.9	25.2	22.3	15.2	4.0	83.6	36.3	52.7	47.3
73718	AMES	95.5	93.7	0.6	0.6	0.0	0.0	4.3	6.5	5.1	6.3	6.1	5.7	3.6	21.5	30.0	19.6	2.2	78.9	46.1	48.2	51.8
73719	AMORITA	96.0	95.5	0.7	0.8	0.0	0.0	1.3	2.3	5.3	6.0	6.0	5.3	4.5	20.3	30.1	19.5	3.0	80.5	46.8	47.4	52.6
73720	BISON	94.4	92.2	0.0	0.0	0.5	1.1	2.0	3.4	4.5	4.5	4.5	5.6	4.5	20.7	35.8	17.9	2.2	83.2	48.1	49.7	50.3
73722	BURLINGTON	96.1	95.2	0.6	0.7	0.0	0.0	1.7	2.3	5.2	5.9	6.2	5.7	4.3	19.4	31.2	19.1	3.0	79.0	47.3	49.0	51.0
73724	CANTON	82.0	80.4	0.0	0.0	0.1	0.1	2.9	3.9	6.0	6.3	6.6	6.4	5.3	22.9	29.4	14.6	2.6	77.3	41.9	49.7	50.3
73726	CARMEN	95.7	94.8	0.2	0.2	0.2	0.2	1.1	1.4	5.8	6.2	5.8	5.4	4.4	21.0	28.3	19.2	3.8	78.6	45.8	50.5	49.5
73727	CARRIER	96.8	95.8	0.6	0.8	0.4	0.4	1.3	1.9	6.7	7.7	7.9	6.3	4.0	21.7	30.3	13.4	1.9	73.7	41.5	49.3	50.7
73728	CHEROKEE	96.0	94.8	0.1	0.1	0.1	0.1	3.0	4.1	5.9	6.1	6.3	5.9	4.3	20.9	27.8	18.6	4.1	77.5	45.3	49.8	50.2
73729	CLEO SPRINGS	96.7	95.9	0.5	0.6	0.2	0.2	1.5	2.2	5.4	6.0	6.0	4.7	4.1	23.5	32.0	16.9	1.5	79.7	45.3	49.0	51.0
73730	COVINGTON	95.5	94.7	0.0	0.0	0.1	0.1	1.2	1.8	5.2	5.6	5.7	5.9	4.8	25.0	29.4	15.8	2.6	79.9	43.5	50.3	49.7
73731	DACOMA	97.4	96.9	0.0	0.0	0.3	0.4	1.6	2.3	3.9	4.2	5.0	6.9	3.9	23.6	29.7	19.7	3.1	82.2	46.6	50.6	49.4
73733	DOUGLAS	95.8	94.6	0.0	0.0	0.0	0.0	1.4	2.0	5.4	5.4	5.4	5.9	5.0	25.2	29.2	15.8	2.5	79.7	43.3	50.0	50.0
73734	DOVER	91.3	88.4	0.9	0.9	0.0	0.0	6.0	8.5	6.3	6.4	6.6	7.2	5.8	27.1	29.2	10.5	0.9	76.3	38.0	49.7	50.3
73735	DRUMMOND	92.9	91.4	1.1	1.3	0.1	0.3	3.2	4.6	6.8	7.3	7.2	6.5	4.7	24.0	30.1	12.2	1.2	74.6	39.9	50.8	49.2
73736	FAIRMONT	96.0	95.1	0.5	0.4	0.6	0.8	1.1	1.6	5.2	5.8	6.4	6.8	4.0	21.6	31.8	17.1	1.4	78.4	45.2	50.0	50.0
73737	FAIRVIEW	96.8	95.9	0.1	0.1	0.1	0.1	1.5	2.2	5.9	6.0	6.0	5.7	5.5	20.8	28.9	16.3	4.8	78.6	45.0	48.4	51.6
73738	GARBER	95.4	94.5	0.2	0.2	0.1	0.1	0.4	0.6	6.8	6.8	7.1	6.3	5.2	21.7	27.8	15.5	2.8	75.2	41.8	49.5	50.5
73739	GOLTRY	95.3	94.3	0.3	0.3	0.3	0.3	1.0	1.4	5.7	6.3	5.7	5.2	4.6	20.6	29.2	18.9	3.7	78.5	46.1	51.0	49.0
73741	HELENA	73.3	69.5	14.4	15.5	0.2	0.4	4.7	6.5	2.5	2.5	2.6	2.7	6.7	45.7	26.0	8.8	2.5	90.8	40.0	76.8	23.2
73742	HENNESSEY	85.3	80.8	2.2	2.3	0.1	0.2	12.3	17.4	6.6	6.9	6.9	6.9	4.8	23.5	28.8	13.4	2.2	75.1	39.9	48.5	51.5
73744	HITCHCOCK	93.0	92.7	0.8	0.9	0.0	0.0	1.2	1.7	6.0	6.9	6.5	6.5	5.2	21.1	30.2	15.1	2.6	75.9	42.9	49.6	50.4
73747	ISABELLA	95.2	93.5	0.3	0.3	0.0	0.0	5.1	7.4	5.6	6.2	6.8	7.6	4.7	21.2	28.2	17.6	2.1	76.5	43.2	51.5	48.5
73749	JET	94.4	92.5	0.2	0.2	0.2	0.4	2.6	3.7	5.3	5.5	5.5	5.3	5.0	19.5	29.2	21.5	3.3	80.3	47.9	48.7	51.3
73750	KINGFISHER	86.9	84.0	1.8	2.0	0.3	0.4	5.7	8.0	6.6	6.6	6.6	6.7	5.7	24.8	26.9	13.2	3.1	75.8	39.4	48.4	51.6
73753	KREMLIN	96.5	95.4	0.6	0.6	0.2	0.4	1.2	2.1	6.5	7.3	7.7	6.7	4.2	21.3	31.1	13.4	1.9	74.5	42.0	49.5	50.5
73754	LAHOMA	93.3	91.5	1.6	1.7	1.3	2.0	1.9	2.8	5.1	5.4	5.6	5.7	4.8	25.1	31.7	15.0	1.7	80.4	43.7	47.8	52.2
73755	LONGDALE	82.4	81.3	0.0	0.0	0.1	0.2	3.2	4.5	5.7	6.0	6.5	6.6	5.6	22.5	29.9	14.5	2.6	77.6	42.1	50.8	49.2
73756	LOYAL	92.6	89.6	1.5	2.1	0.0	0.0	2.2	4.2	5.6	5.6	6.9	6.3	4.2	22.2	33.3	13.9	2.1	78.5	44.5	50.0	50.0
73757	LUCIEN	95.4	94.4	0.0	0.0	0.9	0.9	0.9	0.9	5.6	5.6	5.6	4.7	2.8	24.3	31.8	17.8	1.9	79.4	45.8	52.3	47.7
73758	MANCHESTER	96.5	96.2	0.0	0.0	0.0	0.0	1.0	1.1	3.8	3.8	3.8	6.0	3.8	20.3	33.0	19.2	6.0	84.6	50.3	50.0	50.0
73759	MEDFORD	95.9	94.7	0.2	0.2	0.1	0.2	2.3	3.3	5.4	5.5	5.7	7.0	5.3	21.3	28.5	17.3	4.1	78.9	44.9	47.9	52.1
73760	MENO	87.8	83.6	0.2	0.2	0.2	0.4	12.7	17.8	6.1	6.6	7.2	7.6	3.9	21.3	28.9	15.8	2.5	75.4	42.7	50.0	50.0
73761	NASH	95.9	94.6	0.0	0.0	0.4	0.6	0.2	0.2	5.0	5.4	5.6	6.5	4.6	23.2	30.9	15.7	3.1	79.5	44.8	46.3	53.7
73762	OKARCHE	94.5	92.8	0.2	0.3	0.1	0.2	2.0	3.0	5.8	6.1	6.5	6.7	5.1	24.2	31.8	12.1	1.7	77.5	41.5	50.9	49.1
73763	OKEENE	97.6	97.1	0.4	0.3	0.1	0.1	3.2	4.5	6.8	6.8	7.1	6.6	4.5	20.1	27.1	16.7	4.3	75.1	43.3	49.1	50.9
73764	OMEGA	91.1	91.7	2.2	2.1	0.0	0.0	2.2	2.1	4.2	4.2	4.2	6.3	4.2	16.7	41.7	16.7	2.1	81.3	49.2	50.0	50.0
73766	POND CREEK	93.8	92.1	0.0	0.0	0.3	0.4	1.3	1.8	6.6	6.9	7.3	6.9	4.4	22.7	29.0	14.3	1.9	74.8	41.7	49.1	50.9
73768	RINGWOOD	90.4	87.0	0.3	0.3	0.2	0.2	9.6	13.4	5.8	6.5	6.9	6.7	3.9	22.2	30.0	15.8	2.3	76.7	43.3	49.5	50.5
73770	SOUTHARD	100.0	100.0	0.0	0.0	0.0	0.0	0.0	0.0	0.0	0.0	0.0	0.0	11.1	0.0	88.9	0.0	0.0	100.0	50.8	66.7	33.3
73771	WAKITA	96.7	95.4	0.2	0.2	0.2	0.2	1.2	1.7	3.3	3.8	4.4	5.8	3.5	20.3	32.6	20.0	6.3	84.3	50.9	49.9	50.1
73772	WATONGA	67.5	64.0	11.9	11.7	2.9	3.7	9.7	12.7	4.8	4.5	4.5	5.7	10.2	36.3	21.7	9.8	2.5	83.0	35.2	65.1	34.9
73773	WAUKOMIS	92.9	91.0	0.6	0.7	0.3	0.5	1.5	2.2	5.4	5.5	5.6	6.4	5.4	24.2	31.7	14.2	1.6	79.6	43.0	48.7	51.3
73801	WOODWARD	92.3	90.0	0.5	0.5	0.6	0.9	5.6	8.0	7.1	7.0	6.7	6.2	6.3	26.0	26.4	12.0	2.2	75.4	37.4	49.4	50.6
73832	ARNETT	97.1	96.9	0.2	0.2	0.0	0.0	1.8	1.9	4.9	5.6	6.0	5.8	4.1	21.1	30.6	18.5	3.4	79.7	46.6	50.6	49.4
73834	BUFFALO	94.9	93.0	0.1	0.1	0.1	0.1	7.5	10.8	4.3	4.8	5.2	5.5	4.1	21.7	32.4	18.6	3.4	82.0	47.7	49.7	50.3
73835	CAMARGO	95.7	94.7	0.0	0.0	0.0	0.0	1.4	2.3	4.5	4.5	5.3	6.0	5.3	20.3	35.3	15.8	3.0	82.7	47.5	50.4	49.6
73838	CHESTER	98.0	97.3	0.0	0.0	0.0	0.0	0.4	0.5	5.2	5.7	5.9	5.2	4.3	19.2	33.7	18.5	2.5	79.9	47.4	51.1	48.9
73840	FARGO	94.2	94.1	0.0	0.0	0.0	0.0	3.1	3.1	4.9	5.2	6.2	7.0	4.4	21.9	33.9	13.7	2.8	79.6	45.3	50.2	49.8
73841	FORT SUPPLY	81.7	80.2	11.5	11.5	0.2	0.3	2.5	3.7	3.2	3.2	3.4	10.6	13.5	33.6	21.9	9.5	1.0	87.2	36.0	71.6	28.4
73842	FREEDOM	95.8	94.4	0.0	0.0	0.6	0.7	4.2	6.1	3.5	3.7	4.0	6.8	5.6	22.1	32.9	18.6	2.8	84.6	47.6	46.4	53.6
73843	GAGE	97.8	97.8	0.0	0.0	0.6	0.5	1.7	1.5	4.4	5.1	5.8	6.0	3.5	20.4	32.8	18.8	3.3	80.7	48.5	49.9	50.1
73844	GATE	92.7	90.2	0.0	0.0	0.3	0.3	10.9	15.7	8.0	8.0	8.0	7.7	3.8	23.0	26.8	12.5	2.1	70.7	38.5	48.8	51.2
73848	LAVERNE	97.0	96.1	0.1	0.1	0.1	0.1	3.2	4.7	5.5	5.6	5.8	6.1	5.3	20.3	30.6	17.5	3.3	79.4	45.8	49.5	50.5
73851	MAY	95.8	95.4	0.0	0.0	0.0	0.0	5.6	7.7	4.6	4.6	4.6	6.2	3.1	20.0	33.8	20.0	3.1	81.5	48.8	53.8	46.2
73852	MOORELAND	95.8	94.6	0.1	0.1	0.1	0.2	2.9	4.3	6.0	6.0	6.8	7.2	5.4	21.8	28.2	13.5	4.9	76.0	42.4	47.9	52.1
73853	MUTUAL	94.3	92.8	0.0	0.0	0.4	0.4	3.9	5.1	5.9	6.8	6.8	6.4	3.4	20.8	32.6	16.1	1.3	75.8	45.0	47.5	52.5
73855	ROSSTON	96.8	95.5	0.0	0.0	0.0	0.0	5.9	7.5	4.0	5.0	5.5	7.5	4.0	16.4	35.3	19.9	2.5	80.6	49.3	53.7	46.3
73857	SHARON	96.2	95.3	0.1	0.1	0.2	0.2	2.4	3.6	5.4	6.1	6.4	6.2	4.1	22.4	32.1	15.7	1.6	78.2	44.5	48.6	51.4
73858	SHATTUCK	96.1	96.0	0.0	0.0	0.1	0.1	3.4	3.3	4.7	5.1	5.6	5.6	4.6	20.2	30.6	18.1	5.5	81.1	48.1	48.2	51.8
	OKLAHOMA	76.2	73.0	7.6	7.8	1.4	2.0	5.2	7.0	6.9	6.6	6.5	7.1	7.2	26.2	25.9	11.6	2.0	75.9	36.8	49.3	50.7
	UNITED STATES	75.1	72.0	12.3	12.7	3.8	4.6	12.5	15.7	6.8	6.7	6.6	7.1	6.9	27.0	26.0	10.9	1.9	75.7	36.9	49.2	50.8

ZIP CODE # POST OFFICE NAME	2009 Per Capita Income	2009 HH Income Base	2009 HOUSEHOLD INCOME DISTRIBUTION (%) Less than $25,000	$25,000 to $49,999	$50,000 to $99,999	$100,000 to $149,999	$150,000 or More	MEDIAN HOUSEHOLD INCOME 2009	2014	2009 National Centile	2009 State Centile	2009 Home Value Base	2009 HOME VALUE DISTRIBUTION (%) Less than $50,000	$50,000 to $89,999	$90,000 to $174,999	$175,000 to $399,999	$400,000 or More	2009 Median Home Value
73622 BESSIE	21263	111	29.7	31.5	31.5	5.4	1.8	37338	36537	25	54	90	42.2	17.8	27.8	12.2	0.0	65000
73624 BURNS FLAT	13947	8	37.5	37.5	25.0	0.0	0.0	30000	30000	8	12	5	40.0	60.0	0.0	0.0	0.0	65000
73625 BUTLER	18312	441	29.0	36.1	28.8	3.6	2.5	36696	39333	23	50	366	41.3	19.7	20.5	16.4	2.2	68696
73626 CANUTE	19831	481	33.9	34.1	24.7	3.7	3.5	35085	36690	18	37	394	28.9	27.2	33.5	9.6	0.8	80400
73627 CARTER	18076	249	37.8	41.4	15.3	3.6	2.0	32288	33719	12	23	202	49.5	21.3	20.8	8.4	0.0	50909
73628 CHEYENNE	21298	629	33.4	31.8	26.2	6.4	2.2	36166	37276	21	46	472	37.5	23.7	29.0	7.6	2.1	75385
73632 CORDELL	18778	1608	34.6	32.8	25.8	4.6	2.2	34841	36508	17	35	1201	33.7	31.1	29.3	5.9	0.0	69521
73638 CRAWFORD	19461	56	30.4	30.4	32.1	3.6	3.6	40000	42361	33	68	44	36.4	22.7	31.8	6.8	2.3	77500
73639 CUSTER CITY	21760	275	29.5	29.8	33.5	6.2	1.1	41770	43181	39	73	222	33.8	22.5	28.4	13.5	1.8	75000
73641 DILL CITY	16661	444	35.1	35.4	25.0	3.8	0.7	32918	33524	13	26	349	55.0	24.1	16.0	4.9	0.0	44697
73642 DURHAM	24768	61	32.8	31.1	29.5	3.3	3.3	35755	40000	20	42	48	35.4	22.9	31.3	8.3	2.1	80000
73644 ELK CITY	19674	5451	33.4	31.6	26.9	4.9	3.3	37301	40061	24	53	3775	23.8	23.8	33.7	16.7	2.0	94469
73645 ERICK	17300	674	41.7	30.7	22.8	3.6	1.2	29608	31315	7	11	521	55.7	20.2	17.5	4.2	2.5	43140
73646 FAY	22717	51	33.3	35.3	23.5	5.9	2.0	34419	32786	16	33	43	37.2	23.3	25.6	11.6	2.3	71667
73647 FOSS	18717	895	26.5	35.5	30.2	5.4	2.5	40040	41400	33	68	560	36.1	38.8	20.5	4.6	0.0	63770
73650 HAMMON	19407	273	31.1	32.6	30.0	3.3	2.9	39182	41005	30	63	223	36.3	26.5	24.2	12.6	0.4	67188
73651 HOBART	17937	1729	38.2	27.8	27.0	5.2	1.8	34964	35975	17	36	1259	46.5	30.8	17.9	3.9	1.0	53870
73654 LEEDEY	18803	301	38.5	26.9	29.2	3.3	2.0	36064	38648	21	45	247	46.6	26.7	19.4	7.3	0.0	56071
73655 LONE WOLF	18381	514	38.9	30.5	24.9	4.3	1.4	32243	32693	12	23	405	45.7	28.1	18.5	5.9	1.7	55833
73658 OAKWOOD	20582	111	34.2	35.1	23.4	5.4	1.8	34141	34709	16	31	93	37.6	22.6	30.1	8.6	1.1	70833
73659 PUTNAM	24445	46	23.9	32.6	37.0	2.2	4.3	45000	42951	48	81	36	47.2	22.2	25.0	2.8	2.8	53333
73660 REYDON	21979	180	32.8	31.1	29.4	2.8	3.9	36746	40000	23	51	140	36.4	24.3	29.3	7.9	2.1	76154
73661 ROCKY	19664	107	31.8	36.4	26.2	4.7	0.9	36935	40000	23	51	84	44.0	28.6	20.2	7.1	0.0	57143
73662 SAYRE	17824	1651	39.9	34.5	21.0	3.4	1.2	31302	32451	10	18	1167	44.3	25.1	22.6	7.3	0.7	59638
73663 SEILING	18149	644	35.9	34.5	21.9	5.0	2.8	32384	33305	12	24	495	38.0	30.9	26.7	3.6	0.8	66310
73664 SENTINEL	17363	386	31.1	35.8	27.2	4.7	1.3	38037	39387	27	58	304	44.7	28.6	19.4	7.2	0.0	56154
73666 SWEETWATER	19766	143	34.3	38.5	21.7	3.5	2.1	35716	36196	20	42	117	35.0	25.6	25.6	10.3	3.4	70625
73667 TALOGA	21784	274	28.1	32.1	33.2	2.9	3.6	42738	43683	42	75	219	46.1	24.2	23.7	4.1	1.8	54474
73668 TEXOLA	16652	42	33.3	28.6	33.3	4.8	0.0	40000	38642	33	68	33	30.3	18.2	36.4	12.1	3.0	95000
73669 THOMAS	19150	634	33.1	28.4	31.4	4.6	2.5	38929	41160	30	62	486	40.7	28.2	24.7	5.1	1.2	64419
73673 WILLOW	25123	142	34.5	33.8	26.1	4.2	1.4	34554	36732	17	34	110	42.7	25.5	23.6	7.3	0.9	62857
73701 ENID	16507	9056	35.7	33.9	26.8	2.6	1.1	34883	36945	17	35	5836	41.3	36.9	17.2	4.1	0.5	57202
73703 ENID	26540	11211	20.2	29.6	36.9	8.7	4.7	50200	51595	62	89	8008	8.7	23.0	46.0	19.9	2.4	114270
73705 ENID	2904	0	0.0	0.0	0.0	0.0	0.0	0	0	0	0	0	0.0	0.0	0.0	0.0	0.0	0
73716 ALINE	20795	168	32.7	34.5	28.0	2.4	2.4	35739	37347	20	42	140	57.1	21.4	15.0	5.7	0.7	41667
73717 ALVA	22091	2529	34.6	27.7	29.9	4.2	3.7	37331	40017	25	54	1657	32.8	30.9	29.2	6.5	0.7	71364
73718 AMES	19317	215	32.1	27.9	35.8	2.8	1.4	39176	40563	30	63	182	40.7	30.8	24.2	4.4	0.0	60833
73719 AMORITA	28953	64	32.8	29.7	26.6	4.7	6.3	40000	42978	33	68	50	52.0	16.0	20.0	12.0	0.0	48333
73720 BISON	25020	80	22.5	31.3	41.3	3.8	1.3	47340	48905	55	86	67	16.4	29.9	40.3	11.9	1.5	103125
73722 BURLINGTON	23002	177	33.3	30.5	26.6	4.5	5.1	39350	40745	31	64	139	55.4	16.5	18.7	9.4	0.0	45588
73724 CANTON	17008	460	41.1	27.2	27.2	3.7	0.9	31767	32935	11	21	378	57.4	20.9	20.1	1.6	0.0	44167
73726 CARMEN	18070	203	33.0	34.5	28.6	1.5	2.5	35472	36928	19	40	169	59.2	21.3	13.6	5.3	0.6	39722
73727 CARRIER	19700	194	18.0	37.6	38.7	3.6	2.1	46419	48188	53	84	160	28.8	25.6	31.9	11.9	1.9	78750
73728 CHEROKEE	19639	854	33.0	34.4	26.2	4.6	1.8	36139	36835	21	45	687	49.6	26.5	20.1	3.8	0.0	50521
73729 CLEO SPRINGS	21164	226	28.8	32.3	30.5	3.5	4.9	40344	41130	34	69	192	27.1	25.0	38.5	9.4	0.0	86000
73730 COVINGTON	18307	362	29.3	32.9	34.8	2.2	0.8	39580	42529	31	65	295	43.7	28.5	19.0	8.8	0.0	56167
73731 DACOMA	24113	114	29.8	34.2	23.7	6.1	6.1	38439	40241	28	60	96	41.7	21.9	26.0	7.3	3.1	71111
73733 DOUGLAS	20318	91	29.7	33.0	35.2	2.2	0.0	39594	41976	31	65	74	44.6	25.7	20.3	9.5	0.0	58000
73734 DOVER	25148	240	12.5	38.3	37.9	7.9	3.3	49541	50101	60	88	199	32.2	15.6	27.6	23.1	1.5	95000
73735 DRUMMOND	18796	290	24.8	29.0	42.1	3.8	0.3	46233	47196	52	84	223	21.1	28.3	37.2	13.5	0.0	91500
73736 FAIRMONT	19617	282	22.0	34.8	37.6	5.0	0.7	45000	46809	48	81	250	17.6	22.8	39.2	18.0	2.4	104412
73737 FAIRVIEW	20766	1515	30.5	31.7	31.1	5.0	1.7	37890	39175	26	56	1151	32.2	30.0	29.5	7.0	1.3	72398
73738 GARBER	16966	473	33.4	38.1	26.0	1.9	0.6	33381	35496	14	29	376	51.1	30.9	13.3	4.5	0.3	48400
73739 GOLTRY	19636	156	32.7	34.6	28.2	1.9	2.6	35399	37341	19	39	130	59.2	21.5	12.3	6.2	0.8	39286
73741 HELENA	15046	270	26.7	39.3	31.5	1.5	1.1	40000	40738	33	68	216	53.2	26.9	18.1	1.9	0.0	46818
73742 HENNESSEY	19374	1598	25.6	36.2	28.5	6.8	3.0	39761	41951	32	66	1265	33.0	24.9	26.7	14.5	0.8	76507
73744 HITCHCOCK	17899	88	34.1	28.4	28.4	6.8	2.3	35000	35000	18	36	74	31.1	28.4	28.4	12.2	0.0	70000
73747 ISABELLA	18395	134	21.6	47.0	23.1	8.2	0.0	36309	38075	21	47	110	27.3	44.5	20.9	5.5	1.8	68000
73749 JET	18868	225	41.8	33.3	20.9	3.6	0.4	30852	31591	9	16	184	65.8	20.7	9.8	3.8	0.0	37813
73750 KINGFISHER	23601	2686	22.3	28.7	35.9	9.6	3.5	49147	50297	59	88	2043	20.0	23.4	39.5	16.2	0.9	102104
73753 KREMLIN	22155	189	17.5	35.4	39.2	4.8	3.2	48012	50109	57	87	157	24.8	25.5	33.1	13.4	3.2	89167
73754 LAHOMA	20661	481	20.8	35.3	38.9	3.5	1.5	45592	47274	50	83	365	11.8	26.6	45.5	14.2	1.9	108393
73755 LONGDALE	17569	279	42.7	27.6	25.1	2.9	1.8	29157	30751	7	10	230	63.9	20.4	13.0	2.6	0.0	39063
73756 LOYAL	21935	60	23.3	30.0	40.0	6.7	0.0	45000	45000	48	81	47	29.8	23.4	31.9	12.8	2.1	77500
73757 LUCIEN	24910	49	26.5	22.4	42.9	8.2	0.0	50676	47382	63	90	41	22.0	29.3	34.1	14.6	0.0	87500
73758 MANCHESTER	18791	77	33.8	35.1	27.3	2.6	1.3	35442	37981	19	39	62	74.2	19.4	6.5	0.0	0.0	33333
73759 MEDFORD	19575	711	28.8	33.9	30.7	4.6	2.0	37284	39747	24	53	545	36.0	26.6	30.3	6.6	0.6	72700
73760 MENO	19316	204	27.0	32.8	35.3	2.9	2.0	39144	40682	30	63	176	30.1	27.3	35.2	6.3	1.1	79091
73761 NASH	16980	196	34.2	30.6	30.1	4.1	1.0	33740	34515	15	30	150	34.0	30.0	28.7	5.3	2.0	74000
73762 OKARCHE	21697	847	20.5	33.9	37.1	6.1	2.4	46281	46605	52	84	688	13.7	20.6	45.1	19.8	0.9	118287
73763 OKEENE	21002	625	27.8	37.8	27.4	4.0	3.0	37940	37576	26	57	495	43.8	29.3	23.4	3.2	0.2	58026
73764 OMEGA	16563	17	23.5	35.3	35.3	5.9	0.0	42353	45000	40	74	13	38.5	23.1	30.8	7.7	0.0	65000
73766 POND CREEK	20792	392	30.4	32.9	28.8	3.8	4.1	38628	40340	29	60	314	40.1	28.3	26.1	4.8	0.6	57561
73768 RINGWOOD	19334	514	27.0	33.5	33.5	3.1	2.9	39659	40701	32	65	442	28.5	26.5	36.9	7.2	0.9	82143
73770 SOUTHARD	0	0	0.0	0.0	0.0	0.0	0.0	0	0	0	0	0	0.0	0.0	0.0	0.0	0.0	0
73771 WAKITA	18173	214	34.1	33.6	28.5	2.3	1.4	35590	36729	20	41	173	76.3	17.9	5.2	0.6	0.0	29750
73772 WATONGA	15732	1826	33.2	33.2	27.5	5.1	1.0	34829	35215	17	34	1340	35.1	31.5	26.6	6.7	0.0	65763
73773 WAUKOMIS	19596	633	26.4	33.5	36.2	3.2	0.8	43520	45352	44	77	496	17.3	48.6	27.8	5.2	1.0	74407
73801 WOODWARD	21233	5905	28.4	30.8	31.6	6.8	2.3	42111	44124	40	73	4047	22.1	28.0	39.7	9.3	0.8	89788
73832 ARNETT	18895	505	29.5	42.4	23.0	3.4	1.8	34171	34250	16	32	407	49.9	23.1	19.7	5.2	2.2	50179
73834 BUFFALO	20819	669	25.3	35.0	32.4	6.1	1.2	40312	42228	34	68	523	45.7	28.1	19.3	5.7	1.1	54688
73835 CAMARGO	19907	67	41.8	26.9	28.4	3.0	0.0	31882	34047	11	21	54	37.0	24.1	27.8	11.1	0.0	76000
73838 CHESTER	17814	196	38.3	31.1	26.5	3.6	0.5	32814	34795	13	26	165	30.9	26.1	27.9	8.5	6.7	75000
73840 FARGO	20000	255	31.4	34.5	27.5	4.7	2.0	35326	35697	19	38	202	39.1	31.2	23.3	4.0	2.5	67778
73841 FORT SUPPLY	15535	261	24.5	31.4	35.2	6.9	1.9	45139	46743	49	81	217	24.9	28.1	38.2	7.4	1.4	83500
73842 FREEDOM	21959	187	27.8	36.9	28.3	4.8	2.1	39432	41581	31	64	149	41.6	30.2	16.1	8.7	3.4	60455
73843 GAGE	20823	256	34.8	33.6	25.8	3.9	2.0	35205	36899	18	37	204	48.0	28.4	19.6	2.5	1.5	52857
73844 GATE	19545	120	31.7	32.5	27.5	5.8	2.5	37703	40886	26	56	94	46.8	25.5	21.3	2.1	4.3	55000
73848 LAVERNE	22112	776	29.5	31.3	29.6	6.6	3.0	41795	43573	39	73	613	43.6	25.4	23.7	6.7	0.7	58977
73851 MAY	22659	30	26.7	30.0	40.0	3.3	0.0	45000	45000	48	81	24	29.2	25.0	29.2	12.5	4.2	80000
73852 MOORELAND	19347	861	24.5	40.3	28.6	4.6	2.0	40627	42272	35	69	677	23.9	30.4	36.3	7.7	1.6	81571
73853 MUTUAL	24813	106	17.9	38.7	34.9	5.7	2.8	42704	45577	42	75	91	18.7	20.9	41.8	15.4	3.3	100625
73855 ROSSTON	20609	83	27.7	28.9	36.1	6.0	1.2	45370	47340	49	82	67	28.4	28.4	23.9	13.4	6.0	76250
73857 SHARON	20650	490	20.6	33.7	39.6	4.7	1.4	46487	47449	53	85	434	24.2	24.7	32.9	15.7	2.5	91852
73858 SHATTUCK	21408	776	34.0	33.9	24.4	5.9	1.8	34499	36006	17	33	621	44.9	30.3	20.6	3.5	0.6	56300
OKLAHOMA	22515		27.2	29.2	32.3	7.2	4.0	43746	45901				20.4	25.6	36.1	15.4	2.4	96076
UNITED STATES	27277		20.9	24.4	35.3	11.7	7.6	54719	56938				9.3	13.1	31.6	32.6	13.5	162279

ZIP CODE #	POST OFFICE NAME	FINANCIAL SERVICES: Auto Loan	Home Loan	Invest-ments	Retire-ment Plans	THE HOME: Home Improvements: Home Repair	Lawn & Garden	Furnishings: Comput-ers & Hard-ware-Personal	Major Appli-ances	TV, Radio, Sound Equip-ment	Furni-ture	ENTERTAINMENT: Dine out/ Carry out	Sports Equip-ment	Fees & Tickets	Toys & Games	Travel	Cable TV	PERSONAL: Apparel & Services	Auto Repairs	Health Insur-ance	Pets & Supplies
73622	BESSIE	82	59	84	57	61	83	60	76	67	56	66	57	48	66	59	73	43	70	80	91
73624	BURNS FLAT	49	41	38	42	39	44	49	45	50	44	49	36	44	50	43	51	34	48	49	55
73625	BUTLER	81	55	89	55	58	85	62	77	64	50	63	63	45	63	61	70	41	71	81	94
73626	CANUTE	87	60	94	60	63	91	66	82	69	55	69	67	49	68	66	76	45	77	87	101
73627	CARTER	76	52	84	52	55	80	58	72	60	47	60	60	43	59	58	66	39	67	76	89
73628	CHEYENNE	80	57	83	56	59	84	63	78	69	55	67	59	49	68	61	76	44	72	84	92
73632	CORDELL	78	55	81	54	57	82	61	75	66	52	64	58	47	64	59	72	42	70	81	90
73638	CRAWFORD	87	60	96	60	63	92	66	83	69	54	68	68	49	68	66	75	44	77	87	102
73639	CUSTER CITY	88	61	97	61	64	93	68	84	70	55	69	69	49	69	67	77	45	78	89	103
73641	DILL CITY	70	50	73	49	52	73	54	67	59	47	58	52	42	58	53	65	38	63	73	80
73642	DURHAM	87	60	96	60	63	92	67	83	69	54	68	68	49	68	66	75	44	77	87	102
73644	ELK CITY	78	63	68	62	62	76	68	72	72	64	71	56	59	72	63	76	48	72	78	88
73645	ERICK	70	49	72	48	51	73	54	67	59	47	57	52	42	58	53	65	38	63	72	80
73646	FAY	84	58	93	58	61	89	64	80	67	52	66	66	47	66	64	73	43	75	85	99
73647	FOSS	77	64	63	65	61	71	75	71	76	68	75	56	66	77	67	79	52	74	76	87
73650	HAMMON	87	60	95	60	62	91	66	82	69	54	68	68	48	68	66	75	44	77	87	101
73651	HOBART	71	53	67	52	54	73	59	68	64	53	62	52	48	64	55	70	42	65	75	81
73654	LEEDEY	80	55	87	55	57	84	61	76	63	49	63	63	45	62	61	69	41	71	80	93
73655	LONE WOLF	72	52	74	50	53	73	53	67	59	49	58	51	42	58	52	65	38	62	70	80
73658	OAKWOOD	84	57	92	57	60	88	64	79	66	52	66	66	47	65	63	72	43	74	84	98
73659	PUTNAM	95	65	104	65	68	100	72	90	75	59	74	74	53	74	72	82	48	84	95	111
73660	REYDON	87	60	95	60	63	91	66	82	69	54	68	68	49	68	66	75	44	77	87	101
73661	ROCKY	79	54	87	54	57	83	60	75	63	49	62	62	44	61	60	68	40	70	79	92
73662	SAYRE	67	48	68	47	50	70	53	65	59	47	57	49	42	58	51	65	38	61	71	77
73663	SEILING	75	53	78	52	55	79	58	72	64	50	62	56	45	62	57	70	41	67	78	86
73664	SENTINEL	79	54	86	54	57	83	60	75	62	49	62	62	44	61	60	68	40	70	79	92
73666	SWEETWATER	82	56	90	56	59	86	62	78	65	51	64	64	46	64	62	71	42	73	82	96
73667	TALOGA	91	63	100	63	66	96	70	87	73	57	72	72	51	71	69	79	47	81	92	107
73668	TEXOLA	81	56	89	55	58	85	62	77	64	50	63	63	45	63	61	70	41	72	81	94
73669	THOMAS	84	59	86	58	62	87	65	81	71	57	69	62	51	70	63	78	46	75	87	96
73673	WILLOW	77	53	83	53	56	81	59	73	63	49	61	59	44	61	58	68	40	68	78	89
73701	ENID	63	51	50	52	50	61	58	58	61	53	59	45	51	61	52	64	41	59	64	71
73703	ENID	91	88	86	89	88	97	88	92	90	85	89	69	86	90	88	93	61	90	98	108
73705	ENID	0	0	0	0	0	0	0	0	0	0	0	0	0	0	0	0	0	0	0	0
73716	ALINE	80	55	88	55	58	85	61	76	64	50	63	63	45	62	61	69	41	71	80	94
73717	ALVA	81	61	74	62	63	79	72	76	75	64	73	59	60	74	66	79	50	76	82	91
73718	AMES	79	55	87	54	57	84	61	75	63	49	62	62	44	62	60	69	40	70	80	93
73719	AMORITA	108	74	118	74	77	114	82	102	85	67	84	84	60	84	82	93	55	95	108	126
73720	BISON	100	69	110	69	72	106	76	95	80	62	79	79	56	78	76	87	51	89	100	117
73722	BURLINGTON	101	70	110	70	73	107	78	96	82	64	80	79	58	80	77	89	52	90	102	118
73724	CANTON	72	52	74	50	54	74	53	68	59	50	58	51	43	59	53	65	38	62	70	81
73726	CARMEN	78	54	86	54	56	83	60	74	62	48	62	61	44	61	60	68	40	69	79	92
73727	CARRIER	92	67	100	67	70	98	72	88	75	60	74	73	56	74	73	81	49	83	93	108
73728	CHEROKEE	79	55	85	54	57	83	61	75	64	50	63	61	45	63	60	70	41	70	80	91
73729	CLEO SPRINGS	90	62	99	62	65	95	69	85	71	56	71	71	50	70	68	78	46	80	90	105
73730	COVINGTON	81	55	89	55	58	85	62	77	64	50	63	63	45	63	61	70	41	71	81	94
73731	DACOMA	98	67	108	67	71	103	75	93	78	61	77	77	55	76	74	85	50	87	98	114
73733	DOUGLAS	81	55	89	55	58	85	62	77	64	50	63	63	45	63	61	70	41	71	81	94
73734	DOVER	107	99	87	95	96	101	93	99	97	97	97	72	88	100	89	99	66	95	99	117
73735	DRUMMOND	89	61	97	61	64	93	68	84	70	55	70	69	50	69	67	77	45	78	89	103
73736	FAIRMONT	88	61	97	60	63	93	67	84	70	55	69	69	49	69	67	76	45	78	88	103
73737	FAIRVIEW	78	64	82	62	65	85	65	78	71	59	69	59	57	69	66	77	46	74	86	92
73738	GARBER	68	48	70	47	50	71	53	66	58	46	56	50	42	57	52	64	37	61	71	78
73739	GOLTRY	78	53	85	53	56	82	59	74	62	48	61	61	43	60	59	67	40	69	78	91
73741	HELENA	78	55	81	54	57	80	58	73	63	52	62	56	45	62	57	69	41	67	76	87
73742	HENNESSEY	93	64	96	63	66	95	68	86	75	61	74	68	52	74	67	82	48	80	90	105
73744	HITCHCOCK	84	58	93	58	61	89	64	80	67	52	66	66	47	66	64	73	43	75	85	99
73747	ISABELLA	83	57	92	57	60	88	64	79	66	52	66	66	47	65	63	72	43	74	84	97
73749	JET	65	46	65	45	48	67	51	63	56	45	54	47	40	55	49	62	36	58	68	74
73750	KINGFISHER	90	86	84	85	85	97	82	89	87	80	86	67	81	88	83	92	59	87	98	106
73753	KREMLIN	96	73	103	73	75	102	77	93	79	66	79	76	62	78	78	85	52	87	97	113
73754	LAHOMA	90	66	91	64	68	92	67	85	74	62	73	64	55	74	67	81	48	78	88	100
73755	LONGDALE	74	53	76	52	55	76	55	70	61	51	60	52	44	60	54	67	39	64	72	83
73756	LOYAL	94	65	103	65	68	99	72	89	75	58	74	74	53	73	72	82	48	83	94	110
73757	LUCIEN	97	67	107	67	70	103	74	92	77	60	76	76	54	76	74	84	50	86	98	114
73758	MANCHESTER	76	52	84	52	55	80	58	72	61	47	60	60	43	59	58	66	39	68	76	89
73759	MEDFORD	81	58	84	56	60	85	63	78	69	55	67	60	49	68	62	76	44	73	84	93
73760	MENO	87	60	95	59	62	91	66	82	69	54	68	68	48	68	66	75	44	77	87	101
73761	NASH	74	51	81	51	53	78	57	70	59	46	58	58	42	58	56	64	38	66	74	87
73762	OKARCHE	96	71	100	70	73	99	76	91	79	65	78	73	59	78	75	85	51	85	95	111
73763	OKEENE	87	61	92	60	64	92	67	84	72	57	71	66	51	71	66	79	46	78	89	101
73764	OMEGA	84	58	92	57	60	88	64	79	66	52	66	66	47	65	64	72	43	74	84	98
73766	POND CREEK	92	63	101	63	66	97	70	87	73	57	72	72	51	72	70	80	47	82	92	107
73768	RINGWOOD	88	61	97	61	63	93	67	84	70	55	69	69	49	69	67	76	45	78	88	103
73770	SOUTHARD	0	0	0	0	0	0	0	0	0	0	0	0	0	0	0	0	0	0	0	0
73771	WAKITA	76	52	83	52	55	80	58	72	60	47	60	59	42	59	58	66	39	67	76	89
73772	WATONGA	73	53	71	53	54	75	60	69	64	52	62	54	47	63	56	70	42	66	75	84
73773	WAUKOMIS	81	58	84	57	60	85	63	78	69	55	67	60	49	68	62	76	44	73	85	93
73801	WOODWARD	83	67	73	66	67	82	71	78	76	67	74	59	62	77	66	80	50	76	83	93
73832	ARNETT	76	52	83	52	55	80	58	72	60	47	60	60	42	59	58	66	39	67	76	89
73834	BUFFALO	87	60	95	60	63	92	66	82	69	54	68	68	49	68	66	75	44	77	87	101
73835	CAMARGO	71	49	77	48	51	74	54	67	56	44	56	55	40	55	54	61	36	63	71	82
73838	CHESTER	72	49	79	49	52	76	55	68	57	44	56	56	40	56	55	62	37	64	72	84
73840	FARGO	86	59	94	59	62	91	66	82	68	53	68	67	48	67	65	74	44	76	86	100
73841	FORT SUPPLY	91	66	94	63	68	93	67	86	75	63	73	64	54	74	67	82	48	78	89	102
73842	FREEDOM	90	64	92	62	67	91	66	84	73	62	72	63	53	73	65	81	48	77	88	100
73843	GAGE	80	55	88	55	57	84	61	76	63	49	63	63	45	62	61	69	41	71	80	93
73844	GATE	84	57	92	57	60	88	64	79	66	52	66	66	47	65	64	72	43	74	84	98
73848	LAVERNE	87	62	90	61	64	91	68	84	74	59	72	65	53	73	66	82	48	78	91	100
73851	MAY	88	60	96	60	63	93	67	83	70	54	69	69	49	68	67	76	45	78	88	103
73852	MOORELAND	86	61	90	60	64	89	65	82	71	58	70	63	51	70	64	78	46	76	87	98
73853	MUTUAL	99	68	108	68	71	104	75	94	78	61	78	78	55	77	75	86	50	88	99	115
73855	ROSSTON	89	61	98	61	64	94	68	85	71	55	70	70	50	70	68	77	45	79	89	104
73857	SHARON	95	65	104	65	68	100	72	90	75	59	74	74	53	74	72	82	48	84	95	111
73858	SHATTUCK	78	56	80	55	58	82	61	76	67	54	65	58	48	66	59	74	43	71	82	90
	OKLAHOMA	87	75	78	75	74	84	79	82	82	77	81	63	73	83	75	85	56	82	86	98
	UNITED STATES	100	100	100	100	100	100	100	100	100	100	100	100	100	100	100	100	100	100	100	100

ZIP CODE			POPULATION			2000-2009 ANNUAL RATE		HOUSEHOLDS					FAMILIES		
#	POST OFFICE NAME	COUNTY FIPS CODE	2000	2009	2014	% Rate	State Centile	2000	2009	2014	% Annual Rate 2000-2009	2009 Average HH Size	2000	2009	% Annual Rate 2000-2009
73859	VICI	043	1211	1169	1142	-0.4	22	501	495	487	-0.1	2.25	318	305	-0.5
73860	WAYNOKA	151	1477	1291	1215	-1.4	2	666	592	560	-1.3	2.10	407	351	-1.6
73931	BALKO	007	657	611	589	-0.8	9	271	255	247	-0.7	2.40	212	197	-0.8
73932	BEAVER	007	2034	1968	1920	-0.4	22	796	774	754	-0.3	2.42	583	555	-0.5
73933	BOISE CITY	025	1966	1802	1716	-0.9	8	796	738	705	-0.8	2.39	535	483	-1.1
73937	FELT	025	213	195	186	-0.9	8	79	73	70	-0.9	2.67	59	53	-1.2
73938	FORGAN	007	746	710	689	-0.5	15	274	261	253	-0.5	2.72	206	193	-0.7
73939	GOODWELL	139	2020	2018	2015	0.0	43	687	683	676	-0.1	2.62	451	434	-0.4
73942	GUYMON	139	12429	13342	13660	0.8	78	4338	4544	4622	0.5	2.90	3190	3270	0.3
73944	HARDESTY	139	511	521	518	0.2	55	195	195	193	0.0	2.67	153	151	-0.1
73945	HOOKER	139	2751	2768	2769	0.1	49	1054	1039	1031	-0.2	2.66	791	762	-0.4
73946	KENTON	025	129	118	112	-1.0	7	55	51	49	-0.8	2.31	41	37	-1.1
73947	KEYES	025	718	647	614	-1.1	5	279	253	241	-1.1	2.56	199	177	-1.3
73949	TEXHOMA	025	1616	1615	1609	0.0	43	607	596	590	-0.2	2.70	460	443	-0.4
73950	TURPIN	007	1725	1730	1711	0.0	43	623	627	620	0.1	2.76	482	475	-0.2
73951	TYRONE	139	1273	1255	1248	-0.2	33	458	444	440	-0.3	2.83	351	334	-0.5
74002	BARNSDALL	113	3144	3237	3261	0.3	60	1184	1234	1246	0.4	2.59	872	885	0.2
74003	BARTLESVILLE	113	14944	14861	14849	-0.1	38	6190	6201	6211	0.0	2.37	4030	3923	-0.3
74006	BARTLESVILLE	147	24007	24921	25414	0.4	64	10061	10694	10981	0.7	2.29	7124	7379	0.4
74008	BIXBY	143	16170	20448	22325	2.6	95	5885	7560	8288	2.7	2.69	4663	5878	2.5
74010	BRISTOW	037	10003	10120	10174	0.1	49	3930	4029	4069	0.3	2.49	2825	2825	0.0
74011	BROKEN ARROW	143	23016	25756	27160	1.2	86	8057	9212	9761	1.5	2.79	6664	7441	1.2
74012	BROKEN ARROW	143	47142	54990	58408	1.7	92	16540	19592	20884	1.8	2.78	13160	15119	1.5
74014	BROKEN ARROW	145	22798	30579	35020	3.2	98	7968	10839	12468	3.4	2.82	6775	9114	3.3
74015	CATOOSA	131	7746	8159	8491	0.6	73	2829	2985	3119	0.6	2.70	2192	2244	0.3
74016	CHELSEA	131	5395	5661	5844	0.5	68	2048	2130	2202	0.4	2.64	1505	1518	0.1
74017	CLAREMORE	131	25117	29082	31556	1.6	91	9548	10977	11930	1.5	2.60	6873	7677	1.2
74019	CLAREMORE	131	13577	17719	19846	2.9	96	4793	6242	7019	2.9	2.82	4024	5114	2.6
74020	CLEVELAND	117	9487	9321	9218	-0.2	33	3675	3625	3584	-0.1	2.55	2776	2679	-0.4
74021	COLLINSVILLE	143	12300	15655	17352	2.6	95	4526	5790	6436	2.7	2.68	3534	4417	2.4
74022	COPAN	147	1791	1829	1859	0.2	55	741	776	796	0.5	2.36	542	554	0.2
74023	CUSHING	119	10915	11177	11225	0.3	60	4036	3964	3993	-0.2	2.47	2771	2614	-0.6
74026	DAVENPORT	081	986	803	751	-2.2	1	391	326	306	-1.9	2.46	300	245	-2.2
74027	DELAWARE	105	1226	1370	1427	1.2	86	478	535	557	1.2	2.56	368	403	1.0
74028	DEPEW	037	1932	1906	1906	-0.1	38	720	726	728	0.1	2.63	539	530	-0.2
74029	DEWEY	147	5047	5090	5122	0.1	49	2040	2099	2122	0.3	2.37	1452	1455	0.0
74030	DRUMRIGHT	037	6431	6345	6329	-0.1	38	2571	2556	2556	-0.1	2.45	1808	1749	-0.4
74032	GLENCOE	119	1268	1684	1863	3.1	97	494	648	721	3.0	2.60	373	472	2.6
74033	GLENPOOL	143	8463	9517	10047	1.3	89	2872	3299	3502	1.5	2.86	2351	2637	1.2
74035	HOMINY	113	3518	3322	3260	-0.6	13	1372	1317	1299	-0.4	2.27	919	855	-0.8
74036	INOLA	131	5601	6662	7273	1.9	94	2000	2374	2602	1.9	2.78	1604	1848	1.5
74037	JENKS	143	9555	13890	15728	4.1	99	3475	5080	5764	4.2	2.72	2758	4035	4.2
74038	JENNINGS	117	843	1264	1385	4.5	99	315	477	523	4.6	2.65	242	361	4.4
74039	KELLYVILLE	037	3330	3326	3344	0.0	43	1184	1207	1220	0.2	2.76	931	929	0.0
74041	KIEFER	037	1549	1578	1601	0.2	55	575	599	612	0.4	2.60	451	459	0.2
74042	LENAPAH	105	836	853	856	0.2	55	298	301	301	0.1	2.83	242	242	0.0
74044	MANNFORD	037	6676	7197	7443	0.8	78	2475	2724	2831	1.0	2.61	1915	2060	0.8
74045	MARAMEC	117	304	299	297	-0.2	33	121	120	120	-0.1	2.49	91	88	-0.4
74047	MOUNDS	111	5513	5876	6041	0.7	75	1939	2105	2176	0.9	2.79	1541	1638	0.7
74048	NOWATA	105	6006	6178	6254	0.3	60	2412	2468	2493	0.2	2.42	1648	1642	0.0
74051	OCHELATA	147	1420	1603	1675	1.3	89	504	576	604	1.5	2.78	394	441	1.2
74053	OOLOGAH	131	3812	5123	5795	3.2	98	1382	1847	2094	3.2	2.77	1114	1445	2.9
74054	OSAGE	113	531	549	557	0.4	64	222	235	240	0.6	2.34	155	159	0.3
74055	OWASSO	143	26702	35503	39409	3.1	97	9373	12576	13991	3.2	2.80	7581	10050	3.1
74056	PAWHUSKA	113	5761	5994	6082	0.4	64	2297	2413	2456	0.5	2.42	1550	1577	0.2
74058	PAWNEE	117	4341	4240	4182	-0.3	27	1674	1645	1626	-0.2	2.52	1169	1117	-0.5
74059	PERKINS	119	4102	4888	5281	1.9	94	1615	1908	2068	1.8	2.55	1162	1326	1.4
74060	PRUE	113	1588	1693	1741	0.7	75	573	623	643	0.9	2.72	447	476	0.7
74061	RAMONA	147	1898	2011	2071	0.6	73	742	798	828	0.8	2.52	565	597	0.6
74062	RIPLEY	119	948	1026	1075	0.9	80	342	367	385	0.8	2.80	266	276	0.4
74063	SAND SPRINGS	143	28213	29038	29653	0.3	60	10587	11084	11370	0.5	2.58	8061	8223	0.2
74066	SAPULPA	037	29190	30600	31250	0.5	68	10906	11565	11844	0.6	2.61	8249	8578	0.4
74070	SKIATOOK	113	10603	12582	13390	1.9	94	3807	4586	4903	2.0	2.73	3017	3554	1.8
74072	S COFFEYVILLE	105	1496	1503	1502	0.1	49	579	584	583	0.1	2.57	426	420	-0.2
74073	SPERRY	143	4263	4573	4792	0.8	78	1494	1611	1690	0.8	2.82	1167	1225	0.5
74074	STILLWATER	119	25892	29711	31438	1.5	91	10536	11672	12396	1.1	2.31	5745	6227	0.9
74075	STILLWATER	119	18679	21461	22906	1.5	91	8534	9612	10277	1.3	2.18	4254	4609	0.9
74077	STILLWATER	119	142	187	188	3.0	97	0	0	0	0.0	0.00	0	0	0.0
74078	STILLWATER	119	4206	5422	5448	2.8	96	290	303	314	0.5	2.99	154	152	-0.1
74079	STROUD	081	5048	5143	5182	0.2	55	1972	2035	2057	0.3	2.49	1391	1401	0.1
74080	TALALA	131	1466	1657	1768	1.3	89	525	592	634	1.3	2.80	418	459	1.0
74081	TERLTON	117	1073	1068	1063	-0.1	38	371	373	372	0.1	2.86	303	300	-0.1
74083	WANN	105	868	883	886	0.2	55	333	342	344	0.3	2.58	267	269	0.1
74084	WYNONA	113	2132	2156	2163	0.1	49	386	402	408	0.4	3.10	277	280	0.1
74085	YALE	119	2390	2609	2725	1.0	82	951	1030	1083	0.9	2.48	676	706	0.5
74103	TULSA	143	2173	2075	2078	-0.5	15	60	60	60	0.0	2.55	15	14	-0.7
74104	TULSA	143	14034	14088	14195	0.0	43	5945	6034	6110	0.2	2.10	2735	2592	-0.6
74105	TULSA	143	29190	29305	29580	0.0	43	14381	14575	14751	0.1	2.00	7383	7045	-0.5
74106	TULSA	143	17999	17725	17743	-0.2	33	7055	7047	7086	0.0	2.46	4514	4296	-0.5
74107	TULSA	143	20069	20218	20495	0.1	49	8173	8370	8509	0.3	2.40	5387	5297	-0.2
74108	TULSA	143	7626	7662	7783	0.1	49	2780	2854	2916	0.3	2.68	2110	2099	-0.1
74110	TULSA	143	15685	15800	15927	0.1	49	5766	5772	5810	0.0	2.68	3753	3590	-0.5
74112	TULSA	143	22779	22440	22460	-0.2	33	10334	10296	10332	0.0	2.18	5855	5523	-0.6
74114	TULSA	143	17131	16596	16508	-0.3	27	7769	7651	7639	-0.2	2.14	4668	4370	-0.7
74115	TULSA	143	23633	23617	23801	0.0	43	9092	9138	9221	0.1	2.58	6139	5928	-0.4
74116	TULSA	143	3667	4108	4331	1.2	86	1469	1660	1756	1.3	2.47	967	1044	0.8
74117	TULSA	143	108	127	137	1.8	93	40	48	52	2.0	2.63	30	36	2.0
74119	TULSA	143	3763	3734	3772	-0.1	38	2570	2605	2637	0.1	1.34	633	586	-0.8
74120	TULSA	143	5735	5751	5811	0.0	43	2854	2924	2973	0.3	1.86	1053	997	-0.6
74126	TULSA	113	12456	12113	12105	-0.3	27	4198	4146	4153	-0.1	2.92	3149	3013	-0.5
74127	TULSA	113	17942	17658	17616	-0.2	33	7095	7071	7082	0.0	2.46	4599	4411	-0.5
74128	TULSA	143	11637	11583	11658	-0.1	38	4689	4742	4794	0.1	2.40	3190	3098	-0.3
74129	TULSA	143	17681	17635	17766	0.0	43	7252	7383	7478	0.2	2.35	4678	4542	-0.3
74130	TULSA	143	2352	2260	2240	-0.4	22	870	851	847	-0.2	2.66	603	567	-0.7
74131	TULSA	037	3292	3377	3454	0.3	60	1214	1264	1301	0.4	2.67	955	981	0.3
	OKLAHOMA					0.7					0.8	2.46			0.6
	UNITED STATES					1.0					1.1	2.59			0.9

ZIP CODE #	POST OFFICE NAME	RACE (%) White 2000	White 2009	Black 2000	Black 2009	Asian/Pacific 2000	Asian/Pacific 2009	% Hispanic Origin 2000	% Hispanic Origin 2009	2009 AGE DISTRIBUTION (%) 0-4	5-9	10-14	15-19	20-24	25-44	45-64	65-84	85+	18+	MEDIAN AGE 2009	% 2009 Males	% 2009 Females
73859	VICI	96.1	95.0	0.0	0.0	0.2	0.2	3.0	4.4	5.0	5.6	5.1	5.1	5.3	20.6	29.7	17.6	6.0	81.4	47.0	47.6	52.4
73860	WAYNOKA	93.8	91.9	1.6	1.8	0.1	0.1	4.3	6.0	4.6	5.2	5.0	6.5	5.0	21.4	29.3	18.2	4.7	81.1	46.5	47.9	52.1
73931	BALKO	96.3	95.3	0.3	0.3	0.0	0.0	2.1	3.1	3.9	4.6	5.4	6.2	3.9	19.3	34.9	19.1	2.6	82.2	49.7	50.7	49.3
73932	BEAVER	93.4	91.6	0.5	0.6	0.1	0.2	7.9	11.1	6.1	6.3	6.3	6.6	4.3	23.3	26.3	16.6	4.2	77.0	42.9	50.1	49.9
73933	BOISE CITY	82.9	77.6	0.6	0.6	0.3	0.3	19.0	25.7	6.8	6.8	6.7	6.3	5.1	21.5	27.3	15.6	3.9	75.7	42.3	49.8	50.2
73937	FELT	84.9	80.0	1.9	2.1	0.0	0.0	14.2	20.0	5.1	5.1	6.2	7.7	5.1	22.1	30.8	15.4	2.6	77.9	44.0	54.9	45.1
73938	FORGAN	93.2	90.6	0.0	0.0	0.1	0.3	11.1	15.9	8.0	8.0	7.9	7.9	3.9	22.8	26.1	13.0	2.4	71.0	38.4	49.2	50.8
73939	GOODWELL	86.5	82.0	2.0	2.2	0.6	0.9	13.7	19.8	7.1	5.8	5.2	13.3	20.7	21.9	18.6	6.3	1.0	77.9	24.5	53.3	46.7
73942	GUYMON	72.3	66.5	0.8	0.7	0.9	1.2	36.6	45.3	9.1	8.2	7.4	6.8	7.4	29.2	22.2	8.4	1.3	71.1	31.8	51.4	48.6
73944	HARDESTY	84.3	79.1	0.6	0.6	0.2	0.2	24.1	33.6	8.3	8.1	7.7	8.8	7.3	26.3	23.6	8.6	1.3	69.7	32.0	52.4	47.6
73945	HOOKER	84.5	78.9	0.1	0.1	0.1	0.1	16.5	23.4	7.7	6.7	7.9	7.2	5.5	24.4	27.3	11.7	1.6	73.1	37.8	51.4	48.6
73946	KENTON	84.5	80.5	2.3	1.7	0.0	0.0	14.0	19.5	5.1	5.1	6.8	7.6	5.1	20.3	30.5	16.9	2.5	78.8	45.0	53.4	46.6
73947	KEYES	93.0	90.1	0.0	0.0	0.0	0.0	7.5	10.8	8.3	8.3	8.3	7.3	4.5	23.5	25.2	12.1	2.5	70.0	36.9	49.5	50.5
73949	TEXHOMA	82.9	78.3	0.2	0.2	0.1	0.2	26.6	34.8	8.6	8.5	8.4	7.2	5.1	26.3	23.8	10.3	1.6	69.7	35.2	51.7	48.3
73950	TURPIN	89.3	86.4	0.2	0.2	0.2	0.2	19.2	26.0	6.3	6.6	6.2	9.8	7.3	24.9	29.7	7.3	1.8	74.9	36.3	52.2	47.8
73951	TYRONE	80.0	72.4	0.2	0.2	0.1	0.1	20.9	29.4	8.0	7.6	7.4	7.5	6.5	27.5	25.1	9.6	0.6	72.3	33.8	50.8	49.2
74002	BARNSDALL	74.2	70.3	0.1	0.2	0.4	0.6	1.8	2.4	7.4	7.4	7.4	6.9	5.4	22.8	27.0	13.4	2.3	73.5	39.0	49.8	50.2
74003	BARTLESVILLE	74.8	71.0	5.6	6.0	0.5	0.6	3.8	5.3	7.2	6.7	6.5	6.9	7.0	25.7	26.3	11.5	2.1	75.4	36.8	48.8	51.2
74006	BARTLESVILLE	86.4	83.6	1.2	1.4	1.2	1.8	2.2	3.2	5.1	5.4	5.9	6.6	5.6	20.1	29.8	17.8	3.7	79.5	45.9	47.4	52.6
74008	BIXBY	86.0	83.0	1.2	1.5	0.5	0.8	3.7	5.3	7.1	7.0	7.1	6.9	5.5	27.1	27.4	10.9	1.2	74.5	37.5	49.6	50.4
74010	BRISTOW	78.5	75.6	5.6	6.3	0.1	0.2	1.5	2.1	7.1	6.7	6.7	6.8	6.2	24.3	26.7	13.2	2.2	75.3	38.5	48.8	51.2
74011	BROKEN ARROW	87.8	84.8	3.0	3.7	0.8	1.1	2.9	4.4	7.2	7.5	7.8	7.6	5.4	26.8	27.6	9.1	1.0	72.5	36.6	49.0	51.0
74012	BROKEN ARROW	83.9	79.6	4.1	5.0	2.6	3.9	4.0	6.1	8.0	7.9	7.8	7.2	5.9	29.6	25.6	6.9	1.1	71.7	34.1	48.5	51.5
74014	BROKEN ARROW	86.4	83.0	2.0	2.5	1.0	1.5	2.6	3.8	7.2	7.4	7.7	7.3	5.1	27.3	28.8	8.5	0.6	73.1	37.2	49.6	50.4
74015	CATOOSA	80.8	77.2	0.5	0.6	0.2	0.3	2.6	3.6	7.5	7.6	7.5	7.0	5.4	26.4	26.7	10.6	1.3	73.0	36.9	48.5	51.5
74016	CHELSEA	69.8	65.8	0.2	0.2	0.3	0.4	1.1	1.6	7.8	7.5	7.5	7.2	6.2	25.2	25.2	11.7	1.7	72.6	36.1	48.8	51.2
74017	CLAREMORE	77.2	73.9	1.2	1.3	0.4	0.5	2.2	3.0	7.0	6.9	6.9	6.9	6.1	24.9	26.8	12.6	2.0	75.0	38.3	48.7	51.3
74019	CLAREMORE	81.4	77.8	0.7	0.8	0.3	0.5	1.9	2.8	7.3	7.5	7.7	7.2	5.2	25.7	27.8	10.8	0.9	72.8	37.9	50.0	50.0
74020	CLEVELAND	85.4	83.0	0.2	0.2	0.4	0.5	1.3	1.7	6.5	6.4	6.6	6.5	5.4	23.8	28.3	14.4	2.2	76.6	40.9	49.5	50.5
74021	COLLINSVILLE	83.8	80.6	0.5	0.7	0.5	0.8	1.5	2.3	7.2	7.2	7.2	6.9	5.2	26.9	26.6	11.3	1.5	74.1	37.8	49.7	50.3
74022	COPAN	81.4	78.7	0.2	0.2	0.2	0.3	1.2	1.6	4.5	4.8	5.3	6.5	5.5	21.5	34.3	15.7	1.9	81.5	46.1	50.2	49.8
74023	CUSHING	81.8	78.6	5.6	6.6	0.1	0.2	2.3	3.3	5.7	5.7	5.7	6.1	7.0	27.8	25.6	13.4	3.0	79.2	38.9	53.8	46.2
74026	DAVENPORT	87.3	85.4	2.7	3.0	0.2	0.2	1.8	2.5	7.8	7.5	7.6	6.7	4.9	24.4	25.3	14.1	1.7	72.9	38.2	46.7	53.3
74027	DELAWARE	72.1	69.3	0.8	0.8	0.0	0.1	0.7	0.9	6.4	7.2	7.2	6.2	4.8	23.2	30.3	13.4	1.4	75.5	40.9	51.5	48.5
74028	DEPEW	76.7	73.6	5.9	6.7	0.3	0.4	1.9	2.6	6.1	6.3	7.8	8.3	5.5	24.5	28.8	11.5	1.2	74.4	39.2	49.5	50.5
74029	DEWEY	79.6	76.5	1.5	1.6	0.1	0.1	2.8	3.9	5.6	5.8	6.1	6.2	5.3	22.1	29.2	17.0	2.9	78.6	44.2	48.9	51.1
74030	DRUMRIGHT	85.5	83.0	1.0	1.2	0.1	0.1	1.3	1.9	7.0	7.0	7.2	7.1	5.1	23.4	26.1	14.6	2.6	74.5	39.6	48.1	51.9
74032	GLENCOE	90.5	88.2	0.3	0.4	0.8	1.0	1.0	1.5	6.7	6.1	6.5	6.9	7.7	25.0	28.7	11.0	1.4	76.5	39.0	48.9	51.1
74033	GLENPOOL	77.1	72.8	2.2	2.8	0.9	1.4	3.1	4.6	8.9	8.6	8.1	7.5	6.4	30.8	22.8	5.9	0.9	69.7	31.6	47.3	52.7
74035	HOMINY	68.1	64.2	4.7	6.0	0.1	0.2	2.9	4.0	6.2	6.2	6.1	6.6	6.8	26.7	25.5	13.3	2.5	77.6	38.5	52.9	47.1
74036	INOLA	82.5	79.1	0.6	0.7	0.2	0.3	1.1	1.6	6.9	7.1	7.4	7.3	5.6	26.3	28.0	10.3	1.2	74.0	37.9	49.6	50.4
74037	JENKS	86.9	84.0	1.5	1.9	0.8	1.2	4.1	5.9	7.7	7.5	7.4	7.0	5.8	28.5	26.6	8.7	1.0	73.1	35.8	49.1	50.9
74038	JENNINGS	85.1	83.5	0.6	0.6	0.1	0.1	0.8	1.2	6.6	6.8	7.2	7.4	5.6	25.3	28.1	11.4	1.5	74.8	38.3	47.9	52.1
74039	KELLYVILLE	83.1	80.5	2.1	2.4	0.2	0.2	1.0	1.4	6.8	6.8	7.0	7.4	5.7	26.6	27.8	10.9	0.9	74.8	37.5	50.1	49.9
74041	KIEFER	83.9	81.5	0.5	0.6	0.3	0.4	2.3	3.2	6.5	6.8	7.0	7.5	6.0	28.1	27.9	9.4	0.6	74.6	36.6	48.9	51.1
74042	LENAPAH	66.4	63.0	4.5	4.9	0.0	0.0	1.1	1.6	6.9	6.9	7.2	7.4	6.6	25.3	25.6	12.7	1.5	74.4	37.0	53.2	46.8
74044	MANNFORD	87.2	84.8	0.5	0.6	0.4	0.7	1.3	1.9	6.9	7.1	7.5	6.9	5.5	24.5	28.9	11.3	1.4	73.8	38.6	49.9	50.1
74045	MARAMEC	87.2	85.6	0.3	0.3	0.0	0.0	1.3	2.0	6.0	6.4	6.4	6.0	5.0	22.4	32.4	13.7	1.7	77.6	43.2	50.5	49.5
74047	MOUNDS	80.6	77.4	1.5	1.8	0.1	0.2	2.6	3.9	7.7	7.5	7.4	7.6	5.4	26.0	28.0	9.7	0.8	72.8	36.5	50.1	49.9
74048	NOWATA	70.8	67.3	3.3	3.6	0.1	0.2	1.1	1.4	6.5	6.5	6.7	6.7	5.3	22.2	27.3	15.7	3.2	76.3	41.8	48.7	51.3
74051	OCHELATA	72.7	69.0	0.1	0.2	0.0	0.0	0.8	1.1	8.0	7.8	7.4	7.2	6.6	27.1	24.7	10.2	1.0	72.4	34.3	50.6	49.4
74053	OOLOGAH	78.6	74.5	0.1	0.1	0.2	0.3	0.7	1.0	7.2	7.4	7.6	7.8	6.1	25.4	27.6	10.0	0.8	72.9	36.5	49.8	50.2
74054	OSAGE	80.8	77.4	0.2	0.4	0.2	0.4	1.1	1.5	6.0	6.6	6.6	5.3	4.7	23.3	32.4	13.7	1.5	77.8	42.8	50.3	49.7
74055	OWASSO	87.6	84.8	1.3	1.5	0.8	1.2	3.2	4.3	7.7	7.5	7.6	7.4	5.9	27.7	26.3	8.7	1.3	72.6	35.3	48.9	51.1
74056	PAWHUSKA	64.0	60.2	2.6	3.3	0.2	0.3	1.8	2.4	6.2	6.0	6.5	6.9	6.1	21.5	28.2	15.7	2.8	76.7	42.1	48.4	51.6
74058	PAWNEE	74.3	71.7	2.0	2.1	0.0	0.0	1.1	1.5	6.2	6.2	6.5	7.1	5.8	23.0	27.8	14.4	2.9	76.7	40.9	48.8	51.2
74059	PERKINS	87.4	85.0	2.0	2.2	0.2	0.3	1.1	1.6	7.0	6.8	6.8	6.9	6.4	27.3	26.7	10.6	1.5	75.1	35.9	50.2	49.8
74060	PRUE	84.1	81.0	1.1	1.4	0.3	0.5	1.4	2.0	5.7	6.1	6.6	6.3	4.4	23.2	33.2	13.5	1.0	77.7	43.3	50.9	49.1
74061	RAMONA	75.6	71.9	0.5	0.5	0.3	0.4	1.4	1.8	6.1	6.3	6.5	6.8	4.8	24.0	29.3	14.5	1.7	76.8	41.4	50.1	49.9
74062	RIPLEY	86.4	83.1	1.1	1.2	0.4	0.6	0.8	1.4	6.1	7.9	8.1	9.6	4.9	24.1	25.6	11.9	1.8	71.4	36.8	49.0	51.0
74063	SAND SPRINGS	85.1	82.1	1.7	2.2	0.4	0.5	1.9	2.8	6.7	6.6	6.7	7.3	6.3	25.8	28.1	11.2	1.3	75.3	37.9	49.3	50.7
74066	SAPULPA	81.7	78.9	2.7	2.8	0.3	0.5	2.2	3.2	6.6	6.6	6.8	6.8	5.7	25.1	28.2	12.2	1.9	75.8	39.2	48.8	51.2
74070	SKIATOOK	74.7	71.0	0.5	0.6	0.1	0.2	1.9	2.7	7.6	7.5	7.4	7.3	6.2	26.0	26.5	10.3	1.3	73.1	35.9	49.2	50.8
74072	S COFFEYVILLE	82.0	79.4	0.3	0.3	0.2	0.3	1.9	2.7	6.4	6.3	6.4	6.5	6.3	24.2	29.2	12.7	2.1	77.0	40.7	48.6	51.4
74073	SPERRY	74.4	70.2	2.9	3.4	0.4	0.6	2.6	3.7	7.4	7.4	7.5	7.2	5.8	26.2	26.3	10.9	1.3	73.1	36.4	49.7	50.3
74074	STILLWATER	87.8	85.1	2.8	2.9	2.0	3.0	2.1	3.0	5.3	4.8	4.5	7.8	21.3	25.4	20.5	8.4	2.1	82.4	28.6	50.6	49.4
74075	STILLWATER	83.1	79.7	3.7	3.9	5.1	6.9	2.4	3.3	5.8	4.5	4.2	6.6	21.1	29.1	19.1	8.0	1.6	82.7	28.5	50.7	49.3
74077	STILLWATER	84.4	80.2	3.5	4.3	2.8	4.3	2.1	3.2	0.5	0.5	0.0	64.2	31.0	3.7	0.0	0.0	0.0	98.4	18.8	63.6	36.4
74078	STILLWATER	68.2	62.1	8.1	8.0	13.2	17.9	3.0	4.1	1.6	0.9	0.5	46.5	33.3	15.5	1.3	0.3	0.1	96.5	20.1	51.1	48.9
74079	STROUD	85.0	82.9	2.6	2.8	0.4	0.6	1.5	2.2	6.3	7.0	7.2	7.4	4.7	22.7	27.2	14.5	3.0	74.7	40.5	48.5	51.5
74080	TALALA	76.5	72.5	0.1	0.1	0.4	0.5	0.8	1.0	7.1	7.0	7.1	7.4	6.5	26.2	26.9	11.0	0.8	74.4	36.9	50.0	50.0
74081	TERLTON	81.8	79.2	0.0	0.0	0.3	0.4	0.8	1.2	6.1	6.3	6.6	7.7	6.9	23.2	30.6	12.1	0.5	76.3	39.6	51.5	48.5
74083	WANN	78.6	75.8	0.6	0.6	0.1	0.2	2.3	2.9	5.9	6.1	6.6	7.0	5.7	21.7	31.5	14.0	1.5	77.1	42.7	50.5	49.5
74084	WYNONA	56.0	51.0	13.2	16.1	0.1	0.1	3.6	4.9	3.8	4.0	4.0	4.2	8.0	39.8	26.1	9.0	1.0	85.9	37.6	71.1	28.9
74085	YALE	89.0	86.4	0.0	0.0	0.3	0.5	0.8	1.2	6.4	6.6	6.3	7.1	5.9	22.9	28.4	13.8	2.7	76.5	40.3	49.2	50.8
74103	TULSA	55.0	48.8	30.8	35.3	0.6	0.8	4.6	6.4	1.4	1.9	1.2	4.0	10.2	48.8	27.3	4.7	0.4	94.8	38.5	74.8	25.2
74104	TULSA	75.2	70.8	6.7	7.6	1.8	2.6	13.7	17.5	6.2	5.3	4.7	8.8	15.2	30.5	21.1	6.7	1.6	81.3	30.7	50.9	49.1
74105	TULSA	80.5	75.9	8.1	9.7	1.1	1.5	5.0	7.4	6.2	5.6	5.5	5.6	7.2	27.5	26.8	12.6	2.9	79.5	38.9	47.9	52.1
74106	TULSA	11.7	9.7	78.6	79.5	0.2	0.2	5.1	6.4	8.2	8.1	7.6	8.0	7.2	21.9	23.3	12.8	2.9	71.1	34.7	45.4	54.6
74107	TULSA	73.2	68.2	10.0	11.6	0.8	1.1	4.4	6.3	9.1	7.8	7.0	6.8	7.2	25.6	23.5	11.3	1.7	72.0	33.9	47.4	52.6
74108	TULSA	73.7	68.6	6.1	6.9	2.4	3.3	6.1	8.4	8.5	8.3	7.9	7.9	6.2	27.2	24.5	8.7	0.9	70.3	33.2	48.5	51.5
74110	TULSA	46.8	41.4	29.7	30.8	0.3	0.4	15.5	21.0	9.4	8.4	7.4	8.6	8.1	26.7	21.4	8.3	1.6	69.6	30.4	49.8	50.2
74112	TULSA	77.8	73.1	5.8	6.8	1.4	1.9	9.3	13.2	6.9	6.3	6.0	5.8	6.4	28.5	25.2	12.4	2.4	77.3	38.1	49.1	50.9
74114	TULSA	89.7	87.1	2.4	3.0	0.9	1.3	2.2	3.4	6.0	6.2	6.5	5.4	4.7	23.9	30.2	13.9	3.2	78.0	43.3	47.1	52.9
74115	TULSA	65.1	59.4	15.5	17.4	0.4	0.6	8.6	12.3	9.1	8.5	7.9	7.5	7.0	26.8	22.8	9.2	1.3	70.0	32.3	48.5	51.5
74116	TULSA	68.2	62.3	11.1	12.6	2.2	3.0	10.3	14.3	10.1	6.7	6.0	7.6	10.0	25.8	24.2	8.6	0.9	73.1	31.3	51.0	49.0
74117	TULSA	77.8	74.8	7.4	7.9	0.0	0.8	1.9	3.1	5.5	5.5	6.3	6.3	4.7	22.8	32.3	15.0	1.6	78.7	44.1	51.2	48.8
74119	TULSA	80.4	76.2	9.4	11.4	1.2	1.8	2.7	4.1	3.0	2.4	2.2	3.1	6.7	31.8	30.4	16.0	4.4	90.8	45.5	51.2	48.8
74120	TULSA	71.9	66.9	9.1	10.1	0.9	1.3	9.4	13.0	5.9	5.2	4.7	4.9	9.1	35.2	25.6	7.6	1.8	81.4	35.3	51.9	48.1
74126	TULSA	20.5	18.4	71.4	72.8	0.2	0.2	1.5	2.0	9.3	9.6	9.1	10.0	7.4	23.7	21.7	8.4	0.9	65.8	28.1	45.9	54.1
74127	TULSA	59.0	54.0	24.7	27.1	0.3	0.4	5.3	7.3	6.7	6.6	6.7	7.2	6.2	25.9	27.5	11.6	1.6	75.5	37.8	49.6	50.4
74128	TULSA	73.4	68.1	9.2	10.6	2.0	2.6	11.2	15.4	7.6	7.1	6.8	6.5	6.1	26.2	23.5	14.2	2.0	74.6	37.0	48.1	51.9
74129	TULSA	72.2	66.4	9.6	11.0	3.2	4.3	9.5	13.4	7.7	6.9	6.2	6.1	5.8	27.3	24.1	13.4	2.6	75.5	37.5	47.5	52.5
74130	TULSA	42.5	37.4	42.2	45.6	0.3	0.4	3.0	4.1	7.7	7.2	7.1	8.1	7.8	24.6	26.2	10.1	1.2	73.2	33.8	48.5	51.5
74131	TULSA	83.3	80.9	0.9	1.1	0.3	0.4	3.4	4.5	6.8	7.0	7.2	7.6	6.7	24.7	29.5	9.7	0.8	74.4	36.7	50.7	49.3
	OKLAHOMA	76.2	73.0	7.6	7.8	1.4	2.0	5.2	7.0	6.9	6.6	6.5	7.1	7.2	26.2	25.9	11.6	2.0	75.9	36.8	49.3	50.7
	UNITED STATES	75.1	72.0	12.3	12.7	3.8	4.6	12.5	15.7	6.8	6.7	6.6	7.1	6.9	27.0	26.0	10.9	1.9	75.7	36.9	49.2	50.8

ZIP CODE #	POST OFFICE NAME	2009 Per Capita Income	2009 HH Income Base	2009 HOUSEHOLD INCOME DISTRIBUTION (%) Less than $25,000	$25,000 to $49,999	$50,000 to $99,999	$100,000 to $149,999	$150,000 or More	MEDIAN HOUSEHOLD INCOME 2009	2014	2009 National Centile	2009 State Centile	2009 Home Value Base	2009 HOME VALUE DISTRIBUTION (%) Less than $50,000	$50,000 to $89,999	$90,000 to $174,999	$175,000 to $399,999	$400,000 or More	2009 Median Home Value
73859	VICI	17776	495	37.0	29.5	28.9	3.6	1.0	33214	34519	14	28	378	47.4	24.9	23.3	3.7	0.8	54000
73860	WAYNOKA	18353	592	40.5	34.6	20.1	3.4	1.4	30196	30946	8	14	462	60.2	21.6	14.7	3.2	0.2	40208
73931	BALKO	21764	255	23.5	31.8	36.9	6.3	1.6	45160	46149	49	82	203	16.3	27.6	38.9	16.7	0.5	96579
73932	BEAVER	21922	774	26.6	28.4	36.8	6.1	2.1	45220	45442	49	82	615	27.2	31.1	34.6	7.2	0.0	79868
73933	BOISE CITY	18884	738	34.6	31.2	27.4	4.1	2.8	37123	37566	24	52	542	46.5	27.3	21.6	3.5	1.1	54634
73937	FELT	17197	73	27.4	35.6	30.1	4.1	2.7	39525	40000	31	64	51	37.3	19.6	29.4	7.8	5.9	76250
73938	FORGAN	17231	261	32.2	33.3	26.1	5.4	3.1	37185	41174	24	52	204	47.5	24.0	22.5	2.5	3.4	54167
73939	GOODWELL	18721	683	28.8	30.5	29.6	10.0	1.2	42044	43724	39	73	354	24.9	24.0	32.5	16.4	2.3	93077
73942	GUYMON	19112	4544	24.1	28.5	37.3	7.5	2.6	47371	49372	55	86	2976	17.9	27.3	38.1	13.9	2.8	96636
73944	HARDESTY	17132	195	27.2	35.4	32.8	4.1	0.5	41183	42171	37	71	139	35.3	23.0	28.8	11.5	1.4	73125
73945	HOOKER	19642	1039	24.1	34.1	33.2	6.3	2.4	43950	44907	45	78	804	26.6	29.2	35.0	8.3	0.9	82985
73946	KENTON	19785	51	25.5	33.3	37.3	2.0	2.0	42353	39422	40	74	35	37.1	22.9	31.4	2.9	5.7	75000
73947	KEYES	18432	253	32.8	33.6	27.7	3.2	2.8	36152	36911	21	46	180	47.8	21.1	21.7	9.4	0.0	53333
73949	TEXHOMA	17631	596	31.2	34.1	28.5	3.9	2.3	38133	40528	27	58	414	30.0	33.6	28.5	7.2	0.7	68718
73950	TURPIN	20920	627	16.4	33.5	40.7	6.1	3.3	50059	50712	61	89	486	36.8	19.1	32.5	8.2	3.3	77273
73951	TYRONE	18202	444	23.2	31.3	39.0	5.2	1.4	46730	47963	53	85	343	36.4	29.7	27.1	5.8	0.9	65000
74002	BARNSDALL	18737	1234	27.1	30.5	34.0	7.1	1.4	41585	44189	38	72	1011	55.3	20.1	19.0	4.2	1.5	45466
74003	BARTLESVILLE	18867	6201	36.8	29.6	26.7	4.7	2.2	33898	36033	15	31	3876	44.7	26.9	19.7	7.4	1.3	55687
74006	BARTLESVILLE	33027	10694	18.9	26.0	34.4	11.7	9.2	55247	55427	72	93	8247	8.2	24.0	45.1	19.2	3.5	111631
74008	BIXBY	30366	7560	14.0	21.3	42.1	13.3	9.4	64460	65493	83	97	5977	13.8	12.9	40.6	23.8	8.9	131391
74010	BRISTOW	19252	4029	32.1	30.9	30.3	4.6	2.0	38430	41680	28	59	3007	33.8	27.4	29.1	9.0	0.7	73553
74011	BROKEN ARROW	28384	9212	10.0	20.3	48.0	15.0	6.7	68815	69855	86	97	7405	0.8	11.2	64.5	20.8	2.6	131250
74012	BROKEN ARROW	28993	19592	10.3	21.3	44.3	15.0	9.0	70090	70922	87	98	15007	1.7	17.7	54.8	25.0	0.9	130184
74014	BROKEN ARROW	28548	10839	8.6	19.6	48.4	16.3	7.0	71314	74335	88	98	9523	8.4	8.3	48.5	30.5	4.3	148185
74015	CATOOSA	21667	2985	19.1	27.1	44.3	7.3	2.1	53364	55424	69	92	2400	28.6	16.4	31.6	21.3	2.0	99225
74016	CHELSEA	17636	2130	30.4	31.9	32.4	3.8	1.4	39092	41055	30	62	1604	29.0	24.9	29.9	14.3	1.9	82250
74017	CLAREMORE	21792	10977	24.4	26.4	38.8	7.3	3.2	48975	51769	59	87	7857	16.0	21.8	42.2	18.1	1.9	108589
74019	CLAREMORE	25446	6242	13.2	19.8	50.0	12.9	4.1	66587	67978	85	97	5376	10.6	9.8	53.0	23.6	3.0	136167
74020	CLEVELAND	20184	3625	26.1	33.6	31.4	6.3	2.5	41415	43756	37	71	2866	31.8	26.4	31.1	9.6	1.1	76731
74021	COLLINSVILLE	23885	5790	18.6	26.8	40.4	9.9	4.3	53936	56164	70	92	4792	19.1	22.9	41.5	15.7	0.8	102590
74022	COPAN	21549	776	29.6	30.8	32.2	5.0	2.3	38512	41608	28	60	675	22.4	29.6	35.1	9.9	3.0	87065
74023	CUSHING	16951	3964	36.5	31.8	25.5	5.0	1.2	34909	35848	17	35	2747	27.7	28.9	34.4	6.8	2.3	81322
74026	DAVENPORT	16124	326	36.5	35.6	23.9	3.4	0.6	32644	34701	13	25	238	44.1	28.6	19.3	7.1	0.8	55833
74027	DELAWARE	17092	535	30.8	34.6	30.1	3.7	0.7	37526	38665	25	55	440	42.0	20.2	21.4	12.5	3.9	68077
74028	DEPEW	16196	726	29.8	39.7	25.8	3.7	1.1	36147	38189	21	45	597	47.6	22.6	22.4	7.0	0.3	53718
74029	DEWEY	21267	2099	30.9	30.5	29.3	7.4	1.9	39554	42578	31	65	1596	29.8	32.0	27.6	10.2	0.3	72080
74030	DRUMRIGHT	18240	2556	34.7	31.3	27.7	4.9	1.4	35521	38526	19	40	1897	44.1	29.9	18.3	6.4	1.2	57550
74032	GLENCOE	19755	648	21.3	38.6	30.9	7.4	1.9	42174	43330	40	74	510	29.6	28.0	29.8	10.6	2.0	80488
74033	GLENPOOL	22003	3299	12.8	30.1	46.8	7.6	2.6	56239	58566	73	93	2636	7.1	41.8	46.5	3.8	0.7	90685
74035	HOMINY	18318	1317	38.8	33.9	21.0	3.6	2.7	31825	33030	11	21	929	50.5	31.4	13.5	3.9	0.8	49531
74036	INOLA	21936	2374	16.9	31.7	37.7	9.7	4.0	51219	53155	64	90	1979	11.6	24.3	41.8	19.5	2.9	109481
74037	JENKS	31157	5080	8.2	20.1	44.2	19.0	8.6	74130	76266	89	98	4246	6.0	10.0	50.8	30.2	2.9	140018
74038	JENNINGS	18319	477	22.4	36.9	34.4	5.0	1.3	42986	44787	42	76	401	46.6	28.9	19.7	3.0	1.7	54091
74039	KELLYVILLE	17999	1207	23.8	31.9	38.1	5.2	1.0	45647	47826	50	83	1015	30.5	29.0	31.4	8.2	0.9	80631
74041	KIEFER	21472	599	22.4	27.0	43.9	4.5	2.2	50398	51182	62	89	488	27.5	25.0	32.6	12.7	2.3	87778
74042	LENAPAH	18038	301	28.9	27.9	35.5	4.3	3.3	43764	45489	45	77	251	32.7	24.3	25.9	10.8	6.4	79737
74044	MANNFORD	19565	2724	26.7	30.0	35.1	6.9	1.3	42764	45516	42	75	2234	27.0	28.2	35.6	8.8	0.4	83743
74045	MARAMEC	21625	120	21.7	35.8	35.8	5.0	1.7	43450	45494	44	76	105	41.0	21.0	21.0	16.2	1.0	60833
74047	MOUNDS	21427	2105	21.0	25.9	41.8	7.5	3.8	52534	53697	67	92	1731	23.6	27.0	31.8	14.2	3.4	89266
74048	NOWATA	17605	2468	36.7	32.5	25.2	3.6	2.1	33733	34807	15	30	1796	32.6	27.4	26.7	11.3	2.0	72544
74051	OCHELATA	18677	576	22.6	28.5	41.5	6.1	1.4	49130	50230	59	88	486	40.1	22.0	27.0	10.7	0.2	62222
74053	OOLOGAH	21329	1847	20.3	24.7	45.4	8.0	1.6	53969	55895	70	93	1520	16.5	18.6	41.6	18.3	5.0	107829
74054	OSAGE	17123	235	38.3	33.2	21.3	5.1	2.1	30721	31916	9	15	198	43.9	25.3	17.7	10.1	3.0	64286
74055	OWASSO	28838	12576	10.8	21.7	42.0	17.8	7.8	69242	71357	86	98	10136	4.8	11.2	49.3	31.7	3.0	144595
74056	PAWHUSKA	18032	2413	36.4	30.8	27.4	2.9	2.4	34038	35757	16	31	1766	56.3	21.5	15.6	4.9	1.8	44638
74058	PAWNEE	17227	1645	33.4	34.6	26.9	3.6	1.5	34837	36531	17	35	1230	44.5	25.4	21.5	8.1	0.5	57234
74059	PERKINS	20337	1908	26.6	32.1	33.4	5.4	2.6	41053	42529	36	70	1443	21.3	32.6	34.0	10.8	1.2	86925
74060	PRUE	22778	623	19.9	25.5	40.1	10.6	3.9	53585	55230	69	92	557	22.1	21.0	33.6	19.9	3.4	103664
74061	RAMONA	19975	798	25.6	29.6	39.1	3.8	2.0	44805	47070	48	80	669	24.2	24.5	31.4	18.7	1.2	92576
74062	RIPLEY	15550	367	30.5	33.8	31.6	3.3	0.8	36226	37587	21	46	283	32.2	32.2	24.7	9.9	1.1	76607
74063	SAND SPRINGS	23178	11084	18.6	28.5	41.6	8.3	3.0	52209	54026	66	91	8695	19.4	31.7	36.9	10.8	1.1	88897
74066	SAPULPA	21261	11565	25.6	30.8	33.2	6.8	3.6	44297	46790	46	78	8753	19.7	30.3	35.8	13.8	0.5	90008
74070	SKIATOOK	21568	4586	18.1	29.2	41.1	8.9	2.8	52041	53547	66	91	3747	18.0	27.4	33.4	19.7	1.6	95178
74072	S COFFEYVILLE	19405	584	28.4	33.0	31.7	5.0	1.9	41489	42461	38	72	475	28.4	36.2	26.7	7.2	1.5	70116
74073	SPERRY	18210	1611	25.3	32.0	34.9	5.4	2.4	42154	44034	40	74	1290	27.9	27.0	33.3	10.5	1.4	84706
74074	STILLWATER	23031	11672	35.8	24.5	26.2	8.2	5.3	37962	40429	27	58	6289	17.0	16.8	31.3	30.3	4.5	131382
74075	STILLWATER	22621	9612	36.3	25.9	27.2	6.8	3.8	37725	40152	26	56	4404	11.8	10.1	49.9	26.5	1.7	134452
74077	STILLWATER	11520	0	0.0	0.0	0.0	0.0	0.0	0	0	0	0	0	0.0	0.0	0.0	0.0	0.0	0
74078	STILLWATER	12393	303	61.7	33.3	1.3	3.3	0.3	18249	18896	1	1	27	0.0	0.0	100.0	0.0	0.0	140341
74079	STROUD	17381	2035	36.0	33.6	24.5	3.7	2.2	32978	34782	13	26	1486	30.7	34.8	21.9	11.2	1.4	72484
74080	TALALA	20378	592	21.5	26.7	43.2	5.4	3.2	51418	53300	65	90	518	21.2	21.8	40.9	12.2	3.9	98182
74081	TERLTON	17365	373	22.5	38.1	33.5	4.0	1.9	42094	43428	40	73	340	39.4	30.9	23.2	5.9	0.6	62593
74083	WANN	18265	342	27.8	33.6	33.3	3.2	2.0	41083	42548	36	71	306	26.1	25.2	30.4	13.7	4.6	87778
74084	WYNONA	14245	402	34.1	33.1	26.1	3.7	3.0	35150	37343	18	37	312	54.8	26.9	12.8	3.2	2.2	45313
74085	YALE	17078	1030	33.0	33.4	29.6	3.5	0.5	35000	35786	18	36	762	40.6	32.8	19.2	5.6	1.8	60000
74103	TULSA	10759	60	61.7	30.0	8.3	0.0	0.0	15826	16060	1	1	10	10.0	50.0	40.0	0.0	0.0	85000
74104	TULSA	23198	6034	31.3	30.2	29.4	5.7	3.5	39288	41518	31	64	2909	11.3	30.9	44.4	13.1	0.2	104117
74105	TULSA	33341	14575	23.7	31.3	29.6	7.6	7.8	45344	46726	49	82	7592	3.3	19.7	42.2	26.0	8.9	127090
74106	TULSA	14234	7047	49.5	29.4	17.8	1.9	1.4	25266	25920	3	3	3767	45.8	36.2	15.4	2.2	0.5	53109
74107	TULSA	18961	8370	32.6	31.2	29.5	5.2	1.5	36535	38944	22	49	4810	24.3	47.5	24.1	3.6	0.6	70554
74108	TULSA	19102	2854	23.2	33.3	36.9	5.0	1.5	45509	46835	50	83	1855	13.3	55.6	27.5	3.4	0.1	80370
74110	TULSA	13190	5772	44.4	34.8	18.5	1.4	0.9	28038	28624	6	7	2895	61.3	31.5	6.3	0.9	0.0	45500
74112	TULSA	22853	10296	23.8	35.6	34.2	4.9	1.5	42632	44339	41	75	6130	6.4	52.5	38.8	2.0	0.3	84596
74114	TULSA	41291	7651	15.3	24.8	36.2	10.2	13.4	59170	60921	76	95	5911	2.6	23.4	39.1	20.1	14.7	118287
74115	TULSA	17297	9138	30.1	35.0	30.2	3.5	1.2	37317	39923	25	53	5876	42.0	52.6	4.7	0.7	0.1	53965
74116	TULSA	17624	1660	33.6	34.0	27.7	4.1	0.7	35886	37314	20	44	722	20.5	26.5	33.7	16.2	3.2	94783
74117	TULSA	21520	48	29.2	31.3	31.3	6.3	2.1	41118	45000	36	71	40	22.5	15.0	47.5	12.5	2.5	100000
74119	TULSA	39399	2605	34.8	27.8	26.4	4.7	6.3	35725	39040	20	42	696	5.9	19.4	42.2	25.6	6.9	127692
74120	TULSA	26157	2924	37.4	31.4	21.7	5.1	4.4	32514	33561	12	24	860	19.2	13.8	34.5	22.7	9.8	131034
74126	TULSA	13239	4146	41.8	32.3	21.9	2.1	1.9	30047	30849	8	13	2468	59.7	29.2	9.2	1.7	0.2	45000
74127	TULSA	19297	7071	30.0	31.9	31.4	4.4	2.4	39761	42056	32	66	4563	30.2	35.7	26.7	6.8	0.7	70750
74128	TULSA	21027	4742	18.8	38.7	36.6	4.4	1.5	44693	46097	47	79	3241	7.0	64.5	27.8	0.5	0.1	81421
74129	TULSA	23202	7383	23.1	30.8	36.5	7.6	2.0	46236	49036	52	84	4163	1.2	36.5	58.9	3.4	0.0	98226
74130	TULSA	17541	851	33.1	32.5	28.6	4.3	1.4	37644	40378	26	55	629	45.6	43.9	9.5	1.0	0.0	52806
74131	TULSA	24079	1264	21.2	33.1	27.6	13.2	4.8	46979	48472	54	86	1079	37.8	14.7	21.2	23.2	3.1	82361
	OKLAHOMA	22515		27.2	29.2	32.3	7.2	4.0	43746	45901				20.4	25.6	36.1	15.4	2.4	96076
	UNITED STATES	27277		20.9	24.4	35.3	11.7	7.6	54719	56938				9.3	13.1	31.6	32.6	13.5	162279

ZIP CODE #	POST OFFICE NAME	FINANCIAL SERVICES: Auto Loan	Home Loan	Invest-ments	Retire-ment Plans	THE HOME: Home Improvements: Home Repair	Lawn & Garden	Furnishings: Comput-ers & Hard-ware-Personal	Major Appli-ances	TV, Radio, Sound Equip-ment	Furni-ture	ENTERTAINMENT: Dine out/ Carry out	Sports Equip-ment	Fees & Tickets	Toys & Games	Travel	Cable TV	PERSONAL: Apparel & Services	Auto Repairs	Health Insur-ance	Pets & Supplies
73859	VICI	70	49	72	48	51	73	54	67	59	47	58	52	42	58	53	65	38	63	73	80
73860	WAYNOKA	68	48	72	47	50	71	53	65	56	45	55	52	40	55	52	62	36	61	70	79
73931	BALKO	93	64	102	64	67	98	71	88	74	58	73	73	52	73	71	81	48	83	93	109
73932	BEAVER	95	66	102	66	69	100	73	91	78	61	76	73	55	76	72	85	50	85	97	110
73933	BOISE CITY	79	56	84	55	58	83	61	76	66	52	64	60	47	64	60	72	42	71	81	91
73937	FELT	82	57	90	56	59	87	63	78	65	51	65	64	46	64	62	71	42	73	82	96
73938	FORGAN	84	58	92	58	60	88	64	80	67	52	66	66	47	65	64	73	43	74	84	98
73939	GOODWELL	82	54	68	57	55	70	82	71	78	66	77	62	60	77	66	79	53	77	75	89
73942	GUYMON	87	77	77	76	76	84	79	82	80	77	80	64	72	81	76	82	54	81	84	98
73944	HARDESTY	82	56	90	56	59	86	63	78	65	51	64	64	46	64	62	71	42	73	82	96
73945	HOOKER	90	68	90	67	69	90	73	84	75	65	74	68	58	75	71	79	49	80	87	103
73946	KENTON	82	56	90	56	59	86	63	78	65	51	64	64	46	64	62	71	42	73	82	96
73947	KEYES	84	58	93	58	61	89	64	80	67	52	66	66	47	66	64	73	43	75	85	98
73949	TEXHOMA	85	60	90	59	63	88	64	80	69	56	68	63	49	68	63	75	44	74	84	97
73950	TURPIN	98	77	96	75	77	97	81	91	83	73	82	73	66	83	78	87	55	88	94	111
73951	TYRONE	83	72	72	69	70	78	73	77	74	73	74	60	66	76	70	75	50	76	76	92
74002	BARNSDALL	85	61	78	60	62	85	65	78	73	61	71	59	52	73	61	80	47	74	84	94
74003	BARTLESVILLE	68	58	58	59	57	67	64	65	67	60	65	50	58	67	59	70	45	66	70	78
74006	BARTLESVILLE	109	109	115	110	112	120	105	113	108	105	107	83	106	107	109	112	74	110	120	131
74008	BIXBY	121	125	111	123	121	121	116	119	115	119	116	89	117	119	116	116	81	115	117	139
74010	BRISTOW	79	63	67	62	63	76	67	73	71	64	70	55	58	73	62	76	47	71	77	87
74011	BROKEN ARROW	113	128	111	126	123	114	112	114	108	119	110	87	119	113	116	106	77	110	106	132
74012	BROKEN ARROW	120	126	105	125	119	112	117	115	113	122	115	91	119	119	115	110	80	112	108	134
74014	BROKEN ARROW	116	127	110	127	122	117	115	116	111	119	112	91	120	116	118	109	79	112	110	135
74015	CATOOSA	92	87	78	85	85	89	82	86	84	84	84	63	79	87	79	87	58	84	87	102
74016	CHELSEA	76	63	65	61	62	74	64	71	69	63	67	53	57	70	60	73	46	68	74	84
74017	CLAREMORE	87	80	76	80	78	87	80	84	83	78	82	64	75	84	77	86	56	82	87	100
74019	CLAREMORE	106	110	96	110	107	108	101	105	101	103	102	80	103	104	102	102	70	102	104	124
74020	CLEVELAND	86	69	78	67	69	85	70	80	76	68	74	60	61	77	67	81	50	77	84	96
74021	COLLINSVILLE	98	94	87	93	91	100	90	96	92	88	91	74	86	95	89	95	63	92	98	113
74022	COPAN	85	68	83	68	70	88	69	82	73	63	72	62	59	74	68	79	48	76	85	97
74023	CUSHING	71	54	67	54	55	72	59	68	64	54	62	52	49	63	56	69	42	65	73	81
74026	DAVENPORT	71	51	73	49	53	72	52	66	58	49	57	50	42	57	52	64	38	61	69	79
74027	DELAWARE	78	56	80	54	58	79	58	73	64	53	63	55	46	64	57	70	41	67	76	87
74028	DEPEW	77	53	76	51	54	77	56	70	63	52	61	54	43	63	53	69	41	65	73	85
74029	DEWEY	84	65	82	64	67	88	68	83	75	61	72	62	57	74	67	82	49	77	89	97
74030	DRUMRIGHT	78	56	75	54	57	79	60	73	66	55	65	55	48	66	57	73	43	68	78	87
74032	GLENCOE	81	75	64	72	72	73	73	74	74	76	74	56	69	77	69	75	51	74	73	88
74033	GLENPOOL	96	98	80	95	92	85	92	90	89	98	90	70	91	94	88	85	62	88	82	105
74035	HOMINY	72	53	67	52	53	73	58	68	64	53	62	51	47	64	54	70	42	65	73	81
74036	INOLA	93	93	81	92	90	93	85	90	87	88	87	67	85	90	85	88	60	87	90	106
74037	JENKS	123	136	114	133	129	121	122	122	117	128	119	96	127	124	123	114	83	118	115	141
74038	JENNINGS	88	63	72	61	63	83	65	76	73	64	71	58	52	76	59	79	48	72	80	93
74039	KELLYVILLE	85	68	70	66	68	80	68	76	73	68	72	57	59	76	63	77	49	72	78	91
74041	KIEFER	90	83	73	80	81	85	78	83	81	81	81	60	74	84	74	83	55	80	83	98
74042	LENAPAH	92	66	76	64	66	88	69	80	76	67	75	62	55	80	63	83	50	76	85	98
74044	MANNFORD	90	68	77	66	68	86	69	80	76	68	74	61	58	78	65	81	50	76	83	97
74045	MARAMEC	96	69	98	67	71	97	71	90	79	66	77	67	57	78	70	86	51	82	93	107
74047	MOUNDS	94	88	77	85	85	88	84	87	86	88	86	65	80	90	80	88	59	86	87	104
74048	NOWATA	74	53	74	51	54	75	58	70	63	52	62	53	46	62	55	70	41	66	75	83
74051	OCHELATA	83	77	68	74	75	78	72	77	75	75	75	56	68	78	69	77	51	74	77	91
74053	OOLOGAH	95	87	77	84	85	89	82	87	85	86	85	63	78	89	78	88	58	84	87	104
74054	OSAGE	71	51	73	50	53	73	52	67	58	49	57	50	42	58	52	64	38	61	70	79
74055	OWASSO	117	128	109	126	121	114	117	116	112	122	114	92	121	118	117	109	80	113	108	134
74056	PAWHUSKA	74	54	71	53	55	76	59	70	65	54	63	53	48	65	56	72	42	67	76	84
74058	PAWNEE	76	54	78	53	56	79	58	73	64	51	62	56	46	63	57	70	41	67	78	86
74059	PERKINS	78	74	65	73	70	79	73	75	75	72	75	58	70	77	71	77	51	74	79	90
74060	PRUE	101	87	107	85	89	103	84	99	88	82	87	73	76	88	86	92	59	93	99	116
74061	RAMONA	85	68	79	67	69	86	68	80	73	65	72	60	59	74	66	79	48	75	83	95
74062	RIPLEY	78	56	80	54	58	79	57	73	63	53	62	54	46	63	56	70	41	67	76	86
74063	SAND SPRINGS	93	85	79	84	83	90	85	88	87	84	87	66	80	89	81	90	59	86	91	104
74066	SAPULPA	88	76	77	76	75	88	77	84	81	75	80	63	71	83	74	86	55	81	88	99
74070	SKIATOOK	88	86	73	86	82	90	83	85	85	81	84	65	82	87	81	87	58	84	89	102
74072	S COFFEYVILLE	90	64	79	63	65	87	67	80	74	64	73	61	54	76	62	81	49	75	84	96
74073	SPERRY	84	71	70	70	70	82	71	78	75	70	74	59	64	78	67	79	51	75	81	93
74074	STILLWATER	83	70	66	72	69	72	86	75	83	79	83	60	75	83	74	82	58	80	77	91
74075	STILLWATER	75	57	53	60	55	58	83	64	76	72	77	55	67	77	65	74	54	72	65	79
74077	STILLWATER	0	0	0	0	0	0	0	0	0	0	0	0	0	0	0	0	0	0	0	0
74078	STILLWATER	40	17	17	21	16	20	56	28	45	38	46	30	33	44	30	41	32	39	28	38
74079	STROUD	75	54	76	52	56	78	57	72	64	52	62	54	46	63	56	71	41	67	77	85
74080	TALALA	93	83	76	80	81	87	79	85	83	82	82	62	74	86	75	85	56	82	86	101
74081	TERLTON	90	64	75	63	64	85	67	78	74	65	73	60	54	77	61	81	49	74	82	95
74083	WANN	82	62	82	61	64	84	63	78	68	58	67	58	52	68	62	75	45	71	81	92
74084	WYNONA	86	57	83	54	57	85	61	76	70	57	68	59	46	71	57	78	45	72	81	93
74085	YALE	72	53	68	52	54	72	58	68	63	53	61	51	47	63	55	69	41	64	73	80
74103	TULSA	31	25	26	27	25	28	35	29	37	32	37	23	32	34	31	39	26	35	37	37
74104	TULSA	73	61	56	63	59	60	79	65	76	72	77	54	70	77	68	75	54	73	68	80
74105	TULSA	94	86	86	89	86	87	97	90	97	96	97	71	94	96	93	96	68	96	94	108
74106	TULSA	51	42	40	43	40	49	48	47	53	48	52	34	45	52	44	57	36	50	55	58
74107	TULSA	69	57	54	59	55	64	65	63	68	61	67	50	59	69	59	71	46	66	69	77
74108	TULSA	77	72	61	71	68	72	73	72	75	72	75	55	70	77	68	76	52	73	74	86
74110	TULSA	52	42	38	43	40	48	51	47	54	47	53	37	45	54	44	57	37	51	54	59
74112	TULSA	70	66	58	67	63	69	72	67	73	68	73	53	69	73	68	75	50	71	75	81
74114	TULSA	119	132	129	134	133	132	126	126	125	126	124	96	134	124	131	125	88	125	130	147
74115	TULSA	68	57	51	57	54	64	65	63	67	60	66	49	57	68	57	70	45	65	68	76
74116	TULSA	63	52	47	55	49	51	64	55	64	63	66	46	60	66	58	63	46	63	57	68
74117	TULSA	90	77	84	78	78	96	78	90	82	70	80	68	69	83	77	88	54	84	94	105
74119	TULSA	72	73	74	74	74	76	77	74	79	76	79	55	79	76	78	81	55	78	84	88
74120	TULSA	71	57	53	61	54	57	74	62	75	71	76	51	68	75	65	74	53	71	66	77
74126	TULSA	59	48	43	49	44	54	54	52	58	53	58	40	50	59	48	61	39	55	58	65
74127	TULSA	71	63	61	64	61	72	67	68	70	63	69	52	62	70	63	74	47	69	75	82
74128	TULSA	72	69	60	71	66	74	73	70	74	69	74	55	71	75	70	76	51	73	78	85
74129	TULSA	76	77	71	77	75	78	78	76	79	77	79	58	78	79	77	80	55	78	81	90
74130	TULSA	72	62	55	61	60	67	67	66	69	65	68	51	60	71	61	71	47	68	70	80
74131	TULSA	97	98	89	96	95	95	91	94	90	94	91	73	91	94	90	91	63	91	90	110
	OKLAHOMA	87	75	78	75	74	84	79	82	82	77	81	63	73	83	75	85	56	82	86	98
	UNITED STATES	100	100	100	100	100	100	100	100	100	100	100	100	100	100	100	100	100	100	100	100

ZIP CODE #	POST OFFICE NAME	COUNTY FIPS CODE	POPULATION 2000	POPULATION 2009	POPULATION 2014	2000-2009 ANNUAL RATE % Rate	2000-2009 ANNUAL RATE State Centile	HOUSEHOLDS 2000	HOUSEHOLDS 2009	HOUSEHOLDS 2014	HOUSEHOLDS % Annual Rate 2000-2009	HOUSEHOLDS 2009 Average HH Size	FAMILIES 2000	FAMILIES 2009	FAMILIES % Annual Rate 2000-2009
74132	TULSA	143	6991	7850	8222	1.3	89	2511	2868	3021	1.4	2.73	1986	2208	1.2
74133	TULSA	143	37569	41543	43639	1.1	84	15723	17337	18183	1.1	2.38	9989	10643	0.7
74134	TULSA	143	13014	14518	15349	1.2	86	5237	6070	6490	1.6	2.39	3338	3608	0.8
74135	TULSA	143	20920	20568	20587	-0.2	33	10082	10077	10122	0.0	1.99	5445	5137	-0.6
74136	TULSA	143	30066	30877	31499	0.3	60	14123	14643	14975	0.4	2.02	7278	7138	-0.2
74137	TULSA	143	23301	26416	27919	1.4	90	8655	9935	10534	1.5	2.62	6543	7326	1.2
74145	TULSA	143	17827	17360	17385	-0.3	27	8144	8061	8104	-0.1	2.14	4819	4523	-0.7
74146	TULSA	143	14357	14306	14390	0.0	43	5873	5855	5890	0.0	2.44	3488	3325	-0.5
74171	TULSA	143	2202	2119	2131	-0.4	22	3	3	3	0.0	2.67	2	2	0.0
74301	VINITA	035	10639	10640	10670	0.0	43	3974	3977	3987	0.0	2.40	2682	2609	-0.3
74330	ADAIR	097	5478	5655	5719	0.3	60	2049	2151	2184	0.5	2.63	1644	1699	0.4
74331	AFTON	041	6200	6994	7334	1.3	89	2713	3077	3235	1.4	2.27	1933	2140	1.1
74332	BIG CABIN	035	1571	1736	1809	1.1	84	607	677	707	1.2	2.56	474	517	0.9
74333	BLUEJACKET	035	1225	1346	1393	1.0	82	438	487	505	1.2	2.72	345	375	0.9
74337	CHOUTEAU	097	4513	4626	4676	0.3	60	1661	1712	1732	0.3	2.69	1271	1287	0.1
74338	COLCORD	041	4867	5338	5626	1.0	82	1786	2004	2127	1.3	2.61	1357	1492	1.0
74339	COMMERCE	115	2758	2669	2591	-0.4	22	1005	952	919	-0.6	2.69	719	664	-0.9
74342	EUCHA	041	3686	4039	4275	1.0	82	1430	1601	1704	1.2	2.52	1032	1129	1.0
74343	FAIRLAND	115	2950	2891	2831	-0.2	33	1180	1158	1132	-0.2	2.47	882	847	-0.4
74344	GROVE	041	13168	15080	16054	1.5	91	5625	6509	6955	1.6	2.28	3929	4437	1.3
74346	JAY	041	5865	6226	6475	0.6	73	2210	2370	2470	0.8	2.58	1613	1692	0.5
74347	KANSAS	041	2807	3132	3312	1.2	86	979	1108	1179	1.3	2.79	788	879	1.2
74352	LOCUST GROVE	097	6682	6787	6811	0.2	55	2513	2582	2600	0.3	2.61	1852	1863	0.1
74354	MIAMI	115	17765	17729	17396	0.0	43	7145	7036	6879	-0.2	2.39	4808	4621	-0.4
74358	NORTH MIAMI	115	326	317	309	-0.3	27	121	117	113	-0.4	2.71	92	87	-0.6
74359	OAKS	041	300	324	342	0.8	78	92	102	108	1.1	3.07	73	80	1.0
74360	PICHER	115	2029	1555	1467	-2.8	0	771	578	543	-3.1	2.62	535	384	-3.5
74361	PRYOR	097	12811	13543	13797	0.6	73	5108	5499	5636	0.8	2.41	3562	3738	0.5
74363	QUAPAW	115	2899	2822	2751	-0.3	27	1054	1024	997	-0.3	2.73	820	774	-0.6
74364	ROSE	041	1512	1621	1692	0.8	78	556	607	636	1.0	2.67	438	470	0.8
74365	SALINA	097	4268	4812	5015	1.3	89	1624	1872	1963	1.5	2.53	1157	1304	1.3
74366	SPAVINAW	097	1248	1292	1311	0.4	64	476	495	502	0.4	2.60	335	340	0.2
74367	STRANG	097	2531	2603	2621	0.3	60	1064	1107	1116	0.4	2.26	732	744	0.2
74368	TWIN OAKS	041	555	600	634	0.8	78	185	205	218	1.1	2.83	148	161	0.9
74369	WELCH	035	1834	1867	1884	0.2	55	728	751	760	0.3	2.46	542	543	0.0
74370	WYANDOTTE	115	3075	3483	3531	1.4	90	1168	1329	1348	1.4	2.62	886	986	1.2
74401	MUSKOGEE	101	17983	18430	18566	0.3	60	6933	7103	7172	0.3	2.51	4622	4597	-0.1
74403	MUSKOGEE	101	30122	31284	31747	0.4	64	12215	12688	12900	0.4	2.40	8275	8374	0.1
74421	BEGGS	111	4875	5102	5072	0.5	68	1824	1932	1923	0.6	2.63	1385	1433	0.4
74422	BOYNTON	101	770	775	770	0.1	49	297	301	300	0.1	2.57	222	220	-0.1
74423	BRAGGS	101	663	693	708	0.5	68	260	274	281	0.6	2.53	199	204	0.3
74425	CANADIAN	121	1676	1760	1805	0.5	68	706	757	782	0.8	2.32	526	551	0.5
74426	CHECOTAH	091	11815	12543	12875	0.6	73	4883	5260	5423	0.8	2.35	3485	3657	0.5
74427	COOKSON	021	1647	1740	1770	0.6	73	745	807	827	0.9	2.16	513	535	0.5
74428	COUNCIL HILL	091	1029	1043	1061	0.1	49	403	416	426	0.3	2.51	312	316	0.1
74429	COWETA	145	11046	14132	15705	2.7	96	3980	5177	5778	2.9	2.72	3149	4019	2.7
74432	EUFAULA	091	5623	5585	5610	-0.1	38	2383	2410	2433	0.1	2.25	1566	1544	-0.2
74434	FORT GIBSON	101	7499	8261	8550	1.1	84	2698	3007	3127	1.2	2.72	2131	2327	1.0
74435	GORE	135	1380	1478	1529	0.7	75	559	616	644	1.1	2.37	416	450	0.9
74436	HASKELL	101	3634	3681	3691	0.1	49	1348	1374	1381	0.2	2.65	1017	1013	0.0
74437	HENRYETTA	111	11524	11517	11298	0.0	43	4509	4528	4441	0.0	2.50	3143	3063	-0.3
74441	HULBERT	021	5578	6344	6656	1.4	90	2103	2454	2595	1.7	2.59	1624	1848	1.4
74442	INDIANOLA	121	1109	1145	1166	0.3	60	429	448	458	0.5	2.56	320	327	0.2
74445	MORRIS	111	3396	3568	3545	0.5	68	1227	1302	1297	0.6	2.74	958	994	0.4
74447	OKMULGEE	111	17572	17273	16890	-0.2	33	6950	6885	6725	-0.1	2.41	4575	4409	-0.4
74450	OKTAHA	101	2160	2210	2234	0.2	55	766	790	800	0.3	2.80	614	620	0.1
74451	PARK HILL	021	3884	4362	4538	1.3	89	1548	1770	1852	1.5	2.42	1153	1283	1.2
74452	PEGGS	021	1114	1113	1105	0.0	43	390	400	400	0.3	2.78	306	306	0.0
74454	PORTER	145	3079	3652	4077	1.9	94	1162	1415	1593	2.2	2.56	877	1035	1.8
74455	PORUM	101	3110	3207	3231	0.3	60	1260	1314	1331	0.5	2.44	938	955	0.2
74457	PROCTOR	001	917	1195	1302	2.9	96	328	446	487	3.4	2.68	250	332	3.1
74462	STIGLER	061	5373	5836	6032	0.9	80	2119	2310	2386	0.9	2.47	1484	1578	0.7
74463	TAFT	101	2086	2214	2213	0.6	73	210	215	215	0.3	2.85	145	145	0.0
74464	TAHLEQUAH	021	26985	28357	28898	0.5	68	10205	10817	11080	0.6	2.46	6564	6746	0.3
74467	WAGONER	145	15653	18259	20100	1.7	92	6171	7312	8102	1.9	2.48	4517	5175	1.5
74469	WARNER	101	2626	2750	2801	0.5	68	917	963	987	0.5	2.58	666	682	0.3
74470	WEBBERS FALLS	101	1364	1410	1431	0.4	64	530	552	563	0.4	2.55	402	409	0.2
74471	WELLING	021	1693	1685	1669	-0.1	38	624	638	636	0.2	2.63	475	472	-0.1
74472	WHITEFIELD	061	389	369	362	-0.6	13	162	155	152	-0.5	2.38	122	115	-0.6
74501	MCALESTER	121	29916	30997	31491	0.4	64	11344	11860	12101	0.5	2.38	7787	7946	0.2
74523	ANTLERS	127	6135	6108	6106	0.0	43	2473	2490	2499	0.1	2.37	1717	1685	-0.2
74525	ATOKA	005	9847	10395	10594	0.6	73	3392	3688	3795	0.9	2.54	2337	2481	0.6
74528	BLANCO	121	249	248	248	0.0	43	102	104	104	0.2	2.38	80	79	-0.1
74531	CALVIN	063	1031	986	949	-0.5	15	410	395	382	-0.4	2.50	297	279	-0.7
74533	CANEY	005	1291	1293	1299	0.0	43	503	521	528	0.4	2.48	381	386	0.1
74534	CENTRAHOMA	029	423	410	401	-0.3	27	168	163	159	-0.3	2.52	126	120	-0.5
74536	CLAYTON	127	1703	1764	1786	0.4	64	740	774	787	0.5	2.28	482	491	0.2
74538	COALGATE	029	4031	3916	3841	-0.3	27	1625	1589	1559	-0.2	2.42	1091	1039	-0.5
74540	DAISY	005	164	174	177	0.6	73	68	79	83	1.6	1.71	49	56	1.5
74543	FINLEY	127	217	222	225	0.2	55	95	99	101	0.4	2.24	66	67	0.2
74547	HARTSHORNE	121	4700	4685	4699	0.0	43	1885	1906	1919	0.1	2.36	1313	1292	-0.2
74549	KIAMICHI CHRISTIAN M	079	301	305	306	0.1	49	123	127	128	0.3	2.40	90	90	0.0
74552	KINTA	061	2952	2783	2724	-0.6	13	1193	1133	1111	-0.6	2.46	900	839	-0.8
74553	KIOWA	121	1309	1303	1314	0.0	43	538	546	553	0.2	2.39	398	395	-0.1
74555	LANE	005	1071	1109	1121	0.4	64	418	437	444	0.5	2.10	302	307	0.2
74557	MOYERS	127	170	176	178	0.4	64	66	69	71	0.5	2.55	48	49	0.2
74558	NASHOBA	127	595	611	618	0.3	60	241	252	256	0.5	2.42	171	175	0.3
74560	PITTSBURG	121	552	550	551	0.0	43	209	212	214	0.2	2.59	162	162	0.0
74561	QUINTON	121	4426	4605	4681	0.4	64	1936	2048	2092	0.6	2.23	1352	1392	0.3
74562	RATTAN	127	1628	1666	1686	0.2	55	653	684	696	0.5	2.44	472	483	0.2
74563	RED OAK	077	2160	2140	2104	-0.1	38	848	859	851	0.1	2.49	635	630	-0.1
74567	SNOW	127	298	305	309	0.3	60	128	134	136	0.5	2.28	89	91	0.2
74569	STRINGTOWN	005	602	674	700	1.2	86	233	269	281	1.6	2.42	173	195	1.3
74570	STUART	063	758	763	756	0.1	49	314	320	318	0.2	2.38	240	240	0.0
74571	TALIHINA	079	2974	3032	3046	0.2	55	1099	1142	1154	0.4	2.60	775	787	0.2
	OKLAHOMA					0.7					0.8	2.46			0.6
	UNITED STATES					1.0					1.1	2.59			0.9

ZIP CODE		RACE (%)						% Hispanic Origin		2009 AGE DISTRIBUTION (%)										MEDIAN AGE	% 2009 Males	% 2009 Females
#	POST OFFICE NAME	White 2000	White 2009	Black 2000	Black 2009	Asian/Pacific 2000	Asian/Pacific 2009	2000	2009	0-4	5-9	10-14	15-19	20-24	25-44	45-64	65-84	85+	18+	2009		
74132	TULSA	84.9	81.5	3.6	4.0	0.9	1.2	2.3	3.4	6.6	7.0	7.2	7.0	5.5	25.1	30.4	10.4	0.8	74.5	38.7	49.5	50.5
74133	TULSA	84.0	79.8	4.9	5.8	3.3	4.7	4.6	6.7	6.8	6.2	6.0	6.6	8.6	30.6	24.8	8.6	1.7	77.2	34.2	49.2	50.8
74134	TULSA	72.0	65.9	9.3	10.8	4.7	6.3	9.2	12.8	8.2	6.9	6.1	6.5	10.5	33.2	23.1	5.1	0.4	75.2	29.9	50.6	49.4
74135	TULSA	82.8	78.9	6.3	7.3	1.2	1.7	5.8	8.2	5.5	5.2	5.3	4.9	5.1	25.2	26.3	17.2	5.1	81.2	43.9	46.8	53.2
74136	TULSA	73.4	68.0	13.5	15.4	2.8	3.8	7.3	10.4	6.4	4.9	4.5	6.5	10.9	30.0	23.5	11.0	2.3	81.2	33.8	48.2	51.8
74137	TULSA	89.1	86.1	2.9	3.4	2.3	3.4	2.9	4.2	5.6	6.7	8.0	7.7	4.9	22.1	32.8	10.3	1.9	74.7	41.9	48.4	51.6
74145	TULSA	79.3	74.8	7.4	8.5	2.9	3.9	5.8	8.3	6.1	5.4	5.3	5.3	7.8	27.4	23.8	16.5	2.3	80.1	38.4	48.0	52.0
74146	TULSA	63.2	56.3	11.2	12.2	4.5	6.0	16.7	22.3	8.8	7.2	6.2	7.1	10.1	32.7	20.5	6.6	0.8	73.9	29.3	50.9	49.1
74171	TULSA	76.2	70.2	14.6	17.5	2.4	3.3	5.7	8.4	0.7	0.5	0.8	30.0	48.1	5.0	7.5	6.1	1.3	96.7	21.9	43.3	56.7
74301	VINITA	68.2	63.8	4.1	4.4	0.2	0.4	1.3	2.3	5.8	5.9	5.9	6.0	5.5	25.7	28.4	14.3	2.5	78.8	41.8	51.6	48.4
74330	ADAIR	76.1	72.7	0.2	0.2	0.1	0.2	1.5	1.9	6.7	6.7	6.7	6.1	5.3	23.5	30.4	13.2	1.4	76.1	40.9	49.5	50.5
74331	AFTON	82.1	79.4	0.1	0.1	0.1	0.2	1.0	1.4	5.0	5.3	5.6	5.2	3.8	19.3	32.2	21.6	2.0	80.8	49.5	49.6	50.4
74332	BIG CABIN	68.5	64.5	0.8	0.9	0.4	0.6	1.3	1.8	6.5	6.9	6.7	6.4	5.0	23.1	31.0	13.4	1.1	76.0	41.3	50.1	49.9
74333	BLUEJACKET	64.7	60.0	0.4	0.4	0.0	0.1	0.3	0.4	6.4	6.6	6.8	6.3	5.3	24.2	28.8	13.5	2.0	76.4	40.6	49.8	50.2
74337	CHOUTEAU	78.5	75.3	1.0	1.0	0.4	0.6	1.8	2.5	7.3	7.2	7.3	7.6	6.3	25.6	26.1	11.3	1.3	73.5	36.1	49.8	50.2
74338	COLCORD	72.2	68.6	0.1	0.1	0.1	0.2	1.9	2.7	7.2	7.1	7.4	7.2	5.8	24.8	26.6	11.7	2.2	73.9	37.8	50.2	49.8
74339	COMMERCE	68.6	63.4	0.6	0.6	0.3	0.4	17.6	24.2	9.2	8.1	7.1	6.9	7.3	26.8	19.2	11.4	3.9	71.5	32.6	47.7	52.3
74342	EUCHA	56.2	52.8	0.1	0.1	0.1	0.0	1.8	2.5	6.1	6.6	6.6	6.8	5.1	22.8	30.6	13.9	1.5	76.2	41.5	50.7	49.3
74343	FAIRLAND	74.7	71.7	0.1	0.1	0.2	0.3	0.8	1.1	5.8	5.9	5.9	6.1	5.1	22.8	28.7	17.2	2.5	78.3	43.8	49.3	50.7
74344	GROVE	80.4	77.4	0.1	0.1	0.4	0.6	1.6	2.2	4.9	4.9	4.8	5.1	4.5	18.2	31.2	23.3	3.2	82.1	50.9	48.3	51.7
74346	JAY	60.1	56.5	0.4	0.4	0.1	0.1	2.7	3.8	6.9	6.8	6.8	7.2	6.2	25.2	26.2	13.0	1.8	75.0	38.0	48.7	51.3
74347	KANSAS	55.1	51.6	0.0	0.0	0.1	0.2	1.5	2.0	9.2	8.8	8.4	7.2	6.2	26.0	23.5	9.6	1.1	69.1	33.2	48.9	51.1
74352	LOCUST GROVE	64.0	60.9	0.0	0.0	0.1	0.2	1.3	1.7	7.4	7.3	7.1	6.7	5.8	25.5	26.4	12.2	1.5	74.0	37.0	51.2	48.8
74354	MIAMI	75.1	71.9	0.9	1.0	0.6	0.9	2.2	3.1	6.4	6.1	6.3	8.5	6.9	22.7	25.0	15.4	2.7	77.0	38.9	48.3	51.7
74358	NORTH MIAMI	61.5	57.4	0.3	0.3	0.3	0.3	4.3	6.3	7.6	6.9	6.3	6.3	7.6	22.4	24.0	17.0	1.9	75.4	38.0	47.6	52.4
74359	OAKS	35.0	32.1	0.0	0.0	0.0	0.0	1.7	2.2	9.6	9.9	9.9	6.5	5.6	27.8	21.6	8.6	0.6	66.0	31.1	47.5	52.5
74360	PICHER	76.7	73.2	0.0	0.0	0.2	0.3	1.5	2.1	6.9	6.9	7.1	6.8	5.1	23.3	27.1	14.1	2.6	75.1	40.0	49.3	50.7
74361	PRYOR	77.7	74.7	0.2	0.3	0.5	0.8	2.4	3.3	6.8	6.3	6.3	7.7	5.7	25.2	25.5	13.6	2.8	75.5	38.5	49.0	51.0
74363	QUAPAW	71.4	68.6	0.0	0.0	0.2	0.3	1.6	2.2	7.1	7.2	7.5	6.6	5.0	24.9	28.0	12.1	1.6	74.1	38.4	50.6	49.4
74364	ROSE	48.7	45.7	0.0	0.0	0.0	0.0	1.7	2.3	7.5	8.0	7.7	7.9	6.5	25.4	26.5	9.6	1.0	71.9	34.4	51.4	48.6
74365	SALINA	57.0	54.1	0.2	0.2	0.1	0.1	1.2	1.6	7.4	7.3	7.3	6.6	5.7	25.4	24.9	13.4	2.0	73.9	37.4	49.7	50.3
74366	SPAVINAW	66.9	63.9	0.0	0.0	0.1	0.1	3.1	4.1	6.1	6.3	6.9	7.3	4.8	21.2	30.2	15.7	1.5	75.9	43.0	49.4	50.6
74367	STRANG	75.9	72.8	0.9	0.9	0.2	0.2	2.6	3.7	5.1	5.5	5.7	4.9	3.5	21.4	32.7	19.0	2.2	80.3	47.6	50.4	49.6
74368	TWIN OAKS	35.7	32.8	0.0	0.0	0.0	0.0	1.6	2.0	9.7	10.0	10.0	6.8	5.8	26.5	22.0	8.7	0.5	65.3	30.6	47.7	52.3
74369	WELCH	74.1	70.5	0.2	0.2	0.0	0.0	1.1	1.7	6.6	6.9	6.7	5.9	4.3	24.3	25.9	16.6	2.7	75.9	41.4	49.5	50.5
74370	WYANDOTTE	74.1	71.6	0.0	0.0	0.3	0.3	1.9	2.7	6.4	6.3	7.0	7.2	5.0	22.8	30.4	13.6	1.2	75.6	41.5	50.6	49.4
74401	MUSKOGEE	48.5	45.2	33.6	34.9	0.9	1.1	2.5	3.3	7.6	7.3	7.1	7.3	6.2	23.1	25.9	12.9	2.7	73.7	37.6	48.0	52.0
74403	MUSKOGEE	71.9	68.4	3.9	4.3	0.8	1.0	3.2	4.4	6.7	6.3	6.3	6.6	5.9	24.7	26.6	13.8	3.1	76.7	39.5	48.0	52.0
74421	BEGGS	72.9	69.2	8.8	9.8	0.2	0.2	2.1	2.9	7.3	7.3	7.5	7.1	6.2	24.7	28.2	10.5	1.2	73.2	37.0	49.5	50.5
74422	BOYNTON	59.2	54.7	22.2	24.3	0.0	0.0	1.2	1.7	6.1	6.2	6.3	7.6	6.5	23.2	28.0	13.8	2.3	76.9	40.4	51.0	49.0
74423	BRAGGS	70.0	66.7	0.9	0.9	0.0	0.0	0.9	1.4	6.1	6.3	6.6	6.6	4.9	25.8	29.7	12.7	1.2	76.9	40.5	51.1	48.9
74425	CANADIAN	85.7	83.2	0.3	0.3	0.1	0.2	0.6	0.9	3.9	4.1	5.8	7.2	3.7	17.8	35.4	20.3	1.6	81.9	49.5	49.0	51.0
74426	CHECOTAH	74.9	71.7	4.2	4.4	0.2	0.2	1.3	1.8	5.4	5.5	5.9	5.8	4.6	19.5	29.3	21.3	2.8	79.7	47.6	47.9	52.1
74427	COOKSON	67.9	65.5	0.1	0.1	0.2	0.3	0.4	0.7	3.2	3.6	3.9	4.7	3.9	17.1	36.2	25.4	2.2	86.6	54.1	50.1	49.9
74428	COUNCIL HILL	70.5	67.0	7.4	8.0	0.1	0.1	1.3	1.6	5.8	6.0	6.5	6.9	5.7	21.3	28.9	16.7	2.2	77.2	42.9	49.2	50.8
74429	COWETA	78.5	76.0	3.1	3.0	0.2	0.3	3.0	4.0	7.4	7.5	7.4	7.6	5.6	27.1	26.9	9.5	1.0	72.9	36.2	49.2	50.8
74432	EUFAULA	67.3	64.1	5.1	5.5	0.2	0.2	1.1	1.5	5.1	5.4	5.7	5.4	4.7	20.3	30.0	20.0	3.5	80.3	47.4	47.8	52.2
74434	FORT GIBSON	69.0	65.7	2.1	2.3	0.2	0.2	3.7	5.0	7.1	7.0	7.1	7.4	6.0	26.7	26.5	10.7	1.4	74.2	36.7	50.1	49.9
74435	GORE	66.2	63.1	2.3	2.5	0.1	0.1	1.3	1.8	6.0	6.0	6.4	6.8	5.5	22.0	29.2	16.2	2.0	77.6	42.9	49.7	50.3
74436	HASKELL	70.5	66.9	10.7	11.8	0.1	0.1	1.4	1.9	7.7	7.4	7.4	6.6	5.4	23.2	26.7	12.9	2.7	73.3	38.4	47.9	52.1
74437	HENRYETTA	77.3	74.0	1.8	2.0	0.2	0.3	2.0	2.7	6.5	6.5	6.8	7.4	5.7	22.5	27.5	14.3	2.9	75.7	40.5	48.0	52.0
74441	HULBERT	60.1	57.2	0.4	0.5	0.2	0.3	2.0	2.9	7.2	6.9	7.2	7.5	5.7	24.7	28.1	11.7	1.1	74.3	37.9	50.6	49.4
74442	INDIANOLA	84.7	82.5	0.2	0.2	0.2	0.3	1.4	1.9	5.8	6.0	6.3	6.7	5.7	21.7	30.3	15.8	1.7	77.8	43.1	48.0	52.0
74445	MORRIS	72.4	68.7	3.9	4.6	0.1	0.1	1.9	2.6	6.9	6.6	6.5	7.0	6.8	25.2	27.2	12.4	1.4	75.7	37.7	49.4	50.6
74447	OKMULGEE	62.0	58.8	18.3	19.4	0.3	0.4	1.8	2.4	7.1	6.6	6.5	7.9	7.1	23.0	25.1	14.0	2.7	75.7	37.8	49.2	50.8
74450	OKTAHA	65.7	62.4	10.8	11.9	0.5	0.6	1.6	2.3	6.8	7.1	7.3	7.1	5.3	23.8	29.8	11.4	1.4	74.4	39.1	48.9	51.1
74451	PARK HILL	58.4	55.6	0.4	0.4	0.2	0.3	2.6	3.7	6.6	6.8	6.8	7.4	4.7	22.5	29.3	14.7	1.2	75.1	40.8	49.7	50.3
74452	PEGGS	59.4	56.6	0.1	0.1	0.1	0.2	0.6	1.0	7.6	7.7	7.6	7.2	6.0	25.2	27.2	10.6	0.8	72.6	35.6	51.3	48.7
74454	PORTER	68.1	64.1	14.5	15.6	0.0	0.0	1.3	1.8	6.4	6.6	6.6	6.8	5.9	23.7	29.0	13.5	1.5	76.2	39.9	49.5	50.5
74455	PORUM	68.3	65.6	0.5	0.6	0.1	0.2	1.0	1.4	6.6	6.7	6.6	6.1	5.2	21.1	27.3	18.1	2.1	76.1	42.6	49.4	50.6
74457	PROCTOR	47.8	43.5	0.2	0.2	0.0	0.1	2.0	2.6	7.0	7.4	8.3	8.3	4.8	25.8	26.8	10.6	1.1	72.2	36.8	50.0	50.0
74462	STIGLER	78.7	75.9	0.0	0.1	0.3	0.4	1.9	2.6	7.7	7.4	6.9	6.1	5.4	23.7	25.0	14.3	3.5	74.2	38.7	48.5	51.5
74463	TAFT	42.6	38.5	41.2	44.0	0.3	0.4	2.1	2.8	2.8	2.7	2.6	3.1	8.8	57.0	18.1	4.3	0.6	90.4	36.2	54.0	46.0
74464	TAHLEQUAH	54.8	51.5	1.6	1.7	0.4	0.5	5.4	7.2	7.3	6.5	6.3	9.5	11.9	24.9	21.7	10.0	1.9	75.7	30.6	48.6	51.4
74467	WAGONER	74.0	70.6	5.4	5.8	0.3	0.4	2.0	2.7	6.7	6.7	6.5	6.3	5.6	23.3	27.9	15.1	1.9	76.4	40.8	48.7	51.3
74469	WARNER	65.1	62.1	2.9	3.2	0.0	0.0	1.8	2.4	6.8	6.8	6.4	10.3	7.1	22.4	23.6	13.6	3.0	76.7	35.1	48.6	51.4
74470	WEBBERS FALLS	68.8	66.2	0.5	0.6	0.0	0.0	1.7	2.3	6.9	7.0	7.1	6.4	4.9	23.3	27.8	15.1	1.6	75.0	40.7	48.2	51.8
74471	WELLING	50.3	48.0	0.6	0.7	0.0	0.1	2.1	2.7	7.3	7.0	7.1	7.1	6.1	25.2	27.5	11.5	1.2	74.1	37.6	50.4	49.6
74472	WHITEFIELD	76.9	73.7	0.5	0.5	0.3	0.3	0.3	0.3	5.4	6.0	6.0	6.5	4.6	22.5	28.5	18.7	1.9	78.3	44.2	52.3	47.7
74501	MCALESTER	76.8	73.8	5.5	5.9	0.4	0.5	2.5	3.4	5.7	5.7	5.9	6.3	6.4	26.0	27.1	14.0	2.9	78.8	40.6	51.3	48.7
74523	ANTLERS	79.8	77.2	1.1	1.2	0.2	0.3	1.8	2.4	6.5	6.4	6.5	6.6	5.4	23.1	26.1	16.1	3.4	76.7	41.7	48.1	51.9
74525	ATOKA	75.2	72.1	6.3	6.7	0.3	0.4	1.3	1.8	6.1	6.0	6.2	6.3	5.5	26.6	27.3	13.6	2.5	77.9	40.2	53.1	46.9
74528	BLANCO	69.5	66.1	0.4	0.4	0.0	0.0	3.2	4.4	5.6	5.6	6.0	5.6	5.2	23.8	31.0	14.9	2.0	79.0	43.2	49.2	50.8
74531	CALVIN	82.4	79.2	0.0	0.0	0.5	0.7	2.1	3.1	6.7	7.0	7.1	6.5	4.4	23.5	27.4	15.4	2.0	75.3	41.2	51.8	48.2
74533	CANEY	83.2	81.0	0.7	0.8	0.1	0.1	1.5	2.1	6.4	6.8	6.7	6.1	5.3	23.1	29.6	14.5	1.5	76.4	40.7	50.3	49.7
74534	CENTRAHOMA	73.5	70.7	0.2	0.2	0.2	0.5	1.9	2.7	7.1	7.6	7.3	6.3	4.1	25.9	27.1	12.7	2.0	74.1	38.2	51.2	48.8
74536	CLAYTON	73.7	71.0	1.3	1.4	0.0	0.0	1.3	1.7	7.2	7.0	6.8	6.2	5.6	21.2	26.2	17.3	2.4	74.9	41.6	49.6	50.4
74538	COALGATE	75.5	73.0	0.5	0.5	0.4	0.5	2.2	3.1	6.2	5.9	6.1	7.0	6.1	22.9	27.0	15.6	3.2	77.5	41.6	49.1	50.9
74540	DAISY	66.5	63.2	15.2	16.7	0.0	0.0	3.7	5.2	2.9	2.9	2.9	2.9	9.2	44.8	24.7	8.6	1.1	90.2	38.4	77.6	22.4
74543	FINLEY	81.0	78.4	0.0	0.0	0.0	0.5	1.4	2.3	5.0	5.4	5.4	5.9	5.9	18.9	33.3	18.5	1.8	80.2	47.4	49.5	50.5
74547	HARTSHORNE	70.2	67.2	2.2	2.4	0.2	0.3	1.7	2.3	6.0	7.2	7.9	7.5	4.7	21.5	28.1	14.5	2.8	74.2	40.9	48.9	51.1
74549	KIAMICHI CHRISTIAN M	76.7	74.1	0.7	0.7	0.0	0.0	1.0	1.6	5.6	6.2	6.2	6.6	5.2	20.3	31.1	17.0	1.6	78.0	44.9	47.5	52.5
74552	KINTA	75.7	72.1	2.2	2.6	0.1	0.3	0.5	0.7	5.7	6.0	6.4	6.7	4.3	22.1	28.4	18.3	2.1	77.7	43.9	51.2	48.8
74553	KIOWA	76.4	72.8	0.1	0.1	0.0	0.0	2.5	3.5	6.1	6.2	6.4	5.8	5.0	24.5	30.0	14.0	2.0	77.6	42.2	48.3	51.7
74555	LANE	74.5	70.7	5.2	5.5	0.4	0.5	1.7	2.3	5.4	5.5	5.9	6.0	6.0	31.0	26.0	12.7	1.5	79.6	39.4	58.3	41.7
74557	MOYERS	81.8	80.1	0.0	0.0	0.0	0.0	1.2	1.1	5.7	5.7	6.3	6.3	4.5	25.0	27.8	17.0	1.7	78.4	42.7	49.4	50.6
74558	NASHOBA	78.3	76.1	0.3	0.3	0.2	0.2	1.3	1.8	5.2	5.4	5.7	6.7	5.9	18.8	32.7	17.8	1.6	79.5	46.2	47.3	52.7
74560	PITTSBURG	70.2	66.7	0.2	0.2	0.0	0.0	3.1	4.5	5.6	6.0	6.2	5.8	5.1	23.8	30.5	15.1	1.8	78.5	42.8	50.0	50.0
74561	QUINTON	84.1	82.1	0.2	0.2	0.1	0.1	0.9	1.5	4.2	4.8	5.1	5.6	3.9	18.3	31.7	23.8	2.5	82.1	51.2	50.4	49.6
74562	RATTAN	76.1	73.5	0.1	0.1	0.3	0.4	1.7	2.5	6.3	6.6	6.8	6.4	5.0	20.5	30.5	16.1	1.7	76.4	43.5	49.6	50.4
74563	RED OAK	74.6	71.9	0.2	0.2	0.1	0.1	0.8	1.2	6.8	7.0	6.8	6.4	5.3	22.8	27.9	15.1	1.9	75.4	40.6	51.2	48.8
74567	SNOW	80.3	78.0	0.3	0.3	0.3	0.7	1.3	2.0	4.9	5.2	5.6	5.9	5.9	19.0	33.4	18.0	2.0	81.0	47.1	49.8	50.2
74569	STRINGTOWN	76.4	73.7	6.1	6.7	0.3	0.4	0.7	0.9	6.1	6.1	6.2	6.5	5.8	24.3	30.1	12.9	1.9	77.4	41.5	52.7	47.3
74570	STUART	86.8	84.8	0.1	0.1	0.0	0.0	1.8	2.5	4.6	4.8	5.4	6.4	4.3	22.4	31.6	18.0	2.5	81.1	46.3	49.3	50.7
74571	TALIHINA	64.5	61.8	0.7	0.7	0.1	0.1	1.2	1.6	6.4	6.4	6.4	6.3	5.7	23.1	27.3	16.1	2.4	76.8	41.2	48.3	51.7
	OKLAHOMA	76.2	73.0	7.6	7.8	1.4	2.0	5.2	7.0	6.9	6.6	6.5	7.1	7.2	26.2	25.9	11.6	2.0	75.9	36.8	49.3	50.7
	UNITED STATES	75.1	72.0	12.3	12.7	3.8	4.6	12.5	15.7	6.8	6.7	6.6	7.1	6.9	27.0	26.0	10.9	1.9	75.7	36.9	49.2	50.8

ZIP CODE #	POST OFFICE NAME	2009 Per Capita Income	2009 HH Income Base	2009 Household Income Distribution (%): Less than $25,000	$25,000 to $49,999	$50,000 to $99,999	$100,000 to $149,999	$150,000 or More	Median Household Income: 2009	2014	2009 National Centile	2009 State Centile	2009 Home Value Base	2009 Home Value Distribution (%): Less than $50,000	$50,000 to $89,999	$90,000 to $174,999	$175,000 to $399,999	$400,000 or More	2009 Median Home Value
74132	TULSA	27732	2868	17.0	23.0	38.5	14.4	7.1	61603	61572	80	96	2250	9.5	14.7	48.8	21.6	5.5	122446
74133	TULSA	33382	17337	12.6	23.8	38.4	15.9	9.2	64278	65689	83	96	9310	1.2	3.6	50.9	41.5	2.8	167886
74134	TULSA	24730	6070	18.3	30.0	41.4	7.9	2.5	51247	53131	64	90	3299	0.6	18.6	68.5	10.3	2.0	111152
74135	TULSA	29947	10077	21.7	30.3	34.5	9.0	4.5	48118	50748	57	87	5427	1.6	12.0	62.8	22.7	0.9	136006
74136	TULSA	32496	14643	23.6	30.5	29.3	8.8	7.8	45264	47997	49	82	5254	8.0	9.7	24.2	48.3	9.7	191343
74137	TULSA	52588	9935	8.7	15.3	28.0	17.0	31.0	95789	98105	96	100	7485	2.3	3.5	19.0	52.7	22.5	262070
74145	TULSA	27288	8061	18.4	29.8	41.8	7.7	2.2	51138	52951	64	90	4306	1.0	17.6	74.5	6.6	0.2	113912
74146	TULSA	19905	5855	28.7	33.4	30.8	5.0	2.0	38636	41583	29	61	2298	12.1	42.1	41.6	4.0	0.3	88111
74171	TULSA	10431	3	0.0	0.0	100.0	0.0	0.0	81250	56095	93	99	2	0.0	0.0	0.0	100.0	0.0	200000
74301	VINITA	19479	3977	31.5	34.4	28.0	3.3	2.8	37615	38994	26	55	2874	26.2	27.0	31.7	12.6	2.4	84773
74330	ADAIR	21144	2151	21.3	32.9	35.7	7.2	2.9	46462	46572	53	85	1858	11.7	25.1	41.0	18.3	3.8	116908
74331	AFTON	24867	3077	29.8	30.6	28.6	5.7	5.2	40649	42811	35	69	2480	21.4	21.3	28.5	20.4	8.5	108053
74332	BIG CABIN	20544	677	26.3	36.6	28.5	6.6	1.9	39109	40468	30	63	552	21.6	20.8	34.1	20.3	3.3	99545
74333	BLUEJACKET	16495	487	27.7	38.4	28.5	3.7	1.6	37850	39259	26	56	408	30.4	25.0	33.1	9.8	1.7	81852
74337	CHOUTEAU	18808	1712	29.7	28.2	33.1	6.3	2.8	40682	41724	35	70	1289	17.5	29.2	32.7	17.1	3.4	95667
74338	COLCORD	17529	2004	30.4	34.6	29.1	4.1	1.7	37584	40063	25	55	1550	24.6	24.9	33.0	13.7	3.7	90673
74339	COMMERCE	14733	952	32.6	36.0	28.9	2.4	0.1	35790	37460	20	43	642	51.6	34.4	13.6	0.5	0.0	48529
74342	EUCHA	17039	1601	39.0	32.7	22.7	3.0	2.5	31428	32347	10	19	1335	32.5	28.8	24.8	10.1	3.7	71292
74343	FAIRLAND	17140	1158	30.1	38.2	28.2	2.2	1.4	36470	38660	22	48	899	22.4	30.6	34.0	11.1	1.9	86159
74344	GROVE	21096	6509	31.7	33.1	27.9	4.4	2.8	36435	37974	22	48	5077	16.8	15.1	35.0	26.7	6.4	125223
74346	JAY	17253	2370	36.3	32.2	24.5	4.8	2.2	33706	34759	15	29	1703	23.7	24.3	31.5	15.3	5.2	92659
74347	KANSAS	16973	1108	25.4	38.3	31.2	3.2	1.9	39813	41406	32	66	919	26.3	25.6	35.0	8.7	4.4	86875
74352	LOCUST GROVE	16988	2582	30.1	34.4	30.5	3.8	1.3	36368	37699	22	47	2093	29.5	31.3	28.4	9.3	1.5	75929
74354	MIAMI	19018	7036	33.4	33.5	26.9	3.9	2.3	35212	37065	18	37	4928	27.7	31.6	30.8	8.9	1.1	75841
74358	NORTH MIAMI	14801	117	35.0	35.9	26.5	0.0	2.6	35373	35451	19	39	98	45.9	35.7	12.2	6.1	0.0	54000
74359	OAKS	14389	102	36.3	33.3	26.5	2.9	1.0	35547	37695	19	41	83	27.7	34.9	30.1	4.8	2.4	73571
74360	PICHER	13121	578	48.3	32.7	15.9	2.2	0.9	25969	26581	4	4	423	66.2	19.4	9.0	3.5	1.9	31328
74361	PRYOR	21999	5499	28.1	30.3	31.5	6.5	3.6	40961	42200	36	70	3792	12.4	23.4	45.3	17.4	1.5	108872
74363	QUAPAW	15687	1024	35.2	29.9	29.8	4.2	1.0	36589	39632	22	49	838	34.8	27.9	24.5	11.3	1.4	71406
74364	ROSE	16814	607	31.8	36.9	28.3	0.7	2.3	35687	37573	20	42	508	37.2	29.3	19.7	12.8	1.0	66591
74365	SALINA	18638	1872	31.2	30.7	31.8	4.9	1.4	37932	39873	26	57	1435	26.6	28.6	34.6	9.8	0.5	82475
74366	SPAVINAW	16277	495	40.4	29.3	25.7	3.0	1.6	32411	34804	12	24	387	31.8	33.9	25.8	5.4	3.1	70161
74367	STRANG	20564	1107	32.8	36.5	23.1	5.6	2.0	35773	37546	20	43	921	24.9	23.8	31.5	15.6	4.2	93205
74368	TWIN OAKS	15645	205	33.2	34.1	26.8	3.9	2.0	37313	39253	25	53	168	26.2	33.3	32.1	6.5	1.8	76923
74369	WELCH	18028	751	29.0	37.9	28.1	2.8	2.1	37794	39091	26	56	591	29.8	23.7	27.9	13.2	5.4	84605
74370	WYANDOTTE	16867	1329	31.8	32.7	30.2	4.1	1.3	38645	41151	29	61	1127	30.7	23.6	30.6	12.6	2.5	82302
74401	MUSKOGEE	17419	7103	41.7	29.4	22.4	3.4	3.0	30555	31682	9	15	4512	27.8	31.0	28.2	11.1	1.9	77598
74403	MUSKOGEE	21240	12688	30.7	29.4	31.0	6.2	2.7	39957	41904	32	67	8616	19.4	28.4	40.9	10.4	0.9	92644
74421	BEGGS	19342	1932	26.6	29.6	35.0	6.8	2.0	43512	45314	44	76	1534	29.3	25.3	29.7	13.4	2.4	82473
74422	BOYNTON	18052	301	37.5	28.2	28.6	3.7	2.0	33546	35000	14	29	259	39.8	21.2	27.8	9.7	1.5	70333
74423	BRAGGS	17452	274	33.9	32.1	28.1	4.7	1.1	35663	37341	20	42	218	32.6	33.5	29.4	4.6	0.0	71364
74425	CANADIAN	18605	757	34.1	35.4	24.4	4.8	1.3	35550	36681	19	41	666	28.8	35.0	23.7	11.3	1.2	74167
74426	CHECOTAH	20434	5260	37.8	30.0	24.3	4.9	3.0	33323	34137	14	28	4178	25.3	27.8	32.6	12.6	1.6	85623
74427	COOKSON	19758	807	38.4	33.3	22.9	3.7	1.6	32669	34296	13	25	691	20.0	25.3	41.5	10.3	2.9	96500
74428	COUNCIL HILL	17544	416	37.3	29.3	29.1	3.4	1.0	34299	35864	16	32	351	31.9	25.9	31.6	7.7	2.8	74310
74429	COWETA	21312	5177	18.5	29.4	43.1	7.2	1.9	51637	54261	65	91	3981	15.9	18.5	44.6	18.7	2.3	114216
74432	EUFAULA	19423	2410	43.1	30.6	18.8	4.0	3.5	29611	30132	7	12	1799	31.2	23.3	32.6	11.3	1.6	76524
74434	FORT GIBSON	20214	3007	26.4	25.5	37.6	7.5	2.9	47508	49871	55	86	2256	14.6	22.3	43.5	17.5	2.1	109985
74435	GORE	19082	616	38.0	32.1	22.9	5.2	1.8	35634	36953	20	41	509	25.3	30.8	32.2	10.4	1.2	84375
74436	HASKELL	16751	1374	33.6	31.7	30.1	2.8	1.8	37792	40193	26	56	1087	32.7	29.3	27.3	7.5	3.1	70938
74437	HENRYETTA	15752	4528	41.3	29.8	23.3	4.7	0.8	31065	32220	10	17	3341	45.0	30.4	19.1	5.1	0.5	56456
74441	HULBERT	16972	2454	33.5	31.9	29.1	4.4	1.1	36813	39347	23	51	2016	23.7	28.1	35.3	11.7	1.2	87465
74442	INDIANOLA	17730	448	37.9	32.4	22.1	5.8	1.8	33873	35386	15	30	379	35.9	27.7	25.9	8.7	1.8	71400
74445	MORRIS	17654	1302	30.0	31.8	30.8	5.8	1.7	39406	42084	31	64	1063	26.5	32.5	31.5	8.5	1.0	79225
74447	OKMULGEE	17806	6885	39.5	29.7	24.6	3.8	2.4	32794	34495	13	25	4457	38.5	28.3	24.4	8.0	0.8	63016
74450	OKTAHA	17466	790	30.8	30.3	32.5	4.8	1.6	39260	40882	31	63	684	28.9	21.6	33.2	13.6	2.6	88824
74451	PARK HILL	18698	1770	32.8	31.0	29.8	4.9	1.6	35977	38612	21	44	1437	23.3	26.0	33.8	14.1	2.7	90969
74452	PEGGS	17146	400	30.3	33.5	29.3	5.0	2.0	37920	40304	26	57	346	31.8	24.3	30.6	11.0	2.3	79000
74454	PORTER	18526	1415	35.1	28.8	27.8	6.4	2.0	38270	40560	27	59	1141	40.0	25.2	20.9	13.8	0.3	64036
74455	PORUM	16156	1314	44.3	29.9	20.9	3.9	1.1	28150	28918	6	8	1074	42.2	22.8	24.5	9.6	0.9	61231
74457	PROCTOR	15118	446	37.4	30.7	26.7	4.7	0.4	32337	34418	12	23	359	24.2	33.7	27.9	9.7	4.5	79028
74462	STIGLER	17141	2310	45.2	30.8	18.9	2.4	2.8	27821	28550	5	6	1628	27.5	30.7	28.7	10.3	2.8	76716
74463	TAFT	14038	215	40.0	27.4	24.2	5.1	3.3	34394	35474	16	33	150	28.7	27.3	36.0	5.3	2.7	81818
74464	TAHLEQUAH	17269	10817	39.6	29.0	24.7	4.8	1.9	32607	34611	13	24	6090	15.4	26.3	40.7	15.3	2.3	101168
74467	WAGONER	20111	7312	31.4	28.4	32.5	4.5	3.2	40369	42555	34	69	5256	26.4	30.7	31.6	10.6	0.7	79046
74469	WARNER	15436	963	39.6	27.2	28.5	4.6	0.2	33135	34326	14	27	670	28.1	34.5	28.5	9.0	0.0	71020
74470	WEBBERS FALLS	15250	552	44.4	30.1	20.5	3.4	1.6	29348	30696	7	11	420	39.3	31.7	22.1	6.9	0.0	63750
74471	WELLING	18509	638	35.9	34.0	24.3	3.3	2.5	32915	34593	13	26	510	29.4	32.0	26.7	9.6	2.4	78750
74472	WHITEFIELD	16236	155	37.4	33.5	25.2	2.6	1.3	31191	31496	10	18	135	28.9	31.9	28.9	8.9	1.5	76818
74501	MCALESTER	19358	11860	35.0	28.5	29.1	4.9	2.6	37592	40422	26	55	8603	22.5	29.8	32.2	13.6	1.8	86631
74523	ANTLERS	15586	2490	47.9	29.9	18.0	2.8	1.5	26347	27244	4	4	1866	29.9	33.1	27.5	7.5	2.0	72013
74525	ATOKA	14865	3688	44.1	30.0	21.4	3.0	1.5	28943	29814	7	9	2671	28.8	30.1	29.4	10.2	1.5	80265
74528	BLANCO	16179	104	37.5	30.8	28.8	2.9	0.0	31696	33603	11	20	83	32.5	33.7	20.5	10.8	2.4	75000
74531	CALVIN	15199	395	41.8	30.1	24.6	3.5	0.0	30139	32358	8	13	315	42.9	22.2	26.0	8.3	0.6	61842
74533	CANEY	17277	521	37.8	33.6	23.4	3.1	2.1	32126	33646	12	22	442	34.6	29.0	29.0	6.6	0.9	67879
74534	CENTRAHOMA	15305	163	47.9	23.3	23.9	3.1	1.8	27016	30244	5	5	133	46.6	21.8	21.8	8.3	1.5	57500
74536	CLAYTON	16072	774	50.4	27.4	17.4	2.7	2.1	24728	25537	3	2	582	45.2	25.1	23.7	5.0	1.0	55833
74538	COALGATE	14254	1589	46.4	31.5	19.3	2.2	0.6	28099	29252	6	7	1117	44.9	33.1	16.2	3.3	2.5	54600
74540	DAISY	26094	79	34.2	26.6	32.9	6.3	0.0	35364	36369	19	39	70	32.9	21.4	31.4	12.9	1.4	84000
74543	FINLEY	20178	99	37.4	33.3	25.3	2.0	2.0	34529	37330	17	33	85	36.5	24.7	21.2	12.9	4.7	66250
74547	HARTSHORNE	16775	1906	40.9	30.6	24.0	3.7	0.8	31607	33170	11	20	1453	34.6	33.8	25.5	5.2	0.9	67702
74549	KIAMICHI CHRISTIAN M	13993	127	47.2	29.9	18.9	2.4	1.6	26401	26799	4	4	106	47.2	26.4	20.8	5.7	0.0	54286
74552	KINTA	16477	1133	37.1	34.6	24.2	2.6	1.6	31901	33242	11	21	969	30.0	29.3	27.9	10.7	2.1	76831
74553	KIOWA	16801	546	38.6	33.7	24.4	2.4	0.9	32103	33579	12	22	438	40.6	29.7	19.9	9.1	0.7	61892
74555	LANE	16539	437	46.0	31.1	18.5	3.2	1.1	27286	27731	5	5	349	27.5	23.8	34.7	11.7	2.3	88200
74557	MOYERS	13731	69	49.3	29.0	17.4	1.4	2.9	25546	27950	4	3	59	40.7	22.0	33.9	3.4	0.0	65000
74558	NASHOBA	14001	252	52.0	26.6	19.0	2.0	0.4	23903	24410	3	2	203	40.9	28.6	22.2	7.4	1.0	61154
74560	PITTSBURG	15004	212	37.7	31.1	27.4	2.8	0.9	31698	33272	11	21	168	33.9	31.5	20.2	12.5	1.8	72667
74561	QUINTON	18206	2048	41.7	29.5	23.7	3.6	1.5	31034	31859	10	17	1699	40.3	28.1	20.7	9.2	1.6	59622
74562	RATTAN	16462	684	38.7	36.3	20.0	3.9	1.0	31541	32932	11	20	567	29.8	32.3	22.9	11.8	3.2	72907
74563	RED OAK	16504	859	40.6	29.2	23.7	4.7	1.7	29821	31228	8	12	690	37.7	28.7	25.7	4.8	3.2	62292
74567	SNOW	19789	134	36.6	32.8	25.4	3.0	2.2	35358	36521	19	38	116	35.3	25.0	21.6	12.9	5.2	70000
74569	STRINGTOWN	15119	269	43.1	34.2	18.2	3.0	1.5	28879	29033	7	9	222	43.2	26.1	23.9	5.4	1.4	62000
74570	STUART	17023	320	44.7	27.2	21.9	3.8	2.5	28072	28817	6	7	273	27.1	26.7	29.3	13.9	2.9	81923
74571	TALIHINA	15838	1142	40.1	33.0	21.7	3.4	1.8	31235	32595	10	18	815	41.7	30.6	22.5	4.4	0.9	61172
	OKLAHOMA	22515		27.2	29.2	32.3	7.2	4.0	43746	45901				20.4	25.6	36.1	15.4	2.4	96076
	UNITED STATES	27277		20.9	24.4	35.3	11.7	7.6	54719	56938				9.3	13.1	31.6	32.6	13.5	162279

ZIP CODE #	POST OFFICE NAME	FINANCIAL SERVICES: Auto Loan	FINANCIAL SERVICES: Home Loan	FINANCIAL SERVICES: Invest-ments	FINANCIAL SERVICES: Retire-ment Plans	THE HOME: Home Improvements: Home Repair	THE HOME: Home Improvements: Lawn & Garden	THE HOME: Furnishings: Comput-ers & Hard-ware-Personal	THE HOME: Furnishings: Major Appli-ances	THE HOME: Furnishings: TV, Radio, Sound Equip-ment	THE HOME: Furnishings: Furni-ture	ENTERTAINMENT: Dine out/ Carry out	ENTERTAINMENT: Sports Equip-ment	ENTERTAINMENT: Fees & Tickets	ENTERTAINMENT: Toys & Games	ENTERTAINMENT: Travel	ENTERTAINMENT: Cable TV	PERSONAL: Apparel & Services	PERSONAL: Auto Repairs	PERSONAL: Health Insur-ance	PERSONAL: Pets & Supplies
74132	TULSA	116	117	109	115	113	113	107	112	106	112	107	85	107	110	107	106	74	107	106	131
74133	TULSA	118	109	98	112	104	100	117	106	114	120	116	86	114	118	110	111	82	112	104	127
74134	TULSA	91	74	63	76	69	67	89	76	87	90	89	63	80	91	78	84	62	84	75	93
74135	TULSA	82	80	81	82	81	85	85	83	87	84	87	62	85	84	85	89	60	86	91	98
74136	TULSA	101	79	75	85	76	77	101	85	100	100	101	70	91	101	89	98	71	96	87	104
74137	TULSA	185	217	225	228	224	197	198	196	187	211	189	156	222	189	213	178	139	192	176	225
74145	TULSA	84	76	71	79	74	78	84	78	86	83	86	61	81	86	80	86	60	83	85	94
74146	TULSA	75	60	51	61	56	55	73	62	72	73	73	51	65	74	63	69	51	70	61	76
74171	TULSA	111	117	159	116	135	138	105	124	111	119	109	77	116	100	122	116	75	118	138	140
74301	VINITA	84	60	86	58	62	87	64	80	71	58	69	61	51	70	63	78	46	74	86	95
74330	ADAIR	96	75	90	72	76	94	75	89	81	73	80	66	63	82	72	87	54	83	91	106
74331	AFTON	95	74	111	72	80	100	75	94	81	71	79	69	64	78	78	87	53	87	97	110
74332	BIG CABIN	93	69	93	66	71	94	70	87	77	66	75	65	57	77	69	84	50	80	90	103
74333	BLUEJACKET	80	57	83	56	60	82	59	75	65	54	64	57	47	65	59	72	42	69	79	90
74337	CHOUTEAU	89	68	75	66	67	84	69	78	75	68	74	59	58	78	64	80	50	75	81	95
74338	COLCORD	83	60	68	58	59	79	62	72	69	60	67	55	50	72	56	75	45	68	76	88
74339	COMMERCE	61	49	44	50	47	57	58	56	61	53	59	43	50	62	50	64	41	58	62	68
74342	EUCHA	73	56	77	53	59	76	56	70	62	55	61	51	48	61	57	68	40	65	75	83
74343	FAIRLAND	73	53	76	52	56	76	56	70	62	51	61	53	45	61	55	68	40	65	75	83
74344	GROVE	74	65	86	63	71	80	65	76	69	66	68	52	61	65	68	73	46	73	82	88
74346	JAY	76	57	70	56	58	74	61	70	66	58	65	53	51	67	58	71	44	67	74	84
74347	KANSAS	86	61	71	60	61	81	64	74	71	62	70	57	51	74	58	77	47	70	79	91
74352	LOCUST GROVE	77	57	64	56	56	74	61	68	67	58	65	53	50	68	55	72	44	66	73	83
74354	MIAMI	71	59	67	59	60	74	63	70	68	59	67	52	57	68	61	73	45	68	77	82
74358	NORTH MIAMI	68	49	68	47	51	71	53	66	59	48	57	49	43	58	51	66	38	61	72	77
74359	OAKS	80	57	66	56	57	76	60	69	66	58	65	53	48	69	54	72	44	66	73	85
74360	PICHER	63	42	62	40	42	63	45	56	51	42	50	44	34	52	42	57	33	53	59	69
74361	PRYOR	82	72	74	72	72	84	74	80	78	71	77	60	68	78	72	83	52	78	86	94
74363	QUAPAW	75	56	71	54	57	74	57	69	63	55	62	52	47	64	55	68	41	64	71	82
74364	ROSE	82	56	73	54	56	79	59	72	67	57	66	56	46	69	55	74	44	68	76	88
74365	SALINA	86	61	71	60	61	81	64	74	71	62	69	57	51	74	58	77	47	70	78	90
74366	SPAVINAW	74	54	76	51	56	76	55	69	62	54	61	51	45	62	54	68	40	65	74	83
74367	STRANG	81	62	95	60	66	84	62	79	67	58	66	59	52	65	65	73	44	73	80	93
74368	TWIN OAKS	80	58	66	56	57	76	60	70	67	59	65	54	48	69	55	73	44	66	74	85
74369	WELCH	78	55	82	54	57	82	60	74	64	51	63	59	46	63	59	71	41	69	80	90
74370	WYANDOTTE	77	57	84	55	60	79	58	73	64	55	63	55	48	63	59	69	42	68	75	87
74401	MUSKOGEE	66	56	56	56	55	65	61	62	66	58	64	47	56	65	57	70	44	64	70	75
74403	MUSKOGEE	76	68	68	69	68	78	72	75	76	69	74	56	67	75	69	79	51	75	81	89
74421	BEGGS	84	71	68	69	69	79	71	76	75	71	74	57	64	78	66	78	50	74	78	91
74422	BOYNTON	85	57	84	54	58	85	61	76	69	57	67	59	46	70	58	77	45	71	80	93
74423	BRAGGS	80	57	66	56	57	76	59	69	66	58	65	53	48	69	54	72	43	66	73	84
74425	CANADIAN	68	59	78	55	64	74	57	69	62	60	60	47	54	58	61	66	40	66	76	80
74426	CHECOTAH	78	63	85	60	67	83	64	78	70	63	68	55	57	67	65	76	46	73	84	91
74427	COOKSON	66	58	77	54	64	73	56	68	61	59	59	46	53	57	60	65	40	65	74	79
74428	COUNCIL HILL	79	55	80	53	57	80	58	73	65	54	63	55	45	65	56	71	42	67	76	88
74429	COWETA	87	84	73	85	81	85	83	83	83	82	83	64	80	86	80	84	57	82	84	99
74432	EUFAULA	70	58	77	55	63	75	59	70	64	59	62	49	53	61	61	69	42	67	76	82
74434	FORT GIBSON	85	81	73	80	78	85	77	81	79	77	79	62	74	82	75	82	54	79	83	97
74435	GORE	81	58	83	56	60	82	60	76	66	55	65	57	48	66	59	73	43	70	79	90
74436	HASKELL	76	57	69	55	57	74	61	69	66	57	65	53	50	67	57	71	43	67	74	84
74437	HENRYETTA	67	49	60	48	49	66	53	61	59	50	57	46	44	59	50	64	39	59	67	74
74441	HULBERT	76	57	70	56	58	74	59	70	64	56	63	52	49	65	57	70	42	66	73	83
74442	INDIANOLA	80	58	83	56	61	82	60	75	66	56	65	56	48	65	59	72	43	69	79	89
74445	MORRIS	82	63	78	62	64	82	65	77	71	62	69	57	55	71	63	76	46	72	81	91
74447	OKMULGEE	69	54	61	54	54	69	60	65	65	56	63	49	52	64	56	69	43	64	72	78
74450	OKTAHA	87	63	89	61	65	88	64	82	71	60	70	61	51	71	63	78	46	75	85	97
74451	PARK HILL	78	60	88	58	63	80	60	75	65	58	64	56	51	64	62	70	43	70	76	89
74452	PEGGS	86	62	71	60	61	82	64	75	71	63	70	57	52	74	58	78	47	71	79	91
74454	PORTER	86	61	80	58	61	84	63	77	70	60	69	59	50	72	59	77	46	72	81	93
74455	PORUM	70	49	71	46	50	71	51	64	58	50	57	49	41	58	50	64	38	60	68	78
74457	PROCTOR	73	52	68	50	52	72	54	66	60	51	59	50	43	61	51	66	39	61	69	79
74462	STIGLER	72	52	72	51	54	73	57	69	63	52	61	51	46	62	55	69	41	65	74	81
74463	TAFT	87	57	84	53	56	85	61	76	70	58	68	60	45	71	57	78	45	72	81	94
74464	TAHLEQUAH	67	54	55	54	53	61	64	61	65	59	64	48	55	65	56	67	44	63	64	74
74467	WAGONER	80	66	77	65	67	82	68	77	73	65	72	57	61	73	67	78	48	74	83	91
74469	WARNER	70	50	70	49	52	72	54	67	60	49	58	50	43	59	52	66	38	62	71	78
74470	WEBBERS FALLS	70	50	71	48	52	71	51	65	57	48	56	49	41	56	51	62	37	60	68	77
74471	WELLING	88	63	79	61	64	85	65	78	72	63	71	60	52	74	61	79	47	73	82	94
74472	WHITEFIELD	69	49	71	48	51	70	51	65	56	47	55	48	41	56	50	62	37	59	67	77
74501	MCALESTER	76	61	73	61	63	77	65	73	70	61	68	54	57	69	63	75	46	71	79	86
74523	ANTLERS	64	46	65	45	48	66	49	61	55	45	53	46	39	54	48	60	35	57	65	73
74525	ATOKA	66	47	66	46	49	67	51	62	56	47	55	47	41	56	49	62	37	58	66	74
74528	BLANCO	69	49	71	48	51	70	51	64	56	47	55	48	41	56	50	62	36	59	67	77
74531	CALVIN	68	49	70	47	50	69	50	63	55	46	54	48	40	55	49	61	36	58	66	75
74533	CANEY	77	55	79	53	57	78	56	72	62	52	61	54	45	62	56	69	41	66	75	85
74534	CENTRAHOMA	69	49	71	48	51	70	51	64	56	47	55	48	40	56	50	62	36	59	67	76
74536	CLAYTON	63	45	64	44	47	65	48	60	54	44	52	45	39	53	47	59	35	56	65	71
74538	COALGATE	57	42	56	41	44	57	47	54	51	43	50	40	39	50	45	56	34	52	59	64
74540	DAISY	75	53	77	52	55	76	55	70	61	51	60	52	44	60	54	67	39	64	73	83
74543	FINLEY	81	58	83	56	60	82	59	76	66	55	65	57	48	65	59	73	43	69	79	90
74547	HARTSHORNE	69	50	70	48	51	71	53	66	59	48	57	49	42	58	52	65	38	61	71	78
74549	KIAMICHI CHRISTIAN M	60	43	62	42	45	61	44	56	49	41	48	42	35	49	44	54	32	51	58	67
74552	KINTA	72	52	74	50	54	73	53	68	59	50	58	51	43	59	53	65	38	62	70	80
74553	KIOWA	72	51	74	50	53	73	53	67	58	49	57	50	42	58	52	64	38	61	70	80
74555	LANE	65	46	66	45	48	66	48	61	53	44	52	45	38	52	47	58	34	56	63	72
74557	MOYERS	63	45	64	43	46	64	46	59	51	43	50	44	37	51	46	56	33	54	61	70
74558	NASHOBA	61	43	62	42	45	62	45	57	49	41	49	43	36	49	44	54	32	52	59	67
74560	PITTSBURG	70	50	71	48	52	71	51	65	57	48	56	49	41	56	51	62	37	60	68	77
74561	QUINTON	64	54	72	51	59	70	54	65	58	55	57	46	49	55	56	63	38	62	72	76
74562	RATTAN	72	51	74	50	53	73	53	67	58	49	57	50	42	58	52	64	38	61	70	80
74563	RED OAK	71	51	72	50	53	73	54	68	60	49	59	51	44	60	53	67	39	63	73	80
74567	SNOW	80	58	83	56	60	82	59	75	66	55	64	56	47	65	59	72	43	69	78	89
74569	STRINGTOWN	66	47	67	46	49	67	48	61	54	45	53	46	39	53	48	59	35	56	64	73
74570	STUART	72	52	74	50	54	74	53	68	59	50	58	51	43	59	53	65	38	62	71	81
74571	TALIHINA	71	51	72	50	53	74	55	68	61	50	59	51	44	60	53	67	39	63	73	80
	OKLAHOMA	87	75	78	75	74	84	79	82	82	77	81	63	73	83	75	85	56	82	86	98
	UNITED STATES	100	100	100	100	100	100	100	100	100	100	100	100	100	100	100	100	100	100	100	100

ZIP CODE			POPULATION			2000-2009 ANNUAL RATE		HOUSEHOLDS					FAMILIES		
#	POST OFFICE NAME	COUNTY FIPS CODE	2000	2009	2014	% Rate	State Centile	2000	2009	2014	% Annual Rate 2000-2009	2009 Average HH Size	2000	2009	% Annual Rate 2000-2009
74572	TUPELO	029	1507	1457	1424	-0.4	22	555	536	523	-0.4	2.72	418	395	-0.6
74574	TUSKAHOMA	077	2396	2418	2401	0.1	49	926	955	955	0.3	2.43	677	683	0.1
74576	WARDVILLE	005	345	366	373	0.6	73	140	163	171	1.7	1.71	102	116	1.4
74577	WHITESBORO	079	193	198	198	0.3	60	76	79	80	0.4	2.51	55	56	0.2
74578	WILBURTON	077	6469	6260	6105	-0.4	22	2353	2299	2248	-0.3	2.47	1680	1603	-0.5
74601	PONCA CITY	071	20532	19734	19254	-0.4	22	8368	8100	7912	-0.4	2.41	5403	5078	-0.7
74604	PONCA CITY	113	13246	13109	12975	-0.1	38	5180	5218	5176	0.1	2.45	3917	3857	-0.2
74630	BILLINGS	103	848	774	745	-1.0	7	277	253	243	-1.0	2.49	204	181	-1.3
74631	BLACKWELL	071	8355	7995	7782	-0.5	15	3330	3205	3122	-0.4	2.46	2302	2154	-0.7
74632	BRAMAN	071	602	606	603	0.1	49	251	257	256	0.3	2.36	172	171	-0.1
74633	BURBANK	113	521	520	518	0.0	43	222	227	227	0.2	2.29	160	158	-0.1
74636	DEER CREEK	053	256	236	225	-0.9	8	100	92	88	-0.9	2.57	70	63	-1.1
74637	FAIRFAX	113	2138	2017	1969	-0.6	13	876	832	815	-0.6	2.38	587	539	-0.9
74640	HUNTER	047	449	432	427	-0.4	22	186	182	180	-0.2	2.37	139	133	-0.5
74641	KAW CITY	071	551	534	522	-0.3	27	234	231	226	-0.1	2.31	176	169	-0.4
74643	LAMONT	053	625	577	550	-0.9	8	253	234	223	-0.8	2.47	176	159	-1.1
74644	MARLAND	103	571	582	579	0.2	55	201	211	211	0.5	2.76	155	158	0.2
74646	NARDIN	071	221	227	227	0.3	60	85	88	88	0.4	2.58	69	70	0.2
74647	NEWKIRK	071	3710	3614	3535	-0.3	27	1459	1440	1412	-0.1	2.46	1039	1001	-0.4
74650	RALSTON	117	685	660	649	-0.4	22	279	273	269	-0.2	2.42	206	196	-0.5
74651	RED ROCK	103	717	730	727	0.2	55	245	257	258	0.5	2.84	188	193	0.3
74652	SHIDLER	113	995	997	1001	0.0	43	432	443	447	0.3	2.25	304	303	0.0
74653	TONKAWA	071	3950	3881	3815	-0.2	33	1440	1423	1396	-0.1	2.51	983	945	-0.4
74701	DURANT	013	18871	20754	21680	1.0	82	7461	8213	8603	1.0	2.41	4868	5232	0.8
74723	BENNINGTON	013	1657	1780	1864	0.8	78	628	686	722	1.0	2.59	499	535	0.8
74724	BETHEL	089	1640	1629	1618	-0.1	38	607	621	622	0.2	2.62	462	463	0.0
74726	BOKCHITO	013	2127	2295	2402	0.8	78	851	926	971	0.9	2.48	608	643	0.6
74727	BOSWELL	023	2163	2081	2027	-0.4	22	872	854	837	-0.2	2.44	607	583	-0.4
74728	BROKEN BOW	089	10799	10742	10656	-0.1	38	4108	4207	4211	0.3	2.52	2986	2989	0.0
74729	CADDO	013	2268	2479	2596	1.0	82	867	957	1007	1.1	2.55	624	671	0.8
74730	CALERA	013	3418	3742	3935	1.0	82	1309	1452	1532	1.1	2.53	964	1042	0.8
74731	CARTWRIGHT	013	1490	1638	1713	1.0	82	611	682	717	1.2	2.40	424	459	0.9
74733	COLBERT	013	2941	3211	3356	1.0	82	1143	1264	1325	1.1	2.51	813	873	0.8
74734	EAGLETOWN	089	1133	1254	1276	1.1	84	454	518	533	1.4	2.42	328	367	1.2
74735	FORT TOWSON	023	2367	2278	2223	-0.4	22	938	911	892	-0.3	2.50	690	657	-0.5
74736	GARVIN	089	809	779	766	-0.4	22	310	307	303	-0.1	2.54	239	232	-0.3
74738	GRANT	023	727	705	690	-0.3	27	282	279	275	-0.1	2.53	215	209	-0.3
74740	HAWORTH	089	1752	1693	1667	-0.4	22	676	667	661	-0.1	2.54	477	458	-0.4
74741	HENDRIX	013	1623	1743	1824	0.8	78	632	690	725	1.0	2.53	476	507	0.7
74743	HUGO	023	8553	8700	8625	0.2	55	3487	3642	3637	0.5	2.33	2314	2351	0.2
74745	IDABEL	089	10401	10177	10041	-0.2	33	4059	4055	4028	0.0	2.43	2782	2710	-0.3
74748	KENEFIC	069	497	534	545	0.8	78	202	221	226	1.0	2.42	152	163	0.8
74754	RINGOLD	089	134	131	129	-0.2	33	58	58	58	0.0	2.26	45	45	0.0
74755	RUFE	089	274	276	275	0.1	49	113	116	116	0.3	2.38	91	92	0.1
74756	SAWYER	023	456	446	437	-0.2	33	185	182	178	-0.2	2.45	140	136	-0.3
74759	SOPER	023	945	911	890	-0.4	22	396	391	384	-0.1	2.33	272	263	-0.4
74760	SPENCERVILLE	023	298	291	285	-0.3	27	115	113	111	-0.2	2.58	87	84	-0.4
74764	VALLIANT	089	4310	4340	4310	0.1	49	1646	1692	1692	0.3	2.54	1230	1237	0.1
74766	WRIGHT CITY	089	1840	1781	1757	-0.4	22	670	669	665	0.0	2.66	516	506	-0.2
74801	SHAWNEE	125	21838	22527	22970	0.3	60	8675	8961	9150	0.4	2.48	5945	5982	0.1
74804	SHAWNEE	125	19250	20967	21769	0.9	80	7141	7798	8125	1.0	2.48	5073	5409	0.7
74820	ADA	123	26275	27238	27746	0.4	64	10666	11189	11428	0.5	2.36	6913	7052	0.2
74824	AGRA	081	1525	1504	1493	-0.1	38	554	553	551	0.0	2.72	448	440	-0.2
74825	ALLEN	123	4491	4428	4438	-0.2	33	1630	1628	1637	0.0	2.62	1241	1215	-0.2
74826	ASHER	125	942	1050	1108	1.2	86	366	411	434	1.3	2.55	283	310	1.0
74827	ATWOOD	063	688	653	626	-0.6	13	289	277	266	-0.5	2.36	207	193	-0.8
74829	BOLEY	107	1505	1435	1397	-0.5	15	267	240	226	-1.1	2.67	173	151	-1.5
74831	BYARS	087	1244	1303	1372	0.5	68	480	515	545	0.8	2.53	367	386	0.5
74832	CARNEY	081	691	684	679	-0.1	38	269	270	268	0.0	2.53	200	196	-0.2
74833	CASTLE	107	601	548	521	-1.0	7	225	208	198	-0.8	2.61	173	156	-1.1
74834	CHANDLER	081	6110	6503	6642	0.7	75	2358	2545	2612	0.8	2.50	1724	1817	0.6
74839	DUSTIN	063	893	832	796	-0.8	9	347	328	314	-0.6	2.53	257	237	-0.9
74840	EARLSBORO	125	892	1403	1531	5.0	100	327	504	552	4.8	2.78	273	413	4.6
74842	FITTSTOWN	123	706	731	751	0.4	64	276	288	296	0.5	2.54	220	226	0.3
74843	FITZHUGH	123	207	214	220	0.4	64	76	79	82	0.4	2.71	61	62	0.2
74845	HANNA	091	520	512	518	-0.2	33	192	193	197	0.1	2.65	148	146	-0.1
74848	HOLDENVILLE	063	8394	8232	8026	-0.2	33	3000	2925	2842	-0.3	2.39	2038	1936	-0.6
74849	KONAWA	133	2977	3224	3267	0.9	80	1107	1213	1232	1.0	2.59	797	854	0.7
74850	LAMAR	063	277	261	250	-0.6	13	110	105	101	-0.5	2.49	87	82	-0.6
74851	MCLOUD	125	7722	8728	9198	1.3	89	2468	2844	3023	1.5	2.74	1977	2230	1.3
74852	MACOMB	125	1029	1013	1017	-0.2	33	369	366	370	-0.1	2.77	300	292	-0.3
74854	MAUD	125	4130	4153	4166	0.1	49	1601	1630	1641	0.2	2.52	1179	1172	-0.1
74855	MEEKER	081	4703	4918	4995	0.5	68	1735	1858	1901	0.7	2.61	1359	1428	0.5
74856	MILL CREEK	069	1446	1402	1382	-0.3	27	545	530	523	-0.3	2.65	419	400	-0.5
74857	NEWALLA	027	7580	8385	8904	1.1	84	2674	3066	3289	1.5	2.73	2192	2444	1.2
74859	OKEMAH	107	5758	5421	5212	-0.6	13	2290	2185	2107	-0.5	2.42	1558	1446	-0.8
74860	PADEN	107	1567	1635	1615	0.5	68	591	634	631	0.8	2.50	451	471	0.5
74864	PRAGUE	081	4456	4609	4662	0.4	64	1709	1798	1827	0.6	2.45	1250	1288	0.3
74865	ROFF	123	1418	1437	1460	0.1	49	533	545	555	0.2	2.64	404	404	0.0
74867	SASAKWA	133	730	703	693	-0.4	22	297	292	288	-0.2	2.41	211	202	-0.5
74868	SEMINOLE	133	11637	11202	11016	-0.4	22	4533	4391	4323	-0.3	2.52	3240	3073	-0.6
74869	SPARKS	081	295	288	285	-0.3	27	113	113	112	0.0	2.55	90	88	-0.2
74871	STONEWALL	123	2322	2440	2483	0.5	68	899	957	978	0.7	2.55	669	697	0.4
74872	STRATFORD	049	3106	3229	3278	0.4	64	1225	1275	1295	0.4	2.51	869	883	0.2
74873	TECUMSEH	125	10898	11086	11262	0.2	55	4065	4158	4235	0.2	2.62	3036	3019	-0.1
74875	TRYON	081	1553	1523	1504	-0.2	33	600	597	594	-0.1	2.55	433	421	-0.3
74878	WANETTE	125	1435	1527	1570	0.7	75	555	589	607	0.6	2.59	436	453	0.4
74880	WELEETKA	107	2383	2175	2070	-1.0	7	897	832	794	-0.8	2.51	618	559	-1.1
74881	WELLSTON	081	3702	3660	3637	-0.1	38	1394	1408	1409	0.1	2.60	1055	1046	-0.1
74883	WETUMKA	063	2175	2001	1905	-0.9	8	875	811	772	-0.8	2.32	568	510	-1.2
74884	WEWOKA	133	7408	7630	7674	0.3	60	2787	2912	2939	0.5	2.51	1925	1954	0.2
74901	ARKOMA	079	2186	2169	2162	-0.1	38	879	890	893	0.1	2.39	599	590	-0.2
74902	POCOLA	079	4491	4997	5218	1.2	86	1695	1926	2020	1.4	2.56	1311	1463	1.2
74930	BOKOSHE	079	3336	3431	3470	0.3	60	1269	1320	1335	0.4	2.60	938	953	0.2
74931	BUNCH	001	1719	1764	1796	0.3	60	581	612	628	0.6	2.88	447	461	0.3
	OKLAHOMA					0.7					0.8	2.46			0.6
	UNITED STATES					1.0					1.1	2.59			0.9

ZIP CODE #	POST OFFICE NAME	RACE (%) White 2000	White 2009	Black 2000	Black 2009	Asian/Pacific 2000	Asian/Pacific 2009	% Hispanic Origin 2000	% Hispanic Origin 2009	2009 AGE DISTRIBUTION (%) 0-4	5-9	10-14	15-19	20-24	25-44	45-64	65-84	85+	18+	MEDIAN AGE 2009	% 2009 Males	% 2009 Females
74572	TUPELO	74.9	72.2	0.1	0.1	0.1	0.3	2.1	2.7	8.2	8.2	8.2	7.2	4.0	25.0	25.1	12.3	1.8	70.9	36.8	49.3	50.7
74574	TUSKAHOMA	69.7	66.9	1.3	1.4	0.1	0.1	1.7	2.4	5.8	6.0	6.2	6.3	4.8	20.4	29.1	19.1	2.2	77.9	45.2	51.0	49.0
74576	WARDVILLE	66.3	63.1	15.4	16.7	0.0	0.0	3.8	4.9	2.7	2.7	2.5	3.3	9.6	45.9	24.6	7.9	0.8	89.9	38.0	77.3	22.7
74577	WHITESBORO	76.2	73.7	0.0	0.0	0.0	0.0	1.0	1.5	6.6	6.6	6.6	6.1	5.1	22.7	29.8	14.6	2.0	76.3	42.5	48.5	51.5
74578	WILBURTON	74.1	71.4	1.2	1.3	0.2	0.2	1.8	2.3	7.2	6.5	6.0	9.9	7.8	22.2	24.0	13.8	2.6	76.3	36.3	48.1	51.9
74601	PONCA CITY	79.5	76.3	3.3	3.5	0.5	0.7	5.0	7.0	8.0	7.3	6.7	6.9	6.8	24.9	25.4	11.7	2.3	73.8	36.3	48.4	51.6
74604	PONCA CITY	89.8	87.4	1.1	1.2	0.8	1.2	2.1	3.0	5.2	5.5	6.2	6.7	5.1	18.8	31.4	17.6	3.5	78.9	46.6	49.0	51.0
74630	BILLINGS	90.9	89.1	0.2	0.3	0.0	0.0	2.0	3.0	5.6	5.8	5.7	6.1	4.8	21.7	32.6	15.8	2.1	79.1	45.3	49.6	50.4
74631	BLACKWELL	87.3	84.1	0.1	0.1	0.5	0.7	5.5	7.7	7.4	7.3	7.0	7.0	5.9	22.6	25.5	14.3	3.0	73.9	38.4	48.3	51.7
74632	BRAMAN	90.7	88.3	0.2	0.2	0.0	0.0	2.3	3.3	5.8	5.9	6.1	5.1	5.0	21.8	30.7	17.5	2.1	79.2	45.2	48.7	51.3
74633	BURBANK	79.8	77.5	0.0	0.0	0.4	0.4	1.0	1.2	4.4	4.4	5.2	6.5	4.8	21.0	33.7	17.9	2.1	82.1	47.0	48.8	51.2
74636	DEER CREEK	94.5	92.8	0.0	0.0	0.0	0.0	3.1	4.7	6.8	7.6	6.8	7.2	4.7	21.2	26.7	16.1	3.0	74.2	41.2	49.6	50.4
74637	FAIRFAX	66.9	63.7	1.1	1.4	0.5	0.7	1.7	2.3	6.4	6.3	6.2	6.2	5.8	21.3	27.1	17.2	3.4	76.8	42.8	46.9	53.1
74640	HUNTER	97.5	96.8	0.0	0.0	0.0	0.0	1.6	2.3	5.3	5.8	6.5	5.6	4.4	20.8	32.4	16.2	3.0	78.7	46.1	50.7	49.3
74641	KAW CITY	87.6	86.3	0.0	0.0	0.0	0.0	1.5	2.1	5.1	5.8	6.0	6.7	4.1	18.2	33.5	19.1	1.5	79.2	47.6	48.9	51.1
74643	LAMONT	94.4	92.7	0.0	0.0	0.0	0.0	3.2	4.3	6.6	7.3	6.9	7.1	4.5	21.3	27.9	15.4	2.9	74.9	41.7	50.3	49.7
74644	MARLAND	53.0	50.3	0.5	0.7	0.2	0.2	3.2	4.0	6.5	6.7	7.4	8.4	5.7	21.8	29.6	12.5	1.4	74.1	39.0	48.1	51.9
74646	NARDIN	90.5	88.5	0.0	0.0	0.5	0.4	0.9	1.8	5.3	6.2	6.6	6.2	4.4	19.4	33.9	15.4	2.6	77.5	45.9	50.2	49.8
74647	NEWKIRK	83.7	81.2	0.7	0.7	0.1	0.1	1.9	2.7	5.9	6.2	6.3	6.8	5.3	23.4	28.9	15.1	2.1	77.3	42.1	50.5	49.5
74650	RALSTON	80.5	78.8	0.3	0.3	0.4	0.6	1.2	1.8	4.7	5.2	5.9	7.0	4.7	21.7	31.8	16.4	2.7	80.2	45.5	51.2	48.8
74651	RED ROCK	53.1	50.3	0.6	0.7	0.1	0.3	3.1	4.0	6.6	6.8	7.4	8.4	5.8	22.1	29.0	12.6	1.4	74.0	38.6	48.2	51.8
74652	SHIDLER	82.1	79.4	0.0	0.0	0.4	0.6	2.3	3.2	6.0	6.0	5.9	5.5	5.7	23.5	27.0	17.7	2.7	78.8	42.6	48.5	51.5
74653	TONKAWA	83.4	80.1	0.7	0.7	0.3	0.5	6.2	8.7	6.4	7.2	7.0	11.5	7.5	21.6	23.9	12.2	2.6	75.2	34.8	50.5	49.5
74701	DURANT	79.8	77.1	1.3	1.3	0.7	1.0	3.0	4.2	6.7	6.2	5.9	7.5	8.9	26.7	23.2	12.1	2.7	77.6	34.7	48.7	51.3
74723	BENNINGTON	73.9	71.4	0.2	0.3	0.1	0.2	1.9	2.6	6.7	7.0	7.2	6.3	4.6	22.2	29.2	14.9	1.9	75.2	41.8	49.5	50.5
74724	BETHEL	71.1	68.3	0.2	0.2	0.0	0.0	2.2	2.8	6.9	7.2	7.2	6.2	4.5	24.9	28.4	13.3	1.4	74.8	39.7	51.4	48.6
74726	BOKCHITO	79.8	76.9	0.1	0.1	0.2	0.3	2.3	3.3	6.4	6.4	6.6	6.7	5.2	23.8	27.5	15.2	2.2	76.5	41.1	49.1	50.9
74727	BOSWELL	68.3	65.4	5.3	5.4	0.2	0.3	2.2	3.1	6.6	6.2	7.1	7.4	4.7	22.7	27.8	15.1	2.5	75.4	41.0	49.4	50.6
74728	BROKEN BOW	72.3	69.0	4.9	5.3	0.3	0.4	3.8	5.2	7.8	7.3	7.3	6.9	5.9	23.9	25.6	13.0	2.1	73.2	37.6	48.0	52.0
74729	CADDO	79.5	76.4	0.4	0.4	0.2	0.3	1.7	2.3	6.1	6.2	6.3	6.7	5.4	24.2	26.8	15.2	3.0	77.0	41.0	49.4	50.6
74730	CALERA	82.0	79.1	0.3	0.3	0.2	0.3	2.9	4.2	7.3	7.3	7.2	6.1	5.0	25.1	25.8	13.8	2.4	74.3	39.0	48.2	51.8
74731	CARTWRIGHT	85.8	83.0	1.0	1.1	0.1	0.1	3.0	4.2	6.0	6.4	6.8	6.3	5.1	23.9	29.8	14.4	1.2	76.8	41.7	49.6	50.4
74733	COLBERT	78.8	75.9	7.2	7.7	0.1	0.2	2.4	3.5	6.3	6.4	6.5	6.7	5.3	25.0	27.9	13.4	2.6	76.9	40.5	48.1	51.9
74734	EAGLETOWN	77.9	75.1	5.5	6.3	0.2	0.2	2.5	3.3	6.2	6.3	6.5	6.3	5.6	24.4	28.9	14.2	1.6	77.2	40.9	49.4	50.6
74735	FORT TOWSON	82.8	80.8	2.4	2.5	0.2	0.3	1.2	1.6	5.8	5.7	6.0	5.9	5.0	23.5	29.5	16.6	2.0	78.9	43.6	48.9	51.1
74736	GARVIN	81.0	78.4	4.2	4.7	0.2	0.4	2.0	2.8	5.9	6.0	6.5	7.2	4.9	24.1	28.5	15.3	1.5	77.3	41.6	49.0	51.0
74738	GRANT	68.0	65.5	13.6	13.9	0.1	0.1	1.2	1.7	5.4	5.5	6.2	7.5	6.0	22.8	30.6	14.3	1.6	78.4	42.2	48.7	51.3
74740	HAWORTH	71.7	68.2	19.2	21.2	0.1	0.1	1.3	1.8	5.8	7.0	7.1	8.1	5.1	23.3	28.4	12.8	2.3	75.3	39.7	48.6	51.4
74741	HENDRIX	77.2	74.3	1.8	1.9	0.4	0.5	1.5	2.1	7.2	7.2	7.3	7.1	5.7	24.6	25.8	13.4	1.7	73.8	38.5	49.1	50.9
74743	HUGO	63.5	60.4	16.0	16.9	0.2	0.3	1.7	2.3	6.8	6.6	6.5	6.8	5.8	22.9	26.1	15.0	3.5	76.1	40.6	46.6	53.4
74745	IDABEL	63.2	59.9	19.3	20.2	0.4	0.6	4.0	5.5	7.7	7.3	7.2	7.1	6.0	24.0	25.6	12.8	2.3	73.4	37.3	47.5	52.5
74748	KENEFIC	81.1	80.7	0.4	0.4	0.2	0.2	2.4	2.4	5.6	6.0	6.4	6.6	5.1	24.2	29.8	14.8	1.7	78.1	42.0	50.9	49.1
74754	RINGOLD	81.2	77.9	0.0	0.0	0.0	0.0	2.3	3.1	6.1	6.1	6.1	6.1	6.9	23.7	30.5	13.0	1.5	78.6	40.4	49.6	50.4
74755	RUFE	86.5	84.4	1.1	1.4	0.0	0.0	0.7	1.1	5.4	6.2	6.9	7.6	4.3	24.3	29.7	14.5	1.1	76.8	41.2	50.4	49.6
74756	SAWYER	80.0	78.0	3.3	3.4	0.0	0.2	1.3	1.6	6.1	6.1	6.3	6.7	4.7	23.3	30.3	15.0	1.6	77.6	42.9	50.0	50.0
74759	SOPER	72.0	69.0	1.4	1.4	0.0	0.0	1.0	1.4	6.1	6.0	6.5	6.5	4.7	23.6	28.5	15.8	2.2	77.4	42.0	47.9	52.1
74760	SPENCERVILLE	79.9	78.4	3.4	3.4	0.0	0.0	1.3	1.7	5.8	6.2	6.2	6.9	4.8	24.1	29.6	14.8	1.7	77.7	42.4	50.5	49.5
74764	VALLIANT	81.3	78.7	3.3	3.8	0.1	0.1	1.3	1.9	6.7	6.7	7.1	7.2	5.3	24.7	27.5	12.9	2.0	75.1	39.1	49.7	50.3
74766	WRIGHT CITY	64.2	61.6	3.7	4.1	0.0	0.0	2.1	2.8	7.4	7.2	7.2	7.0	6.0	24.4	27.7	11.7	1.5	74.0	38.0	48.6	51.4
74801	SHAWNEE	77.1	74.5	3.9	4.2	0.6	0.7	2.6	3.5	7.9	7.3	6.8	6.7	6.2	25.9	25.0	12.3	2.0	74.1	36.4	49.2	50.8
74804	SHAWNEE	81.6	78.9	2.3	2.5	1.3	1.9	2.4	3.2	6.4	6.5	6.5	9.2	8.6	24.2	24.3	12.0	2.2	76.8	35.3	49.2	50.8
74820	ADA	75.7	72.8	2.4	2.6	0.6	0.9	2.5	3.4	6.5	6.1	5.9	7.4	8.9	25.3	24.2	13.1	2.6	77.7	36.2	48.4	51.6
74824	AGRA	91.6	89.8	0.0	0.0	0.1	0.1	1.2	1.8	8.2	8.1	7.8	6.1	4.9	24.5	25.9	13.3	1.1	72.0	36.9	50.6	49.4
74825	ALLEN	72.9	69.9	0.8	0.9	0.1	0.2	2.0	2.7	6.1	6.2	6.4	6.9	6.1	26.5	28.3	11.8	1.8	77.0	39.3	49.1	50.9
74826	ASHER	80.7	78.3	0.0	0.0	0.0	0.0	2.8	3.7	6.4	6.6	6.9	6.5	4.9	24.9	28.4	13.9	1.7	76.2	40.5	51.1	48.9
74827	ATWOOD	81.9	78.6	0.0	0.0	0.6	0.8	2.3	3.2	6.7	7.0	7.2	6.6	4.4	23.7	27.1	15.2	2.0	74.9	40.7	51.6	48.4
74829	BOLEY	36.5	33.7	52.5	54.2	0.1	0.1	2.7	3.5	3.7	3.6	3.2	4.0	8.2	44.0	23.7	8.2	1.5	87.0	37.5	73.5	26.5
74831	BYARS	85.7	83.3	2.1	2.3	0.2	0.3	3.2	4.5	6.6	6.9	7.0	5.5	4.8	23.0	29.1	15.0	2.0	76.0	41.8	50.5	49.5
74832	CARNEY	89.0	87.1	1.2	1.3	0.0	0.0	1.0	1.5	7.5	7.5	7.6	7.9	5.3	22.1	28.7	12.6	1.0	72.5	39.3	50.9	49.1
74833	CASTLE	72.5	69.5	6.8	7.3	0.0	0.0	1.2	1.6	6.0	6.4	6.6	7.3	4.9	23.7	28.6	14.8	1.6	76.3	41.1	50.2	49.8
74834	CHANDLER	84.5	82.3	5.5	5.8	0.4	0.6	1.5	2.2	6.6	6.9	6.9	7.2	5.5	23.9	27.5	13.1	2.4	75.3	39.8	49.3	50.7
74839	DUSTIN	61.7	57.6	1.7	1.8	0.1	0.1	1.8	2.4	5.0	5.0	5.6	8.1	5.5	21.9	29.8	16.9	2.0	79.2	44.0	51.1	48.9
74840	EARLSBORO	78.9	75.5	5.4	6.3	0.4	0.8	2.1	3.1	6.1	6.3	6.6	6.8	5.4	23.0	31.2	13.6	1.1	77.0	41.8	49.4	50.6
74842	FITTSTOWN	81.0	78.5	0.0	0.0	0.1	0.1	1.7	2.5	6.3	6.8	7.1	6.7	3.7	23.8	29.5	14.5	1.5	75.6	41.5	48.8	51.2
74843	FITZHUGH	81.2	79.0	0.0	0.0	0.0	0.0	1.9	2.3	6.1	7.0	7.0	6.5	3.7	23.8	29.4	15.0	1.4	74.8	41.8	49.1	50.9
74845	HANNA	61.6	59.2	0.8	0.8	0.0	0.0	2.3	2.9	8.4	7.6	6.8	7.2	7.2	21.1	27.1	12.5	2.0	73.0	38.1	50.6	49.4
74848	HOLDENVILLE	72.8	69.9	6.3	6.6	0.3	0.4	2.7	3.7	5.6	5.4	5.5	6.0	6.4	27.2	26.0	14.2	3.7	80.2	40.5	53.7	46.3
74849	KONAWA	69.8	69.9	1.4	1.6	0.2	0.2	2.0	2.1	6.6	7.1	7.3	6.9	5.9	23.4	25.8	14.3	2.6	74.7	39.3	49.2	50.8
74850	LAMAR	81.6	79.3	0.4	0.4	0.0	0.0	2.5	3.4	5.0	5.4	5.7	6.1	5.0	20.7	33.0	17.2	1.9	80.1	46.4	49.0	51.0
74851	MCLOUD	80.2	77.3	4.0	4.0	0.7	1.0	2.7	3.8	6.0	6.1	6.3	6.4	6.3	30.9	26.7	10.0	1.2	77.6	37.2	44.4	55.6
74852	MACOMB	85.5	82.2	0.7	0.7	0.2	0.3	1.7	2.4	5.9	6.0	6.2	6.1	5.3	21.6	32.3	15.6	0.9	78.1	43.9	50.0	50.0
74854	MAUD	80.1	78.6	0.5	0.6	0.2	0.2	1.7	2.1	6.7	6.2	6.2	6.7	5.1	23.2	28.7	15.1	2.1	76.7	41.4	49.4	50.6
74855	MEEKER	88.0	86.0	0.8	0.9	0.1	0.2	1.4	1.9	6.4	6.3	6.7	7.2	5.8	24.5	28.1	13.0	2.0	75.7	40.0	49.0	51.0
74856	MILL CREEK	73.1	73.0	0.0	0.0	0.6	0.6	1.0	1.1	6.1	6.8	6.3	6.7	4.8	24.3	30.2	12.9	1.9	76.7	41.5	47.8	52.2
74857	NEWALLA	87.2	84.7	1.0	1.1	0.4	0.5	1.9	2.8	5.5	6.7	7.3	7.9	5.2	26.6	32.0	8.4	0.5	75.6	38.8	51.3	48.7
74859	OKEMAH	70.3	67.3	2.8	3.2	0.1	0.1	1.6	2.3	6.9	6.3	6.3	7.1	5.9	22.5	26.2	15.4	3.3	76.2	40.7	47.5	52.5
74860	PADEN	78.8	76.3	3.7	3.9	0.1	0.2	0.8	1.2	6.2	6.5	6.6	6.1	5.0	23.7	29.2	15.0	1.6	76.9	41.5	50.1	49.9
74864	PRAGUE	85.0	82.8	2.4	2.6	0.2	0.3	1.2	1.8	5.6	5.7	6.3	7.6	5.5	22.5	29.0	15.0	2.9	77.3	42.4	48.7	51.3
74865	ROFF	83.4	81.1	0.1	0.1	0.1	0.2	1.4	2.1	6.7	7.0	7.0	6.1	4.7	24.6	27.7	14.2	2.0	75.5	39.9	48.8	51.2
74867	SASAKWA	70.8	70.6	2.5	2.6	0.0	0.0	2.6	2.7	6.1	6.5	7.0	7.4	4.8	20.8	30.2	15.4	1.8	75.7	42.7	49.9	50.1
74868	SEMINOLE	76.0	75.9	3.0	3.1	0.3	0.2	2.3	2.4	7.0	6.7	6.7	6.9	6.2	23.5	26.1	13.9	2.9	75.7	38.9	48.5	51.5
74869	SPARKS	88.5	86.5	2.0	2.1	0.3	0.3	0.3	0.3	4.9	6.9	6.6	9.4	4.2	22.6	32.6	11.8	1.0	75.3	42.3	50.7	49.3
74871	STONEWALL	76.2	73.6	1.9	2.0	0.0	0.0	1.9	2.6	5.8	5.9	6.1	6.9	5.5	23.8	30.1	14.3	1.6	78.0	42.0	48.3	51.7
74872	STRATFORD	84.1	82.0	0.7	0.7	0.1	0.2	1.4	2.0	7.2	7.2	7.0	6.6	5.4	21.9	26.1	15.5	3.2	74.5	40.6	48.3	51.7
74873	TECUMSEH	81.3	78.7	1.9	2.1	0.3	0.4	1.9	2.6	6.4	6.4	6.6	7.7	5.7	24.5	27.9	12.7	2.0	75.6	39.3	49.3	50.7
74875	TRYON	86.8	85.0	0.5	0.6	0.1	0.1	1.5	2.1	6.6	6.6	6.8	7.0	5.1	23.4	28.4	15.0	1.2	75.6	40.8	51.8	48.2
74878	WANETTE	85.9	83.2	0.1	0.1	0.2	0.3	0.8	1.2	5.9	6.2	6.5	6.8	5.2	22.9	29.7	15.2	1.6	77.2	42.0	51.9	48.1
74880	WELEETKA	61.5	57.5	7.4	8.4	0.0	0.0	1.6	2.1	6.7	6.9	6.5	5.8	5.7	22.0	28.6	14.7	3.0	76.2	41.2	49.2	50.8
74881	WELLSTON	87.8	85.4	3.0	3.2	0.1	0.2	2.3	3.1	6.7	7.0	7.3	6.9	5.4	23.0	30.3	12.1	1.2	74.6	39.8	50.2	49.8
74883	WETUMKA	63.3	60.3	4.4	4.6	0.0	0.0	2.4	3.1	6.4	6.3	6.3	7.2	5.2	23.0	25.7	16.2	3.5	76.1	41.0	47.5	52.5
74884	WEWOKA	60.8	61.2	13.0	12.7	0.3	0.4	2.2	2.1	6.7	6.4	6.5	7.3	6.0	22.0	26.8	15.4	2.8	75.7	40.9	48.3	51.7
74901	ARKOMA	89.1	87.0	0.4	0.5	0.3	0.5	1.8	2.6	6.8	6.5	6.0	5.8	5.8	25.2	26.5	15.1	2.2	77.1	40.2	48.4	51.6
74902	POCOLA	86.7	84.3	3.0	3.0	0.3	0.4	1.8	2.7	6.1	6.4	6.9	7.1	5.5	26.0	29.0	11.5	1.5	76.2	38.9	48.9	51.1
74930	BOKOSHE	81.2	78.3	0.1	0.1	0.4	0.5	1.6	2.4	7.8	7.6	7.7	7.3	5.7	25.4	24.6	12.5	1.4	72.3	36.3	49.8	50.2
74931	BUNCH	35.5	32.9	0.0	0.0	0.1	0.1	1.5	1.6	6.2	8.3	8.1	7.9	6.0	23.2	28.2	10.8	1.2	72.3	36.5	50.9	49.1
	OKLAHOMA	76.2	73.0	7.6	7.8	1.4	2.0	5.2	7.0	6.9	6.6	6.5	7.1	7.2	26.2	25.9	11.6	2.0	75.9	36.8	49.3	50.7
	UNITED STATES	75.1	72.0	12.3	12.7	3.8	4.6	12.5	15.7	6.8	6.7	6.6	7.1	6.9	27.0	26.0	10.9	1.9	75.7	36.9	49.2	50.8

#	POST OFFICE NAME	2009 Per Capita Income	2009 HH Income Base	2009 Household Income Distribution (%): Less than $25,000	$25,000 to $49,999	$50,000 to $99,999	$100,000 to $149,999	$150,000 or More	Median Household Income: 2009	2014	2009 National Centile	2009 State Centile	2009 Home Value Base	2009 Home Value Distribution (%): Less than $50,000	$50,000 to $89,999	$90,000 to $174,999	$175,000 to $399,999	$400,000 or More	2009 Median Home Value
74572	TUPELO	15418	536	43.7	26.5	24.4	3.4	2.1	31087	33035	10	17	452	42.0	21.5	25.9	8.2	2.4	65161
74574	TUSKAHOMA	15590	955	43.0	32.4	19.7	3.2	1.7	28915	30045	7	9	760	33.0	31.1	26.3	7.1	2.5	71500
74576	WARDVILLE	25693	163	35.0	27.6	30.7	6.1	0.6	34484	36804	16	33	144	31.9	22.2	32.6	12.5	0.7	83333
74577	WHITESBORO	11439	79	51.9	30.4	16.5	1.3	0.0	23569	24159	3	2	62	45.2	29.0	24.2	1.6	0.0	56000
74578	WILBURTON	16148	2299	44.3	29.1	22.1	2.4	2.0	28284	29151	6	8	1620	33.8	36.5	26.2	3.0	0.5	67045
74601	PONCA CITY	18267	8100	35.9	32.1	26.2	3.9	1.9	34158	36223	16	31	5199	34.3	38.0	22.7	4.7	0.3	63951
74604	PONCA CITY	28213	5218	18.0	23.6	39.2	13.1	6.2	58759	58184	76	94	4312	9.8	15.9	49.3	22.1	2.9	119250
74630	BILLINGS	17273	253	25.3	34.0	35.6	5.1	0.0	45414	46545	49	83	182	44.5	32.4	14.8	3.3	4.9	60000
74631	BLACKWELL	17168	3205	36.2	35.3	23.1	3.6	1.9	33193	34874	14	27	2286	45.1	29.6	20.8	4.1	0.3	54291
74632	BRAMAN	20463	257	26.1	36.2	32.3	2.7	2.7	39530	42203	31	65	202	42.1	21.3	28.2	7.4	1.0	61538
74633	BURBANK	22199	227	31.3	33.0	26.9	5.3	3.5	36115	38011	21	45	190	39.5	18.4	28.9	9.5	3.7	71250
74636	DEER CREEK	15271	92	35.9	39.1	22.8	2.2	0.0	32322	33409	12	23	72	54.2	18.1	19.4	8.3	0.0	45000
74637	FAIRFAX	16781	832	40.4	34.3	20.6	3.1	1.7	31083	32692	10	17	616	61.7	22.4	10.7	2.6	2.6	35781
74640	HUNTER	19975	182	27.5	34.1	33.0	3.8	1.6	37912	39491	26	57	150	32.7	22.7	28.7	14.0	2.0	81111
74641	KAW CITY	21641	231	23.4	33.8	37.7	3.9	1.3	44254	45297	46	78	193	17.1	30.6	39.4	11.9	1.0	92813
74643	LAMONT	15802	234	34.6	38.9	23.5	2.1	0.9	32953	33212	13	26	183	53.0	18.0	21.3	7.7	0.0	46071
74644	MARLAND	13889	211	37.4	30.3	29.9	1.9	0.5	31322	33845	10	18	150	50.0	20.0	19.3	6.0	4.7	50000
74646	NARDIN	20471	88	19.3	35.2	37.5	6.8	1.1	46534	46534	53	85	72	18.1	19.4	43.1	15.3	4.2	126471
74647	NEWKIRK	18657	1440	30.6	33.1	31.2	4.1	1.0	37958	40545	27	58	1115	26.5	34.9	29.8	7.9	0.9	74192
74650	RALSTON	18913	273	28.9	38.8	26.7	2.6	2.9	34274	36235	16	32	233	38.2	19.7	29.2	8.2	4.7	77727
74651	RED ROCK	13497	257	37.7	30.4	29.2	2.3	0.4	31129	33889	10	17	183	49.2	20.8	19.1	7.1	3.8	51154
74652	SHIDLER	20086	443	33.2	31.2	30.2	3.6	1.8	37468	40286	25	55	349	67.3	20.3	7.2	2.9	2.3	34052
74653	TONKAWA	17738	1423	32.5	34.8	27.1	4.0	1.6	36352	38820	22	47	1030	36.5	32.7	26.5	3.7	0.6	62500
74701	DURANT	18730	8213	34.6	30.8	27.6	4.7	2.2	36126	38840	21	45	4977	19.5	24.9	39.0	15.7	0.9	101141
74723	BENNINGTON	15948	686	40.7	33.2	21.3	2.6	2.2	30883	31852	10	16	562	33.3	26.9	26.5	10.1	3.2	74815
74724	BETHEL	14502	621	43.8	27.2	25.8	2.3	1.0	28694	29450	6	8	494	31.6	30.8	26.9	6.9	3.8	71935
74726	BOKCHITO	16572	926	40.8	31.0	22.8	3.5	1.9	30916	31485	10	16	717	36.7	24.8	26.9	10.2	1.4	69300
74727	BOSWELL	13046	854	50.7	31.0	15.6	2.0	0.7	24517	25416	3	2	647	31.1	39.7	20.9	6.5	1.9	70652
74728	BROKEN BOW	15885	4207	41.9	31.2	20.5	4.7	1.7	30180	30899	8	13	3006	30.7	31.6	25.8	10.2	1.7	73798
74729	CADDO	16948	957	33.5	31.8	29.4	4.2	1.1	36677	39122	23	50	735	33.7	26.7	30.1	7.9	1.6	71744
74730	CALERA	17818	1452	32.0	34.7	27.8	3.7	1.9	36638	39274	22	50	1094	27.4	26.4	31.9	12.6	1.6	84000
74731	CARTWRIGHT	16094	682	42.1	28.9	25.4	2.6	1.0	31704	32818	11	21	553	38.5	27.7	25.0	8.5	0.4	61216
74733	COLBERT	17153	1264	37.2	30.4	26.4	4.3	1.7	35295	38220	19	38	962	32.6	31.0	27.2	8.0	1.1	68514
74734	EAGLETOWN	16525	518	39.8	31.9	24.1	3.3	1.0	30772	30913	9	16	407	43.5	28.0	18.7	7.6	2.2	60114
74735	FORT TOWSON	15523	911	45.4	30.2	18.8	4.0	1.6	27806	28763	5	6	723	37.5	30.0	25.4	5.0	2.1	64592
74736	GARVIN	18746	307	37.1	27.4	27.7	5.9	2.0	37901	40250	26	57	250	36.0	22.4	28.4	11.6	1.6	75455
74738	GRANT	17858	279	35.8	27.2	29.7	4.3	2.9	35481	39254	19	40	241	28.6	32.8	24.5	14.1	0.0	71667
74740	HAWORTH	16025	667	46.0	32.8	15.0	3.4	2.7	26987	27811	5	5	562	46.8	26.3	17.4	8.2	1.2	53051
74741	HENDRIX	16308	690	39.4	31.2	25.1	2.9	1.4	32421	34684	12	24	565	35.0	31.9	22.3	8.8	1.9	66463
74743	HUGO	15574	3642	45.4	28.4	23.3	2.0	0.9	28049	28978	6	7	2332	33.8	34.6	24.1	7.3	0.1	66610
74745	IDABEL	16815	4055	45.8	26.1	21.2	4.9	1.9	27702	28284	5	6	2644	30.9	29.7	29.3	7.9	2.2	69825
74748	KENEFIC	15939	221	38.0	38.0	20.4	2.7	0.9	31176	32488	10	18	185	41.1	27.6	19.5	8.1	3.8	59167
74754	RINGOLD	19866	58	29.3	32.8	31.0	6.9	0.0	37330	42383	25	54	47	34.0	40.4	19.1	6.4	0.0	61667
74755	RUFE	25221	116	40.5	18.1	31.0	3.4	6.9	38200	40000	27	59	101	27.7	20.8	29.7	20.8	1.0	95000
74756	SAWYER	15434	182	42.9	29.1	24.7	2.7	0.5	30495	32981	9	15	151	41.7	25.8	25.2	6.0	1.3	60556
74759	SOPER	14336	391	49.6	29.9	16.9	3.3	0.3	25282	26433	3	3	323	36.5	30.7	23.8	8.0	0.9	66739
74760	SPENCERVILLE	14704	113	41.6	30.1	24.8	2.7	0.9	31375	32347	10	19	94	40.4	26.6	26.6	6.4	0.0	61667
74764	VALLIANT	18713	1692	38.5	24.6	30.7	4.1	2.1	36442	38317	22	48	1322	36.9	23.4	25.9	11.6	2.0	68913
74766	WRIGHT CITY	18456	669	34.7	28.7	31.2	3.6	1.8	37280	39915	24	53	545	46.2	29.4	19.4	2.9	2.0	53306
74801	SHAWNEE	18680	8961	34.9	29.7	28.7	4.6	2.2	36336	38954	22	47	5813	24.1	34.5	31.5	8.9	1.0	79133
74804	SHAWNEE	22290	7798	26.0	28.3	35.1	6.5	4.1	44971	47261	48	80	5518	10.3	24.6	42.9	21.2	1.1	116268
74820	ADA	19283	11189	36.3	29.7	27.2	4.4	2.4	35077	37225	18	37	6987	21.4	26.2	36.7	13.5	2.2	93836
74824	AGRA	16589	553	27.8	43.2	23.1	4.3	1.4	36248	38847	21	46	456	31.6	28.5	22.1	17.3	0.4	71071
74825	ALLEN	17369	1628	32.9	32.1	29.4	3.3	2.3	35969	38400	20	44	1327	29.8	25.3	34.6	9.3	1.1	80625
74826	ASHER	14580	411	39.2	33.6	22.9	3.9	0.5	29046	30000	7	10	334	41.9	34.1	20.1	3.9	0.0	56750
74827	ATWOOD	15870	277	41.5	30.0	24.9	3.6	0.0	30224	33209	8	14	218	45.9	21.1	24.8	7.8	0.5	57500
74829	BOLEY	13953	240	47.5	20.8	26.7	3.3	1.7	27324	30000	5	5	187	40.1	27.8	23.5	8.0	0.5	61471
74831	BYARS	16881	515	38.3	33.4	24.7	2.3	1.4	31930	33288	11	22	433	48.3	23.3	20.6	6.0	1.8	53261
74832	CARNEY	17413	270	28.5	37.4	29.3	3.3	1.5	38171	40398	27	58	216	30.1	30.6	31.9	6.9	0.5	78571
74833	CASTLE	16240	208	33.2	40.9	21.2	3.8	1.0	35000	36830	18	36	178	30.9	19.1	38.8	10.1	1.1	90000
74834	CHANDLER	19607	2545	29.6	32.1	28.6	7.1	2.6	38837	40963	29	61	1898	22.1	28.1	36.1	13.2	0.5	89710
74839	DUSTIN	13116	328	44.5	33.5	20.1	1.5	0.3	27676	28577	5	6	265	60.4	20.8	13.6	5.3	0.0	42568
74840	EARLSBORO	18937	504	23.6	33.3	35.9	5.0	2.2	44394	45000	47	79	434	19.1	24.9	35.9	18.4	1.6	101953
74842	FITTSTOWN	18894	288	26.4	33.3	32.6	5.6	2.1	40444	42220	34	69	233	20.6	25.8	30.0	20.2	3.4	99444
74843	FITZHUGH	17771	79	26.6	34.2	31.6	6.3	1.3	40366	42680	34	69	64	21.9	26.6	29.7	18.8	3.1	95000
74845	HANNA	13824	193	44.6	28.0	23.3	3.6	0.5	29288	30199	7	10	146	54.8	19.2	15.8	8.2	2.1	46500
74848	HOLDENVILLE	16333	2925	44.4	30.3	19.1	4.4	1.8	28541	29801	6	8	2157	46.0	25.4	21.4	6.7	0.6	55000
74849	KONAWA	14077	1213	42.6	26.5	28.4	2.1	0.4	30267	31628	8	14	837	40.6	30.6	22.6	5.1	1.1	63250
74850	LAMAR	17465	105	35.2	29.5	31.4	3.8	0.0	35450	39315	19	40	88	31.8	23.9	33.0	9.1	2.3	81667
74851	MCLOUD	20138	2844	20.4	30.5	39.1	7.6	2.5	49063	50467	59	87	2324	15.7	29.0	43.5	11.4	0.4	97029
74852	MACOMB	17439	366	26.8	36.3	30.6	4.6	1.6	38567	41221	28	60	316	25.0	28.8	34.5	10.4	1.3	85200
74854	MAUD	17225	1630	37.1	34.2	22.8	4.2	1.8	33036	34398	13	27	1339	43.2	26.7	21.4	6.7	1.9	57754
74855	MEEKER	19153	1858	26.6	31.5	34.4	5.7	1.7	43475	44628	44	76	1548	24.7	31.4	33.8	9.1	1.0	82857
74856	MILL CREEK	15358	530	37.0	34.5	24.3	2.5	1.7	32248	33148	12	23	418	47.8	26.1	20.3	4.1	1.7	52647
74857	NEWALLA	22297	3066	15.1	27.3	48.6	7.3	1.8	55790	57644	72	93	2718	14.5	30.6	40.0	14.5	0.4	96333
74859	OKEMAH	15443	2185	42.8	33.5	19.6	2.9	1.1	28985	29548	7	10	1527	39.2	25.4	27.6	7.4	0.4	64099
74860	PADEN	17586	634	32.5	35.5	26.0	3.9	2.1	35364	36834	19	39	541	35.1	34.6	21.4	6.8	2.0	64100
74864	PRAGUE	18803	1798	31.5	35.7	25.7	5.2	1.8	37449	40071	25	54	1415	29.5	32.7	28.0	8.1	1.8	73901
74865	ROFF	16369	545	36.7	28.4	29.4	4.6	0.9	34918	36965	17	35	412	45.9	24.0	17.5	10.0	2.7	54250
74867	SASAKWA	13281	292	51.4	32.9	12.3	2.7	0.7	24340	24534	3	2	246	45.5	22.8	22.8	8.5	0.4	55500
74868	SEMINOLE	18347	4391	35.5	32.9	25.3	4.2	2.0	34833	36527	17	34	3119	31.3	31.2	26.4	9.8	1.3	73016
74869	SPARKS	18136	113	31.0	28.3	33.6	6.2	0.9	37361	38909	25	54	99	24.2	33.3	36.4	6.1	0.0	80625
74871	STONEWALL	17502	957	37.2	29.8	27.0	5.0	1.0	32771	34053	13	25	779	38.8	28.2	22.5	7.4	3.1	64855
74872	STRATFORD	16098	1275	41.3	29.5	24.2	2.7	2.2	31195	32804	10	18	965	29.1	29.6	25.7	12.6	2.9	78106
74873	TECUMSEH	17740	4158	30.1	33.9	29.6	4.6	1.8	38864	41290	29	61	3167	21.9	36.3	30.0	10.9	1.0	79208
74875	TRYON	15449	597	35.0	33.7	28.5	2.3	0.5	33186	34436	14	27	483	35.0	30.4	23.6	9.7	1.2	68953
74878	WANETTE	17911	589	30.4	35.5	27.7	3.9	2.5	37210	40213	24	52	493	28.2	31.4	31.2	8.5	0.6	80104
74880	WELEETKA	15287	832	47.8	30.5	15.7	4.0	1.9	26140	26806	4	4	672	51.8	22.9	21.0	3.9	0.4	48125
74881	WELLSTON	18360	1408	26.7	36.6	30.8	4.6	1.3	39068	40898	30	62	1184	30.4	27.7	30.6	10.0	1.4	79302
74883	WETUMKA	14184	811	49.8	28.7	18.7	2.3	0.4	25108	25825	3	3	576	51.4	29.3	12.7	5.7	0.9	48750
74884	WEWOKA	15182	2912	43.4	31.1	20.8	3.3	1.3	28872	30299	7	9	2067	46.9	27.0	19.5	5.6	1.1	52986
74901	ARKOMA	18078	890	38.5	31.9	24.0	3.0	2.5	31406	32390	10	19	577	38.1	34.1	24.6	3.1	0.0	63936
74902	POCOLA	19009	1926	29.7	31.4	31.4	6.0	1.5	42312	44632	40	74	1516	26.5	31.9	35.0	5.0	1.6	80379
74930	BOKOSHE	16620	1320	37.3	31.6	24.7	5.2	1.2	33818	36181	15	30	1011	39.7	30.4	19.6	5.5	4.8	63228
74931	BUNCH	13919	612	38.1	35.6	20.8	4.1	1.5	31431	32057	10	19	515	26.8	36.3	20.6	13.0	3.3	73750
	OKLAHOMA	22515		27.2	29.2	32.3	7.2	4.0	43746	45901				20.4	25.6	36.1	15.4	2.4	96076
	UNITED STATES	27277		20.9	24.4	35.3	11.7	7.6	54719	56938				9.3	13.1	31.6	32.6	13.5	162279

ZIP CODE #	POST OFFICE NAME	FINANCIAL SERVICES: Auto Loan	Home Loan	Invest-ments	Retire-ment Plans	THE HOME: Home Improvements: Home Repair	Lawn & Garden	Furnishings: Comput-ers & Hard-ware-Personal	Major Appli-ances	TV, Radio, Sound Equip-ment	Furni-ture	ENTERTAINMENT: Dine out/ Carry out	Sports Equip-ment	Fees & Tickets	Toys & Games	Travel	Cable TV	PERSONAL: Apparel & Services	Auto Repairs	Health Insur-ance	Pets & Supplies
74572	TUPELO	75	53	79	52	55	77	56	71	60	49	59	55	43	60	56	66	39	65	74	85
74574	TUSKAHOMA	68	49	70	47	51	69	50	64	56	47	55	48	40	55	50	61	36	59	66	76
74576	WARDVILLE	74	53	76	52	55	76	55	70	61	51	60	52	44	60	54	67	39	64	72	83
74577	WHITESBORO	51	36	52	35	38	52	38	48	42	35	41	36	30	42	37	46	27	44	50	57
74578	WILBURTON	70	51	66	49	51	70	55	65	60	51	59	49	44	60	52	66	39	62	69	78
74601	PONCA CITY	67	56	56	57	55	66	63	64	66	58	64	49	56	66	58	70	44	65	70	77
74604	PONCA CITY	104	103	109	102	105	113	95	106	99	97	98	76	96	98	99	102	68	101	110	123
74630	BILLINGS	81	58	83	56	60	82	60	76	66	55	65	57	48	66	59	73	43	70	79	90
74631	BLACKWELL	70	52	63	52	53	70	59	66	63	53	61	50	48	63	54	68	41	64	72	79
74632	BRAMAN	86	59	95	59	62	91	66	82	69	53	68	68	48	67	66	75	44	76	87	101
74633	BURBANK	90	64	93	63	67	92	67	85	74	61	73	65	53	73	66	81	48	78	89	101
74636	DEER CREEK	70	48	77	48	50	74	53	66	56	43	55	55	39	55	53	61	36	62	70	82
74637	FAIRFAX	69	49	70	48	51	72	53	66	59	47	57	51	42	58	52	65	38	62	72	78
74640	HUNTER	83	59	91	60	62	88	65	80	67	53	67	66	49	66	65	73	43	75	84	98
74641	KAW CITY	89	64	92	62	66	91	66	84	73	61	72	63	53	72	65	80	47	77	87	99
74643	LAMONT	70	48	77	48	50	74	53	66	55	43	55	55	39	54	53	60	36	62	70	81
74644	MARLAND	68	49	70	47	51	69	50	64	56	47	55	48	40	55	50	61	36	59	67	76
74646	NARDIN	94	65	104	65	68	100	72	90	75	58	74	74	53	74	72	82	48	84	95	110
74647	NEWKIRK	81	58	83	57	60	83	61	77	67	56	66	58	49	67	60	74	44	71	81	91
74650	RALSTON	82	56	90	56	59	86	62	78	65	51	64	64	46	64	62	71	42	72	82	96
74651	RED ROCK	68	49	70	47	51	70	50	64	56	47	55	48	40	55	50	61	36	59	67	76
74652	SHIDLER	77	55	77	54	57	80	60	74	67	54	65	55	48	66	58	74	43	69	81	87
74653	TONKAWA	78	56	80	55	58	81	60	75	67	54	65	57	48	66	59	74	43	70	81	89
74701	DURANT	70	58	58	59	58	67	66	66	68	62	67	50	58	69	60	71	46	67	70	79
74723	BENNINGTON	74	53	76	51	55	75	54	69	60	51	59	52	43	60	54	66	39	63	72	82
74724	BETHEL	68	48	71	47	50	70	51	64	55	45	54	50	39	54	50	60	36	59	67	77
74726	BOKCHITO	71	52	72	50	54	73	54	68	60	50	59	51	44	60	53	66	39	63	72	80
74727	BOSWELL	56	39	58	39	41	58	42	53	46	37	45	41	33	46	42	51	30	49	56	63
74728	BROKEN BOW	68	50	61	49	50	66	55	62	60	51	59	47	45	60	51	65	40	60	66	75
74729	CADDO	74	56	72	54	57	75	58	70	64	54	62	52	48	63	56	69	41	65	74	83
74730	CALERA	76	60	73	58	61	77	61	72	66	59	65	53	52	66	59	71	43	68	76	85
74731	CARTWRIGHT	69	50	64	48	51	68	51	63	57	49	56	48	41	58	49	62	37	58	66	75
74733	COLBERT	78	55	73	52	55	76	57	69	64	55	63	53	45	65	54	70	42	65	73	84
74734	EAGLETOWN	74	49	72	46	49	73	52	66	60	49	58	51	40	60	49	66	39	61	69	80
74735	FORT TOWSON	68	49	70	47	51	70	51	64	57	47	56	48	41	56	50	63	37	59	68	76
74736	GARVIN	85	61	87	59	63	86	62	79	69	58	68	60	50	69	62	76	45	73	83	94
74738	GRANT	81	58	83	56	60	82	59	75	66	55	65	57	47	65	59	72	43	69	78	90
74740	HAWORTH	76	49	73	46	49	74	53	66	61	50	59	52	39	62	49	68	39	63	70	82
74741	HENDRIX	74	53	70	51	54	73	55	67	61	52	60	51	44	61	52	66	40	62	70	81
74743	HUGO	60	44	57	43	45	60	49	57	54	45	53	42	40	54	46	59	35	55	62	68
74745	IDABEL	68	50	61	50	50	66	56	62	62	52	60	47	47	61	52	67	41	61	68	75
74748	KENEFIC	68	50	68	49	52	68	51	63	56	48	55	47	42	56	50	61	37	59	66	75
74754	RINGOLD	81	58	67	57	58	77	60	70	67	59	66	54	49	70	55	73	44	67	74	86
74755	RUFE	107	77	110	74	80	109	79	100	87	73	86	75	63	87	78	96	57	92	104	119
74756	SAWYER	68	48	69	47	50	69	50	63	55	46	54	47	40	55	49	61	36	58	66	75
74759	SOPER	60	43	61	41	44	61	44	56	49	41	48	42	35	48	43	54	32	51	58	66
74760	SPENCERVILLE	68	48	69	47	50	69	50	63	55	46	54	47	40	55	49	61	36	58	66	75
74764	VALLIANT	86	61	79	60	62	84	63	77	70	60	69	58	51	72	60	77	46	72	81	93
74766	WRIGHT CITY	91	61	83	58	61	88	65	79	73	62	72	62	49	75	60	81	48	75	84	97
74801	SHAWNEE	73	60	60	60	59	71	66	68	69	61	68	52	58	70	60	73	46	68	74	82
74804	SHAWNEE	87	80	81	79	80	88	80	84	82	79	82	63	76	83	78	85	56	83	88	99
74820	ADA	71	58	64	58	58	70	65	68	68	60	67	52	57	68	60	72	46	68	73	81
74824	AGRA	81	58	83	56	60	82	59	75	66	55	65	57	47	65	59	72	43	69	78	90
74825	ALLEN	79	60	74	59	61	79	62	73	67	59	66	55	52	68	59	73	44	69	77	87
74826	ASHER	67	48	68	46	49	68	49	62	54	46	53	47	39	54	48	60	35	57	65	74
74827	ATWOOD	67	48	69	46	50	68	49	63	55	46	54	47	39	54	49	60	35	57	65	74
74829	BOLEY	74	49	73	46	49	73	53	66	59	48	58	52	39	59	50	65	38	62	70	81
74831	BYARS	76	55	78	53	57	77	56	71	62	52	61	54	45	62	55	68	40	65	74	85
74832	CARNEY	79	56	81	55	59	80	58	74	64	54	63	55	46	64	57	71	42	68	77	88
74833	CASTLE	76	54	78	52	56	77	56	71	62	52	61	53	44	62	55	68	40	65	74	84
74834	CHANDLER	83	65	79	63	66	84	66	79	72	63	71	58	56	73	64	78	48	74	83	93
74839	DUSTIN	61	40	59	38	40	60	43	54	50	41	48	42	32	50	40	55	32	51	57	67
74840	EARLSBORO	92	69	92	67	71	93	70	87	77	66	75	65	58	77	69	83	50	80	90	103
74842	FITTSTOWN	86	59	94	59	62	90	65	81	68	53	67	67	48	67	65	74	44	76	86	100
74843	FITZHUGH	86	59	95	59	62	91	66	82	68	53	68	68	48	67	65	75	44	76	86	101
74845	HANNA	68	45	66	42	45	67	48	60	55	45	53	47	36	55	45	61	35	56	63	74
74848	HOLDENVILLE	69	50	68	49	51	71	54	66	60	49	58	49	43	59	52	66	39	62	70	78
74849	KONAWA	60	46	52	45	45	58	51	55	55	47	53	42	43	55	46	59	36	54	60	67
74850	LAMAR	78	56	80	54	58	79	57	73	63	53	62	54	46	63	56	70	41	67	75	86
74851	MCLOUD	93	83	81	80	81	90	79	87	83	81	83	64	74	85	77	86	56	83	87	103
74852	MACOMB	86	62	88	60	64	88	63	81	70	59	69	61	51	70	63	77	46	74	84	96
74854	MAUD	74	55	71	54	56	75	59	70	64	54	63	53	48	64	56	70	42	66	74	83
74855	MEEKER	88	63	82	62	65	88	67	81	74	63	72	61	54	75	63	82	48	76	86	97
74856	MILL CREEK	74	50	74	48	51	74	53	67	60	50	59	51	41	61	51	67	39	62	70	81
74857	NEWALLA	96	91	80	89	89	92	85	90	87	88	88	66	82	91	82	90	60	87	90	106
74859	OKEMAH	63	47	59	46	47	64	51	59	56	47	54	45	42	56	48	61	36	57	64	71
74860	PADEN	79	57	81	55	59	80	58	74	65	54	63	56	46	64	58	71	42	68	77	88
74864	PRAGUE	80	58	81	56	60	83	62	77	69	56	67	58	50	68	60	76	44	71	83	91
74865	ROFF	75	53	78	52	55	78	58	72	63	50	61	56	45	62	57	69	40	67	77	86
74867	SASAKWA	57	41	59	40	42	58	42	53	47	39	46	40	34	46	42	51	30	49	56	63
74868	SEMINOLE	78	58	70	57	58	77	64	72	69	59	67	55	52	70	59	75	45	70	78	87
74869	SPARKS	83	59	85	57	61	84	61	77	67	56	66	58	49	67	60	74	44	71	80	92
74871	STONEWALL	81	56	81	54	58	81	58	74	66	55	64	56	46	66	57	72	42	68	77	89
74872	STRATFORD	68	50	66	49	50	70	56	64	59	48	58	51	44	59	53	64	39	62	70	78
74873	TECUMSEH	80	60	75	58	61	80	63	75	69	59	67	56	52	69	60	75	45	70	79	89
74875	TRYON	70	50	72	49	52	71	52	66	57	48	56	49	41	57	51	63	37	60	68	78
74878	WANETTE	83	59	85	58	62	84	61	78	68	57	66	58	49	67	60	74	44	71	81	92
74880	WELEETKA	67	48	68	47	50	69	51	64	57	46	55	48	41	56	50	62	37	59	68	75
74881	WELLSTON	84	60	86	58	63	86	63	79	70	58	68	59	50	69	62	77	45	73	84	94
74883	WETUMKA	56	40	56	39	42	58	44	54	49	39	47	40	35	48	42	54	31	51	59	64
74884	WEWOKA	65	47	63	46	49	66	51	61	57	47	55	46	42	56	49	62	37	58	67	73
74901	ARKOMA	70	53	59	53	53	69	61	65	66	55	63	50	51	66	55	70	43	65	72	78
74902	POCOLA	89	62	76	60	62	85	65	77	73	63	72	60	52	76	60	80	48	73	82	94
74930	BOKOSHE	78	55	71	53	56	76	57	69	64	55	63	53	46	66	54	70	42	65	73	84
74931	BUNCH	72	51	71	50	53	72	53	66	59	50	58	50	42	59	51	65	38	61	69	79
	OKLAHOMA	87	75	78	75	74	84	79	82	82	77	81	63	73	83	75	85	56	82	86	98
	UNITED STATES	100	100	100	100	100	100	100	100	100	100	100	100	100	100	100	100	100	100	100	100

ZIP CODE			POPULATION			2000-2009 ANNUAL RATE		HOUSEHOLDS					FAMILIES		
#	POST OFFICE NAME	COUNTY FIPS CODE	2000	2009	2014	% Rate	State Centile	2000	2009	2014	% Annual Rate 2000-2009	2009 Average HH Size	2000	2009	% Annual Rate 2000-2009
74932	CAMERON	079	1112	1021	991	-0.9	8	401	376	367	-0.7	2.72	325	300	-0.9
74937	HEAVENER	079	6311	6538	6596	0.4	64	2256	2328	2351	0.3	2.61	1683	1701	0.1
74939	HODGEN	079	960	989	995	0.3	60	113	119	120	0.6	5.51	89	92	0.4
74940	HOWE	079	1656	1766	1815	0.7	75	603	646	665	0.7	2.71	478	503	0.6
74941	KEOTA	061	2006	2229	2323	1.1	84	749	841	877	1.3	2.65	568	628	1.1
74944	MCCURTAIN	061	1086	1022	997	-0.7	10	408	381	371	-0.7	2.68	309	284	-0.9
74948	MULDROW	135	9673	10510	10927	0.9	80	3635	4041	4227	1.2	2.59	2780	3030	0.9
74949	MUSE	079	206	210	210	0.2	55	88	92	92	0.5	2.28	63	65	0.3
74953	POTEAU	079	11662	12330	12620	0.6	73	4382	4697	4827	0.8	2.52	3123	3266	0.5
74954	ROLAND	135	8429	8873	9096	0.6	73	3036	3261	3363	0.8	2.71	2389	2520	0.6
74955	SALLISAW	135	12770	13689	14088	0.8	78	4945	5387	5575	0.9	2.50	3516	3739	0.7
74956	SHADY POINT	079	1426	1503	1539	0.6	73	512	545	560	0.7	2.76	418	439	0.5
74957	SMITHVILLE	089	435	428	423	-0.2	33	168	170	169	0.1	2.52	124	123	-0.1
74959	SPIRO	079	8008	8444	8611	0.6	73	3039	3258	3333	0.8	2.57	2274	2389	0.5
74960	STILWELL	001	11473	12190	12512	0.7	75	4092	4438	4581	0.9	2.72	3012	3199	0.7
74962	VIAN	135	6720	7258	7527	0.8	78	2586	2875	3007	1.2	2.47	1888	2052	0.9
74963	WATSON	089	875	868	861	-0.1	38	347	353	353	0.2	2.46	255	254	0.0
74964	WATTS	001	2569	2575	2600	0.0	43	874	894	909	0.2	2.66	664	665	0.0
74965	WESTVILLE	001	4630	5454	5833	1.8	93	1680	2006	2158	1.9	2.69	1256	1467	1.7
74966	WISTER	079	3910	4134	4231	0.6	73	1514	1617	1661	0.7	2.54	1114	1165	0.5
	OKLAHOMA					0.7					0.8	2.46			0.6
	UNITED STATES					1.0					1.1	2.59			0.9

ZIP CODE #	POST OFFICE NAME	RACE (%) White 2000	White 2009	Black 2000	Black 2009	Asian/Pacific 2000	Asian/Pacific 2009	% Hispanic Origin 2000	% Hispanic Origin 2009	2009 AGE DISTRIBUTION (%) 0-4	5-9	10-14	15-19	20-24	25-44	45-64	65-84	85+	18+	MEDIAN AGE 2009	% 2009 Males	% 2009 Females
74932	CAMERON	87.2	84.8	0.1	0.2	0.3	0.3	2.0	3.0	7.1	7.1	7.3	7.1	5.4	23.8	29.1	11.9	1.2	74.0	38.9	51.6	48.4
74937	HEAVENER	75.2	71.5	1.9	2.0	0.1	0.2	12.2	16.5	7.1	6.7	6.3	6.7	7.4	27.8	24.5	11.4	2.2	76.3	36.0	53.7	46.3
74939	HODGEN	71.8	68.5	9.0	9.5	0.0	0.0	1.7	2.4	3.7	4.0	4.2	4.3	7.1	37.9	27.2	10.3	1.1	85.6	39.4	66.3	33.7
74940	HOWE	78.9	75.0	0.1	0.1	0.2	0.2	4.6	6.7	6.7	7.0	7.1	6.6	5.0	25.0	28.4	12.7	1.4	75.2	38.8	51.3	48.7
74941	KEOTA	81.8	79.6	0.0	0.0	0.3	0.4	2.3	3.4	7.7	7.7	7.5	6.7	5.2	24.4	26.5	12.7	1.5	73.0	37.2	47.7	52.3
74944	MCCURTAIN	77.0	74.1	0.2	0.2	0.6	0.8	0.9	1.3	6.7	6.8	7.0	7.8	5.4	24.1	26.7	13.7	1.8	74.5	39.5	51.6	48.4
74948	MULDROW	73.6	70.0	1.3	1.4	0.3	0.5	2.3	3.1	6.8	6.8	7.0	6.7	5.8	25.1	27.7	12.7	1.4	75.3	38.7	50.1	49.9
74949	MUSE	77.8	74.3	0.0	0.0	0.0	0.0	1.4	2.4	6.7	6.7	6.7	5.7	4.8	22.4	30.0	14.8	2.4	76.2	42.9	47.6	52.4
74953	POTEAU	83.5	81.3	1.5	1.6	0.4	0.5	4.5	6.5	7.3	7.0	6.7	7.5	6.4	25.4	24.7	12.6	2.4	75.1	36.7	48.6	51.4
74954	ROLAND	69.8	66.0	3.2	3.2	0.3	0.4	2.3	3.0	7.8	7.7	7.4	7.5	6.3	25.8	26.0	10.5	1.1	72.5	35.5	49.6	50.4
74955	SALLISAW	65.0	61.4	1.0	1.1	0.3	0.4	2.1	2.7	7.3	7.0	7.1	6.7	5.7	24.8	26.3	13.1	2.0	74.4	38.2	49.5	50.5
74956	SHADY POINT	86.0	83.8	0.1	0.1	0.3	0.4	1.4	2.0	7.1	7.1	7.3	6.7	4.9	24.6	27.9	13.2	1.3	74.3	39.7	48.1	51.9
74957	SMITHVILLE	64.7	61.4	0.9	0.9	0.0	0.0	2.1	2.1	7.0	7.0	7.5	7.2	5.4	23.8	27.6	12.9	1.6	74.3	38.8	50.2	49.8
74959	SPIRO	78.8	75.3	6.3	6.9	0.1	0.2	1.7	2.5	6.8	6.8	7.0	6.7	5.6	25.3	27.4	12.6	1.8	75.3	38.7	48.7	51.3
74960	STILWELL	41.0	38.1	0.2	0.2	0.1	0.1	3.7	4.6	7.8	8.1	7.8	7.8	6.6	26.2	24.1	10.0	1.6	71.5	33.9	49.3	50.7
74962	VIAN	64.5	60.7	2.5	2.8	0.1	0.1	1.4	1.9	6.5	6.2	6.4	6.7	5.2	22.2	28.2	16.3	2.4	76.6	42.4	49.7	50.3
74963	WATSON	69.1	65.7	0.8	0.9	0.1	0.1	1.9	2.4	6.6	6.6	6.9	7.3	5.6	23.5	28.3	13.7	1.5	75.3	40.2	50.0	50.0
74964	WATTS	65.8	62.7	0.2	0.3	0.3	0.4	1.5	2.1	7.7	7.9	8.5	8.1	5.2	24.6	25.6	11.2	1.2	69.9	35.6	50.8	49.2
74965	WESTVILLE	61.7	57.6	0.1	0.1	0.1	0.2	3.3	4.7	7.9	7.7	7.6	7.5	5.9	25.9	24.4	11.3	1.8	72.2	35.3	49.5	50.5
74966	WISTER	79.5	77.2	0.2	0.2	0.4	0.5	1.7	2.5	6.6	6.7	6.8	6.7	5.2	23.7	27.7	14.7	2.0	75.7	40.7	50.5	49.5
	OKLAHOMA	76.2	73.0	7.6	7.8	1.4	2.0	5.2	7.0	6.9	6.6	6.5	7.1	7.2	26.2	25.9	11.6	2.0	75.9	36.8	49.3	50.7
	UNITED STATES	75.1	72.0	12.3	12.7	3.8	4.6	12.5	15.7	6.8	6.7	6.6	7.1	6.9	27.0	26.0	10.9	1.9	75.7	36.9	49.2	50.8

ZIP CODE #	POST OFFICE NAME	2009 Per Capita Income	2009 HH Income Base	2009 HOUSEHOLD INCOME DISTRIBUTION (%) Less than $25,000	$25,000 to $49,999	$50,000 to $99,999	$100,000 to $149,999	$150,000 or More	MEDIAN HOUSEHOLD INCOME 2009	2014	2009 National Centile	2009 State Centile	2009 Home Value Base	2009 HOME VALUE DISTRIBUTION (%) Less than $50,000	$50,000 to $89,999	$90,000 to $174,999	$175,000 to $399,999	$400,000 or More	2009 Median Home Value
74932	CAMERON	15711	376	28.5	39.9	27.4	3.5	0.8	35555	38707	19	41	297	35.7	19.9	29.0	14.8	0.7	82143
74937	HEAVENER	15443	2328	39.6	31.9	23.2	4.0	1.3	31535	33007	11	20	1750	38.9	30.7	21.7	6.5	2.2	62914
74939	HODGEN	9608	119	38.7	31.1	24.4	3.4	2.5	33057	35000	13	27	103	30.1	32.0	21.4	10.7	5.8	72143
74940	HOWE	17408	646	31.3	35.3	26.3	5.7	1.4	35447	37529	19	39	527	34.7	27.5	26.4	9.1	2.3	72500
74941	KEOTA	15496	841	40.8	35.9	18.0	2.5	2.9	30762	31037	9	16	668	45.1	25.1	25.0	4.0	0.7	55690
74944	MCCURTAIN	15419	381	40.4	28.1	25.2	5.2	1.0	33309	35317	14	28	316	41.8	31.6	18.0	5.7	2.8	59630
74948	MULDROW	17113	4041	34.2	31.0	28.9	4.5	1.3	36800	39024	23	51	3213	29.3	29.9	30.5	9.0	1.4	77457
74949	MUSE	14933	92	50.0	30.4	15.2	1.1	3.3	25000	24262	3	3	73	47.9	27.4	23.3	1.4	0.0	53000
74953	POTEAU	17950	4697	34.4	31.5	27.9	4.0	2.3	35344	37990	19	38	3307	27.6	28.6	32.9	9.8	1.1	82118
74954	ROLAND	18282	3261	31.9	29.4	31.0	4.5	3.1	39026	41404	30	62	2539	25.0	33.7	30.9	8.7	1.6	80992
74955	SALLISAW	16989	5387	38.1	28.5	28.0	3.7	1.6	33364	34548	14	29	3593	24.8	32.3	31.1	10.0	1.8	81090
74956	SHADY POINT	18818	545	31.6	25.5	35.0	5.0	2.9	41654	44663	38	72	462	28.1	24.2	32.3	13.4	1.9	86452
74957	SMITHVILLE	14589	170	45.9	28.2	21.8	2.9	1.2	27719	27678	5	6	134	35.8	36.6	17.9	6.7	3.0	65385
74959	SPIRO	16590	3258	35.1	33.5	25.0	4.9	1.4	35000	36631	18	36	2469	36.2	32.5	26.0	4.9	0.4	66609
74960	STILWELL	14474	4438	42.0	30.6	22.7	3.4	1.4	29733	30832	8	12	3170	26.0	36.5	25.7	10.2	1.5	74087
74962	VIAN	17494	2875	40.5	28.7	24.3	4.4	2.2	32214	33701	12	22	2238	31.3	29.7	26.3	11.0	1.7	76857
74963	WATSON	14818	353	45.3	28.9	22.1	2.8	0.8	27855	28047	5	6	282	38.7	34.8	18.1	5.7	2.8	64074
74964	WATTS	16140	894	30.9	34.1	31.3	2.3	1.3	38152	41072	27	58	739	30.4	29.8	26.9	9.2	3.7	75000
74965	WESTVILLE	15319	2006	34.2	32.2	29.4	3.3	0.8	36367	38331	22	47	1375	27.9	30.6	25.1	11.0	5.4	75272
74966	WISTER	16582	1617	40.0	28.6	26.6	3.8	1.0	32855	34368	13	26	1294	35.5	25.6	28.7	8.3	1.9	74588
	OKLAHOMA	22515		27.2	29.2	32.3	7.2	4.0	43746	45901				20.4	25.6	36.1	15.4	2.4	96076
	UNITED STATES	27277		20.9	24.4	35.3	11.7	7.6	54719	56938				9.3	13.1	31.6	32.6	13.5	162279

ZIP CODE		FINANCIAL SERVICES				THE HOME						ENTERTAINMENT						PERSONAL			
						Home Improvements		Furnishings													
#	POST OFFICE NAME	Auto Loan	Home Loan	Invest-ments	Retire-ment Plans	Home Repair	Lawn & Garden	Comput-ers & Hard-ware-Personal	Major Appli-ances	TV, Radio, Sound Equip-ment	Furni-ture	Dine out/ Carry out	Sports Equip-ment	Fees & Tickets	Toys & Games	Travel	Cable TV	Apparel & Services	Auto Repairs	Health Insur-ance	Pets & Supplies
74932	CAMERON	76	55	78	53	57	77	56	71	62	52	61	53	45	62	55	68	40	65	74	85
74937	HEAVENER	69	51	65	50	52	69	56	65	61	51	59	49	45	60	52	66	40	62	69	77
74939	HODGEN	77	55	79	53	57	78	57	72	63	53	62	54	45	62	56	69	41	66	75	86
74940	HOWE	84	60	85	59	62	85	62	78	69	58	68	59	50	69	61	76	45	72	82	93
74941	KEOTA	74	53	68	51	54	72	55	67	61	52	59	50	44	62	52	66	40	62	70	80
74944	MCCURTAIN	74	53	76	51	55	75	54	69	60	51	59	52	43	60	54	66	39	63	72	82
74948	MULDROW	79	57	68	56	57	76	60	70	66	57	65	53	49	68	55	72	43	66	74	84
74949	MUSE	61	44	62	42	45	62	45	57	50	42	49	43	36	49	44	55	32	52	59	68
74953	POTEAU	76	58	69	57	59	76	63	72	68	58	66	54	53	68	59	73	44	69	77	85
74954	ROLAND	84	65	68	64	64	79	69	75	74	67	73	57	58	76	62	79	49	73	79	90
74955	SALLISAW	71	53	65	53	54	70	59	66	63	54	62	50	49	63	55	68	42	64	71	79
74956	SHADY POINT	87	69	81	70	70	90	70	83	76	65	74	63	60	77	69	82	50	77	86	98
74957	SMITHVILLE	68	45	67	43	45	67	48	60	54	44	53	48	36	55	46	60	35	57	64	74
74959	SPIRO	75	55	65	53	55	73	58	67	64	55	62	51	47	65	53	69	42	64	71	81
74960	STILWELL	69	49	59	48	49	66	54	61	59	51	58	47	43	61	49	64	39	59	65	74
74962	VIAN	75	54	76	53	56	76	58	71	64	53	62	53	47	63	56	70	42	66	75	84
74963	WATSON	67	45	66	43	45	66	47	60	54	45	53	46	36	55	45	60	35	56	63	73
74964	WATTS	79	56	65	55	56	75	59	68	65	57	64	53	47	68	53	71	43	65	72	83
74965	WESTVILLE	71	52	59	52	52	68	57	63	62	53	60	49	46	63	52	67	41	62	68	77
74966	WISTER	74	53	75	51	55	76	56	70	62	51	60	52	44	61	55	68	40	65	74	83
	OKLAHOMA	87	75	78	75	74	84	79	82	82	77	81	63	73	83	75	85	56	82	86	98
	UNITED STATES	100	100	100	100	100	100	100	100	100	100	100	100	100	100	100	100	100	100	100	100

ZIP CODE #	POST OFFICE NAME	COUNTY FIPS CODE	POPULATION 2000	POPULATION 2009	POPULATION 2014	2000-2009 ANNUAL RATE % Rate	2000-2009 ANNUAL RATE State Centile	HOUSEHOLDS 2000	HOUSEHOLDS 2009	HOUSEHOLDS 2014	HOUSEHOLDS % Annual Rate 2000-2009	HOUSEHOLDS 2009 Average HH Size	FAMILIES 2000	FAMILIES 2009	FAMILIES % Annual Rate 2000-2009
97001	ANTELOPE	065	184	185	184	0.1	23	72	72	72	0.0	2.51	50	50	0.0
97002	AURORA	047	5798	6045	6211	0.5	43	2154	2234	2290	0.4	2.68	1639	1675	0.2
97004	BEAVERCREEK	005	4380	4536	4622	0.4	39	1536	1577	1609	0.3	2.87	1263	1283	0.2
97005	BEAVERTON	067	22638	24465	25461	0.8	59	9433	10019	10415	0.7	2.39	5149	5301	0.3
97006	BEAVERTON	067	52369	64699	71134	2.3	95	19949	24418	26816	2.2	2.64	13177	15914	2.1
97007	BEAVERTON	067	56721	68994	75611	2.1	93	20457	24764	27149	2.1	2.77	14734	17529	1.9
97008	BEAVERTON	067	28481	31375	32989	1.1	71	11401	12477	13122	1.0	2.50	7327	7860	0.8
97009	BORING	005	7720	8083	8358	0.5	43	2832	2935	3040	0.4	2.74	2268	2321	0.3
97011	BRIGHTWOOD	005	1101	1284	1377	1.7	85	476	548	589	1.5	2.30	321	362	1.3
97013	CANBY	005	19651	22911	24525	1.7	85	6909	7948	8537	1.5	2.86	5293	6007	1.4
97014	CASCADE LOCKS	027	1298	1353	1363	0.4	39	495	506	507	0.2	2.67	363	369	0.2
97015	CLACKAMAS	005	18687	21196	22656	1.4	78	7244	8113	8670	1.2	2.60	4917	5396	1.0
97016	CLATSKANIE	009	6152	6791	7099	1.1	71	2366	2623	2746	1.1	2.58	1719	1883	1.0
97017	COLTON	005	2915	3028	3088	0.4	39	977	1007	1030	0.3	3.01	784	798	0.2
97018	COLUMBIA CITY	009	1571	2016	2216	2.7	97	595	759	837	2.7	2.65	458	581	2.6
97019	CORBETT	051	2962	3035	3122	0.3	32	1043	1082	1116	0.4	2.76	797	820	0.3
97021	DUFUR	065	1130	1119	1119	-0.1	14	459	454	454	-0.1	2.46	334	327	-0.2
97022	EAGLE CREEK	005	3628	3829	3935	0.6	48	1236	1294	1333	0.5	2.96	943	973	0.3
97023	ESTACADA	005	9371	10121	10474	0.8	59	3262	3460	3595	0.6	2.83	2468	2577	0.5
97024	FAIRVIEW	051	8124	9795	10468	2.0	91	3077	3678	3926	1.9	2.65	2074	2455	1.8
97026	GERVAIS	047	3528	4091	4369	1.6	83	905	1016	1079	1.3	3.97	749	835	1.2
97027	GLADSTONE	005	12247	13206	13669	0.8	59	4560	4847	5025	0.7	2.69	3259	3413	0.5
97028	GOVERNMENT CAMP	005	390	475	517	2.2	94	173	208	227	2.0	2.23	94	110	1.7
97029	GRASS VALLEY	055	383	382	373	0.0	19	157	156	153	-0.1	2.45	109	107	-0.2
97030	GRESHAM	051	30431	34732	36824	1.4	78	11734	13430	14242	1.5	2.55	7562	8556	1.3
97031	HOOD RIVER	027	16661	18359	19002	1.1	71	6004	6425	6607	0.7	2.77	4220	4466	0.6
97032	HUBBARD	047	4261	4920	5277	1.6	83	1348	1530	1632	1.4	3.22	1057	1187	1.3
97034	LAKE OSWEGO	005	18679	20454	21178	1.0	66	7405	8015	8321	0.9	2.54	5304	5663	0.7
97035	LAKE OSWEGO	005	22906	23860	24394	0.4	39	9917	10195	10450	0.3	2.33	6227	6264	0.1
97037	MAUPIN	065	1577	1575	1575	0.0	19	565	563	564	0.0	2.78	414	409	-0.1
97038	MOLALLA	005	12860	15076	16135	1.7	85	4482	5195	5578	1.6	2.87	3376	3848	1.4
97039	MORO	055	654	652	639	0.0	19	256	254	249	-0.1	2.57	176	173	-0.2
97040	MOSIER	065	997	1093	1133	1.0	66	394	432	448	1.0	2.52	262	285	0.9
97041	MOUNT HOOD PARKDALE	027	2622	2761	2832	0.6	48	813	838	857	0.3	2.95	638	652	0.2
97042	MULINO	005	2886	2992	3055	0.4	39	1033	1064	1091	0.3	2.80	825	839	0.2
97045	OREGON CITY	005	45229	53475	57376	1.8	87	16357	19029	20495	1.6	2.74	12344	14199	1.5
97048	RAINIER	009	6556	7081	7353	0.8	59	2451	2658	2764	0.9	2.66	1836	1971	0.8
97049	RHODODENDRON	005	1770	2144	2330	2.1	93	749	896	978	2.0	2.34	439	514	1.7
97050	RUFUS	055	264	265	263	0.0	19	130	130	129	0.0	2.04	87	86	-0.1
97051	SAINT HELENS	009	13238	15670	16802	1.8	87	4931	5802	6219	1.8	2.67	3489	4091	1.7
97053	WARREN	009	3144	3437	3583	1.0	66	1152	1257	1310	0.9	2.73	912	979	0.8
97054	DEER ISLAND	009	1300	1334	1354	0.3	32	489	503	511	0.3	2.65	384	392	0.2
97055	SANDY	005	13748	17335	19002	2.5	96	4926	6162	6775	2.4	2.81	3742	4594	2.2
97056	SCAPPOOSE	009	9174	10671	11431	1.6	83	3561	4173	4479	1.7	2.54	2590	2993	1.6
97057	SHANIKO	065	94	94	94	0.0	19	45	45	45	0.0	2.07	31	31	0.0
97058	THE DALLES	065	18871	19220	19395	0.2	26	7442	7537	7604	0.1	2.48	5114	5121	0.0
97060	TROUTDALE	051	17949	20703	22035	1.6	83	6151	7192	7673	1.7	2.82	4725	5470	1.6
97062	TUALATIN	067	24212	28919	31288	1.9	89	9067	10747	11637	1.9	2.68	6219	7255	1.7
97063	TYGH VALLEY	065	938	926	925	-0.1	14	424	418	418	-0.2	2.22	298	291	-0.3
97064	VERNONIA	009	3612	3878	4001	0.8	59	1285	1374	1418	0.7	2.82	973	1031	0.6
97065	WASCO	055	633	632	619	0.0	19	254	252	246	-0.1	2.51	174	170	-0.3
97067	WELCHES	005	1411	1693	1834	2.0	91	541	640	697	1.8	2.58	360	419	1.7
97068	WEST LINN	005	25486	29268	31337	1.5	80	9325	10604	11397	1.4	2.74	7264	8121	1.2
97070	WILSONVILLE	005	15223	18044	19448	1.9	89	6362	7348	7911	1.6	2.44	4133	4699	1.4
97071	WOODBURN	047	25114	30384	32818	2.1	93	7749	9198	9931	1.9	3.23	5670	6630	1.7
97080	GRESHAM	051	36639	43426	46659	1.9	89	13337	15899	17084	1.9	2.72	9906	11780	1.9
97086	HAPPY VALLEY	005	16829	24326	27828	4.1	99	6318	8672	9850	3.5	2.79	4445	6363	4.0
97089	DAMASCUS	005	7560	9193	10011	2.1	93	2558	3084	3367	2.0	2.98	2203	2624	1.9
97101	AMITY	071	3182	3538	3766	1.2	74	1055	1168	1240	1.1	3.02	849	932	1.0
97103	ASTORIA	007	17070	17823	18246	0.5	43	6847	7191	7382	0.5	2.37	4418	4576	0.4
97106	BANKS	067	4163	4984	5449	2.0	91	1413	1687	1845	1.9	2.95	1139	1341	1.8
97107	BAY CITY	057	1398	1536	1618	1.0	66	596	654	689	1.0	2.33	414	450	0.9
97108	BEAVER	057	569	620	652	0.9	62	230	251	263	0.9	2.47	171	185	0.9
97109	BUXTON	067	496	534	557	0.8	59	170	182	190	0.7	2.93	135	143	0.6
97111	CARLTON	071	2916	3370	3640	1.6	83	1005	1176	1271	1.7	2.86	799	928	1.6
97112	CLOVERDALE	057	2988	3238	3372	0.9	62	1257	1359	1416	0.8	2.38	891	951	0.7
97113	CORNELIUS	067	11880	13307	14076	1.2	74	3659	4053	4284	1.1	3.23	2786	3033	0.9
97114	DAYTON	071	4990	5745	6180	1.5	80	1643	1894	2036	1.5	3.02	1293	1474	1.4
97115	DUNDEE	071	3615	4282	4673	1.8	87	1264	1524	1667	2.0	2.79	1014	1212	1.9
97116	FOREST GROVE	067	21476	24923	26756	1.6	83	7670	8859	9533	1.6	2.70	5229	5984	1.5
97117	GALES CREEK	067	508	530	545	0.5	43	195	203	209	0.4	2.61	151	154	0.2
97119	GASTON	067	4693	5164	5452	1.0	66	1569	1728	1826	1.0	2.97	1290	1404	0.9
97121	HAMMOND	007	1261	1457	1552	1.6	83	493	578	620	1.7	2.51	344	397	1.6
97122	HEBO	057	255	276	286	0.9	62	104	112	116	0.8	2.46	75	80	0.7
97123	HILLSBORO	067	36047	44735	49592	2.4	95	11802	14549	16199	2.3	3.04	8893	10755	2.1
97124	HILLSBORO	067	38600	48708	53238	2.5	96	14587	18260	19967	2.5	2.63	9637	12059	2.5
97125	MANNING	067	89	93	96	0.5	43	29	30	31	0.4	3.10	21	22	0.5
97127	LAFAYETTE	071	2445	2530	2616	0.4	39	778	809	837	0.4	3.13	606	625	0.3
97128	MCMINNVILLE	071	29750	35301	38267	1.9	89	10514	12613	13714	2.0	2.67	7407	8831	1.9
97131	NEHALEM	057	2904	3214	3369	1.1	71	1284	1427	1501	1.1	2.18	825	903	1.0
97132	NEWBERG	071	24059	28569	31035	1.9	89	8223	9972	10893	2.1	2.74	6107	7326	2.0
97133	NORTH PLAINS	067	3676	4416	4845	2.0	91	1314	1577	1732	2.0	2.79	1016	1203	1.8
97136	ROCKAWAY BEACH	057	3014	3291	3433	1.0	66	1469	1600	1673	0.9	2.03	873	937	0.8
97137	SAINT PAUL	047	1498	1537	1566	0.3	32	452	461	470	0.2	3.14	333	335	0.1
97138	SEASIDE	007	9989	10485	10795	0.5	43	4418	4673	4828	0.6	2.20	2697	2814	0.5
97140	SHERWOOD	067	16855	22456	25345	3.2	97	6066	7980	8997	3.0	2.81	4767	6155	2.8
97141	TILLAMOOK	057	12673	13666	14181	0.8	59	5039	5412	5622	0.8	2.46	3407	3618	0.7
97144	TIMBER	067	174	183	189	0.5	43	66	69	71	0.5	2.64	49	50	0.2
97145	TOLOVANA PARK	007	1401	1558	1642	1.2	74	623	701	742	1.3	2.16	381	421	1.1
97146	WARRENTON	007	4860	5450	5754	1.2	74	1918	2185	2323	1.4	2.43	1319	1478	1.2
97148	YAMHILL	071	3061	3389	3594	1.1	71	1037	1167	1240	1.3	2.90	864	965	1.2
97149	NESKOWIN	057	429	455	474	0.6	48	201	213	221	0.6	2.14	129	135	0.5
97201	PORTLAND	051	12518	13959	14687	1.2	74	7637	8768	9289	1.5	1.52	2030	2154	0.6
97202	PORTLAND	051	37072	38517	39724	0.4	39	16684	17554	18149	0.6	2.12	8075	8343	0.4
97203	PORTLAND	051	27743	29848	31085	0.8	59	10004	10777	11229	0.8	2.65	6315	6716	0.7
	OREGON					1.3					1.2	2.51			1.1
	UNITED STATES					1.0					1.1	2.59			0.9

#	POST OFFICE NAME	RACE (%) White 2000	White 2009	Black 2000	Black 2009	Asian/Pacific 2000	Asian/Pacific 2009	% Hispanic Origin 2000	% Hispanic Origin 2009	2009 AGE DISTRIBUTION (%) 0-4	5-9	10-14	15-19	20-24	25-44	45-64	65-84	85+	18+	MEDIAN AGE 2009	% 2009 Males	% 2009 Females
97001	ANTELOPE	90.2	88.1	0.0	0.0	1.6	1.6	4.3	5.9	4.9	5.4	6.5	5.9	3.2	20.0	35.7	16.2	2.2	78.4	47.5	54.6	45.4
97002	AURORA	89.9	86.1	0.3	0.3	0.6	0.7	9.4	14.3	5.4	5.9	6.5	6.9	5.3	23.0	32.6	13.1	1.3	77.9	42.8	52.0	48.0
97004	BEAVERCREEK	95.4	94.6	0.3	0.4	0.7	0.8	2.0	3.0	4.8	6.3	6.5	6.7	4.7	22.4	37.7	9.9	1.1	78.2	44.1	50.9	49.1
97005	BEAVERTON	75.1	69.1	1.9	1.9	6.8	7.7	20.3	28.6	7.6	6.3	5.4	5.9	9.0	31.6	21.8	9.3	3.0	77.5	33.7	49.7	50.3
97006	BEAVERTON	75.5	70.4	1.8	1.9	13.1	15.6	10.6	15.0	8.5	7.3	6.6	6.3	8.0	35.4	21.6	5.6	0.7	73.8	31.2	50.4	49.6
97007	BEAVERTON	81.1	76.6	1.5	1.6	9.3	11.4	8.0	11.6	8.0	7.6	7.5	6.9	6.0	31.6	25.4	6.0	0.8	72.4	33.9	49.1	50.9
97008	BEAVERTON	83.3	79.6	1.6	1.6	6.4	7.9	9.9	13.8	6.5	6.1	6.3	6.4	7.3	29.4	26.5	9.6	1.9	77.2	36.3	48.8	51.2
97009	BORING	92.5	90.6	0.3	0.4	1.3	1.7	4.5	6.6	4.6	5.4	6.4	6.7	4.2	22.6	34.8	13.8	1.6	79.4	45.0	51.1	48.9
97011	BRIGHTWOOD	92.5	90.5	0.4	0.4	0.5	0.5	6.4	9.3	5.5	5.9	6.5	7.5	5.0	25.0	33.9	9.7	1.0	77.2	41.7	53.3	46.7
97013	CANBY	89.9	87.2	0.4	0.5	1.1	1.4	12.1	16.5	7.4	7.3	7.3	7.1	5.9	25.9	26.9	10.2	1.9	73.5	36.7	49.8	50.2
97014	CASCADE LOCKS	89.8	88.2	0.2	0.1	0.8	1.0	6.4	9.4	6.3	6.9	7.2	7.3	5.0	26.1	31.3	8.6	1.2	74.9	38.8	50.2	49.8
97015	CLACKAMAS	85.8	82.4	1.4	1.6	6.7	8.6	4.5	6.6	8.2	7.0	6.5	6.3	8.6	30.6	24.4	7.4	0.9	74.6	32.5	48.5	51.5
97016	CLATSKANIE	94.8	93.9	0.1	0.1	0.6	0.7	2.2	3.2	5.8	5.8	6.3	6.9	6.0	22.1	31.6	13.8	1.8	77.8	42.8	50.6	49.4
97017	COLTON	94.8	93.9	0.3	0.3	0.7	0.9	2.0	2.9	5.4	6.0	6.9	7.9	5.4	23.1	34.0	10.2	1.0	76.8	41.6	49.4	50.6
97018	COLUMBIA CITY	94.8	93.7	0.4	0.4	0.7	0.9	3.0	4.3	6.2	6.8	7.6	7.6	4.5	24.7	31.1	10.4	1.1	74.2	40.1	52.1	47.9
97019	CORBETT	94.2	93.0	0.2	0.3	1.5	1.9	2.3	3.5	5.0	5.7	6.5	7.4	4.6	24.3	35.3	10.2	1.0	78.1	42.3	50.6	49.4
97021	DUFUR	93.8	92.7	0.2	0.2	0.1	0.1	1.9	2.9	4.9	5.3	5.9	6.6	5.5	20.8	34.2	14.7	2.1	79.8	45.6	51.7	48.3
97022	EAGLE CREEK	92.9	91.1	0.5	0.6	0.5	0.6	4.9	7.1	5.2	6.0	6.9	7.4	5.1	22.7	34.6	11.0	1.2	77.3	42.9	50.7	49.3
97023	ESTACADA	91.0	88.6	0.5	0.6	0.9	1.1	6.4	9.4	5.4	5.7	6.5	9.2	6.3	23.6	31.4	10.5	1.4	76.9	39.9	51.4	48.6
97024	FAIRVIEW	78.6	74.1	2.8	3.1	3.3	4.2	13.6	18.1	8.0	7.5	7.2	6.9	6.1	30.1	24.7	8.4	1.0	73.3	34.6	50.5	49.5
97026	GERVAIS	54.7	45.9	0.3	0.3	0.5	0.5	47.4	58.1	9.8	9.2	8.5	9.2	7.9	29.3	19.6	5.6	0.9	67.3	28.4	52.7	47.3
97027	GLADSTONE	91.4	89.2	0.7	0.8	2.2	2.7	5.5	8.1	6.2	6.3	6.6	6.7	5.5	26.2	28.6	11.7	2.2	76.6	39.7	48.8	51.2
97028	GOVERNMENT CAMP	94.1	92.8	0.3	0.2	0.8	1.1	5.9	8.8	4.6	4.6	5.1	5.7	6.3	28.0	33.3	11.4	1.1	82.3	41.6	54.3	45.7
97029	GRASS VALLEY	94.8	94.8	0.5	0.5	0.3	0.3	4.2	3.9	4.5	4.7	5.5	6.5	6.0	19.1	34.8	16.5	2.4	80.9	47.1	49.7	50.3
97030	GRESHAM	84.2	80.2	1.9	2.1	3.3	4.1	10.7	15.1	7.7	7.0	6.5	7.0	7.7	28.7	23.4	9.7	2.4	75.0	33.8	48.8	51.2
97031	HOOD RIVER	78.5	72.8	0.7	0.7	1.6	1.9	25.2	33.4	7.5	7.1	7.0	7.2	6.3	26.2	26.2	10.2	2.3	73.8	36.5	49.2	50.8
97032	HUBBARD	78.8	71.0	0.2	0.2	0.7	0.8	21.7	31.4	8.5	8.3	7.8	7.7	6.9	27.2	24.4	8.2	1.0	70.7	32.4	51.3	48.7
97034	LAKE OSWEGO	94.1	92.9	0.5	0.5	2.7	3.5	2.1	3.1	4.2	5.0	6.6	7.2	4.5	18.6	37.9	13.7	2.2	79.4	47.2	48.4	51.6
97035	LAKE OSWEGO	89.4	87.1	0.7	0.8	5.5	7.0	3.0	4.4	5.3	5.9	6.5	6.2	6.0	26.8	32.5	9.3	1.6	78.2	40.8	48.3	51.7
97037	MAUPIN	57.5	55.7	0.1	0.1	0.8	1.0	5.5	6.9	7.6	7.3	7.3	6.6	5.4	20.6	28.5	15.6	1.1	73.6	40.9	52.1	47.9
97038	MOLALLA	91.0	88.5	0.4	0.4	0.7	0.9	7.0	10.2	8.6	7.9	7.5	7.1	5.8	29.2	24.0	8.4	1.5	71.7	33.5	49.5	50.5
97039	MORO	94.0	94.0	0.3	0.3	0.5	0.5	4.6	4.4	4.9	5.2	5.7	6.7	5.8	19.3	33.7	16.1	2.5	80.2	46.3	49.8	50.2
97040	MOSIER	89.1	86.1	0.7	0.7	0.9	1.1	10.8	15.5	5.9	7.0	6.4	6.4	4.9	23.3	32.6	12.7	0.8	76.0	42.4	50.3	49.7
97041	MOUNT HOOD PARKDALE	76.5	71.2	0.0	0.0	1.8	2.1	31.6	40.3	7.0	7.8	7.1	7.5	5.5	25.6	28.4	9.7	1.3	73.4	37.2	52.4	47.6
97042	MULINO	96.2	95.5	0.2	0.2	0.6	0.7	2.1	3.2	4.8	5.4	7.0	7.4	4.6	22.4	34.8	12.3	1.3	78.0	43.9	51.7	48.3
97045	OREGON CITY	93.9	92.4	0.5	0.5	1.0	1.4	3.8	5.7	6.8	6.9	7.0	6.7	5.6	26.9	28.9	9.7	1.6	75.3	38.1	49.5	50.5
97048	RAINIER	94.5	93.7	0.1	0.1	0.6	0.8	1.7	2.5	5.4	5.5	6.3	6.8	5.7	22.4	33.3	13.0	1.5	78.4	43.3	49.2	50.8
97049	RHODODENDRON	93.2	91.7	0.3	0.3	0.7	0.8	6.3	9.2	5.0	5.1	5.6	6.3	5.8	26.9	33.4	10.8	1.0	80.3	41.6	54.0	46.0
97050	RUFUS	93.6	93.2	0.0	0.0	1.1	1.1	4.5	4.9	6.4	6.8	6.4	5.3	4.9	21.5	28.3	17.7	2.6	76.6	44.0	51.3	48.7
97051	SAINT HELENS	93.4	92.4	0.3	0.3	0.8	1.0	3.5	5.0	7.7	7.0	6.9	7.4	7.1	26.7	26.1	9.4	1.6	73.6	35.6	50.1	49.9
97053	WARREN	95.6	94.9	0.2	0.2	0.5	0.7	2.3	3.4	4.6	5.2	6.0	6.6	4.7	21.2	35.6	14.4	1.7	80.1	46.0	50.4	49.6
97054	DEER ISLAND	94.7	93.9	0.1	0.1	0.8	1.2	1.2	1.8	4.9	5.5	6.5	7.5	4.9	21.8	35.6	12.1	1.1	78.5	44.1	51.6	48.4
97055	SANDY	94.2	93.0	0.3	0.3	0.9	1.1	3.4	5.1	6.3	6.9	7.3	7.0	5.1	25.7	30.7	9.6	1.2	74.9	39.0	50.2	49.8
97056	SCAPPOOSE	94.6	93.7	0.3	0.3	0.8	1.0	2.4	3.3	5.9	6.4	6.7	6.4	5.2	25.2	31.8	10.9	1.6	76.8	41.1	49.7	50.3
97057	SHANIKO	90.4	88.3	0.0	0.0	1.1	2.1	4.3	5.3	5.3	6.4	6.4	6.4	3.2	21.3	33.0	16.0	2.1	76.6	45.6	54.3	45.7
97058	THE DALLES	88.1	84.6	0.3	0.3	1.5	1.8	10.3	14.6	6.7	6.3	6.2	6.7	6.2	23.1	28.2	13.6	3.0	76.5	40.5	48.9	51.1
97060	TROUTDALE	86.6	83.4	1.7	2.0	3.7	4.9	6.9	9.7	8.2	7.9	7.6	7.3	6.1	31.0	25.3	5.9	0.6	71.8	33.1	50.1	49.9
97062	TUALATIN	87.6	84.6	0.8	0.8	3.8	4.6	10.8	15.2	7.2	7.0	7.0	7.0	7.5	29.1	27.9	6.3	1.0	74.5	34.9	49.6	50.4
97063	TYGH VALLEY	93.5	91.6	0.2	0.3	0.9	1.1	3.9	5.8	3.6	3.9	3.9	4.2	4.3	12.3	34.7	31.3	1.8	86.3	57.8	50.6	49.4
97064	VERNONIA	95.9	95.3	0.4	0.4	0.5	0.7	1.9	2.7	7.7	7.6	7.7	7.4	5.9	24.8	28.1	9.7	1.1	72.5	36.9	49.9	50.1
97065	WASCO	92.4	92.4	0.0	0.0	0.3	0.3	5.7	5.9	6.0	6.0	6.6	7.0	5.4	19.5	32.8	14.7	2.1	77.1	44.6	49.7	50.3
97067	WELCHES	92.1	90.1	0.4	0.4	0.4	0.5	6.7	9.7	5.6	5.9	6.5	7.5	5.0	25.0	33.3	10.2	1.0	77.1	41.6	53.4	46.6
97068	WEST LINN	93.5	91.9	0.5	0.6	3.0	3.8	2.8	4.1	5.9	6.6	7.8	7.5	4.7	22.9	34.2	9.2	1.2	74.8	41.3	49.8	50.2
97070	WILSONVILLE	90.9	88.4	0.6	0.7	2.3	2.9	6.6	9.7	7.5	6.4	6.0	5.7	7.3	28.5	24.7	11.3	2.6	76.7	36.2	48.6	51.4
97071	WOODBURN	62.3	56.1	0.4	0.4	0.7	0.8	44.1	52.6	8.6	7.9	7.2	8.4	6.8	25.4	18.8	13.3	3.6	71.2	32.8	51.2	48.8
97080	GRESHAM	89.3	86.7	1.0	1.2	3.4	4.5	5.6	8.0	6.9	6.7	6.8	7.1	6.6	27.6	28.7	8.3	1.2	75.2	36.0	49.4	50.6
97086	HAPPY VALLEY	83.2	80.6	1.8	1.7	8.3	10.6	6.7	7.8	6.7	6.5	6.9	7.1	6.7	26.5	28.4	8.9	2.2	75.6	37.3	48.9	51.1
97089	DAMASCUS	94.7	93.6	0.3	0.4	1.9	2.4	2.2	3.2	4.4	5.8	7.7	7.8	4.0	19.8	38.7	10.9	0.9	77.0	45.3	50.3	49.7
97101	AMITY	92.3	90.1	0.3	0.3	0.6	0.8	7.5	11.4	6.9	6.9	7.2	7.1	5.7	25.9	29.3	9.9	1.1	74.5	37.7	50.8	49.2
97103	ASTORIA	92.1	90.6	0.8	0.9	1.6	2.1	4.7	6.7	5.9	5.6	6.3	8.3	7.3	22.9	29.2	12.2	2.4	77.5	40.0	49.5	50.5
97106	BANKS	93.6	91.9	0.3	0.3	1.3	1.8	3.4	5.4	6.9	7.3	8.2	7.9	4.3	25.5	31.1	8.1	0.8	72.5	38.9	50.8	49.2
97107	BAY CITY	93.6	92.3	0.4	0.5	0.9	1.3	3.2	4.4	4.4	4.7	5.1	5.1	3.6	22.3	35.4	17.3	2.1	82.6	47.9	49.2	50.8
97108	BEAVER	96.0	95.5	0.2	0.2	0.2	0.2	5.4	8.2	6.0	6.1	6.8	7.3	5.0	19.5	32.7	14.7	1.9	76.8	44.5	48.2	51.8
97109	BUXTON	95.5	93.6	0.4	0.6	0.2	0.4	3.2	5.2	6.2	5.2	7.3	9.9	4.1	24.5	34.8	7.7	0.2	74.7	40.9	51.3	48.7
97111	CARLTON	93.1	91.0	0.1	0.2	0.4	0.5	4.7	7.0	6.5	7.2	7.8	7.6	5.0	23.7	30.2	10.9	1.2	73.9	39.5	50.5	49.5
97112	CLOVERDALE	93.5	92.2	0.2	0.2	0.6	0.7	2.7	4.1	4.0	4.7	5.3	5.9	3.6	19.0	35.7	19.3	2.4	82.4	49.7	49.7	50.3
97113	CORNELIUS	73.8	66.4	0.6	0.6	1.4	1.6	30.5	40.7	9.1	8.4	7.8	7.3	6.0	31.6	21.2	7.5	1.1	70.2	31.9	51.7	48.3
97114	DAYTON	85.7	81.5	0.9	1.0	0.7	0.8	19.1	26.8	7.6	7.6	7.7	8.0	6.1	25.2	25.5	10.9	1.4	72.1	35.8	49.5	50.5
97115	DUNDEE	92.6	90.4	0.2	0.2	1.1	1.4	6.9	10.3	6.8	7.4	8.0	7.4	4.4	25.3	29.7	9.8	1.1	72.7	39.3	51.2	48.8
97116	FOREST GROVE	83.3	78.4	0.4	0.4	2.1	2.4	15.9	22.2	7.8	7.5	7.5	8.5	6.5	27.2	24.0	8.5	2.5	73.0	34.5	48.8	51.2
97117	GALES CREEK	95.5	94.5	0.2	0.2	0.8	0.9	3.3	5.3	4.5	5.7	6.4	6.4	3.6	23.2	36.0	12.6	1.5	79.2	45.1	50.8	49.2
97119	GASTON	93.2	90.7	0.2	0.2	1.0	1.3	5.7	9.0	5.6	6.5	7.3	7.5	4.8	22.6	34.6	10.1	1.1	75.8	41.9	51.2	48.8
97121	HAMMOND	91.8	89.8	0.2	0.2	1.3	1.7	3.6	5.6	7.9	7.5	7.3	6.5	5.6	27.0	25.4	11.5	1.4	73.0	36.2	50.7	49.3
97122	HEBO	95.3	93.8	0.0	0.0	0.4	0.4	2.4	3.6	3.3	5.1	6.2	8.7	2.5	19.2	37.0	15.6	2.5	80.1	47.7	50.4	49.6
97123	HILLSBORO	77.4	73.1	0.8	0.9	4.5	5.6	23.4	28.6	9.0	8.1	7.6	7.1	6.2	30.8	23.0	7.1	1.2	71.0	32.9	51.3	48.7
97124	HILLSBORO	81.0	76.8	1.1	1.1	7.3	8.9	13.1	17.7	8.4	7.5	7.0	6.4	7.4	34.8	21.9	5.7	0.9	73.3	31.9	51.1	48.9
97125	MANNING	93.3	92.5	0.0	0.0	1.1	1.1	4.4	6.5	4.3	6.5	6.5	6.5	4.3	22.6	39.8	8.6	1.1	78.5	44.6	48.4	51.6
97127	LAFAYETTE	86.1	82.1	0.4	0.5	0.9	1.0	19.9	27.8	9.6	9.5	9.3	7.5	4.8	29.1	23.0	6.5	0.7	66.8	32.5	49.2	50.8
97128	MCMINNVILLE	87.3	84.3	0.6	0.7	1.4	1.7	13.4	18.2	7.2	6.7	6.5	8.4	8.1	26.3	23.6	10.7	2.4	75.4	34.3	48.8	51.2
97131	NEHALEM	95.7	94.7	0.4	0.5	1.0	1.3	2.9	4.2	3.5	4.0	4.3	4.3	3.0	18.1	34.4	24.8	3.7	85.5	54.7	50.0	50.0
97132	NEWBERG	91.5	89.0	0.3	0.4	1.2	1.5	8.9	12.8	7.2	6.7	6.7	8.0	8.3	26.1	25.6	9.6	1.9	75.3	34.9	49.1	50.9
97133	NORTH PLAINS	91.1	87.9	0.1	0.1	1.6	2.0	7.3	11.5	6.0	7.0	8.0	7.5	4.0	23.5	32.4	10.4	1.2	74.1	41.3	51.5	48.5
97136	ROCKAWAY BEACH	94.8	94.0	0.1	0.2	1.0	1.2	1.9	2.8	2.5	3.6	4.0	4.0	3.4	16.4	36.6	26.1	3.5	87.4	55.3	49.7	50.3
97137	SAINT PAUL	71.6	62.3	0.2	0.2	0.2	0.3	29.2	39.8	6.8	7.3	7.3	9.2	6.9	29.2	23.7	8.3	1.3	73.2	33.8	58.4	41.6
97138	SEASIDE	94.1	92.8	0.2	0.3	1.0	1.3	5.2	7.6	4.6	4.6	5.4	6.5	5.1	21.5	34.1	15.4	2.9	81.6	46.6	48.6	51.4
97140	SHERWOOD	92.6	90.2	0.4	0.4	2.1	2.8	4.6	7.4	9.6	9.3	8.8	6.6	4.4	30.3	23.9	6.3	0.8	67.9	34.8	49.3	50.7
97141	TILLAMOOK	93.2	91.6	0.2	0.2	0.9	1.1	7.3	10.5	5.9	6.3	6.4	7.4	5.3	23.2	29.7	13.6	2.1	76.4	41.5	51.3	48.7
97144	TIMBER	93.7	92.3	0.6	0.5	1.1	1.1	4.0	6.6	4.9	6.0	6.6	7.1	4.4	23.5	36.6	9.8	1.1	77.0	43.4	49.7	50.3
97145	TOLOVANA PARK	93.7	91.8	0.3	0.4	0.6	0.7	7.4	11.0	3.9	4.2	4.5	6.2	4.3	17.8	36.7	20.2	2.2	84.3	49.8	48.1	51.9
97146	WARRENTON	94.2	93.0	0.2	0.2	1.7	2.3	2.0	3.0	5.7	5.9	7.1	7.8	5.0	22.4	31.2	13.2	1.7	76.1	42.2	50.9	49.1
97148	YAMHILL	94.6	93.2	0.1	0.1	0.7	0.9	4.3	6.6	5.7	6.6	7.6	8.0	5.5	23.2	32.7	9.3	1.4	74.5	40.2	50.5	49.5
97149	NESKOWIN	95.3	94.5	0.2	0.2	1.2	1.5	3.0	4.6	2.9	4.0	5.3	5.7	1.8	15.2	40.4	20.9	4.0	84.6	52.8	47.9	52.1
97201	PORTLAND	83.3	78.7	1.9	2.3	9.4	12.7	3.5	5.1	2.3	1.8	1.8	5.8	15.0	35.1	22.7	12.1	3.5	92.9	34.4	50.5	49.5
97202	PORTLAND	86.4	83.6	1.9	2.2	5.5	7.0	4.4	6.3	5.1	4.4	4.3	5.7	8.7	33.9	26.4	9.0	2.5	83.7	37.0	49.0	51.0
97203	PORTLAND	68.9	64.0	9.5	10.1	6.4	7.6	13.7	18.6	8.2	7.4	6.6	9.0	8.9	28.5	21.9	7.8	1.4	73.7	31.2	49.8	50.2
	OREGON	86.6	83.7	1.6	1.7	3.2	4.0	8.0	11.2	6.5	6.2	6.3	6.8	6.8	26.7	27.5	11.1	2.1	77.0	38.0	49.6	50.4
	UNITED STATES	75.1	72.0	12.3	12.7	3.8	4.6	12.5	15.7	6.8	6.7	6.6	7.1	6.9	27.0	26.0	10.9	1.9	75.7	36.9	49.2	50.8

#	POST OFFICE NAME	2009 Per Capita Income	2009 HH Income Base	2009 HOUSEHOLD INCOME DISTRIBUTION (%) Less than $25,000	$25,000 to $49,999	$50,000 to $99,999	$100,000 to $149,999	$150,000 or More	MEDIAN HOUSEHOLD INCOME 2009	2014	2009 National Centile	2009 State Centile	2009 Home Value Base	2009 HOME VALUE DISTRIBUTION (%) Less than $50,000	$50,000 to $89,999	$90,000 to $174,999	$175,000 to $399,999	$400,000 or More	2009 Median Home Value
97001	ANTELOPE	19935	72	25.0	34.7	34.7	2.8	2.8	42322	43128	40	36	47	8.5	12.8	38.3	31.9	8.5	148611
97002	AURORA	26437	2234	15.2	24.5	43.8	9.3	7.3	58360	59483	76	80	1806	7.4	3.7	21.3	35.3	32.3	248380
97004	BEAVERCREEK	30153	1577	6.8	13.7	46.0	26.6	6.9	72111	74964	88	96	1392	1.1	1.7	4.6	44.2	48.3	393372
97005	BEAVERTON	24237	10019	19.9	33.9	33.8	9.5	3.0	45897	50038	51	47	4064	7.6	1.2	11.4	71.1	8.8	249572
97006	BEAVERTON	27822	24418	11.9	24.4	41.2	16.7	5.7	63649	65935	82	89	12962	3.1	4.6	11.1	62.8	18.4	290932
97007	BEAVERTON	32087	24764	9.1	18.6	40.4	21.1	10.8	72134	75835	88	96	15600	1.2	0.6	4.5	60.8	32.9	341320
97008	BEAVERTON	29808	12477	12.2	26.7	38.8	15.6	6.7	61377	63477	79	84	6972	1.6	0.3	7.0	74.3	16.8	318673
97009	BORING	29257	2935	10.5	20.1	40.4	22.0	7.1	67829	70867	85	94	2486	5.9	6.1	11.9	36.7	39.3	349811
97011	BRIGHTWOOD	30862	548	16.6	20.1	40.7	17.3	5.3	62962	65155	81	87	428	9.8	2.3	20.6	49.8	17.5	241667
97013	CANBY	25889	7948	14.3	23.1	39.0	17.1	6.5	62107	64332	80	85	5776	3.8	4.4	13.4	52.8	25.6	301055
97014	CASCADE LOCKS	19740	506	26.1	25.5	40.5	6.3	1.6	48070	51548	57	53	350	9.4	6.0	38.9	38.6	7.1	169792
97015	CLACKAMAS	28614	8113	13.7	24.2	37.6	18.1	6.4	62978	65754	81	87	4930	15.1	8.9	7.8	46.7	21.5	307864
97016	CLATSKANIE	22791	2623	24.2	25.3	40.4	7.2	2.9	50547	54091	62	60	2056	8.3	5.3	28.9	50.6	7.0	196291
97017	COLTON	24777	1007	14.7	16.1	50.9	13.1	5.2	65491	67879	84	92	840	1.4	0.2	9.2	52.7	36.4	352893
97018	COLUMBIA CITY	29010	759	11.9	17.4	52.7	11.9	6.2	69347	71033	86	95	632	2.1	2.7	25.3	49.8	20.1	268493
97019	CORBETT	29652	1082	11.1	17.3	44.4	20.0	7.3	73701	75411	89	97	868	2.5	0.8	4.6	49.1	43.0	374370
97021	DUFUR	22664	454	22.7	29.7	38.5	6.2	2.9	46991	46966	54	50	318	3.5	10.4	37.7	36.5	11.9	172642
97022	EAGLE CREEK	22518	1294	14.9	25.1	44.2	12.7	3.1	60037	60726	77	82	1116	7.0	11.4	11.5	39.3	30.8	290000
97023	ESTACADA	24490	3460	17.4	22.7	38.4	16.9	4.7	60511	62182	78	83	2685	6.4	4.7	13.3	47.2	28.4	289255
97024	FAIRVIEW	25319	3678	16.0	25.8	42.5	10.5	5.2	56351	58527	73	76	2317	18.6	10.3	13.1	42.9	15.1	214487
97026	GERVAIS	15886	1016	18.2	24.4	44.2	8.8	4.4	54070	55275	70	71	771	1.9	4.4	19.6	62.8	11.3	221382
97027	GLADSTONE	24918	4847	15.0	23.3	43.8	14.9	3.0	61951	63915	80	85	3365	4.9	3.5	7.1	72.6	11.9	271617
97028	GOVERNMENT CAMP	35735	208	21.6	17.3	35.1	16.3	9.6	64830	68401	83	91	148	0.0	0.7	21.6	52.0	25.7	290000
97029	GRASS VALLEY	22505	156	25.6	27.6	39.7	3.2	3.8	46330	46617	52	47	112	10.7	10.7	49.1	23.2	6.3	132143
97030	GRESHAM	24494	13430	19.9	26.0	40.2	10.1	3.7	53934	57219	70	70	6777	3.5	2.3	6.3	79.3	8.6	264954
97031	HOOD RIVER	21598	6425	20.8	29.0	39.7	5.9	4.7	50154	52461	62	57	4099	5.8	1.9	11.1	57.8	23.4	265303
97032	HUBBARD	20340	1530	15.8	27.5	43.0	9.8	3.9	55572	57419	72	73	1164	8.1	4.9	14.9	57.1	14.9	226523
97034	LAKE OSWEGO	53763	8015	7.3	13.1	28.6	21.4	29.5	102111	104435	97	100	6201	0.2	0.7	0.9	24.6	73.6	560323
97035	LAKE OSWEGO	42074	10195	9.8	19.6	34.4	20.6	15.6	72934	76708	88	97	6617	0.4	0.0	4.1	43.5	52.0	412846
97037	MAUPIN	17283	563	25.6	35.0	34.8	2.5	2.1	41316	42887	37	32	398	8.3	13.6	36.2	33.4	8.5	156395
97038	MOLALLA	23150	5195	16.0	24.6	43.0	12.2	4.2	60662	62568	78	83	3721	5.2	4.6	15.6	51.8	22.7	249608
97039	MORO	20837	254	26.4	29.5	37.0	3.5	3.5	44307	45122	46	43	182	11.0	12.6	46.7	24.2	5.5	131818
97040	MOSIER	23768	432	21.1	29.4	39.8	5.8	3.9	49589	50000	60	56	319	8.5	8.2	23.8	37.0	22.6	238043
97041	MOUNT HOOD PARKDALE	20043	838	17.1	36.9	34.2	8.2	3.6	45134	50785	49	45	588	1.7	1.9	21.3	48.3	26.9	293056
97042	MULINO	29712	1064	11.4	21.2	38.9	20.4	8.1	70641	75332	87	96	924	5.1	1.6	7.1	37.7	48.5	393000
97045	OREGON CITY	27348	19029	12.7	21.6	41.4	18.3	5.9	64492	66834	83	91	13847	4.1	3.3	10.4	54.6	27.5	311277
97048	RAINIER	22925	2658	19.9	23.1	46.0	8.0	2.9	55592	58593	72	73	2079	10.9	3.9	19.2	51.5	14.4	231522
97049	RHODODENDRON	32876	896	19.3	18.6	37.1	16.9	8.1	64287	67126	83	90	659	4.2	1.1	22.0	51.3	21.4	269688
97050	RUFUS	22776	130	33.8	30.8	26.9	3.8	4.6	35000	35741	18	10	84	20.2	21.4	35.7	16.7	6.0	116667
97051	SAINT HELENS	23508	5802	20.7	21.5	45.8	8.6	3.4	57272	60674	74	77	3938	3.0	2.2	18.9	62.7	13.2	237027
97053	WARREN	28180	1257	14.9	21.6	41.0	14.4	8.1	63553	66029	82	89	1094	5.6	1.5	7.0	52.7	33.2	341587
97054	DEER ISLAND	25494	503	15.1	22.9	50.5	7.0	4.6	57319	59786	74	78	410	8.3	2.0	12.0	47.3	30.5	310112
97055	SANDY	25365	6162	16.9	23.3	39.9	14.6	5.4	61096	63058	79	84	4725	7.4	3.7	13.5	47.9	27.4	282090
97056	SCAPPOOSE	27355	4173	15.7	20.1	47.0	13.0	4.2	62199	64092	80	86	3203	6.3	1.6	14.5	54.2	23.4	271096
97057	SHANIKO	24451	45	22.2	35.6	33.3	4.4	4.4	42951	42682	42	38	29	3.4	17.2	34.5	34.5	10.3	162500
97058	THE DALLES	22127	7537	25.8	27.0	37.4	6.7	3.1	46535	47253	53	48	5036	5.5	4.5	34.9	47.7	7.4	185846
97060	TROUTDALE	27516	7192	9.9	18.9	47.7	17.8	5.7	69525	70596	86	95	5142	6.2	2.6	10.2	69.0	11.9	275919
97062	TUALATIN	35167	10747	9.9	21.1	36.0	19.5	13.5	69856	73238	87	95	6098	4.6	2.2	4.9	45.1	43.2	375255
97063	TYGH VALLEY	20792	418	29.4	38.0	28.2	1.7	2.6	37169	40787	24	17	338	11.8	8.6	29.3	40.2	10.1	176000
97064	VERNONIA	20424	1374	20.4	27.6	43.1	6.0	3.0	51164	53833	64	62	1081	3.6	3.6	26.0	52.6	14.2	225125
97065	WASCO	19436	252	28.2	31.7	31.7	6.3	2.0	42196	43185	40	35	184	7.6	20.1	38.0	31.5	2.7	138158
97067	WELCHES	27718	640	15.2	20.2	41.7	17.7	5.3	63504	65364	82	89	499	10.8	2.2	22.4	49.1	15.4	232566
97068	WEST LINN	45403	10604	7.2	13.5	30.8	23.0	25.4	96089	98510	96	100	8293	0.7	0.1	3.7	35.2	60.3	469048
97070	WILSONVILLE	36103	7348	12.1	22.8	35.1	19.6	10.4	67513	72200	85	93	4091	6.9	5.5	7.6	37.2	42.8	368935
97071	WOODBURN	16681	9198	23.8	31.4	36.6	5.5	2.6	43942	50007	45	42	6222	5.0	3.2	32.9	49.6	9.3	198842
97080	GRESHAM	29057	15899	11.9	19.6	43.8	17.5	7.2	68557	70048	86	94	10868	2.2	1.0	4.8	65.3	26.7	326788
97086	HAPPY VALLEY	38122	8672	10.8	17.3	31.3	20.8	19.7	78192	85138	91	98	6199	2.6	1.3	0.7	37.5	57.8	444389
97089	DAMASCUS	34091	3084	4.4	11.3	41.0	28.2	15.1	88820	90553	95	99	2811	1.2	0.1	2.1	40.7	56.0	430651
97101	AMITY	20996	1168	13.4	26.6	48.2	9.5	2.3	58346	60704	76	80	878	0.7	2.7	20.3	50.5	25.9	250000
97103	ASTORIA	23543	7191	23.6	29.2	38.0	6.1	3.1	47296	49533	55	51	4523	3.5	2.7	19.9	61.2	12.7	225388
97106	BANKS	28007	1687	9.8	18.0	39.4	26.3	6.5	74960	78286	89	97	1377	3.3	0.8	4.6	46.8	44.4	374836
97107	BAY CITY	23800	654	24.9	29.5	37.0	5.7	2.9	44692	45124	47	44	486	1.6	3.1	37.7	50.6	7.0	191228
97108	BEAVER	22694	251	21.9	33.9	35.1	5.6	3.6	43142	43860	43	39	203	0.0	12.8	15.8	54.2	17.2	261500
97109	BUXTON	24160	182	16.5	20.3	35.7	22.5	4.9	63778	65999	82	90	152	13.8	3.3	3.9	38.8	40.1	351613
97111	CARLTON	20544	1176	16.8	25.6	51.0	5.3	1.4	56096	60291	73	75	901	4.8	0.8	15.6	53.4	25.4	274485
97112	CLOVERDALE	24180	1359	24.2	27.8	38.3	6.8	2.9	46475	46432	53	48	1062	5.2	2.6	21.8	45.5	25.0	252846
97113	CORNELIUS	21023	4053	14.3	23.2	46.3	12.7	3.5	61621	63153	80	84	3013	11.1	4.7	20.1	53.8	10.3	219577
97114	DAYTON	21008	1894	15.7	27.6	45.6	7.2	4.0	54820	57884	71	72	1390	6.1	6.4	19.6	44.8	23.0	239367
97115	DUNDEE	27599	1524	12.7	20.7	45.5	14.0	7.0	67717	68790	85	94	1272	2.8	1.3	10.0	53.8	32.2	314394
97116	FOREST GROVE	23362	8859	20.5	23.4	39.3	13.6	3.1	56701	59321	74	76	5241	6.0	4.7	11.3	60.0	18.0	267002
97117	GALES CREEK	30302	203	12.3	16.3	45.3	20.2	5.9	69230	72747	86	95	159	5.0	0.6	5.0	47.8	41.5	363514
97119	GASTON	29365	1728	10.6	22.0	43.9	15.5	8.0	65971	68436	84	93	1384	1.9	1.0	9.2	33.1	54.8	442038
97121	HAMMOND	22232	578	27.9	24.2	40.1	4.3	3.5	47571	48942	56	52	367	1.6	0.3	20.2	73.0	4.9	220991
97122	HEBO	26481	112	24.1	20.5	48.2	4.5	2.7	60000	60000	77	82	87	9.2	0.0	29.9	47.1	13.8	210294
97123	HILLSBORO	25510	14549	13.3	20.4	41.1	18.3	6.9	66345	69238	84	93	9877	4.8	1.9	6.8	67.9	18.6	289501
97124	HILLSBORO	31338	18260	10.4	19.4	41.6	21.0	7.7	70128	74284	87	96	9322	0.4	0.6	4.9	69.1	24.9	321937
97125	MANNING	23296	30	20.0	20.0	40.0	13.3	6.7	62351	66479	80	86	24	4.2	4.2	4.2	41.7	45.8	380000
97127	LAFAYETTE	17843	809	20.5	30.3	42.8	4.3	2.1	48801	52957	58	54	618	6.6	7.4	41.3	40.8	3.9	161475
97128	MCMINNVILLE	23529	12613	19.4	24.8	43.4	8.0	4.5	54043	57294	70	70	8087	3.8	5.1	18.4	55.6	17.1	239633
97131	NEHALEM	26293	1427	26.0	33.9	29.1	5.5	5.5	41760	43153	39	33	1149	6.5	2.0	17.1	40.5	33.9	300269
97132	NEWBERG	26256	9972	13.5	23.6	46.3	10.5	6.2	63892	65497	82	90	6843	3.7	5.2	11.6	55.3	24.2	260871
97133	NORTH PLAINS	32807	1577	12.9	18.0	34.3	24.9	9.9	76435	79490	90	98	1222	3.6	1.4	12.8	32.1	50.1	401087
97136	ROCKAWAY BEACH	22261	1600	32.1	32.8	29.6	3.8	1.6	37019	39694	24	16	1147	6.4	4.5	24.3	47.9	16.9	221733
97137	SAINT PAUL	22848	461	17.1	23.0	42.5	9.1	8.2	55739	56380	72	74	287	4.5	2.4	10.8	48.4	33.8	305102
97138	SEASIDE	25869	4673	26.2	26.5	37.3	6.4	3.7	46103	49499	52	47	2800	4.4	3.3	12.7	55.0	24.6	286968
97140	SHERWOOD	37258	7980	7.7	14.6	34.5	27.6	15.6	87428	89852	94	99	6372	2.0	3.0	10.5	49.1	35.3	352000
97141	TILLAMOOK	22099	5412	25.2	29.4	38.2	3.9	3.3	44942	45825	48	45	3626	5.4	2.7	25.3	49.3	17.3	226556
97144	TIMBER	27008	69	18.8	15.9	43.5	14.5	7.2	64188	64651	83	90	56	8.9	3.6	3.6	39.3	44.6	375000
97145	TOLOVANA PARK	27973	701	25.7	24.0	39.2	5.1	6.0	50325	50870	62	59	474	0.8	0.2	1.3	44.7	53.0	419718
97146	WARRENTON	25270	2185	22.7	27.0	38.1	8.0	4.2	50288	50555	62	58	1601	7.3	4.9	16.9	52.0	19.0	222246
97148	YAMHILL	26290	1167	13.3	20.0	49.1	9.5	8.1	65565	66770	84	92	953	3.0	2.4	16.3	31.3	47.0	372857
97149	NESKOWIN	26583	213	18.8	27.7	43.7	9.9	0.0	53142	53057	68	68	176	0.0	0.6	4.0	45.5	50.0	400000
97201	PORTLAND	46106	8768	33.9	21.5	24.1	9.0	11.4	42578	46390	41	37	2175	0.0	1.4	3.5	22.0	73.1	610320
97202	PORTLAND	30586	17554	20.1	26.4	37.8	10.1	5.6	53358	56707	69	69	8944	0.1	0.2	5.5	71.4	22.8	305074
97203	PORTLAND	19848	10777	24.5	27.7	40.1	6.3	1.4	47558	51982	56	51	6052	1.4	1.2	26.6	67.9	2.8	209879
	OREGON	26362		20.3	25.9	37.7	10.2	5.9	53483	55628				4.6	3.5	17.3	54.4	20.2	249991
	UNITED STATES	27277		20.9	24.4	35.3	11.7	7.6	54719	56938				9.3	13.1	31.6	32.6	13.5	162279

ZIP CODE #	POST OFFICE NAME	FINANCIAL SERVICES: Auto Loan	Home Loan	Invest-ments	Retire-ment Plans	THE HOME: Home Improvements: Home Repair	Lawn & Garden	Furnishings: Comput-ers & Hard-ware-Personal	Major Appli-ances	TV, Radio, Sound Equip-ment	Furni-ture	ENTERTAINMENT: Dine out/ Carry out	Sports Equip-ment	Fees & Tickets	Toys & Games	Travel	Cable TV	PERSONAL: Apparel & Services	Auto Repairs	Health Insur-ance	Pets & Supplies
97001	ANTELOPE	84	67	109	66	74	89	67	86	70	63	70	63	58	67	73	75	46	79	85	99
97002	AURORA	106	105	107	103	107	112	98	107	100	101	100	78	98	100	101	103	68	103	110	125
97004	BEAVERCREEK	119	137	127	141	136	134	121	127	118	124	119	97	132	120	130	117	84	121	124	148
97005	BEAVERTON	83	72	67	75	69	69	86	74	85	84	86	61	81	86	79	84	61	83	78	91
97006	BEAVERTON	110	101	89	104	96	90	109	98	105	111	108	81	105	110	101	101	76	103	93	117
97007	BEAVERTON	129	135	118	138	130	119	129	124	124	135	126	100	133	130	128	119	89	123	114	144
97008	BEAVERTON	105	103	96	106	100	96	109	100	106	109	108	81	109	108	105	104	76	105	98	119
97009	BORING	113	125	126	128	126	127	111	120	110	114	110	91	119	110	120	110	77	113	117	139
97011	BRIGHTWOOD	119	95	154	94	105	126	95	121	100	90	99	89	83	95	103	106	66	112	120	141
97013	CANBY	105	113	104	112	110	110	104	107	103	105	104	82	108	106	107	104	73	105	106	125
97014	CASCADE LOCKS	83	78	69	76	77	80	73	78	76	76	76	57	71	79	71	78	52	75	78	92
97015	CLACKAMAS	110	102	94	104	99	95	109	101	107	111	108	81	106	110	104	104	76	105	99	120
97016	CLATSKANIE	91	80	86	82	83	95	82	91	85	77	83	68	75	85	81	89	57	86	95	106
97017	COLTON	104	117	101	120	113	115	104	109	103	105	103	85	111	105	110	103	72	104	107	128
97018	COLUMBIA CITY	107	121	104	124	117	119	108	112	106	108	107	88	115	109	114	106	75	108	111	132
97019	CORBETT	113	132	116	135	129	125	116	120	112	118	113	94	126	115	123	111	80	114	115	139
97021	DUFUR	99	72	103	69	75	101	73	93	81	69	80	70	59	80	73	89	53	86	97	111
97022	EAGLE CREEK	104	96	98	97	96	109	92	103	95	89	94	78	87	96	93	99	64	97	104	121
97023	ESTACADA	95	108	97	109	105	103	99	100	97	98	97	78	105	98	104	97	69	98	99	117
97024	FAIRVIEW	94	99	88	98	96	93	97	94	95	97	96	74	98	97	96	94	67	95	93	111
97026	GERVAIS	99	91	90	84	90	89	91	95	88	93	89	72	82	90	88	87	62	92	89	109
97027	GLADSTONE	90	100	92	102	98	97	95	94	94	94	95	74	101	95	99	94	67	94	95	111
97028	GOVERNMENT CAMP	109	122	117	124	121	114	115	112	111	118	113	88	122	112	119	109	80	112	110	132
97029	GRASS VALLEY	99	68	108	68	71	104	75	94	78	61	77	77	55	77	75	85	50	87	99	115
97030	GRESHAM	88	85	80	87	83	82	91	85	90	90	91	68	89	91	88	89	63	89	86	101
97031	HOOD RIVER	92	82	83	82	81	88	86	88	86	83	86	69	79	87	83	87	59	87	89	104
97032	HUBBARD	101	97	88	92	94	93	94	96	92	97	93	73	89	96	90	92	64	94	91	112
97034	LAKE OSWEGO	171	221	257	228	241	205	193	201	179	211	178	153	226	174	222	170	133	190	181	224
97035	LAKE OSWEGO	137	146	139	151	143	133	142	135	136	146	139	108	148	140	143	132	99	137	128	159
97037	MAUPIN	76	67	85	65	71	79	65	76	68	66	67	54	60	66	68	72	45	72	79	89
97038	MOLALLA	96	102	89	100	98	94	96	95	93	97	94	75	97	97	96	92	66	93	91	111
97039	MORO	96	66	103	66	69	100	72	90	76	61	75	73	54	75	72	84	49	84	95	110
97040	MOSIER	100	80	127	79	88	105	80	101	84	76	83	74	70	80	86	89	55	93	100	117
97041	MOUNT HOOD PARKDALE	101	80	111	79	84	103	81	98	85	76	84	74	69	84	83	90	56	92	99	116
97042	MULINO	120	128	134	130	129	133	115	126	114	116	115	96	120	115	124	116	80	120	124	147
97045	OREGON CITY	103	115	110	117	114	109	107	107	104	110	105	82	114	105	112	103	75	106	104	125
97048	RAINIER	91	88	84	90	88	95	86	92	87	82	86	70	83	89	86	90	60	88	94	107
97049	RHODODENDRON	114	112	132	113	115	119	108	117	108	108	108	89	108	106	114	109	75	113	114	136
97050	RUFUS	83	59	85	58	62	84	61	78	68	57	66	58	49	67	60	74	44	71	81	92
97051	SAINT HELENS	86	91	82	92	88	86	91	87	89	89	90	69	93	90	91	88	63	89	87	103
97053	WARREN	108	120	113	124	120	121	107	114	106	108	106	87	114	107	115	106	74	108	112	133
97054	DEER ISLAND	101	99	93	103	99	109	94	103	96	89	95	79	92	98	96	99	65	97	105	121
97055	SANDY	105	107	101	107	106	108	99	105	100	100	100	79	100	102	101	102	70	101	105	123
97056	SCAPPOOSE	105	104	100	105	103	107	98	105	98	97	98	80	96	100	99	99	68	100	103	122
97057	SHANIKO	84	67	109	66	74	89	67	86	70	63	70	63	58	67	73	75	46	79	85	99
97058	THE DALLES	81	75	74	76	75	83	78	80	80	75	79	60	75	80	76	83	55	80	85	94
97060	TROUTDALE	115	121	103	119	115	107	113	111	109	119	111	87	115	114	112	105	78	109	102	129
97062	TUALATIN	134	135	127	141	133	123	137	127	132	141	134	104	141	136	135	127	96	131	120	151
97063	TYGH VALLEY	68	64	82	59	72	77	61	72	65	66	63	47	61	59	67	69	42	70	81	83
97064	VERNONIA	91	84	77	83	83	90	80	87	83	79	82	64	75	86	78	86	56	83	88	103
97065	WASCO	87	62	89	60	65	88	64	81	71	60	70	61	51	71	63	78	46	75	85	97
97067	WELCHES	120	97	155	95	106	127	97	122	101	91	100	89	84	96	105	108	66	113	121	142
97068	WEST LINN	162	207	211	212	213	183	177	181	164	190	166	143	204	166	198	155	122	171	159	205
97070	WILSONVILLE	130	124	124	128	124	117	127	122	125	134	126	95	127	127	125	122	89	124	118	143
97071	WOODBURN	78	73	77	68	76	78	75	80	76	78	76	57	72	74	76	77	52	79	83	89
97080	GRESHAM	111	119	107	120	115	107	114	110	110	117	112	88	118	113	115	107	79	111	104	129
97086	HAPPY VALLEY	151	159	147	167	156	142	154	146	148	162	150	120	162	154	154	141	108	147	134	171
97089	DAMASCUS	134	166	170	170	170	157	141	149	135	151	137	111	161	134	158	133	98	141	141	171
97101	AMITY	97	95	88	94	93	99	88	94	90	89	90	72	87	92	88	92	62	91	95	112
97103	ASTORIA	83	77	79	77	76	82	80	81	81	77	81	62	76	81	78	83	56	82	85	96
97106	BANKS	113	131	119	135	129	127	115	121	113	118	114	93	125	115	124	112	80	115	118	141
97107	BAY CITY	92	74	119	73	81	98	74	94	78	70	77	69	64	74	80	83	51	87	93	109
97108	BEAVER	100	72	103	70	75	102	74	94	82	69	80	70	59	81	73	90	53	86	97	111
97109	BUXTON	99	111	96	115	108	109	99	103	98	100	98	81	106	100	105	98	69	99	102	122
97111	CARLTON	88	86	81	89	86	95	82	90	83	77	82	69	80	85	83	87	57	84	92	105
97112	CLOVERDALE	96	77	120	75	84	102	77	97	81	73	80	71	67	77	82	87	53	90	97	113
97113	CORNELIUS	105	104	93	98	100	95	98	101	95	103	97	77	95	100	96	93	67	97	92	115
97114	DAYTON	102	91	94	89	90	101	88	96	91	87	90	73	81	93	86	94	61	93	97	115
97115	DUNDEE	108	121	107	124	118	119	108	113	106	108	107	88	115	109	114	106	75	108	111	133
97116	FOREST GROVE	87	92	86	93	91	93	90	91	90	88	90	70	92	90	91	92	63	90	93	106
97117	GALES CREEK	106	128	125	131	129	122	110	116	106	116	107	87	123	107	121	105	76	110	111	134
97119	GASTON	123	137	121	141	133	136	122	128	120	123	121	100	130	123	130	121	85	123	127	151
97121	HAMMOND	73	83	77	81	81	77	80	78	78	78	79	60	84	79	82	78	56	78	77	90
97122	HEBO	109	87	141	86	96	115	87	111	91	82	90	81	76	87	94	97	60	102	109	128
97123	HILLSBORO	111	116	102	114	112	104	112	109	108	115	111	86	114	112	111	106	78	109	103	126
97124	HILLSBORO	122	117	103	120	111	105	122	112	118	125	120	92	120	123	116	114	85	116	106	133
97125	MANNING	101	113	98	117	110	111	101	105	100	102	100	82	108	102	107	100	70	101	104	124
97127	LAFAYETTE	90	82	73	80	80	84	78	82	81	81	81	60	73	84	74	83	55	80	82	98
97128	MCMINNVILLE	87	90	86	90	89	89	91	89	90	89	90	69	92	90	91	91	64	90	91	104
97131	NEHALEM	92	79	122	78	88	101	77	96	81	76	79	68	71	75	85	86	53	89	98	111
97132	NEWBERG	102	109	98	109	106	103	105	103	102	105	103	80	108	104	106	101	73	103	100	121
97133	NORTH PLAINS	124	147	139	151	147	141	128	134	124	133	125	102	141	125	139	123	89	128	130	155
97136	ROCKAWAY BEACH	70	62	88	59	69	77	60	74	64	62	62	51	57	59	66	67	42	69	78	85
97137	SAINT PAUL	122	101	113	98	101	120	101	113	104	96	104	87	87	106	97	110	70	108	116	137
97138	SEASIDE	88	76	102	76	81	92	79	89	81	76	81	65	73	78	81	85	55	86	93	104
97140	SHERWOOD	154	170	147	168	163	144	152	151	143	164	146	120	159	152	153	135	103	144	133	172
97141	TILLAMOOK	89	71	97	72	75	93	75	88	78	68	77	68	64	76	76	83	52	83	90	104
97144	TIMBER	100	112	97	116	109	110	100	104	99	101	99	82	107	101	106	99	69	100	103	123
97145	TOLOVANA PARK	89	87	123	86	98	105	80	96	84	86	83	63	83	77	91	89	56	91	104	110
97146	WARRENTON	97	87	104	85	91	100	85	96	88	85	87	69	80	87	87	92	59	92	99	112
97148	YAMHILL	113	113	114	116	112	124	106	115	106	102	106	92	105	107	111	108	73	110	116	138
97149	NESKOWIN	78	82	112	81	95	97	74	87	78	84	77	54	81	70	85	82	53	83	97	99
97201	PORTLAND	102	75	81	86	74	74	119	85	109	105	112	79	101	109	97	104	80	102	86	108
97202	PORTLAND	89	87	87	90	87	86	96	87	94	94	95	69	96	93	93	94	67	93	92	105
97203	PORTLAND	72	72	66	71	70	67	77	71	75	75	77	56	76	76	75	75	54	75	72	84
	OREGON	96	93	95	94	93	95	95	95	95	94	95	74	93	95	95	95	66	96	96	112
	UNITED STATES	100	100	100	100	100	100	100	100	100	100	100	100	100	100	100	100	100	100	100	100

ZIP CODE			POPULATION			2000-2009 ANNUAL RATE		HOUSEHOLDS					FAMILIES		
#	POST OFFICE NAME	COUNTY FIPS CODE	2000	2009	2014	% Rate	State Centile	2000	2009	2014	% Annual Rate 2000-2009	2009 Average HH Size	2000	2009	% Annual Rate 2000-2009
97204	PORTLAND	051	1259	1291	1308	0.3	32	397	429	445	0.8	1.04	15	16	0.7
97205	PORTLAND	051	7058	7302	7458	0.4	39	4802	5049	5174	0.5	1.30	687	689	0.0
97206	PORTLAND	051	44545	46975	48745	0.6	48	17623	18677	19390	0.6	2.49	10370	10829	0.5
97209	PORTLAND	051	8109	12223	13985	4.5	99	5226	8366	9678	5.2	1.30	670	1049	5.0
97210	PORTLAND	051	9702	10298	10705	0.6	48	5593	5962	6194	0.7	1.71	1715	1799	0.5
97211	PORTLAND	051	31290	32415	33475	0.4	39	11827	12372	12789	0.5	2.55	7025	7244	0.3
97212	PORTLAND	051	23556	24409	25263	0.4	39	10061	10571	10963	0.5	2.30	5482	5651	0.3
97213	PORTLAND	051	29315	30306	31230	0.4	39	12850	13407	13830	0.5	2.23	6957	7123	0.3
97214	PORTLAND	051	23124	23776	24405	0.3	32	11587	12075	12427	0.4	1.89	3839	3913	0.2
97215	PORTLAND	051	16706	17285	17849	0.4	39	7106	7441	7700	0.5	2.25	3823	3934	0.3
97216	PORTLAND	051	13322	15875	17030	1.9	89	5126	6095	6536	1.9	2.59	3243	3816	1.8
97217	PORTLAND	051	29733	31173	32258	0.5	43	12302	13011	13474	0.6	2.38	6804	7075	0.4
97218	PORTLAND	051	14131	14912	15353	0.6	48	5161	5357	5493	0.4	2.72	3190	3266	0.3
97219	PORTLAND	051	37054	38624	39951	0.4	39	15336	16180	16775	0.6	2.32	9075	9419	0.4
97220	PORTLAND	051	29735	32013	33278	0.8	59	10909	11718	12186	0.8	2.54	6601	7001	0.6
97221	PORTLAND	051	11448	11846	12233	0.4	39	4814	5048	5224	0.5	2.31	3098	3208	0.4
97222	PORTLAND	005	35431	37449	38442	0.6	48	14768	15347	15797	0.4	2.38	9097	9242	0.2
97223	PORTLAND	067	41190	46430	49175	1.3	76	16464	18196	19201	1.1	2.54	10646	11588	0.9
97224	PORTLAND	067	27206	32660	35629	2.0	91	11845	13766	14873	1.6	2.35	7342	8369	1.4
97225	PORTLAND	067	22250	24412	25719	1.0	66	10228	11226	11853	1.0	2.17	5811	6173	0.7
97227	PORTLAND	051	3259	3377	3493	0.4	39	1292	1356	1405	0.5	2.43	632	653	0.4
97229	PORTLAND	067	41915	54331	60593	2.8	97	15496	19873	22110	2.7	2.73	11488	14589	2.6
97230	PORTLAND	051	35226	37666	39094	0.7	53	14074	14975	15511	0.7	2.49	9241	9710	0.5
97231	PORTLAND	051	4361	4647	4836	0.7	53	1746	1878	1957	0.8	2.42	1184	1263	0.7
97232	PORTLAND	051	10823	11487	11852	0.6	48	5815	6266	6487	0.8	1.79	2020	2103	0.4
97233	PORTLAND	051	33253	37290	39206	1.2	74	11701	12890	13493	1.1	2.87	7890	8594	0.9
97236	PORTLAND	051	26579	32010	34370	2.0	91	9312	11216	12035	2.0	2.82	6536	7837	2.0
97239	PORTLAND	051	12303	13382	13976	0.9	62	6014	6678	7011	1.1	1.98	2907	3110	0.7
97266	PORTLAND	051	28115	31277	32867	1.2	74	10136	11210	11752	1.1	2.75	6708	7295	0.9
97267	PORTLAND	005	28807	30609	31582	0.7	53	11450	12024	12431	0.5	2.53	7851	8092	0.3
97301	SALEM	047	50375	53990	55848	0.8	59	17170	18043	18604	0.5	2.70	10182	10544	0.4
97302	SALEM	047	37483	40320	42065	0.8	59	15498	16614	17279	0.8	2.39	9809	10361	0.6
97303	SALEM	047	34503	38450	40582	1.2	74	12864	14239	14997	1.1	2.68	9210	10057	1.0
97304	SALEM	053	22512	27219	29890	2.1	93	8743	10296	11314	1.8	2.58	6041	7025	1.6
97305	SALEM	047	34955	39616	42067	1.4	78	12672	14171	14988	1.2	2.78	8849	9739	1.0
97306	SALEM	047	21664	25416	27382	1.7	85	8303	9724	10445	1.7	2.60	6124	7063	1.6
97317	SALEM	047	22021	24712	26104	1.3	76	7163	8017	8484	1.2	2.76	5281	5846	1.1
97321	ALBANY	043	20283	23725	25362	1.7	85	7907	9320	9981	1.8	2.53	5648	6629	1.7
97322	ALBANY	043	28865	33840	36445	1.7	85	11352	13304	14334	1.7	2.50	7652	8881	1.6
97324	ALSEA	003	1167	1229	1279	0.6	48	450	485	508	0.8	2.52	326	346	0.6
97325	AUMSVILLE	047	6037	6748	7145	1.2	74	2043	2287	2418	1.2	2.95	1686	1869	1.1
97326	BLODGETT	041	694	690	688	-0.1	14	273	275	275	0.1	2.51	208	207	-0.1
97327	BROWNSVILLE	043	2826	3011	3139	0.7	53	1042	1120	1171	0.8	2.69	804	859	0.7
97329	CASCADIA	043	76	78	80	0.3	32	31	32	33	0.3	2.44	23	24	0.5
97330	CORVALLIS	003	40580	41903	43130	0.3	32	16528	17559	18181	0.7	2.28	9220	9580	0.4
97331	CORVALLIS	003	2260	1959	1963	-1.5	0	72	75	77	0.4	1.95	14	14	0.0
97333	CORVALLIS	003	16869	19436	20709	1.5	80	6981	8248	8828	1.8	2.28	3797	4412	1.6
97338	DALLAS	053	17454	20353	22118	1.7	85	6480	7410	8059	1.5	2.67	4790	5418	1.3
97341	DEPOE BAY	041	3104	3460	3616	1.2	74	1568	1751	1831	1.2	1.97	951	1047	1.0
97342	DETROIT	047	399	447	475	1.2	74	169	190	203	1.3	2.21	103	114	1.1
97343	EDDYVILLE	041	570	577	569	0.1	23	213	216	212	0.2	2.67	158	158	0.0
97344	FALLS CITY	053	1175	1391	1528	1.8	87	409	474	520	1.6	2.93	319	367	1.5
97345	FOSTER	043	542	554	566	0.2	26	210	216	221	0.3	2.56	163	167	0.3
97346	GATES	043	877	957	1011	0.9	62	365	400	422	1.0	2.39	260	281	0.8
97347	GRAND RONDE	071	1571	1767	1900	1.3	76	574	639	687	1.2	2.77	416	458	1.0
97348	HALSEY	043	1321	1455	1534	1.0	66	464	516	546	1.2	2.82	364	404	1.1
97350	IDANHA	047	272	297	313	1.0	66	101	111	117	1.0	2.57	67	73	0.9
97351	INDEPENDENCE	053	7586	9352	10377	2.3	95	2549	3071	3405	2.0	2.98	1843	2197	1.9
97352	JEFFERSON	047	5204	6004	6445	1.6	83	1795	2065	2210	1.5	2.91	1442	1642	1.4
97355	LEBANON	043	26328	28156	29337	0.7	53	9900	10644	11120	0.8	2.62	7275	7751	0.7
97357	LOGSDEN	041	257	250	248	-0.3	8	105	102	101	-0.3	2.44	81	78	-0.4
97358	LYONS	047	2366	2611	2750	1.1	71	883	982	1037	1.2	2.65	683	754	1.1
97360	MILL CITY	043	1999	2221	2351	1.1	71	750	839	888	1.2	2.65	560	622	1.1
97361	MONMOUTH	053	10222	11749	12620	1.5	80	3626	4046	4356	1.2	2.67	2225	2446	1.0
97362	MOUNT ANGEL	047	4157	4780	5113	1.5	80	1322	1538	1653	1.6	2.86	868	994	1.5
97364	NEOTSU	041	399	398	397	0.0	19	160	159	159	-0.1	2.42	96	94	-0.2
97365	NEWPORT	041	9998	10377	10537	0.4	39	4267	4442	4514	0.4	2.26	2601	2663	0.3
97366	SOUTH BEACH	041	1224	1453	1542	1.9	89	551	660	704	2.0	2.17	352	416	1.8
97367	LINCOLN CITY	041	9285	9176	9096	-0.1	14	4260	4162	4121	-0.3	2.19	2460	2364	-0.4
97368	OTIS	041	3285	3321	3274	0.1	23	1346	1351	1331	0.0	2.45	929	921	-0.1
97369	OTTER ROCK	041	169	186	194	1.0	66	83	92	95	1.1	2.02	51	56	1.0
97370	PHILOMATH	003	8197	9029	9486	1.1	71	2919	3266	3446	1.2	2.76	2212	2437	1.1
97371	RICKREALL	053	585	645	688	1.1	71	206	223	237	0.9	2.89	164	176	0.8
97374	SCIO	043	5132	5363	5530	0.5	43	1893	1995	2063	0.6	2.69	1497	1565	0.5
97375	SCOTTS MILLS	047	1374	1421	1452	0.4	39	441	455	465	0.3	3.10	356	365	0.3
97376	SEAL ROCK	041	1456	1609	1676	1.1	71	671	743	774	1.1	2.16	426	466	1.0
97377	SHEDD	043	844	875	897	0.4	39	317	332	341	0.5	2.64	240	249	0.4
97378	SHERIDAN	071	8103	8617	8954	0.7	53	2205	2378	2498	0.8	2.75	1627	1736	0.7
97380	SILETZ	041	2195	2239	2261	0.2	26	821	840	849	0.2	2.66	630	639	0.2
97381	SILVERTON	047	13240	14954	15888	1.3	76	4624	5227	5542	1.3	2.84	3458	3859	1.2
97383	STAYTON	047	8729	9770	10334	1.2	74	3207	3595	3796	1.2	2.72	2394	2646	1.1
97385	SUBLIMITY	047	2674	2985	3162	1.2	74	882	998	1064	1.3	2.66	668	746	1.2
97386	SWEET HOME	043	12558	13346	13866	0.7	53	4739	5048	5250	0.7	2.63	3477	3672	0.6
97389	TANGENT	043	1496	1578	1634	0.6	48	546	582	603	0.7	2.71	394	415	0.6
97390	TIDEWATER	041	644	703	729	1.0	66	296	325	337	1.0	2.09	184	200	0.9
97391	TOLEDO	041	5586	5704	5701	0.2	26	2132	2181	2181	0.2	2.61	1553	1574	0.1
97392	TURNER	047	4174	4498	4696	0.8	59	1532	1652	1721	0.8	2.72	1200	1279	0.7
97394	WALDPORT	041	4409	4880	5068	1.1	71	1986	2196	2284	1.1	2.22	1256	1369	0.9
97396	WILLAMINA	071	2798	3187	3445	1.4	78	1025	1170	1265	1.4	2.72	756	853	1.3
97401	EUGENE	039	37177	39732	41104	0.7	53	17352	18577	19290	0.7	2.02	7121	7400	0.4
97402	EUGENE	039	45012	49102	51169	0.9	62	18520	20198	21073	0.9	2.40	10910	11782	0.8
97403	EUGENE	039	10395	10470	10561	0.1	23	3713	3751	3801	0.1	2.17	1653	1614	-0.3
97404	EUGENE	039	28590	31623	33194	1.1	71	10843	12115	12768	1.2	2.60	7951	8778	1.1
97405	EUGENE	039	43472	44908	45919	0.4	39	17896	18624	19095	0.4	2.36	11111	11377	0.3
97406	AGNESS	015	133	135	132	0.2	26	69	71	70	0.3	1.90	47	48	0.2
	OREGON					1.3					1.2	2.51			1.1
	UNITED STATES					1.0					1.1	2.59			0.9

ZIP CODE #	POST OFFICE NAME	RACE (%) White 2000	White 2009	Black 2000	Black 2009	Asian/Pacific 2000	Asian/Pacific 2009	% Hispanic Origin 2000	% Hispanic Origin 2009	2009 AGE DISTRIBUTION (%) 0-4	5-9	10-14	15-19	20-24	25-44	45-64	65-84	85+	18+	MEDIAN AGE 2009	% 2009 Males	% 2009 Females
97204	PORTLAND	64.6	59.8	21.4	23.5	2.1	2.6	7.5	10.5	0.4	0.8	0.3	4.2	9.1	51.3	26.1	7.4	0.5	97.8	38.5	76.2	23.8
97205	PORTLAND	84.3	81.0	4.7	5.4	5.0	6.5	4.9	6.9	1.3	1.2	1.2	3.4	9.4	37.9	31.0	12.4	2.3	95.1	42.0	59.2	40.8
97206	PORTLAND	79.7	75.3	1.7	2.0	9.6	12.1	6.5	9.2	6.6	6.2	6.0	6.0	6.5	31.0	26.5	9.3	2.0	77.7	37.3	49.6	50.4
97209	PORTLAND	83.5	80.4	5.3	6.1	3.4	4.4	5.4	7.7	2.1	1.6	1.2	1.9	9.1	47.8	26.2	8.6	1.6	94.6	37.0	56.5	43.5
97210	PORTLAND	90.8	88.8	1.6	1.9	3.6	4.8	2.7	3.9	3.0	2.6	2.9	3.3	8.7	41.6	27.1	8.8	1.9	89.6	37.2	50.5	49.5
97211	PORTLAND	51.6	47.2	33.4	35.4	3.6	4.3	8.0	10.8	6.7	6.4	6.1	6.7	8.0	31.7	25.3	7.9	1.3	77.0	35.2	48.2	51.8
97212	PORTLAND	77.0	73.9	14.5	16.1	2.2	2.8	4.5	6.2	5.3	5.0	5.7	5.7	6.7	29.4	31.4	8.8	2.1	80.5	40.3	48.2	51.8
97213	PORTLAND	80.6	76.6	3.5	3.9	9.5	11.9	4.4	6.3	5.7	5.4	5.3	5.8	6.1	30.7	29.2	9.4	2.3	79.9	39.6	48.7	51.3
97214	PORTLAND	86.2	83.3	2.5	2.9	4.8	6.2	4.2	6.0	3.8	3.0	2.6	3.4	10.2	44.4	24.0	6.9	1.9	88.8	35.2	50.3	49.7
97215	PORTLAND	84.6	81.2	1.7	1.9	8.2	10.4	4.6	6.6	5.1	4.8	4.8	5.0	7.0	32.3	28.2	10.0	2.8	82.7	39.1	47.3	52.7
97216	PORTLAND	78.4	73.4	2.5	3.0	10.6	13.0	7.2	10.4	7.1	6.5	6.2	6.4	7.4	29.5	24.5	10.2	2.2	76.4	35.6	49.1	50.9
97217	PORTLAND	65.0	60.8	17.6	18.8	5.1	6.2	8.8	12.0	6.7	6.2	5.8	6.0	6.7	30.1	28.2	8.7	1.6	77.7	37.6	50.0	50.0
97218	PORTLAND	62.4	56.6	10.0	10.6	8.6	10.1	18.8	24.3	7.4	7.0	6.6	6.7	6.8	30.9	25.0	8.0	1.6	74.9	34.8	51.3	48.7
97219	PORTLAND	88.7	86.2	1.7	2.0	4.0	5.2	4.0	5.8	5.1	5.1	5.3	6.8	6.6	29.0	31.5	9.0	1.6	81.1	39.5	48.9	51.1
97220	PORTLAND	75.9	71.1	4.6	5.1	10.3	12.8	6.5	9.1	6.7	6.2	5.9	6.5	7.7	28.2	25.0	10.7	3.1	77.9	36.8	49.6	50.4
97221	PORTLAND	91.9	89.8	1.1	1.3	2.9	3.8	3.2	4.8	4.9	4.8	5.5	5.7	6.0	22.5	33.8	13.6	3.2	81.1	45.4	47.9	52.1
97222	PORTLAND	89.6	87.2	1.0	1.1	2.7	3.3	5.5	8.1	6.7	6.2	6.1	6.1	6.5	27.6	25.4	11.7	3.8	77.4	38.1	48.2	51.8
97223	PORTLAND	85.2	81.6	1.1	1.2	6.3	7.8	8.4	12.4	7.3	6.8	6.6	6.2	6.7	30.4	26.9	7.9	1.2	75.5	36.1	49.7	50.3
97224	PORTLAND	89.9	87.0	0.9	0.9	3.9	5.1	5.7	8.7	6.5	6.3	6.4	5.5	4.2	26.9	25.2	15.1	3.9	77.3	40.8	47.0	53.0
97225	PORTLAND	88.7	85.6	1.1	1.3	4.1	5.2	5.4	8.3	5.5	5.0	5.1	5.4	7.2	28.9	28.2	12.1	2.6	81.2	39.7	49.1	50.9
97227	PORTLAND	48.7	45.1	34.2	35.3	3.7	4.3	11.0	14.2	7.8	6.2	6.1	6.9	8.9	32.9	22.7	7.0	1.5	76.0	32.8	50.5	49.5
97229	PORTLAND	82.4	78.2	0.9	1.0	12.0	15.4	3.7	5.2	7.9	8.2	8.4	6.9	4.3	28.6	27.9	7.1	0.7	71.1	36.9	49.4	50.6
97230	PORTLAND	77.4	72.3	4.0	4.4	7.3	9.2	10.4	14.4	6.9	6.4	6.2	5.9	6.4	26.6	24.6	14.0	3.0	77.0	38.2	49.0	51.0
97231	PORTLAND	91.2	89.2	0.4	0.5	2.2	3.0	4.8	7.0	4.3	4.8	5.9	6.1	3.5	22.4	40.0	11.5	1.5	80.7	46.3	51.6	48.4
97232	PORTLAND	83.3	80.1	6.7	7.9	3.3	4.2	5.0	7.1	3.7	3.1	3.2	3.8	9.1	37.6	26.1	9.3	4.1	87.9	38.1	49.1	50.9
97233	PORTLAND	74.7	69.2	2.7	2.9	5.9	7.3	16.6	22.3	9.0	8.2	7.2	7.0	7.5	29.6	21.5	8.6	1.5	71.5	31.6	50.4	49.6
97236	PORTLAND	81.8	78.0	2.2	2.5	6.8	8.5	8.3	11.5	7.9	7.3	6.8	6.8	7.0	27.4	25.2	9.6	1.9	73.8	35.0	48.7	51.3
97239	PORTLAND	90.0	87.7	1.4	1.7	4.2	5.5	3.4	5.0	4.3	3.8	4.0	3.9	8.2	33.2	29.2	10.9	2.4	85.6	39.3	48.9	51.1
97266	PORTLAND	76.7	71.4	2.0	2.2	10.0	12.7	9.0	12.3	7.7	7.1	6.8	6.9	6.8	28.5	25.1	9.5	1.7	74.1	35.2	49.7	50.3
97267	PORTLAND	91.5	89.4	0.6	0.7	2.0	2.5	5.6	8.2	6.0	5.8	6.1	6.1	5.8	24.9	29.1	13.7	2.6	78.5	41.5	48.6	51.4
97301	SALEM	76.1	70.4	1.8	1.9	2.8	3.2	23.7	32.2	8.3	7.0	6.1	7.5	9.2	29.6	21.9	8.4	2.1	74.9	32.2	51.8	48.2
97302	SALEM	89.1	86.3	0.8	0.9	2.3	3.0	6.8	10.0	6.3	5.8	5.9	6.7	7.2	25.5	27.6	12.3	2.8	77.8	38.7	48.1	51.9
97303	SALEM	84.7	80.4	0.7	0.8	1.6	2.1	13.5	19.0	8.2	7.5	7.1	6.8	6.3	28.0	24.1	10.0	2.1	72.9	34.9	48.9	51.1
97304	SALEM	91.8	89.9	0.4	0.5	1.7	2.2	8.0	11.2	5.4	5.6	6.1	6.4	5.5	22.3	29.4	14.6	4.6	78.7	43.9	47.6	52.4
97305	SALEM	76.6	70.4	1.0	1.0	4.6	5.4	20.2	28.1	9.5	8.3	7.4	6.9	7.2	29.1	21.2	9.0	1.4	70.7	31.3	50.1	49.9
97306	SALEM	91.3	89.1	0.6	0.7	2.7	3.6	4.5	6.8	6.7	6.5	6.6	6.6	6.6	27.0	27.9	10.4	1.6	75.9	37.5	48.3	51.7
97317	SALEM	83.7	79.5	1.6	1.7	2.1	2.5	12.1	17.4	6.5	6.3	6.2	7.3	8.3	27.3	25.2	11.3	1.5	76.9	35.6	53.3	46.7
97321	ALBANY	93.4	92.1	0.4	0.5	1.4	1.8	3.9	5.5	6.2	6.3	6.6	6.7	5.5	25.0	30.3	11.7	1.8	76.8	40.5	49.1	50.9
97322	ALBANY	91.4	89.4	0.5	0.5	1.2	1.6	6.7	9.5	7.7	6.8	6.6	7.0	7.0	26.9	24.4	10.8	2.8	74.8	35.7	48.7	51.3
97324	ALSEA	96.1	95.2	0.3	0.3	0.4	0.6	2.4	3.7	4.3	5.6	6.1	8.9	4.5	21.1	34.7	13.3	1.5	77.5	44.7	48.8	51.2
97325	AUMSVILLE	90.7	88.2	0.2	0.2	0.8	1.0	7.3	11.0	7.6	7.7	7.7	7.5	5.9	25.2	26.6	10.7	1.1	72.3	36.0	49.0	51.0
97326	BLODGETT	92.1	91.0	0.3	0.4	0.4	0.7	2.6	4.1	4.6	5.1	6.2	7.2	4.5	22.2	36.2	12.8	1.2	79.6	45.1	50.1	49.9
97327	BROWNSVILLE	94.7	93.9	0.2	0.2	0.2	0.3	2.8	4.0	6.0	6.5	7.0	6.4	4.9	23.4	31.5	12.7	1.5	76.4	41.6	50.0	50.0
97329	CASCADIA	96.1	96.2	0.0	0.0	0.0	0.0	1.3	1.3	5.1	5.1	5.1	5.1	3.8	21.8	33.3	17.9	2.6	79.5	47.5	51.3	48.7
97330	CORVALLIS	87.7	84.6	1.0	1.1	6.0	7.9	4.9	7.1	4.9	4.6	5.0	7.6	15.4	26.4	24.3	9.5	2.2	82.0	32.6	49.7	50.3
97331	CORVALLIS	78.0	71.3	2.1	2.2	9.3	12.2	8.0	11.6	0.9	0.5	0.4	56.6	29.5	8.0	3.0	1.1	0.1	86.8	19.3	45.5	54.5
97333	CORVALLIS	88.2	85.8	1.0	1.1	4.8	6.0	5.4	7.5	5.4	4.9	4.8	8.7	15.5	28.8	22.3	8.0	1.5	81.6	30.8	50.1	49.9
97338	DALLAS	93.4	92.1	0.2	0.3	0.7	0.8	3.9	5.8	6.7	6.9	7.1	6.9	5.7	23.3	27.8	12.7	2.9	74.8	39.8	49.2	50.8
97341	DEPOE BAY	93.9	92.7	0.2	0.2	0.8	1.1	2.7	4.2	2.6	3.1	3.5	3.2	2.5	14.2	38.9	28.4	3.6	88.8	57.1	48.6	51.4
97342	DETROIT	94.5	92.6	0.3	0.2	0.0	0.0	5.3	8.3	6.7	4.9	7.4	4.5	4.3	25.7	33.1	11.6	1.8	77.9	43.0	50.6	49.4
97343	EDDYVILLE	96.0	95.5	0.2	0.2	0.4	0.5	2.3	3.6	4.5	4.9	6.1	8.3	3.8	21.3	35.9	13.9	1.4	79.5	45.5	51.3	48.7
97344	FALLS CITY	93.0	92.4	0.7	0.7	0.3	0.4	3.1	4.7	5.9	6.2	7.2	7.5	6.1	21.8	32.6	11.2	1.5	76.1	41.3	49.7	50.3
97345	FOSTER	95.2	94.2	0.2	0.2	1.1	1.4	1.7	2.3	6.0	6.5	7.0	6.3	4.2	22.0	32.9	13.5	1.6	76.5	43.5	52.5	47.5
97346	GATES	89.3	87.0	0.5	0.4	0.1	0.1	5.6	8.5	5.0	6.4	7.2	5.6	3.9	19.3	34.7	15.9	2.0	77.7	46.7	50.1	49.9
97347	GRAND RONDE	79.0	77.8	0.1	0.1	0.9	1.1	2.5	3.7	5.4	5.6	6.4	7.1	5.8	23.7	31.7	12.9	1.4	78.2	41.8	51.2	48.8
97348	HALSEY	93.0	91.3	0.2	0.1	0.3	0.4	4.0	5.9	6.5	7.1	7.1	7.4	7.1	24.8	28.5	9.8	1.7	74.9	36.0	53.1	46.9
97350	IDANHA	94.9	93.3	0.4	0.3	0.0	0.0	5.1	7.4	5.4	4.7	7.4	5.4	4.0	23.9	34.3	13.1	1.7	78.1	44.5	50.2	49.8
97351	INDEPENDENCE	76.6	70.1	0.4	0.4	1.0	1.1	26.5	35.8	8.4	7.5	7.0	7.6	9.2	29.2	21.9	8.0	1.3	72.6	30.6	49.5	50.5
97352	JEFFERSON	87.9	83.8	0.3	0.3	0.8	0.9	12.7	18.9	7.5	7.5	7.8	7.4	5.3	24.0	28.9	10.4	1.1	72.5	37.9	50.1	49.9
97355	LEBANON	94.5	93.5	0.2	0.2	0.8	1.1	2.9	4.2	6.6	6.6	6.8	6.7	5.5	23.8	27.9	13.5	2.5	75.7	40.3	49.4	50.6
97357	LOGSDEN	71.6	70.4	0.0	0.0	0.0	0.4	2.3	3.6	6.4	6.4	6.8	6.8	6.4	22.8	31.6	11.6	1.2	75.2	40.3	50.8	49.2
97358	LYONS	93.1	92.0	0.1	0.1	0.5	0.6	2.7	4.1	5.5	6.2	6.9	6.2	4.4	23.0	32.4	13.8	1.6	77.5	43.5	50.4	49.6
97360	MILL CITY	88.5	85.7	0.3	0.3	0.9	1.1	8.9	12.6	5.9	6.6	7.2	7.4	5.1	22.8	29.6	13.5	1.8	75.6	41.5	49.9	50.1
97361	MONMOUTH	87.3	83.9	0.7	0.8	2.3	2.8	8.5	12.3	5.6	5.0	5.3	12.7	17.7	21.0	22.1	9.1	1.5	80.6	27.8	47.5	52.5
97362	MOUNT ANGEL	76.3	69.4	0.4	0.4	0.7	0.7	26.9	36.9	7.4	6.9	6.9	7.6	7.2	25.3	22.0	12.1	4.6	74.4	35.1	50.0	50.0
97364	NEOTSU	92.9	91.5	0.5	0.8	1.0	1.3	3.5	5.0	4.5	5.0	5.8	5.3	3.8	17.3	34.9	17.8	5.5	81.7	51.5	47.7	52.3
97365	NEWPORT	88.8	86.2	0.4	0.5	1.8	2.3	8.5	12.1	5.3	5.4	5.8	5.6	5.1	22.9	31.2	15.6	3.0	79.8	44.8	49.4	50.6
97366	SOUTH BEACH	95.6	95.1	0.1	0.1	1.0	1.2	2.6	4.0	3.0	3.3	4.0	4.3	3.9	18.9	41.4	19.7	1.7	86.6	52.8	50.4	49.6
97367	LINCOLN CITY	89.7	87.5	0.4	0.4	1.4	1.7	6.9	9.9	4.9	4.8	4.9	5.3	5.0	20.8	32.4	18.7	3.2	82.2	48.3	47.4	52.6
97368	OTIS	93.1	92.1	0.1	0.2	0.4	0.5	2.8	4.2	4.2	4.7	5.6	5.9	3.9	19.8	37.1	16.7	2.0	81.9	48.8	49.6	50.4
97369	OTTER ROCK	93.5	92.5	0.0	0.5	1.8	2.2	2.4	3.2	3.8	4.3	4.8	4.8	3.8	18.3	41.9	16.7	1.6	84.4	51.4	50.0	50.0
97370	PHILOMATH	93.8	92.4	0.2	0.3	1.6	2.1	3.0	4.6	6.0	6.8	7.9	7.8	5.5	25.8	30.2	8.9	1.1	73.9	38.0	49.9	50.1
97371	RICKREALL	93.2	91.3	0.5	0.5	0.3	0.3	5.3	7.9	4.8	5.4	6.0	7.0	4.5	22.2	32.2	15.8	2.0	79.2	45.1	49.9	50.1
97374	SCIO	94.7	94.1	0.1	0.1	0.4	0.6	2.6	3.8	5.5	5.9	6.5	6.8	5.0	22.0	32.5	13.9	1.8	77.6	43.7	49.8	50.2
97375	SCOTTS MILLS	93.9	91.9	0.4	0.6	0.4	0.6	5.4	8.2	6.1	6.8	7.3	7.5	5.0	24.3	30.8	10.9	1.4	74.9	40.0	50.5	49.5
97376	SEAL ROCK	95.2	94.5	0.0	0.0	0.7	0.9	1.6	2.5	2.7	3.0	3.7	4.1	3.4	17.2	42.3	21.4	2.2	88.0	54.9	47.8	52.2
97377	SHEDD	96.3	95.7	0.1	0.1	0.5	0.6	2.4	3.5	5.9	6.4	6.9	6.7	4.8	23.0	32.1	12.2	1.9	76.8	42.2	50.3	49.7
97378	SHERIDAN	83.3	80.7	4.7	5.2	2.0	2.5	6.8	9.7	5.4	5.3	5.2	5.6	7.7	34.7	26.5	8.3	1.4	80.9	36.6	61.6	38.4
97380	SILETZ	76.7	75.7	0.2	0.3	0.4	0.5	2.3	3.2	6.4	6.7	6.9	6.6	5.8	23.4	31.0	12.0	1.3	75.4	40.2	50.6	49.4
97381	SILVERTON	91.3	88.5	0.2	0.2	0.5	0.7	9.0	13.0	7.5	7.2	7.4	7.5	6.1	23.8	27.2	11.2	2.1	73.0	36.7	48.9	51.1
97383	STAYTON	91.7	89.5	0.1	0.1	0.7	0.8	8.0	11.9	8.5	7.4	6.8	7.2	7.5	25.7	24.9	10.4	1.6	72.9	33.7	49.2	50.8
97385	SUBLIMITY	97.0	96.4	0.1	0.1	0.5	0.6	2.2	3.4	5.2	5.5	6.2	7.2	4.7	20.4	26.8	16.9	7.1	78.4	45.5	47.2	52.8
97386	SWEET HOME	94.1	93.2	0.2	0.2	0.6	0.8	2.8	4.1	6.5	6.4	6.6	6.8	5.5	22.4	28.5	14.7	2.5	76.2	41.4	49.6	50.4
97389	TANGENT	95.1	93.8	0.2	0.2	0.6	0.8	3.4	4.9	6.2	6.4	6.7	7.2	5.3	25.6	29.8	11.2	1.6	76.2	39.1	49.4	50.6
97390	TIDEWATER	94.4	94.0	0.5	0.4	0.8	1.0	2.2	3.3	2.4	2.7	3.4	5.5	4.0	11.9	40.1	27.0	2.8	88.2	57.3	49.5	50.5
97391	TOLEDO	91.9	91.0	0.2	0.2	0.7	0.9	2.3	3.6	6.2	6.2	7.5	7.3	5.4	24.3	30.9	10.9	1.2	75.2	40.5	49.8	50.2
97392	TURNER	93.8	92.1	0.1	0.1	0.8	1.0	3.9	6.0	5.0	5.6	6.7	7.2	4.8	20.9	33.6	14.0	2.1	78.1	44.8	49.2	50.8
97394	WALDPORT	93.5	92.6	0.1	0.1	0.8	1.1	2.5	3.8	3.7	4.6	5.7	5.2	3.3	16.9	35.7	22.2	2.6	82.1	52.0	47.8	52.2
97396	WILLAMINA	84.9	83.5	0.1	0.2	0.4	0.5	3.0	4.6	6.6	6.6	6.8	7.2	6.7	25.6	27.9	11.1	1.5	75.7	37.3	50.4	49.6
97401	EUGENE	86.9	83.8	1.5	1.6	5.8	7.6	3.9	5.6	4.0	3.5	3.5	8.0	20.4	26.2	20.9	10.1	3.3	86.4	30.3	49.3	50.7
97402	EUGENE	87.3	85.0	1.3	1.3	2.4	2.9	7.2	10.1	7.1	6.2	6.1	6.4	8.4	30.8	24.1	9.2	1.7	76.9	34.5	49.9	50.1
97403	EUGENE	88.6	86.0	0.9	0.9	5.1	6.6	3.8	5.5	2.5	2.7	3.0	20.9	19.7	20.3	21.4	8.1	1.6	89.6	26.0	50.4	49.6
97404	EUGENE	91.1	89.3	0.8	0.9	1.3	1.8	4.7	6.7	6.5	6.5	6.8	6.6	5.5	26.9	29.0	10.6	1.5	76.0	38.9	48.7	51.3
97405	EUGENE	90.9	88.9	1.0	1.1	3.0	4.0	3.2	4.7	4.2	4.4	5.1	5.9	8.3	24.9	32.4	12.0	2.8	82.8	42.6	48.4	51.6
97406	AGNESS	92.5	90.4	0.0	0.0	0.8	0.7	4.5	5.9	3.0	3.0	3.7	5.2	3.7	15.6	40.7	22.2	3.0	85.9	54.4	51.9	48.1
	OREGON	86.6	83.7	1.6	1.7	3.2	4.0	8.0	11.2	6.5	6.2	6.3	6.8	6.8	26.7	27.5	11.1	2.1	77.0	38.0	49.6	50.4
	UNITED STATES	75.1	72.0	12.3	12.7	3.8	4.6	12.5	15.7	6.8	6.7	6.6	7.1	6.9	27.0	26.0	10.9	1.9	75.7	36.9	49.2	50.8

ZIP CODE #	POST OFFICE NAME	2009 Per Capita Income	2009 HH Income Base	2009 HOUSEHOLD INCOME DISTRIBUTION (%) Less than $25,000	$25,000 to $49,999	$50,000 to $99,999	$100,000 to $149,999	$150,000 or More	MEDIAN HOUSEHOLD INCOME 2009	2014	2009 National Centile	2009 State Centile	2009 Home Value Base	2009 HOME VALUE DISTRIBUTION (%) Less than $50,000	$50,000 to $89,999	$90,000 to $174,999	$175,000 to $399,999	$400,000 or More	2009 Median Home Value
97204	PORTLAND	17311	429	85.8	10.3	3.7	0.2	0.0	12338	12341	1	1	0	0.0	0.0	0.0	0.0	0.0	0
97205	PORTLAND	34259	5049	48.6	24.1	17.3	4.4	5.6	26007	26269	4	2	635	0.0	0.0	1.4	26.6	72.0	613095
97206	PORTLAND	23507	18677	19.5	28.4	42.8	6.5	2.8	51739	54927	65	64	11751	1.8	0.9	21.0	74.2	2.2	218957
97209	PORTLAND	36315	8366	40.8	25.9	21.4	6.4	5.5	32387	34503	12	6	1863	0.3	0.1	0.0	42.2	57.5	442145
97210	PORTLAND	53328	5962	21.5	21.6	27.3	12.7	17.0	60053	62586	77	82	2062	0.3	0.2	0.0	15.5	84.0	662983
97211	PORTLAND	24298	12372	18.8	26.1	42.0	9.6	3.6	54258	56968	70	71	8083	2.2	1.6	17.4	71.1	7.7	235148
97212	PORTLAND	36094	10571	17.2	19.8	35.4	15.0	12.6	66558	67647	85	93	6624	0.2	0.8	4.6	45.9	48.5	394513
97213	PORTLAND	29945	13407	17.8	24.9	41.1	11.4	4.8	58521	60815	76	81	8088	0.0	0.4	7.9	77.3	14.4	274624
97214	PORTLAND	32888	12075	20.6	28.4	36.0	10.1	5.0	50960	54645	63	61	4379	0.8	0.2	5.3	65.6	28.0	343349
97215	PORTLAND	31371	7441	16.0	23.6	40.9	13.7	5.8	62196	63798	80	86	4565	0.6	0.5	4.2	71.6	23.1	319614
97216	PORTLAND	22707	6095	16.9	30.5	43.6	6.4	2.6	52163	55217	66	65	3699	3.5	1.6	18.0	74.4	2.5	220268
97217	PORTLAND	24457	13011	21.5	27.0	40.9	7.6	3.0	51226	54662	64	62	8406	5.4	3.0	22.9	64.4	4.3	212985
97218	PORTLAND	21572	5357	20.6	25.9	42.9	7.6	3.0	52809	55720	68	67	3350	6.9	0.6	19.4	70.0	3.0	219295
97219	PORTLAND	40613	16180	10.9	19.9	38.1	15.9	15.2	72714	73373	88	97	11078	0.2	0.1	4.8	57.8	37.1	359363
97220	PORTLAND	23362	11718	18.8	28.7	41.8	7.3	3.3	52309	55872	67	65	6879	2.0	0.3	14.0	79.0	4.7	231103
97221	PORTLAND	51667	5048	11.7	16.8	30.1	16.8	24.5	81830	83671	93	99	3633	0.2	0.2	1.0	40.2	58.3	456041
97222	PORTLAND	26668	15347	16.9	28.5	39.4	11.3	3.9	54626	57160	71	71	8650	3.0	3.1	14.2	71.4	8.3	244388
97223	PORTLAND	31385	18196	13.1	23.3	37.2	17.4	9.0	64816	67882	83	91	10697	1.2	0.6	4.7	62.9	30.6	347356
97224	PORTLAND	35278	13766	14.3	24.1	33.3	17.3	11.0	63311	66231	82	88	9110	5.8	3.5	6.8	49.7	34.2	337760
97225	PORTLAND	41565	11226	12.3	23.7	35.3	16.7	12.0	64839	67798	83	91	6414	1.0	0.5	8.2	40.0	50.3	402308
97227	PORTLAND	19653	1356	29.9	32.2	30.8	5.3	1.8	40573	42992	35	28	652	0.8	1.5	22.5	67.6	7.5	226776
97229	PORTLAND	46915	19873	7.6	14.1	30.0	22.9	25.4	96070	100560	96	99	14910	0.6	0.6	2.3	35.0	61.5	473048
97230	PORTLAND	26139	14975	15.9	28.7	41.9	9.4	4.1	54734	57674	71	71	9063	2.4	0.9	6.4	78.6	11.8	281906
97231	PORTLAND	39994	1878	11.6	19.6	33.7	19.2	16.0	76896	78564	91	98	1520	2.1	1.0	7.3	29.9	59.7	485057
97232	PORTLAND	39006	6266	21.4	24.6	34.4	11.7	7.9	53646	56360	69	70	2141	0.0	0.8	6.0	52.0	41.1	369287
97233	PORTLAND	19604	12890	22.3	28.8	39.2	7.5	2.2	48871	52890	59	55	6990	6.4	2.3	11.7	77.7	1.9	225053
97236	PORTLAND	22759	11216	16.1	27.2	43.2	9.7	3.8	56803	59839	74	77	6867	3.1	2.1	18.8	64.0	12.0	240365
97239	PORTLAND	49847	6678	12.8	20.1	35.9	13.0	18.3	68391	69587	86	94	3679	0.5	0.3	1.4	39.5	58.4	445102
97266	PORTLAND	20555	11210	22.4	27.0	40.8	7.0	2.8	50444	53431	62	60	6652	2.6	0.9	17.4	73.2	6.0	222711
97267	PORTLAND	29217	12024	14.1	23.1	39.3	17.5	6.0	63295	65781	82	88	8442	7.2	3.2	5.7	68.8	15.0	285220
97301	SALEM	17727	18043	29.2	30.2	35.2	3.8	1.6	40495	44247	34	28	8619	4.4	3.5	46.2	44.8	1.1	170992
97302	SALEM	29122	16614	18.5	26.0	38.9	10.2	6.5	54875	56617	71	72	9820	2.9	1.7	14.7	66.6	14.2	239992
97303	SALEM	25231	14239	16.1	24.5	44.2	9.9	5.3	58433	59157	76	80	9058	3.9	2.6	15.7	69.9	8.0	227035
97304	SALEM	28386	10296	15.6	23.6	40.9	12.8	7.1	62133	63990	80	85	7268	1.2	1.0	11.8	68.5	17.5	264979
97305	SALEM	19955	14171	22.0	30.8	37.8	6.8	2.6	46390	51076	52	48	8017	7.7	4.5	20.3	63.2	4.2	207451
97306	SALEM	29769	9724	8.4	23.1	50.4	11.7	6.4	65720	66918	84	92	6885	0.8	2.5	13.3	67.1	16.3	256718
97317	SALEM	23051	8017	15.7	26.0	45.7	8.6	4.0	55895	57087	73	75	5460	5.7	3.6	16.7	53.9	20.2	230868
97321	ALBANY	28620	9320	16.1	23.0	42.2	12.1	6.6	60368	60420	78	83	6657	2.8	1.1	15.9	60.5	19.7	272497
97322	ALBANY	22371	13304	23.9	25.7	41.1	6.7	2.7	50316	51545	62	58	7882	7.3	5.2	18.8	61.8	7.0	213754
97324	ALSEA	21036	485	21.0	29.9	43.5	4.7	0.8	48650	52162	59	55	370	10.0	3.8	15.9	49.7	20.5	240972
97325	AUMSVILLE	22054	2287	16.4	21.3	51.1	6.8	4.4	57590	58020	75	79	1873	3.0	8.8	27.1	41.7	19.4	212320
97326	BLODGETT	24047	275	21.1	27.3	41.5	5.8	4.4	51539	53417	65	63	206	5.3	3.9	21.8	41.7	27.2	247917
97327	BROWNSVILLE	21604	1120	19.4	28.3	43.1	7.2	2.0	51408	52226	65	63	868	2.1	3.5	18.0	54.7	21.8	245758
97329	CASCADIA	26549	32	15.6	21.9	50.0	9.4	3.1	62744	61704	81	86	24	0.0	4.2	20.8	54.2	20.8	233333
97330	CORVALLIS	28909	17559	25.1	23.3	33.8	10.2	7.7	51609	54316	65	64	9119	5.2	2.9	7.3	60.9	23.8	284263
97331	CORVALLIS	17297	75	84.0	16.0	0.0	0.0	0.0	13868	13872	1	1	0	0.0	0.0	0.0	0.0	0.0	0
97333	CORVALLIS	24914	8248	28.2	24.1	36.4	7.6	3.8	45862	51455	51	46	4134	5.9	3.4	12.6	63.0	15.1	238348
97338	DALLAS	21552	7410	22.3	26.0	42.4	6.8	2.5	51556	55000	65	64	5248	4.5	6.6	20.3	52.4	16.2	224932
97341	DEPOE BAY	28775	1751	22.4	33.2	36.1	4.3	4.0	43511	45821	44	41	1300	6.7	2.4	14.7	46.6	29.6	271429
97342	DETROIT	22288	190	26.3	36.3	32.6	2.6	2.1	41268	42869	37	31	128	3.9	6.3	33.6	46.1	10.2	203704
97343	EDDYVILLE	19747	216	26.9	22.7	44.0	4.6	1.9	50309	51031	62	58	161	8.1	6.2	24.2	46.6	14.9	227083
97344	FALLS CITY	19555	474	18.1	31.2	41.4	7.4	1.9	50416	53172	62	59	371	1.9	5.7	31.3	39.6	21.6	215500
97345	FOSTER	21998	216	22.2	22.7	47.2	5.6	2.3	53557	53827	69	69	162	2.5	1.2	19.1	51.9	25.3	270588
97346	GATES	21383	400	24.0	34.5	36.3	3.5	1.8	43049	46292	43	39	305	10.8	4.9	28.2	45.2	10.8	189015
97347	GRAND RONDE	19625	639	18.3	33.2	41.2	6.3	1.1	48407	52171	58	54	488	8.4	1.4	24.6	44.3	21.3	271429
97348	HALSEY	22936	516	17.2	31.6	39.3	5.6	6.2	50775	51238	63	61	368	3.5	3.3	21.7	59.0	12.5	218421
97350	IDANHA	19848	111	24.3	35.1	35.1	2.7	2.7	43368	45218	43	40	79	1.3	5.1	32.9	46.8	13.9	210938
97351	INDEPENDENCE	18759	3071	23.9	25.8	41.1	6.0	3.3	50228	52949	62	58	1994	10.6	4.5	35.8	38.2	10.9	173680
97352	JEFFERSON	23544	2065	17.9	21.0	47.3	9.1	4.7	59818	60098	77	81	1598	2.6	4.4	24.8	47.1	21.0	238066
97355	LEBANON	20508	10644	25.0	29.7	36.7	6.1	2.5	44262	47690	46	43	7565	3.9	4.1	23.2	56.1	12.7	220648
97357	LOGSDEN	24346	102	24.5	26.5	37.3	6.9	4.9	49088	49602	59	55	78	1.3	7.7	25.6	48.7	16.7	228571
97358	LYONS	19759	982	24.1	27.8	42.1	5.0	1.0	47565	50207	56	51	763	1.3	1.7	25.6	56.5	14.9	231981
97360	MILL CITY	17333	839	26.0	35.0	35.5	3.1	0.4	40587	44557	35	28	623	0.8	2.7	36.6	50.1	9.8	196062
97361	MONMOUTH	21570	4046	26.1	23.2	40.8	6.5	3.5	50852	55257	63	61	2271	4.4	3.9	13.3	61.9	16.5	241033
97362	MOUNT ANGEL	18785	1538	24.8	25.2	41.8	5.7	2.5	50000	52461	61	56	900	6.8	3.1	17.1	57.0	16.0	226098
97364	NEOTSU	23018	159	30.8	20.8	38.4	6.3	3.8	48102	50240	57	53	94	0.0	0.0	8.5	54.3	37.2	336842
97365	NEWPORT	24804	4442	29.1	31.4	28.3	7.1	4.1	41232	42248	37	30	2408	6.4	2.2	21.3	50.1	19.9	235142
97366	SOUTH BEACH	28142	660	23.5	34.7	25.9	9.4	6.5	43040	44693	43	39	480	7.1	2.3	16.7	49.8	24.2	261111
97367	LINCOLN CITY	21179	4162	33.6	30.7	30.3	3.5	1.9	35567	36872	19	11	2294	6.1	3.0	18.4	55.1	17.4	237201
97368	OTIS	22801	1351	20.9	31.2	41.2	4.5	2.2	47464	49875	55	51	1038	7.2	5.1	28.7	47.7	11.3	202222
97369	OTTER ROCK	35111	92	15.2	33.7	37.0	4.3	9.8	50557	51138	62	60	64	3.1	3.1	17.2	50.0	26.6	245455
97370	PHILOMATH	25898	3266	13.7	26.5	43.1	10.0	6.6	57976	58893	75	79	2256	4.9	1.0	18.0	52.6	23.5	246825
97371	RICKREALL	24570	223	14.8	25.1	43.0	10.3	6.7	59254	61630	76	81	174	1.7	2.9	11.5	34.5	49.4	395000
97374	SCIO	25227	1995	15.8	23.8	44.9	10.1	5.4	57834	56802	75	79	1591	1.4	3.1	16.2	50.0	29.4	293436
97375	SCOTTS MILLS	22408	455	13.4	24.4	46.2	12.3	3.7	63246	64248	81	88	375	1.9	3.5	9.1	45.6	40.0	344030
97376	SEAL ROCK	23801	743	23.6	34.6	33.9	6.1	1.9	42571	44024	41	37	607	8.4	2.6	15.0	52.1	21.9	247794
97377	SHEDD	28449	332	16.6	32.5	32.5	8.1	10.2	50608	52061	63	60	252	5.6	4.4	11.1	52.0	27.0	315942
97378	SHERIDAN	20354	2378	22.0	27.1	41.8	5.8	3.4	50812	55053	63	61	1581	3.4	4.9	27.6	46.0	18.2	223300
97380	SILETZ	21384	840	22.0	27.5	41.2	6.5	2.7	50421	51580	62	59	652	10.3	5.4	26.4	48.8	9.2	197414
97381	SILVERTON	23456	5227	17.8	23.6	45.1	8.9	4.6	57505	58310	75	78	3565	2.8	1.9	12.9	52.9	29.6	293927
97383	STAYTON	20687	3595	26.0	25.4	38.8	6.2	3.6	47576	51877	56	52	2296	4.1	5.5	15.7	61.3	13.4	230179
97385	SUBLIMITY	24137	998	15.7	20.1	52.7	8.0	3.4	63724	63371	82	89	771	9.9	2.1	5.1	64.5	18.5	279472
97386	SWEET HOME	19017	5048	29.8	30.2	33.2	4.5	2.3	41273	43968	37	31	3556	7.0	3.8	33.8	42.5	12.9	191638
97389	TANGENT	23688	582	17.7	24.2	43.6	9.3	5.2	55936	57316	73	75	443	8.6	13.8	24.2	40.9	12.6	191848
97390	TIDEWATER	25232	325	22.8	34.8	34.8	5.2	2.5	43822	45718	45	42	259	3.1	1.2	11.2	57.1	27.4	294512
97391	TOLEDO	21211	2181	24.4	26.9	38.1	8.1	2.5	47717	50482	56	52	1562	0.1	4.3	30.0	55.1	10.5	218293
97392	TURNER	24862	1652	16.1	23.0	44.8	12.5	3.6	57586	58798	75	78	1304	4.7	3.6	16.3	47.5	27.8	280726
97394	WALDPORT	22016	2196	30.5	28.7	35.3	3.5	2.0	41895	43460	39	34	1613	7.7	2.8	19.3	54.1	16.1	238857
97396	WILLAMINA	19603	1170	20.2	32.6	41.8	4.0	1.5	46918	51877	54	49	828	2.3	3.3	37.9	41.5	15.0	197131
97401	EUGENE	25949	18577	35.4	26.6	27.3	6.0	4.7	37524	40557	25	18	6371	0.1	0.3	6.4	71.3	21.9	296688
97402	EUGENE	21553	20198	26.8	30.5	36.2	4.2	2.4	43533	47803	44	41	10873	8.2	7.6	22.4	55.7	6.1	198788
97403	EUGENE	27069	3751	35.3	21.4	25.5	9.8	8.0	41998	47537	39	35	2024	15.6	2.7	5.8	44.7	31.3	305013
97404	EUGENE	26168	12115	13.3	25.6	47.1	9.5	4.5	60808	60921	79	84	8993	1.2	0.5	9.1	84.6	4.5	239998
97405	EUGENE	31632	18624	18.8	24.2	36.5	10.9	9.5	56751	57561	74	77	12658	1.0	0.6	8.0	66.9	23.6	293789
97406	AGNESS	27552	71	28.2	35.2	31.0	4.2	1.4	37329	41143	25	17	56	7.1	1.8	19.6	41.1	30.4	271429
	OREGON	26362		20.3	25.9	37.7	10.2	5.9	53483	55628				4.6	3.5	17.3	54.4	20.2	249991
	UNITED STATES	27277		20.9	24.4	35.3	11.7	7.6	54719	56938				9.3	13.1	31.6	32.6	13.5	162279

ZIP CODE		FINANCIAL SERVICES				THE HOME						ENTERTAINMENT						PERSONAL			
						Home Improvements		Furnishings													
#	POST OFFICE NAME	Auto Loan	Home Loan	Invest-ments	Retire-ment Plans	Home Repair	Lawn & Garden	Comput-ers & Hard-ware-Personal	Major Appli-ances	TV, Radio, Sound Equip-ment	Furni-ture	Dine out/ Carry out	Sports Equip-ment	Fees & Tickets	Toys & Games	Travel	Cable TV	Apparel & Services	Auto Repairs	Health Insur-ance	Pets & Supplies
97204	PORTLAND	19	14	17	16	15	17	23	18	25	20	25	14	20	21	20	26	17	23	26	24
97205	PORTLAND	59	46	54	53	47	51	69	55	71	63	71	46	63	65	62	72	50	66	67	70
97206	PORTLAND	77	83	78	83	82	79	84	80	83	82	84	63	87	83	85	83	60	83	82	94
97209	PORTLAND	69	51	54	58	49	51	76	58	76	70	78	52	68	74	66	75	55	70	65	75
97210	PORTLAND	122	113	125	124	115	105	139	116	130	135	135	101	136	130	133	125	98	128	112	140
97211	PORTLAND	83	88	82	88	86	83	90	84	89	87	90	66	92	89	89	89	64	87	86	100
97212	PORTLAND	109	119	125	122	122	112	120	113	115	120	117	90	127	115	124	113	84	116	111	132
97213	PORTLAND	87	96	93	95	95	90	96	91	94	94	95	71	101	94	98	94	68	94	93	107
97214	PORTLAND	88	76	77	82	74	72	96	79	92	91	95	69	90	92	88	90	67	89	80	98
97215	PORTLAND	94	103	103	104	104	98	103	99	100	103	101	77	108	99	106	99	72	100	99	115
97216	PORTLAND	77	83	77	83	81	79	85	79	83	82	84	63	88	83	85	83	60	83	82	94
97217	PORTLAND	78	81	77	81	80	78	84	80	83	82	84	62	85	83	83	83	59	83	82	94
97218	PORTLAND	76	85	79	83	84	78	85	81	82	83	84	64	88	83	86	82	60	83	80	94
97219	PORTLAND	131	140	139	145	140	130	138	132	133	142	134	105	145	134	141	129	96	134	127	155
97220	PORTLAND	79	85	81	84	84	82	86	82	86	84	86	64	89	85	87	86	61	85	86	97
97221	PORTLAND	156	186	203	190	196	172	173	173	162	183	162	133	191	159	189	156	118	169	161	197
97222	PORTLAND	85	91	85	91	89	86	92	87	90	91	91	68	95	91	93	90	65	90	89	103
97223	PORTLAND	111	115	108	118	113	106	116	109	112	118	114	87	119	114	115	109	81	112	105	128
97224	PORTLAND	114	125	123	124	128	122	116	120	115	124	115	88	125	115	123	114	81	117	122	137
97225	PORTLAND	125	127	124	131	126	119	131	122	127	133	129	98	134	128	130	124	91	126	120	145
97227	PORTLAND	68	59	55	61	57	57	71	61	71	68	71	50	66	71	64	70	50	68	64	75
97229	PORTLAND	175	207	195	214	206	181	183	181	172	196	175	146	204	179	193	163	128	174	160	207
97230	PORTLAND	89	90	87	90	90	89	93	89	93	92	94	69	95	92	93	93	66	93	93	105
97231	PORTLAND	135	154	167	157	158	152	136	146	132	142	133	110	148	132	149	131	95	138	138	168
97232	PORTLAND	96	84	89	92	84	80	107	87	102	101	106	76	101	103	99	100	76	99	89	108
97233	PORTLAND	77	77	73	76	75	72	82	77	80	80	81	61	81	81	80	79	58	80	75	89
97236	PORTLAND	85	93	86	92	91	85	93	88	90	91	92	70	96	91	94	89	65	90	86	103
97239	PORTLAND	136	132	137	140	133	124	147	129	141	146	144	107	147	142	143	137	103	138	127	155
97266	PORTLAND	75	80	76	79	79	74	82	77	80	80	81	61	84	80	82	79	58	80	78	90
97267	PORTLAND	98	108	104	108	107	105	105	103	104	104	104	79	110	103	109	104	74	104	105	121
97301	SALEM	69	60	55	61	58	60	70	64	70	68	71	50	65	71	64	70	49	69	66	76
97302	SALEM	97	96	95	98	96	96	100	97	100	100	100	75	100	99	99	100	70	99	99	115
97303	SALEM	96	98	90	97	96	92	98	95	96	98	97	74	98	97	97	95	68	96	94	111
97304	SALEM	101	109	108	110	111	108	105	105	103	107	103	79	110	102	108	103	73	104	107	122
97305	SALEM	83	74	68	75	72	73	80	76	80	80	81	60	76	82	76	80	56	79	76	91
97306	SALEM	108	115	107	117	113	107	111	108	108	114	110	84	115	110	113	106	77	109	105	127
97317	SALEM	92	95	94	95	96	94	92	93	91	95	91	70	94	91	95	91	64	93	94	109
97321	ALBANY	100	108	104	109	107	106	103	103	101	103	102	79	107	102	105	102	72	102	104	121
97322	ALBANY	80	78	73	78	77	77	80	78	80	80	81	60	79	81	78	81	56	80	80	92
97324	ALSEA	87	72	105	71	77	92	72	88	75	66	74	65	63	72	76	79	49	82	88	103
97325	AUMSVILLE	100	98	89	94	96	94	92	96	92	96	92	71	89	94	90	91	64	93	92	111
97326	BLODGETT	93	88	103	88	90	99	83	95	84	81	84	71	80	84	87	87	57	89	94	111
97327	BROWNSVILLE	86	85	80	89	85	94	81	89	82	76	81	68	79	84	83	85	56	83	90	104
97329	CASCADIA	108	86	140	85	95	114	86	110	90	81	89	80	75	86	94	96	59	101	108	127
97330	CORVALLIS	96	89	85	92	87	86	103	90	97	98	98	73	96	98	93	95	69	95	89	108
97331	CORVALLIS	25	11	10	13	10	12	35	17	28	24	28	19	21	27	19	25	20	25	17	23
97333	CORVALLIS	83	71	68	74	69	69	91	75	85	84	86	63	80	85	78	82	61	82	74	91
97338	DALLAS	86	83	90	82	83	90	81	87	82	78	81	67	78	82	83	84	56	85	88	102
97341	DEPOE BAY	89	78	119	77	87	99	75	93	79	76	78	65	71	74	83	84	52	87	96	107
97342	DETROIT	84	66	106	65	73	88	67	85	70	62	69	62	57	67	72	75	46	78	84	98
97343	EDDYVILLE	88	70	113	69	77	93	71	90	74	66	73	65	61	70	76	79	48	83	88	104
97344	FALLS CITY	91	84	76	82	82	88	80	86	82	80	82	63	75	85	77	85	56	82	86	101
97345	FOSTER	88	79	91	81	82	95	78	90	80	72	79	68	71	80	80	85	54	83	91	105
97346	GATES	90	66	99	65	70	92	67	86	74	63	72	64	55	72	69	80	48	79	88	101
97347	GRAND RONDE	86	79	72	78	78	84	75	81	78	76	78	60	71	81	73	81	53	78	82	96
97348	HALSEY	104	89	99	91	91	111	90	103	92	79	91	80	79	93	90	98	61	96	107	122
97350	IDANHA	85	68	110	67	75	90	68	87	71	64	71	63	59	68	74	76	47	80	86	101
97351	INDEPENDENCE	82	80	69	78	77	73	82	78	79	84	80	61	79	82	78	77	56	80	75	91
97352	JEFFERSON	101	105	95	103	104	100	97	100	95	101	96	75	98	98	98	95	67	97	96	116
97355	LEBANON	80	74	78	74	75	84	75	81	77	71	77	61	71	77	75	81	53	78	84	95
97357	LOGSDEN	96	88	79	85	86	90	83	88	86	86	86	64	78	89	79	88	58	85	88	105
97358	LYONS	83	73	82	75	76	89	72	84	75	66	74	63	66	75	73	79	50	77	86	97
97360	MILL CITY	75	62	74	63	64	79	62	74	66	57	65	56	55	66	62	71	44	68	76	87
97361	MONMOUTH	82	73	72	75	72	73	93	77	87	82	87	64	82	87	80	85	62	84	78	94
97362	MOUNT ANGEL	74	76	74	74	77	77	76	77	76	75	76	57	76	75	77	77	53	77	81	88
97364	NEOTSU	93	75	121	74	82	99	75	95	78	70	77	69	65	74	81	84	51	88	94	110
97365	NEWPORT	83	76	92	75	80	88	78	85	81	78	80	61	75	77	80	84	55	84	91	99
97366	SOUTH BEACH	102	82	132	81	90	108	82	104	86	77	85	76	71	81	89	91	56	96	103	121
97367	LINCOLN CITY	71	60	83	59	64	74	63	72	66	60	65	53	57	63	65	70	44	70	76	84
97368	OTIS	93	75	120	74	82	99	75	95	78	70	77	69	65	74	81	83	51	88	94	110
97369	OTTER ROCK	118	95	153	93	104	125	95	121	99	89	98	88	82	94	103	106	65	111	119	140
97370	PHILOMATH	101	105	99	107	103	100	103	101	100	104	101	79	105	102	103	99	71	101	98	118
97371	RICKREALL	113	99	121	101	102	123	98	114	100	89	99	89	88	99	101	105	67	106	116	135
97374	SCIO	104	99	102	100	100	109	94	104	96	91	95	78	90	97	96	99	65	98	105	122
97375	SCOTTS MILLS	97	109	94	112	106	107	97	101	96	98	96	79	104	98	103	96	67	97	100	119
97376	SEAL ROCK	85	69	111	68	76	91	69	87	72	65	71	63	60	68	75	77	47	81	86	101
97377	SHEDD	125	100	132	101	102	133	103	121	106	90	105	99	87	105	105	112	70	114	126	148
97378	SHERIDAN	84	84	85	83	84	86	81	85	82	80	82	65	81	83	83	83	57	83	85	99
97380	SILETZ	91	84	76	81	82	86	79	84	82	82	82	61	75	85	76	84	56	81	84	100
97381	SILVERTON	95	96	108	95	97	103	93	99	93	89	93	78	93	92	98	95	65	97	100	117
97383	STAYTON	84	77	74	77	76	80	81	80	81	79	81	62	76	83	77	82	56	81	82	95
97385	SUBLIMITY	95	102	97	104	101	104	92	99	92	92	92	76	96	93	98	93	64	94	98	116
97386	SWEET HOME	80	66	78	65	67	83	68	78	73	63	71	59	60	72	67	78	48	74	83	92
97389	TANGENT	99	95	86	94	94	95	90	93	92	93	92	69	88	95	88	93	63	91	93	111
97390	TIDEWATER	79	75	109	74	84	92	70	85	74	74	73	57	70	68	79	78	49	80	90	98
97391	TOLEDO	87	76	81	76	76	86	78	84	80	74	79	63	71	81	76	83	54	81	86	99
97392	TURNER	98	101	107	103	103	108	94	102	94	94	94	76	95	94	99	96	65	97	102	119
97394	WALDPORT	75	67	98	65	75	84	65	79	68	66	67	55	62	63	71	72	45	75	83	91
97396	WILLAMINA	81	77	67	77	74	82	75	78	77	73	77	59	73	79	73	79	52	76	82	93
97401	EUGENE	76	59	58	64	58	60	89	66	81	76	82	58	74	80	71	79	58	77	69	82
97402	EUGENE	78	67	63	68	65	68	77	71	76	75	76	56	70	77	69	76	53	75	72	85
97403	EUGENE	91	77	79	81	77	79	103	84	96	92	96	70	90	95	87	95	68	93	87	102
97404	EUGENE	93	105	92	104	101	99	96	96	95	97	96	75	102	97	99	95	67	95	96	113
97405	EUGENE	104	108	109	111	109	107	110	106	106	108	107	82	111	106	109	105	75	107	105	124
97406	AGNESS	87	70	113	69	77	92	70	89	73	66	72	65	61	70	76	78	48	82	88	103
	OREGON	96	93	95	94	93	95	95	95	95	94	95	74	93	95	95	95	66	96	96	112
	UNITED STATES	100	100	100	100	100	100	100	100	100	100	100	100	100	100	100	100	100	100	100	100

#	POST OFFICE NAME	COUNTY FIPS CODE	POPULATION 2000	POPULATION 2009	POPULATION 2014	2000-2009 ANNUAL RATE % Rate	2000-2009 ANNUAL RATE State Centile	HOUSEHOLDS 2000	HOUSEHOLDS 2009	HOUSEHOLDS 2014	HOUSEHOLDS % Annual Rate 2000-2009	HOUSEHOLDS 2009 Average HH Size	FAMILIES 2000	FAMILIES 2009	FAMILIES % Annual Rate 2000-2009
97408	EUGENE	039	9583	11762	12782	2.2	94	3876	4726	5130	2.2	2.48	2704	3247	2.0
97410	AZALEA	019	649	703	727	0.9	62	286	315	329	1.0	2.23	201	219	0.9
97411	BANDON	011	6587	6994	7139	0.7	53	2888	3105	3188	0.8	2.19	1871	1983	0.6
97412	BLACHLY	039	544	520	515	-0.5	4	199	192	190	-0.4	2.62	139	132	-0.6
97413	BLUE RIVER	043	865	912	939	0.6	48	406	433	447	0.7	2.10	268	279	0.4
97414	BROADBENT	011	169	165	162	-0.3	8	67	66	65	-0.2	2.48	47	46	-0.2
97415	BROOKINGS	015	13292	13862	13879	0.5	43	5947	6279	6317	0.6	2.18	3903	4070	0.5
97416	CAMAS VALLEY	019	819	853	863	0.4	39	302	319	324	0.6	2.67	223	232	0.4
97417	CANYONVILLE	019	1664	1725	1756	0.4	39	677	716	734	0.6	2.40	448	466	0.4
97419	CHESHIRE	039	1223	1296	1339	0.6	48	485	520	540	0.8	2.49	368	389	0.6
97420	COOS BAY	011	26845	27165	27202	0.1	23	11209	11454	11518	0.2	2.33	7338	7397	0.1
97423	COQUILLE	011	7449	7615	7608	0.2	26	3050	3154	3164	0.4	2.34	2104	2151	0.2
97424	COTTAGE GROVE	039	16328	17366	17983	0.7	53	6227	6673	6929	0.8	2.58	4443	4689	0.6
97426	CRESWELL	039	7891	8614	9005	1.0	66	2864	3144	3297	1.0	2.72	2145	2318	0.8
97427	CULP CREEK	039	279	303	318	0.9	62	110	121	127	1.0	2.50	83	90	0.9
97429	DAYS CREEK	019	673	677	676	0.1	23	260	267	269	0.3	2.52	190	192	0.1
97430	DEADWOOD	039	550	555	564	0.1	23	195	199	202	0.2	2.72	133	133	0.0
97431	DEXTER	039	2040	2116	2163	0.4	39	706	740	760	0.5	2.85	542	560	0.4
97434	DORENA	039	585	602	613	0.3	32	223	232	238	0.4	2.59	172	177	0.3
97435	DRAIN	019	1983	2038	2053	0.3	32	802	840	852	0.5	2.43	568	586	0.3
97436	ELKTON	019	840	835	826	-0.1	14	348	353	351	0.2	2.36	248	248	0.0
97437	ELMIRA	039	2229	2277	2312	0.2	26	837	864	881	0.3	2.64	659	672	0.2
97438	FALL CREEK	039	1605	1604	1614	0.0	19	582	588	594	0.1	2.72	443	442	0.0
97439	FLORENCE	039	12844	15141	16300	1.8	87	6087	7267	7853	1.9	2.07	3938	4606	1.7
97441	GARDINER	019	12	12	12	0.0	19	7	7	7	0.0	1.71	5	5	0.0
97442	GLENDALE	019	2107	2276	2331	0.8	59	819	891	916	0.9	2.55	591	634	0.8
97443	GLIDE	019	2213	2272	2302	0.3	32	787	823	839	0.5	2.65	585	604	0.3
97444	GOLD BEACH	015	4767	5074	5122	0.7	53	2142	2311	2345	0.8	2.16	1407	1496	0.7
97446	HARRISBURG	043	4270	4872	5201	1.4	78	1518	1740	1859	1.5	2.80	1176	1336	1.4
97447	IDLEYLD PARK	019	793	800	798	0.1	23	306	314	315	0.3	2.38	215	216	0.1
97448	JUNCTION CITY	039	11956	12513	12843	0.5	43	4565	4797	4935	0.5	2.58	3242	3353	0.4
97449	LAKESIDE	011	1578	1622	1653	0.3	32	735	768	787	0.5	2.06	498	514	0.3
97450	LANGLOIS	015	514	512	496	0.0	19	233	236	229	0.1	2.17	156	156	0.0
97451	LORANE	039	482	538	569	1.2	74	180	202	214	1.3	2.66	136	150	1.1
97452	LOWELL	039	1059	1142	1190	0.8	59	406	441	461	0.9	2.59	302	325	0.8
97453	MAPLETON	039	1049	1134	1181	0.8	59	445	486	508	1.0	2.33	318	341	0.8
97454	MARCOLA	039	1376	1413	1466	0.3	32	529	549	573	0.4	2.57	403	413	0.3
97455	PLEASANT HILL	039	3188	3188	3205	0.0	19	1140	1151	1162	0.1	2.75	896	893	0.0
97456	MONROE	003	2783	2841	2906	0.2	26	1028	1070	1101	0.4	2.66	788	809	0.3
97457	MYRTLE CREEK	019	9765	10466	10752	0.8	59	3761	4099	4237	0.9	2.54	2746	2953	0.8
97458	MYRTLE POINT	011	4786	4861	4869	0.2	26	1926	1975	1986	0.3	2.44	1357	1377	0.2
97459	NORTH BEND	011	14367	14222	14129	-0.1	14	5898	5892	5874	0.0	2.35	3964	3913	-0.1
97461	NOTI	039	890	877	877	-0.2	10	336	334	335	-0.1	2.63	258	254	-0.2
97462	OAKLAND	019	3849	4047	4139	0.5	43	1506	1609	1657	0.7	2.50	1138	1200	0.6
97463	OAKRIDGE	039	3756	4025	4187	0.8	59	1582	1712	1789	0.9	2.35	1073	1141	0.7
97465	PORT ORFORD	015	2065	2167	2167	0.5	43	1000	1065	1070	0.7	2.03	566	593	0.5
97466	POWERS	011	998	1026	1039	0.3	32	440	456	463	0.4	2.25	270	276	0.2
97467	REEDSPORT	019	6180	6081	6053	-0.2	10	2767	2775	2781	0.0	2.17	1815	1789	-0.2
97469	RIDDLE	019	2891	2982	3010	0.3	32	1068	1123	1141	0.5	2.60	776	805	0.4
97470	ROSEBURG	019	18475	18273	18185	-0.1	14	7651	7647	7648	0.0	2.33	4919	4840	-0.2
97471	ROSEBURG	019	25927	28816	30102	1.1	71	9971	11265	11836	1.3	2.50	7380	8252	1.2
97473	SCOTTSBURG	019	208	214	216	0.3	32	97	102	103	0.5	2.10	70	72	0.3
97476	SIXES	015	366	366	354	0.0	19	152	154	150	0.1	2.38	101	101	0.0
97477	SPRINGFIELD	039	35725	37134	38038	0.4	39	14507	15132	15540	0.5	2.42	9094	9325	0.3
97478	SPRINGFIELD	039	32011	35395	37152	1.1	71	11814	13180	13889	1.2	2.67	8795	9666	1.0
97479	SUTHERLIN	019	8373	9588	10105	1.5	80	3367	3936	4176	1.7	2.43	2396	2764	1.6
97480	SWISSHOME	039	353	372	385	0.6	48	140	149	155	0.7	2.45	92	96	0.5
97481	TENMILE	019	933	960	968	0.3	32	330	346	351	0.5	2.77	261	271	0.4
97484	TILLER	019	277	274	273	-0.1	14	117	118	118	0.1	2.30	83	83	0.0
97486	UMPQUA	019	837	844	840	0.1	23	335	345	346	0.3	2.42	271	276	0.2
97487	VENETA	039	6924	8404	9079	2.1	93	2484	3025	3275	2.2	2.78	1912	2298	2.0
97488	VIDA	039	1025	1063	1087	0.4	39	422	442	454	0.5	2.40	294	302	0.3
97489	WALTERVILLE	039	896	961	996	0.8	59	372	403	420	0.9	2.38	276	294	0.7
97490	WALTON	039	286	294	301	0.3	32	103	107	110	0.4	2.75	78	80	0.3
97492	WESTFIR	039	639	696	731	0.9	62	247	272	287	1.0	2.56	184	199	0.9
97493	WESTLAKE	039	299	322	336	0.8	59	128	139	146	0.9	2.32	95	101	0.7
97495	WINCHESTER	019	1766	1691	1669	-0.5	4	727	707	702	-0.3	2.38	516	497	-0.4
97496	WINSTON	019	6718	7139	7326	0.7	53	2573	2779	2870	0.8	2.56	1885	2010	0.7
97497	WOLF CREEK	033	1632	1866	1974	1.5	80	677	779	827	1.5	2.39	451	512	1.4
97498	YACHATS	041	1465	1565	1608	0.7	53	666	717	738	0.8	2.01	392	415	0.6
97499	YONCALLA	019	2066	2176	2233	0.6	48	805	863	891	0.8	2.51	583	617	0.6
97501	MEDFORD	029	37065	42197	44405	1.4	78	14274	16359	17277	1.5	2.54	9417	10672	1.4
97502	CENTRAL POINT	029	23485	28327	30654	2.0	91	8610	10359	11205	2.0	2.72	6586	7829	1.9
97503	WHITE CITY	029	8742	10554	11306	2.1	93	2674	3199	3435	2.0	3.05	2114	2490	1.8
97504	MEDFORD	029	40379	44297	46076	1.0	66	16499	18214	18985	1.1	2.38	11087	12084	0.9
97520	ASHLAND	029	23898	26275	27343	1.0	66	10291	11477	12032	1.2	2.17	5706	6191	0.9
97522	BUTTE FALLS	029	630	648	658	0.3	32	234	245	250	0.5	2.64	176	181	0.3
97523	CAVE JUNCTION	033	6536	7232	7562	1.1	71	2768	3073	3218	1.1	2.35	1785	1951	1.0
97524	EAGLE POINT	029	10815	14688	16504	3.4	98	3933	5399	6078	3.5	2.72	3045	4123	3.3
97525	GOLD HILL	029	4791	5362	5635	1.2	74	1940	2213	2337	1.4	2.42	1357	1517	1.2
97526	GRANTS PASS	033	32134	34175	34942	0.7	53	13137	14016	14356	0.7	2.38	8793	9263	0.6
97527	GRANTS PASS	033	27380	31390	33199	1.5	80	11224	12927	13705	1.5	2.41	8046	9145	1.4
97530	JACKSONVILLE	029	6580	7430	7812	1.3	76	2727	3198	3390	1.7	2.31	1973	2266	1.5
97531	KERBY	033	277	313	330	1.3	76	114	129	136	1.3	2.43	70	78	1.2
97532	MERLIN	033	2214	2578	2759	1.7	85	879	1031	1107	1.7	2.50	677	787	1.6
97534	O BRIEN	033	332	350	357	0.6	48	141	150	153	0.7	2.33	89	94	0.6
97535	PHOENIX	029	4200	4737	4987	1.3	76	1812	2075	2189	1.5	2.26	1106	1242	1.3
97536	PROSPECT	029	932	981	1001	0.6	48	384	412	423	0.8	2.38	292	309	0.6
97537	ROGUE RIVER	029	6489	6902	7113	0.7	53	2722	2952	3064	0.9	2.33	1895	2020	0.7
97538	SELMA	033	2476	2962	3227	2.0	91	974	1173	1279	2.0	2.53	683	812	1.9
97539	SHADY COVE	029	2820	3372	3633	2.0	91	1191	1453	1578	2.2	2.32	843	1011	2.0
97540	TALENT	029	7853	8415	8685	0.8	59	3154	3443	3579	1.0	2.39	2043	2184	0.7
97541	TRAIL	029	1303	1427	1494	1.0	66	522	583	615	1.2	2.45	386	426	1.1
97543	WILDERVILLE	033	1477	1728	1861	1.7	85	594	701	757	1.8	2.46	440	513	1.7
97544	WILLIAMS	033	2555	2645	2673	0.4	39	1057	1101	1114	0.4	2.40	725	746	0.3
	OREGON					1.3					1.2	2.51			1.1
	UNITED STATES					1.0					1.1	2.59			0.9

#	POST OFFICE NAME	White 2000	White 2009	Black 2000	Black 2009	Asian/Pacific 2000	Asian/Pacific 2009	% Hispanic Origin 2000	% Hispanic Origin 2009	0-4	5-9	10-14	15-19	20-24	25-44	45-64	65-84	85+	18+	MEDIAN AGE 2009	% 2009 Males	% 2009 Females
97408	EUGENE	93.0	91.4	0.5	0.6	1.8	2.5	2.6	3.8	5.3	5.5	6.1	6.5	5.4	21.9	31.0	15.3	3.0	79.1	44.4	47.7	52.3
97410	AZALEA	94.5	93.7	0.2	0.1	0.3	0.4	2.3	3.6	3.6	4.0	4.3	3.7	3.7	15.2	41.8	21.6	2.1	85.8	54.1	50.6	49.4
97411	BANDON	92.6	91.7	0.2	0.2	0.8	1.1	2.3	3.4	3.7	3.9	4.5	5.0	4.2	17.6	36.0	21.4	3.7	84.6	52.7	47.5	52.5
97412	BLACHLY	92.1	91.3	0.2	0.2	0.9	1.3	1.7	2.5	5.4	6.0	6.2	6.0	3.8	21.3	35.4	14.6	1.3	78.8	45.8	52.1	47.9
97413	BLUE RIVER	96.1	95.5	0.2	0.3	0.5	0.5	2.8	4.3	3.2	3.7	4.7	4.8	3.3	17.1	39.9	20.7	2.5	85.1	52.4	52.1	47.9
97414	BROADBENT	92.9	92.7	0.0	0.0	0.6	0.6	2.4	3.0	4.2	4.8	6.1	6.7	3.6	20.0	35.2	17.0	2.4	80.6	47.7	51.5	48.5
97415	BROOKINGS	92.4	91.3	0.2	0.2	0.9	1.2	3.9	5.6	4.2	4.4	4.6	4.9	4.4	17.0	32.1	24.3	4.1	83.5	52.5	48.9	51.1
97416	CAMAS VALLEY	93.5	93.2	0.1	0.1	0.4	0.4	2.2	3.2	4.9	5.6	6.0	6.3	5.4	22.3	32.5	15.5	1.5	79.5	44.5	51.5	48.5
97417	CANYONVILLE	91.9	90.7	0.2	0.2	0.9	1.2	3.8	5.3	5.4	5.6	5.9	6.0	5.4	21.3	30.1	17.4	2.8	79.3	45.2	48.8	51.2
97419	CHESHIRE	93.1	91.8	0.3	0.4	0.6	0.8	3.3	4.9	4.2	4.5	5.9	6.5	4.6	20.6	39.4	12.7	1.5	81.3	46.7	50.7	49.3
97420	COOS BAY	90.8	89.4	0.3	0.3	1.4	1.8	3.9	5.6	5.2	5.1	5.5	6.5	5.7	22.1	30.8	16.4	2.7	80.5	44.9	49.0	51.0
97423	COQUILLE	93.2	92.2	0.5	0.6	0.6	0.8	3.6	5.3	4.7	4.7	5.1	5.7	5.9	22.0	30.9	18.0	2.9	81.7	46.3	48.7	51.3
97424	COTTAGE GROVE	93.5	92.1	0.2	0.2	0.9	1.3	3.8	5.6	5.9	5.9	6.2	6.5	5.5	23.4	30.3	14.1	2.2	77.9	42.3	49.2	50.8
97426	CRESWELL	91.5	89.5	0.3	0.4	0.7	1.0	4.5	6.8	6.9	6.7	7.2	6.7	5.7	25.9	28.2	10.9	1.7	74.9	38.2	49.3	50.7
97427	CULP CREEK	93.9	92.7	0.4	0.3	0.7	1.3	2.9	4.3	4.0	4.3	5.3	7.3	5.3	21.8	34.7	16.2	1.3	81.8	46.4	51.8	48.2
97429	DAYS CREEK	92.9	92.0	0.1	0.1	0.4	0.6	2.8	4.0	4.6	6.1	6.1	5.6	3.8	17.9	37.8	16.8	1.3	79.8	48.3	49.0	51.0
97430	DEADWOOD	90.4	89.4	0.2	0.2	0.7	0.9	2.4	3.4	5.0	5.2	5.8	5.8	4.9	21.4	34.6	15.7	1.6	80.2	46.2	50.3	49.7
97431	DEXTER	94.2	93.5	0.3	0.3	0.4	0.6	3.5	5.2	5.3	5.8	6.4	7.3	5.9	23.3	33.3	11.7	1.2	78.0	42.0	51.4	48.6
97434	DORENA	92.8	91.2	0.0	0.0	0.7	1.0	3.3	4.7	4.7	5.3	6.5	8.0	2.5	23.9	34.1	14.0	1.2	77.7	44.5	52.0	48.0
97435	DRAIN	92.8	92.0	0.1	0.1	0.5	0.5	2.6	3.9	5.0	5.4	5.9	5.7	5.0	23.0	32.8	15.3	2.0	80.2	45.0	48.8	51.2
97436	ELKTON	95.0	94.6	0.2	0.2	0.2	0.4	1.2	1.6	3.8	4.3	5.9	6.6	4.1	19.0	34.6	19.9	1.8	81.8	49.3	49.3	50.7
97437	ELMIRA	95.6	94.9	0.1	0.1	0.5	0.7	2.4	3.6	4.0	4.4	6.2	7.1	4.2	21.4	36.9	13.9	1.9	80.5	46.3	50.2	49.8
97438	FALL CREEK	91.6	90.5	0.1	0.2	0.5	0.6	3.2	4.9	4.5	5.2	6.2	6.5	4.6	24.0	37.5	10.4	1.0	80.0	44.2	50.4	49.6
97439	FLORENCE	95.9	95.3	0.2	0.2	0.7	0.9	2.2	3.3	3.3	3.5	3.8	4.5	4.0	14.4	31.4	30.5	4.6	86.5	57.1	47.7	52.3
97441	GARDINER	100.0	100.0	0.0	0.0	0.0	0.0	0.0	0.0	0.0	0.0	0.0	0.0	0.0	0.0	100.0	0.0	0.0	100.0	53.0	16.7	83.3
97442	GLENDALE	91.5	90.7	0.1	0.1	1.0	1.2	6.8	9.5	6.1	6.1	6.2	7.0	6.5	22.0	30.4	14.2	1.7	77.4	41.6	49.5	50.5
97443	GLIDE	93.4	92.8	0.2	0.3	0.4	0.5	1.6	2.3	3.9	5.0	7.9	10.7	4.5	19.9	35.1	12.0	1.0	76.3	43.7	52.2	47.8
97444	GOLD BEACH	94.5	93.7	0.1	0.2	0.8	1.0	2.3	3.3	3.4	3.8	4.5	4.9	3.8	15.8	38.2	22.9	2.6	85.0	53.6	48.9	51.1
97446	HARRISBURG	93.3	91.7	0.2	0.2	0.5	0.7	5.2	7.4	8.8	8.9	8.4	6.4	5.0	27.3	25.2	8.9	1.1	70.0	34.9	51.6	48.4
97447	IDLEYLD PARK	90.2	89.4	0.4	0.4	0.6	0.8	3.2	4.4	4.9	5.4	7.3	11.5	6.0	20.4	32.8	10.9	1.0	75.5	40.8	53.4	46.6
97448	JUNCTION CITY	93.0	91.4	0.3	0.3	0.8	1.0	5.0	7.3	6.2	6.2	6.7	7.0	5.5	24.3	30.0	12.1	2.1	76.7	40.5	49.6	50.4
97449	LAKESIDE	92.8	91.9	0.4	0.4	0.4	0.5	3.2	4.5	2.8	3.1	3.3	3.6	4.2	14.1	37.5	28.5	2.8	89.0	56.6	50.4	49.6
97450	LANGLOIS	92.2	90.4	0.2	0.2	0.4	0.6	4.9	7.0	2.5	3.1	3.9	5.5	4.3	14.8	40.6	22.3	2.9	86.9	54.6	51.8	48.2
97451	LORANE	95.7	95.2	0.2	0.2	0.4	0.6	0.8	1.1	5.0	5.8	6.7	7.1	4.5	22.7	35.3	11.9	1.1	78.1	43.8	49.6	50.4
97452	LOWELL	92.3	91.0	0.2	0.3	0.5	0.6	4.5	6.7	5.7	6.3	6.7	6.8	5.3	27.8	32.0	8.5	0.9	77.1	39.2	50.5	49.5
97453	MAPLETON	90.7	89.7	0.1	0.1	0.5	0.7	3.4	4.9	3.7	3.9	6.8	6.3	4.1	18.2	35.5	20.3	1.3	82.0	49.0	49.8	50.2
97454	MARCOLA	93.7	92.6	0.1	0.1	0.4	0.6	3.0	4.5	4.5	5.0	5.1	7.2	4.0	22.7	39.0	11.4	1.1	80.7	45.7	51.4	48.6
97455	PLEASANT HILL	94.6	93.6	0.6	0.7	1.0	1.3	1.7	2.6	4.2	4.8	6.0	6.4	4.7	20.7	35.7	15.6	2.0	80.7	47.2	49.1	50.9
97456	MONROE	95.7	95.0	0.2	0.2	0.6	0.9	5.2	7.8	5.5	5.6	6.3	6.5	5.5	25.0	33.7	10.8	1.1	78.7	42.2	51.4	48.6
97457	MYRTLE CREEK	93.5	92.7	0.1	0.2	0.7	0.9	2.8	4.0	6.1	6.2	6.7	6.5	5.2	22.4	29.0	15.7	2.1	77.0	42.3	48.5	51.5
97458	MYRTLE POINT	93.1	92.4	0.2	0.2	0.3	0.3	3.1	4.5	4.9	5.3	6.3	6.8	4.8	20.1	31.9	17.1	2.8	79.1	46.1	48.7	51.3
97459	NORTH BEND	93.1	92.1	0.4	0.4	1.3	1.6	3.1	4.4	5.0	5.0	5.5	6.1	5.9	23.1	31.5	15.0	2.9	80.7	44.5	49.1	50.9
97461	NOTI	94.3	93.4	0.1	0.1	0.7	0.8	2.4	3.5	5.1	5.7	6.0	5.0	4.7	25.0	37.2	9.9	1.4	79.9	43.8	51.1	48.9
97462	OAKLAND	93.9	93.1	0.3	0.3	0.6	0.8	3.1	4.6	4.6	4.9	5.7	5.9	4.3	19.4	35.6	17.7	1.8	80.9	48.6	50.5	49.5
97463	OAKRIDGE	92.9	91.3	0.3	0.4	0.5	0.6	4.5	6.7	4.9	5.1	5.7	7.0	5.3	20.5	31.9	17.2	2.5	80.0	46.0	51.0	49.0
97465	PORT ORFORD	92.9	91.9	0.0	0.0	0.5	0.6	4.0	5.8	3.0	3.3	3.5	4.5	4.5	13.8	37.2	27.3	2.8	87.4	55.9	50.1	49.9
97466	POWERS	86.4	85.4	0.1	0.1	0.5	0.7	2.1	3.1	4.5	4.9	5.3	5.3	5.3	19.7	33.2	18.9	3.0	82.3	48.5	49.9	50.1
97467	REEDSPORT	94.1	93.0	0.0	0.0	0.5	0.6	4.0	5.8	4.6	4.7	4.7	5.3	5.0	17.8	32.1	22.5	3.3	82.9	51.2	49.6	50.4
97469	RIDDLE	92.7	91.9	0.1	0.1	0.4	0.5	2.6	3.8	6.0	6.4	7.0	7.1	5.0	21.7	29.0	15.3	2.6	76.1	42.2	49.4	50.6
97470	ROSEBURG	93.6	92.4	0.3	0.3	1.0	1.3	3.9	5.6	6.1	5.8	6.0	6.3	6.0	24.8	29.0	13.9	2.2	78.4	41.2	49.4	50.6
97471	ROSEBURG	94.5	93.4	0.2	0.2	0.8	1.1	3.2	4.7	5.2	5.5	6.0	6.4	4.9	22.1	30.8	16.1	3.1	79.1	44.9	48.7	51.3
97473	SCOTTSBURG	94.2	93.5	0.0	0.0	0.5	0.5	3.4	5.6	4.7	5.6	5.6	4.7	3.3	20.6	34.1	19.6	1.9	80.8	48.8	52.8	47.2
97476	SIXES	92.3	90.4	0.0	0.0	0.5	0.5	4.9	6.8	2.5	3.0	3.8	5.5	4.4	15.3	40.7	21.9	3.0	87.4	54.4	51.9	48.1
97477	SPRINGFIELD	88.9	86.4	0.8	0.9	1.6	2.0	7.6	10.9	7.6	6.8	6.3	6.4	7.2	29.1	23.9	10.6	2.1	75.7	34.5	48.8	51.2
97478	SPRINGFIELD	93.1	91.6	0.4	0.4	0.9	1.2	4.1	6.0	6.9	6.7	6.8	6.9	6.0	27.0	27.7	10.3	1.6	75.2	37.6	49.5	50.5
97479	SUTHERLIN	94.2	93.1	0.1	0.2	0.5	0.7	3.8	5.6	6.0	5.9	6.1	6.6	5.9	22.0	28.2	16.5	2.7	77.7	42.9	48.3	51.7
97480	SWISSHOME	88.1	87.1	0.3	0.3	0.6	0.5	3.4	4.6	4.8	4.8	5.4	5.6	5.9	21.5	33.9	16.1	1.9	80.9	46.3	47.8	52.2
97481	TENMILE	94.1	93.5	0.2	0.2	0.4	0.5	2.6	3.5	4.4	5.1	5.7	6.4	5.3	22.9	34.5	14.4	1.4	80.5	45.1	51.4	48.6
97484	TILLER	91.6	90.9	0.0	0.0	0.4	0.7	2.2	2.6	4.4	7.3	7.3	6.6	1.5	18.2	39.4	15.0	0.4	76.3	47.4	48.2	51.8
97486	UMPQUA	95.1	94.2	0.1	0.1	0.8	1.1	2.3	3.3	3.3	3.7	4.5	4.9	3.9	17.2	39.6	21.1	1.9	85.1	54.4	51.7	48.3
97487	VENETA	93.8	92.5	0.2	0.3	0.7	1.0	2.6	4.1	6.3	6.5	7.0	7.0	5.6	24.6	31.3	10.5	1.1	75.8	40.0	49.6	50.4
97488	VIDA	96.0	95.1	0.4	0.5	0.8	1.1	2.6	4.0	3.6	4.7	5.6	5.5	4.0	19.4	41.0	14.4	1.9	82.5	49.1	50.0	50.0
97489	WALTERVILLE	97.3	96.7	0.1	0.1	0.8	1.1	2.0	3.0	3.5	4.1	4.9	5.2	3.7	18.9	38.5	19.0	2.1	84.5	50.8	50.2	49.8
97490	WALTON	94.8	93.9	0.3	0.3	0.7	0.7	1.4	2.0	5.4	6.1	6.8	5.8	4.4	23.8	36.1	10.2	1.4	77.6	43.1	51.0	49.0
97492	WESTFIR	95.5	94.5	0.5	0.6	0.8	1.0	1.9	2.7	4.7	5.5	5.7	6.0	5.0	20.3	35.9	14.8	2.0	80.3	46.7	51.9	48.1
97493	WESTLAKE	96.7	95.7	0.0	0.0	1.0	1.6	1.7	2.5	2.2	2.8	3.4	4.0	3.7	12.7	40.7	27.6	2.8	88.8	57.6	49.4	50.6
97495	WINCHESTER	94.5	93.6	0.2	0.2	0.9	1.2	2.4	3.5	5.0	5.6	6.3	5.7	3.7	20.9	33.1	17.1	2.5	79.8	47.0	48.8	51.2
97496	WINSTON	94.6	93.8	0.2	0.2	0.5	0.6	2.6	3.9	7.2	6.4	6.6	7.1	6.1	23.1	27.5	14.0	2.0	75.4	39.8	49.2	50.8
97497	WOLF CREEK	93.7	92.8	0.2	0.3	0.5	0.6	3.1	4.5	4.3	4.6	5.3	6.3	4.6	18.3	37.6	17.2	1.8	81.2	49.5	51.1	48.9
97498	YACHATS	93.1	92.0	0.9	1.0	1.0	1.2	2.9	4.4	2.6	3.1	3.9	9.5	5.4	13.2	37.6	22.0	2.7	84.9	53.8	49.6	50.4
97499	YONCALLA	94.0	93.4	0.1	0.1	0.8	0.9	2.1	3.0	5.6	5.4	6.5	6.9	4.8	22.2	32.1	14.7	1.8	78.1	44.0	49.7	50.3
97501	MEDFORD	87.6	84.9	0.6	0.6	1.0	1.2	12.5	16.9	7.5	7.1	6.9	6.8	6.2	26.5	26.4	10.8	1.8	74.4	36.9	49.8	50.2
97502	CENTRAL POINT	93.7	92.2	0.2	0.2	0.7	1.0	4.6	6.8	6.4	6.4	6.9	7.1	5.3	24.1	29.2	12.5	2.0	75.7	40.3	49.1	50.9
97503	WHITE CITY	88.2	84.2	0.7	0.8	0.6	0.7	11.4	17.8	6.9	6.9	6.8	7.2	6.4	25.3	29.6	10.1	0.9	75.0	37.9	53.8	46.2
97504	MEDFORD	92.8	90.8	0.4	0.4	1.6	2.1	5.4	7.9	5.8	5.5	5.8	6.4	5.9	22.3	28.0	15.6	4.7	78.7	43.6	46.9	53.1
97520	ASHLAND	92.0	90.4	0.5	0.6	1.8	2.3	3.5	5.1	4.0	4.0	4.7	8.5	10.2	22.2	30.0	13.2	3.2	83.7	41.9	46.7	53.3
97522	BUTTE FALLS	94.6	93.8	0.0	0.0	0.3	0.3	2.2	3.2	5.1	5.4	6.0	6.3	5.6	21.0	33.6	15.6	1.4	79.6	45.4	51.4	48.6
97523	CAVE JUNCTION	92.3	91.3	0.3	0.4	0.8	1.0	4.4	6.4	4.6	5.1	6.1	6.6	5.0	18.5	35.6	16.1	2.4	80.6	47.5	50.6	49.4
97524	EAGLE POINT	93.6	92.3	0.2	0.3	0.6	0.8	4.0	5.9	6.9	7.0	7.2	7.0	5.5	25.4	28.9	11.0	1.2	74.6	38.4	49.8	50.2
97525	GOLD HILL	94.4	93.2	0.2	0.2	0.4	0.6	3.8	5.7	4.6	5.4	6.0	5.8	3.4	19.4	36.3	16.7	2.4	80.1	48.0	49.4	50.6
97526	GRANTS PASS	93.4	92.0	0.3	0.3	0.9	1.2	4.6	6.7	5.9	5.6	6.0	6.5	5.6	21.5	29.4	16.1	3.4	78.4	44.1	48.0	52.0
97527	GRANTS PASS	94.7	93.7	0.2	0.3	0.5	0.7	4.2	6.1	5.3	5.5	5.7	6.0	4.8	20.5	31.6	17.7	2.9	79.8	46.6	48.5	51.5
97530	JACKSONVILLE	95.2	94.2	0.2	0.2	0.6	0.7	2.8	4.3	3.8	4.8	6.0	6.5	3.5	18.0	38.9	16.2	2.4	81.0	48.8	50.0	50.0
97531	KERBY	91.7	90.4	0.4	0.3	0.7	1.0	5.1	7.0	4.2	4.5	5.4	7.0	6.1	18.8	35.5	16.3	2.2	81.5	47.5	51.4	48.6
97532	MERLIN	94.7	93.8	0.3	0.3	0.7	0.9	3.4	5.0	3.6	4.0	4.6	5.2	4.1	18.1	38.6	19.9	1.8	84.5	51.6	50.1	49.9
97534	O BRIEN	91.5	90.0	0.6	0.6	0.9	1.4	4.5	6.6	3.4	4.0	4.6	6.6	4.9	17.7	39.7	17.1	2.0	83.7	51.0	54.3	45.7
97535	PHOENIX	89.9	87.0	0.6	0.7	1.1	1.4	8.7	12.8	5.6	5.8	6.0	5.2	3.9	22.6	31.6	16.3	3.0	79.2	45.7	48.7	51.3
97536	PROSPECT	95.9	95.4	0.1	0.1	0.3	0.4	2.4	3.4	3.9	4.5	5.1	5.4	4.0	18.6	38.3	19.1	1.2	83.2	50.5	51.5	48.5
97537	ROGUE RIVER	94.8	93.6	0.2	0.2	0.6	0.9	3.6	5.5	4.2	4.6	5.2	5.3	3.8	18.1	35.9	19.8	3.1	82.8	50.9	49.2	50.8
97538	SELMA	93.5	92.6	0.2	0.3	0.4	0.5	3.1	4.5	4.3	4.7	5.5	5.7	4.3	18.9	38.3	17.1	1.2	82.0	49.1	50.3	49.7
97539	SHADY COVE	96.0	95.6	0.1	0.2	0.3	0.5	2.7	4.1	5.0	5.5	6.1	5.3	3.7	19.1	34.9	19.2	1.4	80.2	48.4	50.1	49.9
97540	TALENT	89.0	85.7	0.5	0.5	0.5	0.7	10.4	15.0	6.3	6.1	6.3	6.4	6.0	26.6	26.6	13.2	2.6	77.6	38.8	48.8	51.2
97541	TRAIL	95.5	94.6	0.2	0.2	0.4	0.4	3.1	4.6	4.4	5.2	6.0	7.4	3.5	20.9	37.5	13.7	1.5	79.8	46.3	50.9	49.1
97543	WILDERVILLE	95.6	95.0	0.1	0.1	0.4	0.5	2.8	4.1	3.7	4.3	4.9	5.0	3.5	18.3	39.7	18.7	1.9	83.9	51.7	50.3	49.7
97544	WILLIAMS	95.3	94.6	0.2	0.2	0.6	0.8	2.5	3.7	3.7	5.2	5.9	5.5	3.1	18.8	40.0	16.4	1.4	81.7	49.2	50.7	49.3
	OREGON	86.6	83.7	1.6	1.7	3.2	4.0	8.0	11.2	6.5	6.2	6.3	6.8	6.8	26.7	27.5	11.1	2.1	77.0	38.0	49.6	50.4
	UNITED STATES	75.1	72.0	12.3	12.7	3.8	4.6	12.5	15.7	6.8	6.7	6.6	7.1	6.9	27.0	26.0	10.9	1.9	75.7	36.9	49.2	50.8

ZIP CODE #	POST OFFICE NAME	2009 Per Capita Income	2009 HH Income Base	2009 HOUSEHOLD INCOME DISTRIBUTION (%) Less than $25,000	$25,000 to $49,999	$50,000 to $99,999	$100,000 to $149,999	$150,000 or More	MEDIAN HOUSEHOLD INCOME 2009	2014	2009 National Centile	2009 State Centile	2009 Home Value Base	2009 HOME VALUE DISTRIBUTION (%) Less than $50,000	$50,000 to $89,999	$90,000 to $174,999	$175,000 to $399,999	$400,000 or More	2009 Median Home Value
97408	EUGENE	32456	4726	14.7	21.4	42.0	12.4	9.6	63421	63202	82	88	3702	10.0	1.5	11.6	48.6	28.2	273370
97410	AZALEA	20620	315	32.1	27.6	34.6	5.1	0.6	40423	43738	34	27	246	3.7	4.1	19.5	49.2	23.6	243590
97411	BANDON	22692	3105	29.6	31.7	31.7	4.7	2.4	39458	41631	31	23	2176	5.6	4.8	23.9	46.6	19.2	225077
97412	BLACHLY	20802	192	20.3	33.3	40.6	1.6	4.2	47158	50646	55	50	147	13.6	4.1	16.3	48.3	17.7	210417
97413	BLUE RIVER	27678	433	23.1	23.3	48.7	1.2	3.7	52547	53718	67	66	332	4.8	3.0	16.0	60.2	16.0	255970
97414	BROADBENT	14911	66	45.5	22.7	30.3	1.5	0.0	30000	33647	8	4	48	14.6	12.5	37.5	27.1	8.3	143750
97415	BROOKINGS	22102	6279	30.7	34.1	28.9	3.1	3.2	38232	40312	27	20	4494	15.0	4.9	16.4	44.2	19.5	222373
97416	CAMAS VALLEY	16083	319	28.8	37.6	30.1	2.8	0.6	38638	39302	29	21	236	2.1	10.6	26.7	46.6	14.0	208108
97417	CANYONVILLE	18193	716	32.0	35.8	28.2	2.8	1.3	36087	37597	21	14	439	10.5	9.1	41.2	31.9	7.3	158507
97419	CHESHIRE	26640	520	14.0	28.5	44.2	9.0	4.2	58034	58293	75	79	420	5.2	3.6	13.8	37.4	40.0	339130
97420	COOS BAY	21477	11454	32.5	27.0	32.8	4.8	2.9	40282	42088	34	26	7473	9.4	8.8	37.1	36.0	8.6	165042
97423	COQUILLE	21956	3154	29.1	29.5	34.8	3.3	3.3	39907	42492	32	25	2275	5.1	6.5	39.8	43.5	5.2	172398
97424	COTTAGE GROVE	20000	6673	25.3	30.3	37.6	4.9	1.8	44652	48772	47	44	4659	5.5	3.7	19.8	59.7	11.3	224622
97426	CRESWELL	22475	3144	20.5	25.1	44.9	6.0	3.6	53390	54447	69	69	2330	10.0	4.8	18.2	49.6	17.4	228291
97427	CULP CREEK	18117	121	23.1	33.1	42.1	0.8	0.8	42658	45580	41	38	98	7.1	2.0	28.6	54.1	8.2	212500
97429	DAYS CREEK	18854	267	30.3	33.3	30.3	3.7	2.2	39021	40875	30	22	181	8.3	6.6	28.7	38.1	18.2	197115
97430	DEADWOOD	17479	199	32.2	30.7	30.2	3.5	3.5	37871	41023	26	19	144	9.7	2.1	29.2	45.1	13.9	198214
97431	DEXTER	20252	740	29.2	20.7	39.7	6.8	3.6	50114	52485	61	57	595	16.5	2.7	13.6	49.6	17.6	245430
97434	DORENA	16757	232	23.3	45.7	28.9	2.2	0.0	39330	41359	31	23	180	18.3	3.9	17.2	48.9	11.7	210606
97435	DRAIN	18442	840	33.0	32.9	28.6	4.5	1.1	36410	38146	22	15	594	7.1	6.7	31.3	42.3	12.6	192262
97436	ELKTON	20349	353	26.1	35.4	33.1	3.7	1.7	40712	42139	35	29	267	5.6	4.1	21.7	49.4	19.1	244079
97437	ELMIRA	21832	864	13.2	38.3	39.6	7.2	1.7	48643	52151	58	54	719	1.5	1.4	11.7	61.8	23.6	300785
97438	FALL CREEK	24302	588	19.2	23.1	41.8	9.4	6.5	56731	58296	74	77	455	3.3	2.2	21.3	51.0	22.2	264583
97439	FLORENCE	23420	7267	29.5	34.9	29.8	3.0	2.9	40721	44235	35	29	5282	5.3	3.5	30.4	49.1	11.7	208375
97441	GARDINER	25000	7	14.3	57.1	28.6	0.0	0.0	37238	37238	24	17	5	0.0	0.0	40.0	40.0	20.0	275000
97442	GLENDALE	17609	891	33.0	34.3	27.3	3.6	1.8	36068	38177	21	13	633	6.5	7.7	43.9	28.8	13.1	153542
97443	GLIDE	23280	823	18.1	26.4	44.6	6.9	4.0	53409	53896	69	69	608	1.8	6.9	21.5	54.6	15.1	236408
97444	GOLD BEACH	22938	2311	28.7	30.7	34.0	4.9	1.7	41610	44847	38	33	1751	11.5	5.2	19.1	48.0	16.1	227500
97446	HARRISBURG	22460	1740	18.4	27.8	42.1	7.6	4.0	52578	52800	67	66	1303	8.1	7.3	18.5	54.0	12.1	209911
97447	IDLEYLD PARK	22698	314	25.2	26.4	40.4	5.7	2.2	48221	49860	57	53	208	14.4	4.3	19.7	44.7	16.8	218519
97448	JUNCTION CITY	23899	4797	18.4	28.4	42.0	8.1	3.1	52534	54320	67	66	3302	5.6	5.8	14.8	51.9	21.9	260132
97449	LAKESIDE	20442	768	35.9	31.8	27.7	3.8	0.8	35462	37283	19	10	604	5.3	5.5	50.5	35.8	3.0	154518
97450	LANGLOIS	23263	236	29.2	34.7	28.0	5.5	2.5	36054	38359	21	13	184	9.2	2.7	20.7	39.7	27.7	260417
97451	LORANE	25005	202	22.3	24.8	39.6	9.9	3.5	55660	57865	72	74	154	0.6	0.0	16.9	46.1	36.4	327586
97452	LOWELL	21294	441	21.3	28.1	43.3	5.0	2.3	50329	52015	62	59	338	3.3	3.6	32.5	49.4	11.2	202419
97453	MAPLETON	17849	486	32.3	35.2	28.4	3.5	0.6	34735	40510	17	8	353	6.8	6.8	31.4	38.2	16.7	198026
97454	MARCOLA	26596	549	14.9	27.5	45.0	8.4	4.2	59336	60059	77	81	458	3.7	2.0	17.9	52.0	24.5	290196
97455	PLEASANT HILL	27899	1151	13.5	24.2	43.1	10.6	8.7	65347	65219	84	92	937	5.1	4.1	5.5	49.6	35.6	341522
97456	MONROE	22726	1070	18.4	28.5	46.4	3.6	3.1	52932	55239	68	68	789	1.8	4.7	22.6	52.7	18.3	240116
97457	MYRTLE CREEK	19535	4099	28.9	31.4	32.3	5.1	2.2	41505	43970	38	32	2993	6.8	5.9	41.1	41.0	5.2	169682
97458	MYRTLE POINT	17185	1975	37.2	29.7	28.4	3.8	0.9	35253	36909	19	10	1433	7.6	11.3	45.5	31.9	3.7	149507
97459	NORTH BEND	23055	5892	27.4	27.1	36.6	6.2	2.6	44349	46243	46	43	3942	6.2	3.5	35.6	46.0	8.7	187568
97461	NOTI	22437	334	18.9	27.2	44.0	8.4	1.5	52715	54502	67	67	249	1.6	1.2	8.0	60.6	28.5	316406
97462	OAKLAND	20161	1609	25.1	34.7	33.3	5.0	1.9	41279	42840	37	31	1281	3.7	7.7	25.1	48.3	15.2	220775
97463	OAKRIDGE	17766	1712	34.5	37.0	23.5	3.6	1.3	36032	39316	21	13	1241	10.6	9.9	48.6	28.1	2.8	144943
97465	PORT ORFORD	20171	1065	40.1	29.4	25.4	3.2	1.9	31267	33390	10	5	786	5.1	9.0	37.4	33.2	15.3	171203
97466	POWERS	17424	456	40.6	31.6	24.1	2.9	0.9	30490	32819	9	4	321	18.1	17.8	43.3	15.6	5.3	110991
97467	REEDSPORT	20046	2775	34.9	34.2	24.5	4.3	2.1	33315	35355	14	7	1884	10.4	10.2	37.9	34.2	7.3	156395
97469	RIDDLE	19854	1123	28.9	33.4	31.4	3.6	2.8	39137	41105	30	22	786	6.0	6.0	48.6	33.5	6.0	160072
97470	ROSEBURG	20875	7647	30.7	30.5	31.7	4.9	2.1	40580	42017	35	28	4799	10.9	8.5	34.9	36.9	8.8	166307
97471	ROSEBURG	23900	11265	20.7	29.9	38.1	7.7	3.6	49289	50307	59	56	8589	3.5	2.9	28.9	50.8	14.1	215816
97473	SCOTTSBURG	24007	102	25.5	43.1	21.6	8.8	1.0	35547	37871	19	11	74	6.8	1.4	32.4	40.5	18.9	233333
97476	SIXES	21150	154	29.9	34.4	27.9	5.8	1.9	35808	38358	20	12	120	9.2	2.5	21.7	40.0	26.7	256250
97477	SPRINGFIELD	20362	15132	29.7	29.9	34.5	4.0	1.9	41789	45638	39	34	7808	4.4	2.7	29.2	58.7	5.1	205016
97478	SPRINGFIELD	23356	13180	19.2	25.2	44.8	7.8	3.0	54849	56411	71	72	9293	7.2	2.9	20.1	57.4	12.4	218668
97479	SUTHERLIN	18705	3936	30.1	34.2	30.8	3.4	1.6	38098	39964	27	19	2872	12.0	9.9	38.0	35.7	4.4	156807
97480	SWISSHOME	16084	149	46.3	27.5	18.8	4.7	2.7	28809	31014	6	3	100	4.0	2.0	46.0	38.0	10.0	171875
97481	TENMILE	17099	346	23.7	33.5	38.2	4.6	0.0	41898	43827	39	34	271	4.8	11.4	38.0	36.9	8.9	167628
97484	TILLER	22284	118	32.2	28.8	32.2	5.1	1.7	40000	41728	33	25	73	5.5	2.7	26.0	50.7	15.1	208333
97486	UMPQUA	23164	345	17.4	30.1	45.5	6.1	0.9	51408	51219	65	63	292	3.4	7.5	19.5	48.6	20.9	279762
97487	VENETA	22549	3025	16.0	27.9	46.1	6.9	3.0	55070	55593	71	73	2367	5.0	4.7	15.8	53.9	20.6	238327
97488	VIDA	26643	442	20.1	26.9	42.3	7.0	3.6	52379	55080	67	66	333	9.0	0.9	14.1	43.8	32.1	311194
97489	WALTERVILLE	29961	403	12.4	26.3	44.9	11.4	5.0	62923	65466	81	87	324	4.0	1.2	5.9	41.4	47.5	390000
97490	WALTON	21350	107	20.6	27.1	43.0	7.5	1.9	51757	52594	65	65	78	5.1	0.0	11.5	64.1	19.2	281818
97492	WESTFIR	20096	272	22.4	38.2	33.1	2.2	4.0	44185	47325	46	42	222	10.4	6.3	37.8	38.7	6.8	167647
97493	WESTLAKE	26805	139	23.7	32.4	30.9	7.2	5.8	46022	49492	51	47	115	5.2	0.0	10.4	56.5	27.8	295000
97495	WINCHESTER	23173	707	20.2	29.7	43.3	5.0	1.8	50037	50059	61	56	589	22.9	17.8	17.5	28.4	13.4	153348
97496	WINSTON	17857	2779	31.2	30.7	34.3	3.0	0.9	40139	41983	33	26	1876	4.3	5.1	54.1	31.9	4.7	159131
97497	WOLF CREEK	19695	779	37.6	27.7	28.8	2.7	3.2	36715	38701	23	15	589	6.5	11.7	30.4	34.0	17.5	181855
97498	YACHATS	24933	717	28.0	36.7	27.3	5.0	2.9	40633	40878	35	29	544	1.3	1.7	15.1	50.6	31.4	292405
97499	YONCALLA	17735	863	33.0	35.0	27.8	2.9	1.3	36156	37611	21	14	661	6.4	11.8	33.3	38.6	10.0	171558
97501	MEDFORD	18858	16359	29.7	31.9	33.1	3.8	1.6	39379	43424	31	23	10024	9.4	7.2	30.4	47.2	5.8	182470
97502	CENTRAL POINT	23580	10359	16.4	29.2	42.5	7.9	4.0	53326	55213	69	68	7840	4.5	3.5	21.5	59.3	11.1	220620
97503	WHITE CITY	16776	3199	24.9	31.9	36.8	4.0	2.3	43855	47868	45	42	2578	20.4	7.6	33.0	30.6	8.5	154611
97504	MEDFORD	30721	18214	17.8	25.0	39.8	9.5	7.9	56705	57393	74	76	11074	1.2	0.3	10.1	69.9	18.5	265755
97520	ASHLAND	28221	11477	28.3	25.1	31.1	9.1	6.3	45763	50586	51	46	6515	3.6	1.6	5.4	52.5	37.0	343177
97522	BUTTE FALLS	18194	245	26.5	37.1	29.8	4.5	2.0	39868	41686	32	24	176	4.5	7.4	23.3	40.3	24.4	240909
97523	CAVE JUNCTION	16276	3073	47.3	25.5	22.1	4.1	0.9	26763	28109	4	3	2138	7.1	7.2	40.9	37.2	7.6	164798
97524	EAGLE POINT	21407	5399	20.3	32.0	38.5	5.4	3.8	48343	51190	57	53	4038	9.5	3.0	21.4	47.3	18.9	222536
97525	GOLD HILL	21765	2213	28.5	29.9	32.9	4.8	3.8	41526	46213	38	33	1640	9.8	2.3	23.5	53.4	11.1	214706
97526	GRANTS PASS	22047	14016	26.9	33.6	30.9	5.2	3.4	40913	42990	36	30	9193	6.0	3.6	27.9	50.5	12.0	208372
97527	GRANTS PASS	20867	12927	30.0	29.8	32.2	5.4	2.6	40456	42769	34	27	9330	6.3	4.2	20.2	58.0	11.3	221740
97530	JACKSONVILLE	29757	3198	20.5	25.8	38.4	8.8	6.5	52818	54162	68	67	2562	7.3	2.3	11.4	46.2	32.9	317013
97531	KERBY	14426	129	51.9	26.4	17.8	2.3	1.6	24003	25481	3	1	86	12.8	12.8	34.9	32.6	7.0	152500
97532	MERLIN	22128	1031	25.8	28.0	36.4	6.8	3.0	46685	47797	53	49	872	2.9	1.7	14.3	61.4	19.7	249448
97534	O BRIEN	15449	150	48.7	26.7	20.0	2.7	2.0	25877	27313	4	2	103	5.8	17.5	31.1	37.9	7.8	169643
97535	PHOENIX	20731	2075	27.9	35.9	31.2	3.8	1.2	38310	40823	28	20	1422	27.4	13.5	19.6	33.3	6.1	121324
97536	PROSPECT	20981	412	25.2	36.4	30.1	5.8	2.4	39523	42364	31	24	303	9.6	3.6	28.4	42.2	16.2	214362
97537	ROGUE RIVER	23805	2952	27.3	27.8	34.0	7.1	3.7	43398	48500	44	41	2180	3.3	4.1	21.6	53.4	17.5	239588
97538	SELMA	17852	1173	33.9	33.2	25.8	5.2	1.8	36340	37389	22	14	898	2.9	3.5	31.6	46.7	15.4	218067
97539	SHADY COVE	22428	1453	27.1	31.3	34.2	5.0	2.3	43325	47003	43	40	1059	6.6	11.2	16.0	49.4	16.8	218836
97540	TALENT	22849	3443	25.7	33.8	33.0	4.4	3.1	42246	45918	40	36	2164	11.5	6.4	25.9	41.0	15.2	196069
97541	TRAIL	23480	583	22.6	34.3	32.4	6.3	4.3	43039	46718	43	38	448	11.6	1.3	10.0	51.1	25.9	279808
97543	WILDERVILLE	22426	701	29.0	28.5	32.1	6.7	3.7	40354	41558	34	26	559	1.6	4.3	24.0	51.0	19.1	239939
97544	WILLIAMS	21250	1101	30.4	31.6	28.3	6.4	3.2	41276	44780	37	31	835	3.0	2.5	20.8	53.1	20.6	245109
	OREGON	26362		20.3	25.9	37.7	10.2	5.9	53483	55628				4.6	3.5	17.3	54.4	20.2	249991
	UNITED STATES	27277		20.9	24.4	35.3	11.7	7.6	54719	56938				9.3	13.1	31.6	32.6	13.5	162279

ZIP CODE #	POST OFFICE NAME	FINANCIAL SERVICES: Auto Loan	Home Loan	Invest-ments	Retire-ment Plans	THE HOME: Home Improvements: Home Repair	Lawn & Garden	Furnishings: Comput-ers & Hard-ware-Personal	Major Appli-ances	TV, Radio, Sound Equip-ment	Furni-ture	ENTERTAINMENT: Dine out/ Carry out	Sports Equip-ment	Fees & Tickets	Toys & Games	Travel	Cable TV	PERSONAL: Apparel & Services	Auto Repairs	Health Insur-ance	Pets & Supplies
97408	EUGENE	107	121	119	122	122	121	111	115	112	114	112	85	121	110	119	113	79	113	120	133
97410	AZALEA	78	61	97	60	66	82	61	78	65	57	64	57	52	62	65	69	42	72	78	91
97411	BANDON	80	67	97	66	73	85	68	82	71	65	70	59	61	67	72	75	47	77	84	95
97412	BLACHLY	98	67	107	67	70	103	75	93	78	61	77	77	55	76	74	85	50	87	98	114
97413	BLUE RIVER	97	78	125	77	85	103	78	99	81	73	80	72	67	77	84	87	53	91	97	114
97414	BROADBENT	58	50	67	47	55	64	49	59	53	51	52	41	46	50	52	57	34	56	65	69
97415	BROOKINGS	73	66	87	63	71	80	65	76	68	66	67	53	62	64	69	72	45	73	82	88
97416	CAMAS VALLEY	73	57	72	57	59	76	58	70	62	53	61	53	49	62	57	68	41	65	73	83
97417	CANYONVILLE	74	54	75	52	56	77	58	72	64	53	62	53	47	63	56	71	41	67	77	84
97419	CHESHIRE	103	95	121	96	99	111	91	106	92	87	92	80	86	91	97	96	62	99	105	124
97420	COOS BAY	74	66	78	66	69	78	69	75	72	68	71	55	65	70	70	76	49	74	81	88
97423	COQUILLE	81	69	86	68	72	86	71	81	74	66	73	60	64	73	72	79	49	78	86	95
97424	COTTAGE GROVE	77	72	75	73	73	82	72	78	74	68	73	59	69	74	72	77	50	75	82	92
97426	CRESWELL	94	90	94	88	89	95	85	92	86	85	86	71	83	88	86	89	60	88	91	108
97427	CULP CREEK	70	64	63	67	65	75	63	71	65	57	64	54	58	66	63	69	44	66	73	83
97429	DAYS CREEK	82	62	96	61	67	85	63	80	68	59	67	59	53	66	66	73	44	74	81	94
97430	DEADWOOD	83	58	89	58	61	87	64	79	69	54	67	63	49	67	63	75	44	74	85	96
97431	DEXTER	87	88	79	87	86	88	80	85	81	83	82	63	81	84	81	83	56	82	84	100
97434	DORENA	75	57	75	56	59	77	58	72	63	54	62	54	48	63	57	69	41	66	74	85
97435	DRAIN	79	58	85	56	61	81	59	75	65	55	64	56	48	64	59	71	42	69	77	89
97436	ELKTON	80	64	104	63	71	85	64	82	67	60	66	60	56	64	70	72	44	75	81	95
97437	ELMIRA	90	81	107	82	85	97	78	93	80	75	80	69	73	78	84	84	54	87	92	108
97438	FALL CREEK	94	103	89	105	100	102	93	97	92	93	92	75	97	94	97	92	64	93	96	114
97439	FLORENCE	70	67	87	63	75	82	65	76	68	69	67	50	65	63	71	72	45	73	85	87
97441	GARDINER	71	57	92	56	63	76	57	73	60	54	59	53	50	57	62	64	39	67	72	84
97442	GLENDALE	76	57	70	56	57	75	61	71	67	57	65	54	50	67	58	72	44	68	75	85
97443	GLIDE	104	83	133	82	91	110	83	106	87	78	86	77	72	83	90	93	57	97	104	122
97444	GOLD BEACH	75	69	98	67	78	85	66	80	69	69	68	53	65	64	73	73	46	75	85	91
97446	HARRISBURG	99	93	83	91	91	97	88	94	90	89	90	69	84	93	85	93	61	90	94	111
97447	IDLEYLD PARK	94	72	105	71	77	96	74	90	79	70	77	67	62	77	75	85	52	84	91	107
97448	JUNCTION CITY	92	90	94	89	90	95	86	92	87	85	87	70	85	88	88	89	60	90	92	108
97449	LAKESIDE	63	59	77	55	65	71	56	67	59	60	58	45	55	55	61	63	39	64	73	77
97450	LANGLOIS	84	67	109	66	74	89	67	86	71	63	70	63	58	67	73	75	46	79	85	99
97451	LORANE	93	104	90	108	101	103	93	97	92	94	92	76	100	94	99	92	65	93	96	114
97452	LOWELL	85	83	73	82	81	84	77	81	78	79	79	60	76	81	76	80	54	78	81	96
97453	MAPLETON	63	57	76	53	63	71	55	66	59	58	57	45	53	54	60	62	38	63	72	76
97454	MARCOLA	105	99	122	99	102	114	93	109	95	91	95	82	90	94	100	98	64	102	107	127
97455	PLEASANT HILL	105	119	128	120	123	124	105	115	105	109	105	83	114	103	116	107	74	109	117	132
97456	MONROE	95	88	81	88	87	95	84	91	87	83	86	68	79	89	82	90	59	87	92	107
97457	MYRTLE CREEK	82	65	83	63	66	85	67	79	73	62	71	59	57	72	66	79	48	75	85	94
97458	MYRTLE POINT	71	54	77	52	57	74	55	69	61	52	59	51	46	59	56	66	39	64	73	81
97459	NORTH BEND	83	74	85	74	76	87	76	83	78	72	77	61	70	77	76	82	53	81	87	97
97461	NOTI	88	86	81	89	86	96	82	90	83	77	83	69	80	85	84	87	57	85	92	105
97462	OAKLAND	87	66	101	65	71	90	67	85	72	63	71	63	56	70	70	78	47	78	86	99
97463	OAKRIDGE	67	57	69	56	58	73	55	66	60	52	59	49	50	60	57	65	40	62	71	78
97465	PORT ORFORD	60	57	73	53	64	69	55	65	58	59	56	42	54	53	60	61	38	62	72	74
97466	POWERS	70	50	72	49	52	71	51	65	57	48	56	49	41	57	51	63	37	60	68	78
97467	REEDSPORT	66	59	77	56	65	73	59	69	62	60	60	47	56	58	62	66	41	66	75	79
97469	RIDDLE	84	67	81	65	69	85	71	80	76	68	74	59	61	75	68	82	50	78	87	95
97470	ROSEBURG	72	65	69	65	66	74	69	71	71	66	70	53	64	70	67	74	48	71	77	84
97471	ROSEBURG	89	86	94	86	89	95	83	91	85	83	84	66	82	84	85	88	58	87	94	105
97473	SCOTTSBURG	84	67	109	66	74	89	67	86	70	63	70	62	58	67	73	75	46	79	84	99
97476	SIXES	83	67	108	66	74	89	67	85	70	63	69	62	58	67	73	75	46	79	84	99
97477	SPRINGFIELD	71	64	61	66	63	66	72	67	72	69	72	53	68	73	67	73	50	71	71	81
97478	SPRINGFIELD	91	91	84	92	88	91	89	90	88	88	89	70	88	90	88	89	62	89	90	106
97479	SUTHERLIN	75	60	76	57	62	77	61	73	66	59	65	53	53	65	61	71	43	69	77	85
97480	SWISSHOME	67	48	68	47	50	70	52	65	58	46	56	49	41	57	51	64	37	60	70	76
97481	TENMILE	73	67	66	70	68	79	66	74	68	60	67	56	61	69	66	72	46	69	77	86
97484	TILLER	86	69	111	67	75	91	69	87	72	64	71	64	59	68	74	76	47	80	86	101
97486	UMPQUA	94	75	121	74	82	99	75	95	79	70	78	70	65	75	81	84	52	88	94	111
97487	VENETA	95	95	84	95	93	95	87	92	89	90	89	69	87	92	87	90	61	89	92	109
97488	VIDA	107	86	138	84	94	113	86	109	90	80	89	79	74	85	93	96	59	100	107	126
97489	WALTERVILLE	113	101	145	100	108	122	96	117	99	93	98	86	90	95	105	103	66	109	115	136
97490	WALTON	86	88	81	91	87	94	82	89	82	78	82	68	82	84	84	85	57	84	90	104
97492	WESTFIR	79	73	72	76	74	85	71	80	74	65	72	61	67	75	72	78	49	74	83	93
97493	WESTLAKE	97	86	129	84	96	108	82	102	86	83	85	70	78	80	91	91	57	95	105	117
97495	WINCHESTER	99	71	101	68	73	100	72	92	80	67	79	69	58	80	72	89	52	85	96	110
97496	WINSTON	73	58	67	58	58	71	64	68	67	59	66	53	55	67	60	71	45	68	72	82
97497	WOLF CREEK	81	62	91	60	66	84	62	78	67	59	66	57	53	66	64	73	44	72	81	92
97498	YACHATS	86	69	111	67	75	91	69	87	72	64	71	64	59	68	74	77	47	80	86	101
97499	YONCALLA	78	58	78	57	61	78	60	72	65	57	64	54	49	65	59	70	43	68	74	86
97501	MEDFORD	70	65	68	64	65	70	67	69	69	66	69	52	64	69	66	72	48	69	72	82
97502	CENTRAL POINT	94	93	98	93	93	99	89	95	90	88	91	72	89	91	92	93	63	93	96	112
97503	WHITE CITY	80	73	75	69	72	76	71	76	72	73	72	57	66	73	70	74	50	75	75	90
97504	MEDFORD	98	104	109	106	107	106	103	103	103	104	104	77	108	100	108	105	73	104	109	120
97520	ASHLAND	88	84	87	87	85	85	93	86	90	89	90	69	89	89	88	89	63	89	87	103
97522	BUTTE FALLS	86	62	89	60	64	87	63	80	70	59	69	60	51	69	63	77	45	74	83	96
97523	CAVE JUNCTION	59	50	69	48	55	63	51	60	55	51	53	42	47	51	54	58	36	58	65	70
97524	EAGLE POINT	92	85	83	84	84	91	81	88	83	81	83	65	76	85	79	86	56	84	89	104
97525	GOLD HILL	84	71	104	68	77	90	71	86	74	69	73	61	64	70	76	79	49	81	89	100
97526	GRANTS PASS	80	71	86	70	74	84	73	80	76	71	75	58	68	73	74	79	51	78	85	94
97527	GRANTS PASS	81	68	92	66	72	83	69	81	72	67	71	59	61	69	71	76	48	77	82	94
97530	JACKSONVILLE	111	96	143	95	104	119	93	114	96	89	95	84	85	92	101	101	64	106	112	132
97531	KERBY	55	44	58	43	47	57	47	54	51	46	50	39	42	49	47	55	34	53	59	64
97532	MERLIN	92	74	119	73	81	98	74	94	77	69	76	69	64	74	80	83	51	87	93	109
97534	O BRIEN	64	46	66	45	48	65	47	60	53	44	52	45	38	52	47	58	34	55	63	72
97535	PHOENIX	69	67	81	64	72	77	63	73	66	67	65	50	63	62	68	69	44	70	79	84
97536	PROSPECT	84	66	105	65	72	89	67	85	70	62	69	62	57	67	71	75	46	78	84	98
97537	ROGUE RIVER	89	73	110	71	79	94	75	91	79	71	78	66	66	75	79	84	52	86	93	105
97538	SELMA	74	61	95	59	67	79	60	76	63	58	62	54	53	60	65	67	41	70	76	88
97539	SHADY COVE	78	72	96	67	80	88	69	83	73	73	72	55	67	67	76	78	48	79	90	95
97540	TALENT	78	77	80	77	79	82	77	80	78	76	77	60	77	77	79	80	54	79	83	93
97541	TRAIL	91	78	115	75	87	99	77	94	81	77	79	66	71	75	83	86	53	89	98	109
97543	WILDERVILLE	92	74	119	72	81	97	74	94	77	69	76	68	64	73	80	82	51	86	92	108
97544	WILLIAMS	85	68	110	67	75	90	68	87	71	64	71	63	59	68	74	76	47	80	86	100
	OREGON	96	93	95	94	93	95	95	95	95	94	95	74	93	95	95	95	66	96	96	112
	UNITED STATES	100	100	100	100	100	100	100	100	100	100	100	100	100	100	100	100	100	100	100	100

ZIP CODE #	POST OFFICE NAME	COUNTY FIPS CODE	POPULATION 2000	POPULATION 2009	POPULATION 2014	2000-2009 ANNUAL RATE % Rate	2000-2009 ANNUAL RATE State Centile	HOUSEHOLDS 2000	HOUSEHOLDS 2009	HOUSEHOLDS 2014	HOUSEHOLDS % Annual Rate 2000-2009	HOUSEHOLDS 2009 Average HH Size	FAMILIES 2000	FAMILIES 2009	FAMILIES % Annual Rate 2000-2009
97601	KLAMATH FALLS	035	21635	22391	22632	0.4	39	8686	8855	8946	0.2	2.44	5415	5459	0.1
97603	KLAMATH FALLS	035	29323	31177	31871	0.7	53	11505	12167	12448	0.6	2.52	8171	8521	0.5
97620	ADEL	037	111	110	110	-0.1	14	51	52	52	0.2	2.12	38	38	0.0
97621	BEATTY	035	99	104	107	0.5	43	47	50	51	0.7	2.08	31	32	0.3
97623	BONANZA	035	2823	3133	3275	1.1	71	1070	1190	1246	1.2	2.63	828	913	1.1
97624	CHILOQUIN	035	3708	3907	3993	0.6	48	1478	1555	1589	0.6	2.48	1054	1092	0.4
97625	DAIRY	035	194	263	282	3.3	98	62	85	92	3.5	3.09	51	69	3.3
97627	KENO	035	585	663	696	1.4	78	248	282	297	1.4	2.35	179	201	1.3
97630	LAKEVIEW	037	4880	4810	4778	-0.2	10	2018	2024	2026	0.0	2.35	1406	1395	-0.1
97632	MALIN	035	1250	1236	1228	-0.1	14	424	416	413	-0.2	2.89	333	324	-0.3
97633	MERRILL	035	1044	1056	1056	0.1	23	395	400	400	0.1	2.63	296	295	0.0
97635	NEW PINE CREEK	037	180	180	180	0.0	19	77	79	79	0.3	2.28	54	54	0.0
97636	PAISLEY	037	512	509	505	-0.1	14	216	219	219	0.1	2.32	161	161	0.0
97637	PLUSH	037	155	154	153	-0.1	14	64	65	65	0.2	2.37	48	48	0.0
97638	SILVER LAKE	037	1557	1645	1677	0.6	48	646	696	716	0.8	2.36	439	467	0.7
97639	SPRAGUE RIVER	035	309	325	333	0.5	43	124	131	134	0.6	2.48	82	85	0.4
97640	SUMMER LAKE	037	1	1	1	0.0	19	1	1	1	0.0	1.00	1	0	-100.0
97701	BEND	017	45126	63847	75894	3.8	99	18087	26169	31280	4.1	2.41	11916	17072	4.0
97702	BEND	017	28954	42579	50976	4.3	99	11167	16804	20211	4.5	2.52	7986	11835	4.3
97707	BEND	017	5207	7035	8217	3.3	98	2244	3135	3691	3.7	2.24	1682	2324	3.6
97710	FIELDS	025	73	68	66	-0.8	2	30	28	28	-0.7	2.43	22	21	-0.5
97711	ASHWOOD	031	140	173	190	2.3	95	52	64	71	2.3	2.70	40	49	2.2
97712	BROTHERS	017	46	72	80	5.0	100	15	27	30	6.6	2.67	12	22	6.8
97720	BURNS	025	4828	4763	4726	-0.1	14	1946	1927	1916	-0.1	2.40	1284	1257	-0.2
97721	PRINCETON	025	326	304	296	-0.8	2	128	120	117	-0.7	2.53	94	88	-0.7
97730	CAMP SHERMAN	031	359	424	463	1.8	87	143	170	186	1.9	2.49	118	139	1.8
97731	CHEMULT	035	347	350	348	0.1	23	149	151	151	0.1	2.23	104	103	-0.1
97733	CRESCENT	035	1254	1291	1303	0.3	32	512	528	534	0.3	2.45	371	377	0.2
97734	CULVER	031	2189	2625	2862	2.0	91	791	954	1044	2.0	2.74	620	742	2.0
97735	FORT ROCK	037	26	27	28	0.4	39	11	12	12	0.9	2.25	7	8	1.5
97737	GILCHRIST	035	319	334	341	0.5	43	150	158	161	0.6	2.11	112	116	0.4
97738	HINES	025	2111	1934	1878	-0.9	1	819	756	736	-0.9	2.53	610	559	-0.9
97739	LA PINE	017	8442	10208	11475	2.1	93	3431	4236	4781	2.3	2.40	2527	3069	2.1
97741	MADRAS	031	10450	12387	13407	1.9	89	3754	4452	4833	1.9	2.76	2789	3276	1.8
97750	MITCHELL	069	497	487	478	-0.2	10	208	204	201	-0.2	2.37	145	140	-0.4
97751	PAULINA	013	105	134	153	2.7	97	47	60	68	2.7	2.23	33	41	2.4
97752	POST	013	208	266	303	2.7	97	84	107	122	2.7	2.49	58	73	2.5
97753	POWELL BUTTE	013	1839	2541	2938	3.6	98	723	999	1153	3.6	2.54	585	797	3.4
97754	PRINEVILLE	013	16821	21556	24406	2.7	97	6422	8189	9273	2.7	2.60	4687	5919	2.6
97756	REDMOND	017	21539	34753	42387	5.3	100	8310	13690	16770	5.5	2.53	6010	9843	5.5
97758	RILEY	025	107	98	95	-0.9	1	42	39	38	-0.8	2.46	33	30	-1.0
97759	SISTERS	017	4576	6278	7419	3.5	98	1835	2581	3068	3.8	2.43	1412	1957	3.6
97760	TERREBONNE	017	5924	6560	7011	1.1	71	2340	2622	2810	1.2	2.50	1826	2020	1.1
97761	WARM SPRINGS	031	2632	3229	3542	2.2	94	638	792	875	2.4	4.00	541	668	2.3
97801	PENDLETON	059	21944	22256	22121	0.2	26	7999	7899	7846	-0.1	2.47	5312	5178	-0.3
97810	ADAMS	059	569	571	569	0.0	19	207	209	209	0.1	2.72	160	160	0.0
97812	ARLINGTON	021	815	794	775	-0.3	8	340	337	332	-0.1	2.35	230	224	-0.3
97813	ATHENA	059	1524	1543	1544	0.1	23	548	558	560	0.2	2.75	424	428	0.1
97814	BAKER CITY	001	12524	12305	12043	-0.2	10	5076	4970	4874	-0.2	2.37	3444	3332	-0.4
97818	BOARDMAN	049	3780	4419	4740	1.7	85	1172	1325	1413	1.3	3.33	940	1053	1.2
97820	CANYON CITY	023	803	781	764	-0.3	8	313	307	301	-0.2	2.47	228	221	-0.3
97823	CONDON	021	1094	1071	1053	-0.2	10	477	474	469	-0.1	2.21	313	306	-0.2
97824	COVE	061	1409	1559	1617	1.1	71	539	602	629	1.2	2.59	440	488	1.1
97825	DAYVILLE	023	138	129	124	-0.7	3	59	56	54	-0.6	2.29	41	39	-0.5
97826	ECHO	059	1036	1063	1062	0.3	32	382	388	388	0.2	2.59	271	271	0.0
97827	ELGIN	061	2455	2460	2469	0.0	19	979	992	1001	0.1	2.47	708	709	0.0
97828	ENTERPRISE	063	3198	3133	3068	-0.2	10	1351	1335	1312	-0.1	2.30	906	884	-0.3
97830	FOSSIL	069	1024	1016	1004	-0.1	14	437	434	430	-0.1	2.28	295	289	-0.2
97833	HAINES	001	987	955	932	-0.4	6	390	380	373	-0.3	2.51	291	280	-0.4
97834	HALFWAY	001	1102	1088	1067	-0.1	14	473	470	463	-0.1	2.31	308	303	-0.2
97835	HELIX	059	416	411	409	-0.1	14	149	149	148	0.0	2.76	115	113	-0.2
97836	HEPPNER	049	2106	2250	2341	0.7	53	859	890	921	0.4	2.50	613	627	0.2
97837	HEREFORD	001	187	182	177	-0.3	8	74	73	71	-0.1	2.49	51	50	-0.2
97838	HERMISTON	059	21419	23699	24520	1.1	71	7742	8517	8795	1.0	2.76	5560	6038	0.9
97839	LEXINGTON	049	632	685	715	0.9	62	250	263	273	0.5	2.60	187	194	0.4
97840	OXBOW	001	148	152	152	0.3	32	67	70	70	0.5	2.17	48	49	0.2
97841	IMBLER	061	415	444	456	0.7	53	152	165	170	0.9	2.69	121	129	0.7
97842	IMNAHA	063	186	186	183	0.0	19	81	82	81	0.1	2.27	58	58	0.0
97843	IONE	049	503	543	565	0.8	59	190	199	206	0.5	2.73	138	143	0.4
97844	IRRIGON	049	3826	4412	4723	1.6	83	1262	1413	1504	1.2	3.12	1010	1119	1.1
97845	JOHN DAY	023	3565	3439	3347	-0.4	6	1441	1402	1370	-0.3	2.39	987	949	-0.4
97846	JOSEPH	063	1913	1842	1790	-0.4	6	815	793	774	-0.3	2.27	551	531	-0.4
97848	KIMBERLY	023	37	35	33	-0.6	3	11	10	10	-1.0	3.40	8	7	-1.4
97850	LA GRANDE	061	16240	16437	16585	0.1	23	6537	6686	6774	0.2	2.36	4087	4111	0.1
97856	LONG CREEK	023	498	455	433	-1.0	1	217	201	192	-0.8	2.26	145	133	-0.9
97857	LOSTINE	063	427	414	404	-0.3	8	171	167	163	-0.3	2.48	121	116	-0.5
97862	MILTON FREEWATER	059	11200	11309	11270	0.1	23	4058	4030	4006	-0.1	2.71	2891	2838	-0.2
97864	MONUMENT	023	354	323	308	-1.0	1	166	153	147	-0.9	2.11	111	102	-0.9
97865	MOUNT VERNON	023	595	568	550	-0.5	4	248	239	233	-0.4	2.36	163	155	-0.5
97867	NORTH POWDER	061	781	807	819	0.4	39	284	292	296	0.3	2.76	208	211	0.2
97868	PILOT ROCK	059	2473	2445	2422	-0.1	14	936	933	926	0.0	2.60	704	695	-0.1
97869	PRAIRIE CITY	023	1555	1438	1380	-0.8	2	626	584	562	-0.7	2.37	435	401	-0.9
97870	RICHLAND	001	614	593	579	-0.4	6	294	287	281	-0.3	2.07	195	187	-0.5
97873	SENECA	023	361	338	324	-0.7	3	149	141	136	-0.6	2.37	104	98	-0.6
97874	SPRAY	069	26	25	25	-0.4	6	8	8	8	0.0	3.13	6	5	-2.0
97875	STANFIELD	059	2633	2705	2735	0.3	32	910	939	950	0.3	2.87	692	707	0.2
97876	SUMMERVILLE	061	913	933	945	0.2	26	343	355	360	0.4	2.63	279	286	0.3
97877	SUMPTER	001	111	107	104	-0.4	6	57	55	54	-0.4	1.95	39	38	-0.3
97882	UMATILLA	059	6166	7071	7311	1.5	80	1816	2039	2118	1.3	3.03	1381	1532	1.1
97883	UNION	061	2387	2521	2580	0.6	48	927	983	1008	0.6	2.56	685	719	0.5
97884	UNITY	001	237	231	225	-0.3	8	100	98	96	-0.2	2.36	70	69	-0.2
97885	WALLOWA	063	1502	1444	1402	-0.4	6	611	590	574	-0.4	2.45	448	428	-0.5
97886	WESTON	059	1322	1371	1380	0.4	39	493	512	517	0.4	2.67	371	382	0.3
97901	ADRIAN	045	588	592	592	0.1	23	205	204	203	-0.1	2.90	161	159	-0.1
97903	BROGAN	045	186	200	202	0.8	59	67	76	79	1.4	2.55	51	57	1.2
	OREGON					1.3					1.2	2.51			1.1
	UNITED STATES					1.0					1.1	2.59			0.9

ZIP CODE		RACE (%)								2009 AGE DISTRIBUTION (%)										MEDIAN AGE		
#	POST OFFICE NAME	White		Black		Asian/Pacific		% Hispanic Origin														
		2000	2009	2000	2009	2000	2009	2000	2009	0-4	5-9	10-14	15-19	20-24	25-44	45-64	65-84	85+	18+	2009	% 2009 Males	% 2009 Females
97601	KLAMATH FALLS	86.7	84.6	0.8	0.8	1.4	1.8	8.1	11.4	6.8	6.4	6.3	7.7	8.2	25.7	26.3	10.5	2.2	76.5	35.4	50.7	49.3
97603	KLAMATH FALLS	88.9	86.7	0.6	0.7	0.8	1.0	7.1	10.4	6.5	6.5	6.7	6.9	6.0	23.7	28.0	13.4	2.2	75.8	39.9	49.3	50.7
97620	ADEL	97.3	97.3	0.0	0.0	0.0	0.0	1.8	1.8	4.5	5.5	5.5	6.4	4.5	20.9	35.5	15.5	1.8	79.1	47.1	54.5	45.5
97621	BEATTY	85.9	85.6	1.0	1.0	0.0	0.0	3.0	4.8	3.8	4.8	5.8	4.8	5.8	17.3	38.5	17.3	1.9	81.7	50.0	51.0	49.0
97623	BONANZA	90.0	87.5	0.5	0.6	0.6	0.7	7.0	10.6	6.1	6.7	6.4	6.6	5.1	19.7	32.2	15.8	1.3	76.7	44.4	51.3	48.7
97624	CHILOQUIN	76.6	75.3	0.1	0.2	0.5	0.6	4.0	5.9	5.4	5.7	6.9	5.9	4.1	18.1	35.3	16.9	1.7	77.9	47.4	51.3	48.7
97625	DAIRY	89.7	86.7	0.5	0.8	0.5	0.8	9.3	13.7	6.8	6.8	6.8	7.2	6.5	21.3	30.0	12.9	1.5	74.9	40.5	50.6	49.4
97627	KENO	90.4	89.3	0.3	0.3	1.2	1.4	3.8	5.6	3.6	5.1	7.2	4.2	3.5	20.2	38.5	16.6	1.1	81.4	48.3	50.1	49.9
97630	LAKEVIEW	90.2	90.1	0.0	0.0	1.1	1.1	6.7	6.8	4.7	4.9	5.6	7.0	5.5	20.2	32.3	16.7	3.1	80.0	46.3	49.3	50.7
97632	MALIN	75.8	71.0	0.7	0.8	0.5	0.5	33.8	42.6	6.4	7.4	8.0	6.6	6.1	23.3	27.5	12.9	1.7	75.6	36.7	53.0	47.0
97633	MERRILL	81.8	76.0	0.3	0.4	0.5	0.6	21.6	30.1	6.6	6.8	7.1	6.8	4.8	23.1	30.0	13.0	1.7	74.8	40.8	50.1	49.9
97635	NEW PINE CREEK	91.1	90.6	0.0	0.0	0.6	0.6	7.3	7.2	5.0	6.1	6.7	6.7	4.4	19.4	33.3	17.2	1.1	77.8	46.5	48.3	51.7
97636	PAISLEY	96.9	96.9	0.4	0.4	0.4	0.4	1.8	1.8	4.7	5.3	5.9	5.7	4.3	21.6	32.8	17.5	2.2	79.6	46.8	53.0	47.0
97637	PLUSH	96.2	96.1	0.6	0.6	0.6	0.6	1.9	1.9	5.2	5.2	5.8	5.8	4.5	21.4	33.1	16.9	1.9	78.6	46.5	53.2	46.8
97638	SILVER LAKE	90.4	90.3	0.3	0.3	0.3	0.2	3.3	3.5	5.5	6.0	6.4	6.4	4.4	20.9	32.2	16.8	1.3	77.4	45.2	50.8	49.2
97639	SPRAGUE RIVER	86.1	84.6	0.6	0.9	0.6	0.6	2.9	4.0	4.3	4.6	5.2	5.2	5.5	17.5	36.6	19.1	1.8	82.2	50.1	52.0	48.0
97640	SUMMER LAKE	100.0	100.0	0.0	0.0	0.0	0.0	0.0	0.0	0.0	0.0	0.0	0.0	0.0	0.0	100.0	0.0	0.0	100.0	52.5	0.0	100.0
97701	BEND	94.9	93.8	0.3	0.3	1.0	1.3	3.6	5.2	6.2	5.8	6.1	6.5	6.9	27.6	28.8	10.3	1.8	78.1	38.4	49.2	50.8
97702	BEND	94.2	92.8	0.2	0.2	0.9	1.1	4.4	6.5	6.5	6.4	6.9	7.0	5.8	25.1	30.0	10.7	1.6	75.8	39.6	49.7	50.3
97707	BEND	95.9	95.3	0.2	0.2	0.6	0.9	2.2	3.2	4.1	4.2	4.8	4.6	3.1	18.7	35.8	23.3	1.3	83.8	52.3	50.7	49.3
97710	FIELDS	94.5	92.6	0.0	0.0	0.0	0.0	5.5	8.8	5.9	7.4	7.4	7.4	2.9	25.0	26.5	14.7	2.9	73.5	41.0	54.4	45.6
97711	ASHWOOD	88.7	85.5	0.7	0.6	1.4	1.7	7.8	11.6	5.8	5.8	6.4	6.4	4.6	23.1	31.2	15.6	1.2	78.6	43.3	52.0	48.0
97712	BROTHERS	95.7	95.8	0.0	0.0	2.2	1.4	2.2	2.8	4.2	5.6	5.6	6.9	4.2	16.7	40.3	15.3	1.4	79.2	49.2	51.4	48.6
97720	BURNS	90.8	89.4	0.1	0.1	0.5	0.7	4.6	6.6	5.5	6.0	6.5	7.3	5.1	22.3	30.1	14.8	2.3	77.1	42.9	50.4	49.6
97721	PRINCETON	94.5	92.8	0.0	0.0	0.3	0.7	6.2	8.6	6.3	6.9	7.2	7.6	3.6	22.4	31.9	12.8	1.3	74.7	42.1	54.3	45.7
97730	CAMP SHERMAN	95.3	94.6	0.0	0.0	1.1	1.7	1.7	2.6	1.9	2.6	3.3	4.7	4.5	12.7	43.6	25.0	1.7	89.4	56.3	50.9	49.1
97731	CHEMULT	92.2	91.4	0.3	0.3	0.3	0.3	2.9	4.0	4.6	4.0	6.0	9.4	3.1	20.0	39.4	12.3	1.1	79.7	46.4	53.7	46.3
97733	CRESCENT	94.7	93.9	0.2	0.3	0.4	0.5	2.2	3.3	4.6	5.3	6.5	6.1	2.4	20.7	39.6	13.1	1.6	79.4	47.2	51.9	48.1
97734	CULVER	84.6	80.6	0.2	0.2	0.3	0.3	16.2	22.4	7.0	7.0	7.4	7.7	5.7	23.5	27.9	12.3	1.4	73.0	38.8	50.4	49.6
97735	FORT ROCK	92.0	92.6	0.0	0.0	0.0	0.0	4.0	0.0	7.4	7.4	7.4	7.4	7.4	29.6	29.6	3.7	0.0	70.4	33.8	48.1	51.9
97737	GILCHRIST	92.8	91.9	0.3	0.3	0.0	0.0	2.8	4.5	4.2	3.3	5.4	4.2	2.1	18.0	44.3	17.7	0.9	83.8	51.8	52.7	47.3
97738	HINES	94.1	93.1	0.1	0.2	0.7	0.8	2.8	4.1	5.7	6.4	7.0	7.5	5.0	20.8	32.6	13.0	1.8	75.9	43.1	51.9	48.1
97739	LA PINE	95.6	94.7	0.1	0.1	0.4	0.5	2.2	3.3	4.3	5.1	6.2	5.6	3.2	18.5	36.2	19.3	1.6	80.5	49.4	50.7	49.3
97741	MADRAS	73.2	68.7	0.4	0.3	0.6	0.7	26.4	34.8	8.9	8.2	8.0	7.6	6.2	26.5	23.6	9.7	1.4	70.1	33.6	49.8	50.2
97750	MITCHELL	93.2	93.0	0.2	0.2	0.4	0.4	5.2	5.5	4.3	3.9	7.2	8.2	1.2	17.2	35.1	20.5	2.3	77.4	50.5	52.2	47.8
97751	PAULINA	90.6	89.6	0.0	0.0	0.0	0.0	6.6	10.4	6.7	7.5	8.2	6.7	3.7	20.9	29.9	14.9	1.5	73.1	41.9	53.0	47.0
97752	POST	90.9	89.1	0.0	0.0	0.5	0.4	7.2	10.5	6.8	7.5	7.9	6.4	3.8	20.7	32.7	13.5	0.8	73.3	42.5	53.4	46.6
97753	POWELL BUTTE	94.0	92.0	0.1	0.0	0.8	1.0	3.9	5.7	4.4	4.8	5.4	5.2	3.7	19.9	38.8	16.6	1.3	82.3	49.1	50.1	49.9
97754	PRINEVILLE	92.9	90.9	0.0	0.0	0.4	0.6	5.8	8.4	6.7	6.7	6.9	7.3	5.4	23.5	28.5	13.2	1.8	75.4	40.0	49.9	50.1
97756	REDMOND	94.6	93.5	0.1	0.1	0.6	0.8	4.3	6.0	6.8	6.6	7.0	6.9	6.0	25.2	28.3	11.5	1.7	75.0	39.1	49.5	50.5
97758	RILEY	86.8	83.7	0.0	0.0	0.9	2.0	4.7	7.1	5.1	6.1	7.1	7.1	5.1	20.4	34.7	13.3	1.0	76.5	44.0	50.0	50.0
97759	SISTERS	96.5	96.0	0.1	0.1	0.5	0.6	2.2	3.2	3.8	5.0	6.9	6.5	3.3	18.6	36.7	17.4	1.6	79.9	48.1	49.6	50.4
97760	TERREBONNE	95.1	94.3	0.2	0.2	0.5	0.6	3.0	4.5	4.5	5.2	5.6	6.1	4.2	20.3	34.5	18.3	1.4	80.7	47.5	50.5	49.5
97761	WARM SPRINGS	2.7	4.0	0.1	0.1	0.1	0.1	6.2	8.5	10.1	9.2	10.2	10.6	9.6	26.0	19.2	4.6	0.5	63.5	25.2	50.5	49.5
97801	PENDLETON	84.6	82.4	1.2	1.3	0.9	1.1	5.0	7.5	6.3	6.1	6.0	6.6	7.8	28.9	25.6	10.7	2.0	77.7	36.8	53.0	47.0
97810	ADAMS	86.5	84.8	0.0	0.0	0.9	1.1	3.5	5.3	6.5	6.7	8.1	7.9	6.3	23.8	29.4	9.6	1.8	72.7	37.8	50.3	49.7
97812	ARLINGTON	96.1	96.0	0.0	0.0	0.0	0.0	2.6	2.6	4.5	5.0	6.0	7.3	3.9	23.9	33.4	14.1	1.8	78.8	44.5	50.8	49.2
97813	ATHENA	90.1	87.5	0.3	0.3	0.5	0.6	5.1	7.5	8.0	8.2	8.1	6.8	5.2	24.3	27.4	10.5	1.5	70.7	37.5	49.6	50.4
97814	BAKER CITY	95.4	94.4	0.3	0.3	0.5	0.7	2.5	3.6	5.7	5.7	6.1	6.4	5.6	21.7	29.4	15.9	3.4	78.4	44.0	49.3	50.7
97818	BOARDMAN	60.2	52.2	0.3	0.3	0.6	0.7	44.0	54.6	11.3	10.3	8.4	7.5	7.1	28.8	19.6	6.3	0.6	65.4	27.9	52.2	47.8
97820	CANYON CITY	95.4	94.4	0.0	0.0	0.2	0.4	2.5	3.6	6.0	6.5	6.8	7.0	5.8	22.4	29.7	13.3	2.4	75.8	41.1	49.3	50.7
97823	CONDON	97.3	97.2	0.3	0.3	0.3	0.3	1.3	1.3	4.5	5.0	5.5	5.3	4.3	19.6	33.1	18.9	3.8	81.2	48.4	51.7	48.3
97824	COVE	95.0	93.5	0.3	0.4	0.9	1.2	2.8	4.2	5.5	6.0	6.6	6.0	4.4	18.9	34.8	16.2	1.7	78.1	47.1	49.1	50.9
97825	DAYVILLE	95.0	93.8	0.7	0.8	0.7	0.8	2.2	3.9	4.7	5.4	6.2	7.0	4.7	18.6	34.9	17.1	1.6	79.1	47.5	50.4	49.6
97826	ECHO	90.4	87.1	0.4	0.5	0.3	0.4	7.3	10.8	6.4	7.0	7.1	6.3	5.4	25.3	28.1	12.5	2.0	75.8	38.9	52.4	47.6
97827	ELGIN	96.8	96.4	0.0	0.0	0.7	0.9	1.4	2.1	6.1	6.3	6.6	6.5	4.8	20.7	31.4	15.6	2.0	76.9	44.1	50.7	49.3
97828	ENTERPRISE	96.7	96.1	0.0	0.0	0.3	0.4	1.6	2.3	4.6	4.9	6.2	6.7	4.7	19.1	34.8	16.0	3.1	79.9	47.0	49.5	50.5
97830	FOSSIL	93.4	93.3	0.0	0.0	0.3	0.3	5.0	5.0	4.6	4.2	5.6	6.1	3.4	16.0	33.4	23.7	2.9	80.8	53.6	51.1	48.9
97833	HAINES	96.8	95.8	0.1	0.1	0.2	0.3	1.7	2.6	5.4	6.2	7.4	7.1	4.2	19.4	33.6	14.9	1.8	76.2	45.1	51.1	48.9
97834	HALFWAY	97.1	96.8	0.3	0.4	0.0	0.0	1.2	1.8	3.0	4.0	9.0	8.9	1.8	16.0	38.5	15.8	2.8	77.6	48.4	49.9	50.1
97835	HELIX	95.2	94.2	0.2	0.2	0.5	0.5	2.6	3.9	4.4	6.3	10.0	8.5	4.9	22.9	27.0	14.4	1.7	72.5	40.4	52.6	47.4
97836	HEPPNER	96.6	95.6	0.0	0.0	0.3	0.4	2.4	3.9	5.3	5.7	6.1	6.7	4.4	20.0	31.9	17.0	2.8	78.7	46.1	50.7	49.3
97837	HEREFORD	96.8	95.6	0.0	0.0	0.0	0.5	2.2	3.3	4.4	4.9	4.9	4.9	3.8	16.5	37.4	21.4	1.6	83.0	51.5	51.1	48.9
97838	HERMISTON	80.3	74.7	0.6	0.6	1.3	1.5	22.7	30.9	8.2	7.4	6.9	7.4	7.2	25.8	25.3	10.0	1.8	73.0	34.1	49.9	50.1
97839	LEXINGTON	94.1	93.0	0.0	0.0	0.3	0.4	3.8	6.0	6.0	6.9	7.3	7.3	4.2	20.0	32.8	13.9	1.6	75.3	43.5	53.3	46.7
97840	OXBOW	98.6	98.7	0.0	0.0	0.0	0.0	0.7	0.7	3.3	3.9	9.2	9.2	2.0	17.1	40.1	13.2	2.0	77.0	47.0	51.3	48.7
97841	IMBLER	97.1	96.8	0.2	0.2	1.7	1.8	0.7	1.1	4.5	5.2	5.9	8.1	5.6	19.8	35.4	13.3	2.3	79.5	45.5	50.7	49.3
97842	IMNAHA	96.2	95.2	0.0	0.0	0.0	0.0	2.7	3.8	3.2	3.8	4.8	4.8	3.8	15.6	41.4	20.4	2.2	84.9	54.3	52.7	47.3
97843	IONE	96.6	95.9	0.0	0.0	0.2	0.2	3.6	5.9	5.3	6.1	6.8	6.8	4.6	19.2	35.0	14.4	1.8	77.5	45.7	52.5	47.5
97844	IRRIGON	74.6	66.6	0.1	0.1	0.5	0.7	24.1	33.3	8.7	8.0	7.7	7.2	7.3	26.7	24.5	9.1	0.8	71.2	32.0	50.2	49.8
97845	JOHN DAY	96.1	95.3	0.1	0.1	0.3	0.4	2.3	3.3	6.2	6.5	6.6	7.1	5.1	21.6	29.7	14.5	2.7	75.8	42.3	48.9	51.1
97846	JOSEPH	95.8	95.1	0.0	0.0	0.2	0.2	1.4	2.1	4.5	5.0	5.9	5.8	3.9	18.1	35.3	17.9	3.3	80.7	49.6	51.5	48.5
97848	KIMBERLY	97.2	97.1	0.0	0.0	0.0	0.0	2.8	2.9	5.7	5.7	5.7	5.7	5.7	22.9	34.3	14.3	0.0	77.1	43.8	54.3	45.7
97850	LA GRANDE	93.3	92.1	0.7	0.7	1.9	2.3	2.7	3.9	6.1	5.7	5.8	8.0	9.1	24.2	26.5	11.6	3.0	78.5	36.8	48.1	51.9
97856	LONG CREEK	94.4	93.4	0.2	0.2	0.0	0.0	1.8	2.9	4.6	5.1	5.3	4.6	4.0	22.0	35.2	16.7	2.6	82.0	48.1	51.4	48.6
97857	LOSTINE	96.3	95.2	0.0	0.0	0.2	0.5	2.6	3.9	6.0	6.8	7.2	6.8	5.1	17.4	33.8	15.0	1.9	74.6	45.4	49.8	50.2
97862	MILTON FREEWATER	80.0	74.3	0.3	0.3	1.1	1.3	23.4	31.0	8.0	7.7	7.5	7.2	5.7	24.0	25.1	11.9	2.9	72.4	36.6	49.3	50.7
97864	MONUMENT	94.9	93.5	0.0	0.0	0.0	0.0	2.0	2.8	4.6	5.3	5.3	5.0	4.0	22.3	33.7	16.7	3.1	81.7	47.4	51.4	48.6
97865	MOUNT VERNON	95.3	94.5	0.2	0.2	0.2	0.2	1.8	2.5	5.3	5.8	6.3	5.8	5.1	20.8	33.1	15.7	2.1	79.0	45.6	47.9	52.1
97867	NORTH POWDER	96.0	95.7	0.4	0.4	0.5	0.6	4.5	6.6	5.7	5.9	6.2	7.3	6.1	22.1	31.6	13.3	1.9	77.4	41.9	50.7	49.3
97868	PILOT ROCK	93.0	91.7	0.2	0.2	0.4	0.6	2.0	3.1	5.8	6.7	7.2	7.4	4.7	22.3	30.8	13.5	1.7	75.6	42.0	49.4	50.6
97869	PRAIRIE CITY	95.7	95.1	0.0	0.0	0.1	0.1	1.5	2.2	5.1	5.6	6.1	7.0	4.9	17.5	31.6	17.7	4.5	78.3	47.4	50.1	49.9
97870	RICHLAND	94.8	93.8	0.0	0.0	0.5	0.7	2.6	3.7	3.5	3.7	4.2	4.6	3.9	12.8	36.9	27.2	3.2	85.8	56.0	52.1	47.9
97873	SENECA	95.6	94.7	0.6	0.6	0.3	0.6	2.2	3.0	5.0	5.3	6.2	7.1	4.4	18.9	34.6	16.3	2.1	78.4	47.2	50.3	49.7
97874	SPRAY	96.0	96.0	0.0	0.0	0.0	0.0	4.0	4.0	4.0	4.0	8.0	8.0	0.0	20.0	36.0	20.0	0.0	76.0	48.8	52.0	48.0
97875	STANFIELD	73.3	66.1	0.5	0.4	0.5	0.5	25.8	34.3	9.2	9.1	8.5	7.2	5.5	27.5	23.3	8.6	1.2	68.6	32.3	51.9	48.1
97876	SUMMERVILLE	95.3	94.5	0.4	0.5	0.9	1.1	2.0	2.6	4.5	5.3	6.8	7.2	2.7	20.2	39.1	12.8	1.6	79.0	47.0	51.2	48.8
97877	SUMPTER	96.4	95.3	0.0	0.0	0.0	0.0	1.8	1.9	3.7	4.7	5.6	5.6	3.7	16.8	37.4	20.6	1.9	82.2	51.1	50.5	49.5
97882	UMATILLA	75.9	70.9	2.2	2.1	0.5	0.6	28.0	34.9	9.2	8.4	7.4	7.6	7.8	31.2	21.2	6.4	0.8	70.9	30.8	57.3	42.7
97883	UNION	96.4	95.8	0.1	0.1	0.4	0.5	1.1	1.7	5.6	6.1	6.7	6.7	5.7	20.8	31.7	14.5	2.2	77.4	43.7	49.2	50.8
97884	UNITY	96.6	95.7	0.0	0.0	0.0	0.4	1.7	2.2	4.3	5.2	5.2	4.8	3.5	15.6	38.5	21.2	1.7	82.3	51.9	50.6	49.4
97885	WALLOWA	97.1	96.4	0.1	0.1	0.3	0.4	2.2	3.1	5.0	6.0	7.8	6.8	4.4	18.1	34.5	15.7	1.8	76.0	46.1	50.1	49.9
97886	WESTON	87.7	84.1	0.0	0.0	0.2	0.1	10.2	14.8	4.4	6.4	9.3	7.4	3.5	23.6	30.8	13.1	1.5	74.5	41.5	50.2	49.8
97901	ADRIAN	88.1	83.3	0.0	0.0	2.2	2.7	16.0	23.8	5.1	6.1	6.4	7.1	4.7	23.5	31.9	13.7	1.5	78.0	41.7	54.9	45.1
97903	BROGAN	78.9	72.5	8.1	8.0	1.1	1.0	10.8	17.0	1.5	2.0	1.5	3.5	17.0	49.0	21.5	4.0	0.0	94.0	34.8	91.0	9.0
	OREGON	86.6	83.7	1.6	1.7	3.2	4.0	8.0	11.2	6.5	6.2	6.3	6.8	6.8	26.7	27.5	11.1	2.1	77.0	38.0	49.6	50.4
	UNITED STATES	75.1	72.0	12.3	12.7	3.8	4.6	12.5	15.7	6.8	6.7	6.6	7.1	6.9	27.0	26.0	10.9	1.9	75.7	36.9	49.2	50.8

ZIP CODE #	POST OFFICE NAME	2009 Per Capita Income	2009 HH Income Base	2009 HOUSEHOLD INCOME DISTRIBUTION (%) Less than $25,000	$25,000 to $49,999	$50,000 to $99,999	$100,000 to $149,999	$150,000 or More	MEDIAN HOUSEHOLD INCOME 2009	2014	2009 National Centile	2009 State Centile	2009 Home Value Base	2009 HOME VALUE DISTRIBUTION (%) Less than $50,000	$50,000 to $89,999	$90,000 to $174,999	$175,000 to $399,999	$400,000 or More	2009 Median Home Value
97601	KLAMATH FALLS	20302	8855	32.8	30.9	27.8	5.0	3.4	36877	38913	23	15	5013	5.0	15.5	37.7	33.6	8.2	155063
97603	KLAMATH FALLS	21181	12167	27.2	28.5	36.5	5.2	2.7	43200	45874	43	40	8719	8.4	8.6	39.0	37.8	6.2	162858
97620	ADEL	21326	52	32.7	32.7	30.8	1.9	1.9	35000	40000	18	10	32	6.3	21.9	25.0	28.1	18.8	162500
97621	BEATTY	15200	50	50.0	30.0	20.0	0.0	0.0	25000	24267	3	2	42	9.5	9.5	42.9	33.3	4.8	150000
97623	BONANZA	17290	1190	33.2	32.6	27.1	4.3	2.8	36936	38997	23	16	922	5.6	9.8	39.0	32.8	12.8	164541
97624	CHILOQUIN	16750	1555	35.2	31.9	29.1	3.0	0.9	35465	37240	19	11	1212	8.2	13.5	34.8	34.3	9.2	160038
97625	DAIRY	16666	85	29.4	30.6	29.4	7.1	3.5	41225	43612	37	30	64	3.1	12.5	28.1	35.9	20.3	189286
97627	KENO	22390	282	30.1	26.6	34.4	6.4	2.5	42653	44580	41	37	233	3.9	8.6	27.9	52.4	7.3	197500
97630	LAKEVIEW	20430	2024	30.0	30.0	33.7	4.2	2.1	39079	42190	30	22	1385	12.2	16.3	43.0	23.7	4.8	120218
97632	MALIN	18437	416	27.4	32.7	30.8	5.3	3.8	41989	45058	39	34	296	3.4	11.5	35.5	33.8	15.9	174000
97633	MERRILL	22426	400	28.3	24.3	37.3	4.8	5.5	45777	48803	51	46	289	2.4	15.6	31.5	36.3	14.2	176875
97635	NEW PINE CREEK	21226	79	31.6	30.4	30.4	6.3	1.3	34303	38662	16	7	55	3.6	5.5	36.4	43.6	10.9	187500
97636	PAISLEY	19589	219	31.5	33.3	31.1	1.8	2.3	35866	37610	20	12	135	8.9	19.3	25.9	26.7	19.3	159722
97637	PLUSH	19265	65	30.8	32.3	33.8	1.5	1.5	36726	35757	23	15	40	7.5	17.5	27.5	27.5	20.0	166667
97638	SILVER LAKE	16541	696	43.7	29.3	23.4	1.9	1.7	29311	31229	7	3	519	23.3	19.3	29.5	17.3	10.6	110337
97639	SPRAGUE RIVER	12833	131	51.1	27.5	19.1	0.8	1.5	24259	28180	3	1	110	13.6	11.8	35.5	34.5	4.5	151923
97640	SUMMER LAKE	0	0	0.0	0.0	0.0	0.0	0.0	0	0	0	0	0	0.0	0.0	0.0	0.0	0.0	0
97701	BEND	28943	26169	17.1	24.9	42.6	9.4	6.1	56650	59388	74	76	17136	1.8	1.3	9.4	60.4	27.1	281831
97702	BEND	27375	16804	16.6	25.5	42.4	8.7	6.7	55780	57905	72	74	12508	5.4	6.3	18.1	51.5	18.7	232359
97707	BEND	35446	3135	16.3	23.6	38.3	9.3	12.4	57402	59568	74	78	2619	0.0	3.2	19.9	34.1	42.8	346165
97710	FIELDS	19301	28	32.1	35.7	25.0	3.6	3.6	35000	42337	18	10	17	0.0	5.9	17.6	35.3	41.2	275000
97711	ASHWOOD	22917	64	14.1	32.8	45.3	4.7	3.1	51612	51965	65	64	46	4.3	4.3	6.5	50.0	34.8	322222
97712	BROTHERS	38604	27	14.8	14.8	33.3	14.8	22.2	77369	78810	91	98	24	0.0	0.0	0.0	33.3	66.7	500000
97720	BURNS	19648	1927	30.0	38.0	24.3	4.8	2.9	35351	36664	19	10	1355	15.7	19.9	34.2	20.2	10.0	124560
97721	PRINCETON	20721	120	29.2	31.7	30.0	5.0	4.2	38623	40973	29	21	73	6.8	9.6	9.6	38.4	35.6	254167
97730	CAMP SHERMAN	27765	170	20.0	23.5	40.6	8.8	7.1	61652	62787	80	85	137	4.4	4.4	14.6	40.1	36.5	311905
97731	CHEMULT	21850	151	27.8	27.2	39.1	4.0	2.0	43092	47376	43	39	100	8.0	15.0	38.0	33.0	6.0	141667
97733	CRESCENT	18425	528	31.6	29.2	33.9	3.6	1.7	38237	40216	27	20	386	5.7	19.7	46.4	25.6	2.6	122917
97734	CULVER	20803	954	18.0	32.9	39.1	7.2	2.7	48941	50146	59	55	713	4.6	5.9	32.7	40.8	16.0	193945
97735	FORT ROCK	17139	12	33.3	41.7	25.0	0.0	0.0	35000	35000	18	10	9	22.2	22.2	55.6	0.0	0.0	112500
97737	GILCHRIST	21952	158	27.2	34.8	32.9	2.5	2.5	37742	40381	26	18	126	5.6	16.7	42.9	32.5	2.4	126923
97738	HINES	20153	756	20.9	33.2	40.3	4.5	1.1	46761	47619	53	49	605	6.9	11.2	48.4	27.4	6.0	149258
97739	LA PINE	19260	4236	27.9	36.1	31.4	3.1	1.5	37976	39803	27	19	3404	2.6	9.2	44.0	36.0	8.2	164324
97741	MADRAS	19677	4452	21.7	34.3	35.0	6.0	3.0	44770	46859	48	45	2924	10.1	4.9	31.9	43.8	9.4	183244
97750	MITCHELL	18125	204	37.3	33.8	23.5	2.0	3.4	32909	34392	13	6	142	7.7	15.5	26.1	22.5	28.2	178571
97751	PAULINA	18735	60	33.3	38.3	23.3	1.7	3.3	37292	37831	24	17	39	7.7	15.4	25.6	23.1	28.2	179167
97752	POST	16868	107	35.5	36.4	22.4	2.8	2.8	37052	38765	24	16	70	7.1	18.6	21.4	24.3	28.6	185000
97753	POWELL BUTTE	27124	999	8.2	25.6	53.2	8.5	4.5	60155	59761	78	82	831	1.6	2.9	7.0	42.2	46.3	380696
97754	PRINEVILLE	19059	8189	28.6	30.2	35.3	4.2	1.6	41538	44348	38	33	5965	8.5	5.6	36.0	41.4	8.4	174720
97756	REDMOND	23859	13690	19.2	28.7	42.1	6.4	3.5	51250	54005	64	63	10038	2.8	2.8	27.9	51.9	14.6	218301
97758	RILEY	24654	39	12.8	25.6	51.3	10.3	0.0	60792	61160	79	83	29	0.0	6.9	10.3	51.7	31.0	289286
97759	SISTERS	33134	2581	15.9	25.7	37.8	12.6	8.0	58170	60490	75	80	2081	1.2	0.9	8.8	43.0	46.0	380072
97760	TERREBONNE	23741	2622	13.9	36.0	40.4	6.5	3.2	50073	51560	61	57	2253	2.8	3.3	22.4	58.9	12.6	226836
97761	WARM SPRINGS	11283	792	30.2	33.1	31.8	3.5	1.4	39905	42546	32	24	518	14.1	12.9	56.4	14.1	2.5	125000
97801	PENDLETON	22614	7899	22.3	27.6	40.4	6.7	3.0	50061	51877	61	57	4816	7.5	5.7	30.6	49.0	7.3	188678
97810	ADAMS	21453	209	19.1	25.8	47.4	5.3	2.4	53691	55046	69	70	158	3.2	12.0	37.3	39.2	8.2	170652
97812	ARLINGTON	22514	337	21.1	33.5	37.1	5.9	2.4	44662	44641	47	44	221	10.0	18.6	41.2	20.8	9.5	143304
97813	ATHENA	20835	558	23.3	25.3	42.8	6.1	2.5	51132	52922	64	62	391	7.2	8.7	38.1	35.0	11.0	168432
97814	BAKER CITY	19375	4970	29.7	35.6	29.5	3.6	1.6	38891	40352	29	21	3435	5.4	10.6	42.5	30.9	10.6	156781
97818	BOARDMAN	16510	1325	19.2	33.4	40.6	4.8	2.1	46946	49488	54	49	878	25.2	6.9	26.3	37.6	4.0	152711
97820	CANYON CITY	22873	307	21.2	32.2	35.2	8.8	2.6	47096	47862	54	50	225	5.3	5.8	38.2	41.8	8.9	176974
97823	CONDON	22369	474	32.5	27.4	32.1	5.7	2.3	39784	42008	32	24	352	8.0	19.6	41.8	26.7	4.0	135714
97824	COVE	24184	602	21.6	24.6	40.9	8.5	4.5	53145	52916	68	68	480	1.5	5.2	19.6	53.8	20.0	257353
97825	DAYVILLE	18066	56	33.9	37.5	25.0	3.6	0.0	35000	35000	18	10	42	11.9	16.7	28.6	23.8	19.0	141667
97826	ECHO	20319	388	27.8	29.1	35.6	4.9	2.6	43655	46970	44	41	263	7.6	10.6	39.2	28.9	13.7	156250
97827	ELGIN	20170	992	28.1	32.1	32.9	4.2	2.7	41414	43346	37	32	731	9.4	15.0	32.7	32.6	10.3	156514
97828	ENTERPRISE	22152	1335	29.8	29.0	32.9	5.5	2.8	42095	43450	40	35	939	5.4	4.7	26.6	46.0	17.3	218196
97830	FOSSIL	19553	434	30.2	36.4	28.6	2.8	2.1	37159	39080	24	16	321	7.2	20.9	37.7	19.0	15.3	138352
97833	HAINES	21303	380	28.9	31.8	31.3	5.0	2.9	42900	45489	42	38	289	5.9	13.8	25.6	28.7	26.0	202083
97834	HALFWAY	17799	470	36.0	35.7	23.4	3.0	1.9	31972	32951	11	5	323	8.7	5.6	29.1	38.1	18.6	207432
97835	HELIX	21454	149	16.8	25.5	47.7	8.1	2.0	55895	55025	73	75	97	3.1	17.5	26.8	42.3	10.3	190625
97836	HEPPNER	23377	890	24.6	29.1	35.2	6.2	4.9	44467	47170	47	43	630	6.0	16.3	38.6	31.0	8.1	152303
97837	HEREFORD	17464	73	28.8	39.7	26.0	5.5	0.0	37735	39524	26	18	54	3.7	9.3	33.3	38.9	14.8	200000
97838	HERMISTON	21275	8517	22.2	28.8	37.9	7.4	3.7	48847	51251	59	54	5451	9.9	7.6	31.5	44.1	6.9	177621
97839	LEXINGTON	25602	263	14.8	29.7	40.7	8.4	6.5	55344	56314	72	73	196	11.7	14.8	25.0	37.2	11.2	165625
97840	OXBOW	22724	70	20.0	44.3	28.6	4.3	2.9	40735	42843	35	29	51	5.9	2.0	19.6	45.1	27.5	287500
97841	IMBLER	21472	165	19.4	26.1	43.6	8.5	2.4	52761	52175	67	67	131	6.1	12.2	21.4	39.7	20.6	206250
97842	IMNAHA	21827	82	30.5	40.2	18.3	7.3	3.7	36166	37015	21	14	61	6.6	0.0	18.0	34.4	41.0	345000
97843	IONE	21441	199	19.6	26.6	43.7	7.0	3.0	52331	52192	67	65	146	13.7	11.0	32.2	37.0	6.2	154167
97844	IRRIGON	17803	1413	18.3	33.5	40.5	6.0	1.7	47978	48576	57	52	1119	14.3	9.6	37.1	33.8	5.3	155739
97845	JOHN DAY	21208	1402	26.2	34.5	31.3	5.6	2.5	42190	43485	40	35	1030	14.3	9.7	36.4	31.1	8.5	147600
97846	JOSEPH	23522	793	28.6	33.4	28.1	5.2	4.7	41374	43126	37	32	569	2.5	4.0	30.2	43.1	20.2	226293
97848	KIMBERLY	9342	10	40.0	40.0	20.0	0.0	0.0	30000	30000	8	4	7	0.0	0.0	57.1	14.3	28.6	137500
97850	LA GRANDE	22109	6686	29.8	26.8	34.4	5.9	3.1	43147	45169	43	40	4049	8.4	5.9	38.3	40.7	6.8	170807
97856	LONG CREEK	20142	201	32.8	33.8	25.9	3.5	4.0	33997	35746	16	7	137	12.4	20.4	27.0	16.8	23.4	143750
97857	LOSTINE	18555	167	34.1	31.7	27.5	4.2	2.4	37707	39389	26	18	124	7.3	12.9	37.1	33.1	9.7	154545
97862	MILTON FREEWATER	17524	4030	31.9	32.0	28.6	5.9	1.6	37891	40297	26	19	2734	10.0	7.6	40.3	33.5	8.6	159730
97864	MONUMENT	21705	153	33.3	34.0	26.1	3.9	2.6	33245	35746	14	6	104	12.5	20.2	26.0	17.3	24.0	146875
97865	MOUNT VERNON	19204	239	26.8	38.9	30.5	2.9	0.8	41218	42195	37	30	181	22.7	15.5	30.4	22.1	9.4	126875
97867	NORTH POWDER	16406	292	37.7	33.2	21.6	3.8	3.8	34017	35768	16	7	206	9.7	18.0	41.3	17.0	14.1	133824
97868	PILOT ROCK	19093	933	24.0	32.2	38.9	3.4	1.5	44588	47742	47	44	678	8.8	13.7	42.6	28.8	6.0	145413
97869	PRAIRIE CITY	19804	584	29.8	34.2	30.3	3.4	2.2	38290	39576	28	20	442	8.6	17.2	42.3	22.9	9.0	144298
97870	RICHLAND	18941	287	40.1	31.7	22.6	3.8	1.7	29045	31197	7	3	217	13.8	13.8	26.3	27.2	18.9	159821
97873	SENECA	17612	141	34.8	34.8	27.0	3.5	0.0	34758	35666	17	8	106	9.4	18.9	27.4	25.5	18.9	150000
97874	SPRAY	8800	8	50.0	37.5	12.5	0.0	0.0	25000	25000	3	2	6	0.0	0.0	66.7	0.0	33.3	162500
97875	STANFIELD	18763	939	21.0	33.8	37.7	5.5	2.0	46632	48687	53	48	659	8.5	4.4	47.3	30.7	9.1	158617
97876	SUMMERVILLE	25851	355	17.5	26.2	39.4	10.7	6.2	54835	54542	71	72	297	1.3	1.0	11.4	53.2	33.0	327857
97877	SUMPTER	22927	55	25.5	36.4	34.5	3.6	0.0	40434	41127	34	27	43	4.7	11.6	39.5	32.6	11.6	162500
97882	UMATILLA	17010	2039	25.1	31.4	36.2	5.2	2.2	45701	48152	50	46	1331	13.4	7.7	44.0	29.9	5.1	147278
97883	UNION	17467	983	35.0	32.7	27.3	3.7	1.4	38370	41197	28	21	771	6.7	10.6	47.6	24.4	10.6	149540
97884	UNITY	19414	98	26.5	36.7	29.6	6.1	1.0	40385	42034	34	26	74	1.4	8.1	31.1	43.2	16.2	233333
97885	WALLOWA	18860	590	32.2	31.2	30.8	4.1	1.7	39069	40247	30	22	444	5.4	13.7	34.7	37.6	8.6	164634
97886	WESTON	18358	512	20.9	38.3	35.0	5.3	0.6	44875	47301	48	45	389	5.1	9.5	42.2	34.7	8.5	162260
97901	ADRIAN	18467	204	25.5	33.8	28.9	6.4	5.4	42328	45187	40	36	139	15.1	6.5	27.3	38.8	12.2	178409
97903	BROGAN	29389	76	40.8	27.6	27.6	3.9	0.0	33158	36118	14	6	49	14.3	30.6	18.4	22.4	14.3	104167
	OREGON	26362		20.3	25.9	37.7	10.2	5.9	53483	55628				4.6	3.5	17.3	54.4	20.2	249991
	UNITED STATES	27277		20.9	24.4	35.3	11.7	7.6	54719	56938				9.3	13.1	31.6	32.6	13.5	162279

ZIP CODE # POST OFFICE NAME	FINANCIAL SERVICES				THE HOME						ENTERTAINMENT						PERSONAL			
					Home Improvements		Furnishings													
	Auto Loan	Home Loan	Investments	Retirement Plans	Home Repair	Lawn & Garden	Computers & Hardware-Personal	Major Appliances	TV, Radio, Sound Equipment	Furniture	Dine out/ Carry out	Sports Equipment	Fees & Tickets	Toys & Games	Travel	Cable TV	Apparel & Services	Auto Repairs	Health Insurance	Pets & Supplies
97601 KLAMATH FALLS	74	64	64	65	63	71	71	70	73	67	73	54	65	73	66	76	50	72	75	84
97603 KLAMATH FALLS	84	73	81	72	73	84	74	81	77	72	77	61	68	78	73	81	52	79	84	96
97620 ADEL	81	55	89	55	58	85	62	77	64	50	63	63	45	63	61	70	41	72	81	94
97621 BEATTY	56	40	58	39	42	57	41	53	46	39	45	40	33	46	41	51	30	48	55	63
97623 BONANZA	70	65	73	61	68	74	62	70	65	65	64	48	59	63	63	68	43	67	75	82
97624 CHILOQUIN	66	56	75	53	61	72	55	67	59	56	58	46	50	56	58	64	39	63	72	78
97625 DAIRY	82	77	68	74	75	78	72	76	74	75	74	55	69	77	69	76	51	73	76	90
97627 KENO	87	71	106	70	77	91	71	87	74	68	73	64	62	71	75	78	49	81	87	102
97630 LAKEVIEW	79	62	81	61	64	82	65	77	70	60	69	57	56	69	64	76	46	73	82	90
97632 MALIN	86	73	84	68	74	80	76	83	74	74	75	65	65	75	74	75	51	80	79	96
97633 MERRILL	105	75	110	73	78	108	78	99	85	70	84	77	61	84	78	94	55	91	103	119
97635 NEW PINE CREEK	86	62	89	60	64	88	63	81	70	59	69	61	51	70	63	78	46	74	84	96
97636 PAISLEY	81	56	89	56	58	86	62	77	64	50	64	64	45	63	62	70	41	72	81	95
97637 PLUSH	82	56	90	56	59	86	62	77	65	51	64	64	46	64	62	71	42	72	82	95
97638 SILVER LAKE	70	50	72	48	52	71	51	65	57	48	56	49	41	57	51	63	37	60	68	78
97639 SPRAGUE RIVER	57	41	58	39	42	58	42	53	46	39	46	40	33	46	41	51	30	49	55	63
97640 SUMMER LAKE	0	0	0	0	0	0	0	0	0	0	0	0	0	0	0	0	0	0	0	0
97701 BEND	101	101	99	102	100	98	101	99	99	102	99	78	100	100	100	98	70	100	97	117
97702 BEND	100	102	97	102	102	101	98	100	97	100	98	75	99	99	99	97	68	98	99	117
97707 BEND	122	110	163	109	124	138	105	129	110	108	109	88	102	102	117	117	73	121	134	148
97710 FIELDS	84	58	92	58	60	88	64	80	67	52	66	66	47	65	64	73	43	74	84	98
97711 ASHWOOD	111	76	122	76	80	117	85	105	88	69	87	87	62	86	84	96	56	98	111	129
97712 BROTHERS	143	162	176	166	166	164	142	155	138	147	139	117	154	137	157	138	98	146	149	179
97720 BURNS	81	58	83	57	61	84	63	78	69	56	67	60	50	68	62	76	45	73	84	93
97721 PRINCETON	94	65	103	64	68	99	72	89	75	58	74	74	53	73	71	81	48	83	94	110
97730 CAMP SHERMAN	115	92	149	91	102	122	93	118	97	87	96	86	80	92	100	103	64	109	116	136
97731 CHEMULT	81	65	94	63	70	86	65	81	70	63	69	58	57	67	68	75	46	75	84	95
97733 CRESCENT	73	60	82	57	65	79	60	73	65	60	63	51	53	62	62	70	42	69	79	85
97734 CULVER	93	81	89	79	82	91	79	88	82	79	81	65	72	83	78	85	55	84	88	104
97735 FORT ROCK	69	49	71	48	51	70	51	64	56	47	55	48	40	56	50	62	36	59	67	77
97737 GILCHRIST	68	65	83	60	72	78	62	73	65	67	64	48	61	60	68	69	43	70	81	83
97738 HINES	82	70	77	72	72	87	70	81	73	63	72	62	63	74	70	78	49	75	84	95
97739 LA PINE	69	64	85	60	71	78	62	74	65	65	64	49	60	60	67	69	43	70	80	84
97741 MADRAS	88	76	75	74	74	84	76	81	79	76	79	61	69	81	72	82	53	79	83	97
97750 MITCHELL	63	60	77	55	67	72	57	67	61	62	59	44	57	55	62	64	40	65	75	77
97751 PAULINA	75	51	82	51	54	79	57	71	59	46	59	59	42	58	57	65	38	66	75	87
97752 POST	75	52	82	51	54	79	57	71	60	46	59	59	42	58	57	65	38	66	75	88
97753 POWELL BUTTE	115	92	149	91	101	122	92	117	96	86	95	86	80	92	100	103	63	108	116	136
97754 PRINEVILLE	79	65	77	65	67	81	69	77	72	64	70	58	61	71	67	77	48	74	82	91
97756 REDMOND	93	86	89	85	86	90	85	89	86	85	86	67	81	87	84	88	59	88	89	106
97758 RILEY	91	90	92	93	89	99	85	93	85	81	85	74	84	86	88	87	58	88	94	111
97759 SISTERS	123	113	161	112	125	139	107	130	112	109	110	90	105	105	119	118	75	122	134	149
97760 TERREBONNE	97	83	114	81	88	100	80	97	83	78	83	71	73	81	85	88	56	90	96	113
97761 WARM SPRINGS	67	56	46	59	50	61	62	58	67	62	67	45	59	68	56	70	46	63	65	74
97801 PENDLETON	82	81	77	82	79	83	82	81	82	80	82	62	81	83	81	84	57	82	85	97
97810 ADAMS	95	83	84	82	83	93	81	89	84	79	83	67	73	86	79	88	56	85	91	106
97812 ARLINGTON	95	65	104	65	68	100	72	90	75	59	74	74	53	74	72	82	48	84	95	111
97813 ATHENA	99	76	98	75	77	100	79	92	82	71	82	73	65	83	77	88	54	87	96	112
97814 BAKER CITY	76	59	78	58	61	78	63	74	67	57	66	56	53	66	62	72	44	70	78	87
97818 BOARDMAN	85	79	68	75	76	72	80	78	78	83	79	59	75	81	75	77	55	79	74	91
97820 CANYON CITY	91	84	74	81	82	86	79	84	82	82	82	61	75	85	75	84	56	81	84	99
97823 CONDON	89	61	98	61	64	94	68	84	71	55	70	70	50	69	67	77	45	79	89	104
97824 COVE	105	83	134	82	91	111	84	106	88	77	87	79	71	84	90	94	57	98	106	124
97825 DAYVILLE	73	53	75	51	55	74	54	69	60	50	59	51	43	59	53	66	39	63	71	82
97826 ECHO	94	67	97	65	70	96	70	88	77	64	76	67	56	76	69	84	50	81	92	105
97827 ELGIN	87	65	93	63	68	89	66	83	72	62	71	62	54	71	66	78	47	76	85	98
97828 ENTERPRISE	81	69	91	68	72	86	69	82	73	65	72	61	63	71	72	77	48	77	85	95
97830 FOSSIL	65	63	80	58	69	75	59	70	63	64	61	46	59	58	65	67	41	67	78	80
97833 HAINES	95	67	107	66	70	100	73	91	76	60	75	74	55	74	73	82	49	85	95	111
97834 HALFWAY	64	57	80	54	63	70	55	67	58	56	57	46	51	54	60	61	38	63	71	77
97835 HELIX	106	73	116	73	76	112	81	100	84	65	83	83	59	82	80	92	54	94	106	124
97836 HEPPNER	99	75	108	75	79	103	81	96	84	71	83	75	66	82	81	90	55	91	100	115
97837 HEREFORD	73	57	90	56	62	77	58	73	62	54	61	54	50	59	62	66	40	68	74	85
97838 HERMISTON	89	81	75	81	79	85	84	84	85	82	85	65	79	87	80	87	59	85	86	100
97839 LEXINGTON	119	82	131	82	86	126	91	113	95	74	94	94	67	93	91	103	61	106	120	139
97840 OXBOW	82	66	106	65	72	87	66	84	69	62	68	61	57	66	71	74	45	77	83	97
97841 IMBLER	103	71	113	71	74	109	79	98	82	64	81	81	58	80	79	90	53	92	104	121
97842 IMNAHA	83	66	107	65	73	87	66	84	69	62	68	61	57	66	72	74	45	78	83	97
97843 IONE	105	72	115	72	75	110	80	99	83	65	82	82	59	81	79	91	53	93	105	122
97844 IRRIGON	87	81	70	78	78	80	79	80	80	82	80	60	74	84	74	81	55	80	79	95
97845 JOHN DAY	85	70	79	68	70	84	69	80	74	68	73	59	61	75	67	78	49	75	82	94
97846 JOSEPH	92	69	111	68	75	98	72	91	76	64	75	70	58	73	76	81	49	85	93	108
97848 KIMBERLY	57	41	60	40	42	58	42	54	46	38	46	41	33	46	42	51	30	49	56	64
97850 LA GRANDE	78	68	72	70	69	76	77	75	77	72	77	58	70	77	72	79	53	77	79	90
97856 LONG CREEK	82	56	90	56	59	86	62	77	65	50	64	64	46	64	62	71	42	72	82	95
97857 LOSTINE	82	59	86	57	62	83	60	77	67	56	66	58	49	66	60	73	43	71	80	91
97862 MILTON FREEWATER	77	62	72	61	62	76	66	74	69	61	68	56	56	69	63	73	46	71	77	87
97864 MONUMENT	82	56	90	56	59	86	63	78	65	51	64	64	46	64	62	71	42	73	82	96
97865 MOUNT VERNON	81	58	83	56	60	82	59	76	66	55	65	57	48	66	59	73	43	69	79	90
97867 NORTH POWDER	81	58	84	56	60	83	60	76	66	55	65	58	47	65	59	72	43	70	79	90
97868 PILOT ROCK	87	64	93	63	67	89	66	83	72	61	71	62	54	71	66	78	47	76	85	98
97869 PRAIRIE CITY	84	60	86	58	63	85	62	79	69	58	67	59	50	68	61	76	45	72	82	94
97870 RICHLAND	60	54	75	51	60	67	52	63	55	54	54	43	50	51	57	58	36	60	68	72
97873 SENECA	74	53	76	52	55	75	55	69	61	51	60	52	44	60	54	67	39	64	72	83
97874 SPRAY	40	39	49	35	43	46	37	43	39	40	38	28	36	35	40	41	25	42	48	49
97875 STANFIELD	87	76	79	72	76	81	76	82	76	76	77	62	68	78	74	77	52	79	80	96
97876 SUMMERVILLE	104	98	134	99	105	114	92	109	93	91	93	80	90	90	101	96	64	102	106	126
97877 SUMPTER	76	59	92	58	64	79	59	75	63	55	62	55	50	61	63	68	41	69	76	88
97882 UMATILLA	79	70	61	69	67	73	74	72	76	72	75	55	67	78	67	77	51	74	75	87
97883 UNION	79	56	81	55	58	81	59	75	65	54	64	56	47	65	58	72	42	69	79	89
97884 UNITY	76	61	99	60	67	81	61	78	64	57	63	57	53	61	66	68	42	72	77	90
97885 WALLOWA	82	58	86	57	61	84	61	77	67	55	66	60	48	66	61	73	43	71	81	93
97886 WESTON	87	63	93	61	66	89	65	82	71	60	70	62	53	70	65	78	46	76	85	97
97901 ADRIAN	96	66	105	66	69	101	73	91	76	59	75	75	54	75	73	83	49	85	96	112
97903 BROGAN	71	49	78	49	51	75	55	68	57	44	56	56	40	56	54	62	36	63	72	83
OREGON	96	93	95	94	93	95	95	95	95	94	95	74	93	95	95	95	66	96	96	112
UNITED STATES	100	100	100	100	100	100	100	100	100	100	100	100	100	100	100	100	100	100	100	100

97904-97920

#	POST OFFICE NAME	COUNTY FIPS CODE	POPULATION 2000	POPULATION 2009	POPULATION 2014	2000-2009 ANNUAL RATE % Rate	2000-2009 ANNUAL RATE State Centile	HOUSEHOLDS 2000	HOUSEHOLDS 2009	HOUSEHOLDS 2014	HOUSEHOLDS % Annual Rate 2000-2009	HOUSEHOLDS 2009 Average HH Size	FAMILIES 2000	FAMILIES 2009	FAMILIES % Annual Rate 2000-2009
97904	DREWSEY	025	149	138	134	-0.8	2	67	62	61	-0.8	2.23	49	45	-0.9
97906	HARPER	045	288	304	305	0.6	48	109	120	122	1.0	1.73	81	88	0.9
97907	HUNTINGTON	001	810	771	749	-0.5	4	355	342	333	-0.4	2.20	237	226	-0.5
97908	IRONSIDE	045	74	80	80	0.8	59	30	34	34	1.4	2.35	23	26	1.3
97909	JAMIESON	045	73	73	74	0.0	19	24	24	24	0.0	3.04	19	19	0.0
97910	JORDAN VALLEY	045	634	593	582	-0.7	3	263	242	237	-0.9	2.42	181	165	-1.0
97911	JUNTURA	045	96	102	103	0.7	53	38	42	43	1.1	2.43	28	31	1.1
97913	NYSSA	045	5769	5724	5724	-0.1	14	1910	1871	1863	-0.2	3.06	1460	1416	-0.3
97914	ONTARIO	045	19163	19275	19252	0.1	23	5954	5793	5752	-0.3	2.84	4087	3929	-0.4
97917	RIVERSIDE	045	63	63	63	0.0	19	22	22	21	0.0	2.77	16	15	-0.7
97918	VALE	045	4636	4754	4784	0.3	32	1583	1595	1600	0.1	2.87	1227	1225	0.0
97920	WESTFALL	045	25	27	27	0.8	59	8	9	9	1.3	2.56	6	7	1.7
	OREGON					1.3					1.2	2.51			1.1
	UNITED STATES					1.0					1.1	2.59			0.9

ZIP CODE		RACE (%)								2009 AGE DISTRIBUTION (%)										MEDIAN AGE		
#	POST OFFICE NAME	White		Black		Asian/Pacific		% Hispanic Origin														
		2000	2009	2000	2009	2000	2009	2000	2009	0-4	5-9	10-14	15-19	20-24	25-44	45-64	65-84	85+	18+	2009	% 2009 Males	% 2009 Females
97904	DREWSEY	95.3	93.5	0.0	0.0	0.0	0.7	2.7	3.6	3.6	6.5	6.5	5.8	2.9	22.5	37.7	13.8	0.7	79.0	46.2	50.0	50.0
97906	HARPER	81.3	76.0	5.9	5.9	0.7	1.0	9.0	13.8	3.0	3.3	3.3	4.6	11.5	44.1	23.0	6.6	0.7	88.2	36.0	79.9	20.1
97907	HUNTINGTON	96.4	95.6	0.5	0.5	0.1	0.1	3.3	5.1	3.8	4.0	4.4	5.6	6.1	19.8	29.4	24.5	2.3	84.8	50.3	53.6	46.4
97908	IRONSIDE	78.4	72.5	8.1	7.5	1.4	1.3	10.8	16.3	2.5	2.5	2.5	2.5	12.5	51.3	23.8	2.5	0.0	92.5	35.5	88.8	11.2
97909	JAMIESON	97.3	95.9	0.0	0.0	0.0	0.0	6.8	11.0	5.5	5.5	8.2	9.6	5.5	21.9	30.1	12.3	1.4	74.0	41.3	53.4	46.6
97910	JORDAN VALLEY	88.8	86.5	0.0	0.0	0.6	0.7	3.8	5.4	5.9	7.1	7.1	6.4	3.7	23.1	29.8	14.2	2.7	75.2	42.4	51.6	48.4
97911	JUNTURA	80.2	74.5	6.3	6.9	1.0	1.0	9.4	14.7	2.0	2.9	2.9	3.9	14.7	46.1	22.5	4.9	0.0	91.2	35.0	84.3	15.7
97913	NYSSA	68.2	61.6	0.4	0.4	1.2	1.3	42.1	52.0	9.5	9.5	8.6	7.9	5.9	23.4	22.3	11.0	1.8	67.3	31.9	49.6	50.4
97914	ONTARIO	73.9	67.1	1.6	1.6	2.6	3.1	25.1	33.1	7.5	6.9	6.2	7.1	8.4	27.9	22.5	11.1	2.5	75.5	34.3	54.8	45.2
97917	RIVERSIDE	88.9	87.3	0.0	0.0	0.0	0.0	3.2	6.3	6.3	7.9	7.9	6.3	3.2	23.8	27.0	14.3	3.2	71.4	40.6	50.8	49.2
97918	VALE	88.5	84.1	0.2	0.2	1.1	1.3	14.3	21.3	7.1	7.1	8.2	7.6	6.0	23.3	26.8	12.0	1.9	72.7	37.1	51.6	48.4
97920	WESTFALL	83.3	74.1	8.3	7.4	0.0	0.0	12.5	14.8	0.0	0.0	0.0	3.7	22.2	55.6	18.5	0.0	0.0	100.0	32.9	100.0	0.0
	OREGON	86.6	83.7	1.6	1.7	3.2	4.0	8.0	11.2	6.5	6.2	6.3	6.8	6.8	26.7	27.5	11.1	2.1	77.0	38.0	49.6	50.4
	UNITED STATES	75.1	72.0	12.3	12.7	3.8	4.6	12.5	15.7	6.8	6.7	6.6	7.1	6.9	27.0	26.0	10.9	1.9	75.7	36.9	49.2	50.8

ZIP CODE #	POST OFFICE NAME	2009 Per Capita Income	2009 HH Income Base	2009 Household Income Distribution (%): Less than $25,000	$25,000 to $49,999	$50,000 to $99,999	$100,000 to $149,999	$150,000 or More	Median Household Income: 2009	2014	2009 National Centile	2009 State Centile	2009 Home Value Base	2009 Home Value Distribution (%): Less than $50,000	$50,000 to $89,999	$90,000 to $174,999	$175,000 to $399,999	$400,000 or More	2009 Median Home Value
97904	DREWSEY	21322	62	25.8	43.5	21.0	6.5	3.2	35884	37715	20	13	50	6.0	8.0	18.0	40.0	28.0	237500
97906	HARPER	26778	120	35.8	31.7	27.5	5.0	0.0	35000	37049	18	10	78	11.5	25.6	23.1	21.8	17.9	135000
97907	HUNTINGTON	16757	342	35.4	40.1	21.6	2.3	0.6	31049	31998	10	4	238	20.6	23.1	39.1	8.4	8.8	98824
97908	IRONSIDE	16971	34	41.2	32.4	23.5	2.9	0.0	31485	35000	11	5	22	9.1	27.3	18.2	27.3	18.2	150000
97909	JAMIESON	16116	24	33.3	29.2	29.2	8.3	0.0	42322	45000	40	36	17	0.0	0.0	23.5	58.8	17.6	243750
97910	JORDAN VALLEY	18112	242	31.8	32.6	30.6	2.9	2.1	35695	38789	20	11	161	11.2	25.5	39.8	9.9	13.7	115500
97911	JUNTURA	16674	42	38.1	31.0	26.2	4.8	0.0	35000	35741	18	10	27	11.1	25.9	22.2	25.9	14.8	131250
97913	NYSSA	14412	1871	32.7	34.8	28.3	2.4	1.8	35725	37793	20	12	1263	11.6	18.1	42.9	22.1	5.3	127486
97914	ONTARIO	18168	5793	29.7	31.4	30.9	5.2	2.8	39149	41447	30	23	3496	7.8	9.0	40.4	34.8	7.9	161850
97917	RIVERSIDE	15474	22	22.7	40.9	31.8	4.5	0.0	40000	38596	33	25	14	7.1	14.3	35.7	14.3	28.6	162500
97918	VALE	16922	1595	30.6	30.8	31.8	4.5	2.3	40403	42931	34	27	1101	6.5	11.9	39.5	33.0	9.1	155469
97920	WESTFALL	25057	9	44.4	33.3	22.2	0.0	0.0	32265	32265	12	5	6	0.0	0.0	0.0	66.7	33.3	237500
	OREGON	26362		20.3	25.9	37.7	10.2	5.9	53483	55628				4.6	3.5	17.3	54.4	20.2	249991
	UNITED STATES	27277		20.9	24.4	35.3	11.7	7.6	54719	56938				9.3	13.1	31.6	32.6	13.5	162279

ZIP CODE	FINANCIAL SERVICES				THE HOME						ENTERTAINMENT						PERSONAL			
					Home Improvements		Furnishings													
# POST OFFICE NAME	Auto Loan	Home Loan	Invest-ments	Retire-ment Plans	Home Repair	Lawn & Garden	Comput-ers & Hard-ware-Personal	Major Appli-ances	TV, Radio, Sound Equip-ment	Furni-ture	Dine out/ Carry out	Sports Equip-ment	Fees & Tickets	Toys & Games	Travel	Cable TV	Apparel & Services	Auto Repairs	Health Insur-ance	Pets & Supplies
97904 DREWSEY	85	58	93	58	61	90	65	81	67	53	67	67	47	66	64	74	43	75	85	99
97906 HARPER	73	50	80	50	52	77	55	69	58	45	57	57	41	57	55	63	37	64	73	85
97907 HUNTINGTON	61	46	63	44	48	65	49	60	54	45	52	44	40	53	48	59	35	56	66	70
97908 IRONSIDE	71	49	78	49	51	75	55	68	57	44	56	56	40	56	54	62	36	63	72	83
97909 JAMIESON	88	60	96	60	63	93	67	83	70	54	69	69	49	68	67	76	45	78	88	102
97910 JORDAN VALLEY	78	54	86	54	56	83	60	74	62	48	61	61	44	61	59	68	40	69	78	91
97911 JUNTURA	72	50	80	50	52	76	55	69	58	45	57	57	41	56	55	63	37	64	73	85
97913 NYSSA	76	57	70	54	57	73	60	70	64	56	63	54	48	64	57	68	42	67	72	83
97914 ONTARIO	78	66	70	66	66	75	74	74	75	69	75	57	66	75	70	78	52	76	79	88
97917 RIVERSIDE	77	53	84	53	55	81	59	73	61	47	60	60	43	60	58	66	39	68	77	90
97918 VALE	84	63	85	61	64	85	66	79	70	60	69	62	53	70	65	75	46	74	82	95
97920 WESTFALL	58	40	64	40	42	61	44	55	46	36	46	46	33	45	44	50	30	52	58	68
OREGON	96	93	95	94	93	95	95	95	95	94	95	74	93	95	95	95	66	96	96	112
UNITED STATES	100	100	100	100	100	100	100	100	100	100	100	100	100	100	100	100	100	100	100	100

ZIP CODE #	POST OFFICE NAME	COUNTY FIPS CODE	POPULATION 2000	POPULATION 2009	POPULATION 2014	2000-2009 ANNUAL RATE % Rate	2000-2009 ANNUAL RATE State Centile	HOUSEHOLDS 2000	HOUSEHOLDS 2009	HOUSEHOLDS 2014	HOUSEHOLDS % Annual Rate 2000-2009	HOUSEHOLDS 2009 Average HH Size	FAMILIES 2000	FAMILIES 2009	FAMILIES % Annual Rate 2000-2009
15001	ALIQUIPPA	007	36066	34871	33925	-0.4	23	14621	14440	14137	-0.1	2.39	10285	9882	-0.4
15003	AMBRIDGE	007	12927	12114	11663	-0.7	8	5786	5532	5361	-0.5	2.17	3538	3264	-0.9
15005	BADEN	007	9345	9135	8913	-0.2	38	3756	3750	3684	0.0	2.38	2742	2680	-0.2
15007	BAKERSTOWN	003	229	273	280	1.9	94	85	103	107	2.1	2.65	60	70	1.7
15009	BEAVER	007	14965	14765	14497	-0.1	46	6000	6049	5969	0.1	2.29	4079	3993	-0.2
15010	BEAVER FALLS	007	29789	28654	27860	-0.4	23	11608	11359	11090	-0.2	2.38	7996	7587	-0.6
15012	BELLE VERNON	129	17293	16924	16552	-0.2	38	7166	7116	7004	-0.1	2.34	4990	4811	-0.4
15014	BRACKENRIDGE	003	3543	3414	3333	-0.4	23	1507	1466	1437	-0.3	2.25	932	869	-0.8
15015	BRADFORDWOODS	003	1176	1195	1188	0.2	61	471	492	495	0.5	2.43	381	389	0.2
15017	BRIDGEVILLE	003	15539	15761	15756	0.2	61	6598	6813	6843	0.3	2.13	4008	3984	-0.1
15018	BUENA VISTA	003	629	597	580	-0.6	13	266	259	254	-0.3	2.22	208	198	-0.5
15019	BULGER	125	1816	1974	2027	0.9	83	696	770	797	1.1	2.55	506	542	0.7
15021	BURGETTSTOWN	125	9112	9271	9299	0.2	61	3598	3737	3782	0.4	2.43	2590	2605	0.1
15022	CHARLEROI	125	11802	11211	11002	-0.6	13	5147	4967	4907	-0.4	2.21	3244	3019	-0.8
15024	CHESWICK	003	8982	8652	8450	-0.4	23	3604	3537	3480	-0.2	2.39	2495	2376	-0.5
15025	CLAIRTON	003	17937	17062	16623	-0.5	19	7435	7208	7064	-0.3	2.32	4821	4525	-0.7
15026	CLINTON	007	3363	3298	3234	-0.2	38	1235	1245	1230	0.1	2.65	947	930	-0.2
15027	CONWAY	007	2297	2214	2143	-0.4	23	992	985	963	-0.1	2.23	659	631	-0.5
15030	CREIGHTON	003	1127	1053	1022	-0.7	8	500	479	468	-0.5	2.11	292	268	-0.9
15031	CUDDY	003	506	530	530	0.5	70	207	222	224	0.8	2.39	138	142	0.3
15033	DONORA	125	5769	5506	5402	-0.5	19	2515	2429	2400	-0.4	2.19	1470	1353	-0.9
15034	DRAVOSBURG	003	2015	1867	1806	-0.8	6	948	902	879	-0.5	2.07	563	512	-1.0
15035	EAST MC KEESPORT	003	2311	2168	2101	-0.7	8	1062	1025	1003	-0.4	2.12	626	578	-0.9
15037	ELIZABETH	003	11741	11275	11011	-0.4	23	4605	4525	4452	-0.2	2.45	3418	3268	-0.5
15042	FREEDOM	007	8221	8529	8453	0.4	68	3076	3305	3310	0.8	2.58	2375	2484	0.5
15043	GEORGETOWN	007	2858	2739	2669	-0.5	19	1024	1010	991	-0.1	2.71	814	785	-0.4
15044	GIBSONIA	003	23123	25988	26528	1.3	90	8196	9348	9602	1.4	2.74	6393	7132	1.2
15045	GLASSPORT	003	4993	4704	4570	-0.6	13	2187	2119	2074	-0.3	2.20	1356	1260	-0.8
15049	HARWICK	003	982	998	997	0.2	61	473	495	498	0.5	2.02	280	281	0.0
15050	HOOKSTOWN	007	2190	2128	2088	-0.3	29	781	779	770	0.0	2.71	607	591	-0.3
15051	INDIANOLA	003	452	443	434	-0.2	38	190	187	184	-0.2	2.27	147	141	-0.4
15052	INDUSTRY	007	4179	4034	3935	-0.4	23	1597	1588	1562	-0.1	2.51	1236	1199	-0.3
15055	LAWRENCE	125	688	743	769	0.8	80	340	378	394	1.2	1.97	225	240	0.7
15056	LEETSDALE	003	1215	1118	1077	-0.9	4	570	534	519	-0.7	2.09	338	303	-1.2
15057	MC DONALD	125	12499	13328	13476	0.7	77	4832	5223	5309	0.8	2.55	3536	3726	0.6
15059	MIDLAND	007	4811	4421	4241	-0.9	4	2034	1905	1837	-0.7	2.30	1304	1185	-1.0
15060	MIDWAY	125	678	674	668	-0.1	46	277	281	280	0.2	2.40	200	196	-0.2
15061	MONACA	007	13650	13336	13002	-0.3	29	5463	5466	5367	0.0	2.39	3868	3774	-0.3
15062	MONESSEN	129	8673	8088	7820	-0.8	6	3917	3735	3637	-0.5	2.14	2454	2250	-0.9
15063	MONONGAHELA	125	12658	12307	12160	-0.3	29	5279	5233	5207	-0.1	2.31	3610	3459	-0.5
15064	MORGAN	003	432	484	493	1.2	88	201	228	233	1.4	2.12	137	150	1.0
15065	NATRONA HEIGHTS	003	11999	11440	11148	-0.5	19	5205	5074	4979	-0.3	2.24	3447	3248	-0.6
15066	NEW BRIGHTON	007	13675	12933	12489	-0.6	13	5475	5267	5113	-0.4	2.41	3737	3484	-0.8
15067	NEW EAGLE	125	2262	2217	2197	-0.2	38	962	963	960	0.0	2.30	650	627	-0.4
15068	NEW KENSINGTON	129	41726	39401	38257	-0.6	13	17507	16899	16520	-0.4	2.29	11442	10712	-0.7
15071	OAKDALE	003	9886	10799	10914	1.0	85	4068	4528	4602	1.2	2.37	2743	2951	0.8
15074	ROCHESTER	007	9608	9182	8909	-0.5	19	3907	3818	3725	-0.2	2.35	2555	2418	-0.6
15076	RUSSELLTON	003	1014	999	980	-0.2	38	436	443	440	0.2	2.25	321	316	-0.2
15077	SHIPPINGPORT	007	138	135	133	-0.2	38	52	52	52	0.0	2.58	40	39	-0.3
15078	SLOVAN	125	407	441	456	0.9	83	171	190	197	1.1	2.32	118	126	0.7
15083	SUTERSVILLE	129	1207	1161	1137	-0.4	23	516	513	508	-0.1	2.26	363	350	-0.4
15084	TARENTUM	003	10498	10115	9884	-0.4	23	4414	4361	4295	-0.1	2.30	2900	2758	-0.5
15085	TRAFFORD	129	8190	7885	7713	-0.4	23	3386	3364	3323	-0.1	2.34	2399	2313	-0.4
15086	WARRENDALE	003	303	306	305	0.1	57	115	118	118	0.3	2.55	93	93	0.0
15089	WEST NEWTON	129	8276	8009	7834	-0.4	23	3344	3307	3260	-0.1	2.41	2377	2284	-0.4
15090	WEXFORD	003	18352	20215	20471	1.1	87	6341	7039	7151	1.1	2.83	5030	5511	1.0
15101	ALLISON PARK	003	24698	24589	24300	0.0	52	8952	9085	9030	0.2	2.60	6874	6830	-0.1
15102	BETHEL PARK	003	31074	29666	28955	-0.5	19	12227	11957	11759	-0.2	2.45	8828	8388	-0.6
15104	BRADDOCK	003	11324	9744	9266	-1.6	1	4655	4039	3854	-1.5	2.39	2891	2408	-2.0
15106	CARNEGIE	003	18703	17957	17548	-0.4	23	8664	8498	8355	-0.2	2.09	5062	4770	-0.6
15108	CORAOPOLIS	003	39237	40365	40183	0.3	64	15425	16145	16160	0.5	2.36	10410	10606	0.2
15110	DUQUESNE	003	7342	6579	6315	-1.2	1	3183	2918	2822	-0.9	2.22	1857	1620	-1.5
15112	EAST PITTSBURGH	003	4503	4214	4077	-0.7	8	2136	2047	1996	-0.5	2.05	1156	1053	-1.0
15116	GLENSHAW	003	14325	13707	13375	-0.5	19	5622	5511	5416	-0.2	2.48	4230	4044	-0.5
15120	HOMESTEAD	003	20493	19326	18810	-0.6	13	8943	8614	8445	-0.4	2.21	5414	4999	-0.9
15122	WEST MIFFLIN	003	21698	20322	19695	-0.7	8	9170	8795	8587	-0.5	2.29	6250	5787	-0.8
15126	IMPERIAL	003	6805	7121	7168	0.5	70	2649	2832	2870	0.7	2.50	1841	1895	0.3
15129	SOUTH PARK	003	11412	11062	10846	-0.3	29	4308	4281	4230	-0.1	2.56	3170	3066	-0.4
15131	MCKEESPORT	003	8740	8445	8268	-0.4	23	3746	3709	3656	-0.1	2.23	2475	2361	-0.5
15132	MCKEESPORT	003	26131	23941	23093	-0.9	4	10715	9926	9606	-0.8	2.28	6540	5802	-1.3
15133	MCKEESPORT	003	7025	6652	6474	-0.6	13	3004	2927	2872	-0.3	2.26	2002	1879	-0.7
15135	MCKEESPORT	003	5692	5420	5280	-0.5	19	2302	2251	2212	-0.2	2.41	1659	1571	-0.6
15136	MC KEES ROCKS	003	22598	21768	21318	-0.4	23	9458	9244	9101	-0.2	2.30	5981	5655	-0.6
15137	NORTH VERSAILLES	003	11212	10769	10524	-0.4	23	4969	4903	4829	-0.1	2.17	3126	2961	-0.6
15139	OAKMONT	003	6911	6624	6459	-0.5	19	3118	3046	2989	-0.3	2.04	1710	1594	-0.8
15140	PITCAIRN	003	3672	3418	3308	-0.8	6	1671	1594	1553	-0.5	2.14	910	826	-1.0
15142	PRESTO	003	646	1183	1288	6.8	100	233	467	513	7.8	2.53	162	313	7.4
15143	SEWICKLEY	003	18091	18679	18619	0.3	64	7084	7468	7495	0.6	2.46	5081	5232	0.3
15144	SPRINGDALE	003	4648	4412	4296	-0.6	13	2009	1945	1904	-0.3	2.26	1290	1202	-0.8
15145	TURTLE CREEK	003	7613	6934	6672	-1.0	3	3400	3177	3079	-0.7	2.11	1915	1704	-1.3
15146	MONROEVILLE	003	29404	28068	27356	-0.5	19	12399	12090	11864	-0.3	2.24	8056	7579	-0.7
15147	VERONA	003	20451	19246	18698	-0.7	8	8556	8282	8109	-0.4	2.29	5771	5390	-0.7
15148	WILMERDING	003	2860	2615	2519	-1.0	3	1346	1261	1223	-0.7	2.05	705	625	-1.3
15201	PITTSBURGH	003	14441	13168	12680	-1.0	3	6598	6167	5977	-0.7	2.09	3558	3169	-1.2
15202	PITTSBURGH	003	20987	19689	19082	-0.7	8	9957	9546	9317	-0.5	2.03	5027	4572	-1.0
15203	PITTSBURGH	003	9327	9170	9017	-0.2	38	4811	4888	4855	0.2	1.83	1817	1701	-0.7
15204	PITTSBURGH	003	9588	8924	8638	-0.8	6	3854	3667	3574	-0.5	2.43	2553	2340	-0.9
15205	PITTSBURGH	003	22887	21480	20895	-0.7	8	10278	9894	9695	-0.4	2.16	5900	5413	-0.9
15206	PITTSBURGH	003	32729	31238	30503	-0.5	19	14940	14504	14235	-0.3	2.06	7544	6954	-0.9
15207	PITTSBURGH	003	13140	11933	11478	-1.0	3	5626	5205	5032	-0.8	2.25	3425	3046	-1.3
15208	PITTSBURGH	003	13407	11608	11046	-1.5	1	5583	4941	4735	-1.3	2.34	3365	2857	-1.8
15209	PITTSBURGH	003	13019	12258	11921	-0.6	13	5452	5246	5133	-0.4	2.31	3506	3271	-0.7
15210	PITTSBURGH	003	31429	28489	27395	-1.1	2	12770	11859	11486	-0.8	2.39	8003	7112	-1.3
15211	PITTSBURGH	003	12429	11663	11302	-0.7	8	5891	5681	5553	-0.4	2.05	2783	2530	-1.0
15212	PITTSBURGH	003	31556	29305	28356	-0.8	6	13884	13174	12831	-0.6	2.17	7567	6841	-1.1
	PENNSYLVANIA					0.3					0.4	2.45			0.1
	UNITED STATES					1.0					1.1	2.59			0.9

ZIP CODE #	POST OFFICE NAME	RACE (%) White 2000	White 2009	Black 2000	Black 2009	Asian/Pacific 2000	Asian/Pacific 2009	% Hispanic Origin 2000	% Hispanic Origin 2009	2009 AGE DISTRIBUTION (%) 0-4	5-9	10-14	15-19	20-24	25-44	45-64	65-84	85+	18+	MEDIAN AGE 2009	% 2009 Males	% 2009 Females
15001	ALIQUIPPA	86.0	84.9	12.7	13.5	0.3	0.4	0.7	0.9	5.5	5.6	5.9	6.3	5.0	23.3	29.4	16.1	2.7	78.9	43.8	47.5	52.5
15003	AMBRIDGE	90.5	87.6	7.3	9.7	0.4	0.6	1.3	1.7	5.9	5.6	5.3	5.3	5.6	22.7	27.3	18.1	4.1	79.9	44.6	47.6	52.4
15005	BADEN	98.3	97.3	0.7	1.1	0.3	0.6	0.6	0.9	4.7	5.5	6.3	5.8	3.7	21.4	32.6	16.6	3.3	79.7	46.5	47.5	52.5
15007	BAKERSTOWN	97.8	95.6	1.8	2.9	0.0	0.4	1.3	2.2	8.1	6.6	7.7	7.0	5.1	26.0	27.5	10.6	1.5	72.5	39.4	48.4	51.6
15009	BEAVER	97.0	96.0	2.0	2.7	0.4	0.5	0.7	1.0	4.4	4.7	5.5	5.9	4.5	19.9	31.0	19.0	5.0	81.6	48.3	47.0	53.0
15010	BEAVER FALLS	90.8	88.3	7.1	9.0	0.5	0.7	0.6	0.8	5.2	5.4	5.7	7.4	7.1	21.7	28.8	15.6	3.2	79.8	43.1	47.3	52.7
15012	BELLE VERNON	96.9	96.0	2.0	2.5	0.3	0.5	0.5	0.7	5.2	5.5	5.9	5.8	4.5	22.9	29.7	17.0	3.5	79.9	45.2	47.6	52.4
15014	BRACKENRIDGE	95.0	92.3	3.4	5.6	0.3	0.4	0.5	0.7	5.4	5.2	5.2	5.7	5.3	26.4	27.6	14.3	4.9	80.5	42.6	45.9	54.1
15015	BRADFORDWOODS	98.4	97.4	0.1	0.1	1.0	1.8	0.8	1.1	3.9	4.9	6.3	5.7	2.7	17.6	38.0	19.4	1.6	81.2	50.2	48.7	51.3
15017	BRIDGEVILLE	93.6	90.0	4.1	6.4	1.3	2.1	0.8	1.3	5.5	5.5	5.6	5.1	5.2	24.0	28.8	15.1	5.1	80.1	44.4	46.8	53.2
15018	BUENA VISTA	97.0	95.5	2.2	3.5	0.2	0.3	0.2	0.2	5.0	5.4	6.0	5.9	4.5	21.8	31.3	16.4	3.7	79.9	45.9	48.4	51.6
15019	BULGER	97.1	96.5	1.8	2.2	0.1	0.2	0.2	0.3	5.8	6.0	6.4	6.7	5.0	24.2	30.1	13.4	2.4	77.5	42.0	49.1	50.9
15021	BURGETTSTOWN	97.5	96.8	1.4	1.8	0.2	0.2	1.1	1.4	5.4	5.7	6.0	6.3	4.8	23.1	30.7	15.3	2.8	79.1	44.1	49.5	50.5
15022	CHARLEROI	96.8	95.9	2.1	2.7	0.3	0.5	0.7	0.9	5.0	5.1	5.4	5.4	4.4	23.3	29.1	17.7	4.7	81.2	46.0	47.2	52.8
15024	CHESWICK	98.1	97.1	0.6	1.1	0.7	1.1	0.5	0.7	4.9	5.3	5.9	5.7	4.5	22.5	30.8	17.3	3.1	80.1	45.7	48.3	51.7
15025	CLAIRTON	83.7	79.4	14.1	17.7	0.7	1.1	0.7	0.9	5.1	5.5	5.9	6.4	5.4	23.1	30.2	14.8	3.6	79.2	43.9	46.9	53.1
15026	CLINTON	98.5	98.0	0.4	0.6	0.1	0.2	0.9	1.2	5.7	6.5	6.9	7.0	4.8	24.4	32.5	11.0	1.2	76.5	41.5	50.4	49.6
15027	CONWAY	98.3	97.7	1.3	1.8	0.0	0.0	0.5	0.7	4.8	5.1	5.6	5.4	4.2	22.4	29.5	19.8	3.3	81.6	46.7	47.9	52.1
15030	CREIGHTON	97.0	95.4	1.8	2.9	0.2	0.3	0.1	0.1	5.2	5.8	5.9	4.7	3.9	24.9	29.7	13.7	6.2	80.4	44.7	46.2	53.8
15031	CUDDY	95.3	92.5	3.4	5.5	0.2	0.6	0.2	0.2	5.5	5.7	6.0	6.2	4.9	22.6	30.9	15.5	2.6	79.1	44.3	47.9	52.1
15033	DONORA	82.4	78.7	14.6	17.8	0.3	0.4	2.0	2.7	5.9	5.6	5.9	6.5	5.4	22.7	27.3	15.6	5.1	78.7	43.4	45.9	54.1
15034	DRAVOSBURG	98.7	98.1	0.5	0.9	0.0	0.0	0.6	0.9	5.5	5.7	5.9	4.9	3.4	23.9	30.5	17.1	3.0	79.8	45.4	45.8	54.2
15035	EAST MC KEESPORT	95.6	93.3	2.9	4.7	0.1	0.2	0.7	1.0	5.4	5.6	5.7	5.0	4.5	24.9	30.3	15.1	3.5	80.3	44.2	48.8	51.2
15037	ELIZABETH	97.0	95.4	1.9	3.2	0.3	0.4	0.3	0.4	4.6	4.9	5.4	6.1	4.6	21.4	31.0	18.5	3.4	81.2	46.9	47.3	52.7
15042	FREEDOM	97.1	96.4	1.7	2.1	0.2	0.4	0.5	0.6	5.6	6.0	6.5	6.5	5.1	24.8	31.4	12.7	1.5	78.0	41.9	49.3	50.7
15043	GEORGETOWN	97.8	97.2	0.6	0.8	0.1	0.1	0.7	1.1	6.2	6.7	7.1	6.9	5.4	25.6	31.0	9.7	1.2	75.6	39.1	49.8	50.2
15044	GIBSONIA	98.0	96.7	0.5	0.8	1.0	1.6	0.5	0.8	6.8	7.3	8.0	7.4	4.3	22.5	31.0	10.5	2.2	72.6	41.1	48.7	51.3
15045	GLASSPORT	98.2	97.4	0.6	0.9	0.2	0.4	0.8	1.2	4.8	4.7	4.9	6.1	6.1	24.1	28.8	16.9	3.6	81.9	44.4	47.4	52.6
15049	HARWICK	99.8	99.7	0.0	0.0	0.0	0.0	0.1	0.1	3.9	4.2	4.7	5.0	4.0	22.6	31.4	21.0	3.1	84.2	48.2	47.3	52.7
15050	HOOKSTOWN	98.7	98.3	0.2	0.3	0.2	0.3	0.6	0.9	6.4	7.1	7.3	6.9	4.8	26.6	30.3	9.5	1.1	74.6	39.2	50.0	50.0
15051	INDIANOLA	96.0	93.7	1.5	2.5	2.0	3.4	0.7	0.9	4.5	7.4	10.2	7.9	2.9	22.8	29.6	11.3	3.4	72.0	42.3	49.0	51.0
15052	INDUSTRY	97.1	96.0	1.9	2.7	0.1	0.2	1.1	1.5	4.8	5.1	5.7	6.1	5.0	22.5	32.3	16.3	2.2	80.5	45.5	49.1	50.9
15055	LAWRENCE	93.9	91.9	3.9	5.1	1.2	1.7	0.9	1.2	5.1	5.7	6.2	5.4	3.5	28.1	29.7	14.1	2.2	79.8	43.2	45.0	55.0
15056	LEETSDALE	89.3	84.5	7.2	11.1	0.0	0.0	1.6	2.4	5.3	5.0	4.9	5.3	6.7	23.2	28.7	17.2	3.8	81.8	44.7	46.2	53.8
15057	MC DONALD	96.3	95.0	2.6	3.5	0.3	0.5	0.4	0.5	6.1	6.5	6.8	6.3	4.9	24.0	30.2	12.9	2.2	76.5	42.0	49.2	50.8
15059	MIDLAND	83.1	79.6	14.3	17.5	0.0	0.1	2.7	3.4	6.4	6.4	6.4	6.5	5.5	22.8	27.3	15.6	3.2	76.8	42.0	47.5	52.5
15060	MIDWAY	98.7	98.2	0.7	0.9	0.1	0.3	0.6	0.9	5.2	5.2	5.5	5.6	4.7	24.0	31.0	15.7	3.0	80.7	44.8	48.7	51.3
15061	MONACA	96.6	95.3	2.3	3.2	0.3	0.5	0.7	1.0	5.3	5.4	5.7	7.3	5.7	23.9	29.1	15.4	2.3	79.8	42.6	48.6	51.4
15062	MONESSEN	83.7	80.7	14.0	16.7	0.2	0.3	0.8	1.1	5.1	5.4	5.7	5.8	4.6	20.8	27.9	19.2	5.4	80.0	46.8	46.5	53.5
15063	MONONGAHELA	96.9	95.9	2.0	2.6	0.2	0.3	0.7	0.9	4.5	4.7	5.0	5.8	5.1	21.6	30.6	18.5	4.2	82.1	47.2	47.4	52.6
15064	MORGAN	97.2	95.5	2.3	3.9	0.2	0.4	0.2	0.4	7.2	7.2	7.2	6.6	5.8	25.6	27.9	10.3	2.1	74.0	38.9	50.8	49.2
15065	NATRONA HEIGHTS	95.2	92.9	3.4	5.2	0.4	0.7	0.5	0.7	5.4	5.6	5.8	5.3	4.6	23.0	30.1	16.6	3.6	79.9	45.2	47.1	52.9
15066	NEW BRIGHTON	91.8	89.3	6.1	8.2	0.2	0.3	0.4	0.6	5.9	5.9	6.2	6.7	6.3	24.5	29.0	13.3	2.0	77.9	41.0	48.0	52.0
15067	NEW EAGLE	97.0	96.2	1.1	1.4	0.6	0.9	0.1	0.1	4.7	4.9	5.5	6.5	4.6	24.5	30.5	15.8	3.0	81.0	44.5	47.9	52.1
15068	NEW KENSINGTON	92.4	91.0	5.9	6.9	0.3	0.5	0.6	0.8	5.2	5.5	5.7	6.1	5.2	23.1	29.5	16.2	3.5	79.7	44.4	47.7	52.3
15071	OAKDALE	94.0	90.9	2.3	3.7	2.9	4.2	0.9	1.3	6.4	6.2	6.2	5.9	6.0	27.6	28.9	11.4	1.5	77.4	40.0	48.7	51.3
15074	ROCHESTER	91.2	88.5	7.0	9.3	0.1	0.2	0.5	0.7	5.1	5.1	5.4	6.1	5.4	24.9	29.4	15.8	2.8	80.6	43.5	48.2	51.8
15076	RUSSELLTON	98.4	97.8	0.4	0.5	0.4	0.6	0.6	0.9	5.0	5.3	6.0	6.4	4.5	23.9	32.7	13.6	2.5	79.8	44.3	48.9	51.1
15077	SHIPPINGPORT	99.3	98.5	0.0	0.0	0.0	0.0	0.7	0.7	7.4	7.4	8.1	6.7	5.2	25.9	28.1	9.6	1.5	71.9	37.3	49.6	50.4
15078	SLOVAN	98.3	97.7	1.5	2.0	0.0	0.0	0.2	0.5	5.4	5.4	5.7	6.3	5.0	23.1	29.7	16.1	3.2	79.4	44.3	48.5	51.5
15083	SUTERSVILLE	98.9	98.4	0.7	1.1	0.1	0.1	0.2	0.2	4.2	4.1	4.6	5.6	4.7	24.5	30.2	18.8	3.3	83.5	46.3	48.1	51.9
15084	TARENTUM	96.4	94.6	1.9	3.0	0.5	0.8	0.7	0.9	5.1	5.3	5.4	5.8	5.5	25.1	31.4	13.9	2.5	80.8	43.4	47.9	52.1
15085	TRAFFORD	98.6	98.1	0.5	0.7	0.4	0.6	0.4	0.6	5.1	5.5	6.0	6.4	4.9	21.5	30.7	16.8	3.2	79.5	45.4	48.5	51.5
15086	WARRENDALE	97.7	96.7	0.7	1.0	1.3	2.0	0.3	0.3	5.9	6.9	7.8	7.2	4.9	22.9	33.0	9.8	1.6	73.9	41.9	51.6	48.4
15089	WEST NEWTON	98.0	97.5	1.0	1.2	0.2	0.3	0.4	0.6	5.0	5.3	5.8	6.1	4.7	24.3	31.3	14.7	2.9	80.1	44.2	48.1	51.9
15090	WEXFORD	94.4	91.8	1.5	2.4	3.2	4.7	0.8	1.1	6.3	7.7	9.1	8.3	4.5	20.4	33.3	8.8	1.6	71.3	40.9	49.0	51.0
15101	ALLISON PARK	96.6	94.7	1.0	1.6	1.7	2.7	0.6	0.8	5.4	6.1	7.0	7.4	5.4	20.9	30.8	14.5	2.5	76.8	43.4	48.4	51.6
15102	BETHEL PARK	97.1	95.5	1.1	1.7	1.1	1.8	0.5	0.7	5.0	5.6	6.4	6.4	4.5	20.9	31.7	16.5	3.0	78.9	45.7	48.1	51.9
15104	BRADDOCK	46.0	37.3	50.9	59.6	0.3	0.4	1.1	1.3	7.0	7.3	7.5	8.0	6.4	21.8	26.0	13.1	2.8	73.2	38.2	45.6	54.4
15106	CARNEGIE	94.2	91.5	3.3	5.1	1.1	1.8	0.8	1.1	5.1	5.2	5.4	5.2	4.8	24.5	29.6	16.7	3.5	81.1	44.9	47.4	52.6
15108	CORAOPOLIS	92.9	89.7	4.4	6.5	1.4	2.2	0.9	1.2	5.3	5.6	6.1	7.5	6.2	23.9	29.8	13.4	2.3	78.9	42.1	48.4	51.6
15110	DUQUESNE	49.0	38.6	47.7	58.0	0.1	0.2	0.7	0.9	9.1	7.7	6.1	7.0	7.6	21.6	23.7	13.7	3.5	73.2	36.8	44.8	55.2
15112	EAST PITTSBURGH	85.1	78.8	12.1	17.7	0.5	0.8	0.6	0.8	6.0	5.6	5.4	5.7	5.5	25.7	28.3	14.2	3.5	79.5	41.9	47.3	52.7
15116	GLENSHAW	97.4	96.1	0.4	0.7	1.5	2.3	0.6	0.8	4.9	5.4	6.2	6.5	4.4	21.4	31.1	17.5	2.5	79.2	45.7	48.1	51.9
15120	HOMESTEAD	84.8	81.5	12.6	15.3	0.9	1.3	0.7	1.0	5.2	5.3	5.6	6.0	5.3	22.9	28.9	17.1	3.8	80.2	44.8	46.9	53.1
15122	WEST MIFFLIN	89.4	85.4	9.1	12.7	0.3	0.4	0.5	0.7	5.2	5.2	5.5	6.0	5.1	22.5	29.3	17.6	3.7	80.4	45.3	47.0	53.0
15126	IMPERIAL	96.1	93.7	1.9	3.4	0.8	1.3	0.6	0.8	6.4	6.6	6.6	6.3	5.7	27.5	30.0	9.5	1.3	76.4	39.3	48.7	51.3
15129	SOUTH PARK	94.4	91.5	3.8	5.9	0.9	1.4	0.6	0.9	6.5	6.9	7.0	6.5	5.6	25.9	30.2	10.0	1.5	75.4	39.2	48.5	51.5
15131	MCKEESPORT	97.4	96.0	1.7	2.8	0.4	0.6	0.4	0.5	4.0	4.4	4.7	6.2	4.9	21.7	31.7	18.7	3.7	83.6	47.7	47.6	52.4
15132	MCKEESPORT	74.3	68.1	22.7	28.6	0.1	0.2	1.4	1.8	6.6	6.6	6.4	6.4	5.6	22.3	26.1	15.6	4.4	76.3	41.7	46.2	53.8
15133	MCKEESPORT	98.5	97.6	1.0	1.6	0.1	0.2	0.6	0.9	4.2	4.4	4.9	6.5	5.0	23.6	30.4	17.6	3.5	82.5	45.9	47.7	52.3
15135	MCKEESPORT	97.9	96.7	1.1	1.9	0.3	0.5	0.5	0.8	4.9	5.1	5.6	6.2	5.4	23.0	31.2	15.5	3.1	80.8	44.9	48.1	51.9
15136	MC KEES ROCKS	90.7	86.9	7.0	10.0	0.9	1.4	0.7	0.9	5.7	5.8	5.9	6.0	5.4	24.2	29.1	14.4	3.4	78.7	42.8	48.0	52.0
15137	NORTH VERSAILLES	87.9	83.8	9.7	13.0	0.8	1.2	0.5	0.6	5.2	5.0	5.3	5.6	4.8	23.8	29.5	17.4	3.4	81.1	45.2	47.2	52.8
15139	OAKMONT	97.8	96.7	0.9	1.5	0.5	0.8	0.6	0.9	4.5	4.4	5.0	5.1	5.3	21.6	28.1	18.4	7.6	82.9	47.8	44.6	55.4
15140	PITCAIRN	98.1	97.2	0.4	0.7	0.4	0.7	0.5	0.8	6.2	5.9	5.6	5.2	6.4	27.1	28.5	12.9	2.4	79.4	40.3	48.0	52.0
15142	PRESTO	96.7	95.2	1.1	1.7	1.1	1.7	0.5	0.8	4.6	5.2	6.0	5.9	3.6	20.3	35.3	16.2	2.9	80.1	47.5	48.1	51.9
15143	SEWICKLEY	94.4	91.7	3.2	4.8	1.3	2.2	0.6	0.8	5.1	5.9	7.0	6.6	4.2	19.7	33.2	15.3	3.0	77.4	45.8	47.3	52.7
15144	SPRINGDALE	99.1	98.7	0.3	0.4	0.1	0.2	0.2	0.2	4.3	4.4	4.9	6.4	6.1	22.9	31.5	16.2	3.4	82.2	45.6	47.8	52.2
15145	TURTLE CREEK	92.6	88.9	5.0	7.7	0.9	1.5	0.6	0.8	5.5	5.0	4.9	5.2	5.9	25.6	26.9	16.4	4.7	81.5	43.4	45.1	54.9
15146	MONROEVILLE	85.6	79.1	8.3	12.2	4.4	6.7	0.8	1.0	4.6	4.9	5.3	5.5	5.0	23.0	30.0	17.7	4.0	81.6	46.1	46.9	53.1
15147	VERONA	81.0	77.1	17.5	21.1	0.3	0.6	0.4	0.6	5.4	5.6	5.8	6.1	5.4	22.6	29.7	15.8	3.6	79.3	44.3	47.1	52.9
15148	WILMERDING	92.9	89.2	5.2	8.3	0.2	0.3	1.0	1.3	5.7	5.3	5.1	5.8	6.6	25.2	27.9	14.1	4.2	80.2	42.3	47.2	52.8
15201	PITTSBURGH	77.8	70.3	19.0	25.7	1.3	1.9	0.7	0.9	5.0	5.1	5.2	5.7	5.8	23.1	29.1	16.6	4.5	81.2	45.1	46.1	53.9
15202	PITTSBURGH	93.9	90.7	4.1	6.5	0.6	1.0	0.7	1.0	5.3	4.9	5.2	5.7	7.7	28.0	26.6	13.5	3.0	81.0	40.4	47.0	53.0
15203	PITTSBURGH	94.9	92.2	3.0	4.9	0.7	1.1	1.0	1.4	3.1	2.7	2.7	3.5	12.3	30.1	23.8	17.8	3.9	89.7	41.1	49.5	50.5
15204	PITTSBURGH	72.5	62.9	24.5	33.7	0.6	0.9	0.9	1.1	6.6	6.7	6.8	6.8	6.1	24.8	27.5	12.4	2.3	75.5	39.3	47.1	52.9
15205	PITTSBURGH	88.4	86.4	8.8	9.9	1.2	1.9	0.7	1.0	5.9	5.8	5.7	5.4	5.7	27.4	28.7	12.9	2.4	79.3	41.0	46.8	53.2
15206	PITTSBURGH	43.6	37.8	50.8	55.8	2.4	3.2	1.5	1.9	5.6	5.5	5.5	6.7	7.6	26.7	26.2	13.5	2.7	79.3	39.3	46.2	53.8
15207	PITTSBURGH	79.0	73.9	18.9	23.7	0.5	0.8	0.9	1.2	5.3	5.5	5.6	6.1	5.2	23.2	29.2	16.2	3.8	79.9	44.4	46.1	53.9
15208	PITTSBURGH	25.1	23.9	71.9	72.8	0.9	1.3	0.9	1.1	6.4	6.6	6.7	7.6	6.6	22.7	27.8	13.4	2.3	75.4	39.8	45.6	54.4
15209	PITTSBURGH	97.8	96.7	0.6	1.0	0.5	0.9	0.7	0.9	5.4	5.5	5.8	6.1	5.7	24.8	29.4	14.6	2.7	79.5	42.8	47.9	52.1
15210	PITTSBURGH	75.2	70.8	22.2	26.1	0.6	0.9	0.8	1.0	6.3	6.4	6.5	6.7	6.6	26.0	26.7	12.4	2.3	76.7	38.4	47.0	53.0
15211	PITTSBURGH	91.5	87.6	6.0	9.0	0.8	1.3	0.8	1.0	4.4	4.1	4.0	4.6	8.1	32.0	26.7	13.9	2.3	85.1	39.1	49.2	50.8
15212	PITTSBURGH	75.7	68.8	21.7	28.1	0.5	0.7	0.9	1.1	5.9	5.5	5.3	6.5	6.9	25.2	27.8	13.9	2.9	79.8	40.9	48.1	51.9
	PENNSYLVANIA	85.4	83.2	10.0	10.7	1.8	2.7	3.2	4.2	5.8	6.0	6.3	7.1	6.5	24.8	27.8	13.1	2.6	77.8	40.4	48.5	51.5
	UNITED STATES	75.1	72.0	12.3	12.7	3.8	4.6	12.5	15.7	6.8	6.7	6.6	7.1	6.9	27.0	26.0	10.9	1.9	75.7	36.9	49.2	50.8

ZIP CODE #	POST OFFICE NAME	2009 Per Capita Income	2009 HH Income Base	2009 HOUSEHOLD INCOME DISTRIBUTION (%) Less than $25,000	$25,000 to $49,999	$50,000 to $99,999	$100,000 to $149,999	$150,000 or More	MEDIAN HOUSEHOLD INCOME 2009	2014	2009 National Centile	2009 State Centile	2009 Home Value Base	2009 HOME VALUE DISTRIBUTION (%) Less than $50,000	$50,000 to $89,999	$90,000 to $174,999	$175,000 to $399,999	$400,000 or More	2009 Median Home Value
15001	ALIQUIPPA	24315	14440	23.9	26.6	37.7	8.5	3.2	49418	52429	60	60	11166	10.5	15.3	47.2	25.0	2.0	133144
15003	AMBRIDGE	23280	5532	30.6	28.7	32.2	5.8	2.8	41129	44964	36	31	3634	7.4	32.9	44.6	13.1	2.1	103065
15005	BADEN	31197	3750	16.4	26.0	37.0	11.3	9.4	60064	60671	77	78	3074	2.6	12.1	42.4	36.4	6.6	155455
15007	BAKERSTOWN	22762	103	27.2	22.3	33.0	13.6	3.9	50879	54609	63	64	72	2.8	5.6	44.4	45.8	1.4	168750
15009	BEAVER	28249	6049	18.5	24.9	40.7	11.4	4.6	57327	58643	74	75	4372	3.0	8.0	43.3	42.0	3.7	166325
15010	BEAVER FALLS	23996	11359	22.1	28.9	38.5	7.2	3.4	49038	52017	59	59	8114	9.6	19.3	45.1	23.9	2.0	131107
15012	BELLE VERNON	23293	7116	23.8	33.3	33.5	6.3	3.1	43596	46897	44	41	5516	14.4	18.5	41.8	23.0	2.3	116973
15014	BRACKENRIDGE	23323	1466	27.0	30.0	37.1	3.8	2.1	41543	46119	38	33	996	11.6	45.7	41.0	1.7	0.0	80875
15015	BRADFORDWOODS	59718	492	8.7	9.1	21.7	25.4	35.0	115801	117580	98	99	474	0.6	0.8	7.0	65.2	26.4	310400
15017	BRIDGEVILLE	31911	6813	14.6	25.0	42.6	11.5	6.2	60174	61368	78	78	4911	2.6	10.6	48.4	32.6	5.8	149019
15018	BUENA VISTA	29420	259	16.6	23.6	48.3	7.7	3.9	60897	61808	79	80	239	10.5	17.6	51.5	19.7	0.8	122384
15019	BULGER	21077	770	22.2	33.2	37.3	5.2	2.1	46253	49161	52	52	656	24.7	14.5	39.0	20.1	1.7	111957
15021	BURGETTSTOWN	23316	3737	22.3	26.6	42.3	6.3	2.5	50978	53159	64	64	3000	13.6	19.2	40.7	24.3	2.2	122181
15022	CHARLEROI	22792	4967	27.8	30.1	34.5	5.7	1.9	41952	45473	39	35	3539	13.6	36.1	38.8	10.9	0.7	90500
15024	CHESWICK	27337	3537	16.8	28.3	42.3	7.5	5.1	53908	56264	69	70	2910	10.5	14.2	47.9	22.7	4.7	132955
15025	CLAIRTON	24933	7208	27.2	23.8	36.6	8.2	4.3	48718	52362	58	59	5137	20.8	27.7	29.0	19.2	3.3	93148
15026	CLINTON	23075	1245	16.9	28.1	43.9	9.1	2.1	54978	56591	71	71	1080	18.9	9.6	31.4	35.2	4.9	146500
15027	CONWAY	25471	985	23.5	27.4	40.8	5.1	3.2	49039	52263	59	59	741	2.0	19.0	66.1	12.4	0.4	126161
15030	CREIGHTON	23449	479	23.8	34.7	35.5	4.6	1.5	41370	46330	37	32	348	23.9	35.1	37.6	3.4	0.0	75926
15031	CUDDY	21552	222	16.7	39.6	34.7	7.7	1.4	42359	47041	40	36	163	3.1	22.7	46.6	23.9	3.7	122039
15033	DONORA	20608	2429	33.9	29.7	31.6	3.7	1.1	36209	39485	21	11	1546	35.2	41.7	19.1	3.8	0.3	61546
15034	DRAVOSBURG	24064	902	28.7	30.0	36.0	4.1	1.1	41511	45747	38	33	567	21.5	44.8	33.3	0.4	0.0	73765
15035	EAST MC KEESPORT	22235	1025	29.8	33.3	31.8	3.8	1.4	37909	40981	26	17	645	12.9	47.8	36.9	2.5	0.0	79943
15037	ELIZABETH	25667	4525	18.2	28.0	42.7	7.2	3.9	53176	55668	68	69	3849	12.2	18.4	53.0	14.9	1.6	119221
15042	FREEDOM	24756	3305	15.9	25.9	44.2	11.0	3.0	60174	60138	78	78	2911	12.4	12.7	38.7	34.6	1.7	148799
15043	GEORGETOWN	20518	1010	20.5	30.7	40.3	6.8	1.7	48816	51814	58	59	883	14.0	20.5	35.2	24.9	5.3	124856
15044	GIBSONIA	36171	9348	10.1	15.7	43.1	15.3	15.8	76588	77149	90	93	8219	2.2	4.1	29.8	49.2	14.8	215594
15045	GLASSPORT	21307	2119	30.6	27.5	38.4	3.0	0.5	42156	46372	40	36	1386	22.8	48.7	26.0	2.1	0.4	67048
15049	HARWICK	29672	495	19.8	30.9	36.8	8.7	3.8	49484	52017	60	61	395	14.9	16.5	51.9	14.4	2.3	115625
15050	HOOKSTOWN	20819	779	21.3	28.5	40.7	7.3	2.2	50170	52818	62	62	691	15.5	16.9	37.2	27.8	2.6	130491
15051	INDIANOLA	41663	187	15.0	20.9	32.1	16.0	16.0	75751	77797	90	92	168	4.2	7.7	31.0	36.3	20.8	227273
15052	INDUSTRY	24029	1588	14.5	33.9	40.8	8.2	2.5	51621	53990	65	66	1399	5.5	19.3	54.7	19.9	0.6	129472
15055	LAWRENCE	38022	378	9.3	20.6	51.9	11.9	6.3	70857	71695	87	90	311	1.6	1.9	61.1	35.4	0.0	155720
15056	LEETSDALE	24725	534	32.2	30.3	28.1	5.6	3.7	38300	42371	28	19	329	11.9	41.6	33.1	10.9	2.4	86806
15057	MC DONALD	24670	5223	19.2	26.7	40.3	9.5	4.2	53697	55613	69	69	4155	9.7	17.0	38.2	31.3	3.8	134282
15059	MIDLAND	20362	1905	32.9	32.7	27.5	5.1	1.8	36594	38889	22	13	1141	23.6	22.3	40.1	12.6	0.5	95952
15060	MIDWAY	22529	281	19.9	29.9	43.8	3.9	2.5	50110	52263	61	62	209	9.1	20.1	59.8	11.0	0.0	112010
15061	MONACA	25987	5466	18.6	26.9	39.7	10.8	4.0	54643	57100	71	71	3884	6.5	12.8	49.6	29.9	1.2	137986
15062	MONESSEN	21991	3735	34.1	29.0	30.5	3.9	2.4	36452	39104	22	12	2853	24.3	31.4	37.6	6.7	0.0	79650
15063	MONONGAHELA	25164	5233	20.9	29.0	39.9	7.2	3.0	50109	52707	61	62	4159	11.6	23.1	46.1	17.6	1.6	117399
15064	MORGAN	28945	228	17.1	30.3	39.9	11.8	0.9	54641	60194	71	71	174	6.3	22.4	29.3	38.5	3.4	125000
15065	NATRONA HEIGHTS	24073	5074	25.7	27.9	38.4	5.9	2.2	46821	50832	54	54	3694	8.9	21.2	53.7	14.4	1.7	120556
15066	NEW BRIGHTON	19452	5267	28.0	32.0	34.8	4.1	1.0	40131	43637	33	26	3544	12.7	25.8	45.3	15.2	1.0	110370
15067	NEW EAGLE	20922	963	25.0	39.1	29.9	4.7	1.2	40312	43384	34	27	773	24.6	31.7	33.9	9.8	0.0	79297
15068	NEW KENSINGTON	24273	16899	25.3	28.1	36.6	7.2	2.8	46835	50417	54	54	11993	8.7	18.0	47.6	23.8	1.9	127056
15071	OAKDALE	33164	4528	9.5	22.5	46.3	14.0	7.6	67938	68803	86	88	3357	9.3	11.1	46.3	28.7	4.6	144375
15074	ROCHESTER	22320	3818	23.2	31.5	39.2	4.4	1.7	46172	49612	52	52	2649	13.9	28.7	41.3	15.1	1.1	100742
15076	RUSSELLTON	29106	443	14.4	26.4	47.0	8.8	3.4	56938	57995	74	74	346	2.3	14.2	54.6	26.6	2.3	144817
15077	SHIPPINGPORT	21650	52	21.2	25.0	46.2	5.8	1.9	53555	51773	69	69	46	19.6	19.6	32.6	26.1	2.2	118750
15078	SLOVAN	25260	190	23.7	20.5	44.7	9.5	1.6	54255	54488	70	70	154	12.3	20.1	40.9	26.6	0.0	114000
15083	SUTERSVILLE	21023	513	24.0	38.4	31.6	5.3	0.8	38389	41698	28	19	429	11.7	20.7	48.3	17.0	2.3	112652
15084	TARENTUM	22247	4361	27.6	28.6	37.5	4.6	1.8	43194	47582	43	40	3032	14.9	32.1	40.1	11.4	1.5	94044
15085	TRAFFORD	27495	3364	21.8	25.1	39.1	8.7	5.3	52452	54753	67	68	2774	4.4	12.4	50.1	28.4	4.7	143521
15086	WARRENDALE	54132	118	10.2	14.4	26.3	22.9	26.3	97885	101422	96	97	102	0.0	2.9	22.5	53.9	20.6	286364
15089	WEST NEWTON	22659	3307	25.6	30.5	34.3	6.9	2.8	44543	47878	47	44	2670	13.3	20.1	39.3	23.8	3.6	115541
15090	WEXFORD	49630	7039	9.3	12.3	29.4	16.0	33.0	97886	101170	96	97	6060	0.1	1.5	15.5	58.8	24.1	307967
15101	ALLISON PARK	34888	9085	9.3	16.1	45.2	17.5	11.8	76614	76819	90	93	7731	0.9	2.1	33.2	53.6	10.2	207581
15102	BETHEL PARK	32618	11957	11.4	20.2	43.9	16.3	8.2	69165	70053	86	89	9658	1.0	3.1	43.6	49.5	2.7	179810
15104	BRADDOCK	14967	4039	50.3	25.3	21.1	2.5	0.8	24805	25263	3	1	2075	56.5	29.6	13.3	0.5	0.0	44788
15106	CARNEGIE	29088	8498	22.3	27.8	38.6	6.5	4.8	49893	52936	61	62	5445	6.2	21.8	50.6	18.2	3.1	123336
15108	CORAOPOLIS	31520	16145	13.9	21.7	43.3	13.4	7.7	66082	67042	84	87	12071	4.4	8.9	37.3	45.0	4.4	173642
15110	DUQUESNE	14803	2918	51.2	25.2	21.1	2.1	0.3	23953	24751	3	1	1487	45.5	41.0	12.8	0.2	0.5	53778
15112	EAST PITTSBURGH	22586	2047	32.8	29.7	32.3	4.2	1.1	38657	41632	29	20	1091	14.8	46.5	36.7	2.1	0.0	77519
15116	GLENSHAW	32411	5511	11.6	19.0	48.3	14.1	7.0	69311	71017	86	89	4908	1.7	3.5	46.7	44.4	3.7	172151
15120	HOMESTEAD	22392	8614	31.8	27.0	34.7	4.7	1.9	41135	44935	36	31	5678	17.7	33.0	42.4	6.3	0.6	88976
15122	WEST MIFFLIN	24687	8795	24.4	25.6	40.5	7.5	2.1	50083	53527	61	62	6848	9.4	24.0	56.8	9.2	0.5	107419
15126	IMPERIAL	26896	2832	17.7	23.0	45.3	9.1	5.0	58351	60766	76	77	2252	26.8	12.7	29.1	27.9	3.5	127200
15129	SOUTH PARK	27781	4281	9.9	21.6	53.0	11.0	4.6	63995	64535	82	84	3187	0.7	5.4	53.3	39.3	1.3	161557
15131	MCKEESPORT	27400	3709	18.6	27.8	42.5	7.3	3.9	53048	55673	68	68	2863	7.2	21.6	54.6	14.8	1.7	121396
15132	MCKEESPORT	17641	9926	38.4	31.0	26.4	3.3	0.9	31361	32958	10	4	5836	34.9	41.1	21.6	2.2	0.2	59933
15133	MCKEESPORT	23674	2927	22.9	31.8	38.7	4.8	1.8	45644	50295	50	49	2443	14.2	45.7	37.4	2.7	0.0	83678
15135	MCKEESPORT	28141	2251	14.3	23.3	48.2	9.1	5.2	61724	63170	80	81	1724	7.3	16.2	49.3	25.1	2.0	128933
15136	MC KEES ROCKS	24879	9244	26.8	27.6	33.8	7.6	4.3	45335	50109	49	48	6115	15.6	24.8	33.6	23.2	2.8	109920
15137	NORTH VERSAILLES	23591	4903	25.1	32.0	35.9	5.0	2.0	42941	47522	42	39	3462	7.9	35.7	50.0	6.4	0.0	95838
15139	OAKMONT	33323	3046	17.8	25.6	41.8	8.6	6.3	56142	58975	73	73	1768	3.2	10.6	37.4	41.2	7.6	172500
15140	PITCAIRN	20554	1594	33.1	30.5	32.1	4.0	0.4	35777	38398	20	10	786	13.0	52.4	29.6	5.0	0.0	79375
15142	PRESTO	34771	467	7.1	27.0	48.4	7.9	9.6	65263	64900	84	86	399	1.8	14.3	39.3	11.5	33.1	157083
15143	SEWICKLEY	43932	7468	12.0	19.7	34.8	14.1	19.3	73771	75408	89	91	6176	2.7	5.7	25.9	37.3	28.5	242000
15144	SPRINGDALE	25865	1945	20.1	28.6	42.8	6.2	2.3	50869	53380	63	64	1354	4.9	25.3	58.5	10.9	0.4	112630
15145	TURTLE CREEK	24468	3177	30.0	27.6	34.7	4.5	3.2	41842	46156	39	34	1470	18.2	47.3	29.7	4.5	0.3	74815
15146	MONROEVILLE	31030	12090	17.2	23.7	42.0	9.8	7.1	59610	61059	77	78	8375	2.1	9.6	55.7	29.6	3.0	144037
15147	VERONA	25109	8282	21.4	27.3	41.8	6.9	2.6	51083	54035	64	65	6178	5.0	23.9	62.7	8.0	0.4	109507
15148	WILMERDING	19456	1261	33.7	37.4	26.4	1.9	0.6	33643	34830	15	6	592	28.9	49.0	20.6	0.3	1.2	66076
15201	PITTSBURGH	21903	6167	36.1	26.9	30.4	4.7	1.9	35449	37901	19	9	3704	23.9	40.7	30.8	4.0	0.6	72807
15202	PITTSBURGH	26158	9546	25.5	30.2	36.1	5.5	2.8	44647	48899	47	45	4747	4.8	19.6	58.8	15.0	1.8	121517
15203	PITTSBURGH	24203	4888	35.1	31.9	27.3	3.5	2.2	35124	36880	18	9	2361	19.7	31.1	36.3	12.1	0.7	88880
15204	PITTSBURGH	21068	3667	27.0	27.8	38.9	5.1	1.2	45186	49653	49	47	2598	15.9	38.0	43.9	2.2	0.0	86354
15205	PITTSBURGH	28973	9894	20.6	26.6	40.1	8.3	4.4	52347	54944	67	67	6231	5.8	18.8	52.9	19.5	3.0	121529
15206	PITTSBURGH	25361	14504	35.9	26.2	27.8	5.4	4.8	36862	39757	23	13	6189	12.5	30.5	34.5	16.6	6.0	101167
15207	PITTSBURGH	21223	5205	32.9	27.4	34.0	4.2	1.5	38314	42253	28	19	3623	20.6	37.4	38.8	2.9	0.3	80748
15208	PITTSBURGH	23622	4941	40.2	25.4	22.0	5.6	6.7	31685	33338	11	4	2494	20.6	29.0	20.2	21.9	8.2	90851
15209	PITTSBURGH	25972	5246	19.3	29.3	40.5	8.1	2.8	51227	54205	64	65	3786	8.7	19.9	47.6	23.7	0.1	133130
15210	PITTSBURGH	19143	11859	33.0	32.2	29.0	4.1	1.6	35680	37713	20	10	7683	24.0	48.2	26.4	1.4	0.0	69015
15211	PITTSBURGH	27096	5681	27.4	29.1	33.7	5.8	4.0	43378	47521	43	41	3102	17.5	37.2	32.0	9.2	4.1	83318
15212	PITTSBURGH	20699	13174	35.7	28.3	30.1	4.1	1.8	35896	38816	20	11	7426	21.6	32.7	39.8	5.3	0.6	83312
	PENNSYLVANIA	26913		21.5	25.3	36.9	10.2	6.1	53225	55819				7.5	12.2	35.6	36.1	8.5	161438
	UNITED STATES	27277		20.9	24.4	35.3	11.7	7.6	54719	56938				9.3	13.1	31.6	32.6	13.5	162279

ZIP CODE #	POST OFFICE NAME	FINANCIAL SERVICES: Auto Loan	FINANCIAL SERVICES: Home Loan	FINANCIAL SERVICES: Investments	FINANCIAL SERVICES: Retirement Plans	THE HOME: Home Improvements: Home Repair	THE HOME: Home Improvements: Lawn & Garden	THE HOME: Furnishings: Computers & Hardware Personal	THE HOME: Furnishings: Major Appliances	THE HOME: Furnishings: TV, Radio, Sound Equipment	THE HOME: Furnishings: Furniture	ENTERTAINMENT: Dine out/Carry out	ENTERTAINMENT: Sports Equipment	ENTERTAINMENT: Fees & Tickets	ENTERTAINMENT: Toys & Games	ENTERTAINMENT: Travel	ENTERTAINMENT: Cable TV	PERSONAL: Apparel & Services	PERSONAL: Auto Repairs	PERSONAL: Health Insurance	PERSONAL: Pets & Supplies
15001	ALIQUIPPA	82	83	80	83	82	91	79	84	84	78	83	61	81	83	81	88	57	83	92	99
15003	AMBRIDGE	70	66	65	66	66	74	71	71	75	67	73	52	69	73	69	79	51	73	81	84
15005	BADEN	99	117	114	117	118	120	101	110	104	103	104	79	114	103	112	107	73	105	116	125
15007	BAKERSTOWN	76	89	84	87	88	82	86	83	84	84	85	65	92	85	90	84	61	84	83	96
15009	BEAVER	88	99	100	98	101	106	90	97	94	92	93	68	98	90	98	98	65	95	108	111
15010	BEAVER FALLS	84	81	81	81	81	91	81	85	85	77	84	63	80	84	81	89	58	84	93	100
15012	BELLE VERNON	80	77	82	76	78	90	74	83	79	71	78	60	73	78	76	84	53	79	91	96
15014	BRACKENRIDGE	75	74	65	75	71	81	75	75	78	71	77	57	74	78	73	81	53	76	84	89
15015	BRADFORDWOODS	174	242	291	249	269	224	203	217	186	226	184	161	248	179	243	177	139	200	193	237
15017	BRIDGEVILLE	96	101	100	102	101	104	99	100	101	98	101	75	103	100	102	104	71	101	108	117
15018	BUENA VISTA	86	105	95	104	101	106	90	95	92	91	93	70	102	93	99	95	65	93	103	110
15019	BULGER	78	80	73	78	79	84	73	79	77	74	77	56	75	78	75	80	53	76	85	92
15021	BURGETTSTOWN	82	82	79	82	82	93	78	85	82	74	81	63	78	82	80	87	56	82	94	99
15022	CHARLEROI	73	67	74	66	68	81	68	75	74	64	73	55	66	71	69	80	50	74	86	88
15024	CHESWICK	95	95	98	94	96	107	89	99	94	88	93	71	90	94	93	99	64	95	107	114
15025	CLAIRTON	85	79	83	80	80	90	80	85	85	79	83	63	78	83	79	89	57	84	92	101
15026	CLINTON	90	92	83	93	90	95	85	91	86	84	86	68	86	88	87	88	59	87	92	106
15027	CONWAY	75	85	81	83	85	92	75	83	81	74	80	58	83	79	82	86	55	80	95	95
15030	CREIGHTON	84	62	85	61	64	88	67	82	75	60	72	61	55	73	65	82	48	77	90	96
15031	CUDDY	67	77	73	75	77	82	69	74	73	68	72	53	75	71	74	77	50	72	84	85
15033	DONORA	72	55	65	55	56	72	63	69	69	57	66	52	53	68	59	74	45	68	77	82
15034	DRAVOSBURG	77	66	79	64	67	85	66	78	73	61	71	57	60	71	67	79	48	74	87	91
15035	EAST MC KEESPORT	79	57	80	56	59	83	62	77	70	56	67	58	50	68	60	77	45	72	84	91
15037	ELIZABETH	86	93	93	92	93	104	84	94	90	83	89	67	90	88	91	95	61	90	105	108
15042	FREEDOM	91	94	86	96	92	101	89	94	91	85	90	71	90	92	91	94	62	91	99	110
15043	GEORGETOWN	89	82	73	79	80	84	77	82	80	80	80	60	73	83	74	83	55	79	83	98
15044	GIBSONIA	132	162	150	163	159	149	139	143	135	146	137	110	157	138	151	133	98	137	138	164
15045	GLASSPORT	65	63	62	63	63	71	65	67	69	62	68	49	64	68	64	73	47	67	76	78
15049	HARWICK	78	89	85	87	89	97	79	87	85	78	84	61	87	83	86	90	58	84	99	99
15050	HOOKSTOWN	90	83	75	82	82	88	79	85	82	79	81	62	74	84	76	84	55	81	86	100
15051	INDIANOLA	128	159	163	163	163	150	135	143	130	144	131	106	154	129	152	127	94	135	135	164
15052	INDUSTRY	83	90	86	90	90	99	82	90	86	79	85	65	86	85	87	90	59	86	98	103
15055	LAWRENCE	96	119	106	119	114	117	101	106	103	103	104	79	117	104	112	105	73	103	112	123
15056	LEETSDALE	71	67	69	67	68	77	71	73	76	67	75	53	70	74	70	81	52	74	84	85
15057	MC DONALD	89	93	88	92	92	97	86	92	89	86	89	67	89	89	89	92	62	89	97	107
15059	MIDLAND	70	60	64	60	60	73	64	68	70	61	68	50	59	68	61	75	46	68	77	81
15060	MIDWAY	72	81	76	79	80	87	72	79	77	71	76	55	78	75	77	81	52	76	89	90
15061	MONACA	86	92	83	92	89	97	87	89	89	84	89	67	91	89	89	93	62	89	98	105
15062	MONESSEN	67	64	66	64	64	76	62	69	69	61	68	49	63	67	64	74	46	68	79	81
15063	MONONGAHELA	78	83	81	82	83	92	79	84	84	76	83	60	83	82	82	90	58	83	96	97
15064	MORGAN	78	91	86	89	90	84	88	85	86	85	87	66	94	86	91	86	62	86	85	98
15065	NATRONA HEIGHTS	75	76	74	75	76	85	74	79	78	71	77	57	75	77	75	82	53	77	88	91
15066	NEW BRIGHTON	71	63	63	64	62	73	66	69	69	61	68	53	61	69	63	73	46	68	75	82
15067	NEW EAGLE	81	59	82	57	61	85	64	79	71	57	69	59	51	70	62	79	46	74	86	93
15068	NEW KENSINGTON	77	78	76	79	78	86	77	80	81	75	80	59	78	79	78	85	55	80	89	94
15071	OAKDALE	112	117	106	118	113	110	112	110	111	115	112	85	116	114	113	110	79	110	110	129
15074	ROCHESTER	75	73	71	73	72	82	73	77	77	69	76	57	72	76	73	81	52	76	85	90
15076	RUSSELLTON	85	103	93	102	100	104	88	94	91	89	91	69	100	91	97	94	64	91	101	108
15077	SHIPPINGPORT	90	82	73	80	81	84	78	82	81	81	81	60	74	84	74	83	55	80	83	98
15078	SLOVAN	77	87	83	86	88	95	77	85	83	77	82	60	85	81	84	88	57	82	97	97
15083	SUTERSVILLE	66	69	71	68	70	79	63	71	68	61	67	50	66	66	67	72	46	68	80	82
15084	TARENTUM	76	68	68	69	68	80	71	75	76	66	74	57	67	75	69	80	51	75	84	89
15085	TRAFFORD	87	93	90	93	93	100	88	93	92	86	91	68	92	90	92	96	63	91	101	108
15086	WARRENDALE	184	228	233	234	234	216	194	205	186	207	188	153	221	185	217	183	135	194	194	234
15089	WEST NEWTON	79	77	79	77	77	88	74	82	78	71	77	60	74	78	76	83	53	79	88	95
15090	WEXFORD	187	232	235	243	237	210	199	203	188	213	190	159	230	192	219	180	140	193	182	232
15101	ALLISON PARK	121	145	145	147	148	142	129	134	127	134	127	99	144	126	141	126	91	130	134	154
15102	BETHEL PARK	105	124	122	125	126	126	109	116	111	113	111	84	123	109	120	113	78	112	123	133
15104	BRADDOCK	55	42	44	42	41	53	48	50	55	48	53	36	43	53	44	60	36	52	59	61
15106	CARNEGIE	83	87	84	87	87	94	84	88	88	82	87	64	87	86	86	92	60	87	98	102
15108	CORAOPOLIS	103	114	108	115	113	113	108	108	108	108	108	82	115	108	112	109	76	108	112	127
15110	DUQUESNE	49	36	35	37	34	44	45	43	51	44	50	32	40	50	39	55	34	47	51	54
15112	EAST PITTSBURGH	66	58	56	59	57	65	67	64	69	62	68	49	62	68	61	72	47	67	71	77
15116	GLENSHAW	106	124	120	124	124	127	109	116	111	112	111	85	122	110	120	114	78	113	123	134
15120	HOMESTEAD	71	66	69	66	66	78	67	72	73	64	71	53	65	71	67	78	49	72	83	85
15122	WEST MIFFLIN	76	82	80	81	82	90	76	82	81	75	80	58	81	79	81	86	55	80	93	95
15126	IMPERIAL	98	102	91	101	99	98	96	97	95	98	95	75	97	98	96	94	66	95	95	114
15129	SOUTH PARK	99	109	97	109	105	101	101	100	99	104	101	78	107	101	104	98	71	100	98	118
15131	MCKEESPORT	83	91	89	89	91	101	82	91	88	80	87	64	88	86	88	93	60	87	103	104
15132	MCKEESPORT	63	49	55	49	49	62	55	59	61	52	60	44	49	60	52	66	41	60	68	71
15133	MCKEESPORT	76	75	80	74	76	89	71	81	77	68	76	58	72	75	75	83	52	77	91	93
15135	MCKEESPORT	92	101	98	101	101	104	93	97	95	94	95	72	99	94	99	97	66	96	103	113
15136	MC KEES ROCKS	84	77	79	77	76	87	80	83	85	77	83	62	77	84	78	89	58	83	91	98
15137	NORTH VERSAILLES	70	73	70	73	73	81	69	74	74	68	73	53	72	72	72	78	50	73	84	86
15139	OAKMONT	94	102	100	102	102	106	97	100	100	97	99	73	103	97	102	103	69	100	109	116
15140	PITCAIRN	61	57	56	57	57	64	62	62	65	58	64	46	59	64	59	69	44	63	71	73
15142	PRESTO	115	135	140	136	141	143	118	130	121	124	121	90	133	117	132	125	84	124	140	147
15143	SEWICKLEY	142	168	177	170	175	169	149	158	149	157	149	115	168	145	165	151	106	153	163	180
15144	SPRINGDALE	79	80	80	80	81	90	79	84	85	76	84	60	81	82	81	90	58	83	96	97
15145	TURTLE CREEK	74	66	66	67	66	75	75	73	78	69	76	55	69	76	70	82	53	76	83	87
15146	MONROEVILLE	94	102	101	102	102	106	98	100	100	97	100	74	104	98	103	103	70	100	109	117
15147	VERONA	79	82	77	82	81	88	79	82	83	78	83	60	82	82	81	87	57	82	92	96
15148	WILMERDING	58	47	49	47	47	55	57	56	61	52	59	41	50	59	51	65	41	58	64	66
15201	PITTSBURGH	64	57	59	57	57	66	64	63	69	60	68	46	60	66	61	73	47	66	74	76
15202	PITTSBURGH	73	68	65	70	67	71	77	71	79	73	78	55	75	77	73	80	54	76	79	86
15203	PITTSBURGH	65	50	54	52	51	58	68	60	68	60	67	48	57	66	58	70	47	65	67	73
15204	PITTSBURGH	72	71	62	72	68	77	71	71	75	69	74	53	71	74	69	78	51	72	80	86
15205	PITTSBURGH	87	87	82	88	85	91	88	87	90	86	90	67	89	90	88	93	63	89	95	104
15206	PITTSBURGH	74	64	63	67	63	69	76	70	80	73	79	54	72	78	70	82	55	76	79	85
15207	PITTSBURGH	67	62	63	63	62	73	65	68	71	63	69	49	63	68	64	76	48	69	79	81
15208	PITTSBURGH	76	70	72	72	70	76	77	74	82	78	80	55	75	78	74	85	56	78	83	90
15209	PITTSBURGH	83	85	80	85	83	90	84	85	87	81	86	64	85	87	84	90	60	86	93	100
15210	PITTSBURGH	67	58	55	59	56	66	64	63	69	61	67	48	60	68	59	73	46	66	72	77
15211	PITTSBURGH	78	70	68	71	69	76	80	76	82	75	81	58	75	81	74	85	57	80	85	91
15212	PITTSBURGH	64	56	56	56	55	64	64	62	68	59	67	47	59	66	59	71	46	65	71	75
	PENNSYLVANIA	94	95	95	95	95	100	94	96	96	91	95	73	94	96	94	99	67	95	101	113
	UNITED STATES	100	100	100	100	100	100	100	100	100	100	100	100	100	100	100	100	100	100	100	100

ZIP CODE #	POST OFFICE NAME	COUNTY FIPS CODE	POPULATION 2000	POPULATION 2009	POPULATION 2014	2000-2009 ANNUAL RATE % Rate	2000-2009 ANNUAL RATE State Centile	HOUSEHOLDS 2000	HOUSEHOLDS 2009	HOUSEHOLDS 2014	HOUSEHOLDS % Annual Rate 2000-2009	HOUSEHOLDS 2009 Average HH Size	FAMILIES 2000	FAMILIES 2009	FAMILIES % Annual Rate 2000-2009
15213	PITTSBURGH	003	28119	27507	27087	-0.2	38	10368	10182	10027	-0.2	1.81	2817	2545	-1.1
15214	PITTSBURGH	003	17881	15964	15289	-1.2	1	6899	6275	6048	-1.0	2.50	4525	3956	-1.4
15215	PITTSBURGH	003	13733	13276	12987	-0.4	23	5799	5690	5593	-0.2	2.29	3598	3404	-0.6
15216	PITTSBURGH	003	26271	25075	24418	-0.5	19	11758	11460	11235	-0.3	2.17	6663	6207	-0.8
15217	PITTSBURGH	003	25850	24791	24203	-0.5	19	11795	11521	11309	-0.3	2.09	6091	5648	-0.8
15218	PITTSBURGH	003	14793	13988	13596	-0.6	13	7112	6903	6762	-0.3	2.02	3713	3417	-0.9
15219	PITTSBURGH	003	19787	18009	17465	-1.0	3	7043	6283	6050	-1.2	1.92	3237	2705	-1.9
15220	PITTSBURGH	003	18099	17164	16677	-0.6	13	7894	7624	7452	-0.4	2.20	4693	4337	-0.8
15221	PITTSBURGH	003	35635	32224	30964	-1.1	2	16466	15220	14721	-0.8	2.09	8980	7923	-1.3
15222	PITTSBURGH	003	1979	2217	2246	1.2	88	811	976	1004	2.0	1.28	161	195	2.1
15223	PITTSBURGH	003	8204	7781	7581	-0.6	13	3649	3542	3471	-0.3	2.17	2210	2053	-0.8
15224	PITTSBURGH	003	12112	10901	10486	-1.1	2	5617	5220	5066	-0.8	2.06	2683	2320	-1.6
15225	PITTSBURGH	003	1232	1093	1043	-1.3	1	624	563	541	-1.1	1.94	314	268	-1.7
15226	PITTSBURGH	003	14840	14001	13595	-0.6	13	6334	6141	6015	-0.3	2.27	4043	3766	-0.8
15227	PITTSBURGH	003	29531	28028	27258	-0.6	13	12976	12602	12349	-0.3	2.20	8061	7522	-0.7
15228	PITTSBURGH	003	17069	16464	16093	-0.4	23	7062	6912	6789	-0.2	2.32	4505	4249	-0.6
15229	PITTSBURGH	003	14169	13560	13245	-0.5	19	6056	5940	5843	-0.2	2.23	3861	3638	-0.6
15232	PITTSBURGH	003	11343	10986	10748	-0.3	29	6511	6370	6256	-0.2	1.63	1704	1539	-1.1
15233	PITTSBURGH	003	4866	4592	4483	-0.6	13	1436	1318	1271	-0.9	2.09	688	603	-1.4
15234	PITTSBURGH	003	14861	14082	13702	-0.6	13	6378	6214	6096	-0.3	2.24	4131	3868	-0.7
15235	PITTSBURGH	003	37921	35176	34014	-0.8	6	16104	15359	14976	-0.5	2.27	10921	10050	-0.9
15236	PITTSBURGH	003	30638	29579	28967	-0.4	23	12450	12249	12067	-0.2	2.37	8835	8417	-0.5
15237	PITTSBURGH	003	40365	39422	38721	-0.3	29	16454	16478	16313	0.0	2.32	11157	10795	-0.4
15238	PITTSBURGH	003	12770	13042	12937	0.2	61	5024	5178	5158	0.3	2.45	3636	3671	0.1
15239	PITTSBURGH	003	21071	20555	20195	-0.3	29	7940	7942	7860	0.0	2.58	6111	5959	-0.3
15241	PITTSBURGH	003	20695	20053	19619	-0.3	29	7308	7248	7144	-0.1	2.70	5967	5808	-0.3
15243	PITTSBURGH	003	13182	13138	12972	0.0	52	5107	5186	5153	0.2	2.41	3713	3659	-0.2
15260	PITTSBURGH	003	46	44	43	-0.5	19	18	17	17	-0.6	2.47	7	7	0.0
15275	PITTSBURGH	003	69	69	69	0.0	52	30	31	31	0.4	2.23	18	18	0.0
15282	PITTSBURGH	003	1	1	1	0.0	52	1	1	1	0.0	1.00	0	0	0.0
15301	WASHINGTON	125	50025	51006	51200	0.2	61	20171	20779	21016	0.3	2.31	13263	13176	-0.1
15310	ALEPPO	059	355	339	330	-0.5	19	136	134	131	-0.2	2.53	100	95	-0.6
15311	AMITY	125	1337	1333	1320	0.0	52	500	512	512	0.3	2.57	394	393	0.0
15312	AVELLA	125	3789	3744	3694	-0.1	46	1419	1438	1432	0.1	2.59	1109	1095	-0.1
15313	BEALLSVILLE	125	307	306	303	0.0	52	122	124	124	0.2	2.47	92	91	-0.1
15314	BENTLEYVILLE	125	3961	3868	3829	-0.3	29	1649	1639	1633	-0.1	2.33	1116	1071	-0.4
15317	CANONSBURG	125	32657	35707	36757	1.0	85	12642	14058	14582	1.2	2.48	9296	10101	0.9
15320	CARMICHAELS	059	6328	6090	5942	-0.4	23	2591	2562	2522	-0.1	2.34	1761	1686	-0.5
15321	CECIL	125	1553	1611	1639	0.4	68	577	615	631	0.7	2.61	453	470	0.4
15322	CLARKSVILLE	059	3138	2991	2927	-0.5	19	1253	1224	1208	-0.3	2.40	873	825	-0.6
15323	CLAYSVILLE	125	4900	4826	4780	-0.2	38	1774	1782	1779	0.0	2.62	1398	1370	-0.2
15324	COKEBURG	125	543	539	535	-0.1	46	241	245	244	0.2	2.20	161	157	-0.3
15327	DILLINER	059	2335	2250	2205	-0.4	23	959	960	949	0.0	2.34	672	653	-0.3
15329	PROSPERITY	125	2015	1946	1916	-0.4	23	698	685	679	-0.2	2.70	555	532	-0.5
15330	EIGHTY FOUR	125	5020	5446	5700	0.9	83	1923	2142	2259	1.2	2.54	1500	1630	0.9
15331	ELLSWORTH	125	952	956	948	0.0	52	425	436	436	0.3	2.17	256	251	-0.2
15332	FINLEYVILLE	125	8079	7939	7926	-0.2	38	3328	3361	3383	0.1	2.36	2384	2326	-0.3
15333	FREDERICKTOWN	125	2201	2168	2150	-0.2	38	905	910	908	0.1	2.37	637	619	-0.3
15337	GRAYSVILLE	059	1018	1003	986	-0.2	38	379	383	379	0.1	2.48	289	284	-0.2
15338	GREENSBORO	059	2004	1904	1850	-0.6	13	789	773	758	-0.2	2.46	587	561	-0.5
15340	HICKORY	125	1634	1645	1642	0.1	57	622	637	641	0.3	2.58	496	496	0.0
15341	HOLBROOK	059	867	866	852	0.0	52	324	334	332	0.3	2.58	244	245	0.0
15342	HOUSTON	125	4725	4890	4948	0.4	68	2014	2134	2175	0.6	2.27	1343	1376	0.3
15344	JEFFERSON	059	1568	1518	1486	-0.3	29	621	623	616	0.0	2.41	454	444	-0.2
15345	MARIANNA	125	1734	1703	1684	-0.2	38	693	695	693	0.0	2.45	483	467	-0.4
15346	MATHER	059	833	797	776	-0.5	19	339	337	331	-0.1	2.32	227	218	-0.4
15349	MOUNT MORRIS	059	1708	1651	1616	-0.4	23	690	687	677	0.0	2.40	508	493	-0.3
15352	NEW FREEPORT	059	873	830	807	-0.5	19	323	315	307	-0.3	2.63	238	226	-0.6
15353	NINEVEH	059	96	94	93	-0.2	38	1	1	1	0.0	3.00	1	1	0.0
15357	RICES LANDING	059	2189	2043	1980	-0.7	8	880	849	829	-0.4	2.39	637	596	-0.7
15359	ROGERSVILLE	059	199	217	218	0.9	83	74	83	85	1.2	2.58	59	65	1.1
15360	SCENERY HILL	125	2148	2091	2067	-0.3	29	800	799	797	0.0	2.61	600	582	-0.3
15362	SPRAGGS	059	1333	1264	1228	-0.6	13	504	493	485	-0.2	2.56	375	358	-0.5
15363	STRABANE	125	818	865	889	0.6	74	374	407	421	0.9	2.13	233	243	0.5
15364	SYCAMORE	059	762	756	744	-0.1	46	276	283	281	0.3	2.52	216	217	0.0
15367	VENETIA	125	5615	7597	8330	3.3	98	1910	2544	2776	3.1	2.97	1562	2067	3.1
15370	WAYNESBURG	059	15276	15302	15103	0.0	52	5054	5175	5131	0.3	2.38	3388	3381	0.0
15376	WEST ALEXANDER	125	1689	1714	1722	0.2	61	639	663	672	0.4	2.55	488	493	0.1
15377	WEST FINLEY	125	920	894	883	-0.3	29	315	313	312	-0.1	2.83	249	242	-0.3
15380	WIND RIDGE	059	847	817	796	-0.4	23	327	324	318	-0.1	2.52	243	234	-0.4
15401	UNIONTOWN	051	35734	34312	33082	-0.4	23	14781	14166	13742	-0.5	2.28	9594	8905	-0.8
15410	ADAH	051	933	886	856	-0.6	13	368	356	346	-0.4	2.47	253	237	-0.7
15411	ADDISON	111	603	565	543	-0.7	8	266	255	248	-0.5	2.15	185	172	-0.8
15412	ALLENPORT	125	411	405	397	-0.2	38	183	184	182	0.1	2.16	120	116	-0.4
15413	ALLISON	051	514	508	498	-0.1	46	206	207	205	0.1	2.42	143	140	-0.2
15417	BROWNSVILLE	125	9349	9043	8841	-0.4	23	3919	3852	3792	-0.2	2.32	2566	2439	-0.5
15419	CALIFORNIA	125	4023	4374	4359	0.9	83	1407	1433	1435	0.2	2.01	548	516	-0.6
15423	COAL CENTER	125	1886	1909	1919	0.1	57	726	748	757	0.3	2.53	515	511	-0.1
15424	CONFLUENCE	111	2649	2580	2508	-0.3	29	1097	1083	1062	-0.1	2.24	752	719	-0.5
15425	CONNELLSVILLE	051	21785	21195	20613	-0.3	29	8961	8915	8744	-0.1	2.33	6024	5808	-0.4
15427	DAISYTOWN	125	2042	2024	2009	-0.1	46	848	860	859	0.2	2.35	595	583	-0.2
15428	DAWSON	051	2026	1934	1868	-0.5	19	829	815	795	-0.2	2.37	606	580	-0.5
15431	DUNBAR	051	5790	5610	5459	-0.3	29	2267	2254	2212	-0.1	2.46	1617	1563	-0.4
15432	DUNLEVY	125	149	147	145	-0.1	46	68	68	68	0.0	2.09	46	44	-0.5
15433	EAST MILLSBORO	051	1051	1047	1029	0.0	52	412	421	417	0.2	2.47	294	291	-0.1
15434	ELCO	125	56	55	54	-0.2	38	24	24	24	0.0	2.21	18	17	-0.6
15436	FAIRCHANCE	051	3237	3164	3097	-0.2	38	1294	1297	1281	0.0	2.40	906	881	-0.3
15437	FARMINGTON	051	3329	3702	3638	1.2	88	1034	1037	1023	0.0	2.49	769	750	-0.3
15438	FAYETTE CITY	051	2832	2670	2566	-0.6	13	1141	1083	1047	-0.6	2.38	830	764	-0.9
15440	GIBBON GLADE	051	258	282	277	1.0	85	96	97	95	0.1	2.13	73	72	-0.1
15442	GRINDSTONE	051	3745	3668	3579	-0.2	38	1556	1565	1542	0.1	2.32	1061	1031	-0.3
15444	HILLER	051	537	510	492	-0.6	13	224	218	212	-0.3	2.34	153	145	-0.6
15445	HOPWOOD	051	3884	3897	3821	0.0	52	1632	1665	1647	0.2	2.31	1128	1121	-0.1
15446	INDIAN HEAD	051	114	121	121	0.6	74	40	44	44	1.0	2.75	31	34	1.0
15450	LA BELLE	051	349	359	357	0.3	64	142	150	151	0.6	2.39	99	102	0.3
	PENNSYLVANIA					0.3					0.4	2.45			0.1
	UNITED STATES					1.0					1.1	2.59			0.9

ZIP CODE #	POST OFFICE NAME	RACE (%) White 2000	White 2009	Black 2000	Black 2009	Asian/Pacific 2000	Asian/Pacific 2009	% Hispanic Origin 2000	% Hispanic Origin 2009	2009 AGE DISTRIBUTION (%) 0-4	5-9	10-14	15-19	20-24	25-44	45-64	65-84	85+	18+	MEDIAN AGE 2009	% 2009 Males	% 2009 Females
15213	PITTSBURGH	67.2	57.7	15.9	20.1	12.4	17.2	2.3	2.8	1.8	1.4	1.2	22.2	34.0	18.6	9.5	8.9	2.3	94.5	23.4	50.7	49.3
15214	PITTSBURGH	56.3	51.0	41.0	46.0	0.5	0.8	0.9	1.1	7.2	7.8	7.5	7.1	5.9	24.1	25.7	12.1	2.5	72.9	37.4	45.8	54.2
15215	PITTSBURGH	95.9	93.7	1.4	2.3	1.6	2.6	1.4	1.9	5.1	5.4	6.1	6.0	5.4	21.7	30.9	16.2	3.2	79.4	45.2	47.5	52.5
15216	PITTSBURGH	93.4	90.2	2.7	4.2	2.2	3.4	1.2	1.7	5.6	5.2	5.3	5.6	7.0	29.2	27.5	12.1	2.6	80.6	39.7	48.1	51.9
15217	PITTSBURGH	88.4	82.9	3.1	4.8	6.3	9.5	1.9	2.6	4.5	4.0	4.0	4.6	8.2	31.0	25.2	14.1	4.3	84.6	39.8	47.9	52.1
15218	PITTSBURGH	80.4	73.0	16.4	22.9	1.1	1.6	1.1	1.5	5.2	4.8	4.8	5.3	7.1	26.8	30.3	13.0	2.7	82.1	42.2	46.9	53.1
15219	PITTSBURGH	32.5	31.2	63.6	63.3	1.5	2.4	1.3	2.6	4.7	4.0	3.9	15.6	16.7	21.6	19.7	11.4	2.4	84.8	29.1	47.7	52.3
15220	PITTSBURGH	86.4	81.3	6.0	8.0	5.5	8.1	0.9	1.2	5.3	4.8	5.0	5.0	5.3	26.7	27.6	16.7	3.5	81.9	43.4	47.5	52.5
15221	PITTSBURGH	46.8	42.7	49.7	53.5	1.0	1.4	1.0	1.2	6.1	6.3	6.3	6.1	5.7	23.7	28.2	14.5	3.0	77.5	41.8	44.7	55.3
15222	PITTSBURGH	66.8	53.8	30.4	42.9	1.1	1.4	1.1	1.4	1.8	1.4	1.3	14.6	11.3	27.2	23.4	16.8	2.3	95.0	39.7	53.0	47.0
15223	PITTSBURGH	98.0	97.0	0.7	1.2	0.4	0.6	0.8	1.1	5.1	5.2	5.6	6.1	5.5	25.5	28.7	15.2	3.1	80.2	43.1	47.5	52.5
15224	PITTSBURGH	62.7	59.3	32.0	34.0	2.6	3.7	1.4	1.9	5.5	5.7	5.6	5.5	7.0	28.7	25.0	14.1	2.9	79.8	38.9	45.9	54.1
15225	PITTSBURGH	97.3	96.2	1.2	2.0	0.0	0.0	0.9	1.3	4.8	5.2	5.9	5.9	3.0	25.3	30.2	16.2	3.6	80.4	45.0	49.0	51.0
15226	PITTSBURGH	96.0	94.1	1.8	2.9	0.9	1.4	0.8	1.2	5.9	6.0	5.9	5.5	4.9	26.6	28.1	14.1	2.8	78.8	41.8	46.8	53.2
15227	PITTSBURGH	97.1	95.6	1.2	1.9	0.8	1.2	0.7	1.0	4.9	4.8	5.1	5.5	5.8	25.2	29.1	15.9	3.6	81.9	44.0	47.6	52.4
15228	PITTSBURGH	96.2	94.2	0.6	0.9	2.3	3.7	0.9	1.3	5.7	6.1	6.8	6.7	5.2	21.5	30.1	13.7	4.1	76.6	43.7	46.7	53.3
15229	PITTSBURGH	97.2	95.7	1.3	2.1	0.7	1.1	0.5	0.8	5.4	5.5	5.6	5.6	5.4	25.5	28.9	14.8	3.2	79.8	43.0	47.1	52.9
15232	PITTSBURGH	78.8	70.3	7.7	11.1	10.3	14.8	3.1	4.0	2.8	1.9	1.5	2.9	17.2	44.4	17.3	9.3	2.7	92.6	31.5	50.3	49.7
15233	PITTSBURGH	25.0	18.1	71.9	78.7	0.4	0.5	2.7	2.8	4.1	4.2	4.3	4.2	9.2	40.8	24.5	7.6	1.1	84.9	36.7	66.9	33.1
15234	PITTSBURGH	97.1	95.5	1.0	1.7	1.0	1.6	0.9	1.3	5.3	5.5	5.8	5.8	5.3	25.0	28.7	15.6	3.0	79.4	43.2	47.9	52.1
15235	PITTSBURGH	73.9	66.2	23.5	30.6	0.8	1.3	0.7	0.9	5.0	5.4	5.8	5.8	4.7	21.8	30.5	17.7	3.3	80.1	45.9	46.9	53.1
15236	PITTSBURGH	96.6	95.0	1.9	3.0	0.7	1.1	0.5	0.7	4.9	5.3	5.8	5.7	4.5	21.6	30.4	18.1	3.7	80.4	46.4	47.5	52.5
15237	PITTSBURGH	95.9	93.6	0.9	1.5	2.4	3.8	0.7	1.0	4.9	5.4	6.1	5.8	4.0	21.5	31.3	17.1	4.0	79.8	46.5	47.3	52.7
15238	PITTSBURGH	93.8	90.4	0.9	1.5	4.3	6.9	0.7	1.0	4.7	6.0	7.4	7.2	3.9	17.9	33.4	16.7	2.8	77.1	46.7	48.8	51.2
15239	PITTSBURGH	95.4	93.0	2.9	4.6	0.9	1.4	0.7	1.0	6.0	6.3	6.7	6.4	5.1	25.4	29.2	13.6	1.5	77.1	41.3	48.8	51.2
15241	PITTSBURGH	94.7	91.7	0.7	1.1	3.9	6.3	0.8	1.1	5.4	6.6	8.1	7.7	4.0	17.1	32.7	15.0	3.5	74.6	45.7	48.2	51.8
15243	PITTSBURGH	96.6	94.6	0.6	1.0	2.3	3.7	0.5	0.6	4.9	5.6	6.4	6.2	4.0	17.7	30.2	18.8	6.1	78.8	48.2	45.8	54.2
15260	PITTSBURGH	84.8	75.0	2.2	4.5	10.9	15.9	2.2	2.3	4.5	4.5	4.5	4.5	6.8	29.5	20.5	18.2	6.8	86.4	40.0	47.7	52.3
15275	PITTSBURGH	89.9	82.6	2.9	5.8	5.8	10.1	1.4	1.4	7.2	5.8	5.8	5.8	10.1	30.4	26.1	8.7	0.0	75.4	36.3	47.8	52.2
15282	PITTSBURGH	100.0	100.0	0.0	0.0	0.0	0.0	0.0	0.0	0.0	0.0	0.0	0.0	100.0	0.0	0.0	0.0	0.0	100.0	22.5	0.0	100.0
15301	WASHINGTON	92.3	90.8	5.8	6.9	0.3	0.5	0.5	0.7	5.2	5.3	5.6	6.7	6.5	23.1	29.1	15.2	3.4	80.2	43.2	47.5	52.5
15310	ALEPPO	99.2	99.1	0.0	0.0	0.0	0.0	0.0	0.0	5.3	6.2	6.8	6.5	4.7	25.1	30.7	13.3	1.5	77.6	41.6	51.6	48.4
15311	AMITY	98.7	98.4	0.3	0.4	0.1	0.2	0.1	0.2	5.3	5.9	6.4	5.7	4.7	23.5	34.0	12.8	1.7	78.7	44.0	50.1	49.9
15312	AVELLA	98.3	97.9	0.6	0.7	0.1	0.1	0.2	0.3	4.6	5.2	5.9	6.6	4.4	24.3	33.6	13.5	1.9	79.8	44.3	51.1	48.9
15313	BEALLSVILLE	99.3	99.0	0.7	1.0	0.0	0.0	0.0	0.0	6.2	6.9	7.5	6.9	3.9	21.6	32.4	13.1	1.6	74.5	42.6	49.7	50.3
15314	BENTLEYVILLE	97.1	96.4	1.4	1.8	0.1	0.1	0.5	0.6	6.4	5.9	5.8	6.0	5.3	23.3	28.4	15.7	3.1	78.4	42.7	48.4	51.6
15317	CANONSBURG	95.5	94.4	2.8	3.3	0.8	1.1	0.7	0.9	5.8	6.4	7.0	6.2	4.3	21.9	30.7	15.0	2.7	76.6	43.9	48.1	51.9
15320	CARMICHAELS	98.5	98.2	0.2	0.3	0.0	0.0	0.5	0.7	5.8	5.8	5.9	6.4	5.9	25.1	29.2	13.1	2.8	78.4	41.2	49.4	50.6
15321	CECIL	99.4	99.3	0.2	0.3	0.0	0.0	0.5	0.6	5.4	6.1	6.9	6.7	3.9	25.5	33.6	10.4	1.5	76.9	42.3	49.3	50.7
15322	CLARKSVILLE	96.7	95.9	2.2	2.8	0.3	0.4	0.3	0.3	4.9	5.1	5.3	5.8	5.0	24.2	29.3	16.9	3.5	81.1	44.7	48.1	51.9
15323	CLAYSVILLE	99.2	99.0	0.2	0.2	0.1	0.1	0.2	0.2	5.7	6.2	6.7	6.4	4.9	23.3	30.8	13.7	2.4	77.0	42.5	50.1	49.9
15324	COKEBURG	98.9	98.5	0.0	0.0	0.2	0.4	0.0	0.0	5.4	5.4	5.6	5.9	5.0	23.9	26.5	18.7	3.5	80.0	44.2	47.1	52.9
15327	DILLINER	98.9	98.6	0.3	0.4	0.2	0.4	0.6	0.8	5.6	5.8	6.2	6.5	5.0	25.6	30.0	12.8	2.5	78.4	41.7	50.6	49.4
15329	PROSPERITY	98.8	98.4	0.4	0.6	0.1	0.2	0.3	0.5	5.4	6.0	7.8	6.8	4.7	24.8	29.3	12.0	3.3	76.3	41.3	49.5	50.5
15330	EIGHTY FOUR	98.3	97.8	1.0	1.2	0.2	0.3	0.4	0.5	4.8	5.5	6.4	6.2	4.1	22.1	34.6	14.7	1.7	79.4	45.6	50.1	49.9
15331	ELLSWORTH	96.0	95.0	2.3	2.9	0.1	0.2	0.6	0.9	5.8	6.0	5.6	4.7	4.7	25.1	28.9	15.5	3.8	79.6	43.3	48.0	52.0
15332	FINLEYVILLE	97.9	97.3	1.0	1.4	0.2	0.4	0.5	0.7	4.9	5.3	5.9	6.3	4.5	22.7	32.2	15.5	2.6	80.0	45.2	49.1	50.9
15333	FREDERICKTOWN	97.4	96.9	1.3	1.6	0.1	0.1	0.5	0.6	5.4	5.4	5.8	6.4	5.2	25.6	28.1	15.1	2.9	79.5	42.3	48.0	52.0
15337	GRAYSVILLE	98.6	98.3	0.6	0.8	0.0	0.0	0.4	0.5	5.2	6.2	6.1	7.6	6.4	26.8	28.1	12.1	1.6	78.2	39.3	51.4	48.6
15338	GREENSBORO	99.0	98.8	0.2	0.3	0.2	0.3	0.5	0.7	5.4	5.7	6.4	6.4	4.5	24.9	30.9	13.3	2.4	78.5	42.3	49.3	50.7
15340	HICKORY	94.9	93.4	4.6	5.9	0.1	0.1	0.1	0.1	5.2	5.7	6.3	7.1	4.7	23.7	31.9	13.6	1.9	78.4	43.2	50.5	49.5
15341	HOLBROOK	99.1	98.8	0.1	0.1	0.0	0.0	0.2	0.3	5.0	6.2	6.6	6.8	4.7	25.2	30.9	12.9	1.6	77.7	41.7	50.9	49.1
15342	HOUSTON	95.0	93.6	3.9	5.1	0.3	0.4	0.4	0.7	4.7	4.9	5.2	5.6	5.0	22.5	30.3	18.7	3.2	81.8	46.3	48.1	51.9
15344	JEFFERSON	96.8	95.8	2.2	2.9	0.2	0.3	0.6	0.9	4.5	4.9	5.3	5.7	4.9	23.6	32.8	15.4	2.8	82.1	45.7	47.9	52.1
15345	MARIANNA	95.3	94.1	3.6	4.6	0.1	0.1	0.0	0.0	5.9	5.8	6.2	6.9	6.1	25.2	28.4	13.6	2.1	78.0	40.5	47.7	52.3
15346	MATHER	98.3	97.2	0.8	1.8	0.0	0.0	0.2	0.4	5.8	6.0	5.9	4.9	4.5	26.6	28.0	15.8	2.5	79.3	42.7	49.6	50.4
15349	MOUNT MORRIS	99.0	98.8	0.1	0.2	0.0	0.0	0.4	0.4	5.6	5.9	6.2	6.1	4.7	25.4	30.1	13.9	2.1	78.3	42.4	48.3	51.7
15352	NEW FREEPORT	99.2	98.9	0.0	0.0	0.0	0.0	0.0	0.0	5.9	7.7	8.0	6.5	4.9	26.0	27.8	11.2	1.9	74.1	38.1	50.0	50.0
15353	NINEVEH	99.0	98.9	1.0	1.1	0.0	0.0	0.0	0.0	4.3	4.3	4.3	8.5	6.4	27.7	30.9	11.7	2.1	83.0	41.4	55.3	44.7
15357	RICES LANDING	98.5	98.2	0.7	1.0	0.1	0.1	0.1	0.1	5.4	5.8	6.0	5.9	4.5	23.6	30.8	14.8	3.1	79.1	44.0	47.8	52.2
15359	ROGERSVILLE	99.0	98.6	0.0	0.0	0.0	0.0	0.5	0.5	4.6	6.5	6.9	7.4	5.1	25.3	31.3	11.1	1.8	77.0	41.1	50.7	49.3
15360	SCENERY HILL	99.3	99.1	0.2	0.2	0.1	0.2	0.2	0.2	5.2	5.7	6.2	5.7	4.4	24.5	32.6	13.8	2.0	79.5	43.9	49.2	50.8
15362	SPRAGGS	99.1	98.8	0.2	0.3	0.1	0.2	0.8	1.0	5.1	7.2	7.7	6.5	4.6	24.5	31.9	11.0	1.6	75.6	40.7	50.7	49.3
15363	STRABANE	96.2	95.0	2.9	3.8	0.1	0.2	0.9	1.2	4.7	5.0	5.2	5.7	4.7	23.4	29.6	17.3	4.4	81.6	45.8	47.7	52.3
15364	SYCAMORE	98.7	98.4	0.7	0.8	0.0	0.0	0.3	0.4	4.8	5.3	5.8	7.4	6.0	26.3	31.2	11.5	1.7	79.8	41.3	51.5	48.5
15367	VENETIA	97.8	96.4	0.2	0.3	1.4	2.4	0.6	1.0	7.8	10.1	8.6	6.9	2.6	25.9	28.2	8.6	1.2	68.4	38.4	49.0	51.0
15370	WAYNESBURG	89.3	86.9	9.5	10.6	0.5	1.0	1.6	2.5	4.3	4.8	5.0	8.5	10.3	28.2	25.6	10.9	2.5	83.4	37.1	54.5	45.5
15376	WEST ALEXANDER	99.0	98.7	0.2	0.4	0.2	0.3	0.2	0.4	6.0	6.2	6.8	6.8	5.0	25.1	29.5	12.9	1.8	76.2	41.2	50.7	49.3
15377	WEST FINLEY	99.0	98.9	0.1	0.1	0.1	0.1	0.2	0.1	6.2	7.0	7.5	6.9	4.8	24.6	29.5	11.9	1.6	74.6	40.1	51.5	48.5
15380	WIND RIDGE	99.1	98.9	0.0	0.0	0.0	0.0	0.2	0.2	5.6	7.0	6.6	7.0	5.4	25.8	27.7	13.7	1.2	76.5	39.6	50.3	49.7
15401	UNIONTOWN	91.4	89.6	6.8	8.2	0.5	0.8	0.4	0.5	5.6	5.6	5.7	5.6	5.4	23.3	28.2	16.3	4.3	79.7	44.1	46.9	53.1
15410	ADAH	91.6	89.4	7.3	9.1	0.1	0.2	0.3	0.6	5.4	5.4	5.9	7.2	5.6	25.7	27.9	13.9	2.9	78.8	41.1	49.2	50.8
15411	ADDISON	100.0	100.0	0.0	0.0	0.0	0.0	0.3	0.4	4.2	4.6	5.0	5.5	4.1	23.9	30.6	19.5	2.7	82.7	46.8	49.9	50.1
15412	ALLENPORT	99.0	99.0	0.7	0.7	0.0	0.0	0.2	0.2	4.4	4.4	4.7	4.7	4.2	22.0	31.9	19.3	4.4	84.2	48.8	47.9	52.1
15413	ALLISON	91.8	90.0	6.4	8.1	0.0	0.0	0.2	0.2	5.9	6.7	6.7	5.5	4.5	24.0	28.5	15.2	3.0	77.2	42.1	46.7	53.3
15417	BROWNSVILLE	92.7	91.2	5.6	6.7	0.1	0.2	0.5	0.7	5.3	5.5	5.6	5.8	5.1	24.1	29.0	16.2	3.4	79.9	43.8	47.3	52.7
15419	CALIFORNIA	92.9	90.7	4.9	6.2	0.8	1.3	0.5	0.7	2.0	1.7	2.0	21.9	32.4	13.3	13.9	10.4	2.4	92.7	23.5	48.3	51.7
15423	COAL CENTER	97.7	97.2	0.9	1.2	0.4	0.5	0.5	0.8	4.5	4.8	5.3	5.8	6.4	21.6	31.7	16.6	3.2	82.0	46.0	49.0	51.0
15424	CONFLUENCE	99.5	99.3	0.1	0.1	0.1	0.2	0.2	0.3	5.1	5.2	5.5	5.7	4.5	23.7	29.2	17.7	3.4	80.5	45.2	49.4	50.6
15425	CONNELLSVILLE	96.8	96.0	2.1	2.7	0.2	0.3	0.4	0.5	5.6	5.6	5.9	6.1	5.5	24.7	28.9	14.8	2.8	79.0	42.5	48.7	51.3
15427	DAISYTOWN	95.4	94.2	3.1	4.0	0.2	0.3	0.5	0.6	5.1	5.3	5.6	5.4	4.4	24.1	30.8	16.1	3.1	80.4	45.0	48.9	51.1
15428	DAWSON	98.2	97.8	1.3	1.7	0.0	0.0	0.1	0.1	4.9	5.8	6.3	5.6	4.7	25.0	31.4	14.6	1.8	79.4	43.5	50.5	49.5
15431	DUNBAR	98.4	98.0	0.9	1.2	0.2	0.3	0.3	0.4	5.2	5.8	6.4	6.5	4.9	25.3	30.4	13.3	2.2	78.5	42.2	49.1	50.9
15432	DUNLEVY	99.3	99.3	0.7	0.7	0.0	0.0	0.0	0.7	4.8	4.8	4.8	4.8	4.1	19.7	32.0	19.7	5.4	83.7	49.4	50.3	49.7
15433	EAST MILLSBORO	96.4	95.3	2.8	3.5	0.1	0.2	0.2	0.3	5.0	5.0	5.3	5.4	4.6	25.3	30.3	16.1	3.0	81.2	44.5	48.1	51.9
15434	ELCO	98.2	98.2	1.8	1.8	0.0	0.0	0.0	0.0	5.5	5.5	5.5	7.3	3.6	20.0	29.1	16.4	7.3	80.0	46.9	47.3	52.7
15436	FAIRCHANCE	97.0	96.3	1.8	2.3	0.1	0.1	0.5	0.7	5.4	5.8	5.9	5.6	5.3	26.0	28.9	14.5	2.7	79.6	42.1	48.3	51.7
15437	FARMINGTON	99.0	98.6	0.1	0.1	0.2	0.3	0.5	0.8	7.5	8.2	7.8	7.1	5.3	23.9	26.8	11.3	2.2	72.2	37.8	48.5	51.5
15438	FAYETTE CITY	99.3	99.1	0.3	0.3	0.1	0.1	0.4	0.5	5.1	5.2	5.5	5.9	5.2	23.5	29.4	16.1	4.1	80.6	44.7	49.1	50.9
15440	GIBBON GLADE	99.6	98.6	0.0	0.0	0.0	0.4	0.4	0.7	7.4	8.2	7.8	6.7	5.3	24.1	28.0	10.6	1.8	72.3	38.1	48.2	51.8
15442	GRINDSTONE	92.0	90.1	6.5	8.1	0.1	0.1	0.4	0.5	5.6	5.8	6.0	5.9	4.9	24.7	27.8	16.6	2.7	79.0	42.8	48.4	51.6
15444	HILLER	91.4	89.4	6.9	8.6	0.0	0.0	0.6	0.8	4.1	4.1	4.7	6.3	4.9	23.1	31.2	17.3	4.3	83.1	46.8	47.6	52.4
15445	HOPWOOD	98.2	97.8	1.0	1.2	0.3	0.4	0.4	0.6	4.9	5.0	5.3	5.5	5.0	23.8	30.4	17.1	3.0	81.4	45.3	49.4	50.6
15446	INDIAN HEAD	99.1	99.2	0.0	0.0	0.0	0.0	0.0	0.0	7.4	7.4	7.4	6.6	5.0	27.3	25.6	11.6	1.7	73.6	37.8	52.1	47.9
15450	LA BELLE	97.4	96.4	2.3	2.8	0.0	0.3	0.3	0.3	4.7	5.0	5.3	4.7	4.2	24.5	32.9	15.9	2.8	82.2	46.2	48.5	51.5
	PENNSYLVANIA	85.4	83.2	10.0	10.7	1.8	2.7	3.2	4.2	5.8	6.0	6.3	7.1	6.5	24.8	27.8	13.1	2.6	77.8	40.4	48.5	51.5
	UNITED STATES	75.1	72.0	12.3	12.7	3.8	4.6	12.5	15.7	6.8	6.7	6.6	7.1	6.9	27.0	26.0	10.9	1.9	75.7	36.9	49.2	50.8

#	POST OFFICE NAME	2009 Per Capita Income	2009 HH Income Base	2009 Household Income Distribution (%) Less than $25,000	$25,000 to $49,999	$50,000 to $99,999	$100,000 to $149,999	$150,000 or More	Median Household Income 2009	2014	2009 National Centile	2009 State Centile	2009 Home Value Base	2009 Home Value Distribution (%) Less than $50,000	$50,000 to $89,999	$90,000 to $174,999	$175,000 to $399,999	$400,000 or More	2009 Median Home Value
15213	PITTSBURGH	20143	10182	51.0	25.0	16.3	3.8	3.9	24224	24888	3	1	2696	9.6	33.0	28.1	14.2	15.1	103613
15214	PITTSBURGH	20389	6275	30.4	26.9	34.9	5.3	2.5	41634	46215	38	34	3966	13.4	28.5	48.3	9.5	0.4	101186
15215	PITTSBURGH	37037	5690	21.4	23.6	29.7	11.1	14.2	56301	59068	73	73	3812	4.4	12.1	30.0	34.1	19.5	191190
15216	PITTSBURGH	28751	11460	20.0	27.1	40.0	8.5	4.4	52655	55828	67	68	6862	3.7	22.6	49.7	22.3	1.7	126060
15217	PITTSBURGH	37255	11521	22.4	22.5	34.3	9.2	11.6	56377	59217	73	73	5824	0.9	9.7	33.0	34.8	21.6	198910
15218	PITTSBURGH	30663	6903	23.4	28.6	36.2	6.4	5.4	48143	51588	57	57	4026	8.5	29.5	42.3	16.8	3.0	110088
15219	PITTSBURGH	15283	6283	59.2	20.7	16.7	1.6	1.8	18441	18890	1	1	1803	36.9	30.3	25.2	5.9	1.7	60944
15220	PITTSBURGH	29682	7624	18.9	22.7	44.3	9.5	4.6	57566	60009	75	75	5135	6.5	15.6	48.6	27.7	1.6	137022
15221	PITTSBURGH	24723	15220	30.8	28.9	31.5	5.5	3.2	39965	43639	32	25	7895	10.7	29.1	44.3	14.7	1.2	103868
15222	PITTSBURGH	30379	976	53.6	16.6	18.4	5.4	5.9	22432	23625	2	1	281	11.4	21.4	28.8	27.8	10.7	130978
15223	PITTSBURGH	26759	3542	21.6	26.6	42.9	6.1	2.8	51349	53874	64	65	2312	7.0	20.3	58.9	13.6	0.2	124313
15224	PITTSBURGH	18916	5220	42.7	30.1	23.0	2.6	1.6	29350	30791	7	3	2075	25.0	41.4	28.1	5.1	0.3	69460
15225	PITTSBURGH	25337	563	26.3	32.1	36.2	3.7	1.6	41585	46340	38	33	282	11.0	32.6	49.6	5.0	1.8	96207
15226	PITTSBURGH	26476	6141	20.8	26.5	43.3	6.7	2.7	52076	54700	66	67	4749	3.6	27.7	64.4	3.9	0.4	105711
15227	PITTSBURGH	26166	12602	22.8	27.3	39.2	7.6	3.1	49867	53667	61	61	8755	2.7	16.3	63.8	16.8	0.5	126252
15228	PITTSBURGH	39948	6912	13.3	18.5	38.7	14.6	14.8	71908	72590	88	90	4783	1.0	3.2	26.4	55.4	13.9	223948
15229	PITTSBURGH	29237	5940	15.9	25.7	46.6	7.4	4.3	57120	58925	74	74	4294	1.7	10.1	66.4	21.4	0.4	137620
15232	PITTSBURGH	38108	6370	31.8	25.3	28.3	6.6	8.0	41538	46261	38	33	1550	1.0	6.8	23.0	39.2	29.9	263174
15233	PITTSBURGH	17844	1318	37.4	29.0	26.9	4.6	2.1	32659	35045	13	5	505	13.7	22.0	42.0	19.4	3.0	113117
15234	PITTSBURGH	30154	6214	17.8	25.3	42.1	9.3	5.6	56774	58958	74	74	4496	1.2	10.4	66.4	17.9	4.1	134043
15235	PITTSBURGH	29350	15359	18.0	24.7	43.0	9.3	5.1	56728	58809	74	74	12246	2.5	24.3	58.5	13.6	1.1	113720
15236	PITTSBURGH	29907	12249	13.7	23.0	47.0	11.0	5.3	63015	64683	81	83	10099	2.1	4.0	63.7	28.9	1.3	147529
15237	PITTSBURGH	35567	16478	13.2	19.9	42.2	14.6	9.9	67743	68110	85	88	12897	1.0	3.6	33.5	57.3	4.6	200342
15238	PITTSBURGH	48256	5178	13.7	18.8	31.4	12.1	24.0	76716	77860	90	93	4318	2.4	5.4	20.9	33.4	38.0	312162
15239	PITTSBURGH	26964	7942	11.8	22.6	50.9	11.1	3.6	63252	65133	81	83	6348	2.0	8.7	63.2	24.6	1.4	142490
15241	PITTSBURGH	50459	7248	6.1	10.4	32.5	21.4	29.6	101938	103548	97	98	6551	0.3	1.2	13.8	63.6	21.0	276218
15243	PITTSBURGH	39101	5186	8.6	18.5	42.9	15.2	14.8	76219	76796	90	92	4648	0.6	2.4	39.2	47.4	10.3	191822
15260	PITTSBURGH	20144	17	35.3	29.4	23.5	5.9	5.9	37343	42353	25	15	8	0.0	0.0	37.5	50.0	12.5	200000
15275	PITTSBURGH	35347	31	6.5	22.6	48.4	19.4	3.2	73117	69624	88	90	17	0.0	0.0	58.8	41.2	0.0	162500
15282	PITTSBURGH	0	0	0.0	0.0	0.0	0.0	0.0	0	0	0	0	0	0.0	0.0	0.0	0.0	0.0	0
15301	WASHINGTON	23195	20779	27.4	27.6	35.1	6.6	3.2	45230	48680	49	47	14238	13.2	15.5	40.4	26.8	4.0	132119
15310	ALEPPO	16280	134	41.8	23.9	30.6	3.7	0.0	34080	35972	16	7	105	23.8	24.8	39.0	10.5	1.9	92500
15311	AMITY	22201	512	21.1	25.0	46.5	5.3	2.1	52620	53842	67	68	436	10.1	16.1	39.2	29.4	5.3	143254
15312	AVELLA	20288	1438	23.3	32.0	36.9	6.0	1.9	45329	48872	49	48	1209	12.0	18.6	40.3	25.0	4.1	128144
15313	BEALLSVILLE	21196	124	26.6	29.0	37.1	5.6	1.6	44091	47374	46	43	112	17.0	25.9	39.3	17.0	0.9	103571
15314	BENTLEYVILLE	21731	1639	34.5	26.4	30.2	5.6	3.2	36988	40041	24	14	1140	16.0	26.5	41.4	14.1	2.0	101403
15317	CANONSBURG	34453	14058	13.2	21.4	39.7	13.0	12.7	69049	69563	86	89	11623	2.3	7.4	30.9	45.2	14.2	209395
15320	CARMICHAELS	20094	2562	35.2	26.6	31.3	5.5	1.4	37091	38532	24	14	1839	20.4	26.9	40.1	12.0	0.5	93255
15321	CECIL	25194	615	18.5	26.0	41.0	10.1	4.4	58156	59506	75	76	530	0.2	3.6	37.5	53.8	4.9	192424
15322	CLARKSVILLE	20152	1224	28.2	36.1	28.8	4.5	2.5	37436	38891	25	15	1011	24.9	42.0	26.1	5.4	1.5	68984
15323	CLAYSVILLE	19616	1782	23.2	30.4	39.8	5.3	1.2	46820	50330	54	54	1486	14.4	17.4	40.9	23.8	3.4	126206
15324	COKEBURG	21805	245	34.3	27.3	31.8	4.5	2.0	39076	43226	30	22	186	33.9	42.5	17.7	4.8	1.1	59375
15327	DILLINER	19451	960	36.8	31.6	24.4	4.3	3.0	34076	35349	16	7	777	36.6	29.0	25.5	8.6	0.4	62643
15329	PROSPERITY	20014	685	18.7	32.0	42.2	4.5	2.6	49569	51839	60	61	556	13.7	15.3	39.2	27.3	4.5	134021
15330	EIGHTY FOUR	29807	2142	14.7	21.6	45.1	11.3	7.3	64063	64531	82	85	1920	9.0	6.8	29.4	40.0	14.8	193110
15331	ELLSWORTH	21800	436	28.4	30.7	35.1	4.6	1.1	41290	45913	37	32	320	33.4	41.3	20.0	5.3	0.0	63333
15332	FINLEYVILLE	26478	3361	15.9	28.5	44.8	7.7	3.0	55372	56783	72	71	2926	14.5	11.5	41.7	28.3	4.0	137242
15333	FREDERICKTOWN	20234	910	31.9	30.8	29.5	6.4	1.5	37699	41037	26	16	729	21.5	33.3	33.1	11.1	1.0	79917
15337	GRAYSVILLE	19371	383	32.1	27.7	32.6	6.0	1.6	40356	42965	34	27	283	18.0	30.7	32.9	15.2	3.2	91944
15338	GREENSBORO	20820	773	31.0	31.2	27.9	7.0	2.8	38636	40000	29	20	650	28.3	27.8	33.1	10.0	0.8	79184
15340	HICKORY	23172	637	21.2	27.5	40.3	8.3	2.7	51135	53248	64	65	551	4.2	16.2	33.9	39.4	6.4	165962
15341	HOLBROOK	17138	334	34.7	27.2	33.2	4.2	0.6	38027	39732	27	17	257	19.8	23.3	42.8	12.1	1.9	103214
15342	HOUSTON	25741	2134	20.3	28.9	42.0	5.9	3.0	50663	52959	63	63	1602	3.8	9.1	52.6	33.6	0.9	143892
15344	JEFFERSON	21202	623	27.3	30.7	34.2	5.8	2.1	41471	43388	38	33	516	19.2	30.0	39.0	9.3	2.5	91026
15345	MARIANNA	18751	695	32.9	31.1	30.6	3.7	1.6	37357	40715	25	15	551	36.1	26.3	26.7	8.9	2.0	66795
15346	MATHER	22438	337	29.4	27.3	33.8	6.5	3.0	44752	47846	48	45	292	24.3	44.9	24.3	6.2	0.3	67333
15349	MOUNT MORRIS	21743	687	25.2	28.5	39.0	5.5	1.7	45554	50241	50	49	552	19.0	23.9	41.1	15.2	0.7	100556
15352	NEW FREEPORT	14922	315	45.1	26.7	24.1	3.2	1.0	28737	30819	6	2	250	29.2	25.2	30.8	12.8	2.0	81538
15353	NINEVEH	1516	0	0.0	0.0	0.0	0.0	0.0	0	0	0	0	0	0.0	0.0	0.0	0.0	0.0	0
15357	RICES LANDING	23883	849	25.0	30.6	32.5	9.7	2.2	43612	46483	44	41	728	20.6	34.6	37.0	7.6	0.3	81556
15359	ROGERSVILLE	18252	83	30.1	32.5	31.3	4.8	1.2	38039	39592	27	18	63	19.0	19.0	44.4	15.9	1.6	112500
15360	SCENERY HILL	21308	799	22.7	28.8	40.4	6.1	2.0	48813	51330	58	59	683	14.6	15.2	39.2	25.6	5.3	132955
15362	SPRAGGS	17123	493	33.5	31.4	30.0	4.1	1.0	35257	37459	19	9	397	29.7	29.2	32.5	7.3	1.3	76034
15363	STRABANE	20405	407	34.9	30.7	31.0	2.7	0.7	34390	36549	16	7	300	7.7	32.3	53.7	6.3	0.0	99375
15364	SYCAMORE	20185	283	26.5	30.0	35.0	6.0	2.5	44087	47174	46	43	224	14.3	22.3	42.9	16.5	4.0	115000
15367	VENETIA	40087	2544	7.1	13.5	38.2	18.5	22.8	86476	88106	94	96	2366	1.9	2.0	21.0	42.3	32.8	309534
15370	WAYNESBURG	19397	5175	31.0	29.0	31.6	5.9	2.5	40325	42668	34	27	3353	13.5	20.8	43.6	19.7	2.5	116864
15376	WEST ALEXANDER	19340	663	25.2	31.8	37.1	5.0	0.9	44615	47595	47	45	557	19.6	19.2	37.5	21.4	2.3	113225
15377	WEST FINLEY	17048	313	28.4	28.1	38.7	3.8	1.0	45303	48376	49	48	257	18.3	20.6	33.5	25.7	1.9	118500
15380	WIND RIDGE	17719	324	36.4	26.5	32.1	4.6	0.3	36915	39309	23	14	238	20.6	30.7	33.2	13.4	2.1	87500
15401	UNIONTOWN	20987	14166	38.2	25.5	26.5	6.3	3.5	33761	35378	15	6	9206	17.5	22.6	39.4	16.6	3.9	105519
15410	ADAH	18248	356	32.9	35.1	24.4	5.6	2.0	34154	35000	16	7	279	39.8	22.6	33.0	3.9	0.7	68077
15411	ADDISON	20342	255	34.9	32.5	27.5	3.9	1.2	35102	36114	18	8	210	18.6	24.8	48.1	6.2	2.4	102344
15412	ALLENPORT	22255	184	27.7	35.9	30.4	4.9	1.1	38722	41019	29	21	143	26.6	32.2	32.9	8.4	0.0	77222
15413	ALLISON	21805	207	37.2	25.1	30.4	2.4	4.8	33927	36967	15	7	154	30.5	29.9	28.6	7.1	3.9	66000
15417	BROWNSVILLE	20768	3852	36.6	26.9	29.0	4.3	3.2	36740	40185	23	13	2814	27.4	30.2	30.1	11.3	1.0	75543
15419	CALIFORNIA	16956	1433	46.3	26.3	23.1	3.3	1.0	27247	28435	5	2	601	16.0	24.5	42.8	16.8	0.0	104239
15423	COAL CENTER	22329	748	27.5	26.3	36.2	7.4	2.5	46650	49807	53	53	610	17.7	23.9	34.8	16.2	7.4	107143
15424	CONFLUENCE	17881	1083	36.7	33.5	26.1	2.8	0.9	34624	35940	17	8	855	19.9	22.9	45.8	9.5	1.9	103003
15425	CONNELLSVILLE	19474	8915	37.6	27.5	28.0	4.7	2.3	34022	35797	16	7	6096	17.6	24.6	40.8	15.5	1.6	101861
15427	DAISYTOWN	23090	860	26.7	30.0	32.2	8.6	2.4	45147	47849	49	47	746	23.1	37.0	24.4	11.7	3.9	74038
15428	DAWSON	19756	815	31.2	32.0	31.5	2.8	2.5	39647	41946	32	24	675	19.1	30.1	34.4	13.0	3.4	91196
15431	DUNBAR	17400	2254	33.4	32.7	30.5	2.7	0.8	36621	38580	22	13	1805	31.4	25.1	33.4	8.1	1.9	77550
15432	DUNLEVY	21992	68	29.4	36.8	26.5	5.9	1.5	35000	36545	18	8	56	33.9	37.5	21.4	7.1	0.0	61667
15433	EAST MILLSBORO	19727	421	33.3	35.2	24.2	5.5	1.9	33072	34144	13	5	350	33.1	17.1	34.3	14.3	1.1	89091
15434	ELCO	24592	24	25.0	29.2	41.7	4.2	0.0	45000	50000	48	46	21	9.5	38.1	47.6	4.8	0.0	92500
15436	FAIRCHANCE	18226	1297	35.9	30.5	28.2	4.2	1.2	33902	34975	15	6	924	17.6	28.4	41.1	12.7	0.2	95139
15437	FARMINGTON	18654	1037	25.1	32.9	36.4	3.3	2.4	42893	45928	42	38	823	14.0	13.4	45.7	20.9	6.1	138569
15438	FAYETTE CITY	22193	1083	25.4	27.9	38.4	6.2	2.1	46210	50398	52	52	893	18.8	28.3	32.9	17.7	2.2	95100
15440	GIBBON GLADE	20544	97	26.8	35.1	34.0	3.1	1.0	39097	42361	30	22	78	17.9	12.8	50.0	14.1	5.1	130882
15442	GRINDSTONE	18999	1565	37.8	29.0	25.6	5.6	2.0	34214	36113	16	7	1174	36.8	23.1	27.9	10.7	1.5	73000
15444	HILLER	20884	218	26.1	32.6	36.2	4.6	0.5	43334	45696	43	41	179	15.6	50.3	33.0	1.1	0.0	69500
15445	HOPWOOD	20202	1665	33.4	28.8	31.1	5.6	1.1	39190	41721	30	23	1261	11.7	17.2	54.7	14.4	2.0	124544
15446	INDIAN HEAD	15525	44	45.5	22.7	27.3	4.5	0.0	28154	33590	6	2	37	35.1	24.3	29.7	10.8	0.0	77500
15450	LA BELLE	20500	150	33.3	38.0	22.0	5.3	1.3	33134	35377	14	5	128	29.7	19.5	33.6	17.2	0.0	95000
	PENNSYLVANIA	26913		21.5	25.3	36.9	10.2	6.1	53225	55819				7.5	12.2	35.6	36.1	8.5	161438
	UNITED STATES	27277		20.9	24.4	35.3	11.7	7.6	54719	56938				9.3	13.1	31.6	32.6	13.5	162279

ZIP CODE #	POST OFFICE NAME	FINANCIAL SERVICES: Auto Loan	Home Loan	Invest-ments	Retire-ment Plans	THE HOME: Home Improvements: Home Repair	Lawn & Garden	Furnishings: Comput-ers & Hard-ware-Personal	Major Appli-ances	TV, Radio, Sound Equip-ment	Furni-ture	ENTERTAINMENT: Dine out/ Carry out	Sports Equip-ment	Fees & Tickets	Toys & Games	Travel	Cable TV	PERSONAL: Apparel & Services	Auto Repairs	Health Insur-ance	Pets & Supplies
15213	PITTSBURGH	63	40	40	45	38	43	75	50	68	61	68	46	56	67	53	65	48	62	53	64
15214	PITTSBURGH	72	68	60	69	65	74	71	69	76	69	75	52	71	75	68	79	52	72	79	84
15215	PITTSBURGH	114	119	127	122	123	124	120	120	122	120	121	89	125	118	123	124	86	121	128	140
15216	PITTSBURGH	87	84	81	86	83	88	90	86	91	86	90	67	89	90	87	92	63	89	92	103
15217	PITTSBURGH	106	108	110	112	109	106	114	107	112	114	113	84	117	111	115	112	80	111	111	127
15218	PITTSBURGH	87	82	78	83	80	85	90	85	90	86	90	66	87	90	85	92	63	88	91	101
15219	PITTSBURGH	45	34	33	36	33	39	44	40	49	42	48	30	40	47	38	51	33	45	47	50
15220	PITTSBURGH	91	91	91	92	92	98	92	93	95	90	94	69	94	93	93	98	65	94	102	110
15221	PITTSBURGH	72	66	65	68	66	73	72	70	77	71	76	52	71	75	70	80	53	74	79	85
15222	PITTSBURGH	71	54	64	60	55	64	80	67	85	72	85	54	71	77	72	89	59	79	85	86
15223	PITTSBURGH	79	83	78	83	82	91	80	84	84	77	83	61	83	83	82	88	57	83	95	98
15224	PITTSBURGH	55	44	45	45	44	49	58	51	60	52	59	39	51	59	50	63	41	56	58	62
15225	PITTSBURGH	83	60	83	58	62	87	65	81	73	58	70	60	52	72	63	80	47	75	88	95
15226	PITTSBURGH	83	86	79	85	83	94	83	86	87	79	86	64	85	86	84	91	59	85	97	101
15227	PITTSBURGH	79	80	76	80	79	85	80	81	83	78	83	60	82	82	81	87	58	82	90	95
15228	PITTSBURGH	121	144	150	147	149	140	131	134	128	137	129	101	147	126	144	128	93	131	134	153
15229	PITTSBURGH	90	94	89	94	93	101	92	94	95	89	94	70	94	94	93	98	65	94	104	110
15232	PITTSBURGH	90	69	73	79	67	67	100	76	96	92	99	69	89	97	86	93	71	90	78	97
15233	PITTSBURGH	52	54	57	55	54	52	62	54	64	56	66	42	63	62	60	67	48	60	59	66
15234	PITTSBURGH	90	99	93	99	98	101	95	95	96	93	96	72	100	95	98	99	67	96	103	112
15235	PITTSBURGH	89	98	93	97	98	106	90	96	95	89	94	68	97	93	96	100	65	94	109	111
15236	PITTSBURGH	94	108	104	107	108	112	97	103	100	98	100	74	107	99	105	103	70	101	112	119
15237	PITTSBURGH	109	127	129	128	131	130	114	121	116	118	116	87	127	113	125	119	82	118	129	139
15238	PITTSBURGH	158	185	211	189	199	189	166	178	164	174	162	130	187	160	184	164	117	169	176	200
15239	PITTSBURGH	94	107	95	106	103	106	95	99	97	97	98	74	104	99	101	99	68	97	104	115
15241	PITTSBURGH	171	228	252	233	243	214	192	203	182	208	182	151	229	179	223	177	134	191	190	227
15243	PITTSBURGH	121	154	162	153	160	153	132	140	132	136	132	101	154	129	150	134	95	135	145	158
15260	PITTSBURGH	68	60	62	63	61	64	76	65	75	70	76	51	71	72	69	77	53	72	75	79
15275	PITTSBURGH	118	105	94	111	100	95	117	103	113	119	116	87	112	119	108	109	81	110	98	124
15282	PITTSBURGH	0	0	0	0	0	0	0	0	0	0	0	0	0	0	0	0	0	0	0	0
15301	WASHINGTON	79	76	74	76	75	84	77	80	80	73	79	59	75	79	76	84	54	79	87	94
15310	ALEPPO	74	52	75	50	53	75	54	68	61	50	59	52	42	61	52	67	39	63	71	82
15311	AMITY	89	81	80	84	83	95	80	90	82	72	81	68	74	84	80	87	55	83	93	105
15312	AVELLA	82	74	74	77	76	88	73	83	76	66	74	63	68	77	73	80	51	76	85	96
15313	BEALLSVILLE	81	73	74	76	75	87	73	82	75	66	74	62	67	76	72	80	50	76	85	96
15314	BENTLEYVILLE	78	64	75	64	65	81	70	78	75	63	73	58	61	74	67	81	50	75	86	91
15317	CANONSBURG	116	134	128	135	133	131	121	124	120	123	120	93	132	120	129	120	85	121	126	144
15320	CARMICHAELS	74	60	66	61	60	75	66	71	70	60	68	54	58	70	62	75	46	70	78	85
15321	CECIL	91	104	89	106	100	102	92	96	91	93	91	75	99	93	98	91	64	92	95	113
15322	CLARKSVILLE	78	62	80	60	64	84	65	78	71	59	69	57	56	70	64	78	47	73	86	91
15323	CLAYSVILLE	81	73	71	75	73	86	72	80	75	66	74	61	66	77	71	79	50	75	84	94
15324	COKEBURG	81	58	81	57	61	85	64	79	71	57	69	59	51	70	62	78	46	73	86	92
15327	DILLINER	80	57	73	56	58	80	61	73	68	57	66	56	49	69	57	74	44	69	78	88
15329	PROSPERITY	86	78	76	80	79	90	76	85	79	71	78	64	70	81	75	83	53	80	87	100
15330	EIGHTY FOUR	105	117	115	120	118	121	104	113	104	104	104	85	111	105	112	106	73	107	113	130
15331	ELLSWORTH	80	58	81	56	60	84	63	78	70	56	68	58	51	69	61	78	45	73	85	92
15332	FINLEYVILLE	87	92	87	92	92	100	85	92	89	82	88	68	88	89	89	93	61	89	99	107
15333	FREDERICKTOWN	76	63	77	61	64	83	64	76	70	59	68	56	57	69	64	77	46	72	84	89
15337	GRAYSVILLE	88	63	82	61	64	87	65	79	72	62	71	60	52	73	62	79	47	74	83	95
15338	GREENSBORO	90	65	91	63	67	92	68	85	75	62	73	64	54	75	66	83	49	78	90	100
15340	HICKORY	93	84	84	88	86	99	83	94	86	75	84	71	77	87	83	91	58	87	97	109
15341	HOLBROOK	79	57	81	55	59	80	58	74	65	54	63	56	47	64	58	71	42	68	77	88
15342	HOUSTON	79	84	79	83	83	92	79	84	84	77	83	60	83	83	83	89	58	83	96	97
15344	JEFFERSON	81	70	84	68	72	89	68	81	74	65	73	59	63	73	70	80	49	76	87	95
15345	MARIANNA	74	58	66	58	58	75	64	71	68	57	66	54	54	68	59	74	45	68	77	84
15346	MATHER	89	64	89	62	66	92	70	86	78	62	75	64	56	77	67	86	50	80	94	101
15349	MOUNT MORRIS	80	73	82	71	74	89	69	81	75	67	74	58	66	74	71	81	50	76	88	94
15352	NEW FREEPORT	73	48	71	45	48	72	51	64	59	48	57	50	38	60	48	65	38	60	68	79
15353	NINEVEH	0	0	0	0	0	0	0	0	0	0	0	0	0	0	0	0	0	0	0	0
15357	RICES LANDING	86	77	89	75	79	97	76	89	83	71	81	65	72	81	78	90	55	84	99	103
15359	ROGERSVILLE	85	61	87	59	63	86	62	79	69	58	68	59	50	69	62	76	45	73	82	94
15360	SCENERY HILL	86	78	80	80	79	93	77	87	80	70	79	66	71	81	77	85	54	81	91	102
15362	SPRAGGS	79	56	80	54	58	80	57	73	64	54	63	55	46	64	57	71	42	67	76	87
15363	STRABANE	73	53	74	51	55	76	58	71	64	51	62	53	46	63	56	71	41	66	78	83
15364	SYCAMORE	90	69	81	68	70	90	70	83	76	66	75	63	58	78	67	83	50	77	87	99
15367	VENETIA	164	202	187	208	201	175	169	174	158	186	160	139	192	165	183	149	117	161	151	196
15370	WAYNESBURG	80	65	76	64	66	81	68	76	73	64	72	57	60	73	66	78	49	74	81	91
15376	WEST ALEXANDER	83	67	71	68	68	84	68	78	73	64	71	59	59	75	65	78	48	73	81	92
15377	WEST FINLEY	77	67	72	69	68	82	66	77	70	60	68	58	59	71	66	74	46	71	80	90
15380	WIND RIDGE	80	57	82	55	59	81	59	75	65	55	64	56	47	65	58	72	42	68	78	89
15401	UNIONTOWN	73	63	70	63	63	77	66	72	72	63	70	53	62	70	65	77	48	71	81	86
15410	ADAH	76	55	77	54	57	80	60	74	67	54	65	55	48	66	58	74	43	69	81	87
15411	ADDISON	79	56	81	55	59	80	58	74	64	54	63	55	46	64	57	71	42	68	77	88
15412	ALLENPORT	82	59	82	58	61	85	64	79	72	58	69	59	52	71	62	79	46	74	87	93
15413	ALLISON	90	65	90	63	67	94	70	87	79	63	76	65	57	77	68	87	51	81	95	102
15417	BROWNSVILLE	77	61	74	60	62	80	65	75	72	60	70	55	57	70	63	78	47	72	83	88
15419	CALIFORNIA	57	39	38	42	38	43	65	48	60	53	60	42	49	60	48	59	42	56	50	60
15423	COAL CENTER	76	81	79	80	81	90	77	82	81	74	81	59	80	80	80	86	56	80	93	94
15424	CONFLUENCE	71	51	72	50	53	73	54	68	60	49	58	51	43	59	53	66	39	62	72	80
15425	CONNELLSVILLE	72	57	66	57	58	72	63	69	68	58	66	52	55	67	59	73	45	67	75	82
15427	DAISYTOWN	85	71	87	69	73	93	72	86	79	67	77	63	65	78	73	87	52	81	95	100
15428	DAWSON	82	59	83	57	61	84	62	77	69	57	67	58	49	68	60	76	44	72	82	92
15431	DUNBAR	77	54	73	52	54	77	57	70	64	53	62	54	45	65	54	70	41	65	73	84
15432	DUNLEVY	79	57	79	55	59	82	62	77	69	55	67	57	50	68	60	76	44	71	83	90
15433	EAST MILLSBORO	83	59	83	58	62	86	65	80	72	58	70	60	52	71	63	80	47	75	87	94
15434	ELCO	73	83	78	81	83	90	73	80	78	72	78	56	81	77	80	83	54	78	92	92
15436	FAIRCHANCE	75	54	76	53	56	78	58	72	65	53	63	54	47	64	57	71	42	67	78	85
15437	FARMINGTON	90	70	81	70	71	90	71	84	77	66	75	64	60	78	68	83	51	78	87	100
15438	FAYETTE CITY	78	74	73	74	74	86	74	79	78	69	76	59	71	78	73	83	53	77	88	93
15440	GIBBON GLADE	89	64	83	62	65	88	66	80	73	63	72	61	53	74	63	80	48	75	84	97
15442	GRINDSTONE	71	55	70	54	56	75	59	70	66	54	63	51	50	64	57	72	43	66	77	82
15444	HILLER	83	59	83	58	62	86	65	80	72	58	70	60	52	71	63	80	47	75	87	94
15445	HOPWOOD	73	63	74	62	65	79	63	73	68	60	67	53	58	67	64	73	45	69	79	85
15446	INDIAN HEAD	77	55	64	54	55	73	58	67	64	56	63	51	46	67	52	70	42	63	71	81
15450	LA BELLE	83	60	83	58	62	86	65	80	73	58	70	60	52	71	63	80	47	75	88	94
	PENNSYLVANIA	94	95	95	95	95	100	94	96	96	91	95	73	94	96	94	99	67	95	101	113
	UNITED STATES	100	100	100	100	100	100	100	100	100	100	100	100	100	100	100	100	100	100	100	100

ZIP CODE			POPULATION			2000-2009 ANNUAL RATE		HOUSEHOLDS					FAMILIES		
#	POST OFFICE NAME	COUNTY FIPS CODE	2000	2009	2014	% Rate	State Centile	2000	2009	2014	% Annual Rate 2000-2009	2009 Average HH Size	2000	2009	% Annual Rate 2000-2009
15451	LAKE LYNN	051	1175	1168	1155	-0.1	46	458	469	467	0.3	2.49	351	350	0.0
15456	LEMONT FURNACE	051	3452	3396	3311	-0.2	38	1368	1380	1359	0.1	2.45	1005	986	-0.2
15458	MC CLELLANDTOWN	051	2958	2901	2821	-0.2	38	1111	1097	1073	-0.1	2.56	788	756	-0.4
15459	MARKLEYSBURG	051	1808	1839	1809	0.2	61	633	640	634	0.1	2.64	471	463	-0.2
15461	MASONTOWN	051	5065	4848	4685	-0.5	19	2099	2044	1991	-0.3	2.33	1399	1319	-0.6
15462	MELCROFT	051	442	453	450	0.3	64	170	179	179	0.6	2.51	128	132	0.3
15463	MERRITTSTOWN	051	959	914	882	-0.5	19	403	392	382	-0.3	2.33	252	236	-0.7
15464	MILL RUN	051	1537	1571	1553	0.2	61	565	594	593	0.5	2.60	428	439	0.3
15468	NEW SALEM	051	3697	3584	3485	-0.3	29	1459	1449	1421	-0.1	2.46	1035	999	-0.4
15469	NORMALVILLE	051	3180	3257	3222	0.3	64	1190	1255	1253	0.6	2.58	911	937	0.3
15470	OHIOPYLE	051	1017	1058	1047	0.4	68	401	420	418	0.5	2.41	297	304	0.3
15473	PERRYOPOLIS	051	3799	3622	3502	-0.5	19	1571	1536	1499	-0.2	2.32	1064	1006	-0.6
15474	POINT MARION	051	2224	2161	2104	-0.3	29	937	935	918	0.0	2.29	652	631	-0.4
15475	REPUBLIC	051	318	304	294	-0.5	19	128	124	121	-0.3	2.42	94	88	-0.7
15477	ROSCOE	125	1076	1057	1037	-0.2	38	483	486	481	0.1	2.15	310	300	-0.4
15478	SMITHFIELD	051	6176	6088	5981	-0.2	38	2353	2388	2367	0.2	2.54	1735	1714	-0.1
15479	SMITHTON	129	2695	2658	2617	-0.1	46	1083	1094	1085	0.1	2.43	811	797	-0.2
15480	SMOCK	051	2372	2410	2384	0.2	61	929	972	971	0.5	2.46	685	698	0.2
15482	STAR JUNCTION	051	492	482	469	-0.2	38	225	223	218	-0.1	2.04	144	138	-0.5
15483	STOCKDALE	125	493	486	475	-0.2	38	220	223	220	0.1	2.16	144	140	-0.3
15486	VANDERBILT	051	3031	3045	2991	0.0	52	1177	1213	1202	0.3	2.47	849	852	0.0
15488	WALTERSBURG	051	61	64	64	0.5	70	26	28	28	0.8	2.25	20	21	0.5
15490	WHITE	051	554	572	569	0.3	64	201	214	215	0.7	2.67	156	162	0.4
15501	SOMERSET	111	17293	19237	18822	1.2	88	7026	6974	6850	-0.1	2.28	4664	4491	-0.4
15521	ALUM BANK	009	1923	1997	2025	0.4	68	688	739	756	0.8	2.70	537	563	0.5
15522	BEDFORD	009	12190	11866	11706	-0.3	29	5117	5128	5106	0.0	2.26	3496	3414	-0.3
15530	BERLIN	111	7273	5387	5265	-3.2	0	2072	2065	2035	0.0	2.51	1534	1490	-0.3
15531	BOSWELL	111	4788	4689	4590	-0.2	38	1984	2002	1978	0.1	2.33	1391	1364	-0.2
15533	BREEZEWOOD	009	1200	1157	1134	-0.4	23	482	479	474	-0.1	2.42	357	345	-0.4
15534	BUFFALO MILLS	009	783	753	738	-0.4	23	307	304	301	-0.1	2.44	239	231	-0.4
15535	CLEARVILLE	009	2239	2414	2493	0.8	80	839	936	976	1.2	2.58	658	717	0.9
15536	CRYSTAL SPRING	057	448	451	449	0.1	57	183	190	192	0.4	2.35	131	133	0.2
15537	EVERETT	009	8088	7911	7817	-0.2	38	3278	3297	3286	0.1	2.36	2351	2298	-0.2
15538	FAIRHOPE	111	748	736	722	-0.2	38	303	308	305	0.2	2.37	228	226	-0.1
15539	FISHERTOWN	009	483	498	503	0.3	64	196	208	212	0.6	2.39	149	154	0.4
15540	FORT HILL	111	419	400	387	-0.5	19	158	154	151	-0.3	2.53	114	108	-0.6
15541	FRIEDENS	111	4671	4833	4805	0.4	68	1743	1860	1864	0.7	2.59	1334	1389	0.4
15542	GARRETT	111	1203	1164	1132	-0.4	23	439	437	429	0.0	2.66	349	340	-0.3
15545	HYNDMAN	009	3061	3087	3081	0.1	57	1225	1271	1281	0.4	2.42	912	922	0.1
15546	JENNERS	111	344	328	319	-0.5	19	137	135	133	-0.2	2.43	98	94	-0.4
15550	MANNS CHOICE	009	1814	1761	1733	-0.3	29	710	710	706	0.0	2.45	536	522	-0.3
15551	MARKLETON	111	851	835	819	-0.2	38	313	315	313	0.1	2.60	244	241	-0.1
15552	MEYERSDALE	111	6643	6338	6145	-0.5	19	2490	2423	2367	-0.3	2.54	1839	1751	-0.5
15554	NEW PARIS	009	2617	2671	2681	0.2	61	999	1055	1071	0.6	2.53	760	782	0.3
15557	ROCKWOOD	111	3692	3670	3597	-0.1	46	1486	1514	1497	0.2	2.39	1078	1066	-0.1
15558	SALISBURY	111	2232	2214	2175	-0.1	46	845	849	839	0.1	2.57	611	596	-0.3
15559	SCHELLSBURG	009	1894	1885	1872	-0.1	46	736	759	761	0.3	2.48	564	566	0.0
15562	SPRINGS	111	229	224	220	-0.2	38	73	73	73	0.0	3.07	55	54	-0.2
15563	STOYSTOWN	111	3525	3540	3489	0.0	52	1392	1447	1441	0.4	2.45	1027	1039	0.1
15601	GREENSBURG	129	57690	59497	58932	0.3	64	23686	24521	24457	0.4	2.27	15670	15781	0.1
15610	ACME	129	3996	4042	4007	0.1	57	1512	1578	1578	0.5	2.52	1133	1151	0.2
15611	ADAMSBURG	129	180	161	168	-1.2	1	62	58	61	-0.7	2.78	48	44	-0.9
15612	ALVERTON	129	401	367	353	-1.0	3	149	141	137	-0.6	2.60	115	107	-0.8
15613	APOLLO	129	16488	16105	15765	-0.3	29	6485	6479	6387	0.0	2.44	4796	4673	-0.3
15615	ARDARA	129	236	222	215	-0.7	8	91	88	86	-0.4	2.52	69	65	-0.6
15617	ARONA	129	407	398	389	-0.2	38	166	160	157	-0.4	2.48	122	114	-0.7
15618	AVONMORE	005	2765	2674	2616	-0.4	23	1088	1076	1061	-0.1	2.47	812	781	-0.4
15620	BRADENVILLE	129	1137	1204	1223	0.6	74	476	520	532	1.0	2.30	344	364	0.6
15622	CHAMPION	051	907	896	876	-0.1	46	392	401	396	0.2	2.23	279	277	-0.1
15623	CLARIDGE	129	788	765	759	-0.3	29	306	304	303	-0.1	2.50	240	232	-0.4
15625	DARRAGH	129	23	22	22	-0.5	19	10	10	10	0.0	2.20	7	7	0.0
15626	DELMONT	129	4970	4884	4813	-0.2	38	2197	2216	2200	0.1	2.19	1475	1436	-0.3
15627	DERRY	129	8138	8207	8119	0.1	57	3209	3326	3319	0.4	2.45	2315	2330	0.1
15628	DONEGAL	129	501	492	484	-0.2	38	172	175	174	0.2	2.75	121	120	-0.1
15631	EVERSON	051	678	616	590	-1.0	3	281	263	253	-0.7	2.34	189	171	-1.1
15632	EXPORT	129	8325	8544	8529	0.3	64	3206	3370	3385	0.5	2.50	2358	2420	0.3
15634	GRAPEVILLE	129	948	901	878	-0.5	19	368	361	355	-0.2	2.49	282	270	-0.5
15636	HARRISON CITY	129	3248	3566	3606	1.0	85	1083	1204	1222	1.2	2.94	930	1015	0.9
15637	HERMINIE	129	2313	2301	2269	-0.1	46	964	983	978	0.2	2.34	657	646	-0.2
15639	HUNKER	129	1688	1615	1578	-0.5	19	671	665	655	-0.1	2.41	488	469	-0.4
15641	HYDE PARK	129	513	500	492	-0.3	29	212	213	211	0.1	2.34	156	152	-0.3
15642	IRWIN	129	44863	45870	45622	0.2	61	17323	18058	18075	0.5	2.50	13019	13277	0.2
15644	JEANNETTE	129	20883	20769	20457	-0.1	46	8632	8757	8687	0.2	2.34	5935	5852	-0.2
15646	JONES MILLS	129	333	328	323	-0.2	38	138	141	140	0.2	2.33	97	96	-0.1
15647	LARIMER	129	106	101	99	-0.5	19	38	37	37	-0.3	2.70	28	27	-0.4
15650	LATROBE	129	28815	28449	27984	-0.1	46	11574	11657	11556	0.1	2.28	7798	7577	-0.3
15655	LAUGHLINTOWN	129	426	413	405	-0.3	29	192	191	189	-0.1	2.16	137	132	-0.4
15656	LEECHBURG	129	10398	9937	9666	-0.5	19	4287	4204	4121	-0.2	2.34	3073	2940	-0.5
15658	LIGONIER	129	9391	9423	9317	0.0	52	3963	4072	4059	0.3	2.28	2752	2742	0.0
15661	LOYALHANNA	129	340	333	327	-0.2	38	146	146	145	0.0	2.25	104	101	-0.3
15663	MADISON	129	369	357	351	-0.4	23	162	162	161	0.0	2.20	119	116	-0.3
15665	MANOR	129	1180	1291	1305	1.0	85	461	516	525	1.2	2.49	331	356	0.8
15666	MOUNT PLEASANT	129	17706	17503	17221	-0.1	46	7250	7377	7325	0.2	2.33	5063	4998	-0.1
15668	MURRYSVILLE	129	12885	13099	12993	0.2	61	4908	5137	5144	0.5	2.52	3878	3968	0.2
15670	NEW ALEXANDRIA	129	3600	3399	3306	-0.6	13	1407	1366	1340	-0.3	2.47	1038	980	-0.6
15672	NEW STANTON	129	3263	3304	3277	0.1	57	1422	1484	1485	0.5	2.18	941	947	0.1
15675	PENN	129	831	779	755	-0.7	8	329	317	309	-0.4	2.46	237	220	-0.8
15677	RECTOR	129	453	449	444	-0.1	46	191	194	194	0.2	2.31	132	129	-0.2
15678	RILLTON	129	595	583	573	-0.2	38	242	244	242	0.1	2.39	172	168	-0.3
15679	RUFFS DALE	129	4036	3920	3845	-0.3	29	1617	1621	1606	0.0	2.41	1171	1139	-0.3
15681	SALTSBURG	063	4662	4411	4282	-0.6	13	1847	1809	1774	-0.2	2.43	1310	1245	-0.5
15683	SCOTTDALE	129	9222	9072	8909	-0.2	38	3759	3799	3761	0.1	2.35	2605	2557	-0.2
15684	SLICKVILLE	129	491	442	422	-1.1	2	200	185	178	-0.8	2.39	139	124	-1.2
15686	SPRING CHURCH	005	872	877	862	0.1	57	340	352	350	0.4	2.49	260	263	0.1
15687	STAHLSTOWN	129	1816	1789	1762	-0.2	38	720	728	723	0.1	2.37	544	535	-0.2
	PENNSYLVANIA					0.3					0.4	2.45			0.1
	UNITED STATES					1.0					1.1	2.59			0.9

#	POST OFFICE NAME	RACE (%) White 2000	White 2009	Black 2000	Black 2009	Asian/Pacific 2000	Asian/Pacific 2009	% Hispanic Origin 2000	% Hispanic Origin 2009	2009 AGE DISTRIBUTION (%) 0-4	5-9	10-14	15-19	20-24	25-44	45-64	65-84	85+	18+	MEDIAN AGE 2009	% 2009 Males	% 2009 Females
15451	LAKE LYNN	97.5	96.9	1.1	1.5	0.3	0.3	0.6	0.9	6.4	6.8	6.8	6.5	4.8	24.8	29.4	12.7	1.8	75.8	40.5	47.6	52.4
15456	LEMONT FURNACE	98.1	97.5	0.9	1.1	0.2	0.4	0.4	0.5	5.1	5.4	6.1	6.4	4.7	24.7	31.0	14.6	2.0	79.4	43.2	48.5	51.5
15458	MC CLELLANDTOWN	89.9	87.5	9.0	11.1	0.1	0.1	0.4	0.5	5.2	5.3	5.9	7.0	5.0	23.8	30.8	14.1	2.8	78.9	43.3	48.3	51.7
15459	MARKLEYSBURG	99.1	98.6	0.3	0.4	0.1	0.2	0.4	0.5	5.8	6.1	6.5	6.0	4.8	24.5	27.1	14.9	4.4	77.7	42.5	49.0	51.0
15461	MASONTOWN	93.7	92.1	5.2	6.5	0.1	0.1	0.4	0.6	5.8	5.8	6.0	6.5	5.5	22.9	29.3	14.5	3.8	78.5	43.0	46.6	53.4
15462	MELCROFT	99.5	99.3	0.0	0.0	0.0	0.2	0.7	1.1	6.2	6.4	6.6	6.6	6.4	26.9	29.6	9.9	1.3	76.4	38.7	50.3	49.7
15463	MERRITTSTOWN	92.6	90.7	5.5	7.0	0.0	0.0	0.4	0.5	5.5	5.6	5.9	6.5	4.7	24.4	28.2	15.9	3.4	78.9	43.1	45.6	54.4
15464	MILL RUN	99.1	98.8	0.0	0.0	0.0	0.1	0.7	1.0	6.0	6.9	6.4	6.3	4.9	26.5	29.0	12.1	1.9	76.6	40.2	50.0	50.0
15468	NEW SALEM	91.8	89.8	6.8	8.5	0.3	0.4	0.3	0.4	6.1	5.8	5.9	6.2	5.5	23.8	29.2	14.9	2.7	78.4	42.6	46.6	53.4
15469	NORMALVILLE	99.2	98.9	0.0	0.0	0.0	0.1	0.3	0.5	6.4	7.3	6.8	6.5	5.0	27.4	27.5	11.4	1.6	75.2	38.7	51.0	49.0
15470	OHIOPYLE	99.5	99.4	0.2	0.2	0.0	0.0	0.3	0.5	4.8	5.3	5.9	6.1	4.4	24.1	32.3	14.5	2.6	80.2	44.5	48.5	51.5
15473	PERRYOPOLIS	97.8	97.2	1.4	1.7	0.2	0.4	0.3	0.3	4.4	4.7	5.0	5.5	4.3	22.8	30.9	18.7	3.9	82.6	47.2	47.9	52.1
15474	POINT MARION	98.7	98.5	0.2	0.3	0.0	0.0	0.6	0.7	5.8	6.0	5.9	5.8	5.5	25.4	28.6	14.5	2.6	78.8	41.9	50.3	49.7
15475	REPUBLIC	94.7	93.4	3.4	4.6	0.3	0.3	0.3	0.7	4.9	4.9	5.3	6.3	5.3	26.3	27.3	16.1	3.6	80.6	42.8	47.4	52.6
15477	ROSCOE	98.3	97.8	0.9	1.2	0.1	0.2	0.3	0.5	4.7	5.0	5.2	5.1	4.1	21.2	30.7	20.1	3.9	81.6	47.9	46.3	53.7
15478	SMITHFIELD	98.4	97.9	0.6	0.8	0.1	0.2	0.4	0.7	5.5	6.0	6.1	5.9	5.1	25.7	30.3	13.3	2.1	78.6	41.9	48.5	51.5
15479	SMITHTON	97.5	96.9	1.1	1.4	0.1	0.2	0.4	0.5	4.9	5.2	5.7	6.0	4.5	24.1	31.6	15.7	2.4	80.5	44.8	49.4	50.6
15480	SMOCK	98.2	97.6	1.1	1.4	0.0	0.1	0.1	0.2	5.6	5.9	6.4	6.3	4.7	24.7	30.3	14.1	1.9	78.2	42.5	48.8	51.2
15482	STAR JUNCTION	98.6	98.3	0.0	0.0	0.4	0.6	0.2	0.4	4.1	4.1	4.4	5.2	4.8	22.6	30.1	18.7	6.0	83.8	47.7	43.4	56.6
15483	STOCKDALE	99.0	99.0	0.6	0.6	0.2	0.2	0.2	0.2	4.3	4.3	4.7	4.9	4.5	24.1	31.1	17.5	4.5	84.8	47.3	46.3	53.7
15486	VANDERBILT	98.0	97.4	1.3	1.6	0.1	0.1	0.1	0.2	4.7	5.6	6.1	6.2	4.6	24.4	31.5	14.8	2.0	79.6	43.8	49.5	50.5
15488	WALTERSBURG	100.0	98.4	0.0	1.6	0.0	0.0	0.0	0.0	4.7	6.3	6.3	6.3	4.7	25.0	32.8	12.5	1.6	79.7	42.5	51.6	48.4
15490	WHITE	99.1	98.8	0.0	0.0	0.0	0.2	0.0	0.2	5.9	6.3	6.5	6.3	5.1	27.4	29.4	11.7	1.4	77.6	40.1	51.0	49.0
15501	SOMERSET	97.5	91.6	1.2	5.9	0.5	1.1	0.5	1.6	4.7	4.8	5.1	6.6	7.2	27.1	27.7	13.5	3.3	82.1	41.2	52.7	47.3
15521	ALUM BANK	98.1	97.5	0.3	0.4	0.2	0.3	1.0	1.4	6.8	7.0	7.1	7.1	5.5	26.3	26.6	12.2	1.5	74.8	38.8	49.2	50.8
15522	BEDFORD	97.8	97.2	0.8	1.0	0.5	0.9	0.6	0.8	5.1	5.4	5.6	5.8	4.9	23.7	29.5	16.6	3.3	80.2	44.6	49.3	50.7
15530	BERLIN	82.2	89.9	14.1	5.6	0.3	0.7	3.3	4.2	5.3	5.9	5.9	6.3	7.2	26.8	27.0	12.3	3.1	79.9	39.3	52.6	47.4
15531	BOSWELL	99.4	99.3	0.0	0.0	0.1	0.1	0.1	0.2	5.6	5.8	5.6	5.7	4.7	24.1	30.6	15.3	2.6	79.5	43.9	48.8	51.2
15533	BREEZEWOOD	99.1	98.7	0.1	0.2	0.2	0.3	0.6	0.8	5.8	6.2	7.0	6.1	4.7	25.8	30.3	12.3	1.8	76.8	40.7	49.9	50.1
15534	BUFFALO MILLS	98.5	98.1	0.1	0.1	0.1	0.3	0.6	0.9	6.2	6.5	6.6	5.6	4.6	23.1	29.3	15.8	2.1	76.9	43.0	51.3	48.7
15535	CLEARVILLE	98.5	98.2	0.3	0.3	0.1	0.2	0.4	0.6	5.4	5.8	6.0	6.1	5.0	23.9	31.2	15.0	1.5	79.0	43.4	51.6	48.4
15536	CRYSTAL SPRING	98.2	98.0	0.0	0.0	0.0	0.0	0.4	0.9	6.7	7.1	7.1	6.0	4.2	22.2	28.4	16.2	2.2	75.6	42.8	48.6	51.4
15537	EVERETT	98.7	98.4	0.3	0.4	0.2	0.4	0.4	0.6	5.7	5.8	6.0	5.7	4.5	24.1	28.9	16.3	3.0	78.8	43.6	48.7	51.3
15538	FAIRHOPE	98.1	97.6	0.1	0.1	0.5	0.8	0.9	1.2	4.6	5.0	6.4	6.1	4.3	23.0	32.7	15.9	1.9	79.9	45.3	52.0	48.0
15539	FISHERTOWN	98.3	97.8	0.6	0.8	0.6	1.0	0.6	1.0	7.0	7.0	7.0	6.6	5.6	26.7	26.9	11.8	1.2	74.7	38.5	50.2	49.8
15540	FORT HILL	100.0	100.0	0.0	0.0	0.0	0.0	0.2	0.3	5.0	5.3	5.8	5.8	4.3	24.3	29.8	17.5	2.5	80.3	44.8	49.8	50.2
15541	FRIEDENS	99.4	99.1	0.1	0.1	0.2	0.3	0.2	0.3	6.6	6.9	7.0	6.4	5.1	25.9	28.5	11.8	1.7	75.5	39.5	50.0	50.0
15542	GARRETT	99.1	98.9	0.2	0.2	0.1	0.2	0.1	0.1	6.5	6.5	6.6	6.5	4.9	27.5	27.6	12.1	1.7	76.3	39.3	50.8	49.2
15545	HYNDMAN	98.6	98.3	0.1	0.1	0.0	0.0	0.4	0.6	6.2	6.3	6.5	6.0	4.9	23.3	28.7	15.8	2.3	77.2	42.6	50.1	49.9
15546	JENNERS	99.1	99.1	0.0	0.0	0.0	0.0	0.0	0.0	4.0	4.6	4.9	5.8	4.6	24.4	35.1	14.3	2.4	83.2	46.1	51.2	48.8
15550	MANNS CHOICE	99.0	98.6	0.1	0.1	0.3	0.6	0.6	0.8	5.6	6.0	6.4	6.2	4.5	22.7	30.0	16.0	2.6	77.6	44.0	50.3	49.7
15551	MARKLETON	99.2	98.9	0.1	0.1	0.0	0.1	0.2	0.2	5.6	5.7	6.1	6.6	5.1	23.5	31.1	14.4	1.8	78.3	43.1	51.4	48.6
15552	MEYERSDALE	99.2	99.0	0.2	0.2	0.1	0.1	0.4	0.6	5.5	5.6	6.2	6.4	4.7	25.0	28.1	15.2	3.2	78.4	42.5	48.9	51.1
15554	NEW PARIS	98.4	97.8	0.6	0.7	0.5	0.8	0.5	0.7	6.6	6.9	6.9	6.4	5.3	25.7	28.6	12.2	1.4	75.6	39.9	50.4	49.6
15557	ROCKWOOD	99.4	99.3	0.2	0.2	0.1	0.1	0.2	0.2	5.1	5.5	5.9	6.3	4.4	24.6	29.8	16.1	2.3	79.3	43.8	49.1	50.9
15558	SALISBURY	99.5	99.4	0.0	0.0	0.0	0.0	0.6	0.9	6.1	6.4	6.5	6.5	4.6	24.5	28.0	14.8	2.6	76.7	41.5	49.1	50.9
15559	SCHELLSBURG	98.6	98.2	0.4	0.5	0.3	0.4	0.7	1.0	5.4	5.9	6.3	5.9	4.5	23.8	31.5	14.8	1.9	78.6	43.8	50.7	49.3
15562	SPRINGS	100.0	100.0	0.0	0.0	0.0	0.0	0.0	0.0	6.7	7.1	7.1	6.3	4.0	25.4	27.7	12.9	2.7	74.1	40.0	49.6	50.4
15563	STOYSTOWN	99.5	99.4	0.0	0.0	0.1	0.1	0.5	0.6	5.2	5.6	6.0	6.2	4.6	24.0	32.1	14.3	1.9	79.4	43.8	50.2	49.8
15601	GREENSBURG	96.3	94.4	1.9	3.0	0.9	1.3	0.6	0.9	4.6	4.9	5.3	6.8	5.8	23.4	30.3	15.4	3.5	81.6	44.4	47.9	52.1
15610	ACME	99.4	99.2	0.1	0.0	0.2	0.3	0.6	0.8	5.7	6.2	6.5	6.0	4.6	25.2	32.2	12.1	1.5	77.9	42.3	50.2	49.8
15611	ADAMSBURG	97.8	97.5	1.1	1.2	0.6	0.6	0.6	0.6	5.6	6.2	6.8	6.8	3.7	24.2	34.2	10.6	1.9	77.0	42.9	49.1	50.9
15612	ALVERTON	99.0	98.9	0.2	0.3	0.2	0.3	0.0	0.0	5.4	5.4	5.7	5.7	3.8	24.8	31.1	16.3	1.6	79.8	44.4	48.0	52.0
15613	APOLLO	98.1	97.6	1.0	1.3	0.1	0.2	0.4	0.6	5.1	5.5	5.9	6.2	4.8	22.3	32.3	15.1	2.7	79.6	45.0	49.1	50.9
15615	ARDARA	99.6	99.1	0.0	0.0	0.4	0.5	0.4	0.5	5.4	6.3	6.8	6.3	4.1	23.0	31.5	14.4	2.3	77.0	43.7	49.1	50.9
15617	ARONA	98.5	98.5	0.2	0.3	0.2	0.3	0.5	0.5	4.8	5.3	5.8	6.3	4.5	24.4	31.9	14.8	2.3	79.9	44.3	49.7	50.3
15618	AVONMORE	98.1	97.5	1.1	1.4	0.2	0.3	0.3	0.3	5.7	6.0	6.2	5.9	4.3	23.7	30.4	14.8	2.8	78.2	43.6	48.8	51.2
15620	BRADENVILLE	99.1	98.8	0.4	0.4	0.2	0.3	0.4	0.7	5.1	5.1	5.5	6.1	4.5	25.1	29.6	16.7	2.5	80.5	44.2	48.9	51.1
15622	CHAMPION	99.2	99.0	0.0	0.0	0.1	0.2	0.6	0.8	5.5	5.8	5.9	5.9	4.5	26.1	30.4	14.2	1.8	79.1	42.7	51.3	48.7
15623	CLARIDGE	99.0	98.7	0.3	0.3	0.1	0.1	0.5	0.7	4.2	4.4	5.2	6.4	5.2	24.1	32.3	15.2	3.0	82.9	45.3	48.6	51.4
15625	DARRAGH	100.0	100.0	0.0	0.0	0.0	0.0	0.0	0.0	0.0	0.0	9.1	4.5	4.5	36.4	36.4	9.1	0.0	86.4	42.5	54.5	45.5
15626	DELMONT	97.7	96.9	0.8	1.0	0.6	1.0	0.4	0.6	5.7	6.1	6.4	5.5	4.4	20.7	31.4	17.3	2.6	78.2	45.7	48.0	52.0
15627	DERRY	98.7	98.3	0.9	1.1	0.1	0.1	0.6	0.8	5.5	5.7	6.1	6.5	5.1	24.9	30.2	13.5	2.4	78.6	42.4	48.9	51.1
15628	DONEGAL	99.4	99.0	0.0	0.0	0.0	0.2	0.6	1.0	5.3	5.9	6.3	5.7	4.3	24.2	31.7	14.6	2.0	78.9	43.9	50.4	49.6
15631	EVERSON	96.3	95.5	3.1	3.9	0.3	0.3	0.0	0.0	6.0	6.3	6.7	6.2	4.1	25.8	27.3	14.9	2.8	77.1	41.5	51.5	48.5
15632	EXPORT	96.9	95.6	0.6	0.7	1.9	2.9	0.5	0.7	5.2	6.4	7.3	7.1	4.1	22.9	31.7	13.3	2.0	76.3	43.2	49.7	50.3
15634	GRAPEVILLE	99.2	99.1	0.2	0.2	0.2	0.2	0.1	0.2	5.5	5.9	6.1	4.9	4.6	22.4	32.1	16.2	2.3	79.4	45.4	46.6	53.4
15636	HARRISON CITY	98.6	94.5	0.2	3.7	0.6	1.1	0.5	0.8	6.8	8.0	7.9	6.9	3.9	25.7	30.6	8.8	1.5	73.9	39.6	49.9	50.1
15637	HERMINIE	98.7	98.3	0.1	0.2	0.2	0.3	0.7	1.0	5.2	5.4	5.7	5.7	4.8	24.3	31.1	15.1	2.8	80.3	44.3	48.5	51.5
15639	HUNKER	98.0	97.3	0.5	0.7	0.5	0.8	0.3	0.4	5.0	5.4	6.0	5.2	4.1	24.8	33.4	14.2	1.9	80.3	44.7	49.8	50.2
15641	HYDE PARK	97.3	96.8	1.6	2.0	0.0	0.0	0.6	0.6	7.4	7.4	7.4	6.4	4.8	21.2	28.2	14.8	2.4	74.0	40.7	48.0	52.0
15642	IRWIN	98.5	96.6	0.5	1.9	0.5	0.8	0.4	0.6	5.4	5.9	6.3	6.2	4.6	23.9	30.7	14.5	2.5	78.6	43.5	48.3	51.7
15644	JEANNETTE	95.8	94.8	2.6	3.1	0.4	0.6	0.5	0.7	5.5	5.7	6.0	6.2	5.0	24.4	29.7	14.4	3.0	79.3	43.1	48.0	52.0
15646	JONES MILLS	99.4	99.4	0.0	0.0	0.0	0.0	0.6	0.9	5.8	6.7	6.7	5.5	4.3	24.4	31.4	13.4	1.8	77.4	42.7	49.7	50.3
15647	LARIMER	100.0	100.0	0.0	0.0	0.0	0.0	1.0	1.0	5.9	5.9	6.9	5.9	4.0	20.8	34.7	12.9	3.0	76.2	45.3	49.5	50.5
15650	LATROBE	98.6	98.0	0.3	0.5	0.5	0.8	0.4	0.6	4.7	4.9	5.4	7.3	6.5	22.6	28.6	16.6	3.4	81.0	44.0	48.5	51.5
15655	LAUGHLINTOWN	99.3	99.0	0.0	0.2	0.2	0.2	0.5	0.5	4.4	4.8	5.3	5.6	3.6	18.6	37.0	18.4	2.2	81.8	49.6	48.9	51.1
15656	LEECHBURG	98.1	97.6	0.9	1.1	0.2	0.3	0.4	0.5	5.2	5.5	5.8	5.9	4.7	22.7	31.1	15.9	3.1	79.7	45.1	49.0	51.0
15658	LIGONIER	99.4	99.2	0.1	0.1	0.1	0.2	0.3	0.5	4.3	4.4	5.4	5.7	4.4	20.9	33.8	17.6	3.5	82.3	47.9	48.9	51.1
15661	LOYALHANNA	99.4	98.8	0.3	0.3	0.0	0.3	0.3	0.3	5.7	5.7	6.3	6.3	4.5	23.4	27.6	17.4	3.0	78.1	43.6	48.6	51.4
15663	MADISON	98.6	98.3	0.5	0.6	0.3	0.6	0.0	0.0	3.9	4.5	4.8	5.0	4.5	24.1	34.2	16.8	2.2	83.8	47.0	49.3	50.7
15665	MANOR	99.3	99.0	0.1	0.2	0.3	0.5	0.9	1.4	6.7	6.7	6.5	6.2	6.1	26.6	27.2	12.0	1.9	76.4	39.0	49.5	50.5
15666	MOUNT PLEASANT	98.6	98.2	0.7	0.8	0.1	0.2	0.4	0.5	4.9	5.2	5.6	5.6	4.7	24.1	30.3	16.5	3.1	80.7	44.9	48.3	51.7
15668	MURRYSVILLE	95.0	92.9	0.7	0.8	3.5	5.3	0.5	0.7	4.6	5.5	6.6	6.6	3.7	18.1	34.9	17.5	2.4	78.6	47.7	49.4	50.6
15670	NEW ALEXANDRIA	98.9	98.5	0.4	0.5	0.1	0.1	0.3	0.4	4.8	5.7	6.2	6.6	4.7	24.6	32.0	13.8	1.6	79.1	43.2	50.0	50.0
15672	NEW STANTON	97.8	97.0	1.0	1.2	0.4	0.6	0.8	1.2	4.4	4.6	4.8	4.7	4.5	25.8	32.8	16.0	2.3	83.1	45.7	49.2	50.8
15675	PENN	88.3	86.3	9.0	10.7	0.2	0.4	0.2	0.4	6.4	6.3	6.4	6.3	5.9	26.3	27.7	12.5	2.2	76.8	39.8	47.0	53.0
15677	RECTOR	99.6	99.3	0.2	0.2	0.0	0.0	0.0	0.0	4.0	4.7	5.1	5.6	3.8	18.7	38.5	17.4	2.2	82.6	49.9	51.0	49.0
15678	RILLTON	99.0	98.5	0.2	0.3	0.2	0.3	0.7	0.9	5.1	5.5	5.8	6.2	4.8	23.8	31.9	14.4	2.4	79.4	44.1	49.7	50.3
15679	RUFFS DALE	98.7	98.4	0.3	0.4	0.1	0.2	0.3	0.4	5.5	5.7	5.9	6.0	5.1	25.7	30.9	13.5	1.7	79.1	42.5	49.3	50.7
15681	SALTSBURG	98.8	98.5	0.4	0.4	0.2	0.2	0.6	0.8	5.8	6.3	7.0	6.6	4.5	24.7	29.7	13.4	2.2	76.8	41.8	50.0	50.0
15683	SCOTTDALE	98.3	97.8	1.0	1.3	0.2	0.3	0.3	0.4	5.3	5.3	5.7	6.1	4.9	24.6	29.4	15.6	3.1	79.8	43.7	47.8	52.2
15684	SLICKVILLE	98.0	97.1	1.4	1.8	0.0	0.0	0.4	0.7	5.4	5.9	7.7	7.9	4.3	24.4	29.6	12.9	1.8	76.0	41.8	51.4	48.6
15686	SPRING CHURCH	98.5	97.8	0.5	0.6	0.1	0.3	0.5	0.8	5.8	6.2	6.4	5.9	4.4	25.2	32.0	12.7	1.4	78.1	42.3	49.0	51.0
15687	STAHLSTOWN	99.5	99.3	0.1	0.1	0.1	0.1	0.4	0.6	4.6	5.1	5.8	6.3	4.1	23.8	32.4	15.7	2.4	80.8	45.3	50.7	49.3
	PENNSYLVANIA	85.4	83.2	10.0	10.7	1.8	2.7	3.2	4.2	5.8	6.0	6.3	7.1	6.5	24.8	27.8	13.1	2.6	77.8	40.4	48.5	51.5
	UNITED STATES	75.1	72.0	12.3	12.7	3.8	4.6	12.5	15.7	6.8	6.7	6.6	7.1	6.9	27.0	26.0	10.9	1.9	75.7	36.9	49.2	50.8

ZIP CODE #	POST OFFICE NAME	2009 Per Capita Income	2009 HH Income Base	2009 HOUSEHOLD INCOME DISTRIBUTION (%) Less than $25,000	$25,000 to $49,999	$50,000 to $99,999	$100,000 to $149,999	$150,000 or More	MEDIAN HOUSEHOLD INCOME 2009	2014	2009 National Centile	2009 State Centile	2009 Home Value Base	2009 HOME VALUE DISTRIBUTION (%) Less than $50,000	$50,000 to $89,999	$90,000 to $174,999	$175,000 to $399,999	$400,000 or More	2009 Median Home Value
15451	LAKE LYNN	14803	469	42.0	32.0	21.5	4.1	0.4	29923	30943	8	3	356	29.2	24.7	34.0	11.8	0.3	79375
15456	LEMONT FURNACE	18655	1380	36.0	27.8	29.6	4.9	1.8	35551	37607	19	10	1094	21.1	33.9	34.5	8.6	1.9	79204
15458	MC CLELLANDTOWN	20300	1097	31.6	27.6	32.1	4.6	4.0	36596	38966	22	13	870	31.0	24.1	34.7	9.8	0.3	81000
15459	MARKLEYSBURG	15026	640	37.2	33.0	26.6	2.2	1.1	32082	33715	12	4	503	16.9	24.5	42.3	15.3	1.0	107617
15461	MASONTOWN	18167	2044	38.5	33.6	20.4	5.7	1.9	30717	31430	9	3	1428	17.3	32.6	45.0	4.6	0.6	90081
15462	MELCROFT	19598	179	23.5	29.1	44.1	3.4	0.0	48126	50993	57	57	150	19.3	19.3	36.7	19.3	5.3	112000
15463	MERRITTSTOWN	20060	392	37.0	29.8	25.3	3.6	4.3	32712	33937	13	5	279	16.8	42.7	28.7	11.5	0.4	76136
15464	MILL RUN	15815	594	34.3	36.2	26.3	2.2	1.0	35464	36807	19	9	489	25.2	22.9	35.6	13.9	2.5	93800
15468	NEW SALEM	19040	1449	36.9	28.5	26.5	4.8	3.2	34450	36266	16	7	1114	30.2	28.7	31.3	9.2	0.6	75000
15469	NORMALVILLE	17694	1255	35.9	28.0	31.2	3.3	1.5	35884	39138	20	11	1042	24.4	20.5	34.6	17.4	3.1	98833
15470	OHIOPYLE	20660	420	24.8	34.8	35.2	2.9	2.4	43171	45696	43	40	345	9.0	20.9	40.0	26.1	4.1	136919
15473	PERRYOPOLIS	22738	1536	25.6	29.0	36.9	6.4	2.1	45126	49139	49	46	1206	17.6	17.9	39.0	23.5	2.1	120255
15474	POINT MARION	18011	935	39.4	26.5	29.1	4.2	0.9	33458	35652	14	6	657	28.2	26.5	36.4	7.3	1.7	80758
15475	REPUBLIC	20089	124	32.3	30.6	30.6	5.6	0.8	33265	33963	14	6	98	41.8	14.3	30.6	10.2	3.1	80000
15477	ROSCOE	23590	486	26.7	32.1	33.7	5.8	1.6	42095	45271	40	36	374	18.4	36.9	38.2	5.3	1.1	83333
15478	SMITHFIELD	17131	2388	37.4	29.1	27.6	3.9	2.0	33701	35400	15	6	1786	28.1	21.3	36.2	14.1	0.3	91068
15479	SMITHTON	23343	1094	20.1	32.1	39.1	6.4	2.3	48487	51366	58	58	898	16.5	18.2	39.6	22.2	3.6	120361
15480	SMOCK	19365	972	26.0	32.8	35.1	5.1	0.9	41099	44848	36	31	800	28.9	25.5	29.4	14.4	1.9	83396
15482	STAR JUNCTION	21407	223	35.4	28.3	31.8	3.6	0.9	36283	40000	21	12	163	39.3	23.3	24.5	11.0	1.8	61875
15483	STOCKDALE	22737	223	27.4	35.9	31.8	3.1	1.8	39841	42545	32	25	164	19.5	23.2	45.1	11.0	1.2	100000
15486	VANDERBILT	18961	1213	29.1	31.8	34.2	3.6	1.2	40671	43640	35	29	1002	20.0	29.5	35.2	12.9	2.4	90704
15488	WALTERSBURG	21352	28	28.6	32.1	28.6	7.1	3.6	40000	45000	33	26	24	16.7	37.5	29.2	16.7	0.0	85000
15490	WHITE	19132	214	39.3	20.6	33.6	4.2	2.3	35655	39546	20	10	188	18.1	18.1	45.2	18.6	0.0	116071
15501	SOMERSET	21164	6974	27.5	31.6	34.1	4.4	2.4	41561	43760	38	33	4852	12.4	13.6	48.4	21.6	4.0	131434
15521	ALUM BANK	16300	739	29.2	39.0	27.5	3.4	0.9	37255	37906	24	15	639	16.1	18.8	44.4	18.0	2.7	113951
15522	BEDFORD	23199	5128	24.2	32.9	35.3	5.0	2.6	43821	45162	45	42	3821	10.9	9.0	45.4	30.4	4.3	144743
15530	BERLIN	19529	2065	24.8	34.4	35.2	3.8	1.8	43223	45548	43	40	1593	15.0	18.5	46.8	18.0	1.8	118835
15531	BOSWELL	20622	2002	28.0	32.4	33.2	4.8	1.5	40853	42762	35	30	1507	13.5	25.7	43.9	15.5	1.5	108573
15533	BREEZEWOOD	18410	479	32.2	34.0	28.8	3.3	1.7	36949	37761	23	14	406	27.8	12.8	39.7	15.8	3.9	108333
15534	BUFFALO MILLS	17814	304	26.6	36.8	33.9	2.6	0.0	40775	41342	35	29	257	12.1	19.5	44.4	20.6	3.5	121181
15535	CLEARVILLE	18088	936	23.9	40.0	31.3	3.3	1.5	39131	40000	30	22	820	10.6	12.7	45.5	26.5	4.8	135362
15536	CRYSTAL SPRING	17425	190	30.5	36.3	30.0	3.2	0.0	36626	39141	22	13	164	14.6	23.2	40.9	17.7	3.7	113043
15537	EVERETT	20079	3297	29.5	34.7	29.7	4.3	1.9	38257	38964	27	19	2516	13.9	15.8	47.0	20.3	2.9	122649
15538	FAIRHOPE	18953	308	31.8	31.8	31.5	3.6	1.3	37691	39578	26	16	257	16.3	25.7	40.9	13.6	3.5	103629
15539	FISHERTOWN	20744	208	25.0	33.2	35.1	6.3	0.5	42135	44007	40	36	177	19.8	13.6	46.9	18.1	1.7	126103
15540	FORT HILL	17896	154	33.8	31.8	27.9	4.5	1.9	36117	37326	21	11	126	17.5	23.8	45.2	11.1	2.4	105000
15541	FRIEDENS	18501	1860	22.7	39.4	33.0	3.4	1.6	41889	44157	39	35	1570	17.5	17.9	40.5	20.9	3.2	121930
15542	GARRETT	16213	437	31.4	32.0	33.0	2.7	0.9	40089	43336	33	26	376	24.2	26.3	39.1	9.3	1.1	89200
15545	HYNDMAN	18110	1271	33.8	32.0	29.9	3.5	0.7	36983	38006	24	14	1056	13.8	27.7	43.1	13.5	1.8	105000
15546	JENNERS	16932	135	37.0	31.1	25.9	5.9	0.0	32599	33614	13	4	111	27.9	33.3	23.4	12.6	2.7	79583
15550	MANNS CHOICE	18412	710	24.5	39.3	32.4	3.4	0.4	40939	41459	36	30	591	13.7	16.2	44.7	20.8	4.6	125941
15551	MARKLETON	16467	315	29.5	38.7	28.3	3.2	0.3	38112	39193	27	18	272	19.1	21.0	44.1	13.2	2.6	107778
15552	MEYERSDALE	17395	2423	33.7	32.5	28.1	4.5	1.2	35991	37299	21	11	1879	17.0	26.8	43.9	11.3	1.1	98969
15554	NEW PARIS	19130	1055	27.3	35.0	31.6	4.9	1.2	39903	40829	32	25	897	19.0	13.8	42.6	22.2	2.5	124030
15557	ROCKWOOD	19059	1514	32.5	31.8	29.9	4.2	1.6	38836	40516	29	21	1256	14.6	23.0	47.1	13.1	2.2	108761
15558	SALISBURY	18008	849	33.9	29.7	29.2	5.3	1.9	37031	39323	24	14	669	13.8	26.2	43.8	13.9	2.4	104535
15559	SCHELLSBURG	18854	759	27.5	33.3	34.8	3.6	0.8	41284	42405	37	32	641	16.1	12.5	43.4	25.1	3.0	131114
15562	SPRINGS	16382	73	35.6	26.0	28.8	5.5	4.1	36734	39307	23	13	57	12.3	21.1	43.9	21.1	1.8	116250
15563	STOYSTOWN	19401	1447	27.7	32.6	34.3	4.1	1.2	41604	43637	38	33	1227	17.8	24.0	39.0	16.2	3.0	105971
15601	GREENSBURG	27329	24521	21.7	26.8	37.4	8.5	5.5	51484	54134	65	66	17766	7.0	10.5	40.9	34.3	7.3	154634
15610	ACME	19790	1578	23.2	31.9	39.7	4.3	1.0	45315	48916	49	48	1385	13.6	16.2	38.9	24.8	6.5	133450
15611	ADAMSBURG	24341	58	13.8	25.9	43.1	12.1	5.2	61481	57778	79	81	55	1.8	10.9	38.2	38.2	10.9	173214
15612	ALVERTON	19898	141	22.7	29.8	40.4	5.7	1.4	47916	50688	56	57	124	14.5	12.9	49.2	19.4	4.0	125000
15613	APOLLO	22057	6479	24.0	30.5	36.5	6.9	2.2	46397	49790	53	53	5335	13.4	16.5	43.0	24.7	2.4	127660
15615	ARDARA	21161	88	29.5	26.1	35.2	5.7	3.4	41564	45000	38	33	81	14.8	18.5	42.0	22.2	2.5	127679
15617	ARONA	29213	160	13.1	30.6	41.9	6.9	7.5	58954	60248	76	77	141	11.3	18.4	36.9	32.6	0.7	141912
15618	AVONMORE	22131	1076	23.4	30.7	37.6	5.9	2.3	46285	49952	52	52	926	14.1	24.1	38.4	21.1	2.3	107692
15620	BRADENVILLE	21465	520	26.5	31.3	36.7	3.5	1.9	39881	45486	32	25	420	21.2	29.0	38.3	11.0	0.5	89333
15622	CHAMPION	24419	401	27.4	26.9	38.9	4.0	2.7	45937	49220	51	51	329	12.5	13.1	38.6	25.8	10.0	133482
15623	CLARIDGE	22417	304	16.8	41.4	32.6	7.2	2.0	44475	46784	47	44	268	6.0	19.4	50.7	22.4	1.5	120370
15625	DARRAGH	23750	10	20.0	30.0	50.0	0.0	0.0	45000	45000	48	46	9	0.0	0.0	55.6	44.4	0.0	168750
15626	DELMONT	29654	2216	22.0	27.6	32.7	12.3	5.4	50532	54429	62	63	1776	15.2	6.4	38.7	37.3	2.3	154913
15627	DERRY	19984	3326	27.3	33.2	33.3	4.2	2.0	41157	44644	37	31	2644	18.3	20.8	47.0	12.3	1.6	105178
15628	DONEGAL	16173	175	29.7	37.7	28.0	2.9	1.7	35673	38643	20	10	140	22.9	12.1	35.7	18.6	10.7	115789
15631	EVERSON	18678	263	33.1	30.0	31.2	4.9	0.8	37892	41048	26	17	190	24.7	36.3	36.3	2.6	0.0	76667
15632	EXPORT	32903	3370	16.3	25.8	32.6	13.4	11.8	61236	62259	79	80	2846	9.1	8.8	25.8	41.7	14.6	203594
15634	GRAPEVILLE	25869	361	18.6	26.0	45.4	4.4	5.5	56601	58046	73	73	311	3.2	27.0	46.3	21.5	1.9	123611
15636	HARRISON CITY	28330	1204	8.7	20.8	41.9	20.0	8.6	75739	75910	90	92	1124	0.8	3.8	29.7	61.8	3.8	212500
15637	HERMINIE	20753	983	31.4	26.9	35.3	4.2	2.2	38818	43338	29	21	717	13.7	22.6	47.0	15.2	1.5	107097
15639	HUNKER	26919	665	15.5	29.2	43.5	9.0	2.9	55475	57290	72	72	538	9.3	11.3	44.2	32.7	2.4	145703
15641	HYDE PARK	21384	213	31.0	30.0	29.1	7.5	2.3	39861	42148	32	25	157	12.7	15.3	52.9	19.1	0.0	121250
15642	IRWIN	26538	18058	16.3	26.5	42.2	10.3	4.7	57817	59099	75	76	15111	4.2	7.3	47.4	36.9	4.1	159241
15644	JEANNETTE	23833	8757	25.1	28.7	36.7	6.4	3.1	46363	50061	52	53	6676	11.6	20.5	42.1	23.1	2.6	119557
15646	JONES MILLS	19136	141	29.8	37.6	28.4	2.8	1.4	35845	38210	20	10	113	23.9	11.5	35.4	18.6	10.6	114844
15647	LARIMER	21674	37	21.6	27.0	40.5	8.1	2.7	51435	58525	65	65	33	9.1	15.2	48.5	24.2	3.0	137500
15650	LATROBE	24396	11657	22.8	30.2	37.1	6.6	3.4	47306	50675	55	56	8536	7.5	15.3	47.4	24.8	5.0	134337
15655	LAUGHLINTOWN	30082	191	25.1	33.0	27.2	8.9	5.8	43124	46152	43	39	158	5.1	8.9	33.5	39.9	12.7	183333
15656	LEECHBURG	24656	4204	23.9	27.6	37.5	7.1	3.9	48356	51681	57	58	3428	9.2	17.9	44.9	24.9	3.1	127307
15658	LIGONIER	25652	4072	25.1	30.3	33.4	7.0	4.2	45100	48447	49	46	3228	7.2	12.0	38.4	34.3	8.1	154734
15661	LOYALHANNA	22616	146	20.5	34.2	38.4	5.5	1.4	46920	49241	54	55	113	8.8	15.9	59.3	15.9	0.0	123295
15663	MADISON	28575	162	19.8	31.5	35.8	8.6	4.3	48233	52632	57	57	140	13.6	11.4	45.7	25.0	4.3	132500
15665	MANOR	22839	516	20.2	27.5	45.5	4.7	2.1	51779	53654	65	66	390	3.3	23.6	61.0	8.2	3.8	114250
15666	MOUNT PLEASANT	21199	7377	28.3	29.1	36.3	4.8	1.4	42482	46327	41	37	5760	15.7	18.4	46.1	18.7	1.2	114037
15668	MURRYSVILLE	41788	5137	7.0	16.8	38.1	19.3	18.8	82640	83378	93	95	4649	2.4	3.0	23.4	55.1	16.2	233044
15670	NEW ALEXANDRIA	21884	1366	27.1	29.1	34.2	7.3	2.3	45052	47928	48	46	1114	15.5	10.5	44.1	25.1	4.8	130525
15672	NEW STANTON	26478	1484	20.1	33.8	35.7	7.1	3.4	46563	50233	53	53	993	12.6	13.3	42.2	29.8	2.1	139149
15675	PENN	20333	317	22.4	33.8	39.7	2.5	1.6	45508	49563	50	48	247	26.7	30.0	32.0	9.3	2.0	77500
15677	RECTOR	32440	194	24.2	32.0	29.4	5.2	9.3	45000	48054	48	46	146	7.5	9.6	30.8	28.8	23.3	182500
15678	RILLTON	20171	244	30.3	30.3	32.4	5.7	1.2	38669	42144	29	20	187	17.1	20.3	46.5	14.4	1.6	110648
15679	RUFFS DALE	19474	1621	28.0	35.9	30.2	4.9	1.0	38719	41470	29	21	1306	20.9	18.1	38.8	19.0	3.2	106630
15681	SALTSBURG	18999	1809	30.6	33.1	30.5	4.9	1.0	40055	42636	33	26	1414	19.0	20.3	41.7	16.9	2.1	106336
15683	SCOTTDALE	21403	3799	27.7	30.2	35.0	5.1	1.9	41788	45877	39	34	2859	12.8	20.7	50.9	14.2	1.3	113140
15684	SLICKVILLE	17776	185	28.1	40.5	28.6	2.2	0.5	38517	41629	28	19	160	22.5	23.8	41.9	11.9	0.0	93750
15686	SPRING CHURCH	19931	352	28.1	25.9	39.5	5.4	1.1	47048	50000	54	55	301	19.3	15.9	36.5	27.2	1.0	125962
15687	STAHLSTOWN	21116	728	25.4	34.9	33.2	4.0	2.5	41037	44148	36	30	632	17.7	20.6	33.5	19.0	9.2	108712
	PENNSYLVANIA	26913		21.5	25.3	36.9	10.2	6.1	53225	55819				7.5	12.2	35.6	36.1	8.5	161438
	UNITED STATES	27277		20.9	24.4	35.3	11.7	7.6	54719	56938				9.3	13.1	31.6	32.6	13.5	162279

ZIP CODE		FINANCIAL SERVICES				THE HOME						ENTERTAINMENT						PERSONAL			
						Home Improvements		Furnishings													
#	POST OFFICE NAME	Auto Loan	Home Loan	Invest-ments	Retire-ment Plans	Home Repair	Lawn & Garden	Comput-ers & Hard-ware-Personal	Major Appli-ances	TV, Radio, Sound Equip-ment	Furni-ture	Dine out/ Carry out	Sports Equip-ment	Fees & Tickets	Toys & Games	Travel	Cable TV	Apparel & Services	Auto Repairs	Health Insur-ance	Pets & Supplies
15451	LAKE LYNN	68	45	66	42	45	67	48	60	55	45	54	47	36	56	45	61	36	57	64	74
15456	LEMONT FURNACE	75	60	73	58	61	79	61	72	67	57	66	54	53	67	60	73	44	68	78	85
15458	MC CLELLANDTOWN	91	65	92	63	67	94	69	87	78	63	75	65	55	77	67	86	50	80	93	103
15459	MARKLEYSBURG	72	51	74	50	53	73	53	67	58	49	57	50	42	58	52	64	38	61	70	80
15461	MASONTOWN	67	54	63	53	54	70	56	64	63	55	62	47	50	62	54	69	42	63	72	77
15462	MELCROFT	89	64	73	63	64	85	67	77	74	65	72	59	54	77	61	80	49	73	82	94
15463	MERRITTSTOWN	78	57	78	55	59	82	62	76	69	56	67	56	50	68	60	77	45	71	83	89
15464	MILL RUN	75	52	75	50	53	75	54	68	61	51	60	52	42	61	52	67	39	63	72	82
15468	NEW SALEM	78	57	75	56	59	81	63	75	70	57	67	56	52	69	60	77	45	71	82	89
15469	NORMALVILLE	81	59	75	58	60	80	61	74	67	58	66	56	50	69	58	74	44	69	77	89
15470	OHIOPYLE	84	68	81	69	70	88	69	82	73	63	72	62	59	74	68	79	48	75	85	96
15473	PERRYOPOLIS	79	74	82	72	75	90	70	82	76	67	75	59	68	75	73	82	51	77	90	95
15474	POINT MARION	70	51	64	50	51	69	56	65	62	51	60	49	46	62	52	67	40	62	70	78
15475	REPUBLIC	83	59	83	58	62	86	65	80	72	58	70	60	52	71	63	80	47	75	87	94
15477	ROSCOE	82	65	83	64	67	88	68	81	75	62	73	60	59	73	67	82	49	77	90	95
15478	SMITHFIELD	76	55	77	53	56	78	57	71	64	53	62	54	46	64	56	70	41	66	76	85
15479	SMITHTON	81	82	86	80	82	95	75	86	81	73	80	61	77	80	80	87	55	81	95	99
15480	SMOCK	82	63	77	61	64	83	64	76	70	61	69	57	54	71	61	77	46	71	81	91
15482	STAR JUNCTION	76	55	77	53	57	79	59	73	66	53	64	55	47	65	57	73	43	68	80	86
15483	STOCKDALE	83	60	84	58	62	87	65	81	73	58	70	60	53	72	63	81	47	75	88	95
15486	VANDERBILT	82	59	83	57	61	84	62	78	69	57	67	58	50	68	61	76	45	72	83	92
15488	WALTERSBURG	86	62	89	60	64	88	63	81	70	59	69	61	51	70	63	77	46	74	84	96
15490	WHITE	85	70	73	70	70	86	70	80	75	66	73	61	61	77	67	80	50	75	84	95
15501	SOMERSET	81	69	79	69	71	84	71	80	76	67	74	59	65	75	71	81	51	77	86	94
15521	ALUM BANK	77	58	65	57	58	75	60	69	65	57	64	53	49	68	55	71	43	65	73	83
15522	BEDFORD	77	74	73	75	75	85	73	79	76	68	75	58	71	76	74	81	52	76	86	92
15530	BERLIN	81	66	78	66	68	86	67	80	72	61	70	60	58	72	67	78	47	74	84	94
15531	BOSWELL	76	64	70	65	65	80	66	75	70	60	69	56	59	71	65	75	47	71	80	88
15533	BREEZEWOOD	80	57	73	56	58	78	59	72	66	57	65	55	47	67	56	72	43	67	75	86
15534	BUFFALO MILLS	75	58	74	57	60	77	58	72	63	54	62	54	49	63	58	69	42	66	74	84
15535	CLEARVILLE	83	60	84	59	62	84	61	78	68	57	67	58	50	68	61	74	44	71	81	92
15536	CRYSTAL SPRING	73	53	75	51	55	75	54	69	60	50	59	52	43	60	53	66	39	63	71	82
15537	EVERETT	77	63	71	64	64	80	66	75	70	60	68	57	57	70	64	75	46	71	79	88
15538	FAIRHOPE	80	58	83	56	60	82	59	75	66	55	64	56	47	65	58	72	43	69	78	89
15539	FISHERTOWN	90	64	74	63	64	85	67	78	74	65	73	60	54	77	61	81	49	74	82	95
15540	FORT HILL	82	58	85	56	60	84	61	77	66	54	65	59	47	65	60	73	43	71	80	92
15541	FRIEDENS	77	68	69	67	68	77	66	74	69	65	69	54	61	71	64	72	46	70	75	87
15542	GARRETT	75	56	68	56	57	75	59	69	63	54	62	54	48	65	56	69	42	65	72	83
15545	HYNDMAN	77	55	78	54	57	79	58	73	64	53	63	55	46	64	57	71	42	67	77	86
15546	JENNERS	73	53	75	51	55	75	54	69	60	50	59	52	43	60	53	66	39	63	71	82
15550	MANNS CHOICE	76	60	75	60	62	79	61	74	65	56	64	55	52	66	60	71	43	68	76	87
15551	MARKLETON	77	55	79	53	57	78	56	72	63	52	61	54	45	62	56	69	41	66	75	85
15552	MEYERSDALE	78	56	80	54	58	80	59	74	65	53	64	56	47	64	58	72	42	69	79	88
15554	NEW PARIS	84	64	71	64	64	82	66	76	72	63	70	58	55	74	61	77	47	71	80	91
15557	ROCKWOOD	78	59	78	58	61	81	61	75	67	56	65	56	50	66	60	73	43	69	79	88
15558	SALISBURY	81	57	85	56	59	85	62	78	67	53	66	61	48	66	61	74	43	72	83	93
15559	SCHELLSBURG	73	65	66	68	67	78	65	73	67	59	66	56	59	69	64	71	45	68	76	86
15562	SPRINGS	90	62	99	62	65	95	69	85	71	56	71	71	50	70	68	78	46	80	90	105
15563	STOYSTOWN	82	61	87	60	64	85	63	79	69	58	67	59	51	68	63	75	45	73	82	93
15601	GREENSBURG	88	92	92	93	93	98	88	93	91	87	90	68	92	89	92	94	63	91	100	108
15610	ACME	83	70	73	69	70	82	69	78	73	67	72	58	61	75	66	77	49	73	80	92
15611	ADAMSBURG	94	106	91	109	103	104	95	98	93	95	94	77	101	96	100	93	65	95	97	116
15612	ALVERTON	85	71	78	72	72	88	71	83	75	65	74	62	62	76	70	81	50	76	86	97
15613	APOLLO	81	77	76	77	77	88	74	82	78	72	77	61	72	78	75	82	53	78	88	96
15615	ARDARA	83	75	75	78	77	89	74	84	77	67	75	63	68	78	74	81	51	77	86	97
15617	ARONA	96	114	103	114	110	115	99	104	100	99	101	78	110	102	108	103	71	101	110	121
15618	AVONMORE	88	73	83	75	75	93	75	88	80	68	78	66	66	80	74	86	53	81	92	102
15620	BRADENVILLE	77	66	78	65	67	85	66	78	72	61	70	58	60	71	67	78	48	73	85	91
15622	CHAMPION	91	73	87	74	75	95	74	88	79	68	78	66	64	80	73	85	52	81	91	104
15623	CLARIDGE	74	85	79	85	84	90	75	81	79	75	79	59	83	78	82	82	55	79	90	94
15625	DARRAGH	68	78	74	76	78	85	69	76	74	68	73	53	76	72	75	79	51	73	87	87
15626	DELMONT	90	97	100	95	98	103	89	96	91	91	91	69	94	89	95	94	63	94	103	111
15627	DERRY	79	65	73	66	66	83	67	77	72	61	70	59	59	72	65	77	47	73	82	91
15628	DONEGAL	80	57	82	55	59	81	59	75	65	55	64	56	47	65	58	72	42	68	78	89
15631	EVERSON	74	53	74	52	55	77	58	72	65	52	62	53	47	64	56	71	42	67	78	84
15632	EXPORT	120	125	130	126	127	132	114	125	115	117	115	93	118	115	121	117	80	118	125	145
15634	GRAPEVILLE	85	96	91	94	96	105	85	94	91	84	91	66	94	89	93	97	63	91	107	107
15636	HARRISON CITY	115	136	118	139	132	126	117	121	113	122	115	96	129	118	125	111	82	115	114	139
15637	HERMINIE	82	61	83	59	63	86	64	79	71	59	69	59	53	70	63	78	46	74	86	93
15639	HUNKER	87	97	91	97	96	102	89	94	92	88	91	69	96	91	94	95	64	92	102	109
15641	HYDE PARK	85	61	85	59	63	88	66	82	74	59	72	61	53	73	64	82	48	77	90	96
15642	IRWIN	91	101	93	102	99	104	92	96	94	91	94	72	99	94	97	96	65	94	102	112
15644	JEANNETTE	79	81	78	80	79	89	76	82	80	75	80	61	78	80	79	84	55	80	90	96
15646	JONES MILLS	79	57	82	55	59	81	58	74	65	54	64	56	47	64	58	71	42	68	77	88
15647	LARIMER	84	88	83	89	87	95	81	88	83	77	82	66	82	84	84	86	57	83	92	103
15650	LATROBE	82	82	82	81	82	91	78	85	82	76	81	62	79	82	80	87	56	82	93	99
15655	LAUGHLINTOWN	108	87	139	86	95	115	87	110	91	81	90	81	75	86	94	97	60	102	109	128
15656	LEECHBURG	83	82	83	82	83	94	79	87	83	75	82	64	78	82	81	88	56	83	95	101
15658	LIGONIER	92	80	108	79	85	99	79	94	83	75	82	69	73	80	84	89	55	89	98	109
15661	LOYALHANNA	67	77	73	75	77	83	68	75	73	67	72	52	75	71	74	77	50	72	85	85
15663	MADISON	83	94	89	92	94	102	83	91	89	82	88	64	92	87	91	95	61	88	104	105
15665	MANOR	79	82	66	84	76	86	81	79	82	77	82	62	82	84	79	84	56	80	88	96
15666	MOUNT PLEASANT	78	68	78	67	69	84	66	77	72	63	71	57	61	71	67	78	48	73	84	91
15668	MURRYSVILLE	140	169	173	172	174	167	145	156	143	154	144	113	164	141	162	144	102	148	156	178
15670	NEW ALEXANDRIA	86	75	84	75	77	93	73	86	78	68	77	64	67	78	74	84	52	80	90	100
15672	NEW STANTON	82	83	81	82	83	91	80	85	84	78	83	62	81	83	82	88	57	84	94	99
15675	PENN	75	70	69	70	68	80	69	74	72	65	71	56	66	72	68	76	49	72	81	88
15677	RECTOR	127	100	158	98	108	133	100	127	106	94	104	93	86	101	107	113	69	117	127	148
15678	RILLTON	84	61	86	59	63	87	64	80	71	58	69	60	51	70	62	78	46	74	85	95
15679	RUFFS DALE	76	61	69	61	62	77	65	72	69	60	68	55	56	70	62	74	46	70	77	86
15681	SALTSBURG	79	60	79	59	62	82	62	76	67	56	66	57	51	67	61	74	44	70	80	90
15683	SCOTTDALE	76	70	73	70	71	83	68	77	73	65	72	56	66	73	69	78	49	73	84	89
15684	SLICKVILLE	76	55	73	53	56	76	56	69	62	53	61	53	45	63	54	68	41	64	73	83
15686	SPRING CHURCH	85	66	76	66	67	85	67	79	73	63	71	60	57	74	65	79	48	74	83	94
15687	STAHLSTOWN	88	66	89	65	68	90	67	84	74	62	72	63	56	74	67	80	48	77	87	99
	PENNSYLVANIA	94	95	95	95	95	100	94	96	96	91	95	73	94	96	94	99	67	95	101	113
	UNITED STATES	100	100	100	100	100	100	100	100	100	100	100	100	100	100	100	100	100	100	100	100

ZIP CODE #	POST OFFICE NAME	COUNTY FIPS CODE	POPULATION 2000	POPULATION 2009	POPULATION 2014	2000-2009 ANNUAL RATE % Rate	2000-2009 ANNUAL RATE State Centile	HOUSEHOLDS 2000	HOUSEHOLDS 2009	HOUSEHOLDS 2014	HOUSEHOLDS % Annual Rate 2000-2009	HOUSEHOLDS 2009 Average HH Size	FAMILIES 2000	FAMILIES 2009	FAMILIES % Annual Rate 2000-2009
15688	TARRS	129	605	578	565	-0.5	19	258	255	252	-0.1	2.26	183	175	-0.5
15690	VANDERGRIFT	005	9377	9131	8930	-0.3	29	4025	3988	3923	-0.1	2.28	2619	2509	-0.5
15692	WESTMORELAND CITY	129	778	814	814	0.5	70	320	338	340	0.6	2.41	229	232	0.1
15697	YOUNGWOOD	129	4164	3044	2919	-3.3	0	1512	1423	1379	-0.7	2.08	897	807	-1.1
15698	YUKON	129	551	528	515	-0.5	19	244	242	239	-0.1	2.18	159	151	-0.6
15701	INDIANA	063	31685	31280	30685	-0.1	46	12725	12997	12882	0.2	2.20	6953	6813	-0.2
15705	INDIANA	063	2554	2632	2624	0.3	64	146	159	161	0.9	4.24	4	4	0.0
15711	ANITA	065	216	222	220	0.3	64	88	92	92	0.5	2.34	67	68	0.2
15713	AULTMAN	063	337	316	306	-0.7	8	117	115	112	-0.2	2.75	92	88	-0.5
15714	NORTHERN CAMBRIA	021	6437	6071	5862	-0.6	13	2598	2533	2472	-0.3	2.38	1829	1729	-0.6
15716	BLACK LICK	063	210	206	202	-0.2	38	92	94	93	0.2	2.04	64	63	-0.2
15717	BLAIRSVILLE	063	11784	11513	11262	-0.3	29	4675	4691	4631	0.0	2.34	3233	3155	-0.3
15720	BRUSH VALLEY	063	36	34	33	-0.6	13	5	5	5	0.0	6.80	4	4	0.0
15721	BURNSIDE	033	104	103	101	-0.1	46	31	32	32	0.3	3.22	24	24	0.0
15722	CARROLLTOWN	021	2912	2760	2669	-0.6	13	1099	1080	1056	-0.2	2.51	833	797	-0.5
15724	CHERRY TREE	063	2965	2898	2834	-0.2	38	1068	1080	1068	0.1	2.58	839	831	-0.1
15725	CLARKSBURG	063	1585	1566	1539	-0.1	46	651	672	668	0.3	2.33	453	453	0.0
15728	CLYMER	063	4645	4535	4436	-0.3	29	1813	1833	1811	0.1	2.45	1296	1272	-0.2
15729	COMMODORE	063	1514	1482	1451	-0.2	38	539	547	541	0.2	2.64	433	430	-0.1
15730	COOLSPRING	065	45	40	38	-1.3	1	20	18	17	-1.1	2.22	15	14	-0.7
15732	CREEKSIDE	063	1571	1665	1662	0.6	74	597	662	670	1.1	2.51	456	493	0.8
15739	ERNEST	063	97	92	89	-0.6	13	33	33	32	0.0	2.70	26	25	-0.4
15742	GLEN CAMPBELL	063	1409	1352	1317	-0.4	23	516	513	505	-0.1	2.55	384	373	-0.3
15744	HAMILTON	065	49	50	49	0.2	61	18	19	19	0.6	2.63	13	14	0.8
15747	HOME	063	2791	2676	2604	-0.5	19	1028	1022	1006	-0.1	2.59	793	771	-0.3
15748	HOMER CITY	063	7968	7875	7727	-0.1	46	3295	3382	3357	0.3	2.32	2326	2322	0.0
15753	LA JOSE	033	574	569	559	-0.1	46	214	220	218	0.3	2.58	163	163	0.0
15757	MAHAFFEY	033	1938	1927	1890	-0.1	46	718	738	732	0.3	2.61	540	540	0.0
15758	MARCHAND	063	9	9	9	0.0	52	6	6	6	0.0	1.50	5	0	-100.0
15759	MARION CENTER	063	3234	3269	3224	0.1	57	1130	1184	1181	0.5	2.73	861	881	0.2
15760	MARSTELLER	021	168	157	151	-0.7	8	60	58	56	-0.4	2.71	46	43	-0.7
15762	NICKTOWN	021	1210	1205	1185	0.0	52	417	428	425	0.3	2.79	333	335	0.1
15763	NORTHPOINT	063	46	45	45	-0.2	38	19	19	19	0.0	2.37	16	16	0.0
15764	OLIVEBURG	065	26	23	22	-1.3	1	9	8	8	-1.3	2.88	7	6	-1.7
15765	PENN RUN	063	2062	2129	2115	0.3	64	740	792	794	0.7	2.58	580	606	0.5
15767	PUNXSUTAWNEY	065	15703	15523	15269	-0.1	46	6296	6376	6320	0.1	2.37	4292	4219	-0.2
15770	RINGGOLD	065	183	185	184	0.1	57	67	70	70	0.5	2.64	51	52	0.2
15771	ROCHESTER MILLS	063	1036	1022	1001	-0.1	46	398	406	402	0.2	2.49	302	300	-0.1
15772	ROSSITER	063	1708	1617	1568	-0.6	13	601	586	573	-0.3	2.48	435	412	-0.6
15773	SAINT BENEDICT	021	554	518	498	-0.7	8	209	202	196	-0.4	2.46	160	151	-0.6
15774	SHELOCTA	005	5006	4781	4655	-0.5	19	1920	1908	1878	-0.1	2.47	1458	1415	-0.3
15775	SPANGLER	021	487	451	432	-0.8	6	191	184	178	-0.4	2.44	139	130	-0.7
15776	SPRANKLE MILLS	065	131	117	112	-1.2	1	48	45	43	-0.7	2.60	36	33	-0.9
15777	STARFORD	063	307	297	290	-0.4	23	108	108	107	0.0	2.62	87	85	-0.3
15778	TIMBLIN	065	193	196	194	0.2	61	74	78	78	0.6	2.51	56	58	0.4
15780	VALIER	065	180	183	182	0.2	61	73	77	77	0.6	2.38	54	56	0.4
15784	WORTHVILLE	065	147	135	129	-0.9	4	59	55	54	-0.8	2.45	45	42	-0.7
15801	DU BOIS	033	20498	20102	19629	-0.2	38	8310	8361	8228	0.1	2.33	5637	5530	-0.2
15821	BENEZETT	047	196	182	175	-0.8	6	87	83	80	-0.5	2.19	63	58	-0.9
15823	BROCKPORT	047	1546	1430	1370	-0.8	6	651	627	609	-0.4	2.28	452	422	-0.7
15824	BROCKWAY	065	5146	4980	4868	-0.4	23	2038	2042	2017	0.0	2.38	1439	1400	-0.3
15825	BROOKVILLE	065	10590	10498	10331	-0.1	46	4213	4278	4241	0.2	2.36	2916	2889	-0.1
15827	BYRNEDALE	047	159	147	140	-0.8	6	64	61	59	-0.5	2.41	41	38	-0.8
15828	CLARINGTON	065	364	358	351	-0.2	38	168	168	167	0.0	2.10	114	111	-0.3
15829	CORSICA	065	1433	1452	1437	0.1	57	561	586	586	0.5	2.47	410	417	0.2
15832	DRIFTWOOD	023	436	370	342	-1.8	0	182	157	146	-1.6	2.36	128	107	-1.9
15834	EMPORIUM	023	5414	4976	4759	-0.9	4	2229	2081	1998	-0.7	2.35	1458	1319	-1.1
15840	FALLS CREEK	065	1948	1911	1879	-0.2	38	792	804	798	0.2	2.34	565	558	-0.1
15845	JOHNSONBURG	047	3412	3048	2892	-1.2	1	1448	1343	1288	-0.8	2.27	928	832	-1.2
15846	KERSEY	047	3698	3765	3721	0.2	61	1406	1490	1489	0.6	2.53	1044	1077	0.3
15848	LUTHERSBURG	033	1215	1210	1190	0.0	52	439	454	451	0.4	2.67	342	346	0.1
15849	PENFIELD	033	1504	1545	1528	0.3	64	624	665	665	0.7	2.32	431	445	0.3
15851	REYNOLDSVILLE	065	7272	7310	7224	0.1	57	2847	2932	2920	0.3	2.47	2086	2092	0.0
15853	RIDGWAY	047	7599	6974	6651	-0.9	4	3098	2926	2818	-0.6	2.33	2095	1920	-0.9
15856	ROCKTON	033	907	919	907	0.1	57	350	364	362	0.4	2.52	265	269	0.2
15857	SAINT MARYS	047	14567	13720	13206	-0.6	13	5747	5612	5462	-0.3	2.39	4019	3815	-0.6
15860	SIGEL	047	976	983	972	0.1	57	421	439	439	0.5	2.24	304	309	0.2
15861	SINNAMAHONING	023	129	109	101	-1.8	0	57	49	46	-1.6	2.22	40	33	-2.1
15864	SUMMERVILLE	065	1832	1758	1714	-0.4	23	689	683	673	-0.1	2.56	533	516	-0.3
15865	SYKESVILLE	065	1262	1216	1192	-0.4	23	553	551	545	0.0	2.21	345	330	-0.5
15868	WEEDVILLE	047	1960	1818	1740	-0.8	6	822	788	762	-0.5	2.31	554	514	-0.8
15870	WILCOX	047	1463	1330	1267	-1.0	3	583	553	533	-0.6	2.40	407	375	-0.9
15901	JOHNSTOWN	021	5559	4730	4449	-1.7	0	2766	2389	2258	-1.6	1.85	1166	957	-2.1
15902	JOHNSTOWN	021	13526	12272	11697	-1.0	3	5958	5567	5358	-0.7	2.20	3689	3317	-1.1
15904	JOHNSTOWN	021	17155	16861	16451	-0.2	38	6734	6661	6536	-0.1	2.24	4482	4277	-0.5
15905	JOHNSTOWN	021	22751	21447	20690	-0.6	13	9432	9074	8817	-0.4	2.25	6373	5936	-0.8
15906	JOHNSTOWN	021	11985	10939	10456	-1.0	3	5369	5061	4887	-0.6	2.15	3390	3077	-1.0
15909	JOHNSTOWN	021	6088	5610	5381	-0.9	4	2521	2407	2332	-0.5	2.32	1800	1671	-0.8
15920	ARMAGH	063	577	554	541	-0.4	23	225	225	221	0.0	2.46	165	161	-0.3
15923	BOLIVAR	129	1860	1807	1774	-0.3	29	707	705	698	0.0	2.50	540	524	-0.3
15924	CAIRNBROOK	111	1032	982	950	-0.5	19	431	422	413	-0.2	2.32	301	286	-0.6
15926	CENTRAL CITY	111	2941	2872	2809	-0.3	29	1224	1227	1210	0.0	2.34	858	836	-0.3
15927	COLVER	021	1204	1157	1123	-0.4	23	472	467	457	-0.1	2.33	336	323	-0.4
15928	DAVIDSVILLE	111	1649	1690	1672	0.3	64	648	682	682	0.6	2.38	480	493	0.3
15931	EBENSBURG	021	9484	9438	9284	-0.1	46	3333	3378	3343	0.1	2.43	2314	2279	-0.2
15935	HOLLSOPPLE	111	4031	3903	3803	-0.3	29	1585	1578	1550	0.0	2.45	1195	1161	-0.3
15936	HOOVERSVILLE	111	1586	1550	1515	-0.2	38	647	652	644	0.1	2.38	434	423	-0.3
15938	LILLY	021	4288	4255	4165	-0.1	46	1160	1156	1133	0.0	2.67	829	800	-0.4
15940	LORETTO	021	3656	4232	4229	1.6	92	604	667	676	1.1	3.21	447	480	0.8
15942	MINERAL POINT	021	2568	2432	2353	-0.6	13	995	977	954	-0.2	2.47	754	721	-0.5
15943	NANTY GLO	021	4406	4336	4234	-0.2	38	1794	1831	1809	0.2	2.36	1244	1227	-0.1
15944	NEW FLORENCE	129	3770	3657	3578	-0.3	29	1481	1484	1467	0.0	2.45	1101	1074	-0.3
15945	PARKHILL	021	58	55	54	-0.6	13	21	21	20	0.0	2.62	16	15	-0.7
15946	PORTAGE	021	7096	6769	6566	-0.5	19	2826	2784	2730	-0.2	2.37	1939	1849	-0.5
15949	ROBINSON	063	596	586	574	-0.2	38	234	237	234	0.1	2.47	183	181	-0.1
	PENNSYLVANIA					0.3					0.4	2.45			0.1
	UNITED STATES					1.0					1.1	2.59			0.9

#	POST OFFICE NAME	RACE (%) White 2000	White 2009	Black 2000	Black 2009	Asian/Pacific 2000	Asian/Pacific 2009	% Hispanic Origin 2000	% Hispanic Origin 2009	2009 AGE DISTRIBUTION (%) 0-4	5-9	10-14	15-19	20-24	25-44	45-64	65-84	85+	18+	MEDIAN AGE 2009	% 2009 Males	% 2009 Females
15688	TARRS	98.8	98.6	0.2	0.3	0.2	0.2	0.3	0.3	6.2	6.2	6.1	6.1	5.5	26.6	28.4	13.5	1.4	77.5	40.7	47.9	52.1
15690	VANDERGRIFT	95.3	94.0	3.0	3.8	0.1	0.2	0.4	0.6	5.4	5.3	5.6	6.3	5.5	24.0	29.3	15.2	3.4	79.7	43.5	48.0	52.0
15692	WESTMORELAND CITY	97.2	96.3	0.5	0.6	0.4	0.6	0.9	1.2	6.6	6.9	6.8	6.1	5.5	26.7	28.6	10.9	1.8	75.7	39.7	49.8	50.2
15697	YOUNGWOOD	87.8	93.1	11.6	5.0	0.2	0.6	2.4	3.2	4.2	4.3	4.7	6.0	5.7	29.8	27.0	14.3	4.0	84.4	42.1	50.0	50.0
15698	YUKON	99.3	99.1	0.0	0.0	0.2	0.4	0.4	0.4	6.1	6.1	6.4	5.7	3.6	26.1	25.9	16.5	3.6	77.7	42.8	46.8	53.2
15701	INDIANA	94.5	92.7	2.7	3.2	1.7	2.7	0.8	1.1	3.6	3.7	4.1	9.5	19.0	20.1	24.4	12.7	2.9	85.7	34.6	47.2	52.8
15705	INDIANA	84.4	81.0	11.6	13.5	2.3	3.5	1.5	1.9	0.0	0.0	0.1	47.4	48.7	2.7	0.7	0.3	0.0	99.7	20.2	42.1	57.9
15711	ANITA	98.6	98.2	0.0	0.5	0.0	0.0	0.5	0.5	6.3	6.8	6.3	6.3	5.0	23.4	30.2	14.0	1.8	76.1	42.4	49.5	50.5
15713	AULTMAN	98.5	98.4	0.6	0.6	0.3	0.3	0.3	0.3	5.1	5.7	6.0	5.4	4.4	24.7	32.3	14.9	1.6	79.7	44.2	51.9	48.1
15714	NORTHERN CAMBRIA	99.4	99.2	0.1	0.1	0.2	0.3	0.3	0.4	5.7	5.7	5.8	6.0	4.9	25.2	29.1	14.4	3.3	79.1	42.4	49.0	51.0
15716	BLACK LICK	99.0	98.1	0.5	1.0	0.0	0.0	1.0	0.5	5.3	5.8	5.8	5.8	4.9	24.3	25.7	17.5	4.9	79.1	43.5	48.1	51.9
15717	BLAIRSVILLE	96.9	96.1	2.2	2.8	0.2	0.4	0.3	0.5	5.2	5.4	5.8	6.5	4.7	23.8	30.7	15.1	2.6	79.5	44.0	49.8	50.2
15720	BRUSH VALLEY	100.0	100.0	0.0	0.0	0.0	0.0	0.0	0.0	5.9	5.9	5.9	5.9	5.9	32.4	26.5	11.8	0.0	79.4	41.0	50.0	50.0
15721	BURNSIDE	100.0	100.0	0.0	0.0	0.0	0.0	0.0	1.0	5.8	5.8	5.8	5.8	4.9	25.2	30.1	14.6	1.9	78.6	42.8	50.5	49.5
15722	CARROLLTOWN	99.5	99.4	0.1	0.1	0.0	0.0	0.0	0.0	5.1	5.4	5.8	5.7	5.4	24.2	30.8	14.3	3.4	80.2	43.7	50.2	49.8
15724	CHERRY TREE	99.1	98.9	0.1	0.1	0.0	0.0	0.5	0.6	5.7	5.9	6.1	6.0	4.7	24.1	31.0	13.8	2.8	78.6	43.3	49.6	50.4
15725	CLARKSBURG	99.1	99.0	0.3	0.3	0.1	0.1	0.0	0.0	5.4	6.2	6.1	6.4	3.4	27.1	29.2	14.4	1.7	77.9	42.1	50.1	49.9
15728	CLYMER	99.2	99.0	0.2	0.2	0.0	0.1	0.3	0.4	5.7	6.0	6.0	6.1	5.4	25.3	29.1	13.9	2.6	78.6	41.8	49.0	51.0
15729	COMMODORE	98.9	98.8	0.2	0.2	0.0	0.0	0.4	0.5	5.7	6.1	6.5	6.3	4.7	25.4	30.3	12.1	3.0	77.8	41.7	50.7	49.3
15730	COOLSPRING	100.0	100.0	0.0	0.0	0.0	0.0	0.0	0.0	5.0	5.0	5.0	5.0	5.0	25.0	37.5	12.5	0.0	80.0	45.0	50.0	50.0
15732	CREEKSIDE	99.0	98.8	0.3	0.4	0.1	0.1	0.1	0.1	6.4	6.8	6.8	5.4	4.1	26.2	32.3	10.7	1.2	76.5	40.9	51.7	48.3
15739	ERNEST	100.0	100.0	0.0	0.0	0.0	0.0	0.0	0.0	5.4	4.3	6.5	7.6	5.4	23.9	33.7	10.9	2.2	78.3	42.9	51.1	48.9
15742	GLEN CAMPBELL	99.0	98.7	0.0	0.0	0.1	0.3	0.3	0.4	5.0	5.3	5.9	6.1	4.9	24.3	32.2	14.1	2.2	79.8	43.9	51.0	49.0
15744	HAMILTON	100.0	100.0	0.0	0.0	0.0	0.0	0.0	0.0	4.0	6.0	8.0	6.0	4.0	26.0	26.0	16.0	4.0	76.0	42.5	54.0	46.0
15747	HOME	99.2	99.1	0.2	0.2	0.1	0.2	0.1	0.1	6.8	7.1	7.5	7.7	4.9	24.3	28.9	11.1	1.8	73.8	39.4	51.0	49.0
15748	HOMER CITY	99.1	98.9	0.4	0.5	0.1	0.1	0.4	0.6	5.2	5.5	5.8	6.1	4.6	24.8	30.3	15.2	2.6	79.6	43.5	49.4	50.6
15753	LA JOSE	98.8	98.6	0.2	0.2	0.3	0.4	0.5	0.7	6.2	6.3	6.7	6.9	5.4	25.8	27.8	13.2	1.8	76.6	39.9	53.1	46.9
15757	MAHAFFEY	99.4	99.1	0.0	0.0	0.1	0.2	0.3	0.4	6.2	6.6	6.8	6.3	4.9	23.6	29.4	14.4	1.9	76.5	42.0	50.8	49.2
15758	MARCHAND	100.0	100.0	0.0	0.0	0.0	0.0	0.0	0.0	0.0	0.0	0.0	0.0	0.0	44.4	55.6	0.0	0.0	100.0	45.8	55.6	44.4
15759	MARION CENTER	99.1	98.7	0.2	0.2	0.4	0.6	0.1	0.2	6.3	6.8	6.9	6.9	5.2	24.3	30.0	11.6	2.0	75.7	40.2	49.8	50.2
15760	MARSTELLER	100.0	100.0	0.0	0.0	0.0	0.0	0.0	0.0	5.7	5.7	6.4	6.4	4.5	24.2	30.6	14.6	1.9	77.7	42.8	49.0	51.0
15762	NICKTOWN	99.7	99.6	0.0	0.0	0.1	0.1	0.2	0.2	6.1	6.4	7.0	7.0	5.1	23.7	31.3	11.2	2.4	76.3	41.1	48.9	51.1
15763	NORTHPOINT	100.0	100.0	0.0	0.0	0.0	0.0	0.0	0.0	13.3	11.1	11.1	11.1	11.1	22.2	17.8	2.2	0.0	53.3	21.5	51.1	48.9
15764	OLIVEBURG	100.0	100.0	0.0	0.0	0.0	0.0	0.0	0.0	4.3	8.7	8.7	8.7	4.3	30.4	34.8	0.0	0.0	69.6	36.3	47.8	52.2
15765	PENN RUN	99.1	98.9	0.2	0.3	0.1	0.2	0.2	0.2	5.5	5.9	6.3	6.1	4.5	25.4	32.3	12.4	1.6	78.6	42.7	51.7	48.3
15767	PUNXSUTAWNEY	99.0	98.8	0.1	0.1	0.2	0.3	0.5	0.6	5.6	5.9	6.0	6.6	5.5	23.8	28.8	14.5	3.2	78.6	42.3	48.2	51.8
15770	RINGGOLD	100.0	99.5	0.0	0.0	0.0	0.0	0.5	1.1	5.4	5.4	6.5	6.5	4.3	23.8	31.9	14.1	2.2	78.4	43.7	50.8	49.2
15771	ROCHESTER MILLS	98.8	98.6	0.2	0.2	0.2	0.3	0.2	0.2	6.0	6.5	6.7	6.5	5.5	24.5	30.5	12.5	1.5	76.8	40.8	51.4	48.6
15772	ROSSITER	99.6	99.6	0.0	0.0	0.1	0.1	0.4	0.6	4.3	4.4	4.8	6.1	5.7	23.9	30.8	17.5	2.5	82.4	45.5	49.8	50.2
15773	SAINT BENEDICT	99.6	99.6	0.0	0.0	0.0	0.0	0.0	0.0	4.4	4.4	5.0	5.8	6.0	21.6	30.5	17.4	4.8	82.6	46.6	49.8	50.2
15774	SHELOCTA	99.1	98.8	0.2	0.3	0.1	0.1	0.3	0.4	5.4	5.8	6.1	5.7	4.6	25.6	31.7	12.9	2.0	79.0	42.9	49.3	50.7
15775	SPANGLER	99.6	99.6	0.0	0.0	0.0	0.0	0.2	0.2	4.7	4.7	5.1	6.4	4.9	24.8	32.2	14.4	2.9	81.2	44.5	47.9	52.1
15776	SPRANKLE MILLS	98.5	97.4	0.0	0.0	0.0	0.9	0.8	0.9	6.0	6.0	6.0	6.0	4.3	25.6	30.8	13.7	1.7	77.8	42.5	49.6	50.4
15777	STARFORD	99.3	99.3	0.3	0.3	0.0	0.0	0.0	0.0	5.7	5.7	6.1	6.7	5.1	24.6	27.9	13.5	4.7	78.1	42.3	49.2	50.8
15778	TIMBLIN	100.0	99.5	0.0	0.0	0.0	0.0	0.5	1.0	5.1	5.1	6.1	6.6	4.6	24.0	32.7	13.8	2.0	79.1	44.0	51.0	49.0
15780	VALIER	99.4	99.5	0.0	0.0	0.0	0.0	0.0	0.0	4.4	6.6	7.7	6.0	4.9	27.9	27.3	13.1	2.2	77.6	40.2	53.6	46.4
15784	WORTHVILLE	98.6	97.8	0.0	0.0	0.0	0.7	0.0	0.0	6.7	6.7	6.7	6.7	5.9	25.9	28.1	11.9	1.5	75.6	39.1	53.3	46.7
15801	DU BOIS	98.4	97.8	0.2	0.3	0.6	0.9	0.4	0.6	5.6	5.7	6.0	6.2	5.3	23.7	28.8	15.1	3.7	78.9	43.2	48.1	51.9
15821	BENEZETT	99.0	98.9	0.0	0.0	1.0	1.1	0.0	0.5	5.5	6.0	6.6	4.9	3.8	25.8	27.5	17.6	2.2	78.6	43.2	50.0	50.0
15823	BROCKPORT	99.2	99.0	0.1	0.1	0.2	0.3	0.1	0.1	5.0	5.5	5.9	5.9	4.8	25.0	32.1	14.5	1.4	79.9	43.5	51.6	48.4
15824	BROCKWAY	99.3	99.2	0.0	0.0	0.1	0.2	0.3	0.4	5.7	6.0	6.1	6.1	5.2	23.8	28.4	15.1	3.5	78.4	42.7	49.8	50.2
15825	BROOKVILLE	98.7	98.2	0.2	0.2	0.4	0.6	0.3	0.5	5.1	5.3	5.6	6.2	5.1	24.3	29.1	15.7	3.6	80.2	43.8	49.2	50.8
15827	BYRNEDALE	99.4	99.3	0.0	0.0	0.0	0.0	1.3	1.4	6.1	6.1	6.1	6.1	4.8	23.8	27.2	17.0	2.7	78.2	43.1	49.0	51.0
15828	CLARINGTON	98.1	97.2	0.3	0.3	0.3	0.6	0.8	0.8	3.9	3.9	4.5	6.1	5.3	20.1	33.8	20.1	2.2	83.5	48.8	50.8	49.2
15829	CORSICA	99.0	98.8	0.2	0.3	0.2	0.3	0.2	0.3	5.2	5.6	5.9	5.9	4.1	25.8	30.9	14.9	1.7	79.7	43.0	51.0	49.0
15832	DRIFTWOOD	98.4	97.8	0.0	0.0	0.2	0.3	0.5	0.5	4.6	4.6	4.9	6.5	5.4	20.5	34.3	17.0	2.2	81.9	46.8	47.8	52.2
15834	EMPORIUM	98.9	98.7	0.4	0.4	0.2	0.2	0.6	0.8	5.1	5.1	5.4	6.8	5.8	23.1	29.2	16.0	3.5	80.0	44.0	48.9	51.1
15840	FALLS CREEK	99.1	99.0	0.2	0.2	0.1	0.1	0.4	0.4	5.2	5.2	5.3	5.9	5.4	24.4	29.6	16.0	2.9	80.7	43.9	48.6	51.4
15845	JOHNSONBURG	98.9	98.6	0.0	0.0	0.4	0.6	1.2	1.6	6.1	5.9	5.9	6.1	5.6	25.4	27.2	15.1	2.8	78.3	41.4	49.4	50.6
15846	KERSEY	99.5	99.4	0.1	0.1	0.1	0.1	0.1	0.2	6.4	6.6	7.0	6.8	4.6	26.5	28.3	12.4	1.4	75.7	40.5	51.2	48.8
15848	LUTHERSBURG	99.1	98.9	0.0	0.0	0.1	0.1	0.2	0.4	6.0	6.4	6.4	5.9	5.1	24.0	31.6	13.0	1.5	77.4	42.0	50.7	49.3
15849	PENFIELD	99.7	99.5	0.0	0.0	0.1	0.3	0.0	0.0	5.9	6.3	6.5	6.1	3.9	25.8	28.8	15.1	1.6	77.3	42.2	50.9	49.1
15851	REYNOLDSVILLE	99.1	98.7	0.1	0.2	0.1	0.2	0.5	0.8	6.4	6.3	6.6	6.8	5.7	25.0	27.8	13.4	2.0	76.3	40.2	50.1	49.9
15853	RIDGWAY	98.8	98.5	0.2	0.2	0.5	0.7	0.4	0.6	5.9	5.9	6.0	5.9	6.0	24.1	29.2	14.4	2.6	78.6	42.3	49.2	50.8
15856	ROCKTON	99.4	99.3	0.0	0.0	0.0	0.0	0.2	0.3	5.1	6.0	6.5	6.4	5.2	22.4	34.7	12.1	1.5	78.3	43.7	50.1	49.9
15857	SAINT MARYS	98.8	98.3	0.2	0.3	0.5	0.8	0.3	0.4	5.6	5.9	6.1	6.4	5.1	24.9	28.1	14.7	3.3	78.0	42.4	49.1	50.9
15860	SIGEL	98.8	98.5	0.2	0.2	0.2	0.3	0.5	0.6	5.2	5.6	5.9	5.7	4.6	22.7	31.9	16.3	2.1	79.9	45.2	51.3	48.7
15861	SINNAMAHONING	98.4	98.2	0.0	0.0	0.0	0.0	0.8	0.9	4.6	4.6	4.6	6.4	5.5	20.2	34.9	16.5	2.8	83.5	46.9	47.7	52.3
15864	SUMMERVILLE	98.9	98.6	0.1	0.1	0.1	0.2	0.1	0.1	5.1	5.5	5.9	5.9	4.9	25.5	32.2	13.0	1.9	79.6	43.0	50.9	49.1
15865	SYKESVILLE	99.4	99.3	0.2	0.3	0.0	0.0	0.2	0.3	5.3	5.2	5.7	6.6	5.6	24.5	27.5	16.3	3.3	79.9	42.9	49.6	50.4
15868	WEEDVILLE	99.3	99.1	0.1	0.1	0.4	0.6	0.7	1.0	5.8	6.1	6.2	5.7	4.5	24.0	28.1	17.1	2.6	78.4	43.6	49.8	50.2
15870	WILCOX	99.5	99.4	0.1	0.1	0.0	0.0	0.3	0.4	4.4	5.0	5.5	6.2	4.5	24.1	34.5	13.7	2.2	81.0	45.2	52.9	47.1
15901	JOHNSTOWN	75.0	71.8	21.0	23.4	0.2	0.3	2.1	2.7	5.2	5.6	5.1	4.7	4.5	21.5	26.2	21.1	6.2	81.2	48.0	45.9	54.1
15902	JOHNSTOWN	91.6	89.7	6.2	7.6	0.2	0.3	1.2	1.6	5.8	5.7	5.6	6.0	5.6	24.7	27.9	15.8	2.9	79.3	42.3	47.0	53.0
15904	JOHNSTOWN	97.3	96.1	0.8	1.1	1.2	2.0	0.5	0.7	4.0	4.2	4.6	9.5	9.7	18.6	27.1	17.8	4.4	84.0	44.3	46.3	53.7
15905	JOHNSTOWN	97.9	97.2	0.7	0.9	0.7	1.1	0.6	0.8	4.3	4.6	5.2	5.9	5.1	20.5	31.0	18.2	5.2	82.3	47.9	46.9	53.1
15906	JOHNSTOWN	92.9	91.2	5.4	6.6	0.2	0.3	1.1	1.4	5.7	5.8	5.8	5.7	4.8	22.6	29.1	17.3	3.4	79.3	44.8	47.0	53.0
15909	JOHNSTOWN	97.3	96.5	2.1	2.7	0.1	0.1	0.5	0.7	4.3	4.6	5.1	5.8	4.6	23.2	32.0	17.4	2.9	82.4	46.6	48.3	51.7
15920	ARMAGH	99.1	99.1	0.0	0.0	0.2	0.2	0.0	0.0	4.2	4.5	5.1	5.4	4.7	25.3	34.7	14.4	1.8	82.7	45.6	49.6	50.4
15923	BOLIVAR	98.1	97.7	0.5	0.6	0.1	0.1	0.1	0.2	4.6	5.0	5.4	7.1	4.9	22.6	31.5	16.7	2.1	80.5	45.2	51.7	48.3
15924	CAIRNBROOK	99.3	99.2	0.2	0.2	0.0	0.0	0.1	0.1	4.8	5.2	5.5	5.8	4.6	26.0	29.0	15.9	3.3	80.9	43.5	50.8	49.2
15926	CENTRAL CITY	99.4	99.3	0.0	0.0	0.1	0.2	0.3	0.4	5.3	5.7	5.9	5.8	4.8	23.6	31.0	15.0	3.0	79.6	44.2	49.7	50.3
15927	COLVER	98.8	98.1	0.8	1.1	0.3	0.5	0.4	0.6	6.1	6.1	6.2	6.1	4.5	26.5	26.9	13.4	4.2	77.6	41.1	51.8	48.2
15928	DAVIDSVILLE	99.4	99.1	0.1	0.1	0.2	0.4	0.4	0.6	4.6	5.0	5.3	5.5	4.9	22.4	29.9	17.0	5.4	81.8	46.8	46.8	53.2
15931	EBENSBURG	97.1	96.1	1.9	2.5	0.4	0.6	0.5	0.7	4.5	4.8	5.3	5.7	5.7	25.0	29.6	15.2	4.1	81.8	44.3	49.7	50.3
15935	HOLLSOPPLE	99.4	99.3	0.0	0.0	0.1	0.2	0.5	0.7	4.7	5.0	5.5	6.2	5.1	22.3	31.1	17.2	2.9	80.9	45.8	47.8	52.2
15936	HOOVERSVILLE	99.1	99.0	0.1	0.1	0.0	0.1	0.6	0.8	5.0	5.2	5.8	6.8	4.8	23.7	29.9	15.8	2.8	79.7	44.0	49.6	50.4
15938	LILLY	87.8	84.5	9.5	11.8	0.2	0.2	2.5	3.3	3.9	4.0	4.2	6.7	8.0	32.7	26.1	12.3	2.2	84.7	39.2	60.5	39.5
15940	LORETTO	88.3	85.0	9.9	12.5	0.8	1.2	5.9	7.7	2.9	3.2	3.3	12.7	15.8	34.1	20.4	6.7	0.9	87.6	31.6	60.3	39.7
15942	MINERAL POINT	99.0	98.7	0.3	0.4	0.1	0.1	0.1	0.2	4.9	5.1	5.6	6.1	4.9	23.4	31.9	15.8	2.3	80.5	45.0	49.4	50.6
15943	NANTY GLO	99.5	99.3	0.2	0.3	0.0	0.0	0.3	0.4	5.5	5.6	5.8	5.9	4.6	24.0	28.7	16.8	3.2	79.5	44.0	49.0	51.0
15944	NEW FLORENCE	99.0	98.7	0.1	0.1	0.1	0.1	0.6	0.8	5.8	6.0	6.4	5.9	5.1	23.5	31.1	14.4	1.8	78.0	43.0	50.2	49.8
15945	PARKHILL	98.3	98.2	1.7	1.8	0.0	0.0	0.0	0.0	3.6	3.6	5.5	7.3	3.6	21.8	36.4	16.4	1.8	80.0	47.1	49.1	50.9
15946	PORTAGE	99.2	99.0	0.2	0.3	0.1	0.2	0.4	0.5	5.2	5.4	5.6	5.8	4.9	24.6	30.1	15.4	3.0	80.2	43.9	49.4	50.6
15949	ROBINSON	99.2	99.1	0.2	0.2	0.3	0.3	0.5	0.5	6.1	6.7	7.0	6.1	3.9	25.3	31.1	12.1	1.9	76.5	41.2	51.4	48.6
	PENNSYLVANIA	85.4	83.2	10.0	10.7	1.8	2.7	3.2	4.2	5.8	6.0	6.3	7.1	6.5	24.8	27.8	13.1	2.6	77.8	40.4	48.5	51.5
	UNITED STATES	75.1	72.0	12.3	12.7	3.8	4.6	12.5	15.7	6.8	6.7	6.6	7.1	6.9	27.0	26.0	10.9	1.9	75.7	36.9	49.2	50.8

#	POST OFFICE NAME	2009 Per Capita Income	2009 HH Income Base	2009 HOUSEHOLD INCOME DISTRIBUTION (%) Less than $25,000	$25,000 to $49,999	$50,000 to $99,999	$100,000 to $149,999	$150,000 or More	MEDIAN HOUSEHOLD INCOME 2009	2014	2009 National Centile	2009 State Centile	2009 Home Value Base	2009 HOME VALUE DISTRIBUTION (%) Less than $50,000	$50,000 to $89,999	$90,000 to $174,999	$175,000 to $399,999	$400,000 or More	2009 Median Home Value
15688	TARRS	18930	255	30.6	35.3	29.8	3.5	0.8	36056	38641	21	11	198	26.3	15.2	41.9	14.6	2.0	100000
15690	VANDERGRIFT	20107	3988	31.1	31.2	32.2	4.1	1.4	37111	39953	24	14	2801	14.9	39.0	36.8	8.4	0.9	84349
15692	WESTMORELAND CITY	26590	338	18.0	25.7	38.8	13.9	3.6	56881	57985	74	74	283	2.8	20.8	48.1	26.9	1.4	120750
15697	YOUNGWOOD	24998	1423	22.6	32.5	39.5	3.9	1.5	44536	48860	47	44	893	5.5	24.5	47.5	22.5	0.0	120148
15698	YUKON	22425	242	26.9	36.0	28.1	5.8	3.3	41787	45122	39	34	184	25.5	40.2	33.2	1.1	0.0	72778
15701	INDIANA	22631	12997	35.5	25.3	28.7	6.5	4.0	37454	40643	25	16	7471	9.9	11.9	43.7	29.9	4.6	144750
15705	INDIANA	11260	159	87.4	5.7	0.0	0.0	6.9	11850	11823	1	1	2	0.0	0.0	0.0	100.0	0.0	187500
15711	ANITA	20991	92	23.9	42.4	29.3	3.3	1.1	40000	43194	33	26	78	20.5	32.1	37.2	10.3	0.0	86667
15713	AULTMAN	17324	115	24.3	40.0	31.3	3.5	0.9	41585	44374	38	33	97	14.4	26.8	36.1	21.6	1.0	106944
15714	NORTHERN CAMBRIA	17884	2533	34.1	34.2	26.7	3.7	1.3	34394	36138	16	7	1964	29.4	32.2	29.1	8.4	0.9	72467
15716	BLACK LICK	21348	94	31.9	31.9	27.7	6.4	2.1	34190	36748	16	7	69	27.5	20.3	46.4	5.8	0.0	93000
15717	BLAIRSVILLE	21040	4691	27.8	30.5	34.7	5.3	1.7	43508	46430	44	41	3520	13.2	25.3	42.5	16.9	2.0	109725
15720	BRUSH VALLEY	7500	5	0.0	40.0	60.0	0.0	0.0	51667	51667	65	66	4	0.0	0.0	100.0	0.0	0.0	125000
15721	BURNSIDE	13183	32	34.4	34.4	28.1	3.1	0.0	35000	37339	18	8	27	29.6	33.3	29.6	7.4	0.0	72500
15722	CARROLLTOWN	20036	1080	26.3	32.5	34.4	5.0	1.8	44039	46934	45	43	936	22.4	30.4	35.4	10.5	1.3	86351
15724	CHERRY TREE	15823	1080	34.0	35.7	27.1	2.3	0.8	34411	36589	16	7	897	26.8	30.5	31.0	10.1	1.6	77063
15725	CLARKSBURG	18774	672	32.3	35.1	28.7	2.5	1.3	38299	40498	28	19	560	23.8	23.8	35.0	14.3	3.2	94828
15728	CLYMER	17486	1833	34.3	31.5	29.8	3.7	0.7	36436	38713	22	12	1442	27.9	27.4	33.8	9.4	1.5	78455
15729	COMMODORE	14589	547	34.2	39.1	24.1	2.4	0.2	33539	34924	14	6	465	31.8	31.2	27.1	9.0	0.9	65571
15730	COOLSPRING	18563	18	22.2	44.4	33.3	0.0	0.0	37278	38575	24	15	16	12.5	25.0	50.0	12.5	0.0	100000
15732	CREEKSIDE	18169	662	28.5	34.3	32.2	3.9	1.1	39363	42007	31	23	534	15.4	28.1	44.2	11.6	0.7	98974
15739	ERNEST	18699	33	27.3	27.3	42.4	3.0	0.0	43636	51612	44	42	28	3.6	17.9	60.7	17.9	0.0	119444
15742	GLEN CAMPBELL	15120	513	38.4	36.6	22.2	1.8	1.0	31852	33700	11	4	439	29.8	30.1	31.7	8.2	0.2	75323
15744	HAMILTON	17960	19	21.1	47.4	26.3	5.3	0.0	36091	42361	21	11	17	5.9	23.5	58.8	11.8	0.0	112500
15747	HOME	18149	1022	28.7	32.2	35.0	3.1	1.0	40208	43386	33	27	854	17.4	22.6	43.6	15.5	0.9	106560
15748	HOMER CITY	21519	3382	26.6	32.1	34.4	5.3	1.7	42815	45867	42	38	2682	12.8	26.5	47.8	12.4	0.4	104046
15753	LA JOSE	14967	220	37.3	38.6	20.9	1.8	1.4	31112	32003	10	3	182	30.8	25.8	33.5	9.9	0.0	76000
15757	MAHAFFEY	15247	738	35.1	37.5	23.8	2.7	0.8	32791	35201	13	5	632	26.1	29.1	34.2	9.7	0.9	82326
15758	MARCHAND	20278	6	50.0	16.7	33.3	0.0	0.0	25000	37500	3	2	5	0.0	0.0	100.0	0.0	0.0	120833
15759	MARION CENTER	15911	1184	32.3	32.5	31.6	2.7	0.9	36643	39951	22	13	951	20.7	20.5	40.5	17.6	0.7	105018
15760	MARSTELLER	15375	58	36.2	31.0	29.3	1.7	1.7	33188	35000	14	5	49	32.7	20.4	38.8	8.2	0.0	82500
15762	NICKTOWN	16822	428	25.7	33.9	35.3	4.4	0.7	44383	46985	46	44	377	17.2	20.4	41.4	19.1	1.9	113480
15763	NORTHPOINT	15334	19	36.8	42.1	21.1	0.0	0.0	28989	28562	7	3	17	11.8	29.4	35.3	23.5	0.0	104167
15764	OLIVEBURG	13370	8	25.0	50.0	25.0	0.0	0.0	35000	45000	18	8	7	0.0	0.0	100.0	0.0	0.0	131250
15765	PENN RUN	18497	792	23.7	34.3	36.7	4.5	0.6	43127	46302	43	39	684	18.9	18.7	44.3	16.7	1.5	112879
15767	PUNXSUTAWNEY	19557	6376	30.3	34.9	28.8	3.7	2.3	38172	39594	27	18	4694	13.8	26.4	43.7	14.4	1.6	104583
15770	RINGGOLD	15800	70	25.7	47.1	24.3	2.9	0.0	37238	38115	24	15	58	15.5	27.6	43.1	13.8	0.0	98000
15771	ROCHESTER MILLS	16389	406	33.5	34.7	29.1	2.0	0.7	35193	37489	18	9	338	22.5	25.4	36.4	14.2	1.5	93500
15772	ROSSITER	17094	586	32.4	32.6	31.6	2.4	1.0	37270	39909	24	15	498	32.1	29.9	29.3	8.6	0.0	70606
15773	SAINT BENEDICT	18361	202	28.2	37.1	31.7	2.5	0.5	39101	43655	30	22	181	34.3	35.9	24.3	5.0	0.6	62333
15774	SHELOCTA	19063	1908	28.7	29.4	37.2	3.9	0.9	41994	46145	39	35	1582	20.2	16.1	44.6	17.6	1.5	113049
15775	SPANGLER	18637	184	31.0	34.2	27.7	6.0	1.1	36522	39385	22	12	146	24.7	29.5	40.4	5.5	0.0	80000
15776	SPRANKLE MILLS	17527	45	22.2	40.0	35.6	2.2	0.0	40748	39286	35	29	39	15.4	20.5	51.3	12.8	0.0	106250
15777	STARFORD	15797	108	32.4	34.3	31.5	1.9	0.0	33899	39317	15	6	97	29.9	32.0	36.1	2.1	0.0	73500
15778	TIMBLIN	16477	78	26.9	47.4	23.1	2.6	0.0	37016	37765	24	14	65	13.8	27.7	46.2	12.3	0.0	100962
15780	VALIER	19901	77	24.7	40.3	29.9	3.9	1.3	38794	39527	29	21	69	13.0	20.3	46.4	18.8	1.4	117045
15784	WORTHVILLE	18680	55	25.5	40.0	29.1	3.6	1.8	37303	40000	24	15	48	14.6	29.2	43.8	12.5	0.0	97500
15801	DU BOIS	23572	8361	25.7	28.8	36.3	6.0	3.3	45939	48782	51	51	6226	6.3	19.7	45.0	25.8	3.2	131846
15821	BENEZETT	21794	83	24.1	33.7	39.8	2.4	0.0	42321	46567	40	36	76	10.5	27.6	48.7	11.8	1.3	105000
15823	BROCKPORT	21455	627	27.1	37.3	30.5	3.7	1.4	41351	43536	37	32	522	15.5	24.7	49.0	9.6	1.1	104268
15824	BROCKWAY	22708	2042	20.2	33.9	38.9	5.2	1.8	47243	49805	55	55	1569	6.6	22.1	53.3	17.3	0.7	116359
15825	BROOKVILLE	20927	4278	28.1	33.8	31.3	4.2	2.7	40597	42337	35	28	3290	10.3	21.3	50.0	16.9	1.4	114825
15827	BYRNEDALE	20558	61	29.5	27.9	37.7	4.9	0.0	41730	44304	38	34	53	18.9	35.8	30.2	15.1	0.0	81667
15828	CLARINGTON	22219	168	32.7	32.1	30.4	4.2	0.6	37563	38629	25	16	145	13.8	26.2	43.4	15.2	1.4	103472
15829	CORSICA	19459	586	24.7	35.5	35.0	3.4	1.4	41351	42767	37	32	486	14.4	22.6	45.9	15.8	1.2	106522
15832	DRIFTWOOD	17746	157	33.1	35.0	28.0	3.2	0.6	36439	37314	22	12	134	19.4	28.4	43.3	8.2	0.7	96000
15834	EMPORIUM	20242	2081	26.5	34.2	33.8	4.1	1.4	40649	42542	35	29	1527	11.5	25.1	51.7	11.2	0.5	107754
15840	FALLS CREEK	21538	804	24.9	33.8	35.3	4.7	1.2	44702	46389	47	45	671	7.7	27.4	51.4	12.4	1.0	107500
15845	JOHNSONBURG	20706	1343	32.2	28.3	32.4	5.9	1.3	37541	40291	25	16	998	20.4	43.3	30.0	6.2	0.1	76038
15846	KERSEY	19653	1490	20.9	28.7	47.4	2.3	0.5	50157	52088	62	62	1294	8.1	13.8	50.5	25.4	2.2	138519
15848	LUTHERSBURG	18495	454	25.6	37.0	32.4	3.3	1.8	40985	43405	36	30	395	16.7	20.5	47.3	13.7	1.8	109964
15849	PENFIELD	19930	665	28.4	32.3	35.5	3.2	0.6	40897	44433	36	30	579	20.2	25.7	37.8	15.4	0.9	96528
15851	REYNOLDSVILLE	19006	2932	31.2	32.0	30.8	4.4	1.6	39293	40809	31	23	2303	12.1	26.0	47.5	13.2	1.2	108460
15853	RIDGWAY	22893	2926	24.6	29.3	38.9	5.4	1.9	46274	49961	52	52	2213	9.5	32.5	42.9	13.8	1.2	102621
15856	ROCKTON	20233	364	16.8	36.3	42.9	3.3	0.8	47244	50126	55	55	315	10.2	18.4	55.2	16.2	0.0	117708
15857	SAINT MARYS	24779	5612	20.0	24.9	44.2	8.7	2.1	54597	56213	71	71	4330	3.1	10.8	58.8	24.9	2.3	139148
15860	SIGEL	21908	439	26.4	37.1	30.5	4.3	1.6	41014	42535	36	30	383	12.0	24.8	41.8	19.8	1.6	110142
15861	SINNAMAHONING	18782	49	32.7	36.7	28.6	2.0	0.0	36703	37308	23	13	42	19.0	31.0	42.9	7.1	0.0	90000
15864	SUMMERVILLE	19235	683	24.9	36.2	33.4	3.8	1.8	40850	43135	35	29	581	14.1	28.1	41.5	15.1	1.2	100718
15865	SYKESVILLE	20144	551	35.2	30.5	29.6	3.3	1.5	38107	39893	27	18	351	12.5	41.3	44.4	1.7	0.0	86250
15868	WEEDVILLE	21093	788	27.4	30.5	37.6	3.3	1.3	42078	45164	40	36	695	16.0	31.1	37.3	14.5	1.2	94556
15870	WILCOX	21884	553	21.0	30.4	42.5	4.5	1.6	48689	52019	58	59	471	11.7	19.1	52.0	16.3	0.8	114480
15901	JOHNSTOWN	13973	2389	64.8	22.9	10.5	1.3	0.5	17234	17035	1	1	852	70.4	19.0	6.6	2.6	1.4	37528
15902	JOHNSTOWN	19211	5567	35.1	34.0	26.5	3.4	1.0	34190	35471	16	7	3296	26.1	38.6	28.0	6.6	0.7	72215
15904	JOHNSTOWN	24913	6661	23.0	30.6	35.1	6.8	4.5	47112	50292	54	55	4996	6.2	11.6	53.0	25.3	3.9	138795
15905	JOHNSTOWN	28590	9074	20.8	28.4	35.7	9.8	5.3	50809	53658	63	64	7043	8.7	21.8	43.3	21.6	4.6	121893
15906	JOHNSTOWN	17732	5061	41.3	33.4	21.7	2.6	0.9	31021	32228	10	3	3327	30.6	43.4	22.8	3.1	0.0	64724
15909	JOHNSTOWN	21490	2407	24.8	33.6	36.0	3.6	2.0	43109	46925	43	39	1995	25.4	23.0	40.7	10.5	0.5	93916
15920	ARMAGH	17736	225	30.2	35.6	30.7	3.1	0.4	37004	39767	24	14	184	21.7	22.8	42.9	12.5	0.0	100962
15923	BOLIVAR	18507	705	32.1	35.6	27.2	2.7	2.4	36298	37956	21	12	620	22.3	27.7	35.6	11.0	3.4	90000
15924	CAIRNBROOK	18799	422	35.8	33.2	25.8	3.8	1.4	36246	37243	21	11	357	23.5	40.1	34.2	2.2	0.0	67683
15926	CENTRAL CITY	19832	1227	31.5	31.5	32.2	3.4	1.4	39222	40912	30	23	1043	19.3	32.1	36.2	10.2	2.2	87836
15927	COLVER	16486	467	28.1	45.8	24.6	1.3	0.2	32802	33872	13	5	392	16.3	55.4	20.9	5.1	2.3	71837
15928	DAVIDSVILLE	22558	682	22.7	30.2	37.5	7.6	1.9	46560	50078	53	53	559	18.4	11.1	42.0	27.2	1.3	134875
15931	EBENSBURG	21401	3378	22.6	31.3	37.5	6.2	2.3	46837	50260	54	54	2533	9.3	16.7	45.5	24.2	4.3	132906
15935	HOLLSOPPLE	20282	1578	24.8	31.9	38.8	3.4	1.1	43146	45934	43	39	1337	16.8	28.0	36.7	16.5	2.0	100414
15936	HOOVERSVILLE	18455	652	33.7	31.7	29.8	3.8	0.9	37317	38559	25	15	525	22.9	34.5	36.0	6.3	0.4	79490
15938	LILLY	18596	1156	22.8	32.0	35.9	5.8	3.5	45504	49552	50	48	979	16.4	31.1	37.1	14.3	1.1	93403
15940	LORETTO	15238	667	22.3	27.9	41.5	6.1	2.1	49770	52465	60	61	554	13.4	12.1	47.7	23.5	3.4	134862
15942	MINERAL POINT	20422	977	22.6	35.6	35.4	3.8	2.6	44136	47500	46	43	871	19.1	15.4	50.4	14.7	0.5	123103
15943	NANTY GLO	19804	1831	34.1	28.6	30.3	5.1	2.0	37036	39035	24	14	1428	27.2	40.3	21.6	10.2	0.8	72418
15944	NEW FLORENCE	19299	1484	29.5	33.9	30.7	3.6	2.3	38149	40813	27	18	1258	22.0	20.8	43.6	11.8	1.7	100359
15945	PARKHILL	19591	21	19.0	33.3	42.9	4.8	0.0	48610	50000	58	59	19	21.1	21.1	52.6	5.3	0.0	103125
15946	PORTAGE	20336	2784	30.1	31.6	31.0	5.2	2.0	38666	41580	29	20	2231	15.4	33.8	39.2	11.3	0.4	91006
15949	ROBINSON	17271	237	32.5	33.3	32.1	1.7	0.4	36134	37772	21	11	210	22.4	34.3	34.3	8.1	1.0	79130
	PENNSYLVANIA	26913		21.5	25.3	36.9	10.2	6.1	53225	55819				7.5	12.2	35.6	36.1	8.5	161438
	UNITED STATES	27277		20.9	24.4	35.3	11.7	7.6	54719	56938				9.3	13.1	31.6	32.6	13.5	162279

ZIP CODE #	POST OFFICE NAME	FINANCIAL SERVICES: Auto Loan	Home Loan	Invest-ments	Retire-ment Plans	THE HOME: Home Improvements: Home Repair	Lawn & Garden	Furnishings: Comput-ers & Hard-ware-Personal	Major Appli-ances	TV, Radio, Sound Equip-ment	Furni-ture	ENTERTAINMENT: Dine out/ Carry out	Sports Equip-ment	Fees & Tickets	Toys & Games	Travel	Cable TV	PERSONAL: Apparel & Services	Auto Repairs	Health Insur-ance	Pets & Supplies
15688	TARRS	71	54	62	53	54	69	60	65	64	55	62	50	50	64	55	69	42	64	70	79
15690	VANDERGRIFT	75	56	72	56	58	76	63	72	68	57	66	54	52	67	59	74	45	69	79	85
15692	WESTMORELAND CITY	89	95	77	97	89	97	91	90	91	88	91	71	93	93	91	92	63	90	96	108
15697	YOUNGWOOD	78	69	69	70	70	77	76	76	77	72	76	57	70	77	71	80	52	77	82	90
15698	YUKON	83	60	83	58	62	86	65	80	73	58	70	60	52	71	63	80	47	75	88	94
15701	INDIANA	77	62	64	65	63	70	81	71	78	71	77	58	68	77	69	78	54	76	75	86
15705	INDIANA	37	16	15	19	14	18	52	26	41	35	42	28	31	40	28	38	30	36	26	35
15711	ANITA	89	64	91	62	66	90	65	83	72	61	71	62	52	72	65	80	47	76	86	99
15713	AULTMAN	74	67	66	70	69	79	66	75	68	60	67	57	61	70	66	72	46	69	77	87
15714	NORTHERN CAMBRIA	71	54	72	52	56	75	57	69	63	51	61	51	47	62	56	69	41	65	75	81
15716	BLACK LICK	76	55	76	53	57	79	59	74	66	53	64	55	48	65	58	73	43	69	80	86
15717	BLAIRSVILLE	78	67	75	67	68	84	68	78	73	62	71	59	62	73	68	78	48	74	84	92
15720	BRUSH VALLEY	91	65	94	63	68	92	67	85	74	62	73	64	54	74	66	82	48	78	89	101
15721	BURNSIDE	76	54	78	53	56	77	56	71	62	52	61	53	45	61	55	68	40	65	74	84
15722	CARROLLTOWN	76	70	77	69	71	85	68	78	73	64	72	57	65	72	70	79	49	74	86	91
15724	CHERRY TREE	73	52	75	51	54	74	54	69	60	50	59	51	43	59	53	66	39	63	72	81
15725	CLARKSBURG	77	55	79	54	57	79	58	73	64	53	63	55	46	63	57	70	41	67	76	86
15728	CLYMER	70	54	67	54	56	71	58	67	63	53	62	50	50	62	56	68	42	64	72	79
15729	COMMODORE	69	49	70	48	51	70	51	64	56	47	55	48	41	56	50	62	36	59	67	77
15730	COOLSPRING	74	53	76	51	55	75	54	69	60	50	59	52	43	60	54	66	39	63	72	82
15732	CREEKSIDE	82	58	84	57	61	83	60	76	67	56	65	57	48	66	59	73	43	70	79	91
15739	ERNEST	79	72	71	75	73	85	71	80	73	64	72	60	65	74	71	77	49	74	82	93
15742	GLEN CAMPBELL	69	50	71	48	51	70	51	65	56	47	55	49	41	56	50	62	37	59	67	77
15744	HAMILTON	84	60	87	59	63	86	62	79	69	58	68	59	50	68	61	76	45	72	82	94
15747	HOME	81	62	81	61	64	84	63	78	68	57	67	59	52	68	63	74	45	72	81	92
15748	HOMER CITY	77	68	76	68	69	84	67	78	73	63	71	57	63	72	68	78	48	73	85	90
15753	LA JOSE	69	50	61	48	50	67	52	62	57	50	56	47	41	59	48	63	38	58	65	75
15757	MAHAFFEY	71	51	72	49	53	72	52	66	58	49	57	50	42	58	51	64	38	61	69	79
15758	MARCHAND	54	39	56	38	40	55	40	51	44	37	44	38	32	44	39	49	29	47	53	60
15759	MARION CENTER	76	57	76	56	59	78	58	72	63	53	62	54	47	63	57	69	41	66	75	85
15760	MARSTELLER	74	53	76	52	55	75	55	70	61	51	60	52	44	60	54	67	39	64	72	83
15762	NICKTOWN	77	64	73	65	66	81	64	76	68	58	67	57	56	68	64	73	45	70	78	88
15763	NORTHPOINT	65	47	56	46	47	63	49	58	54	47	53	44	39	56	45	59	36	54	61	70
15764	OLIVEBURG	69	49	70	48	51	70	50	64	56	47	55	48	40	56	50	62	36	59	67	76
15765	PENN RUN	79	66	74	67	68	83	66	77	70	60	68	58	58	71	66	75	46	71	80	91
15767	PUNXSUTAWNEY	75	60	71	60	61	77	64	72	69	59	67	54	56	68	62	74	46	70	78	86
15770	RINGGOLD	75	53	77	52	55	76	55	70	61	51	60	52	44	60	54	67	39	64	73	83
15771	ROCHESTER MILLS	73	52	75	51	54	74	54	68	60	50	58	51	43	59	53	65	39	63	71	81
15772	ROSSITER	75	54	75	52	56	77	58	72	64	52	62	54	46	63	56	71	41	66	77	84
15773	SAINT BENEDICT	76	56	77	55	58	80	61	74	68	54	65	55	49	66	59	74	44	70	81	87
15774	SHELOCTA	81	63	79	61	64	82	63	76	69	60	68	57	53	69	62	74	45	71	79	91
15775	SPANGLER	78	56	79	55	58	81	60	75	67	55	65	56	48	66	59	74	43	70	81	89
15776	SPRANKLE MILLS	81	58	84	56	61	83	60	76	66	56	65	57	48	66	59	73	43	70	79	90
15777	STARFORD	75	53	76	52	55	76	55	70	61	51	60	52	44	60	54	67	39	64	72	83
15778	TIMBLIN	74	53	76	51	55	75	54	69	60	51	59	52	43	60	54	66	39	63	72	82
15780	VALIER	84	61	87	59	63	86	62	79	69	58	68	59	50	68	61	76	45	72	82	94
15784	WORTHVILLE	82	59	75	57	60	81	61	74	68	58	66	56	49	69	58	74	44	69	78	89
15801	DU BOIS	81	78	78	78	78	87	77	82	80	74	79	61	75	80	77	84	55	80	88	96
15821	BENEZETT	74	67	67	70	69	79	66	75	69	60	67	57	61	70	66	73	46	69	77	87
15823	BROCKPORT	86	64	72	64	64	83	66	77	73	64	71	59	55	75	61	79	48	72	81	93
15824	BROCKWAY	85	75	78	76	75	91	75	85	79	69	78	65	69	80	74	84	53	80	90	100
15825	BROOKVILLE	81	66	77	66	67	84	69	79	73	63	72	60	60	73	67	78	48	75	83	93
15827	BYRNEDALE	84	60	84	59	63	87	66	81	73	59	71	61	53	72	64	81	47	76	89	95
15828	CLARINGTON	82	59	83	57	61	84	62	78	69	57	67	58	50	68	61	76	44	72	82	92
15829	CORSICA	85	62	86	60	64	87	63	80	70	59	69	60	51	70	63	77	46	73	83	95
15832	DRIFTWOOD	74	54	76	52	56	76	55	70	61	51	60	52	44	61	54	67	40	64	73	83
15834	EMPORIUM	75	62	70	63	64	78	66	74	70	60	68	56	58	70	64	75	47	71	80	87
15840	FALLS CREEK	82	67	78	67	69	87	69	81	74	62	72	61	60	74	68	80	49	75	87	95
15845	JOHNSONBURG	79	58	78	57	60	82	63	77	69	56	67	57	51	68	61	76	45	71	83	90
15846	KERSEY	77	70	69	73	71	83	69	78	71	62	70	59	64	73	69	75	48	72	80	91
15848	LUTHERSBURG	88	63	90	61	66	89	65	82	72	60	71	62	52	71	64	79	47	75	86	98
15849	PENFIELD	82	59	84	58	62	84	61	77	67	57	66	58	49	67	60	74	44	71	80	92
15851	REYNOLDSVILLE	74	61	66	62	62	76	65	72	69	60	68	54	57	70	62	74	46	69	77	85
15853	RIDGWAY	79	74	72	75	74	84	75	79	78	71	77	60	72	78	74	82	53	78	86	94
15856	ROCKTON	79	72	71	75	73	85	71	80	73	64	72	61	65	75	71	78	49	74	83	93
15857	SAINT MARYS	84	87	81	88	86	97	82	89	85	78	84	65	83	85	85	90	58	85	97	103
15860	SIGEL	82	66	79	66	68	85	66	80	71	61	70	60	57	71	66	77	47	73	82	94
15861	SINNAMAHONING	75	53	77	52	55	76	55	70	61	51	60	52	44	60	54	67	39	64	73	83
15864	SUMMERVILLE	85	65	79	65	67	86	66	80	72	62	71	60	56	73	65	78	47	74	83	94
15865	SYKESVILLE	75	54	75	53	56	78	59	73	66	53	64	54	47	65	57	73	42	68	79	86
15868	WEEDVILLE	79	63	76	64	65	84	66	78	71	59	69	59	56	71	65	77	47	73	84	92
15870	WILCOX	81	74	73	77	76	87	73	83	75	66	74	63	67	77	73	80	51	76	85	96
15901	JOHNSTOWN	37	27	30	29	27	34	36	34	40	34	39	25	32	37	32	43	27	37	42	42
15902	JOHNSTOWN	62	54	54	54	53	64	59	61	63	55	61	45	54	62	55	67	42	61	69	72
15904	JOHNSTOWN	79	84	84	83	85	93	79	85	85	78	84	60	84	82	84	90	58	84	98	98
15905	JOHNSTOWN	90	96	100	95	99	107	89	98	93	88	92	70	94	91	95	98	64	94	108	112
15906	JOHNSTOWN	59	47	55	47	47	61	51	57	57	48	55	42	46	56	49	62	38	56	65	68
15909	JOHNSTOWN	74	69	76	68	70	84	67	77	72	63	71	56	64	71	69	78	48	73	85	89
15920	ARMAGH	78	56	80	54	58	79	57	73	64	53	62	55	46	63	57	70	41	67	76	87
15923	BOLIVAR	82	59	83	57	61	84	61	77	68	57	67	58	49	68	60	75	44	71	81	91
15924	CAIRNBROOK	74	53	74	52	55	77	58	72	65	52	62	53	46	64	56	71	42	67	78	84
15926	CENTRAL CITY	78	58	82	57	61	82	62	77	68	56	66	57	50	67	61	75	44	71	82	90
15927	COLVER	65	48	64	47	50	68	52	63	57	46	55	47	42	57	50	63	37	59	69	74
15928	DAVIDSVILLE	81	77	85	75	76	91	73	84	78	70	77	62	71	78	76	83	53	80	90	98
15931	EBENSBURG	80	78	80	78	79	89	75	83	79	72	78	60	74	78	77	83	53	79	90	96
15935	HOLLSOPPLE	72	71	75	70	71	83	67	76	71	64	70	55	67	71	70	76	48	72	83	88
15936	HOOVERSVILLE	76	55	77	53	57	78	58	73	65	53	63	54	46	64	57	71	42	67	78	86
15938	LILLY	83	75	84	75	77	93	74	85	80	69	78	62	70	79	75	86	53	81	94	99
15940	LORETTO	78	81	78	81	81	91	75	83	79	71	78	60	76	78	79	84	54	79	91	96
15942	MINERAL POINT	77	71	79	69	72	86	67	78	73	64	72	57	65	72	70	78	49	74	85	91
15943	NANTY GLO	75	61	77	59	62	81	62	75	68	57	67	55	54	67	62	75	45	70	82	87
15944	NEW FLORENCE	82	62	81	60	63	83	63	77	69	59	68	57	52	69	62	75	45	72	81	91
15945	PARKHILL	67	77	73	75	77	83	68	75	73	67	72	52	75	71	74	77	50	72	85	85
15946	PORTAGE	78	64	79	63	65	84	65	78	71	60	69	57	57	70	65	77	47	73	84	91
15949	ROBINSON	76	55	78	53	57	77	56	71	62	52	61	54	45	62	55	68	40	65	74	85
	PENNSYLVANIA	94	95	95	95	95	100	94	96	96	91	95	73	94	96	94	99	67	95	101	113
	UNITED STATES	100	100	100	100	100	100	100	100	100	100	100	100	100	100	100	100	100	100	100	100

ZIP CODE #	POST OFFICE NAME	COUNTY FIPS CODE	POPULATION 2000	POPULATION 2009	POPULATION 2014	2000-2009 ANNUAL RATE % Rate	2000-2009 ANNUAL RATE State Centile	HOUSEHOLDS 2000	HOUSEHOLDS 2009	HOUSEHOLDS 2014	HOUSEHOLDS % Annual Rate 2000-2009	HOUSEHOLDS 2009 Average HH Size	FAMILIES 2000	FAMILIES 2009	FAMILIES % Annual Rate 2000-2009
15951	SAINT MICHAEL	021	341	312	298	-1.0	3	131	124	120	-0.6	2.45	92	84	-1.0
15952	SALIX	021	1826	1778	1756	-0.3	29	708	717	716	0.1	2.47	546	538	-0.2
15953	SEANOR	111	98	94	91	-0.4	23	43	43	42	0.0	2.19	30	29	-0.4
15954	SEWARD	063	3000	2879	2810	-0.4	23	1218	1209	1193	-0.1	2.37	895	865	-0.4
15955	SIDMAN	021	3263	3093	2993	-0.6	13	1273	1247	1219	-0.2	2.46	923	878	-0.5
15956	SOUTH FORK	021	2984	2893	2820	-0.3	29	1186	1190	1172	0.0	2.41	863	841	-0.3
15957	STRONGSTOWN	063	512	509	501	-0.1	46	211	217	216	0.3	2.35	167	168	0.1
15958	SUMMERHILL	021	2211	2165	2122	-0.2	38	773	783	775	0.1	2.72	583	576	-0.1
15960	TWIN ROCKS	021	5	5	5	0.0	52	1	1	1	0.0	5.00	1	1	0.0
15961	VINTONDALE	063	1531	1464	1419	-0.5	19	588	582	570	-0.1	2.51	435	419	-0.4
15963	WINDBER	111	11949	11372	11016	-0.5	19	4957	4834	4726	-0.3	2.28	3337	3158	-0.6
16001	BUTLER	019	42474	42677	42810	0.1	57	17942	18533	18758	0.4	2.25	11469	11433	0.0
16002	BUTLER	019	16796	16975	16885	0.1	57	6017	6274	6305	0.5	2.58	4560	4619	0.1
16020	BOYERS	019	1073	1112	1123	0.4	68	409	434	442	0.6	2.55	308	317	0.3
16022	BRUIN	019	365	377	376	0.4	68	137	145	146	0.6	2.60	102	105	0.3
16023	CABOT	019	4325	4591	4695	0.6	74	1466	1614	1672	1.0	2.57	1089	1163	0.7
16025	CHICORA	019	5418	5541	5562	0.2	61	1925	2042	2075	0.6	2.64	1445	1487	0.3
16028	EAST BRADY	005	2081	1984	1929	-0.5	19	890	879	863	-0.1	2.18	601	572	-0.5
16030	EAU CLAIRE	019	295	303	304	0.3	64	113	119	120	0.6	2.52	88	90	0.2
16033	EVANS CITY	019	6699	6959	7077	0.4	68	2566	2727	2794	0.7	2.53	1914	1975	0.3
16034	FENELTON	019	1900	1972	1979	0.4	68	645	693	704	0.8	2.67	489	510	0.5
16036	FOXBURG	031	405	405	399	0.0	52	164	166	165	0.1	2.44	123	121	-0.2
16037	HARMONY	019	4354	4520	4560	0.4	68	1592	1703	1735	0.7	2.60	1234	1288	0.5
16038	HARRISVILLE	019	3660	3982	4050	0.9	83	1387	1545	1584	1.2	2.51	1024	1113	0.9
16040	HILLIARDS	019	1063	1090	1091	0.3	64	390	409	412	0.5	2.66	302	308	0.2
16041	KARNS CITY	019	2560	2528	2493	-0.1	46	988	1007	1002	0.2	2.50	743	737	-0.1
16045	LYNDORA	019	944	926	910	-0.2	38	459	465	461	0.1	1.99	289	281	-0.3
16046	MARS	019	10187	14110	15535	3.6	99	3597	5038	5584	3.7	2.73	2744	3749	3.4
16049	PARKER	031	3706	3633	3564	-0.2	38	1428	1437	1423	0.1	2.53	1053	1030	-0.2
16050	PETROLIA	019	1414	1422	1410	0.1	57	508	524	524	0.3	2.71	387	387	0.0
16051	PORTERSVILLE	019	3231	3237	3218	0.0	52	1277	1310	1313	0.3	2.47	957	952	-0.1
16052	PROSPECT	019	2342	2553	2656	0.9	83	908	1020	1072	1.3	2.50	674	733	0.9
16053	RENFREW	019	3510	3711	3784	0.6	74	1326	1438	1479	0.9	2.58	1000	1054	0.6
16055	SARVER	019	8165	8253	8227	0.1	57	2988	3112	3131	0.4	2.61	2358	2393	0.2
16056	SAXONBURG	019	4990	5296	5398	0.6	74	1929	2128	2197	1.1	2.37	1367	1453	0.7
16057	SLIPPERY ROCK	019	13059	13714	13943	0.5	70	4041	4341	4457	0.8	2.54	2477	2559	0.4
16059	VALENCIA	019	7117	7740	7949	0.9	83	2603	2939	3054	1.3	2.57	2010	2172	0.8
16061	WEST SUNBURY	019	2581	2764	2858	0.7	77	939	1035	1081	1.1	2.65	712	762	0.7
16063	ZELIENOPLE	019	6861	6913	6877	0.1	57	3044	3154	3164	0.4	2.17	1872	1866	0.0
16066	CRANBERRY TWP	019	23583	27576	29339	1.7	93	8343	9773	10415	1.7	2.80	6563	7548	1.5
16101	NEW CASTLE	073	36291	35004	34325	-0.4	23	14306	13840	13592	-0.4	2.44	9724	9156	-0.6
16102	NEW CASTLE	073	6270	6179	6091	-0.2	38	2428	2406	2379	-0.1	2.55	1710	1654	-0.4
16105	NEW CASTLE	073	14822	14654	14450	-0.1	46	6196	6185	6131	0.0	2.33	4314	4174	-0.4
16110	ADAMSVILLE	039	315	328	326	0.4	68	126	134	134	0.7	2.45	102	106	0.4
16111	ATLANTIC	039	1387	1437	1427	0.4	68	417	441	441	0.6	3.26	330	342	0.4
16112	BESSEMER	073	1637	1627	1608	-0.1	46	668	671	666	0.0	2.42	494	481	-0.3
16114	CLARKS MILLS	085	709	709	700	0.0	52	261	269	268	0.3	2.62	198	199	0.1
16115	DARLINGTON	007	3567	3392	3281	-0.5	19	1327	1293	1259	-0.3	2.55	961	908	-0.6
16116	EDINBURG	073	3563	3490	3443	-0.2	38	1425	1409	1394	-0.1	2.46	1008	967	-0.4
16117	ELLWOOD CITY	073	18163	17229	16737	-0.6	13	7348	7063	6891	-0.4	2.43	5134	4789	-0.7
16120	ENON VALLEY	073	2603	2511	2456	-0.4	23	924	901	886	-0.3	2.79	721	688	-0.5
16121	FARRELL	085	6766	6146	5885	-1.0	3	2833	2639	2545	-0.8	2.28	1810	1622	-1.2
16123	FOMBELL	007	2389	2293	2227	-0.4	23	877	863	844	-0.2	2.63	659	630	-0.5
16124	FREDONIA	085	2059	2079	2058	0.1	57	738	764	761	0.4	2.68	578	586	0.1
16125	GREENVILLE	085	19210	18701	18265	-0.3	29	7469	7412	7279	-0.1	2.35	5194	5007	-0.4
16127	GROVE CITY	085	15332	15547	15328	0.2	61	5175	5285	5227	0.2	2.37	3546	3522	-0.1
16130	HADLEY	085	2031	2025	1996	0.0	52	792	814	810	0.3	2.46	600	602	0.0
16131	HARTSTOWN	039	950	986	980	0.4	68	351	373	374	0.7	2.64	271	282	0.4
16133	JACKSON CENTER	085	1398	1451	1444	0.4	68	519	555	557	0.7	2.57	405	423	0.5
16134	JAMESTOWN	039	3971	4176	4159	0.5	70	1628	1762	1771	0.9	2.36	1155	1210	0.5
16137	MERCER	085	12581	12501	12294	-0.1	46	4436	4490	4442	0.1	2.50	3228	3182	-0.2
16141	NEW GALILEE	073	1885	1752	1689	-0.8	6	742	704	683	-0.6	2.48	545	502	-0.9
16142	NEW WILMINGTON	085	6566	6315	6164	-0.4	23	2246	2179	2134	-0.3	2.75	1649	1563	-0.6
16143	PULASKI	073	3546	3325	3224	-0.7	8	1301	1233	1200	-0.6	2.62	987	912	-0.9
16145	SANDY LAKE	085	2724	2768	2742	0.2	61	1060	1099	1096	0.4	2.50	798	805	0.1
16146	SHARON	085	16415	15233	14642	-0.8	6	6834	6470	6254	-0.6	2.27	4212	3841	-1.0
16148	HERMITAGE	085	16437	16743	16554	0.2	61	6915	7215	7182	0.5	2.27	4702	4755	0.1
16150	SHARPSVILLE	085	8900	8542	8300	-0.4	23	3641	3584	3508	-0.2	2.38	2596	2490	-0.4
16153	STONEBORO	085	2609	2668	2646	0.2	61	1040	1083	1080	0.4	2.46	750	760	0.1
16154	TRANSFER	085	2938	2940	2893	0.0	52	1143	1175	1166	0.3	2.50	851	852	0.0
16156	VOLANT	073	3078	3002	2940	-0.3	29	1100	1088	1071	-0.1	2.76	856	828	-0.4
16157	WAMPUM	073	5156	4866	4725	-0.6	13	2109	2018	1969	-0.5	2.37	1484	1376	-0.8
16159	WEST MIDDLESEX	085	4143	3958	3848	-0.5	19	1663	1632	1599	-0.2	2.40	1251	1197	-0.5
16172	NEW WILMINGTON	073	840	854	854	0.2	61	11	12	12	0.9	2.25	3	3	0.0
16201	KITTANNING	005	19580	18876	18405	-0.4	23	7830	7765	7623	-0.1	2.37	5425	5223	-0.4
16210	ADRIAN	005	742	703	680	-0.6	13	271	264	258	-0.3	2.66	206	196	-0.5
16212	CADOGAN	005	378	351	337	-0.8	6	169	162	157	-0.5	2.15	122	114	-0.7
16213	CALLENSBURG	031	352	347	340	-0.2	38	140	142	141	0.2	2.44	95	93	-0.2
16214	CLARION	031	9920	9233	9081	-0.8	6	3540	3557	3517	0.1	2.21	1759	1701	-0.4
16217	COOKSBURG	053	45	41	40	-1.0	3	16	15	14	-0.7	2.67	11	10	-1.0
16218	COWANSVILLE	005	1255	1199	1167	-0.5	19	480	474	464	-0.1	2.37	368	355	-0.4
16222	DAYTON	005	2384	2256	2180	-0.6	13	888	854	829	-0.4	2.63	662	622	-0.7
16224	FAIRMOUNT CITY	031	1578	1516	1474	-0.4	23	599	590	580	-0.2	2.57	463	445	-0.4
16225	FISHER	031	100	98	96	-0.2	38	46	47	46	0.2	2.09	33	33	0.0
16226	FORD CITY	005	10066	9996	9772	-0.1	46	4237	4303	4232	0.2	2.31	2879	2849	-0.1
16229	FREEPORT	005	5369	5117	4958	-0.5	19	2146	2095	2045	-0.3	2.44	1540	1468	-0.5
16232	KNOX	031	5048	4980	4897	-0.1	46	2027	2068	2052	0.2	2.41	1497	1484	-0.1
16233	LEEPER	031	1226	1216	1200	-0.1	46	506	522	521	0.3	2.33	347	346	0.0
16234	LIMESTONE	031	141	132	128	-0.7	8	55	53	52	-0.4	2.49	43	40	-0.8
16235	LUCINDA	031	1190	1186	1171	0.0	52	447	461	460	0.3	2.57	330	332	0.1
16238	MANORVILLE	005	401	437	469	0.9	83	180	205	222	1.4	2.13	122	135	1.1
16239	MARIENVILLE	053	1263	2460	2423	7.5	100	512	477	463	-0.8	1.95	333	300	-1.1
16240	MAYPORT	005	1736	1687	1650	-0.3	29	606	608	600	0.0	2.65	465	456	-0.2
16242	NEW BETHLEHEM	031	5281	4979	4827	-0.6	13	2169	2105	2055	-0.3	2.33	1520	1430	-0.7
16248	RIMERSBURG	031	3699	3720	3681	0.1	57	1452	1502	1497	0.4	2.48	1039	1042	0.0
	PENNSYLVANIA					0.3					0.4	2.45			0.1
	UNITED STATES					1.0					1.1	2.59			0.9

# ZIP CODE	POST OFFICE NAME	RACE (%) White 2000	White 2009	Black 2000	Black 2009	Asian/Pacific 2000	Asian/Pacific 2009	% Hispanic Origin 2000	% Hispanic Origin 2009	2009 AGE DISTRIBUTION (%) 0-4	5-9	10-14	15-19	20-24	25-44	45-64	65-84	85+	18+	MEDIAN AGE 2009	% 2009 Males	% 2009 Females
15951	SAINT MICHAEL	98.8	98.4	0.3	0.3	0.0	0.0	0.3	0.3	4.5	4.5	5.4	6.7	6.4	23.7	26.6	18.9	3.2	81.4	44.0	47.1	52.9
15952	SALIX	98.6	98.1	0.1	0.1	0.3	0.6	0.9	1.2	5.1	5.6	6.1	6.4	4.4	25.5	31.4	13.8	1.6	79.2	42.9	50.5	49.5
15953	SEANOR	100.0	98.9	0.0	0.0	0.0	0.0	1.0	2.1	5.3	5.3	5.3	7.4	5.3	23.4	28.7	16.0	3.2	79.8	43.6	52.1	47.9
15954	SEWARD	99.0	98.8	0.1	0.1	0.0	0.0	0.5	0.7	4.9	5.1	5.6	6.1	4.8	22.6	32.3	16.2	2.3	80.7	45.5	49.6	50.4
15955	SIDMAN	99.2	99.1	0.1	0.1	0.1	0.1	0.2	0.4	5.5	5.6	6.1	6.9	5.3	25.0	28.7	14.7	2.3	78.5	41.9	48.4	51.6
15956	SOUTH FORK	99.6	99.6	0.1	0.1	0.0	0.0	0.5	0.6	5.8	5.9	6.3	6.7	4.7	25.0	28.8	14.5	2.4	77.9	41.7	49.9	50.1
15957	STRONGSTOWN	99.2	99.0	0.0	0.0	0.0	0.0	0.2	0.2	5.5	6.1	6.3	5.7	4.5	26.1	33.6	10.8	1.4	78.4	42.2	49.9	50.1
15958	SUMMERHILL	99.1	98.8	0.3	0.4	0.1	0.2	0.2	0.2	5.8	6.1	6.3	6.6	5.5	24.5	29.9	13.6	1.8	77.6	41.7	50.8	49.2
15960	TWIN ROCKS	100.0	100.0	0.0	0.0	0.0	0.0	0.0	0.0	0.0	0.0	0.0	0.0	0.0	0.0	100.0	0.0	0.0	100.0	53.8	60.0	40.0
15961	VINTONDALE	99.7	99.5	0.1	0.1	0.0	0.1	0.5	0.6	4.9	5.1	5.4	5.7	5.4	25.3	30.5	15.2	2.5	81.2	43.7	50.5	49.5
15963	WINDBER	99.2	99.0	0.1	0.1	0.2	0.3	0.6	0.8	4.7	4.9	5.5	6.4	5.2	22.6	29.0	17.5	4.2	81.0	45.4	47.7	52.3
16001	BUTLER	97.4	96.8	1.1	1.3	0.5	0.7	0.7	1.0	5.8	5.7	5.9	5.9	5.4	24.7	28.4	15.1	3.2	79.1	42.6	48.4	51.6
16002	BUTLER	97.9	97.4	1.3	1.6	0.3	0.5	0.5	0.7	5.5	6.1	6.8	8.2	4.6	22.8	30.2	13.0	2.7	75.9	42.3	50.6	49.4
16020	BOYERS	98.6	98.4	0.5	0.5	0.4	0.4	0.3	0.3	6.5	6.8	6.9	6.1	4.7	26.2	30.1	11.4	1.3	75.8	40.4	51.5	48.5
16022	BRUIN	98.6	98.4	0.0	0.0	0.0	0.0	0.5	0.8	5.8	6.1	5.8	6.9	6.9	23.9	30.5	12.2	1.9	78.0	39.9	49.9	50.1
16023	CABOT	99.2	99.0	0.1	0.2	0.1	0.2	0.3	0.4	5.6	6.1	6.6	6.2	4.0	21.5	27.2	15.5	7.4	77.9	45.1	47.0	53.0
16025	CHICORA	99.3	99.2	0.3	0.4	0.0	0.1	0.2	0.3	6.0	6.2	6.7	6.9	4.7	24.3	29.2	13.6	2.6	76.4	41.9	49.2	50.8
16028	EAST BRADY	99.0	98.8	0.5	0.6	0.1	0.2	0.3	0.4	5.3	5.6	5.6	5.1	4.8	22.5	30.2	16.5	4.2	80.1	45.7	49.9	50.1
16030	EAU CLAIRE	99.7	99.3	0.0	0.0	0.0	0.3	0.3	0.0	6.9	7.3	6.6	5.3	5.0	26.4	28.1	13.5	1.0	75.2	40.5	52.5	47.5
16033	EVANS CITY	98.8	98.5	0.2	0.2	0.4	0.6	0.3	0.4	6.1	6.5	7.0	6.7	4.7	25.3	30.2	11.8	1.7	76.2	41.1	49.8	50.2
16034	FENELTON	98.8	98.5	0.2	0.3	0.1	0.2	0.6	0.8	6.5	6.7	6.7	6.1	5.0	25.1	29.2	12.2	2.6	75.9	41.0	50.4	49.6
16036	FOXBURG	99.5	99.3	0.2	0.2	0.0	0.2	0.7	1.0	5.7	5.9	6.4	6.9	4.4	24.2	30.4	14.3	1.7	77.5	42.8	51.9	48.1
16037	HARMONY	98.9	98.7	0.2	0.3	0.3	0.3	0.4	0.5	5.4	6.1	6.4	6.3	4.4	25.7	31.4	12.1	2.3	78.1	42.4	50.3	49.7
16038	HARRISVILLE	98.3	97.8	0.5	0.6	0.3	0.5	0.3	0.4	5.6	6.1	6.5	6.2	4.1	24.6	31.1	13.4	2.4	77.9	42.8	50.3	49.7
16040	HILLIARDS	98.9	98.6	0.1	0.1	0.2	0.3	0.6	0.7	6.8	6.7	6.8	7.0	5.8	25.7	28.5	11.4	1.4	75.2	39.7	49.9	50.1
16041	KARNS CITY	99.3	99.1	0.2	0.3	0.1	0.2	0.1	0.2	5.8	6.1	6.4	6.6	4.7	25.9	30.1	12.7	1.6	77.5	41.5	50.2	49.8
16045	LYNDORA	98.3	97.9	0.4	0.5	0.1	0.2	0.5	0.8	5.1	5.5	5.7	5.5	4.2	24.5	29.9	15.3	4.2	80.2	44.6	49.2	50.8
16046	MARS	97.5	96.4	0.6	0.8	1.2	1.9	0.7	1.0	7.8	8.4	8.6	6.8	3.7	25.8	27.9	9.0	2.1	70.6	38.9	48.2	51.8
16049	PARKER	98.7	98.4	0.6	0.8	0.2	0.3	0.3	0.4	5.8	6.2	6.3	6.4	5.0	24.5	30.4	13.6	1.8	77.6	42.0	49.7	50.3
16050	PETROLIA	98.9	98.7	0.2	0.2	0.2	0.4	0.4	0.6	6.3	6.3	6.5	7.2	5.7	25.4	28.9	12.1	1.5	76.2	40.0	49.2	50.8
16051	PORTERSVILLE	98.8	98.5	0.2	0.2	0.2	0.4	0.3	0.4	5.9	6.2	6.4	6.5	5.6	25.2	30.4	12.6	1.3	77.5	40.9	49.8	50.2
16052	PROSPECT	99.2	99.1	0.0	0.0	0.3	0.3	0.4	0.6	6.0	6.4	6.7	5.9	5.2	26.7	31.5	10.4	1.3	77.3	40.8	50.5	49.5
16053	RENFREW	98.9	98.6	0.3	0.4	0.4	0.5	0.5	0.6	6.3	6.7	7.3	6.5	4.5	24.7	30.5	11.9	1.6	75.6	41.4	50.2	49.8
16055	SARVER	99.0	98.7	0.2	0.3	0.3	0.4	0.3	0.3	5.6	6.1	6.7	6.4	4.4	23.9	31.5	13.2	2.2	77.2	42.9	49.6	50.4
16056	SAXONBURG	99.1	98.8	0.2	0.2	0.0	0.1	0.7	1.1	5.3	5.8	6.2	6.1	4.7	22.8	30.5	14.9	3.8	78.8	44.4	47.2	52.8
16057	SLIPPERY ROCK	95.7	94.5	1.7	2.1	1.3	1.9	0.7	1.0	3.6	4.1	4.4	15.5	23.7	19.0	20.4	8.2	1.2	85.0	24.7	48.1	51.9
16059	VALENCIA	98.5	97.9	0.5	0.7	0.2	0.4	0.8	1.2	5.6	6.7	7.8	7.2	4.4	22.4	31.6	12.2	2.3	75.0	42.2	48.8	51.2
16061	WEST SUNBURY	98.9	98.6	0.3	0.3	0.2	0.4	0.5	0.8	6.3	6.7	6.9	6.7	5.4	26.7	30.2	9.9	1.1	75.6	39.5	50.9	49.1
16063	ZELIENOPLE	98.0	97.3	0.7	0.9	0.5	0.7	0.4	0.5	5.0	5.3	5.9	5.7	4.7	24.3	27.8	15.9	5.3	80.1	44.3	47.3	52.7
16066	CRANBERRY TWP	96.8	95.6	0.9	1.1	1.4	2.1	0.7	1.0	9.3	8.8	8.1	5.9	3.5	30.8	24.7	7.1	1.7	69.6	35.9	49.4	50.6
16101	NEW CASTLE	89.9	87.9	8.1	9.7	0.2	0.3	0.7	1.0	5.9	6.1	6.2	6.9	5.2	23.2	27.5	15.7	3.4	77.6	42.3	48.1	51.9
16102	NEW CASTLE	96.7	95.9	1.9	2.2	0.2	0.4	0.4	0.5	5.6	5.6	6.0	6.5	5.4	23.3	29.2	15.5	3.0	78.8	43.3	47.9	52.1
16105	NEW CASTLE	97.5	96.6	1.1	1.4	0.8	1.2	0.4	0.6	4.8	4.9	5.4	5.7	4.5	20.7	29.8	19.3	4.8	81.1	47.7	46.6	53.4
16110	ADAMSVILLE	97.5	96.6	1.0	1.2	0.3	0.3	1.0	1.2	9.5	9.1	9.8	8.5	6.1	23.5	22.9	9.5	1.2	66.2	31.5	51.2	48.8
16111	ATLANTIC	97.8	97.3	0.8	1.0	0.1	0.3	0.6	1.0	8.8	8.6	8.8	8.2	6.1	25.2	24.2	9.0	1.2	68.8	33.3	50.8	49.2
16112	BESSEMER	98.6	98.1	0.4	0.5	0.4	0.6	0.9	1.2	5.3	5.4	5.8	6.5	4.6	24.1	30.4	14.9	3.0	79.3	43.8	49.2	50.8
16114	CLARKS MILLS	99.4	99.2	0.1	0.1	0.0	0.1	0.1	0.0	5.5	5.9	6.3	6.3	4.4	23.8	31.6	14.5	1.6	78.1	43.4	49.6	50.4
16115	DARLINGTON	98.5	97.9	0.7	1.0	0.2	0.2	0.3	0.5	4.4	4.7	5.2	6.0	4.7	21.4	33.8	16.8	2.7	81.8	46.8	48.0	52.0
16116	EDINBURG	98.8	98.4	0.4	0.5	0.2	0.3	0.3	0.5	5.3	5.6	6.0	6.4	4.9	23.4	31.6	14.6	2.1	78.9	43.8	49.9	50.1
16117	ELLWOOD CITY	98.6	98.1	0.6	0.8	0.2	0.3	0.5	0.7	5.6	5.7	5.9	6.1	5.4	24.4	29.0	14.9	3.1	79.0	42.8	48.3	51.7
16120	ENON VALLEY	99.3	99.1	0.2	0.2	0.1	0.1	0.7	1.1	6.0	6.1	6.7	7.1	5.9	25.2	29.8	12.2	1.1	77.0	40.5	49.2	50.8
16121	FARRELL	54.2	48.7	42.9	48.4	0.2	0.2	0.7	0.8	6.7	6.2	6.3	6.2	5.2	22.0	25.7	18.0	3.7	76.9	42.9	45.5	54.5
16123	FOMBELL	99.2	99.0	0.2	0.2	0.1	0.1	0.8	1.2	5.6	6.1	6.5	6.5	4.8	24.1	31.9	12.6	1.9	77.6	42.6	49.8	50.2
16124	FREDONIA	99.2	98.9	0.1	0.1	0.1	0.1	0.2	0.3	6.6	6.4	6.9	7.7	5.1	23.1	28.6	13.7	1.9	75.1	40.5	50.6	49.4
16125	GREENVILLE	97.9	97.0	0.8	1.2	0.4	0.7	0.5	0.6	5.4	5.5	5.7	7.6	7.0	22.0	27.6	15.6	3.6	79.4	42.4	48.2	51.8
16127	GROVE CITY	96.2	94.6	2.1	3.0	0.9	1.3	0.6	0.9	4.4	4.7	5.6	13.0	13.3	20.2	23.3	12.6	2.9	80.0	34.3	50.4	49.6
16130	HADLEY	99.1	98.9	0.1	0.2	0.1	0.1	0.1	0.1	5.0	5.5	6.0	6.1	4.7	23.7	31.8	15.2	2.1	79.7	44.3	49.9	50.1
16131	HARTSTOWN	97.5	97.1	0.2	0.2	0.1	0.1	0.4	0.5	6.2	6.4	6.8	7.7	5.9	25.1	28.8	12.0	1.2	75.8	39.2	51.5	48.5
16133	JACKSON CENTER	98.6	98.0	0.6	0.9	0.1	0.1	0.8	1.2	5.7	6.3	6.4	6.0	4.8	25.7	31.2	12.3	1.6	77.9	41.7	50.1	49.9
16134	JAMESTOWN	98.9	98.5	0.1	0.1	0.2	0.3	0.1	0.1	4.7	5.1	6.3	5.9	3.9	21.8	32.4	18.1	2.0	79.9	46.6	49.4	50.6
16137	MERCER	95.6	94.0	3.2	4.5	0.3	0.4	1.2	1.7	5.8	5.8	6.1	5.9	5.0	26.8	29.0	13.4	2.1	78.5	41.5	53.4	46.6
16141	NEW GALILEE	98.6	98.2	0.5	0.7	0.1	0.1	0.6	0.9	4.6	5.0	5.4	6.0	5.1	24.5	33.3	14.4	1.8	81.3	44.5	48.9	51.1
16142	NEW WILMINGTON	98.5	98.1	0.5	0.6	0.2	0.3	0.7	0.9	6.5	6.8	7.2	8.0	8.1	21.2	25.7	13.1	3.4	75.1	37.8	46.1	53.9
16143	PULASKI	98.8	98.4	0.5	0.7	0.1	0.2	0.3	0.4	5.6	5.8	6.2	6.6	5.4	24.0	29.7	14.5	2.3	78.4	42.3	48.1	51.9
16145	SANDY LAKE	99.3	99.0	0.2	0.3	0.1	0.3	0.2	0.3	6.2	6.4	6.6	6.0	5.1	25.0	29.6	13.2	2.0	76.9	41.2	49.2	50.8
16146	SHARON	86.4	82.7	10.9	14.1	0.2	0.3	0.9	1.1	6.7	6.4	6.2	6.3	6.1	24.8	26.1	13.9	3.5	76.7	39.9	47.3	52.7
16148	HERMITAGE	95.1	93.2	3.0	4.1	0.8	1.2	0.7	0.9	4.8	5.1	5.5	5.9	4.8	20.4	30.4	18.8	4.3	80.8	47.3	46.8	53.2
16150	SHARPSVILLE	97.3	96.3	1.5	2.1	0.3	0.5	0.7	0.9	5.6	5.8	6.1	6.2	5.2	23.0	29.8	15.5	2.7	78.6	43.6	48.1	51.9
16153	STONEBORO	99.0	98.6	0.1	0.2	0.2	0.2	0.3	0.5	6.6	6.9	7.0	6.4	4.6	24.3	28.4	13.6	2.1	75.5	40.7	49.4	50.6
16154	TRANSFER	98.4	97.8	0.5	0.7	0.2	0.4	0.5	0.6	6.3	6.4	6.9	6.5	4.9	23.6	30.8	12.9	1.7	76.4	41.9	51.3	48.7
16156	VOLANT	99.4	99.2	0.1	0.2	0.2	0.3	0.5	0.7	6.6	6.9	7.4	6.9	4.4	24.4	29.9	11.9	1.6	74.8	40.2	49.4	50.6
16157	WAMPUM	97.7	97.0	1.2	1.7	0.2	0.2	0.5	0.7	4.9	5.2	5.6	5.6	4.5	23.0	31.5	16.6	3.0	80.8	45.7	49.5	50.5
16159	WEST MIDDLESEX	97.5	96.6	1.4	2.0	0.3	0.5	0.4	0.5	5.2	5.4	5.8	6.1	5.1	22.0	31.4	16.5	2.6	79.9	45.3	48.8	51.2
16172	NEW WILMINGTON	97.4	96.4	1.0	1.3	0.6	0.9	0.5	0.6	0.1	0.0	0.0	46.5	51.5	1.3	0.4	0.2	0.0	99.8	20.3	37.4	62.6
16201	KITTANNING	98.7	98.4	0.5	0.6	0.2	0.3	0.5	0.7	5.4	5.6	5.7	6.5	5.3	24.0	30.1	14.6	3.0	79.4	43.3	48.2	51.8
16210	ADRIAN	99.3	99.1	0.1	0.1	0.3	0.4	0.3	0.4	5.8	6.5	7.0	6.8	4.1	22.3	31.4	14.1	1.8	76.5	42.9	50.8	49.2
16212	CADOGAN	99.5	99.4	0.0	0.0	0.3	0.3	0.0	0.0	4.6	4.6	5.4	6.8	4.8	24.2	31.9	14.5	3.1	80.6	44.7	51.3	48.7
16213	CALLENSBURG	99.1	98.8	0.3	0.3	0.0	0.0	0.3	0.6	6.3	6.6	6.9	6.1	4.9	26.8	25.9	14.7	1.7	76.4	39.7	49.0	51.0
16214	CLARION	95.7	94.5	2.6	3.2	0.7	1.1	0.6	0.9	4.0	3.9	3.8	13.9	22.7	19.4	20.0	10.4	2.0	86.1	26.6	45.5	54.5
16217	COOKSBURG	100.0	97.6	0.0	0.0	0.0	0.0	0.0	0.0	4.9	4.9	4.9	7.3	4.9	22.0	29.3	19.5	2.4	78.0	45.6	53.7	46.3
16218	COWANSVILLE	98.7	98.5	0.9	1.1	0.1	0.1	0.4	0.4	5.3	5.8	6.1	6.4	4.2	21.7	31.9	15.1	3.5	78.7	45.3	50.0	50.0
16222	DAYTON	99.4	99.3	0.0	0.0	0.0	0.0	0.3	0.3	6.3	6.5	7.0	6.7	4.9	24.6	27.7	14.2	2.2	75.9	40.9	50.6	49.4
16224	FAIRMOUNT CITY	98.5	98.2	0.5	0.6	0.3	0.5	0.3	0.4	6.0	6.0	6.1	6.2	6.1	24.7	28.6	14.6	1.7	78.1	41.4	49.5	50.5
16225	FISHER	99.0	99.0	0.0	0.0	0.0	0.0	0.0	0.0	4.1	4.1	4.1	6.1	4.1	25.5	31.6	18.4	2.0	84.7	46.0	52.0	48.0
16226	FORD CITY	97.4	96.9	1.6	1.8	0.1	0.2	0.5	0.6	5.5	5.6	5.7	5.8	5.0	22.7	29.1	17.2	3.3	79.4	44.7	48.6	51.4
16229	FREEPORT	98.9	98.6	0.2	0.2	0.1	0.3	0.3	0.4	5.4	5.6	5.9	6.1	5.3	25.5	31.0	12.8	2.4	79.0	42.3	49.2	50.8
16232	KNOX	99.0	98.7	0.0	0.0	0.3	0.4	0.4	0.5	5.7	6.0	6.4	6.3	4.7	24.5	30.2	14.2	2.0	78.1	42.6	49.2	50.8
16233	LEEPER	99.4	99.3	0.2	0.2	0.1	0.2	0.2	0.2	4.9	5.5	6.0	5.8	4.4	23.8	32.7	15.5	1.5	80.3	44.8	50.6	49.4
16234	LIMESTONE	100.0	100.0	0.0	0.0	0.0	0.0	0.0	0.0	4.5	6.1	6.1	6.8	4.5	26.5	31.1	12.9	1.5	78.8	42.0	49.2	50.8
16235	LUCINDA	99.1	98.7	0.2	0.3	0.1	0.2	0.1	0.2	5.6	6.0	6.2	5.8	4.5	24.9	30.7	14.8	1.6	78.8	42.8	49.7	50.3
16238	MANORVILLE	98.8	98.4	0.5	0.7	0.0	0.2	0.2	0.2	5.3	5.3	5.5	6.2	5.5	23.8	29.5	16.2	2.7	79.6	43.8	48.7	51.3
16239	MARIENVILLE	92.1	92.6	5.1	4.5	0.2	0.2	2.3	2.6	1.3	1.4	1.7	11.6	11.3	40.2	20.4	10.7	1.3	87.1	35.7	77.2	22.8
16240	MAYPORT	99.1	98.8	0.1	0.1	0.2	0.3	0.4	0.6	5.0	5.4	5.7	5.9	4.9	24.1	30.9	15.0	3.0	80.0	44.2	48.7	51.3
16242	NEW BETHLEHEM	99.1	98.8	0.3	0.4	0.1	0.2	0.2	0.3	5.6	5.8	6.1	6.2	4.8	23.0	29.2	16.1	3.2	78.7	43.8	48.2	51.8
16248	RIMERSBURG	99.5	99.2	0.2	0.3	0.0	0.0	0.3	0.5	6.1	6.7	6.7	6.9	5.0	24.9	28.4	13.2	2.0	76.0	40.3	48.7	51.3
	PENNSYLVANIA	85.4	83.2	10.0	10.7	1.8	2.7	3.2	4.2	5.8	6.0	6.3	7.1	6.5	24.8	27.8	13.1	2.6	77.8	40.4	48.5	51.5
	UNITED STATES	75.1	72.0	12.3	12.7	3.8	4.6	12.5	15.7	6.8	6.7	6.6	7.1	6.9	27.0	26.0	10.9	1.9	75.7	36.9	49.2	50.8

#	POST OFFICE NAME	2009 Per Capita Income	2009 HH Income Base	2009 Household Income Distribution (%): Less than $25,000	$25,000 to $49,999	$50,000 to $99,999	$100,000 to $149,999	$150,000 or More	Median Household Income: 2009	2014	2009 National Centile	2009 State Centile	2009 Home Value Base	2009 Home Value Distribution (%): Less than $50,000	$50,000 to $89,999	$90,000 to $174,999	$175,000 to $399,999	$400,000 or More	2009 Median Home Value
15951	SAINT MICHAEL	18507	124	33.1	31.5	31.5	1.6	2.4	40439	41519	34	28	96	36.5	20.8	33.3	9.4	0.0	76667
15952	SALIX	19881	717	23.3	38.2	31.4	5.4	1.7	40235	43729	33	27	579	15.9	17.4	38.2	25.6	2.9	133131
15953	SEANOR	20173	43	44.2	25.6	25.6	2.3	2.3	29051	36515	7	3	38	26.3	26.3	34.2	13.2	0.0	86667
15954	SEWARD	19538	1209	28.9	34.7	30.9	3.9	1.5	37847	40920	26	17	1019	20.0	26.9	43.7	9.2	0.2	94257
15955	SIDMAN	18150	1247	30.7	34.9	30.1	3.2	1.1	37542	39963	25	16	1010	29.6	27.4	29.0	12.1	1.9	76714
15956	SOUTH FORK	18836	1190	28.2	34.5	32.3	3.8	1.2	39690	42784	32	24	1001	24.5	31.6	29.0	12.1	2.9	77589
15957	STRONGSTOWN	18410	217	30.0	38.2	27.2	3.7	0.9	37841	40000	26	17	188	27.7	18.6	33.0	20.7	0.0	101667
15958	SUMMERHILL	17783	783	27.5	33.0	32.6	5.7	1.3	40563	44089	35	28	676	17.6	19.5	40.5	21.3	1.0	117208
15960	TWIN ROCKS	0	0	0.0	0.0	0.0	0.0	0.0	0	0	0	0	0	0.0	0.0	0.0	0.0	0.0	0
15961	VINTONDALE	17594	582	32.1	33.3	30.6	3.3	0.7	37792	40000	26	17	503	30.0	26.8	31.6	11.1	0.4	77609
15963	WINDBER	20584	4834	29.1	34.6	30.5	4.2	1.7	38902	41316	29	21	3620	15.9	26.2	43.3	13.5	1.2	101375
16001	BUTLER	24380	18533	25.6	27.1	38.5	6.4	2.5	47432	51595	55	56	12375	7.4	13.4	45.7	31.0	2.5	142201
16002	BUTLER	24261	6274	16.4	26.3	46.3	7.6	3.5	57426	60982	75	75	5301	10.7	8.1	39.2	36.9	5.0	158646
16020	BOYERS	18757	434	26.3	31.8	38.0	3.2	0.7	43065	47361	43	39	372	19.9	22.8	37.9	16.9	2.4	101020
16022	BRUIN	16682	145	25.5	44.8	25.5	4.1	0.0	35320	36548	19	9	110	22.7	36.4	34.5	6.4	0.0	73846
16023	CABOT	21087	1614	19.8	29.5	42.6	6.9	1.2	50641	54523	63	63	1335	11.6	8.5	39.8	36.9	3.2	154297
16025	CHICORA	20690	2042	22.0	28.7	40.8	7.4	1.1	49302	52780	60	60	1716	10.8	16.9	46.3	24.2	1.7	133041
16028	EAST BRADY	20958	879	34.4	29.4	30.0	4.6	1.7	37464	39796	25	16	615	18.7	27.6	43.6	8.9	1.1	95357
16030	EAU CLAIRE	17819	119	28.6	34.5	33.6	2.5	0.8	40276	43631	34	27	97	20.6	20.6	41.2	16.5	1.0	104167
16033	EVANS CITY	24939	2727	15.3	27.8	45.0	8.9	3.0	55844	58683	72	72	2179	7.8	7.1	39.6	39.4	6.1	164152
16034	FENELTON	18572	693	22.9	33.6	36.7	5.6	1.2	44763	49177	48	45	608	18.4	16.4	41.3	22.4	1.5	126214
16036	FOXBURG	18008	166	28.3	39.2	27.7	3.6	1.2	36534	37792	22	12	134	23.9	29.1	33.6	12.7	0.7	85000
16037	HARMONY	24088	1703	16.3	26.0	45.8	9.3	2.6	55923	58213	73	73	1441	12.1	7.2	28.6	41.8	10.3	181197
16038	HARRISVILLE	19005	1545	27.2	32.0	35.7	3.8	1.2	41926	45368	39	35	1258	14.4	21.1	46.4	16.0	2.1	111779
16040	HILLIARDS	17117	409	29.3	33.0	33.5	3.4	0.7	40246	42652	33	27	355	24.5	23.7	36.1	14.1	1.7	94063
16041	KARNS CITY	20794	1007	25.8	29.3	37.2	6.3	1.4	45363	50060	49	48	851	15.9	23.7	41.5	18.1	0.8	108296
16045	LYNDORA	24425	465	30.8	29.9	31.4	6.5	1.5	40890	43640	36	30	349	5.2	22.6	52.7	18.3	1.1	119246
16046	MARS	38701	5038	9.2	16.4	35.5	20.2	18.7	81453	82632	93	95	4125	3.7	3.0	22.4	46.9	24.0	267987
16049	PARKER	18013	1437	29.8	34.9	30.3	3.8	1.2	39193	41112	30	23	1160	20.3	26.6	41.7	10.5	0.8	93846
16050	PETROLIA	18517	524	25.8	33.6	34.0	5.5	1.1	43335	45786	43	41	445	19.6	26.7	40.9	11.2	1.6	95500
16051	PORTERSVILLE	20649	1310	26.3	30.5	37.0	4.4	1.9	44843	47792	48	45	1131	27.3	10.6	34.3	24.8	3.0	120262
16052	PROSPECT	20954	1020	21.7	34.3	37.1	5.0	2.0	45072	49454	48	46	884	17.3	12.0	37.1	29.3	4.3	136250
16053	RENFREW	24459	1438	16.6	30.2	42.5	6.7	4.0	53076	57064	68	68	1212	10.6	8.5	34.1	41.1	5.7	167323
16055	SARVER	24876	3112	15.3	27.5	43.6	9.4	4.1	56801	59567	74	74	2798	14.4	6.5	29.2	44.4	5.5	174656
16056	SAXONBURG	24610	2128	22.7	26.1	39.8	8.1	3.4	50960	53826	63	64	1693	18.0	6.5	34.6	37.3	3.5	153301
16057	SLIPPERY ROCK	17919	4341	33.4	27.3	31.8	5.3	2.2	41162	44290	37	32	2849	14.3	13.9	37.5	30.6	3.8	140436
16059	VALENCIA	26383	2939	14.0	28.2	41.7	11.0	5.2	57170	60077	74	75	2580	10.9	5.9	35.3	39.6	8.3	168973
16061	WEST SUNBURY	19505	1035	24.9	29.9	39.3	4.2	1.7	46341	50628	52	52	899	17.1	17.9	37.6	25.3	2.1	125305
16063	ZELIENOPLE	29510	3154	21.2	24.4	41.1	8.2	5.0	53726	56793	69	69	1885	3.7	2.3	40.3	48.0	5.8	183594
16066	CRANBERRY TWP	37733	9773	6.2	11.4	42.8	21.2	18.4	86463	88293	94	96	8338	6.9	1.2	23.7	54.5	13.7	232621
16101	NEW CASTLE	19149	13840	32.0	29.2	33.0	4.0	1.8	39187	42218	30	23	10167	19.1	30.1	35.4	14.4	1.0	91289
16102	NEW CASTLE	19540	2406	29.6	28.7	34.4	5.1	2.3	41468	44563	38	33	1865	17.7	31.2	33.5	15.8	1.8	91627
16105	NEW CASTLE	27993	6185	22.6	26.1	34.9	10.1	6.3	51425	53512	65	65	4870	2.7	16.8	42.2	32.1	6.2	144173
16110	ADAMSVILLE	18392	134	25.4	41.0	29.1	3.7	0.7	38016	40495	27	17	115	13.0	22.6	43.5	16.5	4.3	115441
16111	ATLANTIC	13721	441	24.9	40.4	31.1	2.7	0.9	39154	41862	30	22	377	15.9	24.9	43.5	12.7	2.9	105943
16112	BESSEMER	21070	671	25.8	30.8	35.9	5.4	2.1	40949	46333	36	30	541	11.6	19.2	56.0	11.8	1.3	115981
16114	CLARKS MILLS	18466	269	21.2	39.4	34.2	3.7	1.5	41769	45529	39	34	239	24.3	20.1	38.1	16.3	1.3	97941
16115	DARLINGTON	21125	1293	20.4	31.9	40.9	4.5	2.2	47958	50940	56	57	1078	16.2	19.2	44.3	19.3	0.9	118793
16116	EDINBURG	18767	1409	31.4	31.4	31.9	4.2	1.1	39409	41608	31	24	1219	24.8	19.7	36.7	17.7	1.1	99375
16117	ELLWOOD CITY	21370	7063	27.2	29.3	36.0	5.0	2.4	43470	46884	44	41	5432	7.1	19.7	52.6	19.6	1.1	126164
16120	ENON VALLEY	18971	901	25.1	32.4	36.2	4.2	2.1	43373	46079	43	41	761	19.4	17.7	37.1	21.0	4.7	119901
16121	FARRELL	17783	2639	41.5	29.7	24.6	3.0	1.2	30740	32010	9	3	1854	39.5	35.3	25.1	0.2	0.0	59898
16123	FOMBELL	22416	863	20.0	27.6	42.2	7.4	2.8	51894	53777	66	67	697	8.5	8.6	39.9	37.9	5.2	161676
16124	FREDONIA	19522	764	21.9	27.7	44.0	4.8	1.6	50311	52749	62	63	628	16.4	28.0	36.6	16.2	2.7	100000
16125	GREENVILLE	22196	7412	23.2	30.0	40.1	4.4	2.3	46831	50603	54	54	5646	15.2	28.1	41.2	13.9	1.6	100524
16127	GROVE CITY	22166	5285	23.2	29.2	38.0	6.4	3.2	47570	51094	56	56	3993	11.7	16.6	48.2	21.2	2.3	120637
16130	HADLEY	19822	814	23.3	37.1	34.4	3.4	1.7	41609	45337	38	34	714	22.4	20.2	40.5	15.8	1.1	101651
16131	HARTSTOWN	16901	373	29.2	34.6	31.9	3.5	0.8	39001	42716	30	22	312	11.9	18.9	48.7	18.9	1.6	118519
16133	JACKSON CENTER	21551	555	17.7	31.4	43.8	5.4	1.8	50613	52788	63	63	485	11.8	20.0	39.4	25.4	3.5	123346
16134	JAMESTOWN	20966	1762	26.7	33.0	33.9	4.7	1.8	41038	44403	36	30	1522	12.7	25.0	42.7	17.7	1.9	109325
16137	MERCER	20655	4490	22.6	32.9	36.4	6.1	2.0	44085	48457	46	43	3633	17.6	18.4	42.1	20.1	1.9	112923
16141	NEW GALILEE	21077	704	22.9	32.7	38.1	5.1	1.3	45923	48497	51	51	599	26.2	18.2	40.6	14.0	1.0	100615
16142	NEW WILMINGTON	20112	2179	24.6	29.9	35.1	7.3	3.1	45818	49090	51	50	1657	7.2	11.5	39.3	35.7	6.2	156922
16143	PULASKI	19478	1233	27.5	28.8	36.2	5.7	1.9	43825	46247	45	42	1074	21.2	12.7	43.7	20.1	2.3	119427
16145	SANDY LAKE	20515	1099	21.9	33.7	36.9	5.4	2.1	44429	49892	47	44	896	16.6	22.0	42.9	16.7	1.8	105114
16146	SHARON	20248	6470	34.9	31.2	27.4	4.2	2.3	35520	36909	19	9	4023	30.7	40.0	23.3	5.1	0.9	65737
16148	HERMITAGE	27925	7215	18.3	30.4	38.7	7.7	4.9	51053	53860	64	64	5411	8.2	15.2	45.0	26.7	4.8	137311
16150	SHARPSVILLE	24389	3584	20.0	31.4	39.8	5.6	3.2	48553	51752	58	59	2842	11.7	23.3	48.1	15.8	1.2	111511
16153	STONEBORO	20322	1083	25.5	31.3	37.0	4.5	1.7	43734	48185	45	42	874	18.8	24.8	38.0	15.6	2.9	99492
16154	TRANSFER	19542	1175	22.6	37.5	34.0	4.9	1.0	42248	45306	40	36	994	19.8	23.8	40.9	14.4	1.0	98514
16156	VOLANT	19507	1088	20.7	33.5	38.8	5.0	2.0	46347	49220	52	52	908	12.3	15.3	40.3	25.8	6.3	134142
16157	WAMPUM	21522	2018	25.3	30.9	37.2	4.9	1.8	44949	47799	48	45	1602	13.5	28.2	44.4	13.4	0.5	100000
16159	WEST MIDDLESEX	22687	1632	20.1	31.1	40.4	6.3	2.1	49092	51550	59	60	1400	12.4	18.4	46.2	22.3	0.7	124227
16172	NEW WILMINGTON	13097	12	58.3	33.3	8.3	0.0	0.0	10000	10000	0	0	3	0.0	0.0	0.0	100.0	0.0	350000
16201	KITTANNING	20036	7765	32.1	29.1	32.0	4.8	2.0	39342	42697	31	23	5620	14.3	24.6	42.7	17.2	1.1	107321
16210	ADRIAN	16041	264	36.7	34.1	26.1	1.9	1.1	33183	35000	14	5	228	28.1	26.3	34.6	9.2	1.8	84118
16212	CADOGAN	23725	162	23.5	27.8	42.0	4.9	1.9	48233	51678	57	57	140	12.1	26.4	50.0	8.6	2.9	104310
16213	CALLENSBURG	18468	142	38.0	33.8	21.8	2.8	3.5	31641	33725	11	4	108	13.9	24.1	46.3	13.9	1.9	107143
16214	CLARION	18636	3557	40.9	24.8	27.9	4.6	1.9	31510	33488	11	4	1867	8.6	9.9	50.5	28.9	2.1	140278
16217	COOKSBURG	16916	15	26.7	26.7	46.7	0.0	0.0	47351	42500	55	56	13	0.0	23.1	69.2	7.7	0.0	127500
16218	COWANSVILLE	19407	474	30.6	34.8	29.1	3.6	1.9	38073	41132	27	18	403	17.9	27.8	40.0	12.2	2.2	95645
16222	DAYTON	16929	854	29.9	36.5	28.3	3.3	2.0	37702	40038	26	16	715	19.9	29.9	35.9	12.4	1.8	90300
16224	FAIRMOUNT CITY	18150	590	27.3	36.6	30.5	4.4	1.2	38746	40436	29	21	449	15.1	39.4	35.9	8.5	1.1	84875
16225	FISHER	26561	47	19.1	31.9	42.6	4.3	2.1	47408	51367	55	56	44	13.6	25.0	38.6	20.5	2.3	112500
16226	FORD CITY	21560	4303	27.7	32.7	33.6	3.5	2.5	41464	44496	38	33	3276	15.2	28.0	39.6	16.7	0.5	97872
16229	FREEPORT	21403	2095	27.3	27.1	37.0	6.3	2.3	45803	50053	51	50	1602	11.7	21.5	37.1	25.5	4.2	127423
16232	KNOX	21142	2068	26.0	32.4	34.9	4.7	2.0	43282	45131	43	40	1641	10.8	20.2	49.8	17.9	1.3	120176
16233	LEEPER	20021	522	28.2	32.4	33.7	4.6	1.1	40225	41066	33	27	446	10.5	24.2	43.5	18.6	3.1	114683
16234	LIMESTONE	20587	53	22.6	30.2	41.5	3.8	1.9	47363	51553	55	56	45	6.7	13.3	48.9	28.9	2.2	138750
16235	LUCINDA	20322	461	21.3	29.5	43.8	4.3	1.1	49136	51266	59	60	410	6.8	14.6	52.9	24.4	1.2	132468
16238	MANORVILLE	24730	205	22.0	33.7	39.0	3.4	2.0	43860	49397	45	42	153	18.3	24.2	35.9	21.6	0.0	98214
16239	MARIENVILLE	16710	477	32.7	31.2	31.2	3.8	1.0	36000	37365	21	11	393	10.7	28.2	48.6	11.5	1.0	108114
16240	MAYPORT	16795	608	27.6	38.3	29.3	3.6	1.2	38662	40457	29	20	493	18.3	28.2	40.2	12.8	0.6	95000
16242	NEW BETHLEHEM	19902	2105	29.7	33.3	31.2	4.4	1.4	38282	40562	28	19	1598	17.7	28.3	41.4	11.8	0.9	95424
16248	RIMERSBURG	16945	1502	34.2	34.8	26.6	3.5	0.9	32984	34426	13	5	1085	23.8	28.8	38.6	8.2	0.6	86474
	PENNSYLVANIA	26913		21.5	25.3	36.9	10.2	6.1	53225	55819				7.5	12.2	35.6	36.1	8.5	161438
	UNITED STATES	27277		20.9	24.4	35.3	11.7	7.6	54719	56938				9.3	13.1	31.6	32.6	13.5	162279

#	POST OFFICE NAME	FINANCIAL SERVICES: Auto Loan	Home Loan	Invest-ments	Retire-ment Plans	THE HOME: Home Improvements: Home Repair	Lawn & Garden	Furnishings: Comput-ers & Hard-ware-Personal	Major Appli-ances	TV, Radio, Sound Equip-ment	Furni-ture	ENTERTAINMENT: Dine out/ Carry out	Sports Equip-ment	Fees & Tickets	Toys & Games	Travel	Cable TV	PERSONAL: Apparel & Services	Auto Repairs	Health Insur-ance	Pets & Supplies
15951	SAINT MICHAEL	77	56	77	54	58	81	61	75	68	54	65	56	49	66	59	75	44	70	82	88
15952	SALIX	77	69	69	72	71	82	68	77	71	62	69	59	63	72	68	75	47	72	80	90
15953	SEANOR	75	58	78	56	60	79	58	72	64	54	63	54	49	63	58	70	42	67	76	85
15954	SEWARD	74	63	76	61	64	80	61	73	67	58	66	54	56	66	63	73	44	69	79	86
15955	SIDMAN	74	58	73	57	59	78	60	73	66	54	64	54	51	65	59	71	43	67	77	85
15956	SOUTH FORK	77	58	76	58	60	80	61	74	67	55	65	56	50	66	60	73	43	69	79	87
15957	STRONGSTOWN	77	55	79	53	57	78	57	72	63	53	62	54	45	63	56	69	41	66	75	86
15958	SUMMERHILL	79	65	78	65	67	84	65	78	70	60	69	58	57	70	65	76	46	72	82	91
15960	TWIN ROCKS	0	0	0	0	0	0	0	0	0	0	0	0	0	0	0	0	0	0	0	0
15961	VINTONDALE	74	57	72	56	59	77	59	71	65	55	63	53	50	65	58	71	43	66	76	84
15963	WINDBER	73	62	73	62	64	80	64	74	69	59	68	54	58	68	64	75	46	70	81	86
16001	BUTLER	78	76	73	77	75	83	77	79	80	74	80	59	77	79	77	84	55	79	87	93
16002	BUTLER	94	95	91	96	94	102	88	96	90	86	90	72	89	92	91	94	62	91	99	112
16020	BOYERS	83	64	81	62	65	83	64	78	70	61	69	58	53	70	62	75	46	72	80	92
16022	BRUIN	78	56	65	55	56	74	58	68	65	57	64	52	47	68	53	71	43	64	72	83
16023	CABOT	86	82	79	82	81	91	77	84	81	76	80	64	75	82	77	84	55	81	88	100
16025	CHICORA	85	78	79	79	79	92	75	85	79	70	78	64	71	80	76	84	53	80	90	100
16028	EAST BRADY	80	58	81	56	60	83	61	77	68	56	66	57	49	67	60	75	44	71	82	90
16030	EAU CLAIRE	80	58	83	56	60	82	59	75	66	55	64	56	47	65	59	72	43	69	78	89
16033	EVANS CITY	93	93	86	95	92	99	89	94	90	86	89	72	88	91	90	93	62	91	97	110
16034	FENELTON	86	69	72	68	69	83	69	78	74	68	73	59	60	77	65	79	50	74	81	93
16036	FOXBURG	78	56	81	54	58	80	58	73	64	54	63	55	46	64	57	70	42	67	76	87
16037	HARMONY	93	95	85	96	93	97	89	93	89	89	89	71	89	91	90	91	62	90	93	110
16038	HARRISVILLE	86	62	88	60	64	87	63	80	70	59	69	60	51	70	63	77	45	74	84	96
16040	HILLIARDS	81	59	72	57	59	79	61	73	67	59	66	55	49	69	57	73	44	68	76	88
16041	KARNS CITY	85	71	78	72	72	88	71	82	76	67	74	62	63	77	70	81	50	77	85	97
16045	LYNDORA	72	67	75	65	68	82	65	75	70	61	69	54	62	69	67	76	47	71	83	87
16046	MARS	148	174	162	177	172	158	151	155	145	162	147	122	167	150	161	140	105	147	144	177
16049	PARKER	80	58	81	56	60	82	60	76	67	55	65	57	48	66	59	73	43	70	79	90
16050	PETROLIA	83	67	72	67	66	84	69	77	74	66	73	59	60	76	65	79	49	74	82	93
16051	PORTERSVILLE	80	73	69	72	72	78	72	77	73	70	73	58	66	76	69	76	50	74	77	90
16052	PROSPECT	83	78	69	76	76	80	73	78	75	75	75	57	70	78	71	77	51	75	78	92
16053	RENFREW	93	94	87	95	93	99	88	94	89	86	89	71	88	91	90	92	61	90	96	110
16055	SARVER	95	100	92	101	99	102	91	97	91	91	92	73	94	94	94	93	64	92	97	113
16056	SAXONBURG	90	85	81	87	85	92	84	89	85	82	85	67	81	87	83	88	58	86	92	104
16057	SLIPPERY ROCK	76	60	60	61	59	67	75	68	73	66	73	55	61	74	63	74	50	71	70	83
16059	VALENCIA	101	103	105	104	103	111	94	104	96	94	96	78	96	96	99	99	66	98	105	121
16061	WEST SUNBURY	85	74	70	72	73	81	72	77	75	73	75	57	66	78	68	79	51	75	79	93
16063	ZELIENOPLE	83	93	90	93	93	94	89	90	90	88	90	67	95	88	94	93	64	90	98	105
16066	CRANBERRY TWP	150	176	152	176	170	151	151	153	143	164	146	122	166	151	157	136	104	144	137	173
16101	NEW CASTLE	70	63	66	64	63	75	65	70	69	61	68	52	61	68	64	73	46	68	77	83
16102	NEW CASTLE	77	64	73	65	66	81	68	77	73	62	71	57	61	72	67	79	49	74	84	90
16105	NEW CASTLE	85	97	96	96	99	104	88	94	92	89	92	67	97	89	96	97	64	92	106	108
16110	ADAMSVILLE	81	58	70	57	58	78	60	71	67	58	66	55	48	69	56	73	44	67	75	87
16111	ATLANTIC	81	58	67	56	58	77	60	70	67	59	66	54	48	70	55	73	44	66	74	85
16112	BESSEMER	76	70	78	68	71	86	68	79	74	64	72	57	65	72	70	80	49	75	87	91
16114	CLARKS MILLS	83	64	82	64	66	86	65	80	70	60	69	60	55	70	64	76	46	73	82	94
16115	DARLINGTON	88	74	89	74	76	94	73	87	78	68	77	65	65	78	74	85	52	81	92	102
16116	EDINBURG	81	60	80	58	61	82	61	76	68	57	66	57	50	68	60	74	44	70	79	90
16117	ELLWOOD CITY	75	72	71	73	72	82	72	77	75	67	74	57	69	75	72	80	51	75	84	90
16120	ENON VALLEY	92	70	80	69	71	91	72	84	78	68	76	64	60	80	68	84	51	78	87	100
16121	FARRELL	63	51	59	50	51	66	54	61	61	52	59	44	48	59	52	66	40	60	70	73
16123	FOMBELL	92	83	83	87	85	98	82	93	85	74	83	70	76	87	82	90	57	86	96	108
16124	FREDONIA	79	74	69	77	73	85	74	79	76	68	75	61	70	77	73	79	51	76	84	94
16125	GREENVILLE	78	75	73	75	75	85	74	79	78	70	77	59	72	78	74	82	53	77	87	93
16127	GROVE CITY	84	79	78	80	79	90	80	85	84	75	82	64	76	83	79	88	57	83	92	100
16130	HADLEY	83	65	82	65	67	86	66	80	71	60	70	60	56	71	65	77	47	74	83	94
16131	HARTSTOWN	80	58	70	56	58	77	60	71	66	58	65	54	48	69	55	73	44	67	75	86
16133	JACKSON CENTER	86	79	78	82	80	93	77	87	80	70	78	66	71	81	77	85	54	81	90	102
16134	JAMESTOWN	78	67	84	65	72	85	66	79	71	66	69	56	61	68	69	76	47	74	86	92
16137	MERCER	85	73	78	74	74	88	74	83	78	69	77	63	67	79	73	83	52	79	87	98
16141	NEW GALILEE	84	71	79	70	72	89	70	81	76	67	75	60	64	77	69	82	51	77	87	96
16142	NEW WILMINGTON	84	80	79	82	80	88	79	84	80	75	80	65	76	81	79	83	55	81	86	99
16143	PULASKI	86	70	77	69	70	88	70	81	76	66	74	61	61	77	67	82	50	76	85	96
16145	SANDY LAKE	82	71	75	72	71	86	71	80	74	65	73	61	64	75	70	79	50	75	84	95
16146	SHARON	67	60	57	61	58	68	65	65	69	62	68	49	62	68	61	73	47	67	74	78
16148	HERMITAGE	90	91	95	90	92	103	86	95	91	84	90	69	88	89	91	97	62	92	105	110
16150	SHARPSVILLE	84	82	83	82	82	93	79	87	83	76	82	63	78	82	81	88	57	84	95	101
16153	STONEBORO	81	66	78	67	68	86	68	80	73	61	71	60	59	73	67	79	48	75	85	94
16154	TRANSFER	80	67	68	67	66	81	67	75	72	64	70	57	60	74	64	76	48	71	79	89
16156	VOLANT	83	76	75	79	77	89	75	84	77	68	76	64	69	79	75	82	52	78	87	98
16157	WAMPUM	80	70	80	69	71	88	69	81	74	64	73	60	63	74	70	80	49	76	87	94
16159	WEST MIDDLESEX	80	79	78	78	79	90	74	82	78	71	77	60	74	78	76	84	53	78	90	96
16172	NEW WILMINGTON	36	15	15	19	14	18	51	25	41	35	41	27	30	40	27	37	29	36	25	34
16201	KITTANNING	74	63	71	63	64	78	65	73	70	61	69	55	59	69	64	75	47	70	79	86
16210	ADRIAN	76	55	78	53	57	77	56	71	62	52	61	54	45	62	55	68	40	65	74	85
16212	CADOGAN	67	77	73	75	77	83	68	75	73	67	72	52	75	71	74	77	50	72	85	85
16213	CALLENSBURG	81	58	83	56	60	82	59	75	66	55	65	57	47	65	59	72	43	69	78	90
16214	CLARION	66	49	53	52	49	58	69	60	66	58	65	50	55	66	56	67	45	64	63	73
16217	COOKSBURG	76	55	76	53	57	79	59	74	66	53	64	55	48	65	57	73	43	68	80	86
16218	COWANSVILLE	84	60	86	58	62	85	62	79	69	57	67	59	49	68	61	75	44	72	82	93
16222	DAYTON	79	56	80	54	58	80	59	74	65	54	64	56	47	65	57	72	42	68	78	88
16224	FAIRMOUNT CITY	77	60	74	60	62	81	63	75	68	56	66	57	53	68	61	74	45	70	81	88
16225	FISHER	99	71	102	69	74	100	73	93	81	68	79	69	58	80	72	89	52	85	96	110
16226	FORD CITY	75	66	72	66	67	80	68	75	73	63	71	56	63	72	67	78	49	73	83	88
16229	FREEPORT	78	72	68	74	72	81	73	77	76	69	75	59	69	77	71	79	51	75	82	91
16232	KNOX	85	67	83	67	69	89	69	83	74	62	72	62	58	74	68	80	49	76	87	97
16233	LEEPER	79	62	77	62	64	82	63	76	68	58	66	57	54	68	62	73	44	70	79	89
16234	LIMESTONE	79	72	72	75	74	85	71	81	74	64	72	61	66	75	71	78	49	74	83	94
16235	LUCINDA	81	73	74	76	75	87	72	82	75	66	74	62	67	76	72	79	50	76	85	96
16238	MANORVILLE	89	64	89	62	66	93	70	86	78	62	75	64	56	77	68	86	50	81	94	101
16239	MARIENVILLE	69	58	77	54	62	76	58	71	64	58	62	49	52	60	60	69	41	67	78	82
16240	MAYPORT	77	59	76	59	61	79	60	74	65	56	64	55	50	66	59	71	43	68	77	87
16242	NEW BETHLEHEM	80	58	80	57	60	83	62	77	68	56	67	57	50	68	60	75	44	71	82	90
16248	RIMERSBURG	74	53	75	51	55	75	55	70	61	51	60	52	44	61	54	68	40	64	74	83
	PENNSYLVANIA	94	95	95	95	95	100	94	96	96	91	95	73	94	96	94	99	67	95	101	113
	UNITED STATES	100	100	100	100	100	100	100	100	100	100	100	100	100	100	100	100	100	100	100	100

ZIP CODE #	POST OFFICE NAME	COUNTY FIPS CODE	POPULATION 2000	POPULATION 2009	POPULATION 2014	2000-2009 ANNUAL RATE % Rate	2000-2009 ANNUAL RATE State Centile	HOUSEHOLDS 2000	HOUSEHOLDS 2009	HOUSEHOLDS 2014	HOUSEHOLDS % Annual Rate 2000-2009	HOUSEHOLDS 2009 Average HH Size	FAMILIES 2000	FAMILIES 2009	FAMILIES % Annual Rate 2000-2009
16249	RURAL VALLEY	005	3218	3006	2899	-0.7	8	1258	1206	1170	-0.5	2.45	920	860	-0.7
16254	SHIPPENVILLE	031	3469	3515	3493	0.1	57	1322	1417	1423	0.8	2.37	937	974	0.4
16255	SLIGO	031	2162	2202	2187	0.2	61	764	812	814	0.7	2.58	567	585	0.3
16256	SMICKSBURG	063	1890	1834	1787	-0.3	29	495	491	482	-0.1	3.73	409	398	-0.3
16258	STRATTANVILLE	031	1949	1912	1880	-0.2	38	820	834	828	0.2	2.29	534	522	-0.2
16259	TEMPLETON	005	1570	1460	1404	-0.8	6	607	580	562	-0.5	2.52	439	409	-0.8
16260	VOWINCKEL	031	322	310	303	-0.4	23	143	142	140	-0.1	2.15	95	91	-0.5
16262	WORTHINGTON	005	2335	2102	2001	-1.1	2	912	849	816	-0.8	2.45	682	620	-1.0
16301	OIL CITY	121	19238	18279	17647	-0.6	13	7842	7641	7440	-0.3	2.35	5228	4936	-0.6
16311	CARLTON	085	553	545	535	-0.2	38	203	206	204	0.2	2.52	157	155	-0.1
16313	CLARENDON	123	1171	1124	1094	-0.4	23	468	463	455	-0.1	2.43	324	311	-0.4
16314	COCHRANTON	039	5236	5270	5197	0.1	57	1990	2058	2047	0.4	2.55	1511	1523	0.1
16316	CONNEAUT LAKE	039	5727	5761	5694	0.1	57	2468	2549	2535	0.3	2.26	1654	1649	0.0
16317	COOPERSTOWN	121	619	619	612	0.0	52	254	264	264	0.4	2.34	201	204	0.2
16319	CRANBERRY	121	1079	1049	1028	-0.3	29	429	431	427	0.1	2.43	324	317	-0.2
16321	EAST HICKORY	053	261	256	252	-0.2	38	113	113	113	0.0	2.27	80	79	-0.1
16323	FRANKLIN	121	17612	16666	16097	-0.6	13	6955	6738	6545	-0.3	2.31	4749	4463	-0.7
16326	FRYBURG	031	847	907	910	0.7	77	314	349	353	1.1	2.60	234	252	0.8
16327	GUYS MILLS	039	2907	2825	2759	-0.3	29	1052	1047	1030	-0.1	2.66	819	796	-0.3
16329	IRVINE	123	286	275	267	-0.4	23	108	107	104	-0.1	2.08	70	67	-0.5
16331	KOSSUTH	031	49	48	48	-0.2	38	21	21	21	0.0	2.29	17	17	0.0
16332	LICKINGVILLE	031	200	200	198	0.0	52	71	74	74	0.4	2.70	51	52	0.2
16333	LUDLOW	083	20	19	18	-0.6	13	10	10	10	0.0	1.90	6	6	0.0
16334	MARBLE	031	201	191	186	-0.6	13	77	76	74	-0.1	2.51	59	57	-0.4
16335	MEADVILLE	039	28991	28423	27800	-0.2	38	11655	11521	11316	-0.1	2.27	7302	6988	-0.5
16340	PITTSFIELD	123	2918	2661	2528	-1.0	3	1140	1076	1030	-0.6	2.40	853	782	-0.9
16341	PLEASANTVILLE	121	2298	2196	2136	-0.5	19	930	918	901	-0.1	2.39	691	666	-0.4
16342	POLK	121	2662	2667	2619	0.0	52	848	886	877	0.5	2.64	640	652	0.2
16345	RUSSELL	123	3614	3709	3652	0.3	64	1426	1516	1508	0.7	2.45	1094	1135	0.4
16346	SENECA	121	3058	2948	2869	-0.4	23	1263	1261	1241	0.0	2.33	918	890	-0.3
16347	SHEFFIELD	123	2346	2182	2091	-0.8	6	955	905	873	-0.6	2.39	665	611	-0.9
16350	SUGAR GROVE	123	3530	3352	3233	-0.6	13	1258	1221	1187	-0.3	2.74	965	914	-0.6
16351	TIDIOUTE	123	2143	1990	1896	-0.8	6	927	882	848	-0.5	2.21	635	586	-0.9
16353	TIONESTA	053	3332	4336	4343	2.9	98	1292	1397	1415	0.8	2.39	877	919	0.5
16354	TITUSVILLE	123	13188	12383	11954	-0.7	8	5235	5024	4883	-0.4	2.38	3569	3317	-0.8
16360	TOWNVILLE	039	1292	1260	1234	-0.3	29	475	473	466	0.0	2.66	369	359	-0.3
16362	UTICA	121	1726	1715	1692	-0.1	46	648	666	663	0.3	2.57	499	501	0.0
16364	VENUS	121	1077	969	920	-1.1	2	390	363	349	-0.8	2.67	296	269	-1.0
16365	WARREN	123	20987	19131	18153	-1.0	3	8867	8310	7941	-0.7	2.21	5650	5117	-1.1
16371	YOUNGSVILLE	123	2560	2436	2343	-0.5	19	992	970	940	-0.2	2.44	691	656	-0.6
16372	CLINTONVILLE	121	251	247	243	-0.2	38	114	115	114	0.1	2.15	85	83	-0.3
16373	EMLENTON	121	3419	3349	3287	-0.2	38	1347	1358	1343	0.1	2.43	962	940	-0.2
16374	KENNERDELL	121	1782	1754	1724	-0.2	38	716	728	722	0.2	2.41	522	514	-0.2
16401	ALBION	049	6304	6401	6365	0.2	61	1709	1720	1714	0.1	2.55	1235	1208	-0.2
16402	BEAR LAKE	123	1074	981	932	-1.0	3	340	318	304	-0.7	3.08	270	247	-1.0
16403	CAMBRIDGE SPRINGS	039	6263	6194	6068	-0.1	46	2154	2135	2100	-0.1	2.53	1538	1479	-0.4
16404	CENTERVILLE	039	3192	3273	3248	0.3	64	1124	1174	1172	0.5	2.77	857	872	0.2
16405	COLUMBUS	123	1095	1075	1048	-0.2	38	416	420	413	0.1	2.56	308	302	-0.2
16406	CONNEAUTVILLE	039	3501	3510	3451	0.0	52	1271	1289	1275	0.2	2.56	937	925	-0.1
16407	CORRY	049	11049	10762	10606	-0.3	29	4205	4151	4110	-0.1	2.54	2979	2852	-0.5
16410	CRANESVILLE	049	1790	1866	1874	0.5	70	629	667	674	0.6	2.80	499	518	0.4
16411	EAST SPRINGFIELD	049	1299	1460	1493	1.3	90	476	543	559	1.4	2.69	358	398	1.2
16412	EDINBORO	049	12609	13305	13330	0.6	74	4112	4266	4283	0.4	2.61	2437	2427	0.0
16415	FAIRVIEW	049	7789	8713	8884	1.2	88	2703	3079	3160	1.4	2.72	2174	2435	1.2
16417	GIRARD	049	8543	8718	8716	0.2	61	3198	3308	3325	0.4	2.62	2361	2369	0.0
16420	GRAND VALLEY	123	58	50	47	-1.6	1	23	21	19	-1.0	2.38	17	15	-1.3
16421	HARBORCREEK	049	2827	2857	2866	0.1	57	1033	1056	1063	0.2	2.59	771	766	-0.1
16423	LAKE CITY	049	4268	4324	4318	0.1	57	1617	1662	1667	0.3	2.59	1197	1196	0.0
16424	LINESVILLE	039	5181	5171	5092	0.0	52	2105	2150	2134	0.2	2.40	1476	1461	-0.1
16426	MC KEAN	049	4156	4186	4168	0.1	57	1507	1544	1548	0.3	2.71	1202	1203	0.0
16428	NORTH EAST	049	14129	12953	12852	-0.9	4	4859	4885	4869	0.1	2.59	3537	3458	-0.2
16430	NORTH SPRINGFIELD	049	163	191	197	1.7	93	60	71	74	1.8	2.69	45	52	1.6
16433	SAEGERTOWN	039	5709	5728	5646	0.0	52	2021	2054	2034	0.2	2.63	1508	1491	-0.1
16434	SPARTANSBURG	039	2969	3182	3192	0.8	80	875	954	962	0.9	3.33	707	755	0.7
16435	SPRINGBORO	039	2063	2136	2123	0.4	68	744	785	785	0.6	2.71	551	566	0.3
16436	SPRING CREEK	123	90	83	79	-0.9	4	35	34	32	-0.3	2.38	26	24	-0.9
16438	UNION CITY	049	8856	8757	8650	-0.1	46	3231	3244	3221	0.0	2.69	2402	2351	-0.2
16440	VENANGO	039	1059	1037	1015	-0.2	38	386	387	382	0.0	2.63	283	276	-0.3
16441	WATERFORD	049	9604	10109	10178	0.6	74	3411	3642	3689	0.7	2.78	2683	2796	0.4
16442	WATTSBURG	049	2959	2999	2990	0.1	57	1003	1034	1036	0.3	2.90	804	810	0.1
16443	WEST SPRINGFIELD	049	1527	1610	1622	0.6	74	565	603	611	0.7	2.67	427	444	0.4
16444	EDINBORO	049	108	107	106	-0.1	46	48	48	47	0.0	2.23	17	16	-0.7
16501	ERIE	049	3045	3134	3121	0.3	64	1367	1389	1388	0.2	1.33	191	175	-0.9
16502	ERIE	049	17470	16674	16315	-0.5	19	7219	6895	6759	-0.5	2.31	3857	3516	-1.0
16503	ERIE	049	18580	17509	17028	-0.6	13	6581	6142	5972	-0.7	2.71	4186	3764	-1.1
16504	ERIE	049	18062	17577	17300	-0.3	29	6654	6475	6389	-0.3	2.38	4220	3934	-0.8
16505	ERIE	049	18202	17728	17508	-0.3	29	7832	7715	7651	-0.2	2.26	4838	4580	-0.6
16506	ERIE	049	22584	23505	23689	0.4	68	9040	9559	9680	0.6	2.44	6278	6413	0.2
16507	ERIE	049	9824	9407	9209	-0.5	19	3851	3688	3619	-0.5	2.32	2020	1835	-1.0
16508	ERIE	049	15643	15099	14846	-0.4	23	6597	6450	6375	-0.2	2.28	4288	4033	-0.7
16509	ERIE	049	25822	26686	26772	0.4	68	10576	11049	11128	0.5	2.35	7022	7095	0.1
16510	ERIE	049	25617	26953	26829	0.6	74	9323	9492	9489	0.2	2.66	6915	6865	-0.1
16511	ERIE	049	11477	11284	11164	-0.2	38	4377	4357	4332	0.0	2.45	3034	2917	-0.4
16565	ERIE	049	2	2	2	0.0	52	1	1	1	0.0	2.00	1	1	0.0
16601	ALTOONA	013	32388	31743	31250	-0.2	38	12757	12768	12653	0.0	2.38	8141	7922	-0.3
16602	ALTOONA	013	31168	29376	28614	-0.6	13	12959	12483	12241	-0.4	2.29	8426	7827	-0.8
16611	ALEXANDRIA	061	2645	2595	2542	-0.2	38	1022	1039	1028	0.2	2.48	753	742	-0.2
16613	ASHVILLE	021	1601	1684	1676	0.5	70	576	619	622	0.8	2.59	428	445	0.4
16616	BECCARIA	033	112	112	110	0.0	52	46	48	47	0.5	2.33	32	32	0.0
16617	BELLWOOD	013	6146	6099	6022	-0.1	46	2403	2439	2425	0.2	2.48	1786	1765	-0.1
16620	BRISBIN	033	336	337	332	0.0	52	137	142	142	0.4	2.37	97	98	0.1
16621	BROAD TOP	061	384	380	372	-0.1	46	162	166	164	0.3	2.29	117	116	-0.1
16622	CALVIN	061	1306	1287	1247	-0.2	38	508	520	510	0.3	2.48	399	399	0.0
16623	CASSVILLE	061	116	114	110	-0.2	38	51	52	51	0.2	2.19	40	40	0.0
16625	CLAYSBURG	013	3697	3676	3653	-0.1	46	1444	1475	1477	0.2	2.48	1052	1044	-0.1
	PENNSYLVANIA					0.3					0.4	2.45			0.1
	UNITED STATES					1.0					1.1	2.59			0.9

ZIP CODE #	POST OFFICE NAME	RACE (%) White 2000	White 2009	Black 2000	Black 2009	Asian/Pacific 2000	Asian/Pacific 2009	% Hispanic Origin 2000	% Hispanic Origin 2009	2009 AGE DISTRIBUTION (%) 0-4	5-9	10-14	15-19	20-24	25-44	45-64	65-84	85+	18+	MEDIAN AGE 2009	% 2009 Males	% 2009 Females
16249	RURAL VALLEY	99.1	98.9	0.2	0.3	0.1	0.2	0.3	0.4	5.5	6.1	6.8	6.6	4.6	24.1	29.1	14.9	2.5	77.5	42.6	50.2	49.8
16254	SHIPPENVILLE	98.4	97.6	0.3	0.5	0.8	1.4	0.5	0.8	5.5	5.9	6.3	6.2	4.4	22.8	30.0	15.8	3.2	78.3	44.3	48.4	51.6
16255	SLIGO	98.3	97.6	0.0	0.0	0.4	0.5	0.6	0.9	5.2	5.3	5.8	6.9	5.4	24.8	27.1	15.8	3.6	79.2	42.3	48.1	51.9
16256	SMICKSBURG	99.3	99.0	0.2	0.3	0.2	0.3	0.0	0.0	12.2	10.9	10.1	8.7	6.3	23.4	19.4	8.1	0.9	61.3	26.3	52.3	47.7
16258	STRATTANVILLE	97.9	97.4	1.0	1.3	0.2	0.3	0.2	0.2	6.1	6.3	6.3	6.3	4.7	27.9	27.0	13.8	1.6	77.6	40.0	49.6	50.4
16259	TEMPLETON	99.0	98.8	0.3	0.3	0.0	0.0	0.5	0.8	6.2	6.3	6.4	6.5	4.9	25.4	29.0	13.2	2.2	77.1	41.0	51.0	49.0
16260	VOWINCKEL	99.4	98.7	0.0	0.0	0.0	0.3	0.0	0.3	4.2	4.8	5.5	6.1	4.2	21.3	33.9	18.1	1.9	81.6	47.5	49.4	50.6
16262	WORTHINGTON	99.2	99.0	0.1	0.1	0.1	0.2	0.6	0.9	5.5	5.7	6.1	6.4	4.7	24.4	31.2	14.0	2.0	78.7	43.1	49.0	51.0
16301	OIL CITY	98.2	97.7	0.7	0.8	0.3	0.4	0.6	0.8	6.0	5.9	6.1	6.8	6.1	23.1	28.6	14.5	2.9	77.8	41.9	48.0	52.0
16311	CARLTON	99.5	99.4	0.2	0.2	0.4	0.4	0.5	0.7	5.7	6.4	6.4	5.5	4.6	24.2	29.7	14.5	2.9	77.2	43.0	49.0	51.0
16313	CLARENDON	98.3	97.9	0.0	0.0	0.5	0.8	0.7	1.0	5.8	6.4	6.5	6.8	4.9	23.4	30.1	14.3	1.9	76.9	42.4	49.4	50.6
16314	COCHRANTON	99.2	99.0	0.2	0.3	0.2	0.3	0.2	0.3	6.1	6.4	6.9	6.4	4.8	25.0	30.3	12.6	1.6	76.5	41.0	49.7	50.3
16316	CONNEAUT LAKE	99.0	98.7	0.1	0.1	0.4	0.6	0.3	0.5	4.8	5.1	5.5	6.1	4.6	23.2	32.8	16.1	1.9	80.8	45.5	49.9	50.1
16317	COOPERSTOWN	99.2	99.0	0.2	0.2	0.2	0.3	0.6	0.8	4.8	5.3	6.0	6.6	5.0	23.4	33.0	14.5	1.3	80.0	44.1	47.8	52.2
16319	CRANBERRY	98.9	98.5	0.2	0.3	0.2	0.3	0.6	1.0	4.7	4.9	5.4	6.0	5.4	20.7	33.7	17.1	2.1	81.4	46.6	49.0	51.0
16321	EAST HICKORY	98.8	98.4	0.0	0.0	0.0	0.0	0.4	0.4	4.3	4.3	5.1	6.3	4.3	21.9	31.6	19.9	2.3	82.4	47.4	50.8	49.2
16323	FRANKLIN	95.9	94.9	2.4	2.9	0.2	0.4	0.7	0.9	5.5	5.6	5.8	7.2	5.4	22.8	29.4	15.7	2.7	78.4	43.2	48.8	51.2
16326	FRYBURG	99.3	99.3	0.1	0.1	0.1	0.1	0.2	0.3	7.6	7.9	8.3	7.5	5.6	23.8	26.1	11.8	1.3	71.6	36.8	50.6	49.4
16327	GUYS MILLS	99.0	98.7	0.3	0.4	0.2	0.3	0.4	0.6	6.4	6.7	7.0	7.0	5.7	24.4	29.2	12.0	1.6	75.7	40.2	51.6	48.4
16329	IRVINE	99.0	98.5	0.0	0.0	0.3	0.4	0.0	0.0	4.4	5.1	4.7	4.0	3.6	17.5	26.9	23.3	10.5	83.3	53.0	46.5	53.5
16331	KOSSUTH	98.0	95.8	0.0	0.0	0.0	2.1	0.0	0.0	6.3	6.3	8.3	4.2	4.2	25.0	27.1	16.7	2.1	75.0	42.5	54.2	45.8
16332	LICKINGVILLE	99.5	99.5	0.5	0.5	0.0	0.0	0.0	0.0	5.0	5.5	6.0	6.0	5.0	25.0	33.0	13.5	1.0	79.5	43.2	52.5	47.5
16333	LUDLOW	100.0	100.0	0.0	0.0	0.0	0.0	0.0	0.0	10.5	10.5	10.5	10.5	0.0	21.1	36.8	0.0	0.0	63.2	38.8	47.4	52.6
16334	MARBLE	99.5	99.5	0.0	0.0	0.0	0.0	0.0	0.0	6.3	6.8	7.3	6.8	4.7	24.1	27.7	14.7	1.6	74.9	41.2	48.2	51.8
16335	MEADVILLE	94.9	93.6	3.0	3.6	0.5	0.8	0.8	1.1	5.4	5.3	5.4	8.7	8.6	22.2	26.9	14.0	3.5	80.3	40.5	47.4	52.6
16340	PITTSFIELD	99.2	99.1	0.1	0.2	0.1	0.1	0.1	0.2	5.4	6.0	6.6	7.1	4.9	22.9	30.1	14.1	2.7	77.3	42.6	51.0	49.0
16341	PLEASANTVILLE	98.6	98.2	0.1	0.1	0.1	0.2	0.3	0.4	4.2	4.6	5.1	6.1	5.4	22.3	32.6	17.7	2.0	82.4	46.5	50.0	50.0
16342	POLK	97.6	97.0	1.1	1.3	0.3	0.4	0.1	0.1	4.1	4.6	5.9	7.5	3.4	21.5	37.1	14.3	1.5	80.1	46.7	50.7	49.3
16345	RUSSELL	98.6	98.0	0.2	0.2	0.4	0.7	0.3	0.4	4.7	5.3	6.0	6.4	4.9	22.2	34.8	14.0	1.5	79.9	45.2	51.0	49.0
16346	SENECA	99.0	98.7	0.3	0.3	0.2	0.2	0.4	0.6	6.1	6.2	6.5	6.3	5.5	23.1	30.4	14.1	1.7	77.2	42.0	49.4	50.6
16347	SHEFFIELD	98.8	98.4	0.3	0.4	0.2	0.3	0.7	0.9	5.7	5.8	6.2	6.4	5.0	23.5	28.4	16.4	2.5	78.2	43.0	49.4	50.6
16350	SUGAR GROVE	99.0	98.8	0.2	0.3	0.1	0.1	0.2	0.3	7.1	7.4	7.5	7.2	6.2	23.7	28.1	11.3	1.4	73.4	37.7	50.8	49.2
16351	TIDIOUTE	99.2	98.8	0.2	0.3	0.1	0.2	0.1	0.2	4.4	4.6	4.9	5.6	4.8	20.2	31.6	21.0	3.0	82.7	48.6	49.6	50.4
16353	TIONESTA	97.3	96.5	1.4	1.8	0.2	0.2	0.9	1.2	3.9	4.1	4.5	8.1	7.3	28.9	26.3	14.9	2.0	82.1	40.4	60.4	39.6
16354	TITUSVILLE	98.4	97.9	0.7	0.8	0.2	0.3	0.5	0.8	5.5	5.6	6.0	8.3	6.4	22.5	28.2	14.9	2.6	78.6	41.6	48.5	51.5
16360	TOWNVILLE	98.7	98.3	0.2	0.2	0.3	0.5	0.8	1.0	6.3	6.4	6.9	7.4	6.1	24.4	29.3	11.8	1.3	75.9	40.2	52.3	47.7
16362	UTICA	99.0	98.8	0.2	0.3	0.1	0.2	0.3	0.4	5.2	5.5	6.1	7.1	5.4	24.0	32.4	13.1	1.3	78.9	42.7	49.7	50.3
16364	VENUS	99.3	99.1	0.1	0.1	0.4	0.5	0.3	0.3	6.2	6.6	6.9	6.8	4.7	22.8	30.0	14.3	1.5	76.0	42.2	49.8	50.2
16365	WARREN	98.5	98.1	0.2	0.3	0.4	0.6	0.4	0.5	5.4	5.6	5.8	5.9	5.4	23.1	30.1	15.8	3.0	79.6	44.2	48.5	51.5
16371	YOUNGSVILLE	99.2	98.9	0.0	0.0	0.1	0.2	0.5	0.7	6.2	6.0	6.0	6.2	5.7	22.9	26.9	16.7	3.3	77.8	42.5	47.2	52.8
16372	CLINTONVILLE	97.2	96.8	1.6	1.6	0.0	0.4	0.0	0.0	6.5	6.5	6.5	6.1	5.3	25.9	28.3	13.0	2.0	76.9	40.1	50.6	49.4
16373	EMLENTON	98.6	98.2	0.4	0.4	0.3	0.4	0.3	0.4	5.2	5.9	6.0	6.2	5.0	24.2	29.1	15.3	3.1	78.7	43.2	49.0	51.0
16374	KENNERDELL	98.4	97.9	0.6	0.7	0.3	0.4	0.4	0.5	5.1	5.6	5.8	5.9	5.1	22.5	32.2	15.8	1.9	79.8	45.0	51.0	49.0
16401	ALBION	82.9	79.6	15.8	18.8	0.3	0.5	3.6	4.7	4.0	4.6	4.7	5.5	10.4	38.7	22.6	8.3	1.0	83.3	35.3	65.4	34.6
16402	BEAR LAKE	99.1	98.8	0.1	0.1	0.1	0.2	0.1	0.1	7.7	9.4	9.4	8.6	3.6	24.3	25.9	9.9	1.3	67.5	35.1	49.9	50.1
16403	CAMBRIDGE SPRINGS	93.8	92.3	4.9	5.9	0.2	0.4	1.3	1.8	5.2	5.4	6.1	7.4	5.4	30.8	27.5	10.5	1.8	78.6	38.9	45.1	54.9
16404	CENTERVILLE	98.8	98.7	0.3	0.4	0.1	0.2	0.3	0.4	8.2	7.3	7.8	7.7	6.2	23.5	26.5	11.3	1.6	71.6	37.0	51.4	48.6
16405	COLUMBUS	98.4	98.0	0.1	0.2	0.0	0.0	0.4	0.6	5.5	5.8	6.1	6.6	5.2	25.2	31.2	12.7	1.8	78.3	42.0	49.5	50.5
16406	CONNEAUTVILLE	98.7	98.3	0.4	0.5	0.1	0.2	0.2	0.3	5.9	6.2	6.5	6.6	5.2	23.7	27.6	13.8	4.4	77.1	42.0	49.8	50.2
16407	CORRY	98.3	97.6	0.2	0.3	0.2	0.4	0.6	1.0	6.6	6.6	6.8	7.2	6.0	24.5	26.8	13.2	2.5	75.2	39.2	48.3	51.7
16410	CRANESVILLE	98.3	97.7	0.2	0.2	0.2	0.2	0.6	1.0	6.9	7.2	7.3	6.9	5.4	26.2	27.6	11.3	1.2	74.3	38.8	49.7	50.3
16411	EAST SPRINGFIELD	97.3	96.2	0.8	1.2	0.3	0.5	0.7	1.2	5.8	6.1	6.7	7.3	5.9	24.3	30.6	11.8	1.4	77.0	40.6	50.4	49.6
16412	EDINBORO	95.0	92.9	2.6	3.7	1.0	1.5	0.8	1.3	4.0	4.1	4.5	15.1	24.0	20.2	20.4	6.8	1.0	84.1	24.7	48.8	51.2
16415	FAIRVIEW	98.4	97.7	0.4	0.5	0.5	0.8	0.7	1.0	4.9	5.9	7.0	7.2	4.2	20.4	33.8	14.1	2.6	77.7	45.3	48.3	51.7
16417	GIRARD	98.6	98.1	0.3	0.4	0.2	0.4	0.4	0.7	6.4	6.5	6.8	7.7	6.1	25.2	28.8	11.0	1.6	75.6	39.1	49.3	50.7
16420	GRAND VALLEY	100.0	100.0	0.0	0.0	0.0	0.0	0.0	0.0	4.0	4.0	4.0	8.0	8.0	24.0	36.0	12.0	0.0	80.0	43.3	54.0	46.0
16421	HARBORCREEK	98.7	98.1	0.4	0.6	0.1	0.2	0.6	1.0	4.5	4.3	6.3	9.2	5.8	21.8	31.9	13.6	2.6	78.9	43.7	48.5	51.5
16423	LAKE CITY	99.3	99.1	0.1	0.1	0.2	0.3	0.6	0.9	6.9	6.9	7.0	6.9	6.1	25.6	27.7	11.6	1.3	74.6	38.0	48.3	51.7
16424	LINESVILLE	98.2	97.7	0.4	0.5	0.1	0.2	0.5	0.8	4.5	4.9	5.5	6.4	4.9	21.1	32.3	18.0	2.4	80.8	46.8	50.6	49.4
16426	MC KEAN	98.3	97.7	0.6	0.8	0.1	0.2	0.6	1.0	6.2	6.6	7.1	7.0	5.4	25.1	31.6	10.2	0.8	75.5	39.4	50.9	49.1
16428	NORTH EAST	97.8	95.1	0.8	3.0	0.3	0.2	1.1	2.0	5.8	6.0	6.6	9.8	7.2	24.5	27.2	10.5	2.3	76.9	37.0	50.7	49.3
16430	NORTH SPRINGFIELD	97.5	95.8	1.2	1.6	0.0	0.5	0.6	1.0	6.3	6.3	7.3	7.9	6.3	24.6	30.4	9.9	1.0	74.3	38.7	49.7	50.3
16433	SAEGERTOWN	97.9	97.4	0.8	1.0	0.2	0.3	0.4	0.5	5.6	6.0	6.7	7.1	5.0	25.6	28.5	13.3	2.1	77.2	40.9	50.3	49.7
16434	SPARTANSBURG	99.3	99.2	0.2	0.2	0.0	0.0	0.2	0.3	10.7	10.1	9.7	8.7	6.7	23.1	21.8	8.3	0.9	63.8	28.0	52.7	47.3
16435	SPRINGBORO	97.5	96.8	1.1	1.4	0.2	0.3	0.5	0.7	6.7	6.8	7.2	7.3	5.5	26.1	28.5	10.5	1.3	74.6	37.6	51.5	48.5
16436	SPRING CREEK	100.0	100.0	0.0	0.0	0.0	0.0	0.0	0.0	3.6	4.8	6.0	6.0	4.8	21.7	36.1	14.5	2.4	80.7	47.1	50.6	49.4
16438	UNION CITY	98.7	98.2	0.2	0.3	0.3	0.5	0.5	0.8	6.8	6.7	6.8	7.3	6.1	25.9	27.9	10.9	1.5	74.8	38.1	50.3	49.7
16440	VENANGO	97.6	97.0	0.7	0.9	0.5	0.7	0.5	0.7	6.3	6.8	7.3	7.2	4.1	26.0	29.3	11.2	1.7	74.9	39.6	50.5	49.5
16441	WATERFORD	98.6	98.1	0.3	0.4	0.1	0.2	0.5	0.8	6.5	6.9	7.1	7.2	5.4	26.2	29.5	10.2	1.0	75.0	38.4	50.5	49.5
16442	WATTSBURG	99.0	98.5	0.1	0.1	0.3	0.5	0.3	0.5	6.2	6.6	7.1	7.2	4.8	26.6	31.4	9.2	0.9	75.6	39.4	50.6	49.4
16443	WEST SPRINGFIELD	98.5	97.8	0.4	0.6	0.1	0.2	0.4	0.6	7.0	7.1	7.3	7.1	5.3	25.7	27.3	11.9	1.2	74.1	38.1	50.4	49.6
16444	EDINBORO	95.4	93.5	1.9	1.9	1.9	3.7	1.9	1.9	2.8	2.8	3.7	5.6	42.1	18.7	14.0	9.3	0.9	90.7	24.2	49.5	50.5
16501	ERIE	86.4	81.7	10.2	13.8	0.9	1.3	1.7	2.5	2.4	2.0	1.5	19.7	21.2	18.2	14.3	16.8	3.9	93.3	28.5	45.4	54.6
16502	ERIE	84.5	80.0	9.7	12.6	0.7	1.2	5.1	7.1	7.3	6.5	6.1	7.5	9.7	28.8	22.5	8.8	2.9	75.7	33.5	48.7	51.3
16503	ERIE	57.4	50.3	33.6	38.7	0.8	1.0	8.7	11.3	9.8	9.0	8.0	8.8	9.1	27.1	20.1	7.0	1.1	68.1	28.3	49.8	50.2
16504	ERIE	90.5	87.2	6.9	9.2	0.7	1.1	1.8	2.6	5.6	5.6	5.7	9.4	9.5	23.9	23.0	13.4	3.9	79.4	37.0	46.3	53.7
16505	ERIE	96.8	95.4	1.2	1.7	0.7	1.1	1.5	2.2	5.3	5.5	6.0	6.4	5.3	21.4	31.0	15.1	4.1	79.0	45.1	47.1	52.9
16506	ERIE	96.4	94.7	0.9	1.3	1.7	2.8	0.9	1.4	5.8	6.1	6.8	6.3	5.0	24.1	30.1	13.5	2.3	77.1	42.1	48.4	51.6
16507	ERIE	72.9	66.8	21.2	25.9	1.0	1.4	4.6	6.1	7.6	6.7	6.0	7.7	9.8	27.9	22.2	10.0	2.1	75.0	32.8	51.2	48.8
16508	ERIE	94.5	92.5	2.8	3.7	0.5	0.8	1.9	2.9	6.6	6.5	6.5	6.1	5.2	26.5	25.6	13.7	3.3	76.6	40.1	47.5	52.5
16509	ERIE	96.5	95.1	1.6	2.1	0.9	1.5	0.8	1.2	5.0	5.1	5.6	6.2	6.0	23.5	29.2	16.0	3.4	80.4	43.9	48.2	51.8
16510	ERIE	87.7	83.9	8.5	11.3	0.9	1.4	2.6	3.5	6.0	6.0	6.1	7.5	7.4	26.5	27.7	11.4	1.3	77.8	37.6	50.8	49.2
16511	ERIE	91.9	90.0	4.9	5.9	0.4	0.6	2.6	3.5	6.0	5.7	5.7	6.6	5.8	22.6	27.3	15.8	4.4	78.3	42.9	46.3	53.7
16565	ERIE	100.0	100.0	0.0	0.0	0.0	0.0	0.0	0.0	0.0	0.0	0.0	0.0	0.0	50.0	50.0	0.0	0.0	100.0	45.0	50.0	50.0
16601	ALTOONA	95.8	94.9	2.7	3.2	0.3	0.4	0.7	0.9	5.9	5.8	5.7	8.6	6.7	25.1	26.9	13.1	2.2	79.2	38.8	48.0	52.0
16602	ALTOONA	97.4	96.7	1.4	1.7	0.4	0.6	0.6	0.8	5.9	5.9	6.0	5.8	5.1	24.8	27.8	15.2	3.3	78.7	42.2	47.4	52.6
16611	ALEXANDRIA	98.8	98.3	0.2	0.2	0.5	0.6	0.9	1.3	5.0	5.5	6.2	6.4	4.8	23.9	32.9	13.4	1.8	79.2	43.6	49.6	50.4
16613	ASHVILLE	97.9	97.0	1.4	1.9	0.1	0.2	1.1	1.5	5.2	5.9	6.5	7.1	4.8	27.6	28.2	12.9	2.0	78.1	40.6	53.5	46.5
16616	BECCARIA	99.1	99.1	0.0	0.0	0.0	0.0	0.0	0.0	5.4	5.4	5.4	6.3	5.4	24.1	29.5	16.1	2.7	81.3	43.8	50.0	50.0
16617	BELLWOOD	99.0	98.7	0.1	0.1	0.2	0.3	0.5	0.7	5.7	5.9	6.0	6.0	5.1	25.5	29.7	13.9	2.1	78.6	42.0	49.1	50.9
16620	BRISBIN	99.4	99.1	0.0	0.0	0.0	0.0	0.0	0.3	5.6	5.9	6.2	6.2	5.0	24.9	30.0	13.9	2.1	78.3	42.4	47.8	52.2
16621	BROAD TOP	99.2	98.9	0.3	0.5	0.3	0.3	0.0	0.3	6.6	6.3	6.6	5.3	5.0	26.6	28.2	13.9	1.6	77.4	40.7	50.8	49.2
16622	CALVIN	99.5	99.3	0.0	0.1	0.0	0.0	0.2	0.3	6.0	6.4	6.8	6.4	4.0	26.1	28.4	14.5	1.6	77.2	40.9	49.1	50.9
16623	CASSVILLE	100.0	100.0	0.0	0.0	0.0	0.0	0.0	0.0	6.1	7.0	7.0	7.0	4.4	26.3	25.4	14.9	1.8	74.6	39.5	47.4	52.6
16625	CLAYSBURG	99.1	98.9	0.1	0.1	0.0	0.1	0.3	0.4	6.1	6.0	6.2	6.6	5.3	26.7	28.7	13.0	1.6	77.7	40.2	48.7	51.3
	PENNSYLVANIA	85.4	83.2	10.0	10.7	1.8	2.7	3.2	4.2	5.8	6.0	6.3	7.1	6.5	24.8	27.8	13.1	2.6	77.8	40.4	48.5	51.5
	UNITED STATES	75.1	72.0	12.3	12.7	3.8	4.6	12.5	15.7	6.8	6.7	6.6	7.1	6.9	27.0	26.0	10.9	1.9	75.7	36.9	49.2	50.8

ZIP CODE #	POST OFFICE NAME	2009 Per Capita Income	2009 HH Income Base	2009 Household Income Distribution (%): Less than $25,000	$25,000 to $49,999	$50,000 to $99,999	$100,000 to $149,999	$150,000 or More	Median Household Income: 2009	2014	2009 National Centile	2009 State Centile	2009 Home Value Base	2009 Home Value Distribution (%): Less than $50,000	$50,000 to $89,999	$90,000 to $174,999	$175,000 to $399,999	$400,000 or More	2009 Median Home Value
16249	RURAL VALLEY	17522	1206	33.3	32.0	29.6	4.0	1.2	35874	38663	20	10	968	19.5	28.6	41.6	8.5	1.8	92500
16254	SHIPPENVILLE	22709	1417	22.9	33.7	34.2	6.4	2.8	44594	46830	47	44	1166	18.4	17.2	37.8	24.0	2.7	125155
16255	SLIGO	19933	812	28.3	32.0	31.8	4.8	3.1	41972	44298	39	35	604	11.8	24.5	44.4	16.9	2.5	112778
16256	SMICKSBURG	10236	491	35.8	39.7	22.2	1.4	0.8	30702	32073	9	3	423	16.3	28.1	34.3	19.1	2.1	101008
16258	STRATTANVILLE	20796	834	29.9	33.5	30.9	3.4	2.4	38218	39552	27	18	579	21.2	18.8	40.8	17.3	1.9	110634
16259	TEMPLETON	17031	580	34.1	31.4	30.3	3.3	0.9	36478	39081	22	12	476	30.7	42.9	21.0	4.0	1.5	63934
16260	VOWINCKEL	20316	142	30.3	34.5	31.0	3.5	0.7	37714	38632	26	16	120	13.3	25.0	42.5	16.7	2.5	103333
16262	WORTHINGTON	19695	849	27.2	33.6	31.7	6.2	1.3	41070	44868	36	31	673	13.8	16.0	48.1	19.6	2.4	125500
16301	OIL CITY	21194	7641	30.5	28.5	33.8	4.8	2.4	41672	44696	38	34	5410	20.2	32.9	37.0	9.1	0.7	85638
16311	CARLTON	19833	206	23.3	35.9	33.5	4.9	2.4	40916	46394	36	30	178	18.5	20.8	44.4	15.7	0.6	108000
16313	CLARENDON	20043	463	29.2	33.0	33.3	3.0	1.5	39768	42022	32	25	388	21.4	35.3	33.2	9.3	0.8	79167
16314	COCHRANTON	20322	2058	23.8	31.6	37.8	5.1	1.7	44576	48175	47	44	1743	13.0	19.4	43.6	21.7	2.2	121309
16316	CONNEAUT LAKE	23744	2549	23.3	31.3	37.5	5.5	2.4	45941	48870	51	51	2012	10.4	11.8	45.6	26.4	5.8	136077
16317	COOPERSTOWN	21129	264	22.7	31.8	40.2	5.3	0.0	46350	49081	52	52	232	9.9	27.2	55.6	6.0	1.3	101923
16319	CRANBERRY	21410	431	22.3	31.1	39.7	4.9	2.1	45679	49839	50	49	381	14.2	23.1	45.9	16.0	0.8	110261
16321	EAST HICKORY	18867	113	31.9	34.5	30.1	3.5	0.0	34680	34734	17	8	101	9.9	29.7	49.5	8.9	2.0	105147
16323	FRANKLIN	22210	6738	29.6	28.4	32.7	6.4	2.9	42068	45530	39	35	4900	15.2	32.3	40.4	10.8	1.3	94261
16326	FRYBURG	16388	349	35.2	29.2	30.7	3.7	1.1	35131	37106	18	9	282	16.0	17.0	45.0	21.3	0.7	120732
16327	GUYS MILLS	19853	1047	20.4	34.3	39.3	4.0	2.0	45598	48752	50	49	930	13.4	22.2	46.2	16.6	1.6	115769
16329	IRVINE	23545	107	25.2	31.8	34.6	5.6	2.8	42776	45000	42	38	86	12.8	26.7	48.8	11.6	0.0	100000
16331	KOSSUTH	19167	21	23.8	42.9	28.6	4.8	0.0	37357	47375	25	15	18	0.0	22.2	55.6	22.2	0.0	133333
16332	LICKINGVILLE	18816	74	27.0	24.3	40.5	6.8	1.4	45000	50000	48	46	64	6.3	21.9	50.0	18.8	3.1	128571
16333	LUDLOW	16842	10	40.0	40.0	20.0	0.0	0.0	30000	35000	8	3	9	22.2	22.2	44.4	11.1	0.0	95000
16334	MARBLE	20810	76	22.4	35.5	35.5	5.3	1.3	43223	46151	43	40	64	7.8	18.8	40.6	29.7	3.1	136364
16335	MEADVILLE	23106	11521	28.7	28.7	32.2	7.1	3.3	42286	45598	40	36	7501	12.6	15.7	48.8	20.3	2.6	126292
16340	PITTSFIELD	19588	1076	26.3	34.6	33.6	4.6	1.0	42153	44629	40	36	925	15.1	27.8	46.6	9.9	0.5	99924
16341	PLEASANTVILLE	20793	918	27.1	29.8	37.0	4.5	1.5	42603	46376	41	38	791	11.6	31.0	45.1	11.8	0.5	99750
16342	POLK	18577	886	25.3	32.6	34.7	5.8	1.7	43437	46374	44	41	748	17.0	24.6	44.4	13.0	1.1	102778
16345	RUSSELL	23525	1516	15.9	31.9	42.5	7.6	2.1	51200	52717	64	65	1339	9.2	13.4	49.2	26.0	2.2	136096
16346	SENECA	22375	1261	26.6	27.6	37.0	6.4	2.3	45810	49619	51	50	1013	13.1	22.0	51.2	12.8	0.8	111643
16347	SHEFFIELD	20870	905	28.8	26.2	38.5	5.2	1.3	45980	48518	51	51	720	20.0	36.9	35.6	5.8	1.7	81935
16350	SUGAR GROVE	18029	1221	24.0	32.6	38.9	3.9	0.6	45185	47834	49	47	1030	17.6	22.3	45.1	13.5	1.5	106646
16351	TIDIOUTE	22228	882	29.4	32.7	31.1	5.0	1.9	39335	41710	31	23	721	15.3	31.5	42.2	9.4	1.7	94352
16353	TIONESTA	17035	1397	34.4	31.5	29.1	3.8	1.3	34402	35357	16	7	1121	11.7	26.9	48.9	11.0	1.6	105175
16354	TITUSVILLE	20203	5024	31.1	32.1	29.5	4.7	2.5	38911	41700	29	22	3575	17.1	30.0	41.2	10.2	1.5	94457
16360	TOWNVILLE	18335	473	23.5	36.2	35.7	3.4	1.3	42264	45418	40	36	407	15.5	22.9	43.5	16.5	1.7	107460
16362	UTICA	18864	666	26.4	30.8	37.1	4.8	0.9	43534	47036	44	41	576	19.4	26.2	41.1	11.6	1.6	96944
16364	VENUS	18893	363	27.5	29.8	37.2	3.9	1.7	43462	46226	44	41	306	10.8	20.6	46.4	21.2	1.0	127315
16365	WARREN	24521	8310	23.2	30.9	37.2	6.0	2.7	46130	49852	52	51	5966	10.1	25.4	50.6	12.7	1.2	110397
16371	YOUNGSVILLE	21130	970	24.0	32.6	36.5	5.5	1.4	43922	46653	45	42	732	11.5	28.8	48.4	11.3	0.0	101307
16372	CLINTONVILLE	20940	115	34.8	29.6	31.3	4.3	0.0	35373	37866	19	9	89	23.6	23.6	40.4	12.4	0.0	94167
16373	EMLENTON	20387	1358	28.4	32.2	31.7	5.4	2.4	40611	42825	35	29	1059	17.3	23.2	40.3	16.1	3.0	107535
16374	KENNERDELL	18949	728	29.1	37.2	28.2	4.1	1.4	37650	40092	26	16	623	17.8	24.7	44.5	11.4	1.6	100128
16401	ALBION	17779	1720	25.9	30.3	37.8	4.4	1.6	45041	48038	48	46	1324	13.5	20.9	50.8	14.0	0.8	109191
16402	BEAR LAKE	14844	318	25.8	38.7	31.1	3.1	1.3	40913	42708	36	30	279	17.6	30.1	43.4	7.5	1.4	93824
16403	CAMBRIDGE SPRINGS	20096	2135	23.3	29.4	39.4	6.0	1.9	47946	50191	56	57	1686	12.5	16.5	47.2	21.8	2.1	123003
16404	CENTERVILLE	16376	1174	28.8	34.7	32.2	2.8	1.5	39190	42203	30	23	990	20.8	21.8	41.7	14.1	1.5	103045
16405	COLUMBUS	20607	420	26.9	29.5	35.7	6.2	1.7	44119	46512	46	43	359	8.6	20.3	54.9	15.6	0.6	122588
16406	CONNEAUTVILLE	18090	1289	27.2	35.2	32.4	3.9	1.2	40434	43712	34	28	1068	17.3	20.8	43.8	16.9	1.2	110736
16407	CORRY	19484	4151	26.8	31.6	36.2	4.0	1.4	42544	45887	41	37	2930	18.2	36.5	36.9	7.5	0.9	85073
16410	CRANESVILLE	19644	667	19.0	31.9	42.9	4.5	1.6	49202	51497	59	60	578	13.5	23.0	43.9	18.3	1.2	110514
16411	EAST SPRINGFIELD	20383	543	22.5	33.3	36.3	5.5	2.4	46899	49281	54	55	491	14.3	25.9	46.2	11.8	1.8	107302
16412	EDINBORO	20540	4266	28.3	23.7	36.4	7.1	4.5	48443	50947	58	58	2620	8.9	8.9	40.8	37.1	4.4	155000
16415	FAIRVIEW	32003	3079	10.4	20.0	43.5	13.5	12.7	72657	73060	88	90	2788	2.3	4.8	31.5	50.5	10.9	200812
16417	GIRARD	21420	3308	16.5	33.1	42.9	6.0	1.4	50191	52302	62	62	2714	17.1	8.7	52.1	20.2	2.0	122169
16420	GRAND VALLEY	18021	21	23.8	42.9	28.6	4.8	0.0	41107	46103	36	31	19	26.3	31.6	31.6	10.5	0.0	75000
16421	HARBORCREEK	23727	1056	15.2	27.1	50.4	5.5	1.8	59072	59648	76	77	850	3.5	9.3	52.6	32.0	2.6	150376
16423	LAKE CITY	22133	1662	17.4	38.1	34.8	6.8	2.9	43627	48426	44	42	1341	19.9	12.1	55.7	10.4	1.9	112307
16424	LINESVILLE	20044	2150	27.8	34.1	32.6	4.2	1.4	40617	43247	35	29	1757	11.8	23.4	50.0	13.3	1.4	112500
16426	MC KEAN	22638	1544	13.4	33.9	42.6	8.2	1.9	52199	54190	66	67	1403	20.5	10.3	32.5	31.8	5.0	135991
16428	NORTH EAST	22798	4885	19.3	27.9	41.6	8.1	3.0	52420	54430	67	67	3772	13.7	10.0	46.6	26.5	3.1	138196
16430	NORTH SPRINGFIELD	22162	71	23.9	29.6	36.6	7.0	2.8	48430	50917	58	58	64	14.1	23.4	43.8	15.6	3.1	110417
16433	SAEGERTOWN	20882	2054	20.2	32.4	38.9	6.4	2.1	47224	50218	55	55	1745	15.4	15.1	43.2	23.8	2.6	127392
16434	SPARTANSBURG	13722	954	28.7	36.5	28.9	4.4	1.5	37251	39907	24	15	812	18.2	25.2	42.5	13.1	1.0	101527
16435	SPRINGBORO	16778	785	30.2	34.0	31.1	3.8	0.9	38785	41171	29	21	623	22.2	17.2	44.3	15.2	1.1	109861
16436	SPRING CREEK	22077	34	14.7	38.2	41.2	5.9	0.0	47361	51052	55	56	29	13.8	20.7	51.7	13.8	0.0	121875
16438	UNION CITY	18551	3244	25.6	32.0	36.4	4.1	1.9	43877	47087	45	42	2467	15.2	30.2	36.8	15.9	1.9	97201
16440	VENANGO	20992	387	21.4	33.3	35.7	7.0	2.6	45891	48480	51	50	317	6.9	18.3	45.1	27.4	2.2	133088
16441	WATERFORD	21080	3642	16.0	29.8	45.4	7.0	1.7	52895	54315	68	68	3091	15.3	14.1	35.4	31.5	3.7	135453
16442	WATTSBURG	21019	1034	15.6	28.5	43.6	10.3	2.0	55649	56890	72	72	878	8.4	14.0	42.3	33.5	1.8	143919
16443	WEST SPRINGFIELD	20656	603	25.0	26.9	40.1	6.5	1.5	48234	51091	57	58	510	11.8	23.3	50.4	13.5	1.0	110119
16444	EDINBORO	16804	48	54.2	20.8	16.7	8.3	0.0	22739	24397	2	1	13	0.0	23.1	46.2	30.8	0.0	137500
16501	ERIE	14038	1389	78.4	16.1	4.8	0.4	0.4	11699	12463	1	0	46	13.0	21.7	37.0	21.7	6.5	128125
16502	ERIE	17585	6895	36.7	32.8	27.3	2.6	0.7	33490	34817	14	6	2723	14.4	45.5	37.7	2.2	0.2	82217
16503	ERIE	12041	6142	46.8	34.3	17.3	1.0	0.6	26354	26807	4	2	2428	48.2	43.4	7.9	0.4	0.1	50915
16504	ERIE	22314	6475	22.5	28.2	40.2	6.7	2.3	49258	52103	59	60	4482	4.2	39.3	51.0	5.4	0.2	94104
16505	ERIE	33504	7715	18.4	27.1	36.3	9.3	8.9	55037	57192	71	71	5744	10.8	9.9	44.2	26.8	8.4	141732
16506	ERIE	31482	9559	12.6	24.8	41.4	13.0	8.2	64051	64621	82	85	6941	7.5	5.7	40.0	40.8	6.0	167677
16507	ERIE	16062	3688	42.2	33.7	20.8	1.9	1.5	28919	30355	7	2	1395	27.7	50.0	16.6	2.4	3.3	58750
16508	ERIE	23555	6450	19.5	31.9	42.1	5.1	1.4	48746	51636	58	59	4699	2.5	29.3	61.6	6.4	0.1	102481
16509	ERIE	27937	11049	15.3	28.8	41.3	9.5	5.1	55340	56845	72	71	8159	9.2	8.5	48.2	30.8	3.3	144373
16510	ERIE	22081	9492	18.5	25.6	45.7	8.1	2.1	55857	57153	72	73	7637	7.7	19.8	52.5	19.8	0.2	117428
16511	ERIE	23244	4357	23.3	26.2	39.1	8.6	2.8	50529	53324	62	63	3166	7.5	21.7	49.2	20.1	1.4	120189
16565	ERIE	0	0	0.0	0.0	0.0	0.0	0.0	0	0	0	0	0	0.0	0.0	0.0	0.0	0.0	0
16601	ALTOONA	20057	12768	32.5	28.5	32.0	5.0	2.1	38415	41743	28	19	8703	13.5	29.6	42.8	13.3	0.8	99975
16602	ALTOONA	21947	12483	29.9	29.2	32.7	6.0	2.2	40241	45218	33	27	8790	15.6	26.0	43.0	13.9	1.4	102576
16611	ALEXANDRIA	20120	1039	27.1	26.9	39.9	5.1	1.0	46131	46915	52	51	846	11.5	17.3	46.7	22.3	2.2	127649
16613	ASHVILLE	17595	619	29.6	34.2	30.9	3.9	1.5	38039	41188	27	18	531	14.1	24.5	41.4	17.1	2.8	109414
16616	BECCARIA	18259	48	35.4	33.3	29.2	2.1	0.0	35000	38646	18	8	42	19.0	28.6	42.9	9.5	0.0	93333
16617	BELLWOOD	21537	2439	20.6	29.7	42.0	6.4	1.4	49732	52168	60	61	1916	8.2	14.4	53.3	23.5	0.5	131268
16620	BRISBIN	18556	142	32.4	32.4	30.3	4.2	0.7	38981	41007	30	22	117	17.9	31.6	37.6	12.8	0.0	90714
16621	BROAD TOP	18125	166	33.7	30.7	31.9	3.6	0.0	38039	40000	27	18	137	14.6	27.0	50.4	8.0	0.0	100431
16622	CALVIN	19131	520	25.0	35.6	35.8	2.7	1.0	40794	42454	35	29	454	11.5	18.3	47.4	20.9	2.0	125000
16623	CASSVILLE	21882	52	26.9	36.5	34.6	1.9	0.0	40000	41715	33	26	45	6.7	20.0	46.7	24.4	2.2	129167
16625	CLAYSBURG	17600	1475	34.4	32.9	27.9	3.7	1.0	35437	37308	19	9	1160	17.3	20.5	45.1	15.4	1.6	112778
	PENNSYLVANIA	26913		21.5	25.3	36.9	10.2	6.1	53225	55819				7.5	12.2	35.6	36.1	8.5	161438
	UNITED STATES	27277		20.9	24.4	35.3	11.7	7.6	54719	56938				9.3	13.1	31.6	32.6	13.5	162279

ZIP CODE #	POST OFFICE NAME	FINANCIAL SERVICES: Auto Loan	FINANCIAL SERVICES: Home Loan	FINANCIAL SERVICES: Invest-ments	FINANCIAL SERVICES: Retire-ment Plans	THE HOME: Home Improvements: Home Repair	THE HOME: Home Improvements: Lawn & Garden	THE HOME: Furnishings: Comput-ers & Hard-ware-Personal	THE HOME: Furnishings: Major Appli-ances	THE HOME: Furnishings: TV, Radio, Sound Equip-ment	THE HOME: Furnishings: Furni-ture	ENTERTAINMENT: Dine out/ Carry out	ENTERTAINMENT: Sports Equip-ment	ENTERTAINMENT: Fees & Tickets	ENTERTAINMENT: Toys & Games	ENTERTAINMENT: Travel	ENTERTAINMENT: Cable TV	PERSONAL: Apparel & Services	PERSONAL: Auto Repairs	PERSONAL: Health Insur-ance	PERSONAL: Pets & Supplies
16249	RURAL VALLEY	76	54	77	52	56	77	57	71	63	52	62	54	45	63	55	70	41	66	75	85
16254	SHIPPENVILLE	95	72	96	70	74	98	73	91	80	67	78	68	60	80	72	87	52	83	94	107
16255	SLIGO	86	67	84	67	70	91	70	85	77	63	74	64	59	76	69	83	50	79	90	99
16256	SMICKSBURG	69	49	63	48	49	67	51	62	56	48	55	48	40	57	48	61	37	58	65	75
16258	STRATTANVILLE	79	59	71	59	60	78	66	74	71	60	69	56	54	71	61	77	46	71	80	88
16259	TEMPLETON	74	54	75	53	56	76	57	71	63	52	61	53	46	62	56	69	41	65	75	84
16260	VOWINCKEL	77	55	79	54	58	79	58	73	64	53	63	55	46	64	57	71	42	67	77	87
16262	WORTHINGTON	77	66	72	67	67	82	66	77	70	60	68	58	59	71	66	75	46	71	81	90
16301	OIL CITY	74	67	68	67	66	79	69	74	74	65	72	55	65	73	67	78	49	73	82	87
16311	CARLTON	79	72	71	75	73	85	71	80	73	64	72	60	65	74	71	77	49	74	82	93
16313	CLARENDON	85	61	86	59	63	87	64	81	71	59	70	60	51	71	63	79	46	74	86	95
16314	COCHRANTON	82	72	73	75	74	87	72	82	75	66	74	62	65	77	71	80	50	76	84	95
16316	CONNEAUT LAKE	87	73	86	73	75	90	74	85	77	69	76	64	65	78	73	82	52	80	87	100
16317	COOPERSTOWN	80	68	71	70	70	83	68	78	72	63	70	59	61	73	67	77	48	72	81	92
16319	CRANBERRY	78	74	79	73	75	88	70	80	75	66	74	59	68	74	72	80	50	76	87	93
16321	EAST HICKORY	76	55	78	53	57	78	56	71	62	52	61	54	45	62	56	68	40	65	74	85
16323	FRANKLIN	85	67	80	67	69	88	72	82	77	66	76	62	62	77	70	84	51	78	89	97
16326	FRYBURG	72	57	62	57	58	72	58	67	63	55	61	51	50	65	55	67	42	63	70	80
16327	GUYS MILLS	83	75	74	77	76	88	74	83	76	67	75	63	68	78	73	81	51	77	86	97
16329	IRVINE	92	67	90	65	69	95	72	88	80	65	78	66	58	80	69	89	52	82	96	104
16331	KOSSUTH	68	62	61	64	63	73	61	69	63	55	62	52	56	64	61	67	42	64	71	80
16332	LICKINGVILLE	79	72	71	75	73	85	71	80	73	64	72	60	65	74	71	77	49	74	82	93
16333	LUDLOW	57	41	59	40	42	58	42	53	47	39	46	40	34	46	42	51	30	49	56	64
16334	MARBLE	81	74	73	77	75	87	73	82	75	66	74	62	67	76	73	79	50	76	85	95
16335	MEADVILLE	79	72	74	73	73	82	77	79	79	72	78	59	72	78	74	83	54	79	86	93
16340	PITTSFIELD	82	62	72	62	63	81	64	75	70	61	69	57	53	72	61	76	46	71	79	90
16341	PLEASANTVILLE	80	65	77	66	67	85	67	80	73	61	71	60	58	72	66	78	48	74	85	93
16342	POLK	90	66	92	64	68	92	67	85	74	62	73	64	54	74	67	82	48	78	88	101
16345	RUSSELL	89	81	80	85	83	96	80	90	83	72	81	68	74	84	80	87	55	83	93	105
16346	SENECA	77	74	69	75	72	83	73	77	75	68	74	59	70	76	72	79	51	75	83	92
16347	SHEFFIELD	81	67	84	65	68	87	66	80	73	62	71	59	59	72	67	79	48	75	86	94
16350	SUGAR GROVE	85	66	72	66	66	84	67	78	73	64	72	59	57	76	63	79	48	73	81	93
16351	TIDIOUTE	86	62	87	60	64	88	65	82	73	59	71	61	52	72	64	80	47	76	87	97
16353	TIONESTA	75	55	75	54	57	77	58	71	64	54	62	53	47	63	56	70	41	66	75	84
16354	TITUSVILLE	79	61	76	61	63	80	66	76	72	61	70	57	56	71	63	78	47	73	82	90
16360	TOWNVILLE	84	65	72	65	65	83	66	77	72	63	71	59	56	74	63	78	48	72	80	92
16362	UTICA	78	67	69	69	68	81	67	76	70	61	69	58	60	72	66	75	47	71	79	90
16364	VENUS	86	67	84	67	69	89	68	82	73	62	72	62	57	73	67	79	48	76	85	97
16365	WARREN	83	75	77	75	75	88	76	82	80	71	79	62	72	80	75	85	54	80	90	97
16371	YOUNGSVILLE	76	74	68	74	71	83	72	76	76	69	75	57	71	76	71	79	51	75	84	90
16372	CLINTONVILLE	80	58	82	56	60	82	59	75	66	55	64	56	47	65	58	72	42	69	78	89
16373	EMLENTON	86	64	92	62	67	89	66	83	72	61	71	62	54	71	66	79	47	77	86	98
16374	KENNERDELL	81	59	85	57	61	83	60	76	66	56	65	57	48	66	60	73	43	70	79	91
16401	ALBION	84	67	73	67	67	85	69	78	74	65	73	60	60	76	66	80	49	74	83	94
16402	BEAR LAKE	82	59	68	58	59	78	62	72	68	60	67	55	50	71	56	74	45	68	76	87
16403	CAMBRIDGE SPRINGS	85	73	75	75	74	88	74	83	78	69	76	62	67	79	72	82	52	78	86	97
16404	CENTERVILLE	80	60	71	59	60	79	61	72	67	58	66	55	50	69	58	73	44	68	76	87
16405	COLUMBUS	82	74	74	77	76	88	73	83	76	66	74	63	68	77	73	80	51	76	85	96
16406	CONNEAUTVILLE	83	62	76	60	62	82	63	76	69	60	68	57	52	71	60	75	45	71	79	91
16407	CORRY	80	65	67	65	64	80	69	75	74	65	72	57	60	75	64	79	49	73	81	89
16410	CRANESVILLE	91	75	79	76	75	93	75	86	80	70	79	66	66	83	72	86	53	81	90	102
16411	EAST SPRINGFIELD	94	73	80	73	73	93	75	86	81	71	79	66	63	84	70	87	54	81	90	103
16412	EDINBORO	85	72	66	75	70	75	91	77	86	81	86	64	78	87	77	85	60	83	79	94
16415	FAIRVIEW	122	138	136	141	140	142	122	132	122	123	122	99	132	123	133	125	86	125	133	153
16417	GIRARD	83	81	73	82	79	87	79	83	81	76	80	63	77	82	78	83	55	80	87	97
16420	GRAND VALLEY	77	56	64	54	55	74	58	67	64	56	63	52	46	67	53	70	42	64	71	82
16421	HARBORCREEK	91	90	87	92	90	98	87	93	89	84	88	70	87	90	89	92	61	90	97	109
16423	LAKE CITY	86	80	77	81	77	91	80	84	83	76	82	66	77	84	78	87	56	83	91	101
16424	LINESVILLE	79	63	83	61	67	84	64	78	70	61	68	57	56	68	65	76	45	73	84	92
16426	MC KEAN	88	95	81	96	91	92	86	89	85	87	86	69	90	88	89	86	60	86	88	105
16428	NORTH EAST	84	86	79	87	85	91	83	86	85	81	85	65	84	86	84	88	59	85	92	101
16430	NORTH SPRINGFIELD	108	77	89	75	77	102	80	93	89	78	87	72	64	93	73	97	59	89	99	114
16433	SAEGERTOWN	89	78	77	80	78	93	78	87	81	72	80	66	71	83	76	86	54	82	91	102
16434	SPARTANSBURG	82	59	68	58	59	78	62	72	68	60	67	55	50	71	56	74	45	68	75	87
16435	SPRINGBORO	81	59	71	58	59	79	61	73	68	59	66	55	49	70	57	74	44	68	76	88
16436	SPRING CREEK	82	75	74	78	76	88	74	83	76	67	75	63	68	78	74	81	51	77	86	97
16438	UNION CITY	78	67	64	68	66	79	71	75	74	65	72	57	63	75	66	78	49	73	80	89
16440	VENANGO	86	78	78	82	80	93	77	87	80	70	78	66	71	81	77	84	54	81	90	102
16441	WATERFORD	88	86	77	88	84	92	82	87	83	79	83	66	80	86	82	86	57	83	89	103
16442	WATTSBURG	89	92	83	95	91	97	85	92	85	82	85	71	86	87	88	88	59	87	92	107
16443	WEST SPRINGFIELD	96	73	81	72	73	94	75	86	82	72	80	66	62	85	70	89	54	81	91	104
16444	EDINBORO	56	36	35	40	35	39	67	45	60	53	60	41	49	60	47	58	42	55	48	58
16501	ERIE	24	18	20	20	18	21	29	23	30	25	30	18	25	27	25	32	21	28	30	29
16502	ERIE	58	50	44	51	47	53	62	54	62	55	61	44	55	62	53	63	43	59	59	66
16503	ERIE	44	37	32	38	34	39	47	40	50	43	49	32	43	49	40	52	35	46	46	51
16504	ERIE	77	78	71	79	76	85	78	78	81	75	80	59	79	81	78	85	56	80	89	93
16505	ERIE	108	109	109	109	110	119	105	111	109	105	108	82	107	107	108	113	75	109	120	130
16506	ERIE	106	116	112	116	116	116	107	111	107	110	108	83	113	107	112	109	75	109	115	129
16507	ERIE	51	44	39	45	41	45	56	48	58	50	58	38	51	57	48	60	41	54	53	59
16508	ERIE	74	77	67	78	74	81	76	75	79	73	78	58	78	79	76	81	54	77	84	90
16509	ERIE	96	94	95	95	94	102	92	96	95	91	95	72	92	95	94	98	66	95	103	113
16510	ERIE	87	86	78	87	84	92	84	87	87	81	86	67	83	88	84	90	59	86	93	103
16511	ERIE	77	83	75	84	81	87	80	81	83	78	83	60	85	82	83	86	58	82	90	95
16565	ERIE	0	0	0	0	0	0	0	0	0	0	0	0	0	0	0	0	0	0	0	0
16601	ALTOONA	68	64	59	65	62	71	68	67	71	64	70	51	66	70	65	75	49	69	76	80
16602	ALTOONA	72	70	70	69	69	79	69	73	74	67	73	54	69	73	70	78	50	73	82	87
16611	ALEXANDRIA	77	71	70	74	72	83	70	79	72	63	70	59	64	73	69	76	48	73	81	91
16613	ASHVILLE	79	60	78	59	62	81	62	76	67	56	66	57	51	67	61	73	44	70	80	89
16616	BECCARIA	74	53	74	51	55	76	56	70	63	51	61	53	45	62	55	69	40	65	75	83
16617	BELLWOOD	79	76	70	79	76	86	75	80	77	69	76	61	72	78	75	81	52	77	86	95
16620	BRISBIN	79	56	81	55	58	80	58	74	64	54	63	55	46	64	57	71	42	67	77	87
16621	BROAD TOP	75	54	62	52	53	71	56	65	62	54	61	50	45	65	51	68	41	62	69	79
16622	CALVIN	85	61	87	59	63	86	62	79	69	58	68	59	50	69	62	76	45	73	82	94
16623	CASSVILLE	86	61	88	59	64	87	63	80	70	59	69	60	50	69	62	77	45	74	83	95
16625	CLAYSBURG	73	57	68	57	58	74	60	69	64	55	63	53	50	65	57	69	42	65	73	82
	PENNSYLVANIA	94	95	95	95	95	100	94	96	96	91	95	73	94	96	94	99	67	95	101	113
	UNITED STATES	100	100	100	100	100	100	100	100	100	100	100	100	100	100	100	100	100	100	100	100

#	POST OFFICE NAME	COUNTY FIPS CODE	POPULATION 2000	POPULATION 2009	POPULATION 2014	2000-2009 ANNUAL RATE % Rate	2000-2009 ANNUAL RATE State Centile	HOUSEHOLDS 2000	HOUSEHOLDS 2009	HOUSEHOLDS 2014	HOUSEHOLDS % Annual Rate 2000-2009	HOUSEHOLDS 2009 Average HH Size	FAMILIES 2000	FAMILIES 2009	FAMILIES % Annual Rate 2000-2009
16627	COALPORT	033	2221	2200	2156	-0.1	46	913	934	925	0.2	2.34	633	627	-0.1
16630	CRESSON	021	4469	4284	4141	-0.5	19	1831	1792	1746	-0.2	2.19	1155	1088	-0.6
16634	DUDLEY	061	596	589	578	-0.1	46	235	240	238	0.2	2.45	169	168	-0.1
16635	DUNCANSVILLE	013	15474	15452	15320	0.0	52	5947	6090	6076	0.3	2.45	4293	4263	-0.1
16636	DYSART	021	820	806	790	-0.2	38	321	328	325	0.2	2.43	243	241	-0.1
16637	EAST FREEDOM	013	2108	2060	2032	-0.2	38	857	858	852	0.0	2.39	627	610	-0.3
16639	FALLENTIMBER	021	1708	1658	1613	-0.3	29	657	649	635	-0.1	2.36	483	463	-0.5
16640	FLINTON	021	717	697	680	-0.3	29	276	275	270	0.0	2.40	201	195	-0.3
16641	GALLITZIN	021	2726	2746	2691	0.1	57	1065	1087	1074	0.2	2.40	748	740	-0.1
16645	GLEN HOPE	033	149	147	144	-0.1	46	55	56	55	0.2	2.63	39	39	0.0
16646	HASTINGS	021	2723	2608	2537	-0.5	19	1041	1031	1012	-0.1	2.44	755	725	-0.4
16647	HESSTON	061	1055	1001	977	-0.6	13	400	391	386	-0.2	2.50	308	294	-0.5
16648	HOLLIDAYSBURG	013	13866	14123	14051	0.2	61	5453	5674	5680	0.4	2.36	3774	3832	0.2
16650	HOPEWELL	009	2187	2116	2072	-0.4	23	875	874	865	0.0	2.42	639	618	-0.4
16651	HOUTZDALE	033	5435	5357	5272	-0.2	38	1508	1522	1501	0.1	2.34	1050	1027	-0.2
16652	HUNTINGDON	061	17199	17148	16972	0.0	52	5543	5544	5515	0.0	2.25	3617	3504	-0.3
16655	IMLER	009	1731	1818	1852	0.5	70	655	716	736	1.0	2.54	496	528	0.7
16656	IRVONA	033	1486	1486	1461	0.0	52	535	553	550	0.4	2.69	401	404	0.1
16657	JAMES CREEK	061	534	506	495	-0.6	13	231	226	223	-0.2	2.19	178	170	-0.5
16659	LOYSBURG	009	343	361	365	0.6	74	133	144	148	0.9	2.49	106	113	0.7
16661	MADERA	033	1156	1147	1122	-0.1	46	468	479	474	0.3	2.39	337	334	-0.1
16662	MARTINSBURG	013	4957	4918	4875	-0.1	46	1911	1942	1938	0.2	2.39	1304	1280	-0.2
16664	NEW ENTERPRISE	009	2251	2384	2426	0.6	74	783	855	879	1.0	2.78	643	688	0.7
16666	OSCEOLA MILLS	033	3196	3450	3376	0.8	80	1301	1305	1286	0.0	2.35	902	876	-0.3
16667	OSTERBURG	009	1192	1230	1243	0.3	64	447	479	489	0.8	2.57	337	352	0.5
16668	PATTON	021	4124	3919	3784	-0.5	19	1604	1555	1515	-0.3	2.40	1096	1027	-0.7
16669	PETERSBURG	061	2214	2405	2428	0.9	83	860	972	991	1.3	2.47	644	709	1.0
16671	RAMEY	033	512	513	503	0.0	52	203	210	208	0.4	2.44	144	144	0.0
16673	ROARING SPRING	013	5215	5271	5240	0.1	57	2070	2156	2163	0.4	2.44	1558	1578	0.1
16674	ROBERTSDALE	061	634	617	594	-0.3	29	246	248	241	0.1	2.49	184	180	-0.2
16678	SAXTON	009	3220	3153	3093	-0.2	38	1325	1337	1324	0.1	2.34	937	913	-0.3
16679	SIX MILE RUN	009	1293	1231	1202	-0.5	19	496	484	477	-0.3	2.53	367	348	-0.6
16680	SMITHMILL	033	651	653	640	0.0	52	279	288	286	0.3	2.27	198	198	0.0
16683	SPRUCE CREEK	061	485	478	468	-0.2	38	209	213	210	0.2	2.24	157	155	-0.1
16685	TODD	061	1004	1003	970	0.0	52	343	352	343	0.3	2.64	271	272	0.0
16686	TYRONE	013	11687	12187	12133	0.5	70	4736	5027	5037	0.6	2.39	3265	3389	0.4
16689	WATERFALL	057	519	587	616	1.3	90	205	235	250	1.5	2.49	149	167	1.2
16691	WELLS TANNERY	057	370	372	371	0.1	57	158	164	166	0.4	2.25	113	115	0.2
16692	WESTOVER	033	803	796	781	-0.1	46	299	307	305	0.3	2.58	230	231	0.0
16693	WILLIAMSBURG	013	4992	4860	4782	-0.3	29	1872	1866	1849	0.0	2.55	1368	1327	-0.3
16695	WOODBURY	009	795	858	880	0.8	80	285	315	325	1.1	2.72	237	256	0.8
16701	BRADFORD	083	18709	17692	17046	-0.6	13	7584	7285	7059	-0.4	2.27	4862	4520	-0.8
16720	AUSTIN	105	1232	1213	1196	-0.2	38	506	514	510	0.2	2.36	359	354	-0.2
16724	CROSBY	083	152	143	138	-0.7	8	58	56	55	-0.4	2.55	40	38	-0.6
16726	CYCLONE	083	385	374	362	-0.3	29	145	139	134	-0.5	2.13	106	99	-0.7
16727	DERRICK CITY	083	365	346	333	-0.6	13	140	136	132	-0.3	2.54	98	93	-0.6
16729	DUKE CENTER	083	827	765	731	-0.8	6	327	312	301	-0.5	2.44	238	221	-0.8
16731	ELDRED	083	3042	2842	2729	-0.7	8	1226	1185	1149	-0.4	2.40	861	807	-0.7
16732	GIFFORD	083	305	301	292	-0.1	46	121	117	114	-0.4	2.09	90	85	-0.6
16734	JAMES CITY	047	509	472	454	-0.8	6	210	203	197	-0.4	2.33	145	136	-0.7
16735	KANE	083	8378	7596	7260	-1.1	2	3562	3320	3197	-0.8	2.25	2353	2130	-1.1
16738	LEWIS RUN	083	2632	2810	2757	0.7	77	545	531	516	-0.3	2.79	374	353	-0.6
16740	MOUNT JEWETT	083	86	81	78	-0.6	13	34	33	32	-0.3	2.45	24	22	-0.9
16743	PORT ALLEGANY	083	4448	4256	4112	-0.5	19	1761	1720	1674	-0.3	2.47	1233	1169	-0.6
16744	REW	083	293	305	298	0.4	68	109	106	103	-0.3	1.78	77	73	-0.6
16745	RIXFORD	083	525	488	468	-0.8	6	210	201	195	-0.5	2.41	154	144	-0.7
16746	ROULETTE	105	1342	1327	1307	-0.1	46	546	556	553	0.2	2.39	389	385	-0.1
16748	SHINGLEHOUSE	105	3357	3184	3090	-0.6	13	1301	1262	1234	-0.3	2.52	917	865	-0.6
16749	SMETHPORT	083	4639	4702	4626	0.1	57	1765	1835	1820	0.4	2.44	1260	1270	0.1
16750	TURTLEPOINT	083	649	612	589	-0.6	13	249	242	235	-0.3	2.53	186	176	-0.6
16801	STATE COLLEGE	027	44049	46240	46569	0.5	70	15802	16440	16693	0.4	2.30	6070	5977	-0.2
16802	UNIVERSITY PARK	027	683	794	794	1.6	92	157	163	163	0.4	2.55	0	0	0.0
16803	STATE COLLEGE	027	23265	26850	27907	1.6	92	7762	9069	9551	1.7	2.40	3974	4339	1.0
16820	AARONSBURG	027	739	773	788	0.5	70	263	283	291	0.8	2.73	199	206	0.4
16821	ALLPORT	033	241	233	227	-0.4	23	93	93	92	0.0	2.51	65	63	-0.3
16822	BEECH CREEK	035	2220	2183	2151	-0.2	38	881	892	887	0.1	2.43	650	640	-0.2
16823	BELLEFONTE	027	24170	25969	26511	0.8	80	8956	9701	9980	0.9	2.38	6107	6396	0.5
16827	BOALSBURG	027	4532	4632	4662	0.2	61	1700	1764	1782	0.4	2.61	1266	1268	0.0
16828	CENTRE HALL	027	4089	4193	4231	0.3	64	1631	1709	1738	0.5	2.38	1189	1199	0.1
16829	CLARENCE	027	699	710	713	0.2	61	271	284	287	0.5	2.50	204	207	0.2
16830	CLEARFIELD	033	14918	14010	13527	-0.7	8	6336	6140	5979	-0.3	2.21	4082	3817	-0.7
16832	COBURN	027	479	523	540	1.0	85	176	197	206	1.2	2.52	141	153	0.9
16833	CURWENSVILLE	033	5181	4940	4790	-0.5	19	2102	2065	2021	-0.2	2.36	1507	1438	-0.5
16836	FRENCHVILLE	033	1426	1444	1422	0.1	57	541	564	561	0.5	2.32	391	395	0.1
16837	GLEN RICHEY	033	334	289	271	-1.6	1	134	121	114	-1.1	2.39	103	90	-1.4
16838	GRAMPIAN	033	1982	1966	1932	-0.1	46	773	795	788	0.3	2.47	577	576	0.0
16839	GRASSFLAT	033	1290	1299	1278	0.1	57	499	518	514	0.4	2.50	372	376	0.1
16840	HAWK RUN	033	258	250	243	-0.3	29	133	133	131	0.0	1.88	92	90	-0.2
16841	HOWARD	027	5402	5420	5414	0.0	52	2051	2116	2133	0.3	2.55	1570	1568	0.0
16844	JULIAN	027	2749	3013	3115	1.0	85	1039	1173	1224	1.3	2.57	801	874	0.9
16845	KARTHAUS	027	985	990	981	0.1	57	297	307	307	0.4	2.87	213	213	0.0
16852	MADISONBURG	027	339	383	401	1.3	90	116	134	141	1.6	2.84	93	104	1.2
16854	MILLHEIM	027	970	977	974	0.1	57	401	413	416	0.3	2.36	275	271	-0.2
16858	MORRISDALE	033	4557	4479	4378	-0.2	38	1733	1764	1744	0.2	2.54	1289	1277	-0.1
16859	MOSHANNON	027	502	554	577	1.1	87	199	226	237	1.4	2.45	156	172	1.1
16860	MUNSON	033	297	299	296	0.1	57	113	116	116	0.3	2.42	77	76	-0.1
16861	NEW MILLPORT	033	402	403	397	0.0	52	165	172	171	0.5	2.34	124	125	0.1
16863	OLANTA	033	337	337	332	0.0	52	138	143	142	0.4	2.36	103	104	0.1
16864	ORVISTON	027	103	101	100	-0.2	38	37	37	37	0.0	2.73	28	27	-0.4
16865	PENNSYLVANIA FURNACE	027	2242	2236	2222	0.0	52	870	892	895	0.3	2.51	681	679	0.0
16866	PHILIPSBURG	027	9470	10479	10349	1.1	87	3984	4031	4007	0.1	2.27	2632	2563	-0.3
16870	PORT MATILDA	027	5817	6742	7206	1.6	92	2114	2511	2710	1.9	2.68	1629	1879	1.6
16871	POTTERSDALE	035	74	74	73	0.0	52	33	34	34	0.3	2.03	22	22	0.0
16872	REBERSBURG	027	1173	1326	1389	1.3	90	392	452	478	1.6	2.90	313	350	1.2
16874	SNOW SHOE	027	1387	1466	1500	0.6	74	524	572	591	1.0	2.56	399	422	0.6
	PENNSYLVANIA					0.3					0.4	2.45			0.1
	UNITED STATES					1.0					1.1	2.59			0.9

ZIP CODE		RACE (%)						% Hispanic Origin		2009 AGE DISTRIBUTION (%)										MEDIAN AGE	% 2009 Males	% 2009 Females
#	POST OFFICE NAME	White 2000	White 2009	Black 2000	Black 2009	Asian/Pacific 2000	Asian/Pacific 2009	2000	2009	0-4	5-9	10-14	15-19	20-24	25-44	45-64	65-84	85+	18+	2009		
16627	COALPORT	99.3	99.0	0.0	0.0	0.2	0.3	0.2	0.3	5.3	5.6	5.9	6.2	4.8	25.6	29.7	14.5	2.4	79.3	42.5	49.0	51.0
16630	CRESSON	96.0	94.7	2.6	3.3	0.3	0.5	1.0	1.4	5.2	5.1	5.4	6.3	6.5	28.1	27.7	13.1	2.5	80.6	40.2	50.4	49.6
16634	DUDLEY	99.2	98.6	0.3	0.5	0.2	0.3	0.2	0.2	6.5	6.5	6.3	5.3	5.1	27.3	28.0	13.6	1.5	77.2	41.0	51.3	48.7
16635	DUNCANSVILLE	98.8	98.3	0.4	0.5	0.3	0.5	0.3	0.4	5.0	5.4	5.8	5.9	4.2	23.8	31.0	16.4	2.5	80.2	45.0	49.7	50.3
16636	DYSART	99.3	99.1	0.1	0.1	0.1	0.1	0.4	0.5	5.7	6.0	6.3	6.0	5.0	25.7	30.3	13.3	1.9	78.3	41.4	51.5	48.5
16637	EAST FREEDOM	98.9	98.6	0.2	0.2	0.0	0.0	0.3	0.5	6.8	6.5	6.6	6.7	5.4	26.3	27.3	12.6	1.8	76.0	38.8	48.1	51.9
16639	FALLENTIMBER	98.3	97.5	0.4	0.5	0.6	1.0	0.4	0.5	4.6	5.1	6.6	7.2	5.0	24.2	29.2	14.9	3.2	78.8	42.9	51.1	48.9
16640	FLINTON	97.9	97.4	0.4	0.4	0.8	1.1	0.3	0.4	4.6	5.3	6.7	7.2	4.9	24.8	30.1	14.3	2.0	78.3	42.2	52.2	47.8
16641	GALLITZIN	97.5	96.5	1.4	2.1	0.1	0.2	1.5	2.1	5.4	5.7	5.9	6.0	5.6	28.9	27.7	12.6	2.2	79.4	39.9	50.7	49.3
16645	GLEN HOPE	99.3	99.3	0.0	0.0	0.0	0.0	0.0	0.0	5.4	5.4	5.4	6.1	6.1	22.4	31.3	14.3	3.4	80.3	44.3	47.6	52.4
16646	HASTINGS	99.5	99.3	0.0	0.1	0.1	0.2	0.4	0.5	5.2	5.4	5.8	6.0	4.7	24.0	29.0	16.1	3.8	79.9	44.1	48.5	51.5
16647	HESSTON	99.2	99.0	0.1	0.2	0.0	0.0	0.7	1.0	4.9	5.3	5.8	5.8	4.8	25.0	31.7	14.8	2.0	80.2	44.0	51.0	49.0
16648	HOLLIDAYSBURG	97.6	96.5	0.6	0.7	1.2	1.9	0.5	0.8	4.5	4.7	5.4	6.1	5.7	22.4	31.0	15.9	4.2	81.5	45.7	48.3	51.7
16650	HOPEWELL	99.2	99.1	0.1	0.1	0.0	0.0	0.5	0.7	6.0	6.3	6.6	6.6	5.0	26.2	28.4	13.3	1.7	77.2	40.5	50.0	50.0
16651	HOUTZDALE	78.8	74.3	17.6	20.9	0.2	0.3	3.2	4.3	3.6	3.5	3.8	7.9	6.7	36.8	24.9	10.8	2.0	85.5	38.7	65.9	34.1
16652	HUNTINGDON	85.9	82.9	11.6	13.7	0.4	0.6	2.1	2.7	4.0	4.1	4.3	7.5	11.2	30.0	25.2	11.4	2.2	84.3	37.7	58.1	41.9
16655	IMLER	99.4	99.2	0.1	0.1	0.0	0.1	0.3	0.4	5.8	5.9	6.1	6.2	4.8	27.8	28.4	13.7	1.4	78.5	40.8	49.9	50.1
16656	IRVONA	99.3	99.2	0.1	0.1	0.1	0.2	0.1	0.2	6.0	5.9	6.4	7.1	5.2	25.8	29.3	12.7	1.6	77.3	40.7	50.1	49.9
16657	JAMES CREEK	99.3	98.8	0.2	0.2	0.0	0.0	0.6	1.0	4.9	5.3	5.7	5.7	4.7	25.3	31.4	14.8	2.0	80.0	44.0	51.0	49.0
16659	LOYSBURG	99.4	99.4	0.0	0.0	0.0	0.0	0.3	0.3	6.9	7.2	7.2	6.1	4.2	27.4	26.6	13.3	1.1	75.6	39.1	50.7	49.3
16661	MADERA	99.1	99.0	0.1	0.1	0.1	0.1	0.1	0.2	5.8	5.8	5.7	5.9	5.8	23.2	29.2	15.7	3.1	79.4	43.5	47.7	52.3
16662	MARTINSBURG	99.2	99.0	0.1	0.1	0.1	0.2	0.4	0.6	5.6	5.7	5.9	5.9	4.8	23.8	26.1	16.0	6.2	78.9	43.7	47.7	52.3
16664	NEW ENTERPRISE	99.3	99.1	0.1	0.1	0.1	0.2	0.4	0.6	7.5	7.8	7.8	6.7	4.5	25.8	27.6	11.2	1.1	73.0	38.3	50.1	49.9
16666	OSCEOLA MILLS	98.8	98.4	0.1	0.1	0.1	0.2	0.8	1.1	4.9	5.1	5.2	5.8	5.8	29.8	28.1	13.3	1.9	81.2	41.0	55.0	45.0
16667	OSTERBURG	99.0	98.6	0.3	0.3	0.3	0.5	0.3	0.3	7.1	6.9	6.9	6.2	5.6	26.8	27.4	11.9	1.2	75.4	38.5	50.4	49.6
16668	PATTON	98.3	97.4	1.2	1.9	0.1	0.2	0.9	1.4	5.5	5.7	5.9	6.3	5.2	25.7	30.0	13.4	2.3	79.1	41.7	50.6	49.4
16669	PETERSBURG	98.8	98.4	0.5	0.7	0.1	0.1	0.3	0.4	6.0	6.4	6.7	5.9	4.2	26.5	29.6	13.2	1.5	77.2	41.2	49.7	50.3
16671	RAMEY	99.4	99.2	0.0	0.0	0.0	0.0	0.2	0.4	5.1	5.1	5.3	6.2	5.8	24.2	28.1	16.4	3.9	81.1	43.9	48.9	51.1
16673	ROARING SPRING	98.8	98.4	0.2	0.2	0.4	0.6	0.3	0.4	5.4	5.7	6.1	6.4	4.9	26.4	29.3	13.7	2.0	78.8	41.2	50.0	50.0
16674	ROBERTSDALE	99.2	99.0	0.0	0.0	0.0	0.0	0.6	1.1	6.2	6.0	6.0	6.5	6.0	26.9	27.4	13.9	1.1	78.0	38.8	51.5	48.5
16678	SAXTON	98.9	98.6	0.2	0.2	0.1	0.2	0.4	0.6	6.0	6.3	6.6	5.9	4.4	24.8	29.0	14.7	2.3	77.1	41.8	48.5	51.5
16679	SIX MILE RUN	99.1	98.9	0.2	0.3	0.2	0.2	0.5	0.7	6.7	6.8	6.7	6.3	5.5	25.8	27.1	13.4	1.7	76.2	39.1	50.1	49.9
16680	SMITHMILL	99.4	99.2	0.0	0.0	0.0	0.0	0.3	0.5	4.9	4.9	5.2	6.4	6.1	24.0	28.5	16.2	3.7	81.3	43.9	49.2	50.8
16683	SPRUCE CREEK	99.0	98.3	0.0	0.0	0.0	0.2	1.0	1.7	6.5	6.9	6.7	5.2	4.2	26.6	29.1	13.2	1.7	76.6	40.9	49.4	50.6
16685	TODD	98.0	97.3	1.4	1.9	0.0	0.0	2.0	3.0	6.9	7.1	6.9	12.9	4.5	22.4	25.0	13.4	1.0	69.1	36.3	56.5	43.5
16686	TYRONE	99.1	98.8	0.2	0.3	0.1	0.2	0.4	0.6	5.5	5.6	5.9	6.4	5.3	24.7	29.2	14.3	3.0	79.0	42.4	48.1	51.9
16689	WATERFALL	99.0	98.5	0.0	0.2	0.0	0.0	0.4	0.5	7.0	7.3	7.0	6.1	4.6	23.0	28.6	14.7	1.7	75.0	41.2	51.1	48.9
16691	WELLS TANNERY	98.4	97.8	0.0	0.0	0.0	0.0	0.5	0.8	6.7	7.3	7.3	5.9	4.0	22.0	28.5	16.1	2.2	75.0	42.8	48.4	51.6
16692	WESTOVER	99.0	98.6	0.1	0.3	0.2	0.4	0.5	0.8	5.8	6.0	6.3	6.7	5.4	25.9	28.6	13.4	1.9	77.8	40.9	52.4	47.6
16693	WILLIAMSBURG	98.6	98.2	0.7	0.9	0.1	0.2	0.3	0.5	6.2	6.4	6.6	6.3	4.7	26.1	28.6	12.7	2.3	77.0	40.5	49.6	50.4
16695	WOODBURY	97.6	96.6	0.0	0.0	0.9	1.4	1.3	1.6	8.4	8.7	8.9	7.5	5.2	23.8	25.3	10.7	1.5	69.5	36.4	48.8	51.2
16701	BRADFORD	97.4	96.7	0.9	1.1	0.5	0.8	0.8	1.1	5.7	5.7	6.0	7.3	6.7	24.4	26.8	14.4	3.0	78.5	40.6	48.4	51.6
16720	AUSTIN	98.2	97.9	0.2	0.2	0.2	0.3	0.6	0.8	7.2	7.1	7.6	6.7	5.0	25.1	27.7	12.2	1.5	73.9	38.6	49.1	50.9
16724	CROSBY	98.0	97.9	0.0	0.0	0.7	0.7	0.7	1.4	6.3	6.3	6.3	7.0	5.6	23.8	28.7	14.0	2.1	76.9	41.3	51.7	48.3
16726	CYCLONE	92.7	90.6	5.2	6.1	0.3	0.5	2.3	2.9	4.5	4.5	4.8	6.1	5.9	26.7	27.8	15.0	4.5	81.8	43.2	55.1	44.9
16727	DERRICK CITY	98.9	98.8	0.3	0.3	0.3	0.3	0.5	0.6	5.2	5.8	5.8	6.1	5.8	24.9	29.5	15.0	2.0	79.5	42.8	48.8	51.2
16729	DUKE CENTER	98.4	98.2	0.4	0.4	0.2	0.4	0.2	0.4	6.7	6.4	6.5	6.9	6.1	25.2	27.6	12.7	1.8	75.6	39.3	49.3	50.7
16731	ELDRED	99.0	98.8	0.1	0.1	0.0	0.1	0.2	0.2	6.2	6.2	6.3	6.4	5.8	24.8	28.7	13.7	1.8	77.2	41.0	49.3	50.7
16732	GIFFORD	89.8	87.7	7.2	8.3	0.3	0.7	2.3	3.3	4.0	4.3	5.0	6.0	5.6	29.6	29.9	13.3	2.3	82.7	42.4	57.1	42.9
16734	JAMES CITY	98.8	98.7	0.2	0.2	0.0	0.0	0.0	0.0	5.9	6.4	6.8	6.4	4.0	22.5	29.2	16.9	1.9	76.9	43.8	51.9	48.1
16735	KANE	99.1	99.0	0.1	0.1	0.1	0.2	0.6	0.8	5.6	5.9	6.2	6.1	4.4	24.2	29.0	15.4	3.2	78.3	43.3	49.2	50.8
16738	LEWIS RUN	71.3	67.3	21.7	23.5	0.8	1.2	7.2	9.1	2.5	2.8	3.3	4.9	7.5	43.4	25.6	8.8	1.1	88.0	37.6	72.5	27.5
16740	MOUNT JEWETT	100.0	100.0	0.0	0.0	0.0	0.0	0.0	0.0	4.9	6.2	7.4	6.2	4.9	24.7	29.6	13.6	2.5	75.3	42.1	50.6	49.4
16743	PORT ALLEGANY	98.7	98.5	0.1	0.1	0.1	0.1	0.4	0.5	6.7	6.7	6.8	7.5	6.4	24.9	27.0	12.1	1.9	74.6	38.1	49.6	50.4
16744	REW	77.5	74.1	16.7	18.7	0.7	1.0	5.5	7.2	3.0	3.3	3.6	5.2	6.9	39.3	26.9	10.2	1.6	86.6	39.0	67.9	32.1
16745	RIXFORD	98.7	98.4	0.4	0.4	0.2	0.4	0.2	0.2	6.4	6.4	6.6	6.8	5.9	25.0	28.5	12.7	1.8	76.0	40.1	49.0	51.0
16746	ROULETTE	98.7	98.5	0.1	0.1	0.3	0.4	1.0	1.4	7.9	8.1	7.8	6.3	4.2	23.4	26.7	13.8	1.7	72.2	38.7	47.7	52.3
16748	SHINGLEHOUSE	98.6	98.3	0.1	0.1	0.2	0.3	0.4	0.6	6.3	6.3	6.5	6.9	5.7	23.5	27.6	15.0	2.2	76.7	41.1	49.7	50.3
16749	SMETHPORT	98.8	98.6	0.2	0.3	0.2	0.2	0.6	0.7	5.4	5.6	6.0	6.3	5.5	22.7	29.4	15.2	3.9	78.6	43.9	48.7	51.3
16750	TURTLEPOINT	98.2	97.9	0.3	0.3	0.2	0.2	0.2	0.2	6.9	6.7	6.7	6.4	5.9	24.7	28.1	13.2	1.5	75.7	40.1	50.0	50.0
16801	STATE COLLEGE	86.5	81.8	3.0	3.4	7.9	11.7	2.4	3.1	2.9	2.4	2.5	12.1	40.3	18.9	13.0	6.4	1.6	90.5	23.7	50.7	49.3
16802	UNIVERSITY PARK	78.8	73.2	10.0	11.2	6.1	9.4	3.7	4.9	0.0	0.0	0.0	38.5	57.1	4.4	0.0	0.0	0.0	100.0	21.0	43.2	56.8
16803	STATE COLLEGE	86.6	81.3	3.7	4.3	6.7	10.7	2.7	3.7	4.0	3.6	3.7	18.0	24.6	21.8	17.0	6.6	0.8	86.5	24.2	52.3	47.7
16820	AARONSBURG	98.9	98.3	0.1	0.1	0.7	1.3	0.7	0.9	6.9	7.1	7.6	7.8	4.9	24.1	28.5	11.5	1.7	73.5	38.9	49.7	50.3
16821	ALLPORT	99.6	99.1	0.0	0.0	0.0	0.4	0.8	0.9	6.0	6.4	6.4	6.0	4.7	25.3	29.2	14.2	1.7	76.8	42.0	49.8	50.2
16822	BEECH CREEK	98.6	98.4	0.2	0.2	0.4	0.5	0.6	0.8	4.4	4.8	5.4	6.3	4.8	25.1	31.8	15.5	1.8	81.4	44.4	50.2	49.8
16823	BELLEFONTE	93.5	91.9	4.6	5.5	0.4	0.6	1.1	1.6	5.3	5.3	5.5	5.8	6.4	30.5	27.3	11.8	2.1	80.3	39.8	53.1	46.9
16827	BOALSBURG	95.1	93.5	1.4	1.6	1.7	2.8	1.2	1.6	5.1	5.7	6.6	7.3	5.3	22.0	33.0	13.4	1.6	77.6	43.6	48.0	52.0
16828	CENTRE HALL	98.8	98.4	0.4	0.5	0.3	0.5	0.4	0.5	5.5	6.3	7.5	7.2	3.9	23.4	30.5	14.1	1.7	75.9	42.3	48.9	51.1
16829	CLARENCE	99.3	98.9	0.0	0.0	0.1	0.4	0.4	0.6	6.1	6.3	6.6	5.8	3.9	24.8	30.6	13.9	2.0	77.2	42.7	51.5	48.5
16830	CLEARFIELD	98.6	98.1	0.5	0.7	0.3	0.4	0.4	0.5	5.2	5.3	5.5	5.7	5.4	24.4	28.7	16.1	3.6	80.4	43.7	48.1	51.9
16832	COBURN	98.3	97.1	0.6	0.8	0.8	1.5	0.6	1.0	6.9	7.3	7.3	6.7	4.2	27.0	27.3	10.5	2.9	74.0	38.6	50.9	49.1
16833	CURWENSVILLE	99.2	98.8	0.2	0.3	0.1	0.2	0.3	0.3	5.7	5.9	6.1	6.4	4.7	24.0	30.5	14.0	2.8	78.5	43.0	48.6	51.4
16836	FRENCHVILLE	93.6	91.6	4.8	6.2	0.1	0.2	1.3	1.7	5.5	5.7	6.0	6.3	8.5	28.0	26.3	12.0	1.7	79.2	37.5	54.4	45.6
16837	GLEN RICHEY	98.8	98.3	0.3	0.3	0.6	1.0	0.3	0.3	5.9	5.9	6.6	6.2	4.5	24.9	31.1	13.1	1.7	77.9	42.1	46.4	53.6
16838	GRAMPIAN	99.4	99.3	0.1	0.1	0.1	0.1	0.4	0.5	5.6	5.6	6.3	6.5	4.7	24.0	31.2	14.0	2.1	78.5	43.2	50.6	49.4
16839	GRASSFLAT	99.7	99.6	0.0	0.0	0.2	0.2	0.3	0.4	6.4	6.5	6.7	6.9	5.5	25.4	28.1	12.5	2.2	75.7	40.6	49.3	50.7
16840	HAWK RUN	99.6	99.2	0.0	0.0	0.0	0.4	0.8	0.8	6.0	6.4	6.8	6.0	4.8	25.6	28.8	13.6	2.0	76.4	41.7	49.2	50.8
16841	HOWARD	99.1	98.9	0.1	0.1	0.1	0.1	0.4	0.5	6.0	6.4	6.7	6.2	4.7	25.5	30.1	12.9	1.5	77.2	41.5	50.9	49.1
16844	JULIAN	98.1	97.5	0.3	0.4	0.3	0.5	1.1	1.6	5.6	5.9	6.4	6.1	5.0	26.6	31.5	11.8	1.1	78.2	41.4	51.2	48.8
16845	KARTHAUS	92.5	90.0	5.5	7.3	0.2	0.3	1.5	2.0	5.3	5.4	5.8	5.9	8.0	27.1	27.7	13.2	1.8	80.3	39.7	56.1	43.9
16852	MADISONBURG	98.8	98.2	0.6	0.8	0.0	0.3	0.0	0.3	9.4	9.4	9.7	8.4	3.9	22.5	23.2	12.0	1.6	66.8	34.4	47.8	52.2
16854	MILLHEIM	99.2	99.0	0.1	0.1	0.2	0.3	0.1	0.2	6.6	6.9	6.6	6.3	6.0	26.4	26.4	12.8	2.0	76.2	38.6	49.3	50.7
16858	MORRISDALE	99.1	98.9	0.0	0.1	0.1	0.2	0.4	0.6	5.7	6.1	6.5	6.4	4.6	25.7	30.0	13.4	1.7	77.5	42.0	50.2	49.8
16859	MOSHANNON	99.8	99.8	0.0	0.0	0.0	0.0	0.4	0.7	5.1	5.2	6.0	6.0	4.5	25.6	32.7	13.4	1.6	80.1	43.7	50.5	49.5
16860	MUNSON	100.0	99.7	0.0	0.0	0.0	0.0	0.7	0.7	5.4	5.4	5.4	5.4	4.3	25.4	27.1	16.4	5.4	80.6	44.2	47.8	52.2
16861	NEW MILLPORT	99.8	99.8	0.0	0.0	0.0	0.0	0.2	0.2	6.0	6.0	6.5	6.2	4.2	25.6	30.3	13.6	1.7	77.4	42.2	51.4	48.6
16863	OLANTA	99.7	99.7	0.0	0.0	0.0	0.0	0.0	0.0	5.6	5.6	6.2	6.5	4.5	25.5	30.9	13.6	1.5	78.6	42.4	51.3	48.7
16864	ORVISTON	100.0	99.0	0.0	0.0	0.0	0.0	0.0	0.0	5.9	5.9	5.9	6.9	4.0	23.8	31.7	13.9	2.0	77.2	43.2	48.5	51.5
16865	PENNSYLVANIA FURNACE	96.3	94.7	0.5	0.7	2.1	3.4	0.5	0.7	5.5	6.5	7.6	7.1	3.5	24.2	33.3	11.3	0.9	75.5	42.3	49.9	50.1
16866	PHILIPSBURG	99.0	98.8	0.1	0.1	0.3	0.4	0.2	0.3	5.1	5.1	5.2	6.0	6.1	29.1	26.2	14.3	3.0	81.2	40.9	52.8	47.2
16870	PORT MATILDA	97.4	96.1	0.5	0.6	1.0	1.9	0.8	1.3	6.4	7.0	7.6	7.7	4.7	26.2	30.7	8.9	0.9	74.2	39.2	51.1	48.9
16871	POTTERSDALE	94.6	93.2	4.1	5.4	0.0	0.0	1.4	1.4	4.1	4.1	5.4	6.8	5.4	24.3	33.8	14.9	1.4	81.1	45.0	54.1	45.9
16872	REBERSBURG	98.7	98.3	0.7	0.8	0.1	0.2	0.1	0.2	9.5	9.5	9.6	8.1	3.8	22.9	23.1	11.8	1.6	66.4	34.3	47.9	52.1
16874	SNOW SHOE	99.6	99.3	0.0	0.0	0.2	0.4	0.4	0.6	5.8	6.1	6.9	6.5	4.0	25.6	30.2	13.3	1.7	77.1	42.1	52.7	47.3
	PENNSYLVANIA	85.4	83.2	10.0	10.7	1.8	2.7	3.2	4.2	5.8	6.0	6.3	7.1	6.5	24.8	27.8	13.1	2.6	77.8	40.4	48.5	51.5
	UNITED STATES	75.1	72.0	12.3	12.7	3.8	4.6	12.5	15.7	6.8	6.7	6.6	7.1	6.9	27.0	26.0	10.9	1.9	75.7	36.9	49.2	50.8

#	POST OFFICE NAME	2009 Per Capita Income	2009 HH Income Base	2009 Household Income Distribution (%): Less than $25,000	$25,000 to $49,999	$50,000 to $99,999	$100,000 to $149,999	$150,000 or More	Median Household Income: 2009	2014	2009 National Centile	2009 State Centile	2009 Home Value Base	2009 Home Value Distribution (%): Less than $50,000	$50,000 to $89,999	$90,000 to $174,999	$175,000 to $399,999	$400,000 or More	2009 Median Home Value
16627	COALPORT	17645	934	32.4	35.1	29.4	2.9	0.1	35792	37821	20	10	783	29.6	32.8	30.9	6.5	0.1	70636
16630	CRESSON	22064	1792	29.2	29.6	33.8	5.1	2.3	41902	46243	39	35	1267	14.8	23.3	47.4	13.0	1.4	106950
16634	DUDLEY	16963	240	33.8	30.4	31.7	3.8	0.4	38078	40843	27	18	198	15.2	27.3	49.0	8.6	0.0	99375
16635	DUNCANSVILLE	21272	6090	23.8	33.1	35.8	5.0	2.4	45269	48276	49	47	4975	16.6	14.1	39.3	27.8	2.3	130229
16636	DYSART	20157	328	25.0	33.2	36.3	4.0	1.5	42806	46682	42	38	290	15.2	20.7	43.1	19.7	1.4	114375
16637	EAST FREEDOM	16966	858	35.3	32.6	29.4	2.3	0.3	34666	36612	17	8	659	17.9	18.5	51.9	11.2	0.5	108413
16639	FALLENTIMBER	15981	649	37.0	36.5	23.3	2.6	0.6	32701	34273	13	5	564	31.9	27.1	30.7	9.2	1.1	75882
16640	FLINTON	16682	275	33.8	36.0	26.5	2.9	0.7	35862	37485	20	10	241	29.9	28.2	29.5	11.6	0.8	78929
16641	GALLITZIN	19375	1087	27.6	31.8	35.1	4.2	1.2	40694	46285	35	29	911	21.4	37.8	31.3	7.6	2.0	78813
16645	GLEN HOPE	16035	56	35.7	28.6	33.9	1.8	0.0	33186	34291	14	5	50	14.0	32.0	48.0	6.0	0.0	93333
16646	HASTINGS	18077	1031	34.5	30.0	30.6	3.8	1.2	36338	39213	22	12	847	21.5	33.1	36.1	8.6	0.7	84077
16647	HESSTON	20356	391	22.5	31.2	39.6	5.1	1.5	47342	47981	55	56	346	8.4	13.3	47.4	28.0	2.9	137324
16648	HOLLIDAYSBURG	27238	5674	18.4	28.4	39.1	8.2	6.0	52892	55163	68	68	4121	3.1	11.0	36.8	38.3	10.7	172930
16650	HOPEWELL	18605	874	32.7	33.0	29.6	3.4	1.3	38148	38703	27	18	701	17.7	24.1	44.8	11.8	1.6	100781
16651	HOUTZDALE	17122	1522	31.7	31.7	30.9	4.9	0.9	37855	40637	26	17	1212	15.2	27.6	46.1	10.6	0.5	99888
16652	HUNTINGDON	20494	5544	25.6	29.9	36.4	5.8	2.3	45143	46327	49	47	3909	6.9	18.8	49.1	22.8	2.4	131005
16655	IMLER	19291	716	29.3	32.7	32.4	3.8	1.8	39901	40887	32	25	609	15.4	19.7	47.0	15.8	2.1	114307
16656	IRVONA	14669	553	33.1	38.2	26.8	1.8	0.2	34924	36521	17	8	482	28.6	32.2	31.7	7.5	0.0	71000
16657	JAMES CREEK	23216	226	22.6	31.4	38.9	5.8	1.3	47036	47655	54	55	200	8.5	12.5	47.0	29.0	3.0	138415
16659	LOYSBURG	22143	144	18.8	38.9	34.0	5.6	2.8	45000	45679	48	46	118	16.1	16.1	44.1	19.5	4.2	121667
16661	MADERA	17381	479	35.1	31.9	28.6	3.3	1.0	33439	35722	14	6	424	18.2	30.2	43.4	8.0	0.2	91556
16662	MARTINSBURG	19896	1942	28.3	32.3	33.0	5.0	1.5	40346	44708	34	27	1435	17.5	14.4	45.4	20.5	2.3	126276
16664	NEW ENTERPRISE	19257	855	20.1	36.4	36.6	5.3	1.6	45592	45983	50	49	718	8.9	11.8	49.3	27.0	2.9	140806
16666	OSCEOLA MILLS	19376	1305	29.1	35.0	30.2	4.1	1.5	39889	42676	32	25	1047	20.3	27.8	42.3	9.1	0.5	92191
16667	OSTERBURG	18592	479	29.9	32.8	31.7	4.0	1.7	39779	40359	32	25	394	20.1	17.3	42.6	18.3	1.8	112981
16668	PATTON	19316	1555	31.3	28.9	33.3	4.9	1.6	39082	43636	30	22	1218	17.0	33.1	35.3	12.9	1.7	89867
16669	PETERSBURG	20868	972	23.0	34.4	36.1	4.9	1.5	45285	46335	49	47	778	9.9	18.1	41.4	26.1	4.5	135537
16671	RAMEY	18916	210	31.0	31.4	31.9	4.8	1.0	38730	41762	29	21	182	15.9	27.5	45.1	11.0	0.5	97500
16673	ROARING SPRING	23478	2156	20.1	30.5	41.9	5.1	2.4	49502	51895	60	61	1663	5.1	18.3	53.9	19.4	3.3	127055
16674	ROBERTSDALE	16391	248	34.7	27.8	34.7	2.8	0.0	36159	40286	21	11	203	41.9	25.6	27.6	3.9	1.0	58250
16678	SAXTON	20485	1337	29.3	35.2	29.6	4.0	1.9	37783	38826	26	16	995	16.1	22.9	49.4	9.9	1.6	104575
16679	SIX MILE RUN	16670	484	35.1	34.5	27.3	2.3	0.8	35836	36542	20	10	382	33.2	30.9	29.3	5.8	0.8	67576
16680	SMITHMILL	20424	288	30.9	31.9	31.6	4.9	0.7	38480	42606	28	19	250	15.6	27.6	45.6	10.8	0.4	97727
16683	SPRUCE CREEK	23132	213	23.0	33.8	35.2	7.0	0.9	45147	46346	49	47	165	5.5	15.2	43.0	27.9	8.5	142578
16685	TODD	17171	352	30.7	32.4	30.1	5.1	1.7	38632	41983	29	20	315	12.4	15.2	45.7	25.1	1.6	135227
16686	TYRONE	20337	5027	28.0	30.1	36.6	3.7	1.6	43257	46960	43	40	3688	10.8	20.8	46.6	19.4	2.5	121911
16689	WATERFALL	17804	235	27.2	33.6	34.9	3.4	0.9	39571	40891	31	24	194	12.4	18.6	45.4	21.1	2.6	120968
16691	WELLS TANNERY	18235	164	30.5	36.0	29.9	3.7	0.0	36914	39489	23	13	141	14.2	23.4	40.4	17.7	4.3	113816
16692	WESTOVER	15040	307	38.1	37.1	22.1	1.6	1.0	30952	32201	10	3	248	29.8	29.4	32.3	8.5	0.0	73125
16693	WILLIAMSBURG	19328	1866	27.1	32.2	33.8	4.8	2.1	41154	45670	37	31	1432	12.4	24.1	38.6	19.9	5.0	115055
16695	WOODBURY	18837	315	22.2	33.0	39.4	3.8	1.6	45376	46424	49	48	267	12.0	12.4	46.4	19.1	10.1	132188
16701	BRADFORD	22911	7285	27.3	28.9	35.0	6.1	2.6	43294	47002	43	41	5074	14.2	30.1	43.8	10.7	1.2	97500
16720	AUSTIN	19500	514	28.4	33.5	34.6	3.1	0.4	40502	41537	34	28	424	14.9	20.0	41.3	20.8	3.1	117788
16724	CROSBY	19273	56	26.8	35.7	32.1	5.4	0.0	41130	44302	36	31	47	23.4	31.9	34.0	10.6	0.0	81667
16726	CYCLONE	21751	139	23.0	33.1	37.4	5.8	0.7	44606	46744	47	44	113	14.2	26.5	45.1	13.3	0.9	104861
16727	DERRICK CITY	21779	136	20.6	33.8	36.8	6.6	2.2	45652	49220	50	49	116	10.3	30.2	50.0	8.6	0.9	100806
16729	DUKE CENTER	19855	312	28.5	32.1	34.9	2.6	1.9	40000	42064	33	26	268	18.7	36.9	39.6	4.5	0.4	82857
16731	ELDRED	19775	1185	28.3	32.0	34.7	4.2	0.8	40935	44218	36	30	950	15.1	32.2	41.8	10.1	0.8	94262
16732	GIFFORD	24828	117	18.8	29.1	42.7	8.5	0.9	51617	53302	65	66	103	12.6	25.2	47.6	12.6	1.9	105147
16734	JAMES CITY	17865	203	34.5	33.5	28.6	2.5	1.0	35795	37604	20	10	179	26.8	30.7	34.1	8.4	0.0	80357
16735	KANE	22493	3320	28.0	29.7	34.9	5.2	2.2	43051	46103	43	39	2509	10.4	32.8	45.6	10.8	0.6	98892
16738	LEWIS RUN	15979	531	24.9	33.3	35.6	3.8	2.4	43342	46684	43	41	435	12.0	32.2	43.4	11.7	0.7	97969
16740	MOUNT JEWETT	19992	33	27.3	33.3	36.4	3.0	0.0	41140	45000	36	31	27	11.1	33.3	48.1	7.4	0.0	97500
16743	PORT ALLEGANY	21427	1720	25.9	27.9	39.4	4.1	2.8	45955	49608	51	51	1275	12.6	30.1	45.8	10.5	0.9	99635
16744	REW	23860	106	22.6	31.1	37.7	6.6	1.9	46546	49540	53	53	90	10.0	30.0	46.7	12.2	1.1	102941
16745	RIXFORD	20045	201	27.9	32.3	35.8	2.5	1.5	40562	43283	35	28	173	17.3	35.8	41.0	5.8	0.0	85769
16746	ROULETTE	17577	556	28.4	42.4	26.3	2.5	0.4	36921	37846	23	14	426	17.1	32.2	38.5	10.8	1.4	90909
16748	SHINGLEHOUSE	18751	1262	29.4	31.6	34.4	3.2	1.4	39929	42169	32	25	975	15.8	32.1	39.2	11.2	1.7	92253
16749	SMETHPORT	20132	1835	25.9	32.9	34.3	5.6	1.3	43023	46328	42	39	1456	19.6	27.7	40.9	10.9	0.8	95135
16750	TURTLEPOINT	19195	242	27.3	30.6	36.4	4.1	1.7	42516	45188	41	37	187	11.8	24.6	53.5	8.6	1.6	106250
16801	STATE COLLEGE	20719	16440	37.5	25.3	25.5	7.7	3.9	35961	37799	20	11	5986	3.0	1.1	20.3	62.6	13.0	238589
16802	UNIVERSITY PARK	18207	163	42.3	33.1	22.7	1.2	0.6	29377	30347	7	3	0	0.0	0.0	0.0	0.0	0.0	0
16803	STATE COLLEGE	25482	9069	22.1	25.1	36.3	9.0	7.6	53906	56332	69	70	4415	5.8	1.2	19.8	61.4	11.7	243553
16820	AARONSBURG	19826	283	19.8	36.0	37.1	4.9	2.1	45966	49036	51	51	243	4.1	9.1	48.6	30.9	7.4	149318
16821	ALLPORT	16724	93	31.2	37.6	29.0	2.2	0.0	38050	41292	27	18	78	14.1	16.7	56.4	12.8	0.0	112500
16822	BEECH CREEK	20002	892	27.0	31.7	35.8	4.1	1.3	42015	46051	39	35	753	14.9	14.2	54.1	15.1	1.7	121077
16823	BELLEFONTE	23056	9701	18.1	29.9	44.3	5.7	2.1	51567	53819	65	66	6978	8.9	6.3	43.2	38.2	3.4	161397
16827	BOALSBURG	33638	1764	10.7	21.7	44.7	12.0	11.0	75429	75541	90	92	1396	2.9	0.3	12.8	62.6	21.4	264260
16828	CENTRE HALL	27503	1709	18.9	24.7	43.8	7.7	4.9	57396	58530	74	75	1412	10.2	3.0	31.1	39.2	16.6	193578
16829	CLARENCE	19586	284	28.9	32.7	35.2	2.1	1.1	38619	42757	28	20	258	13.6	17.4	49.6	17.1	2.3	125962
16830	CLEARFIELD	21580	6140	32.8	28.7	31.7	4.6	2.3	38394	41040	28	19	4252	14.8	23.2	47.8	13.7	0.4	104843
16832	COBURN	20848	197	18.3	32.0	43.7	5.6	0.5	49768	52322	60	61	162	3.1	12.3	43.8	31.5	9.3	156250
16833	CURWENSVILLE	19851	2065	31.0	29.2	34.5	4.0	1.3	41232	44744	37	32	1605	13.9	27.1	42.4	15.6	1.0	105410
16836	FRENCHVILLE	18459	564	32.8	33.5	29.4	3.0	1.2	37267	39909	24	15	482	16.8	25.3	47.1	10.2	0.6	100316
16837	GLEN RICHEY	22538	121	30.6	20.7	40.5	4.1	4.1	46186	50429	52	52	96	5.2	15.6	50.0	27.1	2.1	131250
16838	GRAMPIAN	17409	795	30.4	35.1	30.7	3.4	0.4	38451	41200	28	19	701	15.7	24.3	49.2	9.8	1.0	102946
16839	GRASSFLAT	20540	518	25.9	29.3	39.2	3.7	1.9	46038	48812	51	51	453	9.3	27.6	49.7	12.6	0.9	108724
16840	HAWK RUN	22291	133	30.1	36.8	30.8	2.3	0.0	39157	41263	30	22	112	14.3	16.1	56.3	13.4	0.0	113000
16841	HOWARD	20043	2116	22.4	31.3	41.3	4.0	1.0	46990	50447	54	55	1782	13.6	12.9	45.9	23.6	4.0	136739
16844	JULIAN	20901	1173	22.1	31.1	40.0	4.4	2.4	47145	50728	54	55	1025	12.1	6.0	39.8	32.8	9.3	159795
16845	KARTHAUS	16310	307	30.3	31.9	33.6	2.6	1.6	38813	41595	29	21	269	13.0	23.8	48.0	13.8	1.5	111012
16852	MADISONBURG	15655	134	25.4	40.3	31.3	3.0	0.0	39179	41018	30	23	108	8.3	11.1	45.4	24.1	11.1	153947
16854	MILLHEIM	24967	413	20.6	30.5	41.4	4.6	2.9	49239	52067	59	60	314	5.1	6.7	52.9	30.9	4.5	153302
16858	MORRISDALE	18249	1764	28.3	33.2	34.5	3.1	0.9	41417	44829	37	33	1533	12.9	20.9	51.2	14.5	0.5	112416
16859	MOSHANNON	17949	226	34.5	30.5	30.5	3.5	0.9	36520	40566	22	12	192	22.9	12.0	52.6	10.4	2.1	111702
16860	MUNSON	17826	116	28.4	39.7	29.3	2.6	0.0	38762	41726	29	21	97	21.6	18.6	46.4	13.4	0.0	107500
16861	NEW MILLPORT	17169	172	33.7	37.8	25.0	2.9	0.6	35309	36716	19	9	153	26.1	28.8	34.6	9.8	0.7	76875
16863	OLANTA	16433	143	35.7	38.5	23.1	2.8	0.0	33610	35000	15	6	126	26.2	28.6	36.5	8.7	0.0	76667
16864	ORVISTON	15607	37	32.4	35.1	29.7	2.7	0.0	35733	38635	20	10	31	16.1	16.1	51.6	16.1	0.0	122500
16865	PENNSYLVANIA FURNACE	35267	892	6.1	16.7	45.3	23.7	8.3	81040	80960	92	95	761	0.4	2.4	23.9	56.8	16.6	230085
16866	PHILIPSBURG	19682	4031	28.9	34.2	31.1	4.6	1.2	39596	42279	31	24	2992	16.9	20.9	44.6	16.2	1.4	113471
16870	PORT MATILDA	30054	2511	10.9	22.1	46.0	12.3	8.8	65306	65618	84	86	2042	3.7	5.0	28.0	45.8	17.5	226389
16871	POTTERSDALE	20540	34	32.4	32.4	32.4	2.9	0.0	37343	45000	25	15	29	13.8	27.6	48.3	10.3	0.0	102083
16872	REBERSBURG	15283	452	25.9	40.7	29.9	3.3	0.2	38813	40742	29	21	364	7.7	10.4	47.8	23.9	10.2	151984
16874	SNOW SHOE	20240	572	24.1	32.5	37.8	4.5	1.0	44290	48133	46	43	507	9.3	15.0	57.8	16.6	1.4	130235
	PENNSYLVANIA	26913		21.5	25.3	36.9	10.2	6.1	53225	55819				7.5	12.2	35.6	36.1	8.5	161438
	UNITED STATES	27277		20.9	24.4	35.3	11.7	7.6	54719	56938				9.3	13.1	31.6	32.6	13.5	162279

ZIP CODE #	POST OFFICE NAME	FINANCIAL SERVICES: Auto Loan	Home Loan	Invest-ments	Retire-ment Plans	THE HOME: Home Improvements: Home Repair	Lawn & Garden	Furnishings: Comput-ers & Hard-ware-Personal	Major Appli-ances	TV, Radio, Sound Equip-ment	Furni-ture	ENTERTAINMENT: Dine out/ Carry out	Sports Equip-ment	Fees & Tickets	Toys & Games	Travel	Cable TV	PERSONAL: Apparel & Services	Auto Repairs	Health Insur-ance	Pets & Supplies
16627	COALPORT	73	52	69	51	53	73	55	67	61	51	60	51	44	62	52	67	40	63	71	80
16630	CRESSON	78	63	75	62	64	81	68	77	74	62	72	57	60	73	66	80	49	74	85	90
16634	DUDLEY	75	54	62	52	54	71	56	65	62	55	61	50	45	65	51	68	41	62	69	79
16635	DUNCANSVILLE	82	74	80	74	75	87	72	82	76	69	75	61	67	76	73	80	51	77	85	96
16636	DYSART	80	65	76	66	67	84	67	79	72	60	70	59	58	72	66	77	47	73	83	92
16637	EAST FREEDOM	69	52	58	51	51	66	56	62	61	53	59	48	46	62	51	66	40	60	67	75
16639	FALLENTIMBER	69	48	69	46	49	69	50	63	56	47	55	48	39	57	48	62	37	59	66	76
16640	FLINTON	73	52	74	50	53	74	53	68	59	50	58	51	42	59	52	65	38	62	70	81
16641	GALLITZIN	81	59	81	58	61	84	63	78	70	57	68	58	51	69	61	76	45	72	83	91
16645	GLEN HOPE	71	51	71	50	53	74	56	69	62	50	60	52	45	61	54	69	40	64	75	81
16646	HASTINGS	75	56	76	55	58	79	59	73	65	54	64	54	49	64	58	72	42	68	78	86
16647	HESSTON	80	72	72	76	74	85	72	81	74	65	72	61	66	75	71	78	49	75	83	94
16648	HOLLIDAYSBURG	92	95	94	96	97	102	92	97	94	90	93	71	94	93	95	96	64	94	102	112
16650	HOPEWELL	76	60	65	61	61	76	61	71	66	58	65	54	53	68	58	71	44	66	74	84
16651	HOUTZDALE	76	55	77	53	57	79	59	74	66	53	64	55	47	65	57	73	42	68	79	87
16652	HUNTINGDON	77	70	75	71	72	82	72	79	76	67	74	58	67	75	72	80	51	76	84	92
16655	IMLER	80	67	70	69	68	82	68	77	71	62	70	58	60	73	66	76	47	72	80	91
16656	IRVONA	71	51	64	49	51	69	53	63	58	50	57	48	42	60	49	64	38	59	66	76
16657	JAMES CREEK	80	72	72	75	74	85	71	81	74	65	72	61	66	75	71	78	49	74	83	94
16659	LOYSBURG	86	78	77	81	80	92	77	87	79	70	78	66	71	81	77	84	53	80	90	101
16661	MADERA	71	51	71	50	53	74	55	68	62	50	60	51	44	61	54	68	40	64	74	80
16662	MARTINSBURG	78	64	74	65	66	83	66	78	71	59	69	58	57	71	65	76	46	72	82	91
16664	NEW ENTERPRISE	83	76	75	79	77	89	75	84	77	67	76	64	69	78	74	81	52	78	87	98
16666	OSCEOLA MILLS	83	60	84	58	62	85	62	79	70	57	68	59	50	69	61	77	45	73	83	93
16667	OSTERBURG	85	62	71	61	62	82	65	75	71	62	70	57	53	74	59	77	47	71	79	91
16668	PATTON	76	61	75	61	63	81	63	76	69	57	67	56	55	68	63	75	45	70	81	88
16669	PETERSBURG	80	73	72	76	74	86	72	81	74	65	73	61	66	76	72	78	50	75	84	94
16671	RAMEY	78	56	78	55	58	82	61	76	69	55	66	57	49	67	59	76	44	71	83	89
16673	ROARING SPRING	84	82	74	84	80	91	80	85	82	75	81	65	78	84	80	86	56	82	91	100
16674	ROBERTSDALE	74	53	61	51	53	70	55	64	61	54	60	49	44	64	50	66	40	61	67	78
16678	SAXTON	84	61	84	59	63	86	64	79	71	59	69	60	51	70	62	78	46	73	84	94
16679	SIX MILE RUN	76	55	63	53	54	72	57	66	63	55	62	51	46	66	52	69	42	63	70	81
16680	SMITHMILL	78	56	79	55	58	82	61	76	69	55	66	57	49	67	59	76	44	71	83	89
16683	SPRUCE CREEK	80	73	72	76	75	86	72	82	74	65	73	62	67	76	72	79	50	75	84	95
16685	TODD	82	59	85	57	61	84	61	77	67	56	66	58	48	67	60	74	44	71	80	92
16686	TYRONE	74	66	66	68	66	78	68	74	71	62	70	56	63	72	66	75	48	71	79	87
16689	WATERFALL	79	57	81	55	59	81	58	74	65	54	64	56	47	64	58	71	42	68	77	88
16691	WELLS TANNERY	73	53	75	51	55	75	54	69	60	50	59	52	43	60	53	66	39	63	71	82
16692	WESTOVER	70	50	64	49	51	68	52	63	57	49	56	48	41	59	49	63	38	58	66	75
16693	WILLIAMSBURG	83	64	83	64	66	88	67	81	72	59	70	63	55	71	66	78	47	75	86	96
16695	WOODBURY	79	72	72	75	74	85	71	81	74	65	72	61	66	75	71	78	49	74	83	94
16701	BRADFORD	78	72	74	72	72	84	73	79	78	69	77	58	70	77	73	83	53	78	88	92
16720	AUSTIN	79	62	67	62	62	78	63	72	68	59	66	55	53	70	59	73	45	68	76	86
16724	CROSBY	88	63	86	61	65	88	65	81	72	61	71	61	52	73	63	79	47	75	84	97
16726	CYCLONE	92	66	90	64	68	92	67	84	75	63	74	64	54	75	66	82	49	78	88	101
16727	DERRICK CITY	78	81	79	79	80	91	73	82	79	72	78	58	77	78	78	85	54	79	92	95
16729	DUKE CENTER	87	63	72	61	63	83	65	76	73	64	71	58	53	76	60	79	48	72	80	93
16731	ELDRED	84	60	75	58	61	82	63	76	71	60	69	58	51	72	59	77	46	71	81	91
16732	GIFFORD	93	79	82	81	80	97	79	90	84	73	82	69	71	86	77	89	56	84	94	106
16734	JAMES CITY	74	53	76	51	55	75	55	69	61	51	59	52	44	60	54	67	39	64	72	82
16735	KANE	81	69	80	67	70	87	68	80	74	64	72	59	62	74	68	80	49	75	87	94
16738	LEWIS RUN	92	67	83	65	68	90	69	83	76	66	75	63	56	78	65	83	50	77	87	99
16740	MOUNT JEWETT	88	63	82	61	64	87	65	80	72	62	71	60	52	73	62	79	47	74	83	96
16743	PORT ALLEGANY	86	72	74	71	69	87	73	80	78	70	77	62	65	80	69	83	52	77	86	97
16744	REW	93	72	79	72	73	92	74	85	80	70	78	65	62	83	70	86	53	80	89	102
16745	RIXFORD	86	63	73	62	63	83	65	76	72	63	71	59	53	75	60	78	47	72	80	92
16746	ROULETTE	75	54	76	52	56	76	55	70	61	51	60	52	44	61	54	67	40	64	73	83
16748	SHINGLEHOUSE	82	60	82	58	62	84	63	78	69	57	68	58	51	69	61	76	45	72	83	92
16749	SMETHPORT	87	63	89	61	65	90	66	83	73	60	71	62	53	73	65	81	47	76	88	98
16750	TURTLEPOINT	87	63	75	61	63	84	65	77	72	63	71	59	52	75	60	79	48	72	81	93
16801	STATE COLLEGE	75	55	54	60	54	57	90	64	80	74	81	57	71	79	67	77	57	75	65	80
16802	UNIVERSITY PARK	54	23	23	28	21	27	76	38	61	51	62	41	45	59	41	55	44	53	38	51
16803	STATE COLLEGE	98	83	80	89	81	80	110	87	101	100	103	75	96	102	92	97	73	97	86	107
16820	AARONSBURG	84	76	76	80	78	90	75	85	78	68	76	64	69	79	75	82	52	78	88	99
16821	ALLPORT	75	54	77	52	56	76	55	70	61	51	60	53	44	61	54	67	40	64	73	83
16822	BEECH CREEK	73	69	71	70	70	81	66	75	70	62	69	56	64	70	68	74	47	71	80	87
16823	BELLEFONTE	82	82	76	83	81	86	82	83	83	79	82	64	81	83	82	85	57	82	87	98
16827	BOALSBURG	118	139	130	141	138	136	122	127	120	125	121	96	135	121	133	121	86	123	127	148
16828	CENTRE HALL	94	101	92	100	100	104	91	97	94	92	94	71	96	95	95	96	65	94	102	113
16829	CLARENCE	87	63	90	61	65	89	64	82	71	60	70	61	51	71	64	78	46	75	85	97
16830	CLEARFIELD	76	62	73	62	63	79	66	74	71	61	69	55	58	70	64	76	47	71	81	87
16832	COBURN	83	76	75	79	77	89	75	84	77	67	76	64	69	78	74	81	52	78	87	98
16833	CURWENSVILLE	76	61	70	61	62	79	65	74	69	58	67	56	55	69	62	75	46	70	79	87
16836	FRENCHVILLE	79	57	74	55	58	78	59	72	65	56	64	54	47	66	56	71	43	67	75	86
16837	GLEN RICHEY	83	76	75	79	77	90	75	85	77	68	76	64	69	79	75	82	52	78	87	98
16838	GRAMPIAN	77	55	78	54	57	78	57	72	63	53	62	54	45	62	56	69	41	66	75	85
16839	GRASSFLAT	80	71	73	71	68	84	71	77	75	67	74	60	66	75	69	79	50	75	83	93
16840	HAWK RUN	75	54	77	52	56	76	55	70	61	51	60	53	44	61	54	67	40	64	73	83
16841	HOWARD	82	70	77	71	72	87	69	81	74	65	73	60	63	75	69	79	49	75	85	95
16844	JULIAN	84	77	73	78	77	86	75	82	77	72	76	61	70	79	73	81	52	77	84	96
16845	KARTHAUS	86	61	88	59	64	87	63	80	70	59	69	60	50	69	62	77	45	74	83	95
16852	MADISONBURG	79	55	87	54	57	84	61	75	63	49	62	62	44	62	60	69	40	70	80	93
16854	MILLHEIM	85	84	70	86	80	90	84	84	85	79	84	66	83	87	82	88	58	84	92	101
16858	MORRISDALE	78	62	75	61	63	80	62	74	67	58	66	56	54	67	62	72	44	69	78	88
16859	MOSHANNON	79	56	81	55	58	80	58	74	64	54	63	55	46	64	57	71	42	67	76	87
16860	MUNSON	76	57	75	56	58	77	58	71	64	55	63	54	49	64	58	69	42	66	75	85
16861	NEW MILLPORT	72	51	74	50	53	73	53	67	59	49	58	50	42	58	52	64	38	62	70	80
16863	OLANTA	69	50	70	48	51	70	51	64	56	48	55	48	41	56	50	62	37	59	67	77
16864	ORVISTON	76	54	78	53	57	77	56	71	62	52	61	53	45	62	55	68	40	65	74	85
16865	PENNSYLVANIA FURNACE	117	143	144	147	146	137	122	130	118	129	120	96	139	118	136	117	85	123	125	149
16866	PHILIPSBURG	76	61	77	60	62	80	62	75	68	58	67	55	54	67	62	74	45	70	80	88
16870	PORT MATILDA	113	127	115	128	124	121	114	118	111	114	112	92	121	114	119	110	79	113	113	137
16871	POTTERSDALE	68	57	77	54	62	74	56	69	61	58	59	48	51	58	59	65	40	65	74	80
16872	REBERSBURG	80	55	87	55	57	84	61	75	63	49	62	62	44	62	60	69	41	70	80	93
16874	SNOW SHOE	86	70	82	71	72	90	70	84	75	64	74	63	61	76	70	81	49	77	87	98
	PENNSYLVANIA	94	95	95	95	95	100	94	96	96	91	95	73	94	96	94	99	67	95	101	113
	UNITED STATES	100	100	100	100	100	100	100	100	100	100	100	100	100	100	100	100	100	100	100	100

ZIP CODE			POPULATION			2000-2009 ANNUAL RATE		HOUSEHOLDS					FAMILIES		
#	POST OFFICE NAME	COUNTY FIPS CODE	2000	2009	2014	% Rate	State Centile	2000	2009	2014	% Annual Rate 2000-2009	2009 Average HH Size	2000	2009	% Annual Rate 2000-2009
16875	SPRING MILLS	027	3381	3752	3903	1.1	87	1235	1403	1472	1.4	2.64	954	1048	1.0
16877	WARRIORS MARK	061	2170	2470	2593	1.4	91	801	934	992	1.7	2.64	630	716	1.4
16878	WEST DECATUR	033	2033	1900	1832	-0.7	8	797	771	749	-0.4	2.46	597	562	-0.7
16879	WINBURNE	033	189	190	186	0.1	57	67	69	68	0.3	2.74	50	50	0.0
16881	WOODLAND	033	3033	3176	3153	0.5	70	1109	1195	1198	0.8	2.66	887	935	0.6
16882	WOODWARD	027	552	577	588	0.5	70	188	202	208	0.8	2.86	142	147	0.4
16901	WELLSBORO	117	10490	10184	9970	-0.3	29	4206	4204	4149	0.0	2.34	2909	2834	-0.3
16912	BLOSSBURG	117	1995	1932	1894	-0.3	29	848	847	836	0.0	2.24	543	523	-0.4
16914	COLUMBIA CROSS ROADS	015	2464	2428	2384	-0.2	38	901	917	910	0.2	2.64	719	717	0.0
16915	COUDERSPORT	105	5929	5821	5714	-0.2	38	2298	2312	2284	0.1	2.42	1613	1575	-0.3
16917	COVINGTON	117	1395	1542	1560	1.1	87	549	621	633	1.3	2.48	394	435	1.1
16920	ELKLAND	117	1799	1739	1698	-0.4	23	760	752	740	-0.1	2.31	498	477	-0.5
16921	GAINES	117	428	422	415	-0.2	38	194	198	197	0.2	2.13	131	129	-0.2
16922	GALETON	105	2212	2215	2190	0.0	52	874	891	885	0.2	2.42	617	611	-0.1
16923	GENESEE	105	1483	1534	1528	0.4	68	546	578	580	0.6	2.65	396	408	0.3
16925	GILLETT	015	4521	4444	4362	-0.2	38	1705	1742	1729	0.2	2.52	1287	1285	0.0
16926	GRANVILLE SUMMIT	015	1497	1480	1457	-0.1	46	547	560	557	0.3	2.64	431	432	0.0
16927	HARRISON VALLEY	105	686	844	888	2.3	96	252	320	340	2.6	2.58	186	230	2.3
16928	KNOXVILLE	117	900	997	1008	1.1	87	352	398	405	1.3	2.50	252	278	1.1
16929	LAWRENCEVILLE	117	2264	2142	2074	-0.6	13	889	865	847	-0.3	2.46	657	625	-0.5
16930	LIBERTY	117	1091	1090	1076	0.0	52	419	435	433	0.4	2.50	309	312	0.1
16932	MAINESBURG	117	796	837	838	0.5	70	285	310	313	0.9	2.66	229	244	0.7
16933	MANSFIELD	117	7542	7702	7680	0.2	61	2529	2717	2735	0.8	2.38	1638	1703	0.4
16935	MIDDLEBURY CENTER	117	2286	2213	2167	-0.4	23	849	851	841	0.0	2.60	636	623	-0.2
16936	MILLERTON	117	2054	1935	1882	-0.6	13	777	759	744	-0.3	2.49	600	574	-0.5
16937	MILLS	105	138	142	149	0.3	64	49	51	54	0.4	2.73	36	37	0.3
16938	MORRIS	117	735	721	709	-0.2	38	287	292	290	0.2	2.43	208	206	-0.1
16939	MORRIS RUN	117	462	467	463	0.1	57	176	184	184	0.5	2.48	120	122	0.2
16940	NELSON	117	659	654	643	-0.1	46	258	264	263	0.2	2.48	197	197	0.0
16941	GENESEE	105	38	40	40	0.6	74	15	16	16	0.7	2.50	11	12	0.9
16942	OSCEOLA	117	544	529	521	-0.3	29	211	212	210	0.1	2.49	152	148	-0.3
16943	SABINSVILLE	117	731	650	618	-1.3	1	284	261	250	-0.9	2.49	216	194	-1.2
16946	TIOGA	117	1783	1761	1734	-0.1	46	686	696	691	0.2	2.52	484	478	-0.1
16947	TROY	015	4076	4000	3929	-0.2	38	1458	1463	1446	0.0	2.52	968	942	-0.3
16948	ULYSSES	105	1600	1695	1700	0.6	74	589	636	642	0.8	2.66	449	473	0.6
16950	WESTFIELD	117	3208	3388	3364	0.6	74	1288	1394	1397	0.9	2.41	943	996	0.6
17002	ALLENSVILLE	061	772	802	808	0.4	68	255	271	276	0.7	2.96	206	214	0.4
17003	ANNVILLE	075	12458	13301	13786	0.7	77	4376	4776	4992	1.0	2.52	3196	3399	0.7
17004	BELLEVILLE	087	4988	5335	5337	0.7	77	1610	1695	1710	0.6	2.92	1230	1263	0.3
17005	BERRYSBURG	043	294	307	314	0.5	70	121	129	133	0.7	2.37	93	96	0.3
17006	BLAIN	099	777	825	845	0.7	77	278	303	314	0.9	2.72	207	221	0.7
17007	BOILING SPRINGS	041	5111	5655	5949	1.1	87	1894	2163	2298	1.4	2.60	1545	1723	1.2
17009	BURNHAM	087	1966	1905	1881	-0.3	29	837	830	823	-0.1	2.30	553	530	-0.5
17011	CAMP HILL	041	34047	34446	34775	0.1	57	13448	13868	14124	0.3	2.18	8671	8560	-0.1
17013	CARLISLE	041	31589	33638	34741	0.7	77	12684	13857	14451	1.0	2.21	7842	8281	0.6
17014	COCOLAMUS	067	1021	1026	1016	0.1	57	360	368	366	0.2	2.77	291	293	0.1
17015	CARLISLE	041	20480	22237	23204	0.9	83	7765	8699	9179	1.2	2.49	5881	6393	0.9
17017	DALMATIA	097	1869	1762	1709	-0.6	13	743	719	704	-0.4	2.45	567	537	-0.6
17018	DAUPHIN	043	4022	4171	4231	0.4	68	1583	1675	1708	0.6	2.49	1206	1245	0.3
17019	DILLSBURG	133	15482	18345	19890	1.9	94	5842	7044	7684	2.0	2.59	4498	5284	1.8
17020	DUNCANNON	099	7989	8238	8344	0.3	64	3090	3277	3349	0.6	2.47	2211	2286	0.4
17021	EAST WATERFORD	067	965	958	944	-0.1	46	382	388	385	0.2	2.47	288	286	-0.1
17022	ELIZABETHTOWN	071	27370	30059	31343	1.0	85	10076	11405	12002	1.3	2.46	7178	7919	1.1
17023	ELIZABETHVILLE	043	3136	3223	3261	0.3	64	1218	1278	1300	0.5	2.49	862	875	0.2
17024	ELLIOTTSBURG	099	1906	2035	2097	0.7	77	712	784	814	1.0	2.59	545	586	0.8
17025	ENOLA	041	14337	16479	17479	1.5	92	5925	6999	7489	1.8	2.32	3981	4537	1.4
17026	FREDERICKSBURG	075	2608	2937	3103	1.3	90	948	1085	1151	1.5	2.71	721	803	1.2
17028	GRANTVILLE	043	3084	3273	3356	0.6	74	1180	1289	1334	1.0	2.47	898	951	0.6
17029	GRANVILLE	087	553	592	588	0.7	77	192	196	196	0.2	2.60	151	150	-0.1
17030	GRATZ	043	731	726	724	-0.1	46	285	289	290	0.2	2.51	210	206	-0.2
17032	HALIFAX	043	7616	7852	7940	0.3	64	2910	3056	3109	0.5	2.57	2251	2303	0.2
17033	HERSHEY	043	15048	15070	15114	0.0	52	6354	6426	6465	0.1	2.28	4005	3890	-0.3
17034	HIGHSPIRE	043	2430	2255	2193	-0.8	6	1120	1059	1037	-0.6	2.13	613	551	-1.1
17035	HONEY GROVE	067	942	929	917	-0.2	38	354	357	354	0.1	2.60	267	264	-0.1
17036	HUMMELSTOWN	043	18840	21437	22528	1.4	91	7268	8382	8841	1.6	2.53	5211	5854	1.3
17037	ICKESBURG	099	838	906	937	0.8	80	303	338	353	1.2	2.67	232	254	1.0
17038	JONESTOWN	075	6038	6817	7184	1.3	90	2291	2647	2816	1.6	2.57	1697	1900	1.2
17040	LANDISBURG	099	2271	2354	2393	0.4	68	864	923	948	0.7	2.55	682	715	0.5
17042	LEBANON	075	35063	38575	40220	1.0	85	13683	15302	16057	1.2	2.37	9459	10308	0.9
17043	LEMOYNE	041	5693	5898	6024	0.4	68	2774	2938	3024	0.6	2.00	1434	1432	0.0
17044	LEWISTOWN	087	21050	20693	20339	-0.2	38	8948	8779	8680	-0.2	2.26	5825	5521	-0.6
17045	LIVERPOOL	099	3697	3782	3818	0.2	61	1383	1455	1484	0.6	2.52	1015	1042	0.3
17046	LEBANON	075	29015	30751	31514	0.6	74	11390	12219	12583	0.8	2.50	7838	8181	0.5
17047	LOYSVILLE	099	2512	2455	2441	-0.2	38	875	885	889	0.1	2.66	667	657	-0.2
17048	LYKENS	043	4440	4408	4396	-0.1	46	1790	1801	1802	0.1	2.45	1235	1200	-0.3
17049	MC ALISTERVILLE	067	3158	3967	4269	2.5	97	1202	1532	1656	2.7	2.57	931	1163	2.4
17050	MECHANICSBURG	041	26926	31337	33444	1.7	93	10284	12312	13259	2.0	2.51	7617	8943	1.8
17051	MC VEYTOWN	087	5145	5313	5317	0.3	64	1969	2084	2104	0.6	2.51	1476	1520	0.3
17052	MAPLETON DEPOT	061	1270	1242	1219	-0.2	38	499	507	503	0.2	2.45	373	369	-0.1
17053	MARYSVILLE	099	4545	4652	4711	0.3	64	1856	1967	2010	0.6	2.36	1299	1337	0.3
17055	MECHANICSBURG	041	33045	37367	39322	1.3	90	12497	14537	15481	1.6	2.33	8395	9436	1.3
17057	MIDDLETOWN	043	21707	22105	22283	0.2	61	8783	9122	9248	0.4	2.34	5797	5793	0.0
17058	MIFFLIN	067	1671	1683	1691	0.1	57	675	693	699	0.3	2.35	491	493	0.0
17059	MIFFLINTOWN	067	6220	6259	6252	0.1	57	2345	2408	2416	0.3	2.52	1730	1724	0.0
17060	MILL CREEK	061	982	1048	1066	0.7	77	362	398	409	1.0	2.63	281	301	0.7
17061	MILLERSBURG	043	6855	6925	6973	0.1	57	2775	2850	2880	0.3	2.36	1872	1867	0.0
17062	MILLERSTOWN	099	1708	1816	1862	0.7	77	664	726	752	1.0	2.50	499	531	0.7
17063	MILROY	087	3518	3611	3613	0.3	64	1375	1448	1460	0.6	2.49	1002	1025	0.2
17065	MOUNT HOLLY SPRINGS	041	3710	4129	4350	1.2	88	1500	1722	1833	1.5	2.37	1095	1214	1.1
17066	MOUNT UNION	061	5046	5143	5112	0.2	61	2211	2305	2312	0.5	2.20	1435	1449	0.1
17067	MYERSTOWN	075	13289	14380	14907	0.9	83	4882	5409	5646	1.1	2.60	3624	3913	0.8
17068	NEW BLOOMFIELD	099	3854	3933	3976	0.2	61	1444	1525	1558	0.6	2.45	1068	1100	0.3
17070	NEW CUMBERLAND	133	14872	15525	16003	0.5	70	6481	6912	7168	0.7	2.24	4209	4337	0.3
17071	NEW GERMANTOWN	099	494	524	538	0.6	74	195	213	221	1.0	2.46	145	155	0.7
17073	NEWMANSTOWN	075	4648	4892	5046	0.6	74	1729	1860	1932	0.8	2.63	1297	1357	0.5
	PENNSYLVANIA					0.3					0.4	2.45			0.1
	UNITED STATES					1.0					1.1	2.59			0.9

ZIP CODE		RACE (%)						% Hispanic Origin		2009 AGE DISTRIBUTION (%)										MEDIAN AGE		
#	POST OFFICE NAME	White 2000	White 2009	Black 2000	Black 2009	Asian/Pacific 2000	Asian/Pacific 2009	2000	2009	0-4	5-9	10-14	15-19	20-24	25-44	45-64	65-84	85+	18+	2009	% 2009 Males	% 2009 Females
16875	SPRING MILLS	99.0	98.6	0.1	0.2	0.5	0.7	0.4	0.6	6.4	6.9	7.4	6.9	4.3	24.6	29.9	12.0	1.6	74.9	40.6	50.9	49.1
16877	WARRIORS MARK	98.4	98.0	0.3	0.4	0.7	1.1	0.4	0.6	6.6	7.3	7.7	6.5	4.3	24.7	31.4	10.5	1.1	74.3	40.8	50.0	50.0
16878	WEST DECATUR	99.0	98.7	0.1	0.2	0.2	0.4	0.1	0.2	5.8	5.9	6.6	6.1	5.6	26.8	29.1	12.9	1.2	77.9	40.5	49.2	50.8
16879	WINBURNE	100.0	99.5	0.0	0.0	0.0	0.5	0.5	0.5	6.8	6.8	6.8	6.8	6.3	25.3	26.3	12.6	2.1	73.7	39.6	47.4	52.6
16881	WOODLAND	98.9	98.4	0.2	0.3	0.1	0.2	0.2	0.3	6.0	6.1	6.5	6.9	5.8	25.9	29.4	12.2	1.2	77.1	39.5	49.8	50.2
16882	WOODWARD	99.3	98.8	0.0	0.0	0.7	1.2	0.7	0.9	6.8	7.1	7.5	7.8	4.9	24.1	28.6	11.6	1.7	73.7	39.2	49.9	50.1
16901	WELLSBORO	98.3	97.8	0.3	0.3	0.6	0.9	0.6	0.8	5.0	5.6	6.0	6.5	4.9	22.4	30.1	15.9	3.6	79.0	44.7	48.5	51.5
16912	BLOSSBURG	99.3	99.2	0.2	0.2	0.1	0.1	0.4	0.6	6.0	6.1	6.1	6.1	5.7	23.3	27.3	16.1	3.3	77.8	42.5	48.2	51.8
16914	COLUMBIA CROSS ROADS	98.8	98.6	0.1	0.1	0.1	0.1	0.2	0.4	5.9	6.3	6.6	7.2	5.3	23.0	29.8	14.1	1.8	76.4	42.1	49.6	50.4
16915	COUDERSPORT	97.3	96.3	0.4	0.5	1.1	1.8	0.5	0.7	5.4	5.6	6.3	6.6	5.1	22.6	30.5	14.3	3.6	78.2	43.7	49.6	50.4
16917	COVINGTON	98.1	97.5	0.1	0.1	0.2	0.3	0.6	0.8	6.0	6.2	6.6	6.9	4.6	25.3	29.5	13.5	1.4	76.7	41.4	49.7	50.3
16920	ELKLAND	98.3	98.0	0.9	1.1	0.0	0.0	0.8	1.1	6.0	5.9	6.0	6.4	5.8	24.6	26.5	15.6	3.3	78.6	42.0	48.0	52.0
16921	GAINES	98.4	97.4	0.2	0.5	0.0	0.2	0.0	0.0	4.5	4.7	5.2	5.7	4.3	21.3	32.5	19.7	2.1	81.8	47.6	49.8	50.2
16922	GALETON	97.8	97.2	0.6	0.7	0.5	0.9	0.5	0.7	5.4	5.6	5.5	5.4	4.9	20.9	31.1	17.5	3.7	80.1	46.4	47.9	52.1
16923	GENESEE	98.4	98.0	0.5	0.6	0.0	0.1	0.3	0.5	6.5	6.5	6.8	6.6	5.5	23.2	29.5	13.6	1.8	76.2	41.2	50.6	49.4
16925	GILLETT	98.7	98.4	0.4	0.5	0.1	0.2	0.6	0.8	6.1	6.4	6.6	6.6	5.2	23.2	30.6	13.5	1.9	76.4	42.1	49.7	50.3
16926	GRANVILLE SUMMIT	98.5	98.0	0.4	0.5	0.1	0.1	0.6	0.9	5.6	6.6	8.7	7.3	4.3	23.3	31.9	10.7	1.6	74.5	40.4	52.2	47.8
16927	HARRISON VALLEY	98.5	98.2	0.1	0.2	0.1	0.1	0.6	0.8	6.3	6.2	7.2	8.1	6.3	24.3	28.9	11.7	1.1	75.0	38.3	49.5	50.5
16928	KNOXVILLE	99.4	99.5	0.2	0.2	0.0	0.0	0.4	0.6	6.8	6.5	6.8	7.0	5.5	24.3	25.4	15.1	2.5	75.4	40.0	50.5	49.5
16929	LAWRENCEVILLE	99.3	99.1	0.2	0.3	0.1	0.1	0.4	0.5	6.3	6.4	6.8	7.3	5.7	24.7	27.0	14.1	1.6	75.7	39.8	49.6	50.4
16930	LIBERTY	99.5	99.4	0.0	0.0	0.0	0.0	0.3	0.5	5.8	6.4	6.6	5.7	4.8	24.2	30.5	14.0	2.0	77.7	42.4	51.1	48.9
16932	MAINESBURG	97.9	97.4	0.3	0.2	0.3	0.5	0.4	0.6	5.9	6.6	6.9	6.7	4.3	23.4	29.9	14.8	1.6	76.3	42.2	50.1	49.9
16933	MANSFIELD	95.8	94.8	2.1	2.5	0.6	0.9	0.7	1.0	4.9	4.7	4.7	12.0	15.7	22.6	22.9	11.1	1.5	82.2	30.7	48.3	51.7
16935	MIDDLEBURY CENTER	98.6	98.4	0.1	0.2	0.1	0.2	0.6	0.8	5.5	6.0	7.0	7.7	4.6	23.5	30.0	14.1	1.7	76.7	42.1	50.4	49.6
16936	MILLERTON	98.6	98.3	0.3	0.4	0.1	0.2	0.3	0.4	4.9	5.1	5.7	7.3	5.4	23.4	31.9	14.1	2.0	80.0	43.7	49.6	50.4
16937	MILLS	99.3	98.6	0.0	0.0	0.0	0.0	0.7	0.7	6.3	6.3	7.0	8.5	6.3	25.4	26.8	12.0	1.4	74.6	37.2	48.6	51.4
16938	MORRIS	98.5	98.1	0.3	0.3	0.4	0.6	0.4	0.6	5.3	5.7	6.0	6.0	4.9	20.9	31.5	17.3	2.5	79.2	45.7	51.0	49.0
16939	MORRIS RUN	98.9	98.7	0.0	0.0	0.4	0.6	0.2	0.2	5.8	5.8	6.2	5.8	5.1	22.7	30.8	15.0	2.8	77.9	44.0	49.0	51.0
16940	NELSON	98.9	98.9	0.2	0.2	0.0	0.0	0.2	0.2	5.7	5.8	6.4	7.3	5.2	23.7	30.1	14.1	1.7	77.5	42.6	49.7	50.3
16941	GENESEE	100.0	100.0	0.0	0.0	0.0	0.0	0.0	0.0	10.0	10.0	10.0	7.5	5.0	25.0	20.0	12.5	0.0	62.5	28.8	47.5	52.5
16942	OSCEOLA	97.8	97.2	0.6	0.8	0.2	0.4	0.2	0.2	7.2	6.8	7.0	6.6	6.6	25.5	27.0	11.7	1.5	74.9	38.1	47.1	52.9
16943	SABINSVILLE	98.9	98.6	0.0	0.0	0.3	0.3	0.5	0.9	5.8	6.2	6.5	6.0	4.6	21.4	30.6	17.1	1.8	77.7	44.6	51.4	48.6
16946	TIOGA	99.2	99.0	0.1	0.1	0.1	0.1	0.2	0.3	7.0	6.9	6.6	6.5	5.6	24.8	27.7	13.2	1.6	75.5	38.9	50.8	49.2
16947	TROY	98.7	98.4	0.2	0.3	0.3	0.5	0.5	0.7	5.2	5.4	5.8	6.2	5.2	24.6	29.1	14.8	3.8	80.0	43.4	47.1	52.9
16948	ULYSSES	98.6	98.2	0.1	0.2	0.1	0.2	0.6	0.8	7.6	7.2	7.3	7.3	5.7	24.1	27.0	12.3	1.6	73.5	37.7	50.0	50.0
16950	WESTFIELD	98.5	98.1	0.4	0.5	0.2	0.3	0.6	0.8	5.8	5.5	6.3	7.3	5.1	23.2	29.1	15.4	2.3	77.5	42.6	49.1	50.9
17002	ALLENSVILLE	98.2	97.9	0.9	1.0	0.0	0.0	0.5	0.6	10.0	9.5	9.0	7.6	5.7	25.6	21.1	10.5	1.1	67.0	31.8	50.2	49.8
17003	ANNVILLE	97.1	96.0	0.5	0.7	0.9	1.4	1.5	2.2	5.0	5.2	5.5	9.4	9.0	22.9	28.6	12.1	2.3	80.8	39.4	48.7	51.3
17004	BELLEVILLE	98.8	98.5	0.6	0.7	0.1	0.1	0.3	0.5	8.6	8.4	8.2	7.3	5.3	23.5	22.0	12.7	4.0	70.0	35.7	49.6	50.4
17005	BERRYSBURG	99.3	98.4	0.7	1.0	0.0	0.0	0.0	0.0	6.8	7.5	7.5	5.5	4.2	24.4	28.7	13.4	2.0	73.9	40.8	51.5	48.5
17006	BLAIN	98.5	98.2	0.8	1.0	0.0	0.0	0.1	0.2	6.5	6.5	6.7	7.0	5.3	23.3	27.8	14.9	1.9	75.8	41.0	51.2	48.8
17007	BOILING SPRINGS	98.2	97.5	0.6	0.8	0.7	1.1	0.5	0.8	5.5	6.2	7.0	6.7	4.3	22.0	34.0	13.0	1.2	76.5	43.8	49.6	50.4
17009	BURNHAM	99.2	98.9	0.3	0.4	0.2	0.3	0.3	0.4	4.9	5.0	5.5	6.3	5.6	25.1	30.0	15.4	2.3	80.8	43.5	48.4	51.6
17011	CAMP HILL	89.5	86.6	6.1	7.1	2.9	4.4	2.6	3.4	4.5	4.8	5.3	5.7	6.4	26.0	28.1	15.6	3.6	82.0	43.1	52.4	47.6
17013	CARLISLE	91.0	88.5	5.2	6.4	1.6	2.4	1.7	2.4	5.1	5.0	5.4	8.1	8.4	23.9	26.6	14.3	3.3	80.9	40.5	47.2	52.8
17014	COCOLAMUS	99.5	99.5	0.2	0.2	0.0	0.0	0.2	0.2	7.2	7.4	7.6	6.5	4.5	28.7	26.2	10.4	1.5	73.6	37.4	52.4	47.6
17015	CARLISLE	97.3	96.3	0.7	0.9	0.8	1.3	0.8	1.2	5.4	5.8	6.4	6.5	4.8	23.1	31.6	14.1	2.3	78.2	43.6	49.4	50.6
17017	DALMATIA	99.3	99.1	0.4	0.6	0.1	0.1	0.2	0.2	5.3	5.6	5.6	5.2	4.4	27.1	30.0	14.9	2.0	80.2	42.9	50.7	49.3
17018	DAUPHIN	98.4	95.8	0.2	1.3	0.4	0.7	0.6	1.9	4.1	4.5	5.3	6.4	4.8	23.5	34.6	15.2	1.6	82.0	45.8	49.0	51.0
17019	DILLSBURG	98.1	97.1	0.3	0.5	0.6	1.0	0.7	1.2	6.0	6.6	7.2	7.1	5.0	25.3	31.1	10.5	1.2	75.7	40.5	50.0	50.0
17020	DUNCANNON	98.7	98.4	0.3	0.3	0.1	0.2	0.8	1.1	6.0	6.0	6.4	6.2	5.7	26.1	30.0	11.7	1.8	77.5	40.7	49.2	50.8
17021	EAST WATERFORD	99.0	98.7	0.1	0.1	0.1	0.1	0.4	0.6	5.1	5.3	5.6	6.8	4.6	24.6	29.4	16.6	1.9	79.6	43.4	51.7	48.3
17022	ELIZABETHTOWN	97.1	95.7	0.6	0.8	1.0	1.6	1.2	1.9	5.8	6.0	6.3	8.1	7.5	24.7	25.9	11.8	3.7	78.0	38.9	47.8	52.2
17023	ELIZABETHVILLE	98.2	97.3	0.5	0.8	0.4	0.7	0.9	1.6	6.3	6.5	6.9	6.7	4.6	27.1	26.9	12.8	2.3	76.2	39.6	50.2	49.8
17024	ELLIOTTSBURG	98.4	98.0	0.5	0.6	0.2	0.2	0.6	0.8	6.6	7.0	7.6	7.2	5.1	24.9	29.1	11.3	1.3	74.3	39.9	50.3	49.7
17025	ENOLA	96.0	94.5	0.8	1.1	1.3	2.1	1.2	1.7	5.9	5.8	6.0	7.1	6.3	27.6	28.8	11.0	1.4	78.5	39.5	47.9	52.1
17026	FREDERICKSBURG	97.9	96.7	0.2	0.3	0.2	0.3	1.8	2.9	7.0	7.3	7.5	6.6	4.3	26.4	28.3	11.4	1.1	74.0	39.4	51.3	48.7
17028	GRANTVILLE	95.7	93.3	1.0	1.5	0.5	0.8	2.8	4.7	5.7	6.0	6.6	7.7	6.4	25.9	31.3	9.4	1.0	77.0	39.8	50.0	50.0
17029	GRANVILLE	98.7	98.3	0.5	0.8	0.0	0.0	0.2	0.2	6.6	6.4	6.6	5.1	4.7	23.0	23.5	17.2	6.9	77.5	43.4	51.0	49.0
17030	GRATZ	99.2	98.8	0.1	0.3	0.0	0.0	0.5	1.0	7.4	7.7	7.6	6.1	4.1	26.3	25.6	13.4	1.8	73.6	38.2	52.2	47.8
17032	HALIFAX	98.4	97.5	0.2	0.4	0.4	0.6	0.8	1.4	5.8	6.4	6.8	6.5	4.4	25.4	31.6	11.8	1.4	76.9	41.7	50.0	50.0
17033	HERSHEY	92.8	88.8	1.8	2.8	3.6	5.9	1.4	2.3	5.2	5.4	5.8	5.9	5.9	23.6	27.7	16.2	4.3	79.8	43.6	47.5	52.5
17034	HIGHSPIRE	87.6	81.8	7.5	10.8	0.9	1.4	4.7	7.5	6.0	5.0	4.8	5.4	7.3	27.9	28.1	13.3	2.3	81.2	40.5	48.5	51.5
17035	HONEY GROVE	98.9	98.5	0.2	0.2	0.2	0.4	1.0	1.4	6.4	6.6	6.6	5.6	5.7	26.4	27.9	13.7	1.3	77.0	39.7	50.9	49.1
17036	HUMMELSTOWN	94.6	91.7	1.4	2.0	2.3	3.9	1.5	2.3	5.7	6.1	6.8	6.8	4.9	26.7	30.3	11.1	1.6	76.8	40.4	48.6	51.4
17037	ICKESBURG	98.2	97.8	0.7	0.9	0.2	0.3	0.6	0.9	6.8	7.3	7.8	7.0	4.7	25.4	28.6	11.1	1.2	73.6	39.4	51.5	48.5
17038	JONESTOWN	97.9	97.2	0.6	0.7	0.4	0.6	1.1	1.7	5.3	5.7	6.2	6.6	4.6	26.5	31.0	12.8	1.3	78.5	41.8	51.7	48.3
17040	LANDISBURG	98.5	98.2	0.3	0.4	0.1	0.2	0.6	0.8	6.0	6.5	6.9	6.5	4.6	25.2	31.6	11.6	1.0	76.4	41.6	50.2	49.8
17042	LEBANON	94.4	92.5	1.5	1.9	1.3	1.9	4.1	5.8	5.3	5.5	6.0	6.0	4.8	23.4	29.0	16.1	3.9	79.5	44.2	49.1	50.9
17043	LEMOYNE	95.7	94.2	0.8	1.1	1.8	2.8	1.1	1.6	5.8	5.4	5.4	5.7	6.6	28.5	28.5	11.9	2.3	79.9	40.1	48.0	52.0
17044	LEWISTOWN	98.1	97.6	0.6	0.7	0.4	0.6	0.8	1.1	5.7	5.6	5.8	6.1	5.6	25.2	27.4	15.6	3.0	79.0	42.2	48.9	51.1
17045	LIVERPOOL	98.6	98.3	0.5	0.6	0.2	0.3	0.5	0.6	5.8	6.1	6.4	6.1	4.7	24.7	30.1	13.3	2.7	78.0	42.3	49.3	50.7
17046	LEBANON	88.3	85.1	2.4	2.6	1.0	1.5	13.4	17.7	7.2	6.8	6.9	6.8	6.0	25.6	27.3	11.9	1.6	74.9	38.3	49.0	51.0
17047	LOYSVILLE	96.1	95.3	2.0	2.3	0.2	0.3	1.4	1.9	6.4	6.6	7.3	10.1	5.0	23.9	27.5	11.5	1.7	72.5	37.5	52.6	47.4
17048	LYKENS	98.2	97.3	0.3	0.5	0.5	0.8	0.4	0.7	6.3	6.3	6.4	6.4	5.1	24.6	27.1	15.5	2.4	77.1	41.3	49.4	50.6
17049	MC ALISTERVILLE	98.8	98.4	0.3	0.4	0.3	0.4	0.7	1.0	6.8	7.2	7.4	7.0	4.6	24.6	28.1	12.6	1.8	74.2	39.9	50.4	49.6
17050	MECHANICSBURG	94.4	92.1	0.8	1.0	3.5	5.3	1.0	1.5	5.6	6.2	7.0	6.7	4.7	23.0	32.4	12.5	2.0	76.8	43.0	48.7	51.3
17051	MC VEYTOWN	99.3	99.1	0.2	0.2	0.1	0.2	0.3	0.4	5.7	5.9	6.3	6.3	4.9	24.4	29.8	14.2	2.4	78.1	42.6	49.2	50.8
17052	MAPLETON DEPOT	98.3	97.9	0.3	0.4	0.0	0.0	0.4	0.6	5.1	5.1	6.7	6.0	4.1	24.2	31.6	16.3	1.1	79.4	44.2	48.2	51.8
17053	MARYSVILLE	98.7	98.3	0.2	0.3	0.2	0.3	0.4	0.6	5.0	5.2	5.7	6.4	5.1	25.2	32.3	13.2	1.8	80.2	43.2	48.0	52.0
17055	MECHANICSBURG	96.1	94.5	0.9	1.2	1.6	2.5	1.1	1.6	4.9	4.9	5.3	8.3	8.8	22.5	27.9	14.3	3.0	81.4	41.2	47.2	52.8
17057	MIDDLETOWN	92.1	88.4	4.6	6.7	0.9	1.5	2.3	3.8	5.6	5.5	5.7	6.4	7.3	26.1	28.1	12.8	2.6	79.4	40.4	47.7	52.3
17058	MIFFLIN	94.7	92.9	0.1	0.2	0.7	1.0	6.1	8.5	5.3	5.6	6.0	6.0	4.3	28.0	28.9	12.7	3.1	79.1	41.8	50.1	49.9
17059	MIFFLINTOWN	97.9	97.2	0.3	0.4	0.9	1.3	2.0	2.7	6.6	6.8	6.9	6.4	4.9	24.6	27.4	13.8	2.7	75.8	40.5	49.5	50.5
17060	MILL CREEK	98.8	98.5	0.1	0.2	0.0	0.0	0.5	0.9	7.9	7.3	7.2	6.6	7.0	26.6	24.0	12.2	1.2	73.7	36.2	51.4	48.6
17061	MILLERSBURG	98.7	98.0	0.4	0.6	0.3	0.6	0.7	1.1	5.4	5.6	6.0	6.0	4.9	24.7	28.0	15.7	3.6	79.0	43.0	47.9	52.1
17062	MILLERSTOWN	99.4	99.2	0.2	0.2	0.1	0.1	0.9	1.4	5.5	5.9	6.4	6.7	4.7	24.9	31.1	13.1	1.7	78.0	42.2	48.6	51.4
17063	MILROY	98.8	98.3	0.1	0.1	0.4	0.6	0.6	0.9	6.4	6.4	6.9	7.0	5.1	25.6	27.6	13.5	1.6	76.0	40.2	50.6	49.4
17065	MOUNT HOLLY SPRINGS	97.7	96.9	0.8	1.1	0.5	0.8	0.7	1.0	6.0	6.2	6.5	7.0	5.6	26.3	29.5	11.5	1.4	76.6	40.1	50.5	49.5
17066	MOUNT UNION	92.7	90.6	5.7	7.5	0.1	0.2	0.9	1.3	6.5	6.1	6.3	6.7	5.7	23.4	26.8	15.9	2.7	77.2	41.4	47.0	53.0
17067	MYERSTOWN	98.1	97.3	0.7	0.8	0.4	0.7	1.1	1.7	6.4	6.6	6.8	6.4	4.8	24.7	27.3	13.8	3.2	76.2	40.6	48.8	51.2
17068	NEW BLOOMFIELD	98.9	98.7	0.3	0.4	0.2	0.2	0.5	0.8	5.6	5.8	6.5	7.0	5.3	26.5	29.2	11.2	2.8	77.6	40.3	49.2	50.8
17070	NEW CUMBERLAND	96.1	94.4	1.0	1.4	1.1	1.7	1.6	2.4	5.4	5.6	6.1	5.8	4.9	24.7	31.4	14.1	2.2	79.2	43.5	48.9	51.1
17071	NEW GERMANTOWN	98.8	98.5	0.8	1.0	0.0	0.0	0.2	0.2	6.5	6.5	6.7	7.1	5.5	23.3	28.1	14.5	1.9	76.3	40.9	51.0	49.0
17073	NEWMANSTOWN	98.7	98.2	0.4	0.6	0.2	0.3	0.9	1.3	6.8	7.0	7.2	6.7	5.3	24.9	28.4	12.2	1.5	74.7	39.1	49.9	50.1
	PENNSYLVANIA	85.4	83.2	10.0	10.7	1.8	2.7	3.2	4.2	5.8	6.0	6.3	7.1	6.5	24.8	27.8	13.1	2.6	77.8	40.4	48.5	51.5
	UNITED STATES	75.1	72.0	12.3	12.7	3.8	4.6	12.5	15.7	6.8	6.7	6.6	7.1	6.9	27.0	26.0	10.9	1.9	75.7	36.9	49.2	50.8

INCOME

16875-17073

ZIP CODE #	POST OFFICE NAME	2009 Per Capita Income	2009 HH Income Base	2009 HOUSEHOLD INCOME DISTRIBUTION (%) Less than $25,000	$25,000 to $49,999	$50,000 to $99,999	$100,000 to $149,999	$150,000 or More	MEDIAN HOUSEHOLD INCOME 2009	2014	2009 National Centile	2009 State Centile	2009 Home Value Base	2009 HOME VALUE DISTRIBUTION (%) Less than $50,000	$50,000 to $89,999	$90,000 to $174,999	$175,000 to $399,999	$400,000 or More	2009 Median Home Value
16875	SPRING MILLS	21973	1403	17.8	30.6	42.6	6.6	2.4	51089	53248	64	65	1149	7.7	7.9	35.7	34.6	14.1	171445
16877	WARRIORS MARK	25358	934	15.6	26.0	43.3	9.9	5.2	57112	55566	74	74	780	4.4	5.0	32.6	47.1	11.0	194937
16878	WEST DECATUR	17401	771	30.2	36.2	30.1	3.2	0.3	38235	40644	27	18	688	20.8	25.4	40.7	11.9	1.2	95306
16879	WINBURNE	18979	69	23.2	27.5	44.9	4.3	0.0	49443	51029	60	60	61	6.6	29.5	54.1	9.8	0.0	107500
16881	WOODLAND	17499	1195	29.8	35.0	30.8	2.8	1.7	39132	41193	30	22	1048	17.4	28.3	38.9	11.7	3.6	96818
16882	WOODWARD	18963	202	19.8	36.6	36.1	5.0	2.5	45595	47850	50	49	173	3.5	9.8	48.0	31.2	7.5	150625
16901	WELLSBORO	21689	4204	28.3	29.5	34.5	4.9	2.9	41784	44755	39	34	3193	9.1	13.1	46.8	27.0	4.1	137344
16912	BLOSSBURG	22570	847	29.4	29.3	33.8	5.4	2.1	39748	42020	32	25	612	9.2	25.8	52.1	11.6	1.3	106405
16914	COLUMBIA CROSS ROADS	18942	917	24.9	32.5	36.2	4.6	1.9	44072	45690	46	43	765	12.9	14.8	48.0	20.0	4.3	126349
16915	COUDERSPORT	24703	2312	23.2	27.2	39.1	6.9	3.7	49683	50207	60	61	1742	8.2	14.1	42.3	31.1	4.4	142596
16917	COVINGTON	18627	621	29.8	37.2	28.2	2.7	2.1	38235	39578	27	18	498	14.3	17.5	52.6	14.5	1.2	114474
16920	ELKLAND	19581	752	33.5	32.2	28.6	3.7	2.0	35927	36836	20	11	500	15.6	35.2	43.4	5.8	0.0	88788
16921	GAINES	19973	198	34.3	37.9	24.2	2.5	1.0	32476	34462	12	4	163	14.7	21.5	42.3	19.0	2.5	113068
16922	GALETON	18791	891	30.1	33.1	31.3	3.9	1.6	37180	38253	24	14	673	14.3	28.1	42.2	14.0	1.5	99537
16923	GENESEE	18831	578	29.4	32.5	32.7	3.6	1.7	40000	41321	33	26	456	15.1	23.2	39.7	19.1	2.9	110385
16925	GILLETT	19326	1742	27.1	33.4	34.1	3.6	1.8	41471	43877	38	33	1425	18.0	19.1	43.8	16.8	2.3	115036
16926	GRANVILLE SUMMIT	17489	560	28.9	29.3	36.1	5.2	0.5	43598	45334	44	41	467	14.6	17.6	50.7	14.1	3.0	116896
16927	HARRISON VALLEY	15441	320	32.5	36.3	29.1	2.2	0.0	35381	36942	19	9	258	18.2	23.3	46.9	8.5	3.1	101818
16928	KNOXVILLE	20172	398	25.9	34.4	34.2	3.3	2.3	40787	42997	35	29	293	17.7	42.7	30.7	8.2	0.7	79479
16929	LAWRENCEVILLE	19075	865	24.4	37.2	34.2	3.4	0.8	42119	44106	40	36	692	27.2	15.9	40.6	15.2	1.2	105108
16930	LIBERTY	20378	435	23.9	29.4	41.1	4.1	1.4	47073	50149	54	55	355	8.7	11.0	54.4	20.8	5.1	132321
16932	MAINESBURG	18216	310	19.7	36.5	40.0	2.9	1.0	45000	47709	48	46	272	8.5	15.8	50.0	22.1	3.7	125658
16933	MANSFIELD	19221	2717	29.6	30.4	32.4	6.0	1.7	40144	42030	33	27	1834	12.6	12.1	44.7	27.3	3.2	137102
16935	MIDDLEBURY CENTER	18380	851	28.1	32.7	33.7	3.9	1.6	40821	43108	35	29	694	14.6	17.7	44.8	19.9	3.0	124176
16936	MILLERTON	18518	759	26.7	32.7	36.8	2.6	1.2	41391	44635	37	33	644	16.6	16.9	48.3	16.6	1.6	119505
16937	MILLS	14779	51	33.3	35.3	29.4	2.0	0.0	35547	36120	19	10	41	19.5	22.0	46.3	9.8	2.4	101563
16938	MORRIS	19395	292	29.5	38.7	27.4	2.4	2.1	35617	36667	20	10	252	23.4	17.9	40.5	15.9	2.4	106250
16939	MORRIS RUN	16242	184	35.9	34.8	25.5	2.7	1.1	32469	33870	12	4	157	35.0	20.4	26.8	16.6	1.3	76429
16940	NELSON	18584	264	29.2	31.8	34.1	3.4	1.5	40000	41609	33	26	207	13.5	16.9	46.9	18.8	3.9	121371
16941	GENESEE	15000	16	37.5	31.3	31.3	0.0	0.0	35000	35000	18	8	12	8.3	33.3	50.0	8.3	0.0	100000
16942	OSCEOLA	19194	212	32.1	29.2	31.1	5.7	1.9	40898	42158	36	30	168	22.6	32.1	30.4	14.3	0.6	80000
16943	SABINSVILLE	18058	261	31.0	34.5	29.9	3.1	1.5	38131	39374	27	18	226	15.9	20.4	39.4	20.8	3.5	117241
16946	TIOGA	19514	696	31.2	29.7	32.0	5.2	1.9	38538	40500	28	19	561	27.1	20.0	39.0	13.2	0.7	93837
16947	TROY	19826	1463	26.7	32.9	32.8	5.1	2.5	41044	43904	36	30	1018	12.7	14.4	50.7	19.1	3.1	127404
16948	ULYSSES	16368	636	32.5	32.2	30.3	3.3	1.6	37404	38561	25	15	496	15.9	20.4	44.2	16.7	2.8	110112
16950	WESTFIELD	17790	1394	32.6	32.7	30.6	3.2	0.9	38639	39867	29	20	1039	16.3	30.1	39.3	12.2	2.1	94464
17002	ALLENSVILLE	14701	271	32.1	34.3	28.8	4.1	0.7	36325	38551	21	12	214	14.0	17.8	43.9	19.6	4.7	120833
17003	ANNVILLE	25555	4776	13.8	27.2	43.6	11.3	4.1	58555	58887	76	77	3770	8.3	5.6	32.2	47.5	6.4	183753
17004	BELLEVILLE	15520	1695	29.9	34.2	30.8	3.4	1.8	38651	41665	29	20	1313	6.5	12.6	52.4	23.5	5.0	132374
17005	BERRYSBURG	22145	129	21.7	34.1	39.5	3.9	0.8	46442	50712	53	53	103	5.8	29.1	43.7	13.6	7.8	116346
17006	BLAIN	18485	303	25.4	36.3	31.7	3.6	3.0	40590	44084	35	28	247	11.7	20.2	35.6	25.5	6.9	132212
17007	BOILING SPRINGS	29917	2163	11.0	20.8	45.2	17.0	6.0	72608	76508	88	90	1844	0.9	1.8	28.7	64.6	4.1	217578
17009	BURNHAM	22204	830	23.1	32.2	38.3	5.1	1.3	46322	48887	52	52	625	11.4	23.2	55.4	9.9	0.2	108299
17011	CAMP HILL	33487	13868	13.3	21.8	43.9	12.4	8.6	67051	72549	85	88	9954	0.7	0.9	37.1	53.8	7.5	197359
17013	CARLISLE	27953	13857	21.0	25.3	39.4	9.8	4.4	53912	58567	69	70	8363	5.4	5.8	43.5	40.9	4.4	166451
17014	COCOLAMUS	18646	368	23.4	32.3	38.9	3.3	2.2	46131	46149	52	51	309	8.7	13.9	48.2	25.9	3.2	135045
17015	CARLISLE	27481	8699	12.7	26.4	47.3	9.5	4.1	60277	64768	78	79	7497	14.7	5.1	27.5	44.6	8.1	182556
17017	DALMATIA	21505	719	18.2	33.5	43.5	3.8	1.0	48525	51243	58	58	595	9.7	23.2	38.0	23.2	5.9	129688
17018	DAUPHIN	31183	1675	9.1	21.2	51.5	10.9	7.3	68304	68695	86	89	1419	3.1	6.7	38.2	42.8	9.2	178711
17019	DILLSBURG	27072	7044	12.4	24.6	47.8	10.0	5.2	61153	63004	79	80	5617	6.2	2.7	25.5	56.0	9.6	217953
17020	DUNCANNON	22457	3277	21.3	28.3	40.1	8.4	2.0	50350	53579	62	63	2463	11.2	10.5	42.3	34.0	2.0	150108
17021	EAST WATERFORD	16622	388	30.2	39.4	27.6	2.8	0.0	35130	36272	18	9	329	14.3	22.8	37.7	18.2	7.0	111859
17022	ELIZABETHTOWN	26954	11405	13.2	23.0	48.4	11.6	3.8	62440	65919	81	82	8124	4.9	2.2	32.0	56.0	4.7	192312
17023	ELIZABETHVILLE	21949	1278	23.4	27.2	41.9	6.1	1.4	49485	53193	60	61	929	5.7	14.9	48.3	27.9	3.2	137352
17024	ELLIOTTSBURG	21530	784	20.2	28.4	43.6	5.9	1.9	51035	53867	64	64	652	4.3	9.4	42.6	36.7	7.1	162651
17025	ENOLA	28797	6999	12.1	27.1	46.5	10.8	3.5	60833	64416	79	79	4908	1.3	4.1	47.9	43.4	3.4	169302
17026	FREDERICKSBURG	20706	1085	21.0	27.2	43.8	6.0	2.0	50935	52606	63	64	875	8.3	4.0	38.7	43.0	5.9	173241
17028	GRANTVILLE	27825	1289	10.5	29.4	45.4	8.1	6.6	60388	61269	78	79	1131	17.1	11.2	22.9	41.6	7.2	171208
17029	GRANVILLE	17345	196	19.4	40.8	34.2	5.6	0.0	43285	46524	43	40	162	8.6	19.1	49.4	21.6	1.2	123333
17030	GRATZ	20259	289	23.2	31.8	39.1	3.8	2.1	45150	50170	49	47	223	7.6	18.8	45.7	21.1	6.7	127917
17032	HALIFAX	23725	3056	19.1	24.6	47.3	7.1	1.9	55845	57745	72	72	2548	10.6	10.1	43.1	33.3	2.9	151475
17033	HERSHEY	34074	6426	16.7	22.9	39.0	11.8	9.6	61141	62593	79	80	3801	4.8	1.8	22.0	56.7	14.7	231707
17034	HIGHSPIRE	25177	1059	19.5	37.3	37.9	4.0	1.3	44976	47909	48	45	609	9.9	14.4	66.0	9.7	0.0	124896
17035	HONEY GROVE	18000	357	29.7	34.5	30.8	3.1	2.0	36874	40176	23	13	296	17.9	17.6	38.9	17.2	8.4	117742
17036	HUMMELSTOWN	36510	8382	9.7	19.4	42.6	14.6	13.7	74615	74905	89	91	5995	1.8	2.2	29.0	53.1	13.9	222182
17037	ICKESBURG	19831	338	18.6	32.2	43.5	4.7	0.9	49356	52664	60	60	289	5.2	12.5	43.3	31.5	7.6	154276
17038	JONESTOWN	22778	2647	17.5	30.5	43.0	6.7	2.3	51427	53416	65	65	2039	5.1	4.8	38.6	46.5	5.0	177793
17040	LANDISBURG	22816	923	18.4	27.8	44.4	6.9	2.4	53041	55662	68	68	790	5.6	8.2	41.8	38.9	5.6	164423
17042	LEBANON	26708	15302	16.9	27.1	41.6	9.8	4.6	55637	57116	72	72	11086	1.1	7.2	43.6	40.1	8.0	171773
17043	LEMOYNE	32308	2938	13.7	34.8	40.6	6.0	4.9	51076	54228	64	65	1590	0.1	3.1	59.9	27.9	9.0	153333
17044	LEWISTOWN	20358	8779	32.9	31.0	29.6	4.5	1.9	38237	40484	27	18	5739	10.6	22.2	48.9	16.8	1.5	113113
17045	LIVERPOOL	21393	1163	20.3	30.5	41.0	6.0	2.1	49236	51014	59	60	1127	5.4	11.4	49.0	29.5	4.6	146470
17046	LEBANON	19711	12219	28.0	30.8	35.2	4.7	1.4	41740	45141	38	34	7909	8.0	16.3	43.1	29.6	3.0	137719
17047	LOYSVILLE	18656	885	26.1	30.3	36.5	6.0	1.1	44299	48320	46	44	701	4.4	12.0	46.4	29.2	8.0	148646
17048	LYKENS	21238	1801	24.5	31.0	38.5	4.4	1.6	45674	49234	50	49	1406	14.9	31.8	40.5	11.4	1.4	94340
17049	MC ALISTERVILLE	18271	1532	27.8	39.1	27.0	4.4	1.6	36449	38051	22	12	1199	5.9	15.0	47.5	31.4	0.3	143850
17050	MECHANICSBURG	36632	12312	7.5	19.4	43.8	16.9	12.4	76070	78735	90	92	10364	7.1	1.7	20.1	60.0	11.0	233841
17051	MC VEYTOWN	18789	2084	29.3	31.6	34.1	3.4	1.6	41352	44789	37	32	1776	11.5	19.4	46.5	20.0	2.6	124177
17052	MAPLETON DEPOT	18578	507	27.6	34.3	33.5	4.5	0.0	39452	42013	31	24	443	25.1	29.3	38.4	6.8	0.5	83906
17053	MARYSVILLE	26782	1967	18.4	22.2	46.6	9.2	3.7	58879	60252	76	77	1566	5.3	6.4	47.1	36.5	4.7	161782
17055	MECHANICSBURG	30717	14537	12.3	22.4	46.9	11.9	6.5	66453	71323	85	88	10457	2.3	1.9	32.9	55.8	7.1	200861
17057	MIDDLETOWN	25111	9122	17.2	31.3	41.8	7.5	2.2	51436	54415	65	66	6294	13.3	8.2	49.1	26.9	2.5	142113
17058	MIFFLIN	19534	693	27.3	32.5	35.6	3.8	0.9	40342	42681	34	27	481	10.4	18.9	43.9	21.4	5.4	133971
17059	MIFFLINTOWN	19862	2408	23.2	35.4	34.9	4.2	2.2	42557	43887	41	37	1885	8.3	13.4	42.0	32.8	3.6	147537
17060	MILL CREEK	16203	398	33.9	31.9	28.9	4.3	1.0	34780	36751	17	8	329	21.0	24.3	39.2	14.0	1.5	99688
17061	MILLERSBURG	22527	2850	22.1	29.5	43.4	4.1	0.9	48399	52369	58	58	2014	8.1	14.4	50.3	23.5	3.5	136721
17062	MILLERSTOWN	24713	726	18.5	22.7	48.8	6.9	3.2	56488	58258	73	73	592	2.0	6.1	54.1	32.6	5.2	159071
17063	MILROY	17370	1448	28.5	33.2	36.7	1.4	0.1	42598	45660	41	38	1190	11.8	10.4	57.1	19.8	0.8	125717
17065	MOUNT HOLLY SPRINGS	27148	1722	12.9	26.5	49.6	9.2	1.8	62247	66089	80	82	1343	7.8	6.5	48.6	33.7	3.4	155103
17066	MOUNT UNION	18239	2305	40.3	27.7	28.0	3.3	0.7	33137	35108	14	5	1550	21.0	32.7	38.2	7.2	0.8	84957
17067	MYERSTOWN	22038	5409	17.4	31.7	41.2	7.0	2.6	50623	52908	63	63	4227	7.5	9.0	34.4	42.5	6.7	173421
17068	NEW BLOOMFIELD	23325	1525	17.1	29.6	43.4	8.1	1.8	52590	55290	67	68	1233	8.2	7.0	41.9	39.4	3.5	163364
17070	NEW CUMBERLAND	33288	6912	11.7	24.9	43.6	14.0	5.9	63192	66413	81	83	5220	4.8	2.5	36.6	51.3	4.9	186294
17071	NEW GERMANTOWN	20415	213	24.9	36.2	32.9	3.3	2.8	41135	44785	36	31	174	10.9	19.5	35.6	27.6	6.3	134722
17073	NEWMANSTOWN	25052	1860	14.6	28.0	46.0	7.0	4.4	57275	59073	74	75	1499	0.9	3.7	41.6	43.2	10.6	182646
	PENNSYLVANIA	26913		21.5	25.3	36.9	10.2	6.1	53225	55819				7.5	12.2	35.6	36.1	8.5	161438
	UNITED STATES	27277		20.9	24.4	35.3	11.7	7.6	54719	56938				9.3	13.1	31.6	32.6	13.5	162279

ZIP CODE #	POST OFFICE NAME	FINANCIAL SERVICES Auto Loan	Home Loan	Invest-ments	Retire-ment Plans	THE HOME Home Improvements: Home Repair	Lawn & Garden	Furnishings: Comput-ers & Hard-ware-Personal	Major Appli-ances	TV, Radio, Sound Equip-ment	Furni-ture	ENTERTAINMENT Dine out/ Carry out	Sports Equip-ment	Fees & Tickets	Toys & Games	Travel	Cable TV	PERSONAL Apparel & Services	Auto Repairs	Health Insur-ance	Pets & Supplies
16875	SPRING MILLS	89	84	82	87	85	96	81	90	83	75	82	68	77	85	82	87	56	84	93	105
16877	WARRIORS MARK	100	100	97	103	101	108	93	103	94	89	93	78	92	96	96	97	65	96	103	119
16878	WEST DECATUR	77	55	69	54	56	75	57	69	64	55	62	52	46	65	54	70	42	64	72	83
16879	WINBURNE	73	75	58	76	69	78	75	72	75	71	75	57	75	77	72	77	52	73	80	88
16881	WOODLAND	84	60	69	59	60	80	63	73	70	61	68	56	50	72	57	76	46	69	77	89
16882	WOODWARD	84	76	76	80	78	90	75	85	78	68	76	64	69	79	75	82	52	79	88	99
16901	WELLSBORO	81	70	80	70	72	86	70	81	74	66	73	60	64	74	71	79	49	76	85	94
16912	BLOSSBURG	86	63	85	61	65	90	68	83	75	61	73	62	55	74	66	83	49	78	91	98
16914	COLUMBIA CROSS ROADS	78	71	70	74	72	83	70	79	72	63	71	59	64	73	70	76	48	73	81	91
16915	COUDERSPORT	98	81	102	81	85	101	84	97	88	78	86	72	74	86	84	93	58	92	101	113
16917	COVINGTON	82	59	85	57	61	84	61	77	67	56	66	58	48	67	60	74	44	71	80	92
16920	ELKLAND	76	55	77	54	57	80	60	74	67	54	65	55	48	66	58	74	43	69	81	87
16921	GAINES	76	54	78	53	57	77	56	71	62	52	61	53	45	62	55	68	40	65	74	85
16922	GALETON	77	58	87	57	62	81	61	77	66	56	65	57	51	64	62	72	43	71	80	89
16923	GENESEE	89	64	88	62	66	90	66	82	73	62	72	62	53	73	64	80	48	76	86	98
16925	GILLETT	82	66	80	66	68	85	66	80	71	61	70	60	57	71	66	77	47	73	82	94
16926	GRANVILLE SUMMIT	83	57	91	57	59	87	63	78	66	51	65	65	46	64	63	72	42	73	83	96
16927	HARRISON VALLEY	72	52	60	50	52	69	54	63	60	53	59	48	43	62	49	65	39	59	66	76
16928	KNOXVILLE	84	64	82	64	66	88	68	82	74	61	72	61	57	74	66	81	48	76	88	96
16929	LAWRENCEVILLE	85	61	70	59	61	81	63	74	70	62	69	57	51	73	58	77	46	70	78	90
16930	LIBERTY	79	72	71	75	73	85	71	80	73	64	72	61	65	75	71	77	49	74	83	93
16932	MAINESBURG	76	69	68	71	70	81	68	77	70	61	69	58	62	71	68	74	47	71	79	89
16933	MANSFIELD	77	60	68	61	61	72	71	71	71	64	71	56	60	72	64	74	49	72	74	86
16935	MIDDLEBURY CENTER	84	62	84	61	64	85	63	79	70	59	68	59	52	70	62	76	45	72	82	94
16936	MILLERTON	72	66	65	68	67	77	65	73	67	58	65	55	60	68	65	71	45	67	75	85
16937	MILLS	73	52	60	51	52	69	55	63	60	53	59	49	44	63	50	66	40	60	67	77
16938	MORRIS	83	62	83	61	64	85	63	78	69	58	68	59	52	69	62	75	45	72	81	93
16939	MORRIS RUN	72	52	74	50	54	74	53	68	59	50	58	51	43	59	53	65	38	62	70	81
16940	NELSON	82	59	83	57	61	83	61	76	67	57	66	57	49	67	59	74	44	70	80	91
16941	GENESEE	68	49	56	47	48	64	51	59	56	49	55	45	41	58	46	61	37	56	62	72
16942	OSCEOLA	86	62	71	60	62	82	64	75	72	63	70	58	52	75	59	78	47	71	79	91
16943	SABINSVILLE	80	58	82	56	60	82	59	75	66	55	64	56	47	65	58	72	42	69	78	89
16946	TIOGA	84	62	78	61	63	83	67	78	73	62	71	59	55	73	63	79	48	74	83	93
16947	TROY	86	66	86	66	68	88	70	82	74	64	73	63	59	74	69	80	49	78	87	98
16948	ULYSSES	78	56	71	55	57	76	58	70	65	56	63	53	47	66	55	71	42	66	73	84
16950	WESTFIELD	75	54	74	52	56	76	57	71	63	52	62	53	46	63	55	69	41	65	75	84
17002	ALLENSVILLE	78	55	74	54	56	78	59	71	64	53	63	56	45	65	56	69	41	67	75	86
17003	ANNVILLE	101	95	94	97	95	105	95	101	97	90	96	77	91	98	94	100	66	97	104	118
17004	BELLEVILLE	79	59	81	59	62	82	61	76	66	55	65	58	50	66	61	72	43	70	79	90
17005	BERRYSBURG	81	74	73	77	76	87	73	83	75	66	74	62	67	77	73	80	51	76	85	96
17006	BLAIN	90	64	92	62	67	91	66	84	73	61	72	63	53	73	65	81	48	77	87	100
17007	BOILING SPRINGS	107	123	111	127	121	120	109	114	107	111	107	88	118	109	117	106	75	109	112	133
17009	BURNHAM	80	67	75	67	66	84	70	78	75	64	73	60	62	74	68	80	49	75	86	93
17011	CAMP HILL	105	115	115	116	117	121	108	113	111	109	111	82	116	108	115	115	78	112	123	131
17013	CARLISLE	90	90	86	91	89	94	92	91	93	88	93	70	92	93	91	96	65	92	97	108
17014	COCOLAMUS	80	73	72	76	74	86	72	81	74	65	73	61	66	76	72	79	50	75	84	94
17015	CARLISLE	101	102	97	103	101	109	96	103	98	94	98	77	96	99	98	102	67	99	107	121
17017	DALMATIA	82	74	74	77	76	88	73	83	76	66	74	63	68	77	73	80	51	76	85	96
17018	DAUPHIN	100	123	110	122	118	122	105	110	107	106	108	82	120	108	116	110	76	108	118	128
17019	DILLSBURG	101	106	92	108	102	105	100	101	99	99	99	78	102	102	101	100	69	99	101	120
17020	DUNCANNON	85	77	73	78	77	83	79	82	81	76	80	62	74	82	76	84	55	80	85	97
17021	EAST WATERFORD	73	53	72	51	54	73	54	68	60	51	59	51	43	60	53	66	39	62	71	81
17022	ELIZABETHTOWN	95	100	92	101	98	100	96	96	97	96	97	73	100	97	98	99	68	97	101	114
17023	ELIZABETHVILLE	82	78	72	81	77	88	77	83	79	71	78	64	73	81	76	83	53	79	87	98
17024	ELLIOTTSBURG	86	78	78	81	80	92	78	87	80	71	79	66	72	81	77	85	54	81	90	101
17025	ENOLA	91	97	87	98	93	96	95	92	96	93	96	72	99	96	96	97	67	95	98	110
17026	FREDERICKSBURG	86	80	78	83	81	92	78	87	80	72	79	66	73	82	79	84	54	81	89	101
17028	GRANTVILLE	104	106	93	106	103	106	97	102	98	99	98	77	98	101	98	100	68	99	102	121
17029	GRANVILLE	85	61	70	59	60	80	63	73	70	62	69	56	51	73	57	76	46	70	78	89
17030	GRATZ	79	72	71	75	73	85	71	80	73	64	72	60	65	74	71	77	49	74	82	93
17032	HALIFAX	92	87	84	90	87	100	85	94	87	78	86	71	80	89	85	92	59	88	98	110
17033	HERSHEY	109	111	111	113	112	115	110	111	112	111	112	82	113	110	113	114	78	112	119	130
17034	HIGHSPIRE	78	67	68	68	68	76	77	76	80	72	78	57	70	79	71	83	54	78	83	90
17035	HONEY GROVE	85	61	70	59	60	80	63	73	70	61	69	56	51	73	57	76	46	70	77	89
17036	HUMMELSTOWN	128	137	129	141	135	130	132	129	130	135	131	102	139	132	135	128	93	130	127	152
17037	ICKESBURG	82	75	74	78	76	88	74	83	76	67	75	63	68	77	74	80	51	77	86	97
17038	JONESTOWN	91	83	82	86	84	97	82	92	84	74	83	70	75	86	81	89	56	85	95	107
17040	LANDISBURG	90	82	81	85	84	97	81	91	84	73	82	69	75	85	81	88	56	84	94	106
17042	LEBANON	91	94	89	95	93	100	91	94	93	89	92	71	93	93	93	96	64	93	101	111
17043	LEMOYNE	92	86	80	88	84	90	94	89	95	89	94	69	90	95	88	97	65	93	96	107
17044	LEWISTOWN	72	61	65	61	61	74	65	70	69	60	67	53	58	69	62	73	46	68	76	83
17045	LIVERPOOL	84	76	76	78	77	88	76	84	79	70	77	63	70	80	76	83	53	79	88	98
17046	LEBANON	73	64	62	66	63	72	70	70	73	65	72	54	65	73	66	76	50	71	76	84
17047	LOYSVILLE	84	64	87	65	67	88	69	82	72	60	71	65	56	71	69	77	47	77	86	98
17048	LYKENS	84	66	78	67	68	87	71	82	77	64	74	62	61	77	68	83	50	78	88	96
17049	MC ALISTERVILLE	73	66	66	69	68	78	65	74	68	59	66	56	60	69	65	72	45	68	76	86
17050	MECHANICSBURG	126	145	138	148	144	138	130	133	127	135	128	102	142	128	139	125	91	129	129	155
17051	MC VEYTOWN	80	63	75	64	65	82	64	76	69	59	68	58	55	70	63	75	45	71	80	90
17052	MAPLETON DEPOT	80	57	81	55	59	82	60	76	67	55	65	57	48	66	59	73	43	70	80	89
17053	MARYSVILLE	91	91	83	94	90	96	90	91	90	87	90	70	90	91	90	92	62	90	96	108
17055	MECHANICSBURG	102	110	104	112	109	110	107	106	107	106	107	81	112	106	110	108	75	107	111	124
17057	MIDDLETOWN	87	83	77	83	81	88	85	85	86	82	86	65	82	87	82	89	59	85	90	101
17058	MIFFLIN	72	65	65	68	67	77	65	73	67	58	65	55	59	68	64	70	45	67	75	85
17059	MIFFLINTOWN	79	69	71	71	70	82	71	78	73	64	72	60	64	74	69	77	49	74	81	92
17060	MILL CREEK	77	55	64	54	55	73	58	67	64	56	63	51	46	67	52	70	42	63	71	81
17061	MILLERSBURG	85	72	77	73	73	88	75	84	78	67	77	64	66	79	73	84	52	79	88	98
17062	MILLERSTOWN	90	89	87	91	90	102	84	94	88	79	87	69	84	88	87	93	60	88	101	109
17063	MILROY	75	57	63	57	58	74	59	68	64	56	63	52	49	66	55	69	42	64	71	82
17065	MOUNT HOLLY SPRINGS	91	95	77	97	89	98	92	91	93	88	92	72	93	95	91	95	64	91	98	110
17066	MOUNT UNION	65	49	59	48	50	64	55	61	60	51	59	46	46	60	51	66	40	60	67	73
17067	MYERSTOWN	91	80	84	81	80	96	80	89	83	74	82	68	73	84	79	88	56	84	94	106
17068	NEW BLOOMFIELD	91	82	80	83	83	93	82	89	84	78	83	67	76	86	80	88	57	85	92	104
17070	NEW CUMBERLAND	102	110	104	110	109	112	104	106	105	104	105	79	109	105	108	107	73	105	112	124
17071	NEW GERMANTOWN	90	64	92	62	67	91	66	84	73	61	72	63	53	73	65	80	47	77	87	100
17073	NEWMANSTOWN	98	94	85	97	92	105	93	98	94	86	93	76	89	96	92	98	64	94	104	116
	PENNSYLVANIA	94	95	95	95	95	100	94	96	96	91	95	73	94	96	94	99	67	95	101	113
	UNITED STATES	100	100	100	100	100	100	100	100	100	100	100	100	100	100	100	100	100	100	100	100

ZIP CODE #	POST OFFICE NAME	COUNTY FIPS CODE	POPULATION 2000	POPULATION 2009	POPULATION 2014	2000-2009 ANNUAL RATE % Rate	2000-2009 ANNUAL RATE State Centile	HOUSEHOLDS 2000	HOUSEHOLDS 2009	HOUSEHOLDS 2014	HOUSEHOLDS % Annual Rate 2000-2009	HOUSEHOLDS 2009 Average HH Size	FAMILIES 2000	FAMILIES 2009	FAMILIES % Annual Rate 2000-2009
17074	NEWPORT	099	8857	9486	9754	0.7	77	3446	3794	3938	1.0	2.49	2521	2705	0.8
17076	OAKLAND MILLS	067	490	492	488	0.0	52	163	166	166	0.2	2.88	119	117	-0.2
17078	PALMYRA	075	17552	18865	19548	0.8	80	7341	8020	8359	1.0	2.31	5009	5303	0.6
17080	PILLOW	043	304	318	324	0.5	70	131	140	143	0.7	2.26	100	104	0.4
17082	PORT ROYAL	067	3580	3650	3656	0.2	61	1328	1376	1385	0.4	2.63	1005	1019	0.1
17084	REEDSVILLE	087	4041	4294	4317	0.7	77	1481	1586	1607	0.7	2.64	1138	1188	0.5
17086	RICHFIELD	109	1810	1817	1815	0.0	52	644	657	658	0.2	2.72	518	518	0.0
17087	RICHLAND	011	2833	3043	3165	0.8	80	999	1095	1147	1.0	2.75	775	828	0.7
17090	SHERMANS DALE	099	5350	5921	6177	1.1	87	1979	2267	2388	1.5	2.61	1540	1727	1.2
17094	THOMPSONTOWN	067	2741	2723	2703	-0.1	46	1105	1120	1118	0.1	2.38	801	793	-0.1
17097	WICONISCO	043	67	66	66	-0.2	38	28	28	28	0.0	2.36	20	19	-0.6
17098	WILLIAMSTOWN	043	2568	2488	2458	-0.3	29	1065	1047	1039	-0.2	2.38	745	708	-0.5
17099	YEAGERTOWN	087	1112	1126	1124	0.1	57	453	472	475	0.4	2.38	333	336	0.1
17101	HARRISBURG	043	1901	1900	1899	0.0	52	1444	1483	1497	0.3	1.20	190	177	-0.8
17102	HARRISBURG	043	8266	8209	8199	-0.1	46	4199	4217	4228	0.0	1.82	1381	1309	-0.6
17103	HARRISBURG	043	11176	10813	10679	-0.4	23	4403	4314	4282	-0.2	2.47	2753	2584	-0.7
17104	HARRISBURG	043	21473	20630	20342	-0.4	23	8020	7820	7742	-0.3	2.55	5124	4803	-0.7
17109	HARRISBURG	043	23069	22818	22705	-0.1	46	10364	10384	10376	0.0	2.13	5883	5612	-0.5
17110	HARRISBURG	043	22537	23751	24215	0.6	74	9048	9703	9947	0.8	2.38	5670	5851	0.3
17111	HARRISBURG	043	26311	27450	27951	0.5	70	10597	11216	11459	0.6	2.31	6978	7110	0.2
17112	HARRISBURG	043	30615	32656	33437	0.7	77	11864	12894	13271	0.9	2.52	8868	9396	0.6
17113	HARRISBURG	043	11091	11236	11243	0.1	57	4483	4535	4549	0.1	2.47	2928	2853	-0.3
17201	CHAMBERSBURG	055	22023	24286	25403	1.1	87	9471	10709	11298	1.3	2.16	5632	6129	0.9
17202	CHAMBERSBURG	055	26122	29263	31135	1.2	88	9806	11338	12180	1.6	2.53	7523	8475	1.3
17211	ARTEMAS	009	360	541	580	4.5	99	144	219	237	4.6	2.47	111	165	4.4
17212	BIG COVE TANNERY	057	792	813	820	0.3	64	301	322	329	0.7	2.52	227	235	0.4
17213	BLAIRS MILLS	061	648	651	633	0.0	52	238	244	239	0.3	2.65	180	180	0.0
17214	BLUE RIDGE SUMMIT	055	989	1103	1167	1.2	88	436	503	538	1.6	2.19	277	307	1.1
17215	BURNT CABINS	057	134	145	149	0.9	83	61	69	72	1.3	2.06	45	50	1.1
17217	CONCORD	055	9	10	11	1.1	87	4	5	5	2.4	2.00	3	3	0.0
17219	DOYLESBURG	055	432	486	515	1.3	90	146	169	181	1.6	2.79	111	125	1.3
17220	DRY RUN	055	196	222	237	1.4	91	65	76	81	1.7	2.87	49	56	1.5
17221	FANNETTSBURG	055	619	722	777	1.7	93	245	293	318	2.0	2.46	180	210	1.7
17222	FAYETTEVILLE	055	9010	10496	11161	1.7	93	3550	4279	4604	2.0	2.36	2686	3165	1.8
17223	FORT LITTLETON	057	393	436	454	1.1	87	158	183	193	1.6	2.33	117	132	1.3
17224	FORT LOUDON	055	1583	1815	1937	1.5	92	641	752	808	1.7	2.41	484	553	1.5
17225	GREENCASTLE	055	16164	18308	19482	1.4	91	6131	7123	7636	1.6	2.57	4665	5300	1.4
17228	HARRISONVILLE	057	1050	1092	1122	0.4	68	392	424	440	0.9	2.58	292	308	0.6
17229	HUSTONTOWN	057	1233	1243	1306	0.1	57	478	500	532	0.5	2.46	352	359	0.2
17232	LURGAN	055	45	48	49	0.7	77	19	21	22	1.1	2.29	15	16	0.7
17233	MC CONNELLSBURG	057	4660	4678	4691	0.0	52	1924	1996	2021	0.4	2.31	1315	1324	0.1
17236	MERCERSBURG	055	8017	8756	9177	1.0	85	3094	3479	3675	1.3	2.52	2358	2587	1.0
17237	MONT ALTO	055	1122	1280	1371	1.4	91	452	529	571	1.7	2.41	348	397	1.4
17238	NEEDMORE	057	1758	1963	2040	1.2	88	674	778	820	1.6	2.52	509	574	1.3
17239	NEELYTON	061	923	916	902	-0.1	46	340	349	348	0.3	2.61	256	256	0.0
17240	NEWBURG	041	3067	3316	3447	0.8	80	1009	1098	1146	0.9	3.02	846	905	0.7
17241	NEWVILLE	041	11739	12608	13098	0.8	80	4333	4792	5024	1.1	2.59	3396	3662	0.8
17243	ORBISONIA	061	2147	2164	2167	0.1	57	834	867	876	0.4	2.36	576	582	0.1
17244	ORRSTOWN	055	2535	2765	2893	0.9	83	940	1055	1113	1.3	2.61	745	818	1.0
17246	PLEASANT HALL	055	69	75	78	0.9	83	27	30	32	1.1	2.50	21	23	1.0
17252	SAINT THOMAS	055	3494	3824	4013	1.0	85	1320	1486	1572	1.3	2.56	1022	1124	1.0
17255	SHADE GAP	061	438	434	427	-0.1	46	172	176	175	0.2	2.45	130	129	-0.1
17257	SHIPPENSBURG	041	23108	26845	28519	1.6	92	7852	9259	9942	1.8	2.62	5156	5990	1.6
17260	SHIRLEYSBURG	061	1383	1368	1363	-0.1	46	530	544	547	0.3	2.43	395	394	0.0
17262	SPRING RUN	055	1952	2197	2336	1.3	90	704	815	874	1.6	2.66	534	602	1.3
17264	THREE SPRINGS	061	2679	2926	2912	1.0	85	1079	1224	1230	1.4	2.37	790	871	1.1
17265	UPPERSTRASBURG	055	169	183	192	0.9	83	67	75	79	1.2	2.44	53	58	1.0
17266	WALNUT BOTTOM	041	490	527	554	0.8	80	186	207	220	1.2	2.48	145	156	0.8
17267	WARFORDSBURG	057	2615	2725	2768	0.4	68	1013	1098	1129	0.9	2.48	764	808	0.6
17268	WAYNESBORO	055	26939	29752	31333	1.1	87	10590	12038	12792	1.4	2.41	7494	8305	1.1
17271	WILLOW HILL	055	468	544	584	1.6	92	159	189	205	1.9	2.86	117	136	1.6
17301	ABBOTTSTOWN	001	3403	3804	4015	1.2	88	1210	1375	1460	1.4	2.74	953	1056	1.1
17302	AIRVILLE	133	2843	3157	3339	1.1	87	1004	1132	1203	1.3	2.79	793	873	1.0
17304	ASPERS	001	3183	3562	3766	1.2	88	1115	1262	1340	1.3	2.80	860	948	1.1
17307	BIGLERVILLE	001	5723	6589	7014	1.5	92	2142	2497	2671	1.7	2.61	1625	1843	1.4
17309	BROGUE	133	2176	2329	2424	0.7	77	825	902	946	1.0	2.58	655	700	0.7
17313	DALLASTOWN	133	10620	11531	12061	0.9	83	4342	4772	5018	1.0	2.36	2957	3131	0.6
17314	DELTA	133	5581	6533	7044	1.7	93	1967	2335	2531	1.9	2.79	1520	1756	1.6
17315	DOVER	133	22547	25736	27487	1.4	91	8731	10166	10921	1.7	2.50	6474	7309	1.3
17316	EAST BERLIN	001	7256	7818	8063	0.8	80	2640	2889	2999	1.0	2.70	2070	2208	0.7
17319	ETTERS	133	9551	10893	11675	1.4	91	3508	4065	4377	1.6	2.68	2706	3057	1.3
17320	FAIRFIELD	001	6976	8412	9098	2.0	95	2607	3181	3454	2.2	2.62	2015	2397	1.9
17321	FAWN GROVE	133	1970	2470	2708	2.5	97	704	911	1005	2.8	2.71	567	718	2.6
17322	FELTON	133	5704	6339	6708	1.1	87	2030	2303	2455	1.4	2.75	1639	1817	1.1
17324	GARDNERS	041	4328	4620	4783	0.7	77	1604	1756	1832	1.0	2.62	1233	1312	0.7
17325	GETTYSBURG	001	25238	27516	28466	0.9	83	9247	10194	10632	1.1	2.41	6232	6686	0.8
17327	GLEN ROCK	133	7271	7869	8245	0.9	83	2736	3007	3170	1.0	2.61	2139	2296	0.8
17329	GLENVILLE	133	2152	2359	2490	1.0	85	763	856	910	1.3	2.76	645	712	1.1
17331	HANOVER	133	43990	50922	54450	1.6	92	17404	20415	21933	1.7	2.46	12237	14110	1.6
17339	LEWISBERRY	133	5539	6589	7140	1.9	94	2044	2485	2712	2.1	2.61	1607	1908	1.9
17340	LITTLESTOWN	001	9832	11577	12413	1.8	93	3650	4341	4671	1.9	2.65	2824	3277	1.6
17344	MC SHERRYSTOWN	001	3312	3544	3669	0.7	77	1403	1525	1587	0.9	2.31	912	952	0.5
17345	MANCHESTER	133	7518	8426	9040	1.2	88	2987	3415	3688	1.5	2.46	2195	2434	1.1
17347	MOUNT WOLF	133	3521	4593	5027	2.9	98	1380	1804	1982	2.9	2.54	1013	1288	2.6
17349	NEW FREEDOM	133	7122	7692	8055	0.8	80	2569	2838	2993	1.1	2.68	2038	2197	0.8
17350	NEW OXFORD	001	11999	13078	13538	0.9	83	4359	4809	5004	1.1	2.62	3221	3446	0.7
17352	NEW PARK	133	1250	1452	1593	1.6	92	454	528	581	1.6	2.75	371	423	1.4
17353	ORRTANNA	001	2851	3270	3473	1.5	92	1080	1262	1351	1.7	2.52	818	930	1.4
17356	RED LION	133	18077	22377	24441	2.3	96	7025	8771	9615	2.4	2.54	5142	6288	2.2
17360	SEVEN VALLEYS	133	4800	5106	5318	0.7	77	1784	1941	2038	0.9	2.63	1384	1469	0.6
17361	SHREWSBURY	133	4854	5626	6031	1.6	92	1887	2224	2398	1.8	2.51	1394	1599	1.5
17362	SPRING GROVE	133	12649	13716	14404	0.9	83	4630	5134	5429	1.1	2.66	3707	4020	0.9
17363	STEWARTSTOWN	133	8138	9598	10357	1.8	93	2912	3462	3746	1.9	2.77	2357	2745	1.7
17364	THOMASVILLE	133	2978	3188	3321	0.7	77	1109	1213	1273	1.0	2.61	864	922	0.7
17365	WELLSVILLE	133	2422	2641	2771	0.9	83	958	1068	1131	1.2	2.46	737	801	0.9
	PENNSYLVANIA					0.3					0.4	2.45			0.1
	UNITED STATES					1.0					1.1	2.59			0.9

ZIP CODE #	POST OFFICE NAME	RACE (%) White 2000	White 2009	Black 2000	Black 2009	Asian/Pacific 2000	Asian/Pacific 2009	% Hispanic Origin 2000	% Hispanic Origin 2009	2009 AGE DISTRIBUTION (%) 0-4	5-9	10-14	15-19	20-24	25-44	45-64	65-84	85+	18+	MEDIAN AGE 2009	% 2009 Males	% 2009 Females
17074	NEWPORT	98.3	97.9	0.4	0.5	0.2	0.3	0.8	1.1	5.9	6.1	6.3	6.7	5.7	25.6	30.0	12.2	1.5	77.5	40.8	49.9	50.1
17076	OAKLAND MILLS	98.8	98.2	0.4	0.4	0.2	0.4	0.6	1.0	7.7	7.7	7.7	7.1	4.9	24.8	25.0	12.4	2.6	72.6	38.1	49.2	50.8
17078	PALMYRA	97.1	96.0	0.7	0.9	1.0	1.6	1.1	1.7	5.9	6.2	6.4	6.0	4.9	24.7	28.6	14.0	3.2	77.6	42.3	47.5	52.5
17080	PILLOW	99.3	98.1	0.7	1.3	0.0	0.0	0.0	0.0	6.6	7.2	7.2	6.0	4.4	24.8	28.3	13.5	1.9	74.5	40.8	51.3	48.7
17082	PORT ROYAL	97.0	96.0	0.9	1.0	0.3	0.4	2.5	3.5	6.2	6.4	6.6	6.6	5.1	26.6	28.1	12.7	1.7	76.7	39.8	49.9	50.1
17084	REEDSVILLE	98.7	98.1	0.3	0.4	0.5	0.8	0.3	0.5	6.9	7.2	7.3	6.7	4.8	23.7	26.8	13.8	2.7	74.2	40.3	49.2	50.8
17086	RICHFIELD	99.2	99.0	0.3	0.4	0.1	0.1	0.3	0.4	6.5	6.6	6.8	7.0	5.1	25.9	25.7	14.0	2.4	75.6	40.2	50.7	49.3
17087	RICHLAND	97.7	96.7	0.7	0.9	0.3	0.4	1.2	2.0	6.8	7.2	7.4	6.9	4.7	25.3	27.8	12.0	1.9	74.2	39.4	50.6	49.4
17090	SHERMANS DALE	98.9	98.6	0.2	0.3	0.1	0.1	0.6	0.8	6.7	7.0	7.2	6.4	4.7	29.5	29.4	8.5	0.6	75.1	37.9	49.9	50.1
17094	THOMPSONTOWN	99.3	99.0	0.1	0.1	0.1	0.2	0.3	0.3	6.2	6.5	6.5	5.3	4.1	25.7	28.2	15.0	2.5	77.4	41.8	48.1	51.9
17097	WICONISCO	100.0	98.5	0.0	0.0	0.0	1.5	0.0	0.0	6.1	6.1	6.1	6.1	6.1	24.2	24.2	18.2	3.0	77.3	41.3	48.5	51.5
17098	WILLIAMSTOWN	98.8	98.2	0.2	0.2	0.1	0.2	0.6	1.0	5.2	5.6	6.2	6.3	4.4	25.5	29.5	14.8	2.5	79.1	42.7	49.8	50.2
17099	YEAGERTOWN	98.1	97.5	0.4	0.5	0.4	0.6	0.6	0.8	6.7	6.6	6.6	6.2	5.1	26.3	26.7	14.0	1.9	76.4	39.8	48.9	51.1
17101	HARRISBURG	62.1	51.6	29.7	37.8	2.3	3.3	4.7	6.5	2.4	1.7	1.4	2.2	5.4	29.2	31.8	20.6	5.2	93.9	49.5	51.3	48.7
17102	HARRISBURG	44.3	35.6	46.9	53.7	1.7	2.3	6.1	7.6	5.7	5.0	4.3	4.9	7.2	30.8	27.9	11.0	3.2	82.3	39.7	49.7	50.3
17103	HARRISBURG	30.0	25.3	60.8	64.3	1.3	1.6	7.4	8.7	7.9	7.7	7.4	7.9	7.3	26.5	24.4	9.5	1.3	72.2	34.0	46.1	53.9
17104	HARRISBURG	32.5	25.4	48.3	52.2	4.7	5.7	18.0	20.8	9.6	8.7	7.6	7.7	8.0	25.8	23.2	8.0	1.3	69.4	31.0	46.8	53.2
17109	HARRISBURG	77.7	69.8	15.6	20.8	2.9	4.4	3.2	4.7	5.3	5.1	5.1	5.4	6.5	27.5	26.6	14.9	3.6	81.2	41.3	46.9	53.1
17110	HARRISBURG	57.7	52.8	36.1	39.5	1.9	2.8	3.8	4.6	6.2	6.2	6.3	6.7	6.6	25.4	30.2	10.7	1.7	77.1	39.9	47.1	52.9
17111	HARRISBURG	81.3	75.0	13.1	17.2	2.2	3.4	3.5	5.1	5.7	5.8	6.0	6.4	6.1	27.5	28.6	12.0	2.1	78.5	40.2	48.7	51.3
17112	HARRISBURG	93.3	89.9	3.3	4.9	1.9	3.1	1.3	2.1	5.1	5.6	6.4	6.8	4.7	23.2	33.2	13.1	1.8	78.4	43.7	48.7	51.3
17113	HARRISBURG	68.0	58.8	25.9	33.2	0.8	1.1	7.2	10.0	6.7	6.6	6.6	7.4	7.3	23.7	26.7	12.5	2.5	75.7	38.4	46.4	53.6
17201	CHAMBERSBURG	88.3	85.7	6.5	7.5	0.9	1.3	5.5	7.2	5.9	5.6	5.6	6.1	6.0	24.3	24.9	16.3	5.3	79.3	42.1	45.6	54.4
17202	CHAMBERSBURG	96.0	94.7	1.8	2.3	0.7	1.1	1.3	1.9	6.0	6.3	6.6	6.3	4.7	25.1	28.8	14.1	2.0	77.0	41.5	49.5	50.5
17211	ARTEMAS	99.2	99.1	0.3	0.2	0.0	0.2	0.3	0.4	5.7	6.1	6.1	6.1	4.8	23.5	31.1	15.2	1.5	78.2	43.4	51.9	48.1
17212	BIG COVE TANNERY	98.1	97.7	0.8	0.9	0.3	0.4	0.5	0.6	5.9	6.2	6.4	6.0	5.3	26.4	30.1	12.7	1.0	77.7	40.6	50.8	49.2
17213	BLAIRS MILLS	100.0	100.0	0.0	0.0	0.0	0.0	0.0	0.0	7.4	8.1	8.0	5.7	4.6	27.0	25.3	12.4	1.4	72.5	37.6	48.8	51.2
17214	BLUE RIDGE SUMMIT	94.6	92.8	2.3	2.9	1.1	1.6	1.9	2.6	5.5	5.3	5.5	5.3	5.4	25.0	30.9	14.6	2.3	80.4	43.5	48.9	51.1
17215	BURNT CABINS	99.3	99.3	0.7	0.7	0.0	0.0	0.0	0.0	4.8	5.5	5.5	6.2	4.8	26.9	29.7	14.5	2.1	80.0	42.9	50.3	49.7
17217	CONCORD	100.0	100.0	0.0	0.0	0.0	0.0	0.0	0.0	0.0	0.0	0.0	0.0	10.0	70.0	20.0	0.0	0.0	100.0	37.5	30.0	70.0
17219	DOYLESBURG	98.1	97.5	1.2	1.4	0.2	0.4	0.2	0.4	8.0	8.0	8.4	8.6	4.7	24.3	24.1	11.1	2.7	69.5	35.9	48.1	51.9
17220	DRY RUN	99.0	98.2	0.5	0.9	0.0	0.5	0.5	0.5	8.1	8.1	8.6	8.1	5.0	24.8	24.3	11.3	1.8	68.9	35.3	49.5	50.5
17221	FANNETTSBURG	99.2	98.8	0.3	0.4	0.2	0.3	0.5	0.7	6.0	6.2	6.6	7.1	4.2	25.5	29.4	13.7	1.4	76.6	41.8	50.7	49.3
17222	FAYETTEVILLE	96.0	94.9	1.9	2.3	0.5	0.7	1.2	1.6	5.5	5.7	6.3	6.9	4.2	23.0	28.3	17.6	2.5	77.9	43.9	49.3	50.7
17223	FORT LITTLETON	99.5	99.3	0.5	0.5	0.0	0.2	0.3	0.2	5.0	5.3	5.7	6.4	4.8	24.5	30.5	15.6	2.1	79.6	43.8	46.8	53.2
17224	FORT LOUDON	98.4	98.0	1.0	1.3	0.1	0.2	0.9	1.3	6.5	6.8	7.0	6.3	4.2	25.3	28.7	13.9	1.4	75.8	41.2	50.7	49.3
17225	GREENCASTLE	97.8	97.0	0.8	1.0	0.4	0.5	0.8	1.2	6.2	6.4	6.8	6.8	5.0	26.6	28.9	11.9	1.4	76.2	40.1	49.7	50.3
17228	HARRISONVILLE	98.9	98.5	0.0	0.0	0.2	0.3	0.2	0.3	6.1	6.5	7.1	7.0	4.5	26.0	28.1	13.1	1.6	75.9	40.4	50.6	49.4
17229	HUSTONTOWN	99.4	99.0	0.2	0.3	0.0	0.1	0.2	0.3	6.0	6.4	6.3	6.3	4.7	24.0	29.8	14.8	1.9	77.3	42.5	49.6	50.4
17232	LURGAN	100.0	100.0	0.0	0.0	0.0	0.0	0.0	0.0	8.3	8.3	8.3	6.3	4.2	27.1	25.0	12.5	0.0	68.8	36.3	52.1	47.9
17233	MC CONNELLSBURG	96.9	96.1	1.6	2.1	0.2	0.3	0.5	0.7	5.7	5.6	6.0	6.3	5.8	25.5	27.9	14.9	2.3	78.7	41.3	49.5	50.5
17236	MERCERSBURG	97.3	96.6	1.7	2.1	0.2	0.3	0.9	1.3	6.1	6.3	6.6	6.1	4.9	25.7	29.6	13.1	1.6	77.2	41.3	50.1	49.9
17237	MONT ALTO	97.5	96.7	1.0	1.3	0.8	1.3	0.3	0.3	6.4	6.9	7.2	6.5	3.8	28.4	27.9	11.6	1.4	75.6	39.8	48.7	51.3
17238	NEEDMORE	99.5	99.4	0.1	0.1	0.1	0.2	0.1	0.2	6.9	7.3	7.6	6.5	4.1	26.3	27.1	12.7	1.4	74.0	39.2	51.1	48.9
17239	NEELYTON	98.7	98.4	0.4	0.5	0.0	0.0	0.7	0.9	6.2	6.6	6.7	5.9	3.9	28.8	28.2	12.0	1.7	76.5	40.0	52.1	47.9
17240	NEWBURG	98.2	97.7	0.6	0.7	0.2	0.3	0.5	0.7	7.6	7.9	8.1	7.4	4.7	25.0	27.6	10.7	1.1	71.8	37.6	49.9	50.1
17241	NEWVILLE	98.3	97.8	0.4	0.5	0.3	0.5	0.6	0.9	6.8	7.1	7.2	6.9	4.8	25.7	28.5	11.0	1.9	74.6	39.2	50.2	49.8
17243	ORBISONIA	99.1	98.8	0.3	0.4	0.0	0.1	0.6	0.8	5.8	5.9	6.0	5.5	5.6	23.5	26.7	16.5	4.6	79.0	43.4	47.5	52.5
17244	ORRSTOWN	98.3	97.7	0.9	1.2	0.1	0.2	0.5	0.7	6.8	7.1	7.2	6.2	4.3	26.5	28.6	11.9	1.3	74.8	38.9	51.1	48.9
17246	PLEASANT HALL	98.6	98.7	1.4	1.3	0.0	0.0	0.0	0.0	5.3	6.7	6.7	5.3	4.0	28.0	29.3	13.3	1.3	76.0	40.5	50.7	49.3
17252	SAINT THOMAS	98.0	97.5	0.7	0.8	0.3	0.4	0.8	1.3	6.0	6.3	6.5	6.5	4.8	25.5	30.1	12.8	1.5	77.1	41.3	50.1	49.9
17255	SHADE GAP	98.6	97.9	0.5	0.7	0.0	0.0	0.7	1.2	6.2	6.5	6.7	5.8	3.9	29.0	28.1	12.0	1.8	77.0	40.0	52.1	47.9
17257	SHIPPENSBURG	95.9	94.7	2.1	2.6	0.7	1.1	0.9	1.3	5.8	5.5	5.5	12.0	14.4	22.5	22.2	10.4	1.6	79.5	30.8	48.3	51.7
17260	SHIRLEYSBURG	98.3	97.5	0.6	0.8	0.2	0.4	0.7	1.0	5.6	5.6	5.9	6.0	5.3	23.1	30.0	16.3	2.3	79.5	44.0	50.1	49.9
17262	SPRING RUN	98.9	98.5	0.5	0.6	0.2	0.2	0.5	0.7	8.1	8.1	8.3	7.3	4.9	25.2	25.2	11.1	1.7	70.6	35.9	49.4	50.6
17264	THREE SPRINGS	99.2	98.9	0.1	0.2	0.0	0.1	0.1	0.3	6.2	6.7	6.3	5.8	4.6	24.9	27.5	15.5	2.4	77.1	41.8	50.7	49.3
17265	UPPERSTRASBURG	98.8	97.8	1.2	1.6	0.0	0.0	0.6	1.1	6.0	6.0	6.6	6.0	4.4	28.4	29.5	11.5	1.6	77.6	39.8	52.5	47.5
17266	WALNUT BOTTOM	98.4	97.9	0.4	0.6	0.2	0.4	0.4	0.6	6.3	6.8	7.2	7.2	4.9	24.3	30.6	10.8	1.9	75.0	39.8	49.5	50.5
17267	WARFORDSBURG	98.6	98.4	0.2	0.2	0.1	0.1	0.4	0.5	6.7	6.8	6.9	6.2	5.1	26.1	27.9	13.0	1.4	75.8	39.4	50.9	49.1
17268	WAYNESBORO	96.5	95.4	1.7	2.0	0.7	1.0	1.0	1.5	6.1	5.9	6.2	7.1	5.7	24.7	27.6	14.0	2.7	77.9	40.8	48.4	51.6
17271	WILLOW HILL	98.9	98.5	0.4	0.6	0.2	0.4	0.4	0.6	6.3	6.4	6.8	7.2	4.4	25.4	28.7	13.2	1.7	75.7	41.2	50.0	50.0
17301	ABBOTTSTOWN	97.5	96.5	0.3	0.4	0.4	0.6	2.4	3.4	6.4	6.8	7.4	6.7	4.6	26.4	30.8	9.9	1.1	74.9	39.8	50.3	49.7
17302	AIRVILLE	97.7	96.6	0.6	0.9	0.6	1.0	0.5	0.9	6.5	7.5	8.7	7.9	4.8	26.4	28.4	8.4	1.3	72.2	37.7	51.2	48.8
17304	ASPERS	93.1	90.8	1.3	1.5	0.2	0.3	9.3	12.9	6.6	7.1	7.4	7.0	4.6	26.6	29.2	10.1	1.3	74.7	38.8	50.7	49.3
17307	BIGLERVILLE	93.3	91.1	1.0	1.2	0.1	0.2	8.6	11.9	5.8	6.1	6.5	7.1	5.3	25.3	29.9	12.3	1.8	77.2	41.0	50.3	49.7
17309	BROGUE	97.5	96.4	0.6	0.9	0.5	0.8	0.8	1.2	6.3	6.8	7.1	6.7	4.6	28.0	29.3	9.9	1.3	75.5	39.2	51.4	48.6
17313	DALLASTOWN	97.1	95.7	0.8	1.2	0.7	1.1	1.4	2.3	6.0	6.0	6.0	6.3	6.1	27.2	27.8	12.1	2.5	78.1	39.9	49.1	50.9
17314	DELTA	96.9	95.4	1.7	2.6	0.3	0.5	0.5	0.8	6.9	7.2	7.6	7.5	5.6	25.8	29.4	9.0	1.1	73.7	38.3	51.0	49.0
17315	DOVER	97.2	95.7	1.0	1.6	0.4	0.7	1.0	1.8	5.9	6.2	6.5	6.6	5.2	26.6	29.9	11.5	1.6	77.2	40.6	49.6	50.4
17316	EAST BERLIN	98.1	97.4	0.3	0.3	0.2	0.3	1.5	2.1	7.2	7.6	7.9	7.1	4.7	26.6	28.7	9.2	1.1	72.8	38.3	49.5	50.5
17319	ETTERS	97.2	95.9	0.8	1.2	0.7	1.2	1.3	2.1	6.7	7.0	7.3	7.4	5.3	29.1	29.6	6.9	0.6	74.4	37.7	49.6	50.4
17320	FAIRFIELD	97.2	96.5	0.4	0.5	0.4	0.6	0.9	1.2	6.4	6.6	7.0	6.8	4.8	26.0	29.9	11.0	1.4	75.6	40.3	49.4	50.6
17321	FAWN GROVE	98.4	97.7	0.6	1.0	0.3	0.4	0.5	0.8	6.3	7.0	7.4	6.8	4.1	25.6	31.7	9.9	1.2	74.9	40.6	49.6	50.4
17322	FELTON	98.2	97.3	0.7	1.1	0.3	0.6	0.5	0.8	6.1	6.8	7.3	6.6	4.3	26.8	31.5	9.4	1.1	75.5	40.2	51.0	49.0
17324	GARDNERS	96.9	95.8	0.6	0.8	0.5	0.7	3.7	5.3	5.5	6.3	6.4	6.7	5.0	26.0	31.0	11.6	1.4	77.7	41.3	50.4	49.6
17325	GETTYSBURG	92.3	90.2	2.9	3.4	1.0	1.5	4.5	6.0	4.8	4.9	5.5	9.0	10.5	21.9	26.6	14.0	2.7	81.0	39.4	48.3	51.7
17327	GLEN ROCK	98.4	97.7	0.5	0.7	0.3	0.5	0.4	0.6	5.1	5.4	6.0	7.2	5.6	23.2	33.0	12.9	1.6	78.9	43.1	50.2	49.8
17329	GLENVILLE	98.6	98.0	0.0	0.1	0.3	0.5	0.3	0.4	5.2	5.9	6.8	7.5	5.0	23.1	35.1	10.4	0.9	77.4	42.7	50.8	49.2
17331	HANOVER	97.5	96.4	0.5	0.8	0.7	1.1	1.4	2.2	5.7	6.0	6.4	6.5	5.2	25.3	29.4	13.1	2.4	77.8	41.6	48.9	51.1
17339	LEWISBERRY	97.8	96.8	0.5	0.8	0.7	1.2	0.7	1.1	4.9	5.8	6.5	6.5	4.1	24.4	35.6	10.6	1.6	78.5	43.6	49.8	50.2
17340	LITTLESTOWN	97.8	97.0	0.5	0.6	0.4	0.7	1.1	1.5	6.2	6.3	6.9	7.4	5.7	25.9	28.4	11.7	1.5	75.6	39.7	49.0	51.0
17344	MC SHERRYSTOWN	98.0	97.3	0.5	0.6	0.2	0.4	1.4	2.0	6.6	6.3	6.6	6.1	5.6	27.6	25.8	13.0	2.3	76.7	39.2	47.7	52.3
17345	MANCHESTER	97.3	96.0	0.9	1.3	0.4	0.7	1.3	2.1	6.1	6.3	6.3	6.5	5.1	28.0	29.3	11.1	1.4	77.1	39.8	49.5	50.5
17347	MOUNT WOLF	97.3	96.0	1.1	1.6	0.6	0.9	1.1	1.9	6.3	6.5	6.4	6.4	4.6	28.1	28.6	11.4	1.6	76.7	40.1	49.8	50.2
17349	NEW FREEDOM	97.4	96.1	0.5	0.8	0.9	1.4	0.8	1.3	5.3	6.1	7.1	6.7	4.0	22.2	35.0	11.4	2.1	77.0	43.9	49.0	51.0
17350	NEW OXFORD	95.9	94.3	0.6	0.7	0.5	0.7	4.1	5.8	6.3	6.3	6.5	6.9	5.8	26.0	26.8	11.8	3.7	76.6	39.8	48.9	51.1
17352	NEW PARK	97.5	96.4	0.9	1.4	0.6	0.9	0.4	0.6	5.9	6.5	7.2	7.8	4.3	25.0	32.6	9.6	1.0	75.6	40.7	49.6	50.4
17353	ORRTANNA	95.6	94.2	1.5	2.0	0.1	0.3	2.7	3.8	4.9	5.4	6.0	6.3	4.9	24.5	32.8	12.9	2.4	79.7	43.8	50.4	49.6
17356	RED LION	97.7	96.3	0.5	0.8	0.5	1.0	1.0	1.8	6.5	6.9	7.0	6.9	5.1	26.8	28.7	10.7	1.4	75.1	39.4	49.6	50.4
17360	SEVEN VALLEYS	98.2	97.4	0.3	0.5	0.3	0.5	0.6	0.9	4.9	5.4	6.0	6.6	4.5	25.1	33.6	12.5	1.4	79.6	43.3	50.3	49.7
17361	SHREWSBURY	97.9	96.7	0.6	0.9	0.7	1.2	0.9	1.6	5.7	6.0	6.6	6.8	5.3	21.2	32.3	13.5	2.5	77.5	43.8	49.0	51.0
17362	SPRING GROVE	98.3	97.5	0.3	0.4	0.3	0.5	0.8	1.3	5.4	6.0	6.6	7.0	5.2	25.8	31.6	11.0	1.2	77.6	41.0	50.6	49.4
17363	STEWARTSTOWN	97.7	96.5	0.9	1.4	0.4	0.7	1.0	1.5	6.7	6.9	7.4	7.4	5.5	24.9	30.7	9.3	1.1	74.3	39.3	50.2	49.8
17364	THOMASVILLE	98.8	98.1	0.3	0.5	0.3	0.4	0.5	0.9	5.8	6.3	7.1	6.3	4.4	24.7	32.5	11.7	1.3	76.6	42.2	50.9	49.1
17365	WELLSVILLE	98.3	97.6	0.3	0.5	0.5	0.7	0.8	1.4	5.0	5.6	6.2	6.4	4.4	24.9	34.6	11.8	1.2	79.1	43.5	50.2	49.8
	PENNSYLVANIA	85.4	83.2	10.0	10.7	1.8	2.7	3.2	4.2	5.8	6.0	6.3	7.1	6.5	24.8	27.8	13.1	2.6	77.8	40.4	48.5	51.5
	UNITED STATES	75.1	72.0	12.3	12.7	3.8	4.6	12.5	15.7	6.8	6.7	6.6	7.1	6.9	27.0	26.0	10.9	1.9	75.7	36.9	49.2	50.8

ZIP CODE #	POST OFFICE NAME	2009 Per Capita Income	2009 HH Income Base	2009 HOUSEHOLD INCOME DISTRIBUTION (%) Less than $25,000	$25,000 to $49,999	$50,000 to $99,999	$100,000 to $149,999	$150,000 or More	MEDIAN HOUSEHOLD INCOME 2009	2014	2009 National Centile	2009 State Centile	2009 Home Value Base	2009 HOME VALUE DISTRIBUTION (%) Less than $50,000	$50,000 to $89,999	$90,000 to $174,999	$175,000 to $399,999	$400,000 or More	2009 Median Home Value
17074	NEWPORT	22153	3794	21.4	28.5	42.1	6.3	1.7	50034	52753	61	62	2882	7.3	10.9	45.6	31.9	4.4	153763
17076	OAKLAND MILLS	16529	166	25.9	34.9	33.1	3.6	2.4	40000	42572	33	26	118	5.1	15.3	38.1	40.7	0.8	161111
17078	PALMYRA	29759	8020	13.3	26.3	44.4	11.2	4.7	61104	61670	79	80	5803	2.7	2.9	39.1	51.0	4.2	188015
17080	PILLOW	23143	140	21.4	33.6	40.0	4.3	0.7	46916	49720	54	55	112	5.4	29.5	43.8	13.4	8.0	116071
17082	PORT ROYAL	19212	1376	21.6	34.2	37.7	5.1	1.4	46108	46635	52	51	1071	5.4	16.3	49.4	24.3	4.6	135688
17084	REEDSVILLE	20248	1586	23.7	31.1	35.8	6.8	2.6	45939	48890	51	51	1295	2.0	10.0	54.8	31.7	1.5	147711
17086	RICHFIELD	19172	657	21.9	32.9	38.7	4.3	2.3	45778	46846	51	50	538	7.6	10.0	47.6	30.5	4.3	145430
17087	RICHLAND	22070	1095	14.2	30.0	46.9	6.4	2.6	54244	55801	70	70	879	1.9	4.0	51.0	38.1	5.0	164849
17090	SHERMANS DALE	22662	2267	14.6	31.6	43.8	7.8	2.3	52406	54531	67	67	1947	19.1	9.0	33.2	33.8	4.8	150280
17094	THOMPSONTOWN	21080	1120	22.9	37.7	33.5	4.2	1.8	42344	43803	40	36	819	9.6	12.2	50.4	24.5	3.2	135654
17097	WICONISCO	22431	28	21.4	28.6	42.9	7.1	0.0	50000	52900	61	62	24	20.8	33.3	37.5	8.3	0.0	85000
17098	WILLIAMSTOWN	21141	1047	24.8	31.9	38.2	4.2	0.9	45670	48636	50	49	815	10.6	41.1	38.4	8.8	1.1	87632
17099	YEAGERTOWN	25283	472	13.3	31.8	43.4	9.7	1.7	53389	54891	69	69	353	1.4	20.7	62.0	15.3	0.6	126868
17101	HARRISBURG	30814	1483	45.4	30.1	20.2	3.0	1.3	26845	27126	5	2	83	3.6	18.1	39.8	38.6	0.0	151250
17102	HARRISBURG	21307	4217	41.7	30.0	24.0	3.2	1.1	30672	32475	9	3	1146	10.5	21.6	62.5	5.3	0.1	111567
17103	HARRISBURG	18603	4314	30.8	33.1	31.3	3.5	1.3	38667	41240	29	20	2299	8.9	31.5	51.0	7.6	1.0	98327
17104	HARRISBURG	17574	7820	37.0	30.1	26.3	4.6	2.0	33520	34914	14	6	3610	9.8	40.3	40.6	7.9	1.4	89935
17109	HARRISBURG	29108	10384	14.1	31.1	43.5	7.9	3.4	54233	56756	70	70	5634	1.5	2.3	55.6	39.5	1.1	163922
17110	HARRISBURG	31076	9703	16.5	22.7	39.5	14.0	7.3	60036	62168	77	78	6656	3.0	11.3	39.4	39.9	6.3	167914
17111	HARRISBURG	31373	11216	12.2	25.0	43.2	13.5	6.1	64708	65650	83	85	7863	1.1	3.3	46.8	43.5	5.2	173238
17112	HARRISBURG	33360	12894	9.2	21.3	46.1	14.1	9.3	71194	71661	87	90	10726	1.4	3.1	31.9	53.9	9.8	201193
17113	HARRISBURG	21942	4535	22.9	31.3	38.4	4.7	2.6	46277	50441	52	52	2999	6.2	19.3	59.0	15.5	0.0	124372
17201	CHAMBERSBURG	25792	10709	24.7	30.6	33.7	7.3	3.6	44760	49040	48	45	6019	6.5	8.0	53.9	28.3	3.2	146343
17202	CHAMBERSBURG	25508	11338	15.6	27.5	43.8	9.4	3.8	55803	57142	72	72	9230	11.4	5.1	40.1	39.6	3.8	164546
17211	ARTEMAS	18457	219	23.3	42.0	30.6	2.7	1.4	39051	40138	30	22	194	7.7	12.9	51.0	25.3	3.1	132927
17212	BIG COVE TANNERY	21080	322	23.0	33.9	35.4	5.3	2.5	44222	45065	46	43	255	11.8	10.6	45.9	27.5	4.3	144688
17213	BLAIRS MILLS	17770	244	30.3	33.6	31.1	3.7	1.2	39726	41652	32	24	214	17.3	12.6	39.7	27.6	2.8	136290
17214	BLUE RIDGE SUMMIT	29798	503	10.9	26.0	52.3	6.6	4.2	57931	60168	75	76	349	10.6	5.7	41.3	38.1	4.3	162010
17215	BURNT CABINS	23184	69	27.5	33.3	34.8	2.9	1.4	40764	42322	35	29	55	16.4	14.5	49.1	18.2	1.8	120833
17217	CONCORD	36500	5	0.0	0.0	100.0	0.0	0.0	69801	66333	87	89	0	0.0	0.0	0.0	0.0	0.0	0
17219	DOYLESBURG	17702	169	29.0	29.6	34.3	5.9	1.2	42360	45225	41	37	132	7.6	17.4	40.2	27.3	7.6	133824
17220	DRY RUN	17179	76	26.3	30.3	36.8	5.3	1.3	43644	45570	44	42	60	11.7	15.0	45.0	23.3	5.0	130000
17221	FANNETTSBURG	20822	293	26.6	32.1	35.8	3.4	2.0	42466	46082	41	37	248	14.1	14.1	48.0	17.7	6.0	123649
17222	FAYETTEVILLE	26796	4279	12.7	28.2	47.2	9.0	3.0	58799	60160	76	77	3671	9.0	11.0	40.2	35.1	4.7	154413
17223	FORT LITTLETON	20319	183	27.9	31.7	34.4	3.8	2.2	42365	42914	41	37	145	15.9	15.2	51.0	16.6	1.4	121196
17224	FORT LOUDON	20947	752	28.1	32.6	32.7	4.3	2.4	40000	43798	33	26	608	10.2	9.5	54.1	18.9	7.2	133686
17225	GREENCASTLE	23787	7123	15.4	28.8	45.9	7.6	2.3	55549	56442	72	72	5516	6.1	4.3	43.3	42.7	3.6	169142
17228	HARRISONVILLE	18824	424	22.6	35.4	36.1	4.2	1.7	43128	43542	43	39	342	12.6	18.4	37.4	27.2	4.4	132778
17229	HUSTONTOWN	18806	500	26.8	33.0	35.0	3.6	1.6	40999	42152	36	30	404	14.4	15.8	48.5	19.6	1.7	120290
17232	LURGAN	24567	21	19.0	23.8	52.4	4.8	0.0	57143	56155	74	74	18	5.6	5.6	50.0	33.3	5.6	162500
17233	MC CONNELLSBURG	20569	1996	28.2	31.8	33.4	5.1	1.6	40644	42045	35	29	1443	18.4	11.4	44.9	23.1	2.2	131029
17236	MERCERSBURG	24246	3479	18.4	29.5	39.9	8.4	3.8	51995	53901	66	67	2599	6.5	9.1	42.5	37.2	4.7	159476
17237	MONT ALTO	21623	529	17.8	37.2	38.4	5.5	1.1	46466	49790	53	53	429	4.2	10.7	64.1	21.0	0.0	136335
17238	NEEDMORE	20155	778	20.6	37.3	36.0	4.4	1.8	45269	45354	49	47	650	11.2	12.3	44.5	27.4	4.6	141228
17239	NEELYTON	19378	349	26.9	33.5	33.0	3.7	2.9	40399	42606	34	28	299	13.7	14.7	46.8	22.1	2.7	124734
17240	NEWBURG	19788	1098	16.5	31.1	45.9	4.6	1.8	51889	54544	66	66	947	5.9	5.3	45.4	37.7	5.7	164298
17241	NEWVILLE	21804	4792	15.9	29.8	48.0	5.3	1.1	53092	55972	68	69	3881	8.8	8.8	40.0	37.0	5.4	160923
17243	ORBISONIA	20104	867	28.6	30.8	35.3	3.8	1.5	41877	43901	39	35	695	14.5	23.6	47.9	11.8	2.2	108036
17244	ORRSTOWN	22114	1055	16.4	32.0	42.5	6.3	2.8	51048	52940	64	64	887	10.9	6.8	40.5	37.7	4.2	160950
17246	PLEASANT HALL	23001	30	13.3	33.3	46.7	6.7	0.0	52087	52228	66	67	26	11.5	11.5	42.3	34.6	0.0	150000
17252	SAINT THOMAS	21694	1486	17.6	32.6	41.7	5.7	2.4	49703	52131	60	61	1257	16.3	9.5	45.8	25.3	3.1	137256
17255	SHADE GAP	20646	176	26.1	34.1	33.5	4.0	2.3	40502	43640	34	28	151	13.9	13.9	47.7	21.9	2.6	125463
17257	SHIPPENSBURG	19612	9259	24.6	28.1	40.3	5.2	1.7	47481	50679	55	56	6376	12.6	10.0	41.6	31.0	4.9	148730
17260	SHIRLEYSBURG	17640	544	28.9	34.4	34.6	1.7	0.6	38049	40594	27	18	479	21.3	24.0	42.0	9.0	3.8	100426
17262	SPRING RUN	18961	815	25.8	32.9	34.4	5.0	2.0	42702	46029	41	38	654	11.6	13.8	46.0	22.9	5.7	132692
17264	THREE SPRINGS	19327	1224	29.9	32.8	32.0	3.8	1.5	38980	41335	30	22	1009	16.8	20.8	44.1	17.0	1.2	108252
17265	UPPERSTRASBURG	23378	75	16.0	36.0	40.0	6.7	1.3	48373	51837	57	58	64	17.2	7.8	40.6	32.8	1.6	147222
17266	WALNUT BOTTOM	23909	207	13.0	28.0	51.2	5.8	1.9	56367	58348	73	73	176	4.0	8.5	43.8	36.9	6.8	158824
17267	WARFORDSBURG	19251	1098	21.9	37.7	35.7	3.9	0.8	43737	44213	45	42	889	12.8	14.1	42.5	28.3	2.2	139274
17268	WAYNESBORO	23984	12038	19.9	28.7	41.9	7.1	2.3	51227	53720	64	65	8544	6.7	8.0	49.9	31.8	3.6	150140
17271	WILLOW HILL	17872	189	26.5	31.7	36.0	3.7	2.1	42981	46044	42	39	159	13.8	14.5	47.8	18.2	5.7	123438
17301	ABBOTTSTOWN	23078	1375	14.2	22.0	53.7	7.3	2.8	60679	60742	78	79	1201	10.7	5.4	31.2	47.4	5.2	180625
17302	AIRVILLE	21421	1132	15.9	28.0	47.4	7.0	1.7	55020	57809	71	71	927	4.0	5.6	31.9	48.2	10.2	193690
17304	ASPERS	19458	1262	19.7	29.4	41.4	8.2	1.3	50608	52657	63	63	966	4.7	10.0	46.6	35.3	3.4	153373
17307	BIGLERVILLE	21431	2497	17.9	30.0	43.9	6.4	1.8	51622	53502	65	66	1923	6.9	6.9	37.1	44.8	4.3	173302
17309	BROGUE	25402	902	16.4	21.6	50.0	8.6	3.3	61895	63976	80	81	769	5.3	6.6	39.7	40.8	7.5	172500
17313	DALLASTOWN	27431	4772	16.5	24.7	44.7	10.9	3.2	59287	61989	77	78	3183	5.2	2.1	43.7	45.6	3.4	173766
17314	DELTA	20842	2335	16.3	29.4	46.3	6.1	2.0	52933	55244	68	68	1914	2.7	5.7	39.4	46.8	5.3	179236
17315	DOVER	24930	10166	13.0	27.5	49.4	8.4	1.7	59199	61371	76	78	8415	9.0	4.9	38.7	43.6	3.9	171520
17316	EAST BERLIN	23530	2889	13.0	26.6	49.3	8.8	2.4	60122	60358	77	78	2410	5.1	3.7	36.8	48.9	5.6	185786
17319	ETTERS	27602	4065	9.2	22.4	50.5	12.2	5.8	65905	68997	84	87	3624	9.6	3.1	35.7	45.4	6.3	178330
17320	FAIRFIELD	25846	3181	11.1	23.9	52.0	9.2	3.9	62011	62917	80	81	2734	2.5	4.8	34.9	53.0	4.8	193174
17321	FAWN GROVE	25009	911	10.6	23.7	52.1	11.4	2.1	65511	68779	84	86	765	0.8	2.0	23.8	64.3	9.2	227356
17322	FELTON	24983	2303	12.0	24.1	50.5	9.4	4.0	62858	65224	81	83	2066	3.0	3.6	30.3	54.5	8.8	203659
17324	GARDNERS	24008	1756	14.1	28.1	49.0	5.3	3.6	56232	58352	73	73	1458	7.7	9.6	42.9	34.8	4.9	155497
17325	GETTYSBURG	23401	10194	21.2	28.4	38.7	8.1	3.6	50367	53097	62	63	7064	8.8	6.9	31.7	42.9	9.8	182593
17327	GLEN ROCK	25705	3007	12.1	25.4	49.8	8.7	4.0	62477	65290	81	82	2380	1.6	1.8	26.4	57.2	13.0	219316
17329	GLENVILLE	26393	856	11.6	22.3	51.4	9.9	4.8	64347	66268	83	85	768	0.7	1.6	19.5	65.2	13.0	253716
17331	HANOVER	25505	20415	15.1	25.7	49.3	7.0	2.8	57706	59749	75	75	15127	1.8	2.5	43.9	48.3	3.5	178679
17339	LEWISBERRY	30027	2485	9.6	23.8	45.8	13.0	7.8	65101	67349	83	86	2141	1.6	2.4	26.2	54.8	15.0	219015
17340	LITTLESTOWN	22605	4341	16.0	29.6	45.0	7.2	2.2	53714	55280	69	69	3356	0.7	3.3	38.3	51.9	5.8	192267
17344	MC SHERRYSTOWN	24725	1525	24.2	31.2	33.4	8.1	3.1	46103	48827	52	51	910	2.5	4.7	69.7	23.1	0.0	142123
17345	MANCHESTER	25337	3415	12.0	30.9	46.9	7.6	2.6	57512	60649	75	75	2585	5.5	6.7	52.2	34.5	1.1	156825
17347	MOUNT WOLF	24782	1804	15.4	27.0	46.5	7.9	3.2	58106	61029	75	76	1555	17.4	6.3	35.0	40.4	0.9	158063
17349	NEW FREEDOM	30288	2838	8.7	15.5	49.4	18.6	7.7	75880	77382	90	92	2464	2.4	0.9	14.4	70.0	12.3	250688
17350	NEW OXFORD	22071	4809	16.7	27.6	47.2	6.4	2.1	54338	55630	70	70	3748	10.5	7.0	44.7	33.3	4.6	154704
17352	NEW PARK	25238	528	10.0	23.5	50.4	12.9	3.2	63689	66809	82	84	457	1.5	3.3	20.8	64.6	9.8	241406
17353	ORRTANNA	23536	1262	15.0	27.1	49.2	6.1	2.6	55608	56054	72	72	1027	5.7	9.8	42.7	36.6	5.1	159167
17356	RED LION	25259	8771	14.4	27.0	46.8	7.8	3.9	56949	59523	74	74	6785	2.4	2.6	44.5	43.8	6.7	176131
17360	SEVEN VALLEYS	25115	1941	13.1	25.9	48.8	9.5	2.6	60887	63037	79	79	1616	2.5	2.6	30.1	56.4	8.4	203392
17361	SHREWSBURY	28131	2224	15.6	15.3	54.0	10.2	4.8	65728	67698	84	87	1788	0.3	0.8	15.7	76.6	6.5	233306
17362	SPRING GROVE	24816	5134	10.5	24.9	54.1	8.3	2.2	61797	63481	80	81	4283	1.8	1.4	36.1	54.8	5.9	198585
17363	STEWARTSTOWN	26740	3462	12.3	20.4	44.3	18.5	4.5	68895	73106	86	89	3007	4.1	1.8	17.8	67.6	8.8	238065
17364	THOMASVILLE	23098	1213	15.7	25.5	51.3	5.9	1.6	59623	61353	77	78	1056	9.2	3.2	31.0	50.6	6.1	190217
17365	WELLSVILLE	25704	1068	11.3	30.3	47.9	7.2	3.2	58611	60878	76	77	881	1.7	3.6	34.7	47.7	12.3	203201
	PENNSYLVANIA	26913		21.5	25.3	36.9	10.2	6.1	53225	55819				7.5	12.2	35.6	36.1	8.5	161438
	UNITED STATES	27277		20.9	24.4	35.3	11.7	7.6	54719	56938				9.3	13.1	31.6	32.6	13.5	162279

#	ZIP CODE POST OFFICE NAME	FINANCIAL SERVICES Auto Loan	Home Loan	Invest-ments	Retire-ment Plans	THE HOME Home Improvements Home Repair	Lawn & Garden	Furnishings Comput-ers & Hard-ware-Personal	Major Appli-ances	TV, Radio, Sound Equip-ment	Furni-ture	ENTERTAINMENT Dine out/ Carry out	Sports Equip-ment	Fees & Tickets	Toys & Games	Travel	Cable TV	PERSONAL Apparel & Services	Auto Repairs	Health Insur-ance	Pets & Supplies
17074	NEWPORT	84	76	74	78	76	87	78	83	80	72	79	63	72	82	75	84	54	80	87	98
17076	OAKLAND MILLS	77	66	72	68	68	81	66	76	69	60	68	58	59	70	66	74	46	70	79	89
17078	PALMYRA	98	100	92	102	99	105	98	100	99	94	98	76	99	100	99	102	68	99	106	118
17080	PILLOW	81	74	73	77	75	87	73	82	75	66	74	62	67	77	73	80	50	76	85	96
17082	PORT ROYAL	76	72	66	74	71	82	71	77	73	65	72	59	67	74	70	76	49	73	81	90
17084	REEDSVILLE	85	75	76	78	77	90	75	85	78	68	76	64	68	79	74	83	52	78	88	99
17086	RICHFIELD	81	74	73	77	75	87	73	82	75	66	74	62	67	77	73	80	50	76	85	96
17087	RICHLAND	94	86	85	90	88	101	85	96	87	77	86	72	79	89	85	92	59	88	99	111
17090	SHERMANS DALE	94	86	79	85	85	92	82	89	85	82	85	65	77	88	80	88	58	85	90	105
17094	THOMPSONTOWN	81	68	75	70	70	86	69	81	73	62	72	61	61	74	69	79	48	75	85	94
17097	WICONISCO	89	64	90	63	67	93	70	87	78	63	76	65	56	77	68	86	50	81	95	102
17098	WILLIAMSTOWN	81	67	76	68	69	86	69	80	73	62	71	60	60	73	68	79	48	74	85	94
17099	YEAGERTOWN	87	86	74	88	82	93	85	86	87	80	86	68	84	88	84	90	59	86	94	104
17101	HARRISBURG	49	39	43	43	39	43	56	46	58	51	58	37	51	53	50	60	40	55	58	58
17102	HARRISBURG	54	44	44	47	43	47	58	49	60	53	60	39	53	58	51	63	42	56	58	62
17103	HARRISBURG	61	61	56	60	59	63	64	60	68	60	68	45	65	68	61	72	48	64	68	73
17104	HARRISBURG	62	55	48	56	52	57	65	57	68	60	68	45	61	68	58	71	48	63	65	71
17109	HARRISBURG	87	85	81	86	83	87	90	86	91	88	91	66	90	90	88	92	64	90	93	102
17110	HARRISBURG	100	108	104	108	107	106	105	103	107	104	107	78	111	106	107	109	76	105	107	122
17111	HARRISBURG	103	110	102	111	108	108	106	105	105	106	106	81	110	107	108	106	75	105	108	123
17112	HARRISBURG	114	131	120	133	128	128	117	121	116	118	117	93	128	118	125	117	82	117	122	141
17113	HARRISBURG	77	72	65	73	69	79	76	75	80	73	79	56	74	79	72	84	54	77	85	90
17201	CHAMBERSBURG	78	76	75	77	77	83	80	79	83	77	82	59	79	80	79	86	57	81	89	94
17202	CHAMBERSBURG	95	97	93	97	97	102	90	97	92	89	91	73	91	93	93	95	63	93	100	113
17211	ARTEMAS	81	58	84	56	61	83	60	76	66	56	65	57	48	66	59	73	43	70	79	91
17212	BIG COVE TANNERY	92	71	78	71	71	90	72	83	79	69	77	64	61	81	68	85	52	78	87	100
17213	BLAIRS MILLS	85	61	70	59	61	81	64	74	70	62	69	57	51	73	58	77	46	70	78	90
17214	BLUE RIDGE SUMMIT	98	86	90	88	89	99	93	96	95	89	94	71	85	94	89	99	64	96	103	113
17215	BURNT CABINS	84	63	84	62	65	86	64	80	70	59	69	60	53	70	63	76	46	73	83	94
17217	CONCORD	113	103	102	107	105	121	102	115	105	92	103	87	94	107	101	111	70	106	118	133
17219	DOYLESBURG	79	69	70	72	71	83	69	78	72	63	70	59	63	73	68	76	48	72	81	91
17220	DRY RUN	82	67	71	68	68	83	68	78	72	63	71	59	59	74	65	78	48	73	81	92
17221	FANNETTSBURG	79	72	72	75	74	85	71	81	74	65	72	61	66	75	71	78	49	74	83	94
17222	FAYETTEVILLE	95	94	102	93	95	107	87	99	91	85	91	72	87	90	92	96	62	94	104	115
17223	FORT LITTLETON	85	61	87	59	63	86	63	80	69	58	68	60	50	69	62	76	45	73	83	95
17224	FORT LOUDON	80	70	74	72	72	85	70	80	73	63	71	61	63	74	69	77	48	74	83	94
17225	GREENCASTLE	90	89	82	91	88	94	86	90	87	84	86	68	85	89	86	89	60	87	92	106
17228	HARRISONVILLE	77	68	70	70	69	82	67	77	70	61	68	58	61	71	67	74	47	71	79	89
17229	HUSTONTOWN	83	59	85	57	62	84	61	77	68	57	66	58	49	67	60	74	44	71	81	92
17232	LURGAN	87	79	78	83	81	93	78	88	81	71	79	67	72	82	78	85	54	81	91	102
17233	MC CONNELLSBURG	81	61	69	60	61	78	65	73	71	62	70	55	54	73	60	77	47	71	78	88
17236	MERCERSBURG	93	86	86	89	87	99	85	94	87	80	86	71	80	88	85	91	59	88	97	109
17237	MONT ALTO	81	74	73	77	75	87	73	82	75	66	74	62	67	76	73	79	50	76	85	95
17238	NEEDMORE	79	72	71	75	73	85	71	80	73	64	72	60	65	74	71	77	49	74	82	93
17239	NEELYTON	79	71	71	74	73	85	70	80	73	64	71	60	65	74	70	77	49	74	82	93
17240	NEWBURG	92	84	83	88	86	99	83	94	86	75	84	71	77	87	83	91	57	87	97	109
17241	NEWVILLE	87	81	76	83	81	91	80	86	82	75	81	65	75	84	78	86	55	82	89	102
17243	ORBISONIA	85	61	76	59	62	84	65	77	72	61	70	59	52	73	60	79	47	73	83	93
17244	ORRSTOWN	90	82	81	85	83	96	81	91	83	73	82	69	74	85	80	88	56	84	94	106
17246	PLEASANT HALL	89	81	80	84	83	96	80	90	83	72	81	68	74	84	80	87	55	83	93	105
17252	SAINT THOMAS	88	78	84	78	79	94	76	88	80	71	79	65	69	81	76	86	54	82	91	102
17255	SHADE GAP	79	72	71	75	73	84	71	80	73	64	72	60	65	74	71	77	49	74	82	93
17257	SHIPPENSBURG	82	71	66	72	70	75	79	76	78	74	78	59	70	80	71	80	54	77	78	91
17260	SHIRLEYSBURG	78	56	73	54	57	77	57	70	64	55	63	53	46	65	55	70	42	65	74	84
17262	SPRING RUN	85	68	73	69	69	86	69	80	74	65	73	61	60	77	66	80	49	74	83	95
17264	THREE SPRINGS	81	58	81	56	60	82	61	76	67	56	66	57	49	67	59	74	44	70	80	90
17265	UPPERSTRASBURG	88	80	80	84	82	95	79	90	82	72	80	68	73	83	79	87	55	83	92	104
17266	WALNUT BOTTOM	93	85	84	88	86	100	84	94	86	75	85	71	77	88	83	91	58	87	97	110
17267	WARFORDSBURG	85	62	72	61	63	82	64	75	71	62	70	58	53	73	60	77	47	71	79	91
17268	WAYNESBORO	84	82	78	83	81	90	82	85	84	78	83	64	80	85	81	88	57	84	91	100
17271	WILLOW HILL	79	72	72	75	74	85	71	81	74	65	72	61	66	75	71	78	49	74	83	94
17301	ABBOTTSTOWN	96	95	86	96	93	100	89	95	90	87	90	72	87	93	89	93	62	91	96	112
17302	AIRVILLE	92	87	82	89	87	96	83	92	85	79	84	69	79	87	83	89	58	86	93	107
17304	ASPERS	85	78	75	80	79	89	76	85	79	71	77	64	70	80	75	83	53	79	87	99
17307	BIGLERVILLE	84	80	78	82	81	91	79	86	80	72	79	66	74	82	79	84	54	81	89	100
17309	BROGUE	99	95	91	99	96	107	91	101	93	85	92	77	88	95	93	97	63	94	103	118
17313	DALLASTOWN	90	94	82	96	90	94	94	91	93	91	93	71	96	95	93	94	65	92	95	108
17314	DELTA	90	84	77	84	83	91	81	87	84	79	83	65	77	86	79	87	57	83	90	103
17315	DOVER	96	90	86	91	89	98	88	94	90	85	89	71	84	92	87	93	61	90	96	110
17316	EAST BERLIN	88	98	87	99	96	96	90	92	88	89	89	72	95	90	94	89	62	89	91	108
17319	ETTERS	108	115	99	114	110	106	105	106	103	109	104	82	108	107	106	102	73	104	101	124
17320	FAIRFIELD	102	106	92	106	102	103	97	102	95	97	95	79	97	99	98	95	66	96	97	117
17321	FAWN GROVE	95	106	92	109	103	104	95	99	93	95	94	77	101	96	100	94	66	95	98	116
17322	FELTON	98	106	93	109	104	107	96	102	95	95	96	79	100	98	101	97	67	97	101	119
17324	GARDNERS	97	90	87	93	91	104	88	98	90	81	89	74	82	92	87	95	61	91	101	114
17325	GETTYSBURG	85	84	82	85	84	90	83	86	85	81	84	64	82	84	83	87	58	85	91	101
17327	GLEN ROCK	93	101	93	103	100	105	93	99	94	91	94	75	98	95	98	96	66	95	101	115
17329	GLENVILLE	104	112	99	115	109	114	102	108	101	100	101	84	105	104	106	103	70	103	108	126
17331	HANOVER	89	91	81	93	89	96	89	90	90	85	90	70	90	91	89	93	62	90	96	107
17339	LEWISBERRY	114	122	107	124	119	123	111	116	110	110	110	90	114	113	115	112	77	112	116	137
17340	LITTLESTOWN	83	91	80	92	88	90	85	86	84	83	84	67	89	86	88	85	59	85	87	101
17344	MC SHERRYSTOWN	81	76	69	77	74	84	81	81	84	75	83	62	77	84	77	88	57	82	90	96
17345	MANCHESTER	90	91	87	91	89	98	86	92	89	83	88	70	87	90	88	93	61	89	97	108
17347	MOUNT WOLF	95	92	89	91	89	102	86	93	90	85	90	71	86	92	87	95	62	90	98	110
17349	NEW FREEDOM	111	130	122	134	130	126	114	119	111	117	112	91	125	112	124	111	79	114	117	139
17350	NEW OXFORD	88	84	84	83	83	90	82	88	84	79	83	66	79	85	81	87	58	85	90	103
17352	NEW PARK	97	109	94	112	106	106	98	101	96	99	96	79	104	99	102	95	67	97	99	119
17353	ORRTANNA	91	87	83	90	88	98	84	93	86	77	84	71	80	87	85	90	58	87	95	108
17356	RED LION	93	93	84	95	91	98	91	94	92	87	91	73	90	94	91	94	63	92	97	111
17360	SEVEN VALLEYS	97	98	91	102	98	106	92	100	93	88	92	77	91	95	95	96	64	94	101	117
17361	SHREWSBURY	94	106	98	108	105	106	99	101	99	98	99	77	106	98	104	100	70	99	105	118
17362	SPRING GROVE	95	99	90	101	97	104	93	98	93	89	93	76	94	95	95	95	64	94	100	115
17363	STEWARTSTOWN	103	117	101	116	112	107	106	106	102	108	103	84	111	106	109	101	73	103	102	124
17364	THOMASVILLE	92	87	84	90	88	99	84	94	86	77	85	71	80	88	85	91	58	87	97	109
17365	WELLSVILLE	95	93	88	97	93	103	89	97	90	83	89	74	86	92	90	93	61	91	99	113
	PENNSYLVANIA	94	95	95	95	95	100	94	96	96	91	95	73	94	96	94	99	67	95	101	113
	UNITED STATES	100	100	100	100	100	100	100	100	100	100	100	100	100	100	100	100	100	100	100	100

ZIP CODE #	POST OFFICE NAME	COUNTY FIPS CODE	POPULATION 2000	POPULATION 2009	POPULATION 2014	2000-2009 ANNUAL RATE % Rate	2000-2009 ANNUAL RATE State Centile	HOUSEHOLDS 2000	HOUSEHOLDS 2009	HOUSEHOLDS 2014	HOUSEHOLDS % Annual Rate 2000-2009	HOUSEHOLDS 2009 Average HH Size	FAMILIES 2000	FAMILIES 2009	FAMILIES % Annual Rate 2000-2009
17366	WINDSOR	133	5054	5577	5871	1.1	87	1843	2070	2195	1.3	2.69	1397	1527	1.0
17368	WRIGHTSVILLE	133	7716	8386	8801	0.9	83	3071	3406	3596	1.1	2.46	2194	2358	0.8
17370	YORK HAVEN	133	5598	6853	7437	2.2	96	2109	2626	2865	2.4	2.61	1609	1951	2.1
17372	YORK SPRINGS	001	3390	3819	4024	1.3	90	1236	1418	1504	1.5	2.67	956	1068	1.2
17401	YORK	133	17323	17927	18346	0.4	68	6589	6839	7023	0.4	2.54	3681	3633	-0.1
17402	YORK	133	29874	34073	36421	1.4	91	11784	13699	14758	1.6	2.31	8006	8940	1.2
17403	YORK	133	35636	37877	39262	0.7	77	13881	14989	15652	0.8	2.36	8687	9027	0.4
17404	YORK	133	28172	33099	35509	1.8	93	11591	13607	14608	1.7	2.41	7632	8818	1.6
17406	YORK	133	18736	22189	24112	1.8	93	7660	9274	10138	2.1	2.39	5513	6456	1.7
17407	YORK	133	1659	1804	1894	0.9	83	633	703	743	1.1	2.56	514	559	0.9
17408	YORK	133	20189	22419	23704	1.1	87	8090	9175	9781	1.4	2.38	5728	6278	1.0
17501	AKRON	071	4582	4935	5098	0.8	80	1843	2027	2104	1.0	2.37	1310	1395	0.7
17502	BAINBRIDGE	071	2315	2498	2590	0.8	80	832	919	960	1.1	2.72	653	704	0.8
17505	BIRD IN HAND	071	1683	1777	1829	0.6	74	480	517	534	0.8	3.44	373	392	0.5
17509	CHRISTIANA	071	4395	4735	4897	0.8	80	1270	1394	1448	1.0	3.33	1062	1145	0.8
17512	COLUMBIA	071	17373	17827	18082	0.3	64	6823	7149	7284	0.5	2.45	4581	4672	0.2
17516	CONESTOGA	071	4101	4281	4372	0.5	70	1478	1572	1613	0.7	2.72	1153	1196	0.4
17517	DENVER	071	14255	15567	16194	1.0	85	4966	5509	5758	1.1	2.81	3977	4319	0.9
17518	DRUMORE	071	1350	1428	1466	0.6	74	433	467	482	0.8	3.06	352	372	0.6
17519	EAST EARL	071	5405	6092	6366	1.3	90	1656	1908	2004	1.5	3.17	1397	1581	1.3
17520	EAST PETERSBURG	071	4633	4624	4634	0.0	52	1767	1809	1823	0.3	2.53	1381	1379	0.0
17522	EPHRATA	071	28017	29684	30431	0.6	74	10340	11233	11594	0.9	2.60	7431	7851	0.6
17527	GAP	071	5654	6135	6366	0.9	83	1800	1985	2070	1.1	3.04	1458	1573	0.8
17529	GORDONVILLE	071	3582	3949	4204	1.1	87	1097	1237	1326	1.3	3.19	887	980	1.1
17532	HOLTWOOD	071	3352	3475	3532	0.4	68	1139	1207	1234	0.6	2.88	923	957	0.4
17535	KINZERS	071	2585	2822	2945	1.0	85	731	811	848	1.1	3.46	609	663	0.9
17536	KIRKWOOD	071	2586	2798	2913	0.9	83	793	882	924	1.2	3.17	687	753	1.0
17538	LANDISVILLE	071	6132	6597	6821	0.8	80	2221	2446	2543	1.0	2.67	1785	1927	0.8
17540	LEOLA	071	10142	10816	11172	0.7	77	3507	3810	3955	0.9	2.83	2743	2911	0.6
17543	LITITZ	071	37705	41911	43849	1.1	87	13762	15706	16537	1.4	2.60	10366	11563	1.2
17545	MANHEIM	071	18939	20692	21489	1.0	85	7025	7883	8248	1.3	2.59	5372	5925	1.1
17547	MARIETTA	071	6191	6878	7195	1.1	87	2369	2678	2815	1.3	2.57	1725	1907	1.1
17551	MILLERSVILLE	071	9455	10557	11000	1.2	88	2894	3302	3474	1.4	2.48	1803	1972	1.0
17552	MOUNT JOY	071	14384	17034	18148	1.8	93	5570	6836	7351	2.2	2.48	4009	4778	1.9
17554	MOUNTVILLE	071	5330	6380	6850	2.0	95	2155	2670	2902	2.3	2.30	1561	1869	2.0
17555	NARVON	071	7165	7668	7910	0.7	77	2129	2314	2398	0.9	3.28	1817	1943	0.7
17557	NEW HOLLAND	071	12683	13465	13891	0.6	74	4524	4902	5083	0.9	2.74	3437	3633	0.6
17560	NEW PROVIDENCE	071	4557	4728	4819	0.4	68	1663	1769	1816	0.7	2.66	1253	1295	0.4
17562	PARADISE	071	4159	4457	4612	0.8	80	1277	1400	1456	1.0	3.16	1030	1104	0.8
17563	PEACH BOTTOM	071	3333	3539	3640	0.7	77	1088	1172	1208	0.8	3.02	873	918	0.5
17565	PEQUEA	071	2604	2703	2751	0.4	68	922	980	1004	0.7	2.73	726	754	0.4
17566	QUARRYVILLE	071	10971	11668	12006	0.7	77	3554	3896	4045	1.0	2.91	2846	3049	0.7
17569	REINHOLDS	071	5478	6018	6293	1.0	85	1943	2166	2274	1.2	2.74	1578	1718	0.9
17572	RONKS	071	3856	4089	4233	0.6	74	1225	1327	1380	0.9	3.07	946	1002	0.6
17576	SMOKETOWN	071	239	265	278	1.1	87	84	95	100	1.3	2.79	65	72	1.1
17578	STEVENS	071	6748	7245	7483	0.8	80	2220	2419	2507	0.9	2.92	1738	1853	0.7
17579	STRASBURG	071	5778	5888	6064	0.2	61	2048	2122	2201	0.4	2.77	1599	1617	0.1
17581	TERRE HILL	071	863	924	953	0.7	77	316	346	359	1.0	2.67	269	289	0.8
17582	WASHINGTON BORO	071	2362	2409	2438	0.2	61	815	854	869	0.5	2.78	664	681	0.3
17584	WILLOW STREET	071	8418	9013	9343	0.7	77	3278	3590	3744	1.0	2.46	2405	2537	0.6
17601	LANCASTER	071	45452	48291	49796	0.7	77	17943	19562	20303	0.9	2.41	12761	13503	0.6
17602	LANCASTER	071	46992	50622	52232	0.8	80	17394	19047	19759	1.0	2.54	11386	12114	0.7
17603	LANCASTER	071	57333	60151	61626	0.5	70	23202	24740	25471	0.7	2.34	14002	14390	0.3
17701	WILLIAMSPORT	081	45961	44603	43583	-0.3	29	18560	18517	18232	0.0	2.23	11006	10566	-0.4
17702	WILLIAMSPORT	081	11048	10732	10489	-0.3	29	4516	4521	4458	0.0	2.37	3107	3016	-0.3
17721	AVIS	035	1557	1513	1483	-0.3	29	661	663	657	0.0	2.27	439	426	-0.3
17723	CAMMAL	081	225	218	214	-0.3	29	118	119	118	0.1	1.82	77	75	-0.3
17724	CANTON	117	4700	4612	4533	-0.2	38	1840	1867	1853	0.2	2.45	1300	1283	-0.1
17728	COGAN STATION	081	5121	5005	4907	-0.2	38	1940	1972	1954	0.2	2.54	1503	1492	-0.1
17729	CROSS FORK	105	195	203	203	0.4	68	107	114	115	0.7	1.78	75	77	0.3
17737	HUGHESVILLE	081	6606	6741	6679	0.2	61	2707	2853	2853	0.6	2.36	1903	1948	0.3
17740	JERSEY SHORE	081	12032	11650	11364	-0.3	29	4552	4531	4459	0.0	2.53	3315	3213	-0.3
17742	LAIRDSVILLE	081	83	90	91	0.9	83	34	39	39	1.5	2.31	27	30	1.1
17744	LINDEN	081	3193	3354	3348	0.5	70	1236	1345	1357	0.9	2.48	918	968	0.6
17745	LOCK HAVEN	035	17464	17157	16912	-0.2	38	7097	7203	7154	0.2	2.20	4417	4326	-0.2
17747	LOGANTON	035	2709	2958	2984	1.0	85	924	1033	1051	1.2	2.86	738	807	1.0
17751	MILL HALL	035	8307	8299	8209	0.0	52	2835	2936	2925	0.4	2.59	2109	2126	0.1
17752	MONTGOMERY	081	5259	4557	4510	-1.5	1	1685	1728	1717	0.3	2.64	1267	1267	0.0
17754	MONTOURSVILLE	081	12461	12336	12127	-0.1	46	4946	5052	5011	0.2	2.40	3608	3588	-0.1
17756	MUNCY	081	11191	11249	11104	0.1	57	4075	4205	4181	0.3	2.43	3009	3022	0.0
17758	MUNCY VALLEY	113	1795	1771	1737	-0.1	46	745	756	748	0.2	2.09	513	505	-0.2
17763	RALSTON	081	448	435	426	-0.3	29	173	175	173	0.1	2.42	132	130	-0.2
17764	RENOVO	035	3335	3165	3077	-0.6	13	1449	1415	1388	-0.3	2.21	898	843	-0.7
17765	ROARING BRANCH	081	835	823	810	-0.2	38	315	322	319	0.2	2.54	252	252	0.0
17768	SHUNK	113	332	316	308	-0.5	19	135	134	133	-0.1	2.29	90	87	-0.4
17771	TROUT RUN	081	3926	3829	3756	-0.3	29	1512	1533	1518	0.1	2.49	1108	1091	-0.2
17772	TURBOTVILLE	093	3569	3354	3237	-0.7	8	1260	1213	1179	-0.4	2.75	1016	961	-0.6
17774	UNITYVILLE	081	1340	1428	1431	0.7	77	516	573	579	1.1	2.49	386	418	0.9
17776	WATERVILLE	081	410	406	400	-0.1	46	183	189	188	0.3	2.13	127	128	0.1
17777	WATSONTOWN	097	7046	6511	6252	-0.9	4	2798	2638	2550	-0.6	2.41	1951	1792	-0.9
17778	WESTPORT	035	84	82	81	-0.3	29	40	41	40	0.3	2.00	28	27	-0.4
17779	WOOLRICH	035	1451	1416	1390	-0.3	29	588	594	589	0.1	2.38	429	421	-0.2
17801	SUNBURY	097	16465	17077	16984	0.4	68	6800	7200	7213	0.6	2.30	4424	4462	0.1
17810	ALLENWOOD	081	6011	6392	6378	0.7	77	780	795	798	0.2	2.73	624	620	-0.1
17812	BEAVER SPRINGS	109	1566	1545	1527	-0.1	46	598	607	606	0.2	2.55	452	449	-0.1
17813	BEAVERTOWN	109	2142	2225	2262	0.4	68	834	891	915	0.7	2.50	632	658	0.4
17814	BENTON	037	5733	6064	6178	0.6	74	2305	2512	2582	0.9	2.40	1679	1778	0.6
17815	BLOOMSBURG	037	27903	28898	29042	0.4	68	10182	10664	10797	0.5	2.39	6323	6393	0.1
17820	CATAWISSA	037	5949	6003	6022	0.1	57	2446	2543	2572	0.4	2.36	1767	1787	0.1
17821	DANVILLE	093	19755	19514	19125	-0.1	46	7740	7825	7715	0.1	2.37	5277	5182	-0.2
17823	DORNSIFE	097	435	402	385	-0.8	6	151	143	138	-0.6	2.81	114	105	-0.9
17824	ELYSBURG	097	3764	3889	3863	0.4	68	1497	1595	1597	0.7	2.40	1121	1165	0.4
17827	FREEBURG	109	620	615	606	-0.1	46	254	260	258	0.3	2.37	182	180	-0.1
17830	HERNDON	097	2040	1889	1815	-0.8	6	805	763	739	-0.6	2.44	600	557	-0.8
17832	MARION HEIGHTS	097	735	662	631	-1.1	2	314	290	279	-0.9	2.28	213	191	-1.2
	PENNSYLVANIA					0.3					0.4	2.45			0.1
	UNITED STATES					1.0					1.1	2.59			0.9

ZIP CODE		RACE (%)						% Hispanic Origin		2009 AGE DISTRIBUTION (%)										MEDIAN AGE		
#	POST OFFICE NAME	White		Black		Asian/Pacific																
		2000	2009	2000	2009	2000	2009	2000	2009	0-4	5-9	10-14	15-19	20-24	25-44	45-64	65-84	85+	18+	2009	% 2009 Males	% 2009 Females
17366	WINDSOR	98.6	98.0	0.4	0.6	0.1	0.2	1.0	1.6	7.0	7.0	7.2	7.1	6.0	28.2	27.6	9.1	1.0	74.3	37.1	49.7	50.3
17368	WRIGHTSVILLE	98.0	97.1	0.4	0.6	0.2	0.4	1.4	2.3	5.9	6.1	6.7	6.3	5.0	27.4	30.9	10.4	1.3	77.3	40.3	50.0	50.0
17370	YORK HAVEN	97.5	96.3	0.4	0.7	0.4	0.7	1.4	2.4	7.3	7.2	7.2	7.0	5.7	28.0	28.7	8.1	0.8	73.9	37.4	50.2	49.8
17372	YORK SPRINGS	96.7	95.6	0.3	0.3	0.6	0.9	5.0	7.0	6.2	6.8	7.2	6.6	4.3	26.3	30.2	10.9	1.5	75.5	40.3	50.8	49.2
17401	YORK	52.0	43.6	31.0	35.5	0.9	1.1	20.3	25.4	8.5	7.8	7.1	8.1	10.9	27.7	20.9	7.6	1.4	71.7	29.6	49.3	50.7
17402	YORK	92.4	89.6	3.4	4.4	2.3	3.4	2.5	3.6	4.7	4.9	5.5	6.4	5.9	24.3	28.3	16.4	3.7	81.1	43.8	49.2	50.8
17403	YORK	81.6	77.4	11.2	13.4	1.4	2.0	7.5	9.8	5.9	5.7	5.7	8.6	8.4	22.6	26.0	13.3	3.7	78.8	39.3	47.5	52.5
17404	YORK	88.0	84.6	5.9	7.2	1.3	2.0	5.4	7.1	6.8	7.0	7.1	6.8	5.4	26.2	27.0	11.3	2.3	74.7	38.9	48.2	51.8
17406	YORK	95.6	93.4	1.7	2.6	1.1	1.7	1.5	2.5	5.3	5.6	6.3	6.5	4.6	24.5	31.5	13.9	1.8	78.6	43.1	49.4	50.6
17407	YORK	99.2	99.0	0.1	0.1	0.4	0.6	0.5	0.8	5.0	5.5	6.5	6.4	4.1	21.7	33.7	15.2	1.9	78.9	45.5	50.1	49.9
17408	YORK	96.2	94.2	1.2	1.9	1.1	1.7	1.3	2.1	5.1	5.2	5.6	5.7	4.9	24.0	29.6	16.2	3.6	80.5	44.6	47.8	52.2
17501	AKRON	96.4	94.3	0.5	0.7	1.4	2.5	2.1	3.4	6.1	6.1	6.1	6.0	5.6	25.7	26.6	14.8	3.0	77.5	41.2	48.1	51.9
17502	BAINBRIDGE	98.9	98.4	0.0	0.0	0.2	0.4	0.9	1.5	6.2	7.0	7.7	7.4	5.0	26.9	29.5	9.2	1.1	74.3	39.4	51.2	48.8
17505	BIRD IN HAND	95.3	92.8	1.2	1.7	1.9	3.0	2.6	4.2	9.8	8.7	7.8	7.9	7.4	24.3	22.7	9.9	1.4	68.5	30.8	49.6	50.4
17509	CHRISTIANA	98.2	97.4	0.8	1.1	0.2	0.3	1.0	1.8	9.1	9.2	9.3	8.3	5.1	24.2	23.7	9.1	2.0	67.2	32.9	49.4	50.6
17512	COLUMBIA	91.5	88.0	3.5	4.6	0.7	1.0	5.3	8.3	7.0	6.9	6.9	6.8	6.0	26.4	26.8	11.1	2.2	75.1	37.9	48.4	51.6
17516	CONESTOGA	98.4	97.5	0.3	0.5	0.4	0.6	1.0	1.8	5.3	6.4	7.1	7.5	4.7	24.1	32.9	10.6	1.3	76.4	41.5	50.7	49.3
17517	DENVER	96.9	95.2	0.5	0.8	1.3	2.1	1.4	2.3	7.8	8.0	8.2	7.5	5.0	25.9	26.4	10.0	1.3	71.4	36.8	49.3	50.7
17518	DRUMORE	98.8	98.2	0.2	0.4	0.1	0.1	0.7	1.3	7.8	8.2	8.4	7.6	5.3	23.2	29.3	9.0	1.1	70.7	36.2	50.7	49.3
17519	EAST EARL	98.2	97.3	0.5	0.7	0.4	0.7	0.8	1.4	8.9	8.9	8.8	7.9	5.1	25.4	23.3	10.1	1.4	68.4	33.3	49.9	50.1
17520	EAST PETERSBURG	95.2	92.7	1.3	1.8	1.2	1.9	2.7	4.6	5.5	6.0	6.6	6.8	5.4	24.8	29.2	14.1	1.7	77.5	41.5	48.2	51.8
17522	EPHRATA	96.5	94.6	0.5	0.7	1.4	2.3	2.0	3.4	7.3	7.3	7.3	7.1	5.8	26.2	25.6	11.2	2.2	73.6	36.9	49.4	50.6
17527	GAP	97.1	95.8	0.9	1.3	0.6	1.1	1.4	2.4	9.2	9.0	9.0	7.7	4.9	25.5	23.8	9.5	1.4	67.8	34.0	50.5	49.5
17529	GORDONVILLE	98.0	96.9	0.5	0.8	0.7	1.1	0.7	1.1	10.6	10.1	9.0	8.4	5.9	23.3	20.3	10.8	1.5	65.0	29.8	50.3	49.7
17532	HOLTWOOD	98.3	97.5	0.5	0.7	0.2	0.3	1.2	1.9	6.8	7.5	8.1	8.1	4.7	24.5	31.1	8.5	0.9	72.6	39.1	51.1	48.9
17535	KINZERS	97.7	96.7	0.7	1.0	0.4	0.6	0.9	1.5	10.1	10.0	9.9	8.0	4.6	25.1	22.2	9.3	1.0	65.0	31.7	51.1	48.9
17536	KIRKWOOD	97.8	96.8	0.8	1.1	0.1	0.2	1.0	1.8	10.0	10.0	9.9	7.8	5.4	23.9	23.6	8.4	1.0	65.1	30.8	50.5	49.5
17538	LANDISVILLE	96.6	94.6	0.9	1.4	1.6	2.7	1.3	2.2	5.0	6.4	7.1	7.5	4.0	23.3	32.4	12.6	1.7	76.4	42.9	50.0	50.0
17540	LEOLA	93.3	89.8	0.9	1.2	3.5	5.6	2.8	4.6	8.0	8.0	7.8	7.2	5.7	24.4	26.9	10.6	1.4	71.5	35.7	49.4	50.6
17543	LITITZ	96.8	95.1	0.7	1.0	1.1	1.8	1.6	2.8	6.3	6.7	7.3	7.0	4.7	23.9	29.1	11.6	3.4	75.0	40.8	48.8	51.2
17545	MANHEIM	97.4	96.1	0.5	0.8	0.8	1.3	1.0	1.7	6.3	6.5	7.0	6.9	5.4	24.5	28.6	12.7	2.0	75.7	40.0	49.7	50.3
17547	MARIETTA	96.6	95.1	1.5	2.1	0.4	0.7	1.8	3.1	7.4	7.5	7.5	6.4	5.0	30.4	26.2	8.6	1.0	73.7	36.4	50.1	49.9
17551	MILLERSVILLE	93.6	83.8	3.6	12.0	1.1	2.0	2.0	3.3	3.4	3.6	3.9	11.4	16.2	25.0	22.8	11.7	2.0	86.5	33.4	52.8	47.2
17552	MOUNT JOY	96.2	94.3	1.1	1.5	0.7	1.1	2.4	4.0	6.6	6.8	7.0	6.7	5.5	27.9	28.0	10.0	1.5	75.4	38.5	49.9	50.1
17554	MOUNTVILLE	94.7	92.1	1.7	2.3	1.4	2.1	3.1	4.8	5.7	5.9	6.2	6.3	5.7	24.7	30.4	12.8	2.3	78.1	41.7	47.7	52.3
17555	NARVON	98.4	97.6	0.5	0.8	0.3	0.6	0.7	1.2	9.3	9.6	9.4	8.2	4.7	25.1	23.9	8.4	1.4	66.5	32.6	50.0	50.0
17557	NEW HOLLAND	94.5	91.8	0.8	1.1	2.3	3.4	3.2	5.2	7.5	7.4	7.1	6.8	5.5	23.8	25.3	14.3	2.3	73.8	38.1	49.3	50.7
17560	NEW PROVIDENCE	97.8	96.9	0.5	0.8	0.3	0.5	0.9	1.5	6.0	6.5	7.0	7.2	5.2	24.3	29.8	12.4	1.6	76.1	40.2	49.7	50.3
17562	PARADISE	98.4	97.8	0.6	0.8	0.1	0.2	0.6	0.9	8.5	8.8	8.6	8.1	4.9	25.0	23.9	10.8	1.2	69.1	33.8	50.5	49.5
17563	PEACH BOTTOM	97.6	96.4	1.1	1.8	0.2	0.4	1.1	1.9	8.9	8.8	9.0	8.0	5.5	25.2	24.5	9.2	0.9	68.3	33.9	49.6	50.4
17565	PEQUEA	98.2	97.3	0.6	0.9	0.2	0.3	1.6	2.7	5.8	6.7	7.6	8.1	4.6	24.6	32.3	9.1	1.0	74.5	40.3	51.9	48.1
17566	QUARRYVILLE	98.1	97.1	0.6	0.8	0.2	0.3	1.1	1.9	7.9	8.0	8.0	7.7	5.7	24.8	24.2	11.0	2.7	71.3	35.3	49.0	51.0
17569	REINHOLDS	97.8	96.5	0.6	0.9	0.7	1.1	1.2	2.1	7.2	7.7	8.2	7.8	4.2	25.5	29.3	9.1	0.9	71.9	38.7	50.3	49.7
17572	RONKS	97.3	96.0	0.6	0.9	0.8	1.3	1.2	2.1	9.0	8.7	8.1	7.7	6.2	23.3	23.4	12.0	1.7	69.5	33.5	49.9	50.1
17576	SMOKETOWN	96.2	94.0	0.8	1.1	1.3	2.3	2.9	5.3	7.9	8.3	6.0	7.2	7.9	21.5	24.5	14.3	2.3	72.8	36.8	50.2	49.8
17578	STEVENS	96.8	95.1	0.3	0.4	1.5	2.5	1.3	2.2	7.5	7.9	8.1	7.3	4.5	24.6	27.1	11.2	1.8	71.9	38.2	49.5	50.5
17579	STRASBURG	98.3	97.6	0.4	0.5	0.5	0.7	0.3	0.6	7.7	7.8	8.2	7.5	5.0	25.5	26.6	10.4	1.3	71.5	36.7	49.4	50.6
17581	TERRE HILL	98.6	97.5	0.3	0.5	0.2	0.4	1.0	1.7	9.4	9.0	8.9	9.0	5.7	24.4	22.3	10.2	1.2	66.9	31.6	50.2	49.8
17582	WASHINGTON BORO	98.3	97.3	0.4	0.6	0.5	0.8	1.2	2.0	5.7	6.4	6.9	7.0	4.9	25.1	31.5	10.8	1.8	76.7	40.7	49.8	50.2
17584	WILLOW STREET	97.9	96.9	0.5	0.7	0.5	0.8	1.1	1.9	5.2	5.7	6.2	6.5	4.2	19.4	26.4	20.4	6.0	78.9	47.0	47.9	52.1
17601	LANCASTER	93.2	89.9	1.4	2.0	3.1	4.9	2.8	4.4	5.5	5.8	6.4	6.5	5.3	22.1	29.6	15.6	3.3	78.2	43.8	47.8	52.2
17602	LANCASTER	67.7	63.8	11.7	11.8	2.6	3.5	25.0	29.0	7.5	7.1	6.9	7.4	7.7	26.9	23.4	10.9	2.2	74.1	34.9	49.2	50.8
17603	LANCASTER	81.0	75.1	6.9	8.3	2.0	2.9	14.0	19.4	6.6	6.2	6.0	7.4	8.1	26.4	24.4	12.3	2.7	77.5	36.8	47.9	52.1
17701	WILLIAMSPORT	88.0	84.5	9.2	11.8	0.7	1.1	0.9	1.3	5.7	5.5	5.4	8.7	9.7	23.5	25.4	13.0	3.1	79.7	37.7	49.0	51.0
17702	WILLIAMSPORT	98.8	98.4	0.3	0.4	0.2	0.3	0.5	0.7	5.5	5.5	5.7	6.4	5.8	25.3	28.9	14.5	2.4	79.3	42.0	49.4	50.6
17721	AVIS	98.8	98.3	0.3	0.4	0.6	0.9	0.1	0.1	5.4	5.4	5.7	6.3	5.8	24.4	28.0	16.8	2.4	79.6	42.6	49.1	50.9
17723	CAMMAL	99.6	99.1	0.0	0.0	0.0	0.0	0.4	0.9	3.7	4.1	4.1	4.6	2.8	18.3	34.4	25.2	2.8	84.9	53.2	53.2	46.8
17724	CANTON	98.4	98.0	0.5	0.7	0.1	0.1	0.4	0.5	6.7	6.7	6.8	7.1	5.4	24.0	27.4	13.6	2.4	75.2	40.2	50.2	49.8
17728	COGAN STATION	98.5	98.0	0.4	0.5	0.4	0.6	0.2	0.3	4.9	5.5	6.3	6.8	5.5	23.7	32.8	13.2	1.2	79.0	42.9	50.5	49.5
17729	CROSS FORK	98.5	98.0	0.0	0.0	0.5	0.5	0.0	0.0	3.0	3.4	5.4	5.9	3.0	20.2	39.4	17.7	2.0	83.7	50.6	52.2	47.8
17737	HUGHESVILLE	98.9	98.6	0.2	0.2	0.2	0.3	0.3	0.4	5.8	6.1	6.4	6.2	5.6	25.0	30.0	12.9	2.0	77.9	41.4	49.9	50.1
17740	JERSEY SHORE	98.8	98.4	0.3	0.4	0.3	0.5	0.2	0.3	6.5	6.5	6.7	6.5	6.0	26.0	27.6	12.0	2.1	76.2	39.1	48.8	51.2
17742	LAIRDSVILLE	100.0	100.0	0.0	0.0	0.0	0.0	0.0	0.0	5.6	5.6	5.6	4.4	4.4	32.2	30.0	11.1	1.1	78.9	40.0	52.2	47.8
17744	LINDEN	98.5	97.9	0.6	0.8	0.2	0.3	0.2	0.3	5.5	6.0	6.6	6.8	4.8	26.8	29.7	12.5	1.3	77.6	40.9	50.2	49.8
17745	LOCK HAVEN	97.6	96.9	0.8	1.0	0.6	0.9	0.7	1.0	5.3	4.9	5.0	8.2	11.3	23.2	24.5	14.6	3.0	81.5	38.1	47.7	52.3
17747	LOGANTON	98.9	98.6	0.2	0.2	0.2	0.4	0.8	1.1	8.5	8.1	8.4	7.2	4.9	24.0	25.7	12.1	1.3	70.5	36.5	50.5	49.5
17751	MILL HALL	98.7	98.3	0.4	0.5	0.3	0.5	0.4	0.6	5.0	5.3	5.7	9.8	7.4	23.0	27.5	13.8	2.4	80.1	40.2	49.1	50.9
17752	MONTGOMERY	92.6	86.8	6.4	11.4	0.4	0.9	1.0	1.9	5.8	5.6	6.2	7.0	10.0	26.3	27.7	10.2	1.2	79.4	37.5	52.4	47.6
17754	MONTOURSVILLE	98.5	97.8	0.3	0.5	0.4	0.7	0.5	0.8	5.0	5.3	5.9	6.5	5.4	21.8	30.8	16.2	3.1	79.6	45.1	48.4	51.6
17756	MUNCY	94.2	93.0	4.0	4.7	0.3	0.5	1.0	1.4	5.1	5.4	5.7	6.2	5.7	27.8	28.9	12.8	2.4	80.0	41.0	44.9	55.1
17758	MUNCY VALLEY	93.7	92.4	3.7	4.3	0.1	0.1	1.5	2.0	3.4	3.8	4.0	11.0	4.5	19.1	30.9	19.8	3.5	82.3	48.0	52.2	47.8
17763	RALSTON	96.9	95.9	1.6	2.3	0.0	0.0	0.2	0.2	4.1	5.1	5.7	6.9	3.4	24.6	32.2	16.6	1.4	80.5	45.1	49.0	51.0
17764	RENOVO	99.2	99.1	0.1	0.1	0.1	0.1	0.2	0.3	5.0	5.1	5.5	6.0	5.4	20.3	31.6	17.3	3.9	80.3	46.9	49.0	51.0
17765	ROARING BRANCH	98.4	98.3	0.5	0.6	0.1	0.1	0.1	0.2	4.9	5.3	6.1	6.4	4.7	25.0	30.7	15.1	1.7	79.8	43.4	50.8	49.2
17768	SHUNK	98.8	98.7	0.0	0.0	0.6	0.6	0.3	0.3	4.7	5.4	5.1	4.4	4.4	22.5	33.2	16.8	3.5	82.3	47.1	50.9	49.1
17771	TROUT RUN	99.0	98.7	0.2	0.3	0.1	0.2	0.5	0.7	4.8	5.9	6.3	6.4	4.7	23.8	32.9	13.7	1.4	78.8	43.7	51.1	48.9
17772	TURBOTVILLE	99.1	98.9	0.1	0.1	0.2	0.3	0.3	0.4	6.9	7.1	7.2	6.4	5.2	24.6	29.4	11.9	1.3	74.7	40.1	50.3	49.7
17774	UNITYVILLE	99.6	99.4	0.2	0.4	0.0	0.1	0.0	0.0	6.0	6.0	6.3	5.8	4.4	25.5	29.8	14.6	1.6	78.2	42.4	51.5	48.5
17776	WATERVILLE	99.8	99.0	0.0	0.0	0.0	0.0	0.5	1.0	4.4	4.9	5.4	5.7	3.7	20.7	32.0	20.9	2.2	81.8	48.4	51.5	48.5
17777	WATSONTOWN	98.8	98.4	0.4	0.5	0.2	0.3	0.5	0.6	5.8	5.7	6.2	6.4	5.4	25.0	28.4	14.7	2.4	78.0	41.9	48.2	51.8
17778	WESTPORT	100.0	100.0	0.0	0.0	0.0	0.0	0.0	0.0	4.9	4.9	6.1	4.9	4.9	15.9	35.4	19.5	3.7	79.3	50.6	47.6	52.4
17779	WOOLRICH	99.2	99.1	0.2	0.2	0.2	0.4	0.1	0.1	4.8	5.1	5.9	6.6	5.2	22.8	32.6	15.1	1.8	79.9	44.7	49.2	50.8
17801	SUNBURY	96.4	95.4	0.9	1.2	0.3	0.4	2.2	3.0	5.8	5.5	5.4	6.0	6.9	25.8	27.9	14.0	2.8	79.8	41.0	48.6	51.4
17810	ALLENWOOD	64.7	61.1	28.6	30.5	1.6	2.1	16.1	19.6	2.3	2.5	2.6	2.8	7.0	55.4	22.4	4.7	0.3	91.0	35.9	82.5	17.5
17812	BEAVER SPRINGS	98.5	98.2	0.1	0.2	0.1	0.2	0.3	0.5	6.1	6.3	6.8	7.1	4.5	26.1	28.2	12.9	1.9	76.3	40.3	48.9	51.1
17813	BEAVERTOWN	99.3	99.0	0.1	0.1	0.0	0.0	0.4	0.6	5.8	6.1	6.3	6.5	4.5	26.7	28.2	14.1	1.7	77.7	41.5	48.6	51.4
17814	BENTON	98.7	98.4	0.2	0.3	0.1	0.1	0.4	0.6	5.2	5.6	5.9	6.3	4.9	24.8	30.9	14.4	2.0	79.5	43.3	50.5	49.5
17815	BLOOMSBURG	96.5	95.4	1.3	1.6	0.9	1.4	1.1	1.6	4.3	4.3	4.7	11.9	15.3	21.3	24.3	11.7	2.2	83.7	33.9	46.9	53.1
17820	CATAWISSA	98.9	98.6	0.3	0.4	0.2	0.3	0.6	0.8	5.2	5.6	5.9	5.9	4.7	23.3	32.5	14.6	2.2	79.6	44.5	49.6	50.4
17821	DANVILLE	96.8	95.7	1.0	1.2	1.2	1.9	0.9	1.2	5.5	5.8	6.3	6.7	4.8	23.9	29.3	14.6	3.2	78.1	43.1	47.7	52.3
17823	DORNSIFE	99.8	99.5	0.0	0.0	0.0	0.2	0.0	0.0	5.7	6.2	7.0	8.0	5.0	23.9	28.1	14.2	2.0	76.1	40.6	51.0	49.0
17824	ELYSBURG	99.3	99.1	0.1	0.1	0.3	0.4	0.4	0.6	4.4	5.0	5.8	6.2	4.5	20.6	33.4	17.1	2.9	80.5	47.1	48.8	51.2
17827	FREEBURG	99.4	98.9	0.3	0.5	0.2	0.3	0.0	0.0	5.2	5.2	5.7	6.5	5.5	24.1	29.1	15.9	2.8	80.2	43.2	49.6	50.4
17830	HERNDON	98.8	98.4	0.4	0.5	0.2	0.4	0.4	0.6	5.4	5.6	6.2	5.9	4.3	24.6	30.9	15.5	1.7	79.0	43.5	49.0	51.0
17832	MARION HEIGHTS	99.3	99.2	0.0	0.0	0.0	0.0	0.4	0.6	4.2	4.4	4.7	5.1	5.3	22.4	33.5	16.8	3.6	83.5	47.2	48.5	51.5
	PENNSYLVANIA	85.4	83.2	10.0	10.7	1.8	2.7	3.2	4.2	5.8	6.0	6.3	7.1	6.5	24.8	27.8	13.1	2.6	77.8	40.4	48.5	51.5
	UNITED STATES	75.1	72.0	12.3	12.7	3.8	4.6	12.5	15.7	6.8	6.7	6.6	7.1	6.9	27.0	26.0	10.9	1.9	75.7	36.9	49.2	50.8

ZIP CODE #	POST OFFICE NAME	2009 Per Capita Income	2009 HH Income Base	2009 Household Income Distribution (%): Less than $25,000	$25,000 to $49,999	$50,000 to $99,999	$100,000 to $149,999	$150,000 or More	Median Household Income: 2009	2014	2009 National Centile	2009 State Centile	2009 Home Value Base	2009 Home Value Distribution (%): Less than $50,000	$50,000 to $89,999	$90,000 to $174,999	$175,000 to $399,999	$400,000 or More	2009 Median Home Value
17366	WINDSOR	22110	2070	15.7	26.0	50.3	5.2	2.7	56083	57879	73	73	1687	8.5	9.4	46.5	32.7	2.9	150454
17368	WRIGHTSVILLE	24679	3406	15.6	26.0	49.5	6.5	2.3	56676	59013	74	74	2622	3.5	7.9	47.9	33.9	6.8	160545
17370	YORK HAVEN	25172	2626	12.5	27.8	46.8	9.4	3.5	59256	61315	76	78	2193	16.9	8.8	32.1	38.0	4.3	157844
17372	YORK SPRINGS	22182	1418	14.8	28.1	48.1	6.9	2.0	55854	56826	72	73	1143	5.2	4.7	42.6	39.7	7.8	170313
17401	YORK	14629	6839	41.8	32.3	23.2	1.8	0.9	28937	29690	7	2	2389	15.1	47.2	31.8	5.1	0.8	78503
17402	YORK	31313	13699	11.9	22.7	47.7	11.2	6.6	65960	69057	84	87	9890	3.3	1.4	27.6	60.1	7.6	206963
17403	YORK	26693	14989	23.6	27.6	36.0	6.8	6.0	48895	51959	59	59	9917	3.7	14.5	37.1	35.0	9.6	162571
17404	YORK	28207	13607	16.1	26.4	42.5	9.9	5.1	57833	61069	75	76	9982	2.4	6.8	55.6	28.7	6.5	147411
17406	YORK	29092	9274	13.0	25.4	47.6	9.1	4.9	60665	62646	78	79	7439	4.1	3.8	41.3	44.6	6.2	176507
17407	YORK	34712	703	9.7	19.9	43.5	16.1	10.8	69449	72719	86	89	615	0.5	1.0	25.2	70.2	3.1	209828
17408	YORK	28282	9175	13.4	24.5	49.0	9.0	4.1	62342	64896	80	82	7275	5.9	2.6	36.3	51.8	3.5	183919
17501	AKRON	27124	2027	10.7	24.9	53.6	8.3	2.5	61511	64799	79	81	1378	4.8	1.2	39.3	53.5	1.2	181633
17502	BAINBRIDGE	23843	919	11.6	25.0	52.1	9.1	2.1	58044	61390	75	76	744	3.6	3.8	34.3	56.0	2.3	188964
17505	BIRD IN HAND	19865	517	19.0	24.8	41.8	8.7	5.8	55428	59177	72	72	328	0.3	0.0	13.1	69.5	17.1	248611
17509	CHRISTIANA	19832	1394	15.5	23.5	47.2	9.9	3.9	60327	63268	78	79	1085	2.9	1.9	20.3	62.5	12.4	222736
17512	COLUMBIA	23167	7149	21.0	28.6	41.0	7.1	2.3	50327	53744	62	63	4777	3.1	9.1	50.5	34.9	2.3	147692
17516	CONESTOGA	24513	1572	13.5	23.7	52.3	8.1	2.4	61911	65434	80	81	1303	6.4	1.8	25.3	55.6	10.8	200833
17517	DENVER	25220	5509	10.8	24.0	51.3	9.7	4.2	64023	67859	82	85	4566	3.4	1.5	29.1	60.4	5.5	197525
17518	DRUMORE	20744	467	14.1	28.1	47.8	7.5	2.6	59537	62474	77	78	383	7.6	3.9	19.8	50.9	17.8	209615
17519	EAST EARL	20254	1908	12.4	26.7	51.2	7.2	2.6	57893	61259	75	76	1433	3.1	2.3	26.2	53.3	15.1	202411
17520	EAST PETERSBURG	30071	1809	8.7	18.4	55.5	12.6	4.9	70822	75431	87	89	1525	0.5	0.3	43.6	53.5	2.2	181633
17522	EPHRATA	24692	11233	15.2	26.4	47.2	7.8	3.5	57260	60985	74	75	7794	6.3	3.5	37.3	48.0	5.0	180731
17527	GAP	20073	1985	15.5	30.3	43.1	8.3	2.8	53608	57504	69	69	1519	9.5	7.7	21.4	51.5	9.9	201070
17529	GORDONVILLE	17628	1237	23.0	29.7	35.0	8.5	3.9	48274	50829	57	58	838	8.0	3.3	13.5	54.9	20.3	250781
17532	HOLTWOOD	23374	1207	12.6	22.4	52.9	8.7	3.5	61982	64642	80	81	1050	6.7	1.6	24.9	57.1	9.7	206114
17535	KINZERS	17451	811	15.7	31.6	41.6	8.3	3.0	52508	56326	67	68	579	1.2	0.9	20.9	61.7	15.4	233396
17536	KIRKWOOD	19727	882	17.7	25.1	45.7	8.3	3.3	58054	61209	75	76	700	1.6	2.6	10.4	65.7	19.7	245320
17538	LANDISVILLE	31567	2446	6.8	18.5	45.9	20.4	8.4	75095	78330	89	91	2134	2.4	0.6	19.8	71.7	5.5	234031
17540	LEOLA	26283	3810	11.4	26.0	46.3	10.1	6.2	61631	64785	80	81	2718	3.1	1.2	19.1	67.8	8.9	220543
17543	LITITZ	30224	15706	10.0	22.0	48.8	11.8	7.4	65741	69498	83	86	12135	3.8	1.5	26.7	57.9	10.1	207224
17545	MANHEIM	25716	7883	12.1	23.8	52.0	9.1	2.9	61748	65184	80	81	6096	5.0	1.5	30.3	55.7	7.5	195705
17547	MARIETTA	26233	2678	9.9	23.9	54.8	9.1	2.3	63302	66789	82	84	1997	1.9	3.9	49.8	39.7	4.8	166174
17551	MILLERSVILLE	23432	3302	20.9	22.8	41.4	9.8	5.1	57336	62128	74	75	2387	0.9	1.0	33.3	57.5	7.2	195590
17552	MOUNT JOY	26730	6836	11.3	25.3	51.8	8.7	2.9	61471	64399	79	81	4990	3.0	2.0	35.7	54.4	4.9	188554
17554	MOUNTVILLE	29958	2670	10.6	23.2	53.0	8.6	4.6	63308	67083	82	84	2001	3.2	0.9	34.9	56.7	4.2	190258
17555	NARVON	20050	2314	13.6	26.7	48.9	7.6	3.2	60882	63335	79	79	1936	3.3	3.4	22.9	59.3	11.1	215936
17557	NEW HOLLAND	24118	4902	13.8	29.0	44.1	9.0	4.1	56448	60855	73	73	3450	3.8	2.1	25.9	56.9	11.3	208982
17560	NEW PROVIDENCE	22017	1769	17.0	28.5	45.6	7.5	1.4	54183	58317	70	70	1529	26.0	6.9	21.7	42.3	3.1	164446
17562	PARADISE	18997	1400	17.2	28.9	44.1	6.4	3.4	52450	55456	67	67	1008	0.7	1.7	27.4	56.3	14.0	217907
17563	PEACH BOTTOM	19022	1172	19.5	27.8	45.3	5.5	1.9	52095	54977	66	67	905	5.5	7.1	30.8	45.3	11.3	188281
17565	PEQUEA	25306	980	12.2	20.4	56.0	7.4	3.9	64000	67510	82	84	864	4.6	2.0	27.8	57.5	8.1	206193
17566	QUARRYVILLE	21189	3896	17.1	27.2	43.7	8.8	3.1	55004	59188	71	71	2862	2.0	2.5	24.3	60.7	10.4	214339
17569	REINHOLDS	25851	2166	9.0	24.8	50.9	10.5	4.7	63156	66000	81	83	1910	3.3	1.4	29.4	55.7	10.3	209375
17572	RONKS	19434	1327	21.3	24.8	42.4	8.2	3.3	52522	55086	67	68	873	3.3	2.1	26.5	49.7	18.4	223732
17576	SMOKETOWN	20130	95	27.4	21.1	35.8	13.7	2.1	51019	53328	64	64	58	0.0	0.0	24.1	56.9	19.0	250000
17578	STEVENS	23017	2419	12.3	25.8	49.6	8.4	3.8	60829	63937	79	79	1984	5.7	5.0	25.1	57.7	6.6	195920
17579	STRASBURG	25152	2122	10.7	23.5	52.0	9.9	3.9	64229	68447	83	85	1636	0.5	1.5	21.9	63.0	13.1	227827
17581	TERRE HILL	24823	346	13.3	29.5	46.0	7.2	4.0	56523	60835	73	73	263	0.0	2.3	27.4	52.9	17.5	204412
17582	WASHINGTON BORO	25243	854	10.4	24.4	50.7	9.0	5.5	62094	65842	80	82	709	0.8	0.0	21.9	60.9	16.4	236607
17584	WILLOW STREET	27659	3590	10.3	26.2	48.6	11.0	3.8	61381	66002	79	80	2579	3.3	1.2	25.1	63.6	6.8	207053
17601	LANCASTER	36359	19562	10.1	18.7	45.5	14.4	11.2	71243	75990	87	90	14417	1.6	0.9	21.3	64.2	12.0	222712
17602	LANCASTER	21895	19047	23.6	28.9	37.7	6.5	3.2	47645	51230	56	57	10391	1.4	8.5	45.4	39.5	5.1	160986
17603	LANCASTER	26061	24740	20.9	27.8	38.8	7.8	4.8	51048	54202	64	64	14661	2.8	8.9	48.9	34.1	5.3	154724
17701	WILLIAMSPORT	21925	18517	32.2	29.8	29.7	5.1	3.2	39058	41807	30	22	10138	4.2	17.6	52.0	23.1	3.1	131497
17702	WILLIAMSPORT	23056	4521	21.8	31.0	39.1	5.8	2.3	47335	51082	55	56	3381	3.7	11.6	60.5	22.7	1.5	131343
17721	AVIS	22233	663	25.9	32.1	36.5	3.8	1.7	42759	46627	42	38	507	6.5	11.8	71.2	10.5	0.0	126161
17723	CAMMAL	26874	119	27.7	28.6	37.0	5.9	0.8	44541	48456	47	44	99	0.0	13.1	60.6	25.3	1.0	142130
17724	CANTON	18106	1867	29.7	36.1	29.0	4.0	1.2	37825	39854	26	17	1282	13.5	22.9	50.7	10.5	2.3	112250
17728	COGAN STATION	21673	1972	22.2	31.3	37.6	6.1	2.7	47057	50555	54	55	1709	13.0	9.6	42.4	30.5	4.5	143387
17729	CROSS FORK	27341	114	28.9	33.3	32.5	3.5	1.8	38620	40318	28	20	97	14.4	24.7	44.3	12.4	4.1	104464
17737	HUGHESVILLE	21838	2853	23.6	31.7	38.6	4.5	1.6	44383	49223	46	44	2220	12.3	8.6	48.3	27.5	3.3	139939
17740	JERSEY SHORE	20088	4531	23.3	33.1	37.8	3.7	2.2	44074	48314	46	43	3362	8.0	15.2	51.5	22.7	2.6	130707
17742	LAIRDSVILLE	22405	39	20.5	35.9	41.0	2.6	0.0	45745	52049	51	50	31	0.0	19.4	61.3	19.4	0.0	134722
17744	LINDEN	19635	1345	21.1	36.4	37.9	3.7	0.9	43788	47972	45	42	1156	20.6	11.7	43.6	22.1	2.1	123939
17745	LOCK HAVEN	21007	7203	34.0	30.1	28.0	5.2	2.7	37292	39717	24	15	4550	8.7	15.6	52.6	21.0	2.0	133841
17747	LOGANTON	16796	1033	22.7	36.5	37.6	2.4	0.9	41880	45892	39	35	863	8.8	14.3	50.3	23.6	3.0	134401
17751	MILL HALL	18534	2936	27.2	33.4	33.2	4.5	1.7	41304	44562	37	32	2410	13.7	12.2	50.6	21.3	2.2	131315
17752	MONTGOMERY	19080	1728	22.1	33.4	38.1	5.6	0.8	45537	49266	50	49	1322	5.1	15.5	55.1	22.8	1.5	128600
17754	MONTOURSVILLE	25714	5052	17.6	29.3	40.4	8.2	4.4	52455	54549	67	68	4097	6.6	4.3	44.7	39.7	4.7	165047
17756	MUNCY	21031	4205	23.4	32.3	36.1	6.2	2.0	45415	48790	49	48	3247	9.5	12.1	45.1	28.6	4.7	142833
17758	MUNCY VALLEY	23070	756	28.2	32.0	30.7	7.0	2.1	41866	42186	39	35	653	8.3	17.2	40.7	26.3	7.5	134605
17763	RALSTON	16751	175	34.9	33.7	27.4	2.9	1.1	35182	37352	18	9	145	22.1	24.1	46.9	6.2	0.7	95500
17764	RENOVO	18045	1415	41.1	30.1	25.2	2.4	1.2	31159	32919	10	4	1041	36.7	36.8	23.1	2.8	0.7	59112
17765	ROARING BRANCH	19413	322	24.2	35.4	35.4	4.0	0.9	42464	43988	41	37	271	9.6	21.4	48.3	17.7	3.0	118155
17768	SHUNK	19511	134	32.1	31.3	30.6	4.5	1.5	35000	34646	18	8	110	11.8	18.2	41.8	22.7	5.5	135000
17771	TROUT RUN	20740	1533	22.1	34.8	36.7	4.2	2.2	44476	48381	47	44	1322	10.2	15.1	45.5	24.6	4.5	132639
17772	TURBOTVILLE	21136	1213	15.7	32.6	42.2	6.6	2.9	51299	53454	64	65	1042	3.4	9.5	50.7	31.8	4.7	152258
17774	UNITYVILLE	19664	573	27.7	33.9	33.0	3.5	1.9	42113	45057	40	36	471	12.1	18.5	40.8	25.3	3.4	131964
17776	WATERVILLE	23223	189	23.8	32.8	37.0	5.3	1.1	44723	49007	47	45	163	5.5	15.3	50.9	24.5	3.7	138542
17777	WATSONTOWN	21164	2638	27.2	27.3	37.8	6.0	1.7	45352	48523	49	48	1913	8.1	16.1	45.4	27.5	2.9	136161
17778	WESTPORT	24465	41	29.3	36.6	26.8	4.9	2.4	39283	40000	31	23	36	33.3	30.6	30.6	5.6	0.0	65000
17779	WOOLRICH	23130	594	22.2	33.8	35.5	4.7	3.7	46126	49318	52	51	508	17.7	12.2	36.8	29.7	3.5	135000
17801	SUNBURY	19795	7200	32.0	30.0	33.5	3.3	1.3	39412	41731	31	24	4212	5.2	22.4	49.5	20.2	2.7	121821
17810	ALLENWOOD	15493	795	17.7	34.7	42.0	4.0	1.5	47986	50904	57	57	657	5.8	8.1	55.1	28.2	2.9	144434
17812	BEAVER SPRINGS	17575	607	26.2	37.7	33.1	2.6	0.3	40090	44032	33	26	484	6.4	18.6	48.3	22.7	3.9	131452
17813	BEAVERTOWN	19637	891	22.0	38.3	35.1	2.9	1.7	39420	43793	31	24	701	5.3	16.0	52.6	21.8	4.3	132964
17814	BENTON	20074	2512	24.8	34.0	35.9	4.2	1.1	43001	46421	42	39	2060	7.8	12.4	46.2	28.8	4.8	142440
17815	BLOOMSBURG	21711	10664	27.9	28.9	33.3	6.3	3.7	43911	46985	45	42	7080	11.1	7.9	46.4	30.9	3.6	145936
17820	CATAWISSA	22009	2543	24.2	31.6	37.4	4.9	1.9	45297	48397	49	47	2026	9.3	10.6	46.5	29.2	4.4	141031
17821	DANVILLE	25855	7825	20.6	28.3	39.0	7.2	4.9	50854	53124	63	64	5799	7.7	10.4	46.0	30.7	5.2	147353
17823	DORNSIFE	17125	143	28.7	30.1	34.3	5.6	1.4	42047	44217	39	35	128	5.5	21.1	50.8	21.1	1.6	119444
17824	ELYSBURG	26838	1595	20.5	22.8	42.8	11.1	2.8	58963	60378	76	77	1366	2.9	7.5	40.5	44.1	4.9	173307
17827	FREEBURG	20658	260	24.2	34.6	36.9	3.8	0.4	42388	45602	41	37	213	5.2	13.1	69.5	11.7	0.5	134375
17830	HERNDON	21426	763	23.6	29.1	41.2	3.0	3.1	47367	50514	55	56	657	7.6	19.6	48.4	19.5	4.9	124889
17832	MARION HEIGHTS	22171	290	32.1	27.2	34.1	3.8	2.8	38903	43519	29	21	244	22.1	36.9	34.8	5.7	0.4	75909
	PENNSYLVANIA	26913		21.5	25.3	36.9	10.2	6.1	53225	55819				7.5	12.2	35.6	36.1	8.5	161438
	UNITED STATES	27277		20.9	24.4	35.3	11.7	7.6	54719	56938				9.3	13.1	31.6	32.6	13.5	162279

ZIP CODE #	POST OFFICE NAME	FINANCIAL SERVICES: Auto Loan	FINANCIAL SERVICES: Home Loan	FINANCIAL SERVICES: Investments	FINANCIAL SERVICES: Retirement Plans	THE HOME: Home Improvements: Home Repair	THE HOME: Home Improvements: Lawn & Garden	THE HOME: Furnishings: Computers & Hardware-Personal	THE HOME: Furnishings: Major Appliances	THE HOME: Furnishings: TV, Radio, Sound Equipment	THE HOME: Furnishings: Furniture	ENTERTAINMENT: Dine out/Carry out	ENTERTAINMENT: Sports Equipment	ENTERTAINMENT: Fees & Tickets	ENTERTAINMENT: Toys & Games	ENTERTAINMENT: Travel	ENTERTAINMENT: Cable TV	PERSONAL: Apparel & Services	PERSONAL: Auto Repairs	PERSONAL: Health Insurance	PERSONAL: Pets & Supplies
17366	WINDSOR	91	86	77	86	84	93	83	88	86	81	85	67	80	88	81	89	58	85	92	105
17368	WRIGHTSVILLE	90	89	78	90	86	95	85	89	87	82	86	69	83	89	84	90	59	87	93	106
17370	YORK HAVEN	104	96	85	93	93	97	93	96	95	95	95	72	87	99	88	97	65	94	95	114
17372	YORK SPRINGS	88	88	82	91	88	95	83	90	84	79	83	69	82	86	85	86	57	85	91	105
17401	YORK	49	43	38	44	40	43	55	46	57	49	57	37	51	56	47	59	41	52	51	57
17402	YORK	102	108	106	110	109	111	105	106	106	105	107	79	111	105	109	108	75	107	113	124
17403	YORK	88	87	83	89	86	92	92	89	95	88	94	68	92	93	90	98	66	92	98	106
17404	YORK	95	98	89	100	95	102	96	96	98	93	97	74	98	98	96	100	68	96	103	114
17406	YORK	99	103	97	103	101	108	97	102	98	95	98	77	99	99	99	101	68	99	106	119
17407	YORK	115	143	135	144	141	139	122	128	121	126	122	95	140	121	136	121	86	123	129	148
17408	YORK	93	101	94	100	100	104	93	98	96	94	96	72	99	96	98	99	67	96	106	113
17501	AKRON	88	95	91	95	95	95	92	94	92	88	92	73	95	93	95	93	65	92	94	109
17502	BAINBRIDGE	100	91	91	95	93	108	90	102	93	82	91	77	83	95	90	98	62	94	105	118
17505	BIRD IN HAND	98	97	98	95	97	98	98	100	95	95	96	80	95	95	99	94	67	99	97	116
17509	CHRISTIANA	97	100	92	103	99	106	93	100	93	90	93	77	94	95	96	95	64	95	100	117
17512	COLUMBIA	81	81	69	81	77	82	82	80	82	79	82	62	81	84	79	84	57	81	84	95
17516	CONESTOGA	98	100	92	103	99	107	93	101	94	89	93	77	93	96	96	97	64	95	102	118
17517	DENVER	98	109	97	111	106	107	100	103	99	99	99	80	105	101	104	99	70	100	102	121
17518	DRUMORE	98	89	89	93	91	105	88	100	91	80	89	75	81	93	88	96	61	92	103	116
17519	EAST EARL	98	92	91	96	93	106	90	100	91	83	90	76	85	93	91	96	62	93	102	117
17520	EAST PETERSBURG	107	119	104	116	114	115	106	110	107	109	108	81	113	109	110	108	75	107	113	127
17522	EPHRATA	97	91	87	92	89	98	92	95	93	88	92	74	87	95	89	95	64	93	97	112
17527	GAP	93	91	86	92	90	97	86	92	87	85	87	70	84	89	86	89	59	88	93	109
17529	GORDONVILLE	94	72	95	70	74	92	79	90	79	70	79	74	63	78	78	82	54	87	90	107
17532	HOLTWOOD	96	103	92	107	101	105	94	100	94	93	94	77	98	96	98	95	65	95	99	117
17535	KINZERS	94	86	94	88	87	101	84	94	85	77	84	74	78	86	86	89	57	89	96	112
17536	KIRKWOOD	87	98	85	101	95	96	88	91	86	88	87	71	94	89	93	86	61	88	90	107
17538	LANDISVILLE	114	135	126	137	134	131	117	124	116	120	116	93	130	117	127	116	82	118	123	143
17540	LEOLA	102	113	104	114	111	112	105	108	103	103	104	84	110	105	110	104	73	105	108	126
17543	LITITZ	110	123	114	124	121	121	112	116	110	113	111	88	119	112	118	111	78	112	116	135
17545	MANHEIM	92	100	90	101	98	100	95	96	94	92	94	75	98	96	98	95	66	95	98	113
17547	MARIETTA	99	101	85	102	96	101	96	98	96	94	95	77	96	99	95	96	66	95	99	115
17551	MILLERSVILLE	91	88	84	90	88	90	98	90	95	91	95	71	93	95	92	95	67	94	93	107
17552	MOUNT JOY	92	99	91	99	97	98	94	95	93	92	94	74	97	95	96	94	66	94	95	112
17554	MOUNTVILLE	97	104	95	104	102	103	100	100	99	98	99	78	103	100	102	100	70	100	102	118
17555	NARVON	95	101	90	104	99	104	92	98	92	90	92	76	95	94	96	93	64	93	98	115
17557	NEW HOLLAND	96	94	94	96	95	102	93	99	94	88	93	76	91	95	94	97	65	95	101	115
17560	NEW PROVIDENCE	100	79	97	78	81	102	79	95	85	74	84	71	67	86	78	92	56	88	98	112
17562	PARADISE	96	83	91	86	85	102	83	96	86	74	85	74	74	87	84	91	57	89	99	113
17563	PEACH BOTTOM	90	83	78	84	83	92	80	88	82	77	82	66	75	85	79	86	56	83	89	103
17565	PEQUEA	97	108	94	111	105	108	97	102	96	97	96	79	103	98	102	97	67	98	101	120
17566	QUARRYVILLE	88	93	87	95	92	95	88	91	87	85	87	71	89	89	91	88	61	88	92	107
17569	REINHOLDS	99	111	100	114	110	110	100	104	98	100	99	81	106	100	106	99	69	100	103	122
17572	RONKS	94	82	90	80	83	92	85	92	84	79	84	73	75	85	84	86	58	89	91	107
17576	SMOKETOWN	84	84	72	74	82	68	83	81	77	90	80	61	78	80	80	73	56	81	71	89
17578	STEVENS	102	100	94	103	99	109	95	103	96	91	96	79	93	99	96	99	66	97	104	121
17579	STRASBURG	95	109	96	111	106	104	98	100	96	98	97	79	106	98	104	96	68	98	99	118
17581	TERRE HILL	103	94	93	97	95	110	92	104	95	83	93	79	85	97	92	101	64	96	107	121
17582	WASHINGTON BORO	98	113	98	115	109	108	99	103	97	101	98	81	107	100	105	96	69	99	100	120
17584	WILLOW STREET	89	100	98	101	101	105	93	97	96	93	96	71	101	94	100	100	67	96	108	113
17601	LANCASTER	120	132	128	135	132	130	124	125	124	127	124	95	133	124	130	124	88	125	128	146
17602	LANCASTER	78	74	66	75	71	73	82	75	82	79	83	59	80	82	77	83	59	80	79	90
17603	LANCASTER	86	83	79	84	82	85	89	85	90	86	90	66	88	90	86	92	63	88	90	101
17701	WILLIAMSPORT	71	65	63	66	65	72	72	70	75	68	73	53	68	74	68	77	51	72	77	84
17702	WILLIAMSPORT	77	79	73	79	78	87	75	80	78	71	77	59	76	78	77	82	53	78	88	93
17721	AVIS	86	62	85	60	64	89	67	83	75	60	73	62	54	74	65	83	48	77	90	97
17723	CAMMAL	82	66	106	65	72	87	66	83	69	62	68	61	57	65	71	73	45	77	82	97
17724	CANTON	77	56	78	55	58	79	59	73	65	54	64	55	48	65	58	72	42	68	78	87
17728	COGAN STATION	90	77	79	77	77	91	76	85	80	72	79	65	68	82	74	85	54	80	88	101
17729	CROSS FORK	75	67	94	63	74	83	65	79	68	67	67	54	61	63	71	73	45	75	84	91
17737	HUGHESVILLE	81	71	70	73	71	84	72	78	75	67	74	60	66	77	70	79	50	75	83	93
17740	JERSEY SHORE	77	71	66	73	70	80	72	76	74	67	73	58	68	76	70	77	50	74	80	90
17742	LAIRDSVILLE	80	73	72	76	74	86	72	81	74	65	73	61	66	76	72	79	50	75	84	94
17744	LINDEN	80	67	69	68	68	81	67	76	71	64	70	57	59	73	64	76	47	71	79	90
17745	LOCK HAVEN	72	60	66	61	61	72	67	70	70	62	69	53	60	70	63	74	47	70	76	83
17747	LOGANTON	74	68	67	71	69	80	67	76	69	60	68	57	62	70	67	73	46	70	78	88
17751	MILL HALL	78	67	72	69	69	83	67	77	71	62	70	58	61	72	67	76	48	72	82	90
17752	MONTGOMERY	76	69	65	72	69	80	71	76	73	65	72	58	66	75	69	77	49	73	80	89
17754	MONTOURSVILLE	86	93	86	94	92	97	86	90	88	86	87	67	90	88	90	90	61	88	96	105
17756	MUNCY	81	74	72	75	73	84	74	80	77	69	76	61	69	78	73	80	52	77	84	94
17758	MUNCY VALLEY	79	70	96	69	75	87	68	82	71	64	70	59	64	68	73	76	47	77	85	95
17763	RALSTON	73	52	75	51	54	74	54	68	59	50	58	51	43	59	53	65	39	62	71	81
17764	RENOVO	63	49	60	48	50	64	54	61	60	51	58	44	47	58	51	65	39	60	69	72
17765	ROARING BRANCH	79	68	74	70	70	84	68	79	71	62	70	60	60	72	67	76	47	73	81	92
17768	SHUNK	81	58	83	56	60	82	59	75	66	55	65	57	47	65	59	72	43	69	78	90
17771	TROUT RUN	84	71	74	73	72	87	71	81	75	66	74	62	63	77	70	80	50	75	84	96
17772	TURBOTVILLE	88	82	78	85	82	95	81	89	84	74	82	68	77	85	81	88	56	84	93	104
17774	UNITYVILLE	83	65	82	65	67	86	66	80	71	61	70	60	56	71	65	77	47	74	83	94
17776	WATERVILLE	80	68	89	69	72	85	68	81	70	62	69	60	60	69	71	75	47	75	82	94
17777	WATSONTOWN	82	69	71	70	69	83	71	77	76	67	74	59	64	77	68	80	51	75	83	92
17778	WESTPORT	79	63	84	60	67	85	65	79	71	62	69	57	56	68	66	78	46	75	87	92
17779	WOOLRICH	93	74	80	75	75	93	75	86	81	71	79	66	65	83	72	87	54	81	90	103
17801	SUNBURY	66	58	55	60	57	66	66	64	68	60	67	50	60	68	61	71	46	66	71	77
17810	ALLENWOOD	91	74	79	75	75	92	75	86	80	70	78	65	65	82	72	86	53	80	89	102
17812	BEAVER SPRINGS	69	63	62	66	64	74	62	70	64	56	63	53	57	65	62	68	43	65	72	82
17813	BEAVERTOWN	76	69	68	72	71	82	68	77	70	62	69	58	63	72	68	74	47	71	79	89
17814	BENTON	75	66	66	69	67	79	68	75	70	61	69	57	61	71	66	74	47	70	78	87
17815	BLOOMSBURG	81	70	69	73	70	78	82	78	81	73	80	61	73	81	74	83	55	79	82	93
17820	CATAWISSA	82	70	77	72	72	88	71	83	75	64	73	62	63	76	71	81	50	76	86	96
17821	DANVILLE	92	87	87	89	88	98	87	93	90	83	89	69	84	90	87	95	61	90	99	109
17823	DORNSIFE	75	68	67	71	69	80	67	76	69	61	68	57	62	70	67	73	46	70	78	88
17824	ELYSBURG	89	99	96	100	99	105	88	96	90	88	90	70	95	90	95	94	63	92	102	111
17827	FREEBURG	65	73	69	71	73	79	65	71	69	64	69	50	70	68	70	74	47	69	81	82
17830	HERNDON	81	74	73	77	76	87	73	82	75	66	74	62	67	77	73	80	50	76	85	96
17832	MARION HEIGHTS	86	62	86	60	64	89	67	83	75	60	72	62	54	74	65	83	48	77	91	97
	PENNSYLVANIA	94	95	95	95	95	100	94	96	96	91	95	73	94	96	94	99	67	95	101	113
	UNITED STATES	100	100	100	100	100	100	100	100	100	100	100	100	100	100	100	100	100	100	100	100

ZIP CODE #	POST OFFICE NAME	COUNTY FIPS CODE	POPULATION 2000	POPULATION 2009	POPULATION 2014	2000-2009 ANNUAL RATE % Rate	2000-2009 ANNUAL RATE State Centile
17834	KULPMONT	097	3268	3062	2953	-0.7	8
17835	LAURELTON	119	11	12	12	0.9	83
17836	LECK KILL	097	600	557	536	-0.8	6
17837	LEWISBURG	119	18516	20085	20338	0.9	83
17841	MC CLURE	087	4580	4614	4600	0.1	57
17842	MIDDLEBURG	109	9215	9491	9589	0.3	64
17844	MIFFLINBURG	119	9418	9429	9407	0.0	52
17845	MILLMONT	119	2676	2919	3024	0.9	83
17846	MILLVILLE	037	3920	3931	3918	0.0	52
17847	MILTON	097	11661	11075	10734	-0.6	13
17850	MONTANDON	097	180	171	165	-0.6	13
17851	MOUNT CARMEL	097	8808	8322	8040	-0.6	13
17853	MOUNT PLEASANT MILLS	109	1959	2885	3243	4.3	99
17855	NEW BERLIN	119	938	990	1016	0.6	74
17856	NEW COLUMBIA	119	3699	3879	3956	0.5	70
17857	NORTHUMBERLAND	097	7445	7239	7080	-0.3	29
17859	ORANGEVILLE	037	2877	3020	3092	0.5	70
17860	PAXINOS	097	2159	2109	2068	-0.3	29
17864	PORT TREVORTON	109	2927	2980	2989	0.2	61
17866	COAL TOWNSHIP	097	10625	10160	9874	-0.5	19
17867	REBUCK	097	659	611	589	-0.8	6
17868	RIVERSIDE	097	222	200	191	-1.1	2
17870	SELINSGROVE	109	13874	13356	13217	-0.4	23
17872	SHAMOKIN	097	8698	8606	8431	-0.1	46
17876	SHAMOKIN DAM	109	1539	1544	1548	0.0	52
17877	SNYDERTOWN	097	357	334	322	-0.7	8
17878	STILLWATER	037	759	1099	1198	4.1	99
17881	TREVORTON	097	2538	2337	2246	-0.9	4
17888	WILBURTON	037	506	471	459	-0.8	6
17889	WINFIELD	119	2206	2280	2319	0.4	68
17901	POTTSVILLE	107	27523	25906	25653	-0.7	8
17921	ASHLAND	107	7736	9499	9417	2.2	96
17922	AUBURN	107	4428	4605	4616	0.4	68
17923	BRANCHDALE	107	530	505	496	-0.5	19
17925	BROCKTON	107	1123	1098	1085	-0.2	38
17929	CRESSONA	107	1644	1613	1597	-0.2	38
17931	FRACKVILLE	107	8653	5565	5509	-4.7	0
17935	GIRARDVILLE	107	2037	1902	1851	-0.7	8
17938	HEGINS	107	2329	2424	2433	0.4	68
17941	KLINGERSTOWN	107	565	688	718	2.2	96
17948	MAHANOY CITY	107	5467	7054	6838	2.8	97
17954	MINERSVILLE	107	4697	4643	4596	-0.1	46
17957	MUIR	107	381	366	360	-0.4	23
17959	NEW PHILADELPHIA	107	2498	2430	2394	-0.3	29
17960	NEW RINGGOLD	107	3598	3545	3509	-0.2	38
17961	ORWIGSBURG	107	6575	6795	6804	0.4	68
17963	PINE GROVE	107	9312	9194	9096	-0.1	46
17964	PITMAN	107	790	834	842	0.6	74
17965	PORT CARBON	107	2020	1887	1837	-0.7	8
17967	RINGTOWN	107	2500	2567	2565	0.3	64
17968	SACRAMENTO	107	294	292	291	-0.1	46
17970	SAINT CLAIR	107	3592	3411	3339	-0.6	13
17972	SCHUYLKILL HAVEN	107	10618	10522	10422	-0.1	46
17976	SHENANDOAH	107	9090	8672	8476	-0.5	19
17978	SPRING GLEN	107	344	342	340	-0.1	46
17980	TOWER CITY	107	3302	3369	3366	0.2	61
17981	TREMONT	107	2613	2514	2473	-0.4	23
17983	VALLEY VIEW	107	1868	1856	1846	-0.1	46
17985	ZION GROVE	107	1886	2023	2046	0.8	80
18011	ALBURTIS	011	4661	6159	7012	3.1	98
18013	BANGOR	095	17036	18318	18997	0.8	80
18014	BATH	095	10850	11872	12336	1.0	85
18015	BETHLEHEM	095	30828	33278	34530	0.8	80
18017	BETHLEHEM	095	35400	37739	39057	0.7	77
18018	BETHLEHEM	077	30912	32539	33455	0.6	74
18020	BETHLEHEM	095	18759	21404	22768	1.4	91
18031	BREINIGSVILLE	077	3447	5087	5742	4.3	99
18032	CATASAUQUA	077	9400	9503	9622	0.1	57
18034	CENTER VALLEY	077	6097	7885	8680	2.8	97
18035	CHERRYVILLE	095	242	260	270	0.8	80
18036	COOPERSBURG	077	12353	13355	14260	0.8	80
18037	COPLAY	077	7431	7897	8178	0.7	77
18038	DANIELSVILLE	095	2607	2986	3195	1.5	92
18040	EASTON	095	10225	16097	18817	5.0	99
18041	EAST GREENVILLE	091	5802	5889	6138	0.2	61
18042	EASTON	095	39531	42837	44474	0.9	83
18045	EASTON	095	22117	26976	29124	2.2	96
18049	EMMAUS	077	16976	17658	18289	0.4	68
18051	FOGELSVILLE	077	3118	3330	3533	0.7	77
18052	WHITEHALL	077	24978	26306	27124	0.6	74
18053	GERMANSVILLE	077	2334	2484	2586	0.7	77
18054	GREEN LANE	091	4765	5139	5288	0.8	80
18055	HELLERTOWN	095	10667	11830	12359	1.1	87
18056	HEREFORD	011	1165	1285	1347	1.1	87
18058	KUNKLETOWN	089	8243	10674	11792	2.8	97
18059	LAURYS STATION	077	1354	1518	1603	1.2	88
18062	MACUNGIE	077	14664	22657	26047	4.8	99
18064	NAZARETH	095	21495	24253	25633	1.3	90
18066	NEW TRIPOLI	077	5019	5675	6028	1.3	90
18067	NORTHAMPTON	095	16011	18939	20380	1.8	93
18069	OREFIELD	077	6575	7927	8503	2.0	95
18070	PALM	011	752	798	821	0.6	74
18071	PALMERTON	025	10749	11463	11899	0.7	77
18072	PEN ARGYL	095	6269	6657	6867	0.7	77
18073	PENNSBURG	091	6681	8539	9739	2.7	97
	PENNSYLVANIA					0.3	
	UNITED STATES					1.0	

ZIP CODE #	POST OFFICE NAME	HOUSEHOLDS 2000	HOUSEHOLDS 2009	HOUSEHOLDS 2014	HOUSEHOLDS % Annual Rate 2000-2009	HOUSEHOLDS 2009 Average HH Size	FAMILIES 2000	FAMILIES 2009	FAMILIES % Annual Rate 2000-2009
17834	KULPMONT	1449	1393	1353	-0.4	2.16	913	851	-0.8
17835	LAURELTON	4	5	5	2.4	2.20	3	3	0.0
17836	LECK KILL	224	214	207	-0.5	2.60	171	159	-0.8
17837	LEWISBURG	5918	6378	6534	0.8	2.29	3753	3930	0.5
17841	MC CLURE	1690	1758	1769	0.4	2.62	1307	1329	0.2
17842	MIDDLEBURG	3473	3698	3773	0.7	2.55	2627	2727	0.4
17844	MIFFLINBURG	3508	3638	3669	0.4	2.59	2602	2623	0.1
17845	MILLMONT	976	1110	1164	1.4	2.57	722	797	1.1
17846	MILLVILLE	1476	1519	1526	0.3	2.49	1101	1103	0.0
17847	MILTON	4837	4686	4569	-0.3	2.29	3246	3077	-0.6
17850	MONTANDON	74	72	70	-0.3	2.36	48	46	-0.5
17851	MOUNT CARMEL	4010	3867	3762	-0.4	2.12	2332	2171	-0.8
17853	MOUNT PLEASANT MILLS	681	1029	1166	4.6	2.80	535	792	4.3
17855	NEW BERLIN	375	410	425	1.0	2.41	279	296	0.6
17856	NEW COLUMBIA	1427	1560	1609	1.0	2.48	1100	1172	0.7
17857	NORTHUMBERLAND	3104	3090	3044	0.0	2.26	2104	2033	-0.4
17859	ORANGEVILLE	1126	1226	1269	0.9	2.37	845	894	0.6
17860	PAXINOS	851	851	843	0.0	2.48	648	639	-0.2
17864	PORT TREVORTON	932	971	981	0.4	3.07	737	753	0.2
17866	COAL TOWNSHIP	3731	3537	3429	-0.6	2.21	2369	2177	-0.9
17867	REBUCK	262	250	243	-0.5	2.44	199	187	-0.7
17868	RIVERSIDE	104	96	93	-0.9	2.08	70	63	-1.1
17870	SELINSGROVE	4827	4797	4787	-0.1	2.34	3298	3168	-0.4
17872	SHAMOKIN	4010	4031	3972	0.1	2.13	2240	2177	-0.3
17876	SHAMOKIN DAM	688	714	723	0.4	2.16	456	455	0.0
17877	SNYDERTOWN	136	131	127	-0.4	2.54	99	93	-0.7
17878	STILLWATER	305	457	502	4.5	2.40	229	333	4.1
17881	TREVORTON	1063	1005	973	-0.6	2.33	707	649	-0.9
17888	WILBURTON	213	205	201	-0.4	2.30	149	138	-0.8
17889	WINFIELD	823	880	905	0.7	2.45	654	682	0.5
17901	POTTSVILLE	10589	10735	10707	0.1	2.31	6865	6739	-0.2
17921	ASHLAND	3190	3220	3210	0.1	2.33	2138	2090	-0.2
17922	AUBURN	1669	1782	1800	0.7	2.58	1310	1368	0.5
17923	BRANCHDALE	223	219	217	-0.2	2.31	146	139	-0.5
17925	BROCKTON	503	508	507	0.1	2.16	345	339	-0.2
17929	CRESSONA	665	669	667	0.1	2.41	471	459	-0.3
17931	FRACKVILLE	2465	2493	2490	0.1	2.17	1547	1503	-0.3
17935	GIRARDVILLE	892	855	838	-0.5	2.20	574	528	-0.9
17938	HEGINS	919	990	1003	0.8	2.42	653	682	0.5
17941	KLINGERSTOWN	213	267	280	2.5	2.58	165	202	2.2
17948	MAHANOY CITY	2433	2219	2136	-1.0	2.22	1429	1250	-1.4
17954	MINERSVILLE	2099	2117	2111	0.1	2.19	1272	1233	-0.3
17957	MUIR	156	154	152	-0.1	2.37	121	116	-0.5
17959	NEW PHILADELPHIA	1082	1078	1071	0.0	2.25	680	653	-0.4
17960	NEW RINGGOLD	1386	1408	1406	0.2	2.52	1055	1044	-0.1
17961	ORWIGSBURG	2506	2652	2676	0.6	2.41	1804	1857	0.3
17963	PINE GROVE	3645	3701	3695	0.2	2.46	2670	2643	-0.1
17964	PITMAN	303	330	336	0.9	2.53	233	248	0.7
17965	PORT CARBON	852	818	802	-0.4	2.30	580	540	-0.8
17967	RINGTOWN	993	1044	1052	0.5	2.46	686	700	0.2
17968	SACRAMENTO	112	115	115	0.3	2.54	84	84	0.0
17970	SAINT CLAIR	1652	1618	1599	-0.2	2.11	986	925	-0.7
17972	SCHUYLKILL HAVEN	4398	4462	4450	0.2	2.33	3027	2977	-0.2
17976	SHENANDOAH	4085	3959	3896	-0.3	2.12	2311	2146	-0.8
17978	SPRING GLEN	132	135	136	0.2	2.53	99	99	0.0
17980	TOWER CITY	1409	1477	1488	0.5	2.28	964	980	0.2
17981	TREMONT	1006	989	979	-0.2	2.38	656	622	-0.6
17983	VALLEY VIEW	782	799	799	0.2	2.32	560	557	-0.1
17985	ZION GROVE	748	827	845	1.1	2.44	516	552	0.7
18011	ALBURTIS	1755	2386	2745	3.4	2.57	1320	1717	2.9
18013	BANGOR	6609	7152	7443	0.9	2.55	4732	4950	0.5
18014	BATH	4268	4709	4922	1.1	2.50	3153	3373	0.7
18015	BETHLEHEM	10423	11361	11886	0.9	2.60	6689	7044	0.6
18017	BETHLEHEM	14035	15001	15569	0.7	2.44	9888	10231	0.4
18018	BETHLEHEM	13315	14153	14623	0.7	2.17	7615	7694	0.1
18020	BETHLEHEM	6671	7647	8168	1.5	2.71	5174	5782	1.2
18031	BREINIGSVILLE	1447	2143	2429	4.3	2.35	1035	1475	3.9
18032	CATASAUQUA	3751	3841	3905	0.3	2.46	2540	2496	-0.2
18034	CENTER VALLEY	1944	2616	2916	3.3	2.83	1591	2090	3.0
18035	CHERRYVILLE	89	97	101	0.9	2.65	70	74	0.6
18036	COOPERSBURG	4438	4860	5212	1.0	2.64	3516	3771	0.8
18037	COPLAY	2893	3095	3210	0.7	2.54	2122	2204	0.4
18038	DANIELSVILLE	931	1075	1156	1.6	2.77	738	829	1.3
18040	EASTON	3761	5803	6767	4.8	2.77	2938	4434	4.5
18041	EAST GREENVILLE	2074	2142	2242	0.3	2.75	1581	1592	0.1
18042	EASTON	14810	16119	16830	0.9	2.47	9250	9704	0.5
18045	EASTON	8718	10632	11504	2.2	2.51	6470	7668	1.9
18049	EMMAUS	7060	7441	7718	0.6	2.36	4825	4906	0.2
18051	FOGELSVILLE	1144	1241	1323	0.9	2.68	889	944	0.7
18052	WHITEHALL	10395	11055	11434	0.7	2.35	6831	6967	0.2
18053	GERMANSVILLE	838	906	948	0.8	2.74	663	700	0.6
18054	GREEN LANE	1837	2019	2091	1.0	2.52	1408	1509	0.8
18055	HELLERTOWN	4443	4957	5202	1.2	2.38	3092	3346	0.9
18056	HEREFORD	450	503	528	1.2	2.55	336	366	0.9
18058	KUNKLETOWN	2939	3782	4177	2.8	2.78	2275	2857	2.5
18059	LAURYS STATION	470	524	554	1.2	2.90	370	401	0.9
18062	MACUNGIE	5646	8806	10161	4.9	2.55	4177	6466	4.8
18064	NAZARETH	7699	8723	9258	1.4	2.65	5752	6376	1.1
18066	NEW TRIPOLI	1793	2061	2199	1.5	2.74	1404	1569	1.2
18067	NORTHAMPTON	6394	7570	8166	1.8	2.48	4663	5380	1.6
18069	OREFIELD	2190	2697	2910	2.3	2.85	1711	2062	2.0
18070	PALM	277	299	309	0.8	2.67	222	235	0.6
18071	PALMERTON	4331	4756	4981	1.0	2.40	3005	3200	0.7
18072	PEN ARGYL	2385	2549	2641	0.7	2.57	1734	1793	0.4
18073	PENNSBURG	2425	3159	3624	2.9	2.66	1844	2337	2.6
	PENNSYLVANIA				0.4	2.45			0.1
	UNITED STATES				1.1	2.59			0.9

ZIP CODE #	POST OFFICE NAME	RACE (%) White 2000	White 2009	Black 2000	Black 2009	Asian/Pacific 2000	Asian/Pacific 2009	% Hispanic Origin 2000	% Hispanic Origin 2009	2009 AGE DISTRIBUTION (%) 0-4	5-9	10-14	15-19	20-24	25-44	45-64	65-84	85+	18+	MEDIAN AGE 2009	% 2009 Males	% 2009 Females
17834	KULPMONT	99.0	98.7	0.4	0.5	0.0	0.1	0.5	0.7	4.6	4.9	5.1	5.4	5.1	22.1	28.8	19.6	4.4	82.1	46.9	47.9	52.1
17835	LAURELTON	100.0	100.0	0.0	0.0	0.0	0.0	0.0	0.0	8.3	8.3	8.3	0.0	16.7	58.3	0.0	0.0	0.0	75.0	27.5	33.3	66.7
17836	LECK KILL	99.8	99.8	0.0	0.0	0.0	0.0	0.3	0.4	4.5	5.0	5.6	6.3	5.4	24.6	31.8	14.4	2.5	81.1	44.1	50.4	49.6
17837	LEWISBURG	90.9	87.9	5.8	7.6	1.7	2.5	2.9	4.2	3.9	4.0	4.5	11.2	13.9	23.5	22.9	12.5	3.6	84.3	35.7	53.9	46.1
17841	MC CLURE	99.1	99.0	0.4	0.5	0.1	0.2	0.3	0.4	6.5	6.7	6.8	6.2	5.5	26.1	28.2	12.7	1.4	76.1	39.7	50.7	49.3
17842	MIDDLEBURG	99.1	98.7	0.2	0.3	0.1	0.2	0.5	0.7	6.2	6.4	6.6	6.8	5.6	26.5	28.7	11.7	1.5	76.7	39.9	49.9	50.1
17844	MIFFLINBURG	98.2	97.6	0.5	0.6	0.2	0.4	0.7	1.0	6.9	6.9	7.1	7.3	6.0	26.0	26.9	11.3	1.6	74.5	37.6	49.5	50.5
17845	MILLMONT	98.9	98.5	0.2	0.2	0.2	0.4	0.3	0.4	7.1	7.3	7.6	7.0	4.7	24.5	26.9	13.0	2.0	73.7	39.7	49.6	50.4
17846	MILLVILLE	98.9	98.6	0.1	0.1	0.3	0.4	0.3	0.4	5.5	5.8	6.0	5.7	4.7	25.3	28.5	15.4	3.1	79.3	42.9	48.3	51.7
17847	MILTON	96.2	95.3	1.7	2.1	0.2	0.4	1.5	2.0	5.6	5.5	5.7	6.0	6.2	24.3	28.7	14.8	3.2	79.3	42.5	48.9	51.1
17850	MONTANDON	98.3	98.2	0.6	0.6	0.0	0.0	0.6	0.0	5.8	5.8	5.8	5.8	5.8	24.6	31.6	13.5	1.2	78.9	42.3	51.5	48.5
17851	MOUNT CARMEL	98.8	98.5	0.0	0.0	0.3	0.4	0.7	0.9	4.7	4.7	5.1	5.3	5.0	21.9	29.1	19.2	4.9	82.3	47.3	47.9	52.1
17853	MOUNT PLEASANT MILLS	99.2	99.1	0.1	0.1	0.1	0.2	0.4	0.6	7.2	7.5	7.7	7.2	5.0	25.5	27.5	11.3	1.2	73.1	38.0	51.8	48.2
17855	NEW BERLIN	98.5	97.9	0.2	0.3	0.0	0.0	0.9	1.3	6.4	6.3	6.6	7.6	6.5	26.2	26.5	12.9	1.2	76.2	38.5	48.9	51.1
17856	NEW COLUMBIA	98.2	97.7	0.6	0.7	0.2	0.3	0.7	1.0	5.3	5.9	6.3	6.0	4.5	24.7	32.7	13.1	1.4	78.5	43.1	50.2	49.8
17857	NORTHUMBERLAND	98.5	98.0	0.5	0.7	0.3	0.5	0.7	0.9	4.8	5.0	5.2	5.4	5.6	23.2	30.7	16.1	4.0	81.2	45.5	48.1	51.9
17859	ORANGEVILLE	99.1	98.8	0.2	0.3	0.1	0.3	0.6	0.8	4.8	5.3	6.0	6.4	4.4	23.3	32.2	15.0	2.7	79.7	44.9	49.1	50.9
17860	PAXINOS	99.4	99.1	0.2	0.2	0.2	0.3	0.2	0.3	5.5	6.0	6.2	5.4	4.3	24.2	32.1	14.9	1.5	79.1	44.1	51.3	48.7
17864	PORT TREVORTON	99.4	99.1	0.1	0.1	0.1	0.2	0.6	0.9	8.7	8.8	8.6	7.7	6.0	25.2	24.3	9.5	1.2	69.1	33.2	51.1	48.9
17866	COAL TOWNSHIP	89.5	87.3	9.0	10.7	0.3	0.4	2.1	2.7	3.5	3.5	4.1	6.4	7.4	29.8	24.7	16.4	4.2	84.7	41.8	57.2	42.8
17867	REBUCK	99.5	99.5	0.2	0.2	0.0	0.0	0.5	0.7	4.6	5.2	5.7	6.5	5.4	24.5	31.4	14.1	2.5	80.5	43.6	50.1	49.9
17868	RIVERSIDE	100.0	100.0	0.0	0.0	0.0	0.0	0.5	0.5	5.5	5.5	5.5	5.5	4.5	24.0	28.0	18.5	3.0	80.0	44.6	46.0	54.0
17870	SELINSGROVE	96.0	94.6	1.9	2.4	0.9	1.4	1.9	2.7	4.3	4.6	4.8	9.6	10.5	22.8	27.6	13.1	2.7	83.1	39.8	48.2	51.8
17872	SHAMOKIN	98.8	98.5	0.2	0.2	0.3	0.5	0.7	1.0	5.9	5.3	5.1	5.7	6.9	23.6	27.3	16.3	3.8	80.2	42.9	47.5	52.5
17876	SHAMOKIN DAM	98.1	97.3	0.6	0.8	0.7	1.2	0.7	1.0	4.3	4.6	5.3	6.0	5.1	21.6	29.5	20.0	3.7	82.0	46.9	46.9	53.1
17877	SNYDERTOWN	99.2	98.8	0.0	0.0	0.6	0.9	0.0	0.0	5.7	6.3	6.6	4.8	3.9	24.9	32.3	14.1	1.5	78.4	43.7	50.9	49.1
17878	STILLWATER	99.2	99.1	0.0	0.0	0.1	0.2	0.7	1.0	5.0	5.6	6.2	6.1	4.4	24.7	32.0	14.1	1.8	79.3	43.7	50.0	50.0
17881	TREVORTON	98.9	98.6	0.2	0.2	0.2	0.2	0.4	0.5	5.0	5.3	5.4	5.9	5.3	24.0	29.7	16.4	2.9	80.7	44.3	50.5	49.5
17888	WILBURTON	99.6	99.6	0.0	0.0	0.0	0.0	0.8	1.1	4.5	4.9	5.1	6.2	4.5	22.3	31.4	18.3	3.0	81.5	46.7	48.4	51.6
17889	WINFIELD	97.1	96.1	0.3	0.4	1.1	1.8	0.3	0.4	4.4	5.1	6.0	8.4	5.5	20.6	33.7	13.9	2.3	80.7	45.0	50.9	49.1
17901	POTTSVILLE	94.9	95.4	3.5	2.1	0.5	0.8	1.7	2.2	5.1	5.0	5.4	5.8	6.4	23.8	28.3	16.3	3.8	81.0	43.8	48.8	51.2
17921	ASHLAND	99.2	89.6	0.2	8.3	0.2	0.7	0.2	1.8	4.0	4.2	4.3	4.4	5.5	32.7	28.8	13.5	2.4	84.9	41.6	58.9	41.1
17922	AUBURN	98.3	97.7	0.5	0.6	0.3	0.6	0.5	0.8	5.9	6.4	6.8	6.6	4.6	24.6	31.8	12.2	1.2	76.9	42.0	49.8	50.2
17923	BRANCHDALE	99.6	99.4	0.0	0.0	0.0	0.0	0.2	0.4	6.7	6.5	6.3	6.1	5.1	24.6	27.7	14.1	2.8	76.8	41.6	48.3	51.7
17925	BROCKTON	99.4	99.2	0.1	0.1	0.1	0.2	0.1	0.1	4.1	4.5	4.7	4.5	4.0	21.0	32.1	21.4	3.7	84.1	49.8	47.6	52.4
17929	CRESSONA	98.5	98.0	0.1	0.1	1.0	1.5	0.2	0.2	5.6	5.6	5.8	6.4	5.8	28.7	28.1	11.7	2.2	79.2	39.6	50.7	49.3
17931	FRACKVILLE	77.4	87.3	19.4	8.9	0.8	1.6	3.9	3.2	4.5	4.5	4.6	5.4	6.0	27.8	25.5	17.4	4.2	83.5	42.8	52.7	47.3
17935	GIRARDVILLE	99.4	99.2	0.1	0.2	0.0	0.1	0.1	0.2	4.4	4.5	4.8	6.4	5.6	22.9	30.7	17.4	3.4	82.5	45.9	48.9	51.1
17938	HEGINS	99.3	99.1	0.0	0.0	0.2	0.2	0.4	0.6	4.4	4.8	5.3	6.1	4.5	25.8	30.9	15.3	2.8	81.0	44.4	48.9	51.1
17941	KLINGERSTOWN	100.0	100.0	0.0	0.0	0.0	0.0	0.5	0.9	5.4	5.7	6.0	6.0	4.5	27.0	28.3	14.4	2.8	79.2	42.2	49.7	50.3
17948	MAHANOY CITY	98.9	84.6	0.2	12.4	0.2	1.0	1.1	3.4	3.8	3.8	4.0	8.1	10.3	29.3	23.0	14.1	3.6	85.9	38.5	56.5	43.5
17954	MINERSVILLE	98.5	98.1	0.4	0.5	0.2	0.3	0.6	0.8	5.9	5.6	5.7	6.3	5.6	24.9	25.7	16.1	4.2	78.9	42.2	47.3	52.7
17957	MUIR	99.7	99.7	0.0	0.0	0.3	0.3	0.0	0.0	4.9	4.9	5.5	4.9	4.4	27.6	30.3	15.6	1.9	81.7	43.5	52.2	47.8
17959	NEW PHILADELPHIA	99.4	99.2	0.0	0.0	0.4	0.6	0.3	0.5	4.6	4.8	5.3	6.3	4.7	24.2	29.1	17.5	3.7	81.3	45.2	50.1	49.9
17960	NEW RINGGOLD	98.7	98.4	0.1	0.2	0.3	0.5	0.5	0.8	4.9	5.4	5.9	6.0	4.4	24.8	33.3	13.3	2.0	80.0	44.0	51.0	49.0
17961	ORWIGSBURG	97.2	95.9	0.2	0.3	1.8	2.8	0.4	0.7	5.0	5.3	5.7	5.8	4.8	22.8	29.8	16.0	4.8	80.3	45.4	47.7	52.3
17963	PINE GROVE	99.1	98.8	0.1	0.1	0.3	0.5	0.2	0.3	5.4	5.9	6.4	6.2	4.5	25.7	30.1	13.5	2.2	78.3	42.1	50.4	49.6
17964	PITMAN	99.4	99.3	0.1	0.1	0.5	0.6	0.5	0.6	5.0	5.4	6.0	5.6	3.6	25.4	32.0	14.4	2.5	80.0	44.2	52.8	47.2
17965	PORT CARBON	99.1	98.9	0.5	0.6	0.1	0.1	0.5	0.7	5.0	5.1	5.2	5.3	5.0	25.5	28.4	17.2	3.3	81.6	44.3	47.8	52.2
17967	RINGTOWN	99.2	98.9	0.2	0.3	0.2	0.3	0.8	1.2	4.7	4.9	5.5	6.7	4.6	22.3	33.6	15.2	2.5	80.8	45.8	49.5	50.5
17968	SACRAMENTO	99.3	99.3	0.3	0.3	0.3	0.3	1.0	1.4	4.5	4.8	5.5	6.2	4.8	26.0	30.5	15.4	2.4	81.2	44.0	53.4	46.6
17970	SAINT CLAIR	98.7	98.5	0.6	0.8	0.1	0.1	0.7	0.9	4.8	4.7	5.1	5.9	4.3	24.9	26.8	19.2	4.4	81.7	45.3	48.0	52.0
17972	SCHUYLKILL HAVEN	97.9	97.2	0.6	0.7	0.6	1.0	0.8	1.1	5.7	5.9	6.1	6.4	5.0	24.6	29.2	14.6	2.6	78.2	42.6	48.7	51.3
17976	SHENANDOAH	98.0	97.3	0.3	0.4	0.4	0.6	1.9	2.6	5.1	4.9	5.0	5.7	5.6	23.6	27.1	17.6	5.4	81.6	45.1	47.3	52.7
17978	SPRING GLEN	99.4	99.4	0.3	0.3	0.3	0.3	1.2	1.2	4.4	5.0	5.3	6.1	4.7	26.3	30.7	15.2	2.3	81.9	43.9	52.0	48.0
17980	TOWER CITY	99.2	98.9	0.1	0.1	0.1	0.1	0.7	1.0	5.1	5.0	5.4	6.1	5.3	25.3	29.4	15.8	2.5	80.7	43.5	48.6	51.4
17981	TREMONT	93.8	94.5	5.3	4.0	0.3	0.4	2.1	5.1	4.8	4.7	5.3	6.0	6.9	26.0	25.5	15.9	4.9	82.3	42.1	51.3	48.7
17983	VALLEY VIEW	98.9	98.4	0.2	0.2	0.4	0.5	0.7	0.9	4.8	5.1	5.7	5.7	3.9	24.9	30.3	16.7	3.0	80.9	45.0	49.6	50.4
17985	ZION GROVE	98.4	97.9	0.1	0.1	0.4	0.6	0.5	0.7	4.7	5.5	6.2	6.3	3.8	24.9	31.8	14.8	2.1	79.6	44.0	50.3	49.7
18011	ALBURTIS	97.7	96.3	0.4	0.5	0.9	1.5	0.9	1.6	6.3	6.6	6.9	6.9	5.0	27.3	29.5	10.0	1.4	75.9	39.3	49.2	50.8
18013	BANGOR	98.4	97.7	0.4	0.6	0.3	0.4	1.2	2.0	5.9	6.1	6.4	6.6	5.5	24.3	30.1	12.5	2.7	77.5	41.7	49.2	50.8
18014	BATH	98.0	97.3	0.7	0.9	0.3	0.5	1.3	2.1	5.1	5.4	5.9	6.3	4.6	24.8	31.7	14.3	2.0	79.7	43.7	49.6	50.4
18015	BETHLEHEM	77.3	71.5	4.2	4.5	2.6	3.6	24.0	30.5	5.6	5.7	5.9	11.6	14.2	22.8	22.2	10.2	2.0	78.8	30.8	50.7	49.3
18017	BETHLEHEM	86.8	83.3	2.7	2.9	2.3	3.6	11.5	14.5	5.8	5.9	6.1	6.1	5.1	21.4	28.5	17.2	3.9	78.3	44.8	47.0	53.0
18018	BETHLEHEM	90.0	85.6	2.5	3.2	1.5	2.2	9.0	14.2	5.1	5.0	5.0	6.7	7.7	26.2	26.2	14.5	3.5	81.4	40.9	47.6	52.4
18020	BETHLEHEM	93.8	90.9	2.1	2.7	1.9	3.0	4.0	6.6	5.4	5.9	6.7	7.8	5.2	22.6	31.6	12.0	2.8	77.3	42.6	48.6	51.4
18031	BREINIGSVILLE	96.3	94.5	0.9	1.4	1.5	2.3	1.3	2.2	4.9	5.5	6.0	5.6	3.9	23.0	32.8	16.1	2.1	79.9	45.6	48.5	51.5
18032	CATASAUQUA	96.2	94.4	1.0	1.4	0.6	0.9	3.0	5.0	5.7	5.8	5.7	6.6	6.7	27.3	28.2	12.0	2.1	78.6	39.8	48.4	51.6
18034	CENTER VALLEY	97.1	95.4	0.7	1.0	1.2	1.9	1.1	1.9	5.3	6.1	6.6	8.9	6.3	21.6	31.3	12.3	1.7	78.0	41.9	49.7	50.3
18035	CHERRYVILLE	98.3	97.3	0.4	0.8	0.0	0.4	1.7	2.7	3.8	4.2	5.0	5.4	5.0	24.2	35.8	14.6	1.9	83.5	46.3	52.3	47.7
18036	COOPERSBURG	97.4	96.2	0.6	0.9	0.9	1.4	1.1	1.8	5.1	5.8	6.8	7.4	5.0	22.7	32.4	12.9	2.1	78.1	43.3	49.6	50.4
18037	COPLAY	97.3	96.0	1.0	1.4	0.5	0.7	1.7	2.8	6.1	7.0	6.9	6.8	4.4	26.7	28.3	12.0	1.7	75.3	40.4	49.3	50.7
18038	DANIELSVILLE	98.7	98.0	0.2	0.3	0.2	0.4	0.7	1.3	5.1	5.8	7.1	6.7	4.4	25.1	33.6	10.9	1.3	77.7	42.4	51.8	48.2
18040	EASTON	95.6	93.5	1.9	2.6	1.2	2.0	1.9	3.2	6.5	7.3	7.9	7.5	4.4	23.8	30.7	10.5	1.4	73.3	40.6	48.7	51.3
18041	EAST GREENVILLE	97.2	96.1	0.8	1.0	0.5	0.9	1.8	2.6	6.9	6.9	6.9	7.0	6.0	26.6	29.0	9.4	1.2	74.8	38.0	49.9	50.1
18042	EASTON	84.1	79.8	8.9	10.5	1.6	2.4	7.5	11.0	6.2	5.8	5.7	8.5	10.0	26.6	25.0	10.1	2.1	78.3	35.3	49.4	50.6
18045	EASTON	94.1	91.2	2.3	3.0	2.1	3.4	2.3	4.0	5.4	5.7	6.5	6.4	4.1	22.4	30.7	15.9	3.0	78.2	44.7	48.2	51.8
18049	EMMAUS	96.3	94.4	0.6	0.8	1.8	2.7	1.5	2.5	5.0	5.4	5.9	6.4	5.4	25.9	29.6	13.8	2.6	79.6	42.5	48.6	51.4
18051	FOGELSVILLE	96.5	95.0	0.8	1.2	1.3	1.9	1.5	2.5	6.0	7.0	7.7	6.2	3.7	21.9	35.0	11.2	1.3	75.3	43.5	49.3	50.7
18052	WHITEHALL	90.5	86.7	2.7	3.6	3.7	5.4	4.4	6.8	5.6	5.4	5.5	5.7	5.8	26.4	27.4	15.3	2.9	79.9	41.9	48.0	52.0
18053	GERMANSVILLE	98.7	98.1	0.3	0.4	0.3	0.5	0.9	1.5	6.2	7.1	7.6	6.4	3.8	27.5	31.8	8.8	1.0	74.8	40.0	51.8	48.2
18054	GREEN LANE	97.6	96.8	0.8	1.1	0.3	0.4	0.9	1.4	5.6	6.2	6.7	6.3	4.5	24.2	32.6	12.0	1.8	77.4	42.8	49.7	50.3
18055	HELLERTOWN	97.7	96.4	0.4	0.5	0.5	0.8	2.4	3.9	4.9	5.4	5.9	5.9	4.6	24.0	31.3	14.9	3.2	80.1	44.6	48.7	51.3
18056	HEREFORD	97.2	95.5	0.3	0.5	0.5	0.9	1.8	3.3	4.7	5.1	5.8	7.1	5.4	26.4	31.4	12.8	1.2	80.0	42.0	51.0	49.0
18058	KUNKLETOWN	96.9	96.1	1.3	1.6	0.4	0.7	2.6	3.5	5.6	6.1	6.7	7.1	4.8	24.1	30.8	12.6	2.1	77.2	42.1	49.9	50.1
18059	LAURYS STATION	97.2	95.8	0.8	1.2	0.5	0.9	1.5	2.6	7.2	8.5	9.0	9.2	4.2	23.6	31.0	6.5	0.8	69.3	37.9	50.3	49.7
18062	MACUNGIE	95.1	92.1	0.8	1.1	2.9	5.0	1.5	2.7	5.8	6.4	7.1	6.8	4.6	23.7	31.5	12.3	1.8	76.1	42.2	49.1	50.9
18064	NAZARETH	98.2	97.3	0.5	0.7	0.5	0.7	1.1	1.9	5.0	5.6	6.3	6.6	5.1	22.9	30.6	14.0	4.0	79.1	44.0	48.2	51.8
18066	NEW TRIPOLI	98.1	97.2	0.3	0.4	0.3	0.5	1.0	1.7	5.6	6.6	7.0	6.7	4.1	26.2	32.5	10.0	1.3	76.5	41.4	50.7	49.3
18067	NORTHAMPTON	98.3	97.4	0.3	0.5	0.4	0.6	1.4	2.4	5.0	5.4	6.0	6.3	4.5	24.4	31.8	14.0	2.5	79.4	43.9	48.6	51.4
18069	OREFIELD	94.6	91.9	1.1	1.4	2.3	3.7	2.1	3.4	5.5	6.5	8.4	8.9	4.2	21.8	31.9	11.6	1.2	73.0	41.7	48.8	51.2
18070	PALM	97.7	96.6	0.7	0.9	0.4	0.8	1.1	1.9	5.0	5.5	6.0	6.4	4.8	24.6	33.5	12.8	1.5	79.3	43.4	50.1	49.9
18071	PALMERTON	98.5	98.2	0.1	0.2	0.2	0.3	1.7	2.1	5.7	6.0	6.0	6.1	5.1	26.3	29.5	12.8	2.5	78.4	41.5	49.0	51.0
18072	PEN ARGYL	98.4	97.6	0.4	0.6	0.4	0.6	1.0	1.6	5.4	5.4	5.9	7.0	5.6	25.3	29.5	13.1	2.8	78.6	41.9	48.5	51.5
18073	PENNSBURG	97.7	96.8	0.7	1.0	0.4	0.6	1.2	1.7	6.2	6.5	6.8	6.6	4.8	24.7	30.4	11.8	2.2	76.1	41.3	49.2	50.8
	PENNSYLVANIA	85.4	83.2	10.0	10.7	1.8	2.7	3.2	4.2	5.8	6.0	6.3	7.1	6.5	24.8	27.8	13.1	2.6	77.8	40.4	48.5	51.5
	UNITED STATES	75.1	72.0	12.3	12.7	3.8	4.6	12.5	15.7	6.8	6.7	6.6	7.1	6.9	27.0	26.0	10.9	1.9	75.7	36.9	49.2	50.8

#	POST OFFICE NAME	2009 Per Capita Income	2009 HH Income Base	2009 Household Income Distribution (%): Less than $25,000	$25,000 to $49,999	$50,000 to $99,999	$100,000 to $149,999	$150,000 or More	Median Household Income: 2009	2014	2009 National Centile	2009 State Centile	2009 Home Value Base	2009 Home Value Distribution (%): Less than $50,000	$50,000 to $89,999	$90,000 to $174,999	$175,000 to $399,999	$400,000 or More	2009 Median Home Value
17834	KULPMONT	22321	1393	31.8	31.4	29.4	5.5	1.9	40450	42344	34	28	1131	28.2	37.0	23.9	10.7	0.2	64394
17835	LAURELTON	18881	5	40.0	0.0	60.0	0.0	0.0	54272	56580	70	70	4	0.0	0.0	100.0	0.0	0.0	137500
17836	LECK KILL	18759	214	25.7	29.0	40.7	4.7	0.0	45000	49184	48	46	184	5.4	20.1	41.8	28.3	4.3	133333
17837	LEWISBURG	24583	6378	23.6	22.5	39.0	9.3	5.7	53531	54760	69	69	4148	3.6	5.1	38.4	44.7	8.3	183516
17841	MC CLURE	18770	1758	21.8	34.9	38.3	4.4	0.7	45705	47667	50	50	1465	13.9	16.8	48.1	18.3	3.0	121365
17842	MIDDLEBURG	19407	3698	24.5	34.6	35.6	3.8	1.5	42750	45490	42	38	2867	8.1	12.7	51.7	25.3	2.3	137860
17844	MIFFLINBURG	20778	3638	22.3	31.2	39.1	5.5	1.9	46836	50162	54	54	2801	14.3	5.2	48.0	27.2	5.3	145755
17845	MILLMONT	18517	1110	22.6	36.4	36.9	3.4	0.6	43195	46736	43	40	907	6.9	18.6	50.6	20.7	3.1	130515
17846	MILLVILLE	21017	1519	24.1	31.7	36.2	5.9	2.1	45561	48338	50	49	1177	9.7	12.8	44.8	28.6	4.1	142635
17847	MILTON	22477	4686	25.5	29.9	38.2	4.2	2.1	44906	47915	48	45	3220	10.7	13.0	51.8	22.9	1.6	131229
17850	MONTANDON	20021	72	27.8	34.7	33.3	4.2	0.0	40000	42355	33	26	57	31.6	15.8	42.1	10.5	0.0	95000
17851	MOUNT CARMEL	20772	3867	38.5	28.0	26.6	5.3	1.7	32976	35000	13	5	3010	41.3	35.2	15.1	7.9	0.5	56102
17853	MOUNT PLEASANT MILLS	17932	1029	24.6	33.0	36.6	4.3	1.5	41202	45363	37	32	855	8.3	11.0	54.0	23.9	2.8	136953
17855	NEW BERLIN	22884	410	21.0	33.9	35.1	8.0	2.0	45412	49655	49	48	315	3.5	7.6	68.9	18.1	1.9	140745
17856	NEW COLUMBIA	22371	1560	20.7	28.7	44.0	4.6	2.1	50451	52389	62	63	1334	8.4	12.0	52.6	24.7	2.2	142736
17857	NORTHUMBERLAND	24263	3090	21.4	31.7	40.1	4.5	2.4	47150	49940	54	55	2358	4.8	13.5	52.6	27.7	1.4	140716
17859	ORANGEVILLE	24158	1226	20.7	29.8	39.9	7.3	2.3	49546	51705	60	61	1052	12.4	10.1	36.9	35.3	5.4	154583
17860	PAXINOS	22899	851	18.7	30.6	40.4	8.9	1.4	50670	52737	63	64	746	3.5	10.9	45.2	35.3	5.2	156888
17864	PORT TREVORTON	16078	971	27.4	32.3	34.3	4.3	1.6	41345	45131	37	32	806	8.9	13.4	43.2	29.4	5.1	146134
17866	COAL TOWNSHIP	19650	3537	33.3	30.8	28.4	5.0	2.4	36227	38360	21	11	2850	31.9	34.9	23.7	8.5	1.1	65366
17867	REBUCK	20002	250	25.2	27.6	42.8	4.4	0.0	46707	49318	53	54	214	6.1	20.1	40.2	28.5	5.1	134375
17868	RIVERSIDE	32132	96	24.0	21.9	41.7	6.3	6.3	54564	55661	71	71	79	2.5	10.1	62.0	24.1	1.3	138971
17870	SELINSGROVE	22997	4797	24.7	29.2	36.1	6.3	3.8	46478	48126	53	53	3405	8.3	6.6	47.5	33.0	4.7	152543
17872	SHAMOKIN	17087	4031	45.8	27.7	24.1	1.8	0.6	27914	29445	6	2	2542	45.0	33.7	18.5	2.8	0.0	53075
17876	SHAMOKIN DAM	25589	714	27.0	25.4	38.5	5.9	3.2	47510	48797	55	56	508	3.1	4.7	63.4	27.8	1.0	150455
17877	SNYDERTOWN	19265	131	23.7	32.1	39.7	4.6	0.0	45750	49079	51	50	106	2.8	14.2	49.1	30.2	3.8	150000
17878	STILLWATER	22121	457	22.3	31.9	38.5	5.7	1.5	46715	49835	53	54	396	7.1	8.8	41.7	36.6	5.8	160849
17881	TREVORTON	20676	1005	28.5	31.9	34.7	4.1	0.8	42719	45589	42	38	828	12.3	38.6	39.6	9.1	0.4	88400
17888	WILBURTON	18832	205	33.2	30.7	33.2	2.0	1.0	37169	39397	24	14	182	25.8	35.2	25.8	12.1	1.1	70714
17889	WINFIELD	28709	880	14.4	24.1	45.8	8.9	6.8	61165	60903	79	80	771	4.9	7.0	42.3	35.3	10.5	167034
17901	POTTSVILLE	23572	10735	29.0	25.4	35.0	6.8	3.8	45179	49482	49	47	7745	10.4	30.2	37.7	19.1	2.6	105212
17921	ASHLAND	20777	3220	27.0	30.1	33.5	6.7	2.7	42599	46011	41	38	2560	15.0	29.4	38.8	15.8	1.0	99000
17922	AUBURN	24065	1782	14.6	29.3	46.2	7.4	2.5	55063	56359	71	71	1617	1.9	7.2	47.0	40.4	3.6	162103
17923	BRANCHDALE	20134	219	30.6	29.7	36.1	3.2	0.5	39172	41632	30	23	192	24.0	29.7	38.5	7.8	0.0	83636
17925	BROCKTON	23122	508	26.8	32.1	34.4	5.5	1.2	42784	45898	42	38	458	18.8	39.5	32.5	9.2	0.0	79273
17929	CRESSONA	25006	669	14.1	30.6	46.6	6.7	1.9	53864	55145	69	69	498	4.4	24.5	56.4	13.1	1.6	110714
17931	FRACKVILLE	24591	2493	27.1	31.8	29.8	8.7	2.6	42709	45477	42	38	1870	7.2	38.4	43.5	10.6	0.3	94659
17935	GIRARDVILLE	19113	855	36.3	35.0	24.2	3.6	0.9	33424	34836	14	6	684	42.4	37.6	13.7	5.8	0.4	55200
17938	HEGINS	21022	990	27.8	29.0	35.3	5.2	2.8	42441	47157	41	37	825	5.0	19.8	55.4	18.7	1.2	118894
17941	KLINGERSTOWN	18469	267	27.0	34.5	34.8	3.0	0.7	43209	46176	43	40	223	8.1	17.5	47.5	23.8	3.1	126014
17948	MAHANOY CITY	16969	2219	35.9	34.9	24.6	3.5	1.2	34085	35246	16	7	1737	50.4	35.1	12.7	1.6	0.2	49709
17954	MINERSVILLE	21014	2117	36.8	24.8	32.7	3.9	1.8	38616	43170	28	20	1450	13.2	50.5	26.9	9.4	0.1	74780
17957	MUIR	21894	154	20.8	29.9	44.2	4.5	0.6	48253	51475	57	58	134	12.7	32.8	37.3	13.4	3.7	97500
17959	NEW PHILADELPHIA	22010	1078	32.2	28.7	31.8	5.7	1.7	40000	43040	33	26	806	18.6	42.6	30.1	8.1	0.6	75682
17960	NEW RINGGOLD	21854	1408	23.5	30.9	36.8	6.3	2.5	45142	49553	49	46	1181	4.1	9.1	42.8	35.6	8.4	162411
17961	ORWIGSBURG	29055	2652	18.4	24.9	39.1	8.9	8.7	57166	58236	74	74	2115	2.6	9.5	44.7	36.2	7.1	156382
17963	PINE GROVE	22506	3701	20.6	29.7	41.2	6.8	1.7	49665	52209	60	61	2972	4.4	17.6	43.6	31.2	3.3	143379
17964	PITMAN	20625	330	23.6	39.4	28.8	5.2	3.0	41304	43391	37	32	275	6.9	16.0	47.6	25.8	3.6	135880
17965	PORT CARBON	22655	818	27.4	34.0	31.7	4.2	2.8	42443	44902	41	37	643	6.1	42.5	41.8	9.5	0.2	91939
17967	RINGTOWN	22679	1044	25.0	30.2	36.2	6.1	2.5	44908	48835	48	45	913	8.9	15.4	45.2	27.9	2.5	132899
17968	SACRAMENTO	20807	115	25.2	24.3	42.6	6.1	1.7	50213	52121	62	62	93	8.6	19.4	50.5	15.1	6.5	122115
17970	SAINT CLAIR	21169	1618	33.8	32.8	27.7	4.9	0.8	36903	38274	23	13	1175	9.5	53.1	32.3	5.0	0.0	78677
17972	SCHUYLKILL HAVEN	23102	4462	23.1	29.9	39.1	5.2	2.6	47055	50758	54	55	3418	9.1	16.3	44.9	27.3	2.4	127000
17976	SHENANDOAH	19411	3959	40.4	28.7	27.3	2.7	1.0	32463	34490	12	4	2996	47.9	30.7	16.9	4.5	0.0	51400
17978	SPRING GLEN	20937	135	24.4	24.4	43.0	5.9	2.2	50525	52349	62	63	109	8.3	19.3	51.4	15.6	5.5	122500
17980	TOWER CITY	23722	1477	24.2	29.4	37.8	5.8	2.8	45631	50491	50	49	1154	10.7	37.2	42.5	7.5	2.1	92400
17981	TREMONT	19550	989	28.9	31.0	35.8	3.3	0.9	41705	44948	38	34	800	15.1	45.6	33.3	5.8	0.3	77600
17983	VALLEY VIEW	24904	799	23.0	24.0	41.8	7.4	3.8	51947	53701	66	67	653	6.0	14.2	63.2	15.2	1.4	126716
17985	ZION GROVE	20422	827	25.5	32.5	35.2	5.1	1.7	42703	46424	42	38	684	5.6	13.7	48.5	28.8	3.4	138949
18011	ALBURTIS	27028	2386	9.6	23.0	53.9	10.6	2.8	65076	67579	83	86	2065	4.8	2.6	32.3	53.6	6.8	197240
18013	BANGOR	24224	7152	20.2	24.3	45.0	7.3	3.3	55595	59974	72	72	5144	1.6	3.6	36.5	52.4	6.0	196086
18014	BATH	26201	4709	14.2	28.1	44.6	8.9	4.2	58341	62152	76	77	3885	8.0	9.5	24.2	51.5	6.8	203397
18015	BETHLEHEM	21589	11361	28.2	24.7	34.5	7.5	5.0	46757	50076	53	54	6606	2.5	10.3	45.8	30.9	10.5	155612
18017	BETHLEHEM	30393	15001	16.8	21.6	41.7	12.2	7.8	63370	67814	82	84	10684	0.7	1.9	28.2	59.7	9.5	219703
18018	BETHLEHEM	26825	14153	21.0	27.8	40.5	7.5	3.3	51211	54432	64	65	8233	0.4	4.0	57.4	36.0	2.1	159780
18020	BETHLEHEM	32031	7647	7.4	18.5	44.6	19.1	10.4	77137	79243	91	93	6529	1.5	0.9	17.4	72.1	8.1	238626
18031	BREINIGSVILLE	31050	2143	13.5	25.7	42.8	11.2	6.9	63096	65851	81	83	1848	20.4	15.4	12.6	41.7	9.9	181148
18032	CATASAUQUA	25589	3841	16.6	24.4	48.6	7.2	3.2	56869	59419	74	74	2673	0.0	3.9	62.1	33.3	0.8	155507
18034	CENTER VALLEY	34765	2616	5.1	15.1	44.3	20.5	14.9	79889	81364	92	94	2351	2.3	2.8	9.2	58.6	27.2	275759
18035	CHERRYVILLE	27756	97	6.2	29.9	47.4	9.3	7.2	67145	70616	85	88	88	2.3	1.1	20.5	62.5	13.6	250000
18036	COOPERSBURG	35019	4860	6.9	15.3	46.4	20.2	11.3	77566	79165	91	93	4225	1.1	0.4	8.1	65.9	24.5	279516
18037	COPLAY	26922	3095	15.3	19.7	51.1	9.9	4.0	62547	64426	81	82	2557	3.0	1.8	31.9	56.6	6.7	200989
18038	DANIELSVILLE	22762	1075	10.5	29.5	51.1	7.1	1.9	57741	61142	75	76	990	1.5	4.3	30.4	58.4	5.4	208284
18040	EASTON	32034	5803	6.9	14.0	49.9	19.5	9.6	78659	80626	91	94	5212	0.7	1.4	14.6	72.1	11.2	266276
18041	EAST GREENVILLE	27083	2142	12.3	21.3	46.1	15.7	4.6	66092	67664	84	87	1619	0.7	0.6	33.2	55.0	10.4	221549
18042	EASTON	22253	16119	22.6	30.1	37.4	6.8	3.1	47641	50537	56	57	8898	1.0	7.6	59.7	25.4	6.3	144778
18045	EASTON	34447	10632	11.5	19.6	41.9	16.8	10.2	73961	77376	89	91	9213	0.7	0.6	18.5	73.8	6.4	229950
18049	EMMAUS	32980	7441	13.5	21.6	44.4	12.6	8.0	65419	68718	84	86	5201	0.7	1.3	27.8	59.2	10.9	219873
18051	FOGELSVILLE	35285	1241	9.5	21.1	41.0	13.9	14.4	75152	76935	89	91	1082	7.0	3.7	18.9	47.6	22.7	264706
18052	WHITEHALL	27144	11055	16.0	26.1	45.7	8.8	3.4	58178	61013	75	76	7020	0.8	2.0	33.0	60.9	3.3	199752
18053	GERMANSVILLE	26117	906	14.8	21.0	51.0	8.2	5.1	62457	63978	81	82	787	5.0	2.3	27.3	56.5	8.9	223090
18054	GREEN LANE	34448	2019	9.9	17.8	41.7	23.3	7.3	76051	78377	90	92	1722	1.8	2.8	10.6	68.0	16.8	270235
18055	HELLERTOWN	30932	4957	14.5	23.5	44.4	11.5	6.1	62040	65559	80	81	3976	0.5	1.2	29.0	55.5	13.8	215385
18056	HEREFORD	23377	503	20.3	25.0	43.7	8.0	3.0	54539	57276	70	71	449	34.3	17.1	11.6	30.1	6.9	81875
18058	KUNKLETOWN	21156	3782	20.1	27.3	41.6	8.1	2.9	51820	53487	66	66	3230	4.1	5.4	37.7	48.2	4.6	181337
18059	LAURYS STATION	26598	524	12.0	19.7	49.6	13.0	5.7	67549	72427	85	88	491	30.3	0.4	7.5	49.5	12.2	268103
18062	MACUNGIE	37336	8806	8.0	18.2	40.6	18.1	15.1	78085	80293	91	93	7507	2.6	1.3	21.8	58.5	15.9	236097
18064	NAZARETH	28272	8723	12.1	20.5	46.1	14.3	7.0	67642	72326	85	88	6855	0.9	2.3	22.6	64.0	10.2	234821
18066	NEW TRIPOLI	27263	2061	10.7	23.9	47.5	13.1	4.9	65333	68271	84	86	1755	2.5	1.3	19.7	63.2	13.3	239313
18067	NORTHAMPTON	27676	7570	12.9	25.9	46.5	9.9	4.8	62354	66485	80	82	6172	2.9	3.4	38.7	50.5	4.6	186407
18069	OREFIELD	33532	2697	10.0	19.1	43.2	11.4	16.3	76800	78547	90	93	2291	8.6	2.9	14.8	45.5	28.2	270392
18070	PALM	28919	299	14.0	21.1	41.1	17.4	6.4	64033	65592	82	85	264	11.7	6.1	13.3	55.7	13.3	239773
18071	PALMERTON	23016	4756	20.7	33.2	37.7	5.9	2.4	46755	50253	53	54	3609	5.6	8.6	47.2	36.2	2.4	155637
18072	PEN ARGYL	23667	2549	17.5	27.5	45.9	5.8	3.4	55305	59923	72	71	1826	0.4	4.1	42.1	48.8	4.6	182176
18073	PENNSBURG	29512	3159	11.9	17.7	44.5	21.1	4.8	72786	75069	88	90	2556	0.2	0.5	15.5	71.7	12.1	254586
	PENNSYLVANIA	26913		21.5	25.3	36.9	10.2	6.1	53225	55819				7.5	12.2	35.6	36.1	8.5	161438
	UNITED STATES	27277		20.9	24.4	35.3	11.7	7.6	54719	56938				9.3	13.1	31.6	32.6	13.5	162279

ZIP CODE #	POST OFFICE NAME	FINANCIAL SERVICES: Auto Loan	FINANCIAL SERVICES: Home Loan	FINANCIAL SERVICES: Invest-ments	FINANCIAL SERVICES: Retire-ment Plans	THE HOME: Home Improvements: Home Repair	THE HOME: Home Improvements: Lawn & Garden	THE HOME: Furnishings: Comput-ers & Hard-ware-Personal	THE HOME: Furnishings: Major Appli-ances	THE HOME: Furnishings: TV, Radio, Sound Equip-ment	THE HOME: Furnishings: Furni-ture	ENTERTAINMENT: Dine out/ Carry out	ENTERTAINMENT: Sports Equip-ment	ENTERTAINMENT: Fees & Tickets	ENTERTAINMENT: Toys & Games	ENTERTAINMENT: Travel	ENTERTAINMENT: Cable TV	PERSONAL: Apparel & Services	PERSONAL: Auto Repairs	PERSONAL: Health Insur-ance	PERSONAL: Pets & Supplies
17834	KULPMONT	76	64	78	62	65	83	64	77	71	60	69	56	58	70	65	77	47	72	85	89
17835	LAURELTON	67	61	60	63	62	72	60	68	62	54	61	51	55	63	60	66	42	63	70	79
17836	LECK KILL	76	69	68	72	70	81	68	77	70	61	69	58	63	71	68	74	47	71	79	89
17837	LEWISBURG	92	91	93	94	93	98	93	95	94	90	94	71	93	93	94	97	65	94	101	111
17841	MC CLURE	83	65	74	65	66	84	67	78	73	62	71	59	56	74	64	79	48	73	83	93
17842	MIDDLEBURG	82	66	74	67	67	84	68	79	73	63	71	60	59	74	65	78	48	73	82	93
17844	MIFFLINBURG	82	77	72	77	76	85	75	80	78	72	77	59	71	79	73	82	53	77	85	94
17845	MILLMONT	74	68	67	70	69	80	67	75	69	60	67	57	61	70	67	73	46	69	78	87
17846	MILLVILLE	81	74	74	76	75	86	74	82	76	68	75	62	68	77	73	81	51	77	85	96
17847	MILTON	79	70	68	71	69	81	73	77	76	68	75	59	67	77	70	80	51	76	83	92
17850	MONTANDON	86	61	71	60	61	81	64	74	71	62	70	57	51	74	58	77	47	71	79	91
17851	MOUNT CARMEL	72	55	72	53	56	75	59	71	65	53	63	52	50	64	57	72	43	67	78	83
17853	MOUNT PLEASANT MILLS	78	71	70	74	72	84	70	79	72	63	71	60	64	74	70	76	48	73	81	92
17855	NEW BERLIN	78	79	63	81	74	83	79	77	80	74	79	61	79	81	77	82	55	78	85	94
17856	NEW COLUMBIA	86	78	77	82	80	92	77	87	80	70	78	66	71	81	77	84	53	80	90	101
17857	NORTHUMBERLAND	81	77	73	79	76	86	79	82	81	73	80	62	76	81	77	84	55	80	87	96
17859	ORANGEVILLE	90	84	87	85	84	96	80	91	83	76	82	69	76	84	82	87	56	85	92	106
17860	PAXINOS	88	80	79	83	82	94	79	89	81	71	80	67	73	83	79	86	55	82	92	103
17864	PORT TREVORTON	82	67	71	68	68	83	68	77	72	63	71	59	59	74	65	77	48	72	81	92
17866	COAL TOWNSHIP	75	60	74	59	62	79	64	74	71	59	68	55	56	69	63	77	46	71	82	87
17867	REBUCK	76	69	68	72	70	81	68	77	70	61	69	58	63	72	68	74	47	71	79	89
17868	RIVERSIDE	88	100	95	98	100	109	88	97	95	87	94	68	97	93	96	101	65	94	111	111
17870	SELINSGROVE	86	78	77	81	79	88	84	85	85	77	84	65	78	85	80	88	58	84	90	100
17872	SHAMOKIN	54	44	50	44	45	54	51	53	55	46	53	39	45	53	47	59	37	53	59	62
17876	SHAMOKIN DAM	76	80	77	79	80	87	75	81	79	74	78	58	78	78	79	83	54	79	89	93
17877	SNYDERTOWN	76	69	68	72	71	82	68	77	70	62	69	58	63	72	68	74	47	71	79	89
17878	STILLWATER	82	75	74	78	77	88	74	84	76	67	75	63	68	78	74	81	51	77	86	97
17881	TREVORTON	80	60	79	59	62	84	64	78	71	58	69	59	53	70	63	78	46	73	85	92
17888	WILBURTON	73	53	73	51	55	76	57	71	64	51	62	53	46	63	56	71	41	66	77	83
17889	WINFIELD	108	106	103	110	107	118	101	111	102	95	101	85	99	104	103	106	70	104	113	129
17901	POTTSVILLE	80	74	78	74	75	86	76	81	81	72	79	59	74	79	76	86	55	80	91	95
17921	ASHLAND	82	70	82	69	71	89	71	83	78	66	76	61	65	76	71	84	51	79	91	96
17922	AUBURN	90	93	82	96	91	98	87	92	88	84	87	71	88	90	89	90	60	88	95	109
17923	BRANCHDALE	78	57	79	55	59	82	62	76	69	55	66	57	49	68	60	76	44	71	83	89
17925	BROCKTON	84	61	85	59	63	88	66	82	74	59	71	61	53	73	64	82	48	76	89	96
17929	CRESSONA	84	87	68	89	80	90	86	83	87	82	87	66	87	89	84	89	60	85	92	101
17931	FRACKVILLE	78	73	80	72	74	88	72	81	78	68	77	58	71	76	74	84	53	78	91	94
17935	GIRARDVILLE	69	53	70	52	55	74	56	68	62	51	60	50	47	61	55	68	40	64	75	80
17938	HEGINS	74	74	72	75	75	84	69	78	73	65	72	57	70	73	72	77	49	73	84	89
17941	KLINGERSTOWN	75	66	68	69	68	80	66	75	68	59	67	57	60	69	66	72	46	69	78	88
17948	MAHANOY CITY	68	50	68	49	52	71	55	66	61	50	59	49	45	60	53	67	40	63	73	78
17954	MINERSVILLE	73	56	68	55	57	74	63	71	69	57	67	53	53	68	59	75	45	69	78	83
17957	MUIR	80	73	73	76	75	86	72	82	75	65	73	62	67	76	72	79	50	75	84	95
17959	NEW PHILADELPHIA	84	60	84	59	63	87	66	81	73	59	71	61	53	72	64	81	47	76	89	95
17960	NEW RINGGOLD	85	78	77	81	79	92	77	86	79	69	78	65	71	80	76	84	53	80	89	100
17961	ORWIGSBURG	104	106	101	108	106	114	100	107	103	98	102	81	101	103	103	106	70	103	113	125
17963	PINE GROVE	83	80	76	82	80	90	77	85	79	72	78	64	75	81	78	83	54	80	89	99
17964	PITMAN	91	66	96	67	69	96	71	87	74	59	73	71	55	73	71	80	48	81	92	106
17965	PORT CARBON	86	65	87	63	67	91	69	85	77	62	74	63	57	76	68	85	50	79	93	99
17967	RINGTOWN	84	79	82	80	80	93	76	86	80	71	79	64	72	80	78	85	54	81	92	100
17968	SACRAMENTO	82	75	74	78	76	88	74	83	76	66	74	63	68	77	73	80	51	77	86	96
17970	SAINT CLAIR	75	54	76	53	56	79	59	73	66	53	64	55	48	65	57	73	43	68	80	86
17972	SCHUYLKILL HAVEN	82	74	76	75	74	87	75	81	79	69	77	61	70	79	74	83	53	79	88	96
17976	SHENANDOAH	61	52	57	52	53	63	58	61	62	53	60	45	52	60	55	66	41	61	69	71
17978	SPRING GLEN	82	75	74	78	76	88	74	83	76	67	75	63	68	78	74	81	51	77	86	97
17980	TOWER CITY	81	74	83	73	75	91	72	84	78	68	77	61	69	77	74	84	52	79	92	97
17981	TREMONT	74	63	76	61	64	81	63	75	69	58	68	55	57	68	64	76	46	71	83	87
17983	VALLEY VIEW	81	85	82	85	85	95	78	87	82	74	81	63	80	82	82	87	56	82	95	100
17985	ZION GROVE	77	71	70	73	72	83	69	78	72	63	70	59	64	73	69	76	48	72	81	91
18011	ALBURTIS	102	107	98	106	104	101	99	101	97	102	98	77	101	100	100	96	68	98	97	118
18013	BANGOR	86	90	82	92	88	94	87	89	88	84	87	68	88	88	88	90	61	88	94	105
18014	BATH	92	98	94	99	98	101	92	97	92	90	92	74	95	92	96	94	64	94	99	113
18015	BETHLEHEM	82	77	71	78	75	78	86	79	86	82	86	62	83	86	80	87	61	84	84	95
18017	BETHLEHEM	100	110	108	111	111	112	104	106	106	105	106	78	111	104	110	108	75	106	113	123
18018	BETHLEHEM	81	83	78	83	82	86	84	83	86	82	86	63	86	85	84	89	60	85	91	98
18020	BETHLEHEM	115	142	130	142	139	132	123	126	120	127	122	97	139	122	134	119	87	122	123	146
18031	BREINIGSVILLE	105	108	118	104	113	119	100	112	102	105	101	79	102	98	107	106	69	108	119	129
18032	CATASAUQUA	84	90	82	89	87	92	89	88	90	85	90	67	91	90	90	93	63	89	95	104
18034	CENTER VALLEY	134	166	166	170	169	158	141	149	137	150	138	111	161	137	158	135	99	142	144	171
18035	CHERRYVILLE	102	116	100	119	113	114	103	107	102	104	102	84	111	104	110	102	72	103	107	126
18036	COOPERSBURG	125	152	149	155	153	145	131	137	128	137	129	103	148	128	145	127	92	132	134	158
18037	COPLAY	95	106	92	105	101	100	97	97	96	98	96	75	102	98	99	96	68	96	97	114
18038	DANIELSVILLE	93	94	87	97	93	101	88	95	89	84	88	73	88	91	91	91	61	90	96	112
18040	EASTON	118	146	131	146	142	132	124	128	119	129	121	99	140	123	135	117	87	122	121	147
18041	EAST GREENVILLE	98	114	103	114	111	107	106	105	103	104	104	83	113	105	111	103	74	104	104	123
18042	EASTON	78	75	65	77	71	77	83	76	83	77	83	61	80	83	77	84	58	80	82	92
18045	EASTON	115	135	129	135	135	133	119	125	120	123	120	92	132	119	129	121	85	121	130	144
18049	EMMAUS	103	118	114	120	118	115	109	110	108	111	109	84	119	108	116	108	77	109	112	128
18051	FOGELSVILLE	131	147	144	149	149	148	131	140	129	136	130	104	141	129	142	130	91	134	140	162
18052	WHITEHALL	88	92	86	93	90	93	90	89	91	89	91	68	94	91	92	92	64	90	95	105
18053	GERMANSVILLE	100	112	97	116	109	110	100	104	99	101	99	81	107	101	106	99	69	100	103	123
18054	GREEN LANE	120	135	129	139	136	135	122	129	120	122	120	98	130	121	130	121	85	123	127	149
18055	HELLERTOWN	98	110	108	111	111	113	101	106	103	102	103	78	109	101	108	105	72	104	113	122
18056	HEREFORD	108	77	89	75	77	102	80	94	89	78	88	72	65	93	73	97	59	89	99	114
18058	KUNKLETOWN	90	86	82	89	86	97	82	91	84	77	83	70	79	86	83	88	57	85	93	106
18059	LAURYS STATION	104	130	114	130	125	113	109	111	103	114	105	88	123	107	118	99	75	106	100	128
18062	MACUNGIE	132	148	150	151	149	142	134	138	131	139	132	107	145	132	143	129	94	134	132	160
18064	NAZARETH	102	119	111	120	118	116	107	110	106	107	107	84	117	107	115	107	75	107	112	128
18066	NEW TRIPOLI	104	118	102	121	114	115	105	109	103	105	104	85	112	106	111	103	73	105	108	128
18067	NORTHAMPTON	94	103	97	104	102	107	95	100	97	93	96	74	101	97	100	100	67	97	106	116
18069	OREFIELD	132	155	150	158	156	151	134	141	132	140	133	106	150	134	146	132	95	135	139	163
18070	PALM	118	114	108	115	111	123	107	115	109	106	109	90	104	113	107	113	75	110	117	137
18071	PALMERTON	79	79	74	80	78	87	76	81	80	73	79	61	76	80	77	83	54	79	88	95
18072	PEN ARGYL	86	90	80	92	87	94	86	88	87	82	87	68	88	88	87	89	60	87	93	104
18073	PENNSBURG	106	124	113	124	122	118	111	113	109	112	110	87	121	110	118	108	78	111	112	132
	PENNSYLVANIA	94	95	95	95	95	100	94	96	96	91	95	73	94	96	94	99	67	95	101	113
	UNITED STATES	100	100	100	100	100	100	100	100	100	100	100	100	100	100	100	100	100	100	100	100

#	POST OFFICE NAME	COUNTY FIPS CODE	POPULATION 2000	POPULATION 2009	POPULATION 2014	2000-2009 ANNUAL RATE % Rate	2000-2009 ANNUAL RATE State Centile	HOUSEHOLDS 2000	HOUSEHOLDS 2009	HOUSEHOLDS 2014	HOUSEHOLDS % Annual Rate 2000-2009	HOUSEHOLDS 2009 Average HH Size	FAMILIES 2000	FAMILIES 2009	FAMILIES % Annual Rate 2000-2009
18074	PERKIOMENVILLE	091	5356	5917	6153	1.1	87	1840	2069	2163	1.3	2.78	1450	1592	1.0
18076	RED HILL	091	2313	2936	3172	2.6	97	929	1215	1327	2.9	2.42	611	768	2.5
18077	RIEGELSVILLE	017	2503	2571	2583	0.3	64	986	1029	1039	0.5	2.50	727	736	0.1
18078	SCHNECKSVILLE	077	5999	6648	7008	1.1	87	2257	2518	2660	1.2	2.59	1805	1966	0.9
18080	SLATINGTON	077	11967	12610	13005	0.6	74	4577	4888	5064	0.7	2.57	3384	3506	0.4
18087	TREXLERTOWN	077	465	491	542	0.6	74	209	224	248	0.8	2.18	175	183	0.5
18088	WALNUTPORT	095	8341	9168	9604	1.0	85	3228	3579	3767	1.1	2.53	2407	2584	0.8
18091	WIND GAP	095	5306	5696	5924	0.8	80	2087	2242	2334	0.8	2.50	1479	1546	0.5
18092	ZIONSVILLE	077	2871	3113	3248	0.9	83	1041	1145	1199	1.0	2.72	833	893	0.8
18101	ALLENTOWN	077	3867	4045	4136	0.5	70	1132	1198	1238	0.6	2.73	567	564	-0.1
18102	ALLENTOWN	077	43423	45459	46447	0.5	70	16759	17242	17587	0.3	2.58	9725	9515	-0.2
18103	ALLENTOWN	077	42685	44414	45617	0.4	68	17293	18254	18841	0.6	2.38	11514	11667	0.1
18104	ALLENTOWN	077	39242	42452	44231	0.9	83	15098	16590	17410	1.0	2.34	10002	10590	0.6
18106	ALLENTOWN	077	6123	7458	8098	2.2	96	2314	2822	3073	2.2	2.60	1772	2091	1.8
18109	ALLENTOWN	077	17051	16765	16848	-0.2	38	6961	6930	6997	0.0	2.36	4468	4254	-0.5
18201	HAZLETON	079	24921	24196	23849	-0.3	29	10944	10818	10736	-0.1	2.20	6466	6126	-0.6
18202	HAZLETON	079	11471	11698	11672	0.2	61	4789	5012	5042	0.5	2.21	3012	3038	0.1
18210	ALBRIGHTSVILLE	025	4364	6458	7338	4.3	99	1565	2335	2663	4.4	2.76	1205	1738	4.0
18211	ANDREAS	107	1161	1169	1165	0.1	57	448	465	468	0.4	2.51	348	354	0.2
18214	BARNESVILLE	107	2365	3486	3472	4.3	99	930	955	956	0.3	2.45	695	694	0.0
18216	BEAVER MEADOWS	025	2446	2621	2736	0.7	77	1018	1127	1190	1.1	2.30	697	745	0.7
18218	COALDALE	107	2295	2309	2292	0.1	57	1046	1076	1078	0.3	2.09	607	599	-0.1
18219	CONYNGHAM	079	866	852	844	-0.2	38	371	373	372	0.1	2.28	268	262	-0.2
18220	DELANO	107	331	327	325	-0.1	46	130	133	133	0.2	2.46	94	93	-0.1
18222	DRUMS	079	7011	8408	8740	2.0	95	2463	3084	3250	2.5	2.46	1848	2252	2.2
18224	FREELAND	079	5720	5691	5656	-0.1	46	2459	2504	2506	0.2	2.26	1554	1527	-0.2
18229	JIM THORPE	025	6912	7395	7679	0.7	77	2782	3070	3218	1.1	2.40	1974	2115	0.7
18232	LANSFORD	025	4230	4200	4230	-0.1	46	1878	1903	1931	0.1	2.19	1099	1064	-0.3
18235	LEHIGHTON	025	18535	19540	20256	0.6	74	7394	8065	8445	0.9	2.39	5273	5595	0.6
18237	MCADOO	107	3882	3826	3784	-0.2	38	1732	1756	1751	0.1	2.17	1089	1062	-0.3
18240	NESQUEHONING	025	3873	4145	4280	0.7	77	1590	1761	1842	1.1	2.19	1040	1107	0.7
18246	ROCK GLEN	079	1117	1095	1083	-0.2	38	444	447	446	0.1	2.39	307	299	-0.3
18248	SHEPPTON	107	959	955	948	0.0	52	444	455	455	0.3	2.10	282	278	-0.2
18249	SUGARLOAF	079	4610	4863	4902	0.6	74	1772	1911	1943	0.8	2.42	1361	1434	0.6
18250	SUMMIT HILL	025	2974	2944	2978	-0.1	46	1291	1324	1354	0.3	2.22	844	834	-0.1
18252	TAMAQUA	107	11691	11583	11463	-0.1	46	4806	4869	4856	0.1	2.30	3135	3071	-0.2
18255	WEATHERLY	025	4350	4491	4596	0.3	64	1588	1692	1752	0.7	2.51	1155	1196	0.4
18301	EAST STROUDSBURG	089	23480	29441	32215	2.5	97	7930	9924	10880	2.5	2.72	5548	6822	2.3
18302	EAST STROUDSBURG	089	14037	16782	17957	1.9	94	4879	5765	6154	1.8	2.90	3696	4242	1.5
18321	BARTONSVILLE	089	1446	1648	1735	1.4	91	503	566	595	1.3	2.90	381	417	1.0
18322	BRODHEADSVILLE	089	1758	2131	2438	2.1	95	628	753	857	2.0	2.79	490	572	1.7
18324	BUSHKILL	103	5975	8689	10167	4.1	99	2074	3073	3610	4.3	2.82	1636	2372	4.1
18325	CANADENSIS	089	1868	2521	2739	3.3	98	742	1001	1091	3.3	2.46	512	674	3.0
18326	CRESCO	089	3918	5426	6126	3.6	99	1560	2135	2407	3.5	2.53	1079	1429	3.1
18327	DELAWARE WATER GAP	089	1069	1291	1441	2.1	95	486	582	648	2.0	2.19	289	325	1.3
18328	DINGMANS FERRY	103	6617	7879	8590	1.9	94	2369	2831	3082	1.9	2.78	1840	2153	1.7
18330	EFFORT	089	8669	10816	12079	2.4	96	2879	3561	3971	2.3	3.00	2298	2777	2.1
18331	GILBERT	089	37	38	43	0.3	64	12	12	13	0.0	3.17	9	9	0.0
18332	HENRYVILLE	089	2608	3459	3929	3.1	98	977	1286	1464	3.0	2.63	704	893	2.6
18333	KRESGEVILLE	089	1079	1318	1461	2.2	96	394	475	526	2.0	2.74	311	368	1.8
18334	LONG POND	089	1886	2442	2679	2.8	97	657	879	963	3.2	2.78	511	668	2.9
18336	MATAMORAS	103	3861	4416	4789	1.5	92	1540	1763	1918	1.5	2.48	1072	1189	1.1
18337	MILFORD	103	11611	14730	16760	2.6	97	4195	5360	6078	2.7	2.74	3195	3984	2.4
18340	MILLRIFT	103	236	233	265	-0.1	46	87	87	100	0.0	2.63	62	60	-0.4
18343	MOUNT BETHEL	095	4059	4398	4589	0.9	83	1597	1749	1833	1.0	2.51	1149	1213	0.6
18344	MOUNT POCONO	089	3361	4036	4351	2.0	95	1248	1488	1602	1.9	2.68	854	987	1.6
18346	POCONO SUMMIT	089	1793	2474	2777	3.5	98	635	866	970	3.4	2.86	471	626	3.1
18347	POCONO LAKE	089	2588	3220	3632	2.4	96	1067	1311	1475	2.3	2.45	755	894	1.8
18350	POCONO PINES	089	998	1239	1397	2.4	96	429	529	595	2.3	2.34	304	362	1.9
18352	REEDERS	089	355	402	442	1.4	91	148	167	183	1.3	2.38	113	124	1.0
18353	SAYLORSBURG	089	9806	13349	14713	3.4	98	3416	4579	5040	3.2	2.90	2744	3601	3.0
18354	SCIOTA	089	443	555	611	2.5	97	170	209	230	2.3	2.65	119	141	1.9
18355	SCOTRUN	089	1753	2098	2372	2.0	95	666	793	896	1.9	2.62	484	559	1.6
18360	STROUDSBURG	089	26458	31781	34400	2.0	95	10000	11844	12787	1.8	2.62	6893	7963	1.6
18370	SWIFTWATER	089	678	1308	1485	7.4	100	259	480	544	6.9	2.71	188	337	6.5
18371	TAMIMENT	103	1433	2191	2587	4.7	99	492	742	873	4.5	2.95	392	580	4.3
18372	TANNERSVILLE	089	2569	3082	3379	2.0	95	955	1130	1234	1.8	2.73	721	830	1.5
18403	ARCHBALD	069	6489	6574	6547	0.1	57	2521	2605	2614	0.4	2.52	1811	1818	0.0
18405	BEACH LAKE	127	1521	1439	1410	-0.6	13	579	564	559	-0.3	2.55	431	408	-0.6
18407	CARBONDALE	069	14636	14405	14237	-0.2	38	6017	6022	5990	0.0	2.32	3918	3797	-0.3
18411	CLARKS SUMMIT	069	23004	24027	24174	0.5	70	8562	9063	9169	0.6	2.54	6290	6488	0.3
18414	DALTON	069	6093	6014	5939	-0.1	46	2331	2359	2349	0.1	2.52	1736	1712	-0.2
18415	DAMASCUS	127	1552	1694	1769	1.0	85	634	719	759	1.4	2.34	444	488	1.0
18417	EQUINUNK	127	858	850	850	-0.1	46	324	334	338	0.3	2.54	236	236	0.0
18419	FACTORYVILLE	131	4999	5023	4963	0.1	57	1761	1805	1796	0.3	2.60	1307	1307	0.0
18421	FOREST CITY	127	5173	5435	5518	0.5	70	2093	2244	2292	0.8	2.36	1395	1457	0.5
18424	GOULDSBORO	069	4285	4268	4243	0.0	52	1651	1676	1679	0.2	2.55	1216	1200	-0.1
18425	GREELEY	103	1395	1333	1460	-0.5	19	555	528	581	-0.5	2.49	397	366	-0.9
18426	GREENTOWN	103	3825	4593	5099	2.0	95	1583	1937	2159	2.2	2.34	1126	1337	1.9
18427	HAMLIN	127	1363	1378	1395	0.1	57	537	563	577	0.5	2.45	398	405	0.2
18428	HAWLEY	103	7966	10576	11850	3.1	98	3182	4326	4871	3.4	2.41	2280	3064	3.2
18430	HERRICK CENTER	115	237	243	244	0.3	64	102	109	110	0.7	2.23	71	74	0.4
18431	HONESDALE	127	13806	14133	14179	0.3	64	5563	5765	5845	0.4	2.34	3695	3704	0.0
18433	JERMYN	069	6551	6517	6454	-0.1	46	2608	2643	2638	0.1	2.43	1826	1800	-0.2
18434	JESSUP	069	4238	4172	4134	-0.2	38	1828	1835	1829	0.0	2.27	1199	1160	-0.4
18435	LACKAWAXEN	103	1422	1887	2096	3.1	98	605	806	894	3.1	2.34	421	542	2.8
18436	LAKE ARIEL	127	10461	11859	12376	1.4	91	3885	4510	4759	1.6	2.56	2953	3346	1.4
18437	LAKE COMO	127	351	376	387	0.7	77	151	167	174	1.1	2.22	103	111	0.8
18438	LAKEVILLE	127	2223	2717	2892	2.2	96	888	1095	1177	2.3	2.44	667	801	2.0
18439	LAKEWOOD	127	750	805	834	0.8	80	309	345	362	1.2	2.32	217	234	0.8
18441	LENOXVILLE	115	733	755	757	0.3	64	271	286	289	0.6	2.63	190	195	0.3
18443	MILANVILLE	127	822	805	801	-0.2	38	337	341	343	0.1	2.35	246	242	-0.2
18444	MOSCOW	069	10865	10754	10655	-0.1	46	4002	4039	4031	0.1	2.62	3085	3036	-0.2
18445	NEWFOUNDLAND	127	1676	1820	1933	0.9	83	650	710	763	1.0	2.42	455	480	0.6
18446	NICHOLSON	115	3187	3180	3136	0.0	52	1245	1276	1271	0.3	2.49	911	907	0.0
	PENNSYLVANIA					0.3					0.4	2.45			0.1
	UNITED STATES					1.0					1.1	2.59			0.9

ZIP CODE #	POST OFFICE NAME	RACE (%) White 2000	White 2009	Black 2000	Black 2009	Asian/Pacific 2000	Asian/Pacific 2009	% Hispanic Origin 2000	% Hispanic Origin 2009	2009 AGE DISTRIBUTION (%) 0-4	5-9	10-14	15-19	20-24	25-44	45-64	65-84	85+	18+	MEDIAN AGE 2009	% 2009 Males	% 2009 Females
18074	PERKIOMENVILLE	97.6	96.7	0.8	1.1	0.4	0.7	0.7	1.0	6.4	7.1	7.6	6.7	4.0	23.9	30.3	11.6	2.3	74.6	41.6	49.6	50.4
18076	RED HILL	98.0	97.2	0.3	0.4	0.1	0.2	1.5	2.2	6.0	6.4	6.3	6.5	5.2	25.0	25.2	16.2	3.2	77.5	41.0	48.1	51.9
18077	RIEGELSVILLE	98.7	98.4	0.2	0.2	0.4	0.6	0.8	1.2	5.0	6.2	6.9	6.1	5.0	24.2	33.2	11.9	1.5	78.2	42.9	51.6	48.4
18078	SCHNECKSVILLE	97.5	96.3	0.6	0.8	0.7	1.1	1.4	2.3	4.9	5.7	7.4	8.2	4.3	21.9	34.6	11.6	1.4	76.0	43.3	49.3	50.7
18080	SLATINGTON	97.7	96.7	0.7	0.9	0.4	0.7	1.4	2.3	5.4	5.8	6.3	6.9	5.0	25.6	32.2	11.2	1.6	78.1	41.7	50.2	49.8
18087	TREXLERTOWN	92.7	88.8	0.6	0.8	5.8	9.0	1.3	2.2	6.3	7.5	9.2	8.8	3.7	21.8	32.4	9.4	1.0	70.7	41.1	49.1	50.9
18088	WALNUTPORT	98.4	97.6	0.4	0.5	0.4	0.7	1.0	1.6	4.7	5.2	5.8	5.8	4.4	24.3	33.4	14.3	2.1	80.6	44.8	49.9	50.1
18091	WIND GAP	97.9	96.9	0.4	0.5	0.5	0.8	1.3	2.2	5.5	5.8	6.3	6.6	4.9	24.5	30.5	13.3	2.6	78.2	42.6	48.6	51.4
18092	ZIONSVILLE	98.3	97.4	0.1	0.1	0.5	0.9	0.7	1.2	4.5	5.5	7.1	6.9	4.4	24.9	34.1	11.0	1.7	78.7	43.2	51.4	48.6
18101	ALLENTOWN	53.6	46.2	17.4	17.9	1.4	1.5	43.8	54.2	7.3	6.8	5.9	7.0	10.9	35.3	18.7	6.9	1.2	76.4	31.2	56.6	43.4
18102	ALLENTOWN	62.5	54.2	10.5	11.3	1.9	2.3	35.6	45.9	8.3	7.7	7.3	7.5	8.3	27.2	21.9	9.7	2.1	72.3	32.5	48.6	51.4
18103	ALLENTOWN	83.6	77.9	4.4	5.4	3.3	4.7	12.0	16.8	5.9	5.9	6.1	6.5	5.9	24.8	27.7	14.1	3.0	78.1	41.2	48.3	51.7
18104	ALLENTOWN	93.7	90.2	1.6	2.2	2.5	4.3	2.6	4.2	4.7	4.9	5.5	8.0	7.4	20.7	28.1	15.4	5.4	81.1	44.1	45.9	54.1
18106	ALLENTOWN	93.7	90.4	0.7	0.9	4.0	6.2	1.6	2.7	5.6	6.1	6.8	7.2	5.4	23.1	31.7	12.0	2.1	76.5	42.2	48.0	52.0
18109	ALLENTOWN	76.3	69.7	7.0	8.2	2.5	3.4	20.5	27.0	7.1	6.3	6.2	6.0	6.6	27.1	25.1	12.8	2.7	76.8	38.1	48.3	51.7
18201	HAZLETON	95.0	93.4	0.8	0.9	0.6	1.0	4.6	6.2	5.2	5.0	5.1	5.8	6.1	24.6	26.6	17.5	4.2	81.3	43.8	47.5	52.5
18202	HAZLETON	98.1	97.4	0.4	0.4	0.4	0.7	1.5	2.1	5.1	4.8	5.2	7.1	5.3	22.1	28.3	18.1	4.1	81.7	45.3	48.6	51.4
18210	ALBRIGHTSVILLE	88.7	87.3	5.4	5.5	0.7	1.0	8.3	10.3	7.1	6.9	7.4	6.7	4.1	24.0	29.7	13.5	0.6	74.0	40.6	50.4	49.6
18211	ANDREAS	98.8	98.5	0.2	0.2	0.3	0.3	0.9	1.3	5.0	5.6	6.2	5.9	4.5	22.6	34.8	13.6	1.8	79.6	45.1	50.6	49.4
18214	BARNESVILLE	99.6	83.2	0.1	14.2	0.1	1.0	0.5	3.1	3.4	3.5	4.0	8.3	10.5	30.8	26.9	10.9	1.7	87.9	38.3	58.5	41.5
18216	BEAVER MEADOWS	99.3	99.2	0.2	0.2	0.1	0.2	0.9	1.2	4.7	4.8	5.2	6.3	5.2	22.6	29.4	18.5	3.4	81.0	45.7	48.3	51.7
18218	COALDALE	98.3	97.7	0.3	0.4	0.3	0.4	1.1	1.6	4.5	4.7	5.1	5.5	5.3	23.3	26.4	19.5	5.6	82.2	46.0	47.4	52.6
18219	CONYNGHAM	97.2	95.8	0.1	0.1	2.3	3.6	0.7	1.1	4.7	4.8	5.6	6.1	5.0	20.5	32.4	17.0	3.8	80.8	47.0	46.4	53.6
18220	DELANO	99.4	98.8	0.0	0.0	0.6	1.2	0.0	0.0	4.0	4.3	4.3	4.6	4.0	23.9	32.4	19.6	3.1	84.7	48.4	53.5	46.5
18222	DRUMS	92.7	91.4	5.7	6.3	0.5	0.8	1.8	2.3	4.6	5.1	5.7	10.6	5.5	22.2	30.8	12.6	2.9	78.2	42.6	50.2	49.8
18224	FREELAND	98.7	98.1	0.2	0.2	0.6	0.9	0.7	0.9	5.2	5.3	5.5	5.9	5.2	23.6	28.3	17.6	3.4	80.4	44.5	48.0	52.0
18229	JIM THORPE	97.9	97.5	0.8	0.8	0.4	0.5	1.2	1.5	5.0	5.3	5.6	5.7	4.7	26.0	31.2	14.4	2.0	80.5	43.3	49.5	50.5
18232	LANSFORD	98.2	97.8	0.4	0.4	0.4	0.6	1.4	1.7	6.0	5.6	5.5	6.0	6.7	24.0	25.5	16.3	4.5	79.4	42.2	46.1	53.9
18235	LEHIGHTON	98.4	98.0	0.3	0.3	0.5	0.7	0.7	0.8	5.2	5.3	5.6	5.7	5.1	24.6	30.6	15.2	2.7	80.3	44.1	48.9	51.1
18237	MCADOO	99.4	99.2	0.1	0.1	0.1	0.2	0.4	0.6	4.9	5.0	5.3	5.8	4.5	24.0	27.7	19.2	3.5	81.0	45.2	48.2	51.8
18240	NESQUEHONING	97.0	96.4	1.3	1.4	0.4	0.7	1.6	2.1	4.3	4.5	4.8	6.8	5.4	25.1	27.7	17.8	3.6	83.0	44.3	49.0	51.0
18246	ROCK GLEN	99.3	99.0	0.5	0.7	0.1	0.2	0.3	0.5	4.0	4.2	4.7	5.6	5.8	23.9	31.1	18.0	2.6	83.0	46.2	52.1	47.9
18248	SHEPPTON	99.3	99.0	0.0	0.0	0.1	0.1	0.9	1.3	3.8	4.2	4.9	5.7	4.4	23.6	34.6	16.2	2.7	83.8	47.0	50.5	49.5
18249	SUGARLOAF	98.2	97.3	0.2	0.2	1.2	1.9	0.6	0.8	4.3	5.0	5.9	9.7	4.8	20.6	33.4	14.2	2.1	80.3	44.8	49.7	50.3
18250	SUMMIT HILL	99.0	98.8	0.1	0.1	0.2	0.3	0.4	0.5	4.5	4.8	5.1	5.7	4.6	25.1	29.1	17.6	3.4	81.8	45.1	48.6	51.4
18252	TAMAQUA	98.2	97.6	0.7	0.8	0.3	0.5	1.2	1.6	4.9	4.8	5.0	6.6	6.0	23.6	28.3	17.1	3.9	81.7	44.5	48.1	51.9
18255	WEATHERLY	98.7	98.5	0.2	0.2	0.2	0.2	0.6	0.7	4.7	5.0	5.2	6.1	5.0	22.3	30.0	17.9	3.9	80.8	46.0	47.0	53.0
18301	EAST STROUDSBURG	85.4	81.5	7.4	8.8	1.5	2.3	7.7	10.5	5.7	5.8	6.3	9.8	8.8	24.8	26.4	10.6	1.8	78.1	36.1	48.4	51.6
18302	EAST STROUDSBURG	86.3	83.1	7.1	8.3	1.3	2.0	7.8	10.4	6.8	7.3	7.8	7.6	5.5	25.4	29.3	9.3	0.9	72.9	38.2	50.6	49.4
18321	BARTONSVILLE	90.3	87.6	2.9	3.4	1.9	2.9	5.3	7.0	5.8	6.7	7.3	6.9	4.7	23.5	33.4	10.6	1.2	75.6	42.2	48.7	51.3
18322	BRODHEADSVILLE	94.6	93.1	2.5	3.0	1.0	1.6	3.1	4.3	5.9	6.5	7.3	7.1	4.5	24.3	31.0	11.7	1.7	75.8	41.2	49.4	50.6
18324	BUSHKILL	79.8	76.6	12.3	13.5	1.2	1.8	11.6	14.6	6.0	7.2	8.1	7.2	4.3	25.3	28.8	12.3	0.9	74.2	39.9	49.0	51.0
18325	CANADENSIS	95.9	95.1	1.6	1.6	0.5	0.8	1.6	2.3	4.6	6.1	6.0	6.0	4.4	23.7	32.1	14.8	2.1	79.7	44.4	50.3	49.7
18326	CRESCO	94.2	92.5	2.9	3.5	0.9	1.4	2.3	3.2	4.9	5.5	6.1	6.6	4.7	23.5	32.8	14.3	1.6	79.7	44.1	49.1	50.9
18327	DELAWARE WATER GAP	92.1	90.2	3.9	4.7	1.2	1.9	4.8	6.5	5.5	4.4	4.4	5.2	10.6	29.0	28.1	10.8	1.9	82.8	37.6	49.6	50.4
18328	DINGMANS FERRY	95.1	94.0	2.2	2.6	0.4	0.6	4.9	6.8	7.2	7.4	7.8	8.1	6.1	23.5	29.2	9.8	0.9	72.5	38.1	49.6	50.4
18330	EFFORT	91.5	89.4	4.5	5.3	0.9	1.4	5.7	7.8	6.4	7.1	7.8	8.2	4.9	23.1	31.0	9.9	1.6	73.2	40.2	50.4	49.6
18331	GILBERT	97.2	97.4	2.8	2.6	0.0	0.0	2.8	5.3	5.3	5.3	5.3	5.3	5.3	21.1	39.5	13.2	0.0	78.9	45.8	47.4	52.6
18332	HENRYVILLE	92.0	89.9	3.7	4.4	1.2	1.8	3.9	5.3	5.1	5.6	6.3	6.6	4.4	24.2	33.0	13.3	1.5	78.7	43.6	49.6	50.4
18333	KRESGEVILLE	97.7	97.1	1.0	1.1	0.2	0.3	2.1	2.7	6.3	7.1	7.4	6.4	4.9	23.7	29.7	12.7	2.0	75.5	41.5	49.0	51.0
18334	LONG POND	87.6	84.8	6.7	7.8	0.8	1.3	8.3	11.1	6.3	6.6	7.1	7.9	5.8	24.0	30.3	11.3	0.8	74.9	40.0	50.4	49.6
18336	MATAMORAS	96.5	95.4	0.5	0.6	1.0	1.6	3.0	3.9	5.6	5.6	5.9	6.7	6.1	22.2	30.8	14.2	3.0	78.5	43.5	48.0	52.0
18337	MILFORD	94.8	93.6	2.0	2.3	0.6	1.0	4.4	5.9	6.3	6.9	7.6	7.8	4.7	23.2	31.0	11.1	1.4	74.2	40.7	49.9	50.1
18340	MILLRIFT	96.2	95.3	0.4	0.4	1.3	1.7	2.5	3.9	4.7	5.6	6.4	6.0	3.4	19.3	35.6	15.9	3.0	78.5	47.6	50.6	49.4
18343	MOUNT BETHEL	97.9	96.9	0.7	0.9	0.5	0.8	1.7	2.7	5.0	5.5	6.1	6.5	4.5	22.8	33.0	14.7	1.9	79.3	44.8	50.0	50.0
18344	MOUNT POCONO	83.6	80.5	9.6	10.9	0.9	1.3	9.1	11.7	6.6	6.2	6.1	6.7	7.2	25.8	27.5	12.0	1.8	76.5	38.2	48.4	51.6
18346	POCONO SUMMIT	90.7	88.2	4.8	5.7	0.7	1.0	6.5	8.8	5.5	6.9	7.0	5.9	4.8	25.3	29.7	13.5	1.5	77.1	41.4	49.4	50.6
18347	POCONO LAKE	94.0	92.9	3.2	3.5	0.6	1.0	3.8	4.7	5.3	5.5	5.8	6.2	5.1	21.8	31.8	16.9	1.6	79.2	45.2	48.4	51.6
18350	POCONO PINES	93.7	92.3	3.3	3.8	0.8	1.2	4.2	5.6	5.1	5.8	6.1	5.9	4.2	22.3	31.9	17.2	1.5	79.3	45.4	49.2	50.8
18352	REEDERS	92.1	90.8	3.1	3.5	1.1	1.7	4.5	5.7	5.7	6.2	7.2	7.5	4.5	22.4	33.6	11.4	1.5	75.6	42.9	49.3	50.7
18353	SAYLORSBURG	95.3	93.5	2.2	2.8	0.7	1.2	2.9	4.1	6.0	6.7	7.5	7.7	4.7	23.3	32.7	10.3	1.0	74.7	41.1	50.5	49.5
18354	SCIOTA	95.3	94.1	2.3	2.7	0.7	1.3	2.0	2.9	5.4	6.1	7.0	7.0	3.8	23.8	33.2	12.3	1.4	76.6	43.1	50.5	49.5
18355	SCOTRUN	93.6	91.8	2.5	3.1	1.0	1.4	4.2	5.8	4.7	6.2	6.7	6.3	4.9	24.5	32.6	12.8	1.3	78.3	42.8	50.3	49.7
18360	STROUDSBURG	91.4	89.2	4.0	4.6	1.5	2.2	4.6	6.2	5.4	5.8	6.5	6.8	6.0	23.5	30.2	13.3	2.4	77.7	42.2	49.0	51.0
18370	SWIFTWATER	93.5	91.7	2.4	2.9	1.2	1.7	4.0	5.6	4.9	5.9	6.5	6.6	4.8	24.5	32.3	13.1	1.5	78.5	43.0	50.1	49.9
18371	TAMIMENT	85.6	83.7	7.9	8.5	0.5	0.6	12.2	15.8	7.1	9.8	9.6	7.3	3.4	28.9	25.4	7.9	0.5	69.2	35.9	50.6	49.4
18372	TANNERSVILLE	91.4	89.1	3.7	4.4	1.1	1.8	5.3	7.1	5.2	5.8	7.1	6.6	4.9	25.9	32.7	10.7	1.0	77.5	41.5	49.5	50.5
18403	ARCHBALD	98.6	98.2	0.3	0.4	0.2	0.4	0.4	0.6	5.7	6.1	6.5	6.3	4.6	24.4	29.1	14.9	2.3	77.7	42.6	48.3	51.7
18405	BEACH LAKE	98.2	97.7	0.6	0.6	0.3	0.6	1.6	2.1	5.6	6.3	7.5	7.8	3.8	22.0	29.5	15.3	2.2	75.3	42.7	50.8	49.2
18407	CARBONDALE	98.7	98.2	0.3	0.3	0.2	0.4	1.0	1.4	5.9	5.7	5.7	5.8	5.7	24.0	26.3	16.6	4.2	79.1	42.8	46.8	53.2
18411	CLARKS SUMMIT	97.4	96.0	0.4	0.6	1.5	2.4	0.8	1.2	5.0	5.6	6.6	7.6	5.5	21.2	32.0	14.1	2.5	78.3	44.0	48.5	51.5
18414	DALTON	98.3	97.7	0.2	0.2	0.7	1.1	0.6	0.8	4.9	5.7	6.5	7.0	4.6	23.1	32.9	13.5	1.8	78.3	43.7	50.2	49.8
18415	DAMASCUS	98.1	97.8	0.7	0.8	0.2	0.3	1.3	1.8	5.0	5.4	7.3	6.5	3.6	20.1	34.2	15.6	2.2	77.6	46.2	50.2	49.8
18417	EQUINUNK	99.0	98.8	0.2	0.2	0.0	0.1	0.2	0.2	5.6	6.0	6.1	6.1	4.8	22.1	31.6	15.9	1.6	78.4	44.4	51.2	48.8
18419	FACTORYVILLE	97.4	97.2	1.1	1.2	0.6	0.7	0.8	0.8	5.2	6.1	7.3	10.3	7.0	23.2	29.2	10.0	1.6	76.7	38.4	48.9	51.1
18421	FOREST CITY	99.1	98.9	0.2	0.2	0.2	0.3	0.5	0.7	5.7	5.7	6.2	6.1	5.3	22.4	27.6	16.3	4.7	78.6	44.0	48.7	51.3
18424	GOULDSBORO	96.8	96.0	1.2	1.3	0.6	0.9	2.3	3.2	5.8	6.3	6.6	5.9	4.3	23.3	32.1	14.5	1.3	77.6	43.6	50.2	49.8
18425	GREELEY	94.2	93.1	3.0	3.3	0.6	1.0	2.8	3.6	5.3	6.2	6.5	6.2	4.4	20.3	33.3	15.8	2.0	77.8	45.6	51.3	48.7
18426	GREENTOWN	97.1	96.5	0.5	0.6	0.3	0.5	2.5	3.3	4.7	5.2	5.6	5.8	3.9	18.0	34.4	20.3	1.9	80.9	48.7	51.3	48.7
18427	HAMLIN	96.2	95.8	1.0	1.0	0.2	0.4	1.9	2.4	6.2	6.6	6.6	6.1	3.8	18.8	32.8	17.1	1.9	76.7	46.1	49.6	50.4
18428	HAWLEY	95.5	94.3	1.8	2.2	0.5	0.7	3.0	4.1	4.6	4.8	5.2	5.7	4.6	18.2	32.5	22.1	2.3	81.9	49.7	49.2	50.8
18430	HERRICK CENTER	98.3	97.9	0.4	0.4	0.4	0.8	0.8	0.8	5.3	5.8	5.8	4.9	3.3	22.2	35.4	16.0	1.2	79.4	47.0	52.7	47.3
18431	HONESDALE	97.9	97.3	0.6	0.6	0.6	1.0	1.3	1.8	5.5	5.7	6.3	6.7	4.9	23.4	29.6	15.0	2.8	78.1	43.1	48.9	51.1
18433	JERMYN	98.5	98.0	0.8	1.0	0.3	0.4	0.5	0.7	5.4	6.0	6.5	6.4	4.6	24.1	28.9	15.6	2.5	77.8	42.8	49.6	50.4
18434	JESSUP	98.8	98.4	0.3	0.4	0.3	0.5	0.3	0.4	5.1	5.3	5.7	5.7	4.4	24.9	28.5	16.7	3.8	80.2	44.3	46.7	53.3
18435	LACKAWAXEN	94.9	93.6	2.7	3.4	0.4	0.6	2.8	3.9	4.9	6.0	6.5	5.9	3.9	19.6	32.8	18.1	2.3	78.8	47.0	50.0	50.0
18436	LAKE ARIEL	97.8	97.4	1.0	1.1	0.2	0.3	1.1	1.6	5.5	6.1	6.5	6.2	4.3	24.4	31.1	13.9	1.9	77.8	42.8	50.5	49.5
18437	LAKE COMO	99.1	98.4	0.0	0.0	0.6	1.1	1.4	1.9	4.0	4.3	4.5	4.5	3.5	19.4	37.2	20.5	2.1	84.3	50.6	50.0	50.0
18438	LAKEVILLE	97.3	97.0	1.1	1.0	0.5	0.7	2.7	3.5	4.5	4.6	5.7	7.2	4.2	19.8	33.7	18.5	2.0	80.0	47.5	48.6	51.4
18439	LAKEWOOD	99.1	98.8	0.0	0.0	0.4	0.6	1.5	2.0	4.8	5.1	5.6	4.8	3.1	20.9	35.7	18.0	2.0	81.1	48.5	50.6	49.4
18441	LENOXVILLE	99.0	98.5	0.3	0.4	0.0	0.1	0.8	0.9	6.0	6.2	6.8	7.0	5.2	25.2	30.1	12.3	1.3	76.7	40.8	50.6	49.4
18443	MILANVILLE	98.8	98.4	0.5	0.6	0.4	0.6	0.7	0.9	5.6	5.7	7.8	6.7	4.5	21.1	30.2	16.0	2.4	75.7	43.9	50.4	49.6
18444	MOSCOW	98.7	98.3	0.5	0.5	0.3	0.4	0.6	0.9	5.2	5.5	6.3	7.0	4.6	24.1	31.1	13.5	2.6	78.5	43.2	49.1	50.9
18445	NEWFOUNDLAND	96.6	96.0	1.3	1.5	0.2	0.3	1.5	2.0	5.1	6.5	6.6	5.7	2.9	21.4	32.1	16.9	2.7	78.0	46.2	49.2	50.8
18446	NICHOLSON	98.7	98.6	0.3	0.4	0.2	0.2	0.4	0.5	6.0	6.1	7.6	6.6	5.2	24.1	31.0	11.7	1.8	76.1	40.8	50.0	50.0
	PENNSYLVANIA	85.4	83.2	10.0	10.7	1.8	2.7	3.2	4.2	5.8	6.0	6.3	7.1	6.5	24.8	27.8	13.1	2.6	77.8	40.4	48.5	51.5
	UNITED STATES	75.1	72.0	12.3	12.7	3.8	4.6	12.5	15.7	6.8	6.7	6.6	7.1	6.9	27.0	26.0	10.9	1.9	75.7	36.9	49.2	50.8

ZIP CODE #	POST OFFICE NAME	2009 Per Capita Income	2009 HH Income Base	2009 Household Income Distribution (%): Less than $25,000	$25,000 to $49,999	$50,000 to $99,999	$100,000 to $149,999	$150,000 or More	Median Household Income: 2009	2014	2009 National Centile	2009 State Centile	2009 Home Value Base	2009 Home Value Distribution (%): Less than $50,000	$50,000 to $89,999	$90,000 to $174,999	$175,000 to $399,999	$400,000 or More	2009 Median Home Value
18074	PERKIOMENVILLE	29455	2069	8.3	21.5	41.4	21.6	7.2	74621	76645	89	91	1845	0.7	0.7	7.4	68.3	22.9	281267
18076	RED HILL	28815	1215	19.6	21.0	38.4	17.6	3.4	62703	62692	81	82	873	0.0	2.1	37.9	58.6	1.4	191572
18077	RIEGELSVILLE	38306	1029	8.8	13.8	39.9	27.1	10.3	80042	84196	92	94	844	0.2	0.5	7.6	62.7	29.0	296131
18078	SCHNECKSVILLE	35523	2518	7.3	15.6	47.0	17.7	12.3	77938	79342	91	93	2169	4.6	1.6	13.4	63.3	17.1	263983
18080	SLATINGTON	24046	4888	17.0	24.4	48.2	8.4	2.0	59291	61483	77	78	3807	6.8	6.8	33.9	47.3	5.3	182117
18087	TREXLERTOWN	62024	224	4.5	13.4	37.5	14.3	30.4	93622	94937	96	97	210	7.6	1.0	10.5	41.9	39.0	346512
18088	WALNUTPORT	24204	3579	18.0	27.6	43.9	6.7	3.8	53913	57370	69	70	3158	9.7	6.4	31.7	47.7	4.5	180319
18091	WIND GAP	24728	2242	17.9	27.1	42.8	8.7	3.4	54216	57568	70	70	1545	2.8	3.8	25.0	62.1	6.2	208924
18092	ZIONSVILLE	36680	1145	6.2	14.8	46.0	17.6	15.3	78161	79727	91	93	1021	2.2	0.6	13.1	57.6	26.5	285441
18101	ALLENTOWN	12620	1198	48.3	32.2	16.4	1.8	1.2	25698	24894	4	2	252	5.6	45.2	38.5	10.7	0.0	89500
18102	ALLENTOWN	15744	17242	37.9	32.6	25.4	3.1	1.0	31844	32686	11	4	7155	3.9	30.5	57.1	8.0	0.4	102108
18103	ALLENTOWN	28177	18254	17.9	27.8	39.1	8.7	6.6	54200	57058	70	70	12065	0.6	4.5	46.7	39.9	8.3	172026
18104	ALLENTOWN	32877	16590	14.0	21.3	41.2	13.9	9.7	66938	70420	85	88	12319	0.9	0.7	28.7	58.9	10.8	221933
18106	ALLENTOWN	36547	2822	6.0	18.5	41.9	20.4	13.2	79151	80889	92	94	2352	9.9	4.8	20.3	50.6	14.4	256467
18109	ALLENTOWN	21800	6930	24.6	31.7	37.6	4.0	2.1	45195	47899	49	47	3977	4.6	12.5	59.9	22.3	0.8	132531
18201	HAZLETON	22537	10818	33.6	29.8	29.5	3.9	3.2	37565	40504	25	16	6523	8.4	29.0	42.9	18.5	1.1	111263
18202	HAZLETON	22554	5012	30.9	26.9	33.8	5.2	3.2	41316	46138	37	32	3615	10.9	25.6	36.6	25.7	1.2	122911
18210	ALBRIGHTSVILLE	19490	2335	21.8	32.7	36.4	7.9	1.2	44611	49331	47	44	2006	1.7	2.9	47.4	45.6	2.3	171903
18211	ANDREAS	23954	465	21.7	25.8	40.6	8.2	3.7	51791	53846	65	66	396	1.5	12.4	32.6	43.2	10.4	185294
18214	BARNESVILLE	19571	955	22.7	28.1	39.2	7.4	2.6	49150	51676	59	60	857	6.0	18.8	42.6	30.5	2.2	135840
18216	BEAVER MEADOWS	23238	1127	25.3	29.6	36.9	5.1	3.0	44757	49486	48	45	911	8.2	28.4	46.0	16.7	0.7	116118
18218	COALDALE	18670	1076	40.0	34.0	22.5	2.4	1.1	31365	32479	10	4	822	18.9	51.3	25.7	4.1	0.0	71343
18219	CONYNGHAM	33877	373	13.7	27.3	39.1	11.8	8.0	63153	64564	81	83	293	1.4	1.4	30.0	59.7	7.5	199755
18220	DELANO	20360	133	32.3	24.1	33.8	8.3	1.5	42379	49114	41	37	119	26.9	44.5	24.4	4.2	0.0	64583
18222	DRUMS	25779	3084	14.6	27.8	42.5	10.8	4.3	56814	57817	74	74	2752	3.7	2.9	41.4	46.4	5.6	178696
18224	FREELAND	21967	2504	27.2	31.1	35.1	4.8	1.8	43231	46577	43	40	1892	11.6	29.5	42.7	13.8	2.5	102075
18229	JIM THORPE	23140	3070	24.7	28.2	36.2	8.6	2.3	47349	50779	55	56	2543	2.9	9.1	51.9	32.9	3.3	155855
18232	LANSFORD	19107	1903	40.0	24.8	29.8	4.9	0.5	35102	36315	18	8	1299	30.9	47.6	19.5	2.1	0.0	61061
18235	LEHIGHTON	21948	8065	24.4	29.8	38.2	6.0	1.6	44675	50070	47	45	6025	7.4	7.8	39.9	41.2	3.8	165214
18237	MCADOO	21207	1756	30.1	33.3	31.3	3.9	1.4	37449	39298	25	16	1268	7.9	30.7	50.1	11.0	0.3	102734
18240	NESQUEHONING	23726	1761	23.1	25.3	45.3	4.7	1.7	50985	52869	64	64	1394	5.8	27.5	44.9	20.7	1.0	117822
18246	ROCK GLEN	24633	447	19.5	30.6	38.5	6.7	4.7	49919	52220	61	62	366	7.9	18.0	45.4	26.0	2.7	128333
18248	SHEPPTON	22836	455	28.8	33.2	32.7	3.1	2.2	38483	41721	28	19	377	11.9	25.2	38.2	21.2	3.4	110880
18249	SUGARLOAF	32177	1911	14.3	24.3	36.6	15.8	9.0	63562	64489	82	84	1672	3.7	4.4	29.5	51.3	11.1	199880
18250	SUMMIT HILL	28060	1324	21.8	23.6	44.2	5.4	5.0	53294	54627	69	69	1081	6.2	31.2	44.9	16.9	0.8	109054
18252	TAMAQUA	22050	4869	27.3	30.1	33.9	6.5	2.2	41851	46011	39	34	3643	8.9	29.1	39.7	20.5	1.8	109658
18255	WEATHERLY	21082	1692	24.2	27.1	41.6	4.5	2.7	48573	51612	58	59	1410	5.7	17.9	47.7	26.5	2.3	136870
18301	EAST STROUDSBURG	24629	9924	18.0	20.5	44.1	11.9	5.5	62119	62626	80	82	6889	4.6	1.9	30.5	55.9	7.1	206446
18302	EAST STROUDSBURG	24782	5765	12.8	22.1	48.4	11.5	5.2	64395	64861	83	85	4784	5.1	5.2	36.1	48.0	5.6	184416
18321	BARTONSVILLE	25079	566	12.7	29.2	41.9	10.6	5.7	58653	59599	76	77	479	13.8	1.3	23.6	54.1	7.3	215260
18322	BRODHEADSVILLE	24376	753	19.4	21.5	44.1	9.7	5.3	60454	60654	78	79	604	0.0	2.6	26.2	63.7	7.5	223913
18324	BUSHKILL	26133	3073	11.2	24.7	46.7	11.5	5.9	65137	67577	83	86	2580	0.4	4.0	39.6	51.4	4.6	187831
18325	CANADENSIS	23231	1001	24.0	25.8	38.5	8.9	2.9	50164	52022	62	62	773	9.1	3.1	32.5	45.3	10.1	191468
18326	CRESCO	27004	2135	16.6	23.9	44.8	10.1	4.5	59465	59463	77	78	1616	0.7	3.4	41.0	45.4	9.5	188621
18327	DELAWARE WATER GAP	28907	582	20.3	28.0	38.3	8.4	5.0	51892	54559	66	66	278	1.4	0.0	34.9	55.0	8.6	210317
18328	DINGMANS FERRY	22647	2831	15.4	23.9	51.5	6.5	2.6	59170	60929	76	77	2461	0.2	1.5	49.2	44.8	4.3	173611
18330	EFFORT	22474	3561	12.6	26.0	47.3	10.2	3.9	61186	61186	79	80	3140	1.1	6.5	32.8	57.8	1.8	195584
18331	GILBERT	15329	12	25.0	33.3	33.3	8.3	0.0	45000	47338	48	46	10	0.0	0.0	40.0	60.0	0.0	187500
18332	HENRYVILLE	23838	1286	19.6	22.6	44.6	9.5	3.7	57619	58194	75	75	989	1.9	2.6	33.6	52.2	9.7	208949
18333	KRESGEVILLE	24119	475	14.3	25.9	49.9	6.3	3.6	56559	56825	73	73	401	0.2	1.5	40.9	45.1	12.2	191761
18334	LONG POND	23980	879	15.2	26.1	43.2	11.0	4.4	57636	58744	75	75	758	6.1	6.5	39.7	46.2	1.6	170479
18336	MATAMORAS	24142	1763	20.7	25.9	43.4	7.3	2.7	53135	56716	68	69	1300	5.8	3.5	31.0	53.7	5.9	195292
18337	MILFORD	27477	5360	12.0	21.5	45.6	14.5	6.5	65305	67257	84	86	4540	1.5	0.8	17.6	68.1	12.0	239085
18340	MILLRIFT	23298	87	17.2	28.7	42.5	9.2	2.3	54572	56592	71	71	69	11.6	5.8	18.8	52.2	11.6	212500
18343	MOUNT BETHEL	24948	1749	17.3	25.2	45.3	8.3	3.9	55470	58417	72	72	1340	1.9	7.5	29.5	50.3	10.7	218750
18344	MOUNT POCONO	23841	1488	17.8	25.7	44.0	9.0	3.6	57810	58881	75	76	969	2.0	3.9	38.0	50.3	5.9	187500
18346	POCONO SUMMIT	21067	866	24.8	20.3	40.3	11.4	3.1	54183	56122	70	70	737	0.9	0.0	50.5	46.1	2.4	172321
18347	POCONO LAKE	26656	1311	22.5	22.0	43.9	7.6	4.0	58087	59407	75	76	1073	0.5	4.8	48.3	42.3	4.2	168750
18350	POCONO PINES	24769	529	27.2	20.2	44.6	6.2	1.7	53008	55450	68	68	437	0.2	4.1	47.1	43.5	5.0	172098
18352	REEDERS	29277	167	12.0	24.0	49.1	10.2	4.8	63855	62994	82	84	143	4.2	2.8	24.5	62.2	6.3	221774
18353	SAYLORSBURG	23321	4579	15.4	24.8	45.4	10.0	4.4	60509	60510	78	79	3956	3.9	3.9	25.7	61.6	4.9	211136
18354	SCIOTA	23650	209	15.3	32.5	39.7	7.7	4.8	51932	53340	66	67	159	10.7	6.3	32.7	44.0	6.3	176042
18355	SCOTRUN	22798	793	21.3	28.4	35.1	10.2	5.0	50280	53347	62	62	646	7.1	5.4	34.1	47.7	5.7	187791
18360	STROUDSBURG	25818	11844	18.0	26.1	38.1	11.6	6.1	57910	59163	75	76	8705	6.4	3.0	27.4	54.5	8.7	209139
18370	SWIFTWATER	22100	480	21.3	26.7	37.7	10.4	4.0	52181	54882	66	67	387	5.7	4.1	33.6	51.2	5.4	198611
18371	TAMIMENT	24935	742	10.1	23.6	50.8	11.5	4.0	68373	71762	86	89	622	0.2	2.4	44.2	48.4	4.8	181410
18372	TANNERSVILLE	23968	1130	17.3	24.0	43.5	11.6	3.7	57437	57861	75	75	924	3.4	1.4	27.1	60.0	8.2	223784
18403	ARCHBALD	26036	2605	21.0	25.5	38.2	9.6	5.7	55445	58081	72	72	2091	1.4	8.8	44.5	42.1	3.3	161607
18405	BEACH LAKE	20694	564	25.0	29.3	38.3	4.1	3.4	45789	46528	51	50	491	9.0	5.3	38.1	37.1	10.6	169133
18407	CARBONDALE	21323	6022	30.1	30.5	31.9	5.1	2.5	40134	43912	33	26	4093	6.7	17.0	52.6	21.1	2.5	124238
18411	CLARKS SUMMIT	32325	9063	13.6	22.2	39.0	14.7	10.5	66393	66960	84	87	7348	1.7	2.1	20.6	57.5	18.0	235624
18414	DALTON	28019	2359	17.0	28.7	38.7	8.8	6.9	53731	54922	69	69	2002	5.6	5.1	29.2	46.9	13.2	202464
18415	DAMASCUS	23365	719	25.9	31.4	35.3	4.6	2.8	42012	43641	39	35	621	7.4	10.1	34.0	43.5	5.0	170975
18417	EQUINUNK	18622	334	26.6	34.1	35.0	3.3	0.9	42467	42843	41	37	280	15.0	11.8	38.2	24.6	10.4	136735
18419	FACTORYVILLE	21978	1805	21.2	29.4	38.4	6.4	4.5	49295	50983	60	60	1507	9.0	5.2	35.4	43.5	7.0	176186
18421	FOREST CITY	21285	2244	29.5	30.1	32.9	4.8	2.7	40385	42279	34	27	1768	7.2	19.7	41.1	27.9	4.1	133700
18424	GOULDSBORO	22331	1676	19.9	31.6	39.3	6.0	3.2	48668	50625	58	59	1438	9.7	8.3	36.7	39.3	6.0	163194
18425	GREELEY	20544	528	25.0	32.2	36.7	4.7	1.3	44216	47132	46	43	438	2.1	4.3	31.5	53.7	8.4	208442
18426	GREENTOWN	23532	1937	24.5	29.9	37.8	4.6	3.1	45910	49973	51	50	1621	5.6	6.7	32.6	45.3	9.8	191240
18427	HAMLIN	21058	563	27.5	32.7	32.3	5.5	2.0	39629	41465	32	24	469	5.3	4.3	43.9	39.2	7.2	168238
18428	HAWLEY	23189	4326	26.6	27.2	36.3	6.4	3.5	46357	48701	52	52	3608	1.6	4.1	34.0	48.6	11.7	204145
18430	HERRICK CENTER	19850	109	35.8	24.8	33.9	3.7	1.8	36936	37697	23	14	95	11.6	9.5	34.7	37.9	6.3	159722
18431	HONESDALE	21180	5765	28.5	30.8	33.6	4.2	2.8	40709	42530	35	29	4177	10.0	7.4	41.6	34.9	6.2	153713
18433	JERMYN	23204	2643	24.4	29.9	36.3	5.7	3.7	46637	50000	53	53	2091	4.5	8.7	50.3	32.9	3.6	148883
18434	JESSUP	22918	1835	31.0	25.6	34.8	5.4	3.3	41705	47627	38	34	1387	2.7	9.3	62.3	25.2	0.4	140872
18435	LACKAWAXEN	23153	806	24.8	27.7	39.5	6.7	1.4	47780	51262	56	57	681	1.8	2.2	36.3	46.0	13.8	206250
18436	LAKE ARIEL	21219	4510	22.3	31.4	38.1	5.4	2.8	46828	47410	54	54	3876	7.7	6.7	39.0	40.9	5.8	167563
18437	LAKE COMO	24576	167	29.3	28.7	34.7	3.6	3.6	41162	42086	37	32	139	6.5	13.7	38.8	32.4	8.6	150962
18438	LAKEVILLE	21822	1095	24.6	30.1	35.4	7.7	2.2	45832	45630	51	50	961	1.4	4.5	39.5	45.4	9.3	188735
18439	LAKEWOOD	23432	345	26.7	30.1	35.4	4.3	3.5	42766	43702	42	38	291	7.2	12.7	39.5	32.0	8.6	147917
18441	LENOXVILLE	20488	286	26.6	31.8	33.2	5.6	2.8	42357	44802	40	36	224	14.7	6.3	38.4	34.8	5.8	151136
18443	MILANVILLE	22778	341	25.5	31.1	37.2	2.9	3.2	42554	43393	41	37	300	9.0	2.7	41.3	40.0	7.0	166964
18444	MOSCOW	24403	4039	16.3	27.7	43.6	8.8	3.6	55868	57482	72	73	3538	7.3	4.5	26.9	51.4	10.0	203713
18445	NEWFOUNDLAND	20433	710	27.5	32.0	32.0	6.2	2.4	41243	43010	37	32	595	5.0	5.4	41.8	41.7	6.1	170377
18446	NICHOLSON	21003	1276	25.1	32.4	34.6	5.3	2.7	43234	45576	43	40	1071	10.6	9.2	41.5	33.7	5.0	150706
	PENNSYLVANIA	26913		21.5	25.3	36.9	10.2	6.1	53225	55819				7.5	12.2	35.6	36.1	8.5	161438
	UNITED STATES	27277		20.9	24.4	35.3	11.7	7.6	54719	56938				9.3	13.1	31.6	32.6	13.5	162279

ZIP CODE		FINANCIAL SERVICES				THE HOME						ENTERTAINMENT						PERSONAL			
						Home Improvements		Furnishings													
#	POST OFFICE NAME	Auto Loan	Home Loan	Invest-ments	Retire-ment Plans	Home Repair	Lawn & Garden	Comput-ers & Hard-ware-Personal	Major Appli-ances	TV, Radio, Sound Equip-ment	Furni-ture	Dine out/ Carry out	Sports Equip-ment	Fees & Tickets	Toys & Games	Travel	Cable TV	Apparel & Services	Auto Repairs	Health Insur-ance	Pets & Supplies
18074	PERKIOMENVILLE	112	133	122	134	132	127	116	121	113	117	114	93	127	116	126	113	81	116	118	140
18076	RED HILL	88	103	99	102	103	103	95	97	97	95	97	72	105	95	103	100	69	97	106	112
18077	RIEGELSVILLE	124	151	150	152	152	141	134	137	130	138	131	104	149	129	147	128	94	133	132	158
18078	SCHNECKSVILLE	129	150	144	152	150	142	130	136	126	137	127	103	143	128	140	125	90	130	129	157
18080	SLATINGTON	88	92	82	94	89	96	87	90	87	85	87	69	89	89	88	90	61	87	93	106
18087	TREXLERTOWN	174	230	238	242	238	207	188	196	176	205	178	155	227	180	214	167	134	182	170	221
18088	WALNUTPORT	94	88	90	90	88	101	85	95	88	80	87	72	81	89	86	92	59	89	98	111
18091	WIND GAP	89	89	88	91	88	95	87	91	88	84	88	70	87	89	88	91	61	89	94	107
18092	ZIONSVILLE	134	160	159	165	162	154	138	146	134	146	135	110	154	135	153	133	96	139	140	169
18101	ALLENTOWN	45	39	34	40	37	39	50	42	52	45	52	34	47	51	43	53	37	48	46	52
18102	ALLENTOWN	56	48	44	49	46	51	59	52	62	54	61	41	55	61	52	64	43	58	58	64
18103	ALLENTOWN	93	96	91	97	95	97	96	95	97	95	97	72	98	96	96	98	68	96	100	111
18104	ALLENTOWN	109	119	117	120	120	121	113	115	114	114	114	86	120	113	118	116	80	114	121	133
18106	ALLENTOWN	128	149	148	151	151	143	134	137	131	139	132	103	148	131	144	130	94	134	135	159
18109	ALLENTOWN	72	68	61	70	65	72	75	70	76	71	76	55	73	76	71	78	53	74	78	85
18201	HAZLETON	72	62	68	63	63	75	69	72	74	64	72	53	64	72	66	79	50	73	81	85
18202	HAZLETON	80	65	74	65	66	82	70	78	75	64	73	58	62	75	67	81	50	75	85	92
18210	ALBRIGHTSVILLE	89	73	107	72	79	92	72	89	76	69	75	65	64	73	77	80	50	83	88	104
18211	ANDREAS	93	85	84	89	87	100	84	94	86	76	85	71	78	88	84	91	58	87	97	110
18214	BARNESVILLE	87	77	80	80	79	93	77	88	80	70	79	66	70	81	77	85	53	81	91	102
18216	BEAVER MEADOWS	80	74	82	72	75	91	72	83	78	67	76	60	68	76	74	84	52	78	92	96
18218	COALDALE	65	48	60	47	49	66	54	62	59	48	57	47	44	58	50	64	38	59	68	73
18219	CONYNGHAM	101	119	123	119	124	125	103	114	106	109	106	79	117	103	116	110	74	109	123	129
18220	DELANO	85	61	85	59	63	88	66	82	74	59	72	61	53	73	64	82	48	77	90	96
18222	DRUMS	95	101	93	103	99	107	92	100	94	89	93	75	95	95	97	97	65	95	103	116
18224	FREELAND	78	65	79	64	67	85	66	79	73	61	71	58	60	72	67	79	48	74	86	92
18229	JIM THORPE	83	78	87	79	79	91	76	85	79	72	78	63	74	78	79	83	53	81	90	100
18232	LANSFORD	68	51	63	50	52	68	58	65	63	52	61	49	48	62	54	68	41	63	72	77
18235	LEHIGHTON	79	73	74	73	73	84	73	79	76	69	75	59	69	76	72	80	51	76	84	93
18237	MCADOO	71	61	73	60	63	79	61	72	67	57	66	53	56	66	62	73	44	68	80	84
18240	NESQUEHONING	80	74	83	72	75	90	71	83	77	68	76	60	69	76	74	83	52	78	91	96
18246	ROCK GLEN	78	89	84	87	89	97	79	87	84	78	84	61	87	82	86	90	58	84	99	99
18248	SHEPPTON	86	61	88	59	64	87	63	80	70	59	69	60	50	69	62	77	45	73	83	95
18249	SUGARLOAF	109	125	123	128	127	127	110	119	110	113	110	87	120	109	120	111	77	113	120	137
18250	SUMMIT HILL	82	93	88	91	93	101	82	91	88	81	88	63	91	86	90	94	60	88	103	104
18252	TAMAQUA	75	67	73	67	68	81	70	76	75	65	74	56	66	74	69	81	51	75	85	90
18255	WEATHERLY	76	79	76	79	79	89	73	81	77	69	76	59	75	77	77	82	52	77	89	93
18301	EAST STROUDSBURG	95	105	99	106	103	101	99	99	97	99	98	77	104	98	102	97	69	98	98	116
18302	EAST STROUDSBURG	105	112	100	111	108	106	102	104	100	105	101	80	105	103	104	99	71	101	100	122
18321	BARTONSVILLE	101	114	98	118	111	112	102	106	100	102	101	83	109	103	108	101	71	102	105	125
18322	BRODHEADSVILLE	95	108	93	110	104	106	96	100	94	96	95	78	103	97	101	95	66	96	99	117
18324	BUSHKILL	98	117	103	118	113	115	101	105	101	103	102	80	113	103	110	103	72	103	108	123
18325	CANADENSIS	96	77	124	76	85	102	77	98	81	73	80	71	67	77	84	86	53	90	97	113
18326	CRESCO	100	102	113	103	103	111	94	105	95	92	95	79	96	94	101	98	65	100	105	122
18327	DELAWARE WATER GAP	87	80	79	84	79	79	94	83	92	91	94	67	90	91	89	92	66	91	88	101
18328	DINGMANS FERRY	95	97	85	95	93	93	89	92	88	92	89	70	89	92	88	88	61	89	89	108
18330	EFFORT	94	106	92	109	103	105	95	99	94	95	94	77	101	96	100	94	66	95	98	116
18331	GILBERT	75	68	68	71	70	81	68	76	70	61	68	58	62	71	67	74	47	70	79	89
18332	HENRYVILLE	98	91	104	92	93	105	87	100	89	82	88	75	83	89	91	93	60	94	100	117
18333	KRESGEVILLE	94	103	90	106	101	103	93	98	92	92	92	76	98	94	98	93	64	93	97	115
18334	LONG POND	99	101	90	99	98	102	92	97	94	95	95	71	94	97	93	97	65	94	99	114
18336	MATAMORAS	87	85	104	84	88	92	84	91	84	80	84	69	83	82	89	86	58	89	90	106
18337	MILFORD	107	119	120	119	118	115	106	113	102	108	103	87	112	104	113	102	73	107	105	130
18340	MILLRIFT	103	82	133	81	91	109	82	105	86	77	85	77	71	82	89	92	57	97	103	121
18343	MOUNT BETHEL	89	93	87	95	93	101	86	94	88	83	88	70	88	89	90	92	61	89	98	109
18344	MOUNT POCONO	85	94	96	92	94	92	91	91	89	88	90	71	95	89	95	90	64	91	91	106
18346	POCONO SUMMIT	91	87	111	86	90	101	81	95	84	78	83	70	80	81	88	87	57	90	96	110
18347	POCONO LAKE	99	91	112	91	95	107	89	102	92	86	92	75	85	90	94	97	62	97	105	118
18350	POCONO PINES	95	79	121	78	85	101	78	97	81	73	80	71	69	77	84	86	54	90	96	112
18352	REEDERS	98	110	95	113	107	108	98	102	97	99	97	80	105	99	104	97	68	98	101	120
18353	SAYLORSBURG	96	105	92	108	102	106	95	100	94	94	94	78	99	96	100	95	66	96	99	117
18354	SCIOTA	94	92	87	95	92	102	87	96	89	82	88	73	85	91	89	92	60	90	98	112
18355	SCOTRUN	94	84	101	85	87	102	82	96	85	76	84	72	75	84	85	90	57	89	98	112
18360	STROUDSBURG	94	101	94	103	100	103	97	98	96	95	96	75	100	96	99	98	67	97	101	115
18370	SWIFTWATER	94	84	92	86	87	101	83	96	86	75	84	72	76	86	84	91	57	88	98	111
18371	TAMIMENT	109	120	98	117	113	104	106	107	101	113	103	85	110	108	107	97	72	102	97	123
18372	TANNERSVILLE	96	98	103	100	98	105	90	100	90	89	91	76	91	91	96	92	62	95	99	117
18403	ARCHBALD	86	101	93	100	99	105	88	94	92	88	92	68	98	91	96	96	64	92	104	109
18405	BEACH LAKE	87	71	110	70	77	93	71	89	74	66	73	65	62	71	76	79	49	82	88	103
18407	CARBONDALE	73	68	68	68	67	79	69	74	73	65	72	55	66	72	68	77	49	72	82	86
18411	CLARKS SUMMIT	113	130	130	132	133	131	116	123	115	119	116	91	127	114	127	117	81	118	126	142
18414	DALTON	101	107	105	109	108	115	98	107	99	95	99	80	101	100	103	102	69	101	110	124
18415	DAMASCUS	92	73	117	72	80	97	73	93	77	69	76	68	63	73	79	82	50	86	92	108
18417	EQUINUNK	84	61	87	59	63	86	62	79	69	58	68	59	50	68	62	76	45	73	82	94
18419	FACTORYVILLE	89	86	84	87	85	93	82	88	83	80	83	67	80	85	83	86	57	85	90	104
18421	FOREST CITY	78	67	82	67	70	83	69	79	73	64	72	58	63	72	70	78	49	75	84	92
18424	GOULDSBORO	89	81	96	80	83	94	77	90	80	75	80	66	73	80	80	84	54	84	90	105
18425	GREELEY	86	69	111	68	75	91	69	87	72	64	71	64	60	68	74	77	47	81	86	101
18426	GREENTOWN	92	74	120	73	81	98	74	94	78	69	77	69	64	74	80	83	51	87	93	109
18427	HAMLIN	86	69	111	68	76	91	69	88	72	65	71	64	60	68	75	77	47	81	86	101
18428	HAWLEY	87	75	111	75	84	95	75	90	79	74	78	63	70	74	81	84	53	86	94	104
18430	HERRICK CENTER	74	59	95	58	65	78	59	75	62	55	61	55	51	59	64	66	41	69	74	87
18431	HONESDALE	80	66	87	66	69	84	69	80	73	64	71	59	61	71	70	78	48	76	84	94
18433	JERMYN	84	80	84	80	81	94	77	87	81	72	80	64	75	81	79	87	55	82	94	101
18434	JESSUP	69	78	73	78	78	84	70	76	73	69	73	54	76	72	75	77	51	73	84	87
18435	LACKAWAXEN	90	72	117	71	79	96	72	92	76	68	75	67	63	72	78	81	50	85	91	107
18436	LAKE ARIEL	86	78	88	79	80	91	76	87	78	72	77	65	70	78	77	82	52	81	87	101
18437	LAKE COMO	91	73	118	72	80	97	73	93	77	69	76	68	64	73	79	82	50	86	92	108
18438	LAKEVILLE	89	72	116	70	79	95	72	91	75	67	74	67	62	71	78	80	49	84	90	106
18439	LAKEWOOD	91	73	117	72	80	96	73	92	76	68	75	68	63	72	79	81	50	85	91	107
18441	LENOXVILLE	90	73	87	73	75	94	73	87	78	67	77	66	63	79	73	84	51	80	91	103
18443	MILANVILLE	89	72	116	70	79	95	72	91	75	67	74	66	62	71	78	80	49	84	90	106
18444	MOSCOW	94	97	90	97	96	102	89	96	91	88	90	71	90	92	92	94	62	91	99	112
18445	NEWFOUNDLAND	84	68	105	67	74	89	68	85	71	63	70	62	59	68	73	75	47	79	84	99
18446	NICHOLSON	88	69	93	68	71	91	70	85	75	66	74	64	61	74	71	81	50	79	88	100
	PENNSYLVANIA	94	95	95	95	95	100	94	96	96	91	95	73	94	96	94	99	67	95	101	113
	UNITED STATES	100	100	100	100	100	100	100	100	100	100	100	100	100	100	100	100	100	100	100	100

ZIP CODE #	POST OFFICE NAME	COUNTY FIPS CODE	POPULATION 2000	POPULATION 2009	POPULATION 2014	2000-2009 ANNUAL RATE % Rate	2000-2009 ANNUAL RATE State Centile	HOUSEHOLDS 2000	HOUSEHOLDS 2009	HOUSEHOLDS 2014	HOUSEHOLDS % Annual Rate 2000-2009	HOUSEHOLDS 2009 Average HH Size	FAMILIES 2000	FAMILIES 2009	FAMILIES % Annual Rate 2000-2009
18447	OLYPHANT	069	8895	8688	8576	-0.3	29	3816	3798	3774	-0.1	2.28	2466	2367	-0.4
18451	PAUPACK	103	453	626	733	3.6	99	189	266	313	3.8	2.35	130	177	3.4
18452	PECKVILLE	069	5494	5341	5261	-0.3	29	2173	2139	2118	-0.2	2.30	1437	1367	-0.5
18453	PLEASANT MOUNT	127	1227	1316	1367	0.8	80	488	545	573	1.2	2.40	340	367	0.8
18455	PRESTON PARK	127	293	315	329	0.8	80	120	135	142	1.3	2.33	88	96	0.9
18456	PROMPTON	127	526	595	611	1.3	90	220	242	252	1.0	2.10	155	165	0.7
18458	SHOHOLA	103	2413	4204	4839	6.2	100	965	1628	1880	5.8	2.57	683	1135	5.6
18460	SOUTH STERLING	127	212	226	231	0.7	77	93	99	102	0.7	2.20	65	67	0.3
18461	STARLIGHT	127	315	337	346	0.7	77	143	158	164	1.1	2.09	97	104	0.8
18462	STARRUCCA	127	372	401	418	0.8	80	157	176	186	1.2	2.28	116	127	1.0
18463	STERLING	127	821	909	954	1.1	87	313	360	382	1.5	2.53	248	278	1.2
18464	TAFTON	103	1498	2289	2660	4.7	99	624	940	1101	4.5	2.37	445	650	4.2
18465	THOMPSON	115	1518	1543	1542	0.2	61	583	614	620	0.6	2.49	421	431	0.3
18466	TOBYHANNA	089	15146	20474	23058	3.3	98	5075	6702	7524	3.1	3.05	4031	5186	2.8
18469	TYLER HILL	127	395	425	438	0.8	80	146	163	170	1.2	2.58	104	113	0.9
18470	UNION DALE	115	1561	1614	1621	0.4	68	609	651	660	0.7	2.47	430	446	0.4
18472	WAYMART	127	5059	6411	6657	2.6	97	1469	1719	1836	1.7	2.51	1077	1224	1.4
18503	SCRANTON	069	814	844	842	0.4	68	483	487	487	0.1	1.73	79	73	-0.9
18504	SCRANTON	069	22060	21636	21375	-0.2	38	9403	9375	9317	0.0	2.30	5779	5545	-0.4
18505	SCRANTON	069	20226	19475	19127	-0.4	23	8800	8611	8507	-0.2	2.19	5182	4864	-0.7
18507	MOOSIC	069	5362	5538	5542	0.3	64	1997	2093	2106	0.5	2.43	1410	1433	0.2
18508	SCRANTON	069	11530	11142	10967	-0.4	23	4864	4795	4750	-0.2	2.31	3055	2891	-0.6
18509	SCRANTON	069	14220	13609	13314	-0.5	19	5596	5363	5264	-0.5	2.20	3097	2840	-0.9
18510	SCRANTON	069	14086	13917	13724	-0.1	46	4964	4863	4804	-0.2	2.38	2578	2402	-0.8
18512	SCRANTON	069	12507	12188	12022	-0.3	29	5505	5479	5442	-0.1	2.21	3507	3361	-0.5
18517	TAYLOR	069	5382	5129	5021	-0.5	19	2170	2104	2073	-0.3	2.35	1475	1384	-0.7
18518	OLD FORGE	069	8788	8519	8381	-0.3	29	3744	3694	3662	-0.1	2.28	2455	2336	-0.5
18519	DICKSON CITY	069	5035	4954	4911	-0.2	38	2201	2191	2180	0.0	2.26	1381	1322	-0.5
18603	BERWICK	037	19187	18432	18139	-0.4	23	7941	7796	7724	-0.2	2.32	5232	4964	-0.6
18610	BLAKESLEE	089	2739	3268	3552	1.9	94	907	1032	1117	1.4	3.16	724	807	1.2
18612	DALLAS	079	14142	14067	13955	-0.1	46	5283	5345	5339	0.1	2.43	3758	3684	-0.2
18614	DUSHORE	113	1863	1790	1741	-0.4	23	821	815	801	-0.1	2.18	485	464	-0.5
18615	FALLS	131	1268	1236	1210	-0.3	29	467	473	467	0.1	2.45	361	357	-0.1
18616	FORKSVILLE	113	1163	1113	1084	-0.5	19	453	451	444	0.0	2.31	328	318	-0.3
18617	GLEN LYON	079	2728	2661	2615	-0.3	29	835	801	786	-0.4	2.22	499	458	-0.9
18618	HARVEYS LAKE	079	2721	2797	2796	0.3	64	1095	1157	1170	0.6	2.41	738	753	0.2
18619	HILLSGROVE	113	265	253	246	-0.5	19	113	113	111	0.0	2.17	76	73	-0.4
18621	HUNLOCK CREEK	079	4117	3842	3744	-0.7	8	1516	1451	1425	-0.5	2.65	1176	1100	-0.7
18622	HUNTINGTON MILLS	079	146	144	143	-0.1	46	55	56	56	0.2	2.38	43	43	0.0
18623	LACEYVILLE	015	3651	3635	3586	0.0	52	1391	1431	1427	0.3	2.52	1021	1024	0.0
18624	LAKE HARMONY	025	987	1058	1116	0.8	80	418	459	489	1.0	2.29	290	306	0.6
18628	LOPEZ	113	638	656	647	0.3	64	175	179	177	0.2	2.56	111	110	-0.1
18629	MEHOOPANY	131	1461	1432	1404	-0.2	38	571	580	576	0.2	2.47	403	397	-0.2
18630	MESHOPPEN	115	3047	3333	3323	1.0	85	1142	1293	1303	1.4	2.57	843	936	1.1
18631	MIFFLINVILLE	037	1201	1189	1177	-0.1	46	502	513	513	0.2	2.32	375	373	-0.1
18632	MILDRED	113	564	549	536	-0.3	29	243	245	242	0.1	2.23	170	166	-0.3
18634	NANTICOKE	079	13923	13520	13341	-0.3	29	6089	6052	6018	-0.1	2.17	3724	3551	-0.5
18635	NESCOPECK	079	3890	3975	3976	0.2	61	1558	1644	1661	0.6	2.42	1116	1140	0.2
18636	NOXEN	131	1724	1691	1660	-0.2	38	665	679	674	0.2	2.48	454	450	-0.1
18640	PITTSTON	079	17465	16961	16729	-0.3	29	7168	7115	7071	-0.1	2.33	4765	4570	-0.5
18641	PITTSTON	079	6361	6047	5935	-0.5	19	2728	2672	2644	-0.2	2.26	1809	1710	-0.6
18642	DURYEA	079	4151	4170	4151	0.0	52	1787	1844	1851	0.3	2.24	1159	1151	-0.1
18643	PITTSTON	079	13715	13374	13208	-0.3	29	5714	5738	5720	0.0	2.31	3803	3689	-0.3
18644	WYOMING	079	7704	7548	7455	-0.2	38	3300	3305	3293	0.0	2.27	2179	2109	-0.4
18651	PLYMOUTH	079	10082	9621	9440	-0.5	19	4195	4085	4034	-0.3	2.34	2684	2517	-0.7
18655	SHICKSHINNY	079	6424	6792	6875	0.6	74	2539	2751	2803	0.9	2.43	1812	1925	0.7
18656	SWEET VALLEY	079	2995	2933	2900	-0.2	38	1123	1133	1132	0.1	2.57	831	816	-0.2
18657	TUNKHANNOCK	131	13656	13584	13417	-0.1	46	5335	5504	5497	0.3	2.41	3773	3791	0.1
18660	WAPWALLOPEN	079	1686	2944	3295	6.2	100	628	1169	1327	6.9	2.51	476	832	6.2
18661	WHITE HAVEN	079	5410	5220	5141	-0.4	23	2091	2047	2027	-0.2	2.39	1473	1394	-0.6
18701	WILKES BARRE	079	3955	3927	3868	-0.1	46	1403	1337	1311	-0.5	1.60	255	222	-1.5
18702	WILKES BARRE	079	42701	40398	39461	-0.6	13	17689	17005	16719	-0.4	2.20	10401	9575	-0.9
18704	KINGSTON	079	32745	31138	30496	-0.5	19	14289	13930	13756	-0.3	2.17	8583	8025	-0.7
18705	WILKES BARRE	079	14652	13904	13636	-0.6	13	6350	6205	6141	-0.2	2.23	4065	3821	-0.7
18706	WILKES BARRE	079	17217	16675	16436	-0.3	29	7392	7340	7290	-0.1	2.25	4727	4515	-0.5
18707	MOUNTAIN TOP	079	15972	16509	16577	0.4	68	5830	6175	6249	0.6	2.64	4602	4762	0.4
18708	SHAVERTOWN	079	11263	11364	11304	0.1	57	3609	3687	3693	0.2	2.54	2747	2735	0.0
18709	LUZERNE	079	2952	2829	2778	-0.5	19	1410	1389	1377	-0.2	2.04	767	719	-0.7
18801	MONTROSE	115	6706	6594	6483	-0.2	38	2695	2738	2718	0.2	2.37	1876	1855	-0.1
18810	ATHENS	015	7793	8051	8047	0.4	68	3059	3212	3231	0.5	2.46	2124	2172	0.2
18812	BRACKNEY	115	1812	1837	1826	0.1	57	655	684	686	0.5	2.69	518	530	0.2
18817	EAST SMITHFIELD	015	1538	1524	1499	-0.1	46	567	576	572	0.2	2.64	434	430	-0.1
18818	FRIENDSVILLE	115	1846	1846	1804	0.0	52	713	740	731	0.4	2.49	535	542	0.1
18821	GREAT BEND	115	1599	1556	1516	-0.3	29	705	714	704	0.1	2.18	453	443	-0.2
18822	HALLSTEAD	115	2804	2780	2728	-0.1	46	1130	1163	1155	0.3	2.39	777	776	0.0
18823	HARFORD	115	1268	1305	1307	0.3	64	508	540	547	0.7	2.38	374	388	0.4
18824	HOP BOTTOM	115	1138	1131	1114	-0.1	46	447	460	458	0.3	2.46	327	328	0.0
18825	JACKSON	115	709	717	715	0.1	57	286	301	303	0.6	2.38	213	218	0.3
18826	KINGSLEY	115	1271	1288	1282	0.1	57	487	510	514	0.5	2.52	355	363	0.2
18828	LAWTON	115	1423	1449	1448	0.2	61	536	565	570	0.6	2.55	407	419	0.3
18829	LE RAYSVILLE	015	975	948	928	-0.3	29	344	348	345	0.1	2.72	273	271	-0.1
18830	LITTLE MEADOWS	115	709	711	708	0.0	52	271	282	284	0.4	2.52	203	207	0.2
18831	MILAN	015	485	479	470	-0.1	46	189	192	191	0.2	2.45	140	139	-0.1
18832	MONROETON	015	2469	2451	2416	-0.1	46	921	947	942	0.3	2.59	687	690	0.0
18833	NEW ALBANY	015	1429	1414	1393	-0.1	46	570	586	584	0.3	2.41	418	419	0.0
18834	NEW MILFORD	115	2737	2732	2705	0.0	52	1072	1105	1107	0.3	2.47	768	770	0.0
18837	ROME	015	2005	1970	1938	-0.2	38	763	778	773	0.2	2.53	569	567	0.0
18840	SAYRE	015	10565	10543	10380	0.0	52	4469	4593	4563	0.3	2.28	2903	2890	0.0
18842	SOUTH GIBSON	115	432	434	433	0.0	52	159	166	167	0.5	2.48	119	121	0.2
18844	SPRINGVILLE	115	2217	2254	2243	0.2	61	816	855	860	0.5	2.63	617	631	0.2
18845	STEVENSVILLE	015	409	406	401	-0.1	46	162	167	167	0.3	2.43	120	121	0.1
18846	SUGAR RUN	015	1186	1185	1172	0.0	52	460	478	478	0.4	2.48	343	348	0.2
18847	SUSQUEHANNA	115	5267	5362	5360	0.2	61	2011	2111	2130	0.5	2.50	1405	1432	0.2
18848	TOWANDA	015	7165	7126	7024	-0.1	46	2890	2966	2952	0.3	2.30	1959	1951	0.0
18850	ULSTER	015	2045	2038	2007	0.0	52	762	783	778	0.3	2.58	577	579	0.0
	PENNSYLVANIA					0.3					0.4	2.45			0.1
	UNITED STATES					1.0					1.1	2.59			0.9

ZIP CODE #	POST OFFICE NAME	RACE (%) White 2000	White 2009	Black 2000	Black 2009	Asian/Pacific 2000	Asian/Pacific 2009	% Hispanic Origin 2000	% Hispanic Origin 2009	2009 AGE DISTRIBUTION (%) 0-4	5-9	10-14	15-19	20-24	25-44	45-64	65-84	85+	18+	MEDIAN AGE 2009	% 2009 Males	% 2009 Females
18447	OLYPHANT	98.7	98.1	0.4	0.6	0.3	0.5	0.6	0.8	5.1	5.1	5.3	5.6	5.0	25.2	29.2	16.4	3.2	81.9	44.1	47.7	52.3
18451	PAUPACK	97.8	97.3	0.7	0.8	0.4	0.8	2.2	3.0	3.5	4.0	4.3	5.8	4.0	20.3	36.6	20.0	1.6	84.7	49.2	51.1	48.9
18452	PECKVILLE	98.2	97.6	0.2	0.3	0.5	0.8	0.8	1.1	4.8	4.8	5.0	5.2	5.0	21.0	26.6	19.4	8.2	82.0	48.2	44.1	55.9
18453	PLEASANT MOUNT	99.1	98.8	0.2	0.2	0.2	0.5	1.5	2.1	5.2	5.9	6.0	6.0	3.6	22.3	34.6	14.6	1.9	78.8	45.6	51.1	48.9
18455	PRESTON PARK	98.6	98.7	0.0	0.0	0.3	0.3	0.7	0.6	5.1	5.7	5.7	5.1	3.5	22.2	33.3	17.8	1.6	79.7	46.8	50.2	49.8
18456	PROMPTON	95.4	94.5	2.5	3.0	0.4	0.5	0.9	1.5	4.9	5.2	5.7	5.5	3.9	24.9	30.6	15.5	3.9	80.3	45.0	54.6	45.4
18458	SHOHOLA	97.6	96.4	0.3	0.6	0.3	0.5	3.7	5.0	5.4	5.9	6.8	7.2	3.8	20.5	33.9	14.8	1.8	76.9	45.3	49.2	50.8
18460	SOUTH STERLING	94.3	92.9	3.3	3.5	0.5	0.9	3.8	4.4	5.8	7.1	7.1	6.2	3.1	21.2	31.9	15.5	2.2	75.7	44.7	49.6	50.4
18461	STARLIGHT	98.7	98.2	0.0	0.0	1.0	1.2	1.0	1.2	3.3	3.9	4.2	4.2	3.6	19.0	38.0	21.7	2.4	86.1	51.7	51.0	49.0
18462	STARRUCCA	98.7	98.8	0.0	0.0	0.3	0.2	0.5	0.5	5.5	5.5	5.7	5.2	3.5	22.7	32.4	17.7	1.7	80.0	46.3	50.4	49.6
18463	STERLING	96.5	95.6	1.7	1.9	0.4	0.7	1.8	2.4	5.2	5.7	6.4	6.3	5.1	25.3	31.6	13.3	1.2	78.9	42.5	52.0	48.0
18464	TAFTON	95.9	95.1	1.9	2.1	0.4	0.6	2.1	2.8	4.6	5.2	5.5	5.4	4.1	21.4	34.9	17.2	1.6	81.3	47.3	52.2	47.8
18465	THOMPSON	98.1	97.7	0.3	0.3	0.2	0.3	0.9	1.2	5.3	5.7	6.0	6.0	4.6	22.7	31.7	15.4	2.6	79.1	44.7	50.9	49.1
18466	TOBYHANNA	71.6	67.8	15.7	16.9	1.1	1.5	15.3	18.8	6.8	7.0	7.1	8.0	6.5	25.2	27.9	10.5	1.0	74.1	36.5	48.9	51.1
18469	TYLER HILL	98.0	97.4	1.0	1.2	0.3	0.5	0.5	0.5	4.7	5.6	7.5	6.6	5.9	20.2	31.5	15.8	2.1	76.7	44.6	49.6	50.4
18470	UNION DALE	98.3	97.9	0.4	0.4	0.3	0.4	1.6	2.1	6.1	6.4	7.0	6.3	5.0	24.3	29.9	13.1	1.9	76.5	41.5	51.3	48.7
18472	WAYMART	88.7	86.4	7.8	9.0	0.3	0.5	3.2	4.3	4.1	4.2	4.4	4.6	5.6	33.8	29.2	11.2	3.0	84.3	41.6	63.9	36.1
18503	SCRANTON	85.2	81.6	8.7	10.2	2.6	3.9	3.3	4.3	2.7	1.7	1.9	6.8	13.6	27.3	21.1	20.0	5.0	92.2	41.9	52.6	47.4
18504	SCRANTON	97.6	96.8	0.8	1.0	0.5	0.8	1.1	1.5	5.5	5.3	5.4	6.1	6.0	24.7	27.7	15.7	3.5	80.1	42.6	47.4	52.6
18505	SCRANTON	93.6	91.7	3.0	3.7	0.9	1.3	3.0	4.1	5.5	5.1	5.2	6.0	5.7	23.5	27.3	17.2	4.5	80.8	44.2	46.5	53.5
18507	MOOSIC	98.7	98.0	0.3	0.4	0.5	0.8	0.5	0.8	4.4	4.7	5.1	5.4	3.9	22.8	29.4	19.6	4.7	82.2	47.5	47.7	52.3
18508	SCRANTON	93.7	92.2	2.5	2.9	0.8	1.2	3.7	4.9	6.4	6.1	5.9	6.4	6.0	25.4	26.7	14.1	2.9	77.8	40.0	47.2	52.8
18509	SCRANTON	94.4	92.8	3.1	3.9	0.9	1.3	1.9	2.7	4.9	4.6	4.8	7.7	8.4	24.4	24.6	16.2	4.5	82.3	41.2	46.5	53.5
18510	SCRANTON	88.7	85.7	5.5	6.5	2.6	3.8	3.6	4.8	5.0	4.6	4.5	13.2	14.6	20.9	20.6	12.6	3.9	82.9	32.3	46.7	53.3
18512	SCRANTON	98.9	98.5	0.3	0.4	0.3	0.4	0.7	1.0	5.0	5.1	5.5	5.7	4.9	24.9	27.9	17.3	3.7	80.9	44.2	47.4	52.6
18517	TAYLOR	98.6	98.1	0.2	0.2	0.7	1.1	0.5	0.7	4.7	4.7	5.1	5.7	5.0	24.2	28.7	17.5	4.5	81.7	45.5	47.2	52.8
18518	OLD FORGE	99.0	98.7	0.2	0.2	0.4	0.6	0.3	0.5	5.1	5.3	5.6	5.6	4.3	24.3	28.2	17.0	4.6	80.5	44.9	46.6	53.4
18519	DICKSON CITY	98.7	98.3	0.3	0.3	0.3	0.4	1.0	1.4	5.1	5.1	5.1	5.5	5.6	25.8	28.0	16.2	3.6	81.2	43.5	46.8	53.2
18603	BERWICK	97.8	97.2	0.7	0.8	0.4	0.6	1.2	1.6	5.3	5.3	5.7	6.4	5.4	24.4	28.5	15.6	3.5	79.7	43.3	47.9	52.1
18610	BLAKESLEE	87.0	84.1	6.9	8.0	1.0	1.5	9.0	11.9	6.7	7.0	7.6	8.7	6.1	23.5	30.1	9.6	0.6	73.0	38.0	50.8	49.2
18612	DALLAS	98.5	97.9	0.3	0.4	0.6	0.9	0.6	0.8	4.8	5.0	5.5	7.5	6.6	21.0	29.3	16.2	4.2	80.9	44.7	46.5	53.5
18614	DUSHORE	98.3	97.9	0.3	0.3	0.1	0.1	0.6	0.8	5.4	5.5	5.4	5.8	6.4	20.5	31.5	16.6	3.0	80.3	45.6	47.8	52.2
18615	FALLS	96.4	96.0	2.4	2.7	0.4	0.4	1.5	1.5	5.7	5.7	9.8	9.8	4.4	23.2	29.1	10.8	1.4	71.4	38.5	53.7	46.3
18616	FORKSVILLE	97.2	96.7	0.5	0.6	0.3	0.3	0.3	0.4	4.5	4.7	5.1	5.0	3.1	21.1	31.1	20.8	4.6	82.1	49.4	49.7	50.3
18617	GLEN LYON	82.8	79.6	15.7	18.5	0.4	0.6	3.8	5.0	4.3	4.1	4.0	5.0	10.6	40.8	20.8	8.2	2.3	85.0	34.9	66.8	33.2
18618	HARVEYS LAKE	98.2	97.5	0.1	0.1	0.4	0.7	0.7	1.1	5.1	5.1	5.5	6.1	5.3	26.2	32.1	12.6	2.1	80.2	43.0	49.1	50.9
18619	HILLSGROVE	99.2	99.2	0.0	0.0	0.4	0.4	0.0	0.0	4.7	5.1	5.5	4.3	4.0	22.1	35.6	15.4	3.2	81.8	47.3	51.4	48.6
18621	HUNLOCK CREEK	98.8	98.4	0.1	0.1	0.4	0.7	0.1	0.1	5.3	5.9	6.1	5.9	4.8	25.7	32.0	12.9	1.4	78.9	42.6	51.5	48.5
18622	HUNTINGTON MILLS	97.9	97.9	0.7	0.7	0.0	0.0	0.7	0.7	5.6	5.6	6.3	6.3	4.2	25.0	26.4	15.3	5.6	79.2	43.6	49.3	50.7
18623	LACEYVILLE	98.6	98.5	0.3	0.3	0.2	0.2	0.6	0.6	6.4	6.5	7.1	6.3	4.9	24.7	29.7	12.8	1.6	76.2	40.5	49.1	50.9
18624	LAKE HARMONY	95.2	94.6	1.2	1.2	0.1	0.2	3.6	4.4	3.4	3.8	4.4	6.0	3.0	20.9	34.7	22.2	1.5	84.6	50.7	50.1	49.9
18628	LOPEZ	84.5	82.0	10.4	11.7	0.0	0.0	3.8	4.7	2.3	3.0	3.2	22.3	6.9	13.4	23.6	20.1	5.2	78.2	43.8	55.6	44.4
18629	MEHOOPANY	98.0	98.0	0.2	0.2	0.1	0.1	0.8	0.8	5.9	6.5	6.6	6.5	4.5	25.6	30.2	12.8	1.4	76.9	41.0	51.3	48.7
18630	MESHOPPEN	99.0	98.7	0.1	0.2	0.2	0.2	0.5	0.7	6.4	6.9	7.3	8.0	5.2	25.7	28.3	10.9	1.3	74.2	38.4	49.6	50.4
18631	MIFFLINVILLE	98.9	98.4	0.0	0.0	0.7	1.2	0.3	0.5	4.5	4.9	5.3	6.1	5.0	23.0	31.7	17.1	2.4	81.8	45.7	48.6	51.4
18632	MILDRED	98.9	98.4	0.2	0.2	0.2	0.2	0.7	1.1	5.1	5.5	5.8	6.4	4.7	21.1	33.0	16.6	1.8	79.6	45.8	49.9	50.1
18634	NANTICOKE	98.9	98.5	0.2	0.3	0.2	0.4	0.5	0.6	4.7	4.6	4.7	5.5	5.3	24.5	27.1	18.6	4.8	82.7	45.4	47.5	52.5
18635	NESCOPECK	98.4	97.8	0.2	0.3	0.4	0.6	0.7	1.0	5.9	6.1	6.2	6.1	4.9	25.7	30.1	13.2	1.8	78.0	41.6	49.6	50.4
18636	NOXEN	98.6	98.6	0.3	0.4	0.1	0.1	0.2	0.2	6.8	6.6	6.7	6.5	5.4	25.8	27.5	13.0	1.7	76.0	39.6	50.8	49.2
18640	PITTSTON	98.8	98.5	0.4	0.6	0.2	0.3	0.5	0.7	5.1	5.1	5.4	5.8	5.2	24.5	28.0	16.8	4.2	81.1	44.3	47.2	52.8
18641	PITTSTON	99.2	99.0	0.3	0.4	0.2	0.3	0.2	0.2	4.6	4.9	5.1	5.3	4.2	24.9	29.5	18.2	3.4	82.2	45.7	48.2	51.8
18642	DURYEA	98.9	98.4	0.2	0.3	0.4	0.6	0.3	0.4	4.4	4.4	4.6	5.3	5.1	24.1	30.0	18.3	3.7	83.2	46.3	47.2	52.8
18643	PITTSTON	99.1	98.7	0.3	0.3	0.1	0.2	0.4	0.6	5.2	5.3	5.6	5.8	5.0	24.6	29.1	16.1	3.3	80.2	44.0	47.1	52.9
18644	WYOMING	99.4	99.2	0.2	0.2	0.1	0.2	0.3	0.4	5.0	5.5	6.0	6.0	4.3	22.7	30.0	16.8	3.7	79.7	45.3	47.8	52.2
18651	PLYMOUTH	98.6	98.2	0.6	0.7	0.1	0.2	0.8	1.0	5.9	5.6	5.6	6.3	6.0	25.3	27.4	14.6	3.3	79.0	41.6	47.6	52.4
18655	SHICKSHINNY	98.9	98.6	0.2	0.2	0.2	0.3	0.5	0.6	5.3	5.7	6.2	6.6	4.3	25.2	29.5	14.7	2.4	78.4	42.8	49.8	50.2
18656	SWEET VALLEY	99.2	99.0	0.0	0.0	0.1	0.1	0.3	0.4	5.2	5.6	6.3	6.5	4.2	25.6	32.2	12.4	2.0	78.8	42.8	50.6	49.4
18657	TUNKHANNOCK	98.7	98.6	0.3	0.3	0.3	0.3	0.6	0.6	5.4	5.9	6.4	6.6	4.9	24.5	30.5	13.4	2.4	77.9	42.4	50.0	50.0
18660	WAPWALLOPEN	98.2	97.4	0.5	0.8	0.3	0.7	0.7	1.4	5.4	5.8	6.2	6.5	4.7	24.3	31.8	13.4	1.9	78.3	42.9	50.8	49.2
18661	WHITE HAVEN	97.7	97.0	1.0	1.2	0.4	0.6	1.2	1.7	4.2	4.5	5.2	6.8	4.8	23.8	33.5	15.4	1.9	81.8	45.4	50.4	49.6
18701	WILKES BARRE	91.3	89.0	5.1	6.2	1.3	2.1	2.0	2.6	4.1	3.3	2.5	18.7	22.2	10.0	10.9	18.3	10.0	88.6	24.8	48.2	51.8
18702	WILKES BARRE	92.6	90.6	4.6	5.6	1.2	1.8	1.4	1.9	5.0	4.8	4.8	6.0	7.2	25.1	26.7	16.6	3.9	82.1	42.9	49.1	50.9
18704	KINGSTON	97.6	96.7	0.8	1.0	0.8	1.3	0.7	0.9	4.8	4.7	4.9	6.0	5.4	24.1	28.5	17.1	4.6	82.0	45.1	46.6	53.4
18705	WILKES BARRE	98.1	97.5	1.1	1.4	0.3	0.5	0.6	0.9	4.8	4.8	5.1	5.4	4.6	25.0	29.2	17.6	3.5	82.0	45.2	48.0	52.0
18706	WILKES BARRE	98.2	97.7	0.8	1.0	0.2	0.4	0.6	0.8	5.6	5.3	5.3	5.5	5.8	25.0	27.9	16.2	3.2	80.5	43.0	47.2	52.8
18707	MOUNTAIN TOP	97.1	95.7	0.5	0.6	1.6	2.5	1.0	1.6	5.6	6.2	6.9	7.0	4.3	22.8	32.0	13.1	2.0	76.7	43.1	49.0	51.0
18708	SHAVERTOWN	88.6	86.7	9.9	11.3	0.6	0.9	1.9	2.4	4.1	4.6	5.2	5.6	5.3	29.4	32.5	11.7	1.5	82.7	42.5	58.1	41.9
18709	LUZERNE	98.9	98.6	0.3	0.4	0.1	0.1	0.4	0.6	5.2	5.3	4.9	4.3	5.2	25.1	29.7	16.3	4.0	82.0	45.0	47.7	52.3
18801	MONTROSE	98.4	98.0	0.4	0.5	0.1	0.2	0.5	0.7	5.9	6.1	6.4	6.6	5.2	23.1	29.0	14.9	2.8	77.4	42.6	49.2	50.8
18810	ATHENS	98.0	97.5	0.6	0.7	0.3	0.5	0.7	0.9	6.4	6.6	6.9	6.5	5.2	23.4	28.5	14.0	2.4	76.0	41.0	48.0	52.0
18812	BRACKNEY	98.2	97.6	0.2	0.3	0.1	0.1	0.8	1.1	5.0	5.9	6.5	7.7	5.0	21.7	33.9	13.4	1.0	77.8	43.6	50.2	49.8
18817	EAST SMITHFIELD	98.8	98.6	0.9	1.1	0.1	0.2	0.7	0.9	5.4	5.7	6.4	7.5	4.7	22.2	32.2	14.1	1.7	77.1	43.5	50.4	49.6
18818	FRIENDSVILLE	98.8	98.3	0.1	0.1	0.1	0.2	1.0	1.4	4.8	5.5	6.1	7.0	5.0	22.4	33.1	15.0	1.1	79.4	44.4	51.1	48.9
18821	GREAT BEND	98.6	98.1	0.2	0.2	0.6	1.0	0.2	0.2	4.8	5.1	5.3	5.7	5.2	23.1	31.7	16.5	2.5	81.1	45.4	48.8	51.2
18822	HALLSTEAD	98.3	97.8	0.4	0.5	0.2	0.3	0.4	0.5	6.0	6.5	6.4	6.0	5.3	22.9	31.3	13.9	1.8	77.4	42.7	49.2	50.8
18823	HARFORD	98.9	98.7	0.2	0.2	0.1	0.2	0.6	0.7	5.1	5.7	6.5	7.2	5.1	22.4	30.7	14.5	2.9	78.2	43.8	50.2	49.8
18824	HOP BOTTOM	98.4	98.0	0.7	0.9	0.1	0.2	0.3	0.4	5.1	5.4	6.0	6.9	5.0	23.9	32.3	13.6	1.8	79.2	43.4	51.5	48.5
18825	JACKSON	97.9	97.5	0.6	0.6	0.1	0.3	0.6	0.7	4.2	4.5	4.9	4.2	4.0	19.2	38.4	18.5	2.1	84.0	50.2	49.8	50.2
18826	KINGSLEY	98.7	98.4	0.1	0.2	0.1	0.2	0.3	0.4	5.9	6.4	6.8	7.1	5.1	21.0	31.9	13.7	2.2	76.5	43.5	49.8	50.2
18828	LAWTON	98.5	98.1	0.3	0.4	0.1	0.1	0.5	0.8	5.4	5.9	6.6	7.4	4.6	24.0	31.1	13.5	1.6	77.1	42.2	51.3	48.7
18829	LE RAYSVILLE	98.4	97.9	0.6	0.7	0.0	0.0	1.2	1.8	8.6	8.8	8.1	6.6	4.7	25.6	25.3	10.9	1.3	70.4	35.2	51.5	48.5
18830	LITTLE MEADOWS	97.7	97.3	0.3	0.3	0.4	0.6	0.7	1.1	5.8	6.3	6.8	6.3	3.0	27.3	34.0	10.0	0.6	77.1	41.8	51.5	48.5
18831	MILAN	97.5	96.9	0.4	0.6	0.2	0.2	0.6	1.0	6.3	6.9	7.1	7.1	4.2	25.1	29.9	12.1	1.5	74.5	40.5	48.6	51.4
18832	MONROETON	98.3	97.9	0.1	0.1	0.0	0.0	0.3	0.4	5.8	6.1	6.7	7.6	5.3	25.4	29.2	12.6	1.3	76.7	40.3	50.5	49.5
18833	NEW ALBANY	98.0	97.7	0.0	0.0	0.1	0.1	0.3	0.5	5.7	6.1	6.4	6.2	5.4	24.2	30.8	13.5	1.6	77.9	42.3	52.9	47.1
18834	NEW MILFORD	98.2	97.8	0.7	0.8	0.2	0.3	0.9	1.2	6.5	6.7	6.9	6.9	5.3	23.7	29.5	13.0	1.5	75.7	41.2	50.5	49.5
18837	ROME	98.9	98.6	0.1	0.2	0.1	0.1	0.6	0.9	7.0	7.4	7.5	6.5	5.1	25.9	27.3	11.7	1.7	74.2	38.8	49.3	50.7
18840	SAYRE	96.8	95.8	0.5	0.6	1.5	2.1	0.6	0.9	6.3	6.3	6.4	6.2	5.6	22.8	28.9	14.6	2.8	77.1	42.2	47.4	52.6
18842	SOUTH GIBSON	99.3	98.8	0.2	0.2	0.0	0.2	0.9	1.4	4.8	6.0	6.9	7.4	5.1	21.7	30.2	12.9	5.1	77.4	43.8	51.8	48.2
18844	SPRINGVILLE	98.8	98.6	0.3	0.4	0.2	0.2	0.6	0.8	6.4	6.8	7.3	7.3	4.7	23.8	29.2	12.8	1.6	74.7	40.4	50.1	49.9
18845	STEVENSVILLE	97.1	96.6	0.5	0.5	0.5	0.7	1.0	1.2	5.2	5.4	5.7	6.2	5.2	23.4	32.0	15.3	1.7	79.6	44.3	50.2	49.8
18846	SUGAR RUN	98.2	97.7	0.3	0.4	0.3	0.5	0.5	0.8	5.8	6.3	6.7	6.2	4.8	23.8	30.0	15.0	1.4	77.5	42.6	51.2	48.8
18847	SUSQUEHANNA	98.3	97.8	0.1	0.1	0.7	1.1	1.1	1.4	5.8	5.9	6.2	7.0	5.7	23.6	29.3	14.0	2.5	77.6	41.7	49.3	50.7
18848	TOWANDA	97.6	96.9	0.5	0.5	0.7	1.0	0.9	1.2	5.3	5.3	5.6	6.7	5.8	23.5	28.2	15.6	3.9	79.3	43.2	48.7	51.3
18850	ULSTER	97.9	97.5	0.3	0.4	0.1	0.1	0.3	0.4	6.5	7.2	7.5	6.9	4.7	24.5	29.1	12.4	1.4	74.2	40.1	50.0	50.0
	PENNSYLVANIA	85.4	83.2	10.0	10.7	1.8	2.7	3.2	4.2	5.8	6.0	6.3	7.1	6.5	24.8	27.8	13.1	2.6	77.8	40.4	48.5	51.5
	UNITED STATES	75.1	72.0	12.3	12.7	3.8	4.6	12.5	15.7	6.8	6.7	6.6	7.1	6.9	27.0	26.0	10.9	1.9	75.7	36.9	49.2	50.8

ZIP CODE #	POST OFFICE NAME	2009 Per Capita Income	2009 HH Income Base	2009 HOUSEHOLD INCOME DISTRIBUTION (%) Less than $25,000	$25,000 to $49,999	$50,000 to $99,999	$100,000 to $149,999	$150,000 or More	MEDIAN HOUSEHOLD INCOME 2009	2014	2009 National Centile	2009 State Centile	2009 Home Value Base	2009 HOME VALUE DISTRIBUTION (%) Less than $50,000	$50,000 to $89,999	$90,000 to $174,999	$175,000 to $399,999	$400,000 or More	2009 Median Home Value
18447	OLYPHANT	24255	3798	27.0	25.4	37.3	7.1	3.2	47449	50961	55	56	2635	2.3	7.6	51.8	36.2	2.1	155084
18451	PAUPACK	27832	266	20.3	24.1	45.5	5.6	4.5	55821	59813	72	72	226	0.0	0.9	28.3	55.8	15.0	235000
18452	PECKVILLE	24948	2139	25.6	25.3	37.5	7.2	4.3	48380	52569	58	58	1590	0.5	3.3	53.5	39.9	2.8	161058
18453	PLEASANT MOUNT	22921	545	21.8	29.2	40.7	5.9	2.4	48969	47574	59	59	466	7.1	8.4	39.9	35.8	8.8	161111
18455	PRESTON PARK	22924	135	26.7	33.3	32.6	4.4	3.0	41155	42626	37	31	113	10.6	17.7	42.5	22.1	7.1	133929
18456	PROMPTON	21158	242	29.8	33.5	31.0	4.5	1.2	39667	41570	32	24	200	8.5	8.0	40.5	36.5	6.5	162500
18458	SHOHOLA	25397	1628	18.1	24.8	42.9	10.8	3.5	56882	60032	74	74	1377	1.5	2.5	24.8	53.1	18.1	232129
18460	SOUTH STERLING	21196	99	30.3	30.3	33.3	4.0	2.0	40452	42700	34	28	84	9.5	13.1	40.5	32.1	4.8	144643
18461	STARLIGHT	25843	158	31.6	28.5	33.5	3.2	3.2	39440	41014	31	24	131	6.1	18.3	39.7	29.0	6.9	143750
18462	STARRUCCA	23487	176	27.3	33.5	31.8	4.5	2.8	40569	42148	35	28	147	13.6	19.0	40.1	21.1	6.1	126705
18463	STERLING	21492	360	18.9	33.1	41.1	4.7	2.2	48417	48027	58	58	311	4.2	6.4	38.3	43.7	7.4	177917
18464	TAFTON	23449	940	24.0	28.5	37.4	6.7	3.3	46735	51217	53	54	797	0.5	2.8	32.2	49.3	15.2	220200
18465	THOMPSON	18828	614	33.9	30.1	29.2	4.6	2.3	37578	39229	25	16	510	9.0	11.4	37.8	34.7	7.1	152174
18466	TOBYHANNA	21629	6702	15.9	23.1	47.7	9.9	3.4	63129	63185	81	83	5456	2.8	8.3	52.8	33.7	2.3	146793
18469	TYLER HILL	20122	163	25.8	31.3	37.4	3.1	2.5	42055	42916	39	35	138	8.0	2.9	39.1	47.8	2.2	175000
18470	UNION DALE	20377	651	29.3	31.2	31.0	6.1	2.3	39280	40156	31	23	531	11.3	10.9	36.9	31.8	9.0	153348
18472	WAYMART	18418	1719	23.8	31.5	36.5	5.8	2.4	45661	46325	50	49	1376	6.1	8.1	45.4	35.2	5.2	153686
18503	SCRANTON	12911	487	69.6	20.3	9.0	1.0	0.0	15177	14262	1	1	30	0.0	60.0	20.0	16.7	3.3	80000
18504	SCRANTON	21579	9375	33.0	30.0	28.1	6.2	2.7	38427	41205	28	19	5484	3.4	14.8	60.4	20.0	1.4	130357
18505	SCRANTON	22859	8611	31.4	27.7	33.0	5.6	2.3	39847	44007	32	25	5035	2.8	12.3	59.2	24.2	1.4	136823
18507	MOOSIC	26194	2093	22.6	26.9	36.2	6.9	7.4	50434	52886	62	63	1712	12.8	6.4	38.8	32.8	9.2	154825
18508	SCRANTON	20743	4795	31.8	29.1	33.8	3.4	2.0	40190	43828	33	27	2819	1.7	15.8	70.0	12.4	0.2	124290
18509	SCRANTON	22513	5363	30.7	29.3	30.6	5.4	4.0	39837	43827	32	25	2745	3.4	11.5	50.7	30.4	4.0	144846
18510	SCRANTON	19285	4863	34.9	27.1	29.7	5.7	2.6	36201	39342	21	11	2149	2.0	11.0	61.3	23.3	2.4	135465
18512	SCRANTON	24774	5479	27.7	26.3	37.2	5.6	3.2	46303	50012	52	52	3660	0.6	7.2	53.9	36.7	1.5	155882
18517	TAYLOR	22106	2104	27.6	25.0	40.3	5.7	1.5	46464	51064	53	53	1553	14.8	8.8	50.1	24.9	1.4	140305
18518	OLD FORGE	25521	3694	24.0	27.6	37.5	7.7	3.3	48211	51684	57	57	2656	1.8	8.8	47.7	37.2	4.4	152347
18519	DICKSON CITY	22064	2191	29.7	29.2	34.9	5.1	1.1	41652	45679	38	34	1413	0.7	9.7	67.1	21.7	0.8	134358
18603	BERWICK	20709	7796	27.6	33.6	32.5	4.4	1.9	40020	43414	33	26	5546	12.3	13.0	54.5	18.0	2.3	125322
18610	BLAKESLEE	18680	1032	18.9	27.0	44.7	7.1	2.3	53833	55131	69	69	901	7.8	9.5	38.4	43.0	1.3	161995
18612	DALLAS	29898	5345	18.5	21.5	39.5	12.7	7.8	62128	62759	80	82	4387	6.6	4.0	28.5	49.4	11.5	203019
18614	DUSHORE	21167	815	32.4	30.9	29.6	5.4	1.7	36476	37822	22	12	572	9.1	24.8	49.3	13.5	3.3	119444
18615	FALLS	20983	473	23.7	33.6	34.2	6.8	1.7	43006	45430	42	39	382	4.2	9.9	38.7	42.1	5.0	168605
18616	FORKSVILLE	20031	451	29.5	35.7	28.8	4.0	2.0	34457	36363	16	8	365	10.4	19.2	44.9	21.9	3.6	127148
18617	GLEN LYON	17141	801	40.0	27.7	26.0	4.5	1.9	31501	34166	11	4	472	14.6	31.1	51.7	2.5	0.0	92817
18618	HARVEYS LAKE	25689	1157	19.8	31.5	36.3	7.1	5.3	48538	51805	58	58	938	5.7	7.9	40.7	33.6	12.2	166803
18619	HILLSGROVE	20379	113	35.4	30.1	29.2	5.3	0.0	32348	35570	12	4	93	8.6	17.2	46.2	22.6	5.4	137500
18621	HUNLOCK CREEK	19365	1451	22.5	32.6	38.2	5.5	1.1	45822	49240	51	50	1278	9.5	13.8	44.1	31.1	1.5	145341
18622	HUNTINGTON MILLS	21343	56	19.6	35.7	35.7	7.1	1.8	43207	45000	43	40	48	2.1	8.3	52.1	29.2	8.3	143182
18623	LACEYVILLE	19112	1431	30.7	32.2	29.9	5.2	2.0	38908	41720	29	21	1156	14.0	11.8	45.4	25.2	3.6	133946
18624	LAKE HARMONY	24820	459	27.0	32.5	25.9	7.4	7.2	40107	43787	33	26	382	2.4	2.4	44.0	40.6	10.7	178676
18628	LOPEZ	18655	179	29.6	27.4	32.4	8.4	2.2	40382	42391	34	27	158	5.7	17.7	46.8	25.3	4.4	135714
18629	MEHOOPANY	21741	580	23.1	30.9	36.4	6.7	2.9	45679	48641	50	49	460	8.5	11.1	40.2	34.6	5.7	147468
18630	MESHOPPEN	18545	1293	28.3	31.7	33.8	4.8	1.4	41073	43837	36	31	977	8.4	11.1	46.6	29.3	4.7	143226
18631	MIFFLINVILLE	25536	513	16.6	34.1	38.6	7.2	3.5	49378	51773	60	60	423	9.0	6.4	61.9	22.2	0.5	142330
18632	MILDRED	20748	245	30.6	33.9	29.8	4.1	1.6	37117	38523	24	14	213	12.7	22.5	45.1	15.5	4.2	123295
18634	NANTICOKE	21607	6052	31.6	29.6	31.5	5.6	1.7	38303	41195	28	19	3915	6.9	23.8	54.0	15.2	0.1	113483
18635	NESCOPECK	22330	1644	22.7	29.4	40.3	5.2	2.3	47730	50972	56	57	1277	7.8	8.4	53.0	27.1	3.7	145375
18636	NOXEN	19485	679	29.3	31.8	31.1	5.3	2.5	39382	43207	31	23	535	16.1	14.8	44.1	20.6	4.5	130461
18640	PITTSTON	23302	7115	27.3	28.4	33.4	7.2	3.6	43883	47855	45	42	5048	7.6	12.5	50.4	25.9	3.7	136931
18641	PITTSTON	24183	2672	25.7	28.5	36.3	7.2	2.3	46738	50077	53	54	2063	3.9	10.8	62.9	21.3	1.2	138273
18642	DURYEA	24658	1844	26.6	27.3	35.8	5.9	4.4	45240	50081	49	47	1329	1.4	13.8	59.1	23.7	2.0	136647
18643	PITTSTON	22588	5738	26.0	31.1	34.6	6.4	2.0	43263	46837	43	40	4160	9.4	9.2	51.4	26.0	3.9	143697
18644	WYOMING	26749	3305	21.1	26.7	37.8	10.9	3.6	51826	53997	66	66	2468	1.8	6.4	45.1	40.2	6.4	169666
18651	PLYMOUTH	19856	4085	31.7	30.0	32.0	5.3	1.0	39058	42274	30	22	2657	8.2	29.7	46.8	14.8	0.5	107599
18655	SHICKSHINNY	21760	2751	24.9	28.7	38.6	5.5	2.3	46201	50359	52	52	2249	5.9	15.2	45.1	31.0	2.8	141727
18656	SWEET VALLEY	21543	1133	25.0	25.9	41.1	5.1	2.8	48966	51786	59	59	1024	11.0	11.3	33.4	39.3	5.0	159794
18657	TUNKHANNOCK	21854	5504	25.2	30.3	34.9	6.6	3.0	45454	47135	50	48	4370	7.3	8.8	39.7	39.4	4.6	161732
18660	WAPWALLOPEN	19303	1169	25.7	31.7	36.7	5.6	0.3	44138	47145	46	43	966	2.7	8.6	48.7	35.2	4.9	155165
18661	WHITE HAVEN	23000	2047	20.8	31.9	37.9	5.9	3.6	47823	50996	56	57	1766	8.7	9.1	45.4	31.5	5.3	152067
18701	WILKES BARRE	15468	1337	60.8	25.2	11.1	2.5	0.4	19983	20120	1	1	121	13.2	13.2	44.6	28.1	0.8	139844
18702	WILKES BARRE	21871	17005	32.6	28.9	29.9	5.8	2.8	38761	41716	29	21	10017	7.0	21.1	51.3	17.9	2.7	118660
18704	KINGSTON	25175	13930	28.0	27.5	34.1	6.7	3.7	44252	48103	46	43	8523	2.5	8.7	57.3	28.8	2.7	148351
18705	WILKES BARRE	25384	6205	24.1	29.0	35.9	7.8	3.1	45840	50540	51	50	4365	3.3	16.8	56.7	22.0	1.2	131623
18706	WILKES BARRE	22229	7340	30.2	29.1	32.2	6.5	2.0	41120	44951	36	31	5071	10.3	18.7	51.0	18.3	1.7	120605
18707	MOUNTAIN TOP	28376	6175	12.9	23.9	42.7	13.1	7.3	64269	64421	83	85	5515	2.8	4.3	29.3	54.8	8.8	206483
18708	SHAVERTOWN	29777	3687	13.7	21.1	37.2	17.2	10.8	67698	68583	85	88	3199	3.2	2.9	31.9	48.8	13.3	204099
18709	LUZERNE	22562	1389	32.3	30.2	31.8	3.1	2.6	38624	42453	29	20	805	6.7	20.5	63.6	9.2	0.0	114727
18801	MONTROSE	21432	2738	27.6	30.7	34.4	4.9	2.4	42556	44952	41	37	2128	8.8	12.3	48.9	26.6	3.5	139010
18810	ATHENS	22336	3212	25.6	31.3	34.6	4.9	3.6	43928	45869	45	42	2372	14.0	15.9	48.4	18.1	3.6	121183
18812	BRACKNEY	23329	684	16.5	27.6	44.2	7.5	4.2	54758	56157	71	71	601	6.5	9.2	44.9	33.3	6.2	152641
18817	EAST SMITHFIELD	19364	576	19.6	37.2	36.5	4.5	2.3	44561	46268	47	44	508	10.6	16.3	41.9	25.6	5.5	137798
18818	FRIENDSVILLE	21454	740	22.7	30.9	38.8	5.0	2.6	46427	49237	53	53	637	7.5	12.2	48.8	27.6	3.8	142411
18821	GREAT BEND	21566	714	30.1	33.3	30.8	4.5	1.3	38037	39436	27	17	481	12.1	25.4	46.6	15.0	1.0	108733
18822	HALLSTEAD	19538	1163	28.8	34.0	32.0	4.1	1.1	39466	40844	31	24	842	12.8	22.7	49.3	14.0	1.2	110326
18823	HARFORD	21014	540	22.8	35.4	35.9	4.4	1.5	43033	45405	42	39	460	8.7	10.9	40.2	34.3	5.9	152941
18824	HOP BOTTOM	19226	460	28.7	35.4	29.1	5.2	1.5	38659	39837	29	20	370	13.2	15.7	48.4	18.9	3.8	122596
18825	JACKSON	21380	301	27.9	30.6	33.2	6.0	2.3	42356	43809	40	36	265	4.5	12.8	48.7	27.9	6.0	146398
18826	KINGSLEY	18792	510	24.9	36.7	32.9	4.3	1.2	41734	43454	38	34	429	7.5	10.7	47.1	29.6	5.1	145494
18828	LAWTON	19256	565	24.1	33.5	37.0	3.9	1.6	43178	45000	43	40	470	7.4	10.2	46.8	29.6	6.0	145000
18829	LE RAYSVILLE	20475	348	25.6	25.0	40.8	6.6	2.0	49449	49637	60	60	282	8.5	17.0	48.6	23.8	2.1	129167
18830	LITTLE MEADOWS	20898	282	25.2	24.8	43.6	4.6	1.8	50000	51828	61	62	241	14.1	16.6	49.8	17.0	2.5	118750
18831	MILAN	20400	192	19.3	35.4	41.7	3.1	0.5	46643	47174	53	53	147	8.2	14.3	58.5	17.0	2.0	127652
18832	MONROETON	18488	947	25.7	37.1	31.8	3.8	1.7	41121	43062	36	31	789	14.1	20.8	45.4	17.5	2.3	119482
18833	NEW ALBANY	19728	586	23.4	36.3	35.0	4.6	0.7	43331	45226	43	41	488	13.3	23.2	45.9	16.0	1.6	110915
18834	NEW MILFORD	19922	1105	30.0	30.1	33.2	4.8	1.8	40653	42512	35	29	895	9.6	16.0	49.1	21.9	3.5	128960
18837	ROME	19022	778	28.5	32.5	33.2	3.9	1.9	39554	42241	31	24	658	19.8	19.1	43.0	16.6	1.5	110577
18840	SAYRE	25163	4593	23.7	31.9	33.9	7.0	3.5	45422	46761	50	48	3209	10.9	18.3	51.0	17.2	2.6	123273
18842	SOUTH GIBSON	21906	166	25.3	30.7	34.3	7.8	1.8	44387	47382	46	44	147	9.5	8.8	35.4	38.1	8.2	164423
18844	SPRINGVILLE	18969	855	25.5	32.5	36.1	4.1	1.8	43112	45301	43	39	705	9.4	10.5	46.8	29.1	4.3	142175
18845	STEVENSVILLE	19074	167	30.5	35.9	27.5	4.2	1.8	36836	38510	23	13	145	9.7	22.1	39.3	22.8	6.2	129605
18846	SUGAR RUN	20346	478	24.9	34.5	31.8	6.5	2.3	40540	43820	34	28	402	12.7	10.0	48.8	22.1	6.5	141912
18847	SUSQUEHANNA	18449	2111	32.3	32.7	29.5	3.8	1.6	36823	38427	23	13	1544	16.7	23.3	43.5	15.1	1.4	103893
18848	TOWANDA	23108	2966	24.2	31.5	34.5	6.5	3.3	45538	46623	50	49	2006	9.6	13.5	50.7	23.0	3.1	131555
18850	ULSTER	19228	783	21.3	35.0	38.8	4.0	0.9	45446	46395	50	48	642	14.2	14.8	49.7	18.2	3.1	124010
	PENNSYLVANIA	26913		21.5	25.3	36.9	10.2	6.1	53225	55819				7.5	12.2	35.6	36.1	8.5	161438
	UNITED STATES	27277		20.9	24.4	35.3	11.7	7.6	54719	56938				9.3	13.1	31.6	32.6	13.5	162279

ZIP CODE #	POST OFFICE NAME	FINANCIAL SERVICES: Auto Loan	Home Loan	Invest-ments	Retire-ment Plans	THE HOME: Home Improvements: Home Repair	Lawn & Garden	Furnishings: Comput-ers & Hard-ware-Personal	Major Appli-ances	TV, Radio, Sound Equip-ment	Furni-ture	ENTERTAINMENT: Dine out/ Carry out	Sports Equip-ment	Fees & Tickets	Toys & Games	Travel	Cable TV	PERSONAL: Apparel & Services	Auto Repairs	Health Insur-ance	Pets & Supplies
18447	OLYPHANT	74	81	75	80	79	86	76	79	79	74	78	58	80	78	79	83	54	78	88	92
18451	PAUPACK	109	87	141	86	96	116	88	111	92	82	90	81	76	87	95	98	60	103	110	129
18452	PECKVILLE	80	83	81	83	83	91	82	85	86	79	85	61	84	84	84	91	59	85	96	99
18453	PLEASANT MOUNT	92	74	119	73	81	97	74	94	77	69	76	68	64	73	80	82	51	86	92	109
18455	PRESTON PARK	89	71	115	70	78	94	71	91	75	67	74	66	62	71	77	80	49	84	90	105
18456	PROMPTON	81	62	97	61	67	84	63	80	67	59	66	59	53	65	66	72	44	73	80	93
18458	SHOHOLA	103	94	128	92	99	109	88	106	90	86	90	79	83	88	96	93	61	98	102	122
18460	SOUTH STERLING	79	63	102	62	69	83	63	80	66	59	65	59	55	63	68	70	43	74	79	93
18461	STARLIGHT	91	73	118	72	80	96	73	93	76	68	75	68	63	72	79	81	50	85	91	107
18462	STARRUCCA	89	71	115	70	78	94	72	91	75	67	74	66	62	71	77	80	49	84	90	105
18463	STERLING	84	77	76	80	78	90	76	85	78	68	76	65	70	79	75	82	52	79	88	99
18464	TAFTON	94	75	121	74	82	99	75	96	79	70	78	70	65	75	81	84	52	88	94	111
18465	THOMPSON	81	62	95	60	66	84	62	79	67	58	66	59	52	65	65	72	44	73	80	93
18466	TOBYHANNA	100	102	96	98	98	97	93	97	92	97	93	73	93	95	93	92	64	94	93	113
18469	TYLER HILL	87	70	112	68	76	92	70	88	73	65	72	65	60	69	75	78	48	82	87	102
18470	UNION DALE	86	67	88	67	70	89	68	83	73	62	71	62	57	72	68	79	48	76	85	98
18472	WAYMART	83	71	82	72	74	87	73	83	76	68	74	62	65	75	72	80	50	78	86	97
18503	SCRANTON	26	19	24	22	20	24	32	26	34	28	34	20	28	30	28	37	24	32	36	33
18504	SCRANTON	71	64	67	64	64	76	69	72	73	64	71	53	65	71	67	77	49	72	81	85
18505	SCRANTON	69	68	68	68	69	76	70	72	74	67	73	52	70	72	70	78	51	72	81	84
18507	MOOSIC	100	94	107	92	96	113	88	103	95	85	94	74	86	93	92	102	64	97	112	119
18508	SCRANTON	70	63	64	63	61	73	67	69	70	62	69	53	63	70	64	74	48	69	77	82
18509	SCRANTON	73	68	70	68	68	76	74	74	77	70	76	55	71	75	72	81	53	76	83	87
18510	SCRANTON	69	59	57	61	58	66	72	66	73	65	72	52	65	71	65	75	50	70	74	80
18512	SCRANTON	75	80	79	78	80	89	73	81	78	71	77	57	77	77	78	83	53	78	91	93
18517	TAYLOR	78	74	75	73	74	85	71	78	76	70	75	57	70	76	72	81	52	76	86	92
18518	OLD FORGE	77	86	82	85	85	92	79	84	83	77	82	60	85	82	84	87	57	82	94	97
18519	DICKSON CITY	68	68	65	68	68	76	69	71	72	65	71	52	69	71	69	76	49	71	81	83
18603	BERWICK	75	64	68	64	64	78	67	73	71	62	69	55	60	71	64	76	47	71	79	86
18610	BLAKESLEE	94	88	77	85	86	89	82	87	85	85	85	64	79	88	79	87	58	84	87	103
18612	DALLAS	105	111	111	112	113	119	104	112	107	103	106	81	108	105	110	111	74	108	120	129
18614	DUSHORE	75	57	74	56	59	75	63	72	69	58	67	53	53	67	60	74	45	69	78	85
18615	FALLS	82	74	74	77	76	88	73	83	76	66	74	63	68	77	73	80	51	76	85	96
18616	FORKSVILLE	79	63	102	62	70	84	63	81	66	59	66	59	55	63	69	71	44	74	80	93
18617	GLEN LYON	68	52	59	52	52	68	59	64	64	53	62	49	49	64	54	69	42	63	71	77
18618	HARVEYS LAKE	95	85	86	87	87	98	87	95	90	81	88	71	80	90	86	94	60	90	99	110
18619	HILLSGROVE	80	57	82	55	59	81	59	75	65	55	64	56	47	65	58	72	42	69	78	89
18621	HUNLOCK CREEK	82	71	76	73	73	87	70	81	74	65	72	62	64	75	71	78	49	75	84	95
18622	HUNTINGTON MILLS	81	74	73	77	75	87	73	82	75	66	74	62	67	76	73	79	50	76	85	95
18623	LACEYVILLE	84	64	79	63	65	85	65	78	71	61	69	59	54	71	63	77	46	73	82	93
18624	LAKE HARMONY	95	76	122	75	83	101	76	97	80	71	79	71	66	76	82	85	52	89	96	112
18628	LOPEZ	71	80	76	79	80	87	71	78	76	70	76	55	78	75	78	81	52	76	89	89
18629	MEHOOPANY	83	76	75	79	77	89	75	84	77	68	76	64	69	79	75	82	52	78	87	98
18630	MESHOPPEN	79	65	70	66	66	81	65	75	70	61	68	57	57	72	63	75	46	70	78	89
18631	MIFFLINVILLE	80	88	84	87	88	96	79	87	84	77	83	62	85	83	85	89	57	84	98	100
18632	MILDRED	83	59	85	58	62	84	61	77	68	57	66	58	49	67	60	74	44	71	81	92
18634	NANTICOKE	68	62	67	62	63	74	65	69	70	61	68	50	62	67	64	74	47	69	79	81
18635	NESCOPECK	79	77	69	79	75	85	76	80	78	70	77	62	73	79	75	81	53	77	85	95
18636	NOXEN	84	60	78	59	62	84	65	78	72	60	70	59	52	73	61	79	47	73	84	93
18640	PITTSTON	78	75	76	74	75	86	74	80	80	70	78	59	73	78	75	85	54	79	90	94
18641	PITTSTON	76	79	79	78	80	90	73	81	78	70	77	58	76	77	77	83	53	78	91	94
18642	DURYEA	74	79	77	78	80	87	74	80	80	73	79	57	79	78	78	85	54	79	91	92
18643	PITTSTON	79	70	78	69	71	86	71	80	76	66	75	59	66	75	71	82	51	76	88	93
18644	WYOMING	81	92	88	91	92	98	81	89	85	81	85	63	89	84	89	90	59	85	98	102
18651	PLYMOUTH	71	59	67	59	60	74	64	70	69	59	67	53	57	68	62	74	46	69	78	83
18655	SHICKSHINNY	85	72	79	74	74	90	73	85	77	66	75	64	65	78	72	82	51	78	89	99
18656	SWEET VALLEY	86	78	77	81	80	92	77	87	80	70	78	66	71	81	77	84	53	80	90	101
18657	TUNKHANNOCK	83	74	75	76	75	88	74	83	77	68	75	63	68	78	73	81	51	77	86	97
18660	WAPWALLOPEN	83	64	82	63	66	86	65	79	70	60	69	60	54	70	64	76	46	73	82	94
18661	WHITE HAVEN	86	80	88	79	81	96	76	88	81	72	80	65	72	80	78	86	54	82	94	102
18701	WILKES BARRE	37	25	27	28	25	29	45	32	44	37	44	28	36	41	35	45	31	40	40	42
18702	WILKES BARRE	72	63	67	63	63	74	70	71	73	65	72	53	64	72	66	77	50	72	80	85
18704	KINGSTON	77	75	77	75	76	85	76	80	80	73	79	58	75	78	77	85	55	80	90	93
18705	WILKES BARRE	78	82	81	80	82	91	76	83	81	74	80	60	79	80	80	86	55	81	94	96
18706	WILKES BARRE	75	66	71	65	66	79	69	75	74	65	72	55	64	73	67	78	49	73	83	88
18707	MOUNTAIN TOP	105	117	110	119	117	118	104	111	104	106	104	83	111	105	111	106	73	106	112	129
18708	SHAVERTOWN	110	133	127	134	133	133	115	122	116	118	117	90	130	115	127	118	82	118	127	141
18709	LUZERNE	68	59	61	59	58	70	64	67	68	59	66	51	59	67	61	72	45	67	75	80
18801	MONTROSE	78	70	75	71	72	84	70	79	74	65	72	59	65	73	70	78	49	74	84	92
18810	ATHENS	85	75	75	76	75	88	77	83	81	72	79	63	70	82	74	86	54	80	90	98
18812	BRACKNEY	89	96	85	100	94	98	88	93	87	86	87	72	91	89	92	88	61	88	92	109
18817	EAST SMITHFIELD	79	72	72	75	74	85	71	80	73	64	72	61	66	75	71	78	49	74	83	93
18818	FRIENDSVILLE	82	77	74	80	78	88	75	83	76	68	75	63	70	78	75	80	52	77	85	97
18821	GREAT BEND	81	59	83	57	61	84	62	78	69	56	67	58	50	68	61	76	45	72	83	92
18822	HALLSTEAD	77	61	75	61	63	81	63	76	68	57	66	57	54	68	62	74	45	70	80	89
18823	HARFORD	80	70	82	71	73	85	69	81	72	63	70	61	63	71	71	76	48	75	82	94
18824	HOP BOTTOM	83	61	85	60	63	85	62	79	69	58	68	59	51	68	62	75	45	72	82	93
18825	JACKSON	85	68	110	67	75	90	68	86	71	64	70	63	59	68	74	76	47	80	85	100
18826	KINGSLEY	73	67	66	70	68	79	66	75	68	60	67	56	61	69	66	72	46	69	77	87
18828	LAWTON	76	69	69	72	71	82	68	77	71	62	69	58	63	72	68	75	47	71	80	90
18829	LE RAYSVILLE	86	79	78	82	80	93	78	88	80	70	79	66	72	82	77	85	54	81	90	102
18830	LITTLE MEADOWS	82	74	74	77	76	88	73	83	76	66	74	63	68	77	73	80	51	76	85	96
18831	MILAN	78	71	70	74	72	84	70	79	72	63	71	60	65	74	70	76	48	73	81	92
18832	MONROETON	83	64	70	63	64	81	65	75	71	62	69	57	55	73	61	76	47	71	79	90
18833	NEW ALBANY	76	66	67	68	67	80	66	75	69	60	67	57	60	70	65	73	46	69	77	87
18834	NEW MILFORD	79	66	74	68	68	84	68	79	71	61	70	59	60	72	67	77	47	73	82	91
18837	ROME	80	65	69	66	66	81	66	76	70	62	69	58	57	73	63	76	47	71	79	90
18840	SAYRE	86	77	82	77	78	90	80	86	84	75	82	64	74	83	79	88	56	84	93	101
18842	SOUTH GIBSON	93	74	120	73	81	98	74	94	78	70	77	69	64	74	80	83	51	87	93	109
18844	SPRINGVILLE	78	70	71	73	72	84	69	79	72	63	70	60	63	73	69	76	48	73	81	92
18845	STEVENSVILLE	83	59	85	57	62	84	61	77	68	57	66	58	49	67	60	74	44	71	81	92
18846	SUGAR RUN	78	71	70	74	72	84	70	79	72	63	71	60	65	74	70	77	49	73	82	92
18847	SUSQUEHANNA	80	59	81	57	61	81	62	76	68	57	66	57	50	67	61	74	44	71	80	90
18848	TOWANDA	83	72	80	73	74	87	74	82	78	71	77	61	69	78	74	83	53	79	89	97
18850	ULSTER	78	70	70	72	71	83	69	78	72	63	70	59	63	73	68	76	48	72	81	91
	PENNSYLVANIA	94	95	95	95	95	100	94	96	96	91	95	73	94	96	94	99	67	95	101	113
	UNITED STATES	100	100	100	100	100	100	100	100	100	100	100	100	100	100	100	100	100	100	100	100

ZIP CODE			POPULATION			2000-2009 ANNUAL RATE		HOUSEHOLDS					FAMILIES		
#	POST OFFICE NAME	COUNTY FIPS CODE	2000	2009	2014	% Rate	State Centile	2000	2009	2014	% Annual Rate 2000-2009	2009 Average HH Size	2000	2009	% Annual Rate 2000-2009
18851	WARREN CENTER	015	1019	1017	1005	0.0	52	360	370	369	0.3	2.73	288	290	0.1
18853	WYALUSING	015	3528	3481	3427	-0.1	46	1375	1409	1400	0.3	2.41	958	954	0.0
18854	WYSOX	015	2359	2365	2334	0.0	52	920	947	943	0.3	2.50	668	670	0.0
18901	DOYLESTOWN	017	28234	29752	30262	0.6	74	10703	11299	11526	0.6	2.37	6892	7072	0.3
18902	DOYLESTOWN	017	19266	23923	25721	2.4	96	6498	8139	8785	2.5	2.94	5436	6663	2.2
18913	CARVERSVILLE	017	154	158	158	0.3	64	49	51	52	0.4	3.10	37	39	0.6
18914	CHALFONT	017	17300	19129	19988	1.1	87	6123	6802	7133	1.1	2.80	4794	5212	0.9
18915	COLMAR	091	1537	1610	1643	0.5	70	636	679	697	0.7	2.36	480	499	0.4
18917	DUBLIN	017	2083	2218	2279	0.7	77	851	919	951	0.8	2.41	521	539	0.4
18920	ERWINNA	017	698	751	776	0.8	80	274	300	312	1.0	2.49	191	202	0.6
18923	FOUNTAINVILLE	017	412	919	998	9.1	100	142	333	364	9.7	2.74	109	239	8.9
18925	FURLONG	017	2959	5325	6181	6.6	100	999	1864	2187	7.0	2.84	819	1462	6.5
18927	HILLTOWN	017	382	432	475	1.3	90	135	155	171	1.5	2.79	104	115	1.1
18929	JAMISON	017	7304	8154	8638	1.2	88	2305	2598	2769	1.3	3.14	1916	2121	1.1
18930	KINTNERSVILLE	017	2397	2570	2635	0.8	80	887	966	995	0.9	2.66	677	717	0.6
18932	LINE LEXINGTON	017	502	555	582	1.1	87	184	208	220	1.3	2.62	151	167	1.1
18933	LUMBERVILLE	017	97	99	100	0.2	61	37	39	39	0.6	2.54	28	29	0.4
18934	MECHANICSVILLE	017	162	175	183	0.8	80	57	63	67	1.1	2.78	46	51	1.1
18936	MONTGOMERYVILLE	091	59	74	78	2.5	97	5	6	6	2.0	2.50	4	4	0.0
18938	NEW HOPE	017	13048	14512	15071	1.2	88	5602	6263	6537	1.2	2.28	3685	3976	0.8
18940	NEWTOWN	017	27542	28979	29847	0.6	74	9924	10471	10813	0.6	2.74	7559	7790	0.3
18942	OTTSVILLE	017	3270	3443	3575	0.6	74	1245	1344	1405	0.8	2.56	922	969	0.5
18944	PERKASIE	017	21279	23103	23979	0.9	83	7671	8346	8684	0.9	2.76	5850	6230	0.7
18947	PIPERSVILLE	017	5895	6755	7227	1.5	92	2000	2310	2478	1.6	2.90	1512	1701	1.3
18951	QUAKERTOWN	017	31279	35016	36532	1.2	88	11567	13077	13705	1.3	2.63	8368	9189	1.0
18954	RICHBORO	017	10354	10531	10542	0.2	61	3113	3216	3237	0.4	3.22	2841	2907	0.2
18955	RICHLANDTOWN	017	1517	1600	1639	0.6	74	520	560	577	0.8	2.64	393	411	0.5
18960	SELLERSVILLE	017	11741	12943	13306	1.1	87	4373	4906	5079	1.3	2.59	3145	3454	1.0
18964	SOUDERTON	091	12565	13498	13827	0.8	80	4868	5300	5458	0.9	2.50	3468	3675	0.6
18966	SOUTHAMPTON	017	38480	39234	39413	0.2	61	13953	14394	14522	0.3	2.71	10881	11001	0.1
18969	TELFORD	091	14688	15526	15799	0.6	74	5375	5766	5892	0.8	2.64	3941	4119	0.5
18972	UPPER BLACK EDDY	017	3822	4137	4285	0.9	83	1524	1679	1750	1.1	2.46	1089	1162	0.7
18974	WARMINSTER	017	37809	40690	41620	0.8	80	13583	14840	15265	1.0	2.72	10494	11248	0.8
18976	WARRINGTON	017	16424	20259	21724	2.3	96	5613	7000	7540	2.4	2.87	4371	5381	2.3
18977	WASHINGTON CROSSING	017	3699	4367	4535	1.8	93	1369	1663	1744	2.1	2.62	1162	1385	1.9
19001	ABINGTON	091	18627	18541	18500	-0.1	46	6987	7041	7061	0.1	2.58	4888	4770	-0.3
19002	AMBLER	091	30656	32504	33047	0.6	74	11467	12249	12488	0.7	2.59	8182	8447	0.3
19003	ARDMORE	045	13221	13602	13581	0.3	64	5854	5901	5910	0.1	2.19	3245	3115	-0.4
19004	BALA CYNWYD	091	9431	9448	9445	0.0	52	3798	3895	3926	0.3	2.40	2640	2608	-0.1
19006	HUNTINGDON VALLEY	091	20372	20901	21106	0.3	64	7722	7987	8085	0.4	2.54	5836	5904	0.1
19007	BRISTOL	017	21747	21739	21651	0.0	52	8375	8467	8476	0.1	2.54	5463	5327	-0.3
19008	BROOMALL	045	20705	20567	20430	-0.1	46	7507	7491	7459	0.0	2.63	5684	5526	-0.3
19010	BRYN MAWR	045	21317	21094	21012	-0.1	46	7976	7889	7869	-0.1	2.28	4605	4370	-0.6
19012	CHELTENHAM	091	6623	6599	6562	0.0	52	2294	2284	2273	0.0	2.85	1778	1727	-0.3
19013	CHESTER	045	38912	38031	37593	-0.2	38	13625	13269	13138	-0.3	2.62	8666	8119	-0.7
19014	ASTON	045	20769	21224	21364	0.2	61	7490	7723	7798	0.3	2.65	5506	5496	0.0
19015	BROOKHAVEN	045	15921	15900	15849	0.0	52	6349	6385	6378	0.1	2.48	4258	4144	-0.3
19018	CLIFTON HEIGHTS	045	23569	23007	22759	-0.3	29	9886	9748	9679	-0.2	2.35	6123	5797	-0.6
19020	BENSALEM	017	53667	55212	55827	0.3	64	20749	21593	21933	0.4	2.54	13809	13863	0.0
19021	CROYDON	017	10129	10065	10007	-0.1	46	3788	3816	3812	0.1	2.64	2612	2543	-0.3
19022	CRUM LYNNE	045	3709	3762	3769	0.2	61	1520	1555	1562	0.2	2.42	916	898	-0.2
19023	DARBY	045	21440	20981	20730	-0.2	38	7448	7301	7230	-0.2	2.80	5187	4921	-0.6
19025	DRESHER	091	6069	6049	6042	0.0	52	1966	1990	1996	0.1	2.99	1684	1677	0.0
19026	DREXEL HILL	045	31946	31322	30998	-0.2	38	12847	12689	12592	-0.1	2.46	8232	7831	-0.5
19027	ELKINS PARK	091	19726	19799	19772	0.0	52	8008	8105	8119	0.1	2.43	5309	5186	-0.3
19029	ESSINGTON	045	4353	4252	4200	-0.3	29	1749	1718	1702	-0.2	2.47	1137	1075	-0.6
19030	FAIRLESS HILLS	017	12812	13427	13702	0.5	70	4834	5167	5321	0.7	2.58	3464	3585	0.4
19031	FLOURTOWN	091	4006	4111	4142	0.3	64	1519	1585	1605	0.5	2.43	1055	1064	0.1
19032	FOLCROFT	045	6902	6798	6738	-0.2	38	2507	2494	2481	-0.1	2.72	1851	1788	-0.4
19033	FOLSOM	045	7057	6934	6861	-0.2	38	2700	2679	2661	-0.1	2.58	1897	1821	-0.4
19034	FORT WASHINGTON	091	6103	6233	6269	0.2	61	2131	2203	2223	0.4	2.74	1582	1590	0.1
19035	GLADWYNE	091	4050	4045	4032	0.0	52	1476	1488	1490	0.1	2.50	1090	1067	-0.2
19036	GLENOLDEN	045	13576	13356	13229	-0.2	38	5430	5389	5358	-0.1	2.47	3576	3422	-0.5
19038	GLENSIDE	091	31824	31468	31312	-0.1	46	11785	11794	11766	0.0	2.55	8172	7910	-0.4
19040	HATBORO	091	20218	19913	19766	-0.2	38	7810	7805	7783	0.0	2.54	5380	5209	-0.3
19041	HAVERFORD	045	6977	6544	6616	-0.7	8	2604	2592	2655	0.0	2.24	1502	1426	-0.6
19043	HOLMES	045	2810	2724	2689	-0.3	29	1083	1060	1049	-0.2	2.57	750	710	-0.6
19044	HORSHAM	091	16577	16478	16390	-0.1	46	6566	6595	6584	0.0	2.46	4319	4186	-0.3
19046	JENKINTOWN	091	17876	17789	17724	-0.1	46	7438	7473	7473	0.1	2.34	4746	4590	-0.4
19047	LANGHORNE	017	34214	37590	38813	1.0	85	11724	13027	13516	1.1	2.74	8693	9443	0.9
19050	LANSDOWNE	045	28815	28162	27836	-0.2	38	11676	11478	11376	-0.2	2.41	7171	6767	-0.6
19053	FEASTERVILLE TREVOSE	017	26109	26285	26272	0.1	57	9697	9906	9955	0.2	2.64	7288	7242	-0.1
19054	LEVITTOWN	017	17599	17325	17227	-0.2	38	6368	6374	6373	0.0	2.71	4766	4639	-0.3
19055	LEVITTOWN	017	14064	13719	13598	-0.3	29	4847	4809	4796	-0.1	2.85	3750	3629	-0.4
19056	LEVITTOWN	017	15792	15566	15472	-0.2	38	5745	5748	5743	0.0	2.69	4133	4005	-0.3
19057	LEVITTOWN	017	16490	16260	16188	-0.2	38	5663	5683	5694	0.0	2.85	4394	4296	-0.2
19061	MARCUS HOOK	045	26538	30180	31413	1.4	91	9657	10961	11392	1.4	2.74	6922	7769	1.3
19063	MEDIA	045	37739	38460	38479	0.2	61	14540	14787	14827	0.2	2.37	9252	9077	-0.2
19064	SPRINGFIELD	045	24118	23701	23487	-0.2	38	8691	8617	8569	-0.1	2.71	6801	6589	-0.3
19066	MERION STATION	091	5981	5992	5964	0.0	52	1977	1980	1974	0.0	2.75	1511	1473	-0.3
19067	MORRISVILLE	017	53146	53127	52965	0.0	52	20292	20503	20521	0.1	2.58	14775	14529	-0.2
19070	MORTON	045	7247	7191	7140	-0.1	46	2787	2790	2780	0.0	2.57	1913	1849	-0.4
19072	NARBERTH	091	9596	9509	9445	-0.1	46	4111	4116	4103	0.0	2.31	2523	2425	-0.4
19073	NEWTOWN SQUARE	045	16882	17874	18156	0.6	74	6678	7073	7204	0.6	2.44	4693	4795	0.2
19074	NORWOOD	045	5985	5860	5801	-0.2	38	2286	2272	2261	-0.1	2.58	1537	1472	-0.5
19075	ORELAND	091	7042	6910	6845	-0.2	38	2711	2703	2692	0.0	2.55	2034	1973	-0.3
19076	PROSPECT PARK	045	6594	6511	6450	-0.1	46	2577	2565	2553	-0.1	2.47	1601	1529	-0.5
19078	RIDLEY PARK	045	11713	11508	11387	-0.2	38	4793	4755	4726	-0.1	2.41	3065	2926	-0.5
19079	SHARON HILL	045	8840	8847	8815	0.0	52	3332	3366	3368	0.1	2.62	2292	2244	-0.2
19081	SWARTHMORE	045	10271	10300	10222	0.0	52	3652	3633	3608	-0.1	2.47	2506	2411	-0.4
19082	UPPER DARBY	045	38348	38753	38634	0.1	57	14765	14747	14691	0.0	2.61	9275	8916	-0.4
19083	HAVERTOWN	045	36570	35898	35542	-0.2	38	13453	13318	13230	-0.1	2.68	10036	9662	-0.4
19085	VILLANOVA	045	9134	9321	9263	0.2	61	1844	1833	1822	-0.1	2.99	1528	1489	-0.3
19086	WALLINGFORD	045	11827	11747	11674	-0.1	46	4409	4411	4396	0.0	2.60	3257	3169	-0.3
19087	WAYNE	029	32258	32330	32414	0.0	52	12912	13066	13178	0.1	2.31	8116	7893	-0.3
	PENNSYLVANIA					0.3					0.4	2.45			0.1
	UNITED STATES					1.0					1.1	2.59			0.9

ZIP CODE #	POST OFFICE NAME	RACE (%) White 2000	White 2009	Black 2000	Black 2009	Asian/Pacific 2000	Asian/Pacific 2009	% Hispanic Origin 2000	% Hispanic Origin 2009	2009 AGE DISTRIBUTION (%) 0-4	5-9	10-14	15-19	20-24	25-44	45-64	65-84	85+	18+	MEDIAN AGE 2009	% 2009 Males	% 2009 Females
18851	WARREN CENTER	98.9	98.5	0.2	0.2	0.2	0.3	0.8	1.2	6.5	6.9	7.4	6.9	5.0	24.2	28.8	12.8	1.6	74.6	40.4	52.2	47.8
18853	WYALUSING	97.4	96.7	0.2	0.3	0.2	0.3	1.2	1.7	5.5	5.8	6.1	6.3	4.5	23.9	30.2	15.1	2.7	78.7	43.4	48.8	51.2
18854	WYSOX	97.4	96.7	0.3	0.3	0.5	0.7	0.8	1.1	5.4	5.8	6.3	7.4	5.4	23.8	29.8	14.4	1.7	78.0	42.0	50.4	49.6
18901	DOYLESTOWN	95.6	93.5	2.1	3.0	1.3	2.1	1.4	2.1	4.9	5.2	5.8	7.1	6.3	21.8	28.6	15.2	5.1	80.1	44.2	47.6	52.4
18902	DOYLESTOWN	96.3	94.7	1.0	1.4	1.2	1.9	1.7	2.5	8.7	9.1	8.8	6.9	3.3	26.0	29.2	7.3	0.7	68.7	38.0	49.3	50.7
18913	CARVERSVILLE	97.4	97.5	0.6	0.6	0.6	0.6	1.3	1.3	4.4	5.1	6.3	6.3	3.8	16.5	41.8	14.6	1.3	80.4	49.0	46.8	53.2
18914	CHALFONT	96.0	94.1	1.3	1.7	1.7	2.8	1.1	1.7	8.2	7.9	7.6	6.6	3.4	27.0	27.8	10.4	1.2	71.7	38.7	49.0	51.0
18915	COLMAR	90.0	85.2	2.0	2.6	6.2	9.8	2.0	2.7	5.6	6.0	6.4	7.0	5.8	23.7	31.1	12.6	1.8	77.4	41.4	49.4	50.6
18917	DUBLIN	95.1	93.2	1.5	2.0	1.3	2.1	1.9	2.8	8.5	7.4	6.5	6.5	8.9	33.1	21.4	6.6	1.0	73.8	31.6	48.6	51.4
18920	ERWINNA	98.1	97.2	0.4	0.5	0.4	0.7	1.0	1.6	4.7	5.5	6.5	5.6	3.6	20.8	36.6	14.9	1.9	79.9	46.7	52.7	47.3
18923	FOUNTAINVILLE	96.4	96.1	1.2	1.3	0.7	1.0	1.7	2.0	7.0	7.5	7.9	6.7	3.7	27.2	29.1	9.5	1.4	73.1	39.5	50.4	49.6
18925	FURLONG	97.4	95.9	0.6	0.7	1.3	2.3	0.9	1.4	4.9	5.8	6.7	6.3	3.5	20.0	35.1	15.8	1.9	78.5	46.6	48.7	51.3
18927	HILLTOWN	98.2	97.5	1.3	1.6	0.3	0.5	0.3	0.7	6.7	6.9	6.7	6.0	5.3	23.1	29.6	13.9	1.6	75.2	41.9	48.8	51.2
18929	JAMISON	95.8	93.8	1.0	1.4	2.3	3.7	1.0	1.4	9.1	9.2	9.1	7.2	4.5	29.6	24.8	5.8	0.5	67.6	33.9	48.8	51.2
18930	KINTNERSVILLE	98.7	98.1	0.3	0.4	0.4	0.7	0.7	1.1	4.6	5.7	6.7	6.5	4.0	24.4	35.3	11.5	1.2	78.8	43.7	51.5	48.5
18932	LINE LEXINGTON	97.0	95.9	1.0	1.3	1.0	1.6	1.4	2.0	5.8	6.8	7.6	7.4	4.5	19.6	31.9	13.5	2.9	74.6	43.8	48.8	51.2
18933	LUMBERVILLE	99.0	96.0	1.0	1.0	0.0	1.0	1.0	1.0	4.0	5.1	7.1	6.1	4.0	17.2	40.4	14.1	2.0	78.8	48.6	46.5	53.5
18934	MECHANICSVILLE	97.5	97.1	0.6	1.1	0.6	0.6	1.2	1.1	4.6	6.3	7.4	6.9	3.4	18.3	39.4	12.6	1.1	77.1	46.5	48.6	51.4
18936	MONTGOMERYVILLE	81.7	77.0	5.0	5.4	11.7	16.2	1.7	1.4	8.1	8.1	9.5	8.1	2.7	18.9	27.0	13.5	4.1	66.2	42.1	47.3	52.7
18938	NEW HOPE	96.9	95.7	0.7	1.0	0.9	1.4	2.1	2.9	4.3	5.0	5.9	5.3	3.2	19.1	36.6	18.2	2.5	81.3	49.0	49.3	50.7
18940	NEWTOWN	94.5	91.9	1.0	1.4	3.3	5.3	1.2	1.7	6.7	7.6	8.3	6.8	3.9	24.8	31.8	8.7	1.5	72.7	40.5	48.4	51.6
18942	OTTSVILLE	97.8	97.0	0.3	0.4	0.3	0.5	1.3	1.9	4.9	5.8	6.6	6.2	3.4	23.6	35.4	12.5	1.5	78.7	44.7	50.8	49.2
18944	PERKASIE	97.9	97.0	0.6	0.8	0.5	0.9	1.0	1.5	7.0	7.3	7.6	7.1	4.8	27.0	28.6	9.3	1.3	73.4	38.4	49.6	50.4
18947	PIPERSVILLE	96.5	95.1	1.0	1.3	0.9	1.5	1.7	2.5	7.3	8.1	8.6	6.9	3.5	25.4	30.2	9.0	1.0	71.4	39.8	50.6	49.4
18951	QUAKERTOWN	96.4	94.9	0.9	1.2	1.1	1.8	1.6	2.4	6.7	6.9	6.9	6.6	5.2	27.0	28.5	10.2	2.0	75.2	39.1	49.5	50.5
18954	RICHBORO	97.1	95.6	0.5	0.6	1.8	2.9	0.7	1.0	5.5	6.6	7.9	8.4	4.2	20.9	33.3	11.2	2.1	74.4	42.4	48.9	51.1
18955	RICHLANDTOWN	98.2	97.4	0.5	0.6	0.5	0.8	1.2	1.7	6.2	6.2	6.4	7.0	5.8	25.6	25.4	11.9	5.4	76.1	40.1	46.9	53.1
18960	SELLERSVILLE	97.6	96.8	0.6	0.8	0.4	0.7	1.3	1.8	6.3	6.6	6.9	7.0	5.2	24.9	28.7	11.9	2.6	75.8	40.7	49.8	50.2
18964	SOUDERTON	93.5	90.9	1.2	1.5	3.1	4.7	2.8	3.9	6.5	6.5	6.4	6.1	5.2	25.2	25.1	15.2	3.8	76.7	40.9	48.0	52.0
18966	SOUTHAMPTON	97.0	95.5	0.5	0.7	1.6	2.7	0.8	1.3	5.3	5.8	6.6	6.8	4.6	22.9	31.0	14.4	2.7	78.0	43.7	48.0	52.0
18969	TELFORD	93.9	91.4	1.6	2.0	2.6	4.1	2.3	3.2	7.5	6.7	6.9	6.4	4.8	27.3	25.5	11.8	3.2	74.8	38.8	48.3	51.7
18972	UPPER BLACK EDDY	98.4	97.8	0.5	0.7	0.2	0.4	0.7	1.1	4.8	5.5	6.3	6.0	3.9	23.3	36.5	12.3	1.4	79.7	45.1	51.0	49.0
18974	WARMINSTER	92.0	89.8	2.9	3.3	2.0	3.3	4.0	5.0	6.6	6.7	6.9	6.7	5.3	25.9	26.7	13.3	1.9	75.4	39.5	48.6	51.4
18976	WARRINGTON	94.4	92.1	2.1	2.6	2.3	3.6	1.6	2.2	7.4	7.6	7.6	6.9	4.6	28.3	27.6	8.9	1.1	73.0	37.2	49.7	50.3
18977	WASHINGTON CROSSING	97.1	95.8	0.7	1.1	1.4	2.2	1.0	1.5	5.0	6.1	7.6	7.0	3.6	18.4	37.5	13.7	1.2	76.9	46.3	49.0	51.0
19001	ABINGTON	82.1	77.4	12.4	15.0	3.3	5.1	1.9	2.5	6.2	6.4	6.7	6.4	5.1	24.4	27.2	13.5	4.1	76.5	41.7	47.6	52.4
19002	AMBLER	87.8	83.3	6.2	7.6	4.8	7.6	1.3	1.8	6.0	6.3	7.0	6.8	5.1	21.9	29.8	13.6	3.5	76.0	42.9	47.6	52.4
19003	ARDMORE	83.8	76.7	10.9	15.9	2.9	4.5	2.0	3.0	5.0	4.6	5.2	6.6	9.3	28.5	25.7	12.1	3.0	82.1	38.6	48.1	51.9
19004	BALA CYNWYD	92.6	89.3	2.1	2.8	3.9	6.2	1.4	2.0	5.3	5.8	6.7	6.1	3.8	21.5	29.4	17.3	4.1	78.1	45.5	47.8	52.2
19006	HUNTINGDON VALLEY	94.9	92.3	0.7	0.9	3.5	5.8	1.1	1.5	4.2	4.8	5.6	6.1	4.3	19.4	31.1	20.0	4.5	81.4	48.6	47.8	52.2
19007	BRISTOL	76.3	71.0	14.3	16.5	3.1	4.6	8.8	11.6	6.6	6.4	6.4	6.5	6.9	27.9	25.9	11.2	2.2	76.6	37.2	48.7	51.3
19008	BROOMALL	92.6	88.3	1.0	1.5	5.7	9.3	0.6	0.8	4.9	5.2	6.0	6.2	4.7	21.6	29.4	17.4	4.6	79.9	45.8	47.5	52.5
19010	BRYN MAWR	85.9	77.6	5.4	10.4	6.7	9.7	1.7	2.4	4.2	4.4	5.3	9.2	11.0	23.5	23.5	13.5	5.3	83.0	38.4	46.3	53.7
19012	CHELTENHAM	74.1	67.6	13.8	15.9	9.0	12.9	2.6	3.4	5.4	5.9	6.7	7.2	5.5	23.5	31.0	12.1	2.7	76.9	42.0	47.6	52.4
19013	CHESTER	19.4	14.8	75.4	79.7	0.6	0.8	5.2	5.3	8.3	8.2	7.4	9.2	9.5	23.9	21.5	10.2	1.8	71.4	30.9	47.1	52.9
19014	ASTON	91.4	88.5	6.2	8.0	1.0	1.7	1.1	1.7	6.0	6.2	6.7	7.8	5.4	25.1	28.3	12.5	1.9	77.1	40.1	47.7	52.3
19015	BROOKHAVEN	80.0	75.8	17.2	20.4	0.9	1.5	1.6	2.1	6.4	6.7	6.7	6.4	5.6	26.0	27.4	12.6	2.0	76.0	39.9	47.2	52.8
19018	CLIFTON HEIGHTS	90.5	86.0	4.4	6.4	3.8	5.9	1.1	1.5	6.2	6.0	6.1	6.2	6.2	28.2	26.4	12.2	2.5	77.7	39.3	48.6	51.4
19020	BENSALEM	83.3	77.9	6.0	7.3	7.1	10.4	4.5	5.9	5.8	5.6	5.7	6.0	6.4	30.7	28.0	10.2	1.7	79.2	38.2	49.7	50.3
19021	CROYDON	93.3	91.0	2.9	3.6	1.3	2.0	3.7	5.2	6.2	6.2	6.3	6.4	5.8	29.2	28.0	10.6	1.4	77.4	38.4	50.8	49.2
19022	CRUM LYNNE	87.8	83.0	8.4	11.7	1.1	1.7	2.3	3.3	7.4	7.0	6.6	7.3	7.4	26.9	26.0	9.8	1.8	74.5	35.8	50.4	49.6
19023	DARBY	59.5	53.2	36.8	42.3	1.2	1.8	1.0	1.2	7.7	8.0	7.7	8.3	7.1	25.2	23.7	9.8	2.8	71.6	34.1	47.2	52.8
19025	DRESHER	86.1	80.3	5.1	6.4	7.8	12.2	0.9	1.2	5.3	6.4	8.6	8.6	4.5	18.7	33.1	13.0	1.7	73.2	43.4	49.0	51.0
19026	DREXEL HILL	93.3	90.4	1.9	2.8	3.6	5.4	1.0	1.4	6.7	6.5	6.6	6.5	6.5	27.3	26.2	11.1	2.6	76.2	38.4	47.8	52.2
19027	ELKINS PARK	60.7	55.3	28.8	30.9	7.7	10.8	2.1	2.7	5.0	5.1	5.5	6.3	7.4	24.0	29.4	14.6	2.6	80.4	42.4	47.2	52.8
19029	ESSINGTON	97.1	95.6	0.8	1.2	0.4	0.8	1.3	1.9	6.0	5.8	5.6	6.3	6.4	27.1	27.7	12.9	2.1	78.7	40.1	49.7	50.3
19030	FAIRLESS HILLS	91.8	88.7	3.1	3.9	3.0	4.6	2.7	3.8	6.0	6.1	6.6	6.3	5.1	27.5	28.8	11.8	1.9	77.3	40.2	47.8	52.2
19031	FLOURTOWN	92.9	89.9	3.2	4.4	2.7	4.3	1.0	1.4	5.5	5.8	7.1	6.1	4.4	22.3	29.4	15.3	4.1	77.4	44.2	48.2	51.8
19032	FOLCROFT	93.9	91.0	3.9	5.9	1.0	1.6	1.1	1.6	7.1	6.8	6.6	6.8	6.0	26.8	25.0	13.6	1.4	75.0	37.6	48.9	51.1
19033	FOLSOM	96.0	93.9	2.1	3.3	1.2	2.1	0.7	0.9	5.1	5.4	6.0	6.5	5.0	24.8	29.0	15.3	2.8	79.4	43.1	48.4	51.6
19034	FORT WASHINGTON	89.2	84.6	3.6	4.6	6.2	9.6	1.0	1.3	5.3	5.5	6.5	6.8	5.6	21.9	32.4	13.6	2.4	77.8	43.8	49.1	50.9
19035	GLADWYNE	96.3	94.6	0.6	0.9	2.2	3.5	1.0	1.5	4.8	5.9	7.9	7.1	2.9	16.2	29.1	17.3	8.8	76.1	48.4	46.9	53.1
19036	GLENOLDEN	93.7	90.6	3.8	5.7	1.5	2.4	0.8	1.2	6.3	6.2	6.3	6.4	5.7	27.5	26.6	12.9	2.1	77.3	39.3	47.4	52.6
19038	GLENSIDE	84.4	80.3	11.9	14.6	2.3	3.5	1.3	1.8	5.5	5.7	6.2	6.5	5.5	23.0	28.9	14.4	4.3	78.5	43.3	46.8	53.2
19040	HATBORO	94.3	92.1	2.1	2.7	2.2	3.5	1.4	2.1	5.7	5.7	5.9	6.4	6.1	25.1	28.3	13.9	2.9	78.7	41.6	48.6	51.4
19041	HAVERFORD	89.5	83.9	5.3	9.5	3.6	4.8	1.9	2.5	3.8	4.2	4.9	8.5	8.7	21.6	25.9	16.3	6.1	83.8	43.7	49.3	50.7
19043	HOLMES	96.0	94.1	1.6	2.5	1.2	2.0	0.7	1.1	6.0	6.0	6.3	6.5	5.9	28.2	27.3	11.4	2.5	77.7	39.0	48.9	51.1
19044	HORSHAM	87.9	83.2	4.8	6.1	5.2	8.1	1.8	2.5	6.5	6.5	6.7	7.1	7.0	28.6	28.2	8.4	1.0	75.7	37.4	49.3	50.7
19046	JENKINTOWN	93.4	90.7	2.3	3.0	3.1	4.8	1.1	1.6	4.6	4.8	5.3	6.2	5.7	21.2	29.4	17.9	4.9	81.5	46.4	46.0	54.0
19047	LANGHORNE	92.8	89.9	2.9	3.6	2.8	4.5	1.7	2.3	5.5	6.0	6.8	7.5	6.2	25.6	30.6	9.6	2.2	77.3	39.8	49.1	50.9
19050	LANSDOWNE	50.9	43.7	43.8	49.7	2.5	3.7	1.2	1.5	6.1	6.2	6.4	6.5	6.3	26.2	28.5	11.2	2.7	77.2	39.8	46.7	53.3
19053	FEASTERVILLE TREVOSE	93.1	91.0	4.0	4.7	1.6	2.5	1.5	2.1	5.4	5.9	6.3	6.2	4.8	26.1	30.3	12.7	2.1	78.4	41.9	49.1	50.9
19054	LEVITTOWN	94.3	92.4	2.3	3.0	1.4	2.2	1.7	2.4	6.1	6.2	6.6	6.9	5.7	27.0	28.7	11.2	1.7	77.0	39.4	48.7	51.3
19055	LEVITTOWN	94.5	92.7	2.4	3.1	0.8	1.2	2.4	3.4	6.4	6.5	6.9	6.9	5.3	26.6	27.6	11.7	1.9	75.8	39.5	48.8	51.2
19056	LEVITTOWN	90.3	87.1	4.8	6.0	2.1	3.3	2.9	4.0	6.3	6.2	6.3	6.6	6.6	26.9	27.3	11.9	1.9	77.1	38.6	49.2	50.8
19057	LEVITTOWN	89.1	86.9	7.9	9.0	0.9	1.4	2.5	3.5	6.0	6.7	6.9	6.9	5.6	25.9	27.4	12.9	1.8	76.0	39.4	48.5	51.5
19061	MARCUS HOOK	92.3	88.7	4.6	6.5	1.7	2.9	1.4	2.0	7.0	7.0	7.3	7.0	5.3	27.4	27.4	10.1	1.5	74.3	37.8	48.7	51.3
19063	MEDIA	90.4	86.2	5.9	8.2	2.3	3.8	1.1	1.6	4.5	5.0	5.7	6.0	5.2	21.4	29.5	16.9	5.7	80.9	46.4	46.8	53.2
19064	SPRINGFIELD	96.3	94.2	0.8	1.3	2.1	3.6	0.7	1.0	5.3	5.6	6.2	6.5	5.0	22.4	29.7	15.9	3.4	78.8	44.2	47.7	52.3
19066	MERION STATION	93.7	91.1	2.1	2.7	2.7	4.4	1.4	2.0	5.0	5.7	7.1	10.3	7.0	17.9	31.5	13.5	2.1	77.8	42.3	46.6	53.4
19067	MORRISVILLE	88.2	84.6	6.8	8.0	3.1	4.9	2.4	3.2	6.7	7.2	7.6	6.5	4.5	25.4	29.8	10.8	1.5	74.2	40.6	48.5	51.5
19070	MORTON	86.9	82.9	9.8	12.3	2.2	3.5	0.9	1.2	5.5	5.7	6.2	7.0	6.3	25.2	28.6	13.0	2.6	78.1	41.0	47.8	52.2
19072	NARBERTH	94.5	92.1	1.4	1.8	2.9	4.6	1.3	1.8	5.1	5.3	6.7	6.2	5.0	24.4	31.5	13.7	2.2	79.0	43.4	47.2	52.8
19073	NEWTOWN SQUARE	95.2	92.2	1.2	2.0	2.7	4.6	0.8	1.2	5.3	5.9	7.2	6.5	3.6	19.8	29.7	17.2	4.9	77.0	46.1	47.5	52.5
19074	NORWOOD	97.6	96.1	1.1	1.8	0.7	1.2	0.7	1.1	6.2	6.0	6.3	6.7	7.1	27.4	27.9	10.8	1.6	77.5	38.4	48.3	51.7
19075	ORELAND	90.8	88.0	6.2	7.5	1.9	3.0	1.1	1.6	5.9	6.2	6.9	6.5	4.8	23.2	30.4	13.3	2.7	76.8	42.7	48.4	51.6
19076	PROSPECT PARK	95.4	93.0	1.4	2.1	1.8	3.0	0.9	1.4	6.3	6.0	5.9	6.5	7.1	28.2	26.3	10.7	2.9	77.8	37.8	48.1	51.9
19078	RIDLEY PARK	96.7	95.0	1.0	1.5	1.3	2.3	0.6	0.9	5.7	5.7	5.9	6.0	5.6	26.2	28.0	13.9	3.0	78.9	41.6	47.7	52.3
19079	SHARON HILL	44.7	37.8	51.9	58.2	1.0	1.5	1.3	1.5	6.5	6.9	7.3	7.6	6.6	25.0	26.4	11.9	1.8	74.5	37.6	46.2	53.8
19081	SWARTHMORE	89.8	85.1	3.5	5.1	4.0	6.4	2.3	3.2	4.6	5.1	5.9	11.4	11.9	19.5	26.0	13.3	2.4	80.8	37.6	47.7	52.3
19082	UPPER DARBY	60.2	50.5	20.4	25.0	15.4	20.1	2.4	3.0	7.0	6.9	6.7	7.1	7.2	29.0	25.4	9.1	1.7	75.2	35.4	48.1	51.9
19083	HAVERTOWN	95.1	92.3	1.0	1.5	2.9	4.9	0.8	1.1	6.5	6.8	7.3	6.9	5.2	24.0	28.6	12.1	2.7	75.1	40.8	48.0	52.0
19085	VILLANOVA	92.2	87.9	2.2	3.3	3.8	6.2	2.5	3.7	3.6	4.3	5.3	28.1	18.1	10.4	19.8	9.2	1.3	83.9	22.4	48.9	51.1
19086	WALLINGFORD	92.9	89.3	3.5	5.0	2.3	3.9	1.2	1.8	5.1	5.9	7.0	7.1	4.6	20.6	31.6	15.0	3.1	76.9	44.8	47.8	52.2
19087	WAYNE	91.5	87.5	3.1	4.3	4.2	6.6	1.6	2.2	5.4	5.6	6.2	8.5	7.4	21.8	29.5	13.4	2.2	79.2	41.6	46.6	53.4
	PENNSYLVANIA	85.4	83.2	10.0	10.7	1.8	2.7	3.2	4.2	5.8	6.0	6.3	7.1	6.5	24.8	27.8	13.1	2.6	77.8	40.4	48.5	51.5
	UNITED STATES	75.1	72.0	12.3	12.7	3.8	4.6	12.5	15.7	6.8	6.7	6.6	7.1	6.9	27.0	26.0	10.9	1.9	75.7	36.9	49.2	50.8

#	POST OFFICE NAME	2009 Per Capita Income	2009 HH Income Base	2009 HOUSEHOLD INCOME DISTRIBUTION (%) Less than $25,000	$25,000 to $49,999	$50,000 to $99,999	$100,000 to $149,999	$150,000 or More	MEDIAN HOUSEHOLD INCOME 2009	2014	2009 National Centile	2009 State Centile	2009 Home Value Base	2009 HOME VALUE DISTRIBUTION (%) Less than $50,000	$50,000 to $89,999	$90,000 to $174,999	$175,000 to $399,999	$400,000 or More	2009 Median Home Value
18851	WARREN CENTER	20038	370	18.6	29.5	44.3	6.8	0.8	51318	51267	64	65	300	9.3	17.3	49.0	20.3	4.0	137745
18853	WYALUSING	21653	1409	26.4	31.7	33.4	5.9	2.6	43206	45117	43	40	1096	9.3	18.7	47.1	21.6	3.3	129020
18854	WYSOX	22279	947	21.1	35.6	32.6	7.7	3.0	45412	46502	49	48	773	17.6	12.3	38.9	26.1	5.0	136004
18901	DOYLESTOWN	43452	11299	11.7	14.5	30.6	24.0	19.3	86116	92870	94	96	7960	1.9	0.7	4.9	50.6	41.9	363605
18902	DOYLESTOWN	50657	8139	5.4	10.1	23.3	28.4	32.9	124519	124462	99	99	7497	1.4	1.4	1.1	33.6	62.5	462550
18913	CARVERSVILLE	52009	51	7.8	9.8	19.6	27.5	35.3	122782	127472	99	99	46	0.0	0.0	0.0	8.7	91.3	716667
18914	CHALFONT	39654	6802	4.6	11.2	35.1	31.5	17.7	98511	103324	96	97	6103	0.8	0.9	5.2	66.1	27.0	330945
18915	COLMAR	37451	679	7.1	20.6	35.2	27.8	9.3	79865	84852	92	94	510	0.0	0.0	2.7	89.0	8.2	279825
18917	DUBLIN	30195	919	12.7	22.6	42.2	18.0	4.5	64031	64141	82	85	375	0.0	0.8	17.1	76.0	6.1	274593
18920	ERWINNA	40171	300	11.3	15.0	35.7	25.3	12.7	79556	82480	92	94	253	1.2	1.2	2.0	31.6	64.0	498611
18923	FOUNTAINVILLE	34405	333	8.4	13.8	41.7	25.2	10.8	76642	78686	90	93	269	0.0	1.5	9.3	56.1	33.1	318750
18925	FURLONG	45242	1864	7.0	12.8	30.1	24.0	26.1	100093	105538	97	98	1803	0.6	0.6	1.4	47.3	50.1	400859
18927	HILLTOWN	35107	155	10.3	12.9	49.7	16.1	11.0	76071	80114	90	92	142	0.0	0.0	4.2	66.9	28.9	328571
18929	JAMISON	44215	2598	2.8	6.4	25.9	34.8	30.1	124124	125774	99	99	2491	0.0	0.0	2.3	58.9	38.7	360574
18930	KINTNERSVILLE	34796	966	8.7	16.7	37.5	28.0	9.2	78418	82113	91	93	804	0.1	0.2	5.2	55.3	39.1	347929
18932	LINE LEXINGTON	40621	208	6.7	12.0	37.0	31.3	13.0	92750	96918	96	96	183	0.0	1.1	4.4	59.6	35.0	359559
18933	LUMBERVILLE	62676	39	5.1	7.7	17.9	35.9	33.3	130336	127022	99	100	35	0.0	0.0	0.0	8.6	91.4	715909
18934	MECHANICSVILLE	57786	63	9.5	7.9	20.6	25.4	36.5	126092	129580	99	99	57	0.0	0.0	0.0	14.0	86.0	638158
18936	MONTGOMERYVILLE	9399	6	0.0	0.0	33.3	33.3	33.3	125000	125000	99	99	6	0.0	0.0	33.3	0.0	66.7	450000
18938	NEW HOPE	55631	6263	9.0	16.9	27.8	21.9	24.4	91747	100106	95	96	5185	0.4	0.0	3.0	37.7	58.9	472937
18940	NEWTOWN	50879	10471	4.8	9.1	29.0	27.2	30.0	114107	116898	98	99	8981	0.2	0.2	4.9	53.4	41.4	362716
18942	OTTSVILLE	37188	1344	7.6	20.6	39.9	20.5	11.5	71397	72678	88	90	1069	0.0	0.6	4.6	47.8	47.1	385417
18944	PERKASIE	33305	8346	8.9	15.3	39.9	26.0	9.8	79401	83984	92	94	6709	0.2	0.3	6.9	71.9	20.7	288080
18947	PIPERSVILLE	38194	2310	6.2	14.3	32.5	31.0	15.9	93534	100560	96	97	1990	1.4	1.9	3.6	42.5	50.7	404778
18951	QUAKERTOWN	27453	13077	12.9	21.2	43.8	18.4	3.7	64758	65053	83	86	10240	4.5	3.0	20.7	61.6	10.3	239937
18954	RICHBORO	45228	3216	2.7	8.4	23.9	30.9	34.0	127354	128423	99	100	3139	0.0	0.1	0.6	46.1	53.2	413668
18955	RICHLANDTOWN	26636	560	9.8	25.7	47.1	13.2	4.1	63653	64358	82	84	400	0.0	0.3	39.0	55.0	5.8	206522
18960	SELLERSVILLE	30874	4906	11.3	19.5	40.6	21.6	7.0	69600	71698	87	89	3763	2.2	1.4	12.1	70.8	13.4	262918
18964	SOUDERTON	31989	5300	11.6	20.2	38.5	22.9	6.8	71718	75561	88	90	3734	0.2	0.6	16.6	72.9	9.7	259476
18966	SOUTHAMPTON	40458	14394	6.8	12.7	35.2	27.7	17.7	91627	98711	95	96	12641	0.1	0.1	7.7	65.2	26.9	333882
18969	TELFORD	31271	5766	13.1	15.6	42.1	22.2	7.0	74524	76983	89	91	4180	0.4	0.2	13.7	71.6	14.1	261188
18972	UPPER BLACK EDDY	32851	1679	11.7	22.9	38.9	19.1	7.4	67682	69440	85	88	1408	1.1	1.0	6.0	53.6	38.4	348589
18974	WARMINSTER	33220	14840	9.3	18.4	37.5	25.6	9.2	77456	81464	91	93	11552	0.2	0.9	4.9	81.5	12.6	286235
18976	WARRINGTON	36157	7000	6.3	10.2	38.8	29.6	15.1	89816	97430	95	96	5611	0.0	0.2	5.0	64.1	30.6	347664
18977	WASHINGTON CROSSING	66337	1663	4.9	7.2	23.0	24.5	40.4	132670	134559	99	100	1558	0.0	0.0	0.3	18.2	81.5	610108
19001	ABINGTON	33280	7041	9.2	19.7	37.6	24.6	8.8	75698	78592	90	92	5506	0.3	0.1	9.3	83.3	7.0	234705
19002	AMBLER	48776	12249	7.6	14.9	32.0	20.3	25.2	90629	98681	95	96	9141	0.6	0.4	8.4	42.8	47.8	389398
19003	ARDMORE	43348	5901	13.2	17.7	33.8	20.9	14.4	76088	79246	90	92	3632	0.6	0.4	9.2	66.6	23.2	279766
19004	BALA CYNWYD	57425	3895	8.8	15.5	26.0	19.8	29.9	99390	107089	97	97	3148	0.0	0.6	4.6	38.3	56.5	442213
19006	HUNTINGDON VALLEY	49541	7987	10.1	13.6	27.3	23.0	26.0	97737	104596	96	97	6468	0.6	0.1	2.8	53.3	43.2	377495
19007	BRISTOL	22911	8467	23.1	26.2	36.8	11.0	2.9	50623	52569	63	63	4871	0.7	1.3	55.7	40.4	2.0	168222
19008	BROOMALL	34737	7491	9.5	18.9	38.3	20.1	13.2	75448	78385	90	92	6276	0.2	0.2	3.1	66.6	29.9	339608
19010	BRYN MAWR	52383	7889	15.0	16.0	25.8	15.4	27.7	83051	88822	93	95	4888	0.8	0.8	7.2	27.5	63.6	573581
19012	CHELTENHAM	34189	2284	9.3	13.5	38.8	25.1	13.2	81745	84737	93	95	1960	1.1	0.0	10.6	82.4	5.8	253958
19013	CHESTER	16191	13269	39.6	29.5	23.9	5.2	1.8	33018	33843	13	5	6271	17.8	40.2	37.3	4.5	0.2	81080
19014	ASTON	31436	7723	9.4	16.5	42.3	23.7	8.0	75248	78082	89	91	6630	4.0	2.0	12.7	76.7	4.6	240029
19015	BROOKHAVEN	27035	6385	14.3	26.5	41.7	14.0	3.5	61272	63555	79	80	4836	0.8	9.1	43.3	46.3	0.5	168149
19018	CLIFTON HEIGHTS	28253	9748	15.7	24.8	43.4	12.4	3.7	61244	63632	79	80	6240	0.8	1.6	44.7	51.9	1.1	179762
19020	BENSALEM	29821	21593	14.0	20.5	39.9	20.1	5.6	66315	67435	84	87	11855	3.9	1.4	13.6	77.1	4.0	232583
19021	CROYDON	26427	3816	12.5	22.2	47.6	14.6	3.1	63693	63664	82	84	2739	1.1	2.0	40.5	55.2	1.2	182708
19022	CRUM LYNNE	22055	1555	26.2	28.7	34.1	9.3	1.7	45251	49026	49	47	838	0.8	6.8	70.6	20.4	1.3	136176
19023	DARBY	19675	7301	24.6	26.8	37.4	9.1	2.0	48476	51942	58	58	4818	3.4	23.0	68.9	4.4	0.2	110522
19025	DRESHER	52322	1990	6.3	10.6	24.8	21.5	36.8	121052	126551	99	99	1891	0.4	0.4	0.5	46.6	52.0	410907
19026	DREXEL HILL	32261	12689	13.1	23.8	36.4	18.6	8.2	65608	68986	84	86	8419	0.2	0.5	24.0	70.3	5.0	234744
19027	ELKINS PARK	41961	8105	11.3	19.9	32.8	21.0	15.0	75620	78530	90	92	5124	0.1	0.6	10.1	68.7	20.6	286321
19029	ESSINGTON	25700	1718	14.7	23.6	49.5	11.0	1.2	61564	64024	79	81	1161	0.0	1.1	57.0	41.1	0.8	166622
19030	FAIRLESS HILLS	30578	5167	15.3	17.8	38.8	20.5	7.5	71666	74221	88	90	4088	6.0	2.3	7.6	83.3	0.8	228502
19031	FLOURTOWN	46367	1585	4.6	13.8	34.1	27.7	19.7	94128	101010	96	97	1252	0.0	0.6	4.1	75.2	20.1	319397
19032	FOLCROFT	24123	2494	16.0	20.1	49.6	11.8	2.6	62555	64551	81	82	1932	0.0	2.8	85.7	10.6	0.8	137790
19033	FOLSOM	29292	2679	14.6	19.9	39.4	20.6	5.6	66486	69481	85	88	2255	0.1	1.0	16.9	79.6	2.5	221654
19034	FORT WASHINGTON	49683	2203	6.2	12.8	33.1	22.8	25.1	95772	102806	96	97	1762	0.6	0.6	2.3	43.8	52.7	415016
19035	GLADWYNE	86046	1488	6.5	7.3	15.9	9.6	60.8	205048	209091	100	100	1245	0.0	0.1	3.3	7.6	89.1	994318
19036	GLENOLDEN	27032	5389	15.0	25.3	42.4	13.5	3.8	61420	63609	79	80	4001	1.1	4.4	69.1	25.2	0.1	157399
19038	GLENSIDE	37286	11794	9.2	16.8	36.2	24.4	13.4	81509	85759	93	95	9437	0.4	0.4	8.5	77.5	13.2	265321
19040	HATBORO	30732	7805	10.9	23.3	38.6	21.7	5.5	69171	72310	86	89	5477	1.2	0.3	6.7	81.2	10.7	263931
19041	HAVERFORD	64324	2592	7.7	13.8	25.2	20.7	32.6	109431	115752	98	98	1736	0.9	0.2	3.5	29.1	66.4	576241
19043	HOLMES	26605	1060	12.2	22.8	49.4	11.9	3.7	63271	65448	81	83	789	0.0	0.0	29.5	68.4	2.0	207065
19044	HORSHAM	34430	6595	8.9	19.9	41.1	22.0	8.1	75160	76926	89	91	4343	1.1	0.0	11.2	74.9	12.8	254519
19046	JENKINTOWN	49381	7473	9.8	17.6	33.7	20.8	18.1	80775	84566	92	94	5412	0.1	0.4	11.8	56.5	31.1	306928
19047	LANGHORNE	36479	13027	7.6	13.0	36.0	27.6	15.8	88423	93988	95	96	9828	0.4	0.2	6.2	72.2	21.0	307387
19050	LANSDOWNE	29851	11478	14.6	23.1	41.9	14.4	6.0	63026	65534	81	83	7280	0.8	2.2	58.3	37.5	1.2	162918
19053	FEASTERVILLE TREVOSE	32809	9906	10.3	16.6	41.7	22.6	8.9	74893	76979	89	91	8131	3.4	3.1	8.8	77.0	7.8	257501
19054	LEVITTOWN	28717	6374	10.4	20.6	43.2	20.6	5.1	70532	73309	87	89	4883	1.3	0.0	16.5	81.1	1.1	206366
19055	LEVITTOWN	25748	4809	11.1	19.3	48.2	18.0	3.3	68226	69893	86	88	4223	0.6	0.0	36.7	62.3	0.4	185713
19056	LEVITTOWN	28791	5748	10.3	18.4	43.4	23.2	4.6	68272	69041	86	88	3973	1.1	0.4	10.5	86.9	1.1	234162
19057	LEVITTOWN	25405	5683	12.0	20.8	46.2	17.5	3.5	67596	69169	85	88	4675	0.5	1.8	30.5	66.7	0.5	193756
19061	MARCUS HOOK	32133	10961	14.6	17.8	35.3	19.6	12.7	72729	77111	88	90	8095	0.8	3.6	30.0	47.1	18.4	243130
19063	MEDIA	40629	14787	9.5	17.4	36.5	20.1	16.5	77341	80757	91	93	10443	0.7	1.1	5.3	56.1	36.8	332097
19064	SPRINGFIELD	34414	8617	7.0	16.2	38.8	28.4	9.6	81489	83866	93	95	7944	0.5	0.7	2.2	85.8	10.8	292501
19066	MERION STATION	62719	1980	5.3	5.5	23.7	23.6	41.9	132820	136973	99	100	1698	0.0	0.4	2.3	27.7	69.7	575711
19067	MORRISVILLE	47879	20503	7.9	15.2	30.2	22.4	24.3	92678	100518	96	96	15658	4.8	2.1	8.1	50.4	34.6	327016
19070	MORTON	28903	2790	12.8	22.1	41.6	17.9	5.6	65808	69019	84	87	2102	0.4	1.8	18.0	77.5	2.4	233731
19072	NARBERTH	58779	4116	8.3	14.3	29.9	18.8	28.7	94429	102059	96	97	3031	0.4	0.1	7.4	34.3	57.9	470441
19073	NEWTOWN SQUARE	52266	7073	7.4	15.1	30.2	21.4	25.8	93358	97975	96	97	5780	0.5	1.1	3.4	44.6	50.4	403587
19074	NORWOOD	27252	2272	13.3	26.2	43.3	12.5	4.8	62659	65268	81	82	1668	0.0	0.4	41.7	56.9	1.1	185106
19075	ORELAND	37276	2703	8.3	15.3	36.3	30.1	10.0	82342	88033	93	95	2349	0.1	0.2	3.4	84.1	12.2	277481
19076	PROSPECT PARK	26994	2565	13.4	25.4	46.1	11.1	4.0	62747	65171	81	83	1552	0.5	0.0	43.0	56.0	0.5	182764
19078	RIDLEY PARK	28650	4755	15.4	22.4	42.6	15.9	3.7	63298	66364	82	84	3275	0.5	2.0	25.5	71.1	0.9	209395
19079	SHARON HILL	21914	3366	25.1	26.1	36.7	9.4	2.7	48384	51926	58	58	2280	2.3	14.2	75.1	7.9	0.5	127065
19081	SWARTHMORE	39589	3633	12.7	14.9	34.4	19.6	18.4	79949	83094	92	94	2734	0.0	0.2	10.4	59.9	29.5	288140
19082	UPPER DARBY	21359	14747	23.6	30.0	34.3	9.8	2.3	46546	49808	53	53	8525	1.7	19.0	60.4	18.6	0.2	125736
19083	HAVERTOWN	34314	13318	9.1	16.3	38.7	24.5	11.5	78504	81155	91	93	11583	0.7	0.4	6.7	81.7	10.5	285103
19085	VILLANOVA	48741	1833	5.3	4.2	17.2	15.3	57.9	199788	202173	100	100	1688	0.0	0.0	0.3	6.2	93.5	877907
19086	WALLINGFORD	40829	4411	9.1	18.2	32.2	19.9	20.6	82231	85708	93	95	3801	0.3	0.2	16.8	54.2	28.6	305180
19087	WAYNE	58975	13066	7.6	12.7	27.0	21.4	31.3	105177	110412	97	98	9875	0.3	0.0	6.1	38.8	54.7	434533
	PENNSYLVANIA	26913		21.5	25.3	36.9	10.2	6.1	53225	55819				7.5	12.2	35.6	36.1	8.5	161438
	UNITED STATES	27277		20.9	24.4	35.3	11.7	7.6	54719	56938				9.3	13.1	31.6	32.6	13.5	162279

ZIP CODE		FINANCIAL SERVICES				THE HOME						ENTERTAINMENT						PERSONAL			
						Home Improvements		Furnishings													
#	POST OFFICE NAME	Auto Loan	Home Loan	Invest-ments	Retire-ment Plans	Home Repair	Lawn & Garden	Comput-ers & Hard-ware-Personal	Major Appli-ances	TV, Radio, Sound Equip-ment	Furni-ture	Dine out/ Carry out	Sports Equip-ment	Fees & Tickets	Toys & Games	Travel	Cable TV	Apparel & Services	Auto Repairs	Health Insur-ance	Pets & Supplies
18851	WARREN CENTER	85	77	77	81	79	91	76	86	79	69	77	65	70	80	76	83	53	80	89	100
18853	WYALUSING	85	71	81	72	73	90	72	84	76	65	75	64	63	77	71	82	50	78	88	99
18854	WYSOX	93	75	80	76	76	94	76	87	81	71	80	67	66	84	73	87	54	82	91	104
18901	DOYLESTOWN	143	171	177	173	176	163	155	158	150	162	151	119	172	148	169	149	109	154	156	181
18902	DOYLESTOWN	200	252	244	260	255	219	210	216	195	230	198	172	244	204	230	184	146	200	185	242
18913	CARVERSVILLE	192	269	325	276	300	249	226	241	206	252	204	178	276	198	271	196	154	223	216	264
18914	CHALFONT	149	183	174	185	183	164	157	161	149	166	151	125	177	153	170	144	109	153	147	183
18915	COLMAR	106	149	154	138	154	132	123	128	118	123	119	94	145	119	141	118	88	123	121	140
18917	DUBLIN	111	95	82	97	90	86	110	96	106	110	108	79	101	111	98	102	75	104	93	116
18920	ERWINNA	136	160	151	165	160	155	140	147	136	145	137	112	154	138	152	135	97	140	142	171
18923	FOUNTAINVILLE	133	151	133	154	147	143	134	138	130	137	131	107	143	134	141	128	92	132	133	161
18925	FURLONG	168	210	224	216	220	200	178	190	171	193	172	141	206	169	203	167	124	179	179	216
18927	HILLTOWN	117	164	170	152	170	145	136	141	130	135	131	104	160	132	155	131	97	136	133	155
18929	JAMISON	203	235	198	235	225	192	200	201	186	222	190	164	217	201	205	173	137	187	169	226
18930	KINTNERSVILLE	126	148	137	152	147	143	129	135	126	133	127	104	142	127	140	125	89	129	131	157
18932	LINE LEXINGTON	138	177	182	177	182	164	149	157	143	156	145	116	172	143	169	142	105	150	149	178
18933	LUMBERVILLE	190	265	321	272	297	246	223	238	204	249	201	176	273	196	268	193	152	220	213	260
18934	MECHANICSVILLE	199	270	301	281	290	246	223	236	207	246	207	180	272	205	261	197	156	218	208	262
18936	MONTGOMERYVILLE	140	194	207	186	203	174	159	166	151	163	152	123	189	154	182	150	113	157	156	182
18938	NEW HOPE	164	205	240	210	224	196	179	191	169	196	169	141	207	163	205	164	123	180	177	213
18940	NEWTOWN	186	233	231	240	237	206	198	203	185	214	187	160	228	190	218	176	138	191	179	229
18942	OTTSVILLE	130	151	138	156	149	147	133	139	130	136	131	107	145	132	143	129	92	133	136	162
18944	PERKASIE	124	149	136	149	147	135	130	133	125	135	126	103	144	129	139	122	90	127	125	152
18947	PIPERSVILLE	151	184	176	189	185	166	156	162	148	168	150	126	177	153	170	143	109	152	146	184
18951	QUAKERTOWN	105	112	101	110	108	107	103	105	102	105	103	81	106	105	105	101	72	103	102	123
18954	RICHBORO	187	250	260	259	259	225	204	213	191	220	193	166	246	195	233	183	145	198	188	239
18955	RICHLANDTOWN	93	110	104	109	109	102	104	102	101	103	103	79	113	102	110	101	73	102	101	118
18960	SELLERSVILLE	106	124	119	124	124	118	113	115	111	114	112	88	123	112	121	111	80	113	115	133
18964	SOUDERTON	104	122	118	121	122	117	113	114	112	114	113	86	124	111	121	113	80	113	117	131
18966	SOUTHAMPTON	139	176	181	176	182	166	152	158	147	158	148	118	175	147	170	147	108	152	154	178
18969	TELFORD	108	129	123	127	128	121	117	118	115	119	116	89	128	115	125	115	82	116	119	135
18972	UPPER BLACK EDDY	112	127	111	131	124	125	113	118	111	114	112	92	122	114	120	111	78	113	116	139
18974	WARMINSTER	116	143	138	139	143	130	127	128	124	129	125	97	142	125	137	123	90	126	125	145
18976	WARRINGTON	143	173	155	171	168	149	149	150	140	157	143	119	164	147	157	135	103	143	134	171
18977	WASHINGTON CROSSING	208	292	352	302	325	271	242	259	223	270	221	193	301	217	289	212	168	238	229	282
19001	ABINGTON	110	134	130	133	134	129	120	123	119	122	120	92	135	118	131	121	86	121	127	141
19002	AMBLER	163	202	216	205	212	187	181	184	172	191	173	140	206	170	201	168	126	178	174	208
19003	ARDMORE	130	134	139	138	136	130	143	131	139	141	141	105	147	138	142	138	101	138	134	156
19004	BALA CYNWYD	169	217	252	222	237	207	194	201	184	208	183	150	226	177	221	179	135	192	193	224
19006	HUNTINGDON VALLEY	158	204	232	206	220	198	177	188	171	190	170	136	208	164	205	169	124	179	186	210
19007	BRISTOL	79	82	76	81	80	81	84	80	84	81	84	62	85	84	83	85	59	83	84	95
19008	BROOMALL	114	151	162	147	158	145	128	135	126	131	127	98	150	125	147	128	92	130	136	151
19010	BRYN MAWR	174	190	216	199	202	181	199	184	186	199	188	147	209	184	203	181	138	188	176	213
19012	CHELTENHAM	122	159	163	156	163	147	137	141	132	140	133	106	158	132	154	131	96	136	136	159
19013	CHESTER	55	57	56	54	56	57	58	55	64	54	64	39	61	63	57	69	46	59	64	67
19014	ASTON	114	130	123	130	128	128	118	121	118	120	119	92	128	119	126	119	84	119	124	141
19015	BROOKHAVEN	86	101	94	99	99	99	92	93	95	90	95	68	101	95	97	99	68	93	100	109
19018	CLIFTON HEIGHTS	87	96	90	96	94	95	93	92	94	92	95	70	99	94	97	95	67	93	97	108
19020	BENSALEM	102	111	104	112	109	103	109	104	106	109	108	82	114	108	110	105	77	106	103	122
19021	CROYDON	92	106	95	105	102	101	97	97	97	98	98	74	106	99	102	97	69	97	99	113
19022	CRUM LYNNE	73	71	57	73	66	73	77	70	79	72	78	57	76	79	72	80	55	75	78	87
19023	DARBY	72	79	71	76	76	80	76	74	81	71	81	54	80	81	75	86	57	77	84	89
19025	DRESHER	195	265	296	272	285	240	222	232	205	241	205	177	267	203	258	195	154	216	206	257
19026	DREXEL HILL	102	117	116	116	118	110	112	109	111	111	112	84	122	111	118	111	80	111	110	126
19027	ELKINS PARK	135	148	156	150	153	141	145	142	141	149	143	108	155	140	152	140	102	144	140	163
19029	ESSINGTON	82	94	86	92	92	90	90	88	89	87	90	68	96	90	93	90	64	89	92	103
19030	FAIRLESS HILLS	103	125	114	124	122	118	110	112	108	111	110	86	123	110	119	109	78	110	113	130
19031	FLOURTOWN	145	190	209	187	201	175	165	169	157	170	158	127	192	157	187	155	116	164	161	189
19032	FOLCROFT	89	96	83	96	91	98	92	91	94	89	94	70	96	95	93	96	65	92	100	109
19033	FOLSOM	98	118	109	117	116	119	102	108	105	104	105	79	116	105	113	108	74	105	116	125
19034	FORT WASHINGTON	173	221	247	223	237	199	200	202	184	211	185	156	227	181	224	176	137	195	182	226
19035	GLADWYNE	272	389	478	408	436	367	313	337	294	349	291	253	407	293	377	282	228	308	296	367
19036	GLENOLDEN	87	99	90	98	97	99	93	94	94	91	95	71	100	94	97	97	66	94	101	110
19038	GLENSIDE	126	153	152	152	155	147	136	139	134	139	135	104	153	133	149	134	96	136	140	159
19040	HATBORO	101	117	112	116	116	114	109	109	109	109	110	82	119	108	116	110	78	109	114	127
19041	HAVERFORD	201	241	295	248	268	237	224	232	211	241	211	171	253	202	252	205	154	224	220	260
19043	HOLMES	87	105	96	104	102	101	95	95	95	95	96	73	106	95	102	96	68	95	99	111
19044	HORSHAM	115	127	118	128	124	116	123	118	119	124	121	93	129	121	126	117	86	120	115	138
19046	JENKINTOWN	148	174	184	175	181	173	162	166	161	167	161	122	179	155	177	162	115	164	174	189
19047	LANGHORNE	138	162	156	166	161	148	146	145	140	152	142	114	162	143	156	137	103	142	137	168
19050	LANSDOWNE	98	105	97	105	102	103	103	100	103	102	104	77	107	103	104	104	73	102	105	119
19053	FEASTERVILLE TREVOSE	113	137	135	136	137	131	120	124	118	123	119	94	134	120	131	119	86	121	123	143
19054	LEVITTOWN	102	121	110	121	117	116	108	109	108	109	109	83	120	109	116	108	77	108	112	127
19055	LEVITTOWN	94	114	103	114	110	113	100	103	102	101	103	77	113	102	109	104	72	102	110	120
19056	LEVITTOWN	100	117	111	115	116	112	109	108	108	108	109	82	119	108	115	109	78	109	111	125
19057	LEVITTOWN	93	113	103	112	109	112	98	102	100	100	101	76	111	101	108	103	71	101	109	119
19061	MARCUS HOOK	116	134	124	135	132	128	123	123	123	124	123	95	135	124	129	123	88	122	126	143
19063	MEDIA	131	154	162	156	160	149	144	144	141	147	141	109	159	138	155	140	102	143	145	165
19064	SPRINGFIELD	116	153	161	148	160	146	128	137	126	131	127	98	150	125	147	128	92	131	136	152
19066	MERION STATION	225	304	365	313	339	276	265	276	239	291	238	210	315	232	310	225	180	258	240	303
19067	MORRISVILLE	164	195	194	198	197	178	176	175	167	184	169	137	195	170	188	163	123	171	163	201
19070	MORTON	97	112	106	112	110	109	103	103	103	104	104	78	113	103	109	105	74	104	108	121
19072	NARBERTH	171	210	239	218	226	192	195	193	180	206	181	152	221	178	215	172	135	187	174	218
19073	NEWTOWN SQUARE	158	211	241	212	229	201	180	191	173	193	172	139	215	167	210	171	127	181	185	212
19074	NORWOOD	91	104	95	104	101	101	98	96	98	98	100	74	106	99	103	99	70	98	101	114
19075	ORELAND	120	151	155	150	155	147	130	137	129	134	130	100	150	128	146	130	93	133	139	155
19076	PROSPECT PARK	85	100	94	98	99	92	97	93	94	94	95	73	104	95	101	94	68	95	93	108
19078	RIDLEY PARK	88	103	97	102	101	101	95	96	96	95	97	72	105	95	102	98	69	96	102	112
19079	SHARON HILL	76	82	75	80	80	83	79	78	83	76	83	58	83	83	80	87	58	80	86	93
19081	SWARTHMORE	134	167	177	168	174	159	150	153	145	155	145	116	171	142	166	143	105	149	151	173
19082	UPPER DARBY	72	77	74	76	76	75	79	75	81	74	81	56	81	80	78	84	58	78	80	88
19083	HAVERTOWN	112	152	157	145	157	140	127	133	123	128	124	98	149	124	145	124	91	128	129	147
19085	VILLANOVA	260	370	454	387	415	348	300	323	281	335	278	242	386	278	361	269	216	296	285	352
19086	WALLINGFORD	137	171	178	171	177	165	149	156	146	155	146	115	171	145	166	146	105	150	154	176
19087	WAYNE	180	221	252	228	238	205	206	206	191	219	192	159	232	187	229	184	141	200	190	233
	PENNSYLVANIA	94	95	95	95	95	100	94	96	96	91	95	73	94	96	94	99	67	95	101	113
	UNITED STATES	100	100	100	100	100	100	100	100	100	100	100	100	100	100	100	100	100	100	100	100

ZIP CODE #	POST OFFICE NAME	COUNTY FIPS CODE	POPULATION 2000	POPULATION 2009	POPULATION 2014	2000-2009 ANNUAL RATE % Rate	2000-2009 ANNUAL RATE State Centile	HOUSEHOLDS 2000	HOUSEHOLDS 2009	HOUSEHOLDS 2014	HOUSEHOLDS % Annual Rate 2000-2009	HOUSEHOLDS 2009 Average HH Size	FAMILIES 2000	FAMILIES 2009	FAMILIES % Annual Rate 2000-2009
19090	WILLOW GROVE	091	19318	18993	18817	-0.2	38	7476	7458	7426	0.0	2.47	5162	4984	-0.4
19094	WOODLYN	045	4778	4909	4927	0.3	64	1886	1942	1953	0.3	2.52	1257	1248	-0.1
19095	WYNCOTE	091	6555	6648	6765	0.2	61	2762	2837	2940	0.3	1.99	1681	1658	-0.1
19096	WYNNEWOOD	091	12768	12828	12805	0.1	57	4968	5022	5032	0.1	2.47	3516	3441	-0.2
19102	PHILADELPHIA	101	4303	4481	4463	0.4	68	2544	2669	2667	0.5	1.41	536	525	-0.2
19103	PHILADELPHIA	101	18882	18860	18617	0.0	52	12928	12926	12806	0.0	1.39	2680	2517	-0.7
19104	PHILADELPHIA	101	49437	48968	47980	-0.1	46	16756	16426	16014	-0.2	2.17	5871	5373	-1.0
19106	PHILADELPHIA	101	8036	8793	8896	1.0	85	5202	5785	5889	1.2	1.46	1433	1458	0.2
19107	PHILADELPHIA	101	11865	13730	14020	1.6	92	6369	7035	7134	1.1	1.58	1200	1438	2.0
19111	PHILADELPHIA	101	59042	56164	54546	-0.5	19	24071	22898	22252	-0.5	2.40	14998	13810	-0.9
19114	PHILADELPHIA	101	31083	29280	28290	-0.6	13	13365	12776	12403	-0.5	2.26	8175	7570	-0.8
19115	PHILADELPHIA	101	30759	29353	28587	-0.5	19	13196	12679	12383	-0.4	2.25	8447	7874	-0.8
19116	PHILADELPHIA	101	33617	32168	31475	-0.5	19	13059	12591	12295	-0.4	2.49	9067	8509	-0.7
19118	PHILADELPHIA	101	9732	9337	9091	-0.4	23	4355	4204	4099	-0.4	2.04	2305	2140	-0.8
19119	PHILADELPHIA	101	28825	27422	26664	-0.5	19	11907	11449	11161	-0.4	2.27	7073	6572	-0.8
19120	PHILADELPHIA	101	67909	64678	62672	-0.5	19	22016	20696	20025	-0.7	3.12	16491	15167	-0.9
19121	PHILADELPHIA	101	35015	34950	34452	0.0	52	12667	12714	12555	0.0	2.67	7714	7479	-0.3
19122	PHILADELPHIA	101	19713	20132	19977	0.2	61	5720	6009	6006	0.5	2.79	3779	3811	0.1
19123	PHILADELPHIA	101	9429	9969	10131	0.6	74	3954	4234	4316	0.7	2.18	1900	1936	0.2
19124	PHILADELPHIA	101	63166	61059	59373	-0.4	23	22369	21337	20719	-0.5	2.83	15125	14032	-0.8
19125	PHILADELPHIA	101	23389	22493	21988	-0.4	23	8438	8207	8047	-0.3	2.69	5454	5139	-0.6
19126	PHILADELPHIA	101	16699	15991	15570	-0.5	19	6007	5773	5629	-0.4	2.62	3945	3682	-0.7
19127	PHILADELPHIA	101	5733	5736	5702	0.0	52	2644	2689	2683	0.2	2.12	1085	1056	-0.3
19128	PHILADELPHIA	101	35706	34977	34319	-0.2	38	15669	15612	15386	0.0	2.20	8505	8124	-0.5
19129	PHILADELPHIA	101	12436	11781	11559	-0.6	13	5085	4847	4767	-0.5	2.18	2486	2264	-1.0
19130	PHILADELPHIA	101	22402	21804	21355	-0.3	29	11364	11168	10965	-0.2	1.84	4006	3732	-0.8
19131	PHILADELPHIA	101	47047	45379	44245	-0.4	23	19131	18517	18082	-0.4	2.27	10112	9442	-0.7
19132	PHILADELPHIA	101	41565	38069	36567	-0.9	4	15559	14460	13940	-0.8	2.60	9825	8853	-1.1
19133	PHILADELPHIA	101	27087	24323	23223	-1.2	1	8305	7564	7249	-1.0	3.18	6106	5438	-1.2
19134	PHILADELPHIA	101	58434	55854	54176	-0.5	19	20052	18941	18371	-0.6	2.92	13754	12644	-0.9
19135	PHILADELPHIA	101	30486	28581	27600	-0.7	8	12036	11396	11038	-0.6	2.49	7716	7081	-0.9
19136	PHILADELPHIA	101	40579	38812	37827	-0.5	19	13608	12930	12575	-0.6	2.43	8645	7952	-0.9
19137	PHILADELPHIA	101	7976	7455	7190	-0.7	8	3144	2983	2889	-0.6	2.49	2042	1882	-0.9
19138	PHILADELPHIA	101	34502	32262	31148	-0.7	8	12345	11725	11374	-0.6	2.72	8900	8246	-0.8
19139	PHILADELPHIA	101	43668	40264	38726	-0.9	4	17350	16157	15584	-0.8	2.44	10259	9213	-1.2
19140	PHILADELPHIA	101	57501	53578	51683	-0.8	6	19113	17957	17364	-0.7	2.91	13175	12085	-0.9
19141	PHILADELPHIA	101	35852	34371	33513	-0.5	19	12423	11961	11677	-0.4	2.67	8033	7523	-0.7
19142	PHILADELPHIA	101	29115	28115	27314	-0.4	23	9926	9435	9153	-0.5	2.96	7007	6485	-0.8
19143	PHILADELPHIA	101	72052	65275	62466	-1.1	2	26958	24721	23743	-0.9	2.59	17091	15228	-1.2
19144	PHILADELPHIA	101	45367	42978	41672	-0.6	13	18771	17912	17405	-0.5	2.30	9999	9196	-0.9
19145	PHILADELPHIA	101	45542	42947	41615	-0.6	13	18059	17136	16638	-0.6	2.49	11641	10736	-0.9
19146	PHILADELPHIA	101	37047	36477	35879	-0.2	38	15635	15586	15398	0.0	2.31	7960	7557	-0.6
19147	PHILADELPHIA	101	33513	33613	33268	0.0	52	16377	16590	16471	0.1	2.01	6882	6671	-0.3
19148	PHILADELPHIA	101	48619	47084	45953	-0.3	29	19180	18698	18296	-0.3	2.50	12267	11592	-0.6
19149	PHILADELPHIA	101	48683	46623	45277	-0.5	19	19068	18177	17655	-0.5	2.56	12750	11803	-0.8
19150	PHILADELPHIA	101	25332	23733	22948	-0.7	8	10009	9554	9282	-0.5	2.48	6970	6483	-0.8
19151	PHILADELPHIA	101	31255	29765	28833	-0.5	19	11983	11349	10996	-0.6	2.58	7827	7196	-0.9
19152	PHILADELPHIA	101	31324	29984	29149	-0.5	19	13299	12734	12384	-0.5	2.26	8188	7584	-0.8
19153	PHILADELPHIA	101	12272	11675	11356	-0.5	19	5207	5039	4925	-0.4	2.31	3247	3040	-0.7
19154	PHILADELPHIA	101	35606	33163	32214	-0.8	6	12868	12200	11919	-0.6	2.69	9669	8971	-0.8
19301	PAOLI	029	7449	7539	7617	0.1	57	2985	3080	3138	0.3	2.40	2016	2005	-0.1
19310	ATGLEN	029	2892	3282	3488	1.4	91	952	1099	1174	1.6	2.98	753	846	1.3
19311	AVONDALE	029	5227	8339	9604	5.2	99	1577	2532	2926	5.3	3.18	1259	1983	5.0
19312	BERWYN	029	10851	11077	11244	0.2	61	4128	4290	4386	0.4	2.53	3086	3110	0.1
19317	CHADDS FORD	029	8496	10445	11158	2.3	96	3200	3886	4164	2.1	2.66	2506	2994	1.9
19319	CHEYNEY	045	190	217	224	1.4	91	69	84	89	2.1	1.86	60	72	2.0
19320	COATESVILLE	029	43114	52851	57744	2.2	96	15282	19069	20997	2.4	2.70	11233	13664	2.1
19330	COCHRANVILLE	029	4596	5511	5997	2.0	95	1552	1897	2081	2.2	2.84	1230	1462	1.9
19333	DEVON	029	6447	6625	6736	0.3	64	2690	2805	2872	0.5	2.31	1717	1718	0.0
19335	DOWNINGTOWN	029	40963	47770	52161	1.7	93	14301	17113	18809	2.0	2.77	10995	12747	1.6
19341	EXTON	029	14341	17680	18821	2.3	96	5964	7361	7882	2.3	2.39	3912	4689	2.0
19342	GLEN MILLS	045	13960	17509	18843	2.5	97	4571	5873	6401	2.7	2.62	3647	4591	2.5
19343	GLENMOORE	029	8190	9047	9510	1.1	87	2576	2903	3078	1.3	3.01	2167	2389	1.1
19344	HONEY BROOK	029	9784	11195	11959	1.5	92	3311	3853	4147	1.7	2.81	2534	2862	1.3
19348	KENNETT SQUARE	029	18925	21969	23508	1.6	92	6791	7990	8617	1.8	2.67	4845	5506	1.4
19350	LANDENBERG	029	10034	12064	13091	2.0	95	3215	3874	4222	2.0	3.06	2759	3272	1.9
19352	LINCOLN UNIVERSITY	029	7444	9338	10098	2.5	97	1892	2435	2674	2.8	3.25	1620	2043	2.5
19355	MALVERN	029	23060	25503	26683	1.1	87	8216	9142	9618	1.2	2.65	5934	6398	0.8
19362	NOTTINGHAM	029	5252	5616	5848	0.7	77	1825	1989	2082	0.9	2.82	1458	1554	0.7
19363	OXFORD	029	13254	16776	18497	2.6	97	4619	5864	6477	2.6	2.82	3423	4243	2.3
19365	PARKESBURG	029	6327	6707	7048	0.6	74	2277	2440	2577	0.8	2.74	1680	1741	0.4
19372	THORNDALE	029	1222	1328	1403	0.9	83	470	545	586	1.6	2.43	356	394	1.1
19373	THORNTON	045	3572	4939	5454	3.6	99	672	1090	1241	5.4	3.69	584	931	5.2
19374	TOUGHKENAMON	029	1456	1729	1900	1.9	94	382	444	490	1.6	3.63	298	340	1.4
19380	WEST CHESTER	029	45359	49270	51334	0.9	83	17436	19175	20082	1.0	2.52	11903	12746	0.7
19382	WEST CHESTER	029	51485	55961	58074	0.9	83	18062	19955	20936	1.1	2.52	12038	12818	0.7
19383	WEST CHESTER	029	766	820	844	0.7	77	139	151	157	0.9	4.50	116	123	0.6
19390	WEST GROVE	029	10034	13562	15217	3.3	98	3323	4617	5242	3.6	2.88	2631	3510	3.2
19401	NORRISTOWN	091	37875	38956	39211	0.3	64	14850	15243	15364	0.3	2.46	8853	8697	-0.2
19403	NORRISTOWN	091	41413	42465	42967	0.3	64	15730	16297	16547	0.4	2.47	10738	10768	0.0
19405	BRIDGEPORT	091	5022	4952	4919	-0.2	38	2195	2198	2193	0.0	2.25	1233	1179	-0.5
19406	KING OF PRUSSIA	091	21418	21799	21904	0.2	61	9477	9779	9866	0.3	2.21	5554	5545	0.0
19422	BLUE BELL	091	18333	18950	19176	0.4	68	7001	7341	7465	0.5	2.55	5136	5229	0.2
19425	CHESTER SPRINGS	029	8074	12979	14868	5.3	100	2859	4506	5159	5.0	2.86	2269	3590	5.1
19426	COLLEGEVILLE	091	30530	36684	38952	2.0	95	9419	11554	12390	2.2	2.75	7219	8698	2.0
19428	CONSHOHOCKEN	091	16508	18223	18901	1.1	87	7015	7790	8090	1.1	2.33	4119	4350	0.6
19435	FREDERICK	091	222	233	239	0.5	70	84	90	92	0.7	2.59	67	71	0.6
19436	GWYNEDD	091	497	535	550	0.8	80	295	324	336	1.0	1.57	211	186	-1.4
19438	HARLEYSVILLE	091	21164	23628	24621	1.2	88	7477	8431	8814	1.3	2.78	5869	6462	1.0
19440	HATFIELD	091	17630	18684	19055	0.6	74	6564	6991	7157	0.7	2.63	4551	4686	0.3
19444	LAFAYETTE HILL	091	10462	10761	10851	0.3	64	3834	4005	4058	0.5	2.56	2828	2867	0.1
19446	LANSDALE	091	50971	52934	53620	0.4	68	19627	20579	20915	0.5	2.53	13566	13795	0.2
19453	MONT CLARE	091	1174	1262	1393	0.8	80	562	626	691	1.2	2.02	387	410	0.6
19454	NORTH WALES	091	24541	26361	27017	0.8	80	9614	10266	10548	0.7	2.55	6901	7148	0.4
19460	PHOENIXVILLE	029	33853	38762	41125	1.5	92	13263	15389	16428	1.6	2.45	8763	9842	1.3
	PENNSYLVANIA					0.3					0.4	2.45			0.1
	UNITED STATES					1.0					1.1	2.59			0.9

#	POST OFFICE NAME	RACE (%) White 2000	White 2009	Black 2000	Black 2009	Asian/Pacific 2000	Asian/Pacific 2009	% Hispanic Origin 2000	% Hispanic Origin 2009	2009 AGE DISTRIBUTION (%) 0-4	5-9	10-14	15-19	20-24	25-44	45-64	65-84	85+	18+	MEDIAN AGE 2009	% 2009 Males	% 2009 Females
19090	WILLOW GROVE	79.8	75.8	15.4	17.5	2.7	4.2	1.7	2.2	6.2	6.3	6.4	6.2	5.6	25.0	26.8	13.9	3.6	77.1	41.1	46.8	53.2
19094	WOODLYN	87.2	81.8	9.9	14.1	1.1	1.8	1.2	1.7	6.1	6.4	6.6	7.3	5.4	25.4	26.6	13.5	2.7	76.4	40.1	48.3	51.7
19095	WYNCOTE	72.2	67.1	23.8	27.5	2.4	3.6	1.2	1.5	3.6	3.8	4.5	8.6	7.5	16.5	25.2	20.6	9.8	84.9	49.7	42.2	57.8
19096	WYNNEWOOD	92.9	89.8	2.4	3.2	3.2	5.2	1.3	1.8	5.6	6.2	7.4	6.2	4.2	19.9	30.2	15.7	4.7	76.4	45.4	47.1	52.9
19102	PHILADELPHIA	78.7	66.7	7.8	12.4	10.1	15.7	3.1	5.3	1.4	0.8	0.5	2.7	13.3	48.3	19.3	10.3	3.5	96.8	33.0	48.6	51.4
19103	PHILADELPHIA	81.8	72.3	7.0	10.8	8.4	13.0	3.6	5.6	1.9	1.2	1.1	3.9	10.0	40.4	21.4	14.4	5.7	95.2	37.6	46.6	53.4
19104	PHILADELPHIA	32.8	26.5	50.9	51.8	12.3	16.8	3.0	4.4	4.1	3.9	3.6	19.2	27.2	20.6	13.4	6.5	1.4	86.1	23.5	49.6	50.4
19106	PHILADELPHIA	87.0	78.7	6.7	10.8	4.0	7.2	2.9	4.8	1.8	1.2	0.9	1.3	5.8	44.3	30.8	12.2	1.8	95.4	41.0	51.8	48.2
19107	PHILADELPHIA	62.1	46.3	11.8	15.4	22.1	34.0	3.9	5.2	2.0	1.5	1.4	5.6	20.3	43.3	16.9	7.6	1.4	94.1	29.9	54.2	45.8
19111	PHILADELPHIA	84.0	76.4	6.0	8.7	4.8	7.5	6.3	9.7	6.1	5.9	5.9	6.0	6.3	26.0	25.3	14.1	4.5	78.4	40.5	47.0	53.0
19114	PHILADELPHIA	87.9	82.0	6.8	9.9	2.6	4.3	3.4	5.4	5.6	5.4	5.3	5.0	4.8	27.1	25.4	17.2	4.1	80.6	42.6	46.8	53.2
19115	PHILADELPHIA	87.0	79.8	3.5	5.3	7.1	11.5	3.2	5.2	4.3	4.1	4.4	4.6	5.0	22.2	27.4	21.7	6.4	84.4	49.2	45.7	54.3
19116	PHILADELPHIA	84.6	76.6	4.0	6.0	8.3	13.2	3.2	5.1	5.4	5.3	5.3	5.5	5.4	26.9	27.2	15.4	3.6	80.7	42.2	47.4	52.6
19118	PHILADELPHIA	79.4	72.7	15.3	19.9	2.4	3.6	2.3	3.5	4.9	4.8	5.0	5.6	6.4	24.2	29.8	15.3	3.9	82.6	44.3	42.7	57.3
19119	PHILADELPHIA	27.5	20.4	67.7	74.4	1.0	1.3	1.9	2.3	5.3	5.6	5.9	5.9	6.1	24.5	29.1	14.4	3.1	79.3	42.7	43.6	56.4
19120	PHILADELPHIA	25.9	20.0	40.9	43.2	14.2	15.9	23.7	26.8	8.5	8.8	8.4	9.0	8.1	27.0	22.9	6.5	1.0	68.8	30.1	46.6	53.4
19121	PHILADELPHIA	2.0	1.4	95.7	96.3	0.6	0.7	1.5	1.7	8.2	8.9	8.5	8.7	8.2	23.9	21.7	10.1	1.9	69.2	31.2	44.4	55.6
19122	PHILADELPHIA	23.0	18.2	49.2	52.6	2.0	2.5	32.9	34.1	7.2	7.5	7.1	15.1	12.8	20.6	18.8	9.6	1.3	74.1	25.3	44.6	55.4
19123	PHILADELPHIA	26.0	22.7	64.5	65.3	1.7	2.3	11.2	14.8	6.2	6.9	6.4	6.7	7.2	30.0	23.5	10.9	2.3	76.5	35.9	48.3	51.7
19124	PHILADELPHIA	54.9	44.4	25.9	30.8	4.4	5.5	18.8	24.9	8.5	8.4	8.1	8.2	7.5	26.9	22.0	8.8	1.6	70.0	31.6	47.2	52.8
19125	PHILADELPHIA	81.4	75.6	4.2	5.5	5.3	6.9	10.7	14.5	7.8	7.9	7.3	7.6	7.1	27.2	24.2	9.4	1.4	72.3	34.1	48.7	51.3
19126	PHILADELPHIA	11.7	8.0	80.5	83.4	3.8	4.6	2.8	3.4	5.9	6.4	6.4	7.2	7.0	24.8	26.7	13.1	2.5	76.9	39.0	45.2	54.8
19127	PHILADELPHIA	93.7	90.0	3.3	5.3	1.4	2.4	1.1	1.8	3.9	3.7	3.5	3.6	13.0	40.5	20.2	9.9	1.7	86.9	32.4	50.9	49.1
19128	PHILADELPHIA	88.9	83.0	6.6	10.0	2.5	4.1	1.9	3.1	4.9	4.6	4.7	5.0	6.9	32.0	26.5	12.2	3.1	82.8	39.5	47.7	52.3
19129	PHILADELPHIA	53.8	47.5	40.3	44.5	3.2	4.8	2.2	3.2	4.5	4.6	5.1	10.3	12.9	29.7	21.8	9.6	1.5	82.8	31.8	45.5	54.5
19130	PHILADELPHIA	58.9	50.6	31.0	36.0	3.5	5.0	7.6	10.3	4.3	3.9	3.6	4.3	9.8	38.9	22.4	10.6	2.3	85.8	35.5	49.0	51.0
19131	PHILADELPHIA	17.8	13.6	76.9	80.4	2.4	3.2	1.7	2.1	5.5	5.7	5.7	8.8	9.3	24.0	23.0	13.8	4.2	79.4	37.2	43.6	56.4
19132	PHILADELPHIA	1.0	0.6	96.9	97.4	0.3	0.3	1.3	1.4	7.5	8.0	8.0	8.1	6.9	23.8	23.9	11.8	1.8	71.5	35.2	44.1	55.9
19133	PHILADELPHIA	15.2	13.9	42.2	41.5	0.6	0.6	57.5	59.4	9.6	9.8	9.2	9.4	7.9	24.7	21.3	7.3	0.7	65.7	27.9	46.3	53.7
19134	PHILADELPHIA	58.7	51.6	14.1	16.0	2.1	2.6	32.5	38.3	10.0	9.9	8.7	8.6	7.8	25.8	20.4	7.6	1.3	66.1	28.6	47.1	52.9
19135	PHILADELPHIA	92.3	87.8	3.5	5.5	0.9	1.6	3.8	6.5	6.8	6.6	6.4	6.8	6.7	27.1	25.6	11.7	2.3	76.0	37.3	48.3	51.7
19136	PHILADELPHIA	76.7	70.5	18.0	21.9	1.3	2.0	5.0	7.2	5.3	5.3	5.3	6.8	9.3	31.5	22.6	11.3	2.6	80.5	36.3	54.3	45.7
19137	PHILADELPHIA	95.6	93.0	1.1	1.7	0.4	0.8	2.8	4.7	5.9	6.1	6.3	6.9	6.5	25.9	26.9	12.8	2.7	77.4	39.6	47.6	52.4
19138	PHILADELPHIA	1.6	1.1	95.6	96.5	0.3	0.4	1.2	1.3	6.6	7.2	7.5	8.2	6.8	23.2	26.5	12.8	1.3	73.7	37.5	43.6	56.4
19139	PHILADELPHIA	3.1	2.1	93.4	94.4	1.1	1.3	1.2	1.4	7.3	7.6	7.4	8.1	7.2	24.1	23.7	12.0	2.5	72.7	35.4	43.8	56.2
19140	PHILADELPHIA	13.0	11.5	60.9	60.6	1.3	1.4	34.4	36.5	8.8	8.8	8.4	8.8	8.0	24.6	22.6	8.9	1.2	68.8	30.2	46.1	53.9
19141	PHILADELPHIA	9.3	8.1	83.4	84.4	3.8	4.2	2.9	3.2	6.4	6.6	6.8	9.8	10.0	23.0	23.8	10.8	2.7	75.6	33.8	44.6	55.4
19142	PHILADELPHIA	32.1	23.0	54.5	61.4	10.2	12.3	2.3	2.7	8.8	9.3	8.9	9.2	7.4	26.3	21.0	7.7	1.2	67.1	29.6	46.2	53.8
19143	PHILADELPHIA	5.8	3.9	90.4	92.2	1.2	1.4	1.4	1.6	7.3	7.5	7.4	7.8	7.5	24.8	24.2	11.8	1.6	73.1	34.7	44.2	55.8
19144	PHILADELPHIA	14.0	9.8	81.6	85.7	1.0	1.3	1.7	2.0	7.2	7.2	6.7	7.4	7.9	27.0	24.6	10.1	2.0	74.7	34.7	45.2	54.8
19145	PHILADELPHIA	50.9	45.7	38.0	41.0	8.6	10.5	1.8	2.5	6.4	6.6	6.8	7.4	6.3	24.9	25.1	13.8	2.6	75.6	38.8	45.2	54.8
19146	PHILADELPHIA	24.2	19.7	69.4	73.0	3.4	4.2	2.4	3.0	6.9	6.9	6.6	6.9	7.5	29.4	23.5	10.2	2.1	75.5	34.3	46.7	53.3
19147	PHILADELPHIA	67.4	57.4	16.4	20.7	11.7	16.3	4.9	6.8	4.4	4.1	4.0	4.6	8.0	34.6	26.5	11.6	2.1	84.8	38.5	49.5	50.5
19148	PHILADELPHIA	73.4	65.7	10.9	13.3	11.0	15.0	4.8	6.8	6.3	6.7	6.6	7.1	6.2	25.8	25.8	12.9	2.6	76.1	38.6	46.4	53.6
19149	PHILADELPHIA	81.5	73.3	6.8	9.4	5.7	8.6	7.6	11.5	7.1	6.9	6.9	6.9	6.0	27.8	24.5	11.2	2.6	74.9	37.1	47.5	52.5
19150	PHILADELPHIA	2.2	1.3	95.3	96.5	0.2	0.2	1.0	1.1	5.4	6.2	6.8	7.1	5.6	23.0	30.5	14.1	1.2	77.2	41.8	43.5	56.5
19151	PHILADELPHIA	22.9	16.4	72.0	78.0	1.8	2.2	1.9	2.3	7.1	7.2	7.1	8.2	8.1	25.1	24.7	10.3	2.1	73.8	35.4	45.1	54.9
19152	PHILADELPHIA	87.3	80.5	4.1	6.1	5.0	8.0	4.7	7.6	5.1	5.0	5.1	4.8	4.7	23.2	25.3	19.8	6.9	81.8	46.5	45.8	54.2
19153	PHILADELPHIA	35.7	26.3	59.5	68.2	1.9	2.3	1.9	2.3	6.0	6.0	6.0	6.1	6.8	25.8	28.1	13.4	1.8	78.3	40.1	45.6	54.4
19154	PHILADELPHIA	89.5	84.1	5.6	8.3	2.3	3.8	3.2	5.2	6.7	6.6	6.6	6.1	5.4	28.7	25.3	13.3	1.4	76.4	38.5	48.7	51.3
19301	PAOLI	91.7	88.6	4.1	5.1	3.2	5.1	0.9	1.3	5.4	5.9	6.9	6.3	4.5	20.9	31.1	15.6	3.3	77.5	45.0	48.2	51.8
19310	ATGLEN	92.1	89.5	5.3	7.0	0.2	0.4	2.9	4.3	7.9	7.9	7.9	7.9	5.9	26.4	26.1	8.9	1.1	71.4	34.9	49.5	50.5
19311	AVONDALE	84.9	81.8	6.1	6.7	0.7	1.2	20.4	24.0	8.8	8.6	8.1	6.5	5.2	30.9	24.5	6.8	0.7	70.0	34.6	52.6	47.4
19312	BERWYN	93.2	90.4	2.8	3.6	3.0	4.8	1.0	1.4	5.8	6.7	8.2	7.1	3.9	18.9	31.5	15.5	2.5	74.5	44.7	48.6	51.4
19317	CHADDS FORD	95.0	92.4	1.2	1.7	2.4	4.2	2.6	3.6	5.5	6.3	7.4	7.0	4.0	19.8	33.9	14.3	1.6	76.0	44.9	49.2	50.8
19319	CHEYNEY	49.2	40.1	45.0	53.0	1.6	1.8	3.7	5.1	4.6	5.5	5.5	35.9	13.8	15.7	13.8	4.6	0.5	63.1	19.8	61.3	38.7
19320	COATESVILLE	73.5	70.7	22.1	24.1	0.5	0.8	4.5	5.4	7.1	7.4	7.7	7.7	5.2	25.0	27.9	10.3	1.7	72.6	38.1	49.5	50.5
19330	COCHRANVILLE	95.0	93.3	1.8	2.3	0.4	0.6	5.1	7.6	6.7	7.2	7.9	7.8	4.6	25.0	29.6	10.2	1.1	73.2	39.1	50.2	49.8
19333	DEVON	90.0	86.1	2.4	3.0	6.4	9.4	1.3	1.8	6.0	6.1	6.9	6.0	6.7	23.8	28.6	13.3	2.7	76.7	41.1	48.1	51.9
19335	DOWNINGTOWN	91.0	87.9	5.0	6.2	2.2	3.6	1.8	2.6	7.2	7.6	7.9	7.4	5.2	25.9	29.7	7.8	1.2	72.1	37.9	49.2	50.8
19341	EXTON	91.2	88.0	2.9	3.5	4.3	6.5	1.5	2.0	6.6	6.5	6.9	6.5	4.7	29.8	28.4	9.4	1.1	75.7	38.5	48.6	51.4
19342	GLEN MILLS	86.5	81.2	9.7	13.1	2.1	3.3	1.4	2.3	5.7	6.5	7.6	12.2	6.0	20.8	27.9	11.3	1.9	72.8	38.8	51.7	48.3
19343	GLENMOORE	96.8	95.5	1.6	2.1	0.8	1.3	1.1	1.6	6.7	8.1	10.1	8.0	4.5	22.0	32.3	7.6	0.8	69.6	39.4	50.6	49.4
19344	HONEY BROOK	97.2	96.2	1.2	1.6	0.3	0.5	1.0	1.4	7.4	7.6	7.8	7.5	5.4	25.3	25.8	9.9	3.4	72.6	37.3	48.9	51.1
19348	KENNETT SQUARE	86.7	83.6	4.3	4.7	1.7	2.6	14.7	18.5	6.3	6.6	7.2	6.9	5.2	23.5	28.8	11.8	3.6	75.2	40.9	49.8	50.2
19350	LANDENBERG	94.8	92.8	1.5	2.0	1.2	2.0	5.7	7.9	6.1	7.5	9.0	9.0	4.7	20.8	33.8	8.4	0.8	71.2	40.7	51.5	48.5
19352	LINCOLN UNIVERSITY	77.8	78.1	19.4	18.1	0.5	0.8	3.1	4.2	7.2	8.2	8.5	12.2	13.0	23.8	21.6	5.0	0.6	71.2	26.3	49.1	50.9
19355	MALVERN	92.8	89.9	2.5	3.2	3.3	5.1	1.5	2.0	5.7	6.6	7.4	7.4	4.8	21.6	31.1	13.1	2.3	75.6	42.8	47.5	52.5
19362	NOTTINGHAM	95.7	94.3	1.5	1.9	0.3	0.4	3.3	4.9	7.8	8.0	7.9	7.5	5.3	27.2	26.2	9.3	0.9	71.7	35.9	50.4	49.6
19363	OXFORD	87.8	85.5	6.1	6.8	0.5	0.7	8.9	11.1	8.4	8.0	7.8	7.4	5.7	26.5	24.3	9.9	1.9	71.1	35.4	49.7	50.3
19365	PARKESBURG	92.2	89.8	5.9	7.6	0.3	0.5	2.5	3.5	6.9	6.8	7.1	7.7	6.3	26.2	27.3	10.2	1.5	74.0	37.3	49.4	50.6
19372	THORNDALE	87.0	82.8	8.3	10.6	2.5	3.8	3.0	4.2	6.9	7.4	7.5	6.3	4.1	28.6	28.6	9.3	1.2	73.8	38.6	47.4	52.6
19373	THORNTON	78.6	78.3	18.5	17.7	1.1	1.8	1.6	3.2	5.3	6.3	6.7	8.2	8.8	26.8	26.2	10.0	1.8	79.6	37.6	54.2	45.8
19374	TOUGHKENAMON	75.1	69.9	4.7	5.0	1.0	1.3	40.5	50.0	10.1	7.3	6.9	7.4	8.6	33.5	18.4	6.8	1.0	71.5	30.6	56.9	43.1
19380	WEST CHESTER	88.7	85.6	6.5	7.7	2.5	3.9	3.3	4.2	6.3	6.8	7.5	6.9	5.4	25.7	27.3	12.1	1.9	74.7	39.5	49.2	50.8
19382	WEST CHESTER	88.5	85.2	7.0	8.4	2.6	4.0	2.7	3.5	5.0	5.3	5.9	10.3	11.5	24.2	26.5	9.8	1.6	79.7	35.9	48.5	51.5
19383	WEST CHESTER	93.1	90.2	4.3	5.7	1.8	3.0	1.0	1.7	5.6	6.5	7.7	8.2	13.5	19.3	27.1	9.1	3.0	75.2	37.1	44.8	55.2
19390	WEST GROVE	89.0	86.8	3.9	4.4	0.3	0.5	11.4	14.1	7.1	7.6	7.9	7.2	4.7	26.7	27.8	9.4	1.6	72.5	38.0	50.4	49.6
19401	NORRISTOWN	60.0	54.0	29.9	33.4	3.3	4.7	8.9	10.8	6.6	6.2	6.0	6.3	7.3	28.9	24.5	11.6	2.6	77.4	37.0	48.3	51.7
19403	NORRISTOWN	87.7	83.5	6.9	8.5	3.8	6.0	1.7	2.4	5.6	5.8	6.4	6.4	5.1	27.2	29.0	12.7	1.9	78.1	41.2	50.4	49.6
19405	BRIDGEPORT	92.2	89.2	2.5	3.2	2.3	3.7	3.6	5.1	5.4	5.0	4.9	5.5	6.7	31.8	26.6	11.8	2.3	81.4	39.1	49.3	50.7
19406	KING OF PRUSSIA	83.4	76.9	4.4	5.5	9.8	14.8	1.9	2.5	5.3	5.2	5.2	4.6	5.9	33.2	24.8	13.7	2.3	81.5	39.5	49.7	50.3
19422	BLUE BELL	86.1	80.5	5.0	6.1	7.8	12.0	1.4	2.0	5.5	6.1	7.0	6.7	4.2	21.5	32.0	14.1	2.9	76.9	44.3	47.8	52.2
19425	CHESTER SPRINGS	96.2	95.3	1.3	1.2	1.5	2.2	1.0	1.3	7.2	8.5	9.6	7.8	3.3	22.1	32.8	7.9	0.8	69.4	40.2	49.9	50.1
19426	COLLEGEVILLE	85.3	83.7	10.1	10.1	2.3	3.6	2.3	3.1	7.7	7.7	7.4	6.9	5.7	31.7	24.4	7.1	1.3	73.6	36.1	52.8	47.2
19428	CONSHOHOCKEN	89.3	83.6	5.8	9.2	3.4	5.3	1.3	1.9	5.8	5.3	5.3	5.6	7.4	32.8	24.7	11.0	2.1	80.1	37.2	49.3	50.7
19435	FREDERICK	98.6	98.3	0.0	0.0	0.9	1.3	0.5	0.4	5.2	5.6	5.6	5.6	6.0	24.0	32.2	14.2	1.7	81.1	43.7	50.2	49.8
19436	GWYNEDD	89.9	85.2	2.8	3.6	6.0	9.5	1.2	1.7	4.7	5.6	6.7	8.0	5.2	18.1	34.2	13.8	3.6	77.8	45.9	46.4	53.6
19438	HARLEYSVILLE	93.3	90.6	2.7	3.5	2.7	4.2	1.3	1.9	7.5	8.0	8.2	7.0	4.7	26.6	28.1	8.6	1.3	71.4	37.7	48.5	51.5
19440	HATFIELD	82.9	76.5	3.3	3.9	10.6	15.8	2.4	3.3	6.5	6.5	6.7	6.6	5.9	26.9	27.8	10.9	2.4	75.9	38.7	50.0	50.0
19444	LAFAYETTE HILL	94.0	91.3	2.6	3.4	2.8	4.5	0.9	1.3	6.7	7.1	7.7	5.9	3.4	25.0	27.5	12.8	3.9	74.4	41.7	47.4	52.6
19446	LANSDALE	87.3	82.2	3.5	4.3	7.3	11.1	2.0	2.7	6.2	6.5	6.9	6.3	5.0	25.9	29.1	11.5	2.7	76.4	40.7	48.2	51.8
19453	MONT CLARE	93.2	89.4	2.7	3.7	3.2	5.5	1.8	2.5	7.6	7.1	6.5	5.8	3.8	33.4	27.3	7.7	0.8	75.0	36.8	48.4	51.6
19454	NORTH WALES	85.4	79.2	4.5	5.7	8.6	13.3	1.3	1.8	7.1	7.5	8.0	7.0	4.7	24.8	28.8	10.3	1.8	72.6	39.6	48.5	51.5
19460	PHOENIXVILLE	91.3	88.4	4.4	5.4	2.4	3.9	2.0	2.7	6.5	6.5	6.8	6.8	6.1	26.6	28.1	10.9	1.7	75.9	39.3	49.2	50.8
	PENNSYLVANIA	85.4	83.2	10.0	10.7	1.8	2.7	3.2	4.2	5.8	6.0	6.3	7.1	6.5	24.8	27.8	13.1	2.6	77.8	40.4	48.5	51.5
	UNITED STATES	75.1	72.0	12.3	12.7	3.8	4.6	12.5	15.7	6.8	6.7	6.6	7.1	6.9	27.0	26.0	10.9	1.9	75.7	36.9	49.2	50.8

#	POST OFFICE NAME	2009 Per Capita Income	2009 HH Income Base	2009 Household Income Distribution (%): Less than $25,000	$25,000 to $49,999	$50,000 to $99,999	$100,000 to $149,999	$150,000 or More	Median Household Income: 2009	2014	2009 National Centile	2009 State Centile	2009 Home Value Base	2009 Home Value Distribution (%): Less than $50,000	$50,000 to $89,999	$90,000 to $174,999	$175,000 to $399,999	$400,000 or More	2009 Median Home Value
19090	WILLOW GROVE	31845	7458	10.6	21.1	40.4	21.4	6.5	68858	70596	86	89	5226	0.5	0.3	12.0	82.6	4.6	238540
19094	WOODLYN	25878	1942	22.7	21.6	38.7	12.8	4.3	58261	60798	75	77	1344	0.4	1.0	32.5	64.4	1.8	203492
19095	WYNCOTE	44682	2837	11.6	18.0	30.0	25.3	15.2	81578	85989	93	95	1492	0.5	3.7	6.0	64.7	25.1	311848
19096	WYNNEWOOD	63774	5022	7.1	12.1	23.2	21.4	36.2	116260	119280	98	99	4119	0.1	0.1	2.8	40.0	57.0	456509
19102	PHILADELPHIA	44028	2669	22.0	28.6	26.1	13.8	9.5	49562	52205	60	61	497	0.0	0.6	19.5	43.5	36.4	304930
19103	PHILADELPHIA	51460	12926	27.6	22.5	31.1	7.6	11.2	49880	52855	61	61	4095	7.7	13.0	17.9	20.6	40.7	304375
19104	PHILADELPHIA	14376	16426	56.5	23.0	16.7	2.3	1.5	20466	21015	2	1	3698	33.9	26.7	22.9	14.3	2.2	72879
19106	PHILADELPHIA	73925	5785	11.3	15.3	35.4	15.9	22.2	76006	76412	90	92	2597	0.0	0.6	6.9	38.9	53.6	432578
19107	PHILADELPHIA	26935	7035	42.2	23.4	24.7	5.5	4.2	32690	34300	13	5	980	2.1	3.8	12.2	51.0	30.8	284906
19111	PHILADELPHIA	24649	22898	22.1	25.5	40.4	8.6	3.4	52306	54860	67	67	14572	0.7	2.6	52.3	43.4	0.9	168394
19114	PHILADELPHIA	28145	12776	18.5	24.2	44.3	9.2	3.8	57507	59148	75	75	8040	0.8	1.3	43.4	51.9	2.6	179211
19115	PHILADELPHIA	27122	12679	24.1	23.9	36.9	10.9	4.1	52451	55558	67	67	7906	0.9	2.0	17.4	75.5	4.2	233106
19116	PHILADELPHIA	26346	12591	19.9	21.2	42.1	11.6	5.2	60577	61289	78	79	7842	0.5	1.2	13.8	82.4	2.1	226842
19118	PHILADELPHIA	51453	4204	10.7	17.5	37.3	14.0	20.5	74904	75136	89	91	2079	0.5	0.2	3.8	42.6	53.0	426974
19119	PHILADELPHIA	34041	11449	18.0	22.6	36.9	11.9	10.6	61622	62527	80	81	7247	1.7	8.8	28.7	47.9	12.9	199184
19120	PHILADELPHIA	15719	20696	30.2	29.2	33.6	4.9	2.1	41527	45394	38	33	14334	2.6	30.0	62.8	4.1	0.5	104501
19121	PHILADELPHIA	11984	12714	56.4	23.0	17.5	2.0	1.1	20818	21263	2	1	5152	55.6	28.0	11.9	4.5	0.1	45217
19122	PHILADELPHIA	12856	6009	51.7	23.2	21.0	3.1	1.0	23478	24389	2	1	2633	28.5	27.6	39.6	4.3	0.0	79652
19123	PHILADELPHIA	19174	4234	44.0	23.8	25.4	3.7	3.0	29394	31611	7	3	1378	5.4	15.2	49.9	26.2	3.2	146538
19124	PHILADELPHIA	16262	21337	34.4	28.2	31.1	4.8	1.6	37656	41093	26	16	14370	5.9	36.9	51.4	5.3	0.4	95232
19125	PHILADELPHIA	16886	8207	34.9	27.5	31.9	4.0	1.7	37841	40442	26	17	5672	21.9	32.0	40.6	5.0	0.4	85099
19126	PHILADELPHIA	21006	5773	24.5	30.0	33.9	7.6	4.1	45878	49532	51	50	3630	2.1	15.0	54.2	26.7	2.0	133212
19127	PHILADELPHIA	31539	2689	20.8	21.1	40.0	12.1	6.0	59658	60329	77	78	1419	1.1	4.4	66.7	27.4	0.5	153527
19128	PHILADELPHIA	30815	15612	17.1	23.5	42.9	11.2	5.3	60221	60595	78	79	9712	0.7	2.0	37.9	55.9	3.5	191186
19129	PHILADELPHIA	25087	4847	30.4	23.4	33.7	7.1	5.4	46667	50178	53	53	2396	7.9	18.5	43.1	21.2	9.3	136435
19130	PHILADELPHIA	34874	11168	25.9	22.5	35.1	9.8	6.7	51683	54105	65	66	4138	5.8	6.4	26.8	42.4	18.6	218614
19131	PHILADELPHIA	21151	18517	34.7	26.1	30.7	5.8	2.7	39229	42847	30	23	9620	13.3	25.2	43.3	16.5	1.7	110146
19132	PHILADELPHIA	13577	14460	51.0	26.1	19.2	2.2	1.5	24186	24909	3	1	8892	52.3	36.4	10.1	0.8	0.4	47233
19133	PHILADELPHIA	9476	7564	59.7	20.9	16.0	2.2	1.2	18514	18959	1	1	3741	63.2	26.1	9.4	1.1	0.2	37325
19134	PHILADELPHIA	12674	18941	46.4	26.7	23.1	2.9	0.8	27468	28965	5	2	12543	22.8	47.7	27.6	1.3	0.5	71298
19135	PHILADELPHIA	22265	11396	24.1	27.1	38.8	7.1	2.8	48660	51972	58	59	8445	1.3	16.2	76.7	5.2	0.5	118818
19136	PHILADELPHIA	21750	12930	23.6	25.7	40.4	7.5	2.9	50683	53588	63	64	8734	3.2	7.6	70.5	18.4	0.3	137584
19137	PHILADELPHIA	20946	2983	26.8	29.6	35.4	5.6	2.7	45104	48083	49	46	2467	5.5	25.6	63.7	4.1	1.1	109320
19138	PHILADELPHIA	18395	11725	26.9	30.0	36.2	5.1	1.8	44007	47469	45	43	8987	6.4	25.7	59.1	8.3	0.5	112921
19139	PHILADELPHIA	15482	16157	46.0	27.8	22.6	2.5	1.2	27690	29059	5	2	8280	24.0	44.5	28.3	2.6	0.6	72150
19140	PHILADELPHIA	12149	17957	49.1	27.4	19.8	2.8	1.0	25555	26217	4	2	10422	37.2	47.7	13.6	1.2	0.3	58709
19141	PHILADELPHIA	16779	11961	33.1	30.5	30.3	4.4	1.7	37789	40940	26	17	7013	4.9	30.2	57.6	6.4	0.9	104701
19142	PHILADELPHIA	14260	9435	38.4	29.7	27.3	3.2	1.4	34802	36371	17	8	6302	14.7	41.7	41.1	2.4	0.1	85012
19143	PHILADELPHIA	16887	24721	38.4	28.6	27.1	4.0	1.9	33818	35618	15	6	14973	17.9	43.2	30.5	7.2	1.2	78489
19144	PHILADELPHIA	20888	17912	36.5	27.0	28.0	5.1	3.4	36350	39096	22	12	7596	10.2	28.0	44.9	14.0	3.0	107463
19145	PHILADELPHIA	18892	17136	38.3	24.9	28.8	5.3	2.7	36277	39013	21	12	11413	11.2	29.1	40.8	17.2	1.7	104784
19146	PHILADELPHIA	19536	15586	39.8	27.3	24.8	5.1	3.0	33958	35725	15	7	7715	32.5	25.7	19.2	13.9	8.8	73443
19147	PHILADELPHIA	30176	16590	28.9	24.3	32.2	8.0	6.6	46725	50582	53	54	8366	3.8	14.2	39.0	27.9	15.1	157963
19148	PHILADELPHIA	18322	18698	37.1	27.5	28.8	4.9	1.8	35874	38254	20	10	13296	8.8	26.3	56.2	8.5	0.2	109282
19149	PHILADELPHIA	23122	18177	20.8	26.7	42.0	7.6	2.9	52505	54947	67	68	14165	0.6	6.4	88.0	4.7	0.3	129656
19150	PHILADELPHIA	25690	9554	15.9	25.3	47.1	8.4	3.3	57733	59122	75	75	7434	0.6	4.5	67.0	27.6	0.2	151103
19151	PHILADELPHIA	20779	11349	26.3	27.7	36.9	6.1	3.0	46270	50066	52	52	7889	4.8	16.0	66.7	10.4	2.2	127895
19152	PHILADELPHIA	25963	12734	22.6	25.7	39.0	9.2	3.5	51752	54770	65	66	8417	0.2	2.2	38.8	58.3	0.5	181940
19153	PHILADELPHIA	24841	5039	24.4	26.2	38.4	7.4	3.6	49423	52464	60	60	3043	2.1	10.1	61.2	26.4	0.2	153009
19154	PHILADELPHIA	27993	12200	10.8	21.7	46.9	14.6	5.9	68447	68762	86	89	9863	0.3	0.6	43.8	54.2	1.0	178804
19301	PAOLI	47989	3080	10.6	14.8	28.3	24.3	22.0	91898	101911	95	96	2404	0.1	0.4	2.2	54.9	42.4	368930
19310	ATGLEN	23700	1099	17.0	21.8	40.7	15.7	4.8	65663	67262	84	86	814	2.8	1.1	20.6	66.6	8.8	233333
19311	AVONDALE	39035	2532	7.3	9.4	30.9	28.8	23.6	103297	108833	97	98	1908	2.5	0.5	8.3	52.9	35.8	336019
19312	BERWYN	57579	4290	6.7	11.1	23.2	23.3	35.6	118434	122305	98	99	3593	0.1	0.4	0.8	30.7	68.0	520511
19317	CHADDS FORD	56293	3886	5.0	10.2	28.2	23.9	32.7	112709	116000	98	99	3507	0.1	0.6	8.1	36.3	54.9	434154
19319	CHEYNEY	63895	84	4.8	11.9	17.9	27.4	38.1	128374	130584	99	100	73	0.0	0.0	0.0	20.5	79.5	564024
19320	COATESVILLE	27881	19069	16.8	19.9	38.2	19.2	5.9	66396	67655	84	87	14271	3.5	3.6	25.1	59.4	8.4	225743
19330	COCHRANVILLE	26256	1897	15.7	22.4	39.2	16.9	5.9	66818	69259	85	88	1579	5.8	3.1	9.1	63.6	18.4	266053
19333	DEVON	56767	2805	8.3	13.0	26.0	23.6	29.1	104337	109169	97	98	1961	0.3	0.0	6.4	30.1	63.2	487374
19335	DOWNINGTOWN	42914	17113	6.5	12.0	31.6	28.3	21.6	99797	104801	97	98	13718	1.1	1.0	12.3	60.2	25.5	295800
19341	EXTON	49432	7361	5.7	11.6	32.4	29.0	21.4	100494	105923	97	98	4654	0.9	0.5	2.8	66.5	29.4	334915
19342	GLEN MILLS	45677	5873	5.5	10.6	30.7	25.0	28.3	105551	106766	97	98	5291	0.3	0.2	4.4	32.2	62.9	460790
19343	GLENMOORE	42261	2903	7.0	10.8	29.0	24.9	28.2	105409	110093	97	98	2678	4.1	2.9	4.0	49.4	39.6	362701
19344	HONEY BROOK	25417	3853	15.8	19.9	43.3	15.9	5.0	66181	67050	84	87	3091	13.1	5.5	13.4	55.5	12.5	240123
19348	KENNETT SQUARE	45841	7990	7.7	15.2	29.0	23.1	24.9	96202	103405	96	97	5567	0.4	1.0	8.6	45.8	44.3	371628
19350	LANDENBERG	51036	3874	4.2	7.5	26.1	24.7	37.5	126268	128215	99	99	3507	0.6	0.6	1.8	48.6	48.4	393491
19352	LINCOLN UNIVERSITY	31607	2435	6.7	9.4	34.5	28.9	20.5	99020	104031	97	97	2161	0.6	0.8	7.9	68.6	22.1	309791
19355	MALVERN	50062	9142	6.5	11.9	31.2	22.4	28.0	100813	107452	97	98	7252	2.1	0.3	4.7	47.1	45.8	381292
19362	NOTTINGHAM	23448	1989	14.3	27.2	45.0	10.1	3.4	58412	59678	76	77	1699	11.8	6.0	16.5	55.0	10.7	221576
19363	OXFORD	24700	5864	16.6	23.1	40.4	15.7	4.2	61441	61739	79	80	4212	1.7	1.3	16.9	69.8	10.3	253539
19365	PARKESBURG	25972	2440	14.0	21.9	44.4	15.5	4.2	64743	64864	83	85	1782	3.0	1.2	28.9	60.3	6.6	212712
19372	THORNDALE	41401	545	3.1	9.9	50.3	23.7	13.0	85634	86854	94	96	414	1.0	0.5	21.3	73.7	3.6	237981
19373	THORNTON	33640	1090	3.8	7.8	27.3	27.5	33.6	120334	120517	98	99	1028	0.0	0.0	2.3	34.6	63.0	446528
19374	TOUGHKENAMON	26349	444	12.2	14.0	36.9	20.9	16.0	83517	86052	93	95	279	4.7	4.3	6.8	62.4	21.9	314674
19380	WEST CHESTER	46484	19175	7.5	15.0	32.4	23.2	21.9	91861	100012	95	96	14129	0.6	0.6	6.2	55.3	37.3	347534
19382	WEST CHESTER	45041	19955	9.3	14.0	30.0	23.0	23.8	93650	101176	96	97	14003	0.5	0.7	10.6	48.0	40.2	361464
19383	WEST CHESTER	37602	151	0.0	6.6	24.5	19.2	49.7	149113	154822	100	100	145	0.0	0.7	0.0	44.1	55.2	434091
19390	WEST GROVE	32075	4617	10.2	16.8	39.2	23.4	10.4	79826	83843	92	94	3813	6.4	2.0	8.8	64.4	18.4	277575
19401	NORRISTOWN	24894	15243	22.9	27.2	34.8	11.2	3.9	49909	52069	61	62	7747	1.1	5.4	52.3	39.0	2.2	164841
19403	NORRISTOWN	36774	16297	8.3	16.1	38.4	26.0	11.3	80625	84894	92	94	12709	1.8	1.0	12.3	70.0	14.8	271269
19405	BRIDGEPORT	27405	2198	16.8	29.0	42.1	9.9	2.2	53943	54907	70	70	1197	0.6	1.5	49.3	45.9	2.7	173825
19406	KING OF PRUSSIA	42308	9779	8.2	16.8	37.8	26.5	10.7	81396	85960	93	95	5978	0.4	0.5	7.7	81.1	10.3	272610
19422	BLUE BELL	56162	7341	5.5	10.7	25.8	27.0	31.0	112475	115734	98	98	5750	0.0	0.2	6.2	38.3	55.3	432334
19425	CHESTER SPRINGS	58110	4506	4.5	7.7	25.6	23.6	38.6	125829	129205	99	99	4115	0.0	0.1	2.7	42.3	55.0	429724
19426	COLLEGEVILLE	41532	11554	4.1	9.9	30.1	30.5	25.5	108701	112061	98	98	9871	0.1	0.2	4.7	67.3	27.6	314806
19428	CONSHOHOCKEN	35269	7790	14.2	22.2	37.3	16.8	9.5	66010	66620	84	87	4721	0.5	1.6	22.0	61.6	14.2	227001
19435	FREDERICK	33929	90	7.8	24.4	35.6	24.4	7.8	75000	76447	89	91	82	3.7	2.4	4.9	51.2	37.8	300000
19436	GWYNEDD	97517	324	2.2	10.8	27.5	21.6	38.0	123166	125532	99	99	235	1.7	0.0	1.3	23.4	73.6	614583
19438	HARLEYSVILLE	38424	8431	7.3	10.9	34.9	31.1	15.9	94587	101437	96	97	6775	0.3	0.1	6.6	65.7	27.3	304913
19440	HATFIELD	30687	6991	10.0	21.5	40.2	21.2	7.1	71853	74831	88	90	4409	1.8	2.0	6.6	79.5	10.0	267618
19444	LAFAYETTE HILL	55942	4005	5.6	11.0	27.5	25.0	30.8	110486	114584	98	98	3410	0.4	0.6	2.5	57.1	39.4	359756
19446	LANSDALE	39916	20579	8.8	16.4	35.7	22.5	16.6	82523	87301	93	95	14526	0.5	0.4	12.9	67.2	19.0	283493
19453	MONT CLARE	45909	626	6.1	16.1	42.5	25.2	10.1	81058	82441	92	95	524	0.0	1.0	22.1	56.5	20.4	252907
19454	NORTH WALES	45937	10266	7.2	16.8	31.1	24.2	20.7	90129	98897	95	96	8608	0.7	2.9	14.0	51.2	31.2	297269
19460	PHOENIXVILLE	40518	15389	11.5	19.0	32.8	21.8	14.9	78436	82212	91	93	11149	1.7	0.9	20.0	53.8	23.6	266292
	PENNSYLVANIA	26913		21.5	25.3	36.9	10.2	6.1	53225	55819				7.5	12.2	35.6	36.1	8.5	161438
	UNITED STATES	27277		20.9	24.4	35.3	11.7	7.6	54719	56938				9.3	13.1	31.6	32.6	13.5	162279

ZIP CODE #	POST OFFICE NAME	FINANCIAL SERVICES: Auto Loan	FINANCIAL SERVICES: Home Loan	FINANCIAL SERVICES: Invest-ments	FINANCIAL SERVICES: Retire-ment Plans	THE HOME: Home Improvements: Home Repair	THE HOME: Home Improvements: Lawn & Garden	THE HOME: Furnishings: Comput-ers & Hard-ware-Personal	THE HOME: Furnishings: Major Appli-ances	THE HOME: Furnishings: TV, Radio, Sound Equip-ment	THE HOME: Furnishings: Furni-ture	ENTERTAINMENT: Dine out/ Carry out	ENTERTAINMENT: Sports Equip-ment	ENTERTAINMENT: Fees & Tickets	ENTERTAINMENT: Toys & Games	ENTERTAINMENT: Travel	ENTERTAINMENT: Cable TV	PERSONAL: Apparel & Services	PERSONAL: Auto Repairs	PERSONAL: Health Insur-ance	PERSONAL: Pets & Supplies
19090	WILLOW GROVE	104	119	115	118	119	114	112	111	111	112	112	84	121	111	118	112	80	112	115	129
19094	WOODLYN	86	93	92	93	93	96	91	92	93	89	92	68	95	91	94	96	65	92	99	107
19095	WYNCOTE	124	144	154	145	151	150	135	140	139	139	139	100	150	131	148	143	98	140	157	161
19096	WYNNEWOOD	194	269	314	273	295	245	227	238	209	246	208	179	274	205	267	200	157	223	213	262
19102	PHILADELPHIA	99	74	76	85	71	71	109	82	105	101	109	75	96	106	93	102	78	98	85	105
19103	PHILADELPHIA	100	82	88	91	81	82	111	89	109	104	112	77	103	107	100	108	80	104	98	112
19104	PHILADELPHIA	45	31	31	33	30	33	55	38	51	44	52	33	42	50	39	51	37	46	41	48
19106	PHILADELPHIA	146	133	151	150	136	125	168	137	159	161	165	121	164	159	159	154	120	153	135	167
19107	PHILADELPHIA	65	49	52	56	48	49	74	55	72	66	74	49	65	71	63	71	53	67	60	71
19111	PHILADELPHIA	79	83	78	83	81	85	84	82	86	81	86	62	86	84	84	88	60	84	91	97
19114	PHILADELPHIA	82	92	90	91	92	92	89	89	90	87	91	66	95	88	93	93	64	90	96	103
19115	PHILADELPHIA	78	85	88	85	88	90	85	85	88	84	88	62	90	84	89	91	61	87	98	99
19116	PHILADELPHIA	85	96	93	96	95	95	92	92	93	91	94	69	99	92	97	95	67	93	97	107
19118	PHILADELPHIA	147	156	166	162	161	151	161	153	156	163	157	119	169	153	165	154	113	157	154	179
19119	PHILADELPHIA	104	113	113	113	113	111	111	108	114	110	115	80	118	112	113	117	82	111	114	128
19120	PHILADELPHIA	61	68	67	64	67	67	66	64	72	61	72	45	71	71	65	78	52	67	71	76
19121	PHILADELPHIA	41	40	39	38	39	41	43	40	48	40	48	28	44	47	40	52	34	44	47	49
19122	PHILADELPHIA	45	45	45	43	44	46	49	45	54	45	53	32	49	52	46	58	38	49	52	54
19123	PHILADELPHIA	57	49	48	51	48	51	61	53	64	57	64	42	58	62	55	67	45	60	61	66
19124	PHILADELPHIA	58	63	61	60	61	62	63	60	68	58	68	43	66	67	61	73	49	63	67	72
19125	PHILADELPHIA	56	64	63	59	64	63	60	60	67	56	67	40	66	66	61	73	49	62	67	70
19126	PHILADELPHIA	70	77	76	75	76	76	77	73	82	72	82	53	82	80	77	87	59	77	81	88
19127	PHILADELPHIA	93	84	83	89	82	84	99	87	98	95	99	71	94	97	92	97	70	95	92	106
19128	PHILADELPHIA	91	94	91	95	93	93	98	92	98	96	99	72	100	97	98	99	69	97	98	110
19129	PHILADELPHIA	78	70	70	73	69	70	84	73	85	79	86	58	80	85	77	87	61	81	79	89
19130	PHILADELPHIA	91	80	81	85	78	78	98	83	98	93	100	69	94	97	90	98	71	93	88	103
19131	PHILADELPHIA	63	64	65	63	64	66	68	64	73	64	73	46	70	70	66	77	52	69	73	77
19132	PHILADELPHIA	43	48	48	45	48	48	47	46	52	43	52	31	50	51	46	57	38	48	52	54
19133	PHILADELPHIA	39	39	37	36	38	39	40	39	45	38	45	26	41	44	38	49	33	41	43	46
19134	PHILADELPHIA	47	48	47	46	47	48	50	48	55	47	55	33	52	54	48	59	40	51	53	57
19135	PHILADELPHIA	75	77	68	76	74	81	78	76	81	73	80	57	78	81	76	85	56	78	86	91
19136	PHILADELPHIA	77	82	74	81	79	86	80	80	84	76	83	59	83	83	80	88	58	81	90	95
19137	PHILADELPHIA	67	75	71	72	74	78	70	72	76	66	75	51	75	74	72	81	53	72	81	84
19138	PHILADELPHIA	63	71	69	67	69	71	66	66	73	63	73	45	72	71	67	79	52	69	76	79
19139	PHILADELPHIA	47	50	51	47	50	50	51	49	56	46	56	33	53	55	49	61	41	52	55	58
19140	PHILADELPHIA	45	47	46	44	47	47	47	46	52	44	52	31	49	51	46	57	38	49	52	54
19141	PHILADELPHIA	55	62	62	58	62	62	60	59	67	56	67	40	65	65	60	73	48	62	68	70
19142	PHILADELPHIA	51	59	60	55	59	59	56	55	62	51	62	37	61	61	56	68	45	57	63	65
19143	PHILADELPHIA	54	59	60	56	59	58	59	57	65	54	65	40	63	64	58	70	47	60	63	67
19144	PHILADELPHIA	62	61	62	60	60	61	68	61	73	62	73	45	68	71	64	77	52	67	69	75
19145	PHILADELPHIA	59	65	65	62	65	67	63	63	69	59	69	44	67	67	64	74	49	65	72	74
19146	PHILADELPHIA	57	58	60	57	58	58	63	58	67	58	68	42	64	66	60	71	49	62	64	69
19147	PHILADELPHIA	80	76	79	78	76	76	87	78	89	82	91	61	86	88	83	92	65	85	84	94
19148	PHILADELPHIA	56	64	65	60	64	65	61	61	67	56	67	41	66	66	62	74	48	63	69	71
19149	PHILADELPHIA	80	85	73	84	81	88	82	82	86	78	85	62	85	86	82	89	59	83	92	98
19150	PHILADELPHIA	86	91	85	92	88	97	85	87	91	88	92	61	91	88	87	96	63	89	99	106
19151	PHILADELPHIA	67	74	72	71	73	73	74	71	79	67	79	51	78	78	73	85	57	74	78	84
19152	PHILADELPHIA	77	85	83	84	85	89	81	83	85	80	85	60	87	82	86	89	59	84	95	97
19153	PHILADELPHIA	81	73	72	75	72	80	80	78	85	78	84	58	77	83	76	88	58	82	88	94
19154	PHILADELPHIA	99	115	103	114	111	111	105	105	105	105	106	81	115	107	111	106	75	106	109	123
19301	PAOLI	146	178	194	179	188	176	160	166	159	166	159	121	183	154	178	160	115	162	171	188
19310	ATGLEN	94	108	97	109	106	103	100	100	98	99	99	79	107	100	105	98	70	99	100	117
19311	AVONDALE	174	212	192	214	209	180	181	183	169	196	172	148	203	179	193	159	126	171	158	205
19312	BERWYN	178	239	285	246	264	223	207	216	192	225	191	163	249	187	241	184	144	203	196	238
19317	CHADDS FORD	185	250	284	253	270	229	212	223	196	228	196	167	252	193	247	189	146	209	201	246
19319	CHEYNEY	191	253	261	266	262	227	207	216	193	225	196	170	250	197	236	184	147	200	187	243
19320	COATESVILLE	104	114	103	115	111	110	107	107	107	108	108	82	113	108	110	108	76	106	108	126
19330	COCHRANVILLE	105	118	102	122	115	116	106	110	104	106	105	86	113	107	112	104	73	106	109	129
19333	DEVON	170	196	224	206	210	182	193	185	180	202	182	147	212	178	207	172	134	185	171	212
19335	DOWNINGTOWN	161	190	178	193	188	170	170	169	162	178	164	134	187	166	180	156	118	164	156	195
19341	EXTON	165	181	171	188	178	162	170	164	162	178	165	133	182	168	175	156	119	163	151	192
19342	GLEN MILLS	162	220	234	221	230	201	181	190	172	190	174	143	217	174	208	169	129	179	176	211
19343	GLENMOORE	176	214	212	220	217	198	181	189	174	194	175	146	206	178	198	169	128	178	172	217
19344	HONEY BROOK	104	111	101	111	109	109	102	107	101	102	102	82	105	104	105	102	71	103	104	124
19348	KENNETT SQUARE	159	198	206	198	207	187	173	181	168	183	169	134	199	166	194	166	122	173	176	203
19350	LANDENBERG	202	268	276	280	277	240	219	228	205	237	208	179	264	210	250	196	156	212	200	257
19352	LINCOLN UNIVERSITY	161	190	166	194	185	163	162	165	152	176	154	133	179	162	170	143	112	153	143	186
19355	MALVERN	178	219	227	225	226	201	195	197	184	205	186	153	221	185	214	178	136	190	182	224
19362	NOTTINGHAM	99	101	88	101	98	100	93	97	93	95	94	73	93	97	93	94	65	93	96	114
19363	OXFORD	98	106	91	106	101	100	100	99	99	101	99	77	103	101	100	98	70	98	98	116
19365	PARKESBURG	94	108	98	109	106	103	101	101	99	100	100	79	108	100	106	99	71	100	100	118
19372	THORNDALE	136	162	148	163	158	145	143	143	136	149	139	113	157	140	152	132	99	139	133	166
19373	THORNTON	172	239	259	239	253	217	195	205	184	204	185	154	237	186	227	180	139	192	187	226
19374	TOUGHKENAMON	133	165	154	150	171	125	149	151	128	162	131	117	156	130	159	115	97	141	117	157
19380	WEST CHESTER	158	182	185	186	186	169	169	168	161	177	163	130	185	162	180	157	117	165	160	193
19382	WEST CHESTER	162	181	188	188	186	170	179	170	169	180	170	135	190	169	183	164	124	170	161	197
19383	WEST CHESTER	245	325	336	342	337	292	266	277	249	289	251	218	321	254	303	236	189	257	241	313
19390	WEST GROVE	129	150	130	152	145	139	132	135	127	136	129	107	143	132	139	125	91	129	128	157
19401	NORRISTOWN	82	82	78	82	80	82	89	82	91	85	91	63	89	90	85	93	65	88	89	99
19403	NORRISTOWN	121	146	144	146	147	137	131	132	128	134	130	101	146	129	142	128	93	131	132	152
19405	BRIDGEPORT	80	86	82	86	84	81	89	83	87	86	88	66	92	87	89	87	63	87	85	98
19406	KING OF PRUSSIA	127	131	133	136	132	125	136	126	132	135	135	101	141	133	137	130	96	131	125	149
19422	BLUE BELL	178	236	267	240	255	217	204	212	189	220	189	160	240	185	235	181	140	200	192	236
19425	CHESTER SPRINGS	215	280	287	293	288	252	232	240	218	251	221	189	277	222	262	208	164	225	212	272
19426	COLLEGEVILLE	174	210	192	214	208	180	180	182	168	195	171	147	202	177	191	158	125	170	158	205
19428	CONSHOHOCKEN	112	115	107	117	112	109	119	111	117	118	118	89	121	118	118	116	84	116	112	132
19435	FREDERICK	105	148	153	137	153	130	122	127	116	121	118	93	143	118	139	117	87	122	120	139
19436	GWYNEDD	191	267	323	274	298	248	224	240	205	250	202	177	274	197	269	195	153	221	214	262
19438	HARLEYSVILLE	144	172	164	175	171	155	152	152	145	159	147	119	169	148	162	141	106	148	141	175
19440	HATFIELD	111	125	115	124	122	112	117	113	112	119	114	90	124	116	120	110	82	113	107	131
19444	LAFAYETTE HILL	192	249	255	251	258	220	209	216	195	225	197	168	245	201	234	187	146	202	192	239
19446	LANSDALE	134	157	153	160	157	147	144	143	140	148	141	111	158	141	153	138	101	141	139	166
19453	MONT CLARE	126	141	132	144	139	134	131	131	128	133	129	102	140	130	137	126	91	129	128	154
19454	NORTH WALES	155	191	187	190	192	170	166	168	158	174	160	130	187	163	180	154	116	162	155	190
19460	PHOENIXVILLE	136	152	148	155	152	143	144	141	140	147	141	110	154	141	150	138	101	141	138	164
	PENNSYLVANIA	94	95	95	95	95	100	94	96	96	91	95	73	94	96	94	99	67	95	101	113
	UNITED STATES	100	100	100	100	100	100	100	100	100	100	100	100	100	100	100	100	100	100	100	100

ZIP CODE			POPULATION			2000-2009 ANNUAL RATE		HOUSEHOLDS					FAMILIES		
#	POST OFFICE NAME	COUNTY FIPS CODE	2000	2009	2014	% Rate	State Centile	2000	2009	2014	% Annual Rate 2000-2009	2009 Average HH Size	2000	2009	% Annual Rate 2000-2009
19462	PLYMOUTH MEETING	091	13631	13903	13992	0.2	61	5419	5611	5674	0.4	2.43	3840	3940	0.3
19464	POTTSTOWN	091	42236	44619	45783	0.6	74	16570	17650	18138	0.7	2.50	11182	11639	0.4
19465	POTTSTOWN	029	14120	16243	17323	1.5	92	5422	6338	6802	1.7	2.53	3958	4495	1.4
19468	ROYERSFORD	091	21752	25786	27459	1.9	94	8288	9935	10586	2.0	2.57	5770	6758	1.7
19473	SCHWENKSVILLE	091	13605	15404	16111	1.4	91	4859	5513	5780	1.4	2.72	3619	4005	1.1
19475	SPRING CITY	029	9518	11249	12069	1.8	93	3621	4344	4696	2.0	2.48	2512	2914	1.6
19477	SPRING HOUSE	091	2	2	3	0.0	52	1	1	1	0.0	2.00	1	1	0.0
19492	ZIEGLERVILLE	091	182	208	218	1.5	92	74	86	91	1.6	2.37	57	65	1.4
19501	ADAMSTOWN	071	849	984	1049	1.6	92	347	410	439	1.8	2.40	243	278	1.5
19503	BALLY	011	1034	1144	1199	1.1	87	404	453	475	1.2	2.53	298	326	1.0
19504	BARTO	011	4626	4680	4769	0.1	57	1647	1693	1732	0.3	2.76	1324	1332	0.1
19505	BECHTELSVILLE	011	3716	3969	4463	0.7	77	1349	1463	1654	0.9	2.71	1070	1132	0.6
19506	BERNVILLE	011	7202	8234	8700	1.5	92	2641	3055	3239	1.6	2.66	2008	2265	1.3
19507	BETHEL	011	4225	4516	4651	0.7	77	1447	1567	1623	0.9	2.78	1113	1176	0.6
19508	BIRDSBORO	011	15539	16889	17463	0.9	83	5778	6352	6597	1.0	2.65	4387	4711	0.8
19510	BLANDON	011	5403	6940	7531	2.7	97	1865	2395	2598	2.7	2.90	1528	1921	2.5
19512	BOYERTOWN	011	16973	17297	17558	0.2	61	6655	6893	7024	0.4	2.48	4761	4780	0.0
19518	DOUGLASSVILLE	011	10444	13544	14851	2.8	97	3805	4947	5429	2.9	2.73	2953	3749	2.6
19520	ELVERSON	029	5317	5675	5959	0.7	77	2029	2204	2326	0.9	2.55	1582	1670	0.6
19522	FLEETWOOD	011	13699	14526	14948	0.6	74	5167	5542	5720	0.8	2.61	3908	4086	0.5
19525	GILBERTSVILLE	091	10360	13178	14146	2.6	97	3536	4575	4936	2.8	2.88	2910	3700	2.6
19526	HAMBURG	011	11003	11514	11729	0.5	70	4278	4512	4608	0.6	2.47	3049	3119	0.2
19529	KEMPTON	011	2979	3420	3628	1.5	92	1083	1262	1346	1.7	2.70	839	951	1.4
19530	KUTZTOWN	011	14953	16231	16640	0.9	83	4719	5127	5304	0.9	2.55	2980	3139	0.6
19533	LEESPORT	011	7112	8174	8565	1.5	92	2034	2361	2517	1.6	2.61	1538	1737	1.3
19534	LENHARTSVILLE	011	1990	2164	2236	0.9	83	755	830	861	1.0	2.53	567	606	0.7
19539	MERTZTOWN	011	4855	5119	5255	0.6	74	1792	1910	1971	0.7	2.59	1380	1432	0.4
19540	MOHNTON	011	10982	11889	12335	0.9	83	4087	4471	4646	1.0	2.65	3159	3373	0.7
19541	MOHRSVILLE	011	3779	4013	4124	0.7	77	1373	1477	1522	0.8	2.72	1046	1097	0.5
19543	MORGANTOWN	011	3891	4935	5304	2.6	97	1344	1742	1882	2.8	2.82	1042	1310	2.5
19547	OLEY	011	4367	4590	4822	0.5	70	1682	1788	1882	0.7	2.56	1259	1303	0.4
19549	PORT CLINTON	107	288	284	281	-0.2	38	132	135	135	0.2	2.10	91	90	-0.1
19551	ROBESONIA	011	4761	5205	5400	1.0	85	1768	1955	2035	1.1	2.59	1333	1436	0.8
19555	SHOEMAKERSVILLE	011	4281	4497	4574	0.5	70	1453	1520	1557	0.5	2.42	1046	1061	0.2
19560	TEMPLE	011	6535	6956	7139	0.7	77	2793	3001	3091	0.8	2.26	1885	1957	0.4
19562	TOPTON	011	2245	2385	2436	0.7	77	823	879	902	0.7	2.45	589	610	0.4
19565	WERNERSVILLE	011	7370	8334	8771	1.3	90	2892	3303	3493	1.4	2.38	2029	2202	0.9
19567	WOMELSDORF	011	4913	5363	5648	1.0	85	1832	2011	2120	1.0	2.58	1305	1388	0.7
19601	READING	011	30767	32926	33750	0.7	77	11481	12131	12420	0.6	2.68	7005	7087	0.1
19602	READING	011	17104	17893	18174	0.5	70	6717	6944	7048	0.4	2.53	3689	3614	-0.2
19604	READING	011	24295	25966	26405	0.7	77	8475	8740	8864	0.3	2.84	5607	5569	-0.1
19605	READING	011	17244	19393	20356	1.3	90	6914	7789	8181	1.3	2.46	4926	5412	1.0
19606	READING	011	30478	33673	35225	1.1	87	11999	13290	13898	1.1	2.52	8609	9292	0.8
19607	READING	011	20579	21341	21648	0.4	68	9122	9507	9675	0.4	2.17	5671	5669	0.0
19608	READING	011	17020	22480	24752	3.1	98	6298	8418	9304	3.2	2.63	4682	6085	2.9
19609	READING	011	9836	10057	10175	0.2	61	4213	4350	4405	0.3	2.31	2886	2886	0.0
19610	READING	011	14216	14796	14981	0.4	68	5708	5966	6069	0.5	2.26	3762	3788	0.1
19611	READING	011	10000	10112	10125	0.1	57	3928	3969	3984	0.1	2.32	2316	2243	-0.3
	PENNSYLVANIA					0.3					0.4	2.45			0.1
	UNITED STATES					1.0					1.1	2.59			0.9

ZIP CODE		RACE (%)						% Hispanic Origin		2009 AGE DISTRIBUTION (%)										MEDIAN AGE	% 2009 Males	% 2009 Females
#	POST OFFICE NAME	White		Black		Asian/Pacific																
		2000	2009	2000	2009	2000	2009	2000	2009	0-4	5-9	10-14	15-19	20-24	25-44	45-64	65-84	85+	18+	2009		
19462	PLYMOUTH MEETING	90.8	83.8	3.7	8.1	4.4	6.6	1.1	1.7	4.5	5.0	5.7	5.4	4.5	24.5	29.5	17.8	3.1	81.7	45.2	48.6	51.4
19464	POTTSTOWN	84.9	82.2	10.9	12.5	0.8	1.3	3.0	3.8	7.2	7.2	7.0	6.7	5.7	26.5	26.1	11.3	2.3	74.3	38.0	48.5	51.5
19465	POTTSTOWN	97.2	96.3	1.3	1.6	0.6	0.9	0.8	1.2	5.0	5.6	6.2	6.2	4.8	23.3	32.7	13.9	2.3	79.2	44.3	49.2	50.8
19468	ROYERSFORD	95.0	93.1	2.2	2.8	1.4	2.2	1.2	1.8	8.2	7.9	7.5	6.2	4.9	29.6	25.4	8.7	1.6	72.3	37.1	48.9	51.1
19473	SCHWENKSVILLE	95.0	93.2	2.0	2.6	1.2	2.0	1.5	2.2	7.8	8.3	8.4	7.7	5.1	27.3	26.6	7.7	1.0	71.0	36.9	49.2	50.8
19475	SPRING CITY	94.1	92.1	3.4	4.5	0.9	1.4	1.1	1.6	7.0	6.8	6.6	6.7	5.3	24.5	28.4	12.2	2.5	75.2	40.3	50.3	49.7
19477	SPRING HOUSE	100.0	100.0	0.0	0.0	0.0	0.0	0.0	0.0	0.0	0.0	0.0	0.0	0.0	0.0	100.0	0.0	0.0	100.0	50.0	0.0	100.0
19492	ZIEGLERVILLE	97.8	95.7	0.6	1.0	0.6	1.0	0.6	0.5	6.7	7.7	8.2	6.7	3.8	24.5	31.3	9.6	1.4	72.1	40.8	51.0	49.0
19501	ADAMSTOWN	99.2	98.8	0.1	0.1	0.2	0.4	0.9	1.5	7.2	7.0	6.6	5.9	5.9	27.5	26.6	11.1	2.1	75.7	38.8	49.0	51.0
19503	BALLY	98.7	98.2	0.5	0.7	0.5	0.8	0.3	0.5	5.5	5.7	6.3	7.0	4.5	26.8	26.5	15.1	2.6	78.2	41.5	50.7	49.3
19504	BARTO	98.7	98.1	0.3	0.5	0.3	0.4	0.5	0.9	6.1	6.9	7.4	6.5	4.3	24.7	32.1	10.9	1.2	75.6	41.5	50.4	49.6
19505	BECHTELSVILLE	98.3	97.4	0.5	0.8	0.3	0.4	0.7	1.3	6.4	7.0	7.5	6.8	4.2	25.4	30.6	11.1	1.1	74.8	40.6	50.8	49.2
19506	BERNVILLE	97.4	96.0	0.8	1.2	0.4	0.6	1.8	3.1	5.7	6.2	6.8	7.1	4.6	25.2	31.7	11.3	1.5	76.8	41.5	51.0	49.0
19507	BETHEL	95.7	93.4	1.7	2.3	0.5	0.9	2.2	3.9	6.3	6.7	7.1	7.1	4.7	27.6	28.9	10.4	1.2	75.5	39.3	53.2	46.8
19508	BIRDSBORO	96.5	94.8	1.3	2.0	0.5	0.9	1.3	2.3	6.4	6.9	7.3	7.0	4.6	25.1	30.3	10.9	1.6	75.0	40.6	49.8	50.2
19510	BLANDON	96.6	94.6	0.8	1.3	1.3	2.1	2.4	4.2	8.2	8.2	8.1	6.6	4.7	29.4	26.7	7.4	0.7	71.4	36.2	49.8	50.2
19512	BOYERTOWN	97.0	95.4	2.0	2.9	0.4	0.6	0.6	1.1	5.2	5.7	6.3	7.2	4.6	25.3	31.0	12.8	2.0	78.2	42.2	49.8	50.2
19518	DOUGLASSVILLE	96.0	94.0	1.8	2.7	0.6	1.0	0.8	1.5	6.8	6.8	7.0	6.9	5.2	25.4	29.2	11.4	1.3	75.0	39.9	49.4	50.6
19520	ELVERSON	97.8	97.0	0.5	0.7	0.6	1.0	0.7	1.0	5.5	6.2	7.0	6.7	4.0	22.5	32.1	14.4	1.5	76.9	43.7	50.1	49.9
19522	FLEETWOOD	98.3	97.2	0.3	0.4	0.4	0.6	1.3	2.4	5.8	6.3	6.8	6.7	4.8	25.2	31.0	11.8	1.7	76.9	41.6	49.5	50.5
19525	GILBERTSVILLE	97.8	96.9	0.7	0.8	0.9	1.4	0.6	0.9	6.8	7.3	8.2	7.7	4.5	25.1	29.5	9.7	1.2	72.6	39.2	49.6	50.4
19526	HAMBURG	97.9	96.7	0.4	0.6	0.2	0.4	1.1	2.1	5.7	6.0	6.3	5.8	4.4	25.9	29.7	13.5	2.6	78.4	42.3	49.4	50.6
19529	KEMPTON	98.6	97.9	0.2	0.3	0.4	0.6	0.7	1.2	5.5	6.2	7.0	7.5	4.3	24.6	33.4	10.1	1.3	76.3	41.6	50.9	49.1
19530	KUTZTOWN	97.0	95.4	1.2	1.8	0.7	1.1	1.2	2.1	3.8	4.0	4.4	15.6	19.1	19.3	21.9	9.8	2.0	85.1	28.4	47.1	52.9
19533	LEESPORT	93.6	91.7	4.0	4.9	1.1	1.6	7.3	10.9	4.1	4.5	5.2	6.2	6.1	29.7	27.1	12.9	4.3	82.7	41.5	55.7	44.3
19534	LENHARTSVILLE	98.3	97.6	0.4	0.5	0.1	0.2	0.9	1.5	5.3	5.8	6.3	6.0	4.3	26.7	33.2	11.3	1.2	78.9	42.5	51.0	49.0
19539	MERTZTOWN	98.6	97.9	0.3	0.5	0.3	0.5	0.9	1.7	5.4	6.0	6.6	6.8	5.1	24.5	31.1	11.9	2.6	77.9	42.1	48.9	51.1
19540	MOHNTON	97.3	95.8	0.8	1.2	0.5	0.8	1.3	2.4	5.4	5.8	6.5	7.1	5.0	23.5	33.5	11.8	1.5	77.8	42.8	49.6	50.4
19541	MOHRSVILLE	97.8	96.5	0.6	0.9	0.4	0.6	1.6	2.8	5.4	5.9	6.7	6.5	4.0	27.2	32.5	10.6	1.2	77.9	41.8	50.5	49.5
19543	MORGANTOWN	98.1	97.1	0.4	0.6	0.6	1.1	0.7	1.2	6.8	7.0	7.4	7.5	5.5	24.9	28.3	11.2	1.5	74.2	38.7	50.0	50.0
19547	OLEY	98.8	98.2	0.2	0.3	0.3	0.5	0.8	1.5	4.9	5.7	6.3	6.5	4.6	25.6	31.8	13.0	1.7	79.0	42.8	50.4	49.6
19549	PORT CLINTON	97.6	97.5	0.3	0.4	0.0	0.0	1.4	2.5	3.2	3.9	4.2	6.0	4.2	22.2	37.7	16.5	2.1	85.6	48.3	52.5	47.5
19551	ROBESONIA	96.6	94.6	1.3	1.9	0.4	0.7	1.8	3.2	5.4	5.9	7.0	7.8	4.8	23.0	32.4	12.2	1.7	76.6	42.6	50.1	49.9
19555	SHOEMAKERSVILLE	95.4	92.9	1.7	2.4	0.4	0.7	4.0	7.1	4.7	4.6	5.0	5.2	5.2	27.5	27.7	16.0	4.1	82.6	43.5	51.6	48.4
19560	TEMPLE	96.8	94.7	0.8	1.2	0.4	0.6	4.1	7.2	4.5	4.9	5.4	5.8	4.5	22.6	30.2	18.0	4.1	81.6	46.3	48.2	51.8
19562	TOPTON	99.1	98.4	0.1	0.2	0.2	0.4	1.2	2.2	5.2	5.4	5.8	5.5	4.2	23.1	26.7	15.4	8.6	79.7	45.4	45.8	54.2
19565	WERNERSVILLE	97.1	95.3	1.3	1.9	0.5	0.8	1.3	2.4	5.0	5.4	6.1	6.9	4.3	23.4	30.4	14.2	4.3	78.8	44.4	49.5	50.5
19567	WOMELSDORF	95.7	93.2	1.5	2.1	0.9	1.5	2.2	4.0	6.3	6.5	7.0	7.1	5.1	26.1	28.2	12.0	1.7	75.7	39.9	51.3	48.7
19601	READING	50.5	42.6	17.6	17.6	1.4	1.8	42.6	52.8	9.5	8.2	7.2	7.8	8.6	26.9	21.4	8.8	1.5	70.3	30.5	48.6	51.4
19602	READING	57.1	48.3	11.4	11.9	1.7	2.0	42.3	53.3	9.2	7.8	7.0	7.6	8.5	27.8	20.4	9.5	2.1	71.6	31.5	49.8	50.2
19604	READING	68.9	59.4	7.7	8.8	1.8	2.4	29.3	40.0	8.3	7.6	6.9	9.4	9.7	26.4	20.7	8.9	1.9	72.7	30.5	48.9	51.1
19605	READING	94.5	91.4	1.4	2.1	0.8	1.3	4.6	7.7	5.1	5.4	5.8	6.2	4.7	23.5	29.8	16.4	3.0	79.8	44.5	48.5	51.5
19606	READING	94.6	91.9	1.9	2.7	1.1	1.8	3.3	5.4	5.9	6.2	6.7	6.7	4.9	25.4	29.5	12.5	2.2	76.9	41.2	49.0	51.0
19607	READING	94.0	90.8	1.9	2.7	1.6	2.6	3.0	5.2	4.7	4.6	4.9	5.8	5.4	24.8	28.7	16.9	4.1	82.6	44.8	47.4	52.6
19608	READING	93.9	90.7	2.2	3.1	1.8	2.8	2.9	5.0	6.1	6.4	6.8	6.9	5.1	25.3	29.3	12.0	2.1	76.3	40.9	48.6	51.4
19609	READING	95.9	93.5	1.1	1.6	1.2	2.0	2.1	3.8	5.2	5.6	6.1	5.9	4.0	23.9	29.2	17.1	3.1	79.4	44.6	47.8	52.2
19610	READING	94.2	90.9	1.4	2.0	2.7	4.4	1.9	3.3	3.5	3.9	4.8	9.6	4.9	17.0	28.8	20.3	7.2	84.3	49.8	46.6	53.4
19611	READING	73.3	67.9	6.2	7.3	1.6	2.3	25.0	30.5	8.0	7.6	6.7	6.4	5.8	25.6	20.9	13.7	5.4	74.2	37.3	45.4	54.6
	PENNSYLVANIA	85.4	83.2	10.0	10.7	1.8	2.7	3.2	4.2	5.8	6.0	6.3	7.1	6.5	24.8	27.8	13.1	2.6	77.8	40.4	48.5	51.5
	UNITED STATES	75.1	72.0	12.3	12.7	3.8	4.6	12.5	15.7	6.8	6.7	6.6	7.1	6.9	27.0	26.0	10.9	1.9	75.7	36.9	49.2	50.8

INCOME

ZIP CODE #	POST OFFICE NAME	2009 Per Capita Income	2009 HH Income Base	2009 Household Income Distribution (%): Less than $25,000	$25,000 to $49,999	$50,000 to $99,999	$100,000 to $149,999	$150,000 or More	Median Household Income: 2009	2014	2009 National Centile	2009 State Centile	2009 Home Value Base	2009 Home Value Distribution (%): Less than $50,000	$50,000 to $89,999	$90,000 to $174,999	$175,000 to $399,999	$400,000 or More	2009 Median Home Value
19462	PLYMOUTH MEETING	40280	5611	9.1	16.9	37.0	24.2	12.8	79021	83236	92	94	4555	0.0	0.3	7.2	76.3	16.2	286779
19464	POTTSTOWN	28210	17650	16.9	24.7	37.3	15.9	5.2	59127	59718	76	77	12019	1.7	1.8	44.8	48.1	3.7	179512
19465	POTTSTOWN	36525	6338	9.2	20.0	33.9	25.7	11.2	79629	84220	92	94	4932	1.6	0.4	11.0	69.4	17.5	275974
19468	ROYERSFORD	35775	9935	6.7	16.3	40.9	25.9	10.2	80287	83994	92	94	7405	1.4	0.7	17.0	67.9	12.9	257380
19473	SCHWENKSVILLE	35155	5513	6.9	13.5	42.0	26.2	11.4	81937	86144	93	95	4533	0.2	1.2	13.5	66.1	19.0	261256
19475	SPRING CITY	33761	4344	16.7	18.6	31.9	23.3	9.4	74597	78083	89	91	3014	3.6	2.6	21.5	55.4	16.9	243696
19477	SPRING HOUSE	0	0	0.0	0.0	0.0	0.0	0.0	0	0	0	0	0	0.0	0.0	0.0	0.0	0.0	0
19492	ZIEGLERVILLE	34795	86	7.0	20.9	44.2	19.8	8.1	73179	75600	88	90	74	0.0	0.0	6.8	67.6	25.7	296667
19501	ADAMSTOWN	27406	410	11.0	22.2	55.4	8.8	2.7	60409	62704	78	79	294	0.7	3.1	45.2	46.3	4.8	176415
19503	BALLY	29644	453	12.8	24.7	48.8	7.9	5.7	66450	70215	85	87	362	0.0	2.2	34.0	63.3	0.6	188587
19504	BARTO	25180	1693	12.5	24.2	47.3	11.5	4.5	62748	64709	81	83	1469	5.3	1.6	15.2	64.1	13.9	252778
19505	BECHTELSVILLE	24511	1463	12.4	21.5	54.5	9.0	2.7	62933	64449	81	83	1201	2.1	0.7	25.9	64.1	7.2	215830
19506	BERNVILLE	25013	3055	14.2	24.5	48.9	8.3	4.0	61033	62830	79	80	2519	2.1	3.3	30.8	55.3	8.6	199405
19507	BETHEL	21449	1567	15.1	26.2	50.7	5.6	2.5	57103	59444	74	74	1276	2.1	7.8	31.0	52.7	6.3	189520
19508	BIRDSBORO	26455	6352	12.7	21.8	50.3	11.5	3.8	64269	66565	83	85	5356	3.8	4.5	33.4	53.3	5.1	190231
19510	BLANDON	29183	2395	7.8	12.3	53.2	18.6	8.1	74546	76545	89	91	2128	4.3	1.4	27.0	65.0	2.3	203465
19512	BOYERTOWN	28049	6893	12.8	22.7	51.3	8.5	4.7	62840	64550	81	83	5218	1.7	1.4	32.4	58.1	6.4	200328
19518	DOUGLASSVILLE	30129	4947	11.4	18.0	46.3	15.5	8.7	73002	76014	88	90	4053	3.3	2.6	18.0	65.0	11.1	231885
19520	ELVERSON	34086	2204	10.1	20.9	37.3	22.6	9.1	75825	78737	90	92	1831	2.1	1.6	11.2	61.6	23.5	296148
19522	FLEETWOOD	27791	5542	12.5	22.4	46.6	13.4	5.2	64455	67063	83	85	4684	2.3	3.1	31.3	55.4	8.0	203480
19525	GILBERTSVILLE	33026	4575	7.4	14.8	39.7	28.1	10.0	83724	87641	93	96	3942	0.5	0.3	8.7	79.5	10.9	267949
19526	HAMBURG	25315	4512	15.5	26.2	47.7	8.2	2.5	59182	61708	76	77	3388	5.5	7.6	44.1	38.1	4.8	161902
19529	KEMPTON	25420	1262	11.8	28.2	45.5	9.7	4.8	59722	62118	77	78	1065	1.1	3.1	22.8	56.6	16.3	237024
19530	KUTZTOWN	22994	5127	20.6	25.6	40.7	7.9	5.2	54012	57328	70	70	3536	9.4	3.7	32.6	45.0	9.3	185215
19533	LEESPORT	24471	2361	10.8	23.3	49.2	12.9	3.9	64650	67039	83	85	2005	1.9	2.5	39.2	49.7	6.7	186811
19534	LENHARTSVILLE	26655	830	12.0	27.3	48.6	8.1	4.0	60390	62316	78	79	682	6.9	4.7	24.2	50.7	13.5	208182
19539	MERTZTOWN	26749	1910	13.4	22.6	48.3	11.6	4.2	63751	66743	82	84	1598	4.8	4.4	29.1	53.0	8.7	203406
19540	MOHNTON	30026	4471	10.7	24.6	45.6	11.7	7.4	65874	69409	84	87	3787	0.6	3.7	29.1	55.4	11.3	214864
19541	MOHRSVILLE	24195	1477	11.0	26.5	52.6	8.1	1.7	62427	64606	81	82	1257	5.4	5.0	26.1	58.3	5.2	192956
19543	MORGANTOWN	24600	1742	11.7	23.0	50.2	11.4	3.7	63463	65870	82	84	1367	3.0	0.7	18.8	64.4	13.2	234851
19547	OLEY	26656	1788	12.1	20.9	53.5	10.6	2.9	64863	67215	83	86	1408	1.0	1.8	26.8	58.5	11.9	215678
19549	PORT CLINTON	25906	135	17.0	36.3	34.1	12.6	0.0	47351	50555	55	56	96	3.1	10.4	60.4	25.0	1.0	123148
19551	ROBESONIA	27232	1955	13.3	23.6	49.0	9.7	4.4	63565	65866	82	84	1605	0.9	5.0	41.1	43.2	9.8	180793
19555	SHOEMAKERSVILLE	23371	1520	16.0	25.9	47.0	9.1	2.0	58235	61092	75	76	1186	2.5	5.7	49.3	39.2	3.2	161994
19560	TEMPLE	27175	3001	16.0	29.0	44.2	7.7	3.1	55799	59518	72	72	2443	2.0	3.9	61.4	29.6	3.1	152616
19562	TOPTON	26535	879	13.1	24.1	48.7	10.2	3.9	62152	64359	80	82	656	5.6	2.0	46.6	43.4	2.3	167857
19565	WERNERSVILLE	29336	3303	13.0	22.8	45.9	13.8	4.5	64475	67819	83	85	2695	6.5	3.1	36.4	48.3	5.7	182359
19567	WOMELSDORF	25391	2011	13.0	27.3	48.8	7.4	3.5	61103	63543	79	80	1511	1.0	5.3	51.4	36.9	5.5	160116
19601	READING	15230	12131	40.9	29.8	23.6	4.2	1.4	30885	31606	10	3	5345	17.9	44.3	28.3	7.5	2.0	76196
19602	READING	14023	6944	47.4	28.5	21.2	2.0	0.9	26736	26978	4	2	2851	31.5	47.4	16.0	4.7	0.5	60785
19604	READING	17581	8740	27.9	31.5	33.4	4.4	2.7	40436	43049	34	28	5426	12.6	53.8	25.7	7.1	0.8	74750
19605	READING	28435	7789	14.6	22.2	46.1	12.6	4.5	63374	66259	82	84	6778	3.8	5.9	43.2	44.5	2.6	169338
19606	READING	29759	13290	11.5	22.8	46.5	13.1	6.0	65197	68420	83	86	10951	3.8	6.4	36.7	49.2	3.9	180047
19607	READING	33040	9507	15.3	22.9	45.0	10.0	6.8	61940	64183	80	81	6754	0.9	2.9	53.3	38.6	4.3	164963
19608	READING	31076	8418	10.3	21.2	44.8	14.7	9.0	70614	74197	87	89	6221	1.2	1.8	27.8	58.6	10.5	216010
19609	READING	32488	4350	10.1	24.4	48.1	10.6	6.7	65729	68642	84	87	3646	1.0	2.1	53.2	42.5	1.3	167007
19610	READING	42441	5966	10.9	19.8	36.4	17.0	15.7	75270	78088	89	92	4445	0.3	2.5	24.4	54.7	18.2	239266
19611	READING	21250	3969	27.4	28.5	37.7	3.9	2.5	43784	46496	45	42	2131	1.1	18.3	69.4	10.5	0.8	119690
	PENNSYLVANIA	26913		21.5	25.3	36.9	10.2	6.1	53225	55819				7.5	12.2	35.6	36.1	8.5	161438
	UNITED STATES	27277		20.9	24.4	35.3	11.7	7.6	54719	56938				9.3	13.1	31.6	32.6	13.5	162279

ZIP CODE #	POST OFFICE NAME	FINANCIAL SERVICES: Auto Loan	FINANCIAL SERVICES: Home Loan	FINANCIAL SERVICES: Invest-ments	FINANCIAL SERVICES: Retire-ment Plans	THE HOME: Home Improvements: Home Repair	THE HOME: Home Improvements: Lawn & Garden	THE HOME: Furnishings: Comput-ers & Hard-ware-Personal	THE HOME: Furnishings: Major Appli-ances	THE HOME: Furnishings: TV, Radio, Sound Equip-ment	THE HOME: Furnishings: Furni-ture	ENTERTAINMENT: Dine out/ Carry out	ENTERTAINMENT: Sports Equip-ment	ENTERTAINMENT: Fees & Tickets	ENTERTAINMENT: Toys & Games	ENTERTAINMENT: Travel	ENTERTAINMENT: Cable TV	PERSONAL: Apparel & Services	PERSONAL: Auto Repairs	PERSONAL: Health Insur-ance	PERSONAL: Pets & Supplies
19462	PLYMOUTH MEETING	126	154	160	152	159	151	136	142	135	140	136	103	154	133	151	137	97	139	146	161
19464	POTTSTOWN	97	103	93	102	100	100	101	99	101	100	101	76	104	102	101	102	71	100	102	116
19465	POTTSTOWN	123	145	142	147	146	139	130	134	127	133	128	102	143	128	141	126	91	130	131	155
19468	ROYERSFORD	128	143	128	143	138	129	132	130	128	136	130	103	140	132	135	125	92	128	124	151
19473	SCHWENKSVILLE	133	160	142	160	155	141	138	140	131	144	133	111	152	136	147	127	95	134	127	161
19475	SPRING CITY	113	130	126	131	130	123	122	122	119	121	120	95	131	120	128	118	86	120	119	141
19477	SPRING HOUSE	0	0	0	0	0	0	0	0	0	0	0	0	0	0	0	0	0	0	0	0
19492	ZIEGLERVILLE	116	131	113	135	127	129	117	122	115	117	116	95	125	118	124	115	81	117	120	143
19501	ADAMSTOWN	83	97	92	95	96	89	94	90	92	92	93	71	101	92	98	91	67	92	90	105
19503	BALLY	96	119	106	119	115	117	101	106	103	103	104	79	117	104	112	105	73	104	112	123
19504	BARTO	98	109	95	112	106	108	97	102	96	98	97	79	103	99	103	97	67	98	101	120
19505	BECHTELSVILLE	97	100	91	103	99	106	93	100	93	89	93	77	93	96	96	96	64	95	101	117
19506	BERNVILLE	99	99	92	103	99	107	93	101	94	89	93	78	93	96	96	97	65	95	103	119
19507	BETHEL	92	87	84	90	88	99	84	94	86	77	85	71	80	88	85	90	58	87	96	109
19508	BIRDSBORO	102	106	97	107	104	110	97	103	99	97	99	79	100	101	100	101	69	99	105	122
19510	BLANDON	124	137	113	135	130	121	122	123	116	128	118	97	126	123	123	113	83	117	113	142
19512	BOYERTOWN	96	105	94	107	102	108	97	101	98	96	98	77	102	99	101	100	68	99	106	119
19518	DOUGLASSVILLE	117	128	115	127	125	121	116	119	114	120	115	91	122	118	119	114	81	115	115	138
19520	ELVERSON	118	139	133	142	140	136	121	128	119	126	120	96	134	119	133	119	84	122	126	148
19522	FLEETWOOD	103	110	97	112	107	112	102	106	102	100	102	82	106	104	105	103	71	102	107	125
19525	GILBERTSVILLE	127	155	137	156	150	142	133	136	129	137	131	107	149	133	143	127	93	131	130	157
19526	HAMBURG	92	93	86	93	92	101	87	94	91	85	90	69	88	92	89	95	62	90	100	110
19529	KEMPTON	96	108	93	111	105	106	96	100	95	97	95	78	103	97	102	95	67	96	99	118
19530	KUTZTOWN	97	86	82	89	86	93	96	92	95	89	94	73	87	96	88	96	65	93	95	110
19533	LEESPORT	102	114	99	117	111	113	103	106	102	103	102	82	109	104	108	103	71	103	108	125
19534	LENHARTSVILLE	101	104	93	106	102	107	96	102	96	94	96	78	97	99	98	98	66	97	102	120
19539	MERTZTOWN	98	110	96	112	106	109	98	103	98	98	98	79	105	100	104	99	68	99	103	121
19540	MOHNTON	110	122	110	124	119	121	112	115	111	111	111	89	118	113	117	112	78	112	116	135
19541	MOHRSVILLE	93	102	89	105	99	102	92	96	91	92	91	75	97	93	96	92	64	92	96	113
19543	MORGANTOWN	94	107	95	108	104	103	98	99	96	97	97	78	105	98	103	96	68	97	99	116
19547	OLEY	94	107	94	109	104	106	95	99	94	95	95	77	102	96	101	96	66	96	101	116
19549	PORT CLINTON	84	77	76	80	78	91	76	86	78	69	77	65	70	80	76	83	52	79	88	99
19551	ROBESONIA	100	108	99	110	106	113	99	105	100	96	100	80	103	102	104	103	69	101	109	123
19555	SHOEMAKERSVILLE	91	89	79	91	87	98	87	92	89	82	88	71	85	91	86	92	60	88	97	108
19560	TEMPLE	87	91	88	91	92	102	84	93	89	80	88	68	86	88	88	94	60	89	102	107
19562	TOPTON	89	107	93	107	102	106	94	96	95	94	96	73	105	96	101	97	67	95	103	113
19565	WERNERSVILLE	95	111	102	111	109	114	97	104	100	97	100	76	108	100	106	104	70	101	112	120
19567	WOMELSDORF	95	97	88	99	95	106	92	98	95	88	94	74	93	96	94	99	65	95	105	115
19601	READING	56	49	44	50	46	51	59	52	62	54	62	41	55	61	52	64	44	58	58	64
19602	READING	48	41	38	42	39	44	52	45	54	46	54	36	47	53	45	57	38	50	51	56
19604	READING	70	63	57	63	60	68	73	67	76	67	75	52	68	76	65	79	53	72	75	81
19605	READING	95	106	95	106	103	110	97	101	99	95	99	76	103	99	102	102	69	99	109	118
19606	READING	104	113	105	113	111	115	105	108	105	104	105	83	110	107	109	107	74	106	112	127
19607	READING	99	106	103	106	106	110	101	104	104	100	103	77	106	102	105	107	72	103	112	121
19608	READING	114	125	117	127	124	122	116	118	114	118	115	91	123	116	121	114	81	115	117	137
19609	READING	101	111	107	110	111	119	102	109	106	101	105	78	109	104	108	111	73	106	120	126
19610	READING	131	153	160	153	159	161	137	147	141	143	141	103	154	135	153	146	99	144	163	168
19611	READING	72	67	58	67	64	69	73	69	74	70	75	54	71	75	69	75	52	73	74	82
	PENNSYLVANIA	94	95	95	95	95	100	94	96	96	91	95	73	94	96	94	99	67	95	101	113
	UNITED STATES	100	100	100	100	100	100	100	100	100	100	100	100	100	100	100	100	100	100	100	100

POPULATION CHANGE

ZIP CODE			POPULATION			2000-2009 ANNUAL RATE		HOUSEHOLDS					FAMILIES		
#	POST OFFICE NAME	COUNTY FIPS CODE	2000	2009	2014	% Rate	State Centile	2000	2009	2014	% Annual Rate 2000-2009	2009 Average HH Size	2000	2009	% Annual Rate 2000-2009
02804	ASHAWAY	009	2885	3199	3327	1.1	91	1064	1204	1261	1.3	2.66	797	885	1.1
02806	BARRINGTON	001	16825	16684	16560	-0.1	25	6014	6039	6022	0.0	2.69	4718	4679	-0.1
02807	BLOCK ISLAND	009	1010	1062	1070	0.5	76	472	507	516	0.8	2.09	250	260	0.4
02808	BRADFORD	009	2112	2355	2450	1.2	95	716	807	844	1.3	2.91	574	639	1.2
02809	BRISTOL	001	22469	22677	22657	0.1	44	8314	8591	8646	0.4	2.40	5650	5735	0.2
02812	CAROLINA	009	1483	1559	1578	0.5	76	516	554	565	0.8	2.81	411	434	0.6
02813	CHARLESTOWN	009	7890	8878	9266	1.3	96	3192	3652	3829	1.5	2.42	2290	2564	1.2
02814	CHEPACHET	007	7576	7978	8013	0.6	83	2728	2856	2876	0.5	2.79	2151	2220	0.3
02815	CLAYVILLE	007	242	251	251	0.4	67	86	88	89	0.2	2.84	70	71	0.2
02816	COVENTRY	003	30951	31730	31658	0.3	53	11743	12176	12197	0.4	2.57	8558	8725	0.2
02817	WEST GREENWICH	003	5131	6110	6407	1.9	100	1765	2087	2191	1.8	2.92	1465	1713	1.7
02818	EAST GREENWICH	003	18266	19037	19113	0.4	67	7339	7707	7764	0.5	2.45	4993	5183	0.4
02822	EXETER	009	5542	5664	5702	0.2	48	1938	2018	2047	0.4	2.69	1486	1521	0.3
02825	FOSTER	007	4908	5165	5193	0.6	83	1752	1833	1845	0.5	2.81	1387	1431	0.3
02827	GREENE	003	2094	2195	2217	0.5	76	689	733	745	0.7	2.93	569	598	0.5
02828	GREENVILLE	007	6421	6633	6623	0.4	67	2521	2602	2608	0.3	2.47	1800	1823	0.1
02830	HARRISVILLE	007	6648	6885	6893	0.4	67	2439	2511	2517	0.3	2.73	1870	1900	0.2
02831	HOPE	007	4426	4647	4671	0.5	76	1507	1568	1577	0.4	2.95	1236	1274	0.3
02832	HOPE VALLEY	009	4612	5004	5172	0.9	87	1769	1956	2033	1.1	2.55	1313	1426	0.9
02833	HOPKINTON	009	334	353	361	0.6	83	115	124	128	0.8	2.85	73	76	0.4
02835	JAMESTOWN	005	5622	5519	5395	-0.2	11	2359	2301	2254	-0.3	2.39	1625	1547	-0.5
02836	KENYON	009	45	47	47	0.5	76	18	19	19	0.6	2.47	14	15	0.7
02837	LITTLE COMPTON	005	3593	3597	3558	0.0	35	1475	1470	1455	0.0	2.45	1041	1014	-0.3
02838	MANVILLE	007	3592	3633	3610	0.1	44	1471	1479	1472	0.1	2.43	946	930	-0.2
02839	MAPLEVILLE	007	1500	1466	1442	-0.2	11	526	511	503	-0.3	2.72	420	402	-0.5
02840	NEWPORT	005	25663	24308	23296	-0.6	3	11549	10505	10045	-1.0	2.09	5635	4917	-1.5
02841	NEWPORT	005	1009	1155	1128	1.5	97	62	56	54	-1.1	2.55	58	52	-1.2
02842	MIDDLETOWN	005	17137	16540	16048	-0.4	5	6948	6636	6457	-0.5	2.42	4599	4273	-0.8
02852	NORTH KINGSTOWN	009	23461	23566	23584	0.0	35	9094	9276	9334	0.2	2.51	6484	6493	0.0
02857	NORTH SCITUATE	007	8818	9126	9128	0.4	67	3263	3359	3367	0.3	2.70	2502	2537	0.2
02858	OAKLAND	007	743	768	769	0.4	67	269	277	277	0.3	2.77	207	210	0.2
02859	PASCOAG	007	6835	6947	6913	0.2	48	2287	2307	2299	0.1	2.84	1726	1718	-0.1
02860	PAWTUCKET	007	46516	46110	45548	-0.1	25	19089	18770	18564	-0.2	2.43	11338	10888	-0.4
02861	PAWTUCKET	007	26604	26348	26032	-0.1	25	11038	10873	10758	-0.2	2.40	7219	6953	-0.4
02863	CENTRAL FALLS	007	18789	18661	18453	-0.1	25	6638	6494	6417	-0.2	2.78	4320	4132	-0.5
02864	CUMBERLAND	007	31848	33347	33474	0.5	76	12219	12720	12791	0.4	2.60	9050	9271	0.3
02865	LINCOLN	007	17289	17798	17762	0.3	53	6724	6857	6852	0.2	2.57	4787	4806	0.0
02871	PORTSMOUTH	005	17061	16847	16479	-0.1	25	6705	6585	6464	-0.2	2.55	4845	4656	-0.4
02872	PRUDENCE ISLAND	005	88	75	70	-1.7	1	53	45	42	-1.8	1.67	21	17	-2.3
02873	ROCKVILLE	009	171	183	188	0.7	84	64	69	72	0.8	2.65	47	50	0.7
02874	SAUNDERSTOWN	009	4722	5472	5705	1.6	99	1758	2058	2154	1.7	2.65	1300	1504	1.6
02877	SLOCUM	009	105	101	100	-0.4	5	34	33	33	-0.3	2.94	25	24	-0.4
02878	TIVERTON	005	15260	15826	15753	0.4	67	6077	6260	6238	0.3	2.52	4408	4452	0.1
02879	WAKEFIELD	009	19274	20932	21492	0.9	87	7636	8442	8735	1.1	2.46	5196	5614	0.8
02881	KINGSTON	009	6458	6707	6803	0.4	67	912	1008	1046	1.1	2.81	637	695	0.9
02882	NARRAGANSETT	009	14841	14898	14817	0.0	35	6233	6368	6372	0.2	2.33	3447	3417	-0.1
02885	WARREN	001	11360	11250	11174	-0.1	25	4708	4754	4753	0.1	2.31	2995	2968	-0.1
02886	WARWICK	003	30352	30145	29780	-0.1	25	13169	13291	13214	0.1	2.23	8035	7887	-0.2
02888	WARWICK	003	20757	20443	20180	-0.2	11	8611	8593	8524	0.0	2.35	5551	5417	-0.3
02889	WARWICK	003	29289	29158	28774	0.0	35	11328	11442	11359	0.1	2.54	7908	7838	-0.1
02891	WESTERLY	009	21316	22147	22417	0.4	67	8866	9345	9507	0.6	2.33	5691	5885	0.4
02892	WEST KINGSTON	009	4722	5280	5495	1.2	95	1661	1890	1981	1.4	2.72	1308	1465	1.2
02893	WEST WARWICK	003	29372	29932	29935	0.2	48	12410	12837	12902	0.4	2.32	7653	7729	0.1
02894	WOOD RIVER JUNCTION	009	984	1079	1118	1.0	89	331	370	387	1.2	2.92	260	286	1.0
02895	WOONSOCKET	007	43224	42830	42311	-0.1	25	17750	17487	17303	-0.2	2.39	10768	10355	-0.4
02896	NORTH SMITHFIELD	007	10515	10865	10849	0.4	67	3928	4041	4048	0.3	2.61	2934	2969	0.1
02898	WYOMING	009	1621	1774	1839	1.0	89	528	589	615	1.2	2.99	425	468	1.0
02903	PROVIDENCE	007	9190	9490	9484	0.3	53	4374	4546	4560	0.4	1.71	1213	1198	-0.1
02904	PROVIDENCE	007	28502	28819	28637	0.1	44	12961	13025	12970	0.1	2.18	7183	7015	-0.3
02905	PROVIDENCE	007	25289	25408	25208	0.1	44	8613	8553	8483	-0.1	2.82	5833	5698	-0.3
02906	PROVIDENCE	007	30701	30795	30572	0.0	35	12033	12029	11954	0.0	2.09	5066	4867	-0.4
02907	PROVIDENCE	007	26456	27866	27983	0.6	83	8241	8591	8633	0.5	3.18	5888	6023	0.2
02908	PROVIDENCE	007	35687	37703	37916	0.6	83	13055	13532	13604	0.4	2.67	8238	8340	0.1
02909	PROVIDENCE	007	41036	42825	42764	0.5	76	14621	14801	14764	0.1	2.87	9270	9189	-0.1
02910	CRANSTON	007	20790	20454	20170	-0.2	11	8583	8393	8291	-0.2	2.43	5502	5257	-0.5
02911	NORTH PROVIDENCE	007	15538	15353	15155	-0.1	25	6730	6614	6541	-0.2	2.28	3999	3829	-0.5
02912	PROVIDENCE	007	393	397	398	0.1	44	0	0	0	0.0	0.00	0	0	0.0
02914	EAST PROVIDENCE	007	22056	21793	21505	-0.1	25	9085	8923	8823	-0.2	2.41	5799	5563	-0.4
02915	RIVERSIDE	007	18429	18419	18232	0.0	35	7920	7893	7837	0.0	2.28	4855	4719	-0.3
02916	RUMFORD	007	8220	8246	8179	0.0	35	3531	3518	3495	0.0	2.34	2199	2140	-0.3
02917	SMITHFIELD	007	14249	14612	14606	0.3	53	4696	4811	4816	0.3	2.49	3206	3218	0.0
02918	PROVIDENCE	007	3113	3134	3132	0.1	44	135	136	136	0.1	6.62	71	70	-0.2
02919	JOHNSTON	007	28223	28478	28300	0.1	44	11211	11247	11198	0.0	2.49	7740	7613	-0.2
02920	CRANSTON	007	37622	37385	37004	-0.1	25	14647	14435	14293	-0.2	2.30	9308	8961	-0.4
02921	CRANSTON	007	10444	11630	11831	1.2	95	3518	3868	3935	1.0	2.99	2938	3219	1.0
	RHODE ISLAND					0.2					0.1	2.48			-0.1
	UNITED STATES					1.0					1.1	2.59			0.9

ZIP CODE		RACE (%)						% Hispanic Origin		2009 AGE DISTRIBUTION (%)										MEDIAN AGE		
#	POST OFFICE NAME	White		Black		Asian/Pacific																
		2000	2009	2000	2009	2000	2009	2000	2009	0-4	5-9	10-14	15-19	20-24	25-44	45-64	65-84	85+	18+	2009	% 2009 Males	% 2009 Females
02804	ASHAWAY	96.5	95.6	0.7	0.9	0.7	1.0	1.1	1.6	5.9	6.3	6.8	6.9	4.8	26.1	30.0	11.5	1.7	76.7	41.2	50.0	50.0
02806	BARRINGTON	96.4	96.3	0.7	0.7	1.8	1.8	1.0	1.1	5.4	6.5	8.0	8.5	5.6	18.6	32.9	12.3	2.2	74.6	43.2	49.0	51.0
02807	BLOCK ISLAND	97.8	97.0	0.6	0.8	0.8	1.2	1.2	1.9	5.5	5.7	5.7	4.7	3.6	23.4	33.2	16.3	1.9	80.0	45.8	47.8	52.2
02808	BRADFORD	96.4	95.4	0.6	0.8	0.5	0.8	1.5	2.4	8.3	7.9	7.7	8.0	7.1	26.2	25.7	8.0	1.1	70.5	33.7	49.7	50.3
02809	BRISTOL	97.1	97.0	0.6	0.7	0.7	0.7	1.3	1.3	5.1	5.0	5.3	9.5	8.7	22.7	25.6	14.9	3.3	81.3	40.0	48.2	51.8
02812	CAROLINA	96.6	95.5	0.2	0.3	0.7	1.0	2.0	3.1	6.3	7.1	7.6	6.5	4.2	26.5	32.4	8.4	1.0	74.8	40.3	50.0	50.0
02813	CHARLESTOWN	96.3	95.2	0.4	0.5	0.6	0.9	1.1	1.7	5.3	5.6	6.0	5.6	4.4	23.6	32.7	14.9	1.7	79.3	44.6	49.1	50.9
02814	CHEPACHET	98.4	97.6	0.3	0.5	0.3	0.5	0.7	1.3	5.5	6.2	6.8	7.2	5.3	24.3	34.1	9.6	1.1	77.1	41.7	49.9	50.1
02815	CLAYVILLE	98.3	97.2	0.0	0.4	0.8	1.2	0.8	1.6	6.4	7.2	8.0	7.6	4.0	23.1	32.7	10.0	1.2	74.1	40.9	48.2	51.8
02816	COVENTRY	97.6	96.8	0.4	0.5	0.6	0.8	1.2	1.9	6.1	6.3	6.7	6.6	5.0	25.6	29.3	12.1	2.2	76.7	41.1	48.3	51.7
02817	WEST GREENWICH	97.7	97.0	0.3	0.4	0.6	0.9	0.7	1.0	6.2	7.2	7.8	7.2	4.5	23.9	34.1	8.4	0.8	74.2	40.8	49.6	50.4
02818	EAST GREENWICH	95.9	94.3	0.6	0.8	2.3	3.4	1.0	1.5	5.1	5.9	7.1	7.4	4.6	19.7	33.0	14.2	3.0	76.8	45.1	48.1	51.9
02822	EXETER	96.4	95.4	0.7	0.9	0.8	1.1	1.3	2.0	5.4	6.1	7.1	7.3	4.4	24.6	32.9	9.9	2.2	76.5	41.8	48.9	51.1
02825	FOSTER	97.4	96.0	0.2	0.3	0.7	1.2	0.8	1.6	5.2	6.2	6.9	7.4	5.0	22.5	35.2	10.1	1.5	76.9	43.0	49.1	50.9
02827	GREENE	97.7	97.0	0.6	0.7	0.3	0.5	0.7	1.1	6.6	7.4	7.8	7.0	4.4	24.9	31.6	8.7	1.5	73.7	39.9	50.8	49.2
02828	GREENVILLE	98.5	97.6	0.2	0.4	0.6	1.0	0.5	1.0	4.5	5.1	5.6	6.5	4.5	21.0	31.9	16.7	4.2	80.5	46.6	47.4	52.6
02830	HARRISVILLE	98.9	98.4	0.1	0.1	0.2	0.3	0.6	1.1	5.7	6.1	6.4	7.0	5.8	26.5	31.8	9.3	1.5	77.5	40.3	49.1	50.9
02831	HOPE	97.8	96.7	0.4	0.6	0.8	1.3	0.7	1.4	6.5	7.4	8.0	7.4	4.2	24.5	31.8	9.1	1.1	73.4	40.6	49.6	50.4
02832	HOPE VALLEY	97.0	96.2	0.6	0.7	0.3	0.5	1.1	1.8	6.2	6.8	7.3	6.8	4.6	25.6	31.7	9.7	1.3	75.4	41.0	49.7	50.3
02833	HOPKINTON	97.6	97.5	0.3	0.3	0.3	0.3	0.9	1.4	5.4	5.7	6.2	6.8	5.4	24.1	31.7	12.5	2.3	78.2	42.9	47.9	52.1
02835	JAMESTOWN	97.5	96.6	0.8	1.1	0.4	0.6	0.9	1.5	3.5	4.7	5.8	6.1	4.7	20.1	38.7	14.4	2.0	81.9	47.8	48.3	51.7
02836	KENYON	97.7	97.9	0.0	0.0	0.0	0.0	2.3	2.1	4.3	6.4	8.5	6.4	4.3	25.5	36.2	8.5	0.0	74.5	41.9	46.8	53.2
02837	LITTLE COMPTON	98.7	98.3	0.1	0.1	0.3	0.4	0.9	1.5	4.4	5.2	6.1	5.8	3.3	20.3	34.8	17.6	2.6	80.7	48.0	49.5	50.5
02838	MANVILLE	94.2	91.1	1.6	2.4	1.6	2.6	2.4	4.5	6.0	5.7	5.9	7.3	7.0	26.5	26.3	12.2	3.1	78.0	39.3	47.4	52.6
02839	MAPLEVILLE	98.5	97.5	0.1	0.2	0.3	0.4	0.9	1.8	5.0	5.8	6.2	5.9	4.2	26.7	32.3	11.5	2.3	78.9	42.6	49.0	51.0
02840	NEWPORT	84.9	81.3	7.3	8.8	1.3	1.8	5.4	7.7	5.7	5.0	4.6	8.4	9.1	29.4	24.4	10.8	2.5	81.7	36.1	47.3	52.7
02841	NEWPORT	64.5	56.9	20.1	23.9	5.8	7.3	9.2	13.1	4.1	3.0	2.8	15.9	27.6	37.5	8.0	1.0	0.1	87.1	24.4	72.4	27.6
02842	MIDDLETOWN	89.2	85.8	4.7	6.0	2.2	3.1	2.9	4.5	6.9	6.7	6.1	5.8	6.3	25.7	26.7	12.3	3.6	76.6	39.5	48.7	51.3
02852	NORTH KINGSTOWN	95.6	94.2	1.0	1.3	1.0	1.4	1.9	2.9	6.2	6.6	6.9	6.7	5.2	23.7	31.4	11.3	2.0	75.8	41.3	48.3	51.7
02857	NORTH SCITUATE	98.3	97.4	0.3	0.4	0.4	0.7	0.7	1.3	5.3	6.0	6.7	6.7	4.3	22.3	34.1	12.7	1.9	77.6	44.2	48.8	51.2
02858	OAKLAND	99.1	98.7	0.0	0.1	0.1	0.1	0.7	1.3	5.6	5.9	6.1	6.6	6.1	26.0	32.2	10.2	1.3	78.5	40.8	48.7	51.3
02859	PASCOAG	98.2	97.2	0.4	0.6	0.3	0.5	1.1	2.0	5.7	5.9	6.2	7.5	6.0	27.0	29.2	9.6	2.9	77.5	39.8	49.1	50.9
02860	PAWTUCKET	66.5	59.0	10.3	12.2	1.0	1.4	18.6	27.6	7.5	6.8	6.2	7.1	8.2	28.7	23.2	10.1	2.1	75.3	34.2	48.2	51.8
02861	PAWTUCKET	91.1	87.0	2.1	2.9	0.7	1.2	5.8	10.2	5.8	5.6	5.7	6.3	5.9	26.7	27.4	13.5	3.1	79.0	40.9	47.5	52.5
02863	CENTRAL FALLS	57.2	48.7	5.8	5.8	0.7	0.8	47.8	62.0	8.9	7.9	6.9	7.9	9.0	29.5	18.9	9.0	2.1	71.7	30.4	50.2	49.8
02864	CUMBERLAND	96.7	94.8	0.6	0.9	0.9	1.4	2.1	3.9	6.0	6.3	6.8	6.4	4.6	24.3	29.4	13.5	2.7	76.9	42.2	47.7	52.3
02865	LINCOLN	95.6	93.1	0.7	1.1	1.8	3.0	1.7	3.1	5.4	5.6	6.2	6.8	5.7	23.0	30.6	13.6	3.2	78.2	43.2	48.0	52.0
02871	PORTSMOUTH	95.8	94.2	1.2	1.6	1.4	2.1	1.5	2.3	5.7	5.8	6.7	6.9	4.1	22.4	33.1	13.3	2.1	77.4	44.0	49.0	51.0
02872	PRUDENCE ISLAND	98.9	98.7	1.1	1.3	0.0	0.0	0.0	0.0	2.7	1.3	4.0	4.0	1.3	9.3	41.3	32.0	4.0	89.3	58.4	45.3	54.7
02873	ROCKVILLE	97.6	96.7	0.0	0.0	0.0	0.5	1.2	1.6	6.0	6.6	6.6	7.1	5.5	24.6	32.2	9.8	1.6	76.0	40.9	50.3	49.7
02874	SAUNDERSTOWN	96.6	95.6	0.6	0.7	1.1	1.6	0.8	1.2	6.9	7.5	8.1	6.8	4.3	26.2	30.1	9.0	1.2	73.2	39.1	49.3	50.7
02877	SLOCUM	95.3	95.0	0.9	1.0	0.9	1.0	0.9	1.0	5.0	5.9	6.9	7.9	4.0	24.8	32.7	9.9	3.0	77.2	42.2	48.5	51.5
02878	TIVERTON	98.0	97.2	0.4	0.6	0.4	0.6	0.7	1.1	5.2	5.4	5.9	6.4	5.1	23.7	31.1	14.6	2.5	79.5	43.9	48.5	51.5
02879	WAKEFIELD	92.7	90.7	1.2	1.5	2.3	3.3	1.1	1.7	5.8	6.2	6.9	6.9	5.4	23.2	30.9	12.1	2.6	76.7	42.0	48.1	51.9
02881	KINGSTON	85.6	81.3	3.0	3.5	6.3	8.8	3.9	5.7	2.4	2.7	3.3	40.2	23.4	11.3	12.2	3.8	0.7	89.3	20.3	46.2	53.8
02882	NARRAGANSETT	95.7	94.5	0.7	1.0	0.8	1.2	1.3	2.0	3.8	3.9	3.9	5.4	16.6	22.9	28.1	13.5	1.9	85.6	39.2	48.5	51.5
02885	WARREN	96.8	96.8	0.8	0.8	0.5	0.5	0.9	0.9	5.1	4.9	5.3	6.0	6.7	25.3	29.0	14.1	3.7	81.1	42.7	47.6	52.4
02886	WARWICK	95.3	93.8	1.0	1.3	2.0	2.8	1.5	2.2	4.8	5.0	5.4	5.6	5.0	24.8	29.4	16.0	3.9	81.2	44.5	47.2	52.8
02888	WARWICK	95.3	93.9	1.2	1.5	1.2	1.6	1.9	2.9	5.3	5.4	5.7	5.9	5.3	25.1	30.0	13.8	3.5	79.9	43.2	47.5	52.5
02889	WARWICK	94.7	93.2	1.4	1.7	1.3	1.8	1.6	2.5	5.9	6.0	6.3	6.5	5.8	26.3	29.6	11.8	1.9	77.8	40.7	48.4	51.6
02891	WESTERLY	95.1	93.5	0.7	0.9	2.1	3.0	1.1	1.7	5.8	5.9	6.2	6.2	5.2	24.5	28.7	14.0	3.4	78.2	42.4	48.4	51.6
02892	WEST KINGSTON	95.5	94.3	0.5	0.7	0.8	1.1	1.0	1.5	6.0	6.7	7.4	7.9	5.0	25.5	31.4	8.7	1.5	74.8	39.9	49.4	50.6
02893	WEST WARWICK	93.8	91.8	1.1	1.4	1.5	2.1	3.1	4.6	6.5	6.1	5.9	6.0	6.2	28.9	26.6	11.6	2.2	78.0	38.4	48.4	51.6
02894	WOOD RIVER JUNCTION	96.9	96.0	0.4	0.5	0.7	1.0	1.5	2.3	8.0	8.5	8.8	6.7	3.6	26.1	28.8	8.4	1.0	70.4	38.4	49.1	50.9
02895	WOONSOCKET	83.1	76.3	4.4	5.6	4.1	5.8	9.3	15.0	7.8	6.9	6.2	6.8	7.3	27.1	23.5	11.6	2.8	75.0	35.8	48.3	51.7
02896	NORTH SMITHFIELD	98.3	97.4	0.4	0.7	0.5	0.9	0.5	0.9	5.1	5.5	6.1	6.3	4.9	22.0	31.4	14.3	4.3	79.2	45.0	47.4	52.6
02898	WYOMING	97.2	96.5	0.6	0.7	0.2	0.4	0.8	1.2	7.1	7.7	8.2	7.0	4.1	26.6	30.3	8.2	0.7	72.3	39.3	49.8	50.2
02903	PROVIDENCE	61.8	52.3	15.3	17.7	6.0	7.8	19.3	26.8	3.9	3.5	2.9	13.9	15.3	25.1	18.6	13.2	3.6	87.8	31.1	49.4	50.6
02904	PROVIDENCE	82.8	76.3	7.3	9.3	2.2	3.2	8.4	13.7	5.4	5.3	5.1	5.5	6.1	26.9	26.5	15.4	3.9	80.9	42.0	47.1	52.9
02905	PROVIDENCE	53.3	47.0	18.3	18.8	3.4	4.1	26.5	33.6	7.6	6.9	6.7	10.9	9.9	27.2	21.7	7.5	1.6	74.1	30.1	48.0	52.0
02906	PROVIDENCE	77.7	70.4	7.4	9.2	7.0	10.3	5.0	8.0	3.9	3.5	3.3	12.3	21.5	25.8	19.6	8.0	2.0	87.1	28.0	47.8	52.2
02907	PROVIDENCE	26.7	23.2	23.4	21.5	9.7	9.9	50.5	58.1	9.8	8.9	7.7	9.0	10.4	28.0	19.3	6.0	0.9	68.2	27.1	49.6	50.4
02908	PROVIDENCE	61.9	53.7	13.0	14.1	4.7	5.8	25.6	35.1	7.8	7.2	6.5	9.2	11.7	28.0	19.6	7.8	2.1	73.9	29.7	48.3	51.7
02909	PROVIDENCE	48.2	40.7	11.9	11.7	6.8	7.0	44.3	55.6	9.7	8.8	7.4	8.3	9.8	30.1	18.0	6.7	1.3	69.3	28.2	49.5	50.5
02910	CRANSTON	88.3	82.4	2.5	3.5	4.6	7.1	4.0	7.1	5.8	5.7	5.8	6.5	6.9	27.8	28.2	10.9	2.6	78.9	39.5	47.6	52.4
02911	NORTH PROVIDENCE	93.0	89.3	2.0	2.9	1.7	2.6	3.8	7.0	4.7	4.5	4.8	5.7	7.0	27.0	28.4	14.2	3.7	82.6	42.5	46.6	53.4
02912	PROVIDENCE	77.0	67.5	2.8	3.8	14.5	20.9	4.8	8.3	0.0	0.0	0.0	59.2	36.0	3.3	1.3	0.0	0.3	100.0	19.2	42.6	57.4
02914	EAST PROVIDENCE	80.2	73.7	7.0	9.7	1.3	1.9	2.3	4.1	5.8	5.6	5.3	6.0	6.6	27.6	25.5	14.2	3.4	79.7	40.1	47.1	52.9
02915	RIVERSIDE	91.5	87.9	3.5	5.1	1.3	2.1	1.6	2.8	5.0	5.1	5.4	5.7	5.6	24.5	28.9	15.7	4.1	80.9	44.1	46.0	54.0
02916	RUMFORD	92.2	88.6	3.2	4.7	0.8	1.2	1.5	2.8	5.4	5.5	5.8	6.1	5.4	23.4	29.7	14.8	3.9	79.3	43.9	47.0	53.0
02917	SMITHFIELD	96.8	95.2	1.1	1.5	1.0	1.7	1.1	2.1	4.0	4.4	5.0	12.2	11.4	20.3	26.6	12.0	4.0	83.1	39.6	49.3	50.7
02918	PROVIDENCE	88.3	83.0	4.1	5.6	1.5	2.2	6.7	11.6	1.6	1.8	1.8	38.4	39.3	7.4	5.4	3.8	0.4	93.6	20.8	41.9	58.1
02919	JOHNSTON	96.5	94.5	0.7	1.0	1.1	1.9	2.0	3.7	5.4	5.5	5.8	6.2	5.1	24.7	28.8	14.8	3.8	79.6	43.3	46.9	53.1
02920	CRANSTON	88.3	83.5	4.9	6.2	3.2	4.8	5.5	9.0	4.6	4.6	4.9	6.0	6.2	27.7	26.5	15.6	4.0	82.3	42.4	51.0	49.0
02921	CRANSTON	96.5	94.4	0.5	0.8	2.0	3.3	1.2	2.2	6.3	7.7	8.7	7.8	3.8	23.1	32.0	8.8	1.8	71.8	41.0	49.0	51.0
	RHODE ISLAND	85.0	81.4	4.5	5.1	2.3	3.1	8.7	12.0	6.1	6.0	6.1	7.6	7.5	25.6	26.8	11.8	2.6	77.9	38.6	48.3	51.7
	UNITED STATES	75.1	72.0	12.3	12.7	3.8	4.6	12.5	15.7	6.8	6.7	6.6	7.1	6.9	27.0	26.0	10.9	1.9	75.7	36.9	49.2	50.8

ZIP CODE				2009 HOUSEHOLD INCOME DISTRIBUTION (%)					MEDIAN HOUSEHOLD INCOME					2009 HOME VALUE DISTRIBUTION (%)					
#	POST OFFICE NAME	2009 Per Capita Income	2009 HH Income Base	Less than $25,000	$25,000 to $49,999	$50,000 to $99,999	$100,000 to $149,999	$150,000 or More	2009	2014	2009 National Centile	2009 State Centile	2009 Home Value Base	Less than $50,000	$50,000 to $89,999	$90,000 to $174,999	$175,000 to $399,999	$400,000 or More	2009 Median Home Value
02804	ASHAWAY	32064	1204	10.0	18.4	43.9	16.8	11.0	69328	72037	86	60	1001	0.0	0.0	9.0	80.4	10.6	239955
02806	BARRINGTON	46457	6039	8.5	13.7	25.3	27.2	25.3	104073	106700	97	100	5285	0.1	0.1	3.3	55.5	41.1	360294
02807	BLOCK ISLAND	41109	507	14.8	25.0	29.2	19.1	11.8	64055	67656	82	45	345	0.0	0.0	0.3	6.4	93.3	907839
02808	BRADFORD	23849	807	11.4	23.8	43.4	17.8	3.6	62518	63878	81	43	591	0.0	0.0	18.8	76.8	4.4	220305
02809	BRISTOL	28536	8591	20.6	21.6	33.4	17.6	6.7	60023	63002	77	35	5717	0.2	0.3	4.0	78.2	17.4	277235
02812	CAROLINA	32485	554	4.7	17.0	43.5	23.8	11.0	80183	82446	92	84	483	0.6	2.9	7.7	75.2	13.7	256250
02813	CHARLESTOWN	33918	3652	11.9	18.9	42.4	18.7	8.1	67598	70811	85	51	3043	1.0	1.6	6.7	67.7	23.0	280155
02814	CHEPACHET	29332	2856	9.8	13.0	52.3	19.3	5.5	75903	77179	90	71	2409	2.4	2.0	8.7	71.3	15.6	284794
02815	CLAYVILLE	32352	88	9.1	10.2	47.7	22.7	10.2	82913	83411	93	88	79	0.0	0.0	2.5	58.2	39.2	363043
02816	COVENTRY	27367	12176	15.7	20.0	46.7	13.5	4.1	64868	69444	83	47	9752	2.5	4.8	14.8	67.2	10.7	246551
02817	WEST GREENWICH	31205	2087	8.4	12.5	45.6	22.3	11.2	81542	83767	93	85	1871	0.0	1.5	10.2	50.6	37.7	357236
02818	EAST GREENWICH	45109	7707	13.3	17.0	35.6	12.7	21.4	76476	80122	90	72	5600	0.4	0.5	3.2	37.0	58.9	477449
02822	EXETER	35383	2018	7.8	13.3	36.1	30.0	12.8	86176	89654	94	93	1718	3.0	0.6	6.9	59.6	29.9	303889
02825	FOSTER	29857	1833	7.9	18.0	45.5	19.9	8.7	78185	78195	91	80	1600	0.0	0.9	4.2	69.9	25.0	320160
02827	GREENE	29102	733	4.4	14.9	54.2	19.5	7.1	77605	79638	91	77	674	0.0	0.0	5.2	71.4	23.4	328968
02828	GREENVILLE	31422	2602	11.9	21.6	40.2	18.4	7.8	70321	69591	87	61	2151	0.6	1.1	4.1	82.7	11.6	275898
02830	HARRISVILLE	27244	2511	13.9	19.4	46.3	14.1	6.3	67971	69259	86	53	1953	1.2	1.5	11.0	76.4	9.9	262248
02831	HOPE	32988	1568	4.9	15.5	47.4	20.5	11.6	80144	80274	92	83	1368	0.0	0.0	7.4	58.6	34.1	338244
02832	HOPE VALLEY	31173	1956	15.6	18.3	38.5	19.2	8.4	68425	72696	86	55	1566	0.0	0.3	7.6	79.3	12.8	264732
02833	HOPKINTON	27428	124	29.0	12.9	30.6	15.3	12.1	62460	67145	81	41	88	0.0	0.0	3.4	79.5	17.0	279167
02835	JAMESTOWN	47284	2301	9.0	12.6	34.5	23.2	20.7	84910	89796	94	89	1805	0.0	0.0	2.5	46.9	50.6	407047
02836	KENYON	38748	19	0.0	15.8	47.4	26.3	10.5	84960	84960	94	91	17	0.0	0.0	5.9	82.4	11.8	256250
02837	LITTLE COMPTON	42403	1470	11.6	15.7	35.2	21.3	16.2	74671	79978	89	67	1174	0.4	0.0	2.6	46.0	51.0	408571
02838	MANVILLE	22692	1479	24.0	28.4	38.2	6.6	2.8	47892	50921	56	19	629	0.0	0.0	4.9	75.2	19.9	275893
02839	MAPLEVILLE	29142	511	8.2	19.8	48.5	16.2	7.2	73656	72494	89	65	435	9.2	9.7	16.1	54.5	10.6	252083
02840	NEWPORT	32923	10505	24.2	22.1	30.6	14.2	8.9	55403	60279	72	29	4445	0.2	0.0	6.5	62.5	30.8	295674
02841	NEWPORT	11831	56	14.3	10.7	19.6	48.2	7.1	101538	102930	97	99	0	0.0	0.0	0.0	0.0	0.0	0
02842	MIDDLETOWN	33679	6636	12.0	22.6	37.6	18.0	9.9	65028	68492	83	48	3755	1.3	1.0	3.8	75.3	18.6	282722
02852	NORTH KINGSTOWN	37874	9276	15.6	14.4	31.1	23.3	15.6	78127	82404	91	79	6779	2.2	0.1	4.4	67.7	25.7	290498
02857	NORTH SCITUATE	33962	3359	8.2	17.3	43.4	20.7	10.3	77354	77691	91	73	2847	1.5	1.3	2.9	64.0	30.2	338750
02858	OAKLAND	27282	277	14.1	19.5	43.7	15.9	6.9	68958	70897	86	57	213	0.5	1.4	10.3	77.9	9.9	268229
02859	PASCOAG	24951	2307	12.6	19.4	51.7	11.7	4.7	67626	68501	85	52	1676	0.9	0.7	9.1	82.0	7.3	253333
02860	PAWTUCKET	18879	18770	37.4	28.6	27.4	4.6	2.0	34625	38295	17	11	6401	1.0	1.7	33.8	60.8	2.7	193745
02861	PAWTUCKET	23402	10873	23.1	26.4	41.5	6.5	2.5	50413	52730	62	23	6926	2.8	1.8	26.3	68.1	1.1	194344
02863	CENTRAL FALLS	12612	6494	45.3	30.4	21.1	2.7	0.6	27615	29795	5	7	1485	1.4	1.4	48.4	47.9	0.9	173561
02864	CUMBERLAND	31967	12720	13.8	18.9	41.5	16.2	9.6	69285	69229	86	59	9598	0.7	0.3	5.5	74.2	19.3	279793
02865	LINCOLN	33831	6857	15.3	19.9	39.6	13.8	11.5	68791	69580	86	56	4884	0.8	0.6	3.1	64.8	30.7	312870
02871	PORTSMOUTH	38451	6585	9.8	15.8	37.1	21.2	16.0	77376	81307	91	75	4841	2.4	0.7	4.8	65.1	26.9	291954
02872	PRUDENCE ISLAND	22533	45	48.9	22.2	28.9	0.0	0.0	25334	25675	3	4	40	0.0	0.0	17.5	67.5	15.0	262500
02873	ROCKVILLE	33113	69	7.2	21.7	37.7	20.3	13.0	79269	80427	92	81	57	0.0	0.0	7.0	82.5	10.5	276563
02874	SAUNDERSTOWN	40723	2058	4.6	12.0	36.3	29.8	17.3	94321	96640	96	96	1748	0.3	0.3	2.6	62.9	33.9	328861
02877	SLOCUM	33881	33	3.0	15.2	33.3	36.4	12.1	96111	100888	96	97	26	0.0	0.0	7.7	73.1	19.2	320000
02878	TIVERTON	29494	6260	17.6	19.1	39.1	18.2	6.0	65181	68971	83	49	4963	1.0	0.9	8.6	73.5	15.9	252608
02879	WAKEFIELD	37534	8442	12.2	18.3	33.6	22.3	13.6	73316	77109	88	64	6223	0.2	0.2	6.4	64.0	29.2	313948
02881	KINGSTON	22487	1008	13.1	17.6	25.1	23.1	21.1	85683	89322	94	92	710	0.0	0.0	1.7	57.0	41.3	371028
02882	NARRAGANSETT	36429	6368	17.9	23.9	27.9	19.2	11.1	63900	69162	82	44	3848	0.2	0.2	2.3	64.9	32.3	316359
02885	WARREN	28780	4754	21.8	25.6	33.0	14.1	5.6	53267	58388	68	28	2830	0.4	0.4	11.6	77.1	10.6	243046
02886	WARWICK	29547	13291	18.8	24.4	42.2	9.9	4.7	58135	62311	75	32	8842	1.4	0.5	17.4	67.6	13.1	229212
02888	WARWICK	28734	8593	16.3	22.6	45.8	10.7	4.7	60703	64324	78	39	6577	0.6	1.0	25.8	67.4	5.2	207816
02889	WARWICK	26755	11442	16.1	23.3	46.1	10.0	4.5	61293	65260	79	40	8873	0.2	1.4	28.7	62.3	7.4	203630
02891	WESTERLY	31498	9345	18.8	23.0	36.0	14.8	7.4	60222	62833	78	36	6004	0.4	0.1	4.7	73.8	21.0	278358
02892	WEST KINGSTON	34066	1890	4.1	17.8	39.3	28.2	10.6	82852	85470	93	87	1663	0.1	1.3	7.9	74.4	16.4	278343
02893	WEST WARWICK	24731	12837	23.6	26.7	39.2	7.2	3.3	49707	51612	60	21	7010	1.6	1.0	27.7	67.4	2.4	204615
02894	WOOD RIVER JUNCTION	27591	370	13.2	15.9	44.1	19.7	7.0	75543	77937	90	69	319	0.0	0.0	8.2	80.9	11.0	246684
02895	WOONSOCKET	19337	17487	33.8	29.4	30.5	4.6	1.7	38324	42131	28	13	6238	1.1	0.5	19.0	77.9	1.5	217288
02896	NORTH SMITHFIELD	31013	4041	13.4	17.5	43.6	16.6	8.8	75272	75806	89	68	3152	0.0	0.0	5.1	73.4	21.4	292996
02898	WYOMING	28631	589	6.3	13.8	46.0	27.5	6.5	77568	80434	91	76	537	0.0	1.7	9.9	80.1	8.4	261653
02903	PROVIDENCE	18730	4546	60.2	18.8	15.5	2.9	2.6	17113	18516	1	3	566	0.0	0.0	35.0	44.7	20.3	196684
02904	PROVIDENCE	24105	13025	31.5	24.9	35.1	5.6	2.9	43279	47361	43	16	6532	0.5	1.7	22.4	70.5	5.1	216499
02905	PROVIDENCE	19371	8553	29.7	26.9	32.4	6.8	4.2	42403	46452	41	15	4307	0.7	2.7	32.6	54.7	9.3	196401
02906	PROVIDENCE	38221	12029	23.7	20.2	29.1	11.0	16.0	59314	61154	77	33	5040	0.0	0.0	7.9	43.9	48.2	391659
02907	PROVIDENCE	12686	8591	44.5	27.8	22.3	3.9	1.5	28232	30143	6	8	2596	2.5	3.6	51.3	39.5	3.0	167711
02908	PROVIDENCE	17388	13532	34.4	29.0	29.8	4.8	1.9	36953	40811	23	12	5837	0.0	1.2	38.4	58.5	1.9	188814
02909	PROVIDENCE	12924	14801	47.0	26.7	21.9	3.0	1.5	26905	28905	5	5	4477	1.2	1.7	54.6	40.3	2.1	167850
02910	CRANSTON	25265	8393	17.6	29.9	40.7	8.4	3.4	52337	54197	67	27	5525	0.4	0.8	21.0	76.9	1.0	203821
02911	NORTH PROVIDENCE	25293	6614	22.7	29.2	37.5	7.2	3.4	47977	51053	57	20	3928	0.7	2.1	16.7	77.7	2.7	223525
02912	PROVIDENCE	10626	0	0.0	0.0	0.0	0.0	0.0	0	0	0	0	0	0.0	0.0	0.0	0.0	0.0	0
02914	EAST PROVIDENCE	20620	8923	29.1	26.0	38.5	5.2	1.1	44162	48450	46	17	4820	0.5	0.1	15.4	80.8	3.1	224350
02915	RIVERSIDE	24620	7893	21.4	26.5	43.3	6.9	1.9	51845	54103	66	25	4844	0.5	0.3	16.4	80.0	2.8	224708
02916	RUMFORD	31806	3518	18.1	20.6	43.4	9.9	8.0	60540	61128	78	37	2379	1.3	2.1	8.8	74.2	13.5	254359
02917	SMITHFIELD	28981	4811	14.8	17.0	41.5	18.1	8.6	71867	72253	88	63	3593	0.1	0.0	10.1	74.0	15.8	272599
02918	PROVIDENCE	10712	136	40.4	28.7	26.5	0.7	3.7	32078	36161	12	9	50	0.0	0.0	52.0	48.0	0.0	172500
02919	JOHNSTON	26042	11247	22.7	22.3	38.2	11.5	5.3	56643	58646	74	31	7994	0.0	1.0	11.8	79.1	8.0	248149
02920	CRANSTON	25242	14435	22.6	25.9	39.1	8.7	3.7	51528	53815	65	24	9201	0.6	0.5	12.5	79.9	6.6	237809
02921	CRANSTON	35345	3868	7.0	11.2	40.7	22.5	18.6	88869	89914	95	95	3440	0.2	0.4	2.6	56.7	40.2	368386
	RHODE ISLAND	27186		22.7	22.9	35.9	11.7	6.7	54939	57605				0.8	1.0	14.8	67.1	16.3	247721
	UNITED STATES	27277		20.9	24.4	35.3	11.7	7.6	54719	56938				9.3	13.1	31.6	32.6	13.5	162279

ZIP CODE #	POST OFFICE NAME	FINANCIAL SERVICES: Auto Loan	FINANCIAL SERVICES: Home Loan	FINANCIAL SERVICES: Invest-ments	FINANCIAL SERVICES: Retire-ment Plans	THE HOME: Home Improvements: Home Repair	THE HOME: Home Improvements: Lawn & Garden	THE HOME: Furnishings: Comput-ers & Hard-ware-Personal	THE HOME: Furnishings: Major Appli-ances	THE HOME: Furnishings: TV, Radio, Sound Equip-ment	THE HOME: Furnishings: Furni-ture	ENTERTAINMENT: Dine out/ Carry out	ENTERTAINMENT: Sports Equip-ment	ENTERTAINMENT: Fees & Tickets	ENTERTAINMENT: Toys & Games	ENTERTAINMENT: Travel	ENTERTAINMENT: Cable TV	PERSONAL: Apparel & Services	PERSONAL: Auto Repairs	PERSONAL: Health Insur-ance	PERSONAL: Pets & Supplies
02804	ASHAWAY	108	140	133	135	139	129	118	122	115	119	116	92	135	117	131	116	84	118	120	139
02806	BARRINGTON	154	212	238	211	228	197	176	186	167	186	167	137	213	166	205	164	124	175	174	205
02807	BLOCK ISLAND	109	133	159	135	148	120	126	127	113	136	113	99	138	108	141	105	83	123	111	142
02808	BRADFORD	91	106	97	105	103	98	99	97	96	97	97	77	106	98	104	96	69	97	96	113
02809	BRISTOL	89	107	111	104	110	101	101	100	100	99	101	75	111	98	108	102	73	101	102	113
02812	CAROLINA	124	152	133	153	147	135	129	132	123	134	125	105	144	127	139	119	89	126	121	152
02813	CHARLESTOWN	117	124	125	124	126	126	114	120	114	119	115	88	119	114	120	116	80	117	122	140
02814	CHEPACHET	106	134	127	131	134	123	115	119	110	115	111	90	129	113	126	110	80	114	113	135
02815	CLAYVILLE	123	154	142	155	152	137	130	134	123	137	125	104	147	126	142	119	90	127	122	153
02816	COVENTRY	91	112	104	110	110	104	99	100	97	99	98	77	111	98	107	97	70	98	100	115
02817	WEST GREENWICH	124	152	133	152	146	135	129	132	122	134	125	104	143	127	138	119	89	126	121	152
02818	EAST GREENWICH	141	170	181	175	178	164	154	158	150	162	151	119	175	147	170	149	109	154	156	180
02822	EXETER	137	161	142	160	156	144	138	142	132	145	135	111	151	138	146	129	96	135	130	164
02825	FOSTER	106	140	140	136	142	126	117	122	111	121	113	91	135	113	131	110	82	116	114	137
02827	GREENE	116	146	128	146	141	126	122	124	115	129	117	99	138	120	132	110	84	118	111	143
02828	GREENVILLE	98	124	126	120	127	121	108	113	108	109	108	81	123	106	120	111	77	110	119	128
02830	HARRISVILLE	95	121	115	117	121	108	105	106	101	106	102	82	118	103	114	100	74	103	101	120
02831	HOPE	129	162	151	163	160	144	137	140	130	144	132	110	156	134	150	126	96	134	128	161
02832	HOPE VALLEY	111	125	120	124	125	124	111	119	110	108	110	91	117	112	118	111	78	112	116	136
02833	HOPKINTON	94	131	135	122	135	116	108	113	104	108	105	83	127	105	124	104	77	108	106	124
02835	JAMESTOWN	143	182	204	186	196	164	163	167	148	176	149	129	184	145	184	140	109	159	148	187
02836	KENYON	129	162	142	162	156	140	136	138	127	143	130	110	153	133	147	123	94	131	123	158
02837	LITTLE COMPTON	138	165	180	168	173	164	142	154	139	153	140	110	160	135	160	139	99	146	152	176
02838	MANVILLE	71	82	78	81	81	76	79	76	77	78	78	60	85	77	82	76	56	77	76	89
02839	MAPLEVILLE	113	132	114	134	128	124	115	119	111	117	113	93	125	115	123	110	80	114	114	139
02840	NEWPORT	97	97	103	101	99	90	109	98	103	107	106	81	108	102	108	100	76	104	95	116
02841	NEWPORT	166	88	67	101	79	75	157	109	148	146	156	108	120	175	114	137	109	139	100	134
02842	MIDDLETOWN	106	122	126	121	126	112	119	114	115	118	116	89	129	116	125	113	84	116	112	130
02852	NORTH KINGSTOWN	126	150	147	150	151	137	136	136	131	139	132	105	149	133	145	128	95	133	129	156
02857	NORTH SCITUATE	118	151	152	150	155	141	128	134	123	132	124	100	146	124	143	122	90	128	128	152
02858	OAKLAND	93	124	123	117	126	110	106	108	101	105	103	81	121	103	118	101	75	105	103	121
02859	PASCOAG	94	116	108	113	114	103	104	103	100	104	101	80	115	101	111	98	73	101	98	118
02860	PAWTUCKET	61	55	52	56	54	53	68	58	67	64	69	47	64	67	62	67	49	65	61	70
02861	PAWTUCKET	73	82	78	81	81	80	79	78	80	77	80	60	84	79	82	81	57	79	82	91
02863	CENTRAL FALLS	49	37	34	38	36	33	53	43	51	51	54	36	46	52	46	49	39	51	40	50
02864	CUMBERLAND	108	131	128	129	132	124	116	119	114	118	115	89	129	114	126	115	82	116	120	136
02865	LINCOLN	108	138	143	134	142	128	122	124	118	123	119	93	139	118	135	119	87	122	123	140
02871	PORTSMOUTH	132	152	153	155	155	149	137	142	134	142	135	106	150	134	148	134	96	138	140	164
02872	PRUDENCE ISLAND	52	54	74	54	63	64	49	58	52	55	51	36	54	46	56	54	35	55	64	65
02873	ROCKVILLE	105	147	153	137	153	130	122	127	116	121	118	93	143	118	139	117	87	122	120	139
02874	SAUNDERSTOWN	146	180	174	183	181	159	153	158	143	165	145	125	174	148	167	136	106	148	139	178
02877	SLOCUM	137	173	152	172	166	149	145	147	136	152	139	117	163	142	156	131	100	140	131	169
02878	TIVERTON	92	119	120	114	121	114	102	107	101	101	102	78	116	101	114	104	73	104	110	120
02879	WAKEFIELD	122	145	154	145	149	138	130	135	125	133	126	103	143	125	142	124	91	130	129	154
02881	KINGSTON	137	157	159	165	160	145	151	143	140	152	142	116	162	143	154	135	104	141	131	166
02882	NARRAGANSETT	118	120	137	122	125	123	122	123	118	122	119	94	123	116	126	118	84	123	122	143
02885	WARREN	86	97	95	96	98	95	95	93	95	93	95	70	101	93	98	96	68	95	98	107
02886	WARWICK	85	99	96	99	99	99	91	93	92	92	93	69	101	91	98	95	66	93	100	108
02888	WARWICK	87	102	99	101	103	102	94	96	94	94	95	71	103	93	101	96	67	95	102	111
02889	WARWICK	87	104	97	103	102	99	95	95	94	94	95	73	105	95	102	95	68	95	97	110
02891	WESTERLY	97	108	112	107	111	107	104	105	104	103	104	78	110	102	109	105	74	105	107	121
02892	WEST KINGSTON	127	158	139	158	153	137	134	135	126	140	128	108	150	131	144	121	92	129	121	156
02893	WEST WARWICK	76	79	76	78	78	77	82	78	82	79	83	61	83	82	82	83	58	81	82	92
02894	WOOD RIVER JUNCTION	112	127	109	130	123	124	113	117	111	114	111	92	121	114	119	111	78	113	115	138
02895	WOONSOCKET	61	59	57	60	58	59	67	61	68	63	68	48	66	67	64	69	49	66	66	73
02896	NORTH SMITHFIELD	100	134	139	127	139	123	114	118	111	114	111	86	132	110	129	112	81	115	116	131
02898	WYOMING	117	143	126	144	138	127	122	125	115	126	117	99	135	120	130	112	84	118	114	144
02903	PROVIDENCE	46	34	35	37	33	36	53	41	53	47	53	35	45	51	44	53	38	49	47	52
02904	PROVIDENCE	68	68	68	69	68	70	75	70	77	72	77	54	75	74	74	79	54	75	78	84
02905	PROVIDENCE	74	76	71	74	75	68	81	75	79	80	81	59	81	79	79	77	58	79	72	86
02906	PROVIDENCE	124	114	121	122	115	110	144	118	134	133	136	100	134	133	130	130	98	130	117	143
02907	PROVIDENCE	55	47	43	47	46	42	60	51	58	58	61	42	55	59	54	56	44	58	49	59
02908	PROVIDENCE	63	58	53	59	56	56	69	60	69	65	70	49	66	69	64	69	50	67	62	72
02909	PROVIDENCE	50	42	39	42	41	39	55	47	55	52	56	38	50	54	49	54	41	53	47	55
02910	CRANSTON	78	91	86	89	90	85	87	85	86	85	87	66	94	86	91	86	62	86	86	99
02911	NORTH PROVIDENCE	77	79	79	80	80	79	83	79	83	80	83	61	85	82	83	84	59	82	84	93
02912	PROVIDENCE	0	0	0	0	0	0	0	0	0	0	0	0	0	0	0	0	0	0	0	0
02914	EAST PROVIDENCE	66	68	66	68	67	67	71	68	71	69	72	53	72	71	71	72	51	71	71	80
02915	RIVERSIDE	73	82	79	81	82	84	78	79	80	77	80	58	84	78	83	82	56	80	87	92
02916	RUMFORD	93	113	114	110	114	108	104	104	103	102	103	78	115	102	112	105	74	104	108	119
02917	SMITHFIELD	104	126	126	126	128	121	113	115	111	115	112	86	126	110	123	112	80	113	117	132
02918	PROVIDENCE	70	46	44	51	45	50	83	57	75	66	75	52	62	75	59	73	53	69	60	73
02919	JOHNSTON	80	100	100	96	101	96	89	91	90	88	91	67	101	89	98	93	65	91	97	104
02920	CRANSTON	79	89	89	88	90	90	86	87	87	84	87	64	92	85	90	90	62	87	93	100
02921	CRANSTON	136	175	176	180	179	159	147	152	140	157	141	118	173	141	164	135	104	144	139	172
	RHODE ISLAND	90	98	97	98	98	94	98	94	96	96	98	73	103	96	100	97	70	97	96	110
	UNITED STATES	100	100	100	100	100	100	100	100	100	100	100	100	100	100	100	100	100	100	100	100

29001-29205

ZIP CODE			POPULATION			2000-2009 ANNUAL RATE		HOUSEHOLDS					FAMILIES		
#	POST OFFICE NAME	COUNTY FIPS CODE	2000	2009	2014	% Rate	State Centile	2000	2009	2014	% Annual Rate 2000-2009	2009 Average HH Size	2000	2009	% Annual Rate 2000-2009
29001	ALCOLU	027	2616	2674	2651	0.2	34	914	974	975	0.7	2.73	694	715	0.3
29003	BAMBERG	009	7281	6779	6465	-0.8	5	2713	2652	2558	-0.2	2.42	1933	1817	-0.7
29006	BATESBURG	081	10917	11561	11885	0.6	50	4266	4692	4869	1.0	2.45	3102	3270	0.6
29009	BETHUNE	055	2225	2418	2558	0.9	64	879	1011	1084	1.5	2.39	622	683	1.0
29010	BISHOPVILLE	061	14434	14305	14018	-0.1	21	4860	5035	4984	0.4	2.47	3434	3417	-0.1
29014	BLACKSTOCK	039	1665	1666	1640	0.0	25	630	662	660	0.5	2.52	474	481	0.2
29015	BLAIR	039	1684	1651	1619	-0.2	18	558	581	577	0.4	2.81	400	401	0.0
29016	BLYTHEWOOD	079	9853	13650	15521	3.6	95	3524	5044	5818	4.0	2.67	2807	3821	3.4
29018	BOWMAN	075	4133	4122	4099	0.0	25	1519	1583	1593	0.4	2.60	1105	1105	0.0
29020	CAMDEN	055	21426	22845	23889	0.7	56	8571	9508	10059	1.1	2.35	6001	6357	0.6
29030	CAMERON	017	3030	3048	2998	0.1	29	1258	1339	1335	0.7	2.27	900	921	0.2
29031	CARLISLE	023	1452	1325	1269	-1.0	2	574	554	538	-0.4	2.39	400	369	-0.9
29032	CASSATT	055	3788	4148	4397	1.0	69	1359	1548	1660	1.4	2.68	1029	1128	1.0
29033	CAYCE	063	11391	11892	12254	0.5	47	4917	5354	5588	0.9	2.21	3085	3096	0.0
29036	CHAPIN	063	12274	16188	18337	3.0	93	4655	6393	7348	3.5	2.46	3727	4928	3.1
29037	CHAPPELLS	071	578	625	648	0.8	61	236	267	280	1.3	2.34	179	195	0.9
29038	COPE	075	2626	2817	2835	0.8	61	966	1076	1095	1.2	2.62	727	779	0.7
29039	CORDOVA	075	4010	3922	3857	-0.2	18	1479	1502	1495	0.2	2.61	1124	1099	-0.2
29040	DALZELL	085	7018	7715	7801	1.0	69	2586	2961	3030	1.5	2.61	1962	2173	1.1
29042	DENMARK	009	6349	5965	5747	-0.7	7	2202	2176	2113	-0.1	2.43	1489	1407	-0.6
29044	EASTOVER	079	6064	6344	6638	0.5	47	2213	2447	2601	1.1	2.56	1651	1706	0.4
29045	ELGIN	055	14168	19441	22643	3.5	95	5039	7223	8520	4.0	2.69	4055	5578	3.5
29046	ELLIOTT	061	112	110	108	-0.2	18	34	36	36	0.6	3.06	25	26	0.4
29047	ELLOREE	075	2878	2887	2874	0.0	25	1194	1254	1262	0.5	2.30	804	805	0.0
29048	EUTAWVILLE	075	4748	4983	4989	0.5	47	1801	1969	1996	1.0	2.53	1301	1363	0.5
29051	GABLE	027	2381	2416	2384	0.2	34	448	458	452	0.2	2.64	348	345	-0.1
29052	GADSDEN	079	2264	2281	2368	0.1	29	751	803	847	0.7	2.84	594	601	0.1
29053	GASTON	063	15547	16684	17465	0.8	61	5560	6145	6497	1.1	2.71	4136	4380	0.6
29054	GILBERT	063	7768	9409	10326	2.1	87	2924	3649	4053	2.4	2.55	2287	2754	2.0
29055	GREAT FALLS	023	4974	4817	4676	-0.3	15	1917	1928	1894	0.1	2.50	1376	1334	-0.3
29056	GREELEYVILLE	089	2632	2425	2350	-0.9	3	995	987	968	-0.1	2.46	706	673	-0.5
29058	HEATH SPRINGS	057	4847	5104	5388	0.6	50	1904	2116	2271	1.1	2.27	1395	1481	0.6
29059	HOLLY HILL	075	6192	6045	5976	-0.3	15	2304	2348	2355	0.2	2.53	1697	1661	-0.2
29061	HOPKINS	079	13056	14091	14947	0.8	61	4610	5259	5658	1.4	2.67	3560	3826	0.8
29063	IRMO	079	23904	31699	35471	3.1	93	8444	11684	13260	3.6	2.70	6832	8996	3.0
29065	JENKINSVILLE	039	750	802	802	0.7	56	296	337	341	1.4	2.38	216	236	1.0
29067	KERSHAW	057	9879	10427	10902	0.6	50	3431	3779	4026	1.0	2.45	2487	2618	0.6
29069	LAMAR	031	4893	5054	5065	0.4	43	1837	1903	1914	0.4	2.66	1354	1350	0.0
29070	LEESVILLE	063	11556	13728	14933	1.9	85	4443	5494	6049	2.3	2.49	3302	3907	1.8
29072	LEXINGTON	063	30895	43776	49780	3.8	96	11182	16302	18758	4.2	2.61	8626	12109	3.7
29073	LEXINGTON	063	28999	35598	39162	2.2	88	10905	13788	15291	2.6	2.58	8219	10013	2.2
29075	LITTLE MOUNTAIN	071	2804	2984	3114	0.7	56	1088	1201	1267	1.1	2.48	835	887	0.7
29078	LUGOFF	055	11976	14733	16180	2.3	89	4435	5673	6305	2.7	2.59	3441	4251	2.3
29080	LYNCHBURG	061	3814	3699	3611	-0.3	15	1330	1362	1347	0.3	2.72	976	964	-0.1
29081	EHRHARDT	009	1451	1304	1232	-1.1	2	577	555	531	-0.4	2.34	396	364	-0.9
29082	LODGE	029	645	612	596	-0.6	8	243	238	235	-0.2	2.41	170	160	-0.7
29101	MC BEE	025	3151	3228	3205	0.3	38	1135	1202	1206	0.6	2.63	862	883	0.3
29102	MANNING	027	15792	16468	16549	0.5	47	5996	6623	6740	1.1	2.46	4313	4583	0.7
29104	MAYESVILLE	085	2266	2193	2144	-0.4	12	779	793	785	0.2	2.77	587	577	-0.2
29105	MONETTA	003	1430	1443	1441	0.1	29	518	535	539	0.3	2.68	393	391	-0.1
29107	NEESES	075	3039	3087	3062	0.2	34	1215	1270	1274	0.5	2.43	898	902	0.0
29108	NEWBERRY	071	19716	20229	20429	0.3	38	7385	7782	7934	0.6	2.47	5024	5058	0.1
29111	NEW ZION	027	1189	1140	1106	-0.5	9	413	418	410	0.1	2.73	326	320	-0.2
29112	NORTH	075	4547	4637	4628	0.2	34	1758	1868	1886	0.7	2.48	1234	1252	0.2
29113	NORWAY	075	1689	1648	1624	-0.3	15	608	622	621	0.2	2.65	451	443	-0.2
29114	OLANTA	041	2243	2163	2136	-0.4	12	776	775	773	0.0	2.68	583	561	-0.4
29115	ORANGEBURG	075	30154	28997	28372	-0.4	12	11743	11645	11503	-0.1	2.38	7589	7192	-0.6
29117	ORANGEBURG	075	2437	2235	2202	-0.9	3	37	35	34	-0.6	2.54	21	19	-1.1
29118	ORANGEBURG	075	13614	14024	13957	0.3	38	5089	5435	5474	0.7	2.51	3767	3864	0.3
29123	PELION	063	5794	6710	7202	1.6	80	2071	2484	2696	2.0	2.68	1560	1788	1.5
29125	PINEWOOD	085	4090	4124	4056	0.1	29	1474	1542	1532	0.5	2.63	1090	1100	0.1
29126	POMARIA	071	2405	2515	2574	0.5	47	942	1030	1065	1.0	2.44	679	712	0.5
29127	PROSPERITY	071	6917	7812	8191	1.3	76	2801	3307	3504	1.8	2.35	2072	2354	1.4
29128	REMBERT	085	6069	6085	6049	0.0	25	1939	2062	2076	0.7	2.63	1397	1428	0.2
29129	RIDGE SPRING	081	3654	3857	3911	0.6	50	1335	1446	1479	0.9	2.67	965	1007	0.5
29130	RIDGEWAY	039	5975	6699	6860	1.2	73	2242	2667	2769	1.9	2.42	1660	1899	1.5
29133	ROWESVILLE	075	1057	1063	1053	0.1	29	400	419	421	0.5	2.53	288	289	0.0
29135	SAINT MATTHEWS	017	11127	11391	11307	0.3	38	4238	4577	4604	0.8	2.45	3072	3194	0.4
29137	SALLEY	003	2759	2897	2936	0.5	47	1059	1138	1162	0.8	2.54	767	790	0.3
29138	SALUDA	081	11265	11188	11046	-0.1	21	4060	4116	4088	0.1	2.65	3032	2968	-0.2
29142	SANTEE	075	4595	4883	4902	0.7	56	1736	1937	1974	1.2	2.52	1279	1372	0.8
29145	SILVERSTREET	071	941	1000	1031	0.7	56	339	377	392	1.2	2.64	250	267	0.7
29146	SPRINGFIELD	075	1744	1711	1690	-0.2	18	671	684	684	0.2	2.41	468	456	-0.3
29148	SUMMERTON	027	6298	6733	6835	0.7	56	2501	2884	2977	1.6	2.30	1772	1972	1.2
29150	SUMTER	085	38171	37610	36810	-0.2	18	14581	14953	14801	0.3	2.44	9876	9715	-0.2
29152	SHAW A F B	085	6216	4697	4371	-3.0	0	1616	1227	1143	-2.9	3.23	1500	1139	-2.9
29153	SUMTER	085	14888	15073	14882	0.1	29	5328	5623	5621	0.6	2.63	4004	4086	0.2
29154	SUMTER	085	24063	25642	25746	0.7	56	8769	9706	9864	1.1	2.62	6679	7160	0.8
29160	SWANSEA	063	6237	7204	7755	1.6	80	2391	2856	3108	1.9	2.52	1745	1996	1.5
29161	TIMMONSVILLE	041	11179	11622	11876	0.4	43	4088	4361	4498	0.7	2.66	3096	3187	0.3
29162	TURBEVILLE	027	2507	2529	2527	0.1	29	914	975	987	0.7	2.56	695	715	0.3
29163	VANCE	075	2096	2139	2127	0.2	34	746	797	803	0.7	2.68	539	551	0.2
29164	WAGENER	003	4273	4669	4819	1.0	69	1673	1868	1940	1.2	2.50	1203	1285	0.7
29166	WARD	081	1086	1129	1127	0.4	43	414	443	445	0.7	2.55	297	306	0.3
29168	WEDGEFIELD	085	3562	3686	3655	0.4	43	1293	1390	1396	0.8	2.65	946	983	0.4
29169	WEST COLUMBIA	063	21705	22941	24095	0.6	50	9566	10469	11118	1.0	2.08	5087	5138	0.1
29170	WEST COLUMBIA	063	18763	20024	20995	0.7	56	7323	8078	8552	1.1	2.48	5403	5716	0.6
29172	WEST COLUMBIA	063	8870	9279	9680	0.5	47	3299	3597	3797	0.9	2.58	2418	2521	0.5
29175	WESTVILLE	055	459	501	528	1.0	69	177	202	216	1.4	2.48	131	143	1.0
29178	WHITMIRE	071	3662	3502	3435	-0.5	9	1541	1525	1511	-0.1	2.29	1023	962	-0.7
29180	WINNSBORO	039	14495	14110	13774	-0.3	15	5508	5646	5584	0.3	2.47	3973	3919	-0.1
29201	COLUMBIA	079	15800	18909	20216	2.0	86	5699	7276	8082	2.7	1.82	1905	2198	1.6
29203	COLUMBIA	079	43518	44053	44723	0.1	29	15056	15722	16217	0.5	2.54	10323	9947	-0.4
29204	COLUMBIA	079	21404	20637	20612	-0.4	12	8598	8567	8689	0.0	2.08	4822	4300	-1.2
29205	COLUMBIA	079	25412	24640	24725	-0.3	15	12014	12069	12289	0.0	1.93	5253	4583	-1.5
	SOUTH CAROLINA					1.3					1.7	2.45			1.2
	UNITED STATES					1.0					1.1	2.59			0.9

ZIP CODE # POST OFFICE NAME	RACE (%) White 2000	White 2009	Black 2000	Black 2009	Asian/Pacific 2000	Asian/Pacific 2009	% Hispanic Origin 2000	% Hispanic Origin 2009	2009 AGE DISTRIBUTION (%) 0-4	5-9	10-14	15-19	20-24	25-44	45-64	65-84	85+	18+	MEDIAN AGE 2009	% 2009 Males	% 2009 Females
29001 ALCOLU	41.4	38.1	57.3	59.9	0.0	0.1	1.1	1.8	5.5	6.6	7.0	8.4	5.8	24.8	30.2	10.5	1.2	75.6	39.0	48.9	51.1
29003 BAMBERG	43.9	42.4	55.2	56.4	0.2	0.3	0.6	0.8	5.9	6.4	6.5	9.5	6.9	22.6	27.0	12.9	2.3	75.9	38.6	46.8	53.2
29006 BATESBURG	72.5	70.0	25.3	26.8	0.1	0.2	2.2	3.4	6.6	6.6	6.6	6.4	5.2	25.0	28.4	13.4	1.8	76.2	40.5	49.4	50.6
29009 BETHUNE	66.7	64.7	32.2	33.8	0.1	0.1	1.0	1.4	6.4	6.6	6.9	6.1	4.4	24.9	29.9	13.1	1.7	76.2	40.7	49.5	50.5
29010 BISHOPVILLE	37.7	36.4	61.2	62.1	0.2	0.3	1.1	1.5	6.1	6.4	6.3	6.8	7.0	28.1	26.9	10.5	1.9	77.2	37.2	52.8	47.2
29014 BLACKSTOCK	62.0	59.9	36.6	38.3	0.2	0.4	0.3	0.4	6.0	6.3	6.7	7.1	5.8	25.8	29.1	11.9	1.2	76.7	40.0	50.0	50.0
29015 BLAIR	15.0	13.9	84.0	84.9	0.1	0.2	0.9	1.1	5.7	5.8	6.2	7.6	5.9	23.9	30.2	12.8	1.9	77.4	41.4	45.9	54.1
29016 BLYTHEWOOD	60.3	54.4	36.9	41.5	0.7	1.0	1.8	2.7	7.2	7.6	7.8	7.2	4.5	29.4	28.1	7.5	0.8	72.7	37.1	48.7	51.3
29018 BOWMAN	34.5	32.7	64.4	65.9	0.1	0.2	1.0	1.4	6.0	6.8	6.8	7.1	6.4	24.2	29.5	11.6	1.6	76.5	39.8	47.8	52.2
29020 CAMDEN	61.9	59.7	36.3	37.9	0.4	0.5	1.6	2.3	5.8	5.9	6.2	6.4	5.5	23.1	28.8	15.3	3.0	78.2	42.7	47.3	52.7
29030 CAMERON	49.3	47.5	50.2	51.7	0.1	0.1	0.8	1.0	5.6	5.9	6.2	6.4	4.9	21.5	32.1	15.4	2.0	78.3	44.7	48.2	51.8
29031 CARLISLE	24.9	23.9	74.2	75.0	0.1	0.2	0.4	0.6	5.1	5.8	6.7	7.8	5.9	25.1	29.9	12.2	1.5	77.1	40.3	46.8	53.2
29032 CASSATT	65.1	62.8	33.2	34.8	0.1	0.2	1.6	2.5	6.2	6.2	6.6	7.8	6.7	27.2	28.8	9.5	0.9	76.2	36.9	49.8	50.2
29033 CAYCE	73.0	70.0	24.2	25.9	1.0	1.5	1.3	2.0	5.9	5.8	5.7	6.2	7.1	27.2	26.8	13.2	2.2	79.2	39.1	47.5	52.5
29036 CHAPIN	95.2	94.2	3.7	4.1	0.3	0.5	0.8	1.2	4.8	5.5	6.5	6.4	3.9	20.2	34.7	15.0	3.0	79.0	46.5	49.0	51.0
29037 CHAPPELLS	69.2	67.4	30.1	31.8	0.0	0.0	1.2	1.8	5.3	5.6	5.8	6.1	5.9	24.6	31.5	13.8	1.4	79.8	42.7	51.7	48.3
29038 COPE	62.8	60.3	36.2	38.4	0.2	0.2	0.5	0.7	6.1	6.2	6.7	7.7	6.5	25.6	30.1	9.9	1.1	76.3	38.8	49.0	51.0
29039 CORDOVA	55.2	53.0	43.4	45.1	0.2	0.3	1.0	1.4	7.4	7.0	6.5	7.1	7.8	28.8	25.6	9.0	0.8	74.9	33.8	48.7	51.3
29040 DALZELL	51.5	48.1	44.3	46.2	1.4	1.9	2.0	2.9	7.5	7.4	7.2	7.3	7.1	28.7	25.8	8.3	0.7	73.6	34.2	49.2	50.8
29042 DENMARK	17.7	17.2	81.3	81.5	0.3	0.4	0.5	0.6	6.5	6.7	6.6	10.1	11.1	22.0	24.4	10.9	1.5	76.1	33.3	47.9	52.1
29044 EASTOVER	33.9	29.4	64.1	67.9	0.2	0.3	1.1	1.6	6.8	7.1	7.4	7.6	5.5	24.1	29.5	10.7	1.2	73.8	38.5	47.7	52.3
29045 ELGIN	75.7	72.2	20.6	22.4	0.9	1.3	2.5	4.1	7.9	7.7	7.8	7.1	5.8	28.9	27.2	7.1	0.5	72.0	35.6	49.1	50.9
29046 ELLIOTT	13.5	12.7	86.5	86.4	0.0	0.9	0.9	0.9	5.5	5.5	5.5	6.4	7.3	25.5	30.9	12.7	0.9	80.9	40.0	48.2	51.8
29047 ELLOREE	45.1	43.0	53.5	55.1	0.0	0.0	1.5	2.1	5.7	6.0	6.5	6.5	4.7	21.7	30.2	16.6	2.0	77.8	44.1	47.2	52.8
29048 EUTAWVILLE	36.5	34.6	61.8	63.1	0.1	0.1	0.8	1.2	5.7	5.9	6.1	7.1	5.9	20.9	30.8	16.0	1.6	77.7	43.6	48.1	51.9
29051 GABLE	35.2	32.0	62.8	65.3	0.1	0.1	1.1	1.7	3.2	3.3	3.4	14.7	27.2	24.8	16.0	6.7	0.8	86.2	24.7	74.7	25.3
29052 GADSDEN	6.8	5.6	92.4	93.5	0.0	0.0	0.9	0.9	6.8	7.6	8.3	8.3	6.0	23.2	29.2	9.5	1.1	72.6	36.3	44.4	55.6
29053 GASTON	82.5	79.8	14.4	16.0	0.3	0.5	1.8	2.7	8.2	7.7	7.2	7.5	7.8	29.3	24.8	7.0	0.5	72.2	32.7	49.6	50.4
29054 GILBERT	92.6	90.1	4.1	4.6	0.2	0.4	3.5	5.6	6.1	6.4	6.6	6.7	5.4	27.3	29.8	10.7	0.9	76.6	39.5	51.3	48.7
29055 GREAT FALLS	65.8	63.3	33.1	35.1	0.2	0.3	0.7	1.0	6.7	6.5	6.4	6.6	6.4	25.6	27.6	12.7	1.6	76.5	39.1	49.6	50.4
29056 GREELEYVILLE	23.4	23.2	75.7	75.8	0.2	0.2	1.2	1.3	6.8	6.9	7.1	6.3	6.4	22.9	29.1	12.7	1.8	75.3	39.5	46.6	53.4
29058 HEATH SPRINGS	68.3	63.4	30.9	35.5	0.1	0.1	0.5	0.7	5.5	5.7	5.9	6.2	6.1	27.0	28.6	13.1	1.8	79.2	40.4	51.6	48.4
29059 HOLLY HILL	28.1	26.0	69.4	70.7	0.0	0.1	0.7	1.1	6.7	7.1	7.2	7.4	6.1	24.1	28.5	11.5	1.4	75.6	38.1	47.2	52.8
29061 HOPKINS	35.0	30.7	61.2	64.0	0.7	0.9	2.8	4.0	6.4	6.7	7.0	7.5	6.3	26.6	29.9	8.8	0.8	75.3	37.3	48.1	51.9
29063 IRMO	77.5	74.8	19.4	21.0	1.4	2.0	1.4	2.1	8.1	8.1	8.1	7.2	5.1	30.6	26.4	5.7	0.7	70.8	35.2	48.7	51.3
29065 JENKINSVILLE	15.4	14.6	84.0	84.5	0.1	0.1	0.5	0.6	6.4	6.5	6.9	7.5	6.0	24.1	29.8	11.2	1.7	75.8	39.7	47.1	52.9
29067 KERSHAW	73.8	69.5	24.6	28.3	0.2	0.3	1.0	1.5	5.3	5.6	5.8	6.5	7.1	29.2	26.6	12.3	1.6	79.4	38.3	55.1	44.9
29069 LAMAR	50.1	48.1	48.9	50.6	0.1	0.1	0.6	0.7	6.7	6.9	6.9	7.0	5.9	24.7	28.8	11.5	1.6	75.2	38.8	48.3	51.7
29070 LEESVILLE	83.8	82.0	13.9	14.5	0.2	0.3	2.0	3.1	6.6	6.6	6.6	6.5	5.8	26.3	29.5	10.7	1.3	76.2	39.0	50.8	49.2
29072 LEXINGTON	91.3	89.2	5.9	6.4	1.1	1.7	2.0	3.2	7.5	7.6	7.7	6.7	4.6	28.3	27.8	8.7	1.2	72.9	37.5	49.3	50.7
29073 LEXINGTON	90.8	89.0	6.6	7.3	0.6	0.9	1.6	2.5	7.6	7.4	7.3	7.0	5.7	30.3	26.9	7.2	0.6	73.3	35.6	49.2	50.8
29075 LITTLE MOUNTAIN	79.1	76.9	19.6	20.9	0.1	0.2	1.0	1.6	5.4	5.9	6.8	6.5	4.1	24.8	33.0	12.1	1.5	77.8	42.8	49.8	50.2
29078 LUGOFF	80.3	78.3	17.2	18.3	0.5	0.7	1.8	2.7	7.3	7.4	7.5	6.9	5.3	26.7	28.2	9.7	0.9	73.4	37.6	48.5	51.5
29080 LYNCHBURG	20.5	19.4	77.0	76.9	0.0	0.0	2.8	4.2	6.1	6.8	7.1	7.8	6.3	23.0	29.8	11.2	1.9	75.2	38.9	48.4	51.6
29081 EHRHARDT	57.4	55.7	41.4	42.5	0.0	0.0	1.5	2.2	5.2	5.3	6.0	7.1	4.8	24.0	30.8	14.7	2.1	79.2	43.3	47.1	52.9
29082 LODGE	63.8	59.0	27.5	27.0	0.0	0.0	10.7	16.3	4.9	5.1	5.6	6.5	7.2	26.6	29.1	13.1	2.0	81.4	40.4	52.8	47.2
29101 MC BEE	65.0	63.3	32.7	33.4	0.2	0.3	3.7	5.3	6.2	6.1	6.5	7.3	6.0	28.0	29.2	9.7	1.0	76.5	37.5	49.8	50.2
29102 MANNING	46.5	44.9	51.4	52.1	0.3	0.5	2.0	2.9	6.3	6.4	6.6	6.8	5.8	22.7	29.2	14.4	1.7	76.4	41.2	47.9	52.1
29104 MAYESVILLE	19.1	17.8	79.4	80.0	0.3	0.4	1.0	1.4	6.4	7.6	8.6	9.0	6.0	22.8	28.4	9.9	1.5	72.9	36.6	45.2	54.8
29105 MONETTA	64.1	61.7	33.2	34.5	0.1	0.1	3.4	5.1	6.7	6.7	7.1	7.6	5.5	27.6	27.9	9.8	1.1	74.6	37.5	49.8	50.2
29107 NEESES	63.2	60.4	33.4	35.2	0.1	0.2	0.8	1.2	7.2	7.2	7.4	7.0	5.6	25.9	27.1	11.2	1.3	73.8	37.9	49.4	50.6
29108 NEWBERRY	56.6	54.9	39.2	38.9	0.5	0.6	6.9	10.2	7.0	6.7	6.4	7.6	7.4	25.6	25.3	11.3	2.7	76.2	36.4	48.4	51.6
29111 NEW ZION	51.5	47.6	47.5	50.7	0.2	0.3	0.8	1.3	6.1	6.7	6.7	6.1	5.8	24.5	29.3	13.3	1.5	76.8	39.7	50.6	49.4
29112 NORTH	51.8	49.5	46.2	47.9	0.2	0.3	0.4	0.5	6.5	6.8	6.8	6.5	5.4	24.0	30.0	12.2	1.8	75.9	40.3	47.2	52.8
29113 NORWAY	46.9	44.7	49.7	51.2	0.1	0.2	0.6	0.7	7.1	7.2	7.4	6.7	5.2	26.0	26.7	12.4	1.3	74.2	38.3	48.1	51.9
29114 OLANTA	46.3	42.6	52.3	55.3	0.0	0.0	1.7	2.6	6.1	6.1	6.4	7.0	5.7	25.2	29.0	12.6	1.8	77.1	40.4	47.9	52.1
29115 ORANGEBURG	28.6	27.5	69.7	70.3	0.4	0.5	1.0	1.5	6.9	6.6	6.5	7.7	8.8	24.6	24.0	12.3	2.8	75.8	35.5	45.9	54.1
29117 ORANGEBURG	0.9	0.9	96.4	95.7	0.2	0.3	1.6	2.3	1.3	0.9	1.6	37.9	42.5	7.0	5.1	2.9	0.8	94.9	21.0	42.1	57.9
29118 ORANGEBURG	45.2	43.5	52.0	52.8	1.8	2.5	0.8	1.2	6.8	6.8	7.0	7.2	6.2	25.2	27.8	11.5	1.4	74.9	38.3	47.8	52.2
29123 PELION	92.1	90.1	5.2	6.1	0.3	0.4	1.2	1.9	7.7	7.1	6.8	7.7	8.0	27.9	26.2	7.9	0.7	73.7	33.9	49.5	50.5
29125 PINEWOOD	41.5	39.9	57.0	58.0	0.2	0.2	1.1	1.7	6.8	6.7	6.6	7.3	6.4	24.8	27.4	11.9	2.1	75.4	37.7	47.3	52.7
29126 POMARIA	71.9	69.8	26.9	28.7	0.2	0.2	0.8	1.2	6.1	6.4	6.8	5.8	4.4	27.0	30.0	11.8	1.7	77.1	40.6	51.0	49.0
29127 PROSPERITY	74.7	72.7	23.8	25.2	0.4	0.6	1.1	1.6	5.8	6.0	6.2	5.8	4.6	23.5	32.2	14.4	1.5	78.3	43.7	49.2	50.8
29128 REMBERT	23.8	22.5	74.6	75.2	0.3	0.4	1.2	1.7	5.7	6.1	6.2	8.0	8.1	27.3	27.8	9.7	1.1	77.5	36.8	53.8	46.2
29129 RIDGE SPRING	54.5	52.2	42.9	44.1	0.3	0.4	4.4	6.2	6.7	6.7	6.8	7.3	5.3	26.6	27.6	11.6	1.5	75.3	38.2	48.7	51.3
29130 RIDGEWAY	53.5	52.6	44.9	45.0	0.2	0.3	1.1	1.6	5.3	5.6	5.9	5.8	4.6	23.1	32.6	14.7	2.4	79.6	44.7	48.6	51.4
29133 ROWESVILLE	39.2	37.0	60.0	62.0	0.0	0.0	0.9	1.3	7.4	7.5	7.4	6.1	4.7	24.7	29.3	11.2	1.6	73.7	38.7	47.9	52.1
29135 SAINT MATTHEWS	47.3	45.7	51.2	52.2	0.2	0.3	1.6	2.1	6.2	6.5	6.8	6.6	5.1	24.4	30.1	12.5	1.9	76.3	40.9	47.5	52.5
29137 SALLEY	57.9	55.2	40.2	42.2	0.2	0.3	1.0	1.3	7.1	7.1	7.1	6.5	5.3	24.7	28.1	12.4	1.7	74.7	39.2	48.3	51.7
29138 SALUDA	61.4	58.8	33.2	32.8	0.1	0.1	9.7	14.5	6.7	6.8	6.8	7.0	5.8	26.3	25.8	12.4	2.3	75.6	37.8	50.3	49.7
29142 SANTEE	32.7	30.8	65.2	66.4	0.1	0.2	1.5	2.2	6.2	6.7	7.1	6.3	5.2	22.5	27.7	16.1	2.1	76.5	41.6	46.5	53.5
29145 SILVERSTREET	59.6	57.3	39.3	41.0	0.0	0.1	1.6	2.4	6.1	6.4	6.5	6.3	5.6	25.8	30.1	11.7	1.5	77.0	40.2	50.4	49.6
29146 SPRINGFIELD	41.5	39.1	57.0	59.0	0.1	0.1	1.5	2.0	5.9	6.3	6.4	6.7	5.2	24.6	29.8	13.2	2.0	77.2	41.3	48.3	51.7
29148 SUMMERTON	37.6	37.9	60.2	59.0	0.4	0.5	1.7	2.3	5.3	5.6	5.5	5.7	5.1	18.8	30.7	20.8	2.5	80.2	48.1	46.9	53.1
29150 SUMTER	45.9	44.8	51.6	51.5	0.9	1.3	1.5	2.3	7.1	7.1	6.9	7.3	7.2	24.6	25.4	12.2	2.3	74.7	36.6	46.5	53.5
29152 SHAW A F B	65.7	61.1	23.0	23.1	3.3	4.5	5.7	8.7	14.0	10.8	7.0	8.0	22.1	34.0	3.4	0.5	0.2	65.2	22.3	55.3	44.7
29153 SUMTER	45.9	44.0	51.7	52.4	0.4	0.7	1.8	2.8	7.2	7.4	7.5	7.4	6.0	26.9	25.6	10.7	1.3	73.4	36.2	48.9	51.1
29154 SUMTER	66.4	64.1	30.4	31.4	1.1	1.6	1.6	2.4	7.2	7.2	7.2	7.0	6.1	26.8	27.5	9.8	1.2	73.9	36.9	49.2	50.8
29160 SWANSEA	73.8	71.4	24.1	25.7	0.3	0.4	0.9	1.5	7.2	7.1	7.3	7.2	6.1	26.5	27.7	10.0	1.0	74.1	37.0	49.4	50.6
29161 TIMMONSVILLE	49.8	47.7	48.9	50.5	0.2	0.2	1.0	1.4	6.7	7.0	7.1	6.9	5.9	27.7	27.7	9.8	1.3	75.1	37.0	48.6	51.4
29162 TURBEVILLE	67.9	65.0	29.9	31.5	0.2	0.2	2.6	4.1	6.8	7.5	7.8	7.9	5.6	25.3	26.7	11.0	1.5	73.1	37.1	47.3	52.7
29163 VANCE	21.4	20.0	77.6	78.8	0.0	0.0	1.0	1.2	6.1	6.5	7.0	8.1	6.1	22.6	28.9	13.3	1.4	75.9	39.0	47.3	52.7
29164 WAGENER	64.2	60.9	33.6	35.9	0.2	0.2	2.0	3.0	6.3	6.2	6.6	7.2	6.0	26.2	28.5	11.5	1.5	76.5	39.0	49.1	50.9
29166 WARD	66.2	63.3	29.7	30.7	0.1	0.1	5.2	7.5	7.7	7.7	7.6	6.9	6.3	26.4	26.5	9.6	1.3	72.7	35.9	49.3	50.7
29168 WEDGEFIELD	40.4	38.5	57.2	58.2	0.4	0.7	1.0	1.5	8.2	7.3	7.2	7.3	8.6	27.2	26.1	7.5	0.7	73.0	32.4	49.4	50.6
29169 WEST COLUMBIA	78.5	75.9	16.4	17.1	1.9	2.5	3.5	5.0	5.1	4.8	4.7	5.5	9.8	25.6	23.7	15.7	5.0	82.7	40.3	45.8	54.2
29170 WEST COLUMBIA	89.4	87.1	7.4	8.3	1.1	1.8	1.8	2.8	6.9	6.9	6.9	6.5	5.4	28.5	27.4	10.5	1.0	75.4	37.9	48.2	51.8
29172 WEST COLUMBIA	68.5	65.8	28.2	29.6	0.8	1.1	2.3	3.4	6.8	6.6	6.4	7.5	7.0	27.9	28.6	8.6	0.7	75.8	36.2	48.6	51.4
29175 WESTVILLE	79.5	77.0	18.8	20.2	0.2	0.4	1.3	2.0	6.0	6.0	6.2	7.2	6.2	23.0	32.9	11.0	1.6	77.6	41.4	49.5	50.5
29178 WHITMIRE	71.3	69.4	27.4	28.8	0.2	0.3	0.7	1.1	5.8	6.1	6.0	6.3	5.3	23.5	29.3	15.0	2.7	78.1	42.6	48.1	51.9
29180 WINNSBORO	40.7	38.8	57.9	59.3	0.2	0.3	1.2	1.6	7.4	7.5	7.3	7.0	5.8	25.3	27.4	10.8	1.5	73.5	37.2	47.6	52.4
29201 COLUMBIA	57.2	53.7	37.5	39.1	2.7	3.5	2.4	3.6	3.3	2.9	2.9	17.5	23.7	24.3	16.3	7.3	1.6	88.8	24.9	49.2	50.8
29203 COLUMBIA	15.5	14.9	82.3	82.0	0.7	1.0	1.6	2.1	6.9	7.1	7.2	8.8	7.7	25.3	24.7	10.7	1.6	73.9	34.8	46.7	53.3
29204 COLUMBIA	38.3	36.3	59.4	60.6	0.5	0.7	1.6	2.2	5.3	5.4	5.6	9.5	10.9	21.6	25.0	13.1	3.6	80.0	37.6	45.3	54.7
29205 COLUMBIA	72.5	69.0	22.9	24.4	2.2	3.0	2.3	3.6	4.9	4.2	4.1	6.5	14.9	32.0	22.9	8.7	1.7	84.2	32.7	48.9	51.1
SOUTH CAROLINA	67.2	65.9	29.5	29.4	0.9	1.4	2.4	3.6	6.5	6.5	6.5	7.2	6.9	26.6	26.8	11.3	1.6	76.4	37.6	48.9	51.1
UNITED STATES	75.1	72.0	12.3	12.7	3.8	4.6	12.5	15.7	6.8	6.7	6.6	7.1	6.9	27.0	26.0	10.9	1.9	75.7	36.9	49.2	50.8

#	POST OFFICE NAME	2009 Per Capita Income	2009 HH Income Base	2009 Household Income Distribution (%): Less than $25,000	$25,000 to $49,999	$50,000 to $99,999	$100,000 to $149,999	$150,000 or More	Median Household Income: 2009	2014	2009 National Centile	2009 State Centile	2009 Home Value Base	2009 Home Value Distribution (%): Less than $50,000	$50,000 to $89,999	$90,000 to $174,999	$175,000 to $399,999	$400,000 or More	2009 Median Home Value
29001	ALCOLU	17227	974	30.2	30.7	32.4	5.5	1.1	40424	42689	34	44	777	31.7	26.1	35.9	5.9	0.4	82882
29003	BAMBERG	16869	2652	44.8	24.0	24.9	4.3	2.0	30066	31575	8	5	2013	32.6	32.6	27.4	6.7	0.7	71846
29006	BATESBURG	21925	4692	25.9	30.7	34.3	6.6	2.6	44043	46842	46	60	3702	23.1	27.1	35.1	13.5	1.2	89705
29009	BETHUNE	18686	1011	30.7	33.3	30.3	4.9	0.8	39262	42078	31	38	877	29.3	29.5	36.7	4.0	0.5	81484
29010	BISHOPVILLE	17691	5035	39.4	27.9	25.4	5.2	2.0	33884	35147	15	15	3896	31.6	36.0	26.7	5.2	0.4	68093
29014	BLACKSTOCK	19542	662	30.7	31.3	29.8	6.2	2.1	41558	43252	38	50	575	24.9	32.9	34.1	5.7	2.4	80532
29015	BLAIR	14239	581	37.3	28.7	31.3	2.4	0.2	34626	36228	17	18	515	27.2	33.4	32.8	5.2	1.4	76900
29016	BLYTHEWOOD	29822	5044	12.2	22.7	43.4	13.7	8.0	63793	64381	82	93	4369	8.4	14.9	42.4	28.7	5.5	137029
29018	BOWMAN	16959	1583	39.5	28.8	25.5	4.0	2.1	34571	36002	17	18	1255	32.6	28.7	32.7	5.3	0.6	72945
29020	CAMDEN	23186	9508	29.8	26.9	32.5	7.4	3.5	43454	46758	44	58	7252	15.4	25.8	37.2	17.9	3.6	102778
29030	CAMERON	23607	1339	33.8	25.6	28.8	7.8	4.0	40032	42323	33	43	1142	25.5	29.4	29.7	13.9	1.5	83708
29031	CARLISLE	20047	554	34.5	29.4	28.2	5.8	2.2	38762	41333	29	35	475	28.4	38.5	26.9	5.5	0.6	68509
29032	CASSATT	19733	1548	28.0	25.8	39.3	4.8	2.1	46338	49396	52	68	1306	27.3	26.6	38.6	5.7	1.8	86269
29033	CAYCE	23554	5354	25.5	30.7	35.3	6.8	1.7	44308	46621	46	61	3481	10.4	27.4	52.1	10.1	0.0	102747
29036	CHAPIN	38770	6393	10.1	16.5	40.2	19.2	14.0	78180	80231	91	98	5850	4.4	9.8	27.0	42.4	16.3	205137
29037	CHAPPELLS	24590	267	22.5	26.2	39.0	9.4	3.0	50580	50373	63	78	225	19.1	21.3	34.2	19.6	5.8	113068
29038	COPE	19752	1076	30.0	26.9	34.7	5.9	2.6	42994	44765	42	56	906	28.0	35.1	27.4	8.3	1.2	73421
29039	CORDOVA	19430	1502	27.8	29.0	36.0	5.2	1.9	42935	44398	42	56	1170	28.2	37.3	30.1	3.9	0.5	74776
29040	DALZELL	20136	2961	26.3	27.1	39.1	5.7	1.8	46885	48541	54	69	2267	22.4	35.1	36.2	6.2	0.1	84619
29042	DENMARK	14729	2176	48.3	26.6	20.2	3.4	1.5	26262	27599	4	2	1487	36.4	36.0	22.3	5.3	0.0	62043
29044	EASTOVER	18495	2447	31.9	30.3	30.8	4.7	2.3	39424	42891	31	39	2011	25.0	32.2	35.3	7.0	0.5	81399
29045	ELGIN	25990	7223	15.5	21.8	45.4	11.7	5.6	60051	61140	77	90	6238	10.3	18.5	48.0	19.9	3.3	121252
29046	ELLIOTT	12942	36	36.1	30.6	30.6	2.8	0.0	35000	35000	18	20	31	48.4	35.5	16.1	0.0	0.0	51250
29047	ELLOREE	19485	1254	42.4	28.8	20.8	5.4	2.6	30823	33069	9	6	1015	31.3	30.7	28.2	7.9	1.9	72778
29048	EUTAWVILLE	17962	1969	38.8	25.9	29.3	4.2	1.8	35856	38827	20	24	1746	27.7	26.2	33.4	11.4	1.4	84885
29051	GABLE	13897	458	33.6	25.8	36.5	3.7	0.4	42570	45779	41	54	385	31.4	26.8	35.3	5.5	1.0	78478
29052	GADSDEN	18357	803	25.3	26.9	40.1	5.0	2.7	46542	50674	53	69	673	24.7	35.4	34.6	3.7	1.6	78141
29053	GASTON	17980	6145	25.2	35.4	33.6	4.6	1.1	42264	45181	40	52	4920	32.4	31.1	31.4	4.9	0.3	71747
29054	GILBERT	27219	3649	18.4	21.7	42.3	13.0	4.7	60737	64169	78	91	3188	17.4	16.9	36.9	21.9	6.9	120220
29055	GREAT FALLS	18993	1928	36.2	29.8	27.2	4.1	2.7	37644	39726	26	30	1511	39.3	32.4	23.8	3.9	0.7	64279
29056	GREELEYVILLE	17945	987	44.3	26.1	23.1	1.2	5.3	29330	29798	7	4	827	37.5	31.9	26.8	3.3	0.5	63362
29058	HEATH SPRINGS	20654	2116	29.5	30.0	33.4	5.4	1.6	41495	43161	38	49	1816	13.4	31.6	43.2	10.8	1.0	94946
29059	HOLLY HILL	16581	2348	42.6	25.3	25.6	5.0	1.5	31021	34239	10	7	1898	33.4	29.8	29.9	6.2	0.7	67134
29061	HOPKINS	21083	5259	21.6	30.5	38.6	6.6	2.7	47857	50935	56	72	4113	17.1	31.2	39.8	11.2	0.7	91870
29063	IRMO	34901	11684	6.1	14.8	49.2	19.5	10.4	79482	80160	92	98	10528	1.1	5.4	57.0	31.3	5.2	145532
29065	JENKINSVILLE	17937	337	36.5	23.1	34.4	5.6	0.3	39481	42096	31	40	296	25.3	31.1	34.1	7.4	2.0	80500
29067	KERSHAW	19545	3779	29.2	28.6	35.4	5.2	1.6	42866	45089	42	55	3050	21.4	32.6	38.8	6.4	0.8	86013
29069	LAMAR	17239	1903	37.7	29.3	25.6	4.8	2.6	33750	36093	15	14	1563	31.6	28.8	32.6	6.0	1.0	78636
29070	LEESVILLE	24638	5494	18.9	28.3	40.7	8.4	3.8	52736	55651	67	83	4545	19.9	25.8	36.5	14.9	3.0	95255
29072	LEXINGTON	35758	16302	9.8	15.9	38.1	22.2	14.0	82252	85025	93	99	13590	8.2	5.1	34.9	45.3	6.5	179217
29073	LEXINGTON	24977	13788	14.6	28.0	45.3	8.9	3.1	56934	60167	74	88	11517	17.4	17.3	51.8	12.9	0.6	110073
29075	LITTLE MOUNTAIN	27367	1201	16.4	24.9	41.0	12.9	4.7	56555	57174	73	88	1051	12.5	19.4	37.3	26.3	4.6	125450
29078	LUGOFF	23856	5673	18.5	26.7	41.9	9.5	3.4	53689	55485	69	84	4799	16.2	18.9	45.4	18.4	1.1	114840
29080	LYNCHBURG	16883	1362	41.7	26.7	24.7	3.8	3.2	33065	35321	13	11	1078	42.9	28.9	22.4	4.7	0.9	60989
29081	EHRHARDT	19305	555	34.1	34.4	23.2	5.6	2.7	35155	36179	18	20	453	26.3	33.6	32.5	7.7	0.0	77976
29082	LODGE	18173	238	36.1	30.7	25.2	7.6	0.4	35452	37986	19	22	190	43.7	22.6	24.7	8.9	0.0	59231
29101	MC BEE	18889	1202	34.7	27.0	28.7	6.5	3.2	39463	41467	31	40	1047	33.9	35.1	21.9	8.9	0.2	69293
29102	MANNING	19080	6623	39.7	24.2	28.0	5.5	2.5	34505	35323	17	17	5106	24.3	26.9	34.6	12.7	1.6	88471
29104	MAYESVILLE	16720	793	43.4	27.4	21.8	4.3	3.2	31558	32963	11	7	656	34.8	36.1	20.7	6.7	1.7	63333
29105	MONETTA	17922	535	28.0	32.0	34.0	4.9	1.1	41969	45153	39	51	441	41.7	27.4	24.3	4.5	2.0	58295
29107	NEESES	20930	1270	33.0	28.7	29.9	5.0	3.4	38340	40479	28	32	1058	32.2	33.9	28.2	5.5	0.2	71525
29108	NEWBERRY	18866	7782	33.8	28.2	29.5	5.9	2.5	38801	42060	29	35	5389	20.7	32.8	36.5	9.4	0.6	86044
29111	NEW ZION	17754	418	32.1	27.0	34.7	5.0	1.2	45411	46674	49	65	356	27.8	32.0	32.3	7.9	0.0	79630
29112	NORTH	17486	1868	38.5	29.1	27.0	3.7	1.6	34353	36763	16	17	1534	33.6	29.7	31.4	4.8	0.6	72422
29113	NORWAY	17902	622	35.5	30.4	26.4	5.9	1.8	35270	37868	19	21	516	34.7	27.9	30.6	6.8	0.0	71333
29114	OLANTA	16542	775	38.5	29.5	26.8	3.1	2.1	34822	38042	17	19	633	36.3	36.5	19.9	5.1	2.2	64643
29115	ORANGEBURG	18520	11645	39.2	26.6	27.9	4.5	1.9	34913	36932	17	19	7468	24.2	33.6	34.2	7.2	0.7	81422
29117	ORANGEBURG	9191	35	37.1	25.7	22.9	14.3	0.0	29391	30000	7	4	9	11.1	44.4	44.4	0.0	0.0	85000
29118	ORANGEBURG	25379	5435	24.7	23.8	35.8	10.1	5.5	51489	49716	65	81	4245	12.5	20.8	48.2	16.3	2.1	111261
29123	PELION	19521	2484	23.9	32.8	36.0	4.5	2.7	43764	46223	45	59	2165	33.3	26.6	34.6	4.8	0.6	74152
29125	PINEWOOD	15854	1542	40.8	29.2	24.1	4.4	1.4	32992	35055	13	10	1234	34.7	31.9	30.4	2.6	0.4	68387
29126	POMARIA	21128	1030	28.3	24.7	39.8	5.1	2.1	47361	46846	55	71	911	16.4	25.9	38.3	18.2	1.2	102016
29127	PROSPERITY	24473	3307	21.1	28.7	36.9	10.8	2.5	50129	49273	61	78	2880	16.6	21.7	33.9	24.1	3.9	116167
29128	REMBERT	16325	2062	38.2	27.6	27.6	4.3	2.3	35125	38887	18	20	1784	34.5	34.2	23.3	6.1	1.8	67606
29129	RIDGE SPRING	18230	1446	31.5	28.1	33.4	5.1	1.9	39559	44276	31	40	1161	27.4	26.6	30.1	11.9	4.0	83451
29130	RIDGEWAY	22433	2667	29.4	22.5	36.5	8.1	3.5	46846	47231	54	69	2286	17.5	25.4	35.5	19.6	2.0	98907
29133	ROWESVILLE	16524	419	40.3	28.6	27.0	2.1	1.9	33626	36631	15	13	341	32.8	32.6	29.3	5.0	0.3	73382
29135	SAINT MATTHEWS	20915	4577	32.5	26.3	31.9	6.1	3.1	40768	43238	35	45	3789	23.6	34.7	30.5	10.0	1.2	81091
29137	SALLEY	17741	1138	32.2	32.0	30.3	4.2	1.2	36437	38627	22	27	945	39.5	26.7	30.5	2.5	0.8	65508
29138	SALUDA	19513	4116	28.9	28.2	34.0	6.7	2.2	43192	46161	43	57	3179	20.0	31.9	35.6	11.0	1.5	87877
29142	SANTEE	18977	1937	39.5	26.0	26.6	4.3	3.6	33359	36063	14	12	1583	27.9	24.3	27.2	17.8	2.8	86034
29145	SILVERSTREET	19514	377	28.1	29.7	32.9	7.4	1.9	42145	44536	40	52	311	22.2	25.1	36.0	14.5	2.3	96071
29146	SPRINGFIELD	18829	684	38.0	28.1	26.0	5.0	2.9	33022	34761	13	11	574	41.5	29.1	26.3	2.4	0.7	62927
29148	SUMMERTON	19209	2884	41.5	28.9	21.8	4.4	3.5	30289	31882	9	5	2367	28.0	21.5	33.7	15.0	1.8	91157
29150	SUMTER	20840	14953	32.8	27.9	29.6	6.0	3.8	38488	42549	28	33	9269	20.3	33.1	34.9	10.8	0.9	85981
29152	SHAW A F B	14043	1227	20.5	50.7	24.1	2.8	2.0	37541	39770	25	30	89	52.8	23.6	23.6	0.0	0.0	39107
29153	SUMTER	16883	5623	32.5	31.5	31.8	3.0	1.2	36853	39461	23	28	4493	25.6	35.7	31.6	6.5	0.6	77910
29154	SUMTER	24547	9706	18.8	25.9	42.2	8.4	4.7	53604	53603	69	84	7427	14.5	23.7	48.7	12.2	1.0	104637
29160	SWANSEA	20365	2856	30.0	26.2	35.7	6.3	1.8	43685	46721	44	59	2432	25.9	33.2	32.4	7.7	0.8	77396
29161	TIMMONSVILLE	17892	4361	33.1	26.3	33.2	5.4	1.9	39437	44017	31	39	3511	29.1	32.6	30.6	7.4	0.3	75549
29162	TURBEVILLE	17702	975	33.9	29.8	29.6	5.4	1.1	36646	37302	22	28	714	35.2	26.8	31.2	5.5	1.4	79016
29163	VANCE	15083	797	43.2	27.5	24.3	3.0	2.0	29072	31136	7	4	677	40.0	32.8	20.7	5.8	0.7	58333
29164	WAGENER	18221	1868	33.7	29.4	30.5	5.4	1.0	37007	39681	24	29	1541	29.9	29.0	36.5	4.2	0.4	78564
29166	WARD	21245	443	30.5	24.8	35.7	6.1	2.9	41312	45966	37	49	359	31.5	33.7	30.4	1.9	2.5	69324
29168	WEDGEFIELD	16757	1390	32.3	33.1	29.7	2.9	2.0	35665	37090	20	23	1064	31.6	41.2	22.4	4.5	0.4	67714
29169	WEST COLUMBIA	24693	10469	29.5	29.3	31.3	6.6	3.3	41492	44750	38	49	5598	11.9	18.0	52.1	16.3	1.7	115132
29170	WEST COLUMBIA	26515	8078	14.1	26.7	45.7	9.7	3.8	58378	61186	76	89	6375	13.4	12.2	58.9	14.9	0.4	119255
29172	WEST COLUMBIA	20782	3597	26.3	27.8	38.0	6.3	1.6	46198	48407	52	67	2766	24.5	23.0	45.3	7.1	0.1	92438
29175	WESTVILLE	21405	202	29.7	21.8	44.1	3.0	1.5	48392	50904	58	75	183	29.0	40.4	26.8	3.8	0.0	66481
29178	WHITMIRE	18049	1525	40.2	26.8	27.9	4.2	0.9	32447	34764	12	8	1196	43.6	30.7	21.2	4.3	0.2	56160
29180	WINNSBORO	19237	5646	37.0	26.9	27.6	5.5	2.9	35907	38499	20	25	4031	24.2	31.0	33.1	9.7	2.0	82869
29201	COLUMBIA	18539	7276	47.2	27.2	20.1	3.6	2.0	27186	28847	5	2	2334	6.6	35.7	40.6	13.1	4.1	97298
29203	COLUMBIA	16320	15722	38.8	29.8	25.9	3.7	1.7	33521	35547	14	13	8437	14.7	39.8	40.8	4.0	0.7	86057
29204	COLUMBIA	24605	8567	35.1	25.3	28.7	5.0	5.9	39212	42231	30	37	4571	5.5	19.9	54.7	16.0	3.9	117639
29205	COLUMBIA	30814	12069	29.7	28.6	29.1	6.0	6.7	41114	44259	36	47	5523	2.7	13.8	40.0	34.9	8.7	153949
	SOUTH CAROLINA	24352		25.1	26.4	35.2	8.4	4.8	48210	50493				16.4	20.9	37.4	20.6	4.8	112284
	UNITED STATES	27277		20.9	24.4	35.3	11.7	7.6	54719	56938				9.3	13.1	31.6	32.6	13.5	162279

ZIP CODE #	POST OFFICE NAME	FINANCIAL SERVICES: Auto Loan	Home Loan	Investments	Retirement Plans	THE HOME: Home Improvements: Home Repair	Lawn & Garden	Furnishings: Computers & Hardware-Personal	Major Appliances	TV, Radio, Sound Equipment	Furniture	ENTERTAINMENT: Dine out/Carry out	Sports Equipment	Fees & Tickets	Toys & Games	Travel	Cable TV	PERSONAL: Apparel & Services	Auto Repairs	Health Insurance	Pets & Supplies
29001	ALCOLU	87	59	79	56	58	84	62	76	71	60	69	59	48	72	57	78	46	72	80	93
29003	BAMBERG	69	51	64	50	51	69	55	63	62	53	61	47	47	62	52	68	41	62	71	77
29006	BATESBURG	93	69	88	67	70	93	72	86	79	68	78	65	59	80	69	86	52	81	91	103
29009	BETHUNE	80	57	75	56	58	79	59	73	66	56	65	55	47	67	57	72	43	68	76	87
29010	BISHOPVILLE	81	57	74	55	56	79	61	72	69	59	68	55	49	70	57	76	45	69	78	88
29014	BLACKSTOCK	89	63	79	60	63	86	65	79	73	63	72	60	52	75	61	80	48	74	83	96
29015	BLAIR	75	49	72	46	49	73	52	66	60	49	59	51	39	61	49	67	39	62	69	81
29016	BLYTHEWOOD	125	124	107	121	119	117	114	118	113	120	114	89	112	119	111	113	79	113	112	138
29018	BOWMAN	82	54	77	51	54	80	58	72	66	55	64	56	44	67	53	73	43	67	76	88
29020	CAMDEN	88	74	83	73	74	91	75	84	81	72	79	63	68	81	73	86	54	81	90	100
29030	CAMERON	94	69	93	68	71	96	71	88	79	66	77	67	58	79	70	86	51	81	92	105
29031	CARLISLE	89	59	83	56	59	86	63	78	72	60	70	60	47	73	58	80	46	73	82	95
29032	CASSATT	92	70	76	68	69	87	72	81	78	71	77	62	61	81	67	84	52	78	85	98
29033	CAYCE	72	73	65	74	71	75	74	72	75	72	75	55	75	76	73	77	52	74	78	86
29036	CHAPIN	130	156	151	159	156	151	135	142	132	141	133	107	150	133	148	131	94	136	139	164
29037	CHAPPELLS	103	75	87	73	75	99	78	90	86	76	84	69	63	89	71	93	56	86	96	109
29038	COPE	93	67	78	65	67	89	70	81	77	68	76	62	56	80	64	84	51	77	86	99
29039	CORDOVA	80	74	64	70	70	73	72	73	73	75	73	55	68	77	68	74	50	73	72	87
29040	DALZELL	87	74	75	71	72	82	73	79	76	74	76	60	65	79	69	79	51	77	80	95
29042	DENMARK	64	45	58	43	44	63	48	57	56	47	54	43	39	55	45	61	36	56	63	70
29044	EASTOVER	83	63	75	61	62	80	64	74	70	63	69	56	54	72	60	75	46	71	77	90
29045	ELGIN	109	107	92	103	102	102	99	102	99	104	100	78	96	104	96	99	69	99	99	120
29046	ELLIOTT	74	48	71	45	48	72	51	65	59	49	58	50	38	60	48	66	38	61	68	80
29047	ELLOREE	81	56	82	54	57	82	59	74	66	55	65	57	46	66	57	73	43	69	78	90
29048	EUTAWVILLE	80	57	82	54	59	81	59	74	67	58	65	55	48	66	58	74	43	70	79	89
29051	GABLE	83	55	77	52	55	81	59	73	67	56	66	56	45	69	54	74	44	68	77	89
29052	GADSDEN	78	72	75	71	70	84	69	75	75	70	75	54	68	74	69	81	51	75	84	92
29053	GASTON	76	71	61	68	68	68	70	70	70	73	71	53	66	73	66	70	49	70	68	83
29054	GILBERT	107	105	97	104	104	106	97	103	99	101	99	76	96	102	97	101	68	99	102	122
29055	GREAT FALLS	83	60	69	58	59	79	65	73	71	62	70	56	52	73	58	77	47	71	78	89
29056	GREELEYVILLE	82	53	79	50	53	80	57	72	66	54	64	56	43	67	53	74	43	68	76	89
29058	HEATH SPRINGS	86	62	77	61	63	84	65	77	72	62	70	59	52	74	61	78	47	72	81	93
29059	HOLLY HILL	74	51	69	49	51	73	55	66	63	53	62	50	44	63	52	70	41	64	72	81
29061	HOPKINS	84	84	74	82	80	84	78	81	80	81	81	60	78	82	77	82	55	80	83	96
29063	IRMO	140	154	129	150	146	131	137	137	130	146	132	107	141	138	137	124	93	131	123	157
29065	JENKINSVILLE	79	52	77	49	52	78	55	70	64	53	62	54	41	65	52	71	41	66	74	86
29067	KERSHAW	88	66	77	65	66	87	68	80	75	65	73	61	56	77	64	81	49	75	84	96
29069	LAMAR	84	57	79	53	56	81	60	74	68	58	67	57	46	70	56	75	44	70	77	90
29070	LEESVILLE	100	85	94	84	86	98	85	95	89	83	88	71	77	90	83	92	60	91	96	112
29072	LEXINGTON	139	152	136	151	148	138	135	139	131	144	132	109	142	137	138	127	93	132	128	160
29073	LEXINGTON	100	99	84	95	94	92	92	94	92	97	92	71	89	96	88	91	63	91	90	110
29075	LITTLE MOUNTAIN	104	99	93	101	99	109	95	104	97	91	96	78	91	99	95	101	66	98	105	121
29078	LUGOFF	95	92	83	90	89	95	86	91	88	88	88	68	84	92	85	91	61	88	92	108
29080	LYNCHBURG	85	56	82	52	55	84	59	75	69	57	67	58	45	70	55	77	44	71	79	92
29081	EHRHARDT	81	58	83	56	60	82	59	75	66	55	65	57	47	65	59	72	43	69	79	90
29082	LODGE	84	55	81	51	54	82	58	74	67	55	66	57	44	68	54	75	44	69	78	90
29101	MC BEE	89	66	77	63	65	85	67	78	74	66	73	60	55	77	62	81	49	74	82	95
29102	MANNING	81	59	79	57	61	82	62	74	70	61	68	56	52	69	60	76	46	71	80	90
29104	MAYESVILLE	86	56	82	53	56	84	60	75	69	57	68	59	45	70	56	77	45	71	80	93
29105	MONETTA	87	62	73	61	62	83	65	76	72	63	70	58	52	75	59	78	47	72	80	92
29107	NEESES	91	66	82	63	65	87	68	80	75	66	74	62	55	77	64	82	50	76	84	98
29108	NEWBERRY	78	61	69	60	60	76	66	72	71	62	69	55	56	71	61	75	47	70	76	86
29111	NEW ZION	90	59	87	55	59	88	63	79	72	60	71	62	47	74	59	81	47	74	84	97
29112	NORTH	80	53	77	50	53	78	57	70	65	54	63	55	43	66	53	72	42	66	74	87
29113	NORWAY	87	59	86	56	59	86	62	78	70	58	69	60	47	71	59	78	45	73	82	95
29114	OLANTA	84	55	81	51	54	82	58	74	67	55	66	57	44	68	54	75	44	69	78	90
29115	ORANGEBURG	70	58	59	57	57	67	61	64	67	61	66	48	56	67	58	71	45	65	70	78
29117	ORANGEBURG	70	50	48	53	48	58	73	60	74	65	72	48	59	72	57	76	50	68	68	75
29118	ORANGEBURG	95	91	94	91	91	98	90	94	93	90	92	71	88	93	90	96	64	93	97	111
29123	PELION	82	77	65	73	73	73	76	75	76	79	76	57	71	79	71	76	52	75	73	89
29125	PINEWOOD	74	54	66	52	53	70	56	65	62	55	61	50	46	64	52	67	41	63	68	80
29126	POMARIA	89	69	75	68	69	88	70	81	76	67	75	62	59	79	66	82	50	76	85	97
29127	PROSPERITY	99	76	104	75	79	100	77	94	83	73	82	71	65	83	78	90	55	88	96	112
29128	REMBERT	82	55	78	53	55	81	58	73	66	55	65	56	45	68	55	74	43	68	77	89
29129	RIDGE SPRING	88	62	77	60	62	85	65	77	72	62	71	60	52	75	60	79	47	73	82	94
29130	RIDGEWAY	99	71	100	68	73	99	73	91	81	69	80	69	59	81	71	89	53	85	94	109
29133	ROWESVILLE	78	51	74	48	51	76	55	68	63	52	61	53	41	64	51	70	41	64	72	84
29135	SAINT MATTHEWS	92	66	86	64	66	91	69	83	77	66	75	64	55	78	65	84	50	78	87	101
29137	SALLEY	84	55	79	52	55	82	59	73	68	56	66	57	44	69	55	75	44	69	78	90
29138	SALUDA	92	67	83	65	67	91	70	83	78	66	76	64	57	79	66	85	51	79	88	101
29142	SANTEE	87	60	87	58	62	87	63	79	70	59	69	60	49	70	61	78	46	73	83	95
29145	SILVERSTREET	93	67	82	65	67	90	69	83	77	66	75	63	55	79	64	84	50	77	87	100
29146	SPRINGFIELD	86	56	83	53	56	84	60	75	69	57	67	59	45	70	56	77	45	71	80	93
29148	SUMMERTON	72	57	75	54	60	75	59	69	65	59	63	49	52	63	59	71	42	67	77	83
29150	SUMTER	76	68	66	69	67	76	71	72	76	71	75	54	68	75	68	79	52	74	79	87
29152	SHAW A F B	83	43	32	50	39	37	78	54	73	73	77	54	59	88	56	67	54	69	49	66
29153	SUMTER	77	58	68	57	57	74	60	69	66	59	65	53	51	68	56	71	44	66	72	84
29154	SUMTER	100	96	87	93	92	97	90	94	92	93	92	72	88	96	88	94	64	92	94	112
29160	SWANSEA	87	71	73	68	69	81	71	78	75	72	75	59	62	78	66	79	51	75	79	93
29161	TIMMONSVILLE	83	62	71	60	61	79	64	73	71	64	70	56	54	73	59	76	47	71	77	89
29162	TURBEVILLE	83	57	82	55	58	83	60	75	67	56	66	57	46	68	57	74	44	70	79	91
29163	VANCE	75	49	73	46	49	74	53	66	61	50	59	52	39	62	49	68	39	62	70	81
29164	WAGENER	83	57	75	55	57	81	60	73	68	58	67	56	47	70	55	75	44	69	77	89
29166	WARD	98	70	81	68	70	93	73	85	81	71	79	65	58	84	66	88	53	80	90	103
29168	WEDGEFIELD	76	60	67	56	58	71	61	68	65	61	65	52	52	67	57	69	44	66	69	82
29169	WEST COLUMBIA	77	67	70	68	67	74	77	74	78	72	78	57	70	77	71	80	54	77	80	88
29170	WEST COLUMBIA	99	100	87	97	96	95	93	95	93	97	94	72	92	97	91	93	65	93	93	111
29172	WEST COLUMBIA	85	79	71	75	75	78	76	78	77	79	77	59	72	80	72	78	53	77	77	93
29175	WESTVILLE	96	69	79	67	68	91	72	83	79	70	78	64	57	83	65	87	52	79	88	101
29178	WHITMIRE	71	51	63	50	51	70	56	65	62	52	60	50	45	63	52	67	40	62	70	78
29180	WINNSBORO	80	58	70	58	58	76	64	71	72	62	70	54	54	72	59	78	48	71	78	87
29201	COLUMBIA	57	43	40	46	41	45	65	49	61	56	61	42	53	61	51	60	43	57	53	62
29203	COLUMBIA	62	56	49	57	53	59	59	57	63	60	63	43	58	63	56	66	43	60	64	70
29204	COLUMBIA	77	72	71	74	72	79	77	76	82	76	81	56	76	79	75	85	56	79	86	91
29205	COLUMBIA	88	76	75	80	75	77	95	81	91	88	92	66	86	91	84	90	64	88	84	99
	SOUTH CAROLINA	95	83	86	82	82	92	85	89	88	84	88	68	79	90	81	91	60	88	92	106
	UNITED STATES	100	100	100	100	100	100	100	100	100	100	100	100	100	100	100	100	100	100	100	100

29206-29511

ZIP CODE			POPULATION			2000-2009 ANNUAL RATE		HOUSEHOLDS					FAMILIES		
#	POST OFFICE NAME	COUNTY FIPS CODE	2000	2009	2014	% Rate	State Centile	2000	2009	2014	% Annual Rate 2000-2009	2009 Average HH Size	2000	2009	% Annual Rate 2000-2009
29206	COLUMBIA	079	21608	21356	21507	-0.1	21	8557	8590	8767	0.0	2.06	5701	5223	-0.9
29207	COLUMBIA	079	6345	6450	6350	0.2	34	42	43	44	0.3	2.56	29	27	-0.8
29208	COLUMBIA	079	747	839	839	1.3	76	2	2	2	0.0	1.00	1	0	-100.0
29209	COLUMBIA	079	27935	31600	33968	1.3	76	10937	13058	14275	1.9	2.34	7415	8113	1.0
29210	COLUMBIA	079	34920	34845	35453	0.0	25	16631	17187	17721	0.4	1.98	8167	7607	-0.8
29212	COLUMBIA	063	32213	34702	36217	0.8	61	10606	11828	12592	1.2	2.52	7831	8295	0.6
29223	COLUMBIA	079	43839	47851	51014	1.0	69	16705	19365	20980	1.6	2.41	11826	12856	0.9
29229	COLUMBIA	079	18053	38345	46419	8.5	98	6149	13787	16923	9.1	2.78	5159	11138	8.7
29301	SPARTANBURG	083	28838	31071	32604	0.8	61	11170	12240	12911	1.0	2.49	7590	7886	0.4
29302	SPARTANBURG	083	16991	16920	17120	0.0	25	6888	6996	7127	0.2	2.31	4561	4397	-0.4
29303	SPARTANBURG	083	25046	25039	25292	0.0	25	9225	9319	9478	0.1	2.35	5634	5319	-0.6
29306	SPARTANBURG	083	16160	15828	15915	-0.2	18	6500	6515	6590	0.0	2.40	4141	3940	-0.5
29307	SPARTANBURG	083	20008	20646	21208	0.3	38	8295	8791	9117	0.6	2.27	5460	5467	0.0
29316	BOILING SPRINGS	083	14548	19640	22033	3.3	94	5433	7590	8605	3.7	2.57	4269	5714	3.2
29321	BUFFALO	087	2533	2602	2578	0.3	38	1023	1093	1099	0.7	2.38	738	758	0.3
29322	CAMPOBELLO	083	7860	8878	9462	1.3	76	3007	3495	3758	1.6	2.53	2305	2570	1.2
29323	CHESNEE	083	13648	14967	15734	1.0	69	5201	5865	6222	1.3	2.54	3914	4238	0.9
29325	CLINTON	059	15981	15480	15191	-0.3	15	5693	5596	5527	-0.2	2.41	3883	3642	-0.7
29330	COWPENS	021	8337	9250	9714	1.1	70	3237	3688	3914	1.4	2.50	2381	2594	0.9
29332	CROSS HILL	059	2250	2331	2344	0.4	43	920	991	1010	0.8	2.35	678	702	0.4
29334	DUNCAN	083	8220	10801	11810	3.0	93	3109	4164	4586	3.2	2.59	2369	3064	2.8
29335	ENOREE	083	5820	6221	6451	0.7	56	1752	1921	2015	1.0	2.87	1325	1393	0.5
29340	GAFFNEY	021	21286	20599	20382	-0.4	12	8290	8328	8328	0.0	2.40	5805	5585	-0.4
29341	GAFFNEY	021	16889	18501	19117	1.0	69	6570	7435	7762	1.3	2.46	4713	5138	0.9
29349	INMAN	083	23596	28280	30511	2.0	86	8985	11059	12034	2.3	2.52	6827	8083	1.8
29351	JOANNA	059	2307	2256	2224	-0.2	18	949	952	948	0.0	2.36	674	648	-0.4
29353	JONESVILLE	087	4494	4362	4260	-0.3	15	1784	1812	1794	0.2	2.39	1282	1249	-0.3
29355	KINARDS	071	411	421	429	0.3	38	168	180	185	0.7	2.34	125	129	0.3
29356	LANDRUM	045	7987	8703	9174	0.9	64	3281	3670	3899	1.2	2.37	2372	2529	0.7
29360	LAURENS	059	22012	21498	21139	-0.3	15	8513	8468	8383	-0.1	2.45	5963	5683	-0.5
29365	LYMAN	083	7287	9182	10000	2.5	90	2933	3753	4113	2.7	2.44	2185	2701	2.3
29369	MOORE	083	10657	13717	15093	2.8	92	3837	5095	5668	3.1	2.67	3142	4035	2.7
29370	MOUNTVILLE	059	1358	1412	1426	0.4	43	492	527	536	0.7	2.65	370	381	0.3
29372	PACOLET	021	5185	5564	5819	0.8	61	2057	2283	2416	1.1	2.38	1438	1514	0.6
29374	PAULINE	083	3344	3620	3769	0.9	64	1284	1426	1505	1.1	2.08	995	1063	0.7
29376	ROEBUCK	083	5661	6624	7164	1.7	83	2242	2717	2965	2.1	2.44	1690	1953	1.6
29379	UNION	087	20644	19039	18287	-0.9	3	8425	8127	7905	-0.4	2.29	5867	5430	-0.8
29384	WATERLOO	059	4163	4171	4141	0.0	25	1750	1803	1806	0.3	2.31	1246	1230	-0.1
29385	WELLFORD	083	6751	7283	7656	0.8	61	2576	2846	3014	1.1	2.55	1876	1983	0.6
29388	WOODRUFF	083	13222	14094	14751	0.7	56	5055	5509	5808	0.9	2.53	3759	3929	0.5
29401	CHARLESTON	019	10115	9924	9825	-0.2	18	4690	4711	4737	0.0	1.82	1786	1591	-1.2
29403	CHARLESTON	019	23635	23711	23872	0.0	25	8984	9393	9619	0.5	2.16	4351	4125	-0.6
29404	CHARLESTON AFB	019	4380	3591	3407	-2.1	1	1207	1000	955	-2.0	3.07	1139	929	-2.2
29405	NORTH CHARLESTON	019	31228	30011	29604	-0.4	12	11187	11039	11035	-0.1	2.41	7111	6536	-0.9
29406	CHARLESTON	019	24278	26178	27013	0.8	61	9624	10793	11343	1.2	2.30	5495	5634	0.3
29407	CHARLESTON	019	36510	36795	37164	0.1	29	16103	17045	17486	0.6	2.11	9114	8821	-0.4
29410	NORTH CHARLESTON	015	12983	12647	12755	-0.3	15	5266	5326	5446	0.1	2.24	3356	3203	-0.5
29412	CHARLESTON	019	33871	39027	41617	1.5	78	14299	17390	18839	2.1	2.23	9073	10298	1.4
29414	CHARLESTON	019	23761	30567	33394	2.8	92	9697	12817	14140	3.1	2.38	6351	8154	2.7
29418	NORTH CHARLESTON	019	21007	22410	23685	0.7	56	8571	9508	10152	1.1	2.35	5492	5678	0.4
29420	NORTH CHARLESTON	035	15414	20910	24088	3.4	94	5179	7134	8253	3.5	2.93	4087	5437	3.1
29426	ADAMS RUN	019	1812	2038	2168	1.3	76	658	780	842	1.9	2.61	495	558	1.3
29429	AWENDAW	019	2640	2855	3096	0.9	64	913	1025	1126	1.3	2.78	727	784	0.8
29431	BONNEAU	015	5487	6111	6562	1.2	73	2089	2429	2646	1.6	2.51	1556	1736	1.2
29432	BRANCHVILLE	075	2534	2569	2566	0.1	29	1020	1078	1089	0.6	2.37	710	715	0.1
29434	CORDESVILLE	015	691	705	735	0.2	34	243	259	274	0.7	2.69	180	184	0.2
29435	COTTAGEVILLE	029	3778	4081	4194	0.8	61	1413	1604	1671	1.4	2.54	1046	1145	1.0
29436	CROSS	015	4485	4694	4948	0.5	47	1649	1803	1925	1.0	2.60	1229	1288	0.5
29437	DORCHESTER	035	1955	2295	2560	1.7	83	726	873	981	2.0	2.63	544	629	1.6
29438	EDISTO ISLAND	019	2301	2689	2880	1.7	83	989	1223	1326	2.3	2.20	687	804	1.7
29440	GEORGETOWN	043	29520	31862	32457	0.8	61	10704	12110	12460	1.3	2.59	8001	8779	1.0
29445	GOOSE CREEK	015	48672	53565	56990	1.0	69	15999	18352	19842	1.5	2.76	12447	13763	1.1
29446	GREEN POND	029	1911	1965	1988	0.3	38	691	753	772	0.9	2.61	499	523	0.5
29448	HARLEYVILLE	035	2508	2833	3122	1.3	76	968	1119	1244	1.6	2.53	714	793	1.1
29449	HOLLYWOOD	019	7344	8295	8829	1.3	76	2630	3145	3397	2.0	2.63	1970	2234	1.4
29450	HUGER	015	2870	3105	3330	0.9	64	982	1110	1206	1.3	2.80	743	782	0.6
29451	ISLE OF PALMS	019	4569	4125	3980	-1.1	2	1939	1827	1791	-0.6	2.26	1382	1228	-1.3
29453	JAMESTOWN	015	1435	1545	1644	0.8	61	528	594	642	1.3	2.60	381	410	0.8
29455	JOHNS ISLAND	019	13680	16986	18791	2.4	89	5349	6943	7775	2.9	2.44	3951	4836	2.2
29456	LADSON	019	16333	22780	26566	3.7	96	5686	8238	9742	4.1	2.75	4396	6145	3.7
29458	MC CLELLANVILLE	019	3021	3342	3540	1.1	70	1075	1258	1356	1.7	2.65	778	861	1.1
29461	MONCKS CORNER	015	23408	26245	28502	1.2	73	8561	9913	10918	1.6	2.60	6443	7166	1.2
29464	MOUNT PLEASANT	019	39506	44988	47592	1.4	76	16098	19136	20535	1.9	2.31	10398	11596	1.2
29466	MOUNT PLEASANT	019	12912	26084	31134	7.9	98	4672	9962	12069	8.5	2.62	3677	7718	8.3
29468	PINEVILLE	015	2226	2210	2283	-0.1	21	839	870	912	0.4	2.54	595	588	-0.1
29469	PINOPOLIS	015	1336	1490	1609	1.2	73	506	590	647	1.7	2.42	382	428	1.2
29470	RAVENEL	019	4038	4444	4678	1.0	69	1469	1693	1809	1.5	2.62	1127	1239	1.0
29471	REEVESVILLE	035	1406	1626	1801	1.6	80	550	648	724	1.8	2.50	398	449	1.3
29472	RIDGEVILLE	035	9230	10662	11564	1.6	80	2534	3053	3410	2.0	2.72	1924	2235	1.6
29474	ROUND O	029	1966	2080	2113	0.6	50	755	835	860	1.1	2.49	565	604	0.7
29475	RUFFIN	029	2306	2366	2366	0.3	38	900	968	981	0.8	2.44	659	683	0.4
29477	SAINT GEORGE	035	6911	7526	8144	0.9	64	2682	2987	3264	1.2	2.44	1871	1990	0.7
29479	SAINT STEPHEN	015	7174	7551	7978	0.6	50	2547	2791	2992	1.0	2.67	1876	1969	0.5
29481	SMOAKS	029	2112	2119	2090	0.0	25	762	803	802	0.6	2.64	566	577	0.2
29482	SULLIVANS ISLAND	019	1911	2073	2149	0.9	64	797	903	951	1.4	2.30	484	506	0.5
29483	SUMMERVILLE	015	48218	61903	70129	2.7	91	17438	23061	26394	3.1	2.67	13391	17133	2.7
29485	SUMMERVILLE	035	29949	44092	51949	4.3	97	10809	16362	19470	4.6	2.67	8303	12067	4.1
29487	WADMALAW ISLAND	019	2611	2890	3049	1.1	70	960	1126	1209	1.7	2.50	718	799	1.2
29488	WALTERBORO	029	21948	22168	21885	0.1	29	8267	8699	8698	0.6	2.52	5970	6047	0.1
29492	CHARLESTON	015	2103	9199	11666	17.3	100	727	3314	4257	17.8	2.78	601	2592	17.1
29501	FLORENCE	041	38623	41456	42902	0.8	61	15575	17096	17834	1.0	2.36	10301	10833	0.5
29505	FLORENCE	041	18828	21950	23356	1.7	83	7142	8547	9183	2.0	2.52	5417	6238	1.5
29506	FLORENCE	041	21324	21101	21210	-0.1	21	7420	7535	7638	0.2	2.60	5244	5112	-0.3
29510	ANDREWS	089	10686	10715	10553	0.0	25	3913	4157	4142	0.7	2.57	2939	3021	0.3
29511	AYNOR	051	4320	5043	5644	1.7	83	1649	2028	2300	2.3	2.47	1217	1429	1.8
	SOUTH CAROLINA					1.3					1.7	2.45			1.2
	UNITED STATES					1.0					1.1	2.59			0.9

ZIP CODE #	POST OFFICE NAME	RACE (%) White 2000	White 2009	Black 2000	Black 2009	Asian/Pacific 2000	Asian/Pacific 2009	% Hispanic Origin 2000	% Hispanic Origin 2009	2009 AGE DISTRIBUTION (%) 0-4	5-9	10-14	15-19	20-24	25-44	45-64	65-84	85+	18+	MEDIAN AGE 2009	% 2009 Males	% 2009 Females
29206	COLUMBIA	74.0	70.7	19.9	20.5	1.8	2.4	4.9	7.2	5.2	5.3	5.4	11.4	11.6	22.5	23.3	12.4	2.8	80.4	34.2	49.3	50.7
29207	COLUMBIA	48.8	42.1	35.7	36.3	3.3	4.2	13.1	18.7	4.9	4.9	3.4	28.0	31.7	25.2	1.7	0.3	0.0	83.4	21.4	58.4	41.6
29208	COLUMBIA	73.2	68.1	22.1	25.3	2.5	3.7	1.9	2.7	0.0	0.0	0.0	61.3	38.0	0.6	0.0	0.1	0.0	99.8	19.1	31.5	68.5
29209	COLUMBIA	53.7	50.1	41.8	43.6	1.9	2.7	2.1	3.1	6.5	6.4	6.2	6.6	7.5	27.8	26.3	11.5	1.1	76.9	37.0	48.2	51.8
29210	COLUMBIA	53.6	49.1	41.6	44.4	2.5	3.5	1.8	2.7	5.9	4.8	4.6	5.8	13.5	33.1	22.1	9.1	1.1	81.6	31.6	47.6	52.4
29212	COLUMBIA	72.3	68.2	24.3	27.0	1.8	2.6	1.3	1.9	5.8	5.6	6.3	8.5	7.2	31.1	27.2	7.3	0.9	76.5	35.5	53.1	46.9
29223	COLUMBIA	49.1	45.3	43.5	44.4	3.4	4.7	4.4	6.3	6.0	6.1	6.5	6.8	6.4	27.5	28.6	10.6	1.3	77.0	38.3	46.9	53.1
29229	COLUMBIA	59.4	55.5	34.7	36.8	2.9	3.7	3.1	4.5	8.7	8.4	8.1	7.2	5.4	31.5	25.3	4.9	0.4	70.2	33.2	48.1	51.9
29301	SPARTANBURG	61.7	58.1	30.6	30.6	3.0	4.2	5.8	8.8	6.4	6.6	6.6	7.4	7.2	27.2	26.6	10.5	1.5	76.4	36.5	48.7	51.3
29302	SPARTANBURG	76.8	73.5	18.0	19.5	3.8	4.9	1.2	1.8	5.8	6.0	6.3	7.3	7.0	25.0	28.6	11.9	2.0	78.0	39.5	46.6	53.4
29303	SPARTANBURG	64.5	59.8	28.7	30.3	1.9	2.7	5.9	8.7	6.2	5.9	5.6	8.7	10.0	27.5	22.7	11.1	2.4	79.0	34.8	49.6	50.4
29306	SPARTANBURG	31.6	31.1	66.2	66.0	0.7	1.0	1.4	2.0	7.3	7.2	7.1	7.5	6.6	24.5	25.9	11.9	2.1	73.9	37.1	45.3	54.7
29307	SPARTANBURG	83.4	80.4	13.7	15.3	1.1	1.6	1.8	2.9	5.6	5.5	5.8	6.0	5.3	23.8	27.8	16.2	4.0	79.4	43.4	46.8	53.2
29316	BOILING SPRINGS	88.8	86.1	7.5	8.4	2.2	3.3	1.4	2.2	7.1	6.9	6.9	6.4	5.0	30.0	26.0	10.4	1.2	75.0	37.4	49.8	50.2
29321	BUFFALO	83.2	81.6	15.9	17.1	0.3	0.4	0.6	1.0	6.3	6.5	6.8	6.5	4.8	25.9	29.2	12.5	1.5	76.4	40.3	48.0	52.0
29322	CAMPOBELLO	91.9	89.6	5.9	6.9	0.8	1.2	1.5	2.5	6.1	6.3	6.8	6.5	4.9	25.5	30.4	12.2	1.2	76.8	41.0	50.8	49.2
29323	CHESNEE	86.6	83.8	10.6	12.0	1.2	1.8	1.6	2.5	6.9	6.9	7.1	6.7	5.2	27.6	27.9	10.4	1.2	75.0	38.2	50.3	49.7
29325	CLINTON	65.8	61.3	32.6	36.3	0.3	0.4	0.8	1.6	5.7	5.8	5.9	8.5	7.5	24.4	25.9	13.4	3.0	78.0	39.2	47.2	52.8
29330	COWPENS	89.1	86.5	8.6	10.0	0.3	0.4	1.7	2.9	6.7	6.7	6.8	6.9	5.7	26.4	27.5	11.9	1.4	75.6	38.6	49.5	50.5
29332	CROSS HILL	64.0	63.1	34.5	35.1	0.2	0.2	0.5	0.8	5.6	5.7	5.9	6.6	4.6	21.2	35.4	13.7	1.3	78.6	45.3	49.3	50.7
29334	DUNCAN	77.2	73.4	19.5	21.5	1.0	1.6	2.6	4.1	8.3	8.1	7.3	6.8	5.4	27.0	26.1	10.0	1.0	72.1	36.2	49.7	50.3
29335	ENOREE	78.9	76.0	19.2	21.4	0.4	0.7	1.0	1.6	6.0	6.0	6.4	6.2	6.6	30.9	27.1	9.5	1.2	77.8	37.6	55.3	44.7
29340	GAFFNEY	77.5	75.9	20.8	21.7	0.2	0.3	1.7	2.6	7.1	7.0	7.0	7.3	6.3	26.4	25.2	11.5	2.2	75.0	36.9	48.3	51.7
29341	GAFFNEY	66.0	65.0	30.6	30.2	0.6	0.9	2.8	4.1	7.1	7.1	7.1	6.8	5.7	26.8	26.9	11.0	1.5	74.5	37.8	48.6	51.4
29349	INMAN	85.7	83.1	11.4	12.4	1.1	1.6	1.7	2.8	6.4	6.6	6.7	6.4	4.9	27.1	28.9	11.1	1.8	76.1	39.5	48.8	51.2
29351	JOANNA	84.9	82.4	13.3	14.8	0.2	0.4	1.5	2.3	6.0	6.1	6.1	6.0	5.9	24.4	29.3	14.2	2.0	78.1	41.6	48.5	51.5
29353	JONESVILLE	70.8	68.9	28.2	29.7	0.1	0.1	0.8	1.1	6.0	6.4	6.9	6.5	5.2	25.8	29.3	12.3	1.6	76.5	40.3	48.8	51.2
29355	KINARDS	69.3	67.2	30.2	32.1	0.0	0.0	0.7	1.2	5.0	5.5	5.7	5.9	5.7	25.7	32.5	12.4	1.7	80.0	42.7	51.5	48.5
29356	LANDRUM	92.5	90.9	6.0	6.8	0.3	0.4	1.2	1.9	5.6	5.8	6.1	6.1	4.8	23.1	31.9	14.7	1.9	78.7	43.9	49.7	50.3
29360	LAURENS	63.9	61.6	33.1	34.0	0.2	0.3	2.8	4.2	6.6	6.4	6.5	6.5	5.9	26.0	26.5	13.0	2.8	76.5	39.3	48.3	51.7
29365	LYMAN	88.6	86.1	8.9	10.0	0.6	0.9	1.6	2.7	6.4	6.6	6.9	6.2	4.6	27.0	28.8	12.0	1.5	76.3	40.2	49.1	50.9
29369	MOORE	80.5	78.3	16.3	17.2	2.0	2.8	1.2	1.8	6.3	6.8	7.4	7.3	5.0	25.8	31.2	9.4	0.8	74.8	39.5	49.3	50.7
29370	MOUNTVILLE	65.6	63.3	32.9	34.5	0.1	0.2	1.1	1.7	6.8	6.7	7.2	7.2	5.3	24.0	30.2	11.3	1.3	74.6	39.8	50.3	49.7
29372	PACOLET	77.6	73.8	20.6	23.7	0.5	0.7	1.0	1.6	5.7	5.9	6.2	6.3	4.9	24.8	28.5	15.6	2.2	78.5	42.3	48.0	52.0
29374	PAULINE	80.7	77.9	17.5	19.7	0.4	0.7	0.6	1.0	5.1	5.2	5.9	6.1	6.7	34.0	27.1	8.8	1.0	80.1	37.7	59.1	40.9
29376	ROEBUCK	85.3	82.6	12.5	14.2	1.0	1.4	1.6	2.5	6.2	6.4	6.9	6.8	4.8	26.2	29.6	11.9	1.2	76.4	40.5	48.8	51.2
29379	UNION	67.7	66.1	31.0	32.2	0.3	0.4	0.7	1.0	6.3	6.3	6.5	6.4	5.0	24.3	27.8	14.7	2.6	76.9	41.4	47.3	52.7
29384	WATERLOO	82.9	80.6	16.2	18.1	0.1	0.2	0.8	1.2	6.2	6.4	6.6	5.8	4.6	24.1	30.4	14.8	1.1	77.1	42.4	49.8	50.2
29385	WELLFORD	71.1	67.4	24.5	26.0	1.5	2.2	2.7	4.3	7.0	7.0	7.2	6.8	5.9	27.7	26.8	10.6	1.1	74.7	37.5	48.2	51.8
29388	WOODRUFF	81.7	78.6	15.3	16.9	0.3	0.4	2.6	4.2	6.8	7.1	7.2	6.7	5.1	26.1	27.4	11.9	1.6	74.8	39.0	49.1	50.9
29401	CHARLESTON	89.5	87.5	8.6	9.7	0.9	1.4	1.0	1.6	2.7	2.3	2.3	14.1	17.7	21.3	21.8	14.4	3.4	90.9	32.5	44.5	55.5
29403	CHARLESTON	32.5	31.1	65.3	65.7	0.7	1.0	1.6	2.4	4.8	5.0	5.1	13.9	17.1	21.4	20.2	10.5	2.0	81.7	28.1	49.7	50.3
29404	CHARLESTON AFB	74.6	69.5	17.3	18.6	1.6	2.3	6.5	10.1	15.0	9.3	6.4	5.6	22.3	36.4	3.7	1.2	0.1	66.8	23.1	54.1	45.9
29405	NORTH CHARLESTON	28.5	26.5	68.5	69.3	0.8	1.1	2.4	3.5	7.0	7.0	6.8	8.3	9.2	26.7	22.8	10.2	1.9	74.5	33.2	50.3	49.7
29406	CHARLESTON	53.0	49.4	39.3	39.8	1.7	2.5	5.7	8.1	8.3	7.5	6.8	8.2	8.5	31.6	19.4	8.2	1.5	74.0	31.1	48.7	51.3
29407	CHARLESTON	66.4	63.1	30.3	32.1	1.6	2.3	1.6	2.4	5.3	5.0	4.9	6.5	9.2	27.9	25.6	13.2	2.4	81.6	37.8	47.2	52.8
29410	NORTH CHARLESTON	81.5	78.5	12.9	13.0	2.1	3.1	3.2	5.2	5.4	5.0	5.0	6.3	9.7	30.0	25.4	12.0	1.1	81.4	36.2	52.9	47.1
29412	CHARLESTON	79.1	74.9	18.8	22.1	0.6	0.9	1.2	1.9	5.2	5.2	5.4	5.4	6.0	27.6	29.1	13.9	2.2	80.9	41.7	48.2	51.8
29414	CHARLESTON	76.0	71.8	20.2	22.9	1.8	2.6	1.6	2.3	6.5	6.5	6.4	6.0	6.3	30.9	27.0	9.2	1.3	76.8	36.9	48.0	52.0
29418	NORTH CHARLESTON	52.1	48.5	40.8	41.8	3.0	4.1	3.4	4.9	7.8	7.0	6.5	7.0	8.3	31.9	23.7	7.1	0.7	74.6	32.6	48.6	51.4
29420	NORTH CHARLESTON	56.3	55.5	36.1	34.7	2.8	3.8	4.3	5.6	8.4	7.8	7.6	7.6	6.7	32.1	23.7	5.7	0.4	71.6	32.0	48.6	51.4
29426	ADAMS RUN	31.9	28.4	66.7	69.7	0.2	0.2	0.9	1.5	6.7	6.8	7.0	7.9	6.0	23.1	30.0	11.0	1.4	74.7	38.9	47.8	52.2
29429	AWENDAW	45.1	41.9	53.4	56.0	0.3	0.5	0.8	1.2	6.8	6.9	7.1	6.9	5.3	25.1	29.8	11.2	0.9	74.7	39.3	48.5	51.5
29431	BONNEAU	79.0	77.9	19.6	20.0	0.1	0.2	1.3	2.1	6.7	6.6	6.8	7.1	5.9	24.6	28.4	12.5	1.3	75.5	39.1	49.0	51.0
29432	BRANCHVILLE	55.1	52.7	43.3	45.3	0.1	0.1	0.8	1.1	6.7	6.8	7.0	6.9	5.5	22.9	28.7	13.7	1.9	75.5	40.8	47.6	52.4
29434	CORDESVILLE	67.5	66.1	31.4	32.3	0.1	0.3	1.0	1.6	5.7	5.8	6.1	7.0	6.2	24.5	31.1	12.3	1.3	77.9	40.8	49.1	50.9
29435	COTTAGEVILLE	70.8	68.6	25.0	26.1	0.4	0.6	1.0	1.3	6.5	6.8	7.0	6.6	5.0	25.3	30.1	11.6	1.1	75.6	39.9	49.3	50.7
29436	CROSS	35.3	33.8	63.1	63.9	0.1	0.1	1.1	1.7	5.9	6.4	7.0	7.4	6.2	22.5	30.5	12.7	1.3	76.2	41.0	48.0	52.0
29437	DORCHESTER	55.0	50.6	43.1	47.1	0.1	0.1	0.4	0.5	5.8	5.9	6.4	7.3	6.1	24.4	30.5	12.2	1.5	77.5	40.7	48.8	51.2
29438	EDISTO ISLAND	59.6	56.9	39.1	41.1	0.1	0.1	1.4	1.9	4.1	4.4	5.1	5.0	4.8	18.2	39.1	17.7	1.6	83.5	50.3	47.8	52.2
29440	GEORGETOWN	48.4	44.5	49.5	52.3	0.3	0.4	2.2	3.3	7.1	7.1	7.5	7.2	6.2	24.5	27.0	11.8	1.7	73.8	37.5	47.9	52.1
29445	GOOSE CREEK	72.4	69.1	18.7	18.3	4.0	5.8	4.2	6.2	8.3	7.2	6.4	9.7	9.5	30.5	21.2	6.6	0.5	74.2	29.4	51.8	48.2
29446	GREEN POND	25.6	24.5	73.5	74.3	0.0	0.0	0.8	1.0	6.6	6.6	7.0	7.9	6.2	22.9	29.3	11.9	1.6	75.0	38.9	48.0	52.0
29448	HARLEYVILLE	50.5	46.0	47.7	51.7	0.1	0.1	0.4	0.5	6.0	6.1	6.6	7.6	6.1	24.1	29.4	12.6	1.5	76.7	40.2	48.3	51.7
29449	HOLLYWOOD	37.4	33.6	60.4	63.1	0.2	0.3	2.3	3.6	5.8	5.9	6.3	7.2	6.1	22.9	31.9	12.7	1.3	77.9	41.5	48.1	51.9
29450	HUGER	26.6	25.4	72.3	72.9	0.3	0.5	0.8	1.3	7.0	7.4	8.5	9.3	6.0	24.9	27.5	8.0	1.3	70.9	35.4	48.5	51.5
29451	ISLE OF PALMS	98.1	97.0	0.5	0.9	0.5	0.8	1.2	1.9	4.5	5.1	6.0	5.1	3.1	22.5	34.1	17.7	1.8	81.1	47.3	49.3	50.7
29453	JAMESTOWN	48.5	46.9	50.1	51.2	0.1	0.1	0.6	0.7	5.6	5.9	6.1	6.2	5.8	25.0	31.3	12.8	1.4	78.7	41.3	49.0	51.0
29455	JOHNS ISLAND	62.5	58.1	32.9	34.8	0.5	0.7	5.6	8.8	5.3	5.4	5.8	6.0	5.0	22.7	31.1	17.1	1.6	79.7	44.8	48.5	51.5
29456	LADSON	73.7	70.3	20.4	21.5	1.9	2.8	2.8	4.2	7.4	7.3	7.2	7.5	6.5	30.0	25.9	7.7	0.6	73.3	34.4	49.7	50.3
29458	MC CLELLANVILLE	33.9	30.6	65.0	67.9	0.1	0.1	1.0	1.3	5.5	5.7	6.2	6.8	6.0	22.4	32.6	13.0	1.7	78.2	42.6	49.0	51.0
29461	MONCKS CORNER	65.4	62.7	31.0	31.9	0.4	0.6	2.1	3.4	6.8	6.8	6.8	7.0	6.2	25.9	28.1	11.0	1.4	75.1	38.0	48.8	51.2
29464	MOUNT PLEASANT	87.8	85.4	9.7	10.9	1.1	1.7	1.3	2.1	6.5	6.5	6.5	5.7	5.6	29.5	27.6	9.9	2.0	76.8	38.5	47.8	52.2
29466	MOUNT PLEASANT	76.1	73.7	21.4	23.0	1.3	1.6	1.6	2.5	9.2	8.7	8.1	6.1	3.4	32.3	24.9	6.6	0.5	70.0	36.1	48.9	51.1
29468	PINEVILLE	15.7	15.0	83.5	83.8	0.0	0.0	0.9	1.3	5.2	6.7	6.9	7.9	5.7	22.7	30.7	12.4	1.8	76.5	40.9	48.6	51.4
29469	PINOPOLIS	67.1	65.5	31.7	32.8	0.1	0.2	0.6	0.9	5.5	5.7	6.0	6.3	5.8	24.6	31.7	13.2	1.1	79.0	42.4	52.8	47.2
29470	RAVENEL	53.5	49.6	45.3	48.6	0.1	0.2	1.1	1.8	6.0	6.2	6.6	7.2	6.0	24.6	30.7	11.5	1.2	77.5	40.1	48.2	51.8
29471	REEVESVILLE	50.5	46.4	48.3	52.2	0.1	0.0	1.2	1.4	6.3	6.4	6.5	7.1	6.2	23.7	28.9	12.9	2.1	76.5	41.0	50.1	49.9
29472	RIDGEVILLE	48.5	44.9	47.2	49.6	0.2	0.2	1.2	1.7	4.9	5.0	5.2	6.3	7.8	33.8	26.3	9.7	1.0	81.8	37.4	60.1	39.9
29474	ROUND O	59.4	57.4	35.6	36.3	0.4	0.5	1.1	1.5	6.7	6.9	7.0	6.7	5.3	23.9	30.1	12.1	1.4	75.4	40.1	49.0	51.0
29475	RUFFIN	60.4	58.1	37.8	39.3	0.4	0.5	1.0	1.6	6.0	6.3	6.6	7.2	5.4	25.2	29.0	12.7	1.6	76.8	39.8	49.1	50.9
29477	SAINT GEORGE	45.6	41.5	53.1	56.8	0.4	0.5	0.8	1.0	5.8	6.0	6.4	7.2	5.5	24.0	28.8	14.1	2.4	77.5	41.6	49.0	51.0
29479	SAINT STEPHEN	39.4	38.9	59.2	58.9	0.1	0.2	1.2	1.8	7.2	7.1	7.3	7.6	6.4	23.4	27.3	11.6	2.0	73.6	37.6	47.6	52.4
29481	SMOAKS	40.8	38.8	57.7	59.3	0.2	0.2	0.9	1.1	7.3	7.3	7.5	7.9	5.6	23.2	26.9	12.9	1.5	73.1	38.1	47.3	52.7
29482	SULLIVANS ISLAND	98.7	98.4	0.6	0.7	0.2	0.2	0.8	1.3	4.3	4.1	5.2	7.1	6.6	24.3	34.8	11.8	1.8	82.1	43.7	50.9	49.1
29483	SUMMERVILLE	76.7	74.8	19.3	19.9	0.9	1.2	2.1	3.1	7.1	7.1	7.3	7.4	6.4	28.0	27.1	8.7	1.0	73.9	35.7	48.8	51.2
29485	SUMMERVILLE	81.5	78.4	14.9	16.5	1.2	1.7	1.8	2.8	6.8	6.8	7.1	7.6	6.4	26.8	27.8	9.5	1.2	74.4	37.1	48.5	51.5
29487	WADMALAW ISLAND	37.7	34.9	60.9	63.1	0.1	0.1	4.1	5.7	4.3	5.3	6.4	7.1	5.2	22.0	33.6	14.3	1.8	79.5	44.8	49.0	51.0
29488	WALTERBORO	55.4	53.6	42.7	43.7	0.3	0.5	1.4	2.1	7.4	7.3	7.1	7.1	6.4	24.8	26.6	11.7	1.7	73.7	37.0	47.4	52.6
29492	CHARLESTON	57.6	56.5	41.5	42.2	0.5	0.8	0.7	0.9	9.8	8.8	8.0	6.4	5.3	33.5	22.3	5.5	0.5	69.4	31.8	48.3	51.7
29501	FLORENCE	69.6	67.9	27.9	28.7	1.2	1.6	1.0	1.5	6.3	6.3	6.5	6.5	6.3	27.2	27.8	11.1	2.2	76.9	38.8	47.2	52.8
29505	FLORENCE	72.9	70.0	24.6	26.5	1.5	2.1	0.8	1.1	6.7	6.6	6.9	6.9	5.7	27.3	28.0	10.6	1.3	75.5	38.1	47.4	52.6
29506	FLORENCE	33.8	31.7	64.4	65.9	0.3	0.4	1.2	1.7	6.8	6.8	6.7	9.0	9.4	24.4	24.6	10.4	1.7	75.2	33.7	46.2	53.8
29510	ANDREWS	49.0	46.4	49.6	51.7	0.1	0.2	1.6	2.2	6.8	7.2	8.0	8.0	6.1	24.6	27.2	10.3	1.4	72.9	36.6	47.5	52.5
29511	AYNOR	85.3	83.4	13.4	14.5	0.1	0.1	1.5	2.3	6.8	6.5	7.9	7.1	6.2	27.1	26.9	10.3	1.1	74.3	37.3	49.0	51.0
	SOUTH CAROLINA	67.2	65.9	29.5	29.4	0.9	1.4	2.4	3.6	6.5	6.5	6.5	7.2	6.9	26.6	26.8	11.3	1.6	76.4	37.6	48.9	51.1
	UNITED STATES	75.1	72.0	12.3	12.7	3.8	4.6	12.5	15.7	6.8	6.7	6.6	7.1	6.9	27.0	26.0	10.9	1.9	75.7	36.9	49.2	50.8

29206-29511

#	POST OFFICE NAME	2009 Per Capita Income	2009 HH Income Base	2009 Household Income Distribution (%) Less than $25,000	$25,000 to $49,999	$50,000 to $99,999	$100,000 to $149,999	$150,000 or More	Median Household Income 2009	2014	2009 National Centile	2009 State Centile	2009 Home Value Base	2009 Home Value Distribution (%) Less than $50,000	$50,000 to $89,999	$90,000 to $174,999	$175,000 to $399,999	$400,000 or More	2009 Median Home Value
29206	COLUMBIA	32817	8590	14.2	30.2	38.6	8.7	8.3	55106	57230	71	86	5324	1.3	6.7	40.6	41.6	9.7	177299
29207	COLUMBIA	8242	43	4.7	23.3	37.2	4.7	30.2	78483	79776	91	98	23	0.0	0.0	4.3	34.8	60.9	462500
29208	COLUMBIA	10858	2	50.0	50.0	0.0	0.0	0.0	27500	27500	5	2	0	0.0	0.0	0.0	0.0	0.0	0
29209	COLUMBIA	27563	13058	19.9	30.2	36.2	8.8	4.9	49943	52356	61	78	7966	3.4	15.0	54.1	23.1	4.3	132659
29210	COLUMBIA	25922	17187	22.4	35.1	34.4	6.5	1.6	43440	46518	44	58	6279	2.5	17.5	59.9	20.1	0.1	125699
29212	COLUMBIA	31660	11828	10.6	18.1	41.5	18.8	10.9	75738	77507	90	96	8743	0.6	5.2	53.3	36.5	4.5	157625
29223	COLUMBIA	32782	19365	15.7	24.9	38.7	10.7	10.0	59106	62268	76	90	12222	6.7	14.0	46.6	24.3	8.3	136563
29229	COLUMBIA	34326	13787	6.9	12.9	47.6	20.2	12.4	80078	80477	92	99	11796	2.6	9.4	51.1	32.9	4.1	145963
29301	SPARTANBURG	25726	12240	24.0	26.2	35.4	8.3	6.2	49824	51538	61	77	7406	15.7	23.3	43.4	15.2	2.4	103831
29302	SPARTANBURG	31626	6996	19.7	25.2	35.0	11.3	8.8	55271	55677	72	86	5054	8.4	23.7	39.8	22.0	6.1	115633
29303	SPARTANBURG	18152	9319	35.2	28.7	30.2	3.9	2.0	35609	39029	20	23	5200	22.2	37.0	35.1	5.4	0.3	81987
29306	SPARTANBURG	16977	6515	45.5	25.7	23.2	3.1	2.5	28798	30824	6	3	3109	21.7	41.5	28.0	6.0	2.8	76457
29307	SPARTANBURG	27897	8791	24.3	27.1	33.7	9.1	5.8	48202	50171	57	73	5905	13.2	19.7	45.7	20.1	1.4	114240
29316	BOILING SPRINGS	27211	7590	13.4	25.1	44.5	12.3	4.7	61928	61652	80	92	6170	6.7	17.0	65.2	10.6	0.5	112311
29321	BUFFALO	21003	1093	20.8	34.9	39.4	3.9	1.0	45909	46610	51	66	872	31.4	38.6	26.7	3.2	0.0	67849
29322	CAMPOBELLO	22931	3495	22.2	29.2	36.9	8.5	3.2	48150	50494	57	73	3025	21.9	26.4	32.1	15.6	4.0	92333
29323	CHESNEE	21091	5865	25.7	27.9	37.6	6.5	2.3	45333	48698	49	64	4606	23.3	25.1	41.4	9.4	0.7	91610
29325	CLINTON	18542	5596	32.8	31.0	27.9	6.0	2.3	38198	41334	27	32	3834	26.8	31.0	33.0	8.7	0.4	81671
29330	COWPENS	20546	3688	29.2	26.2	35.1	7.0	2.5	43164	46648	43	57	2852	24.8	31.6	34.6	8.4	0.6	82789
29332	CROSS HILL	21413	991	31.2	31.2	28.3	6.7	2.7	42014	45640	39	51	887	28.4	23.1	35.6	11.4	1.5	87891
29334	DUNCAN	23090	4164	24.6	24.1	38.6	9.0	3.7	50969	52759	64	80	2969	18.1	25.1	38.1	16.2	2.6	98654
29335	ENOREE	17737	1921	26.6	26.7	37.6	7.0	2.1	44336	48121	46	61	1659	32.1	32.4	27.7	6.9	1.0	73690
29340	GAFFNEY	20641	8328	30.2	29.9	31.9	5.3	2.8	40767	42684	35	45	6122	20.4	30.4	41.7	6.9	0.5	88891
29341	GAFFNEY	21797	7435	27.4	26.2	36.9	7.1	2.4	46392	47344	53	68	5309	14.4	22.7	45.0	16.6	1.3	105226
29349	INMAN	24750	11059	17.1	27.4	41.7	9.7	4.0	54026	54593	70	85	9111	14.3	25.2	43.7	15.9	1.0	102914
29351	JOANNA	20606	952	33.3	28.7	30.1	5.6	2.3	41452	45594	38	49	781	30.7	37.9	23.8	5.4	2.2	65063
29353	JONESVILLE	20442	1812	28.1	31.8	32.5	6.0	1.5	41739	44136	38	50	1492	33.0	30.1	30.8	5.4	0.7	69538
29355	KINARDS	20402	180	28.3	35.6	27.8	7.2	1.1	38515	41105	28	33	150	25.3	31.3	28.7	12.0	2.7	84737
29356	LANDRUM	23789	3670	25.9	26.6	37.7	6.7	3.1	46292	50265	52	67	2947	20.1	21.4	35.6	18.4	4.5	104594
29360	LAURENS	19739	8468	31.4	28.7	32.1	5.6	2.1	40778	45212	35	45	5932	21.0	29.8	36.2	12.0	1.0	88973
29365	LYMAN	24606	3753	21.8	23.4	42.6	9.6	2.6	53676	54501	69	84	3111	13.6	31.9	41.5	12.4	0.6	95000
29369	MOORE	29660	5095	10.8	21.0	44.5	15.3	8.4	65628	65798	84	94	4518	7.3	13.2	40.9	36.9	1.7	141427
29370	MOUNTVILLE	18795	527	26.4	30.9	35.9	4.7	2.1	42691	46900	41	55	456	32.9	21.7	31.1	12.3	2.0	85116
29372	PACOLET	19708	2283	33.5	27.2	33.7	4.7	0.9	39622	42747	32	41	1753	34.0	37.1	24.6	4.1	0.2	70322
29374	PAULINE	27843	1426	18.7	23.0	46.4	7.5	4.5	55626	56068	72	87	1283	20.7	29.0	34.0	15.0	1.3	90511
29376	ROEBUCK	26496	2717	19.0	23.3	45.0	8.6	4.0	56257	56638	73	87	2169	14.5	16.6	47.9	18.7	2.3	111977
29379	UNION	20938	8127	32.5	29.9	29.4	6.4	1.9	38921	41569	30	35	5996	29.4	32.7	31.1	6.2	0.7	74976
29384	WATERLOO	21146	1803	28.2	26.8	40.9	3.1	1.0	44059	47366	46	60	1511	26.7	25.2	38.6	8.8	0.6	87993
29385	WELLFORD	20944	2846	24.2	27.7	40.5	5.8	1.8	47686	50207	56	72	2229	16.8	41.5	32.1	9.1	0.4	80533
29388	WOODRUFF	21947	5509	27.7	24.7	37.7	6.8	3.2	46291	49962	52	67	4284	19.5	29.2	38.2	11.4	1.8	91505
29401	CHARLESTON	44892	4711	30.7	20.6	24.6	8.0	16.0	47587	51287	56	71	1990	0.4	0.6	5.1	17.6	76.3	707229
29403	CHARLESTON	16268	9393	55.1	21.4	17.6	3.4	2.5	21176	21935	2	0	3073	6.5	17.8	41.9	24.7	9.1	137153
29404	CHARLESTON AFB	15970	1000	12.5	46.3	37.5	2.5	1.2	44210	47146	46	61	96	50.0	14.6	17.7	8.3	9.4	55000
29405	NORTH CHARLESTON	14576	11039	46.8	28.3	22.2	2.1	0.7	27753	29443	5	3	4686	15.7	45.4	34.1	3.9	0.9	80681
29406	CHARLESTON	19229	10793	34.3	31.0	28.1	5.4	1.3	36859	39939	23	28	4312	32.7	23.1	37.8	5.3	1.1	80386
29407	CHARLESTON	27343	17045	25.3	29.3	34.1	7.0	4.2	45110	48621	49	64	9207	4.2	12.8	46.9	29.1	6.9	148295
29410	NORTH CHARLESTON	26096	5326	18.6	31.3	37.8	8.4	3.8	50063	52172	61	78	2835	12.1	12.1	37.8	37.2	0.9	155228
29412	CHARLESTON	31231	17390	17.9	23.1	42.9	10.3	5.8	57086	58662	74	88	12048	2.4	7.1	44.1	36.4	10.0	168064
29414	CHARLESTON	30138	12817	14.3	22.8	45.1	11.8	6.0	60798	61807	79	91	8676	2.6	7.5	43.8	42.2	3.8	168786
29418	NORTH CHARLESTON	23046	9508	20.9	34.7	35.0	7.1	2.3	44455	49085	47	62	4884	23.6	20.0	33.3	22.3	0.8	99968
29420	NORTH CHARLESTON	25365	7134	13.3	22.1	44.7	14.1	5.7	65256	67300	84	93	5043	11.3	14.8	35.0	32.0	6.9	150375
29426	ADAMS RUN	17475	780	35.8	28.3	28.7	5.9	1.3	36319	38932	21	26	692	27.7	30.3	31.8	7.9	2.2	77571
29429	AWENDAW	25748	1025	27.8	22.5	31.6	8.3	9.8	49115	52549	59	77	949	20.2	15.7	26.8	24.3	13.0	123676
29431	BONNEAU	20867	2429	25.4	28.5	37.5	7.0	1.6	46009	50026	51	67	2134	26.6	24.6	31.7	15.2	1.9	88120
29432	BRANCHVILLE	20212	1078	34.7	30.3	28.9	3.3	2.7	35531	37018	19	22	864	34.1	29.6	29.4	6.6	0.2	71096
29434	CORDESVILLE	18694	259	31.3	31.3	29.7	5.0	2.7	39850	41950	32	42	224	27.7	36.6	26.8	5.8	3.1	68889
29435	COTTAGEVILLE	19370	1604	31.2	29.3	33.0	3.9	2.6	38668	39506	29	34	1386	24.0	29.5	35.8	10.1	0.6	84674
29436	CROSS	14862	1803	38.7	28.7	30.6	1.7	0.4	35138	36603	18	20	1587	32.4	22.9	36.5	6.2	1.9	76062
29437	DORCHESTER	17867	873	32.3	32.3	28.9	5.2	1.4	35738	38649	20	24	781	26.5	30.5	28.4	13.4	1.2	79030
29438	EDISTO ISLAND	32622	1223	34.1	20.3	26.5	10.5	8.6	42995	45675	42	56	1047	13.8	9.5	18.3	27.9	30.6	237798
29440	GEORGETOWN	20141	12110	32.1	27.8	31.4	5.5	3.2	39414	43342	31	39	9528	25.6	22.1	36.2	12.3	3.8	92964
29445	GOOSE CREEK	23332	18352	16.1	24.7	43.3	11.3	4.5	57867	60319	75	89	12056	6.5	15.1	49.3	28.1	1.0	139181
29446	GREEN POND	17795	753	42.4	28.6	21.9	3.2	4.0	32145	35000	12	8	620	25.8	33.9	29.5	10.3	0.5	75435
29448	HARLEYVILLE	19718	1119	32.4	27.5	33.3	4.6	2.1	39213	42761	30	37	964	34.6	22.7	27.8	13.5	1.3	76613
29449	HOLLYWOOD	20795	3145	33.6	26.9	28.6	6.7	4.2	39339	42334	31	38	2771	24.1	26.6	26.3	15.6	7.4	89102
29450	HUGER	15569	1110	28.0	35.5	32.6	3.1	0.8	39076	42202	30	36	978	22.6	19.0	32.9	22.4	3.1	106081
29451	ISLE OF PALMS	57553	1827	5.9	11.9	35.0	19.2	28.1	95867	95907	96	100	1453	0.1	0.8	2.4	24.7	72.1	589735
29453	JAMESTOWN	15791	594	39.7	31.3	23.2	5.2	0.5	33661	35000	15	14	530	37.2	23.4	27.2	11.3	0.9	62703
29455	JOHNS ISLAND	28059	6943	23.8	27.6	32.3	9.2	7.1	48378	50822	57	75	5881	15.5	17.6	26.1	16.8	23.9	127610
29456	LADSON	22858	8238	15.2	27.7	45.1	8.7	3.3	54800	56937	71	85	6040	13.6	15.8	53.3	16.5	0.8	121284
29458	MC CLELLANVILLE	18197	1258	37.5	22.9	32.2	4.4	3.0	37138	40292	24	29	1106	26.9	20.3	32.3	14.0	6.4	94762
29461	MONCKS CORNER	21126	9913	24.9	29.4	34.0	8.9	2.8	45485	49242	50	65	7758	18.4	21.1	36.1	21.8	2.6	115201
29464	MOUNT PLEASANT	38370	19136	11.1	19.3	43.4	15.7	10.6	74973	75202	89	96	13119	1.3	2.2	26.5	55.3	14.8	228703
29466	MOUNT PLEASANT	43403	9962	9.6	15.3	34.6	18.7	21.7	87086	88202	94	100	8957	4.6	4.4	16.1	53.4	21.6	269712
29468	PINEVILLE	15914	870	42.9	32.1	18.3	4.5	2.3	29566	30281	7	5	781	46.4	28.6	16.1	7.2	1.8	52568
29469	PINOPOLIS	25068	590	24.9	25.9	33.7	10.3	5.1	48351	52158	57	75	510	28.0	21.0	22.9	22.9	5.1	95000
29470	RAVENEL	20298	1693	30.5	26.2	34.7	5.8	2.8	42417	46490	41	53	1502	29.8	22.1	28.7	13.1	6.3	86979
29471	REEVESVILLE	19568	648	31.5	34.6	27.5	2.9	3.5	39802	41847	32	41	572	34.3	25.7	24.5	13.3	2.3	72000
29472	RIDGEVILLE	16562	3053	30.8	25.5	36.0	5.9	1.8	42091	46323	40	51	2724	32.3	23.2	27.3	16.0	1.2	79542
29474	ROUND O	18971	835	32.7	31.0	29.3	4.2	2.8	37793	38817	26	31	717	25.5	30.1	34.2	9.1	1.1	81563
29475	RUFFIN	18470	968	36.4	29.4	27.1	5.0	2.2	37207	38478	24	30	803	27.4	30.1	29.6	11.1	1.7	81597
29477	SAINT GEORGE	17832	2987	38.1	30.5	25.2	3.8	2.3	33817	35749	15	15	2417	33.6	26.8	27.8	11.5	0.2	73816
29479	SAINT STEPHEN	16716	2791	39.8	25.2	28.3	4.7	2.0	34237	36882	16	16	2262	35.4	20.9	32.4	10.7	0.6	79756
29481	SMOAKS	15054	803	46.3	24.3	24.8	2.9	1.7	27294	28939	5	2	686	30.2	27.3	32.8	9.5	0.3	77333
29482	SULLIVANS ISLAND	55943	903	10.3	14.4	33.2	17.8	24.3	86435	87268	94	99	636	0.0	0.0	2.7	13.5	83.8	810680
29483	SUMMERVILLE	22928	23061	19.1	26.8	41.7	9.0	3.4	53023	56175	68	83	17298	14.8	14.5	42.3	22.7	5.7	126987
29485	SUMMERVILLE	26201	16362	13.9	23.6	44.9	12.5	5.1	60589	62900	78	91	11975	8.1	8.5	34.8	44.7	3.9	172351
29487	WADMALAW ISLAND	22045	1126	37.1	22.6	30.4	5.0	4.9	37899	41308	26	31	987	21.2	21.6	28.0	12.4	16.9	103005
29488	WALTERBORO	19034	8699	33.8	26.9	31.5	5.7	2.2	39054	40240	30	36	6613	21.7	32.6	34.4	10.5	0.9	85299
29492	CHARLESTON	29666	3314	13.0	20.1	38.9	17.3	10.7	66500	66579	85	94	3054	2.3	7.8	30.5	41.3	18.1	223111
29501	FLORENCE	28528	17096	23.1	25.4	34.7	9.9	6.9	51201	51817	64	81	11458	10.5	20.9	41.0	22.2	5.4	120238
29505	FLORENCE	26253	8547	18.7	24.4	41.3	10.7	5.0	55517	54871	72	86	6827	10.6	16.8	51.5	19.8	1.3	118240
29506	FLORENCE	16473	7535	38.9	28.3	27.1	3.4	2.3	33348	35973	14	12	4919	30.9	32.3	30.1	4.7	2.0	72192
29510	ANDREWS	15445	4157	43.5	26.8	24.8	3.7	1.2	30295	31446	9	6	3412	34.8	29.7	29.2	5.8	0.5	67250
29511	AYNOR	20184	2028	30.5	28.4	32.6	6.0	2.5	39423	44863	31	39	1592	37.6	20.0	23.7	17.3	1.4	76543
	SOUTH CAROLINA	24352		25.1	26.4	35.2	8.4	4.8	48210	50493				16.4	20.9	37.4	20.6	4.8	112284
	UNITED STATES	27277		20.9	24.4	35.3	11.7	7.6	54719	56938				9.3	13.1	31.6	32.6	13.5	162279

#	POST OFFICE NAME	FINANCIAL SERVICES: Auto Loan	FINANCIAL SERVICES: Home Loan	FINANCIAL SERVICES: Invest-ments	FINANCIAL SERVICES: Retire-ment Plans	THE HOME: Home Improvements: Home Repair	THE HOME: Home Improvements: Lawn & Garden	THE HOME: Furnishings: Comput-ers & Hard-ware-Personal	THE HOME: Furnishings: Major Appli-ances	THE HOME: Furnishings: TV, Radio, Sound Equip-ment	THE HOME: Furnishings: Furni-ture	ENTERTAINMENT: Dine out/ Carry out	ENTERTAINMENT: Sports Equip-ment	ENTERTAINMENT: Fees & Tickets	ENTERTAINMENT: Toys & Games	ENTERTAINMENT: Travel	ENTERTAINMENT: Cable TV	PERSONAL: Apparel & Services	PERSONAL: Auto Repairs	PERSONAL: Health Insur-ance	PERSONAL: Pets & Supplies
29206	COLUMBIA	106	108	109	110	111	109	109	107	108	111	109	81	113	109	112	108	77	109	111	124
29207	COLUMBIA	164	216	257	223	239	200	189	197	173	209	173	148	225	170	220	164	129	185	176	216
29208	COLUMBIA	42	18	18	22	16	21	59	29	47	40	48	31	35	46	32	43	34	42	29	40
29209	COLUMBIA	92	92	86	93	90	92	93	90	94	94	95	69	94	94	92	95	66	93	95	108
29210	COLUMBIA	79	59	54	64	56	60	78	65	78	76	79	54	69	80	67	77	55	75	69	81
29212	COLUMBIA	125	134	120	134	129	120	128	123	123	132	125	98	132	127	128	119	88	123	116	144
29223	COLUMBIA	115	115	107	117	112	109	116	110	114	119	115	86	117	116	114	112	81	113	109	131
29229	COLUMBIA	145	157	127	151	147	129	139	138	131	151	134	109	142	141	137	124	94	131	121	158
29301	SPARTANBURG	96	88	88	89	86	94	91	92	94	90	93	71	88	95	88	96	65	93	95	110
29302	SPARTANBURG	105	108	102	111	107	110	108	106	107	106	106	83	110	107	108	107	75	106	109	126
29303	SPARTANBURG	70	55	56	56	54	65	65	63	68	60	67	49	56	68	58	71	46	66	70	77
29306	SPARTANBURG	60	48	47	50	46	56	57	54	62	55	61	42	52	61	51	66	42	58	62	68
29307	SPARTANBURG	93	90	93	89	91	99	89	94	93	88	92	69	88	92	90	97	64	93	102	110
29316	BOILING SPRINGS	104	109	95	107	105	104	99	103	98	101	99	79	100	103	100	98	69	99	100	120
29321	BUFFALO	90	64	80	62	64	87	67	80	74	64	73	61	53	76	62	81	49	75	84	97
29322	CAMPOBELLO	103	76	89	75	76	100	78	92	86	76	85	70	64	89	73	94	57	86	96	111
29323	CHESNEE	95	71	80	69	70	90	73	84	80	71	78	64	60	83	67	86	53	79	87	101
29325	CLINTON	78	59	69	58	59	76	64	71	71	62	69	54	55	71	60	76	47	70	77	86
29330	COWPENS	90	67	78	65	67	87	70	81	76	67	75	61	57	78	65	83	50	77	85	97
29332	CROSS HILL	82	67	90	62	71	87	66	81	73	68	71	57	59	70	68	79	47	77	88	95
29334	DUNCAN	93	85	78	85	83	92	84	89	87	82	86	67	79	89	81	90	59	86	91	105
29335	ENOREE	96	69	80	67	69	92	72	84	80	70	78	64	58	83	65	87	53	79	88	102
29340	GAFFNEY	83	65	68	64	63	79	69	75	75	67	74	57	59	77	63	80	50	74	80	91
29341	GAFFNEY	83	73	70	73	72	81	75	78	79	74	78	59	70	80	71	83	54	78	83	94
29349	INMAN	100	89	88	89	87	101	87	95	91	85	90	72	80	93	84	95	61	91	98	114
29351	JOANNA	82	61	70	60	61	80	67	75	73	62	71	57	55	74	61	79	48	73	81	90
29353	JONESVILLE	90	61	81	59	61	87	65	79	73	62	72	61	50	75	60	81	48	74	83	96
29355	KINARDS	86	62	72	60	62	82	64	75	71	62	70	58	52	74	59	78	47	71	79	91
29356	LANDRUM	99	73	99	71	75	99	75	92	82	71	81	69	62	83	73	90	54	86	95	109
29360	LAURENS	79	64	65	64	63	77	68	73	73	66	72	55	60	75	63	78	49	72	79	88
29365	LYMAN	97	84	85	84	84	97	83	93	87	80	86	69	75	89	81	92	58	88	96	109
29369	MOORE	117	123	108	123	119	120	112	116	111	115	112	89	114	115	113	112	78	112	114	137
29370	MOUNTVILLE	88	63	86	60	65	88	66	80	74	65	72	60	53	74	63	81	48	76	86	97
29372	PACOLET	83	59	81	58	61	84	63	78	70	58	68	58	50	70	61	77	45	72	83	92
29374	PAULINE	107	92	93	92	91	108	90	101	95	87	94	77	82	98	87	101	64	95	104	120
29376	ROEBUCK	101	91	89	92	91	102	90	97	93	87	92	73	84	95	88	97	63	93	100	115
29379	UNION	83	60	73	59	60	81	65	75	73	62	71	57	54	73	60	79	48	72	81	91
29384	WATERLOO	89	62	82	60	62	87	65	79	73	62	71	61	51	74	61	80	47	74	83	96
29385	WELLFORD	89	75	74	72	73	84	74	80	78	75	78	60	66	81	69	82	53	78	82	96
29388	WOODRUFF	95	74	81	72	73	92	76	86	83	73	81	66	64	85	71	89	55	83	91	104
29401	CHARLESTON	122	114	130	122	120	111	144	120	132	134	133	101	135	129	132	127	97	130	116	143
29403	CHARLESTON	52	39	38	42	38	44	58	46	58	51	58	37	49	56	46	59	40	53	52	58
29404	CHARLESTON AFB	91	47	35	55	42	40	85	59	80	80	85	59	65	97	62	74	59	75	53	72
29405	NORTH CHARLESTON	52	44	40	45	42	49	50	48	55	49	54	36	47	54	46	58	37	51	55	59
29406	CHARLESTON	68	58	50	59	54	56	67	60	67	66	67	48	61	69	59	66	47	65	61	73
29407	CHARLESTON	83	74	72	77	73	78	86	78	86	82	86	61	81	85	79	87	60	83	84	95
29410	NORTH CHARLESTON	85	80	78	82	79	84	87	83	88	83	88	65	84	87	84	89	61	86	89	100
29412	CHARLESTON	98	101	98	102	101	103	99	100	99	99	99	75	101	99	100	100	69	99	103	116
29414	CHARLESTON	103	105	95	105	101	97	104	99	101	106	102	80	104	104	102	99	72	101	96	118
29418	NORTH CHARLESTON	82	73	63	73	69	69	80	73	79	81	80	59	74	82	73	77	55	77	73	88
29420	NORTH CHARLESTON	111	119	98	115	111	102	108	106	103	114	105	84	110	110	106	99	73	103	97	123
29426	ADAMS RUN	85	55	82	52	55	83	59	75	68	56	67	58	44	69	55	76	44	70	79	92
29429	AWENDAW	122	99	115	98	99	121	97	113	103	95	102	87	85	106	95	110	69	105	114	134
29431	BONNEAU	92	69	84	66	69	89	71	83	77	69	76	63	58	79	67	83	51	79	86	100
29432	BRANCHVILLE	89	58	86	55	58	88	62	78	72	59	70	61	47	73	58	80	46	74	83	97
29434	CORDESVILLE	94	61	91	58	61	92	66	83	76	62	74	64	49	77	61	84	49	78	87	102
29435	COTTAGEVILLE	86	66	76	64	66	83	66	77	72	65	71	58	56	75	63	78	48	73	80	93
29436	CROSS	72	47	69	44	47	71	50	63	58	48	57	49	38	59	47	65	37	59	67	78
29437	DORCHESTER	85	60	73	58	60	82	63	74	70	61	69	57	50	73	57	77	46	70	78	91
29438	EDISTO ISLAND	120	93	133	90	99	128	93	115	104	95	102	83	82	101	95	113	68	108	123	137
29440	GEORGETOWN	87	69	80	67	68	87	71	80	77	69	76	60	62	78	68	83	51	77	86	97
29445	GOOSE CREEK	100	96	79	96	90	87	98	92	95	100	96	74	95	101	91	92	67	93	88	108
29446	GREEN POND	86	56	83	53	56	85	60	76	69	57	68	59	45	71	56	78	45	71	80	93
29448	HARLEYVILLE	92	62	85	59	62	89	66	81	75	63	73	63	50	77	61	83	49	76	85	99
29449	HOLLYWOOD	98	71	94	68	71	96	72	88	81	70	79	67	59	82	69	88	53	83	92	107
29450	HUGER	81	53	78	50	53	79	57	71	65	54	64	55	43	66	53	72	42	67	75	87
29451	ISLE OF PALMS	157	213	255	219	237	195	185	194	167	204	166	146	220	161	218	158	124	181	171	213
29453	JAMESTOWN	76	50	74	47	50	75	53	67	61	51	60	52	40	62	50	69	40	63	71	83
29455	JOHNS ISLAND	112	93	112	91	95	116	92	107	99	91	98	79	83	99	92	106	66	102	113	127
29456	LADSON	97	97	82	93	92	89	90	91	89	95	90	68	88	93	87	88	62	89	87	106
29458	MC CLELLANVILLE	88	60	88	58	62	88	63	80	71	59	70	61	49	71	61	79	46	74	84	96
29461	MONCKS CORNER	90	77	80	75	75	88	76	83	80	76	80	63	69	82	73	84	54	81	86	100
29464	MOUNT PLEASANT	121	138	132	141	137	126	129	126	123	133	124	100	138	125	134	119	89	124	119	146
29466	MOUNT PLEASANT	160	189	165	194	184	163	162	164	152	176	154	134	180	161	170	143	112	153	143	186
29468	PINEVILLE	75	49	73	46	49	74	52	66	61	50	59	52	39	62	49	68	39	62	70	81
29469	PINOPOLIS	111	78	119	75	81	112	82	103	91	77	89	78	65	90	81	100	59	96	107	124
29470	RAVENEL	89	75	76	72	74	85	73	81	78	74	77	60	65	80	69	82	52	78	82	97
29471	REEVESVILLE	91	59	88	56	59	89	64	80	73	60	72	63	48	75	59	82	47	75	85	99
29472	RIDGEVILLE	88	64	80	61	64	85	66	78	73	65	72	60	54	75	62	80	48	74	81	95
29474	ROUND O	84	61	81	58	61	83	63	76	69	60	68	58	50	70	60	76	45	72	79	92
29475	RUFFIN	81	58	76	55	58	79	60	72	67	58	66	55	48	68	57	73	44	68	75	88
29477	SAINT GEORGE	82	54	79	50	53	80	57	72	66	54	64	56	43	67	53	74	43	68	76	89
29479	SAINT STEPHEN	83	55	79	52	55	81	58	73	67	56	66	57	44	68	54	75	44	69	77	90
29481	SMOAKS	74	48	71	46	49	72	52	65	59	49	58	51	39	60	48	66	38	61	69	80
29482	SULLIVANS ISLAND	160	201	235	205	221	173	191	189	167	205	168	151	209	162	213	153	125	182	159	210
29483	SUMMERVILLE	94	90	79	88	86	89	87	88	88	89	88	67	84	91	84	88	61	87	88	105
29485	SUMMERVILLE	106	104	95	103	101	102	100	102	100	102	100	77	98	103	98	100	69	100	100	120
29487	WADMALAW ISLAND	100	71	102	69	74	101	73	93	81	68	80	70	59	81	73	89	53	86	97	111
29488	WALTERBORO	78	65	68	63	64	75	66	72	71	66	70	54	59	72	63	74	47	71	75	86
29492	CHARLESTON	126	137	110	131	127	111	121	120	113	131	116	95	123	123	118	106	81	113	103	136
29501	FLORENCE	99	96	88	97	94	96	97	95	98	98	98	73	96	99	94	99	69	97	98	113
29505	FLORENCE	100	101	92	99	98	100	94	97	95	97	95	73	94	97	93	96	66	95	97	114
29506	FLORENCE	67	57	54	57	55	63	61	61	65	61	65	46	57	65	56	68	44	63	67	75
29510	ANDREWS	72	49	66	47	49	70	52	63	60	50	58	49	40	61	48	66	39	60	68	78
29511	AYNOR	87	67	77	65	67	84	68	78	73	67	72	59	57	75	64	79	49	74	81	94
	SOUTH CAROLINA	95	83	86	82	82	92	85	89	88	84	88	68	79	90	81	91	60	88	92	106
	UNITED STATES	100	100	100	100	100	100	100	100	100	100	100	100	100	100	100	100	100	100	100	100

ZIP CODE			POPULATION			2000-2009 ANNUAL RATE		HOUSEHOLDS					FAMILIES		
#	POST OFFICE NAME	COUNTY FIPS CODE	2000	2009	2014	% Rate	State Centile	2000	2009	2014	% Annual Rate 2000-2009	2009 Average HH Size	2000	2009	% Annual Rate 2000-2009
29512	BENNETTSVILLE	069	19280	19638	18926	0.2	34	6860	6593	6387	-0.4	2.46	4775	4404	-0.9
29516	BLENHEIM	069	654	633	621	-0.4	12	282	289	287	0.3	2.19	182	177	-0.3
29518	CADES	089	1234	1150	1116	-0.8	5	453	449	440	-0.1	2.46	341	328	-0.4
29520	CHERAW	025	13735	13640	13468	-0.1	21	5384	5561	5548	0.4	2.38	3754	3721	-0.1
29525	CLIO	069	2041	1901	1830	-0.8	5	755	747	729	-0.1	2.54	535	509	-0.5
29526	CONWAY	051	30465	39788	46096	2.9	93	11456	15708	18514	3.5	2.45	8342	10956	3.0
29527	CONWAY	051	18279	22365	25415	2.2	88	6670	8631	9957	2.8	2.54	4942	6119	2.3
29530	COWARD	041	2167	2543	2713	1.7	83	845	1019	1099	2.0	2.50	632	734	1.6
29532	DARLINGTON	031	19851	19627	19423	-0.1	21	7649	7550	7495	-0.1	2.52	5263	4976	-0.6
29536	DILLON	033	17031	16646	16383	-0.2	18	6202	6326	6307	0.2	2.60	4380	4294	-0.2
29540	DARLINGTON	031	5703	5790	5786	0.2	34	2042	2079	2086	0.2	2.77	1531	1504	-0.2
29541	EFFINGHAM	041	8415	9011	9348	0.7	56	2912	3213	3369	1.1	2.68	2237	2383	0.7
29543	FORK	033	711	692	684	-0.3	15	238	243	243	0.2	2.39	173	170	-0.2
29544	GALIVANTS FERRY	051	4439	5272	5890	1.9	85	1677	2102	2381	2.5	2.50	1234	1479	2.0
29545	GREEN SEA	051	1333	1631	1835	2.2	88	527	680	776	2.8	2.40	379	466	2.3
29546	GRESHAM	067	2838	2901	2864	0.2	34	982	1050	1051	0.7	2.76	730	753	0.3
29547	HAMER	033	2987	3256	3331	0.9	64	997	1142	1185	1.5	2.85	779	864	1.1
29550	HARTSVILLE	031	31807	31635	31385	-0.1	21	12398	12371	12327	0.0	2.49	8850	8491	-0.4
29554	HEMINGWAY	043	10209	10007	9902	-0.2	18	3790	3906	3906	0.3	2.56	2827	2815	0.0
29555	JOHNSONVILLE	041	6200	6460	6611	0.4	43	2243	2397	2478	0.7	2.69	1733	1789	0.3
29556	KINGSTREE	089	15495	14538	14067	-0.7	7	5753	5735	5628	0.0	2.50	4138	3971	-0.4
29560	LAKE CITY	041	13952	13282	13096	-0.5	9	5123	5040	5015	-0.2	2.62	3776	3578	-0.6
29563	LAKE VIEW	033	2549	2570	2562	0.1	29	989	1050	1063	0.6	2.39	693	705	0.2
29564	LANE	089	875	931	928	0.7	56	326	360	364	1.1	2.59	242	259	0.7
29565	LATTA	033	6235	6171	6088	-0.1	21	2343	2421	2424	0.4	2.55	1728	1718	-0.1
29566	LITTLE RIVER	051	11477	15911	18786	3.6	95	5051	7361	8810	4.2	2.16	3561	4936	3.6
29567	LITTLE ROCK	033	432	479	491	1.1	70	132	153	159	1.6	3.00	102	115	1.3
29568	LONGS	051	7593	14472	17867	7.2	98	2862	5794	7242	7.9	2.50	2099	4106	7.5
29569	LORIS	051	13834	16898	19243	2.2	88	5187	6657	7678	2.7	2.52	3821	4692	2.2
29570	MC COLL	069	4282	3922	3736	-0.9	3	1617	1554	1501	-0.4	2.52	1142	1053	-0.9
29571	MARION	067	17726	17242	16801	-0.3	15	6642	6758	6673	0.2	2.53	4785	4686	-0.2
29572	MYRTLE BEACH	051	8045	9577	10705	1.9	85	4109	5116	5792	2.4	1.84	2128	2473	1.6
29574	MULLINS	067	12654	11826	11403	-0.7	7	4816	4717	4610	-0.2	2.47	3383	3179	-0.7
29575	MYRTLE BEACH	051	15430	16866	18385	1.0	69	7148	8240	9097	1.5	2.04	4679	5113	1.0
29576	MURRELLS INLET	043	16186	25281	29596	4.9	97	7745	12380	14603	5.2	2.04	5080	8052	5.1
29577	MYRTLE BEACH	051	22897	25768	28198	1.3	76	10247	11996	13295	1.7	2.13	5457	5910	0.9
29579	MYRTLE BEACH	051	9192	21184	27027	9.4	99	3795	9422	12206	10.3	2.25	2395	5484	9.4
29580	NESMITH	089	1942	1840	1792	-0.6	8	635	643	635	0.1	2.86	491	482	-0.2
29581	NICHOLS	051	5112	5451	5722	0.7	56	1993	2215	2357	1.1	2.46	1409	1495	0.6
29582	NORTH MYRTLE BEACH	051	12183	15266	17459	2.5	90	5864	7796	9059	3.1	1.96	3447	4281	2.4
29583	PAMPLICO	041	5317	5730	5961	0.8	61	1989	2198	2309	1.1	2.59	1523	1623	0.7
29584	PATRICK	025	2242	2317	2324	0.4	43	873	945	960	0.9	2.44	617	642	0.4
29585	PAWLEYS ISLAND	043	10266	13217	14575	2.8	92	4516	6106	6804	3.3	2.16	3313	4330	2.9
29588	MYRTLE BEACH	051	23909	33382	39832	3.7	96	9419	13823	16741	4.2	2.41	6677	9317	3.7
29590	SALTERS	089	2862	4457	4374	4.9	97	1026	1021	1002	-0.1	2.66	748	716	-0.5
29591	SCRANTON	041	5402	5613	5757	0.4	43	1990	2130	2207	0.7	2.56	1492	1539	0.3
29592	SELLERS	033	865	879	874	0.2	34	326	349	352	0.7	2.52	236	243	0.3
29593	SOCIETY HILL	031	2806	3019	3061	0.8	61	1049	1153	1177	1.0	2.61	778	823	0.6
29596	WALLACE	069	2453	2465	2437	0.1	29	925	979	981	0.6	2.52	680	692	0.2
29601	GREENVILLE	045	9696	9678	9890	0.0	25	4262	4410	4575	0.4	1.90	1888	1743	-0.9
29605	GREENVILLE	045	30850	33510	35241	0.9	64	12989	14394	15226	1.1	2.33	8215	8621	0.5
29607	GREENVILLE	045	28939	32414	34524	1.2	73	12617	14463	15532	1.5	2.18	7412	7904	0.7
29609	GREENVILLE	045	29207	31130	32673	0.7	56	11035	12084	12831	1.0	2.36	7035	7261	0.3
29611	GREENVILLE	045	28366	29248	30209	0.3	38	11084	11708	12190	0.6	2.47	7529	7543	0.0
29613	GREENVILLE	045	2315	2376	2386	0.3	38	9	10	11	1.1	2.60	7	7	0.0
29615	GREENVILLE	045	32132	36725	39561	1.5	78	14660	17024	18440	1.6	2.13	8395	9101	0.9
29617	GREENVILLE	045	23620	25824	27332	1.0	69	9567	10608	11293	1.1	2.40	6411	6719	0.5
29620	ABBEVILLE	001	13128	12760	12455	-0.3	15	5170	5183	5107	0.0	2.42	3691	3557	-0.4
29621	ANDERSON	007	32191	37752	40405	1.7	83	12641	15068	16241	1.9	2.41	8907	10227	1.5
29624	ANDERSON	007	15729	15518	15568	-0.1	21	6269	6288	6351	0.0	2.38	4034	3837	-0.5
29625	ANDERSON	007	23525	26348	27797	1.2	73	9682	11055	11739	1.4	2.34	6603	7222	1.0
29626	ANDERSON	007	11726	12378	12790	0.6	50	4648	4992	5191	0.8	2.48	3483	3597	0.3
29627	BELTON	007	17859	18771	19430	0.5	47	7090	7587	7906	0.7	2.45	5272	5417	0.3
29628	CALHOUN FALLS	001	3136	2952	2859	-0.7	7	1233	1200	1174	-0.3	2.45	898	841	-0.7
29630	CENTRAL	077	11854	13524	14298	1.4	76	4836	5660	6027	1.7	2.33	2785	3054	1.0
29631	CLEMSON	077	11707	12474	12875	0.7	56	4890	5358	5569	1.0	2.30	2258	2340	0.4
29632	CLEMSON	077	6067	5521	5523	-1.0	2	18	20	21	1.1	2.20	11	12	0.9
29635	CLEVELAND	045	1341	1514	1614	1.3	76	545	632	679	1.6	2.37	399	443	1.1
29638	DONALDS	001	3225	3389	3398	0.5	47	1282	1378	1391	0.8	2.24	913	942	0.3
29639	DUE WEST	001	1602	1655	1644	0.4	43	448	470	469	0.5	2.95	320	323	0.1
29640	EASLEY	077	29214	30261	30966	0.4	43	11439	12202	12573	0.7	2.47	8428	8661	0.3
29642	EASLEY	007	24313	28609	30811	1.8	83	9127	11051	11976	2.1	2.57	7061	8291	1.8
29643	FAIR PLAY	073	2472	2840	3028	1.5	78	1043	1222	1312	1.7	2.31	780	880	1.3
29644	FOUNTAIN INN	059	15604	18079	19331	1.6	80	5813	6956	7517	2.0	2.57	4380	5013	1.5
29645	GRAY COURT	059	10737	11738	12041	1.0	69	3940	4423	4572	1.3	2.65	3012	3263	0.9
29646	GREENWOOD	047	28006	28005	28081	0.0	25	10723	10708	10750	0.0	2.53	7361	7041	-0.5
29649	GREENWOOD	047	23549	25784	26662	1.0	69	9230	10079	10454	1.0	2.41	6177	6457	0.5
29650	GREER	045	22075	28308	31325	2.7	91	8172	10725	11950	3.0	2.62	6147	7794	2.6
29651	GREER	045	34657	42152	46183	2.1	87	13295	16491	18191	2.4	2.54	9754	11596	1.9
29653	HODGES	047	4275	4628	4780	0.9	64	1631	1770	1833	0.9	2.59	1228	1284	0.5
29654	HONEA PATH	007	9477	9660	9777	0.2	34	3834	4006	4086	0.5	2.40	2793	2797	0.0
29655	IVA	007	7577	8131	8404	0.8	61	3042	3345	3479	1.0	2.41	2208	2323	0.6
29657	LIBERTY	077	14443	15286	15812	0.6	50	5460	5961	6215	1.0	2.55	4142	4355	0.5
29658	LONG CREEK	073	285	302	312	0.6	50	131	141	146	0.8	2.14	89	91	0.2
29659	LOWNDESVILLE	001	94	94	93	0.0	25	43	45	44	0.5	2.09	29	29	0.0
29661	MARIETTA	045	5983	6619	7038	1.1	70	2309	2618	2808	1.4	2.49	1676	1807	0.8
29662	MAULDIN	045	12175	14726	16115	2.1	87	4859	6085	6726	2.5	2.41	3449	4088	1.9
29664	MOUNTAIN REST	073	1470	1695	1804	1.6	80	658	773	829	1.8	2.19	468	528	1.3
29666	NINETY SIX	047	5889	6089	6195	0.4	43	2376	2463	2508	0.4	2.47	1731	1727	0.0
29667	NORRIS	077	372	410	429	1.1	70	152	172	182	1.3	2.38	115	125	0.9
29669	PELZER	045	11727	12828	13508	1.0	69	4617	5190	5518	1.3	2.41	3417	3675	0.8
29670	PENDLETON	007	7662	8358	8777	0.9	64	3300	3688	3905	1.2	2.26	2213	2349	0.6
29671	PICKENS	077	18096	19098	19693	0.6	50	7127	7778	8084	0.9	2.43	5204	5457	0.5
29672	SENECA	073	9445	11062	11820	1.7	83	3924	4677	5030	1.9	2.32	2867	3289	1.5
29673	PIEDMONT	045	21875	25511	27525	1.7	83	8331	9983	10867	2.0	2.54	6346	7321	1.6
	SOUTH CAROLINA					1.3					1.7	2.45			1.2
	UNITED STATES					1.0					1.1	2.59			0.9

ZIP CODE #	POST OFFICE NAME	RACE (%) White 2000	White 2009	Black 2000	Black 2009	Asian/Pacific 2000	Asian/Pacific 2009	% Hispanic Origin 2000	% Hispanic Origin 2009	2009 AGE DISTRIBUTION (%) 0-4	5-9	10-14	15-19	20-24	25-44	45-64	65-84	85+	18+	MEDIAN AGE 2009	% 2009 Males	% 2009 Females
29512	BENNETTSVILLE	39.8	38.3	57.4	58.0	0.3	0.5	0.7	0.9	5.8	5.9	5.9	6.8	7.8	31.2	25.2	9.9	1.6	78.3	36.1	55.2	44.8
29516	BLENHEIM	65.9	64.6	31.2	31.4	0.0	0.0	0.5	0.5	5.4	5.7	6.2	7.0	4.9	22.9	32.9	13.6	1.6	78.4	43.5	46.0	54.0
29518	CADES	50.7	50.6	48.5	48.6	0.0	0.0	1.1	1.0	6.0	6.3	7.0	6.9	5.1	24.3	29.8	12.2	2.4	76.4	40.6	48.0	52.0
29520	CHERAW	55.0	52.9	43.2	44.6	0.6	0.9	0.7	1.0	6.5	6.6	6.5	7.1	6.0	24.2	28.7	12.3	2.1	75.8	39.9	46.6	53.4
29525	CLIO	33.0	31.9	60.9	60.1	0.0	0.1	0.7	1.2	6.9	8.5	7.9	7.6	5.2	23.8	27.7	10.8	1.7	71.9	36.8	46.0	54.0
29526	CONWAY	80.0	77.7	16.7	17.5	0.6	0.9	2.6	4.1	6.4	6.3	6.2	7.9	7.0	26.2	26.5	12.2	1.2	77.1	37.6	49.0	51.0
29527	CONWAY	64.1	62.1	33.9	35.1	0.3	0.4	1.4	2.1	7.0	6.9	6.8	7.2	6.9	27.4	26.0	10.2	1.5	74.9	36.1	48.9	51.1
29530	COWARD	78.6	75.3	20.0	22.7	0.3	0.4	1.2	1.8	6.6	6.8	6.8	6.4	4.8	26.8	28.7	12.2	0.9	75.8	39.6	49.4	50.6
29532	DARLINGTON	51.1	50.0	47.7	48.7	0.2	0.2	1.0	1.0	6.5	6.6	6.8	7.0	5.8	26.1	26.9	12.1	2.2	75.8	38.3	47.2	52.8
29536	DILLON	48.2	46.2	47.3	47.8	0.5	0.7	1.8	2.7	7.7	7.7	7.5	7.8	6.9	25.1	25.3	10.4	1.6	72.1	34.7	46.7	53.3
29540	DARLINGTON	41.0	39.2	58.1	59.7	0.1	0.1	0.6	0.7	7.1	7.5	7.3	7.0	6.9	26.3	27.8	9.0	1.0	73.8	35.9	48.2	51.8
29541	EFFINGHAM	64.2	60.0	34.4	38.3	0.2	0.3	0.8	1.1	6.0	6.2	6.2	6.7	6.3	28.8	29.1	9.4	1.4	77.6	38.0	50.3	49.7
29543	FORK	67.0	65.5	31.5	32.8	0.0	0.0	0.4	0.6	2.9	3.0	3.5	5.1	4.2	22.5	30.8	21.5	6.5	87.6	50.8	43.9	56.1
29544	GALIVANTS FERRY	88.3	86.9	9.6	10.0	0.0	0.0	2.2	3.5	6.9	6.5	6.6	6.5	6.5	29.0	26.3	10.5	1.1	75.9	36.7	50.1	49.9
29545	GREEN SEA	74.7	72.5	22.9	24.0	0.0	0.0	1.5	2.4	5.7	6.4	6.6	7.5	6.3	24.3	27.8	13.2	2.3	76.8	39.4	48.6	51.4
29546	GRESHAM	37.9	36.3	56.3	55.1	0.2	0.2	9.6	13.7	6.5	6.3	6.1	6.3	7.2	30.0	27.0	9.4	1.2	77.4	35.5	49.9	50.1
29547	HAMER	47.4	44.9	45.5	45.9	0.1	0.2	2.9	4.3	8.8	8.0	7.4	7.8	8.4	28.2	23.7	7.2	0.6	71.3	31.4	48.1	51.9
29550	HARTSVILLE	67.3	66.9	31.2	31.5	0.3	0.3	1.2	1.4	6.5	6.7	6.9	7.2	5.9	25.0	28.1	12.0	1.7	75.6	38.8	47.8	52.2
29554	HEMINGWAY	45.8	43.0	52.9	55.4	0.1	0.1	1.1	1.3	7.0	7.3	7.5	7.5	5.7	24.5	27.7	11.3	1.5	73.6	37.6	48.2	51.8
29555	JOHNSONVILLE	65.8	61.7	32.6	36.1	0.2	0.2	1.0	1.3	7.1	7.1	7.5	7.4	6.0	25.9	27.8	10.1	1.2	73.6	36.9	48.2	51.8
29556	KINGSTREE	28.4	29.3	70.6	69.7	0.3	0.3	0.5	0.6	7.0	7.2	7.6	8.1	6.6	22.8	26.7	12.4	1.7	74.1	37.2	46.3	53.7
29560	LAKE CITY	40.8	39.0	57.8	59.2	0.4	0.5	1.3	1.8	7.0	7.0	7.4	7.6	6.5	24.4	27.1	11.2	1.8	73.9	37.2	46.0	54.0
29563	LAKE VIEW	55.6	53.6	42.2	43.5	0.2	0.3	1.5	1.9	6.3	6.5	6.7	6.6	5.6	24.2	28.7	13.1	2.1	76.4	40.3	46.2	53.8
29564	LANE	11.2	11.5	88.5	88.2	0.0	0.0	0.3	0.3	6.8	7.3	7.5	7.7	6.2	24.1	28.2	10.6	1.5	73.7	36.3	46.1	53.9
29565	LATTA	52.5	50.9	44.7	45.3	0.2	0.3	1.2	1.8	7.0	7.2	7.3	7.0	6.0	25.7	28.3	10.3	1.2	73.9	36.9	47.0	53.0
29566	LITTLE RIVER	81.5	79.0	16.8	18.7	0.3	0.4	1.1	1.6	4.6	4.9	5.3	4.9	3.2	21.3	33.0	21.2	1.7	82.0	48.9	48.7	51.3
29567	LITTLE ROCK	25.8	23.4	56.4	55.3	0.2	0.4	1.2	1.5	6.7	7.7	8.4	9.8	9.8	24.2	24.0	8.4	1.0	71.2	32.1	49.1	50.9
29568	LONGS	53.5	57.2	42.4	37.3	0.4	0.7	4.1	4.9	7.1	7.0	7.0	6.7	5.8	27.9	26.2	11.3	1.0	74.7	36.8	49.2	50.8
29569	LORIS	65.6	63.3	31.9	32.9	0.3	0.5	2.3	3.5	6.8	7.1	7.1	6.7	5.8	26.4	27.3	11.3	1.6	75.0	37.8	48.6	51.4
29570	MC COLL	57.9	54.5	27.4	26.7	0.1	0.1	1.1	1.5	7.4	7.2	7.7	7.2	6.1	25.0	27.9	10.0	1.6	73.3	36.7	47.9	52.1
29571	MARION	39.1	37.8	59.5	60.2	0.3	0.4	0.9	1.4	7.2	7.2	7.0	7.6	6.9	25.6	27.0	10.2	1.5	74.0	35.9	46.7	53.3
29572	MYRTLE BEACH	95.2	94.0	1.8	1.8	1.2	1.9	1.7	2.6	3.3	3.2	3.5	3.2	5.0	20.8	32.6	24.7	3.6	88.0	53.0	48.5	51.5
29574	MULLINS	44.6	43.0	53.6	54.5	0.4	0.5	1.3	1.9	6.5	6.8	7.0	6.9	5.7	23.8	29.2	11.9	2.1	75.5	39.2	46.1	53.9
29575	MYRTLE BEACH	95.7	94.2	1.5	1.6	1.2	1.8	1.5	2.4	3.8	3.5	3.8	4.1	4.8	21.6	32.0	24.4	2.0	86.5	51.1	48.5	51.5
29576	MURRELLS INLET	94.3	92.5	4.0	5.1	0.4	0.7	0.9	1.3	3.8	3.8	4.3	4.3	3.3	20.3	32.5	25.4	2.3	85.4	51.8	48.5	51.5
29577	MYRTLE BEACH	78.7	75.8	14.9	15.1	1.6	2.2	4.7	7.1	5.5	5.0	4.8	5.2	7.1	31.5	26.7	12.3	1.8	81.6	38.9	50.6	49.4
29579	MYRTLE BEACH	88.3	86.1	7.9	7.8	1.1	1.6	2.5	4.1	7.5	5.9	5.1	6.2	11.8	35.2	20.7	7.0	0.7	78.5	30.5	49.4	50.6
29580	NESMITH	23.6	24.0	75.3	74.8	0.4	0.4	0.5	0.5	6.7	6.9	7.2	7.0	6.5	24.3	28.8	11.1	1.5	75.1	37.3	48.3	51.7
29581	NICHOLS	64.1	62.4	33.7	34.4	0.1	0.1	2.0	3.0	6.0	6.3	6.4	6.4	5.4	24.7	30.1	13.1	1.6	77.5	40.9	48.0	52.0
29582	NORTH MYRTLE BEACH	90.3	89.4	6.1	5.6	0.7	1.0	2.6	3.9	3.7	3.6	3.9	3.8	3.3	21.2	34.8	23.4	2.3	86.4	52.3	49.5	50.5
29583	PAMPLICO	59.2	56.0	38.6	40.9	0.1	0.1	1.5	2.4	5.9	6.2	6.6	6.7	4.7	24.7	30.2	13.3	1.6	77.1	41.2	48.2	51.8
29584	PATRICK	83.2	81.9	15.3	16.1	0.0	0.0	2.2	3.1	6.1	6.0	6.1	7.9	4.9	26.2	30.6	11.5	0.8	77.1	40.2	50.4	49.6
29585	PAWLEYS ISLAND	84.8	82.6	14.3	15.9	0.3	0.4	0.6	1.0	4.0	4.4	4.8	4.6	2.6	17.6	37.0	23.1	1.9	83.6	53.0	47.9	52.1
29588	MYRTLE BEACH	86.5	83.7	8.5	9.3	1.6	2.2	3.8	5.6	6.3	6.2	6.1	5.9	5.9	28.8	27.5	12.2	1.0	77.7	38.8	49.6	50.4
29590	SALTERS	9.3	9.5	90.5	90.3	0.0	0.0	0.3	0.3	3.9	4.0	4.2	6.8	11.2	39.5	22.3	6.9	1.2	83.7	34.3	65.7	34.3
29591	SCRANTON	72.1	69.2	26.1	28.2	0.1	0.1	2.0	2.9	6.2	6.3	6.5	6.8	5.5	26.2	28.7	12.3	1.5	76.6	39.8	48.3	51.7
29592	SELLERS	58.7	57.1	38.6	39.0	0.1	0.1	2.0	3.0	7.2	7.4	7.1	6.0	5.6	26.8	29.6	9.3	1.0	74.4	37.5	48.7	51.3
29593	SOCIETY HILL	43.3	41.5	55.6	57.1	0.0	0.0	0.5	0.6	6.2	7.1	6.5	7.5	6.2	25.7	29.9	9.8	1.1	75.3	37.8	48.4	51.6
29596	WALLACE	61.1	59.9	36.3	36.5	0.0	0.0	0.6	0.9	5.9	6.0	6.5	6.7	5.5	26.0	30.5	11.8	1.2	77.4	40.0	47.5	52.5
29601	GREENVILLE	47.8	45.9	50.0	50.9	0.6	0.8	2.0	2.9	4.5	4.4	4.3	5.7	7.0	29.6	27.9	13.5	3.0	83.5	41.2	50.9	49.1
29605	GREENVILLE	51.6	51.2	45.7	45.0	0.4	0.6	2.6	3.9	6.8	6.7	6.6	6.5	6.3	26.1	27.3	11.7	2.0	75.9	38.5	47.1	52.9
29607	GREENVILLE	62.5	61.4	33.1	32.3	1.8	2.6	3.3	5.0	6.5	6.2	6.0	6.5	7.8	29.4	25.0	10.6	2.0	77.6	36.3	48.1	51.9
29609	GREENVILLE	80.5	76.9	14.7	16.2	1.7	2.4	4.4	6.7	6.0	5.8	5.8	8.5	10.0	25.5	25.0	11.2	2.3	78.9	36.1	48.1	51.9
29611	GREENVILLE	65.2	61.6	30.0	31.2	0.3	0.4	6.0	9.1	7.0	7.2	6.8	6.6	6.1	26.6	26.1	11.6	1.8	74.9	37.4	48.3	51.7
29613	GREENVILLE	93.2	91.3	4.7	5.6	1.3	1.9	1.1	1.8	0.2	0.4	0.6	40.9	53.3	1.7	1.7	1.1	0.3	98.1	20.7	43.8	56.2
29615	GREENVILLE	84.5	80.8	8.9	9.7	3.3	4.5	5.2	7.8	5.5	5.1	5.1	5.4	7.6	30.4	25.4	12.8	2.7	81.2	38.2	49.6	50.4
29617	GREENVILLE	80.8	76.8	11.8	12.2	1.4	1.9	10.6	15.2	6.9	6.6	6.3	6.1	6.1	28.8	24.6	12.5	2.0	76.7	37.4	47.9	52.1
29620	ABBEVILLE	63.8	62.0	35.0	36.4	0.3	0.4	0.6	0.9	7.0	6.9	7.0	6.7	5.8	24.2	27.7	12.4	2.4	75.0	39.2	47.5	52.5
29621	ANDERSON	79.1	78.2	18.4	18.4	1.0	1.4	1.2	1.7	6.8	6.6	6.6	7.1	6.6	24.8	26.6	12.6	2.4	76.1	38.7	47.7	52.3
29624	ANDERSON	57.2	55.3	41.1	42.4	0.2	0.2	1.0	1.6	7.0	6.8	6.7	6.6	5.9	24.0	26.3	13.9	2.7	75.6	39.4	47.6	52.4
29625	ANDERSON	81.9	80.5	16.1	16.8	0.7	0.9	0.9	1.3	6.2	6.3	6.5	6.3	5.0	27.5	27.6	12.8	1.9	77.1	40.0	48.8	51.2
29626	ANDERSON	79.5	76.8	18.9	21.1	0.3	0.4	0.9	1.3	6.6	6.6	6.5	6.1	5.5	26.1	28.2	13.2	1.3	76.7	39.8	48.7	51.3
29627	BELTON	83.6	81.5	14.8	16.5	0.2	0.2	1.1	1.7	6.7	6.9	7.0	6.2	4.8	25.9	27.9	13.2	1.6	75.6	39.8	49.0	51.0
29628	CALHOUN FALLS	51.1	49.3	47.0	48.1	0.2	0.3	1.5	2.2	6.5	6.1	7.2	7.5	5.7	23.6	28.6	12.7	2.1	75.4	40.1	49.3	50.7
29630	CENTRAL	86.5	83.7	9.3	10.1	1.9	2.8	2.3	3.6	5.3	5.0	5.5	7.3	19.9	24.4	22.1	9.0	1.4	80.9	29.5	51.8	48.2
29631	CLEMSON	80.2	76.3	11.1	11.7	6.7	9.3	1.8	2.6	3.8	3.8	4.0	6.0	30.0	21.1	18.0	10.1	3.2	85.8	26.5	51.7	48.3
29632	CLEMSON	86.0	83.8	11.0	11.8	1.7	2.5	1.1	1.7	0.0	0.0	0.0	58.2	39.9	1.4	0.3	0.1	0.0	99.7	19.3	52.6	47.4
29635	CLEVELAND	96.2	95.2	2.1	2.4	0.1	0.1	1.0	1.6	5.1	5.9	6.2	5.9	4.7	24.6	32.9	13.4	1.3	78.9	43.3	50.7	49.3
29638	DONALDS	76.4	74.0	22.0	23.7	0.2	0.4	0.9	1.3	5.9	6.1	6.7	9.4	9.4	22.9	26.3	11.6	1.8	77.7	36.6	48.4	51.6
29639	DUE WEST	79.0	76.9	20.0	21.6	0.4	0.6	1.1	1.5	4.4	4.5	5.3	11.2	12.1	18.2	25.4	14.9	4.2	81.4	39.5	46.1	53.9
29640	EASLEY	89.7	88.8	8.0	8.0	0.2	0.4	2.1	3.2	7.0	7.0	7.0	6.3	5.4	27.2	27.7	11.0	1.4	75.1	38.3	49.7	50.3
29642	EASLEY	93.2	91.9	4.8	5.4	0.5	0.8	1.6	2.4	6.8	6.8	7.0	6.4	5.1	27.3	28.8	10.3	1.4	75.3	38.8	48.7	51.3
29643	FAIR PLAY	96.4	95.2	2.1	2.3	0.3	0.5	1.3	2.2	5.6	6.1	5.9	5.3	3.7	22.7	34.6	14.9	1.2	79.2	45.4	51.2	48.8
29644	FOUNTAIN INN	79.5	76.5	18.6	20.7	0.2	0.3	1.9	3.1	7.6	7.2	7.3	6.8	5.9	28.5	26.6	9.1	1.0	73.6	36.6	49.1	50.9
29645	GRAY COURT	80.0	77.9	17.3	18.0	0.1	0.2	3.0	4.6	7.0	6.8	6.9	6.7	6.2	27.6	28.1	9.7	0.9	75.2	37.7	50.4	49.6
29646	GREENWOOD	54.1	52.7	42.7	42.6	0.4	0.6	5.0	7.1	7.2	7.0	7.0	7.6	7.5	25.1	24.4	12.0	2.2	74.3	36.0	47.5	52.5
29649	GREENWOOD	72.9	70.6	24.0	25.0	1.5	2.1	1.8	3.1	6.6	6.3	6.1	8.2	8.5	26.8	24.3	11.3	1.8	76.6	35.6	46.3	53.7
29650	GREER	86.5	83.8	7.4	7.4	3.3	4.6	3.9	6.1	6.5	6.8	7.2	7.0	5.5	27.3	29.6	8.7	1.3	74.9	38.0	48.9	51.1
29651	GREER	84.7	83.0	11.1	10.8	0.7	1.1	4.0	5.9	7.0	7.0	7.1	6.5	5.1	27.3	27.4	10.9	1.6	74.7	38.6	49.5	50.5
29653	HODGES	75.8	72.8	23.0	25.5	0.3	0.4	0.4	0.6	5.9	6.2	6.7	6.8	5.1	25.2	29.8	12.6	1.6	76.8	40.9	48.6	51.4
29654	HONEA PATH	86.4	84.5	12.2	13.5	0.2	0.3	1.0	1.5	6.4	6.5	6.7	6.2	5.1	25.0	28.3	13.9	2.0	76.6	40.6	49.1	50.9
29655	IVA	85.6	83.5	13.2	15.0	0.1	0.1	0.4	0.5	6.3	6.5	6.8	6.6	4.8	25.0	28.7	13.5	1.9	76.4	40.8	48.9	51.1
29657	LIBERTY	93.0	91.9	5.5	6.1	0.1	0.2	1.0	1.5	7.1	7.2	7.4	6.8	5.3	27.7	27.0	10.1	1.4	74.0	37.5	50.1	49.9
29658	LONG CREEK	98.6	98.0	0.0	0.0	0.0	0.3	0.4	0.7	5.6	6.0	6.3	5.6	4.3	25.8	31.8	12.9	1.7	78.1	42.7	52.6	47.4
29659	LOWNDESVILLE	90.4	89.4	7.4	7.4	0.0	0.0	1.1	1.1	7.4	7.4	7.4	5.3	5.3	24.5	29.8	11.7	1.1	73.4	38.3	48.9	51.1
29661	MARIETTA	94.3	92.3	3.5	4.1	0.2	0.2	3.7	6.1	6.4	6.6	6.8	6.1	4.8	28.0	28.2	11.4	1.7	76.3	39.4	51.0	49.0
29662	MAULDIN	74.3	70.1	21.2	23.5	2.0	2.7	2.8	4.4	7.2	6.9	6.7	5.9	5.7	30.0	25.9	10.4	1.2	75.5	37.1	48.2	51.8
29664	MOUNTAIN REST	98.4	97.9	0.3	0.4	0.3	0.3	0.9	1.4	4.7	5.1	5.4	5.1	3.7	20.9	35.9	17.5	1.6	81.6	48.0	50.9	49.1
29666	NINETY SIX	77.2	74.3	21.8	24.4	0.1	0.1	0.6	1.1	6.3	6.3	6.5	6.3	5.2	24.9	28.8	13.8	1.8	76.9	41.1	48.0	52.0
29667	NORRIS	93.8	92.7	4.6	4.9	0.0	0.2	0.8	1.2	6.8	6.8	7.1	6.3	5.1	26.6	26.8	12.9	1.5	75.4	39.2	48.0	52.0
29669	PELZER	86.6	83.7	11.6	13.8	0.2	0.3	1.0	1.6	6.3	6.5	6.7	6.3	5.3	28.0	28.3	11.4	1.4	76.6	39.1	51.6	48.4
29670	PENDLETON	74.1	71.7	24.1	25.9	0.4	0.6	0.9	1.3	6.1	5.9	6.5	6.2	5.4	27.4	27.2	13.3	1.9	77.7	39.8	49.0	51.0
29671	PICKENS	94.7	94.0	3.9	4.0	0.2	0.3	1.3	2.0	6.2	6.3	6.7	6.6	5.1	26.0	28.1	13.3	1.7	76.8	40.3	49.4	50.6
29672	SENECA	93.3	91.9	4.4	4.7	0.9	1.3	1.4	2.3	4.7	5.2	5.7	5.4	3.6	23.0	31.8	18.1	2.3	80.9	46.5	49.4	50.6
29673	PIEDMONT	80.6	78.3	17.2	18.7	0.4	0.6	1.6	2.3	6.6	6.8	7.0	6.6	5.2	26.7	29.1	10.7	1.2	75.4	38.9	49.2	50.8
	SOUTH CAROLINA	67.2	65.9	29.5	29.4	0.9	1.4	2.4	3.6	6.5	6.5	6.5	7.2	6.9	26.6	26.8	11.3	1.6	76.4	37.6	48.9	51.1
	UNITED STATES	75.1	72.0	12.3	12.7	3.8	4.6	12.5	15.7	6.8	6.7	6.6	7.1	6.9	27.0	26.0	10.9	1.9	75.7	36.9	49.2	50.8

SOUTH CAROLINA — INCOME

C 29512-29673

# (ZIP Code)	Post Office Name	2009 Per Capita Income	2009 HH Income Base	2009 Household Income Distribution (%): Less than $25,000	$25,000 to $49,999	$50,000 to $99,999	$100,000 to $149,999	$150,000 or More	Median Household Income: 2009	2014	2009 National Centile	2009 State Centile	2009 Home Value Base	2009 Home Value Distribution (%): Less than $50,000	$50,000 to $89,999	$90,000 to $174,999	$175,000 to $399,999	$400,000 or More	2009 Median Home Value
29512	BENNETTSVILLE	16593	6593	40.3	27.7	26.4	3.7	1.8	31625	32769	11	7	4573	31.1	40.5	25.1	3.0	0.3	67998
29516	BLENHEIM	21185	289	38.1	29.8	28.0	2.8	1.4	34220	36605	16	16	237	47.3	33.8	12.7	5.5	0.8	51970
29518	CADES	17020	449	39.0	24.9	29.4	5.6	1.1	35602	38114	20	23	379	33.0	37.5	22.4	5.8	1.3	71923
29520	CHERAW	19204	5561	35.2	25.6	31.0	6.1	2.0	37861	39861	26	31	3983	20.7	30.8	38.3	8.9	1.2	88287
29525	CLIO	17289	747	40.7	27.8	24.9	4.3	2.3	32461	33082	12	9	518	35.3	41.3	18.3	3.5	1.5	63438
29526	CONWAY	22939	15708	24.3	29.3	36.1	6.5	3.8	45856	47914	51	66	12086	14.9	17.9	31.7	32.0	3.5	136230
29527	CONWAY	19113	8631	31.1	30.4	31.2	4.8	2.5	39643	42908	32	41	6380	24.9	21.6	35.6	16.6	1.3	95796
29530	COWARD	16854	1019	31.1	38.8	27.1	1.4	1.7	32668	33996	13	10	882	35.5	41.2	20.0	3.4	0.0	63529
29532	DARLINGTON	18963	7550	34.4	29.2	28.5	5.0	2.9	36966	39979	23	29	5537	30.8	32.5	28.9	7.3	0.6	74107
29536	DILLON	16491	6326	40.9	27.3	26.2	3.8	1.9	32525	34615	12	9	4284	32.6	31.8	28.6	6.8	0.3	72493
29540	DARLINGTON	17062	2079	37.1	26.4	27.8	5.2	3.4	35279	39089	19	21	1759	30.6	35.1	26.9	6.7	0.7	70041
29541	EFFINGHAM	20860	3213	23.7	27.8	39.0	5.4	4.0	48653	49410	58	76	2681	28.0	29.0	34.2	7.2	1.6	82788
29543	FORK	17944	243	31.7	30.5	32.9	4.1	0.8	41062	41923	36	47	202	23.8	43.6	29.2	3.5	0.0	72381
29544	GALIVANTS FERRY	19311	2102	30.1	28.2	35.5	4.3	1.9	42129	45894	40	51	1635	27.5	22.9	30.0	18.3	1.3	89217
29545	GREEN SEA	16920	680	38.1	29.7	26.3	5.1	0.7	32614	35249	13	9	516	36.8	34.7	22.1	5.2	1.2	63725
29546	GRESHAM	16579	1050	35.3	31.1	29.2	2.7	1.6	36537	38611	22	27	849	40.5	32.4	23.1	4.0	0.0	61474
29547	HAMER	15821	1142	32.0	32.8	29.2	4.5	1.4	37580	40611	25	30	948	37.8	34.4	24.8	2.7	0.3	64630
29550	HARTSVILLE	21236	12371	32.3	26.3	30.8	6.5	4.1	41201	45231	37	48	9435	27.1	27.3	33.5	10.9	1.1	84584
29554	HEMINGWAY	17333	3906	35.5	31.8	26.4	5.0	1.4	36187	37973	21	26	3189	34.6	32.7	26.8	5.4	0.5	66080
29555	JOHNSONVILLE	18451	2397	33.3	28.4	33.1	3.0	2.1	38960	44921	30	36	1945	32.9	38.4	24.2	4.3	0.3	64581
29556	KINGSTREE	17326	5735	45.4	23.7	24.6	3.7	2.5	29308	30428	7	4	4303	29.7	35.9	26.6	7.6	0.2	71794
29560	LAKE CITY	16605	5040	41.8	24.0	28.1	3.8	2.2	33598	36378	15	13	3669	32.1	36.4	24.0	6.8	0.7	68640
29563	LAKE VIEW	18469	1050	40.1	26.8	25.7	5.3	2.1	33775	36000	15	14	810	30.6	32.3	32.3	4.3	0.4	73607
29564	LANE	12937	360	55.0	21.9	20.6	1.4	1.1	21943	22748	2	1	307	45.3	30.9	13.4	9.8	0.7	55800
29565	LATTA	17432	2421	38.3	29.7	25.5	4.3	2.1	33027	34840	13	11	1816	36.6	31.7	25.6	5.5	0.7	65366
29566	LITTLE RIVER	29827	7361	17.8	29.6	38.6	7.7	6.2	51712	52406	65	82	6042	5.0	14.8	35.7	38.4	6.2	164258
29567	LITTLE ROCK	16096	153	34.0	22.9	37.9	3.3	2.0	45555	47783	50	65	128	35.9	26.6	33.6	3.9	0.0	66667
29568	LONGS	20674	5794	28.4	27.3	36.1	6.1	2.2	43134	46797	43	57	5060	17.5	13.0	36.8	28.2	4.5	132204
29569	LORIS	17768	6657	35.7	29.4	28.4	4.6	1.9	36260	39540	21	26	5145	25.9	22.3	34.0	16.9	0.9	92393
29570	MC COLL	15873	1554	38.2	29.7	27.9	3.4	0.7	34196	36016	16	16	1097	32.9	42.1	23.1	1.9	0.0	65699
29571	MARION	18178	6758	38.7	26.1	27.8	5.1	2.3	33780	35268	15	14	4857	29.7	33.8	30.3	5.8	0.4	73329
29572	MYRTLE BEACH	42311	5116	16.8	28.6	32.9	11.3	10.5	55385	54427	72	86	3312	4.0	5.0	26.0	34.1	31.0	273077
29574	MULLINS	17357	4717	40.5	28.9	23.7	5.0	1.8	31691	33203	11	8	3421	28.9	32.7	29.2	8.8	0.5	78463
29575	MYRTLE BEACH	34808	8240	13.9	30.6	37.6	9.7	8.2	54203	54368	70	85	6170	6.9	7.2	29.0	50.3	6.5	195982
29576	MURRELLS INLET	30706	12380	16.1	33.0	39.4	7.2	4.4	50716	52221	63	79	10504	13.5	8.2	38.4	31.1	8.8	151103
29577	MYRTLE BEACH	27202	11996	24.5	31.8	32.7	6.2	4.8	44512	47154	47	62	6181	12.8	11.0	35.0	30.0	11.2	152278
29579	MYRTLE BEACH	24387	9422	20.6	34.2	36.8	5.2	3.1	45645	47736	50	66	5931	4.1	10.1	42.2	40.5	3.2	164173
29580	NESMITH	13888	643	41.8	24.1	31.3	2.0	0.8	31744	32912	11	8	579	43.0	25.9	26.4	4.5	0.2	59419
29581	NICHOLS	18763	2215	35.6	28.1	28.1	6.0	2.1	35972	39053	20	25	1695	31.8	33.2	26.0	8.7	0.4	71327
29582	NORTH MYRTLE BEACH	32812	7796	19.2	29.4	37.0	8.5	5.9	50919	51816	63	80	5598	9.1	7.1	29.0	42.8	12.0	189386
29583	PAMPLICO	17891	2198	34.3	27.8	31.3	4.4	2.3	40405	45277	34	44	1790	25.8	37.5	30.8	5.6	0.3	71824
29584	PATRICK	17464	945	36.2	32.7	24.6	4.3	2.2	34007	34720	16	15	831	39.6	30.7	25.3	3.5	1.0	63554
29585	PAWLEYS ISLAND	39767	6106	16.7	20.1	38.6	13.8	10.8	64379	62839	83	93	5096	5.7	5.0	22.1	47.8	19.5	241875
29588	MYRTLE BEACH	23459	13823	17.3	31.8	41.2	7.6	2.1	50595	51127	63	79	10274	13.1	11.4	42.5	30.1	2.9	146118
29590	SALTERS	12259	1021	49.0	25.2	22.9	2.4	0.6	25642	27326	4	1	863	51.6	27.5	15.3	5.6	0.1	47589
29591	SCRANTON	17567	2130	31.2	29.8	33.9	3.7	1.4	38443	42320	28	33	1706	35.3	35.5	23.8	5.2	0.2	64890
29592	SELLERS	16930	349	37.0	29.8	27.5	4.9	0.9	35711	38491	20	24	281	38.8	32.4	24.2	3.6	1.1	62708
29593	SOCIETY HILL	16556	1153	38.5	26.7	29.6	2.9	2.3	34324	37218	16	17	949	36.4	30.7	27.4	5.4	0.2	64722
29596	WALLACE	17927	979	32.1	32.6	27.8	6.0	1.5	38715	41538	29	34	808	33.2	43.7	22.9	0.2	0.0	62870
29601	GREENVILLE	22691	4410	46.7	26.0	17.8	4.6	4.9	28192	29727	6	3	1695	10.5	25.2	24.8	23.4	16.1	131865
29605	GREENVILLE	25725	14394	29.7	28.7	29.4	6.7	5.5	41230	44822	37	48	9394	16.2	26.2	32.4	19.1	6.0	99528
29607	GREENVILLE	28844	14463	24.7	26.1	33.2	10.1	5.8	49014	52493	59	76	6947	3.7	15.3	47.1	27.7	6.2	137779
29609	GREENVILLE	23462	12084	27.8	27.6	32.0	7.7	4.8	44043	47599	46	60	7624	8.8	22.3	40.5	24.6	3.8	127332
29611	GREENVILLE	18224	11708	35.3	30.0	27.9	5.1	1.6	35992	38442	21	25	7231	25.4	39.7	27.5	6.6	0.9	75193
29613	GREENVILLE	10551	10	0.0	40.0	30.0	20.0	10.0	75000	66742	89	96	7	0.0	14.3	57.1	28.6	0.0	145833
29615	GREENVILLE	37288	17024	15.9	25.1	37.7	11.2	10.1	58707	61015	76	89	8903	1.3	5.4	36.6	46.5	10.3	192109
29617	GREENVILLE	20835	10608	28.3	32.0	32.5	5.2	2.0	39852	43416	32	42	6556	16.3	26.2	45.3	11.1	1.1	96188
29620	ABBEVILLE	19655	5183	30.7	30.3	31.6	5.4	2.0	40467	42081	34	44	4045	25.8	25.9	34.0	13.3	1.0	87545
29621	ANDERSON	27123	15068	22.0	24.4	37.1	10.4	6.1	53009	52598	68	83	10802	6.7	14.2	44.2	30.9	4.0	136651
29624	ANDERSON	15292	6288	45.8	27.8	23.0	2.6	0.9	28181	30320	6	3	3730	38.3	39.7	19.2	2.8	0.0	61937
29625	ANDERSON	23981	11055	25.3	25.8	38.0	7.2	3.6	48883	50412	59	76	7913	10.7	21.9	51.4	14.2	1.7	110968
29626	ANDERSON	20746	4992	27.4	31.4	32.2	6.2	2.7	41651	45403	38	50	4207	16.5	26.8	39.3	14.8	2.5	98962
29627	BELTON	20806	7587	28.9	28.9	33.8	6.1	2.2	42521	45817	41	54	6093	19.8	32.6	35.5	10.1	2.1	87416
29628	CALHOUN FALLS	16480	1200	36.8	30.5	28.7	3.3	0.8	35711	37235	20	24	950	37.7	35.1	22.5	3.4	1.4	63012
29630	CENTRAL	19788	5660	34.3	27.9	30.6	5.2	2.0	38056	41629	27	32	3207	18.6	23.8	38.3	17.2	2.1	99625
29631	CLEMSON	25142	5358	37.9	21.3	23.6	8.6	8.5	37011	41508	24	29	2563	6.9	8.4	43.9	35.5	5.3	158082
29632	CLEMSON	10899	20	20.0	45.0	30.0	0.0	5.0	42301	43604	40	53	12	16.7	0.0	41.7	33.3	8.3	162500
29635	CLEVELAND	25097	632	24.2	23.7	42.7	6.3	3.0	51133	52571	64	80	533	21.0	20.1	32.5	19.9	6.6	100212
29638	DONALDS	21171	1378	29.9	29.1	33.3	6.2	1.5	42262	43989	40	52	1126	20.6	32.7	36.2	10.1	0.4	86300
29639	DUE WEST	16830	470	26.2	25.3	39.6	6.6	2.3	48141	49263	57	73	380	19.5	27.6	35.5	17.4	0.0	94074
29640	EASLEY	22300	12202	24.7	28.2	38.0	6.1	3.0	46982	49360	54	70	9590	19.1	26.9	37.7	15.3	0.9	95873
29642	EASLEY	27642	11051	17.0	21.3	42.2	13.5	5.9	61934	60862	80	92	9035	9.4	10.6	48.4	28.6	2.9	137918
29643	FAIR PLAY	24015	1222	23.2	34.3	31.8	7.1	3.7	43985	46312	45	60	1074	21.9	17.8	34.4	23.0	3.0	106985
29644	FOUNTAIN INN	22629	6956	20.9	27.8	41.4	7.3	2.7	50978	52352	64	80	5637	15.4	19.1	48.8	14.1	2.5	110330
29645	GRAY COURT	20550	4423	23.0	28.9	39.1	6.7	2.3	48238	49382	57	74	3818	19.6	26.5	42.6	10.4	0.9	94000
29646	GREENWOOD	19729	10708	33.1	28.9	30.0	4.7	3.4	38490	41679	28	33	6715	16.0	34.7	34.8	12.4	2.0	89204
29649	GREENWOOD	24102	10079	23.7	27.9	35.3	8.5	4.5	48236	48303	57	74	6931	10.1	19.2	46.9	21.3	2.5	121214
29650	GREER	36641	10725	14.5	15.6	37.6	16.8	15.5	76509	77279	90	97	8166	2.7	7.7	39.9	43.2	6.5	174438
29651	GREER	23994	16491	22.7	27.5	36.8	8.2	4.8	49799	52369	61	77	12766	16.3	18.0	41.3	22.4	2.0	111991
29653	HODGES	20969	1770	23.5	32.1	35.3	6.8	2.3	45445	46244	50	65	1527	23.2	25.6	34.6	15.4	1.2	91667
29654	HONEA PATH	20279	4006	31.3	28.0	33.9	4.8	2.1	40985	45284	36	46	3248	22.2	35.7	33.6	7.5	1.0	79730
29655	IVA	18842	3345	34.8	26.2	34.3	2.9	1.9	40241	42594	33	43	2761	28.7	30.1	31.8	8.3	1.2	78184
29657	LIBERTY	19969	5961	23.4	31.0	39.2	4.9	1.5	45349	47831	49	64	4946	24.8	28.3	36.0	10.3	0.5	85575
29658	LONG CREEK	20746	141	35.5	39.0	14.9	7.8	2.8	35197	39214	18	21	120	21.7	20.0	44.2	14.2	0.0	102381
29659	LOWNDESVILLE	23574	45	31.1	26.7	33.3	4.4	4.4	38644	45000	29	34	36	38.9	30.6	19.4	8.3	2.8	58000
29661	MARIETTA	20300	2618	26.4	30.3	37.1	4.4	1.8	42637	46551	41	55	2052	28.1	28.3	29.3	12.0	2.3	80576
29662	MAULDIN	31412	6085	13.3	19.0	44.9	16.6	6.2	66941	68084	85	95	4172	1.4	5.9	63.5	28.5	0.7	146543
29664	MOUNTAIN REST	23316	773	28.2	32.2	29.2	7.5	2.8	39859	42838	32	42	670	18.7	24.6	35.8	18.1	2.8	99783
29666	NINETY SIX	21615	2463	26.5	28.9	36.7	5.7	2.2	45147	45670	49	64	1991	16.0	36.8	35.9	9.9	1.5	86847
29667	NORRIS	19591	172	23.3	37.2	36.6	2.3	0.6	42325	45647	40	53	146	39.0	33.6	21.9	5.5	0.0	60909
29669	PELZER	21982	5190	24.9	29.4	37.3	6.2	2.2	45573	48706	50	66	4271	24.0	28.2	34.4	12.4	1.1	87188
29670	PENDLETON	22385	3688	31.1	28.7	30.9	5.9	3.4	40915	45255	36	46	2591	16.8	29.9	37.6	13.0	2.7	93817
29671	PICKENS	20764	7778	27.1	29.3	36.7	5.0	1.9	43717	47080	44	59	6249	22.9	26.1	34.1	14.9	2.1	91312
29672	SENECA	30468	4677	16.1	25.2	39.8	11.6	7.3	58776	55493	76	90	3821	14.3	11.9	33.7	27.4	12.7	144899
29673	PIEDMONT	22015	9983	22.6	25.0	43.1	7.1	2.1	51633	52700	65	82	8128	19.3	25.0	39.0	15.6	1.1	99209
	SOUTH CAROLINA	24352		25.1	26.4	35.2	8.4	4.8	48210	50493				16.4	20.9	37.4	20.6	4.8	112284
	UNITED STATES	27277		20.9	24.4	35.3	11.7	7.6	54719	56938				9.3	13.1	31.6	32.6	13.5	162279

ZIP CODE		FINANCIAL SERVICES				THE HOME						ENTERTAINMENT						PERSONAL			
						Home Improvements		Furnishings													
#	POST OFFICE NAME	Auto Loan	Home Loan	Invest-ments	Retire-ment Plans	Home Repair	Lawn & Garden	Comput-ers & Hard-ware-Personal	Major Appli-ances	TV, Radio, Sound Equip-ment	Furni-ture	Dine out/ Carry out	Sports Equip-ment	Fees & Tickets	Toys & Games	Travel	Cable TV	Apparel & Services	Auto Repairs	Health Insur-ance	Pets & Supplies
29512	BENNETTSVILLE	75	54	66	53	53	73	59	67	66	56	64	51	49	66	54	71	43	65	72	82
29516	BLENHEIM	86	56	83	53	56	85	60	76	69	57	68	59	45	71	56	77	45	71	80	93
29518	CADES	79	52	76	49	51	78	55	69	64	52	62	54	41	65	51	71	41	65	73	85
29520	CHERAW	74	60	65	59	59	73	63	69	69	62	68	51	56	69	59	74	46	68	74	83
29525	CLIO	81	54	79	51	54	80	57	72	66	54	64	56	43	66	54	73	42	68	76	88
29526	CONWAY	89	81	78	79	80	86	80	84	83	82	82	62	75	84	77	85	56	83	87	100
29527	CONWAY	77	68	63	67	65	73	68	70	71	69	71	53	64	73	64	74	49	70	73	85
29530	COWARD	77	52	71	50	52	75	55	68	63	53	62	53	42	65	51	70	41	64	72	83
29532	DARLINGTON	79	64	67	63	63	76	66	72	72	66	71	54	59	73	62	76	48	71	77	87
29536	DILLON	69	55	59	54	54	67	58	63	64	58	63	47	52	64	55	69	43	63	69	76
29540	DARLINGTON	85	60	77	57	59	82	63	75	71	61	69	58	50	72	59	77	46	71	79	92
29541	EFFINGHAM	94	81	80	78	79	89	79	86	83	80	83	64	72	86	75	86	56	83	87	103
29543	FORK	83	59	83	57	61	83	61	77	67	57	66	58	48	67	60	74	44	71	80	91
29544	GALIVANTS FERRY	82	66	70	64	65	77	67	74	71	67	70	56	58	73	63	75	47	71	76	89
29545	GREEN SEA	75	50	73	47	50	74	53	66	61	50	59	52	40	61	50	67	39	62	70	81
29546	GRESHAM	77	62	68	59	60	72	63	69	67	63	67	53	55	69	59	70	45	68	70	84
29547	HAMER	79	59	71	56	57	75	61	70	67	60	66	54	50	69	57	72	44	68	73	86
29550	HARTSVILLE	88	72	77	70	71	86	73	81	79	72	78	61	65	80	69	84	53	78	86	97
29554	HEMINGWAY	81	55	78	52	55	80	58	72	66	55	65	56	45	67	55	73	43	68	76	88
29555	JOHNSONVILLE	90	63	85	60	62	89	65	80	74	63	72	62	52	75	62	81	48	75	84	98
29556	KINGSTREE	74	53	70	52	54	74	57	68	65	55	63	51	47	65	54	71	42	65	74	82
29560	LAKE CITY	74	53	67	52	53	73	57	67	66	56	64	50	47	65	53	72	43	65	74	82
29563	LAKE VIEW	82	55	77	52	55	80	58	72	67	56	65	56	45	68	54	74	43	68	76	89
29564	LANE	62	41	60	38	40	61	43	55	50	41	49	43	32	51	40	56	32	51	58	67
29565	LATTA	79	56	74	53	56	78	59	71	66	56	65	55	47	67	55	73	43	67	75	86
29566	LITTLE RIVER	102	89	128	87	97	110	86	105	90	86	89	74	80	86	93	95	60	98	107	121
29567	LITTLE ROCK	90	60	86	57	60	88	64	79	73	61	71	62	49	74	60	81	47	75	83	97
29568	LONGS	82	74	67	72	73	76	73	76	75	75	75	56	68	77	69	76	51	74	76	90
29569	LORIS	76	59	68	56	58	75	60	69	67	59	65	52	51	68	57	72	44	67	73	84
29570	MC COLL	75	49	72	46	48	73	52	65	60	49	59	51	39	61	48	67	39	62	69	81
29571	MARION	76	58	65	57	57	72	63	68	69	61	68	52	54	70	58	74	46	68	73	83
29572	MYRTLE BEACH	108	106	126	106	115	117	108	112	111	115	111	78	113	105	114	114	77	114	124	130
29574	MULLINS	77	53	72	50	52	76	56	69	65	54	63	53	44	65	53	71	42	65	73	84
29575	MYRTLE BEACH	100	102	123	100	111	114	96	107	99	103	98	72	100	93	104	103	67	104	116	123
29576	MURRELLS INLET	91	90	113	87	97	105	84	98	87	87	86	68	85	82	92	91	58	93	104	112
29577	MYRTLE BEACH	85	75	76	76	75	78	84	80	85	83	85	62	79	84	79	86	59	84	84	96
29579	MYRTLE BEACH	85	63	56	68	59	61	83	69	82	82	83	58	72	85	70	80	58	79	70	86
29580	NESMITH	74	48	71	45	48	72	52	65	59	49	58	51	39	60	48	66	38	61	69	80
29581	NICHOLS	85	57	81	54	57	83	60	75	69	57	67	58	46	70	56	77	45	71	79	92
29582	NORTH MYRTLE BEACH	95	87	116	87	96	105	87	99	91	89	89	69	85	85	93	95	61	96	106	115
29583	PAMPLICO	84	58	84	56	60	84	61	77	68	57	67	58	48	69	59	76	44	71	80	92
29584	PATRICK	79	52	75	49	52	77	56	69	64	53	62	54	42	65	52	71	41	65	73	85
29585	PAWLEYS ISLAND	132	119	178	117	134	150	114	140	119	116	118	96	110	111	127	126	79	131	145	161
29588	MYRTLE BEACH	86	81	78	79	81	83	80	82	81	83	81	60	77	82	78	82	56	81	84	97
29590	SALTERS	65	43	63	40	42	64	45	57	52	43	51	45	34	53	42	59	34	54	61	70
29591	SCRANTON	83	57	75	55	57	81	60	73	68	58	67	56	47	70	56	75	44	69	77	89
29592	SELLERS	78	53	70	51	53	76	56	68	64	54	62	53	44	66	52	70	42	64	72	84
29593	SOCIETY HILL	80	53	74	51	53	78	57	70	65	54	63	54	43	66	52	72	42	66	74	86
29596	WALLACE	82	57	73	55	57	79	60	72	68	58	66	56	47	70	55	74	44	68	76	88
29601	GREENVILLE	64	53	54	56	53	61	65	60	70	63	69	45	61	66	60	74	48	66	72	75
29605	GREENVILLE	88	80	78	81	78	88	83	84	87	82	87	63	80	87	80	91	60	86	92	102
29607	GREENVILLE	93	82	77	85	79	82	92	85	94	92	94	67	88	94	86	94	66	91	89	102
29609	GREENVILLE	83	79	73	80	77	81	82	80	84	82	84	62	80	84	79	86	58	83	85	96
29611	GREENVILLE	73	57	60	57	56	70	63	67	68	60	66	51	54	68	58	72	45	66	72	81
29613	GREENVILLE	119	148	132	148	143	146	126	132	128	128	129	99	145	129	140	131	91	129	139	153
29615	GREENVILLE	115	105	101	110	103	102	117	106	116	117	117	85	114	117	111	114	82	113	108	128
29617	GREENVILLE	77	65	64	66	64	75	72	73	75	67	73	56	64	75	66	78	50	73	78	87
29620	ABBEVILLE	81	61	73	60	61	79	65	74	71	62	70	56	55	72	61	77	47	71	79	89
29621	ANDERSON	98	94	90	95	93	98	94	96	96	94	96	73	92	97	92	98	66	95	99	113
29624	ANDERSON	59	45	46	45	44	56	50	53	56	50	54	39	44	56	45	60	37	54	59	65
29625	ANDERSON	85	79	74	79	77	88	79	83	82	76	81	63	75	83	77	86	56	82	89	99
29626	ANDERSON	82	70	72	70	70	81	72	77	75	69	74	59	65	76	69	78	50	75	80	92
29627	BELTON	86	68	77	66	68	86	69	79	75	67	74	60	60	77	66	81	50	76	84	95
29628	CALHOUN FALLS	72	50	66	49	51	71	54	65	60	50	59	50	42	61	50	66	39	61	70	78
29630	CENTRAL	74	55	56	57	54	63	72	64	71	64	70	53	59	72	60	72	49	68	67	79
29631	CLEMSON	85	64	62	68	62	67	98	73	90	83	90	64	79	89	76	87	63	85	76	91
29632	CLEMSON	71	58	60	60	59	66	73	67	71	65	70	52	62	70	63	72	48	70	71	80
29635	CLEVELAND	100	81	99	81	83	103	81	96	87	76	85	72	70	87	81	93	57	90	99	114
29638	DONALDS	89	64	80	62	65	87	66	80	74	63	72	61	53	75	62	80	48	75	84	96
29639	DUE WEST	88	69	82	69	71	87	73	82	78	69	76	62	62	78	70	83	52	79	87	98
29640	EASLEY	90	76	75	74	75	86	77	82	81	76	80	62	69	83	72	85	54	80	86	98
29642	EASLEY	105	108	97	108	105	106	101	104	100	103	101	79	102	103	101	101	70	101	102	122
29643	FAIR PLAY	90	75	99	72	81	95	74	89	80	75	78	63	67	77	77	85	52	84	95	104
29644	FOUNTAIN INN	94	83	76	81	80	88	82	86	85	83	85	64	76	89	77	88	58	84	87	103
29645	GRAY COURT	94	74	77	72	73	88	75	83	81	75	80	63	64	84	69	85	54	80	86	100
29646	GREENWOOD	78	65	67	65	64	76	70	73	75	68	74	55	64	75	66	79	51	74	79	88
29649	GREENWOOD	90	81	75	82	79	84	88	84	88	85	88	65	81	89	81	89	61	86	87	101
29650	GREER	136	149	139	151	147	138	138	139	133	143	134	109	145	137	141	130	95	134	130	160
29651	GREER	95	87	82	86	85	94	85	90	89	85	88	67	81	91	82	92	60	88	94	107
29653	HODGES	92	74	80	74	74	92	74	85	80	71	78	65	64	82	71	86	53	80	89	102
29654	HONEA PATH	83	64	75	62	64	84	65	76	72	63	71	57	56	73	62	78	48	72	82	91
29655	IVA	82	58	77	56	59	81	60	74	68	58	66	56	48	69	57	74	44	69	77	89
29657	LIBERTY	89	69	73	67	68	84	69	78	75	69	74	59	59	79	64	81	50	75	81	95
29658	LONG CREEK	80	57	78	55	59	80	59	73	65	55	64	55	47	65	57	71	42	68	76	88
29659	LOWNDESVILLE	89	64	73	62	63	84	66	77	74	65	72	59	53	77	60	80	49	73	81	94
29661	MARIETTA	91	66	78	65	67	87	69	80	76	67	74	61	56	78	64	82	50	76	84	97
29662	MAULDIN	107	115	101	114	110	106	109	106	106	111	108	83	112	110	109	105	75	106	104	124
29664	MOUNTAIN REST	88	67	100	66	72	90	68	85	73	64	72	63	57	72	70	79	48	79	86	100
29666	NINETY SIX	90	71	86	69	71	91	72	84	78	69	77	64	62	79	70	85	52	80	89	101
29667	NORRIS	84	61	69	59	60	80	63	73	70	62	68	56	51	73	57	76	46	69	77	89
29669	PELZER	92	71	77	70	71	89	73	83	79	71	78	63	62	82	68	85	53	79	87	100
29670	PENDLETON	82	65	74	64	65	82	70	77	75	65	73	59	60	75	66	80	50	75	83	92
29671	PICKENS	88	66	77	65	66	87	68	80	75	65	74	61	56	77	64	82	50	75	85	96
29672	SENECA	110	101	126	101	105	120	97	112	101	95	100	83	93	99	102	106	68	106	115	131
29673	PIEDMONT	92	79	80	77	77	89	77	85	81	77	81	64	70	84	74	85	55	82	87	102
	SOUTH CAROLINA	95	83	86	82	82	92	85	89	88	84	88	68	79	90	81	91	60	88	92	106
	UNITED STATES	100	100	100	100	100	100	100	100	100	100	100	100	100	100	100	100	100	100	100	100

ZIP CODE			POPULATION			2000-2009 ANNUAL RATE		HOUSEHOLDS					FAMILIES		
#	POST OFFICE NAME	COUNTY FIPS CODE	2000	2009	2014	% Rate	State Centile	2000	2009	2014	% Annual Rate 2000-2009	2009 Average HH Size	2000	2009	% Annual Rate 2000-2009
29676	SALEM	073	4818	5006	5070	0.4	43	2241	2361	2408	0.6	2.09	1743	1780	0.2
29678	SENECA	073	19062	21296	22380	1.2	73	7855	8926	9444	1.4	2.36	5336	5814	0.9
29680	SIMPSONVILLE	045	20272	25642	28594	2.6	90	6977	9017	10125	2.8	2.77	5492	6853	2.4
29681	SIMPSONVILLE	045	29977	43340	49257	4.1	96	10862	15906	18166	4.2	2.71	8762	12423	3.8
29682	SIX MILE	077	3434	3877	4097	1.3	76	1269	1482	1577	1.7	2.59	987	1114	1.3
29684	STARR	007	4455	4667	4816	0.5	47	1670	1782	1848	0.7	2.62	1265	1295	0.3
29685	SUNSET	077	880	1006	1066	1.5	78	378	450	481	1.9	2.21	280	320	1.5
29686	TAMASSEE	073	1084	1209	1270	1.2	73	418	476	505	1.4	2.52	309	339	1.0
29687	TAYLORS	045	35614	40523	43413	1.4	76	14205	16550	17863	1.7	2.44	10195	11325	1.1
29688	TIGERVILLE	045	82	98	106	1.9	85	31	38	42	2.2	2.58	23	27	1.7
29689	TOWNVILLE	007	3841	4390	4686	1.5	78	1599	1870	2013	1.7	2.35	1163	1300	1.2
29690	TRAVELERS REST	045	17662	19678	20988	1.2	73	6368	7316	7881	1.5	2.59	4829	5306	1.0
29691	WALHALLA	073	11064	11563	11820	0.5	47	4406	4653	4781	0.6	2.46	3166	3214	0.2
29692	WARE SHOALS	059	4956	5092	5111	0.3	38	2020	2104	2123	0.4	2.40	1403	1398	0.0
29693	WESTMINSTER	073	13434	14108	14489	0.5	47	5434	5806	6007	0.7	2.42	3930	4049	0.3
29696	WEST UNION	073	3350	3917	4182	1.7	83	1318	1565	1681	1.9	2.50	1001	1147	1.5
29697	WILLIAMSTON	007	10409	11653	12359	1.2	73	3966	4489	4783	1.3	2.60	3038	3317	1.0
29702	BLACKSBURG	021	9704	9906	10018	0.2	34	3845	4077	4171	0.6	2.43	2743	2793	0.2
29704	CATAWBA	091	3292	3867	4298	1.8	83	1170	1427	1603	2.2	2.67	933	1099	1.8
29706	CHESTER	023	21000	19644	18908	-0.7	7	7939	7726	7526	-0.3	2.51	5701	5338	-0.7
29707	FORT MILL	057	5241	12256	15013	9.6	100	2003	4860	6025	10.1	2.52	1519	3546	9.6
29708	FORT MILL	091	10617	22833	28761	8.6	99	3812	8390	10605	8.9	2.72	2942	6218	8.4
29709	CHESTERFIELD	025	6028	6562	6710	0.9	64	2454	2785	2887	1.4	2.33	1692	1839	0.9
29710	CLOVER	091	21488	27574	31568	2.7	91	8277	11042	12785	3.2	2.49	6324	8056	2.7
29712	EDGEMOOR	023	2147	2302	2335	0.8	61	806	903	926	1.2	2.55	616	665	0.8
29714	FORT LAWN	023	2736	2793	2759	0.2	34	1005	1074	1075	0.7	2.57	742	762	0.3
29715	FORT MILL	091	14700	22011	26340	4.5	97	5713	8601	10339	4.5	2.55	4321	6268	4.1
29717	HICKORY GROVE	091	1174	1349	1493	1.5	78	432	510	571	1.8	2.65	341	388	1.4
29718	JEFFERSON	025	3607	3606	3538	0.0	25	1383	1424	1415	0.3	2.52	1007	999	-0.1
29720	LANCASTER	057	44026	45306	46928	0.3	38	16922	18173	19076	0.8	2.46	12222	12590	0.3
29726	MC CONNELLS	091	1532	1828	2043	1.9	85	532	655	739	2.3	2.78	413	488	1.8
29727	MOUNT CROGHAN	025	1321	1363	1356	0.3	38	509	550	555	0.8	2.48	376	393	0.5
29728	PAGELAND	025	9226	9271	9168	0.1	29	3388	3542	3545	0.5	2.60	2390	2402	0.1
29729	RICHBURG	023	2222	2313	2297	0.4	43	817	890	894	0.9	2.60	628	662	0.6
29730	ROCK HILL	091	45915	55297	61772	2.0	86	16751	20932	23687	2.4	2.53	11741	14098	2.0
29732	ROCK HILL	091	39570	53491	61852	3.3	94	15035	20818	24267	3.6	2.51	10733	14376	3.2
29741	RUBY	025	1427	1449	1430	0.2	34	585	619	618	0.6	2.33	414	422	0.2
29742	SHARON	091	2104	2651	2995	2.5	90	753	979	1114	2.9	2.70	584	730	2.4
29743	SMYRNA	091	1275	1562	1739	2.2	88	485	610	685	2.5	2.56	381	462	2.1
29745	YORK	091	23255	29045	32844	2.4	89	8195	10575	12098	2.8	2.69	6278	7794	2.4
29801	AIKEN	003	26394	26878	26985	0.2	34	10264	10645	10761	0.4	2.40	6810	6720	-0.1
29803	AIKEN	003	30321	36763	39438	2.1	87	11904	14678	15849	2.3	2.49	8829	10466	1.9
29805	AIKEN	003	4775	5258	5459	1.0	69	1781	1999	2089	1.3	2.63	1351	1461	0.8
29808	AIKEN	011	76	83	83	1.0	69	26	30	30	1.6	2.77	20	22	1.0
29809	NEW ELLENTON	003	2386	2298	2269	-0.4	12	926	911	905	-0.2	2.49	647	599	-0.8
29810	ALLENDALE	005	5772	5357	5131	-0.8	5	2183	2121	2059	-0.3	2.50	1448	1344	-0.8
29812	BARNWELL	011	12202	12087	11897	-0.1	21	4706	4873	4860	0.4	2.46	3351	3340	0.0
29817	BLACKVILLE	011	5187	4806	4655	-0.8	5	1938	1900	1865	-0.2	2.47	1392	1312	-0.6
29819	BRADLEY	047	1543	1643	1690	0.7	56	567	605	624	0.7	2.64	430	443	0.3
29821	CLARKS HILL	065	956	1017	1029	0.7	56	354	394	403	1.2	2.58	273	296	0.9
29824	EDGEFIELD	037	8645	8943	8852	0.4	43	2589	2656	2649	0.3	2.43	1879	1851	-0.2
29827	FAIRFAX	005	4260	4048	3909	-0.6	8	1237	1177	1134	-0.5	2.40	836	761	-1.0
29828	GLOVERVILLE	003	1030	1081	1102	0.5	47	435	466	479	0.7	2.32	301	304	0.1
29829	GRANITEVILLE	003	7123	7582	7763	0.7	56	2715	2952	3046	0.9	2.55	1992	2096	0.6
29831	JACKSON	003	3102	3364	3479	0.9	64	1238	1364	1417	1.1	2.46	879	925	0.6
29832	JOHNSTON	037	4934	4904	4864	-0.1	21	1880	1949	1957	0.4	2.50	1340	1330	-0.1
29835	MC CORMICK	065	6912	7212	7234	0.5	47	2372	2639	2682	1.2	2.22	1722	1845	0.7
29836	MARTIN	005	488	451	431	-0.8	5	197	192	186	-0.3	2.33	130	122	-0.7
29838	MODOC	065	397	367	363	-0.8	5	186	178	178	-0.5	2.06	139	128	-0.9
29840	MOUNT CARMEL	065	1011	970	941	-0.4	12	337	350	343	0.4	2.43	270	273	0.1
29841	NORTH AUGUSTA	003	30135	31171	31567	0.4	43	12226	12871	13114	0.6	2.40	8311	8343	0.0
29842	BEECH ISLAND	003	9010	9617	9858	0.7	56	3367	3660	3779	0.9	2.63	2444	2551	0.5
29843	OLAR	009	1653	1493	1416	-1.1	2	663	639	615	-0.4	2.34	463	428	-0.8
29845	PLUM BRANCH	065	1291	1212	1179	-0.7	7	529	531	524	0.0	2.28	380	367	-0.4
29847	TRENTON	037	3879	4126	4250	0.7	56	1264	1412	1478	1.2	2.55	951	1023	0.8
29848	TROY	065	855	869	876	0.2	34	312	321	324	0.3	2.56	236	235	0.0
29849	ULMER	005	800	759	726	-0.6	8	336	334	324	-0.1	2.27	230	219	-0.5
29851	WARRENVILLE	003	8535	9220	9513	0.8	61	3476	3828	3977	1.0	2.41	2374	2474	0.4
29853	WILLISTON	011	6821	6947	6935	0.2	34	2652	2819	2847	0.7	2.44	1885	1921	0.2
29856	WINDSOR	003	2605	3097	3319	1.9	85	925	1121	1210	2.1	2.76	699	816	1.7
29860	NORTH AUGUSTA	037	10945	13493	14500	2.3	89	3791	4829	5246	2.7	2.76	3107	3856	2.4
29902	BEAUFORT	013	18387	18655	19152	0.2	34	5741	6189	6437	0.8	2.40	3844	3913	0.2
29906	BEAUFORT	013	21719	24497	26032	1.3	76	6586	7740	8314	1.8	2.96	5326	6032	1.4
29907	LADYS ISLAND	013	9321	12460	14097	3.2	94	3521	4741	5377	3.3	2.63	2690	3468	2.8
29909	OKATIE	013	5135	11505	14462	9.1	99	2505	6082	7747	10.1	1.89	1994	4540	9.3
29910	BLUFFTON	013	12422	26437	32554	8.5	98	4653	10353	12821	9.0	2.55	3419	7314	8.6
29911	BRUNSON	049	1545	1520	1499	-0.2	18	584	602	601	0.3	2.52	423	419	-0.1
29915	DAUFUSKIE ISLAND	013	279	251	288	-1.1	2	138	135	156	-0.2	1.86	101	92	-1.0
29916	EARLY BRANCH	049	1578	1651	1663	0.5	47	604	664	677	1.0	2.49	452	479	0.6
29918	ESTILL	049	7386	7017	6910	-0.6	8	2080	2107	2096	0.1	2.61	1495	1456	-0.3
29920	SAINT HELENA ISLAND	013	9486	12387	13916	2.9	93	3761	5130	5825	3.4	2.40	2755	3577	2.9
29922	GARNETT	049	578	588	585	0.2	34	189	202	204	0.7	2.91	136	141	0.4
29924	HAMPTON	049	4225	4138	4069	-0.2	18	1723	1756	1748	0.2	2.35	1173	1147	-0.2
29926	HILTON HEAD ISLAND	013	18763	23921	26530	2.7	91	7633	9720	10759	2.6	2.45	5722	7085	2.3
29927	HARDEEVILLE	053	6555	7043	7268	0.8	61	2317	2558	2663	1.1	2.75	1645	1745	0.6
29928	HILTON HEAD ISLAND	013	17169	18046	18700	0.5	47	7798	8276	8595	0.6	2.15	5012	4994	0.0
29929	ISLANDTON	029	1283	1242	1205	-0.4	12	474	480	472	0.1	2.55	329	319	-0.3
29932	LURAY	049	556	532	521	-0.5	9	203	202	200	-0.1	2.56	155	149	-0.4
29934	PINELAND	053	1251	1286	1303	0.3	38	471	506	517	0.8	2.54	339	350	0.3
29935	PORT ROYAL	013	3056	3499	3732	1.5	78	1343	1606	1729	2.0	2.09	849	949	1.2
29936	RIDGELAND	053	9821	11457	12150	1.7	83	3112	3811	4108	2.2	2.64	2260	2665	1.8
29940	SEABROOK	013	4175	4984	5461	1.9	85	1450	1784	1973	2.3	2.79	1079	1262	1.7
29941	SHELDON	013	183	394	442	8.6	99	85	188	213	9.0	2.10	60	126	8.4
29943	TILLMAN	053	2026	2145	2187	0.6	50	754	834	859	1.1	2.57	560	597	0.7
29944	VARNVILLE	049	4666	4720	4668	0.1	29	1752	1839	1844	0.5	2.55	1266	1278	0.1
	SOUTH CAROLINA					1.3					1.7	2.45			1.2
	UNITED STATES					1.0					1.1	2.59			0.9

ZIP CODE #	POST OFFICE NAME	RACE (%) White 2000	White 2009	Black 2000	Black 2009	Asian/Pacific 2000	Asian/Pacific 2009	% Hispanic Origin 2000	% Hispanic Origin 2009	2009 AGE DISTRIBUTION (%) 0-4	5-9	10-14	15-19	20-24	25-44	45-64	65-84	85+	18+	MEDIAN AGE 2009	% 2009 Males	% 2009 Females
29676	SALEM	98.4	97.8	0.5	0.7	0.2	0.3	0.7	1.2	2.9	3.3	4.0	3.9	2.6	15.4	27.4	37.7	2.8	87.4	59.6	49.6	50.4
29678	SENECA	77.1	75.8	20.7	21.1	0.4	0.6	1.3	2.0	6.8	6.8	6.7	6.1	5.4	27.5	26.5	12.3	1.8	75.8	38.2	48.5	51.5
29680	SIMPSONVILLE	83.3	80.7	13.4	14.5	1.1	1.5	2.8	4.1	8.6	8.2	7.9	6.7	6.1	32.1	24.5	5.4	0.4	70.9	33.6	50.8	49.2
29681	SIMPSONVILLE	88.2	85.3	8.7	9.9	1.4	2.2	2.4	3.7	7.9	8.2	8.5	7.2	4.4	27.0	27.8	8.1	1.0	70.7	37.1	48.8	51.2
29682	SIX MILE	98.5	98.0	0.4	0.5	0.2	0.3	0.7	1.0	6.3	6.3	6.7	6.4	5.5	25.6	29.8	11.9	1.5	76.8	40.3	50.7	49.3
29684	STARR	84.7	82.1	14.0	16.1	0.1	0.1	1.1	1.6	6.4	6.5	6.8	6.5	5.7	26.6	28.4	12.0	1.0	76.3	39.1	49.2	50.8
29685	SUNSET	97.6	96.8	0.9	1.0	0.2	0.3	0.5	0.7	5.8	5.8	6.4	6.2	5.8	25.6	31.1	12.0	1.4	78.4	41.5	51.3	48.7
29686	TAMASSEE	98.0	97.4	0.7	0.8	0.1	0.1	0.8	1.3	4.9	5.4	6.1	6.1	4.4	24.2	32.3	15.2	1.3	79.7	44.2	50.5	49.5
29687	TAYLORS	83.5	80.2	11.9	13.4	2.0	2.7	3.4	5.2	6.6	6.7	6.9	6.6	5.6	27.5	27.5	11.2	1.3	75.6	38.2	48.9	51.1
29688	TIGERVILLE	97.6	98.0	1.2	1.0	0.0	0.0	1.2	1.0	6.1	6.1	7.1	6.1	4.1	24.5	33.7	11.2	1.0	76.5	42.1	49.0	51.0
29689	TOWNVILLE	93.3	91.8	5.6	6.6	0.3	0.4	1.1	1.6	5.4	5.6	5.9	5.2	3.7	23.5	33.9	15.4	1.3	79.7	45.3	51.3	48.7
29690	TRAVELERS REST	89.5	87.1	8.4	9.7	0.5	0.7	1.7	2.8	6.4	6.5	6.7	8.2	7.2	25.5	28.0	10.2	1.2	76.3	37.1	50.3	49.7
29691	WALHALLA	91.6	88.9	3.3	3.2	0.3	0.4	7.3	11.1	6.3	6.4	6.7	6.5	5.5	25.8	27.9	13.1	1.6	76.5	39.7	49.8	50.2
29692	WARE SHOALS	81.9	80.0	16.7	18.0	0.2	0.3	0.9	1.5	6.7	6.8	7.0	6.7	5.5	24.4	27.6	13.1	2.2	75.1	39.5	48.0	52.0
29693	WESTMINSTER	93.4	92.2	4.9	5.2	0.2	0.3	1.3	2.2	6.4	6.5	7.0	6.3	5.0	26.1	28.2	12.9	1.5	76.2	39.8	49.5	50.5
29696	WEST UNION	95.2	94.2	2.4	2.2	0.2	0.2	3.5	5.2	5.2	5.6	6.1	6.1	4.6	25.2	31.5	14.5	1.2	79.3	43.0	49.4	50.6
29697	WILLIAMSTON	89.0	86.8	8.6	9.7	0.2	0.2	2.4	3.6	7.0	7.1	7.2	6.7	5.1	27.1	27.3	11.2	1.3	74.5	38.3	50.0	50.0
29702	BLACKSBURG	87.5	85.1	9.7	10.5	0.1	0.1	2.0	3.4	6.9	6.8	6.8	6.4	5.6	27.5	27.6	11.1	1.2	75.6	38.3	49.7	50.3
29704	CATAWBA	81.6	77.9	14.9	17.4	0.3	0.4	0.9	1.4	6.7	6.9	7.1	6.7	5.4	27.2	29.6	9.8	0.7	75.2	38.9	50.9	49.1
29706	CHESTER	54.0	52.6	44.7	45.7	0.3	0.4	0.7	0.9	6.8	7.0	7.0	7.2	5.9	25.6	27.1	11.8	1.7	74.8	37.8	48.3	51.7
29707	FORT MILL	94.3	92.2	3.6	4.7	0.2	0.3	1.5	2.4	6.9	7.0	7.2	6.7	5.3	27.2	29.0	9.7	1.0	74.6	38.3	50.7	49.3
29708	FORT MILL	91.6	87.7	5.1	7.6	1.5	1.9	1.4	2.5	7.2	7.1	7.4	7.1	5.0	29.2	28.7	7.6	0.7	73.7	36.7	48.9	51.1
29709	CHESTERFIELD	68.8	66.9	30.1	31.6	0.2	0.3	0.7	0.9	6.0	6.0	6.5	6.8	5.4	26.2	29.2	12.3	1.5	77.2	40.6	49.2	50.8
29710	CLOVER	87.7	85.3	9.5	10.6	0.8	1.1	1.4	2.2	5.9	6.1	6.3	6.5	5.1	25.5	30.4	13.0	1.1	77.5	41.3	49.9	50.1
29712	EDGEMOOR	77.3	74.8	20.7	22.2	0.0	0.1	1.5	2.4	6.7	6.9	6.9	6.2	5.3	27.9	28.7	10.2	1.2	75.7	38.5	50.9	49.1
29714	FORT LAWN	67.3	64.7	30.8	32.9	0.1	0.1	0.7	1.1	7.0	6.9	7.2	6.8	6.1	26.8	28.2	9.7	1.3	75.0	37.8	48.4	51.6
29715	FORT MILL	88.6	86.5	8.9	9.5	0.8	1.4	1.4	2.3	6.9	7.0	7.3	7.3	5.5	26.1	28.6	10.1	1.3	74.3	38.5	48.5	51.5
29717	HICKORY GROVE	83.0	79.4	15.8	18.8	0.1	0.1	0.9	1.4	6.2	6.3	6.9	6.7	5.3	27.5	28.6	11.3	1.3	76.5	39.1	51.9	48.1
29718	JEFFERSON	71.3	69.5	26.9	27.9	0.1	0.1	3.1	3.9	7.4	7.4	7.4	6.7	5.4	25.3	28.1	10.9	1.4	73.6	38.4	50.1	49.9
29720	LANCASTER	68.6	64.4	29.1	32.2	0.3	0.5	1.9	2.8	6.7	6.7	7.0	7.1	5.7	26.4	27.3	11.5	1.7	75.4	38.4	48.6	51.4
29726	MC CONNELLS	78.6	74.3	19.4	22.8	0.1	0.2	1.1	1.8	6.5	6.7	6.8	6.3	5.5	28.3	30.3	8.8	0.8	76.1	37.6	48.0	52.0
29727	MOUNT CROGHAN	72.2	70.1	26.2	27.6	0.2	0.1	1.3	1.8	7.2	7.0	7.0	6.2	5.1	25.7	29.2	11.2	1.5	75.1	39.0	50.3	49.7
29728	PAGELAND	60.6	58.1	34.0	33.6	0.3	0.5	5.1	7.9	7.9	7.8	7.6	7.5	6.8	27.6	24.4	9.2	1.2	72.2	34.1	49.0	51.0
29729	RICHBURG	68.4	65.1	29.8	32.4	0.8	1.1	1.0	1.4	6.3	6.2	6.5	6.7	5.8	26.5	29.2	11.5	1.3	77.0	39.6	50.2	49.8
29730	ROCK HILL	58.9	55.5	36.6	38.4	0.8	1.1	2.1	3.1	6.9	6.7	6.7	8.4	8.6	27.9	24.3	9.4	1.2	75.1	34.1	47.5	52.5
29732	ROCK HILL	83.0	79.8	13.2	14.9	1.5	2.0	2.2	3.3	6.9	6.8	6.9	6.8	5.6	27.4	27.8	9.9	1.9	75.0	38.1	48.6	51.4
29741	RUBY	76.5	74.7	22.3	23.7	0.1	0.3	1.1	1.3	6.8	6.8	6.9	6.1	4.9	26.5	27.5	12.9	1.7	75.8	39.5	50.2	49.8
29742	SHARON	78.9	76.2	19.5	21.5	0.1	0.1	0.9	1.4	6.7	6.9	6.9	6.2	5.6	27.0	28.5	11.1	1.2	75.7	38.5	50.6	49.4
29743	SMYRNA	89.6	86.9	8.5	10.4	0.1	0.1	1.0	1.6	6.4	6.5	6.9	6.7	5.4	27.0	29.1	11.0	1.1	76.0	39.0	51.2	48.8
29745	YORK	77.9	75.3	18.6	19.6	0.3	0.5	2.8	4.1	6.9	7.0	7.0	7.2	6.1	27.5	27.3	9.8	1.3	74.5	37.4	49.7	50.3
29801	AIKEN	54.7	52.7	42.9	44.1	0.4	0.5	1.5	2.2	6.1	6.5	6.6	7.6	6.5	25.0	26.0	12.9	2.8	76.5	38.4	47.3	52.7
29803	AIKEN	81.1	78.6	15.3	16.1	1.2	1.7	2.1	3.3	6.0	6.3	6.6	6.6	5.5	24.5	30.3	12.7	1.6	77.0	40.9	48.3	51.7
29805	AIKEN	79.7	76.9	18.0	19.9	0.3	0.5	1.1	1.7	7.1	7.3	7.5	7.1	5.3	27.6	27.8	9.4	0.9	73.7	36.9	49.7	50.3
29808	AIKEN	60.5	59.0	36.8	38.6	0.0	0.0	1.3	2.4	7.2	7.2	7.2	7.2	10.8	24.1	27.7	8.4	0.0	74.7	31.9	49.4	50.6
29809	NEW ELLENTON	61.8	58.7	34.3	35.9	0.4	0.6	2.6	3.8	5.6	5.8	6.1	6.5	5.3	26.2	29.4	13.5	1.5	78.1	40.8	47.8	52.2
29810	ALLENDALE	24.3	23.3	73.6	73.4	0.2	0.4	2.4	3.6	8.0	7.7	7.4	7.8	6.4	22.8	26.7	11.2	1.9	71.8	36.2	48.5	51.5
29812	BARNWELL	59.3	57.0	37.7	38.8	0.6	0.9	2.0	2.8	7.5	7.0	7.4	7.3	6.7	26.1	26.3	10.1	1.5	73.5	36.0	48.9	51.1
29817	BLACKVILLE	40.5	39.1	58.4	59.5	0.2	0.3	0.7	0.8	6.9	6.7	8.2	7.6	6.0	24.2	27.2	11.6	1.6	73.2	37.7	47.9	52.1
29819	BRADLEY	67.6	64.3	31.2	34.1	0.1	0.1	0.5	0.9	6.6	6.8	7.1	6.6	5.0	26.0	27.9	11.6	2.4	75.2	39.6	50.9	49.1
29821	CLARKS HILL	70.2	68.9	28.1	28.7	0.2	0.4	0.8	1.4	5.5	5.9	6.4	6.6	4.7	24.3	33.0	12.2	1.4	78.2	42.6	48.3	51.7
29824	EDGEFIELD	48.4	46.0	50.3	52.2	0.2	0.3	2.7	4.0	4.5	4.6	4.7	4.9	6.6	36.1	26.2	10.4	2.0	83.6	37.9	60.2	39.8
29827	FAIRFAX	27.5	26.0	71.5	72.8	0.1	0.2	0.4	0.6	5.0	5.2	5.2	6.0	8.5	34.8	23.9	9.4	2.1	81.2	35.8	63.1	36.9
29828	GLOVERVILLE	84.9	82.7	12.6	14.1	0.2	0.2	1.0	1.5	8.1	8.2	8.0	6.4	4.3	25.4	26.1	11.8	1.5	71.7	37.4	48.7	51.3
29829	GRANITEVILLE	67.7	66.3	28.4	28.6	0.4	0.5	2.3	3.5	7.9	7.1	6.8	7.0	6.0	24.9	26.8	11.9	1.5	74.0	37.4	48.2	51.8
29831	JACKSON	76.3	73.3	21.4	23.7	0.3	0.4	2.1	3.1	6.0	6.7	6.5	7.0	6.3	26.7	27.3	12.2	1.3	76.5	38.5	47.9	52.1
29832	JOHNSTON	46.3	43.9	52.0	53.7	0.2	0.3	2.5	3.5	7.0	7.7	6.7	6.4	6.3	24.2	28.8	11.2	1.7	75.1	38.3	48.7	51.3
29835	MC CORMICK	39.9	38.4	58.6	59.6	0.3	0.5	0.8	1.2	4.4	4.5	5.0	5.9	6.9	28.5	27.1	15.7	2.1	82.5	41.3	56.2	43.8
29836	MARTIN	22.7	21.7	75.4	75.8	0.0	0.0	1.6	2.7	5.3	6.0	6.4	6.4	4.4	22.8	36.1	10.0	2.4	78.9	43.8	48.1	51.9
29838	MODOC	65.0	62.7	33.8	35.7	0.0	0.3	0.5	0.8	4.6	5.2	5.7	6.0	4.4	22.9	34.6	15.0	1.6	80.7	45.8	46.9	53.1
29840	MOUNT CARMEL	62.0	60.7	36.6	37.4	0.6	0.8	0.9	1.1	2.7	2.8	4.7	5.9	1.4	10.9	28.1	38.9	4.5	85.3	62.4	47.5	52.5
29841	NORTH AUGUSTA	74.8	72.4	21.8	22.8	0.9	1.2	2.8	4.1	7.0	6.8	6.8	6.5	6.1	27.0	26.6	11.7	1.7	75.5	37.9	48.0	52.0
29842	BEECH ISLAND	63.8	60.3	33.5	35.9	0.4	0.5	2.6	3.7	6.5	6.4	6.6	7.7	6.7	27.2	28.0	9.7	1.2	75.8	36.9	49.2	50.8
29843	OLAR	65.5	64.4	33.3	34.1	0.2	0.4	1.1	1.5	6.3	6.6	6.6	5.8	5.1	23.2	30.3	14.2	1.9	76.8	42.0	51.6	48.4
29845	PLUM BRANCH	40.3	39.5	59.2	59.7	0.2	0.2	1.0	1.2	5.0	5.5	7.2	5.9	4.5	24.0	33.4	13.3	1.2	78.2	43.4	46.4	53.6
29847	TRENTON	50.1	46.8	47.2	49.4	0.2	0.2	2.6	3.8	5.4	5.6	5.9	9.5	11.9	25.0	27.3	8.5	1.0	78.6	34.0	55.9	44.1
29848	TROY	71.9	69.2	26.9	29.2	0.1	0.2	0.6	0.9	6.2	6.2	6.8	6.3	5.1	25.1	28.1	14.0	2.2	76.6	41.0	51.8	48.2
29849	ULMER	54.9	53.1	43.6	44.9	0.1	0.1	1.9	2.6	6.5	6.7	6.9	7.0	5.3	21.9	31.4	12.5	2.0	75.6	41.8	49.0	51.0
29851	WARRENVILLE	85.3	83.2	12.4	13.7	0.2	0.4	1.1	1.7	7.1	7.2	7.2	6.5	4.8	25.9	27.7	12.2	1.5	74.5	38.8	49.5	50.5
29853	WILLISTON	57.7	55.7	40.2	41.4	0.1	0.2	1.0	1.5	6.6	7.1	7.5	7.5	5.4	25.3	27.4	11.5	1.8	74.2	37.9	48.2	51.8
29856	WINDSOR	79.2	75.8	15.2	16.3	0.2	0.3	6.2	9.3	8.4	7.7	7.4	8.2	8.0	27.8	25.4	6.7	0.5	71.7	32.2	50.2	49.8
29860	NORTH AUGUSTA	81.6	80.7	16.3	16.4	0.7	1.0	0.9	1.5	6.9	7.3	7.7	7.3	5.4	26.0	29.2	9.1	1.1	73.6	38.2	49.2	50.8
29902	BEAUFORT	68.5	63.1	24.3	26.0	1.5	2.3	6.1	9.5	6.8	6.1	5.3	14.0	13.4	26.4	18.1	8.3	1.6	78.4	27.6	54.5	45.5
29906	BEAUFORT	59.2	53.9	33.9	35.5	1.2	1.8	6.5	10.1	11.4	8.8	7.1	6.9	12.7	31.7	16.2	4.6	0.6	68.9	26.4	52.1	47.9
29907	LADYS ISLAND	75.6	72.1	20.7	22.1	1.2	1.9	3.1	5.0	7.9	7.5	7.3	6.3	5.5	28.1	26.2	9.9	1.2	73.2	36.2	48.5	51.5
29909	OKATIE	85.7	84.5	12.4	12.2	0.3	0.4	1.8	3.5	3.5	3.8	4.2	3.8	2.4	14.8	34.5	30.5	2.6	86.1	56.7	48.4	51.6
29910	BLUFFTON	81.6	78.8	13.9	14.6	0.5	0.6	6.5	9.2	6.2	5.7	5.6	5.5	6.1	23.2	27.5	18.5	1.8	79.3	43.2	48.5	51.5
29911	BRUNSON	50.4	47.8	47.6	49.2	0.1	0.1	1.6	2.6	6.8	6.7	6.8	7.6	6.1	25.3	26.4	12.6	1.6	74.9	37.6	48.2	51.8
29915	DAUFUSKIE ISLAND	87.1	84.1	10.8	12.4	0.4	0.4	3.2	5.6	4.4	5.2	6.4	7.2	4.0	22.7	35.9	13.1	1.2	79.3	45.1	49.4	50.6
29916	EARLY BRANCH	45.1	43.4	53.7	54.7	0.1	0.1	1.2	2.0	7.0	7.2	7.5	7.2	6.2	24.1	27.4	11.9	1.5	73.9	37.9	47.2	52.8
29918	ESTILL	31.6	32.0	67.1	66.1	0.1	0.1	5.5	7.6	5.9	6.4	6.7	6.8	6.2	33.2	24.6	8.4	1.8	76.5	34.8	58.1	41.9
29920	SAINT HELENA ISLAND	42.0	42.1	56.0	54.9	0.3	0.5	3.6	5.0	5.3	5.4	5.7	6.5	5.3	19.7	29.2	21.0	1.9	79.4	46.5	47.7	52.3
29922	GARNETT	13.3	12.4	86.0	86.7	0.0	0.0	0.5	0.7	7.0	7.3	7.8	10.0	6.8	23.1	29.6	7.0	1.4	71.6	33.8	47.6	52.4
29924	HAMPTON	58.9	56.3	39.5	41.4	0.3	0.5	0.7	1.2	6.5	6.3	6.5	6.9	6.5	23.9	27.4	14.0	1.9	76.4	40.1	47.5	52.5
29926	HILTON HEAD ISLAND	81.3	76.6	12.1	12.6	0.6	0.9	11.5	18.0	4.7	4.7	4.8	4.6	4.8	19.3	29.9	24.3	2.9	82.9	50.6	49.7	50.3
29927	HARDEEVILLE	41.1	39.4	50.3	48.0	0.9	1.2	11.3	16.3	8.2	7.7	7.0	7.4	7.9	29.2	23.2	8.6	0.8	72.9	32.3	51.9	48.1
29928	HILTON HEAD ISLAND	91.3	88.2	3.2	3.4	0.5	0.8	10.2	15.1	3.3	3.2	3.5	4.3	5.6	20.3	30.8	25.3	3.7	87.6	52.7	49.9	50.1
29929	ISLANDTON	60.5	57.9	36.8	38.0	0.0	0.0	3.0	4.4	6.3	6.5	6.7	6.3	5.7	23.3	29.8	13.3	2.1	76.7	41.3	48.7	51.3
29932	LURAY	44.1	42.5	54.0	55.1	0.2	0.2	2.5	3.8	7.9	8.3	8.1	7.5	5.8	23.5	27.6	10.3	0.9	71.1	36.3	49.1	50.9
29934	PINELAND	16.9	16.6	82.3	82.2	0.1	0.1	0.9	1.2	6.9	6.9	7.5	8.0	5.8	22.7	28.3	11.6	2.3	73.7	38.6	48.3	51.7
29935	PORT ROYAL	64.3	59.6	29.8	31.3	1.6	2.5	3.8	6.2	7.8	7.0	6.0	6.3	9.0	32.0	21.1	8.9	1.9	75.9	32.4	48.1	51.9
29936	RIDGELAND	44.6	41.8	51.7	52.3	0.4	0.5	3.8	6.2	6.7	6.7	6.7	6.9	6.9	30.2	24.4	10.0	1.5	76.1	35.6	55.0	45.0
29940	SEABROOK	30.0	26.2	67.9	70.7	0.2	0.3	2.2	3.0	7.1	7.9	8.2	8.6	7.1	24.5	24.9	10.4	1.3	71.4	33.4	48.4	51.6
29941	SHELDON	36.1	32.0	62.3	65.5	0.0	0.0	1.1	2.3	5.6	5.8	6.3	7.1	5.6	23.1	29.4	15.2	1.8	77.9	42.0	49.2	50.8
29943	TILLMAN	47.2	46.2	50.0	49.5	0.4	0.5	2.7	4.2	7.6	7.6	7.5	6.9	5.5	25.5	26.7	11.5	1.3	73.0	37.5	49.9	50.1
29944	VARNVILLE	50.6	48.5	48.2	49.8	0.2	0.3	0.9	1.3	7.2	7.3	7.4	7.5	6.0	25.1	27.4	10.9	1.3	73.5	37.1	47.9	52.1
	SOUTH CAROLINA	67.2	65.9	29.5	29.4	0.9	1.4	2.4	3.6	6.5	6.5	6.5	7.2	6.9	26.6	26.8	11.3	1.6	76.4	37.6	48.9	51.1
	UNITED STATES	75.1	72.0	12.3	12.7	3.8	4.6	12.5	15.7	6.8	6.7	6.6	7.1	6.9	27.0	26.0	10.9	1.9	75.7	36.9	49.2	50.8

ZIP CODE #	POST OFFICE NAME	2009 Per Capita Income	2009 HH Income Base	2009 HOUSEHOLD INCOME DISTRIBUTION (%) Less than $25,000	$25,000 to $49,999	$50,000 to $99,999	$100,000 to $149,999	$150,000 or More	MEDIAN HOUSEHOLD INCOME 2009	2014	2009 National Centile	2009 State Centile	2009 Home Value Base	2009 HOME VALUE DISTRIBUTION (%) Less than $50,000	$50,000 to $89,999	$90,000 to $174,999	$175,000 to $399,999	$400,000 or More	2009 Median Home Value
29676	SALEM	40229	2361	16.3	21.4	38.3	11.7	12.2	61213	55588	79	91	2100	13.8	14.9	18.9	30.5	21.9	186792
29678	SENECA	21774	8926	28.9	26.7	35.1	6.7	2.6	43933	46185	45	59	6354	16.6	24.6	41.0	15.9	1.9	103014
29680	SIMPSONVILLE	29733	9017	9.4	18.1	46.4	17.9	8.2	74160	75885	89	95	7553	6.4	6.6	49.9	35.1	2.0	147987
29681	SIMPSONVILLE	37616	15906	9.1	16.2	38.2	19.3	17.2	80700	81509	92	99	13971	4.6	5.2	37.9	44.0	8.3	180563
29682	SIX MILE	21948	1482	21.3	27.3	44.1	4.4	2.9	50844	51225	63	79	1304	21.0	22.9	31.2	22.1	2.8	101678
29684	STARR	18793	1782	26.5	32.5	34.8	3.8	2.4	41215	45196	37	48	1545	25.2	33.7	31.8	8.0	1.4	80646
29685	SUNSET	23305	450	22.0	34.4	36.7	5.6	1.3	43542	46729	44	58	399	20.6	31.3	30.1	14.5	3.5	87794
29686	TAMASSEE	21130	476	29.2	29.2	33.2	5.7	2.7	42426	45038	41	54	407	25.3	19.9	31.2	22.4	1.2	97800
29687	TAYLORS	26910	16550	17.3	25.6	42.2	10.3	4.7	56295	58581	73	88	11765	9.1	13.0	52.4	24.1	1.3	130537
29688	TIGERVILLE	19209	38	21.1	23.7	52.6	2.6	0.0	51431	52310	65	81	34	17.6	14.7	32.4	26.5	8.8	133333
29689	TOWNVILLE	25423	1870	27.2	26.0	32.4	9.4	5.0	47226	49022	55	70	1593	22.7	19.1	32.3	21.0	5.0	101332
29690	TRAVELERS REST	22305	7316	23.9	28.4	37.1	7.1	3.5	47261	50862	55	71	5759	19.9	24.7	36.2	14.3	4.9	96571
29691	WALHALLA	20360	4653	32.1	28.0	31.8	6.2	1.8	41057	44670	36	46	3530	23.3	23.4	36.9	14.7	1.7	95514
29692	WARE SHOALS	19738	2104	33.9	28.5	30.1	6.0	1.5	36743	38733	23	28	1656	28.0	37.0	30.1	4.0	1.0	73916
29693	WESTMINSTER	20686	5806	26.3	33.1	32.6	6.2	1.8	41964	45175	39	50	4641	23.5	24.6	37.3	13.0	1.7	92934
29696	WEST UNION	23398	1565	19.9	26.9	42.6	8.3	2.2	52524	52238	67	83	1343	16.6	21.1	36.0	20.8	5.4	111334
29697	WILLIAMSTON	20536	4489	24.5	28.0	39.4	5.7	2.4	47668	49585	56	71	3673	20.9	26.8	38.2	12.1	2.0	92522
29702	BLACKSBURG	20505	4077	32.0	29.3	31.2	5.1	2.4	39638	42828	32	41	3123	26.7	28.0	33.5	11.0	0.8	82358
29704	CATAWBA	23345	1427	19.9	22.6	45.7	7.9	3.9	56198	57958	73	87	1196	17.1	20.7	43.8	18.1	0.3	110085
29706	CHESTER	18506	7726	31.7	30.8	30.2	6.1	1.3	39014	40020	30	36	5776	23.4	34.1	35.2	6.5	0.9	82530
29707	FORT MILL	23581	4860	20.8	26.5	40.7	9.4	2.7	52226	50889	66	82	3964	12.3	14.9	35.6	34.0	3.2	144946
29708	FORT MILL	34624	8390	9.4	15.5	42.5	19.4	13.2	77047	77122	91	97	6652	4.9	5.5	25.8	51.1	12.7	210017
29709	CHESTERFIELD	20488	2785	32.5	28.8	31.2	6.0	1.6	40569	42204	35	44	2216	28.1	32.2	30.5	8.5	0.8	76867
29710	CLOVER	29114	11042	18.8	20.7	41.8	11.7	7.0	59646	61240	77	90	8872	14.6	15.6	30.8	28.3	10.5	139613
29712	EDGEMOOR	24197	903	17.6	29.9	39.5	9.6	3.3	51707	52099	65	82	792	16.4	27.0	38.4	16.8	1.4	99286
29714	FORT LAWN	19127	1074	27.0	31.7	35.3	4.9	1.1	43367	43842	43	57	904	26.8	32.6	33.8	6.7	0.0	77500
29715	FORT MILL	27942	8601	18.5	21.4	38.8	15.5	5.8	62179	64265	80	92	6947	9.3	8.2	36.4	40.1	6.0	163691
29717	HICKORY GROVE	20704	510	26.3	25.9	38.6	7.5	1.8	47674	50794	56	72	441	24.5	30.4	30.4	13.6	1.1	82833
29718	JEFFERSON	16349	1424	39.1	26.6	30.3	2.7	1.3	34438	36406	16	17	1152	32.2	31.9	28.9	6.3	0.8	72283
29720	LANCASTER	20551	18173	28.4	29.6	33.7	6.2	2.1	42241	43803	40	52	13088	14.3	25.2	45.7	13.7	1.0	103804
29726	MC CONNELLS	22510	655	20.8	23.1	47.0	7.3	1.8	54399	55956	70	85	558	19.5	26.5	38.0	10.9	5.0	96471
29727	MOUNT CROGHAN	15836	550	35.6	36.4	25.6	1.6	0.7	35000	36033	18	20	438	47.9	30.4	15.1	4.3	2.3	51698
29728	PAGELAND	17470	3542	35.2	28.1	30.5	4.3	1.8	35872	36832	20	24	2420	30.0	30.0	30.8	8.7	0.5	77576
29729	RICHBURG	20350	890	22.7	31.0	37.4	8.0	0.9	46863	47331	54	69	755	23.3	29.5	30.5	16.3	0.4	83485
29730	ROCK HILL	21002	20932	26.6	28.3	35.6	7.2	2.4	44571	48397	47	62	12906	13.6	22.0	45.4	17.6	1.5	112130
29732	ROCK HILL	29724	20818	14.0	22.5	44.6	11.5	7.3	62723	64387	81	93	14930	6.5	9.9	41.9	36.8	4.9	156085
29741	RUBY	18425	619	38.1	25.4	30.4	5.7	0.5	35418	37641	19	22	521	36.5	31.7	20.0	10.7	1.2	69828
29742	SHARON	19330	979	24.6	29.9	38.3	5.2	1.9	44712	48372	47	63	855	25.4	27.0	35.3	9.5	2.8	86058
29743	SMYRNA	20749	610	28.9	27.7	34.9	6.4	2.1	42952	46653	42	56	527	21.6	26.2	37.8	12.1	2.3	92556
29745	YORK	20978	10575	24.6	25.8	38.7	8.4	2.5	49456	52220	60	77	8196	16.8	21.1	37.5	19.4	5.1	109619
29801	AIKEN	20921	10645	33.4	25.1	31.9	6.2	3.4	40038	43865	33	43	7342	16.6	26.9	41.2	13.6	1.6	98404
29803	AIKEN	32072	14678	15.6	20.9	38.2	15.3	10.0	66507	67002	85	94	11544	9.8	12.9	37.9	33.0	6.5	145058
29805	AIKEN	20987	1999	26.8	25.2	38.9	6.4	2.8	46948	50617	54	70	1649	26.8	23.0	37.1	10.9	2.2	90315
29808	AIKEN	20020	30	30.0	23.3	36.7	10.0	0.0	45000	42343	48	63	26	50.0	23.1	19.2	7.7	0.0	50000
29809	NEW ELLENTON	21061	911	26.8	28.1	37.4	4.9	2.7	46394	48301	53	68	709	24.8	36.5	34.3	4.2	0.1	80183
29810	ALLENDALE	14177	2121	51.1	25.0	19.0	3.5	1.4	24075	24410	3	1	1488	35.4	37.8	22.5	3.8	0.5	61257
29812	BARNWELL	21088	4873	34.2	23.7	31.7	7.0	3.4	39260	41834	31	38	3727	31.4	27.7	32.8	7.5	0.6	74750
29817	BLACKVILLE	16997	1900	44.3	25.6	22.3	6.0	1.8	30522	32241	9	6	1439	39.5	29.0	25.6	5.8	0.0	62841
29819	BRADLEY	20011	605	27.1	24.5	40.0	6.6	1.8	47989	47189	57	72	528	22.3	27.3	39.0	11.4	0.0	90426
29821	CLARKS HILL	20380	394	27.7	24.6	40.1	6.1	1.5	48257	47892	57	74	350	23.7	25.4	28.3	17.7	4.9	92000
29824	EDGEFIELD	18028	2656	32.1	28.1	29.9	6.0	4.0	40105	43048	33	43	2045	17.6	28.8	37.5	14.9	1.4	95551
29827	FAIRFAX	14980	1177	50.6	26.3	16.0	4.4	2.6	24458	25076	3	1	850	40.9	36.2	19.1	3.6	0.1	59625
29828	GLOVERVILLE	16488	466	43.3	25.8	27.0	3.4	0.4	30557	32868	9	6	322	46.9	30.4	20.5	2.2	0.0	53030
29829	GRANITEVILLE	20250	2952	30.3	25.4	34.7	7.6	2.0	44575	48294	47	62	2206	20.8	26.3	36.4	16.0	0.5	94638
29831	JACKSON	21913	1364	29.8	24.6	34.8	8.5	2.3	44906	48157	48	63	1094	22.1	33.6	36.4	7.7	0.2	84375
29832	JOHNSTON	18377	1949	35.5	28.0	29.6	5.0	1.9	36466	39311	22	27	1330	20.4	30.8	33.2	13.5	2.0	88609
29835	MC CORMICK	20685	2639	36.5	25.0	28.8	5.7	4.0	38762	40330	29	35	2039	25.8	36.1	21.3	12.1	4.7	77313
29836	MARTIN	17549	192	40.1	27.6	29.2	3.1	0.0	41193	43062	37	48	152	48.7	48.0	2.6	0.7	0.0	50909
29838	MODOC	22427	178	33.7	26.4	34.3	3.9	1.7	41154	42642	37	47	156	26.3	32.7	23.1	13.5	4.5	71429
29840	MOUNT CARMEL	27630	350	18.0	21.7	40.9	11.1	8.3	55978	57175	73	87	312	22.1	11.2	14.4	37.5	14.7	196875
29841	NORTH AUGUSTA	25372	12871	23.3	25.3	37.6	9.9	4.0	51341	53045	64	81	9018	8.0	23.1	55.0	12.9	1.0	111659
29842	BEECH ISLAND	19892	3660	31.3	26.5	32.1	7.7	2.4	41003	45265	36	46	2858	23.0	33.1	35.0	8.3	0.6	80695
29843	OLAR	18027	639	41.5	27.9	25.5	4.1	1.1	33489	36156	14	12	548	47.3	27.4	18.1	7.3	0.0	55556
29845	PLUM BRANCH	20470	531	43.1	18.8	31.5	5.3	1.3	32451	36478	12	9	471	41.0	35.0	18.0	4.9	1.1	57083
29847	TRENTON	20381	1412	27.3	28.2	34.0	7.4	3.0	44060	46252	46	61	1169	23.5	30.1	30.2	13.8	2.4	85707
29848	TROY	20976	321	26.2	25.2	39.3	6.5	2.8	48395	47002	58	75	280	24.6	26.4	35.0	11.8	2.1	88636
29849	ULMER	19928	334	35.9	33.8	24.3	2.4	3.6	33322	35378	14	12	283	37.1	35.3	16.6	8.8	2.1	65370
29851	WARRENVILLE	17992	3828	37.4	30.5	27.1	4.1	0.9	33948	35968	15	15	2881	40.1	32.5	24.3	3.0	0.1	60063
29853	WILLISTON	18033	2819	40.1	24.5	28.9	4.6	1.8	34748	35978	17	18	2148	36.1	31.1	28.9	3.6	0.3	65143
29856	WINDSOR	17343	1121	28.9	33.5	32.5	3.3	1.9	38839	41905	29	35	978	40.9	31.6	22.6	4.3	0.6	59082
29860	NORTH AUGUSTA	25792	4829	17.3	19.4	44.7	12.6	5.9	62380	61535	80	92	4304	11.9	15.8	41.5	28.4	2.4	136052
29902	BEAUFORT	22596	6189	23.9	27.7	35.9	6.6	5.8	48177	49297	57	73	3293	7.0	7.3	53.9	19.2	12.6	141751
29906	BEAUFORT	18051	7740	18.9	34.1	39.1	5.9	2.0	47075	48617	54	70	4343	22.5	19.0	43.9	12.4	2.3	102854
29907	LADYS ISLAND	32206	4741	15.4	20.6	40.1	12.9	10.9	66515	69127	85	94	3732	5.4	9.2	26.8	37.2	21.4	200795
29909	OKATIE	50717	6082	9.1	20.3	41.0	15.3	14.2	75080	77317	89	96	5596	2.8	4.2	17.0	50.5	25.5	273030
29910	BLUFFTON	32625	10353	12.8	23.0	40.4	13.3	10.6	68631	71716	86	95	7893	4.8	7.7	17.4	46.8	23.3	248151
29911	BRUNSON	17580	602	37.4	29.7	27.4	3.7	1.8	34739	35361	17	18	510	35.7	31.6	26.7	5.3	0.8	65000
29915	DAUFUSKIE ISLAND	45083	135	5.9	19.3	54.1	14.8	5.9	76489	77393	90	97	107	6.5	12.1	31.8	29.0	20.6	174107
29916	EARLY BRANCH	17900	664	35.2	33.0	25.3	4.7	1.8	36519	37938	22	27	571	38.5	24.0	28.9	6.3	2.3	66429
29918	ESTILL	15870	2107	41.0	25.3	26.1	4.7	2.9	32918	34458	13	10	1612	38.2	35.0	20.8	5.3	0.7	61216
29920	SAINT HELENA ISLAND	28503	5130	26.3	24.7	32.9	9.4	6.8	48828	50076	59	76	4374	17.1	12.4	23.0	20.1	27.4	164700
29922	GARNETT	15048	202	38.6	31.2	25.7	2.5	2.0	33620	35569	15	13	169	42.0	39.1	13.6	3.6	1.8	55870
29924	HAMPTON	22442	1756	31.3	27.2	32.0	6.0	3.4	40830	42740	35	45	1288	26.0	30.7	32.5	9.9	0.9	81650
29926	HILTON HEAD ISLAND	42471	9720	8.6	19.7	37.1	17.8	16.8	76147	78693	90	97	7710	2.8	4.0	10.7	27.2	55.3	437125
29927	HARDEEVILLE	20248	2558	34.0	22.8	30.4	8.3	4.5	42464	44696	41	54	1899	23.0	19.1	39.2	16.3	2.5	99774
29928	HILTON HEAD ISLAND	51070	8276	9.5	18.7	35.3	15.6	20.9	78869	80458	92	98	6102	2.3	1.0	12.1	24.7	59.9	496172
29929	ISLANDTON	16806	480	41.9	23.5	30.2	2.3	2.1	35000	37480	18	20	403	32.3	36.0	17.1	14.6	0.0	73525
29932	LURAY	18381	202	35.1	29.2	29.7	3.0	3.0	36040	37122	21	25	173	29.5	42.8	23.7	4.0	0.0	69667
29934	PINELAND	18384	506	29.1	37.2	25.9	4.9	3.0	39293	40447	31	38	438	26.3	38.4	29.2	5.3	0.9	67333
29935	PORT ROYAL	25406	1606	21.0	37.1	32.0	6.8	3.0	42790	45776	42	55	703	9.4	10.5	64.3	11.7	4.1	120793
29936	RIDGELAND	17823	3811	33.2	28.7	29.9	5.7	2.4	38005	39060	27	31	2914	24.8	20.8	38.5	11.5	4.5	96515
29940	SEABROOK	18336	1784	43.4	24.9	22.9	4.7	4.0	30941	33239	10	7	1404	32.1	22.5	29.8	9.8	5.8	83333
29941	SHELDON	27459	188	41.5	23.4	23.4	5.9	5.9	35500	38324	19	22	161	23.6	18.0	36.6	6.8	14.9	97941
29943	TILLMAN	21351	834	30.7	26.3	33.2	4.9	4.9	39129	39478	30	37	701	30.7	27.4	28.5	10.6	2.9	79815
29944	VARNVILLE	19534	1839	31.5	28.3	31.3	6.6	2.3	39540	41111	31	40	1422	26.9	31.8	34.4	6.0	1.0	81338
	SOUTH CAROLINA	24352		25.1	26.4	35.2	8.4	4.8	48210	50493				16.4	20.9	37.4	20.6	4.8	112284
	UNITED STATES	27277		20.9	24.4	35.3	11.7	7.6	54719	56938				9.3	13.1	31.6	32.6	13.5	162279

ZIP CODE #	POST OFFICE NAME	FINANCIAL SERVICES: Auto Loan	Home Loan	Invest-ments	Retire-ment Plans	THE HOME: Home Improvements: Home Repair	Lawn & Garden	Furnishings: Comput-ers & Hard-ware-Personal	Major Appli-ances	TV, Radio, Sound Equip-ment	Furni-ture	ENTERTAINMENT: Dine out/ Carry out	Sports Equip-ment	Fees & Tickets	Toys & Games	Travel	Cable TV	PERSONAL: Apparel & Services	Auto Repairs	Health Insur-ance	Pets & Supplies
29676	SALEM	130	118	157	116	130	147	111	133	120	119	118	90	110	114	120	128	80	126	145	154
29678	SENECA	86	68	73	67	67	84	71	78	77	69	75	60	62	78	66	82	51	76	84	94
29680	SIMPSONVILLE	128	131	109	128	123	113	122	120	117	130	119	95	122	125	118	112	83	116	108	138
29681	SIMPSONVILLE	150	163	145	164	158	150	145	149	141	154	142	118	152	148	148	137	101	141	137	172
29682	SIX MILE	98	78	81	76	77	93	78	87	84	78	83	66	68	88	73	90	56	83	90	105
29684	STARR	88	64	74	62	64	84	66	77	73	65	72	59	53	76	61	80	48	73	81	94
29685	SUNSET	93	67	77	65	67	89	70	81	77	68	76	62	56	81	63	84	51	77	86	99
29686	TAMASSEE	96	69	92	67	70	95	71	88	78	67	77	66	57	79	68	86	51	81	91	105
29687	TAYLORS	95	97	87	97	94	96	93	93	93	94	94	71	94	95	92	94	65	93	95	110
29688	TIGERVILLE	79	73	65	71	71	75	69	73	72	72	72	53	65	74	66	73	49	71	73	87
29689	TOWNVILLE	104	78	114	76	82	106	79	100	86	74	84	74	66	84	81	93	56	92	102	117
29690	TRAVELERS REST	95	82	80	82	81	93	82	89	86	80	85	67	74	88	78	90	58	85	91	106
29691	WALHALLA	89	65	76	63	65	86	68	79	75	65	73	60	55	77	63	82	49	75	84	95
29692	WARE SHOALS	84	60	75	58	61	82	64	76	71	60	69	58	51	72	59	78	46	71	81	91
29693	WESTMINSTER	90	65	77	63	65	87	67	79	75	65	73	61	54	77	62	82	49	75	83	96
29696	WEST UNION	97	81	93	80	82	97	80	92	85	78	84	68	71	86	79	89	56	87	94	109
29697	WILLIAMSTON	89	71	75	70	71	86	74	82	79	70	77	62	64	81	69	84	52	78	86	98
29702	BLACKSBURG	87	66	73	64	65	82	68	77	74	67	73	59	57	77	63	79	49	74	79	93
29704	CATAWBA	102	92	83	89	90	96	87	93	91	90	91	68	82	95	83	94	62	90	94	111
29706	CHESTER	78	61	64	60	59	75	63	70	70	62	68	53	55	71	59	75	46	68	75	85
29707	FORT MILL	95	88	78	85	86	90	83	88	86	86	86	64	78	89	79	88	58	85	88	104
29708	FORT MILL	134	154	139	152	150	135	135	137	128	145	130	106	144	133	140	123	92	130	124	156
29709	CHESTERFIELD	86	62	75	60	62	83	64	76	71	62	70	58	52	74	59	78	47	72	80	92
29710	CLOVER	112	105	107	103	106	113	100	109	104	102	103	79	97	105	100	107	71	105	111	128
29712	EDGEMOOR	101	89	82	86	87	95	85	92	90	88	89	68	79	93	81	93	61	89	93	110
29714	FORT LAWN	89	64	74	62	64	85	67	78	74	65	72	60	53	77	61	81	49	73	82	94
29715	FORT MILL	101	111	100	111	107	105	101	102	99	103	100	80	106	102	104	98	70	100	100	120
29717	HICKORY GROVE	99	71	82	69	71	94	74	86	82	72	80	66	59	85	67	89	54	81	91	105
29718	JEFFERSON	77	50	73	48	50	75	54	67	62	51	60	52	41	63	50	69	40	63	71	83
29720	LANCASTER	83	67	70	66	66	82	70	76	75	68	74	58	61	77	65	81	50	74	82	92
29726	MC CONNELLS	105	89	86	86	87	99	86	94	91	88	91	70	78	95	81	96	62	91	96	113
29727	MOUNT CROGHAN	72	49	65	47	49	70	52	63	59	50	57	49	40	60	48	65	38	59	67	77
29728	PAGELAND	80	58	68	56	57	76	62	70	68	60	67	54	50	70	56	74	45	68	74	86
29729	RICHBURG	88	74	73	73	74	84	73	80	77	73	76	60	65	80	69	81	52	77	82	96
29730	ROCK HILL	82	73	66	73	70	77	77	76	80	76	79	58	72	81	72	82	55	78	80	91
29732	ROCK HILL	109	110	100	112	108	109	108	108	107	108	108	83	108	109	107	108	75	107	108	127
29741	RUBY	78	55	66	54	55	74	58	68	64	56	63	52	46	67	53	70	42	64	71	83
29742	SHARON	94	68	79	66	67	90	70	82	78	69	77	63	57	81	64	85	51	78	87	100
29743	SMYRNA	95	69	79	67	69	90	72	83	79	70	78	64	58	83	65	86	52	79	87	101
29745	YORK	92	79	79	77	78	88	79	85	83	79	82	63	72	85	75	87	56	83	88	102
29801	AIKEN	79	69	72	68	68	81	70	75	75	70	74	56	65	75	68	80	51	75	82	91
29803	AIKEN	115	119	115	120	118	119	112	115	112	115	113	88	115	114	114	113	79	113	115	136
29805	AIKEN	93	78	76	75	76	87	76	83	81	77	80	62	68	84	71	85	54	80	85	100
29808	AIKEN	86	81	69	77	77	77	80	79	80	83	80	60	75	83	75	80	55	80	77	94
29809	NEW ELLENTON	87	72	79	72	72	89	72	83	77	67	75	64	63	78	70	82	51	78	86	99
29810	ALLENDALE	59	43	52	42	42	58	47	53	54	46	52	40	40	53	43	59	35	53	59	65
29812	BARNWELL	87	69	76	67	67	84	71	79	77	70	76	61	61	79	67	82	51	77	82	96
29817	BLACKVILLE	79	52	75	49	51	77	55	69	63	52	62	54	41	65	51	71	41	65	73	85
29819	BRADLEY	96	70	79	68	70	91	72	84	80	71	78	64	59	83	66	87	53	79	88	102
29821	CLARKS HILL	90	71	86	69	72	89	71	84	76	69	76	62	61	77	69	82	50	78	86	100
29824	EDGEFIELD	82	65	75	65	65	82	69	77	75	65	73	59	60	75	66	80	49	75	83	93
29827	FAIRFAX	70	48	64	46	48	69	52	62	61	51	59	47	42	61	49	67	39	61	68	77
29828	GLOVERVILLE	71	46	69	44	46	70	50	62	57	47	56	49	37	58	46	64	37	59	66	77
29829	GRANITEVILLE	83	67	70	67	66	79	71	76	77	70	76	57	64	78	66	81	52	75	81	91
29831	JACKSON	82	80	71	77	77	81	75	78	78	77	78	58	74	80	74	80	53	77	81	92
29832	JOHNSTON	78	58	70	57	58	77	63	71	69	59	67	55	52	69	58	74	45	69	76	87
29835	MC CORMICK	86	64	85	62	66	88	67	79	75	67	74	58	57	74	65	82	49	76	87	96
29836	MARTIN	76	50	74	47	50	75	53	67	61	51	60	52	40	62	50	69	40	63	71	82
29838	MODOC	81	60	81	59	62	83	61	76	67	57	66	57	50	67	61	73	44	70	79	90
29840	MOUNT CARMEL	100	105	143	104	121	124	95	112	100	107	98	70	104	90	110	105	67	107	125	127
29841	NORTH AUGUSTA	90	85	82	86	84	91	87	88	88	85	88	67	84	89	85	90	61	88	92	104
29842	BEECH ISLAND	84	74	68	71	72	79	73	77	76	74	76	57	67	79	68	79	52	75	79	92
29843	OLAR	77	52	72	50	52	75	55	68	63	53	62	53	43	64	52	69	41	64	71	83
29845	PLUM BRANCH	86	57	83	55	58	85	61	76	70	58	68	59	46	71	57	77	45	72	81	93
29847	TRENTON	100	72	84	70	71	95	75	87	83	73	81	67	60	86	68	90	55	83	92	106
29848	TROY	97	72	86	70	73	95	74	86	82	73	80	65	62	84	69	89	54	82	92	104
29849	ULMER	84	55	81	52	55	83	59	74	68	56	66	58	44	69	55	76	44	70	78	91
29851	WARRENVILLE	79	54	73	52	54	77	57	69	65	55	63	54	45	66	53	71	42	66	73	85
29853	WILLISTON	81	55	74	52	55	79	58	71	66	56	65	55	45	68	54	73	43	67	75	87
29856	WINDSOR	75	70	60	66	66	67	69	69	69	72	69	52	65	72	65	69	48	69	67	82
29860	NORTH AUGUSTA	107	111	100	109	107	108	101	105	100	104	101	81	103	104	102	100	70	101	101	123
29902	BEAUFORT	91	83	77	84	81	84	89	86	89	87	89	67	84	91	84	89	62	88	88	101
29906	BEAUFORT	89	72	61	72	68	68	82	75	81	82	82	60	73	88	72	79	57	79	72	89
29907	LADYS ISLAND	131	128	132	125	126	127	120	128	118	123	119	98	117	121	121	117	82	121	120	148
29909	OKATIE	132	140	185	139	159	162	125	147	132	141	129	93	138	119	144	137	89	140	162	166
29910	BLUFFTON	119	118	128	120	122	120	117	119	117	124	117	87	119	115	120	117	82	119	121	139
29911	BRUNSON	83	54	80	51	54	81	58	72	66	55	65	57	43	68	54	74	43	68	77	89
29915	DAUFUSKIE ISLAND	117	132	113	135	128	129	118	122	116	118	116	95	125	119	124	116	81	117	121	144
29916	EARLY BRANCH	82	56	73	53	55	79	59	71	67	57	65	55	46	69	54	73	43	67	75	87
29918	ESTILL	84	55	79	52	55	81	59	73	67	56	66	57	45	69	55	75	44	69	77	90
29920	SAINT HELENA ISLAND	118	88	127	85	92	123	89	111	100	89	98	82	76	98	90	110	65	104	118	133
29922	GARNETT	81	53	79	50	53	80	57	72	66	54	64	56	43	67	53	73	42	67	76	88
29924	HAMPTON	89	67	84	66	68	88	72	82	78	69	76	62	60	78	68	84	51	79	87	99
29926	HILTON HEAD ISLAND	150	146	182	147	160	163	142	155	146	154	145	106	146	138	152	149	100	152	165	178
29927	HARDEEVILLE	85	78	67	75	74	77	80	78	81	81	82	59	75	84	74	82	57	79	79	93
29928	HILTON HEAD ISLAND	153	157	193	157	172	174	150	163	155	162	153	110	159	144	163	159	106	161	178	188
29929	ISLANDTON	80	52	77	49	52	79	56	70	64	53	63	55	42	66	52	72	42	66	74	87
29932	LURAY	89	58	85	54	58	87	62	78	71	59	70	61	46	73	58	80	46	73	82	96
29934	PINELAND	86	57	81	55	57	84	61	76	70	58	68	59	46	71	57	78	45	71	80	93
29935	PORT ROYAL	79	69	61	71	66	72	81	73	81	75	80	58	74	82	72	82	56	78	78	89
29936	RIDGELAND	86	65	77	63	64	83	67	77	73	65	72	59	56	75	63	79	49	74	81	94
29940	SEABROOK	91	66	84	62	64	87	69	81	76	67	75	63	55	78	64	82	50	77	84	98
29941	SHELDON	107	70	103	66	70	105	75	94	86	71	84	73	56	88	70	96	56	88	99	116
29943	TILLMAN	101	69	90	66	69	97	73	88	82	70	80	68	57	85	67	91	54	83	93	107
29944	VARNVILLE	90	63	82	60	63	87	66	80	74	64	73	61	52	76	61	82	49	75	84	97
	SOUTH CAROLINA	95	83	86	82	82	92	85	89	88	84	88	68	79	90	81	91	60	88	92	106
	UNITED STATES	100	100	100	100	100	100	100	100	100	100	100	100	100	100	100	100	100	100	100	100

POPULATION CHANGE

ZIP CODE			POPULATION			2000-2009 ANNUAL RATE		HOUSEHOLDS					FAMILIES		
#	POST OFFICE NAME	COUNTY FIPS CODE	2000	2009	2014	% Rate	State Centile	2000	2009	2014	% Annual Rate 2000-2009	2009 Average HH Size	2000	2009	% Annual Rate 2000-2009
29945	YEMASSEE	013	3919	4137	4239	0.6	50	1442	1592	1649	1.1	2.59	1014	1070	0.6
	SOUTH CAROLINA					1.3					1.7	2.45			1.2
	UNITED STATES					1.0					1.1	2.59			0.9

ZIP CODE #	POST OFFICE NAME	RACE (%) White 2000	White 2009	Black 2000	Black 2009	Asian/Pacific 2000	Asian/Pacific 2009	% Hispanic Origin 2000	% Hispanic Origin 2009	2009 AGE DISTRIBUTION (%) 0-4	5-9	10-14	15-19	20-24	25-44	45-64	65-84	85+	18+	MEDIAN AGE 2009	% 2009 Males	% 2009 Females
29945	YEMASSEE	26.6	24.6	72.2	73.8	0.2	0.2	0.9	1.4	7.0	7.3	8.0	7.8	6.8	22.7	27.4	11.3	1.7	72.8	37.0	47.0	53.0
	SOUTH CAROLINA	67.2	65.9	29.5	29.4	0.9	1.4	2.4	3.6	6.5	6.5	6.5	7.2	6.9	26.6	26.8	11.3	1.6	76.4	37.6	48.9	51.1
	UNITED STATES	75.1	72.0	12.3	12.7	3.8	4.6	12.5	15.7	6.8	6.7	6.6	7.1	6.9	27.0	26.0	10.9	1.9	75.7	36.9	49.2	50.8

29945-29945

#	POST OFFICE NAME	2009 Per Capita Income	2009 HH Income Base	2009 HOUSEHOLD INCOME DISTRIBUTION (%) Less than $25,000	$25,000 to $49,999	$50,000 to $99,999	$100,000 to $149,999	$150,000 or More	MEDIAN HOUSEHOLD INCOME 2009	2014	2009 National Centile	2009 State Centile	2009 Home Value Base	2009 HOME VALUE DISTRIBUTION (%) Less than $50,000	$50,000 to $89,999	$90,000 to $174,999	$175,000 to $399,999	$400,000 or More	2009 Median Home Value
29945	YEMASSEE	17607	1592	40.3	26.3	24.9	6.1	2.3	32967	34329	13	10	1293	31.6	29.9	30.8	5.4	2.4	73353
	SOUTH CAROLINA	24352		25.1	26.4	35.2	8.4	4.8	48210	50493				16.4	20.9	37.4	20.6	4.8	112284
	UNITED STATES	27277		20.9	24.4	35.3	11.7	7.6	54719	56938				9.3	13.1	31.6	32.6	13.5	162279

ZIP CODE	FINANCIAL SERVICES				THE HOME						ENTERTAINMENT						PERSONAL			
					Home Improvements		Furnishings													
# POST OFFICE NAME	Auto Loan	Home Loan	Invest-ments	Retire-ment Plans	Home Repair	Lawn & Garden	Comput-ers & Hard-ware-Personal	Major Appli-ances	TV, Radio, Sound Equip-ment	Furni-ture	Dine out/ Carry out	Sports Equip-ment	Fees & Tickets	Toys & Games	Travel	Cable TV	Apparel & Services	Auto Repairs	Health Insur-ance	Pets & Supplies
29945 YEMASSEE	85	55	82	52	55	83	59	75	68	56	67	58	44	69	55	76	44	70	79	92
SOUTH CAROLINA	95	83	86	82	82	92	85	89	88	84	88	68	79	90	81	91	60	88	92	106
UNITED STATES	100	100	100	100	100	100	100	100	100	100	100	100	100	100	100	100	100	100	100	100

ZIP CODE #	POST OFFICE NAME	COUNTY FIPS CODE	POPULATION 2000	POPULATION 2009	POPULATION 2014	2000-2009 ANNUAL RATE % Rate	2000-2009 ANNUAL RATE State Centile	HOUSEHOLDS 2000	HOUSEHOLDS 2009	HOUSEHOLDS 2014	HOUSEHOLDS % Annual Rate 2000-2009	HOUSEHOLDS 2009 Average HH Size	FAMILIES 2000	FAMILIES 2009	FAMILIES % Annual Rate 2000-2009
57001	ALCESTER	127	2051	2199	2311	0.8	84	799	893	953	1.2	2.38	563	634	1.3
57002	AURORA	011	895	901	916	0.1	64	355	375	385	0.6	2.40	258	276	0.7
57003	BALTIC	099	1654	2072	2308	2.5	95	606	787	885	2.9	2.63	484	626	2.8
57004	BERESFORD	083	3221	3254	3352	0.1	64	1290	1335	1381	0.4	2.40	893	933	0.5
57005	BRANDON	099	6988	9641	10975	3.5	97	2348	3417	3933	4.1	2.80	1963	2851	4.1
57006	BROOKINGS	011	19134	20178	20604	0.6	78	7926	8590	8847	0.9	2.20	4160	4608	1.1
57007	BROOKINGS	011	1904	2117	2112	1.2	88	4	4	4	0.0	2.50	3	3	0.0
57010	BURBANK	027	439	452	456	0.3	70	172	182	185	0.6	2.48	131	140	0.7
57012	CANISTOTA	087	1319	1397	1399	0.6	78	474	506	506	0.7	2.66	348	375	0.8
57013	CANTON	083	4294	4389	4679	0.2	67	1627	1693	1812	0.4	2.53	1164	1205	0.4
57014	CENTERVILLE	125	1473	1461	1447	-0.1	55	613	628	626	0.3	2.27	418	434	0.4
57015	CHANCELLOR	125	873	878	874	0.1	64	323	332	331	0.3	2.61	239	249	0.4
57016	CHESTER	079	946	989	1014	0.5	75	344	369	382	0.8	2.68	270	292	0.9
57017	COLMAN	101	1263	1337	1367	0.6	78	470	517	532	1.0	2.59	349	386	1.1
57018	COLTON	099	1384	1591	1726	1.5	92	509	606	665	1.9	2.59	383	453	1.8
57020	CROOKS	099	1222	1494	1694	2.2	94	410	540	621	3.0	2.66	338	446	3.0
57021	DAVIS	125	294	301	298	0.3	70	123	128	127	0.4	2.35	88	93	0.6
57022	DELL RAPIDS	099	4137	4845	5232	1.7	93	1509	1832	2004	2.1	2.57	1102	1332	2.1
57024	EGAN	101	654	655	654	0.0	59	240	249	251	0.4	2.62	165	174	0.6
57025	ELK POINT	127	3027	3460	3716	1.5	92	1166	1370	1482	1.8	2.48	837	992	1.9
57026	ELKTON	011	1291	1378	1416	0.7	81	470	518	537	1.1	2.65	344	385	1.2
57027	FAIRVIEW	083	170	173	183	0.2	67	51	52	55	0.2	3.23	36	36	0.0
57028	FLANDREAU	101	3538	3476	3445	-0.2	47	1395	1412	1410	0.1	2.42	929	954	0.3
57029	FREEMAN	067	2161	2073	2019	-0.4	38	899	882	862	-0.2	2.26	603	601	0.0
57030	GARRETSON	099	2692	3039	3321	1.3	90	909	1136	1254	2.4	2.61	698	869	2.4
57031	GAYVILLE	135	715	701	695	-0.2	47	283	286	286	0.1	2.45	201	206	0.3
57032	HARRISBURG	083	2640	4380	5880	5.6	100	924	1579	2138	6.0	2.77	748	1281	6.0
57033	HARTFORD	099	3829	4984	5581	2.9	97	1308	1779	2017	3.4	2.77	1086	1472	3.3
57034	HUDSON	083	786	801	846	0.2	67	292	300	318	0.3	2.59	202	206	0.2
57035	HUMBOLDT	099	1083	1269	1387	1.7	93	394	482	532	2.2	2.63	310	377	2.1
57036	HURLEY	125	885	894	882	0.1	64	352	364	360	0.4	2.45	259	271	0.5
57037	IRENE	135	1058	1028	1012	-0.3	42	396	396	393	0.0	2.49	283	286	0.1
57038	JEFFERSON	127	1347	1658	1825	2.3	94	505	637	706	2.5	2.60	369	471	2.7
57039	LENNOX	083	3125	3985	4775	2.7	97	1213	1610	1953	3.1	2.43	855	1119	3.0
57040	LESTERVILLE	135	429	428	430	0.0	59	160	166	168	0.4	2.58	127	133	0.5
57042	MADISON	079	7831	7775	7827	-0.1	55	3074	3194	3243	0.4	2.26	1860	1960	0.6
57043	MARION	125	1543	1549	1525	0.0	59	581	594	587	0.2	2.51	417	432	0.4
57045	MENNO	067	1327	1262	1226	-0.5	33	519	507	495	-0.3	2.37	362	358	-0.1
57046	MISSION HILL	135	708	698	694	-0.2	47	265	270	270	0.2	2.59	194	200	0.3
57047	MONROE	125	219	217	214	-0.1	55	94	96	95	0.2	2.23	75	77	0.3
57048	MONTROSE	087	1123	1172	1174	0.5	75	407	436	438	0.7	2.69	312	337	0.8
57049	NORTH SIOUX CITY	127	4268	5516	6182	2.8	97	1669	2242	2532	3.2	2.46	1206	1639	3.4
57050	NUNDA	079	314	310	313	-0.1	55	123	128	130	0.4	2.31	88	92	0.5
57051	OLDHAM	077	392	356	340	-1.0	15	168	158	153	-0.7	2.22	112	107	-0.5
57052	OLIVET	067	484	462	448	-0.5	33	163	159	156	-0.3	2.90	128	126	-0.2
57053	PARKER	125	1789	1796	1778	0.0	59	706	725	720	0.3	2.45	518	538	0.4
57054	RAMONA	079	577	576	583	0.0	59	237	247	253	0.4	2.28	174	183	0.5
57055	RENNER	099	933	1171	1330	2.5	95	337	426	489	2.6	2.75	266	336	2.6
57057	RUTLAND	079	107	106	107	-0.1	55	39	41	41	0.5	2.46	28	29	0.4
57058	SALEM	087	2059	2048	2017	-0.1	55	806	820	810	0.2	2.42	539	556	0.3
57059	SCOTLAND	009	1531	1451	1386	-0.6	29	608	566	540	-0.8	2.21	397	374	-0.6
57062	SPRINGFIELD	009	2074	2223	2177	0.8	84	545	535	519	-0.2	2.38	383	381	-0.1
57063	TABOR	009	906	940	938	0.4	73	349	372	374	0.7	2.52	255	274	0.8
57064	TEA	083	2850	3582	4533	2.5	95	936	1207	1540	2.8	2.97	774	1000	2.8
57065	TRENT	101	679	708	721	0.5	75	253	275	283	0.9	2.53	191	210	1.0
57066	TYNDALL	009	1793	1687	1616	-0.7	26	722	686	660	-0.6	2.31	467	449	-0.4
57067	UTICA	135	633	612	607	-0.4	38	214	215	216	0.1	2.85	164	166	0.1
57068	VALLEY SPRINGS	099	1590	1857	2021	1.7	93	544	657	722	2.1	2.82	435	527	2.1
57069	VERMILLION	027	11562	11277	11159	-0.3	42	4150	4153	4131	0.0	2.20	2186	2234	0.2
57070	VIBORG	125	1426	1419	1398	-0.1	55	585	601	596	0.3	2.26	374	390	0.5
57071	VOLGA	011	2456	2645	2732	0.8	84	950	1063	1109	1.2	2.49	713	808	1.4
57072	VOLIN	135	664	655	653	-0.1	55	250	256	257	0.3	2.56	193	199	0.3
57073	WAKONDA	027	756	725	713	-0.5	33	269	263	260	-0.2	2.48	190	188	-0.1
57075	WENTWORTH	079	1032	1307	1419	2.6	96	413	550	603	3.1	2.37	301	405	3.3
57076	WINFRED	079	539	532	535	-0.1	55	178	182	185	0.2	2.92	140	144	0.3
57077	WORTHING	083	1049	1461	1804	3.6	98	381	540	667	3.8	2.71	302	427	3.8
57078	YANKTON	135	17972	18419	18519	0.3	70	6828	7111	7196	0.4	2.31	4381	4638	0.6
57103	SIOUX FALLS	099	32841	36885	39611	1.3	90	12639	14624	15832	1.6	2.50	8672	9999	1.6
57104	SIOUX FALLS	099	26028	28218	29486	0.9	86	11262	12381	13119	1.0	2.05	5372	5929	1.1
57105	SIOUX FALLS	099	24194	25167	26198	0.4	73	10214	11109	11722	0.9	2.14	6261	6752	0.8
57106	SIOUX FALLS	099	27526	39036	44989	3.8	98	10988	15710	18132	3.9	2.45	7058	10384	4.3
57107	SIOUX FALLS	099	5125	7864	9096	4.7	99	1922	3012	3503	5.0	2.60	1430	2299	5.3
57108	SIOUX FALLS	083	6097	16361	22895	11.3	100	2225	6217	8763	11.7	2.63	1712	4798	11.8
57110	SIOUX FALLS	099	8446	11922	13583	3.8	98	2853	4185	4810	4.2	2.82	2334	3416	4.2
57197	SIOUX FALLS	099	773	1245	1252	5.3	99	5	5	6	0.0	2.60	4	4	0.0
57201	WATERTOWN	029	23497	24377	24827	0.4	73	9494	10161	10428	0.7	2.36	6188	6730	0.9
57212	ARLINGTON	077	2171	2246	2246	0.4	73	871	925	931	0.7	2.37	597	641	0.8
57213	ASTORIA	039	421	410	403	-0.3	42	167	170	168	0.2	2.40	113	116	0.3
57216	BIG STONE CITY	051	890	840	809	-0.6	29	361	356	347	-0.2	2.32	249	249	0.0
57217	BRADLEY	025	394	355	335	-1.1	12	145	133	126	-0.9	2.59	103	96	-0.8
57218	BRANDT	039	609	598	588	-0.2	47	238	244	242	0.3	2.45	166	172	0.4
57219	BRISTOL	037	619	624	619	0.1	64	262	277	278	0.6	2.12	164	177	0.8
57220	BRUCE	011	854	862	868	0.1	64	333	349	355	0.5	2.47	258	273	0.6
57221	BRYANT	057	749	761	763	0.2	67	277	282	281	0.2	2.60	187	193	0.3
57223	CASTLEWOOD	057	1352	1435	1471	0.6	78	471	511	526	0.9	2.76	360	394	1.0
57224	CLAIRE CITY	109	324	305	295	-0.7	26	128	124	120	-0.3	2.46	101	98	-0.3
57225	CLARK	025	2060	1891	1799	-0.9	18	807	753	717	-0.7	2.42	532	503	-0.6
57226	CLEAR LAKE	039	1939	1906	1870	-0.2	47	795	802	794	0.1	2.29	525	538	0.3
57227	CORONA	109	772	763	752	-0.1	55	313	319	316	0.2	2.39	217	225	0.4
57231	DE SMET	077	1842	1763	1715	-0.5	33	789	786	770	0.0	2.15	500	506	0.1
57232	EDEN	091	299	292	286	-0.3	42	123	124	122	0.1	2.35	88	90	0.2
57233	ERWIN	077	177	170	166	-0.4	38	69	69	68	0.0	2.46	52	53	0.2
57234	ESTELLINE	057	1202	1281	1319	0.7	81	499	547	565	1.0	2.26	338	376	1.2
57235	FLORENCE	029	823	845	861	0.3	70	290	311	320	0.8	2.71	226	243	0.8
57236	GARDEN CITY	025	156	142	134	-1.0	15	62	57	54	-0.9	2.49	47	44	-0.7
	SOUTH DAKOTA					0.8					1.2	2.43			1.3
	UNITED STATES					1.0					1.1	2.59			0.9

ZIP CODE		RACE (%)						% Hispanic Origin		2009 AGE DISTRIBUTION (%)										MEDIAN AGE		
#	POST OFFICE NAME	White		Black		Asian/Pacific															%	%
		2000	2009	2000	2009	2000	2009	2000	2009	0-4	5-9	10-14	15-19	20-24	25-44	45-64	65-84	85+	18+	2009	2009 Males	2009 Females
57001	ALCESTER	98.7	98.3	0.0	0.0	0.6	0.9	0.2	0.2	4.8	5.4	6.5	7.8	3.9	22.3	29.1	15.8	4.5	77.6	44.5	48.6	51.4
57002	AURORA	98.1	97.4	0.0	0.0	0.1	0.2	1.0	1.6	6.2	7.0	6.8	6.1	4.8	27.5	30.2	10.4	1.0	76.1	38.9	51.9	48.1
57003	BALTIC	98.9	98.6	0.0	0.0	0.2	0.2	0.1	0.2	7.4	7.7	8.3	7.6	4.6	28.8	26.3	8.3	1.1	71.8	36.5	51.7	48.3
57004	BERESFORD	98.9	98.5	0.1	0.1	0.3	0.5	0.5	0.8	6.5	6.3	6.7	6.7	5.2	24.1	26.9	13.7	3.8	76.2	40.6	49.1	50.9
57005	BRANDON	98.3	97.7	0.3	0.4	0.3	0.4	0.4	0.7	9.2	8.3	8.4	7.5	5.4	29.1	24.4	6.8	0.8	69.1	32.8	49.1	50.9
57006	BROOKINGS	95.4	93.5	0.4	0.6	1.9	3.1	0.9	1.3	5.8	5.0	4.9	7.7	22.0	24.5	19.4	8.2	2.5	81.2	27.8	50.2	49.8
57007	BROOKINGS	99.0	98.6	0.1	0.1	0.4	0.6	0.2	0.2	0.6	0.6	0.6	53.1	38.9	2.3	2.8	1.1	0.0	97.8	19.5	49.7	50.3
57010	BURBANK	97.0	96.2	0.2	0.2	0.7	1.1	0.7	0.9	6.9	7.3	7.5	6.4	4.0	23.7	31.6	11.3	1.3	74.3	41.1	51.8	48.2
57012	CANISTOTA	98.3	97.9	0.1	0.1	0.2	0.1	1.0	1.4	7.2	7.2	8.2	7.9	5.1	20.9	26.5	12.8	4.2	72.4	40.6	51.1	48.9
57013	CANTON	97.8	97.2	0.3	0.3	0.5	0.7	0.4	0.5	7.2	6.8	6.8	6.9	6.6	24.8	26.2	11.6	3.1	74.5	37.6	49.6	50.4
57014	CENTERVILLE	99.2	99.0	0.1	0.1	0.1	0.2	0.5	0.7	5.3	5.3	5.5	6.4	6.3	21.5	29.1	16.4	4.3	79.8	44.8	49.2	50.8
57015	CHANCELLOR	98.2	97.9	0.3	0.3	0.1	0.2	0.5	0.5	6.0	7.2	7.7	6.8	4.3	24.4	27.9	12.8	2.8	74.3	40.5	50.8	49.2
57016	CHESTER	98.3	97.7	0.0	0.0	0.3	0.5	0.2	0.3	6.0	6.7	6.8	6.7	4.6	23.0	30.8	14.1	1.5	76.4	42.2	49.5	50.5
57017	COLMAN	97.0	96.6	0.3	0.4	0.5	0.5	0.7	0.7	6.1	6.9	9.0	8.6	4.7	25.0	27.5	10.2	2.0	72.4	37.7	51.1	48.9
57018	COLTON	99.2	99.0	0.0	0.0	0.1	0.2	0.8	1.2	7.2	6.9	7.4	7.2	5.1	24.2	25.3	14.0	2.8	74.2	39.2	51.0	49.0
57020	CROOKS	96.6	95.4	0.7	0.7	0.2	0.3	1.0	1.5	7.2	7.4	8.6	9.7	6.0	28.2	26.0	6.2	0.8	69.9	32.8	52.1	47.9
57021	DAVIS	99.3	99.3	0.0	0.0	0.3	0.3	0.0	0.0	7.3	8.0	7.6	6.3	3.7	22.9	28.6	13.0	2.7	73.1	40.1	50.5	49.5
57022	DELL RAPIDS	98.5	97.9	0.1	0.2	0.2	0.4	0.6	0.9	7.3	6.9	7.2	7.3	6.6	24.5	25.3	11.0	3.8	73.8	37.5	48.8	51.2
57024	EGAN	80.3	77.6	0.2	0.2	0.2	0.2	0.8	0.8	6.9	7.3	7.9	7.8	5.5	24.6	27.0	10.8	2.1	72.7	37.3	49.6	50.4
57025	ELK POINT	98.4	98.0	0.3	0.3	0.3	0.5	0.8	1.2	7.3	7.6	8.0	7.4	4.5	24.4	27.5	11.0	2.4	72.6	38.5	49.7	50.3
57026	ELKTON	98.4	97.9	0.1	0.1	0.1	0.1	1.0	1.5	5.8	6.3	6.5	7.3	6.4	24.0	30.2	10.7	2.8	76.6	40.1	50.4	49.6
57027	FAIRVIEW	98.8	98.3	0.0	0.0	0.0	0.0	0.6	1.2	6.4	6.9	7.5	7.5	5.2	22.0	28.9	12.1	3.5	72.8	41.0	49.7	50.3
57028	FLANDREAU	77.3	74.0	0.3	0.3	0.8	0.8	0.8	0.9	6.8	6.5	6.3	6.8	7.2	23.5	26.9	12.5	3.7	76.2	39.0	49.4	50.6
57029	FREEMAN	99.3	99.2	0.1	0.1	0.1	0.1	0.2	0.3	5.5	5.7	5.8	6.0	5.1	19.5	28.2	17.4	6.8	79.0	46.7	48.0	52.0
57030	GARRETSON	98.0	96.2	0.1	1.6	0.2	0.2	0.3	0.3	6.4	6.8	7.3	7.1	5.0	22.4	31.2	11.1	2.8	78.2	41.6	50.1	49.9
57031	GAYVILLE	97.5	96.4	0.0	0.0	0.3	0.4	0.4	0.7	6.7	7.6	7.8	6.8	4.3	22.7	31.4	11.0	1.7	73.6	40.6	52.5	47.5
57032	HARRISBURG	98.1	97.6	0.3	0.2	0.5	0.7	0.6	0.7	7.3	7.3	7.4	7.2	6.2	28.1	28.2	7.4	0.9	75.1	35.6	49.8	50.2
57033	HARTFORD	98.4	97.7	0.1	0.1	0.1	0.1	0.4	0.6	7.0	7.9	8.7	8.9	4.9	27.1	26.4	7.7	1.4	70.3	35.7	49.8	50.2
57034	HUDSON	98.9	98.6	0.0	0.0	0.0	0.0	0.6	0.6	6.7	7.0	7.4	7.7	4.9	22.5	28.3	12.0	3.5	73.2	40.7	50.3	49.7
57035	HUMBOLDT	97.9	97.2	0.0	0.0	0.6	0.9	0.2	0.2	7.8	8.0	8.0	8.1	4.6	25.1	26.8	10.2	1.3	74.6	37.6	49.7	50.3
57036	HURLEY	99.5	99.6	0.0	0.0	0.2	0.2	0.1	0.1	6.9	7.4	7.8	6.8	3.8	22.1	29.8	13.1	2.2	73.4	40.9	51.2	48.8
57037	IRENE	99.0	98.6	0.0	0.0	0.0	0.0	0.8	1.2	5.6	5.8	6.2	6.7	5.4	21.3	29.6	15.1	4.2	78.1	44.1	50.1	49.9
57038	JEFFERSON	96.3	95.0	0.7	0.7	1.2	2.0	1.6	2.3	6.5	6.6	7.0	7.4	5.4	26.5	29.5	9.9	1.2	75.3	38.9	50.7	49.3
57039	LENNOX	98.8	98.4	0.2	0.1	0.1	0.1	0.7	1.0	6.4	6.7	7.0	6.9	4.9	24.6	28.2	12.2	3.2	75.2	40.4	48.7	51.3
57040	LESTERVILLE	98.1	97.9	0.0	0.0	0.2	0.2	0.9	1.4	6.3	7.0	7.9	8.4	4.0	20.8	31.1	13.1	1.4	73.6	41.5	51.6	48.4
57042	MADISON	97.4	96.4	0.2	0.3	0.7	1.1	0.9	1.4	5.5	5.4	6.0	10.8	10.3	21.1	23.8	13.4	3.7	78.7	36.7	49.3	50.7
57043	MARION	98.6	98.5	0.2	0.2	0.2	0.2	1.0	1.0	5.1	5.6	6.8	7.1	5.4	19.9	28.9	16.5	4.8	77.5	45.1	50.2	49.8
57045	MENNO	98.9	98.7	0.1	0.1	0.1	0.1	0.2	0.2	4.9	5.9	5.9	6.1	3.4	17.7	25.8	23.5	6.7	79.0	49.7	49.4	50.6
57046	MISSION HILL	97.5	96.4	0.0	0.0	0.1	0.4	0.4	0.6	6.6	7.3	7.7	7.3	4.4	22.6	31.4	10.9	1.7	73.8	40.5	52.0	48.0
57047	MONROE	98.2	98.2	0.5	0.5	0.5	0.5	0.5	0.9	5.1	6.5	8.8	7.8	5.1	24.0	27.2	13.4	2.3	74.2	39.8	53.0	47.0
57048	MONTROSE	99.3	99.0	0.0	0.1	0.1	0.1	0.6	0.9	7.6	7.9	8.4	7.8	4.4	23.3	27.5	11.2	2.0	71.4	38.2	49.7	50.3
57049	NORTH SIOUX CITY	94.0	92.1	0.5	0.6	3.0	4.4	2.3	3.2	7.5	7.2	7.1	6.8	5.8	27.5	27.2	9.8	1.0	74.0	36.8	50.0	50.0
57050	NUNDA	98.4	97.7	0.3	0.3	0.3	0.6	0.3	0.3	5.5	6.5	6.1	5.2	4.5	22.6	31.6	15.2	2.9	77.4	44.8	51.0	49.0
57051	OLDHAM	98.5	98.0	0.3	0.3	0.3	0.6	1.0	1.4	6.2	6.2	7.0	6.5	4.8	17.1	28.4	20.8	3.1	76.4	46.6	49.4	50.6
57052	OLIVET	99.2	99.1	0.0	0.0	0.2	0.2	0.2	0.2	7.1	8.0	8.0	7.4	4.5	21.6	29.2	13.0	1.1	72.1	39.2	52.6	47.4
57053	PARKER	98.2	98.1	0.3	0.3	0.2	0.2	0.4	0.4	6.3	7.2	7.8	6.3	4.0	24.2	28.1	13.3	2.7	74.2	40.9	50.6	49.4
57054	RAMONA	99.1	99.0	0.2	0.2	0.2	0.3	0.2	0.3	5.9	6.6	7.3	7.5	3.6	22.2	31.9	13.0	1.9	74.7	43.0	52.8	47.2
57055	RENNER	97.7	97.2	0.2	0.3	0.2	0.3	1.1	1.6	6.3	6.8	7.3	6.7	4.2	26.7	31.4	9.6	0.9	75.3	39.9	50.5	49.5
57057	RUTLAND	98.1	97.2	0.0	0.0	0.0	0.9	0.0	0.0	5.7	5.7	5.7	5.7	4.7	22.6	32.1	15.1	2.8	78.3	45.0	50.9	49.1
57058	SALEM	99.0	98.7	0.0	0.0	0.2	0.2	0.4	0.6	6.6	6.8	6.8	6.6	4.8	22.3	25.8	15.5	4.6	75.3	41.8	49.1	50.9
57059	SCOTLAND	95.8	95.7	0.7	0.6	0.3	0.3	1.2	1.3	4.4	4.8	5.9	8.6	5.7	17.0	24.9	19.6	9.1	78.2	47.9	50.5	49.5
57062	SPRINGFIELD	90.5	89.6	1.1	1.1	0.0	0.0	0.5	0.4	3.4	3.7	3.9	5.9	12.1	35.9	24.4	9.3	1.4	85.7	36.7	71.7	28.3
57063	TABOR	98.6	98.6	0.3	0.3	0.0	0.0	0.4	0.5	6.9	7.1	7.2	6.7	4.1	23.3	28.5	13.4	2.7	74.5	40.8	49.3	50.7
57064	TEA	96.2	95.4	0.6	0.5	0.7	0.9	1.0	1.3	10.7	9.6	8.5	6.3	5.0	37.2	18.8	3.6	0.3	67.2	31.0	50.9	49.1
57065	TRENT	98.4	98.2	0.1	0.1	0.0	0.0	0.4	0.4	5.5	7.1	8.2	9.0	3.4	24.0	30.1	10.9	1.8	72.7	40.2	52.3	47.7
57066	TYNDALL	98.4	98.4	0.4	0.4	0.0	0.0	0.5	0.5	5.9	5.6	6.5	7.6	5.4	19.3	27.7	16.4	5.7	76.7	44.8	50.0	50.0
57067	UTICA	98.3	97.9	0.2	0.2	0.0	0.0	0.5	0.7	7.5	8.0	8.7	8.0	4.2	22.1	29.6	10.8	1.1	70.6	38.6	52.0	48.0
57068	VALLEY SPRINGS	98.1	97.3	0.4	0.5	0.4	0.6	0.7	1.1	7.8	8.1	8.2	6.9	4.7	27.5	28.3	7.6	0.9	71.5	36.6	50.1	49.9
57069	VERMILLION	91.8	88.9	1.2	1.5	2.2	3.6	1.0	1.4	5.1	4.4	3.9	13.0	26.0	21.3	16.9	7.6	1.7	83.8	24.5	48.5	51.5
57070	VIBORG	99.6	99.6	0.0	0.0	0.1	0.1	0.1	0.1	5.4	5.6	6.0	6.5	5.1	20.3	28.0	16.8	6.3	78.4	45.7	47.5	52.5
57071	VOLGA	98.1	97.5	0.0	0.0	0.3	0.4	0.6	0.9	6.6	7.0	7.3	6.3	4.5	27.7	28.1	10.9	1.7	75.1	38.6	50.5	49.5
57072	VOLIN	97.4	96.9	0.0	0.0	0.2	0.2	0.3	0.5	6.6	7.2	7.3	7.2	4.6	22.6	31.9	11.1	1.5	74.5	41.1	51.9	48.1
57073	WAKONDA	99.3	98.9	0.0	0.1	0.1	0.3	0.3	0.4	5.9	5.9	6.3	6.6	4.8	19.7	26.5	17.2	6.9	78.1	45.5	47.4	52.6
57075	WENTWORTH	98.4	97.6	0.3	0.5	0.2	0.3	0.5	0.8	4.1	5.7	5.7	8.6	5.0	21.2	37.1	12.0	0.5	78.0	44.8	53.9	46.1
57076	WINFRED	99.3	98.9	0.0	0.0	0.2	0.2	0.9	1.3	7.0	7.7	7.7	6.6	4.3	21.2	32.7	11.8	0.9	73.7	40.9	52.4	47.6
57077	WORTHING	99.0	98.6	0.1	0.1	0.2	0.3	0.4	0.5	7.5	7.2	7.6	8.5	5.7	29.7	24.0	8.8	1.0	72.5	34.0	52.6	47.4
57078	YANKTON	94.6	92.8	1.4	1.9	0.5	0.8	2.1	3.0	6.1	6.2	6.4	7.0	6.8	26.6	26.3	11.7	2.9	77.1	38.2	50.8	49.2
57103	SIOUX FALLS	91.1	88.2	2.0	2.2	1.6	2.6	2.9	4.3	7.4	7.3	7.5	7.1	6.5	28.0	26.4	8.7	1.1	74.5	35.3	49.6	50.4
57104	SIOUX FALLS	85.3	81.1	3.5	3.8	1.3	2.0	4.6	6.7	6.7	5.8	5.2	6.0	9.5	33.8	22.0	8.5	2.5	79.2	33.6	53.5	46.5
57105	SIOUX FALLS	95.2	93.3	1.0	1.2	0.8	1.3	1.4	2.2	5.5	5.4	5.6	6.8	7.2	25.0	25.7	15.2	3.5	80.8	40.5	47.3	52.7
57106	SIOUX FALLS	95.3	93.7	0.9	1.0	1.2	1.8	1.3	2.0	8.1	7.4	6.9	6.5	7.2	33.4	22.5	6.5	1.5	74.8	32.4	48.3	51.7
57107	SIOUX FALLS	95.2	94.5	1.0	0.9	0.4	0.5	1.7	2.4	7.5	7.5	7.7	7.2	5.3	29.3	26.4	8.4	0.7	72.7	36.0	50.5	49.5
57108	SIOUX FALLS	97.1	96.5	0.5	0.4	0.7	1.0	0.9	1.2	6.9	6.6	6.7	6.7	6.1	27.1	29.6	9.0	1.2	79.0	37.6	48.5	51.5
57110	SIOUX FALLS	94.1	91.8	1.6	1.8	1.2	2.0	1.8	2.8	10.3	9.9	9.2	7.3	5.4	28.6	23.4	5.3	0.7	67.3	30.6	48.8	51.2
57197	SIOUX FALLS	96.5	93.6	0.8	1.1	1.8	2.7	0.8	1.6	2.0	1.8	1.6	31.3	46.7	7.9	4.7	3.5	0.5	91.0	21.4	40.3	59.7
57201	WATERTOWN	96.6	95.4	0.1	0.2	0.3	0.5	1.1	1.7	7.2	6.9	6.7	6.8	6.1	27.3	25.2	11.1	2.7	75.0	36.2	49.3	50.7
57212	ARLINGTON	98.7	98.0	0.0	0.0	0.4	0.7	0.6	0.9	6.1	6.3	6.4	6.2	5.0	21.5	28.8	15.3	4.5	77.3	43.8	50.2	49.8
57213	ASTORIA	98.3	98.3	0.2	0.2	0.2	0.2	0.5	0.5	6.8	7.3	7.3	6.3	4.1	21.7	29.3	14.4	2.7	74.6	41.4	52.4	47.6
57216	BIG STONE CITY	99.0	98.6	0.0	0.0	0.0	0.0	0.3	0.5	5.4	5.8	6.1	6.1	5.2	20.4	34.5	14.2	2.4	78.3	45.6	51.4	48.6
57217	BRADLEY	98.7	98.6	0.0	0.0	0.3	0.3	0.3	0.3	4.2	4.5	5.4	7.0	4.5	22.0	30.1	16.6	5.6	81.1	46.5	51.3	48.7
57218	BRANDT	98.7	98.7	0.2	0.2	0.2	0.2	0.8	0.8	5.9	6.5	6.5	6.7	4.5	21.7	30.6	15.2	2.3	76.8	43.6	50.7	49.3
57219	BRISTOL	99.7	99.7	0.3	0.3	0.0	0.0	0.0	0.0	5.3	6.1	6.3	5.9	3.8	18.6	28.8	19.1	6.1	77.7	47.6	50.2	49.8
57220	BRUCE	97.8	97.0	0.0	0.0	0.4	0.5	2.0	2.9	6.0	6.7	7.2	7.0	3.9	24.4	31.7	11.6	1.5	75.6	41.4	53.0	47.0
57221	BRYANT	99.3	99.1	0.1	0.1	0.1	0.3	0.3	0.4	8.1	8.5	7.8	7.1	4.9	20.5	25.1	13.4	4.6	70.6	38.0	49.9	50.1
57223	CASTLEWOOD	98.7	98.4	0.1	0.1	0.3	0.5	0.6	0.8	6.1	7.2	9.1	10.6	4.2	23.2	25.2	11.4	3.1	70.2	37.6	50.8	49.2
57224	CLAIRE CITY	86.8	84.6	0.0	0.0	0.0	0.0	0.0	0.0	4.3	6.9	4.9	9.8	3.6	21.6	31.8	15.4	1.6	76.1	44.0	55.4	44.6
57225	CLARK	98.9	98.7	0.1	0.2	0.2	0.2	0.4	0.6	5.6	5.9	6.0	6.1	5.1	19.8	28.7	17.6	5.2	78.3	46.0	48.0	52.0
57226	CLEAR LAKE	98.8	98.7	0.0	0.0	0.3	0.3	0.4	0.4	6.0	5.8	6.0	6.9	5.4	21.2	26.7	16.4	5.6	78.2	43.9	48.6	51.4
57227	CORONA	97.7	97.2	0.0	0.0	0.4	0.4	0.0	0.0	5.9	6.7	7.2	7.1	4.1	18.6	30.8	17.4	2.2	75.8	45.3	50.5	49.5
57231	DE SMET	98.4	98.0	0.1	0.1	0.2	0.3	0.7	1.0	5.6	5.2	6.1	6.2	4.0	19.6	28.0	19.2	6.2	79.4	47.4	47.4	52.6
57232	EDEN	83.3	81.2	0.3	0.3	0.0	0.0	0.7	0.3	6.5	6.8	7.2	7.2	4.8	20.2	29.5	15.4	2.4	74.7	42.9	51.7	48.3
57233	ERWIN	99.4	99.4	0.0	0.0	0.0	0.0	0.0	0.0	4.7	5.9	6.5	7.1	4.7	18.8	34.7	15.3	2.4	78.2	46.3	51.8	48.2
57234	ESTELLINE	97.4	96.9	0.2	0.2	0.2	0.4	1.2	1.8	4.1	4.2	4.9	6.3	4.4	21.6	30.5	19.0	4.9	82.0	47.9	50.0	50.0
57235	FLORENCE	98.4	97.9	0.1	0.1	0.1	0.1	0.2	0.2	6.7	7.9	9.6	7.1	4.6	25.2	25.6	12.1	1.2	70.9	37.5	50.4	49.6
57236	GARDEN CITY	98.7	98.6	0.0	0.0	0.0	0.0	1.3	1.4	7.7	7.7	7.7	7.0	5.6	22.5	28.9	10.6	2.1	72.5	38.9	48.6	51.4
	SOUTH DAKOTA	88.7	87.0	0.6	0.8	0.6	1.0	1.4	2.0	6.9	6.7	6.9	7.6	7.3	25.0	25.9	11.3	2.4	75.3	36.7	49.7	50.3
	UNITED STATES	75.1	72.0	12.3	12.7	3.8	4.6	12.5	15.7	6.8	6.7	6.6	7.1	6.9	27.0	26.0	10.9	1.9	75.7	36.9	49.2	50.8

ZIP CODE #	POST OFFICE NAME	2009 Per Capita Income	2009 HH Income Base	2009 HOUSEHOLD INCOME DISTRIBUTION (%) Less than $25,000	$25,000 to $49,999	$50,000 to $99,999	$100,000 to $149,999	$150,000 or More	MEDIAN HOUSEHOLD INCOME 2009	2014	2009 National Centile	2009 State Centile	2009 Home Value Base	2009 HOME VALUE DISTRIBUTION (%) Less than $50,000	$50,000 to $89,999	$90,000 to $174,999	$175,000 to $399,999	$400,000 or More	2009 Median Home Value
57001	ALCESTER	19889	893	25.9	31.1	39.5	2.8	0.7	42910	45522	42	68	664	26.1	32.8	33.1	6.8	1.2	81918
57002	AURORA	21782	375	20.5	32.3	42.7	2.4	2.1	47907	47786	56	85	285	11.6	19.6	50.9	16.1	1.8	118490
57003	BALTIC	24069	787	14.5	24.7	52.7	6.1	2.0	60330	62328	78	95	678	23.5	13.4	34.7	25.2	3.2	120833
57004	BERESFORD	22451	1335	21.1	31.4	41.6	3.5	2.4	47133	49390	54	83	1013	18.2	25.3	43.1	12.2	1.2	101730
57005	BRANDON	30724	3417	7.0	12.3	50.8	22.7	7.3	77707	81233	91	100	2752	2.8	5.1	49.5	39.3	3.4	165299
57006	BROOKINGS	24430	8590	27.8	26.3	35.6	6.6	3.5	45217	47730	49	77	4374	11.6	9.2	48.7	27.8	2.5	140733
57007	BROOKINGS	9786	4	0.0	0.0	100.0	0.0	0.0	60000	60000	77	95	3	0.0	0.0	0.0	100.0	0.0	225000
57010	BURBANK	22822	182	23.6	26.9	40.1	7.1	2.2	49393	50885	60	87	138	13.0	21.0	41.3	20.3	4.3	114130
57012	CANISTOTA	17263	506	26.9	32.4	36.2	3.0	1.6	41638	43692	38	62	410	20.5	30.0	37.1	12.0	0.5	89412
57013	CANTON	24693	1693	16.6	27.2	43.0	10.2	3.0	55612	56127	72	94	1315	19.5	23.4	38.9	17.2	1.0	101890
57014	CENTERVILLE	20068	628	26.6	36.1	32.2	3.8	1.3	40393	42620	34	55	479	21.9	32.6	33.2	11.5	0.8	86228
57015	CHANCELLOR	20911	332	22.3	27.4	43.7	4.2	2.4	50154	49636	62	88	265	14.0	25.3	41.5	17.4	1.9	107552
57016	CHESTER	22318	369	16.8	32.5	42.5	4.6	3.5	50436	49712	62	88	311	15.4	15.4	37.6	27.0	4.5	128819
57017	COLMAN	21717	517	19.7	31.1	42.6	4.3	2.3	49024	49330	59	86	409	11.2	21.8	42.8	19.6	4.6	119556
57018	COLTON	24361	606	14.7	24.8	53.1	5.0	2.5	60091	62838	77	95	487	20.5	27.3	38.2	12.7	1.2	95250
57020	CROOKS	27047	540	8.7	20.6	56.5	10.6	3.7	67171	72661	85	98	462	5.6	6.9	61.5	24.7	1.3	136688
57021	DAVIS	21139	128	24.2	31.3	39.1	3.1	2.3	42718	42518	42	67	105	18.1	32.4	38.1	10.5	1.0	89545
57022	DELL RAPIDS	24449	1832	17.5	20.6	51.0	8.2	2.6	62266	65688	80	96	1379	11.2	18.9	45.5	22.8	1.6	121520
57024	EGAN	18374	249	28.9	33.3	32.5	2.8	2.4	40582	42557	35	56	166	24.1	23.5	38.6	12.7	1.2	93636
57025	ELK POINT	22198	1370	21.8	26.4	45.1	5.1	1.6	51628	54091	65	89	1040	16.2	24.6	47.9	10.4	1.0	103837
57026	ELKTON	20292	518	27.4	26.4	40.5	2.7	2.9	46437	47493	53	81	389	21.6	26.2	38.8	11.8	1.5	92742
57027	FAIRVIEW	15181	52	21.2	36.5	38.5	3.8	0.0	43138	43341	43	69	44	38.6	43.2	13.6	4.5	0.0	65000
57028	FLANDREAU	21424	1412	25.4	29.5	38.4	4.5	2.2	44729	45809	47	76	974	16.8	31.8	41.0	9.1	1.2	91494
57029	FREEMAN	19120	882	31.0	36.1	29.4	1.6	2.0	36966	38930	23	36	680	23.1	25.9	36.0	14.3	0.7	92000
57030	GARRETSON	21873	1136	16.4	30.5	45.3	5.9	1.9	52264	53032	66	91	895	15.9	24.8	34.1	20.7	4.6	110520
57031	GAYVILLE	19539	286	23.8	31.1	40.9	3.5	0.7	44631	48457	47	76	223	13.9	33.6	44.4	5.8	2.2	92037
57032	HARRISBURG	30123	1579	10.6	16.8	48.3	16.4	7.9	70328	75170	87	99	1264	6.0	13.8	32.7	38.8	8.7	170032
57033	HARTFORD	25619	1779	8.7	23.3	53.9	10.9	3.2	64219	68427	83	98	1487	13.5	10.3	47.6	27.4	1.2	135012
57034	HUDSON	18753	300	22.0	37.7	35.7	3.7	1.0	42672	43803	41	66	249	40.6	35.7	16.1	5.6	2.0	63571
57035	HUMBOLDT	20866	482	22.6	25.1	46.3	4.1	1.9	51716	51034	65	90	383	16.7	25.1	37.1	19.3	1.8	103233
57036	HURLEY	20890	364	24.2	30.8	39.0	3.0	3.0	43451	43684	44	70	296	17.6	32.4	37.8	11.5	0.7	90000
57037	IRENE	18398	396	29.5	32.3	32.1	4.8	1.3	40457	43193	34	56	306	25.2	23.2	37.3	14.1	0.3	91923
57038	JEFFERSON	27057	637	15.7	22.9	48.0	7.4	6.0	61423	62377	79	96	494	19.4	23.3	39.5	13.4	4.5	102000
57039	LENNOX	21910	1610	19.3	30.7	42.9	6.1	1.1	50000	48935	61	87	1303	20.3	24.4	36.6	17.8	0.9	101193
57040	LESTERVILLE	20238	166	24.7	30.7	39.2	3.6	1.8	45822	48054	51	79	135	22.2	24.4	28.1	19.3	5.9	99000
57042	MADISON	20778	3194	26.7	32.0	36.3	3.3	1.7	42248	45389	40	65	2066	10.2	20.0	49.2	20.0	0.6	115851
57043	MARION	20508	594	24.9	30.3	37.7	4.5	2.5	45516	46019	50	78	459	26.1	31.6	32.2	9.4	0.7	81548
57045	MENNO	18082	507	33.3	30.2	33.1	2.0	1.4	36707	39328	23	34	408	41.2	26.7	19.9	11.5	0.7	60714
57046	MISSION HILL	18736	270	23.7	32.6	38.9	4.1	0.7	43553	47219	44	71	210	18.6	31.0	40.5	8.6	1.4	90417
57047	MONROE	25590	96	21.9	28.1	42.7	4.2	3.1	50000	50449	61	87	76	14.5	21.1	38.2	22.4	3.9	115385
57048	MONTROSE	18701	436	25.2	28.4	39.4	5.7	1.1	46548	45981	53	81	348	20.4	23.0	40.2	16.4	0.0	102941
57049	NORTH SIOUX CITY	38148	2242	11.5	22.3	38.8	13.7	13.7	68866	70416	86	99	1597	21.9	11.0	30.3	25.0	11.8	123425
57050	NUNDA	20182	128	27.3	35.9	31.3	4.7	0.8	36516	40000	22	32	103	21.4	25.2	35.0	16.5	1.9	95833
57051	OLDHAM	20418	158	34.2	31.0	27.8	3.8	3.2	32494	37087	12	17	121	40.5	16.5	24.0	14.9	4.1	71250
57052	OLIVET	16172	159	30.2	36.5	26.4	3.8	3.1	36882	38022	23	36	126	34.9	22.2	19.8	17.5	5.6	68889
57053	PARKER	21959	725	22.8	28.3	43.2	3.4	2.3	48873	48845	59	86	577	14.9	27.6	42.6	13.9	1.0	102741
57054	RAMONA	22955	247	23.1	32.0	39.7	4.0	1.2	44082	46384	46	73	202	15.3	20.8	48.0	13.9	2.0	111429
57055	RENNER	23656	426	9.4	20.7	61.3	6.8	1.9	61527	64223	79	96	366	23.8	13.4	36.9	23.8	2.2	126596
57057	RUTLAND	18748	41	26.8	39.0	29.3	4.9	0.0	35738	39067	20	30	33	18.2	24.2	45.5	12.1	0.0	101563
57058	SALEM	20887	820	26.6	30.0	36.8	4.4	2.2	43478	45339	44	70	629	20.7	33.4	36.1	8.7	1.1	86357
57059	SCOTLAND	16645	566	34.6	36.2	27.2	1.6	0.4	34424	34661	16	24	435	42.1	29.7	20.5	7.4	0.5	58023
57062	SPRINGFIELD	15193	535	28.8	33.1	33.5	4.7	0.0	39912	44286	32	52	395	23.5	24.3	41.3	10.6	0.3	91848
57063	TABOR	17670	372	28.8	36.0	31.2	3.0	1.1	40408	42111	34	56	288	25.7	31.6	32.6	8.7	1.4	82500
57064	TEA	26115	1207	4.1	10.6	71.7	11.1	2.4	69991	74360	87	99	1106	4.1	13.3	49.5	32.7	0.5	153959
57065	TRENT	21832	275	18.9	39.6	32.7	3.6	5.1	44700	45063	47	76	214	13.1	20.6	39.7	25.2	1.4	115116
57066	TYNDALL	18224	686	34.0	35.9	25.5	2.5	2.2	34916	35299	17	25	502	28.1	32.5	32.3	7.2	0.0	79744
57067	UTICA	17182	215	33.0	28.4	32.6	3.7	2.3	41468	46152	38	61	163	20.2	27.6	31.3	17.2	3.7	93500
57068	VALLEY SPRINGS	23841	657	11.4	23.3	53.6	9.0	2.7	62830	64767	81	97	552	15.0	16.1	38.9	27.2	2.7	116009
57069	VERMILLION	19286	4153	38.7	23.8	30.3	4.4	2.8	35011	36812	18	27	2072	18.2	15.2	44.8	19.1	2.7	113456
57070	VIBORG	20308	601	31.3	35.6	26.1	4.5	2.5	36495	40767	22	32	422	20.4	31.3	41.9	5.2	1.2	88772
57071	VOLGA	22609	1063	19.8	25.9	47.9	5.4	1.0	53105	52901	68	92	840	12.7	15.6	46.9	22.0	2.7	123921
57072	VOLIN	19895	256	23.8	33.6	35.5	5.1	2.0	43188	46335	43	69	200	22.0	23.0	36.5	15.5	3.0	94762
57073	WAKONDA	18036	263	32.7	28.5	31.9	5.3	1.5	39842	43084	32	52	201	34.3	24.9	26.9	12.4	1.5	74231
57075	WENTWORTH	27976	550	14.2	32.0	41.6	6.4	5.8	52387	51234	67	92	450	8.9	22.2	33.3	27.6	8.0	134524
57076	WINFRED	17603	182	25.8	22.0	48.9	2.2	1.1	51789	52417	65	90	145	11.7	20.7	44.8	21.4	1.4	118750
57077	WORTHING	21148	540	12.4	32.4	47.8	6.5	0.9	54918	54572	71	93	472	11.9	21.4	51.9	13.3	1.5	110659
57078	YANKTON	22203	7111	24.7	29.5	38.5	4.1	3.2	45886	48615	51	80	4791	12.3	16.7	48.1	19.8	3.0	119378
57103	SIOUX FALLS	29757	14624	14.1	23.7	43.5	11.7	7.0	63492	67428	82	97	9626	5.5	11.2	48.2	31.7	3.4	145760
57104	SIOUX FALLS	22510	12381	26.4	34.1	34.0	3.8	1.7	40819	42860	35	58	5004	11.9	31.8	47.4	7.3	1.7	97965
57105	SIOUX FALLS	30694	11109	16.6	27.6	43.3	7.2	5.3	55513	57602	72	94	7463	3.2	12.5	55.5	24.1	4.7	135401
57106	SIOUX FALLS	29369	15710	12.7	23.5	45.8	12.1	5.9	63726	68145	82	97	9883	11.2	6.6	45.8	34.4	2.0	157104
57107	SIOUX FALLS	24926	3012	10.1	26.8	52.0	9.0	2.3	62657	65873	81	97	2568	34.0	16.5	26.4	21.3	1.7	88506
57108	SIOUX FALLS	37550	6217	11.3	16.2	37.4	20.8	14.4	76456	78948	90	99	4478	0.7	4.3	23.2	51.8	20.0	233041
57110	SIOUX FALLS	31244	4185	7.1	16.5	46.3	21.0	9.2	77532	81005	91	100	3375	9.1	1.8	27.9	58.3	2.8	192949
57197	SIOUX FALLS	9635	5	0.0	20.0	60.0	20.0	0.0	66333	65822	84	98	4	0.0	0.0	75.0	25.0	0.0	150000
57201	WATERTOWN	23007	10161	24.8	28.7	38.4	4.8	3.3	46713	49277	53	82	6958	10.0	16.7	47.8	23.0	2.4	128258
57212	ARLINGTON	21424	925	25.4	32.2	35.9	4.3	2.2	43916	46151	45	72	697	25.4	25.1	33.9	13.5	2.2	89364
57213	ASTORIA	17587	170	34.1	30.0	32.4	2.9	0.6	36555	38618	22	33	142	35.9	23.2	24.6	14.1	2.1	70000
57216	BIG STONE CITY	19442	356	29.2	37.4	30.6	2.2	0.6	38441	39744	28	46	300	30.7	26.0	31.3	11.0	1.0	79333
57217	BRADLEY	18708	133	38.3	27.1	29.3	3.0	2.3	33817	34044	15	22	112	49.1	17.9	24.1	5.4	3.6	53333
57218	BRANDT	18300	244	32.0	32.0	30.7	3.3	2.0	37095	39112	24	38	203	34.0	17.2	26.6	20.2	2.0	87222
57219	BRISTOL	19595	277	30.0	35.0	31.4	2.9	0.7	38052	40348	27	44	216	53.7	20.8	19.9	5.1	0.5	45789
57220	BRUCE	25395	349	17.5	29.8	43.3	5.4	4.0	51293	51094	64	89	279	14.7	18.6	37.3	25.4	3.9	120357
57221	BRYANT	19703	282	34.8	30.9	25.5	5.0	3.9	36872	38689	23	35	222	32.4	29.3	31.1	7.2	0.0	66316
57223	CASTLEWOOD	19260	511	20.9	32.7	40.9	2.5	2.9	46059	46992	51	80	422	13.0	23.5	45.3	14.5	3.8	110145
57224	CLAIRE CITY	20429	124	15.3	47.6	31.5	2.4	3.2	42783	45803	42	67	99	42.4	29.3	18.2	9.1	1.0	56250
57225	CLARK	17586	753	31.5	33.2	31.2	2.9	1.2	37041	39250	24	37	588	36.2	30.6	28.2	2.9	2.0	69070
57226	CLEAR LAKE	19052	802	28.2	37.5	30.5	2.4	1.4	38880	40812	29	48	603	23.2	28.9	37.3	9.8	0.8	85690
57227	CORONA	20854	319	30.1	31.7	30.4	5.6	2.2	38871	41711	29	48	281	30.6	14.6	26.7	21.0	7.1	99643
57231	DE SMET	20147	786	32.8	30.8	31.0	3.3	2.0	37170	39473	24	38	590	30.7	28.8	28.0	10.7	1.9	74681
57232	EDEN	17870	124	33.9	32.3	29.8	3.2	0.8	35000	37355	18	27	99	34.3	20.2	28.3	14.1	3.0	79167
57233	ERWIN	19639	69	27.5	36.2	29.0	5.8	1.4	38604	41141	28	47	59	37.3	20.3	18.6	20.3	3.4	75000
57234	ESTELLINE	21390	547	26.7	32.9	34.0	4.2	2.2	41292	43268	37	61	465	22.6	21.9	38.9	15.5	1.1	98500
57235	FLORENCE	19575	311	23.8	31.5	39.2	1.9	3.5	45792	48319	51	79	264	23.1	16.3	42.0	14.8	3.8	103500
57236	GARDEN CITY	19947	57	26.3	29.8	36.8	3.5	3.5	45559	48630	50	78	50	50.0	14.0	18.0	6.0	12.0	50000
	SOUTH DAKOTA	22885		24.5	28.5	37.1	6.5	3.5	46883	49493				19.9	18.0	38.6	20.2	3.3	113473
	UNITED STATES	27277		20.9	24.4	35.3	11.7	7.6	54719	56938				9.3	13.1	31.6	32.6	13.5	162279

ZIP CODE #	POST OFFICE NAME	FINANCIAL SERVICES: Auto Loan	FINANCIAL SERVICES: Home Loan	FINANCIAL SERVICES: Investments	FINANCIAL SERVICES: Retirement Plans	THE HOME: Home Improvements: Home Repair	THE HOME: Home Improvements: Lawn & Garden	THE HOME: Furnishings: Computers & Hardware-Personal	THE HOME: Furnishings: Major Appliances	THE HOME: Furnishings: TV, Radio, Sound Equipment	THE HOME: Furnishings: Furniture	ENTERTAINMENT: Dine out/Carry out	ENTERTAINMENT: Sports Equipment	ENTERTAINMENT: Fees & Tickets	ENTERTAINMENT: Toys & Games	ENTERTAINMENT: Travel	ENTERTAINMENT: Cable TV	PERSONAL: Apparel & Services	PERSONAL: Auto Repairs	PERSONAL: Health Insurance	PERSONAL: Pets & Supplies
57001	ALCESTER	83	59	87	58	61	87	65	80	70	55	68	63	50	69	63	77	45	75	86	96
57002	AURORA	84	72	80	74	73	90	72	84	75	64	74	65	64	76	72	80	50	77	87	98
57003	BALTIC	95	94	96	96	93	103	88	96	88	84	88	76	87	89	92	90	60	92	97	115
57004	BERESFORD	89	69	90	70	72	92	76	86	78	67	77	67	63	77	74	83	51	83	91	103
57005	BRANDON	130	143	116	138	134	118	126	126	118	136	121	100	130	128	125	112	85	119	110	143
57006	BROOKINGS	84	65	63	68	64	69	90	74	85	79	85	61	74	85	73	84	59	81	76	90
57007	BROOKINGS	87	102	96	100	101	94	99	95	96	96	97	75	106	97	103	96	70	97	95	110
57010	BURBANK	101	70	110	70	73	106	78	96	81	63	80	79	57	79	77	88	52	90	101	118
57012	CANISTOTA	80	57	84	56	59	84	62	77	68	54	66	60	48	67	61	75	44	72	83	93
57013	CANTON	94	87	82	89	85	98	90	92	92	84	91	71	85	92	87	95	62	92	100	110
57014	CENTERVILLE	79	56	81	55	58	83	62	76	68	54	66	58	48	66	60	74	43	71	83	91
57015	CHANCELLOR	97	68	106	68	71	103	75	92	78	62	77	76	56	76	75	85	50	86	97	114
57016	CHESTER	107	74	118	74	78	113	82	102	85	67	84	83	60	83	82	93	55	95	107	125
57017	COLMAN	100	69	110	69	72	106	77	95	80	62	79	79	56	78	76	87	51	89	101	117
57018	COLTON	100	86	95	87	83	106	89	96	91	79	90	78	79	92	87	96	61	95	105	118
57020	CROOKS	114	113	102	110	107	107	105	108	103	108	105	83	102	107	103	102	72	104	103	127
57021	DAVIS	89	61	98	61	64	94	68	84	71	55	70	70	50	69	68	77	45	79	89	104
57022	DELL RAPIDS	96	86	88	88	86	99	90	94	92	85	91	72	84	92	88	96	62	93	102	112
57024	EGAN	83	59	86	58	61	87	65	80	70	56	68	62	50	69	63	77	45	75	86	96
57025	ELK POINT	94	73	91	72	74	95	76	89	80	69	79	68	63	81	74	86	53	84	93	107
57026	ELKTON	86	74	81	77	76	92	75	86	77	66	76	66	66	78	74	82	51	79	89	101
57027	FAIRVIEW	89	61	97	61	64	93	68	84	70	55	70	69	50	69	67	77	45	78	89	103
57028	FLANDREAU	84	67	82	67	69	86	72	82	76	66	75	62	62	75	70	81	50	79	87	97
57029	FREEMAN	76	54	78	53	56	79	59	73	64	51	63	56	46	63	57	71	41	68	79	87
57030	GARRETSON	88	83	80	86	84	95	81	90	83	74	81	68	76	84	81	87	56	84	92	105
57031	GAYVILLE	86	59	94	59	62	90	65	81	68	53	67	67	48	67	65	74	44	76	86	100
57032	HARRISBURG	121	128	115	127	124	118	119	119	116	123	118	91	122	120	120	115	82	117	114	139
57033	HARTFORD	107	111	97	109	106	104	101	104	99	105	101	80	102	103	101	98	70	101	99	122
57034	HUDSON	88	60	97	60	63	93	67	83	70	54	69	69	49	68	67	76	45	78	88	103
57035	HUMBOLDT	86	77	79	80	78	92	76	87	79	68	77	66	69	80	76	83	53	80	89	101
57036	HURLEY	92	63	100	63	66	97	70	87	73	57	72	72	51	71	70	80	47	81	92	107
57037	IRENE	81	57	85	56	59	85	63	78	68	53	66	61	48	66	61	74	44	73	83	93
57038	JEFFERSON	103	102	100	105	103	110	99	106	99	94	99	81	97	101	100	102	69	101	107	123
57039	LENNOX	85	73	82	74	74	91	73	85	78	67	76	64	66	78	73	83	52	79	89	99
57040	LESTERVILLE	93	64	102	64	67	98	71	89	74	58	73	73	52	73	71	81	48	83	94	109
57042	MADISON	75	62	71	62	63	76	68	73	71	63	70	56	60	70	65	75	48	72	79	87
57043	MARION	90	64	94	63	67	95	70	87	76	61	74	68	55	75	69	84	49	81	94	104
57045	MENNO	78	54	86	54	56	82	60	74	62	48	61	61	44	61	59	68	40	69	78	91
57046	MISSION HILL	87	60	95	59	62	91	66	82	69	54	68	68	48	67	66	75	44	77	87	101
57047	MONROE	103	71	113	71	74	108	79	98	82	64	81	81	58	80	78	89	52	91	103	120
57048	MONTROSE	90	62	98	62	65	95	69	85	71	56	71	70	51	70	68	78	46	79	90	105
57049	NORTH SIOUX CITY	127	142	136	144	140	132	134	131	129	137	131	102	142	131	139	127	93	131	127	154
57050	NUNDA	85	59	94	59	61	90	65	81	68	53	67	67	48	66	65	74	43	76	85	100
57051	OLDHAM	82	56	90	56	59	86	62	77	65	50	64	64	46	64	62	71	42	72	82	95
57052	OLIVET	84	58	92	58	60	89	64	80	67	52	66	66	47	65	64	73	43	74	84	98
57053	PARKER	97	67	106	66	70	102	74	92	77	60	76	76	54	75	73	84	49	86	97	113
57054	RAMONA	95	65	104	65	68	100	72	90	75	59	74	74	53	74	72	82	48	84	95	111
57055	RENNER	91	101	89	104	99	101	91	95	90	91	90	75	96	92	96	90	63	91	94	112
57057	RUTLAND	84	58	93	58	61	89	64	80	67	52	66	66	47	66	64	73	43	75	85	99
57058	SALEM	88	63	91	61	65	92	69	85	75	60	73	65	54	74	67	83	48	79	92	101
57059	SCOTLAND	66	47	67	46	49	69	52	64	57	46	55	48	41	56	50	63	37	60	69	75
57062	SPRINGFIELD	78	54	86	54	56	83	60	74	62	48	62	61	44	61	60	68	40	69	79	92
57063	TABOR	79	55	87	55	57	84	61	75	63	49	63	62	45	62	60	69	41	70	80	93
57064	TEA	118	128	104	123	119	105	113	113	106	122	109	90	115	115	111	101	76	107	98	128
57065	TRENT	100	69	109	68	72	105	76	95	79	62	78	78	56	78	76	86	51	88	100	116
57066	TYNDALL	74	53	75	51	55	77	58	71	64	51	62	54	46	62	56	70	41	66	77	84
57067	UTICA	87	60	96	60	63	92	67	83	69	54	69	69	49	68	66	76	45	78	88	102
57068	VALLEY SPRINGS	95	106	91	109	103	103	95	98	93	96	93	77	101	96	99	92	65	94	96	115
57069	VERMILLION	71	52	53	55	51	58	78	61	72	65	72	53	61	72	61	71	50	69	64	76
57070	VIBORG	80	57	82	56	59	84	63	77	69	55	67	59	49	68	61	76	44	72	84	92
57071	VOLGA	89	83	78	82	81	88	78	84	80	79	80	63	74	83	77	82	55	81	85	100
57072	VOLIN	91	63	100	62	66	96	70	86	72	56	71	71	51	71	69	79	46	81	91	106
57073	WAKONDA	80	57	83	56	59	84	63	77	68	54	66	60	49	67	61	75	44	72	84	92
57075	WENTWORTH	111	88	142	87	96	118	89	113	93	82	92	83	76	89	96	99	61	104	112	131
57076	WINFRED	92	63	101	63	66	97	70	87	73	57	72	72	51	72	70	80	47	82	92	107
57077	WORTHING	92	83	78	82	82	89	80	86	82	80	82	63	74	85	77	85	56	82	86	102
57078	YANKTON	82	75	70	75	74	80	78	78	79	76	79	59	73	80	74	81	54	78	82	93
57103	SIOUX FALLS	108	108	95	109	104	102	109	104	106	109	107	82	108	109	105	105	75	105	102	123
57104	SIOUX FALLS	71	58	52	61	56	60	73	63	73	68	73	51	66	73	64	74	51	70	68	78
57105	SIOUX FALLS	92	96	91	97	95	100	96	95	97	94	97	71	98	96	96	100	68	96	104	112
57106	SIOUX FALLS	110	103	89	104	98	93	107	99	104	110	105	80	103	109	100	100	74	102	94	118
57107	SIOUX FALLS	96	98	84	97	94	95	92	94	92	95	92	72	93	95	92	92	64	92	92	111
57108	SIOUX FALLS	134	149	143	152	148	139	141	138	136	144	138	107	150	138	146	134	98	138	134	162
57110	SIOUX FALLS	132	145	119	140	136	121	129	128	122	138	125	101	132	130	128	116	87	122	113	146
57197	SIOUX FALLS	91	113	101	113	109	111	96	100	97	98	99	75	111	99	107	100	69	98	106	117
57201	WATERTOWN	80	75	74	76	74	82	77	79	79	74	78	61	74	79	76	82	54	79	84	94
57212	ARLINGTON	88	64	92	63	66	93	69	85	75	60	73	66	54	73	68	82	48	79	91	102
57213	ASTORIA	76	52	83	52	54	80	58	72	60	47	59	59	42	59	57	66	39	67	76	88
57216	BIG STONE CITY	81	58	84	56	60	83	60	76	66	55	65	58	47	65	59	72	43	70	79	91
57217	BRADLEY	88	60	96	60	63	93	67	83	70	54	69	69	49	68	67	76	45	78	88	103
57218	BRANDT	80	55	88	55	58	85	61	76	64	50	63	63	45	62	61	69	41	71	80	94
57219	BRISTOL	76	52	84	52	55	80	58	72	61	47	60	60	43	59	58	66	39	68	76	89
57220	BRUCE	112	77	123	77	81	118	86	106	89	69	88	88	63	87	85	97	57	99	112	131
57221	BRYANT	93	64	102	64	67	98	71	88	74	58	73	73	52	73	71	81	47	83	93	109
57223	CASTLEWOOD	96	66	105	66	69	101	73	91	76	60	75	75	54	75	73	83	49	85	96	112
57224	CLAIRE CITY	90	62	99	62	65	95	69	85	71	56	71	71	50	70	68	78	46	80	90	105
57225	CLARK	76	53	80	52	55	79	58	72	62	49	61	58	44	61	57	68	40	68	77	87
57226	CLEAR LAKE	76	54	78	53	56	79	59	73	65	52	63	56	47	64	58	72	42	68	79	87
57227	CORONA	89	61	98	61	64	94	68	85	71	55	70	70	50	69	68	77	45	79	89	104
57231	DE SMET	77	55	80	54	57	80	59	74	65	52	63	56	46	64	58	71	42	68	78	88
57232	EDEN	75	52	83	52	54	79	57	71	60	47	59	59	42	59	57	65	38	67	75	88
57233	ERWIN	87	60	95	59	62	91	66	82	69	54	68	68	48	67	66	75	44	77	87	101
57234	ESTELLINE	88	63	91	61	65	89	65	82	72	60	70	62	51	71	64	79	46	76	86	98
57235	FLORENCE	95	65	104	65	68	100	73	90	75	59	75	75	53	74	72	82	48	84	95	111
57236	GARDEN CITY	89	61	98	61	64	94	68	84	71	55	70	70	50	69	68	77	45	79	89	104
	SOUTH DAKOTA	88	76	83	76	75	87	80	84	82	76	82	66	72	82	77	85	56	83	88	101
	UNITED STATES	100	100	100	100	100	100	100	100	100	100	100	100	100	100	100	100	100	100	100	100

57237-57424

#	POST OFFICE NAME	COUNTY FIPS CODE	POPULATION 2000	POPULATION 2009	POPULATION 2014	2000-2009 ANNUAL RATE % Rate	2000-2009 ANNUAL RATE State Centile	HOUSEHOLDS 2000	HOUSEHOLDS 2009	HOUSEHOLDS 2014	HOUSEHOLDS % Annual Rate 2000-2009	HOUSEHOLDS 2009 Average HH Size	FAMILIES 2000	FAMILIES 2009	FAMILIES % Annual Rate 2000-2009
57237	GARY	039	567	557	547	-0.2	47	259	266	264	0.3	2.09	186	193	0.4
57238	GOODWIN	039	568	571	575	0.1	64	211	220	223	0.5	2.60	155	164	0.6
57239	GRENVILLE	037	311	283	271	-1.0	15	139	133	128	-0.5	2.13	103	100	-0.3
57241	HAYTI	057	858	931	962	0.9	86	300	330	340	1.0	2.82	228	253	1.1
57242	HAZEL	057	466	490	499	0.5	75	162	172	175	0.6	2.80	116	125	0.8
57243	HENRY	029	562	596	614	0.6	78	208	231	241	1.1	2.58	163	183	1.3
57245	KRANZBURG	029	180	172	187	-0.5	33	62	62	68	0.0	2.76	52	52	0.0
57246	LABOLT	051	215	201	192	-0.7	26	81	78	75	-0.4	2.58	57	56	-0.2
57247	LAKE CITY	091	417	407	399	-0.3	42	155	156	154	0.1	2.61	115	118	0.3
57248	LAKE NORDEN	057	1016	1083	1112	0.7	81	378	407	418	0.8	2.53	254	277	0.9
57249	LAKE PRESTON	077	1120	1070	1038	-0.5	33	468	459	448	-0.2	2.21	294	293	0.0
57251	MARVIN	051	147	128	120	-1.5	5	52	47	45	-1.1	2.64	39	36	-0.9
57252	MILBANK	051	5049	4691	4493	-0.8	22	2020	1957	1894	-0.3	2.29	1360	1336	-0.2
57255	NEW EFFINGTON	109	398	386	378	-0.3	42	162	159	155	-0.2	2.43	111	111	0.0
57256	ORTLEY	051	223	214	208	-0.4	38	77	75	74	-0.3	2.85	61	60	-0.2
57257	PEEVER	109	998	975	954	-0.3	42	302	302	298	0.0	3.20	235	237	0.1
57258	RAYMOND	025	345	311	294	-1.1	12	116	107	101	-0.9	2.90	90	83	-0.9
57259	REVILLO	051	481	454	435	-0.6	29	196	190	185	-0.3	2.39	142	140	-0.2
57260	ROSHOLT	109	857	827	807	-0.4	38	317	309	301	-0.3	2.50	222	220	-0.1
57261	ROSLYN	037	413	367	349	-1.3	8	161	149	143	-0.8	2.40	113	106	-0.7
57262	SISSETON	109	5035	5061	4994	0.1	64	1806	1838	1814	0.2	2.68	1285	1322	0.3
57263	SOUTH SHORE	029	557	538	532	-0.4	38	205	207	206	0.1	2.54	163	165	0.1
57264	STOCKHOLM	051	212	199	191	-0.7	26	92	90	87	-0.2	2.21	69	68	-0.2
57265	STRANDBURG	051	220	206	198	-0.7	26	84	81	79	-0.4	2.54	58	56	-0.4
57266	SUMMIT	109	641	621	608	-0.3	42	242	239	236	-0.1	2.60	181	182	0.1
57268	TORONTO	039	430	420	413	-0.3	42	175	178	177	0.2	2.35	122	126	0.3
57269	TWIN BROOKS	051	416	379	362	-1.0	15	154	147	142	-0.5	2.55	117	112	-0.5
57270	VEBLEN	091	625	613	604	-0.2	47	269	272	269	0.1	2.25	176	181	0.3
57271	VIENNA	025	422	382	363	-1.1	12	141	130	123	-0.9	2.92	100	93	-0.8
57272	WALLACE	029	160	165	169	0.3	70	66	71	73	0.8	2.32	51	55	0.8
57273	WAUBAY	037	1249	1158	1110	-0.8	22	464	447	432	-0.4	2.57	310	302	-0.3
57274	WEBSTER	037	3067	2797	2663	-1.0	15	1297	1222	1175	-0.6	2.22	825	790	-0.5
57276	WHITE	011	1338	1267	1236	-0.6	29	497	484	477	-0.3	2.53	384	379	-0.1
57278	WILLOW LAKE	025	625	557	526	-1.2	9	251	229	217	-1.0	2.43	181	167	-0.9
57279	WILMOT	109	1042	1122	1129	0.8	84	433	484	490	1.2	2.27	285	325	1.4
57301	MITCHELL	035	17319	17863	18068	0.3	70	7058	7468	7598	0.6	2.30	4369	4702	0.8
57311	ALEXANDRIA	061	1452	1742	1875	2.0	93	496	606	654	2.2	2.87	367	454	2.3
57312	ALPENA	005	584	547	531	-0.7	26	237	232	228	-0.2	2.36	175	175	0.0
57313	ARMOUR	043	1303	1193	1142	-0.9	18	526	499	482	-0.6	2.30	361	348	-0.4
57314	ARTESIAN	111	627	586	553	-0.7	26	251	240	228	-0.5	2.44	188	183	-0.3
57315	AVON	009	1046	1001	962	-0.5	33	447	436	422	-0.3	2.19	316	312	-0.1
57317	BONESTEEL	053	655	609	591	-0.8	22	252	245	240	-0.3	2.46	174	171	-0.2
57319	BRIDGEWATER	087	1189	1214	1202	0.2	67	433	448	444	0.4	2.61	300	314	0.5
57321	CANOVA	097	493	483	479	-0.2	47	192	198	198	0.3	2.44	144	150	0.4
57322	CARPENTER	005	193	172	164	-1.2	9	80	74	71	-0.8	2.32	65	60	-0.9
57323	CARTHAGE	097	339	306	296	-1.1	12	169	161	158	-0.5	1.90	104	101	-0.3
57324	CAVOUR	005	405	375	365	-0.8	22	165	158	156	-0.5	2.37	126	122	-0.3
57325	CHAMBERLAIN	015	3057	2963	2950	-0.3	42	1146	1146	1149	0.0	2.28	721	732	0.2
57328	CORSICA	043	1249	1191	1157	-0.5	33	454	450	442	-0.1	2.50	323	324	0.0
57329	DANTE	023	329	366	372	1.2	88	109	124	126	1.4	2.95	88	101	1.5
57330	DELMONT	043	687	623	593	-1.1	12	244	230	221	-0.6	2.71	183	174	-0.5
57331	DIMOCK	067	454	437	426	-0.4	38	170	169	166	-0.1	2.59	136	136	0.0
57332	EMERY	061	862	915	932	0.6	78	342	371	378	0.9	2.46	255	280	1.0
57334	ETHAN	035	937	1004	1033	0.7	81	327	359	371	1.0	2.78	255	283	1.1
57335	FAIRFAX	053	342	319	310	-0.7	26	145	141	138	-0.3	2.23	100	99	-0.1
57337	FEDORA	097	193	174	168	-1.1	12	81	77	75	-0.5	2.26	50	48	-0.4
57339	FORT THOMPSON	017	1833	1929	1978	0.6	78	444	479	494	0.8	4.00	367	398	0.9
57340	FULTON	061	335	363	375	0.9	86	123	136	141	1.1	2.67	103	116	1.3
57341	GANN VALLEY	017	199	191	190	-0.4	38	82	82	82	0.0	2.33	55	56	0.2
57342	GEDDES	023	622	596	578	-0.5	33	257	253	246	-0.2	2.36	170	170	0.0
57344	HARRISON	043	283	271	265	-0.5	33	106	106	106	0.0	2.56	83	83	0.0
57345	HIGHMORE	069	1524	1507	1493	-0.1	55	623	628	624	0.1	2.34	409	419	0.3
57348	HITCHCOCK	005	581	545	529	-0.7	26	221	216	211	-0.2	2.52	162	159	-0.2
57349	HOWARD	097	1753	1633	1589	-0.8	22	734	712	701	-0.3	2.22	460	452	-0.2
57350	HURON	005	13987	12978	12649	-0.8	22	6008	5787	5695	-0.4	2.17	3621	3546	-0.2
57353	IROQUOIS	077	904	829	798	-0.9	18	330	315	305	-0.5	2.63	256	246	-0.4
57355	KIMBALL	015	1460	1449	1454	-0.1	55	531	544	551	0.3	2.66	363	377	0.4
57356	LAKE ANDES	023	2448	2405	2351	-0.2	47	790	787	770	0.0	2.99	551	556	0.1
57359	LETCHER	111	926	869	827	-0.7	26	312	302	289	-0.4	2.85	229	224	-0.2
57362	MILLER	059	2300	2043	1915	-1.3	8	995	920	871	-0.8	2.16	635	597	-0.7
57363	MOUNT VERNON	035	1015	999	982	-0.2	47	364	367	363	0.1	2.72	281	287	0.2
57364	NEW HOLLAND	043	50	48	47	-0.4	38	25	25	25	0.0	1.92	19	20	0.6
57365	OACOMA	085	505	523	534	0.4	73	210	226	233	0.8	2.31	140	152	0.9
57366	PARKSTON	067	2500	2416	2359	-0.4	38	962	951	932	-0.1	2.42	662	663	0.0
57368	PLANKINTON	003	1224	1175	1145	-0.4	38	467	462	454	-0.1	2.28	318	320	0.1
57369	PLATTE	023	2551	2435	2363	-0.5	33	989	978	955	-0.1	2.43	693	694	0.0
57370	PUKWANA	015	662	642	640	-0.3	42	259	261	262	0.1	2.41	191	195	0.2
57371	REE HEIGHTS	059	278	243	226	-1.4	7	100	92	87	-0.9	2.64	79	74	-0.7
57373	SAINT LAWRENCE	059	447	396	370	-1.3	8	177	163	155	-0.9	2.37	120	113	-0.6
57374	SPENCER	087	467	488	489	0.5	75	177	187	188	0.6	2.61	133	143	0.8
57375	STICKNEY	003	824	776	754	-0.6	29	340	331	323	-0.3	2.30	237	234	-0.1
57376	TRIPP	067	1260	1211	1179	-0.4	38	540	528	515	-0.2	2.17	352	350	-0.1
57379	VIRGIL	005	112	109	108	-0.3	42	46	47	47	0.2	2.32	35	36	0.3
57380	WAGNER	023	3329	3285	3220	-0.1	55	1176	1169	1145	-0.1	2.75	813	818	0.1
57381	WESSINGTON	059	640	589	567	-0.9	18	268	258	251	-0.4	2.28	202	196	-0.3
57382	WESSINGTON SPRINGS	073	1664	1573	1527	-0.6	29	724	717	705	-0.1	2.14	459	462	0.1
57383	WHITE LAKE	003	855	861	853	0.1	64	309	319	318	0.3	2.52	224	234	0.5
57384	WOLSEY	005	874	846	837	-0.4	38	353	356	356	0.1	2.38	269	274	0.2
57385	WOONSOCKET	111	1551	1468	1413	-0.6	29	634	623	604	-0.2	2.30	431	430	0.0
57386	YALE	005	246	225	219	-1.0	15	87	82	81	-0.6	2.74	67	64	-0.5
57401	ABERDEEN	013	28946	28773	28776	-0.1	55	12104	12586	12721	0.4	2.19	7426	7854	0.6
57420	AKASKA	129	31	29	29	-0.7	26	16	16	16	0.0	1.81	12	12	0.0
57421	AMHERST	091	202	197	193	-0.3	42	60	60	59	0.0	3.28	42	42	0.0
57422	ANDOVER	037	311	305	300	-0.2	47	130	134	133	0.3	2.18	84	88	0.5
57424	ASHTON	115	389	360	343	-0.8	22	156	148	142	-0.6	2.43	117	112	-0.5
	SOUTH DAKOTA					0.8					1.2	2.43			1.3
	UNITED STATES					1.0					1.1	2.59			0.9

#	POST OFFICE NAME	RACE (%) White 2000	White 2009	Black 2000	Black 2009	Asian/Pacific 2000	Asian/Pacific 2009	% Hispanic Origin 2000	% Hispanic Origin 2009	2009 AGE DISTRIBUTION (%) 0-4	5-9	10-14	15-19	20-24	25-44	45-64	65-84	85+	18+	MEDIAN AGE 2009	% 2009 Males	% 2009 Females
57237	GARY	98.2	98.2	0.2	0.2	0.0	0.0	1.2	1.3	5.4	5.9	6.3	6.8	4.5	22.3	30.9	16.0	2.0	78.1	44.2	50.6	49.4
57238	GOODWIN	97.7	97.5	0.0	0.0	0.2	0.2	1.2	1.2	6.3	6.7	7.2	7.2	4.4	23.3	28.7	14.7	1.6	75.3	41.3	51.8	48.2
57239	GRENVILLE	76.8	71.4	0.0	0.0	0.0	0.0	0.3	0.4	6.4	6.7	6.7	7.1	6.0	18.7	31.8	15.2	1.4	76.0	43.5	52.3	47.7
57241	HAYTI	98.8	98.6	0.0	0.0	0.0	0.0	0.0	0.0	9.2	9.3	8.6	7.1	4.8	24.5	24.4	10.2	1.8	68.4	34.3	51.6	48.4
57242	HAZEL	99.1	99.0	0.0	0.0	0.0	0.0	0.2	0.2	8.6	8.4	8.0	7.1	4.7	22.9	25.5	11.8	3.1	70.4	36.9	50.8	49.2
57243	HENRY	98.4	97.8	0.2	0.3	0.0	0.0	0.5	1.0	6.9	7.6	7.9	6.5	4.2	24.3	29.9	11.7	1.0	73.5	40.3	51.2	48.8
57245	KRANZBURG	98.3	98.3	0.0	0.0	0.6	0.6	0.6	0.6	8.1	7.6	9.3	10.5	3.5	26.7	25.0	8.7	0.6	68.0	35.0	52.3	47.7
57246	LABOLT	98.6	97.5	0.0	0.0	0.0	0.0	0.9	1.0	6.5	6.5	7.5	8.0	4.5	21.9	30.8	12.4	2.0	74.1	41.3	51.2	48.8
57247	LAKE CITY	70.2	66.3	0.5	0.5	0.0	0.0	0.7	0.5	7.9	8.4	7.9	6.4	4.9	18.7	28.5	15.2	2.2	71.5	41.3	51.4	48.6
57248	LAKE NORDEN	98.0	97.5	0.1	0.1	0.2	0.3	1.1	1.6	8.1	7.8	7.6	7.5	4.7	21.5	23.9	14.2	4.6	70.8	39.3	49.4	50.6
57249	LAKE PRESTON	99.0	98.9	0.0	0.0	0.1	0.1	0.7	1.0	5.0	5.1	5.7	7.1	5.0	19.1	29.8	18.4	4.9	79.3	46.8	49.7	50.3
57251	MARVIN	98.6	98.4	0.0	0.0	0.0	0.0	0.0	0.0	4.7	6.3	6.3	6.3	3.9	19.5	38.3	13.3	1.6	78.1	46.8	56.3	43.7
57252	MILBANK	98.7	98.2	0.0	0.0	0.3	0.5	0.6	0.8	6.2	6.2	6.1	6.3	5.6	20.6	28.5	15.6	4.9	77.1	44.0	48.1	51.9
57255	NEW EFFINGTON	80.9	77.2	0.0	0.0	0.0	0.0	0.0	0.0	6.7	6.0	7.0	6.7	2.8	19.7	26.4	21.2	3.4	76.9	45.8	50.5	49.5
57256	ORTLEY	90.1	88.8	0.0	0.0	0.0	0.0	0.0	0.0	5.6	5.6	7.5	6.5	4.2	23.4	29.4	14.0	3.7	76.6	42.3	54.7	45.3
57257	PEEVER	50.9	47.5	0.0	0.0	0.2	0.2	0.8	0.8	7.7	7.9	9.1	9.3	6.2	21.4	25.6	11.1	1.6	69.6	34.3	50.1	49.9
57258	RAYMOND	99.1	99.0	0.0	0.0	0.0	0.0	0.9	1.3	6.1	6.8	6.8	6.4	5.1	23.2	29.3	13.8	2.6	76.5	41.6	50.5	49.5
57259	REVILLO	97.7	96.9	0.0	0.0	0.0	0.0	1.5	2.0	6.4	6.8	7.3	7.7	4.6	21.8	30.8	12.8	1.8	74.9	41.4	50.9	49.1
57260	ROSHOLT	95.7	94.8	0.6	0.6	0.1	0.1	0.5	0.5	6.7	7.5	7.6	6.2	2.9	19.7	27.0	14.9	7.6	73.9	44.5	47.6	52.4
57261	ROSLYN	98.3	97.3	0.5	0.8	0.2	0.3	0.5	0.8	4.6	4.9	5.4	6.0	4.6	19.1	33.2	17.4	4.6	80.9	48.4	50.7	49.3
57262	SISSETON	55.7	50.8	0.1	0.1	0.2	0.2	0.9	0.9	7.3	7.4	8.1	8.7	5.7	22.1	24.5	13.3	2.9	71.8	36.7	49.0	51.0
57263	SOUTH SHORE	98.9	98.5	0.2	0.2	0.0	0.2	0.2	0.2	6.9	7.4	7.8	6.7	3.7	21.7	30.7	12.8	2.2	73.0	42.0	50.9	49.1
57264	STOCKHOLM	98.6	97.0	0.0	0.0	0.0	0.5	0.5	1.0	5.5	5.5	6.5	7.5	4.5	23.6	29.1	15.6	2.0	76.9	42.8	50.8	49.2
57265	STRANDBURG	99.1	98.5	0.0	0.0	0.0	0.0	0.5	0.0	6.3	6.8	6.8	7.8	4.4	22.3	30.6	12.6	2.4	74.8	41.8	51.5	48.5
57266	SUMMIT	68.7	64.9	0.0	0.0	0.0	0.0	0.2	0.2	6.3	6.3	7.6	8.7	6.3	23.5	25.1	13.2	3.1	74.2	37.6	51.7	48.3
57268	TORONTO	98.4	98.3	0.2	0.2	0.2	0.2	0.9	1.0	6.2	6.9	6.9	6.7	4.3	21.9	29.5	15.0	2.6	75.7	42.7	51.4	48.6
57269	TWIN BROOKS	98.1	97.6	0.0	0.0	0.2	0.3	0.5	1.1	5.0	5.5	6.1	7.4	4.5	22.4	32.2	14.8	2.1	78.4	44.4	52.5	47.5
57270	VEBLEN	81.4	78.5	0.0	0.0	0.2	0.2	1.4	1.5	7.3	5.2	7.2	8.3	3.8	15.8	27.7	20.6	4.1	74.2	46.7	50.4	49.6
57271	VIENNA	97.9	97.4	0.0	0.0	0.0	0.0	0.5	0.5	6.8	7.6	7.9	7.6	4.7	20.4	27.5	14.7	2.9	73.0	40.9	52.1	47.9
57272	WALLACE	98.7	98.2	0.0	0.0	0.0	0.0	0.0	0.0	6.7	7.9	8.5	7.3	4.8	25.5	26.1	12.1	1.2	72.1	37.8	51.5	48.5
57273	WAUBAY	69.4	61.3	0.0	0.0	0.1	0.1	0.7	0.9	7.0	6.9	7.5	7.3	4.7	17.4	29.3	17.4	2.5	73.7	44.1	48.5	51.5
57274	WEBSTER	97.7	96.7	0.1	0.1	0.1	0.2	0.2	0.2	5.7	5.9	6.2	6.4	5.0	20.1	29.0	16.8	5.0	77.9	45.5	48.9	51.1
57276	WHITE	98.1	97.6	0.1	0.1	0.1	0.2	1.3	2.0	6.8	7.3	7.6	7.5	3.6	22.7	27.8	13.7	3.2	73.8	40.7	50.8	49.2
57278	WILLOW LAKE	97.8	97.1	0.0	0.0	0.0	0.0	0.5	0.7	6.6	7.2	7.4	7.4	4.8	20.6	28.4	14.9	2.7	74.3	41.6	51.9	48.1
57279	WILMOT	93.8	92.7	0.0	0.0	0.5	0.4	0.6	0.6	6.0	6.7	6.9	6.1	4.3	20.4	29.9	15.7	4.2	75.8	44.8	51.4	48.6
57301	MITCHELL	96.1	94.8	0.3	0.4	0.5	0.8	0.7	1.0	6.7	6.3	6.2	7.7	7.8	25.3	24.4	12.4	3.2	76.8	36.2	48.8	51.2
57311	ALEXANDRIA	99.2	99.1	0.0	0.0	0.3	0.3	0.1	0.1	7.1	8.2	7.5	8.7	6.2	23.0	25.8	11.9	1.6	71.7	36.7	50.9	49.1
57312	ALPENA	98.6	98.4	0.0	0.0	0.2	0.2	0.5	0.4	3.7	5.3	7.1	8.4	4.6	21.4	32.7	15.0	1.8	77.7	44.7	53.0	47.0
57313	ARMOUR	96.5	95.5	0.0	0.0	0.1	0.2	0.5	0.6	5.0	5.3	5.5	6.7	5.5	18.7	30.2	17.4	5.7	79.6	47.2	48.7	51.3
57314	ARTESIAN	99.5	99.3	0.0	0.0	0.0	0.0	1.0	1.5	6.5	7.2	7.5	7.0	5.1	21.5	29.5	14.2	1.5	74.2	41.4	53.2	46.8
57315	AVON	97.6	97.3	0.1	0.1	0.1	0.1	0.2	0.2	5.7	6.5	6.7	6.5	4.9	21.9	29.7	15.2	3.0	77.0	43.5	54.5	45.5
57317	BONESTEEL	85.2	81.4	0.0	0.0	0.2	0.2	0.9	1.0	6.9	7.4	7.6	6.6	4.6	18.1	27.6	17.4	3.9	73.2	44.0	50.9	49.1
57319	BRIDGEWATER	98.7	98.5	0.1	0.1	0.3	0.2	1.4	2.1	6.1	6.2	7.3	7.7	5.1	20.6	26.0	15.8	5.2	75.3	42.6	49.4	50.6
57321	CANOVA	98.6	97.9	1.0	1.4	0.0	0.0	0.0	0.0	6.6	6.6	6.8	6.4	5.4	21.1	30.8	13.9	2.3	75.8	42.7	52.0	48.0
57322	CARPENTER	99.5	99.4	0.0	0.0	0.0	0.0	0.0	0.6	6.4	7.0	7.6	7.0	5.2	21.5	30.8	13.4	1.2	74.4	40.6	53.5	46.5
57323	CARTHAGE	99.1	99.0	0.3	0.3	0.0	0.0	0.6	1.0	4.6	5.2	5.6	5.9	4.2	18.6	32.7	19.6	3.6	81.0	48.9	52.3	47.7
57324	CAVOUR	98.5	98.1	0.2	0.3	0.0	0.3	0.2	0.3	6.7	6.7	7.7	8.0	3.5	24.3	29.3	13.1	0.8	73.9	40.8	50.9	49.1
57325	CHAMBERLAIN	84.0	79.6	0.5	0.6	0.5	0.7	0.6	0.7	5.6	7.0	8.7	8.3	7.2	21.2	25.5	13.1	3.4	72.9	37.9	46.4	53.6
57328	CORSICA	99.2	98.9	0.2	0.2	0.0	0.0	0.2	0.3	6.9	6.8	6.5	6.3	5.6	19.1	26.5	15.9	6.3	75.7	43.9	49.0	51.0
57329	DANTE	79.1	72.1	0.3	0.3	0.3	0.3	0.9	1.1	8.2	6.8	9.8	10.7	3.6	21.3	26.2	13.1	0.3	66.4	36.6	53.0	47.0
57330	DELMONT	95.5	94.1	0.0	0.0	0.4	0.6	0.3	0.3	6.7	7.5	7.9	7.7	5.0	19.9	29.2	13.8	2.2	73.2	40.5	49.0	51.0
57331	DIMOCK	99.1	98.6	0.0	0.0	0.2	0.2	1.3	2.1	8.5	8.7	8.5	6.2	4.6	22.9	26.5	12.6	1.6	70.7	37.7	52.6	47.4
57332	EMERY	99.8	99.7	0.0	0.0	0.0	0.0	0.1	0.1	7.4	8.1	8.1	6.7	4.2	20.8	27.9	14.4	2.5	72.0	41.2	50.1	49.9
57334	ETHAN	98.6	98.1	0.1	0.2	0.3	0.5	0.5	0.7	6.7	7.5	9.2	8.5	4.3	24.1	27.6	10.6	1.7	70.9	37.8	51.2	48.8
57335	FAIRFAX	84.5	80.6	0.0	0.0	0.0	0.0	0.9	0.9	7.2	7.5	7.5	6.3	4.4	17.2	28.5	17.2	4.1	72.7	44.8	50.5	49.5
57337	FEDORA	99.0	98.9	0.5	0.6	0.0	0.0	0.5	1.1	4.6	4.6	5.2	5.7	4.0	17.2	36.2	19.0	3.4	82.8	50.5	52.9	47.1
57339	FORT THOMPSON	7.3	8.8	0.1	0.1	0.0	0.0	1.0	0.9	12.4	11.8	9.3	11.3	8.6	22.4	17.8	5.8	0.5	59.4	23.0	49.3	50.7
57340	FULTON	100.0	100.0	0.0	0.0	0.0	0.0	0.0	0.0	8.0	8.3	7.7	7.7	4.4	24.2	24.5	14.0	1.1	71.1	38.1	49.3	50.7
57341	GANN VALLEY	99.5	99.5	0.0	0.0	0.0	0.0	0.0	0.0	5.2	5.8	6.8	6.8	4.2	23.6	29.8	15.2	2.6	78.0	42.8	55.5	44.5
57342	GEDDES	96.6	95.3	0.0	0.0	0.2	0.3	1.4	2.2	5.9	6.5	6.7	6.9	4.5	23.2	29.0	14.1	3.2	76.5	41.8	51.8	48.2
57344	HARRISON	98.9	98.5	0.0	0.0	0.0	0.0	0.7	0.7	8.1	7.7	7.7	7.7	5.5	21.4	24.7	14.4	2.6	71.6	38.6	51.7	48.3
57345	HIGHMORE	90.4	89.1	0.1	0.1	0.1	0.1	0.5	0.5	7.2	6.8	6.7	5.7	5.7	20.3	26.5	16.3	4.7	75.2	42.6	50.6	49.4
57348	HITCHCOCK	99.3	98.9	0.2	0.2	0.0	0.2	0.2	0.2	5.9	6.4	7.2	7.5	5.0	20.4	31.7	13.9	2.0	75.6	43.2	52.7	47.3
57349	HOWARD	98.6	98.2	0.5	0.6	0.2	0.2	0.9	1.2	5.6	5.8	5.9	6.7	5.5	20.6	27.7	16.4	5.9	78.3	45.0	48.3	51.7
57350	HURON	96.4	95.3	0.8	1.1	0.4	0.6	1.1	1.6	5.7	5.7	5.8	6.9	5.8	22.7	27.9	15.1	4.3	78.5	42.7	48.7	51.3
57353	IROQUOIS	97.6	97.0	0.2	0.4	0.4	0.7	1.1	1.3	5.9	6.2	6.8	7.5	4.8	22.9	30.0	14.5	1.4	76.5	42.1	50.1	49.9
57355	KIMBALL	98.5	98.0	0.0	0.0	0.5	0.7	0.3	0.3	6.7	7.2	7.2	7.2	4.7	22.8	27.9	13.1	3.2	74.3	40.1	49.6	50.4
57356	LAKE ANDES	46.7	38.7	0.2	0.3	0.1	0.1	2.0	2.2	11.1	9.0	8.6	8.6	6.7	21.5	20.5	12.0	1.8	65.7	29.6	48.7	51.3
57359	LETCHER	98.7	98.4	0.0	0.0	0.1	0.3	1.3	1.7	6.0	6.7	7.1	6.9	4.3	21.6	31.0	13.8	2.6	75.7	42.8	53.7	46.3
57362	MILLER	99.2	99.1	0.0	0.0	0.1	0.1	0.3	0.3	5.3	5.7	6.5	6.3	4.5	18.1	28.0	20.3	5.2	78.1	47.3	48.4	51.6
57363	MOUNT VERNON	98.6	98.1	0.2	0.3	0.0	0.0	0.8	1.1	6.9	7.4	7.6	7.7	4.5	23.0	29.2	12.1	1.5	73.2	39.5	52.9	47.1
57364	NEW HOLLAND	100.0	100.0	0.0	0.0	0.0	0.0	0.0	0.0	8.3	8.3	8.3	8.3	4.2	22.9	22.9	14.6	2.1	66.7	37.5	52.1	47.9
57365	OACOMA	92.7	88.3	0.0	0.0	0.0	0.0	0.2	0.2	6.1	6.7	7.3	6.7	4.6	22.9	31.0	13.2	1.5	75.5	42.0	51.6	48.4
57366	PARKSTON	98.3	97.8	0.1	0.2	0.0	0.1	0.6	0.9	6.1	6.2	7.0	7.4	5.0	20.3	25.3	16.5	6.2	75.4	43.3	49.0	51.0
57368	PLANKINTON	91.4	90.6	0.6	0.6	0.2	0.2	4.2	4.3	4.7	5.3	8.3	12.5	4.3	18.6	28.2	14.8	3.2	72.2	41.3	53.2	46.8
57369	PLATTE	99.1	98.7	0.0	0.0	0.2	0.5	0.6	0.9	5.8	6.2	6.4	7.2	5.4	20.8	27.7	15.5	4.9	76.4	43.5	49.0	51.0
57370	PUKWANA	95.9	94.5	0.0	0.0	0.5	0.8	0.6	0.8	5.9	6.5	7.0	7.5	4.2	22.6	30.4	12.8	3.1	75.9	42.4	50.0	50.0
57371	REE HEIGHTS	99.3	99.2	0.0	0.0	0.0	0.0	0.4	0.0	4.9	6.2	9.1	9.1	3.3	20.2	30.0	16.5	0.8	73.3	43.2	52.7	47.3
57373	SAINT LAWRENCE	99.1	99.0	0.0	0.0	0.0	0.0	0.2	0.5	5.3	5.8	6.8	6.6	4.3	18.2	29.0	19.4	4.5	77.5	46.8	49.0	51.0
57374	SPENCER	99.6	99.6	0.0	0.0	0.2	0.2	0.0	0.0	8.0	8.6	8.8	7.8	4.5	20.5	27.9	12.5	1.4	69.9	38.3	50.8	49.2
57375	STICKNEY	99.6	99.6	0.0	0.0	0.0	0.0	0.1	0.1	6.6	7.2	7.5	7.5	4.1	19.1	28.5	15.7	3.9	73.5	43.3	51.8	48.2
57376	TRIPP	98.9	98.7	0.0	0.0	0.2	0.3	0.9	1.3	6.5	4.5	5.9	5.9	3.4	18.8	26.0	23.1	5.8	78.9	48.5	47.6	52.4
57379	VIRGIL	100.0	100.0	0.0	0.0	0.0	0.0	0.0	0.0	4.6	6.4	6.4	6.4	3.7	20.2	33.9	16.5	1.8	78.0	46.1	51.4	48.6
57380	WAGNER	58.0	49.5	0.2	0.2	0.1	0.1	3.0	3.5	9.5	8.1	8.3	7.5	4.9	20.3	23.6	13.8	4.0	69.0	37.0	47.8	52.2
57381	WESSINGTON	99.5	99.5	0.0	0.0	0.0	0.0	0.3	0.3	5.1	5.9	7.8	7.8	4.2	19.7	32.3	15.3	1.9	75.9	44.6	52.8	47.2
57382	WESSINGTON SPRINGS	99.2	99.0	0.0	0.0	0.1	0.2	0.2	0.3	4.5	4.6	5.0	5.7	4.9	20.2	28.8	19.7	6.7	82.2	48.7	48.6	51.4
57383	WHITE LAKE	97.9	97.7	0.2	0.2	0.1	0.1	0.7	0.8	6.4	7.0	7.5	7.9	3.7	19.0	26.2	16.3	5.9	74.1	43.7	51.1	48.9
57384	WOLSEY	99.5	99.4	0.0	0.0	0.0	0.0	0.2	0.4	5.2	5.9	6.4	6.1	4.1	20.6	34.0	15.5	2.1	78.6	45.9	51.8	48.2
57385	WOONSOCKET	98.5	97.8	0.0	0.0	0.6	1.1	1.0	1.4	5.2	5.8	5.9	5.7	4.9	22.1	29.8	17.1	3.6	79.5	45.3	51.2	48.8
57386	YALE	98.4	98.2	0.4	0.4	0.0	0.0	0.0	0.0	7.6	7.1	8.4	8.4	3.6	23.1	28.9	12.0	0.9	71.6	38.8	52.0	48.0
57401	ABERDEEN	94.7	93.1	0.3	0.5	0.6	0.9	0.7	1.1	6.2	6.1	6.1	7.4	7.5	25.4	26.1	12.3	3.0	77.9	37.9	47.8	52.2
57420	AKASKA	96.8	96.6	0.0	0.0	0.0	0.0	0.0	0.0	6.9	6.9	6.9	6.9	6.9	27.6	27.6	10.3	0.0	72.4	36.3	48.3	51.7
57421	AMHERST	99.0	99.0	0.0	0.0	0.0	0.0	0.5	0.0	5.6	5.6	6.6	8.1	4.6	20.8	29.9	16.2	2.5	76.6	44.2	52.8	47.2
57422	ANDOVER	99.4	99.0	0.0	0.0	0.0	0.0	0.6	0.7	5.6	5.9	6.2	5.9	3.9	19.7	29.5	18.0	5.2	78.0	46.8	51.1	48.9
57424	ASHTON	98.7	98.3	0.0	0.0	0.0	0.0	0.5	0.6	5.8	6.9	7.8	7.8	4.4	19.4	31.9	13.6	2.2	74.4	43.3	49.4	50.6
	SOUTH DAKOTA	88.7	87.0	0.6	0.8	0.6	1.0	1.4	2.0	6.9	6.7	6.9	7.6	7.3	25.0	25.9	11.3	2.4	75.3	36.7	49.7	50.3
	UNITED STATES	75.1	72.0	12.3	12.7	3.8	4.6	12.5	15.7	6.8	6.7	6.6	7.1	6.9	27.0	26.0	10.9	1.9	75.7	36.9	49.2	50.8

ZIP CODE #	POST OFFICE NAME	2009 Per Capita Income	2009 HH Income Base	2009 HOUSEHOLD INCOME DISTRIBUTION (%) Less than $25,000	$25,000 to $49,999	$50,000 to $99,999	$100,000 to $149,999	$150,000 or More	MEDIAN HOUSEHOLD INCOME 2009	2014	2009 National Centile	2009 State Centile	2009 Home Value Base	2009 HOME VALUE DISTRIBUTION (%) Less than $50,000	$50,000 to $89,999	$90,000 to $174,999	$175,000 to $399,999	$400,000 or More	2009 Median Home Value
57237	GARY	22616	266	29.3	32.3	33.8	2.6	1.9	40466	41436	34	56	219	29.2	17.4	29.2	21.0	3.2	96818
57238	GOODWIN	19330	220	27.3	30.0	37.3	3.2	2.3	44340	46169	46	75	183	23.0	21.3	34.4	15.3	6.0	102500
57239	GRENVILLE	22341	133	29.3	27.8	37.6	3.0	2.3	42666	46891	41	66	105	32.4	20.0	25.7	19.0	2.9	87500
57241	HAYTI	17831	330	23.0	36.1	36.4	2.4	2.1	43765	45477	45	72	265	17.7	26.8	41.9	13.2	0.4	101359
57242	HAZEL	18328	172	28.5	32.6	32.6	4.1	2.3	41131	43276	36	60	137	25.5	27.0	36.5	10.2	0.7	85000
57243	HENRY	20122	231	18.6	29.0	48.5	3.5	0.4	51638	51556	65	90	195	21.0	19.5	42.6	14.4	2.6	104167
57245	KRANZBURG	22198	62	16.1	27.4	46.8	4.8	4.8	54450	53182	70	93	53	5.7	9.4	50.9	30.2	3.8	142708
57246	LABOLT	19725	78	24.4	33.3	37.2	3.8	1.3	43181	42747	43	69	65	44.6	23.1	21.5	10.8	0.0	55833
57247	LAKE CITY	15691	156	39.7	29.5	26.9	2.6	1.3	29648	31725	8	10	123	27.6	17.1	29.3	22.0	4.1	102885
57248	LAKE NORDEN	17653	407	27.5	33.9	33.7	3.2	1.7	40246	42349	33	54	326	31.3	34.0	24.2	9.2	1.2	67917
57249	LAKE PRESTON	19760	459	34.4	28.1	31.8	4.4	1.3	36713	38847	23	34	346	40.2	24.6	24.0	8.1	3.2	62353
57251	MARVIN	18600	47	23.4	29.8	42.6	2.1	2.1	47354	47690	55	83	41	26.8	24.4	36.6	9.8	2.4	88333
57252	MILBANK	20707	1957	29.8	31.5	32.1	4.3	2.2	38908	39825	29	48	1440	18.0	25.8	43.1	12.2	0.8	98241
57255	NEW EFFINGTON	18851	159	35.2	30.2	28.9	2.5	3.1	40729	44084	35	57	114	47.4	26.3	14.9	11.4	0.0	53000
57256	ORTLEY	14915	75	34.7	30.7	29.3	4.0	1.3	37367	35000	25	41	60	46.7	21.7	18.3	6.7	6.7	56667
57257	PEEVER	11451	302	44.4	28.8	24.2	1.7	1.0	30376	31617	9	12	197	36.5	25.4	23.9	11.7	2.5	69615
57258	RAYMOND	16910	107	28.0	32.7	34.6	2.8	1.9	40969	43009	36	59	91	42.9	19.8	23.1	5.5	8.8	59286
57259	REVILLO	20641	190	26.3	34.7	34.2	3.7	1.1	41708	42661	38	63	156	42.3	21.8	23.1	10.9	1.9	59231
57260	ROSHOLT	16247	309	32.0	34.6	29.8	2.3	1.3	38229	40372	27	45	232	27.6	23.3	31.5	15.1	2.6	88333
57261	ROSLYN	18020	149	35.6	32.2	26.8	3.4	2.0	35245	35245	18	28	126	48.4	21.4	19.0	7.1	4.0	52000
57262	SISSETON	15245	1838	37.1	30.4	28.0	3.5	1.0	34018	36021	16	22	1142	25.4	29.4	31.4	12.0	1.8	81912
57263	SOUTH SHORE	21968	207	22.7	28.5	41.1	3.4	4.3	48866	50000	59	86	180	16.1	26.1	37.8	16.7	3.3	102273
57264	STOCKHOLM	23261	90	22.2	33.3	40.0	1.1	3.3	46297	45885	52	81	75	37.3	16.0	36.0	10.7	0.0	81667
57265	STRANDBURG	20613	81	25.9	32.1	35.8	4.9	1.2	42754	43622	42	67	68	44.1	25.0	20.6	8.8	1.5	55714
57266	SUMMIT	16558	239	38.5	30.1	25.1	3.8	2.5	33924	33890	15	22	171	35.7	29.8	19.3	13.5	1.8	67188
57268	TORONTO	19010	178	31.5	31.5	32.0	2.8	2.2	38462	39781	28	47	148	34.5	19.6	25.7	18.9	1.4	81429
57269	TWIN BROOKS	19713	147	22.4	32.7	40.8	1.4	2.7	46719	46530	53	82	125	32.0	16.8	40.0	10.4	0.8	91364
57270	VEBLEN	15334	272	47.1	28.7	22.8	1.5	0.0	27162	28841	5	6	191	41.4	23.6	27.2	4.7	3.1	67917
57271	VIENNA	14569	130	34.6	35.4	26.9	2.3	0.8	35000	35738	18	27	102	47.1	32.4	16.7	2.9	1.0	53333
57272	WALLACE	22863	71	23.9	32.4	39.4	1.4	2.8	45446	48262	50	78	60	23.3	15.0	43.3	15.0	3.3	104167
57273	WAUBAY	15491	447	36.0	32.9	27.5	2.2	1.3	33165	34210	14	20	324	49.7	17.6	21.0	9.9	1.9	50714
57274	WEBSTER	19348	1222	33.8	30.4	31.4	3.4	1.1	37316	39427	25	39	898	40.3	26.2	25.3	7.5	0.8	63621
57276	WHITE	20653	484	19.6	33.3	41.5	2.3	3.3	47666	48028	56	84	392	14.0	26.3	36.7	17.6	5.4	106383
57278	WILLOW LAKE	17400	229	33.6	36.2	27.1	2.2	0.9	35120	35741	18	27	181	45.9	32.0	16.6	3.9	1.7	55000
57279	WILMOT	18928	484	32.6	35.3	26.7	3.7	1.7	34740	36304	17	25	390	34.1	29.7	24.6	10.0	1.5	67381
57301	MITCHELL	24090	7468	26.2	27.8	35.6	6.8	3.5	45780	48660	51	79	4509	12.9	20.1	44.3	20.1	2.6	114750
57311	ALEXANDRIA	16454	606	30.2	29.9	34.2	4.1	1.7	40831	42228	35	58	467	16.9	29.1	39.0	13.9	1.1	98409
57312	ALPENA	18527	232	31.0	31.5	33.6	2.6	1.3	40788	43644	35	58	184	33.2	28.8	28.8	7.6	1.6	70714
57313	ARMOUR	17109	499	34.1	34.5	28.5	2.0	1.0	34567	36665	17	24	394	35.8	29.7	27.9	4.6	2.0	65769
57314	ARTESIAN	22096	240	28.3	30.4	32.1	5.0	4.2	42354	45000	40	65	192	41.7	17.2	29.7	10.4	1.0	70000
57315	AVON	19243	436	28.7	36.0	32.3	2.1	0.9	37571	39516	25	41	346	29.5	33.2	27.2	9.2	0.9	79063
57317	BONESTEEL	13427	245	46.9	33.1	18.8	1.2	0.0	27310	27814	5	7	179	61.5	17.9	16.2	3.9	0.6	35750
57319	BRIDGEWATER	17796	448	28.3	31.5	36.4	1.8	2.0	41474	43639	38	61	340	30.0	30.3	28.2	11.2	0.3	73793
57321	CANOVA	19410	198	24.7	34.8	35.4	3.5	1.5	41518	44450	38	62	164	53.7	19.5	16.5	8.5	1.8	44545
57322	CARPENTER	20047	74	35.1	27.0	35.1	1.4	1.4	36549	38660	22	32	56	25.0	25.0	33.9	12.5	3.6	90000
57323	CARTHAGE	18830	161	44.7	31.7	20.5	2.5	0.6	29682	30330	8	10	125	52.0	16.8	17.6	13.6	0.0	48077
57324	CAVOUR	22563	158	24.7	27.8	40.5	4.4	2.5	47025	47523	54	82	131	29.0	23.7	31.3	14.5	1.5	83000
57325	CHAMBERLAIN	23029	1146	22.4	31.0	38.5	4.6	3.5	47253	47686	55	83	754	16.0	19.4	48.8	13.1	2.7	107547
57328	CORSICA	16564	450	31.6	39.8	24.7	2.7	1.3	33756	34131	15	22	351	31.9	26.2	31.6	8.8	1.4	74250
57329	DANTE	14795	124	29.8	29.0	36.3	3.2	1.6	39301	45927	31	50	105	34.3	18.1	31.4	12.4	3.8	83750
57330	DELMONT	13082	230	40.4	35.7	22.2	1.7	0.0	31260	31681	10	14	189	43.4	25.9	23.3	4.2	3.2	55952
57331	DIMOCK	21493	169	27.8	28.4	35.5	5.9	2.4	45559	48043	50	78	138	21.0	31.2	37.7	10.1	0.0	88421
57332	EMERY	18038	371	27.8	34.5	33.7	3.2	0.8	39494	40718	31	51	301	28.6	25.6	31.6	13.6	0.7	83056
57334	ETHAN	21362	359	19.2	30.1	42.1	5.6	3.1	50511	50604	62	88	289	10.4	23.9	41.2	22.8	1.7	116964
57335	FAIRFAX	14621	141	46.8	34.0	17.7	1.4	0.0	27630	28607	5	8	102	61.8	18.6	15.7	3.9	0.0	35833
57337	FEDORA	15709	77	45.5	31.2	20.8	1.3	1.3	29294	30359	7	9	60	55.0	16.7	16.7	11.7	0.0	45714
57339	FORT THOMPSON	5182	479	66.8	22.3	10.6	0.2	0.0	11540	12022	1	0	180	49.4	17.8	22.8	8.3	1.7	50833
57340	FULTON	21860	136	24.3	27.2	38.2	4.4	5.9	47892	48108	56	84	109	16.5	17.4	41.3	20.2	4.6	120536
57341	GANN VALLEY	20288	82	37.8	39.0	13.4	3.7	6.1	33403	33403	14	21	59	39.0	20.3	16.9	6.8	16.9	59286
57342	GEDDES	16293	253	38.3	29.6	28.5	3.6	0.0	31359	33040	10	14	192	43.8	18.2	20.8	10.9	6.3	60000
57344	HARRISON	18575	106	32.1	34.0	28.3	3.8	1.9	35549	36295	19	29	90	45.6	18.9	21.1	10.0	4.4	54444
57345	HIGHMORE	19708	628	31.4	32.0	30.4	4.5	1.8	37923	38794	26	43	448	43.8	21.7	27.2	4.7	2.7	62258
57348	HITCHCOCK	17464	216	31.9	33.8	29.6	2.8	1.9	36983	38605	24	36	170	45.3	22.4	18.2	11.2	2.9	57273
57349	HOWARD	18510	712	33.3	33.7	29.1	2.7	1.3	35205	36338	18	28	527	46.7	23.7	21.4	6.5	1.7	55000
57350	HURON	21471	5787	32.4	30.3	32.1	3.2	2.0	37839	39615	26	42	3774	20.5	30.2	39.0	9.8	0.5	89059
57353	IROQUOIS	18601	315	25.4	34.0	34.3	3.8	2.5	42002	43705	39	64	254	36.6	20.1	29.1	12.6	1.6	74545
57355	KIMBALL	16539	544	30.3	37.9	27.9	3.3	0.6	37370	39581	25	41	416	35.8	30.0	24.5	5.3	4.3	68000
57356	LAKE ANDES	11294	787	46.3	28.8	22.7	2.2	0.0	27481	28403	5	7	512	40.8	24.6	23.4	6.1	5.1	63158
57359	LETCHER	17049	302	26.8	37.1	30.5	3.3	2.3	41651	43143	38	63	242	36.0	16.9	33.5	11.6	2.1	84615
57362	MILLER	21525	920	33.7	31.6	29.5	2.6	2.6	38099	39747	27	44	671	36.4	32.2	24.9	5.4	1.2	68091
57363	MOUNT VERNON	17621	367	27.2	30.8	34.9	6.0	1.1	42695	47718	41	66	303	31.0	32.7	26.7	8.3	1.3	72885
57364	NEW HOLLAND	21458	25	32.0	36.0	28.0	4.0	0.0	36115	36115	21	31	21	52.4	19.0	19.0	9.5	0.0	45000
57365	OACOMA	23628	226	31.4	29.6	32.3	4.0	2.7	40295	42624	34	55	178	30.9	25.3	32.6	7.9	3.4	71667
57366	PARKSTON	17963	951	33.1	32.4	29.4	3.9	1.2	37244	38167	24	39	726	25.2	27.7	34.6	11.3	1.2	86500
57368	PLANKINTON	17709	462	31.0	34.2	32.0	2.6	0.2	37904	38811	26	43	346	35.0	29.2	28.9	4.6	2.3	71379
57369	PLATTE	18215	978	30.2	36.5	29.6	1.8	1.9	37277	39961	24	39	740	21.9	24.5	39.7	9.6	4.3	94219
57370	PUKWANA	18446	261	26.8	36.4	33.7	3.1	0.0	39874	42582	32	52	203	24.6	19.7	35.0	14.3	6.4	98214
57371	REE HEIGHTS	22488	92	28.3	33.7	26.1	5.4	6.5	41494	43053	38	61	66	37.9	21.2	24.2	13.6	3.0	76000
57373	SAINT LAWRENCE	20823	163	31.3	31.3	31.3	3.1	3.1	39763	41806	32	52	120	39.2	28.3	23.3	6.7	2.5	67500
57374	SPENCER	19613	187	23.5	29.9	42.2	2.7	1.6	46289	47177	52	80	151	27.8	18.5	29.8	23.2	0.7	95000
57375	STICKNEY	19582	331	29.6	31.1	34.4	3.6	1.2	38954	39367	30	48	262	45.0	22.1	26.7	5.0	1.1	56842
57376	TRIPP	18543	528	37.3	35.8	22.9	2.1	1.9	32237	33331	12	15	426	52.3	22.8	16.4	6.8	1.6	47143
57379	VIRGIL	20301	47	23.4	34.0	40.4	2.1	0.0	44080	44080	46	73	38	31.6	28.9	26.3	7.9	5.3	75000
57380	WAGNER	13028	1169	42.9	29.7	24.6	2.2	0.6	29765	30096	8	10	713	29.6	26.2	34.9	6.5	2.8	82170
57381	WESSINGTON	21318	258	31.8	32.6	28.3	3.9	3.5	38297	39863	28	46	199	40.2	22.6	20.6	12.6	4.0	68125
57382	WESSINGTON SPRINGS	20791	717	36.1	30.8	27.3	3.3	2.4	35790	36432	20	30	504	32.9	32.5	32.1	2.4	0.0	71163
57383	WHITE LAKE	14704	319	37.3	34.2	25.1	3.4	0.0	32793	33721	13	19	247	51.8	24.3	19.4	3.2	1.2	46538
57384	WOLSEY	19678	356	26.4	33.4	36.2	2.8	1.1	42023	44722	39	64	290	31.7	26.6	27.2	9.7	4.8	76875
57385	WOONSOCKET	20571	623	33.7	34.0	27.1	2.7	2.4	38995	40458	30	49	470	44.9	26.2	23.6	4.7	0.6	54898
57386	YALE	17908	82	29.3	28.0	39.0	2.4	1.2	43902	45269	45	72	66	30.3	21.2	34.8	12.1	1.5	86667
57401	ABERDEEN	24066	12586	25.6	27.8	39.3	4.7	2.6	46141	48331	52	80	7944	14.5	18.9	46.7	18.0	2.0	114460
57420	AKASKA	27191	16	25.0	25.0	43.8	6.3	0.0	47500	50000	55	84	14	42.9	21.4	21.4	14.3	0.0	60000
57421	AMHERST	13323	60	26.7	35.0	33.3	5.0	0.0	40000	42363	33	54	48	43.8	22.9	25.0	6.3	2.1	63333
57422	ANDOVER	19727	134	29.9	35.1	31.3	3.0	0.7	38008	39739	27	44	108	50.9	20.4	20.4	6.5	1.9	48889
57424	ASHTON	20561	148	22.3	35.8	36.5	4.1	1.4	42847	46326	42	67	125	44.0	23.2	20.8	8.8	3.2	57500
	SOUTH DAKOTA	22885		24.5	28.5	37.1	6.5	3.5	46883	49493				19.9	18.0	38.6	20.2	3.3	113473
	UNITED STATES	27277		20.9	24.4	35.3	11.7	7.6	54719	56938				9.3	13.1	31.6	32.6	13.5	162279

ZIP CODE #	POST OFFICE NAME	FINANCIAL SERVICES: Auto Loan	FINANCIAL SERVICES: Home Loan	FINANCIAL SERVICES: Invest-ments	FINANCIAL SERVICES: Retire-ment Plans	THE HOME: Home Improvements: Home Repair	THE HOME: Home Improvements: Lawn & Garden	THE HOME: Furnishings: Comput-ers & Hard-ware-Personal	THE HOME: Furnishings: Major Appli-ances	THE HOME: Furnishings: TV, Radio, Sound Equip-ment	THE HOME: Furnishings: Furni-ture	ENTERTAINMENT: Dine out/ Carry out	ENTERTAINMENT: Sports Equip-ment	ENTERTAINMENT: Fees & Tickets	ENTERTAINMENT: Toys & Games	ENTERTAINMENT: Travel	ENTERTAINMENT: Cable TV	PERSONAL: Apparel & Services	PERSONAL: Auto Repairs	PERSONAL: Health Insur-ance	PERSONAL: Pets & Supplies
57237	GARY	85	58	93	58	61	89	65	80	67	52	67	66	47	66	64	73	43	75	85	99
57238	GOODWIN	90	62	99	62	65	95	69	85	71	56	70	70	50	70	68	78	46	80	90	105
57239	GRENVILLE	85	58	93	58	61	90	65	81	68	53	67	67	48	66	65	74	43	75	85	99
57241	HAYTI	90	62	99	62	65	95	69	85	71	56	71	70	50	70	68	78	46	80	90	105
57242	HAZEL	92	64	101	63	67	97	71	88	73	57	73	72	52	72	70	80	47	82	93	108
57243	HENRY	93	64	102	64	67	98	71	88	74	57	73	73	52	72	71	80	47	82	93	108
57245	KRANZBURG	110	76	121	75	79	116	84	104	87	68	86	86	61	86	83	95	56	97	110	128
57246	LABOLT	91	63	100	62	65	96	69	86	72	56	71	71	51	71	69	79	46	81	91	106
57247	LAKE CITY	73	50	80	50	53	77	56	69	58	45	57	57	41	57	56	63	37	65	73	86
57248	LAKE NORDEN	81	58	84	56	60	83	60	76	66	55	65	58	48	66	59	73	43	70	79	91
57249	LAKE PRESTON	77	55	79	54	57	80	60	74	66	52	64	57	47	65	58	72	42	69	80	88
57251	MARVIN	89	61	98	61	64	94	68	84	71	55	70	70	50	69	68	77	45	79	89	104
57252	MILBANK	77	63	79	62	64	83	65	77	71	60	69	58	57	69	65	76	46	73	84	90
57255	NEW EFFINGTON	82	56	90	56	59	86	63	78	65	51	64	64	46	64	62	71	42	73	82	96
57256	ORTLEY	76	52	84	52	55	80	58	72	60	47	60	60	43	59	58	66	39	67	76	89
57257	PEEVER	65	45	70	45	47	68	50	62	53	42	52	50	37	52	49	58	34	58	65	75
57258	RAYMOND	88	60	96	60	63	93	67	83	70	54	69	69	49	68	67	76	45	78	88	102
57259	REVILLO	88	61	97	61	63	93	67	84	70	55	69	69	49	69	67	76	45	78	88	103
57260	ROSHOLT	74	51	82	51	53	78	57	70	59	46	58	58	42	58	56	64	38	66	74	87
57261	ROSLYN	78	54	86	54	56	82	60	74	62	48	61	61	44	61	59	68	40	69	78	91
57262	SISSETON	70	50	71	49	52	72	56	67	60	48	59	52	44	59	54	66	39	63	73	80
57263	SOUTH SHORE	101	69	111	69	73	107	77	96	80	63	79	79	56	79	77	88	51	90	101	118
57264	STOCKHOLM	92	63	101	63	66	97	70	87	73	57	72	72	51	72	70	80	47	82	92	107
57265	STRANDBURG	94	64	103	64	67	99	72	89	74	58	74	74	52	73	71	81	48	83	94	110
57266	SUMMIT	74	53	76	51	55	77	58	71	63	50	61	55	45	62	56	69	41	66	77	85
57268	TORONTO	80	55	88	55	58	84	61	76	64	50	63	63	45	62	61	69	41	71	80	94
57269	TWIN BROOKS	90	62	99	62	65	95	69	86	72	56	71	71	50	70	69	78	46	80	90	105
57270	VEBLEN	60	42	63	42	44	63	46	58	50	40	49	45	36	49	45	55	32	54	62	69
57271	VIENNA	76	52	84	52	55	81	58	72	61	47	60	60	43	59	58	66	39	68	76	89
57272	WALLACE	95	65	104	65	68	100	73	90	75	59	75	75	53	74	72	82	48	84	95	111
57273	WAUBAY	69	49	72	48	51	72	54	66	58	46	57	52	42	57	53	64	37	62	72	80
57274	WEBSTER	75	53	78	52	55	79	58	72	64	50	62	56	45	62	57	70	41	68	78	87
57276	WHITE	95	65	104	65	68	100	73	90	75	59	75	75	53	74	72	82	48	84	95	111
57278	WILLOW LAKE	76	52	83	52	54	80	58	72	60	47	59	59	42	59	58	66	39	67	76	88
57279	WILMOT	78	53	85	53	56	82	59	74	62	48	61	61	43	60	59	67	40	69	78	90
57301	MITCHELL	83	74	72	75	73	82	81	80	83	76	82	62	75	83	76	86	56	82	87	96
57311	ALEXANDRIA	85	58	93	58	61	89	65	80	67	52	66	66	47	66	64	73	43	75	85	99
57312	ALPENA	78	54	86	54	56	82	60	74	62	48	61	61	44	61	59	68	40	69	78	91
57313	ARMOUR	69	49	72	48	51	73	54	67	58	46	57	52	42	57	53	64	37	62	72	80
57314	ARTESIAN	96	66	106	66	69	102	74	92	77	60	76	76	54	75	73	84	49	86	97	113
57315	AVON	77	53	85	53	55	81	59	73	61	48	60	60	43	60	59	67	39	68	77	90
57317	BONESTEEL	59	41	65	41	43	62	45	56	47	37	46	46	33	46	45	51	30	52	59	69
57319	BRIDGEWATER	81	58	84	56	60	85	63	78	69	55	67	60	49	68	62	76	44	73	84	93
57321	CANOVA	85	58	93	58	61	89	65	80	67	52	66	66	47	66	64	73	43	75	85	99
57322	CARPENTER	83	57	91	57	60	88	64	79	66	52	65	65	47	65	63	72	42	74	84	97
57323	CARTHAGE	64	44	70	44	46	68	49	61	51	40	50	50	36	50	49	55	33	57	64	75
57324	CAVOUR	96	66	105	66	69	101	73	91	76	59	75	75	54	75	73	83	49	85	96	112
57325	CHAMBERLAIN	85	71	80	72	73	85	79	83	83	74	81	62	71	81	76	87	55	83	91	98
57328	CORSICA	73	52	76	51	54	76	57	70	62	49	60	54	44	61	55	68	40	65	76	84
57329	DANTE	78	54	86	54	56	82	60	74	62	48	61	61	44	61	59	68	40	69	78	91
57330	DELMONT	63	44	70	43	46	67	48	60	50	39	50	50	35	49	48	55	32	56	64	74
57331	DIMOCK	99	68	109	68	72	105	76	94	79	62	78	78	56	77	76	86	51	88	100	116
57332	EMERY	79	55	87	54	57	84	61	75	63	49	62	62	44	62	60	69	40	70	80	93
57334	ETHAN	107	73	117	73	77	112	81	101	85	66	84	84	60	83	81	92	54	94	107	125
57335	FAIRFAX	59	40	64	40	42	62	45	56	47	36	46	46	33	46	45	51	30	52	59	68
57337	FEDORA	63	44	70	44	46	67	48	60	50	39	50	50	36	49	48	55	32	56	64	74
57339	FORT THOMPSON	30	21	20	23	20	25	28	25	32	28	31	19	25	31	24	35	22	29	31	33
57340	FULTON	104	72	115	72	75	110	80	99	83	65	82	82	58	81	79	90	53	92	105	122
57341	GANN VALLEY	85	58	93	58	61	89	65	80	67	52	66	66	47	66	64	73	43	75	85	99
57342	GEDDES	69	47	75	47	49	72	52	65	55	42	54	54	38	53	52	59	35	61	69	80
57344	HARRISON	85	58	93	58	61	90	65	81	67	53	67	67	48	66	65	74	43	75	85	99
57345	HIGHMORE	79	58	80	57	60	82	63	76	68	56	66	59	50	67	61	74	44	72	82	91
57348	HITCHCOCK	79	54	87	54	57	83	60	75	63	49	62	62	44	61	60	68	40	70	79	92
57349	HOWARD	72	51	74	50	53	75	56	69	61	48	59	53	43	60	54	67	39	64	75	82
57350	HURON	74	60	74	60	62	78	64	73	69	59	68	55	57	68	63	74	46	71	81	86
57353	IROQUOIS	88	60	96	60	63	92	67	83	70	54	69	69	49	68	67	76	45	78	88	102
57355	KIMBALL	79	54	86	54	57	83	60	75	62	49	62	62	44	61	60	68	40	70	79	92
57356	LAKE ANDES	55	42	50	42	41	55	46	51	50	42	49	40	39	50	43	54	33	50	56	62
57359	LETCHER	87	60	96	60	63	92	67	83	69	54	68	68	49	68	66	75	44	77	87	102
57362	MILLER	81	57	83	56	60	84	63	78	69	55	67	59	49	68	61	76	44	73	84	92
57363	MOUNT VERNON	86	59	94	59	62	90	65	81	68	53	67	67	48	67	65	74	44	76	86	100
57364	NEW HOLLAND	74	51	81	51	53	78	56	70	59	46	58	58	41	57	56	64	38	65	74	86
57365	OACOMA	98	70	100	68	73	99	72	91	80	67	78	69	57	79	71	88	52	84	95	109
57366	PARKSTON	76	54	78	53	56	80	59	73	65	52	63	56	47	64	58	72	42	68	79	87
57368	PLANKINTON	73	52	75	51	54	76	57	70	62	49	60	54	44	61	55	68	40	65	76	83
57369	PLATTE	77	55	80	54	57	81	60	74	65	52	63	58	47	64	59	72	42	69	80	89
57370	PUKWANA	80	55	88	55	58	84	61	76	64	50	63	63	45	63	61	70	41	71	80	93
57371	REE HEIGHTS	106	73	117	73	76	112	81	101	84	66	83	83	59	83	81	92	54	94	106	124
57373	SAINT LAWRENCE	87	61	90	60	64	91	67	83	73	58	71	65	52	71	66	80	47	78	89	100
57374	SPENCER	92	63	101	63	66	97	70	87	73	57	72	72	51	71	70	79	47	81	92	107
57375	STICKNEY	81	56	89	56	58	86	62	77	65	50	64	64	45	63	62	70	41	72	81	95
57376	TRIPP	71	50	74	49	52	75	55	69	60	48	59	53	43	59	54	66	39	64	74	82
57379	VIRGIL	84	58	92	58	61	89	64	80	67	52	66	66	47	66	64	73	43	75	84	98
57380	WAGNER	58	43	56	43	44	58	49	55	53	44	52	42	41	52	47	58	35	54	61	66
57381	WESSINGTON	87	60	96	60	63	92	66	83	69	54	68	68	49	68	66	75	44	77	87	102
57382	WESSINGTON SPRINGS	77	55	80	54	57	81	60	75	66	52	64	57	47	65	59	72	42	70	81	89
57383	WHITE LAKE	67	46	74	46	49	71	52	64	54	42	53	53	38	53	51	58	34	60	68	79
57384	WOLSEY	84	58	92	57	60	88	64	79	66	52	66	66	47	65	64	72	43	74	84	98
57385	WOONSOCKET	83	59	87	58	61	87	64	80	69	55	68	63	49	68	63	76	45	74	86	96
57386	YALE	88	60	96	60	63	93	67	83	70	54	69	69	49	68	67	76	45	78	88	103
57401	ABERDEEN	79	73	69	74	71	79	77	77	79	73	78	59	73	79	73	81	54	78	82	92
57420	AKASKA	88	61	97	60	63	93	67	84	70	55	69	69	49	69	67	76	45	78	88	103
57421	AMHERST	78	54	86	54	56	83	60	74	62	48	61	61	44	61	59	68	40	69	78	91
57422	ANDOVER	78	54	86	54	56	83	60	74	62	49	62	62	44	61	60	68	40	70	79	92
57424	ASHTON	89	62	98	61	64	94	68	85	71	55	70	70	50	70	68	77	46	79	90	104
	SOUTH DAKOTA	88	76	83	76	75	87	80	84	82	76	82	66	72	82	77	85	56	83	88	101
	UNITED STATES	100	100	100	100	100	100	100	100	100	100	100	100	100	100	100	100	100	100	100	100

ZIP CODE #	POST OFFICE NAME	COUNTY FIPS CODE	POPULATION 2000	POPULATION 2009	POPULATION 2014	2000-2009 ANNUAL RATE % Rate	2000-2009 ANNUAL RATE State Centile	HOUSEHOLDS 2000	HOUSEHOLDS 2009	HOUSEHOLDS 2014	HOUSEHOLDS % Annual Rate 2000-2009	HOUSEHOLDS 2009 Average HH Size	FAMILIES 2000	FAMILIES 2009	FAMILIES % Annual Rate 2000-2009
57427	BATH	013	523	545	549	0.4	73	204	220	225	0.8	2.48	164	178	0.9
57428	BOWDLE	045	841	800	775	-0.5	33	340	328	318	-0.4	2.31	233	227	-0.3
57429	BRENTFORD	115	78	68	64	-1.5	5	33	30	28	-1.0	2.27	23	21	-1.0
57430	BRITTON	091	2406	2378	2337	-0.1	55	970	982	971	0.1	2.33	646	663	0.3
57432	CLAREMONT	013	434	444	446	0.2	67	176	188	191	0.7	2.36	127	137	0.8
57433	COLUMBIA	013	433	453	457	0.5	75	182	198	202	0.9	2.29	139	153	1.0
57434	CONDE	115	635	567	536	-1.2	9	281	260	248	-0.8	2.17	200	188	-0.7
57435	CRESBARD	049	300	296	294	-0.1	55	122	121	120	-0.1	2.43	95	95	0.0
57436	DOLAND	115	824	765	731	-0.8	22	284	272	262	-0.5	2.81	209	203	-0.3
57437	EUREKA	089	1638	1473	1402	-1.1	12	736	681	652	-0.8	2.06	459	431	-0.7
57438	FAULKTON	049	1613	1624	1628	0.1	64	605	622	626	0.3	2.53	392	410	0.5
57440	FRANKFORT	115	556	517	494	-0.8	22	192	185	178	-0.4	2.79	142	137	-0.4
57441	FREDERICK	013	665	652	647	-0.2	47	278	282	284	0.2	2.31	203	208	0.3
57442	GETTYSBURG	107	1704	1556	1491	-1.0	15	740	707	687	-0.5	2.12	473	459	-0.3
57445	GROTON	013	1951	1971	1967	0.1	64	754	784	791	0.4	2.43	549	576	0.5
57446	HECLA	013	608	589	586	-0.3	42	264	269	271	0.2	2.19	179	184	0.3
57448	HOSMER	089	436	419	406	-0.4	38	173	168	163	-0.3	2.36	122	119	-0.3
57449	HOUGHTON	013	166	161	160	-0.3	42	72	73	74	0.1	2.21	48	50	0.4
57450	HOVEN	107	863	747	707	-1.5	5	342	311	298	-1.0	2.38	248	229	-0.9
57451	IPSWICH	045	2440	2421	2384	-0.1	55	900	916	907	0.2	2.58	677	696	0.3
57452	JAVA	129	375	326	309	-1.5	5	166	151	144	-1.0	2.16	118	109	-0.9
57454	LANGFORD	091	568	552	542	-0.3	42	245	245	241	0.0	2.25	169	172	0.2
57455	LEBANON	107	172	148	140	-1.6	3	69	63	60	-1.0	2.33	50	46	-0.9
57456	LEOLA	089	938	856	817	-1.0	15	391	365	350	-0.7	2.35	282	266	-0.6
57457	LONGLAKE	089	154	141	135	-0.9	18	71	67	65	-0.6	2.10	59	56	-0.6
57460	MANSFIELD	013	389	388	385	0.0	59	133	137	137	0.3	2.82	105	110	0.5
57461	MELLETTE	115	462	430	410	-0.8	22	174	166	158	-0.5	2.59	131	126	-0.4
57465	NORTHVILLE	115	348	332	321	-0.5	33	132	128	124	-0.3	2.59	101	99	-0.2
57466	ONAKA	049	124	120	119	-0.4	38	54	53	52	-0.2	2.26	41	41	0.0
57467	ORIENT	059	357	328	315	-0.9	18	135	129	125	-0.5	2.54	107	103	-0.4
57468	PIERPONT	037	271	246	236	-1.0	15	122	116	113	-0.5	2.11	82	79	-0.4
57469	REDFIELD	115	3821	3495	3324	-1.0	15	1466	1344	1274	-0.9	2.21	921	856	-0.8
57470	ROCKHAM	059	225	215	210	-0.5	33	83	81	80	-0.3	2.65	66	65	-0.2
57471	ROSCOE	045	684	576	540	-1.8	2	291	250	235	-1.6	2.28	198	172	-1.5
57472	SELBY	129	1248	1178	1143	-0.6	29	499	484	473	-0.3	2.29	350	345	-0.2
57473	SENECA	049	202	202	202	0.0	59	81	82	82	0.1	2.46	63	64	0.2
57474	STRATFORD	013	338	319	310	-0.6	29	105	103	101	-0.2	3.10	82	80	-0.3
57475	TOLSTOY	107	150	127	120	-1.8	2	64	57	54	-1.2	2.21	46	41	-1.2
57476	TULARE	115	521	480	456	-0.9	18	209	200	192	-0.5	2.40	156	151	-0.4
57477	TURTON	115	113	98	92	-1.5	5	54	49	46	-1.0	2.00	37	34	-0.9
57479	WARNER	013	593	602	603	0.2	67	202	213	216	0.6	2.83	161	171	0.7
57481	WESTPORT	013	700	705	701	0.1	64	220	232	234	0.6	3.03	172	184	0.7
57501	PIERRE	065	15593	16071	16241	0.3	70	6195	6562	6699	0.6	2.30	4064	4366	0.8
57520	AGAR	119	162	152	147	-0.7	26	72	70	68	-0.3	2.17	52	51	-0.2
57521	BELVIDERE	071	176	173	170	-0.2	47	72	73	72	0.1	2.37	47	48	0.2
57522	BLUNT	065	506	550	565	0.9	86	206	227	235	1.1	2.42	161	179	1.2
57523	BURKE	053	1158	1084	1053	-0.7	26	512	500	491	-0.3	2.13	307	304	-0.1
57528	COLOME	123	743	748	735	0.1	64	292	310	309	0.6	2.41	217	233	0.8
57529	DALLAS	123	303	291	284	-0.4	38	126	127	125	0.1	2.27	92	93	0.1
57531	DRAPER	075	272	254	247	-0.7	26	116	114	112	-0.2	2.23	75	75	0.0
57532	FORT PIERRE	117	2634	2780	2812	0.6	78	1056	1167	1197	1.1	2.37	733	820	1.2
57533	GREGORY	053	2279	2100	2027	-0.9	18	968	928	906	-0.5	2.20	612	596	-0.3
57534	HAMILL	123	119	107	101	-1.1	12	43	41	39	-0.5	2.61	33	31	-0.7
57536	HARROLD	065	606	669	691	1.1	87	198	221	230	1.2	3.03	149	167	1.2
57537	HAYES	117	138	148	150	0.8	84	55	61	62	1.1	2.43	42	48	1.5
57538	HERRICK	053	264	242	234	-0.9	18	105	100	98	-0.5	2.41	72	70	-0.3
57540	HOLABIRD	069	135	124	120	-0.9	18	53	51	49	-0.4	2.43	44	43	-0.2
57541	IDEAL	123	378	331	310	-1.4	7	125	115	110	-0.9	2.88	95	89	-0.7
57543	KADOKA	071	990	957	937	-0.4	38	400	394	387	-0.2	2.37	248	249	0.0
57544	KENNEBEC	085	504	503	500	0.0	59	195	201	202	0.3	2.50	142	148	0.4
57547	LONG VALLEY	071	220	218	214	-0.1	55	68	68	67	0.0	3.21	57	57	0.0
57548	LOWER BRULE	085	1360	1410	1436	0.4	73	358	385	395	0.8	3.65	278	302	0.9
57551	MARTIN	007	2365	2342	2315	-0.1	55	800	795	784	-0.1	2.89	556	559	0.1
57552	MIDLAND	055	688	613	568	-1.2	9	264	250	236	-0.6	2.45	204	195	-0.5
57553	MILESVILLE	055	147	129	119	-1.4	7	53	50	47	-0.6	2.58	44	42	-0.5
57555	MISSION	121	3550	4032	4290	1.4	91	1107	1304	1399	1.8	3.04	829	988	1.9
57559	MURDO	075	755	704	685	-0.8	22	328	322	318	-0.2	2.19	211	211	0.0
57560	NORRIS	095	369	371	372	0.1	64	123	129	130	0.5	2.88	88	93	0.6
57562	OKATON	075	166	155	151	-0.7	26	65	64	63	-0.2	2.42	42	42	0.0
57564	ONIDA	119	1182	1226	1227	0.4	73	474	507	512	0.7	2.42	330	358	0.9
57566	PARMELEE	121	1419	1610	1708	1.4	91	337	394	421	1.7	4.07	269	317	1.8
57567	PHILIP	055	1361	1171	1082	-1.6	3	553	507	473	-0.9	2.21	372	346	-0.8
57568	PRESHO	085	803	795	792	-0.1	55	333	339	341	0.2	2.32	237	244	0.3
57569	RELIANCE	085	373	383	388	0.3	70	157	167	171	0.7	2.29	107	116	0.9
57571	SAINT CHARLES	053	71	66	64	-0.8	22	32	31	30	-0.3	2.10	22	21	-0.5
57572	SAINT FRANCIS	121	4081	4611	4936	1.3	90	1018	1182	1275	1.6	3.85	819	959	1.7
57574	TUTHILL	007	258	249	245	-0.4	38	100	99	98	-0.1	2.52	75	75	0.0
57576	VIVIAN	085	202	200	199	-0.1	55	82	84	84	0.3	2.36	58	60	0.4
57577	WANBLEE	071	1383	1361	1334	-0.2	47	330	332	326	0.1	4.10	274	278	0.2
57579	WHITE RIVER	095	1408	1417	1413	0.1	64	452	470	474	0.4	2.92	323	340	0.6
57580	WINNER	123	4954	4555	4354	-0.9	18	1991	1904	1838	-0.5	2.34	1299	1257	-0.4
57584	WITTEN	123	101	87	82	-1.6	3	44	40	38	-1.0	2.18	34	31	-1.0
57585	WOOD	095	309	303	300	-0.2	47	121	124	123	0.3	2.44	89	92	0.4
57601	MOBRIDGE	129	3968	3706	3590	-0.7	26	1692	1634	1596	-0.4	2.20	1063	1043	-0.2
57620	BISON	105	589	514	474	-1.5	5	261	236	221	-1.1	2.18	182	167	-0.9
57622	CHERRY CREEK	137	652	635	637	-0.3	42	155	160	162	0.3	3.97	123	128	0.4
57623	DUPREE	137	1602	1713	1751	0.7	81	502	544	558	0.9	3.15	403	440	1.0
57625	EAGLE BUTTE	041	4075	4179	4216	0.3	70	1238	1313	1334	0.6	3.10	912	980	0.8
57626	FAITH	093	718	714	693	-0.1	55	282	296	291	0.5	2.41	205	218	0.7
57630	GLENCROSS	041	47	46	46	-0.2	47	16	16	16	0.0	2.88	12	12	0.0
57631	GLENHAM	129	270	251	242	-0.8	22	106	102	100	-0.4	2.46	79	77	-0.3
57632	HERREID	021	756	624	560	-2.1	1	293	250	226	-1.7	2.46	205	177	-1.6
57633	ISABEL	041	1129	1179	1195	0.5	75	345	365	371	0.6	3.23	274	292	0.7
57634	KELDRON	031	116	124	126	0.7	81	46	50	51	0.9	2.46	32	36	1.3
57638	LEMMON	105	1946	1720	1608	-1.3	8	832	762	716	-0.9	2.17	515	479	-0.8
	SOUTH DAKOTA					0.8					1.2	2.43			1.3
	UNITED STATES					1.0					1.1	2.59			0.9

ZIP CODE #	POST OFFICE NAME	RACE (%) White 2000	White 2009	Black 2000	Black 2009	Asian/Pacific 2000	Asian/Pacific 2009	% Hispanic Origin 2000	% Hispanic Origin 2009	2009 AGE DISTRIBUTION (%) 0-4	5-9	10-14	15-19	20-24	25-44	45-64	65-84	85+	18+	MEDIAN AGE 2009	% 2009 Males	% 2009 Females
57427	BATH	98.7	97.8	0.2	0.2	0.0	0.2	0.2	0.2	6.2	7.0	7.9	7.3	3.9	21.7	32.8	12.1	1.1	74.1	42.4	51.9	48.1
57428	BOWDLE	99.3	98.9	0.1	0.1	0.1	0.3	0.5	0.8	5.4	5.6	6.3	7.0	4.0	18.6	26.1	20.5	6.5	78.0	47.0	48.3	51.7
57429	BRENTFORD	98.7	98.5	0.0	0.0	0.0	0.0	0.0	0.0	2.9	2.9	5.9	5.9	4.4	20.6	39.7	14.7	2.9	82.4	49.2	54.4	45.6
57430	BRITTON	98.5	98.2	0.0	0.0	0.1	0.1	0.7	0.7	5.4	5.6	6.1	7.1	5.1	20.1	28.6	16.4	5.4	77.8	45.3	48.7	51.3
57432	CLAREMONT	99.3	99.1	0.0	0.0	0.0	0.0	0.2	0.2	5.4	5.9	6.8	7.2	3.8	20.9	31.5	16.4	2.0	77.3	45.0	51.8	48.2
57433	COLUMBIA	99.3	99.1	0.0	0.0	0.0	0.0	0.0	0.2	5.7	6.6	7.3	7.3	3.8	20.8	32.5	14.6	1.5	75.5	44.0	52.1	47.9
57434	CONDE	99.2	98.6	0.0	0.0	0.0	0.2	0.2	0.2	4.9	5.5	5.8	6.0	4.4	21.5	33.2	15.3	3.4	79.9	46.2	52.4	47.6
57435	CRESBARD	99.3	99.3	0.0	0.0	0.0	0.0	0.3	0.3	6.8	7.1	7.1	7.4	5.1	22.0	27.7	14.9	2.0	74.3	40.8	51.7	48.3
57436	DOLAND	99.3	99.1	0.1	0.1	0.0	0.0	0.2	0.4	7.1	7.8	7.8	6.8	4.4	22.2	29.0	13.2	1.6	72.9	39.5	49.2	50.8
57437	EUREKA	99.1	98.9	0.0	0.0	0.2	0.3	0.1	0.2	4.2	4.9	5.3	5.1	2.8	14.0	25.5	30.0	8.2	82.4	56.6	47.8	52.2
57438	FAULKTON	99.5	99.5	0.1	0.1	0.0	0.0	0.2	0.2	5.6	5.8	6.0	6.3	5.4	19.2	27.9	19.1	4.8	78.6	46.2	48.6	51.4
57440	FRANKFORT	99.1	99.0	0.2	0.2	0.0	0.0	0.2	0.4	7.2	7.5	7.9	6.8	4.6	22.2	28.8	13.3	1.5	73.3	39.5	49.1	50.9
57441	FREDERICK	97.7	96.9	0.0	0.0	0.0	0.0	1.2	1.7	6.9	7.5	7.7	6.3	3.7	21.6	28.7	15.5	2.1	73.9	42.1	51.2	48.8
57442	GETTYSBURG	98.0	97.5	0.0	0.0	0.1	0.2	0.2	0.2	5.2	5.3	5.7	6.6	5.3	15.6	31.4	18.8	6.1	79.4	48.6	48.7	51.3
57445	GROTON	99.0	98.8	0.0	0.0	0.0	0.0	0.4	0.6	7.3	7.0	7.0	6.8	6.2	22.1	25.0	14.2	4.5	73.9	40.1	48.7	51.3
57446	HECLA	99.0	98.8	0.0	0.0	0.0	0.0	0.5	0.5	4.8	5.4	6.1	5.4	4.1	20.4	32.6	18.2	3.1	80.1	47.6	52.0	48.0
57448	HOSMER	99.3	99.0	0.0	0.0	0.2	0.2	0.7	1.0	5.7	5.7	6.4	6.9	3.8	18.6	26.3	20.0	6.4	77.6	46.8	48.2	51.8
57449	HOUGHTON	99.4	99.4	0.0	0.0	0.0	0.0	0.0	0.0	4.3	5.0	6.2	5.6	4.3	19.3	33.5	18.6	3.1	80.7	48.5	53.4	46.6
57450	HOVEN	98.4	97.9	0.0	0.0	0.2	0.4	0.2	0.3	4.0	4.6	5.1	5.8	4.3	18.2	33.6	20.9	3.6	82.3	49.4	51.5	48.5
57451	IPSWICH	98.9	98.6	0.1	0.1	0.1	0.2	0.5	0.8	6.1	6.4	6.9	7.6	5.5	19.6	29.2	15.5	3.3	75.5	43.3	49.6	50.4
57452	JAVA	98.4	97.9	0.3	0.3	0.0	0.0	0.3	0.3	4.3	4.6	5.5	6.7	4.3	17.2	33.7	20.6	3.1	81.3	49.3	54.6	45.4
57454	LANGFORD	98.8	98.6	0.0	0.0	0.0	0.0	0.5	0.4	5.4	5.6	6.5	8.2	4.3	20.8	30.3	16.1	2.7	77.2	44.4	52.7	47.3
57455	LEBANON	98.3	98.0	0.0	0.0	0.6	0.7	0.0	0.0	4.1	4.1	4.7	6.1	4.1	18.9	33.8	20.3	4.1	83.1	49.3	52.0	48.0
57456	LEOLA	99.6	99.5	0.0	0.0	0.0	0.0	0.3	0.5	6.8	7.5	7.4	6.2	3.9	21.4	27.2	17.3	2.5	74.4	42.5	50.2	49.8
57457	LONGLAKE	100.0	99.3	0.0	0.0	0.0	0.0	0.7	0.7	7.1	7.8	7.8	7.1	4.3	19.1	27.7	17.7	1.4	73.0	42.5	51.8	48.2
57460	MANSFIELD	99.0	98.5	0.0	0.0	0.0	0.0	0.3	0.5	6.7	7.2	8.0	8.2	4.6	20.9	32.0	10.8	1.5	72.9	40.9	51.0	49.0
57461	MELLETTE	98.7	98.4	0.0	0.0	0.0	0.0	0.4	0.7	6.3	7.0	7.9	7.7	4.2	19.3	32.6	13.0	2.1	74.0	43.3	49.3	50.7
57465	NORTHVILLE	98.9	98.5	0.0	0.0	0.0	0.0	0.6	0.6	6.6	7.2	8.1	7.8	4.5	19.6	30.7	13.3	2.1	72.9	42.0	49.7	50.3
57466	ONAKA	100.0	100.0	0.0	0.0	0.0	0.0	0.0	0.0	7.5	7.5	7.5	7.5	5.0	22.5	24.2	15.8	2.5	72.5	39.2	52.5	47.5
57467	ORIENT	100.0	100.0	0.0	0.0	0.0	0.0	0.3	0.3	5.8	6.4	6.4	7.0	4.9	19.8	30.5	17.4	1.8	76.8	44.8	50.6	49.4
57468	PIERPONT	96.7	95.9	0.0	0.0	0.7	0.8	1.8	2.4	4.5	4.5	4.9	5.7	4.9	21.5	33.3	17.5	3.3	82.5	47.5	51.6	48.4
57469	REDFIELD	96.3	94.9	0.3	0.5	0.1	0.6	0.5	0.7	4.7	4.7	4.9	7.7	8.1	24.1	26.3	15.4	4.0	83.1	41.7	51.4	48.6
57470	ROCKHAM	100.0	100.0	0.0	0.0	0.0	0.0	0.4	0.5	6.0	6.0	7.0	7.0	4.7	20.9	29.8	16.7	1.9	75.8	43.8	51.6	48.4
57471	ROSCOE	99.9	99.8	0.0	0.0	0.0	0.0	0.1	0.2	6.8	6.9	7.1	6.8	4.3	19.4	27.6	17.4	3.6	74.8	44.0	51.2	48.8
57472	SELBY	98.0	97.5	0.0	0.0	0.1	0.1	0.3	0.3	4.9	5.5	5.9	6.4	4.1	18.4	29.5	19.9	5.3	79.3	48.2	49.8	50.2
57473	SENECA	100.0	99.5	0.0	0.0	0.0	0.0	0.5	0.5	6.9	6.9	6.9	7.4	5.0	22.8	26.2	15.8	2.0	73.8	40.7	51.0	49.0
57474	STRATFORD	98.5	98.1	0.0	0.0	0.0	0.0	0.3	0.3	9.1	9.1	9.1	6.3	3.8	24.8	24.1	12.5	1.3	68.7	37.1	52.7	47.3
57475	TOLSTOY	99.3	99.2	0.0	0.0	0.0	0.0	0.0	0.0	4.7	5.5	5.5	6.3	4.7	18.9	32.3	18.9	3.1	80.3	47.3	52.8	47.2
57476	TULARE	98.7	98.3	0.2	0.2	0.2	0.4	0.0	0.0	5.8	6.7	7.1	7.3	4.8	21.7	30.4	14.6	1.7	75.6	42.6	53.5	46.5
57477	TURTON	99.1	99.0	0.0	0.0	0.0	0.0	0.0	0.0	4.1	4.1	5.1	6.1	5.1	19.4	37.8	15.3	3.1	84.7	48.8	54.1	45.9
57479	WARNER	98.8	98.2	0.0	0.0	0.0	0.2	0.3	0.5	6.8	7.3	8.0	8.1	4.7	21.9	32.2	9.6	1.3	72.8	40.2	51.2	48.8
57481	WESTPORT	98.7	98.3	0.1	0.1	0.0	0.0	0.1	0.1	6.1	6.8	7.2	6.7	4.1	21.8	30.9	14.6	1.7	75.6	42.9	50.5	49.5
57501	PIERRE	89.6	86.6	0.2	0.3	0.4	0.7	1.2	1.7	6.3	6.4	7.6	6.5	6.2	23.5	28.2	12.2	3.1	75.6	39.9	47.6	52.4
57520	AGAR	97.5	97.4	0.0	0.0	0.0	0.0	1.2	1.3	4.6	5.3	5.3	5.9	4.6	21.7	30.9	19.1	2.6	81.6	46.5	51.3	48.7
57521	BELVIDERE	86.9	83.2	0.0	0.0	0.0	0.0	1.1	1.2	5.8	6.4	6.4	7.5	4.0	23.7	29.5	15.0	1.7	76.3	43.0	50.3	49.7
57522	BLUNT	95.5	94.4	0.2	0.2	0.2	0.2	1.0	1.3	6.5	6.9	7.6	8.0	5.6	21.5	31.6	11.3	0.9	74.0	40.8	50.4	49.6
57523	BURKE	96.5	95.4	0.0	0.0	0.3	0.6	0.3	0.5	5.2	5.4	6.1	6.7	5.1	19.1	30.4	17.1	5.1	79.0	46.8	47.0	53.0
57528	COLOME	96.8	95.7	0.0	0.0	0.1	0.3	0.3	0.4	5.6	5.9	6.6	7.4	4.4	22.6	30.9	14.3	2.4	76.3	43.0	51.3	48.7
57529	DALLAS	95.7	94.5	0.0	0.0	0.7	1.0	0.7	0.7	4.8	5.2	5.8	7.6	4.1	20.6	32.3	16.8	2.7	79.4	46.1	53.6	46.4
57531	DRAPER	96.0	95.7	0.0	0.0	0.0	0.0	0.4	0.0	5.1	5.9	5.9	5.9	4.7	22.0	32.7	15.0	2.8	78.7	45.3	49.6	50.4
57532	FORT PIERRE	92.8	90.8	0.2	0.3	0.3	0.4	0.4	0.6	5.9	6.0	6.4	7.2	5.6	25.7	30.0	11.9	1.3	76.9	40.5	50.3	49.7
57533	GREGORY	95.3	93.8	0.0	0.0	0.2	0.3	1.0	1.0	4.8	4.9	5.6	6.7	5.8	19.5	28.3	18.4	6.0	80.6	46.9	48.2	51.8
57534	HAMILL	83.9	79.4	0.0	0.0	0.0	0.0	0.0	0.0	6.5	8.4	8.4	8.4	3.7	21.5	30.8	10.3	1.9	71.0	39.6	49.5	50.5
57536	HARROLD	67.8	65.5	0.0	0.1	0.0	0.0	1.2	1.6	7.9	7.3	7.6	8.5	6.9	22.4	27.1	11.1	1.2	72.0	35.7	51.3	48.7
57537	HAYES	97.1	95.9	0.0	0.0	0.7	0.7	0.7	1.4	5.4	5.4	6.8	7.4	3.4	24.3	33.8	12.2	1.4	77.7	43.2	51.4	48.6
57538	HERRICK	92.4	90.1	0.4	0.4	0.0	0.4	1.1	1.2	4.1	4.5	8.3	9.1	5.0	23.6	29.3	14.5	1.7	76.4	43.0	54.1	45.9
57540	HOLABIRD	97.8	97.6	0.0	0.0	0.0	0.0	0.0	0.0	6.5	6.5	8.1	7.3	4.0	18.5	30.6	16.9	1.6	75.0	44.2	55.6	44.4
57541	IDEAL	82.3	77.6	0.0	0.0	0.0	0.0	0.0	0.0	7.6	8.2	8.5	8.5	3.9	20.2	29.9	11.5	1.8	70.4	39.0	48.9	51.1
57543	KADOKA	85.2	81.1	0.1	0.1	0.1	0.1	0.4	0.4	6.2	6.4	6.3	6.4	6.1	20.7	28.0	16.2	3.9	76.9	43.4	47.6	52.4
57544	KENNEBEC	93.7	90.3	0.0	0.0	0.6	0.6	0.4	0.4	6.4	6.8	6.8	6.2	4.2	21.1	28.6	17.5	2.6	76.5	44.0	52.3	47.7
57547	LONG VALLEY	64.5	57.3	0.0	0.0	0.0	0.0	0.0	0.0	7.8	6.4	7.8	11.0	2.3	19.3	33.0	11.9	0.5	70.2	41.7	52.8	47.2
57548	LOWER BRULE	9.3	5.8	0.1	0.1	0.0	0.0	0.5	0.5	13.8	13.5	11.1	9.7	6.8	24.0	16.6	4.3	0.4	55.1	21.5	47.7	52.3
57551	MARTIN	47.2	43.3	0.4	0.4	0.2	0.2	2.3	2.4	9.4	9.0	8.4	8.9	6.1	22.6	22.6	10.7	2.4	67.6	31.7	48.7	51.3
57552	MIDLAND	96.8	96.1	0.0	0.0	0.0	0.0	0.0	0.0	6.0	7.0	7.5	6.9	3.8	22.7	31.0	13.4	1.8	75.2	41.7	50.4	49.6
57553	MILESVILLE	96.6	96.1	0.0	0.0	0.0	0.0	0.0	0.0	6.2	6.2	6.2	6.2	5.4	22.5	31.8	14.0	1.6	77.5	43.1	51.9	48.1
57555	MISSION	22.8	22.8	0.1	0.1	0.0	0.0	1.7	1.6	11.0	11.1	10.3	9.4	6.9	24.0	19.9	6.7	0.7	61.4	25.9	49.1	50.9
57559	MURDO	95.9	95.3	0.0	0.0	0.1	0.1	0.4	0.3	5.0	5.8	5.8	6.1	4.8	22.4	32.2	15.3	2.4	79.7	45.0	49.7	50.3
57560	NORRIS	36.1	32.3	0.0	0.0	0.0	0.0	1.9	1.6	9.7	10.0	9.7	9.4	6.7	24.0	19.9	9.2	1.3	63.6	30.6	50.7	49.3
57562	OKATON	95.8	95.5	0.0	0.0	0.0	0.0	0.6	0.0	5.2	5.2	5.8	5.8	4.5	21.9	33.5	15.5	2.6	80.0	46.0	50.3	49.7
57564	ONIDA	98.1	98.0	0.0	0.0	0.1	0.1	0.7	0.7	6.4	7.0	7.0	6.5	4.2	22.4	29.7	14.4	2.2	75.4	42.4	51.5	48.5
57566	PARMELEE	4.4	4.5	0.1	0.1	0.0	0.0	0.6	0.5	14.6	12.9	10.4	9.9	9.4	22.4	15.3	4.7	0.4	56.0	21.2	47.0	53.0
57567	PHILIP	96.1	95.1	0.0	0.0	0.1	0.2	1.0	1.5	4.7	5.4	5.5	5.4	4.9	21.4	33.4	14.3	5.0	81.1	46.8	48.8	51.2
57568	PRESHO	96.9	96.0	0.2	0.3	0.5	0.5	0.7	0.9	5.3	6.0	6.5	6.3	4.3	19.5	32.2	16.4	3.5	77.6	46.1	54.3	45.7
57569	RELIANCE	92.0	88.0	0.0	0.0	0.3	0.3	0.3	0.3	6.3	6.8	7.3	6.5	4.4	23.0	30.3	13.8	1.6	75.2	41.9	52.0	48.0
57571	SAINT CHARLES	88.7	84.8	0.0	0.0	0.0	0.0	1.4	1.5	6.1	6.1	7.6	9.1	4.5	19.7	27.3	16.7	3.0	72.7	42.5	51.5	48.5
57572	SAINT FRANCIS	6.5	6.5	0.1	0.1	0.3	0.4	1.7	1.6	13.4	12.3	11.8	11.2	7.8	22.3	16.2	4.5	0.4	55.3	20.8	48.6	51.4
57574	TUTHILL	77.1	75.1	0.0	0.0	0.8	0.8	0.8	0.4	6.0	7.6	8.0	7.2	3.2	22.1	29.7	14.5	1.6	73.1	42.2	49.0	51.0
57576	VIVIAN	97.0	96.0	0.0	0.0	0.5	0.5	1.0	0.5	5.0	6.5	6.5	6.5	4.5	20.0	31.5	16.0	3.5	77.0	45.6	54.0	46.0
57577	WANBLEE	13.7	10.9	0.0	0.0	0.0	0.0	0.4	0.4	11.0	11.7	12.9	12.4	7.8	20.9	17.8	5.1	0.5	56.1	21.3	50.8	49.2
57579	WHITE RIVER	39.8	36.1	0.0	0.0	0.1	0.1	2.0	2.0	9.0	9.7	10.0	8.5	5.2	21.2	23.1	10.9	2.5	65.8	32.6	50.0	50.0
57580	WINNER	86.4	82.9	0.0	0.0	0.1	0.1	1.0	1.1	6.9	7.1	7.0	6.9	5.1	21.2	26.8	15.2	3.8	74.4	41.4	49.0	51.0
57584	WITTEN	81.4	75.9	0.0	0.0	0.0	0.0	0.0	0.0	8.0	8.0	8.0	8.0	4.6	19.5	28.7	12.6	2.3	70.1	39.4	47.1	52.9
57585	WOOD	77.9	74.9	0.0	0.0	0.0	0.0	0.0	0.0	6.6	9.9	7.9	5.3	3.6	19.1	30.4	15.2	2.0	71.6	42.9	50.8	49.2
57601	MOBRIDGE	80.8	76.2	0.0	0.0	0.3	0.3	0.8	0.9	7.0	6.7	6.7	6.0	5.6	20.9	26.3	17.1	3.6	75.7	42.1	47.3	52.7
57620	BISON	97.6	97.3	0.3	0.4	0.0	0.0	1.0	1.4	6.4	7.6	7.8	6.2	3.9	18.9	31.3	14.6	3.3	74.3	44.4	51.6	48.4
57622	CHERRY CREEK	7.8	7.6	0.0	0.0	0.0	0.0	1.1	0.9	16.5	14.5	9.6	8.0	10.4	21.4	15.3	4.1	0.2	54.8	20.6	49.0	51.0
57623	DUPREE	36.3	34.6	0.0	0.0	0.1	0.2	0.7	0.9	7.7	9.3	9.5	9.7	5.3	22.8	25.8	9.0	0.8	67.5	31.8	48.8	51.2
57625	EAGLE BUTTE	11.3	9.5	0.0	0.0	0.1	0.1	1.0	1.0	11.5	10.5	9.9	10.3	8.0	25.2	17.7	6.1	0.6	61.3	24.8	49.0	51.0
57626	FAITH	93.9	92.0	0.1	0.3	0.0	0.0	0.3	0.4	5.7	6.3	6.9	7.0	4.5	20.7	31.0	15.1	2.8	76.9	44.1	51.8	48.2
57630	GLENCROSS	66.0	63.0	0.0	0.0	0.0	0.0	0.0	0.0	6.5	6.5	6.5	8.7	6.5	21.7	28.3	15.2	0.0	71.7	38.3	45.7	54.3
57631	GLENHAM	97.4	96.4	0.0	0.0	0.0	0.0	0.4	0.8	5.2	6.0	6.4	6.0	4.8	19.5	33.5	17.1	1.6	78.5	46.4	51.8	48.2
57632	HERREID	99.3	99.0	0.0	0.0	0.0	0.2	0.3	0.3	5.4	6.1	6.4	7.1	4.3	18.1	30.4	18.3	3.8	76.6	46.3	50.6	49.4
57633	ISABEL	39.0	34.4	0.0	0.0	0.1	0.1	1.1	1.1	10.6	10.3	8.9	8.3	8.1	22.3	23.4	7.0	1.0	65.1	27.6	44.4	55.6
57634	KELDRON	87.8	84.7	0.0	0.0	0.0	0.0	0.9	0.8	5.6	6.5	7.3	7.3	4.0	20.2	30.6	16.1	2.4	75.8	44.4	53.2	46.8
57638	LEMMON	95.7	94.7	0.1	0.1	0.4	0.4	0.6	0.6	5.3	5.6	5.8	6.2	5.3	20.8	28.5	17.6	4.9	79.4	45.6	47.3	52.7
	SOUTH DAKOTA	88.7	87.0	0.6	0.8	0.6	1.0	1.4	2.0	6.9	6.7	6.9	7.6	7.3	25.0	25.9	11.3	2.4	75.3	36.7	49.7	50.3
	UNITED STATES	75.1	72.0	12.3	12.7	3.8	4.6	12.5	15.7	6.8	6.7	6.6	7.1	6.9	27.0	26.0	10.9	1.9	75.7	36.9	49.2	50.8

INCOME

ZIP CODE #	POST OFFICE NAME	2009 Per Capita Income	2009 HH Income Base	2009 HOUSEHOLD INCOME DISTRIBUTION (%) Less than $25,000	$25,000 to $49,999	$50,000 to $99,999	$100,000 to $149,999	$150,000 or More	MEDIAN HOUSEHOLD INCOME 2009	2014	2009 National Centile	2009 State Centile	2009 Home Value Base	2009 HOME VALUE DISTRIBUTION (%) Less than $50,000	$50,000 to $89,999	$90,000 to $174,999	$175,000 to $399,999	$400,000 or More	2009 Median Home Value
57427	BATH	24147	220	13.2	34.1	45.9	4.5	2.3	52356	52578	67	91	191	16.2	18.8	38.2	25.1	1.6	115761
57428	BOWDLE	16618	328	35.7	33.5	27.7	2.4	0.6	35000	37055	18	27	273	63.4	19.8	13.9	1.5	1.5	37237
57429	BRENTFORD	22689	30	26.7	30.0	36.7	6.7	0.0	42343	45000	40	65	25	40.0	28.0	20.0	12.0	0.0	62500
57430	BRITTON	19516	982	29.9	31.6	33.5	3.5	1.5	39436	42131	31	50	763	27.9	30.7	34.2	6.3	0.9	76636
57432	CLAREMONT	19545	188	31.4	31.4	31.4	3.7	2.1	37757	42064	26	42	154	40.3	26.6	21.4	9.7	1.9	64545
57433	COLUMBIA	22836	198	24.7	33.3	34.8	4.0	3.0	42351	46417	40	65	168	29.8	22.6	28.6	17.3	1.8	86364
57434	CONDE	22958	260	29.6	32.7	30.0	5.4	2.3	38268	39480	27	45	215	43.7	23.7	20.9	9.3	2.3	61667
57435	CRESBARD	17563	121	33.9	33.1	28.1	3.3	1.7	34755	35000	17	25	102	46.1	17.6	25.5	4.9	5.9	55714
57436	DOLAND	16634	272	29.4	36.0	27.2	4.0	3.3	41064	43004	36	59	210	55.7	20.0	17.6	5.2	1.4	41429
57437	EUREKA	16247	681	49.3	28.5	19.2	1.9	1.0	25518	26507	4	4	555	57.5	20.9	15.9	4.0	1.8	38875
57438	FAULKTON	16873	622	33.9	32.5	28.6	4.0	1.0	35736	36795	20	30	496	40.3	27.2	26.0	4.6	1.8	63684
57440	FRANKFORT	16629	185	29.7	36.8	26.5	3.8	3.2	40852	43727	35	58	142	54.9	19.7	17.6	5.6	2.1	42222
57441	FREDERICK	19315	282	27.3	36.2	32.3	3.2	1.1	40220	45000	33	54	235	33.6	33.2	23.0	8.5	1.7	68250
57442	GETTYSBURG	20577	707	33.2	33.2	28.4	3.3	1.8	36627	37711	22	33	536	39.6	31.9	24.4	3.9	0.2	63947
57445	GROTON	22689	784	24.5	26.3	40.9	4.6	3.7	48926	50761	59	86	598	19.2	26.9	39.3	13.5	1.0	96389
57446	HECLA	19361	269	33.1	32.3	30.5	3.0	1.1	36653	41050	23	33	205	43.4	29.8	18.0	7.8	1.0	57941
57448	HOSMER	16109	168	37.5	33.3	26.8	2.4	0.0	34128	36651	16	23	141	61.0	19.1	15.6	2.1	2.1	38750
57449	HOUGHTON	19329	73	34.2	32.9	30.1	2.7	0.0	35441	39062	19	29	55	49.1	27.3	16.4	7.3	0.0	51250
57450	HOVEN	20126	311	30.2	34.4	27.7	4.5	3.2	37079	39026	24	37	264	41.3	26.1	24.6	6.1	1.9	62500
57451	IPSWICH	20779	916	28.6	28.7	35.3	4.7	2.7	43221	45235	43	70	736	23.9	21.6	35.2	16.2	3.1	96735
57452	JAVA	20420	151	28.5	33.8	33.1	4.0	0.7	37526	38775	25	41	127	55.1	15.7	17.3	2.4	9.4	41875
57454	LANGFORD	19400	245	27.3	35.9	32.2	4.5	0.0	39177	41348	30	49	199	43.7	23.1	23.6	7.5	2.0	62083
57455	LEBANON	20736	63	30.2	36.5	25.4	4.8	3.2	36724	36538	23	35	53	37.7	28.3	28.3	5.7	0.0	71250
57456	LEOLA	16485	365	41.4	31.8	23.0	1.9	1.9	30549	31706	9	12	301	53.8	17.6	17.3	5.3	6.0	45208
57457	LONGLAKE	19137	67	44.8	26.9	23.9	3.0	1.5	30751	31151	9	13	58	36.2	10.3	34.5	8.6	10.3	100000
57460	MANSFIELD	20099	137	16.8	27.7	49.6	5.1	0.7	53630	54599	69	92	117	22.2	21.4	37.6	15.4	3.4	99375
57461	MELLETTE	19204	166	21.7	35.5	38.0	3.6	1.2	43511	45570	44	71	141	44.7	22.7	21.3	7.8	3.5	56818
57465	NORTHVILLE	18195	128	24.2	35.2	35.9	3.1	1.6	41525	43213	38	62	109	45.0	20.2	22.9	6.4	5.5	56111
57466	ONAKA	18136	53	35.8	35.8	26.4	1.9	0.0	32684	35000	13	18	45	46.7	15.6	28.9	2.2	6.7	55000
57467	ORIENT	20992	129	25.6	28.7	37.2	6.2	2.3	44688	46438	47	76	103	50.5	19.4	15.5	9.7	4.9	49375
57468	PIERPONT	21451	116	30.2	37.1	26.7	3.4	2.6	37815	37557	26	42	101	46.5	19.8	23.8	5.9	4.0	55000
57469	REDFIELD	18745	1344	33.0	33.3	27.8	4.2	1.8	36607	39048	22	33	895	40.4	32.2	23.4	3.8	0.2	58301
57470	ROCKHAM	19594	81	28.4	28.4	35.8	4.9	2.5	43624	45746	44	71	65	47.7	16.9	16.9	12.3	6.2	55000
57471	ROSCOE	18940	250	29.2	37.2	28.4	3.2	2.0	36728	38531	23	35	202	55.4	21.8	17.3	3.5	2.0	43889
57472	SELBY	19012	484	29.3	35.3	29.3	4.5	1.4	37901	40143	26	42	390	46.7	25.6	23.6	4.1	0.0	54063
57473	SENECA	18062	82	34.1	31.7	28.0	3.7	2.4	36848	38896	23	35	68	45.6	14.7	25.0	10.3	4.4	57500
57474	STRATFORD	15670	103	28.2	34.0	31.1	2.9	3.9	39057	40373	30	49	86	25.6	20.9	34.9	15.1	3.5	96000
57475	TOLSTOY	21287	57	29.8	36.8	28.1	3.5	1.8	36716	38616	23	34	48	43.8	27.1	22.9	6.3	0.0	57500
57476	TULARE	20342	200	22.0	42.5	29.5	4.5	1.5	40689	41296	35	57	156	46.2	25.0	21.2	7.7	0.0	56000
57477	TURTON	25761	49	26.5	34.7	30.6	6.1	2.0	39292	42372	31	50	40	47.5	27.5	15.0	7.5	2.5	53333
57479	WARNER	21245	213	13.6	25.4	53.5	6.1	1.4	59278	60171	77	94	181	12.2	23.2	44.2	18.2	2.2	108013
57481	WESTPORT	18342	232	20.7	32.8	39.7	3.4	3.4	46795	49729	54	82	198	23.2	17.2	32.3	24.2	3.0	112500
57501	PIERRE	26540	6562	18.7	24.5	45.6	6.6	4.5	54728	54830	71	93	4304	11.3	11.9	50.4	25.5	0.9	135530
57520	AGAR	20341	70	31.4	38.6	24.3	4.3	1.4	37310	37649	24	39	53	32.1	17.0	28.3	13.2	9.4	92500
57521	BELVIDERE	18739	73	34.2	37.0	21.9	4.1	2.7	32284	32823	12	16	55	54.5	9.1	18.2	7.3	10.9	39167
57522	BLUNT	24149	227	18.9	23.8	49.3	6.2	1.8	54755	54610	71	93	193	20.2	16.6	37.3	24.4	1.6	115948
57523	BURKE	17157	500	44.4	28.8	24.4	1.4	1.0	28999	31260	7	8	374	41.4	26.2	25.1	5.9	1.3	64828
57528	COLOME	17408	310	32.9	28.7	36.1	1.0	1.3	40000	45461	33	54	260	39.2	23.8	21.9	8.8	6.2	65789
57529	DALLAS	16845	127	41.7	28.3	26.8	1.6	1.6	31770	32877	11	15	105	38.1	25.7	20.0	10.5	5.7	66429
57531	DRAPER	19610	114	36.0	30.7	28.1	3.5	1.8	36987	38618	24	37	83	39.8	22.9	26.5	9.6	1.2	66250
57532	FORT PIERRE	24837	1167	20.9	27.1	43.3	5.3	3.4	50981	51519	64	89	895	17.2	18.1	38.0	22.0	4.7	122875
57533	GREGORY	17433	928	44.0	29.0	22.4	3.2	1.4	29284	30414	7	9	699	41.2	23.6	26.0	8.0	1.1	64868
57534	HAMILL	13302	41	41.5	36.6	22.0	0.0	0.0	32312	32913	12	17	32	50.0	21.9	18.8	9.4	0.0	50000
57536	HARROLD	20546	221	27.6	32.6	32.1	4.1	3.6	37927	41573	26	43	162	32.7	27.8	22.8	14.2	2.5	76364
57537	HAYES	21538	61	19.7	37.7	32.8	6.6	3.3	44435	48166	47	75	46	17.4	10.9	30.4	26.1	15.2	140000
57538	HERRICK	15253	100	49.0	24.0	24.0	2.0	1.0	25469	26675	4	4	78	50.0	12.8	25.6	7.7	3.8	50000
57540	HOLABIRD	22163	51	23.5	33.3	35.3	5.9	2.0	44298	44082	46	74	40	40.0	17.5	27.5	5.0	10.0	76667
57541	IDEAL	11826	115	41.7	37.4	19.1	0.9	0.9	32328	32797	12	17	90	47.8	23.3	16.7	10.0	2.2	52222
57543	KADOKA	17618	394	36.3	34.5	26.4	1.3	1.5	33092	35948	13	20	289	47.1	29.1	16.6	3.5	3.8	53696
57544	KENNEBEC	20842	201	30.3	27.9	34.8	3.0	4.0	41038	43009	36	59	168	19.6	30.4	32.7	16.1	1.2	90000
57547	LONG VALLEY	13381	68	27.9	33.8	35.3	2.9	0.0	29232	29388	7	9	54	35.2	40.7	24.1	0.0	0.0	55333
57548	LOWER BRULE	9060	385	46.8	32.2	18.7	2.1	0.3	26748	28903	4	5	150	21.3	25.3	42.0	11.3	0.0	100658
57551	MARTIN	13722	795	39.0	30.1	26.7	3.8	0.5	32587	35461	13	18	483	37.7	26.3	28.0	7.2	0.8	68472
57552	MIDLAND	19794	250	28.4	44.0	22.4	2.0	3.2	34692	35274	17	24	187	44.4	24.1	18.2	7.5	5.9	59545
57553	MILESVILLE	19459	50	32.0	36.0	22.0	6.0	4.0	35000	33735	18	27	37	18.9	24.3	21.6	18.9	16.2	112500
57555	MISSION	12011	1304	42.8	32.4	20.2	3.5	1.1	28330	29215	6	8	689	43.7	14.8	31.5	7.7	2.3	65811
57559	MURDO	20006	322	35.7	31.1	27.6	3.7	1.9	37091	38793	24	38	235	40.9	22.1	25.5	9.8	1.7	64091
57560	NORRIS	11171	129	49.6	28.7	18.6	3.1	0.0	25311	26110	3	4	78	56.4	14.1	19.2	10.3	0.0	31667
57562	OKATON	18007	64	35.9	31.3	26.6	4.7	1.6	37339	40560	25	40	47	42.6	19.1	25.5	10.6	2.1	62500
57564	ONIDA	20898	507	23.1	37.7	32.9	3.6	2.8	41065	42520	36	60	387	26.4	25.8	37.0	6.5	4.4	83929
57566	PARMELEE	5087	394	74.6	16.8	7.1	1.0	0.5	13167	13896	1	1	186	40.9	14.5	26.3	8.6	9.7	65000
57567	PHILIP	21630	507	28.2	34.3	29.8	4.3	3.4	37360	38581	25	40	397	33.5	30.0	30.5	3.5	2.5	67564
57568	PRESHO	18219	339	33.3	31.6	31.3	2.9	0.9	38313	41158	28	46	270	35.6	35.2	18.1	8.1	3.0	60000
57569	RELIANCE	23552	167	31.1	29.3	31.7	4.2	3.6	40610	43099	35	57	133	27.8	26.3	32.3	10.5	3.0	80833
57571	SAINT CHARLES	16312	31	48.4	29.0	22.6	0.0	0.0	26108	23094	4	5	23	60.9	17.4	17.4	4.3	0.0	32500
57572	SAINT FRANCIS	8823	1182	51.4	26.6	18.5	2.4	1.0	23797	25192	3	2	440	50.2	10.7	24.3	5.9	8.9	49474
57574	TUTHILL	15369	99	38.4	32.3	28.3	1.0	0.0	33580	35895	15	21	73	35.6	30.1	27.4	5.5	1.4	68750
57576	VIVIAN	17835	84	32.1	31.0	33.3	3.6	0.0	40000	41152	33	54	67	35.8	37.3	17.9	6.0	3.0	58636
57577	WANBLEE	6974	332	53.3	34.3	9.3	1.5	1.5	21184	22322	2	2	148	47.3	4.7	21.6	13.5	12.8	84000
57579	WHITE RIVER	12488	470	47.9	24.5	23.8	3.2	0.6	27212	27218	5	6	293	50.9	22.9	18.1	6.1	2.0	48750
57580	WINNER	18548	1904	38.4	28.7	27.7	2.3	2.8	34488	35497	16	24	1382	33.6	27.8	27.6	9.0	2.0	72917
57584	WITTEN	15232	40	45.0	37.5	17.5	0.0	0.0	30000	31496	8	11	31	48.4	22.6	19.4	9.7	0.0	51667
57585	WOOD	17680	124	41.9	20.2	33.1	4.0	0.8	34077	36389	16	23	99	39.4	23.2	15.2	13.1	9.1	61667
57601	MOBRIDGE	18098	1634	38.4	31.3	26.6	3.1	0.6	32883	34660	13	19	1072	32.3	30.5	26.9	9.4	0.9	68444
57620	BISON	19813	236	37.7	28.8	28.0	3.0	2.5	33529	34782	14	21	186	43.5	24.7	10.2	5.9	15.6	60000
57622	CHERRY CREEK	5026	160	72.5	20.6	6.3	0.6	0.0	14566	15437	1	1	61	34.4	29.5	36.1	0.0	0.0	65357
57623	DUPREE	11657	544	41.9	34.9	19.7	2.0	1.5	30000	31936	8	11	401	30.7	25.9	26.7	9.5	7.2	76563
57625	EAGLE BUTTE	10840	1313	46.6	32.1	18.2	2.4	0.7	26997	28166	5	6	581	42.7	26.3	25.0	3.6	2.4	59659
57626	FAITH	18970	296	33.1	35.8	24.7	1.7	4.7	35981	37445	21	31	214	43.9	21.0	17.8	5.1	12.1	61818
57630	GLENCROSS	13031	16	43.8	31.3	25.0	0.0	0.0	30000	40000	8	11	12	58.3	25.0	16.7	0.0	0.0	40000
57631	GLENHAM	19750	102	32.4	28.4	32.4	5.9	1.0	38612	40000	28	47	87	46.0	24.1	20.7	9.2	0.0	57000
57632	HERREID	16686	250	35.2	31.2	30.0	3.2	0.4	35374	37091	19	29	204	53.9	26.5	12.7	4.9	2.0	45556
57633	ISABEL	10157	365	44.9	34.0	20.3	0.3	0.5	27491	28457	5	7	238	37.8	26.9	26.1	6.7	2.5	59667
57634	KELDRON	15166	50	40.0	30.0	28.0	2.0	0.0	33179	42402	14	20	40	67.5	15.0	12.5	5.0	0.0	22500
57638	LEMMON	19683	762	36.9	33.2	24.7	2.1	3.1	32768	33472	13	18	564	53.2	24.5	13.5	6.2	2.7	46538
	SOUTH DAKOTA	22885		24.5	28.5	37.1	6.5	3.5	46883	49493				19.9	18.0	38.6	20.2	3.3	113473
	UNITED STATES	27277		20.9	24.4	35.3	11.7	7.6	54719	56938				9.3	13.1	31.6	32.6	13.5	162279

ZIP CODE #	POST OFFICE NAME	FINANCIAL SERVICES: Auto Loan	Home Loan	Invest-ments	Retire-ment Plans	THE HOME: Home Improvements: Home Repair	Lawn & Garden	Furnishings: Comput-ers & Hard-ware-Personal	Major Appli-ances	TV, Radio, Sound Equip-ment	Furni-ture	ENTERTAINMENT: Dine out/ Carry out	Sports Equip-ment	Fees & Tickets	Toys & Games	Travel	Cable TV	PERSONAL: Apparel & Services	Auto Repairs	Health Insur-ance	Pets & Supplies
57427	BATH	107	74	117	73	77	113	82	102	85	66	84	84	60	83	81	93	55	95	107	125
57428	BOWDLE	70	48	77	48	50	74	53	66	56	43	55	55	39	54	53	61	36	62	70	82
57429	BRENTFORD	92	63	101	63	66	97	70	87	73	57	72	72	51	72	70	80	47	82	92	107
57430	BRITTON	79	57	82	55	59	83	62	77	68	54	66	59	48	67	60	75	44	72	83	91
57432	CLAREMONT	83	57	91	57	59	87	63	78	66	51	65	65	46	64	63	72	42	73	83	96
57433	COLUMBIA	93	64	103	64	67	99	71	89	74	58	73	73	52	73	71	81	48	83	94	109
57434	CONDE	89	61	98	61	64	94	68	85	71	55	70	70	50	69	68	77	45	79	89	104
57435	CRESBARD	77	53	84	53	55	81	59	73	61	47	60	60	43	60	58	66	39	68	77	90
57436	DOLAND	84	58	92	57	60	88	64	79	66	52	66	66	47	65	64	72	43	74	84	98
57437	EUREKA	58	42	60	41	43	61	46	56	50	40	48	43	36	49	44	55	32	53	61	67
57438	FAULKTON	74	53	77	52	55	78	58	72	63	50	61	55	45	62	57	69	41	67	77	85
57440	FRANKFORT	83	57	91	57	60	88	63	79	66	51	65	65	46	65	63	72	42	74	83	97
57441	FREDERICK	79	55	87	55	58	84	61	76	63	50	63	62	45	62	61	69	41	71	80	93
57442	GETTYSBURG	76	54	77	53	56	79	59	73	65	52	63	56	47	64	58	72	42	68	79	87
57445	GROTON	89	73	87	73	75	91	79	87	81	72	80	66	68	80	77	86	54	84	92	103
57446	HECLA	76	52	83	52	55	80	58	72	60	47	60	59	42	59	58	66	39	67	76	89
57448	HOSMER	69	48	76	48	50	73	53	66	55	43	54	54	39	54	53	60	35	61	69	81
57449	HOUGHTON	76	52	84	52	55	80	58	72	61	47	60	60	43	59	58	66	39	68	76	89
57450	HOVEN	86	59	94	59	62	91	66	82	68	53	68	67	48	67	65	75	44	76	86	100
57451	IPSWICH	94	67	99	66	70	99	73	90	78	62	77	71	57	77	72	86	50	84	96	109
57452	JAVA	79	54	87	54	57	83	60	75	63	49	62	62	44	61	60	68	40	70	79	92
57454	LANGFORD	78	54	86	54	56	82	60	74	62	48	61	61	44	61	59	68	40	69	78	91
57455	LEBANON	87	60	95	59	62	91	66	82	69	54	68	68	48	67	66	75	44	77	87	101
57456	LEOLA	69	48	76	47	50	73	53	66	55	43	54	54	39	54	53	60	35	61	69	81
57457	LONGLAKE	72	50	79	49	52	76	55	68	57	45	57	57	40	56	55	62	37	64	72	84
57460	MANSFIELD	101	70	111	70	73	107	78	96	81	63	80	79	57	79	77	88	52	90	101	118
57461	MELLETTE	89	61	98	61	64	94	68	84	71	55	70	70	50	69	68	77	45	79	89	104
57465	NORTHVILLE	84	58	93	58	61	89	64	80	67	52	66	66	47	66	64	73	43	75	85	99
57466	ONAKA	73	51	81	50	53	77	56	70	58	45	58	58	41	57	56	64	37	65	74	86
57467	ORIENT	95	66	105	66	69	101	73	91	76	59	75	75	53	74	73	83	49	85	96	111
57468	PIERPONT	81	56	89	56	58	86	62	77	64	50	64	64	45	63	62	70	41	72	81	95
57469	REDFIELD	72	53	72	53	55	74	61	70	66	54	64	53	49	64	58	72	43	68	77	83
57470	ROCKHAM	93	64	102	64	67	98	71	88	74	58	73	73	52	72	71	81	47	82	93	109
57471	ROSCOE	78	53	85	53	56	82	59	74	62	48	61	61	43	60	59	67	40	69	78	91
57472	SELBY	80	55	88	55	58	84	61	76	63	49	63	63	45	62	61	69	41	71	80	93
57473	SENECA	80	55	87	55	57	84	61	76	63	49	62	62	45	62	60	69	41	71	80	93
57474	STRATFORD	87	60	95	60	62	92	66	82	69	54	68	68	49	68	66	75	44	77	87	101
57475	TOLSTOY	84	58	93	58	61	89	65	80	67	52	66	66	47	66	64	73	43	75	85	99
57476	TULARE	87	60	96	60	63	92	67	83	69	54	69	69	49	68	66	76	44	77	88	102
57477	TURTON	92	63	101	63	66	97	70	87	73	57	72	72	52	72	70	80	47	82	92	108
57479	WARNER	107	74	118	74	77	113	82	102	85	66	84	84	60	84	82	93	55	95	108	125
57481	WESTPORT	95	73	102	73	75	101	76	92	79	65	78	75	62	78	77	84	51	86	96	112
57501	PIERRE	93	90	86	90	89	93	89	91	91	89	91	69	88	91	88	92	63	90	94	108
57520	AGAR	79	54	87	54	57	83	60	75	63	49	62	62	44	62	60	68	40	70	79	92
57521	BELVIDERE	79	55	87	55	57	84	61	75	63	49	62	62	44	62	60	69	40	70	80	93
57522	BLUNT	95	85	81	82	83	91	81	88	84	82	84	65	75	87	78	87	57	85	89	105
57523	BURKE	63	45	65	44	47	66	49	61	54	43	52	47	39	53	48	59	35	57	66	72
57528	COLOME	75	52	82	52	54	79	57	71	60	46	59	59	42	58	57	65	38	67	75	88
57529	DALLAS	69	47	75	47	49	72	52	65	54	42	54	54	38	53	52	59	35	61	69	80
57531	DRAPER	78	54	86	54	56	82	60	74	62	48	61	61	44	61	59	68	40	69	78	91
57532	FORT PIERRE	97	85	83	82	84	93	82	89	85	82	85	66	75	88	79	88	57	86	90	107
57533	GREGORY	67	47	69	46	49	70	52	64	57	45	55	49	41	56	51	62	36	60	69	76
57534	HAMILL	62	43	68	43	45	66	47	59	49	38	49	49	35	48	47	54	32	55	62	73
57536	HARROLD	107	80	110	79	82	109	86	101	89	75	88	82	68	89	84	95	58	96	105	123
57537	HAYES	93	64	103	64	67	99	71	89	74	58	73	73	52	73	71	81	48	83	94	109
57538	HERRICK	66	45	72	45	47	70	50	63	52	41	52	52	37	51	50	57	34	58	66	77
57540	HOLABIRD	96	66	106	66	69	102	74	91	77	60	76	76	54	75	73	83	49	85	97	113
57541	IDEAL	61	42	67	42	44	64	46	58	48	38	48	48	34	47	46	53	31	54	61	71
57543	KADOKA	72	51	74	50	53	76	56	70	62	49	60	53	44	61	55	68	40	65	75	83
57544	KENNEBEC	93	64	102	64	67	98	71	88	74	58	73	73	52	73	71	81	48	82	93	109
57547	LONG VALLEY	77	53	84	53	55	81	59	73	61	47	60	60	43	60	58	66	39	68	77	90
57548	LOWER BRULE	50	42	37	43	38	47	46	44	49	45	49	35	43	50	42	52	33	47	49	56
57551	MARTIN	68	48	70	48	50	71	53	66	58	46	57	51	42	57	52	64	37	61	71	78
57552	MIDLAND	87	60	95	60	62	92	66	82	69	54	68	68	49	68	66	75	44	77	87	101
57553	MILESVILLE	90	62	99	62	65	95	69	85	71	56	71	70	50	70	68	78	46	80	90	105
57555	MISSION	57	46	46	47	43	54	51	51	54	48	54	41	46	55	47	57	37	53	56	64
57559	MURDO	78	54	86	54	56	83	60	74	62	48	61	61	44	61	59	68	40	69	78	91
57560	NORRIS	57	40	63	39	41	61	44	55	46	36	45	45	32	45	44	50	29	51	58	67
57562	OKATON	78	54	86	54	56	82	60	74	62	48	61	61	44	61	59	68	40	69	78	91
57564	ONIDA	90	62	99	62	65	95	69	86	72	56	71	71	51	70	69	78	46	80	91	106
57566	PARMELEE	30	21	18	23	19	23	29	24	33	28	32	19	26	32	24	34	22	29	29	32
57567	PHILIP	87	62	91	60	65	89	65	82	71	59	70	63	51	70	64	78	46	75	86	98
57568	PRESHO	76	52	83	52	55	80	58	72	60	47	60	60	42	59	58	66	39	67	76	89
57569	RELIANCE	96	68	100	67	71	99	72	90	78	65	77	70	56	77	71	86	51	83	94	108
57571	SAINT CHARLES	62	43	68	42	45	65	47	59	49	38	49	49	35	48	47	54	32	55	62	72
57572	SAINT FRANCIS	51	43	35	44	38	46	47	44	51	47	51	34	45	52	42	53	35	48	50	56
57574	TUTHILL	69	48	76	47	50	73	53	66	55	43	54	54	39	54	53	60	35	61	69	81
57576	VIVIAN	76	52	83	52	54	80	58	72	60	47	59	59	42	59	57	65	38	67	76	88
57577	WANBLEE	45	37	36	37	34	42	40	40	42	39	42	32	36	43	37	44	28	41	44	50
57579	WHITE RIVER	58	46	48	47	43	56	51	52	54	48	54	41	45	54	47	57	36	53	57	65
57580	WINNER	77	54	81	53	56	80	59	73	63	50	62	58	45	62	58	70	41	68	79	88
57584	WITTEN	59	41	65	41	43	63	45	56	47	37	47	46	33	46	45	51	30	52	59	69
57585	WOOD	77	53	85	53	56	82	59	73	61	48	61	61	43	60	59	67	39	68	77	90
57601	MOBRIDGE	66	49	65	48	51	67	54	64	60	49	58	48	45	59	52	65	39	61	70	75
57620	BISON	77	53	85	53	56	81	59	73	61	48	61	61	43	60	59	67	39	68	77	90
57622	CHERRY CREEK	29	18	16	21	17	21	29	23	32	27	31	18	24	31	22	34	22	28	28	30
57623	DUPREE	64	47	67	46	48	66	51	60	52	44	52	49	39	52	50	56	34	57	63	74
57625	EAGLE BUTTE	54	43	44	43	40	50	47	48	50	45	49	38	41	51	43	52	34	49	52	60
57626	FAITH	82	56	90	56	59	86	62	78	65	51	64	64	46	64	62	71	42	73	82	96
57630	GLENCROSS	63	45	64	43	46	64	46	59	51	43	50	44	37	51	45	56	33	54	61	70
57631	GLENHAM	87	60	95	60	63	92	66	82	69	54	68	68	49	68	66	75	44	77	87	102
57632	HERREID	74	51	81	51	53	78	56	70	59	46	58	58	41	58	56	64	38	65	74	86
57633	ISABEL	52	41	45	42	39	51	45	47	48	42	48	38	40	48	42	51	32	48	52	59
57634	KELDRON	67	46	74	46	48	71	51	64	53	42	53	53	38	52	51	58	34	59	67	78
57638	LEMMON	74	53	76	52	55	78	58	72	64	51	62	55	46	63	57	70	41	67	78	85
	SOUTH DAKOTA	88	76	83	76	75	87	80	84	82	76	82	66	72	82	77	85	56	83	88	101
	UNITED STATES	100	100	100	100	100	100	100	100	100	100	100	100	100	100	100	100	100	100	100	100

57640-57799

#	POST OFFICE NAME	COUNTY FIPS CODE	POPULATION 2000	POPULATION 2009	POPULATION 2014	2000-2009 ANNUAL RATE % Rate	2000-2009 ANNUAL RATE State Centile	HOUSEHOLDS 2000	HOUSEHOLDS 2009	HOUSEHOLDS 2014	HOUSEHOLDS % Annual Rate 2000-2009	HOUSEHOLDS 2009 Average HH Size	FAMILIES 2000	FAMILIES 2009	FAMILIES % Annual Rate 2000-2009
57640	LODGEPOLE	105	194	166	153	-1.7	2	87	78	73	-1.2	2.13	64	58	-1.1
57641	MC INTOSH	031	409	432	437	0.6	78	170	183	185	0.8	2.35	121	132	0.9
57642	MC LAUGHLIN	031	2591	2578	2565	-0.1	55	732	727	721	-0.1	3.55	558	559	0.0
57644	MEADOW	105	443	401	378	-1.1	12	173	162	154	-0.7	2.48	124	118	-0.5
57645	MORRISTOWN	031	154	164	167	0.7	81	54	59	60	1.0	2.78	38	42	1.1
57646	MOUND CITY	021	312	258	231	-2.0	1	122	104	94	-1.7	2.44	85	74	-1.5
57648	POLLOCK	021	458	378	339	-2.1	1	208	177	160	-1.7	2.11	146	126	-1.6
57649	PRAIRIE CITY	105	165	143	132	-1.5	5	68	61	57	-1.2	2.34	49	44	-1.2
57650	RALPH	063	68	60	56	-1.3	8	31	29	27	-0.7	2.07	22	21	-0.5
57651	REVA	063	276	242	226	-1.4	7	91	84	79	-0.9	2.81	62	58	-0.7
57656	TIMBER LAKE	041	840	842	838	0.0	59	296	301	301	0.2	2.80	217	224	0.3
57657	TRAIL CITY	041	92	94	94	0.2	67	35	36	37	0.3	2.61	27	28	0.4
57658	WAKPALA	031	727	739	740	0.2	67	199	205	205	0.3	3.60	151	157	0.4
57660	WATAUGA	031	91	97	99	0.7	81	29	31	32	0.7	3.13	20	22	1.0
57701	RAPID CITY	093	40421	43362	44970	0.8	84	15928	17699	18565	1.1	2.34	9743	10994	1.3
57702	RAPID CITY	103	28899	31430	32898	0.9	86	11582	13093	13860	1.3	2.37	8312	9474	1.4
57703	RAPID CITY	103	10615	13500	14860	2.6	96	3905	5145	5723	3.0	2.62	2910	3851	3.1
57706	ELLSWORTH AFB	093	4569	3687	3557	-2.3	0	1178	1006	976	-1.7	3.21	1091	921	-1.8
57714	ALLEN	007	946	946	940	0.0	59	222	227	227	0.2	4.17	187	193	0.3
57716	BATESLAND	113	556	578	596	0.4	73	145	157	163	0.9	3.57	123	134	0.9
57717	BELLE FOURCHE	019	7145	7584	7834	0.6	78	2759	2988	3097	0.9	2.50	1905	2089	1.0
57718	BLACK HAWK	093	4643	5747	6186	2.3	94	1648	2150	2350	2.9	2.67	1327	1744	3.0
57719	BOX ELDER	093	4058	5133	5595	2.6	96	1462	1892	2078	2.8	2.71	1117	1453	2.9
57720	BUFFALO	063	728	639	596	-1.4	7	310	287	270	-0.8	2.11	204	191	-0.7
57722	BUFFALO GAP	033	336	426	462	2.6	96	147	187	207	2.6	2.26	108	139	2.8
57724	CAMP CROOK	063	230	205	192	-1.2	9	85	79	75	-0.8	2.54	61	57	-0.7
57725	CAPUTA	103	198	198	201	0.0	59	80	83	85	0.4	2.39	62	64	0.3
57730	CUSTER	033	5426	5767	5916	0.7	81	2241	2507	2612	1.2	2.19	1530	1730	1.3
57732	DEADWOOD	081	2353	2528	2607	0.8	84	1048	1167	1219	1.2	2.03	655	745	1.4
57735	EDGEMONT	047	1403	1406	1396	0.0	59	631	664	666	0.6	2.11	427	455	0.7
57737	ENNING	093	162	167	165	0.3	70	61	66	66	0.9	2.53	48	52	0.9
57738	FAIRBURN	033	238	365	398	4.7	99	88	152	169	6.1	2.38	65	113	6.2
57741	FORT MEADE	093	126	125	136	-0.1	55	49	52	58	0.6	2.21	38	41	0.8
57744	HERMOSA	033	1367	1643	1784	2.0	93	529	672	742	2.6	2.42	391	501	2.7
57745	HILL CITY	103	1915	2157	2280	1.3	90	752	877	940	1.7	2.46	531	622	1.7
57747	HOT SPRINGS	047	5617	5586	5561	-0.1	55	2317	2426	2437	0.5	2.15	1421	1514	0.7
57748	HOWES	093	120	122	119	0.2	67	52	56	55	0.8	2.18	38	41	0.8
57750	INTERIOR	071	152	149	147	-0.2	47	70	71	70	0.2	2.10	46	47	0.2
57751	KEYSTONE	103	658	971	1054	4.3	99	270	431	474	5.2	2.19	190	316	5.7
57752	KYLE	113	1786	1916	1999	0.8	84	418	466	491	1.2	4.02	339	382	1.3
57754	LEAD	081	3647	3776	3817	0.4	73	1564	1689	1732	0.8	2.20	1009	1106	1.0
57755	LUDLOW	063	113	99	93	-1.4	7	39	36	34	-0.9	2.75	28	26	-0.8
57756	MANDERSON	113	1270	1353	1408	0.7	81	271	302	317	1.2	4.41	230	257	1.2
57758	MUD BUTTE	093	248	246	239	-0.1	55	94	98	96	0.5	2.51	71	75	0.6
57759	NEMO	081	467	522	552	1.2	88	110	130	141	1.8	3.43	80	96	2.0
57760	NEWELL	019	1244	1384	1448	1.2	88	492	560	588	1.4	2.47	350	403	1.5
57761	NEW UNDERWOOD	093	1197	1343	1406	1.3	90	426	493	523	1.6	2.63	322	374	1.6
57762	NISLAND	019	354	374	388	0.6	78	134	145	151	0.9	2.52	107	117	1.0
57763	OELRICHS	047	257	255	250	-0.1	55	111	116	115	0.5	2.19	79	83	0.5
57766	ORAL	047	263	261	257	-0.1	55	103	107	107	0.4	2.44	76	80	0.6
57767	OWANKA	103	111	120	123	0.8	84	40	45	47	1.3	2.67	30	34	1.4
57769	PIEDMONT	093	3150	3587	3769	1.4	91	1176	1408	1502	2.0	2.54	945	1143	2.1
57770	PINE RIDGE	113	7597	8464	8923	1.2	88	1660	1889	2002	1.4	4.37	1415	1620	1.5
57772	PORCUPINE	113	434	467	488	0.8	84	114	128	135	1.3	3.58	97	110	1.4
57775	QUINN	103	101	107	110	0.6	78	31	34	35	1.0	3.15	23	26	1.3
57779	SAINT ONGE	081	397	465	496	1.7	93	157	193	208	2.3	2.41	126	154	2.2
57780	SCENIC	103	134	149	157	1.2	88	57	66	70	1.6	2.26	41	47	1.5
57782	SMITHWICK	047	20	20	20	0.0	59	8	8	8	0.0	2.50	6	6	0.0
57783	SPEARFISH	081	12073	13089	13495	0.9	86	5084	5748	6009	1.3	2.15	3032	3488	1.5
57785	STURGIS	093	8987	8980	9067	0.0	59	3654	3816	3892	0.5	2.31	2426	2588	0.7
57787	UNION CENTER	093	223	230	226	0.3	70	87	95	95	1.0	2.42	69	76	1.1
57788	VALE	093	466	534	559	1.5	92	173	203	214	1.7	2.57	138	164	1.9
57790	WALL	103	1273	1392	1453	1.0	86	526	597	632	1.4	2.31	340	384	1.3
57791	WASTA	093	212	230	237	0.9	86	83	95	100	1.5	2.42	61	70	1.5
57792	WHITE OWL	093	140	142	139	0.2	67	51	54	54	0.6	2.63	37	40	0.8
57793	WHITEWOOD	081	1793	2172	2326	2.1	93	685	876	952	2.7	2.43	517	662	2.7
57794	WOUNDED KNEE	113	805	883	926	1.0	86	174	196	206	1.3	4.43	146	166	1.4
57799	SPEARFISH	081	888	896	893	0.1	64	151	156	157	0.4	4.29	92	96	0.5
	SOUTH DAKOTA					0.8					1.2	2.43			1.3
	UNITED STATES					1.0					1.1	2.59			0.9

ZIP CODE #	POST OFFICE NAME	RACE (%) White 2000	White 2009	Black 2000	Black 2009	Asian/Pacific 2000	Asian/Pacific 2009	% Hispanic Origin 2000	% Hispanic Origin 2009	2009 AGE DISTRIBUTION (%) 0-4	5-9	10-14	15-19	20-24	25-44	45-64	65-84	85+	18+	MEDIAN AGE 2009	% 2009 Males	% 2009 Females
57640	LODGEPOLE	96.4	95.8	0.0	0.0	0.5	0.6	1.0	1.2	5.4	6.6	6.6	5.4	4.2	18.7	30.1	19.3	3.6	78.3	47.3	51.8	48.2
57641	MC INTOSH	80.2	77.5	0.2	0.2	0.2	0.2	1.0	0.7	6.0	6.9	7.9	7.9	4.6	20.4	28.5	15.5	2.3	73.8	41.9	52.8	47.2
57642	MC LAUGHLIN	28.3	23.4	0.1	0.1	0.0	0.0	2.5	2.6	10.6	10.7	9.5	8.7	7.8	23.2	20.4	8.3	0.7	63.9	26.9	49.7	50.3
57644	MEADOW	88.9	87.3	0.2	0.2	0.0	0.0	0.9	1.2	6.5	7.2	7.5	6.5	4.2	20.0	30.7	14.7	2.7	74.6	43.4	50.6	49.4
57645	MORRISTOWN	87.7	84.8	0.0	0.0	0.0	0.0	0.6	0.6	5.5	6.7	7.9	7.9	4.3	20.1	28.7	16.5	2.4	73.8	43.0	52.4	47.6
57646	MOUND CITY	99.4	99.2	0.0	0.0	0.0	0.0	0.3	0.4	5.4	5.8	6.6	7.0	4.3	18.2	30.6	18.2	3.9	76.4	46.3	50.4	49.6
57648	POLLOCK	99.3	98.9	0.0	0.0	0.0	0.3	0.2	0.3	5.6	6.1	6.3	7.1	4.2	17.7	30.7	18.5	3.7	76.7	46.4	50.8	49.2
57649	PRAIRIE CITY	97.6	97.2	0.0	0.0	0.0	0.0	1.2	0.7	5.6	7.0	7.0	6.3	3.5	18.2	32.9	16.8	2.8	76.2	46.8	51.7	48.3
57650	RALPH	98.5	98.3	0.0	0.0	1.5	1.7	1.5	1.7	5.0	8.3	10.0	8.3	3.3	23.3	30.0	10.0	1.7	68.3	38.8	43.3	56.7
57651	REVA	97.5	96.7	0.4	0.4	0.7	0.8	1.4	2.1	4.1	7.0	7.9	9.9	4.1	20.2	33.1	11.6	2.1	72.7	42.3	50.4	49.6
57656	TIMBER LAKE	58.1	53.1	0.0	0.0	0.6	0.6	0.2	0.2	6.9	7.6	8.4	9.1	5.7	23.5	26.1	11.3	1.3	71.3	35.8	48.7	51.3
57657	TRAIL CITY	30.4	28.7	0.0	0.0	0.0	0.0	0.0	0.0	7.4	9.6	9.6	7.4	10.6	24.5	18.1	12.8	0.0	69.1	30.0	48.9	51.1
57658	WAKPALA	14.7	11.8	0.0	0.0	0.0	0.0	2.1	2.2	10.6	10.4	9.3	10.0	8.8	24.5	17.7	8.4	0.3	63.3	25.7	50.6	49.4
57660	WATAUGA	87.9	84.5	0.0	0.0	0.0	0.0	1.1	1.0	6.2	6.2	7.2	7.2	4.1	22.7	28.9	15.5	2.1	76.3	42.1	52.6	47.4
57701	RAPID CITY	80.4	75.7	1.2	1.5	1.2	1.8	3.5	4.5	7.7	6.6	6.2	7.6	9.6	28.1	23.1	9.2	2.0	75.5	32.6	49.9	50.1
57702	RAPID CITY	93.4	90.9	0.4	0.5	0.6	1.0	1.5	2.3	5.6	6.0	6.6	6.6	5.4	23.1	31.4	13.4	2.0	77.6	42.6	49.1	50.9
57703	RAPID CITY	90.2	87.3	0.6	0.9	0.7	1.1	2.2	3.2	8.0	7.7	7.6	7.2	6.4	28.5	25.9	8.1	0.6	72.3	34.3	49.8	50.2
57706	ELLSWORTH AFB	82.2	75.3	6.5	9.1	2.5	4.2	6.2	9.5	15.2	9.1	7.5	8.0	20.3	33.2	5.3	1.1	0.2	64.6	22.5	53.8	46.2
57714	ALLEN	15.2	13.1	0.1	0.1	0.0	0.0	1.6	1.6	9.2	11.9	11.7	13.1	8.1	21.8	18.4	5.1	0.6	58.5	22.5	51.7	48.3
57716	BATESLAND	14.2	18.2	0.5	0.5	0.0	0.0	0.4	0.5	10.9	10.4	9.3	10.2	8.5	25.6	19.0	5.5	0.5	62.1	25.4	47.6	52.4
57717	BELLE FOURCHE	95.3	93.8	0.1	0.1	0.3	0.4	3.4	4.9	6.6	6.6	7.2	8.0	6.0	23.1	27.4	12.7	2.4	74.3	39.9	49.1	50.9
57718	BLACK HAWK	94.9	93.1	0.3	0.5	0.3	0.6	1.2	1.9	6.8	6.9	7.2	7.1	6.2	27.2	30.7	7.4	0.5	74.3	37.1	48.6	51.4
57719	BOX ELDER	86.0	81.6	2.0	2.7	1.7	2.7	3.1	4.6	9.7	8.3	7.8	7.6	8.4	28.9	22.8	6.1	0.5	69.6	29.3	50.3	49.7
57720	BUFFALO	97.3	96.1	0.4	0.6	0.4	0.6	1.5	1.9	3.8	5.5	6.3	12.1	4.5	20.0	34.3	11.4	2.2	74.2	43.1	53.4	46.6
57722	BUFFALO GAP	94.3	93.4	0.3	0.5	0.3	0.2	1.5	2.1	4.0	4.7	6.8	7.7	3.3	20.2	38.5	12.7	2.1	78.6	46.4	50.2	49.8
57724	CAMP CROOK	97.8	97.1	0.0	0.0	0.9	1.0	1.3	2.0	4.4	6.8	7.8	8.8	3.9	21.5	32.2	12.7	2.0	73.7	42.5	49.3	50.7
57725	CAPUTA	93.4	90.9	0.0	0.0	0.5	1.0	0.5	1.0	5.6	6.1	7.1	6.1	4.5	23.7	31.8	13.6	1.5	77.3	42.5	50.0	50.0
57730	CUSTER	94.0	92.3	0.3	0.3	0.2	0.3	1.5	2.2	4.5	4.5	5.9	9.1	3.9	18.7	35.7	15.1	2.6	78.6	47.1	51.6	48.4
57732	DEADWOOD	94.9	93.2	0.1	0.1	0.3	0.5	1.9	2.6	3.8	4.4	5.5	10.5	4.7	21.8	34.3	13.4	1.5	79.6	44.5	51.4	48.6
57735	EDGEMONT	93.9	93.2	0.1	0.1	0.1	0.1	1.5	1.6	4.3	4.7	5.7	6.1	2.9	18.1	35.5	20.1	2.6	80.9	49.8	51.9	48.1
57737	ENNING	91.4	89.2	1.8	2.4	0.6	1.2	1.2	2.4	8.4	6.0	7.8	7.8	9.6	25.7	24.6	9.0	1.2	72.5	33.1	53.3	46.7
57738	FAIRBURN	94.5	93.4	0.4	0.5	0.0	0.3	1.7	1.9	4.1	4.9	7.1	7.9	3.3	20.5	37.8	12.1	2.2	78.1	45.9	50.7	49.3
57741	FORT MEADE	94.5	93.6	0.8	0.8	0.8	0.8	0.8	0.8	4.0	5.6	7.2	8.0	2.4	18.4	36.0	16.0	2.4	76.8	47.3	56.0	44.0
57744	HERMOSA	93.0	91.7	0.3	0.4	0.2	0.3	1.5	2.0	4.4	4.9	7.2	7.7	3.5	20.5	37.8	12.0	2.0	77.8	45.8	50.1	49.9
57745	HILL CITY	93.3	90.8	0.1	0.1	0.1	0.2	4.9	7.2	4.2	4.9	7.5	6.8	4.5	24.5	33.1	13.8	0.8	79.0	43.6	49.7	50.3
57747	HOT SPRINGS	89.7	88.6	0.3	0.3	0.4	0.4	1.8	1.8	4.9	5.1	6.0	6.6	5.3	18.0	31.3	19.4	3.4	79.6	48.1	52.5	47.5
57748	HOWES	93.3	91.8	0.0	0.0	0.0	0.0	0.0	0.0	5.7	5.7	6.6	7.4	4.1	19.7	32.8	15.6	2.5	77.9	45.4	50.0	50.0
57750	INTERIOR	86.8	83.2	0.0	0.0	0.0	0.0	0.7	1.3	6.0	6.0	7.4	7.4	4.0	21.5	29.5	16.1	2.0	75.8	43.5	50.3	49.7
57751	KEYSTONE	95.3	93.6	0.3	0.4	0.0	0.1	1.8	2.5	4.9	5.9	7.2	6.4	3.6	21.4	38.2	11.5	0.8	77.4	45.2	50.8	49.2
57752	KYLE	4.8	6.3	0.1	0.1	0.0	0.0	1.5	1.2	11.4	10.6	10.7	10.9	8.7	25.4	16.2	5.9	0.2	60.0	23.7	49.7	50.3
57754	LEAD	95.8	94.6	0.2	0.2	0.2	0.3	2.5	3.6	5.3	5.9	6.4	6.9	6.3	25.8	29.7	12.1	1.6	77.9	40.5	51.1	48.9
57755	LUDLOW	99.1	99.0	0.0	0.0	0.9	1.0	1.8	2.0	4.0	9.1	10.1	7.1	3.0	24.2	29.3	11.1	2.0	71.7	39.6	47.5	52.5
57756	MANDERSON	2.8	3.6	0.0	0.0	0.0	0.0	1.6	1.3	10.6	11.0	13.3	12.3	7.2	22.8	17.1	5.2	0.4	56.7	21.9	51.6	48.4
57758	MUD BUTTE	96.0	94.7	0.0	0.0	0.0	0.0	0.4	0.8	5.3	6.1	6.9	7.3	3.7	21.5	31.7	15.4	2.0	76.8	44.4	52.0	48.0
57759	NEMO	91.6	89.1	0.2	0.2	0.4	0.6	1.5	2.1	3.4	4.6	4.4	17.6	3.8	19.7	32.4	12.6	1.3	75.7	42.5	55.0	45.0
57760	NEWELL	96.9	96.0	0.1	0.1	0.1	0.1	1.0	1.5	5.3	5.5	6.2	7.3	6.0	22.0	30.2	15.0	2.5	78.5	43.1	48.8	51.2
57761	NEW UNDERWOOD	92.6	90.0	0.7	1.0	0.3	0.5	1.2	1.9	7.3	6.4	7.2	7.9	6.6	23.2	26.6	11.2	3.6	73.6	38.3	49.1	50.9
57762	NISLAND	94.1	92.5	0.0	0.0	0.3	0.3	2.0	3.2	5.3	5.9	10.4	10.2	2.9	24.3	29.1	10.7	1.1	71.1	40.1	54.3	45.7
57763	OELRICHS	91.9	91.0	0.8	0.8	0.0	0.0	1.6	1.6	2.7	3.1	3.9	5.9	3.9	17.6	39.6	20.0	3.1	85.9	52.5	51.8	48.2
57766	ORAL	91.6	90.8	0.8	0.8	0.0	0.0	1.9	1.5	2.3	2.7	3.4	6.1	4.6	18.8	39.8	19.2	3.1	88.5	51.9	50.2	49.8
57767	OWANKA	90.3	87.5	1.8	2.5	0.9	1.7	1.8	2.5	8.3	6.7	8.3	7.5	8.3	23.3	25.8	10.0	1.7	72.5	34.2	52.5	47.5
57769	PIEDMONT	95.4	93.8	0.4	0.6	0.3	0.6	0.9	1.4	5.9	6.2	6.6	6.7	6.2	24.9	33.3	9.5	0.7	77.0	40.1	50.4	49.6
57770	PINE RIDGE	4.0	5.3	0.1	0.1	0.1	0.1	1.4	1.3	12.0	12.0	11.7	11.6	8.5	23.5	16.1	4.2	0.4	56.5	21.6	49.0	51.0
57772	PORCUPINE	1.6	2.1	0.0	0.0	0.0	0.0	1.6	1.5	10.7	11.1	13.7	12.4	7.3	22.3	17.1	4.9	0.4	55.9	21.4	51.6	48.4
57775	QUINN	96.0	94.4	0.0	0.0	0.0	0.0	0.0	0.0	5.6	6.5	7.5	7.5	5.6	23.4	29.9	12.1	1.9	75.7	40.9	51.4	48.6
57779	SAINT ONGE	97.7	96.6	0.0	0.2	0.8	1.3	1.0	1.5	4.9	6.0	7.7	10.5	4.3	20.4	33.8	11.4	0.9	74.0	42.6	52.0	48.0
57780	SCENIC	94.7	92.6	0.0	0.0	0.0	0.0	0.8	0.0	6.0	7.4	8.1	7.4	4.0	20.8	31.5	13.4	1.3	73.8	41.6	51.0	49.0
57782	SMITHWICK	94.7	95.0	0.0	0.0	0.0	0.0	0.0	0.0	0.0	0.0	0.0	10.0	10.0	10.0	55.0	15.0	0.0	90.0	53.3	40.0	60.0
57783	SPEARFISH	95.9	94.6	0.3	0.4	0.5	0.7	1.7	2.5	5.1	5.2	5.5	9.1	9.4	25.5	24.9	11.7	3.6	80.0	36.0	47.7	52.3
57785	STURGIS	95.3	93.7	0.2	0.3	0.3	0.6	1.6	2.7	5.8	6.1	6.4	6.4	5.8	22.5	29.5	14.4	3.0	77.4	42.4	48.8	51.2
57787	UNION CENTER	95.9	93.9	0.0	0.4	0.5	0.4	0.5	1.3	5.7	5.7	7.0	7.8	4.3	22.6	31.3	14.3	1.3	77.0	42.7	53.0	47.0
57788	VALE	96.8	95.5	0.2	0.4	0.2	0.4	1.3	2.1	4.7	5.4	7.1	7.7	3.9	21.5	33.1	14.8	1.7	77.3	44.7	52.6	47.4
57790	WALL	92.6	90.2	0.2	0.2	0.4	0.4	0.6	0.9	5.7	5.9	6.4	6.5	6.5	22.3	29.5	14.9	2.4	77.9	42.0	49.4	50.6
57791	WASTA	91.9	88.3	1.4	2.2	0.5	1.3	1.4	2.2	8.3	7.0	7.8	7.4	7.0	23.9	26.5	11.3	0.9	72.2	36.0	51.3	48.7
57792	WHITE OWL	92.9	91.5	0.0	0.0	0.0	0.0	0.0	0.7	5.6	6.3	7.0	7.0	4.9	21.1	31.0	14.1	2.8	76.8	43.5	52.1	47.9
57793	WHITEWOOD	96.7	95.4	0.2	0.3	0.3	0.6	1.6	2.5	5.0	5.7	6.5	7.4	4.7	21.4	34.2	13.5	1.6	77.5	44.5	51.2	48.8
57794	WOUNDED KNEE	6.6	8.0	0.0	0.0	0.0	0.0	1.4	1.1	11.8	10.8	9.7	11.1	9.4	25.5	16.1	5.2	0.5	60.2	23.5	49.2	50.8
57799	SPEARFISH	95.6	94.4	0.4	0.6	0.3	0.4	0.9	1.3	3.5	4.0	5.5	22.7	19.4	16.6	21.3	6.3	0.8	82.5	23.7	49.1	50.9
	SOUTH DAKOTA	88.7	87.0	0.6	0.8	0.6	1.0	1.4	2.0	6.9	6.7	6.9	7.6	7.3	25.0	25.9	11.3	2.4	75.3	36.7	49.7	50.3
	UNITED STATES	75.1	72.0	12.3	12.7	3.8	4.6	12.5	15.7	6.8	6.7	6.6	7.1	6.9	27.0	26.0	10.9	1.9	75.7	36.9	49.2	50.8

#	POST OFFICE NAME	2009 Per Capita Income	2009 HH Income Base	2009 HOUSEHOLD INCOME DISTRIBUTION (%) Less than $25,000	$25,000 to $49,999	$50,000 to $99,999	$100,000 to $149,999	$150,000 or More	MEDIAN HOUSEHOLD INCOME 2009	2014	2009 National Centile	2009 State Centile	2009 Home Value Base	2009 HOME VALUE DISTRIBUTION (%) Less than $50,000	$50,000 to $89,999	$90,000 to $174,999	$175,000 to $399,999	$400,000 or More	2009 Median Home Value
57640	LODGEPOLE	19346	78	35.9	35.9	23.1	2.6	2.6	32652	32318	13	18	65	41.5	12.3	20.0	13.8	12.3	77500
57641	MC INTOSH	15762	183	42.1	28.4	26.2	1.6	1.6	31129	28910	10	14	142	62.7	16.9	14.1	6.3	0.0	28125
57642	MC LAUGHLIN	9239	727	52.1	26.3	19.3	1.8	0.6	23889	23842	3	3	369	51.2	23.8	18.2	6.8	0.0	48448
57644	MEADOW	16879	162	37.7	30.9	27.2	2.5	1.9	33025	35000	13	20	126	44.4	21.4	14.3	7.1	12.7	60000
57645	MORRISTOWN	13428	59	42.4	27.1	27.1	1.7	1.7	30747	45000	9	12	48	58.3	18.8	14.6	8.3	0.0	30000
57646	MOUND CITY	16803	104	35.6	31.7	27.9	3.8	1.0	35000	36149	18	27	85	52.9	25.9	12.9	5.9	2.4	46429
57648	POLLOCK	19530	177	35.6	30.5	29.9	3.4	0.6	35281	35648	19	28	145	54.5	26.2	12.4	4.8	2.1	45000
57649	PRAIRIE CITY	18121	61	37.7	32.8	26.2	1.6	1.6	32301	34292	12	16	49	40.8	22.4	14.3	8.2	14.3	65000
57650	RALPH	15754	29	44.8	37.9	17.2	0.0	0.0	28596	28592	6	8	22	36.4	22.7	18.2	4.5	18.2	70000
57651	REVA	13654	84	42.9	31.0	22.6	2.4	1.2	30619	30439	9	12	63	34.9	28.6	19.0	4.8	12.7	67500
57656	TIMBER LAKE	14295	301	38.2	35.5	22.3	2.0	2.0	34048	36861	16	23	220	43.6	30.0	18.6	5.0	2.7	57000
57657	TRAIL CITY	11481	36	50.0	27.8	22.2	0.0	0.0	25000	24028	3	3	25	32.0	16.0	12.0	4.0	36.0	112500
57658	WAKPALA	8037	205	52.7	30.7	16.1	0.5	0.0	22670	24756	2	2	116	49.1	13.8	24.1	12.9	0.0	51429
57660	WATAUGA	10825	31	41.9	29.0	29.0	0.0	0.0	31120	37500	10	13	25	60.0	16.0	16.0	8.0	0.0	32500
57701	RAPID CITY	22512	17699	25.9	30.8	34.7	5.8	2.9	43194	47560	43	69	9712	20.4	19.1	42.6	16.0	2.0	107017
57702	RAPID CITY	31893	13093	13.1	24.0	43.2	12.6	7.1	60411	60567	78	95	9555	5.5	4.4	41.6	41.6	6.9	172410
57703	RAPID CITY	22830	5145	15.5	30.5	44.4	5.9	3.6	52459	53722	67	92	4324	26.9	12.0	51.2	9.1	0.8	107666
57706	ELLSWORTH AFB	14684	1006	15.3	50.1	30.5	1.9	2.2	41958	45409	39	63	109	39.4	19.3	19.3	17.4	4.6	78333
57714	ALLEN	6494	227	46.7	41.0	11.0	0.0	1.3	25737	25977	4	5	116	46.6	27.6	18.1	7.8	0.0	53636
57716	BATESLAND	7877	157	69.4	19.7	5.1	5.1	0.6	19421	20149	1	1	91	59.3	16.5	20.9	3.3	0.0	37500
57717	BELLE FOURCHE	17721	2988	32.8	32.1	29.7	4.0	1.5	38083	39640	27	44	2145	25.5	21.3	36.1	14.5	2.6	99648
57718	BLACK HAWK	22298	2150	14.4	32.8	43.9	6.7	2.2	51700	51350	65	90	1893	17.2	17.2	45.9	18.2	1.6	118319
57719	BOX ELDER	19862	1892	17.9	34.2	41.0	4.8	2.2	47611	51075	56	84	1180	49.0	19.7	25.3	5.1	0.9	51818
57720	BUFFALO	18936	287	42.2	28.2	25.1	2.4	2.1	31000	31639	10	13	210	34.3	33.3	20.5	2.9	9.0	68500
57722	BUFFALO GAP	21176	187	26.2	32.1	37.4	3.7	0.5	43121	45910	43	68	156	21.2	15.4	28.8	25.6	9.0	123438
57724	CAMP CROOK	13926	79	41.8	34.2	20.3	2.5	1.3	31598	31352	11	14	59	32.2	23.7	15.3	5.1	23.7	75000
57725	CAPUTA	22856	83	18.1	34.9	39.8	4.8	2.4	48056	49680	57	85	65	36.9	12.3	26.2	21.5	3.1	95000
57730	CUSTER	22378	2507	25.9	29.5	37.5	4.9	2.1	44747	46723	47	77	1869	13.3	12.1	37.3	27.5	9.8	148349
57732	DEADWOOD	24749	1167	22.0	38.1	34.0	4.3	1.5	43055	43210	43	68	812	12.1	12.7	43.1	24.9	7.3	139286
57735	EDGEMONT	21336	664	33.3	31.0	30.1	4.4	1.2	38384	40912	28	46	534	44.9	16.5	18.7	12.7	7.1	60909
57737	ENNING	20117	66	25.8	37.9	31.8	1.5	3.0	40000	43636	33	54	36	36.1	25.0	22.2	8.3	8.3	73333
57738	FAIRBURN	20184	152	25.7	31.6	38.8	3.3	0.7	44313	45875	46	75	127	21.3	15.7	25.2	27.6	10.2	130682
57741	FORT MEADE	23324	52	19.2	32.7	44.2	1.9	1.9	48627	49270	58	85	35	17.1	0.0	45.7	31.4	5.7	162500
57744	HERMOSA	20009	672	25.3	32.1	37.8	3.6	1.2	44153	46010	46	74	557	20.8	15.1	28.0	26.9	9.2	127250
57745	HILL CITY	22935	877	23.7	32.5	35.2	4.9	3.6	43963	48230	45	73	680	24.6	7.8	32.6	28.2	6.8	137143
57747	HOT SPRINGS	21073	2426	31.9	31.5	30.2	3.9	2.5	37060	38533	24	37	1615	27.6	18.9	38.8	11.1	3.7	96389
57748	HOWES	20993	56	32.1	35.7	25.0	1.8	5.4	36475	37702	22	31	40	45.0	20.0	20.0	5.0	10.0	60000
57750	INTERIOR	21153	71	35.2	35.2	22.5	4.2	2.8	32281	33622	12	16	53	56.6	9.4	17.0	7.5	9.4	35833
57751	KEYSTONE	31494	431	19.3	30.6	31.3	10.0	8.8	50100	52185	61	88	348	17.2	5.2	27.0	38.2	12.4	176282
57752	KYLE	10559	466	32.8	30.3	33.9	2.4	0.6	39571	44428	31	51	284	46.1	24.3	13.0	10.9	5.6	53235
57754	LEAD	21852	1689	25.3	34.6	36.2	2.7	1.2	41051	41573	36	59	1167	21.2	31.9	33.1	11.7	2.1	84621
57755	LUDLOW	10379	36	47.2	38.9	13.9	0.0	0.0	27317	28131	5	7	27	37.0	22.2	18.5	3.7	18.5	67500
57756	MANDERSON	7636	302	49.7	26.2	21.2	2.0	1.0	25226	27051	3	3	175	49.7	18.9	17.1	12.0	2.3	50250
57758	MUD BUTTE	17122	98	39.8	30.6	23.5	3.1	3.1	32937	34067	13	19	72	34.7	33.3	16.7	4.2	11.1	67500
57759	NEMO	14686	130	21.5	37.7	35.4	4.6	0.8	44312	44817	46	74	113	8.8	11.5	38.9	34.5	6.2	154808
57760	NEWELL	16341	560	37.3	35.0	25.0	1.4	1.3	32105	33126	12	15	425	33.2	30.1	21.4	10.6	4.7	68778
57761	NEW UNDERWOOD	18993	493	22.3	40.2	30.2	4.7	2.6	41270	45699	37	60	335	39.4	32.5	20.0	6.6	1.5	63966
57762	NISLAND	18501	145	30.3	32.4	33.1	2.8	1.4	37322	37526	25	40	121	30.6	18.2	14.9	27.3	9.1	97500
57763	OELRICHS	19248	116	29.3	38.8	27.6	4.3	0.0	35433	35274	19	29	92	42.4	15.2	30.4	3.3	8.7	66667
57766	ORAL	17531	107	27.1	43.0	26.2	3.7	0.0	34785	36412	17	25	85	35.3	15.3	34.1	3.5	11.8	88333
57767	OWANKA	20529	45	20.0	37.8	33.3	4.4	4.4	44078	49298	46	73	28	39.3	14.3	25.0	14.3	7.1	80000
57769	PIEDMONT	24122	1408	16.3	30.8	43.6	6.8	2.5	52061	51789	66	91	1214	15.2	11.5	37.9	28.5	6.9	134965
57770	PINE RIDGE	8115	1889	46.5	28.0	21.8	3.2	0.6	26664	27246	4	5	846	52.6	14.9	23.2	6.6	2.7	45849
57772	PORCUPINE	8661	128	50.8	27.3	21.1	0.8	0.0	24053	26234	3	3	73	53.4	17.8	13.7	12.3	2.7	45000
57775	QUINN	14189	34	29.4	32.4	35.3	2.9	0.0	38159	39059	27	45	28	46.4	10.7	21.4	10.7	10.7	65000
57779	SAINT ONGE	22060	193	29.0	32.1	30.1	6.7	2.1	39721	41389	32	51	160	21.9	16.9	28.1	30.0	3.1	129688
57780	SCENIC	22649	66	24.2	30.3	36.4	7.6	1.5	45000	48646	48	77	53	41.5	13.2	24.5	15.1	5.7	77500
57782	SMITHWICK	13625	8	37.5	37.5	25.0	0.0	0.0	30000	35000	8	11	6	0.0	0.0	66.7	0.0	33.3	137500
57783	SPEARFISH	23444	5748	33.3	25.7	32.4	4.7	3.8	40254	41384	34	54	3378	13.6	10.5	40.6	30.3	5.0	146827
57785	STURGIS	21232	3816	29.4	31.1	33.9	3.6	2.0	41838	45517	39	63	2494	20.6	23.8	39.7	14.0	1.9	102836
57787	UNION CENTER	17526	95	41.1	29.5	23.2	4.2	2.1	32285	33799	12	16	67	29.9	40.3	17.9	1.5	10.4	69375
57788	VALE	18157	203	29.1	36.5	30.0	2.0	2.5	40385	42159	34	55	158	22.8	13.3	28.5	25.3	10.1	132692
57790	WALL	21906	597	30.0	32.3	29.5	6.0	2.2	39304	43465	31	50	446	49.1	20.2	18.4	9.6	2.7	51818
57791	WASTA	22229	95	21.1	35.8	33.7	5.3	4.2	44536	48174	47	75	63	42.9	12.7	23.8	15.9	4.8	75000
57792	WHITE OWL	17690	54	31.5	37.0	24.1	1.9	5.6	36471	37278	22	31	39	43.6	20.5	20.5	5.1	10.3	62500
57793	WHITEWOOD	22029	876	25.5	32.6	33.9	3.4	4.6	43607	45214	44	71	691	16.1	12.4	38.5	24.9	8.1	140954
57794	WOUNDED KNEE	5659	196	67.3	17.9	13.3	1.5	0.0	14788	16658	1	1	103	56.3	8.7	33.0	1.9	0.0	40714
57799	SPEARFISH	12210	156	32.1	25.6	30.8	8.3	3.2	42079	43977	40	64	97	10.3	9.3	42.3	36.1	2.1	154464
	SOUTH DAKOTA	22885		24.5	28.5	37.1	6.5	3.5	46883	49493				19.9	18.0	38.6	20.2	3.3	113473
	UNITED STATES	27277		20.9	24.4	35.3	11.7	7.6	54719	56938				9.3	13.1	31.6	32.6	13.5	162279

ZIP CODE #	POST OFFICE NAME	FINANCIAL SERVICES: Auto Loan	Home Loan	Investments	Retirement Plans	THE HOME: Home Improvements: Home Repair	Lawn & Garden	Furnishings: Computers & Hardware-Personal	Major Appliances	TV, Radio, Sound Equipment	Furniture	ENTERTAINMENT: Dine out/Carry out	Sports Equipment	Fees & Tickets	Toys & Games	Travel	Cable TV	PERSONAL: Apparel & Services	Auto Repairs	Health Insurance	Pets & Supplies
57640	LODGEPOLE	74	51	81	51	53	78	56	70	58	46	58	58	41	57	56	64	38	65	74	86
57641	MC INTOSH	66	46	73	46	48	70	51	63	53	41	52	52	37	52	50	58	34	59	67	78
57642	MC LAUGHLIN	51	41	39	43	38	48	45	45	49	44	48	35	42	49	41	51	33	47	50	57
57644	MEADOW	75	51	82	51	54	79	57	71	59	46	59	59	42	58	57	65	38	66	75	87
57645	MORRISTOWN	67	46	73	46	48	70	51	63	53	41	52	52	37	52	51	58	34	59	67	78
57646	MOUND CITY	74	51	81	51	53	78	56	70	59	46	58	58	41	58	56	64	38	66	74	86
57648	POLLOCK	74	51	81	51	53	78	57	70	59	46	58	58	41	58	56	64	38	66	74	86
57649	PRAIRIE CITY	76	52	83	52	55	80	58	72	60	47	60	60	42	59	58	66	39	67	76	89
57650	RALPH	58	40	64	40	42	62	45	55	46	36	46	46	33	45	44	50	30	52	58	68
57651	REVA	69	47	76	47	50	73	53	65	55	43	54	54	38	54	52	60	35	61	69	80
57656	TIMBER LAKE	71	51	74	49	53	73	53	67	58	48	57	51	41	57	52	63	37	62	70	80
57657	TRAIL CITY	43	30	39	29	29	41	32	37	36	31	35	29	26	37	29	40	24	36	40	46
57658	WAKPALA	43	37	30	38	33	39	40	37	44	40	43	29	39	44	36	45	30	41	42	48
57660	WATAUGA	61	42	67	42	44	64	46	57	48	37	48	48	34	47	46	52	31	54	61	71
57701	RAPID CITY	80	69	63	71	67	71	80	73	79	76	80	58	73	81	72	80	55	77	76	88
57702	RAPID CITY	106	112	111	114	113	113	107	110	107	108	107	83	111	106	111	107	75	108	111	128
57703	RAPID CITY	93	90	79	87	86	86	85	87	85	89	86	66	82	89	82	85	59	85	84	103
57706	ELLSWORTH AFB	86	48	48	54	45	51	77	62	74	70	77	59	58	86	60	71	53	73	59	76
57714	ALLEN	43	31	34	32	30	38	38	38	41	36	41	29	32	41	33	44	28	39	41	47
57716	BATESLAND	42	35	29	37	31	38	39	36	42	39	41	28	37	42	35	43	28	39	41	46
57717	BELLE FOURCHE	74	59	68	58	59	72	61	69	65	58	64	53	53	66	59	69	43	66	72	82
57718	BLACK HAWK	96	88	78	85	86	90	83	88	86	86	86	64	78	90	79	88	59	85	88	104
57719	BOX ELDER	86	75	70	73	72	77	78	78	78	78	78	61	70	82	72	79	54	79	77	93
57720	BUFFALO	73	50	80	50	53	77	56	70	58	45	58	57	41	57	56	63	37	65	73	86
57722	BUFFALO GAP	80	64	103	63	70	85	64	82	67	60	66	60	56	64	70	72	44	75	80	94
57724	CAMP CROOK	64	44	70	44	46	67	49	60	51	39	50	50	36	50	48	55	32	56	64	74
57725	CAPUTA	86	76	80	78	77	92	76	87	78	67	77	66	68	79	76	83	52	80	90	101
57730	CUSTER	84	66	104	65	72	89	67	85	71	62	70	62	57	68	71	76	46	78	85	99
57732	DEADWOOD	84	68	97	68	72	85	72	83	74	67	74	62	63	72	73	78	50	80	84	98
57735	EDGEMONT	79	57	91	56	60	83	61	76	64	52	63	61	47	62	62	69	41	71	79	93
57737	ENNING	91	63	100	62	66	96	70	86	72	56	71	71	51	71	69	79	46	81	91	106
57738	FAIRBURN	80	64	104	63	71	85	64	82	67	60	67	60	56	64	70	72	44	76	81	95
57741	FORT MEADE	97	66	106	66	69	102	74	92	77	60	76	76	54	75	73	84	49	86	97	113
57744	HERMOSA	81	65	103	64	71	85	65	82	68	61	67	60	57	65	70	73	45	76	81	95
57745	HILL CITY	92	79	98	77	82	92	77	90	80	76	80	65	70	80	78	84	54	84	89	105
57747	HOT SPRINGS	76	59	82	57	63	81	63	76	68	58	66	55	53	66	63	74	45	72	82	89
57748	HOWES	82	56	90	56	59	86	62	78	65	51	64	64	46	64	62	71	42	72	82	96
57750	INTERIOR	79	55	87	54	57	84	61	75	63	49	62	62	44	62	60	69	40	70	80	93
57751	KEYSTONE	106	103	136	104	110	117	96	112	96	95	96	82	95	93	105	99	66	105	109	129
57752	KYLE	66	59	48	56	55	58	60	59	62	62	62	44	56	64	55	63	43	61	60	71
57754	LEAD	73	65	70	65	64	75	69	71	70	64	70	55	63	70	67	73	47	71	76	86
57755	LUDLOW	51	35	56	35	37	54	39	48	41	32	40	40	29	40	39	44	26	45	51	60
57756	MANDERSON	50	43	35	44	39	46	47	44	50	47	50	34	45	51	42	52	34	47	49	55
57758	MUD BUTTE	77	53	84	53	55	81	59	73	61	48	60	60	43	60	58	67	39	68	77	90
57759	NEMO	88	70	113	69	77	93	70	89	74	66	73	65	61	70	76	78	48	82	88	104
57760	NEWELL	70	49	73	48	51	73	54	67	59	47	57	52	42	58	53	65	38	63	72	80
57761	NEW UNDERWOOD	90	64	95	63	67	93	68	85	73	60	72	66	52	72	67	80	47	79	89	103
57762	NISLAND	84	58	93	58	61	89	64	80	67	52	66	66	47	66	64	73	43	75	85	98
57763	OELRICHS	72	55	89	54	60	76	57	72	59	51	59	54	47	57	60	64	39	66	72	85
57766	ORAL	71	57	92	56	63	75	57	73	60	54	59	53	50	57	62	64	39	67	72	84
57767	OWANKA	98	67	107	67	70	103	75	93	78	61	77	77	55	76	74	85	50	87	98	114
57769	PIEDMONT	97	91	81	89	89	93	85	91	88	88	88	67	82	92	83	90	60	88	91	108
57770	PINE RIDGE	53	45	37	46	40	48	49	46	53	49	52	36	47	53	44	55	36	50	51	58
57772	PORCUPINE	46	39	32	40	35	42	43	40	46	43	46	31	41	47	39	48	32	43	45	51
57775	QUINN	80	55	88	55	57	84	61	76	63	49	63	63	45	62	61	69	41	71	80	93
57779	SAINT ONGE	95	65	104	65	68	100	73	90	75	59	75	75	53	74	72	82	48	84	95	111
57780	SCENIC	91	63	100	63	66	96	70	87	73	57	72	72	51	71	69	79	47	81	92	107
57782	SMITHWICK	57	45	73	45	50	60	45	58	48	43	47	42	39	45	49	51	31	53	57	67
57783	SPEARFISH	78	67	70	68	67	74	75	73	76	72	76	57	68	75	70	78	52	76	78	88
57785	STURGIS	78	67	75	66	68	79	68	76	72	66	71	56	62	71	67	76	48	73	80	89
57787	UNION CENTER	76	52	83	52	55	80	58	72	60	47	60	60	42	59	58	66	39	67	76	89
57788	VALE	84	58	92	58	61	89	64	80	67	52	66	66	47	66	64	73	43	75	84	98
57790	WALL	88	62	91	61	65	92	68	85	74	59	72	66	53	73	67	81	48	79	91	101
57791	WASTA	96	66	106	66	69	102	74	91	76	60	76	76	54	75	73	83	49	85	96	112
57792	WHITE OWL	83	57	91	57	60	88	64	79	66	51	65	65	47	65	63	72	42	74	83	97
57793	WHITEWOOD	97	68	101	67	71	99	72	91	78	64	77	70	56	77	71	86	50	84	95	109
57794	WOUNDED KNEE	37	31	25	32	28	34	34	32	37	34	37	25	33	38	31	39	25	35	36	41
57799	SPEARFISH	82	72	75	73	74	82	77	80	79	74	78	59	71	79	74	83	53	80	86	94
	SOUTH DAKOTA	88	76	83	76	75	87	80	84	82	76	82	66	72	82	77	85	56	83	88	101
	UNITED STATES	100	100	100	100	100	100	100	100	100	100	100	100	100	100	100	100	100	100	100	100

POPULATION CHANGE

37010-37172

ZIP CODE #	POST OFFICE NAME	COUNTY FIPS CODE	POPULATION 2000	POPULATION 2009	POPULATION 2014	2000-2009 ANNUAL RATE % Rate	2000-2009 ANNUAL RATE State Centile	HOUSEHOLDS 2000	HOUSEHOLDS 2009	HOUSEHOLDS 2014	HOUSEHOLDS % Annual Rate 2000-2009	HOUSEHOLDS 2009 Average HH Size	FAMILIES 2000	FAMILIES 2009	FAMILIES % Annual Rate 2000-2009
37010	ADAMS	147	3363	4325	4868	2.8	94	1189	1568	1778	3.0	2.73	968	1250	2.8
37012	ALEXANDRIA	041	2007	2232	2334	1.2	72	805	906	952	1.3	2.45	589	646	1.0
37013	ANTIOCH	037	54001	68146	74041	2.5	93	22090	28195	30745	2.7	2.37	13068	16189	2.3
37014	ARRINGTON	187	1253	1455	1617	1.6	82	464	551	617	1.9	2.64	374	429	1.5
37015	ASHLAND CITY	021	16394	18309	19246	1.2	72	5957	6777	7159	1.4	2.66	4538	5046	1.2
37016	AUBURNTOWN	189	938	1049	1119	1.2	72	351	399	427	1.4	2.62	274	304	1.1
37018	BEECHGROVE	031	1631	1959	2116	2.0	90	675	833	909	2.3	2.35	500	602	2.0
37019	BELFAST	117	812	848	871	0.5	41	288	304	313	0.6	2.78	220	226	0.3
37020	BELL BUCKLE	003	3534	5206	5941	4.3	98	1316	1935	2211	4.3	2.68	1001	1452	4.1
37022	BETHPAGE	165	4573	5347	5855	1.7	84	1703	2055	2269	2.1	2.59	1328	1562	1.8
37023	BIG ROCK	161	1691	1835	1897	0.9	63	627	688	714	1.0	2.67	472	506	0.8
37025	BON AQUA	081	5371	6208	6517	1.6	82	1979	2323	2451	1.7	2.67	1508	1729	1.5
37026	BRADYVILLE	015	2033	2207	2281	0.9	63	755	831	864	1.0	2.66	586	630	0.8
37027	BRENTWOOD	187	36243	47241	54220	2.9	95	12992	17206	19778	3.1	2.73	10228	13354	2.9
37028	BUMPUS MILLS	161	590	636	656	0.8	60	239	258	267	0.8	2.47	179	189	0.6
37029	BURNS	043	4273	4883	5201	1.5	81	1613	1886	2021	1.7	2.58	1280	1468	1.5
37030	CARTHAGE	159	6658	6855	6946	0.3	31	2678	2808	2857	0.5	2.39	1839	1867	0.2
37031	CASTALIAN SPRINGS	165	2639	3508	4010	3.1	96	995	1340	1539	3.3	2.62	801	1054	3.0
37032	CEDAR HILL	147	3311	3924	4256	1.9	88	1173	1412	1540	2.0	2.76	951	1121	1.8
37033	CENTERVILLE	081	7649	7678	7694	0.0	18	2973	3034	3054	0.2	2.46	2091	2070	-0.1
37034	CHAPEL HILL	117	4974	6618	7406	3.1	96	1821	2446	2744	3.2	2.71	1426	1870	3.0
37035	CHAPMANSBORO	021	2922	3284	3495	1.3	76	1012	1147	1225	1.4	2.86	821	912	1.1
37036	CHARLOTTE	043	5477	6031	6284	1.0	66	2031	2269	2375	1.2	2.59	1537	1677	0.9
37037	CHRISTIANA	149	3951	6421	7803	5.4	99	1406	2356	2881	5.7	2.73	1126	1838	5.4
37040	CLARKSVILLE	125	30479	39846	44351	2.9	95	11684	15492	17276	3.1	2.49	7885	10331	3.0
37042	CLARKSVILLE	125	53823	65280	70998	2.1	91	18754	23250	25381	2.4	2.81	14553	17599	2.1
37043	CLARKSVILLE	125	31734	36943	40118	1.7	84	12336	14860	16227	2.0	2.44	8894	10501	1.8
37046	COLLEGE GROVE	187	3271	3861	4323	1.8	86	1174	1416	1597	2.0	2.73	944	1108	1.7
37047	CORNERSVILLE	117	2269	2498	2623	1.0	66	853	954	1006	1.2	2.61	635	690	0.9
37048	COTTONTOWN	165	5361	6098	6749	1.4	78	1945	2277	2538	1.7	2.67	1587	1818	1.5
37049	CROSS PLAINS	147	2783	3189	3446	1.5	81	1030	1206	1312	1.7	2.64	843	969	1.5
37050	CUMBERLAND CITY	161	1455	1647	1731	1.3	76	573	657	694	1.5	2.49	425	475	1.2
37051	CUMBERLAND FURNACE	043	3081	3317	3449	0.8	60	1166	1284	1342	1.0	2.57	909	978	0.8
37052	CUNNINGHAM	125	2567	2705	2813	0.6	47	961	1049	1099	1.0	2.58	775	825	0.7
37055	DICKSON	043	24265	27720	29397	1.4	78	9357	10867	11579	1.6	2.51	6728	7623	1.4
37057	DIXON SPRINGS	169	919	1001	1040	0.9	63	342	377	393	1.1	2.65	259	279	0.8
37058	DOVER	161	6570	7051	7270	0.8	60	2652	2886	2986	0.9	2.41	1936	2058	0.7
37059	DOWELLTOWN	041	1744	1817	1859	0.4	36	680	721	742	0.6	2.50	499	516	0.4
37060	EAGLEVILLE	149	2078	2435	2679	1.7	84	778	932	1033	2.0	2.59	613	710	1.6
37061	ERIN	083	5254	5419	5502	0.3	31	2066	2173	2220	0.5	2.41	1474	1511	0.3
37062	FAIRVIEW	187	9117	11478	13178	2.5	93	3345	4329	5011	2.8	2.65	2607	3275	2.5
37064	FRANKLIN	187	37367	46927	53793	2.5	93	13541	17495	20241	2.8	2.64	10493	13163	2.5
37066	GALLATIN	165	34120	42053	46633	2.3	92	12932	16436	18412	2.6	2.51	9496	11833	2.4
37067	FRANKLIN	187	15124	20827	24669	3.5	97	5947	8259	9818	3.6	2.52	4293	5822	3.3
37069	FRANKLIN	187	16503	20352	22772	2.3	92	5511	6954	7828	2.5	2.93	4740	5880	2.4
37072	GOODLETTSVILLE	037	27287	30369	32342	1.2	72	10751	12238	13112	1.4	2.47	7761	8595	1.1
37073	GREENBRIER	147	11157	13137	14257	1.8	86	4097	4928	5379	2.0	2.66	3292	3880	1.8
37074	HARTSVILLE	169	6453	7139	7475	1.1	69	2453	2741	2877	1.2	2.54	1773	1931	0.9
37075	HENDERSONVILLE	165	47778	57377	63021	2.0	90	18214	22426	24829	2.3	2.55	13600	16381	2.0
37076	HERMITAGE	037	30189	34814	37112	1.6	82	12756	15130	16242	1.9	2.26	7968	9048	1.4
37078	HURRICANE MILLS	085	890	879	865	-0.1	13	351	357	354	0.2	2.42	244	241	-0.1
37079	INDIAN MOUND	161	2311	2439	2505	0.6	47	905	972	1001	0.8	2.51	687	719	0.5
37080	JOELTON	037	7179	7654	7927	0.7	53	2688	2933	3060	0.9	2.60	2083	2222	0.7
37082	KINGSTON SPRINGS	021	5886	6441	6697	1.0	66	2130	2383	2495	1.2	2.70	1735	1904	1.0
37083	LAFAYETTE	111	12217	13373	13849	1.0	66	4863	5376	5579	1.1	2.47	3555	3836	0.8
37085	LASCASSAS	149	2761	3914	4630	3.8	97	994	1450	1731	4.2	2.65	801	1136	3.8
37086	LA VERGNE	149	18808	30253	37327	5.3	99	6578	10924	13565	5.6	2.77	5221	8366	5.2
37087	LEBANON	189	31403	39259	43868	2.4	92	12037	15283	17209	2.6	2.49	8573	10638	2.4
37090	LEBANON	189	12000	14085	15386	1.7	84	4466	5336	5864	1.9	2.64	3536	4129	1.7
37091	LEWISBURG	117	18682	20567	21630	1.0	66	7307	8114	8547	1.1	2.49	5165	5577	0.8
37095	LIBERTY	041	1986	2094	2160	0.6	47	795	851	880	0.7	2.46	604	632	0.5
37096	LINDEN	135	5462	5801	5922	0.7	53	2182	2368	2433	0.9	2.39	1555	1644	0.6
37097	LOBELVILLE	135	1916	1718	1641	-1.2	0	774	709	682	-0.9	2.42	558	499	-1.2
37098	LYLES	081	4620	5109	5394	1.1	69	1719	1939	2058	1.3	2.63	1319	1453	1.1
37101	MC EWEN	085	5813	6084	6163	0.5	41	2288	2453	2504	0.8	2.47	1662	1735	0.5
37110	MC MINNVILLE	177	30845	31994	32439	0.4	36	12382	13126	13397	0.6	2.39	8689	8962	0.3
37115	MADISON	037	34342	36517	37922	0.7	53	15144	16357	17078	0.8	2.20	8549	8893	0.4
37118	MILTON	149	1397	1590	1788	1.4	78	414	491	559	1.9	3.04	332	382	1.5
37122	MOUNT JULIET	189	33557	45579	52421	3.4	97	11914	16548	19171	3.6	2.75	9940	13540	3.4
37127	MURFREESBORO	149	11039	14847	17397	3.3	97	3843	5346	6312	3.6	2.75	3062	4097	3.2
37128	MURFREESBORO	149	18769	38302	48519	8.0	100	6694	14157	18044	8.4	2.70	5219	10711	8.1
37129	MURFREESBORO	149	39333	50775	58155	2.8	94	14264	19083	22056	3.2	2.61	10648	13849	2.9
37130	MURFREESBORO	149	40129	51046	58286	2.6	93	16623	21715	24975	2.9	2.29	8992	11035	2.2
37132	MURFREESBORO	149	2941	3042	3060	0.4	36	21	25	27	1.9	3.96	11	12	0.9
37134	NEW JOHNSONVILLE	085	3018	3293	3393	0.9	63	1210	1364	1421	1.3	2.41	912	1004	1.0
37135	NOLENSVILLE	187	4325	7719	9745	6.5	99	1442	2608	3302	6.6	2.96	1221	2144	6.3
37137	NUNNELLY	081	2370	2803	2953	1.8	86	923	1101	1160	1.9	2.26	683	798	1.7
37138	OLD HICKORY	037	20583	22162	23360	0.8	60	8113	8908	9434	1.0	2.48	5860	6281	0.8
37140	ONLY	081	1281	1268	1260	-0.1	13	76	78	77	0.3	2.55	55	55	0.0
37141	ORLINDA	147	730	815	861	1.2	72	283	323	344	1.4	2.52	220	245	1.2
37142	PALMYRA	125	1675	1828	1921	0.9	63	572	643	681	1.3	2.79	457	500	1.0
37143	PEGRAM	021	3424	3709	3859	0.9	63	1238	1373	1437	1.1	2.63	972	1054	0.9
37144	PETERSBURG	103	2999	3288	3429	1.0	66	1159	1299	1363	1.2	2.52	880	962	1.0
37145	PLEASANT SHADE	159	2784	3176	3345	1.4	78	1062	1227	1298	1.6	2.58	822	929	1.3
37146	PLEASANT VIEW	021	4959	7172	7919	4.1	98	1731	2562	2843	4.3	2.80	1437	2090	4.1
37148	PORTLAND	165	17014	22061	24858	2.8	94	6361	8388	9511	3.0	2.62	4879	6289	2.8
37149	READYVILLE	149	2392	2703	2902	1.3	76	904	1059	1146	1.7	2.53	706	804	1.4
37150	RED BOILING SPRINGS	111	4698	4786	4776	0.2	27	1840	1905	1908	0.4	2.45	1321	1333	0.1
37151	RIDDLETON	159	407	466	494	1.5	81	160	187	200	1.7	2.49	124	141	1.4
37153	ROCKVALE	149	4255	5222	5915	2.2	92	1462	1846	2105	2.6	2.82	1198	1475	2.3
37160	SHELBYVILLE	003	27126	32882	35977	2.1	91	10087	12166	13289	2.0	2.66	7381	8685	1.8
37166	SMITHVILLE	041	12393	13187	13606	0.7	53	4902	5306	5499	0.9	2.43	3478	3668	0.6
37167	SMYRNA	149	34872	47105	55026	3.3	97	12708	17930	21114	3.8	2.61	9697	13242	3.4
37171	SOUTHSIDE	125	1039	1094	1138	0.6	47	388	425	446	1.0	2.57	304	324	0.7
37172	SPRINGFIELD	147	25261	30699	33617	2.1	91	9372	11565	12723	2.3	2.62	6941	8377	2.1
	TENNESSEE					1.1					1.3	2.44			1.0
	UNITED STATES					1.0					1.1	2.59			0.9

ZIP CODE		RACE (%)						% Hispanic Origin		2009 AGE DISTRIBUTION (%)										MEDIAN AGE		
#	POST OFFICE NAME	White		Black		Asian/Pacific																
		2000	2009	2000	2009	2000	2009	2000	2009	0-4	5-9	10-14	15-19	20-24	25-44	45-64	65-84	85+	18+	2009	% 2009 Males	% 2009 Females
37010	ADAMS	92.1	89.8	5.2	6.1	0.7	1.0	2.1	3.5	6.1	6.7	7.2	7.2	5.0	25.1	31.2	10.1	1.4	75.3	40.5	50.9	49.1
37012	ALEXANDRIA	94.5	93.5	3.7	4.2	0.0	0.1	0.8	1.3	6.8	6.8	7.0	6.4	5.2	27.1	27.5	11.4	1.9	75.4	39.0	49.6	50.4
37013	ANTIOCH	64.8	60.4	26.0	27.5	4.0	5.2	5.7	8.3	7.2	6.3	6.0	6.2	10.2	35.0	23.0	5.6	0.6	77.0	32.4	49.9	50.1
37014	ARRINGTON	92.3	90.8	6.5	7.4	0.3	0.5	1.1	1.9	5.5	6.0	7.1	7.0	3.9	23.0	34.2	12.0	1.3	76.9	43.4	51.3	48.7
37015	ASHLAND CITY	96.1	95.1	1.9	2.2	0.2	0.3	1.4	2.3	6.7	6.8	6.8	6.7	5.5	28.4	28.3	9.4	1.4	75.5	37.9	50.3	49.7
37016	AUBURNTOWN	97.5	96.8	1.4	1.6	0.0	0.2	1.1	1.9	6.3	6.3	6.7	6.9	5.2	26.1	29.3	11.8	1.4	76.5	40.5	50.6	49.4
37018	BEECHGROVE	97.2	96.3	1.2	1.4	0.6	0.9	1.1	1.8	6.0	6.2	6.5	6.3	5.3	25.4	30.2	12.9	1.2	77.4	41.3	51.3	48.7
37019	BELFAST	93.0	90.8	4.3	5.2	0.2	0.4	2.3	4.0	6.5	6.5	6.8	6.4	5.5	27.0	29.8	10.4	1.1	76.2	39.2	49.2	50.8
37020	BELL BUCKLE	94.7	92.6	3.5	4.5	0.6	0.8	1.6	2.7	6.9	7.0	7.2	7.1	5.0	28.6	27.3	9.8	1.1	74.4	37.5	50.2	49.8
37022	BETHPAGE	96.6	95.8	1.7	1.9	0.1	0.2	0.9	1.5	5.6	5.8	6.2	6.6	5.1	27.1	30.7	11.8	1.2	78.4	40.7	50.1	49.9
37023	BIG ROCK	97.3	96.7	0.4	0.4	0.2	0.3	1.2	1.9	7.0	7.0	7.1	6.8	5.4	26.3	27.7	11.4	1.4	74.8	38.6	50.2	49.8
37025	BON AQUA	97.0	96.1	1.1	1.5	0.1	0.2	1.1	1.7	7.4	7.4	7.6	7.1	5.3	28.2	26.5	9.7	0.9	73.2	37.0	51.3	48.7
37026	BRADYVILLE	97.1	96.3	1.5	1.7	0.0	0.1	1.1	1.7	7.4	7.3	7.5	7.3	5.3	27.3	26.0	10.9	1.0	73.3	37.3	50.6	49.4
37027	BRENTWOOD	93.4	91.1	2.7	3.4	2.6	3.8	1.4	2.2	5.4	6.6	7.7	7.5	4.2	22.7	34.5	10.3	1.1	75.4	42.2	48.6	51.4
37028	BUMPUS MILLS	96.6	95.8	0.7	0.8	0.3	0.6	1.2	1.7	6.9	6.9	6.9	7.1	5.2	26.4	28.0	11.3	1.3	75.0	38.4	50.9	49.1
37029	BURNS	93.4	92.0	4.5	5.1	0.3	0.4	1.1	1.9	6.7	7.0	7.1	6.9	4.8	27.3	28.9	10.3	1.0	74.9	39.2	49.3	50.7
37030	CARTHAGE	94.7	93.6	3.3	3.7	0.3	0.4	1.2	1.9	6.7	6.7	6.7	6.2	5.5	25.1	27.6	12.9	2.6	76.1	40.0	48.3	51.7
37031	CASTALIAN SPRINGS	92.8	90.8	4.5	5.4	0.6	0.9	1.6	2.6	5.7	6.0	6.5	7.0	5.6	26.5	30.9	10.9	1.0	77.5	40.1	50.4	49.6
37032	CEDAR HILL	94.5	92.5	3.5	4.5	0.3	0.4	1.3	2.4	6.3	6.9	7.3	7.5	5.6	26.1	29.3	9.7	1.2	74.7	38.5	51.5	48.5
37033	CENTERVILLE	95.6	94.7	2.8	3.3	0.1	0.1	0.8	1.4	6.2	6.3	6.5	6.1	5.4	23.5	28.0	15.1	2.8	77.4	41.9	49.6	50.4
37034	CHAPEL HILL	95.8	94.5	2.5	3.0	0.1	0.1	1.6	3.0	6.8	7.1	7.3	6.8	5.0	28.1	28.3	9.4	1.1	74.6	37.7	49.8	50.2
37035	CHAPMANSBORO	96.4	95.6	1.7	2.0	0.3	0.4	1.1	1.8	7.3	7.3	7.4	6.9	5.6	28.2	27.2	9.3	0.8	73.4	37.4	50.6	49.4
37036	CHARLOTTE	92.9	91.5	5.7	6.6	0.1	0.2	0.8	1.3	6.1	6.2	6.6	7.0	5.8	28.3	27.6	11.0	1.3	76.7	38.7	51.7	48.3
37037	CHRISTIANA	92.7	90.5	4.8	5.9	0.7	1.1	0.9	1.5	7.4	7.3	7.3	6.8	5.0	30.3	26.8	8.3	0.9	73.8	36.1	49.7	50.3
37040	CLARKSVILLE	70.1	66.7	24.7	25.6	1.0	1.7	3.3	5.8	8.1	7.5	6.9	7.5	7.9	31.7	22.1	7.4	0.9	73.4	32.6	49.6	50.4
37042	CLARKSVILLE	62.9	58.9	25.4	26.1	3.1	4.2	8.0	11.6	10.5	9.1	7.8	7.0	8.0	35.5	17.2	4.6	0.3	68.3	28.8	50.1	49.9
37043	CLARKSVILLE	86.6	84.1	9.1	9.9	1.6	2.4	2.4	3.8	6.5	6.6	6.7	6.4	5.4	28.3	27.3	10.8	2.0	76.2	38.2	49.1	50.9
37046	COLLEGE GROVE	92.2	90.8	6.5	7.4	0.2	0.3	1.0	1.7	5.2	5.7	6.4	7.0	4.8	24.7	32.9	11.8	1.4	78.3	42.4	50.6	49.4
37047	CORNERSVILLE	97.0	96.0	1.9	2.4	0.2	0.3	0.7	1.1	6.2	6.8	7.1	7.4	5.2	26.7	27.4	11.4	1.8	75.0	39.0	49.2	50.8
37048	COTTONTOWN	96.9	96.0	1.3	1.6	0.2	0.3	1.0	1.7	6.3	6.8	7.1	6.3	4.3	25.9	31.3	10.7	1.2	75.6	40.6	50.9	49.1
37049	CROSS PLAINS	94.2	92.3	4.0	5.1	0.2	0.3	1.2	2.1	6.6	6.9	7.2	7.1	5.2	26.3	29.9	9.9	0.8	74.8	39.0	49.8	50.2
37050	CUMBERLAND CITY	93.2	92.0	4.3	4.7	0.3	0.5	1.1	1.6	6.3	6.6	7.1	6.8	4.5	24.5	30.2	12.4	1.6	75.7	40.8	50.2	49.8
37051	CUMBERLAND FURNACE	96.0	95.0	1.9	2.3	0.3	0.5	0.7	1.3	5.9	6.2	6.6	6.9	5.7	25.7	29.7	11.9	1.4	77.1	40.1	50.9	49.1
37052	CUNNINGHAM	96.0	95.2	2.1	2.4	0.2	0.3	1.1	1.9	5.6	5.9	6.3	6.9	5.8	24.8	31.1	12.3	1.2	78.0	41.3	50.9	49.1
37055	DICKSON	91.4	90.0	6.0	6.6	0.3	0.5	1.4	2.2	7.1	7.1	7.1	6.7	5.9	26.9	26.5	10.9	1.7	74.5	37.4	49.0	51.0
37057	DIXON SPRINGS	95.1	93.7	2.5	2.9	0.2	0.3	1.6	2.6	7.0	6.9	7.2	6.9	5.4	26.3	27.7	11.1	1.6	74.6	38.7	50.0	50.0
37058	DOVER	94.7	93.3	1.5	1.6	2.0	2.8	0.9	1.5	5.3	5.5	5.9	6.1	4.7	23.9	30.2	16.0	2.2	79.4	43.9	49.1	50.9
37059	DOWELLTOWN	95.7	94.1	1.1	1.2	0.1	0.1	3.2	5.1	5.2	5.3	6.1	6.7	5.7	27.4	30.4	11.9	1.4	79.3	41.1	50.6	49.4
37060	EAGLEVILLE	93.1	91.7	5.4	6.3	0.2	0.4	1.2	2.1	5.9	6.3	6.7	6.8	4.9	24.5	30.6	12.6	1.5	76.8	41.5	49.2	50.8
37061	ERIN	93.9	92.9	4.4	4.9	0.2	0.3	0.8	1.2	6.8	6.7	7.1	6.3	5.0	23.8	26.5	15.0	2.8	75.4	40.6	49.4	50.6
37062	FAIRVIEW	97.4	96.6	0.6	0.7	0.2	0.4	1.3	2.1	7.0	7.1	7.2	7.1	6.3	27.4	28.2	8.9	0.9	74.3	36.9	49.2	50.8
37064	FRANKLIN	86.3	84.2	10.2	10.9	0.8	1.2	3.3	5.1	7.5	7.7	8.0	6.8	4.9	27.7	28.3	7.9	1.2	72.5	37.2	48.8	51.2
37066	GALLATIN	82.8	81.6	13.7	13.9	0.5	0.6	2.7	4.1	6.6	6.7	6.8	6.3	5.2	26.3	28.4	11.9	1.9	76.0	39.4	48.7	51.3
37067	FRANKLIN	89.2	86.7	5.0	5.5	2.3	3.6	5.5	7.2	7.3	6.9	7.3	6.5	4.9	34.7	26.5	5.1	0.8	74.3	35.0	50.0	50.0
37069	FRANKLIN	96.0	94.7	1.8	2.1	1.1	1.7	1.7	2.8	7.2	8.7	9.9	8.6	3.7	23.3	31.3	6.7	0.6	68.6	38.3	49.1	50.9
37072	GOODLETTSVILLE	89.7	87.1	7.3	8.7	1.1	1.7	1.3	2.1	6.4	6.5	6.9	6.5	5.5	27.0	28.7	11.1	1.5	76.2	39.2	48.9	51.1
37073	GREENBRIER	97.2	96.2	0.9	1.2	0.3	0.4	0.9	1.7	6.9	7.1	7.3	6.9	5.0	28.9	27.4	9.6	0.9	74.4	37.7	50.0	50.0
37074	HARTSVILLE	86.8	84.8	11.2	12.4	0.2	0.2	1.4	2.3	6.1	6.3	6.5	6.6	5.2	25.7	28.4	13.0	2.1	77.1	40.4	49.1	50.9
37075	HENDERSONVILLE	93.5	91.4	3.7	4.7	1.0	1.6	1.6	2.6	6.2	6.3	6.5	6.6	6.0	27.0	29.2	10.7	1.4	76.7	39.1	48.7	51.3
37076	HERMITAGE	83.6	79.3	11.3	13.3	1.3	2.0	3.7	6.0	7.3	6.5	6.2	5.9	7.6	32.4	23.9	8.3	1.8	76.5	34.8	48.2	51.8
37078	HURRICANE MILLS	96.5	96.0	1.9	2.2	0.3	0.5	1.1	1.7	5.8	5.8	6.4	7.4	6.0	24.0	29.7	13.8	1.1	76.8	40.9	52.7	47.3
37079	INDIAN MOUND	96.0	95.0	1.3	1.6	0.5	0.8	1.2	2.0	6.6	6.8	7.1	6.8	5.3	26.7	28.5	10.9	1.2	75.2	39.1	52.3	47.7
37080	JOELTON	97.2	96.3	1.5	1.9	0.2	0.3	1.0	1.7	5.9	6.5	6.8	6.2	4.5	25.6	31.8	11.5	1.1	76.8	41.3	50.1	49.9
37082	KINGSTON SPRINGS	97.8	97.1	0.9	1.0	0.4	0.6	0.8	1.3	6.9	7.0	7.2	6.8	5.3	28.1	30.7	7.4	0.5	74.7	37.9	49.8	50.2
37083	LAFAYETTE	97.9	97.1	0.2	0.2	0.3	0.5	1.6	2.6	6.8	6.7	6.9	6.3	5.3	27.4	26.6	12.1	1.9	75.7	38.8	49.6	50.4
37085	LASCASSAS	91.7	89.8	6.8	8.2	0.1	0.2	1.1	1.8	8.0	7.6	7.3	7.2	5.5	33.2	23.8	6.6	0.8	73.1	34.0	49.2	50.8
37086	LA VERGNE	85.2	81.3	10.5	12.3	1.3	1.9	3.4	5.9	9.9	9.0	8.1	6.4	5.2	34.8	21.2	5.1	0.4	68.9	32.0	49.0	51.0
37087	LEBANON	86.8	85.3	10.4	11.0	0.6	0.8	1.8	2.7	7.0	6.7	6.7	6.8	6.4	26.8	26.6	11.2	2.0	75.7	37.9	48.9	51.1
37090	LEBANON	94.0	92.7	4.1	4.9	0.3	0.4	1.1	1.7	6.0	6.3	6.6	6.5	5.1	26.9	30.5	10.9	1.2	77.0	40.3	49.7	50.3
37091	LEWISBURG	86.6	83.9	10.1	11.2	0.4	0.6	3.5	5.5	6.6	6.6	6.6	6.6	5.5	27.4	27.5	11.3	2.0	76.3	38.5	49.0	51.0
37095	LIBERTY	96.9	95.8	1.0	1.1	0.2	0.2	1.9	3.0	6.9	6.8	7.1	6.3	5.7	25.4	29.5	11.2	1.3	75.5	39.3	49.7	50.3
37096	LINDEN	96.1	95.5	2.3	2.5	0.2	0.2	0.8	1.2	5.7	5.7	6.3	6.3	5.2	23.8	27.7	16.6	2.7	78.1	42.7	49.1	50.9
37097	LOBELVILLE	97.7	96.9	0.3	0.3	0.4	0.5	0.9	1.4	6.7	6.8	7.2	6.6	4.9	23.3	29.5	13.6	1.4	75.1	40.2	50.8	49.2
37098	LYLES	95.8	94.8	2.1	2.5	0.1	0.2	1.0	1.5	7.2	7.2	7.4	6.9	5.6	27.5	27.3	10.1	0.9	74.0	37.2	51.3	48.7
37101	MC EWEN	97.7	97.2	0.7	0.7	0.2	0.3	0.6	0.9	6.4	6.5	6.9	6.9	5.4	26.6	27.3	12.5	1.4	75.9	38.9	50.0	50.0
37110	MC MINNVILLE	91.4	88.3	3.3	3.5	0.5	0.7	5.1	8.1	6.6	6.4	6.4	6.2	5.8	26.9	26.8	12.8	2.1	76.8	39.0	49.4	50.6
37115	MADISON	73.1	67.8	19.7	21.9	1.1	1.6	6.1	9.8	6.6	5.8	5.3	5.9	7.7	29.0	24.7	12.3	2.6	79.0	37.0	48.1	51.9
37118	MILTON	92.6	91.0	5.8	6.9	0.4	0.5	0.5	0.8	6.0	6.6	7.0	9.6	7.1	23.9	29.1	9.6	1.2	76.2	37.7	47.8	52.2
37122	MOUNT JULIET	94.1	92.6	3.9	4.7	0.5	0.8	1.0	1.7	6.6	7.1	7.5	6.9	4.5	27.1	30.7	8.6	0.8	74.4	39.2	49.7	50.3
37127	MURFREESBORO	83.9	79.2	8.7	10.3	5.3	7.7	1.3	2.2	7.9	7.7	7.4	6.3	5.3	30.9	25.5	8.0	1.0	73.1	35.4	49.3	50.7
37128	MURFREESBORO	87.6	84.8	7.5	8.1	3.1	4.7	1.4	2.3	8.9	8.0	7.3	6.4	5.4	36.9	21.7	4.9	0.4	71.8	32.5	49.1	50.9
37129	MURFREESBORO	88.8	86.4	6.7	7.3	1.9	2.6	2.5	4.1	6.9	7.0	7.1	7.1	5.6	30.1	27.1	8.0	1.1	74.7	36.3	49.9	50.1
37130	MURFREESBORO	78.2	74.9	15.9	16.8	2.1	2.9	3.9	6.0	6.7	5.8	5.2	6.9	14.6	31.7	19.1	8.4	1.6	79.2	30.0	50.2	49.8
37132	MURFREESBORO	70.1	65.7	27.2	30.6	1.3	1.8	1.2	2.0	0.1	0.0	0.3	48.3	46.4	3.4	1.4	0.1	0.0	99.1	20.1	54.1	45.9
37134	NEW JOHNSONVILLE	97.8	97.2	1.2	1.4	0.2	0.3	0.6	1.0	6.0	6.3	6.7	6.4	5.0	24.7	30.0	13.6	1.3	77.0	41.0	49.5	50.5
37135	NOLENSVILLE	93.3	91.0	5.1	6.3	0.3	0.7	1.3	2.5	6.8	7.2	8.0	7.7	4.5	26.0	31.3	7.8	0.7	73.1	38.7	49.5	50.5
37137	NUNNELLY	90.0	89.0	8.0	8.4	0.1	0.1	1.0	1.5	5.8	5.9	6.2	6.6	6.4	29.9	27.2	10.7	1.4	78.0	38.5	56.0	44.0
37138	OLD HICKORY	92.1	89.4	5.1	6.5	0.9	1.4	1.5	2.6	6.2	6.6	6.8	6.4	4.7	26.5	30.0	11.3	1.4	76.4	40.6	48.7	51.3
37140	ONLY	73.1	69.2	25.6	29.1	0.2	0.3	1.6	2.2	2.2	2.4	3.4	5.4	9.8	45.2	24.1	6.9	0.6	88.5	37.0	77.4	22.6
37141	ORLINDA	94.4	92.9	4.4	5.6	0.1	0.1	0.7	1.1	6.4	6.6	6.9	6.1	4.7	27.6	29.3	11.2	1.2	76.4	39.8	48.6	51.4
37142	PALMYRA	95.9	94.8	1.9	2.4	0.3	0.4	1.0	1.5	6.1	6.4	6.7	7.0	5.6	24.9	30.4	11.5	1.3	76.3	40.1	50.8	49.2
37143	PEGRAM	95.9	95.0	2.6	3.0	0.3	0.4	1.3	2.0	7.1	7.4	7.4	5.7	4.7	26.4	30.0	9.7	1.5	74.1	39.5	50.7	49.3
37144	PETERSBURG	94.8	93.3	3.0	3.7	0.2	0.3	1.5	2.4	5.7	5.8	6.2	6.2	5.2	25.0	31.1	13.0	1.8	78.3	42.1	49.9	50.1
37145	PLEASANT SHADE	97.1	96.3	1.1	1.3	0.0	0.1	1.3	2.1	6.7	6.6	6.8	6.3	5.7	26.9	28.5	10.9	1.6	75.9	38.9	50.7	49.3
37146	PLEASANT VIEW	97.5	96.7	1.0	1.2	0.2	0.2	1.1	1.8	7.7	7.6	7.6	7.1	5.3	29.8	26.6	7.6	0.7	72.5	35.8	50.3	49.7
37148	PORTLAND	95.4	93.9	2.3	3.0	0.2	0.3	1.6	2.6	7.4	7.3	7.1	6.7	5.5	28.4	25.9	10.3	1.4	74.1	36.7	49.4	50.6
37149	READYVILLE	97.1	96.1	1.5	1.8	0.3	0.4	0.8	1.4	6.4	6.5	6.8	6.5	5.1	27.0	28.9	11.6	1.2	76.2	39.3	51.0	49.0
37150	RED BOILING SPRINGS	97.5	96.7	0.1	0.1	0.2	0.3	2.5	3.4	6.5	6.6	6.7	6.2	4.9	25.7	27.3	13.6	2.4	76.2	40.3	49.1	50.9
37151	RIDDLETON	91.9	89.7	4.9	5.6	0.0	0.0	3.0	4.5	7.9	7.1	7.3	6.4	5.6	26.4	26.2	10.7	2.4	73.4	37.9	48.5	51.5
37153	ROCKVALE	94.9	93.4	3.1	3.7	0.7	1.1	1.0	1.7	7.9	7.5	7.4	7.0	5.4	31.6	25.3	7.1	0.7	72.7	35.0	49.1	50.9
37160	SHELBYVILLE	83.8	80.7	10.4	11.0	0.6	0.8	9.8	14.9	7.5	7.2	6.9	6.4	5.7	28.0	25.0	11.5	1.8	74.6	36.7	49.4	50.6
37166	SMITHVILLE	95.2	93.4	1.3	1.4	0.2	0.2	4.7	7.6	6.2	6.2	6.2	5.8	5.2	27.3	28.1	12.9	2.1	77.9	40.4	49.8	50.2
37167	SMYRNA	88.5	85.3	7.0	8.1	1.3	1.8	3.6	5.8	8.1	7.7	7.3	7.0	7.1	30.1	25.1	6.9	0.7	72.8	33.1	49.1	50.9
37171	SOUTHSIDE	94.7	93.7	3.8	4.4	0.1	0.1	1.3	2.0	6.0	6.3	6.8	6.4	4.7	27.1	29.3	12.3	1.2	77.0	40.8	51.3	48.7
37172	SPRINGFIELD	81.1	78.9	16.2	17.3	0.4	0.6	4.5	6.7	6.7	6.8	6.9	6.5	5.6	27.7	27.2	10.9	1.8	75.7	38.1	49.3	50.7
	TENNESSEE	80.2	78.4	16.4	16.9	1.0	1.5	2.2	3.4	6.5	6.4	6.5	6.8	6.5	27.2	27.0	11.4	1.7	76.6	38.0	49.0	51.0
	UNITED STATES	75.1	72.0	12.3	12.7	3.8	4.6	12.5	15.7	6.8	6.7	6.6	7.1	6.9	27.0	26.0	10.9	1.9	75.7	36.9	49.2	50.8

ZIP CODE #	POST OFFICE NAME	2009 Per Capita Income	2009 HH Income Base	2009 HOUSEHOLD INCOME DISTRIBUTION (%) Less than $25,000	$25,000 to $49,999	$50,000 to $99,999	$100,000 to $149,999	$150,000 or More	MEDIAN HOUSEHOLD INCOME 2009	2014	2009 National Centile	2009 State Centile	2009 Home Value Base	2009 HOME VALUE DISTRIBUTION (%) Less than $50,000	$50,000 to $89,999	$90,000 to $174,999	$175,000 to $399,999	$400,000 or More	2009 Median Home Value
37010	ADAMS	27789	1568	14.2	22.5	43.1	11.9	8.2	60719	62650	78	90	1296	6.9	14.0	33.7	38.0	7.3	163095
37012	ALEXANDRIA	19935	906	26.6	31.5	35.2	6.0	0.8	42830	45474	42	62	736	9.0	23.2	48.9	16.7	2.2	111378
37013	ANTIOCH	30158	28195	11.0	25.9	43.9	14.5	4.6	62355	63524	80	91	15569	4.0	3.2	59.9	30.4	2.4	148989
37014	ARRINGTON	34685	551	16.2	14.5	36.1	23.0	10.2	76987	79219	91	97	475	3.4	11.8	24.4	39.4	21.1	224554
37015	ASHLAND CITY	22366	6777	16.4	30.1	43.6	7.0	2.9	53069	56721	68	83	5386	9.5	14.6	48.3	25.0	2.5	131481
37016	AUBURNTOWN	22564	399	20.1	31.3	37.1	8.0	3.5	48061	48782	57	76	336	15.8	22.9	33.0	24.4	3.9	110606
37018	BEECHGROVE	21933	833	28.6	29.3	33.7	5.8	2.6	40510	42625	34	52	695	26.3	17.4	36.5	17.0	2.7	99886
37019	BELFAST	19378	304	24.7	27.0	41.4	5.9	1.0	48416	48243	58	76	248	15.3	21.4	41.1	19.8	2.4	112500
37020	BELL BUCKLE	23505	1935	18.2	25.9	44.2	7.8	3.9	55077	55441	71	85	1632	9.7	11.9	44.5	26.2	7.7	140640
37022	BETHPAGE	23234	2055	20.4	26.5	45.0	4.7	3.4	52375	52556	67	82	1727	14.4	22.4	32.5	24.9	5.8	122483
37023	BIG ROCK	18143	688	25.9	31.3	36.9	4.4	1.6	42781	45569	42	61	541	15.0	24.6	45.8	14.2	0.4	101856
37025	BON AQUA	19150	2323	25.4	31.0	36.4	5.4	1.7	44043	45528	46	65	1911	11.7	22.5	43.9	18.9	2.9	114745
37026	BRADYVILLE	18016	831	26.1	31.6	36.8	4.3	1.1	41827	43655	39	57	694	20.7	15.7	45.2	16.6	1.7	110926
37027	BRENTWOOD	59787	17206	4.6	9.0	25.1	24.6	36.7	119489	123006	98	100	14501	0.4	0.5	6.3	49.1	43.8	374235
37028	BUMPUS MILLS	21075	258	27.1	22.9	43.0	3.5	3.5	50000	49335	61	78	207	12.1	23.2	44.9	19.8	0.0	106250
37029	BURNS	24471	1886	16.6	27.6	45.7	7.4	2.8	56887	58434	74	88	1565	5.4	11.6	44.7	35.1	3.1	147296
37030	CARTHAGE	21244	2808	30.8	31.6	29.2	4.5	4.0	39137	43236	30	46	1975	11.4	19.9	43.8	21.6	3.2	122450
37031	CASTALIAN SPRINGS	21509	1340	21.0	26.9	44.8	5.1	2.2	51289	51496	64	81	1171	10.3	22.4	41.2	25.0	1.1	124071
37032	CEDAR HILL	21099	1412	18.2	27.8	45.4	6.4	2.3	54232	57169	70	84	1187	6.1	9.0	44.1	36.3	4.5	156871
37033	CENTERVILLE	17491	3034	36.8	29.8	28.3	3.2	2.0	35304	37527	19	26	2304	16.4	23.1	45.7	13.1	1.6	109328
37034	CHAPEL HILL	22878	2446	20.0	25.5	42.4	8.5	3.7	54430	54173	70	84	2044	9.7	13.8	55.3	17.3	3.9	123197
37035	CHAPMANSBORO	19886	1147	15.9	26.1	52.7	3.3	2.0	54678	56996	71	85	991	5.5	5.8	56.3	29.5	2.9	143691
37036	CHARLOTTE	21499	2269	21.9	32.3	37.6	4.8	3.4	46177	49522	52	73	1852	10.5	18.9	48.3	18.3	4.0	118827
37037	CHRISTIANA	24968	2356	11.5	25.1	50.6	9.6	3.2	61509	64832	79	90	2044	7.3	9.0	41.4	37.3	5.0	164477
37040	CLARKSVILLE	21476	15492	25.3	30.1	35.1	7.2	2.4	44802	48917	48	67	9460	5.2	20.6	57.1	15.9	1.2	122126
37042	CLARKSVILLE	20955	23250	15.7	31.7	43.4	6.9	2.3	51998	54697	66	82	13980	5.9	12.1	71.2	10.4	0.4	125319
37043	CLARKSVILLE	29109	14860	15.2	26.4	41.4	10.1	6.9	58214	59169	75	89	10333	3.3	10.2	49.7	31.3	5.6	150844
37046	COLLEGE GROVE	27163	1416	18.1	24.4	35.0	15.7	6.7	60095	59373	77	90	1152	7.7	10.0	31.7	33.7	16.9	178500
37047	CORNERSVILLE	22778	954	23.2	25.4	39.9	8.4	3.1	51371	50560	65	81	753	8.5	22.8	46.3	17.1	5.2	120465
37048	COTTONTOWN	24924	2277	15.8	22.3	50.1	8.8	3.1	62663	67410	81	92	1963	4.5	14.9	35.3	41.7	3.7	162292
37049	CROSS PLAINS	23751	1206	16.3	26.9	45.4	9.3	2.2	57177	59262	74	88	1020	7.7	15.5	35.1	36.5	5.2	152151
37050	CUMBERLAND CITY	19522	657	28.2	29.8	35.3	4.1	2.6	42538	45639	41	60	513	15.4	27.1	44.2	11.9	1.4	99625
37051	CUMBERLAND FURNACE	20406	1284	24.1	29.8	38.9	4.4	2.8	46063	50000	52	72	1078	17.6	20.5	41.1	18.3	2.5	108436
37052	CUNNINGHAM	20263	1049	24.6	31.5	37.0	4.8	2.2	43778	47612	45	64	892	10.8	29.8	44.3	12.8	2.4	110437
37055	DICKSON	22771	10867	23.7	27.0	38.6	7.5	3.2	49328	51929	60	78	7761	7.4	13.7	47.0	27.9	4.1	136609
37057	DIXON SPRINGS	19889	377	31.3	31.0	29.2	6.4	2.1	38214	40578	27	42	309	22.3	19.4	41.1	14.9	2.3	105398
37058	DOVER	19379	2886	30.3	32.2	31.8	3.4	2.3	38731	40876	29	44	2268	19.6	25.9	41.2	12.4	0.8	96516
37059	DOWELLTOWN	18832	721	32.6	32.9	28.6	3.3	2.6	36182	37229	21	31	564	15.6	22.3	45.4	14.5	2.1	102664
37060	EAGLEVILLE	26580	932	18.8	24.8	41.0	8.9	6.5	55862	56559	72	87	750	4.5	11.7	37.2	38.3	8.3	167169
37061	ERIN	18112	2173	36.7	29.0	28.3	4.3	1.7	36503	37725	22	33	1621	22.7	30.2	34.6	11.9	0.6	86092
37062	FAIRVIEW	26666	4329	15.7	29.1	38.3	11.4	5.6	55587	54357	72	86	3391	8.1	10.2	51.5	27.1	3.2	139266
37064	FRANKLIN	38296	17495	11.9	18.6	27.4	24.5	17.6	81466	84557	93	97	13390	5.4	4.7	21.6	53.8	14.5	253239
37066	GALLATIN	26904	16436	20.1	24.6	39.1	10.5	5.6	56714	60725	74	87	11673	8.9	9.7	33.2	39.9	8.4	169973
37067	FRANKLIN	51278	8259	6.2	12.9	26.6	28.3	25.9	105212	108595	97	99	4959	0.5	2.2	9.0	53.0	35.4	335683
37069	FRANKLIN	51939	6954	4.0	7.6	23.1	29.9	35.5	124131	128035	99	100	6477	0.5	0.4	6.1	60.0	33.1	334223
37072	GOODLETTSVILLE	28667	12238	14.4	24.4	43.1	12.6	5.5	61949	63841	80	91	8605	6.9	5.0	40.9	41.9	5.3	169665
37073	GREENBRIER	23318	4928	15.8	28.4	43.8	9.5	2.4	55085	56998	71	86	4009	5.0	9.3	48.0	34.5	3.2	156560
37074	HARTSVILLE	19172	2741	31.5	30.2	31.8	4.6	1.9	39075	41294	30	46	2050	14.9	23.2	45.8	14.0	2.1	104379
37075	HENDERSONVILLE	32997	22426	11.1	21.6	41.9	15.0	10.4	70681	76752	87	95	16553	1.3	2.3	38.3	48.9	9.2	195733
37076	HERMITAGE	31927	15130	11.6	24.8	44.3	13.6	5.7	62976	64187	81	92	8488	0.3	5.1	59.0	33.9	1.7	151655
37078	HURRICANE MILLS	20743	357	24.4	31.4	38.7	2.8	2.8	42075	43895	40	59	286	17.5	27.6	40.6	14.3	0.0	94667
37079	INDIAN MOUND	20510	972	22.8	35.0	36.4	2.7	3.1	42687	43921	41	61	761	20.5	18.9	41.3	18.4	0.9	108718
37080	JOELTON	24980	2933	15.2	28.1	41.8	11.6	3.3	54593	57371	71	85	2453	6.6	10.2	48.9	31.9	2.4	147342
37082	KINGSTON SPRINGS	30285	2383	10.6	17.5	49.6	13.7	8.5	69583	76272	87	95	2098	2.5	8.7	25.3	57.8	5.7	204167
37083	LAFAYETTE	18620	5376	34.1	28.6	31.7	4.0	1.6	37409	39796	25	38	4176	20.0	25.4	41.0	11.7	1.9	96978
37085	LASCASSAS	27517	1450	14.4	18.1	51.2	11.0	5.4	68596	75362	86	94	1275	2.0	8.9	38.1	39.0	12.0	177170
37086	LA VERGNE	27201	10924	7.5	22.9	51.7	12.8	5.1	69406	75386	86	94	9186	14.1	7.5	42.9	34.5	1.0	157718
37087	LEBANON	25046	15283	21.3	25.1	40.9	7.8	4.9	53705	54718	69	84	10618	7.3	11.2	38.1	36.5	6.8	158602
37090	LEBANON	25070	5336	15.4	23.4	49.0	8.8	3.4	60148	61265	78	90	4444	7.4	11.2	33.8	39.5	8.1	168568
37091	LEWISBURG	21630	8114	25.6	26.9	38.1	6.7	2.6	46618	48871	53	74	5627	10.8	21.7	48.4	16.0	3.1	113385
37095	LIBERTY	19167	851	27.6	34.0	34.3	2.1	2.0	41124	43223	36	55	688	14.8	22.1	40.8	19.0	3.2	109750
37096	LINDEN	19524	2368	35.8	31.0	27.0	4.2	1.9	34254	35065	16	22	2004	28.0	31.6	31.4	8.3	0.7	77066
37097	LOBELVILLE	18430	709	35.8	35.1	22.0	4.7	2.4	34497	34063	17	22	613	31.0	31.0	23.7	14.2	0.2	71413
37098	LYLES	17826	1939	28.3	34.5	31.9	3.9	1.4	40144	41824	33	51	1622	14.0	26.0	42.0	16.2	1.7	105568
37101	MC EWEN	20500	2453	25.6	32.5	35.2	4.5	2.2	43505	44846	44	64	1943	16.4	22.9	45.5	13.0	2.2	101186
37110	MC MINNVILLE	19528	13126	34.2	28.5	30.4	4.3	2.5	37702	39150	26	40	9222	13.3	27.3	43.5	14.0	1.9	99227
37115	MADISON	24556	16357	25.9	30.1	34.1	7.3	2.6	43330	47906	43	63	8101	7.1	12.8	59.9	18.8	1.4	122777
37118	MILTON	20641	491	22.8	23.4	38.1	10.0	5.7	55214	57241	72	86	420	8.1	18.8	23.1	26.9	23.1	175000
37122	MOUNT JULIET	30848	16548	7.9	16.8	49.7	17.0	8.6	73592	77953	89	96	14724	6.6	4.4	27.4	55.5	6.1	203038
37127	MURFREESBORO	28413	5346	11.7	16.9	51.4	12.5	7.5	69176	75241	86	94	4511	5.1	3.8	37.0	48.0	6.1	184009
37128	MURFREESBORO	29998	14157	7.3	15.4	55.7	15.2	6.4	74407	77664	89	96	10535	0.7	0.9	39.8	55.5	3.2	185962
37129	MURFREESBORO	28755	19083	12.2	20.3	47.9	13.1	6.6	66941	71778	85	93	14128	4.1	3.7	38.7	47.7	5.7	182191
37130	MURFREESBORO	23869	21715	30.9	26.0	32.2	6.6	4.3	41375	44736	37	56	9926	6.8	6.0	43.3	38.1	5.8	163350
37132	MURFREESBORO	13005	25	40.0	12.0	48.0	0.0	0.0	42376	42380	41	60	11	0.0	18.2	36.4	45.5	0.0	168750
37134	NEW JOHNSONVILLE	25740	1364	20.5	26.1	43.2	6.6	3.6	52492	51176	67	82	1139	13.7	30.0	41.4	14.0	0.9	97079
37135	NOLENSVILLE	33910	2608	8.9	12.0	36.2	30.5	12.4	84382	88015	94	98	2404	1.0	4.5	24.8	52.0	17.7	236923
37137	NUNNELLY	19533	1101	32.6	33.8	28.1	3.4	2.2	37810	40000	26	40	871	19.6	24.7	36.4	16.9	2.4	99167
37138	OLD HICKORY	33316	8908	14.5	18.2	43.5	14.1	9.6	67868	70983	85	94	7275	5.1	8.0	44.0	36.1	6.9	162249
37140	ONLY	10058	78	30.8	34.6	25.6	5.1	3.8	38893	40366	29	45	60	30.0	16.7	35.0	15.0	3.3	100000
37141	ORLINDA	22128	323	20.4	24.5	45.2	9.3	0.6	53505	55131	69	84	271	13.3	17.7	39.1	22.1	7.7	127315
37142	PALMYRA	18877	643	20.8	32.0	39.3	7.2	0.6	46800	50943	54	74	540	13.0	30.4	41.9	14.6	0.2	101359
37143	PEGRAM	26516	1373	14.7	22.9	47.1	10.2	5.0	62450	67742	81	91	1157	3.3	8.9	37.9	44.8	5.2	174905
37144	PETERSBURG	22998	1299	25.4	29.8	34.6	6.6	3.6	44833	45508	48	67	1096	19.6	20.2	37.9	19.0	3.4	111641
37145	PLEASANT SHADE	18581	1227	30.9	30.8	32.9	2.7	2.7	40537	43953	34	53	1028	16.2	23.2	43.9	12.9	3.8	112273
37146	PLEASANT VIEW	25777	2562	11.2	20.9	51.5	11.8	4.6	64258	67713	83	92	2259	3.1	5.5	49.4	39.8	2.2	161158
37148	PORTLAND	20919	8388	20.1	30.0	43.0	5.7	1.2	49908	50159	61	78	6399	10.2	18.5	49.4	20.3	1.5	117939
37149	READYVILLE	21203	1059	21.5	30.9	41.4	4.4	1.8	47325	47266	55	75	886	12.6	20.1	36.1	26.4	4.7	125568
37150	RED BOILING SPRINGS	17922	1905	38.6	31.5	24.3	2.9	2.7	33106	35340	13	19	1483	30.9	29.3	28.2	8.7	2.9	75550
37151	RIDDLETON	20846	187	29.9	28.9	29.9	8.6	2.7	39164	40833	30	46	156	15.4	16.0	49.4	18.6	0.6	126974
37153	ROCKVALE	27302	1846	10.7	19.6	50.9	11.9	6.8	67609	73960	85	94	1617	4.9	5.3	40.8	41.9	7.1	173578
37160	SHELBYVILLE	20002	12166	26.2	28.9	36.4	5.9	2.6	45193	47533	49	68	8456	9.9	22.0	49.2	16.0	3.0	112936
37166	SMITHVILLE	19638	5306	36.9	28.0	27.8	4.3	3.0	35560	36538	19	27	3885	10.1	24.4	46.6	15.6	3.3	110666
37167	SMYRNA	27091	17930	13.3	22.6	48.0	11.0	5.1	63723	68418	82	92	12455	5.5	4.3	39.2	47.3	3.6	177030
37171	SOUTHSIDE	22880	425	12.2	37.6	39.3	7.3	3.5	50098	52337	61	79	357	12.9	24.9	36.4	21.0	4.8	132176
37172	SPRINGFIELD	23612	11565	22.0	25.6	39.9	8.1	4.4	52489	55558	67	82	8033	6.2	13.6	44.7	31.8	3.8	143481
	TENNESSEE	24986		24.9	27.0	34.7	8.2	5.2	47751	50104				12.0	19.9	40.9	22.7	4.6	120455
	UNITED STATES	27277		20.9	24.4	35.3	11.7	7.6	54719	56938				9.3	13.1	31.6	32.6	13.5	162279

ZIP CODE		FINANCIAL SERVICES				THE HOME						ENTERTAINMENT						PERSONAL			
						Home Improvements		Furnishings													
#	POST OFFICE NAME	Auto Loan	Home Loan	Invest-ments	Retire-ment Plans	Home Repair	Lawn & Garden	Comput-ers & Hard-ware-Personal	Major Appli-ances	TV, Radio, Sound Equip-ment	Furni-ture	Dine out/ Carry out	Sports Equip-ment	Fees & Tickets	Toys & Games	Travel	Cable TV	Apparel & Services	Auto Repairs	Health Insur-ance	Pets & Supplies
37010	ADAMS	115	114	108	115	112	120	106	114	107	105	107	88	105	110	108	110	74	109	115	135
37012	ALEXANDRIA	86	65	72	64	65	83	66	77	73	64	71	59	55	75	62	79	48	72	81	93
37013	ANTIOCH	112	91	78	94	85	83	109	93	106	110	108	77	98	111	95	103	75	103	91	114
37014	ARRINGTON	126	144	142	149	146	143	127	136	125	130	125	103	138	126	138	125	88	128	132	157
37015	ASHLAND CITY	92	88	77	87	85	90	84	87	86	85	86	65	81	89	81	88	59	85	89	104
37016	AUBURNTOWN	100	80	86	80	80	100	81	93	87	76	85	71	70	90	77	93	58	87	97	111
37018	BEECHGROVE	93	67	77	65	67	88	70	81	77	68	76	62	56	80	63	84	51	77	85	98
37019	BELFAST	90	76	74	74	75	85	74	81	79	76	78	60	67	82	70	83	53	78	83	97
37020	BELL BUCKLE	100	92	84	91	91	98	88	95	91	88	90	70	82	94	85	94	62	91	96	112
37022	BETHPAGE	97	85	84	86	85	98	83	93	87	80	86	70	76	90	81	92	59	88	96	110
37023	BIG ROCK	83	66	71	64	66	80	66	75	71	65	70	56	57	73	62	76	47	71	77	90
37025	BON AQUA	87	70	72	68	69	83	70	78	75	70	74	59	61	78	65	80	50	75	81	94
37026	BRADYVILLE	86	62	71	60	62	82	64	75	72	63	70	58	52	75	59	78	47	71	79	91
37027	BRENTWOOD	216	268	266	276	272	242	230	235	218	246	220	184	264	222	253	209	161	223	212	268
37028	BUMPUS MILLS	83	77	68	74	75	78	72	77	75	75	75	56	68	78	69	77	51	74	77	91
37029	BURNS	100	92	85	91	91	99	88	96	91	87	90	71	83	94	85	95	62	91	97	113
37030	CARTHAGE	89	66	75	64	65	86	70	79	77	67	75	61	57	79	64	83	50	76	84	96
37031	CASTALIAN SPRINGS	91	81	76	79	80	87	78	84	82	80	81	62	72	85	74	85	55	81	85	100
37032	CEDAR HILL	94	83	82	83	83	93	81	89	84	79	83	67	74	86	79	88	57	85	91	106
37033	CENTERVILLE	75	54	73	53	56	77	58	71	64	53	62	53	46	64	55	71	42	66	76	84
37034	CHAPEL HILL	100	88	84	88	88	98	86	94	90	84	89	70	79	93	83	94	60	89	96	111
37035	CHAPMANSBORO	91	84	74	81	82	86	79	84	82	82	82	61	75	85	75	84	56	81	84	100
37036	CHARLOTTE	96	77	80	76	76	92	77	87	83	75	81	65	67	86	72	88	55	82	90	104
37037	CHRISTIANA	106	102	92	101	100	103	96	102	97	96	97	78	92	101	94	98	66	97	100	119
37040	CLARKSVILLE	84	75	67	74	71	75	79	76	79	78	79	60	73	82	72	80	55	77	77	91
37042	CLARKSVILLE	90	80	67	81	75	72	88	79	85	89	87	65	82	90	79	82	60	83	75	94
37043	CLARKSVILLE	106	104	94	105	102	103	102	103	102	103	102	79	101	105	101	102	71	102	103	121
37046	COLLEGE GROVE	110	110	102	114	110	119	103	112	104	99	104	86	102	107	106	108	71	106	114	131
37047	CORNERSVILLE	101	80	86	80	81	100	81	93	87	77	86	71	70	90	77	94	58	87	97	111
37048	COTTONTOWN	100	99	91	102	98	106	93	101	94	89	94	77	91	96	95	97	64	95	102	118
37049	CROSS PLAINS	99	93	83	91	91	96	87	93	90	90	90	68	83	94	84	93	62	90	93	110
37050	CUMBERLAND CITY	86	63	83	62	65	86	65	80	71	61	70	60	53	72	63	78	47	74	83	95
37051	CUMBERLAND FURNACE	90	70	76	70	71	89	72	82	78	69	76	63	61	80	67	84	51	77	86	99
37052	CUNNINGHAM	86	72	74	72	72	86	72	81	76	69	75	61	63	79	69	81	51	76	84	96
37055	DICKSON	86	80	74	80	78	84	81	83	84	79	83	62	77	85	77	86	58	82	86	98
37057	DIXON SPRINGS	91	70	77	70	70	90	72	83	78	68	76	63	60	81	67	84	52	78	87	99
37058	DOVER	83	60	83	58	62	84	62	77	69	58	67	58	50	69	60	75	45	71	81	92
37059	DOWELLTOWN	84	61	73	59	61	81	63	75	70	61	69	57	51	73	59	76	46	70	78	90
37060	EAGLEVILLE	106	100	96	103	100	113	96	107	99	89	97	81	91	101	97	103	67	100	109	125
37061	ERIN	79	55	72	53	56	77	59	71	66	55	64	54	46	67	55	72	43	67	76	86
37062	FAIRVIEW	105	103	92	105	100	104	101	102	100	100	101	80	99	104	99	101	70	100	102	121
37064	FRANKLIN	144	162	149	165	160	148	145	147	139	153	141	117	156	145	151	135	101	141	135	169
37066	GALLATIN	99	99	91	100	97	102	96	98	97	95	97	75	95	98	95	100	67	97	102	116
37067	FRANKLIN	187	201	178	209	194	172	187	180	177	201	180	149	199	188	188	166	130	175	158	207
37069	FRANKLIN	204	259	248	269	261	224	214	220	199	235	202	177	250	208	235	186	150	203	186	247
37072	GOODLETTSVILLE	101	102	95	104	101	103	101	101	100	101	101	77	102	102	101	101	70	101	102	119
37073	GREENBRIER	99	91	82	90	90	95	86	93	89	88	89	68	82	93	83	92	61	89	93	110
37074	HARTSVILLE	86	63	76	62	63	84	66	78	73	63	71	60	54	75	62	80	48	74	82	94
37075	HENDERSONVILLE	116	126	118	127	124	120	120	118	117	122	119	91	125	119	123	116	84	118	117	138
37076	HERMITAGE	109	99	86	101	94	92	108	98	105	108	107	79	102	109	99	103	74	103	97	117
37078	HURRICANE MILLS	91	65	75	64	65	87	68	79	76	66	74	61	55	79	62	82	50	75	84	96
37079	INDIAN MOUND	91	68	75	66	68	86	70	80	76	69	75	61	58	80	64	83	51	76	83	97
37080	JOELTON	100	96	88	96	95	103	90	98	93	89	92	73	87	96	90	96	63	93	100	115
37082	KINGSTON SPRINGS	122	133	112	129	126	116	117	119	113	125	115	93	121	120	117	109	80	113	108	137
37083	LAFAYETTE	82	59	72	57	59	80	62	73	69	59	67	56	49	71	57	75	45	69	78	89
37085	LASCASSAS	111	119	99	116	112	105	106	108	102	112	103	85	108	109	106	99	72	102	98	124
37086	LA VERGNE	116	121	100	116	114	104	109	110	105	117	107	86	109	112	106	101	74	105	98	126
37087	LEBANON	92	88	81	89	86	91	90	89	91	88	91	69	88	93	87	93	63	90	93	107
37090	LEBANON	100	97	89	98	96	102	93	99	94	91	94	75	90	97	92	96	64	94	99	116
37091	LEWISBURG	84	74	70	74	73	83	76	80	80	73	79	60	70	81	72	84	54	78	85	95
37095	LIBERTY	84	61	70	60	61	81	64	74	70	62	69	57	52	73	58	77	46	70	78	90
37096	LINDEN	83	60	78	58	61	83	63	76	70	59	68	58	50	70	59	76	45	71	81	91
37097	LOBELVILLE	80	57	78	56	59	80	59	73	66	56	64	55	47	66	57	72	43	68	77	88
37098	LYLES	84	61	69	60	61	80	63	73	70	62	69	56	52	73	58	76	46	70	77	89
37101	MC EWEN	91	66	75	64	66	87	68	79	76	66	74	61	55	79	62	82	50	75	84	97
37110	MC MINNVILLE	76	60	64	61	60	73	66	70	70	61	68	54	57	71	61	74	47	69	74	84
37115	MADISON	78	69	64	71	67	72	79	73	80	76	80	57	74	80	73	81	56	78	79	88
37118	MILTON	95	97	88	99	95	102	89	96	90	88	90	74	90	93	92	92	62	91	97	113
37122	MOUNT JULIET	120	136	117	137	131	126	120	123	116	124	118	97	128	121	125	114	83	118	117	144
37127	MURFREESBORO	115	120	103	119	115	112	113	113	110	114	111	89	114	115	112	109	77	110	109	132
37128	MURFREESBORO	124	133	107	127	124	109	119	117	112	128	114	93	120	121	116	105	80	112	102	134
37129	MURFREESBORO	111	114	101	113	110	107	108	108	107	112	108	83	109	110	107	106	75	107	105	127
37130	MURFREESBORO	82	67	61	69	64	66	87	72	83	80	84	60	75	84	73	82	58	80	74	88
37132	MURFREESBORO	71	55	51	58	53	57	82	62	75	69	75	53	67	76	64	74	53	71	65	77
37134	NEW JOHNSONVILLE	104	85	88	85	85	103	85	96	91	82	90	73	75	94	81	97	61	91	100	115
37135	NOLENSVILLE	137	168	152	168	164	147	142	145	134	151	137	114	158	139	153	129	98	138	131	167
37137	NUNNELLY	82	59	79	57	60	82	61	75	68	58	66	57	49	68	59	74	44	70	79	90
37138	OLD HICKORY	119	127	117	126	124	122	117	120	116	120	116	93	121	119	119	115	81	116	117	139
37140	ONLY	92	66	94	64	68	93	67	86	75	63	74	64	54	74	67	82	49	79	89	102
37141	ORLINDA	87	79	77	82	80	91	78	87	80	72	79	65	72	82	77	84	54	81	89	101
37142	PALMYRA	89	72	76	72	72	89	73	83	78	68	76	63	63	80	69	83	52	78	87	99
37143	PEGRAM	112	106	94	103	103	105	99	104	101	104	102	77	95	106	95	103	69	100	103	123
37144	PETERSBURG	98	79	90	78	80	98	79	92	84	75	83	69	68	86	77	90	56	86	95	109
37145	PLEASANT SHADE	87	62	73	60	62	83	65	76	72	63	70	58	52	74	59	78	47	71	80	92
37146	PLEASANT VIEW	110	113	96	110	108	104	103	105	101	108	102	81	103	107	101	100	71	101	99	123
37148	PORTLAND	88	76	71	75	74	86	77	82	81	74	79	62	69	83	72	85	54	79	85	98
37149	READYVILLE	92	73	77	72	73	89	73	83	79	72	78	63	63	82	69	85	53	79	87	100
37150	RED BOILING SPRINGS	81	56	70	54	56	77	59	70	66	57	65	54	46	68	54	73	43	66	74	86
37151	RIDDLETON	94	67	77	65	67	89	70	81	78	68	76	63	56	81	64	85	51	77	86	99
37153	ROCKVALE	119	122	104	119	116	111	111	115	108	115	109	89	110	114	109	106	75	108	106	131
37160	SHELBYVILLE	85	71	69	72	70	83	75	79	79	71	78	61	67	81	70	84	53	78	84	95
37166	SMITHVILLE	85	61	80	60	63	84	64	78	71	61	69	59	52	72	61	78	46	73	82	93
37167	SMYRNA	106	103	88	103	98	94	103	98	101	106	102	78	101	105	98	99	71	100	94	117
37171	SOUTHSIDE	92	83	83	86	84	98	82	93	85	74	83	70	75	86	81	90	57	85	95	108
37172	SPRINGFIELD	93	86	85	87	85	95	87	91	90	84	89	70	83	91	85	93	62	89	95	108
	TENNESSEE	95	84	85	84	82	93	87	90	90	85	89	69	80	91	83	93	61	89	93	107
	UNITED STATES	100	100	100	100	100	100	100	100	100	100	100	100	100	100	100	100	100	100	100	100

37174-37374

ZIP CODE #	POST OFFICE NAME	COUNTY FIPS CODE	POPULATION 2000	POPULATION 2009	POPULATION 2014	2000-2009 ANNUAL RATE % Rate	2000-2009 ANNUAL RATE State Centile	HOUSEHOLDS 2000	HOUSEHOLDS 2009	HOUSEHOLDS 2014	HOUSEHOLDS % Annual Rate 2000-2009	HOUSEHOLDS 2009 Average HH Size	FAMILIES 2000	FAMILIES 2009	FAMILIES % Annual Rate 2000-2009
37174	SPRING HILL	119	8186	23270	29729	12.0	100	2943	8220	10514	11.7	2.82	2310	6487	11.8
37175	STEWART	083	1244	1355	1406	0.9	63	535	598	625	1.2	2.26	367	399	0.9
37178	TENNESSEE RIDGE	083	1850	1832	1830	-0.1	13	727	738	743	0.2	2.46	550	548	0.0
37179	THOMPSONS STATION	187	6100	12308	15972	7.9	100	2038	4137	5376	8.0	2.98	1710	3380	7.6
37180	UNIONVILLE	003	2387	3135	3535	3.0	95	824	1092	1231	3.1	2.87	659	856	2.9
37181	VANLEER	043	1284	1387	1440	0.8	60	480	527	549	1.0	2.63	369	396	0.8
37183	WARTRACE	003	2892	3218	3401	1.2	72	1085	1216	1287	1.2	2.61	842	922	1.0
37184	WATERTOWN	189	4804	5518	5943	1.5	81	1844	2142	2320	1.6	2.58	1404	1588	1.3
37185	WAVERLY	085	8250	8242	8168	0.0	18	3404	3491	3486	0.3	2.30	2338	2328	0.0
37186	WESTMORELAND	165	8834	9696	10214	1.0	66	3222	3604	3823	1.2	2.67	2451	2671	0.9
37187	WHITE BLUFF	043	5645	6411	6782	1.4	78	2152	2504	2668	1.7	2.55	1608	1827	1.4
37188	WHITE HOUSE	147	10284	13855	15542	3.3	97	3563	4891	5521	3.5	2.83	2910	3918	3.3
37189	WHITES CREEK	037	2791	3179	3341	1.4	78	1068	1269	1346	1.9	2.48	773	894	1.6
37190	WOODBURY	015	7812	8249	8461	0.6	47	3114	3354	3459	0.8	2.41	2196	2305	0.5
37191	WOODLAWN	125	3896	4025	4145	0.4	36	1390	1486	1543	0.7	2.71	1082	1121	0.4
37201	NASHVILLE	037	1438	1733	1890	2.0	90	324	509	577	5.0	1.82	35	46	3.0
37203	NASHVILLE	037	11282	11419	11636	0.1	22	4981	5224	5416	0.5	1.91	1947	1878	-0.4
37204	NASHVILLE	037	10772	11126	11428	0.4	36	5094	5387	5574	0.6	2.05	2685	2690	0.0
37205	NASHVILLE	037	25140	25673	26252	0.2	27	11853	12352	12710	0.4	2.05	6460	6429	-0.1
37206	NASHVILLE	037	27767	28378	29005	0.2	27	11001	11540	11898	0.5	2.40	6604	6619	0.0
37207	NASHVILLE	037	36092	37517	38741	0.4	36	13182	13966	14508	0.6	2.67	9460	9708	0.3
37208	NASHVILLE	037	15527	16538	17179	0.7	53	5844	6240	6514	0.7	2.40	3248	3339	0.3
37209	NASHVILLE	037	35196	36353	37128	0.4	36	13264	13964	14415	0.6	2.22	7469	7542	0.1
37210	NASHVILLE	037	16192	17094	17545	0.6	47	6650	6928	7082	0.4	2.38	3620	3688	0.2
37211	NASHVILLE	037	63374	69262	72615	1.0	66	27663	30353	31870	1.0	2.27	15246	16070	0.6
37212	NASHVILLE	037	16694	16671	16733	0.0	18	7175	7243	7327	0.1	1.82	2403	2269	-0.6
37213	NASHVILLE	037	180	280	315	4.9	98	11	20	24	6.7	2.55	10	18	6.6
37214	NASHVILLE	037	26370	29377	30970	1.2	72	11790	13514	14372	1.5	2.11	6726	7394	1.0
37215	NASHVILLE	037	22713	23236	23864	0.2	27	10151	10579	10951	0.4	2.06	5573	5571	0.0
37216	NASHVILLE	037	19527	19627	19932	0.1	22	8180	8428	8626	0.3	2.32	5205	5158	-0.1
37217	NASHVILLE	037	27243	29334	30320	0.8	60	11679	12548	13013	0.8	2.27	6343	6483	0.2
37218	NASHVILLE	037	14929	15539	16077	0.4	36	5036	5379	5627	0.7	2.61	3652	3792	0.4
37219	NASHVILLE	037	580	1066	1188	6.8	99	463	850	1000	6.8	1.25	54	93	6.1
37220	NASHVILLE	037	5727	6017	6246	0.5	41	2343	2520	2635	0.8	2.39	1764	1845	0.5
37221	NASHVILLE	037	31844	36017	38448	1.3	76	13557	15528	16636	1.5	2.31	8698	9766	1.3
37228	NASHVILLE	037	422	717	792	5.9	99	279	501	569	6.5	1.38	116	188	5.4
37240	NASHVILLE	037	2811	3039	3078	0.8	60	159	220	245	3.6	1.56	28	32	1.5
37301	ALTAMONT	061	1693	1710	1713	0.1	22	588	617	624	0.5	2.71	449	461	0.3
37302	APISON	065	2534	2596	2626	0.3	31	980	1034	1055	0.6	2.51	748	769	0.3
37303	ATHENS	107	24355	25665	26356	0.6	47	9899	10678	11046	0.8	2.36	7003	7355	0.5
37305	BEERSHEBA SPRINGS	061	853	848	843	-0.1	13	338	345	346	0.2	2.45	258	258	0.0
37306	BELVIDERE	051	2500	2739	2879	1.0	66	924	1035	1098	1.2	2.64	750	825	1.0
37307	BENTON	139	4752	4746	4708	0.0	18	1879	1954	1961	0.4	2.40	1401	1423	0.2
37308	BIRCHWOOD	065	2251	2458	2574	1.0	66	823	923	973	1.2	2.66	670	734	1.0
37309	CALHOUN	107	1845	2125	2249	1.5	81	691	821	875	1.9	2.57	542	631	1.7
37310	CHARLESTON	011	3633	4318	4684	1.9	88	1394	1712	1876	2.2	2.52	1073	1279	1.9
37311	CLEVELAND	011	24710	25841	26722	0.5	41	10076	10880	11359	0.8	2.24	6135	6362	0.4
37312	CLEVELAND	011	27735	31150	33102	1.3	76	10654	12346	13235	1.6	2.48	7956	8972	1.3
37313	COALMONT	061	1277	1297	1297	0.2	27	489	516	523	0.6	2.51	373	386	0.4
37317	COPPERHILL	139	3217	3176	3137	-0.1	13	1343	1370	1369	0.2	2.22	914	904	-0.1
37318	COWAN	051	1981	2120	2172	0.7	53	821	907	938	1.1	2.33	579	623	0.8
37321	DAYTON	143	16330	18441	19409	1.3	76	6225	7180	7625	1.6	2.46	4545	5118	1.3
37322	DECATUR	121	7323	7719	7909	0.6	47	2845	3069	3167	0.8	2.48	2124	2235	0.6
37323	CLEVELAND	011	25637	29452	31473	1.5	81	9677	11457	12358	1.8	2.57	7598	8789	1.6
37324	DECHERD	051	5208	5692	5862	1.0	66	2134	2403	2494	1.3	2.36	1501	1645	1.0
37325	DELANO	139	1706	1730	1731	0.2	27	660	693	701	0.5	2.48	507	521	0.3
37327	DUNLAP	153	8990	10660	11648	1.9	88	3528	4319	4765	2.2	2.44	2600	3109	2.0
37328	ELORA	103	1321	1346	1360	0.2	27	543	570	581	0.5	2.36	403	411	0.2
37329	ENGLEWOOD	107	5112	5743	6064	1.3	76	2035	2344	2493	1.5	2.42	1516	1702	1.3
37330	ESTILL SPRINGS	051	6768	7157	7234	0.6	47	2590	2810	2868	0.9	2.53	2066	2199	0.7
37331	ETOWAH	107	7851	8231	8423	0.5	41	3265	3510	3622	0.8	2.30	2247	2343	0.5
37332	EVENSVILLE	143	2102	2310	2421	1.0	66	816	923	976	1.3	2.50	630	697	1.1
37333	FARNER	139	651	646	635	-0.1	13	248	255	254	0.3	2.53	195	197	0.1
37334	FAYETTEVILLE	103	20745	21458	21791	0.4	36	8385	8857	9057	0.6	2.37	5950	6127	0.3
37335	FLINTVILLE	103	2604	2715	2765	0.5	41	991	1061	1090	0.7	2.56	750	783	0.5
37336	GEORGETOWN	121	3881	4240	4441	1.0	66	1454	1637	1729	1.3	2.58	1177	1296	1.0
37337	GRANDVIEW	035	1315	1386	1420	0.6	47	563	614	635	0.9	2.26	400	424	0.6
37338	GRAYSVILLE	007	2518	2542	2575	0.1	22	982	1008	1028	0.3	2.52	733	739	0.1
37339	GRUETLI LAAGER	061	1836	1836	1828	0.0	18	699	728	734	0.4	2.52	525	535	0.2
37340	GUILD	115	1113	1188	1210	0.7	53	451	497	512	1.1	2.39	340	367	0.8
37341	HARRISON	065	12038	12765	13252	0.6	47	4392	4792	5017	0.9	2.66	3560	3799	0.7
37342	HILLSBORO	031	3157	3586	3806	1.4	78	1149	1325	1412	1.6	2.71	919	1039	1.3
37343	HIXSON	065	36219	38561	39960	0.7	53	13919	15264	15940	1.0	2.52	10605	11350	0.7
37345	HUNTLAND	051	2298	2471	2552	0.8	60	880	975	1016	1.1	2.52	658	712	0.9
37347	JASPER	115	7641	8114	8255	0.7	53	3056	3365	3461	1.0	2.38	2242	2408	0.8
37348	KELSO	103	1076	1217	1278	1.3	76	399	461	487	1.6	2.64	314	354	1.3
37350	LOOKOUT MOUNTAIN	065	1928	1943	1976	0.1	22	761	774	789	0.2	2.51	564	556	-0.2
37352	LYNCHBURG	127	2918	3240	3388	1.1	69	1142	1313	1389	1.5	2.44	838	943	1.3
37353	MC DONALD	011	4481	4691	4848	0.5	41	1779	1918	2001	0.8	2.44	1321	1378	0.5
37354	MADISONVILLE	123	14110	16740	18208	1.9	88	5572	6809	7481	2.2	2.42	4034	4808	1.9
37355	MANCHESTER	031	22169	24819	26065	1.2	72	8546	9794	10358	1.5	2.48	6217	6932	1.2
37356	MONTEAGLE	115	2465	2553	2574	0.4	36	985	1054	1076	0.7	2.31	705	736	0.5
37357	MORRISON	177	5109	5661	5909	1.1	69	1947	2210	2323	1.4	2.54	1492	1655	1.1
37359	MULBERRY	103	788	815	828	0.4	36	302	320	328	0.6	2.54	240	249	0.4
37360	NORMANDY	003	1603	1743	1828	0.9	63	629	694	730	1.1	2.45	481	517	0.8
37361	OCOEE	139	1162	1239	1260	0.7	53	472	525	540	1.2	2.36	354	385	0.9
37362	OLDFORT	139	3219	3299	3310	0.3	31	1245	1326	1347	0.7	2.48	948	988	0.4
37363	OOLTEWAH	065	24515	29430	31495	2.0	90	8455	10467	11314	2.3	2.67	6861	8320	2.1
37365	PALMER	061	1529	1468	1446	-0.4	5	614	614	612	0.0	2.39	443	432	-0.3
37366	PELHAM	061	763	764	763	0.0	18	307	320	323	0.4	2.37	224	228	0.2
37367	PIKEVILLE	007	9889	10398	10683	0.5	41	3479	3757	3897	0.8	2.50	2587	2730	0.6
37369	RELIANCE	139	1016	1007	996	-0.1	13	429	442	441	0.3	2.28	324	326	0.1
37370	RICEVILLE	107	4006	4219	4333	0.6	47	1538	1660	1717	0.8	2.53	1218	1288	0.6
37373	SALE CREEK	065	2655	3247	3482	2.2	92	1069	1355	1464	2.6	2.40	847	1046	2.3
37374	SEQUATCHIE	115	1393	1367	1329	-0.2	10	531	541	533	0.2	2.53	412	411	0.0
	TENNESSEE					1.1					1.3	2.44			1.0
	UNITED STATES					1.0					1.1	2.59			0.9

#	POST OFFICE NAME	RACE (%) White 2000	White 2009	Black 2000	Black 2009	Asian/Pacific 2000	Asian/Pacific 2009	% Hispanic Origin 2000	% Hispanic Origin 2009	2009 AGE DISTRIBUTION (%) 0-4	5-9	10-14	15-19	20-24	25-44	45-64	65-84	85+	18+	MEDIAN AGE 2009	% 2009 Males	% 2009 Females
37174	SPRING HILL	89.4	87.5	7.0	7.3	0.5	0.8	3.4	5.7	8.6	8.4	8.1	6.8	4.9	31.1	25.5	6.1	0.6	70.6	34.6	50.0	50.0
37175	STEWART	92.1	89.2	0.5	0.5	2.6	3.4	3.6	5.8	3.8	3.8	4.2	4.7	4.0	21.0	33.9	22.5	2.1	85.3	51.1	50.9	49.1
37178	TENNESSEE RIDGE	97.7	97.1	1.0	1.1	0.4	0.5	0.8	1.4	6.5	6.5	6.8	6.5	5.2	24.6	27.6	14.6	1.7	76.0	40.5	48.2	51.8
37179	THOMPSONS STATION	92.3	89.7	5.0	5.8	0.5	0.9	2.8	5.2	9.6	9.0	8.4	6.7	4.8	32.4	23.3	5.2	0.5	68.7	33.0	49.8	50.2
37180	UNIONVILLE	95.3	93.7	2.7	3.3	0.0	0.1	1.7	3.0	8.1	8.0	7.9	7.0	5.0	28.7	25.2	9.0	1.1	71.5	35.5	50.0	50.0
37181	VANLEER	96.3	95.4	1.5	1.7	0.2	0.4	0.5	1.0	6.2	6.2	6.6	6.8	6.0	25.8	29.0	12.0	1.4	76.9	39.7	51.0	49.0
37183	WARTRACE	93.8	92.1	4.2	5.0	0.2	0.4	1.5	2.6	6.1	6.4	6.8	6.7	4.9	26.4	29.3	11.9	1.5	76.6	40.5	50.8	49.2
37184	WATERTOWN	93.7	92.3	4.5	5.3	0.1	0.2	1.0	1.7	6.4	6.6	6.8	6.4	5.0	25.8	29.7	11.7	1.5	76.2	40.4	50.2	49.8
37185	WAVERLY	92.8	91.5	5.5	6.2	0.3	0.5	1.1	1.7	5.6	5.6	5.9	6.0	4.9	24.4	29.7	15.6	2.4	79.2	43.2	49.2	50.8
37186	WESTMORELAND	98.4	97.8	0.1	0.1	0.2	0.3	1.0	1.7	7.8	7.7	7.6	6.7	5.5	26.4	26.2	10.6	1.5	72.8	36.8	49.6	50.4
37187	WHITE BLUFF	98.4	98.0	0.4	0.5	0.2	0.3	0.6	1.0	6.3	7.0	7.0	6.5	5.1	28.7	28.1	10.3	1.0	75.4	37.9	50.0	50.0
37188	WHITE HOUSE	96.8	95.8	1.6	2.1	0.4	0.6	1.1	1.9	8.1	7.7	7.6	7.2	5.5	31.1	25.1	7.1	0.7	72.2	34.6	50.5	49.5
37189	WHITES CREEK	73.4	67.0	24.7	30.5	0.3	0.5	0.7	1.1	5.3	5.9	6.4	6.2	4.6	25.1	31.4	13.5	1.7	78.5	42.3	48.7	51.3
37190	WOODBURY	96.5	95.7	1.7	1.8	0.2	0.2	1.3	2.0	6.4	6.3	6.4	6.3	5.6	25.5	27.2	14.0	2.3	77.0	40.2	48.9	51.1
37191	WOODLAWN	89.3	86.7	5.1	5.9	1.2	1.7	3.1	4.9	8.5	7.9	7.3	6.4	5.4	34.6	22.3	6.9	0.7	72.3	33.6	50.8	49.2
37201	NASHVILLE	54.6	48.8	41.5	45.5	0.9	1.2	5.1	8.0	0.8	0.5	0.4	4.3	14.9	58.3	16.8	3.5	0.5	97.9	33.0	77.9	22.1
37203	NASHVILLE	37.6	35.1	55.9	56.0	3.5	5.1	3.2	4.7	7.4	6.2	5.6	6.1	10.8	31.4	20.3	9.5	2.7	77.2	31.6	49.7	50.3
37204	NASHVILLE	65.8	62.0	31.0	33.2	1.6	2.5	1.2	2.3	5.1	4.6	4.7	5.3	7.1	29.6	29.4	11.6	2.4	82.2	40.4	48.0	52.0
37205	NASHVILLE	93.2	90.7	2.9	3.7	2.3	3.5	1.2	2.2	5.2	5.2	5.5	5.1	6.3	27.0	28.7	13.4	3.5	81.0	42.0	47.3	52.7
37206	NASHVILLE	49.3	44.7	44.7	47.4	1.2	1.6	3.2	4.9	8.2	7.0	6.3	7.6	7.9	26.7	25.5	9.3	1.5	74.4	34.9	48.1	51.9
37207	NASHVILLE	26.1	22.9	69.9	72.1	0.7	1.0	2.6	3.8	8.0	8.3	7.8	8.0	6.9	25.5	24.6	9.6	1.2	70.9	33.2	46.3	53.7
37208	NASHVILLE	5.1	4.2	92.3	92.8	0.5	0.6	0.9	1.1	6.5	6.3	6.0	8.6	12.2	22.7	23.7	11.7	2.2	77.0	33.5	44.9	55.1
37209	NASHVILLE	61.1	57.5	31.0	31.6	3.5	5.0	4.1	6.1	5.9	5.5	5.1	9.3	9.9	31.3	22.6	9.2	1.4	80.5	33.7	52.0	48.0
37210	NASHVILLE	50.6	44.1	34.0	35.4	3.5	4.3	12.8	18.1	8.7	7.2	6.0	8.1	9.8	27.6	20.9	9.5	2.2	74.4	31.2	49.4	50.6
37211	NASHVILLE	69.4	63.4	17.5	18.8	3.6	4.9	10.1	14.7	7.2	6.1	5.4	5.7	8.6	34.1	23.1	8.5	1.4	78.2	33.8	49.2	50.8
37212	NASHVILLE	75.5	70.8	15.9	17.1	6.0	8.7	2.1	3.5	3.2	2.7	2.6	10.4	22.7	31.6	18.4	6.5	1.9	89.3	28.7	48.6	51.4
37213	NASHVILLE	33.1	28.2	61.9	65.7	0.0	0.0	3.3	5.7	10.4	8.9	10.0	22.1	5.7	18.9	20.4	3.2	0.4	51.1	19.7	61.1	38.9
37214	NASHVILLE	86.4	81.9	9.1	11.4	1.6	2.5	2.7	4.8	5.8	5.6	5.5	5.6	6.8	30.0	27.1	11.6	2.0	79.8	39.4	48.3	51.7
37215	NASHVILLE	95.6	93.9	1.6	2.0	1.6	2.5	1.0	1.8	3.8	4.2	5.0	7.5	7.5	22.9	30.0	15.0	4.0	83.9	44.3	46.1	53.9
37216	NASHVILLE	67.3	62.4	28.8	32.3	0.9	1.3	1.8	3.1	6.5	5.9	5.9	6.3	6.3	26.1	28.7	12.0	2.3	78.0	40.0	48.0	52.0
37217	NASHVILLE	63.4	57.1	21.3	22.9	3.2	4.2	14.2	19.9	6.7	5.7	5.1	5.4	9.2	36.5	22.9	7.6	0.9	79.6	33.7	52.8	47.2
37218	NASHVILLE	25.9	23.5	71.5	73.2	0.4	0.6	1.1	1.6	5.4	5.5	5.9	7.0	5.4	24.8	27.5	15.3	3.2	78.6	41.5	44.8	55.2
37219	NASHVILLE	68.7	61.3	26.1	31.5	2.1	2.9	3.6	6.0	1.3	0.9	0.8	2.7	10.0	54.1	22.5	6.5	1.1	96.6	35.9	68.4	31.6
37220	NASHVILLE	96.7	95.4	1.2	1.5	1.1	1.7	0.9	1.7	5.1	5.9	6.8	6.0	3.6	19.3	34.4	15.7	3.1	78.3	46.9	48.6	51.4
37221	NASHVILLE	90.4	87.3	4.2	4.9	3.3	5.0	1.8	3.0	6.4	6.6	6.9	5.7	5.4	28.2	28.5	10.5	1.7	76.5	39.3	47.1	52.9
37228	NASHVILLE	14.7	15.5	82.0	81.5	0.7	0.6	0.5	0.7	7.1	6.1	5.0	6.4	8.5	20.6	21.2	19.9	5.0	78.1	41.0	40.7	59.3
37240	NASHVILLE	82.4	76.2	4.4	5.1	9.4	13.4	4.3	7.2	0.4	0.5	0.2	56.9	36.1	5.0	0.8	0.1	0.0	98.5	19.3	47.0	53.0
37301	ALTAMONT	97.6	97.5	0.1	0.1	0.1	0.1	2.8	2.9	8.0	8.1	8.1	6.9	4.7	27.5	24.7	10.9	1.1	71.3	35.6	51.0	49.0
37302	APISON	93.8	91.4	1.3	1.6	1.4	2.0	3.1	5.1	5.2	5.6	6.2	6.2	4.1	28.0	30.5	12.4	1.8	79.2	41.4	50.8	49.2
37303	ATHENS	91.0	89.0	5.5	6.2	1.1	1.6	2.2	3.5	6.4	6.3	6.4	6.5	5.9	25.7	27.5	13.3	2.1	77.1	39.9	47.9	52.1
37305	BEERSHEBA SPRINGS	99.4	99.4	0.0	0.0	0.0	0.0	0.7	0.8	6.6	6.5	6.7	6.6	5.0	26.7	26.9	13.2	1.9	76.1	39.0	48.8	51.2
37306	BELVIDERE	94.3	93.1	3.6	4.0	0.2	0.3	2.0	3.3	6.3	6.4	6.6	6.4	5.2	25.6	29.1	12.9	1.4	76.9	40.5	50.0	50.0
37307	BENTON	98.9	98.9	0.1	0.1	0.0	0.0	0.9	0.9	6.5	6.7	6.9	6.2	5.0	27.7	27.4	12.4	1.3	76.0	39.2	49.0	51.0
37308	BIRCHWOOD	97.2	96.5	1.2	1.5	0.1	0.1	0.5	0.9	6.1	6.4	7.0	6.5	4.6	26.7	29.5	12.1	1.2	76.5	40.3	50.4	49.6
37309	CALHOUN	95.0	93.7	2.4	2.8	0.3	0.5	2.7	4.3	5.8	6.0	6.7	6.5	5.0	26.4	29.6	12.6	1.3	77.1	40.3	51.1	48.9
37310	CHARLESTON	91.2	89.2	6.4	7.6	0.2	0.3	1.2	2.0	6.5	6.9	7.2	6.3	4.0	26.5	29.6	11.7	1.3	75.5	40.2	49.1	50.9
37311	CLEVELAND	88.6	86.3	7.3	8.0	0.7	1.0	3.0	4.7	6.7	5.9	5.6	8.3	10.1	26.8	23.9	11.1	1.8	78.5	34.3	48.1	51.9
37312	CLEVELAND	93.2	91.5	3.7	4.2	0.9	1.3	2.1	3.4	6.1	6.3	6.5	6.0	4.7	27.5	27.6	13.2	2.1	77.3	40.1	48.6	51.4
37313	COALMONT	98.4	98.4	0.0	0.0	0.1	0.1	0.9	1.0	7.1	6.8	6.9	6.6	5.9	28.1	25.4	11.6	1.5	75.1	37.0	49.5	50.5
37317	COPPERHILL	97.6	97.5	0.3	0.3	0.4	0.4	0.8	0.9	5.3	5.4	5.6	5.1	4.1	22.6	27.9	20.0	4.0	80.6	46.4	47.7	52.3
37318	COWAN	90.1	88.1	7.2	8.3	0.0	0.1	1.3	2.1	6.8	6.8	6.7	6.3	5.8	24.4	27.8	13.3	2.2	75.8	39.1	46.2	53.8
37321	DAYTON	94.4	93.0	2.5	2.7	0.5	0.7	2.1	3.4	6.7	6.6	6.7	7.5	6.7	26.2	26.1	11.7	1.8	76.0	37.3	48.6	51.4
37322	DECATUR	98.1	97.6	0.9	1.0	0.2	0.3	0.6	1.0	6.7	6.7	6.9	6.2	5.2	26.6	27.9	12.3	1.5	75.7	39.2	50.1	49.9
37323	CLEVELAND	96.1	94.9	1.6	1.9	0.3	0.5	1.5	2.4	6.6	6.8	6.9	6.6	5.2	28.7	27.7	10.7	1.0	75.7	38.3	49.7	50.3
37324	DECHERD	90.1	88.5	8.1	9.0	0.2	0.2	1.4	2.2	6.4	6.6	6.7	5.9	4.6	25.8	27.8	14.3	2.0	76.7	40.8	49.3	50.7
37325	DELANO	97.7	97.4	0.5	0.6	0.1	0.2	0.6	0.8	5.8	6.1	6.5	6.1	4.4	26.3	30.5	12.8	1.5	77.6	41.6	50.9	49.1
37327	DUNLAP	98.7	98.4	0.2	0.2	0.2	0.3	0.7	1.1	7.0	7.0	7.1	6.4	5.0	26.9	27.0	12.1	1.6	75.1	38.4	50.0	50.0
37328	ELORA	96.6	95.5	0.9	1.1	0.2	0.3	1.7	2.8	6.1	6.3	6.7	6.8	5.4	26.4	29.1	11.8	1.3	76.7	39.7	50.9	49.1
37329	ENGLEWOOD	96.9	96.0	0.9	1.0	0.2	0.3	1.2	1.9	6.4	6.5	6.8	6.6	5.3	25.6	27.5	13.4	1.9	76.2	39.9	50.1	49.9
37330	ESTILL SPRINGS	96.6	95.5	1.5	1.7	0.7	1.0	1.3	2.2	5.8	6.2	6.5	6.4	5.0	25.2	30.1	13.3	1.5	77.2	41.3	50.7	49.3
37331	ETOWAH	91.7	90.0	6.0	6.8	0.2	0.3	1.4	2.3	5.5	5.6	5.9	6.2	4.5	24.0	28.1	17.1	3.2	79.3	43.8	47.9	52.1
37332	EVENSVILLE	97.3	96.4	0.4	0.5	0.1	0.3	1.0	1.7	6.7	6.8	7.0	6.4	5.2	27.7	28.1	11.0	1.0	75.6	38.1	49.2	50.8
37333	FARNER	97.4	97.4	0.0	0.0	0.0	0.0	0.2	0.2	7.3	7.4	7.9	6.7	5.0	25.7	25.4	13.6	1.1	73.2	37.4	50.9	49.1
37334	FAYETTEVILLE	87.3	85.5	10.4	11.6	0.4	0.6	0.9	1.5	6.1	6.3	6.4	6.0	4.9	24.7	28.0	14.8	2.7	77.4	41.7	48.1	51.9
37335	FLINTVILLE	96.6	95.7	0.8	1.0	0.2	0.3	1.4	2.2	6.4	6.4	6.7	6.7	5.5	26.6	28.9	11.6	1.3	76.3	39.5	50.4	49.6
37336	GEORGETOWN	97.2	96.5	1.8	2.1	0.2	0.2	0.5	0.8	5.9	6.2	6.7	6.3	4.4	27.1	29.6	12.5	1.2	77.1	40.9	49.9	50.1
37337	GRANDVIEW	97.9	97.3	0.3	0.4	0.3	0.4	0.8	1.3	4.5	4.9	5.4	6.1	5.3	25.1	32.5	14.6	1.6	81.5	44.1	51.2	48.8
37338	GRAYSVILLE	97.4	96.7	0.4	0.4	0.0	0.1	1.4	2.2	6.1	6.2	6.6	6.7	5.1	28.2	29.0	10.7	1.3	76.9	39.3	49.7	50.3
37339	GRUETLI LAAGER	98.9	98.9	0.0	0.0	0.2	0.2	0.7	0.7	7.5	7.2	7.2	6.5	5.8	27.2	25.5	11.7	1.4	74.1	36.9	49.7	50.3
37340	GUILD	95.2	93.7	1.7	2.0	0.5	0.9	1.1	1.8	4.7	5.1	5.2	5.5	4.7	23.9	34.1	15.2	1.5	81.7	45.5	49.7	50.3
37341	HARRISON	93.6	91.2	4.4	6.0	0.4	0.7	0.8	1.4	5.7	6.2	6.8	6.6	4.7	26.8	31.6	10.6	1.0	77.2	40.8	49.4	50.6
37342	HILLSBORO	98.1	96.9	0.0	0.0	0.2	0.3	1.9	3.3	6.9	6.9	7.2	6.9	5.8	25.7	28.1	11.5	1.0	74.7	38.5	50.2	49.8
37343	HIXSON	93.3	90.6	3.0	4.0	2.1	3.1	1.4	2.3	5.7	5.9	6.3	6.4	5.0	25.8	30.9	12.5	1.3	78.1	41.3	48.3	51.7
37345	HUNTLAND	94.6	93.4	2.8	3.1	0.1	0.1	2.6	4.2	6.4	6.2	6.2	6.2	6.0	26.5	27.7	12.7	2.0	77.2	39.2	49.2	50.8
37347	JASPER	93.1	91.4	5.0	5.9	0.4	0.6	0.8	1.4	5.6	5.8	6.2	6.0	5.0	27.0	30.3	12.8	1.3	78.6	41.1	49.7	50.3
37348	KELSO	97.0	96.1	0.9	1.2	0.3	0.3	0.7	1.0	7.1	6.9	6.8	5.9	5.8	26.9	28.1	11.5	1.1	75.6	39.0	49.6	50.4
37350	LOOKOUT MOUNTAIN	96.9	95.7	2.1	2.9	0.6	0.9	0.4	0.7	6.6	7.6	9.1	7.1	3.7	16.8	31.1	14.8	3.2	72.2	44.3	48.7	51.3
37352	LYNCHBURG	94.8	94.0	3.8	4.3	0.1	0.2	0.6	0.9	5.6	5.9	6.1	6.2	4.8	24.0	29.5	15.6	2.2	78.4	43.0	49.6	50.4
37353	MC DONALD	96.9	95.7	0.6	0.7	0.2	0.3	1.6	2.7	5.8	6.1	6.3	5.8	4.5	26.7	30.9	12.7	1.2	78.3	41.5	51.5	48.5
37354	MADISONVILLE	96.0	94.8	1.5	1.7	0.2	0.3	1.8	2.9	6.5	6.5	6.7	7.2	5.7	26.9	26.8	12.2	1.6	76.2	38.5	50.1	49.9
37355	MANCHESTER	95.1	93.5	2.2	2.5	0.7	1.1	2.7	4.2	6.5	6.4	6.4	6.3	5.6	26.1	26.8	13.8	2.0	76.8	39.8	49.3	50.7
37356	MONTEAGLE	97.4	97.1	0.6	0.6	0.3	0.4	0.7	1.0	5.3	5.6	5.8	5.7	4.5	23.3	29.2	17.6	3.0	79.7	44.8	49.6	50.4
37357	MORRISON	93.9	91.9	2.7	3.1	0.4	0.6	2.9	4.6	6.6	6.8	7.0	7.1	5.2	27.6	27.5	11.1	1.1	75.4	38.1	50.4	49.6
37359	MULBERRY	95.9	95.0	2.9	3.6	0.3	0.4	0.5	0.6	5.2	5.5	5.6	5.8	4.8	24.8	31.8	15.1	1.5	80.0	43.8	51.2	48.8
37360	NORMANDY	93.9	92.2	3.4	4.0	0.7	1.0	1.4	2.4	5.8	6.1	6.3	6.1	5.3	25.2	29.7	13.8	1.7	78.1	41.4	50.6	49.4
37361	OCOEE	98.5	98.4	0.0	0.0	0.1	0.1	0.8	0.8	6.7	6.9	6.9	5.5	4.8	27.4	28.5	12.3	1.0	76.1	39.5	51.2	48.8
37362	OLDFORT	98.7	98.5	0.1	0.1	0.2	0.2	0.7	0.8	7.1	7.2	7.2	6.2	5.1	28.2	27.9	10.3	0.8	74.7	38.1	51.1	48.9
37363	OOLTEWAH	90.0	86.5	5.5	7.3	1.4	2.0	3.0	4.8	6.1	6.3	6.6	7.9	7.2	26.5	28.4	9.7	1.3	77.1	37.6	48.5	51.5
37365	PALMER	99.0	99.0	0.0	0.0	0.1	0.1	0.4	0.4	6.9	6.9	7.2	6.4	4.9	25.2	26.6	13.9	1.8	74.9	39.5	49.6	50.4
37366	PELHAM	99.2	99.2	0.1	0.1	0.1	0.1	1.3	1.3	6.0	6.3	6.8	6.5	5.1	25.0	28.5	13.5	2.2	77.1	40.8	50.9	49.1
37367	PIKEVILLE	94.1	93.1	4.1	4.6	0.2	0.3	1.1	1.7	5.6	5.8	6.1	7.1	5.4	28.5	28.0	12.2	1.3	78.0	39.4	55.0	45.0
37369	RELIANCE	98.9	98.8	0.0	0.0	0.0	0.0	0.8	0.8	5.2	5.6	5.9	5.5	4.3	25.2	31.9	14.9	1.7	79.8	43.9	49.6	50.4
37370	RICEVILLE	95.4	94.2	2.1	2.4	0.6	1.0	1.7	2.7	6.4	6.6	6.8	6.2	4.8	25.9	29.7	12.3	1.2	76.4	40.2	49.8	50.2
37373	SALE CREEK	97.6	96.6	1.3	1.8	0.3	0.4	0.6	1.0	5.3	5.5	5.9	6.1	4.5	24.2	33.4	13.5	1.6	79.5	44.0	49.7	50.3
37374	SEQUATCHIE	97.2	96.4	1.1	1.4	0.2	0.4	0.7	1.2	6.4	6.4	6.5	6.5	5.9	28.3	27.7	11.3	1.0	76.7	38.2	49.7	50.3
	TENNESSEE	80.2	78.4	16.4	16.9	1.0	1.5	2.2	3.4	6.5	6.4	6.5	6.8	6.5	27.2	27.0	11.4	1.7	76.6	38.0	49.0	51.0
	UNITED STATES	75.1	72.0	12.3	12.7	3.8	4.6	12.5	15.7	6.8	6.7	6.6	7.1	6.9	27.0	26.0	10.9	1.9	75.7	36.9	49.2	50.8

#	POST OFFICE NAME	2009 Per Capita Income	2009 HH Income Base	2009 Household Income Distribution (%): Less than $25,000	$25,000 to $49,999	$50,000 to $99,999	$100,000 to $149,999	$150,000 or More
37174	SPRING HILL	29360	8220	9.0	15.1	46.7	23.1	6.1
37175	STEWART	20660	598	38.3	30.6	23.2	5.0	2.8
37178	TENNESSEE RIDGE	18836	738	29.3	31.6	33.9	4.7	0.5
37179	THOMPSONS STATION	29586	4137	9.5	13.8	41.5	28.1	7.0
37180	UNIONVILLE	19581	1092	22.0	27.3	41.1	7.3	2.3
37181	VANLEER	19707	527	24.9	28.8	39.7	4.0	2.7
37183	WARTRACE	20241	1216	24.1	29.6	38.4	6.3	1.6
37184	WATERTOWN	22105	2142	24.7	25.1	41.3	6.0	2.8
37185	WAVERLY	21975	3491	28.3	29.1	34.4	6.3	2.0
37186	WESTMORELAND	17859	3604	30.0	29.9	35.0	3.6	1.4
37187	WHITE BLUFF	21962	2504	22.1	27.2	41.3	7.5	1.8
37188	WHITE HOUSE	25598	4891	11.2	22.1	48.7	14.5	3.4
37189	WHITES CREEK	27817	1269	12.9	27.0	42.6	12.4	5.0
37190	WOODBURY	19844	3354	32.3	28.3	33.1	4.5	1.8
37191	WOODLAWN	23783	1486	16.3	22.4	52.0	5.5	3.8
37201	NASHVILLE	20743	509	22.2	45.8	26.3	4.7	1.0
37203	NASHVILLE	18936	5224	47.6	28.9	18.4	3.0	2.1
37204	NASHVILLE	36661	5387	18.1	26.4	34.0	12.8	8.8
37205	NASHVILLE	61236	12352	10.7	15.6	31.6	17.9	24.3
37206	NASHVILLE	20364	11540	34.1	28.3	29.0	5.8	2.7
37207	NASHVILLE	18455	13966	33.5	30.4	27.7	5.7	2.6
37208	NASHVILLE	14276	6240	52.1	26.8	16.4	3.6	1.2
37209	NASHVILLE	24315	13964	24.6	29.2	34.5	8.3	3.5
37210	NASHVILLE	17464	6928	41.8	27.4	25.1	4.1	1.5
37211	NASHVILLE	27513	30353	18.9	29.7	37.5	9.9	3.9
37212	NASHVILLE	32291	7243	28.0	25.3	27.7	12.2	6.8
37213	NASHVILLE	8190	20	0.0	60.0	40.0	0.0	0.0
37214	NASHVILLE	32230	13514	11.7	27.3	45.7	10.9	4.4
37215	NASHVILLE	64150	10579	9.3	16.0	27.6	18.3	28.8
37216	NASHVILLE	25080	8428	22.0	29.3	38.0	7.7	3.0
37217	NASHVILLE	26207	12548	18.4	29.5	39.5	9.5	3.1
37218	NASHVILLE	22487	5379	25.4	23.0	37.3	10.5	3.8
37219	NASHVILLE	39822	850	33.6	32.7	21.6	8.5	3.5
37220	NASHVILLE	55101	2520	4.8	14.2	36.7	22.4	21.9
37221	NASHVILLE	43874	15528	8.3	17.6	38.1	19.4	16.6
37228	NASHVILLE	20423	501	58.9	26.1	12.6	0.6	1.8
37240	NASHVILLE	13417	220	46.4	52.3	1.4	0.0	0.0
37301	ALTAMONT	13507	617	43.8	32.1	19.8	3.9	0.5
37302	APISON	25908	1034	17.4	27.1	44.2	7.8	3.5
37303	ATHENS	21614	10678	30.2	27.8	33.5	5.9	2.6
37305	BEERSHEBA SPRINGS	17321	345	45.2	28.1	19.4	3.5	3.8
37306	BELVIDERE	20823	1035	24.4	29.8	37.1	5.4	3.3
37307	BENTON	20039	1954	30.7	33.8	29.1	3.9	2.5
37308	BIRCHWOOD	19547	923	23.6	31.3	39.9	3.6	1.6
37309	CALHOUN	20574	821	24.5	29.2	38.7	5.2	2.3
37310	CHARLESTON	24431	1712	22.2	24.5	41.0	9.0	3.3
37311	CLEVELAND	19514	10880	41.4	28.0	23.7	4.3	2.6
37312	CLEVELAND	27052	12346	19.1	25.7	39.4	10.6	5.2
37313	COALMONT	13763	516	46.9	32.0	18.6	2.1	0.4
37317	COPPERHILL	17852	1370	42.9	28.8	23.4	3.7	1.2
37318	COWAN	19311	907	34.2	30.3	30.0	4.4	1.1
37321	DAYTON	18704	7180	33.2	31.3	28.9	4.6	2.0
37322	DECATUR	18451	3069	33.0	30.3	31.5	3.7	1.5
37323	CLEVELAND	20415	11457	23.0	32.3	38.1	4.5	2.1
37324	DECHERD	18700	2403	33.3	31.5	29.6	4.1	1.5
37325	DELANO	21824	693	26.0	33.2	31.6	5.8	3.5
37327	DUNLAP	19907	4319	32.5	30.9	29.2	5.2	2.2
37328	ELORA	20808	570	33.5	30.7	25.8	6.0	4.0
37329	ENGLEWOOD	18645	2344	34.0	29.9	30.4	4.6	1.1
37330	ESTILL SPRINGS	22552	2810	20.9	28.4	40.8	7.2	2.7
37331	ETOWAH	19126	3510	35.7	31.3	26.8	5.1	1.1
37332	EVENSVILLE	18882	923	28.9	30.7	33.6	5.9	1.0
37333	FARNER	15415	255	47.1	34.1	15.7	2.0	1.2
37334	FAYETTEVILLE	22314	8857	30.2	28.1	31.0	7.4	3.2
37335	FLINTVILLE	20341	1061	29.3	31.3	29.9	5.2	4.3
37336	GEORGETOWN	22887	1637	24.0	27.2	38.5	7.3	3.0
37337	GRANDVIEW	20061	614	34.2	29.5	30.1	4.7	1.5
37338	GRAYSVILLE	18578	1008	28.1	32.3	34.6	4.0	1.0
37339	GRUETLI LAAGER	14322	728	44.1	33.0	19.6	2.5	0.8
37340	GUILD	23756	497	38.6	28.6	19.3	7.2	6.2
37341	HARRISON	27814	4792	12.7	23.4	48.5	10.4	4.9
37342	HILLSBORO	19513	1325	23.6	30.9	37.8	6.8	0.9
37343	HIXSON	31272	15264	12.9	23.7	41.6	13.2	8.6
37345	HUNTLAND	20313	975	31.7	25.5	34.1	5.7	3.0
37347	JASPER	21085	3365	25.1	33.6	32.8	6.9	1.6
37348	KELSO	20716	461	24.1	29.7	39.0	4.3	2.8
37350	LOOKOUT MOUNTAIN	63107	774	9.2	9.4	23.9	19.3	38.2
37352	LYNCHBURG	22130	1313	28.4	30.8	30.5	5.9	4.3
37353	MC DONALD	23473	1918	27.9	28.1	34.6	5.0	4.4
37354	MADISONVILLE	18865	6809	30.4	35.0	28.9	3.9	1.8
37355	MANCHESTER	21678	9794	26.0	27.7	37.4	6.4	2.5
37356	MONTEAGLE	19024	1054	41.1	30.3	20.2	5.1	3.3
37357	MORRISON	20190	2210	27.0	28.9	35.2	6.7	2.2
37359	MULBERRY	20868	320	25.0	28.1	39.4	4.4	3.1
37360	NORMANDY	22130	694	26.8	25.9	38.0	6.9	2.3
37361	OCOEE	21422	525	23.0	31.4	39.0	5.9	0.6
37362	OLDFORT	20252	1326	29.6	29.6	32.8	4.8	3.1
37363	OOLTEWAH	30667	10467	12.9	18.4	44.8	14.3	9.7
37365	PALMER	14428	614	46.7	31.8	18.4	2.4	0.7
37366	PELHAM	16917	320	33.4	33.8	27.8	5.0	0.0
37367	PIKEVILLE	17205	3757	36.7	30.9	26.5	3.8	2.0
37369	RELIANCE	23619	442	24.4	33.7	31.4	5.7	4.8
37370	RICEVILLE	21371	1660	23.9	31.7	36.3	6.1	1.9
37373	SALE CREEK	22432	1355	22.3	32.9	35.8	7.7	1.3
37374	SEQUATCHIE	16707	541	27.4	42.7	26.1	2.6	1.3
	TENNESSEE	24986		24.9	27.0	34.7	8.2	5.2
	UNITED STATES	27277		20.9	24.4	35.3	11.7	7.6

#	POST OFFICE NAME	Median Household Income: 2009	2014	2009 National Centile	2009 State Centile
37174	SPRING HILL	75740	75930	90	96
37175	STEWART	31217	32628	10	15
37178	TENNESSEE RIDGE	39183	41575	30	47
37179	THOMPSONS STATION	78799	81952	92	97
37180	UNIONVILLE	50546	51259	62	80
37181	VANLEER	46286	50226	52	73
37183	WARTRACE	45767	47235	51	70
37184	WATERTOWN	50150	50655	62	79
37185	WAVERLY	42625	45129	41	60
37186	WESTMORELAND	40772	43159	35	53
37187	WHITE BLUFF	50662	53051	63	80
37188	WHITE HOUSE	65712	68684	84	93
37189	WHITES CREEK	57330	58934	74	88
37190	WOODBURY	40573	43481	35	53
37191	WOODLAWN	61860	62201	80	91
37201	NASHVILLE	40443	40788	34	52
37203	NASHVILLE	26352	27613	4	5
37204	NASHVILLE	55359	57281	72	86
37205	NASHVILLE	84656	85216	94	98
37206	NASHVILLE	38194	41106	27	42
37207	NASHVILLE	37208	39577	24	37
37208	NASHVILLE	23593	24141	3	3
37209	NASHVILLE	45481	50215	50	69
37210	NASHVILLE	30753	32538	9	14
37211	NASHVILLE	51194	54179	64	80
37212	NASHVILLE	45356	50193	49	69
37213	NASHVILLE	45000	45000	48	68
37214	NASHVILLE	59359	61221	77	89
37215	NASHVILLE	92700	93906	96	99
37216	NASHVILLE	48241	51972	57	76
37217	NASHVILLE	51665	54667	65	81
37218	NASHVILLE	51439	54110	65	81
37219	NASHVILLE	35727	36851	20	28
37220	NASHVILLE	90456	91115	95	98
37221	NASHVILLE	79108	79436	92	97
37228	NASHVILLE	16836	17291	1	3
37240	NASHVILLE	28494	28694	6	9
37301	ALTAMONT	29648	31508	8	11
37302	APISON	56493	58229	73	87
37303	ATHENS	41952	44330	39	58
37305	BEERSHEBA SPRINGS	27852	28669	5	8
37306	BELVIDERE	46322	46249	52	73
37307	BENTON	38045	39440	27	41
37308	BIRCHWOOD	44878	48960	48	67
37309	CALHOUN	45703	46360	50	70
37310	CHARLESTON	52504	52272	67	82
37311	CLEVELAND	30766	33306	9	14
37312	CLEVELAND	54884	55007	71	85
37313	COALMONT	26704	27459	4	6
37317	COPPERHILL	30496	32103	9	13
37318	COWAN	35766	40573	20	28
37321	DAYTON	37645	39475	26	40
37322	DECATUR	37615	39768	26	39
37323	CLEVELAND	45333	47882	49	69
37324	DECHERD	36395	40840	22	32
37325	DELANO	41976	44905	39	58
37327	DUNLAP	39413	41280	31	48
37328	ELORA	36524	38583	22	33
37329	ENGLEWOOD	36099	38137	21	30
37330	ESTILL SPRINGS	50432	49271	62	80
37331	ETOWAH	35294	37313	19	26
37332	EVENSVILLE	40966	43082	36	54
37333	FARNER	26195	27888	4	5
37334	FAYETTEVILLE	41561	42621	38	56
37335	FLINTVILLE	39338	40586	31	48
37336	GEORGETOWN	48799	50725	58	77
37337	GRANDVIEW	35723	37597	20	28
37338	GRAYSVILLE	39930	42848	32	50
37339	GRUETLI LAAGER	28686	30874	6	9
37340	GUILD	32244	34844	12	17
37341	HARRISON	64383	64783	83	93
37342	HILLSBORO	45993	46363	51	71
37343	HIXSON	65142	65877	83	93
37345	HUNTLAND	42894	43397	42	62
37347	JASPER	42266	44272	40	60
37348	KELSO	44691	44166	47	67
37350	LOOKOUT MOUNTAIN	127864	128390	99	100
37352	LYNCHBURG	42072	44563	39	59
37353	MC DONALD	43124	46654	43	62
37354	MADISONVILLE	37389	38889	25	37
37355	MANCHESTER	45436	46777	50	69
37356	MONTEAGLE	31260	35142	10	15
37357	MORRISON	44127	45104	46	66
37359	MULBERRY	46931	46189	54	74
37360	NORMANDY	47081	47550	54	74
37361	OCOEE	45867	47586	51	71
37362	OLDFORT	42026	45438	39	59
37363	OOLTEWAH	72611	73163	88	95
37365	PALMER	26755	27892	4	6
37366	PELHAM	35127	36812	18	25
37367	PIKEVILLE	34654	35117	17	23
37369	RELIANCE	42013	44818	39	58
37370	RICEVILLE	44018	45769	45	65
37373	SALE CREEK	46587	49253	53	73
37374	SEQUATCHIE	36813	40048	23	34
	TENNESSEE	47751	50104		
	UNITED STATES	54719	56938		

#	POST OFFICE NAME	2009 Home Value Base	2009 Home Value Distribution (%): Less than $50,000	$50,000 to $89,999	$90,000 to $174,999	$175,000 to $399,999	$400,000 or More	2009 Median Home Value
37174	SPRING HILL	7293	1.9	5.9	28.4	55.9	7.8	197081
37175	STEWART	503	24.7	24.9	38.6	10.3	1.6	90500
37178	TENNESSEE RIDGE	605	16.9	33.4	43.0	6.3	0.5	89681
37179	THOMPSONS STATION	3842	3.4	7.1	17.2	59.8	12.5	213214
37180	UNIONVILLE	927	12.7	18.4	54.3	10.1	4.4	113259
37181	VANLEER	438	19.2	21.7	37.7	18.3	3.2	102308
37183	WARTRACE	1012	13.9	20.0	37.7	22.9	5.4	126296
37184	WATERTOWN	1768	11.7	23.6	34.7	23.0	7.1	119167
37185	WAVERLY	2601	18.3	24.3	37.4	18.0	2.0	101501
37186	WESTMORELAND	2889	21.9	29.6	34.5	12.7	1.2	88041
37187	WHITE BLUFF	1985	7.4	18.9	48.9	22.7	2.2	128070
37188	WHITE HOUSE	4070	2.0	4.7	52.7	37.6	2.9	161203
37189	WHITES CREEK	1005	7.2	8.9	49.3	31.3	3.4	143392
37190	WOODBURY	2508	12.5	22.3	45.4	18.1	1.7	113855
37191	WOODLAWN	1115	10.2	15.3	54.5	18.3	1.6	132959
37201	NASHVILLE	174	0.0	0.0	24.1	58.0	17.8	237179
37203	NASHVILLE	1282	6.4	26.4	45.4	18.1	3.7	113420
37204	NASHVILLE	3117	1.8	4.4	26.4	56.1	11.3	228365
37205	NASHVILLE	7768	0.5	1.5	10.7	47.7	39.6	337827
37206	NASHVILLE	5718	4.7	24.0	54.4	15.9	1.0	115442
37207	NASHVILLE	7887	10.8	24.1	55.4	9.1	0.6	104047
37208	NASHVILLE	2179	19.2	45.2	30.7	3.4	1.5	76011
37209	NASHVILLE	6899	3.1	16.3	50.3	27.5	2.8	138144
37210	NASHVILLE	2391	7.6	25.7	61.2	4.5	1.0	103807
37211	NASHVILLE	13959	2.0	7.9	59.2	29.8	1.2	144968
37212	NASHVILLE	2565	1.6	5.8	23.7	57.5	11.5	233820
37213	NASHVILLE	0	0.0	0.0	0.0	0.0	0.0	0
37214	NASHVILLE	8692	0.4	8.2	66.6	24.2	0.6	136628
37215	NASHVILLE	7625	0.1	1.6	10.4	41.0	46.9	382060
37216	NASHVILLE	5743	1.9	15.0	73.5	9.0	0.6	116388
37217	NASHVILLE	5014	2.2	7.1	64.7	25.1	0.8	142672
37218	NASHVILLE	4015	5.8	20.0	54.9	17.8	1.6	114650
37219	NASHVILLE	219	0.0	5.0	4.6	67.6	22.8	273649
37220	NASHVILLE	2237	0.0	0.5	18.6	55.7	25.2	263610
37221	NASHVILLE	11094	0.6	2.3	26.0	63.9	7.3	217441
37228	NASHVILLE	134	22.4	49.3	24.6	3.7	0.0	68000
37240	NASHVILLE	0	0.0	0.0	0.0	0.0	0.0	0
37301	ALTAMONT	533	36.6	34.7	23.1	4.3	1.3	67121
37302	APISON	776	9.4	17.9	30.7	35.1	7.0	143403
37303	ATHENS	7579	13.3	23.2	44.1	16.7	2.6	107156
37305	BEERSHEBA SPRINGS	280	38.9	32.5	25.4	2.5	0.7	61579
37306	BELVIDERE	887	13.5	20.9	40.8	18.9	5.9	109873
37307	BENTON	1528	27.4	26.2	34.8	8.4	3.1	85299
37308	BIRCHWOOD	797	15.4	24.7	33.6	21.7	4.5	108724
37309	CALHOUN	684	15.5	28.1	40.6	13.7	2.0	97719
37310	CHARLESTON	1416	14.3	18.1	39.2	22.4	6.1	125419
37311	CLEVELAND	5350	14.0	28.1	36.4	16.2	5.3	100974
37312	CLEVELAND	8634	5.2	7.5	52.9	30.8	3.6	143509
37313	COALMONT	433	32.8	31.4	29.8	5.5	0.5	70143
37317	COPPERHILL	1113	20.3	30.0	38.3	10.2	1.2	89657
37318	COWAN	632	23.6	29.0	35.1	10.4	1.9	86444
37321	DAYTON	5244	19.6	24.3	41.5	12.8	1.8	97589
37322	DECATUR	2455	23.8	23.7	36.5	14.5	1.5	93956
37323	CLEVELAND	9307	11.4	23.4	51.5	12.8	1.0	104303
37324	DECHERD	1760	20.3	28.5	40.8	8.7	1.8	91594
37325	DELANO	583	22.1	25.4	32.6	18.4	1.5	96905
37327	DUNLAP	3267	19.3	20.5	41.0	15.0	4.3	102531
37328	ELORA	449	23.2	28.7	35.2	10.7	2.2	87344
37329	ENGLEWOOD	1860	20.1	28.7	36.9	12.1	2.2	91597
37330	ESTILL SPRINGS	2378	13.2	18.2	47.7	17.0	3.9	115167
37331	ETOWAH	2640	18.1	32.4	38.3	8.7	2.5	89336
37332	EVENSVILLE	774	29.5	23.5	37.6	8.7	0.8	84524
37333	FARNER	210	43.8	31.9	22.4	1.9	0.0	54815
37334	FAYETTEVILLE	6485	15.6	25.6	40.0	17.0	1.9	99132
37335	FLINTVILLE	847	20.2	29.8	39.7	9.1	1.3	90052
37336	GEORGETOWN	1414	12.0	17.1	38.6	26.3	6.0	125989
37337	GRANDVIEW	512	27.7	22.5	35.9	10.7	3.1	89730
37338	GRAYSVILLE	829	29.3	25.9	34.0	9.7	1.1	80745
37339	GRUETLI LAAGER	623	26.8	36.3	30.3	5.5	1.1	72589
37340	GUILD	399	40.9	22.3	19.5	9.3	8.0	62125
37341	HARRISON	4096	5.7	10.4	55.0	24.0	4.9	134815
37342	HILLSBORO	1081	18.8	22.9	41.3	14.5	2.5	100690
37343	HIXSON	11738	3.2	8.6	59.2	25.9	3.1	137195
37345	HUNTLAND	785	15.2	35.2	36.8	10.3	2.5	89648
37347	JASPER	2666	18.1	24.0	42.3	14.4	1.2	100475
37348	KELSO	371	10.0	31.0	50.1	8.9	0.0	94718
37350	LOOKOUT MOUNTAIN	686	0.7	1.7	8.9	32.8	55.8	456338
37352	LYNCHBURG	1060	10.2	22.7	39.2	21.0	6.9	116346
37353	MC DONALD	1485	15.2	20.3	39.7	20.1	4.7	112670
37354	MADISONVILLE	5200	19.5	21.5	42.9	14.2	2.0	104497
37355	MANCHESTER	7098	13.9	21.4	45.4	17.3	2.0	110480
37356	MONTEAGLE	830	19.2	28.1	36.0	13.5	3.3	92949
37357	MORRISON	1778	16.5	22.3	41.6	16.8	2.8	105378
37359	MULBERRY	275	8.7	24.4	36.7	25.8	4.4	114939
37360	NORMANDY	559	17.4	18.1	35.4	24.2	5.0	120395
37361	OCOEE	389	19.3	19.8	47.6	10.8	2.6	104490
37362	OLDFORT	1075	21.6	33.7	33.3	11.2	0.3	81929
37363	OOLTEWAH	8740	11.4	7.5	40.5	33.6	7.1	152623
37365	PALMER	531	34.7	36.9	23.4	4.1	0.9	62700
37366	PELHAM	280	21.4	43.9	22.1	11.4	1.1	78182
37367	PIKEVILLE	2994	23.7	29.6	31.8	12.2	2.7	84624
37369	RELIANCE	375	22.1	31.2	31.2	12.0	3.5	84792
37370	RICEVILLE	1396	12.5	20.2	41.6	20.7	5.0	116139
37373	SALE CREEK	1184	17.7	22.9	40.5	14.1	4.8	101435
37374	SEQUATCHIE	449	23.2	30.5	40.5	4.5	1.3	85976
	TENNESSEE		12.0	19.9	40.9	22.7	4.6	120455
	UNITED STATES		9.3	13.1	31.6	32.6	13.5	162279

#	POST OFFICE NAME	FINANCIAL SERVICES: Auto Loan	FINANCIAL SERVICES: Home Loan	FINANCIAL SERVICES: Invest-ments	FINANCIAL SERVICES: Retire-ment Plans	THE HOME: Home Improvements: Home Repair	THE HOME: Home Improvements: Lawn & Garden	THE HOME: Furnishings: Comput-ers & Hard-ware-Personal	THE HOME: Furnishings: Major Appli-ances	THE HOME: Furnishings: TV, Radio, Sound Equip-ment	THE HOME: Furnishings: Furni-ture	ENTERTAINMENT: Dine out/ Carry out	ENTERTAINMENT: Sports Equip-ment	ENTERTAINMENT: Fees & Tickets	ENTERTAINMENT: Toys & Games	ENTERTAINMENT: Travel	ENTERTAINMENT: Cable TV	PERSONAL: Apparel & Services	PERSONAL: Auto Repairs	PERSONAL: Health Insur-ance	PERSONAL: Pets & Supplies
37174	SPRING HILL	125	131	109	128	124	119	119	121	116	125	117	94	120	123	117	114	81	116	113	140
37175	STEWART	75	63	84	59	68	81	62	75	67	63	65	52	56	64	65	72	44	71	81	88
37178	TENNESSEE RIDGE	82	59	74	58	60	81	62	74	69	59	67	56	50	70	58	76	45	70	79	89
37179	THOMPSONS STATION	133	143	118	138	135	124	128	129	122	135	124	102	129	130	126	117	86	122	116	148
37180	UNIONVILLE	96	77	79	75	76	91	77	86	83	77	82	64	67	86	72	88	55	82	89	103
37181	VANLEER	94	67	77	65	67	89	70	81	78	68	76	62	56	81	64	85	51	77	86	99
37183	WARTRACE	84	76	73	77	76	86	74	82	77	70	76	61	68	79	72	81	52	77	84	96
37184	WATERTOWN	95	78	82	78	78	96	78	89	83	73	82	68	68	86	75	89	55	83	93	106
37185	WAVERLY	84	67	76	67	69	85	70	80	75	66	73	59	60	76	67	81	50	76	85	94
37186	WESTMORELAND	85	61	73	60	61	82	64	75	71	62	70	58	52	74	59	78	47	71	80	91
37187	WHITE BLUFF	90	83	73	80	81	85	78	83	81	81	81	60	74	84	74	83	55	80	83	98
37188	WHITE HOUSE	110	117	96	113	110	102	104	106	101	111	102	82	106	107	103	97	71	101	96	122
37189	WHITES CREEK	95	105	91	105	100	106	96	98	98	96	98	74	103	100	99	100	68	97	104	116
37190	WOODBURY	81	61	70	61	62	79	66	74	72	62	70	56	55	73	61	78	47	71	80	89
37191	WOODLAWN	100	103	85	99	98	90	93	94	90	100	91	73	93	96	90	87	63	90	85	108
37201	NASHVILLE	72	51	52	59	49	49	77	58	75	72	78	53	67	76	65	73	55	70	60	75
37203	NASHVILLE	53	39	39	43	37	43	56	45	58	52	58	38	49	56	47	60	41	53	53	58
37204	NASHVILLE	104	103	103	106	103	102	110	104	108	108	108	81	109	107	108	107	76	107	106	123
37205	NASHVILLE	167	182	196	190	188	172	182	173	175	187	177	137	195	174	189	171	128	176	169	201
37206	NASHVILLE	70	61	54	63	58	65	71	65	74	67	73	51	67	73	64	77	51	70	73	80
37207	NASHVILLE	72	65	55	66	60	69	69	66	73	69	73	51	67	74	64	76	50	70	73	82
37208	NASHVILLE	50	38	36	40	36	44	49	44	53	47	52	33	43	51	42	56	36	49	53	56
37209	NASHVILLE	83	73	68	76	71	76	84	77	86	82	86	61	80	86	78	87	60	83	84	94
37210	NASHVILLE	59	50	45	52	48	53	61	54	63	58	62	43	56	62	54	64	43	60	61	67
37211	NASHVILLE	93	77	70	81	73	76	93	81	92	91	93	67	85	94	83	91	65	89	84	99
37212	NASHVILLE	96	78	77	84	75	78	107	84	102	97	103	73	94	101	91	100	73	97	88	106
37213	NASHVILLE	68	43	37	48	39	49	67	53	75	63	73	43	57	73	52	79	52	65	64	71
37214	NASHVILLE	99	93	86	95	91	94	100	95	100	98	100	74	97	101	96	101	70	99	100	113
37215	NASHVILLE	178	202	223	209	212	196	197	192	191	203	192	148	216	187	209	189	139	193	193	222
37216	NASHVILLE	81	81	69	82	76	85	82	80	85	79	84	62	82	85	80	88	58	82	89	97
37217	NASHVILLE	92	71	65	75	68	69	91	77	90	89	91	64	81	92	79	88	63	87	79	95
37218	NASHVILLE	86	87	83	87	84	94	84	87	88	83	88	64	86	87	85	92	60	87	96	104
37219	NASHVILLE	71	52	54	60	50	50	77	58	75	71	77	53	68	75	66	72	55	70	60	75
37220	NASHVILLE	165	210	228	212	223	208	179	194	176	192	175	140	210	171	207	176	126	183	194	217
37221	NASHVILLE	144	145	136	151	143	137	146	139	143	150	144	111	149	146	144	140	102	141	136	163
37228	NASHVILLE	34	25	29	28	25	30	40	32	43	36	43	25	35	38	35	46	30	40	44	42
37240	NASHVILLE	39	17	16	21	15	19	55	27	44	37	45	30	33	43	30	40	32	39	27	37
37301	ALTAMONT	66	47	56	46	47	63	49	58	55	48	54	44	39	57	45	60	36	55	61	70
37302	APISON	94	98	89	102	97	103	91	97	91	88	91	75	92	93	94	93	63	92	98	114
37303	ATHENS	80	68	68	69	67	80	72	76	76	67	74	58	65	77	68	80	51	75	82	91
37305	BEERSHEBA SPRINGS	79	52	75	49	52	77	55	69	64	53	62	54	42	65	51	71	41	65	73	85
37306	BELVIDERE	95	73	87	72	74	95	74	88	81	70	79	67	62	82	71	87	53	82	92	105
37307	BENTON	87	63	72	61	62	83	65	76	72	63	71	58	52	75	59	79	48	72	80	92
37308	BIRCHWOOD	85	72	74	73	72	87	72	81	75	67	74	62	64	78	70	80	51	76	84	96
37309	CALHOUN	96	69	79	67	68	91	71	83	79	70	78	64	57	83	65	86	52	79	88	101
37310	CHARLESTON	95	89	85	91	89	100	86	94	88	81	87	72	81	90	86	92	60	89	96	111
37311	CLEVELAND	66	55	54	56	54	62	65	62	67	60	66	48	57	67	58	70	46	65	68	75
37312	CLEVELAND	99	98	93	100	98	103	95	99	96	93	96	75	94	97	96	98	66	97	102	117
37313	COALMONT	63	44	55	42	44	61	46	55	52	44	51	43	36	53	42	57	34	52	58	67
37317	COPPERHILL	70	50	68	49	52	71	53	66	59	49	58	49	43	59	51	65	38	61	70	78
37318	COWAN	79	57	72	55	57	78	60	72	67	56	65	55	48	68	57	74	44	68	78	86
37321	DAYTON	83	60	69	58	60	79	63	73	70	61	68	56	51	72	57	76	46	69	77	88
37322	DECATUR	83	59	68	58	59	79	62	72	69	60	67	55	50	72	56	75	45	68	76	88
37323	CLEVELAND	90	70	76	69	70	87	72	81	78	69	76	62	61	80	67	83	51	77	85	98
37324	DECHERD	78	55	74	53	56	78	59	72	66	55	64	54	47	66	56	72	43	67	77	86
37325	DELANO	98	70	89	68	71	96	72	88	80	69	79	67	58	82	68	88	53	82	92	106
37327	DUNLAP	88	63	73	61	63	84	66	76	73	64	71	59	53	76	60	79	48	72	81	93
37328	ELORA	89	64	73	62	63	84	66	77	73	64	72	59	53	77	60	80	48	73	81	94
37329	ENGLEWOOD	79	59	67	58	59	77	61	71	67	59	66	54	50	69	57	73	44	67	75	86
37330	ESTILL SPRINGS	94	79	83	80	80	95	79	89	83	75	82	67	70	85	76	88	56	84	92	106
37331	ETOWAH	76	55	74	53	57	78	59	72	66	54	64	54	47	65	57	72	42	67	78	86
37332	EVENSVILLE	85	61	70	60	61	81	64	74	71	62	69	57	51	74	58	77	47	70	78	90
37333	FARNER	70	51	58	49	50	67	53	61	58	51	57	47	42	61	48	64	38	58	65	75
37334	FAYETTEVILLE	86	71	78	72	72	89	73	83	78	68	76	63	64	79	71	84	52	79	88	98
37335	FLINTVILLE	94	68	77	66	67	89	70	82	78	68	76	63	57	81	64	85	51	77	86	99
37336	GEORGETOWN	93	85	83	86	84	96	82	90	85	79	84	69	77	87	81	89	58	85	92	107
37337	GRANDVIEW	81	58	73	57	59	79	60	73	67	58	66	55	48	69	57	73	44	68	76	88
37338	GRAYSVILLE	84	61	70	59	61	80	63	73	70	61	69	56	51	73	58	76	46	69	77	89
37339	GRUETLI LAAGER	65	47	55	45	46	62	49	57	54	47	53	44	39	56	44	59	36	54	60	69
37340	GUILD	103	71	107	67	72	103	74	94	84	70	82	72	58	84	72	92	54	88	97	114
37341	HARRISON	105	115	101	115	111	113	103	108	103	104	104	81	108	106	107	105	72	104	108	126
37342	HILLSBORO	95	68	79	67	68	91	71	83	79	69	77	64	57	82	65	86	52	78	87	101
37343	HIXSON	112	119	112	118	117	118	110	114	110	112	111	86	114	112	113	112	77	111	115	133
37345	HUNTLAND	92	66	76	65	66	88	69	80	77	67	75	62	55	80	63	84	50	76	85	98
37347	JASPER	86	68	76	67	68	85	69	79	74	66	73	60	59	76	65	80	49	75	83	95
37348	KELSO	98	71	82	70	71	94	74	86	81	71	80	66	60	85	68	89	54	81	91	104
37350	LOOKOUT MOUNTAIN	189	264	320	271	295	245	222	237	203	248	200	175	271	195	267	193	151	219	212	259
37352	LYNCHBURG	92	70	91	69	72	96	72	89	79	66	77	67	60	79	71	86	52	82	94	105
37353	MC DONALD	96	78	83	78	78	96	78	89	84	75	82	68	68	87	75	90	56	84	93	107
37354	MADISONVILLE	79	58	67	57	58	77	62	71	69	59	67	54	51	70	57	74	45	68	76	86
37355	MANCHESTER	88	72	75	72	72	86	75	82	80	72	79	62	66	81	71	85	53	79	87	98
37356	MONTEAGLE	79	56	80	54	57	80	59	74	66	54	64	56	46	65	57	72	42	68	78	88
37357	MORRISON	87	70	73	69	70	85	70	79	75	69	74	60	61	78	66	80	50	75	82	95
37359	MULBERRY	93	69	95	67	71	95	70	88	77	65	76	66	57	77	70	85	50	81	92	105
37360	NORMANDY	90	75	77	75	75	91	75	85	80	71	79	65	66	82	72	85	53	80	88	101
37361	OCOEE	91	65	75	64	65	87	68	79	76	66	74	61	55	79	62	82	50	75	84	96
37362	OLDFORT	91	65	75	63	65	86	68	79	75	66	74	61	54	78	62	82	50	75	83	96
37363	OOLTEWAH	124	132	122	131	129	125	119	124	117	124	118	95	123	121	122	116	83	118	118	144
37365	PALMER	63	43	57	41	43	61	46	55	52	44	50	43	35	53	42	57	34	52	58	68
37366	PELHAM	72	52	60	50	52	69	54	63	60	52	59	48	43	62	49	65	39	60	67	77
37367	PIKEVILLE	79	57	67	55	57	76	59	70	66	57	64	53	48	68	54	72	43	66	74	84
37369	RELIANCE	97	69	87	67	70	94	72	87	80	69	78	66	58	82	68	87	52	81	91	104
37370	RICEVILLE	94	72	79	72	72	92	74	85	80	70	79	65	62	83	69	87	53	80	89	102
37373	SALE CREEK	95	70	91	68	71	95	71	88	79	67	77	66	58	80	69	86	51	81	92	105
37374	SEQUATCHIE	76	55	63	53	54	72	57	66	63	55	62	51	46	66	52	69	42	63	70	81
	TENNESSEE	95	84	85	84	82	93	87	90	90	85	89	69	80	91	83	93	61	89	93	107
	UNITED STATES	100	100	100	100	100	100	100	100	100	100	100	100	100	100	100	100	100	100	100	100

POPULATION CHANGE

ZIP CODE #	POST OFFICE NAME	COUNTY FIPS CODE	POPULATION 2000	POPULATION 2009	POPULATION 2014	2000-2009 ANNUAL RATE % Rate	2000-2009 ANNUAL RATE State Centile	HOUSEHOLDS 2000	HOUSEHOLDS 2009	HOUSEHOLDS 2014	HOUSEHOLDS % Annual Rate 2000-2009	HOUSEHOLDS 2009 Average HH Size	FAMILIES 2000	FAMILIES 2009	FAMILIES % Annual Rate 2000-2009
37375	SEWANEE	051	3643	4202	4375	1.6	82	1026	1237	1325	2.0	2.22	667	778	1.7
37376	SHERWOOD	051	502	554	580	1.1	69	211	241	255	1.4	2.30	154	172	1.2
37377	SIGNAL MOUNTAIN	065	15881	16749	17357	0.6	47	6346	6875	7182	0.9	2.42	4497	4728	0.5
37379	SODDY DAISY	065	23316	26745	28197	1.5	81	8864	10476	11135	1.8	2.54	6942	8010	1.6
37380	SOUTH PITTSBURG	115	6229	6222	6159	0.0	18	2469	2531	2528	0.3	2.40	1725	1717	-0.1
37381	SPRING CITY	143	8565	9283	9610	0.9	63	3548	3952	4130	1.2	2.31	2529	2741	0.9
37385	TELLICO PLAINS	123	7653	9082	9864	1.9	88	2999	3677	4031	2.2	2.47	2253	2698	2.0
37387	TRACY CITY	061	4563	4545	4513	0.0	18	1802	1868	1881	0.4	2.42	1284	1297	0.1
37388	TULLAHOMA	031	23899	25370	26087	0.6	47	9541	10309	10658	0.8	2.43	6809	7178	0.6
37391	TURTLETOWN	139	1284	1252	1235	-0.3	7	547	555	554	0.2	2.26	403	399	-0.1
37397	WHITWELL	115	9758	10877	11351	1.2	72	3854	4470	4721	1.6	2.43	2885	3266	1.4
37398	WINCHESTER	051	13195	14110	14409	0.7	53	5249	5746	5915	1.0	2.40	3826	4103	0.8
37402	CHATTANOOGA	065	4185	4452	4575	0.7	53	2377	2514	2604	0.6	1.53	607	582	-0.5
37403	CHATTANOOGA	065	3937	4593	4804	1.7	84	1253	1533	1653	2.2	1.71	405	460	1.4
37404	CHATTANOOGA	065	14773	14610	14545	-0.1	13	5441	5385	5376	-0.1	2.52	3375	3196	-0.6
37405	CHATTANOOGA	115	13727	14172	14483	0.3	31	6506	6882	7096	0.6	2.00	3293	3288	0.0
37406	CHATTANOOGA	065	14327	13939	13886	-0.3	7	5535	5521	5547	0.0	2.49	3819	3672	-0.4
37407	CHATTANOOGA	065	7807	7992	8173	0.3	31	3180	3284	3370	0.3	2.43	1989	1968	-0.1
37408	CHATTANOOGA	065	1935	1922	1912	-0.1	13	708	684	680	-0.4	2.68	388	355	-1.0
37409	CHATTANOOGA	065	3199	3243	3311	0.1	22	1268	1300	1330	0.3	2.49	790	776	-0.2
37410	CHATTANOOGA	065	4502	4351	4310	-0.4	5	1680	1655	1650	-0.2	2.58	1131	1072	-0.6
37411	CHATTANOOGA	065	17372	17569	17866	0.1	22	7390	7620	7792	0.3	2.30	4729	4681	-0.1
37412	CHATTANOOGA	065	20471	20684	21096	0.1	22	9201	9553	9816	0.4	2.14	5693	5663	-0.1
37415	CHATTANOOGA	065	22728	23790	24510	0.5	41	10592	11398	11834	0.8	2.08	6259	6416	0.3
37416	CHATTANOOGA	065	14577	15198	15666	0.5	41	5987	6425	6679	0.8	2.36	4234	4388	0.4
37419	CHATTANOOGA	065	5523	5915	6152	0.7	53	2334	2592	2720	1.1	2.28	1627	1743	0.7
37421	CHATTANOOGA	065	39642	44675	46926	1.3	76	16287	18894	20017	1.6	2.27	10730	12076	1.3
37601	JOHNSON CITY	179	33216	35677	36754	0.8	60	14380	15475	16048	0.8	2.22	9061	9373	0.4
37604	JOHNSON CITY	179	33205	34839	35966	0.5	41	13790	14658	15227	0.7	2.18	7960	8111	0.2
37615	JOHNSON CITY	179	15164	18211	19582	2.0	90	6166	7515	8135	2.2	2.40	4460	5266	1.8
37616	AFTON	059	4857	5322	5533	1.0	66	1814	2035	2136	1.3	2.50	1317	1440	1.0
37617	BLOUNTVILLE	163	13151	13637	13929	0.4	36	5085	5495	5679	0.8	2.41	3850	4059	0.6
37618	BLUFF CITY	163	12067	12823	13166	0.7	53	4812	5313	5516	1.1	2.41	3647	3921	0.8
37620	BRISTOL	163	38809	38733	38834	0.0	18	16276	16848	17058	0.4	2.23	11040	11110	0.1
37640	BUTLER	091	3720	3960	4042	0.7	53	1573	1730	1785	1.0	2.24	1138	1220	0.8
37641	CHUCKEY	059	7289	7794	8027	0.7	53	2910	3174	3298	0.9	2.43	2153	2284	0.6
37642	CHURCH HILL	073	13752	14696	15166	0.7	53	5620	6204	6474	1.1	2.35	4188	4511	0.8
37643	ELIZABETHTON	019	33608	34448	34561	0.3	31	14042	14455	14630	0.3	2.28	9793	9815	0.0
37645	MOUNT CARMEL	073	6453	6679	6806	0.4	36	2648	2823	2906	0.7	2.33	1920	1995	0.4
37650	ERWIN	171	12180	11957	11774	-0.2	10	5221	5291	5261	0.1	2.21	3564	3505	-0.2
37656	FALL BRANCH	179	3299	3558	3724	0.8	60	1365	1495	1575	1.0	2.38	1051	1119	0.7
37657	FLAG POND	171	1045	961	928	-0.9	1	453	434	424	-0.5	2.21	322	300	-0.8
37658	HAMPTON	019	4305	4578	4702	0.7	53	1831	2013	2087	1.0	2.27	1306	1398	0.7
37659	JONESBOROUGH	179	23677	27622	29730	1.7	84	9287	10966	11875	1.8	2.49	7075	8111	1.5
37660	KINGSPORT	163	39432	40335	40838	0.2	27	16879	17931	18357	0.7	2.21	11395	11733	0.3
37663	KINGSPORT	163	14779	15259	15582	0.3	31	5841	6227	6420	0.7	2.43	4501	4681	0.4
37664	KINGSPORT	163	26301	26760	27012	0.2	27	11050	11622	11846	0.5	2.27	7758	7953	0.3
37665	KINGSPORT	163	4651	4629	4622	-0.1	13	2032	2098	2118	0.3	2.20	1383	1382	0.0
37680	LAUREL BLOOMERY	091	911	1038	1088	1.4	78	373	435	460	1.7	2.39	271	308	1.4
37681	LIMESTONE	179	5465	6054	6407	1.1	69	2129	2404	2566	1.3	2.47	1585	1737	1.0
37683	MOUNTAIN CITY	091	12120	12782	12851	0.6	47	4568	4915	5001	0.8	2.26	3133	3276	0.5
37686	PINEY FLATS	163	6913	7540	7811	0.9	63	2741	3074	3211	1.2	2.45	2067	2260	1.0
37687	ROAN MOUNTAIN	019	5231	6115	6360	1.7	84	2024	2341	2468	1.6	2.36	1477	1665	1.3
37688	SHADY VALLEY	091	1123	1169	1175	0.4	36	477	518	526	0.9	2.26	349	370	0.6
37690	TELFORD	179	3601	4211	4553	1.7	84	1394	1654	1801	1.9	2.55	1085	1251	1.6
37691	TRADE	091	885	998	1044	1.3	76	366	428	453	1.7	2.33	255	290	1.4
37692	UNICOI	171	4487	4806	4839	0.7	53	1853	2050	2085	1.1	2.34	1351	1456	0.8
37694	WATAUGA	019	1651	1715	1743	0.4	36	653	696	714	0.7	2.46	492	512	0.4
37701	ALCOA	009	6223	6507	6774	0.5	41	2769	2932	3068	0.6	2.22	1766	1789	0.1
37705	ANDERSONVILLE	001	5768	6229	6429	0.8	60	2235	2447	2535	1.0	2.53	1667	1781	0.7
37708	BEAN STATION	057	6146	6473	6693	0.6	47	2471	2702	2823	1.0	2.39	1852	1980	0.7
37709	BLAINE	057	3182	3270	3358	0.3	31	1259	1341	1391	0.7	2.44	949	989	0.4
37710	BRICEVILLE	001	1744	1791	1806	0.3	31	659	689	700	0.5	2.60	502	513	0.2
37711	BULLS GAP	073	4550	5093	5345	1.2	72	1796	2060	2179	1.5	2.47	1332	1490	1.2
37713	BYBEE	029	1532	1621	1658	0.6	47	619	674	698	0.9	2.41	464	493	0.7
37714	CARYVILLE	013	4368	4622	4725	0.6	47	1754	1931	1999	1.0	2.39	1272	1361	0.7
37715	CLAIRFIELD	025	1100	1127	1114	0.3	31	415	444	444	0.7	2.54	327	344	0.5
37716	CLINTON	001	24227	25336	25840	0.5	41	9994	10606	10874	0.6	2.37	7098	7345	0.4
37721	CORRYTON	093	9876	11721	12610	1.9	88	3801	4633	5025	2.2	2.53	3004	3565	1.9
37722	COSBY	029	4706	5296	5590	1.3	76	1895	2199	2344	1.6	2.41	1380	1557	1.3
37723	CRAB ORCHARD	035	1011	1114	1180	1.1	69	403	464	496	1.5	2.40	307	344	1.2
37724	CUMBERLAND GAP	025	3157	3241	3226	0.3	31	1137	1213	1222	0.7	2.44	869	907	0.5
37725	DANDRIDGE	089	13229	16490	18244	2.4	92	5210	6618	7372	2.6	2.44	3932	4877	2.4
37726	DEER LODGE	129	1691	1748	1779	0.4	36	636	678	696	0.7	2.52	471	490	0.4
37727	DEL RIO	029	1995	2116	2177	0.6	47	813	895	930	1.0	2.36	580	621	0.7
37729	DUFF	013	1657	1745	1783	0.6	47	635	699	725	1.0	2.50	473	507	0.8
37731	EIDSON	073	710	716	730	0.1	22	297	311	320	0.5	2.30	202	205	0.2
37737	FRIENDSVILLE	009	5500	6473	7130	1.8	86	2118	2516	2780	1.9	2.57	1673	1937	1.6
37738	GATLINBURG	155	4362	4950	5291	1.4	78	1971	2257	2422	1.5	2.17	1296	1433	1.1
37742	GREENBACK	105	4342	5696	6265	3.0	95	1671	2209	2441	3.1	2.58	1320	1711	2.8
37743	GREENEVILLE	059	23924	25705	26447	0.8	60	9817	10765	11167	1.0	2.32	6866	7325	0.7
37745	GREENEVILLE	059	16795	17727	18107	0.6	47	7250	7794	8015	0.8	2.19	4841	5052	0.5
37748	HARRIMAN	145	19063	19330	19530	0.2	27	7759	8096	8251	0.5	2.36	5473	5562	0.2
37752	HARROGATE	025	5226	5544	5566	0.6	47	2040	2246	2280	1.0	2.42	1522	1639	0.8
37753	HARTFORD	029	807	834	850	0.4	36	330	355	365	0.8	2.35	233	243	0.5
37754	HEISKELL	001	4550	4913	5115	0.8	60	1697	1870	1960	1.1	2.60	1346	1447	0.8
37755	HELENWOOD	151	3351	3453	3509	0.3	31	1301	1401	1442	0.8	2.42	965	1017	0.6
37756	HUNTSVILLE	151	2752	2829	2877	0.3	31	1020	1100	1132	0.8	2.50	770	815	0.6
37757	JACKSBORO	013	8371	9126	9424	0.9	63	3303	3758	3934	1.4	2.39	2491	2764	1.1
37760	JEFFERSON CITY	089	12248	13866	14825	1.4	78	4619	5390	5816	1.7	2.36	3132	3555	1.4
37762	JELLICO	013	3255	3388	3428	0.4	36	1345	1443	1476	0.8	2.27	894	930	0.4
37763	KINGSTON	145	13961	15055	15543	0.8	60	5762	6363	6624	1.1	2.34	4183	4504	0.8
37764	KODAK	155	7828	9310	10146	1.9	88	2970	3549	3881	1.9	2.62	2335	2728	1.7
37765	KYLES FORD	067	846	815	803	-0.4	5	346	345	343	0.0	2.36	242	236	-0.3
37766	LA FOLLETTE	013	18982	18995	19011	0.0	18	7798	8116	8225	0.4	2.31	5485	5559	0.1
	TENNESSEE					1.1					1.3	2.44			1.0
	UNITED STATES					1.0					1.1	2.59			0.9

#	POST OFFICE NAME	RACE (%) White 2000	White 2009	Black 2000	Black 2009	Asian/Pacific 2000	Asian/Pacific 2009	% Hispanic Origin 2000	% Hispanic Origin 2009	2009 AGE DISTRIBUTION (%) 0-4	5-9	10-14	15-19	20-24	25-44	45-64	65-84	85+	18+	MEDIAN AGE 2009	% 2009 Males	% 2009 Females
37375	SEWANEE	94.4	93.5	3.8	4.1	0.7	1.0	1.4	2.2	3.4	3.4	3.5	16.6	23.5	15.2	22.4	10.3	1.7	87.4	24.9	47.7	52.3
37376	SHERWOOD	98.2	97.8	0.0	0.0	0.0	0.0	1.0	1.4	5.4	6.0	5.8	5.1	4.2	22.7	34.5	13.9	2.5	79.8	45.6	48.2	51.8
37377	SIGNAL MOUNTAIN	97.5	96.4	0.9	1.2	0.5	0.8	0.9	1.5	5.3	5.8	6.9	6.5	4.5	23.1	30.7	13.8	3.5	77.9	43.5	48.8	51.2
37379	SODDY DAISY	97.4	96.3	1.4	2.0	0.3	0.4	0.7	1.2	6.2	6.4	6.7	6.2	4.5	27.0	29.7	11.9	1.4	76.9	40.3	48.9	51.1
37380	SOUTH PITTSBURG	88.6	87.1	9.9	11.0	0.2	0.3	0.6	0.9	5.8	5.9	6.4	6.4	5.4	24.1	29.1	14.5	2.4	78.1	41.8	48.5	51.5
37381	SPRING CITY	96.6	95.8	1.8	2.0	0.1	0.2	1.0	1.7	5.2	5.4	5.8	5.6	4.6	23.0	31.7	16.2	2.4	80.0	45.2	49.1	50.9
37385	TELLICO PLAINS	98.1	97.6	0.2	0.2	0.2	0.3	0.9	1.4	6.1	6.2	6.5	6.5	5.3	26.4	28.6	12.9	1.4	77.2	40.1	50.4	49.6
37387	TRACY CITY	98.1	98.1	0.1	0.1	0.2	0.2	0.6	0.7	6.6	6.7	6.8	6.4	4.9	26.0	28.0	13.0	1.7	76.0	39.5	49.3	50.7
37388	TULLAHOMA	91.4	89.7	5.4	6.0	0.9	1.4	1.5	2.4	6.6	6.6	6.7	6.8	5.7	24.9	27.6	13.2	2.0	75.9	39.6	48.5	51.5
37391	TURTLETOWN	97.9	97.8	0.2	0.2	0.1	0.1	0.5	0.6	5.5	5.8	6.1	5.1	3.7	23.2	30.7	17.9	2.1	79.3	45.5	50.9	49.1
37397	WHITWELL	98.0	97.5	1.1	1.3	0.1	0.1	0.7	1.2	6.2	6.4	6.6	6.3	5.0	26.8	29.1	12.3	1.3	76.8	39.7	49.3	50.7
37398	WINCHESTER	88.7	86.7	8.5	9.3	0.5	0.7	1.9	2.9	6.1	6.3	6.3	5.9	5.0	23.9	28.7	15.2	2.7	77.6	42.3	48.2	51.8
37402	CHATTANOOGA	37.0	30.4	59.8	66.0	1.0	1.1	2.6	3.3	6.3	4.6	2.8	4.6	9.5	25.4	23.8	16.8	6.2	84.7	42.2	46.8	53.2
37403	CHATTANOOGA	44.0	34.4	51.6	60.2	1.8	2.3	1.7	2.5	2.6	2.2	2.4	18.5	24.6	19.7	17.9	9.4	2.7	91.0	24.9	47.9	52.1
37404	CHATTANOOGA	30.6	25.8	63.0	66.1	1.3	1.6	6.0	8.0	6.3	6.6	6.7	8.6	8.9	24.1	24.7	10.9	3.3	76.0	35.3	47.9	52.1
37405	CHATTANOOGA	85.5	81.0	10.8	13.9	1.5	2.2	1.4	2.4	5.1	4.7	4.5	5.2	9.2	31.7	24.9	11.9	2.9	83.1	37.4	48.3	51.7
37406	CHATTANOOGA	17.8	14.6	80.4	83.5	0.2	0.3	0.9	1.1	7.5	7.5	7.2	7.6	6.6	22.9	26.2	12.3	2.1	73.1	37.0	44.4	55.6
37407	CHATTANOOGA	65.4	57.9	29.9	35.9	0.7	1.0	2.6	4.1	7.7	6.6	6.5	6.6	7.5	25.2	26.5	11.5	1.8	75.5	37.1	47.7	52.3
37408	CHATTANOOGA	10.3	8.5	83.4	83.5	1.1	1.3	6.3	8.4	9.6	12.2	9.7	7.2	7.4	22.5	20.5	9.4	1.6	63.9	27.5	52.3	47.7
37409	CHATTANOOGA	54.5	47.5	40.5	46.3	0.6	0.7	4.1	5.9	6.2	6.2	6.1	6.2	6.5	28.2	27.7	11.0	1.8	77.8	37.9	50.5	49.5
37410	CHATTANOOGA	6.1	4.7	91.5	92.6	0.5	0.5	1.9	2.2	10.0	10.5	8.7	7.8	7.6	21.7	21.6	10.3	1.7	65.8	29.1	43.9	56.1
37411	CHATTANOOGA	42.9	36.9	54.2	59.5	0.9	1.1	1.3	1.9	6.0	5.9	6.2	6.5	6.8	27.2	28.3	11.1	2.1	77.9	38.8	47.2	52.8
37412	CHATTANOOGA	93.4	90.7	3.1	4.2	1.7	2.6	1.1	1.9	5.3	5.2	5.1	5.3	5.7	27.6	26.8	15.7	3.2	81.2	41.9	47.5	52.5
37415	CHATTANOOGA	89.5	85.4	6.4	8.7	1.2	1.8	2.2	3.6	5.8	5.6	5.5	5.5	6.2	27.9	26.6	14.4	2.6	80.0	40.1	48.3	51.7
37416	CHATTANOOGA	59.8	53.0	37.3	43.3	1.2	1.6	1.1	1.8	5.9	5.9	6.1	6.3	5.7	27.1	28.4	13.1	1.5	78.4	40.1	47.2	52.8
37419	CHATTANOOGA	98.0	97.2	0.3	0.4	0.6	0.9	0.5	0.7	5.1	5.4	5.6	5.3	4.8	24.0	31.2	16.7	2.0	80.5	44.9	48.7	51.3
37421	CHATTANOOGA	81.5	76.1	13.4	16.7	2.8	4.1	1.7	2.7	5.4	5.5	5.7	5.8	5.6	27.6	28.2	13.5	2.8	79.9	41.1	48.5	51.5
37601	JOHNSON CITY	92.6	90.8	4.7	5.4	0.6	0.9	1.5	2.5	5.9	5.6	5.3	6.7	7.2	27.3	26.5	13.0	2.5	79.7	38.9	47.8	52.2
37604	JOHNSON CITY	90.1	87.9	6.3	7.0	1.4	2.1	1.9	3.1	4.9	4.7	4.7	7.5	10.0	26.5	25.5	13.5	2.8	82.7	38.2	48.8	51.2
37615	JOHNSON CITY	97.3	96.3	0.9	1.1	0.7	1.1	0.9	1.5	6.3	6.1	6.2	5.6	5.5	29.7	28.6	10.7	1.2	77.8	39.0	49.3	50.7
37616	AFTON	97.4	96.7	1.2	1.3	0.3	0.5	1.3	2.0	5.6	5.7	6.0	6.4	5.5	27.6	28.8	13.1	1.3	79.1	40.6	50.6	49.4
37617	BLOUNTVILLE	98.5	98.0	0.5	0.5	0.2	0.4	0.7	1.2	5.6	5.9	6.2	6.1	4.6	27.1	29.5	13.5	1.6	78.6	41.6	50.6	49.4
37618	BLUFF CITY	98.4	98.0	0.5	0.6	0.3	0.4	0.4	0.7	5.4	5.8	6.2	6.1	4.6	26.9	30.6	13.1	1.2	78.8	41.7	50.6	49.4
37620	BRISTOL	96.1	95.2	2.4	2.7	0.5	0.7	0.6	1.0	5.3	5.4	5.7	6.5	5.6	24.7	29.1	15.6	2.2	80.0	42.7	48.8	51.2
37640	BUTLER	98.4	98.0	0.6	0.6	0.1	0.2	0.6	1.0	5.2	5.4	5.6	5.3	4.5	26.8	30.4	15.0	1.8	80.6	43.1	52.1	47.9
37641	CHUCKEY	98.1	97.3	0.5	0.7	0.2	0.3	1.4	2.3	5.6	5.7	6.1	6.2	5.0	27.1	29.7	13.0	1.6	78.7	41.3	49.8	50.2
37642	CHURCH HILL	97.9	97.4	1.2	1.4	0.2	0.2	0.6	1.0	6.0	6.1	6.4	6.0	4.8	27.2	28.9	13.0	1.6	77.8	41.0	48.8	51.2
37643	ELIZABETHTON	97.3	96.5	1.2	1.3	0.3	0.5	0.9	1.4	5.4	5.5	5.7	5.8	5.3	26.7	28.2	15.0	2.4	79.8	42.0	49.2	50.8
37645	MOUNT CARMEL	95.2	94.1	2.9	3.3	0.7	1.1	0.9	1.4	6.6	6.6	6.8	6.3	4.8	25.8	27.9	12.7	2.4	75.8	40.3	47.3	52.7
37650	ERWIN	97.9	97.8	0.1	0.1	0.1	0.1	2.0	2.1	5.5	5.6	5.7	5.0	4.6	23.7	29.0	17.7	3.2	80.2	44.9	48.3	51.7
37656	FALL BRANCH	99.1	98.7	0.2	0.2	0.1	0.1	0.5	0.8	5.4	5.8	6.3	5.9	4.3	24.1	33.5	13.1	1.5	78.8	43.9	49.9	50.1
37657	FLAG POND	99.0	99.0	0.0	0.0	0.0	0.0	0.7	0.7	4.6	4.9	5.3	5.1	5.2	24.6	31.7	16.4	2.2	82.0	45.2	49.6	50.4
37658	HAMPTON	99.0	98.6	0.0	0.0	0.1	0.1	0.7	1.0	5.4	5.6	5.9	5.5	4.5	27.5	30.4	13.7	1.6	79.7	42.4	50.0	50.0
37659	JONESBOROUGH	97.2	96.4	1.5	1.8	0.3	0.5	0.8	1.3	6.1	6.4	6.8	6.1	4.4	27.1	30.0	11.7	1.4	76.9	40.6	49.9	50.1
37660	KINGSPORT	94.5	93.5	3.5	3.8	0.6	0.9	0.9	1.5	5.5	5.4	5.6	5.8	5.1	23.9	28.7	17.0	2.9	79.9	44.0	47.3	52.7
37663	KINGSPORT	97.8	97.2	0.7	0.8	0.6	0.8	0.6	1.0	5.3	5.8	6.5	6.3	3.9	24.1	31.6	14.8	1.8	78.3	43.8	48.8	51.2
37664	KINGSPORT	96.8	96.0	1.5	1.7	0.5	0.7	0.8	1.3	5.4	5.7	6.1	5.8	4.5	23.5	29.9	16.2	2.9	79.1	44.2	47.2	52.8
37665	KINGSPORT	97.9	97.3	0.8	1.0	0.1	0.1	0.7	1.1	5.7	5.5	5.6	5.9	5.2	25.0	27.9	16.7	2.6	79.7	43.1	47.8	52.2
37680	LAUREL BLOOMERY	97.4	96.9	1.2	1.3	0.2	0.4	0.7	1.3	6.2	6.5	6.6	5.8	4.7	24.8	30.6	13.6	1.3	77.3	42.0	49.0	51.0
37681	LIMESTONE	98.0	97.4	0.8	1.0	0.1	0.2	1.3	2.2	5.6	5.8	6.1	6.0	4.8	26.6	29.9	13.2	2.1	78.8	42.0	49.8	50.2
37683	MOUNTAIN CITY	95.6	94.8	3.2	3.6	0.2	0.2	0.8	1.3	4.6	4.8	5.0	5.1	4.9	30.0	28.8	14.6	2.2	82.5	42.3	55.5	44.5
37686	PINEY FLATS	98.8	98.5	0.3	0.3	0.2	0.2	0.5	0.8	5.8	6.2	6.6	5.8	4.0	27.3	31.3	11.9	1.2	77.8	41.5	50.1	49.9
37687	ROAN MOUNTAIN	97.7	97.3	1.3	1.5	0.0	0.1	0.8	1.3	5.3	5.4	5.6	5.2	5.0	28.4	28.6	13.9	2.5	80.4	41.9	53.3	46.7
37688	SHADY VALLEY	98.8	98.6	0.2	0.2	0.1	0.2	0.9	1.5	4.9	5.0	5.3	5.0	4.2	20.4	33.2	19.6	2.5	81.8	48.2	49.4	50.6
37690	TELFORD	98.4	97.8	0.5	0.6	0.1	0.1	1.1	1.9	6.1	6.3	6.6	6.2	4.9	27.4	30.0	11.4	1.2	77.3	40.3	51.1	48.9
37691	TRADE	98.9	98.4	0.0	0.0	0.2	0.3	2.4	3.8	5.8	5.9	6.1	6.2	5.1	25.4	30.2	13.5	1.8	78.4	42.2	51.0	49.0
37692	UNICOI	98.0	98.1	0.0	0.0	0.2	0.2	1.9	1.9	5.5	5.9	6.3	5.8	4.5	27.4	31.3	11.9	1.5	78.5	41.4	50.8	49.2
37694	WATAUGA	98.5	98.1	0.4	0.5	0.2	0.3	1.1	1.6	5.2	5.7	5.9	5.5	4.3	27.1	32.0	12.9	1.3	79.7	42.6	50.9	49.1
37701	ALCOA	78.5	76.6	18.9	20.0	0.3	0.5	1.8	2.8	5.8	5.9	6.1	6.4	5.1	25.6	27.5	14.6	3.0	78.1	41.4	47.4	52.6
37705	ANDERSONVILLE	98.6	98.2	0.1	0.1	0.2	0.3	0.8	1.3	5.7	5.9	6.3	6.2	4.6	24.7	31.0	13.7	1.9	78.2	42.7	48.4	51.6
37708	BEAN STATION	98.7	98.3	0.2	0.2	0.1	0.2	0.7	1.2	6.1	6.1	6.5	6.2	5.4	27.6	29.0	12.1	1.0	77.3	39.9	50.6	49.4
37709	BLAINE	98.1	97.7	0.6	0.6	0.1	0.1	0.8	1.2	6.4	6.6	6.9	5.9	4.8	27.4	29.1	11.7	1.1	76.4	39.7	50.3	49.7
37710	BRICEVILLE	98.7	98.2	0.1	0.1	0.1	0.3	1.4	2.3	5.8	6.0	6.2	5.8	5.2	26.0	31.0	12.5	1.5	78.3	40.7	49.2	50.8
37711	BULLS GAP	98.5	98.1	0.6	0.8	0.1	0.1	0.4	0.6	6.2	6.3	6.6	6.4	5.3	26.9	28.7	12.5	1.2	77.0	40.2	50.2	49.8
37713	BYBEE	97.4	96.7	0.1	0.2	0.1	0.2	1.8	2.7	5.2	5.4	5.8	6.3	5.4	24.3	32.3	13.9	1.4	79.8	43.3	50.6	49.4
37714	CARYVILLE	97.8	97.3	0.1	0.1	0.4	0.5	1.4	2.3	6.2	6.4	6.4	5.8	4.4	27.7	28.9	13.0	1.3	77.5	40.6	50.1	49.9
37715	CLAIRFIELD	99.7	99.7	0.0	0.0	0.2	0.2	0.5	0.8	7.0	7.0	6.9	6.6	5.6	26.2	28.0	11.4	1.3	75.1	38.3	50.6	49.4
37716	CLINTON	96.4	95.6	1.8	2.1	0.3	0.5	0.7	1.2	5.7	5.8	6.1	6.1	4.9	25.9	29.6	13.9	2.0	78.5	41.9	48.6	51.4
37721	CORRYTON	98.2	97.6	0.8	1.0	0.2	0.3	0.4	0.7	6.3	6.6	6.7	6.1	4.6	26.8	30.3	11.4	1.2	76.5	40.5	49.7	50.3
37722	COSBY	98.3	97.8	0.3	0.3	0.1	0.2	0.9	1.5	5.6	5.9	6.1	5.9	4.9	26.8	30.9	12.6	1.2	78.7	41.4	48.5	51.5
37723	CRAB ORCHARD	99.0	98.7	0.0	0.0	0.1	0.2	0.4	0.6	5.7	5.8	6.1	6.2	4.8	24.3	29.6	16.0	1.5	78.5	43.1	50.1	49.9
37724	CUMBERLAND GAP	95.3	94.2	0.9	0.9	0.7	1.0	0.9	1.3	4.8	4.7	5.2	10.2	9.3	23.2	30.5	10.4	1.7	79.3	39.0	47.9	52.1
37725	DANDRIDGE	97.1	96.3	1.8	2.1	0.2	0.2	0.7	1.2	5.7	6.0	6.4	6.6	4.2	25.7	29.7	14.1	1.6	77.6	41.9	50.3	49.7
37726	DEER LODGE	98.5	98.2	0.4	0.4	0.1	0.2	0.7	1.0	5.3	6.0	6.4	8.0	5.3	25.6	29.9	11.9	1.7	77.0	40.3	52.5	47.5
37727	DEL RIO	97.8	97.1	0.6	0.7	0.0	0.0	0.7	1.1	4.8	5.1	5.4	6.3	5.3	24.4	32.1	15.2	1.4	80.9	44.1	50.2	49.8
37729	DUFF	98.3	97.9	0.0	0.0	0.1	0.1	0.8	1.4	6.2	6.0	6.3	7.3	6.0	25.1	28.8	13.0	1.4	77.0	39.9	49.8	50.2
37731	EIDSON	98.0	97.6	0.4	0.4	0.6	0.7	0.3	0.4	5.9	6.3	6.4	6.3	4.9	27.0	28.8	13.5	1.0	77.5	40.9	52.0	48.0
37737	FRIENDSVILLE	97.6	96.8	0.6	0.7	0.5	0.7	0.8	1.3	5.9	6.3	6.6	6.1	4.5	26.9	30.7	11.5	1.3	77.3	41.0	49.9	50.1
37738	GATLINBURG	96.3	94.7	0.2	0.2	1.5	2.3	1.6	2.6	3.3	3.5	3.7	4.3	3.9	22.4	38.4	18.3	2.2	86.8	50.3	50.0	50.0
37742	GREENBACK	97.7	96.8	0.3	0.4	0.4	0.6	0.7	1.3	5.8	6.3	6.6	6.1	4.7	26.3	30.5	12.4	1.4	77.5	41.1	50.0	50.0
37743	GREENEVILLE	95.2	94.4	3.2	3.5	0.3	0.5	0.9	1.4	5.6	5.6	6.0	6.2	4.8	25.2	28.9	15.2	2.5	78.9	42.6	48.9	51.1
37745	GREENEVILLE	95.9	94.9	2.5	2.8	0.4	0.6	1.1	1.7	5.5	5.5	5.8	6.3	5.4	25.6	28.4	15.3	2.1	79.6	42.0	48.2	51.8
37748	HARRIMAN	94.6	93.7	3.5	3.9	0.2	0.3	0.6	0.9	5.9	6.1	6.1	5.8	5.0	25.6	28.9	14.7	2.1	78.4	42.0	48.6	51.4
37752	HARROGATE	98.7	98.3	0.2	0.3	0.4	0.6	0.2	0.3	5.0	5.3	5.6	6.4	5.0	27.0	30.2	13.2	2.3	80.0	41.9	48.4	51.6
37753	HARTFORD	98.0	97.4	0.0	0.0	0.1	0.2	1.4	2.0	4.9	5.8	6.4	6.5	4.8	25.8	31.8	13.1	1.1	78.8	42.0	51.4	48.6
37754	HEISKELL	97.8	97.1	0.2	0.2	0.4	0.6	0.6	1.0	6.0	6.1	6.5	6.8	5.4	26.6	29.8	11.2	1.5	77.1	40.2	49.8	50.2
37755	HELENWOOD	98.2	97.7	0.3	0.3	0.1	0.1	0.4	0.7	6.7	6.6	6.7	6.7	6.1	26.8	27.3	11.5	1.6	75.9	37.9	49.4	50.6
37756	HUNTSVILLE	98.8	98.5	0.1	0.1	0.1	0.2	0.7	1.1	6.4	6.7	6.4	7.1	7.1	26.7	27.8	10.3	1.5	76.2	37.0	50.3	49.7
37757	JACKSBORO	98.2	97.6	0.2	0.2	0.2	0.3	0.8	1.2	6.4	6.4	6.6	6.1	5.3	28.5	27.3	12.1	1.2	76.9	38.9	48.5	51.5
37760	JEFFERSON CITY	92.7	91.0	4.5	5.0	0.6	0.9	2.2	3.5	6.2	5.8	5.7	9.0	10.1	26.0	23.3	12.0	2.0	78.8	34.9	48.6	51.4
37762	JELLICO	96.7	95.9	1.5	1.6	0.5	0.8	0.4	0.6	5.7	5.8	5.9	6.0	5.1	24.9	26.1	17.1	3.3	78.8	42.3	46.9	53.1
37763	KINGSTON	96.3	95.5	1.5	1.6	0.4	0.5	0.8	1.3	5.5	5.9	6.2	5.7	4.6	24.6	30.5	14.8	2.1	78.9	43.1	49.7	50.3
37764	KODAK	97.9	97.1	0.3	0.4	0.3	0.4	0.9	1.5	7.3	7.4	7.4	6.1	4.5	28.9	26.4	11.1	0.9	74.1	37.5	48.6	51.4
37765	KYLES FORD	98.6	98.5	0.1	0.1	0.1	0.1	0.6	0.6	6.0	6.4	6.3	5.4	5.4	22.6	29.9	16.0	2.1	77.9	43.4	50.8	49.2
37766	LA FOLLETTE	98.4	98.0	0.2	0.3	0.1	0.2	0.5	0.8	5.6	5.5	5.8	6.1	5.5	25.0	28.0	16.1	2.5	79.4	42.5	47.8	52.2
	TENNESSEE	80.2	78.4	16.4	16.9	1.0	1.5	2.2	3.4	6.5	6.4	6.5	6.8	6.5	27.2	27.0	11.4	1.7	76.6	38.0	49.0	51.0
	UNITED STATES	75.1	72.0	12.3	12.7	3.8	4.6	12.5	15.7	6.8	6.7	6.6	7.1	6.9	27.0	26.0	10.9	1.9	75.7	36.9	49.2	50.8

#	POST OFFICE NAME	2009 Per Capita Income	2009 HH Income Base	2009 Household Income Distribution (%) Less than $25,000	$25,000 to $49,999	$50,000 to $99,999	$100,000 to $149,999	$150,000 or More	Median Household Income 2009	2014	2009 National Centile	2009 State Centile	2009 Home Value Base	2009 Home Value Distribution (%) Less than $50,000	$50,000 to $89,999	$90,000 to $174,999	$175,000 to $399,999	$400,000 or More	2009 Median Home Value
37375	SEWANEE	26067	1237	24.7	21.4	33.1	10.4	10.3	53095	49794	68	83	895	15.1	20.8	21.3	31.6	11.2	132102
37376	SHERWOOD	13275	241	41.9	42.7	15.4	0.0	0.0	30402	32377	9	13	213	56.3	28.6	11.7	0.0	3.3	45781
37377	SIGNAL MOUNTAIN	40342	6875	13.3	20.0	35.1	15.1	16.5	71885	71238	88	95	5006	6.4	6.8	26.3	46.3	14.2	208494
37379	SODDY DAISY	23827	10476	19.8	27.7	40.2	8.9	3.3	52237	54801	66	82	8769	17.1	18.8	42.3	19.2	2.6	111757
37380	SOUTH PITTSBURG	19121	2531	36.8	29.1	26.5	4.7	2.9	35707	38142	20	28	1880	21.1	25.4	39.9	12.4	1.1	94286
37381	SPRING CITY	20532	3952	33.2	30.0	27.9	5.8	3.0	37485	39441	25	38	3132	19.2	22.4	38.6	17.7	2.2	100998
37385	TELLICO PLAINS	17310	3677	37.1	29.8	28.7	3.0	1.4	35861	37171	20	29	3037	29.8	23.4	30.4	14.9	1.6	82904
37387	TRACY CITY	14892	1868	46.0	30.0	20.7	2.0	1.2	26785	27377	4	6	1456	32.8	31.8	28.2	6.5	0.7	71008
37388	TULLAHOMA	24352	10309	26.9	26.1	35.6	7.1	4.3	46147	47618	52	72	7252	11.3	24.4	43.3	17.8	3.3	109881
37391	TURTLETOWN	19025	555	44.1	25.8	23.4	4.5	2.2	30062	31855	8	12	469	26.0	20.0	38.8	12.6	2.6	93558
37397	WHITWELL	18025	4470	32.6	34.7	28.5	2.7	1.5	36349	38859	22	32	3688	27.6	23.1	37.2	11.3	0.9	88972
37398	WINCHESTER	21393	5746	29.9	26.1	34.8	6.9	2.3	43496	44443	44	63	4376	13.7	23.2	40.6	19.0	3.4	109318
37402	CHATTANOOGA	16134	2514	69.8	17.5	9.7	1.9	1.0	14172	15144	1	2	28	3.6	3.6	53.6	14.3	25.0	122727
37403	CHATTANOOGA	17872	1533	54.5	23.4	18.6	1.4	2.1	21758	22085	2	3	319	19.1	43.3	19.7	10.7	7.2	76371
37404	CHATTANOOGA	15611	5385	44.4	29.9	21.3	2.1	2.3	27713	28995	5	7	2478	28.9	41.9	22.2	5.4	1.6	68393
37405	CHATTANOOGA	30209	6882	26.2	30.8	31.1	5.9	6.0	43376	46799	43	63	3653	13.5	21.6	35.4	20.6	8.8	118490
37406	CHATTANOOGA	16330	5521	43.3	25.2	26.9	2.8	1.8	29080	31325	7	10	2989	14.6	46.2	35.6	3.6	0.1	79950
37407	CHATTANOOGA	16533	3284	46.1	28.6	20.5	2.4	2.4	27155	28625	5	7	1723	41.4	42.5	11.9	3.4	0.8	56095
37408	CHATTANOOGA	9975	684	67.4	24.4	6.4	0.0	1.8	13611	14670	1	2	108	35.2	49.1	13.0	2.8	0.0	60000
37409	CHATTANOOGA	21397	1300	31.3	29.6	31.4	3.6	4.1	41139	45044	36	55	876	18.5	49.7	26.1	3.4	2.3	72205
37410	CHATTANOOGA	10749	1655	65.1	20.5	12.1	0.7	1.6	16190	16811	1	2	545	36.5	50.3	11.7	1.5	0.0	58855
37411	CHATTANOOGA	26049	7620	24.5	28.6	36.5	5.5	5.0	45941	50513	51	71	4925	5.3	37.6	47.4	8.8	0.8	95551
37412	CHATTANOOGA	27903	9553	18.2	31.6	40.1	6.6	3.6	50194	52595	62	79	5799	3.7	24.4	61.5	10.3	0.2	106282
37415	CHATTANOOGA	29728	11398	20.3	31.0	37.5	6.2	5.0	48804	51754	58	77	6940	5.7	19.2	57.6	14.1	3.3	114887
37416	CHATTANOOGA	28381	6425	16.0	26.5	45.1	7.7	4.8	56070	57854	73	87	4245	2.9	15.5	65.5	12.9	3.3	121215
37419	CHATTANOOGA	28011	2592	21.1	28.7	37.0	7.6	5.6	50166	52182	62	79	1958	14.7	19.7	48.8	10.6	6.2	106895
37421	CHATTANOOGA	34802	18894	14.3	22.6	40.9	12.6	9.5	64527	66040	83	93	12277	2.9	6.8	51.6	32.5	6.3	152104
37601	JOHNSON CITY	23424	15475	32.5	29.6	28.5	5.4	4.0	39207	43269	30	47	9395	10.9	19.8	46.8	19.4	3.2	121044
37604	JOHNSON CITY	23990	14658	31.9	29.1	28.0	6.0	5.0	39035	42826	30	46	8350	10.2	17.4	42.0	27.3	3.1	122687
37615	JOHNSON CITY	27407	7515	21.3	24.4	39.5	9.7	5.1	53483	54030	69	84	5544	7.7	11.5	47.4	27.6	5.8	139110
37616	AFTON	19338	2035	29.7	35.0	29.3	3.3	2.6	40473	41966	34	52	1643	21.2	22.8	41.8	11.6	2.6	96396
37617	BLOUNTVILLE	23004	5495	23.4	29.3	37.6	6.6	3.1	47014	49498	54	74	4532	17.1	14.2	40.4	23.1	5.2	127176
37618	BLUFF CITY	20686	5313	28.5	31.9	33.0	4.6	2.1	41973	45456	39	58	4424	22.8	18.3	39.7	17.1	2.1	101594
37620	BRISTOL	23033	16848	30.4	30.9	31.1	4.8	2.9	41100	44729	36	54	12441	20.1	24.0	39.0	14.9	1.9	98228
37640	BUTLER	15939	1730	45.9	32.7	17.3	2.7	1.4	27130	29213	5	7	1494	34.6	26.0	29.5	8.1	1.9	76222
37641	CHUCKEY	19060	3174	30.5	30.4	33.6	3.8	1.7	40799	43296	35	53	2641	20.1	22.7	39.9	15.0	2.3	98626
37642	CHURCH HILL	21436	6204	27.4	30.6	34.8	5.3	2.0	42826	45139	42	61	5009	17.2	15.7	48.6	17.7	0.9	125790
37643	ELIZABETHTON	17905	14455	37.4	33.1	24.7	3.5	1.3	34004	37122	16	21	10739	16.6	26.2	42.6	13.6	1.0	98934
37645	MOUNT CARMEL	24458	2823	23.8	30.5	34.6	7.2	3.9	45127	46589	49	68	2036	12.5	17.9	47.1	18.2	4.3	130704
37650	ERWIN	19206	5291	34.5	33.2	27.0	4.0	1.3	35866	37781	20	29	3990	17.6	27.4	39.8	14.6	0.6	96177
37656	FALL BRANCH	23141	1495	23.1	29.7	40.6	4.3	2.3	47394	49613	55	75	1268	15.1	16.1	44.1	23.1	1.7	118341
37657	FLAG POND	20657	434	33.2	35.5	22.8	5.5	3.0	35350	37834	19	26	362	25.4	18.5	41.2	14.9	0.0	97097
37658	HAMPTON	16009	2013	40.5	34.3	22.8	1.6	0.8	30224	33993	8	12	1605	28.1	31.7	32.0	7.9	0.3	76914
37659	JONESBOROUGH	22313	10966	24.5	30.3	37.0	5.6	2.6	45068	47559	48	68	8886	10.0	15.1	46.7	23.3	4.9	129125
37660	KINGSPORT	23696	17931	33.6	29.1	27.5	5.8	4.0	38913	42047	29	45	12355	12.9	23.9	41.7	17.2	4.2	107751
37663	KINGSPORT	28571	6227	17.4	23.0	43.5	9.3	6.8	58273	57792	75	89	5109	4.8	6.6	51.2	34.1	3.4	155293
37664	KINGSPORT	25782	11622	26.2	27.5	34.5	7.3	4.5	46011	48889	51	72	8928	9.3	15.6	45.6	25.3	4.2	133783
37665	KINGSPORT	17486	2098	40.5	32.2	22.9	3.9	0.6	30627	32689	9	13	1446	18.3	33.2	43.6	4.6	0.4	88279
37680	LAUREL BLOOMERY	17267	435	36.8	35.9	23.0	2.5	1.8	32925	35770	13	18	369	30.6	28.5	36.3	3.5	1.1	79038
37681	LIMESTONE	19265	2404	29.3	31.7	33.4	3.7	1.9	39616	42493	32	49	1991	15.4	20.5	45.0	16.2	3.0	108322
37683	MOUNTAIN CITY	16985	4915	46.0	28.6	20.8	2.5	2.0	27751	28498	5	8	3778	28.1	22.4	35.8	12.2	1.6	89224
37686	PINEY FLATS	25238	3074	22.2	34.1	34.4	5.3	4.1	44815	47520	48	67	2521	15.3	11.6	37.8	27.1	8.3	130483
37687	ROAN MOUNTAIN	15894	2341	46.2	32.6	17.0	2.3	1.9	26985	29232	5	7	1993	28.9	27.5	36.4	5.8	1.4	79553
37688	SHADY VALLEY	14981	518	41.7	38.8	17.2	1.4	1.0	27179	27196	5	7	459	25.1	21.1	37.7	13.3	2.8	93804
37690	TELFORD	19828	1654	30.5	29.4	32.4	5.1	2.5	38783	41960	29	44	1377	16.2	22.9	43.3	14.5	3.1	106646
37691	TRADE	13933	428	37.1	51.6	11.2	0.0	0.0	32863	34554	13	18	331	24.8	26.9	37.8	7.9	2.7	87105
37692	UNICOI	19051	2050	31.4	31.1	32.1	3.4	2.0	36275	38110	21	31	1600	17.4	18.6	42.8	17.4	3.8	115728
37694	WATAUGA	16667	696	33.6	35.8	26.9	3.3	0.4	35833	38742	20	29	551	22.7	19.8	43.4	13.1	1.1	103059
37701	ALCOA	23299	2932	30.9	28.4	30.6	6.5	3.6	39502	43366	31	48	1995	11.8	26.3	44.8	12.0	5.1	108425
37705	ANDERSONVILLE	23432	2447	23.3	28.1	37.8	7.4	3.4	48373	49930	57	76	2049	9.5	12.5	41.0	30.0	7.0	141980
37708	BEAN STATION	17329	2702	35.0	32.5	28.2	2.6	1.7	36447	38934	22	32	2246	19.5	29.1	35.4	14.6	1.5	92075
37709	BLAINE	19680	1341	32.4	29.2	32.7	3.5	2.2	39580	41358	31	49	1110	18.4	22.6	41.1	15.0	2.9	104645
37710	BRICEVILLE	11780	689	50.7	29.6	19.2	0.6	0.0	24578	26287	3	4	521	48.6	31.1	19.4	1.0	0.0	51316
37711	BULLS GAP	17189	2060	32.6	31.1	32.9	3.0	0.5	38432	40051	28	42	1724	18.2	29.9	37.5	13.5	1.0	92957
37713	BYBEE	18495	674	40.9	29.7	25.2	1.6	2.5	33483	36273	14	19	565	23.4	27.6	37.0	9.4	2.7	87800
37714	CARYVILLE	18148	1931	33.1	36.1	25.2	4.1	1.5	36381	38387	22	32	1472	22.7	26.1	40.4	7.5	3.3	91259
37715	CLAIRFIELD	9783	444	64.0	24.8	11.3	0.0	0.0	20232	20882	1	3	376	76.3	14.1	9.3	0.3	0.0	30000
37716	CLINTON	21909	10606	27.6	27.6	36.3	6.3	2.2	43967	47184	45	65	7804	13.8	18.0	43.9	21.9	2.3	118920
37721	CORRYTON	22135	4633	20.9	30.3	40.9	6.2	1.6	48596	51819	58	77	3886	11.7	15.2	48.9	21.3	2.8	121748
37722	COSBY	16938	2199	37.7	35.5	23.0	2.3	1.6	32914	34169	13	18	1771	21.1	26.4	33.8	15.9	2.8	93739
37723	CRAB ORCHARD	16699	464	34.1	35.6	27.4	2.2	0.9	35128	37981	18	25	402	30.6	27.9	25.6	13.9	2.0	73846
37724	CUMBERLAND GAP	17623	1213	35.5	30.4	28.9	3.6	1.5	34808	36431	17	24	987	23.2	21.2	41.3	13.4	0.9	97603
37725	DANDRIDGE	21413	6618	25.9	31.8	34.3	5.1	2.8	43142	44867	43	62	5510	21.3	16.7	34.5	22.4	5.1	116945
37726	DEER LODGE	13840	678	45.9	36.4	14.2	2.2	1.3	26411	27591	4	5	577	28.1	38.5	27.2	5.4	0.9	72197
37727	DEL RIO	13996	895	42.9	38.7	16.9	1.3	0.2	28874	28886	7	9	722	42.0	23.4	27.3	6.1	1.2	68000
37729	DUFF	11889	699	51.1	33.3	13.4	0.9	1.3	24239	25211	3	4	563	65.4	24.2	9.4	1.1	0.0	37888
37731	EIDSON	14922	311	41.8	29.9	26.7	1.6	0.0	28686	30701	6	9	274	43.4	17.5	19.0	19.0	1.1	60833
37737	FRIENDSVILLE	24655	2516	17.4	29.3	41.3	7.1	4.9	52648	54530	67	83	2134	13.0	13.5	37.8	26.3	9.4	137391
37738	GATLINBURG	26641	2257	19.0	36.0	35.4	5.6	3.9	45866	46060	51	70	1577	8.8	6.6	30.5	48.1	6.1	188206
37742	GREENBACK	22818	2209	21.5	27.3	41.8	7.0	2.4	51027	53274	64	80	1875	11.1	12.1	43.0	26.8	7.0	135990
37743	GREENEVILLE	20118	10765	34.3	29.5	30.3	3.7	2.2	37076	38552	24	36	8055	16.0	23.7	42.7	14.6	3.0	104564
37745	GREENEVILLE	21413	7794	33.1	31.8	27.4	5.3	2.4	37696	39165	26	40	5597	18.0	21.2	43.9	15.2	1.8	105239
37748	HARRIMAN	19674	8096	32.6	30.0	31.9	4.0	1.5	37890	39759	26	41	6040	22.6	25.8	40.1	10.4	1.1	92160
37752	HARROGATE	18472	2246	31.2	31.1	31.9	4.1	1.7	38211	41196	27	42	1764	21.1	22.3	44.6	10.4	1.6	97697
37753	HARTFORD	12021	355	50.7	38.6	8.7	2.0	0.0	24610	25289	3	4	284	34.5	32.7	29.9	2.1	0.7	75517
37754	HEISKELL	20420	1870	23.3	30.8	38.5	5.2	2.2	45578	48613	50	70	1588	19.0	17.5	38.5	20.0	4.9	112906
37755	HELENWOOD	16590	1401	41.4	30.8	23.5	2.4	1.9	29048	29764	7	10	1080	25.1	33.1	34.0	6.0	1.9	78018
37756	HUNTSVILLE	12710	1100	52.6	29.8	15.4	1.5	0.7	23722	24314	3	3	900	47.2	25.9	22.0	4.2	0.7	52717
37757	JACKSBORO	19661	3758	33.6	31.9	28.3	4.3	1.9	37495	40462	25	39	2794	12.0	25.6	50.6	10.6	1.2	105193
37760	JEFFERSON CITY	20834	5390	33.3	26.3	31.2	5.7	3.4	40236	42720	33	51	3527	11.0	17.7	48.9	18.8	3.6	121277
37762	JELLICO	15109	1443	48.0	31.5	17.0	1.4	2.1	26638	27978	4	6	997	40.4	39.1	16.9	3.5	0.1	58843
37763	KINGSTON	24306	6363	24.7	28.9	34.8	8.5	3.1	46199	46081	52	73	5086	13.8	20.9	40.5	21.4	3.4	114445
37764	KODAK	19773	3549	22.6	34.3	38.1	3.7	1.3	43522	44286	44	64	2908	26.8	13.0	30.9	25.8	3.5	123467
37765	KYLES FORD	11037	345	66.7	22.9	9.0	0.0	1.4	16307	16575	1	2	286	29.7	41.3	25.9	3.1	0.0	61707
37766	LA FOLLETTE	16058	8116	46.0	30.3	19.8	2.7	1.2	28056	29059	6	8	5742	22.6	33.8	33.4	9.5	0.8	80691
	TENNESSEE	24986		24.9	27.0	34.7	8.2	5.2	47751	50104				12.0	19.9	40.9	22.7	4.6	120455
	UNITED STATES	27277		20.9	24.4	35.3	11.7	7.6	54719	56938				9.3	13.1	31.6	32.6	13.5	162279

ZIP CODE		FINANCIAL SERVICES				THE HOME						ENTERTAINMENT						PERSONAL			
						Home Improvements		Furnishings													
#	POST OFFICE NAME	Auto Loan	Home Loan	Invest-ments	Retire-ment Plans	Home Repair	Lawn & Garden	Comput-ers & Hard-ware-Personal	Major Appli-ances	TV, Radio, Sound Equip-ment	Furni-ture	Dine out/ Carry out	Sports Equip-ment	Fees & Tickets	Toys & Games	Travel	Cable TV	Apparel & Services	Auto Repairs	Health Insur-ance	Pets & Supplies
37375	SEWANEE	118	98	124	98	100	119	100	114	105	97	104	86	90	104	100	110	71	109	116	135
37376	SHERWOOD	57	37	55	35	37	56	40	50	46	38	45	39	30	46	37	51	29	47	53	61
37377	SIGNAL MOUNTAIN	136	143	151	148	148	145	137	140	136	142	136	106	144	135	144	136	96	138	140	163
37379	SODDY DAISY	96	88	87	87	87	97	84	93	87	83	86	71	79	89	83	90	59	88	93	109
37380	SOUTH PITTSBURG	81	58	76	56	59	81	62	75	69	57	67	56	49	69	58	76	45	70	80	89
37381	SPRING CITY	81	62	82	59	65	83	63	77	70	61	68	57	53	69	63	76	45	72	83	91
37385	TELLICO PLAINS	77	55	66	54	55	74	57	68	64	55	62	52	46	66	53	70	42	64	71	82
37387	TRACY CITY	66	44	64	42	45	65	47	59	54	45	52	46	36	54	44	60	35	55	62	72
37388	TULLAHOMA	88	82	79	83	81	90	84	86	87	81	86	65	80	87	81	90	59	85	91	102
37391	TURTLETOWN	77	55	76	53	57	77	57	71	63	53	62	53	45	63	55	69	41	65	74	85
37397	WHITWELL	80	56	68	54	56	76	59	69	66	57	64	53	46	68	54	72	43	66	73	85
37398	WINCHESTER	85	68	81	68	69	88	70	82	76	65	74	62	60	76	68	82	50	77	87	97
37402	CHATTANOOGA	31	22	26	26	23	27	37	29	39	33	39	23	32	35	32	41	27	36	40	38
37403	CHATTANOOGA	49	35	38	39	35	40	56	44	57	49	57	36	47	53	46	59	40	53	54	56
37404	CHATTANOOGA	59	49	45	50	46	56	55	54	60	54	59	40	51	60	50	64	41	57	62	67
37405	CHATTANOOGA	87	77	75	79	76	82	89	82	91	85	90	64	83	90	82	93	63	88	91	100
37406	CHATTANOOGA	59	52	46	53	49	58	56	54	61	56	60	40	54	60	52	65	41	58	63	68
37407	CHATTANOOGA	60	47	42	49	45	54	58	53	62	54	60	41	51	62	50	65	42	58	61	66
37408	CHATTANOOGA	38	25	22	28	23	28	38	30	42	36	41	24	32	41	30	44	29	37	37	40
37409	CHATTANOOGA	82	68	69	69	67	83	75	78	79	69	77	60	66	80	69	84	53	78	86	94
37410	CHATTANOOGA	41	29	27	31	27	34	38	34	43	38	42	26	34	42	32	46	29	39	41	44
37411	CHATTANOOGA	85	80	70	81	76	85	85	81	88	82	87	63	82	88	80	91	60	85	91	100
37412	CHATTANOOGA	83	82	77	82	80	87	85	84	87	81	86	64	84	87	83	90	60	86	92	100
37415	CHATTANOOGA	86	85	80	86	84	89	88	86	89	85	89	65	87	89	86	92	62	88	93	102
37416	CHATTANOOGA	94	96	86	98	93	100	95	95	96	92	95	73	95	97	94	98	66	95	102	113
37419	CHATTANOOGA	95	89	102	87	89	107	85	99	91	81	90	72	82	90	89	98	61	94	107	115
37421	CHATTANOOGA	111	116	111	119	115	113	115	112	114	116	115	86	119	114	117	114	81	114	114	132
37601	JOHNSON CITY	80	68	70	68	68	76	75	75	78	72	77	57	68	78	70	81	53	77	81	90
37604	JOHNSON CITY	80	69	72	70	69	77	80	77	80	74	80	59	72	80	73	83	55	79	82	91
37615	JOHNSON CITY	101	94	91	94	94	100	93	98	95	93	94	72	89	96	90	98	65	95	100	115
37616	AFTON	87	65	72	63	64	82	67	76	73	65	72	58	55	76	61	79	48	73	80	92
37617	BLOUNTVILLE	88	80	80	79	79	91	77	85	81	75	80	64	72	83	76	85	55	81	89	101
37618	BLUFF CITY	85	67	73	67	67	84	68	78	73	65	72	59	58	76	64	79	49	73	81	93
37620	BRISTOL	80	70	76	69	70	84	71	79	76	68	75	58	65	76	70	81	51	76	86	93
37640	BUTLER	64	46	62	44	47	64	47	59	53	45	52	44	38	53	46	58	34	54	61	70
37641	CHUCKEY	84	60	70	58	60	80	62	73	69	61	68	56	50	72	57	76	46	69	77	89
37642	CHURCH HILL	87	67	74	65	67	84	69	78	75	67	73	59	58	77	64	80	50	75	82	94
37643	ELIZABETHTON	71	52	65	51	53	70	56	65	61	52	60	50	46	62	52	67	40	62	70	78
37645	MOUNT CARMEL	89	78	79	79	79	90	81	86	83	77	82	64	74	84	78	87	56	84	91	101
37650	ERWIN	73	54	71	52	55	75	57	69	63	52	61	52	46	63	55	69	41	65	74	82
37656	FALL BRANCH	95	74	88	72	75	94	74	88	80	71	79	66	63	82	71	87	53	82	91	105
37657	FLAG POND	83	59	68	58	59	78	62	72	68	60	67	55	49	71	56	75	45	68	76	87
37658	HAMPTON	67	45	63	43	45	65	48	59	54	46	53	46	37	56	44	60	35	56	62	72
37659	JONESBOROUGH	89	79	78	79	79	90	77	85	81	75	80	64	71	83	75	84	54	81	87	101
37660	KINGSPORT	82	67	78	67	69	84	72	80	78	68	76	59	64	76	70	83	52	78	87	94
37663	KINGSPORT	100	104	101	106	105	112	96	105	98	94	97	78	98	99	100	102	67	99	108	121
37664	KINGSPORT	87	83	87	83	83	95	81	89	84	78	83	66	78	84	82	89	57	85	95	104
37665	KINGSPORT	64	46	62	45	48	65	52	62	57	46	55	46	42	56	49	63	37	58	68	73
37680	LAUREL BLOOMERY	74	53	76	51	55	75	54	69	60	50	59	52	43	60	54	66	39	63	72	82
37681	LIMESTONE	86	62	76	60	63	84	64	77	71	61	70	58	52	73	60	78	47	72	80	92
37683	MOUNTAIN CITY	71	50	71	48	51	72	52	66	59	49	57	50	41	59	51	65	38	61	69	79
37686	PINEY FLATS	100	87	90	87	87	102	85	96	89	81	88	72	77	91	83	95	60	90	99	114
37687	ROAN MOUNTAIN	69	49	70	47	50	69	50	64	56	47	55	48	40	56	49	62	36	59	66	76
37688	SHADY VALLEY	60	43	62	42	45	61	44	56	49	41	48	42	35	49	44	54	32	52	59	67
37690	TELFORD	91	65	80	63	66	88	68	81	75	65	73	62	54	77	63	82	49	76	85	98
37691	TRADE	59	42	48	41	42	56	44	51	49	43	48	39	35	51	40	53	32	48	54	62
37692	UNICOI	76	62	62	60	61	72	61	68	66	62	65	51	53	68	57	70	44	65	70	82
37694	WATAUGA	74	53	73	51	54	74	54	68	60	51	59	51	43	60	53	66	39	63	71	81
37701	ALCOA	79	69	73	68	69	82	71	77	76	68	74	57	66	75	69	81	51	75	85	91
37705	ANDERSONVILLE	92	85	88	85	86	97	81	90	85	80	84	67	78	86	82	89	58	86	94	107
37708	BEAN STATION	75	53	64	51	53	72	55	66	62	54	61	51	44	64	51	68	41	62	69	80
37709	BLAINE	87	62	71	60	62	82	65	75	72	63	70	58	52	75	59	78	47	71	79	92
37710	BRICEVILLE	57	37	55	35	37	56	40	50	46	38	45	39	30	47	37	51	30	47	53	62
37711	BULLS GAP	77	55	63	54	55	73	57	67	64	56	62	51	46	66	52	69	42	63	70	81
37713	BYBEE	80	57	72	56	58	78	59	71	66	57	65	54	48	68	56	72	43	67	75	86
37714	CARYVILLE	79	55	69	54	55	76	58	69	65	56	63	53	46	67	53	71	42	65	73	84
37715	CLAIRFIELD	46	30	45	28	30	45	32	41	37	31	36	32	24	38	30	41	24	38	43	50
37716	CLINTON	82	71	77	70	71	84	71	79	76	69	75	59	65	76	69	80	51	76	83	94
37721	CORRYTON	89	79	77	80	80	91	78	86	81	73	80	65	71	83	76	85	54	81	89	101
37722	COSBY	73	52	69	51	53	72	54	66	60	52	59	50	43	61	52	66	39	62	69	80
37723	CRAB ORCHARD	71	52	64	50	53	70	53	64	59	52	58	48	44	61	50	65	39	60	68	77
37724	CUMBERLAND GAP	76	57	69	57	58	76	59	70	65	56	64	54	50	66	57	71	43	66	73	84
37725	DANDRIDGE	88	73	80	72	74	87	72	83	76	70	75	61	64	78	70	81	51	78	84	98
37726	DEER LODGE	64	43	59	41	43	62	46	56	52	44	51	44	35	54	43	58	34	53	59	69
37727	DEL RIO	61	42	54	40	41	58	44	53	49	42	48	41	34	51	40	55	32	50	56	65
37729	DUFF	55	36	53	34	36	54	39	48	44	37	43	38	29	45	36	50	29	46	51	60
37731	EIDSON	62	44	51	43	44	59	46	54	51	45	50	41	37	54	42	56	34	51	57	66
37737	FRIENDSVILLE	100	92	95	91	93	100	87	96	90	89	90	71	83	92	87	93	62	91	96	113
37738	GATLINBURG	93	78	115	78	86	99	78	95	82	76	81	68	71	78	84	86	54	89	97	110
37742	GREENBACK	94	83	81	84	83	96	81	91	85	77	84	68	74	87	79	90	57	85	93	107
37743	GREENEVILLE	79	61	72	60	62	79	64	74	70	60	68	56	54	71	61	75	46	70	78	88
37745	GREENEVILLE	76	63	71	62	64	77	65	72	70	63	69	54	58	70	63	74	47	70	77	86
37748	HARRIMAN	77	60	71	59	61	77	63	72	69	60	67	54	54	69	60	74	45	69	77	86
37752	HARROGATE	77	59	71	58	60	77	61	72	66	57	65	54	51	67	58	71	43	67	75	86
37753	HARTFORD	53	34	51	32	34	51	37	46	42	35	41	36	27	43	34	47	27	43	49	57
37754	HEISKELL	90	75	74	73	74	86	73	81	78	73	77	61	65	81	69	82	52	78	83	97
37755	HELENWOOD	73	51	65	49	51	71	53	64	60	52	59	50	42	62	49	66	39	61	68	78
37756	HUNTSVILLE	59	39	57	36	38	58	41	52	48	39	46	41	31	48	39	53	31	49	55	64
37757	JACKSBORO	83	61	73	59	61	81	64	75	70	61	69	57	52	72	60	76	46	71	79	90
37760	JEFFERSON CITY	79	65	67	65	64	74	73	73	75	69	74	56	64	76	66	79	51	74	78	88
37762	JELLICO	61	41	58	39	41	60	46	55	52	43	50	42	36	52	42	57	34	52	59	67
37763	KINGSTON	90	79	82	79	79	92	79	87	83	76	82	65	72	84	77	87	56	83	91	103
37764	KODAK	84	75	70	73	74	80	72	77	75	74	75	57	67	78	68	78	51	75	78	92
37765	KYLES FORD	49	32	47	30	32	48	34	43	39	32	38	33	25	40	32	44	25	40	45	52
37766	LA FOLLETTE	63	46	60	45	47	63	50	59	55	46	54	44	41	55	47	60	36	56	63	70
	TENNESSEE	95	84	85	84	82	93	87	90	90	85	89	69	80	91	83	93	61	89	93	107
	UNITED STATES	100	100	100	100	100	100	100	100	100	100	100	100	100	100	100	100	100	100	100	100

ZIP CODE #	POST OFFICE NAME	COUNTY FIPS CODE	POPULATION 2000	POPULATION 2009	POPULATION 2014	2000-2009 ANNUAL RATE % Rate	2000-2009 ANNUAL RATE State Centile	HOUSEHOLDS 2000	HOUSEHOLDS 2009	HOUSEHOLDS 2014	HOUSEHOLDS % Annual Rate 2000-2009	HOUSEHOLDS 2009 Average HH Size	FAMILIES 2000	FAMILIES 2009	FAMILIES % Annual Rate 2000-2009
37769	LAKE CITY	001	6001	6404	6593	0.7	53	2474	2701	2801	1.0	2.33	1745	1848	0.6
37770	LANCING	129	2545	2627	2662	0.3	31	965	1023	1047	0.6	2.55	729	755	0.4
37771	LENOIR CITY	105	13219	14876	15830	1.3	76	5320	6097	6525	1.5	2.41	3701	4112	1.1
37772	LENOIR CITY	105	8853	10682	11682	2.1	91	3575	4408	4848	2.3	2.42	2731	3282	2.0
37774	LOUDON	105	14180	17271	18969	2.2	92	5927	7497	8339	2.6	2.27	4502	5568	2.3
37777	LOUISVILLE	009	10731	11589	12184	0.8	60	4727	5139	5419	0.9	2.22	3004	3154	0.5
37778	LOWLAND	063	17	18	19	0.6	47	8	9	9	1.3	2.00	6	7	1.7
37779	LUTTRELL	173	3849	4125	4251	0.8	60	1422	1568	1630	1.1	2.60	1126	1221	0.9
37801	MARYVILLE	009	19183	23160	25359	2.1	91	7880	9568	10506	2.1	2.40	5610	6642	1.8
37803	MARYVILLE	009	27521	31834	34337	1.6	82	10681	12462	13514	1.7	2.48	8025	9138	1.4
37804	MARYVILLE	009	21151	23580	25177	1.2	72	8239	9283	9962	1.3	2.45	5883	6433	1.0
37806	MASCOT	093	2860	3086	3245	0.8	60	1166	1290	1369	1.1	2.39	834	887	0.7
37807	MAYNARDVILLE	173	9049	9869	10209	0.9	63	3419	3815	3976	1.2	2.57	2630	2877	1.0
37809	MIDWAY	059	1906	1940	1946	0.2	27	723	747	753	0.4	2.60	548	553	0.1
37810	MOHAWK	059	1722	1893	1968	1.0	66	690	771	806	1.2	2.46	518	565	0.9
37811	MOORESBURG	073	3071	3621	3842	1.8	86	1232	1496	1603	2.1	2.42	916	1086	1.9
37813	MORRISTOWN	063	16850	18033	18717	0.7	53	6759	7382	7709	1.0	2.42	4743	5034	0.6
37814	MORRISTOWN	063	30575	32597	33756	0.7	53	12224	13301	13868	0.9	2.41	8588	9095	0.6
37818	MOSHEIM	059	4642	5119	5330	1.1	69	1881	2113	2218	1.3	2.42	1387	1519	1.0
37819	NEWCOMB	013	918	944	952	0.3	31	356	381	390	0.7	2.48	266	277	0.4
37820	NEW MARKET	089	6835	7734	8329	1.3	76	2556	2958	3202	1.6	2.58	1983	2243	1.3
37821	NEWPORT	029	21792	22582	22995	0.4	36	9015	9653	9934	0.7	2.30	6224	6477	0.4
37825	NEW TAZEWELL	025	7821	8359	8483	0.7	53	3169	3503	3591	1.1	2.37	2305	2485	0.8
37826	NIOTA	107	3759	3966	4071	0.6	47	1511	1634	1692	0.8	2.43	1179	1249	0.6
37829	OAKDALE	129	1730	1753	1766	0.1	22	629	659	669	0.5	2.65	497	510	0.3
37830	OAK RIDGE	001	27723	28313	28672	0.2	27	12203	12664	12903	0.4	2.20	7824	7836	0.0
37840	OLIVER SPRINGS	129	10518	10527	10572	0.0	18	4188	4305	4362	0.3	2.45	3100	3106	0.0
37841	ONEIDA	151	8699	9496	9816	1.0	66	3515	3991	4185	1.4	2.37	2475	2736	1.1
37843	PARROTTSVILLE	029	3485	3864	4032	1.1	69	1376	1583	1671	1.5	2.44	1049	1178	1.3
37846	PHILADELPHIA	105	3939	4440	4722	1.3	76	1452	1670	1788	1.5	2.66	1141	1282	1.3
37847	PIONEER	013	2581	2705	2764	0.5	41	936	1024	1060	1.0	2.64	721	771	0.7
37848	POWDER SPRINGS	057	226	230	233	0.2	27	95	100	102	0.6	2.29	72	74	0.3
37849	POWELL	093	22383	25907	27807	1.6	82	8650	10262	11101	1.9	2.48	6511	7477	1.5
37852	ROBBINS	151	2836	2907	2956	0.3	31	1088	1162	1198	0.7	2.50	823	860	0.5
37853	ROCKFORD	009	3513	3928	4185	1.2	72	1426	1615	1731	1.4	2.42	1013	1113	1.0
37854	ROCKWOOD	035	11717	12249	12549	0.5	41	4845	5199	5370	0.8	2.30	3392	3537	0.5
37857	ROGERSVILLE	073	19090	20704	21527	0.9	63	7941	8902	9349	1.2	2.30	5597	6115	1.0
37860	RUSSELLVILLE	063	3228	3716	3946	1.5	81	1278	1514	1623	1.8	2.43	968	1121	1.6
37861	RUTLEDGE	057	7323	8593	9222	1.7	84	2969	3596	3904	2.1	2.35	2168	2562	1.8
37862	SEVIERVILLE	155	17335	20394	22038	1.8	86	7243	8581	9307	1.8	2.33	4905	5621	1.5
37863	PIGEON FORGE	155	5501	5925	6198	0.8	60	2174	2355	2475	0.9	2.46	1542	1621	0.5
37865	SEYMOUR	155	16857	20488	22587	2.1	91	6465	7926	8770	2.2	2.58	5054	6054	2.0
37866	SHARPS CHAPEL	173	1465	1790	1914	2.2	92	605	767	828	2.6	2.33	429	531	2.3
37869	SNEEDVILLE	067	5293	5358	5418	0.1	22	2173	2314	2373	0.7	2.25	1507	1562	0.4
37870	SPEEDWELL	025	4516	4997	5187	1.1	69	1819	2072	2174	1.4	2.41	1384	1543	1.2
37871	STRAWBERRY PLAINS	093	8477	9719	10352	1.5	81	3276	3824	4098	1.7	2.54	2474	2808	1.4
37872	SUNBRIGHT	129	2019	2165	2223	0.8	60	775	861	894	1.1	2.50	575	624	0.9
37873	SURGOINSVILLE	073	4286	4824	5076	1.3	76	1765	2060	2191	1.7	2.34	1331	1518	1.4
37874	SWEETWATER	123	14001	15853	16927	1.4	78	5457	6308	6794	1.6	2.46	3977	4484	1.3
37876	SEVIERVILLE	155	21250	28077	31326	3.1	96	8377	11137	12471	3.1	2.52	6308	8204	2.9
37877	TALBOTT	089	7744	8776	9322	1.4	78	3052	3555	3803	1.7	2.47	2383	2715	1.4
37878	TALLASSEE	009	632	746	819	1.8	86	287	343	379	1.9	2.17	210	243	1.6
37879	TAZEWELL	025	9263	9954	10148	0.8	60	3746	4170	4299	1.2	2.34	2656	2880	0.9
37880	TEN MILE	121	3437	3801	3971	1.1	69	1413	1589	1669	1.3	2.39	1079	1187	1.0
37881	THORN HILL	057	2057	2291	2407	1.2	72	806	928	986	1.5	2.47	603	679	1.3
37882	TOWNSEND	009	2438	3204	3593	3.0	95	1085	1452	1638	3.2	2.21	770	995	2.8
37885	VONORE	123	3687	4816	5284	2.9	95	1491	2023	2241	3.4	2.38	1122	1499	3.2
37886	WALLAND	009	3817	4537	4950	1.9	88	1548	1859	2038	2.0	2.44	1174	1367	1.7
37887	WARTBURG	129	6348	6401	6435	0.1	22	1830	1919	1954	0.5	2.50	1360	1393	0.3
37888	WASHBURN	057	2605	2755	2869	0.6	47	1017	1104	1160	0.9	2.50	781	831	0.7
37890	WHITE PINE	089	5818	6653	7142	1.5	81	2354	2743	2959	1.7	2.43	1734	1969	1.4
37891	WHITESBURG	063	3224	3576	3748	1.1	69	1278	1462	1547	1.5	2.44	969	1081	1.2
37892	WINFIELD	151	1935	2080	2152	0.8	60	752	831	868	1.1	2.50	566	612	0.8
37902	KNOXVILLE	093	1216	1406	1504	1.6	82	734	904	988	2.3	1.08	62	68	1.0
37909	KNOXVILLE	093	13700	14769	15536	0.8	60	6476	7183	7629	1.1	1.97	3021	3113	0.3
37912	KNOXVILLE	093	18483	19948	21086	0.8	60	8739	9670	10297	1.1	2.05	5025	5241	0.5
37914	KNOXVILLE	093	20161	21161	21960	0.5	41	8349	8960	9365	0.8	2.34	5505	5660	0.3
37915	KNOXVILLE	093	5507	5814	6042	0.6	47	2708	2929	3069	0.9	1.97	1326	1334	0.1
37916	KNOXVILLE	093	11672	11863	12104	0.2	27	2765	3005	3162	0.9	1.67	324	314	-0.3
37917	KNOXVILLE	093	25796	26326	26928	0.2	27	11965	12415	12774	0.4	2.06	6105	5976	-0.2
37918	KNOXVILLE	093	35978	41235	44144	1.5	81	14710	17204	18538	1.7	2.34	9933	11161	1.3
37919	KNOXVILLE	093	27302	29521	30957	0.8	60	12962	14250	15035	1.0	2.03	6691	6934	0.4
37920	KNOXVILLE	093	37946	40408	42252	0.7	53	16155	17603	18557	0.9	2.25	10003	10416	0.4
37921	KNOXVILLE	093	26254	28142	29543	0.8	60	10540	11571	12251	1.0	2.41	7106	7487	0.6
37922	KNOXVILLE	093	24942	33187	37077	3.1	96	9020	12096	13573	3.2	2.74	7249	9505	3.0
37923	KNOXVILLE	093	27765	30855	32766	1.1	69	12328	13989	14958	1.4	2.19	7296	7831	0.8
37924	KNOXVILLE	093	8645	10198	10978	1.8	86	3653	4390	4761	2.0	2.32	2630	3033	1.6
37931	KNOXVILLE	093	15908	20917	23119	3.0	95	6237	8396	9352	3.3	2.48	4725	6138	2.9
37932	KNOXVILLE	093	11129	13260	14371	1.9	88	4238	5173	5650	2.2	2.56	3184	3757	1.8
37934	KNOXVILLE	093	20702	24597	26657	1.9	88	7457	9038	9854	2.1	2.70	6024	7102	1.8
37938	KNOXVILLE	093	13738	16648	18105	2.1	91	5159	6393	7007	2.3	2.59	4171	5032	2.0
38001	ALAMO	033	4703	4554	4458	-0.3	7	1820	1775	1738	-0.3	2.47	1264	1197	-0.6
38002	ARLINGTON	157	17592	29737	34199	5.8	99	6386	10778	12444	5.8	2.72	5051	8427	5.7
38004	ATOKA	167	5930	9173	10604	4.8	98	2030	3183	3697	5.0	2.88	1707	2633	4.8
38006	BELLS	075	4893	5198	5225	0.7	53	1845	1973	1985	0.7	2.57	1341	1397	0.4
38008	BOLIVAR	069	10451	10172	9966	-0.3	7	3905	3931	3887	0.1	2.35	2742	2685	-0.2
38011	BRIGHTON	167	7565	9101	9791	2.0	90	2650	3232	3496	2.2	2.80	2176	2596	1.9
38012	BROWNSVILLE	075	15245	14897	14539	-0.2	10	5782	5810	5722	0.1	2.52	4121	4035	-0.2
38015	BURLISON	167	2693	2819	2879	0.5	41	1034	1111	1145	0.8	2.54	777	808	0.4
38016	CORDOVA	157	28931	42092	46805	4.1	98	11757	16964	18866	4.0	2.47	8067	11763	4.2
38017	COLLIERVILLE	157	35790	42949	45840	2.0	90	11789	14624	15751	2.4	2.93	10122	12183	2.0
38018	CORDOVA	157	24028	32064	34701	3.2	96	9401	12593	13644	3.2	2.51	6605	8711	3.0
38019	COVINGTON	167	15674	16600	17087	0.6	47	5847	6356	6597	0.9	2.56	4241	4459	0.5
38023	DRUMMONDS	167	4638	6054	6670	2.9	95	1622	2183	2425	3.3	2.77	1302	1711	3.0
38024	DYERSBURG	045	28130	28356	28237	0.1	22	11124	11331	11312	0.2	2.45	7734	7666	-0.1
	TENNESSEE					1.1					1.3	2.44			1.0
	UNITED STATES					1.0					1.1	2.59			0.9

POPULATION COMPOSITION

ZIP CODE #	POST OFFICE NAME	RACE (%) White		Black		Asian/Pacific		% Hispanic Origin		2009 AGE DISTRIBUTION (%) 0-4	5-9	10-14	15-19	20-24	25-44	45-64	65-84	85+	18+	MEDIAN AGE	% 2009 Males	% 2009 Females
		2000	2009	2000	2009	2000	2009	2000	2009											2009		
37769	LAKE CITY	98.7	98.3	0.2	0.2	0.1	0.2	0.5	0.8	5.6	5.6	5.8	6.1	5.2	23.8	29.0	15.9	3.0	79.2	43.5	48.4	51.6
37770	LANCING	98.2	97.8	0.4	0.4	0.2	0.2	0.5	0.8	5.9	6.1	6.6	6.9	5.2	27.0	29.0	12.0	1.3	77.1	39.8	50.0	50.0
37771	LENOIR CITY	94.6	92.1	0.9	1.1	0.2	0.3	3.9	6.5	6.7	6.7	6.6	6.3	5.9	27.1	27.1	11.6	2.0	76.2	38.6	48.6	51.4
37772	LENOIR CITY	97.2	96.3	0.8	0.9	0.2	0.3	1.2	2.0	5.2	5.7	6.3	5.8	3.9	23.0	34.0	14.6	1.5	79.1	45.1	49.8	50.2
37774	LOUDON	96.1	95.0	1.5	1.6	0.3	0.4	1.8	2.8	4.7	4.8	5.0	4.8	3.8	19.8	29.0	25.7	2.4	82.5	50.5	48.6	51.4
37777	LOUISVILLE	92.9	91.0	4.7	5.9	0.4	0.6	1.3	2.1	5.0	5.1	5.6	6.2	6.2	30.0	29.4	11.2	1.2	80.5	39.7	50.1	49.9
37778	LOWLAND	94.1	94.4	0.0	0.0	0.0	0.0	5.9	11.1	5.6	5.6	5.6	11.1	11.1	38.9	22.2	0.0	0.0	72.2	30.0	61.1	38.9
37779	LUTTRELL	97.9	97.3	0.2	0.2	0.2	0.1	1.0	1.6	7.5	7.2	7.1	6.4	6.2	27.0	27.5	9.8	1.4	74.1	36.7	49.6	50.4
37801	MARYVILLE	94.9	93.5	2.4	2.9	0.6	0.9	1.3	2.1	6.4	6.4	6.6	6.5	5.4	27.2	27.8	12.1	1.5	76.7	39.4	48.4	51.6
37803	MARYVILLE	96.5	95.2	1.1	1.3	1.3	1.9	0.8	1.3	5.3	5.7	6.2	6.8	5.4	23.7	30.6	13.9	2.5	78.9	42.9	48.3	51.7
37804	MARYVILLE	95.5	94.1	2.2	2.8	0.8	1.3	1.0	1.6	5.8	5.9	6.2	6.8	5.7	25.4	27.6	13.8	2.9	78.2	41.1	47.8	52.2
37806	MASCOT	96.6	95.4	2.0	2.7	0.1	0.1	0.6	0.9	5.8	6.0	6.4	6.0	4.8	26.2	30.7	12.8	1.3	77.8	41.7	48.8	51.2
37807	MAYNARDVILLE	98.7	98.5	0.1	0.1	0.2	0.2	0.7	1.1	6.7	6.7	6.7	6.3	5.7	28.0	28.0	10.7	1.2	76.1	38.7	50.1	49.9
37809	MIDWAY	98.1	97.3	0.4	0.5	0.1	0.2	1.2	2.0	6.6	6.6	6.8	6.2	5.4	27.0	27.6	12.8	1.1	76.2	39.0	49.5	50.5
37810	MOHAWK	98.2	97.6	0.9	1.0	0.0	0.0	0.8	1.4	6.1	6.3	6.6	6.3	5.5	28.2	27.7	12.2	1.2	77.2	39.4	50.0	50.0
37811	MOORESBURG	98.8	98.3	0.2	0.3	0.2	0.3	0.7	1.2	6.3	6.4	6.5	6.1	5.0	26.8	29.4	12.3	1.1	77.0	40.5	50.4	49.6
37813	MORRISTOWN	89.9	86.8	4.6	5.1	0.4	0.6	6.4	10.1	6.8	6.6	6.4	6.2	5.8	27.6	26.1	12.8	1.8	76.5	38.3	48.9	51.1
37814	MORRISTOWN	89.0	85.5	4.9	5.2	0.9	1.3	6.9	10.8	6.4	6.5	6.4	6.0	5.0	27.9	26.6	13.4	1.8	77.1	39.4	49.9	50.1
37818	MOSHEIM	98.6	98.3	0.5	0.6	0.1	0.2	0.6	1.0	6.0	6.1	6.5	6.1	4.4	26.5	29.5	13.6	1.2	77.5	41.0	49.7	50.3
37819	NEWCOMB	98.1	97.7	0.5	0.6	0.1	0.2	0.9	1.5	6.6	6.5	7.4	7.0	6.0	25.7	28.4	11.4	1.0	75.4	38.0	50.1	49.9
37820	NEW MARKET	96.2	94.9	1.3	1.5	0.3	0.6	1.5	2.5	6.3	6.5	6.7	6.8	5.1	26.4	28.2	12.5	1.5	76.2	40.0	50.1	49.9
37821	NEWPORT	95.4	94.5	2.7	3.0	0.2	0.2	1.1	1.8	6.0	6.0	6.1	6.0	5.2	26.3	29.0	13.8	1.7	78.4	41.1	48.5	51.5
37825	NEW TAZEWELL	97.8	97.1	0.7	0.8	0.3	0.4	0.7	1.1	6.2	6.2	6.4	6.3	5.6	26.8	28.0	13.1	1.4	77.4	40.2	49.0	51.0
37826	NIOTA	94.5	93.3	3.6	4.0	0.7	1.1	0.9	1.4	6.4	6.5	7.0	6.7	4.8	26.5	29.2	11.7	1.2	76.0	39.8	49.8	50.2
37829	OAKDALE	98.9	98.6	0.0	0.0	0.2	0.3	0.1	0.3	7.3	7.5	7.4	6.5	4.9	26.8	27.9	10.6	1.1	73.6	37.3	50.9	49.1
37830	OAK RIDGE	87.2	84.3	8.0	9.0	2.1	3.1	1.9	3.0	4.9	4.9	5.4	6.4	5.9	21.6	30.4	16.7	3.7	80.8	45.6	47.1	52.9
37840	OLIVER SPRINGS	96.8	96.1	1.8	2.1	0.2	0.3	0.4	0.7	6.1	6.4	6.4	6.0	4.9	25.9	29.6	13.0	1.7	77.4	40.8	49.0	51.0
37841	ONEIDA	98.5	98.1	0.0	0.1	0.2	0.3	0.6	0.9	7.1	7.2	7.3	6.5	5.2	27.1	26.4	11.6	1.6	74.5	37.6	48.5	51.5
37843	PARROTTSVILLE	96.8	96.1	1.6	1.9	0.3	0.5	0.5	0.9	5.8	6.0	6.3	6.0	5.2	25.0	30.4	13.8	1.4	78.2	41.8	50.5	49.5
37846	PHILADELPHIA	96.1	94.8	1.3	1.6	0.2	0.3	1.6	2.7	7.1	7.4	7.2	6.1	5.5	26.9	27.7	11.0	1.2	74.6	38.1	50.7	49.3
37847	PIONEER	98.3	97.9	0.2	0.2	0.1	0.2	0.7	1.1	7.3	7.5	7.2	7.0	6.8	26.1	27.4	9.8	0.9	74.0	36.1	51.5	48.5
37848	POWDER SPRINGS	99.1	98.3	0.0	0.0	0.0	0.0	0.9	1.3	6.5	7.0	7.0	5.7	4.8	27.8	27.8	12.2	1.3	75.7	39.4	49.1	50.9
37849	POWELL	97.0	96.0	1.3	1.6	0.5	0.8	0.7	1.1	6.0	5.9	6.3	6.9	5.6	25.8	29.7	12.4	1.4	77.9	40.5	48.6	51.4
37852	ROBBINS	98.6	98.2	0.0	0.0	0.0	0.0	0.6	1.0	6.3	6.8	6.7	6.9	6.9	26.4	28.1	10.9	1.2	76.0	37.2	51.3	48.7
37853	ROCKFORD	94.9	93.7	3.3	4.0	0.3	0.5	0.9	1.4	5.3	5.8	6.2	6.2	4.9	26.6	30.5	13.1	1.5	79.0	41.5	49.3	50.7
37854	ROCKWOOD	95.4	94.5	3.1	3.5	0.2	0.3	0.5	0.8	5.8	6.1	6.2	5.7	4.7	23.3	29.0	16.4	2.7	78.3	43.6	47.8	52.2
37857	ROGERSVILLE	96.9	96.3	1.8	2.1	0.2	0.3	0.8	1.3	6.0	6.1	6.3	5.8	5.1	26.5	28.1	14.0	2.0	78.0	41.1	49.0	51.0
37860	RUSSELLVILLE	96.7	95.8	2.2	2.6	0.1	0.2	0.9	1.5	6.1	6.2	6.4	6.0	4.7	27.3	28.6	13.0	1.6	77.5	41.1	50.9	49.1
37861	RUTLEDGE	98.1	97.4	0.4	0.4	0.1	0.1	1.8	2.9	5.6	5.9	6.2	5.8	4.6	26.6	29.4	14.0	1.9	78.7	42.0	50.5	49.5
37862	SEVIERVILLE	96.5	95.3	0.9	0.9	0.8	1.2	1.7	2.8	5.6	5.6	5.8	5.7	5.3	26.1	28.9	14.8	2.3	79.7	42.0	48.6	51.4
37863	PIGEON FORGE	95.5	93.4	0.7	0.7	1.1	1.7	3.3	5.4	6.3	6.1	6.1	6.1	5.6	27.5	26.8	13.5	2.0	77.7	39.2	48.6	51.4
37865	SEYMOUR	97.8	97.1	0.5	0.6	0.4	0.6	0.7	1.3	5.8	6.3	6.7	6.6	4.6	26.7	30.3	11.9	1.2	77.1	40.6	49.4	50.6
37866	SHARPS CHAPEL	98.8	98.5	0.0	0.0	0.1	0.1	0.5	0.9	4.9	5.4	5.6	5.3	4.0	22.6	33.0	17.7	1.5	80.9	46.3	50.9	49.1
37869	SNEEDVILLE	97.8	97.8	0.5	0.5	0.1	0.1	0.4	0.4	5.4	5.5	5.8	6.4	5.4	25.7	29.4	14.2	2.2	79.5	41.9	48.6	51.4
37870	SPEEDWELL	98.8	98.5	0.1	0.1	0.1	0.1	1.0	1.6	4.9	5.2	5.7	6.5	4.6	24.9	31.5	15.0	1.6	80.2	43.8	49.6	50.4
37871	STRAWBERRY PLAINS	96.6	95.7	1.8	2.0	0.2	0.3	0.7	1.2	6.1	6.3	6.5	6.1	4.8	26.7	29.1	12.9	1.3	77.3	40.8	49.6	50.4
37872	SUNBRIGHT	98.2	97.6	0.1	0.1	0.1	0.1	0.9	1.4	6.8	7.1	7.0	6.3	5.5	26.9	27.7	11.5	1.2	75.1	38.4	50.1	49.9
37873	SURGOINSVILLE	98.5	98.1	0.4	0.5	0.0	0.0	1.7	2.8	5.8	5.8	6.2	6.3	5.1	27.9	28.9	12.8	1.2	78.3	40.8	49.8	50.2
37874	SWEETWATER	91.8	89.9	5.0	5.6	0.7	1.0	1.7	2.8	6.2	6.4	6.5	6.7	5.6	25.7	27.7	13.0	2.2	77.0	39.9	48.5	51.5
37876	SEVIERVILLE	98.1	97.5	0.4	0.4	0.3	0.4	0.8	1.3	5.7	6.1	6.4	6.2	4.9	26.6	31.2	11.8	1.2	77.9	41.2	49.8	50.2
37877	TALBOTT	97.2	96.2	0.7	0.9	0.3	0.5	1.3	2.2	6.1	6.6	6.8	5.9	4.1	25.8	29.8	13.7	1.2	76.8	41.3	49.8	50.2
37878	TALLASSEE	98.4	97.9	0.2	0.3	0.5	0.8	0.8	1.1	4.7	5.2	5.6	5.0	3.9	22.3	37.0	15.0	1.3	81.2	47.0	50.9	49.1
37879	TAZEWELL	97.5	96.9	1.4	1.5	0.2	0.4	0.6	1.0	6.0	5.9	6.2	6.4	5.3	26.6	27.9	13.6	2.0	78.0	40.5	47.6	52.4
37880	TEN MILE	98.0	97.4	0.6	0.7	0.1	0.2	0.5	0.8	6.4	6.4	6.6	5.6	4.3	25.7	29.4	14.4	1.2	77.2	41.5	51.0	49.0
37881	THORN HILL	98.6	98.4	0.7	0.7	0.1	0.2	0.3	0.6	5.8	6.0	6.3	6.1	5.1	26.7	29.6	13.2	1.2	78.1	40.6	50.5	49.5
37882	TOWNSEND	97.8	97.1	0.1	0.1	0.3	0.4	1.0	1.7	4.1	4.5	4.8	4.3	3.1	20.3	37.5	19.4	2.0	83.9	50.1	50.0	50.0
37885	VONORE	95.8	94.6	0.2	0.2	0.2	0.3	2.4	3.6	6.5	6.5	6.6	6.1	4.8	24.9	28.4	15.0	1.2	76.6	41.0	50.4	49.6
37886	WALLAND	97.6	96.9	0.2	0.2	0.3	0.5	0.9	1.5	5.2	6.2	6.4	5.7	4.5	25.8	32.2	12.7	1.4	78.6	42.2	49.9	50.1
37887	WARTBURG	92.8	91.7	6.5	7.5	0.1	0.1	0.8	1.3	4.9	5.0	5.5	5.7	7.5	36.1	25.0	8.7	1.6	81.1	36.9	60.6	39.4
37888	WASHBURN	98.6	98.2	0.1	0.1	0.2	0.3	0.7	1.2	6.0	6.2	6.5	6.5	5.4	27.8	28.2	12.3	1.2	77.4	39.6	48.9	51.1
37890	WHITE PINE	97.0	95.8	0.8	0.9	0.2	0.3	1.5	2.6	6.7	6.9	7.0	6.0	4.8	25.8	28.3	13.2	1.4	75.7	40.0	49.8	50.2
37891	WHITESBURG	98.0	97.4	1.1	1.2	0.1	0.2	0.8	1.3	6.2	6.3	6.7	6.2	5.0	26.9	29.3	12.1	1.3	77.0	40.4	50.0	50.0
37892	WINFIELD	98.9	98.6	0.0	0.0	0.1	0.0	0.3	0.4	7.7	7.5	7.6	6.4	5.0	30.3	25.0	9.3	1.0	73.1	35.9	48.9	51.1
37902	KNOXVILLE	80.7	75.7	15.9	20.0	0.8	1.1	1.2	1.8	0.4	0.5	0.3	3.0	25.6	31.2	25.2	12.4	1.6	98.4	36.8	56.9	43.1
37909	KNOXVILLE	88.8	85.0	6.2	8.0	2.0	3.0	2.2	3.5	5.1	4.1	4.2	5.4	16.2	30.6	20.1	11.1	3.1	83.7	32.4	47.3	52.7
37912	KNOXVILLE	89.2	85.8	6.8	8.7	1.6	2.3	1.2	2.1	6.5	6.0	5.6	5.1	7.2	29.6	24.7	13.1	2.2	79.1	37.9	47.6	52.4
37914	KNOXVILLE	56.5	54.0	41.4	43.5	0.3	0.4	0.8	1.2	5.5	5.5	5.9	6.3	5.4	23.0	30.3	15.5	2.7	79.2	43.8	47.3	52.7
37915	KNOXVILLE	13.2	10.8	84.4	86.7	0.1	0.1	1.0	1.2	11.0	7.7	5.5	8.8	9.9	23.7	23.7	8.3	1.5	72.0	29.9	42.3	57.7
37916	KNOXVILLE	84.7	79.8	7.4	9.3	5.6	8.0	1.4	2.3	0.5	0.3	0.2	36.4	47.0	11.2	2.7	1.2	0.5	98.7	21.3	51.8	48.2
37917	KNOXVILLE	82.3	78.2	14.1	16.9	0.5	0.8	1.7	2.6	5.8	5.7	5.3	5.7	7.0	27.6	26.8	13.1	3.0	79.8	40.1	48.2	51.8
37918	KNOXVILLE	94.8	93.2	3.2	4.1	0.5	0.9	1.1	1.6	6.3	6.1	6.1	5.6	5.4	28.2	27.5	12.5	2.3	78.0	39.6	48.4	51.6
37919	KNOXVILLE	90.9	87.8	4.3	5.4	2.7	3.8	1.9	3.0	5.2	4.8	4.9	5.4	9.0	27.4	27.0	13.2	3.1	81.7	39.3	47.8	52.2
37920	KNOXVILLE	93.4	91.5	4.0	4.9	0.5	0.8	1.1	1.9	5.6	5.5	5.6	6.1	8.7	25.8	26.9	13.5	2.2	79.8	39.4	49.0	51.0
37921	KNOXVILLE	76.5	72.4	20.1	23.1	0.7	1.0	1.4	2.2	7.9	7.8	7.2	6.9	6.7	28.8	24.1	9.4	1.3	73.1	34.9	47.7	52.3
37922	KNOXVILLE	94.0	91.8	2.3	2.9	2.2	3.2	1.4	2.2	7.0	7.6	8.3	7.3	4.4	25.4	30.9	8.2	0.8	72.3	39.0	49.2	50.8
37923	KNOXVILLE	90.3	87.0	5.1	6.5	2.4	3.6	2.0	3.1	6.1	5.4	5.1	5.8	8.6	31.3	25.7	10.3	1.6	80.0	36.3	48.6	51.4
37924	KNOXVILLE	92.1	89.4	6.0	7.8	0.5	0.7	1.1	1.9	5.4	5.8	6.1	5.6	4.1	26.0	30.8	14.5	1.8	79.1	43.0	49.3	50.7
37931	KNOXVILLE	95.8	94.3	2.1	2.7	0.8	1.3	0.8	1.3	6.5	6.8	7.1	6.4	4.4	26.3	30.3	11.0	1.2	75.4	40.5	49.4	50.6
37932	KNOXVILLE	93.9	91.5	3.2	4.3	1.4	2.2	1.0	1.7	6.2	6.5	6.9	6.2	4.7	26.7	32.3	9.7	0.9	76.6	40.8	49.0	51.0
37934	KNOXVILLE	93.5	90.7	2.2	2.9	3.0	4.7	1.1	1.8	5.2	6.1	7.0	7.1	4.3	21.8	34.9	11.8	1.7	76.9	43.9	49.2	50.8
37938	KNOXVILLE	98.4	97.8	0.2	0.3	0.3	0.4	0.5	0.8	5.8	6.2	6.9	6.6	4.4	24.8	31.6	12.3	1.4	76.8	42.1	49.3	50.7
38001	ALAMO	83.0	81.8	14.7	15.9	0.1	0.1	2.6	2.6	6.3	6.2	6.4	6.8	5.3	24.5	26.0	15.2	3.4	76.9	40.9	47.5	52.5
38002	ARLINGTON	82.4	73.2	15.4	23.5	0.9	1.3	1.1	1.9	7.1	7.4	7.5	6.6	4.3	28.6	28.5	9.0	0.9	73.6	38.0	49.2	50.8
38004	ATOKA	85.9	82.2	11.4	14.1	0.6	0.8	1.9	3.0	8.3	7.7	7.5	7.2	6.0	30.2	25.3	7.2	0.7	72.2	33.8	49.7	50.3
38006	BELLS	77.4	76.7	15.7	16.4	0.1	0.1	12.1	12.0	7.3	7.1	7.2	6.7	5.3	27.2	24.5	11.9	2.9	74.3	37.6	49.3	50.7
38008	BOLIVAR	51.0	49.3	47.7	49.4	0.4	0.4	0.7	0.7	6.2	6.4	6.6	6.9	6.5	26.3	26.5	12.1	2.6	76.5	38.4	49.6	50.4
38011	BRIGHTON	86.4	83.1	11.6	14.3	0.3	0.5	1.2	1.8	6.9	7.1	7.3	7.6	5.9	27.1	27.8	9.1	1.2	74.0	36.9	49.4	50.6
38012	BROWNSVILLE	44.2	40.9	53.3	55.5	0.2	0.2	3.1	4.5	7.1	7.4	7.4	7.4	6.1	26.1	25.9	10.5	2.1	73.7	36.0	46.7	53.3
38015	BURLISON	93.9	91.9	5.1	6.6	0.1	0.1	0.7	1.1	6.5	6.7	6.9	6.6	5.2	26.0	29.6	11.5	1.1	75.8	39.1	50.3	49.7
38016	CORDOVA	86.4	77.9	8.2	14.6	3.6	4.9	1.9	3.3	7.7	7.4	7.1	6.1	5.0	32.1	26.5	7.1	1.0	73.6	35.8	48.6	51.4
38017	COLLIERVILLE	87.9	82.6	9.4	13.2	1.4	2.3	1.5	2.6	7.1	7.9	8.5	8.1	4.6	25.2	30.8	7.2	0.8	71.3	37.7	49.3	50.7
38018	CORDOVA	86.8	79.9	7.5	12.0	3.8	5.3	1.8	3.4	8.0	6.9	6.7	5.6	6.2	32.4	25.2	7.6	1.4	74.7	34.7	48.6	51.4
38019	COVINGTON	66.1	61.6	32.2	36.3	0.4	0.5	0.8	1.1	7.4	7.2	7.0	7.3	6.3	25.0	25.7	11.8	2.2	73.8	36.7	47.2	52.8
38023	DRUMMONDS	80.4	77.7	17.6	19.7	0.4	0.5	0.8	1.3	6.9	6.9	7.5	7.7	6.0	27.5	27.5	9.1	0.9	73.8	36.5	49.0	51.0
38024	DYERSBURG	83.1	80.9	15.1	16.5	0.4	0.6	1.2	1.9	6.9	6.8	6.8	6.8	5.9	26.3	26.6	11.9	2.2	75.4	38.2	48.0	52.0
	TENNESSEE	80.2	78.4	16.4	16.9	1.0	1.5	2.2	3.4	6.5	6.4	6.5	6.8	6.5	27.2	27.0	11.4	1.7	76.6	38.0	49.0	51.0
	UNITED STATES	75.1	72.0	12.3	12.7	3.8	4.6	12.5	15.7	6.8	6.7	6.6	7.1	6.9	27.0	26.0	10.9	1.9	75.7	36.9	49.2	50.8

ZIP CODE				2009 HOUSEHOLD INCOME DISTRIBUTION (%)					MEDIAN HOUSEHOLD INCOME					2009 HOME VALUE DISTRIBUTION (%)					
#	POST OFFICE NAME	2009 Per Capita Income	2009 HH Income Base	Less than $25,000	$25,000 to $49,999	$50,000 to $99,999	$100,000 to $149,999	$150,000 or More	2009	2014	2009 National Centile	2009 State Centile	2009 Home Value Base	Less than $50,000	$50,000 to $89,999	$90,000 to $174,999	$175,000 to $399,999	$400,000 or More	2009 Median Home Value
37769	LAKE CITY	16266	2701	40.9	33.0	22.6	2.5	1.1	31574	34128	11	16	1883	25.5	24.7	39.4	9.2	1.2	89631
37770	LANCING	14253	1023	40.4	34.7	22.1	2.8	0.0	30593	31987	9	13	878	30.3	29.2	35.6	4.2	0.7	75517
37771	LENOIR CITY	22404	6097	23.6	30.4	38.3	5.7	2.0	45597	48888	50	70	4320	14.4	26.8	41.8	14.4	2.6	101549
37772	LENOIR CITY	31212	4408	16.1	23.3	41.9	11.1	7.5	61971	62919	80	91	3757	6.5	10.2	49.5	24.3	9.4	143880
37774	LOUDON	29002	7497	20.2	24.6	39.3	9.7	6.2	54693	58251	71	85	6075	8.0	15.8	33.7	26.4	16.1	147078
37777	LOUISVILLE	27020	5139	21.5	31.4	34.3	7.7	5.1	47122	50086	54	75	3217	16.5	10.8	29.5	35.3	7.9	154583
37778	LOWLAND	20000	9	33.3	33.3	33.3	0.0	0.0	42288	47295	40	60	7	0.0	28.6	42.9	28.6	0.0	131250
37779	LUTTRELL	17563	1568	33.7	33.9	26.9	2.8	2.6	35416	37595	19	27	1259	25.7	19.6	41.3	12.8	0.6	95000
37801	MARYVILLE	21778	9568	25.2	31.1	35.7	5.6	2.4	43188	47179	43	63	6953	18.8	11.2	43.3	23.9	2.7	126088
37803	MARYVILLE	27764	12462	17.7	24.1	41.3	10.3	6.6	57453	58225	75	88	10073	7.1	9.7	40.9	36.5	5.8	160218
37804	MARYVILLE	20893	9283	25.5	28.9	38.3	5.5	1.7	45312	48768	49	68	6959	10.7	17.6	44.5	25.5	1.6	127738
37806	MASCOT	17395	1290	28.5	38.4	30.6	2.2	0.2	36925	40158	23	35	1035	29.0	26.6	29.2	13.7	1.5	80726
37807	MAYNARDVILLE	16494	3815	36.6	30.7	27.5	4.0	1.2	35371	38038	19	26	3025	23.4	18.0	43.4	14.0	1.2	100140
37809	MIDWAY	15601	747	31.2	36.5	30.4	1.2	0.7	36795	39537	23	34	597	21.3	33.0	31.8	10.7	3.2	85887
37810	MOHAWK	16268	771	31.5	39.7	24.1	4.3	0.4	34956	36889	17	24	609	18.7	29.2	38.6	11.8	1.6	92315
37811	MOORESBURG	16031	1496	38.0	33.2	25.3	2.9	0.5	30627	34485	9	13	1279	23.0	28.2	33.5	12.8	2.4	87817
37813	MORRISTOWN	18846	7382	32.6	29.8	32.9	3.3	1.4	38689	42265	29	44	5070	12.5	30.0	46.6	10.1	0.9	98268
37814	MORRISTOWN	23621	13301	28.0	30.2	31.4	5.9	4.5	41014	44187	36	54	9403	10.6	17.9	49.2	19.3	3.0	119571
37818	MOSHEIM	18614	2113	27.1	33.9	35.0	3.0	0.9	39843	40791	32	50	1736	16.9	30.2	42.2	9.6	1.1	93125
37819	NEWCOMB	11604	381	46.5	38.1	15.0	0.3	0.3	27750	28452	5	8	312	45.2	39.7	9.9	5.1	0.0	53488
37820	NEW MARKET	19703	2958	26.3	35.1	32.0	4.4	2.1	41363	43095	37	56	2417	17.1	22.1	42.9	14.9	3.0	107615
37821	NEWPORT	17598	9653	42.4	29.4	23.1	3.3	1.8	30985	31702	10	15	6967	26.1	24.2	38.4	10.3	1.0	89518
37825	NEW TAZEWELL	17317	3503	40.2	28.7	26.3	3.3	1.6	32631	34640	13	17	2734	25.9	23.5	38.7	10.2	1.8	91063
37826	NIOTA	19996	1634	26.9	31.5	36.0	3.9	1.8	42296	44316	40	60	1353	16.1	20.6	46.0	14.0	3.3	108967
37829	OAKDALE	17362	659	26.6	36.3	32.8	2.3	2.1	39208	42454	30	47	577	18.2	37.4	34.3	9.5	0.5	81216
37830	OAK RIDGE	32466	12664	20.2	24.5	33.9	12.7	8.6	56047	55030	73	87	8656	2.4	17.8	47.5	27.1	5.1	133790
37840	OLIVER SPRINGS	19627	4305	29.9	31.4	32.3	5.1	1.2	40373	42211	34	51	3460	23.2	24.2	41.7	9.5	1.4	93132
37841	ONEIDA	17538	3991	41.2	32.5	22.3	2.5	1.5	30764	31444	9	14	2877	24.6	29.1	34.7	10.2	1.5	83817
37843	PARROTTSVILLE	17143	1583	36.5	32.5	26.1	3.6	1.3	35824	37519	20	29	1289	24.7	21.7	41.6	8.9	3.1	94844
37846	PHILADELPHIA	18310	1670	27.2	31.6	34.9	4.0	2.3	42017	43412	39	58	1370	13.4	24.0	45.2	13.0	4.4	107481
37847	PIONEER	12577	1024	51.3	31.3	14.6	2.0	0.9	24400	24827	3	4	855	49.5	25.4	19.9	3.9	1.4	50608
37848	POWDER SPRINGS	17053	100	53.0	26.0	15.0	3.0	3.0	23273	27362	2	3	86	34.9	26.7	25.6	9.3	3.5	71429
37849	POWELL	25711	10262	18.3	27.6	41.0	8.9	4.2	55252	57180	72	86	8482	13.4	12.7	46.8	25.6	1.5	132037
37852	ROBBINS	14865	1162	42.9	33.2	21.3	1.5	1.1	29117	30355	7	10	950	34.3	32.5	27.5	5.3	0.4	64815
37853	ROCKFORD	21535	1615	28.2	30.0	33.9	5.8	2.2	41957	45764	39	58	1188	23.6	17.2	33.8	21.1	4.4	111417
37854	ROCKWOOD	18748	5199	37.6	28.6	29.2	3.3	1.3	35651	37901	20	27	3940	24.5	29.4	32.8	11.6	1.7	82094
37857	ROGERSVILLE	18883	8902	36.2	29.9	28.9	3.2	1.8	36219	38638	21	31	6785	16.4	27.8	37.0	16.7	2.1	98110
37860	RUSSELLVILLE	21408	1514	24.4	32.3	35.9	5.2	2.3	44394	47779	47	66	1214	7.7	17.6	52.6	21.4	0.7	124085
37861	RUTLEDGE	18799	3596	37.3	29.5	27.6	3.6	2.0	32970	34305	13	19	2952	20.3	26.1	35.4	15.2	3.1	95459
37862	SEVIERVILLE	23131	8581	29.6	30.4	30.0	5.9	4.1	41633	43181	38	56	5247	11.6	12.5	34.7	35.0	6.2	154061
37863	PIGEON FORGE	19744	2355	30.5	34.8	27.2	4.7	2.8	38199	40556	27	42	1449	22.0	10.9	30.0	34.0	3.0	139711
37865	SEYMOUR	21818	7926	19.4	30.7	41.1	6.9	2.0	49918	49574	61	78	6395	9.3	11.8	48.6	26.2	4.1	139182
37866	SHARPS CHAPEL	16851	767	47.2	25.7	20.1	5.2	1.8	29873	31330	8	11	656	17.7	30.3	27.7	12.5	11.7	92097
37869	SNEEDVILLE	15090	2314	50.4	28.0	18.6	2.0	0.9	24477	25249	3	4	1783	38.2	26.8	27.3	6.6	1.2	66085
37870	SPEEDWELL	15354	2072	41.6	33.2	22.4	2.0	0.9	30980	33738	10	14	1732	23.2	22.1	39.1	11.8	3.9	96103
37871	STRAWBERRY PLAINS	20013	3824	25.4	33.6	34.7	4.7	1.6	42037	45154	39	59	3113	19.4	22.9	40.1	15.8	1.9	105173
37872	SUNBRIGHT	15045	861	41.9	33.8	20.0	3.3	1.0	30133	31579	8	12	706	32.7	35.3	25.2	4.8	2.0	67792
37873	SURGOINSVILLE	20024	2060	28.5	33.3	32.5	4.5	1.2	41943	44497	39	57	1712	18.8	25.5	37.3	16.3	2.1	98818
37874	SWEETWATER	18929	6308	31.6	32.1	29.1	4.7	2.6	37776	39540	26	40	4844	18.6	24.4	41.9	12.1	3.0	99687
37876	SEVIERVILLE	20836	11137	25.9	32.8	33.8	4.9	2.6	42630	43396	41	61	8965	15.0	17.1	35.4	27.4	5.1	131250
37877	TALBOTT	21991	3555	22.1	30.1	39.9	5.3	2.6	47245	48705	55	75	3018	10.1	16.6	54.2	15.8	3.3	122683
37878	TALLASSEE	24672	343	27.7	33.5	28.0	5.0	5.8	42137	45545	40	59	288	21.2	20.8	28.5	20.1	9.4	108871
37879	TAZEWELL	16106	4170	45.3	29.3	21.4	2.7	1.3	28244	29169	6	9	3127	26.8	29.8	34.3	7.8	1.2	80935
37880	TEN MILE	18725	1589	29.5	35.7	28.3	5.0	1.4	37200	39207	24	37	1350	24.3	23.9	26.0	18.4	7.5	94098
37881	THORN HILL	14509	928	42.3	34.6	20.4	2.2	0.5	29477	31567	7	10	795	29.6	28.7	30.1	11.1	0.6	77676
37882	TOWNSEND	24091	1452	26.8	30.7	32.8	6.3	3.4	42754	47033	42	61	1177	13.9	12.7	29.2	31.3	12.8	146875
37885	VONORE	21960	2023	24.4	32.8	34.7	6.0	2.1	43838	46293	45	64	1652	11.7	18.6	36.3	24.5	9.0	130191
37886	WALLAND	21383	1859	24.0	30.0	38.0	6.2	1.8	46140	49413	52	72	1557	18.6	21.1	32.8	22.0	5.5	110688
37887	WARTBURG	15909	1919	36.7	31.9	26.5	3.4	1.4	33993	35900	15	21	1482	17.8	38.1	38.5	5.6	0.0	83759
37888	WASHBURN	16133	1104	43.2	32.6	17.6	3.3	3.4	31019	32856	10	15	955	31.9	26.7	31.9	5.5	3.9	77381
37890	WHITE PINE	18711	2743	30.2	32.7	31.3	4.0	1.7	39498	42057	31	48	2161	21.5	20.3	38.0	16.7	3.5	105195
37891	WHITESBURG	18382	1462	34.7	29.8	29.4	5.3	0.8	37994	40896	27	41	1187	17.3	23.2	44.4	12.7	2.4	99956
37892	WINFIELD	17276	831	42.7	33.9	19.0	1.9	2.4	29597	30858	7	11	629	27.7	32.6	30.8	7.3	1.6	75096
37902	KNOXVILLE	18023	904	78.0	9.4	10.2	1.1	1.3	13361	13870	1	1	81	0.0	0.0	34.6	63.0	2.5	191447
37909	KNOXVILLE	28294	7183	25.4	30.5	31.8	7.8	4.5	44423	48007	47	66	3025	2.0	9.4	55.2	30.8	2.6	147740
37912	KNOXVILLE	24527	9670	26.7	33.3	33.4	4.7	2.0	41506	45122	38	56	5355	6.4	20.8	62.3	9.9	0.6	112529
37914	KNOXVILLE	20051	8960	33.4	29.3	30.7	4.7	1.8	37869	41472	26	41	6215	13.6	31.2	38.9	15.7	0.7	96739
37915	KNOXVILLE	12279	2929	70.0	16.4	11.5	1.2	1.0	13216	13859	1	1	684	17.8	50.4	26.3	5.1	0.3	77304
37916	KNOXVILLE	12884	3005	71.0	21.2	7.3	0.2	0.2	14357	14784	1	2	193	13.0	7.8	45.6	33.7	0.0	140132
37917	KNOXVILLE	19149	12415	41.5	31.8	22.3	2.9	1.5	30348	31999	9	12	6256	9.4	44.6	40.9	5.1	0.1	86780
37918	KNOXVILLE	25775	17204	20.5	29.5	38.4	7.5	4.1	50032	52894	61	79	12184	6.4	13.9	56.7	20.7	2.2	125542
37919	KNOXVILLE	39717	14250	25.6	22.5	29.6	10.1	12.3	52594	55653	67	83	7695	4.4	6.9	34.2	32.4	22.0	194012
37920	KNOXVILLE	22991	17603	30.7	29.4	30.8	6.2	2.8	39766	43266	32	49	11570	9.7	27.0	43.1	17.1	3.2	109100
37921	KNOXVILLE	20916	11571	30.5	27.3	34.8	5.3	2.1	41878	45986	39	57	7250	11.5	22.3	57.0	8.8	0.3	107811
37922	KNOXVILLE	46063	12096	6.2	11.6	35.7	20.4	26.1	94162	95582	96	99	10693	1.4	2.1	30.4	47.8	18.3	223060
37923	KNOXVILLE	33310	13989	13.2	25.1	43.6	11.8	6.2	62108	63425	80	91	7979	2.4	4.5	48.3	43.2	1.6	166366
37924	KNOXVILLE	23268	4390	23.9	29.0	39.3	5.6	2.1	46879	50348	54	74	3367	11.4	21.1	47.1	18.1	2.2	114504
37931	KNOXVILLE	27569	8396	12.7	27.0	43.4	12.4	4.5	60063	61651	77	90	6965	13.5	10.4	42.6	31.1	2.5	140722
37932	KNOXVILLE	32480	5173	8.8	22.1	43.9	17.3	7.9	70481	70399	87	95	4388	9.3	6.6	41.5	35.6	7.0	162403
37934	KNOXVILLE	45413	9038	7.3	11.0	33.3	22.4	25.9	96946	97968	96	99	7803	1.3	2.4	28.0	52.5	15.8	243378
37938	KNOXVILLE	27819	6393	13.5	24.2	44.8	13.0	4.5	63444	64219	82	92	5550	7.7	7.8	46.8	35.4	2.3	151582
38001	ALAMO	18788	1775	37.0	27.7	28.3	4.3	2.7	35525	36544	19	27	1289	15.3	30.0	42.7	11.5	0.5	94840
38002	ARLINGTON	31066	10778	9.7	15.9	50.1	16.7	7.6	75520	76056	90	96	9272	4.8	17.7	38.8	33.5	5.2	145450
38004	ATOKA	26298	3183	10.8	19.4	45.0	19.9	4.9	69112	71057	86	94	2701	6.4	11.3	55.0	27.0	0.4	137137
38006	BELLS	17540	1973	33.2	31.2	30.4	3.5	1.7	36919	37840	23	35	1426	19.4	31.1	38.8	10.0	0.8	89483
38008	BOLIVAR	17966	3931	38.0	27.9	29.2	3.5	1.4	35554	36577	19	27	2678	16.2	38.8	36.6	7.7	0.6	85467
38011	BRIGHTON	21279	3232	17.1	25.5	48.4	6.7	2.3	57308	60011	74	88	2605	8.1	18.9	52.9	19.2	1.0	117327
38012	BROWNSVILLE	18006	5810	37.1	28.1	28.0	4.5	2.3	34785	37410	17	23	3702	11.7	34.6	40.7	11.8	1.2	93333
38015	BURLISON	21479	1111	24.4	26.3	40.1	6.6	2.7	49187	51871	59	77	898	18.4	26.5	41.8	12.5	0.9	97931
38016	CORDOVA	40356	16964	6.8	13.9	45.3	19.5	14.4	82553	83001	93	98	12372	0.2	12.5	44.7	38.8	3.8	154291
38017	COLLIERVILLE	40105	14624	7.4	13.2	34.8	20.0	24.6	91506	93469	95	99	12295	2.0	6.7	23.2	56.9	11.2	218113
38018	CORDOVA	40523	12593	6.3	13.4	45.6	19.4	15.3	82240	82537	93	97	9445	0.5	3.8	55.6	34.3	5.9	156230
38019	COVINGTON	20308	6356	31.5	23.3	36.5	5.6	3.1	43708	48085	44	64	4183	15.3	30.6	40.0	12.9	1.1	95313
38023	DRUMMONDS	21795	2183	20.0	28.4	42.0	5.7	3.8	51209	53775	64	80	1745	17.2	23.8	41.6	17.0	0.5	100280
38024	DYERSBURG	20918	11331	31.4	27.1	32.5	6.1	2.9	41022	42798	36	54	7216	12.3	29.6	42.8	13.6	1.7	99151
	TENNESSEE	24986		24.9	27.0	34.7	8.2	5.2	47751	50104				12.0	19.9	40.9	22.7	4.6	120455
	UNITED STATES	27277		20.9	24.4	35.3	11.7	7.6	54719	56938				9.3	13.1	31.6	32.6	13.5	162279

ZIP CODE #	POST OFFICE NAME	FINANCIAL SERVICES: Auto Loan	Home Loan	Investments	Retirement Plans	THE HOME: Home Improvements: Home Repair	Lawn & Garden	Furnishings: Computers & Hardware-Personal	Major Appliances	TV, Radio, Sound Equipment	Furniture	ENTERTAINMENT: Dine out/Carry out	Sports Equipment	Fees & Tickets	Toys & Games	Travel	Cable TV	PERSONAL: Apparel & Services	Auto Repairs	Health Insurance	Pets & Supplies
37769	LAKE CITY	63	47	60	46	48	63	51	59	56	47	55	45	43	56	49	61	37	57	64	71
37770	LANCING	65	47	59	45	47	64	48	58	54	46	53	44	39	55	45	59	35	55	61	70
37771	LENOIR CITY	84	74	72	73	73	82	76	79	80	74	79	60	70	81	72	83	54	79	84	95
37772	LENOIR CITY	115	107	124	110	112	124	104	119	106	99	105	88	99	106	108	111	72	111	120	137
37774	LOUDON	103	91	112	90	96	112	89	103	95	89	93	73	84	93	92	101	63	98	111	121
37777	LOUISVILLE	92	84	79	84	81	85	86	85	87	87	88	66	82	89	83	88	61	87	86	102
37778	LOWLAND	72	52	60	50	52	69	54	63	60	52	59	48	43	62	49	65	39	59	66	76
37779	LUTTRELL	79	61	65	60	60	75	63	70	68	62	67	54	53	71	58	72	45	67	73	85
37801	MARYVILLE	84	72	72	72	72	83	73	79	76	71	76	60	66	78	70	80	51	76	82	94
37803	MARYVILLE	104	101	103	102	101	111	97	105	99	95	99	79	95	100	99	103	68	101	108	123
37804	MARYVILLE	79	71	70	72	70	81	72	77	75	69	74	58	68	76	70	79	51	75	82	91
37806	MASCOT	75	54	62	52	54	71	56	65	62	55	61	50	45	65	51	68	41	62	69	79
37807	MAYNARDVILLE	74	56	62	54	55	71	58	66	63	56	62	50	48	65	53	68	42	63	69	79
37809	MIDWAY	73	52	60	51	52	69	55	64	61	53	59	49	44	63	50	66	40	60	67	77
37810	MOHAWK	72	52	59	50	51	68	54	63	60	52	59	48	43	62	49	65	39	59	66	76
37811	MOORESBURG	70	50	58	49	50	67	52	61	58	51	57	47	42	60	48	63	38	58	64	74
37813	MORRISTOWN	72	60	59	60	58	71	64	67	68	60	67	52	57	69	59	72	46	66	73	81
37814	MORRISTOWN	89	77	76	78	77	89	81	85	84	77	83	65	74	85	76	88	57	83	90	101
37818	MOSHEIM	81	59	67	57	59	77	61	71	67	59	66	54	49	70	56	73	44	67	75	86
37819	NEWCOMB	53	35	52	33	35	52	37	47	43	35	42	37	28	44	35	48	28	44	50	58
37820	NEW MARKET	89	68	76	67	68	86	70	80	75	67	74	61	58	78	65	81	50	76	83	96
37821	NEWPORT	69	51	61	51	52	68	55	64	61	52	59	48	45	61	51	66	40	61	68	76
37825	NEW TAZEWELL	72	52	61	51	52	69	56	64	61	54	60	49	45	63	51	67	41	61	68	77
37826	NIOTA	84	64	71	64	64	83	66	76	72	63	70	58	55	74	62	78	48	72	80	92
37829	OAKDALE	83	60	70	58	59	79	62	73	69	60	67	56	50	71	57	75	45	69	77	88
37830	OAK RIDGE	101	101	101	102	102	108	100	103	103	99	102	77	101	102	102	107	71	103	111	121
37840	OLIVER SPRINGS	81	63	75	61	63	81	64	75	71	62	69	56	55	72	62	77	47	71	80	90
37841	ONEIDA	75	53	66	51	53	72	55	66	62	53	61	51	44	64	51	68	41	62	70	80
37843	PARROTTSVILLE	75	54	65	53	54	73	56	66	62	54	61	51	45	64	52	68	41	63	70	80
37846	PHILADELPHIA	88	63	75	61	63	84	65	77	73	63	71	59	52	75	60	79	48	73	81	93
37847	PIONEER	62	40	59	38	40	60	43	54	50	41	49	42	32	51	40	55	32	51	57	67
37848	POWDER SPRINGS	71	51	58	49	50	67	53	61	59	51	57	47	42	61	48	64	39	58	65	75
37849	POWELL	96	93	90	94	93	101	89	95	92	88	91	72	88	93	90	95	63	92	99	112
37852	ROBBINS	68	46	61	44	46	66	49	60	56	47	54	46	38	57	45	61	36	56	63	73
37853	ROCKFORD	85	71	75	71	71	85	72	81	76	68	75	61	64	78	70	80	51	77	83	95
37854	ROCKWOOD	73	55	69	55	56	74	58	69	64	54	63	51	49	64	56	70	42	65	74	82
37857	ROGERSVILLE	77	56	66	54	56	75	59	69	65	57	64	52	47	67	54	71	43	65	73	83
37860	RUSSELLVILLE	89	70	77	70	70	89	71	82	77	67	75	63	60	79	67	83	51	77	86	98
37861	RUTLEDGE	80	57	71	55	57	78	59	71	66	57	65	54	47	68	55	72	43	67	75	86
37862	SEVIERVILLE	82	73	81	74	75	84	76	81	78	73	77	61	71	78	75	82	53	80	86	96
37863	PIGEON FORGE	77	69	70	66	69	75	68	73	71	69	70	54	63	72	66	73	48	72	75	87
37865	SEYMOUR	88	82	78	81	81	89	78	85	81	77	80	63	74	83	77	84	55	81	87	100
37866	SHARPS CHAPEL	70	50	72	49	52	71	52	66	57	48	56	49	41	57	51	63	37	60	68	78
37869	SNEEDVILLE	63	42	61	40	42	62	44	56	51	42	50	43	34	51	42	56	33	52	59	68
37870	SPEEDWELL	66	48	64	46	49	66	49	61	54	46	53	46	39	55	47	60	35	56	63	73
37871	STRAWBERRY PLAINS	90	66	80	65	67	88	68	81	75	65	74	62	56	77	65	82	49	76	85	98
37872	SUNBRIGHT	68	48	59	46	48	65	50	60	56	49	55	46	40	58	46	62	37	56	63	73
37873	SURGOINSVILLE	85	61	70	59	60	81	63	74	70	61	69	57	51	73	58	76	46	70	78	90
37874	SWEETWATER	83	60	72	59	61	81	63	74	70	60	68	57	51	72	58	76	46	70	79	90
37876	SEVIERVILLE	86	73	82	72	73	87	71	82	76	70	75	62	64	77	71	80	51	77	84	97
37877	TALBOTT	89	74	80	75	75	92	75	86	79	69	77	65	66	81	73	84	52	80	89	101
37878	TALLASSEE	93	70	105	68	74	96	71	90	77	66	76	67	59	75	73	84	50	83	92	106
37879	TAZEWELL	66	47	58	46	47	64	51	59	57	49	55	45	41	58	47	62	37	57	63	72
37880	TEN MILE	81	58	71	56	58	78	60	71	67	58	65	55	48	68	56	73	44	67	75	86
37881	THORN HILL	65	46	57	45	46	62	48	57	53	46	52	44	38	55	45	58	35	54	60	69
37882	TOWNSEND	89	71	115	70	78	94	71	90	74	67	73	66	62	71	77	79	49	83	89	105
37885	VONORE	93	68	80	66	69	90	70	82	78	69	76	62	58	80	65	85	51	78	87	99
37886	WALLAND	90	70	85	68	72	88	71	83	76	69	75	62	60	77	68	81	50	78	85	99
37887	WARTBURG	77	53	68	51	53	74	56	67	63	54	62	52	44	65	51	69	41	64	71	82
37888	WASHBURN	73	52	60	51	52	69	54	63	60	53	59	49	44	63	49	66	40	60	67	77
37890	WHITE PINE	80	60	68	58	59	77	61	71	67	60	66	54	51	70	57	73	44	67	75	86
37891	WHITESBURG	81	58	70	57	58	78	60	71	67	58	66	55	48	69	56	73	44	67	75	86
37892	WINFIELD	78	56	64	54	56	74	58	68	65	57	63	52	47	67	53	70	43	64	72	83
37902	KNOXVILLE	28	20	25	24	21	25	33	27	36	30	36	21	30	31	30	39	25	33	38	35
37909	KNOXVILLE	84	65	61	69	63	65	92	72	86	82	87	62	77	87	75	84	61	82	74	89
37912	KNOXVILLE	73	63	61	65	62	67	74	69	75	70	74	54	68	75	67	76	52	73	74	83
37914	KNOXVILLE	72	61	70	61	62	76	63	70	69	61	68	51	58	68	62	74	46	69	78	84
37915	KNOXVILLE	35	24	21	26	22	27	34	28	38	33	38	22	30	37	28	40	26	34	35	37
37916	KNOXVILLE	32	14	13	17	13	16	46	22	36	31	37	24	27	35	24	33	26	32	22	30
37917	KNOXVILLE	58	47	47	49	46	55	57	54	60	52	59	42	51	59	51	63	41	58	62	66
37918	KNOXVILLE	91	85	81	86	85	90	86	88	88	85	88	66	83	89	84	90	60	88	92	104
37919	KNOXVILLE	111	107	111	112	109	106	122	109	117	118	118	88	119	116	116	116	84	116	111	130
37920	KNOXVILLE	77	68	69	69	68	77	76	75	77	70	76	57	69	77	70	80	53	76	80	89
37921	KNOXVILLE	75	66	60	67	63	69	72	69	75	71	74	53	67	76	66	77	51	72	74	84
37922	KNOXVILLE	173	208	199	214	209	185	178	183	168	194	170	144	201	175	191	160	124	171	162	206
37923	KNOXVILLE	107	97	89	100	94	92	108	97	106	108	107	79	104	108	101	103	75	104	97	117
37924	KNOXVILLE	88	72	84	73	74	91	74	86	78	68	77	65	64	79	73	84	52	80	89	101
37931	KNOXVILLE	101	103	97	103	102	104	96	100	96	98	97	75	97	98	97	98	67	97	100	118
37932	KNOXVILLE	116	128	121	130	127	123	117	119	115	121	116	91	124	117	122	116	82	116	116	140
37934	KNOXVILLE	165	202	200	208	205	185	173	179	164	185	166	138	196	167	190	158	120	169	163	204
37938	KNOXVILLE	103	110	107	112	110	115	100	108	101	99	101	81	104	102	105	103	70	102	109	125
38001	ALAMO	82	59	79	57	60	83	62	76	69	58	68	58	50	70	59	76	45	71	81	91
38002	ARLINGTON	124	138	123	136	134	124	121	125	117	128	118	96	127	122	125	114	83	118	114	143
38004	ATOKA	117	122	101	117	115	106	109	111	105	117	107	86	109	113	107	102	74	105	101	127
38006	BELLS	79	59	64	58	58	75	62	69	68	60	66	53	51	70	56	73	45	67	74	84
38008	BOLIVAR	72	55	63	54	54	70	58	65	65	57	63	49	50	65	54	70	43	64	71	79
38011	BRIGHTON	94	88	79	87	87	91	83	88	86	85	86	65	80	89	81	88	58	85	89	105
38012	BROWNSVILLE	75	58	61	58	56	72	63	67	68	60	67	52	54	69	58	73	45	67	73	82
38015	BURLISON	90	75	77	76	76	90	75	84	79	72	78	64	67	82	72	84	53	79	87	100
38016	CORDOVA	145	159	137	159	152	136	145	141	137	154	140	114	152	145	146	130	99	137	126	163
38017	COLLIERVILLE	162	194	178	199	191	173	166	170	157	177	159	135	186	164	177	151	116	160	152	194
38018	CORDOVA	151	160	140	162	154	137	149	144	141	159	144	117	155	150	148	134	103	141	129	167
38019	COVINGTON	82	68	68	68	67	80	73	77	78	70	76	58	65	79	68	82	52	76	83	92
38023	DRUMMONDS	100	86	84	83	84	95	83	91	88	85	87	67	76	91	79	92	59	88	92	109
38024	DYERSBURG	81	68	66	69	67	78	73	75	76	70	75	58	66	78	68	80	52	75	80	90
	TENNESSEE	95	84	85	84	82	93	87	90	90	85	89	69	80	91	83	93	61	89	93	107
	UNITED STATES	100	100	100	100	100	100	100	100	100	100	100	100	100	100	100	100	100	100	100	100

POPULATION CHANGE

ZIP CODE #	POST OFFICE NAME	COUNTY FIPS CODE	POPULATION 2000	POPULATION 2009	POPULATION 2014	2000-2009 ANNUAL RATE % Rate	2000-2009 ANNUAL RATE State Centile	HOUSEHOLDS 2000	HOUSEHOLDS 2009	HOUSEHOLDS 2014	HOUSEHOLDS % Annual Rate 2000-2009	HOUSEHOLDS 2009 Average HH Size	FAMILIES 2000	FAMILIES 2009	FAMILIES % Annual Rate 2000-2009
38028	EADS	047	4911	6322	7719	2.8	94	1757	2371	2926	3.3	2.66	1458	1915	3.0
38030	FINLEY	045	341	366	374	0.8	60	138	151	156	1.0	2.42	104	112	0.8
38034	FRIENDSHIP	033	3505	3426	3376	-0.2	10	1463	1450	1432	-0.1	2.36	1057	1021	-0.4
38037	GATES	075	2134	2134	2108	0.0	18	735	755	753	0.3	2.62	560	564	0.1
38039	GRAND JUNCTION	069	1991	2146	2173	0.8	60	699	777	795	1.2	2.76	535	580	0.9
38040	HALLS	097	5212	4998	4888	-0.5	3	2096	2052	2019	-0.2	2.43	1501	1430	-0.5
38041	HENNING	097	5178	5407	5429	0.5	41	1082	1193	1214	1.1	2.52	773	830	0.8
38042	HICKORY VALLEY	069	960	983	975	0.3	31	347	367	367	0.6	2.68	264	273	0.4
38044	HORNSBY	069	1039	1042	1036	0.0	18	420	433	434	0.3	2.37	312	314	0.1
38049	MASON	047	4848	5169	5423	0.7	53	1534	1717	1835	1.2	2.68	1165	1266	0.9
38052	MIDDLETON	069	3613	3756	3742	0.4	36	1453	1565	1576	0.8	2.39	1047	1099	0.5
38053	MILLINGTON	157	28437	29797	30633	0.5	41	9943	10704	11069	0.8	2.72	7825	8205	0.5
38057	MOSCOW	047	3553	4232	4715	1.9	88	1239	1517	1711	2.2	2.79	958	1144	1.9
38058	MUNFORD	167	8588	10838	11894	2.5	93	2997	3889	4306	2.9	2.79	2407	3046	2.6
38059	NEWBERN	045	6843	7081	7126	0.4	36	2671	2815	2846	0.6	2.51	2035	2092	0.3
38060	OAKLAND	047	3904	8436	10584	8.7	100	1418	3256	4143	9.4	2.59	1140	2556	9.1
38061	POCAHONTAS	109	1002	1037	1038	0.4	36	413	440	445	0.7	2.36	304	316	0.4
38063	RIPLEY	097	16280	16411	16278	0.1	22	6312	6529	6529	0.4	2.49	4476	4506	0.1
38066	ROSSVILLE	047	2228	2669	2993	2.0	90	822	1038	1180	2.6	2.57	623	765	2.2
38067	SAULSBURY	069	1275	1297	1287	0.2	27	528	556	557	0.6	2.33	387	396	0.2
38068	SOMERVILLE	047	9952	11701	13113	1.8	86	3602	4419	5030	2.2	2.58	2682	3197	1.9
38069	STANTON	075	2860	2931	2916	0.3	31	1110	1182	1188	0.7	2.47	806	837	0.4
38075	WHITEVILLE	069	6730	6879	6899	0.2	27	1230	1320	1339	0.8	2.99	902	945	0.5
38076	WILLISTON	047	620	711	789	1.5	81	218	261	293	2.0	2.72	171	199	1.7
38079	TIPTONVILLE	095	5641	5291	5056	-0.7	2	1486	1312	1218	-1.3	2.24	964	823	-1.7
38080	RIDGELY	095	2693	2470	2331	-0.9	1	1083	1014	964	-0.7	2.34	770	702	-1.0
38103	MEMPHIS	157	7743	10028	10906	2.8	94	3556	5007	5529	3.8	1.59	977	1268	2.9
38104	MEMPHIS	157	24422	22875	22369	-0.7	2	12961	12423	12212	-0.5	1.77	4666	4088	-1.4
38105	MEMPHIS	157	8002	7418	7257	-0.8	2	3343	3161	3109	-0.6	2.08	1442	1240	-1.6
38106	MEMPHIS	157	33676	29883	28762	-1.3	0	12351	11228	10866	-1.0	2.61	8091	7032	-1.5
38107	MEMPHIS	157	23913	21487	20759	-1.1	1	8511	7770	7531	-1.0	2.62	5346	4638	-1.5
38108	MEMPHIS	157	22533	20514	19872	-1.0	1	8511	7908	7696	-0.8	2.57	5586	4953	-1.3
38109	MEMPHIS	157	52307	49944	49193	-0.5	3	17580	17222	17078	-0.2	2.89	13303	12659	-0.5
38111	MEMPHIS	157	43841	42933	42483	-0.2	10	18307	18094	17941	-0.1	2.25	9934	9294	-0.7
38112	MEMPHIS	157	18426	17495	17107	-0.6	3	7618	7292	7154	-0.5	2.39	4205	3790	-1.1
38114	MEMPHIS	157	34382	31900	31066	-0.8	2	12845	12234	11991	-0.5	2.59	8532	7762	-1.0
38115	MEMPHIS	157	40328	41134	41093	0.2	27	17165	17243	17203	0.0	2.37	9790	9263	-0.6
38116	MEMPHIS	157	51126	48493	47526	-0.6	3	18105	17278	16969	-0.5	2.78	12934	11887	-0.9
38117	MEMPHIS	157	25743	25108	24823	-0.3	7	11744	11689	11620	-0.1	2.14	7272	6869	-0.6
38118	MEMPHIS	157	47261	45268	44402	-0.5	3	16113	15149	14830	-0.7	2.94	11631	10551	-1.0
38119	MEMPHIS	157	22019	22060	22087	0.0	18	9750	9965	10036	0.2	2.16	6068	5903	-0.3
38120	MEMPHIS	157	13700	14465	14757	0.6	47	5985	6474	6653	0.9	2.22	3871	3960	0.2
38122	MEMPHIS	157	24611	23741	23353	-0.4	5	10591	10271	10132	-0.3	2.31	6265	5744	-0.9
38125	MEMPHIS	157	23067	31846	35042	3.5	97	8357	11812	13071	3.8	2.69	6643	9099	3.5
38126	MEMPHIS	157	8481	8343	8434	-0.2	10	2952	2956	3049	0.0	2.63	1667	1513	-1.0
38127	MEMPHIS	157	50929	49168	48402	-0.4	5	17271	16831	16619	-0.3	2.91	13104	12353	-0.6
38128	MEMPHIS	157	43834	44579	44754	0.2	27	15992	16371	16478	0.3	2.70	11321	11171	-0.1
38131	MEMPHIS	157	1	1	1	0.0	18	0	1	1	0.0	1.00	0	0	0.0
38132	MEMPHIS	157	2	2	2	0.0	18	1	1	1	0.0	2.00	0	1	0.0
38133	MEMPHIS	157	18834	19876	20384	0.6	47	6553	7061	7281	0.8	2.81	5324	5608	0.6
38134	MEMPHIS	157	41692	42399	42471	0.2	27	14509	14979	15080	0.3	2.47	9900	9784	-0.1
38135	MEMPHIS	157	25079	28203	29467	1.3	76	8673	10042	10562	1.6	2.80	7192	8116	1.3
38138	GERMANTOWN	157	23966	24186	24300	0.1	22	8914	9256	9375	0.4	2.61	6938	6999	0.1
38139	GERMANTOWN	157	14482	16159	16788	1.2	72	4647	5288	5518	1.4	3.06	4235	4794	1.3
38141	MEMPHIS	157	21995	21377	21148	-0.3	7	7697	7572	7514	-0.2	2.82	5901	5621	-0.5
38152	MEMPHIS	157	479	472	468	-0.2	10	11	11	11	0.0	2.55	3	3	0.0
38201	MC KENZIE	017	9851	9814	9642	0.0	18	3910	3935	3887	0.1	2.35	2733	2678	-0.2
38220	ATWOOD	017	2032	2007	1970	-0.1	13	827	831	821	0.1	2.42	592	580	-0.2
38221	BIG SANDY	005	3246	3256	3243	0.0	18	1391	1424	1426	0.3	2.29	1021	1018	0.0
38222	BUCHANAN	079	2274	2534	2620	1.2	72	967	1103	1147	1.4	2.29	726	804	1.1
38224	COTTAGE GROVE	079	1062	1063	1052	0.0	18	399	409	407	0.3	2.60	300	300	0.0
38225	DRESDEN	183	6453	6187	6037	-0.5	3	2560	2525	2477	-0.1	2.36	1810	1739	-0.4
38226	DUKEDOM	183	443	433	422	-0.2	10	187	185	181	-0.1	2.34	138	133	-0.4
38229	GLEASON	183	2971	2857	2776	-0.4	5	1200	1182	1158	-0.2	2.42	875	842	-0.4
38230	GREENFIELD	183	3922	3703	3594	-0.6	3	1583	1514	1476	-0.5	2.45	1127	1050	-0.8
38231	HENRY	079	1882	1980	2008	0.6	47	707	762	778	0.8	2.60	542	570	0.5
38232	HORNBEAK	131	2165	2278	2278	0.6	47	885	960	968	0.9	2.37	652	689	0.6
38233	KENTON	053	2931	2820	2772	-0.4	5	1217	1201	1190	-0.1	2.35	868	832	-0.5
38236	MANSFIELD	079	815	850	859	0.5	41	341	365	372	0.7	2.33	246	255	0.4
38237	MARTIN	183	15763	15143	14900	-0.4	5	5855	5912	5839	0.1	2.27	3573	3485	-0.3
38238	MARTIN	183	11	10	10	-1.0	1	0	0	0	0.0	0.00	0	0	0.0
38240	OBION	131	2347	2338	2303	0.0	18	946	963	955	0.2	2.43	690	684	-0.1
38241	PALMERSVILLE	183	993	968	944	-0.3	7	403	400	392	-0.1	2.42	311	302	-0.3
38242	PARIS	079	18992	18897	18703	-0.1	13	7984	8060	8009	0.1	2.28	5338	5235	-0.2
38251	PURYEAR	079	2840	2992	3035	0.6	47	1149	1240	1267	0.8	2.39	841	881	0.5
38253	RIVES	131	1136	1103	1080	-0.3	7	431	430	424	0.0	2.53	336	328	-0.3
38255	SHARON	183	2325	2304	2268	-0.1	13	995	1010	1003	0.2	2.28	699	691	-0.1
38256	SPRINGVILLE	079	3073	3274	3331	0.7	53	1400	1523	1561	0.9	2.15	958	1007	0.5
38257	SOUTH FULTON	131	4794	4390	4225	-0.9	1	1967	1843	1785	-0.7	2.36	1440	1314	-1.0
38258	TREZEVANT	017	1880	1879	1856	0.0	18	796	809	803	0.2	2.32	559	553	-0.1
38259	TRIMBLE	131	947	968	972	0.2	27	393	409	412	0.4	2.37	276	278	0.1
38260	TROY	131	4102	4511	4564	1.0	66	1582	1784	1817	1.3	2.53	1220	1341	1.0
38261	UNION CITY	131	16594	16114	15756	-0.3	7	6798	6766	6666	-0.1	2.31	4652	4499	-0.4
38301	JACKSON	113	40268	39381	38987	-0.2	10	15843	15783	15715	0.0	2.36	10211	9711	-0.5
38305	JACKSON	113	39872	46482	48948	1.7	84	15297	18139	19213	1.9	2.49	10998	12755	1.6
38310	ADAMSVILLE	109	5565	6139	6387	1.1	69	2262	2562	2690	1.4	2.34	1603	1766	1.1
38311	BATH SPRINGS	039	746	757	751	0.2	27	316	331	330	0.5	2.29	238	243	0.2
38313	BEECH BLUFF	113	2966	3194	3287	0.8	60	1126	1251	1298	1.1	2.55	889	961	0.8
38315	BETHEL SPRINGS	109	3761	4045	4183	0.8	60	1497	1648	1715	1.0	2.41	1101	1181	0.8
38316	BRADFORD	053	2979	3091	3147	0.4	36	1205	1280	1313	0.7	2.41	875	903	0.3
38317	BRUCETON	017	2552	2529	2482	-0.1	13	1049	1050	1035	0.0	2.28	737	717	-0.3
38318	BUENA VISTA	017	562	564	557	0.0	18	229	235	234	0.3	2.38	166	166	0.0
38320	CAMDEN	005	10820	10857	10788	0.0	18	4461	4582	4585	0.3	2.31	3106	3105	0.0
38321	CEDAR GROVE	017	2570	2571	2553	0.0	18	1047	1070	1069	0.2	2.39	775	774	0.0
38326	COUNCE	071	2365	2781	2941	1.8	86	1043	1259	1343	2.1	2.21	748	880	1.8
	TENNESSEE					1.1					1.3	2.44			1.0
	UNITED STATES					1.0					1.1	2.59			0.9

ZIP CODE		RACE (%)						% Hispanic Origin		2009 AGE DISTRIBUTION (%)										MEDIAN AGE		
#	POST OFFICE NAME	White		Black		Asian/Pacific																
		2000	2009	2000	2009	2000	2009	2000	2009	0-4	5-9	10-14	15-19	20-24	25-44	45-64	65-84	85+	18+	2009	% 2009 Males	% 2009 Females
38028	EADS	79.4	73.0	18.2	23.7	0.8	1.2	1.5	2.5	6.1	6.8	7.5	7.0	4.3	24.8	32.0	10.4	1.0	74.9	40.7	49.8	50.2
38030	FINLEY	90.4	87.4	8.5	10.9	0.0	0.0	0.9	1.6	5.5	5.5	6.0	5.7	5.5	28.1	29.2	13.1	1.4	79.5	40.6	52.5	47.5
38034	FRIENDSHIP	86.5	85.4	11.6	12.4	0.0	0.1	2.4	2.5	6.0	6.3	6.5	6.3	5.1	25.5	29.1	13.1	2.0	77.3	40.8	50.1	49.9
38037	GATES	67.7	64.2	30.6	33.5	0.1	0.1	1.8	2.7	7.3	7.1	7.3	6.7	4.9	23.6	25.3	13.2	4.8	74.0	40.0	45.8	54.2
38039	GRAND JUNCTION	38.4	35.6	60.8	63.5	0.0	0.0	0.5	0.5	7.5	7.4	7.5	7.9	5.9	24.4	26.0	11.5	1.7	72.7	36.2	45.8	54.2
38040	HALLS	82.4	80.8	16.2	17.5	0.0	0.0	1.0	1.5	6.7	6.7	6.8	6.6	5.6	25.7	27.8	12.1	1.9	75.6	39.2	48.5	51.5
38041	HENNING	42.1	38.5	54.7	57.9	0.2	0.2	1.1	1.5	4.2	4.4	4.4	4.9	10.8	43.5	20.3	6.6	1.0	84.4	34.0	71.8	28.2
38042	HICKORY VALLEY	49.5	46.6	49.2	52.1	0.2	0.2	1.0	1.0	7.8	7.7	7.7	6.9	5.7	24.0	27.6	11.2	1.3	72.5	37.2	47.1	52.9
38044	HORNSBY	94.7	94.1	3.9	4.3	0.0	0.0	0.5	0.6	5.6	5.9	6.1	6.3	5.0	25.0	30.5	14.4	1.2	78.6	42.3	48.7	51.3
38049	MASON	44.4	38.7	53.0	58.4	0.3	0.3	1.8	2.2	6.0	6.2	6.5	6.9	8.0	29.6	25.0	10.2	1.6	77.0	36.2	54.2	45.8
38052	MIDDLETON	90.8	89.9	8.1	8.9	0.5	0.6	0.4	0.5	6.4	6.4	6.5	6.4	5.8	24.8	28.4	13.7	1.7	76.9	40.2	47.9	52.1
38053	MILLINGTON	77.2	68.9	18.4	25.1	1.4	1.8	3.0	4.8	7.3	7.2	6.9	6.7	5.7	27.7	26.3	10.9	1.2	74.4	36.5	49.7	50.3
38057	MOSCOW	58.6	52.9	39.4	44.6	0.3	0.3	1.6	2.4	7.0	7.0	7.2	6.8	6.2	23.3	28.9	12.1	1.4	74.6	38.4	48.2	51.8
38058	MUNFORD	87.8	85.3	9.4	10.8	0.7	1.0	1.3	2.0	7.1	7.1	7.2	7.6	6.2	27.3	27.6	9.1	0.8	74.0	36.5	49.8	50.2
38059	NEWBERN	91.9	90.3	6.6	7.7	0.3	0.4	1.0	1.6	6.4	6.3	6.6	7.0	5.2	27.1	28.7	11.2	1.6	76.5	39.3	48.4	51.6
38060	OAKLAND	72.5	70.7	25.4	26.6	0.5	0.7	1.3	1.9	6.3	6.8	7.2	6.5	4.5	25.9	30.4	11.2	1.1	75.5	40.1	49.7	50.3
38061	POCAHONTAS	94.4	93.7	4.1	4.7	0.8	0.9	0.7	0.9	6.8	7.1	7.0	5.8	5.2	25.5	28.3	12.8	1.4	75.4	39.2	49.9	50.1
38063	RIPLEY	66.0	63.2	32.0	34.2	0.2	0.3	1.2	1.8	7.4	7.1	7.2	7.1	6.3	26.1	26.0	11.0	1.8	74.0	36.5	48.0	52.0
38066	ROSSVILLE	60.8	55.3	37.5	42.6	0.2	0.3	1.0	1.4	6.0	6.6	6.9	5.8	4.1	24.0	31.2	13.6	1.7	76.8	42.6	50.4	49.6
38067	SAULSBURY	55.0	52.2	43.8	46.6	0.1	0.1	0.5	0.5	6.8	7.0	7.5	8.1	5.2	24.4	26.4	12.9	1.7	73.7	38.0	46.6	53.4
38068	SOMERVILLE	61.0	56.2	37.9	42.5	0.1	0.1	0.7	1.0	6.8	6.8	6.9	7.5	5.3	24.1	28.4	12.1	2.0	74.6	39.1	49.4	50.6
38069	STANTON	43.0	39.6	56.1	59.2	0.0	0.0	0.8	1.1	6.5	6.9	7.4	7.4	5.0	24.6	28.8	11.7	1.7	74.5	38.9	49.4	50.6
38075	WHITEVILLE	40.9	38.5	55.9	58.3	0.3	0.2	1.8	1.7	3.7	4.0	4.3	4.9	10.3	41.5	23.9	6.3	1.2	85.0	35.6	70.5	29.5
38076	WILLISTON	67.7	62.6	30.5	35.6	0.3	0.3	0.8	1.1	7.2	7.7	7.7	6.3	4.8	24.8	29.1	11.0	1.4	73.3	38.9	48.7	51.3
38079	TIPTONVILLE	59.2	55.6	38.5	41.4	0.2	0.2	1.4	2.1	3.6	3.7	3.8	5.9	13.4	36.6	21.8	9.6	1.6	86.3	34.7	69.0	31.0
38080	RIDGELY	86.6	85.7	11.8	12.2	0.0	0.0	1.2	1.9	6.4	6.4	6.5	6.4	5.1	23.9	26.0	16.4	3.0	76.7	41.7	48.0	52.0
38103	MEMPHIS	54.4	47.3	40.7	45.6	3.1	5.0	1.7	2.4	2.8	1.3	1.3	3.4	13.7	43.1	23.8	9.1	1.4	93.5	34.3	57.3	42.7
38104	MEMPHIS	62.0	54.9	29.4	35.1	4.8	5.3	3.4	4.6	5.6	4.6	3.9	4.4	8.9	34.4	25.9	10.0	2.4	83.7	37.0	49.3	50.7
38105	MEMPHIS	12.5	8.8	83.6	86.8	2.4	2.7	1.7	2.2	8.1	7.5	7.5	8.3	9.5	26.3	22.9	8.2	1.7	71.4	30.7	48.9	51.1
38106	MEMPHIS	2.3	1.5	96.5	97.1	0.2	0.2	1.0	1.1	7.5	7.4	7.1	8.5	7.0	21.6	24.8	13.7	2.3	73.2	37.0	45.8	54.2
38107	MEMPHIS	16.1	13.9	81.7	83.4	0.9	1.1	1.1	1.4	7.5	7.9	7.5	10.1	9.5	23.4	22.8	9.5	1.7	72.2	30.7	46.1	53.9
38108	MEMPHIS	25.9	23.0	70.1	70.6	0.6	0.9	4.4	7.5	7.6	7.7	7.2	7.4	6.7	25.0	24.7	11.8	1.9	72.9	35.8	48.0	52.0
38109	MEMPHIS	3.1	2.2	96.1	96.8	0.1	0.1	0.6	0.8	7.3	7.6	7.8	8.3	6.7	22.6	26.7	11.6	1.4	72.3	36.0	45.4	54.6
38111	MEMPHIS	50.0	42.4	45.1	51.2	1.7	2.1	3.9	5.4	6.8	6.4	5.9	8.2	10.3	27.4	22.0	9.8	3.2	77.3	33.2	47.0	53.0
38112	MEMPHIS	36.2	30.7	57.8	61.9	2.9	3.3	3.2	4.5	7.2	7.0	6.5	7.4	7.4	26.8	26.0	9.6	2.1	74.9	35.5	46.9	53.1
38114	MEMPHIS	4.3	3.2	94.3	95.3	0.1	0.1	1.2	1.4	8.3	8.5	7.9	7.8	6.6	24.2	24.3	10.6	1.7	70.5	33.7	45.3	54.7
38115	MEMPHIS	31.1	22.2	60.0	67.1	3.2	3.5	6.2	8.3	8.1	7.0	6.2	6.8	10.9	33.8	18.4	6.5	2.4	75.0	29.9	47.9	52.1
38116	MEMPHIS	7.2	4.7	90.8	93.1	0.2	0.3	1.5	1.8	9.4	8.8	8.0	8.3	8.7	26.8	22.7	6.3	1.0	68.8	29.2	46.0	54.0
38117	MEMPHIS	92.7	88.9	4.9	7.4	1.1	1.7	1.7	3.0	5.5	5.8	6.3	5.6	4.0	23.3	28.6	16.6	4.3	78.8	44.7	46.8	53.2
38118	MEMPHIS	17.5	12.5	76.4	79.8	1.5	1.7	5.6	7.5	9.3	8.5	8.0	9.3	9.8	28.9	20.0	5.4	0.8	68.6	27.9	48.0	52.0
38119	MEMPHIS	83.8	75.8	11.3	17.0	2.9	4.2	2.0	3.5	4.9	4.8	5.0	5.0	6.7	27.3	28.0	15.2	3.1	82.4	41.9	46.9	53.1
38120	MEMPHIS	93.4	89.6	2.9	4.6	2.4	3.7	1.4	2.6	4.9	5.1	5.8	5.5	5.1	22.7	30.4	17.4	3.1	80.5	45.6	48.5	51.5
38122	MEMPHIS	74.4	66.8	18.3	22.5	2.4	3.4	8.0	12.7	6.9	6.7	6.6	6.3	6.0	29.3	25.1	11.0	2.3	76.0	37.2	49.4	50.6
38125	MEMPHIS	53.4	42.1	41.9	51.7	2.7	3.6	1.4	2.3	7.5	7.3	7.3	6.7	5.6	31.0	28.2	5.9	0.5	73.6	35.8	48.6	51.4
38126	MEMPHIS	2.7	1.9	96.4	97.2	0.1	0.1	1.1	1.2	10.8	10.8	8.8	8.9	8.5	23.1	19.3	8.1	1.5	64.3	26.6	48.4	51.6
38127	MEMPHIS	25.8	18.2	72.2	79.5	0.3	0.4	1.3	1.7	9.5	9.1	8.5	9.2	8.3	25.1	22.6	6.8	0.9	67.3	28.6	45.5	54.5
38128	MEMPHIS	35.8	26.8	59.1	66.6	1.0	1.3	4.3	6.1	9.0	8.3	7.6	7.9	8.2	28.7	21.5	7.5	1.3	70.3	30.2	46.8	53.2
38131	MEMPHIS	100.0	100.0	0.0	0.0	0.0	0.0	0.0	0.0	0.0	0.0	0.0	0.0	0.0	0.0	100.0	0.0	0.0	100.0	62.5	100.0	0.0
38132	MEMPHIS	100.0	100.0	0.0	0.0	0.0	0.0	0.0	0.0	0.0	0.0	0.0	0.0	0.0	0.0	100.0	0.0	0.0	100.0	62.5	100.0	0.0
38133	MEMPHIS	86.9	79.5	9.2	14.6	1.9	2.8	2.1	3.7	8.3	8.1	8.1	7.6	5.9	28.8	26.4	6.2	0.5	70.6	34.3	48.6	51.4
38134	MEMPHIS	72.1	63.0	22.5	29.2	2.3	3.2	3.4	5.7	5.9	5.3	5.0	6.2	9.8	33.8	24.0	8.9	1.3	80.6	34.3	52.0	48.0
38135	MEMPHIS	88.7	81.7	8.6	14.0	1.2	1.9	1.4	2.7	7.4	7.7	7.9	7.4	4.8	27.3	28.4	8.2	0.9	72.2	36.9	48.8	51.2
38138	GERMANTOWN	91.7	87.1	3.3	5.2	3.6	5.7	1.1	2.2	4.7	5.4	6.4	6.6	4.5	21.6	35.5	13.8	1.4	79.3	45.4	48.4	51.6
38139	GERMANTOWN	93.0	88.7	2.1	3.4	3.8	6.2	1.1	2.2	5.0	6.6	8.4	9.1	4.5	17.3	39.1	9.3	0.8	74.2	44.3	49.0	51.0
38141	MEMPHIS	35.1	24.4	60.3	69.9	1.7	2.0	3.2	4.4	8.4	8.3	8.1	7.7	6.7	31.8	24.4	4.2	0.3	70.4	32.3	47.7	52.3
38152	MEMPHIS	67.0	54.9	22.1	30.7	8.8	11.9	1.5	2.5	1.5	1.7	1.7	21.6	41.7	16.7	11.4	3.0	0.6	93.6	22.8	41.9	58.1
38201	MC KENZIE	89.0	87.6	8.7	9.3	0.3	0.4	1.8	2.6	6.3	6.3	6.3	7.0	6.2	25.0	25.8	14.3	2.9	77.3	39.7	48.3	51.7
38220	ATWOOD	84.3	82.1	14.0	15.8	0.0	0.0	1.5	2.1	5.2	5.4	5.8	6.0	5.6	25.5	28.8	15.0	2.7	79.9	42.7	49.4	50.6
38221	BIG SANDY	98.8	98.4	0.1	0.1	0.1	0.2	0.8	1.3	5.3	5.5	5.6	6.3	4.4	21.3	32.9	16.8	2.0	79.8	46.1	49.6	50.4
38222	BUCHANAN	98.4	97.9	0.4	0.4	0.3	0.5	0.2	0.3	4.5	5.3	5.7	4.8	4.6	20.2	37.2	16.4	1.3	81.3	48.2	50.2	49.8
38224	COTTAGE GROVE	95.5	94.1	2.8	3.6	0.0	0.0	1.1	1.8	5.7	5.9	6.2	6.8	5.3	24.7	29.4	14.6	1.4	78.1	41.7	50.1	49.9
38225	DRESDEN	95.3	94.2	3.5	4.1	0.2	0.3	0.4	0.8	6.4	6.4	6.3	5.8	5.3	26.5	26.8	13.4	3.2	77.5	40.2	48.8	51.2
38226	DUKEDOM	98.2	97.9	0.0	0.0	0.2	0.2	0.2	0.5	6.2	6.2	6.7	6.7	5.3	25.2	28.9	12.9	1.8	76.7	41.0	50.6	49.4
38229	GLEASON	97.5	96.9	1.2	1.5	0.0	0.1	1.1	1.8	6.9	6.8	6.8	6.5	5.8	27.7	25.7	12.4	1.4	75.6	38.2	49.8	50.2
38230	GREENFIELD	93.6	92.2	5.1	6.0	0.0	0.1	1.2	2.0	6.8	6.9	6.8	6.3	4.9	25.5	27.3	13.5	1.9	75.7	39.7	48.5	51.5
38231	HENRY	90.5	87.6	6.9	8.4	0.1	0.2	3.3	5.5	6.5	6.5	6.8	6.4	5.6	26.7	28.3	11.7	1.6	76.3	39.2	49.9	50.1
38232	HORNBEAK	99.4	99.2	0.1	0.2	0.0	0.0	0.4	0.7	5.7	5.7	6.2	6.5	5.7	25.5	29.0	14.0	1.8	78.2	41.4	50.8	49.2
38233	KENTON	91.6	89.3	7.3	9.1	0.1	0.1	1.2	2.0	6.5	6.6	6.9	6.5	5.0	25.0	26.6	14.9	2.2	76.0	40.4	47.9	52.1
38236	MANSFIELD	88.6	85.5	9.8	12.2	0.1	0.2	1.5	2.4	5.6	6.0	6.1	5.3	5.1	25.2	31.9	13.2	1.6	78.8	42.7	51.8	48.2
38237	MARTIN	83.8	80.7	11.4	12.4	2.8	4.2	1.6	2.5	5.3	4.9	5.0	10.2	14.1	24.4	23.0	10.9	2.3	81.6	32.8	48.7	51.3
38238	MARTIN	72.7	70.0	18.2	20.0	9.1	10.0	0.0	0.0	0.0	0.0	0.0	30.0	70.0	0.0	0.0	0.0	0.0	100.0	21.4	40.0	60.0
38240	OBION	95.7	94.8	3.2	3.7	0.1	0.2	0.4	0.7	6.6	6.8	6.8	5.7	4.8	26.4	28.1	13.1	1.8	76.3	39.9	49.3	50.7
38241	PALMERSVILLE	98.4	97.9	0.0	0.0	0.1	0.1	0.6	1.0	5.7	5.8	6.0	6.0	4.8	25.8	30.0	13.8	2.2	78.9	42.4	51.0	49.0
38242	PARIS	85.7	83.7	12.3	13.7	0.4	0.6	0.9	1.4	5.9	5.9	6.0	5.9	4.9	24.3	28.2	15.7	3.1	78.6	42.8	48.3	51.7
38251	PURYEAR	93.9	92.3	4.1	5.0	0.2	0.3	0.9	1.5	6.1	6.4	6.5	6.0	4.9	24.7	28.2	15.3	2.1	77.4	41.8	51.2	48.8
38253	RIVES	94.8	92.7	2.3	2.7	0.2	0.4	2.5	4.1	6.5	7.0	7.2	6.1	5.1	26.0	28.9	11.7	1.5	75.3	40.0	50.1	49.9
38255	SHARON	94.1	92.9	5.3	6.3	0.1	0.1	0.8	1.3	6.3	6.5	6.5	5.7	4.0	25.7	26.0	16.6	2.6	77.2	41.7	50.7	49.3
38256	SPRINGVILLE	96.9	96.1	2.2	2.7	0.0	0.0	0.5	0.9	3.7	4.0	4.3	4.5	3.8	18.3	34.5	24.7	2.2	85.3	52.8	49.6	50.4
38257	SOUTH FULTON	87.8	85.6	11.1	13.0	0.1	0.2	0.4	0.6	5.9	6.4	6.7	6.1	4.1	23.1	30.3	14.9	2.5	76.9	43.0	48.4	51.6
38258	TREZEVANT	83.7	81.5	14.8	16.7	0.0	0.0	1.3	1.9	5.7	5.7	6.0	7.2	6.0	25.1	28.7	13.8	1.9	78.2	41.3	49.1	50.9
38259	TRIMBLE	98.2	97.6	0.8	1.0	0.0	0.0	0.8	1.3	6.2	6.4	6.5	5.5	5.7	25.6	29.0	13.0	2.1	77.7	40.0	48.5	51.5
38260	TROY	98.8	98.4	0.8	1.0	0.1	0.1	0.8	1.3	6.1	6.3	6.6	6.4	4.9	26.8	28.6	12.7	1.4	76.9	39.9	49.5	50.5
38261	UNION CITY	82.2	79.2	14.9	16.6	0.4	0.5	3.0	4.7	6.3	6.2	6.1	5.9	5.4	26.1	27.6	13.6	2.8	77.6	40.4	48.1	51.9
38301	JACKSON	49.6	45.3	48.6	52.4	0.2	0.3	1.4	2.1	7.0	6.9	6.6	8.0	8.2	25.1	24.5	11.4	2.3	75.3	35.3	47.8	52.2
38305	JACKSON	76.7	72.4	20.2	23.4	1.2	1.6	2.2	3.3	6.7	6.8	6.8	7.4	6.8	28.0	26.1	9.7	1.7	75.7	36.1	48.4	51.6
38310	ADAMSVILLE	97.3	96.7	1.3	1.5	0.1	0.2	0.8	1.3	5.7	5.8	6.2	6.3	4.7	23.9	27.7	16.6	3.1	78.3	43.0	47.9	52.1
38311	BATH SPRINGS	94.5	94.3	3.2	3.4	0.5	0.5	1.9	2.0	5.7	5.9	6.1	4.9	4.4	26.7	29.1	15.3	2.0	79.3	42.1	49.5	50.5
38313	BEECH BLUFF	93.1	90.9	5.5	7.1	0.1	0.2	0.9	1.6	6.4	6.5	6.8	6.4	5.1	27.3	29.7	10.7	1.1	76.5	39.3	51.7	48.3
38315	BETHEL SPRINGS	94.1	92.9	4.5	5.2	0.1	0.2	0.9	1.4	6.8	7.0	7.0	6.6	5.2	25.7	27.6	12.7	1.3	75.2	38.7	48.8	51.2
38316	BRADFORD	94.9	93.2	4.1	5.3	0.0	0.1	0.6	1.0	5.4	5.4	5.8	6.7	5.7	25.9	29.5	13.5	2.0	79.2	41.7	48.6	51.4
38317	BRUCETON	91.8	90.4	6.8	7.6	0.1	0.2	0.6	0.9	5.5	5.5	5.8	6.0	4.9	24.0	25.8	17.7	4.8	79.5	43.6	46.5	53.5
38318	BUENA VISTA	88.4	86.3	9.8	11.0	0.2	0.5	0.7	1.1	5.7	5.9	6.4	6.9	5.0	25.5	28.7	14.2	1.8	77.8	41.3	50.4	49.6
38320	CAMDEN	95.6	94.7	2.9	3.2	0.3	0.4	1.0	1.6	5.0	5.4	5.7	6.1	4.6	23.9	29.7	16.4	3.2	80.0	44.4	48.1	51.9
38321	CEDAR GROVE	90.1	88.6	9.0	10.2	0.0	0.0	0.7	1.1	5.4	5.5	6.0	6.3	4.9	27.3	29.2	13.5	1.9	79.3	41.6	49.6	50.4
38326	COUNCE	98.2	97.9	1.2	1.4	0.1	0.1	0.6	0.8	4.7	5.0	5.4	4.9	3.7	21.8	35.3	17.8	1.4	81.9	48.0	51.2	48.8
	TENNESSEE	80.2	78.4	16.4	16.9	1.0	1.5	2.2	3.4	6.5	6.4	6.5	6.8	6.5	27.2	27.0	11.4	1.7	76.6	38.0	49.0	51.0
	UNITED STATES	75.1	72.0	12.3	12.7	3.8	4.6	12.5	15.7	6.8	6.7	6.6	7.1	6.9	27.0	26.0	10.9	1.9	75.7	36.9	49.2	50.8

ZIP CODE #	POST OFFICE NAME	2009 Per Capita Income	2009 HH Income Base	2009 Household Income Distribution (%): Less than $25,000	$25,000 to $49,999	$50,000 to $99,999	$100,000 to $149,999	$150,000 or More	Median Household Income: 2009	2014	2009 National Centile	2009 State Centile	2009 Home Value Base	2009 Home Value Distribution (%): Less than $50,000	$50,000 to $89,999	$90,000 to $174,999	$175,000 to $399,999	$400,000 or More	2009 Median Home Value
38028	EADS	33547	2371	13.7	17.8	41.1	14.3	13.0	72428	72729	88	95	2119	7.0	22.9	31.3	28.2	10.6	132431
38030	FINLEY	17696	151	31.8	29.8	36.4	2.0	0.0	42133	43042	40	59	108	25.9	30.6	38.9	4.6	0.0	81250
38034	FRIENDSHIP	17571	1450	38.7	29.3	27.2	3.5	1.3	34555	36314	17	23	1137	26.5	34.1	33.6	5.8	0.0	78299
38037	GATES	17256	755	32.8	30.1	31.8	4.2	1.1	36928	38497	23	35	548	18.6	37.4	39.8	3.3	0.9	82979
38039	GRAND JUNCTION	15285	777	36.4	31.0	27.5	4.2	0.8	33694	35068	15	20	630	29.8	34.9	26.0	8.3	1.0	70980
38040	HALLS	18169	2052	32.2	34.4	28.5	3.4	1.6	35374	36477	19	26	1440	19.0	36.4	34.7	8.0	1.9	83500
38041	HENNING	15581	1193	38.6	26.7	29.4	3.2	2.2	33528	35239	14	20	825	25.5	37.5	31.3	4.7	1.1	73359
38042	HICKORY VALLEY	14462	367	45.5	26.4	24.3	2.7	1.1	30250	31171	8	12	285	29.1	38.6	20.7	10.9	0.7	70179
38044	HORNSBY	19821	433	30.9	35.1	29.6	2.3	2.1	37489	38450	25	39	356	36.5	27.5	24.7	11.2	0.0	74545
38049	MASON	19107	1717	31.2	29.1	31.0	5.3	3.4	41200	44401	37	55	1261	24.7	30.0	34.2	8.2	2.9	82200
38052	MIDDLETON	18580	1565	33.4	34.2	26.8	3.8	1.7	37188	38394	24	36	1234	20.0	27.7	41.0	9.8	1.5	92545
38053	MILLINGTON	24146	10704	15.0	25.4	45.6	10.4	3.5	59815	61136	77	89	7491	9.2	26.8	47.6	15.3	1.1	98339
38057	MOSCOW	20766	1517	27.0	24.5	34.9	10.6	3.0	48160	51205	57	76	1186	10.0	29.8	30.4	21.7	8.2	103632
38058	MUNFORD	22603	3889	19.4	24.8	45.1	7.4	3.3	55747	58914	72	87	2943	9.7	10.4	58.9	19.9	1.1	122362
38059	NEWBERN	20713	2815	25.0	28.1	40.1	4.8	2.0	46203	46674	52	73	2042	8.2	36.7	44.3	10.4	0.3	95124
38060	OAKLAND	27671	3256	16.1	22.9	43.6	10.2	7.1	57673	60976	75	88	2984	6.7	21.0	38.9	25.5	7.8	130607
38061	POCAHONTAS	18165	440	32.5	39.5	24.1	2.3	1.6	36989	38152	24	36	361	34.9	26.6	31.3	6.4	0.8	73125
38063	RIPLEY	18059	6529	34.4	26.7	33.7	2.7	2.5	39030	40523	30	46	4150	18.7	34.5	38.5	7.6	0.7	86749
38066	ROSSVILLE	22262	1038	27.5	19.9	39.3	9.8	3.5	51974	54676	66	81	861	9.6	19.4	37.4	26.5	7.1	121851
38067	SAULSBURY	17724	556	39.7	28.2	29.0	1.8	1.3	33500	36446	14	19	451	31.7	36.8	24.6	6.7	0.2	69878
38068	SOMERVILLE	19807	4419	30.3	27.2	34.0	5.9	2.7	41719	46144	38	57	3202	15.2	30.7	32.4	16.8	4.9	95462
38069	STANTON	17804	1182	40.9	29.3	25.0	2.5	2.3	30828	33346	9	14	840	26.4	36.4	31.0	6.0	0.2	74227
38075	WHITEVILLE	13664	1320	34.4	34.7	26.8	2.1	2.0	35700	37033	20	28	989	26.2	34.7	31.5	6.6	1.0	77887
38076	WILLISTON	20054	261	26.4	23.8	39.5	9.2	1.1	49616	52347	60	78	210	9.0	29.5	35.7	20.5	5.2	105556
38079	TIPTONVILLE	14708	1312	47.5	27.5	21.0	3.1	0.9	26436	25652	4	5	793	26.5	43.8	25.7	3.2	0.9	71552
38080	RIDGELY	16287	1014	42.6	26.5	28.6	1.5	0.8	29636	37162	8	11	628	26.6	43.8	24.0	4.3	1.3	71029
38103	MEMPHIS	39871	5007	28.0	19.1	32.5	10.5	9.8	53424	55533	69	83	1148	5.3	7.1	20.5	53.0	14.0	218696
38104	MEMPHIS	30409	12423	33.8	27.9	27.8	5.6	5.0	38495	40941	28	43	3911	5.7	21.0	47.5	21.8	4.0	115869
38105	MEMPHIS	12026	3161	68.3	20.2	9.2	1.5	0.8	13685	13927	1	2	456	39.5	42.3	13.6	3.5	1.1	56154
38106	MEMPHIS	13373	11228	50.4	29.0	17.1	2.0	1.4	24672	25056	3	4	6112	46.3	48.5	4.7	0.4	0.2	51960
38107	MEMPHIS	14894	7770	47.2	27.3	20.2	3.5	1.8	26829	27731	5	6	3692	30.1	46.4	22.0	1.4	0.2	64536
38108	MEMPHIS	14408	7908	46.8	27.0	23.1	2.0	1.1	26886	28098	5	6	4401	42.2	53.1	4.5	0.2	0.0	53832
38109	MEMPHIS	15783	17222	34.4	29.4	30.9	4.0	1.3	36920	39714	23	35	12848	26.3	61.7	10.8	1.0	0.2	62848
38111	MEMPHIS	23864	18094	31.1	30.0	28.7	5.9	4.3	40004	42619	33	50	10159	11.0	50.9	26.8	7.2	4.1	78450
38112	MEMPHIS	21381	7292	37.7	27.5	25.3	4.7	4.8	35301	37352	19	26	3425	27.5	33.2	25.1	11.9	2.2	73564
38114	MEMPHIS	14216	12234	45.4	31.3	19.7	2.4	1.2	27504	28726	5	7	6100	34.9	54.7	9.5	0.8	0.1	57823
38115	MEMPHIS	23617	17243	17.9	32.9	42.2	5.1	1.9	49151	51791	59	77	6084	2.7	29.3	67.2	0.7	0.0	97145
38116	MEMPHIS	18519	17278	27.7	30.5	33.7	5.7	2.4	41797	44936	39	57	8072	5.5	47.5	44.4	2.4	0.2	88191
38117	MEMPHIS	39153	11689	13.7	27.6	37.4	10.9	10.4	59485	59954	77	89	9520	0.8	28.8	44.7	18.4	7.2	111598
38118	MEMPHIS	17197	15149	23.4	33.6	38.2	3.8	1.1	43582	47039	44	64	8159	7.0	72.6	19.6	0.6	0.2	77479
38119	MEMPHIS	43158	9965	8.1	17.4	46.5	16.1	11.8	76566	75702	90	96	5934	0.5	13.5	46.6	34.3	5.1	151278
38120	MEMPHIS	58421	6474	8.5	15.1	33.4	16.9	26.0	86764	84971	94	98	4642	0.9	8.8	26.5	43.6	20.2	226201
38122	MEMPHIS	20734	10271	28.4	34.2	32.2	3.9	1.3	39526	41989	31	48	6505	12.1	69.0	17.2	1.5	0.2	71741
38125	MEMPHIS	37334	11812	4.9	11.3	47.4	24.1	12.3	84679	84972	94	98	10141	0.3	2.3	71.3	22.2	3.9	143797
38126	MEMPHIS	8710	2956	71.0	19.0	8.5	1.3	0.2	13098	13443	1	1	500	45.4	45.0	7.8	1.4	0.4	53151
38127	MEMPHIS	13920	16831	36.7	33.9	26.1	2.6	0.8	33508	35025	14	20	10574	24.0	66.1	8.4	1.3	0.1	62496
38128	MEMPHIS	19816	16371	23.8	30.2	38.7	5.2	2.1	46006	49663	51	71	9791	6.8	51.2	40.1	1.8	0.1	85149
38131	MEMPHIS	0	0	0.0	0.0	0.0	0.0	0.0	0	0	0	0	0	0.0	0.0	0.0	0.0	0.0	0
38132	MEMPHIS	0	0	0.0	0.0	0.0	0.0	0.0	0	0	0	0	0	0.0	0.0	0.0	0.0	0.0	0
38133	MEMPHIS	30124	7061	8.0	16.7	49.5	17.9	7.9	75636	75704	90	96	6205	5.7	10.4	61.4	19.2	3.3	118494
38134	MEMPHIS	25258	14979	11.1	27.2	48.8	9.7	3.2	60436	61023	78	90	8466	0.8	20.0	74.3	4.8	0.1	109358
38135	MEMPHIS	30669	10042	7.0	11.1	57.0	18.1	6.8	77878	77994	91	97	8853	0.7	8.0	66.8	23.8	0.6	132288
38138	GERMANTOWN	50851	9256	4.5	10.0	39.8	18.6	27.1	94008	94499	96	99	7243	0.6	4.5	25.7	56.8	12.3	215632
38139	GERMANTOWN	62788	5288	4.0	4.9	21.7	19.3	50.1	150160	150805	100	100	5071	0.3	1.8	6.8	63.7	27.3	303484
38141	MEMPHIS	25055	7572	7.5	24.6	54.0	11.0	2.9	66474	66925	85	93	6410	0.1	27.1	71.1	1.5	0.2	99805
38152	MEMPHIS	6982	11	63.6	27.3	9.1	0.0	0.0	12135	12135	1	1	3	0.0	0.0	100.0	0.0	0.0	112500
38201	MC KENZIE	20754	3935	31.9	31.3	29.4	4.5	2.9	38307	39143	28	42	2916	20.1	32.7	34.0	11.1	2.1	86940
38220	ATWOOD	17057	831	35.7	31.6	28.2	3.6	0.8	34844	35770	17	24	696	23.7	35.9	33.0	7.2	0.1	77606
38221	BIG SANDY	17513	1424	34.3	37.2	25.0	2.2	1.3	32733	33697	13	18	1209	26.5	27.7	31.1	13.1	1.7	83988
38222	BUCHANAN	20516	1103	30.5	33.7	28.7	5.9	1.2	39957	42188	32	50	932	18.2	24.2	32.5	20.1	4.9	100000
38224	COTTAGE GROVE	16349	409	33.0	33.5	29.8	2.9	0.7	35254	37707	19	25	339	22.7	29.8	32.2	13.3	2.1	87258
38225	DRESDEN	19538	2525	32.4	29.9	32.5	3.8	1.5	38511	40574	28	43	1819	19.8	38.8	33.9	6.6	0.9	83369
38226	DUKEDOM	19913	185	27.0	39.5	27.0	2.2	4.3	38520	38771	28	43	158	29.7	25.3	32.9	12.0	0.0	76667
38229	GLEASON	17524	1182	29.5	38.2	28.2	3.6	0.6	36512	36673	22	33	870	25.6	34.3	32.5	6.1	1.5	79254
38230	GREENFIELD	17311	1514	34.5	31.8	29.0	2.9	1.8	34672	36644	17	23	1165	31.8	34.2	26.7	7.0	0.3	67871
38231	HENRY	17723	762	29.3	33.1	31.9	3.8	2.0	38920	41607	29	45	607	22.6	31.1	34.8	9.1	2.5	86786
38232	HORNBEAK	18388	960	30.6	38.4	26.0	3.5	1.4	36311	37785	21	31	787	26.4	42.1	21.9	8.5	1.1	72228
38233	KENTON	19091	1201	32.5	28.0	35.1	3.3	1.1	39812	42242	32	49	915	16.5	42.0	33.8	6.0	1.7	82476
38236	MANSFIELD	19348	365	27.4	33.4	34.0	3.6	1.6	40084	42026	33	51	309	24.6	29.4	33.7	12.0	0.3	85968
38237	MARTIN	20133	5912	36.3	25.4	30.9	5.4	2.0	38501	39648	28	43	3605	11.5	23.7	50.2	13.3	1.2	104921
38238	MARTIN	6115	0	0.0	0.0	0.0	0.0	0.0	0	0	0	0	0	0.0	0.0	0.0	0.0	0.0	0
38240	OBION	18149	963	33.7	31.4	30.1	3.5	1.2	37395	39495	25	38	737	25.1	36.9	32.2	4.9	0.9	74786
38241	PALMERSVILLE	21897	400	33.3	31.5	28.3	3.3	3.8	35983	36030	21	30	339	22.1	38.6	33.0	6.2	0.0	79318
38242	PARIS	19588	8060	33.5	31.8	28.6	4.4	1.7	36615	39074	22	33	5856	17.0	28.0	39.6	13.8	1.7	95940
38251	PURYEAR	18978	1240	27.8	36.8	30.6	3.5	1.4	39243	41154	30	47	1011	22.7	33.3	33.7	8.5	1.7	83724
38253	RIVES	19463	430	29.1	30.5	34.7	3.3	2.6	41255	43131	37	55	363	19.0	31.1	39.1	8.3	2.5	89783
38255	SHARON	19436	1010	33.5	30.4	33.1	1.7	1.4	37655	38304	26	40	754	27.1	32.1	34.5	6.4	0.0	76071
38256	SPRINGVILLE	20391	1523	32.7	35.2	26.9	4.6	0.7	37518	39894	25	39	1318	19.0	28.8	38.3	12.6	1.3	92231
38257	SOUTH FULTON	20796	1843	32.4	30.3	28.8	6.3	2.2	38825	40937	29	45	1429	20.7	34.5	32.8	10.5	1.5	82972
38258	TREZEVANT	17794	809	36.1	28.9	31.1	3.2	0.6	35633	37519	20	27	663	32.4	32.6	29.7	5.3	0.0	71308
38259	TRIMBLE	21370	409	27.6	29.6	35.2	6.4	1.2	43168	45071	43	63	296	21.6	37.2	32.4	7.8	1.0	82571
38260	TROY	20199	1784	25.3	31.1	37.7	3.7	2.2	43901	45982	45	65	1449	23.1	32.0	36.0	8.4	0.6	82723
38261	UNION CITY	23905	6766	28.6	25.6	35.9	6.3	3.6	44591	46015	47	66	4356	11.6	31.0	43.7	12.1	1.5	97312
38301	JACKSON	18750	15783	37.6	30.1	26.5	3.8	2.0	33908	35923	15	21	8970	26.8	37.3	31.4	4.0	0.5	73843
38305	JACKSON	31421	18139	14.1	22.7	42.9	11.9	8.4	62941	63445	81	92	12762	5.6	15.5	55.8	19.8	3.3	120798
38310	ADAMSVILLE	19516	2562	34.6	33.7	25.8	3.4	2.4	36392	37918	22	32	2018	23.3	29.6	34.0	12.6	0.5	85323
38311	BATH SPRINGS	20019	331	31.4	29.6	35.3	1.8	1.8	39434	41876	31	48	288	27.1	33.7	27.8	8.3	3.1	78125
38313	BEECH BLUFF	20283	1251	22.6	31.9	39.6	5.0	0.9	46130	47815	52	72	1059	18.9	31.4	39.3	8.2	2.3	89699
38315	BETHEL SPRINGS	19161	1648	34.6	30.5	29.7	2.3	2.9	36896	39087	23	35	1367	33.4	28.8	29.8	7.2	0.7	69960
38316	BRADFORD	18817	1280	32.1	29.2	33.9	3.6	1.2	39243	41445	30	47	1070	23.6	32.1	38.2	5.9	0.2	82179
38317	BRUCETON	19490	1050	34.0	34.8	26.2	3.7	1.3	36143	36967	21	30	833	30.5	37.7	27.5	3.4	1.0	71298
38318	BUENA VISTA	19282	235	30.6	35.7	28.9	3.4	1.3	38613	39338	28	44	198	27.8	35.9	30.3	5.1	1.0	75000
38320	CAMDEN	17809	4582	35.1	34.5	25.6	4.0	0.9	34882	35789	17	24	3559	21.3	30.9	37.2	9.1	1.4	87312
38321	CEDAR GROVE	20444	1070	31.8	30.3	32.1	3.8	2.0	39722	39660	32	49	902	30.9	30.2	27.7	9.9	1.3	74512
38326	COUNCE	26812	1259	25.5	32.8	27.6	9.6	4.4	42859	44287	42	62	1057	17.4	25.0	37.2	14.7	5.8	102417
	TENNESSEE	24986		24.9	27.0	34.7	8.2	5.2	47751	50104				12.0	19.9	40.9	22.7	4.6	120455
	UNITED STATES	27277		20.9	24.4	35.3	11.7	7.6	54719	56938				9.3	13.1	31.6	32.6	13.5	162279

ZIP CODE	FINANCIAL SERVICES				THE HOME						ENTERTAINMENT						PERSONAL			
					Home Improvements		Furnishings													
# POST OFFICE NAME	Auto Loan	Home Loan	Invest-ments	Retire-ment Plans	Home Repair	Lawn & Garden	Comput-ers & Hard-ware-Personal	Major Appli-ances	TV, Radio, Sound Equip-ment	Furni-ture	Dine out/ Carry out	Sports Equip-ment	Fees & Tickets	Toys & Games	Travel	Cable TV	Apparel & Services	Auto Repairs	Health Insur-ance	Pets & Supplies
38028 EADS	131	139	135	139	138	137	124	132	124	130	124	99	129	126	129	124	87	126	128	154
38030 FINLEY	77	56	64	54	55	74	58	67	64	56	63	52	46	67	53	70	42	64	71	82
38034 FRIENDSHIP	76	52	67	50	52	73	55	66	62	53	61	51	43	64	51	68	41	62	70	81
38037 GATES	84	58	79	55	58	82	61	75	69	58	67	57	47	70	57	76	45	70	79	91
38039 GRAND JUNCTION	78	52	75	49	51	77	55	69	63	52	62	54	41	64	51	70	41	65	73	85
38040 HALLS	78	56	67	54	55	75	60	69	66	57	65	53	48	68	55	72	43	66	74	84
38041 HENNING	83	54	79	51	54	81	58	72	67	55	65	56	44	68	54	74	43	68	77	89
38042 HICKORY VALLEY	72	47	69	44	47	71	50	63	58	48	57	49	38	59	47	65	37	60	67	78
38044 HORNSBY	85	61	70	60	61	81	64	74	71	62	69	57	51	74	58	77	47	70	78	90
38049 MASON	97	67	86	64	67	93	71	85	80	68	78	66	55	82	65	88	52	80	90	104
38052 MIDDLETON	79	56	69	55	57	77	60	71	66	57	65	54	48	68	55	73	43	67	76	85
38053 MILLINGTON	96	99	87	98	95	96	94	94	94	95	95	72	96	97	94	95	66	94	95	111
38057 MOSCOW	100	78	93	75	78	98	78	92	85	76	84	69	66	86	75	91	56	86	94	110
38058 MUNFORD	101	92	83	90	91	96	88	94	91	89	91	69	83	94	84	94	62	90	95	111
38059 NEWBERN	85	69	72	69	69	84	73	80	77	67	75	61	63	78	68	82	51	77	84	95
38060 OAKLAND	111	107	106	105	107	112	99	108	101	102	101	79	97	104	99	104	70	103	107	127
38061 POCAHONTAS	77	55	66	54	55	74	57	68	64	55	62	52	46	66	53	70	42	64	71	82
38063 RIPLEY	76	56	63	56	55	72	62	67	68	59	66	53	51	69	56	73	45	67	72	83
38066 ROSSVILLE	90	80	82	83	82	96	79	90	82	72	81	68	72	84	79	87	55	83	93	105
38067 SAULSBURY	77	50	74	47	50	75	54	68	62	51	60	53	40	63	50	69	40	64	71	83
38068 SOMERVILLE	90	66	86	64	67	90	68	82	76	66	75	62	56	77	66	83	50	78	87	99
38069 STANTON	81	54	76	52	54	79	58	71	66	55	64	55	44	67	53	73	43	67	75	87
38075 WHITEVILLE	78	52	75	50	52	76	55	69	63	52	62	53	42	64	52	70	41	65	73	84
38076 WILLISTON	89	76	79	76	76	89	75	84	79	73	78	63	67	82	72	84	53	80	86	100
38079 TIPTONVILLE	58	43	56	42	44	58	49	55	54	45	52	41	40	53	46	59	36	54	61	66
38080 RIDGELY	67	47	59	46	47	65	52	60	58	49	56	46	41	59	47	63	38	58	64	73
38103 MEMPHIS	103	76	81	88	74	76	114	86	112	105	115	78	101	111	98	110	82	104	93	111
38104 MEMPHIS	76	63	62	68	61	65	82	69	82	77	83	57	75	80	73	82	58	78	76	86
38105 MEMPHIS	34	24	24	26	23	29	35	30	39	33	38	23	31	36	29	41	26	35	38	38
38106 MEMPHIS	51	41	39	42	40	49	46	46	53	48	52	33	44	51	42	57	35	50	56	58
38107 MEMPHIS	57	46	42	48	44	52	55	51	60	54	59	38	51	59	49	63	41	56	59	64
38108 MEMPHIS	56	44	42	45	43	53	51	50	57	50	55	37	46	56	46	61	38	53	59	62
38109 MEMPHIS	65	60	55	61	58	67	61	62	68	63	67	44	61	65	59	72	46	64	72	76
38111 MEMPHIS	78	70	65	72	67	74	80	73	81	77	81	57	76	80	73	83	56	78	80	89
38112 MEMPHIS	72	62	59	64	60	68	71	67	77	71	76	50	68	75	66	80	53	72	76	83
38114 MEMPHIS	54	44	40	45	42	51	50	48	56	51	55	35	47	55	45	60	38	52	57	60
38115 MEMPHIS	85	66	59	70	62	63	84	71	84	82	85	58	75	86	73	82	59	80	73	87
38116 MEMPHIS	75	65	57	67	60	68	72	67	77	73	77	51	70	77	66	79	53	73	74	83
38117 MEMPHIS	110	124	124	125	127	129	115	120	117	117	116	88	125	114	124	120	82	118	130	139
38118 MEMPHIS	76	61	55	64	57	63	73	65	75	72	76	52	67	76	65	76	53	73	70	81
38119 MEMPHIS	132	135	134	139	135	130	136	130	133	139	134	101	140	134	137	131	95	133	131	153
38120 MEMPHIS	166	197	218	203	209	186	186	185	176	195	177	143	206	172	204	170	128	182	176	211
38122 MEMPHIS	71	63	60	63	60	71	68	68	71	63	70	53	63	71	63	74	48	69	75	82
38125 MEMPHIS	146	165	142	162	158	138	146	145	137	157	139	116	153	145	148	129	99	138	127	165
38126 MEMPHIS	32	22	21	24	21	26	31	27	35	30	34	20	27	33	26	37	24	31	33	34
38127 MEMPHIS	60	50	42	52	45	54	57	52	61	56	61	41	54	61	50	63	42	57	59	66
38128 MEMPHIS	79	70	61	72	66	70	77	71	79	77	79	56	74	80	71	79	55	76	75	87
38131 MEMPHIS	0	0	0	0	0	0	0	0	0	0	0	0	0	0	0	0	0	0	0	0
38132 MEMPHIS	0	0	0	0	0	0	0	0	0	0	0	0	0	0	0	0	0	0	0	0
38133 MEMPHIS	125	136	117	133	130	117	122	122	117	131	119	96	127	123	122	112	84	117	109	140
38134 MEMPHIS	98	87	77	91	82	83	98	87	97	97	99	71	94	100	91	96	69	94	89	106
38135 MEMPHIS	123	140	122	138	134	123	123	125	117	129	119	97	130	123	127	114	84	119	114	143
38138 GERMANTOWN	175	213	217	219	218	199	186	192	177	197	179	147	210	178	205	173	129	184	180	220
38139 GERMANTOWN	245	325	336	342	337	292	266	277	248	289	251	218	321	254	303	236	189	257	241	312
38141 MEMPHIS	108	109	89	106	102	94	103	100	99	109	101	78	101	105	98	96	70	99	92	117
38152 MEMPHIS	30	19	18	21	19	21	35	24	32	28	31	22	26	32	25	31	22	29	25	31
38201 MC KENZIE	84	65	74	64	65	84	68	78	74	64	72	59	57	75	64	80	49	74	83	93
38220 ATWOOD	72	52	65	50	53	72	55	66	61	52	60	50	44	62	52	67	40	62	71	79
38221 BIG SANDY	68	53	70	50	55	70	53	65	58	52	57	47	45	57	53	63	38	61	69	77
38222 BUCHANAN	76	63	84	60	68	81	62	76	67	64	66	53	57	64	65	73	44	71	82	88
38224 COTTAGE GROVE	76	55	71	53	56	75	57	69	63	54	62	52	45	64	54	69	41	64	72	83
38225 DRESDEN	82	59	73	58	60	81	63	75	70	59	68	57	50	71	58	76	46	70	80	90
38226 DUKEDOM	84	60	69	59	60	80	63	73	70	61	68	56	50	73	57	76	46	69	77	89
38229 GLEASON	76	55	63	53	55	73	57	66	63	56	62	51	46	66	52	69	42	63	70	81
38230 GREENFIELD	75	54	65	53	54	73	57	67	63	54	62	51	46	65	52	69	41	63	71	81
38231 HENRY	83	60	69	58	59	79	62	72	69	60	67	56	50	71	57	75	45	69	76	88
38232 HORNBEAK	79	56	65	55	56	75	59	68	65	57	64	53	47	68	53	71	43	65	72	83
38233 KENTON	79	57	69	56	57	77	60	71	67	57	65	54	48	69	56	73	44	67	76	86
38236 MANSFIELD	81	58	79	56	59	81	60	74	66	56	65	56	48	66	58	73	43	69	77	89
38237 MARTIN	74	61	61	62	61	69	70	69	71	64	70	53	61	72	63	73	48	70	72	82
38238 MARTIN	0	0	0	0	0	0	0	0	0	0	0	0	0	0	0	0	0	0	0	0
38240 OBION	79	57	68	55	57	76	59	70	66	57	64	53	47	68	54	72	43	66	73	85
38241 PALMERSVILLE	95	68	86	66	69	93	71	85	78	68	77	65	57	80	66	86	51	80	89	103
38242 PARIS	74	57	68	57	58	75	61	71	67	57	65	53	52	67	58	72	44	67	76	84
38251 PURYEAR	82	59	73	57	59	80	61	73	67	58	66	56	49	69	57	74	44	68	77	88
38253 RIVES	89	64	76	62	64	85	66	78	74	64	72	60	53	76	61	80	48	74	82	95
38255 SHARON	77	56	70	54	57	77	59	71	66	55	64	54	48	67	56	72	43	67	76	85
38256 SPRINGVILLE	71	59	79	56	64	76	58	71	63	59	61	50	52	60	61	68	41	67	76	82
38257 SOUTH FULTON	84	63	83	62	65	87	66	81	72	60	70	60	54	72	64	79	47	75	85	95
38258 TREZEVANT	75	54	62	52	53	71	56	65	62	54	61	50	45	64	51	67	41	61	68	79
38259 TRIMBLE	91	65	76	64	65	87	68	80	76	66	74	61	55	78	62	82	50	75	84	97
38260 TROY	92	66	79	64	66	88	69	81	76	66	75	62	55	79	63	83	50	76	85	98
38261 UNION CITY	88	73	75	73	72	88	78	83	83	74	81	63	69	84	73	89	56	82	90	99
38301 JACKSON	68	55	55	56	53	65	63	63	68	60	66	48	56	67	57	72	46	65	70	77
38305 JACKSON	113	116	108	118	114	112	114	112	112	115	113	87	115	114	113	111	79	112	110	131
38310 ADAMSVILLE	82	59	75	57	60	81	61	74	68	58	67	56	49	69	58	75	44	69	79	89
38311 BATH SPRINGS	83	59	68	58	59	78	62	72	68	60	67	55	49	71	56	75	45	68	76	87
38313 BEECH BLUFF	92	68	76	67	68	88	70	81	77	68	75	62	57	80	64	83	51	76	85	98
38315 BETHEL SPRINGS	84	60	70	58	60	80	63	73	70	61	68	56	50	72	57	76	46	69	77	89
38316 BRADFORD	81	58	70	57	58	78	61	72	68	58	66	55	49	70	56	74	44	68	76	87
38317 BRUCETON	78	56	73	55	58	79	60	73	67	56	65	55	48	68	57	74	44	68	79	87
38318 BUENA VISTA	83	60	69	58	59	79	62	72	69	60	67	55	50	72	56	75	45	68	76	88
38320 CAMDEN	73	52	70	51	54	73	55	68	61	51	60	51	44	61	53	67	40	63	72	81
38321 CEDAR GROVE	88	63	79	61	64	86	65	78	72	63	71	60	52	74	61	79	47	73	82	95
38326 COUNCE	102	78	115	76	83	105	79	99	85	74	84	73	66	83	81	92	56	91	100	116
TENNESSEE	95	84	85	84	82	93	87	90	90	85	89	69	80	91	83	93	61	89	93	107
UNITED STATES	100	100	100	100	100	100	100	100	100	100	100	100	100	100	100	100	100	100	100	100

POPULATION CHANGE

38327-38554

#	POST OFFICE NAME	COUNTY FIPS CODE	POPULATION 2000	POPULATION 2009	POPULATION 2014	2000-2009 ANNUAL RATE % Rate	2000-2009 ANNUAL RATE State Centile	HOUSEHOLDS 2000	HOUSEHOLDS 2009	HOUSEHOLDS 2014	HOUSEHOLDS % Annual Rate 2000-2009	HOUSEHOLDS 2009 Average HH Size	FAMILIES 2000	FAMILIES 2009	FAMILIES % Annual Rate 2000-2009
38327	CRUMP	071	508	549	566	0.8	60	222	246	256	1.1	2.23	163	176	0.8
38328	DARDEN	077	852	878	887	0.3	31	354	375	382	0.6	2.34	255	263	0.3
38329	DECATURVILLE	039	3266	3336	3310	0.2	27	1344	1413	1413	0.5	2.30	959	982	0.3
38330	DYER	053	4330	4156	4103	-0.4	5	1747	1714	1702	-0.2	2.36	1254	1196	-0.5
38332	ENVILLE	023	1024	1106	1146	0.8	60	413	452	470	1.0	2.45	302	321	0.7
38333	EVA	005	562	609	623	0.9	63	241	269	278	1.2	2.26	178	193	0.9
38334	FINGER	109	1770	1929	1995	0.9	63	668	741	770	1.1	2.60	518	562	0.9
38337	GADSDEN	033	1581	1624	1615	0.3	31	611	639	638	0.5	2.54	467	477	0.2
38339	GUYS	109	620	614	613	-0.1	13	253	258	259	0.2	2.38	187	186	-0.1
38340	HENDERSON	023	11580	12023	12243	0.4	36	4120	4418	4519	0.8	2.51	3013	3154	0.5
38341	HOLLADAY	005	2225	2282	2288	0.3	31	899	941	950	0.5	2.43	668	682	0.2
38342	HOLLOW ROCK	017	1573	1587	1569	0.1	22	634	654	651	0.3	2.42	459	461	0.0
38343	HUMBOLDT	053	16665	16722	16879	0.0	18	6650	6841	6953	0.3	2.39	4695	4705	0.0
38344	HUNTINGDON	017	9314	9190	9001	-0.1	13	3667	3641	3582	-0.1	2.43	2648	2564	-0.3
38345	HURON	077	1611	1726	1784	0.7	53	620	678	706	1.0	2.54	469	502	0.7
38347	JACKS CREEK	023	375	402	414	0.8	60	153	166	172	0.9	2.42	115	121	0.6
38348	LAVINIA	017	1103	1158	1156	0.5	41	421	451	453	0.7	2.52	311	325	0.5
38351	LEXINGTON	077	16381	17491	18034	0.7	53	6692	7307	7584	1.0	2.35	4760	5067	0.7
38352	LURAY	023	588	650	677	1.1	69	208	233	244	1.2	2.78	162	178	1.0
38355	MEDINA	113	2584	4043	4477	5.0	98	1046	1602	1777	4.7	2.52	791	1186	4.5
38356	MEDON	113	2261	2367	2414	0.5	41	875	947	972	0.9	2.49	654	686	0.5
38357	MICHIE	109	2736	2890	2968	0.6	47	1107	1202	1243	0.9	2.40	817	866	0.6
38358	MILAN	053	11748	12035	12257	0.3	31	4760	4980	5096	0.5	2.36	3292	3344	0.2
38359	MILLEDGEVILLE	071	315	333	342	0.6	47	148	159	164	0.8	2.09	105	110	0.5
38361	MORRIS CHAPEL	071	1034	1110	1142	0.8	60	401	435	450	0.9	2.55	303	321	0.6
38362	OAKFIELD	113	1335	1420	1524	0.7	53	502	548	593	1.0	2.59	394	418	0.6
38363	PARSONS	039	5841	5751	5645	-0.2	10	2435	2450	2422	0.1	2.29	1644	1606	-0.3
38366	PINSON	113	2244	2506	2606	1.2	72	834	968	1017	1.6	2.57	652	735	1.3
38367	RAMER	109	2859	2878	2884	0.1	22	1157	1194	1205	0.3	2.41	843	848	0.1
38368	REAGAN	077	1737	1796	1826	0.4	36	702	742	759	0.6	2.42	520	536	0.3
38369	RUTHERFORD	053	2125	2077	2061	-0.2	10	878	877	877	0.0	2.37	617	597	-0.4
38370	SALTILLO	071	693	713	723	0.3	31	311	329	337	0.6	2.17	205	210	0.3
38371	SARDIS	077	1261	1254	1256	-0.1	13	533	543	548	0.2	2.31	375	372	-0.1
38372	SAVANNAH	071	17180	17012	17021	-0.1	13	6953	7124	7204	0.3	2.32	4928	4912	0.0
38374	SCOTTS HILL	077	1843	1876	1888	0.2	27	759	792	803	0.5	2.36	558	567	0.2
38375	SELMER	109	8459	8652	8734	0.2	27	3427	3576	3633	0.5	2.34	2358	2391	0.2
38376	SHILOH	071	404	445	460	1.1	69	164	186	194	1.4	2.39	124	137	1.1
38379	STANTONVILLE	109	1197	1335	1395	1.2	72	487	553	581	1.4	2.41	367	407	1.1
38380	SUGAR TREE	039	528	512	501	-0.3	7	247	246	243	0.0	2.08	170	164	-0.4
38381	TOONE	069	1781	1780	1759	0.0	18	666	682	678	0.3	2.56	471	470	0.0
38382	TRENTON	053	9693	9689	9706	0.0	18	3930	3991	4021	0.2	2.36	2685	2645	-0.2
38387	WESTPORT	017	373	376	372	0.1	22	138	142	142	0.3	2.59	106	107	0.1
38388	WILDERSVILLE	077	1739	1941	2031	1.2	72	682	780	823	1.5	2.47	512	571	1.2
38390	YUMA	017	875	892	890	0.2	27	343	358	360	0.5	2.45	257	263	0.2
38391	DENMARK	113	1160	1135	1123	-0.2	10	431	437	436	0.1	2.59	311	303	-0.3
38392	MERCER	113	759	737	728	-0.3	7	298	300	299	0.1	2.46	215	208	-0.4
38401	COLUMBIA	119	50545	57936	62545	1.5	81	19333	22654	24585	1.7	2.51	13903	15849	1.4
38425	CLIFTON	181	3585	3767	3783	0.5	41	713	766	781	0.8	2.50	504	528	0.5
38449	ARDMORE	055	3261	3531	3593	0.9	63	1282	1438	1475	1.2	2.41	949	1037	1.0
38450	COLLINWOOD	181	2660	2717	2724	0.2	27	1057	1120	1136	0.6	2.43	767	791	0.3
38451	CULLEOKA	119	4189	4914	5357	1.7	84	1481	1791	1967	2.1	2.74	1193	1408	1.8
38452	CYPRESS INN	181	1004	1026	1028	0.2	27	390	409	415	0.5	2.51	315	325	0.3
38453	DELLROSE	103	340	366	376	0.8	60	135	150	156	1.1	2.44	104	113	0.9
38454	DUCK RIVER	081	1166	1240	1266	0.7	53	451	487	499	0.8	2.53	337	355	0.6
38456	ETHRIDGE	099	4110	4309	4376	0.5	41	1333	1417	1446	0.7	3.04	1026	1066	0.4
38457	FIVE POINTS	099	856	895	913	0.5	41	335	360	369	0.8	2.49	261	273	0.5
38459	FRANKEWING	103	333	371	387	1.2	72	133	152	161	1.5	2.44	103	115	1.2
38460	GOODSPRING	055	1118	1131	1117	0.1	22	441	459	457	0.4	2.46	335	340	0.2
38461	HAMPSHIRE	101	1130	1273	1356	1.3	76	412	473	505	1.5	2.69	324	363	1.2
38462	HOHENWALD	101	9908	10247	10394	0.4	36	3839	4017	4086	0.5	2.49	2793	2852	0.2
38463	IRON CITY	181	2883	3013	3058	0.5	41	1096	1185	1215	0.8	2.54	836	882	0.6
38464	LAWRENCEBURG	099	21643	21653	21632	0.0	18	8746	8914	8951	0.2	2.39	6155	6097	-0.1
38468	LEOMA	099	4809	5050	5142	0.5	41	1798	1922	1968	0.7	2.63	1423	1489	0.5
38469	LORETTO	099	3982	4288	4397	0.8	60	1556	1713	1768	1.0	2.50	1172	1260	0.8
38471	LUTTS	181	626	625	620	0.0	18	244	253	254	0.4	2.47	190	193	0.2
38472	LYNNVILLE	055	2722	2764	2729	0.2	27	1027	1072	1068	0.5	2.58	779	794	0.2
38473	MINOR HILL	055	1064	1126	1121	0.6	47	425	460	462	0.9	2.45	324	343	0.6
38474	MOUNT PLEASANT	119	7105	7914	8436	1.2	72	2791	3202	3439	1.5	2.45	2039	2265	1.1
38475	OLIVEHILL	071	640	647	649	0.1	22	229	240	244	0.5	2.51	173	177	0.2
38476	PRIMM SPRINGS	081	1023	1190	1293	1.6	82	368	438	478	1.9	2.72	287	327	1.4
38477	PROSPECT	055	2678	2780	2760	0.4	36	1028	1101	1103	0.7	2.51	790	827	0.5
38478	PULASKI	055	18312	17840	17403	-0.3	7	7422	7391	7254	0.0	2.35	5119	4951	-0.4
38481	SAINT JOSEPH	099	884	952	979	0.8	60	363	401	416	1.1	2.37	269	289	0.8
38482	SANTA FE	119	1629	1927	2106	1.8	86	621	761	836	2.2	2.53	468	556	1.9
38483	SUMMERTOWN	099	4339	4675	4806	0.8	60	1573	1724	1784	1.0	2.71	1240	1332	0.8
38485	WAYNESBORO	181	6783	6673	6571	-0.2	10	2708	2744	2729	0.1	2.28	1922	1895	-0.2
38486	WESTPOINT	099	897	977	1005	0.9	63	344	386	400	1.3	2.53	260	285	1.0
38487	WILLIAMSPORT	119	963	1063	1127	1.1	69	371	422	450	1.4	2.52	293	324	1.1
38488	TAFT	103	2001	2183	2270	0.9	63	757	849	890	1.2	2.57	584	640	1.0
38501	COOKEVILLE	141	31550	35842	38115	1.4	78	13174	15032	16058	1.4	2.28	7888	8690	1.1
38504	ALLARDT	049	843	947	997	1.3	76	315	366	390	1.6	2.59	246	280	1.4
38505	COOKEVILLE	141	990	1078	1089	0.9	63	3	3	3	0.0	2.67	1	1	0.0
38506	COOKEVILLE	141	22431	25882	27924	1.6	82	8776	10240	11105	1.7	2.50	6486	7353	1.4
38541	ALLONS	027	1397	1489	1523	0.7	53	585	644	665	1.0	2.31	443	477	0.8
38542	ALLRED	133	42	44	45	0.5	41	15	16	17	0.7	2.75	12	13	0.9
38543	ALPINE	133	860	805	785	-0.7	2	355	343	338	-0.4	2.35	258	243	-0.6
38544	BAXTER	141	6254	7201	7765	1.5	81	2533	2946	3186	1.6	2.44	1821	2055	1.3
38545	BLOOMINGTON SPRINGS	087	1078	1178	1220	1.0	66	402	443	460	1.1	2.64	299	322	0.8
38547	BRUSH CREEK	159	1447	1515	1537	0.5	41	549	589	602	0.8	2.57	425	445	0.5
38548	BUFFALO VALLEY	141	706	748	774	0.6	47	272	292	303	0.8	2.55	204	213	0.5
38549	BYRDSTOWN	137	3557	3589	3537	0.1	22	1523	1593	1587	0.5	2.21	1051	1069	0.2
38551	CELINA	027	4237	4373	4341	0.3	31	1842	1976	1984	0.8	2.17	1231	1284	0.5
38552	CHESTNUT MOUND	159	614	646	655	0.6	47	227	243	248	0.7	2.66	173	181	0.5
38553	CLARKRANGE	049	2189	2415	2520	1.1	69	827	944	996	1.4	2.56	632	705	1.2
38554	CRAWFORD	133	886	1001	1050	1.3	76	352	410	435	1.7	2.44	280	319	1.4
	TENNESSEE					1.1					1.3	2.44			1.0
	UNITED STATES					1.0					1.1	2.59			0.9

ZIP CODE #	POST OFFICE NAME	RACE (%) White 2000	White 2009	Black 2000	Black 2009	Asian/Pacific 2000	Asian/Pacific 2009	% Hispanic Origin 2000	% Hispanic Origin 2009	2009 AGE DISTRIBUTION (%) 0-4	5-9	10-14	15-19	20-24	25-44	45-64	65-84	85+	18+	MEDIAN AGE 2009	% 2009 Males	% 2009 Females
38327	CRUMP	98.0	97.4	0.2	0.4	0.0	0.0	1.0	1.6	6.2	6.2	6.9	7.1	4.9	24.6	28.1	14.6	1.5	76.3	40.6	49.9	50.1
38328	DARDEN	97.7	97.5	0.5	0.5	0.1	0.1	1.4	1.6	5.8	6.2	6.3	5.8	4.3	24.7	30.6	14.5	1.8	78.0	42.8	48.9	51.1
38329	DECATURVILLE	94.0	93.9	4.2	4.3	0.2	0.2	0.9	0.9	5.5	5.9	6.1	5.6	4.3	24.4	29.0	16.2	3.1	79.1	43.7	48.3	51.7
38330	DYER	87.2	83.9	11.7	14.6	0.1	0.1	0.6	1.0	5.8	5.8	6.1	6.0	5.2	25.4	27.1	14.9	3.7	78.6	41.8	46.6	53.4
38332	ENVILLE	97.1	96.6	2.0	2.3	0.0	0.0	0.6	1.0	5.7	5.8	6.1	6.3	5.6	25.3	29.4	14.1	1.6	78.6	41.5	49.9	50.1
38333	EVA	98.8	98.2	0.0	0.0	0.4	0.5	0.5	1.0	4.3	5.6	5.9	5.9	4.4	22.5	34.0	15.8	1.6	80.1	46.0	50.2	49.8
38334	FINGER	95.9	95.2	1.9	2.1	0.1	0.2	0.5	0.8	6.7	6.6	6.9	6.9	5.3	27.6	26.4	12.0	1.6	75.6	37.9	49.9	50.1
38337	GADSDEN	83.5	82.5	14.5	15.5	0.0	0.0	1.0	1.0	5.3	6.2	7.0	6.3	4.6	25.9	31.4	11.5	1.8	77.2	41.1	50.2	49.8
38339	GUYS	89.2	87.3	9.4	10.7	0.0	0.0	1.0	1.6	6.5	6.7	7.0	6.2	5.2	24.9	28.0	14.0	1.5	75.9	40.0	49.2	50.8
38340	HENDERSON	86.4	84.6	11.6	12.9	0.3	0.4	1.1	1.8	6.9	6.5	6.4	8.9	9.7	23.9	23.7	11.7	2.3	76.5	34.5	48.6	51.4
38341	HOLLADAY	96.8	95.9	1.6	1.9	0.2	0.3	1.3	1.8	5.7	6.0	6.4	6.3	5.1	23.6	30.5	14.9	1.4	78.0	42.7	49.3	50.7
38342	HOLLOW ROCK	92.1	90.7	6.2	6.9	0.1	0.1	0.8	1.2	6.3	6.2	6.6	6.7	5.3	25.8	26.9	14.5	1.7	76.8	40.2	49.6	50.4
38343	HUMBOLDT	69.8	67.5	28.4	30.1	0.2	0.2	1.2	1.8	6.4	6.6	6.7	6.4	4.9	24.5	28.2	13.8	2.6	76.5	41.0	48.4	51.6
38344	HUNTINGDON	86.5	84.5	11.4	12.8	0.2	0.2	1.2	1.8	6.1	5.7	6.0	6.6	5.6	24.8	26.8	15.5	3.1	78.0	41.6	47.7	52.3
38345	HURON	95.2	94.2	2.6	3.0	0.1	0.2	0.7	1.2	6.7	6.7	7.0	6.4	5.2	28.6	28.0	10.1	1.2	75.6	38.0	49.7	50.3
38347	JACKS CREEK	88.5	86.3	9.1	10.4	0.0	0.2	0.8	1.0	6.7	7.0	7.0	7.2	6.0	26.6	26.6	11.7	1.2	74.9	37.5	48.8	51.2
38348	LAVINIA	93.8	92.9	5.1	5.8	0.2	0.2	0.7	1.1	6.0	6.2	6.5	5.9	4.9	26.9	28.5	12.8	2.3	77.5	40.8	50.1	49.9
38351	LEXINGTON	88.5	87.0	9.8	10.7	0.2	0.3	1.0	1.7	6.4	6.5	6.6	6.4	5.3	26.6	27.6	12.7	2.0	76.4	39.4	48.4	51.6
38352	LURAY	91.0	89.1	7.1	8.5	0.2	0.3	0.7	1.1	7.1	7.1	7.2	6.8	5.2	27.1	27.5	10.8	1.2	74.5	37.5	49.7	50.3
38355	MEDINA	94.5	93.2	4.1	4.9	0.2	0.3	0.7	1.3	7.1	7.4	7.6	7.0	4.7	27.4	28.2	9.4	1.3	73.6	37.9	48.7	51.3
38356	MEDON	69.2	62.9	29.1	35.0	0.1	0.2	1.1	1.5	6.6	6.8	6.8	6.8	5.5	25.3	28.6	12.0	1.5	75.5	39.1	49.6	50.4
38357	MICHIE	94.6	93.7	4.6	5.2	0.0	0.0	1.0	1.7	5.8	6.0	6.3	6.0	5.2	25.3	30.0	13.7	1.7	78.2	41.5	50.2	49.8
38358	MILAN	81.1	78.2	17.0	19.2	0.2	0.4	1.4	2.1	6.6	6.4	6.4	6.3	5.7	24.5	26.5	14.7	3.0	76.7	40.4	46.9	53.1
38359	MILLEDGEVILLE	94.9	93.7	3.8	4.2	0.0	0.3	0.6	1.5	5.4	5.7	6.0	6.3	5.1	24.3	29.7	15.3	2.1	79.0	42.6	49.8	50.2
38361	MORRIS CHAPEL	89.2	87.2	9.0	10.6	0.2	0.3	0.7	1.1	5.7	6.2	6.2	6.0	4.7	24.1	30.2	14.9	2.1	78.2	42.7	49.3	50.7
38362	OAKFIELD	88.0	83.7	10.6	14.2	0.2	0.4	0.7	1.1	7.0	7.3	7.3	6.7	5.5	29.7	27.6	8.0	0.8	74.2	36.6	49.6	50.4
38363	PARSONS	93.2	92.8	4.0	4.3	0.2	0.2	2.4	2.4	5.6	5.8	5.9	6.1	4.7	24.4	27.6	16.5	3.4	78.9	43.2	48.5	51.5
38366	PINSON	91.4	88.9	7.3	9.2	0.0	0.1	1.1	1.9	6.0	6.4	6.9	6.5	4.7	26.9	29.4	11.8	1.2	76.5	40.1	51.1	48.9
38367	RAMER	92.5	91.2	6.3	7.2	0.1	0.2	0.9	1.5	6.4	6.7	7.1	6.3	4.7	25.5	28.0	13.6	1.6	75.8	40.1	49.4	50.6
38368	REAGAN	97.1	96.4	1.6	1.9	0.1	0.2	0.9	1.4	6.7	6.7	6.8	6.3	5.3	25.6	27.8	13.0	1.7	75.8	39.6	50.0	50.0
38369	RUTHERFORD	85.1	81.5	13.9	17.3	0.0	0.0	0.6	0.8	6.2	6.2	6.5	6.8	5.2	23.6	28.2	15.1	2.3	76.9	41.8	47.6	52.4
38370	SALTILLO	90.5	88.6	8.4	10.0	0.1	0.1	1.2	1.7	3.8	4.2	4.9	5.9	3.6	22.7	33.2	19.1	2.5	83.6	48.5	50.5	49.5
38371	SARDIS	96.9	96.3	2.5	3.0	0.1	0.1	0.8	1.1	5.8	6.1	6.5	6.1	4.6	24.7	29.1	14.8	2.4	77.8	42.3	49.5	50.5
38372	SAVANNAH	94.5	93.5	4.0	4.5	0.2	0.3	1.0	1.6	6.1	6.1	6.3	6.2	5.2	25.3	27.7	14.8	2.5	77.7	41.3	49.0	51.0
38374	SCOTTS HILL	98.8	98.7	0.4	0.5	0.1	0.1	1.5	1.7	6.2	6.2	6.4	5.3	4.9	26.0	27.9	14.9	2.1	77.8	41.4	48.2	51.8
38375	SELMER	87.2	85.1	10.8	12.2	0.2	0.3	1.1	1.8	6.0	6.1	6.4	6.3	4.8	25.2	27.9	14.9	2.3	77.3	41.5	48.9	51.1
38376	SHILOH	95.5	94.6	3.5	4.0	0.2	0.2	1.2	2.0	6.3	6.3	6.5	6.3	5.4	26.1	29.2	12.8	1.1	76.9	40.2	49.9	50.1
38379	STANTONVILLE	96.2	95.5	2.4	2.8	0.1	0.1	0.7	1.2	5.7	5.9	6.1	5.9	4.9	26.1	28.2	15.2	1.9	78.6	41.7	51.4	48.6
38380	SUGAR TREE	97.2	97.1	0.9	1.0	0.2	0.2	1.1	1.2	5.5	5.7	5.9	5.5	4.9	22.1	29.5	19.5	1.6	79.5	45.4	51.4	48.6
38381	TOONE	79.2	77.4	19.6	21.5	0.3	0.3	1.5	1.5	7.0	7.2	7.4	6.8	4.7	24.9	27.6	12.8	1.6	74.2	39.6	50.7	49.3
38382	TRENTON	78.7	74.7	19.6	23.0	0.2	0.3	1.4	2.2	6.1	6.0	6.2	6.3	5.4	24.9	27.6	14.7	2.7	77.9	41.4	48.7	51.3
38387	WESTPORT	82.4	80.3	15.0	16.8	0.8	0.8	0.3	0.3	5.9	5.9	6.4	7.2	5.3	26.6	27.1	13.3	2.4	76.9	40.2	50.3	49.7
38388	WILDERSVILLE	86.1	84.1	12.5	14.1	0.1	0.2	1.3	2.1	6.7	6.7	7.0	6.4	5.3	26.2	28.7	11.7	1.4	75.7	39.1	49.9	50.1
38390	YUMA	87.1	84.8	10.4	11.8	0.5	0.7	1.1	1.8	5.9	6.1	6.4	6.6	4.7	27.5	27.7	13.1	2.0	77.6	40.2	49.6	50.4
38391	DENMARK	38.7	31.0	59.5	66.8	0.1	0.1	0.7	1.0	6.0	6.3	6.5	7.0	5.6	24.4	30.3	11.9	2.0	76.7	40.9	51.7	48.3
38392	MERCER	48.4	40.4	50.0	57.7	0.0	0.0	0.5	0.7	6.1	6.4	6.5	7.2	5.8	24.4	30.0	11.7	1.9	76.3	40.3	51.4	48.6
38401	COLUMBIA	80.1	76.9	16.1	17.8	0.4	0.6	3.8	5.9	6.8	6.8	6.9	6.7	5.8	26.0	28.3	10.8	1.8	75.3	38.3	48.8	51.2
38425	CLIFTON	71.6	69.2	27.3	29.5	0.1	0.1	0.9	1.4	3.0	3.0	3.2	4.0	9.4	45.9	21.2	9.4	1.1	88.9	36.2	74.6	25.4
38449	ARDMORE	91.9	91.1	6.4	6.9	0.2	0.2	0.8	1.1	5.9	6.1	6.3	5.6	4.9	23.7	30.3	15.1	2.2	78.4	43.4	49.4	50.6
38450	COLLINWOOD	98.5	97.8	0.0	0.1	0.2	0.3	0.8	1.3	6.0	6.1	6.4	6.6	5.6	26.4	28.7	12.7	1.6	77.4	39.9	48.6	51.4
38451	CULLEOKA	94.3	93.0	3.7	4.5	0.3	0.4	1.1	1.9	6.7	6.9	7.1	7.1	5.7	26.9	29.9	9.0	0.8	74.8	38.2	49.6	50.4
38452	CYPRESS INN	99.3	99.2	0.1	0.1	0.0	0.0	0.5	0.8	6.6	6.6	6.9	7.0	5.5	25.3	28.4	12.6	1.1	75.6	39.7	49.5	50.5
38453	DELLROSE	92.6	91.8	5.0	5.2	0.3	0.3	0.6	0.5	4.6	4.9	5.2	4.9	5.7	26.8	32.0	14.2	1.6	82.2	43.5	51.4	48.6
38454	DUCK RIVER	95.1	94.3	3.4	4.0	0.1	0.1	0.9	1.6	6.6	6.9	7.3	6.0	5.2	24.0	29.8	12.3	1.8	75.5	40.5	51.2	48.8
38456	ETHRIDGE	98.5	98.2	0.8	1.0	0.1	0.2	0.4	0.5	9.5	9.0	9.0	8.7	6.3	25.1	22.4	9.0	1.0	67.1	30.8	49.7	50.3
38457	FIVE POINTS	97.9	97.1	0.0	0.0	0.7	1.0	0.4	0.7	6.7	6.5	6.6	6.5	5.9	28.4	24.6	13.2	1.7	76.2	38.6	49.2	50.8
38459	FRANKEWING	96.1	94.6	1.2	1.9	0.3	0.5	0.6	0.8	4.0	4.6	4.6	4.9	5.9	27.2	32.6	14.6	1.6	83.8	44.2	51.8	48.2
38460	GOODSPRING	94.2	93.7	4.2	4.7	0.0	0.0	0.5	0.4	7.3	7.3	7.5	6.9	5.4	25.6	27.1	11.6	1.3	73.6	37.6	49.8	50.2
38461	HAMPSHIRE	92.2	89.7	5.5	6.9	0.2	0.3	1.6	2.5	5.9	6.0	6.5	6.8	5.7	27.3	31.1	9.6	1.0	77.4	38.9	49.6	50.4
38462	HOHENWALD	97.2	96.6	1.3	1.5	0.2	0.3	1.1	1.9	6.6	6.4	6.7	6.9	5.7	25.1	27.7	13.0	1.9	75.7	39.3	49.6	50.4
38463	IRON CITY	98.6	98.3	0.6	0.7	0.0	0.0	1.0	1.7	6.4	6.2	6.5	6.6	6.0	27.4	27.9	11.6	1.3	76.9	39.1	50.2	49.8
38464	LAWRENCEBURG	95.5	94.4	2.4	2.7	0.4	0.6	1.2	2.0	6.4	6.4	6.5	6.5	5.4	25.7	26.6	13.9	2.5	76.8	40.1	48.2	51.8
38468	LEOMA	98.0	97.4	0.5	0.5	0.1	0.3	0.5	0.8	6.9	6.8	7.0	6.8	5.7	27.2	26.3	11.9	1.4	75.2	38.2	50.3	49.7
38469	LORETTO	98.1	97.5	0.4	0.4	0.2	0.2	1.1	1.9	6.3	6.4	6.6	6.7	5.7	26.5	27.2	13.0	1.6	76.7	39.5	49.4	50.6
38471	LUTTS	99.4	99.4	0.0	0.0	0.2	0.2	0.2	0.2	5.8	5.8	6.1	6.6	6.1	25.0	30.1	12.8	1.9	78.2	41.5	48.5	51.5
38472	LYNNVILLE	93.2	92.6	4.9	5.4	0.3	0.4	0.8	0.9	5.4	6.1	6.8	7.5	5.3	25.2	30.4	11.6	1.7	77.1	40.7	50.4	49.6
38473	MINOR HILL	97.7	97.6	0.8	0.8	0.0	0.0	0.9	1.0	6.1	6.1	6.5	7.2	6.2	23.9	28.8	13.5	1.7	76.9	40.1	48.6	51.4
38474	MOUNT PLEASANT	83.8	81.4	14.5	16.4	0.2	0.2	1.0	1.6	6.3	6.1	6.3	6.7	6.2	25.5	28.0	12.9	1.9	77.1	39.7	47.7	52.3
38475	OLIVEHILL	95.0	94.1	3.8	4.3	0.0	0.0	1.3	1.9	6.0	6.2	6.3	6.3	5.6	28.6	26.1	13.0	1.9	77.6	39.0	53.5	46.5
38476	PRIMM SPRINGS	96.9	96.1	1.6	1.8	0.0	0.1	0.8	1.3	5.9	6.2	6.7	6.2	5.0	25.8	31.8	11.2	1.2	77.3	40.8	51.1	48.9
38477	PROSPECT	88.4	87.2	10.1	11.3	0.0	0.0	0.7	0.7	6.3	6.3	6.7	6.3	5.6	25.1	29.9	12.3	1.6	77.0	40.5	50.4	49.6
38478	PULASKI	83.0	82.0	15.1	16.1	0.5	0.5	1.0	1.0	6.3	6.3	6.5	6.5	5.6	25.2	27.6	13.6	2.4	77.0	40.3	49.1	50.9
38481	SAINT JOSEPH	98.3	98.0	0.9	1.1	0.0	0.0	1.4	2.3	6.2	6.1	6.3	6.1	6.1	29.0	27.3	11.4	1.5	77.6	39.1	50.2	49.8
38482	SANTA FE	97.0	96.1	1.7	2.1	0.0	0.0	0.8	1.3	6.9	7.1	7.2	6.3	4.5	28.1	28.1	10.7	1.1	74.8	38.6	50.9	49.1
38483	SUMMERTOWN	97.9	97.3	0.8	0.9	0.1	0.2	1.1	1.8	7.0	6.9	7.3	7.1	5.6	27.5	27.0	10.5	1.0	74.4	37.4	50.7	49.3
38485	WAYNESBORO	96.3	95.5	2.1	2.3	0.5	0.7	0.9	1.5	5.4	5.4	5.8	6.6	5.0	26.2	27.3	15.5	2.8	79.2	41.9	50.1	49.9
38486	WESTPOINT	96.7	95.7	2.0	2.5	0.1	0.3	0.2	0.4	5.8	5.9	5.8	5.5	6.0	26.9	29.6	12.9	1.4	79.3	40.8	51.1	48.9
38487	WILLIAMSPORT	92.7	91.2	6.0	7.2	0.1	0.1	1.1	1.7	5.7	6.1	6.5	6.8	5.0	25.2	31.7	11.7	1.3	77.6	41.3	50.0	50.0
38488	TAFT	95.9	94.5	1.1	1.4	0.5	0.8	1.4	2.4	5.8	6.0	6.4	6.2	5.5	24.9	31.5	12.6	1.1	77.9	41.4	50.2	49.8
38501	COOKEVILLE	93.4	91.2	2.1	2.3	1.4	2.1	3.2	5.0	5.8	5.2	5.3	8.2	13.5	25.7	22.8	11.6	1.8	80.3	33.8	50.1	49.9
38504	ALLARDT	98.8	98.5	0.0	0.0	0.0	0.0	0.0	0.0	6.3	6.8	7.2	6.8	3.9	25.6	28.5	13.4	1.6	75.6	40.9	50.3	49.7
38505	COOKEVILLE	86.0	82.2	7.3	8.1	3.5	5.3	3.0	4.9	3.3	1.1	0.6	41.0	39.9	10.3	2.5	1.0	0.3	94.7	20.5	56.9	43.1
38506	COOKEVILLE	96.6	95.6	1.3	1.5	0.6	0.9	1.3	2.1	6.3	6.5	6.8	6.3	4.7	26.3	28.7	12.7	1.8	76.6	40.5	48.9	51.1
38541	ALLONS	99.6	99.5	0.1	0.1	0.0	0.0	0.4	0.6	5.6	5.7	5.8	5.6	4.5	25.0	29.1	17.1	1.5	79.4	43.5	50.7	49.3
38542	ALLRED	100.0	97.7	0.0	0.0	0.0	0.0	2.4	4.5	4.5	4.5	4.5	4.5	4.5	27.3	36.4	13.6	0.0	81.8	45.0	52.3	47.7
38543	ALPINE	98.0	97.4	0.1	0.1	0.2	0.2	1.0	1.6	6.2	6.5	6.6	6.3	4.7	24.3	27.2	16.3	1.9	76.9	41.7	51.2	48.8
38544	BAXTER	98.1	97.4	0.1	0.1	0.1	0.2	1.2	2.1	5.9	6.0	6.3	6.3	5.4	26.3	29.2	13.1	1.6	77.9	40.9	50.2	49.8
38545	BLOOMINGTON SPRINGS	98.6	98.5	0.3	0.3	0.1	0.1	1.0	1.0	6.6	6.6	6.9	6.8	5.1	27.0	27.8	11.8	1.4	75.6	39.0	50.0	50.0
38547	BRUSH CREEK	96.3	95.9	1.7	1.9	0.1	0.1	0.5	0.9	5.7	6.2	6.5	6.2	4.8	27.5	31.4	10.6	1.1	77.8	40.7	51.7	48.3
38548	BUFFALO VALLEY	97.6	97.2	1.3	1.5	0.3	0.4	1.1	1.9	5.2	5.3	5.7	6.0	4.7	24.9	31.4	15.1	1.6	80.1	43.7	50.5	49.5
38549	BYRDSTOWN	99.0	99.0	0.1	0.1	0.0	0.0	1.0	0.9	5.7	5.8	5.6	4.8	4.5	22.9	29.4	18.7	2.7	80.1	45.5	49.5	50.5
38551	CELINA	95.6	95.5	2.4	2.5	0.3	0.3	0.7	0.7	5.1	5.0	5.3	5.8	5.2	24.8	29.3	16.8	2.7	81.3	44.2	47.7	52.3
38552	CHESTNUT MOUND	95.6	94.7	2.9	3.4	0.0	0.0	0.3	0.5	6.3	6.3	7.0	7.1	5.3	26.3	28.9	11.3	1.4	76.0	39.8	51.9	48.1
38553	CLARKRANGE	99.5	99.4	0.0	0.0	0.1	0.2	0.4	0.5	6.7	6.7	6.8	6.7	5.8	26.6	27.5	12.0	1.1	75.6	38.7	50.4	49.6
38554	CRAWFORD	97.7	97.3	0.8	0.9	0.0	0.0	0.8	1.2	6.8	6.8	7.1	6.8	5.2	27.5	27.1	11.6	1.2	75.1	37.9	49.7	50.3
	TENNESSEE	80.2	78.4	16.4	16.9	1.0	1.5	2.2	3.4	6.5	6.4	6.5	6.8	6.5	27.2	27.0	11.4	1.7	76.6	38.0	49.0	51.0
	UNITED STATES	75.1	72.0	12.3	12.7	3.8	4.6	12.5	15.7	6.8	6.7	6.6	7.1	6.9	27.0	26.0	10.9	1.9	75.7	36.9	49.2	50.8

#	POST OFFICE NAME	2009 Per Capita Income	2009 HH Income Base	2009 HOUSEHOLD INCOME DISTRIBUTION (%) Less than $25,000	$25,000 to $49,999	$50,000 to $99,999	$100,000 to $149,999	$150,000 or More	MEDIAN HOUSEHOLD INCOME 2009	2014	2009 National Centile	2009 State Centile	2009 Home Value Base	2009 HOME VALUE DISTRIBUTION (%) Less than $50,000	$50,000 to $89,999	$90,000 to $174,999	$175,000 to $399,999	$400,000 or More	2009 Median Home Value
38327	CRUMP	18721	246	31.7	35.8	28.5	3.3	0.8	36958	39019	23	35	206	26.2	31.6	30.6	11.7	0.0	78800
38328	DARDEN	19441	375	33.9	32.0	27.5	4.5	2.1	36781	38996	23	34	316	22.8	29.4	32.9	12.7	2.2	86818
38329	DECATURVILLE	20233	1413	33.5	34.3	26.6	2.8	2.8	35667	38137	20	28	1181	21.2	35.6	32.5	9.6	1.2	81167
38330	DYER	19220	1714	30.5	33.9	29.2	4.9	1.5	37371	40346	25	37	1319	17.2	42.5	31.2	8.2	1.0	79297
38332	ENVILLE	17051	452	38.3	27.4	28.5	5.3	0.4	32431	33308	12	17	385	33.5	24.2	35.8	6.2	0.3	80781
38333	EVA	19904	269	28.3	36.8	28.6	4.5	1.9	38921	40496	30	45	228	19.3	23.7	39.5	16.7	0.9	98889
38334	FINGER	17043	741	35.1	29.0	31.4	3.2	1.2	37645	40913	26	40	622	28.1	33.1	30.5	7.7	0.5	75556
38337	GADSDEN	19583	639	24.6	29.7	40.2	3.9	1.6	44901	48846	48	68	533	18.2	33.2	36.0	12.0	0.6	88256
38339	GUYS	18795	258	32.9	31.0	29.1	5.4	1.6	36962	39078	23	36	215	22.3	30.7	36.3	9.3	1.4	86389
38340	HENDERSON	20052	4418	28.1	27.0	36.9	5.9	2.0	44707	46387	47	67	3265	18.4	29.0	39.6	12.3	0.8	92990
38341	HOLLADAY	16942	941	36.2	31.9	28.1	3.1	0.7	33806	35000	15	20	801	37.6	25.1	30.1	7.0	0.2	65196
38342	HOLLOW ROCK	18908	654	32.3	37.6	25.1	3.1	2.0	35900	36070	20	29	536	33.2	36.4	23.9	5.2	1.3	72051
38343	HUMBOLDT	20791	6841	28.9	30.4	32.3	6.3	2.2	40308	43638	34	51	4974	19.3	26.5	40.7	12.6	1.0	94592
38344	HUNTINGDON	20035	3641	34.1	28.3	30.2	4.6	2.9	37988	38973	27	41	2832	22.0	31.3	37.8	8.4	0.6	85446
38345	HURON	19029	678	23.6	31.9	40.6	2.5	1.5	45439	46618	50	69	568	21.8	26.6	41.0	10.0	0.5	91667
38347	JACKS CREEK	21058	166	24.1	30.7	38.0	6.0	1.2	45911	46185	51	71	136	22.1	19.1	47.8	10.3	0.7	97500
38348	LAVINIA	18886	451	35.3	27.3	31.9	3.3	2.2	40469	40540	34	52	368	37.8	25.5	26.6	9.8	0.3	65000
38351	LEXINGTON	20551	7307	30.5	31.8	31.0	4.4	2.3	40056	41127	33	50	5565	19.3	26.4	38.8	14.3	1.3	95118
38352	LURAY	17413	233	27.0	29.6	38.2	4.7	0.4	44079	45613	46	65	197	22.8	22.8	45.7	8.1	0.5	94048
38355	MEDINA	24567	1602	16.4	25.8	45.8	9.7	2.3	55322	53570	72	86	1258	11.8	21.5	43.2	21.5	2.1	112808
38356	MEDON	19797	947	30.9	26.8	35.3	5.6	1.4	41743	45545	38	57	773	23.5	28.7	35.6	11.4	0.8	87308
38357	MICHIE	18281	1202	34.1	31.1	28.8	4.4	1.6	36121	37459	21	30	996	24.7	31.9	34.0	8.4	0.9	80571
38358	MILAN	21093	4980	27.1	32.6	32.3	5.2	2.8	41035	43601	36	54	3499	15.6	30.4	42.7	10.5	0.7	93908
38359	MILLEDGEVILLE	22068	159	37.7	32.7	22.6	3.8	3.1	32435	32783	12	17	131	32.8	29.8	32.8	3.1	1.5	72778
38361	MORRIS CHAPEL	14782	435	36.1	37.7	23.7	2.3	0.2	34070	35412	16	21	366	39.9	25.7	23.5	10.9	0.0	63333
38362	OAKFIELD	24733	548	13.1	26.1	50.4	8.6	1.8	57991	58578	75	89	484	12.2	24.6	52.3	10.7	0.2	99014
38363	PARSONS	20053	2450	38.7	29.4	25.6	3.5	2.9	32593	34084	13	17	1833	28.4	30.3	33.3	6.8	1.2	77645
38366	PINSON	21517	968	22.3	28.1	43.0	5.0	1.7	49415	51346	60	78	794	18.1	35.1	37.5	7.1	2.1	86176
38367	RAMER	18269	1194	30.7	36.3	28.2	3.6	1.3	36341	36852	22	32	966	29.6	29.5	32.2	7.0	1.7	76842
38368	REAGAN	19440	742	36.3	28.7	29.2	4.2	1.6	35915	37517	20	30	633	29.5	27.3	31.4	10.9	0.8	78143
38369	RUTHERFORD	17622	877	31.7	34.8	29.5	3.2	0.8	37069	39505	24	36	707	23.1	37.6	31.7	5.7	2.0	76176
38370	SALTILLO	20862	329	41.3	29.2	22.5	5.2	1.8	31297	32412	10	15	268	36.2	30.2	31.0	2.6	0.0	71667
38371	SARDIS	20005	543	37.6	26.5	29.3	5.3	1.3	36774	38089	23	34	443	35.2	30.0	29.1	5.4	0.2	68472
38372	SAVANNAH	18580	7124	39.1	30.6	24.3	4.2	1.8	32966	34212	13	18	5251	24.3	27.8	35.3	11.1	1.4	86217
38374	SCOTTS HILL	19923	792	29.9	30.1	35.7	2.8	1.5	40747	41978	35	53	669	28.0	26.3	36.6	7.5	1.6	83523
38375	SELMER	19777	3576	35.0	29.3	30.5	4.0	1.3	37280	39201	24	37	2699	22.1	32.9	34.8	8.9	1.3	83292
38376	SHILOH	16337	186	42.5	35.5	16.7	4.3	1.1	32003	33501	11	16	160	24.4	31.9	35.0	7.5	1.3	78000
38379	STANTONVILLE	18827	553	31.5	32.9	29.1	5.2	1.3	38520	40329	28	43	481	28.9	27.7	31.6	10.2	1.7	77424
38380	SUGAR TREE	19969	246	29.3	41.5	23.2	4.5	1.6	34350	34915	16	22	216	42.1	22.7	32.9	2.3	0.0	58947
38381	TOONE	18075	682	36.4	30.1	26.4	5.1	2.1	35097	35247	18	25	524	22.7	27.7	42.6	6.7	0.4	89459
38382	TRENTON	19277	3991	31.2	31.7	31.1	4.7	1.3	37419	39317	25	38	2765	16.5	29.7	41.8	10.5	1.6	94271
38387	WESTPORT	17287	142	31.7	31.7	32.4	3.5	0.7	38633	40649	29	44	125	29.6	31.2	36.0	2.4	0.8	75500
38388	WILDERSVILLE	20606	780	30.0	28.8	33.5	4.2	3.5	41183	41771	37	55	649	24.7	19.3	40.5	13.6	2.0	99634
38390	YUMA	18037	358	32.7	32.4	30.4	3.1	1.4	37862	38656	26	41	303	31.7	29.0	32.3	6.6	0.3	74833
38391	DENMARK	16263	437	34.8	37.8	22.4	3.9	1.1	33998	35636	16	21	348	35.1	37.1	22.7	4.9	0.3	64815
38392	MERCER	16703	300	37.0	33.0	27.3	2.3	0.3	36291	38629	21	31	237	35.4	35.0	23.6	5.5	0.4	66724
38401	COLUMBIA	25024	22654	22.0	25.0	37.8	10.3	4.8	53204	54169	68	83	15866	8.1	14.8	44.9	27.6	4.6	137077
38425	CLIFTON	15366	766	35.0	35.9	25.2	1.8	2.1	32784	34412	13	18	617	30.0	26.7	32.4	9.4	1.5	82170
38449	ARDMORE	21170	1438	26.2	32.1	32.8	6.7	2.2	43083	43816	43	62	1172	16.4	25.9	43.3	12.5	2.0	98835
38450	COLLINWOOD	16832	1120	42.5	33.4	19.9	2.5	1.7	28981	30311	7	10	920	32.8	36.1	25.3	5.5	0.2	67670
38451	CULLEOKA	23050	1791	18.8	26.5	42.6	8.4	3.7	54973	54858	71	85	1471	9.7	16.4	42.8	26.8	4.3	139583
38452	CYPRESS INN	14899	409	35.2	34.5	29.6	0.5	0.2	33686	36084	15	20	359	23.4	21.4	45.4	8.1	1.7	97708
38453	DELLROSE	20498	150	26.7	33.3	34.7	3.3	2.0	40000	40741	33	50	132	31.1	24.2	34.1	9.1	1.5	80000
38454	DUCK RIVER	15706	487	37.0	29.4	30.0	3.5	0.2	31378	34344	10	15	406	29.3	18.5	44.3	7.6	0.2	94737
38456	ETHRIDGE	14815	1417	32.7	28.6	32.7	4.7	1.3	36751	39468	23	34	1132	16.8	23.7	44.3	13.9	1.4	102210
38457	FIVE POINTS	19582	360	31.7	34.7	28.3	2.5	2.8	36078	38319	21	30	291	23.0	28.5	37.5	10.3	0.7	87500
38459	FRANKEWING	20153	152	27.6	32.9	34.2	3.3	2.0	39236	39557	30	47	136	33.8	24.3	31.6	8.8	1.5	76667
38460	GOODSPRING	19044	459	26.4	37.9	30.7	3.3	1.7	40677	42460	35	53	381	17.8	32.5	41.7	6.8	1.0	89500
38461	HAMPSHIRE	19784	473	22.0	29.0	40.2	6.8	2.1	48941	50931	59	77	388	17.5	21.9	35.8	21.4	3.4	111957
38462	HOHENWALD	17678	4017	34.1	30.8	30.1	3.9	1.0	37266	38144	24	37	3148	22.8	29.3	37.7	9.8	0.4	87956
38463	IRON CITY	16754	1185	33.6	33.3	29.5	1.9	1.8	34971	37314	18	25	1013	27.3	30.8	34.3	7.3	0.3	78678
38464	LAWRENCEBURG	20612	8914	32.5	33.1	28.3	3.5	2.6	37409	38968	25	38	6505	11.7	27.4	46.8	12.7	1.4	102093
38468	LEOMA	18424	1922	26.4	36.6	31.4	3.7	1.9	40066	41840	33	51	1580	17.6	22.8	44.7	14.4	0.4	103906
38469	LORETTO	20256	1713	29.4	34.4	29.8	4.1	2.3	38820	40999	29	45	1393	17.3	29.8	40.5	11.1	1.4	93164
38471	LUTTS	13980	253	39.5	45.1	13.8	0.4	1.2	33394	33167	14	19	221	45.2	29.4	18.1	6.3	0.9	58750
38472	LYNNVILLE	22170	1072	24.4	27.6	38.4	7.1	2.4	47944	47212	56	76	884	18.3	25.2	38.3	16.1	2.0	96552
38473	MINOR HILL	19008	460	28.0	29.8	37.4	4.1	0.7	43497	42975	44	63	368	15.8	30.7	45.1	6.8	1.6	93421
38474	MOUNT PLEASANT	20250	3202	27.9	28.7	37.1	4.5	1.7	44266	47065	46	66	2326	14.1	25.2	46.8	12.7	1.1	103702
38475	OLIVEHILL	16435	240	35.8	35.4	23.8	4.2	0.8	34644	36304	17	23	201	32.8	25.4	28.9	11.4	1.5	79583
38476	PRIMM SPRINGS	19666	438	25.6	32.2	34.7	4.6	3.0	44043	46237	46	65	372	16.9	22.8	31.7	20.4	8.1	113194
38477	PROSPECT	19850	1101	24.7	34.8	32.8	5.2	2.5	40937	41972	36	54	933	17.7	26.8	40.0	13.5	2.0	96131
38478	PULASKI	22030	7391	29.0	28.1	33.9	6.5	2.5	42680	44231	41	61	5253	11.2	26.2	47.1	13.1	2.4	101544
38481	SAINT JOSEPH	18313	401	34.4	35.4	28.2	1.0	1.0	34907	36522	17	24	323	31.3	36.8	26.6	4.6	0.6	69839
38482	SANTA FE	23500	761	18.5	31.4	41.7	4.6	3.8	50067	51405	61	79	628	12.4	22.8	40.9	18.2	5.7	113235
38483	SUMMERTOWN	17820	1724	23.7	37.3	32.6	4.4	2.0	40435	42939	34	52	1439	20.0	24.0	38.8	16.3	0.8	97185
38485	WAYNESBORO	18147	2744	38.0	36.8	20.9	2.5	1.7	31537	32402	11	16	2202	33.4	31.4	28.9	5.6	0.7	67778
38486	WESTPOINT	15894	386	34.5	38.3	24.1	2.6	0.5	32313	33625	12	17	319	35.1	25.7	35.4	3.8	0.0	70333
38487	WILLIAMSPORT	23612	422	23.2	29.6	38.4	5.2	3.6	47143	48550	54	75	361	15.2	18.3	40.4	21.3	4.7	115962
38488	TAFT	20432	849	27.6	30.9	31.3	7.5	2.7	41231	41420	37	55	702	23.4	21.2	32.8	20.4	2.3	96786
38501	COOKEVILLE	21749	15032	35.7	28.1	27.3	5.3	3.5	37133	39359	24	36	8544	6.5	15.0	49.2	23.9	5.3	132300
38504	ALLARDT	16483	366	29.5	37.2	27.3	4.4	1.6	34464	37203	16	22	323	40.6	24.1	28.5	6.8	0.0	55083
38505	COOKEVILLE	9096	3	100.0	0.0	0.0	0.0	0.0	7500	7500	0	1	0	0.0	0.0	0.0	0.0	0.0	0
38506	COOKEVILLE	21580	10240	24.9	31.1	34.7	6.4	2.9	44180	46100	46	66	7934	11.3	16.6	46.2	22.3	3.5	125821
38541	ALLONS	15543	644	45.5	27.3	25.6	1.6	0.0	33481	35410	14	19	561	31.9	23.9	32.1	10.9	1.2	72391
38542	ALLRED	11591	16	50.0	31.3	18.8	0.0	0.0	25000	27313	3	5	14	28.6	21.4	35.7	14.3	0.0	90000
38543	ALPINE	16960	343	43.1	27.4	26.2	0.6	2.6	28141	28012	6	9	294	40.5	26.5	23.1	9.9	0.0	59333
38544	BAXTER	18012	2946	33.1	35.9	25.6	4.1	1.3	35808	37455	20	29	2301	15.9	24.2	41.8	15.1	3.1	98655
38545	BLOOMINGTON SPRINGS	18715	443	30.5	32.1	29.6	4.7	3.2	39162	41878	30	46	374	19.0	26.2	42.0	11.2	1.6	96000
38547	BRUSH CREEK	22166	589	18.2	28.0	45.2	6.8	1.9	51997	51511	66	81	516	11.6	18.8	39.5	24.6	5.4	119412
38548	BUFFALO VALLEY	16908	292	29.5	38.4	28.8	2.7	0.7	37446	39614	25	38	245	13.5	19.2	44.1	21.2	2.0	111607
38549	BYRDSTOWN	17860	1593	40.1	34.2	21.0	2.9	1.8	30367	31401	9	12	1307	22.6	30.1	32.7	11.4	3.2	85203
38551	CELINA	17129	1976	45.0	32.9	17.0	3.0	2.1	27828	28280	5	8	1507	27.0	31.9	33.7	6.5	0.9	80254
38552	CHESTNUT MOUND	20235	243	22.2	32.5	38.3	6.2	0.8	45813	46319	51	70	200	10.5	25.0	39.5	21.5	3.5	117500
38553	CLARKRANGE	15052	944	39.9	34.5	21.8	2.0	1.7	31642	32321	11	16	791	25.4	30.6	35.1	7.8	1.0	82578
38554	CRAWFORD	14821	410	39.5	39.5	19.8	1.2	0.0	29168	30621	7	10	348	38.2	25.9	29.3	6.0	0.6	63000
	TENNESSEE	24986		24.9	27.0	34.7	8.2	5.2	47751	50104				12.0	19.9	40.9	22.7	4.6	120455
	UNITED STATES	27277		20.9	24.4	35.3	11.7	7.6	54719	56938				9.3	13.1	31.6	32.6	13.5	162279

ZIP CODE		FINANCIAL SERVICES				THE HOME						ENTERTAINMENT						PERSONAL			
						Home Improvements		Furnishings													
#	POST OFFICE NAME	Auto Loan	Home Loan	Invest-ments	Retire-ment Plans	Home Repair	Lawn & Garden	Comput-ers & Hard-ware-Personal	Major Appli-ances	TV, Radio, Sound Equip-ment	Furni-ture	Dine out/ Carry out	Sports Equip-ment	Fees & Tickets	Toys & Games	Travel	Cable TV	Apparel & Services	Auto Repairs	Health Insur-ance	Pets & Supplies
38327	CRUMP	75	54	62	53	54	72	56	65	62	55	61	50	45	65	51	68	41	62	69	80
38328	DARDEN	82	57	82	55	59	83	60	75	67	56	66	57	47	67	58	74	43	70	79	91
38329	DECATURVILLE	83	60	78	58	61	83	62	76	69	59	68	58	50	70	59	76	45	71	80	91
38330	DYER	79	58	67	57	58	77	62	71	69	59	67	54	51	70	57	74	45	68	76	86
38332	ENVILLE	75	54	62	53	54	72	56	65	62	55	61	50	45	65	51	68	41	62	69	80
38333	EVA	80	58	83	56	60	82	59	75	66	55	64	56	47	65	59	72	43	69	78	89
38334	FINGER	80	57	66	56	57	76	60	70	66	58	65	53	48	69	54	72	44	66	73	85
38337	GADSDEN	86	65	84	65	67	88	66	81	72	62	71	61	56	73	66	79	47	75	85	96
38339	GUYS	81	58	67	56	58	77	60	70	67	59	66	54	48	70	55	73	44	66	74	85
38340	HENDERSON	85	67	70	66	67	81	72	77	77	69	76	59	62	79	66	82	51	76	83	93
38341	HOLLADAY	74	53	68	51	53	72	55	66	61	52	60	50	44	62	52	67	40	62	70	80
38342	HOLLOW ROCK	82	59	69	57	59	79	62	72	68	59	67	55	49	71	56	75	45	68	76	87
38343	HUMBOLDT	82	66	73	66	66	83	68	77	74	65	72	58	60	75	65	79	49	74	82	92
38344	HUNTINGDON	82	64	70	63	64	81	67	75	73	65	72	57	58	75	62	79	49	72	81	90
38345	HURON	87	63	72	61	62	83	65	76	72	64	71	58	52	75	59	79	48	72	80	92
38347	JACKS CREEK	92	66	76	64	66	87	69	80	76	67	75	61	55	79	62	83	50	76	84	97
38348	LAVINIA	86	62	75	60	62	83	64	76	71	62	70	58	52	74	59	78	47	72	80	92
38351	LEXINGTON	83	63	70	62	63	80	67	74	72	64	71	57	56	74	61	78	48	72	79	90
38352	LURAY	87	63	72	61	62	83	65	76	72	64	71	58	52	76	59	79	48	72	80	92
38355	MEDINA	89	93	78	94	89	94	87	89	88	87	88	69	89	90	88	89	61	87	92	106
38356	MEDON	84	69	72	66	68	80	67	76	72	68	72	56	59	75	64	76	48	72	77	91
38357	MICHIE	79	57	67	55	57	76	59	69	66	57	64	53	47	68	54	72	43	66	73	84
38358	MILAN	81	65	70	65	64	81	70	76	74	65	73	58	60	75	65	79	49	74	82	91
38359	MILLEDGEVILLE	83	60	75	58	60	81	62	74	68	59	67	57	49	70	58	75	45	70	78	90
38361	MORRIS CHAPEL	68	48	66	47	50	67	50	62	55	47	54	47	40	56	48	61	36	57	65	74
38362	OAKFIELD	100	98	83	95	94	92	91	93	91	96	92	69	88	95	87	91	63	90	90	110
38363	PARSONS	83	57	78	55	58	82	61	75	69	57	67	57	48	70	57	76	45	70	80	90
38366	PINSON	98	73	92	71	74	96	74	89	81	71	80	67	61	82	71	88	53	83	93	107
38367	RAMER	79	57	69	55	57	77	59	70	65	57	64	54	47	67	55	71	43	66	74	85
38368	REAGAN	85	61	70	59	61	81	63	74	70	62	69	57	51	73	58	77	46	70	78	90
38369	RUTHERFORD	73	52	67	51	53	73	56	67	62	52	60	51	45	63	52	68	40	63	72	80
38370	SALTILLO	81	58	83	56	60	82	59	75	66	55	65	57	47	66	59	72	43	69	78	90
38371	SARDIS	83	60	73	58	60	80	62	74	69	59	67	56	50	71	58	75	45	69	77	89
38372	SAVANNAH	74	56	63	56	56	72	60	67	65	56	63	51	50	66	55	70	43	65	72	81
38374	SCOTTS HILL	85	61	70	59	61	81	63	74	70	62	69	57	51	73	58	77	46	70	78	90
38375	SELMER	83	59	77	57	60	82	62	76	69	59	68	58	49	71	58	76	45	71	80	91
38376	SHILOH	71	51	58	49	50	67	53	61	58	51	57	47	42	61	48	64	39	58	65	75
38379	STANTONVILLE	82	59	68	57	59	78	61	71	68	59	66	55	49	70	56	74	45	67	75	87
38380	SUGAR TREE	75	54	63	52	54	72	56	66	62	54	61	50	45	64	51	68	41	62	69	80
38381	TOONE	83	60	80	58	61	83	62	76	68	58	67	58	49	69	59	75	45	71	79	91
38382	TRENTON	75	58	66	58	59	75	63	70	68	58	66	53	53	68	59	74	45	68	76	84
38387	WESTPORT	81	58	67	57	58	77	61	71	67	59	66	54	49	70	55	73	44	67	75	86
38388	WILDERSVILLE	92	66	78	64	66	88	69	80	76	67	75	62	55	79	63	83	50	76	85	98
38390	YUMA	80	58	67	56	57	76	60	70	66	58	65	54	48	69	55	72	44	66	74	85
38391	DENMARK	78	51	76	49	51	77	55	69	63	52	62	54	41	64	51	70	41	65	73	85
38392	MERCER	76	50	73	47	50	75	53	67	61	51	60	52	40	63	50	68	40	63	71	82
38401	COLUMBIA	93	90	84	90	88	94	89	91	91	88	91	69	87	92	87	93	63	90	94	108
38425	CLIFTON	76	55	74	53	56	78	59	72	65	54	63	54	47	65	56	72	42	67	77	85
38449	ARDMORE	92	66	84	64	67	90	68	83	76	65	75	63	55	78	65	83	50	77	87	100
38450	COLLINWOOD	75	51	66	49	51	72	54	65	61	52	60	50	42	63	50	67	40	62	69	80
38451	CULLEOKA	102	92	84	90	90	97	88	94	91	90	91	69	82	95	84	95	62	91	95	112
38452	CYPRESS INN	67	48	56	47	48	64	50	59	56	49	55	45	40	58	46	61	37	56	62	71
38453	DELLROSE	90	65	74	63	64	86	67	78	75	66	73	60	54	78	61	82	49	74	83	95
38454	DUCK RIVER	71	51	60	50	51	68	53	63	59	51	58	48	43	61	49	65	39	59	66	76
38456	ETHRIDGE	81	58	67	57	58	77	61	71	67	59	66	54	49	70	55	73	44	67	75	86
38457	FIVE POINTS	88	63	73	61	63	83	66	76	73	64	71	59	53	76	60	79	48	72	81	93
38459	FRANKEWING	89	64	73	62	63	84	66	77	74	65	72	59	53	77	60	80	48	73	81	94
38460	GOODSPRING	85	61	70	59	60	80	63	74	70	62	69	57	51	73	57	77	46	70	78	90
38461	HAMPSHIRE	89	75	73	73	74	84	73	80	78	74	77	60	65	81	69	82	52	77	82	96
38462	HOHENWALD	77	56	66	55	56	75	60	69	66	57	65	53	49	68	55	72	44	66	74	84
38463	IRON CITY	77	55	63	54	55	73	57	67	64	56	62	51	46	66	52	69	42	63	70	81
38464	LAWRENCEBURG	82	64	70	64	64	81	68	76	74	64	72	58	58	75	63	79	49	73	81	91
38468	LEOMA	87	63	72	61	63	83	65	76	72	63	71	58	53	75	60	79	48	72	80	92
38469	LORETTO	92	66	76	64	65	87	68	79	76	67	74	61	55	79	62	83	50	75	84	97
38471	LUTTS	62	45	51	43	44	59	47	54	52	45	51	42	37	54	42	56	34	51	57	66
38472	LYNNVILLE	102	74	95	72	75	101	76	93	84	72	83	70	61	86	72	92	55	86	97	111
38473	MINOR HILL	84	60	69	59	60	80	63	73	70	61	68	56	50	73	57	76	46	69	77	89
38474	MOUNT PLEASANT	79	66	65	66	65	78	69	74	74	66	72	56	62	75	65	78	49	72	79	88
38475	OLIVEHILL	75	54	63	52	54	72	56	66	63	54	61	51	45	65	52	68	41	62	70	80
38476	PRIMM SPRINGS	88	74	76	74	74	88	73	83	78	70	77	63	65	80	70	83	52	78	86	98
38477	PROSPECT	90	65	76	63	65	86	67	79	75	65	73	60	54	77	62	81	49	74	83	96
38478	PULASKI	88	68	77	68	69	88	72	82	77	67	76	63	60	79	67	84	51	78	87	98
38481	SAINT JOSEPH	78	56	65	55	56	75	59	68	65	57	64	52	47	68	53	71	43	65	72	83
38482	SANTA FE	97	86	82	83	85	92	82	89	86	84	86	65	76	89	79	89	58	86	90	106
38483	SUMMERTOWN	87	63	72	61	62	83	65	76	72	63	71	58	52	75	59	79	48	72	80	92
38485	WAYNESBORO	75	52	71	50	53	75	56	68	63	52	61	52	44	63	53	69	41	64	73	83
38486	WESTPOINT	73	52	60	51	52	69	54	63	60	53	59	48	44	63	49	66	40	60	67	77
38487	WILLIAMSPORT	101	79	95	79	81	103	80	96	87	75	85	72	68	88	78	94	57	89	100	113
38488	TAFT	94	68	84	66	68	92	70	84	78	67	76	64	56	80	66	85	51	79	88	102
38501	COOKEVILLE	79	61	62	63	61	70	77	71	76	69	75	56	64	77	65	78	52	74	74	86
38504	ALLARDT	76	55	78	53	57	77	56	71	62	52	61	53	45	62	55	68	40	65	74	85
38505	COOKEVILLE	11	5	5	6	4	6	16	8	13	11	13	9	10	13	9	12	9	11	8	11
38506	COOKEVILLE	89	74	80	74	75	89	75	84	79	72	78	63	66	80	72	84	53	80	87	99
38541	ALLONS	65	45	65	43	46	65	47	60	53	44	52	45	37	53	45	58	34	55	62	72
38542	ALLRED	58	41	47	40	41	55	43	50	48	42	47	38	34	50	39	52	31	47	53	61
38543	ALPINE	74	49	69	46	49	72	52	65	60	50	58	50	39	61	48	66	39	61	68	79
38544	BAXTER	79	56	70	55	57	76	59	70	65	57	64	54	47	67	55	71	43	66	74	85
38545	BLOOMINGTON SPRINGS	88	65	75	64	65	84	67	78	73	65	72	59	55	76	62	79	48	74	81	94
38547	BRUSH CREEK	91	79	81	82	81	95	79	90	82	72	81	68	71	84	78	88	55	83	93	105
38548	BUFFALO VALLEY	77	55	76	54	57	77	57	71	63	54	62	54	46	64	55	69	41	66	74	85
38549	BYRDSTOWN	68	51	75	49	54	71	53	66	57	48	56	49	43	56	53	63	37	61	69	78
38551	CELINA	66	47	59	46	48	65	50	60	56	47	54	45	40	57	47	61	36	56	64	71
38552	CHESTNUT MOUND	97	70	80	68	69	92	72	84	80	71	79	65	58	84	66	88	53	80	89	103
38553	CLARKRANGE	70	49	62	47	48	68	51	61	58	49	56	47	40	60	47	63	38	58	65	75
38554	CRAWFORD	65	47	54	46	47	62	49	57	54	47	53	44	39	56	44	59	36	54	60	69
	TENNESSEE	95	84	85	84	82	93	87	90	90	85	89	69	80	91	83	93	61	89	93	107
	UNITED STATES	100	100	100	100	100	100	100	100	100	100	100	100	100	100	100	100	100	100	100	100

TENNESSEE

POPULATION CHANGE

38555-42223

ZIP CODE #	POST OFFICE NAME	COUNTY FIPS CODE	POPULATION 2000	POPULATION 2009	POPULATION 2014	2000-2009 ANNUAL RATE % Rate	2000-2009 ANNUAL RATE State Centile	HOUSEHOLDS 2000	HOUSEHOLDS 2009	HOUSEHOLDS 2014	HOUSEHOLDS % Annual Rate 2000-2009	HOUSEHOLDS 2009 Average HH Size	FAMILIES 2000	FAMILIES 2009	FAMILIES % Annual Rate 2000-2009
38555	CROSSVILLE	035	16514	17624	18452	0.7	53	6808	7491	7921	1.0	2.29	4771	5108	0.7
38556	JAMESTOWN	049	11960	12637	12926	0.6	47	4908	5381	5569	1.0	2.32	3453	3686	0.7
38558	CROSSVILLE	035	5061	6855	7703	3.3	97	2589	3616	4111	3.7	1.89	2062	2816	3.4
38559	DOYLE	175	1071	1127	1157	0.6	47	463	499	515	0.8	2.25	338	354	0.5
38560	ELMWOOD	159	1166	1227	1244	0.6	47	449	481	491	0.7	2.55	343	358	0.5
38562	GAINESBORO	087	6657	6515	6358	-0.2	10	2757	2757	2707	0.0	2.31	1909	1855	-0.3
38563	GORDONSVILLE	159	2203	2559	2670	1.6	82	870	1027	1078	1.8	2.49	644	743	1.6
38564	GRANVILLE	087	416	472	479	1.4	78	181	208	211	1.5	2.27	128	144	1.3
38565	GRIMSLEY	049	518	584	614	1.3	76	194	226	241	1.7	2.58	150	170	1.4
38567	HICKMAN	159	722	786	817	0.9	63	284	317	331	1.2	2.48	214	233	0.9
38568	HILHAM	133	1637	1746	1785	0.7	53	679	750	774	1.1	2.33	471	506	0.8
38569	LANCASTER	041	366	389	401	0.7	53	145	156	162	0.8	2.49	109	115	0.6
38570	LIVINGSTON	133	8824	8755	8806	-0.1	13	3671	3754	3809	0.2	2.29	2531	2507	-0.1
38571	CROSSVILLE	035	11373	13542	14864	1.9	88	4439	5470	6075	2.3	2.47	3417	4093	2.0
38572	CROSSVILLE	035	9322	11143	12197	1.9	88	3822	4742	5254	2.4	2.32	2893	3490	2.0
38573	MONROE	133	2141	2130	2126	-0.1	13	869	892	900	0.3	2.39	644	645	0.0
38574	MONTEREY	141	7224	8389	8977	1.6	82	2729	3187	3424	1.7	2.59	2043	2325	1.4
38575	MOSS	027	1163	1144	1122	-0.2	10	477	485	481	0.2	2.36	337	334	-0.1
38577	PALL MALL	137	1240	1203	1179	-0.3	7	507	510	506	0.1	2.36	372	365	-0.2
38578	PLEASANT HILL	035	53	62	68	1.7	84	25	30	34	2.0	2.03	17	20	1.8
38579	QUEBECK	185	1260	1386	1447	1.0	66	495	555	582	1.2	2.50	373	408	1.0
38580	RICKMAN	133	1574	1775	1860	1.3	76	623	720	762	1.6	2.46	484	547	1.3
38581	ROCK ISLAND	175	4187	4116	4079	-0.2	10	1602	1624	1626	0.1	2.50	1209	1197	-0.1
38582	SILVER POINT	141	1266	1305	1339	0.3	31	519	542	558	0.5	2.36	380	385	0.1
38583	SPARTA	185	21363	23061	24023	0.8	60	8543	9456	9931	1.1	2.41	6234	6731	0.8
38585	SPENCER	175	4016	4218	4273	0.5	41	1561	1704	1748	1.0	2.44	1159	1235	0.7
38587	WALLING	185	1097	1164	1209	0.6	47	449	488	511	0.9	2.35	333	353	0.6
38588	WHITLEYVILLE	087	1098	1081	1059	-0.2	10	454	458	453	0.1	2.36	307	301	-0.2
38589	WILDER	049	197	196	197	-0.1	13	68	70	72	0.3	2.80	51	51	0.0
42223	FORT CAMPBELL	125	21693	22121	22643	0.2	27	3920	4064	4236	0.4	3.68	3830	3956	0.4
	TENNESSEE					1.1					1.3	2.44			1.0
	UNITED STATES					1.0					1.1	2.59			0.9

ZIP CODE #	POST OFFICE NAME	RACE (%) White 2000	White 2009	Black 2000	Black 2009	Asian/Pacific 2000	Asian/Pacific 2009	% Hispanic Origin 2000	% Hispanic Origin 2009	2009 AGE DISTRIBUTION (%) 0-4	5-9	10-14	15-19	20-24	25-44	45-64	65-84	85+	18+	MEDIAN AGE 2009	% 2009 Males	% 2009 Females
38555	CROSSVILLE	97.6	96.6	0.1	0.1	0.4	0.6	1.8	2.9	6.1	5.9	6.0	6.2	5.5	24.2	26.6	17.0	2.6	78.4	42.1	47.1	52.9
38556	JAMESTOWN	99.2	99.0	0.1	0.2	0.1	0.1	0.6	1.0	6.0	6.1	6.3	6.1	5.1	25.0	29.2	14.2	2.0	78.0	41.7	49.3	50.7
38558	CROSSVILLE	98.6	98.1	0.4	0.5	0.2	0.3	0.5	0.8	2.1	2.2	2.3	2.4	2.0	9.5	26.1	49.4	4.0	92.1	66.2	47.6	52.4
38559	DOYLE	98.7	98.3	0.3	0.4	0.1	0.2	0.8	1.4	5.2	5.3	5.8	5.9	5.3	26.2	30.1	14.6	1.7	80.3	42.3	50.2	49.8
38560	ELMWOOD	95.5	94.7	2.9	3.3	0.0	0.0	0.3	0.4	6.4	6.4	7.0	7.3	5.3	26.3	28.8	11.2	1.4	75.9	39.5	51.8	48.2
38562	GAINESBORO	98.6	98.5	0.2	0.2	0.1	0.1	0.7	0.7	5.4	5.7	5.9	5.6	4.6	25.5	29.5	15.3	2.4	79.7	43.1	49.1	50.9
38563	GORDONSVILLE	95.7	95.0	2.6	3.0	0.1	0.2	0.9	1.5	6.6	6.9	6.8	6.0	5.3	27.6	29.2	10.4	1.3	76.2	38.9	50.2	49.8
38564	GRANVILLE	98.1	98.1	0.0	0.0	0.0	0.0	1.4	1.5	5.7	6.1	6.8	6.1	4.4	21.8	31.6	15.9	1.5	77.3	44.2	51.5	48.5
38565	GRIMSLEY	99.6	99.5	0.0	0.0	0.0	0.2	0.0	0.2	7.4	7.4	7.2	6.3	5.7	26.4	27.2	11.3	1.2	74.1	38.0	51.0	49.0
38567	HICKMAN	95.9	94.7	0.7	0.8	0.6	0.9	1.8	2.7	5.5	5.7	5.7	6.0	6.1	25.8	30.8	13.0	1.4	79.6	41.3	50.1	49.9
38568	HILHAM	98.7	98.3	0.2	0.2	0.2	0.3	0.2	0.3	5.4	5.6	6.0	5.8	5.6	26.6	29.9	13.5	1.5	79.4	41.7	50.8	49.2
38569	LANCASTER	96.4	94.9	0.0	0.0	0.5	1.0	1.9	2.8	5.1	5.1	5.7	6.2	5.9	25.7	30.3	14.4	1.5	80.5	42.2	50.6	49.4
38570	LIVINGSTON	98.7	98.3	0.3	0.4	0.2	0.3	0.5	0.8	5.7	5.8	5.9	5.4	4.8	25.4	28.0	16.3	2.9	79.4	42.8	47.9	52.1
38571	CROSSVILLE	98.3	97.7	0.1	0.1	0.1	0.2	1.3	2.2	5.7	5.9	6.3	5.8	4.5	23.3	28.8	18.0	1.8	78.4	43.9	49.7	50.3
38572	CROSSVILLE	97.8	97.2	0.5	0.5	0.3	0.5	0.9	1.5	5.3	5.4	6.0	6.0	4.7	22.3	30.2	18.1	2.0	79.5	45.2	49.8	50.2
38573	MONROE	99.2	99.0	0.0	0.0	0.0	0.0	0.7	1.0	6.0	6.1	6.5	6.2	4.7	25.1	27.7	15.9	1.8	77.6	41.9	50.2	49.8
38574	MONTEREY	94.5	91.9	0.5	0.6	0.2	0.2	7.5	11.9	6.4	6.6	6.8	6.4	5.2	26.3	27.8	12.7	1.8	76.0	39.4	49.9	50.1
38575	MOSS	98.4	98.3	0.4	0.5	0.3	0.3	1.5	1.5	5.1	5.2	5.7	6.1	4.2	25.1	31.6	15.1	1.8	80.2	44.1	48.2	51.8
38577	PALL MALL	99.6	99.5	0.1	0.1	0.1	0.2	0.2	0.4	6.1	6.4	6.3	5.0	4.1	24.8	30.6	15.1	1.7	78.1	43.1	50.5	49.5
38578	PLEASANT HILL	100.0	98.4	0.0	0.0	0.0	0.0	0.0	0.0	6.5	6.5	6.5	6.5	6.5	24.2	25.8	14.5	3.2	77.4	40.0	48.4	51.6
38579	QUEBECK	99.0	98.8	0.1	0.1	0.1	0.1	0.7	1.2	5.0	5.2	5.6	6.3	4.8	24.6	31.1	15.6	1.7	80.4	44.0	50.4	49.6
38580	RICKMAN	98.4	98.0	0.2	0.2	0.1	0.1	1.1	1.7	6.8	7.0	7.2	6.0	5.0	27.1	28.3	11.5	1.2	75.3	39.2	50.0	50.0
38581	ROCK ISLAND	94.4	92.2	1.8	2.0	0.1	0.1	3.4	5.6	6.3	6.4	6.7	6.1	5.4	27.2	28.9	11.7	1.3	76.8	39.2	51.6	48.4
38582	SILVER POINT	97.2	96.3	1.7	1.9	0.6	0.9	1.3	2.1	5.0	5.5	5.7	5.8	4.2	24.4	31.3	16.1	1.9	79.9	44.6	51.9	48.1
38583	SPARTA	96.4	95.5	1.8	2.0	0.3	0.5	1.1	1.9	6.1	6.1	6.4	6.1	5.3	25.4	28.2	14.2	2.1	77.6	41.1	49.3	50.7
38585	SPENCER	99.1	98.9	0.1	0.2	0.1	0.1	0.3	0.5	5.9	6.1	6.4	6.2	5.2	26.1	28.8	13.6	1.7	77.9	40.4	50.0	50.0
38587	WALLING	97.8	97.2	0.2	0.2	0.1	0.1	0.9	1.5	6.2	6.5	7.0	6.4	4.6	25.3	28.8	14.1	1.3	76.6	40.9	50.1	49.9
38588	WHITLEYVILLE	97.9	97.8	0.3	0.3	0.2	0.2	1.6	1.9	5.3	5.6	5.6	5.5	4.6	23.9	30.8	16.5	2.2	80.1	44.6	49.0	51.0
38589	WILDER	98.5	98.0	0.0	0.0	0.0	0.5	1.0	1.0	6.6	6.6	7.1	6.6	4.6	25.5	27.0	14.3	1.5	75.0	40.6	51.5	48.5
42223	FORT CAMPBELL	61.7	56.2	24.1	24.9	2.7	3.2	12.6	19.0	14.2	10.2	5.8	8.8	27.0	32.6	1.4	0.1	0.0	67.9	22.1	62.8	37.2
	TENNESSEE	80.2	78.4	16.4	16.9	1.0	1.5	2.2	3.4	6.5	6.4	6.5	6.8	6.5	27.2	27.0	11.4	1.7	76.6	38.0	49.0	51.0
	UNITED STATES	75.1	72.0	12.3	12.7	3.8	4.6	12.5	15.7	6.8	6.7	6.6	7.1	6.9	27.0	26.0	10.9	1.9	75.7	36.9	49.2	50.8

ZIP CODE #	POST OFFICE NAME	2009 Per Capita Income	2009 HH Income Base	2009 Household Income Distribution (%): Less than $25,000	$25,000 to $49,999	$50,000 to $99,999	$100,000 to $149,999	$150,000 or More	Median Household Income: 2009	2014	2009 National Centile	2009 State Centile	2009 Home Value Base	2009 Home Value Distribution (%): Less than $50,000	$50,000 to $89,999	$90,000 to $174,999	$175,000 to $399,999	$400,000 or More	2009 Median Home Value
38555	CROSSVILLE	21216	7491	35.9	29.4	26.3	5.9	2.6	36747	38577	23	33	5113	8.7	21.6	47.1	18.3	4.2	115653
38556	JAMESTOWN	15551	5381	47.8	28.7	19.3	2.8	1.4	26385	26866	4	5	4111	31.7	30.0	27.6	9.4	1.3	73685
38558	CROSSVILLE	34632	3616	15.8	28.7	42.4	8.1	5.0	54165	54429	70	84	3197	5.4	10.6	35.6	41.7	6.8	171372
38559	DOYLE	19668	499	35.7	32.5	25.5	4.6	1.8	33986	34950	15	21	413	19.1	29.3	40.4	9.9	1.2	91667
38560	ELMWOOD	21096	481	22.0	32.4	38.5	6.2	0.8	45932	46591	51	71	397	11.3	24.9	39.3	20.9	3.5	115064
38562	GAINESBORO	17897	2757	40.0	32.9	21.8	3.0	2.3	30662	32576	9	13	2163	22.9	30.8	36.7	8.5	1.1	85763
38563	GORDONSVILLE	20877	1027	24.2	27.9	39.9	6.6	1.3	47896	48517	56	75	832	10.3	18.0	45.0	22.7	4.0	121207
38564	GRANVILLE	18536	208	36.1	27.9	30.8	5.3	0.0	34383	40783	16	22	180	17.8	24.4	41.1	12.8	3.9	100000
38565	GRIMSLEY	14440	226	38.9	32.7	26.5	1.3	0.4	33524	33781	14	20	194	27.8	30.4	34.0	6.2	1.5	80000
38567	HICKMAN	20515	317	21.5	33.1	39.4	5.0	0.9	46084	46711	52	72	259	6.6	29.0	34.0	28.2	2.3	113988
38568	HILHAM	14994	750	40.8	38.7	18.3	2.0	0.3	29600	31264	7	11	636	25.8	29.4	33.6	10.2	0.9	83654
38569	LANCASTER	20014	156	21.2	33.3	41.0	3.8	0.6	45569	46869	50	69	127	11.0	26.0	33.9	27.6	1.6	112500
38570	LIVINGSTON	17064	3754	39.6	31.4	25.9	2.1	1.0	30942	32034	10	14	2832	24.5	21.3	43.2	9.8	1.2	95930
38571	CROSSVILLE	18142	5470	29.9	35.8	29.4	3.4	1.5	37571	39335	25	39	4642	17.2	21.7	40.0	17.9	3.1	104353
38572	CROSSVILLE	20282	4742	30.8	36.0	26.8	4.5	1.9	36887	38551	23	34	4045	15.4	27.2	38.8	17.0	1.6	99134
38573	MONROE	18569	892	38.3	33.7	24.8	1.7	1.5	31858	33492	11	16	755	21.2	27.9	33.8	12.6	4.5	91250
38574	MONTEREY	16210	3187	36.1	33.3	26.3	3.5	0.9	34930	36804	17	24	2371	21.5	25.4	37.6	12.8	2.7	93104
38575	MOSS	15918	485	34.8	42.5	19.6	1.6	1.4	31750	32542	11	16	398	43.7	21.1	23.1	11.8	0.3	64444
38577	PALL MALL	14746	510	43.3	31.6	21.6	2.5	1.0	27794	28655	5	8	448	30.1	19.9	35.9	13.2	0.9	90000
38578	PLEASANT HILL	20960	30	30.0	43.3	23.3	3.3	0.0	36483	36496	22	33	23	13.0	39.1	43.5	4.3	0.0	87500
38579	QUEBECK	17908	555	30.1	34.2	29.9	5.2	0.5	38628	40758	29	44	464	16.2	27.6	35.8	17.2	3.2	97250
38580	RICKMAN	18024	720	30.1	34.2	31.7	2.6	1.4	38591	42280	28	43	603	21.2	26.2	35.3	15.6	1.7	93780
38581	ROCK ISLAND	18546	1624	25.8	36.0	34.1	3.4	0.7	41601	42390	38	56	1398	16.5	29.3	42.6	10.0	1.6	93353
38582	SILVER POINT	19900	542	30.4	33.9	30.1	3.0	2.6	40408	41942	34	52	468	23.3	18.6	39.1	15.4	3.6	102941
38583	SPARTA	18364	9456	34.2	32.3	27.9	3.8	1.7	36276	37770	21	31	7450	16.4	24.1	44.4	13.0	2.1	101920
38585	SPENCER	17936	1704	36.3	30.5	29.2	2.3	1.7	34303	35343	16	22	1426	25.2	35.2	32.7	6.1	0.8	77355
38587	WALLING	19986	488	33.6	35.2	25.6	3.1	2.5	35099	34769	18	25	413	14.5	28.6	40.7	14.3	1.9	97917
38588	WHITLEYVILLE	18588	458	35.4	38.2	21.0	2.4	3.1	34534	35070	17	23	352	27.6	28.4	31.8	11.1	1.1	83226
38589	WILDER	13758	70	41.4	28.6	28.6	0.0	1.4	30000	29042	8	11	60	36.7	28.3	26.7	8.3	0.0	62500
42223	FORT CAMPBELL	12860	4064	15.9	48.7	30.9	3.3	1.2	39734	42449	32	49	65	33.8	6.2	49.2	9.2	1.5	117188
	TENNESSEE	24986		24.9	27.0	34.7	8.2	5.2	47751	50104				12.0	19.9	40.9	22.7	4.6	120455
	UNITED STATES	27277		20.9	24.4	35.3	11.7	7.6	54719	56938				9.3	13.1	31.6	32.6	13.5	162279

ZIP CODE #	POST OFFICE NAME	FINANCIAL SERVICES				THE HOME						ENTERTAINMENT						PERSONAL			
						Home Improvements		Furnishings													
		Auto Loan	Home Loan	Investments	Retirement Plans	Home Repair	Lawn & Garden	Computers & Hardware-Personal	Major Appliances	TV, Radio, Sound Equipment	Furniture	Dine out/ Carry out	Sports Equipment	Fees & Tickets	Toys & Games	Travel	Cable TV	Apparel & Services	Auto Repairs	Health Insurance	Pets & Supplies
38555	CROSSVILLE	80	61	77	61	63	80	67	76	72	63	71	57	57	72	64	78	48	74	82	90
38556	JAMESTOWN	64	45	60	44	46	63	48	58	54	46	53	44	38	54	45	59	35	55	61	70
38558	CROSSVILLE	87	94	124	87	109	114	85	102	91	96	88	61	93	80	100	97	59	97	121	114
38559	DOYLE	80	57	68	56	57	77	60	70	66	58	65	54	48	68	55	72	43	66	74	85
38560	ELMWOOD	97	70	80	68	69	92	73	84	80	71	79	65	58	84	66	88	53	80	89	103
38562	GAINESBORO	74	53	67	51	53	73	56	67	62	53	61	51	44	63	52	68	40	63	71	80
38563	GORDONSVILLE	88	71	74	70	71	86	71	81	76	69	75	61	61	79	67	82	51	76	84	97
38564	GRANVILLE	75	54	77	52	56	76	55	70	61	51	60	53	44	61	55	67	40	64	73	83
38565	GRIMSLEY	68	47	59	46	47	65	50	59	56	48	55	46	39	58	46	61	37	56	63	72
38567	HICKMAN	90	67	75	65	66	87	69	80	76	66	74	61	56	79	63	82	50	75	84	97
38568	HILHAM	63	45	53	44	45	60	47	55	52	46	51	42	38	54	43	57	34	52	58	67
38569	LANCASTER	90	65	74	63	64	86	67	78	75	66	73	60	54	78	61	81	49	74	83	95
38570	LIVINGSTON	67	50	63	49	51	68	53	63	58	48	56	48	43	58	50	63	38	59	68	75
38571	CROSSVILLE	78	58	78	56	60	79	59	73	66	57	64	54	49	65	58	72	43	68	77	87
38572	CROSSVILLE	80	62	85	59	65	83	62	77	68	60	67	56	53	67	63	74	44	72	82	91
38573	MONROE	80	57	72	55	58	78	59	71	66	56	64	54	47	67	56	72	43	67	75	86
38574	MONTEREY	76	55	65	53	55	73	57	67	63	55	62	51	46	65	52	68	41	63	70	81
38575	MOSS	67	48	66	47	49	67	50	62	55	47	54	47	40	55	48	60	36	57	64	74
38577	PALL MALL	62	44	64	43	46	63	46	58	51	43	50	44	37	50	45	56	33	53	60	69
38578	PLEASANT HILL	72	52	72	51	54	75	57	70	63	51	61	52	45	62	55	70	41	65	76	82
38579	QUEBECK	80	57	80	55	59	81	59	74	65	55	64	56	47	65	58	72	42	68	77	88
38580	RICKMAN	80	58	66	56	57	76	60	70	66	58	65	54	48	69	55	72	44	66	73	85
38581	ROCK ISLAND	84	60	70	59	60	80	63	73	70	61	68	56	50	73	57	76	46	69	77	89
38582	SILVER POINT	84	61	88	59	64	85	62	79	69	58	67	59	51	68	62	75	45	73	81	93
38583	SPARTA	77	57	67	56	57	75	60	70	66	57	65	53	49	68	56	72	43	66	74	84
38585	SPENCER	79	57	65	55	57	75	59	69	66	58	64	53	47	68	54	72	43	65	73	84
38587	WALLING	85	61	74	59	61	82	63	75	70	61	69	57	51	73	59	77	46	71	79	91
38588	WHITLEYVILLE	77	55	75	54	57	78	58	72	65	54	63	54	47	65	56	71	42	67	76	85
38589	WILDER	71	48	65	45	48	69	51	62	58	48	56	48	39	59	47	64	37	59	66	76
42223	FORT CAMPBELL	85	44	33	51	40	38	80	55	75	74	79	55	61	90	58	69	55	70	50	67
	TENNESSEE	95	84	85	84	82	93	87	90	90	85	89	69	80	91	83	93	61	89	93	107
	UNITED STATES	100	100	100	100	100	100	100	100	100	100	100	100	100	100	100	100	100	100	100	100

75001-75160

ZIP CODE			POPULATION			2000-2009 ANNUAL RATE		HOUSEHOLDS					FAMILIES		
#	POST OFFICE NAME	COUNTY FIPS CODE	2000	2009	2014	% Rate	State Centile	2000	2009	2014	% Annual Rate 2000-2009	2009 Average HH Size	2000	2009	% Annual Rate 2000-2009
75001	ADDISON	113	13718	14655	15219	0.7	49	7407	7864	8152	0.6	1.86	2883	2852	-0.1
75002	ALLEN	085	37289	63352	80858	5.9	95	12276	21025	27003	6.0	3.01	10371	17147	5.6
75006	CARROLLTON	113	47198	48896	49716	0.4	37	17128	17398	17629	0.2	2.79	11900	11777	-0.1
75007	CARROLLTON	121	50357	58304	64562	1.6	71	17616	19827	21844	1.3	2.93	13650	14889	0.9
75009	CELINA	085	5271	8245	10748	5.0	94	1816	2852	3723	5.0	2.88	1485	2232	4.5
75010	CARROLLTON	121	12853	21219	26281	5.6	95	4852	7808	9650	5.3	2.71	3505	5372	4.7
75013	ALLEN	085	11624	28794	39579	10.3	98	3735	9307	12870	10.4	3.09	3264	7975	10.1
75019	COPPELL	113	35959	39556	41004	1.0	58	12212	13122	13554	0.8	3.01	9753	10174	0.5
75020	DENISON	181	21633	22549	22998	0.4	37	8726	8997	9172	0.3	2.45	5896	5969	0.1
75021	DENISON	181	7907	8448	8713	0.7	49	3073	3248	3346	0.6	2.58	2279	2376	0.5
75022	FLOWER MOUND	121	14287	22528	28062	5.0	94	4573	6900	8543	4.5	3.25	4066	6045	4.4
75023	PLANO	085	45433	50907	58115	1.2	63	16780	19331	22286	1.5	2.62	12715	13824	0.9
75024	PLANO	085	19721	32675	41413	5.6	95	7853	13587	17463	6.1	2.40	5147	8085	5.0
75025	PLANO	085	40898	58441	71492	3.9	91	13897	19166	23434	3.5	3.05	11362	14918	3.0
75028	FLOWER MOUND	121	36715	45492	51988	2.3	81	11737	14203	16163	2.1	3.20	10201	12083	1.8
75032	ROCKWALL	397	14152	29733	40037	8.4	97	4787	9841	13199	8.1	3.02	3952	8115	8.1
75034	FRISCO	121	16858	65980	91415	15.9	99	5957	22409	31015	15.4	2.94	4768	17577	15.1
75035	FRISCO	085	19302	48868	65509	10.6	98	6891	17143	23103	10.4	2.84	5653	13924	10.2
75038	IRVING	113	26254	27579	28301	0.5	42	13013	13422	13680	0.3	2.05	5978	5953	0.0
75039	IRVING	113	2816	7293	9052	10.8	98	1881	4534	5590	10.0	1.61	632	1527	10.0
75040	GARLAND	113	55123	56995	58084	0.4	37	16823	17104	17326	0.2	3.32	13738	13807	0.1
75041	GARLAND	113	31076	31885	32254	0.3	34	10587	10543	10594	0.0	3.00	7737	7549	-0.3
75042	GARLAND	113	38234	38900	39252	0.2	30	12108	11923	11922	-0.2	3.25	9318	9036	-0.3
75043	GARLAND	113	53919	58202	60398	0.8	52	20002	21198	21829	0.6	2.71	14292	14837	0.4
75044	GARLAND	113	37192	40638	42347	1.0	58	13676	14666	15149	0.8	2.77	10151	10777	0.6
75048	SACHSE	113	9750	17662	21406	6.6	96	3220	5837	7090	6.6	3.03	2720	4817	6.4
75050	GRAND PRAIRIE	113	37771	39793	41088	0.6	46	14118	14644	15094	0.4	2.70	9194	9180	0.0
75051	GRAND PRAIRIE	113	29090	33847	36054	1.7	73	9435	10746	11370	1.4	3.14	7195	8031	1.2
75052	GRAND PRAIRIE	113	58414	86206	98982	4.3	92	19335	28042	32073	4.1	3.07	15478	22152	4.0
75054	GRAND PRAIRIE	439	82	4175	5568	52.9	100	35	1569	2092	50.9	2.65	32	1348	49.8
75056	THE COLONY	121	28841	46810	58625	5.4	95	9152	15376	19311	5.8	3.03	7499	11738	5.0
75057	LEWISVILLE	121	11871	13627	15014	1.5	69	4507	5062	5571	1.3	2.67	2789	2917	0.5
75058	GUNTER	181	2118	2674	2881	2.6	83	604	759	820	2.5	3.19	479	591	2.3
75060	IRVING	113	45724	46659	47678	0.2	30	15057	15086	15323	0.0	3.09	11422	11258	-0.2
75061	IRVING	113	53362	54841	55423	0.3	34	18778	18693	18748	0.0	2.90	12711	12385	-0.3
75062	IRVING	113	40451	41029	41820	0.2	30	15461	15401	15590	0.0	2.62	10035	9773	-0.3
75063	IRVING	113	24454	30777	33402	2.5	82	12662	15007	16089	1.9	2.05	5784	6736	1.7
75065	LAKE DALLAS	121	8099	9614	11091	1.9	76	2971	3480	3990	1.7	2.76	2200	2446	1.2
75067	LEWISVILLE	121	49017	62974	72987	2.7	84	19746	25437	29689	2.8	2.47	12363	14854	2.0
75068	LITTLE ELM	121	6929	31302	43383	17.7	100	2381	10180	14075	17.0	3.07	1887	7794	16.6
75069	MCKINNEY	085	25739	36661	45402	3.9	91	8885	12796	15987	4.0	2.79	6067	8490	3.7
75070	MCKINNEY	085	26556	75741	102759	12.0	99	8727	25160	34338	12.1	3.01	7605	21365	11.8
75071	MCKINNEY	085	10464	31219	42498	12.5	99	3463	11176	15426	13.5	2.72	2754	8710	13.3
75074	PLANO	085	37288	47854	56689	2.7	84	12876	17027	20402	3.1	2.79	9350	11648	2.4
75075	PLANO	085	35969	39561	44756	1.0	58	13667	15273	17371	1.2	2.58	10144	10620	0.5
75076	POTTSBORO	181	6763	7660	8080	1.4	67	2835	3202	3382	1.3	2.39	2049	2264	1.1
75077	LEWISVILLE	121	30654	39726	46122	2.8	85	10208	12838	14847	2.5	3.09	8922	11019	2.3
75078	PROSPER	085	2948	7572	10513	10.7	98	937	2449	3416	10.9	3.09	809	2017	10.4
75080	RICHARDSON	113	41105	43523	45432	0.6	46	15895	16644	17353	0.5	2.58	10961	11080	0.1
75081	RICHARDSON	113	32737	34422	35358	0.5	42	12426	12882	13160	0.4	2.65	8800	8922	0.1
75082	RICHARDSON	085	15358	21727	27287	3.8	90	5461	7918	9997	4.1	2.74	4377	5913	3.3
75087	ROCKWALL	397	16601	29810	39299	6.5	96	5842	10346	13627	6.4	2.84	4674	8284	6.4
75088	ROWLETT	113	24856	26753	28044	0.8	52	7918	8425	8790	0.7	3.14	6879	7257	0.6
75089	ROWLETT	113	18667	26398	30282	3.8	90	6059	8395	9558	3.6	3.14	5196	7129	3.5
75090	SHERMAN	181	22312	23830	24500	0.7	49	7958	8375	8612	0.6	2.70	5537	5731	0.4
75092	SHERMAN	181	20382	22414	23325	1.0	58	8483	9203	9558	0.9	2.37	5463	5845	0.7
75093	PLANO	085	44683	56710	67124	2.6	83	16958	21763	25919	2.7	2.59	12268	14920	2.1
75094	PLANO	085	3499	16618	22849	18.3	100	1152	5793	8030	19.1	2.87	1017	4818	18.3
75098	WYLIE	085	20722	44582	59744	8.6	98	6995	15271	20602	8.8	2.91	5777	12079	8.3
75102	BARRY	349	824	906	948	1.0	58	307	336	351	1.0	2.70	243	263	0.9
75103	CANTON	467	14584	16107	16799	1.1	61	5613	6189	6459	1.1	2.54	4231	4605	0.9
75104	CEDAR HILL	113	32071	43167	47975	3.3	88	10743	14216	15680	3.1	3.02	8729	11382	2.9
75105	CHATFIELD	349	344	382	403	1.1	61	132	146	154	1.1	2.62	104	113	0.9
75109	CORSICANA	349	2585	3754	4278	4.1	92	904	1307	1490	4.1	2.84	736	1038	3.8
75110	CORSICANA	349	28231	30304	31183	0.8	52	10119	10589	10872	0.5	2.70	7098	7296	0.3
75114	CRANDALL	257	3953	4840	5617	2.2	80	1268	1525	1775	2.0	3.17	1045	1226	1.7
75115	DESOTO	113	37793	48615	53659	2.8	85	13763	17238	18870	2.5	2.80	10700	13259	2.3
75116	DUNCANVILLE	113	18252	18896	19234	0.4	37	6580	6688	6751	0.2	2.81	5121	5120	0.0
75117	EDGEWOOD	467	3967	5058	5547	2.7	84	1534	1967	2159	2.7	2.57	1191	1504	2.6
75119	ENNIS	139	23990	28888	32020	2.0	78	8033	9543	10561	1.9	2.99	6160	7158	1.6
75124	EUSTACE	213	3246	3751	3950	1.6	71	1230	1397	1468	1.4	2.68	897	1004	1.2
75125	FERRIS	139	6151	7345	8601	1.9	76	1931	2269	2645	1.8	3.21	1512	1744	1.6
75126	FORNEY	257	11048	31528	42691	12.0	99	3661	9996	13500	11.5	3.15	3082	8284	11.3
75127	FRUITVALE	467	1993	2282	2422	1.5	69	722	825	875	1.5	2.76	567	639	1.3
75134	LANCASTER	113	12666	19514	22166	4.8	93	4379	6464	7254	4.3	2.96	3302	4668	3.8
75135	CADDO MILLS	231	4376	5123	5398	1.7	73	1540	1751	1838	1.4	2.93	1237	1390	1.3
75137	DUNCANVILLE	113	17760	19560	20515	1.0	58	6284	6813	7100	0.9	2.85	4957	5294	0.7
75140	GRAND SALINE	467	5823	6226	6400	0.7	49	2132	2252	2312	0.6	2.68	1544	1619	0.5
75141	HUTCHINS	113	2862	2930	2941	0.3	34	961	997	1017	0.4	2.23	691	703	0.2
75142	KAUFMAN	257	16970	19029	20658	1.2	63	5710	6242	6782	1.0	2.99	4522	4834	0.7
75143	KEMP	257	12272	13648	14458	1.2	63	4799	5236	5536	0.9	2.60	3562	3810	0.7
75144	KERENS	349	3077	3348	3490	0.9	55	1199	1300	1353	0.9	2.58	849	902	0.7
75146	LANCASTER	113	15188	19187	21385	2.6	83	5355	6605	7294	2.3	2.82	4017	4917	2.2
75147	MABANK	257	3348	4194	4781	2.5	82	1232	1516	1733	2.3	2.72	862	1026	1.9
75148	MALAKOFF	213	5700	6230	6343	1.0	58	2301	2476	2520	0.8	2.47	1646	1748	0.7
75149	MESQUITE	113	54808	56389	57429	0.3	34	18654	18926	19159	0.2	2.96	14602	14583	0.0
75150	MESQUITE	113	55022	60020	62466	0.9	55	20832	22483	23278	0.8	2.66	14454	15237	0.6
75152	PALMER	139	3160	3462	3733	1.0	58	999	1081	1165	0.9	3.20	835	890	0.7
75153	POWELL	349	192	218	231	1.4	67	71	80	85	1.3	2.73	59	67	1.4
75154	RED OAK	139	25546	36699	42899	4.0	91	8410	11946	13938	3.9	3.07	7053	9868	3.7
75155	RICE	349	2380	2643	2788	1.1	61	827	914	963	1.1	2.89	651	710	0.9
75156	MABANK	213	15265	17252	17980	1.3	65	6363	7073	7353	1.2	2.43	4525	4955	1.0
75158	SCURRY	257	4323	5237	5989	2.1	79	1478	1743	1991	1.8	3.00	1227	1414	1.5
75159	SEAGOVILLE	113	14354	18483	20197	2.8	85	4517	5468	6008	2.1	2.92	3483	4153	1.9
75160	TERRELL	257	19642	25022	28806	2.7	84	6678	8300	9565	2.4	2.91	4983	6050	2.1
	TEXAS					1.9					1.8	2.78			1.7
	UNITED STATES					1.0					1.1	2.59			0.9

ZIP CODE #	POST OFFICE NAME	RACE (%) White 2000	White 2009	Black 2000	Black 2009	Asian/Pacific 2000	Asian/Pacific 2009	% Hispanic Origin 2000	% Hispanic Origin 2009	2009 AGE DISTRIBUTION (%) 0-4	5-9	10-14	15-19	20-24	25-44	45-64	65-84	85+	18+	MEDIAN AGE 2009	% 2009 Males	% 2009 Females
75001	ADDISON	68.4	63.9	9.3	9.0	8.0	9.3	23.0	29.8	6.3	4.5	3.6	3.6	11.2	44.2	21.2	5.1	0.4	83.9	32.0	51.9	48.1
75002	ALLEN	87.1	82.5	4.5	5.0	3.2	5.4	7.5	10.7	9.5	9.5	9.0	7.2	4.7	30.7	24.9	4.4	0.3	67.4	33.6	49.7	50.3
75006	CARROLLTON	68.7	63.4	5.7	5.9	9.1	10.5	31.7	38.9	7.8	7.3	7.0	6.6	6.8	30.8	24.8	8.0	0.9	74.0	34.5	50.0	50.0
75007	CARROLLTON	74.0	67.0	6.8	7.9	12.2	16.5	11.3	14.7	7.2	7.6	7.9	7.5	5.8	29.7	28.7	5.3	0.4	72.6	35.7	49.0	51.0
75009	CELINA	87.2	83.8	3.7	3.7	0.5	0.9	12.8	17.1	7.0	7.5	8.0	8.1	5.4	26.0	28.5	8.3	1.3	72.4	37.0	50.4	49.6
75010	CARROLLTON	74.4	62.5	7.3	8.5	10.5	16.8	11.1	18.7	9.2	8.0	7.2	6.0	7.0	36.8	21.5	3.8	0.4	71.8	31.9	49.7	50.3
75013	ALLEN	88.0	83.4	3.2	3.6	5.5	8.3	4.8	7.1	11.0	11.2	10.6	7.4	3.5	29.5	23.6	2.9	0.2	62.3	31.7	49.6	50.4
75019	COPPELL	83.4	77.9	3.2	3.8	9.2	12.3	6.9	11.1	9.4	10.0	9.1	6.9	3.7	32.5	24.9	3.2	0.3	66.7	34.4	49.6	50.4
75020	DENISON	85.7	82.5	7.6	8.7	0.5	0.7	4.6	6.7	6.0	5.8	6.0	6.8	5.9	23.5	27.9	14.9	3.2	78.2	41.7	48.0	52.0
75021	DENISON	88.4	85.7	5.0	5.8	0.4	0.5	4.4	6.2	6.3	6.1	6.1	6.2	5.5	23.5	30.1	14.3	2.0	77.8	42.2	48.0	52.0
75022	FLOWER MOUND	91.8	87.9	2.2	3.0	3.1	5.2	5.0	7.2	11.0	9.4	8.9	6.4	2.5	33.6	24.3	3.5	0.6	66.0	34.9	49.7	50.3
75023	PLANO	82.2	75.3	4.9	5.7	7.9	12.3	7.2	10.2	6.6	7.0	7.6	7.0	5.1	27.0	31.5	7.3	0.8	74.2	38.6	49.4	50.6
75024	PLANO	72.5	65.7	4.9	5.7	18.6	23.4	5.6	8.2	8.3	8.0	7.5	6.1	6.0	34.7	25.3	3.8	0.3	72.5	34.3	49.6	50.4
75025	PLANO	76.5	67.5	4.9	5.9	14.8	21.6	5.0	7.2	10.9	10.5	9.3	6.2	3.8	34.2	22.2	2.7	0.2	65.1	33.4	49.6	50.4
75028	FLOWER MOUND	89.2	85.3	3.5	4.5	3.1	4.7	6.2	8.7	10.0	9.9	9.6	7.1	3.9	31.7	24.7	2.8	0.2	65.5	32.8	49.3	50.7
75032	ROCKWALL	89.1	87.2	1.5	1.9	1.3	1.7	14.4	16.4	7.2	7.9	8.3	7.2	4.3	25.6	30.7	8.2	0.7	72.1	38.7	50.4	49.6
75034	FRISCO	83.9	80.8	3.3	3.7	1.4	2.4	18.7	20.7	9.0	8.8	8.4	6.8	4.5	30.3	25.5	6.1	0.6	69.2	34.5	49.6	50.4
75035	FRISCO	88.9	84.7	4.0	4.9	2.9	3.7	6.2	10.3	11.2	11.3	10.0	5.9	2.6	34.0	21.5	3.3	0.3	63.7	35.0	49.2	50.8
75038	IRVING	50.7	46.0	23.1	22.2	14.5	16.9	19.1	25.6	7.6	5.5	4.3	5.3	13.8	42.6	17.6	3.1	0.2	80.1	29.2	51.9	48.1
75039	IRVING	78.5	73.7	3.7	3.9	14.1	17.4	7.6	11.6	3.5	2.4	2.0	2.6	9.3	46.7	23.7	8.3	1.3	91.0	35.8	53.0	47.0
75040	GARLAND	62.5	57.2	14.2	13.6	6.2	7.8	30.8	38.8	8.8	8.6	8.4	7.9	6.4	29.3	23.7	6.3	0.7	69.3	31.8	49.5	50.5
75041	GARLAND	67.2	61.9	10.6	10.0	1.4	1.5	38.6	49.5	9.4	8.6	7.7	7.4	7.8	29.5	19.6	8.8	1.3	69.8	30.5	50.5	49.5
75042	GARLAND	54.0	48.3	7.8	7.3	13.9	14.7	37.1	46.1	9.0	8.1	7.3	7.5	7.7	30.9	21.1	7.6	0.8	71.2	30.9	51.5	48.5
75043	GARLAND	71.6	65.1	14.8	15.9	3.5	4.7	14.8	21.9	7.5	6.7	6.5	7.1	8.2	28.6	25.8	8.1	1.4	74.9	34.0	48.1	51.9
75044	GARLAND	70.3	64.0	9.1	9.6	13.1	16.5	10.5	15.3	6.7	6.8	7.0	6.9	5.9	29.6	29.4	7.1	0.6	75.3	36.5	48.6	51.4
75048	SACHSE	86.7	81.8	4.7	5.0	2.4	3.3	8.6	14.3	8.8	8.5	8.1	7.1	5.4	31.1	24.8	5.8	0.5	70.2	33.8	49.3	50.7
75050	GRAND PRAIRIE	65.6	59.0	8.5	8.7	2.2	2.6	39.1	49.2	8.6	7.6	7.0	7.0	8.4	31.7	21.0	7.5	1.1	72.6	31.1	50.3	49.7
75051	GRAND PRAIRIE	58.1	51.5	11.7	11.5	2.5	2.6	45.3	56.6	9.6	8.8	8.0	8.1	7.8	27.4	20.8	8.3	1.0	68.6	29.9	49.0	51.0
75052	GRAND PRAIRIE	61.0	54.0	18.0	19.6	7.0	8.5	23.5	30.2	9.0	8.5	7.9	7.1	6.1	32.1	23.9	4.9	0.4	70.1	32.0	49.1	50.9
75054	GRAND PRAIRIE	90.2	62.9	3.7	17.4	2.4	7.6	6.1	18.7	9.0	8.6	8.3	6.9	4.9	31.3	25.2	5.4	0.5	69.7	33.8	49.5	50.5
75056	THE COLONY	83.3	78.8	5.2	6.3	2.7	4.7	13.4	16.7	8.7	8.3	7.8	6.9	5.7	33.3	24.4	4.4	0.5	71.0	32.9	49.5	50.5
75057	LEWISVILLE	70.4	64.3	5.7	6.8	1.6	2.3	30.7	37.6	7.9	6.3	5.4	6.5	11.6	35.4	19.2	6.6	1.0	77.0	29.8	52.1	47.9
75058	GUNTER	87.6	84.0	0.4	0.4	0.4	0.5	17.0	22.2	6.9	6.9	7.1	8.0	6.2	25.5	25.3	10.3	3.8	74.0	37.2	48.8	51.2
75060	IRVING	68.4	62.2	5.3	5.0	5.3	6.1	38.3	49.1	8.8	8.3	7.5	7.7	7.2	29.4	22.8	7.5	0.8	70.8	31.6	50.5	49.5
75061	IRVING	62.7	57.6	9.0	8.5	4.1	4.5	45.7	55.8	8.9	7.9	6.9	7.1	9.0	32.6	19.4	6.9	1.3	72.2	30.1	51.8	48.2
75062	IRVING	67.6	62.0	9.6	9.3	7.5	8.5	27.1	36.5	7.1	6.1	5.8	7.2	9.4	31.3	22.8	9.5	0.9	77.3	33.1	50.4	49.6
75063	IRVING	67.5	60.8	9.9	10.4	17.3	21.8	8.5	12.8	7.3	5.7	4.7	3.8	9.2	45.4	20.8	2.9	0.2	80.1	31.6	49.9	50.1
75065	LAKE DALLAS	90.6	87.4	2.4	3.1	0.9	1.4	9.2	12.9	7.5	7.3	7.1	6.8	6.6	28.8	27.3	7.9	0.6	73.9	36.0	50.5	49.5
75067	LEWISVILLE	78.1	72.0	7.7	9.3	4.6	7.1	16.1	20.2	8.8	7.9	7.0	5.9	7.9	38.6	19.4	4.1	0.5	73.0	30.8	50.0	50.0
75068	LITTLE ELM	85.0	76.0	1.8	2.8	0.4	0.7	16.5	27.7	9.2	8.5	8.0	6.8	5.0	31.8	23.6	6.5	0.6	70.0	33.3	50.0	50.0
75069	MCKINNEY	66.0	62.9	10.2	8.9	1.1	1.7	30.7	35.2	8.6	7.9	7.4	8.5	8.1	29.5	22.0	6.8	1.3	71.4	31.0	51.1	48.9
75070	MCKINNEY	92.2	88.6	2.7	3.7	2.1	3.2	5.3	8.7	10.4	10.2	9.5	7.0	3.3	31.6	23.5	4.3	0.4	64.9	33.8	49.4	50.6
75071	MCKINNEY	85.2	81.6	6.2	7.0	1.2	1.9	11.0	14.1	9.3	9.0	8.5	6.9	4.5	31.6	23.6	5.9	0.8	68.9	33.5	50.3	49.7
75074	PLANO	72.4	65.9	7.7	8.3	3.9	6.1	26.9	32.7	7.9	7.4	6.9	7.3	7.2	31.9	23.5	7.1	0.8	73.7	33.0	50.9	49.1
75075	PLANO	81.3	74.3	3.6	4.1	8.7	12.9	10.4	14.1	6.1	6.2	6.6	6.6	5.6	27.6	30.0	10.4	1.1	77.0	39.2	50.0	50.0
75076	POTTSBORO	96.5	95.4	0.1	0.1	0.3	0.4	1.8	2.7	4.1	4.3	4.8	5.7	4.6	20.3	36.6	18.1	1.5	83.3	48.5	49.6	50.4
75077	LEWISVILLE	88.5	84.2	4.4	5.8	2.9	4.5	5.7	8.2	7.8	8.3	8.6	7.3	4.2	28.1	29.3	5.8	0.5	70.3	36.8	49.1	50.9
75078	PROSPER	92.5	89.2	0.3	0.4	0.4	0.7	16.3	24.3	9.7	9.0	8.3	7.1	5.8	30.3	23.8	5.5	0.6	68.7	31.4	50.2	49.8
75080	RICHARDSON	80.3	75.3	5.0	5.0	7.2	9.5	13.3	19.1	6.1	6.0	6.2	7.2	9.3	25.1	25.0	13.0	2.2	77.9	37.5	49.5	50.5
75081	RICHARDSON	70.8	64.4	7.9	8.2	14.3	18.3	9.4	13.3	6.2	6.2	6.4	6.3	6.5	27.7	29.8	9.9	1.0	77.2	38.4	48.8	51.2
75082	RICHARDSON	71.8	61.4	6.2	7.0	17.2	25.0	6.3	9.1	8.2	8.1	8.1	6.5	4.6	30.5	27.6	6.0	0.5	71.5	36.1	49.9	50.1
75087	ROCKWALL	90.8	88.4	3.3	3.5	1.4	1.9	7.4	10.9	7.1	7.2	7.6	7.0	5.2	27.7	28.1	8.8	1.2	73.6	36.9	49.8	50.2
75088	ROWLETT	82.2	77.2	8.6	9.7	3.7	5.1	8.2	12.7	7.8	8.1	8.3	7.9	5.2	28.1	27.6	5.9	1.0	70.6	35.1	49.0	51.0
75089	ROWLETT	81.4	76.5	9.5	10.4	2.8	3.7	9.7	15.5	9.2	8.8	8.7	7.7	4.9	30.7	24.8	4.6	0.4	68.3	33.4	49.4	50.6
75090	SHERMAN	75.4	71.1	12.7	13.9	1.0	1.2	15.2	19.9	7.6	6.8	6.6	8.9	8.5	26.3	23.6	9.7	2.0	74.7	33.5	49.5	50.5
75092	SHERMAN	87.8	84.6	5.9	7.0	0.9	1.3	5.3	7.6	6.7	5.9	5.9	6.8	7.2	26.7	25.4	12.6	2.9	77.5	37.6	47.8	52.2
75093	PLANO	81.3	74.3	3.9	4.5	11.3	16.5	4.6	6.8	7.5	7.7	7.9	7.0	5.0	29.0	29.6	5.3	0.9	72.2	37.1	49.1	50.9
75094	PLANO	77.1	71.5	8.5	7.3	9.1	13.1	6.0	11.8	10.0	9.8	9.1	6.6	3.5	32.4	23.4	5.0	0.4	66.9	34.2	49.3	50.7
75098	WYLIE	90.7	85.8	2.2	3.1	0.8	1.3	9.5	15.5	8.7	8.2	8.0	7.3	5.3	31.1	24.4	6.3	0.7	70.5	33.6	49.3	50.7
75102	BARRY	87.7	83.3	4.7	5.8	0.8	1.0	8.7	13.2	6.8	6.8	7.0	7.1	6.2	25.4	27.7	11.7	1.3	75.2	38.6	51.0	49.0
75103	CANTON	93.3	91.4	2.1	2.3	0.3	0.4	4.6	6.6	6.0	6.1	6.3	6.1	5.2	22.7	28.9	16.3	2.6	77.9	43.2	49.3	50.7
75104	CEDAR HILL	56.6	52.1	33.5	34.2	2.0	2.5	12.0	18.0	8.3	8.0	7.8	7.6	6.5	30.1	25.7	5.4	0.6	71.3	32.8	47.9	52.1
75105	CHATFIELD	81.6	74.6	5.8	6.8	0.3	0.3	16.3	24.3	8.1	7.6	7.6	7.9	6.5	25.1	26.7	9.7	0.8	72.0	35.8	51.0	49.0
75109	CORSICANA	88.4	84.5	5.9	7.4	1.2	1.5	5.1	8.0	6.9	6.8	7.2	7.7	5.9	25.7	26.2	12.2	1.4	74.0	38.1	50.8	49.2
75110	CORSICANA	63.5	57.8	20.9	22.0	1.0	1.3	20.3	26.5	7.7	7.2	6.8	8.7	7.4	25.5	22.9	11.1	2.7	73.9	34.3	49.1	50.9
75114	CRANDALL	87.8	82.0	5.3	7.0	0.3	0.4	7.8	13.1	7.5	7.5	7.5	7.9	6.5	28.6	26.0	7.6	0.9	72.6	33.8	49.6	50.4
75115	DESOTO	48.7	44.3	45.2	46.9	1.3	1.7	8.2	12.8	7.1	7.2	7.5	7.2	5.9	26.3	28.6	9.0	1.3	73.8	37.0	47.9	52.1
75116	DUNCANVILLE	66.8	60.8	20.1	20.8	1.9	2.3	18.7	27.5	7.1	6.8	6.8	7.2	6.8	26.5	25.7	11.8	1.5	74.9	36.1	47.5	52.5
75117	EDGEWOOD	93.0	90.2	3.7	4.9	0.1	0.1	4.0	5.9	6.3	6.4	6.5	6.4	5.0	22.2	28.7	16.2	2.2	76.8	42.7	48.7	51.3
75119	ENNIS	72.4	66.7	11.0	11.6	0.3	0.3	28.6	36.9	8.4	7.9	7.6	7.5	7.1	26.2	23.6	9.9	1.9	71.7	33.3	49.7	50.3
75124	EUSTACE	95.9	94.2	0.5	0.6	0.3	0.5	4.1	6.3	6.0	6.2	6.5	6.7	5.1	23.9	29.5	14.3	1.7	77.0	41.6	49.5	50.5
75125	FERRIS	77.6	72.0	11.2	13.2	0.2	0.2	26.8	35.9	8.4	8.0	7.5	7.7	8.1	25.7	25.2	8.6	0.9	71.6	32.3	49.7	50.3
75126	FORNEY	87.9	85.6	5.9	6.5	0.3	0.4	7.4	11.0	7.8	7.8	7.8	7.6	5.8	29.1	26.7	6.8	0.6	71.8	34.5	49.4	50.6
75127	FRUITVALE	95.3	93.2	0.3	0.4	0.1	0.0	4.3	6.3	7.0	7.1	7.4	6.9	5.0	22.8	27.5	14.8	1.4	73.9	40.1	49.8	50.2
75134	LANCASTER	30.9	31.0	57.2	48.8	0.4	0.4	15.1	27.7	8.4	8.1	7.7	7.8	7.7	28.2	23.0	7.7	1.3	71.1	31.6	47.9	52.1
75135	CADDO MILLS	91.8	88.4	3.3	4.4	0.2	0.3	6.8	10.6	7.2	7.1	7.3	7.4	5.8	27.1	26.8	10.1	1.1	73.8	37.1	49.2	50.8
75137	DUNCANVILLE	62.3	56.7	28.3	30.5	2.3	2.9	11.3	16.8	6.0	6.3	6.7	7.1	6.1	25.8	30.5	10.2	1.2	76.4	39.0	47.2	52.8
75140	GRAND SALINE	93.8	91.8	0.4	0.4	0.2	0.3	10.3	14.0	6.9	6.9	6.8	6.6	6.0	23.6	25.6	14.3	3.3	75.2	39.3	50.5	49.5
75141	HUTCHINS	40.1	35.0	42.6	42.0	0.2	0.2	21.5	29.9	6.6	6.5	6.7	7.6	9.9	34.8	21.2	6.1	0.7	75.7	32.1	60.6	39.4
75142	KAUFMAN	81.4	75.7	6.8	7.7	0.4	0.5	17.1	24.3	7.6	7.5	7.5	7.3	6.0	26.8	25.7	9.8	1.6	72.8	35.7	49.5	50.5
75143	KEMP	93.8	91.3	2.0	2.7	0.2	0.2	4.4	7.1	5.7	5.8	6.2	6.4	5.2	22.1	30.5	16.4	1.8	78.4	43.9	49.7	50.3
75144	KERENS	66.4	60.5	27.0	30.2	0.1	0.1	7.1	10.4	7.1	6.8	6.8	6.7	6.2	23.7	26.7	13.5	2.5	75.2	39.6	48.5	51.5
75146	LANCASTER	45.9	39.6	45.5	49.0	0.5	0.6	10.3	14.7	8.0	7.4	7.1	7.3	7.5	28.6	25.0	7.8	1.3	73.0	33.9	47.3	52.7
75147	MABANK	90.5	86.0	4.4	5.7	0.2	0.3	5.6	9.7	7.1	6.6	7.0	7.7	6.3	23.2	24.5	14.6	3.1	74.6	38.4	46.7	53.3
75148	MALAKOFF	84.7	81.6	11.2	13.0	0.2	0.3	6.1	8.7	6.1	5.6	5.8	6.4	4.9	20.7	28.1	19.2	3.3	78.4	45.4	48.0	52.0
75149	MESQUITE	70.5	64.0	15.8	16.8	3.1	3.9	16.9	25.1	8.5	8.1	7.8	7.9	7.3	28.9	23.2	7.4	0.9	70.6	31.9	48.3	51.7
75150	MESQUITE	76.5	70.7	10.5	11.4	4.2	5.4	16.2	23.8	7.0	6.5	6.3	7.1	8.3	30.3	25.5	8.2	0.9	76.1	33.5	48.3	51.7
75152	PALMER	86.5	81.3	2.1	2.7	0.2	0.2	23.9	33.9	8.0	7.7	7.5	7.2	7.0	27.7	26.5	7.7	0.8	72.5	33.8	51.2	48.8
75153	POWELL	81.7	77.5	13.1	14.7	0.0	0.0	7.3	10.6	6.4	6.9	6.9	6.0	6.0	22.9	29.4	14.2	1.4	75.7	41.8	51.4	48.6
75154	RED OAK	80.8	75.4	11.4	13.6	0.6	0.8	13.0	19.1	8.0	7.9	7.9	7.7	6.3	27.9	26.9	6.8	0.6	71.5	34.2	49.2	50.8
75155	RICE	81.3	74.5	6.0	6.9	0.3	0.4	16.3	24.0	8.1	7.6	7.7	7.8	6.4	25.3	26.8	9.4	0.9	71.9	35.8	50.7	49.3
75156	MABANK	94.5	92.5	1.7	2.2	0.4	0.6	3.5	5.4	5.7	5.4	5.6	5.6	4.3	20.1	31.7	19.5	2.0	79.6	47.4	49.8	50.2
75158	SCURRY	93.6	90.6	2.4	3.2	0.1	0.2	4.2	7.2	6.6	6.7	7.0	7.8	6.2	25.7	29.4	9.8	0.9	74.9	37.9	50.0	50.0
75159	SEAGOVILLE	81.2	76.0	8.2	8.4	0.5	0.7	16.4	24.7	6.7	6.6	6.4	6.2	6.8	33.2	25.0	8.1	1.0	76.6	35.3	55.9	44.1
75160	TERRELL	65.8	59.0	23.4	26.6	1.0	1.2	14.5	19.3	8.1	7.8	7.4	7.4	6.8	26.4	24.3	9.9	1.9	72.2	34.1	48.5	51.5
	TEXAS	71.0	67.6	11.5	11.4	2.8	3.5	32.0	37.4	7.9	7.5	7.2	7.5	7.4	28.3	24.0	8.8	1.4	73.0	33.6	49.7	50.3
	UNITED STATES	75.1	72.0	12.3	12.7	3.8	4.6	12.5	15.7	6.8	6.7	6.6	7.1	6.9	27.0	26.0	10.9	1.9	75.7	36.9	49.2	50.8

#	POST OFFICE NAME	2009 Per Capita Income	2009 HH Income Base	2009 Household Income Distribution (%): Less than $25,000	$25,000 to $49,999	$50,000 to $99,999	$100,000 to $149,999	$150,000 or More	Median Household Income: 2009	2014	2009 National Centile	2009 State Centile	2009 Home Value Base	2009 Home Value Distribution (%): Less than $50,000	$50,000 to $89,999	$90,000 to $174,999	$175,000 to $399,999	$400,000 or More	2009 Median Home Value
75001	ADDISON	48621	7864	9.0	23.0	41.8	13.5	12.6	67097	68841	85	88	1431	0.0	2.7	19.3	73.9	4.1	241882
75002	ALLEN	42742	21025	4.8	11.2	28.1	30.9	25.0	107189	112979	98	98	17554	1.5	1.9	32.9	53.5	10.1	205719
75006	CARROLLTON	29044	17398	9.6	22.3	45.1	13.9	9.1	67426	69026	85	89	9745	6.1	13.3	58.9	21.2	0.5	124416
75007	CARROLLTON	36276	19827	5.4	13.1	38.5	26.6	16.4	88777	101119	95	96	13208	0.7	0.8	46.7	49.5	2.2	177927
75009	CELINA	31832	2852	14.3	23.7	31.1	19.3	11.5	64599	59368	83	87	2147	9.5	15.4	28.0	30.3	16.7	162093
75010	CARROLLTON	38138	7808	6.5	11.2	39.9	28.5	13.9	88487	101297	95	96	4592	8.5	3.8	24.6	60.5	2.6	196454
75013	ALLEN	54950	9307	3.0	7.8	15.1	30.7	43.4	138627	139838	99	100	7909	1.5	1.6	6.5	65.4	24.9	290247
75019	COPPELL	52823	13122	3.6	8.7	29.0	18.8	39.9	125046	121957	99	99	9322	2.4	2.7	25.3	55.1	14.6	238406
75020	DENISON	22954	8997	26.0	28.9	33.4	8.2	3.5	45217	48698	49	59	6099	25.0	37.9	28.3	8.1	0.8	71589
75021	DENISON	19516	3248	33.4	26.6	31.1	5.9	3.0	39387	43958	31	40	2489	32.5	29.8	28.0	8.8	0.8	70746
75022	FLOWER MOUND	58549	6900	3.4	5.3	18.2	25.2	47.9	145492	145951	100	100	6208	4.2	1.4	5.2	66.5	22.7	309989
75023	PLANO	43418	19331	6.0	11.8	33.6	29.4	19.2	96664	101813	96	97	12869	1.5	1.5	39.0	54.8	3.3	192185
75024	PLANO	59933	13587	5.2	9.5	28.8	25.2	31.4	110148	114606	98	98	6983	3.8	0.6	3.0	73.6	19.0	294443
75025	PLANO	52762	19166	3.5	7.4	19.4	28.3	41.4	133110	136306	99	99	14194	2.3	0.8	7.2	73.4	16.4	284475
75028	FLOWER MOUND	44080	14203	3.2	5.6	27.0	32.9	31.3	125226	126436	99	99	12372	4.2	1.5	25.4	62.1	6.9	214300
75032	ROCKWALL	39773	9841	6.9	17.9	30.6	22.9	21.7	88780	96443	95	96	8235	7.1	4.8	21.9	42.9	23.3	240462
75034	FRISCO	40042	22409	7.8	15.1	28.8	25.7	22.6	95872	102950	96	97	17728	1.6	6.2	35.6	40.6	15.9	194352
75035	FRISCO	46827	17143	2.2	5.7	26.4	40.4	25.2	116992	123186	98	99	14764	0.6	0.5	15.8	76.0	7.0	225893
75038	IRVING	34576	13422	12.6	29.2	43.1	9.6	5.5	57329	60385	74	81	1536	3.7	9.8	43.4	21.1	21.9	158886
75039	IRVING	73637	4534	4.9	12.4	42.5	22.8	17.4	82650	84889	93	95	1694	0.5	13.0	24.9	21.7	39.9	317788
75040	GARLAND	22245	17104	11.3	23.5	44.9	14.4	5.9	64739	66506	83	87	12931	7.2	34.0	53.9	4.7	0.2	101128
75041	GARLAND	19252	10543	17.5	33.3	38.6	7.7	2.9	49299	52897	60	68	5872	5.9	44.5	45.0	4.4	0.3	89723
75042	GARLAND	18254	11923	18.6	29.7	40.6	8.2	2.9	51529	55108	65	73	6573	1.9	42.9	51.9	2.9	0.3	93416
75043	GARLAND	26610	21198	11.3	26.0	44.1	13.2	5.3	63348	65084	82	86	12183	1.9	22.6	65.4	9.7	0.4	112580
75044	GARLAND	35276	14666	6.8	17.0	42.3	19.3	14.6	78897	79300	92	93	10157	0.4	10.1	62.7	24.8	2.0	123061
75048	SACHSE	30908	5837	7.2	13.9	43.2	25.0	10.8	81808	83336	93	94	4899	7.8	7.3	55.8	28.1	0.9	141533
75050	GRAND PRAIRIE	23445	14644	17.3	30.3	39.0	8.7	4.7	52358	55742	67	75	6778	21.8	34.2	33.8	9.1	1.1	77415
75051	GRAND PRAIRIE	16526	10746	28.1	28.2	34.8	6.9	2.0	44339	47789	46	57	5820	17.0	57.1	23.6	2.0	0.3	71466
75052	GRAND PRAIRIE	28102	28042	8.2	16.1	46.5	20.1	9.1	75624	77828	90	92	20457	2.1	18.6	65.8	13.2	0.3	118433
75054	GRAND PRAIRIE	46564	1569	3.3	10.5	40.7	24.0	21.5	92763	90688	96	97	1409	1.4	3.7	56.8	34.3	3.8	148464
75056	THE COLONY	36430	15376	5.0	11.3	39.7	26.7	17.3	90162	101202	95	96	10920	1.2	6.2	56.9	29.9	5.8	145996
75057	LEWISVILLE	25092	5062	15.7	27.1	41.4	11.8	4.0	57868	55762	75	82	2000	36.6	18.3	32.9	11.1	1.3	76471
75058	GUNTER	18061	759	20.7	29.2	39.0	7.9	3.2	50056	51099	61	70	567	14.1	28.0	33.7	19.8	4.4	104808
75060	IRVING	20348	15086	17.8	26.6	42.6	10.6	2.4	56154	60057	73	80	8904	11.1	31.3	54.5	2.7	0.4	97841
75061	IRVING	20157	18693	18.1	33.2	37.2	8.2	3.3	48766	52235	58	68	6994	10.9	26.2	48.9	13.5	0.4	105469
75062	IRVING	27306	15401	12.0	27.4	44.5	10.8	5.3	60401	62433	78	84	7108	1.6	21.3	65.4	10.9	0.8	111718
75063	IRVING	51962	15007	5.4	14.4	44.5	17.8	17.9	79448	80699	92	94	4973	1.1	0.9	20.8	68.4	8.8	232023
75065	LAKE DALLAS	28191	3480	12.9	24.5	37.1	18.4	7.1	63021	58241	81	86	2399	20.3	8.7	40.5	26.6	4.0	133648
75067	LEWISVILLE	34935	25437	8.7	19.2	41.2	21.4	9.5	72436	74319	88	91	10057	2.5	3.2	53.7	39.6	0.9	157793
75068	LITTLE ELM	25966	10180	13.5	21.6	38.4	19.3	7.1	64989	59866	83	87	9173	4.8	12.7	43.6	29.2	9.6	148322
75069	MCKINNEY	28247	12796	18.3	27.3	30.1	14.2	10.2	56850	55560	74	81	6756	12.8	16.3	30.0	28.6	12.3	144512
75070	MCKINNEY	55689	25160	1.3	6.3	23.1	32.3	37.0	128162	131732	99	99	21523	0.0	0.3	15.2	68.8	15.7	244935
75071	MCKINNEY	44073	11176	8.1	16.9	27.8	25.8	21.5	93329	100900	96	97	8788	3.3	4.1	32.8	47.9	11.8	202751
75074	PLANO	31475	17027	10.8	22.1	35.6	21.7	9.8	68617	66191	86	89	9704	3.8	6.9	54.0	32.4	3.0	147247
75075	PLANO	40843	15273	7.8	15.3	33.4	27.6	15.9	86136	89639	94	96	9160	1.0	1.8	28.5	66.7	2.1	198944
75076	POTTSBORO	25922	3202	18.2	28.3	40.6	8.4	4.4	52465	53137	67	75	2602	18.7	37.1	26.0	16.8	1.3	81556
75077	LEWISVILLE	43632	12838	2.9	7.5	31.6	32.6	25.3	110422	114325	98	98	11019	0.9	0.6	26.6	61.2	10.7	215233
75078	PROSPER	32610	2449	11.5	18.6	31.4	23.7	14.8	76063	79588	90	92	2217	3.2	8.8	38.6	36.5	12.9	173117
75080	RICHARDSON	31865	16644	11.3	22.3	40.3	16.8	9.2	67974	68788	86	89	9960	1.9	6.8	56.7	32.4	2.2	145285
75081	RICHARDSON	32391	12882	9.6	18.7	42.0	20.1	9.5	72748	74528	88	91	7734	2.0	6.9	73.6	16.8	0.7	140535
75082	RICHARDSON	53529	7918	4.1	9.3	24.8	27.4	34.4	120136	123281	98	99	5553	3.5	2.1	17.1	65.7	11.6	247573
75087	ROCKWALL	36548	10346	9.4	15.0	32.8	25.7	17.1	86594	94998	94	96	7996	3.3	6.6	19.9	59.8	10.4	232363
75088	ROWLETT	34026	8425	5.0	10.1	43.1	24.9	16.8	88705	90255	95	96	7268	1.6	5.1	59.8	31.1	2.3	143988
75089	ROWLETT	30577	8395	4.2	8.7	52.0	24.6	10.5	82641	83649	93	94	7416	1.9	5.1	70.1	22.1	0.8	138429
75090	SHERMAN	18165	8375	31.0	28.3	32.1	6.8	1.8	40518	45447	34	44	5406	35.0	34.2	24.4	5.6	0.8	64775
75092	SHERMAN	26846	9203	20.4	29.1	35.4	9.9	5.2	50387	51589	62	71	5372	10.5	24.3	48.3	15.0	1.9	111035
75093	PLANO	71470	21763	5.0	11.2	24.3	18.3	41.2	123162	129633	99	99	12675	0.5	0.9	8.4	38.9	51.4	409852
75094	PLANO	46676	5793	3.6	12.3	25.9	30.4	27.9	111485	116753	98	98	5428	3.1	2.4	13.6	72.0	8.9	238052
75098	WYLIE	31463	15271	8.0	16.7	40.1	25.6	9.6	76254	74638	90	93	12582	7.6	7.7	44.0	35.4	5.4	158592
75102	BARRY	18729	336	23.8	31.3	39.6	4.5	0.9	47308	46743	55	65	278	26.3	27.7	36.7	9.4	0.0	80000
75103	CANTON	20174	6189	28.6	29.3	33.4	5.9	2.7	42240	43485	40	51	5102	15.8	21.8	37.5	20.3	4.6	111268
75104	CEDAR HILL	28115	14216	7.4	17.8	47.9	19.1	7.8	74195	76721	89	91	11125	2.2	19.9	65.6	10.4	1.9	115812
75105	CHATFIELD	17596	146	26.0	35.6	32.9	3.4	2.1	41848	43180	39	49	118	29.7	28.0	28.8	10.2	3.4	78000
75109	CORSICANA	20037	1307	24.9	27.5	34.6	8.6	4.5	47061	46673	54	64	1113	21.7	23.4	28.7	19.6	6.7	97500
75110	CORSICANA	17360	10589	36.5	27.8	27.7	5.3	2.7	35649	38514	20	26	6653	25.0	26.5	36.2	10.6	1.7	87372
75114	CRANDALL	21951	1525	13.8	20.8	48.8	12.2	4.4	59563	59530	77	84	1240	12.1	24.9	45.6	16.3	1.0	108852
75115	DESOTO	30066	17238	11.4	19.8	41.4	17.7	9.7	71422	73619	88	90	12249	4.3	10.9	63.7	19.3	1.7	126073
75116	DUNCANVILLE	24111	6688	13.2	28.8	41.8	11.8	4.4	58209	60982	75	82	4243	3.3	37.0	54.9	4.2	0.4	101219
75117	EDGEWOOD	20575	1967	29.3	24.7	34.8	7.5	3.8	46986	46686	54	64	1509	17.3	26.6	35.5	18.4	2.2	104473
75119	ENNIS	19761	9543	23.1	27.0	38.1	7.8	3.9	49881	49640	61	70	6354	18.4	30.6	36.7	12.1	2.2	91491
75124	EUSTACE	18566	1397	28.7	28.9	35.1	4.7	2.5	43901	45699	45	56	1093	27.4	26.0	28.7	15.2	2.7	83852
75125	FERRIS	22231	2269	16.9	26.6	39.5	8.8	8.2	57145	58023	74	81	1782	22.7	42.4	26.6	5.7	2.5	74449
75126	FORNEY	27295	9996	9.4	17.5	43.3	19.4	10.3	75659	75893	90	92	8771	3.3	11.9	46.0	36.8	1.9	146037
75127	FRUITVALE	16423	825	32.5	33.1	28.7	4.5	1.2	38400	41495	28	35	669	22.1	24.5	35.3	14.2	3.9	94891
75134	LANCASTER	18609	6464	20.9	31.0	38.8	6.7	2.5	48566	51428	58	67	4165	7.8	54.4	34.8	2.5	0.6	82083
75135	CADDO MILLS	20178	1751	19.3	27.9	42.9	7.3	2.6	52229	52554	66	74	1412	22.3	32.0	39.2	6.2	0.3	84245
75137	DUNCANVILLE	30596	6813	7.1	23.1	41.8	18.3	9.7	71907	73729	88	90	4884	3.0	21.6	57.9	16.5	0.9	119531
75140	GRAND SALINE	17368	2252	32.2	30.2	31.6	4.4	1.5	39259	42100	31	39	1685	18.9	31.9	34.6	10.9	3.7	88858
75141	HUTCHINS	22534	997	22.0	29.3	38.7	7.5	2.5	48808	52623	58	68	757	50.9	37.5	11.0	0.7	0.0	49476
75142	KAUFMAN	19767	6242	20.1	26.9	42.4	7.1	3.4	51720	53991	65	74	4806	17.7	29.8	39.5	11.1	1.9	93667
75143	KEMP	20547	5236	28.0	27.7	34.5	6.9	2.9	44902	47133	48	58	4324	28.9	26.9	30.7	11.7	1.8	81336
75144	KERENS	17303	1300	33.9	30.5	30.0	3.8	1.7	36584	39139	22	29	932	29.8	31.4	29.8	8.7	0.2	74000
75146	LANCASTER	24492	6605	11.6	24.9	46.7	12.4	4.4	61593	63564	79	85	4519	11.4	24.9	56.7	6.7	0.4	104298
75147	MABANK	18802	1516	28.1	25.3	38.5	6.1	2.0	45806	50141	51	61	1040	30.9	28.8	34.3	5.2	0.8	71406
75148	MALAKOFF	21121	2476	33.8	29.6	25.6	6.7	4.2	37964	40023	27	34	1894	29.0	23.7	27.1	17.3	2.9	85189
75149	MESQUITE	23281	18926	13.4	24.7	45.6	11.5	4.7	61717	63545	80	85	12398	7.5	41.2	45.4	5.3	0.6	91667
75150	MESQUITE	26612	22483	11.8	26.8	43.5	12.8	5.1	61268	63199	79	85	12021	2.5	32.2	60.9	4.2	0.2	104423
75152	PALMER	21000	1081	16.2	27.8	42.6	9.0	4.3	56241	58260	73	80	879	24.5	32.9	26.7	14.0	1.9	80077
75153	POWELL	19624	80	28.8	33.8	26.3	6.3	5.0	40905	42759	36	46	67	17.9	20.9	44.8	14.9	1.5	101042
75154	RED OAK	26277	11946	10.9	19.5	46.8	15.6	7.1	69579	73941	87	89	9440	8.8	16.0	54.5	18.3	2.6	123313
75155	RICE	15933	914	26.5	34.8	33.6	3.5	1.6	41771	42986	39	49	737	29.7	27.1	30.0	10.2	3.0	78939
75156	MABANK	23092	7073	28.8	29.9	31.2	5.6	4.5	42263	44946	40	51	5873	26.5	22.4	32.3	16.1	2.8	91819
75158	SCURRY	22093	1743	15.0	24.2	47.1	9.5	4.1	57338	57944	74	81	1508	16.4	27.9	38.1	14.9	2.7	99053
75159	SEAGOVILLE	20265	5468	19.5	27.0	41.0	9.4	3.2	53165	56627	68	76	4236	31.7	34.5	21.9	10.0	1.8	71089
75160	TERRELL	19779	8300	27.5	23.9	36.1	8.4	4.2	47841	51215	56	66	5347	16.1	30.8	36.7	15.1	1.3	95376
	TEXAS	24551		22.3	25.0	34.3	11.1	7.3	52382	54495				16.5	22.7	36.5	19.7	4.6	109784
	UNITED STATES	27277		20.9	24.4	35.3	11.7	7.6	54719	56938				9.3	13.1	31.6	32.6	13.5	162279

ZIP CODE		FINANCIAL SERVICES				THE HOME						ENTERTAINMENT						PERSONAL			
						Home Improvements		Furnishings													
#	POST OFFICE NAME	Auto Loan	Home Loan	Investments	Retirement Plans	Home Repair	Lawn & Garden	Computers & Hardware-Personal	Major Appliances	TV, Radio, Sound Equipment	Furniture	Dine out/Carry out	Sports Equipment	Fees & Tickets	Toys & Games	Travel	Cable TV	Apparel & Services	Auto Repairs	Health Insurance	Pets & Supplies
75001	ADDISON	137	107	98	117	100	98	138	111	134	136	137	98	125	139	119	128	97	127	109	139
75002	ALLEN	184	212	185	216	206	180	185	184	173	202	176	150	202	185	190	162	128	174	158	209
75006	CARROLLTON	120	114	101	114	110	103	119	111	115	122	118	88	116	119	113	112	83	115	105	130
75007	CARROLLTON	153	167	147	169	161	145	154	149	146	163	149	120	162	154	155	140	106	146	134	173
75009	CELINA	132	147	129	144	142	134	130	133	126	136	128	103	137	131	134	124	90	128	124	154
75010	CARROLLTON	157	155	131	156	145	131	153	142	145	161	149	117	151	155	145	138	105	143	128	167
75013	ALLEN	242	290	250	299	282	239	244	245	225	273	229	204	274	243	255	206	168	225	202	274
75019	COPPELL	228	255	225	264	248	216	230	224	215	249	220	186	249	230	234	201	159	215	193	256
75020	DENISON	83	77	78	77	76	88	79	83	83	75	81	62	75	82	77	87	56	82	91	98
75021	DENISON	79	68	70	68	68	82	70	76	74	65	73	58	63	75	67	79	50	74	82	91
75022	FLOWER MOUND	269	327	289	336	320	272	272	276	252	304	256	228	309	270	289	232	188	253	229	309
75023	PLANO	160	180	168	184	178	161	163	162	155	173	158	127	176	161	169	149	113	157	147	187
75024	PLANO	212	211	187	221	202	183	212	195	201	222	206	164	215	213	204	191	147	197	175	229
75025	PLANO	231	264	229	273	255	219	232	228	216	255	220	190	254	232	237	200	161	215	192	258
75028	FLOWER MOUND	203	241	205	244	232	198	203	204	188	226	191	168	225	203	210	173	139	188	169	229
75032	ROCKWALL	165	192	189	197	195	180	168	173	162	178	164	133	186	166	180	159	118	165	161	200
75034	FRISCO	174	192	171	190	187	169	167	172	161	182	163	134	178	170	171	155	116	162	153	196
75035	FRISCO	188	227	202	231	222	190	191	193	177	211	180	157	214	189	201	164	131	178	162	217
75038	IRVING	112	73	65	82	67	70	110	84	108	106	111	74	92	112	88	105	77	102	86	107
75039	IRVING	158	138	154	156	140	130	179	144	171	171	177	128	172	171	167	165	129	163	143	178
75040	GARLAND	109	113	96	109	108	100	106	106	103	112	105	80	106	107	104	100	73	104	98	121
75041	GARLAND	84	77	67	75	74	72	84	78	83	85	85	61	80	85	79	82	59	83	78	92
75042	GARLAND	86	84	71	81	80	75	87	82	84	89	86	64	84	86	83	81	60	85	78	95
75043	GARLAND	109	100	87	101	95	94	106	99	104	108	106	78	101	108	99	103	74	103	97	118
75044	GARLAND	144	153	132	152	146	133	141	138	135	150	138	108	145	142	139	130	97	135	125	161
75048	SACHSE	141	152	127	148	144	131	134	136	129	144	131	106	138	137	134	124	92	129	122	156
75050	GRAND PRAIRIE	95	81	71	82	78	75	94	84	92	95	94	67	87	95	85	89	66	91	81	99
75051	GRAND PRAIRIE	76	71	62	68	69	66	75	72	74	77	75	55	71	76	71	73	53	75	70	83
75052	GRAND PRAIRIE	129	136	113	133	129	115	126	123	119	135	122	98	127	127	123	114	86	120	110	141
75054	GRAND PRAIRIE	179	207	181	204	199	173	178	180	167	194	170	143	192	178	183	158	122	169	155	203
75056	THE COLONY	166	181	149	177	171	151	161	160	152	175	155	127	166	163	159	143	109	152	139	182
75057	LEWISVILLE	105	83	72	85	78	77	101	87	99	102	101	71	90	103	88	96	70	97	85	106
75058	GUNTER	89	90	78	89	87	90	82	87	83	84	84	65	83	86	82	85	58	84	86	102
75060	IRVING	92	88	75	85	84	80	91	87	89	93	92	67	88	92	86	88	64	90	84	101
75061	IRVING	86	73	66	73	71	67	87	77	85	87	87	62	80	87	79	82	62	85	74	90
75062	IRVING	104	93	84	97	89	89	107	94	105	105	107	77	102	107	99	103	75	102	95	114
75063	IRVING	161	135	123	146	128	123	160	136	155	161	158	116	149	162	143	149	112	149	131	166
75065	LAKE DALLAS	117	118	103	117	114	107	112	111	109	117	111	86	112	114	110	107	77	109	104	130
75067	LEWISVILLE	134	111	93	115	103	99	130	112	126	132	129	94	119	133	114	121	90	122	107	135
75068	LITTLE ELM	122	127	106	123	120	114	114	117	111	121	113	90	115	118	112	109	78	111	108	135
75069	MCKINNEY	119	113	102	112	110	106	115	111	114	119	115	86	112	117	110	112	81	113	107	130
75070	MCKINNEY	236	287	252	295	281	237	239	242	221	267	225	201	271	238	253	203	166	222	200	271
75071	MCKINNEY	179	202	174	200	194	172	175	177	166	191	168	140	186	176	178	157	120	167	155	201
75074	PLANO	127	129	114	130	124	116	128	122	124	132	126	97	128	129	124	120	89	123	114	142
75075	PLANO	145	161	154	166	159	148	150	147	145	157	147	116	161	148	156	141	105	146	139	172
75076	POTTSBORO	100	85	110	82	91	104	84	99	88	84	87	71	76	86	86	94	58	94	102	116
75077	LEWISVILLE	189	227	204	227	221	193	192	195	180	208	184	155	213	190	203	171	132	184	170	222
75078	PROSPER	152	167	135	160	156	137	147	146	138	159	141	116	151	149	145	130	99	139	127	166
75080	RICHARDSON	114	113	111	116	113	110	124	112	118	120	120	89	121	118	118	116	85	117	112	133
75081	RICHARDSON	122	129	119	132	127	119	123	121	120	128	122	94	128	123	125	117	86	120	116	141
75082	RICHARDSON	206	232	213	242	228	201	211	206	199	226	203	169	229	209	217	188	147	199	181	236
75087	ROCKWALL	152	167	151	169	164	151	149	152	143	160	145	118	158	150	153	139	103	144	139	174
75088	ROWLETT	155	178	153	177	171	152	154	155	146	166	148	123	166	154	158	139	106	147	137	177
75089	ROWLETT	140	160	133	156	151	133	139	139	130	150	133	111	147	139	141	124	94	132	121	158
75090	SHERMAN	75	65	60	65	63	71	70	70	73	68	73	54	64	74	65	76	50	72	75	84
75092	SHERMAN	94	87	82	89	85	91	92	90	93	90	93	70	89	94	89	95	65	92	95	107
75093	PLANO	260	286	273	299	285	253	267	258	253	285	257	210	289	265	274	241	187	253	231	297
75094	PLANO	195	224	194	228	218	192	191	195	180	211	183	158	209	193	197	169	132	180	166	220
75098	WYLIE	139	147	122	143	139	130	132	134	128	140	129	104	133	135	130	124	90	128	123	154
75102	BARRY	83	72	71	70	72	79	69	76	73	71	73	56	64	75	67	76	49	73	77	91
75103	CANTON	88	68	86	66	69	89	69	83	75	66	74	62	58	75	68	82	49	78	87	99
75104	CEDAR HILL	126	135	115	132	128	117	123	122	118	131	120	95	125	124	122	113	84	118	111	141
75105	CHATFIELD	83	60	69	58	59	79	62	72	69	60	67	55	50	72	56	75	45	68	76	88
75109	CORSICANA	92	84	75	82	82	86	79	84	82	83	83	61	75	86	76	85	56	82	84	100
75110	CORSICANA	72	62	58	61	61	69	66	67	70	65	69	50	61	70	62	73	48	68	73	80
75114	CRANDALL	108	108	90	104	102	99	99	101	98	105	100	75	97	103	95	98	68	98	96	118
75115	DESOTO	119	130	117	130	126	118	120	119	117	125	118	93	126	121	122	114	84	117	113	139
75116	DUNCANVILLE	97	100	88	99	97	94	98	95	96	100	97	73	98	98	96	94	68	96	94	111
75117	EDGEWOOD	92	66	94	64	69	95	70	88	78	64	76	66	56	77	68	86	50	81	93	104
75119	ENNIS	91	84	75	81	82	84	85	86	86	86	86	64	79	88	80	87	59	85	86	101
75124	EUSTACE	82	68	84	65	71	84	67	79	72	67	71	57	60	70	67	77	47	75	83	93
75125	FERRIS	111	101	88	99	96	103	101	102	104	103	104	78	96	107	95	106	71	103	104	123
75126	FORNEY	126	140	118	137	133	121	124	124	118	132	120	97	129	125	125	114	84	119	112	143
75127	FRUITVALE	81	58	83	56	60	82	59	76	66	55	65	57	48	66	59	73	43	69	79	90
75134	LANCASTER	83	79	66	76	75	72	80	77	79	83	80	59	77	81	76	78	56	79	74	90
75135	CADDO MILLS	96	82	84	80	81	93	81	90	86	81	85	66	73	88	77	90	58	86	93	106
75137	DUNCANVILLE	125	136	123	136	132	124	125	124	121	131	123	96	131	125	127	118	86	122	117	145
75140	GRAND SALINE	78	60	74	59	61	79	63	74	69	59	67	55	54	69	61	75	45	70	79	88
75141	HUTCHINS	88	78	78	75	76	86	78	84	82	78	81	62	72	83	75	85	55	82	87	99
75142	KAUFMAN	94	87	76	83	84	86	84	87	85	87	86	64	79	88	79	87	59	85	86	102
75143	KEMP	86	74	84	71	76	87	73	83	77	74	76	60	66	77	72	81	51	79	86	97
75144	KERENS	76	55	73	54	57	77	60	72	66	55	64	54	49	66	57	72	43	68	77	85
75146	LANCASTER	104	101	86	101	96	95	102	97	100	103	101	77	99	104	97	98	70	99	95	116
75147	MABANK	82	72	70	69	71	77	72	76	75	73	74	57	66	77	68	77	51	75	77	90
75148	MALAKOFF	81	70	83	67	74	85	72	81	76	72	74	57	66	73	72	81	50	79	89	95
75149	MESQUITE	101	101	85	99	96	90	101	96	97	104	99	75	99	101	97	95	69	98	91	112
75150	MESQUITE	105	97	83	98	92	90	104	95	102	105	104	76	100	106	97	100	72	100	94	114
75152	PALMER	105	100	87	97	97	100	94	98	96	98	97	73	91	100	91	98	66	96	98	117
75153	POWELL	95	68	98	66	71	97	70	89	78	65	77	67	56	77	69	86	51	82	93	106
75154	RED OAK	119	127	109	125	122	114	115	116	112	122	114	90	119	117	115	109	79	112	108	135
75155	RICE	83	60	69	58	59	79	62	72	69	60	68	56	50	72	56	75	45	68	76	88
75156	MABANK	85	78	100	73	85	93	76	89	80	79	78	60	72	75	81	84	52	85	95	102
75158	SCURRY	106	98	87	95	95	100	92	98	96	96	96	71	87	100	88	98	65	95	98	116
75159	SEAGOVILLE	98	89	85	87	87	94	87	92	89	88	89	69	81	92	84	91	61	90	92	109
75160	TERRELL	87	79	69	79	76	81	82	80	85	82	85	61	78	87	77	87	59	82	85	97
	TEXAS	104	96	90	94	93	94	99	97	99	101	100	75	94	101	94	99	70	99	96	114
	UNITED STATES	100	100	100	100	100	100	100	100	100	100	100	100	100	100	100	100	100	100	100	100

ZIP CODE #	POST OFFICE NAME	COUNTY FIPS CODE	POPULATION 2000	POPULATION 2009	POPULATION 2014	2000-2009 ANNUAL RATE % Rate	2000-2009 ANNUAL RATE State Centile	HOUSEHOLDS 2000	HOUSEHOLDS 2009	HOUSEHOLDS 2014	HOUSEHOLDS % Annual Rate 2000-2009	HOUSEHOLDS 2009 Average HH Size	FAMILIES 2000	FAMILIES 2009	FAMILIES % Annual Rate 2000-2009
75161	TERRELL	257	5695	6651	7392	1.7	73	2012	2283	2531	1.4	2.90	1636	1813	1.1
75163	TRINIDAD	213	2552	2700	2700	0.6	46	1112	1161	1160	0.5	2.33	774	793	0.3
75165	WAXAHACHIE	139	29339	37959	43010	2.8	85	9911	12816	14555	2.8	2.86	7677	9867	2.8
75166	LAVON	085	569	2239	2973	16.0	99	196	815	1090	16.7	2.75	157	621	16.0
75167	WAXAHACHIE	139	5174	9090	11169	6.3	96	1660	2908	3578	6.2	3.09	1398	2418	6.1
75169	WILLS POINT	467	12536	13206	13502	0.6	46	4730	4952	5060	0.5	2.64	3515	3624	0.3
75172	WILMER	113	2817	3037	3173	0.8	52	871	926	962	0.7	3.28	653	683	0.5
75173	NEVADA	085	4452	5493	6966	2.3	81	1491	1864	2378	2.4	2.95	1208	1435	1.9
75180	MESQUITE	113	18852	21339	22532	1.3	65	5918	6594	6915	1.2	3.22	4680	5147	1.0
75181	MESQUITE	113	17096	23920	26947	3.7	90	5363	7320	8167	3.4	3.27	4611	6245	3.3
75182	SUNNYVALE	113	2991	3762	4315	2.5	82	1038	1279	1454	2.3	2.94	854	1042	2.2
75189	ROYSE CITY	231	10155	19713	26378	7.4	97	3400	6461	8610	7.2	3.04	2785	5153	6.9
75201	DALLAS	113	2855	5157	5825	6.6	96	1673	2906	3328	6.2	1.60	352	710	7.9
75202	DALLAS	113	1696	2347	2647	3.6	90	693	1092	1263	5.0	1.60	138	230	5.7
75203	DALLAS	113	19671	20983	21586	0.7	49	5933	6180	6302	0.4	3.34	4060	4144	0.2
75204	DALLAS	113	21514	26672	28916	2.4	82	10121	12925	14159	2.7	2.01	3574	4057	1.4
75205	DALLAS	113	24181	24292	24359	0.0	25	9943	9617	9570	-0.4	2.21	4962	4658	-0.7
75206	DALLAS	113	39801	40748	41345	0.3	34	20463	20644	20829	0.1	1.97	6802	6514	-0.5
75207	DALLAS	113	8116	9052	9053	1.2	63	4	5	5	2.4	2.20	1	1	0.0
75208	DALLAS	113	35977	35925	35973	0.0	25	11112	10775	10690	-0.3	3.31	7264	6900	-0.6
75209	DALLAS	113	14899	15482	15934	0.4	37	6596	6655	6771	0.1	2.31	3482	3457	-0.1
75210	DALLAS	113	9360	8724	8602	-0.8	6	3352	3075	3008	-0.9	2.84	2182	1953	-1.2
75211	DALLAS	113	68702	75805	78784	1.1	61	18809	20217	20903	0.8	3.73	14506	15310	0.6
75212	DALLAS	113	22167	24029	24985	0.9	55	5883	6294	6508	0.7	3.77	4724	4996	0.6
75214	DALLAS	113	35500	36373	36860	0.3	34	16091	16119	16204	0.0	2.21	8048	7805	-0.3
75215	DALLAS	113	18728	21059	22017	1.3	65	6925	7535	7792	0.9	2.71	4093	4267	0.5
75216	DALLAS	113	49080	50924	51982	0.4	37	16199	16527	16753	0.2	3.05	11868	11894	0.0
75217	DALLAS	113	68171	72489	74311	0.7	49	19280	19858	20203	0.3	3.65	15725	15984	0.2
75218	DALLAS	113	21732	22348	22805	0.3	34	9747	10019	10219	0.3	2.21	5710	5666	-0.1
75219	DALLAS	113	22488	24857	26158	1.1	61	10963	12174	12820	1.1	2.04	3853	4037	0.5
75220	DALLAS	113	50432	54176	54535	0.8	52	14907	14695	14692	-0.2	3.68	10785	10408	-0.4
75223	DALLAS	113	15633	18124	19250	1.6	71	4546	5086	5340	1.2	3.54	3218	3551	1.1
75224	DALLAS	113	32415	34267	34918	0.6	46	9702	9814	9915	0.1	3.46	7240	7198	-0.1
75225	DALLAS	113	20413	20535	20682	0.1	27	8529	8316	8300	-0.3	2.45	5519	5284	-0.5
75226	DALLAS	113	2808	3108	3183	1.1	61	1107	1240	1285	1.2	1.97	461	467	0.1
75227	DALLAS	113	50873	58194	60989	1.5	69	15958	17396	18084	0.9	3.30	11923	12783	0.8
75228	DALLAS	113	65757	68398	69729	0.4	37	24131	24377	24664	0.1	2.77	15742	15531	-0.1
75229	DALLAS	113	32007	32969	33417	0.3	34	11639	11561	11603	-0.1	2.82	8276	8076	-0.3
75230	DALLAS	113	27311	27707	27969	0.2	30	13386	13169	13175	-0.2	2.09	6720	6501	-0.4
75231	DALLAS	113	52907	53973	53653	0.2	30	22352	20764	20443	-0.8	2.56	11314	10217	-1.1
75232	DALLAS	113	28453	29717	30588	0.5	42	9732	9973	10167	0.3	2.98	7494	7596	0.1
75233	DALLAS	113	13685	16093	17148	1.8	75	4166	4690	4946	1.3	3.39	3101	3440	1.1
75234	DALLAS	113	27774	27840	27998	0.0	25	9740	9542	9521	-0.2	2.90	6980	6711	-0.4
75235	DALLAS	113	17544	20683	21773	1.8	75	5649	6390	6681	1.3	3.08	3208	3650	1.4
75236	DALLAS	113	7205	11412	13198	5.1	94	2605	3932	4510	4.6	2.74	1877	2788	4.4
75237	DALLAS	113	15463	17697	18595	1.5	69	6755	7492	7801	1.1	2.36	3943	4267	0.9
75238	DALLAS	113	31770	31693	31824	0.0	25	12997	12559	12504	-0.4	2.49	8412	8002	-0.5
75240	DALLAS	113	30520	31331	31659	0.3	34	10966	10828	10936	-0.1	2.89	6370	6137	-0.4
75241	DALLAS	113	26787	33831	36857	2.6	83	8247	10356	11267	2.5	3.04	6388	7880	2.3
75243	DALLAS	113	58748	60024	60512	0.2	30	26853	26394	26348	-0.2	2.24	13723	13097	-0.5
75244	DALLAS	113	12006	12673	13094	0.6	46	4955	5110	5243	0.3	2.47	3322	3370	0.2
75246	DALLAS	113	4037	3958	3948	-0.2	19	1161	1089	1073	-0.7	3.30	620	568	-0.9
75247	DALLAS	113	254	282	282	1.1	61	23	22	22	-0.5	1.86	13	12	-0.9
75248	DALLAS	113	33759	34582	35111	0.3	34	15793	15943	16089	0.1	2.17	9290	9119	-0.2
75249	DALLAS	113	9181	12790	14404	3.6	90	2865	3984	4474	3.6	3.19	2406	3295	3.5
75251	DALLAS	113	1542	2339	2666	4.6	93	919	1370	1555	4.4	1.66	332	516	4.9
75252	DALLAS	085	22491	24940	28123	1.1	61	11646	13096	14855	1.3	1.90	5458	5414	-0.1
75253	DALLAS	113	15655	17388	18275	1.1	61	5109	5607	5859	1.0	3.09	3876	4172	0.8
75254	DALLAS	113	18518	18821	19025	0.2	30	9800	9622	9610	-0.2	1.94	3787	3676	-0.3
75261	DALLAS	439	3	3	4	0.0	25	1	1	1	0.0	3.00	1	1	0.0
75287	DALLAS	085	44631	51314	57862	1.5	69	24283	27813	31468	1.5	1.84	9551	9563	0.0
75401	GREENVILLE	231	17399	17681	17768	0.2	30	6248	6227	6257	0.0	2.78	4342	4235	-0.3
75402	GREENVILLE	231	14399	16345	17037	1.4	67	5831	6445	6704	1.1	2.47	4167	4535	0.9
75407	PRINCETON	085	9721	13787	16942	3.8	90	3424	5010	6213	4.2	2.74	2674	3697	3.6
75409	ANNA	085	4802	11894	16126	10.3	98	1660	4102	5577	10.3	2.90	1367	3227	9.7
75410	ALBA	499	4808	5823	6235	2.1	79	1911	2315	2483	2.1	2.52	1430	1706	1.9
75411	ARTHUR CITY	277	196	168	159	-1.7	1	86	75	71	-1.5	2.24	70	60	-1.7
75412	BAGWELL	387	953	901	869	-0.6	9	393	375	363	-0.5	2.40	299	282	-0.6
75414	BELLS	181	2803	3145	3317	1.3	65	1076	1198	1262	1.2	2.61	823	901	1.0
75415	BEN FRANKLIN	119	147	140	137	-0.5	11	51	49	48	-0.4	2.86	36	33	-0.9
75416	BLOSSOM	277	3713	3586	3528	-0.4	13	1418	1387	1371	-0.2	2.58	1108	1067	-0.4
75417	BOGATA	387	2785	2655	2575	-0.5	11	1168	1118	1087	-0.5	2.31	784	736	-0.7
75418	BONHAM	147	12974	13903	14277	0.8	52	4076	4367	4512	0.7	2.43	2770	2916	0.6
75420	BRASHEAR	223	267	302	317	1.3	65	120	136	143	1.4	2.22	90	101	1.3
75421	BROOKSTON	277	558	909	976	5.4	95	203	339	367	5.7	2.68	162	268	5.6
75422	CAMPBELL	231	2485	2667	2724	0.8	52	937	986	1006	0.6	2.70	724	751	0.4
75423	CELESTE	231	2359	2564	2639	0.9	55	848	902	927	0.7	2.84	670	703	0.5
75424	BLUE RIDGE	085	2884	3561	4200	2.3	81	1002	1271	1510	2.6	2.80	815	985	2.1
75426	CLARKSVILLE	387	6320	6195	6054	-0.2	19	2508	2456	2401	-0.2	2.43	1735	1672	-0.4
75428	COMMERCE	231	9425	10371	10600	1.0	58	3546	3737	3824	0.6	2.40	2050	2105	0.3
75431	COMO	223	2938	3323	3492	1.3	65	1017	1143	1202	1.3	2.87	788	876	1.2
75432	COOPER	119	3804	3910	3921	0.3	34	1475	1510	1511	0.3	2.52	1028	1037	0.1
75433	CUMBY	223	3348	3919	4165	1.7	73	1340	1570	1671	1.7	2.50	981	1132	1.6
75435	DEPORT	277	2066	1966	1917	-0.5	11	813	780	764	-0.4	2.43	627	595	-0.6
75436	DETROIT	387	1639	1569	1519	-0.5	11	644	621	604	-0.4	2.53	473	450	-0.5
75437	DIKE	223	254	272	278	0.7	49	96	103	105	0.8	2.64	77	81	0.5
75438	DODD CITY	147	1345	1510	1597	1.3	65	524	585	617	1.2	2.58	396	435	1.0
75439	ECTOR	147	857	955	1003	1.2	63	343	380	399	1.1	2.51	244	265	0.9
75440	EMORY	379	4206	5345	5878	2.6	83	1678	2139	2356	2.7	2.47	1231	1547	2.5
75442	FARMERSVILLE	085	7495	9620	11327	2.7	84	2651	3481	4135	3.0	2.74	2073	2581	2.4
75446	HONEY GROVE	147	2751	3619	4005	3.0	86	1089	1416	1565	2.9	2.49	751	961	2.7
75447	IVANHOE	147	873	981	1036	1.3	65	349	390	412	1.2	2.51	276	306	1.1
75448	KLONDIKE	119	709	677	663	-0.5	11	293	279	273	-0.5	2.43	205	192	-0.7
75449	LADONIA	147	1124	1060	1050	-0.6	9	446	414	409	-0.8	2.56	322	295	-0.9
75450	LAKE CREEK	119	51	55	56	0.8	52	19	20	21	0.6	2.75	14	15	0.7
	TEXAS					1.9					1.8	2.78			1.7
	UNITED STATES					1.0					1.1	2.59			0.9

ZIP CODE #	POST OFFICE NAME	RACE (%) White 2000	White 2009	Black 2000	Black 2009	Asian/Pacific 2000	Asian/Pacific 2009	% Hispanic Origin 2000	% Hispanic Origin 2009	2009 AGE DISTRIBUTION (%) 0-4	5-9	10-14	15-19	20-24	25-44	45-64	65-84	85+	18+	MEDIAN AGE 2009	% 2009 Males	% 2009 Females
75161	TERRELL	86.8	81.4	7.7	10.2	0.5	0.8	6.8	11.0	6.4	6.8	7.6	7.4	5.2	25.2	29.8	10.6	1.0	74.4	39.4	51.0	49.0
75163	TRINIDAD	91.0	88.3	5.2	6.4	0.1	0.1	4.4	6.6	4.5	4.7	4.9	5.2	4.6	17.4	30.4	25.5	2.7	82.8	51.9	48.7	51.3
75165	WAXAHACHIE	75.7	72.1	13.1	13.2	0.4	0.5	18.0	24.1	7.4	7.1	6.9	7.6	7.7	27.6	25.3	8.9	1.5	74.2	33.9	49.2	50.8
75166	LAVON	91.9	88.3	1.8	2.2	0.5	0.8	9.1	14.1	6.9	7.1	7.5	7.7	5.9	26.0	29.5	8.7	0.8	73.8	37.5	50.9	49.1
75167	WAXAHACHIE	88.0	84.0	2.3	3.1	0.2	0.2	15.3	20.6	8.4	8.4	8.3	7.6	5.6	28.4	25.2	7.1	1.0	70.0	33.4	50.2	49.8
75169	WILLS POINT	89.6	87.2	4.8	5.3	0.2	0.2	7.3	10.3	6.4	6.6	6.6	6.5	5.3	23.8	28.4	14.3	2.2	76.5	40.9	49.3	50.7
75172	WILMER	47.9	42.3	22.0	22.5	0.0	0.0	46.9	54.8	9.4	8.5	7.8	8.6	8.7	28.4	21.0	7.0	0.7	69.2	29.3	51.3	48.7
75173	NEVADA	92.0	88.5	1.4	1.9	0.3	0.5	9.6	14.5	7.3	7.2	7.4	7.5	5.9	27.3	28.3	8.4	0.7	73.5	36.3	50.5	49.5
75180	MESQUITE	61.1	55.0	19.8	19.3	0.7	0.8	26.5	36.7	9.5	8.6	8.0	8.7	8.7	29.4	20.6	6.0	0.6	68.8	28.7	48.8	51.2
75181	MESQUITE	70.5	64.2	16.7	18.4	5.1	6.1	11.3	17.5	9.7	9.2	8.8	7.9	5.6	31.7	23.3	3.7	0.3	67.4	31.3	48.4	51.6
75182	SUNNYVALE	86.3	83.5	6.5	6.6	2.3	3.0	7.0	10.4	5.1	5.7	6.4	7.6	5.8	22.8	34.2	11.4	1.0	78.0	42.5	48.5	51.5
75189	ROYSE CITY	87.9	82.4	3.4	4.6	0.6	1.0	14.4	22.0	7.3	7.5	7.7	7.5	5.7	27.0	27.9	8.5	0.9	72.8	36.4	50.6	49.4
75201	DALLAS	71.7	63.6	17.6	20.7	3.3	4.1	11.5	19.3	3.9	2.3	1.7	3.1	13.9	49.2	19.2	5.6	1.0	90.4	32.4	51.9	48.1
75202	DALLAS	71.7	66.5	18.5	19.6	1.8	2.3	13.2	20.7	1.9	1.4	1.1	3.4	10.1	54.5	21.5	5.2	0.9	94.5	35.5	55.5	44.5
75203	DALLAS	27.2	26.6	36.0	31.8	0.3	0.4	60.2	65.6	10.1	9.1	7.5	8.2	9.0	31.0	17.2	6.6	1.2	68.6	28.0	54.0	46.0
75204	DALLAS	55.7	54.7	11.6	10.9	5.1	4.9	44.2	47.5	6.1	5.1	4.1	4.8	11.0	44.0	18.1	5.7	1.1	82.0	31.2	54.9	45.1
75205	DALLAS	92.1	89.1	1.7	2.0	2.3	3.2	6.3	10.0	4.6	5.1	6.5	12.4	11.1	24.5	25.6	8.3	1.9	80.0	33.4	47.3	52.7
75206	DALLAS	70.5	66.0	4.9	4.8	3.5	4.4	36.5	43.4	5.9	4.3	3.3	4.1	14.0	46.3	16.3	4.6	1.2	84.5	29.7	55.1	44.9
75207	DALLAS	54.3	51.0	37.4	37.8	0.2	0.5	18.2	26.0	0.9	0.3	0.2	5.2	15.3	66.6	10.5	0.6	0.5	97.5	33.9	71.6	28.4
75208	DALLAS	53.5	49.6	4.5	3.7	0.5	0.5	71.6	79.0	9.6	8.6	7.6	7.9	8.3	29.9	20.7	6.2	1.2	69.5	29.7	52.3	47.7
75209	DALLAS	65.3	60.8	22.9	23.2	1.3	1.9	24.3	29.3	7.2	6.7	6.4	5.1	4.5	31.1	26.0	10.7	2.3	76.6	38.8	48.8	51.2
75210	DALLAS	7.1	8.3	83.4	79.6	0.2	0.3	15.4	19.4	9.8	9.2	8.0	8.0	7.4	25.2	21.4	9.2	1.7	68.2	30.3	46.3	53.7
75211	DALLAS	46.1	43.1	7.9	7.2	1.1	1.1	76.9	82.9	10.8	9.7	8.3	8.7	8.9	29.9	17.6	5.3	0.9	66.1	27.0	51.7	48.3
75212	DALLAS	26.5	26.9	34.2	30.9	1.1	1.0	62.1	66.5	11.1	10.3	9.4	9.9	8.1	24.7	18.5	7.1	0.9	62.7	25.8	48.9	51.1
75214	DALLAS	76.8	72.4	4.4	4.2	1.3	1.6	26.7	34.0	6.9	6.2	5.5	4.9	6.3	33.7	24.0	9.0	3.6	78.5	36.9	49.9	50.1
75215	DALLAS	7.3	9.3	85.6	79.1	0.3	0.3	10.6	17.4	7.7	7.6	7.1	7.5	7.6	24.5	24.7	11.2	2.1	73.2	34.9	47.5	52.5
75216	DALLAS	9.3	10.1	77.5	73.8	0.1	0.1	19.7	24.1	7.6	7.8	7.6	7.8	6.9	24.1	24.0	12.4	1.8	72.2	35.2	46.7	53.3
75217	DALLAS	35.2	32.8	33.4	29.5	0.3	0.3	47.4	56.9	10.2	9.6	8.8	9.0	8.1	27.6	19.8	6.2	0.7	66.0	27.7	49.4	50.6
75218	DALLAS	84.7	81.5	5.3	5.0	1.0	1.4	16.9	23.6	5.9	5.8	5.9	5.0	4.7	26.5	29.7	12.6	3.8	79.3	42.7	47.6	52.4
75219	DALLAS	60.2	58.1	8.5	7.2	7.1	7.0	41.4	48.0	6.7	5.2	4.2	4.7	8.6	40.9	22.7	6.1	0.8	81.1	33.3	57.2	42.8
75220	DALLAS	59.3	57.8	5.2	3.9	0.6	0.6	77.3	82.5	11.4	9.3	7.1	7.8	10.1	34.9	15.0	3.8	0.6	67.9	27.0	55.9	44.1
75223	DALLAS	38.5	37.0	20.1	18.1	0.8	0.7	64.3	70.8	10.2	9.4	8.1	8.4	8.3	29.6	19.4	5.7	1.0	67.3	28.3	51.3	48.7
75224	DALLAS	34.8	33.3	35.0	31.2	0.8	0.9	48.5	56.5	9.9	9.0	8.3	8.9	9.4	27.9	19.6	6.0	1.0	67.7	27.7	49.3	50.7
75225	DALLAS	97.6	96.6	0.4	0.5	0.9	1.3	2.1	3.6	6.1	7.5	8.8	7.1	3.0	18.0	31.4	13.8	4.3	72.9	44.7	47.1	52.9
75226	DALLAS	40.1	36.1	13.3	14.8	0.9	1.3	57.1	60.2	7.1	6.0	4.5	4.8	8.0	38.7	20.7	7.9	2.2	79.6	34.1	58.6	41.4
75227	DALLAS	36.1	33.8	36.7	33.8	1.5	1.7	42.9	51.5	9.7	9.1	8.3	8.5	8.1	29.1	19.7	6.4	1.2	67.8	28.7	48.9	51.1
75228	DALLAS	51.6	47.7	25.2	23.4	4.4	4.9	32.1	41.0	8.9	7.9	7.1	7.2	8.0	29.0	20.6	9.4	1.9	72.0	31.8	48.7	51.3
75229	DALLAS	81.8	78.8	4.3	4.0	3.1	3.4	32.1	40.2	7.2	7.3	7.3	6.6	5.3	23.7	27.1	12.6	2.9	74.1	39.8	50.6	49.4
75230	DALLAS	83.9	80.6	6.1	6.1	2.9	3.6	11.3	16.2	5.9	6.1	6.3	5.0	5.3	25.2	28.0	14.2	4.0	78.5	42.4	47.7	52.3
75231	DALLAS	48.0	46.3	27.2	24.0	1.7	1.9	40.3	49.3	9.8	8.1	6.5	6.5	10.3	37.1	16.9	3.7	1.0	72.1	28.6	52.8	47.2
75232	DALLAS	14.3	13.6	77.9	76.3	0.2	0.2	12.8	16.6	7.0	7.1	7.3	8.0	6.8	24.3	27.0	11.4	1.3	73.8	36.4	45.8	54.2
75233	DALLAS	27.3	25.3	39.7	34.2	0.2	0.2	45.4	54.7	9.7	8.5	7.3	7.5	8.0	28.3	19.7	9.2	1.9	70.1	30.1	49.0	51.0
75234	DALLAS	76.9	71.8	2.5	2.4	3.1	3.5	38.7	48.6	7.2	6.9	6.9	7.1	6.2	25.9	24.9	13.1	1.8	74.8	37.2	49.6	50.4
75235	DALLAS	57.7	54.8	10.0	10.3	3.0	2.7	69.4	73.4	8.7	7.8	6.6	7.4	8.3	35.5	18.9	5.8	0.9	72.6	30.6	56.2	43.8
75236	DALLAS	39.8	38.7	40.1	34.2	5.7	6.3	20.7	31.7	8.3	7.9	7.5	11.0	11.9	27.5	19.9	5.4	0.6	71.2	26.9	48.6	51.4
75237	DALLAS	8.2	9.0	84.3	80.9	0.3	0.4	10.5	14.4	10.2	8.3	7.4	8.6	12.3	31.3	17.5	4.0	0.4	69.2	26.6	44.9	55.1
75238	DALLAS	66.4	63.1	21.7	20.9	1.5	1.9	16.3	23.1	8.1	7.3	6.9	6.5	7.2	27.5	23.8	10.7	1.9	73.6	35.3	47.8	52.2
75240	DALLAS	65.2	62.9	9.0	7.9	3.3	3.6	55.3	62.7	9.2	7.4	6.1	6.9	11.1	35.7	16.4	6.4	0.7	73.5	28.8	53.9	46.1
75241	DALLAS	6.9	7.3	88.2	84.8	0.1	0.2	6.2	10.4	7.1	7.4	7.3	8.2	7.6	24.9	23.5	12.7	1.3	73.3	34.9	48.6	51.4
75243	DALLAS	45.5	41.3	33.6	33.0	9.9	11.7	14.6	20.0	7.8	6.4	5.8	6.0	9.9	35.3	21.3	6.4	1.3	77.0	31.4	48.7	51.3
75244	DALLAS	76.3	71.7	7.5	7.4	4.8	5.8	20.2	27.7	7.0	6.7	6.5	5.7	6.6	25.0	26.4	14.2	1.8	76.3	39.3	49.0	51.0
75246	DALLAS	38.8	34.9	12.8	11.2	2.9	2.9	58.3	65.3	7.9	6.5	5.3	6.2	9.6	37.0	18.0	7.7	1.7	76.9	31.5	56.7	43.3
75247	DALLAS	32.7	29.4	55.1	55.0	2.8	3.2	15.7	22.0	1.4	3.2	2.8	4.3	2.5	41.8	22.3	14.5	7.1	89.4	42.6	66.3	33.7
75248	DALLAS	85.7	81.4	3.6	4.0	6.0	8.1	6.9	10.7	4.4	4.7	5.1	4.9	5.0	27.0	32.7	15.0	1.3	82.9	44.3	49.0	51.0
75249	DALLAS	35.7	33.4	51.3	48.6	2.6	3.5	16.5	23.1	8.1	8.2	8.0	7.8	6.3	30.0	25.8	5.4	0.4	70.7	32.5	47.4	52.6
75251	DALLAS	87.7	83.6	4.1	4.7	4.7	6.5	5.9	9.8	2.9	1.5	1.7	2.2	13.8	39.3	27.6	10.2	0.9	92.6	34.9	50.4	49.6
75252	DALLAS	76.7	67.7	5.9	6.6	12.7	19.7	6.6	8.9	5.4	4.7	4.6	4.5	9.6	33.8	25.8	6.6	0.5	82.9	34.6	49.8	50.2
75253	DALLAS	76.0	69.7	9.9	9.9	0.4	0.6	23.3	34.4	9.8	9.0	8.2	7.6	7.2	29.5	21.7	6.4	0.6	68.3	30.3	50.0	50.0
75254	DALLAS	72.2	68.1	11.3	11.2	7.3	8.8	17.1	23.5	5.5	4.5	3.9	4.0	10.4	43.5	20.1	6.8	1.2	84.1	32.2	49.9	50.1
75261	DALLAS	100.0	66.7	0.0	0.0	0.0	0.0	0.0	0.0	0.0	0.0	0.0	0.0	0.0	100.0	0.0	0.0	0.0	100.0	27.5	66.7	33.3
75287	DALLAS	76.0	68.6	9.8	11.9	7.1	10.5	10.8	14.6	5.9	4.7	4.0	4.4	11.3	45.6	20.4	3.4	0.3	83.1	31.5	50.0	50.0
75401	GREENVILLE	62.8	57.4	23.5	25.0	0.3	0.4	18.4	23.6	8.3	7.7	7.2	7.4	7.5	27.8	22.2	9.7	2.1	72.3	33.1	49.5	50.5
75402	GREENVILLE	90.6	87.1	5.0	6.7	0.8	1.1	4.7	7.2	5.9	6.0	6.1	6.1	5.5	23.7	28.8	15.1	2.8	78.0	42.5	49.2	50.8
75407	PRINCETON	91.9	88.0	0.8	0.9	0.4	0.6	10.1	15.5	7.2	7.2	7.3	7.1	6.0	26.9	28.4	9.2	1.0	74.0	37.1	50.0	50.0
75409	ANNA	89.9	83.4	0.7	0.8	0.5	0.9	13.0	22.8	7.1	7.1	7.3	7.1	5.7	27.3	28.0	9.5	1.0	74.2	37.2	50.8	49.2
75410	ALBA	95.0	93.2	0.6	0.8	0.0	0.1	5.3	7.7	5.4	5.8	6.1	6.0	4.3	21.4	31.5	17.8	1.7	78.9	45.7	50.7	49.3
75411	ARTHUR CITY	95.4	94.0	2.6	3.6	0.0	0.0	1.0	1.8	6.5	7.1	7.1	6.5	4.8	24.4	29.2	13.1	1.2	75.0	41.1	50.0	50.0
75412	BAGWELL	89.3	87.8	8.9	10.2	0.0	0.0	2.3	3.2	5.8	6.1	6.4	6.2	4.1	22.6	29.4	17.2	2.1	77.8	44.0	49.3	50.7
75414	BELLS	94.4	92.7	1.3	1.7	0.4	0.5	1.8	2.8	6.3	6.3	6.6	6.6	5.6	25.7	29.3	11.9	1.8	76.7	40.0	48.4	51.6
75415	BEN FRANKLIN	92.5	91.4	4.1	4.3	0.0	0.0	4.1	4.3	5.0	5.0	5.0	6.4	5.0	23.6	31.4	16.4	2.1	81.4	45.0	52.1	47.9
75416	BLOSSOM	93.5	91.4	3.4	4.5	0.1	0.1	3.7	5.5	6.3	6.6	6.9	6.9	4.8	25.0	29.3	12.5	1.6	75.9	40.6	51.0	49.0
75417	BOGATA	93.2	91.6	3.4	4.0	0.1	0.2	2.8	3.9	5.3	5.4	5.4	5.6	4.9	22.9	28.7	17.7	4.1	80.4	45.3	48.5	51.5
75418	BONHAM	80.7	77.7	13.1	14.4	0.4	0.6	7.5	10.1	5.0	4.8	4.9	5.9	8.7	30.0	24.2	13.5	3.0	82.4	38.7	59.1	40.9
75420	BRASHEAR	92.5	89.4	0.7	1.0	0.0	0.3	8.2	11.6	5.6	6.0	6.3	6.0	3.6	23.8	30.5	16.6	1.7	78.1	43.9	49.7	50.3
75421	BROOKSTON	90.3	88.1	7.0	8.9	0.0	0.1	2.2	2.6	5.5	5.8	6.4	7.3	5.3	23.4	30.9	14.1	1.3	77.8	42.6	48.8	51.2
75422	CAMPBELL	93.3	90.6	2.1	2.8	0.3	0.4	3.9	6.1	5.5	5.9	6.1	6.5	5.6	22.8	31.0	15.1	1.5	78.2	43.1	50.7	49.3
75423	CELESTE	94.2	91.7	1.7	2.2	0.1	0.2	4.1	6.5	6.9	7.0	7.1	7.6	6.3	25.0	28.0	10.6	1.5	74.5	37.2	49.6	50.4
75424	BLUE RIDGE	94.6	91.7	0.2	0.3	0.2	0.4	6.3	10.1	7.0	7.1	7.4	7.6	5.9	25.1	29.1	9.9	1.0	73.9	38.3	49.9	50.1
75426	CLARKSVILLE	65.0	61.3	30.8	33.7	0.2	0.2	6.4	8.2	6.4	6.3	6.3	6.3	5.9	23.5	26.4	15.0	3.9	77.1	40.8	47.7	52.3
75428	COMMERCE	75.1	69.2	17.4	20.8	2.3	3.0	7.3	10.4	6.0	5.4	5.0	10.9	17.7	24.9	19.5	8.5	2.1	79.9	27.8	49.7	50.3
75431	COMO	89.9	86.6	1.7	2.0	0.1	0.1	14.8	20.3	7.0	7.1	7.7	7.6	5.3	24.7	26.0	13.2	1.5	73.2	37.9	50.3	49.7
75432	COOPER	86.3	85.9	10.0	10.3	0.1	0.1	2.7	2.9	6.7	6.5	6.5	7.2	6.0	23.6	25.6	14.6	3.4	75.9	39.7	47.3	52.7
75433	CUMBY	93.6	91.4	0.4	0.4	0.5	0.6	6.1	8.7	6.0	6.4	6.5	6.1	4.4	23.6	29.8	15.6	1.7	77.3	42.9	50.8	49.2
75435	DEPORT	94.8	93.6	2.0	2.5	0.1	0.1	1.3	1.9	6.2	6.4	6.4	6.2	4.7	22.9	27.4	16.5	3.4	77.1	43.1	48.3	51.7
75436	DETROIT	86.6	84.4	9.6	10.8	0.2	0.3	2.3	2.9	6.6	6.6	6.9	7.1	5.2	24.1	27.6	13.8	2.0	75.5	39.8	46.8	53.2
75437	DIKE	89.4	86.0	3.9	4.8	0.0	0.0	8.3	11.8	6.3	6.3	7.0	6.6	5.1	25.4	30.5	11.4	1.5	76.5	39.7	50.0	50.0
75438	DODD CITY	93.2	91.3	3.0	3.8	0.1	0.1	1.0	1.4	5.3	5.4	6.0	6.8	4.9	22.0	30.1	17.4	2.1	79.1	44.7	50.5	49.5
75439	ECTOR	96.0	94.9	0.0	0.0	0.4	0.5	1.6	2.3	5.9	5.7	6.1	7.9	6.7	22.9	27.6	14.6	2.7	77.8	42.0	48.1	51.9
75440	EMORY	90.8	88.8	4.0	4.3	0.2	0.2	6.6	9.1	5.5	5.8	6.0	6.0	5.2	22.6	29.6	17.0	2.4	78.9	44.1	49.8	50.2
75442	FARMERSVILLE	88.8	85.4	4.9	5.5	0.1	0.2	10.8	15.6	7.5	7.1	7.0	7.4	6.6	27.6	25.6	9.3	1.8	73.8	35.3	49.0	51.0
75446	HONEY GROVE	84.8	80.4	10.7	13.5	0.3	0.4	5.2	7.5	6.2	5.9	5.8	6.6	6.2	23.1	26.5	15.6	3.9	77.9	41.6	47.2	52.8
75447	IVANHOE	95.9	94.7	1.1	1.4	0.0	0.1	2.5	3.7	5.1	5.4	5.8	6.0	4.2	21.3	31.5	19.1	1.6	79.7	46.5	49.7	50.3
75448	KLONDIKE	91.9	91.4	4.1	4.3	0.1	0.1	4.1	4.6	4.6	4.7	5.2	6.4	5.0	24.4	31.2	16.7	1.9	81.7	44.8	52.6	47.4
75449	LADONIA	77.3	74.2	18.1	19.5	0.5	0.8	3.3	5.4	7.2	7.5	7.5	6.2	4.7	22.5	29.2	13.0	2.2	73.7	40.5	48.6	51.4
75450	LAKE CREEK	96.1	94.5	2.0	1.8	0.0	0.0	0.0	0.0	5.5	5.5	7.3	7.3	5.5	23.6	29.1	14.5	1.8	76.4	41.9	47.3	52.7
	TEXAS	71.0	67.6	11.5	11.4	2.8	3.5	32.0	37.4	7.9	7.5	7.2	7.5	7.4	28.3	24.0	8.8	1.4	73.0	33.6	49.7	50.3
	UNITED STATES	75.1	72.0	12.3	12.7	3.8	4.6	12.5	15.7	6.8	6.7	6.6	7.1	6.9	27.0	26.0	10.9	1.9	75.7	36.9	49.2	50.8

#	POST OFFICE NAME	2009 Per Capita Income	2009 HH Income Base	2009 Household Income Distribution (%): Less than $25,000	$25,000 to $49,999	$50,000 to $99,999	$100,000 to $149,999	$150,000 or More	Median Household Income: 2009	2014	2009 National Centile	2009 State Centile	2009 Home Value Base	2009 Home Value Distribution (%): Less than $50,000	$50,000 to $89,999	$90,000 to $174,999	$175,000 to $399,999	$400,000 or More	2009 Median Home Value
75161	TERRELL	18685	2283	23.0	26.7	42.3	6.7	1.3	50172	52126	62	71	1926	32.7	25.6	32.8	8.0	0.8	77168
75163	TRINIDAD	21274	1161	30.8	28.3	35.1	3.4	2.4	40418	43975	34	44	962	22.5	17.7	27.2	28.0	4.7	110924
75165	WAXAHACHIE	25197	12816	17.2	22.1	41.3	12.7	6.7	62326	65984	80	85	8780	9.7	20.4	47.9	19.9	2.0	121039
75166	LAVON	24768	815	17.5	24.9	41.3	11.8	4.4	58311	55693	76	83	688	9.6	26.7	42.7	18.3	2.6	113384
75167	WAXAHACHIE	25409	2908	12.7	20.9	44.6	13.3	8.5	67842	73818	85	89	2467	16.4	16.9	35.7	24.2	6.8	127051
75169	WILLS POINT	19625	4952	29.1	26.7	35.2	6.3	2.7	45106	45751	49	59	3914	26.7	24.9	33.9	12.6	2.0	87549
75172	WILMER	15623	926	24.5	33.4	35.4	4.9	1.8	43410	47190	44	54	605	63.0	28.8	7.1	1.2	0.0	38910
75173	NEVADA	22943	1864	16.2	26.0	40.6	13.5	3.7	58906	55734	76	83	1551	14.4	24.4	42.4	16.4	2.5	108650
75180	MESQUITE	17307	6594	17.8	33.2	41.5	6.2	1.3	48937	53116	59	68	3845	20.3	58.0	20.3	1.1	0.2	69430
75181	MESQUITE	30895	7320	5.8	10.3	43.7	27.6	12.5	87506	89686	94	96	6426	7.0	5.5	71.5	15.5	0.4	132327
75182	SUNNYVALE	38576	1279	6.6	15.2	42.2	18.0	18.0	80093	82296	92	94	1040	1.4	12.7	35.1	40.9	9.9	176887
75189	ROYSE CITY	24690	6461	15.7	24.3	38.5	14.5	7.0	61557	59099	79	85	5577	8.9	18.3	38.7	26.6	7.4	133903
75201	DALLAS	76417	2906	17.6	12.2	31.8	16.2	22.2	79319	81706	92	93	230	0.0	11.3	35.7	28.3	24.8	184211
75202	DALLAS	49750	1092	15.5	17.5	35.4	15.9	15.7	71463	75237	88	90	46	0.0	17.4	23.9	41.3	17.4	195000
75203	DALLAS	10563	6180	47.2	31.6	16.9	3.2	1.1	26437	27331	4	5	1919	47.7	31.9	15.0	4.4	1.0	52514
75204	DALLAS	38138	12925	20.9	23.7	33.4	12.8	9.2	57265	61783	74	81	2451	7.1	19.3	27.6	34.7	11.3	160404
75205	DALLAS	59852	9617	11.9	14.9	29.5	13.1	30.6	86092	86654	94	95	4873	1.3	4.4	6.5	17.1	70.7	665205
75206	DALLAS	35697	20644	17.2	25.4	40.0	10.8	6.6	57776	60860	75	82	4409	3.8	16.7	38.7	35.6	5.1	147725
75207	DALLAS	14010	5	0.0	0.0	100.0	0.0	0.0	54084	54084	70	77	2	0.0	0.0	100.0	0.0	0.0	112500
75208	DALLAS	18093	10775	27.9	28.9	29.3	8.1	5.8	43700	47011	44	55	5449	18.1	35.6	26.4	16.5	3.4	84643
75209	DALLAS	45033	6655	17.6	22.7	30.1	10.0	19.5	63063	65689	81	86	4078	5.5	18.3	22.1	25.6	28.5	214583
75210	DALLAS	10070	3075	59.9	24.7	12.7	2.0	0.7	19778	20059	1	2	883	60.9	35.0	3.6	0.5	0.0	41384
75211	DALLAS	13484	20217	27.4	32.3	32.6	5.5	2.2	41315	44992	37	47	10740	19.3	58.5	21.0	1.1	0.1	68652
75212	DALLAS	9504	6294	47.0	29.6	19.7	2.4	1.4	26669	27606	4	5	3069	62.8	29.6	7.3	0.3	0.0	40309
75214	DALLAS	40846	16119	14.7	23.6	33.4	13.6	14.7	63830	65954	82	87	8210	2.4	5.7	32.9	45.9	13.0	197635
75215	DALLAS	11724	7535	56.5	25.0	14.2	3.2	1.1	20401	20868	1	2	2522	57.5	28.6	9.0	3.4	1.5	44107
75216	DALLAS	13679	16527	39.7	31.4	24.1	3.1	1.6	30921	32863	10	12	10004	46.9	44.5	7.9	0.5	0.1	51723
75217	DALLAS	12887	19858	30.6	32.5	31.1	3.9	1.9	39195	42348	30	39	13004	28.1	60.6	10.7	0.6	0.1	59800
75218	DALLAS	38536	10019	12.9	23.4	38.0	15.3	10.5	64585	66370	83	87	6325	2.2	14.4	52.1	27.5	3.8	141350
75219	DALLAS	41665	12174	16.7	25.4	37.2	10.4	10.3	59785	62247	77	84	3546	7.4	8.9	33.4	28.1	22.2	176345
75220	DALLAS	17522	14695	24.3	34.5	28.2	6.5	6.6	42765	45964	42	52	4537	7.8	19.2	41.7	16.8	14.5	120655
75223	DALLAS	15298	5086	35.5	28.4	23.4	7.8	4.9	35129	37466	18	23	2610	29.6	42.3	12.3	15.5	0.3	67848
75224	DALLAS	14507	9814	27.5	33.0	31.4	5.5	2.6	41436	45003	37	48	5526	13.5	55.9	27.4	3.3	0.0	74147
75225	DALLAS	68286	8316	9.8	10.9	25.3	13.2	40.8	113082	113443	98	99	6074	1.5	0.9	8.9	23.8	65.0	543850
75226	DALLAS	39535	1240	27.3	19.0	29.3	12.8	11.7	56283	61620	73	80	83	36.1	1.2	31.3	16.9	14.5	114423
75227	DALLAS	15350	17396	27.1	31.3	34.3	5.2	2.2	41728	46055	38	49	9688	14.4	49.2	35.1	1.3	0.0	77467
75228	DALLAS	19263	24377	25.1	32.5	33.6	6.1	2.6	43247	46866	43	54	11978	4.2	45.1	46.7	3.7	0.3	90757
75229	DALLAS	37941	11561	13.3	20.5	30.7	14.7	20.9	74962	75758	89	92	8019	1.5	4.4	38.6	39.5	16.0	192339
75230	DALLAS	52586	13169	14.7	23.0	28.1	11.1	23.1	66323	68812	84	88	6896	3.4	10.4	13.1	39.5	33.7	304418
75231	DALLAS	21732	20764	25.7	38.1	25.2	5.9	5.0	39762	42430	32	41	2941	11.1	16.7	17.6	45.8	8.8	188715
75232	DALLAS	20748	9973	20.8	28.4	36.1	10.8	3.9	50905	54954	63	72	6770	12.0	37.1	47.9	2.9	0.1	90944
75233	DALLAS	16655	4690	25.9	28.9	35.2	6.1	3.9	46067	49212	52	62	2618	4.1	35.0	57.3	3.4	0.2	100563
75234	DALLAS	27583	9542	12.5	24.3	40.7	13.3	9.4	63385	64886	82	86	6419	1.5	21.8	59.4	15.1	2.2	115674
75235	DALLAS	17048	6390	27.5	33.1	30.5	6.2	2.8	41171	44451	37	47	2222	23.7	39.8	30.4	5.1	0.9	77594
75236	DALLAS	20332	3932	17.8	36.1	35.5	8.4	2.2	47281	49951	55	65	2026	13.9	22.7	52.4	9.6	1.4	105611
75237	DALLAS	17452	7492	30.6	41.0	25.3	2.2	1.0	35183	36995	18	23	932	9.2	33.2	49.1	8.5	0.0	101406
75238	DALLAS	30107	12559	15.1	29.1	34.2	12.5	9.0	56227	60035	73	80	6103	0.8	3.7	55.0	38.4	2.1	161922
75240	DALLAS	24852	10828	20.0	29.8	33.9	7.4	8.8	50165	54131	62	70	2570	2.8	20.7	32.9	27.1	16.5	154952
75241	DALLAS	16152	10356	31.7	30.5	29.1	6.5	2.1	38677	41666	29	37	6835	18.7	59.9	20.5	0.8	0.1	70174
75243	DALLAS	29866	26394	16.7	33.1	34.8	8.1	7.3	50171	53826	62	70	7211	9.0	18.1	33.2	36.2	3.6	145159
75244	DALLAS	42280	5110	9.0	20.7	34.5	16.8	18.9	75491	75667	90	92	2936	5.8	3.9	26.5	58.1	5.8	206897
75246	DALLAS	14425	1089	37.8	30.2	20.8	8.4	2.8	30790	33233	9	12	156	11.5	38.5	26.3	20.5	3.2	90000
75247	DALLAS	13669	22	77.3	9.1	13.6	0.0	0.0	18692	18692	1	1	14	71.4	28.6	0.0	0.0	0.0	40000
75248	DALLAS	53948	15943	8.1	16.8	34.8	17.8	22.4	81740	82153	93	94	8387	1.0	5.5	21.1	61.1	11.3	220461
75249	DALLAS	24030	3984	8.8	18.6	49.0	18.6	5.0	70060	70824	87	90	3183	1.3	32.9	59.9	5.8	0.0	102921
75251	DALLAS	73607	1370	6.9	10.0	41.9	21.2	19.9	85642	86538	94	95	299	0.0	0.0	0.0	55.5	44.5	350000
75252	DALLAS	57197	13096	10.2	22.4	29.2	19.5	18.8	71900	69146	88	90	4704	2.1	3.0	11.6	62.3	21.0	271397
75253	DALLAS	18352	5607	20.7	32.4	38.7	5.7	2.6	47494	51133	55	66	4083	51.8	32.7	13.3	1.8	0.4	47786
75254	DALLAS	43728	9622	10.5	25.7	42.8	10.2	10.7	63536	65157	82	86	2054	1.6	15.1	24.1	25.8	33.3	286260
75261	DALLAS	0	0	0.0	0.0	0.0	0.0	0.0	0	0	0	0	0	0.0	0.0	0.0	0.0	0.0	0
75287	DALLAS	47403	27813	10.2	24.4	39.8	15.7	9.9	63331	62835	82	86	5443	0.6	1.8	27.4	47.0	23.3	238051
75401	GREENVILLE	17467	6227	32.0	29.0	32.2	4.4	2.5	39513	44877	31	40	3678	50.3	29.2	16.8	3.4	0.3	49707
75402	GREENVILLE	25866	6445	18.4	25.9	39.9	11.5	4.4	54730	54791	71	78	4412	13.1	29.4	46.3	10.4	0.8	101106
75407	PRINCETON	22756	5010	18.0	28.1	38.4	12.9	2.6	54539	53315	70	78	3764	20.5	27.0	40.0	11.3	1.2	93827
75409	ANNA	23587	4102	15.2	28.5	37.8	13.8	4.7	57117	54550	74	81	3553	5.6	19.0	43.2	24.5	7.6	130343
75410	ALBA	18776	2315	29.3	33.8	30.0	4.9	1.9	38879	40987	29	38	1947	17.2	19.0	40.1	19.5	4.3	113439
75411	ARTHUR CITY	26078	75	25.3	22.7	42.7	8.0	1.3	51582	49530	65	73	64	25.0	17.2	35.9	21.9	0.0	97143
75412	BAGWELL	17503	375	32.5	36.8	25.9	2.9	1.9	33471	36991	14	18	306	50.3	28.8	11.4	7.8	1.6	49677
75414	BELLS	20454	1198	25.9	27.9	37.1	7.4	1.7	46213	49098	52	62	948	19.1	29.4	39.0	11.4	1.1	92222
75415	BEN FRANKLIN	15403	49	32.7	28.6	32.7	6.1	0.0	39292	37794	31	40	41	56.1	24.4	17.1	2.4	0.0	47222
75416	BLOSSOM	17784	1387	34.0	29.9	30.7	4.5	0.8	36765	39615	23	30	1098	29.8	27.4	30.9	10.2	1.7	77536
75417	BOGATA	20156	1118	34.6	29.9	27.6	4.0	3.8	35156	36318	18	23	848	48.6	25.0	18.9	5.8	1.8	52105
75418	BONHAM	18179	4367	33.3	29.6	29.6	4.9	2.7	37927	41546	26	34	2957	24.1	26.9	34.5	13.0	1.5	88007
75420	BRASHEAR	24071	136	29.4	31.6	27.9	8.1	2.9	41317	43973	37	48	113	26.5	24.8	32.7	13.3	2.7	87500
75421	BROOKSTON	18775	339	26.0	28.0	41.0	4.1	0.9	46920	46273	54	64	290	20.3	33.4	35.5	10.3	0.3	85926
75422	CAMPBELL	20529	986	24.9	28.7	36.7	6.2	3.4	47376	49662	55	65	815	21.7	36.3	31.9	9.0	1.1	82012
75423	CELESTE	19675	902	22.2	27.2	40.1	8.2	2.3	50474	51691	62	71	742	30.1	33.3	27.1	8.9	0.7	69762
75424	BLUE RIDGE	22890	1271	17.2	29.6	36.6	13.4	3.2	53861	52139	69	77	1009	17.7	27.8	34.7	17.2	2.6	99286
75426	CLARKSVILLE	16714	2456	37.3	35.0	23.2	3.4	1.2	32134	34320	12	15	1723	55.0	25.9	14.6	3.1	1.3	46272
75428	COMMERCE	19168	3737	41.2	24.8	24.6	6.5	2.9	32609	34717	13	16	1842	32.2	32.8	29.5	5.2	0.2	72316
75431	COMO	18789	1143	31.1	34.5	26.7	5.7	2.1	36319	38959	21	28	864	29.2	24.4	29.7	13.2	3.5	82791
75432	COOPER	18338	1510	36.1	27.4	29.9	4.6	2.0	36447	39074	22	29	1108	44.0	31.3	21.0	3.6	0.0	55280
75433	CUMBY	20737	1570	28.7	31.7	30.3	7.2	2.1	41421	44587	37	48	1221	26.4	25.7	31.2	13.7	3.0	86136
75435	DEPORT	15986	780	37.7	36.9	21.0	3.5	0.9	33349	36520	14	17	603	34.5	27.0	26.4	10.8	1.3	72674
75436	DETROIT	18027	621	34.0	27.1	32.7	4.7	1.6	38925	43829	30	38	452	44.7	33.6	13.9	4.2	3.5	55581
75437	DIKE	20197	103	25.2	35.0	29.1	7.8	2.9	43820	45447	45	55	86	18.6	26.7	32.6	18.6	3.5	95714
75438	DODD CITY	20560	585	28.2	28.9	34.2	5.3	3.4	42593	44032	41	52	488	21.3	25.0	37.5	14.3	1.8	94615
75439	ECTOR	20567	380	22.9	27.4	43.4	5.8	0.5	49659	49756	60	69	278	30.2	21.2	34.9	11.9	1.8	86364
75440	EMORY	19213	2139	30.4	32.0	29.2	6.7	1.7	38300	39422	28	35	1711	19.9	23.7	35.9	15.7	4.8	101633
75442	FARMERSVILLE	23063	3481	20.3	26.1	37.7	12.2	3.6	53813	52549	69	77	2540	17.3	27.3	40.8	12.8	1.8	98193
75446	HONEY GROVE	19020	1416	34.0	28.2	29.0	7.1	1.6	38797	41293	29	37	1007	29.4	29.7	32.5	7.5	0.9	77115
75447	IVANHOE	23468	390	24.1	29.0	36.7	6.7	3.6	47627	47313	56	66	337	16.9	19.6	40.4	20.8	2.4	114946
75448	KLONDIKE	18299	279	34.4	29.4	30.8	4.7	0.7	37709	38805	26	33	233	57.5	24.0	15.9	2.6	0.0	46196
75449	LADONIA	16438	414	37.7	32.1	24.9	3.6	1.7	35830	39895	20	26	326	33.1	35.9	23.3	6.7	0.9	63571
75450	LAKE CREEK	19143	20	25.0	25.0	45.0	5.0	0.0	50000	46113	61	70	17	23.5	29.4	41.2	5.9	0.0	75000
	TEXAS	24551		22.3	25.0	34.3	11.1	7.3	52382	54495				16.5	22.7	36.5	19.7	4.6	109784
	UNITED STATES	27277		20.9	24.4	35.3	11.7	7.6	54719	56938				9.3	13.1	31.6	32.6	13.5	162279

ZIP CODE #	POST OFFICE NAME	FINANCIAL SERVICES: Auto Loan	Home Loan	Invest-ments	Retire-ment Plans	THE HOME: Home Improvements: Home Repair	Lawn & Garden	Furnishings: Comput-ers & Hard-ware-Personal	Major Appli-ances	TV, Radio, Sound Equip-ment	Furni-ture	ENTERTAINMENT: Dine out/ Carry out	Sports Equip-ment	Fees & Tickets	Toys & Games	Travel	Cable TV	PERSONAL: Apparel & Services	Auto Repairs	Health Insur-ance	Pets & Supplies
75161	TERRELL	91	75	83	73	76	89	74	85	79	73	78	62	65	80	71	83	52	80	86	100
75163	TRINIDAD	80	66	89	61	70	86	65	79	71	67	70	56	58	68	67	77	47	75	86	93
75165	WAXAHACHIE	108	106	95	105	102	105	104	104	104	105	105	80	102	107	101	105	73	104	105	123
75166	LAVON	109	100	89	97	98	103	95	100	98	99	98	73	90	102	90	101	67	97	101	119
75167	WAXAHACHIE	119	122	104	120	117	115	112	115	111	117	112	88	113	116	111	110	77	111	110	134
75169	WILLS POINT	87	70	83	68	71	87	70	82	76	68	74	61	61	76	68	81	50	77	86	97
75172	WILMER	81	66	58	62	63	64	73	71	74	75	76	53	65	76	66	74	53	75	69	82
75173	NEVADA	107	102	89	98	99	100	95	99	97	100	97	74	91	101	91	98	66	96	97	117
75180	MESQUITE	84	78	66	74	75	68	82	77	79	86	81	60	77	82	76	77	57	80	72	89
75181	MESQUITE	149	166	138	164	158	138	146	145	138	159	140	117	154	148	146	129	100	137	125	165
75182	SUNNYVALE	158	182	173	183	181	167	160	165	154	170	156	123	173	157	169	151	110	158	155	190
75189	ROYSE CITY	116	113	101	111	110	113	105	110	107	109	107	82	104	111	103	109	74	106	109	130
75201	DALLAS	185	144	153	165	141	138	204	157	197	191	204	143	186	198	180	191	146	185	161	199
75202	DALLAS	140	104	108	120	100	100	153	115	148	142	154	106	136	150	131	144	109	139	120	148
75203	DALLAS	52	39	34	39	37	39	50	45	52	51	54	34	44	52	43	53	38	51	47	53
75204	DALLAS	112	80	80	90	77	76	119	91	116	113	121	82	104	118	102	112	86	111	93	115
75205	DALLAS	190	200	231	217	212	188	217	194	203	217	207	161	229	203	218	195	154	202	181	226
75206	DALLAS	103	77	74	84	74	73	108	86	105	104	108	75	95	106	92	101	76	101	86	106
75207	DALLAS	17	11	10	12	10	10	17	13	17	16	17	11	14	17	14	16	12	16	13	16
75208	DALLAS	87	76	69	72	75	70	86	81	86	89	88	60	80	86	80	84	63	87	78	92
75209	DALLAS	140	148	155	150	153	138	150	144	144	156	147	111	157	143	154	140	106	147	137	166
75210	DALLAS	42	30	28	32	29	35	39	36	45	39	44	27	35	43	33	47	30	41	43	45
75211	DALLAS	75	63	53	58	61	55	73	68	72	76	75	51	65	73	66	70	53	74	63	76
75212	DALLAS	57	43	34	40	41	44	48	48	54	52	53	32	42	53	42	56	37	51	51	56
75214	DALLAS	126	120	122	125	121	114	133	122	129	134	132	97	132	129	130	126	95	130	120	143
75215	DALLAS	46	34	33	36	33	40	43	40	49	43	48	30	39	47	38	52	33	45	48	51
75216	DALLAS	62	53	47	52	50	58	56	56	62	58	62	39	54	61	52	66	42	59	64	68
75217	DALLAS	73	65	53	58	62	58	67	66	67	72	69	47	61	68	62	67	48	68	63	75
75218	DALLAS	115	120	120	123	121	118	122	118	121	123	122	91	126	119	124	120	86	121	121	138
75219	DALLAS	120	94	97	103	93	87	129	103	124	125	129	90	117	125	115	119	93	121	101	126
75220	DALLAS	92	76	71	77	75	67	95	83	92	96	97	67	88	94	87	87	70	94	76	95
75223	DALLAS	84	71	59	65	69	65	77	75	78	82	80	54	70	79	70	78	56	79	72	85
75224	DALLAS	75	66	57	62	64	59	73	69	72	76	74	51	67	73	67	70	52	73	65	78
75225	DALLAS	206	261	316	272	289	255	231	241	223	250	222	179	276	216	265	218	166	231	231	269
75226	DALLAS	131	97	97	105	94	91	139	111	135	133	141	96	122	137	120	131	101	131	111	136
75227	DALLAS	75	68	58	64	65	61	74	70	73	76	74	53	68	74	68	71	52	73	66	80
75228	DALLAS	77	68	61	69	66	66	78	71	78	78	79	56	73	79	72	77	56	77	73	85
75229	DALLAS	140	159	167	160	165	151	151	151	147	158	149	114	166	146	162	144	108	151	147	171
75230	DALLAS	146	150	169	158	159	145	159	149	154	164	155	117	167	151	163	150	112	155	147	173
75231	DALLAS	85	58	54	63	55	55	85	67	84	84	87	58	73	86	71	81	61	81	67	83
75232	DALLAS	87	83	76	84	81	88	84	84	90	86	90	60	85	88	83	93	62	87	94	101
75233	DALLAS	82	74	63	72	71	73	80	77	82	80	83	57	76	83	75	83	59	81	79	89
75234	DALLAS	109	116	107	114	114	114	113	113	113	114	114	85	117	113	115	113	80	114	116	130
75235	DALLAS	81	59	51	59	56	56	78	67	78	78	81	53	67	80	66	77	57	77	67	80
75236	DALLAS	85	75	65	73	72	66	85	77	82	87	83	61	78	84	77	78	59	82	72	89
75237	DALLAS	62	42	40	46	40	42	62	50	62	60	64	42	53	63	52	61	44	60	52	62
75238	DALLAS	106	101	97	104	99	97	110	101	108	110	109	80	109	109	106	107	77	107	102	120
75240	DALLAS	108	79	74	85	76	74	109	88	106	107	110	75	96	109	94	102	77	104	87	108
75241	DALLAS	71	65	59	65	62	70	67	67	73	69	73	48	67	71	64	77	50	70	76	82
75243	DALLAS	104	75	68	81	70	71	102	83	101	101	103	70	89	104	86	98	72	97	84	103
75244	DALLAS	144	149	150	153	151	140	152	144	146	156	148	113	156	147	154	143	105	148	141	169
75246	DALLAS	68	49	47	52	47	45	72	58	71	69	74	49	62	71	62	68	52	69	58	70
75247	DALLAS	32	25	25	26	25	31	29	29	33	30	32	20	27	32	26	36	22	31	35	36
75248	DALLAS	158	165	171	173	167	156	169	158	163	173	165	126	177	163	172	159	119	163	154	187
75249	DALLAS	117	122	99	117	114	106	110	110	107	118	110	83	110	113	107	104	75	107	102	129
75251	DALLAS	156	165	195	183	175	151	185	161	172	182	178	138	195	171	189	166	133	170	150	189
75252	DALLAS	158	139	135	151	135	128	162	139	157	162	161	119	157	162	150	151	115	151	134	169
75253	DALLAS	88	83	71	78	79	79	82	82	81	85	82	62	77	84	77	81	56	82	80	96
75254	DALLAS	129	92	89	103	88	88	130	102	128	127	131	90	115	131	110	124	92	121	104	129
75261	DALLAS	0	0	0	0	0	0	0	0	0	0	0	0	0	0	0	0	0	0	0	0
75287	DALLAS	133	98	92	109	93	92	133	106	130	130	134	93	118	135	114	126	94	124	106	133
75401	GREENVILLE	75	63	56	62	60	69	70	68	73	67	72	52	62	74	62	76	50	71	73	83
75402	GREENVILLE	96	89	90	91	90	99	91	96	93	87	92	72	87	93	89	97	63	94	100	112
75407	PRINCETON	98	90	79	88	87	93	88	91	91	89	90	67	83	94	83	93	62	89	93	109
75409	ANNA	109	101	90	98	99	103	95	101	98	99	99	74	91	102	91	101	67	98	101	120
75410	ALBA	82	61	92	60	65	85	62	79	68	58	67	59	51	66	64	74	44	73	81	93
75411	ARTHUR CITY	93	83	93	84	83	98	79	91	83	77	82	70	75	84	81	87	56	86	93	108
75412	BAGWELL	75	54	77	52	56	76	55	70	61	51	60	53	44	61	55	67	40	64	73	84
75414	BELLS	86	77	73	76	77	84	74	81	77	74	77	60	69	80	72	80	52	77	82	96
75415	BEN FRANKLIN	79	56	81	55	58	80	58	74	64	54	63	55	46	64	57	71	42	67	76	87
75416	BLOSSOM	80	61	77	59	62	79	61	74	67	59	66	55	52	67	60	72	44	69	77	88
75417	BOGATA	81	59	83	57	61	84	62	78	69	56	67	58	50	68	61	76	45	72	83	92
75418	BONHAM	77	60	74	58	61	78	64	74	70	59	68	55	55	69	62	76	46	71	80	87
75420	BRASHEAR	95	68	98	66	71	97	70	89	78	65	76	67	56	77	69	86	50	82	93	106
75421	BROOKSTON	82	69	78	70	70	87	69	81	73	63	71	61	60	73	68	78	48	75	84	95
75422	CAMPBELL	99	71	97	69	73	99	73	91	81	69	80	69	59	82	71	89	53	84	95	109
75423	CELESTE	85	81	70	81	78	86	79	81	81	77	80	62	76	83	76	83	55	80	86	97
75424	BLUE RIDGE	103	95	84	91	92	97	89	95	93	93	93	69	84	96	85	95	63	92	95	112
75426	CLARKSVILLE	72	51	68	49	51	71	55	66	61	51	59	50	43	61	51	67	40	62	70	79
75428	COMMERCE	72	53	54	56	52	61	76	64	74	65	73	53	61	74	61	75	51	70	68	78
75431	COMO	97	69	94	67	71	97	72	89	79	67	78	68	57	80	70	87	52	83	93	107
75432	COOPER	78	58	73	57	59	79	63	74	69	58	67	56	52	69	60	75	45	70	79	88
75433	CUMBY	92	66	95	64	69	94	68	86	75	63	74	65	54	75	67	83	49	79	90	103
75435	DEPORT	68	49	70	48	51	70	51	65	57	47	56	49	41	57	51	63	37	60	69	77
75436	DETROIT	83	56	82	54	57	83	59	75	67	56	66	58	46	68	57	75	44	70	79	91
75437	DIKE	91	72	87	70	73	90	72	85	77	70	77	63	62	78	70	83	51	80	87	101
75438	DODD CITY	95	68	97	66	70	96	70	89	77	65	76	67	56	77	69	85	50	81	92	105
75439	ECTOR	86	64	85	63	67	90	69	84	76	62	74	63	57	75	67	84	49	78	91	99
75440	EMORY	84	60	85	58	62	86	63	79	70	58	68	59	50	69	62	77	45	73	84	94
75442	FARMERSVILLE	97	92	78	91	88	92	91	91	92	91	91	70	87	96	85	93	63	90	92	108
75446	HONEY GROVE	80	59	74	58	60	80	65	75	71	59	69	57	53	71	61	77	46	72	81	89
75447	IVANHOE	103	77	114	74	81	106	78	99	85	73	84	74	64	83	79	92	55	91	101	117
75448	KLONDIKE	79	57	81	55	59	81	58	74	65	54	64	56	47	64	58	71	42	68	77	88
75449	LADONIA	78	52	76	49	52	77	55	69	63	52	61	53	42	63	52	70	40	65	73	84
75450	LAKE CREEK	94	67	97	65	70	95	69	88	77	64	75	66	55	76	68	84	50	81	91	105
	TEXAS	104	96	90	94	93	94	99	97	99	101	100	75	94	101	94	99	70	99	96	114
	UNITED STATES	100	100	100	100	100	100	100	100	100	100	100	100	100	100	100	100	100	100	100	100

POPULATION CHANGE

75451-75703

ZIP CODE			POPULATION			2000-2009 ANNUAL RATE		HOUSEHOLDS					FAMILIES		
#	POST OFFICE NAME	COUNTY FIPS CODE	2000	2009	2014	% Rate	State Centile	2000	2009	2014	% Annual Rate 2000-2009	2009 Average HH Size	2000	2009	% Annual Rate 2000-2009
75451	LEESBURG	063	1356	1525	1612	1.3	65	543	609	643	1.2	2.50	407	451	1.1
75452	LEONARD	147	4313	5078	5448	1.8	75	1615	1890	2026	1.7	2.67	1210	1396	1.6
75453	LONE OAK	231	2378	2473	2490	0.4	37	911	927	931	0.2	2.67	689	690	0.0
75454	MELISSA	085	2288	5111	6838	9.1	98	815	1868	2512	9.4	2.74	642	1395	8.8
75455	MOUNT PLEASANT	449	20711	22636	23684	1.0	58	6896	7356	7644	0.7	3.00	5094	5362	0.6
75457	MOUNT VERNON	159	6552	7758	8419	1.8	75	2520	3014	3285	2.0	2.52	1828	2154	1.8
75459	HOWE	181	3859	4226	4464	1.0	58	1418	1544	1630	0.9	2.74	1120	1202	0.8
75460	PARIS	277	25095	24497	24134	-0.3	16	10209	10013	9893	-0.2	2.34	6503	6223	-0.5
75462	PARIS	277	7842	9649	10282	2.3	81	2991	3724	3984	2.4	2.58	2331	2833	2.1
75468	PATTONVILLE	277	249	247	245	-0.1	21	79	80	79	0.1	3.09	67	66	-0.2
75469	PECAN GAP	119	508	485	475	-0.5	11	217	207	203	-0.5	2.34	152	142	-0.7
75470	PETTY	277	258	262	259	0.2	30	98	100	100	0.2	2.62	77	78	0.1
75471	PICKTON	223	902	1036	1094	1.5	69	343	388	409	1.3	2.67	258	287	1.2
75472	POINT	379	3665	4209	4445	1.5	69	1449	1660	1750	1.5	2.53	1079	1219	1.3
75473	POWDERLY	277	3942	3590	3459	-1.0	4	1456	1348	1306	-0.8	2.66	1173	1072	-1.0
75474	QUINLAN	231	14034	16060	16882	1.5	69	5278	5913	6203	1.2	2.70	3885	4290	1.1
75476	RAVENNA	147	1987	2238	2370	1.3	65	786	881	931	1.2	2.54	599	663	1.1
75477	ROXTON	277	1147	1147	1137	0.0	25	455	455	452	0.0	2.52	327	322	-0.2
75478	SALTILLO	223	428	480	503	1.2	63	167	187	196	1.2	2.57	129	143	1.1
75479	SAVOY	147	1897	2037	2116	0.8	52	706	754	783	0.7	2.57	537	567	0.6
75480	SCROGGINS	159	2368	2791	3041	1.8	75	991	1171	1279	1.8	2.38	755	880	1.7
75481	SULPHUR BLUFF	223	106	119	125	1.3	65	40	45	47	1.3	2.64	31	35	1.3
75482	SULPHUR SPRINGS	223	23716	24863	25414	0.5	42	9162	9621	9844	0.5	2.54	6530	6750	0.4
75486	SUMNER	277	3589	3741	3807	0.4	37	1335	1407	1440	0.6	2.66	1078	1123	0.4
75487	TALCO	449	1230	1347	1419	1.0	58	473	511	536	0.8	2.64	349	372	0.7
75488	TELEPHONE	147	1023	1016	1023	-0.1	21	397	393	395	-0.1	2.59	302	295	-0.3
75490	TRENTON	147	1727	1900	1986	1.0	58	643	699	728	0.9	2.72	483	519	0.8
75491	WHITEWRIGHT	181	4894	5380	5619	1.0	58	1806	1969	2056	0.9	2.68	1388	1490	0.8
75492	WINDOM	147	327	362	379	1.1	61	134	147	154	1.0	2.46	99	107	0.8
75493	WINFIELD	449	2095	2286	2403	0.9	55	729	786	822	0.8	2.91	564	600	0.7
75494	WINNSBORO	499	8479	9861	10528	1.6	71	3272	3820	4106	1.7	2.38	2337	2694	1.5
75495	VAN ALSTYNE	181	5527	6461	6943	1.7	73	1968	2266	2435	1.5	2.83	1552	1760	1.4
75496	WOLFE CITY	231	2640	2768	2798	0.5	42	1016	1041	1051	0.3	2.58	726	730	0.1
75497	YANTIS	499	2210	2740	2993	2.4	82	940	1189	1303	2.6	2.30	700	873	2.4
75501	TEXARKANA	037	37478	38563	38961	0.3	34	13599	14259	14500	0.5	2.50	9470	9752	0.3
75503	TEXARKANA	037	20834	22322	22860	0.7	49	8271	8972	9226	0.9	2.41	5853	6304	0.8
75550	ANNONA	387	883	842	818	-0.5	11	370	355	345	-0.4	2.37	255	240	-0.7
75551	ATLANTA	067	9238	8836	8598	-0.5	11	3643	3543	3469	-0.3	2.44	2642	2532	-0.5
75554	AVERY	387	1578	1503	1460	-0.5	11	678	648	630	-0.5	2.32	470	441	-0.7
75555	BIVINS	067	2001	1866	1811	-0.8	6	764	724	708	-0.6	2.58	578	541	-0.7
75556	BLOOMBURG	067	846	829	815	-0.2	19	341	342	338	0.0	2.42	252	249	-0.1
75558	COOKVILLE	449	2422	2564	2655	0.6	46	894	934	962	0.5	2.75	690	710	0.3
75559	DE KALB	037	6520	6921	7066	0.6	46	2623	2838	2916	0.9	2.41	1882	2001	0.7
75560	DOUGLASSVILLE	067	1479	1358	1305	-0.9	5	606	569	551	-0.7	2.39	422	390	-0.8
75561	HOOKS	037	5956	6380	6570	0.7	49	2343	2563	2657	1.0	2.49	1713	1843	0.8
75563	LINDEN	067	5735	5461	5317	-0.5	11	2379	2312	2264	-0.3	2.29	1584	1513	-0.5
75566	MARIETTA	067	1347	1297	1266	-0.4	13	565	557	548	-0.2	2.33	386	375	-0.3
75567	MAUD	037	3613	3799	3888	0.5	42	1375	1471	1514	0.7	2.56	1016	1068	0.5
75568	NAPLES	343	2733	2640	2587	-0.4	13	1121	1093	1075	-0.3	2.38	762	734	-0.4
75569	NASH	037	2162	2537	2706	1.7	73	894	1059	1137	1.8	2.40	637	739	1.6
75570	NEW BOSTON	037	11222	11302	11334	0.1	27	3367	3442	3475	0.2	2.41	2410	2417	0.0
75571	OMAHA	343	1891	2226	2328	1.8	75	741	894	942	2.0	2.45	535	630	1.8
75572	QUEEN CITY	067	4638	4642	4582	0.0	25	1817	1851	1836	0.2	2.51	1309	1314	0.0
75574	SIMMS	037	1492	1453	1438	-0.3	16	585	583	582	0.0	2.48	444	436	-0.2
75599	TEXARKANA	037	24	26	26	0.9	55	0	0	0	0.0	0.00	0	0	0.0
75601	LONGVIEW	183	14043	15273	15800	0.9	55	5599	6035	6254	0.8	2.36	3534	3746	0.6
75602	LONGVIEW	203	22052	23129	23523	0.5	42	7614	7866	8000	0.4	2.80	5451	5539	0.2
75603	LONGVIEW	183	5136	5638	5843	1.0	58	2047	2253	2340	1.0	2.50	1563	1694	0.9
75604	LONGVIEW	183	27307	29435	30463	0.8	52	10373	11136	11540	0.8	2.63	7594	8037	0.6
75605	LONGVIEW	183	24874	26780	27802	0.8	52	10316	11106	11561	0.8	2.36	6940	7346	0.6
75630	AVINGER	067	2318	2208	2144	-0.5	11	1061	1027	1002	-0.4	2.12	725	695	-0.5
75631	BECKVILLE	365	2606	2469	2420	-0.6	9	1013	974	960	-0.4	2.53	758	718	-0.6
75633	CARTHAGE	365	13915	14229	14348	0.2	30	5363	5539	5611	0.3	2.48	3871	3945	0.2
75638	DAINGERFIELD	343	6128	6151	6117	0.0	25	2428	2482	2485	0.2	2.44	1782	1797	0.1
75639	DE BERRY	365	3413	3802	3949	1.2	63	1304	1477	1541	1.4	2.57	948	1058	1.2
75640	DIANA	203	3712	4155	4349	1.2	63	1357	1532	1609	1.3	2.71	1092	1220	1.2
75643	GARY	365	1348	1334	1325	-0.1	21	535	537	536	0.0	2.48	380	375	-0.1
75644	GILMER	459	10848	11349	11592	0.5	42	4101	4313	4417	0.5	2.58	3028	3140	0.4
75645	GILMER	459	8251	9323	9827	1.3	65	3159	3604	3814	1.4	2.57	2378	2676	1.3
75647	GLADEWATER	183	11856	12934	13499	0.9	55	4377	4779	4999	1.0	2.63	3244	3490	0.8
75650	HALLSVILLE	203	7247	8073	8345	1.2	63	2597	2925	3037	1.3	2.75	2025	2246	1.1
75651	HARLETON	203	1783	2027	2103	1.4	67	668	767	799	1.5	2.64	520	590	1.4
75652	HENDERSON	401	14578	14706	14676	0.1	27	4944	4965	4973	0.0	2.54	3583	3540	-0.1
75654	HENDERSON	401	10884	12144	12639	1.2	63	4219	4703	4899	1.2	2.55	3056	3376	1.1
75656	HUGHES SPRINGS	067	4687	5369	5511	1.5	69	1839	2179	2260	1.9	2.43	1325	1540	1.6
75657	JEFFERSON	315	9282	9572	9470	0.3	34	3885	4039	4011	0.4	2.34	2644	2709	0.3
75661	KARNACK	203	2265	2219	2178	-0.2	19	972	963	948	-0.1	2.30	682	662	-0.3
75662	KILGORE	183	23126	24805	25720	0.8	52	8801	9397	9753	0.7	2.59	6307	6634	0.5
75667	LANEVILLE	401	3264	3292	3306	0.1	27	1289	1313	1323	0.2	2.48	912	912	0.0
75668	LONE STAR	343	1747	1768	1754	0.1	27	712	734	731	0.3	2.41	506	515	0.2
75669	LONG BRANCH	365	1156	1230	1252	0.7	49	483	518	531	0.8	2.37	347	366	0.6
75670	MARSHALL	203	17603	17344	17131	-0.2	19	6093	5948	5882	-0.3	2.64	4197	4022	-0.5
75672	MARSHALL	203	16886	17017	16890	0.1	27	6715	6826	6805	0.2	2.47	4834	4828	0.0
75681	MOUNT ENTERPRISE	401	1906	1905	1910	0.0	25	749	758	764	0.1	2.51	548	546	0.0
75683	ORE CITY	459	4786	5177	5353	0.9	55	1761	1914	1982	0.9	2.70	1322	1421	0.8
75684	OVERTON	401	6485	6765	6868	0.5	42	2273	2364	2410	0.4	2.58	1676	1716	0.3
75686	PITTSBURG	063	12472	13851	14643	1.1	61	4607	5081	5361	1.1	2.68	3397	3694	0.9
75687	PRICE	073	5	5	5	0.0	25	2	2	2	0.0	2.50	1	1	0.0
75689	SELMAN CITY	401	425	433	436	0.2	30	155	157	158	0.1	2.73	117	117	0.0
75691	TATUM	401	2909	2740	2728	-0.6	9	1054	996	992	-0.6	2.75	803	751	-0.7
75692	WASKOM	203	5279	5350	5283	0.1	27	1935	1976	1957	0.2	2.71	1489	1498	0.1
75693	WHITE OAK	183	5835	6568	6905	1.3	65	2056	2304	2426	1.2	2.83	1637	1807	1.1
75701	TYLER	423	30358	33041	34521	0.9	55	12448	13260	13870	0.7	2.40	8055	8360	0.4
75702	TYLER	423	26372	28167	29118	0.7	49	8241	8511	8787	0.3	3.16	5919	6005	0.2
75703	TYLER	423	30094	35097	37955	1.7	73	12802	14599	15768	1.4	2.37	8235	9224	1.2
	TEXAS					1.9					1.8	2.78			1.7
	UNITED STATES					1.0					1.1	2.59			0.9

ZIP CODE #	POST OFFICE NAME	RACE (%) White 2000	White 2009	Black 2000	Black 2009	Asian/Pacific 2000	Asian/Pacific 2009	% Hispanic Origin 2000	% Hispanic Origin 2009	2009 AGE DISTRIBUTION (%) 0-4	5-9	10-14	15-19	20-24	25-44	45-64	65-84	85+	18+	MEDIAN AGE 2009	% 2009 Males	% 2009 Females
75451	LEESBURG	81.6	77.1	12.5	14.6	0.2	0.3	6.3	8.7	6.0	6.4	6.5	5.5	4.4	22.8	30.2	16.3	1.8	77.6	43.7	49.6	50.4
75452	LEONARD	90.3	86.9	3.0	3.7	0.1	0.2	5.8	8.5	7.4	7.4	7.5	7.4	5.9	24.9	26.1	11.2	2.0	72.9	37.1	49.4	50.6
75453	LONE OAK	93.4	90.7	3.2	4.1	0.4	0.5	4.2	6.5	5.9	6.3	6.6	7.0	5.5	23.1	29.8	14.4	1.4	76.9	41.8	50.6	49.4
75454	MELISSA	91.1	85.6	0.5	0.6	0.3	0.5	11.1	18.5	7.1	7.2	7.5	7.5	5.7	25.7	28.7	9.6	0.9	73.4	37.2	50.9	49.1
75455	MOUNT PLEASANT	65.3	60.0	12.5	12.5	0.6	0.7	33.3	41.4	9.4	8.7	8.1	7.5	6.7	27.4	20.7	9.4	2.2	69.3	31.8	49.8	50.2
75457	MOUNT VERNON	87.5	84.4	5.3	5.9	0.2	0.2	9.6	13.2	5.9	6.0	6.3	6.5	5.0	23.4	28.7	15.5	2.7	77.8	42.6	48.5	51.5
75459	HOWE	95.2	93.3	0.4	0.5	0.2	0.3	4.4	6.6	8.0	8.0	7.8	7.4	6.1	27.4	25.7	8.6	0.9	71.6	34.8	49.0	51.0
75460	PARIS	73.2	68.9	22.1	25.3	0.6	0.8	4.1	5.6	7.5	6.6	6.2	6.9	7.0	24.8	23.5	13.6	3.8	75.8	37.5	46.8	53.2
75462	PARIS	90.9	88.8	5.1	5.6	0.6	0.9	2.7	3.9	7.0	7.2	7.3	6.7	5.0	25.9	27.6	11.5	1.7	74.2	38.7	48.4	51.6
75468	PATTONVILLE	96.8	95.5	1.6	2.0	0.0	0.0	1.2	1.6	6.9	7.3	7.3	6.1	4.5	24.3	28.7	13.4	1.6	74.5	41.3	48.2	51.8
75469	PECAN GAP	91.7	91.3	4.1	4.3	0.2	0.2	4.1	4.5	4.5	4.7	5.2	6.4	4.9	24.3	31.5	16.5	1.9	81.9	44.9	53.0	47.0
75470	PETTY	90.3	87.0	6.6	8.4	0.0	0.0	2.7	3.8	6.1	6.1	6.5	7.6	5.3	23.3	29.0	14.1	1.9	76.7	41.9	48.5	51.5
75471	PICKTON	82.8	77.7	5.2	6.3	0.0	0.0	17.6	23.7	6.8	6.5	6.7	7.6	6.4	27.3	25.6	11.9	1.4	75.4	36.7	50.0	50.0
75472	POINT	92.6	90.5	2.1	2.4	0.7	1.0	4.2	5.7	5.7	6.0	6.2	6.1	4.8	22.9	30.3	16.3	1.7	78.2	43.7	50.2	49.8
75473	POWDERLY	94.4	92.8	2.8	3.6	0.0	0.0	1.2	1.7	6.6	6.9	7.2	6.7	4.5	23.4	30.5	13.0	1.2	75.1	41.3	49.5	50.5
75474	QUINLAN	94.3	92.0	1.0	1.3	0.2	0.3	5.0	7.7	6.7	6.5	6.8	6.6	6.5	24.5	29.2	12.2	1.1	75.9	39.4	50.1	49.9
75476	RAVENNA	94.6	92.9	1.4	1.7	0.1	0.0	3.4	5.0	5.7	6.1	6.5	6.4	4.5	23.1	30.6	15.5	1.5	77.3	43.2	51.1	48.9
75477	ROXTON	80.9	76.5	15.6	19.1	0.0	0.0	2.8	4.0	7.4	7.3	7.1	7.0	6.3	22.2	24.5	15.7	2.4	73.8	39.4	45.1	54.9
75478	SALTILLO	94.2	91.7	0.7	0.8	0.0	0.2	12.4	17.3	6.9	7.3	7.5	7.1	5.2	24.4	27.1	13.3	1.3	74.0	38.9	51.7	48.3
75479	SAVOY	96.0	94.8	0.3	0.3	0.3	0.3	2.2	3.3	5.6	5.7	6.3	7.2	4.6	22.0	29.2	16.0	3.4	77.9	44.0	49.4	50.6
75480	SCROGGINS	94.2	92.2	0.6	0.7	0.1	0.1	6.8	9.6	5.0	5.2	5.3	5.0	4.1	21.7	32.0	19.9	1.9	81.4	47.3	49.4	50.6
75481	SULPHUR BLUFF	95.2	91.6	1.0	1.7	0.0	0.0	4.8	6.7	5.9	6.7	6.7	6.7	5.0	26.1	28.6	12.6	1.7	75.6	39.7	47.9	52.1
75482	SULPHUR SPRINGS	83.1	79.6	10.2	11.5	0.3	0.4	8.7	11.9	6.7	6.5	6.4	6.6	6.1	25.6	26.5	12.7	2.9	76.3	38.8	48.7	51.3
75486	SUMNER	94.8	93.2	1.9	2.6	0.1	0.1	2.8	4.1	6.6	6.8	7.1	7.1	5.1	23.5	28.3	14.1	1.3	75.0	40.6	51.8	48.2
75487	TALCO	78.5	73.5	13.9	15.8	0.1	0.1	9.2	13.1	6.4	6.2	6.6	7.6	5.9	24.1	27.5	13.5	2.1	76.0	40.0	50.1	49.9
75488	TELEPHONE	94.9	93.2	1.3	1.6	0.0	0.0	3.5	5.2	5.7	5.9	5.9	5.5	4.4	24.9	30.1	15.8	1.7	78.8	43.3	50.3	49.7
75490	TRENTON	89.1	85.9	3.0	3.4	0.1	0.2	8.5	11.9	8.3	7.9	8.3	7.7	5.2	24.5	26.4	10.3	1.4	70.8	36.7	48.8	51.2
75491	WHITEWRIGHT	91.7	89.2	3.8	4.6	0.5	0.7	3.8	5.8	6.7	6.8	7.2	7.0	5.8	25.0	26.9	12.3	2.2	74.7	39.1	48.6	51.4
75492	WINDOM	94.8	93.9	2.7	3.3	0.0	0.0	0.3	0.6	6.4	6.4	6.9	7.2	4.4	23.8	28.2	14.9	1.9	75.7	41.8	49.4	50.6
75493	WINFIELD	83.2	77.3	2.0	2.1	0.1	0.1	20.4	28.2	8.3	8.2	8.3	7.4	4.8	26.9	24.3	10.7	1.0	70.6	35.5	49.8	50.2
75494	WINNSBORO	90.5	88.0	4.3	5.0	0.5	0.7	5.3	7.5	5.1	5.1	5.4	6.0	6.0	24.5	27.9	16.6	3.4	80.9	43.4	52.0	48.0
75495	VAN ALSTYNE	92.8	90.1	2.2	2.6	0.3	0.4	6.1	9.4	7.0	6.9	7.1	7.0	5.9	24.3	28.2	11.7	1.9	74.5	39.2	50.1	49.9
75496	WOLFE CITY	85.6	81.4	10.0	12.8	0.3	0.4	3.9	5.8	7.3	7.1	6.9	7.0	6.3	24.7	24.4	13.3	3.1	74.5	37.8	49.6	50.4
75497	YANTIS	93.4	91.4	2.4	2.7	0.1	0.1	6.9	10.2	4.6	4.8	5.1	4.8	3.4	18.7	34.5	22.4	1.8	82.6	50.9	50.6	49.4
75501	TEXARKANA	62.4	59.5	34.4	36.6	0.4	0.5	5.3	7.0	6.8	6.6	6.5	6.8	6.9	28.5	25.6	10.5	1.7	76.1	36.3	51.0	49.0
75503	TEXARKANA	82.4	79.2	14.3	16.3	0.9	1.3	2.3	3.3	6.1	5.9	6.4	6.6	5.6	24.0	28.3	13.7	3.3	77.4	41.6	46.7	53.3
75550	ANNONA	77.3	74.0	14.6	16.0	0.0	0.0	6.8	8.9	5.7	5.9	6.3	6.1	4.4	22.7	29.3	17.1	2.5	78.1	44.0	49.4	50.6
75551	ATLANTA	76.8	74.4	20.8	22.5	0.2	0.4	1.6	2.2	6.2	6.1	6.3	6.8	5.4	22.4	28.3	15.3	3.1	77.1	42.1	47.3	52.7
75554	AVERY	86.8	84.7	7.9	8.8	0.0	0.0	3.9	5.2	5.6	5.9	6.3	6.3	4.5	22.9	28.4	17.5	2.7	78.4	43.7	49.1	50.9
75555	BIVINS	85.8	84.1	11.2	11.9	0.1	0.2	2.0	2.7	6.5	6.9	7.2	6.8	4.7	24.4	28.1	13.9	1.6	75.2	40.5	50.7	49.3
75556	BLOOMBURG	92.0	90.3	6.3	7.2	0.2	0.5	1.5	2.3	5.8	6.0	6.0	5.9	5.1	22.9	32.1	14.1	2.1	78.4	43.6	48.4	51.6
75558	COOKVILLE	88.0	83.3	1.8	2.1	0.0	0.1	12.9	18.5	7.8	7.4	6.9	6.4	6.3	26.8	26.0	11.2	1.2	74.0	36.3	49.8	50.2
75559	DE KALB	80.5	76.8	15.9	18.8	0.1	0.1	2.8	4.1	6.4	6.6	6.8	6.9	5.3	22.4	27.9	14.8	3.0	76.1	41.4	48.9	51.1
75560	DOUGLASSVILLE	60.5	56.6	37.1	40.7	0.1	0.1	0.6	0.7	5.6	5.9	6.2	5.7	4.9	23.3	32.2	14.0	2.1	78.9	43.6	49.7	50.3
75561	HOOKS	80.7	76.0	14.5	17.7	0.4	0.6	3.0	4.3	7.0	7.0	7.1	6.9	5.3	24.5	28.3	12.2	1.8	74.7	38.6	47.5	52.5
75563	LINDEN	75.9	72.6	22.0	24.8	0.1	0.2	1.6	2.1	5.3	5.5	5.6	5.8	5.5	22.0	29.4	17.4	3.5	80.1	45.2	49.5	50.5
75566	MARIETTA	73.6	70.2	25.4	28.5	0.1	0.2	0.5	0.7	4.9	5.0	5.5	5.8	4.4	21.0	30.8	19.5	3.2	81.0	47.6	49.8	50.2
75567	MAUD	89.1	85.9	8.7	11.2	0.1	0.1	1.4	2.2	6.4	6.6	6.8	7.0	5.6	24.6	29.8	11.6	1.5	75.9	39.6	50.8	49.2
75568	NAPLES	70.0	67.0	27.2	29.4	0.1	0.2	1.8	2.4	6.1	6.2	6.5	6.6	5.1	22.2	27.2	16.6	3.6	77.0	42.4	48.5	51.5
75569	NASH	79.1	73.6	16.5	20.6	0.4	0.5	3.9	5.8	7.2	7.0	6.9	6.7	5.8	27.4	26.6	11.0	1.4	74.8	36.9	48.3	51.7
75570	NEW BOSTON	75.8	71.8	21.5	24.9	0.3	0.4	9.0	12.2	5.3	4.9	4.9	5.3	10.2	34.4	22.2	10.8	2.0	81.8	34.8	60.3	39.7
75571	OMAHA	74.7	71.2	21.5	23.9	0.3	0.4	4.1	5.6	6.4	6.7	6.8	6.8	4.9	22.5	27.7	15.3	3.0	75.9	41.5	48.1	51.9
75572	QUEEN CITY	81.2	78.1	16.5	19.0	0.2	0.2	1.7	2.2	6.8	6.9	6.9	6.4	5.5	25.2	28.3	12.3	1.7	75.4	39.1	47.9	52.1
75574	SIMMS	92.5	90.3	4.6	5.8	0.1	0.2	2.3	3.4	5.4	5.8	6.1	7.1	4.7	23.9	30.9	13.8	2.1	78.3	42.6	48.5	51.5
75599	TEXARKANA	62.5	57.7	33.3	38.5	0.0	0.0	4.2	3.8	7.7	7.7	7.7	7.7	7.7	30.8	26.9	3.8	0.0	76.9	32.5	46.2	53.8
75601	LONGVIEW	70.9	66.0	20.4	22.4	0.8	1.0	11.2	15.2	6.7	6.5	6.4	6.6	6.1	25.6	24.6	14.1	3.4	76.8	38.7	48.4	51.6
75602	LONGVIEW	45.1	41.8	45.2	46.2	0.4	0.5	15.1	19.0	8.3	8.1	7.6	9.3	8.5	25.8	22.3	8.9	1.4	71.3	31.1	49.6	50.4
75603	LONGVIEW	58.4	53.1	36.5	40.4	0.3	0.4	5.9	7.7	5.5	6.0	6.4	6.1	4.4	23.4	32.6	14.4	1.3	78.3	43.7	49.0	51.0
75604	LONGVIEW	83.4	79.2	9.0	10.5	0.9	1.3	9.3	13.2	7.6	7.2	7.1	7.1	7.1	27.3	25.4	10.0	1.2	73.6	34.7	48.6	51.4
75605	LONGVIEW	88.3	84.9	8.1	10.1	0.8	1.1	3.3	5.1	5.7	5.6	5.8	6.0	6.4	25.9	28.6	13.4	2.6	79.3	40.6	47.7	52.3
75630	AVINGER	79.2	77.9	17.4	18.3	0.0	0.0	2.3	2.8	4.9	4.3	5.1	4.8	3.8	17.9	34.9	21.4	2.7	82.4	50.9	50.1	49.9
75631	BECKVILLE	76.8	72.6	16.7	18.6	0.1	0.1	5.7	7.9	6.6	7.1	7.1	5.8	4.5	26.6	28.8	12.2	1.5	75.6	39.2	49.8	50.2
75633	CARTHAGE	79.5	76.7	17.1	18.6	0.3	0.4	3.5	5.0	6.1	6.2	6.2	7.0	6.2	23.5	27.7	14.0	3.0	77.3	40.2	47.6	52.4
75638	DAINGERFIELD	69.8	65.6	25.8	28.5	0.3	0.3	3.8	5.1	5.6	5.7	6.0	6.2	5.9	22.2	29.5	16.4	2.6	78.9	43.6	49.2	50.8
75639	DE BERRY	71.2	67.0	26.4	30.1	0.1	0.2	2.6	3.5	5.7	5.8	7.1	6.9	6.1	23.8	31.4	11.8	1.4	77.1	40.9	50.0	50.0
75640	DIANA	89.4	87.4	8.0	9.2	0.1	0.2	2.5	3.5	6.3	6.3	6.7	7.2	6.2	26.5	28.7	11.0	1.1	76.3	38.9	49.8	50.2
75643	GARY	87.9	85.5	9.2	10.6	0.1	0.1	2.9	4.1	6.8	7.0	7.4	6.5	5.0	21.7	28.2	15.1	2.2	74.7	41.3	50.2	49.8
75644	GILMER	83.6	80.6	12.2	13.8	0.2	0.2	4.2	5.8	6.8	6.7	6.7	6.6	5.8	23.4	26.9	14.5	2.6	75.7	40.0	48.4	51.6
75645	GILMER	86.8	84.3	9.5	10.8	0.1	0.2	3.8	5.3	6.3	6.6	6.9	6.8	5.2	24.0	29.5	13.0	1.7	76.0	40.5	50.3	49.7
75647	GLADEWATER	83.9	80.8	12.5	14.2	0.3	0.4	3.2	4.7	6.6	6.7	6.9	6.8	5.9	24.7	28.0	12.3	2.1	75.5	38.8	48.8	51.2
75650	HALLSVILLE	90.6	87.7	7.0	8.9	0.2	0.3	2.2	3.5	7.1	7.1	7.3	7.7	6.3	26.3	28.9	8.4	0.9	73.8	36.3	49.2	50.8
75651	HARLETON	87.8	84.7	9.9	12.1	0.1	0.1	1.6	2.6	6.2	6.3	6.5	7.2	6.3	26.1	28.8	11.3	1.3	76.6	38.8	50.0	50.0
75652	HENDERSON	67.8	64.0	26.6	28.7	0.3	0.4	8.4	11.1	5.7	5.7	5.6	5.5	5.7	30.7	27.3	11.7	2.0	79.6	39.0	55.4	44.6
75654	HENDERSON	80.7	76.8	11.2	12.1	0.4	0.5	11.2	15.8	6.7	6.5	6.7	6.7	5.3	23.5	27.2	14.3	3.1	75.9	40.6	48.2	51.8
75656	HUGHES SPRINGS	82.4	77.1	15.1	19.5	0.1	0.1	2.7	3.9	6.9	5.9	5.9	6.5	6.2	21.6	27.9	16.4	2.8	77.4	42.5	47.1	52.9
75657	JEFFERSON	71.0	69.8	25.8	26.8	0.3	0.3	2.2	2.4	5.5	5.6	6.0	5.9	4.8	20.6	30.9	17.9	2.8	79.3	46.1	48.8	51.2
75661	KARNACK	65.4	59.5	32.5	37.9	0.2	0.3	1.8	2.5	4.2	5.0	5.2	7.0	4.8	19.9	33.8	17.8	2.3	81.0	47.5	49.5	50.5
75662	KILGORE	78.6	74.0	14.4	16.8	0.5	0.6	8.1	11.0	6.6	6.5	6.4	7.4	6.5	25.1	27.2	12.2	2.0	76.4	38.0	49.2	50.8
75667	LANEVILLE	65.4	60.4	26.9	29.7	0.1	0.1	9.9	13.1	6.2	6.1	6.6	7.0	5.4	22.3	27.6	16.3	2.5	76.5	42.2	50.1	49.9
75668	LONE STAR	74.7	70.5	19.2	21.3	0.3	0.4	6.2	8.5	6.8	7.4	7.2	6.5	5.3	23.0	27.9	14.5	1.4	74.3	39.1	46.9	53.1
75669	LONG BRANCH	86.2	84.5	11.9	13.1	0.1	0.1	1.6	2.2	5.4	5.8	6.1	6.9	4.8	21.2	30.9	16.8	2.1	78.5	44.9	47.7	52.3
75670	MARSHALL	45.5	40.9	47.1	49.6	0.3	0.4	10.3	13.3	7.3	7.1	6.7	9.5	9.8	24.3	22.7	10.1	2.5	74.6	32.2	47.9	52.1
75672	MARSHALL	75.4	69.8	20.5	24.6	0.6	0.7	3.9	5.7	5.8	5.8	6.1	6.3	5.7	23.6	29.9	14.5	2.3	78.4	42.3	48.7	51.3
75681	MOUNT ENTERPRISE	66.7	62.0	31.2	35.4	0.1	0.1	3.4	4.6	5.9	6.1	6.6	7.5	5.1	24.4	28.1	14.1	2.3	76.8	41.0	49.2	50.8
75683	ORE CITY	84.4	81.7	9.9	11.0	0.2	0.3	5.5	7.4	7.0	6.9	7.1	6.9	5.7	24.3	28.2	12.5	1.4	74.8	39.4	49.5	50.5
75684	OVERTON	80.2	76.1	16.4	19.3	0.1	0.1	5.5	7.5	6.2	6.4	6.7	6.1	5.4	26.7	27.3	12.7	2.6	76.8	39.5	52.1	47.9
75686	PITTSBURG	70.3	65.6	18.6	19.7	0.2	0.3	14.8	19.7	7.4	7.2	7.3	7.1	5.8	23.9	26.0	13.1	2.1	73.9	37.9	49.1	50.9
75687	PRICE	100.0	100.0	0.0	0.0	0.0	0.0	25.0	0.0	0.0	0.0	0.0	0.0	0.0	100.0	0.0	0.0	0.0	100.0	38.8	40.0	60.0
75689	SELMAN CITY	83.3	78.8	5.6	6.5	0.2	0.2	11.1	15.0	7.9	8.1	7.9	6.7	6.2	27.0	24.7	10.2	1.4	71.8	34.7	50.3	49.7
75691	TATUM	73.6	67.9	15.6	17.8	0.0	0.0	18.1	23.5	7.0	7.0	6.9	6.6	6.1	27.9	27.0	9.8	1.5	74.6	36.4	50.1	49.9
75692	WASKOM	75.1	69.0	19.8	23.8	0.2	0.2	5.1	7.7	7.1	7.2	6.9	6.1	5.9	24.2	29.3	12.0	1.3	75.1	38.8	50.4	49.6
75693	WHITE OAK	93.6	91.3	2.6	3.4	0.1	0.2	3.5	5.3	7.0	7.1	7.1	7.3	6.3	27.2	27.2	9.9	1.0	74.3	36.7	49.9	50.1
75701	TYLER	72.5	66.5	20.4	23.4	0.6	0.8	11.1	15.9	6.8	6.3	6.2	7.3	6.7	23.4	23.9	15.0	4.4	76.8	39.1	45.3	54.7
75702	TYLER	29.7	26.6	47.0	45.2	0.3	0.3	34.2	41.2	9.5	9.0	8.1	8.5	8.4	26.5	20.1	8.1	1.7	68.3	29.1	49.1	50.9
75703	TYLER	85.8	81.8	9.8	12.1	1.7	2.1	3.3	5.5	6.4	6.3	6.3	6.3	6.7	27.5	26.0	12.0	2.5	77.2	37.5	48.0	52.0
	TEXAS	71.0	67.6	11.5	11.4	2.8	3.5	32.0	37.4	7.9	7.5	7.2	7.5	7.4	28.3	24.0	8.8	1.4	73.0	33.6	49.7	50.3
	UNITED STATES	75.1	72.0	12.3	12.7	3.8	4.6	12.5	15.7	6.8	6.7	6.6	7.1	6.9	27.0	26.0	10.9	1.9	75.7	36.9	49.2	50.8

#	POST OFFICE NAME	2009 Per Capita Income	2009 HH Income Base	2009 Household Income Distribution (%): Less than $25,000	$25,000 to $49,999	$50,000 to $99,999	$100,000 to $149,999	$150,000 or More	Median Household Income: 2009	2014	2009 National Centile	2009 State Centile	2009 Home Value Base	2009 Home Value Distribution (%): Less than $50,000	$50,000 to $89,999	$90,000 to $174,999	$175,000 to $399,999	$400,000 or More	2009 Median Home Value
75451	LEESBURG	18391	609	28.2	38.1	28.1	4.1	1.5	40402	41437	34	44	514	31.7	23.5	27.0	17.7	0.0	78750
75452	LEONARD	19833	1890	25.8	28.9	37.0	6.8	1.4	46385	46549	52	63	1395	17.9	25.8	38.9	15.7	1.7	99021
75453	LONE OAK	17247	927	28.5	36.9	28.8	4.5	1.3	38113	43803	27	34	737	35.1	32.6	22.0	10.2	0.1	63909
75454	MELISSA	30914	1868	16.6	22.9	34.2	15.8	10.5	63339	60834	82	86	1578	14.3	18.6	35.2	21.7	10.1	121919
75455	MOUNT PLEASANT	16849	7356	31.4	31.4	28.6	5.5	3.0	38990	41286	30	38	4951	18.5	32.2	33.7	13.2	2.4	89119
75457	MOUNT VERNON	21612	3014	31.2	28.3	29.8	5.9	4.8	41146	42896	36	46	2313	24.0	20.8	35.5	15.3	4.5	98934
75459	HOWE	21605	1544	22.3	26.1	39.0	8.9	3.7	51170	52139	64	73	1180	18.6	30.1	36.7	12.8	1.8	92308
75460	PARIS	18663	10013	39.8	28.5	25.8	3.5	2.3	32754	36067	13	16	5410	33.7	33.3	27.4	4.9	0.7	67646
75462	PARIS	24650	3724	19.1	30.1	37.4	9.2	4.2	50682	48677	63	72	2933	7.0	21.7	48.3	20.3	2.8	116979
75468	PATTONVILLE	12092	80	36.3	42.5	17.5	3.8	0.0	33581	36118	15	18	66	25.8	22.7	33.3	15.2	3.0	95000
75469	PECAN GAP	18918	207	34.3	28.5	30.9	5.3	1.0	38016	38956	27	34	173	58.4	23.7	15.6	2.3	0.0	46081
75470	PETTY	19232	100	28.0	31.0	36.0	4.0	1.0	43200	43438	43	54	85	31.8	31.8	24.7	10.6	1.2	70833
75471	PICKTON	19565	388	30.2	34.5	27.6	4.1	3.6	40000	42792	33	42	278	29.1	27.3	32.4	4.3	6.8	83571
75472	POINT	18930	1660	28.8	29.4	35.4	4.4	2.0	42232	42905	40	50	1373	16.5	33.4	35.9	12.8	1.4	90138
75473	POWDERLY	20429	1348	22.3	27.5	42.4	5.3	2.5	50119	47683	61	70	1133	20.8	25.1	34.7	17.8	1.6	94947
75474	QUINLAN	19858	5913	24.0	31.6	35.0	6.8	2.6	45047	48210	48	59	4781	37.4	30.3	23.2	8.3	0.8	63736
75476	RAVENNA	20724	881	29.1	28.4	35.2	4.9	2.5	43873	45145	45	55	751	22.4	29.3	33.7	11.6	3.1	86951
75477	ROXTON	17521	455	37.1	26.8	30.5	4.4	1.1	35538	38065	19	25	340	41.5	32.4	20.3	5.6	0.3	60000
75478	SALTILLO	17202	187	29.4	33.2	34.2	2.7	0.5	36578	38810	22	29	152	28.3	28.9	27.0	11.8	3.9	74286
75479	SAVOY	20231	754	23.7	34.4	36.1	3.8	2.0	45000	45648	48	59	580	22.8	32.8	28.1	12.4	4.0	83191
75480	SCROGGINS	20894	1171	24.7	39.6	26.5	6.4	2.8	40919	41942	36	46	984	16.5	17.2	32.3	27.7	6.3	122336
75481	SULPHUR BLUFF	18972	45	26.7	31.1	35.6	6.7	0.0	44078	42347	46	56	37	37.8	21.6	29.7	10.8	0.0	72500
75482	SULPHUR SPRINGS	19926	9621	30.6	31.8	29.4	5.1	3.1	39904	42217	32	41	6565	19.1	27.7	38.8	11.6	2.8	94873
75486	SUMNER	18311	1407	30.1	26.1	38.2	4.1	1.6	41928	42995	39	50	1132	23.4	31.2	31.7	11.1	2.6	82973
75487	TALCO	14390	511	40.1	32.3	23.9	3.7	0.0	30424	35915	9	11	417	51.8	21.1	20.9	6.2	0.0	47917
75488	TELEPHONE	18743	393	33.8	23.9	35.4	5.6	1.3	40825	43331	35	45	317	21.8	29.0	31.9	15.5	1.9	88864
75490	TRENTON	21509	699	23.0	25.3	38.9	10.4	2.3	51096	50366	64	72	547	17.6	23.0	31.8	25.6	2.0	108705
75491	WHITEWRIGHT	20118	1969	22.4	28.6	39.9	7.2	1.9	49064	50786	59	68	1512	20.1	27.9	36.5	13.1	2.4	94000
75492	WINDOM	23626	147	27.9	27.9	33.3	5.4	5.4	42795	45404	42	52	112	32.1	26.8	29.5	9.8	1.8	72500
75493	WINFIELD	18872	786	24.2	35.4	28.8	9.7	2.0	43662	45325	44	55	627	23.3	15.6	34.1	22.5	4.5	109844
75494	WINNSBORO	19380	3820	34.1	33.9	25.2	4.4	2.5	35611	38026	20	26	2987	14.2	27.4	39.4	15.1	4.0	100025
75495	VAN ALSTYNE	22515	2266	18.7	27.5	38.3	11.1	4.3	53514	53444	69	77	1801	11.1	22.4	36.1	28.0	2.4	127324
75496	WOLFE CITY	18764	1041	31.3	29.6	30.8	5.9	2.4	40039	44532	33	42	749	42.9	25.9	25.8	4.9	0.5	57868
75497	YANTIS	24339	1189	26.3	32.7	33.1	4.3	3.5	42360	43892	41	51	998	15.3	17.7	34.1	24.5	8.3	121303
75501	TEXARKANA	17523	14259	36.6	28.5	28.5	5.0	1.3	35469	39826	19	25	9276	34.2	33.7	28.1	3.8	0.1	65613
75503	TEXARKANA	29437	8972	19.9	24.8	35.4	12.6	7.3	55439	54011	72	79	6255	12.2	22.3	44.7	17.3	3.4	112984
75550	ANNONA	17754	355	39.7	30.7	25.4	2.8	1.4	33556	34741	14	18	295	47.5	28.5	14.9	7.8	1.4	53750
75551	ATLANTA	19530	3543	33.0	30.4	29.1	5.4	2.1	36432	38451	22	29	2696	24.0	32.4	34.2	8.3	1.1	81925
75554	AVERY	17461	648	41.2	31.2	23.3	2.9	1.4	31594	32996	11	13	512	50.6	27.9	14.5	5.9	1.2	49231
75555	BIVINS	14874	724	36.5	34.1	27.2	1.9	0.3	37734	40274	26	33	628	38.2	28.7	28.5	4.1	0.5	64318
75556	BLOOMBURG	20348	342	33.6	28.4	30.7	5.3	2.0	38751	40351	29	37	270	30.7	21.5	37.4	8.5	1.9	86000
75558	COOKVILLE	18493	934	34.8	29.0	27.8	5.9	2.5	38836	41374	29	37	780	18.3	24.6	33.5	19.2	4.4	103713
75559	DE KALB	17294	2838	38.4	28.4	29.0	3.0	1.2	33646	36924	15	19	2162	43.9	24.5	25.7	4.2	1.6	57939
75560	DOUGLASSVILLE	17658	569	37.3	43.2	13.9	2.6	3.0	29876	32226	8	10	481	30.6	33.1	28.9	5.6	1.9	65889
75561	HOOKS	19685	2563	29.7	31.2	32.4	5.0	1.7	41783	45286	39	49	1968	39.6	32.5	23.0	4.3	0.6	59152
75563	LINDEN	18289	2312	37.2	29.5	27.9	3.8	1.6	33931	34868	15	19	1824	34.3	31.0	24.4	8.5	1.8	67975
75566	MARIETTA	16728	557	41.7	36.4	18.7	1.4	1.8	28489	31067	6	7	483	47.4	26.5	21.5	3.3	1.2	53205
75567	MAUD	19285	1471	30.5	29.7	32.7	5.3	1.8	41609	45000	38	49	1199	37.1	31.2	23.6	7.6	0.5	64406
75568	NAPLES	19064	1093	37.3	30.8	25.0	4.6	2.3	32435	33340	12	15	849	33.1	31.4	30.0	5.1	0.4	68839
75569	NASH	19085	1059	30.3	32.7	32.0	3.5	1.5	38230	41545	27	35	739	40.1	37.3	20.8	1.8	0.0	57903
75570	NEW BOSTON	18174	3442	32.7	26.6	35.4	3.5	1.8	39286	44428	31	40	2537	35.6	34.7	25.0	4.1	0.6	64059
75571	OMAHA	17681	894	36.7	30.8	27.2	4.0	1.3	32260	33377	12	15	696	32.8	37.2	24.9	3.9	1.3	66981
75572	QUEEN CITY	17215	1851	37.8	28.1	28.7	4.3	1.1	33335	34503	14	17	1449	33.7	29.8	30.0	6.0	0.4	69312
75574	SIMMS	20264	583	24.4	36.7	31.2	3.8	3.9	40272	45199	34	43	481	35.1	31.2	27.2	6.0	0.4	65648
75599	TEXARKANA	565	0	0.0	0.0	0.0	0.0	0.0	0	0	0	0	0	0.0	0.0	0.0	0.0	0.0	0
75601	LONGVIEW	22763	6035	28.2	28.8	31.8	6.9	4.3	43509	46839	44	54	3695	18.2	23.1	45.5	12.0	1.3	103482
75602	LONGVIEW	15417	7866	37.9	31.0	25.3	4.1	1.7	33264	36122	14	17	4862	37.1	36.4	19.9	5.4	1.3	60151
75603	LONGVIEW	22347	2253	24.0	30.0	35.1	8.3	2.6	46581	48699	53	63	1935	23.8	27.2	31.9	16.1	1.0	88646
75604	LONGVIEW	23368	11136	23.0	29.5	35.2	8.2	4.1	48095	50080	57	67	7008	15.7	25.8	42.6	14.1	1.8	103223
75605	LONGVIEW	27173	11106	20.7	27.5	37.3	9.0	5.4	51469	51947	65	73	6923	7.7	12.8	54.1	22.5	2.9	131069
75630	AVINGER	22263	1027	35.2	28.7	28.4	5.4	2.2	35413	37377	19	24	855	40.7	29.8	22.7	5.8	0.9	59464
75631	BECKVILLE	18665	974	30.7	30.8	30.7	6.5	1.3	39555	41658	31	41	783	35.8	23.9	28.5	10.6	1.3	72111
75633	CARTHAGE	19191	5539	31.3	31.1	28.4	7.1	2.0	40101	41547	33	43	4274	29.6	24.4	34.6	10.4	1.0	81748
75638	DAINGERFIELD	19213	2482	32.4	29.7	30.9	4.6	2.3	39829	44729	32	41	1991	39.7	27.9	26.4	5.8	0.2	59424
75639	DE BERRY	18743	1477	33.0	29.5	30.3	5.3	1.9	37811	40287	26	33	1240	36.0	32.8	23.8	6.9	0.6	63333
75640	DIANA	18034	1532	27.3	32.7	34.2	4.1	1.7	41465	43450	38	48	1299	28.7	31.8	31.2	7.4	0.9	77278
75643	GARY	16768	537	41.3	30.0	23.6	3.4	1.7	31147	33939	10	13	454	39.9	25.1	23.8	8.6	2.6	65625
75644	GILMER	18506	4313	32.0	31.2	29.2	5.5	2.1	38748	40600	29	37	3402	28.2	30.3	32.8	6.7	2.0	78297
75645	GILMER	18810	3604	29.6	30.4	32.8	5.3	1.9	41508	42860	38	48	2943	29.2	29.4	30.0	10.2	1.1	76988
75647	GLADEWATER	17807	4779	30.9	31.8	30.7	4.5	2.1	38898	42585	29	38	3548	29.0	29.2	32.1	8.8	1.0	77280
75650	HALLSVILLE	20353	2925	21.5	28.4	41.1	7.4	1.6	50039	47973	61	70	2262	18.2	22.4	40.3	17.1	2.0	101525
75651	HARLETON	17636	767	31.9	32.3	30.0	3.7	2.1	37566	41565	25	33	651	30.9	27.5	27.8	11.8	2.0	76628
75652	HENDERSON	19655	4965	26.7	34.3	29.6	6.1	3.2	40303	43742	34	43	3718	25.9	27.1	33.7	11.6	1.6	85212
75654	HENDERSON	20445	4703	29.2	31.1	31.6	5.3	2.8	41386	45129	37	48	3701	26.3	28.7	34.1	8.6	2.3	82904
75656	HUGHES SPRINGS	18255	2179	36.3	29.5	28.2	4.2	1.8	37304	39746	24	32	1536	33.0	32.9	28.7	4.9	0.5	66183
75657	JEFFERSON	18579	4039	39.8	26.9	26.7	4.5	2.1	33600	35263	15	18	3261	44.1	24.3	23.6	6.6	1.3	57881
75661	KARNACK	21862	963	34.7	27.6	30.0	3.9	3.7	37654	40596	26	33	814	25.4	27.8	29.6	15.5	1.7	85000
75662	KILGORE	20302	9397	27.8	29.4	33.2	6.7	3.0	44741	47169	47	58	6950	30.4	26.8	33.6	9.0	0.3	78168
75667	LANEVILLE	15857	1313	43.9	25.7	24.3	4.9	1.3	28846	32306	6	8	1080	45.8	23.3	24.4	6.0	0.5	54592
75668	LONE STAR	17715	734	37.5	30.5	26.4	3.7	1.9	32631	33963	13	16	453	37.5	23.0	34.7	4.4	0.4	73148
75669	LONG BRANCH	17566	518	33.2	34.2	28.0	3.9	0.8	37330	39564	25	32	456	32.2	23.7	34.0	8.3	1.8	73500
75670	MARSHALL	15099	5948	40.4	30.8	23.6	3.9	1.3	30166	34463	8	11	3816	39.5	30.5	23.8	5.8	0.5	60259
75672	MARSHALL	21983	6826	28.5	26.3	34.7	7.4	3.0	45232	45909	49	59	5362	22.0	22.8	37.3	16.0	1.9	96231
75681	MOUNT ENTERPRISE	16093	758	38.8	31.0	24.5	4.7	0.9	32819	35713	13	16	632	52.1	25.0	19.9	2.5	0.5	48860
75683	ORE CITY	17987	1914	31.9	30.3	31.5	4.2	2.1	38848	41205	29	37	1559	39.2	29.7	26.9	4.0	0.2	59629
75684	OVERTON	18566	2364	32.1	31.0	30.1	4.1	2.6	38851	42677	29	37	1851	36.2	33.0	24.3	5.8	0.8	62782
75686	PITTSBURG	17990	5081	34.0	29.8	27.9	6.1	2.2	38315	40323	28	35	3772	19.9	30.8	31.9	14.3	3.1	89146
75687	PRICE	0	0	0.0	0.0	0.0	0.0	0.0	0	0	0	0	0	0.0	0.0	0.0	0.0	0.0	0
75689	SELMAN CITY	15899	157	29.3	33.8	33.1	3.2	0.6	39762	45000	32	41	126	46.0	34.1	16.7	3.2	0.0	52778
75691	TATUM	17275	996	31.9	31.4	30.1	5.1	1.4	36672	39616	23	30	772	40.9	26.0	25.8	7.3	0.0	58537
75692	WASKOM	17022	1976	29.4	32.9	30.5	6.0	1.3	38994	41543	30	38	1568	27.9	27.6	30.5	12.7	1.2	82091
75693	WHITE OAK	21152	2304	22.6	27.3	38.1	8.1	3.9	50103	51851	61	70	1716	15.5	15.2	56.9	12.4	0.1	111482
75701	TYLER	24414	13260	28.4	28.6	29.5	8.4	5.2	44622	47125	47	57	8318	11.3	30.3	41.3	14.9	2.2	99006
75702	TYLER	12702	8511	41.1	30.1	24.1	2.9	1.7	31385	34113	10	13	4725	38.8	39.3	20.6	1.2	0.2	58666
75703	TYLER	31512	14599	19.4	26.7	34.3	11.1	8.4	54369	54323	70	78	8041	4.6	8.0	49.6	31.1	6.7	148368
	TEXAS	24551		22.3	25.0	34.3	11.1	7.3	52382	54495				16.5	22.7	36.5	19.7	4.6	109784
	UNITED STATES	27277		20.9	24.4	35.3	11.7	7.6	54719	56938				9.3	13.1	31.6	32.6	13.5	162279

ZIP CODE		FINANCIAL SERVICES				THE HOME						ENTERTAINMENT						PERSONAL			
						Home Improvements		Furnishings													
#	POST OFFICE NAME	Auto Loan	Home Loan	Investments	Retirement Plans	Home Repair	Lawn & Garden	Computers & Hardware-Personal	Major Appliances	TV, Radio, Sound Equipment	Furniture	Dine out/ Carry out	Sports Equipment	Fees & Tickets	Toys & Games	Travel	Cable TV	Apparel & Services	Auto Repairs	Health Insurance	Pets & Supplies
75451	LEESBURG	82	59	84	57	61	84	60	77	67	56	66	58	48	67	60	74	44	71	80	91
75452	LEONARD	83	73	68	74	72	82	75	79	78	71	76	59	68	80	70	81	52	77	82	93
75453	LONE OAK	82	59	82	57	61	83	61	76	67	57	66	57	49	67	59	74	44	70	79	91
75454	MELISSA	135	125	111	121	122	128	118	125	122	122	122	91	112	127	113	125	83	121	125	148
75455	MOUNT PLEASANT	79	68	63	66	67	73	71	73	75	71	74	54	65	76	66	77	51	73	75	86
75457	MOUNT VERNON	95	69	101	67	73	98	72	91	80	66	78	68	59	78	72	88	52	84	96	107
75459	HOWE	91	88	77	86	85	88	83	86	84	86	85	65	81	88	81	85	58	84	85	102
75460	PARIS	67	55	58	56	55	67	62	64	66	58	64	48	55	65	57	70	44	64	71	76
75462	PARIS	95	96	86	96	94	98	89	93	90	90	90	70	89	92	89	92	62	90	94	110
75468	PATTONVILLE	67	48	68	46	50	68	49	62	54	46	53	47	39	54	48	60	35	57	65	74
75469	PECAN GAP	79	57	81	55	59	80	58	74	65	54	63	56	47	64	58	71	42	68	77	88
75470	PETTY	90	64	93	62	67	91	66	84	73	61	72	63	53	73	66	81	48	77	88	100
75471	PICKTON	94	68	78	66	67	90	70	82	78	69	77	63	56	81	64	85	51	78	86	100
75472	POINT	86	61	88	59	64	87	63	80	70	59	69	60	50	69	62	77	45	74	83	95
75473	POWDERLY	90	75	91	74	76	94	73	87	78	70	77	66	65	78	74	83	52	81	89	103
75474	QUINLAN	88	76	73	73	74	83	75	80	78	76	78	60	68	81	70	81	53	78	81	96
75476	RAVENNA	93	68	96	66	70	95	69	88	77	64	75	66	56	76	69	84	50	80	91	104
75477	ROXTON	76	55	77	53	57	79	58	73	65	53	63	54	47	64	57	72	42	68	78	86
75478	SALTILLO	79	56	84	54	58	82	59	74	64	52	63	58	45	63	59	70	41	69	78	90
75479	SAVOY	88	71	85	72	73	92	71	85	76	65	75	64	62	77	71	82	50	79	89	100
75480	SCROGGINS	84	66	105	65	72	88	66	84	70	62	69	62	57	67	71	75	46	78	84	98
75481	SULPHUR BLUFF	90	64	92	62	67	91	66	84	73	61	72	63	53	73	65	80	47	77	87	100
75482	SULPHUR SPRINGS	81	66	72	66	66	80	70	76	75	67	74	57	62	75	66	80	50	75	82	91
75486	SUMNER	85	63	82	63	65	86	66	79	71	60	70	61	53	71	64	77	46	74	83	95
75487	TALCO	69	47	69	45	48	69	49	63	56	47	55	48	38	57	47	62	36	58	66	76
75488	TELEPHONE	87	60	93	60	63	91	66	82	69	55	68	66	49	68	65	76	45	76	86	100
75490	TRENTON	96	79	87	77	79	95	80	91	85	78	84	67	70	87	76	91	57	86	95	107
75491	WHITEWRIGHT	88	75	78	73	75	86	74	83	79	74	78	61	67	81	71	83	53	79	86	98
75492	WINDOM	104	74	107	72	77	106	76	97	85	71	83	73	61	84	76	93	55	89	101	116
75493	WINFIELD	88	81	72	78	79	83	76	81	79	80	79	59	72	82	73	81	54	78	81	96
75494	WINNSBORO	81	60	88	58	63	84	63	79	69	57	67	58	51	67	63	75	44	73	82	92
75495	VAN ALSTYNE	97	92	86	92	91	97	90	94	91	90	91	70	87	93	88	94	62	92	96	111
75496	WOLFE CITY	77	64	63	65	63	76	69	73	73	63	71	56	61	74	64	77	48	71	78	87
75497	YANTIS	92	75	118	74	83	98	75	94	79	72	77	68	66	74	81	84	52	87	95	109
75501	TEXARKANA	70	57	59	57	56	67	61	64	66	60	65	48	55	66	57	70	44	65	70	78
75503	TEXARKANA	103	103	101	105	103	105	102	102	102	103	102	78	103	103	102	103	71	102	104	120
75550	ANNONA	75	54	77	52	56	76	55	70	61	51	60	53	44	61	55	67	40	65	73	84
75551	ATLANTA	80	60	77	60	62	82	65	76	71	59	69	57	54	70	62	77	46	72	82	91
75554	AVERY	71	51	72	49	53	73	53	67	59	49	58	50	43	59	52	65	38	62	71	79
75555	BIVINS	68	49	70	47	51	70	50	64	56	47	55	48	40	55	50	61	36	59	67	76
75556	BLOOMBURG	88	63	90	61	65	89	65	82	72	60	71	62	52	71	64	79	47	76	86	98
75558	COOKVILLE	81	75	66	72	73	76	71	75	73	74	73	54	67	76	67	75	50	72	75	89
75559	DE KALB	73	52	66	51	53	72	55	66	62	53	61	50	45	63	52	68	41	63	71	80
75560	DOUGLASSVILLE	75	54	77	52	56	76	55	70	61	52	60	53	44	61	55	68	40	65	73	84
75561	HOOKS	84	63	81	61	64	84	66	79	72	62	70	59	54	72	63	78	47	74	82	93
75563	LINDEN	72	52	72	51	54	73	56	68	62	51	61	51	46	61	55	68	40	64	73	81
75566	MARIETTA	70	50	71	48	52	71	51	65	57	48	56	49	41	56	51	62	37	60	68	77
75567	MAUD	85	67	80	65	68	84	66	79	72	65	71	58	57	73	65	77	48	74	81	94
75568	NAPLES	79	57	80	55	59	81	60	75	67	55	65	56	48	66	59	74	43	70	81	89
75569	NASH	74	59	62	58	58	72	64	69	68	60	66	52	55	69	59	73	45	68	74	82
75570	NEW BOSTON	78	61	69	60	61	77	65	73	70	62	69	55	56	71	61	75	47	70	78	87
75571	OMAHA	75	54	76	53	56	78	58	72	64	52	62	54	46	63	56	71	41	67	77	85
75572	QUEEN CITY	78	55	69	53	55	75	58	69	64	55	63	53	46	66	53	70	42	65	73	84
75574	SIMMS	90	64	92	62	66	91	66	84	74	61	72	63	53	73	65	81	48	77	88	100
75599	TEXARKANA	0	0	0	0	0	0	0	0	0	0	0	0	0	0	0	0	0	0	0	0
75601	LONGVIEW	79	72	70	73	72	80	78	77	81	75	80	58	74	80	74	85	55	80	86	92
75602	LONGVIEW	66	56	52	55	54	61	60	60	64	60	64	45	56	64	56	67	44	62	66	73
75603	LONGVIEW	96	76	91	73	76	94	75	89	81	73	80	66	65	82	73	87	54	83	91	106
75604	LONGVIEW	91	87	79	87	84	87	88	87	89	88	89	66	86	91	84	89	62	88	88	103
75605	LONGVIEW	93	90	86	91	89	93	91	91	93	91	93	68	91	93	90	95	65	92	96	108
75630	AVINGER	72	64	84	60	70	80	63	75	68	65	66	51	60	63	67	72	44	72	84	87
75631	BECKVILLE	86	60	78	58	60	84	63	76	70	60	69	58	49	72	59	77	46	71	80	92
75633	CARTHAGE	79	63	75	62	64	80	65	75	70	63	69	56	56	71	63	76	47	72	79	89
75638	DAINGERFIELD	82	59	78	58	61	82	63	76	70	58	68	57	51	70	60	76	45	71	81	91
75639	DE BERRY	87	62	84	60	63	86	64	79	71	60	70	60	51	72	61	78	46	73	83	95
75640	DIANA	85	66	77	64	66	83	66	77	72	64	71	58	56	73	63	77	47	73	80	93
75643	GARY	76	52	75	49	52	76	54	69	62	51	60	53	42	62	52	68	40	64	72	83
75644	GILMER	80	62	79	60	63	83	64	77	70	60	69	57	54	70	63	77	46	72	82	91
75645	GILMER	83	65	79	63	66	82	65	77	70	63	70	57	56	71	63	76	46	72	80	92
75647	GLADEWATER	78	64	69	62	63	77	64	72	69	63	68	54	57	70	62	73	46	69	76	87
75650	HALLSVILLE	91	82	75	79	80	86	78	83	81	80	81	61	73	84	74	84	55	80	84	99
75651	HARLETON	84	60	70	59	60	80	63	73	70	61	68	56	50	73	57	76	46	69	77	89
75652	HENDERSON	86	68	82	68	69	88	72	82	77	66	75	63	61	77	69	82	51	78	87	98
75654	HENDERSON	87	68	86	66	69	90	70	84	77	65	75	63	60	76	69	83	50	79	89	99
75656	HUGHES SPRINGS	73	56	66	55	57	73	62	68	66	57	64	52	52	66	57	71	44	67	74	82
75657	JEFFERSON	72	57	77	54	61	76	58	71	63	56	62	51	50	61	59	69	41	66	76	83
75661	KARNACK	88	64	91	61	66	90	66	82	74	64	72	61	54	73	65	81	48	77	87	99
75662	KILGORE	85	71	77	69	71	84	73	80	77	71	76	60	65	78	69	82	52	78	85	95
75667	LANEVILLE	72	48	70	46	49	71	52	64	59	49	57	50	40	59	49	65	38	60	68	78
75668	LONE STAR	72	52	73	51	54	75	57	70	63	51	61	52	45	62	55	70	41	65	76	82
75669	LONG BRANCH	74	53	76	52	55	76	55	70	61	51	60	52	44	60	54	67	39	64	72	83
75670	MARSHALL	65	49	53	49	48	62	55	58	61	53	59	44	47	61	49	65	40	59	65	72
75672	MARSHALL	88	72	86	71	73	91	74	85	79	70	78	63	65	79	73	85	53	81	90	100
75681	MOUNT ENTERPRISE	74	50	73	48	51	74	53	67	60	50	59	51	40	60	50	67	39	62	70	81
75683	ORE CITY	84	65	79	62	66	83	65	77	71	65	70	57	55	72	63	77	47	73	81	92
75684	OVERTON	86	62	86	60	64	88	65	81	72	60	70	61	52	72	63	79	47	75	86	96
75686	PITTSBURG	82	62	76	61	63	81	65	76	72	62	70	57	55	72	62	77	47	73	81	91
75687	PRICE	0	0	0	0	0	0	0	0	0	0	0	0	0	0	0	0	0	0	0	0
75689	SELMAN CITY	78	56	65	55	56	74	59	68	65	57	64	52	47	68	53	71	43	65	72	83
75691	TATUM	86	61	75	58	60	83	63	75	71	61	70	58	50	73	58	78	47	71	80	92
75692	WASKOM	79	63	69	61	62	75	62	71	67	63	67	53	54	70	59	72	45	68	73	85
75693	WHITE OAK	88	89	77	90	86	92	84	88	85	82	85	67	84	88	84	87	59	85	90	104
75701	TYLER	84	79	78	80	79	86	83	83	87	82	86	62	82	85	81	90	59	85	92	99
75702	TYLER	62	51	43	49	48	52	55	55	59	57	59	39	50	60	50	61	41	58	58	65
75703	TYLER	106	102	98	106	101	99	109	101	107	109	108	80	108	108	106	106	76	106	103	121
	TEXAS	104	96	90	94	93	94	99	97	99	101	100	75	94	101	94	99	70	99	96	114
	UNITED STATES	100	100	100	100	100	100	100	100	100	100	100	100	100	100	100	100	100	100	100	100

POPULATION CHANGE

ZIP CODE #	POST OFFICE NAME	COUNTY FIPS CODE	POPULATION 2000	POPULATION 2009	POPULATION 2014	2000-2009 ANNUAL RATE % Rate	2000-2009 ANNUAL RATE State Centile	HOUSEHOLDS 2000	HOUSEHOLDS 2009	HOUSEHOLDS 2014	HOUSEHOLDS % Annual Rate 2000-2009	HOUSEHOLDS 2009 Average HH Size	FAMILIES 2000	FAMILIES 2009	FAMILIES % Annual Rate 2000-2009
75704	TYLER	423	6680	7940	8645	1.9	76	2545	2970	3243	1.7	2.56	1896	2174	1.5
75705	TYLER	423	2051	2396	2596	1.7	73	705	808	876	1.5	2.92	528	595	1.3
75706	TYLER	423	6429	8037	8861	2.4	82	2227	2733	3016	2.2	2.86	1691	2038	2.0
75707	TYLER	423	11330	13475	14501	1.9	76	4433	5175	5567	1.7	2.59	3158	3611	1.5
75708	TYLER	423	5338	6476	7089	2.1	79	1837	2171	2377	1.8	2.96	1397	1624	1.6
75709	TYLER	423	3680	4324	4693	1.8	75	1392	1604	1742	1.5	2.67	1063	1205	1.4
75750	ARP	423	3102	3555	3823	1.5	69	1154	1296	1392	1.3	2.72	895	991	1.1
75751	ATHENS	213	15457	16427	16602	0.7	49	5585	5809	5861	0.4	2.67	4047	4152	0.3
75752	ATHENS	213	6054	6685	6914	1.1	61	2339	2546	2634	0.9	2.58	1760	1891	0.8
75754	BEN WHEELER	467	5264	5984	6315	1.4	67	1959	2236	2366	1.4	2.60	1483	1666	1.3
75755	BIG SANDY	459	4948	5189	5349	0.5	42	2051	2176	2261	0.6	2.38	1526	1596	0.5
75756	BROWNSBORO	213	2217	2525	2630	1.4	67	830	935	973	1.3	2.70	647	718	1.1
75757	BULLARD	073	6614	8293	9022	2.5	82	2605	3176	3445	2.2	2.61	2053	2475	2.0
75758	CHANDLER	213	8288	9286	9666	1.2	63	3283	3629	3775	1.1	2.53	2425	2645	0.9
75760	CUSHING	347	2224	2106	2063	-0.6	9	900	849	829	-0.6	2.43	640	594	-0.8
75762	FLINT	423	7840	10168	11484	2.9	86	2988	3803	4282	2.6	2.67	2413	3031	2.5
75763	FRANKSTON	001	5729	5994	6111	0.5	42	2272	2362	2408	0.4	2.51	1663	1704	0.3
75765	HAWKINS	499	6107	7397	7920	2.1	79	2307	2855	3086	2.3	2.41	1707	2078	2.1
75766	JACKSONVILLE	073	21369	22150	22315	0.4	37	7776	7960	7997	0.3	2.70	5555	5619	0.1
75770	LARUE	213	2661	2896	2985	0.9	55	1009	1082	1114	0.8	2.67	781	826	0.6
75771	LINDALE	423	14835	17858	19424	2.0	78	5311	6251	6827	1.8	2.65	4109	4762	1.6
75773	MINEOLA	499	9714	11381	12084	1.7	73	3805	4465	4758	1.7	2.51	2770	3213	1.6
75778	MURCHISON	213	3274	3539	3634	0.8	52	1340	1433	1470	0.7	2.47	1017	1071	0.6
75783	QUITMAN	499	7086	8541	9260	2.0	78	2890	3503	3814	2.1	2.36	2083	2486	1.9
75784	REKLAW	073	503	513	510	0.2	30	184	186	184	0.1	2.76	132	131	-0.1
75785	RUSK	073	12097	12804	13035	0.6	46	3948	4239	4327	0.8	2.56	2856	2999	0.5
75789	TROUP	073	9662	11324	11929	1.7	73	3561	4115	4327	1.6	2.74	2691	3094	1.5
75790	VAN	467	5048	5719	5985	1.4	67	1875	2102	2197	1.2	2.67	1385	1527	1.1
75791	WHITEHOUSE	423	11710	13771	15058	1.8	75	4057	4651	5084	1.5	2.94	3274	3706	1.3
75792	WINONA	423	2815	3133	3327	1.2	63	1039	1136	1205	1.0	2.76	807	868	0.8
75798	TYLER	423	309	340	341	1.0	58	0	0	0	0.0	0.00	0	0	0.0
75799	TYLER	423	278	336	366	2.1	79	145	168	183	1.6	1.98	77	87	1.3
75801	PALESTINE	001	15637	16073	16225	0.3	34	6040	6266	6347	0.4	2.52	4112	4195	0.2
75803	PALESTINE	001	15071	15454	15608	0.3	34	5163	5381	5463	0.4	2.61	3907	4016	0.3
75831	BUFFALO	289	4345	4825	5036	1.1	61	1658	1859	1948	1.2	2.57	1243	1376	1.1
75833	CENTERVILLE	289	3017	3275	3397	0.9	55	1280	1396	1450	0.9	2.31	899	966	0.8
75835	CROCKETT	225	12197	12456	12503	0.2	30	4749	4883	4915	0.3	2.44	3246	3286	0.1
75838	DONIE	161	411	430	439	0.5	42	169	179	183	0.6	2.40	125	130	0.4
75839	ELKHART	001	5311	5697	5850	0.8	52	2048	2224	2297	0.9	2.52	1535	1643	0.7
75840	FAIRFIELD	161	6655	6927	7116	0.4	37	2597	2719	2801	0.5	2.51	1846	1903	0.3
75844	GRAPELAND	225	4860	4864	4855	0.0	25	2003	2021	2023	0.1	2.38	1414	1405	-0.1
75845	GROVETON	455	2676	2745	2777	0.3	34	1092	1124	1139	0.3	2.37	753	763	0.1
75846	JEWETT	289	2028	2205	2279	0.9	55	813	886	915	0.9	2.49	592	634	0.7
75847	KENNARD	225	1928	1878	1845	-0.3	16	771	754	742	-0.2	2.49	550	531	-0.4
75850	LEONA	289	600	595	591	-0.1	21	239	236	234	-0.1	2.52	170	166	-0.3
75851	LOVELADY	225	4772	4828	4825	0.1	27	963	992	993	0.3	2.47	721	733	0.2
75852	MIDWAY	313	4181	4085	4080	-0.3	16	602	586	583	-0.3	2.48	436	419	-0.4
75853	MONTALBA	001	1193	1499	1596	2.5	82	467	570	609	2.2	2.62	350	422	2.0
75855	OAKWOOD	289	2429	2522	2559	0.4	37	1012	1058	1077	0.5	2.38	722	743	0.3
75856	PENNINGTON	455	330	346	358	0.5	42	137	144	149	0.5	2.40	98	101	0.3
75859	STREETMAN	161	1001	1547	1685	4.8	93	450	685	746	4.6	2.24	327	500	4.7
75860	TEAGUE	161	6803	7365	7606	0.9	55	2186	2418	2521	1.1	2.47	1534	1667	0.9
75861	TENNESSEE COLONY	001	14677	14947	14983	0.2	30	720	761	777	0.6	2.59	527	547	0.4
75862	TRINITY	455	9480	9725	9831	0.3	34	3998	4106	4159	0.3	2.29	2791	2821	0.1
75901	LUFKIN	005	25125	25288	25123	0.1	27	9089	9309	9284	0.3	2.65	6615	6660	0.1
75904	LUFKIN	005	30399	32563	33126	0.7	49	11300	12258	12491	0.9	2.61	8153	8765	0.8
75925	ALTO	073	3312	3246	3205	-0.2	19	1258	1225	1207	-0.3	2.58	892	856	-0.4
75926	APPLE SPRINGS	455	1225	1283	1322	0.5	42	481	506	523	0.5	2.47	347	359	0.4
75928	BON WIER	351	2348	2215	2131	-0.6	9	854	822	797	-0.4	2.69	655	623	-0.5
75929	BROADDUS	405	1986	1865	1789	-0.7	7	876	834	804	-0.5	2.24	618	581	-0.7
75930	BRONSON	403	2181	2140	2134	-0.2	19	902	888	885	-0.2	2.41	632	613	-0.3
75931	BROOKELAND	241	2389	2280	2208	-0.5	11	1001	961	934	-0.4	2.36	754	716	-0.6
75932	BURKEVILLE	351	2412	2291	2208	-0.6	9	1004	971	942	-0.4	2.36	699	665	-0.5
75933	CALL	351	1878	1750	1679	-0.8	6	722	686	662	-0.6	2.55	553	519	-0.7
75935	CENTER	419	13461	14171	14412	0.6	46	4931	5157	5229	0.5	2.69	3547	3658	0.3
75936	CHESTER	457	1685	1634	1604	-0.3	16	660	642	632	-0.3	2.55	504	485	-0.4
75937	CHIRENO	347	3051	3536	3752	1.6	71	1172	1361	1444	1.6	2.60	892	1022	1.5
75938	COLMESNEIL	457	1255	1218	1200	-0.3	16	484	467	460	-0.4	2.61	362	347	-0.5
75939	CORRIGAN	373	4122	4544	4611	1.1	61	1458	1624	1655	1.2	2.76	1087	1195	1.0
75941	DIBOLL	005	8877	8918	8845	0.0	25	2578	2649	2637	0.3	2.96	2081	2115	0.2
75943	DOUGLASS	347	992	1053	1083	0.6	46	379	401	412	0.6	2.61	279	291	0.5
75946	GARRISON	347	3621	3960	4090	1.0	58	1361	1492	1541	1.0	2.61	987	1067	0.8
75948	HEMPHILL	403	4751	5024	5164	0.6	46	2078	2221	2290	0.7	2.24	1482	1559	0.5
75949	HUNTINGTON	005	7827	7919	7895	0.1	27	2907	2997	2998	0.3	2.64	2264	2302	0.2
75951	JASPER	241	16137	16110	15817	0.0	25	6023	6097	6009	0.1	2.52	4329	4335	0.0
75954	JOAQUIN	419	3252	3270	3268	0.1	27	1241	1240	1236	0.0	2.64	916	902	-0.2
75956	KIRBYVILLE	241	6791	7082	7036	0.5	42	2636	2798	2792	0.6	2.50	1933	2010	0.4
75959	MILAM	403	2406	2409	2410	0.0	25	1085	1091	1094	0.1	2.21	738	730	-0.1
75960	MOSCOW	373	1180	1271	1338	0.8	52	430	470	497	1.0	2.70	323	347	0.8
75961	NACOGDOCHES	347	12707	14578	15333	1.5	69	5070	5857	6179	1.6	2.47	3185	3534	1.1
75962	NACOGDOCHES	347	2863	2798	2794	-0.2	19	2	2	2	0.0	2.50	1	0	-100.0
75964	NACOGDOCHES	347	18816	19674	19975	0.5	42	6594	6838	6939	0.4	2.80	4699	4799	0.2
75965	NACOGDOCHES	347	15741	16151	16334	0.3	34	6838	7019	7100	0.3	2.17	3583	3633	0.1
75966	NEWTON	351	4941	4655	4497	-0.6	9	1687	1610	1558	-0.5	2.53	1211	1139	-0.7
75968	PINELAND	403	1296	1267	1267	-0.2	19	499	494	495	-0.1	2.49	358	350	-0.2
75969	POLLOK	005	5237	5384	5391	0.3	34	1701	1779	1788	0.5	2.79	1346	1391	0.4
75972	SAN AUGUSTINE	405	6539	6806	6722	0.4	37	2498	2614	2593	0.5	2.48	1762	1815	0.3
75973	SHELBYVILLE	419	3271	3295	3292	0.1	27	1340	1338	1333	0.0	2.46	974	959	-0.2
75974	TENAHA	419	1798	1847	1854	0.3	34	702	717	720	0.2	2.57	509	513	0.1
75975	TIMPSON	419	3442	3721	3806	0.8	52	1381	1476	1507	0.7	2.52	961	1011	0.5
75976	WELLS	073	1697	1671	1653	-0.2	19	637	623	614	-0.2	2.58	468	452	-0.4
75977	WIERGATE	351	280	266	257	-0.6	9	112	109	105	-0.3	2.44	78	75	-0.4
75979	WOODVILLE	457	11813	12146	12236	0.3	34	4272	4438	4489	0.4	2.38	2993	3063	0.3
75980	ZAVALLA	005	2665	3587	3926	3.3	88	1110	1496	1634	3.3	2.40	803	1064	3.1
76001	ARLINGTON	439	21388	31089	36635	4.1	92	6847	9808	11539	4.0	3.16	5868	8183	3.7
	TEXAS					1.9					1.8	2.78			1.7
	UNITED STATES					1.0					1.1	2.59			0.9

ZIP CODE #	POST OFFICE NAME	RACE (%) White 2000	White 2009	Black 2000	Black 2009	Asian/Pacific 2000	Asian/Pacific 2009	% Hispanic Origin 2000	% Hispanic Origin 2009	2009 AGE DISTRIBUTION (%) 0-4	5-9	10-14	15-19	20-24	25-44	45-64	65-84	85+	18+	MEDIAN AGE 2009	% 2009 Males	% 2009 Females
75704	TYLER	68.2	61.1	24.6	28.5	0.5	0.6	9.8	14.8	6.5	6.5	6.8	6.6	5.8	27.3	26.6	12.3	1.4	76.0	37.8	49.8	50.2
75705	TYLER	45.2	38.6	50.4	55.2	0.2	0.2	6.7	9.7	6.7	6.8	7.0	7.0	5.8	23.9	28.4	12.7	1.6	75.0	38.9	49.0	51.0
75706	TYLER	64.4	55.5	20.4	22.7	0.3	0.4	20.5	29.5	7.1	6.9	7.2	7.4	6.2	27.1	25.8	11.1	1.2	74.3	36.5	51.0	49.0
75707	TYLER	85.3	80.6	10.4	12.8	1.1	1.6	4.9	8.2	7.1	6.5	6.4	7.0	7.6	27.2	25.6	11.3	1.3	76.2	35.5	49.2	50.8
75708	TYLER	64.4	56.0	17.7	18.7	0.3	0.4	27.5	38.7	8.7	8.1	7.6	7.5	7.2	27.7	23.5	8.5	1.0	70.8	32.0	49.5	50.5
75709	TYLER	66.7	59.3	29.0	34.8	0.6	0.7	5.0	8.0	6.5	6.7	6.9	6.5	5.4	26.2	28.8	11.8	1.2	75.8	39.2	49.0	51.0
75750	ARP	85.3	80.5	12.5	16.3	0.1	0.2	2.5	4.2	6.4	6.7	7.3	6.8	5.3	25.0	28.6	12.4	1.5	75.2	39.4	50.5	49.5
75751	ATHENS	78.5	76.2	14.1	14.6	0.5	0.7	14.7	18.5	7.4	7.0	6.7	7.5	6.5	24.5	23.8	13.4	3.3	74.8	37.0	48.7	51.3
75752	ATHENS	90.4	87.0	3.7	4.7	0.1	0.2	7.6	11.5	6.3	6.6	6.7	5.5	4.4	23.1	29.7	15.6	2.2	76.9	42.7	48.9	51.1
75754	BEN WHEELER	87.7	85.2	5.7	6.3	0.1	0.2	8.7	12.0	6.1	6.4	6.8	6.1	4.5	22.2	30.5	15.8	1.7	76.9	43.4	50.8	49.2
75755	BIG SANDY	88.8	86.9	7.1	7.7	0.5	0.6	3.6	5.2	6.3	6.1	6.1	5.7	5.5	21.3	29.0	18.1	1.8	78.1	44.0	49.8	50.2
75756	BROWNSBORO	90.3	87.0	4.6	5.9	0.1	0.1	8.2	12.2	7.1	7.4	7.2	6.6	5.0	24.9	27.6	12.9	1.3	74.1	38.7	49.2	50.8
75757	BULLARD	91.3	87.5	5.2	7.3	0.5	0.8	3.0	5.2	6.2	6.4	6.6	6.3	4.7	23.5	28.8	16.0	1.6	76.9	42.4	48.0	52.0
75758	CHANDLER	89.9	87.0	6.5	8.0	0.4	0.6	4.4	6.7	6.4	6.3	6.5	5.9	5.0	22.2	28.2	17.0	2.5	77.1	43.2	48.8	51.2
75760	CUSHING	92.9	90.6	4.3	5.2	0.3	0.4	3.7	5.7	6.1	6.3	6.6	6.5	4.6	22.2	29.3	15.7	2.6	77.0	43.0	49.3	50.7
75762	FLINT	91.2	88.3	5.9	7.5	0.8	1.0	2.6	4.4	6.4	6.8	7.2	6.5	4.3	22.8	30.2	14.6	1.3	75.5	42.4	49.7	50.3
75763	FRANKSTON	87.9	84.2	9.1	11.8	0.2	0.2	3.4	5.2	5.8	5.9	6.2	5.6	4.9	22.0	30.5	16.7	2.5	78.6	44.7	48.9	51.1
75765	HAWKINS	82.3	79.7	14.8	16.6	0.1	0.1	2.8	4.1	4.4	4.4	4.7	6.7	7.7	18.2	29.3	22.5	2.2	83.8	48.3	48.2	51.8
75766	JACKSONVILLE	69.4	65.6	17.7	17.6	0.6	0.8	18.2	23.8	8.0	7.2	7.1	7.7	6.9	24.1	23.9	12.3	2.8	73.4	35.8	48.7	51.3
75770	LARUE	79.0	74.9	17.4	20.2	0.2	0.2	4.7	6.9	5.9	6.3	6.5	6.4	4.9	23.9	29.8	14.5	1.8	77.4	42.0	50.6	49.4
75771	LINDALE	89.5	85.5	6.7	8.6	0.4	0.6	3.8	6.7	5.7	5.9	6.1	8.5	6.6	21.0	27.0	16.5	2.6	78.4	41.6	48.0	52.0
75773	MINEOLA	86.1	83.3	7.1	7.6	0.3	0.3	8.7	11.7	6.4	6.4	6.4	6.4	5.2	22.0	27.5	16.9	2.8	77.0	42.7	48.4	51.6
75778	MURCHISON	92.0	89.2	1.8	2.2	0.2	0.3	6.2	9.3	6.1	6.4	6.6	5.8	4.4	23.4	29.8	16.0	1.5	77.1	42.8	49.5	50.5
75783	QUITMAN	91.7	89.3	4.1	4.9	0.2	0.3	5.0	7.2	5.1	5.2	5.4	5.6	4.2	20.9	29.9	20.0	3.9	80.7	47.6	49.1	50.9
75784	REKLAW	72.8	66.1	16.1	18.1	0.2	0.2	12.1	17.5	6.8	6.8	7.0	6.0	4.5	25.1	28.8	13.1	1.8	75.8	39.3	49.1	50.9
75785	RUSK	76.7	71.7	17.6	20.5	0.5	0.7	7.0	9.8	5.6	5.6	5.7	6.2	6.0	30.3	25.4	12.9	2.4	79.4	39.1	55.0	45.0
75789	TROUP	80.7	76.6	11.0	13.2	0.3	0.4	11.8	14.6	7.1	7.1	7.3	7.1	5.5	25.8	26.6	11.7	1.9	74.1	37.8	49.3	50.7
75790	VAN	94.5	92.8	1.0	1.1	0.2	0.3	7.4	10.6	6.7	6.7	6.6	6.7	6.3	23.5	26.3	14.5	2.8	75.7	40.0	48.5	51.5
75791	WHITEHOUSE	91.6	88.1	5.0	6.8	0.6	0.8	3.1	5.4	7.3	7.3	7.5	7.8	6.5	27.0	26.9	8.7	1.2	73.1	35.9	48.4	51.6
75792	WINONA	77.5	71.6	19.6	23.7	0.1	0.1	5.3	8.6	6.4	6.5	6.7	6.6	5.9	26.7	28.0	11.9	1.3	76.4	38.7	49.6	50.4
75798	TYLER	60.7	52.4	34.4	40.0	0.3	0.6	8.8	13.2	3.2	4.1	2.6	39.4	21.5	11.8	8.8	7.9	0.6	87.4	20.1	47.1	52.9
75799	TYLER	82.0	76.2	12.6	16.4	2.9	3.6	2.9	5.1	6.3	3.6	4.2	10.7	14.6	25.0	24.1	10.4	1.2	83.0	32.5	47.6	52.4
75801	PALESTINE	70.4	65.4	21.1	23.3	0.8	1.1	11.7	15.6	7.9	7.4	7.1	7.1	6.3	24.4	24.9	12.2	2.6	73.2	36.3	48.3	51.7
75803	PALESTINE	73.0	68.3	18.5	20.4	0.4	0.5	11.0	15.2	7.0	6.8	6.6	6.5	6.5	27.7	25.4	11.4	2.1	75.5	36.5	51.5	48.5
75831	BUFFALO	81.1	77.1	9.9	11.1	0.4	0.5	11.7	15.7	6.9	6.4	6.5	7.0	6.2	22.8	28.6	13.3	2.3	75.9	40.3	48.7	51.3
75833	CENTERVILLE	82.7	80.0	14.1	15.9	0.2	0.2	3.7	5.1	4.2	4.6	5.2	6.3	4.5	19.8	32.5	19.9	3.0	81.7	48.6	49.5	50.5
75835	CROCKETT	61.4	58.3	33.3	34.9	0.5	0.6	8.1	10.9	6.4	6.2	6.6	7.9	5.7	20.8	26.6	16.3	3.5	75.7	41.8	47.7	52.3
75838	DONIE	83.7	80.2	10.7	12.1	0.2	0.5	6.8	9.3	4.4	4.4	4.9	6.5	5.1	22.6	32.6	17.2	2.3	82.3	46.3	49.5	50.5
75839	ELKHART	92.5	90.2	5.4	7.1	0.2	0.2	2.3	3.6	6.5	6.7	6.9	6.4	5.2	22.5	28.4	14.9	2.5	75.9	41.8	47.5	52.5
75840	FAIRFIELD	77.9	74.4	16.0	17.5	0.4	0.5	8.4	11.5	6.3	6.6	6.7	6.5	5.6	22.8	28.5	14.3	2.7	76.3	41.1	49.5	50.5
75844	GRAPELAND	84.1	80.9	13.9	16.3	0.1	0.1	2.4	3.5	5.5	5.7	6.0	6.3	5.1	21.7	28.6	17.8	3.2	78.8	44.7	49.0	51.0
75845	GROVETON	84.6	81.0	10.4	12.3	0.1	0.1	6.7	9.4	6.7	6.7	6.7	6.2	4.9	22.1	26.5	17.2	3.1	76.1	42.3	48.5	51.5
75846	JEWETT	84.2	79.6	5.4	6.0	0.0	0.0	13.8	19.0	6.6	6.5	6.6	7.9	4.8	22.4	28.0	15.1	2.1	75.6	41.5	50.8	49.2
75847	KENNARD	78.9	74.8	19.3	22.9	0.2	0.2	1.7	2.3	6.6	6.8	7.0	6.7	4.8	23.2	27.7	15.3	2.1	75.5	40.9	49.2	50.8
75850	LEONA	85.4	83.2	12.0	13.6	0.2	0.2	3.7	5.0	4.9	5.0	5.4	6.4	5.5	19.8	29.6	21.0	2.4	80.8	47.1	51.9	48.1
75851	LOVELADY	70.2	67.5	28.7	31.1	0.0	0.0	12.8	16.3	2.9	2.9	3.1	3.3	3.1	45.3	28.6	9.4	1.4	89.1	41.4	74.2	25.8
75852	MIDWAY	47.4	42.0	38.8	40.5	0.7	0.9	21.5	27.1	2.2	2.6	2.6	3.8	21.0	47.5	13.7	5.7	1.1	91.1	29.1	80.9	19.1
75853	MONTALBA	88.5	86.4	8.2	8.8	0.5	0.8	3.8	5.7	6.4	6.7	6.7	6.1	4.7	24.1	29.3	14.4	1.7	76.3	41.2	51.1	48.9
75855	OAKWOOD	64.4	59.5	32.4	36.4	0.1	0.1	4.1	5.6	5.0	5.2	5.4	5.6	4.7	19.6	31.4	20.5	2.5	80.9	47.9	49.6	50.4
75856	PENNINGTON	91.2	87.9	5.5	6.9	0.3	0.6	4.3	6.1	6.4	6.6	6.9	5.8	4.0	21.1	28.0	18.2	2.9	76.0	44.2	50.9	49.1
75859	STREETMAN	86.0	83.1	10.0	11.1	0.4	0.5	4.8	7.3	5.9	6.2	6.6	6.5	5.1	23.0	29.5	15.3	1.9	77.3	42.4	49.6	50.4
75860	TEAGUE	72.9	69.5	21.0	22.3	0.2	0.3	10.5	14.1	4.9	5.1	5.4	6.3	9.4	30.5	23.3	12.5	2.6	81.0	36.3	58.0	42.0
75861	TENNESSEE COLONY	39.6	32.7	41.9	43.0	0.4	0.5	20.1	26.3	1.0	1.1	1.1	1.8	10.8	66.7	15.6	1.9	0.2	96.2	34.7	93.5	6.5
75862	TRINITY	82.3	79.7	13.3	14.5	0.3	0.4	5.2	7.1	5.3	5.0	5.3	6.0	5.1	19.4	28.4	22.7	2.8	80.9	48.2	49.2	50.8
75901	LUFKIN	70.7	64.7	16.8	19.0	1.0	1.4	16.9	22.0	8.1	7.3	7.0	7.2	7.3	26.3	24.1	10.9	1.8	73.4	34.6	48.6	51.4
75904	LUFKIN	71.6	67.8	18.9	19.3	0.8	1.1	12.9	18.0	7.7	7.4	7.0	6.9	6.8	26.6	24.5	11.0	2.2	73.6	35.4	48.0	52.0
75925	ALTO	68.9	63.0	23.8	26.7	0.2	0.3	8.4	12.3	7.3	6.1	6.7	7.1	5.4	22.1	27.2	14.9	3.4	75.7	41.2	47.6	52.4
75926	APPLE SPRINGS	81.4	77.6	15.0	17.8	0.0	0.0	2.9	4.0	6.7	6.9	6.6	8.5	4.9	22.5	25.7	16.1	1.9	73.7	39.9	52.1	47.9
75928	BON WIER	75.0	70.8	22.7	26.3	0.1	0.1	2.0	2.8	6.6	7.0	6.8	6.8	6.1	23.5	28.9	12.8	1.5	75.3	39.7	50.0	50.0
75929	BROADDUS	96.3	95.1	2.4	2.9	0.0	0.0	2.0	2.7	4.6	4.7	5.0	5.4	4.2	18.6	30.2	25.0	2.5	82.4	51.0	49.6	50.4
75930	BRONSON	97.2	96.5	1.4	1.6	0.0	0.0	1.4	2.0	7.2	7.4	7.1	6.0	4.3	22.2	27.1	16.6	1.9	74.5	41.6	48.7	51.3
75931	BROOKELAND	89.0	86.7	8.0	9.3	0.2	0.2	2.6	3.8	4.8	5.1	6.0	5.8	3.9	19.4	33.5	19.9	1.6	79.9	48.2	49.7	50.3
75932	BURKEVILLE	75.3	72.7	22.0	24.0	0.2	0.3	1.9	2.5	5.3	5.4	5.4	5.5	4.9	19.2	30.0	21.8	2.3	80.5	48.3	49.2	50.8
75933	CALL	72.2	67.6	26.6	30.9	0.1	0.1	2.0	2.7	6.6	6.9	6.7	7.1	6.7	23.9	28.2	12.5	1.5	75.4	38.9	48.7	51.3
75935	CENTER	69.0	64.7	19.9	20.6	0.4	0.5	13.7	18.1	7.3	7.1	7.1	7.0	6.1	24.7	24.6	13.2	2.9	74.2	37.6	48.6	51.4
75936	CHESTER	96.4	95.5	2.4	3.0	0.1	0.1	1.7	2.3	6.4	6.5	6.7	5.8	4.1	23.2	28.9	16.3	2.1	76.6	42.8	49.6	50.4
75937	CHIRENO	92.6	90.1	4.9	6.0	0.0	0.1	3.3	5.2	6.3	6.5	6.9	6.9	5.1	23.8	28.7	14.4	1.5	76.0	41.0	49.9	50.1
75938	COLMESNEIL	91.3	88.7	5.8	7.1	0.1	0.1	3.2	4.8	6.7	6.7	6.9	6.7	5.2	22.2	28.0	15.8	2.0	75.6	41.9	47.9	52.1
75939	CORRIGAN	64.2	57.7	22.4	25.4	0.3	0.4	20.8	26.6	8.7	8.6	8.5	7.7	6.2	24.1	23.7	10.7	1.9	69.7	33.4	49.1	50.9
75941	DIBOLL	66.7	61.0	15.5	15.9	0.2	0.2	30.8	39.8	8.1	8.0	7.4	7.0	6.4	31.7	22.1	8.0	1.4	72.3	33.2	54.5	45.5
75943	DOUGLASS	85.3	81.6	11.0	13.3	0.0	0.0	3.9	6.1	5.3	5.7	6.5	7.4	5.4	21.7	32.4	14.0	1.7	77.6	43.4	49.9	50.1
75946	GARRISON	74.9	70.9	22.4	25.5	0.3	0.4	2.8	4.1	6.4	6.7	6.8	6.7	5.6	23.9	28.0	13.2	2.7	75.9	40.2	49.2	50.8
75948	HEMPHILL	88.6	87.0	8.7	9.6	0.0	0.0	2.1	3.0	4.5	4.6	4.6	4.6	4.0	16.0	29.4	29.0	3.3	83.2	54.5	47.4	52.6
75949	HUNTINGTON	94.1	91.5	3.1	4.3	0.1	0.1	2.7	4.3	7.4	7.5	7.7	6.9	5.6	25.1	26.6	11.9	1.4	73.1	37.6	49.3	50.7
75951	JASPER	63.0	59.0	31.2	33.5	0.6	0.7	6.1	8.0	7.1	7.2	6.9	6.4	6.0	24.3	26.2	13.7	2.2	74.8	38.7	49.0	51.0
75954	JOAQUIN	86.8	83.5	8.7	10.3	0.2	0.2	5.9	8.4	7.4	7.2	7.3	7.0	6.0	24.8	25.8	12.8	1.6	74.0	37.9	49.0	51.0
75956	KIRBYVILLE	85.5	82.5	12.0	14.2	0.2	0.3	2.2	3.2	6.5	6.6	6.7	6.7	5.4	23.0	27.9	14.7	2.4	76.2	41.2	48.1	51.9
75959	MILAM	84.5	81.6	13.9	16.5	0.3	0.5	1.3	1.7	4.2	4.2	4.0	4.3	4.5	15.4	30.3	30.1	2.9	84.9	55.4	49.8	50.2
75960	MOSCOW	68.0	63.2	25.8	28.9	0.2	0.2	8.8	11.9	7.1	7.4	7.7	6.9	5.1	23.0	27.3	13.9	1.6	73.4	38.8	49.6	50.4
75961	NACOGDOCHES	64.3	62.1	29.3	29.2	0.4	0.6	8.9	12.2	6.6	6.6	6.6	7.1	14.0	23.3	23.9	10.0	1.8	76.0	32.3	48.2	51.8
75962	NACOGDOCHES	72.3	66.7	21.5	24.8	1.4	1.9	6.5	9.3	0.1	0.1	0.0	59.8	35.6	4.0	0.4	0.0	0.0	99.5	19.2	43.9	56.1
75964	NACOGDOCHES	66.7	61.4	17.9	18.7	0.5	0.7	23.0	30.0	8.7	8.3	7.9	7.5	7.3	27.3	21.3	9.8	2.0	70.7	32.2	49.9	50.1
75965	NACOGDOCHES	86.2	82.8	9.1	10.8	1.6	2.1	4.5	6.5	4.9	4.5	4.7	8.1	20.9	21.6	22.2	10.9	2.1	82.7	29.9	47.1	52.9
75966	NEWTON	65.0	60.3	28.9	31.8	0.6	0.9	7.6	10.3	6.7	6.6	6.6	7.0	7.7	26.7	24.7	11.9	2.0	76.0	36.1	53.7	46.3
75968	PINELAND	80.5	77.0	16.7	19.3	0.2	0.2	2.2	2.9	6.1	6.1	6.2	7.3	5.2	23.5	25.7	16.5	3.4	76.8	41.9	47.5	52.5
75969	POLLOK	90.6	86.4	4.0	5.5	0.3	0.4	6.2	9.8	6.7	6.6	6.8	7.0	5.7	29.8	26.8	9.7	1.0	75.7	37.2	51.6	48.4
75972	SAN AUGUSTINE	59.3	55.7	37.4	40.0	0.3	0.4	4.2	5.5	6.3	6.4	6.5	6.5	5.4	22.1	26.1	16.6	4.2	76.9	42.4	47.5	52.5
75973	SHELBYVILLE	71.4	66.4	25.1	28.7	0.2	0.3	4.1	5.7	6.3	6.4	6.6	6.1	5.0	22.4	28.1	17.0	2.1	76.9	42.8	47.7	52.3
75974	TENAHA	67.7	63.0	26.0	28.8	0.0	0.0	8.2	11.2	7.3	7.1	7.4	7.7	5.9	24.6	26.2	12.0	1.7	73.6	37.2	47.9	52.1
75975	TIMPSON	77.4	73.5	19.0	21.6	0.1	0.1	5.0	7.0	6.7	6.7	6.7	6.6	5.3	23.0	27.8	14.5	2.6	75.8	40.7	47.8	52.2
75976	WELLS	81.4	76.6	13.0	15.2	0.0	0.0	5.4	8.2	7.1	7.1	7.3	6.2	4.0	24.1	27.5	14.2	2.5	75.4	40.5	50.6	49.4
75977	WIERGATE	40.7	35.3	55.4	59.8	0.0	0.0	4.3	5.6	8.3	8.3	6.4	7.1	5.3	22.2	24.8	15.4	2.3	72.6	38.1	49.2	50.8
75979	WOODVILLE	75.5	71.8	18.7	20.6	0.3	0.5	4.9	6.7	5.6	5.8	5.9	5.6	6.2	27.7	24.7	15.8	2.8	79.3	39.7	53.3	46.7
75980	ZAVALLA	97.9	96.8	0.3	0.4	0.0	0.1	2.2	3.4	6.0	6.2	6.6	6.2	4.3	21.2	29.4	18.1	1.9	77.2	44.5	49.0	51.0
76001	ARLINGTON	78.3	70.7	10.5	13.0	4.3	5.2	10.1	17.0	9.6	9.4	8.9	7.4	4.6	31.0	24.1	4.6	0.3	67.0	33.0	49.4	50.6
	TEXAS	71.0	67.6	11.5	11.4	2.8	3.5	32.0	37.4	7.9	7.5	7.2	7.5	7.4	28.3	24.0	8.8	1.4	73.0	33.6	49.7	50.3
	UNITED STATES	75.1	72.0	12.3	12.7	3.8	4.6	12.5	15.7	6.8	6.7	6.6	7.1	6.9	27.0	26.0	10.9	1.9	75.7	36.9	49.2	50.8

75704-76001

ZIP CODE #	POST OFFICE NAME	2009 Per Capita Income	2009 HH Income Base	2009 HOUSEHOLD INCOME DISTRIBUTION (%) Less than $25,000	$25,000 to $49,999	$50,000 to $99,999	$100,000 to $149,999	$150,000 or More	MEDIAN HOUSEHOLD INCOME 2009	2014	2009 National Centile	2009 State Centile	2009 Home Value Base	2009 HOME VALUE DISTRIBUTION (%) Less than $50,000	$50,000 to $89,999	$90,000 to $174,999	$175,000 to $399,999	$400,000 or More	2009 Median Home Value
75704	TYLER	19347	2970	26.9	33.5	32.7	4.4	2.4	41283	45900	37	47	2338	23.1	31.9	38.0	5.6	1.4	84867
75705	TYLER	15883	808	32.2	30.8	30.1	5.2	1.7	37991	42066	27	34	639	27.1	33.5	34.6	4.5	0.3	77417
75706	TYLER	16304	2733	27.4	34.8	33.0	3.5	1.3	41015	46207	36	46	2149	32.9	33.8	27.0	5.6	0.7	71742
75707	TYLER	24671	5175	22.8	25.0	38.0	9.9	4.3	52012	52777	66	74	3575	18.7	20.9	42.2	15.9	2.5	104772
75708	TYLER	15578	2171	29.7	32.2	33.1	3.5	1.5	41011	45960	36	46	1632	39.4	38.8	18.5	2.6	0.7	63473
75709	TYLER	20050	1604	27.4	29.7	32.9	6.9	3.0	43798	46617	45	55	1274	18.8	22.8	46.3	10.4	1.6	99554
75750	ARP	19971	1296	25.1	31.1	35.4	5.7	2.7	46198	48059	52	62	1081	30.4	28.6	31.0	6.7	3.3	76690
75751	ATHENS	19166	5809	32.2	29.1	28.7	6.1	3.8	39187	41884	30	39	3912	22.4	20.4	36.4	17.9	2.8	99338
75752	ATHENS	20748	2546	26.6	29.5	33.7	7.9	2.4	45444	46600	50	60	2007	16.8	22.3	33.0	20.6	7.2	111301
75754	BEN WHEELER	19027	2236	29.5	28.9	34.3	5.6	1.7	42531	43763	41	52	1889	23.2	21.0	33.3	17.9	4.6	99775
75755	BIG SANDY	21338	2176	29.0	31.8	30.4	7.1	1.8	42129	45029	40	50	1736	22.4	26.3	35.0	13.8	2.5	92255
75756	BROWNSBORO	18576	935	29.1	31.2	31.8	5.0	2.9	40206	42505	33	43	788	24.7	27.7	28.6	16.2	2.8	86724
75757	BULLARD	22716	3176	19.7	28.8	39.2	8.2	4.1	50810	52473	63	72	2678	20.1	21.7	32.6	22.2	3.4	108844
75758	CHANDLER	20960	3629	25.1	31.9	33.4	6.7	2.9	43618	45622	44	55	2981	26.1	20.5	34.3	18.3	0.8	96506
75760	CUSHING	16273	849	37.0	37.6	19.9	4.7	0.8	31661	33092	11	13	661	28.4	32.2	28.9	9.8	0.6	75313
75762	FLINT	25767	3803	16.4	27.5	39.3	11.6	5.3	56197	55664	73	80	3177	13.7	12.5	40.7	29.3	3.8	136997
75763	FRANKSTON	20010	2362	29.1	32.0	30.9	5.5	2.5	41251	44223	37	47	1932	27.9	27.2	26.8	16.3	1.9	82033
75765	HAWKINS	21490	2855	22.1	33.8	35.3	6.3	2.6	45633	46736	50	60	2383	20.1	24.7	34.8	17.9	2.5	99291
75766	JACKSONVILLE	16933	7960	35.1	32.2	25.8	4.3	2.6	35229	37401	18	24	5405	26.1	31.0	29.3	11.8	1.8	77687
75770	LARUE	18185	1082	29.7	31.6	30.8	5.6	2.3	39655	43201	32	41	921	28.9	26.3	29.9	11.1	3.9	79921
75771	LINDALE	21125	6251	21.5	31.4	35.9	7.8	3.4	47835	49880	56	66	5179	21.8	18.1	39.2	19.1	1.8	107371
75773	MINEOLA	19658	4465	29.5	32.7	29.2	5.7	2.9	40599	42703	35	45	3425	17.2	23.4	36.8	20.6	2.0	110372
75778	MURCHISON	19270	1433	28.6	32.0	32.5	5.4	1.4	40342	42346	34	43	1220	25.4	25.8	32.0	13.4	3.4	88171
75783	QUITMAN	23085	3503	27.1	32.6	31.3	5.3	3.6	41448	43001	38	48	2804	12.4	20.3	40.2	19.3	4.6	115389
75784	REKLAW	15160	186	31.2	36.0	29.0	3.8	0.0	38745	41041	29	37	154	45.5	29.9	13.6	7.8	3.2	53182
75785	RUSK	16020	4239	31.9	36.4	27.5	3.3	1.0	35474	37811	19	25	3120	31.9	29.2	29.1	8.4	1.3	74728
75789	TROUP	18329	4115	30.2	28.3	33.2	5.9	2.5	44252	47576	46	57	3275	32.9	26.5	26.8	11.6	2.2	74482
75790	VAN	19858	2102	25.6	35.2	28.6	7.5	3.1	41460	43074	38	48	1629	16.5	27.9	37.7	16.1	1.9	97839
75791	WHITEHOUSE	22495	4651	15.8	22.9	46.2	10.5	4.5	59213	58995	76	83	3773	16.9	18.2	49.6	12.6	2.7	108631
75792	WINONA	17853	1136	28.0	29.4	36.6	4.3	1.7	44852	47287	48	58	925	29.0	30.1	32.5	8.1	0.3	78409
75798	TYLER	7968	0	0.0	0.0	0.0	0.0	0.0	0	0	0	0	0	0.0	0.0	0.0	0.0	0.0	0
75799	TYLER	40303	168	28.0	23.2	24.4	13.1	11.3	49002	49840	59	68	78	1.3	2.6	29.5	62.8	3.8	220588
75801	PALESTINE	18023	6266	33.8	32.5	27.8	4.1	1.9	36751	39222	23	30	4099	22.4	33.0	31.5	11.2	1.8	82500
75803	PALESTINE	18935	5381	30.2	31.0	30.7	5.3	2.7	40826	43580	35	45	4087	23.5	29.6	32.1	12.6	2.2	85450
75831	BUFFALO	18761	1859	31.6	30.4	29.6	6.2	2.1	39072	40075	30	38	1480	27.6	25.3	32.0	13.9	1.1	84634
75833	CENTERVILLE	21453	1396	38.3	26.1	25.6	5.4	4.6	34022	36633	16	20	1160	32.2	21.6	28.4	14.1	3.9	83175
75835	CROCKETT	17379	4883	38.2	30.2	25.8	3.9	2.0	33925	34744	15	19	3483	29.6	34.5	23.7	10.5	1.6	69730
75838	DONIE	21905	179	38.0	19.0	30.7	9.5	2.8	34688	36403	17	22	152	24.3	17.8	43.4	12.5	2.0	101786
75839	ELKHART	18331	2224	31.0	30.9	31.7	5.0	1.4	38410	41196	28	35	1807	33.1	26.7	26.2	12.9	1.1	72356
75840	FAIRFIELD	19538	2719	32.2	28.6	31.6	5.2	2.4	38675	39628	29	36	2087	21.8	29.7	33.3	12.7	2.4	88342
75844	GRAPELAND	18434	2021	39.4	26.8	27.4	5.1	1.2	32933	34010	13	17	1588	26.4	35.3	26.5	9.5	2.3	74627
75845	GROVETON	16121	1124	44.6	30.2	21.3	3.0	1.0	27970	30568	6	7	861	38.7	32.3	24.4	3.1	1.5	63475
75846	JEWETT	21845	886	30.4	25.2	34.3	6.9	3.3	44111	45555	46	56	690	28.7	27.0	32.6	9.7	2.0	82353
75847	KENNARD	17349	754	38.9	27.6	27.2	4.1	2.3	35520	36389	19	25	631	44.7	25.0	20.9	7.0	2.4	58816
75850	LEONA	19078	236	29.7	34.7	25.8	6.8	3.0	37524	38277	25	33	209	27.8	24.4	28.2	13.9	5.7	85000
75851	LOVELADY	16724	992	23.3	34.6	37.1	3.0	2.0	42846	48204	42	53	810	28.6	36.4	24.9	10.0	0.0	67647
75852	MIDWAY	15552	586	32.9	31.6	29.9	2.6	3.1	35000	35571	18	23	455	32.7	22.6	34.7	6.8	3.1	78125
75853	MONTALBA	18849	570	30.0	29.8	32.1	5.8	2.3	40547	43688	34	44	465	30.3	19.6	34.0	11.6	4.5	90385
75855	OAKWOOD	18008	1058	39.3	30.2	23.8	5.6	1.1	34041	35960	16	20	885	23.4	25.8	33.6	13.1	4.2	91071
75856	PENNINGTON	15871	144	41.7	40.3	15.3	2.1	0.7	27424	28244	5	6	119	27.7	36.1	24.4	5.9	5.9	73750
75859	STREETMAN	23336	685	30.1	27.7	32.4	7.0	2.8	42423	42811	41	51	578	25.4	26.5	28.7	15.4	4.0	87885
75860	TEAGUE	18918	2418	33.6	26.6	31.2	6.5	2.2	38565	38987	28	36	1859	33.0	24.9	30.2	11.3	0.6	74375
75861	TENNESSEE COLONY	14861	761	26.5	28.5	38.2	4.7	2.0	45566	47181	50	60	532	30.3	16.7	35.3	14.8	2.8	94000
75862	TRINITY	20102	4106	33.6	30.7	29.4	4.3	2.1	36916	38851	23	31	3262	32.2	31.9	27.3	6.8	1.7	71480
75901	LUFKIN	19720	9309	29.4	29.0	31.8	6.3	3.5	42401	45086	41	51	6316	21.4	32.5	33.9	10.1	2.2	85647
75904	LUFKIN	20747	12258	26.8	30.5	32.6	6.9	3.2	44289	46473	46	57	8425	20.8	26.5	38.4	12.9	1.5	94484
75925	ALTO	16868	1225	36.7	32.8	25.2	3.5	1.7	34825	37109	17	22	925	41.3	20.2	27.0	9.8	1.6	67614
75926	APPLE SPRINGS	15931	506	39.1	31.4	25.1	3.6	0.8	33905	37376	15	19	437	38.9	27.2	25.9	7.3	0.7	69464
75928	BON WIER	14410	822	41.1	30.4	24.8	2.3	1.3	31933	33698	11	14	710	46.9	34.8	14.1	4.2	0.0	52716
75929	BROADDUS	19250	834	34.5	36.5	23.7	3.0	2.3	34316	35092	16	21	725	38.3	28.1	24.4	8.8	0.3	62361
75930	BRONSON	16794	888	36.1	33.4	26.8	2.4	1.2	35288	36132	19	24	749	42.9	23.6	27.6	5.7	0.1	60648
75931	BROOKELAND	23330	961	25.4	31.9	32.9	5.6	4.2	43254	45803	43	54	823	27.2	26.5	30.9	13.5	1.9	83900
75932	BURKEVILLE	19201	971	34.2	31.0	28.5	4.8	1.4	36428	36599	22	28	830	41.7	25.7	22.0	7.7	2.9	62593
75933	CALL	15754	686	40.1	32.2	23.0	3.2	1.5	31790	33239	11	14	596	44.6	34.6	16.4	4.2	0.2	54051
75935	CENTER	17149	5157	32.4	34.2	26.4	5.0	2.0	36539	38435	22	29	3807	34.8	25.5	28.2	9.3	2.3	72822
75936	CHESTER	23752	642	29.1	27.9	32.9	4.5	5.6	40923	42521	36	46	550	35.6	28.0	23.1	11.5	1.8	65135
75937	CHIRENO	18070	1361	33.8	32.0	28.0	4.1	2.1	36721	39581	23	30	1112	35.0	31.0	23.2	6.7	4.0	71319
75938	COLMESNEIL	16065	467	37.7	30.0	27.4	3.2	1.7	32872	34323	13	16	398	35.9	29.4	25.6	7.5	1.5	62941
75939	CORRIGAN	14507	1624	39.0	32.9	22.1	4.6	1.4	31976	34580	11	14	1219	37.7	29.3	22.1	9.6	1.3	61691
75941	DIBOLL	15099	2649	30.8	31.1	33.0	3.9	1.3	40285	43268	34	43	1872	31.1	30.9	30.1	7.1	0.7	69469
75943	DOUGLASS	20322	401	22.4	34.4	33.2	7.2	2.7	46235	48758	52	62	328	18.3	19.5	32.6	25.3	4.3	119000
75946	GARRISON	18899	1492	34.7	28.2	29.3	4.8	3.1	38507	41180	28	35	1167	32.9	23.1	28.5	12.9	2.6	79453
75948	HEMPHILL	19663	2221	34.5	35.6	23.6	4.5	1.8	33919	34660	15	19	1922	30.8	26.3	31.8	9.7	1.3	74659
75949	HUNTINGTON	17985	2997	28.3	32.3	33.0	5.5	0.9	40189	42765	33	43	2408	29.5	28.4	30.7	10.5	0.9	79017
75951	JASPER	17897	6097	37.9	25.8	29.6	4.4	2.3	36474	38565	22	29	4593	29.2	28.0	32.5	9.7	0.6	79241
75954	JOAQUIN	16092	1240	36.5	31.2	26.4	4.7	1.3	34492	36322	17	21	1003	35.3	29.5	25.9	5.9	3.4	68750
75956	KIRBYVILLE	16831	2798	34.8	33.7	26.6	3.6	1.3	34548	35481	17	21	2224	34.8	32.9	27.0	4.9	0.4	67056
75959	MILAM	22131	1091	31.9	34.6	26.6	2.8	4.0	36208	37535	21	28	961	32.4	28.0	29.8	8.0	1.9	70865
75960	MOSCOW	15031	470	37.0	33.4	24.0	4.7	0.9	33372	35883	14	17	382	35.9	31.2	22.0	10.5	0.5	65652
75961	NACOGDOCHES	16858	5857	43.7	26.5	22.8	4.6	2.4	29754	32468	8	9	3266	24.6	25.4	35.3	12.4	2.3	89953
75962	NACOGDOCHES	13661	2	100.0	0.0	0.0	0.0	0.0	5000	5000	0	1	0	0.0	0.0	0.0	0.0	0.0	0
75964	NACOGDOCHES	16014	6838	36.5	32.2	24.8	4.3	2.2	35061	36207	18	23	4432	33.2	22.4	33.6	9.0	1.8	80159
75965	NACOGDOCHES	25176	7019	36.4	22.7	27.0	9.0	5.0	39610	42333	32	41	3528	9.6	9.8	41.1	35.7	3.9	148563
75966	NEWTON	15916	1610	38.9	30.1	26.3	2.8	1.9	32812	34274	13	16	1242	44.5	34.2	17.4	3.5	0.4	57234
75968	PINELAND	16861	494	44.5	27.7	22.9	3.0	1.8	30109	31859	8	10	381	44.9	25.7	25.5	3.4	0.5	55735
75969	POLLOK	17818	1779	25.1	32.2	36.1	4.7	1.9	44899	45409	48	58	1496	38.6	28.7	24.8	6.1	1.7	65319
75972	SAN AUGUSTINE	17677	2614	39.7	29.3	24.4	4.6	2.0	32792	34527	13	16	2021	39.5	28.3	24.3	7.1	0.8	66926
75973	SHELBYVILLE	18736	1338	33.6	33.4	24.4	7.2	1.5	35545	36951	19	25	1159	33.5	27.3	28.0	9.7	1.5	73176
75974	TENAHA	15182	717	39.6	30.5	25.0	3.6	1.3	31490	33451	11	13	551	34.8	25.0	29.8	5.6	4.7	70156
75975	TIMPSON	17115	1476	38.8	30.0	24.7	3.9	2.6	33902	34892	15	19	1168	33.0	23.6	31.7	10.3	1.5	77500
75976	WELLS	15212	623	36.8	34.2	25.0	3.0	1.0	33940	36680	15	19	474	43.0	24.9	23.0	8.0	1.1	61667
75977	WIERGATE	13026	109	52.3	32.1	11.9	3.7	0.0	23770	24723	3	3	87	66.7	13.8	18.4	1.1	0.0	32917
75979	WOODVILLE	17318	4438	36.4	30.3	28.1	3.6	1.5	35117	35893	18	23	3548	38.8	24.9	26.4	7.8	2.2	67208
75980	ZAVALLA	17934	1496	35.4	33.5	24.7	5.3	1.1	34688	38218	17	22	1239	39.3	30.2	23.6	6.9	0.0	62865
76001	ARLINGTON	31336	9808	4.4	11.1	48.3	21.8	14.4	82700	83608	93	95	8339	2.2	6.9	59.2	30.1	1.5	137396
	TEXAS	24551		22.3	25.0	34.3	11.1	7.3	52382	54495				16.5	22.7	36.5	19.7	4.6	109784
	UNITED STATES	27277		20.9	24.4	35.3	11.7	7.6	54719	56938				9.3	13.1	31.6	32.6	13.5	162279

ZIP CODE #	POST OFFICE NAME	FINANCIAL SERVICES: Auto Loan	Home Loan	Invest-ments	Retire-ment Plans	THE HOME: Home Improvements: Home Repair	Lawn & Garden	Furnishings: Comput-ers & Hard-ware-Personal	Major Appli-ances	TV, Radio, Sound Equip-ment	Furni-ture	ENTERTAINMENT: Dine out/ Carry out	Sports Equip-ment	Fees & Tickets	Toys & Games	Travel	Cable TV	PERSONAL: Apparel & Services	Auto Repairs	Health Insur-ance	Pets & Supplies
75704	TYLER	86	66	76	65	66	85	68	78	74	65	73	60	57	76	64	79	49	74	82	94
75705	TYLER	82	60	76	58	60	80	62	74	68	60	67	56	51	70	59	74	45	70	77	89
75706	TYLER	83	62	70	59	61	78	63	73	69	62	68	55	52	72	58	75	46	70	76	88
75707	TYLER	97	90	81	90	87	88	91	89	92	93	93	69	88	95	87	92	64	91	89	107
75708	TYLER	75	65	59	62	63	67	65	67	67	67	67	50	59	70	61	69	46	67	67	80
75709	TYLER	86	76	76	74	75	84	74	81	78	74	77	60	68	79	71	81	52	78	83	96
75750	ARP	93	74	88	71	74	93	73	86	79	71	78	65	63	80	71	85	52	81	89	103
75751	ATHENS	78	72	71	70	72	78	71	76	75	72	75	54	68	75	70	79	51	75	81	89
75752	ATHENS	92	71	99	69	74	94	72	89	78	68	76	66	60	77	73	84	51	82	91	105
75754	BEN WHEELER	88	64	94	62	67	90	66	84	72	61	71	62	53	71	66	79	47	77	86	99
75755	BIG SANDY	82	67	82	66	70	85	69	79	74	68	72	57	61	73	68	79	49	76	85	93
75756	BROWNSBORO	86	68	81	66	69	85	67	80	73	66	72	59	58	74	66	78	48	75	82	95
75757	BULLARD	90	88	89	86	90	93	81	88	84	86	84	62	81	84	83	87	57	85	92	103
75758	CHANDLER	84	72	86	70	76	88	72	83	77	72	75	59	66	75	73	82	51	80	89	97
75760	CUSHING	71	51	73	49	53	72	52	66	58	48	57	50	42	57	51	63	37	61	69	79
75762	FLINT	103	102	104	102	103	111	94	104	97	95	97	77	95	97	98	100	66	99	106	122
75763	FRANKSTON	82	67	93	63	72	88	67	82	72	66	71	58	59	69	70	78	47	77	88	96
75765	HAWKINS	86	70	97	68	76	93	70	86	76	70	74	60	63	73	73	82	50	80	93	100
75766	JACKSONVILLE	75	59	63	59	59	72	64	69	68	61	67	52	55	69	59	73	46	68	73	82
75770	LARUE	88	61	88	59	63	88	64	81	71	60	70	61	50	71	62	79	46	75	84	97
75771	LINDALE	90	80	92	78	83	95	77	88	82	79	81	63	73	81	78	87	55	84	94	104
75773	MINEOLA	82	64	86	63	66	84	67	80	72	63	71	59	57	71	67	78	47	76	83	94
75778	MURCHISON	81	64	87	62	67	82	64	78	68	61	67	58	54	67	65	73	45	72	79	92
75783	QUITMAN	90	73	108	71	79	96	74	91	78	69	77	66	65	75	78	84	51	85	94	106
75784	REKLAW	75	53	77	52	56	76	55	70	61	51	60	52	44	61	54	67	40	64	73	83
75785	RUSK	73	53	71	52	55	74	56	68	61	52	60	51	45	61	54	67	40	64	72	81
75789	TROUP	86	68	77	66	68	84	68	79	74	67	73	59	58	75	65	79	49	74	82	94
75790	VAN	89	68	89	67	71	91	72	86	78	67	76	64	61	77	70	84	51	81	91	101
75791	WHITEHOUSE	101	102	86	99	97	96	94	96	93	98	94	72	93	98	92	93	65	93	92	113
75792	WINONA	82	70	68	68	69	77	68	74	72	69	71	55	62	74	64	75	48	71	75	88
75798	TYLER	0	0	0	0	0	0	0	0	0	0	0	0	0	0	0	0	0	0	0	0
75799	TYLER	121	107	95	113	100	96	119	105	116	121	119	88	113	122	109	111	83	112	100	127
75801	PALESTINE	71	59	61	58	58	68	63	66	67	61	66	49	57	67	59	71	45	66	71	79
75803	PALESTINE	80	69	72	68	68	80	70	76	74	68	73	57	64	74	68	77	50	74	80	90
75831	BUFFALO	81	66	75	63	66	78	66	75	70	66	69	56	58	71	64	74	47	72	76	89
75833	CENTERVILLE	84	66	91	63	70	88	66	82	72	64	70	59	56	70	67	78	47	76	87	96
75835	CROCKETT	70	52	67	52	54	69	58	66	63	55	62	48	49	62	55	69	42	64	72	79
75838	DONIE	94	67	96	65	70	95	69	88	77	64	75	66	55	76	68	84	50	81	91	104
75839	ELKHART	83	59	84	57	61	84	61	77	68	56	66	58	48	68	60	75	44	71	81	92
75840	FAIRFIELD	83	65	80	63	66	83	66	78	72	64	71	58	57	72	64	77	47	74	82	93
75844	GRAPELAND	77	55	79	54	58	79	58	73	64	53	63	55	46	64	57	71	42	67	77	86
75845	GROVETON	68	49	70	46	50	69	50	63	56	48	55	47	40	56	49	62	36	59	67	76
75846	JEWETT	88	76	84	73	76	84	76	83	78	76	78	62	69	79	74	80	53	81	83	98
75847	KENNARD	78	54	79	52	55	79	56	72	64	53	62	55	44	64	55	70	41	66	75	86
75850	LEONA	86	62	88	60	64	87	63	80	70	59	69	60	51	70	62	77	45	74	84	96
75851	LOVELADY	80	63	87	60	67	84	63	78	69	62	67	56	55	66	65	75	45	73	83	92
75852	MIDWAY	82	58	82	55	59	82	60	75	67	56	66	57	47	67	58	74	44	70	78	90
75853	MONTALBA	88	63	91	61	66	90	65	83	72	60	71	62	52	72	64	79	47	76	86	98
75855	OAKWOOD	74	56	78	54	59	77	56	71	62	54	61	52	47	61	57	68	40	66	75	84
75856	PENNINGTON	68	49	70	47	51	69	50	64	56	47	55	48	40	55	50	61	36	58	66	76
75859	STREETMAN	86	74	75	72	73	83	72	80	76	72	76	59	65	78	69	80	51	76	82	95
75860	TEAGUE	83	63	82	62	65	85	66	79	73	61	71	59	56	72	64	79	48	75	85	94
75861	TENNESSEE COLONY	89	74	81	71	74	86	73	83	77	73	77	61	64	79	70	81	52	78	84	98
75862	TRINITY	71	63	78	59	67	77	63	72	67	64	65	50	59	63	65	71	44	70	80	84
75901	LUFKIN	83	70	70	69	69	77	75	76	77	73	77	59	67	79	69	79	53	76	78	91
75904	LUFKIN	82	75	68	75	72	79	77	77	80	76	79	59	73	81	73	82	54	78	81	93
75925	ALTO	79	55	80	53	56	79	57	72	64	54	63	55	45	64	55	71	42	67	76	87
75926	APPLE SPRINGS	72	49	71	47	50	72	51	65	58	48	57	50	40	59	49	65	38	61	68	79
75928	BON WIER	72	48	70	45	48	71	51	64	58	48	56	49	38	58	48	64	37	60	67	78
75929	BROADDUS	72	57	78	54	61	76	57	70	62	56	61	50	49	60	58	67	40	66	75	82
75930	BRONSON	70	53	74	50	55	72	53	67	59	51	58	49	44	58	54	64	38	62	70	79
75931	BROOKELAND	87	75	99	69	81	95	73	88	79	76	77	61	67	75	77	85	52	84	96	103
75932	BURKEVILLE	72	61	81	56	65	78	60	72	65	62	64	50	55	62	62	70	42	69	79	85
75933	CALL	74	49	69	47	49	72	53	65	60	50	59	51	40	61	49	67	39	61	69	80
75935	CENTER	81	58	78	56	59	81	62	75	68	57	67	57	49	68	59	75	44	70	80	90
75936	CHESTER	100	80	110	76	86	106	80	99	87	79	85	70	70	84	82	94	57	92	105	115
75937	CHIRENO	84	60	86	58	62	85	62	78	68	57	67	59	49	68	61	75	44	72	82	93
75938	COLMESNEIL	73	54	77	52	57	75	55	69	61	53	60	51	46	60	55	66	39	64	73	82
75939	CORRIGAN	73	50	66	48	50	71	53	64	60	51	59	50	41	62	49	66	39	61	68	78
75941	DIBOLL	72	62	61	59	61	67	63	67	65	64	65	50	57	67	60	68	45	66	68	79
75943	DOUGLASS	95	68	97	66	71	96	70	89	78	65	76	67	56	77	69	85	50	81	92	106
75946	GARRISON	89	63	87	60	63	88	65	81	73	62	72	62	51	74	62	80	48	75	84	98
75948	HEMPHILL	68	60	79	56	66	75	59	70	63	61	61	48	55	59	62	67	41	67	77	81
75949	HUNTINGTON	83	63	75	61	63	81	64	75	70	62	69	57	53	71	61	75	46	71	78	90
75951	JASPER	78	57	75	56	58	77	61	72	67	58	66	54	50	67	58	73	44	69	77	86
75954	JOAQUIN	77	54	68	51	53	75	56	68	63	54	62	52	44	65	52	70	41	64	71	83
75956	KIRBYVILLE	75	53	73	51	54	75	56	69	62	52	61	52	44	62	54	69	40	64	73	83
75959	MILAM	72	68	87	63	76	82	65	77	69	70	67	50	64	63	71	73	45	74	86	88
75960	MOSCOW	74	51	71	49	52	73	54	66	60	51	59	51	42	61	51	66	39	62	70	80
75961	NACOGDOCHES	65	49	51	50	49	57	62	58	63	57	62	46	52	63	53	65	43	61	62	71
75962	NACOGDOCHES	8	3	3	4	3	4	11	5	9	7	9	6	6	9	6	8	6	7	5	7
75964	NACOGDOCHES	71	60	57	58	58	63	64	64	66	64	66	49	57	68	59	68	45	65	66	77
75965	NACOGDOCHES	84	65	65	69	64	71	92	74	85	79	85	63	75	85	74	84	60	82	76	91
75966	NEWTON	74	50	73	48	51	74	54	67	61	50	59	51	41	61	51	67	39	63	71	81
75968	PINELAND	78	52	76	49	52	77	55	69	63	52	62	54	41	64	52	70	41	65	73	85
75969	POLLOK	89	68	73	66	67	84	69	78	75	68	74	59	58	78	63	81	50	74	81	95
75972	SAN AUGUSTINE	76	54	74	53	55	77	58	71	66	55	64	53	47	65	56	72	43	67	77	85
75973	SHELBYVILLE	85	57	83	54	58	84	60	76	68	57	67	58	46	69	57	76	44	71	80	92
75974	TENAHA	72	49	66	46	48	70	51	63	58	49	57	49	39	60	48	65	38	59	67	77
75975	TIMPSON	78	54	79	52	56	78	56	72	63	53	62	54	44	63	55	70	41	66	75	86
75976	WELLS	70	50	72	49	52	71	52	66	57	48	56	49	41	57	51	63	37	60	68	78
75977	WIERGATE	59	39	57	36	38	58	41	52	48	39	46	41	31	48	38	53	31	49	55	64
75979	WOODVILLE	74	53	72	51	54	74	56	68	63	53	61	51	45	62	54	69	41	64	73	82
75980	ZAVALLA	72	57	78	54	61	76	57	70	62	56	61	50	50	60	58	67	40	66	75	82
76001	ARLINGTON	145	165	138	162	157	138	143	143	135	155	137	115	152	144	146	127	98	136	125	163
	TEXAS	104	96	90	94	93	94	99	97	99	101	100	75	94	101	94	99	70	99	96	114
	UNITED STATES	100	100	100	100	100	100	100	100	100	100	100	100	100	100	100	100	100	100	100	100

ZIP CODE			POPULATION			2000-2009 ANNUAL RATE		HOUSEHOLDS					FAMILIES		
#	POST OFFICE NAME	COUNTY FIPS CODE	2000	2009	2014	% Rate	State Centile	2000	2009	2014	% Annual Rate 2000-2009	2009 Average HH Size	2000	2009	% Annual Rate 2000-2009
76002	ARLINGTON	439	7350	25454	32952	14.4	99	2316	7841	10142	14.1	3.24	2010	6738	14.0
76006	ARLINGTON	439	24328	25149	26300	0.4	37	12848	13114	13691	0.2	1.91	5337	4977	-0.8
76008	ALEDO	367	8455	12134	14553	4.0	91	2913	4058	4870	3.6	2.99	2457	3397	3.6
76009	ALVARADO	251	18842	22389	24137	1.9	76	6284	7277	7836	1.6	3.04	5041	5750	1.4
76010	ARLINGTON	439	53697	55828	58371	0.4	37	18390	18562	19327	0.1	2.97	12268	11857	-0.4
76011	ARLINGTON	439	29917	30430	31684	0.2	30	12296	12317	12827	0.0	2.44	6513	6057	-0.8
76012	ARLINGTON	439	25457	26259	27489	0.3	34	9949	10221	10717	0.3	2.50	7101	7014	-0.1
76013	ARLINGTON	439	32071	34213	36479	0.7	49	13716	14623	15606	0.7	2.32	8338	8369	0.0
76014	ARLINGTON	439	31127	33762	36162	0.9	55	10320	11167	11962	0.9	3.02	7772	8079	0.4
76015	ARLINGTON	439	15960	17253	18456	0.8	52	6229	6755	7245	0.9	2.53	4299	4444	0.4
76016	ARLINGTON	439	30917	32972	35122	0.7	49	10779	11486	12237	0.7	2.87	9023	9372	0.4
76017	ARLINGTON	439	41450	45401	49077	1.0	58	15329	16792	18184	1.0	2.70	11585	12209	0.6
76018	ARLINGTON	439	24069	28322	31911	1.8	75	7529	8718	9807	1.6	3.24	6335	7157	1.3
76019	ARLINGTON	439	4	4	5	0.0	25	3	3	4	0.0	1.33	2	0	-100.0
76020	AZLE	367	23463	27013	29588	1.5	69	8743	9957	10907	1.4	2.70	6632	7348	1.1
76021	BEDFORD	439	33513	35730	37916	0.7	49	14299	15392	16428	0.8	2.30	8952	9037	0.1
76022	BEDFORD	439	13742	13937	14482	0.2	30	5994	6085	6342	0.2	2.25	3628	3437	-0.6
76023	BOYD	497	5359	6663	7446	2.4	82	1933	2403	2683	2.4	2.77	1549	1902	2.2
76028	BURLESON	251	39916	56802	65318	3.9	91	14292	19782	22693	3.6	2.86	11497	15672	3.4
76031	CLEBURNE	251	16410	18951	20081	1.6	71	5429	6106	6466	1.3	3.05	4207	4667	1.1
76033	CLEBURNE	251	21679	24806	26188	1.5	69	8160	9082	9580	1.2	2.68	6018	6612	1.0
76034	COLLEYVILLE	439	19581	22983	25623	1.7	73	6384	7495	8364	1.7	3.07	5776	6648	1.5
76035	CRESSON	221	1004	1556	1874	4.9	94	357	550	661	4.8	2.83	283	427	4.5
76036	CROWLEY	439	12620	19543	24643	4.8	93	4546	7115	8971	5.0	2.74	3563	5449	4.7
76039	EULESS	439	28066	33271	36936	1.9	76	12202	14497	16136	1.9	2.29	7115	7870	1.1
76040	EULESS	439	23174	27121	30145	1.7	73	9913	11673	13013	1.8	2.32	5551	5961	0.8
76041	FORRESTON	139	185	241	273	2.9	86	59	76	86	2.8	3.17	48	60	2.4
76043	GLEN ROSE	425	5297	6363	6948	2.0	78	1883	2260	2473	2.0	2.75	1407	1667	1.9
76044	GODLEY	251	3390	3811	4019	1.3	65	1134	1240	1305	1.0	3.05	922	995	0.8
76048	GRANBURY	221	19433	23392	25583	2.0	78	7601	9209	10135	2.1	2.46	5390	6403	1.9
76049	GRANBURY	221	17563	23372	26693	3.1	87	7020	9402	10768	3.2	2.49	5548	7348	3.1
76050	GRANDVIEW	251	5635	6503	6911	1.6	71	1955	2204	2344	1.3	2.90	1593	1774	1.2
76051	GRAPEVINE	439	41504	46594	50849	1.3	65	15518	17643	19377	1.4	2.63	11181	12043	0.8
76052	HASLET	439	2884	13846	18609	18.5	100	970	4615	6190	18.4	3.00	826	3814	18.0
76053	HURST	439	24449	27888	30009	1.4	67	9657	10842	11635	1.3	2.56	6687	7259	0.9
76054	HURST	439	12045	12988	13693	0.8	52	4455	4756	5003	0.7	2.70	3629	3792	0.5
76055	ITASCA	217	2637	2764	2825	0.5	42	949	989	1010	0.4	2.71	700	720	0.3
76058	JOSHUA	251	13952	17836	19835	2.7	84	4653	5800	6443	2.4	3.07	3793	4664	2.3
76059	KEENE	251	4743	5423	5705	1.5	69	1565	1754	1851	1.2	2.85	1108	1216	1.0
76060	KENNEDALE	439	5851	6894	7536	1.8	75	2083	2453	2685	1.8	2.79	1472	1672	1.4
76063	MANSFIELD	439	31621	57743	70827	6.7	96	10063	18742	23073	7.0	3.04	8557	15744	6.8
76064	MAYPEARL	139	1185	1755	2074	4.3	92	397	573	677	4.0	3.06	316	450	3.9
76065	MIDLOTHIAN	139	17456	27741	33643	5.1	94	5842	9143	11053	5.0	3.03	4851	7509	4.8
76066	MILLSAP	367	2658	3284	3674	2.3	81	1003	1212	1357	2.1	2.71	790	937	1.9
76067	MINERAL WELLS	363	21647	21562	21449	0.0	25	7504	7431	7372	-0.1	2.69	5246	5118	-0.3
76070	NEMO	425	436	534	588	2.2	80	156	190	210	2.2	2.81	127	153	2.0
76071	NEWARK	497	2981	3533	3827	1.9	76	1047	1230	1330	1.8	2.87	804	926	1.5
76073	PARADISE	497	4662	6147	6844	3.0	86	1635	2142	2387	3.0	2.87	1339	1733	2.8
76077	RAINBOW	425	643	785	861	2.2	80	243	297	326	2.2	2.59	188	226	2.0
76078	RHOME	497	5233	7325	8272	3.7	90	1800	2488	2802	3.6	2.94	1458	2000	3.5
76082	SPRINGTOWN	367	14378	18158	20521	2.6	83	4845	5993	6760	2.3	3.03	3926	4789	2.2
76084	VENUS	251	6664	8620	11788	2.8	85	1832	2397	3402	2.9	3.23	1526	1969	2.8
76085	WEATHERFORD	367	7489	9989	11329	3.2	87	2662	3468	3929	2.9	2.87	2118	2704	2.7
76086	WEATHERFORD	367	16403	19217	21153	1.7	73	6412	7421	8195	1.6	2.49	4279	4818	1.3
76087	WEATHERFORD	367	18037	24618	28637	3.4	89	6521	8725	10136	3.2	2.82	5334	7059	3.1
76088	WEATHERFORD	367	8734	11564	13182	3.1	87	3121	4073	4654	2.9	2.68	2503	3217	2.8
76092	SOUTHLAKE	439	21799	27596	31263	2.6	83	6508	8136	9233	2.4	3.39	6029	7434	2.3
76093	RIO VISTA	251	1823	2486	2773	3.4	89	650	865	963	3.1	2.87	517	676	2.9
76102	FORT WORTH	439	8526	9344	9932	1.0	58	2341	2659	2957	1.4	2.06	1059	1087	0.3
76103	FORT WORTH	439	14465	15196	15887	0.5	42	5257	5361	5597	0.2	2.75	3350	3228	-0.4
76104	FORT WORTH	439	17391	17494	18049	0.1	27	5863	5855	6072	0.0	2.71	3607	3396	-0.6
76105	FORT WORTH	439	22415	23576	24833	0.5	42	6623	6972	7380	0.6	3.32	4968	5012	0.1
76106	FORT WORTH	439	33008	36193	38660	1.0	58	8305	9053	9713	0.9	3.85	6739	7112	0.6
76107	FORT WORTH	439	26629	27063	28253	0.2	30	12093	12184	12674	0.1	2.21	6383	6001	-0.7
76108	FORT WORTH	439	26307	35861	41386	3.4	89	9658	13135	15171	3.4	2.69	7061	9386	3.1
76109	FORT WORTH	439	22219	22373	23078	0.1	27	10381	10418	10781	0.0	2.05	5300	4927	-0.8
76110	FORT WORTH	439	32968	33380	34331	0.1	27	10346	10182	10437	-0.2	3.26	7188	6778	-0.6
76111	FORT WORTH	439	20386	20777	21576	0.2	30	6944	6936	7179	0.0	2.96	4742	4505	-0.6
76112	FORT WORTH	439	38855	41157	43647	0.6	46	16442	17289	18321	0.5	2.36	9961	9904	-0.1
76114	FORT WORTH	439	24491	25598	26671	0.5	42	8834	8957	9344	0.1	2.61	5955	5745	-0.4
76115	FORT WORTH	439	19409	19916	20567	0.3	34	5659	5640	5808	0.0	3.47	4472	4312	-0.4
76116	FORT WORTH	439	45283	48446	51964	0.7	49	20153	21323	22829	0.6	2.27	11451	11352	-0.1
76117	HALTOM CITY	439	29411	30948	32743	0.6	46	11354	11902	12592	0.5	2.59	7662	7663	0.0
76118	FORT WORTH	439	12647	14407	16327	1.4	67	4700	5236	5885	1.2	2.70	3433	3738	0.9
76119	FORT WORTH	439	40271	42448	44475	0.6	46	12522	13035	13694	0.4	3.08	9480	9502	0.0
76120	FORT WORTH	439	10209	15184	17947	4.4	93	4953	7121	8362	4.0	2.13	2454	3448	3.7
76122	FORT WORTH	439	269	274	279	0.2	30	2	2	2	0.0	2.50	1	1	0.0
76123	FORT WORTH	439	11641	28844	36157	10.3	98	3577	8954	11217	10.4	3.22	3141	7575	10.0
76126	FORT WORTH	439	15414	18989	21082	2.3	81	5986	7373	8178	2.3	2.56	4599	5485	1.9
76127	NAVAL AIR STATION/ J	439	520	639	704	2.3	81	73	97	112	3.1	4.69	55	72	3.0
76129	FORT WORTH	439	1834	1976	1976	0.8	52	1	1	1	0.0	2.00	0	1	0.0
76131	FORT WORTH	439	7204	26260	34365	15.0	99	2320	8208	10736	14.6	3.20	1925	6288	13.7
76132	FORT WORTH	439	21542	24496	26603	1.4	67	10678	11896	12900	1.2	2.01	4929	5115	0.4
76133	FORT WORTH	439	46118	47333	49699	0.3	34	17806	18250	19199	0.3	2.57	12810	12571	-0.2
76134	FORT WORTH	439	18213	20606	23067	1.3	65	6498	7296	8161	1.3	2.82	4972	5377	0.9
76135	FORT WORTH	439	14357	18197	21005	2.6	83	5724	7171	8267	2.5	2.50	3923	4807	2.2
76137	FORT WORTH	439	39818	51588	58909	2.8	85	13904	17802	20322	2.7	2.89	10683	13372	2.5
76140	FORT WORTH	439	18774	25114	28693	3.2	87	6206	8316	9505	3.2	2.99	4906	6287	2.7
76148	FORT WORTH	439	24702	25185	26317	0.2	30	8093	8240	8617	0.2	3.04	6665	6627	-0.1
76155	FORT WORTH	439	2626	2668	2780	0.2	30	1699	1702	1767	0.0	1.57	463	399	-1.6
76164	FORT WORTH	439	18736	18778	19278	0.0	25	4890	4841	4965	-0.1	3.84	3933	3778	-0.4
76177	FORT WORTH	439	134	2686	3835	38.3	100	47	1244	1875	42.5	2.16	39	1022	42.3
76179	FORT WORTH	439	20591	40248	49496	7.5	97	7310	14251	17512	7.5	2.82	5875	11125	7.1
76180	NORTH RICHLAND HILLS	439	54354	64005	70894	1.8	75	20309	23710	26186	1.7	2.69	14946	16933	1.4
76201	DENTON	121	24682	27274	29050	1.1	61	10122	10897	11778	0.8	1.98	3668	3541	-0.4
	TEXAS					1.9					1.8	2.78			1.7
	UNITED STATES					1.0					1.1	2.59			0.9

ZIP CODE #	POST OFFICE NAME	RACE (%) White 2000	White 2009	Black 2000	Black 2009	Asian/Pacific 2000	Asian/Pacific 2009	% Hispanic Origin 2000	% Hispanic Origin 2009	2009 AGE DISTRIBUTION (%) 0-4	5-9	10-14	15-19	20-24	25-44	45-64	65-84	85+	18+	MEDIAN AGE 2009	% 2009 Males	% 2009 Females
76002	ARLINGTON	63.5	60.7	19.2	18.4	7.9	8.2	13.5	19.0	10.5	9.9	9.0	7.0	4.1	34.8	21.2	3.1	0.2	66.0	32.3	49.2	50.8
76006	ARLINGTON	70.5	61.9	15.1	18.4	6.7	8.3	11.2	17.7	6.3	4.6	4.0	5.1	14.3	41.5	20.0	3.8	0.4	82.6	30.3	50.8	49.2
76008	ALEDO	95.2	93.6	0.8	0.9	0.7	0.8	4.8	6.9	6.4	7.3	8.2	8.2	4.5	24.5	31.5	8.6	0.8	72.9	38.8	49.4	50.6
76009	ALVARADO	87.1	83.0	2.9	3.4	0.4	0.5	15.0	21.0	7.7	7.2	6.9	7.2	7.6	27.6	26.5	8.4	0.8	73.8	34.5	50.8	49.2
76010	ARLINGTON	50.3	42.7	16.0	15.7	6.3	6.3	39.6	51.4	10.7	9.0	7.6	8.8	10.4	31.5	16.0	5.4	0.6	68.1	26.8	51.8	48.2
76011	ARLINGTON	55.3	48.1	18.3	19.5	4.1	4.4	34.9	44.3	9.5	7.3	5.7	6.6	12.7	36.6	16.4	4.5	0.8	74.2	28.1	51.6	48.4
76012	ARLINGTON	79.9	73.9	8.0	9.3	3.4	4.5	13.2	19.4	6.6	6.2	6.3	6.6	6.8	24.5	27.4	13.6	2.1	77.1	39.9	48.4	51.6
76013	ARLINGTON	78.1	71.5	8.9	11.0	5.5	6.6	10.2	16.0	6.5	5.8	5.7	7.0	9.5	28.2	23.0	12.2	2.1	78.6	35.0	48.9	51.1
76014	ARLINGTON	52.2	43.9	22.5	24.8	12.3	13.5	19.6	27.9	9.1	8.1	7.4	7.6	8.7	31.9	21.2	5.6	0.4	70.9	29.9	49.3	50.7
76015	ARLINGTON	76.6	68.7	10.6	13.2	4.8	5.9	12.0	19.3	7.3	6.8	6.5	6.6	8.1	30.2	24.0	9.2	1.3	75.5	34.2	48.7	51.3
76016	ARLINGTON	85.1	79.4	6.7	9.0	4.0	5.3	5.8	10.0	5.4	6.0	6.9	7.4	5.1	24.4	34.5	9.4	0.9	77.0	41.3	49.1	50.9
76017	ARLINGTON	80.2	73.2	9.6	12.5	4.4	5.5	8.1	13.6	7.4	7.5	7.4	7.1	6.0	29.7	28.3	6.1	0.4	73.2	35.3	49.3	50.7
76018	ARLINGTON	59.7	51.1	20.2	23.3	10.3	11.6	14.6	22.2	9.5	9.1	8.7	7.8	5.7	32.9	23.1	3.1	0.2	67.6	31.2	49.1	50.9
76019	ARLINGTON	100.0	100.0	0.0	0.0	0.0	0.0	0.0	0.0	0.0	0.0	0.0	0.0	0.0	100.0	0.0	0.0	0.0	100.0	35.0	75.0	25.0
76020	AZLE	95.2	92.6	0.4	0.6	0.5	0.7	5.4	9.0	6.4	6.7	7.0	6.9	5.4	25.6	29.9	10.7	1.4	75.5	39.3	49.6	50.4
76021	BEDFORD	88.1	82.9	3.5	4.8	4.2	5.7	6.7	11.8	5.5	5.5	5.9	6.4	7.1	29.0	30.3	8.8	1.4	79.2	38.6	48.2	51.8
76022	BEDFORD	86.6	80.4	4.0	5.4	3.1	4.1	8.4	14.7	6.3	5.7	5.6	5.4	6.7	29.8	26.0	12.5	2.0	79.2	38.1	47.5	52.5
76023	BOYD	93.8	91.6	0.4	0.5	0.3	0.4	7.1	10.4	6.3	6.4	6.6	6.9	6.0	27.2	28.7	10.9	0.9	76.4	38.6	49.9	50.1
76028	BURLESON	94.9	92.6	1.0	1.3	0.5	0.6	5.6	9.1	6.9	7.1	7.3	7.1	5.4	25.8	28.5	10.5	1.4	74.3	38.3	49.1	50.9
76031	CLEBURNE	84.3	81.7	5.2	5.4	0.8	1.0	22.1	27.8	8.2	7.7	7.2	7.0	6.9	27.8	24.6	9.4	1.1	72.8	33.9	50.2	49.8
76033	CLEBURNE	90.8	87.9	2.4	2.8	0.6	0.9	12.8	17.9	7.3	6.9	6.7	6.9	6.4	25.4	25.8	11.9	2.6	74.7	37.5	48.2	51.8
76034	COLLEYVILLE	93.2	90.4	1.3	1.8	3.2	4.4	3.4	6.0	5.2	7.3	9.1	8.8	3.6	19.6	37.8	8.2	0.5	72.4	42.9	49.3	50.7
76035	CRESSON	94.9	93.0	0.4	0.4	0.7	1.0	6.8	9.5	7.1	7.3	7.5	6.9	5.5	26.7	28.6	9.6	0.9	73.8	37.2	49.6	50.4
76036	CROWLEY	92.4	89.0	1.7	2.3	1.0	1.2	8.0	13.2	7.2	7.1	7.1	7.2	6.1	26.4	27.3	10.0	1.6	74.1	36.9	48.3	51.7
76039	EULESS	77.3	70.7	5.1	6.5	9.6	11.4	11.0	17.5	6.7	6.5	6.2	6.0	7.6	35.6	24.8	6.2	0.5	77.1	34.5	49.2	50.8
76040	EULESS	71.2	63.4	10.1	12.1	8.6	10.4	16.1	23.7	8.2	6.4	5.6	6.0	10.2	34.8	21.7	6.5	0.7	76.5	31.3	51.0	49.0
76041	FORRESTON	80.4	73.9	4.3	5.4	0.0	0.0	29.9	40.7	7.5	7.1	6.6	7.1	7.1	26.1	28.2	9.1	1.2	74.7	36.2	51.5	48.5
76043	GLEN ROSE	92.2	89.8	0.3	0.3	0.3	0.4	13.1	17.8	6.4	6.4	6.7	7.0	6.1	25.2	28.2	11.4	2.5	76.1	39.0	50.2	49.8
76044	GODLEY	92.9	89.8	0.6	0.8	0.1	0.1	9.5	14.4	7.8	7.9	7.7	6.8	5.8	27.0	27.1	9.1	0.8	72.3	35.9	49.8	50.2
76048	GRANBURY	93.9	92.0	0.4	0.4	0.3	0.4	9.1	12.8	6.0	6.0	6.2	6.4	5.9	23.8	28.1	14.9	2.6	77.7	41.5	48.9	51.1
76049	GRANBURY	95.6	94.2	0.2	0.3	0.4	0.5	5.8	8.2	5.1	5.3	5.7	5.7	4.4	19.0	31.3	21.5	2.1	80.4	48.2	48.8	51.2
76050	GRANDVIEW	92.9	90.4	3.0	3.8	0.1	0.2	7.4	11.1	7.1	7.3	7.3	7.0	5.6	25.2	27.6	10.9	2.1	74.0	38.0	49.3	50.7
76051	GRAPEVINE	88.2	83.0	2.3	3.1	2.6	3.5	11.5	18.1	7.0	7.4	7.4	6.9	5.7	31.0	28.5	5.5	0.8	73.8	35.9	49.9	50.1
76052	HASLET	91.6	91.2	1.8	2.1	1.2	1.0	8.0	12.1	9.8	9.3	8.4	6.6	3.7	33.7	23.9	4.2	0.4	68.2	33.8	49.2	50.8
76053	HURST	84.0	76.2	5.1	6.9	1.9	3.1	12.6	20.8	7.7	6.9	6.7	6.5	7.0	28.0	24.0	11.6	1.5	74.8	35.6	48.8	51.2
76054	HURST	90.5	86.4	2.0	2.8	2.9	3.9	6.6	10.8	5.8	6.4	7.0	6.5	4.5	21.3	33.1	13.7	1.7	76.7	43.9	48.1	51.9
76055	ITASCA	75.0	69.9	10.7	11.3	0.1	0.1	20.1	27.0	7.2	7.4	7.6	7.1	5.3	24.8	26.0	12.1	2.5	73.3	37.6	49.3	50.7
76058	JOSHUA	92.5	89.6	0.9	1.1	0.3	0.5	8.9	13.2	8.0	8.0	7.9	7.6	6.3	27.3	26.2	8.0	0.8	71.4	34.2	50.4	49.6
76059	KEENE	77.9	72.8	5.8	6.5	4.4	5.5	22.2	29.8	7.4	7.0	6.1	9.4	10.0	26.3	19.7	10.3	3.8	75.5	31.3	47.4	52.6
76060	KENNEDALE	85.9	79.0	5.7	7.9	1.4	2.0	10.4	17.9	7.7	7.6	7.1	6.6	6.6	30.5	25.2	7.7	1.1	73.6	34.7	49.5	50.5
76063	MANSFIELD	86.2	78.6	4.5	6.8	1.2	2.4	12.8	19.1	8.3	8.3	8.2	7.5	5.4	28.7	26.4	6.4	0.6	70.3	34.6	50.1	49.9
76064	MAYPEARL	84.3	78.7	5.9	7.2	0.5	0.6	17.0	24.1	7.4	7.7	7.9	7.6	6.0	28.1	27.5	6.8	0.9	72.2	34.3	49.8	50.2
76065	MIDLOTHIAN	91.6	88.7	2.4	2.9	0.5	0.5	10.2	15.2	7.4	7.5	7.6	7.5	6.0	27.9	27.5	7.9	0.8	72.9	35.5	49.8	50.2
76066	MILLSAP	94.1	91.8	0.4	0.5	0.3	0.4	6.2	9.0	6.4	6.5	6.9	6.9	6.0	24.5	30.2	11.6	1.1	76.1	39.8	50.6	49.4
76067	MINERAL WELLS	83.5	78.8	5.5	6.5	0.6	0.7	15.8	21.4	6.6	6.4	6.3	6.5	6.6	27.0	25.6	12.6	2.3	76.6	38.0	52.3	47.7
76070	NEMO	95.9	93.6	0.5	0.6	0.0	0.4	7.8	11.4	6.7	6.9	6.9	7.1	6.4	24.3	30.1	10.3	1.1	74.9	38.7	50.0	50.0
76071	NEWARK	93.7	91.2	0.3	0.4	0.1	0.2	6.2	9.4	6.9	6.8	7.1	7.5	6.4	26.6	27.6	10.1	0.9	74.5	37.5	49.1	50.9
76073	PARADISE	95.6	94.0	0.2	0.2	0.2	0.2	5.3	8.1	6.7	6.8	6.9	7.2	6.5	25.9	29.5	9.8	0.7	75.3	37.9	50.2	49.8
76077	RAINBOW	91.1	88.3	0.3	0.3	0.3	0.4	16.8	22.7	6.9	7.1	7.3	7.1	6.0	26.1	27.5	10.2	1.8	74.3	36.3	49.2	50.8
76078	RHOME	92.1	89.0	1.0	1.3	0.3	0.4	7.1	10.8	7.5	7.6	7.8	7.5	5.8	27.6	27.9	7.6	0.6	72.5	36.5	50.5	49.5
76082	SPRINGTOWN	94.7	92.7	0.5	0.7	0.3	0.4	5.8	8.6	7.1	7.0	7.2	7.6	6.5	26.9	27.9	9.0	0.8	74.1	36.5	50.2	49.8
76084	VENUS	80.8	75.9	7.2	8.2	2.0	2.5	16.3	22.6	7.2	7.0	7.0	6.7	6.7	31.9	26.1	6.9	0.5	74.4	34.8	55.6	44.4
76085	WEATHERFORD	93.9	91.2	0.7	1.0	0.3	0.6	6.6	10.0	7.2	7.3	7.4	7.1	5.9	26.1	28.6	9.5	0.9	73.7	37.2	49.5	50.5
76086	WEATHERFORD	90.2	86.8	2.2	3.0	0.7	1.0	11.1	15.2	7.0	6.5	6.3	7.2	6.5	26.6	23.7	13.0	3.1	76.3	37.1	48.0	52.0
76087	WEATHERFORD	95.0	93.1	0.4	0.6	0.3	0.4	5.2	7.6	5.5	6.2	7.1	7.4	4.7	23.4	33.4	11.3	0.9	76.5	42.0	50.2	49.8
76088	WEATHERFORD	90.3	88.3	3.5	3.5	0.1	0.2	8.0	11.1	6.2	6.4	6.7	7.0	6.0	28.5	27.7	10.3	1.1	76.3	37.6	53.1	46.9
76092	SOUTHLAKE	94.2	91.5	1.5	2.2	1.8	2.5	3.9	6.9	7.5	10.1	10.6	8.6	2.5	24.5	31.5	4.4	0.4	65.6	38.3	50.2	49.8
76093	RIO VISTA	96.1	94.3	0.2	0.2	0.1	0.1	5.1	7.8	7.4	7.3	7.3	7.0	6.6	25.7	27.2	10.6	0.9	73.7	37.1	51.6	48.4
76102	FORT WORTH	54.4	49.9	34.6	36.6	1.1	1.3	26.1	31.2	6.7	5.5	3.9	6.5	10.6	37.1	17.4	7.7	4.6	81.1	33.0	58.2	41.8
76103	FORT WORTH	54.8	47.8	24.5	25.6	3.0	3.2	29.9	39.3	8.5	8.1	7.7	7.2	6.4	26.7	23.3	9.4	2.7	71.3	34.6	49.0	51.0
76104	FORT WORTH	24.6	22.9	57.3	55.6	2.5	2.2	26.1	31.9	7.7	7.5	6.7	7.2	6.3	24.7	23.5	13.1	3.2	73.3	36.9	48.8	51.2
76105	FORT WORTH	26.5	24.7	50.5	48.9	0.6	0.6	40.7	45.6	10.3	9.7	9.1	8.9	7.6	26.2	19.6	7.7	1.0	65.7	28.1	49.4	50.6
76106	FORT WORTH	51.8	47.7	6.3	5.5	0.4	0.4	78.1	84.9	10.6	9.7	8.5	8.6	8.8	30.0	16.9	6.0	0.9	66.1	27.2	53.2	46.8
76107	FORT WORTH	68.3	62.5	17.2	17.8	0.8	0.9	23.2	31.7	7.2	6.5	5.9	5.8	6.9	28.4	26.1	10.9	2.4	77.1	37.5	48.6	51.4
76108	FORT WORTH	86.2	79.9	4.1	5.5	1.8	2.6	12.3	20.3	7.8	7.2	7.0	7.0	6.8	27.5	26.1	9.3	1.3	73.7	35.4	48.9	51.1
76109	FORT WORTH	91.1	87.2	2.9	3.7	1.7	2.2	6.9	11.7	5.4	4.6	4.6	6.6	11.4	27.7	24.0	12.4	3.3	82.7	34.8	47.5	52.5
76110	FORT WORTH	53.2	47.1	5.0	4.7	3.0	2.8	62.1	71.3	10.0	9.2	8.0	7.7	8.3	30.2	19.9	5.8	0.9	68.3	28.9	52.2	47.8
76111	FORT WORTH	61.5	53.6	5.9	5.7	5.3	5.1	46.5	59.9	9.0	8.5	7.8	7.5	6.8	29.1	21.7	7.9	1.7	70.0	32.0	51.8	48.2
76112	FORT WORTH	43.7	36.6	46.1	50.1	2.7	3.1	10.6	15.5	8.0	7.0	6.6	6.7	7.9	28.5	23.6	9.8	1.9	74.4	33.8	46.9	53.1
76114	FORT WORTH	80.4	72.0	3.2	4.2	0.8	1.0	28.1	41.9	7.1	6.8	6.3	6.4	7.0	29.6	24.3	10.5	2.0	75.9	35.7	45.9	54.1
76115	FORT WORTH	50.1	44.0	9.4	8.5	4.0	3.7	61.3	72.0	11.0	9.9	8.2	8.2	8.7	30.6	16.9	5.8	0.8	66.0	27.2	50.5	49.5
76116	FORT WORTH	76.7	70.0	10.7	12.2	1.9	2.3	18.4	27.5	7.9	6.7	6.1	6.0	8.2	29.1	23.1	11.0	1.9	76.0	34.3	49.2	50.8
76117	HALTOM CITY	77.2	68.6	2.2	2.7	7.7	9.1	21.0	32.4	7.9	7.2	6.7	6.8	7.7	28.4	22.7	10.9	1.8	74.2	33.8	50.4	49.6
76118	FORT WORTH	82.3	74.6	5.0	7.0	4.5	6.3	12.2	19.5	8.6	8.0	7.3	6.2	5.9	28.7	23.1	9.8	2.3	72.3	35.5	47.6	52.4
76119	FORT WORTH	30.3	26.7	55.5	55.6	0.9	1.0	23.3	29.3	8.8	8.3	7.9	8.0	7.3	26.4	22.8	9.4	1.1	70.2	32.1	49.7	50.3
76120	FORT WORTH	61.8	53.2	27.7	32.7	4.0	5.3	9.3	13.9	7.9	6.8	6.1	6.3	10.9	35.9	21.0	4.7	0.5	75.9	30.4	47.8	52.2
76122	FORT WORTH	61.9	51.8	3.3	3.3	5.9	5.8	44.1	59.1	8.4	6.6	5.5	5.8	15.0	39.1	15.7	3.3	0.7	76.3	27.6	52.9	47.1
76123	FORT WORTH	65.1	63.1	22.8	22.2	5.0	6.1	10.8	14.9	9.0	8.4	8.0	7.4	6.1	31.7	24.9	4.2	0.4	69.7	31.7	48.7	51.3
76126	FORT WORTH	90.9	86.7	2.8	3.7	1.8	2.5	6.3	11.1	5.6	6.0	6.7	6.7	4.7	22.9	31.7	14.0	1.6	77.5	43.2	48.2	51.8
76127	NAVAL AIR STATION/ J	73.1	64.9	15.4	19.2	1.9	2.3	10.7	17.5	5.6	6.3	5.3	5.9	17.1	34.9	17.7	6.4	0.8	80.4	29.4	59.8	40.2
76129	FORT WORTH	85.9	79.4	5.3	7.2	3.5	4.8	6.3	11.2	0.0	0.0	0.0	64.3	35.4	0.3	0.1	0.0	0.0	100.0	18.9	35.1	64.9
76131	FORT WORTH	81.9	77.5	2.6	3.1	1.7	2.2	20.7	28.4	9.3	8.7	8.1	7.1	5.2	33.4	23.1	4.8	0.4	69.5	32.5	49.5	50.5
76132	FORT WORTH	80.4	73.0	9.2	12.0	3.8	5.0	9.6	15.7	6.0	4.8	4.5	5.6	13.6	34.1	20.7	8.7	2.1	81.9	31.3	48.3	51.7
76133	FORT WORTH	70.4	62.5	16.2	19.1	3.2	3.7	17.0	25.1	7.1	6.7	6.5	6.4	6.7	26.5	25.9	12.2	1.9	75.7	37.3	47.4	52.6
76134	FORT WORTH	56.8	49.4	30.8	33.2	2.1	2.5	17.1	25.1	7.4	7.4	7.3	7.4	6.5	27.1	24.8	10.9	1.2	73.2	35.2	48.0	52.0
76135	FORT WORTH	87.5	81.1	2.0	2.7	1.1	1.6	12.8	20.9	7.2	6.7	6.6	6.6	7.4	27.3	26.2	10.5	1.6	75.6	36.4	49.3	50.7
76137	FORT WORTH	80.2	73.2	4.9	6.1	6.5	8.0	12.0	19.5	9.8	9.2	8.5	7.0	5.8	33.8	22.4	3.3	0.2	68.1	31.5	49.6	50.4
76140	FORT WORTH	49.2	46.1	39.1	37.2	1.1	1.4	15.4	22.8	7.9	7.8	7.8	7.7	6.8	26.4	25.0	9.3	1.4	71.8	33.9	48.3	51.7
76148	FORT WORTH	86.6	80.5	2.2	3.0	4.2	5.5	10.9	18.7	8.3	8.1	7.8	7.7	6.0	30.5	24.8	6.1	0.8	71.0	33.4	49.2	50.8
76155	FORT WORTH	59.6	51.2	15.7	18.2	15.6	17.8	14.8	22.2	6.1	2.2	0.8	2.4	18.1	54.0	15.8	0.7	0.0	90.4	28.9	56.9	43.1
76164	FORT WORTH	52.2	48.6	1.8	1.5	0.3	0.3	90.3	94.2	9.9	9.3	8.3	8.8	8.5	30.0	18.3	6.2	0.8	67.2	28.0	52.9	47.1
76177	FORT WORTH	86.6	80.9	2.2	3.5	4.5	3.4	9.7	17.0	8.7	8.0	7.5	6.6	5.3	34.1	23.6	5.6	0.5	71.6	33.2	49.5	50.5
76179	FORT WORTH	86.3	76.9	1.3	2.0	5.1	8.9	10.7	18.0	7.6	7.5	7.5	7.0	5.8	29.4	26.6	7.9	0.7	73.1	35.1	49.0	51.0
76180	NORTH RICHLAND HILLS	88.6	83.6	2.7	3.7	2.7	3.6	9.4	15.6	7.1	6.9	7.0	7.1	6.9	28.3	27.5	8.2	1.1	74.8	35.6	49.3	50.7
76201	DENTON	73.2	66.6	8.6	10.2	6.6	9.2	16.8	20.9	4.1	3.0	2.7	14.9	27.6	26.8	12.0	6.4	2.5	87.5	24.6	50.3	49.7
	TEXAS	71.0	67.6	11.5	11.4	2.8	3.5	32.0	37.4	7.9	7.5	7.2	7.5	7.4	28.3	24.0	8.8	1.4	73.0	33.6	49.7	50.3
	UNITED STATES	75.1	72.0	12.3	12.7	3.8	4.6	12.5	15.7	6.8	6.7	6.6	7.1	6.9	27.0	26.0	10.9	1.9	75.7	36.9	49.2	50.8

#	POST OFFICE NAME	2009 Per Capita Income	2009 HH Income Base	2009 Household Income Distribution (%): Less than $25,000	$25,000 to $49,999	$50,000 to $99,999	$100,000 to $149,999	$150,000 or More	Median Household Income: 2009	2014	2009 National Centile	2009 State Centile	2009 Home Value Base	2009 Home Value Distribution (%): Less than $50,000	$50,000 to $89,999	$90,000 to $174,999	$175,000 to $399,999	$400,000 or More	2009 Median Home Value
76002	ARLINGTON	33083	7841	1.8	7.0	45.5	29.6	16.0	94426	94005	96	97	6959	0.5	4.1	57.5	35.4	2.6	152812
76006	ARLINGTON	38461	13114	10.6	30.2	41.2	10.6	7.4	58406	60542	76	83	2701	16.0	13.9	23.6	39.3	7.3	164536
76008	ALEDO	32440	4058	8.8	15.6	42.9	18.7	14.1	72665	73582	88	91	3556	13.2	11.1	30.2	33.6	12.0	160881
76009	ALVARADO	20880	7277	17.0	23.7	45.7	9.5	4.2	56527	58911	73	80	6063	23.9	31.3	33.1	10.7	0.9	82942
76010	ARLINGTON	15237	18562	30.2	33.5	31.8	3.4	1.1	38821	40374	29	37	5893	11.7	67.5	19.3	1.2	0.3	71267
76011	ARLINGTON	21356	12317	25.2	34.1	32.6	5.3	2.8	42533	44673	41	52	2298	19.5	43.5	13.1	22.8	1.2	75507
76012	ARLINGTON	31110	10221	14.9	23.6	40.3	12.4	8.9	63002	68804	81	86	6291	6.4	12.4	44.8	33.8	2.7	149014
76013	ARLINGTON	26388	14623	23.8	28.5	33.5	9.0	5.2	47574	48766	56	66	6842	1.5	16.5	59.8	20.1	2.0	122221
76014	ARLINGTON	21136	11167	13.3	27.2	47.9	9.4	2.3	59344	61181	77	83	5679	3.3	41.2	54.7	0.8	0.0	92444
76015	ARLINGTON	26307	6755	11.6	29.0	44.8	10.8	3.8	60197	62588	78	84	3296	4.8	24.1	62.2	8.6	0.3	106570
76016	ARLINGTON	34963	11486	5.7	13.5	44.8	22.5	13.4	81636	83771	93	94	9155	2.6	6.5	59.1	27.0	4.9	137697
76017	ARLINGTON	32116	16792	7.2	17.4	46.9	19.0	9.4	74522	77906	89	91	11673	5.1	11.1	64.7	17.1	2.0	124853
76018	ARLINGTON	26085	8718	3.4	14.0	58.3	18.6	5.7	77257	79287	91	93	7257	0.7	11.8	79.6	7.7	0.2	115926
76019	ARLINGTON	60625	3	0.0	0.0	100.0	0.0	0.0	81250	83333	93	94	2	0.0	0.0	100.0	0.0	0.0	112500
76020	AZLE	22692	9957	19.9	27.1	40.1	9.4	3.5	52614	55500	67	75	7490	16.5	29.7	37.4	13.7	2.6	96919
76021	BEDFORD	36080	15392	10.9	22.4	39.7	16.9	10.2	69141	75020	86	89	8110	1.0	2.0	58.9	37.7	0.4	155994
76022	BEDFORD	30321	6085	10.4	30.8	42.8	10.8	5.2	58164	60721	75	82	2979	1.3	18.9	67.6	12.1	0.0	113527
76023	BOYD	20188	2403	22.7	27.0	40.0	8.2	2.1	50136	52415	61	70	1989	20.8	25.3	33.8	16.2	3.8	98693
76028	BURLESON	24857	19782	13.0	23.5	43.8	14.4	5.3	62471	63481	81	85	15856	7.1	23.7	52.7	14.8	1.7	112788
76031	CLEBURNE	17618	6106	26.0	27.8	36.8	6.9	2.5	45908	50443	51	61	4462	26.8	30.2	32.7	9.4	0.9	79085
76033	CLEBURNE	22868	9082	21.1	27.1	38.6	8.9	4.3	51370	54489	65	73	6361	11.4	34.4	40.3	11.9	2.0	96358
76034	COLLEYVILLE	54361	7495	4.1	8.6	23.3	21.0	43.0	135245	134642	99	100	6782	0.5	3.3	13.9	50.3	32.0	316553
76035	CRESSON	21182	550	15.3	30.2	43.8	6.9	3.8	53076	53907	68	76	442	13.8	22.6	37.3	17.0	9.3	125862
76036	CROWLEY	26328	7115	16.5	21.3	42.0	13.1	7.1	61259	63596	79	84	5143	5.7	41.3	42.5	9.3	1.2	92728
76039	EULESS	33046	14497	8.1	21.7	50.6	14.5	5.1	67618	73972	85	89	5786	1.6	20.6	64.0	13.8	0.0	117633
76040	EULESS	27291	11673	14.4	32.5	38.6	10.7	3.8	53130	54445	68	76	4009	9.5	17.8	57.0	15.5	0.2	113984
76041	FORRESTON	17629	76	17.1	34.2	43.4	2.6	2.6	49074	48752	59	68	58	31.0	27.6	29.3	6.9	5.2	72500
76043	GLEN ROSE	19776	2260	23.7	30.5	34.3	8.8	2.7	46203	47339	52	62	1667	15.1	15.9	32.9	25.5	10.7	139514
76044	GODLEY	19467	1240	21.6	24.6	42.8	7.7	3.3	53377	56494	69	76	972	14.4	27.2	38.8	16.7	3.0	103767
76048	GRANBURY	23339	9209	22.0	29.4	37.5	7.8	3.3	48096	50940	57	67	6883	18.4	16.3	39.0	21.0	5.4	119044
76049	GRANBURY	30742	9402	11.8	25.4	42.2	12.7	7.9	59731	57851	77	84	8033	5.4	8.9	28.3	47.2	10.2	200554
76050	GRANDVIEW	21466	2204	21.1	23.7	42.0	9.2	4.1	54605	57158	71	78	1775	15.4	24.1	39.7	17.2	3.7	107936
76051	GRAPEVINE	39542	17643	8.9	17.0	35.0	20.0	19.2	81539	83578	93	94	10656	4.6	5.0	34.9	51.0	4.5	186299
76052	HASLET	37427	4615	7.3	12.6	34.6	25.2	20.2	93396	97205	96	97	4142	1.2	12.3	34.2	43.6	8.7	182736
76053	HURST	24062	10842	15.9	28.7	43.5	9.6	2.3	55394	58260	72	79	6054	2.6	31.6	60.5	4.9	0.3	105145
76054	HURST	37264	4756	5.4	14.1	42.3	24.7	13.4	83336	86560	93	95	3848	3.5	1.9	53.6	38.8	2.2	160889
76055	ITASCA	17920	989	27.7	32.3	33.7	5.2	1.2	41347	43295	37	48	754	30.8	30.1	26.9	9.8	2.4	75185
76058	JOSHUA	20624	5800	15.1	25.8	47.7	7.8	3.6	56066	58839	73	80	4822	15.1	29.6	42.1	12.8	0.4	98050
76059	KEENE	18603	1754	23.7	29.6	36.0	7.6	3.1	47099	50429	54	64	928	19.5	35.8	36.6	7.4	0.6	84674
76060	KENNEDALE	24511	2453	16.9	25.8	39.4	11.9	6.0	57211	59474	74	81	1408	24.7	17.5	33.2	22.7	1.8	106675
76063	MANSFIELD	34857	18742	8.1	15.4	40.4	18.5	17.6	79706	82799	92	94	15554	8.5	12.4	40.0	34.9	4.3	146980
76064	MAYPEARL	21468	573	16.8	26.9	42.8	8.6	5.1	60192	63114	78	84	426	17.8	20.2	37.3	22.5	2.1	114706
76065	MIDLOTHIAN	27411	9143	10.4	16.9	46.8	17.7	8.3	75287	78335	90	92	7648	4.5	13.5	47.1	29.9	5.0	141117
76066	MILLSAP	19903	1212	21.8	30.9	38.5	6.8	1.9	47290	51133	55	65	1017	27.1	25.6	29.2	14.2	3.9	83452
76067	MINERAL WELLS	16657	7431	31.0	33.9	29.4	4.2	1.5	37406	40000	25	32	4979	35.8	32.1	24.5	6.9	0.7	63442
76070	NEMO	22902	190	18.4	23.7	40.5	14.2	3.2	53891	52859	69	77	157	10.8	12.1	31.2	30.6	15.3	162500
76071	NEWARK	17985	1230	27.6	26.3	36.6	7.3	2.3	46812	50930	54	64	960	29.4	26.0	26.4	16.8	1.5	80545
76073	PARADISE	20212	2142	19.3	26.2	43.1	9.3	2.1	52145	53788	66	74	1852	11.7	26.0	38.6	21.9	1.8	113317
76077	RAINBOW	20659	297	21.9	31.6	36.0	8.4	2.0	46600	47888	53	63	224	10.7	15.6	36.2	26.3	11.2	144853
76078	RHOME	20479	2488	16.9	29.1	40.8	10.0	3.3	52254	54391	66	74	2126	11.6	20.2	45.1	19.9	3.2	116899
76082	SPRINGTOWN	19133	5993	19.2	26.6	43.3	8.4	2.4	52513	55078	67	75	5007	12.7	29.6	42.2	13.3	2.2	101574
76084	VENUS	19299	2397	13.5	24.4	48.8	10.2	3.0	57952	60456	75	82	2075	16.1	35.7	38.5	9.0	0.8	88440
76085	WEATHERFORD	20243	3468	18.2	29.4	40.7	8.7	2.9	51463	54285	65	73	2789	16.2	28.7	37.2	15.0	2.9	98636
76086	WEATHERFORD	21797	7421	25.1	28.2	36.8	6.7	3.2	44881	51111	48	58	4505	12.9	25.2	47.4	13.1	1.5	102642
76087	WEATHERFORD	27663	8725	13.8	21.8	41.2	15.2	8.1	62453	63294	81	85	7628	12.1	13.7	35.3	35.0	4.0	145668
76088	WEATHERFORD	21869	4073	17.8	29.0	42.4	8.0	2.8	52125	54993	66	74	3329	17.7	24.1	37.8	17.0	3.4	104740
76092	SOUTHLAKE	58005	8136	3.9	7.1	17.6	17.7	53.7	158726	158172	100	100	7289	4.8	3.6	8.7	31.3	51.6	407685
76093	RIO VISTA	17959	865	26.0	29.2	37.2	5.4	2.1	45234	48817	49	59	706	25.1	33.4	27.9	9.5	4.1	80625
76102	FORT WORTH	18450	2659	49.7	23.2	17.8	5.3	4.1	25229	25778	3	4	337	50.7	28.5	10.4	7.1	3.3	48864
76103	FORT WORTH	17269	5361	29.0	35.4	28.8	5.2	1.6	38470	40332	28	35	2964	25.8	42.5	28.9	2.7	0.1	71701
76104	FORT WORTH	11774	5855	55.8	27.2	14.3	1.8	0.9	21434	21560	2	3	2676	68.5	26.0	4.6	0.4	0.6	40481
76105	FORT WORTH	10355	6972	47.8	32.5	16.6	1.9	1.1	26113	26084	4	5	4010	73.5	24.6	1.7	0.2	0.1	38392
76106	FORT WORTH	11145	9053	34.8	33.5	27.2	3.2	1.3	34995	35483	18	22	5025	58.6	38.8	2.4	0.1	0.1	46088
76107	FORT WORTH	28111	12184	27.6	29.8	29.9	6.4	6.2	42714	44658	42	52	6196	18.7	33.6	24.4	13.3	10.0	86478
76108	FORT WORTH	22720	13135	18.0	28.0	41.8	9.3	2.9	53521	55418	69	77	8581	19.3	34.3	38.3	7.0	1.1	86074
76109	FORT WORTH	41032	10418	18.1	22.4	35.0	12.0	12.5	62824	68345	81	86	5140	4.1	12.9	27.9	39.2	15.9	193679
76110	FORT WORTH	15701	10182	31.6	31.5	28.1	5.5	3.3	39133	41018	30	38	5504	40.1	37.8	12.1	7.7	2.4	55680
76111	FORT WORTH	16377	6936	27.5	34.7	31.7	4.2	1.9	40394	42449	34	44	4201	30.8	51.6	16.0	1.5	0.2	59012
76112	FORT WORTH	22188	17289	27.1	31.2	32.9	6.1	2.8	42735	45175	42	52	8026	15.7	42.5	35.3	6.1	0.4	82693
76114	FORT WORTH	17887	8957	27.9	34.4	32.5	3.6	1.6	39313	40967	31	40	5604	35.9	50.0	13.1	0.8	0.1	58376
76115	FORT WORTH	12016	5640	32.5	38.8	25.2	2.3	1.2	35238	36029	18	24	2860	44.5	48.5	6.9	0.1	0.0	52101
76116	FORT WORTH	26344	21323	24.9	30.1	31.8	8.2	5.0	45573	46878	50	60	7913	8.9	28.2	43.2	16.4	3.3	107305
76117	HALTOM CITY	20604	11902	22.1	32.5	37.6	5.6	2.2	45847	47246	51	61	6803	16.6	56.5	23.8	2.9	0.3	73053
76118	FORT WORTH	26009	5236	14.0	19.7	47.7	14.4	4.1	65645	73401	84	88	3726	3.0	26.3	65.8	4.8	0.2	112394
76119	FORT WORTH	13615	13035	37.8	31.7	26.0	2.9	1.6	33421	34253	14	17	8031	50.1	42.4	6.7	0.7	0.1	49975
76120	FORT WORTH	29067	7121	13.3	32.4	42.5	8.6	3.2	53476	55604	69	76	2414	15.2	27.8	45.1	11.5	0.4	98622
76122	FORT WORTH	2966	0	0.0	0.0	0.0	0.0	0.0	0	0	0	0	0	0.0	0.0	0.0	0.0	0.0	0
76123	FORT WORTH	30611	8954	6.9	12.3	43.7	20.7	16.5	83573	86177	93	95	7546	0.2	13.1	71.4	14.2	1.2	121890
76126	FORT WORTH	30690	7373	9.2	21.2	45.7	18.0	5.8	68245	74138	86	89	5721	6.8	15.6	61.2	14.8	1.6	113924
76127	NAVAL AIR STATION/ J	13550	97	15.5	27.8	45.4	7.2	4.1	57853	60781	75	82	34	14.7	35.3	20.6	29.4	0.0	95000
76129	FORT WORTH	13982	0	0.0	0.0	0.0	0.0	0.0	0	0	0	0	0	0.0	0.0	0.0	0.0	0.0	0
76131	FORT WORTH	27194	8208	8.7	16.2	47.5	18.9	8.7	76045	79203	90	92	6671	4.2	30.8	35.5	25.2	4.3	126117
76132	FORT WORTH	36036	11896	19.5	26.9	36.2	9.0	8.5	53241	54683	68	76	3196	1.2	8.0	24.2	50.0	16.6	219147
76133	FORT WORTH	25276	18250	16.3	27.4	41.2	11.4	3.9	56285	58589	73	80	11617	4.0	31.2	57.9	6.8	0.1	101423
76134	FORT WORTH	21541	7296	15.2	29.5	44.5	8.9	1.9	55011	57437	71	78	5191	8.7	42.3	47.7	1.2	0.1	89374
76135	FORT WORTH	23772	7171	20.9	28.1	39.4	8.3	3.3	50998	52639	64	72	4613	17.3	36.0	38.4	7.0	1.3	86429
76137	FORT WORTH	33154	17802	6.0	14.4	42.8	22.9	13.9	82463	83965	93	94	13130	4.5	11.4	58.7	25.1	0.4	135152
76140	FORT WORTH	19396	8316	17.3	32.1	40.8	7.3	2.5	50588	51473	63	71	6048	19.0	53.8	23.2	3.2	0.7	73688
76148	FORT WORTH	24444	8240	7.9	18.3	56.3	13.9	3.6	69830	75361	87	90	6451	2.2	36.6	60.3	0.9	0.0	96625
76155	FORT WORTH	38279	1702	11.5	32.3	47.4	7.5	1.4	55516	58543	72	79	13	0.0	100.0	0.0	0.0	0.0	62500
76164	FORT WORTH	11714	4841	30.1	35.7	30.2	2.6	1.3	37866	39249	26	34	2530	52.1	42.1	5.2	0.6	0.0	49080
76177	FORT WORTH	42053	1244	7.7	15.4	44.7	24.3	7.9	80401	81244	92	94	1098	1.3	8.1	55.0	30.8	4.8	145813
76179	FORT WORTH	27619	14251	11.3	17.5	49.2	15.6	6.4	68265	74072	86	89	11052	4.3	22.4	53.5	15.8	4.1	114055
76180	NORTH RICHLAND HILLS	30696	23710	10.1	21.1	44.6	15.0	9.2	68804	75235	86	89	14916	5.8	13.7	58.4	20.7	1.4	124057
76201	DENTON	18963	10897	44.9	28.1	20.2	5.1	1.7	28184	30012	6	7	2309	3.8	13.6	69.8	11.8	1.0	125444
	TEXAS	24551		22.3	25.0	34.3	11.1	7.3	52382	54495				16.5	22.7	36.5	19.7	4.6	109784
	UNITED STATES	27277		20.9	24.4	35.3	11.7	7.6	54719	56938				9.3	13.1	31.6	32.6	13.5	162279

ZIP CODE #	POST OFFICE NAME	FINANCIAL SERVICES: Auto Loan	Home Loan	Invest-ments	Retire-ment Plans	THE HOME: Home Improvements: Home Repair	Lawn & Garden	Furnishings: Comput-ers & Hard-ware-Personal	Major Appli-ances	TV, Radio, Sound Equip-ment	Furni-ture	ENTERTAINMENT: Dine out/ Carry out	Sports Equip-ment	Fees & Tickets	Toys & Games	Travel	Cable TV	PERSONAL: Apparel & Services	Auto Repairs	Health Insur-ance	Pets & Supplies
76002	ARLINGTON	157	182	153	182	174	149	155	156	144	172	147	127	168	156	158	134	106	144	130	175
76006	ARLINGTON	118	73	65	83	67	70	114	86	113	110	116	77	94	117	90	109	81	106	88	110
76008	ALEDO	135	161	141	161	155	141	138	140	130	146	133	111	151	136	146	126	95	133	127	161
76009	ALVARADO	99	93	81	91	90	92	91	92	92	93	92	70	86	95	86	93	63	91	91	109
76010	ARLINGTON	68	54	47	53	51	48	68	58	66	68	68	48	60	68	60	63	48	66	56	69
76011	ARLINGTON	82	53	48	58	50	50	80	62	79	79	82	54	67	82	65	76	57	76	63	78
76012	ARLINGTON	110	111	108	114	111	109	113	109	111	114	112	84	114	112	113	111	79	112	111	129
76013	ARLINGTON	89	78	76	81	77	81	91	83	90	87	90	65	84	90	84	90	63	88	87	100
76014	ARLINGTON	97	90	76	89	85	80	95	87	91	97	93	69	89	96	87	88	65	90	82	103
76015	ARLINGTON	99	92	80	92	88	84	98	90	96	100	97	71	94	99	92	93	68	95	88	107
76016	ARLINGTON	137	163	152	164	160	146	141	144	135	150	137	111	157	139	151	131	98	138	133	166
76017	ARLINGTON	128	137	117	134	130	119	126	123	120	133	122	97	129	126	124	115	86	121	113	143
76018	ARLINGTON	129	138	111	132	129	115	123	122	117	133	120	95	124	125	120	112	83	117	109	140
76019	ARLINGTON	121	107	111	108	110	122	115	119	118	110	116	88	106	117	110	123	79	118	128	140
76020	AZLE	94	91	85	90	89	94	85	91	87	87	87	68	83	90	85	90	60	87	92	107
76021	BEDFORD	121	115	107	120	111	107	122	111	118	124	120	90	121	122	117	115	85	117	108	133
76022	BEDFORD	97	91	82	94	88	90	100	91	100	98	100	73	98	100	95	99	70	98	97	111
76023	BOYD	90	83	73	80	81	84	78	82	81	81	81	60	74	84	74	83	55	80	83	98
76028	BURLESON	104	109	96	109	105	105	101	103	100	102	100	79	102	103	101	100	70	100	101	121
76031	CLEBURNE	87	74	69	71	72	80	75	79	79	75	78	58	68	81	70	82	54	78	81	94
76033	CLEBURNE	90	86	80	86	83	93	87	88	89	84	88	68	85	90	85	92	61	88	94	105
76034	COLLEYVILLE	214	281	290	294	290	254	231	241	217	251	219	189	276	220	262	207	163	224	213	273
76035	CRESSON	96	89	79	86	87	90	83	88	86	87	86	64	79	90	80	89	59	86	88	105
76036	CROWLEY	104	109	96	109	106	108	102	104	102	104	102	80	105	104	103	102	71	102	106	122
76039	EULESS	117	98	84	102	91	89	113	98	111	114	113	81	104	116	100	107	79	107	96	120
76040	EULESS	97	74	65	79	69	71	96	79	94	94	96	67	85	98	82	92	67	90	81	98
76041	FORRESTON	99	74	81	72	74	94	76	87	83	75	82	66	63	87	70	90	55	82	91	105
76043	GLEN ROSE	90	77	77	74	76	87	75	83	80	75	79	61	68	82	71	84	53	80	86	99
76044	GODLEY	92	89	78	88	87	90	83	87	85	86	85	65	81	88	82	86	58	85	87	104
76048	GRANBURY	93	80	87	78	81	91	81	88	84	80	83	65	73	85	78	88	57	86	91	104
76049	GRANBURY	112	112	120	110	117	122	104	114	108	110	107	79	106	105	109	111	73	110	121	133
76050	GRANDVIEW	95	94	84	93	92	95	88	92	89	89	89	69	87	92	87	90	61	89	92	109
76051	GRAPEVINE	149	158	143	163	154	141	151	144	144	158	147	117	157	150	150	138	105	143	133	169
76052	HASLET	161	191	164	195	186	158	161	163	149	179	152	134	179	161	167	138	111	149	135	182
76053	HURST	88	84	75	85	81	84	89	84	89	87	90	66	87	91	85	90	63	88	89	100
76054	HURST	136	159	153	162	159	149	142	144	138	149	139	110	157	139	152	135	99	140	139	167
76055	ITASCA	82	66	74	64	66	80	66	76	72	65	71	57	58	73	63	77	48	72	79	91
76058	JOSHUA	99	93	83	91	90	94	89	92	91	92	91	70	86	94	86	92	62	91	92	110
76059	KEENE	81	72	64	72	69	72	83	74	80	78	80	59	75	82	73	80	56	78	75	89
76060	KENNEDALE	103	101	86	100	96	95	99	97	97	102	98	76	97	102	95	96	68	97	93	115
76063	MANSFIELD	155	173	153	170	168	152	153	155	146	164	148	121	161	153	156	140	105	148	139	177
76064	MAYPEARL	100	99	87	99	97	100	92	96	93	94	93	72	91	97	91	95	64	93	96	114
76065	MIDLOTHIAN	122	132	113	130	126	120	119	120	115	124	116	93	123	120	119	113	82	116	113	140
76066	MILLSAP	91	76	75	73	75	86	74	82	79	75	78	61	66	82	70	83	53	78	83	98
76067	MINERAL WELLS	75	57	69	56	57	75	62	70	67	57	66	53	52	67	58	73	44	68	76	84
76070	NEMO	104	94	87	91	92	99	89	96	93	92	93	70	83	96	85	96	63	92	97	114
76071	NEWARK	88	71	72	69	70	83	71	78	76	71	75	59	62	79	66	80	51	75	81	94
76073	PARADISE	93	86	76	83	84	87	81	85	84	84	84	62	76	87	77	86	57	83	86	102
76077	RAINBOW	87	80	70	77	78	81	75	79	78	78	78	58	71	81	71	80	53	77	80	94
76078	RHOME	97	89	79	86	87	91	84	89	87	87	87	65	79	91	80	89	59	86	89	106
76082	SPRINGTOWN	94	85	77	82	83	88	80	86	84	83	84	63	75	87	76	87	57	83	86	102
76084	VENUS	105	91	87	89	89	99	90	96	93	91	93	72	82	97	85	97	63	93	97	115
76085	WEATHERFORD	93	85	76	83	83	88	81	86	84	84	84	62	77	87	77	86	57	83	86	102
76086	WEATHERFORD	81	75	71	75	75	82	78	79	80	75	79	59	74	80	75	83	54	79	86	94
76087	WEATHERFORD	112	121	111	122	120	119	109	114	108	112	109	86	114	111	113	109	76	110	113	134
76088	WEATHERFORD	97	87	81	84	85	92	83	89	86	85	86	65	77	90	79	90	59	86	90	106
76092	SOUTHLAKE	266	334	318	345	336	289	277	285	258	306	262	229	322	271	302	242	193	263	244	320
76093	RIO VISTA	91	68	75	67	68	87	70	80	77	69	75	61	58	80	64	83	51	76	84	97
76102	FORT WORTH	65	47	45	51	44	48	66	53	68	63	69	44	58	68	55	69	49	63	59	68
76103	FORT WORTH	70	63	54	61	61	64	67	66	70	67	70	48	64	70	63	72	49	68	70	77
76104	FORT WORTH	46	35	33	36	34	41	43	41	48	43	47	30	39	47	38	51	33	45	48	51
76105	FORT WORTH	54	43	36	40	41	44	46	47	51	50	51	32	42	51	42	53	35	49	50	55
76106	FORT WORTH	69	55	43	48	52	50	59	60	62	64	63	40	52	63	53	62	45	62	56	66
76107	FORT WORTH	88	81	79	83	80	81	90	83	90	90	90	65	87	89	85	90	64	89	87	100
76108	FORT WORTH	92	86	74	86	82	85	89	85	89	88	89	67	85	92	83	89	62	87	87	102
76109	FORT WORTH	121	110	112	117	110	109	129	113	126	125	127	92	124	125	121	124	90	123	117	137
76110	FORT WORTH	78	68	57	63	66	63	73	71	74	76	75	51	67	75	67	74	53	74	68	80
76111	FORT WORTH	74	66	56	61	63	65	69	69	71	70	71	51	63	72	64	72	49	71	70	79
76112	FORT WORTH	77	65	57	67	61	66	77	68	78	75	78	55	71	79	69	78	54	75	73	84
76114	FORT WORTH	72	62	58	62	60	69	68	68	71	64	69	52	62	71	63	73	48	69	74	81
76115	FORT WORTH	65	53	43	48	51	49	59	57	60	62	62	41	53	61	53	60	44	61	55	64
76116	FORT WORTH	85	73	70	77	71	73	88	77	88	85	89	63	83	88	81	87	62	85	81	94
76117	HALTOM CITY	77	70	59	71	66	72	77	72	79	74	78	57	73	80	71	80	54	76	78	87
76118	FORT WORTH	103	103	90	102	99	101	101	100	102	101	102	77	100	104	98	102	71	100	103	117
76119	FORT WORTH	63	54	47	52	52	56	58	57	62	60	62	41	54	62	53	64	43	60	61	68
76120	FORT WORTH	99	70	60	75	65	66	94	77	94	94	95	65	80	98	78	91	66	89	77	96
76122	FORT WORTH	0	0	0	0	0	0	0	0	0	0	0	0	0	0	0	0	0	0	0	0
76123	FORT WORTH	146	162	135	160	153	134	143	142	134	156	137	114	150	144	143	126	97	134	123	161
76126	FORT WORTH	109	123	113	122	121	120	109	114	109	113	110	84	118	111	115	110	77	110	115	132
76127	NAVAL AIR STATION/ J	95	80	73	85	78	73	95	81	91	93	93	70	89	99	86	87	66	89	77	97
76129	FORT WORTH	0	0	0	0	0	0	0	0	0	0	0	0	0	0	0	0	0	0	0	0
76131	FORT WORTH	131	144	118	140	135	119	126	126	119	137	122	100	131	128	125	112	86	119	109	143
76132	FORT WORTH	114	81	73	89	76	77	112	89	111	110	113	77	97	114	94	107	79	105	91	112
76133	FORT WORTH	93	93	85	93	91	92	93	91	93	94	93	69	93	94	92	93	65	92	94	107
76134	FORT WORTH	89	91	80	88	87	87	86	87	86	89	87	65	86	88	85	86	60	86	87	102
76135	FORT WORTH	90	84	73	84	80	84	86	84	86	86	87	65	82	89	81	87	60	85	86	100
76137	FORT WORTH	144	151	127	150	143	129	139	136	133	150	135	109	142	142	136	126	95	132	121	157
76140	FORT WORTH	87	85	75	83	82	85	82	84	83	84	83	62	80	85	80	84	57	83	85	98
76148	FORT WORTH	113	117	95	113	110	102	107	107	104	114	106	81	107	110	104	101	73	104	99	124
76155	FORT WORTH	98	55	48	64	49	54	94	68	94	90	96	62	74	97	71	91	66	87	71	89
76164	FORT WORTH	73	60	46	51	58	54	62	64	65	68	66	42	54	66	56	66	47	66	61	70
76177	FORT WORTH	140	148	120	141	138	125	132	132	126	142	128	104	133	135	129	121	89	126	118	151
76179	FORT WORTH	115	125	106	121	118	109	112	112	108	119	110	86	115	113	112	105	76	108	104	130
76180	NORTH RICHLAND HILLS	120	121	106	122	116	111	120	114	117	123	118	91	120	121	116	114	83	116	110	134
76201	DENTON	60	40	38	43	38	43	70	49	64	57	64	44	53	63	50	62	45	59	52	62
	TEXAS	104	96	90	94	93	94	99	97	99	101	100	75	94	101	94	99	70	99	96	114
	UNITED STATES	100	100	100	100	100	100	100	100	100	100	100	100	100	100	100	100	100	100	100	100

POPULATION CHANGE

ZIP CODE #	POST OFFICE NAME	COUNTY FIPS CODE	POPULATION 2000	POPULATION 2009	POPULATION 2014	2000-2009 ANNUAL RATE % Rate	2000-2009 ANNUAL RATE State Centile	HOUSEHOLDS 2000	HOUSEHOLDS 2009	HOUSEHOLDS 2014	HOUSEHOLDS % Annual Rate 2000-2009	HOUSEHOLDS 2009 Average HH Size	FAMILIES 2000	FAMILIES 2009	FAMILIES % Annual Rate 2000-2009
76205	DENTON	121	16162	18641	20557	1.6	71	6393	7162	7910	1.2	2.44	3215	3246	0.1
76207	DENTON	121	6758	8888	10631	3.0	86	2633	3438	4105	2.9	2.57	1655	1902	1.5
76208	DENTON	121	11328	17893	21771	5.1	94	3953	6089	7394	4.8	2.93	2895	4320	4.4
76209	DENTON	121	22770	27164	30381	1.9	76	8291	9655	10784	1.7	2.73	5426	5931	1.0
76210	DENTON	121	19385	36799	46439	7.2	97	6643	12709	16119	7.3	2.81	5350	9844	6.8
76225	ALVORD	497	2470	3356	3763	3.4	89	960	1289	1446	3.2	2.60	728	965	3.1
76226	ARGYLE	121	7112	19589	29427	11.6	99	2454	6531	9734	11.2	3.00	2076	5438	11.0
76227	AUBREY	121	6696	21536	30854	13.5	99	2396	7407	10559	13.0	2.91	1906	5623	12.4
76228	BELLEVUE	077	1579	1583	1553	0.0	25	614	622	613	0.1	2.55	477	478	0.0
76230	BOWIE	337	9469	9959	10227	0.5	42	3807	4022	4138	0.6	2.42	2701	2810	0.4
76233	COLLINSVILLE	181	2163	2512	2673	1.6	71	824	948	1006	1.5	2.62	640	721	1.3
76234	DECATUR	497	12709	15174	16678	1.9	76	4463	5324	5855	1.9	2.80	3478	4102	1.8
76238	ERA	097	365	373	377	0.2	30	124	127	128	0.3	2.94	99	100	0.1
76239	FORESTBURG	337	1182	1287	1338	0.9	55	482	530	554	1.0	2.42	369	401	0.9
76240	GAINESVILLE	097	25474	27462	28297	0.8	52	9696	10392	10708	0.8	2.56	6953	7346	0.6
76245	GORDONVILLE	181	1604	1848	1973	1.5	69	728	834	888	1.5	2.22	508	570	1.3
76247	JUSTIN	121	5628	12563	17509	9.1	98	1880	4103	5768	8.8	3.03	1519	3226	8.5
76248	KELLER	439	27550	85008	109040	13.0	99	8826	27688	35544	13.2	3.07	7718	23287	12.7
76249	KRUM	121	4446	6541	7710	4.3	92	1517	2148	2521	3.8	3.02	1259	1707	3.3
76250	LINDSAY	097	856	936	975	1.0	58	287	314	327	1.0	2.98	227	244	0.8
76251	MONTAGUE	337	587	626	648	0.7	49	237	257	267	0.9	2.33	173	185	0.7
76252	MUENSTER	097	2996	3277	3408	1.0	58	1099	1204	1255	1.0	2.68	805	867	0.8
76255	NOCONA	337	5342	5622	5762	0.6	46	2211	2329	2391	0.6	2.36	1500	1553	0.4
76258	PILOT POINT	121	5760	7654	8941	3.1	87	2004	2616	3060	2.9	2.88	1515	1869	2.3
76259	PONDER	121	2913	4407	7868	4.6	93	977	1448	2594	4.3	3.04	790	1125	3.9
76261	RINGGOLD	337	198	203	206	0.3	34	81	84	85	0.4	2.42	56	57	0.2
76262	ROANOKE	121	14869	23269	27876	5.0	94	5360	8334	9988	4.9	2.78	4363	6551	4.5
76263	ROSSTON	097	156	159	161	0.2	30	67	69	69	0.3	2.30	54	54	0.0
76264	SADLER	181	1441	1735	1862	2.0	78	564	669	717	1.9	2.59	437	509	1.7
76265	SAINT JO	337	1798	1786	1806	-0.1	21	734	734	744	0.0	2.43	526	519	-0.1
76266	SANGER	121	10095	13097	15237	2.9	86	3600	4587	5332	2.7	2.84	2824	3420	2.1
76270	SUNSET	497	1231	1496	1599	2.1	79	484	588	628	2.1	2.51	368	442	2.0
76271	TIOGA	181	1089	1244	1324	1.4	67	424	482	513	1.4	2.58	306	338	1.1
76272	VALLEY VIEW	097	4395	4841	5044	1.1	61	1585	1743	1816	1.0	2.78	1246	1353	0.9
76273	WHITESBORO	181	8465	9309	9715	1.0	58	3226	3524	3677	1.0	2.61	2401	2580	0.8
76301	WICHITA FALLS	485	17529	16419	15984	-0.7	7	7246	6837	6664	-0.6	2.32	4133	3812	-0.9
76302	WICHITA FALLS	485	10631	11179	11185	0.5	42	4189	4544	4587	0.9	2.33	2939	3117	0.6
76305	WICHITA FALLS	485	7204	7804	7774	0.9	55	1366	1617	1620	1.8	2.76	999	1150	1.5
76306	WICHITA FALLS	485	16721	15746	15259	-0.6	9	6232	5988	5834	-0.4	2.60	4478	4235	-0.6
76308	WICHITA FALLS	485	19198	18910	18590	-0.2	19	7939	7959	7851	0.0	2.27	4902	4840	-0.1
76309	WICHITA FALLS	485	13599	13167	12866	-0.3	16	5649	5527	5412	-0.2	2.34	3581	3436	-0.4
76310	WICHITA FALLS	009	16078	16710	16687	0.4	37	6286	6678	6705	0.7	2.46	4536	4741	0.5
76311	SHEPPARD AFB	485	9393	8809	8609	-0.7	7	1342	1164	1112	-1.5	3.45	1292	1121	-1.5
76351	ARCHER CITY	009	1853	1910	1919	0.3	34	759	781	785	0.3	2.39	514	519	0.1
76354	BURKBURNETT	485	11316	11028	10783	-0.3	16	4281	4249	4176	-0.1	2.57	3224	3162	-0.2
76357	BYERS	077	647	646	634	0.0	25	257	259	255	0.1	2.49	196	196	0.0
76360	ELECTRA	487	3794	3533	3414	-0.8	6	1533	1435	1389	-0.7	2.43	1054	970	-0.9
76363	GOREE	275	386	352	334	-1.0	4	148	136	130	-0.9	2.58	108	99	-0.9
76364	HARROLD	487	261	250	249	-0.5	11	107	103	102	-0.4	2.43	79	75	-0.6
76365	HENRIETTA	077	6117	6155	6037	0.1	27	2422	2454	2413	0.1	2.47	1743	1742	0.0
76366	HOLLIDAY	009	3001	3124	3179	0.4	37	1176	1230	1253	0.5	2.54	874	902	0.3
76367	IOWA PARK	485	9551	9387	9227	-0.2	19	3603	3612	3566	0.0	2.45	2755	2727	-0.1
76371	MUNDAY	275	1872	1654	1560	-1.3	2	742	667	630	-1.1	2.42	512	452	-1.3
76372	NEWCASTLE	503	982	1023	1040	0.4	37	394	412	420	0.5	2.48	287	296	0.3
76373	OKLAUNION	487	185	178	176	-0.4	13	63	61	60	-0.3	2.92	46	44	-0.5
76374	OLNEY	503	4453	4538	4566	0.2	30	1828	1878	1892	0.3	2.37	1219	1228	0.1
76377	PETROLIA	077	1597	1594	1564	0.0	25	615	620	610	0.1	2.57	454	451	-0.1
76379	SCOTLAND	009	587	615	626	0.5	42	214	224	229	0.5	2.75	162	167	0.3
76380	SEYMOUR	023	4544	4321	4250	-0.5	11	1969	1864	1832	-0.6	2.29	1283	1192	-0.8
76384	VERNON	487	14077	13816	13848	-0.2	19	5312	5244	5259	-0.1	2.48	3579	3474	-0.3
76388	WEINERT	207	224	195	182	-1.5	1	100	88	83	-1.4	2.20	70	61	-1.5
76389	WINDTHORST	009	1122	1169	1185	0.4	37	380	397	403	0.5	2.94	285	294	0.3
76401	STEPHENVILLE	143	23024	25998	27303	1.3	65	8941	9876	10363	1.1	2.42	5417	5915	1.0
76424	BRECKENRIDGE	429	9165	8971	8857	-0.2	19	3446	3334	3291	-0.4	2.49	2426	2310	-0.5
76426	BRIDGEPORT	497	9517	10932	11726	1.5	69	3196	3697	3985	1.6	2.73	2424	2767	1.4
76427	BRYSON	237	1014	1045	1045	0.3	34	421	433	433	0.3	2.41	308	312	0.1
76429	CADDO	429	161	176	178	1.0	58	68	71	72	0.5	1.93	52	54	0.4
76430	ALBANY	417	2512	2615	2657	0.4	37	983	1011	1024	0.3	2.54	708	716	0.1
76431	CHICO	497	3016	3663	4077	2.1	79	1155	1406	1567	2.1	2.56	881	1054	2.0
76432	BLANKET	049	1405	1439	1465	0.3	34	540	558	568	0.4	2.58	412	419	0.2
76433	BLUFF DALE	143	2092	2179	2264	0.4	37	857	887	921	0.4	2.46	648	660	0.2
76435	CARBON	133	515	513	513	0.0	25	226	224	224	-0.1	2.29	163	160	-0.2
76436	CARLTON	093	540	608	625	1.3	65	218	244	250	1.2	2.43	157	173	1.1
76437	CISCO	133	5421	5547	5594	0.2	30	2149	2184	2204	0.2	2.41	1466	1465	0.0
76442	COMANCHE	093	7539	7389	7360	-0.2	19	2904	2829	2814	-0.3	2.53	2106	2024	-0.4
76443	CROSS PLAINS	059	1821	1952	2027	0.8	52	756	812	844	0.8	2.36	530	559	0.6
76444	DE LEON	093	4176	3921	3867	-0.7	7	1711	1591	1565	-0.8	2.41	1155	1051	-1.0
76445	DESDEMONA	133	425	452	461	0.7	49	176	187	191	0.7	2.41	127	133	0.5
76446	DUBLIN	143	6804	7348	7535	0.8	52	2386	2527	2584	0.6	2.84	1733	1804	0.4
76448	EASTLAND	133	5825	5732	5699	-0.2	19	2345	2290	2272	-0.3	2.43	1671	1609	-0.4
76449	GRAFORD	363	2271	2430	2463	0.7	49	988	1069	1089	0.9	2.27	674	714	0.6
76450	GRAHAM	503	12636	12639	12641	0.0	25	5017	5067	5081	0.1	2.44	3618	3603	0.0
76453	GORDON	363	863	1003	1050	1.6	71	376	436	457	1.6	2.30	268	304	1.4
76454	GORMAN	133	1698	1789	1815	0.6	46	674	706	717	0.5	2.48	461	476	0.3
76455	GUSTINE	093	1093	1167	1209	0.7	49	445	473	489	0.7	2.47	321	334	0.4
76457	HICO	143	3860	3602	3539	-0.7	7	1493	1372	1342	-0.9	2.59	1071	965	-1.1
76458	JACKSBORO	237	6160	6258	6225	0.2	30	2042	2062	2048	0.1	2.50	1451	1442	-0.1
76459	JERMYN	237	138	142	142	0.3	34	53	55	55	0.4	2.58	39	39	0.0
76460	LOVING	503	228	235	238	0.3	34	96	99	101	0.3	2.37	75	77	0.3
76462	LIPAN	221	2016	2380	2601	1.8	75	769	915	1003	1.9	2.60	575	672	1.7
76463	MINGUS	363	253	296	310	1.7	73	116	135	142	1.7	2.19	80	91	1.4
76464	MORAN	417	466	494	509	0.6	46	203	213	219	0.5	2.32	145	149	0.3
76470	RANGER	133	3446	3593	3628	0.5	42	1351	1405	1421	0.4	2.34	893	915	0.3
76471	RISING STAR	133	1739	1649	1627	-0.6	9	735	688	677	-0.7	2.33	504	465	-0.9
76472	SANTO	363	1322	1512	1579	1.5	69	486	558	582	1.5	2.70	373	421	1.3
	TEXAS					1.9					1.8	2.78			1.7
	UNITED STATES					1.0					1.1	2.59			0.9

ZIP CODE #	POST OFFICE NAME	RACE (%) White 2000	White 2009	Black 2000	Black 2009	Asian/Pacific 2000	Asian/Pacific 2009	% Hispanic Origin 2000	% Hispanic Origin 2009	2009 AGE DISTRIBUTION (%) 0-4	5-9	10-14	15-19	20-24	25-44	45-64	65-84	85+	18+	MEDIAN AGE 2009	% 2009 Males	% 2009 Females
76205	DENTON	69.9	63.9	13.9	15.7	2.8	4.1	17.3	21.7	5.4	4.5	4.6	8.3	22.7	28.4	19.0	6.2	0.9	81.7	27.0	51.0	49.0
76207	DENTON	81.2	75.2	6.6	8.5	2.0	3.1	12.4	17.2	8.2	6.8	6.2	6.6	10.9	35.0	19.9	5.8	0.7	75.3	29.8	48.2	51.8
76208	DENTON	82.2	78.2	5.2	6.0	1.0	1.4	17.3	22.2	9.2	8.6	7.7	7.3	8.9	29.3	22.7	5.8	0.5	70.2	30.1	50.6	49.4
76209	DENTON	78.0	72.0	7.9	9.8	1.5	2.2	18.4	24.3	7.6	6.8	6.4	7.4	11.9	30.1	21.3	7.2	1.2	75.3	29.9	47.3	52.7
76210	DENTON	88.6	84.7	4.3	5.2	2.1	3.1	6.6	9.3	9.4	8.9	8.1	5.9	4.7	33.9	22.7	5.6	0.7	69.9	34.0	49.1	50.9
76225	ALVORD	94.4	91.8	0.4	0.5	0.2	0.2	7.0	11.2	6.8	7.0	7.4	7.0	5.3	24.4	28.8	11.5	1.7	74.4	39.0	50.2	49.8
76226	ARGYLE	91.5	91.8	0.9	1.0	0.5	0.6	8.7	9.3	6.2	7.2	7.9	7.8	4.4	23.0	34.4	8.3	0.8	73.6	41.0	50.3	49.7
76227	AUBREY	91.2	84.9	1.3	0.9	0.3	0.5	8.7	17.5	6.9	7.2	7.6	7.1	5.1	27.1	29.0	9.1	1.0	74.1	38.0	50.3	49.7
76228	BELLEVUE	96.5	96.4	0.1	0.1	0.1	0.1	2.7	3.0	5.8	6.4	6.8	6.4	3.9	21.9	31.1	16.0	1.6	76.9	44.1	50.6	49.4
76230	BOWIE	96.6	95.5	0.1	0.1	0.3	0.5	4.0	5.6	6.2	6.2	6.4	6.2	5.2	21.8	28.1	16.5	3.4	77.3	43.3	48.2	51.8
76233	COLLINSVILLE	94.6	92.2	0.2	0.2	0.1	0.2	5.4	8.4	6.5	6.6	6.9	7.1	5.3	27.0	26.6	11.9	2.0	75.0	39.0	49.6	50.4
76234	DECATUR	88.0	83.9	1.2	1.4	0.4	0.5	14.8	20.3	7.3	7.2	7.2	6.9	6.4	26.5	26.7	10.0	1.8	74.0	36.4	50.0	50.0
76238	ERA	95.1	93.0	0.3	0.3	0.5	0.5	5.5	8.8	6.2	6.4	6.7	7.2	5.4	22.5	31.4	12.3	1.9	76.1	42.1	50.4	49.6
76239	FORESTBURG	95.0	93.2	0.1	0.1	0.1	0.1	5.0	7.2	5.4	5.7	5.9	6.3	5.1	21.0	33.1	16.0	1.6	79.1	45.5	47.2	52.8
76240	GAINESVILLE	86.0	82.4	4.2	4.7	0.4	0.5	12.4	16.9	6.9	6.4	6.4	8.0	6.2	23.2	25.9	14.4	2.7	75.6	38.9	49.2	50.8
76245	GORDONVILLE	96.0	94.8	0.1	0.2	0.4	0.5	2.2	3.4	3.7	3.8	4.2	4.9	3.7	16.4	34.5	26.2	2.5	85.3	53.9	50.9	49.1
76247	JUSTIN	92.0	88.1	0.9	1.2	0.9	1.5	7.3	11.1	7.3	7.4	7.5	7.3	5.7	27.1	28.2	8.2	1.2	73.1	36.6	50.1	49.9
76248	KELLER	92.2	84.8	1.6	2.1	2.6	5.5	5.7	13.4	8.7	8.5	8.1	7.2	5.0	30.3	25.5	6.0	0.6	70.1	33.8	49.4	50.6
76249	KRUM	91.6	86.5	1.1	1.9	0.4	0.9	8.1	14.8	7.1	7.3	8.0	7.8	5.5	27.7	27.8	8.1	0.7	72.2	36.2	49.2	50.8
76250	LINDSAY	98.6	97.9	0.2	0.3	0.1	0.1	1.5	2.5	6.3	6.7	7.1	7.8	6.2	25.3	29.6	9.7	1.3	75.1	38.0	50.5	49.5
76251	MONTAGUE	95.4	93.6	0.7	0.8	0.3	0.6	4.6	6.7	4.5	4.6	5.1	5.8	5.4	23.6	32.3	17.1	1.6	81.9	45.6	50.6	49.4
76252	MUENSTER	97.8	96.9	0.1	0.1	0.3	0.5	2.3	3.6	6.6	6.9	7.1	7.3	5.4	23.1	28.5	12.3	2.9	74.7	40.3	49.0	51.0
76255	NOCONA	94.7	93.1	0.4	0.4	0.3	0.3	8.9	12.3	6.4	6.4	6.5	6.4	4.5	21.5	26.4	17.8	4.0	76.5	43.6	47.8	52.2
76258	PILOT POINT	86.8	82.4	2.9	3.6	0.2	0.3	12.7	17.7	7.1	7.1	7.3	7.3	5.6	26.6	27.8	9.7	1.5	74.0	37.5	49.8	50.2
76259	PONDER	92.5	90.0	0.8	1.0	0.6	0.9	7.0	9.9	7.4	7.4	7.6	7.3	5.8	27.0	28.5	8.1	0.8	72.9	36.5	50.1	49.9
76261	RINGGOLD	97.5	96.1	0.0	0.0	0.0	0.0	3.6	4.4	6.9	7.4	6.9	3.9	3.9	23.2	29.1	16.3	2.5	76.8	43.1	49.8	50.2
76262	ROANOKE	93.7	88.9	1.2	1.5	1.1	3.3	5.6	10.1	7.4	7.6	7.7	7.2	4.6	27.3	29.6	8.0	0.7	72.7	37.6	50.3	49.7
76263	ROSSTON	95.5	93.1	0.0	0.0	0.6	0.6	5.8	8.8	6.3	6.3	6.9	6.9	5.0	22.0	32.7	11.9	1.9	76.1	42.7	50.9	49.1
76264	SADLER	95.8	94.1	0.3	0.3	0.1	0.1	3.1	4.7	6.2	6.3	6.5	6.3	5.1	23.3	29.6	15.3	1.3	77.0	42.2	50.3	49.7
76265	SAINT JO	96.5	95.5	0.2	0.2	0.1	0.2	4.5	6.4	5.0	5.0	5.4	6.5	4.7	19.4	32.0	19.6	2.4	80.6	47.6	48.8	51.2
76266	SANGER	91.8	88.6	1.6	2.3	0.3	0.6	8.6	12.7	7.0	7.0	7.1	7.2	6.1	27.2	28.2	9.1	1.1	74.3	37.0	49.8	50.2
76270	SUNSET	96.2	94.7	0.1	0.1	0.4	0.5	3.3	5.2	5.7	5.9	6.5	6.6	5.6	22.7	31.6	14.0	1.3	77.8	42.7	51.6	48.4
76271	TIOGA	93.7	91.0	0.4	0.5	0.9	1.3	11.3	16.3	7.6	8.0	7.7	6.3	4.4	27.7	27.7	9.4	1.3	72.7	37.2	51.5	48.5
76272	VALLEY VIEW	94.1	91.5	0.4	0.6	0.3	0.5	5.9	9.1	7.0	7.0	7.1	6.9	6.0	25.8	28.4	10.9	0.9	74.7	38.0	50.7	49.3
76273	WHITESBORO	95.7	94.1	0.4	0.5	0.2	0.4	3.3	5.0	6.3	6.4	6.6	7.1	5.5	24.3	28.3	13.1	2.4	76.2	40.3	49.5	50.5
76301	WICHITA FALLS	60.3	55.5	22.4	22.4	1.3	1.6	22.6	29.4	7.8	7.3	6.8	7.1	7.4	25.2	24.7	11.4	2.3	74.1	35.4	48.9	51.1
76302	WICHITA FALLS	85.7	81.4	5.8	7.1	1.1	1.4	11.7	16.2	8.3	6.6	6.1	6.7	8.1	24.9	23.8	12.9	2.5	75.2	35.8	48.0	52.0
76305	WICHITA FALLS	74.0	68.4	22.5	26.8	0.4	0.5	17.7	21.7	3.6	3.8	3.9	8.0	13.8	36.4	20.1	8.8	1.4	84.5	33.4	70.2	29.8
76306	WICHITA FALLS	63.1	58.0	20.0	21.1	3.5	4.3	16.4	20.8	8.1	7.7	7.2	7.3	7.1	26.2	24.1	11.1	1.2	72.7	34.5	49.2	50.8
76308	WICHITA FALLS	87.4	83.6	3.9	4.6	2.7	3.6	6.8	9.8	5.8	5.2	5.5	7.8	10.8	25.3	24.9	12.3	2.4	80.0	35.7	48.2	51.8
76309	WICHITA FALLS	80.3	74.8	4.3	4.8	2.1	2.9	15.6	21.2	6.8	6.7	6.6	6.4	5.8	25.6	26.7	12.6	2.9	76.0	38.6	48.4	51.6
76310	WICHITA FALLS	89.9	86.6	2.6	3.2	2.1	2.9	6.7	9.8	6.9	6.6	6.5	7.1	6.3	26.6	27.6	10.8	1.5	75.5	37.7	48.0	52.0
76311	SHEPPARD AFB	70.2	64.2	16.3	18.3	3.6	4.6	10.2	14.1	7.6	6.5	4.7	30.1	25.2	24.5	1.3	0.1	0.0	79.1	20.2	66.8	33.2
76351	ARCHER CITY	97.1	96.1	0.0	0.0	0.0	0.0	2.9	4.1	6.4	6.7	6.8	6.6	5.0	23.0	27.7	14.6	3.2	75.8	41.7	47.2	52.8
76354	BURKBURNETT	90.9	88.0	2.9	3.4	0.7	0.9	6.2	9.0	6.7	6.9	7.2	7.4	5.4	24.2	27.2	13.1	1.8	74.5	39.3	48.3	51.7
76357	BYERS	92.7	92.1	0.0	0.0	0.0	0.0	6.3	7.0	5.3	5.7	7.3	7.7	4.5	21.1	33.0	13.6	1.9	76.9	43.7	49.7	50.3
76360	ELECTRA	88.8	85.6	4.1	4.6	0.1	0.1	8.1	11.7	6.7	6.8	7.3	7.4	5.7	22.2	26.5	14.3	3.0	74.5	40.3	48.6	51.4
76363	GOREE	75.7	69.9	3.6	3.7	0.0	0.0	27.4	35.5	6.8	6.8	7.4	7.1	4.0	20.2	25.6	19.3	2.8	73.9	43.2	48.6	51.4
76364	HARROLD	88.8	84.0	0.8	0.8	0.0	0.0	8.8	12.8	4.8	5.6	6.8	7.2	4.0	21.6	32.0	16.4	1.6	78.0	45.0	51.2	48.8
76365	HENRIETTA	95.7	95.5	0.6	0.6	0.1	0.1	3.2	3.5	5.8	6.1	6.4	6.5	5.2	22.0	30.5	15.0	2.4	77.6	43.5	48.4	51.6
76366	HOLLIDAY	96.3	95.2	0.1	0.1	0.2	0.3	3.3	4.7	6.4	6.6	6.7	7.4	6.4	23.9	29.1	12.0	1.5	75.8	39.0	49.6	50.4
76367	IOWA PARK	93.9	92.1	2.1	2.3	0.5	0.6	5.5	7.9	5.9	6.2	6.6	7.1	6.8	25.8	26.8	12.9	1.9	76.9	38.7	51.2	48.8
76371	MUNDAY	70.7	64.8	7.6	7.6	0.2	0.2	29.9	38.0	7.8	7.4	7.4	7.8	6.1	21.2	22.7	15.2	4.4	71.5	38.6	46.3	53.7
76372	NEWCASTLE	94.6	92.8	0.8	1.0	0.1	0.1	4.3	6.4	5.9	6.2	6.6	6.5	4.8	23.3	29.2	15.8	1.7	77.1	42.3	50.7	49.3
76373	OKLAUNION	88.6	84.3	0.5	1.1	0.0	0.0	8.6	12.4	5.1	5.6	6.2	6.7	3.9	20.8	35.4	15.2	1.1	78.7	46.3	49.4	50.6
76374	OLNEY	90.9	88.1	2.2	2.5	0.3	0.4	12.3	17.1	6.5	6.1	6.6	7.0	5.4	20.6	26.0	17.3	4.4	76.4	43.2	47.1	52.9
76377	PETROLIA	94.0	93.8	0.4	0.4	0.0	0.0	4.7	5.1	6.5	6.6	7.3	7.1	4.5	23.0	28.9	14.1	2.1	75.0	40.7	47.1	52.9
76379	SCOTLAND	89.6	85.5	0.0	0.0	0.2	0.3	14.7	20.3	8.6	8.8	8.8	8.0	4.2	24.4	24.7	10.9	1.6	68.8	35.8	51.9	48.1
76380	SEYMOUR	91.0	88.8	3.2	3.5	0.7	0.8	9.8	13.3	5.2	5.3	5.6	6.5	5.3	19.0	29.3	19.6	4.2	79.8	47.1	48.0	52.0
76384	VERNON	77.7	73.5	9.2	9.6	0.7	0.9	21.0	27.4	6.9	6.5	6.7	9.1	6.2	23.1	24.7	13.5	3.3	74.2	37.4	49.5	50.5
76388	WEINERT	76.3	69.2	2.7	3.1	0.4	0.5	27.2	35.4	5.1	5.6	5.6	6.2	3.6	23.6	30.8	16.4	3.1	79.0	45.2	49.2	50.8
76389	WINDTHORST	91.3	88.0	0.0	0.0	0.3	0.3	12.0	16.7	8.0	8.4	8.6	7.7	4.2	23.8	26.1	11.5	1.8	70.1	37.0	51.3	48.7
76401	STEPHENVILLE	91.2	88.3	1.1	1.1	0.5	0.7	11.7	16.5	6.3	5.8	5.8	9.6	11.4	27.3	21.5	9.8	2.5	78.5	32.2	49.3	50.7
76424	BRECKENRIDGE	86.5	82.6	2.9	3.2	0.3	0.4	15.3	20.8	5.8	5.8	5.6	7.0	7.3	23.5	26.4	15.6	2.9	78.6	40.4	51.4	48.6
76426	BRIDGEPORT	86.4	82.8	3.2	3.5	0.2	0.2	17.6	23.4	6.7	6.8	6.9	6.8	6.5	26.9	25.9	11.6	1.8	75.4	37.5	50.6	49.4
76427	BRYSON	95.7	94.6	0.4	0.4	0.2	0.3	3.1	4.5	5.3	5.5	5.6	6.0	5.7	22.1	30.9	16.9	1.9	80.1	44.8	50.1	49.9
76429	CADDO	89.4	88.1	6.2	6.3	0.0	0.0	5.0	6.8	3.4	3.4	4.0	6.3	10.8	25.6	29.5	15.3	1.7	86.4	42.0	63.6	36.4
76430	ALBANY	93.5	91.4	0.6	0.6	0.0	0.0	8.4	11.6	5.9	6.5	7.0	7.6	4.8	21.6	30.1	13.5	2.9	75.8	42.3	47.3	52.7
76431	CHICO	94.0	91.9	1.2	1.3	0.1	0.1	6.2	9.3	5.9	5.9	6.5	7.7	6.8	24.0	29.8	12.1	1.3	77.1	40.2	51.2	48.8
76432	BLANKET	93.8	91.6	0.5	0.6	0.1	0.2	8.0	11.0	6.0	6.3	6.4	6.5	5.4	21.4	30.4	16.1	1.5	77.4	43.4	50.5	49.5
76433	BLUFF DALE	95.9	94.3	0.2	0.2	0.1	0.2	6.5	9.7	4.7	5.6	6.5	6.2	3.3	24.0	32.7	15.1	1.8	79.4	44.8	53.3	46.7
76435	CARBON	93.8	91.6	0.0	0.0	0.0	0.0	8.1	11.7	6.6	7.4	7.6	6.0	2.5	18.3	30.4	18.9	2.1	74.7	46.1	54.2	45.8
76436	CARLTON	87.2	83.9	0.2	0.2	0.2	0.2	15.7	20.4	5.8	6.3	6.9	6.1	4.6	21.2	28.8	17.1	3.3	77.5	44.3	51.6	48.4
76437	CISCO	92.0	90.3	2.8	2.9	0.2	0.3	8.2	11.1	5.7	5.5	5.5	8.7	6.3	19.5	27.8	17.5	3.3	79.3	43.7	48.3	51.7
76442	COMANCHE	85.4	85.0	0.8	0.8	0.2	0.2	21.6	22.7	6.9	6.9	7.2	6.5	4.9	22.6	24.8	16.5	3.7	74.8	40.9	49.0	51.0
76443	CROSS PLAINS	96.9	95.6	0.1	0.1	0.0	0.0	3.8	5.6	5.1	5.0	5.2	5.8	5.6	20.0	29.2	19.8	4.1	80.7	47.2	48.0	52.0
76444	DE LEON	89.9	89.3	0.1	0.1	0.0	0.1	19.6	21.3	6.5	6.1	6.4	6.9	5.4	21.6	26.1	17.0	4.1	77.0	42.7	49.2	50.8
76445	DESDEMONA	90.3	86.1	0.0	0.2	0.2	0.4	14.9	20.1	6.4	6.4	6.4	6.2	5.1	21.9	27.7	17.3	2.7	76.8	43.0	49.8	50.2
76446	DUBLIN	81.7	76.8	0.2	0.2	0.1	0.1	28.7	36.6	8.0	7.5	8.0	8.1	5.9	23.5	23.5	12.7	2.8	71.2	36.1	49.3	50.7
76448	EASTLAND	93.2	91.0	1.2	1.3	0.1	0.2	10.6	14.6	6.1	6.1	5.9	5.8	5.5	22.0	27.8	17.3	3.5	78.4	43.8	48.0	52.0
76449	GRAFORD	95.0	92.8	0.0	0.0	0.4	0.7	4.9	7.4	4.2	4.5	4.9	5.6	4.1	19.2	34.2	21.4	1.9	83.0	50.4	50.6	49.4
76450	GRAHAM	90.7	87.8	0.9	1.0	0.3	0.4	10.5	14.4	5.9	5.9	6.2	6.3	5.7	21.7	29.1	16.4	3.0	78.0	43.7	48.4	51.6
76453	GORDON	94.4	92.0	0.2	0.2	0.3	0.6	5.9	9.1	5.0	5.4	5.6	5.4	3.7	20.2	34.4	18.1	2.2	80.7	48.2	48.2	51.8
76454	GORMAN	85.2	80.7	0.1	0.1	0.1	0.2	21.4	28.1	6.9	6.9	6.8	6.7	5.4	21.0	25.5	16.4	4.4	75.0	41.5	48.0	52.0
76455	GUSTINE	88.1	87.0	0.0	0.0	0.0	0.0	21.8	24.2	6.4	6.8	6.8	5.8	4.2	22.7	27.2	17.7	2.3	76.4	42.6	51.2	48.8
76457	HICO	90.8	87.2	0.2	0.2	0.1	0.2	14.8	20.5	6.4	6.9	7.0	6.5	4.8	23.6	26.6	15.2	3.2	75.7	41.0	50.2	49.8
76458	JACKSBORO	85.5	82.1	7.8	8.7	0.3	0.4	9.4	13.0	5.7	5.8	5.8	6.7	8.5	28.4	24.4	12.1	2.6	79.2	37.5	55.9	44.1
76459	JERMYN	96.4	94.4	0.0	0.7	0.0	0.0	2.9	4.2	4.9	5.6	5.6	6.3	5.6	22.5	30.3	16.9	2.1	80.3	44.4	49.3	50.7
76460	LOVING	93.9	92.3	1.3	1.3	0.9	1.3	5.2	7.2	5.1	5.1	6.0	6.0	4.3	19.1	31.5	20.0	3.0	79.6	47.5	51.9	48.1
76462	LIPAN	95.3	93.5	0.2	0.3	0.3	0.4	5.1	7.6	6.3	6.7	7.1	6.2	4.5	22.9	30.8	14.1	1.3	76.1	42.0	49.8	50.2
76463	MINGUS	94.5	91.6	0.0	0.3	0.4	0.7	5.9	8.8	4.7	5.1	5.4	5.4	3.4	19.9	35.1	18.6	2.4	81.4	49.1	46.6	53.4
76464	MORAN	96.6	95.3	0.0	0.0	0.0	0.0	4.9	6.9	4.0	4.5	5.3	5.7	4.0	21.1	30.0	22.7	2.8	83.0	49.2	47.8	52.2
76470	RANGER	87.2	84.2	5.1	5.7	0.5	0.6	11.5	15.6	5.8	6.0	5.9	9.9	7.3	20.5	25.4	15.9	3.3	78.0	39.5	49.8	50.2
76471	RISING STAR	95.3	93.6	0.1	0.1	0.2	0.2	5.3	7.8	5.2	5.3	5.2	5.2	5.0	19.3	28.4	22.0	4.5	81.2	49.1	49.8	50.2
76472	SANTO	94.8	92.7	0.2	0.3	0.5	0.6	5.7	8.7	5.8	6.2	6.2	5.4	3.9	21.2	33.3	16.5	1.6	78.4	45.9	52.3	47.7
	TEXAS	71.0	67.6	11.5	11.4	2.8	3.5	32.0	37.4	7.9	7.5	7.2	7.5	7.4	28.3	24.0	8.8	1.4	73.0	33.6	49.7	50.3
	UNITED STATES	75.1	72.0	12.3	12.7	3.8	4.6	12.5	15.7	6.8	6.7	6.6	7.1	6.9	27.0	26.0	10.9	1.9	75.7	36.9	49.2	50.8

#	POST OFFICE NAME	2009 Per Capita Income	2009 HH Income Base	2009 Household Income Distribution (%): Less than $25,000	$25,000 to $49,999	$50,000 to $99,999	$100,000 to $149,999	$150,000 or More	Median Household Income: 2009	2014	2009 National Centile	2009 State Centile	2009 Home Value Base	2009 Home Value Distribution (%): Less than $50,000	$50,000 to $89,999	$90,000 to $174,999	$175,000 to $399,999	$400,000 or More	2009 Median Home Value
76205	DENTON	25382	7162	28.0	28.2	26.5	10.1	7.1	42834	46400	42	53	2176	14.7	13.3	23.6	45.2	3.1	169737
76207	DENTON	27077	3438	16.4	26.9	36.8	14.6	5.2	57275	54787	74	81	1497	12.8	5.2	59.0	19.6	3.5	138163
76208	DENTON	24655	6089	16.9	26.7	32.7	17.6	6.1	55928	55032	73	79	4129	30.7	8.9	25.0	31.6	3.9	134399
76209	DENTON	22850	9655	20.5	24.2	40.0	12.2	3.1	54468	53923	70	78	4695	8.0	12.3	62.6	16.4	0.7	126613
76210	DENTON	37888	12709	5.4	12.3	36.8	30.3	15.2	93100	102568	96	97	10853	11.0	2.8	29.0	52.6	4.6	188910
76225	ALVORD	21482	1289	25.2	27.9	36.4	7.5	3.0	47555	51146	56	66	1043	26.5	27.1	28.1	13.7	4.6	84141
76226	ARGYLE	41981	6531	9.6	12.9	29.0	24.8	23.8	96663	103682	96	97	5669	6.2	6.3	14.6	50.4	22.5	263371
76227	AUBREY	26175	7407	15.4	26.1	36.1	15.3	7.2	59035	55636	76	83	6189	5.3	11.1	42.9	28.6	12.0	149475
76228	BELLEVUE	21067	622	27.3	31.0	32.2	6.4	3.1	42761	44726	42	52	519	39.5	25.4	20.0	12.9	2.1	63085
76230	BOWIE	20444	4022	31.8	31.6	28.6	5.1	2.9	39490	40926	31	40	3103	24.1	31.3	30.5	12.0	2.1	83340
76233	COLLINSVILLE	20548	948	23.4	32.6	35.4	6.0	2.5	44680	47738	47	57	727	17.2	31.9	33.7	13.8	3.4	91300
76234	DECATUR	22193	5324	20.9	27.9	36.1	10.5	4.6	50829	53473	63	72	4063	15.4	17.5	41.4	20.9	4.8	116472
76238	ERA	20681	127	19.7	30.7	40.9	6.3	2.4	49544	50542	60	69	100	10.0	21.0	40.0	24.0	5.0	122222
76239	FORESTBURG	23080	530	27.5	35.7	26.2	6.2	4.3	39415	40370	31	40	423	18.2	21.0	31.0	18.9	10.9	108631
76240	GAINESVILLE	20746	10392	28.3	27.5	33.8	7.6	2.8	44544	47457	47	57	7079	17.1	26.3	34.1	18.1	4.4	104439
76245	GORDONVILLE	24021	834	37.2	26.0	28.8	4.1	4.0	36110	40429	21	27	717	41.6	29.8	19.7	8.6	0.3	59918
76247	JUSTIN	22086	4103	15.0	24.8	44.7	12.7	2.9	57568	55830	75	82	3575	4.1	15.4	48.3	28.9	3.3	134518
76248	KELLER	34867	27688	5.6	13.4	38.4	25.6	17.1	88989	88303	95	96	23971	2.5	6.1	40.6	46.6	4.2	176534
76249	KRUM	24405	2148	12.2	24.1	42.6	16.8	4.3	63174	61782	81	86	1693	14.7	12.1	45.0	24.6	3.6	127773
76250	LINDSAY	20724	314	13.7	25.2	50.3	9.6	1.3	58769	55877	76	83	257	14.0	20.6	37.0	28.0	0.4	128526
76251	MONTAGUE	21896	257	31.5	30.0	30.4	3.9	4.3	39179	40880	30	39	221	27.6	24.0	23.1	18.1	7.2	86500
76252	MUENSTER	22007	1204	21.6	27.8	40.9	6.6	3.1	50392	50788	62	71	948	8.1	21.7	44.8	23.1	2.2	119342
76255	NOCONA	18909	2329	37.1	29.0	27.2	4.8	2.0	36751	39124	23	30	1763	33.8	24.5	30.6	9.2	1.9	73550
76258	PILOT POINT	22568	2616	18.8	24.5	41.9	11.2	3.6	54581	53216	71	78	1745	11.7	19.5	35.4	23.3	10.0	127487
76259	PONDER	23119	1448	16.1	22.7	41.9	15.1	4.2	60000	58869	77	84	1287	6.8	15.1	45.1	28.7	4.3	134872
76261	RINGGOLD	16071	84	40.5	35.7	20.2	3.6	0.0	33166	32389	14	17	69	37.7	14.5	29.0	14.5	4.3	77500
76262	ROANOKE	38117	8334	8.6	16.6	33.9	23.9	17.0	83724	86926	93	95	6368	10.0	5.8	25.4	49.0	9.8	198534
76263	ROSSTON	26215	69	20.3	31.9	37.7	5.8	4.3	47380	49443	55	66	55	10.9	21.8	38.2	23.6	5.5	123438
76264	SADLER	21073	669	20.0	30.2	42.3	4.8	2.7	49735	51407	60	69	571	23.3	27.7	38.9	9.5	0.7	88690
76265	SAINT JO	20381	734	30.1	26.6	36.5	5.2	1.6	42191	43919	40	50	597	25.1	27.3	32.2	13.2	2.2	86705
76266	SANGER	24174	4587	15.7	26.6	40.2	12.9	4.6	56186	54594	73	80	3144	17.9	22.2	31.4	24.0	4.5	111207
76270	SUNSET	20088	588	26.9	32.3	32.8	6.0	2.0	44510	46141	47	57	502	26.3	22.5	30.1	17.1	4.0	91765
76271	TIOGA	21339	482	15.8	39.4	35.9	6.4	2.5	46302	48656	52	63	357	17.1	30.8	37.5	11.5	3.1	93571
76272	VALLEY VIEW	21432	1743	20.8	27.9	39.7	8.4	3.2	51127	51075	64	72	1360	19.3	17.8	36.4	18.1	8.4	113547
76273	WHITESBORO	20637	3524	28.0	26.4	36.0	6.5	3.1	45058	48555	48	59	2726	24.7	26.5	32.2	14.3	2.2	87643
76301	WICHITA FALLS	17662	6837	39.5	35.4	20.4	2.6	2.1	30813	33249	9	12	3564	66.2	21.9	7.4	3.2	1.4	39294
76302	WICHITA FALLS	21937	4544	29.1	31.1	30.6	6.1	3.0	40902	45350	36	46	2773	16.9	43.4	35.4	3.6	0.6	80087
76305	WICHITA FALLS	15881	1617	30.9	34.5	27.5	5.5	1.6	37482	40761	25	32	1168	46.3	22.5	26.0	4.5	0.6	57288
76306	WICHITA FALLS	18258	5988	26.7	33.0	34.3	4.7	1.3	40601	45403	35	45	3656	39.1	39.1	20.2	1.3	0.3	60210
76308	WICHITA FALLS	27991	7959	19.9	33.6	31.8	7.5	7.2	47298	49325	55	65	4750	12.9	31.7	38.1	15.0	2.3	98431
76309	WICHITA FALLS	24218	5527	22.8	34.1	31.4	7.8	3.9	45086	47942	48	59	3292	33.5	25.5	30.0	10.3	0.6	71955
76310	WICHITA FALLS	25178	6678	15.8	31.1	41.5	8.6	3.1	52489	53308	67	75	4536	6.6	42.6	45.5	4.6	0.7	90794
76311	SHEPPARD AFB	14325	1164	7.9	47.4	42.6	1.6	0.4	46586	50361	53	63	12	0.0	66.7	33.3	0.0	0.0	87500
76351	ARCHER CITY	22383	781	29.8	34.1	28.4	4.1	3.6	38547	45025	28	36	585	50.9	31.6	11.6	4.3	1.5	49167
76354	BURKBURNETT	22425	4249	22.8	28.5	36.8	9.7	2.3	48682	50833	58	68	3199	32.9	33.5	30.2	3.0	0.4	68040
76357	BYERS	19907	259	23.9	34.0	35.1	5.4	1.5	43773	45202	45	55	207	36.2	27.1	29.0	6.3	1.4	69615
76360	ELECTRA	18386	1435	36.7	32.4	23.9	4.0	2.9	34139	38884	16	20	1043	64.5	24.0	9.2	2.0	0.3	35321
76363	GOREE	16670	136	38.2	30.1	26.5	4.4	0.7	33592	35918	15	18	107	56.1	25.2	13.1	3.7	1.9	38438
76364	HARROLD	24325	103	26.2	34.0	29.1	2.9	7.8	40453	42353	34	44	77	36.4	33.8	27.3	0.0	2.6	62500
76365	HENRIETTA	19811	2454	24.7	31.3	36.1	6.3	1.6	45363	46089	49	60	2003	40.1	30.5	24.8	4.0	0.5	60254
76366	HOLLIDAY	21000	1230	26.5	29.9	34.6	6.3	2.7	43071	47292	43	54	956	45.2	28.8	19.0	6.1	0.9	54842
76367	IOWA PARK	22389	3612	18.5	30.8	42.5	6.6	1.6	50389	51414	62	71	2809	28.3	45.4	22.4	3.7	0.1	66004
76371	MUNDAY	15216	667	43.6	30.6	21.1	3.9	0.7	30390	30798	9	11	478	62.6	27.0	8.6	1.5	0.4	36714
76372	NEWCASTLE	19276	412	33.0	38.6	23.8	1.9	2.7	34686	36711	17	22	311	47.6	21.9	22.8	6.1	1.6	52778
76373	OKLAUNION	20115	61	24.6	36.1	29.5	3.3	6.6	40760	43211	35	45	46	34.8	34.8	28.3	0.0	2.2	63333
76374	OLNEY	17540	1878	41.2	31.0	21.7	3.6	2.4	31238	35080	10	13	1297	45.9	30.3	16.2	6.9	0.7	53567
76377	PETROLIA	17020	620	31.5	35.5	28.1	3.5	1.5	36861	40226	23	30	500	51.6	27.4	16.6	3.6	0.8	48750
76379	SCOTLAND	19210	224	24.6	30.4	36.6	8.0	0.4	44500	47960	47	57	180	30.6	31.7	29.4	7.8	0.6	76429
76380	SEYMOUR	17542	1864	40.0	32.0	23.4	3.3	1.3	30965	31474	10	12	1341	53.1	27.1	15.0	3.8	1.0	47422
76384	VERNON	19960	5244	32.2	31.9	27.7	4.9	3.1	36755	39365	23	30	3419	41.0	29.9	23.3	5.0	0.8	59611
76388	WEINERT	18431	88	47.7	29.5	17.0	3.4	2.3	26824	28593	4	6	71	64.8	25.4	7.0	2.8	0.0	35625
76389	WINDTHORST	17487	397	25.7	30.5	35.5	7.1	1.3	43515	47313	44	54	317	33.1	30.3	27.4	7.9	1.3	73696
76401	STEPHENVILLE	19863	9876	33.6	30.9	25.9	6.9	2.7	37652	40071	26	33	5875	17.2	22.8	38.7	17.7	3.6	104886
76424	BRECKENRIDGE	18627	3334	30.4	33.5	29.2	4.6	2.4	37472	39334	25	32	2343	45.8	27.0	18.1	6.5	2.6	55412
76426	BRIDGEPORT	18534	3697	23.9	30.9	36.0	7.3	1.9	46097	50522	52	62	2803	22.8	26.3	33.1	15.8	2.0	92217
76427	BRYSON	18941	433	34.2	32.1	28.2	2.5	3.0	36492	39253	22	29	326	39.9	30.1	20.6	6.4	3.1	60882
76429	CADDO	22879	71	29.6	33.8	28.2	5.6	2.8	35759	38212	20	26	58	29.3	24.1	29.3	15.5	1.7	83333
76430	ALBANY	18945	1011	30.7	32.6	29.6	5.3	1.8	37097	38418	24	31	788	43.3	28.6	21.4	5.8	0.9	58983
76431	CHICO	19738	1406	23.8	33.1	34.5	6.1	2.4	46044	49403	51	62	1146	31.5	26.4	29.5	9.9	2.8	78209
76432	BLANKET	19227	558	25.4	31.0	37.5	4.7	1.4	45727	46757	50	61	464	27.6	23.7	32.3	14.0	2.4	87273
76433	BLUFF DALE	23734	887	22.1	32.0	33.7	8.8	3.4	46102	46966	52	62	713	22.0	20.2	27.5	20.1	10.2	106157
76435	CARBON	20660	224	26.3	36.2	32.1	2.2	3.1	40971	46338	36	46	182	38.5	24.2	22.5	13.2	1.6	73333
76436	CARLTON	20911	244	30.7	31.1	28.3	6.6	3.3	37775	41562	26	33	192	26.0	24.5	27.1	15.6	6.8	89231
76437	CISCO	17589	2184	38.2	33.7	22.6	3.3	2.2	32147	34070	12	15	1701	54.0	24.0	15.9	5.3	0.8	45823
76442	COMANCHE	16904	2829	34.1	34.0	26.7	3.9	1.3	37018	38268	24	31	2102	38.7	27.1	24.8	7.1	2.2	65126
76443	CROSS PLAINS	17554	812	36.9	31.8	26.7	3.8	0.7	31982	35121	11	14	640	41.3	25.8	20.0	10.5	2.5	63333
76444	DE LEON	16349	1591	42.4	25.5	27.4	3.8	0.9	30140	32831	8	11	1205	41.8	25.3	22.2	6.6	4.1	58074
76445	DESDEMONA	17429	187	35.8	33.2	24.6	5.3	1.1	33742	35223	15	19	149	31.5	29.5	27.5	8.7	2.7	72917
76446	DUBLIN	15359	2527	35.9	34.9	22.4	4.3	2.6	34505	36701	17	21	1732	37.0	25.3	25.9	9.2	2.6	68938
76448	EASTLAND	19896	2290	32.2	34.1	26.6	3.8	3.3	37384	40035	25	32	1706	39.9	29.2	22.0	6.2	2.8	62481
76449	GRAFORD	21828	1069	28.6	30.8	32.9	5.1	2.5	42785	44712	42	52	866	31.1	21.5	23.3	17.8	6.4	83529
76450	GRAHAM	20858	5067	28.6	32.3	30.5	5.4	3.2	40939	42740	36	46	3750	30.0	27.5	29.6	11.0	1.9	76238
76453	GORDON	22834	436	31.4	27.3	32.6	5.5	3.2	41474	43640	38	48	353	32.9	19.0	26.6	15.3	6.2	85667
76454	GORMAN	15982	706	37.8	35.3	22.1	3.8	1.0	32633	33787	13	16	533	47.8	31.3	15.4	4.9	0.6	52347
76455	GUSTINE	16875	473	38.7	31.5	24.7	3.8	1.3	32354	34032	12	15	360	38.3	23.1	21.9	11.4	5.3	66842
76457	HICO	18173	1372	32.7	30.2	30.0	4.6	2.6	38185	40392	27	35	1014	26.6	26.0	26.3	16.2	4.8	85781
76458	JACKSBORO	18804	2062	29.6	33.8	29.7	4.5	2.5	39669	41138	32	41	1558	35.0	28.8	23.2	8.7	4.2	69386
76459	JERMYN	17548	55	32.7	30.9	32.7	1.8	1.8	37960	41162	27	34	41	41.5	29.3	22.0	4.9	2.4	58750
76460	LOVING	22367	99	28.3	39.4	24.2	6.1	2.0	40213	41104	33	43	83	20.5	20.5	33.7	22.9	2.4	111458
76462	LIPAN	21269	915	22.6	30.5	38.6	5.5	2.8	45861	49451	51	61	772	27.7	19.3	29.0	18.8	5.2	94792
76463	MINGUS	25281	135	31.1	25.9	32.6	5.9	4.4	42791	42989	42	52	108	36.1	18.5	25.9	12.0	7.4	77500
76464	MORAN	18140	213	34.7	37.1	22.1	5.6	0.5	34169	36113	16	20	174	54.6	23.0	7.5	13.2	1.7	45789
76470	RANGER	16015	1405	39.6	37.3	18.8	2.7	1.6	30244	31870	8	11	1014	60.2	18.2	14.0	6.3	1.3	38507
76471	RISING STAR	18738	688	39.1	27.9	25.9	5.1	2.0	33479	35404	14	18	539	52.1	21.9	18.4	6.5	1.1	47830
76472	SANTO	17313	558	30.5	27.8	36.7	3.9	1.1	42029	43932	39	50	465	26.2	20.6	26.5	22.8	3.9	97632
	TEXAS	24551		22.3	25.0	34.3	11.1	7.3	52382	54495				16.5	22.7	36.5	19.7	4.6	109784
	UNITED STATES	27277		20.9	24.4	35.3	11.7	7.6	54719	56938				9.3	13.1	31.6	32.6	13.5	162279

ZIP CODE #	POST OFFICE NAME	FINANCIAL SERVICES: Auto Loan	FINANCIAL SERVICES: Home Loan	FINANCIAL SERVICES: Invest-ments	FINANCIAL SERVICES: Retire-ment Plans	THE HOME: Home Improvements: Home Repair	THE HOME: Home Improvements: Lawn & Garden	THE HOME: Furnishings: Comput-ers & Hard-ware-Personal	THE HOME: Furnishings: Major Appli-ances	THE HOME: Furnishings: TV, Radio, Sound Equip-ment	THE HOME: Furnishings: Furni-ture	ENTERTAINMENT: Dine out/ Carry out	ENTERTAINMENT: Sports Equip-ment	ENTERTAINMENT: Fees & Tickets	ENTERTAINMENT: Toys & Games	ENTERTAINMENT: Travel	ENTERTAINMENT: Cable TV	PERSONAL: Apparel & Services	PERSONAL: Auto Repairs	PERSONAL: Health Insur-ance	PERSONAL: Pets & Supplies
76205	DENTON	97	73	66	76	70	72	101	81	97	94	98	67	84	98	82	95	68	92	82	100
76207	DENTON	109	87	74	90	81	80	105	90	103	105	105	75	94	108	91	100	73	99	88	110
76208	DENTON	112	107	91	103	102	99	106	103	104	109	105	80	100	109	99	102	72	103	98	122
76209	DENTON	94	83	75	84	81	79	94	85	91	93	93	68	87	94	86	90	65	90	84	101
76210	DENTON	160	178	151	175	169	149	159	157	148	171	151	125	165	158	158	140	107	149	136	178
76225	ALVORD	96	76	89	74	77	94	75	89	81	74	80	66	65	83	73	87	54	83	91	106
76226	ARGYLE	171	204	204	210	208	192	175	184	169	187	170	139	197	171	191	165	123	173	170	211
76227	AUBREY	115	115	101	115	112	116	106	112	108	109	108	84	106	111	106	109	74	108	111	132
76228	BELLEVUE	96	66	105	66	69	101	73	91	76	59	75	75	54	75	73	83	49	85	96	112
76230	BOWIE	82	64	83	62	66	86	66	80	73	62	71	59	57	72	66	80	48	75	87	94
76233	COLLINSVILLE	84	81	71	79	79	82	75	79	77	78	77	59	73	80	74	79	53	77	79	94
76234	DECATUR	96	91	81	89	88	93	88	91	90	89	90	68	84	93	85	92	62	89	92	108
76238	ERA	94	86	85	89	87	101	85	95	87	76	86	72	78	89	84	92	58	88	98	111
76239	FORESTBURG	99	72	100	70	75	101	74	93	81	69	80	70	60	81	73	89	53	85	97	110
76240	GAINESVILLE	83	72	76	71	72	83	75	79	79	72	77	59	69	78	72	83	53	78	85	94
76245	GORDONVILLE	82	73	99	69	81	91	71	85	75	74	73	58	67	70	77	80	49	81	92	98
76247	JUSTIN	106	100	88	98	98	102	94	99	96	97	96	73	90	100	91	99	66	96	99	117
76248	KELLER	161	174	148	170	167	151	153	156	147	166	149	122	159	157	153	142	105	147	139	178
76249	KRUM	111	114	97	113	110	109	104	108	104	109	105	81	105	108	104	104	72	104	104	127
76250	LINDSAY	96	87	86	91	89	103	86	97	89	78	87	73	79	90	86	94	59	90	100	113
76251	MONTAGUE	92	66	95	64	69	94	68	86	75	63	74	65	54	75	67	83	49	79	90	103
76252	MUENSTER	90	86	82	89	87	97	83	92	84	77	83	70	79	86	84	88	57	85	93	107
76255	NOCONA	75	57	79	56	59	77	61	73	65	55	64	54	50	64	60	71	43	69	77	86
76258	PILOT POINT	97	98	83	98	94	99	92	94	93	92	93	72	92	96	91	95	64	92	97	113
76259	PONDER	113	104	92	100	101	106	98	104	102	102	102	75	93	106	93	104	69	100	104	123
76261	RINGGOLD	69	50	71	48	52	70	51	65	57	47	56	49	41	56	50	62	37	60	67	77
76262	ROANOKE	155	167	154	168	165	155	150	154	146	159	148	118	158	152	154	143	105	147	143	178
76263	ROSSTON	94	85	84	89	87	100	84	95	87	76	85	72	77	88	84	92	58	88	98	110
76264	SADLER	95	73	93	70	74	95	73	89	79	70	78	66	61	80	71	86	52	82	91	105
76265	SAINT JO	82	64	96	63	69	87	66	83	71	61	69	61	56	68	68	76	46	77	85	96
76266	SANGER	100	102	86	103	97	103	97	98	98	97	98	76	98	101	96	99	68	97	101	117
76270	SUNSET	90	66	83	64	67	88	67	81	74	65	73	62	55	76	64	81	49	76	85	98
76271	TIOGA	86	82	72	81	80	83	77	81	79	79	79	60	74	82	75	81	54	78	81	96
76272	VALLEY VIEW	93	88	78	87	86	90	83	88	85	85	85	65	80	88	81	87	58	85	88	104
76273	WHITESBORO	90	72	86	70	73	90	73	86	79	70	77	63	63	79	71	84	52	81	89	101
76301	WICHITA FALLS	61	51	47	51	49	57	59	56	62	56	61	43	53	62	52	65	42	60	63	68
76302	WICHITA FALLS	76	65	61	67	63	68	76	70	77	73	77	55	70	77	69	78	53	75	75	84
76305	WICHITA FALLS	82	60	83	59	62	84	63	78	70	58	68	59	51	69	62	77	45	73	83	93
76306	WICHITA FALLS	72	64	57	63	61	65	68	66	70	67	70	51	63	71	63	71	48	68	69	79
76308	WICHITA FALLS	90	88	81	90	86	89	95	88	94	91	94	69	93	94	90	95	66	92	94	106
76309	WICHITA FALLS	83	76	77	77	76	86	81	82	84	77	82	62	77	83	78	87	57	83	89	97
76310	WICHITA FALLS	90	92	82	91	88	88	89	88	89	90	89	68	89	91	88	88	62	88	88	104
76311	SHEPPARD AFB	89	46	35	54	41	39	84	58	79	78	83	58	64	95	61	72	58	74	52	71
76351	ARCHER CITY	94	67	98	65	70	98	72	90	79	64	77	69	56	78	71	87	51	83	96	107
76354	BURKBURNETT	84	82	78	82	80	90	81	84	84	78	83	64	79	84	80	87	57	83	90	100
76357	BYERS	89	61	97	61	64	94	68	84	71	55	70	70	50	69	67	77	45	79	89	104
76360	ELECTRA	74	56	69	55	57	76	61	71	67	55	64	54	51	66	58	72	43	68	77	84
76363	GOREE	77	53	85	53	55	81	59	73	61	48	61	60	43	60	59	67	39	68	77	90
76364	HARROLD	106	73	116	72	76	111	81	100	84	65	83	83	59	82	80	91	54	94	106	123
76365	HENRIETTA	80	65	81	64	68	84	67	79	71	63	70	58	58	70	67	76	47	74	84	93
76366	HOLLIDAY	88	74	81	72	73	86	75	82	76	71	76	64	65	78	72	79	51	79	83	99
76367	IOWA PARK	86	80	80	79	78	91	77	84	81	74	80	63	74	82	77	85	55	81	90	100
76371	MUNDAY	63	45	65	44	47	66	49	61	54	43	53	47	39	53	48	60	35	57	66	72
76372	NEWCASTLE	85	61	88	59	63	87	63	80	70	58	68	60	50	69	62	76	45	73	83	95
76373	OKLAUNION	105	72	115	72	76	111	80	100	83	65	82	82	59	82	80	91	53	93	105	123
76374	OLNEY	66	50	61	50	51	66	58	63	62	52	60	49	48	61	54	67	41	63	70	76
76377	PETROLIA	78	55	83	54	57	81	58	74	63	51	62	58	45	62	58	69	41	68	77	89
76379	SCOTLAND	94	65	104	65	68	100	72	90	75	58	74	74	53	73	72	82	48	84	95	110
76380	SEYMOUR	68	49	68	48	51	71	55	65	59	48	57	51	43	58	52	65	38	62	71	78
76384	VERNON	80	64	75	63	65	81	69	77	74	65	73	58	60	73	66	79	49	75	83	91
76388	WEINERT	73	50	80	50	52	77	56	69	58	45	57	57	41	57	55	63	37	64	73	85
76389	WINDTHORST	92	63	101	63	66	97	70	87	73	57	72	72	52	72	70	80	47	81	92	107
76401	STEPHENVILLE	75	64	63	65	63	70	73	70	73	68	72	55	65	73	66	74	50	72	73	85
76424	BRECKENRIDGE	75	60	70	60	61	75	66	72	70	62	68	54	57	69	63	74	46	71	78	85
76426	BRIDGEPORT	83	74	77	69	74	76	72	79	73	74	74	57	66	74	71	75	50	76	76	91
76427	BRYSON	82	58	84	57	61	83	60	76	67	56	65	57	48	66	59	73	43	70	79	91
76429	CADDO	86	62	99	62	66	90	66	83	69	57	69	65	52	67	68	75	45	77	86	100
76430	ALBANY	85	60	89	59	63	88	64	81	70	57	69	62	50	69	64	77	45	75	85	97
76431	CHICO	90	67	81	65	67	87	68	81	75	66	74	61	56	77	65	81	49	76	84	97
76432	BLANKET	89	63	91	61	66	90	65	83	72	61	71	62	52	72	64	79	47	76	86	98
76433	BLUFF DALE	101	75	117	74	80	106	79	98	82	69	81	76	63	80	81	89	54	91	101	118
76435	CARBON	84	59	92	58	62	89	65	80	67	53	66	65	48	66	65	73	43	75	85	98
76436	CARLTON	91	65	94	63	68	93	67	86	75	63	73	64	54	74	67	82	48	78	89	102
76437	CISCO	72	54	72	53	55	73	58	69	63	53	61	52	48	62	56	69	41	65	73	81
76442	COMANCHE	75	53	76	52	55	77	58	71	62	51	61	55	45	62	56	68	40	66	76	85
76443	CROSS PLAINS	73	52	74	51	54	75	55	69	61	50	60	52	44	60	54	67	39	64	73	82
76444	DE LEON	69	48	69	48	50	70	54	64	58	47	57	51	42	58	52	63	37	61	69	78
76445	DESDEMONA	73	51	76	51	54	76	56	70	61	49	60	54	44	60	55	67	39	65	75	84
76446	DUBLIN	75	55	69	53	56	73	60	70	64	55	63	53	48	63	57	68	42	67	73	83
76448	EASTLAND	81	60	84	59	63	84	65	79	72	59	70	59	54	70	64	78	47	74	85	93
76449	GRAFORD	81	66	95	63	72	87	66	82	71	65	69	58	58	67	69	76	46	76	86	95
76450	GRAHAM	85	65	84	64	67	88	69	82	75	63	73	62	58	74	68	81	49	78	88	97
76453	GORDON	88	70	113	69	77	93	70	89	73	66	73	65	61	70	76	78	48	82	88	103
76454	GORMAN	67	48	68	47	50	70	53	65	59	47	57	49	42	58	51	65	38	61	71	77
76455	GUSTINE	74	52	80	51	54	77	56	70	60	48	59	56	42	59	56	65	38	65	74	85
76457	HICO	83	58	86	57	61	86	63	79	69	55	67	61	49	67	62	75	44	73	84	95
76458	JACKSBORO	83	63	82	63	64	87	68	80	72	59	71	63	55	72	66	78	47	76	86	96
76459	JERMYN	81	58	83	56	60	82	59	76	66	55	65	57	48	66	59	73	43	69	79	90
76460	LOVING	95	65	104	65	68	100	73	90	75	59	75	75	53	74	72	82	48	84	95	111
76462	LIPAN	96	73	102	71	76	98	73	91	80	69	79	68	61	79	74	86	52	85	94	108
76463	MINGUS	92	74	119	73	81	98	74	94	78	69	77	69	64	74	80	83	51	87	93	109
76464	MORAN	75	54	78	52	56	76	55	70	61	51	60	53	44	61	55	67	40	65	73	83
76470	RANGER	65	47	66	46	49	68	50	63	56	45	54	47	40	55	49	61	36	58	67	74
76471	RISING STAR	71	57	77	54	61	76	58	71	64	57	62	51	51	61	59	69	41	67	78	83
76472	SANTO	78	62	100	61	68	83	62	79	65	58	65	58	54	62	67	70	43	73	78	92
	TEXAS	104	96	90	94	93	94	99	97	99	101	100	75	94	101	94	99	70	99	96	114
	UNITED STATES	100	100	100	100	100	100	100	100	100	100	100	100	100	100	100	100	100	100	100	100

POPULATION CHANGE

ZIP CODE #	POST OFFICE NAME	COUNTY FIPS CODE	POPULATION 2000	POPULATION 2009	POPULATION 2014	2000-2009 ANNUAL RATE % Rate	2000-2009 ANNUAL RATE State Centile	HOUSEHOLDS 2000	HOUSEHOLDS 2009	HOUSEHOLDS 2014	HOUSEHOLDS % Annual Rate 2000-2009	HOUSEHOLDS 2009 Average HH Size	FAMILIES 2000	FAMILIES 2009	FAMILIES % Annual Rate 2000-2009
76474	SIDNEY	093	96	110	114	1.5	69	36	41	42	1.4	2.68	29	33	1.4
76475	STRAWN	363	1029	1071	1068	0.4	37	418	435	433	0.4	2.46	275	279	0.2
76476	TOLAR	221	2225	2673	2992	2.0	78	834	1006	1129	2.0	2.61	625	740	1.8
76483	THROCKMORTON	447	1303	1148	1090	-1.4	2	546	474	448	-1.5	2.40	380	324	-1.7
76484	PALO PINTO	363	1105	1241	1288	1.3	65	426	483	503	1.4	2.40	331	369	1.2
76486	PERRIN	237	1648	1725	1733	0.5	42	616	643	649	0.5	2.54	494	509	0.3
76487	POOLVILLE	367	1935	2582	2935	3.2	87	676	897	1019	3.1	2.85	551	720	2.9
76490	WHITT	367	112	118	122	0.6	46	44	47	51	0.7	1.79	35	37	0.6
76491	WOODSON	447	495	493	485	0.0	25	196	193	188	-0.2	2.49	139	134	-0.4
76501	TEMPLE	027	16068	17257	18302	0.8	52	6189	6798	7259	1.0	2.51	4228	4516	0.7
76502	TEMPLE	027	22163	28428	31869	2.7	84	8799	11390	12825	2.8	2.44	6237	7978	2.7
76504	TEMPLE	027	22463	24064	25512	0.7	49	8850	9697	10375	1.0	2.35	5466	5773	0.6
76511	BARTLETT	027	3151	3792	4241	2.0	78	759	963	1126	2.6	2.76	541	671	2.4
76513	BELTON	027	28263	32062	34889	1.4	67	9787	11483	12662	1.7	2.62	7275	8324	1.5
76518	BUCKHOLTS	331	1196	1195	1191	0.0	25	437	437	436	0.0	2.73	323	318	-0.2
76519	BURLINGTON	331	1269	1318	1337	0.4	37	519	542	551	0.5	2.43	368	377	0.3
76520	CAMERON	331	7366	7873	8048	0.7	49	2789	2979	3043	0.7	2.56	1918	2013	0.5
76522	COPPERAS COVE	281	34197	36386	36801	0.7	49	11977	12420	12545	0.4	2.91	9363	9623	0.3
76523	DAVILLA	331	1355	1459	1501	0.8	52	516	557	574	0.8	2.62	396	421	0.7
76524	EDDY	145	2621	3205	3452	2.2	80	893	1082	1165	2.1	2.96	722	857	1.9
76525	EVANT	193	1116	1120	1115	0.0	25	462	454	451	-0.2	2.47	343	333	-0.3
76526	FLAT	099	86	77	74	-1.2	3	32	28	27	-1.4	2.75	25	21	-1.9
76527	FLORENCE	491	3039	4195	5227	3.5	89	1046	1431	1782	3.4	2.93	832	1099	3.1
76528	GATESVILLE	099	23071	23392	23409	0.1	27	4987	4956	4947	-0.1	2.72	3616	3543	-0.2
76530	GRANGER	491	2470	3315	3998	3.2	87	933	1249	1510	3.2	2.61	644	826	2.7
76531	HAMILTON	193	4946	5115	5150	0.4	37	2039	2070	2074	0.2	2.39	1393	1390	0.0
76534	HOLLAND	027	2246	2631	2926	1.7	73	818	991	1110	2.1	2.65	627	742	1.8
76537	JARRELL	491	2166	2673	3140	2.3	81	741	903	1060	2.2	2.96	571	678	1.9
76538	JONESBORO	099	531	576	587	0.9	55	195	210	219	0.8	1.79	156	166	0.7
76539	KEMPNER	281	4719	5727	6352	2.1	79	1651	2003	2223	2.1	2.86	1347	1612	2.0
76541	KILLEEN	027	21246	20601	20897	-0.3	16	9040	9044	9256	0.0	2.27	5363	5100	-0.5
76542	KILLEEN	027	24251	31559	35996	2.9	86	8584	11364	12998	3.1	2.77	6584	8497	2.8
76543	KILLEEN	027	28992	32482	35043	1.2	63	10541	12155	13225	1.6	2.66	7814	8785	1.3
76544	KILLEEN	099	33992	35934	37037	0.6	46	5893	6304	6613	0.7	3.91	5739	6127	0.7
76548	HARKER HEIGHTS	027	17609	23935	27195	3.4	89	6322	8676	9921	3.5	2.74	4800	6515	3.4
76549	KILLEEN	027	19379	38194	46488	7.6	97	6700	12859	15627	7.3	2.97	5212	9869	7.1
76550	LAMPASAS	281	9939	11511	12540	1.6	71	3695	4269	4651	1.6	2.63	2635	2992	1.4
76554	LITTLE RIVER ACADEMY	027	1787	2062	2277	1.6	71	632	746	828	1.8	2.76	497	574	1.6
76556	MILANO	331	2120	2160	2163	0.2	30	822	840	840	0.2	2.57	611	615	0.1
76557	MOODY	309	4340	4923	5243	1.4	67	1594	1813	1936	1.4	2.69	1210	1348	1.2
76559	NOLANVILLE	027	2218	3724	4470	5.8	95	802	1394	1685	6.2	2.67	602	1023	5.9
76561	OGLESBY	099	951	960	955	0.1	27	361	355	352	-0.2	2.55	273	265	-0.3
76565	POTTSVILLE	193	273	275	274	0.1	27	108	107	107	-0.1	2.57	81	80	-0.1
76566	PURMELA	099	270	265	260	-0.2	19	109	103	101	-0.6	2.57	88	82	-0.8
76567	ROCKDALE	331	8607	9175	9361	0.7	49	3219	3419	3490	0.7	2.63	2324	2441	0.5
76569	ROGERS	027	2400	2698	2949	1.3	65	871	1011	1114	1.6	2.67	664	751	1.3
76570	ROSEBUD	145	2761	2499	2370	-1.1	3	1066	955	904	-1.2	2.57	747	658	-1.4
76571	SALADO	027	5253	5407	5632	0.3	34	2044	2152	2257	0.6	2.51	1633	1685	0.3
76574	TAYLOR	491	16210	18673	21333	1.5	69	5732	6566	7540	1.5	2.75	4209	4658	1.1
76577	THORNDALE	331	2507	2659	2717	0.6	46	969	1028	1053	0.6	2.59	711	743	0.5
76578	THRALL	491	1479	1917	2282	2.8	85	537	687	818	2.7	2.79	419	519	2.3
76579	TROY	027	3086	3557	3890	1.5	69	1087	1286	1417	1.8	2.77	896	1039	1.6
76621	ABBOTT	217	966	1127	1206	1.7	73	373	432	460	1.6	2.61	280	321	1.5
76622	AQUILLA	217	1149	1213	1244	0.6	46	443	464	475	0.5	2.61	352	365	0.4
76624	AXTELL	309	2271	2412	2470	0.7	49	840	887	909	0.6	2.69	648	671	0.4
76626	BLOOMING GROVE	349	1796	1965	2060	1.0	58	710	771	806	0.9	2.53	520	556	0.7
76627	BLUM	217	2370	2726	2902	1.5	69	897	1025	1087	1.5	2.66	694	784	1.3
76629	BREMOND	395	1836	1805	1766	-0.2	19	748	742	727	-0.1	2.36	508	495	-0.3
76630	BRUCEVILLE	309	1089	1203	1235	1.1	61	377	419	432	1.1	2.87	311	339	0.9
76631	BYNUM	217	518	585	620	1.3	65	182	204	216	1.2	2.87	143	158	1.1
76632	CHILTON	145	2138	2180	2175	0.2	30	765	778	776	0.2	2.76	574	576	0.0
76633	CHINA SPRING	309	3508	4187	4545	1.9	76	1195	1417	1539	1.9	2.95	1004	1175	1.7
76634	CLIFTON	035	7424	7954	8166	0.7	49	2930	3133	3215	0.7	2.43	2056	2166	0.6
76635	COOLIDGE	293	1202	1255	1250	0.5	42	445	461	459	0.4	2.72	313	319	0.2
76636	COVINGTON	217	883	940	953	0.7	49	323	342	345	0.6	2.71	247	258	0.5
76637	CRANFILLS GAP	035	720	799	837	1.1	61	294	325	340	1.1	2.46	228	249	1.0
76638	CRAWFORD	309	2361	2562	2644	0.9	55	843	906	934	0.8	2.83	687	726	0.6
76639	DAWSON	349	1826	2063	2193	1.3	65	733	820	867	1.2	2.52	516	566	1.0
76640	ELM MOTT	309	3095	3477	3642	1.3	65	1154	1289	1351	1.2	2.69	882	962	0.9
76641	FROST	349	2056	2185	2261	0.7	49	788	830	856	0.6	2.62	600	623	0.4
76642	GROESBECK	293	6280	6285	6238	0.0	25	2037	2041	2020	0.0	2.57	1445	1425	-0.2
76643	HEWITT	309	10916	13343	14342	2.2	80	3873	4700	5049	2.1	2.84	3168	3783	1.9
76645	HILLSBORO	217	10875	11966	12414	1.0	58	3888	4216	4370	0.9	2.71	2697	2881	0.7
76648	HUBBARD	217	2186	2459	2589	1.3	65	854	952	999	1.2	2.51	582	639	1.0
76649	IREDELL	035	892	991	1036	1.1	61	380	421	439	1.1	2.35	276	301	0.9
76651	ITALY	139	2968	4002	4676	3.3	88	1006	1346	1572	3.2	2.94	788	1031	2.9
76652	KOPPERL	035	992	975	966	-0.2	19	384	376	372	-0.2	2.59	296	287	-0.3
76653	KOSSE	293	929	971	970	0.5	42	359	374	373	0.4	2.55	259	266	0.3
76655	LORENA	309	6762	7413	7746	1.0	58	2370	2576	2689	0.9	2.88	1970	2106	0.7
76656	LOTT	145	2201	2140	2067	-0.3	16	841	817	790	-0.3	2.62	589	562	-0.5
76657	MC GREGOR	309	7465	8243	8586	1.1	61	2682	2933	3049	1.0	2.75	2026	2166	0.7
76660	MALONE	217	434	481	503	1.1	61	169	186	194	1.0	2.59	120	131	1.0
76661	MARLIN	145	9240	8643	8342	-0.7	7	2930	2699	2577	-0.9	2.50	1867	1683	-1.1
76664	MART	293	3319	3447	3480	0.4	37	1219	1253	1265	0.3	2.61	846	847	0.0
76665	MERIDIAN	035	2669	2848	2901	0.7	49	995	1054	1070	0.6	2.59	722	754	0.5
76666	MERTENS	217	421	476	504	1.3	65	167	187	198	1.2	2.55	131	145	1.1
76667	MEXIA	293	10551	11020	10987	0.5	42	3801	3935	3914	0.4	2.61	2676	2727	0.2
76670	MILFORD	139	1144	1562	1821	3.4	89	434	584	680	3.3	2.67	306	403	3.0
76671	MORGAN	035	1595	1716	1764	0.8	52	658	702	721	0.7	2.44	474	497	0.5
76673	MOUNT CALM	217	559	670	724	2.0	78	215	257	276	1.9	2.58	156	183	1.7
76676	PENELOPE	217	741	821	859	1.1	61	281	309	323	1.0	2.66	200	217	0.9
76678	PRAIRIE HILL	293	546	572	571	0.5	42	223	234	233	0.5	2.44	163	169	0.4
76679	PURDON	349	939	1113	1200	1.9	76	346	408	440	1.8	2.73	261	303	1.6
76680	REAGAN	145	734	664	628	-1.1	3	311	281	266	-1.1	2.36	206	182	-1.3
76681	RICHLAND	349	652	776	839	1.9	76	262	310	335	1.8	2.50	197	229	1.6
	TEXAS					1.9					1.8	2.78			1.7
	UNITED STATES					1.0					1.1	2.59			0.9

ZIP CODE #	POST OFFICE NAME	RACE (%) White 2000	White 2009	Black 2000	Black 2009	Asian/Pacific 2000	Asian/Pacific 2009	% Hispanic Origin 2000	% Hispanic Origin 2009	2009 AGE DISTRIBUTION (%) 0-4	5-9	10-14	15-19	20-24	25-44	45-64	65-84	85+	18+	MEDIAN AGE 2009	% 2009 Males	% 2009 Females
76474	SIDNEY	93.8	93.6	0.0	0.0	0.0	0.0	7.3	8.2	4.5	5.5	6.4	5.5	4.5	23.6	28.2	20.0	1.8	80.9	45.0	52.7	47.3
76475	STRAWN	84.6	79.2	0.2	0.3	0.6	0.7	19.3	26.6	6.7	6.9	6.5	6.7	5.9	23.5	28.1	13.1	2.5	75.6	39.3	49.3	50.7
76476	TOLAR	94.6	92.9	0.6	0.6	0.2	0.3	5.1	7.4	6.7	7.0	7.1	6.6	5.0	24.3	28.1	13.2	1.9	75.2	39.7	48.8	51.2
76483	THROCKMORTON	91.5	88.2	0.1	0.1	0.1	0.1	10.4	14.5	5.9	6.1	6.4	6.9	5.5	20.0	27.6	18.3	3.3	77.3	44.3	50.4	49.6
76484	PALO PINTO	93.5	90.9	0.6	0.8	0.3	0.3	7.1	10.9	6.3	6.8	6.6	6.7	5.2	23.7	28.9	14.3	1.6	76.5	41.1	53.5	46.5
76486	PERRIN	93.0	90.9	2.6	3.2	0.4	0.5	5.9	8.5	6.3	6.4	6.6	7.2	5.7	25.9	27.2	13.4	1.3	76.5	39.7	54.0	46.0
76487	POOLVILLE	94.7	92.9	1.3	1.6	0.3	0.4	5.7	8.1	7.1	7.1	7.3	7.6	6.4	26.5	27.0	10.2	0.9	73.9	36.8	50.7	49.3
76490	WHITT	59.8	50.8	25.9	31.4	0.0	0.0	14.3	18.6	1.7	1.7	2.5	4.2	9.3	50.0	22.0	7.6	0.8	91.5	37.0	78.0	22.0
76491	WOODSON	93.5	91.1	0.0	0.0	0.0	0.0	7.1	10.1	5.7	6.1	6.3	6.5	4.5	19.5	28.0	19.3	4.3	77.7	45.8	48.9	51.1
76501	TEMPLE	61.9	57.3	23.4	23.8	0.5	0.6	20.5	26.5	7.7	7.4	7.1	7.0	6.3	24.2	26.1	11.9	2.4	73.5	37.4	48.5	51.5
76502	TEMPLE	82.8	79.8	8.0	7.8	1.8	2.3	10.8	15.2	7.0	6.8	6.7	6.5	5.5	25.9	26.3	12.4	2.9	75.5	38.9	47.6	52.4
76504	TEMPLE	67.9	63.1	16.2	16.6	1.8	2.3	21.2	27.1	7.9	6.8	6.4	7.0	8.1	28.1	22.4	10.8	2.7	75.0	33.9	49.6	50.4
76511	BARTLETT	59.3	53.5	22.2	23.0	0.2	0.2	26.9	34.6	4.9	4.7	5.0	6.6	11.0	31.0	22.0	10.5	4.2	82.5	35.5	62.2	37.8
76513	BELTON	80.5	76.6	5.5	5.5	1.1	1.4	17.9	22.8	7.2	6.8	6.8	8.5	9.0	26.0	24.3	9.6	1.7	75.1	33.6	49.2	50.8
76518	BUCKHOLTS	87.5	83.3	0.8	0.8	0.1	0.2	25.1	33.4	6.2	6.2	6.6	7.7	5.4	24.4	27.8	13.4	2.3	76.2	40.4	50.0	50.0
76519	BURLINGTON	83.0	78.9	7.8	8.9	0.1	0.2	16.3	21.9	4.2	4.5	5.2	6.5	5.2	21.7	31.3	18.4	2.9	82.1	46.8	50.9	49.1
76520	CAMERON	72.5	68.3	16.7	17.6	0.1	0.2	23.1	30.0	7.1	6.9	7.0	7.2	5.6	22.0	25.1	14.7	4.5	74.5	39.8	48.1	51.9
76522	COPPERAS COVE	68.3	64.2	18.2	19.0	3.0	3.8	11.2	14.8	9.9	8.5	7.4	6.8	8.2	32.1	19.8	6.6	0.6	70.0	29.6	49.3	50.7
76523	DAVILLA	86.1	82.0	4.7	5.5	0.0	0.0	16.8	22.9	6.4	6.6	6.8	6.5	5.6	25.9	28.6	11.9	1.6	76.1	38.7	51.4	48.6
76524	EDDY	87.4	81.1	1.9	2.1	0.2	0.2	14.6	23.2	7.4	7.3	7.6	7.8	6.3	25.0	27.6	10.0	1.0	72.9	37.4	50.0	50.0
76525	EVANT	93.7	91.7	0.4	0.5	0.4	0.4	7.3	10.4	4.3	4.5	5.0	6.3	4.9	18.9	31.4	21.9	2.9	82.4	48.5	49.9	50.1
76526	FLAT	94.3	92.2	0.0	0.0	0.0	0.0	5.7	9.1	7.8	7.8	7.8	5.2	3.9	24.7	27.3	13.0	2.6	71.4	39.6	50.6	49.4
76527	FLORENCE	91.9	88.0	0.6	0.8	0.1	0.2	13.6	20.6	7.8	7.8	7.7	7.1	5.9	27.3	26.1	9.1	1.2	72.2	35.4	50.2	49.8
76528	GATESVILLE	71.3	67.0	19.8	21.2	0.5	0.7	12.3	16.3	3.9	3.9	4.0	5.0	9.0	43.4	21.6	7.8	1.4	85.7	36.1	44.3	55.7
76530	GRANGER	86.5	82.8	4.9	5.4	0.6	0.8	20.7	28.9	6.3	6.5	6.7	6.7	5.5	24.2	27.5	13.7	3.0	76.0	40.6	49.3	50.7
76531	HAMILTON	95.9	94.3	0.1	0.1	0.2	0.3	5.5	7.9	5.7	5.9	6.3	6.3	4.2	20.7	26.5	19.4	5.1	78.1	45.8	47.8	52.2
76534	HOLLAND	89.9	87.1	3.1	3.4	0.8	1.0	14.6	19.9	7.9	6.4	6.7	7.6	5.7	23.7	28.7	11.7	1.6	73.6	38.3	49.7	50.3
76537	JARRELL	85.2	79.5	1.3	1.5	0.2	0.2	23.1	32.8	7.0	6.9	7.0	7.4	5.9	28.4	26.0	10.1	1.3	74.6	36.2	52.5	47.5
76538	JONESBORO	75.9	70.1	15.1	17.5	1.5	1.9	7.9	11.5	3.3	3.6	3.8	11.8	21.2	25.7	20.0	9.4	1.2	86.6	28.3	64.1	35.9
76539	KEMPNER	84.7	80.9	5.4	5.9	1.5	2.0	10.1	14.5	6.7	6.8	6.8	6.8	5.9	27.1	29.1	10.2	0.6	75.6	37.9	49.8	50.2
76541	KILLEEN	48.2	43.0	29.2	29.5	4.4	5.3	21.3	26.7	10.9	8.4	6.5	6.3	10.3	34.2	16.0	6.7	0.8	71.0	28.0	50.2	49.8
76542	KILLEEN	54.7	49.2	26.3	27.6	5.6	6.8	15.0	19.0	8.8	7.6	6.9	6.9	8.9	34.8	21.1	4.6	0.3	72.4	30.1	49.9	50.1
76543	KILLEEN	44.2	39.9	36.5	36.9	4.8	5.8	16.4	20.6	10.6	7.8	6.4	7.2	13.2	33.4	16.1	4.6	0.5	71.3	27.0	49.5	50.5
76544	KILLEEN	50.7	45.3	31.6	32.8	3.0	3.7	16.7	21.5	12.7	11.0	7.3	10.2	25.0	32.1	1.6	0.1	0.0	66.4	21.8	61.6	38.4
76548	HARKER HEIGHTS	71.1	65.4	14.8	16.5	4.0	5.0	12.3	16.8	9.3	8.3	7.5	6.9	7.6	30.8	22.3	6.5	0.7	70.8	31.1	49.7	50.3
76549	KILLEEN	47.6	44.4	32.6	32.0	5.3	5.5	17.3	22.8	9.7	8.4	7.6	7.3	8.2	33.0	20.1	5.3	0.4	69.9	29.6	49.6	50.4
76550	LAMPASAS	86.9	83.4	2.0	2.1	0.6	0.7	18.6	24.6	7.3	6.9	6.8	6.8	6.2	24.4	25.5	13.0	3.0	74.7	38.4	48.4	51.6
76554	LITTLE RIVER ACADEMY	87.3	82.5	0.4	0.5	0.7	0.9	13.8	19.6	7.3	7.2	7.0	7.0	6.9	28.0	26.0	9.4	1.2	74.2	36.2	50.0	50.0
76556	MILANO	89.2	86.8	8.3	9.8	0.1	0.2	6.1	8.5	5.3	5.3	5.5	7.3	5.5	22.0	30.7	16.5	1.8	79.4	44.3	49.6	50.4
76557	MOODY	87.2	82.1	4.3	5.1	0.1	0.2	12.2	18.7	6.7	6.9	6.9	6.7	5.8	24.7	28.0	12.4	1.9	75.3	39.1	49.7	50.3
76559	NOLANVILLE	81.5	76.9	6.2	6.9	0.9	1.2	16.1	22.7	8.9	8.3	7.5	7.2	7.8	28.3	23.8	7.5	0.7	71.0	31.8	50.2	49.8
76561	OGLESBY	88.7	85.2	2.3	2.6	0.2	0.2	9.3	13.5	6.7	6.7	6.6	6.9	8.8	26.4	25.7	11.0	1.4	75.9	35.6	52.3	47.7
76565	POTTSVILLE	97.1	95.6	0.0	0.0	0.0	0.0	5.5	7.6	3.6	4.4	4.7	5.8	4.0	16.0	34.2	24.7	2.5	83.6	51.1	53.1	46.9
76566	PURMELA	93.3	91.7	1.9	2.3	0.4	0.8	3.7	5.3	6.4	6.8	7.2	7.5	4.5	22.6	29.8	13.2	1.9	75.1	41.3	50.6	49.4
76567	ROCKDALE	76.1	72.6	11.6	11.6	0.4	0.6	19.2	24.8	7.6	7.2	7.2	7.7	5.7	22.7	25.7	13.4	2.7	73.0	37.8	49.4	50.6
76569	ROGERS	84.3	79.4	2.9	3.1	0.1	0.1	18.5	25.3	7.3	7.3	7.5	7.6	6.4	23.6	27.8	10.7	1.7	73.2	37.8	49.3	50.7
76570	ROSEBUD	70.6	65.4	14.5	15.1	0.2	0.2	20.3	26.5	6.2	6.7	6.5	6.8	5.4	21.1	27.2	15.5	4.4	76.2	42.5	49.4	50.6
76571	SALADO	92.4	89.6	0.4	0.5	0.7	0.9	8.4	12.1	5.6	6.1	6.6	6.3	4.3	23.2	29.9	15.9	1.9	77.6	43.3	50.5	49.5
76574	TAYLOR	72.2	68.6	12.0	11.8	0.3	0.4	30.1	37.4	7.6	7.5	7.3	7.1	6.6	26.8	24.3	10.5	2.3	73.3	35.5	49.9	50.1
76577	THORNDALE	89.7	87.1	4.1	4.9	0.1	0.1	12.2	16.8	6.4	6.7	7.0	7.1	5.7	23.8	28.9	12.7	1.8	75.5	39.9	51.4	48.6
76578	THRALL	83.0	77.4	4.3	4.9	0.1	0.1	23.2	32.8	7.0	6.8	6.7	7.4	6.4	24.8	26.4	12.7	1.7	75.0	38.0	49.8	50.2
76579	TROY	89.2	84.8	1.3	1.6	0.4	0.6	13.7	19.5	7.0	7.2	7.3	7.3	6.2	25.6	28.5	9.8	1.0	74.0	37.0	49.5	50.5
76621	ABBOTT	93.5	90.7	1.1	1.5	0.1	0.1	8.3	12.9	6.2	6.7	7.0	6.2	4.2	23.3	30.3	13.7	2.4	76.2	42.4	52.3	47.7
76622	AQUILLA	93.8	90.9	1.0	1.4	0.2	0.2	5.7	9.0	6.2	6.5	6.8	6.3	4.7	22.2	30.3	15.3	1.6	76.4	42.8	49.6	50.4
76624	AXTELL	93.0	89.5	3.2	4.4	0.1	0.2	5.3	8.8	6.5	6.9	7.2	6.5	5.4	24.9	29.1	12.2	1.2	75.0	38.9	49.6	50.4
76626	BLOOMING GROVE	92.2	89.5	4.1	5.2	0.2	0.2	4.3	6.6	5.6	5.6	5.7	6.3	6.4	23.5	29.6	14.8	2.5	78.8	42.9	48.9	51.1
76627	BLUM	94.4	91.7	0.8	0.9	0.0	0.0	6.3	10.1	6.6	6.6	6.6	5.8	5.2	23.7	29.9	14.3	1.3	76.6	41.6	50.3	49.7
76629	BREMOND	81.0	78.5	15.5	17.7	0.1	0.1	3.2	3.5	6.5	6.6	6.8	6.6	5.5	20.6	27.3	16.0	4.0	75.5	42.6	49.4	50.6
76630	BRUCEVILLE	91.8	87.1	0.8	1.1	0.6	0.7	8.9	15.1	6.9	7.1	7.1	7.3	6.7	25.5	29.6	8.6	1.2	74.6	37.3	48.5	51.5
76631	BYNUM	90.9	86.5	1.9	2.4	0.2	0.2	8.9	14.2	6.0	6.3	6.7	6.0	4.4	23.4	30.3	14.5	2.4	77.4	42.7	52.3	47.7
76632	CHILTON	72.3	67.3	13.2	14.4	0.1	0.1	22.8	28.7	7.3	7.6	7.8	7.9	5.3	23.0	27.3	11.9	1.7	71.7	37.9	50.4	49.6
76633	CHINA SPRING	94.6	91.8	1.2	1.6	0.1	0.2	6.5	10.5	5.9	6.8	7.8	7.0	5.2	26.8	30.3	9.4	0.8	74.9	38.6	50.3	49.7
76634	CLIFTON	90.9	88.5	1.9	2.0	0.2	0.2	11.5	15.5	5.6	5.6	5.7	5.6	4.8	20.1	29.9	18.1	4.6	79.5	46.8	48.9	51.1
76635	COOLIDGE	68.1	63.0	17.1	18.0	0.1	0.1	23.5	29.8	8.1	7.6	7.3	7.0	7.3	26.0	23.7	11.2	1.8	72.6	34.1	48.8	51.2
76636	COVINGTON	88.1	83.1	3.4	4.4	0.1	0.2	13.9	21.1	7.8	7.9	8.0	7.2	5.7	24.9	25.4	11.8	1.3	71.6	35.9	49.3	50.7
76637	CRANFILLS GAP	94.0	92.1	1.7	2.0	0.1	0.1	6.0	9.0	5.1	5.4	5.6	6.0	4.9	19.6	34.3	16.5	2.5	79.7	47.0	50.2	49.8
76638	CRAWFORD	92.0	87.8	2.2	3.0	0.1	0.2	6.5	10.8	6.4	7.1	7.8	7.4	4.8	22.5	31.1	11.5	1.4	74.0	40.8	50.2	49.8
76639	DAWSON	85.6	81.1	10.1	12.6	0.1	0.0	5.8	8.8	5.9	6.2	6.6	6.5	4.9	22.6	29.7	15.3	2.3	77.4	43.0	50.0	50.0
76640	ELM MOTT	90.6	86.3	3.8	5.1	0.5	0.7	6.7	10.9	7.0	7.2	7.2	6.9	5.9	26.7	27.9	10.1	1.1	74.2	36.5	51.1	48.9
76641	FROST	85.3	80.5	7.5	9.1	0.4	0.6	8.8	13.0	6.7	7.0	6.6	5.8	5.7	22.4	29.0	15.1	1.7	76.1	41.5	51.0	49.0
76642	GROESBECK	68.4	63.6	18.0	18.5	0.0	0.0	14.4	19.4	5.9	5.9	5.6	6.5	9.2	27.9	23.6	12.5	2.9	78.8	36.1	56.1	43.9
76643	HEWITT	85.5	80.0	6.8	8.8	2.3	3.0	8.8	13.7	7.4	7.6	7.6	7.1	5.3	28.3	28.2	7.9	0.7	73.0	36.4	49.1	50.9
76645	HILLSBORO	74.7	70.8	12.6	13.1	0.5	0.6	23.6	29.9	8.1	7.4	6.8	7.8	6.6	24.8	22.8	12.3	3.4	73.5	35.4	50.2	49.8
76648	HUBBARD	79.5	74.7	15.5	18.5	0.5	0.7	4.2	6.3	7.2	7.0	7.0	6.5	5.4	21.1	26.9	15.3	3.5	74.4	41.6	45.8	54.2
76649	IREDELL	95.5	93.3	0.0	0.0	0.0	0.0	6.3	9.5	6.6	6.7	6.2	5.0	3.7	20.1	31.7	17.5	2.6	77.5	46.0	51.8	48.2
76651	ITALY	76.5	70.0	15.8	19.5	0.1	0.1	13.5	19.2	7.4	7.1	7.1	6.9	6.6	27.4	25.7	9.8	2.0	73.9	35.5	48.6	51.4
76652	KOPPERL	97.7	96.6	0.1	0.1	0.1	0.1	7.1	10.6	5.5	5.9	6.8	7.5	4.5	21.0	31.3	16.2	1.2	77.0	44.2	50.9	49.1
76653	KOSSE	83.4	79.8	10.1	11.4	0.2	0.3	8.2	11.1	5.7	5.9	5.9	5.9	4.6	21.9	30.2	17.7	2.3	78.4	45.1	52.5	47.5
76655	LORENA	90.4	86.0	3.8	4.9	0.5	0.7	7.8	12.5	5.8	6.2	6.7	7.4	5.8	25.6	31.5	9.7	1.1	76.6	39.8	49.6	50.4
76656	LOTT	80.1	75.2	13.1	15.3	0.1	0.1	8.8	12.5	5.4	5.6	6.2	8.2	6.5	21.8	30.0	14.2	2.2	78.0	42.1	50.6	49.4
76657	MC GREGOR	79.1	71.7	8.1	10.1	0.5	0.6	19.6	28.2	7.2	7.0	7.1	7.3	6.0	23.7	26.0	12.5	3.2	74.0	37.8	47.5	52.5
76660	MALONE	85.2	79.8	6.9	8.3	0.0	0.0	12.7	19.3	6.4	6.2	7.7	8.1	5.2	24.7	24.9	14.6	2.1	74.6	39.7	50.5	49.5
76661	MARLIN	45.9	41.2	42.6	44.1	0.2	0.2	16.6	21.3	6.1	5.8	6.9	10.3	6.8	27.5	21.1	12.6	3.0	74.1	34.6	42.1	57.9
76664	MART	75.0	68.2	21.0	26.0	0.0	0.0	5.8	8.6	7.2	7.0	7.1	8.8	5.3	21.7	25.5	14.1	3.2	72.3	38.8	47.3	52.7
76665	MERIDIAN	88.6	85.7	3.2	3.4	0.1	0.1	16.3	22.0	5.5	5.4	5.6	6.5	5.3	21.5	29.1	17.4	3.7	79.2	45.1	48.8	51.2
76666	MERTENS	91.2	86.8	1.9	2.3	0.0	0.2	8.8	14.1	5.9	6.3	6.7	6.1	4.4	23.5	29.8	14.7	2.5	77.3	42.6	51.9	48.1
76667	MEXIA	65.7	60.8	24.8	26.7	0.2	0.2	13.1	17.3	7.1	6.9	6.8	7.3	6.0	23.7	26.2	13.1	2.9	74.6	38.4	48.6	51.4
76670	MILFORD	68.8	60.8	21.3	25.9	0.6	0.8	13.2	18.4	6.9	7.1	7.1	7.0	5.6	25.2	28.2	11.4	1.6	74.6	37.8	49.3	50.7
76671	MORGAN	88.9	86.0	1.3	1.4	0.1	0.1	15.1	20.2	5.2	5.4	5.6	6.0	4.8	19.6	31.6	19.8	2.0	80.1	47.5	51.9	48.1
76673	MOUNT CALM	85.1	80.6	11.3	14.2	0.5	0.7	3.0	4.8	6.7	6.9	7.0	6.4	4.8	21.6	30.1	14.0	2.4	75.1	42.3	46.6	53.4
76676	PENELOPE	85.0	79.8	7.0	8.4	0.0	0.0	12.7	19.2	6.6	6.1	7.6	8.0	5.1	25.2	25.1	14.4	1.9	74.7	39.7	50.3	49.7
76678	PRAIRIE HILL	82.1	78.3	12.1	13.8	0.0	0.0	11.0	15.2	5.8	6.1	6.5	6.1	5.1	22.4	30.8	15.2	2.1	77.4	43.5	49.3	50.7
76679	PURDON	91.8	88.1	2.6	3.3	0.2	0.3	7.6	11.5	6.4	6.8	7.0	6.7	4.5	22.5	29.1	15.2	1.8	75.5	41.8	50.8	49.2
76680	REAGAN	85.1	81.0	9.5	11.4	0.0	0.0	6.9	10.1	4.2	4.2	5.0	6.8	5.4	22.7	31.0	17.9	2.7	82.5	45.9	50.8	49.2
76681	RICHLAND	91.4	87.8	2.6	3.4	0.3	0.3	8.1	12.5	6.6	7.0	7.2	6.7	4.5	22.7	28.6	15.1	1.7	75.0	41.2	50.8	49.2
	TEXAS	71.0	67.6	11.5	11.4	2.8	3.5	32.0	37.4	7.9	7.5	7.2	7.5	7.4	28.3	24.0	8.8	1.4	73.0	33.6	49.7	50.3
	UNITED STATES	75.1	72.0	12.3	12.7	3.8	4.6	12.5	15.7	6.8	6.7	6.6	7.1	6.9	27.0	26.0	10.9	1.9	75.7	36.9	49.2	50.8

ZIP CODE #	POST OFFICE NAME	2009 Per Capita Income	2009 HH Income Base	2009 Household Income Distribution (%): Less than $25,000	$25,000 to $49,999	$50,000 to $99,999	$100,000 to $149,999	$150,000 or More	Median Household Income: 2009	2014	2009 National Centile	2009 State Centile	2009 Home Value Base	2009 Home Value Distribution (%): Less than $50,000	$50,000 to $89,999	$90,000 to $174,999	$175,000 to $399,999	$400,000 or More	2009 Median Home Value
76474	SIDNEY	16227	41	26.8	31.7	39.0	2.4	0.0	44073	50000	46	56	33	12.1	42.4	33.3	9.1	3.0	86250
76475	STRAWN	20147	435	34.3	28.7	29.0	4.4	3.7	38980	41140	30	38	325	56.3	17.5	17.8	6.2	2.2	45341
76476	TOLAR	23457	1006	22.9	24.8	41.0	7.1	4.4	51144	51954	64	73	798	13.8	19.7	34.3	23.1	9.1	123684
76483	THROCKMORTON	19428	474	35.0	32.7	25.9	3.6	2.7	34284	34869	16	20	362	59.7	25.7	11.9	1.9	0.8	42391
76484	PALO PINTO	21632	483	24.0	31.5	36.4	4.6	3.5	47105	47375	54	65	386	25.1	17.6	28.2	22.8	6.2	111765
76486	PERRIN	18384	643	29.7	31.7	32.5	4.2	1.9	39516	42855	31	40	509	30.8	25.9	25.0	11.6	6.7	76964
76487	POOLVILLE	20180	897	21.5	26.4	41.7	7.8	2.6	51132	53614	64	73	775	16.6	29.8	32.1	18.5	3.0	97051
76490	WHITT	29310	47	23.4	29.8	38.3	8.5	0.0	46162	54430	52	62	39	30.8	23.1	25.6	12.8	7.7	82500
76491	WOODSON	18864	193	32.1	38.9	23.3	2.6	3.1	34158	34415	16	20	145	51.0	23.4	14.5	6.9	4.1	49250
76501	TEMPLE	19117	6798	33.6	29.3	29.3	5.6	2.0	37538	42005	25	33	4326	27.9	32.2	30.7	8.3	0.9	73652
76502	TEMPLE	29646	11390	16.7	25.8	38.8	10.7	8.0	56736	57245	74	81	7621	5.4	12.6	56.5	21.2	4.3	124565
76504	TEMPLE	20521	9697	28.3	34.6	29.4	5.3	2.4	39660	45134	32	41	4327	18.5	37.6	37.2	6.1	0.6	82871
76511	BARTLETT	16248	963	36.9	27.5	26.3	7.4	2.0	35464	37866	19	24	658	25.2	33.3	33.0	7.3	1.2	78372
76513	BELTON	23417	11483	22.0	28.7	35.0	9.4	4.9	49493	51163	60	69	7795	20.6	22.9	34.8	18.3	3.5	104363
76518	BUCKHOLTS	20513	437	26.5	28.6	34.8	5.3	4.8	43889	45817	45	56	343	28.3	23.6	33.2	11.7	3.2	86389
76519	BURLINGTON	17695	542	36.5	28.8	28.6	4.8	1.3	34607	39862	17	21	436	29.4	18.3	25.0	25.0	2.3	100820
76520	CAMERON	18381	2979	38.0	27.1	27.8	5.1	2.1	34584	37153	17	21	2041	33.5	32.5	25.9	6.1	2.1	70266
76522	COPPERAS COVE	20216	12420	15.5	34.9	39.0	7.7	2.8	49638	51220	60	69	7215	10.9	37.3	44.5	6.9	0.4	91809
76523	DAVILLA	18089	557	28.7	27.3	39.7	3.2	1.1	44250	46498	46	56	425	21.9	20.5	30.1	23.1	4.5	110417
76524	EDDY	16988	1082	25.4	34.2	33.7	4.9	1.8	42383	46063	41	51	891	37.1	34.6	23.5	4.8	0.0	65781
76525	EVANT	19669	454	32.2	32.4	26.9	6.2	2.4	39011	42438	30	38	356	30.1	23.6	15.4	18.5	12.4	84583
76526	FLAT	19273	28	32.1	21.4	39.3	7.1	0.0	47345	50596	55	65	22	36.4	9.1	40.9	13.6	0.0	125000
76527	FLORENCE	22332	1431	15.9	30.3	36.0	13.5	4.3	55287	52353	72	79	1099	16.7	16.2	35.4	24.1	7.6	118530
76528	GATESVILLE	16666	4956	29.3	30.6	32.2	5.5	2.4	42243	45849	40	51	3456	24.0	34.7	31.9	7.9	1.5	78222
76530	GRANGER	20109	1249	29.9	28.3	30.5	8.6	2.6	41711	43333	38	49	895	26.5	28.8	28.2	13.5	3.0	84477
76531	HAMILTON	19863	2070	31.5	31.2	30.2	4.7	2.4	38416	39711	28	35	1593	31.8	27.9	22.0	13.2	5.1	74350
76534	HOLLAND	19795	991	30.8	26.4	32.6	6.7	3.5	41978	46752	39	50	753	27.0	29.5	27.4	14.9	1.3	79018
76537	JARRELL	20518	903	15.8	34.9	35.0	11.6	2.7	49288	48322	59	68	700	19.6	16.4	42.0	17.6	4.4	118224
76538	JONESBORO	26378	210	18.6	37.6	36.2	3.8	3.8	46856	48088	54	64	167	21.0	31.1	31.1	12.6	4.2	87308
76539	KEMPNER	20904	2003	16.4	34.4	38.3	7.3	3.5	49379	50989	60	69	1590	16.7	16.2	53.1	12.4	1.5	114892
76541	KILLEEN	18082	9044	30.9	42.5	22.2	3.2	1.1	34325	36222	16	21	2728	10.1	55.5	30.2	4.0	0.2	77113
76542	KILLEEN	24075	11364	12.3	27.2	45.2	11.7	3.5	57113	57644	74	81	6926	7.4	11.8	71.4	8.6	0.8	116804
76543	KILLEEN	20039	12155	17.5	39.4	35.2	5.7	2.3	46674	48659	53	64	5779	9.7	31.1	52.5	5.8	0.8	95985
76544	KILLEEN	12849	6304	12.7	50.2	33.4	3.1	0.6	43787	47038	45	55	122	0.0	36.1	63.9	0.0	0.0	95152
76548	HARKER HEIGHTS	27635	8676	13.3	28.7	33.9	15.9	8.1	58949	57486	76	83	5110	13.1	12.5	44.9	28.7	0.8	140755
76549	KILLEEN	19335	12859	14.2	34.0	42.8	7.3	1.7	51249	52412	64	73	7181	3.8	22.1	71.8	2.0	0.2	106544
76550	LAMPASAS	19065	4269	28.2	31.1	33.1	5.7	2.0	41742	46214	38	49	2941	19.3	32.5	35.4	9.9	2.8	87247
76554	LITTLE RIVER ACADEMY	20004	746	22.3	28.6	41.0	5.6	2.5	49507	50720	60	69	558	26.5	25.8	34.9	9.5	3.2	86667
76556	MILANO	19019	840	29.6	29.6	33.7	4.9	2.1	41206	43168	37	47	699	27.6	28.9	28.0	11.0	4.4	77889
76557	MOODY	19199	1813	26.4	32.2	34.1	5.5	1.8	43669	46790	44	55	1395	27.9	29.7	31.0	9.7	1.6	76500
76559	NOLANVILLE	21469	1394	17.8	33.2	39.0	7.5	2.4	49359	50814	60	69	952	40.7	27.2	23.0	8.2	0.9	59674
76561	OGLESBY	21180	355	22.3	31.5	36.6	6.8	2.8	46658	49252	53	64	268	32.8	27.2	33.2	5.2	1.5	72500
76565	POTTSVILLE	23156	107	24.3	30.8	31.8	5.6	7.5	43641	43822	44	55	88	12.5	4.5	44.3	31.8	6.8	160294
76566	PURMELA	19713	103	26.2	34.0	33.0	4.9	1.9	42644	45654	41	52	83	22.9	14.5	41.0	16.9	4.8	113542
76567	ROCKDALE	20014	3419	25.4	30.2	36.1	6.2	2.2	45622	46939	50	60	2396	28.0	29.8	30.4	10.8	1.0	77727
76569	ROGERS	18841	1011	34.2	23.6	33.9	5.9	2.3	44784	46993	48	58	760	28.6	33.4	26.4	8.7	2.9	69423
76570	ROSEBUD	16862	955	36.2	32.5	24.6	5.5	1.2	36607	37555	22	29	692	50.4	29.6	15.5	4.5	0.0	49538
76571	SALADO	31200	2152	12.9	24.3	40.5	14.7	7.6	62976	60515	81	86	1771	12.0	10.7	29.4	41.8	6.2	167542
76574	TAYLOR	21754	6566	24.8	26.1	33.6	11.0	4.5	49053	49070	59	68	4341	10.1	21.5	43.6	21.6	3.2	124980
76577	THORNDALE	21714	1028	25.9	32.2	31.8	6.9	3.2	41827	43307	39	49	773	20.3	24.7	37.5	15.5	1.9	96754
76578	THRALL	21487	687	21.8	29.1	36.2	9.6	3.2	49150	48312	59	68	542	19.4	23.1	32.5	18.3	6.8	107979
76579	TROY	22042	1286	18.0	31.2	38.6	8.5	3.8	50673	51534	63	72	991	16.1	26.0	43.2	11.9	2.7	102334
76621	ABBOTT	19424	432	31.9	24.3	35.2	6.9	1.6	44637	46137	47	57	347	18.2	27.7	32.9	17.9	3.5	96905
76622	AQUILLA	19716	464	26.7	28.9	37.1	5.2	2.2	46065	46776	52	62	367	20.7	27.8	32.4	15.5	3.5	92500
76624	AXTELL	19806	887	17.9	33.6	42.4	4.6	1.5	48903	50670	59	68	733	27.1	31.0	34.1	6.8	1.0	76702
76626	BLOOMING GROVE	20650	771	28.7	25.7	35.3	8.2	2.2	46174	46144	52	62	609	17.9	34.8	39.4	7.1	0.8	87250
76627	BLUM	18438	1025	28.9	28.6	35.6	5.7	1.3	44856	46021	48	58	840	21.3	27.1	26.4	19.6	5.5	93714
76629	BREMOND	20929	742	35.6	26.8	26.1	7.4	4.0	36910	38603	23	30	561	32.6	30.3	27.5	9.6	0.0	70625
76630	BRUCEVILLE	20455	419	18.4	31.0	39.9	7.4	3.3	50455	51181	62	71	334	22.5	30.2	36.2	9.9	1.2	86897
76631	BYNUM	18871	204	28.4	25.5	35.3	8.8	2.0	46995	47893	54	64	167	21.6	23.4	34.1	16.8	4.2	98500
76632	CHILTON	16332	778	31.9	33.0	29.4	3.7	1.9	37285	39513	24	32	623	43.3	29.7	19.4	6.4	1.1	57981
76633	CHINA SPRING	21420	1417	17.1	29.9	40.0	9.0	4.0	52428	53108	67	75	1176	11.6	23.6	41.5	20.2	3.1	110683
76634	CLIFTON	21053	3133	29.1	29.7	32.0	6.0	3.1	41295	42370	37	47	2368	22.0	26.3	35.1	13.6	3.0	92031
76635	COOLIDGE	14977	461	39.3	31.2	25.8	2.0	1.7	32914	34419	13	16	325	55.7	18.5	14.5	10.2	1.2	44861
76636	COVINGTON	19263	342	25.4	28.4	39.2	5.8	1.2	46285	47739	52	63	268	20.9	28.0	30.6	16.4	4.1	92000
76637	CRANFILLS GAP	25327	325	22.5	23.7	42.2	7.7	4.0	52672	50842	67	75	263	11.8	18.3	44.5	16.0	9.5	115570
76638	CRAWFORD	22784	906	17.4	31.1	37.9	8.7	4.9	51979	53318	66	74	743	12.9	22.7	40.6	20.2	3.5	113469
76639	DAWSON	16062	820	35.5	29.1	32.2	2.4	0.7	36642	40275	22	30	646	41.6	26.5	23.2	7.3	1.4	60789
76640	ELM MOTT	22545	1289	22.5	29.3	38.4	5.4	4.3	48560	50569	58	67	1032	27.2	29.5	37.6	5.6	0.1	79200
76641	FROST	18398	830	31.9	28.1	33.1	5.2	1.7	41587	43738	38	48	671	30.6	31.4	29.5	8.3	0.1	70102
76642	GROESBECK	16849	2041	34.2	29.4	30.3	4.2	1.9	36115	38463	21	27	1502	31.0	31.6	28.0	8.9	0.4	69843
76643	HEWITT	26630	4700	8.5	19.4	50.9	16.4	4.8	66445	65316	84	88	3379	2.7	19.5	72.6	5.0	0.3	113050
76645	HILLSBORO	16641	4216	33.2	34.1	26.3	4.4	2.0	36339	38143	22	28	2711	24.0	29.0	30.9	14.2	1.9	85934
76648	HUBBARD	18381	952	36.6	27.6	28.2	5.7	2.0	36557	38850	22	29	722	36.0	24.9	29.5	8.4	1.1	69111
76649	IREDELL	18251	421	37.8	27.3	30.4	2.9	1.7	34336	37247	16	21	334	23.7	26.9	19.5	20.1	9.9	89231
76651	ITALY	20370	1346	18.4	29.0	41.8	8.2	2.5	52148	53078	66	74	989	17.8	37.0	34.4	8.3	2.5	83403
76652	KOPPERL	18152	376	29.0	34.3	29.8	5.6	1.3	40559	41956	35	44	302	29.1	26.8	26.2	13.6	4.3	82174
76653	KOSSE	18152	374	35.6	26.5	32.1	4.0	1.9	38995	41307	30	38	296	34.1	32.8	24.0	8.4	0.7	67500
76655	LORENA	24063	2576	13.4	24.2	47.0	10.2	5.2	58959	58758	76	83	2077	14.0	24.5	46.8	13.5	1.3	106941
76656	LOTT	17994	817	34.6	29.1	31.0	3.9	1.3	36479	38563	22	29	629	42.0	23.7	22.6	9.5	2.2	61196
76657	MC GREGOR	24969	2933	26.2	24.0	34.4	7.4	8.0	49761	51319	60	70	2169	31.7	24.6	22.6	16.0	5.1	76573
76660	MALONE	16417	186	35.5	31.7	26.9	5.4	0.5	36035	38608	21	27	148	35.1	27.0	25.7	10.8	1.4	70000
76661	MARLIN	15894	2699	44.9	27.5	21.6	4.1	2.0	28751	30127	6	8	1679	52.9	31.0	10.1	4.6	1.4	47805
76664	MART	18142	1253	36.2	28.5	26.8	5.3	3.2	35582	39288	19	25	901	43.7	30.6	19.1	6.3	0.2	55045
76665	MERIDIAN	20964	1054	27.7	28.7	34.3	5.7	3.6	44698	44469	47	58	790	23.8	22.5	31.6	17.5	4.6	96170
76666	MERTENS	21281	187	28.3	25.7	34.8	9.1	2.1	46967	47648	54	64	153	21.6	24.2	32.7	17.0	4.6	97222
76667	MEXIA	16850	3935	36.1	30.5	26.8	5.3	1.3	34566	35191	17	21	2785	39.9	31.2	22.1	6.0	0.8	60300
76670	MILFORD	18635	584	36.5	25.2	27.6	8.4	2.4	40335	42612	34	43	437	38.0	25.6	24.7	7.6	4.1	63833
76671	MORGAN	19210	702	32.2	30.9	31.3	4.0	1.6	38231	39953	27	35	577	35.2	23.2	29.3	10.2	2.1	68939
76673	MOUNT CALM	18722	257	33.1	26.5	32.3	6.2	1.9	40956	43087	36	46	203	28.1	25.1	35.5	10.3	1.0	80714
76676	PENELOPE	16006	309	34.6	32.0	26.9	5.2	1.3	36633	38405	22	29	246	34.6	27.2	26.4	10.6	1.2	70625
76678	PRAIRIE HILL	17245	234	39.3	29.1	29.1	0.9	1.7	34533	37064	17	21	185	31.9	21.6	23.2	21.1	2.2	81875
76679	PURDON	17414	408	26.5	33.8	34.3	3.9	1.5	42068	43580	39	50	338	21.9	24.0	36.7	13.3	4.1	95833
76680	REAGAN	13166	281	52.3	27.8	16.7	2.5	0.7	22989	25623	2	3	226	50.9	20.8	19.9	4.9	3.5	49412
76681	RICHLAND	18811	310	27.1	33.5	34.2	3.5	1.6	41611	42889	38	49	256	23.0	23.0	35.2	14.1	4.7	95556
	TEXAS	24551		22.3	25.0	34.3	11.1	7.3	52382	54495				16.5	22.7	36.5	19.7	4.6	109784
	UNITED STATES	27277		20.9	24.4	35.3	11.7	7.6	54719	56938				9.3	13.1	31.6	32.6	13.5	162279

#	POST OFFICE NAME	FINANCIAL SERVICES: Auto Loan	FINANCIAL SERVICES: Home Loan	FINANCIAL SERVICES: Invest-ments	FINANCIAL SERVICES: Retire-ment Plans	THE HOME: Home Improvements: Home Repair	THE HOME: Home Improvements: Lawn & Garden	THE HOME: Furnishings: Comput-ers & Hard-ware-Personal	THE HOME: Furnishings: Major Appli-ances	THE HOME: Furnishings: TV, Radio, Sound Equip-ment	THE HOME: Furnishings: Furni-ture	ENTERTAINMENT: Dine out/ Carry out	ENTERTAINMENT: Sports Equip-ment	ENTERTAINMENT: Fees & Tickets	ENTERTAINMENT: Toys & Games	ENTERTAINMENT: Travel	ENTERTAINMENT: Cable TV	PERSONAL: Apparel & Services	PERSONAL: Auto Repairs	PERSONAL: Health Insur-ance	PERSONAL: Pets & Supplies
76474	SIDNEY	78	54	85	53	56	82	59	74	62	48	61	61	44	61	59	67	40	69	78	91
76475	STRAWN	84	62	89	60	65	87	66	82	73	60	70	61	54	71	66	79	47	76	87	96
76476	TOLAR	104	85	96	83	86	102	84	97	89	83	89	71	74	91	81	95	60	91	99	115
76483	THROCKMORTON	80	57	83	56	59	84	63	78	68	54	67	60	49	67	61	75	44	72	84	92
76484	PALO PINTO	93	69	103	67	73	96	70	89	76	65	75	66	58	75	71	83	50	82	91	105
76486	PERRIN	84	60	87	59	63	86	62	79	69	58	68	59	50	68	61	76	45	72	82	94
76487	POOLVILLE	93	84	77	81	83	88	80	86	83	83	83	63	75	86	76	86	56	83	86	102
76490	WHITT	95	68	98	66	71	97	70	89	78	65	76	67	56	77	69	85	50	82	93	106
76491	WOODSON	85	58	93	58	61	89	65	80	67	52	66	66	47	66	64	73	43	75	85	99
76501	TEMPLE	72	61	61	62	60	70	67	68	71	65	70	51	62	70	63	75	48	69	75	82
76502	TEMPLE	105	107	102	108	106	105	104	104	103	106	104	79	105	104	105	103	72	104	104	122
76504	TEMPLE	75	60	57	62	58	64	72	66	73	69	73	53	64	74	64	74	50	71	70	81
76511	BARTLETT	83	59	81	57	60	84	63	77	70	58	68	59	50	70	60	77	46	73	83	93
76513	BELTON	95	89	79	88	86	89	91	89	91	91	91	69	87	93	86	92	63	90	90	106
76518	BUCKHOLTS	100	72	103	69	74	102	74	94	82	69	80	70	59	81	73	90	53	86	97	111
76519	BURLINGTON	76	56	77	54	58	77	57	71	63	53	61	54	46	62	56	69	41	66	74	85
76520	CAMERON	78	60	71	58	59	79	65	73	71	60	69	55	54	71	60	77	46	71	80	88
76522	COPPERAS COVE	92	80	70	80	75	75	87	80	85	88	87	65	80	90	79	84	60	84	78	96
76523	DAVILLA	76	70	62	68	68	71	66	70	68	69	68	51	62	71	63	70	47	68	70	83
76524	EDDY	81	73	68	71	72	77	70	75	73	72	73	55	65	75	67	75	49	72	75	89
76525	EVANT	84	63	96	61	67	87	64	82	69	59	68	61	53	68	66	75	45	75	83	97
76526	FLAT	95	68	97	66	70	96	70	89	77	65	76	66	56	77	69	85	50	81	92	105
76527	FLORENCE	104	98	86	95	95	97	92	96	94	96	94	71	88	98	88	96	64	93	95	114
76528	GATESVILLE	86	66	84	64	67	88	68	82	74	63	72	61	57	74	66	80	48	76	86	97
76530	GRANGER	93	65	94	63	67	95	70	87	77	62	75	68	54	77	68	85	50	81	93	105
76531	HAMILTON	79	61	84	60	63	85	64	78	70	57	68	59	54	68	64	76	45	73	84	92
76534	HOLLAND	81	70	65	72	69	81	75	78	78	69	76	59	67	79	70	82	52	76	83	92
76537	JARRELL	97	90	79	87	88	92	84	90	88	88	88	65	80	91	81	90	60	87	90	106
76538	JONESBORO	103	71	111	71	75	108	78	97	82	65	81	79	58	81	77	90	53	91	102	119
76539	KEMPNER	95	89	78	86	86	90	83	88	86	86	86	64	80	89	80	88	59	85	88	105
76541	KILLEEN	62	45	41	48	42	45	62	51	62	60	63	43	54	63	53	61	44	59	53	63
76542	KILLEEN	105	95	78	95	89	83	100	92	95	103	98	75	94	104	91	91	68	94	84	107
76543	KILLEEN	84	71	58	72	66	64	80	71	78	81	79	59	73	84	71	75	55	76	68	85
76544	KILLEEN	85	44	33	51	39	38	80	55	75	74	79	55	60	90	58	69	55	70	50	67
76548	HARKER HEIGHTS	116	113	96	110	107	102	111	107	108	116	109	84	107	114	105	105	76	107	101	126
76549	KILLEEN	89	83	69	82	78	75	84	80	82	87	84	64	80	88	78	80	58	81	76	94
76550	LAMPASAS	77	68	71	67	68	79	70	75	74	66	72	56	65	74	68	78	50	73	81	89
76554	LITTLE RIVER ACADEMY	86	83	73	82	81	84	77	81	79	79	79	60	75	82	76	81	54	79	81	96
76556	MILANO	87	63	89	61	65	89	64	82	71	60	70	61	51	71	64	78	46	75	85	97
76557	MOODY	89	71	78	69	71	86	70	80	76	70	75	60	61	78	67	81	50	76	83	96
76559	NOLANVILLE	89	84	71	80	80	80	83	82	83	86	83	62	78	86	77	83	57	82	80	97
76561	OGLESBY	99	72	83	70	71	95	74	86	82	72	81	66	60	85	68	90	54	82	91	105
76565	POTTSVILLE	99	79	128	78	87	105	80	101	83	75	82	74	69	79	86	89	55	93	100	117
76566	PURMELA	91	65	93	63	67	92	67	85	74	62	73	64	53	73	66	81	48	78	88	101
76567	ROCKDALE	86	71	77	70	71	86	73	81	77	69	76	62	64	79	70	82	51	78	85	97
76569	ROGERS	88	67	80	64	66	85	67	79	74	66	73	60	56	76	64	80	49	75	82	96
76570	ROSEBUD	73	54	66	53	54	72	59	68	65	55	63	51	49	64	55	70	42	65	73	81
76571	SALADO	111	120	111	121	120	122	108	115	109	111	109	85	114	110	114	111	76	110	117	134
76574	TAYLOR	89	86	82	84	85	89	85	88	86	85	87	66	82	87	84	88	60	87	89	102
76577	THORNDALE	101	72	95	70	74	100	74	92	83	71	81	69	60	84	71	91	54	85	96	110
76578	THRALL	93	79	74	81	78	92	86	88	89	78	87	68	76	91	79	94	60	87	95	105
76579	TROY	98	90	80	87	88	92	85	90	88	88	88	65	80	92	81	90	60	87	90	107
76621	ABBOTT	91	64	96	62	66	94	68	85	73	59	72	67	52	72	67	80	47	79	89	103
76622	AQUILLA	92	66	95	64	68	94	68	86	75	63	74	65	54	75	67	83	49	79	90	102
76624	AXTELL	86	79	70	76	77	81	74	79	77	77	77	57	70	80	71	79	52	76	79	94
76626	BLOOMING GROVE	90	65	90	63	67	93	69	86	77	63	75	64	56	76	68	85	50	80	92	102
76627	BLUM	83	67	81	65	68	83	66	78	71	65	70	58	57	72	65	76	47	73	80	93
76629	BREMOND	86	62	87	60	64	89	66	83	73	60	71	62	53	72	64	81	47	76	88	97
76630	BRUCEVILLE	94	87	77	84	85	88	82	87	85	85	85	63	77	88	78	87	58	84	87	103
76631	BYNUM	97	69	99	67	72	98	71	90	79	66	77	68	57	78	70	87	51	83	94	107
76632	CHILTON	82	56	82	54	57	82	59	75	67	55	65	57	46	67	57	74	43	69	78	90
76633	CHINA SPRING	93	97	85	97	94	97	88	93	89	90	89	71	90	91	90	90	62	89	92	110
76634	CLIFTON	86	67	97	66	72	89	70	85	75	65	73	63	60	72	72	80	49	80	88	100
76635	COOLIDGE	67	51	57	51	50	65	57	61	61	52	59	47	48	62	52	65	40	61	67	74
76636	COVINGTON	84	77	69	75	76	79	73	77	76	76	76	56	69	79	70	78	52	75	78	92
76637	CRANFILLS GAP	104	83	134	82	91	110	83	106	87	78	86	77	72	83	90	93	57	98	104	122
76638	CRAWFORD	93	98	88	101	96	102	90	96	90	88	90	74	92	92	93	92	62	91	96	113
76639	DAWSON	72	52	74	50	54	73	53	68	59	49	58	51	42	58	52	65	38	62	70	80
76640	ELM MOTT	97	90	79	87	87	91	85	89	88	88	88	65	80	91	81	90	60	87	90	106
76641	FROST	87	62	82	60	63	86	64	79	71	61	70	60	51	72	61	78	46	73	82	94
76642	GROESBECK	73	57	68	56	57	74	61	69	66	57	65	52	52	66	58	71	44	67	75	83
76643	HEWITT	111	119	100	118	113	106	108	108	105	113	106	84	112	110	109	102	74	105	101	126
76645	HILLSBORO	75	58	65	56	58	72	63	70	68	59	66	52	53	68	58	72	45	68	74	83
76648	HUBBARD	81	58	82	56	60	83	61	77	68	56	67	58	49	67	60	75	44	71	82	91
76649	IREDELL	71	57	92	56	63	76	57	73	60	54	59	53	50	57	62	64	39	67	72	84
76651	ITALY	93	87	76	86	84	91	84	87	87	85	87	65	80	90	80	89	59	86	90	105
76652	KOPPERL	83	61	90	59	64	85	62	79	68	58	67	59	51	67	63	74	44	73	81	93
76653	KOSSE	78	59	88	58	63	82	62	77	67	56	65	57	51	65	63	73	44	72	81	90
76655	LORENA	104	106	97	105	104	106	96	102	97	99	97	77	98	100	98	98	68	98	100	120
76656	LOTT	83	59	85	58	62	85	62	78	69	57	67	59	50	68	61	76	45	72	83	93
76657	MC GREGOR	106	98	87	98	95	106	98	101	101	94	100	77	92	104	93	105	68	99	106	121
76660	MALONE	76	54	78	53	56	77	56	71	62	52	61	53	45	61	55	68	40	65	74	84
76661	MARLIN	67	49	63	49	50	68	54	64	62	51	59	47	46	60	52	68	40	62	72	76
76664	MART	82	60	83	58	62	85	64	79	71	58	69	59	51	70	62	78	46	73	85	93
76665	MERIDIAN	92	71	104	69	75	97	73	92	80	68	78	67	62	77	75	86	52	85	96	107
76666	MERTENS	97	69	99	67	72	98	71	90	79	66	78	68	57	78	70	87	51	83	94	108
76667	MEXIA	75	56	67	54	56	73	60	69	66	57	65	51	50	66	56	71	43	67	74	82
76670	MILFORD	88	65	81	62	64	86	66	79	74	65	73	60	54	76	62	80	48	75	82	96
76671	MORGAN	76	63	86	59	68	81	62	76	67	63	66	53	56	64	65	72	44	72	81	88
76673	MOUNT CALM	86	62	89	60	64	88	64	81	71	59	69	61	51	70	63	78	46	74	84	96
76676	PENELOPE	76	54	78	53	56	77	56	71	62	52	61	53	45	62	55	68	40	65	74	84
76678	PRAIRIE HILL	75	54	77	52	56	76	55	70	61	52	60	53	44	61	55	68	40	65	73	84
76679	PURDON	85	61	87	59	63	86	62	79	69	58	68	60	50	69	62	76	45	73	83	94
76680	REAGAN	56	40	57	39	41	56	41	52	45	38	45	39	33	45	40	50	29	48	54	62
76681	RICHLAND	84	60	86	58	63	85	62	79	69	58	67	59	50	68	61	75	45	72	82	93
	TEXAS	104	96	90	94	93	94	99	97	99	101	100	75	94	101	94	99	70	99	96	114
	UNITED STATES	100	100	100	100	100	100	100	100	100	100	100	100	100	100	100	100	100	100	100	100

ZIP CODE			POPULATION			2000-2009 ANNUAL RATE		HOUSEHOLDS					FAMILIES		
#	POST OFFICE NAME	COUNTY FIPS CODE	2000	2009	2014	% Rate	State Centile	2000	2009	2014	% Annual Rate 2000-2009	2009 Average HH Size	2000	2009	% Annual Rate 2000-2009
76682	RIESEL	145	2932	3197	3312	0.9	55	1112	1204	1245	0.9	2.63	837	891	0.7
76687	THORNTON	293	1810	1909	1916	0.6	46	742	786	788	0.6	2.43	564	589	0.5
76689	VALLEY MILLS	035	3682	4534	4786	2.3	81	1359	1665	1764	2.2	2.54	1049	1272	2.1
76690	WALNUT SPRINGS	035	924	997	1021	0.8	52	327	351	358	0.8	2.84	243	257	0.6
76691	WEST	309	6262	6497	6604	0.4	37	2354	2413	2446	0.3	2.63	1724	1734	0.1
76692	WHITNEY	217	8224	9336	9866	1.4	67	3342	3773	3979	1.3	2.43	2334	2588	1.1
76693	WORTHAM	161	1800	1891	1928	0.5	42	689	720	734	0.5	2.59	479	492	0.3
76701	WACO	309	2209	2204	2198	0.0	25	463	447	444	-0.4	2.42	204	184	-1.1
76704	WACO	309	7917	7840	7824	-0.1	21	3080	3037	3036	-0.2	2.49	1922	1835	-0.5
76705	WACO	309	27589	29066	29646	0.6	46	9980	10375	10587	0.4	2.70	6822	6948	0.2
76706	WACO	309	32408	35609	36885	1.0	58	11263	12328	12805	1.0	2.58	5847	6311	0.8
76707	WACO	309	17404	17097	16919	-0.2	19	5637	5388	5317	-0.5	3.11	3971	3695	-0.8
76708	WACO	309	20939	23386	24288	1.2	63	7808	8512	8816	0.9	2.64	5196	5649	0.9
76710	WACO	309	22556	22331	22193	-0.1	21	10591	10399	10338	-0.2	2.10	5826	5505	-0.6
76711	WACO	309	8619	8927	9059	0.4	37	2852	2918	2962	0.2	2.92	2101	2102	0.0
76712	WOODWAY	309	19172	21602	22625	1.3	65	7510	8399	8793	1.2	2.53	5560	6040	0.9
76801	BROWNWOOD	049	25584	26288	26673	0.3	34	9641	9906	10061	0.3	2.45	6504	6572	0.1
76802	EARLY	049	4821	5016	5103	0.4	37	1754	1823	1861	0.4	2.69	1346	1380	0.3
76820	ART	319	32	33	34	0.3	34	16	17	17	0.7	1.94	12	13	0.9
76821	BALLINGER	399	5285	5042	4913	-0.5	11	2012	1918	1866	-0.5	2.51	1410	1323	-0.7
76823	BANGS	049	2796	3025	3138	0.9	55	1093	1191	1239	0.9	2.47	771	824	0.7
76825	BRADY	307	6932	6782	6689	-0.2	19	2741	2694	2662	-0.2	2.47	1870	1808	-0.4
76827	BROOKESMITH	049	389	412	424	0.6	46	157	170	176	0.9	1.91	129	138	0.7
76828	BURKETT	083	204	221	223	0.9	55	99	108	109	0.9	1.80	72	77	0.7
76831	CASTELL	299	100	100	99	0.0	25	44	44	43	0.0	2.27	34	33	-0.3
76832	CHEROKEE	411	609	599	590	-0.2	19	219	217	213	-0.1	2.08	163	159	-0.3
76834	COLEMAN	083	6530	6130	5929	-0.7	7	2734	2555	2469	-0.7	2.36	1816	1669	-0.9
76836	DOOLE	307	54	49	48	-1.0	4	23	21	21	-1.0	2.33	17	15	-1.3
76837	EDEN	095	2844	2845	2751	0.0	25	609	534	499	-1.4	2.51	418	361	-1.6
76841	FORT MC KAVETT	327	36	37	37	0.3	34	16	16	16	0.0	2.31	11	11	0.0
76842	FREDONIA	319	83	87	87	0.5	42	32	33	33	0.3	2.64	25	26	0.4
76844	GOLDTHWAITE	333	2942	3019	3029	0.3	34	1223	1245	1245	0.2	2.30	813	813	0.0
76845	GOULDBUSK	083	182	190	191	0.5	42	77	81	81	0.5	2.35	55	56	0.2
76848	HEXT	327	70	71	71	0.2	30	31	31	31	0.0	2.29	22	22	0.0
76849	JUNCTION	267	4015	4139	4177	0.3	34	1658	1745	1772	0.6	2.36	1149	1190	0.4
76852	LOHN	307	291	267	257	-0.9	5	113	104	101	-0.9	2.57	83	76	-0.9
76853	LOMETA	281	1453	1661	1812	1.5	69	579	664	727	1.5	2.43	407	456	1.2
76854	LONDON	267	416	423	424	0.2	30	186	194	196	0.5	2.14	123	126	0.3
76856	MASON	319	3443	3585	3642	0.4	37	1486	1554	1581	0.5	2.29	1017	1046	0.3
76857	MAY	049	1689	1788	1843	0.6	46	720	768	793	0.7	2.33	538	565	0.5
76858	MELVIN	307	305	286	277	-0.7	7	133	122	117	-0.9	2.07	98	89	-1.0
76859	MENARD	327	2224	2135	2080	-0.4	13	933	896	874	-0.4	2.33	624	589	-0.6
76861	MILES	399	1889	1819	1785	-0.4	13	670	646	634	-0.4	2.82	529	505	-0.5
76862	MILLERSVIEW	095	150	138	131	-0.9	5	70	64	60	-1.0	2.05	53	47	-1.3
76864	MULLIN	333	1562	1627	1649	0.4	37	545	561	567	0.3	2.66	407	413	0.2
76865	NORTON	399	286	270	262	-0.6	9	124	117	114	-0.6	2.27	91	85	-0.7
76866	PAINT ROCK	095	628	573	542	-1.0	4	240	218	207	-1.0	2.59	182	163	-1.2
76869	PONTOTOC	319	145	152	153	0.5	42	56	58	59	0.4	2.62	43	45	0.5
76870	PRIDDY	333	130	133	130	0.2	30	41	41	40	0.0	3.20	30	30	0.0
76871	RICHLAND SPRINGS	411	1220	1211	1191	-0.1	21	513	510	501	-0.1	2.37	363	355	-0.2
76872	ROCHELLE	307	799	768	754	-0.4	13	347	336	331	-0.3	2.29	253	242	-0.5
76873	ROCKWOOD	083	54	51	50	-0.6	9	31	30	29	-0.4	1.70	21	20	-0.5
76874	ROOSEVELT	267	22	22	22	0.0	25	12	12	12	0.0	1.83	8	8	0.0
76875	ROWENA	399	639	676	683	0.6	46	268	284	286	0.6	2.38	187	196	0.5
76877	SAN SABA	411	4154	4085	4013	-0.2	19	1468	1436	1407	-0.2	2.57	1029	990	-0.4
76878	SANTA ANNA	083	1579	1366	1297	-1.6	1	659	569	540	-1.6	2.34	434	365	-1.9
76880	STAR	333	512	523	514	0.2	30	191	193	190	0.1	2.68	147	147	0.0
76882	TALPA	083	249	264	267	0.6	46	114	121	122	0.6	2.17	83	86	0.4
76883	TELEGRAPH	267	19	19	20	0.0	25	9	9	10	0.0	2.11	6	6	0.0
76884	VALERA	083	111	120	122	0.8	52	49	53	54	0.9	2.26	35	37	0.6
76885	VALLEY SPRING	299	289	285	282	-0.2	19	127	125	124	-0.2	2.28	99	96	-0.3
76887	VOCA	307	123	115	112	-0.7	7	55	52	51	-0.6	2.21	42	39	-0.8
76888	VOSS	083	107	116	118	0.9	55	47	51	52	0.9	2.27	34	36	0.6
76890	ZEPHYR	049	889	1020	1077	1.5	69	343	397	420	1.6	2.57	270	308	1.4
76901	SAN ANGELO	451	25675	25893	25966	0.1	27	10046	10250	10320	0.2	2.49	7009	7038	0.0
76903	SAN ANGELO	451	31764	30837	30475	-0.3	16	11768	11576	11498	-0.2	2.58	7815	7564	-0.4
76904	SAN ANGELO	451	30210	31523	32009	0.5	42	12696	13536	13853	0.7	2.25	8090	8474	0.5
76905	SAN ANGELO	451	10664	10661	10666	0.0	25	3710	3768	3786	0.2	2.83	2890	2899	0.0
76908	GOODFELLOW AFB	451	1752	1899	1896	0.9	55	104	104	104	0.0	3.14	97	97	0.0
76909	SAN ANGELO	451	441	486	485	1.1	61	2	2	2	0.0	6.50	2	1	-7.2
76930	BARNHART	235	165	170	174	0.3	34	65	68	70	0.5	2.50	50	51	0.2
76932	BIG LAKE	383	3326	3043	2967	-1.0	4	1107	1049	1035	-0.6	2.86	872	817	-0.7
76933	BRONTE	081	1652	1649	1615	0.0	25	578	570	557	-0.2	2.43	403	391	-0.3
76934	CARLSBAD	451	1724	1754	1754	0.2	30	543	556	560	0.3	2.70	414	418	0.1
76935	CHRISTOVAL	451	654	666	677	0.2	30	256	267	274	0.5	2.41	175	179	0.2
76936	ELDORADO	413	2935	2856	2857	-0.3	16	1115	1115	1127	0.0	2.52	817	806	-0.1
76937	EOLA	095	459	448	439	-0.3	16	163	155	151	-0.5	2.69	128	121	-0.6
76940	MERETA	451	163	173	177	0.6	46	61	65	66	0.7	2.66	49	51	0.4
76941	MERTZON	235	1542	1580	1595	0.3	34	602	629	640	0.5	2.51	454	468	0.3
76943	OZONA	105	4094	4019	4027	-0.2	19	1522	1508	1517	-0.1	2.62	1113	1087	-0.3
76945	ROBERT LEE	081	1887	1825	1765	-0.4	13	801	784	762	-0.2	2.26	547	527	-0.4
76949	SILVER	081	20	20	19	0.0	25	11	11	11	0.0	1.82	8	8	0.0
76950	SONORA	435	4072	4199	4269	0.3	34	1513	1581	1615	0.5	2.64	1144	1180	0.3
76951	STERLING CITY	431	1399	1268	1202	-1.1	3	515	479	457	-0.8	2.60	387	356	-0.9
76955	VANCOURT	451	167	177	180	0.6	46	53	56	57	0.6	3.14	45	47	0.5
76957	WALL	451	37	39	40	0.6	46	14	15	15	0.7	2.60	12	12	0.0
77002	HOUSTON	201	13181	15259	15863	1.6	71	1743	2389	2762	3.5	1.48	308	392	2.6
77003	HOUSTON	201	9749	13657	15690	3.7	90	2633	3764	4351	3.9	3.42	1861	2576	3.6
77004	HOUSTON	201	30230	36800	40161	2.1	79	11519	14245	15757	2.3	2.26	5852	6786	1.6
77005	HOUSTON	201	22303	23374	24157	0.5	42	9396	9709	10001	0.4	2.39	5809	5815	0.0
77006	HOUSTON	201	19060	20661	21741	0.9	55	11050	11932	12572	0.8	1.63	2762	2758	0.0
77007	HOUSTON	201	22360	32521	38089	4.1	92	9220	13538	15875	4.2	2.36	4504	6238	3.6
77008	HOUSTON	201	28849	32743	35142	1.4	67	12621	14137	15083	1.2	2.29	6457	6940	0.8
77009	HOUSTON	201	42406	44203	45699	0.4	37	14244	14744	15197	0.4	2.96	9086	9094	0.0
77010	HOUSTON	201	80	89	90	1.2	63	54	60	63	1.1	1.48	5	5	0.0
	TEXAS					1.9					1.8	2.78			1.7
	UNITED STATES					1.0					1.1	2.59			0.9

#	POST OFFICE NAME	RACE (%) White 2000	White 2009	Black 2000	Black 2009	Asian/Pacific 2000	Asian/Pacific 2009	% Hispanic Origin 2000	% Hispanic Origin 2009	2009 AGE DISTRIBUTION (%) 0-4	5-9	10-14	15-19	20-24	25-44	45-64	65-84	85+	18+	MEDIAN AGE 2009	% 2009 Males	% 2009 Females
76682	RIESEL	88.3	83.7	6.1	7.8	0.4	0.5	6.4	10.2	5.9	6.2	6.4	7.0	5.5	24.5	29.3	13.6	1.6	77.0	40.9	50.2	49.8
76687	THORNTON	91.8	89.5	3.5	4.1	0.3	0.4	6.0	8.6	4.8	4.9	5.1	5.8	4.5	20.0	32.9	20.4	1.7	81.4	48.0	50.8	49.2
76689	VALLEY MILLS	88.2	83.8	4.2	5.5	0.3	0.5	8.2	12.2	6.0	6.4	6.9	7.5	6.9	23.8	28.9	11.3	2.4	76.8	39.5	51.7	48.3
76690	WALNUT SPRINGS	88.5	85.4	0.1	0.1	0.0	0.1	25.0	33.4	6.7	7.1	8.6	7.8	5.7	21.7	27.2	13.3	1.8	71.6	37.5	51.5	48.5
76691	WEST	94.2	91.5	2.4	3.2	0.2	0.3	6.1	9.9	6.6	6.8	6.8	6.5	5.5	23.8	27.2	13.3	3.4	75.8	40.0	49.4	50.6
76692	WHITNEY	93.6	91.2	2.1	2.6	0.2	0.2	5.7	9.0	5.6	5.9	5.9	5.7	4.5	20.2	30.5	19.0	2.7	79.0	46.4	48.4	51.6
76693	WORTHAM	81.3	77.0	15.4	18.4	0.0	0.0	3.7	5.2	7.3	7.3	7.4	6.7	5.3	23.5	26.7	13.1	2.7	74.1	38.8	48.0	52.0
76701	WACO	55.3	46.2	25.1	27.5	0.7	0.7	26.0	35.0	4.0	3.6	2.7	6.0	11.3	40.2	16.9	9.0	6.4	87.3	34.7	62.0	38.0
76704	WACO	14.6	12.3	78.1	78.9	0.4	0.4	8.5	10.6	10.4	8.7	7.2	8.2	10.3	20.2	20.1	12.3	2.6	69.2	29.0	44.9	55.1
76705	WACO	73.1	66.3	15.8	18.6	0.7	0.8	15.3	21.5	8.0	7.2	6.6	9.0	9.7	27.0	22.1	9.2	1.2	74.1	30.6	52.0	48.0
76706	WACO	68.0	63.6	12.4	12.8	2.8	3.4	25.8	31.2	5.8	5.3	5.1	16.2	24.2	18.9	16.2	7.3	1.1	80.4	23.6	47.3	52.7
76707	WACO	43.5	38.6	33.9	33.6	0.4	0.5	35.7	43.7	10.4	9.4	8.1	8.0	8.2	27.8	19.9	6.7	1.7	67.4	28.5	48.7	51.3
76708	WACO	67.9	64.9	19.7	19.9	0.6	0.6	21.6	26.7	7.6	7.3	7.4	7.8	6.7	25.0	23.5	11.5	3.2	72.8	35.7	47.7	52.3
76710	WACO	78.8	72.4	10.8	13.0	1.2	1.4	13.0	18.9	6.3	5.5	5.1	5.0	6.7	26.6	23.7	16.6	4.5	80.4	40.1	46.6	53.4
76711	WACO	57.0	49.4	11.3	11.8	0.3	0.3	49.1	59.6	9.1	8.2	7.5	7.7	7.4	26.9	21.4	10.1	1.6	70.5	31.5	50.9	49.1
76712	WOODWAY	89.4	85.0	4.6	6.1	2.0	2.8	6.9	11.0	6.3	6.1	6.6	6.9	5.5	24.9	28.9	12.7	2.1	76.5	40.3	48.5	51.5
76801	BROWNWOOD	84.7	81.1	5.2	5.6	0.5	0.6	18.5	24.6	6.4	5.9	6.2	9.5	7.8	22.4	25.3	13.6	2.7	76.0	37.7	49.7	50.3
76802	EARLY	93.8	91.5	0.7	0.8	0.4	0.5	9.6	13.8	6.6	6.7	6.8	6.8	5.5	23.9	28.1	13.0	2.8	75.4	39.9	49.1	50.9
76820	ART	96.8	93.9	0.0	0.0	0.0	0.0	12.9	18.2	6.1	6.1	6.1	6.1	6.1	24.2	24.2	21.2	0.0	75.8	41.3	48.5	51.5
76821	BALLINGER	81.3	76.4	1.7	1.8	0.4	0.5	29.0	37.3	6.5	6.5	6.5	6.5	5.9	22.1	26.2	15.2	4.5	76.1	41.4	48.4	51.6
76823	BANGS	88.3	84.8	4.3	5.0	0.0	0.0	11.3	16.0	6.2	6.3	6.5	6.4	5.6	21.8	28.6	15.2	3.3	77.1	42.6	47.8	52.2
76825	BRADY	83.4	79.3	1.9	1.9	0.2	0.3	29.0	37.1	7.5	7.1	7.2	6.4	5.7	20.8	26.6	15.1	3.5	74.2	40.6	47.1	52.9
76827	BROOKESMITH	90.7	88.8	6.9	8.0	0.0	0.0	10.0	14.3	3.2	3.6	5.1	9.7	6.8	25.0	32.8	12.4	1.5	83.0	42.6	60.4	39.6
76828	BURKETT	95.6	93.7	0.0	0.0	0.0	0.0	5.4	7.2	4.1	4.5	4.5	5.0	2.7	19.9	28.1	21.7	9.5	83.7	51.0	49.3	50.7
76831	CASTELL	97.0	97.0	0.0	0.0	0.0	0.0	5.0	7.0	2.0	4.0	4.0	4.0	4.0	15.0	40.0	25.0	2.0	86.0	55.5	48.0	52.0
76832	CHEROKEE	84.1	83.6	8.4	8.5	0.2	0.2	17.5	18.9	3.5	3.8	6.7	25.7	3.7	15.4	26.4	12.9	2.0	69.9	34.6	62.1	37.9
76834	COLEMAN	87.0	83.1	2.3	2.6	0.3	0.3	14.8	20.3	6.1	6.3	6.3	6.2	5.3	20.5	26.5	18.3	4.5	77.6	44.4	47.9	52.1
76836	DOOLE	87.0	83.7	0.0	0.0	0.0	0.0	22.2	30.6	4.1	4.1	4.1	6.1	6.1	18.4	34.7	18.4	4.1	81.6	49.4	51.0	49.0
76837	EDEN	90.1	90.0	1.3	1.3	0.2	0.2	47.0	49.2	3.0	3.3	3.0	4.3	11.1	45.2	19.1	8.8	2.0	88.3	34.1	72.9	27.1
76841	FORT MC KAVETT	94.4	94.6	0.0	0.0	0.0	0.0	13.9	16.2	5.4	5.4	5.4	5.4	5.4	18.9	29.7	24.3	0.0	78.4	48.8	51.4	48.6
76842	FREDONIA	95.1	93.1	0.0	0.0	0.0	0.0	12.2	17.2	4.6	5.7	6.9	5.7	3.4	19.5	28.7	23.0	2.3	79.3	47.5	49.4	50.6
76844	GOLDTHWAITE	88.4	84.5	0.3	0.4	0.2	0.2	16.3	21.9	6.4	6.3	6.4	6.0	5.0	18.8	27.5	17.8	5.8	76.7	45.8	48.0	52.0
76845	GOULDBUSK	94.5	92.6	0.5	0.5	0.0	0.0	8.2	12.1	5.3	5.3	5.8	6.3	4.2	20.0	30.5	19.5	3.2	79.5	46.9	51.1	48.9
76848	HEXT	94.3	94.4	0.0	0.0	0.0	0.0	14.3	15.5	2.8	4.2	4.2	2.8	2.8	14.1	39.4	26.8	2.8	85.9	55.9	52.1	47.9
76849	JUNCTION	89.6	86.4	0.1	0.1	0.5	0.7	21.9	28.8	6.1	6.2	6.3	5.9	4.9	20.5	30.3	17.3	2.6	77.8	45.1	48.2	51.8
76852	LOHN	87.3	82.8	0.0	0.0	0.0	0.0	22.3	30.3	3.7	4.9	5.6	6.7	5.2	17.6	35.6	18.0	2.6	81.3	49.3	49.8	50.2
76853	LOMETA	89.0	85.9	1.3	1.3	0.2	0.2	18.1	24.3	5.1	5.4	7.8	7.3	4.8	19.9	29.9	17.1	2.8	76.9	44.9	50.2	49.8
76854	LONDON	95.9	94.8	0.0	0.0	0.0	0.2	10.1	13.7	4.5	4.7	5.4	4.0	3.1	17.0	33.3	24.3	3.5	82.5	53.1	49.6	50.4
76856	MASON	91.3	88.8	0.1	0.1	0.1	0.1	21.7	28.6	5.4	5.7	5.9	5.7	4.5	19.4	30.3	19.4	3.7	79.4	47.6	47.9	52.1
76857	MAY	96.8	95.4	0.1	0.1	0.1	0.1	4.5	6.7	4.3	4.6	4.8	4.9	4.4	17.8	31.5	25.6	2.2	83.5	52.2	50.8	49.2
76858	MELVIN	88.2	84.3	0.3	0.3	0.0	0.0	26.5	34.3	3.5	4.2	4.5	6.3	6.6	24.1	32.2	16.4	2.1	83.9	45.5	56.3	43.7
76859	MENARD	87.2	86.6	0.5	0.6	0.4	0.4	32.6	34.9	5.0	5.2	5.3	5.9	6.0	19.8	30.7	18.2	3.9	80.3	46.9	49.8	50.2
76861	MILES	82.6	76.9	0.1	0.1	0.3	0.4	27.4	36.4	5.8	6.8	7.1	7.8	5.3	24.0	30.2	11.3	1.6	75.3	40.3	49.9	50.1
76862	MILLERSVIEW	83.9	81.9	0.0	0.0	0.0	0.0	26.2	28.3	5.1	5.1	5.1	5.1	4.3	25.4	31.9	15.9	2.2	81.9	45.0	52.9	47.1
76864	MULLIN	89.4	86.3	3.2	3.5	0.2	0.2	7.7	11.0	4.7	5.7	8.2	7.5	4.8	18.2	31.5	17.1	2.2	75.6	45.6	54.6	45.4
76865	NORTON	91.6	88.1	0.7	0.7	0.0	0.0	13.3	19.3	4.8	5.6	5.6	5.2	4.4	19.3	33.7	18.5	3.0	81.1	48.9	51.9	48.1
76866	PAINT ROCK	82.5	80.6	0.0	0.0	0.2	0.2	25.0	27.1	4.9	5.4	5.8	5.8	3.8	23.6	30.7	17.5	2.6	80.1	45.6	50.1	49.9
76869	PONTOTOC	94.5	92.1	0.0	0.0	0.0	0.0	12.4	17.8	5.3	5.9	5.9	5.9	3.9	18.4	29.6	22.4	2.6	78.9	47.9	49.3	50.7
76870	PRIDDY	93.8	91.7	0.8	0.8	0.0	0.0	5.4	6.8	5.3	5.3	5.3	7.5	5.3	21.1	30.1	18.0	2.3	78.2	45.3	50.4	49.6
76871	RICHLAND SPRINGS	92.9	92.5	0.1	0.1	0.1	0.1	12.0	13.0	5.0	5.7	5.9	6.0	4.5	19.8	31.0	19.3	2.7	79.5	47.3	52.5	47.5
76872	ROCHELLE	94.0	92.2	0.0	0.0	0.1	0.1	11.4	15.2	4.3	4.7	5.2	5.7	3.9	18.2	34.6	21.0	2.3	82.4	51.1	49.2	50.8
76873	ROCKWOOD	92.6	88.2	1.9	2.0	0.0	0.0	7.4	11.8	3.9	3.9	3.9	5.9	3.9	19.6	35.3	19.6	3.9	82.4	50.6	51.0	49.0
76874	ROOSEVELT	95.5	95.5	0.0	0.0	0.0	0.0	13.6	18.2	9.1	9.1	9.1	0.0	0.0	18.2	36.4	18.2	0.0	72.7	47.5	50.0	50.0
76875	ROWENA	88.3	83.9	0.0	0.0	0.0	0.0	20.0	27.8	5.9	6.2	6.5	7.2	3.7	20.7	29.4	17.0	3.3	76.6	44.7	51.9	48.1
76877	SAN SABA	81.7	80.7	2.8	2.9	0.1	0.1	25.4	27.2	5.8	5.8	6.6	12.1	5.1	20.1	25.2	15.2	4.1	74.2	40.1	50.5	49.5
76878	SANTA ANNA	90.3	87.8	3.1	3.4	0.1	0.1	15.2	20.6	5.8	6.3	6.1	5.9	5.1	20.1	27.5	18.1	5.2	78.1	45.6	48.4	51.6
76880	STAR	92.4	89.9	0.8	0.8	0.0	0.0	12.9	18.2	5.7	6.5	6.7	6.1	4.0	17.6	30.6	19.3	3.4	77.2	47.2	52.8	47.2
76882	TALPA	95.2	92.8	0.4	0.4	0.0	0.0	9.3	13.3	5.3	5.7	6.1	6.4	4.2	20.1	31.1	18.9	2.3	78.8	46.2	52.3	47.7
76883	TELEGRAPH	100.0	94.7	0.0	0.0	0.0	0.0	11.1	15.8	0.0	0.0	10.5	0.0	0.0	10.5	42.1	36.8	0.0	89.5	58.8	47.4	52.6
76884	VALERA	95.5	94.2	0.0	0.0	0.0	0.0	8.1	11.7	5.8	5.8	5.8	6.7	4.2	19.2	32.5	18.3	1.7	77.5	46.1	51.7	48.3
76885	VALLEY SPRING	96.9	95.4	0.3	0.7	0.3	0.7	4.8	7.0	2.8	3.2	3.9	4.6	3.5	17.9	37.5	24.9	1.8	87.0	54.3	49.1	50.9
76887	VOCA	96.7	94.8	0.0	0.0	0.0	0.0	10.7	15.7	3.5	4.3	5.2	7.0	4.3	19.1	36.5	17.4	2.6	82.6	48.8	50.4	49.6
76888	VOSS	95.3	94.0	0.0	0.0	0.0	0.0	8.4	12.1	6.0	6.0	6.0	6.9	3.4	19.0	31.9	19.0	1.7	76.7	46.3	50.9	49.1
76890	ZEPHYR	94.9	92.7	0.0	0.0	0.1	0.1	7.2	10.4	5.8	6.5	6.7	5.6	4.9	21.8	33.3	13.7	1.8	77.5	44.0	50.6	49.4
76901	SAN ANGELO	83.1	78.2	3.3	3.4	0.6	0.7	27.0	36.8	7.3	6.8	6.7	7.0	6.8	28.2	25.3	10.1	1.9	75.0	35.4	48.6	51.4
76903	SAN ANGELO	67.8	63.4	5.5	5.1	0.7	0.8	50.4	59.1	7.8	7.3	7.0	7.6	7.3	25.5	22.2	12.2	3.2	73.4	34.7	48.2	51.8
76904	SAN ANGELO	88.0	83.9	3.3	3.8	1.3	1.7	13.9	20.8	5.9	5.6	5.7	7.7	9.3	25.1	25.8	12.7	2.2	79.4	36.7	47.6	52.4
76905	SAN ANGELO	74.6	69.3	3.8	3.7	1.2	1.4	37.6	47.3	8.0	7.9	7.9	8.5	6.8	27.0	24.4	8.5	0.9	70.7	32.9	49.5	50.5
76908	GOODFELLOW AFB	74.8	68.5	11.7	13.3	2.5	3.2	12.6	18.3	4.5	1.8	1.2	28.2	42.1	21.5	0.4	0.1	0.1	91.6	21.7	71.6	28.4
76909	SAN ANGELO	76.4	70.0	10.4	11.5	1.4	1.6	17.7	25.7	0.6	0.6	0.6	55.1	40.1	2.7	0.2	0.0	0.0	97.5	19.4	44.2	55.8
76930	BARNHART	95.2	95.3	0.0	0.0	0.0	0.0	16.4	17.1	5.9	6.5	7.1	5.3	4.1	18.8	32.9	17.6	1.8	77.6	46.3	50.0	50.0
76932	BIG LAKE	64.6	58.3	3.0	3.3	0.3	0.3	49.5	58.5	8.6	8.4	8.0	7.6	7.5	25.1	24.9	8.4	1.4	69.8	31.9	49.9	50.1
76933	BRONTE	86.9	86.4	4.4	4.4	0.2	0.2	19.6	21.2	4.7	4.7	5.0	18.4	4.8	17.7	23.2	17.3	4.2	74.5	40.4	53.9	46.1
76934	CARLSBAD	89.9	86.3	2.7	3.1	0.2	0.2	13.8	20.9	4.6	5.7	6.4	7.3	4.5	25.4	31.4	13.3	1.4	78.8	42.6	53.5	46.5
76935	CHRISTOVAL	95.0	92.6	0.5	0.5	0.2	0.2	10.9	16.8	4.1	4.7	5.3	4.7	4.5	18.0	36.9	16.8	5.1	82.9	50.1	49.8	50.2
76936	ELDORADO	76.6	75.8	1.5	1.6	0.2	0.2	43.5	45.8	6.1	6.2	7.5	7.9	5.2	20.9	29.4	13.4	3.5	75.1	41.6	49.6	50.4
76937	EOLA	87.1	85.0	0.2	0.2	0.2	0.2	22.7	26.3	4.9	6.5	6.7	6.7	4.5	26.3	28.3	14.1	2.0	77.0	40.8	53.6	46.4
76940	MERETA	85.3	79.2	0.0	0.0	0.0	0.0	25.8	35.8	6.4	7.5	8.7	8.7	4.6	23.1	30.6	9.8	0.6	70.5	39.0	50.9	49.1
76941	MERTZON	90.0	89.7	0.5	0.4	0.0	0.0	25.9	27.6	5.4	6.5	8.2	7.2	4.2	21.6	29.4	15.6	2.0	74.8	42.6	50.1	49.9
76943	OZONA	76.3	75.8	0.7	0.7	0.3	0.3	54.7	57.1	6.8	6.7	7.4	7.7	6.4	22.5	28.6	11.8	2.2	74.2	38.8	49.8	50.2
76945	ROBERT LEE	89.0	88.3	0.2	0.2	0.1	0.1	17.2	18.6	4.8	5.4	5.9	6.1	4.5	18.9	29.0	21.3	4.1	80.0	47.9	47.5	52.5
76949	SILVER	90.0	90.0	0.0	0.0	0.0	0.0	15.0	15.0	0.0	5.0	5.0	10.0	0.0	20.0	40.0	20.0	0.0	85.0	50.0	55.0	45.0
76950	SONORA	75.3	70.8	0.2	0.2	0.2	0.2	51.7	60.8	7.1	6.9	7.1	7.6	6.3	24.1	27.9	11.5	1.5	74.0	38.2	50.2	49.8
76951	STERLING CITY	85.8	82.1	0.1	0.1	0.1	0.1	31.0	39.1	5.1	6.9	8.8	9.1	3.4	25.9	25.2	13.0	2.4	72.7	39.3	49.5	50.5
76955	VANCOURT	92.9	89.8	0.0	0.0	0.6	0.6	13.1	19.8	5.6	8.5	9.0	7.9	3.4	23.7	29.4	10.7	1.7	70.6	39.4	52.0	48.0
76957	WALL	94.4	89.7	0.0	0.0	0.0	0.0	13.9	20.5	5.1	10.3	10.3	10.3	5.1	25.6	25.6	5.1	2.6	64.1	33.8	46.2	53.8
77002	HOUSTON	56.3	54.2	39.0	39.6	1.7	2.2	23.4	30.7	1.5	0.9	0.8	8.7	16.9	52.0	15.5	3.4	0.4	94.6	32.4	79.0	21.0
77003	HOUSTON	37.2	35.1	20.3	19.8	1.4	1.5	72.5	74.9	10.5	9.1	7.5	8.7	9.4	28.0	19.2	6.5	1.1	67.6	27.7	52.5	47.5
77004	HOUSTON	16.0	15.8	73.2	70.1	2.8	4.2	11.7	15.2	6.4	5.7	5.3	9.9	12.0	26.6	22.0	10.1	2.0	78.9	32.1	49.4	50.6
77005	HOUSTON	91.7	87.7	1.0	1.3	4.6	6.8	5.5	9.8	6.2	7.3	8.7	6.3	3.9	23.9	32.9	8.7	2.0	73.7	41.3	49.2	50.8
77006	HOUSTON	80.0	72.2	4.5	5.6	4.2	5.7	20.2	31.2	3.1	2.4	2.1	3.4	9.8	45.4	26.9	6.2	0.7	90.9	36.0	56.9	43.1
77007	HOUSTON	59.9	54.7	7.6	7.4	1.9	2.2	53.8	63.5	6.8	6.1	5.5	5.9	8.1	34.9	24.1	7.5	1.2	78.1	34.1	53.1	46.9
77008	HOUSTON	68.5	60.4	4.5	4.5	1.1	1.3	43.4	57.0	6.3	5.9	5.5	5.3	6.3	31.1	26.7	10.3	2.5	79.0	38.2	50.6	49.4
77009	HOUSTON	58.8	55.7	6.2	5.2	0.7	0.7	72.6	80.1	8.1	7.5	7.1	7.4	7.3	30.9	22.7	7.7	1.3	72.9	32.7	52.1	47.9
77010	HOUSTON	55.0	51.7	40.0	42.7	1.3	1.1	23.8	31.5	2.2	1.1	0.0	6.7	13.5	58.4	16.9	1.1	0.0	95.5	34.8	74.2	25.8
	TEXAS	71.0	67.6	11.5	11.4	2.8	3.5	32.0	37.4	7.9	7.5	7.2	7.5	7.4	28.3	24.0	8.8	1.4	73.0	33.6	49.7	50.3
	UNITED STATES	75.1	72.0	12.3	12.7	3.8	4.6	12.5	15.7	6.8	6.7	6.6	7.1	6.9	27.0	26.0	10.9	1.9	75.7	36.9	49.2	50.8

#	POST OFFICE NAME	2009 Per Capita Income	2009 HH Income Base	2009 Household Income Distribution (%) Less than $25,000	$25,000 to $49,999	$50,000 to $99,999	$100,000 to $149,999	$150,000 or More	Median Household Income 2009	2014	2009 National Centile	2009 State Centile	2009 Home Value Base	2009 Home Value Distribution (%) Less than $50,000	$50,000 to $89,999	$90,000 to $174,999	$175,000 to $399,999	$400,000 or More	2009 Median Home Value
76682	RIESEL	18514	1204	27.7	32.0	34.3	4.6	1.5	42108	46345	40	50	952	32.0	29.5	29.9	6.6	1.9	72034
76687	THORNTON	21297	786	28.9	30.3	33.0	4.7	3.2	44586	47095	47	57	657	25.1	29.1	34.1	10.5	1.2	85089
76689	VALLEY MILLS	22609	1665	20.3	30.9	37.8	7.6	3.4	48994	49492	59	68	1310	16.3	26.3	34.0	19.4	4.0	101970
76690	WALNUT SPRINGS	14668	351	36.8	36.2	21.7	3.7	1.7	31345	37993	10	13	279	50.5	21.9	17.9	7.2	2.5	49516
76691	WEST	19895	2413	26.9	28.1	36.6	5.6	2.7	46074	49017	52	62	1799	27.0	33.6	31.7	7.6	0.2	72983
76692	WHITNEY	19856	3773	34.1	29.6	28.0	5.9	2.5	38110	39830	27	34	2970	27.7	28.6	26.9	15.0	1.9	82076
76693	WORTHAM	17065	720	33.8	29.4	32.8	2.9	1.1	38492	40715	28	35	535	37.0	27.3	28.6	6.0	1.1	68429
76701	WACO	15472	447	49.9	28.0	13.4	5.1	3.6	25066	26154	3	4	113	63.7	10.6	16.8	6.2	2.7	37917
76704	WACO	10916	3037	60.8	24.4	12.3	2.3	0.2	17845	18875	1	1	1213	73.2	20.7	6.1	0.0	0.0	31964
76705	WACO	17141	10375	32.1	31.4	30.5	4.2	1.9	38173	43240	27	34	6114	38.3	35.8	20.8	4.8	0.3	61123
76706	WACO	14771	12328	48.8	24.2	21.9	3.3	1.8	26153	30180	4	5	5264	30.1	34.0	31.5	4.3	0.2	72273
76707	WACO	12390	5388	42.3	32.6	21.3	2.8	1.1	30446	32889	9	11	2652	62.3	30.7	5.8	1.1	0.2	44181
76708	WACO	18885	8512	30.0	31.6	29.6	6.0	2.7	39564	44328	31	41	5136	31.0	30.5	28.1	9.3	1.1	69280
76710	WACO	28139	10399	25.3	30.1	31.8	7.3	5.4	45446	48332	50	60	5195	7.3	37.9	37.4	13.4	4.1	96095
76711	WACO	13373	2918	35.1	38.9	23.3	2.5	0.3	34266	36472	16	20	1829	58.2	39.9	1.5	0.3	0.1	46833
76712	WOODWAY	33777	8399	11.5	23.7	39.5	14.1	11.2	64195	62084	83	87	5477	3.7	15.6	50.8	27.3	2.6	129608
76801	BROWNWOOD	18491	9906	34.7	29.4	28.4	5.5	2.1	37081	39552	24	31	6675	35.8	29.2	25.1	8.7	1.3	67296
76802	EARLY	19657	1823	26.9	31.0	33.2	5.0	3.8	42537	44841	41	52	1402	21.5	33.9	32.4	11.3	0.9	83504
76820	ART	28894	17	17.6	35.3	29.4	17.6	0.0	47361	37343	55	65	14	7.1	14.3	35.7	14.3	28.6	125000
76821	BALLINGER	16326	1918	37.9	32.4	24.8	3.5	1.4	33512	34114	14	18	1467	44.7	27.3	21.7	5.0	1.3	54403
76823	BANGS	17809	1191	34.3	30.1	31.4	2.4	1.8	35407	38087	19	24	892	38.1	29.5	26.1	5.9	0.3	64943
76825	BRADY	15804	2694	41.9	31.8	22.6	2.4	1.2	31149	32578	10	13	1879	52.1	20.6	19.4	6.2	1.6	47158
76827	BROOKESMITH	33254	170	15.3	22.4	44.1	11.2	7.1	59446	56722	77	84	149	12.8	16.8	37.6	26.2	6.7	122500
76828	BURKETT	23241	108	35.2	36.1	20.4	7.4	0.9	35319	32369	19	24	87	32.2	18.4	27.6	19.5	2.3	89000
76831	CASTELL	27862	44	20.5	29.5	38.6	6.8	4.5	50000	47347	61	70	38	7.9	18.4	31.6	26.3	15.8	150000
76832	CHEROKEE	21303	217	36.9	28.1	27.6	2.8	4.6	35185	36281	18	23	160	25.0	26.9	23.1	16.3	8.8	86250
76834	COLEMAN	17563	2555	40.0	32.1	22.1	3.2	2.6	31064	31937	10	12	1821	56.0	24.1	12.7	5.2	2.0	44954
76836	DOOLE	17806	21	38.1	28.6	23.8	9.5	0.0	36100	32344	21	27	17	35.3	17.6	29.4	17.6	0.0	85000
76837	EDEN	16951	534	34.5	28.8	29.8	3.2	3.7	37608	40090	26	33	378	45.0	32.5	16.1	4.2	2.1	54222
76841	FORT MC KAVETT	24171	16	25.0	37.5	25.0	6.3	6.3	40000	45000	33	42	12	16.7	8.3	8.3	25.0	41.7	300000
76842	FREDONIA	19310	33	24.2	30.3	30.3	15.2	0.0	37379	38629	25	32	28	7.1	25.0	32.1	21.4	14.3	118750
76844	GOLDTHWAITE	19706	1245	35.7	30.4	26.4	4.8	2.7	35786	37028	20	26	964	26.8	25.8	28.4	16.4	2.6	85763
76845	GOULDBUSK	21278	81	33.3	30.9	24.7	6.2	4.9	36367	39093	22	28	67	43.3	17.9	22.4	9.0	7.5	65000
76848	HEXT	21585	31	25.8	45.2	16.1	9.7	3.2	37296	37296	24	32	23	39.1	13.0	13.0	21.7	13.0	85000
76849	JUNCTION	19896	1745	34.7	32.0	26.5	4.1	2.6	35593	36678	20	25	1269	29.2	22.6	18.5	17.2	12.5	86642
76852	LOHN	20539	104	39.4	23.1	25.0	8.7	3.8	36118	45576	21	27	85	31.8	20.0	28.2	15.3	4.7	87000
76853	LOMETA	18250	664	36.3	30.9	25.6	5.4	1.8	36174	40602	21	28	484	34.7	23.6	22.3	15.1	4.3	73462
76854	LONDON	22278	194	29.9	27.3	36.6	5.7	0.5	40000	43474	33	42	148	23.0	14.9	20.3	20.9	20.9	136842
76856	MASON	22073	1554	33.1	31.1	27.8	5.1	2.9	36920	38656	23	31	1227	20.2	26.0	27.7	17.5	8.6	99688
76857	MAY	20743	768	31.1	30.6	31.6	4.4	2.2	39126	42368	30	38	653	36.8	28.5	21.4	10.0	3.4	67685
76858	MELVIN	25055	122	36.9	23.8	25.4	8.2	5.7	37604	39101	26	33	98	29.6	20.4	30.6	14.3	5.1	90000
76859	MENARD	17067	896	43.4	31.4	19.4	4.0	1.8	30142	31586	8	11	663	58.4	18.4	10.7	6.8	5.7	43833
76861	MILES	19018	646	27.2	33.0	30.8	5.4	3.6	41343	45000	37	48	503	29.0	29.0	31.2	8.7	2.0	79103
76862	MILLERSVIEW	24924	64	29.7	34.4	26.6	4.7	4.7	37299	38146	24	32	51	41.2	23.5	21.6	9.8	3.9	61667
76864	MULLIN	17834	561	33.0	33.3	26.0	4.3	3.4	37029	38303	24	31	467	24.2	26.1	29.1	15.6	4.9	89400
76865	NORTON	20275	117	28.2	37.6	30.8	2.6	0.9	39647	41544	32	41	95	44.2	17.9	29.5	5.3	3.2	59167
76866	PAINT ROCK	20008	218	28.9	35.3	28.4	4.1	3.2	37415	38460	25	32	173	41.6	23.7	22.0	8.7	4.0	60500
76869	PONTOTOC	18914	58	25.9	31.0	29.3	13.8	0.0	37374	42405	25	32	48	14.6	25.0	27.1	18.8	14.6	108333
76870	PRIDDY	14122	41	36.6	31.7	26.8	2.4	2.4	36684	40000	23	30	34	35.3	23.5	26.5	14.7	0.0	75000
76871	RICHLAND SPRINGS	19673	510	28.8	31.8	32.0	6.1	1.4	41265	44869	37	47	403	31.8	18.4	31.8	13.2	5.0	89583
76872	ROCHELLE	18377	336	33.6	31.5	32.1	2.1	0.6	35247	39815	18	24	270	34.4	17.4	31.1	13.3	3.7	86429
76873	ROCKWOOD	22794	30	43.3	23.3	26.7	6.7	0.0	28118	46137	6	7	25	44.0	16.0	20.0	12.0	8.0	65000
76874	ROOSEVELT	24773	12	33.3	25.0	33.3	8.3	0.0	35000	45000	18	23	9	0.0	22.2	11.1	22.2	44.4	350000
76875	ROWENA	15095	284	40.5	29.2	28.2	2.1	0.0	29787	32316	8	9	213	24.9	35.7	25.8	10.8	2.8	75000
76877	SAN SABA	17423	1436	31.1	37.9	24.8	3.7	2.6	35291	35138	19	24	1056	41.1	30.1	16.6	9.2	3.0	62391
76878	SANTA ANNA	16303	569	42.0	27.1	26.5	3.2	1.2	31636	32203	11	13	417	56.4	19.7	15.1	6.5	2.4	45583
76880	STAR	19690	193	22.3	39.4	29.5	4.1	4.7	42142	45410	40	50	156	26.9	7.1	35.3	23.1	7.7	116667
76882	TALPA	24651	121	28.9	33.9	27.3	6.6	3.3	39153	41881	30	39	100	37.0	23.0	25.0	8.0	7.0	71667
76883	TELEGRAPH	14605	9	44.4	33.3	22.2	0.0	0.0	27247	42500	5	6	7	0.0	0.0	28.6	42.9	28.6	325000
76884	VALERA	23007	53	30.2	34.0	26.4	5.7	3.8	37957	37370	27	34	44	38.6	22.7	18.2	9.1	11.4	70000
76885	VALLEY SPRING	25932	125	18.4	36.8	34.4	6.4	4.0	45322	48892	49	60	109	19.3	22.9	31.2	17.4	9.2	129375
76887	VOCA	25436	52	15.4	25.0	50.0	5.8	3.8	53038	53053	68	76	43	16.3	18.6	41.9	18.6	4.7	114063
76888	VOSS	22829	51	29.4	35.3	25.5	5.9	3.9	37954	40000	27	34	42	40.5	19.0	19.0	9.5	11.9	70000
76890	ZEPHYR	20488	397	27.0	32.7	31.7	6.8	1.8	42904	45189	42	53	333	18.3	29.4	34.5	14.7	3.0	93409
76901	SAN ANGELO	21864	10250	24.1	32.6	35.2	5.3	2.6	45347	47716	49	60	7027	15.1	45.5	31.7	6.5	1.3	78436
76903	SAN ANGELO	15897	11576	39.4	32.7	23.1	3.4	1.4	31775	34521	11	14	7115	35.8	41.5	19.5	2.2	1.0	59801
76904	SAN ANGELO	27906	13536	22.9	27.4	34.7	9.6	5.4	49712	50940	60	69	7756	3.6	14.9	59.3	19.6	2.6	126721
76905	SAN ANGELO	18169	3768	23.5	34.6	34.5	5.8	1.6	43846	46911	45	55	2657	21.3	37.6	32.8	7.1	1.3	79447
76908	GOODFELLOW AFB	14086	104	21.2	35.6	43.3	0.0	0.0	45000	48178	48	59	8	0.0	0.0	100.0	0.0	0.0	114286
76909	SAN ANGELO	13647	2	100.0	0.0	0.0	0.0	0.0	5000	5000	0	1	0	0.0	0.0	0.0	0.0	0.0	0
76930	BARNHART	25474	68	25.0	27.9	32.4	7.4	7.4	47361	49069	55	65	52	25.0	17.3	36.5	17.3	3.8	107500
76932	BIG LAKE	16101	1049	22.9	40.2	30.9	4.8	1.2	39162	41346	30	39	813	45.8	29.4	19.2	4.4	1.2	56053
76933	BRONTE	18796	570	36.3	30.7	24.6	5.3	3.2	34667	35433	17	21	433	42.5	32.1	21.9	2.1	1.4	58553
76934	CARLSBAD	18590	556	23.7	33.3	35.6	5.6	1.8	45110	47175	49	59	462	24.5	32.0	32.5	9.3	1.7	80909
76935	CHRISTOVAL	22229	267	23.6	31.5	37.8	4.5	2.6	45936	47971	51	61	204	12.3	17.6	48.0	18.1	3.9	114796
76936	ELDORADO	18519	1115	33.8	28.3	30.0	6.0	1.8	35773	36909	20	26	834	42.8	24.9	18.1	8.2	6.0	61765
76937	EOLA	20593	155	25.8	32.9	31.6	6.5	3.2	40985	43838	36	46	120	29.2	20.8	30.8	15.8	3.3	90000
76940	MERETA	23116	65	23.1	27.7	38.5	6.2	4.6	49311	50000	60	69	51	17.6	27.5	35.3	11.8	7.8	98333
76941	MERTZON	22867	629	27.5	28.3	34.2	5.2	4.8	43945	46820	45	56	487	25.9	29.4	32.0	9.9	2.9	83108
76943	OZONA	16874	1508	33.0	30.1	31.2	4.0	1.7	35000	36030	18	23	1066	41.5	24.4	25.9	6.3	2.0	62468
76945	ROBERT LEE	20494	784	35.2	29.6	27.2	5.7	2.3	35741	37223	20	26	609	41.1	31.5	20.7	4.1	2.6	59561
76949	SILVER	21125	11	36.4	36.4	27.3	0.0	0.0	37303	32290	24	32	9	33.3	33.3	33.3	0.0	0.0	75000
76950	SONORA	20251	1581	30.0	28.9	31.4	6.3	3.3	42857	45093	42	53	1132	38.8	28.2	21.2	7.2	4.6	62653
76951	STERLING CITY	19887	479	28.8	31.5	31.5	5.4	2.7	41739	42733	38	49	362	34.0	36.7	19.9	7.7	1.7	62059
76955	VANCOURT	19772	56	17.9	30.4	41.1	8.9	1.8	51719	51531	65	74	42	7.1	14.3	45.2	31.0	2.4	139286
76957	WALL	18526	15	26.7	33.3	33.3	6.7	0.0	42343	42343	40	51	11	0.0	9.1	54.5	36.4	0.0	143750
77002	HOUSTON	23159	2389	30.6	14.0	33.0	9.4	13.0	55300	60517	72	79	303	17.8	11.2	32.0	29.4	9.6	143611
77003	HOUSTON	10443	3764	51.2	24.6	19.5	3.4	1.3	24149	24276	3	4	1275	28.2	37.5	30.1	4.1	0.1	69792
77004	HOUSTON	19454	14245	46.9	20.0	23.2	5.9	4.0	27504	30441	5	7	4717	10.2	20.8	39.6	22.9	6.6	125664
77005	HOUSTON	67223	9709	9.7	11.7	23.2	13.7	41.6	125215	125712	99	99	6795	1.6	1.3	7.0	28.9	61.1	497742
77006	HOUSTON	48338	11932	18.6	19.5	39.1	11.7	11.0	58585	61245	76	83	3740	3.6	6.8	21.0	45.6	23.0	250559
77007	HOUSTON	30445	13538	26.3	19.9	33.9	10.4	9.5	52691	54708	67	75	6238	7.1	19.1	29.5	32.3	12.0	152645
77008	HOUSTON	28008	14137	20.6	24.5	40.1	9.1	5.7	53026	55578	68	76	7281	5.8	14.8	42.1	33.4	3.8	146407
77009	HOUSTON	18063	14744	29.8	26.0	33.3	7.4	3.4	41163	44368	37	47	7721	20.0	30.9	31.0	15.6	2.5	88665
77010	HOUSTON	25816	60	90.0	5.0	0.0	0.0	5.0	10893	10476	0	1	3	0.0	0.0	0.0	0.0	100.0	475000
	TEXAS	24551		22.3	25.0	34.3	11.1	7.3	52382	54495				16.5	22.7	36.5	19.7	4.6	109784
	UNITED STATES	27277		20.9	24.4	35.3	11.7	7.6	54719	56938				9.3	13.1	31.6	32.6	13.5	162279

ZIP CODE #	POST OFFICE NAME	FINANCIAL SERVICES: Auto Loan	FINANCIAL SERVICES: Home Loan	FINANCIAL SERVICES: Invest-ments	FINANCIAL SERVICES: Retire-ment Plans	THE HOME: Home Improvements: Home Repair	THE HOME: Home Improvements: Lawn & Garden	THE HOME: Furnishings: Comput-ers & Hard-ware-Personal	THE HOME: Furnishings: Major Appli-ances	THE HOME: Furnishings: TV, Radio, Sound Equip-ment	THE HOME: Furnishings: Furni-ture	ENTERTAINMENT: Dine out/ Carry out	ENTERTAINMENT: Sports Equip-ment	ENTERTAINMENT: Fees & Tickets	ENTERTAINMENT: Toys & Games	ENTERTAINMENT: Travel	ENTERTAINMENT: Cable TV	PERSONAL: Apparel & Services	PERSONAL: Auto Repairs	PERSONAL: Health Insur-ance	PERSONAL: Pets & Supplies
76682	RIESEL	84	66	80	64	67	83	65	78	71	63	70	58	56	72	64	76	47	73	80	93
76687	THORNTON	88	68	107	67	74	92	69	87	73	64	72	64	58	70	73	79	48	80	88	102
76689	VALLEY MILLS	96	80	101	80	82	101	80	95	84	75	83	72	71	84	81	90	56	89	98	112
76690	WALNUT SPRINGS	73	54	79	52	57	75	55	70	60	51	59	52	45	59	55	66	39	64	72	83
76691	WEST	86	72	78	71	72	86	72	82	77	69	75	61	64	78	70	82	51	77	86	97
76692	WHITNEY	81	64	90	61	68	86	64	80	70	62	68	58	55	67	66	76	45	74	84	94
76693	WORTHAM	77	55	78	54	57	79	58	73	65	53	63	55	47	64	57	72	42	68	78	87
76701	WACO	56	46	43	49	44	47	63	51	62	57	63	42	56	61	54	63	44	58	56	63
76704	WACO	40	28	26	30	27	34	37	34	42	37	41	25	33	41	31	45	28	38	41	43
76705	WACO	72	60	53	60	57	64	68	64	69	65	69	50	61	71	61	70	48	67	67	78
76706	WACO	58	41	38	43	39	44	64	49	60	54	60	41	50	59	48	59	42	56	51	60
76707	WACO	57	46	40	46	44	50	55	51	58	53	57	39	49	58	48	61	40	55	56	62
76708	WACO	73	69	61	69	67	71	71	70	73	71	73	53	69	73	68	74	51	72	74	83
76710	WACO	85	76	76	78	76	81	85	81	87	84	87	62	82	86	82	88	60	86	89	97
76711	WACO	63	50	41	46	48	53	55	55	58	55	58	39	47	59	48	61	40	57	58	64
76712	WOODWAY	125	129	119	129	127	122	123	123	121	128	122	94	126	124	123	119	85	121	119	143
76801	BROWNWOOD	72	59	67	59	60	73	64	69	68	60	67	52	57	67	61	73	45	68	75	83
76802	EARLY	91	72	86	70	73	90	71	85	77	70	76	63	61	78	70	83	51	79	87	101
76820	ART	100	69	110	69	72	106	77	95	80	62	79	79	56	78	76	87	51	89	101	117
76821	BALLINGER	71	51	67	49	53	70	55	67	61	51	59	50	44	60	53	66	40	63	71	78
76823	BANGS	79	55	80	53	57	80	58	73	65	54	64	55	46	65	57	72	42	68	77	87
76825	BRADY	64	49	58	47	49	63	53	60	58	50	57	45	45	57	50	63	38	59	65	71
76827	BROOKESMITH	122	98	158	96	108	129	98	125	103	92	101	91	85	97	106	109	67	115	123	144
76828	BURKETT	79	54	86	54	57	83	60	75	63	49	62	62	44	61	60	68	40	70	79	92
76831	CASTELL	106	84	135	83	92	112	85	108	89	78	88	79	72	84	91	95	58	99	107	125
76832	CHEROKEE	82	66	106	65	72	87	66	84	69	62	68	61	57	65	71	73	45	77	83	97
76834	COLEMAN	69	51	67	50	52	70	56	66	62	51	60	50	46	61	54	67	40	63	72	78
76836	DOOLE	74	51	82	51	53	78	57	71	59	46	58	58	42	58	56	64	38	66	74	87
76837	EDEN	87	62	89	61	64	91	68	84	75	59	72	64	53	73	66	82	48	78	91	100
76841	FORT MC KAVETT	93	75	121	73	82	99	75	95	78	70	77	69	65	74	81	83	51	88	94	110
76842	FREDONIA	91	63	100	62	66	96	70	86	72	56	71	71	51	71	69	79	46	81	91	106
76844	GOLDTHWAITE	78	58	86	57	62	82	61	77	67	56	65	57	50	65	62	73	43	71	81	90
76845	GOULDBUSK	89	61	98	61	64	94	68	85	71	55	70	70	50	70	68	77	45	79	89	104
76848	HEXT	82	66	107	65	73	87	66	84	69	62	68	61	57	66	72	74	45	77	83	97
76849	JUNCTION	81	60	91	58	63	84	62	78	68	58	66	58	51	66	63	74	44	73	81	92
76852	LOHN	94	65	104	65	68	99	72	89	75	58	74	74	53	73	72	82	48	84	95	110
76853	LOMETA	75	57	85	55	61	79	59	74	64	54	63	55	49	62	61	70	42	69	78	87
76854	LONDON	80	64	104	63	70	85	64	82	67	60	66	60	56	64	70	72	44	75	81	95
76856	MASON	89	63	97	62	66	92	68	85	73	59	72	66	53	72	68	80	47	79	89	102
76857	MAY	76	66	87	61	71	83	64	78	69	66	67	53	59	65	68	74	45	73	84	90
76858	MELVIN	98	67	108	67	71	103	75	93	78	61	77	77	55	76	74	85	50	87	98	114
76859	MENARD	69	50	74	48	52	71	53	66	59	49	57	50	42	58	52	64	38	62	70	78
76861	MILES	91	72	93	71	73	94	72	87	77	67	76	67	62	77	72	83	51	81	90	104
76862	MILLERSVIEW	94	64	103	64	67	99	72	89	74	58	74	73	52	73	71	81	48	83	94	109
76864	MULLIN	87	60	95	59	62	91	66	82	69	54	68	68	48	67	66	75	44	77	87	101
76865	NORTON	83	57	91	57	60	87	63	79	66	51	65	65	46	65	63	72	42	73	83	97
76866	PAINT ROCK	93	64	102	64	67	98	71	88	74	58	73	73	52	73	71	81	47	83	93	109
76869	PONTOTOC	89	61	97	61	64	94	68	84	70	55	70	70	50	69	67	77	45	79	89	104
76870	PRIDDY	81	56	89	56	58	86	62	77	64	50	64	64	45	63	62	70	41	72	81	95
76871	RICHLAND SPRINGS	84	57	92	57	60	88	64	79	66	52	66	66	47	65	63	72	43	74	84	98
76872	ROCHELLE	72	55	88	54	59	76	56	71	59	51	58	54	47	57	60	63	38	66	72	84
76873	ROCKWOOD	69	48	76	48	50	73	53	66	55	43	54	54	39	54	53	60	35	61	69	81
76874	ROOSEVELT	77	60	96	59	65	81	61	77	64	56	63	58	51	61	65	68	42	71	77	90
76875	ROWENA	64	44	71	44	46	68	49	61	51	40	50	50	36	50	49	56	33	57	64	75
76877	SAN SABA	77	57	83	55	60	81	61	76	67	55	65	56	49	65	60	73	43	70	81	89
76878	SANTA ANNA	64	47	59	47	47	64	53	60	57	47	55	47	43	56	50	61	37	58	65	72
76880	STAR	95	65	104	65	68	100	72	90	75	59	74	74	53	74	72	82	48	84	95	111
76882	TALPA	96	66	105	66	69	101	73	91	76	59	75	75	54	75	73	83	49	85	96	112
76883	TELEGRAPH	51	41	66	41	45	54	41	52	43	39	43	38	36	41	45	46	28	48	52	61
76884	VALERA	93	64	102	64	67	98	71	88	74	58	73	73	52	73	71	81	47	83	93	109
76885	VALLEY SPRING	99	79	127	78	87	104	79	100	83	74	82	73	68	78	86	88	54	93	99	116
76887	VOCA	100	70	112	70	74	105	77	95	80	63	79	78	57	78	77	87	51	89	100	117
76888	VOSS	93	64	102	64	67	98	71	88	74	57	73	73	52	72	71	80	47	82	93	108
76890	ZEPHYR	94	67	97	65	70	95	69	88	77	64	75	66	55	76	68	84	50	81	91	105
76901	SAN ANGELO	83	74	71	74	72	79	79	78	80	76	79	61	73	81	74	81	55	79	81	93
76903	SAN ANGELO	63	53	47	50	51	55	57	58	61	58	61	41	52	61	53	63	42	60	61	67
76904	SAN ANGELO	92	86	87	88	86	89	92	89	92	90	92	68	89	91	89	93	64	91	93	106
76905	SAN ANGELO	80	72	69	69	70	72	74	76	73	74	74	58	67	74	71	73	51	75	73	88
76908	GOODFELLOW AFB	80	42	32	49	38	36	75	52	71	70	75	52	57	85	55	65	52	67	48	64
76909	SAN ANGELO	9	4	4	5	3	4	12	6	10	8	10	7	7	10	7	9	7	9	6	8
76930	BARNHART	114	78	125	78	82	120	87	108	90	70	89	89	64	89	87	99	58	101	114	133
76932	BIG LAKE	77	64	68	61	63	72	64	71	66	64	66	54	56	68	61	69	45	68	70	84
76933	BRONTE	81	60	87	58	63	84	64	79	70	58	68	59	52	68	64	76	45	74	84	93
76934	CARLSBAD	93	67	96	65	69	95	69	87	76	64	75	65	55	76	68	84	49	80	91	104
76935	CHRISTOVAL	90	73	117	71	80	96	73	92	76	68	75	67	63	72	79	81	50	85	91	107
76936	ELDORADO	82	61	71	56	61	75	63	74	68	61	68	53	51	68	60	73	46	71	76	86
76937	EOLA	101	70	111	70	73	107	77	96	81	63	80	80	57	79	77	88	52	90	102	119
76940	MERETA	110	76	121	76	79	116	84	104	87	68	86	86	62	86	84	95	56	98	110	129
76941	MERTZON	103	72	109	71	75	106	77	97	83	67	81	76	59	82	76	91	53	89	101	117
76943	OZONA	77	58	64	53	57	70	60	69	65	59	64	50	49	65	56	69	43	67	71	81
76945	ROBERT LEE	79	59	88	58	63	82	62	78	68	57	66	57	51	66	63	74	44	72	81	91
76949	SILVER	64	51	83	50	56	68	51	65	54	48	53	48	44	51	56	57	35	60	64	76
76950	SONORA	89	73	75	67	71	80	74	81	77	74	77	60	64	78	71	79	52	80	81	95
76951	STERLING CITY	93	66	97	64	69	95	69	87	75	62	74	67	54	75	68	83	49	80	91	104
76955	VANCOURT	112	77	123	77	80	118	85	106	89	69	88	88	62	87	85	97	57	99	112	130
76957	WALL	86	59	95	59	62	91	66	82	68	53	68	68	48	67	65	75	44	76	86	101
77002	HOUSTON	110	82	86	94	80	82	121	93	119	112	122	83	107	117	104	117	87	111	101	119
77003	HOUSTON	55	42	34	38	40	39	49	47	51	52	53	33	43	52	43	51	37	51	45	53
77004	HOUSTON	65	54	53	56	53	57	67	59	69	63	68	47	61	68	59	70	48	65	65	73
77005	HOUSTON	202	245	286	261	265	228	230	224	215	242	217	178	266	215	252	206	164	219	203	254
77006	HOUSTON	113	92	99	104	91	86	127	99	120	119	125	89	116	121	114	116	90	115	99	124
77007	HOUSTON	103	93	89	93	91	85	106	96	104	107	107	76	101	104	100	102	76	103	93	112
77008	HOUSTON	90	87	83	86	86	83	94	88	92	94	93	68	91	91	90	91	65	92	89	103
77009	HOUSTON	82	73	61	67	71	69	75	75	77	80	78	53	70	78	70	78	55	77	74	86
77010	HOUSTON	45	33	41	38	35	41	54	44	59	49	58	34	48	50	48	63	40	54	62	57
	TEXAS	104	96	90	94	93	94	99	97	99	101	100	75	94	101	94	99	70	99	96	114
	UNITED STATES	100	100	100	100	100	100	100	100	100	100	100	100	100	100	100	100	100	100	100	100

ZIP CODE			POPULATION			2000-2009 ANNUAL RATE		HOUSEHOLDS					FAMILIES		
#	POST OFFICE NAME	COUNTY FIPS CODE	2000	2009	2014	% Rate	State Centile	2000	2009	2014	% Annual Rate 2000-2009	2009 Average HH Size	2000	2009	% Annual Rate 2000-2009
77011	HOUSTON	201	22662	23261	23837	0.3	34	6226	6362	6508	0.2	3.58	4884	4881	0.0
77012	HOUSTON	201	25094	25979	26656	0.4	37	6669	6783	6934	0.2	3.81	5398	5383	0.0
77013	HOUSTON	201	18394	19501	20276	0.6	46	5339	5595	5811	0.5	3.38	4184	4288	0.3
77014	HOUSTON	201	20375	28597	32877	3.7	90	7716	10241	11672	3.1	2.79	4891	6244	2.7
77015	HOUSTON	201	50647	56496	60019	1.2	63	16418	17925	18938	1.0	3.15	12454	13256	0.7
77016	HOUSTON	201	29743	30659	31593	0.3	34	9683	9941	10224	0.3	3.06	7349	7369	0.0
77017	HOUSTON	201	32843	35848	37519	1.0	58	9661	10289	10745	0.7	3.46	7446	7712	0.4
77018	HOUSTON	201	26540	27675	28610	0.5	42	10601	10953	11284	0.4	2.51	6749	6732	0.0
77019	HOUSTON	201	16062	19751	21698	2.3	81	8082	9721	10613	2.0	1.98	3240	3629	1.2
77020	HOUSTON	201	28697	30361	31517	0.6	46	8275	8675	8984	0.5	3.38	6180	6331	0.3
77021	HOUSTON	201	24434	29094	31534	1.9	76	8755	10778	11760	2.3	2.61	5831	6686	1.5
77022	HOUSTON	201	31417	32914	34099	0.5	42	9856	10225	10572	0.4	3.18	6915	6970	0.1
77023	HOUSTON	201	33023	34715	35879	0.5	42	9654	10041	10348	0.4	3.41	7199	7304	0.2
77024	HOUSTON	201	32488	34928	36285	0.8	52	13931	14713	15210	0.6	2.36	8979	9223	0.3
77025	HOUSTON	201	24383	25683	26695	0.6	46	11645	12174	12621	0.5	2.09	6006	5980	0.0
77026	HOUSTON	201	27481	28019	28691	0.2	30	9503	9635	9843	0.1	2.89	6422	6300	-0.2
77027	HOUSTON	201	13752	14491	15109	0.6	46	8222	8582	8905	0.5	1.68	2864	2865	0.0
77028	HOUSTON	201	16473	17601	18387	0.7	49	5505	5856	6107	0.7	2.98	4012	4156	0.4
77029	HOUSTON	201	18147	19023	19660	0.5	42	5709	5917	6095	0.4	3.19	4334	4390	0.1
77030	HOUSTON	201	11133	11784	12310	0.6	46	5054	5233	5492	0.4	1.96	2375	2321	-0.2
77031	HOUSTON	201	16825	18454	19332	1.0	58	6063	6455	6726	0.7	2.86	4119	4232	0.3
77032	HOUSTON	201	10835	12546	13813	1.6	71	3434	3943	4339	1.5	3.11	2604	2914	1.2
77033	HOUSTON	201	27678	29510	30803	0.7	49	8877	9470	9889	0.7	3.10	6759	7029	0.4
77034	HOUSTON	201	26807	31653	34429	1.8	75	9532	11037	11937	1.6	2.87	6580	7310	1.1
77035	HOUSTON	201	37417	39086	40199	0.5	42	13637	13922	14269	0.2	2.79	9135	9028	-0.1
77036	HOUSTON	201	76146	83545	86812	1.0	58	28311	29483	30445	0.4	2.81	18012	18079	0.0
77037	HOUSTON	201	17681	18366	18836	0.4	37	5112	5174	5277	0.1	3.52	4185	4158	-0.1
77038	HOUSTON	201	21488	27002	30095	2.5	82	6320	7690	8548	2.1	3.50	5054	6062	2.0
77039	HOUSTON	201	27782	29212	30399	0.5	42	7694	8006	8296	0.4	3.64	6340	6489	0.3
77040	HOUSTON	201	39161	43791	46704	1.2	63	14443	15922	16912	1.1	2.74	10112	10933	0.8
77041	HOUSTON	201	25238	34571	39418	3.5	89	7656	10381	11815	3.3	3.33	6305	8432	3.2
77042	HOUSTON	201	35630	37429	38872	0.5	42	17708	18517	19204	0.5	2.01	8373	8282	-0.1
77043	HOUSTON	201	24353	25797	26801	0.6	46	8134	8534	8851	0.5	2.99	6014	6158	0.3
77044	HOUSTON	201	13368	22691	27144	5.9	95	4187	7047	8406	5.8	3.22	3404	5648	5.6
77045	HOUSTON	201	24721	28293	30806	1.5	69	7246	8220	8938	1.4	3.43	5940	6705	1.3
77046	HOUSTON	201	471	503	523	0.7	49	307	327	341	0.7	1.53	122	123	0.1
77047	HOUSTON	201	11105	18375	21868	5.6	95	3675	5961	7057	5.4	3.08	2857	4565	5.2
77048	HOUSTON	201	14274	16598	18026	1.6	71	4729	5465	5914	1.6	3.04	3633	4075	1.2
77049	HOUSTON	201	16567	22024	24786	3.1	87	5109	6846	7723	3.2	3.22	4103	5383	3.0
77050	HOUSTON	201	4357	4686	4890	0.8	52	1286	1370	1424	0.7	3.42	1047	1095	0.5
77051	HOUSTON	201	13233	15324	16559	1.6	71	4876	5622	6062	1.6	2.72	3226	3593	1.2
77053	HOUSTON	157	26112	30537	33989	1.7	73	7302	8288	9195	1.4	3.65	6199	6935	1.2
77054	HOUSTON	201	16381	19902	21628	2.1	79	9277	10986	11915	1.8	1.77	3478	4093	1.8
77055	HOUSTON	201	41608	45003	47253	0.9	55	13560	14465	15135	0.7	3.07	9632	9968	0.4
77056	HOUSTON	201	14031	16834	18467	2.0	78	7427	8968	9867	2.1	1.82	3251	3696	1.4
77057	HOUSTON	201	33979	36202	37698	0.7	49	19178	20293	21119	0.6	1.78	6910	6789	-0.2
77058	HOUSTON	201	14926	15832	16673	0.6	46	7878	8351	8764	0.6	1.89	3783	3790	0.0
77059	HOUSTON	201	15068	16294	17072	0.8	52	4736	5088	5308	0.8	3.20	4180	4428	0.6
77060	HOUSTON	201	37171	41982	44524	1.3	65	11988	12961	13642	0.8	3.23	8516	8940	0.5
77061	HOUSTON	201	25467	27562	28538	0.9	55	8908	9195	9455	0.3	2.98	6282	6287	0.0
77062	HOUSTON	201	28382	29422	30285	0.4	37	10296	10568	10838	0.3	2.78	7998	8065	0.1
77063	HOUSTON	201	28768	31030	32495	0.8	52	15456	16485	17234	0.7	1.87	6203	6221	0.0
77064	HOUSTON	201	35833	43915	48548	2.2	80	11676	14234	15716	2.2	3.07	9197	11035	2.0
77065	HOUSTON	201	27155	32312	35444	1.9	76	10368	12183	13292	1.8	2.63	7159	8261	1.6
77066	HOUSTON	201	27991	31507	33678	1.3	65	8945	9959	10610	1.2	3.16	7210	7876	1.0
77067	HOUSTON	201	23489	29689	32569	2.6	83	7472	9120	9953	2.2	3.24	5552	6529	1.8
77068	HOUSTON	201	9140	9805	10250	0.8	52	3266	3493	3639	0.7	2.80	2629	2756	0.5
77069	HOUSTON	201	14734	15878	16814	0.8	52	6799	7267	7655	0.7	2.18	4211	4350	0.4
77070	HOUSTON	201	33429	44732	51046	3.2	87	12413	16706	19096	3.3	2.66	9185	11875	2.8
77071	HOUSTON	201	24924	26070	26937	0.5	42	9178	9503	9785	0.4	2.74	6433	6467	0.1
77072	HOUSTON	201	51318	57675	60979	1.3	65	15761	17249	18158	1.0	3.33	12169	12989	0.7
77073	HOUSTON	201	12809	28924	35796	9.2	98	5281	10869	13217	8.1	2.66	3259	6808	8.3
77074	HOUSTON	201	41059	43738	45099	0.7	49	14738	15148	15555	0.3	2.82	9493	9412	-0.1
77075	HOUSTON	201	22675	31351	35866	3.6	90	7609	10265	11677	3.3	3.05	5496	7104	2.8
77076	HOUSTON	201	29038	32548	34567	1.2	63	8221	8969	9473	0.9	3.62	6550	6998	0.7
77077	HOUSTON	201	42947	49582	53438	1.6	71	20464	23266	24948	1.4	2.12	11033	12188	1.1
77078	HOUSTON	201	14496	15772	16680	0.9	55	4145	4479	4717	0.8	3.49	3452	3674	0.7
77079	HOUSTON	201	31922	33172	34258	0.4	37	12584	13057	13457	0.4	2.54	9225	9321	0.1
77080	HOUSTON	201	47869	50797	52673	0.6	46	15501	16158	16693	0.4	3.12	11086	11208	0.1
77081	HOUSTON	201	48932	53793	55937	1.0	58	17102	18034	18761	0.6	2.97	10466	10588	0.1
77082	HOUSTON	201	35881	46083	51683	2.7	84	15386	19506	21853	2.6	2.35	8649	10519	2.1
77083	HOUSTON	201	52140	64004	71954	2.2	80	15660	18517	20699	1.8	3.45	13016	15102	1.6
77084	HOUSTON	201	63163	84765	96455	3.2	87	21687	28756	32601	3.1	2.94	16435	21406	2.9
77085	HOUSTON	201	7786	12577	15174	5.3	95	2296	3725	4494	5.4	3.37	1869	2976	5.2
77086	HOUSTON	201	19864	25988	29227	2.9	86	5867	7592	8509	2.8	3.42	4809	6124	2.6
77087	HOUSTON	201	36263	39522	41411	0.9	55	10373	11074	11563	0.7	3.53	8035	8380	0.5
77088	HOUSTON	201	50309	53592	56036	0.7	49	16479	17417	18172	0.6	3.07	12774	13182	0.3
77089	HOUSTON	201	36824	48644	54223	3.1	87	12295	16060	17846	2.9	3.02	9689	12583	2.9
77090	HOUSTON	201	26115	30328	32868	1.6	71	11636	13533	14675	1.6	2.20	6237	6832	1.0
77091	HOUSTON	201	23110	25277	26661	1.0	58	8290	8753	9169	0.6	2.87	5613	5799	0.4
77092	HOUSTON	201	37872	39520	40823	0.5	42	14159	14454	14841	0.2	2.73	9276	9148	-0.2
77093	HOUSTON	201	45903	49128	51255	0.7	49	12372	13060	13585	0.6	3.73	9897	10222	0.3
77094	HOUSTON	201	7830	9264	10704	1.8	75	2346	2780	3210	1.9	3.33	2185	2569	1.8
77095	HOUSTON	201	39275	64814	76159	5.6	95	13302	21711	25412	5.4	2.98	10745	16616	4.8
77096	HOUSTON	201	35491	37246	38531	0.5	42	14617	15222	15729	0.4	2.44	9714	9738	0.0
77098	HOUSTON	201	12325	12703	13101	0.3	34	7309	7507	7729	0.3	1.68	2235	2148	-0.4
77099	HOUSTON	201	43755	48950	52111	1.2	63	14347	15666	16592	1.0	3.10	10615	11295	0.7
77301	CONROE	339	25022	31203	35795	2.4	82	8118	9843	11282	2.1	3.08	5726	6786	1.9
77302	CONROE	339	12030	17599	21490	4.2	92	4175	6058	7400	4.1	2.90	3396	4820	3.9
77303	CONROE	339	11257	14936	17744	3.1	87	3950	5172	6134	3.0	2.88	3065	3938	2.7
77304	CONROE	339	15288	21228	25606	3.6	90	6383	8776	10590	3.5	2.40	4139	5516	3.2
77306	CONROE	339	8332	11984	14465	4.0	91	2718	3815	4584	3.7	3.13	2106	2888	3.5
77316	MONTGOMERY	339	9783	14111	17056	4.0	91	3542	5050	6108	3.9	2.78	2698	3754	3.6
77318	WILLIS	339	9900	14515	17809	4.2	92	3796	5514	6769	4.1	2.63	3007	4266	3.9
77320	HUNTSVILLE	471	33141	34059	33977	0.3	34	8431	8544	8549	0.1	2.52	5731	5722	0.0
	TEXAS					1.9					1.8	2.78			1.7
	UNITED STATES					1.0					1.1	2.59			0.9

ZIP CODE #	POST OFFICE NAME	RACE (%) White 2000	White 2009	Black 2000	Black 2009	Asian/Pacific 2000	Asian/Pacific 2009	% Hispanic Origin 2000	% Hispanic Origin 2009	2009 AGE DISTRIBUTION (%) 0-4	5-9	10-14	15-19	20-24	25-44	45-64	65-84	85+	18+	MEDIAN AGE 2009	% 2009 Males	% 2009 Females
77011	HOUSTON	49.1	47.4	1.5	1.3	0.3	0.2	94.5	96.5	9.9	9.4	8.3	7.9	7.1	30.2	19.5	6.9	0.8	67.6	29.7	52.2	47.8
77012	HOUSTON	50.9	49.5	3.4	2.8	1.2	1.1	91.9	94.4	11.0	10.0	8.7	8.7	8.9	29.8	17.3	5.0	0.6	65.0	26.5	53.2	46.8
77013	HOUSTON	42.2	39.5	25.1	23.4	1.1	1.1	59.5	66.0	10.3	9.4	8.1	8.1	8.2	31.2	18.1	5.7	0.8	67.2	28.2	52.5	47.5
77014	HOUSTON	38.8	34.4	36.2	36.0	10.4	11.2	26.0	34.6	9.6	8.0	7.0	7.1	9.3	36.5	19.2	3.0	0.2	71.6	28.9	49.8	50.2
77015	HOUSTON	56.4	50.0	18.5	18.5	2.2	2.5	43.9	55.1	9.5	8.8	7.9	7.8	8.1	29.7	21.4	6.3	0.5	69.1	29.4	50.0	50.0
77016	HOUSTON	10.3	10.5	79.0	76.8	0.3	0.3	17.4	20.8	7.1	7.8	7.6	8.0	6.5	23.4	25.5	12.9	1.2	72.6	36.2	47.0	53.0
77017	HOUSTON	48.4	43.7	3.0	2.8	4.1	3.7	74.3	82.2	10.2	9.2	8.1	8.6	8.7	28.8	18.4	6.8	1.3	67.4	28.1	50.8	49.2
77018	HOUSTON	70.1	63.2	11.4	11.3	0.9	1.1	31.5	44.1	6.6	6.5	6.5	6.0	5.4	26.6	28.1	11.8	2.4	76.8	40.1	49.6	50.4
77019	HOUSTON	81.6	72.8	6.0	8.2	3.3	4.2	18.9	31.8	4.9	4.1	4.6	5.4	7.6	35.6	27.5	9.1	1.4	83.0	37.2	52.1	47.9
77020	HOUSTON	42.0	41.6	30.7	28.7	0.2	0.3	65.2	69.0	9.4	8.9	8.1	8.6	7.7	27.4	20.5	8.0	1.2	68.3	29.7	51.0	49.0
77021	HOUSTON	9.0	11.9	82.2	77.0	1.2	2.1	12.2	14.9	7.7	7.4	6.5	7.0	7.1	24.6	24.3	13.5	2.1	74.4	36.4	46.3	53.7
77022	HOUSTON	43.2	41.0	24.3	22.8	0.5	0.5	64.1	70.4	9.1	8.8	8.1	8.1	7.1	27.5	21.6	8.3	1.4	69.1	31.2	50.7	49.3
77023	HOUSTON	53.8	50.7	1.9	1.6	1.5	1.3	86.0	91.3	9.9	9.1	8.0	8.2	8.5	30.9	19.1	5.6	0.8	68.4	28.5	52.0	48.0
77024	HOUSTON	88.3	81.7	0.8	1.1	8.1	11.2	5.4	12.2	4.4	5.3	6.6	6.9	4.6	18.4	33.5	16.6	3.7	79.3	47.3	47.1	52.9
77025	HOUSTON	68.3	62.2	11.9	12.7	10.8	13.3	18.0	24.7	6.4	5.8	5.7	5.3	7.1	31.0	26.1	9.9	2.8	78.9	37.1	49.0	51.0
77026	HOUSTON	16.5	18.1	67.5	63.3	0.3	0.4	31.1	35.8	8.2	8.4	8.0	7.9	6.6	24.0	23.7	11.1	2.0	70.5	34.2	48.5	51.5
77027	HOUSTON	89.3	85.0	2.7	3.5	3.7	5.0	9.0	15.1	3.5	2.9	2.9	2.7	8.1	40.4	26.8	10.4	2.1	89.1	37.7	48.9	51.1
77028	HOUSTON	7.1	7.0	84.8	82.9	0.2	0.2	11.7	14.7	7.1	7.7	7.4	7.9	6.7	23.2	25.5	13.0	1.4	73.0	36.4	47.2	52.8
77029	HOUSTON	44.2	41.9	30.3	29.5	0.2	0.2	55.6	62.1	8.7	8.3	7.9	8.1	7.1	25.7	21.8	10.5	2.0	70.2	32.2	48.8	51.2
77030	HOUSTON	72.2	65.4	5.4	6.2	17.0	20.9	8.7	13.8	5.3	4.1	4.0	7.5	13.4	34.4	22.2	7.4	1.6	84.7	32.6	48.8	51.2
77031	HOUSTON	38.2	34.1	36.8	36.3	6.4	7.3	32.4	39.0	9.5	8.2	7.1	7.0	8.5	30.9	21.2	6.6	0.9	71.0	30.2	49.7	50.3
77032	HOUSTON	46.4	41.0	34.1	33.8	1.3	1.3	34.0	44.6	12.0	9.1	7.4	7.8	10.4	28.0	18.9	5.9	0.5	67.0	26.9	48.5	51.5
77033	HOUSTON	6.1	6.5	84.3	82.0	0.8	0.8	13.7	16.6	7.5	7.7	7.8	8.4	6.6	23.0	24.8	12.9	1.4	71.9	35.6	45.9	54.1
77034	HOUSTON	60.8	55.4	9.8	8.7	4.6	4.9	47.1	58.6	9.1	8.4	7.4	7.4	8.1	30.9	20.6	7.4	0.7	70.8	30.5	49.9	50.1
77035	HOUSTON	39.7	36.1	39.7	39.4	5.1	5.4	28.2	34.7	9.2	8.4	7.5	7.5	8.2	29.0	21.7	7.2	1.2	70.4	30.6	47.8	52.2
77036	HOUSTON	37.2	35.6	25.0	23.1	15.0	14.8	44.7	52.5	10.4	8.6	6.9	7.0	9.4	33.5	17.3	5.7	1.1	70.2	28.9	50.5	49.5
77037	HOUSTON	65.8	60.2	4.0	3.7	2.8	2.8	62.4	74.4	9.7	9.1	8.3	8.6	7.3	29.1	19.9	7.4	0.7	67.6	29.3	51.5	48.5
77038	HOUSTON	38.5	36.4	24.6	22.3	6.9	7.1	52.2	60.1	10.8	9.5	8.3	8.2	9.2	30.9	18.1	4.5	0.4	66.4	27.0	50.1	49.9
77039	HOUSTON	48.8	45.0	16.9	15.1	1.8	1.8	60.7	70.5	9.9	9.1	8.1	8.8	8.9	30.1	18.7	5.9	0.5	67.7	27.7	50.4	49.6
77040	HOUSTON	68.2	62.0	11.1	11.4	6.8	8.5	28.8	38.1	7.5	7.3	7.2	7.1	7.4	30.1	26.7	6.1	0.6	73.6	33.9	50.2	49.8
77041	HOUSTON	56.4	50.0	9.8	9.3	13.5	13.9	36.2	48.3	9.1	8.9	8.4	7.3	5.6	30.9	23.9	5.4	0.5	69.0	32.1	49.9	50.1
77042	HOUSTON	62.0	55.9	16.5	17.6	9.7	11.4	21.4	29.3	7.1	5.8	5.2	5.2	9.8	38.2	20.8	7.0	0.9	79.2	32.8	49.3	50.7
77043	HOUSTON	63.2	56.3	5.9	5.8	7.9	9.2	39.3	49.7	7.9	7.6	7.1	7.0	7.2	28.0	23.6	10.3	1.3	73.2	34.1	50.3	49.7
77044	HOUSTON	53.5	48.2	28.1	29.3	0.9	1.6	26.9	32.6	8.6	8.6	8.4	8.6	6.9	28.0	24.5	5.8	0.6	68.9	31.3	49.3	50.7
77045	HOUSTON	17.8	17.9	61.0	56.9	0.8	0.9	33.3	39.2	8.0	8.5	8.6	8.9	7.5	25.9	23.7	8.0	0.7	69.2	30.9	46.9	53.1
77046	HOUSTON	93.2	90.3	1.7	2.2	2.3	3.6	9.3	15.9	2.2	1.6	1.0	0.6	2.8	25.0	39.8	23.3	3.8	95.2	54.5	46.3	53.7
77047	HOUSTON	17.4	16.0	71.5	69.6	0.7	0.6	17.5	23.3	7.5	7.7	7.8	7.7	5.9	25.3	24.8	12.0	1.3	72.3	36.2	46.7	53.3
77048	HOUSTON	5.8	6.7	88.2	83.3	0.4	0.6	7.7	12.9	8.7	9.0	8.7	9.4	7.3	24.0	23.2	8.9	0.8	67.9	30.3	44.7	55.3
77049	HOUSTON	46.8	46.1	27.7	23.0	3.4	3.5	38.1	46.7	8.5	8.3	8.1	8.3	7.9	28.8	23.6	5.9	0.5	69.9	30.1	49.5	50.5
77050	HOUSTON	23.4	21.7	52.5	48.9	0.3	0.3	35.8	43.7	9.9	9.1	8.4	8.0	6.8	24.4	23.3	9.3	0.6	67.7	31.7	49.2	50.8
77051	HOUSTON	2.1	2.7	93.8	92.6	1.1	1.1	3.9	5.4	7.8	7.8	7.7	8.4	6.9	21.7	24.1	13.3	2.3	71.6	35.5	45.7	54.3
77053	HOUSTON	22.0	21.9	53.1	49.6	1.3	1.4	40.2	45.8	8.6	9.0	9.1	9.5	8.4	27.6	22.5	4.9	0.3	67.3	28.3	48.3	51.7
77054	HOUSTON	35.5	27.5	37.2	41.3	19.4	20.7	9.5	14.3	6.5	3.9	3.0	3.5	15.2	46.9	16.1	3.7	1.2	84.9	29.3	47.4	52.6
77055	HOUSTON	68.6	63.6	4.0	3.7	3.6	3.8	55.0	65.3	9.4	8.6	7.5	7.6	7.7	29.6	21.1	7.3	1.3	70.1	30.5	51.9	48.1
77056	HOUSTON	88.3	82.9	2.1	2.7	3.8	5.3	11.2	18.9	3.8	3.6	3.8	3.6	7.1	30.0	29.0	14.3	4.9	86.8	43.7	48.9	51.1
77057	HOUSTON	75.4	69.7	4.6	5.0	5.2	6.5	22.9	30.3	4.9	3.9	3.3	3.7	10.1	40.9	23.2	8.8	1.3	86.2	34.9	51.0	49.0
77058	HOUSTON	78.0	70.5	5.0	6.0	8.0	10.5	12.6	19.8	5.3	4.5	4.0	4.7	10.6	33.9	24.7	11.2	1.0	83.7	35.9	50.4	49.6
77059	HOUSTON	80.8	73.3	2.5	3.3	13.5	19.0	6.0	10.1	7.5	8.9	9.0	7.5	3.2	24.4	31.8	7.3	0.4	69.3	39.5	50.6	49.4
77060	HOUSTON	38.2	35.4	26.5	24.2	1.5	1.4	56.8	65.2	11.4	10.0	8.2	8.6	9.7	32.5	15.6	3.8	0.3	65.4	26.1	51.5	48.5
77061	HOUSTON	34.4	31.5	29.0	26.1	6.8	6.7	47.8	57.1	10.3	9.1	7.8	7.8	8.7	29.9	19.2	6.3	1.1	68.3	28.6	50.0	50.0
77062	HOUSTON	77.5	69.9	4.0	5.0	12.1	16.2	10.0	15.8	7.0	7.6	8.0	7.1	5.2	25.9	29.7	8.8	0.7	72.7	38.5	49.3	50.7
77063	HOUSTON	69.6	63.7	12.1	12.6	6.4	8.0	22.4	31.2	5.8	4.5	3.8	4.1	8.9	39.5	22.5	8.5	2.4	84.0	35.0	49.9	50.1
77064	HOUSTON	64.0	56.1	9.5	10.4	12.4	14.3	25.8	35.6	8.9	8.0	7.5	7.2	6.8	32.9	23.6	4.5	0.5	71.0	32.0	49.5	50.5
77065	HOUSTON	76.4	68.4	8.0	9.8	7.8	10.6	14.3	22.0	8.2	7.5	6.9	6.5	6.8	34.2	23.9	5.3	0.7	73.2	32.9	49.8	50.2
77066	HOUSTON	50.3	45.0	21.2	21.2	12.5	13.9	27.7	35.5	7.2	7.1	7.1	7.4	6.8	30.1	26.6	7.0	0.5	74.0	33.9	49.5	50.5
77067	HOUSTON	27.9	28.6	44.9	40.7	9.2	8.9	35.7	43.5	10.2	9.0	7.9	8.1	9.9	31.9	19.4	3.3	0.3	68.2	27.4	48.8	51.2
77068	HOUSTON	71.7	63.0	12.8	15.4	7.0	9.3	13.2	20.3	5.7	5.8	6.6	6.8	5.4	25.0	32.8	11.0	0.8	77.5	40.6	47.6	52.4
77069	HOUSTON	88.7	83.8	3.6	4.8	4.4	6.3	6.0	10.2	5.0	4.8	5.2	5.3	5.8	24.4	32.5	15.6	1.4	81.8	44.6	48.0	52.0
77070	HOUSTON	82.8	75.7	5.8	7.3	4.7	6.5	12.7	21.0	7.4	7.0	7.1	7.2	6.6	29.4	26.4	7.7	1.2	73.9	34.9	48.8	51.2
77071	HOUSTON	28.7	24.1	54.4	55.8	8.7	9.7	13.6	17.9	7.9	7.5	7.1	7.0	6.4	28.2	26.4	8.5	0.9	73.2	34.4	46.4	53.6
77072	HOUSTON	33.2	30.7	28.6	27.0	18.2	18.3	35.9	43.6	9.1	8.4	7.4	8.3	9.6	30.8	20.4	5.5	0.5	70.1	28.7	49.0	51.0
77073	HOUSTON	66.1	55.3	16.4	19.1	4.6	7.5	25.0	36.4	8.6	7.2	6.3	6.5	9.4	33.4	22.2	5.9	0.6	74.3	30.5	49.5	50.5
77074	HOUSTON	46.0	41.0	21.4	20.6	7.0	7.3	43.2	52.8	9.4	8.4	7.3	7.2	8.4	31.0	19.7	6.9	1.8	70.7	30.3	49.5	50.5
77075	HOUSTON	46.8	43.0	18.2	16.0	5.4	6.4	50.3	58.9	9.4	8.5	7.6	7.3	9.0	31.8	20.6	5.4	0.5	70.2	29.2	50.1	49.9
77076	HOUSTON	61.3	57.4	5.8	5.2	0.7	0.7	74.2	83.2	10.5	9.8	8.7	8.6	7.9	29.3	18.4	6.0	0.9	66.0	27.7	51.6	48.4
77077	HOUSTON	74.8	68.4	9.2	10.1	7.7	10.5	14.5	21.4	6.4	5.9	5.8	5.6	7.5	30.2	28.2	9.1	1.3	78.7	37.6	48.7	51.3
77078	HOUSTON	15.1	14.1	69.5	67.1	0.2	0.3	23.9	28.9	9.4	9.6	9.4	9.8	7.9	25.4	21.7	6.3	0.5	65.5	27.7	47.1	52.9
77079	HOUSTON	82.2	76.1	3.1	3.6	9.0	12.1	10.1	15.9	5.5	5.9	6.7	6.9	6.2	21.8	31.5	14.1	1.4	77.6	42.6	47.9	52.1
77080	HOUSTON	59.7	54.1	5.2	5.1	4.7	5.0	57.9	68.1	9.6	8.5	7.2	7.4	8.4	31.3	18.7	7.7	1.3	70.4	29.8	51.9	48.1
77081	HOUSTON	48.4	45.9	9.1	8.1	4.7	4.6	71.5	77.6	10.5	9.1	7.4	7.6	9.9	37.6	15.1	2.6	0.2	68.5	27.4	54.0	46.0
77082	HOUSTON	53.0	46.3	19.7	20.9	14.3	16.4	22.2	30.2	7.4	6.3	5.7	5.6	9.3	37.2	22.8	5.1	0.7	77.3	31.8	48.7	51.3
77083	HOUSTON	39.5	33.9	24.2	24.2	21.2	23.7	26.3	32.6	8.0	7.7	7.6	8.0	7.5	29.5	26.0	5.3	0.4	71.7	31.8	48.7	51.3
77084	HOUSTON	70.6	62.0	9.1	10.4	5.9	7.4	24.3	35.3	8.5	8.0	7.7	7.5	7.1	31.5	24.7	4.6	0.4	71.0	31.5	49.1	50.9
77085	HOUSTON	25.5	23.0	52.7	54.6	0.9	0.9	38.8	40.4	8.7	8.5	8.2	8.6	7.6	27.8	23.5	6.6	0.6	69.4	30.3	49.6	50.4
77086	HOUSTON	41.8	38.5	26.2	25.4	10.5	10.8	39.2	48.4	9.0	8.3	7.8	8.9	9.2	29.9	21.4	5.1	0.5	69.6	28.7	50.2	49.8
77087	HOUSTON	42.9	40.4	16.2	14.7	0.9	0.8	72.4	78.6	9.5	9.0	8.2	8.5	7.9	28.5	20.1	7.0	1.2	68.2	29.2	50.8	49.2
77088	HOUSTON	25.5	21.7	55.5	56.4	5.8	6.0	21.7	26.5	8.2	8.2	7.8	8.1	7.3	27.4	24.3	7.8	0.9	70.8	31.9	47.3	52.7
77089	HOUSTON	61.2	53.9	12.6	12.6	10.9	14.0	28.2	37.0	7.1	7.2	7.1	7.1	6.3	28.8	26.8	8.8	0.8	74.2	35.3	49.4	50.6
77090	HOUSTON	68.2	59.8	17.5	21.0	4.7	5.8	18.5	27.2	7.4	5.9	5.3	5.9	11.2	35.2	20.5	7.6	1.0	78.2	31.0	49.6	50.4
77091	HOUSTON	21.0	19.1	65.5	64.4	0.7	0.7	21.7	27.1	8.7	7.9	7.5	8.2	8.9	26.1	22.3	9.1	1.3	71.0	30.5	47.1	52.9
77092	HOUSTON	52.4	47.2	19.1	17.8	1.5	1.6	46.6	57.7	9.6	7.9	7.1	7.3	9.2	29.9	20.8	7.4	0.8	71.2	29.9	49.8	50.2
77093	HOUSTON	53.9	51.6	13.0	11.5	0.5	0.5	72.6	80.2	10.2	9.7	8.8	8.7	7.3	28.0	19.3	7.3	0.7	66.0	28.6	51.4	48.6
77094	HOUSTON	84.5	78.0	2.4	3.2	10.8	15.4	5.5	9.6	8.2	9.8	11.1	8.9	1.7	26.8	29.6	3.4	0.4	64.2	37.4	50.2	49.8
77095	HOUSTON	78.9	70.1	6.6	8.8	7.5	10.4	12.2	18.8	9.0	9.1	8.6	7.2	4.5	32.6	24.9	3.7	0.3	68.3	33.8	49.1	50.9
77096	HOUSTON	65.9	61.2	17.1	16.9	5.9	7.8	18.7	24.9	7.0	6.7	6.5	6.8	6.8	25.0	26.1	12.9	2.4	75.7	38.4	47.9	52.1
77098	HOUSTON	85.9	80.2	2.0	2.5	3.5	4.9	16.3	24.6	4.0	2.7	2.3	2.6	8.7	43.8	25.6	8.5	1.7	89.6	36.7	51.5	48.5
77099	HOUSTON	31.9	28.3	29.7	29.4	22.7	23.6	25.9	32.3	8.6	8.2	7.6	7.7	8.3	31.2	22.4	5.5	0.4	70.9	30.4	49.0	51.0
77301	CONROE	63.6	58.5	13.4	13.2	0.7	0.9	41.6	50.0	9.6	8.5	7.5	8.2	8.4	30.2	19.2	7.3	1.2	69.8	29.4	51.5	48.5
77302	CONROE	92.6	89.5	0.9	1.3	0.5	0.6	9.3	13.8	7.5	7.3	7.1	7.0	6.2	24.8	27.4	11.7	1.1	73.7	37.4	49.5	50.5
77303	CONROE	89.8	85.9	1.8	2.1	0.4	0.5	12.7	18.5	7.8	7.5	7.3	7.2	6.7	28.5	25.3	8.6	0.9	72.7	34.2	49.6	50.4
77304	CONROE	89.6	86.0	5.1	6.4	1.1	1.5	10.0	13.8	6.2	5.8	5.7	5.9	6.7	28.8	26.3	12.2	2.3	78.7	37.7	48.5	51.5
77306	CONROE	86.2	78.7	0.5	0.6	0.4	0.5	18.7	29.3	8.7	8.1	7.7	7.6	7.0	27.9	24.0	8.2	0.8	70.9	32.2	50.8	49.2
77316	MONTGOMERY	90.2	86.7	4.2	5.2	0.3	0.4	7.2	11.1	7.0	7.2	7.3	6.9	5.7	26.1	29.1	9.7	1.0	74.2	37.7	49.5	50.5
77318	WILLIS	94.0	91.3	1.5	2.0	0.5	0.7	5.8	9.3	6.0	6.2	6.8	6.7	4.6	23.2	31.5	13.8	1.1	76.6	42.4	49.2	50.8
77320	HUNTSVILLE	66.2	63.5	27.6	29.0	0.6	0.7	15.5	18.9	4.4	4.1	4.1	9.4	12.4	35.1	22.2	7.4	0.9	84.2	33.3	66.5	33.5
	TEXAS	71.0	67.6	11.5	11.4	2.8	3.5	32.0	37.4	7.9	7.5	7.2	7.5	7.4	28.3	24.0	8.8	1.4	73.0	33.6	49.7	50.3
	UNITED STATES	75.1	72.0	12.3	12.7	3.8	4.6	12.5	15.7	6.8	6.7	6.6	7.1	6.9	27.0	26.0	10.9	1.9	75.7	36.9	49.2	50.8

#	POST OFFICE NAME	2009 Per Capita Income	2009 HH Income Base	2009 HOUSEHOLD INCOME DISTRIBUTION (%) Less than $25,000	$25,000 to $49,999	$50,000 to $99,999	$100,000 to $149,999	$150,000 or More	MEDIAN HOUSEHOLD INCOME 2009	2014	2009 National Centile	2009 State Centile	2009 Home Value Base	2009 HOME VALUE DISTRIBUTION (%) Less than $50,000	$50,000 to $89,999	$90,000 to $174,999	$175,000 to $399,999	$400,000 or More	2009 Median Home Value
77011	HOUSTON	10229	6362	43.1	30.2	23.4	2.4	0.9	28786	30341	6	8	2700	37.0	54.6	7.6	0.8	0.0	54473
77012	HOUSTON	10273	6783	40.6	32.6	23.3	1.8	1.7	29011	30656	7	8	2636	35.2	54.3	10.4	0.2	0.0	57514
77013	HOUSTON	14163	5595	28.1	27.8	37.6	5.1	1.3	40526	45958	34	44	2738	16.0	51.9	29.8	2.2	0.0	75072
77014	HOUSTON	22856	10241	13.8	28.7	43.9	9.4	4.1	54493	59302	70	78	4134	9.0	9.5	62.2	19.0	0.3	130812
77015	HOUSTON	19075	17925	20.7	24.9	42.1	9.4	2.8	52315	54631	67	75	10451	18.6	28.8	47.7	4.3	0.6	93044
77016	HOUSTON	13629	9941	41.7	26.4	26.5	3.9	1.5	29569	31776	7	9	6768	42.0	46.5	10.4	0.9	0.3	54202
77017	HOUSTON	14286	10289	27.8	28.2	37.8	4.1	2.1	40695	44911	35	45	5586	15.6	57.7	25.0	1.6	0.1	69662
77018	HOUSTON	26614	10953	20.5	22.8	40.9	9.5	6.2	54669	57041	71	78	7616	6.3	13.4	55.8	23.3	1.3	130977
77019	HOUSTON	58134	9721	16.8	14.8	32.9	14.0	21.4	71704	69475	88	90	3905	1.0	5.9	15.2	25.2	52.6	433065
77020	HOUSTON	10676	8675	48.3	24.9	22.9	3.1	0.8	25998	27125	4	5	4098	45.0	47.1	7.6	0.3	0.0	52276
77021	HOUSTON	18334	10778	44.8	21.8	24.7	4.9	3.9	29354	32097	7	9	5778	35.8	34.3	16.9	9.6	3.4	60038
77022	HOUSTON	11536	10225	45.1	27.3	23.4	3.5	0.8	27507	29286	5	7	4786	32.9	50.6	15.1	0.6	0.8	58738
77023	HOUSTON	13715	10041	34.7	27.2	30.6	5.3	2.2	36220	38935	21	28	4774	13.2	52.0	28.1	6.3	0.4	71670
77024	HOUSTON	61416	14713	11.7	13.6	29.5	12.4	32.8	88989	85300	95	96	10357	2.1	7.6	12.7	20.8	56.8	475485
77025	HOUSTON	41422	12174	19.1	19.0	34.9	14.4	12.5	59983	61654	77	84	5386	3.9	7.5	27.9	49.6	11.2	207386
77026	HOUSTON	10806	9635	57.1	23.4	16.9	1.4	1.2	20711	21199	2	2	4183	61.5	29.4	8.2	0.8	0.0	41450
77027	HOUSTON	69931	8582	9.4	13.4	39.7	17.5	20.0	77878	75217	91	93	2948	5.5	6.4	9.6	33.3	45.1	369313
77028	HOUSTON	12078	5856	48.8	25.5	22.1	1.8	1.7	25681	26710	4	5	4034	54.5	37.0	7.4	0.7	0.5	47635
77029	HOUSTON	13857	5917	32.8	29.4	32.9	3.6	1.3	36772	40471	23	30	4001	33.9	55.7	10.0	0.3	0.0	56946
77030	HOUSTON	48335	5233	16.1	12.5	40.0	12.2	19.2	72537	69997	88	91	1996	4.4	7.7	11.8	32.4	43.7	358553
77031	HOUSTON	20105	6455	23.2	26.7	38.3	8.6	3.3	50088	53266	61	70	2692	1.7	6.7	87.4	4.0	0.2	122304
77032	HOUSTON	13431	3943	41.6	24.9	28.0	3.0	2.5	30599	33176	9	11	1684	28.7	46.3	22.9	1.0	1.1	64684
77033	HOUSTON	13272	9470	40.9	26.9	27.5	3.0	1.7	32310	34386	12	15	6507	50.4	41.5	7.3	0.6	0.2	49822
77034	HOUSTON	21197	11037	18.4	27.1	43.0	7.5	4.0	52009	54263	66	74	5623	4.0	46.7	40.8	7.5	0.9	89508
77035	HOUSTON	20457	13922	25.0	25.5	37.0	9.0	3.4	48115	51378	57	67	6261	6.9	21.0	59.1	12.3	0.7	114329
77036	HOUSTON	15909	29483	33.7	32.6	27.6	4.1	1.9	35049	36742	18	23	5573	19.5	12.7	61.8	5.5	0.5	110780
77037	HOUSTON	13847	5174	26.8	29.3	37.6	5.3	1.0	42079	50035	40	50	3885	24.0	46.8	27.9	1.1	0.1	72400
77038	HOUSTON	15595	7690	20.2	29.9	41.8	5.9	2.2	49736	52261	60	70	4006	31.4	42.7	24.9	1.0	0.0	68918
77039	HOUSTON	13449	8006	28.8	26.6	38.4	4.8	1.4	41168	45638	37	47	4922	18.5	52.3	26.7	2.4	0.2	74025
77040	HOUSTON	28499	15922	12.5	21.0	43.1	14.5	8.9	61656	63742	80	85	9631	4.7	19.1	54.1	20.7	1.3	115681
77041	HOUSTON	29039	10381	11.8	16.5	41.7	14.8	15.2	70655	68679	87	90	8878	10.9	21.3	40.0	19.7	8.2	114139
77042	HOUSTON	35279	18517	14.6	24.8	43.5	9.5	7.5	55555	57636	72	79	4495	10.3	9.5	21.4	44.9	13.9	211966
77043	HOUSTON	22632	8534	16.7	23.3	43.9	11.0	5.1	55974	58248	73	80	5102	8.7	17.6	58.0	15.4	0.3	118815
77044	HOUSTON	19335	7047	19.0	20.8	46.2	10.0	4.0	54600	56733	71	78	5569	21.6	35.7	30.0	10.5	2.1	81539
77045	HOUSTON	16114	8220	23.4	26.2	40.9	7.1	2.4	50216	52502	62	71	5882	12.1	61.7	25.7	0.2	0.2	74665
77046	HOUSTON	96132	327	10.4	11.0	20.8	23.5	34.3	122348	123205	99	99	230	0.0	0.0	32.6	45.7	21.7	219048
77047	HOUSTON	18613	5961	24.2	23.6	38.8	10.7	2.6	51114	53717	64	72	4641	20.7	46.8	30.5	1.9	0.0	71476
77048	HOUSTON	14673	5465	38.1	24.5	31.6	4.0	1.7	35923	39535	20	26	3324	21.1	52.3	24.7	1.6	0.2	65279
77049	HOUSTON	17535	6846	18.2	32.9	38.8	8.0	2.1	47934	51563	56	66	4748	10.6	46.7	39.8	3.0	0.0	85341
77050	HOUSTON	15510	1370	26.6	33.6	30.2	5.5	4.1	40331	42302	34	43	1059	38.6	40.2	19.5	0.8	0.8	59640
77051	HOUSTON	12525	5622	54.6	21.8	19.4	3.0	1.3	22195	22856	2	3	3141	59.4	31.7	7.7	0.8	0.4	45296
77053	HOUSTON	15177	8288	19.6	29.3	41.4	8.3	1.4	50673	51756	63	72	5914	15.1	50.5	33.2	1.2	0.0	77099
77054	HOUSTON	30975	10986	25.9	22.6	42.3	6.2	3.0	50696	53097	63	72	2349	19.7	45.6	32.5	1.7	0.5	75506
77055	HOUSTON	21621	14465	24.4	24.6	35.0	8.1	7.9	50556	52738	62	71	6700	8.5	21.5	31.6	29.4	9.0	126345
77056	HOUSTON	73738	8968	10.0	10.8	37.1	13.7	28.3	85786	83547	94	95	3892	1.5	4.4	9.6	24.3	60.2	497311
77057	HOUSTON	50213	20293	14.7	18.0	41.9	12.5	12.9	60868	62394	79	84	6738	5.0	12.8	28.7	25.1	28.5	194104
77058	HOUSTON	42169	8351	11.0	20.0	46.0	13.3	9.6	62484	63298	81	86	3230	6.9	10.1	40.2	36.8	5.9	159766
77059	HOUSTON	48485	5088	3.0	3.6	27.7	25.0	40.7	132486	132536	99	99	4541	1.8	0.4	23.1	63.2	11.5	246220
77060	HOUSTON	13552	12961	31.3	33.4	31.1	3.1	1.1	35426	38027	19	24	3794	13.2	46.0	38.3	1.8	0.7	83750
77061	HOUSTON	17182	9195	29.4	30.0	31.6	6.5	2.5	38638	41500	29	36	3584	10.6	26.9	56.1	5.5	0.9	103911
77062	HOUSTON	39943	10568	7.6	12.8	37.9	19.5	22.3	86968	84984	94	96	7886	1.6	2.8	53.6	35.2	6.8	162976
77063	HOUSTON	41239	16485	18.2	21.6	39.9	10.6	9.7	56980	59969	74	81	4479	7.1	18.3	25.8	33.8	15.0	171373
77064	HOUSTON	28994	14234	7.5	14.2	48.7	18.5	11.2	76129	74484	90	93	10585	4.0	15.2	56.9	23.0	0.9	124840
77065	HOUSTON	32074	12183	8.9	14.0	47.3	20.9	8.9	72180	70523	88	90	7039	0.5	6.0	65.8	27.4	0.3	136251
77066	HOUSTON	24686	9959	13.3	17.5	44.3	18.2	6.7	66136	66231	84	88	7261	3.3	21.9	58.4	15.9	0.5	127723
77067	HOUSTON	16983	9120	19.4	28.2	45.2	5.2	2.0	51032	53262	64	72	4299	6.6	38.6	54.1	0.7	0.0	93309
77068	HOUSTON	40613	3493	14.1	12.6	31.7	19.2	22.4	84010	80609	94	95	2607	1.0	1.5	40.2	49.8	7.4	192482
77069	HOUSTON	52283	7267	9.8	15.4	36.8	16.5	21.6	78797	75295	92	93	4573	1.9	6.8	17.7	57.0	16.7	234236
77070	HOUSTON	34270	16706	8.7	16.0	45.3	17.7	12.4	72652	70975	88	91	10374	1.3	8.1	54.6	34.1	1.9	153265
77071	HOUSTON	24507	9503	18.9	22.4	40.4	12.7	5.6	55499	57982	72	79	5745	5.5	14.6	65.9	13.0	1.0	122243
77072	HOUSTON	15548	17249	24.8	29.3	38.0	6.1	1.8	42801	50327	42	53	7896	12.1	41.2	46.0	0.6	0.1	87276
77073	HOUSTON	24852	10869	13.8	24.1	46.9	11.0	4.3	56760	59151	74	81	6126	0.1	13.1	64.7	18.5	3.6	131232
77074	HOUSTON	18055	15148	26.6	30.2	35.2	5.5	2.4	40097	43611	33	42	5236	11.3	32.2	52.7	3.3	0.4	95168
77075	HOUSTON	19240	10265	17.8	26.8	46.4	7.0	2.0	52764	55476	67	76	5860	10.3	33.3	53.5	2.7	0.2	95179
77076	HOUSTON	11824	8969	31.3	32.4	32.5	2.8	0.9	35700	38688	20	26	5412	22.4	57.6	19.3	0.4	0.2	65479
77077	HOUSTON	42039	23266	9.9	18.7	43.2	15.3	12.9	66659	67102	85	88	10116	0.9	3.8	40.4	47.0	7.9	185501
77078	HOUSTON	12155	4479	38.4	23.0	34.7	2.6	1.3	35261	39433	19	24	2716	29.1	54.7	15.2	0.7	0.3	59545
77079	HOUSTON	43566	13057	10.5	14.7	35.9	16.7	22.3	79086	74987	92	93	8401	1.8	5.3	21.8	51.4	19.7	271230
77080	HOUSTON	17478	16158	24.4	28.6	36.6	7.6	2.7	43920	50759	45	56	6498	8.6	19.4	64.9	6.0	1.1	112218
77081	HOUSTON	14672	18034	35.6	32.3	26.2	3.8	2.1	33688	35468	15	19	1231	23.2	11.0	39.9	24.2	1.8	123516
77082	HOUSTON	30434	19506	11.7	22.7	47.7	11.6	6.2	58123	59250	75	82	7476	3.5	14.8	59.8	20.9	1.1	122850
77083	HOUSTON	22101	18517	11.7	20.2	45.5	16.5	6.1	65497	65909	84	87	12858	3.0	16.5	69.7	10.8	0.1	118141
77084	HOUSTON	27243	28756	9.5	17.0	49.4	15.9	8.2	66772	66388	85	88	19171	1.1	15.6	68.2	14.0	1.1	118663
77085	HOUSTON	17964	3725	18.1	22.3	49.3	8.3	2.0	55341	57585	72	79	2702	10.2	42.6	46.3	0.5	0.4	87623
77086	HOUSTON	16782	7592	20.2	28.9	41.1	6.8	3.0	50477	53109	62	71	4854	5.5	47.8	45.4	1.0	0.4	88279
77087	HOUSTON	12871	11074	33.2	28.2	33.0	4.2	1.4	36964	39978	23	31	6535	16.6	61.0	21.3	0.7	0.4	67810
77088	HOUSTON	18295	17417	27.9	21.6	38.4	8.9	3.3	50320	52306	62	71	11248	15.9	30.3	50.5	3.3	0.1	94227
77089	HOUSTON	26627	16060	10.6	18.0	47.1	16.3	8.0	67979	68836	86	89	11505	0.3	13.6	71.7	12.8	1.6	117505
77090	HOUSTON	31847	13533	13.3	23.3	46.8	10.2	6.4	57034	58709	74	81	3316	2.6	10.2	59.6	25.8	1.8	141705
77091	HOUSTON	15809	8753	36.8	27.3	27.3	5.8	2.8	33631	35790	15	18	4186	26.4	31.4	36.0	6.0	0.2	76318
77092	HOUSTON	18558	14454	25.2	31.3	35.8	5.7	2.0	40797	44466	35	45	5553	9.9	31.0	56.3	2.9	0.0	99082
77093	HOUSTON	10845	13060	39.5	28.3	27.8	3.0	1.4	31467	33472	10	13	8032	46.9	43.3	9.0	0.6	0.2	51727
77094	HOUSTON	63345	2780	4.0	5.5	13.6	11.3	65.5	181426	182957	100	100	2623	3.2	0.0	2.0	73.9	20.9	281662
77095	HOUSTON	37282	21711	5.6	10.8	37.0	24.5	22.1	93646	94216	96	97	17302	0.5	2.5	45.2	50.5	1.4	178642
77096	HOUSTON	32681	15222	19.0	22.1	32.9	13.8	12.2	56609	59118	74	80	7627	2.3	3.2	35.3	52.8	6.5	198585
77098	HOUSTON	55582	7507	15.5	19.8	36.7	14.5	13.5	64079	65148	82	87	2263	0.9	1.7	19.6	42.6	35.1	296619
77099	HOUSTON	18055	15666	19.7	26.3	44.6	7.2	2.1	51547	53176	65	73	7546	6.7	30.2	61.6	1.4	0.1	100194
77301	CONROE	15268	9843	30.4	35.4	28.2	4.2	1.8	37457	39113	25	32	4962	27.2	25.9	39.2	6.5	1.1	84254
77302	CONROE	24293	6058	13.5	26.9	41.9	12.6	5.1	62238	64009	80	85	5233	15.3	18.5	40.8	22.2	3.2	123588
77303	CONROE	19697	5172	18.7	32.1	40.3	6.8	2.1	49332	49400	60	69	3835	18.4	29.2	42.0	9.4	1.0	93671
77304	CONROE	31253	8776	16.8	24.4	37.8	13.1	8.0	61397	62761	79	85	4986	9.2	8.5	41.0	31.5	9.9	156860
77306	CONROE	17834	3815	25.7	29.4	35.3	6.9	2.7	46038	47219	51	62	3028	36.7	31.9	25.4	5.8	0.2	59157
77316	MONTGOMERY	21104	5050	22.2	27.9	38.9	8.5	2.5	49920	51400	61	70	4296	14.2	23.2	40.5	17.0	5.2	111866
77318	WILLIS	29652	5514	15.5	20.7	42.3	13.0	8.4	65968	69505	84	88	4708	11.3	12.5	33.6	30.8	11.7	157237
77320	HUNTSVILLE	17712	8544	29.3	28.3	33.8	6.5	2.2	42657	45192	41	52	5578	26.2	25.3	33.8	13.3	1.4	87109
	TEXAS	24551		22.3	25.0	34.3	11.1	7.3	52382	54495				16.5	22.7	36.5	19.7	4.6	109784
	UNITED STATES	27277		20.9	24.4	35.3	11.7	7.6	54719	56938				9.3	13.1	31.6	32.6	13.5	162279

SPENDING POTENTIAL INDICES

ZIP CODE		FINANCIAL SERVICES				THE HOME						ENTERTAINMENT						PERSONAL			
						Home Improvements		Furnishings													
#	POST OFFICE NAME	Auto Loan	Home Loan	Invest-ments	Retire-ment Plans	Home Repair	Lawn & Garden	Comput-ers & Hard-ware-Personal	Major Appli-ances	TV, Radio, Sound Equip-ment	Furni-ture	Dine out/ Carry out	Sports Equip-ment	Fees & Tickets	Toys & Games	Travel	Cable TV	Apparel & Services	Auto Repairs	Health Insur-ance	Pets & Supplies
77011	HOUSTON	60	48	37	41	46	44	50	52	53	55	54	33	44	53	45	53	38	53	49	57
77012	HOUSTON	63	48	38	43	46	44	55	54	57	59	59	36	47	58	48	57	42	57	51	59
77013	HOUSTON	71	61	54	57	60	53	70	65	68	73	71	51	64	69	65	65	50	70	59	73
77014	HOUSTON	99	79	67	81	73	70	96	81	94	98	96	69	86	98	83	90	67	91	78	99
77015	HOUSTON	91	84	70	80	80	76	87	83	86	90	87	63	82	89	81	84	61	86	80	97
77016	HOUSTON	62	55	51	54	52	61	55	58	62	58	61	40	54	60	53	66	42	59	65	70
77017	HOUSTON	74	65	55	59	64	55	72	68	70	76	73	51	66	71	67	67	52	72	61	75
77018	HOUSTON	92	97	89	97	95	99	93	94	95	94	95	70	97	95	95	97	66	95	100	110
77019	HOUSTON	153	150	169	163	156	138	174	151	164	172	169	128	177	164	172	157	125	163	142	178
77020	HOUSTON	57	44	36	40	42	45	48	49	54	52	53	32	43	53	43	56	37	52	52	57
77021	HOUSTON	69	59	56	61	57	66	66	63	72	66	71	47	63	70	61	76	49	68	73	79
77022	HOUSTON	60	48	38	41	46	47	49	52	54	54	54	33	43	54	44	56	38	53	52	58
77023	HOUSTON	72	61	50	54	59	54	67	65	67	70	69	46	60	69	60	67	49	68	61	72
77024	HOUSTON	179	225	265	232	246	216	203	209	193	217	192	157	237	187	230	189	143	201	198	233
77025	HOUSTON	118	112	117	118	114	107	129	114	124	128	126	94	127	122	125	120	90	123	114	136
77026	HOUSTON	47	37	34	36	36	43	42	42	48	43	47	29	38	46	37	51	32	45	49	51
77027	HOUSTON	156	150	169	165	155	142	176	151	167	173	171	128	177	166	172	161	125	163	147	181
77028	HOUSTON	53	44	41	44	42	51	48	48	55	49	53	34	46	53	44	59	36	51	57	60
77029	HOUSTON	69	59	50	54	57	59	60	62	65	65	65	42	56	64	56	67	45	64	64	72
77030	HOUSTON	137	134	151	146	139	122	158	135	147	155	151	116	158	146	155	140	110	146	127	161
77031	HOUSTON	87	70	62	72	66	64	86	74	84	86	86	60	77	87	76	81	60	82	71	89
77032	HOUSTON	60	51	44	51	49	49	61	54	62	60	62	42	56	63	54	63	44	59	56	65
77033	HOUSTON	60	52	48	52	50	59	55	56	61	57	61	39	53	60	52	65	41	58	64	68
77034	HOUSTON	90	79	68	78	75	72	90	81	87	91	90	65	83	90	82	85	63	87	78	95
77035	HOUSTON	83	71	66	73	69	68	84	75	83	84	85	60	79	84	77	81	60	82	75	89
77036	HOUSTON	67	47	43	50	45	44	67	55	66	66	69	46	58	68	57	64	49	65	54	66
77037	HOUSTON	74	70	59	62	69	59	71	70	68	77	70	51	66	70	67	66	49	71	63	77
77038	HOUSTON	82	68	59	66	65	60	81	72	79	83	82	58	73	81	73	76	57	80	68	84
77039	HOUSTON	72	66	56	60	64	55	72	67	69	75	72	51	66	71	67	66	51	71	61	75
77040	HOUSTON	117	110	98	111	106	98	115	106	111	119	113	85	111	115	108	107	79	110	100	126
77041	HOUSTON	145	156	130	150	149	131	140	140	133	152	135	109	143	140	138	126	95	134	123	159
77042	HOUSTON	110	79	74	87	75	75	109	87	107	107	109	75	95	110	92	103	76	102	87	109
77043	HOUSTON	98	95	86	93	93	86	99	94	96	102	98	73	97	98	96	93	69	97	89	108
77044	HOUSTON	97	93	80	89	90	88	88	90	89	93	89	67	85	92	85	89	61	89	87	106
77045	HOUSTON	80	78	68	75	74	76	77	77	79	81	80	56	76	79	75	80	55	78	79	91
77046	HOUSTON	184	195	231	216	207	179	219	191	204	215	211	163	230	202	223	196	157	200	177	224
77047	HOUSTON	82	84	74	83	80	85	78	80	82	82	82	58	81	82	78	84	56	80	86	96
77048	HOUSTON	64	56	49	57	53	59	62	58	66	63	66	43	60	65	57	69	46	63	65	72
77049	HOUSTON	87	82	74	74	81	74	82	83	79	87	81	62	75	82	78	77	56	82	75	93
77050	HOUSTON	82	74	66	68	71	75	72	76	76	77	77	52	68	76	69	79	53	76	79	88
77051	HOUSTON	50	40	38	41	38	47	46	45	52	47	51	32	43	50	41	56	35	48	54	56
77053	HOUSTON	84	81	67	76	77	73	79	78	79	84	80	58	76	81	75	78	56	79	75	91
77054	HOUSTON	84	57	54	64	53	56	85	65	84	81	87	58	73	86	70	82	61	79	68	84
77055	HOUSTON	93	85	80	84	84	75	98	89	94	99	98	71	93	95	93	89	71	96	81	101
77056	HOUSTON	183	174	196	191	180	170	202	176	195	199	200	147	205	194	197	191	145	190	176	212
77057	HOUSTON	126	103	109	114	103	96	136	110	130	133	134	96	126	132	123	125	96	126	108	135
77058	HOUSTON	121	94	88	101	90	93	119	101	119	118	120	83	108	121	105	116	84	114	104	124
77059	HOUSTON	207	265	255	276	267	229	218	224	203	240	206	181	257	212	240	190	153	207	190	252
77060	HOUSTON	65	50	45	50	49	43	66	56	63	67	66	46	58	65	58	60	47	64	51	65
77061	HOUSTON	76	61	54	61	58	56	76	66	74	76	77	53	68	76	68	72	54	74	64	78
77062	HOUSTON	153	171	160	176	169	155	158	155	152	166	154	123	171	156	164	147	111	153	145	180
77063	HOUSTON	112	85	87	94	84	83	117	94	115	113	118	81	106	116	103	112	83	110	97	118
77064	HOUSTON	135	140	117	135	133	118	130	128	124	140	126	100	130	131	126	118	89	124	113	146
77065	HOUSTON	128	121	104	123	114	106	125	115	121	130	123	94	122	127	117	115	86	118	106	136
77066	HOUSTON	113	120	104	117	115	106	113	111	108	118	110	85	115	112	112	105	77	110	103	128
77067	HOUSTON	84	70	61	69	67	61	83	73	80	85	82	59	74	82	74	76	57	79	68	85
77068	HOUSTON	152	179	177	184	181	166	161	161	154	168	156	125	178	156	173	150	112	157	152	187
77069	HOUSTON	161	157	157	164	157	151	165	154	162	168	163	122	167	162	163	159	116	161	154	183
77070	HOUSTON	132	138	124	139	133	122	133	127	127	139	130	101	136	133	131	122	92	127	118	149
77071	HOUSTON	98	98	86	97	93	89	97	93	95	100	97	72	97	98	94	93	67	94	90	110
77072	HOUSTON	75	67	59	64	65	57	77	69	73	79	76	55	71	75	71	70	54	75	63	79
77073	HOUSTON	102	85	73	87	80	77	100	86	97	100	99	71	90	101	88	93	68	94	84	105
77074	HOUSTON	76	61	54	61	59	56	76	66	74	76	77	54	68	76	68	72	54	74	64	78
77075	HOUSTON	90	79	67	76	75	69	87	79	84	91	86	63	80	88	79	81	60	84	74	93
77076	HOUSTON	68	55	43	48	53	49	60	59	62	65	64	41	53	63	54	62	45	63	56	66
77077	HOUSTON	131	115	110	123	112	109	132	116	129	133	131	96	127	132	123	126	93	126	115	141
77078	HOUSTON	65	54	44	53	50	56	58	56	63	60	63	41	54	63	52	66	44	60	62	69
77079	HOUSTON	146	170	181	173	178	157	158	157	150	167	150	121	174	150	170	145	109	154	147	179
77080	HOUSTON	77	67	61	66	65	61	80	71	78	80	81	57	75	79	74	76	58	79	69	83
77081	HOUSTON	65	44	40	46	42	39	66	52	64	65	68	45	56	66	56	61	48	64	50	62
77082	HOUSTON	111	90	77	94	84	82	108	92	105	109	107	77	98	110	94	102	75	101	89	112
77083	HOUSTON	114	117	98	114	110	101	111	107	107	117	109	84	110	112	107	103	76	107	98	125
77084	HOUSTON	121	119	101	119	113	104	117	111	113	123	115	88	116	119	112	109	81	112	103	131
77085	HOUSTON	92	88	73	84	83	79	86	85	86	92	88	63	84	89	82	84	61	86	80	98
77086	HOUSTON	86	78	68	72	77	65	85	80	81	90	83	61	78	83	79	76	59	83	71	89
77087	HOUSTON	71	59	49	54	57	54	64	63	65	68	67	44	58	66	58	65	47	66	60	71
77088	HOUSTON	82	78	68	77	75	74	80	77	81	83	81	59	78	82	76	81	57	80	78	91
77089	HOUSTON	117	120	105	119	115	109	116	113	113	121	115	87	117	116	114	110	80	113	107	132
77090	HOUSTON	109	80	73	87	76	77	107	88	106	106	108	74	94	109	91	103	75	101	89	109
77091	HOUSTON	67	55	50	56	53	57	64	59	67	65	68	45	59	67	58	68	47	65	64	72
77092	HOUSTON	75	59	54	61	57	58	75	65	75	74	76	53	67	76	66	74	54	74	66	79
77093	HOUSTON	67	54	41	46	52	51	55	58	59	61	60	37	48	60	49	60	42	59	56	64
77094	HOUSTON	300	363	313	373	353	298	302	305	279	339	284	254	341	302	317	255	208	279	250	341
77095	HOUSTON	157	180	162	185	176	155	160	158	150	173	153	129	174	159	165	141	111	150	137	180
77096	HOUSTON	108	106	109	110	109	104	115	108	113	116	115	84	116	112	115	111	82	113	109	126
77098	HOUSTON	126	108	118	121	109	103	143	115	136	135	141	101	134	135	132	132	101	131	116	142
77099	HOUSTON	85	75	64	73	71	66	83	75	81	86	83	60	77	84	76	78	58	80	71	89
77301	CONROE	71	60	54	59	58	60	68	64	69	68	70	49	62	70	62	70	49	68	65	76
77302	CONROE	106	105	98	103	104	106	99	103	100	103	100	76	98	102	98	101	69	100	103	121
77303	CONROE	88	81	70	79	78	81	81	81	82	82	82	61	76	85	76	84	57	81	82	97
77304	CONROE	107	106	99	107	104	103	108	104	107	110	108	80	108	108	106	106	75	106	105	123
77306	CONROE	90	80	72	77	77	82	79	82	81	81	81	62	73	85	74	83	55	81	81	98
77316	MONTGOMERY	96	86	78	83	84	90	82	87	85	84	85	64	76	89	77	88	58	84	88	104
77318	WILLIS	118	118	117	117	118	120	108	116	109	112	110	85	108	112	110	111	76	111	114	136
77320	HUNTSVILLE	77	65	64	65	64	69	73	70	74	71	74	54	65	75	66	75	51	73	73	85
	TEXAS	104	96	90	94	93	94	99	97	99	101	100	75	94	101	94	99	70	99	96	114
	UNITED STATES	100	100	100	100	100	100	100	100	100	100	100	100	100	100	100	100	100	100	100	100

POPULATION CHANGE

ZIP CODE			POPULATION			2000-2009 ANNUAL RATE		HOUSEHOLDS					FAMILIES		
#	POST OFFICE NAME	COUNTY FIPS CODE	2000	2009	2014	% Rate	State Centile	2000	2009	2014	% Annual Rate 2000-2009	2009 Average HH Size	2000	2009	% Annual Rate 2000-2009
77327	CLEVELAND	291	19891	22352	23152	1.3	65	6959	7670	7934	1.1	2.83	5150	5614	0.9
77328	CLEVELAND	407	11609	15653	17832	3.3	88	4026	5321	6037	3.1	2.94	3197	4163	2.9
77331	COLDSPRING	407	6235	7081	7427	1.4	67	2584	2951	3101	1.4	2.38	1846	2077	1.3
77335	GOODRICH	373	2089	2229	2311	0.7	49	822	870	901	0.6	2.56	599	624	0.4
77336	HUFFMAN	201	8807	11703	13312	3.1	87	3057	4047	4597	3.1	2.89	2463	3196	2.9
77338	HUMBLE	201	20234	29225	33911	4.1	92	7396	10558	12210	3.9	2.75	5221	7403	3.8
77339	KINGWOOD	201	31116	37506	41230	2.0	78	11509	14162	15691	2.3	2.65	9063	10669	1.8
77340	HUNTSVILLE	471	25209	26964	27267	0.7	49	8585	9124	9242	0.7	2.36	4735	4938	0.5
77345	KINGWOOD	201	22652	28150	31217	2.4	82	7292	8938	9851	2.2	3.15	6410	7774	2.1
77346	HUMBLE	201	27984	52478	63210	7.0	96	9279	17621	21254	7.2	2.98	7959	14853	7.0
77351	LIVINGSTON	373	29866	34117	35507	1.4	67	10656	12360	12924	1.6	2.49	7716	8833	1.5
77354	MAGNOLIA	339	16324	29130	37195	6.5	96	5389	9448	12046	6.3	3.08	4527	7919	6.2
77355	MAGNOLIA	339	13904	23397	29559	5.8	95	4574	7672	9697	5.8	3.05	3751	6164	5.5
77356	MONTGOMERY	339	14176	23300	29441	5.5	95	5869	9590	12126	5.5	2.43	4523	7207	5.2
77357	NEW CANEY	339	17314	20916	23975	2.1	79	5788	6953	7984	2.0	3.00	4622	5428	1.8
77358	NEW WAVERLY	471	3949	3953	4005	0.0	25	1483	1497	1522	0.1	2.55	1068	1062	-0.1
77359	OAKHURST	407	357	384	395	0.8	52	145	157	162	0.9	2.45	107	114	0.7
77360	ONALASKA	373	3876	4644	4898	2.0	78	1753	2118	2242	2.1	2.19	1195	1417	1.9
77362	PINEHURST	339	3239	4499	5492	3.6	90	1139	1554	1893	3.4	2.89	910	1212	3.1
77363	PLANTERSVILLE	185	2355	2562	2661	0.9	55	877	963	1001	1.0	2.66	653	707	0.9
77364	POINTBLANK	407	2621	3261	3486	2.4	82	1164	1468	1576	2.5	2.22	837	1040	2.4
77365	PORTER	339	15613	24999	31407	5.2	94	5362	8541	10733	5.2	2.91	4163	6557	5.0
77371	SHEPHERD	407	7638	8572	8997	1.3	65	2736	3084	3244	1.3	2.75	2043	2273	1.2
77372	SPLENDORA	339	9620	11218	12845	1.7	73	3317	3873	4436	1.7	2.89	2619	2986	1.4
77373	SPRING	201	36385	50161	57679	3.5	89	12302	16990	19528	3.6	2.95	9831	13232	3.3
77375	TOMBALL	201	18005	28354	33846	5.0	94	6435	9744	11514	4.6	2.86	4678	7155	4.7
77377	TOMBALL	201	16369	28548	34260	6.2	96	5432	9410	11261	6.1	3.03	4414	7444	5.8
77378	WILLIS	339	10352	14076	16662	3.4	89	3413	4593	5439	3.3	3.03	2644	3473	3.0
77379	SPRING	201	45973	70129	80871	4.7	93	15093	22923	26374	4.6	3.05	12841	19163	4.4
77380	SPRING	339	19320	25750	29972	3.2	87	7745	10202	11882	3.0	2.52	5346	6855	2.7
77381	SPRING	339	35861	41080	46000	1.5	69	12255	13834	15492	1.3	2.94	9994	11079	1.1
77382	SPRING	339	13541	35710	46446	11.1	98	4392	11630	15069	11.1	3.07	3776	9936	11.0
77384	CONROE	339	4293	14607	19045	14.2	99	1513	4787	6276	13.3	3.05	1291	4003	13.0
77385	CONROE	339	10004	18115	23067	6.6	96	3282	5852	7429	6.5	3.09	2773	4838	6.2
77386	SPRING	339	13498	28377	36727	8.4	97	4669	9563	12329	8.1	2.97	3715	7569	8.0
77388	SPRING	201	26646	37919	43876	3.9	91	8938	12812	14805	4.0	2.96	7588	10685	3.8
77389	SPRING	201	13219	18595	21551	3.8	90	4306	6028	6965	3.7	3.08	3666	5066	3.6
77396	HUMBLE	201	23214	33125	38411	3.9	91	6693	9826	11544	4.2	3.05	5348	7649	3.9
77401	BELLAIRE	201	15569	16450	17004	0.6	46	5983	6212	6392	0.4	2.63	4294	4330	0.1
77406	RICHMOND	157	20588	30326	36978	4.3	92	6102	8750	10742	4.0	3.21	5197	7404	3.9
77407	RICHMOND	157	2252	19856	28324	26.5	100	753	5944	8443	25.0	3.34	655	5111	24.9
77414	BAY CITY	321	24697	24010	23344	-0.3	16	9205	9026	8809	-0.2	2.61	6444	6219	-0.4
77417	BEASLEY	157	2358	3080	3683	2.9	86	838	1045	1244	2.4	2.95	624	760	2.2
77418	BELLVILLE	015	8386	9025	9365	0.8	52	3153	3356	3475	0.7	2.62	2281	2391	0.5
77419	BLESSING	321	1422	1370	1327	-0.4	13	493	476	462	-0.4	2.88	376	359	-0.5
77420	BOLING	481	2166	2277	2284	0.5	42	744	778	781	0.5	2.91	572	592	0.4
77422	BRAZORIA	039	13908	15002	16101	0.8	52	4635	5119	5551	1.1	2.71	3556	3860	0.9
77423	BROOKSHIRE	473	7779	9256	10022	1.9	76	2558	3055	3314	1.9	2.94	1884	2215	1.8
77426	CHAPPELL HILL	477	1804	1937	2011	0.8	52	719	774	805	0.8	2.50	523	555	0.6
77429	CYPRESS	201	35084	64634	78637	6.8	96	11889	21538	26062	6.6	3.00	9963	18194	6.7
77430	DAMON	039	2280	2743	3150	2.0	78	842	1007	1158	2.0	2.72	651	766	1.8
77432	DANEVANG	481	347	354	352	0.2	30	88	90	90	0.2	3.93	73	74	0.1
77433	CYPRESS	201	10329	35858	46755	14.4	99	3219	11226	14612	14.5	3.18	2798	9264	13.8
77434	EAGLE LAKE	089	4445	4523	4583	0.2	30	1602	1631	1654	0.2	2.74	1154	1159	0.0
77435	EAST BERNARD	481	6183	6311	6317	0.2	30	2146	2192	2196	0.2	2.83	1620	1632	0.1
77437	EL CAMPO	481	16004	16345	16280	0.2	30	5677	5794	5774	0.2	2.79	4196	4222	0.1
77440	ELMATON	321	92	89	86	-0.4	13	36	35	34	-0.3	2.54	26	25	-0.4
77441	FULSHEAR	157	2216	2964	3663	3.2	87	827	1083	1333	3.0	2.74	684	893	2.9
77442	GARWOOD	089	2140	2213	2263	0.4	37	827	859	879	0.4	2.58	593	607	0.3
77444	GUY	157	674	845	949	2.5	82	247	308	347	2.4	2.74	189	228	2.0
77445	HEMPSTEAD	473	9742	11521	12224	1.8	75	3550	4158	4402	1.7	2.73	2500	2881	1.5
77447	HOCKLEY	201	8794	10976	12211	2.4	82	2938	3651	4063	2.4	2.99	2387	2917	2.2
77449	KATY	201	38225	76541	95697	7.8	97	11997	23695	29497	7.6	3.22	10044	19509	7.4
77450	KATY	201	47772	73529	87387	4.8	93	15463	23001	27100	4.4	3.20	13271	19863	4.5
77455	LOUISE	481	2409	2178	2083	-1.1	3	839	759	727	-1.1	2.87	644	575	-1.2
77456	MARKHAM	321	840	808	782	-0.4	13	305	297	289	-0.3	2.72	222	214	-0.4
77457	MATAGORDA	321	887	860	838	-0.3	16	424	415	405	-0.2	2.05	272	263	-0.4
77458	MIDFIELD	321	261	251	243	-0.4	13	94	91	88	-0.4	2.76	72	69	-0.5
77459	MISSOURI CITY	157	33020	53134	66601	5.3	95	10804	16167	20033	4.5	3.28	9404	14022	4.4
77461	NEEDVILLE	157	8119	9611	10991	1.8	75	2779	3150	3594	1.4	3.03	2198	2446	1.2
77465	PALACIOS	321	6546	6565	6457	0.0	25	2179	2194	2162	0.1	2.97	1626	1618	-0.1
77468	PLEDGER	321	262	253	245	-0.4	13	97	95	92	-0.2	2.66	75	72	-0.4
77469	RICHMOND	157	21116	33205	40724	5.0	94	6062	9691	12043	5.2	3.24	4896	7735	5.1
77471	ROSENBERG	157	28589	34721	40126	2.1	79	9310	10710	12268	1.5	3.22	7170	8142	1.4
77474	SEALY	015	10293	12446	13495	2.1	79	3693	4393	4743	1.9	2.81	2772	3253	1.7
77477	STAFFORD	157	27759	36092	42333	2.9	86	9695	12032	14023	2.4	2.99	7054	8505	2.0
77478	SUGAR LAND	157	24675	28646	32434	1.6	71	8476	9314	10466	1.0	3.03	6877	7449	0.9
77479	SUGAR LAND	157	54769	71614	85588	2.9	86	16310	20599	24677	2.6	3.42	14725	18437	2.5
77480	SWEENY	039	7603	8534	9305	1.3	65	2704	3086	3376	1.4	2.74	2101	2357	1.3
77482	VAN VLECK	321	2548	2465	2397	-0.4	13	915	895	873	-0.2	2.75	702	680	-0.3
77483	WADSWORTH	321	215	207	202	-0.4	13	76	74	72	-0.3	2.62	53	51	-0.4
77484	WALLER	473	13104	14689	15566	1.2	63	3705	4269	4572	1.5	2.81	2744	3099	1.3
77485	WALLIS	157	3952	4501	4998	1.4	67	1436	1592	1764	1.1	2.83	1096	1195	0.9
77486	WEST COLUMBIA	039	7104	7264	7583	0.2	30	2685	2799	2937	0.5	2.57	1979	2023	0.2
77488	WHARTON	481	14422	14482	14352	0.0	25	5431	5453	5407	0.0	2.57	3732	3687	-0.1
77489	MISSOURI CITY	157	32835	37540	42170	1.5	69	10144	11073	12395	1.0	3.38	8545	9194	0.8
77493	KATY	201	15050	22184	25510	4.3	92	4715	6894	7896	4.2	3.21	3973	5748	4.1
77494	KATY	157	11918	48816	67344	16.5	100	3788	14927	20499	16.0	3.27	3282	12217	15.3
77498	SUGAR LAND	157	29003	50226	63230	6.1	95	8980	14725	18418	5.5	3.41	7731	12502	5.3
77502	PASADENA	201	35355	37500	38874	0.6	46	11534	12007	12392	0.4	3.10	8852	8991	0.2
77503	PASADENA	201	24912	26533	27799	0.7	49	8388	8835	9230	0.6	2.98	6180	6345	0.3
77504	PASADENA	201	18938	21218	22734	1.2	63	7430	8222	8777	1.1	2.53	4825	5180	0.8
77505	PASADENA	201	17342	22117	24946	2.7	84	5713	7269	8187	2.6	3.04	4806	6016	2.5
77506	PASADENA	201	40232	42236	43570	0.5	42	12041	12223	12531	0.2	3.45	9159	9083	-0.1
77510	SANTA FE	167	12803	14107	14758	1.1	61	4590	5099	5355	1.1	2.77	3621	3943	0.9
	TEXAS					1.9					1.8	2.78			1.7
	UNITED STATES					1.0					1.1	2.59			0.9

ZIP CODE #	POST OFFICE NAME	RACE (%) White 2000	White 2009	Black 2000	Black 2009	Asian/Pacific 2000	Asian/Pacific 2009	% Hispanic Origin 2000	% Hispanic Origin 2009	2009 AGE DISTRIBUTION (%) 0-4	5-9	10-14	15-19	20-24	25-44	45-64	65-84	85+	18+	MEDIAN AGE 2009	% 2009 Males	% 2009 Females
77327	CLEVELAND	79.5	76.5	11.8	12.2	0.3	0.5	11.8	15.7	7.5	7.3	7.2	7.2	6.4	26.7	25.3	10.7	1.7	73.7	35.8	50.4	49.6
77328	CLEVELAND	87.4	84.2	3.4	3.6	0.4	0.5	13.1	17.8	8.3	7.9	7.5	7.3	6.6	26.7	25.3	9.6	0.9	71.9	34.1	50.0	50.0
77331	COLDSPRING	81.0	78.3	17.1	19.3	0.2	0.2	3.2	4.5	5.1	5.7	5.9	5.6	4.4	20.7	32.8	17.9	1.9	79.7	46.9	50.6	49.4
77335	GOODRICH	77.1	71.8	15.6	18.3	0.6	0.8	8.9	12.7	6.7	6.6	6.6	6.3	5.3	21.2	27.6	17.9	1.8	76.3	42.6	49.0	51.0
77336	HUFFMAN	94.0	90.3	1.0	1.4	0.7	1.1	6.0	10.9	6.6	6.8	7.0	7.1	6.1	26.1	30.0	9.5	0.8	75.3	38.0	50.3	49.7
77338	HUMBLE	68.5	61.3	16.7	18.7	3.5	4.2	21.8	30.7	8.0	7.5	7.2	7.3	7.2	30.2	24.1	7.6	0.9	72.7	32.6	49.2	50.8
77339	KINGWOOD	92.5	88.5	1.9	2.8	2.2	3.3	7.7	13.6	6.7	6.8	7.0	6.8	5.8	27.3	28.9	9.9	0.9	75.4	37.7	48.9	51.1
77340	HUNTSVILLE	72.5	68.4	19.3	20.5	1.2	1.5	13.2	18.6	5.3	4.7	4.2	11.2	21.0	25.1	18.1	8.6	1.8	83.2	27.4	53.7	46.3
77345	KINGWOOD	93.5	90.1	1.3	1.8	2.9	4.5	5.2	9.3	6.6	7.8	8.9	8.8	4.4	22.1	34.4	6.4	0.7	70.9	39.5	49.4	50.6
77346	HUMBLE	83.8	77.3	8.0	10.3	2.9	3.9	10.1	16.3	8.5	8.1	8.0	7.0	5.3	31.7	25.7	5.3	0.4	70.9	33.8	49.2	50.8
77351	LIVINGSTON	80.4	77.3	12.6	13.7	0.4	0.5	8.7	12.0	5.7	5.6	5.7	5.8	6.4	25.4	26.9	16.3	2.2	79.5	41.2	52.9	47.1
77354	MAGNOLIA	91.8	88.8	2.6	2.8	0.3	0.6	9.3	14.1	8.6	8.5	8.1	7.1	5.2	30.8	24.9	6.3	0.5	70.3	33.2	49.7	50.3
77355	MAGNOLIA	93.0	90.2	0.7	1.0	0.2	0.3	11.0	15.7	7.3	7.3	7.5	7.8	6.4	26.9	28.6	7.4	0.7	72.9	35.7	49.4	50.6
77356	MONTGOMERY	93.3	91.5	4.0	4.6	0.7	1.1	4.0	6.3	4.2	4.5	5.0	5.1	3.6	18.5	34.6	22.7	1.8	83.1	51.1	49.2	50.8
77357	NEW CANEY	90.9	87.4	1.7	2.1	0.3	0.5	10.6	16.0	8.6	8.1	7.6	7.4	7.2	26.8	25.4	8.4	0.7	71.1	32.6	49.9	50.1
77358	NEW WAVERLY	75.9	73.1	19.3	20.7	0.4	0.6	6.3	8.6	6.1	6.4	6.9	9.6	5.1	22.5	27.9	13.6	1.9	73.8	39.9	50.0	50.0
77359	OAKHURST	78.4	75.3	19.9	22.7	0.0	0.0	1.7	2.1	5.5	6.3	6.5	5.7	4.2	22.7	30.5	16.7	2.1	78.1	44.3	50.3	49.7
77360	ONALASKA	95.1	93.5	2.5	3.3	0.3	0.4	2.8	4.3	4.0	4.2	4.1	4.2	4.0	16.0	31.9	29.0	2.5	85.1	55.1	48.3	51.7
77362	PINEHURST	93.5	89.4	1.1	1.5	0.2	0.4	9.3	15.2	6.3	6.5	6.9	7.4	6.1	26.2	30.7	9.0	0.8	75.6	38.2	50.1	49.9
77363	PLANTERSVILLE	88.9	85.3	6.0	7.2	0.3	0.4	6.9	11.2	6.5	6.4	6.6	6.5	5.3	25.5	30.9	11.3	1.2	76.7	40.2	49.5	50.5
77364	POINTBLANK	83.6	81.5	14.4	16.0	0.2	0.2	2.4	3.4	4.0	4.3	4.5	4.5	3.8	17.2	32.3	27.1	2.4	84.5	54.2	49.3	50.7
77365	PORTER	89.1	84.2	1.3	1.7	0.6	0.9	15.9	23.5	8.6	8.1	7.5	7.3	7.1	27.7	24.2	8.5	0.9	71.4	32.7	49.4	50.6
77371	SHEPHERD	84.0	81.1	10.3	11.4	0.5	0.8	7.5	10.3	7.1	6.8	7.1	7.8	6.3	23.7	27.4	12.0	1.6	74.0	38.1	49.7	50.3
77372	SPLENDORA	93.6	90.6	0.3	0.4	0.4	0.6	8.4	13.0	8.4	7.8	7.4	7.8	7.6	27.0	24.5	8.8	0.8	71.7	32.4	49.6	50.4
77373	SPRING	83.0	76.4	7.0	9.0	1.6	2.1	16.1	25.1	7.3	7.3	7.3	7.5	6.3	29.8	27.1	6.7	0.6	73.4	34.6	48.4	51.6
77375	TOMBALL	86.4	78.3	5.3	6.8	0.9	1.5	11.9	22.0	8.2	7.5	7.1	6.6	6.5	30.5	23.7	8.0	2.0	73.1	33.8	48.7	51.3
77377	TOMBALL	88.2	80.4	2.2	3.2	2.2	3.4	12.0	22.2	8.8	8.3	8.0	6.9	5.1	31.7	25.0	5.5	0.6	70.4	33.4	49.5	50.5
77378	WILLIS	78.1	73.1	10.8	11.9	0.3	0.4	17.8	24.5	8.3	7.9	7.5	7.6	7.3	28.2	24.1	8.1	1.0	71.5	32.4	50.4	49.6
77379	SPRING	85.7	78.6	4.0	5.1	5.2	6.7	8.9	17.4	7.2	8.0	8.9	8.4	4.6	27.2	29.2	5.8	0.5	70.3	36.2	49.6	50.4
77380	SPRING	89.6	85.6	2.9	3.6	2.8	3.8	9.3	14.2	6.6	6.0	6.1	6.5	7.6	28.0	28.5	9.5	1.3	77.4	36.7	47.8	52.2
77381	SPRING	93.0	90.2	1.6	2.0	2.6	3.8	5.9	9.2	6.6	7.9	9.2	8.6	4.1	23.4	31.5	7.1	1.6	70.3	39.4	48.4	51.6
77382	SPRING	92.5	91.3	1.2	1.8	3.5	2.7	6.7	10.1	9.4	9.7	9.6	7.6	4.2	30.0	24.5	4.4	0.4	66.2	33.3	49.5	50.5
77384	CONROE	94.5	90.5	1.2	1.7	1.0	2.1	6.4	10.6	6.6	6.9	7.5	7.4	4.8	25.4	30.2	10.1	1.2	74.4	39.6	49.2	50.8
77385	CONROE	85.9	81.8	6.5	7.5	1.6	2.1	12.4	18.5	8.4	8.2	7.9	7.1	5.2	29.2	25.4	8.0	0.7	71.1	34.9	49.3	50.7
77386	SPRING	87.4	83.4	3.2	3.9	1.5	1.9	13.5	19.0	9.5	8.1	7.5	6.7	6.0	33.5	22.3	5.9	0.5	70.8	32.3	49.6	50.4
77388	SPRING	87.5	81.8	3.9	5.2	3.6	5.2	10.7	18.2	7.3	7.6	7.9	7.4	5.1	27.7	29.3	7.0	0.6	72.5	36.5	49.1	50.9
77389	SPRING	91.7	86.9	1.9	2.9	0.7	1.1	10.3	17.8	8.0	7.8	7.9	7.8	5.6	27.3	27.6	7.4	0.5	71.3	34.6	48.8	51.2
77396	HUMBLE	57.8	51.3	24.2	24.1	2.0	2.1	25.2	36.1	7.8	7.4	7.0	8.3	8.8	32.2	22.1	5.7	0.7	73.2	31.1	54.1	45.9
77401	BELLAIRE	89.1	84.0	0.8	1.1	6.4	9.3	7.8	13.5	6.2	7.3	8.8	7.4	3.9	21.0	33.8	9.1	2.5	72.7	42.1	48.7	51.3
77406	RICHMOND	82.9	78.4	7.7	8.2	1.1	1.6	15.3	24.5	6.1	6.8	7.5	7.7	5.7	26.7	32.0	7.0	0.6	74.8	38.6	53.4	46.6
77407	RICHMOND	57.7	45.9	19.0	22.7	11.2	15.5	17.6	23.5	10.5	10.0	8.8	6.2	3.1	35.3	22.2	3.5	0.3	66.5	33.9	49.4	50.6
77414	BAY CITY	65.9	61.5	16.0	16.0	0.8	1.1	30.4	37.8	7.6	7.2	6.9	7.7	7.3	24.5	26.2	10.7	1.9	73.7	35.5	49.5	50.5
77417	BEASLEY	49.8	43.4	30.2	30.6	0.5	0.6	32.2	41.7	7.8	7.6	7.7	7.4	5.7	25.6	25.9	11.0	1.3	72.2	35.7	50.4	49.6
77418	BELLVILLE	83.1	79.5	10.5	11.7	0.3	0.4	10.3	14.5	5.9	6.0	6.3	6.8	6.1	23.7	28.8	13.3	3.2	77.5	41.1	48.9	51.1
77419	BLESSING	81.3	76.6	3.1	3.0	0.0	0.0	34.1	43.9	7.2	7.4	7.8	8.4	5.2	24.3	27.2	11.2	1.4	72.4	37.6	53.6	46.4
77420	BOLING	73.4	68.6	6.8	6.9	0.0	0.0	41.7	51.3	6.5	6.5	6.6	7.6	7.1	26.7	27.1	10.4	1.4	75.6	35.3	52.0	48.0
77422	BRAZORIA	74.5	71.1	15.6	16.6	0.4	0.4	12.7	16.3	6.6	6.6	6.8	9.1	7.7	25.3	26.7	10.1	1.0	75.1	35.6	53.0	47.0
77423	BROOKSHIRE	51.4	44.0	26.9	29.7	0.4	0.4	31.5	38.3	8.6	7.5	6.9	7.3	6.8	27.0	25.1	9.5	1.2	72.6	34.2	50.0	50.0
77426	CHAPPELL HILL	73.8	68.9	22.6	26.1	0.6	0.7	5.8	8.0	5.0	5.4	6.0	6.8	4.9	21.5	33.0	15.7	1.7	79.4	45.3	49.9	50.1
77429	CYPRESS	89.0	83.1	3.1	4.0	2.5	3.4	9.4	17.2	8.8	9.1	8.8	6.8	4.2	30.2	26.5	5.2	0.4	68.8	35.2	49.5	50.5
77430	DAMON	88.6	84.4	1.3	1.6	0.5	0.7	15.4	21.8	6.0	6.4	6.9	6.8	5.0	24.4	31.3	11.9	1.2	76.4	40.9	51.1	48.9
77432	DANEVANG	75.4	70.1	3.5	3.4	0.6	0.8	43.4	53.4	8.2	8.2	7.9	7.9	6.5	28.0	23.4	8.8	1.1	70.6	31.8	50.8	49.2
77433	CYPRESS	81.6	67.8	5.4	8.3	3.6	5.2	16.0	31.8	9.6	9.8	9.6	8.2	4.9	30.0	23.3	4.3	0.4	65.2	31.8	49.4	50.6
77434	EAGLE LAKE	55.6	52.6	23.5	23.0	0.0	0.0	39.7	47.1	8.0	7.6	7.2	7.2	6.4	23.1	25.2	12.9	2.4	72.8	36.5	48.7	51.3
77435	EAST BERNARD	69.7	65.6	18.3	18.7	0.3	0.4	19.7	26.0	6.8	7.1	7.0	7.2	5.8	24.4	28.1	11.8	1.7	74.7	38.4	50.7	49.3
77437	EL CAMPO	73.4	69.8	9.0	8.7	0.3	0.3	36.5	44.6	7.8	7.5	7.5	7.8	6.5	24.3	25.0	11.3	2.3	72.4	35.9	49.2	50.8
77440	ELMATON	90.2	85.4	1.1	1.1	0.0	0.0	14.1	21.3	4.5	5.6	6.7	9.0	3.4	22.5	31.5	15.7	1.1	77.5	43.8	52.8	47.2
77441	FULSHEAR	75.6	70.3	16.1	17.9	1.0	1.6	10.2	14.7	4.5	5.4	6.7	7.2	4.3	18.0	36.7	15.9	1.3	78.9	47.3	48.9	51.1
77442	GARWOOD	75.8	70.3	13.9	15.5	0.1	0.1	17.0	24.0	6.3	6.6	6.6	6.9	5.2	22.1	28.1	15.7	2.7	76.3	42.3	51.5	48.5
77444	GUY	83.7	78.0	6.2	6.9	0.1	0.2	15.7	23.8	6.6	6.9	7.2	7.2	5.7	24.7	29.3	11.1	1.2	75.0	38.5	49.3	50.7
77445	HEMPSTEAD	52.7	47.3	33.5	36.0	0.4	0.5	20.3	24.7	7.4	7.1	6.9	7.2	8.4	27.0	24.5	10.1	1.5	74.5	33.8	50.5	49.5
77447	HOCKLEY	81.2	76.7	8.8	9.4	0.5	0.6	16.2	23.7	7.6	7.8	8.2	7.7	5.5	28.0	27.2	7.3	0.7	71.5	35.0	49.9	50.1
77449	KATY	73.0	63.8	8.7	10.8	3.8	5.0	25.3	37.0	9.6	9.1	8.7	7.7	5.9	32.0	22.7	4.0	0.4	67.7	31.0	49.1	50.9
77450	KATY	85.4	77.8	3.3	4.4	6.2	10.4	10.7	16.6	8.0	8.8	9.4	8.1	4.2	28.2	28.2	4.6	0.3	68.3	35.5	48.9	51.1
77455	LOUISE	84.1	79.5	3.5	3.8	0.0	0.0	28.4	37.6	6.9	7.5	8.3	7.3	5.9	25.8	25.1	11.7	1.5	72.7	36.3	51.1	48.9
77456	MARKHAM	89.5	86.1	2.0	2.1	0.1	0.1	18.1	24.9	5.7	6.1	6.9	8.0	5.3	24.3	30.0	12.1	1.6	76.6	40.1	53.1	46.9
77457	MATAGORDA	88.4	85.0	2.6	2.9	0.1	0.1	8.4	12.4	4.0	4.7	5.2	5.0	3.6	19.5	37.2	19.0	1.9	83.0	50.1	51.4	48.6
77458	MIDFIELD	80.0	75.3	3.5	3.2	0.0	0.0	37.7	47.8	7.6	7.6	7.2	8.4	5.6	24.7	26.7	10.8	1.6	72.5	37.0	53.4	46.6
77459	MISSOURI CITY	60.3	50.6	18.9	21.9	13.8	16.3	12.2	19.2	8.1	8.2	8.4	6.9	4.3	28.6	28.4	6.6	0.5	70.7	35.8	49.2	50.8
77461	NEEDVILLE	79.5	72.1	6.4	7.8	0.5	0.6	23.3	33.8	6.9	6.8	7.0	7.3	6.2	26.8	28.3	9.4	1.4	74.7	36.6	49.4	50.6
77465	PALACIOS	62.2	57.4	4.0	3.5	10.8	12.4	45.1	52.1	9.4	8.4	8.9	8.3	5.8	22.9	23.8	10.9	1.5	67.9	32.7	50.1	49.9
77468	PLEDGER	77.2	74.3	17.1	18.2	0.0	0.0	13.7	19.4	5.1	4.7	5.1	6.7	7.9	26.1	32.4	11.1	0.8	81.8	40.5	51.8	48.2
77469	RICHMOND	57.5	55.2	15.1	15.1	2.0	4.5	44.8	45.3	8.3	8.4	8.0	7.6	6.3	29.5	23.5	7.3	1.1	70.6	33.3	50.6	49.4
77471	ROSENBERG	67.5	62.5	7.8	7.9	0.4	0.5	51.8	61.7	8.4	8.1	7.7	7.5	6.7	28.1	23.5	8.7	1.2	71.1	33.0	49.4	50.6
77474	SEALY	77.2	73.6	11.5	12.0	0.3	0.4	21.6	27.7	7.5	7.4	7.3	6.9	5.7	25.6	27.0	10.8	1.8	73.4	36.8	49.3	50.7
77477	STAFFORD	49.5	41.3	17.1	18.5	18.5	21.3	25.4	32.9	7.7	7.1	6.8	6.9	7.5	32.2	24.7	6.4	0.7	74.2	32.8	49.1	50.9
77478	SUGAR LAND	60.9	49.5	6.6	7.9	27.4	36.0	7.7	11.0	6.5	6.8	7.2	6.7	4.6	26.2	30.5	9.8	1.6	74.9	39.6	48.6	51.4
77479	SUGAR LAND	65.0	55.2	6.3	7.5	23.7	30.9	7.5	10.7	7.9	8.7	9.4	8.4	4.7	26.5	29.8	4.2	0.4	68.2	35.6	50.3	49.7
77480	SWEENY	79.0	74.9	13.0	14.9	0.3	0.4	11.6	15.1	6.4	6.7	7.0	7.4	6.1	24.5	28.6	11.8	1.6	75.3	38.1	49.2	50.8
77482	VAN VLECK	74.8	71.6	16.4	16.8	0.1	0.2	20.9	27.7	5.8	5.9	6.1	6.9	6.7	24.1	30.1	12.9	1.4	78.1	40.7	49.9	50.1
77483	WADSWORTH	83.2	76.8	3.7	4.3	0.0	0.0	15.4	22.2	4.8	5.8	8.2	8.2	5.8	25.1	29.5	10.6	1.9	75.8	40.7	56.5	43.5
77484	WALLER	57.9	54.6	33.4	33.3	0.5	0.6	14.2	20.2	5.9	5.6	5.7	13.6	16.0	22.6	21.9	7.8	0.8	79.1	27.6	49.2	50.8
77485	WALLIS	77.9	72.6	9.7	10.6	0.2	0.3	19.6	27.1	7.0	7.2	7.3	6.8	5.0	24.5	30.0	10.8	1.5	74.2	39.2	50.1	49.9
77486	WEST COLUMBIA	78.4	74.5	13.4	15.1	0.4	0.4	13.8	17.9	6.7	6.3	6.3	7.0	6.5	23.3	28.4	13.3	2.1	76.3	39.8	47.9	52.1
77488	WHARTON	60.8	56.7	23.4	23.6	0.6	0.7	28.8	35.7	6.7	6.8	6.7	7.8	6.7	24.7	25.4	12.5	2.7	75.2	36.8	48.6	51.4
77489	MISSOURI CITY	12.8	10.9	76.7	76.8	2.8	3.2	11.2	13.6	6.8	7.2	7.6	8.6	6.9	27.7	29.5	5.4	0.4	73.0	33.7	47.4	52.6
77493	KATY	83.0	75.5	3.7	4.6	0.8	1.2	25.2	38.3	8.2	8.1	8.0	7.8	6.0	29.2	25.5	6.4	0.8	70.9	32.8	49.9	50.1
77494	KATY	86.6	79.7	4.4	6.1	4.3	4.6	8.9	17.1	8.1	8.7	9.0	7.7	4.0	29.4	27.5	5.1	0.5	69.2	35.7	49.3	50.7
77498	SUGAR LAND	62.6	49.6	12.0	19.0	13.2	16.2	21.3	26.8	8.3	8.3	8.1	7.5	5.6	29.7	26.7	5.2	0.5	70.5	33.7	49.0	51.0
77502	PASADENA	71.4	63.2	1.4	1.5	0.9	1.0	50.6	65.6	9.2	8.4	7.6	7.7	7.6	27.9	20.7	9.6	1.4	70.3	30.8	49.5	50.5
77503	PASADENA	73.0	65.2	2.0	2.0	1.1	1.2	46.5	61.4	9.6	8.8	7.8	7.9	8.1	30.1	20.2	6.8	0.8	69.1	29.3	50.0	50.0
77504	PASADENA	78.1	70.4	2.0	2.3	2.3	2.9	33.3	46.2	8.1	7.2	6.5	6.4	8.1	30.5	22.8	8.6	2.0	74.5	32.6	48.8	51.2
77505	PASADENA	85.6	79.2	0.8	0.9	4.9	6.8	19.4	30.3	7.6	7.5	7.5	7.3	5.8	31.0	27.2	5.7	0.4	72.9	34.1	49.0	51.0
77506	PASADENA	58.9	53.2	1.5	1.3	0.9	0.8	73.8	83.5	11.5	10.2	8.6	8.6	8.6	29.4	17.2	5.1	0.7	64.6	26.4	51.3	48.7
77510	SANTA FE	94.2	92.1	0.5	0.6	0.3	0.3	10.6	16.2	6.8	6.9	7.1	7.2	5.7	26.5	28.5	10.2	1.0	74.6	37.6	49.5	50.5
	TEXAS	71.0	67.6	11.5	11.4	2.8	3.5	32.0	37.4	7.9	7.5	7.2	7.5	7.4	28.3	24.0	8.8	1.4	73.0	33.6	49.7	50.3
	UNITED STATES	75.1	72.0	12.3	12.7	3.8	4.6	12.5	15.7	6.8	6.7	6.6	7.1	6.9	27.0	26.0	10.9	1.9	75.7	36.9	49.2	50.8

ZIP CODE #	POST OFFICE NAME	2009 Per Capita Income	2009 HH Income Base	2009 Household Income Distribution (%): Less than $25,000	$25,000 to $49,999	$50,000 to $99,999	$100,000 to $149,999	$150,000 or More	Median Household Income: 2009	2014	2009 National Centile	2009 State Centile	2009 Home Value Base	2009 Home Value Distribution (%): Less than $50,000	$50,000 to $89,999	$90,000 to $174,999	$175,000 to $399,999	$400,000 or More	2009 Median Home Value
77327	CLEVELAND	17453	7670	31.8	25.3	35.5	5.4	1.9	42226	46904	40	50	5706	36.9	29.6	27.0	6.0	0.4	63807
77328	CLEVELAND	18557	5321	24.6	29.4	36.2	7.9	2.0	46475	47448	53	63	4507	32.4	29.5	29.2	8.2	0.7	72195
77331	COLDSPRING	22577	2951	29.9	29.8	31.6	5.1	3.7	41266	43231	37	47	2534	29.4	26.4	28.7	12.7	2.8	82663
77335	GOODRICH	16911	870	34.7	33.9	26.7	3.4	1.3	35000	37039	18	23	725	41.7	28.0	22.5	5.8	2.1	58897
77336	HUFFMAN	24015	4047	16.1	18.4	48.3	12.8	4.4	60818	62148	79	84	3423	20.4	28.0	40.2	10.3	1.2	92678
77338	HUMBLE	22729	10558	18.0	20.4	47.4	11.4	2.7	56618	60468	74	80	6234	5.4	20.6	66.7	6.4	0.8	109149
77339	KINGWOOD	36778	14162	7.4	12.1	47.5	19.7	13.2	80081	79534	92	94	10569	0.7	5.3	61.4	28.3	4.3	150617
77340	HUNTSVILLE	19818	9124	34.0	29.4	26.7	6.5	3.4	37096	39340	24	31	4555	20.4	19.9	34.5	22.7	2.5	107445
77345	KINGWOOD	49874	8938	4.5	6.0	26.4	23.7	39.4	129591	131063	99	99	8041	2.6	1.7	19.2	61.1	15.3	249339
77346	HUMBLE	36430	17621	4.6	7.5	43.9	27.5	16.5	91285	94215	95	96	15076	0.3	4.0	59.3	34.8	1.5	151558
77351	LIVINGSTON	19543	12360	29.6	32.1	29.9	5.7	2.7	39210	41143	30	39	9929	26.0	26.2	32.5	13.1	2.2	85962
77354	MAGNOLIA	30284	9448	10.5	18.9	40.3	16.6	13.7	74208	78340	89	91	8552	7.5	18.8	29.3	31.9	12.5	155442
77355	MAGNOLIA	25384	7672	14.7	20.6	41.7	15.2	7.8	65201	67721	83	87	6624	11.2	20.6	35.8	25.7	6.8	132319
77356	MONTGOMERY	41403	9590	11.0	17.0	42.2	16.2	13.6	74569	78389	89	91	8501	6.5	9.7	27.0	35.2	21.7	207447
77357	NEW CANEY	19825	6953	22.2	26.4	39.2	8.9	3.3	51647	51354	65	73	5322	29.7	30.8	31.6	7.4	0.6	71573
77358	NEW WAVERLY	20611	1497	32.5	27.0	30.9	5.9	3.8	40421	43008	34	44	1201	26.7	24.1	29.0	17.8	2.3	88500
77359	OAKHURST	20024	157	30.6	35.7	25.5	4.5	3.8	40222	42911	33	43	131	34.4	32.1	23.7	9.9	0.0	69500
77360	ONALASKA	22395	2118	31.0	27.7	32.5	6.9	1.8	39109	41188	30	38	1830	29.1	27.9	27.0	14.8	1.3	80922
77362	PINEHURST	26075	1554	17.8	19.7	38.5	16.9	7.0	64999	67688	83	87	1331	19.5	20.4	26.4	24.8	8.9	124659
77363	PLANTERSVILLE	20285	963	27.6	33.4	29.1	6.0	3.8	38493	39317	28	35	847	23.0	24.7	36.1	15.3	0.8	94875
77364	POINTBLANK	21613	1468	29.7	31.7	31.6	4.2	2.8	40288	42953	34	43	1296	28.9	30.0	30.4	10.7	0.0	81288
77365	PORTER	20732	8541	18.8	30.9	38.4	9.1	2.9	50412	51539	62	71	6356	24.8	25.4	41.6	7.9	0.3	89601
77371	SHEPHERD	15360	3084	37.4	29.4	27.7	4.4	1.1	36130	39085	21	27	2573	47.1	26.9	20.6	4.0	1.2	54375
77372	SPLENDORA	18712	3873	23.1	30.2	37.6	7.1	1.9	47469	48245	55	66	3140	37.1	29.3	27.8	5.5	0.2	61809
77373	SPRING	26243	16990	7.6	15.8	56.2	15.7	4.7	69446	68787	86	89	12956	2.4	27.5	60.9	8.5	0.7	105830
77375	TOMBALL	27119	9744	13.0	17.8	46.7	14.2	8.2	62882	66117	81	86	7013	9.7	15.6	44.3	25.0	5.5	131442
77377	TOMBALL	32317	9410	8.1	12.7	45.0	19.9	14.3	77705	77832	91	93	8010	6.5	10.4	40.0	35.6	7.5	149786
77378	WILLIS	18326	4593	22.6	33.2	34.5	6.9	2.8	45886	46981	51	61	3437	26.5	32.8	30.4	8.5	1.8	76467
77379	SPRING	38985	22923	5.6	9.5	38.3	22.6	24.0	93555	91319	96	97	19242	1.4	4.4	45.7	40.7	7.7	171356
77380	SPRING	36466	10202	17.5	20.0	34.1	15.7	12.7	66295	70227	84	88	5726	1.0	2.8	52.4	30.4	13.4	163454
77381	SPRING	47755	13834	11.0	10.1	25.0	20.1	33.7	109199	107911	98	98	10889	0.5	1.5	24.1	50.1	23.8	247680
77382	SPRING	50476	11630	2.8	7.2	23.7	25.9	40.3	132279	129192	99	99	10574	0.8	1.3	6.3	66.7	24.9	286408
77384	CONROE	32763	4787	14.0	16.1	32.9	20.8	16.1	80099	82338	92	94	4149	3.3	5.8	36.9	43.6	10.4	187315
77385	CONROE	25972	5852	12.3	19.3	42.7	18.2	7.5	70250	74521	87	90	5024	10.6	17.9	47.0	23.7	0.7	127885
77386	SPRING	29186	9563	8.2	15.9	48.9	18.7	8.3	74939	77634	89	92	7251	2.2	8.6	59.4	28.9	0.9	144624
77388	SPRING	33997	12812	5.4	9.5	47.2	23.0	14.9	83951	83306	93	95	11121	2.1	5.5	58.9	31.8	1.6	145187
77389	SPRING	31509	6028	7.1	17.9	43.7	17.8	13.5	76913	75635	91	93	5413	16.6	20.0	35.8	23.0	4.6	116811
77396	HUMBLE	20946	9826	15.5	21.7	47.9	11.7	3.3	57977	60468	75	82	7288	17.8	32.4	45.7	3.0	1.1	89799
77401	BELLAIRE	54456	6212	6.5	9.9	32.2	19.0	32.3	102643	102802	97	98	5081	1.8	1.4	15.6	40.5	40.8	302391
77406	RICHMOND	35083	8750	7.2	13.2	32.7	26.3	20.6	93651	100614	96	97	7295	4.2	4.8	32.9	42.7	15.4	199686
77407	RICHMOND	34492	5944	3.0	7.5	32.8	37.9	18.8	109764	112053	98	98	5324	0.5	0.1	48.8	44.4	6.2	175994
77414	BAY CITY	18737	9026	31.9	28.2	29.8	7.7	2.4	40165	41563	33	43	5414	25.3	33.5	33.1	7.3	0.8	81034
77417	BEASLEY	17149	1045	30.6	28.6	29.6	9.7	1.5	39503	43364	31	40	783	32.8	33.1	27.2	6.1	0.8	65462
77418	BELLVILLE	21610	3356	21.1	32.7	32.9	10.3	3.2	47231	49419	55	65	2580	18.5	13.6	35.6	25.7	6.6	122473
77419	BLESSING	16215	476	35.1	31.3	25.8	5.3	2.5	34790	38001	17	22	376	26.3	39.6	26.6	6.9	0.5	70238
77420	BOLING	17592	778	26.3	34.6	31.5	4.2	3.3	40410	42002	34	44	595	37.6	27.4	28.7	3.7	2.5	65242
77422	BRAZORIA	20792	5119	22.4	28.5	36.7	9.8	2.6	49013	49993	59	68	4045	27.6	30.5	31.8	8.8	1.4	78565
77423	BROOKSHIRE	18813	3055	29.5	26.3	30.5	9.9	3.8	43259	47120	43	54	2109	33.9	23.3	22.5	14.9	5.4	75792
77426	CHAPPELL HILL	20287	774	34.5	22.0	32.9	8.0	2.6	40199	42148	33	43	622	21.1	10.3	24.8	35.0	8.8	154348
77429	CYPRESS	42240	21538	5.6	11.0	33.6	23.2	26.6	99687	100404	97	97	18987	1.9	5.5	45.1	38.4	9.1	169943
77430	DAMON	22631	1007	19.3	27.8	38.8	12.2	1.9	52961	53782	68	76	829	27.6	22.4	30.6	16.3	3.0	89861
77432	DANEVANG	12682	90	25.6	32.2	33.3	6.7	2.2	45000	45315	48	59	68	36.8	16.2	36.8	5.9	4.4	83333
77433	CYPRESS	30132	11226	5.8	13.8	45.9	19.9	14.7	79318	72739	92	93	9914	0.9	15.8	50.2	27.6	5.5	138387
77434	EAGLE LAKE	17024	1631	33.7	31.1	28.6	3.0	3.6	35601	36980	20	25	1147	42.7	29.2	17.7	8.3	2.1	62848
77435	EAST BERNARD	18470	2192	26.4	30.8	32.5	8.0	2.3	44834	45666	48	58	1685	24.6	26.5	35.4	10.1	3.3	88221
77437	EL CAMPO	17458	5794	30.4	31.3	28.5	7.4	2.4	39189	41184	30	39	3906	28.0	28.3	31.4	11.1	1.2	80996
77440	ELMATON	22210	35	28.6	34.3	25.7	8.6	2.9	40735	42279	35	45	30	26.7	30.0	26.7	16.7	0.0	70000
77441	FULSHEAR	46332	1083	11.4	12.4	27.6	23.7	24.9	96719	103027	96	97	949	14.4	6.0	10.7	38.8	30.0	294940
77442	GARWOOD	16474	859	41.3	29.0	23.7	4.0	2.0	31249	33090	10	13	684	36.1	30.3	26.8	6.9	0.0	71803
77444	GUY	21209	308	24.7	25.3	37.0	10.7	2.3	50000	50508	61	70	245	26.1	28.2	29.8	13.5	2.4	83000
77445	HEMPSTEAD	19540	4158	34.3	23.1	31.2	7.0	4.4	42925	46776	42	53	2814	22.3	27.7	29.4	15.8	4.8	90000
77447	HOCKLEY	23152	3651	16.4	23.9	41.4	13.4	4.9	58871	60197	76	83	2992	11.2	30.3	35.8	18.3	4.4	109430
77449	KATY	26118	23695	6.7	12.4	54.5	18.5	7.8	75157	74208	89	92	19658	3.2	18.9	68.4	9.2	0.2	120685
77450	KATY	44737	23001	4.3	6.5	30.4	27.1	31.7	117941	121290	98	99	19670	0.4	4.2	37.7	48.1	9.6	199675
77455	LOUISE	17365	759	28.1	27.8	35.6	6.7	1.8	45493	46324	50	60	555	20.4	31.2	29.5	18.2	0.7	87927
77456	MARKHAM	19899	297	22.9	34.3	32.7	9.1	1.0	43564	43005	44	55	241	33.2	26.1	26.1	13.3	1.2	67381
77457	MATAGORDA	22801	415	35.7	28.2	25.3	8.2	2.7	35838	38314	20	26	340	27.1	29.4	29.1	14.1	0.3	79355
77458	MIDFIELD	16172	91	36.3	30.8	25.3	4.4	3.3	33359	35903	14	17	71	26.8	42.3	25.4	5.6	0.0	69375
77459	MISSOURI CITY	39705	16167	5.5	9.5	28.2	30.6	26.2	110514	113317	98	98	14487	4.8	3.8	31.7	50.4	9.3	203231
77461	NEEDVILLE	21303	3150	18.9	25.2	38.5	14.4	3.0	56715	54812	74	81	2422	17.6	28.5	39.6	12.8	1.6	97705
77465	PALACIOS	16120	2194	33.8	28.6	27.6	8.6	1.4	39214	41686	30	39	1600	35.1	26.8	23.6	14.3	0.4	70652
77468	PLEDGER	18031	95	17.9	33.7	42.1	6.3	0.0	48013	45550	57	67	79	24.1	44.3	26.6	5.1	0.0	77917
77469	RICHMOND	25142	9691	17.3	24.3	30.4	17.2	10.7	61632	58463	80	85	6938	14.9	15.0	39.5	23.8	6.7	124650
77471	ROSENBERG	17667	10710	23.7	30.3	33.1	10.3	2.6	45754	47845	51	61	6459	23.1	25.7	42.9	6.5	1.8	91713
77474	SEALY	20755	4393	22.9	29.2	36.5	7.0	4.5	48119	50617	57	67	3279	15.6	22.4	37.3	20.5	4.1	110057
77477	STAFFORD	25408	12032	11.7	25.4	38.1	18.9	5.9	64706	62730	83	87	6247	8.8	8.9	62.9	18.9	0.5	127764
77478	SUGAR LAND	38103	9314	8.7	13.2	29.7	26.2	22.2	96444	101848	96	97	7004	1.7	1.2	38.9	45.9	12.3	213375
77479	SUGAR LAND	45249	20599	4.5	8.3	24.0	28.5	34.7	125993	125636	99	99	17995	2.3	2.4	22.5	54.3	18.4	250128
77480	SWEENY	20108	3086	25.4	25.9	37.9	9.0	1.7	48401	49323	58	67	2321	22.2	31.7	37.8	7.3	1.0	83912
77482	VAN VLECK	19201	895	28.0	28.5	32.4	8.5	2.6	41773	41677	39	49	732	28.1	39.2	27.2	5.3	0.1	74091
77483	WADSWORTH	19861	74	31.1	28.4	28.4	8.1	4.1	30000	37347	8	10	62	24.2	41.9	21.0	12.9	0.0	71667
77484	WALLER	19456	4269	24.3	26.9	34.6	10.5	3.7	48655	50971	58	67	3184	16.9	22.8	35.0	21.2	4.1	109696
77485	WALLIS	23179	1592	22.9	27.8	30.5	12.8	6.0	49344	50902	60	69	1256	20.9	20.7	35.8	18.9	3.7	107500
77486	WEST COLUMBIA	22842	2799	26.1	27.0	33.1	10.4	3.4	47601	48824	56	66	1928	15.1	34.0	37.9	12.4	0.6	91391
77488	WHARTON	18695	5453	34.7	27.9	29.2	5.6	2.7	36809	38906	23	30	3481	28.8	28.8	32.2	8.1	2.1	79291
77489	MISSOURI CITY	22691	11073	9.2	23.6	41.4	21.3	4.5	67714	67499	85	89	8861	3.0	23.0	69.0	4.9	0.1	109574
77493	KATY	24715	6894	12.1	18.6	42.7	19.0	7.7	66328	65742	84	88	5457	8.0	18.4	57.7	14.4	1.5	116718
77494	KATY	35868	14927	12.6	11.9	26.6	24.7	24.1	97118	101998	96	97	13327	0.9	2.9	21.5	65.4	9.3	242359
77498	SUGAR LAND	30672	14725	6.5	13.7	37.2	26.5	16.1	87560	94578	94	96	12276	3.2	10.5	59.3	25.3	1.7	135465
77502	PASADENA	17819	12007	23.6	24.3	43.0	6.9	2.2	50992	52725	64	72	7655	14.0	42.1	42.7	1.2	0.0	84811
77503	PASADENA	17025	8835	25.6	25.0	43.2	4.8	1.5	48309	51898	57	67	4810	12.0	49.4	36.7	1.6	0.3	81828
77504	PASADENA	23566	8222	20.7	27.9	39.1	9.0	3.4	50774	52966	63	72	3790	18.3	19.9	49.5	11.3	1.0	108420
77505	PASADENA	32623	7269	7.5	10.6	42.4	24.3	15.2	85124	83522	94	95	6123	5.0	6.7	59.9	27.2	1.1	138494
77506	PASADENA	12599	12223	32.2	32.9	30.6	3.0	1.3	36480	39084	22	29	5181	29.9	60.6	8.4	0.8	0.2	57724
77510	SANTA FE	23594	5099	19.2	21.8	43.7	11.0	4.4	56622	58349	74	80	4076	17.0	21.2	44.2	15.9	1.7	109312
	TEXAS	24551		22.3	25.0	34.3	11.1	7.3	52382	54495				16.5	22.7	36.5	19.7	4.6	109784
	UNITED STATES	27277		20.9	24.4	35.3	11.7	7.6	54719	56938				9.3	13.1	31.6	32.6	13.5	162279

ZIP CODE		FINANCIAL SERVICES				THE HOME						ENTERTAINMENT						PERSONAL			
						Home Improvements		Furnishings													
#	POST OFFICE NAME	Auto Loan	Home Loan	Investments	Retirement Plans	Home Repair	Lawn & Garden	Computers & Hardware-Personal	Major Appliances	TV, Radio, Sound Equipment	Furniture	Dine out/ Carry out	Sports Equipment	Fees & Tickets	Toys & Games	Travel	Cable TV	Apparel & Services	Auto Repairs	Health Insurance	Pets & Supplies
77327	CLEVELAND	81	66	69	64	65	77	68	74	73	67	72	55	60	74	64	78	49	73	78	89
77328	CLEVELAND	90	76	75	73	75	84	76	82	79	77	79	61	68	82	71	83	54	80	83	97
77331	COLDSPRING	89	71	102	68	76	95	71	88	77	71	76	63	62	74	74	84	50	83	93	104
77335	GOODRICH	73	56	78	52	59	76	57	70	63	58	62	50	49	61	57	69	41	66	75	83
77336	HUFFMAN	110	103	96	100	100	105	97	103	99	100	99	77	92	103	94	101	68	99	102	122
77338	HUMBLE	94	88	75	87	83	81	91	86	90	93	91	67	87	93	85	89	63	89	84	102
77339	KINGWOOD	138	151	138	152	147	135	140	137	134	147	136	108	147	139	142	130	97	135	128	160
77340	HUNTSVILLE	76	58	57	60	57	62	81	66	76	71	77	55	66	76	65	75	54	73	68	81
77345	KINGWOOD	212	262	250	271	263	230	221	226	208	241	211	181	254	216	240	196	155	212	198	256
77346	HUMBLE	159	181	151	177	172	150	157	157	147	170	150	126	166	158	159	139	107	148	136	178
77351	LIVINGSTON	83	66	85	63	69	85	67	80	73	67	71	58	59	71	67	79	48	76	85	94
77354	MAGNOLIA	143	150	126	146	143	132	134	136	129	144	131	106	136	138	132	125	92	129	123	157
77355	MAGNOLIA	117	120	104	117	115	112	110	112	109	115	110	86	110	114	109	108	76	109	107	131
77356	MONTGOMERY	142	149	171	147	160	165	134	152	140	144	139	102	143	133	147	145	95	145	164	174
77357	NEW CANEY	91	88	76	85	84	85	85	85	85	89	85	65	82	88	82	85	59	85	84	101
77358	NEW WAVERLY	88	70	90	67	73	91	71	85	77	69	76	62	62	76	70	84	51	80	90	100
77359	OAKHURST	85	64	89	61	67	88	64	81	71	62	70	59	54	69	65	77	46	75	85	96
77360	ONALASKA	72	69	88	63	76	82	65	77	69	71	67	51	65	63	71	73	45	74	86	88
77362	PINEHURST	119	113	100	110	110	113	105	111	108	110	108	81	101	113	102	110	74	107	110	131
77363	PLANTERSVILLE	95	71	83	69	71	92	73	85	80	71	78	64	60	82	68	86	53	80	89	102
77364	POINTBLANK	74	66	86	61	72	82	64	77	68	67	67	52	60	64	68	73	45	73	84	89
77365	PORTER	94	89	75	85	84	86	86	87	87	90	87	66	82	91	82	88	60	87	86	103
77371	SHEPHERD	73	56	67	54	56	71	57	66	62	56	61	51	48	64	54	67	41	63	68	80
77372	SPLENDORA	87	78	71	74	75	80	77	79	79	79	79	60	70	82	72	80	54	78	79	95
77373	SPRING	114	121	103	119	115	107	111	110	108	118	110	85	113	112	110	105	76	108	102	129
77375	TOMBALL	113	119	104	118	114	106	113	110	109	118	111	87	115	113	112	106	78	109	104	128
77377	TOMBALL	146	161	134	156	152	135	142	142	134	153	137	112	147	143	142	128	96	135	125	162
77378	WILLIS	88	81	70	78	77	80	79	80	81	82	81	60	74	84	74	82	55	80	80	96
77379	SPRING	166	195	177	198	191	169	170	170	160	183	163	136	187	168	178	152	118	162	150	195
77380	SPRING	129	131	127	135	130	122	133	125	129	137	131	99	136	131	132	126	93	129	122	148
77381	SPRING	192	228	214	234	227	203	200	201	190	215	192	160	223	196	212	182	140	192	183	229
77382	SPRING	226	257	217	257	246	217	222	224	210	243	214	178	239	224	226	198	153	210	193	254
77384	CONROE	140	157	146	159	155	148	142	145	137	146	138	113	151	141	148	135	98	139	138	167
77385	CONROE	118	129	110	126	123	115	114	116	111	121	113	89	119	117	115	109	79	112	109	134
77386	SPRING	130	135	113	132	127	114	127	122	121	135	123	98	128	129	123	115	86	120	110	141
77388	SPRING	146	165	145	165	160	144	144	146	136	155	139	115	154	144	148	130	99	138	130	167
77389	SPRING	143	157	139	154	152	139	139	141	133	149	135	109	145	140	141	129	95	134	128	162
77396	HUMBLE	100	99	83	94	94	89	96	94	94	101	95	72	93	98	91	92	66	94	89	110
77401	BELLAIRE	180	235	263	244	253	211	204	210	187	221	188	163	240	186	232	177	141	197	183	234
77406	RICHMOND	162	191	178	192	189	172	166	170	159	175	161	132	183	164	177	155	116	163	155	195
77407	RICHMOND	164	198	171	204	193	162	165	167	152	185	155	139	187	165	173	139	114	152	136	186
77414	BAY CITY	77	64	61	63	63	68	70	69	72	70	72	52	63	73	64	74	50	71	71	83
77417	BEASLEY	85	70	74	67	69	81	69	77	74	70	73	58	61	76	65	78	49	74	79	93
77418	BELLVILLE	89	80	82	80	80	91	79	86	82	77	81	65	74	83	78	86	56	83	90	102
77419	BLESSING	83	60	86	58	62	85	61	78	68	57	67	59	49	68	61	75	44	72	81	93
77420	BOLING	81	66	66	67	65	80	73	76	76	66	74	59	63	77	67	81	51	75	82	91
77422	BRAZORIA	93	82	84	81	81	92	80	88	83	79	83	66	73	85	78	87	56	84	90	105
77423	BROOKSHIRE	89	79	80	74	78	82	79	84	79	80	80	64	71	81	76	80	54	82	81	98
77426	CHAPPELL HILL	82	70	87	71	73	87	69	83	72	64	71	62	62	72	71	77	48	76	84	96
77429	CYPRESS	179	211	184	215	205	179	181	182	170	198	173	148	200	181	189	159	125	171	157	206
77430	DAMON	95	90	86	91	89	99	85	92	88	85	87	72	83	90	85	91	60	88	94	110
77432	DANEVANG	90	65	74	63	64	86	67	78	75	65	73	60	54	78	61	81	49	74	83	95
77433	CYPRESS	143	157	131	155	149	133	138	138	131	150	134	108	145	140	138	125	94	131	122	158
77434	EAGLE LAKE	80	60	69	55	60	74	62	74	69	61	68	52	51	68	59	74	46	70	76	85
77435	EAST BERNARD	89	70	84	69	71	91	71	84	77	66	75	64	60	78	69	83	50	78	88	100
77437	EL CAMPO	77	66	66	63	65	75	67	73	71	66	70	54	60	71	64	74	48	72	76	86
77440	ELMATON	101	72	104	70	75	102	74	94	82	69	81	71	59	82	73	91	53	87	98	112
77441	FULSHEAR	176	202	200	204	204	195	176	186	172	187	174	138	192	174	190	171	123	177	179	215
77442	GARWOOD	77	53	80	51	54	79	57	71	62	50	61	57	43	61	55	68	40	66	75	87
77444	GUY	96	83	81	81	81	93	80	88	84	80	84	66	73	88	77	89	57	84	90	105
77445	HEMPSTEAD	87	72	76	70	71	83	74	80	79	74	78	59	66	80	70	83	53	78	83	96
77447	HOCKLEY	108	105	91	102	102	102	97	101	99	102	99	75	95	103	94	99	68	98	99	120
77449	KATY	127	138	113	132	130	114	122	122	116	133	118	96	125	124	121	110	83	116	107	139
77450	KATY	202	242	214	246	236	204	204	207	190	225	194	167	228	203	214	178	141	192	175	233
77455	LOUISE	89	63	88	62	64	90	68	82	72	59	71	66	52	73	65	79	47	77	86	100
77456	MARKHAM	97	70	90	68	71	95	72	88	80	69	78	67	58	81	68	88	52	82	92	105
77457	MATAGORDA	79	62	99	61	67	84	63	80	66	57	65	60	53	63	67	70	43	74	80	93
77458	MIDFIELD	80	57	82	55	59	81	59	75	65	54	64	56	47	65	58	71	42	68	78	89
77459	MISSOURI CITY	182	220	196	224	216	189	185	189	173	203	176	152	208	183	197	163	128	176	164	213
77461	NEEDVILLE	99	95	83	94	92	99	91	95	93	90	93	71	88	96	88	96	63	92	98	113
77465	PALACIOS	80	65	68	60	65	71	66	74	69	67	69	53	57	69	63	71	47	71	72	85
77468	PLEDGER	87	62	72	60	62	82	65	75	72	63	70	58	52	75	59	78	47	71	79	92
77469	RICHMOND	124	123	109	120	120	114	118	119	117	124	119	90	118	121	116	115	84	118	111	136
77471	ROSENBERG	89	80	69	76	77	79	80	82	82	83	83	59	75	84	75	83	57	82	81	95
77474	SEALY	93	83	81	82	82	91	81	88	84	81	84	66	76	87	79	88	57	85	89	104
77477	STAFFORD	114	112	97	112	106	100	110	105	107	115	109	83	109	112	106	104	77	106	98	124
77478	SUGAR LAND	160	190	180	192	189	166	166	167	156	179	158	132	184	162	177	149	115	159	149	190
77479	SUGAR LAND	216	264	240	271	261	225	222	225	207	244	211	183	252	219	237	194	154	210	192	254
77480	SWEENY	91	75	80	74	74	91	76	85	81	72	80	65	66	83	72	86	54	81	90	102
77482	VAN VLECK	92	69	83	68	69	91	71	84	78	68	77	64	59	80	67	85	51	79	88	101
77483	WADSWORTH	95	65	104	65	68	100	73	90	75	59	75	75	53	74	72	82	48	84	95	111
77484	WALLER	91	81	75	80	80	86	82	84	85	82	84	63	76	87	77	87	58	84	86	101
77485	WALLIS	105	94	104	93	95	107	89	101	93	90	93	75	84	94	90	97	63	95	102	119
77486	WEST COLUMBIA	88	79	78	80	79	90	83	86	86	79	84	64	77	86	80	90	58	86	94	102
77488	WHARTON	75	64	66	63	63	74	67	71	71	65	70	53	60	71	63	75	48	71	77	85
77489	MISSOURI CITY	115	122	101	118	115	107	110	110	107	117	109	83	112	112	108	104	75	107	102	128
77493	KATY	119	128	105	124	120	110	114	114	110	122	112	88	116	116	113	106	78	110	104	132
77494	KATY	163	198	173	201	192	168	167	169	156	182	159	138	187	166	177	147	115	158	145	191
77498	SUGAR LAND	154	172	145	168	163	146	150	151	143	162	146	118	158	151	152	136	103	143	134	173
77502	PASADENA	80	76	66	73	73	70	80	77	79	82	80	59	76	80	76	77	56	80	75	88
77503	PASADENA	77	68	61	64	66	62	75	71	72	77	74	55	68	75	69	70	52	74	66	81
77504	PASADENA	90	77	68	77	73	70	90	79	87	91	89	64	82	90	81	84	62	86	77	95
77505	PASADENA	144	162	139	162	156	139	142	142	135	154	137	114	152	143	145	128	98	135	125	163
77506	PASADENA	67	53	44	49	50	47	63	58	63	65	65	43	55	64	55	62	46	63	55	66
77510	SANTA FE	102	98	86	96	95	99	91	96	93	94	93	71	88	97	89	95	64	93	96	114
	TEXAS	104	96	90	94	93	94	99	97	99	101	100	75	94	101	94	99	70	99	96	114
	UNITED STATES	100	100	100	100	100	100	100	100	100	100	100	100	100	100	100	100	100	100	100	100

ZIP CODE #	POST OFFICE NAME	COUNTY FIPS CODE	POPULATION 2000	POPULATION 2009	POPULATION 2014	2000-2009 ANNUAL RATE % Rate	2000-2009 ANNUAL RATE State Centile	HOUSEHOLDS 2000	HOUSEHOLDS 2009	HOUSEHOLDS 2014	HOUSEHOLDS % Annual Rate 2000-2009	HOUSEHOLDS 2009 Average HH Size	FAMILIES 2000	FAMILIES 2009	FAMILIES % Annual Rate 2000-2009
77511	ALVIN	039	42250	47448	51579	1.3	65	14667	16651	18154	1.4	2.84	11156	12472	1.2
77514	ANAHUAC	071	4138	5100	5587	2.3	81	1523	1890	2079	2.4	2.67	1111	1351	2.1
77515	ANGLETON	039	28686	31520	34024	1.0	58	9447	10611	11556	1.3	2.76	7225	7976	1.1
77517	SANTA FE	167	4854	5545	5912	1.4	67	1687	1945	2081	1.6	2.85	1358	1538	1.4
77518	BACLIFF	167	6869	8380	9165	2.2	80	2483	3064	3368	2.3	2.73	1717	2058	2.0
77519	BATSON	199	1200	1248	1281	0.4	37	456	483	498	0.6	2.58	349	364	0.5
77520	BAYTOWN	201	38275	40878	42697	0.7	49	13069	13957	14593	0.7	2.89	9491	9850	0.4
77521	BAYTOWN	201	37506	45576	50718	2.1	79	13528	16393	18207	2.1	2.77	10042	11952	1.9
77523	BAYTOWN	071	10052	16011	18761	5.2	94	3462	5523	6480	5.2	2.90	2837	4492	5.1
77530	CHANNELVIEW	201	27574	33657	37110	2.2	80	8543	10272	11258	2.0	3.27	6795	8068	1.9
77531	CLUTE	039	14277	16030	17401	1.3	65	5120	5787	6301	1.3	2.74	3637	4028	1.1
77532	CROSBY	201	19880	25430	28628	2.7	84	7018	8959	10065	2.7	2.84	5540	6927	2.4
77534	DANBURY	039	2652	3130	3571	1.8	75	895	1074	1233	2.0	2.85	713	839	1.8
77535	DAYTON	291	28229	31113	32199	1.1	61	8308	9087	9429	1.0	2.98	6652	7182	0.8
77536	DEER PARK	201	28540	32760	35273	1.5	69	9624	10955	11749	1.4	2.96	7946	8947	1.3
77538	DEVERS	291	834	928	963	1.2	63	297	325	337	1.0	2.86	237	256	0.8
77539	DICKINSON	167	27426	37068	41608	3.3	88	10047	13686	15418	3.4	2.70	7240	9693	3.2
77541	FREEPORT	039	18766	19839	20988	0.6	46	6548	7006	7435	0.7	2.82	4777	5004	0.5
77545	FRESNO	157	6855	18983	26010	11.6	99	1960	5205	7102	11.1	3.65	1689	4465	11.1
77546	FRIENDSWOOD	167	39034	48168	52249	2.3	81	13318	16319	17663	2.2	2.93	10737	12812	1.9
77547	GALENA PARK	201	9603	10020	10349	0.5	42	2745	2836	2919	0.4	3.53	2214	2242	0.1
77550	GALVESTON	167	30090	31615	32395	0.5	42	12306	13018	13419	0.6	2.30	6799	6884	0.1
77551	GALVESTON	167	20809	21894	22339	0.6	46	8942	9404	9610	0.5	2.33	5428	5541	0.2
77554	GALVESTON	167	8906	10190	10940	1.5	69	3774	4373	4736	1.6	2.14	2326	2606	1.2
77560	HANKAMER	071	326	394	429	2.1	79	115	141	154	2.2	2.79	87	104	1.9
77562	HIGHLANDS	201	10185	11146	11776	1.0	58	3617	3942	4155	0.9	2.82	2837	3027	0.7
77563	HITCHCOCK	167	8640	9475	9927	1.0	58	3461	3824	4019	1.1	2.47	2416	2593	0.8
77564	HULL	291	3670	4012	4143	1.0	58	1349	1450	1495	0.8	2.77	1048	1112	0.6
77565	KEMAH	167	6205	7042	7531	1.4	67	2706	3084	3301	1.4	2.27	1772	1966	1.1
77566	LAKE JACKSON	039	28120	30434	32517	0.9	55	10179	11199	12019	1.0	2.71	7880	8522	0.9
77568	LA MARQUE	167	13734	14122	14370	0.3	34	5252	5437	5550	0.4	2.58	3713	3741	0.1
77571	LA PORTE	201	33752	37703	40255	1.2	63	11609	12889	13720	1.1	2.90	9095	9922	0.9
77573	LEAGUE CITY	167	41741	59680	68273	3.9	91	14652	20908	23953	3.9	2.84	11299	15951	3.8
77575	LIBERTY	291	15540	16494	16755	0.6	46	5597	5835	5918	0.5	2.75	4152	4263	0.3
77577	LIVERPOOL	039	1000	1245	1429	2.4	82	402	510	589	2.6	2.42	289	359	2.4
77578	MANVEL	039	5558	11946	14691	8.6	98	1930	3754	4583	7.5	3.18	1589	3025	7.2
77581	PEARLAND	039	29184	38724	44532	3.1	87	10387	13857	15958	3.2	2.78	8281	10865	3.0
77583	ROSHARON	039	17002	26725	32083	5.0	94	3260	5710	7150	6.2	3.53	2643	4570	6.1
77584	PEARLAND	039	30400	63662	80004	8.3	97	10571	22596	28525	8.6	2.82	8604	17954	8.3
77585	SARATOGA	199	1702	1746	1785	0.3	34	647	676	696	0.5	2.58	498	512	0.3
77586	SEABROOK	201	18809	22534	24608	2.0	78	7764	9151	9941	1.8	2.45	5109	5754	1.3
77587	SOUTH HOUSTON	201	15833	17434	18391	1.0	58	4593	5019	5278	1.0	3.47	3696	3960	0.7
77590	TEXAS CITY	167	30172	31414	32054	0.4	37	11095	11615	11892	0.5	2.68	8062	8223	0.2
77591	TEXAS CITY	167	10408	13596	15020	2.9	86	4018	5312	5909	3.1	2.45	2669	3410	2.7
77597	WALLISVILLE	071	1336	1636	1789	2.2	80	483	598	658	2.3	2.74	377	459	2.2
77598	WEBSTER	201	19208	23297	26119	2.1	79	8899	10691	11841	2.0	2.15	4434	5088	1.5
77611	BRIDGE CITY	361	8881	8767	8897	-0.1	21	3280	3307	3377	0.1	2.65	2541	2527	-0.1
77612	BUNA	241	9641	8920	8550	-0.8	6	3577	3346	3220	-0.7	2.65	2778	2576	-0.8
77614	DEWEYVILLE	351	2489	2392	2328	-0.4	13	940	922	902	-0.2	2.59	702	679	-0.4
77616	FRED	457	1353	1381	1388	0.2	30	510	523	525	0.3	2.64	394	399	0.1
77619	GROVES	245	16625	16045	15761	-0.4	13	6560	6371	6268	-0.3	2.49	4768	4563	-0.5
77622	HAMSHIRE	245	915	885	870	-0.4	13	366	357	351	-0.3	2.48	282	272	-0.4
77624	HILLISTER	457	132	152	158	1.5	69	52	60	62	1.6	2.52	38	43	1.3
77625	KOUNTZE	199	8726	9117	9470	0.5	42	3287	3488	3642	0.6	2.57	2571	2691	0.5
77627	NEDERLAND	245	21536	21666	21547	0.1	27	8423	8503	8465	0.1	2.48	6203	6174	-0.1
77630	ORANGE	361	29506	29318	29755	-0.1	21	11333	11426	11647	0.1	2.51	8043	8010	0.0
77632	ORANGE	361	20804	20991	21451	0.1	27	7652	7907	8140	0.4	2.65	6017	6137	0.2
77640	PORT ARTHUR	245	20599	18538	17839	-1.1	3	8048	7277	7015	-1.1	2.52	5476	4879	-1.2
77642	PORT ARTHUR	245	36875	35579	34921	-0.4	13	13658	13122	12901	-0.4	2.67	9120	8560	-0.7
77650	PORT BOLIVAR	167	3853	4715	5169	2.2	80	1801	2224	2447	2.3	2.12	1139	1360	1.9
77651	PORT NECHES	245	13594	13206	13012	-0.3	16	5280	5147	5075	-0.3	2.56	3975	3834	-0.4
77656	SILSBEE	199	16826	17756	18203	0.6	46	6282	6728	6942	0.7	2.59	4660	4916	0.6
77657	LUMBERTON	199	14734	17504	18516	1.9	76	5359	6456	6861	2.0	2.71	4206	5014	1.9
77659	SOUR LAKE	199	4767	5096	5244	0.7	49	1731	1856	1916	0.8	2.74	1328	1402	0.6
77660	SPURGER	457	1788	1785	1779	0.0	25	655	657	655	0.0	2.72	496	492	-0.1
77662	VIDOR	361	27401	27123	27394	-0.1	21	9976	10114	10297	0.1	2.66	7654	7652	0.0
77664	WARREN	457	2902	2906	2922	0.0	25	1161	1172	1181	0.1	2.48	901	900	0.0
77665	WINNIE	071	6764	7915	8494	1.7	73	2442	2889	3120	1.8	2.67	1822	2114	1.6
77701	BEAUMONT	245	16501	15673	15289	-0.6	9	5785	5449	5313	-0.6	2.71	3751	3467	-0.8
77702	BEAUMONT	245	3051	2898	2830	-0.6	9	1310	1236	1204	-0.6	2.33	722	666	-0.9
77703	BEAUMONT	245	14930	14030	13683	-0.7	7	5535	5187	5055	-0.7	2.69	3727	3432	-0.9
77705	BEAUMONT	245	40527	40515	40249	0.0	25	10599	10561	10466	0.0	2.70	7329	7214	-0.2
77706	BEAUMONT	245	26047	26162	26013	0.0	25	11740	11898	11857	0.1	2.19	7194	7144	-0.1
77707	BEAUMONT	245	16430	16251	16075	-0.1	21	6345	6317	6260	0.0	2.50	4500	4417	-0.2
77708	BEAUMONT	245	11784	11729	11657	-0.1	21	4467	4483	4459	0.0	2.61	3219	3179	-0.1
77710	BEAUMONT	245	12	14	14	1.7	73	5	6	6	2.0	2.33	3	3	0.0
77713	BEAUMONT	245	11328	12328	12489	0.9	55	4295	4735	4813	1.1	2.57	3178	3421	0.8
77801	BRYAN	041	13226	13800	14117	0.5	42	5439	5683	5826	0.5	2.41	2565	2530	-0.1
77802	BRYAN	041	19932	21959	23157	1.1	61	8197	9235	9754	1.3	2.32	5109	5650	1.1
77803	BRYAN	041	27954	28090	28320	0.1	27	8546	8769	8889	0.3	3.04	6192	6170	0.0
77807	BRYAN	041	7021	7905	8359	1.3	65	2471	2852	3034	1.6	2.58	1622	1812	1.2
77808	BRYAN	041	7539	9637	10624	2.7	84	2675	3532	3918	3.1	2.73	2085	2683	2.8
77830	ANDERSON	185	2678	3066	3213	1.5	69	1054	1214	1273	1.5	2.49	756	858	1.4
77831	BEDIAS	185	2545	3045	3229	2.0	78	915	1079	1142	1.8	2.82	694	806	1.6
77833	BRENHAM	477	25080	27137	28244	0.9	55	9170	9966	10399	0.9	2.55	6415	6868	0.7
77835	BURTON	477	2131	2331	2443	1.0	58	909	996	1044	1.0	2.34	631	679	0.8
77836	CALDWELL	051	10212	11319	11741	1.1	61	3877	4283	4448	1.1	2.61	2841	3090	0.9
77837	CALVERT	395	1693	1707	1686	0.1	27	682	691	684	0.1	2.44	453	451	0.0
77840	COLLEGE STATION	041	47415	50936	53018	0.8	52	17213	19529	20634	1.4	2.09	5540	5799	0.5
77845	COLLEGE STATION	041	29076	41232	46606	3.8	90	10613	15005	16897	3.8	2.73	7219	10073	3.7
77850	CONCORD	289	94	101	105	0.8	52	35	38	39	0.9	2.66	25	27	0.8
77853	DIME BOX	287	907	995	1041	1.0	58	362	392	409	0.9	2.54	259	277	0.7
77856	FRANKLIN	395	4796	4966	4933	0.4	37	1891	1976	1968	0.5	2.45	1361	1401	0.3
77859	HEARNE	395	7046	6775	6577	-0.4	13	2601	2523	2457	-0.3	2.66	1845	1764	-0.5
77861	IOLA	185	2005	2122	2142	0.6	46	766	824	836	0.8	2.58	572	606	0.6
	TEXAS					1.9					1.8	2.78			1.7
	UNITED STATES					1.0					1.1	2.59			0.9

ZIP CODE #	POST OFFICE NAME	RACE (%) White 2000	White 2009	Black 2000	Black 2009	Asian/Pacific 2000	Asian/Pacific 2009	% Hispanic Origin 2000	% Hispanic Origin 2009	2009 AGE DISTRIBUTION (%) 0-4	5-9	10-14	15-19	20-24	25-44	45-64	65-84	85+	18+	MEDIAN AGE 2009	% 2009 Males	% 2009 Females
77511	ALVIN	82.2	78.5	1.8	2.1	0.8	0.8	27.5	34.2	8.3	7.9	7.4	7.2	7.1	27.9	24.7	8.6	0.9	72.1	33.0	50.0	50.0
77514	ANAHUAC	65.3	59.6	16.3	18.1	2.6	2.7	20.1	25.2	6.2	6.3	6.6	6.5	5.1	24.8	29.9	13.0	1.7	76.9	41.0	50.3	49.7
77515	ANGLETON	75.0	71.2	11.9	12.6	0.9	0.9	23.4	29.4	7.0	6.8	7.0	7.6	6.6	28.3	26.6	8.7	1.3	74.4	35.8	52.4	47.6
77517	SANTA FE	93.7	91.2	0.4	0.6	0.3	0.3	11.3	17.3	6.7	7.1	7.2	7.0	5.3	25.4	30.6	9.8	0.9	74.7	38.6	50.2	49.8
77518	BACLIFF	83.4	78.9	1.6	2.1	2.8	2.8	22.7	31.1	7.8	7.8	7.5	7.1	5.9	27.8	26.5	8.7	0.8	72.5	35.2	52.2	47.8
77519	BATSON	98.0	97.0	0.1	0.2	0.1	0.2	2.3	3.4	7.5	7.0	6.5	6.8	7.7	27.6	25.2	10.6	1.2	74.9	33.7	49.4	50.6
77520	BAYTOWN	66.7	61.2	11.3	11.3	0.7	0.9	42.7	52.6	9.0	8.2	7.6	7.7	7.4	26.9	21.4	9.6	2.2	70.6	31.7	48.5	51.5
77521	BAYTOWN	67.6	60.8	17.2	18.0	1.5	2.1	23.4	33.1	8.5	7.7	7.2	7.2	7.2	29.5	24.1	7.6	1.0	72.3	32.4	48.5	51.5
77523	BAYTOWN	87.7	84.7	5.8	6.6	0.4	0.4	9.0	13.2	7.0	7.0	7.3	7.6	6.1	28.0	28.8	7.6	0.7	73.9	35.7	49.3	50.7
77530	CHANNELVIEW	63.9	54.0	12.4	14.4	2.0	2.4	37.3	50.5	9.2	8.9	8.4	8.3	6.9	29.8	22.4	5.6	0.5	68.6	30.2	49.7	50.3
77531	CLUTE	68.4	65.0	7.6	7.6	0.9	0.8	41.2	47.4	9.6	8.5	7.5	7.5	8.5	29.9	20.6	6.8	1.1	70.0	29.3	50.1	49.9
77532	CROSBY	77.4	70.9	15.6	18.7	0.4	0.6	9.9	15.5	6.7	7.0	7.3	7.3	5.7	26.1	29.6	9.3	0.9	74.4	37.3	49.4	50.6
77534	DANBURY	88.8	85.7	2.2	2.3	0.3	0.3	15.0	19.8	7.5	7.6	7.3	7.2	6.3	28.0	26.2	9.1	0.8	72.8	34.2	50.4	49.6
77535	DAYTON	80.1	76.7	12.6	13.7	0.3	0.4	9.9	13.4	6.8	6.5	6.4	7.0	7.9	32.8	25.0	7.1	0.7	76.2	34.4	47.7	52.3
77536	DEER PARK	90.0	85.9	1.3	1.5	1.3	1.7	15.2	24.2	6.4	6.7	6.9	7.4	6.0	28.1	29.1	8.4	0.9	75.4	36.5	49.6	50.4
77538	DEVERS	80.0	74.1	8.0	9.4	0.1	0.1	12.9	18.3	7.8	7.3	7.8	6.5	5.4	25.2	28.1	10.9	1.1	73.1	37.8	50.8	49.2
77539	DICKINSON	72.7	66.7	10.9	13.3	2.4	2.5	22.2	29.8	7.6	7.5	7.1	7.2	6.6	27.7	26.4	8.9	0.9	73.3	35.0	49.8	50.2
77541	FREEPORT	70.4	67.4	9.8	9.6	0.4	0.4	39.8	45.8	9.0	8.4	7.9	8.1	7.6	26.1	23.5	8.4	0.9	69.6	30.6	50.9	49.1
77545	FRESNO	40.9	35.5	33.7	34.7	2.4	3.3	39.4	44.6	10.2	9.4	8.8	7.4	5.4	31.8	22.1	4.5	0.4	66.9	30.8	49.6	50.4
77546	FRIENDSWOOD	85.7	80.4	4.3	5.7	4.7	6.2	9.9	15.8	7.3	7.7	8.2	7.4	5.1	27.8	28.2	7.2	1.0	71.8	36.5	48.7	51.3
77547	GALENA PARK	62.2	58.5	8.4	7.8	0.4	0.4	70.8	79.7	10.0	9.4	8.4	8.1	7.7	27.1	20.3	7.6	1.2	67.2	28.7	49.6	50.4
77550	GALVESTON	46.8	43.2	36.1	37.5	3.6	3.5	25.0	30.7	6.9	6.3	5.8	6.7	8.2	28.2	24.5	11.5	2.0	77.4	35.9	48.9	51.1
77551	GALVESTON	68.6	65.0	15.5	16.5	3.1	3.0	30.6	38.5	6.7	6.2	6.1	6.4	7.9	24.9	26.3	13.2	2.2	77.2	38.0	47.4	52.6
77554	GALVESTON	86.2	83.5	6.0	6.8	2.0	2.1	11.2	16.0	4.9	5.2	5.0	8.0	8.4	21.8	31.7	13.5	1.5	82.3	42.5	49.8	50.2
77560	HANKAMER	61.0	54.1	36.2	42.6	0.0	0.0	3.4	4.3	7.6	7.6	7.9	6.9	5.1	23.1	27.7	12.7	1.5	72.3	38.4	48.2	51.8
77562	HIGHLANDS	81.0	73.2	10.5	13.5	0.5	0.6	13.3	21.9	7.3	7.2	7.3	7.4	6.0	27.2	27.4	9.0	1.1	73.6	35.8	49.6	50.4
77563	HITCHCOCK	66.7	62.3	24.6	27.1	0.4	0.4	14.0	18.4	5.7	6.3	6.4	6.5	4.9	23.8	30.2	14.2	2.0	77.6	42.3	48.7	51.3
77564	HULL	90.7	88.5	5.5	6.5	0.0	0.0	4.5	6.5	8.1	7.6	7.4	7.1	6.6	25.2	25.7	10.8	1.5	72.7	35.6	48.5	51.5
77565	KEMAH	86.2	82.6	2.4	3.1	2.1	2.3	14.7	20.4	6.0	6.1	6.2	5.7	5.3	26.9	32.3	10.3	1.1	78.2	40.7	50.8	49.2
77566	LAKE JACKSON	86.6	83.9	3.8	4.3	2.4	2.6	14.4	18.6	7.1	7.2	7.4	7.7	6.4	25.2	28.3	9.3	1.3	73.5	36.5	48.8	51.2
77568	LA MARQUE	56.0	50.4	34.5	38.0	0.5	0.4	15.6	20.6	7.0	7.0	6.7	6.7	6.0	24.4	26.8	13.1	2.4	75.3	38.3	47.3	52.7
77571	LA PORTE	82.0	75.0	6.0	6.8	1.2	1.6	19.8	31.1	7.6	7.5	7.4	7.0	6.0	29.5	26.4	7.6	1.0	73.2	34.7	49.5	50.5
77573	LEAGUE CITY	83.6	79.1	5.2	6.8	3.3	3.6	13.7	19.5	8.0	7.9	7.8	7.1	5.5	29.7	26.8	6.3	0.8	71.7	35.0	49.2	50.8
77575	LIBERTY	73.5	67.9	17.8	20.5	0.4	0.6	10.2	13.9	7.1	6.9	7.1	7.2	6.4	25.0	26.7	11.8	1.9	74.5	37.3	49.3	50.7
77577	LIVERPOOL	91.6	89.1	1.0	1.2	0.1	0.1	7.0	9.6	5.5	5.7	6.0	5.9	5.3	25.7	31.5	13.3	1.1	78.7	42.2	51.4	48.6
77578	MANVEL	83.5	73.3	5.1	6.7	2.0	4.0	18.7	30.5	8.4	8.3	8.0	6.6	5.1	28.9	26.7	7.3	0.6	71.2	35.7	50.1	49.9
77581	PEARLAND	84.1	80.4	4.0	4.7	3.2	3.9	17.0	22.1	7.4	7.4	7.3	6.8	5.6	28.1	27.5	8.8	1.1	73.7	36.5	49.1	50.9
77583	ROSHARON	56.8	55.2	24.3	19.9	2.7	3.0	26.8	37.7	6.3	6.1	6.0	5.8	5.0	37.1	27.4	5.8	0.5	77.9	37.6	62.5	37.5
77584	PEARLAND	73.0	67.9	10.7	10.7	6.6	6.4	18.7	28.6	9.4	9.0	8.2	6.3	5.1	31.9	22.9	6.7	0.7	69.5	34.1	49.2	50.8
77585	SARATOGA	97.5	96.7	0.1	0.1	0.0	0.0	1.8	2.6	5.6	5.9	6.0	6.1	5.2	24.5	30.6	14.5	1.7	78.9	42.5	49.5	50.5
77586	SEABROOK	90.4	85.5	2.2	3.0	2.8	4.2	8.5	14.7	6.0	5.9	6.5	6.8	6.1	27.9	30.0	9.9	0.8	77.2	39.2	50.9	49.1
77587	SOUTH HOUSTON	65.3	61.7	1.0	0.9	0.8	0.7	77.9	86.3	10.3	9.8	8.9	8.6	7.3	28.5	19.5	6.5	0.6	65.7	28.2	51.3	48.7
77590	TEXAS CITY	68.7	63.9	17.7	19.4	0.8	0.8	24.5	32.1	7.4	7.2	6.9	7.4	6.8	26.6	25.6	10.5	1.6	74.0	35.1	48.1	51.9
77591	TEXAS CITY	36.4	36.5	57.0	55.5	1.2	1.6	9.6	12.8	5.8	5.8	5.9	6.6	6.8	25.9	26.8	14.0	2.4	78.6	39.6	45.4	54.6
77597	WALLISVILLE	72.6	67.3	24.8	29.6	0.1	0.1	3.4	4.6	6.5	6.7	7.2	6.9	5.1	25.5	29.6	11.2	1.2	75.2	38.9	48.7	51.3
77598	WEBSTER	71.2	62.9	10.4	11.5	5.2	6.3	19.8	30.3	8.4	6.5	5.5	5.8	11.2	38.1	19.0	4.6	0.8	76.3	29.5	50.5	49.5
77611	BRIDGE CITY	95.2	94.2	0.2	0.3	1.4	1.5	3.7	5.2	6.8	6.8	6.8	6.8	5.8	27.2	27.5	11.0	1.2	75.3	37.1	49.4	50.6
77612	BUNA	94.6	93.3	3.1	3.8	0.2	0.2	1.9	2.7	7.2	7.0	7.2	6.8	5.7	26.1	26.8	11.8	1.3	74.4	37.8	48.9	51.1
77614	DEWEYVILLE	97.3	96.5	0.3	0.4	0.1	0.2	1.7	2.5	6.9	6.8	6.9	6.6	5.6	27.5	27.4	11.4	0.9	75.5	37.9	49.9	50.1
77616	FRED	96.6	95.5	1.0	1.2	0.0	0.0	1.6	2.3	7.7	7.7	7.6	6.3	5.3	25.7	26.3	12.2	1.2	73.1	36.9	50.9	49.1
77619	GROVES	89.9	87.0	4.2	5.1	2.2	2.5	8.1	12.5	6.6	6.3	5.8	5.9	6.5	25.0	26.8	14.1	3.0	77.9	40.1	47.4	52.6
77622	HAMSHIRE	90.5	86.3	5.4	7.3	0.2	0.5	4.6	7.5	6.1	6.2	6.3	6.4	5.6	28.1	29.3	10.5	1.4	77.6	37.9	50.6	49.4
77624	HILLISTER	71.2	65.1	25.0	28.9	0.0	0.7	3.0	3.9	5.9	5.9	5.9	5.9	5.3	22.4	29.6	17.1	2.0	78.9	43.8	50.7	49.3
77625	KOUNTZE	89.0	85.7	8.6	11.1	0.3	0.3	2.3	3.1	6.4	6.4	6.8	7.3	5.8	24.9	28.5	12.4	1.5	75.8	39.6	50.5	49.5
77627	NEDERLAND	92.6	89.9	2.3	2.9	1.8	2.2	5.9	9.5	6.2	6.4	6.4	6.5	6.1	26.8	27.8	12.2	1.6	77.0	38.6	50.0	50.0
77630	ORANGE	73.9	72.8	21.6	21.9	1.3	1.3	4.1	5.7	6.7	6.6	6.5	6.9	6.2	25.2	26.6	13.2	2.1	76.0	38.7	48.7	51.3
77632	ORANGE	93.4	92.3	3.5	3.9	0.5	0.5	3.2	4.5	6.3	6.5	6.9	7.1	5.5	25.1	29.9	11.5	1.1	75.7	39.5	49.6	50.4
77640	PORT ARTHUR	28.3	26.5	65.0	65.5	1.4	1.5	7.0	9.1	6.5	6.5	6.3	6.8	6.1	22.7	27.6	15.2	2.4	76.7	41.0	47.4	52.6
77642	PORT ARTHUR	44.8	40.1	32.0	33.9	8.4	8.3	23.4	28.8	8.8	8.0	7.6	7.8	7.2	24.4	22.0	11.4	2.9	71.1	33.4	47.3	52.7
77650	PORT BOLIVAR	93.7	91.8	0.5	0.6	0.6	0.6	7.0	10.2	2.8	3.2	3.9	4.9	4.0	15.5	39.4	24.7	1.6	87.1	54.7	51.2	48.8
77651	PORT NECHES	94.8	93.0	0.9	1.2	1.6	2.1	5.0	8.2	5.9	6.0	6.3	6.5	5.6	25.2	29.0	13.8	1.7	77.9	40.6	49.0	51.0
77656	SILSBEE	83.5	81.0	14.4	16.4	0.3	0.4	2.5	3.3	7.3	7.4	7.3	6.6	5.3	25.8	26.1	12.1	2.2	73.8	37.5	49.0	51.0
77657	LUMBERTON	97.7	96.8	0.1	0.1	0.2	0.3	2.8	4.1	7.3	7.4	7.4	7.1	5.7	27.8	27.3	9.2	0.9	73.6	36.0	49.5	50.5
77659	SOUR LAKE	94.8	93.0	2.7	3.8	0.3	0.4	2.9	4.0	6.1	6.3	7.4	8.6	5.8	22.7	30.8	10.6	1.5	74.5	40.6	49.8	50.2
77660	SPURGER	95.8	94.6	1.2	1.4	0.1	0.1	1.6	2.4	7.8	7.8	7.6	6.1	5.1	24.6	26.0	13.6	1.4	73.1	37.5	49.9	50.1
77662	VIDOR	97.2	96.6	0.1	0.1	0.3	0.3	3.3	4.7	7.3	7.1	7.0	6.7	5.9	27.3	26.3	11.1	1.4	74.5	36.8	49.2	50.8
77664	WARREN	94.5	93.1	3.6	4.3	0.1	0.1	1.6	2.2	5.3	5.5	6.0	6.7	5.2	21.3	29.5	18.5	2.0	79.0	45.0	49.2	50.8
77665	WINNIE	82.3	77.5	10.5	12.7	0.3	0.3	9.0	12.7	6.8	6.8	6.5	6.9	5.8	25.8	27.8	11.7	1.7	75.6	38.6	50.7	49.3
77701	BEAUMONT	20.9	17.9	64.4	65.5	2.7	2.6	18.2	21.5	7.2	7.5	7.3	9.5	6.8	24.5	23.6	10.8	2.8	72.0	34.2	49.4	50.6
77702	BEAUMONT	55.8	49.4	30.1	33.0	1.8	1.9	18.6	24.4	7.7	6.6	6.0	6.0	8.1	30.0	24.5	9.2	1.7	76.3	34.6	49.4	50.6
77703	BEAUMONT	19.5	16.3	75.9	78.4	0.8	0.8	6.3	7.9	7.7	8.0	7.9	8.6	7.4	24.1	24.0	10.1	2.1	71.1	33.2	46.4	53.6
77705	BEAUMONT	42.7	39.2	51.6	54.1	1.4	1.5	12.3	15.6	5.3	5.2	5.1	7.0	10.6	36.5	21.6	7.6	1.1	80.9	33.3	62.1	37.9
77706	BEAUMONT	82.0	76.6	10.7	14.0	3.9	5.0	5.0	7.6	5.4	5.4	5.8	6.1	6.4	24.7	29.3	13.8	3.1	79.7	42.1	47.3	52.7
77707	BEAUMONT	69.0	62.0	24.0	29.0	3.1	3.7	7.1	10.3	7.1	7.0	6.9	6.6	5.7	25.9	25.5	12.7	2.6	75.0	38.5	46.3	53.7
77708	BEAUMONT	44.7	38.6	50.6	55.8	1.3	1.4	5.0	7.0	8.9	7.5	6.9	7.3	8.3	26.5	24.6	8.7	1.3	72.0	32.5	46.5	53.5
77710	BEAUMONT	27.3	21.4	72.7	78.6	0.0	0.0	9.1	7.1	14.3	14.3	0.0	7.1	21.4	35.7	7.1	0.0	0.0	64.3	23.3	50.0	50.0
77713	BEAUMONT	77.9	71.9	17.5	21.6	1.1	1.5	4.7	7.5	6.3	6.5	6.9	6.9	5.7	26.3	28.6	11.3	1.5	76.0	39.0	49.0	51.0
77801	BRYAN	62.2	54.5	12.6	14.2	5.6	6.2	30.9	39.8	9.1	6.3	4.7	7.8	23.7	33.0	11.4	3.4	0.6	77.0	24.7	52.8	47.2
77802	BRYAN	86.9	82.0	5.9	7.4	1.0	1.3	10.8	16.9	6.5	6.0	5.8	6.8	9.5	27.5	22.7	11.8	3.4	78.3	35.1	47.5	52.5
77803	BRYAN	48.7	43.8	28.5	28.6	0.4	0.4	40.3	48.4	9.2	8.3	7.6	8.5	9.8	30.6	18.8	6.2	1.1	70.1	28.5	49.5	50.5
77807	BRYAN	75.8	68.2	12.0	14.4	1.3	1.6	20.5	29.4	7.3	5.8	4.9	13.2	14.7	26.5	20.7	6.1	0.8	73.3	27.2	54.0	46.0
77808	BRYAN	85.4	80.8	8.1	9.5	0.3	0.4	9.8	15.1	6.8	6.7	6.8	6.8	5.9	29.2	27.7	9.2	1.0	75.4	36.4	50.1	49.9
77830	ANDERSON	83.8	79.5	11.3	13.3	0.1	0.3	6.4	9.8	5.2	5.5	6.0	6.4	5.1	24.2	30.9	14.7	1.9	79.5	43.1	50.3	49.7
77831	BEDIAS	87.2	83.0	8.3	10.3	0.0	0.1	6.4	9.8	5.9	6.8	8.6	6.6	5.6	23.7	29.2	12.0	1.6	74.3	40.0	51.2	48.8
77833	BRENHAM	75.3	71.7	17.5	18.8	1.4	1.8	9.5	12.7	6.4	6.2	6.0	7.9	6.9	25.2	25.9	12.4	3.0	77.7	37.8	49.0	51.0
77835	BURTON	79.8	75.5	14.9	17.2	0.5	0.7	5.7	8.0	5.9	6.2	6.3	6.3	4.2	21.4	29.9	17.2	2.6	77.6	44.7	50.5	49.5
77836	CALDWELL	76.0	71.3	12.1	13.1	0.2	0.2	15.6	20.7	6.9	6.7	6.6	7.0	6.1	24.0	27.1	13.3	2.4	75.7	39.2	49.4	50.6
77837	CALVERT	41.0	38.8	47.8	49.4	0.1	0.1	15.7	16.8	6.2	8.1	8.5	6.6	5.0	20.5	25.6	15.6	3.8	72.6	40.5	46.9	53.1
77840	COLLEGE STATION	78.0	70.9	6.4	7.8	7.9	10.0	11.2	17.2	3.3	2.3	1.8	20.6	45.2	16.9	6.8	2.6	0.4	91.0	22.4	51.8	48.2
77845	COLLEGE STATION	87.3	82.6	3.5	4.5	4.5	6.0	7.6	12.0	7.4	6.7	6.5	7.5	13.3	29.2	22.8	5.9	0.7	75.4	29.8	49.8	50.2
77850	CONCORD	89.4	86.1	4.3	5.0	0.0	0.0	6.4	9.9	5.0	5.0	5.0	5.9	5.0	21.8	31.7	17.8	3.0	81.2	46.8	52.5	47.5
77853	DIME BOX	57.6	53.2	35.7	38.1	0.1	0.1	10.2	13.9	5.8	5.8	6.1	7.4	6.6	21.4	30.3	14.5	2.0	77.8	42.5	48.5	51.5
77856	FRANKLIN	88.6	87.5	7.5	8.4	0.4	0.3	6.3	7.1	6.2	6.4	6.8	6.5	4.5	20.7	29.9	16.2	2.8	76.3	44.1	48.9	51.1
77859	HEARNE	51.3	50.0	33.7	34.1	0.2	0.2	23.5	25.3	8.4	7.9	7.9	8.0	6.1	24.1	23.8	11.6	2.2	70.6	34.9	47.0	53.0
77861	IOLA	94.0	91.7	1.7	2.3	0.1	0.1	7.6	11.9	6.4	6.6	6.7	6.4	5.3	22.5	29.8	14.6	1.8	76.3	42.4	48.8	51.2
	TEXAS	71.0	67.6	11.5	11.4	2.8	3.5	32.0	37.4	7.9	7.5	7.2	7.5	7.4	28.3	24.0	8.8	1.4	73.0	33.6	49.7	50.3
	UNITED STATES	75.1	72.0	12.3	12.7	3.8	4.6	12.5	15.7	6.8	6.7	6.6	7.1	6.9	27.0	26.0	10.9	1.9	75.7	36.9	49.2	50.8

ZIP CODE #	POST OFFICE NAME	2009 Per Capita Income	2009 HH Income Base	2009 HOUSEHOLD INCOME DISTRIBUTION (%) Less than $25,000	$25,000 to $49,999	$50,000 to $99,999	$100,000 to $149,999	$150,000 or More	MEDIAN HOUSEHOLD INCOME 2009	2014	2009 National Centile	2009 State Centile	2009 Home Value Base	2009 HOME VALUE DISTRIBUTION (%) Less than $50,000	$50,000 to $89,999	$90,000 to $174,999	$175,000 to $399,999	$400,000 or More	2009 Median Home Value
77511	ALVIN	21535	16651	20.7	26.0	40.9	9.2	3.3	53679	55657	69	77	11163	22.8	25.0	38.9	12.2	1.1	93502
77514	ANAHUAC	19318	1890	34.3	23.5	31.7	7.7	2.8	41945	45863	39	50	1531	44.2	27.0	20.6	6.9	1.2	56604
77515	ANGLETON	21812	10611	20.3	26.5	38.5	11.5	3.2	54104	56662	70	77	7546	24.6	31.4	35.6	7.4	0.9	81366
77517	SANTA FE	23130	1945	16.2	21.2	47.3	12.2	3.0	59186	60372	76	83	1640	19.1	22.1	40.1	17.4	1.3	105682
77518	BACLIFF	18613	3064	26.9	32.5	31.5	6.3	2.8	40367	43123	34	44	2019	36.8	31.6	20.1	7.7	3.8	59981
77519	BATSON	22055	483	21.3	33.3	32.7	6.6	6.0	46362	48721	52	63	424	44.6	30.2	16.7	8.5	0.0	56571
77520	BAYTOWN	18981	13957	27.0	24.6	38.0	7.3	3.2	44838	51547	48	58	8370	27.7	39.3	29.0	3.8	0.2	67128
77521	BAYTOWN	24927	16393	18.3	19.0	43.5	13.5	5.7	59423	61599	77	84	10345	16.7	24.2	46.0	11.3	1.9	101547
77523	BAYTOWN	27071	5523	13.7	16.9	43.2	19.2	7.0	68802	72047	86	89	4674	18.4	14.9	37.3	26.1	3.2	127536
77530	CHANNELVIEW	18565	10272	17.0	22.5	49.3	9.0	2.2	55285	57906	72	79	7358	17.2	39.5	41.1	2.0	0.1	83710
77531	CLUTE	19105	5787	23.4	34.1	33.7	6.8	2.0	44687	46062	47	57	2836	25.2	41.1	28.0	5.2	0.5	72343
77532	CROSBY	24119	8959	18.8	19.2	44.2	13.3	4.6	59517	61656	77	84	7187	15.5	22.2	50.7	10.6	1.0	105314
77534	DANBURY	21536	1074	20.9	25.6	38.0	12.4	3.1	54275	56161	70	77	823	15.1	32.7	42.2	9.5	0.6	92229
77535	DAYTON	19569	9087	19.3	23.6	43.9	10.5	2.6	56029	55756	73	80	7380	24.3	26.6	36.4	11.9	0.9	88565
77536	DEER PARK	28931	10955	9.3	14.4	46.1	22.9	7.3	75617	74594	90	92	8692	3.3	13.1	70.0	12.9	0.7	124810
77538	DEVERS	23328	325	24.0	20.6	42.2	7.7	5.5	53439	53693	69	76	277	31.8	22.7	26.4	18.4	0.7	78333
77539	DICKINSON	24686	13686	21.1	22.7	37.5	13.6	5.0	54117	56366	70	77	9635	15.7	22.4	44.5	15.5	1.9	107756
77541	FREEPORT	17425	7006	30.8	31.4	30.0	5.4	2.3	40986	43207	36	46	4281	41.3	35.2	19.7	3.3	0.6	56413
77545	FRESNO	23094	5205	11.2	20.5	37.9	21.8	8.6	73860	72724	89	91	4636	13.5	8.8	44.9	31.4	1.5	146287
77546	FRIENDSWOOD	34009	16319	6.6	11.1	44.2	23.5	14.6	83017	82169	93	95	12649	1.1	4.6	55.0	34.1	5.2	150210
77547	GALENA PARK	13261	2836	34.5	26.6	34.0	3.3	1.6	37281	40948	24	32	2009	27.7	59.9	12.0	0.4	0.0	58625
77550	GALVESTON	18280	13018	43.6	26.2	23.0	4.6	2.6	29885	31417	8	10	4886	17.9	37.4	34.6	8.0	2.0	84524
77551	GALVESTON	24314	9404	29.0	24.7	34.0	8.1	4.2	43542	50087	44	54	4465	11.8	31.7	38.9	14.5	3.1	100880
77554	GALVESTON	35425	4373	21.6	21.8	31.7	14.4	10.5	56701	59044	74	81	2716	7.6	11.0	32.5	34.3	14.5	169326
77560	HANKAMER	16188	141	32.6	23.4	38.3	4.3	1.4	43022	47085	42	53	126	42.9	19.8	24.6	12.7	0.0	67500
77562	HIGHLANDS	20734	3942	19.9	26.5	41.7	10.1	1.8	52313	54175	67	74	3092	26.5	33.3	34.7	5.2	0.2	77900
77563	HITCHCOCK	22324	3824	28.7	24.4	34.2	9.6	3.0	44187	50919	46	56	2709	20.6	32.7	34.8	11.1	0.8	84100
77564	HULL	17704	1450	27.7	32.0	32.6	6.6	1.0	41604	46182	38	49	1180	45.0	27.3	23.0	3.6	1.2	54214
77565	KEMAH	42517	3084	11.6	16.8	37.9	18.5	15.2	75210	72088	89	92	1996	3.9	13.5	37.1	34.6	10.9	154911
77566	LAKE JACKSON	31291	11199	13.1	18.7	39.1	19.1	10.0	72133	76727	88	90	7755	3.2	17.3	49.3	25.3	4.9	133535
77568	LA MARQUE	20770	5437	27.8	27.9	33.4	7.9	3.0	42447	46543	41	51	3804	20.0	45.7	31.0	3.1	0.3	76019
77571	LA PORTE	25984	12889	12.0	14.9	51.9	15.7	5.4	68118	69005	86	89	9950	10.6	18.0	62.9	7.6	0.9	111120
77573	LEAGUE CITY	33490	20908	7.6	12.5	43.9	22.5	13.5	81304	80936	93	94	15675	4.0	9.6	50.8	33.2	2.3	139661
77575	LIBERTY	18743	5835	30.3	29.2	30.0	7.8	2.7	42398	46316	41	51	4421	32.0	29.0	31.2	7.6	0.2	74003
77577	LIVERPOOL	22663	510	21.8	30.6	38.0	7.6	2.0	47154	49139	55	65	405	27.2	27.4	34.8	9.4	1.2	80263
77578	MANVEL	27984	3754	10.6	19.9	38.2	19.0	12.2	74042	77678	89	91	3232	12.3	13.1	36.0	35.1	3.6	146065
77581	PEARLAND	31942	13857	9.8	18.1	40.3	20.7	11.1	73648	78077	89	91	10381	6.2	6.7	51.3	33.3	2.4	147045
77583	ROSHARON	20926	5710	14.5	22.3	38.1	16.1	9.0	65530	69607	84	88	4861	15.3	15.8	31.8	29.8	7.4	130785
77584	PEARLAND	35983	22596	8.1	14.1	36.9	23.9	16.9	85139	86556	94	95	19519	7.8	7.9	40.8	40.5	3.0	161141
77585	SARATOGA	15133	676	32.2	40.8	23.5	2.5	0.9	34298	38626	16	21	610	50.3	25.6	20.0	2.3	1.8	49592
77586	SEABROOK	38262	9151	7.9	14.1	45.5	19.6	12.9	75254	71173	89	92	5861	0.6	9.3	44.0	41.3	4.7	167824
77587	SOUTH HOUSTON	13730	5019	31.5	26.8	35.3	4.9	1.5	39427	43204	31	40	3007	27.7	55.1	15.6	1.2	0.3	61430
77590	TEXAS CITY	20224	11615	27.9	24.6	35.9	9.3	2.3	44870	50594	48	58	7079	17.7	40.4	35.3	6.2	0.4	82340
77591	TEXAS CITY	21938	5312	28.0	24.9	35.5	7.8	3.7	42854	50533	42	53	3287	13.6	34.5	41.5	9.3	1.1	92461
77597	WALLISVILLE	18513	598	31.1	29.3	28.9	7.7	3.0	41228	45000	37	47	524	35.9	23.9	25.2	13.5	1.5	72258
77598	WEBSTER	27821	10691	16.1	25.5	47.1	9.0	2.3	54020	56327	70	77	3052	4.5	16.4	77.4	1.5	0.1	114663
77611	BRIDGE CITY	21977	3307	20.8	28.5	38.0	10.6	2.1	50674	52167	63	72	2526	18.4	36.3	36.9	7.9	0.5	85496
77612	BUNA	17086	3346	28.7	33.5	32.2	4.8	0.8	38807	39456	29	37	2841	32.6	28.1	28.5	10.6	0.2	73920
77614	DEWEYVILLE	16424	922	29.6	37.2	30.6	1.7	0.9	40000	41593	33	42	793	46.9	32.0	18.2	2.3	0.6	54224
77616	FRED	16620	523	30.4	35.6	28.1	4.6	1.3	35745	35724	20	26	462	45.2	26.0	19.3	7.4	2.2	55946
77619	GROVES	24977	6371	20.8	26.8	37.9	10.0	4.6	51976	52755	66	74	4706	17.7	46.8	32.7	2.7	0.0	76238
77622	HAMSHIRE	24726	357	19.9	29.4	39.5	7.0	4.2	50656	51586	63	71	301	19.6	42.2	28.9	9.3	0.0	73500
77624	HILLISTER	15615	60	40.0	30.0	25.0	5.0	0.0	30000	32809	8	10	51	31.4	15.7	33.3	15.7	3.9	95000
77625	KOUNTZE	20500	3488	26.6	28.7	35.3	7.1	2.3	45553	47490	50	60	2947	26.3	28.0	31.5	13.9	0.3	80839
77627	NEDERLAND	25550	8503	16.9	27.1	41.8	9.4	4.7	55146	55443	71	79	6357	13.0	38.7	40.3	7.6	0.4	88297
77630	ORANGE	20276	11426	33.0	26.9	30.1	7.1	3.0	40619	45396	35	45	7896	35.2	30.8	27.5	5.9	0.5	63980
77632	ORANGE	23932	7907	19.8	24.6	40.6	11.0	4.0	55142	54623	71	79	6485	23.0	22.9	39.4	14.4	0.4	98546
77640	PORT ARTHUR	15585	7277	46.0	24.6	23.9	3.6	2.0	27717	30769	5	7	5035	60.5	24.2	12.7	1.9	0.8	40268
77642	PORT ARTHUR	17470	13122	37.6	27.0	27.7	5.5	2.2	36346	40703	22	28	7302	48.9	31.9	16.8	2.2	0.3	50871
77650	PORT BOLIVAR	28474	2224	30.6	23.8	33.3	7.7	4.6	42505	48644	41	52	1800	33.8	31.6	25.2	8.9	0.5	66800
77651	PORT NECHES	26108	5147	17.2	24.3	39.4	14.5	4.7	58211	56652	75	83	3937	15.8	26.9	46.7	10.1	0.4	101530
77656	SILSBEE	20000	6728	26.4	31.6	32.2	7.7	2.1	42896	45985	42	53	5272	33.4	29.0	29.9	6.6	1.1	70966
77657	LUMBERTON	20921	6456	17.8	33.8	36.9	9.6	1.8	48658	49925	58	67	5239	21.2	23.1	39.7	14.8	1.1	100576
77659	SOUR LAKE	22555	1856	24.9	28.4	29.9	12.0	4.8	46639	48418	53	64	1576	24.4	24.7	32.7	17.1	1.2	91974
77660	SPURGER	15482	657	36.1	32.6	25.6	4.7	1.1	32841	33707	13	16	572	49.8	24.5	17.7	6.8	1.2	50227
77662	VIDOR	18710	10114	27.6	32.1	32.0	6.1	2.2	41047	45535	36	46	8101	37.0	33.8	25.3	3.7	0.2	61904
77664	WARREN	20265	1172	26.3	34.1	29.2	8.4	2.0	41109	44233	36	46	1016	30.1	21.6	32.3	15.0	1.1	86222
77665	WINNIE	18637	2889	25.5	31.8	34.9	6.0	1.7	42277	45611	40	51	2227	30.6	32.6	26.9	8.9	1.0	68333
77701	BEAUMONT	14724	5449	46.2	28.0	20.2	3.6	2.1	27236	29562	5	6	3004	55.4	31.9	9.9	2.2	0.7	46501
77702	BEAUMONT	23329	1236	36.4	29.8	23.8	5.2	4.9	34842	40127	17	22	542	17.0	28.6	37.3	14.8	2.4	97059
77703	BEAUMONT	13354	5187	46.9	28.6	21.8	1.9	0.9	27014	29779	5	6	2809	62.8	30.5	6.1	0.6	0.0	43349
77705	BEAUMONT	15954	10561	38.1	27.6	27.6	4.5	2.3	35544	39752	19	25	6531	42.6	29.4	22.2	5.3	0.6	57543
77706	BEAUMONT	35118	11898	17.5	25.8	34.6	13.0	9.1	58538	57100	76	83	7431	3.3	16.5	57.2	18.2	4.9	124740
77707	BEAUMONT	26849	6317	20.0	22.8	40.1	9.8	7.3	57712	56226	75	82	4408	7.8	44.9	34.5	11.2	1.6	87952
77708	BEAUMONT	20140	4483	31.1	28.4	30.3	6.2	4.0	41180	46425	37	47	2635	22.6	39.6	32.7	4.9	0.2	75584
77710	BEAUMONT	14754	6	50.0	16.7	33.3	0.0	0.0	30000	37500	8	10	2	100.0	0.0	0.0	0.0	0.0	45000
77713	BEAUMONT	22235	4735	21.1	27.4	40.8	7.5	3.1	51118	52131	64	72	3672	21.8	23.3	44.4	9.5	0.9	96953
77801	BRYAN	15938	5683	42.4	31.9	21.8	2.9	1.1	29862	33691	8	10	1201	28.4	25.8	40.8	5.0	0.0	78295
77802	BRYAN	27292	9235	23.3	23.9	37.2	10.5	5.1	52678	52963	67	75	5278	3.7	14.1	61.3	19.7	1.2	126590
77803	BRYAN	14073	8769	34.8	33.3	28.0	2.7	1.2	36096	38158	21	27	4720	42.8	39.7	16.2	1.1	0.1	55576
77807	BRYAN	22223	2852	23.8	25.0	40.7	6.7	3.8	50814	51030	63	72	1853	27.9	21.4	41.2	7.9	1.6	91311
77808	BRYAN	22196	3532	18.9	28.4	42.1	8.4	2.2	52162	52103	66	74	2710	24.6	18.9	32.2	20.0	4.3	106467
77830	ANDERSON	20080	1214	32.8	28.9	30.4	5.5	2.4	40072	41586	33	42	1002	22.9	24.7	28.9	18.6	5.0	94808
77831	BEDIAS	17161	1079	29.7	28.5	34.5	5.5	1.8	39400	40108	31	40	929	19.7	35.1	29.3	14.5	1.4	85215
77833	BRENHAM	20938	9966	28.1	27.9	33.7	6.8	3.5	45066	45878	48	59	7036	13.7	17.9	39.7	22.4	6.4	121551
77835	BURTON	20247	996	31.3	28.1	33.9	5.1	1.5	40964	43389	36	46	810	16.4	11.4	32.2	27.9	12.1	148947
77836	CALDWELL	19229	4283	28.2	32.1	31.6	6.2	2.0	41757	43664	39	49	3304	31.8	25.8	29.4	11.3	1.8	75787
77837	CALVERT	15559	691	50.5	23.7	21.0	1.9	2.9	24579	26656	3	4	432	47.5	28.9	20.4	3.2	0.0	52037
77840	COLLEGE STATION	15203	19529	61.0	21.4	12.4	3.0	2.3	18718	19524	1	2	3263	12.7	19.5	46.8	18.7	2.3	116574
77845	COLLEGE STATION	30504	15005	20.6	17.8	34.2	15.6	11.8	64287	62796	83	87	9824	10.0	5.5	37.6	40.4	6.6	167955
77850	CONCORD	14431	38	44.7	23.7	26.3	5.3	0.0	30000	39065	8	10	32	25.0	25.0	31.3	15.6	3.1	90000
77853	DIME BOX	16113	392	40.3	25.0	29.3	4.3	1.0	32212	37082	12	15	322	31.7	26.7	29.2	10.2	2.2	81000
77856	FRANKLIN	20746	1976	29.8	27.1	32.6	7.9	2.5	44760	47605	48	58	1538	28.0	33.7	25.6	10.1	2.6	72432
77859	HEARNE	14877	2523	41.1	26.2	28.2	3.7	0.8	32717	34194	13	16	1650	34.8	31.3	29.2	3.9	0.8	65267
77861	IOLA	19121	824	25.5	34.5	32.2	5.5	2.4	40204	40828	33	43	690	23.3	23.6	31.6	19.3	2.2	94773
	TEXAS	24551		22.3	25.0	34.3	11.1	7.3	52382	54495				16.5	22.7	36.5	19.7	4.6	109784
	UNITED STATES	27277		20.9	24.4	35.3	11.7	7.6	54719	56938				9.3	13.1	31.6	32.6	13.5	162279

ZIP CODE		FINANCIAL SERVICES				THE HOME						ENTERTAINMENT						PERSONAL			
						Home Improvements		Furnishings													
#	POST OFFICE NAME	Auto Loan	Home Loan	Investments	Retirement Plans	Home Repair	Lawn & Garden	Computers & Hardware-Personal	Major Appliances	TV, Radio, Sound Equipment	Furniture	Dine out/ Carry out	Sports Equipment	Fees & Tickets	Toys & Games	Travel	Cable TV	Apparel & Services	Auto Repairs	Health Insurance	Pets & Supplies
77511	ALVIN	93	87	76	85	84	85	88	87	88	89	89	66	83	91	83	89	61	87	87	103
77514	ANAHUAC	93	66	90	63	67	92	68	84	76	65	75	64	55	77	66	83	50	79	88	102
77515	ANGLETON	95	90	81	88	86	91	87	90	89	89	89	68	84	92	84	90	61	88	90	106
77517	SANTA FE	102	99	87	98	97	101	92	97	94	94	94	73	90	97	91	96	64	94	97	115
77518	BACLIFF	82	73	69	70	71	77	71	76	74	73	73	56	66	76	68	76	50	74	75	90
77519	BATSON	89	83	71	79	79	80	82	81	82	85	83	62	77	86	77	82	57	82	80	97
77520	BAYTOWN	83	73	64	70	71	72	78	77	80	80	81	56	72	81	72	81	56	79	78	89
77521	BAYTOWN	103	99	87	98	95	92	100	96	98	103	100	75	98	102	96	97	70	98	93	113
77523	BAYTOWN	121	122	107	118	117	114	111	116	110	116	111	88	110	116	109	110	77	111	109	135
77530	CHANNELVIEW	93	92	77	87	88	82	88	87	86	93	87	66	85	89	84	84	60	86	82	101
77531	CLUTE	79	69	61	68	67	63	78	71	76	79	77	56	71	78	71	74	54	76	68	84
77532	CROSBY	104	104	94	101	100	102	96	100	97	99	97	76	95	100	95	97	67	97	98	118
77534	DANBURY	100	91	83	88	89	94	86	92	89	89	89	67	81	93	82	92	61	89	92	109
77535	DAYTON	97	88	79	84	85	90	85	89	88	88	88	66	80	91	81	90	60	87	89	106
77536	DEER PARK	121	138	119	134	132	122	122	123	118	128	120	95	130	122	126	115	85	120	115	142
77538	DEVERS	109	96	91	93	94	103	92	100	97	95	96	73	85	100	87	100	65	96	101	119
77539	DICKINSON	101	97	89	95	93	97	94	96	95	96	96	72	91	98	91	96	66	95	96	114
77541	FREEPORT	77	67	64	63	66	67	70	72	71	72	71	53	64	72	66	71	49	72	70	83
77545	FRESNO	125	140	115	135	131	116	122	122	115	132	118	97	127	123	122	109	83	116	107	139
77546	FRIENDSWOOD	144	161	142	160	156	141	144	144	137	153	139	113	152	143	147	131	98	138	130	165
77547	GALENA PARK	74	63	50	56	60	60	64	66	68	70	69	43	58	68	59	70	48	68	66	74
77550	GALVESTON	61	49	46	51	47	54	62	55	64	59	64	43	56	64	54	66	44	61	62	68
77551	GALVESTON	83	69	65	71	67	72	82	75	84	80	84	58	75	84	74	85	58	81	81	91
77554	GALVESTON	124	102	121	107	104	112	114	115	115	112	115	90	105	114	111	116	80	118	114	137
77560	HANKAMER	84	55	81	52	55	82	59	74	68	56	66	58	44	69	55	76	44	70	78	91
77562	HIGHLANDS	96	82	79	80	80	90	81	87	85	82	85	65	74	88	76	89	58	84	89	104
77563	HITCHCOCK	82	77	81	77	77	87	75	81	79	75	78	60	73	79	76	83	54	79	86	97
77564	HULL	86	65	72	62	64	81	67	76	73	66	72	58	55	75	61	78	48	73	79	92
77565	KEMAH	137	148	137	149	145	136	138	137	134	144	136	107	144	138	141	131	96	135	131	160
77566	LAKE JACKSON	119	127	114	128	123	121	121	119	119	123	120	93	126	121	122	117	84	119	118	140
77568	LA MARQUE	77	73	66	74	70	80	74	75	79	73	78	56	73	78	72	82	53	76	84	90
77571	LA PORTE	112	117	98	114	111	106	108	108	106	113	107	83	109	110	107	104	75	106	103	126
77573	LEAGUE CITY	141	152	129	150	144	130	138	136	131	147	134	108	142	139	137	125	94	131	122	157
77575	LIBERTY	88	68	80	65	68	84	71	80	76	69	75	61	60	77	67	81	51	77	83	96
77577	LIVERPOOL	93	76	85	74	76	91	75	86	80	74	79	64	66	81	72	85	53	81	88	102
77578	MANVEL	133	139	120	138	135	130	126	129	124	133	125	100	129	130	126	122	88	124	122	151
77581	PEARLAND	127	141	124	139	136	127	127	128	123	134	125	99	134	128	130	120	88	124	120	148
77583	ROSHARON	125	125	108	123	121	117	117	118	115	123	116	91	116	121	114	114	81	115	112	138
77584	PEARLAND	152	164	137	160	156	140	147	147	140	159	142	116	151	150	145	133	100	140	130	168
77585	SARATOGA	71	49	71	46	49	71	51	65	58	48	57	49	39	58	49	64	37	60	68	78
77586	SEABROOK	131	135	127	140	133	125	136	128	132	139	134	102	140	134	135	128	95	131	124	151
77587	SOUTH HOUSTON	75	65	53	57	63	56	68	68	68	74	70	47	61	69	62	67	49	70	62	74
77590	TEXAS CITY	78	73	63	74	69	76	77	74	80	75	79	57	75	80	73	81	55	77	80	89
77591	TEXAS CITY	80	71	67	72	69	76	77	75	80	76	80	56	73	80	72	83	55	78	82	91
77597	WALLISVILLE	87	68	78	65	67	84	68	79	74	68	74	59	58	77	64	80	49	75	81	95
77598	WEBSTER	95	65	56	70	60	61	92	73	91	91	93	63	78	95	75	88	65	87	74	92
77611	BRIDGE CITY	88	85	77	84	83	90	81	85	84	81	83	64	79	86	80	86	57	83	89	101
77612	BUNA	82	58	72	56	58	79	61	72	68	58	66	55	48	70	56	74	44	68	76	88
77614	DEWEYVILLE	77	55	63	54	55	73	57	67	64	56	62	51	46	66	52	69	42	63	70	81
77616	FRED	79	57	65	55	57	75	59	69	66	58	64	53	47	68	54	72	43	65	73	84
77619	GROVES	87	88	79	88	84	96	87	88	90	83	89	68	87	90	87	94	62	89	99	106
77622	HAMSHIRE	99	90	80	87	88	93	85	90	89	89	89	66	80	92	81	91	60	88	91	108
77624	HILLISTER	70	50	72	49	52	71	52	66	57	48	56	49	41	57	51	63	37	60	68	78
77625	KOUNTZE	92	71	86	69	72	90	71	84	77	70	76	63	61	79	68	83	51	79	87	101
77627	NEDERLAND	92	93	87	93	90	100	89	93	92	86	91	71	90	92	90	95	63	92	99	110
77630	ORANGE	79	67	68	67	67	80	70	75	76	68	74	56	64	76	67	81	51	74	82	90
77632	ORANGE	97	92	87	93	91	99	88	95	91	87	90	72	85	93	88	94	62	91	97	112
77640	PORT ARTHUR	60	48	51	48	48	60	52	56	59	52	58	40	48	58	49	64	39	57	65	68
77642	PORT ARTHUR	69	59	55	58	58	63	66	64	69	65	69	47	61	68	61	71	48	67	70	76
77650	PORT BOLIVAR	91	83	108	77	92	102	80	96	86	85	83	64	77	79	86	91	56	91	106	110
77651	PORT NECHES	93	99	88	100	96	104	93	96	95	90	95	73	97	96	96	98	65	95	103	113
77656	SILSBEE	86	70	74	69	69	84	71	79	77	70	76	60	63	79	67	82	51	76	83	95
77657	LUMBERTON	90	84	74	81	82	85	79	83	82	82	82	61	76	85	76	84	56	81	83	99
77659	SOUR LAKE	98	86	105	85	87	104	83	97	88	82	87	73	77	88	85	94	60	91	99	114
77660	SPURGER	76	54	66	52	53	73	56	67	63	54	62	51	44	65	51	69	41	63	70	81
77662	VIDOR	82	69	69	67	67	79	69	75	73	68	72	56	62	75	65	77	49	73	78	90
77664	WARREN	90	64	92	62	67	91	66	84	73	61	72	63	53	73	65	81	48	77	87	100
77665	WINNIE	86	68	73	65	67	81	68	76	74	69	73	58	59	76	64	78	49	74	78	92
77701	BEAUMONT	60	49	46	49	47	56	55	54	61	55	59	39	50	59	50	64	41	57	63	66
77702	BEAUMONT	76	68	60	70	65	69	81	71	81	75	81	57	76	81	72	82	57	77	76	87
77703	BEAUMONT	53	43	40	44	41	50	49	48	55	49	53	35	46	54	44	58	37	51	56	60
77705	BEAUMONT	69	58	52	59	55	63	63	62	67	63	67	47	59	68	58	70	46	65	67	76
77706	BEAUMONT	109	105	105	109	105	105	111	106	110	111	110	82	110	110	109	109	78	110	108	126
77707	BEAUMONT	96	99	90	99	96	97	96	95	96	98	97	73	98	98	96	97	68	96	97	112
77708	BEAUMONT	77	71	60	73	66	71	75	70	77	75	77	56	73	79	70	77	53	74	74	86
77710	BEAUMONT	53	34	31	37	32	32	53	41	52	51	54	35	44	53	43	50	38	50	41	51
77713	BEAUMONT	87	82	77	83	80	85	81	83	82	81	82	64	78	84	79	83	57	82	84	99
77801	BRYAN	57	38	35	41	36	38	65	46	60	55	61	41	50	60	48	58	43	56	47	58
77802	BRYAN	93	85	81	86	84	86	96	88	94	92	94	69	89	94	88	93	65	92	91	104
77803	BRYAN	66	56	48	53	54	54	61	59	62	63	63	44	56	64	56	63	44	62	58	69
77807	BRYAN	91	83	72	82	78	77	86	81	85	89	86	64	81	89	80	84	60	84	79	97
77808	BRYAN	96	89	80	87	87	91	85	90	87	87	87	67	80	91	82	89	59	86	89	106
77830	ANDERSON	90	64	92	62	66	91	66	84	73	61	72	63	52	73	65	81	48	77	87	100
77831	BEDIAS	86	62	89	60	64	88	64	81	70	59	69	61	51	70	63	77	46	74	84	96
77833	BRENHAM	86	72	78	73	73	85	76	82	80	72	79	62	68	80	73	84	54	80	87	97
77835	BURTON	83	60	92	60	64	87	64	80	68	56	67	62	50	66	65	73	44	74	83	96
77836	CALDWELL	85	65	79	63	65	85	68	79	74	64	73	60	57	75	65	81	49	76	85	95
77837	CALVERT	61	45	54	45	46	61	50	57	57	48	55	41	43	56	47	63	37	56	65	68
77840	COLLEGE STATION	49	25	24	29	23	27	66	36	54	47	55	37	42	53	38	50	39	48	36	48
77845	COLLEGE STATION	122	120	108	124	116	108	127	114	119	126	120	95	123	123	118	113	86	117	105	135
77850	CONCORD	68	49	70	48	51	70	50	64	56	47	55	48	40	56	50	61	36	59	67	76
77853	DIME BOX	76	50	74	47	50	75	53	67	61	50	60	52	40	62	50	68	39	63	71	82
77856	FRANKLIN	90	66	98	64	70	92	68	86	74	63	73	64	55	73	68	81	48	79	88	102
77859	HEARNE	65	49	54	48	48	62	53	58	60	52	58	43	46	60	49	64	39	58	64	71
77861	IOLA	88	63	90	61	65	89	65	82	72	60	70	62	52	71	64	79	47	75	86	98
	TEXAS	104	96	90	94	93	94	99	97	99	101	100	75	94	101	94	99	70	99	96	114
	UNITED STATES	100	100	100	100	100	100	100	100	100	100	100	100	100	100	100	100	100	100	100	100

 77864-78132

ZIP CODE #	POST OFFICE NAME	COUNTY FIPS CODE	POPULATION 2000	POPULATION 2009	POPULATION 2014	2000-2009 ANNUAL RATE % Rate	2000-2009 ANNUAL RATE State Centile	HOUSEHOLDS 2000	HOUSEHOLDS 2009	HOUSEHOLDS 2014	HOUSEHOLDS % Annual Rate 2000-2009	HOUSEHOLDS 2009 Average HH Size	FAMILIES 2000	FAMILIES 2009	FAMILIES % Annual Rate 2000-2009
77864	MADISONVILLE	313	6454	7089	7433	1.0	58	2379	2598	2723	1.0	2.66	1712	1842	0.8
77865	MARQUEZ	289	1710	1796	1838	0.5	42	666	703	722	0.6	2.55	499	519	0.4
77868	NAVASOTA	185	14397	15422	15831	0.7	49	4266	4684	4836	1.0	2.75	3078	3331	0.9
77871	NORMANGEE	289	3344	3585	3693	0.8	52	1424	1531	1580	0.8	2.34	1052	1116	0.6
77872	NORTH ZULCH	313	1978	2198	2321	1.1	61	797	882	929	1.1	2.49	588	641	0.9
77873	RICHARDS	339	882	1210	1371	3.5	89	379	500	563	3.0	2.42	272	356	3.0
77879	SOMERVILLE	051	6252	6294	6264	0.1	27	2485	2500	2489	0.1	2.52	1730	1714	-0.1
77880	WASHINGTON	477	1395	1465	1508	0.5	42	539	567	586	0.5	2.58	378	391	0.4
77901	VICTORIA	469	41046	41856	42286	0.2	30	14676	15195	15414	0.4	2.69	10168	10340	0.2
77904	VICTORIA	469	23667	24948	25584	0.6	46	8881	9614	9923	0.9	2.57	6774	7236	0.7
77905	VICTORIA	469	15036	16054	16546	0.7	49	5146	5618	5824	1.0	2.81	4150	4475	0.8
77951	BLOOMINGTON	469	2981	3186	3283	0.7	49	900	975	1008	0.9	3.27	724	774	0.7
77954	CUERO	123	11284	11307	11198	0.0	25	3818	3829	3790	0.0	2.54	2694	2662	-0.1
77957	EDNA	239	9157	9163	9174	0.0	25	3426	3428	3437	0.0	2.61	2440	2404	-0.2
77962	GANADO	239	3232	3306	3339	0.2	30	1161	1180	1192	0.2	2.76	875	878	0.0
77963	GOLIAD	175	6116	6444	6622	0.6	46	2345	2499	2582	0.7	2.53	1742	1834	0.6
77964	HALLETTSVILLE	285	7074	7466	7658	0.6	46	2826	3011	3096	0.7	2.41	1972	2066	0.5
77968	INEZ	469	1967	2172	2264	1.1	61	690	784	822	1.4	2.73	554	621	1.2
77971	LOLITA	239	2908	2955	2984	0.2	30	1085	1100	1110	0.1	2.68	831	831	0.0
77974	MEYERSVILLE	123	350	367	372	0.5	42	135	143	146	0.6	2.57	109	114	0.5
77975	MOULTON	285	2114	2031	1994	-0.4	13	862	827	813	-0.4	2.39	593	560	-0.6
77979	PORT LAVACA	057	17672	18031	18186	0.2	30	6351	6472	6535	0.2	2.76	4774	4802	0.1
77983	SEADRIFT	057	2073	2147	2191	0.4	37	757	787	802	0.4	2.72	545	558	0.3
77984	SHINER	285	3650	3511	3452	-0.4	13	1507	1462	1440	-0.3	2.35	1052	1005	-0.5
77990	TIVOLI	391	991	921	889	-0.8	6	397	374	363	-0.6	2.46	296	275	-0.8
77994	WESTHOFF	123	387	427	435	1.1	61	154	171	173	1.1	2.50	110	120	0.9
77995	YOAKUM	285	9832	9750	9662	-0.1	21	3771	3740	3708	-0.1	2.55	2708	2650	-0.2
78002	ATASCOSA	029	6446	7521	8265	1.7	73	1986	2284	2518	1.5	3.28	1576	1768	1.3
78003	BANDERA	019	7243	8791	9655	2.1	79	2922	3515	3852	2.0	2.48	2087	2473	1.9
78004	BERGHEIM	259	456	529	657	1.6	71	158	183	227	1.6	2.88	131	150	1.5
78005	BIGFOOT	163	308	467	500	4.6	93	112	176	190	5.0	2.64	84	130	4.8
78006	BOERNE	259	19109	27887	33251	4.2	92	7025	10233	12204	4.2	2.69	5490	7890	4.0
78007	CALLIHAM	311	314	322	325	0.3	34	134	140	142	0.5	2.30	90	92	0.2
78008	CAMPBELLTON	013	422	472	505	1.2	63	169	190	203	1.3	2.48	126	139	1.1
78009	CASTROVILLE	325	6607	7660	8255	1.6	71	2204	2569	2777	1.7	2.95	1784	2055	1.5
78010	CENTER POINT	265	3523	3839	4005	0.9	55	1361	1487	1554	1.0	2.55	983	1058	0.8
78011	CHARLOTTE	013	2128	2412	2589	1.4	67	712	811	872	1.4	2.97	542	609	1.3
78013	COMFORT	259	4013	5045	5703	2.5	82	1467	1828	2072	2.4	2.70	1104	1349	2.2
78014	COTULLA	283	4954	5142	5219	0.4	37	1503	1585	1622	0.6	2.87	1116	1162	0.4
78015	BOERNE	259	6694	9816	11632	4.2	92	2328	3370	3988	4.1	2.90	2057	2934	3.9
78016	DEVINE	325	9045	10593	11425	1.7	73	3068	3598	3887	1.7	2.89	2366	2741	1.6
78017	DILLEY	163	5229	5145	5130	-0.2	19	1228	1236	1239	0.1	2.92	943	939	0.0
78019	ENCINAL	283	829	817	814	-0.2	19	279	280	281	0.0	2.90	208	206	-0.1
78021	FOWLERTON	283	91	94	94	0.4	37	39	40	40	0.3	1.73	28	29	0.4
78022	GEORGE WEST	297	4609	4513	4427	-0.2	19	1682	1677	1655	0.0	2.62	1241	1220	-0.2
78023	HELOTES	029	8133	20060	25520	10.3	98	2851	6845	8727	9.9	2.93	2402	5704	9.8
78024	HUNT	265	672	764	804	1.4	67	256	292	309	1.4	2.36	187	210	1.3
78025	INGRAM	265	5789	6423	6722	1.1	61	2273	2522	2647	1.1	2.48	1657	1811	1.0
78026	JOURDANTON	013	5356	6070	6439	1.4	67	1764	1999	2128	1.4	2.92	1379	1542	1.2
78027	KENDALIA	259	343	482	590	3.7	90	141	198	242	3.7	2.43	105	145	3.6
78028	KERRVILLE	265	33700	37130	38664	1.1	61	13952	15367	16045	1.0	2.31	9511	10315	0.9
78039	LA COSTE	325	1710	1986	2138	1.6	71	592	687	741	1.6	2.83	476	546	1.5
78040	LAREDO	479	43333	46467	47874	0.8	52	11911	12855	13314	0.8	3.50	9514	10059	0.6
78041	LAREDO	479	39990	48737	53235	2.2	80	11377	14129	15551	2.4	3.35	9327	11370	2.2
78043	LAREDO	479	35384	42883	46951	2.1	79	9616	11660	12765	2.1	3.68	8150	9777	2.0
78045	LAREDO	479	29140	48929	59039	5.8	95	7762	13281	16154	6.0	3.65	6964	11695	5.8
78046	LAREDO	479	43364	59607	68712	3.5	89	9536	13218	15303	3.6	4.50	9039	12481	3.5
78052	LYTLE	013	5111	6281	6843	2.3	81	1639	2019	2202	2.3	3.11	1311	1594	2.1
78055	MEDINA	019	2062	2432	2653	1.8	75	823	965	1054	1.7	2.38	581	671	1.6
78056	MICO	325	802	1235	1337	4.8	93	325	492	532	4.6	2.51	262	394	4.5
78057	MOORE	163	866	996	1067	1.5	69	335	396	428	1.8	2.50	250	292	1.7
78058	MOUNTAIN HOME	265	270	309	325	1.5	69	115	132	140	1.5	2.11	84	95	1.3
78059	NATALIA	325	5081	6111	6644	2.0	78	1618	1932	2098	1.9	3.16	1298	1533	1.8
78061	PEARSALL	163	9849	9882	9869	0.0	25	3068	3143	3164	0.3	2.97	2366	2398	0.1
78063	LAKEHILLS	019	7733	9284	10106	2.0	78	3012	3582	3891	1.9	2.59	2208	2590	1.7
78064	PLEASANTON	013	13424	14973	15796	1.2	63	4677	5231	5530	1.2	2.84	3573	3943	1.1
78065	POTEET	013	9718	11669	12673	2.0	78	3123	3778	4114	2.1	3.08	2483	2972	2.0
78066	RIO MEDINA	325	682	664	735	-0.3	16	240	235	260	-0.2	2.83	196	190	-0.3
78067	SAN YGNACIO	505	1037	1235	1329	1.9	76	322	392	425	2.1	3.15	247	297	2.0
78069	SOMERSET	013	4198	5135	5598	2.2	80	1318	1611	1757	2.2	3.19	1048	1260	2.0
78070	SPRING BRANCH	091	7410	13793	17481	6.9	96	2615	4867	6171	6.9	2.83	2099	3835	6.7
78071	THREE RIVERS	297	5079	4841	4747	-0.5	11	1399	1326	1296	-0.6	2.60	1032	964	-0.7
78072	TILDEN	311	529	543	549	0.3	34	219	229	233	0.5	2.37	148	152	0.3
78073	VON ORMY	029	7188	8330	9042	1.6	71	2203	2541	2763	1.6	3.28	1779	2000	1.3
78074	WARING	259	31	34	38	1.0	58	13	14	16	0.8	2.43	10	10	0.0
78075	WHITSETT	297	179	181	180	0.1	27	73	75	75	0.3	1.73	54	55	0.2
78076	ZAPATA	505	11111	13024	13893	1.7	73	3591	4258	4564	1.9	3.05	2911	3418	1.8
78101	ADKINS	029	5922	7463	8272	2.5	82	2034	2577	2869	2.6	2.90	1647	2048	2.4
78102	BEEVILLE	025	29981	30759	30786	0.3	34	8246	8410	8464	0.2	2.68	5944	5974	0.1
78108	CIBOLO	187	7635	21052	26793	11.6	99	2777	7282	9238	11.0	2.89	2186	5758	11.0
78109	CONVERSE	029	22684	30731	34927	3.3	88	7312	9809	11183	3.2	3.11	6075	7998	3.0
78111	ECLETO	255	3	3	3	0.0	25	3	3	3	0.0	1.00	2	0	-100.0
78112	ELMENDORF	029	6770	7906	8501	1.7	73	2018	2331	2513	1.6	3.39	1666	1880	1.3
78113	FALLS CITY	255	1270	1402	1459	1.1	61	490	545	569	1.2	2.57	368	403	1.0
78114	FLORESVILLE	493	15626	18781	20808	2.0	78	5228	6345	7075	2.1	2.89	4214	5060	2.0
78116	GILLETT	255	616	600	592	-0.3	16	253	250	249	-0.1	2.40	181	176	-0.3
78117	HOBSON	255	393	430	443	1.0	58	146	161	166	1.1	2.66	110	119	0.9
78118	KARNES CITY	255	4457	4413	4393	-0.1	21	1387	1401	1404	0.1	2.70	1007	1002	-0.1
78119	KENEDY	255	7433	7261	7196	-0.3	16	1698	1674	1663	-0.2	2.57	1232	1197	-0.3
78121	LA VERNIA	493	7143	10686	12535	4.5	93	2430	3659	4317	4.5	2.89	1978	2943	4.4
78122	LEESVILLE	177	267	287	293	0.8	52	93	99	101	0.7	2.90	72	76	0.6
78123	MC QUEENEY	187	2034	2364	2647	1.6	71	811	938	1050	1.6	2.49	597	668	1.2
78124	MARION	187	5431	6925	7908	2.7	84	1832	2323	2652	2.6	2.98	1485	1837	2.3
78130	NEW BRAUNFELS	187	43680	61131	72687	3.7	90	15956	22181	26403	3.6	2.71	11493	15661	3.4
78132	NEW BRAUNFELS	091	11769	20670	26193	6.3	96	4160	7213	9138	6.1	2.85	3444	5909	6.0
	TEXAS					1.9					1.8	2.78			1.7
	UNITED STATES					1.0					1.1	2.59			0.9

ZIP CODE #	POST OFFICE NAME	RACE (%) White 2000	White 2009	Black 2000	Black 2009	Asian/Pacific 2000	Asian/Pacific 2009	% Hispanic Origin 2000	% Hispanic Origin 2009	2009 AGE DISTRIBUTION (%) 0-4	5-9	10-14	15-19	20-24	25-44	45-64	65-84	85+	18+	MEDIAN AGE 2009	% 2009 Males	% 2009 Females
77864	MADISONVILLE	68.7	62.6	20.5	23.0	0.4	0.5	16.4	22.1	7.5	7.1	7.0	6.8	5.5	23.6	25.3	13.9	3.3	74.2	38.8	48.9	51.1
77865	MARQUEZ	91.9	89.6	3.5	4.0	0.1	0.2	5.4	7.7	5.3	6.0	6.2	6.3	4.6	21.7	30.5	17.3	2.0	78.4	44.9	51.3	48.7
77868	NAVASOTA	61.5	57.6	27.6	28.7	0.5	0.6	22.4	28.7	6.6	6.6	6.4	6.2	5.4	29.0	27.1	10.8	2.0	76.6	38.4	56.1	43.9
77871	NORMANGEE	90.4	88.4	5.5	6.1	0.1	0.2	5.3	7.4	5.0	5.2	5.4	5.2	4.6	17.9	28.8	25.2	2.7	81.1	50.0	48.2	51.8
77872	NORTH ZULCH	95.7	93.9	1.2	1.5	0.1	0.1	3.9	6.4	5.7	6.0	6.3	6.2	5.0	21.7	31.2	15.9	2.1	78.3	44.3	49.0	51.0
77873	RICHARDS	79.0	74.0	17.7	21.7	0.2	0.4	3.4	4.5	6.0	6.4	6.9	6.5	4.6	22.5	30.7	14.4	2.0	76.5	42.8	50.3	49.7
77879	SOMERVILLE	71.0	66.7	19.9	21.5	0.2	0.3	13.1	17.0	6.5	6.7	6.7	6.4	5.8	22.6	29.0	14.5	1.8	76.2	41.4	48.9	51.1
77880	WASHINGTON	59.4	54.1	38.4	42.9	0.2	0.3	2.9	3.9	5.5	5.8	6.3	7.4	5.4	21.1	30.5	16.0	2.0	77.8	43.6	49.4	50.6
77901	VICTORIA	64.0	59.7	9.5	9.1	0.6	0.6	53.5	62.5	8.7	7.9	7.4	7.5	7.4	27.1	22.4	9.8	1.8	71.6	32.4	48.8	51.2
77904	VICTORIA	87.4	83.4	3.2	3.6	1.7	2.1	18.8	26.7	6.5	6.6	6.9	6.9	5.5	24.1	29.4	12.2	1.9	75.7	40.1	47.8	52.2
77905	VICTORIA	83.5	78.9	3.1	3.4	0.1	0.2	29.3	38.9	7.1	7.3	8.1	7.0	5.2	25.5	28.0	10.7	1.1	73.1	37.4	49.9	50.1
77951	BLOOMINGTON	55.3	50.2	6.2	5.7	0.2	0.2	65.9	74.8	10.5	9.6	9.0	9.2	7.2	25.5	19.9	8.2	0.8	65.1	28.2	48.8	51.2
77954	CUERO	70.0	69.3	15.7	15.9	0.4	0.4	27.8	29.5	5.6	5.5	5.7	5.9	4.9	28.3	27.5	13.7	2.8	79.3	41.3	54.0	46.0
77957	EDNA	72.6	67.7	10.7	11.1	0.6	0.7	24.5	31.1	7.3	7.1	7.3	6.6	5.6	23.7	26.7	13.1	2.6	74.1	38.9	49.1	50.9
77962	GANADO	80.2	74.8	3.3	3.7	0.2	0.2	29.3	38.1	6.8	7.0	7.0	6.5	5.0	24.8	27.8	12.4	2.7	75.3	39.0	50.9	49.1
77963	GOLIAD	81.7	78.5	4.8	4.7	0.2	0.3	37.5	46.1	5.9	6.0	6.4	6.6	4.9	21.7	30.4	15.5	2.5	77.4	43.8	50.1	49.9
77964	HALLETTSVILLE	87.5	86.8	8.1	8.5	0.1	0.1	7.1	7.9	5.6	5.8	6.0	5.9	5.1	21.2	29.6	16.5	4.3	79.0	45.3	49.3	50.7
77968	INEZ	89.9	85.9	1.9	2.3	0.3	0.4	15.7	23.3	6.4	6.9	7.3	8.6	5.3	24.1	29.6	10.9	1.0	73.5	39.0	49.6	50.4
77971	LOLITA	89.0	85.1	0.7	0.8	0.7	0.8	17.9	25.0	6.8	6.9	7.1	6.9	5.7	24.4	27.7	12.8	1.7	75.0	39.4	49.7	50.3
77974	MEYERSVILLE	94.3	92.6	1.1	1.4	0.0	0.0	8.9	12.3	5.4	6.0	6.5	7.1	4.1	23.2	32.4	13.9	1.4	77.4	43.2	49.6	50.4
77975	MOULTON	95.6	95.2	0.5	0.6	0.0	0.0	11.0	12.3	5.5	5.9	6.0	6.0	5.2	20.8	28.4	17.1	5.2	78.7	45.5	50.2	49.8
77979	PORT LAVACA	76.9	73.3	2.9	2.8	3.0	3.5	44.3	52.7	7.9	7.6	7.3	7.3	5.7	24.6	25.9	12.2	1.4	72.6	37.0	50.6	49.4
77983	SEADRIFT	82.0	77.3	0.6	0.7	7.1	8.3	22.2	30.3	7.5	7.7	7.8	7.3	5.3	21.4	27.7	13.9	1.5	72.7	38.7	50.3	49.7
77984	SHINER	88.6	88.0	8.1	8.4	0.2	0.3	5.3	6.0	5.2	5.5	5.8	6.0	4.5	21.0	28.9	18.1	4.9	79.6	46.3	47.8	52.2
77990	TIVOLI	83.5	81.7	2.3	2.1	0.4	0.4	62.8	71.3	6.0	6.3	6.5	6.2	5.4	22.0	31.4	13.8	2.4	77.4	43.2	52.0	48.0
77994	WESTHOFF	85.5	84.8	5.2	5.4	0.3	0.2	21.4	23.2	4.9	5.4	6.1	6.3	4.9	21.1	29.7	19.0	2.6	79.6	45.9	49.9	50.1
77995	YOAKUM	82.3	81.7	7.7	7.8	0.2	0.2	22.8	24.6	7.0	7.1	7.1	6.6	5.2	23.1	26.3	14.3	3.2	74.4	39.7	48.7	51.3
78002	ATASCOSA	70.5	65.2	0.5	0.4	0.4	0.3	68.5	80.8	8.2	8.0	7.7	7.5	7.1	26.0	25.1	9.5	1.1	71.5	33.6	50.8	49.2
78003	BANDERA	93.9	92.2	0.2	0.3	0.3	0.4	15.3	20.6	5.6	5.9	6.2	6.1	5.1	22.0	31.4	15.9	1.9	78.5	44.4	49.2	50.8
78004	BERGHEIM	97.4	96.0	0.0	0.2	0.0	0.0	9.7	14.4	5.3	6.2	7.6	7.2	4.0	20.2	35.9	12.3	1.3	76.0	44.7	49.3	50.7
78005	BIGFOOT	84.7	81.2	0.3	0.4	0.6	0.4	45.1	56.1	5.6	5.8	6.6	7.5	4.5	22.7	31.0	14.6	1.7	77.3	43.0	50.7	49.3
78006	BOERNE	94.4	92.3	0.3	0.3	0.3	0.4	15.3	21.6	5.7	6.4	7.2	7.0	4.5	21.3	33.0	12.9	2.1	76.1	43.5	48.7	51.3
78007	CALLIHAM	88.3	87.9	1.3	1.2	0.0	0.0	32.1	34.2	4.7	4.7	5.0	5.9	5.3	19.6	34.5	18.3	2.2	82.0	47.9	49.7	50.3
78008	CAMPBELLTON	82.5	78.4	0.2	0.2	0.7	1.1	41.9	52.1	7.6	7.8	7.6	5.9	4.7	22.9	26.5	15.0	1.9	73.1	39.7	51.3	48.7
78009	CASTROVILLE	82.4	78.0	0.5	0.5	0.6	0.7	35.2	44.8	7.4	7.4	7.5	7.2	5.9	25.0	27.7	10.1	1.8	73.2	37.3	50.7	49.3
78010	CENTER POINT	88.8	85.3	0.1	0.2	0.3	0.4	23.7	31.5	6.4	5.7	6.6	6.6	4.3	22.1	31.2	15.0	2.2	76.9	43.8	50.4	49.6
78011	CHARLOTTE	70.5	67.7	0.1	0.1	0.0	0.0	73.5	80.4	9.3	8.0	7.8	8.7	6.5	22.3	25.5	10.4	1.5	69.9	33.7	50.4	49.6
78013	COMFORT	83.9	79.0	0.4	0.4	0.4	0.4	32.2	41.3	7.1	6.8	6.8	7.2	6.1	23.2	27.8	12.6	2.2	75.1	39.4	50.3	49.7
78014	COTULLA	82.4	81.2	3.9	3.9	0.4	0.4	75.9	76.2	7.0	6.9	7.8	8.9	6.8	25.5	24.7	10.6	1.7	72.2	34.6	53.3	46.7
78015	BOERNE	95.8	94.1	0.5	0.6	0.5	0.6	10.6	17.8	4.7	5.6	7.0	7.2	3.8	17.5	36.5	16.2	1.5	78.0	47.4	49.5	50.5
78016	DEVINE	80.6	76.8	0.8	0.9	0.3	0.3	44.5	54.0	7.3	7.2	7.5	8.0	5.8	24.5	26.0	11.8	1.9	72.7	37.0	50.1	49.9
78017	DILLEY	66.2	64.0	14.3	14.7	0.8	0.9	65.5	70.7	6.3	6.7	6.4	6.2	12.4	37.2	17.1	6.7	0.9	76.6	29.6	64.0	36.0
78019	ENCINAL	76.2	74.1	0.5	0.5	0.0	0.0	87.6	87.9	8.0	6.7	8.6	10.0	6.4	22.0	23.7	12.1	2.4	70.7	33.9	49.8	50.2
78021	FOWLERTON	80.4	80.9	13.0	12.8	0.0	0.0	47.8	48.9	4.3	4.3	5.3	7.4	9.6	36.2	22.3	9.6	1.1	83.0	35.6	70.2	29.8
78022	GEORGE WEST	87.1	84.4	0.2	0.2	0.2	0.2	43.5	52.1	6.5	6.5	7.0	6.5	5.3	21.0	29.9	14.5	2.6	75.7	42.6	48.7	51.3
78023	HELOTES	88.5	83.7	1.6	1.9	1.6	2.1	26.1	40.2	5.9	6.5	7.3	6.7	4.0	23.4	34.0	11.2	1.1	75.9	42.6	49.2	50.8
78024	HUNT	94.3	92.7	2.7	3.3	0.3	0.4	14.9	20.8	3.1	4.1	5.6	7.9	6.2	17.7	35.1	18.6	1.8	82.3	49.0	52.9	47.1
78025	INGRAM	94.7	92.8	0.4	0.5	0.5	0.6	10.7	15.3	4.4	4.6	5.2	5.9	4.7	17.2	31.9	22.9	3.2	81.9	50.9	48.7	51.3
78026	JOURDANTON	78.2	74.3	1.0	0.9	0.3	0.3	49.8	59.7	8.0	7.6	7.6	8.0	6.7	25.9	24.2	10.1	1.8	71.5	34.0	49.7	50.3
78027	KENDALIA	93.9	91.1	0.3	0.4	0.3	0.4	12.0	17.8	4.8	5.4	6.0	5.6	3.7	19.1	38.6	15.1	1.7	80.3	48.1	51.2	48.8
78028	KERRVILLE	87.8	84.7	2.2	2.3	0.6	0.8	20.1	26.4	5.3	5.2	5.4	6.2	5.8	19.0	27.2	21.1	4.8	80.1	47.3	47.7	52.3
78039	LA COSTE	81.1	77.9	1.8	1.7	0.3	0.3	46.9	57.3	7.7	7.3	7.4	8.0	6.6	28.5	24.5	9.0	1.2	72.8	34.6	50.6	49.4
78040	LAREDO	82.6	82.3	0.4	0.3	0.2	0.2	96.7	97.7	10.1	9.7	8.5	8.5	7.3	25.5	18.1	10.3	2.0	66.7	29.2	47.8	52.2
78041	LAREDO	84.1	83.7	0.5	0.4	0.9	0.8	91.2	93.6	9.1	8.6	8.0	8.1	7.4	29.9	20.5	7.5	1.0	69.5	30.3	48.8	51.2
78043	LAREDO	81.2	80.5	0.3	0.3	0.3	0.3	95.1	96.8	10.7	10.2	9.3	8.7	7.1	27.9	18.0	7.2	0.9	64.5	27.6	48.5	51.5
78045	LAREDO	81.9	81.3	0.3	0.3	1.0	1.0	90.0	92.7	10.9	10.0	9.1	8.4	6.4	31.9	19.1	3.9	0.4	64.8	28.1	49.0	51.0
78046	LAREDO	80.9	80.7	0.3	0.3	0.1	0.1	97.0	98.0	12.4	11.8	10.8	10.6	8.1	26.0	15.9	4.2	0.4	58.4	22.8	49.0	51.0
78052	LYTLE	71.6	67.4	0.6	0.5	0.4	0.4	60.1	69.3	8.1	8.2	8.2	8.7	6.2	25.9	24.0	9.8	1.0	69.9	33.7	48.7	51.3
78055	MEDINA	95.1	93.8	1.0	1.0	0.2	0.3	8.1	11.2	4.6	5.0	7.3	7.5	4.6	17.4	32.4	18.3	2.9	77.5	47.6	48.2	51.8
78056	MICO	90.1	87.0	0.5	0.6	0.5	0.7	20.6	28.4	6.6	7.0	7.2	7.0	5.7	24.5	30.7	10.2	1.1	74.8	39.2	51.1	48.9
78057	MOORE	84.8	81.2	0.3	0.3	0.2	0.3	44.9	55.9	5.6	5.8	6.6	7.3	4.3	23.0	30.4	15.2	1.7	77.2	43.0	50.8	49.2
78058	MOUNTAIN HOME	90.8	88.3	1.1	1.3	0.4	0.3	12.9	18.1	4.5	5.2	6.8	7.4	5.2	17.5	31.4	19.1	2.9	78.0	47.5	49.8	50.2
78059	NATALIA	70.3	66.1	0.7	0.7	0.4	0.4	62.3	71.7	8.5	8.5	8.6	8.4	5.7	24.6	24.5	10.2	1.1	68.9	33.7	49.8	50.2
78061	PEARSALL	73.3	71.0	0.4	0.4	0.3	0.3	81.6	86.8	8.8	8.5	8.1	8.3	7.3	25.3	22.3	9.7	1.8	69.6	31.6	51.0	49.0
78063	LAKEHILLS	93.8	92.0	0.2	0.3	0.4	0.5	13.5	18.3	5.5	6.1	6.5	6.4	4.5	22.1	33.6	14.0	1.2	77.8	44.2	50.2	49.8
78064	PLEASANTON	78.8	75.0	0.8	0.8	0.6	0.7	48.7	57.6	8.4	8.1	8.0	7.4	6.3	25.6	24.6	10.0	1.6	70.8	34.2	49.1	50.9
78065	POTEET	66.6	63.3	0.4	0.4	0.3	0.3	71.7	78.0	8.8	8.4	8.3	8.3	6.6	25.2	23.8	9.5	1.2	69.4	32.2	49.5	50.5
78066	RIO MEDINA	89.9	86.6	0.6	0.8	0.9	1.1	20.8	28.8	6.8	7.1	7.2	7.2	5.9	24.7	30.4	9.6	1.1	74.5	38.3	51.7	48.3
78067	SAN YGNACIO	80.0	79.6	1.4	1.2	0.1	0.1	90.2	93.0	8.7	8.3	7.8	7.7	8.1	25.3	21.9	10.6	1.5	70.5	30.9	53.4	46.6
78069	SOMERSET	71.6	67.3	0.2	0.2	0.2	0.2	66.8	76.5	8.5	8.1	8.2	8.1	6.3	25.9	23.7	10.0	1.1	70.0	32.8	49.9	50.1
78070	SPRING BRANCH	93.0	90.0	0.7	0.9	0.3	0.4	13.4	20.5	5.6	6.3	7.1	6.9	4.5	22.1	34.6	11.9	1.1	76.8	43.5	49.1	50.9
78071	THREE RIVERS	84.6	81.9	5.4	6.1	0.3	0.3	42.3	52.0	4.4	4.4	4.5	5.7	12.6	30.5	26.5	10.0	1.5	83.5	35.8	62.9	37.1
78072	TILDEN	88.3	88.0	1.3	1.3	0.0	0.0	33.6	35.7	4.4	4.6	5.0	5.7	5.7	20.3	34.1	18.0	2.2	82.7	47.5	49.4	50.6
78073	VON ORMY	67.7	63.0	0.6	0.5	0.6	0.5	73.1	83.6	9.1	8.4	7.8	8.4	8.3	26.8	22.4	8.1	0.8	69.9	29.8	50.1	49.9
78074	WARING	93.5	94.1	0.0	0.0	0.0	0.0	16.1	23.5	5.9	5.9	5.9	5.9	5.9	23.5	32.4	14.7	0.0	76.5	42.5	47.1	52.9
78075	WHITSETT	83.7	80.7	9.0	9.9	0.0	0.0	44.9	54.1	2.8	2.8	3.3	5.0	16.6	34.3	25.4	8.8	1.1	88.4	34.6	70.7	29.3
78076	ZAPATA	84.4	83.5	0.3	0.3	0.2	0.2	84.3	88.5	9.7	9.1	8.5	8.4	6.6	23.6	20.8	11.6	1.7	67.5	30.9	48.8	51.2
78101	ADKINS	86.3	81.7	3.8	3.8	0.5	0.6	20.4	31.4	6.2	6.6	7.0	7.2	5.3	26.0	30.6	10.1	1.0	75.7	39.4	50.2	49.8
78102	BEEVILLE	66.5	62.7	10.6	10.9	0.6	0.6	54.0	60.8	5.9	5.6	5.5	6.9	10.5	35.6	19.8	8.7	1.5	79.6	31.8	61.4	38.6
78108	CIBOLO	83.0	78.1	5.1	7.5	1.5	2.0	18.7	24.0	6.8	7.3	7.7	7.6	5.2	26.3	29.7	8.5	0.9	73.4	38.2	49.2	50.8
78109	CONVERSE	64.0	57.3	18.6	19.4	2.8	2.9	28.6	41.5	8.2	7.9	7.7	7.6	6.6	30.4	24.9	6.1	0.6	71.3	32.5	48.1	51.9
78111	ECLETO	100.0	100.0	0.0	0.0	0.0	0.0	0.0	0.0	0.0	0.0	0.0	0.0	0.0	0.0	100.0	0.0	0.0	100.0	53.8	33.3	66.7
78112	ELMENDORF	67.1	61.6	2.1	1.6	0.4	0.4	64.6	77.7	9.9	8.6	8.0	8.3	8.4	27.5	22.8	6.1	0.4	68.4	29.4	49.5	50.5
78113	FALLS CITY	92.8	89.9	0.2	0.1	0.1	0.1	16.9	24.4	6.6	6.9	7.3	7.0	4.4	23.3	29.5	12.7	2.4	75.0	41.1	50.4	49.6
78114	FLORESVILLE	76.4	71.3	1.5	1.5	0.4	0.5	47.7	58.5	7.1	7.0	7.2	7.4	6.0	25.7	27.3	10.5	1.9	74.0	37.3	49.5	50.5
78116	GILLETT	94.5	91.8	0.0	0.0	0.0	0.0	8.3	12.8	3.8	4.3	4.7	5.7	5.3	20.2	34.0	19.2	2.8	83.5	48.8	49.0	51.0
78117	HOBSON	93.6	90.9	0.3	0.2	0.0	0.0	15.0	22.1	6.7	6.7	7.2	7.2	4.7	23.3	29.1	12.6	2.6	74.7	40.8	50.2	49.8
78118	KARNES CITY	74.8	71.6	4.7	4.2	0.4	0.5	56.8	66.3	6.8	6.6	6.3	6.7	8.6	28.0	22.1	12.2	2.7	76.4	34.5	54.7	45.3
78119	KENEDY	56.9	53.1	19.3	18.7	0.7	0.8	48.5	56.9	4.4	3.9	4.3	5.1	12.1	40.4	18.3	9.1	2.4	84.8	32.7	67.9	32.1
78121	LA VERNIA	89.2	85.6	1.5	1.5	0.3	0.3	16.8	24.5	6.8	6.9	7.2	7.9	6.4	25.6	28.6	9.2	1.4	73.9	36.7	49.9	50.1
78122	LEESVILLE	83.1	78.7	4.9	5.6	0.4	0.3	25.8	34.5	5.6	5.9	6.6	7.0	4.2	20.9	30.7	16.7	2.4	77.0	44.9	52.3	47.7
78123	MC QUEENEY	85.6	79.5	1.4	1.4	0.5	0.6	23.9	35.7	6.7	6.9	6.9	5.9	4.6	25.4	30.5	11.9	1.1	75.8	40.3	51.4	48.6
78124	MARION	83.9	77.8	3.1	3.4	1.0	1.1	23.0	34.1	6.5	6.7	6.9	7.1	5.9	25.8	29.1	10.7	1.2	75.4	38.4	49.7	50.3
78130	NEW BRAUNFELS	84.6	80.5	1.3	1.4	0.6	0.7	33.8	44.2	7.4	7.0	6.9	6.7	6.0	26.8	24.9	11.6	2.6	74.6	37.0	48.5	51.5
78132	NEW BRAUNFELS	90.6	87.2	0.7	0.7	0.4	0.6	16.4	23.5	6.0	6.5	7.3	7.2	4.7	22.8	32.4	11.9	1.2	75.7	41.9	50.0	50.0
	TEXAS	71.0	67.6	11.5	11.4	2.8	3.5	32.0	37.4	7.9	7.5	7.2	7.5	7.4	28.3	24.0	8.8	1.4	73.0	33.6	49.7	50.3
	UNITED STATES	75.1	72.0	12.3	12.7	3.8	4.6	12.5	15.7	6.8	6.7	6.6	7.1	6.9	27.0	26.0	10.9	1.9	75.7	36.9	49.2	50.8

#	POST OFFICE NAME	2009 Per Capita Income	2009 HH Income Base	2009 HOUSEHOLD INCOME DISTRIBUTION (%) Less than $25,000	$25,000 to $49,999	$50,000 to $99,999	$100,000 to $149,999	$150,000 or More	MEDIAN HOUSEHOLD INCOME 2009	2014	2009 National Centile	2009 State Centile	2009 Home Value Base	2009 HOME VALUE DISTRIBUTION (%) Less than $50,000	$50,000 to $89,999	$90,000 to $174,999	$175,000 to $399,999	$400,000 or More	2009 Median Home Value
77864	MADISONVILLE	17175	2598	33.4	36.7	22.7	4.2	2.8	33848	34572	15	19	1895	29.2	26.0	28.2	13.6	3.0	80529
77865	MARQUEZ	20042	703	30.6	27.5	33.3	6.0	2.7	41717	43657	38	49	596	29.7	21.0	29.2	16.1	4.0	88857
77868	NAVASOTA	17384	4684	32.0	27.8	32.5	4.7	3.0	40822	42777	35	45	3256	29.0	23.6	26.0	18.5	3.0	85591
77871	NORMANGEE	23732	1531	25.1	31.1	33.1	8.4	2.4	44063	46138	46	56	1292	19.7	12.5	38.1	26.3	3.4	117857
77872	NORTH ZULCH	19945	882	29.4	34.8	28.3	4.8	2.7	40493	43220	34	44	740	24.2	23.5	31.9	16.9	3.5	92931
77873	RICHARDS	21840	500	29.0	31.0	30.6	7.2	2.2	40645	43889	35	45	419	32.0	22.2	23.2	18.6	4.1	83000
77879	SOMERVILLE	19750	2500	32.6	28.7	31.0	4.9	2.8	38677	41207	29	37	2036	39.3	33.7	20.1	5.8	1.0	60188
77880	WASHINGTON	22026	567	30.2	26.5	32.6	6.7	4.1	45058	45448	48	59	468	19.0	16.2	29.1	22.0	13.7	122581
77901	VICTORIA	17835	15195	30.4	32.3	30.0	5.2	2.2	39025	44351	30	38	8466	27.7	40.8	27.4	3.5	0.6	68785
77904	VICTORIA	30894	9614	14.7	21.8	39.5	14.7	9.3	64176	62534	82	87	6973	5.9	11.5	55.0	24.9	2.8	133240
77905	VICTORIA	19353	5618	21.8	28.3	41.3	6.6	2.0	49925	51046	61	70	4693	22.9	26.9	39.7	9.2	1.3	90304
77951	BLOOMINGTON	12484	975	37.8	30.9	26.4	4.3	0.6	36351	40065	22	28	742	52.8	30.7	15.4	0.9	0.1	47640
77954	CUERO	17065	3829	37.2	30.0	26.0	4.8	2.0	33972	34883	15	19	2835	38.9	25.3	24.8	9.2	1.9	64529
77957	EDNA	19210	3428	30.2	27.8	33.9	6.1	2.0	42223	44400	40	50	2414	27.3	33.3	27.5	10.8	1.0	74667
77962	GANADO	18198	1180	25.9	31.5	34.1	5.4	3.1	43967	45092	45	56	886	27.7	33.9	28.6	8.5	1.5	74737
77963	GOLIAD	19403	2499	31.9	29.8	30.0	6.1	2.3	40050	42287	33	42	1961	32.2	23.8	28.0	11.6	4.3	78553
77964	HALLETTSVILLE	19061	3011	36.9	28.1	27.0	5.7	2.2	36001	38327	21	27	2339	24.6	24.3	31.5	14.9	4.7	92772
77968	INEZ	24128	784	12.9	24.4	47.8	11.6	3.3	60226	58176	78	84	654	21.9	19.7	40.2	16.8	1.4	105242
77971	LOLITA	20942	1100	24.1	29.1	38.4	5.7	2.7	47087	47391	54	64	832	30.5	33.4	29.6	5.0	1.4	68095
77974	MEYERSVILLE	21108	143	20.3	32.2	38.5	7.7	1.4	48511	50000	58	67	124	12.9	18.5	49.2	16.9	2.4	118182
77975	MOULTON	18377	827	35.3	33.0	26.2	3.6	1.8	35460	36571	19	24	661	23.4	27.5	31.9	14.4	2.7	87292
77979	PORT LAVACA	19027	6472	28.0	29.0	33.2	6.7	3.0	43670	47725	44	55	4644	28.3	34.3	29.4	7.7	0.2	72521
77983	SEADRIFT	16225	787	31.6	35.2	27.7	3.7	1.8	36725	41235	23	30	644	49.4	23.3	21.4	5.1	0.8	50645
77984	SHINER	18269	1462	33.8	32.0	30.0	3.1	1.2	36163	37735	21	28	1184	23.1	31.3	31.5	12.4	1.7	83810
77990	TIVOLI	19145	374	33.7	30.7	28.9	3.5	3.2	36532	38706	22	29	268	57.8	25.0	15.3	1.1	0.7	43000
77994	WESTHOFF	19913	171	30.4	32.7	28.1	4.7	4.1	37456	39720	25	32	133	33.8	29.3	15.8	15.8	5.3	67500
77995	YOAKUM	18551	3740	33.5	33.7	24.8	5.2	2.8	35572	35601	19	25	2810	29.5	27.7	30.0	11.4	1.5	79055
78002	ATASCOSA	13442	2284	31.3	35.6	27.7	4.0	1.4	35804	38478	20	26	1724	35.3	35.1	24.3	4.9	0.3	68878
78003	BANDERA	21621	3515	27.1	30.1	31.8	7.8	3.1	42808	47524	42	53	2835	16.5	19.6	36.7	23.5	3.6	116081
78004	BERGHEIM	36337	183	7.1	16.4	41.0	17.5	18.0	79584	82321	92	94	156	0.6	1.9	22.4	53.2	21.8	237097
78005	BIGFOOT	17847	176	33.5	28.4	27.8	9.1	1.1	38674	43519	29	36	144	36.8	25.0	20.1	13.2	4.9	65000
78006	BOERNE	31526	10233	15.4	20.8	37.7	14.5	11.7	67971	72979	86	89	8131	8.8	6.5	29.3	40.3	15.1	193966
78007	CALLIHAM	24821	140	31.4	31.4	26.4	5.7	5.0	40000	40000	33	42	112	34.8	31.3	15.2	6.3	12.5	65000
78008	CAMPBELLTON	21530	190	41.1	21.6	26.8	6.3	4.2	36541	43032	22	29	153	37.3	27.5	22.9	11.1	1.3	55909
78009	CASTROVILLE	19367	2569	19.6	31.0	37.6	9.1	2.6	49401	51321	60	69	2108	13.0	25.2	39.7	20.0	2.1	106908
78010	CENTER POINT	22125	1487	26.5	29.3	33.8	5.6	4.8	45765	46212	51	61	1175	21.5	19.4	27.5	23.7	7.9	111927
78011	CHARLOTTE	12943	811	42.5	32.3	20.7	3.1	1.4	30681	32752	9	11	646	58.8	20.6	16.1	2.9	1.5	41857
78013	COMFORT	19968	1828	27.5	32.3	30.8	5.6	3.8	41274	44260	37	47	1421	23.8	24.3	21.5	18.4	12.0	97162
78014	COTULLA	12766	1585	45.3	33.0	16.8	3.7	1.2	28020	29594	6	7	1141	55.5	21.2	17.2	3.9	2.3	41667
78015	BOERNE	43599	3370	7.1	11.3	32.6	20.4	28.6	98064	101915	96	97	3042	4.3	9.3	5.3	49.5	31.5	315083
78016	DEVINE	18306	3598	27.2	31.4	31.3	6.4	3.7	41882	46039	39	50	2722	31.4	28.7	27.3	9.9	2.7	74639
78017	DILLEY	12191	1236	46.5	32.4	18.8	1.3	1.1	26427	27771	4	5	823	62.9	21.0	13.2	1.9	0.9	38450
78019	ENCINAL	9304	280	59.6	26.4	12.9	1.1	0.0	20941	21519	2	2	223	64.6	18.4	13.9	1.8	1.3	33269
78021	FOWLERTON	22522	40	42.5	30.0	20.0	7.5	0.0	28567	32341	6	7	32	34.4	18.8	21.9	12.5	12.5	80000
78022	GEORGE WEST	18751	1677	32.9	31.7	28.3	4.0	3.2	38551	40147	28	36	1347	31.7	35.6	22.4	9.4	0.9	69181
78023	HELOTES	34062	6845	5.3	14.5	42.3	24.3	13.5	82995	85668	93	95	6236	2.7	10.4	42.5	40.2	4.2	159007
78024	HUNT	25906	292	19.5	33.2	37.7	3.8	5.8	46563	47008	53	63	193	4.7	10.4	25.4	32.6	26.9	221875
78025	INGRAM	21978	2522	23.4	32.0	35.6	5.6	3.3	45692	46681	50	61	2058	12.8	18.9	36.7	22.6	9.0	126167
78026	JOURDANTON	17725	1999	31.1	30.7	32.1	2.7	3.4	42997	46182	42	53	1571	35.6	34.5	20.5	6.5	2.9	58779
78027	KENDALIA	25015	198	28.8	24.2	33.8	8.6	4.5	43474	48487	44	54	163	18.4	12.3	25.2	19.6	24.5	153409
78028	KERRVILLE	24364	15367	26.7	31.5	30.8	6.2	4.8	42647	44561	41	52	10914	13.6	17.0	36.5	25.9	7.1	128850
78039	LA COSTE	17304	687	23.7	34.4	34.6	6.1	1.2	44830	47659	48	58	578	28.2	31.1	32.7	7.4	0.5	76667
78040	LAREDO	9024	12855	54.2	28.0	15.3	1.7	0.7	22463	23184	2	3	5897	18.9	46.7	30.5	3.7	0.3	76768
78041	LAREDO	16836	14129	31.7	25.3	31.2	7.3	4.6	42912	47443	42	53	7881	6.3	20.4	52.8	16.5	3.9	124898
78043	LAREDO	11186	11660	40.1	34.3	20.5	3.7	1.5	30997	32495	10	12	7111	22.1	33.2	38.5	5.8	0.4	82899
78045	LAREDO	19717	13281	13.4	23.9	43.9	12.4	6.4	61309	61487	79	85	10908	4.9	7.8	58.7	25.9	2.7	143263
78046	LAREDO	7840	13218	42.7	35.7	18.8	2.3	0.5	29031	31062	7	8	10496	25.1	42.5	29.6	2.7	0.1	73058
78052	LYTLE	16413	2019	24.9	32.3	34.3	6.6	1.8	43972	47304	45	56	1590	29.1	28.5	32.5	8.1	1.9	79099
78055	MEDINA	22568	965	29.4	27.9	31.2	8.2	3.3	43154	47469	43	54	757	19.8	16.4	35.3	22.2	6.3	118575
78056	MICO	23891	492	17.3	28.7	41.7	9.6	2.8	52983	52924	68	76	403	10.7	13.4	39.5	32.5	4.0	138347
78057	MOORE	18823	396	32.6	28.8	28.5	9.3	0.8	39265	44311	31	40	325	37.5	24.3	19.1	14.2	4.9	64412
78058	MOUNTAIN HOME	21535	132	26.5	30.3	40.9	2.3	0.0	45443	45713	50	60	105	3.8	22.9	40.0	22.9	10.5	134821
78059	NATALIA	15986	1932	28.6	30.8	32.4	6.1	2.1	42464	46274	41	51	1598	35.4	26.1	26.3	11.6	0.7	73697
78061	PEARSALL	12869	3143	41.5	34.0	20.6	2.3	1.6	29089	29418	7	8	2094	46.0	30.2	19.3	3.5	1.0	52923
78063	LAKEHILLS	23125	3582	21.6	26.5	39.7	8.8	3.4	50996	51511	64	72	3023	15.7	20.7	36.8	24.5	2.2	114419
78064	PLEASANTON	17479	5231	32.4	25.6	33.9	6.4	1.8	41598	46531	38	48	3810	26.1	29.2	32.2	10.8	1.6	80973
78065	POTEET	15698	3778	32.1	29.3	31.9	4.4	2.4	40424	45608	34	44	2993	40.3	29.6	24.7	4.7	0.7	59222
78066	RIO MEDINA	21735	235	14.9	30.2	42.1	10.2	2.6	54112	54017	70	77	187	9.6	13.4	37.4	36.4	3.2	143229
78067	SAN YGNACIO	10245	392	53.3	27.0	15.3	1.8	2.6	22794	24552	2	3	300	48.0	21.3	27.7	0.0	3.0	52308
78069	SOMERSET	15030	1611	29.0	29.6	34.0	5.6	1.8	40562	46136	35	45	1271	39.4	30.1	24.9	4.9	0.7	62816
78070	SPRING BRANCH	27012	4867	13.2	19.6	45.9	13.2	8.2	64909	68989	83	87	4487	5.4	15.1	33.3	33.7	12.5	158764
78071	THREE RIVERS	18091	1326	31.9	26.4	33.0	5.6	3.2	41289	42645	37	47	1004	35.3	32.0	27.3	4.9	0.6	71739
78072	TILDEN	23188	229	31.9	32.8	25.8	5.7	3.9	39073	40129	30	38	182	35.2	31.3	15.9	6.0	11.5	65000
78073	VON ORMY	14524	2541	26.2	34.6	33.5	4.3	1.4	43033	46246	42	53	1995	48.3	30.4	17.8	3.3	0.2	51215
78074	WARING	25447	14	14.3	35.7	42.9	0.0	7.1	50000	47278	61	70	11	0.0	0.0	18.2	45.5	36.4	262500
78075	WHITSETT	26683	75	38.7	20.0	33.3	4.0	4.0	35761	39438	20	26	60	41.7	30.0	25.0	3.3	0.0	65000
78076	ZAPATA	13073	4258	40.7	31.2	23.8	2.2	2.0	30850	31810	9	12	3484	39.6	28.1	25.8	5.8	0.7	63080
78101	ADKINS	21760	2577	19.6	26.9	41.4	9.4	2.8	52567	53591	67	75	2190	18.0	26.1	33.7	21.8	0.5	102674
78102	BEEVILLE	15453	8410	35.7	30.4	28.8	3.9	1.2	35593	38120	20	25	5345	29.3	34.8	27.4	7.0	1.4	71951
78108	CIBOLO	27387	7282	11.8	15.5	48.6	16.3	7.8	67220	68347	85	88	6241	8.9	12.2	35.4	41.7	1.7	160040
78109	CONVERSE	22558	9809	10.0	22.2	51.1	12.9	3.8	61654	62893	80	85	7241	9.2	22.1	65.0	3.4	0.3	108045
78111	ECLETO	0	0	0.0	0.0	0.0	0.0	0.0	0	0	0	0	0	0.0	0.0	0.0	0.0	0.0	0
78112	ELMENDORF	16022	2331	18.6	34.4	38.3	6.6	2.1	47588	50624	56	66	1956	30.4	43.1	24.3	1.7	0.5	68400
78113	FALLS CITY	20306	545	29.5	27.7	33.6	6.2	2.9	43941	48194	45	56	444	32.9	23.6	30.6	11.7	1.1	78400
78114	FLORESVILLE	18831	6345	22.8	32.7	34.3	7.2	3.0	46014	49167	51	62	5215	19.2	25.8	36.2	18.1	0.7	101270
78116	GILLETT	23210	250	35.6	27.2	24.4	2.8	10.0	35000	33319	18	23	210	37.1	28.6	22.4	11.9	0.0	72222
78117	HOBSON	19072	161	28.6	29.2	33.5	6.2	2.5	43841	47828	45	55	131	35.1	22.9	30.5	10.7	0.8	75833
78118	KARNES CITY	15371	1401	35.4	32.0	26.6	5.2	0.8	33481	35120	14	18	1012	50.9	28.7	15.3	4.3	0.8	48929
78119	KENEDY	15158	1674	40.6	32.1	22.2	3.9	1.3	30128	30597	8	10	1176	47.4	32.1	15.1	3.8	1.5	52500
78121	LA VERNIA	21677	3659	16.4	28.7	40.8	10.1	4.0	52414	53011	67	75	3232	14.6	22.1	40.7	20.7	1.9	113947
78122	LEESVILLE	16942	99	33.3	35.4	26.3	4.0	1.0	33440	34768	14	17	81	29.6	25.9	29.6	12.3	2.5	83571
78123	MC QUEENEY	23790	938	18.2	29.5	42.3	6.3	3.6	51211	53112	64	73	697	15.4	28.1	31.9	13.6	11.0	98922
78124	MARION	20510	2323	16.9	32.4	40.1	6.8	3.8	50461	52578	62	71	1869	17.5	24.9	42.0	13.7	1.8	102238
78130	NEW BRAUNFELS	22147	22181	20.5	28.7	39.1	7.7	3.9	50652	53139	63	71	14791	11.1	18.8	43.7	23.3	3.1	129317
78132	NEW BRAUNFELS	29078	7213	12.7	24.2	37.1	15.5	10.5	66136	70521	84	88	6136	9.3	8.7	24.1	46.5	11.4	201837
	TEXAS	24551		22.3	25.0	34.3	11.1	7.3	52382	54495				16.5	22.7	36.5	19.7	4.6	109784
	UNITED STATES	27277		20.9	24.4	35.3	11.7	7.6	54719	56938				9.3	13.1	31.6	32.6	13.5	162279

ZIP CODE		FINANCIAL SERVICES				THE HOME						ENTERTAINMENT						PERSONAL			
						Home Improvements		Furnishings													
#	POST OFFICE NAME	Auto Loan	Home Loan	Invest-ments	Retire-ment Plans	Home Repair	Lawn & Garden	Comput-ers & Hard-ware-Personal	Major Appli-ances	TV, Radio, Sound Equip-ment	Furni-ture	Dine out/ Carry out	Sports Equip-ment	Fees & Tickets	Toys & Games	Travel	Cable TV	Apparel & Services	Auto Repairs	Health Insur-ance	Pets & Supplies
77864	MADISONVILLE	82	57	85	55	59	83	60	76	67	56	66	58	48	67	59	74	44	71	79	91
77865	MARQUEZ	91	66	94	63	68	93	67	86	75	63	73	64	54	74	67	82	48	78	89	102
77868	NAVASOTA	83	66	70	62	66	77	67	76	72	68	72	54	58	73	64	77	49	73	78	88
77871	NORMANGEE	91	74	101	70	79	97	73	90	80	73	78	64	65	76	76	86	52	85	97	106
77872	NORTH ZULCH	89	64	91	62	66	90	65	83	72	61	71	62	52	72	65	80	47	76	86	99
77873	RICHARDS	95	67	96	64	69	96	69	88	77	65	76	66	55	77	68	85	50	81	92	105
77879	SOMERVILLE	85	65	87	61	67	87	66	80	72	65	71	59	55	72	65	79	47	76	84	96
77880	WASHINGTON	101	73	106	71	76	103	75	95	83	70	81	71	60	82	75	90	54	87	98	113
77901	VICTORIA	73	64	54	61	61	63	69	67	70	70	71	49	63	72	63	71	49	69	68	78
77904	VICTORIA	114	119	115	121	120	119	112	115	111	115	112	86	116	113	115	112	78	112	115	134
77905	VICTORIA	87	79	77	78	78	86	76	83	78	76	78	62	71	80	74	81	53	79	83	98
77951	BLOOMINGTON	67	56	44	48	54	52	56	59	59	62	60	38	50	60	51	60	42	60	56	65
77954	CUERO	79	55	77	53	56	79	60	72	66	55	65	56	46	66	56	73	43	68	77	88
77957	EDNA	85	64	81	63	65	87	68	81	74	61	72	62	56	74	66	81	48	76	87	96
77962	GANADO	90	64	92	62	67	91	66	84	73	62	72	63	53	73	65	81	48	77	88	100
77963	GOLIAD	87	62	94	61	65	89	65	83	71	59	70	63	52	70	66	78	46	76	86	99
77964	HALLETTSVILLE	82	59	84	57	61	84	61	77	68	56	66	58	49	67	60	74	44	71	81	92
77968	INEZ	97	99	91	102	98	106	93	100	93	89	93	77	92	95	95	96	64	94	101	117
77971	LOLITA	95	74	86	73	74	95	76	88	82	72	81	67	65	84	73	89	54	83	93	106
77974	MEYERSVILLE	87	75	91	76	76	93	75	86	76	68	76	69	67	76	77	80	51	81	88	104
77975	MOULTON	78	56	79	54	58	80	58	73	65	53	63	55	47	64	57	71	42	68	78	87
77979	PORT LAVACA	86	70	75	69	70	83	73	81	77	70	76	61	63	78	69	81	52	78	83	95
77983	SEADRIFT	79	57	74	55	58	78	59	72	65	56	64	54	47	66	56	71	43	67	75	86
77984	SHINER	75	53	77	52	55	78	58	72	63	51	61	55	45	62	56	69	41	67	77	85
77990	TIVOLI	84	60	86	58	63	85	62	79	69	58	67	59	50	68	61	76	45	72	82	94
77994	WESTHOFF	89	64	91	62	66	90	65	83	72	61	71	62	52	72	65	80	47	76	86	99
77995	YOAKUM	81	61	79	60	62	83	64	76	70	59	68	58	53	70	62	76	46	72	82	91
78002	ATASCOSA	74	61	56	56	59	65	60	66	64	63	64	46	53	66	56	67	44	64	66	77
78003	BANDERA	90	73	92	71	75	90	73	86	78	70	77	63	63	77	72	83	51	81	88	102
78004	BERGHEIM	138	171	175	176	175	162	145	154	139	155	141	114	166	139	163	137	101	146	145	176
78005	BIGFOOT	84	60	86	58	63	85	62	79	69	58	67	59	49	68	61	75	44	72	82	94
78006	BOERNE	118	132	134	135	134	133	119	126	117	122	117	95	127	117	128	117	82	121	124	146
78007	CALLIHAM	102	72	107	70	75	105	76	96	82	67	81	74	59	82	75	90	53	89	100	115
78008	CAMPBELLTON	96	68	98	66	71	97	70	89	78	65	77	67	56	77	69	86	51	82	93	106
78009	CASTROVILLE	90	85	76	82	83	87	79	84	82	82	82	61	76	85	77	85	56	82	86	100
78010	CENTER POINT	94	77	99	74	79	94	77	90	81	75	80	67	67	81	77	86	54	86	91	107
78011	CHARLOTTE	68	50	52	44	48	58	51	59	57	53	57	41	42	58	46	61	39	58	59	68
78013	COMFORT	89	74	97	72	77	89	74	87	77	72	77	65	66	76	76	81	52	82	86	102
78014	COTULLA	59	50	45	44	49	48	50	54	52	54	53	37	44	53	47	53	36	53	51	60
78015	BOERNE	157	210	240	215	228	196	177	189	165	195	164	140	211	160	208	158	121	176	172	209
78016	DEVINE	90	72	85	69	71	87	72	83	77	71	77	63	62	79	69	82	52	79	85	99
78017	DILLEY	59	43	46	38	42	51	44	51	49	46	49	36	36	50	40	53	33	50	52	60
78019	ENCINAL	45	36	27	30	35	34	36	39	39	41	40	24	32	40	32	41	28	39	38	43
78021	FOWLERTON	72	51	74	50	53	73	53	67	59	49	58	50	42	58	52	64	38	62	70	80
78022	GEORGE WEST	85	65	84	61	67	82	66	80	71	64	71	57	55	70	65	77	47	75	81	93
78023	HELOTES	134	163	161	166	165	152	139	146	133	149	135	110	156	134	153	130	96	138	137	167
78024	HUNT	106	86	138	85	95	113	86	109	90	81	89	79	75	85	93	96	59	100	108	126
78025	INGRAM	83	77	104	75	85	92	73	87	77	77	76	59	72	72	80	81	51	83	92	100
78026	JOURDANTON	86	72	66	66	70	75	71	78	76	75	76	54	64	78	67	78	52	76	77	90
78027	KENDALIA	102	81	131	80	89	107	81	103	85	76	84	76	71	81	88	91	56	95	102	120
78028	KERRVILLE	88	76	97	74	81	94	78	89	82	77	81	63	72	79	79	88	55	86	95	103
78039	LA COSTE	79	72	64	70	71	74	68	72	71	71	71	52	65	74	65	73	48	70	73	86
78040	LAREDO	52	42	32	35	40	39	42	45	45	46	46	28	37	46	38	47	32	45	44	49
78041	LAREDO	86	83	71	76	81	73	81	81	80	87	81	58	77	81	78	78	57	81	75	91
78043	LAREDO	66	56	45	49	54	51	57	59	59	63	60	39	51	60	52	59	42	60	56	65
78045	LAREDO	107	116	97	110	111	96	105	105	99	114	101	82	107	105	105	93	71	101	91	118
78046	LAREDO	58	48	38	41	47	44	48	51	51	54	52	33	43	52	44	51	36	51	48	56
78052	LYTLE	80	75	65	70	73	71	73	75	73	77	73	55	68	75	69	73	51	73	71	86
78055	MEDINA	95	72	110	70	77	98	73	93	78	68	77	69	61	76	76	85	51	85	94	109
78056	MICO	96	88	78	86	86	90	83	88	87	87	87	64	79	90	80	89	59	86	89	105
78057	MOORE	84	60	86	58	63	85	62	79	69	58	67	59	49	68	61	75	44	72	82	94
78058	MOUNTAIN HOME	79	63	102	62	69	83	63	80	66	59	65	59	55	63	68	70	43	74	79	93
78059	NATALIA	81	72	69	68	69	75	71	75	73	73	73	57	65	75	68	74	50	73	74	89
78061	PEARSALL	65	50	47	44	49	54	51	57	55	54	56	38	43	56	47	58	38	56	57	64
78063	LAKEHILLS	95	86	102	85	88	98	82	94	84	81	84	70	77	84	85	88	57	89	93	110
78064	PLEASANTON	82	71	63	66	69	73	68	73	72	72	72	52	62	75	64	75	49	72	74	86
78065	POTEET	79	67	58	61	65	67	67	71	70	71	71	49	60	72	62	72	49	70	70	81
78066	RIO MEDINA	99	91	80	88	88	93	85	91	89	89	89	66	81	92	81	91	60	88	91	108
78067	SAN YGNACIO	54	43	33	36	42	41	43	47	47	49	48	29	38	48	39	49	33	47	45	51
78069	SOMERSET	76	69	61	63	67	66	68	70	68	72	69	51	63	70	64	68	48	70	67	81
78070	SPRING BRANCH	110	118	126	119	121	120	106	115	105	110	105	85	111	105	113	105	74	109	111	133
78071	THREE RIVERS	85	67	77	67	67	86	71	80	76	65	74	61	60	76	67	81	50	77	85	96
78072	TILDEN	98	70	103	68	72	101	73	92	80	66	78	71	57	79	72	87	51	85	96	111
78073	VON ORMY	77	67	60	62	64	68	67	69	69	70	69	51	61	72	62	70	48	69	68	81
78074	WARING	103	83	133	81	91	109	83	105	86	77	85	77	72	82	89	92	57	97	104	122
78075	WHITSETT	87	63	90	61	65	89	64	82	71	60	70	61	51	71	64	79	46	75	85	97
78076	ZAPATA	66	54	51	47	54	57	53	60	58	58	58	39	47	57	51	61	40	59	61	67
78101	ADKINS	97	94	84	94	92	97	88	94	90	89	90	70	86	93	87	92	61	90	94	110
78102	BEEVILLE	69	57	59	54	57	64	59	64	62	59	62	47	53	63	56	65	42	63	66	75
78108	CIBOLO	111	128	114	126	123	117	111	115	108	116	110	89	120	112	117	107	77	110	108	133
78109	CONVERSE	107	110	91	106	103	96	102	101	99	108	100	78	101	104	98	96	70	98	93	117
78111	ECLETO	0	0	0	0	0	0	0	0	0	0	0	0	0	0	0	0	0	0	0	0
78112	ELMENDORF	85	79	68	76	76	77	78	78	78	81	79	59	73	82	73	79	54	78	77	93
78113	FALLS CITY	93	66	96	65	69	95	69	87	76	63	75	66	55	75	68	83	49	80	91	104
78114	FLORESVILLE	90	76	77	73	75	85	75	83	80	75	79	61	68	81	72	83	53	80	85	98
78116	GILLETT	99	71	102	69	74	101	73	93	81	68	80	70	58	81	72	89	53	85	97	111
78117	HOBSON	91	65	93	63	68	92	67	85	74	62	73	64	53	74	66	82	48	78	88	101
78118	KARNES CITY	72	54	60	49	54	66	56	66	62	56	61	46	47	62	53	66	41	63	68	75
78119	KENEDY	70	53	59	50	52	65	56	63	61	54	60	46	47	62	51	65	41	61	66	75
78121	LA VERNIA	100	95	82	91	92	93	88	92	90	92	90	68	85	94	84	91	62	89	91	109
78122	LEESVILLE	88	63	90	61	65	89	64	82	72	60	70	62	52	71	64	79	46	75	85	98
78123	MC QUEENEY	97	83	107	81	86	98	81	95	84	80	84	70	73	83	83	88	56	90	94	112
78124	MARION	96	90	85	88	88	95	84	91	88	86	87	67	81	90	83	90	60	88	92	108
78130	NEW BRAUNFELS	90	87	82	85	85	89	85	88	86	86	86	66	83	87	83	88	59	86	90	102
78132	NEW BRAUNFELS	117	130	127	132	130	128	116	123	114	120	115	92	123	115	123	114	80	117	119	143
	TEXAS	104	96	90	94	93	94	99	97	99	101	100	75	94	101	94	99	70	99	96	114
	UNITED STATES	100	100	100	100	100	100	100	100	100	100	100	100	100	100	100	100	100	100	100	100

ZIP CODE #	POST OFFICE NAME	COUNTY FIPS CODE	POPULATION 2000	POPULATION 2009	POPULATION 2014	2000-2009 ANNUAL RATE % Rate	2000-2009 ANNUAL RATE State Centile	HOUSEHOLDS 2000	HOUSEHOLDS 2009	HOUSEHOLDS 2014	HOUSEHOLDS % Annual Rate 2000-2009	HOUSEHOLDS 2009 Average HH Size	FAMILIES 2000	FAMILIES 2009	FAMILIES % Annual Rate 2000-2009
78133	CANYON LAKE	091	13256	17634	20991	3.1	87	5540	7357	8766	3.1	2.39	4026	5199	2.8
78140	NIXON	177	3301	3359	3345	0.2	30	1124	1146	1145	0.2	2.85	845	852	0.1
78141	NORDHEIM	123	621	650	652	0.5	42	253	265	266	0.5	2.45	182	189	0.4
78147	POTH	493	3068	3676	4073	2.0	78	1072	1300	1448	2.1	2.83	849	1015	1.9
78148	UNIVERSAL CITY	029	18654	20616	22306	1.1	61	7015	7778	8467	1.1	2.57	5059	5428	0.8
78150	UNIVERSAL CITY	029	13	14	14	0.8	52	5	5	5	0.0	2.80	4	4	0.0
78151	RUNGE	255	1469	1405	1383	-0.5	11	557	544	539	-0.3	2.58	406	391	-0.4
78152	SAINT HEDWIG	029	1852	2115	2259	1.4	67	649	738	791	1.4	2.85	530	589	1.1
78154	SCHERTZ	187	19158	26212	30833	3.4	89	6761	9088	10656	3.2	2.87	5409	7118	3.0
78155	SEGUIN	187	40186	46087	51077	1.5	69	14022	15964	17740	1.4	2.79	10375	11512	1.1
78159	SMILEY	177	926	972	988	0.5	42	364	383	389	0.6	2.51	262	272	0.4
78160	STOCKDALE	493	3598	4199	4615	1.7	73	1314	1556	1723	1.8	2.63	976	1135	1.6
78161	SUTHERLAND SPRINGS	493	997	1192	1352	1.9	76	343	417	475	2.1	2.86	272	325	1.9
78163	BULVERDE	091	7304	10998	13651	4.5	93	2523	3743	4652	4.4	2.93	2117	3088	4.2
78164	YORKTOWN	123	3775	3658	3589	-0.3	16	1489	1445	1416	-0.3	2.48	1063	1017	-0.5
78201	SAN ANTONIO	029	46034	45712	46328	-0.1	21	16314	16051	16320	-0.2	2.81	10908	10302	-0.6
78202	SAN ANTONIO	029	11925	11639	11700	-0.3	16	4066	3919	3949	-0.4	2.88	2620	2416	-0.9
78203	SAN ANTONIO	029	5352	5706	5820	0.7	49	1737	1841	1883	0.6	3.08	1218	1232	0.1
78204	SAN ANTONIO	029	11957	12056	12273	0.1	27	3832	3846	3933	0.0	3.05	2706	2615	-0.4
78205	SAN ANTONIO	029	1599	1578	1584	-0.1	21	1016	970	975	-0.5	1.23	177	152	-1.6
78207	SAN ANTONIO	029	56719	57122	58093	0.1	27	15546	15527	15869	0.0	3.36	11815	11464	-0.3
78208	SAN ANTONIO	029	5079	4767	4724	-0.7	7	1628	1505	1493	-0.8	3.06	1118	997	-1.2
78209	SAN ANTONIO	029	39124	38326	38531	-0.2	19	17423	16876	17025	-0.3	2.17	9580	8791	-0.9
78210	SAN ANTONIO	029	38558	39127	39792	0.2	30	13024	13122	13378	0.1	2.93	9013	8725	-0.4
78211	SAN ANTONIO	029	30637	31516	32436	0.3	34	8479	8673	8952	0.2	3.63	7076	7102	0.0
78212	SAN ANTONIO	029	30927	30298	30449	-0.2	19	12036	11609	11697	-0.4	2.34	6233	5691	-1.0
78213	SAN ANTONIO	029	39048	39526	40253	0.1	27	15969	15960	16293	0.0	2.48	9775	9329	-0.5
78214	SAN ANTONIO	029	23653	24133	24785	0.2	30	7511	7622	7853	0.2	3.14	5665	5588	-0.1
78215	SAN ANTONIO	029	1376	1367	1378	-0.1	21	645	635	645	-0.2	1.88	245	222	-1.1
78216	SAN ANTONIO	029	34756	36838	38317	0.6	46	15649	16462	17197	0.5	2.23	8622	8514	-0.1
78217	SAN ANTONIO	029	30322	30899	31670	0.2	30	12848	12975	13335	0.1	2.37	7867	7595	-0.4
78218	SAN ANTONIO	029	30627	32845	34486	0.8	52	12392	12970	13565	0.5	2.51	7789	7860	0.1
78219	SAN ANTONIO	029	14143	15680	16573	1.1	61	5021	5552	5890	1.1	2.82	3755	3994	0.7
78220	SAN ANTONIO	029	17246	17434	17788	0.1	27	6197	6204	6344	0.0	2.75	4414	4263	-0.4
78221	SAN ANTONIO	029	34915	36656	37922	0.5	42	10604	11093	11532	0.5	3.27	8592	8770	0.2
78222	SAN ANTONIO	029	14627	16814	18121	1.5	69	4937	5647	6107	1.5	2.92	3785	4209	1.2
78223	SAN ANTONIO	029	42118	46677	49519	1.1	61	14571	15909	16875	1.0	2.88	10544	11196	0.7
78224	SAN ANTONIO	029	15201	18793	20770	2.3	81	4202	5180	5747	2.3	3.56	3579	4309	2.0
78225	SAN ANTONIO	029	13523	13345	13478	-0.1	21	4329	4251	4309	-0.2	3.14	3388	3236	-0.5
78226	SAN ANTONIO	029	8220	8656	8956	0.6	46	2539	2652	2760	0.5	3.08	2088	2147	0.3
78227	SAN ANTONIO	029	40280	45979	49375	1.4	67	12639	14346	15461	1.4	3.17	9903	10999	1.1
78228	SAN ANTONIO	029	59803	62430	64329	0.5	42	18860	19483	20132	0.4	3.08	14334	14443	0.1
78229	SAN ANTONIO	029	29126	30203	31010	0.4	37	14053	14395	14812	0.3	2.03	6196	5941	-0.5
78230	SAN ANTONIO	029	36352	39772	42097	1.0	58	15827	17111	18151	0.8	2.32	9750	10066	0.3
78231	SAN ANTONIO	029	8890	8924	9167	0.0	25	3599	3596	3702	0.0	2.48	2490	2404	-0.4
78232	SAN ANTONIO	029	34708	36487	37809	0.5	42	14504	15096	15679	0.4	2.39	9589	9599	0.0
78233	SAN ANTONIO	029	36107	41904	45159	1.6	71	12996	15068	16316	1.6	2.77	9752	11009	1.3
78234	SAN ANTONIO	029	5509	5393	5374	-0.2	19	923	865	863	-0.7	3.82	902	843	-0.7
78235	SAN ANTONIO	029	787	737	732	-0.7	7	207	193	193	-0.8	3.35	190	173	-1.0
78236	SAN ANTONIO	029	8017	8357	8426	0.5	42	337	347	359	0.3	4.23	305	310	0.2
78237	SAN ANTONIO	029	36810	39435	41075	0.7	49	10322	10960	11441	0.7	3.53	8403	8722	0.4
78238	SAN ANTONIO	029	21084	23230	24565	1.1	61	8065	8951	9550	1.1	2.58	5402	5685	0.6
78239	SAN ANTONIO	029	26279	28727	30250	1.0	58	9681	10692	11365	1.1	2.66	7184	7666	0.7
78240	SAN ANTONIO	029	42010	48319	51915	1.5	69	18077	20597	22208	1.4	2.32	10320	11170	0.9
78242	SAN ANTONIO	029	27932	31203	33231	1.2	63	7802	8644	9224	1.1	3.61	6461	7046	0.9
78244	SAN ANTONIO	029	18736	25700	29507	3.5	89	5799	7865	9058	3.3	3.27	4912	6519	3.1
78245	SAN ANTONIO	029	31885	45940	53221	4.0	91	10630	15569	18206	4.2	2.94	8216	11520	3.7
78247	SAN ANTONIO	029	38854	48019	52534	2.3	81	13579	16095	17580	1.9	2.97	10743	12440	1.6
78248	SAN ANTONIO	029	13346	15183	16236	1.4	67	5068	5773	6207	1.4	2.63	3752	4121	1.0
78249	SAN ANTONIO	029	33474	44319	49935	3.1	87	12047	15708	17709	2.9	2.78	8630	10789	2.4
78250	SAN ANTONIO	029	50744	56246	59423	1.1	61	16152	17807	18883	1.1	3.15	13445	14506	0.8
78251	SAN ANTONIO	029	24889	46352	56081	7.0	96	8636	15611	18876	6.6	2.97	6449	11545	6.5
78252	SAN ANTONIO	029	4606	5401	5757	1.7	73	769	967	1072	2.5	3.43	625	773	2.3
78253	SAN ANTONIO	029	9646	20689	26309	8.6	98	3162	6738	8583	8.5	3.07	2685	5625	8.3
78254	SAN ANTONIO	029	17103	36150	43625	8.4	97	5735	12419	15068	8.7	2.91	4779	10281	8.6
78255	SAN ANTONIO	029	4908	8894	10679	6.6	96	1353	3314	3982	6.5	2.68	1369	2455	6.5
78256	SAN ANTONIO	029	2747	4131	4846	4.5	93	1166	1638	1897	3.7	2.52	627	841	3.2
78257	SAN ANTONIO	029	2310	3797	4516	5.5	95	898	1431	1702	5.2	2.65	696	998	4.0
78258	SAN ANTONIO	029	13272	36934	47870	11.7	99	4526	12230	15878	11.3	3.02	3738	9876	11.1
78259	SAN ANTONIO	029	9311	19252	23623	8.2	97	2953	6245	7712	8.4	3.06	2644	5422	8.1
78260	SAN ANTONIO	029	6785	21148	26873	13.1	99	2286	7063	8994	13.0	2.99	1963	5885	12.6
78261	SAN ANTONIO	029	1167	8202	10848	23.5	100	383	2649	3512	23.3	3.10	343	2303	22.9
78263	SAN ANTONIO	029	4491	5096	5463	1.4	67	1552	1752	1884	1.3	2.91	1246	1371	1.0
78264	SAN ANTONIO	029	9264	10888	11853	1.8	75	2856	3339	3646	1.7	3.26	2320	2652	1.5
78266	SAN ANTONIO	091	2712	4427	5265	5.4	95	996	1725	2066	6.1	2.57	859	1436	5.7
78332	ALICE	249	27673	29129	29841	0.6	46	9063	9641	9914	0.7	2.97	7096	7469	0.6
78336	ARANSAS PASS	409	11868	12593	12871	0.6	46	4292	4635	4758	0.8	2.70	3140	3342	0.7
78338	ARMSTRONG	261	136	126	121	-0.8	6	44	41	40	-0.8	3.05	35	33	-0.6
78340	BAYSIDE	391	420	384	370	-1.0	4	172	160	155	-0.8	2.40	118	108	-1.0
78343	BISHOP	355	4879	4784	4745	-0.2	19	1639	1646	1642	0.0	2.90	1283	1276	-0.1
78344	BRUNI	479	469	602	666	2.7	84	148	191	213	2.8	3.13	119	150	2.5
78349	CONCEPCION	131	3249	2928	2785	-1.1	3	1188	1102	1059	-0.8	2.65	865	791	-1.0
78353	ENCINO	047	650	609	589	-0.7	7	238	227	221	-0.5	2.68	178	167	-0.7
78355	FALFURRIAS	047	7326	7084	6921	-0.4	13	2473	2431	2385	-0.2	2.90	1902	1848	-0.3
78357	FREER	131	3977	3677	3524	-0.8	6	1373	1293	1250	-0.6	2.84	1036	963	-0.8
78360	GUERRA	247	67	58	55	-1.5	1	27	24	23	-1.3	2.38	19	17	-1.2
78361	HEBBRONVILLE	247	5248	5024	4899	-0.5	11	1796	1745	1712	-0.3	2.85	1347	1292	-0.4
78362	INGLESIDE	409	10277	10368	10627	0.1	27	3320	3555	3669	0.7	2.80	2494	2631	0.6
78363	KINGSVILLE	273	29743	29013	28433	-0.3	16	10248	10138	9971	-0.1	2.75	7167	6985	-0.3
78368	MATHIS	409	10650	10499	10470	-0.2	19	3598	3574	3571	-0.1	2.93	2787	2742	-0.2
78369	MIRANDO CITY	479	1437	2051	2402	3.9	91	390	552	647	3.8	3.71	323	445	3.5
78370	ODEM	409	4415	5135	5442	1.6	71	1399	1654	1764	1.8	3.10	1145	1338	1.7
78372	ORANGE GROVE	249	5581	6087	6327	0.9	55	1850	2044	2136	1.1	2.98	1441	1572	0.9
78373	PORT ARANSAS	355	3450	3671	3733	0.7	49	1583	1726	1769	0.9	2.12	1029	1100	0.7
78374	PORTLAND	409	18222	20267	20719	1.2	63	6034	6779	6954	1.3	2.99	4884	5433	1.2
	TEXAS					1.9					1.8	2.78			1.7
	UNITED STATES					1.0					1.1	2.59			0.9

ZIP CODE #	POST OFFICE NAME	RACE (%) White		RACE (%) Black		RACE (%) Asian/Pacific		% Hispanic Origin		2009 AGE DISTRIBUTION (%)										MEDIAN AGE	% 2009 Males	% 2009 Females
		2000	2009	2000	2009	2000	2009	2000	2009	0-4	5-9	10-14	15-19	20-24	25-44	45-64	65-84	85+	18+	2009		
78133	CANYON LAKE	94.9	92.6	0.3	0.3	0.2	0.3	9.8	15.4	4.8	4.9	5.7	5.7	4.0	21.1	33.7	18.1	1.9	81.0	47.2	49.8	50.2
78140	NIXON	75.2	71.4	3.1	3.1	0.1	0.1	51.9	59.7	8.0	7.8	7.4	7.9	6.9	24.5	23.0	12.1	2.4	72.2	34.6	50.3	49.7
78141	NORDHEIM	86.8	85.8	0.0	0.0	0.0	0.0	25.2	27.5	4.9	4.9	5.5	6.3	4.5	22.9	29.5	17.8	3.5	80.6	45.7	49.4	50.6
78147	POTH	77.9	71.7	0.6	0.7	0.1	0.1	40.5	52.4	7.0	7.1	7.3	7.0	5.7	25.3	28.1	11.0	1.5	73.8	37.9	50.0	50.0
78148	UNIVERSAL CITY	78.4	73.2	8.6	9.2	3.1	3.6	20.3	31.5	7.1	7.1	6.7	6.6	8.0	29.3	23.6	10.4	1.2	75.0	33.9	50.0	50.0
78150	UNIVERSAL CITY	83.3	78.6	8.3	7.1	0.0	0.0	33.3	42.9	14.3	7.1	7.1	14.3	21.4	21.4	14.3	0.0	0.0	64.3	21.7	50.0	50.0
78151	RUNGE	72.5	68.4	1.6	1.4	0.0	0.0	62.6	72.5	7.5	7.8	7.3	8.0	3.9	21.5	25.2	15.9	2.8	72.0	39.1	48.7	51.3
78152	SAINT HEDWIG	89.8	85.0	3.2	3.8	0.2	0.2	13.7	23.2	6.1	6.6	7.0	6.7	4.9	25.4	31.2	11.0	1.0	75.7	40.4	51.6	48.4
78154	SCHERTZ	82.6	78.2	6.3	6.8	1.9	2.2	20.0	30.7	7.5	7.2	7.1	6.7	6.4	28.0	27.3	8.7	1.0	73.7	35.9	48.4	51.6
78155	SEGUIN	73.4	68.8	6.4	5.3	0.7	0.7	40.5	51.0	7.3	7.2	7.1	8.0	6.9	25.0	25.2	11.2	2.0	74.1	35.6	49.1	50.9
78159	SMILEY	83.7	79.2	0.2	0.2	0.0	0.0	40.8	51.9	6.7	7.0	6.9	7.0	5.2	22.7	25.9	15.4	3.1	74.2	39.7	50.0	50.0
78160	STOCKDALE	86.0	81.4	1.2	1.2	0.1	0.2	29.3	39.6	6.2	6.4	6.5	6.4	5.0	22.6	29.4	14.4	3.0	77.1	42.5	49.9	50.1
78161	SUTHERLAND SPRINGS	83.5	77.8	1.0	1.1	0.2	0.2	26.5	37.7	7.0	7.1	7.2	6.8	6.3	24.4	29.6	10.7	0.8	74.5	37.5	48.8	51.2
78163	BULVERDE	93.6	91.1	0.3	0.3	0.5	0.7	13.0	19.7	5.5	6.4	7.7	7.3	3.4	23.0	35.3	10.4	1.0	75.3	43.0	50.6	49.4
78164	YORKTOWN	85.0	84.4	1.9	1.9	0.1	0.1	28.3	30.3	5.3	5.4	5.7	6.5	5.4	21.6	29.8	16.0	4.3	79.4	45.1	49.2	50.8
78201	SAN ANTONIO	69.7	67.5	1.9	1.6	0.6	0.5	83.1	89.9	8.4	7.6	7.0	7.1	7.3	27.1	23.4	10.2	2.0	72.8	34.1	48.9	51.1
78202	SAN ANTONIO	33.3	35.2	43.0	36.8	0.3	0.3	52.0	60.0	8.7	8.7	7.8	7.9	6.4	23.1	22.3	12.2	2.9	69.9	34.3	48.5	51.5
78203	SAN ANTONIO	32.9	31.8	33.8	27.1	0.1	0.2	61.5	70.2	9.4	9.2	8.1	8.1	7.4	25.0	21.8	8.9	2.1	68.3	30.4	48.4	51.6
78204	SAN ANTONIO	59.0	57.1	1.0	0.9	0.2	0.2	91.2	94.6	8.0	7.8	7.5	7.6	6.6	26.8	22.4	11.3	2.0	71.9	34.3	49.8	50.2
78205	SAN ANTONIO	75.7	71.9	7.4	6.7	0.9	1.0	51.5	65.7	2.5	2.2	2.0	2.5	6.0	30.4	28.9	21.6	3.9	92.3	48.1	59.9	40.1
78207	SAN ANTONIO	62.2	61.4	3.1	2.5	0.2	0.2	92.8	95.2	9.4	8.4	7.6	8.4	8.3	27.3	19.5	9.4	1.7	69.6	30.0	51.6	48.4
78208	SAN ANTONIO	55.8	55.6	15.0	12.0	1.0	0.9	74.4	81.6	10.6	9.8	8.7	8.1	7.9	25.5	19.9	8.1	1.6	66.1	28.4	52.5	47.5
78209	SAN ANTONIO	87.8	84.7	3.4	3.3	1.2	1.3	23.7	34.3	5.8	5.6	5.9	6.2	6.2	22.9	27.3	14.9	5.2	79.2	43.0	45.9	54.1
78210	SAN ANTONIO	56.0	54.2	8.1	6.7	0.4	0.3	79.1	85.4	8.0	7.8	7.6	7.8	6.9	26.2	23.4	10.4	1.9	71.6	33.6	49.0	51.0
78211	SAN ANTONIO	60.2	58.8	0.4	0.4	0.2	0.2	95.7	97.5	9.3	9.0	8.4	8.3	7.3	26.9	20.6	9.0	1.1	68.2	30.1	50.0	50.0
78212	SAN ANTONIO	74.1	71.0	2.5	2.2	1.3	1.4	61.0	70.7	6.0	5.4	5.0	8.5	9.9	27.6	23.7	11.0	3.0	80.4	35.7	49.2	50.8
78213	SAN ANTONIO	76.2	71.8	2.7	2.5	1.3	1.3	57.5	70.2	7.5	6.6	6.2	6.8	8.9	29.2	22.0	10.8	2.1	75.9	33.1	47.7	52.3
78214	SAN ANTONIO	57.3	54.4	0.7	0.5	0.3	0.3	88.9	93.6	8.9	8.5	8.0	8.1	7.0	25.9	21.7	10.4	1.6	69.6	31.9	49.1	50.9
78215	SAN ANTONIO	66.3	62.5	9.2	8.0	1.6	1.6	56.3	69.1	5.9	5.1	4.2	4.6	8.1	40.2	21.8	8.2	1.8	82.7	33.9	51.9	48.1
78216	SAN ANTONIO	78.8	74.2	3.8	3.7	1.8	1.9	42.5	55.5	6.7	5.8	5.4	5.6	7.7	31.4	24.1	11.2	2.1	79.0	35.7	48.6	51.4
78217	SAN ANTONIO	75.2	69.2	8.4	8.7	2.7	2.9	31.0	45.0	7.1	6.2	5.7	6.2	8.6	29.5	23.8	10.9	1.9	77.3	34.6	48.5	51.5
78218	SAN ANTONIO	62.1	57.7	16.6	15.6	4.2	4.2	38.7	52.2	8.5	7.3	6.6	6.9	8.1	29.1	22.0	10.2	1.5	73.7	32.6	48.2	51.8
78219	SAN ANTONIO	51.2	45.5	28.7	28.6	2.3	2.7	37.3	48.0	7.5	7.2	7.3	7.6	6.8	24.7	25.3	12.2	1.3	73.3	36.2	47.5	52.5
78220	SAN ANTONIO	27.7	27.8	54.9	50.0	0.2	0.2	31.6	40.7	8.0	7.8	7.4	7.6	6.4	21.7	23.7	14.4	3.0	72.1	36.8	44.6	55.4
78221	SAN ANTONIO	62.9	59.2	0.7	0.6	0.4	0.4	83.6	90.6	8.9	8.6	8.1	8.1	7.1	26.4	21.5	10.0	1.2	69.4	31.5	48.6	51.4
78222	SAN ANTONIO	56.6	53.0	22.8	20.4	0.4	0.4	44.8	57.7	7.5	7.4	7.1	7.3	7.2	26.2	25.2	10.5	1.7	73.6	34.4	47.3	52.7
78223	SAN ANTONIO	64.0	59.5	4.3	3.5	0.5	0.4	67.1	78.3	8.5	8.1	7.8	7.9	7.4	26.8	23.0	9.2	1.3	70.8	32.1	48.7	51.3
78224	SAN ANTONIO	62.4	60.6	1.0	0.8	0.2	0.2	91.6	94.9	9.6	9.0	8.1	8.4	8.0	28.1	19.8	7.9	1.1	68.1	29.1	49.5	50.5
78225	SAN ANTONIO	67.2	65.8	0.4	0.3	0.3	0.3	94.6	96.9	8.3	8.1	7.7	7.6	6.9	26.3	22.6	10.6	2.0	71.4	33.4	49.3	50.7
78226	SAN ANTONIO	62.2	59.3	4.8	5.7	1.1	1.2	78.0	80.0	10.7	9.4	7.9	8.3	11.5	27.5	15.8	8.1	0.8	67.5	26.2	50.0	50.0
78227	SAN ANTONIO	57.8	54.7	6.4	5.6	1.2	1.1	71.5	79.3	9.3	8.8	8.2	8.3	7.7	26.2	20.1	10.1	1.2	68.8	30.1	48.4	51.6
78228	SAN ANTONIO	70.8	67.8	2.4	2.1	0.6	0.9	83.6	89.4	8.2	7.7	7.3	8.3	8.4	25.7	21.2	10.8	2.4	72.2	32.2	47.9	52.1
78229	SAN ANTONIO	67.0	61.9	7.3	6.7	4.1	3.9	49.2	63.2	7.6	5.8	4.8	5.6	11.6	38.3	16.1	7.8	2.4	79.2	30.2	49.1	50.9
78230	SAN ANTONIO	81.2	76.0	3.5	3.6	3.0	3.3	34.2	48.7	6.1	5.5	5.5	5.7	7.6	29.8	25.9	12.1	1.8	79.5	36.9	48.1	51.9
78231	SAN ANTONIO	89.0	85.3	2.3	2.6	2.2	2.6	23.0	36.3	6.2	6.4	6.9	6.6	5.7	26.2	29.9	10.8	1.2	76.4	39.6	47.9	52.1
78232	SAN ANTONIO	88.0	83.4	2.5	2.9	2.2	2.7	19.8	32.2	5.3	5.3	6.0	6.2	6.1	26.6	31.3	11.6	1.7	79.5	41.2	48.5	51.5
78233	SAN ANTONIO	75.5	69.6	8.4	8.8	2.2	2.5	32.7	46.5	7.5	7.3	7.2	7.2	6.5	28.5	25.8	9.0	0.9	73.6	35.0	48.1	51.9
78234	SAN ANTONIO	56.4	48.9	27.3	29.4	4.0	4.4	17.0	26.1	8.4	9.3	7.8	15.3	19.1	34.9	5.1	0.2	0.1	70.9	22.4	54.5	45.5
78235	SAN ANTONIO	62.1	54.8	14.4	15.2	5.7	6.2	26.1	36.9	15.6	10.6	6.9	7.9	13.7	37.2	6.8	1.2	0.1	63.2	23.3	51.6	48.4
78236	SAN ANTONIO	65.2	57.7	18.8	21.3	4.0	4.5	15.4	23.9	2.5	2.6	1.8	38.1	36.9	16.5	1.3	0.2	0.0	91.0	20.7	69.6	30.4
78237	SAN ANTONIO	63.0	62.3	2.8	2.2	0.2	0.2	94.3	96.2	9.1	8.7	8.1	8.9	7.8	25.5	20.4	10.0	1.4	69.0	30.2	49.0	51.0
78238	SAN ANTONIO	67.5	62.5	4.9	4.6	2.1	2.1	61.2	72.7	8.1	7.5	6.8	6.4	7.4	31.5	22.1	9.0	1.2	73.9	32.4	48.4	51.6
78239	SAN ANTONIO	63.9	59.6	19.6	18.8	2.8	2.9	28.4	40.1	7.1	7.1	6.9	7.0	5.7	24.8	24.3	14.2	2.8	74.5	37.9	46.5	53.5
78240	SAN ANTONIO	71.9	65.9	5.2	4.9	4.0	4.0	41.9	56.8	7.4	6.4	5.9	5.8	8.9	35.6	21.1	7.3	1.6	77.2	32.2	48.2	51.8
78242	SAN ANTONIO	59.0	56.3	4.8	3.8	0.9	0.7	80.6	87.7	10.8	10.1	9.4	9.8	8.3	27.0	18.0	6.2	0.4	63.7	26.0	49.3	50.7
78244	SAN ANTONIO	47.7	43.8	28.4	26.5	3.5	3.2	37.4	49.4	8.7	8.5	8.3	8.9	8.1	28.3	24.0	4.9	0.4	69.0	29.5	49.1	50.9
78245	SAN ANTONIO	58.8	54.8	11.3	9.7	3.0	2.8	52.0	63.9	8.6	8.1	7.7	7.7	6.7	30.3	22.4	7.6	1.0	70.8	32.0	48.9	51.1
78247	SAN ANTONIO	81.9	76.1	5.2	5.8	2.2	2.4	27.1	41.6	8.3	8.3	8.0	6.9	5.1	31.0	26.2	5.7	0.7	70.9	35.1	47.7	52.3
78248	SAN ANTONIO	90.7	87.1	1.6	1.9	2.9	3.6	17.4	29.3	7.1	7.8	7.7	6.8	4.4	28.4	30.6	6.6	0.5	73.0	37.5	48.4	51.6
78249	SAN ANTONIO	77.5	72.2	4.0	4.2	4.0	4.1	35.6	50.0	7.6	7.0	6.8	8.2	7.9	30.8	24.9	6.2	0.6	74.5	32.6	48.2	51.8
78250	SAN ANTONIO	70.2	65.3	7.3	6.9	2.3	2.3	47.4	61.6	8.8	8.6	8.3	7.8	6.4	30.0	24.9	4.7	0.4	69.4	31.8	48.2	51.8
78251	SAN ANTONIO	61.0	58.1	11.1	9.8	2.9	3.0	51.7	63.1	9.3	8.2	7.3	6.6	7.2	35.2	21.2	4.8	0.3	71.2	30.9	48.5	51.5
78252	SAN ANTONIO	65.9	63.5	14.3	10.9	0.7	0.7	61.5	73.7	6.6	6.3	5.5	6.9	12.2	42.8	13.7	5.6	0.5	77.5	29.5	69.1	30.9
78253	SAN ANTONIO	77.3	70.7	5.9	6.2	2.9	3.1	32.1	47.3	8.5	7.8	7.5	7.0	5.9	31.6	25.2	5.9	0.5	71.5	32.6	48.5	51.5
78254	SAN ANTONIO	79.2	73.4	4.9	3.8	2.4	2.5	33.8	49.4	8.1	7.8	7.6	6.8	5.4	29.9	27.2	6.7	0.6	72.3	35.2	48.8	51.2
78255	SAN ANTONIO	86.8	83.8	1.8	1.8	2.5	2.5	22.2	33.7	4.8	5.6	6.6	7.3	7.0	21.2	34.5	11.9	1.2	78.7	43.3	49.7	50.3
78256	SAN ANTONIO	75.6	72.2	3.5	3.7	5.3	5.2	29.7	41.6	6.0	6.6	6.9	8.7	15.2	24.3	26.4	5.4	0.4	76.7	29.4	50.5	49.5
78257	SAN ANTONIO	89.7	85.7	1.2	1.5	1.2	1.2	26.0	40.8	5.5	6.4	7.2	5.9	3.1	20.0	34.7	15.4	1.9	77.2	46.2	48.1	51.9
78258	SAN ANTONIO	89.3	85.4	2.7	3.2	3.0	3.6	15.9	26.5	8.4	8.8	9.0	7.4	3.9	26.6	29.0	6.1	0.8	68.8	36.8	49.1	50.9
78259	SAN ANTONIO	88.1	85.2	2.7	2.5	2.6	2.8	18.8	29.8	7.6	8.2	8.8	7.6	4.4	26.4	30.5	6.1	0.5	70.1	36.8	48.3	51.7
78260	SAN ANTONIO	90.2	85.9	1.2	1.7	1.4	2.2	19.9	31.3	8.0	8.5	8.8	7.5	4.2	28.0	29.1	5.5	0.4	69.9	36.2	49.2	50.8
78261	SAN ANTONIO	91.8	88.1	0.7	0.8	2.3	2.9	16.5	27.7	6.5	7.9	8.8	7.9	3.5	23.1	35.2	6.6	0.6	71.8	40.8	49.6	50.4
78263	SAN ANTONIO	84.6	79.3	6.4	7.2	0.3	0.4	21.1	33.7	6.3	6.6	6.9	6.8	5.3	24.2	31.6	11.0	1.3	76.0	40.3	48.3	51.7
78264	SAN ANTONIO	66.6	60.8	0.9	0.8	0.7	0.7	69.1	80.8	9.1	7.9	7.2	7.9	9.5	26.3	23.9	7.6	0.6	71.2	29.5	49.7	50.3
78266	SAN ANTONIO	93.0	89.5	2.0	2.1	1.1	1.4	9.4	18.8	4.2	5.1	6.3	7.0	4.4	17.7	37.4	16.5	1.3	80.0	48.0	49.4	50.6
78332	ALICE	76.7	74.7	0.7	0.8	0.6	0.6	79.2	84.5	8.6	8.4	8.0	8.0	6.9	25.1	22.9	10.3	1.8	70.0	32.4	49.0	51.0
78336	ARANSAS PASS	83.1	79.2	2.7	2.6	0.4	0.5	32.9	43.2	7.8	7.6	7.1	7.3	6.4	23.9	26.3	12.3	1.3	73.0	36.5	50.5	49.5
78338	ARMSTRONG	64.7	64.3	0.7	0.8	0.7	0.8	78.7	76.2	8.7	7.9	5.6	7.9	5.6	23.0	30.2	10.3	0.8	72.2	37.1	51.6	48.4
78340	BAYSIDE	89.3	86.5	1.9	2.1	0.0	0.0	27.4	35.7	6.5	7.0	6.5	5.2	3.6	20.3	34.9	14.1	1.8	76.3	45.4	50.3	49.7
78343	BISHOP	79.4	76.0	1.3	1.1	0.1	0.1	63.8	73.9	7.4	7.7	7.4	8.2	7.5	25.1	24.5	10.6	1.6	72.5	33.5	49.1	50.9
78344	BRUNI	77.8	77.2	0.6	0.5	0.0	0.0	90.8	93.9	8.8	8.6	9.1	8.8	6.0	21.9	23.1	12.3	1.3	67.3	32.6	48.7	51.3
78349	CONCEPCION	82.0	81.4	0.1	0.1	0.1	0.1	93.8	95.4	6.8	6.8	6.8	6.6	5.4	22.4	26.3	15.9	3.0	75.6	40.5	49.8	50.2
78353	ENCINO	86.9	86.2	0.2	0.2	0.0	0.0	93.1	92.8	7.1	6.6	6.1	6.2	6.9	19.2	29.7	16.1	2.1	76.7	42.6	50.6	49.4
78355	FALFURRIAS	74.9	73.8	0.2	0.2	0.2	0.2	91.4	91.1	8.7	7.9	7.9	8.6	6.2	21.6	24.6	12.7	1.9	70.2	35.3	48.6	51.4
78357	FREER	81.8	80.0	0.4	0.5	0.2	0.2	74.0	80.1	8.8	8.4	8.1	8.9	7.3	23.0	24.0	10.3	1.2	68.8	32.1	48.8	51.2
78360	GUERRA	80.9	79.3	1.5	1.7	0.0	0.0	86.8	87.9	6.9	6.9	6.9	6.9	8.6	24.1	22.4	13.8	3.4	74.1	36.7	51.7	48.3
78361	HEBBRONVILLE	80.5	79.6	0.4	0.4	0.2	0.2	90.0	89.5	8.4	8.0	8.0	8.0	6.7	22.4	23.9	12.1	2.4	70.2	34.8	49.4	50.6
78362	INGLESIDE	78.9	73.6	5.1	5.1	2.0	2.2	27.0	37.7	9.2	8.0	7.2	8.0	9.0	30.6	20.8	6.6	0.6	71.2	29.8	51.7	48.3
78363	KINGSVILLE	71.6	69.0	3.9	3.5	1.6	1.8	65.8	72.4	8.1	7.3	6.6	8.0	10.3	28.6	20.4	9.2	1.5	74.0	30.4	50.7	49.3
78368	MATHIS	67.3	63.7	0.9	0.7	0.3	0.3	67.3	75.3	7.7	7.7	7.4	8.0	6.1	23.3	24.7	13.2	1.7	72.1	36.1	49.1	50.9
78369	MIRANDO CITY	84.3	84.1	0.4	0.3	0.1	0.1	93.0	95.5	9.8	9.3	9.1	9.5	7.6	25.1	20.4	8.3	1.0	66.0	28.7	49.6	50.4
78370	ODEM	75.7	72.1	0.4	0.4	0.1	0.1	67.0	76.3	8.5	7.9	8.0	7.8	6.7	25.6	25.3	9.2	1.2	70.7	33.1	48.7	51.3
78372	ORANGE GROVE	85.3	82.8	0.3	0.4	0.6	0.7	56.0	65.2	8.3	8.0	7.8	7.5	6.4	25.0	25.3	10.4	1.3	70.9	34.5	48.7	51.3
78373	PORT ARANSAS	94.0	91.3	0.4	0.6	0.9	1.1	6.0	10.1	3.7	3.8	4.9	6.3	3.7	20.3	39.6	16.7	1.0	83.1	48.7	52.5	47.5
78374	PORTLAND	82.0	78.7	3.4	3.4	1.1	1.2	36.0	44.5	8.6	8.2	8.0	7.7	6.3	28.3	23.5	8.3	1.1	70.2	32.5	49.7	50.3
	TEXAS	71.0	67.6	11.5	11.4	2.8	3.5	32.0	37.4	7.9	7.5	7.2	7.5	7.4	28.3	24.0	8.8	1.4	73.0	33.6	49.7	50.3
	UNITED STATES	75.1	72.0	12.3	12.7	3.8	4.6	12.5	15.7	6.8	6.7	6.6	7.1	6.9	27.0	26.0	10.9	1.9	75.7	36.9	49.2	50.8

#	POST OFFICE NAME	2009 Per Capita Income	2009 HH Income Base	2009 HOUSEHOLD INCOME DISTRIBUTION (%) Less than $25,000	$25,000 to $49,999	$50,000 to $99,999	$100,000 to $149,999	$150,000 or More	MEDIAN HOUSEHOLD INCOME 2009	2014	2009 National Centile	2009 State Centile	2009 Home Value Base	2009 HOME VALUE DISTRIBUTION (%) Less than $50,000	$50,000 to $89,999	$90,000 to $174,999	$175,000 to $399,999	$400,000 or More	2009 Median Home Value
78133	CANYON LAKE	25774	7357	18.4	29.7	40.1	8.2	3.5	51796	54530	65	74	5996	11.8	19.8	42.3	21.4	4.7	124749
78140	NIXON	13889	1146	41.1	32.6	21.6	3.8	0.9	29163	31483	7	8	807	52.8	20.7	17.1	7.1	2.4	47581
78141	NORDHEIM	18034	265	31.3	29.4	34.3	4.9	0.0	40879	45280	36	45	222	34.2	32.9	23.9	7.2	1.8	66957
78147	POTH	17572	1300	30.5	26.6	33.8	7.0	2.1	45093	47908	49	59	1038	20.8	30.1	33.3	14.5	1.3	88200
78148	UNIVERSAL CITY	25931	7778	12.2	28.9	42.2	12.0	4.6	57559	58405	75	82	4080	6.0	21.5	58.5	13.6	0.3	116064
78150	UNIVERSAL CITY	23654	5	0.0	0.0	100.0	0.0	0.0	69801	66333	87	90	0	0.0	0.0	0.0	0.0	0.0	0
78151	RUNGE	13541	544	45.2	33.1	17.6	2.9	1.1	27039	27403	5	6	389	59.9	20.3	13.9	3.6	2.3	36711
78152	SAINT HEDWIG	21070	738	19.2	26.8	42.8	8.7	2.4	53313	53470	69	76	636	26.7	18.6	40.7	11.9	2.0	100000
78154	SCHERTZ	28005	9088	11.7	17.2	46.2	16.9	7.9	68564	70099	86	89	7117	6.8	12.0	43.8	34.6	2.7	153336
78155	SEGUIN	18501	15964	25.9	28.9	37.1	5.8	2.2	44382	49139	46	57	10966	18.7	28.4	39.3	11.6	1.9	94992
78159	SMILEY	14784	383	48.6	31.9	13.3	2.9	3.4	26172	28543	4	5	292	46.6	25.7	16.4	11.3	0.0	54167
78160	STOCKDALE	19859	1556	26.5	30.7	32.6	7.0	3.2	41560	48020	38	48	1215	31.2	26.7	27.7	11.9	2.6	76209
78161	SUTHERLAND SPRINGS	17259	417	20.6	44.6	28.1	4.8	1.9	39257	44378	31	39	355	22.8	27.9	23.7	20.8	4.8	87917
78163	BULVERDE	33464	3743	7.2	16.9	42.7	20.2	13.0	79045	80928	92	93	3344	4.2	8.5	21.9	47.8	17.6	227076
78164	YORKTOWN	17669	1445	34.7	33.1	25.3	5.0	1.9	34037	35000	16	20	1135	41.1	33.7	18.0	5.8	1.4	58664
78201	SAN ANTONIO	15073	16051	36.9	32.4	24.8	4.5	1.3	32458	34974	12	15	8193	18.5	58.7	20.6	2.0	0.1	65709
78202	SAN ANTONIO	9990	3919	54.8	30.5	13.3	0.9	0.4	22476	22869	2	3	1966	47.0	48.7	3.7	0.6	0.1	51199
78203	SAN ANTONIO	9831	1841	53.0	28.6	16.3	1.4	0.7	23264	23976	2	3	944	48.2	45.0	6.7	0.1	0.0	50977
78204	SAN ANTONIO	11903	3846	43.6	32.2	20.9	2.8	0.5	28498	30367	6	7	2202	53.1	36.8	5.9	2.0	2.2	48329
78205	SAN ANTONIO	23470	970	55.6	24.0	16.4	1.3	2.7	20551	21466	2	2	63	4.8	22.2	4.8	47.6	20.6	272917
78207	SAN ANTONIO	9477	15527	51.3	30.7	15.9	1.6	0.5	24153	24989	3	4	7732	57.5	39.4	3.1	0.1	0.0	45716
78208	SAN ANTONIO	10161	1505	53.8	26.9	17.1	1.5	0.7	23053	23576	2	3	547	57.8	34.6	7.1	0.5	0.0	45225
78209	SAN ANTONIO	34752	16876	19.4	24.6	33.5	13.3	9.2	55704	56979	72	79	9200	2.7	13.2	38.1	32.1	13.9	161691
78210	SAN ANTONIO	13430	13122	39.5	31.7	24.3	3.4	1.1	31071	33306	10	12	7422	32.9	53.8	12.1	1.0	0.2	57641
78211	SAN ANTONIO	10018	8673	41.2	33.6	22.4	2.2	0.4	29431	31345	7	9	5771	50.3	43.9	5.7	0.1	0.1	49882
78212	SAN ANTONIO	22884	11609	33.5	30.2	24.9	5.9	5.5	36986	40208	24	31	5022	13.6	41.5	23.1	10.9	10.9	83100
78213	SAN ANTONIO	21073	15960	22.8	35.4	33.9	5.3	2.5	43963	47677	45	56	7565	5.4	50.3	33.4	9.6	1.3	85854
78214	SAN ANTONIO	11926	7622	42.4	32.3	21.2	2.9	1.2	28630	30425	6	8	4472	40.7	52.1	6.1	1.1	0.0	54097
78215	SAN ANTONIO	21213	635	43.1	31.8	20.0	3.0	2.0	28972	31186	7	8	79	13.9	40.5	41.8	3.8	0.0	83000
78216	SAN ANTONIO	27384	16462	22.2	32.9	31.4	8.1	5.4	45516	48884	50	60	6162	1.3	21.6	47.9	24.6	4.6	120589
78217	SAN ANTONIO	25637	12975	15.8	31.7	41.4	7.8	3.2	51542	53145	65	73	5788	2.2	26.7	65.1	5.1	0.9	108977
78218	SAN ANTONIO	19550	12970	27.1	34.5	31.3	4.9	2.2	41227	44905	37	47	5976	11.1	57.6	22.6	6.6	2.0	77636
78219	SAN ANTONIO	17194	5552	26.5	32.3	34.8	5.3	1.1	40890	44632	36	46	3591	19.7	61.4	18.2	0.6	0.2	67935
78220	SAN ANTONIO	14650	6204	39.6	33.8	22.6	2.8	1.2	32219	34102	12	15	3987	30.9	54.9	13.4	0.7	0.1	59460
78221	SAN ANTONIO	12350	11093	34.7	35.8	25.7	3.0	0.8	33668	35775	15	19	7338	27.3	60.3	11.6	0.8	0.1	60559
78222	SAN ANTONIO	18730	5647	22.9	33.5	33.3	7.9	2.5	44766	47042	48	58	3862	21.9	47.7	29.2	1.1	0.2	74167
78223	SAN ANTONIO	15352	15909	30.7	34.8	29.8	3.7	1.0	37817	41791	26	33	9698	25.6	55.3	16.9	1.9	0.2	62325
78224	SAN ANTONIO	12107	5180	31.2	35.9	29.0	3.5	0.4	38331	41604	28	35	3472	19.8	66.8	11.9	1.2	0.3	62012
78225	SAN ANTONIO	11924	4251	38.5	36.0	22.3	2.7	0.5	29908	32180	8	10	2834	35.0	60.0	4.9	0.1	0.0	55261
78226	SAN ANTONIO	13123	2652	36.7	34.3	24.7	2.6	1.8	33410	36068	14	17	1081	28.1	64.4	7.4	0.0	0.1	57081
78227	SAN ANTONIO	13840	14346	31.2	34.4	29.9	3.3	1.2	36901	41240	23	30	8071	21.2	64.8	13.7	0.2	0.1	64316
78228	SAN ANTONIO	14441	19483	33.2	31.7	29.3	4.7	1.1	37200	40698	24	31	11714	16.8	56.3	25.5	1.3	0.1	71346
78229	SAN ANTONIO	23587	14395	28.1	37.0	28.4	4.3	2.2	38858	41726	29	37	2123	4.6	22.9	53.6	15.4	3.5	113821
78230	SAN ANTONIO	35094	17111	15.4	26.2	35.2	12.0	11.3	57646	57478	75	82	8841	0.6	8.0	45.6	38.3	7.6	164258
78231	SAN ANTONIO	40289	3596	7.5	19.0	38.4	20.1	15.0	78225	73621	91	93	2411	2.8	5.7	41.9	44.3	5.3	174042
78232	SAN ANTONIO	36773	15096	9.2	20.6	40.1	19.1	11.1	73165	70439	88	91	9142	2.2	4.1	50.9	39.7	3.1	163434
78233	SAN ANTONIO	23023	15068	13.5	28.6	44.3	11.1	2.5	55741	57114	72	79	9688	4.7	31.6	62.8	0.9	0.1	99105
78234	SAN ANTONIO	16049	865	5.0	35.8	46.5	9.5	3.2	54718	54861	71	78	19	21.1	15.8	15.8	15.8	31.6	168750
78235	SAN ANTONIO	17013	193	10.4	37.3	44.6	5.7	2.1	51919	53883	66	74	16	37.5	62.5	0.0	0.0	0.0	65000
78236	SAN ANTONIO	13572	347	13.0	46.4	36.9	2.6	1.2	43191	46798	43	54	44	20.5	72.7	6.8	0.0	0.0	65000
78237	SAN ANTONIO	9967	10960	44.7	33.4	18.6	2.6	0.6	27468	28547	5	6	6887	51.1	44.3	4.6	0.0	0.0	49472
78238	SAN ANTONIO	20399	8951	24.1	30.3	37.5	5.8	2.2	45880	50088	51	61	4097	7.8	36.3	54.1	1.5	0.3	94773
78239	SAN ANTONIO	23562	10692	16.2	28.6	40.8	11.0	3.5	53982	55151	70	77	6970	15.2	25.7	48.3	10.6	0.1	101069
78240	SAN ANTONIO	26450	20597	18.6	28.9	38.6	9.7	4.1	51657	53234	65	73	8703	3.4	8.1	79.0	9.1	0.5	123062
78242	SAN ANTONIO	11197	8644	35.1	33.9	27.3	2.9	0.9	33479	36159	14	18	4926	29.5	60.6	9.9	0.0	0.0	57581
78244	SAN ANTONIO	18851	7865	12.5	30.2	46.2	8.9	2.1	54841	56478	71	78	5637	2.4	33.6	61.1	2.7	0.1	103155
78245	SAN ANTONIO	20936	15569	11.8	29.8	47.9	8.2	2.3	55140	56185	71	78	9723	6.6	44.0	47.3	1.8	0.3	89673
78247	SAN ANTONIO	27223	16095	5.5	16.7	54.7	17.8	5.3	72943	71459	88	91	12872	0.7	12.8	75.1	11.1	0.2	125371
78248	SAN ANTONIO	49871	5773	7.3	11.3	30.2	19.6	31.6	103299	95298	97	98	3999	1.0	2.6	14.7	65.2	16.5	255430
78249	SAN ANTONIO	27080	15708	14.8	19.4	42.1	17.0	6.7	67260	66950	85	88	10788	2.2	9.9	69.3	18.0	0.6	130683
78250	SAN ANTONIO	22837	17807	8.1	20.9	53.9	13.5	3.7	64803	64681	83	87	13357	1.4	21.4	73.1	4.1	0.0	112693
78251	SAN ANTONIO	24781	15611	7.7	23.8	49.6	14.2	4.7	63464	66167	82	86	10455	0.9	17.6	73.5	7.6	0.4	114452
78252	SAN ANTONIO	12782	967	33.3	34.4	29.7	1.7	0.9	36040	39916	21	27	720	64.4	27.4	6.0	2.2	0.0	40459
78253	SAN ANTONIO	28242	6738	7.4	15.7	47.4	20.5	8.9	76436	75963	90	93	6056	8.6	26.6	47.2	16.3	1.3	111257
78254	SAN ANTONIO	31421	12419	3.1	13.9	53.2	21.1	8.6	79899	80881	92	94	10479	0.3	3.5	69.3	24.3	2.6	146225
78255	SAN ANTONIO	39612	3314	9.9	13.9	33.9	23.3	19.0	85555	87382	94	95	2619	9.4	6.8	24.5	50.3	9.0	200860
78256	SAN ANTONIO	28796	1638	28.1	20.8	26.5	16.5	8.1	52357	56715	67	75	866	0.0	5.7	20.4	56.9	17.0	237143
78257	SAN ANTONIO	42751	1431	15.4	24.1	33.1	6.6	20.7	58156	60530	75	82	1170	15.5	13.0	6.8	12.8	51.9	422222
78258	SAN ANTONIO	47987	12230	4.5	9.5	30.6	22.6	32.8	111142	112439	98	98	10203	1.0	2.4	20.4	60.4	15.8	232028
78259	SAN ANTONIO	41940	6245	4.7	5.4	31.9	28.6	29.5	115609	116986	98	99	5661	0.7	1.6	28.8	60.7	8.1	198740
78260	SAN ANTONIO	41775	7063	6.2	12.7	30.6	24.9	25.6	100944	104632	97	98	6322	3.3	7.6	20.0	60.8	8.3	211839
78261	SAN ANTONIO	44402	2649	6.6	10.6	31.8	23.1	27.8	101404	101307	97	98	2393	0.0	6.2	28.5	44.6	20.7	222643
78263	SAN ANTONIO	21018	1752	14.8	30.4	44.1	9.0	1.7	53743	53775	69	77	1466	20.1	30.7	35.7	13.0	0.5	88776
78264	SAN ANTONIO	15837	3339	27.8	31.2	33.2	5.2	2.6	42508	46686	41	52	2693	45.2	35.9	17.0	1.7	0.1	53866
78266	SAN ANTONIO	43755	1725	9.2	16.3	32.9	20.1	21.4	83829	87725	93	95	1553	7.0	2.8	11.8	53.1	25.3	283737
78332	ALICE	14847	9641	36.0	30.1	27.2	4.9	1.8	35483	36478	19	25	7023	37.5	30.3	25.3	6.1	0.8	63056
78336	ARANSAS PASS	17223	4635	33.5	28.7	31.7	4.6	1.5	38786	43255	29	37	3193	38.6	28.6	25.5	7.0	0.3	59468
78338	ARMSTRONG	13735	41	34.1	43.9	17.1	0.0	4.9	34060	31500	16	20	14	42.9	21.4	28.6	0.0	7.1	65000
78340	BAYSIDE	18019	160	37.5	25.6	28.1	8.1	0.6	36318	37788	21	28	124	46.8	28.2	20.2	2.4	2.4	53636
78343	BISHOP	17443	1646	29.6	30.3	32.3	5.8	2.1	40796	45696	35	45	1238	39.3	37.1	18.9	4.4	0.3	57348
78344	BRUNI	12265	191	39.8	32.5	22.5	4.2	1.0	30670	33834	9	11	142	51.4	29.6	16.9	0.0	2.1	48571
78349	CONCEPCION	14603	1102	49.1	25.1	21.6	2.5	1.6	25416	25486	4	4	943	66.8	19.0	9.1	5.0	0.1	36227
78353	ENCINO	16887	227	34.4	38.3	23.8	1.8	1.8	33301	37366	14	17	179	56.4	24.6	19.0	0.0	0.0	40417
78355	FALFURRIAS	11149	2431	54.9	24.0	17.7	2.2	1.1	20928	21205	2	2	1733	53.8	28.3	14.3	3.5	0.0	44805
78357	FREER	14657	1293	38.4	31.2	24.7	3.7	2.0	29861	32102	8	10	1020	61.8	21.9	13.2	3.1	0.0	39700
78360	GUERRA	12659	24	54.2	20.8	25.0	0.0	0.0	22257	27332	2	3	16	68.8	31.3	0.0	0.0	0.0	37500
78361	HEBBRONVILLE	14173	1745	41.7	31.3	21.7	3.7	1.6	30939	31971	10	12	1328	58.5	25.4	13.5	2.6	0.0	43274
78362	INGLESIDE	20439	3555	16.8	34.0	38.6	7.3	3.3	49388	51108	60	69	2261	15.7	24.3	53.3	6.5	0.1	102726
78363	KINGSVILLE	16653	10138	37.0	27.6	27.3	5.6	2.4	36200	38384	21	28	5730	37.9	30.8	25.6	5.1	0.6	64244
78368	MATHIS	15952	3574	38.6	28.9	25.3	4.1	3.1	32913	37060	13	16	2706	47.4	28.2	21.3	2.7	0.4	52236
78369	MIRANDO CITY	10493	552	44.2	29.5	19.9	5.1	1.3	30919	33730	10	12	431	48.0	27.1	23.9	0.5	0.5	52500
78370	ODEM	15271	1654	31.9	30.7	31.2	4.5	1.6	38865	44283	29	37	1248	34.8	31.3	28.8	5.0	0.2	65054
78372	ORANGE GROVE	14754	2044	34.5	33.0	26.2	4.5	1.7	35392	36326	19	24	1639	33.6	29.8	25.6	8.8	2.2	68986
78373	PORT ARANSAS	27618	1726	26.0	27.2	35.1	7.0	4.8	47503	49407	55	66	1174	16.4	16.7	39.7	19.2	8.0	117766
78374	PORTLAND	22872	6779	14.4	26.7	42.2	11.6	5.1	57967	57479	75	82	4411	9.9	18.5	56.4	13.5	1.7	118024
	TEXAS	24551		22.3	25.0	34.3	11.1	7.3	52382	54495				16.5	22.7	36.5	19.7	4.6	109784
	UNITED STATES	27277		20.9	24.4	35.3	11.7	7.6	54719	56938				9.3	13.1	31.6	32.6	13.5	162279

#	POST OFFICE NAME	FINANCIAL SERVICES: Auto Loan	FINANCIAL SERVICES: Home Loan	FINANCIAL SERVICES: Invest-ments	FINANCIAL SERVICES: Retire-ment Plans	THE HOME: Home Improvements: Home Repair	THE HOME: Home Improvements: Lawn & Garden	THE HOME: Furnishings: Comput-ers & Hard-ware-Personal	THE HOME: Furnishings: Major Appli-ances	THE HOME: Furnishings: TV, Radio, Sound Equip-ment	THE HOME: Furnishings: Furni-ture	ENTERTAINMENT: Dine out/ Carry out	ENTERTAINMENT: Sports Equip-ment	ENTERTAINMENT: Fees & Tickets	ENTERTAINMENT: Toys & Games	ENTERTAINMENT: Travel	ENTERTAINMENT: Cable TV	PERSONAL: Apparel & Services	PERSONAL: Auto Repairs	PERSONAL: Health Insur-ance	PERSONAL: Pets & Supplies
78133	CANYON LAKE	98	86	114	84	91	102	84	99	87	82	86	72	77	85	88	91	58	93	99	115
78140	NIXON	67	53	48	46	52	56	53	59	58	57	58	39	46	58	49	60	40	58	59	67
78141	NORDHEIM	79	56	81	55	59	80	58	74	64	54	63	55	46	64	57	71	42	68	77	88
78147	POTH	89	64	80	62	64	87	67	80	73	63	72	62	53	75	62	80	48	75	84	97
78148	UNIVERSAL CITY	100	95	84	96	92	89	99	93	97	100	98	74	96	101	94	95	68	96	91	109
78150	UNIVERSAL CITY	103	97	82	92	92	92	95	95	96	99	96	72	90	100	89	96	66	95	93	112
78151	RUNGE	61	45	45	40	44	51	46	53	52	49	52	36	39	52	42	55	35	52	53	61
78152	SAINT HEDWIG	88	92	82	94	89	94	84	89	84	84	84	69	86	87	86	85	58	85	88	105
78154	SCHERTZ	120	125	108	122	120	114	116	117	113	121	114	91	116	118	114	110	79	113	110	135
78155	SEGUIN	83	72	66	69	71	77	72	77	76	73	75	55	66	78	68	79	52	75	79	90
78159	SMILEY	69	45	67	42	45	68	48	61	56	46	54	47	36	56	45	62	36	57	64	75
78160	STOCKDALE	94	68	95	66	70	95	69	87	77	65	75	66	56	76	69	84	50	80	91	104
78161	SUTHERLAND SPRINGS	79	73	64	70	71	74	69	73	71	71	71	53	65	74	65	73	48	70	73	86
78163	BULVERDE	129	160	164	165	164	152	136	144	131	146	132	107	155	130	153	128	95	136	136	165
78164	YORKTOWN	79	56	80	53	57	80	58	73	64	54	63	55	45	64	56	71	42	67	76	88
78201	SAN ANTONIO	65	54	46	51	52	54	60	59	63	61	63	41	53	63	54	64	44	61	61	68
78202	SAN ANTONIO	43	33	31	33	32	39	38	38	44	39	42	26	34	42	34	47	29	41	45	47
78203	SAN ANTONIO	49	39	31	35	37	39	41	42	45	44	45	28	36	45	36	47	31	44	44	48
78204	SAN ANTONIO	58	48	38	41	46	45	49	51	53	54	53	33	44	53	45	54	37	53	51	57
78205	SAN ANTONIO	39	29	36	33	31	36	46	38	50	42	49	29	41	43	41	53	34	46	52	49
78207	SAN ANTONIO	49	39	30	34	37	37	41	42	45	45	45	27	36	45	37	47	32	44	43	48
78208	SAN ANTONIO	46	36	29	35	34	36	43	40	47	43	47	29	39	46	37	48	33	44	42	47
78209	SAN ANTONIO	103	107	113	110	110	107	110	107	109	112	109	81	114	106	113	109	78	109	110	124
78210	SAN ANTONIO	62	52	42	47	50	51	54	55	58	57	58	37	49	58	49	60	40	57	57	63
78211	SAN ANTONIO	61	49	37	41	47	46	49	53	53	55	54	33	43	54	44	55	37	53	51	58
78212	SAN ANTONIO	79	70	67	70	69	69	81	74	82	80	82	57	76	80	75	82	58	80	77	88
78213	SAN ANTONIO	77	66	59	67	63	66	76	69	76	75	77	55	71	78	70	76	54	75	72	83
78214	SAN ANTONIO	61	50	39	43	48	47	51	53	55	56	55	34	45	55	46	56	39	54	52	59
78215	SAN ANTONIO	60	44	41	48	41	43	63	50	63	59	65	43	55	64	53	62	46	60	52	63
78216	SAN ANTONIO	88	78	74	81	76	77	89	80	89	88	90	64	85	90	83	88	63	87	83	97
78217	SAN ANTONIO	89	76	68	79	72	74	90	79	89	88	90	64	83	91	81	89	63	87	82	97
78218	SAN ANTONIO	72	63	56	64	60	61	72	65	72	72	73	52	67	73	66	71	51	70	67	78
78219	SAN ANTONIO	71	68	60	66	65	70	67	68	70	69	70	50	66	70	65	72	48	69	73	81
78220	SAN ANTONIO	59	52	48	52	50	59	54	55	60	55	59	39	53	59	51	64	40	57	64	68
78221	SAN ANTONIO	66	56	45	48	54	52	55	59	58	61	59	38	50	59	51	59	41	59	56	65
78222	SAN ANTONIO	86	75	73	74	73	82	77	80	80	77	80	61	71	82	73	83	54	80	84	96
78223	SAN ANTONIO	67	59	52	56	57	60	62	62	65	63	65	45	57	65	58	66	45	64	63	73
78224	SAN ANTONIO	68	57	49	51	55	53	61	61	62	64	63	44	54	63	56	62	44	63	58	69
78225	SAN ANTONIO	63	50	38	42	48	47	50	54	55	56	55	33	44	55	45	56	39	55	53	59
78226	SAN ANTONIO	66	49	38	45	46	46	57	54	60	59	61	38	49	63	49	60	43	58	53	62
78227	SAN ANTONIO	67	60	52	55	59	59	61	63	63	64	64	43	57	64	58	64	44	64	64	71
78228	SAN ANTONIO	68	59	51	55	57	58	62	62	65	64	65	44	58	65	58	66	46	64	63	71
78229	SAN ANTONIO	76	49	44	54	45	48	74	57	74	72	76	50	62	76	60	72	53	70	60	73
78230	SAN ANTONIO	116	111	108	115	110	107	118	110	116	120	117	87	118	118	115	114	83	115	110	131
78231	SAN ANTONIO	140	149	146	157	149	135	144	138	137	151	140	111	153	142	147	132	101	138	127	161
78232	SAN ANTONIO	121	130	129	135	131	124	126	123	123	130	124	96	133	123	130	120	88	123	120	144
78233	SAN ANTONIO	94	94	79	92	89	87	92	89	91	95	92	69	91	94	88	89	64	90	87	105
78234	SAN ANTONIO	116	61	45	70	54	52	109	76	103	102	108	76	83	124	79	95	76	97	68	92
78235	SAN ANTONIO	97	56	44	63	51	50	94	68	90	87	94	65	75	104	71	85	66	84	65	83
78236	SAN ANTONIO	86	48	36	52	43	42	79	58	75	75	79	54	61	89	58	70	55	71	53	70
78237	SAN ANTONIO	59	47	35	39	45	44	47	50	51	53	52	31	41	52	42	53	36	51	49	55
78238	SAN ANTONIO	77	70	61	70	67	68	77	71	76	77	77	56	73	78	72	76	54	75	73	85
78239	SAN ANTONIO	90	91	83	90	89	92	88	89	90	90	90	66	89	90	88	91	62	89	94	105
78240	SAN ANTONIO	94	76	68	81	72	72	92	79	91	92	92	66	84	94	82	88	64	88	79	97
78242	SAN ANTONIO	64	53	42	48	51	49	57	56	59	60	60	39	51	60	51	60	42	59	55	64
78244	SAN ANTONIO	93	94	78	89	90	80	90	88	86	96	88	67	87	90	86	83	61	87	80	101
78245	SAN ANTONIO	94	90	80	87	86	83	89	87	87	94	89	66	86	90	85	86	61	88	84	102
78247	SAN ANTONIO	120	133	110	129	125	112	117	117	111	126	113	92	121	118	117	106	79	112	104	134
78248	SAN ANTONIO	188	207	183	214	201	177	190	183	179	204	182	152	203	190	192	168	131	177	161	211
78249	SAN ANTONIO	111	115	101	114	110	101	112	106	106	116	108	85	112	111	108	102	76	106	98	124
78250	SAN ANTONIO	109	114	93	110	107	98	104	103	100	111	102	79	104	106	101	97	71	100	94	120
78251	SAN ANTONIO	113	112	91	109	104	94	109	103	104	115	106	83	106	111	102	99	74	102	93	120
78252	SAN ANTONIO	67	58	49	52	55	57	57	60	60	61	60	42	52	62	53	61	42	60	59	69
78253	SAN ANTONIO	132	143	115	137	133	117	127	126	119	137	122	100	129	129	124	113	85	119	110	143
78254	SAN ANTONIO	132	149	132	147	143	129	131	132	124	141	127	103	139	130	135	119	90	126	119	151
78255	SAN ANTONIO	142	163	166	169	167	157	153	152	145	156	146	116	164	145	161	142	105	149	146	176
78256	SAN ANTONIO	101	97	98	104	98	93	115	97	105	106	105	81	108	106	103	101	76	102	92	115
78257	SAN ANTONIO	135	188	228	193	211	175	158	169	145	177	143	125	194	139	190	137	108	156	151	185
78258	SAN ANTONIO	199	244	225	251	242	212	205	211	192	225	195	168	233	201	221	181	142	196	183	238
78259	SAN ANTONIO	178	220	201	227	218	187	183	187	170	203	173	152	210	180	197	158	127	172	158	210
78260	SAN ANTONIO	173	214	186	217	207	179	178	181	165	195	169	147	201	176	190	155	123	168	154	204
78261	SAN ANTONIO	176	233	241	245	241	209	190	198	178	207	180	157	230	182	217	169	135	184	172	224
78263	SAN ANTONIO	93	91	82	92	90	95	85	91	87	85	87	68	84	90	85	89	60	87	91	107
78264	SAN ANTONIO	80	75	64	71	72	72	74	74	75	77	75	56	70	78	70	74	52	74	72	88
78266	SAN ANTONIO	151	181	183	186	185	173	156	165	151	166	152	122	174	151	172	149	108	156	157	189
78332	ALICE	72	60	52	54	58	60	61	64	64	65	65	44	54	65	56	66	45	65	63	73
78336	ARANSAS PASS	74	64	64	61	63	70	65	69	68	65	67	51	58	69	61	70	46	68	71	82
78338	ARMSTRONG	70	56	42	47	54	53	56	60	61	63	62	37	49	62	50	63	43	61	59	66
78340	BAYSIDE	77	55	79	54	57	78	57	72	63	53	62	54	45	63	56	69	41	66	75	86
78343	BISHOP	76	74	63	66	72	68	71	73	71	76	73	51	69	72	69	71	51	73	71	82
78344	BRUNI	65	52	39	43	49	49	52	56	56	58	57	34	45	57	46	58	40	56	54	61
78349	CONCEPCION	66	51	48	45	50	55	52	58	57	55	57	38	44	57	48	59	39	57	58	66
78353	ENCINO	84	55	81	52	55	83	59	74	68	56	66	58	44	69	55	76	44	70	78	91
78355	FALFURRIAS	55	43	38	37	42	45	43	48	47	47	47	31	37	48	40	49	33	48	48	54
78357	FREER	71	56	47	48	54	56	56	62	61	61	61	39	48	61	51	63	42	61	61	69
78360	GUERRA	51	41	30	34	39	38	40	44	44	45	45	27	35	45	36	45	31	44	42	48
78361	HEBBRONVILLE	69	54	47	46	52	55	54	60	59	59	59	39	46	60	49	62	41	60	59	67
78362	INGLESIDE	89	84	77	81	81	77	85	83	82	88	83	65	80	85	81	80	58	83	77	96
78363	KINGSVILLE	72	60	55	58	59	60	67	65	67	67	68	48	59	69	60	68	47	67	65	76
78368	MATHIS	76	64	63	57	65	69	63	70	68	68	67	46	57	67	61	71	46	69	73	80
78369	MIRANDO CITY	66	52	39	44	50	49	52	56	57	59	58	35	46	58	47	59	40	57	55	62
78370	ODEM	77	66	58	59	65	65	66	70	68	70	69	48	59	70	61	69	48	69	67	79
78372	ORANGE GROVE	74	59	62	57	59	70	60	67	64	60	64	49	52	66	56	69	43	65	70	80
78373	PORT ARANSAS	97	79	126	78	87	103	78	99	82	74	81	72	69	77	85	87	54	91	98	114
78374	PORTLAND	100	103	89	100	99	95	97	97	96	102	97	74	98	99	96	95	68	96	94	112
	TEXAS	104	96	90	94	93	94	99	97	99	101	100	75	94	101	94	99	70	99	96	114
	UNITED STATES	100	100	100	100	100	100	100	100	100	100	100	100	100	100	100	100	100	100	100	100

#	POST OFFICE NAME	COUNTY FIPS CODE	POPULATION 2000	POPULATION 2009	POPULATION 2014	2000-2009 ANNUAL RATE % Rate	2000-2009 ANNUAL RATE State Centile	HOUSEHOLDS 2000	HOUSEHOLDS 2009	HOUSEHOLDS 2014	HOUSEHOLDS % Annual Rate 2000-2009	HOUSEHOLDS 2009 Average HH Size	FAMILIES 2000	FAMILIES 2009	FAMILIES % Annual Rate 2000-2009
78375	PREMONT	249	3872	4024	4122	0.4	37	1316	1387	1429	0.6	2.87	999	1038	0.4
78376	REALITOS	131	476	429	409	-1.1	3	183	169	163	-0.9	2.50	139	126	-1.1
78377	REFUGIO	391	3903	3897	3851	0.0	25	1466	1472	1459	0.0	2.56	1057	1045	-0.1
78379	RIVIERA	273	1800	1620	1550	-1.1	3	646	588	564	-1.0	2.69	515	465	-1.1
78380	ROBSTOWN	355	26380	26339	26237	0.0	25	7912	8111	8129	0.3	3.21	6579	6672	0.2
78382	ROCKPORT	007	19464	22609	24010	1.6	71	7998	9387	10027	1.7	2.37	5589	6459	1.6
78383	SANDIA	297	2910	3075	3118	0.6	46	1133	1207	1228	0.7	2.52	844	888	0.6
78384	SAN DIEGO	131	6343	6448	6408	0.2	30	1897	1944	1946	0.3	2.96	1443	1459	0.1
78385	SARITA	261	278	257	246	-0.8	6	94	88	84	-0.7	2.89	76	70	-0.9
78387	SINTON	409	9486	9558	9521	0.1	27	3089	3210	3212	0.4	2.92	2375	2436	0.3
78389	SKIDMORE	025	2210	2184	2174	-0.1	21	779	777	776	0.0	2.81	601	592	-0.2
78390	TAFT	409	6286	6218	6232	-0.1	21	1954	1965	1977	0.1	3.13	1543	1534	-0.1
78391	TYNAN	025	320	312	310	-0.3	16	99	98	97	-0.1	3.18	79	77	-0.3
78393	WOODSBORO	391	2514	2303	2214	-0.9	5	950	881	852	-0.8	2.61	704	645	-0.9
78401	CORPUS CHRISTI	355	4633	4351	4232	-0.7	7	1828	1761	1723	-0.4	2.17	859	789	-0.9
78402	CORPUS CHRISTI	355	455	447	443	-0.2	19	254	254	252	0.0	1.76	112	108	-0.4
78404	CORPUS CHRISTI	355	17217	16710	16433	-0.3	16	6401	6331	6256	-0.1	2.56	4071	3944	-0.3
78405	CORPUS CHRISTI	355	17340	16508	16117	-0.5	11	5139	4972	4872	-0.4	3.17	3839	3661	-0.5
78406	CORPUS CHRISTI	355	1904	1956	1934	0.3	34	332	338	333	0.2	3.23	259	260	0.0
78407	CORPUS CHRISTI	355	3702	3416	3300	-0.9	5	1153	1061	1023	-0.9	3.05	858	778	-1.1
78408	CORPUS CHRISTI	355	11173	11036	10950	-0.1	21	3660	3684	3672	0.1	2.95	2692	2670	-0.1
78409	CORPUS CHRISTI	355	3257	3251	3242	0.0	25	1056	1078	1081	0.2	2.88	829	837	0.1
78410	CORPUS CHRISTI	355	22963	24360	24760	0.6	46	7840	8509	8695	0.9	2.83	6252	6712	0.8
78411	CORPUS CHRISTI	355	27705	27153	26764	-0.2	19	10535	10523	10428	0.0	2.55	7392	7255	-0.2
78412	CORPUS CHRISTI	355	34046	35320	35612	0.4	37	13400	14234	14441	0.7	2.43	8793	9144	0.4
78413	CORPUS CHRISTI	355	33397	35903	36712	0.8	52	12644	13688	14006	0.9	2.61	8892	9505	0.7
78414	CORPUS CHRISTI	355	15623	24446	27786	5.0	94	5987	9371	10675	5.0	2.59	4153	6612	5.2
78415	CORPUS CHRISTI	355	38665	37664	37135	-0.3	16	12770	12636	12502	-0.1	2.93	9657	9447	-0.2
78416	CORPUS CHRISTI	355	16344	15578	15251	-0.5	11	4995	4916	4846	-0.2	3.16	4033	3927	-0.3
78417	CORPUS CHRISTI	355	3597	3895	3997	0.9	55	1060	1173	1209	1.1	3.31	868	950	1.0
78418	CORPUS CHRISTI	355	24454	26712	27447	1.0	58	9553	10818	11224	1.4	2.47	6676	7409	1.1
78419	CORPUS CHRISTI	355	2085	1694	1607	-2.2	0	487	375	351	-2.8	3.57	452	347	-2.8
78501	MCALLEN	215	57848	63118	66347	0.9	55	18523	21227	22544	1.5	2.94	14169	15904	1.3
78503	MCALLEN	215	17328	22875	25837	3.0	86	4529	6264	7135	3.6	3.63	3856	5313	3.5
78504	MCALLEN	215	32071	45924	52698	4.0	91	10296	15057	17361	4.2	3.04	8263	12056	4.2
78516	ALAMO	215	25919	32644	36180	2.5	82	7251	9338	10408	2.8	3.50	6221	7897	2.6
78520	BROWNSVILLE	061	48808	58428	63156	2.0	78	14006	16999	18444	2.1	3.34	11182	13533	2.1
78521	BROWNSVILLE	061	84714	99264	106418	1.7	73	22204	26201	28147	1.8	3.78	19255	22559	1.7
78526	BROWNSVILLE	061	26381	41237	47674	4.9	94	6771	10636	12327	5.0	3.88	6141	9587	4.9
78536	DELMITA	427	201	237	251	1.8	75	75	91	97	2.1	2.60	57	68	1.9
78537	DONNA	215	32576	47592	55906	4.2	92	8791	13297	15715	4.6	3.58	7638	11391	4.4
78538	EDCOUCH	215	21421	28063	32050	3.0	86	5406	7474	8619	3.6	3.74	4796	6559	3.4
78539	EDINBURG	215	23125	29522	32976	2.7	84	7069	9570	10817	3.3	3.00	5661	7548	3.2
78541	EDINBURG	215	24893	36663	42411	4.3	92	6371	10238	12059	5.3	3.43	5187	8193	5.1
78542	EDINBURG	215	37253	48811	54752	3.0	86	9122	12497	14262	3.5	3.75	8254	11207	3.4
78547	GARCIASVILLE	427	23	41	46	6.4	96	8	13	15	5.4	3.15	7	12	6.0
78548	GRULLA	427	207	229	260	1.1	61	49	55	63	1.3	4.16	46	51	1.1
78549	HARGILL	215	1343	1746	1996	2.9	86	400	548	633	3.5	3.19	325	437	3.3
78550	HARLINGEN	061	50483	58274	62082	1.6	71	16265	19124	20513	1.8	2.97	12265	14169	1.6
78552	HARLINGEN	061	29779	34756	37575	1.7	73	9741	11566	12578	1.9	2.99	7960	9315	1.7
78557	HIDALGO	215	7330	11227	13213	4.7	93	1749	2807	3332	5.2	4.00	1584	2521	5.2
78559	LA FERIA	061	10793	12734	13786	1.8	75	3439	4114	4478	2.0	3.10	2786	3275	1.8
78560	LA JOYA	215	5486	6972	7860	2.6	83	1445	1938	2203	3.2	3.60	1284	1704	3.1
78563	LINN	215	1765	2348	2717	3.1	87	589	837	981	3.9	2.76	469	652	3.6
78566	LOS FRESNOS	061	12499	16001	17763	2.7	84	3330	4322	4822	2.9	3.58	2847	3655	2.7
78569	LYFORD	489	3281	3487	3576	0.7	49	957	1020	1046	0.7	3.42	812	859	0.6
78570	MERCEDES	215	26776	31866	34843	1.9	76	7118	8810	9679	2.3	3.62	6055	7422	2.2
78572	MISSION	215	62746	83171	94133	3.1	87	18148	25062	28670	3.6	3.31	15470	21141	3.4
78573	MISSION	215	23088	35941	41984	4.9	94	5742	9161	10784	5.2	3.92	5210	8282	5.1
78574	MISSION	215	34292	49362	57711	4.0	91	8244	12497	14764	4.6	3.95	7460	11097	4.4
78575	OLMITO	061	3231	4432	5077	3.5	89	1101	1538	1770	3.7	2.88	863	1183	3.5
78577	PHARR	215	48392	67209	77356	3.6	90	13289	19051	22040	4.0	3.53	11287	16172	4.0
78578	PORT ISABEL	061	10121	12992	14398	2.7	84	3421	4455	4970	2.9	2.89	2610	3348	2.7
78580	RAYMONDVILLE	489	12976	13332	13416	0.3	34	3457	3572	3604	0.4	3.43	2819	2885	0.3
78582	RIO GRANDE CITY	427	34563	41332	44605	2.0	78	9160	11164	12130	2.2	3.67	8060	9768	2.1
78583	RIO HONDO	061	5538	6975	7773	2.5	82	1757	2255	2530	2.7	3.09	1435	1813	2.6
78584	ROMA	427	18169	21867	23690	2.0	78	4957	6086	6643	2.2	3.59	4368	5324	2.2
78586	SAN BENITO	061	44846	53465	58197	1.9	76	12425	14937	16302	2.0	3.57	10525	12510	1.9
78588	SAN ISIDRO	427	269	318	336	1.8	75	103	125	133	2.1	2.54	78	93	1.9
78589	SAN JUAN	215	28960	36187	39974	2.4	82	7241	9310	10349	2.8	3.87	6543	8359	2.7
78590	SAN PERLITA	489	1022	1132	1186	1.1	61	277	310	326	1.2	3.65	223	246	1.1
78591	SANTA ELENA	427	165	191	199	1.6	71	58	69	72	1.9	2.77	46	54	1.7
78593	SANTA ROSA	061	5174	5791	6208	1.2	63	1379	1578	1704	1.5	3.67	1190	1344	1.3
78594	SEBASTIAN	489	2412	2642	2758	1.0	58	716	787	822	1.0	3.36	587	639	0.9
78595	SULLIVAN CITY	215	4511	6308	7304	3.7	90	1152	1687	1972	4.2	3.74	1040	1512	4.1
78596	WESLACO	215	52342	68961	77596	3.0	86	14349	19339	21817	3.3	3.55	12088	16190	3.2
78597	SOUTH PADRE ISLAND	061	2836	3874	4427	3.4	89	1418	1983	2277	3.7	1.95	878	1189	3.3
78598	PORT MANSFIELD	489	415	458	478	1.1	61	187	208	217	1.2	2.20	151	166	1.0
78602	BASTROP	021	18467	23561	25994	2.7	84	6376	8175	9071	2.7	2.68	4603	5802	2.5
78605	BERTRAM	053	3566	5102	6024	3.9	91	1286	1822	2147	3.8	2.75	1002	1400	3.7
78606	BLANCO	031	4094	4541	4720	1.1	61	1595	1756	1824	1.0	2.52	1133	1228	0.9
78607	BLUFFTON	299	237	279	299	1.8	75	123	144	154	1.7	1.94	84	98	1.7
78608	BRIGGS	053	1282	1842	2196	4.0	91	496	706	837	3.9	2.61	387	544	3.7
78609	BUCHANAN DAM	299	2169	2594	2775	2.0	78	1060	1264	1350	1.9	2.05	695	814	1.7
78610	BUDA	209	14614	21172	25847	4.1	92	4729	7001	8592	4.3	3.02	3963	5665	3.9
78611	BURNET	053	11348	14728	16576	2.9	86	4336	5588	6312	2.8	2.49	3155	4010	2.6
78612	CEDAR CREEK	021	9134	13042	15436	3.9	91	3079	4336	5130	3.8	3.00	2362	3283	3.6
78613	CEDAR PARK	491	35030	59171	75504	5.8	95	11627	19733	25235	5.9	2.99	9629	15997	5.6
78614	COST	177	473	496	503	0.5	42	167	175	177	0.5	2.79	126	131	0.4
78615	COUPLAND	491	1148	1336	1559	1.7	73	427	496	580	1.6	2.69	334	376	1.3
78616	DALE	055	5319	7001	7755	3.0	86	1791	2316	2560	2.8	3.01	1396	1781	2.7
78617	DEL VALLE	453	13882	19126	21841	3.5	89	3680	5214	6035	3.8	3.26	2798	3873	3.6
78618	DOSS	171	64	79	88	2.3	81	31	39	43	2.5	2.03	22	28	2.6
78619	DRIFTWOOD	209	1347	1669	2099	2.3	81	504	638	808	2.6	2.54	403	489	2.1
78620	DRIPPING SPRINGS	209	9643	13990	17059	4.1	92	3331	4942	6063	4.4	2.81	2718	3866	3.9
	TEXAS					1.9					1.8	2.78			1.7
	UNITED STATES					1.0					1.1	2.59			0.9

ZIP CODE #	POST OFFICE NAME	RACE (%) White 2000	White 2009	Black 2000	Black 2009	Asian/Pacific 2000	Asian/Pacific 2009	% Hispanic Origin 2000	% Hispanic Origin 2009	2009 AGE DISTRIBUTION (%) 0-4	5-9	10-14	15-19	20-24	25-44	45-64	65-84	85+	18+	MEDIAN AGE 2009	% 2009 Males	% 2009 Females
78375	PREMONT	78.2	76.7	0.4	0.4	0.1	0.0	80.9	86.2	7.5	7.4	7.7	8.0	6.2	22.4	24.8	13.8	2.2	72.3	36.8	50.2	49.8
78376	REALITOS	81.9	80.7	0.0	0.0	0.0	0.0	88.0	91.4	5.4	5.8	6.1	7.2	5.8	16.8	28.2	20.0	4.7	78.8	48.0	51.0	49.0
78377	REFUGIO	77.9	76.3	11.1	10.4	0.5	0.6	41.4	50.0	6.6	6.5	6.4	6.8	6.1	22.6	26.0	15.9	3.2	76.3	41.1	48.2	51.8
78379	RIVIERA	75.8	71.7	0.9	0.9	0.6	0.7	58.5	67.5	6.2	6.3	6.4	7.3	7.2	24.3	29.1	12.2	1.0	76.3	39.2	52.0	48.0
78380	ROBSTOWN	71.8	69.4	0.9	0.8	0.2	0.2	76.3	82.1	8.5	8.2	7.8	8.3	7.2	24.8	23.7	10.0	1.5	70.3	32.3	49.4	50.6
78382	ROCKPORT	87.6	84.5	1.4	1.5	3.2	4.0	19.4	25.4	5.1	5.2	5.4	5.9	4.9	19.4	31.1	20.5	2.7	80.6	48.0	49.1	50.9
78383	SANDIA	88.0	85.4	0.3	0.4	0.4	0.5	36.9	45.6	5.8	5.6	5.9	6.1	5.4	19.6	31.6	18.3	1.8	78.5	46.2	50.1	49.9
78384	SAN DIEGO	75.3	74.3	0.9	1.1	0.1	0.1	94.9	96.0	8.3	7.7	7.4	8.7	8.7	26.9	21.6	9.0	1.8	71.2	31.2	52.0	48.0
78385	SARITA	64.4	64.2	0.7	0.8	0.4	0.4	79.1	76.7	8.9	7.4	5.1	9.7	5.4	23.0	30.4	8.9	1.2	72.8	37.3	52.1	47.9
78387	SINTON	74.9	71.8	2.5	2.1	0.1	0.1	67.0	76.4	8.2	8.0	7.8	8.0	6.5	25.0	24.3	10.7	1.7	71.2	34.0	49.6	50.4
78389	SKIDMORE	84.1	81.2	1.4	1.4	0.4	0.4	51.9	61.5	6.6	7.2	7.6	7.7	5.6	23.2	27.7	12.8	1.5	73.4	38.2	51.6	48.4
78390	TAFT	73.0	70.3	2.0	1.7	0.2	0.2	71.0	78.0	9.1	9.0	8.9	8.6	6.6	25.0	21.9	9.7	1.4	67.7	30.3	50.1	49.9
78391	TYNAN	87.5	84.9	0.9	1.0	0.0	0.0	45.1	54.2	5.8	6.4	8.3	8.0	4.5	21.8	27.9	15.4	1.9	73.7	41.3	51.6	48.4
78393	WOODSBORO	81.1	77.9	2.6	2.5	0.1	0.1	45.1	54.0	5.9	6.5	6.3	7.5	6.2	23.8	28.6	13.5	1.8	76.8	40.2	49.3	50.7
78401	CORPUS CHRISTI	55.8	53.7	18.5	17.3	0.5	0.5	57.0	63.8	7.8	6.9	6.1	6.0	7.1	26.3	22.8	12.1	4.8	75.9	36.9	49.0	51.0
78402	CORPUS CHRISTI	83.3	77.6	1.5	1.8	5.5	6.3	21.8	32.7	2.0	1.8	2.9	5.1	3.6	25.1	39.8	19.0	0.7	89.9	50.1	54.6	45.4
78404	CORPUS CHRISTI	69.9	66.2	2.1	1.9	0.5	0.5	65.0	73.6	8.0	7.5	6.8	6.5	6.8	26.8	24.9	10.4	2.3	73.8	35.3	48.7	51.3
78405	CORPUS CHRISTI	58.4	57.2	4.8	4.1	0.1	0.1	88.8	92.0	9.0	8.3	7.7	8.4	7.2	25.0	21.0	11.0	2.3	69.8	32.0	48.1	51.9
78406	CORPUS CHRISTI	51.0	45.0	5.2	4.7	0.2	0.2	73.5	82.1	3.7	3.2	3.6	9.6	14.3	38.7	19.7	6.2	1.0	86.1	32.3	72.6	27.4
78407	CORPUS CHRISTI	52.2	51.3	23.4	20.1	0.2	0.2	58.1	67.3	9.3	8.7	8.3	8.3	6.9	25.3	22.9	9.0	1.4	68.9	31.0	49.5	50.5
78408	CORPUS CHRISTI	58.4	56.0	7.3	6.0	0.6	0.6	74.5	81.5	8.8	8.2	7.3	7.5	7.1	24.8	24.2	10.3	1.8	71.2	33.2	48.6	51.4
78409	CORPUS CHRISTI	68.6	64.2	2.4	2.1	0.8	0.9	60.3	70.8	7.3	7.1	7.0	7.8	7.4	27.5	26.1	8.2	1.5	73.6	33.9	49.3	50.7
78410	CORPUS CHRISTI	81.6	76.1	1.5	1.6	0.5	0.6	37.9	51.1	7.4	7.3	7.2	7.6	6.7	28.1	26.6	8.1	1.0	73.3	34.0	48.8	51.2
78411	CORPUS CHRISTI	75.7	71.2	2.3	2.2	0.9	0.9	53.0	64.4	7.5	7.2	6.9	6.3	6.1	26.5	25.4	11.8	2.4	74.6	36.2	47.6	52.4
78412	CORPUS CHRISTI	77.1	71.8	3.9	4.0	1.6	1.6	42.6	55.2	7.3	6.7	6.3	7.2	8.2	27.9	23.9	10.8	1.8	76.1	33.7	48.0	52.0
78413	CORPUS CHRISTI	77.6	73.1	4.1	4.1	2.8	2.9	40.0	52.6	7.0	6.6	6.5	6.9	7.6	29.7	26.5	8.2	1.0	75.7	34.1	48.4	51.6
78414	CORPUS CHRISTI	76.7	72.0	4.7	4.8	3.2	3.5	37.2	49.3	8.8	8.0	7.7	6.6	5.9	31.3	23.8	6.3	1.6	71.5	34.0	48.4	51.6
78415	CORPUS CHRISTI	67.5	64.8	3.7	3.3	0.7	0.6	74.6	82.4	8.9	8.0	7.6	7.7	7.8	27.2	22.6	9.0	1.3	70.9	31.0	48.9	51.1
78416	CORPUS CHRISTI	56.4	56.3	11.3	9.6	0.2	0.2	85.3	88.3	8.1	8.0	7.9	8.4	6.6	24.2	22.5	12.6	1.6	70.7	33.4	48.4	51.6
78417	CORPUS CHRISTI	57.5	55.9	5.5	4.6	0.3	0.2	83.9	89.4	8.6	8.7	8.3	8.9	7.7	28.8	22.6	5.8	0.6	68.9	29.6	49.5	50.5
78418	CORPUS CHRISTI	82.6	78.4	3.2	3.5	3.1	3.4	19.9	28.4	6.2	6.2	6.4	6.5	6.0	26.8	29.6	11.5	0.9	77.3	39.1	50.3	49.7
78419	CORPUS CHRISTI	64.0	57.4	18.6	20.7	3.8	4.1	20.9	29.4	14.8	11.6	7.9	6.3	16.8	39.5	3.0	0.2	0.0	63.1	22.8	56.7	43.3
78501	MCALLEN	79.7	78.8	0.5	0.5	1.3	1.4	84.1	87.6	9.0	8.6	8.0	7.4	6.5	28.5	20.6	9.6	1.7	69.8	31.9	47.7	52.3
78503	MCALLEN	73.1	72.8	0.5	0.4	1.2	1.2	91.3	93.5	8.8	8.5	8.1	8.4	7.5	27.6	21.0	8.6	1.3	69.4	30.4	48.2	51.8
78504	MCALLEN	79.0	76.3	0.8	0.7	3.3	3.3	68.0	76.6	8.6	8.3	8.1	8.1	6.8	29.1	23.7	6.5	0.9	70.1	31.7	48.4	51.6
78516	ALAMO	86.1	85.2	0.2	0.2	0.1	0.1	85.6	89.6	10.4	9.8	9.1	9.1	7.1	25.0	18.3	9.7	1.4	65.0	28.2	49.0	51.0
78520	BROWNSVILLE	84.0	83.3	0.4	0.4	0.5	0.6	89.6	92.0	9.4	8.6	8.1	8.3	7.1	26.1	20.4	10.1	1.8	68.9	30.9	47.6	52.4
78521	BROWNSVILLE	80.2	79.3	0.3	0.3	0.3	0.3	93.5	95.6	10.5	10.0	9.1	9.1	7.9	26.4	18.9	7.2	0.9	64.8	27.2	48.0	52.0
78526	BROWNSVILLE	83.1	83.1	0.5	0.5	1.2	1.1	89.2	92.7	11.0	10.4	9.3	8.9	7.4	28.1	18.8	5.5	0.6	63.9	26.9	48.8	51.2
78536	DELMITA	85.6	84.4	0.0	0.0	0.0	0.4	95.0	95.4	5.9	5.9	5.9	7.2	5.9	23.2	28.7	15.2	2.1	78.1	41.8	50.2	49.8
78537	DONNA	80.7	78.9	0.2	0.2	0.1	0.1	88.4	91.9	10.3	9.4	8.7	8.9	7.6	23.9	18.9	11.1	1.3	66.2	28.7	48.8	51.2
78538	EDCOUCH	76.6	76.5	0.5	0.3	0.1	0.1	96.5	97.6	11.0	10.3	9.5	9.5	7.9	25.9	18.1	6.8	0.9	63.4	26.1	49.3	50.7
78539	EDINBURG	79.4	78.3	0.5	0.4	1.0	1.1	85.2	88.9	9.1	8.7	8.1	7.8	7.6	29.4	20.7	7.5	1.2	69.5	30.6	48.7	51.3
78541	EDINBURG	65.5	64.3	2.6	1.7	0.3	0.3	89.9	92.9	9.6	8.8	8.1	9.2	9.7	28.5	18.8	6.5	0.8	68.5	27.7	50.9	49.1
78542	EDINBURG	73.1	72.1	1.2	1.3	0.2	0.2	93.3	94.8	11.2	10.5	9.5	9.8	8.1	27.9	17.0	5.3	0.6	62.8	25.5	51.2	48.8
78547	GARCIASVILLE	95.5	92.7	0.0	0.0	0.0	0.0	100.0	97.6	12.2	12.2	9.8	12.2	9.8	24.4	19.5	0.0	0.0	53.7	21.9	46.3	53.7
78548	GRULLA	93.7	93.0	0.0	0.0	0.0	0.0	98.1	97.8	11.8	11.8	11.4	11.4	7.4	25.8	15.3	5.2	0.0	57.2	22.5	49.8	50.2
78549	HARGILL	79.8	78.9	0.4	0.4	0.1	0.1	87.6	91.5	9.5	9.0	8.6	9.4	7.5	24.6	20.4	9.6	1.3	67.0	29.6	49.7	50.3
78550	HARLINGEN	78.2	76.4	0.9	0.8	1.0	1.0	75.1	81.2	9.3	8.4	7.8	8.4	7.3	25.4	20.9	10.2	2.3	69.4	31.3	48.0	52.0
78552	HARLINGEN	81.6	79.3	0.6	0.6	0.4	0.4	70.0	77.3	8.1	7.8	7.5	7.7	6.1	22.7	23.2	14.8	2.0	71.7	36.0	48.6	51.4
78557	HIDALGO	83.4	82.9	0.1	0.1	0.1	0.1	97.7	98.5	10.5	10.0	9.5	9.8	7.9	26.2	18.8	6.6	0.8	64.3	26.6	48.3	51.7
78559	LA FERIA	76.2	74.1	0.3	0.2	0.4	0.3	76.3	82.9	8.3	7.9	7.8	8.2	6.5	21.8	22.6	15.0	1.9	70.8	35.2	47.8	52.2
78560	LA JOYA	66.8	66.2	0.1	0.1	0.3	0.3	95.5	96.9	10.3	9.8	8.9	8.6	7.1	27.1	18.5	8.9	1.0	65.8	28.6	47.5	52.5
78563	LINN	77.1	75.2	0.2	0.2	0.1	0.1	78.3	84.2	8.3	7.9	7.8	8.0	5.8	23.5	22.8	13.9	2.0	70.9	35.8	48.1	51.9
78566	LOS FRESNOS	81.9	80.8	0.6	0.5	0.3	0.3	83.0	88.7	9.0	9.0	8.8	9.6	8.0	26.2	20.5	7.9	0.9	67.1	28.7	50.6	49.4
78569	LYFORD	67.3	65.6	0.2	0.2	0.0	0.0	89.2	92.5	8.5	8.5	7.9	8.2	7.8	25.6	22.3	10.0	1.1	70.1	30.9	47.8	52.2
78570	MERCEDES	79.3	78.8	0.3	0.3	0.1	0.1	93.3	94.8	10.8	10.3	9.5	9.5	7.6	24.1	18.3	8.5	1.4	63.7	26.6	48.8	51.2
78572	MISSION	72.1	71.3	0.3	0.2	0.4	0.4	85.4	88.9	10.2	9.5	8.7	8.4	7.0	25.4	18.9	10.5	1.5	66.5	29.5	48.7	51.3
78573	MISSION	84.6	84.1	0.2	0.2	0.5	0.4	91.4	94.7	10.8	10.3	9.5	9.5	7.9	26.7	18.9	5.7	0.6	63.6	26.3	49.3	50.7
78574	MISSION	75.9	75.1	0.3	0.2	0.3	0.4	92.1	93.2	11.7	10.9	9.9	9.3	7.4	27.2	17.5	5.4	0.7	61.7	25.5	49.2	50.8
78575	OLMITO	91.7	90.8	0.2	0.2	2.3	2.5	70.6	77.7	8.1	8.0	8.1	8.1	6.2	24.7	23.8	11.4	1.6	70.9	34.6	48.5	51.5
78577	PHARR	79.6	78.3	0.2	0.2	0.3	0.3	90.5	92.9	10.5	9.8	8.9	8.6	7.1	25.8	18.5	9.5	1.3	65.5	28.6	48.4	51.6
78578	PORT ISABEL	79.1	76.5	0.8	0.8	0.3	0.4	69.5	75.9	8.7	8.2	7.8	7.7	6.3	25.4	23.6	11.3	1.1	70.4	33.8	48.8	51.2
78580	RAYMONDVILLE	69.8	68.4	3.1	3.1	0.2	0.2	86.1	89.0	8.8	8.3	7.9	8.9	9.1	27.4	19.6	8.7	1.4	69.9	29.4	53.4	46.6
78582	RIO GRANDE CITY	86.4	86.1	0.2	0.1	0.5	0.5	97.5	97.7	10.8	10.3	9.5	9.5	7.5	25.9	18.4	7.1	0.9	63.6	26.6	49.8	50.2
78583	RIO HONDO	80.2	78.5	0.1	0.1	0.5	0.6	80.5	85.9	8.3	8.0	7.6	8.2	6.3	23.4	23.6	13.1	1.5	71.1	34.8	48.7	51.3
78584	ROMA	90.8	90.7	0.1	0.1	0.1	0.1	97.6	97.7	10.3	9.7	9.1	9.7	7.6	25.0	19.3	8.3	1.1	65.0	27.5	47.8	52.2
78586	SAN BENITO	76.5	75.1	0.3	0.2	0.2	0.2	88.9	92.3	9.9	9.4	8.9	9.0	7.2	25.0	19.9	9.3	1.3	66.1	29.0	48.9	51.1
78588	SAN ISIDRO	85.2	84.6	0.0	0.0	0.4	0.3	94.4	95.0	5.7	6.0	6.0	6.9	6.0	23.3	29.6	14.5	2.2	78.0	42.0	50.9	49.1
78589	SAN JUAN	81.8	82.2	0.3	0.3	0.1	0.1	95.7	97.0	10.7	10.4	9.4	9.4	7.8	26.4	18.2	6.7	0.9	63.7	26.4	48.9	51.1
78590	SAN PERLITA	80.4	77.8	1.1	1.0	0.1	0.2	63.2	71.8	7.5	7.7	7.3	6.7	4.7	24.1	24.6	15.9	1.4	73.1	38.0	47.7	52.3
78591	SANTA ELENA	84.2	83.8	0.0	0.0	0.0	0.0	96.4	96.3	5.2	5.8	5.8	7.9	5.8	22.5	29.3	15.7	2.1	79.1	43.0	50.3	49.7
78593	SANTA ROSA	69.1	67.4	0.5	0.4	0.1	0.1	91.3	94.4	10.0	9.6	9.0	9.0	7.4	26.1	19.8	8.2	0.9	65.8	28.3	49.1	50.9
78594	SEBASTIAN	71.8	70.5	0.5	0.4	0.0	0.0	91.7	94.2	9.3	9.0	8.6	8.6	7.5	24.8	21.8	9.4	1.1	67.9	29.6	49.8	50.2
78595	SULLIVAN CITY	65.9	65.1	0.1	0.1	0.0	0.0	98.5	99.0	10.3	9.4	8.8	9.2	7.9	26.5	19.1	7.8	0.9	66.0	27.8	48.0	52.0
78596	WESLACO	80.4	80.0	0.2	0.2	0.7	0.7	88.3	91.8	10.5	9.8	9.0	9.0	7.7	25.2	18.1	9.0	1.7	65.2	27.8	48.6	51.4
78597	SOUTH PADRE ISLAND	95.5	94.3	0.5	0.4	0.2	0.3	18.5	27.1	2.5	2.6	2.8	2.1	1.5	15.8	34.4	35.9	2.2	90.5	60.1	51.0	49.0
78598	PORT MANSFIELD	80.6	77.7	1.0	1.1	0.0	0.0	64.2	72.5	7.6	7.9	7.4	6.8	4.8	24.5	24.0	15.5	1.5	72.9	37.2	47.8	52.2
78602	BASTROP	79.0	75.4	10.7	11.5	0.7	0.9	19.1	25.2	6.8	6.8	7.1	6.4	5.3	28.0	28.5	9.6	1.4	75.1	38.0	52.6	47.4
78605	BERTRAM	91.8	88.9	0.7	0.8	0.3	0.3	12.4	17.5	6.3	6.5	6.7	6.0	4.8	24.1	30.6	13.0	2.1	77.0	41.9	49.5	50.5
78606	BLANCO	89.6	86.8	1.2	1.3	0.2	0.3	17.8	23.7	5.6	6.1	6.3	5.9	4.9	22.8	31.5	13.9	3.1	78.5	43.9	49.8	50.2
78607	BLUFFTON	97.5	96.4	0.0	0.4	0.0	0.4	2.1	3.2	2.2	2.9	3.2	3.2	2.9	11.8	35.1	34.8	3.9	90.0	60.7	49.8	50.2
78608	BRIGGS	90.2	86.6	0.7	0.8	0.2	0.4	13.2	18.6	7.0	7.2	7.4	6.7	5.5	26.2	28.9	10.0	1.1	74.2	38.3	50.3	49.7
78609	BUCHANAN DAM	96.7	95.5	0.3	0.3	0.0	0.1	5.5	8.1	2.9	3.2	3.8	3.4	2.6	12.3	37.9	30.7	3.2	87.9	58.2	49.5	50.5
78610	BUDA	81.5	77.7	2.3	2.4	0.7	1.0	30.2	36.4	7.3	7.4	7.7	7.6	6.0	27.2	29.5	6.7	0.6	73.0	35.7	49.5	50.5
78611	BURNET	90.3	87.8	2.6	2.8	0.4	0.5	11.8	15.9	5.4	5.7	5.9	6.3	5.0	21.9	29.8	17.2	2.8	79.2	44.8	47.3	52.7
78612	CEDAR CREEK	79.4	75.2	7.5	8.3	0.5	0.6	28.1	35.7	7.6	7.4	7.3	7.3	6.7	26.8	28.0	8.0	0.8	73.1	35.4	50.6	49.4
78613	CEDAR PARK	86.5	82.6	3.3	3.6	2.8	3.4	13.0	18.7	10.1	9.6	9.0	6.8	4.5	32.7	22.5	4.3	0.5	66.6	32.3	49.5	50.5
78614	COST	83.7	79.4	1.7	1.8	0.6	0.6	29.2	37.3	6.9	7.1	7.1	6.7	4.6	24.4	27.6	13.1	2.6	74.8	40.1	51.6	48.4
78615	COUPLAND	89.5	85.7	2.4	2.9	0.3	0.3	14.1	20.9	7.6	7.8	7.7	6.7	5.2	25.8	28.2	9.9	1.2	72.8	37.4	49.6	50.4
78616	DALE	76.4	70.7	5.9	6.3	0.2	0.3	30.8	40.6	7.5	7.4	7.9	7.5	6.4	25.0	28.7	8.9	0.7	72.3	36.1	51.1	48.9
78617	DEL VALLE	59.2	54.1	12.5	11.0	1.7	1.9	46.2	57.6	8.3	7.8	7.2	7.8	9.0	32.8	21.1	5.5	0.5	72.3	30.5	55.2	44.8
78618	DOSS	96.9	96.2	0.0	0.0	0.0	0.0	3.1	5.1	2.5	2.5	3.8	5.1	3.8	16.5	40.5	22.8	2.5	88.6	54.6	48.1	51.9
78619	DRIFTWOOD	94.4	92.8	0.6	0.8	0.7	0.9	7.2	9.8	5.5	6.4	7.5	7.0	4.1	23.1	33.0	11.1	2.3	76.1	42.7	49.7	50.3
78620	DRIPPING SPRINGS	93.9	91.9	0.4	0.4	0.6	0.9	8.1	10.8	5.8	6.7	7.6	7.6	4.9	23.3	34.7	8.3	1.1	75.0	41.1	50.1	49.9
	TEXAS	71.0	67.6	11.5	11.4	2.8	3.5	32.0	37.4	7.9	7.5	7.2	7.5	7.4	28.3	24.0	8.8	1.4	73.0	33.6	49.7	50.3
	UNITED STATES	75.1	72.0	12.3	12.7	3.8	4.6	12.5	15.7	6.8	6.7	6.6	7.1	6.9	27.0	26.0	10.9	1.9	75.7	36.9	49.2	50.8

ZIP CODE #	POST OFFICE NAME	2009 Per Capita Income	2009 HH Income Base	2009 HOUSEHOLD INCOME DISTRIBUTION (%) Less than $25,000	$25,000 to $49,999	$50,000 to $99,999	$100,000 to $149,999	$150,000 or More	MEDIAN HOUSEHOLD INCOME 2009	2014	2009 National Centile	2009 State Centile	2009 Home Value Base	2009 HOME VALUE DISTRIBUTION (%) Less than $50,000	$50,000 to $89,999	$90,000 to $174,999	$175,000 to $399,999	$400,000 or More	2009 Median Home Value
78375	PREMONT	12809	1387	46.5	26.3	23.6	2.6	1.0	27103	30565	5	6	1084	55.5	25.5	15.7	3.3	0.0	44000
78376	REALITOS	13015	169	55.0	21.9	20.1	2.4	0.6	22367	23513	2	3	145	69.0	18.6	9.0	2.8	0.7	36563
78377	REFUGIO	17876	1472	35.3	27.3	31.4	4.6	1.5	36381	37885	22	28	1075	43.3	29.1	19.9	5.8	1.9	55958
78379	RIVIERA	20387	588	31.3	25.7	29.8	10.5	2.7	41269	45168	37	47	475	38.1	16.8	28.6	14.1	2.3	78810
78380	ROBSTOWN	14441	8111	35.9	29.3	27.2	5.8	1.9	35987	39543	21	27	6081	47.0	28.5	16.4	6.7	1.4	52550
78382	ROCKPORT	23479	9387	30.7	28.7	28.3	7.9	4.5	40658	45137	35	45	6940	25.4	22.5	33.3	14.4	4.4	95122
78383	SANDIA	19419	1207	29.0	33.6	30.2	5.4	1.8	40552	41599	35	44	1031	34.2	34.2	21.3	9.0	1.2	64323
78384	SAN DIEGO	11658	1944	50.8	27.1	18.6	2.7	0.8	24469	24557	3	4	1521	63.2	20.8	12.0	3.6	0.4	34794
78385	SARITA	14379	88	40.9	43.2	12.5	1.1	2.3	28832	31838	6	8	30	40.0	20.0	30.0	0.0	10.0	67500
78387	SINTON	16389	3210	37.7	27.4	27.5	5.1	2.2	35127	37335	18	23	2177	37.9	35.6	23.2	3.4	0.0	57689
78389	SKIDMORE	13582	777	42.5	24.1	29.5	4.0	0.0	30542	34711	9	11	634	47.6	28.2	17.8	4.7	1.6	52679
78390	TAFT	14175	1965	37.7	29.3	26.0	4.6	2.4	32289	36122	12	15	1388	39.9	33.4	20.5	6.1	0.1	57254
78391	TYNAN	12910	98	41.8	25.5	23.5	9.2	0.0	31549	35567	11	13	80	37.5	26.3	27.5	5.0	3.8	67143
78393	WOODSBORO	18367	881	31.6	31.6	28.7	5.6	2.6	37487	38160	25	32	667	53.4	27.6	15.6	3.4	0.0	47606
78401	CORPUS CHRISTI	13345	1761	60.8	24.2	11.3	2.0	1.6	18275	19651	1	1	307	54.7	26.7	14.7	2.9	1.0	45735
78402	CORPUS CHRISTI	32029	254	30.7	29.1	26.0	12.6	1.6	37071	38626	24	31	98	8.2	23.5	60.2	8.2	0.0	105233
78404	CORPUS CHRISTI	19967	6331	34.7	29.0	27.7	4.8	3.7	35965	38962	20	27	3345	17.5	42.7	26.8	10.2	2.8	77601
78405	CORPUS CHRISTI	9802	4972	50.4	32.8	14.3	1.8	0.7	24684	25981	3	4	2772	68.8	27.8	2.8	0.6	0.0	38883
78406	CORPUS CHRISTI	13420	338	32.0	34.0	30.8	3.3	0.0	39631	43351	32	41	236	44.9	45.3	9.7	0.0	0.0	52353
78407	CORPUS CHRISTI	11604	1061	57.8	18.9	17.5	4.6	1.1	20509	18679	2	2	486	51.0	40.7	8.2	0.0	0.0	49398
78408	CORPUS CHRISTI	12876	3684	40.9	34.5	20.5	2.6	1.5	30433	31625	9	11	2249	40.2	53.4	4.3	2.1	0.0	54518
78409	CORPUS CHRISTI	16960	1078	25.6	33.9	34.7	4.8	1.0	44649	47043	47	57	732	33.1	25.0	41.0	1.0	0.0	78478
78410	CORPUS CHRISTI	23395	8509	20.1	22.0	41.1	12.5	4.3	57533	56385	75	81	5714	9.8	24.3	53.9	10.8	1.2	106707
78411	CORPUS CHRISTI	23041	10523	24.9	28.0	35.7	7.5	4.0	47658	49667	56	66	6342	3.5	39.9	47.2	7.5	1.9	97221
78412	CORPUS CHRISTI	24763	14234	22.5	31.9	33.2	7.1	5.3	47254	48566	55	65	7420	5.0	42.0	41.0	8.9	3.1	93259
78413	CORPUS CHRISTI	29616	13688	12.9	22.6	42.0	15.1	7.3	64622	62005	83	87	7984	1.0	6.6	66.3	24.7	1.5	137774
78414	CORPUS CHRISTI	31690	9371	12.9	18.3	42.6	16.3	9.8	70798	70338	87	90	6292	1.2	8.0	68.1	19.5	3.2	135643
78415	CORPUS CHRISTI	15711	12636	31.5	31.5	31.2	4.4	1.4	38589	45175	28	36	7460	15.2	54.1	29.1	1.3	0.3	72683
78416	CORPUS CHRISTI	12564	4916	39.0	35.2	21.9	3.0	0.9	30437	32372	9	11	3428	41.0	55.2	3.9	0.0	0.0	53531
78417	CORPUS CHRISTI	11792	1173	33.6	38.2	24.9	3.3	0.0	34040	36591	16	20	848	34.6	51.2	14.3	0.0	0.0	57939
78418	CORPUS CHRISTI	27601	10818	18.1	26.2	39.6	10.6	5.4	54827	54767	71	78	6968	13.3	24.0	39.6	21.2	2.0	110816
78419	CORPUS CHRISTI	15139	375	9.3	52.8	29.6	4.8	3.5	41934	45054	39	50	24	62.5	0.0	37.5	0.0	0.0	46667
78501	MCALLEN	14934	21227	40.1	26.6	25.9	5.0	2.3	33466	38475	14	18	12003	21.2	33.5	38.3	6.0	1.0	84545
78503	MCALLEN	13805	6264	36.8	31.6	23.6	3.8	4.3	34675	38650	17	22	4203	20.1	48.7	22.2	4.8	4.2	72089
78504	MCALLEN	24388	15057	16.1	24.4	38.5	13.8	7.2	58263	56974	75	83	10847	6.9	13.5	57.1	20.1	2.4	125798
78516	ALAMO	9821	9338	48.4	32.1	16.6	2.1	0.8	25800	27711	4	5	7252	48.5	31.7	17.8	1.7	0.3	50967
78520	BROWNSVILLE	12209	16999	45.6	26.2	21.4	4.9	1.9	28537	31933	6	7	9788	34.7	36.5	23.5	4.8	0.6	61652
78521	BROWNSVILLE	10194	26201	43.9	30.1	21.2	3.3	1.5	29188	31726	7	9	15844	40.2	37.9	17.8	3.7	0.4	56150
78526	BROWNSVILLE	12017	10636	35.6	29.1	28.5	4.3	2.5	36724	39244	23	30	8296	18.1	34.0	38.3	8.0	1.6	87846
78536	DELMITA	13005	91	47.3	28.6	19.8	4.4	0.0	26374	28788	4	5	74	50.0	18.9	17.6	10.8	2.7	50000
78537	DONNA	9898	13297	46.3	31.7	18.7	2.4	0.9	27099	29261	5	6	9917	35.2	34.2	23.0	6.8	0.8	64820
78538	EDCOUCH	8045	7474	53.4	29.5	15.4	1.3	0.4	23101	23979	2	3	5740	52.0	36.0	10.7	0.9	0.3	48490
78539	EDINBURG	17861	9570	30.0	24.3	34.9	7.2	3.6	44210	50122	46	56	5885	15.2	30.3	43.2	9.4	1.8	99905
78541	EDINBURG	11200	10238	44.4	29.7	21.6	3.2	1.2	29218	32954	7	9	6542	25.5	35.2	30.7	6.9	1.7	75694
78542	EDINBURG	9529	12497	46.9	29.1	21.0	2.5	0.6	26856	29890	5	6	9371	40.6	35.9	18.9	3.7	0.8	56613
78547	GARCIASVILLE	5549	13	76.9	15.4	7.7	0.0	0.0	13400	18481	1	1	12	33.3	50.0	16.7	0.0	0.0	56667
78548	GRULLA	5621	55	65.5	21.8	10.9	1.8	0.0	17898	17143	1	1	50	36.0	44.0	14.0	6.0	0.0	57778
78549	HARGILL	10105	548	52.2	29.4	15.9	2.0	0.5	23743	24949	3	3	449	59.2	24.1	12.5	3.3	0.9	44236
78550	HARLINGEN	16262	19124	35.8	27.5	28.5	5.1	3.1	36775	41223	23	30	10967	29.8	35.1	28.6	5.9	0.7	68694
78552	HARLINGEN	16987	11566	29.4	31.0	31.7	4.8	3.1	40008	45620	33	42	9101	37.3	26.9	25.7	9.3	0.8	65657
78557	HIDALGO	7460	2807	52.1	32.1	14.1	1.5	0.3	23868	25062	3	4	1974	21.9	48.5	27.4	2.2	0.0	74926
78559	LA FERIA	12861	4114	40.5	30.9	24.2	3.5	0.9	31798	34812	11	14	3109	51.5	27.8	18.1	2.3	0.2	48855
78560	LA JOYA	9448	1938	47.3	30.9	18.6	2.2	1.1	26915	30548	5	6	1419	39.0	36.9	22.6	1.4	0.1	58639
78563	LINN	12848	837	46.6	33.5	14.8	5.1	0.0	27347	29609	5	6	693	53.5	23.7	22.7	0.1	0.0	46111
78566	LOS FRESNOS	10975	4322	41.3	30.7	23.4	3.6	1.1	31023	32682	10	12	3366	38.4	34.1	20.7	6.1	0.7	58478
78569	LYFORD	11559	1020	38.5	32.5	24.2	3.2	1.6	31668	35390	11	13	818	48.8	32.3	15.4	3.5	0.0	51000
78570	MERCEDES	8941	8810	48.9	31.3	17.1	1.9	0.8	25611	27377	4	5	6434	50.7	31.2	15.3	2.6	0.2	49438
78572	MISSION	12983	25062	41.4	28.5	23.5	4.3	2.3	31425	34668	10	13	19202	32.8	33.7	23.7	8.1	1.7	65514
78573	MISSION	9509	9161	46.9	28.7	19.4	3.5	1.5	27049	28876	5	6	7142	37.8	30.8	21.7	7.6	2.1	62475
78574	MISSION	10060	12497	44.8	27.5	21.3	4.6	1.8	28520	31448	6	7	9977	38.8	28.5	25.5	6.1	1.2	59916
78575	OLMITO	22897	1538	32.7	20.6	30.1	8.6	8.0	46615	49223	53	63	1147	22.6	15.5	36.7	20.4	4.8	116071
78577	PHARR	11345	19051	41.5	29.6	23.9	3.4	1.6	30733	33860	9	12	13793	38.4	39.0	19.7	2.4	0.6	57324
78578	PORT ISABEL	16019	4455	37.2	31.8	23.4	4.6	3.0	32782	34537	13	16	2715	27.4	26.0	32.3	12.1	2.2	83015
78580	RAYMONDVILLE	10017	3572	50.0	29.5	17.5	2.5	0.5	25015	24968	3	4	2582	49.7	30.4	16.5	3.4	0.0	50236
78582	RIO GRANDE CITY	8074	11164	57.6	26.8	12.7	2.4	0.5	20477	20974	2	2	8953	38.6	33.7	22.4	5.1	0.3	60058
78583	RIO HONDO	12373	2255	44.5	27.1	24.2	3.0	1.2	29931	32332	8	10	1782	48.0	31.4	14.6	4.9	1.1	51935
78584	ROMA	7671	6086	62.7	24.1	10.2	1.7	1.3	17743	18288	1	1	4637	33.0	33.8	26.0	6.5	0.6	65584
78586	SAN BENITO	10993	14937	43.2	29.8	22.2	3.3	1.4	30185	32860	8	11	11183	51.2	29.2	15.3	3.8	0.6	48974
78588	SAN ISIDRO	13311	125	48.8	28.0	19.2	4.0	0.0	25526	27543	4	5	101	48.5	19.8	18.8	10.9	2.0	51667
78589	SAN JUAN	9391	9310	45.9	30.8	19.1	2.6	1.6	27438	30492	5	6	6932	40.4	38.4	20.2	0.5	0.4	57230
78590	SAN PERLITA	10533	310	40.6	35.2	21.0	1.9	1.3	31060	34408	10	12	246	50.8	26.4	20.3	2.4	0.0	49355
78591	SANTA ELENA	10981	69	60.9	18.8	14.5	5.8	0.0	16280	20000	1	1	52	44.2	25.0	17.3	13.5	0.0	55000
78593	SANTA ROSA	10713	1578	43.9	31.0	21.5	2.6	1.1	29612	32794	7	9	1194	54.5	27.7	15.0	2.6	0.2	46966
78594	SEBASTIAN	10727	787	48.3	35.5	11.2	3.2	1.9	25539	25634	4	5	648	46.9	34.7	11.7	5.2	1.4	51802
78595	SULLIVAN CITY	7123	1687	57.1	28.5	13.5	0.7	0.3	21028	21925	2	2	1284	48.1	42.3	7.8	1.2	0.6	51064
78596	WESLACO	10712	19339	42.8	33.2	19.7	2.8	1.5	29863	32371	8	10	13863	41.3	31.0	21.6	5.6	0.5	57828
78597	SOUTH PADRE ISLAND	38273	1983	20.5	23.7	36.5	12.1	7.3	55124	55206	71	78	1412	8.6	20.0	31.3	33.4	6.7	142935
78598	PORT MANSFIELD	17281	208	40.4	36.1	20.2	1.9	1.4	31126	34351	10	12	165	52.1	25.5	20.0	2.4	0.0	48333
78602	BASTROP	22141	8175	20.6	26.2	40.2	9.1	4.0	52665	55876	67	75	6322	12.6	12.9	40.6	29.8	4.0	143659
78605	BERTRAM	21657	1822	20.0	30.6	35.9	8.8	4.6	49348	48256	60	69	1530	8.2	10.6	38.7	25.8	16.7	154787
78606	BLANCO	21178	1756	27.7	28.5	32.9	6.9	3.9	45910	47276	51	61	1349	6.7	14.8	40.1	27.9	10.5	142235
78607	BLUFFTON	20751	144	34.0	38.2	23.6	2.8	1.4	35000	38215	18	23	125	24.0	24.8	34.4	14.4	2.4	95000
78608	BRIGGS	21512	706	23.7	32.4	33.4	5.7	4.8	45101	45815	49	59	594	8.6	9.3	43.1	23.2	15.8	151103
78609	BUCHANAN DAM	27837	1264	19.3	36.5	36.2	4.4	3.7	45634	47286	50	60	993	13.9	13.6	39.8	23.7	9.1	135982
78610	BUDA	29099	7001	9.0	15.5	43.7	22.3	9.5	75679	80827	90	92	5798	10.4	8.7	26.3	48.5	6.1	190146
78611	BURNET	21735	5588	26.6	26.8	36.7	6.8	3.1	46266	46803	52	62	4292	10.6	15.1	37.0	26.1	11.3	142254
78612	CEDAR CREEK	21948	4336	14.9	24.9	44.0	12.1	4.1	58829	60655	76	83	3632	12.4	14.5	46.4	23.1	3.6	132655
78613	CEDAR PARK	36934	19733	4.3	10.5	36.1	32.1	17.0	98136	102498	96	97	16459	0.7	2.5	26.9	65.3	4.6	211206
78614	COST	16241	175	30.9	33.7	29.7	4.6	1.1	37496	38633	25	33	133	27.1	15.0	34.6	15.0	8.3	107237
78615	COUPLAND	24515	496	15.3	29.0	39.3	12.5	3.8	56102	54523	73	80	397	6.5	14.6	38.8	30.5	9.6	150313
78616	DALE	20433	2316	18.6	30.4	39.4	6.7	4.8	50564	51884	63	71	1968	12.9	24.5	44.6	14.6	3.4	110682
78617	DEL VALLE	18226	5214	17.5	29.0	43.7	6.9	2.9	53957	57726	70	77	3790	24.4	20.8	43.4	9.7	1.7	97931
78618	DOSS	23970	39	23.1	30.8	41.0	2.6	2.6	47338	49423	55	65	32	3.1	15.6	37.5	34.4	9.4	150000
78619	DRIFTWOOD	40111	638	11.0	17.2	32.0	20.2	19.6	78710	82592	91	93	537	2.2	4.7	17.5	49.7	25.9	283631
78620	DRIPPING SPRINGS	35366	4942	9.8	14.7	37.3	24.1	14.1	81139	85466	92	94	4062	4.0	5.9	16.2	46.8	27.1	287650
	TEXAS	24551		22.3	25.0	34.3	11.1	7.3	52382	54495				16.5	22.7	36.5	19.7	4.6	109784
	UNITED STATES	27277		20.9	24.4	35.3	11.7	7.6	54719	56938				9.3	13.1	31.6	32.6	13.5	162279

ZIP CODE		FINANCIAL SERVICES				THE HOME						ENTERTAINMENT						PERSONAL			
						Home Improvements		Furnishings													
#	POST OFFICE NAME	Auto Loan	Home Loan	Invest-ments	Retire-ment Plans	Home Repair	Lawn & Garden	Comput-ers & Hard-ware-Personal	Major Appli-ances	TV, Radio, Sound Equip-ment	Furni-ture	Dine out/ Carry out	Sports Equip-ment	Fees & Tickets	Toys & Games	Travel	Cable TV	Apparel & Services	Auto Repairs	Health Insur-ance	Pets & Supplies
78375	PREMONT	63	47	55	43	47	59	49	58	54	48	53	42	40	53	47	57	36	56	60	67
78376	REALITOS	55	44	34	37	42	42	44	47	48	49	48	29	38	48	39	49	33	48	46	52
78377	REFUGIO	75	58	70	57	59	77	62	72	68	57	66	54	53	67	59	75	45	69	79	86
78379	RIVIERA	99	71	101	68	73	100	72	92	80	67	79	69	58	80	72	88	52	85	96	110
78380	ROBSTOWN	75	65	53	58	63	62	64	67	67	69	67	45	58	68	59	68	47	67	65	76
78382	ROCKPORT	90	74	102	71	80	95	75	90	80	74	79	64	67	77	77	86	53	85	95	105
78383	SANDIA	80	67	81	63	71	83	66	77	71	68	70	55	60	70	66	76	47	74	83	91
78384	SAN DIEGO	57	45	34	38	43	43	45	49	49	51	50	30	40	50	41	51	35	49	47	54
78385	SARITA	70	56	42	47	54	53	56	60	61	63	62	37	49	62	50	63	43	61	58	66
78387	SINTON	80	65	63	58	64	70	65	73	70	68	70	50	56	70	61	73	48	71	73	83
78389	SKIDMORE	70	46	69	44	46	70	50	63	57	46	55	49	37	57	47	63	37	59	66	77
78390	TAFT	71	61	55	56	60	61	62	66	64	65	64	46	56	65	58	65	44	65	64	74
78391	TYNAN	75	50	78	49	52	77	55	69	59	47	59	56	41	59	54	65	38	64	73	85
78393	WOODSBORO	81	60	75	60	61	80	65	75	71	60	69	57	54	71	61	77	47	72	80	90
78401	CORPUS CHRISTI	40	30	28	31	29	33	41	35	44	39	44	27	36	42	35	46	31	41	41	44
78402	CORPUS CHRISTI	69	75	80	74	78	83	75	76	80	75	80	53	81	74	80	85	55	79	95	89
78404	CORPUS CHRISTI	77	70	60	67	67	68	73	72	75	74	75	52	69	75	68	76	53	74	73	83
78405	CORPUS CHRISTI	51	41	31	34	39	38	41	44	45	46	45	27	36	45	37	46	32	45	42	48
78406	CORPUS CHRISTI	70	56	42	47	54	53	56	61	61	63	62	37	49	62	50	63	43	61	59	66
78407	CORPUS CHRISTI	55	42	36	39	41	45	47	47	53	50	52	32	42	52	41	55	36	50	52	56
78408	CORPUS CHRISTI	60	50	41	46	48	49	53	53	56	56	56	37	47	57	47	57	39	55	54	61
78409	CORPUS CHRISTI	80	71	55	63	67	64	68	71	71	75	72	48	63	73	63	71	50	71	68	80
78410	CORPUS CHRISTI	101	100	87	98	96	93	95	96	94	100	95	73	94	97	92	92	66	94	91	111
78411	CORPUS CHRISTI	82	83	75	83	81	83	84	82	84	83	85	63	85	84	83	85	59	84	86	97
78412	CORPUS CHRISTI	86	81	75	82	79	80	88	82	87	87	88	65	85	88	84	87	61	87	86	98
78413	CORPUS CHRISTI	112	113	101	114	109	103	112	107	109	116	111	84	113	113	109	106	78	108	102	125
78414	CORPUS CHRISTI	121	127	109	127	121	109	120	115	114	127	116	93	123	121	118	109	82	114	105	134
78415	CORPUS CHRISTI	72	62	52	57	59	57	66	64	67	69	68	47	60	68	60	67	47	67	62	74
78416	CORPUS CHRISTI	66	52	44	45	50	52	54	58	58	58	58	38	47	59	49	60	41	58	57	64
78417	CORPUS CHRISTI	61	56	45	48	54	48	55	57	55	61	56	39	51	56	52	54	40	57	52	62
78418	CORPUS CHRISTI	98	101	93	100	99	97	97	97	96	100	97	74	98	97	97	95	68	96	95	113
78419	CORPUS CHRISTI	97	50	38	58	45	43	91	63	86	85	90	63	69	103	66	79	63	80	57	77
78501	MCALLEN	68	61	54	56	60	57	62	63	63	66	64	45	57	64	58	63	44	64	61	71
78503	MCALLEN	79	70	57	62	68	65	69	72	72	75	73	48	64	73	65	73	51	73	70	81
78504	MCALLEN	110	113	98	109	109	101	107	106	104	113	105	81	107	108	105	101	74	104	99	122
78516	ALAMO	57	46	41	40	46	47	46	51	50	51	50	33	41	50	43	52	35	51	51	57
78520	BROWNSVILLE	65	55	46	49	53	53	56	58	59	60	60	39	51	59	52	60	41	59	58	65
78521	BROWNSVILLE	62	51	41	45	49	48	53	55	56	58	57	36	47	57	48	57	40	56	53	61
78526	BROWNSVILLE	73	66	54	61	63	59	66	66	66	71	68	47	62	69	61	66	47	67	62	75
78536	DELMITA	63	41	61	39	41	62	44	55	51	42	49	43	33	52	41	57	33	52	58	68
78537	DONNA	59	48	38	40	47	46	47	52	52	53	52	32	42	52	44	53	36	52	51	57
78538	EDCOUCH	51	40	30	34	39	38	40	43	44	45	44	27	35	44	36	45	31	44	42	48
78539	EDINBURG	83	77	65	72	74	70	77	76	77	81	78	56	73	79	73	76	54	77	72	87
78541	EDINBURG	60	50	42	46	49	48	55	53	56	57	56	38	48	57	48	56	39	55	52	61
78542	EDINBURG	58	48	37	40	46	44	48	50	51	53	52	32	42	52	43	52	36	51	48	55
78547	GARCIASVILLE	29	24	18	20	23	22	24	25	26	26	26	16	21	26	21	26	18	26	25	28
78548	GRULLA	39	32	24	26	30	30	31	34	34	35	35	21	27	35	28	35	24	34	33	37
78549	HARGILL	54	43	32	36	41	41	43	47	47	49	48	29	38	48	39	49	33	47	45	51
78550	HARLINGEN	75	66	57	60	64	63	68	69	70	72	71	48	63	70	63	71	49	70	68	78
78552	HARLINGEN	81	71	74	65	72	76	69	77	72	74	72	53	64	72	69	75	50	75	78	88
78557	HIDALGO	50	40	30	34	38	38	40	43	44	45	44	27	35	44	36	45	31	44	42	47
78559	LA FERIA	70	52	56	46	51	61	53	62	59	55	58	43	44	59	49	63	40	60	62	71
78560	LA JOYA	57	46	35	38	44	43	46	49	50	51	50	30	40	50	41	51	35	50	48	54
78563	LINN	65	43	62	40	43	63	46	57	53	44	52	44	35	54	43	59	34	54	60	70
78566	LOS FRESNOS	63	54	46	47	53	51	54	57	56	59	57	38	48	57	50	57	39	57	55	64
78569	LYFORD	66	53	40	44	51	50	53	57	58	59	58	35	46	59	48	60	41	58	56	63
78570	MERCEDES	54	44	35	37	43	42	44	47	47	49	48	29	39	47	40	49	33	47	46	52
78572	MISSION	70	60	52	52	59	58	58	63	62	65	62	41	53	62	55	64	43	63	63	70
78573	MISSION	61	51	40	44	49	47	51	54	54	57	55	35	45	55	47	55	38	54	52	59
78574	MISSION	65	56	44	49	53	52	54	58	57	60	58	38	49	59	50	58	40	57	55	64
78575	OLMITO	103	93	79	85	90	88	91	94	94	98	96	64	86	95	87	96	67	95	92	106
78577	PHARR	66	54	48	47	53	54	54	59	58	59	59	39	48	59	51	60	40	59	58	66
78578	PORT ISABEL	73	63	65	58	64	66	64	69	67	67	67	48	58	66	62	68	46	68	69	79
78580	RAYMONDVILLE	56	44	36	38	43	44	45	49	49	49	49	31	39	49	40	51	34	49	48	54
78582	RIO GRANDE CITY	50	40	30	33	38	38	40	43	43	44	44	27	34	44	36	44	30	43	42	47
78583	RIO HONDO	63	52	43	44	51	51	51	56	56	57	56	35	46	56	48	58	39	56	56	62
78584	ROMA	46	37	28	31	35	35	37	40	40	41	41	25	32	41	33	42	28	40	39	44
78586	SAN BENITO	64	54	46	46	52	53	53	58	57	58	57	37	47	57	49	59	40	57	57	64
78588	SAN ISIDRO	63	41	61	39	41	62	44	55	51	42	49	43	33	52	41	57	33	52	58	68
78589	SAN JUAN	59	50	39	43	48	45	50	53	52	55	53	34	44	53	46	53	37	53	50	58
78590	SAN PERLITA	68	49	70	48	51	70	51	64	56	47	55	48	41	55	50	61	36	59	67	76
78591	SANTA ELENA	57	37	55	35	37	55	39	50	45	37	44	39	30	46	37	51	29	47	53	61
78593	SANTA ROSA	66	53	44	45	51	52	53	58	57	58	58	37	46	58	48	59	40	58	57	64
78594	SEBASTIAN	61	49	36	41	46	46	48	52	53	54	53	32	42	53	43	54	37	53	51	57
78595	SULLIVAN CITY	45	36	27	30	34	34	36	39	39	40	39	24	31	39	32	40	27	39	37	42
78596	WESLACO	61	51	43	45	50	49	52	55	55	57	55	36	47	55	48	56	39	55	54	61
78597	SOUTH PADRE ISLAND	103	108	147	107	125	128	97	115	103	110	101	72	107	92	112	107	69	110	128	130
78598	PORT MANSFIELD	68	49	70	47	51	69	50	64	55	46	54	48	40	55	49	61	36	58	66	76
78602	BASTROP	94	90	81	88	89	91	85	90	87	88	87	66	83	90	84	89	60	87	90	105
78605	BERTRAM	101	83	98	80	84	100	81	95	86	80	86	70	71	87	80	92	57	89	96	112
78606	BLANCO	90	72	103	70	76	93	72	89	77	68	76	65	63	75	75	82	50	83	90	104
78607	BLUFFTON	59	56	72	52	62	67	54	63	57	58	55	41	53	52	58	60	37	61	70	72
78608	BRIGGS	90	83	73	80	81	85	78	83	81	81	81	60	74	84	74	83	55	80	83	98
78609	BUCHANAN DAM	82	81	105	76	90	96	76	89	80	83	78	58	77	73	84	84	53	86	99	102
78610	BUDA	127	142	122	139	136	126	126	127	121	133	123	99	132	127	128	117	86	122	116	147
78611	BURNET	92	72	107	70	77	98	73	91	79	69	77	67	62	76	76	86	52	85	95	107
78612	CEDAR CREEK	105	97	85	93	94	97	93	96	95	97	95	71	88	99	88	97	65	94	96	114
78613	CEDAR PARK	164	183	154	181	174	152	160	160	150	175	153	128	169	162	161	141	109	151	137	181
78614	COST	81	57	82	55	59	81	62	75	65	54	65	59	47	64	60	71	42	71	79	91
78615	COUPLAND	104	97	87	96	96	101	92	98	95	94	95	72	88	98	89	98	65	94	99	116
78616	DALE	99	90	83	86	87	93	86	91	89	88	89	67	80	92	82	92	60	89	92	109
78617	DEL VALLE	94	90	76	83	86	82	89	88	87	93	88	66	84	90	84	85	61	88	83	102
78618	DOSS	81	65	105	64	71	86	65	82	68	61	67	60	56	64	70	72	45	76	81	96
78619	DRIFTWOOD	139	173	162	175	171	155	146	151	138	155	140	117	165	142	160	134	101	143	138	173
78620	DRIPPING SPRINGS	137	165	147	167	161	148	141	145	134	148	136	115	156	139	151	130	97	137	132	167
	TEXAS	104	96	90	94	93	94	99	97	99	101	100	75	94	101	94	99	70	99	96	114
	UNITED STATES	100	100	100	100	100	100	100	100	100	100	100	100	100	100	100	100	100	100	100	100

ZIP CODE #	POST OFFICE NAME	COUNTY FIPS CODE	POPULATION 2000	POPULATION 2009	POPULATION 2014	2000-2009 ANNUAL RATE % Rate	2000-2009 ANNUAL RATE State Centile	HOUSEHOLDS 2000	HOUSEHOLDS 2009	HOUSEHOLDS 2014	HOUSEHOLDS % Annual Rate 2000-2009	HOUSEHOLDS 2009 Average HH Size	FAMILIES 2000	FAMILIES 2009	FAMILIES % Annual Rate 2000-2009
78621	ELGIN	021	14762	19975	22604	3.3	88	4996	6818	7754	3.4	2.91	3754	5021	3.2
78623	FISCHER	091	671	866	1058	2.8	85	262	340	416	2.9	2.55	190	241	2.6
78624	FREDERICKSBURG	171	18287	21127	22843	1.6	71	7495	8783	9552	1.7	2.34	5310	6112	1.5
78626	GEORGETOWN	491	19189	25588	30807	3.2	87	6017	8114	9898	3.3	2.88	4440	5806	2.9
78628	GEORGETOWN	491	18758	23988	29435	2.7	84	6962	8808	10803	2.6	2.72	5625	6935	2.3
78629	GONZALES	177	12000	12488	12555	0.4	37	4404	4582	4608	0.4	2.68	3130	3213	0.3
78631	HARPER	171	1554	2301	2611	4.3	92	628	927	1054	4.3	2.48	458	673	4.2
78632	HARWOOD	177	429	464	476	0.9	55	170	183	188	0.8	2.52	127	135	0.7
78633	GEORGETOWN	491	7545	16860	22549	9.1	98	3226	6997	9398	8.7	2.41	2716	5781	8.5
78634	HUTTO	491	4032	18168	25355	17.7	100	1318	5846	8160	17.5	3.11	1102	4633	16.8
78635	HYE	031	224	267	286	1.9	76	95	113	120	1.9	2.36	68	80	1.8
78636	JOHNSON CITY	031	3063	3507	3677	1.5	69	1206	1365	1428	1.3	2.52	883	986	1.2
78638	KINGSBURY	187	1846	2192	2454	1.9	76	682	801	897	1.8	2.73	530	606	1.5
78639	KINGSLAND	299	5163	6031	6385	1.7	73	2350	2722	2877	1.6	2.18	1520	1727	1.4
78640	KYLE	209	15134	37720	49737	10.4	98	4351	11216	14925	10.8	3.30	3626	8970	10.3
78641	LEANDER	453	20147	42499	55509	8.4	97	6825	14209	18499	8.3	2.99	5511	11082	7.8
78642	LIBERTY HILL	491	5759	8648	10946	4.5	93	1876	2757	3491	4.3	3.11	1573	2262	4.0
78643	LLANO	299	5592	6058	6270	0.9	55	2366	2579	2673	0.9	2.30	1633	1753	0.8
78644	LOCKHART	055	15099	16616	17135	1.0	58	4837	5383	5569	1.2	2.81	3649	4007	1.0
78645	LEANDER	453	7554	9562	10804	2.6	83	3202	4129	4683	2.8	2.32	2231	2723	2.2
78648	LULING	055	7321	8075	8366	1.1	61	2618	2867	2968	1.0	2.76	1838	1975	0.8
78650	MC DADE	021	1186	1361	1443	1.5	69	465	522	553	1.3	2.60	325	358	1.1
78652	MANCHACA	453	3388	3669	4126	0.9	55	1117	1240	1395	1.1	2.95	934	1022	1.0
78653	MANOR	453	6292	12930	15721	8.1	97	2124	4351	5311	8.1	2.97	1645	3263	7.7
78654	MARBLE FALLS	053	14972	19469	21980	2.9	86	5859	7516	8455	2.7	2.57	4247	5359	2.5
78655	MARTINDALE	055	2775	3274	3505	1.8	75	961	1132	1214	1.8	2.89	750	869	1.6
78656	MAXWELL	055	2323	2744	2909	1.8	75	778	918	974	1.8	2.98	586	680	1.6
78657	HORSESHOE BAY	299	4317	5716	6427	3.1	87	1995	2581	2875	2.8	2.21	1460	1863	2.7
78659	PAIGE	021	2415	2814	3006	1.7	73	934	1067	1137	1.4	2.63	699	786	1.3
78660	PFLUGERVILLE	453	35267	65610	80695	6.9	96	11291	21448	26499	7.2	3.05	9329	17226	6.9
78662	RED ROCK	021	1818	2267	2471	2.4	82	648	797	868	2.3	2.84	492	596	2.1
78663	ROUND MOUNTAIN	031	439	505	532	1.5	69	184	210	221	1.4	2.40	137	155	1.3
78664	ROUND ROCK	491	36752	51919	64042	3.8	90	12816	17614	21665	3.5	2.93	9471	12923	3.4
78665	ROUND ROCK	491	9763	28863	39614	12.4	99	3188	9605	13189	12.7	2.99	2470	7109	12.1
78666	SAN MARCOS	209	51251	65252	75443	2.6	83	17544	22372	26466	2.7	2.51	9307	10888	1.7
78669	SPICEWOOD	453	5554	6889	7816	2.4	82	2266	2836	3228	2.5	2.43	1678	2019	2.0
78671	STONEWALL	171	576	687	750	1.9	76	220	266	292	2.1	2.58	163	193	1.8
78672	TOW	299	1066	1257	1343	1.8	75	528	620	663	1.8	2.03	362	421	1.6
78675	WILLOW CITY	171	145	177	194	2.2	80	53	65	72	2.2	2.72	43	53	2.3
78676	WIMBERLEY	209	9428	12438	14920	3.0	86	3874	5184	6251	3.2	2.38	2790	3512	2.5
78677	WRIGHTSBORO	177	20	21	22	0.5	42	9	10	10	1.1	2.10	7	7	0.0
78681	ROUND ROCK	491	31879	51712	65186	5.4	95	10366	16708	21035	5.3	3.09	8733	13715	5.0
78701	AUSTIN	453	3855	4947	5487	2.7	84	1811	2572	2971	3.9	1.44	385	491	2.7
78702	AUSTIN	453	22601	24955	27002	1.1	61	7270	8105	8805	1.2	3.01	4802	5039	0.5
78703	AUSTIN	453	17449	18008	18819	0.3	34	8679	9215	9713	0.6	1.90	3814	3640	-0.5
78704	AUSTIN	453	43120	45726	48560	0.6	46	20563	22206	23718	0.8	2.00	8278	8029	-0.3
78705	AUSTIN	453	25376	26986	28042	0.7	49	9409	10060	10682	0.7	1.75	1203	1115	-0.8
78712	AUSTIN	453	400	427	427	0.7	49	0	0	0	0.0	0.00	0	0	0.0
78717	AUSTIN	491	8210	23405	32426	12.0	99	2692	7615	10531	11.9	3.06	2229	6157	11.6
78719	AUSTIN	453	2025	2151	2306	0.7	49	604	650	702	0.8	3.30	490	511	0.5
78721	AUSTIN	453	10124	13188	15022	2.9	86	3099	4102	4687	3.1	3.19	2275	2863	2.5
78722	AUSTIN	453	6101	6443	6832	0.6	46	2782	2979	3174	0.7	2.09	1110	1073	-0.4
78723	AUSTIN	453	30307	32914	35150	0.9	55	10506	11336	12125	0.8	2.88	6517	6564	0.1
78724	AUSTIN	453	13141	18296	21293	3.6	90	3601	4970	5779	3.5	3.66	2967	3985	3.2
78725	AUSTIN	453	4155	6578	7830	5.1	94	960	1721	2119	6.5	3.21	763	1312	6.0
78726	AUSTIN	453	5192	14320	18267	11.6	99	1761	4924	6287	11.8	2.91	1407	3901	11.7
78727	AUSTIN	453	23036	27519	30850	1.9	76	9837	12312	13927	2.5	2.23	5719	6577	1.5
78728	AUSTIN	453	17290	20307	22500	1.8	75	7939	9192	10133	1.6	2.21	4057	4419	0.9
78729	AUSTIN	491	23646	28863	33555	2.2	80	9446	11349	13184	2.0	2.53	5955	6843	1.5
78730	AUSTIN	453	4686	7432	8995	5.1	94	1909	3071	3708	5.3	2.42	1320	2011	4.7
78731	AUSTIN	453	25926	26978	28409	0.4	37	12649	13376	14141	0.6	1.98	6368	6260	-0.2
78732	AUSTIN	453	3824	12646	16563	13.8	99	1434	4299	5579	12.6	2.94	1120	3342	12.5
78733	AUSTIN	453	7015	8596	9720	2.2	80	2255	2797	3175	2.4	3.07	1830	2152	1.8
78734	AUSTIN	453	13111	17572	20246	3.2	87	5170	6987	8069	3.3	2.51	3784	4850	2.7
78735	AUSTIN	453	9598	13809	16171	4.0	91	4194	6067	7112	4.1	2.26	2528	3531	3.7
78736	AUSTIN	453	6103	6717	7301	1.0	58	2251	2538	2772	1.3	2.61	1653	1769	0.7
78737	AUSTIN	209	7089	10748	12925	4.6	93	2441	3790	4582	4.9	2.83	2061	3094	4.5
78738	AUSTIN	453	5054	9220	11226	6.7	96	1811	3404	4174	7.1	2.69	1501	2707	6.6
78739	AUSTIN	453	8621	13722	16355	5.2	94	2641	4287	5149	5.4	3.15	2403	3852	5.2
78741	AUSTIN	453	40663	48870	54315	2.0	78	17081	20508	22765	2.0	2.38	6680	7304	1.0
78742	AUSTIN	453	1071	1034	1032	-0.4	13	377	366	366	-0.3	2.83	258	236	-1.0
78744	AUSTIN	453	33791	40593	45034	2.0	78	10086	11931	13189	1.8	3.40	7271	8326	1.5
78745	AUSTIN	453	53172	60398	66006	1.4	67	20655	23932	26271	1.6	2.50	12617	13703	0.9
78746	AUSTIN	453	28079	30959	33416	1.1	61	10827	12097	13082	1.2	2.55	7582	8160	0.8
78747	AUSTIN	453	4554	9027	11015	7.7	97	1744	3248	3938	7.0	2.78	1325	2383	6.6
78748	AUSTIN	453	25304	37273	43872	4.3	92	9202	13793	16303	4.5	2.69	6779	9912	4.2
78749	AUSTIN	453	28601	36310	40877	2.6	83	10830	14230	16164	3.0	2.54	7583	9511	2.5
78750	AUSTIN	453	24288	28441	31907	1.7	73	9274	10910	12261	1.8	2.59	6810	7748	1.4
78751	AUSTIN	453	14167	15366	16468	0.9	55	7394	8199	8853	1.1	1.82	2036	1992	-0.2
78752	AUSTIN	453	17733	20802	22800	1.7	73	6678	7604	8293	1.4	2.70	3366	3539	0.5
78753	AUSTIN	453	38486	51707	58470	3.2	87	14648	19052	21434	2.9	2.70	8920	11031	2.3
78754	AUSTIN	453	5304	10136	12724	7.3	97	2251	4263	5318	7.1	2.37	1338	2416	6.6
78756	AUSTIN	453	7983	8489	9076	0.7	49	4410	4770	5113	0.9	1.77	1510	1454	-0.4
78757	AUSTIN	453	23129	24287	25753	0.5	42	10600	11315	12048	0.7	2.13	5405	5300	-0.2
78758	AUSTIN	453	45916	49779	53163	0.9	55	19203	20896	22381	0.9	2.35	9863	9807	-0.1
78759	AUSTIN	453	37694	40375	43126	0.7	49	18235	19744	21128	0.9	2.03	8971	9065	0.1
78801	UVALDE	463	22061	23085	23503	0.5	42	7120	7509	7668	0.6	3.00	5582	5818	0.4
78827	ASHERTON	127	1699	1601	1540	-0.6	9	546	529	514	-0.3	3.02	440	422	-0.5
78828	BARKSDALE	137	350	326	313	-0.8	6	151	144	139	-0.5	2.26	108	102	-0.6
78829	BATESVILLE	507	1414	1382	1374	-0.2	19	409	411	412	0.1	3.36	350	349	0.0
78830	BIG WELLS	127	833	800	773	-0.4	13	290	289	283	0.0	2.76	216	213	-0.2
78832	BRACKETTVILLE	271	3379	3305	3239	-0.2	19	1314	1287	1263	-0.2	2.55	941	908	-0.4
78833	CAMP WOOD	385	1301	1339	1372	0.3	34	485	521	538	0.8	2.54	347	367	0.6
78834	CARRIZO SPRINGS	127	7699	7472	7277	-0.3	16	2464	2477	2442	0.1	2.97	1982	1973	0.0
78837	COMSTOCK	465	565	619	648	1.0	58	241	268	282	1.2	2.31	172	189	1.0
	TEXAS					1.9					1.8	2.78			1.7
	UNITED STATES					1.0					1.1	2.59			0.9

ZIP CODE #	POST OFFICE NAME	RACE (%) White 2000	White 2009	Black 2000	Black 2009	Asian/Pacific 2000	Asian/Pacific 2009	% Hispanic Origin 2000	% Hispanic Origin 2009	2009 AGE DISTRIBUTION (%) 0-4	5-9	10-14	15-19	20-24	25-44	45-64	65-84	85+	18+	MEDIAN AGE 2009	% 2009 Males	% 2009 Females
78621	ELGIN	77.1	74.3	9.7	9.2	0.5	0.6	30.5	37.0	8.0	7.7	7.7	7.2	6.2	25.3	26.7	9.9	1.5	72.2	35.8	50.2	49.8
78623	FISCHER	93.7	91.1	0.7	0.9	0.3	0.5	11.3	17.6	6.4	6.5	6.8	6.4	5.0	23.8	30.6	13.3	1.4	76.2	41.9	49.7	50.3
78624	FREDERICKSBURG	92.6	90.1	0.2	0.2	0.2	0.3	16.8	22.9	5.2	5.4	5.7	5.6	4.2	19.7	30.2	19.5	4.5	80.1	47.9	47.5	52.5
78626	GEORGETOWN	80.0	75.4	4.0	4.3	0.7	0.9	26.0	33.1	8.3	7.5	6.9	8.6	8.7	29.3	20.6	7.8	2.3	73.2	31.4	49.4	50.6
78628	GEORGETOWN	92.3	89.9	2.0	2.3	0.7	1.0	9.1	13.2	5.5	5.7	6.2	6.3	4.8	21.4	31.3	17.0	1.8	78.5	45.1	48.7	51.3
78629	GONZALES	71.6	67.5	9.7	9.4	0.5	0.5	35.8	44.2	7.3	7.1	7.1	7.0	5.9	24.7	25.5	12.8	2.7	74.1	37.6	50.1	49.9
78631	HARPER	95.1	93.4	0.1	0.1	0.1	0.2	7.4	10.4	4.3	4.5	4.8	4.8	3.8	17.3	35.7	22.2	2.6	83.4	51.6	48.9	51.1
78632	HARWOOD	82.5	77.2	4.4	5.0	0.2	0.2	22.1	30.0	5.8	6.0	6.0	6.0	5.4	23.7	29.5	15.3	2.2	78.2	42.7	50.2	49.8
78633	GEORGETOWN	95.5	94.3	0.6	0.7	0.4	0.6	6.7	9.3	4.7	4.8	5.1	5.2	4.0	17.7	31.7	24.7	2.2	82.0	50.9	48.8	51.2
78634	HUTTO	85.4	77.3	3.0	4.0	0.9	0.7	16.9	28.0	8.5	8.0	7.9	7.2	5.2	31.0	25.2	6.3	0.7	71.1	34.0	49.8	50.2
78635	HYE	97.3	95.9	0.4	0.7	0.0	0.0	5.4	7.5	4.9	5.6	6.4	4.9	3.0	18.4	39.3	15.7	1.9	79.8	49.2	52.4	47.6
78636	JOHNSON CITY	92.6	90.2	0.2	0.2	0.2	0.4	13.3	18.0	6.5	6.7	6.7	5.7	4.4	21.1	32.1	14.1	2.7	76.3	44.1	49.2	50.8
78638	KINGSBURY	82.4	74.9	2.1	2.1	0.3	0.3	27.9	41.1	6.3	6.5	6.8	6.3	6.2	24.9	31.3	10.3	1.5	76.4	40.0	51.5	48.5
78639	KINGSLAND	95.8	94.4	0.2	0.2	0.5	0.6	5.9	8.3	3.9	4.3	4.6	4.3	3.4	15.5	32.4	26.3	5.2	84.4	54.7	48.8	51.2
78640	KYLE	65.7	62.2	4.7	4.5	0.3	0.4	52.5	61.3	10.0	9.1	8.1	7.6	7.3	31.5	20.4	5.3	0.6	68.1	29.5	50.8	49.2
78641	LEANDER	88.1	82.7	2.3	3.2	1.1	1.9	13.7	20.6	9.4	8.7	8.1	6.9	5.5	32.2	23.7	5.1	0.4	69.4	32.3	50.2	49.8
78642	LIBERTY HILL	93.3	90.8	0.7	0.8	0.3	0.4	9.7	14.5	7.0	7.2	7.6	8.2	6.0	25.3	29.1	8.7	0.9	72.8	36.9	49.5	50.5
78643	LLANO	95.5	94.2	0.4	0.5	0.2	0.3	6.7	9.2	4.8	4.8	5.0	5.3	4.8	18.0	31.2	22.4	3.8	82.1	50.4	49.3	50.7
78644	LOCKHART	68.6	65.4	10.6	10.0	0.4	0.5	43.2	51.2	7.3	6.7	6.6	7.1	7.5	29.5	23.6	9.5	2.2	74.9	34.9	49.5	50.5
78645	LEANDER	93.6	90.6	0.8	1.0	0.7	0.9	8.0	12.7	5.0	5.3	5.8	5.3	4.2	21.7	33.6	16.8	2.2	80.7	46.5	49.6	50.4
78648	LULING	70.7	65.7	8.7	9.2	0.4	0.5	36.8	45.7	8.0	7.6	7.3	7.1	6.0	24.3	24.2	12.8	2.9	72.8	36.8	48.6	51.4
78650	MC DADE	89.9	86.6	2.5	2.9	0.1	0.1	14.4	20.4	6.2	6.6	7.1	6.5	4.2	24.0	32.4	11.8	1.2	75.8	41.5	51.1	48.9
78652	MANCHACA	86.6	80.8	1.6	1.9	1.6	1.9	18.4	27.5	5.4	6.1	6.8	6.7	4.2	25.6	34.0	10.4	0.8	77.4	42.0	50.5	49.5
78653	MANOR	70.0	62.6	11.5	11.9	0.8	1.9	28.1	37.7	8.2	8.1	7.8	7.1	5.6	28.2	26.3	7.9	0.8	71.5	34.9	49.9	50.1
78654	MARBLE FALLS	87.9	84.2	1.2	1.4	0.4	0.5	18.4	24.6	6.9	6.6	6.7	6.3	5.3	22.0	27.8	16.0	2.4	75.8	42.0	49.3	50.7
78655	MARTINDALE	67.1	61.9	3.2	3.1	0.2	0.2	53.6	63.4	9.0	7.9	7.7	7.4	6.0	29.0	24.0	8.0	1.0	70.8	33.2	51.1	48.9
78656	MAXWELL	67.3	62.1	5.0	4.8	0.3	0.3	50.5	60.8	8.3	7.9	7.2	6.8	7.7	30.6	24.3	6.5	0.6	72.6	32.3	52.6	47.4
78657	HORSESHOE BAY	94.8	92.4	0.5	0.6	0.7	0.9	7.2	11.1	4.1	4.3	4.3	3.6	2.9	16.0	31.4	30.7	2.9	85.1	56.9	48.8	51.2
78659	PAIGE	89.5	86.5	2.7	3.0	0.2	0.3	16.2	22.5	6.9	7.1	7.5	6.8	5.1	24.7	30.7	10.3	0.9	74.2	39.2	49.9	50.1
78660	PFLUGERVILLE	71.8	66.3	11.9	12.9	4.6	5.2	21.8	28.9	9.6	9.1	8.5	7.2	5.4	33.5	22.7	3.6	0.4	68.2	31.8	49.1	50.9
78662	RED ROCK	90.4	87.2	3.3	4.2	0.1	0.1	16.3	22.5	7.7	7.8	7.5	6.7	6.5	26.0	29.1	7.9	0.7	72.5	36.0	51.0	49.0
78663	ROUND MOUNTAIN	91.6	87.7	0.0	0.0	0.0	0.2	10.5	14.9	5.3	5.7	6.1	4.6	3.0	17.8	39.0	16.2	2.2	79.8	49.3	48.9	51.1
78664	ROUND ROCK	73.9	68.0	9.0	10.1	2.8	3.6	25.5	32.8	9.9	9.0	8.3	7.2	6.7	34.1	20.5	3.7	0.6	68.3	30.4	49.5	50.5
78665	ROUND ROCK	78.0	74.2	8.5	8.8	3.4	3.9	17.2	23.2	10.4	9.3	8.2	6.3	6.0	35.2	20.2	3.7	0.7	67.9	31.2	48.7	51.3
78666	SAN MARCOS	72.5	67.5	5.2	6.3	1.1	1.4	37.5	43.3	5.6	4.8	4.5	10.2	23.4	26.6	17.3	6.4	1.2	81.2	25.8	51.7	48.3
78669	SPICEWOOD	95.6	93.4	0.3	0.3	0.4	0.6	6.1	9.7	5.1	5.3	6.7	5.8	3.4	23.0	37.9	11.8	1.0	79.1	45.3	51.2	48.8
78671	STONEWALL	91.7	88.8	0.3	0.3	0.2	0.1	17.9	24.6	4.9	5.4	6.0	5.8	2.9	20.2	32.6	19.8	2.3	80.1	48.5	50.1	49.9
78672	TOW	97.8	97.1	0.2	0.2	0.2	0.2	1.8	2.7	2.4	2.7	2.7	2.9	3.0	11.7	34.7	36.0	3.9	90.5	61.3	49.6	50.4
78675	WILLOW CITY	93.1	89.8	0.0	0.0	0.0	0.0	10.4	14.7	5.1	5.6	6.8	6.2	4.0	16.9	33.3	19.8	2.3	78.5	48.4	52.0	48.0
78676	WIMBERLEY	93.9	91.6	0.3	0.4	0.3	0.5	7.6	10.6	4.3	4.9	6.3	6.3	4.0	20.5	33.9	17.4	2.3	80.1	47.1	49.4	50.6
78677	WRIGHTSBORO	89.5	85.7	0.0	0.0	0.0	0.0	21.1	28.6	9.5	9.5	9.5	9.5	4.8	33.3	23.8	0.0	0.0	61.9	31.3	52.4	47.6
78681	ROUND ROCK	82.5	77.1	4.7	5.5	3.9	5.2	15.0	20.7	9.1	8.9	8.6	7.2	5.3	30.4	25.2	4.9	0.5	68.7	33.0	49.6	50.4
78701	AUSTIN	72.0	66.1	12.0	12.3	3.7	4.3	18.4	25.5	1.8	1.4	1.1	3.4	12.4	41.7	22.1	13.5	2.7	94.9	37.8	62.0	38.0
78702	AUSTIN	30.1	27.4	24.0	21.8	0.4	0.4	67.4	72.7	9.2	8.3	7.4	8.2	8.3	26.8	20.6	9.3	1.9	70.3	30.6	50.2	49.8
78703	AUSTIN	91.2	87.6	1.5	1.8	3.0	3.8	7.1	11.6	4.8	4.3	4.4	4.3	7.8	36.2	27.6	8.3	2.2	83.8	37.7	49.8	50.2
78704	AUSTIN	71.9	64.9	4.9	5.0	1.4	1.7	33.9	44.4	6.3	4.8	4.1	5.6	11.1	40.1	21.2	5.6	1.2	82.1	32.1	51.9	48.1
78705	AUSTIN	74.7	67.9	2.7	3.2	15.1	18.5	10.0	15.0	0.8	0.5	0.3	29.3	46.0	17.3	4.6	1.0	0.2	97.9	22.1	52.8	47.2
78712	AUSTIN	61.8	53.6	6.3	7.0	20.9	24.4	15.1	21.5	0.0	0.0	0.0	75.4	23.7	0.7	0.2	0.0	0.0	99.5	18.3	60.2	39.8
78717	AUSTIN	82.7	78.2	4.3	4.8	8.4	10.8	9.3	13.1	10.2	10.3	9.9	7.1	3.5	31.1	24.5	3.2	0.4	64.8	32.9	49.2	50.8
78719	AUSTIN	65.2	58.4	6.2	5.9	0.8	0.8	54.1	66.0	9.5	9.3	8.6	8.7	7.9	28.2	20.5	6.7	0.6	67.4	28.7	51.5	48.5
78721	AUSTIN	23.4	22.8	44.8	41.8	0.2	0.1	50.8	55.5	9.3	8.7	8.3	8.7	7.6	25.4	21.1	9.5	1.4	68.7	30.6	48.9	51.1
78722	AUSTIN	62.7	56.4	22.2	23.6	2.2	2.5	20.0	27.8	4.5	3.4	3.3	4.3	15.3	39.2	17.6	9.7	2.7	86.7	32.0	52.2	47.8
78723	AUSTIN	41.0	36.2	31.6	30.4	1.3	1.3	42.3	50.7	9.1	7.8	6.6	6.9	10.3	32.4	19.1	6.8	1.0	72.6	29.5	51.8	48.2
78724	AUSTIN	28.9	25.9	40.3	36.4	0.3	0.3	45.3	54.0	10.4	10.0	9.1	9.9	9.1	28.5	18.4	4.2	0.3	64.5	25.8	49.5	50.5
78725	AUSTIN	38.4	34.3	38.9	35.1	1.2	1.5	33.7	44.5	7.3	7.3	7.1	7.3	8.3	35.5	21.5	5.1	0.5	74.0	32.2	56.5	43.5
78726	AUSTIN	86.4	81.1	1.7	2.1	8.8	12.4	5.5	8.7	8.1	8.4	8.8	8.0	3.8	29.5	28.9	4.1	0.3	69.6	35.5	49.7	50.3
78727	AUSTIN	75.7	68.8	6.3	7.4	9.1	11.0	14.6	21.6	6.8	6.1	5.7	5.3	7.9	38.8	24.1	4.7	0.5	78.2	33.9	50.7	49.3
78728	AUSTIN	69.2	61.4	9.6	11.0	11.2	13.7	17.1	24.5	7.8	6.5	5.7	5.2	9.2	42.7	19.2	3.3	0.3	77.2	31.6	50.7	49.3
78729	AUSTIN	80.4	74.9	5.0	5.8	7.4	9.2	11.7	17.0	7.4	6.6	6.4	6.5	8.3	36.0	23.8	4.2	0.8	75.5	32.8	49.9	50.1
78730	AUSTIN	91.3	87.9	1.2	1.5	4.8	6.5	6.1	9.9	7.9	9.1	9.5	5.8	2.0	29.2	30.2	6.0	0.3	69.6	39.3	52.0	48.0
78731	AUSTIN	89.6	86.2	1.0	1.3	5.6	7.1	6.5	10.2	4.0	4.0	4.5	4.6	11.4	28.2	27.6	12.3	3.3	84.9	39.9	49.0	51.0
78732	AUSTIN	90.3	86.3	1.5	1.9	4.6	6.6	7.5	12.4	11.0	11.2	10.2	6.1	2.5	32.3	23.1	3.3	0.2	63.4	35.0	50.9	49.1
78733	AUSTIN	91.3	87.5	0.5	0.7	3.8	5.1	7.4	12.2	7.4	9.1	9.8	8.2	3.4	26.2	31.4	4.1	0.3	67.9	37.5	50.1	49.9
78734	AUSTIN	93.3	89.2	0.5	0.7	0.8	1.1	9.5	16.2	5.2	6.0	6.8	6.7	4.6	22.3	35.5	11.4	1.6	77.7	43.9	50.8	49.2
78735	AUSTIN	89.1	84.2	1.3	1.7	3.9	4.6	10.8	18.5	6.7	6.4	6.2	4.6	4.6	34.6	27.2	8.3	1.5	77.9	37.9	49.8	50.2
78736	AUSTIN	88.8	83.5	1.5	1.8	1.4	1.8	14.2	22.2	5.4	6.0	6.5	7.0	5.2	27.0	32.7	8.6	1.5	77.3	40.1	48.3	51.7
78737	AUSTIN	94.2	91.9	0.7	0.9	1.2	1.7	9.4	12.8	5.6	6.7	7.9	7.9	3.9	22.7	36.1	8.3	0.9	74.6	42.3	50.3	49.7
78738	AUSTIN	93.1	90.4	0.7	1.0	3.1	4.0	4.6	7.5	7.1	7.3	7.6	6.2	2.8	24.3	32.0	11.2	1.5	73.6	41.9	49.6	50.4
78739	AUSTIN	87.0	82.3	2.2	2.7	6.0	8.0	10.1	15.8	9.2	9.4	9.2	7.5	2.8	29.3	27.8	4.4	0.4	66.7	36.2	50.8	49.2
78741	AUSTIN	49.5	42.5	8.8	8.6	5.9	6.2	51.6	61.0	6.8	4.8	3.7	8.2	27.7	35.4	10.6	2.6	0.3	82.3	24.8	55.2	44.8
78742	AUSTIN	49.4	41.5	11.9	10.9	0.3	0.3	55.8	67.1	9.4	8.5	7.8	7.4	7.2	31.3	21.5	6.6	0.3	69.7	31.3	53.4	46.6
78744	AUSTIN	46.5	41.2	11.6	10.5	1.4	1.4	64.9	73.6	10.4	9.6	8.6	8.6	10.1	31.3	17.5	3.6	0.3	66.2	26.3	51.3	48.7
78745	AUSTIN	66.4	57.8	5.8	6.0	1.7	1.8	40.3	52.3	7.3	6.6	6.2	6.3	8.0	34.2	23.0	7.3	1.1	76.1	32.9	50.1	49.9
78746	AUSTIN	88.1	85.2	0.6	0.8	7.6	9.0	5.7	8.7	5.5	6.1	7.6	7.6	6.1	24.6	33.6	7.8	1.2	75.7	39.3	50.1	49.9
78747	AUSTIN	79.2	67.9	5.3	7.7	1.0	1.2	31.1	49.2	7.4	6.9	6.7	5.6	4.2	27.9	26.6	13.3	1.3	75.4	38.8	48.8	51.2
78748	AUSTIN	72.9	66.4	5.4	5.5	3.1	3.6	30.3	40.0	8.1	7.5	6.8	6.1	6.3	34.3	24.6	5.7	0.5	73.8	33.4	49.1	50.9
78749	AUSTIN	80.3	73.9	4.1	4.4	5.1	6.7	18.1	25.9	8.0	7.7	7.4	6.2	6.5	35.2	23.9	4.4	0.7	72.9	33.7	49.5	50.5
78750	AUSTIN	84.9	80.4	2.8	3.3	7.1	9.1	9.6	14.0	6.2	6.5	6.9	6.5	5.6	28.1	30.5	8.6	1.1	76.2	38.8	49.5	50.5
78751	AUSTIN	78.5	72.3	2.9	3.3	6.6	8.2	19.3	26.6	3.4	2.6	2.1	4.1	25.8	42.8	14.3	3.9	1.1	90.6	28.2	54.9	45.1
78752	AUSTIN	49.7	44.0	13.3	12.3	2.5	2.5	55.2	65.0	8.8	7.3	6.0	6.6	12.7	36.8	15.0	5.1	1.7	74.7	28.3	54.3	45.7
78753	AUSTIN	49.8	42.8	19.4	18.1	5.8	9.3	36.9	43.2	9.3	7.9	6.9	6.8	9.1	34.4	19.6	5.3	0.8	72.2	29.7	50.7	49.3
78754	AUSTIN	65.8	59.7	15.8	16.7	5.1	5.7	20.1	27.7	7.6	7.1	6.6	6.2	6.9	31.6	25.0	8.1	0.8	75.1	34.9	49.3	50.7
78756	AUSTIN	83.5	77.8	3.2	3.7	2.6	3.2	16.5	24.3	4.9	3.8	3.2	3.8	10.2	39.2	24.7	7.6	2.5	86.3	35.6	50.8	49.2
78757	AUSTIN	81.3	75.1	2.7	2.9	2.1	2.5	22.2	31.0	5.5	4.7	4.5	5.0	8.3	34.1	25.2	10.3	2.3	82.5	37.2	50.4	49.6
78758	AUSTIN	57.0	50.4	11.8	11.8	8.2	9.1	33.3	42.0	7.6	5.9	4.9	5.6	12.4	40.0	17.8	5.0	0.7	78.7	29.4	53.1	46.9
78759	AUSTIN	85.0	79.8	2.6	3.2	7.4	9.8	8.8	13.6	5.2	4.7	4.7	4.6	8.8	37.0	26.2	7.6	1.2	82.7	35.1	50.1	49.9
78801	UVALDE	74.3	71.6	0.4	0.4	0.5	0.6	69.8	76.9	9.0	8.6	8.3	8.5	6.8	23.9	22.0	10.7	2.2	68.9	32.0	48.9	51.1
78827	ASHERTON	76.9	75.5	0.1	0.1	0.1	0.1	90.6	89.8	8.4	7.7	8.4	8.4	6.3	21.5	24.5	12.1	2.6	69.9	34.9	48.1	51.9
78828	BARKSDALE	94.3	91.7	0.0	0.0	0.0	0.0	8.6	13.5	3.1	3.1	3.7	5.8	4.6	12.9	36.2	28.5	2.1	86.5	55.6	50.0	50.0
78829	BATESVILLE	53.6	52.1	0.4	0.4	0.0	0.0	87.6	87.3	8.8	9.0	8.3	8.0	8.2	26.6	22.1	7.8	1.2	69.1	29.8	49.9	50.1
78830	BIG WELLS	79.4	78.0	0.2	0.3	0.4	0.4	88.1	87.6	6.5	7.8	7.8	8.8	3.8	18.4	30.6	13.9	2.6	72.3	42.7	48.1	51.9
78832	BRACKETTVILLE	75.8	75.2	1.7	1.7	0.1	0.1	50.5	52.9	6.1	5.8	6.2	6.6	4.9	18.2	26.2	23.2	2.8	77.7	46.9	49.9	50.1
78833	CAMP WOOD	89.9	89.6	0.4	0.4	0.2	0.2	31.5	33.8	6.3	6.1	6.3	6.9	5.2	20.6	27.6	19.0	1.8	77.1	43.6	49.1	50.9
78834	CARRIZO SPRINGS	76.7	75.3	1.1	1.2	0.9	1.0	83.4	82.8	8.8	8.2	7.8	8.9	7.6	23.5	23.2	10.3	1.8	69.6	31.4	48.7	51.3
78837	COMSTOCK	84.4	79.6	0.0	0.0	0.2	0.2	35.8	47.8	5.0	5.3	5.8	5.0	4.4	19.9	31.2	21.2	2.3	80.6	48.3	52.3	47.7
	TEXAS	71.0	67.6	11.5	11.4	2.8	3.5	32.0	37.4	7.9	7.5	7.2	7.5	7.4	28.3	24.0	8.8	1.4	73.0	33.6	49.7	50.3
	UNITED STATES	75.1	72.0	12.3	12.7	3.8	4.6	12.5	15.7	6.8	6.7	6.6	7.1	6.9	27.0	26.0	10.9	1.9	75.7	36.9	49.2	50.8

ZIP CODE #	POST OFFICE NAME	2009 Per Capita Income	2009 HH Income Base	2009 HOUSEHOLD INCOME DISTRIBUTION (%) Less than $25,000	$25,000 to $49,999	$50,000 to $99,999	$100,000 to $149,999	$150,000 or More	MEDIAN HOUSEHOLD INCOME 2009	2014	2009 National Centile	2009 State Centile	2009 Home Value Base	2009 HOME VALUE DISTRIBUTION (%) Less than $50,000	$50,000 to $89,999	$90,000 to $174,999	$175,000 to $399,999	$400,000 or More	2009 Median Home Value
78621	ELGIN	21539	6818	20.9	25.8	41.0	8.7	3.6	52706	56069	67	76	5397	12.3	22.1	39.2	22.9	3.5	125205
78623	FISCHER	27806	340	8.2	33.8	44.7	8.2	5.0	56895	60211	74	81	285	11.2	19.3	51.2	15.1	3.2	121726
78624	FREDERICKSBURG	23875	8783	22.6	32.1	35.2	6.7	3.4	46392	48904	53	63	6661	7.1	10.3	34.4	34.3	13.8	168750
78626	GEORGETOWN	24630	8114	16.3	22.8	38.5	15.8	6.7	62059	59424	80	85	5337	7.0	13.3	35.6	38.7	5.3	160692
78628	GEORGETOWN	36205	8808	9.8	16.0	33.1	26.4	14.6	82800	88081	93	95	6737	1.2	1.5	17.2	65.2	14.9	251482
78629	GONZALES	17133	4582	33.0	30.8	29.7	5.0	1.6	37146	39370	24	31	3065	26.1	25.0	30.3	15.4	3.2	87853
78631	HARPER	25239	927	24.8	29.0	34.6	5.2	6.4	46646	49719	53	64	767	9.3	15.9	33.0	27.4	14.5	143875
78632	HARWOOD	18798	183	35.5	30.1	25.7	4.4	4.4	34762	38464	17	22	148	23.6	24.3	27.7	18.9	5.4	100000
78633	GEORGETOWN	45883	6997	5.8	12.4	35.3	28.2	18.3	92619	100617	96	96	6533	1.4	1.8	7.7	63.9	25.3	299077
78634	HUTTO	29216	5846	7.5	22.7	38.0	20.9	11.0	71496	73216	88	90	4997	0.9	5.1	39.7	41.4	12.9	185803
78635	HYE	26475	113	19.5	24.8	44.2	8.0	3.5	53258	52070	68	76	90	4.4	12.2	44.4	27.8	11.1	155769
78636	JOHNSON CITY	22667	1365	23.4	29.7	35.4	8.5	3.1	47203	48325	55	65	1066	7.7	18.0	37.6	25.9	10.8	144725
78638	KINGSBURY	22606	801	17.7	28.7	41.4	8.7	3.4	52665	54484	67	75	619	16.2	31.0	36.8	10.3	5.7	96034
78639	KINGSLAND	23153	2722	28.0	34.5	30.0	4.3	3.2	40555	44774	35	44	2150	19.9	16.8	34.0	24.1	5.1	116968
78640	KYLE	21701	11216	13.0	23.7	44.0	14.6	4.7	63091	67307	81	86	9471	9.7	15.4	46.6	22.3	6.0	135203
78641	LEANDER	29934	14209	8.8	16.7	43.7	20.7	10.1	73475	76737	89	91	11894	4.1	6.8	39.3	41.5	8.3	174772
78642	LIBERTY HILL	24010	2757	11.2	28.1	37.8	17.2	5.7	62311	58295	80	85	2317	9.9	17.7	28.2	30.7	13.5	153852
78643	LLANO	24305	2579	22.6	32.9	36.3	5.3	2.9	45661	47771	50	61	2019	13.9	23.7	31.8	23.1	7.5	125152
78644	LOCKHART	18429	5383	24.5	27.7	39.2	7.0	1.6	48192	50462	57	67	3517	15.1	24.5	42.5	14.4	3.5	104468
78645	LEANDER	32808	4129	12.4	27.1	36.4	16.8	7.3	61948	63888	80	85	3026	5.8	8.9	31.6	40.0	13.7	185316
78648	LULING	16665	2867	31.3	33.8	27.6	5.5	1.9	37137	41238	24	31	1876	31.2	29.2	29.5	8.2	1.8	72761
78650	MC DADE	21599	522	25.1	27.6	34.1	10.9	2.3	47672	51041	56	66	412	24.5	23.1	31.6	18.2	2.7	94762
78652	MANCHACA	35791	1240	4.7	12.3	40.7	29.8	12.5	86522	86899	94	96	1055	2.5	2.9	36.4	53.4	4.8	190337
78653	MANOR	25866	4351	14.5	23.3	40.5	16.2	5.6	62821	66587	81	86	3492	12.7	15.1	34.4	33.7	4.2	148704
78654	MARBLE FALLS	22507	7516	24.2	31.4	32.7	7.1	4.7	44792	45935	48	58	5597	11.5	14.2	30.6	33.4	10.2	153102
78655	MARTINDALE	18548	1132	22.6	32.4	34.2	8.6	2.2	46432	48959	53	63	830	28.6	22.9	34.1	12.4	2.0	86471
78656	MAXWELL	18727	918	21.1	32.0	33.9	10.5	2.5	47772	49770	56	66	605	30.9	28.9	32.4	4.8	3.0	69146
78657	HORSESHOE BAY	36946	2581	14.5	26.4	34.2	13.3	11.7	57932	57053	75	82	2134	4.8	11.0	23.9	37.5	22.9	221815
78659	PAIGE	22718	1067	19.1	27.2	41.4	7.4	4.9	52399	54723	67	75	887	16.0	21.4	34.8	24.0	3.7	120072
78660	PFLUGERVILLE	32150	21448	4.0	11.7	45.1	28.4	10.8	84094	86064	94	95	18013	4.6	6.3	49.6	38.3	1.2	162005
78662	RED ROCK	21959	797	18.6	20.3	44.5	14.6	2.0	57763	59541	75	82	686	9.6	29.9	37.8	17.9	4.8	113636
78663	ROUND MOUNTAIN	28818	210	22.9	25.2	29.5	17.6	4.8	52051	50512	66	74	177	5.6	10.7	24.9	34.5	24.3	214063
78664	ROUND ROCK	32717	17614	6.5	17.0	42.9	21.5	12.2	77599	81586	91	93	11327	1.0	2.0	42.3	48.2	6.4	182620
78665	ROUND ROCK	36107	9605	3.9	7.8	43.6	30.5	14.2	91566	100676	95	96	7571	0.2	0.2	27.2	67.2	5.3	211584
78666	SAN MARCOS	19995	22372	33.2	27.7	27.7	7.9	3.5	39836	42195	32	41	8995	16.7	19.6	29.6	30.3	3.9	129749
78669	SPICEWOOD	41000	2836	11.7	19.6	35.2	17.2	16.2	72767	76187	88	91	2365	6.6	6.3	21.5	35.6	30.0	236966
78671	STONEWALL	21471	266	22.2	40.6	26.7	7.5	3.0	43594	46102	44	55	214	8.4	13.1	27.1	21.5	29.9	180357
78672	TOW	18977	620	36.3	39.2	21.3	2.1	1.1	31920	35419	11	14	543	23.9	25.4	33.9	14.5	2.2	92917
78675	WILLOW CITY	23288	65	16.9	35.4	36.9	7.7	3.1	48363	50910	57	67	56	8.9	12.5	17.9	26.8	33.9	233333
78676	WIMBERLEY	31871	5184	14.7	22.9	39.6	15.2	7.6	61220	64333	79	84	3820	5.8	5.3	25.7	48.3	14.9	221107
78677	WRIGHTSBORO	14286	10	40.0	50.0	10.0	0.0	0.0	30000	35000	8	10	8	0.0	0.0	100.0	0.0	0.0	125000
78681	ROUND ROCK	38169	16708	5.6	11.6	30.0	30.4	22.5	104018	107888	97	98	12686	2.9	1.7	17.2	68.7	9.4	243635
78701	AUSTIN	47623	2572	32.5	21.7	18.0	12.8	15.0	45715	48059	50	61	1018	0.0	5.4	18.5	54.9	21.2	256522
78702	AUSTIN	12122	8105	46.0	31.0	18.3	3.6	1.1	27582	28876	5	7	3551	22.3	44.7	29.0	2.8	1.3	73711
78703	AUSTIN	56459	9215	14.5	20.4	27.5	18.2	19.4	71870	77139	88	90	4607	0.2	1.5	7.4	34.5	56.3	441715
78704	AUSTIN	30064	22206	20.4	32.3	32.6	10.2	4.5	47770	48676	56	66	6232	4.3	6.1	33.3	47.8	8.5	197960
78705	AUSTIN	17284	10060	59.5	22.5	11.6	3.9	2.5	19110	19581	1	2	1125	2.7	8.5	31.2	38.0	19.6	216339
78712	AUSTIN	13986	0	0.0	0.0	0.0	0.0	0.0	0	0	0	0	0	0.0	0.0	0.0	0.0	0.0	0
78717	AUSTIN	46812	7615	2.5	7.7	23.8	30.6	35.4	126815	128910	99	99	5430	0.0	0.9	14.3	69.2	15.6	292818
78719	AUSTIN	17337	650	19.7	29.4	40.8	8.8	1.4	51213	53316	64	73	468	13.2	33.8	41.0	11.8	0.2	94118
78721	AUSTIN	13365	4102	38.9	28.4	26.8	4.2	1.7	33914	35276	15	19	2252	21.7	46.4	29.6	2.3	0.0	69875
78722	AUSTIN	27724	2979	24.7	27.9	34.5	9.1	3.8	47337	48367	55	65	1219	5.4	10.3	45.0	38.5	0.9	156500
78723	AUSTIN	18255	11336	25.9	31.3	33.6	7.4	1.8	44271	46250	46	57	4600	2.4	14.5	75.6	7.3	0.3	118369
78724	AUSTIN	14728	4970	21.3	31.9	39.5	5.7	1.6	47462	48568	55	66	3129	24.4	28.8	40.0	4.3	2.5	85000
78725	AUSTIN	22561	1721	8.1	24.4	43.8	18.4	5.3	62492	65086	81	86	1381	6.9	13.8	67.8	7.7	3.9	126139
78726	AUSTIN	57688	4924	3.6	7.5	18.6	25.9	44.4	139511	140090	99	100	3026	1.0	1.5	4.4	64.7	28.4	340991
78727	AUSTIN	39886	12312	6.5	16.2	45.1	22.9	9.3	74633	78632	89	92	6095	0.5	1.0	54.7	41.9	1.8	166440
78728	AUSTIN	36201	9192	9.4	21.1	42.6	19.3	7.6	67396	70589	85	88	3357	2.2	2.2	45.6	49.7	0.3	174946
78729	AUSTIN	37190	11349	7.2	16.2	40.4	24.8	11.4	78990	82643	92	93	5873	2.3	0.7	19.4	76.0	1.5	218555
78730	AUSTIN	80601	3071	3.7	11.0	21.0	17.0	47.3	143549	145280	100	100	2105	0.0	0.5	4.1	15.9	79.5	561367
78731	AUSTIN	54594	13376	13.7	18.2	28.0	19.8	20.3	74942	80270	89	92	7169	0.3	1.5	9.8	46.2	42.2	362932
78732	AUSTIN	64158	4299	0.9	5.0	16.4	26.6	51.0	151279	153587	100	100	3849	0.1	3.8	28.1	47.5	20.5	255452
78733	AUSTIN	51050	2797	6.0	9.8	27.7	23.0	33.4	111299	109591	98	98	2304	2.5	2.9	10.8	44.0	39.9	342752
78734	AUSTIN	40862	6987	7.4	19.4	35.4	21.8	16.0	75443	80355	90	92	5418	4.5	2.9	22.8	44.4	25.2	268732
78735	AUSTIN	58995	6067	12.9	13.4	23.4	25.3	25.1	100653	98366	97	98	3848	2.0	2.3	21.2	53.9	20.6	247991
78736	AUSTIN	34714	2538	9.1	15.7	45.7	19.7	9.9	70478	75178	87	90	1938	3.4	3.1	56.0	30.2	7.3	161404
78737	AUSTIN	42877	3790	8.1	10.4	32.7	24.7	24.0	97225	95759	96	97	3360	2.5	3.7	10.9	55.5	27.4	300132
78738	AUSTIN	58427	3404	5.4	11.2	22.9	24.1	36.3	121591	119128	99	99	2942	0.7	1.7	7.3	39.1	51.2	406757
78739	AUSTIN	56119	4287	1.4	4.4	19.6	29.1	45.6	142469	142747	99	100	3866	1.6	0.0	2.7	78.4	17.4	289764
78741	AUSTIN	16993	20508	39.6	31.7	23.6	3.8	1.2	32723	34173	13	16	2847	26.3	29.9	34.1	9.2	0.5	79124
78742	AUSTIN	17484	366	23.8	46.4	23.0	4.1	2.7	39190	40971	30	39	169	55.6	17.2	15.4	4.1	7.7	42083
78744	AUSTIN	16380	11931	17.9	34.1	39.5	6.5	2.0	48552	48995	58	67	6010	14.7	30.6	50.5	3.3	1.0	94965
78745	AUSTIN	25687	23932	15.3	28.7	39.6	13.0	3.4	56373	57572	73	80	11453	3.3	10.3	76.8	8.9	0.7	126767
78746	AUSTIN	59157	12097	11.3	12.8	23.2	16.2	36.5	106547	105812	97	98	7661	0.7	0.5	2.2	31.4	65.2	497611
78747	AUSTIN	36905	3248	7.1	17.9	39.6	20.4	15.0	73412	77716	89	91	2766	3.2	8.5	27.0	48.7	12.7	228280
78748	AUSTIN	32257	13793	6.6	17.1	44.9	22.8	8.6	73832	79205	89	91	9802	1.8	1.7	49.8	43.7	2.9	170045
78749	AUSTIN	41862	14230	6.0	11.6	36.8	29.3	16.2	91768	92784	95	96	9523	0.9	0.3	30.0	66.7	2.1	208188
78750	AUSTIN	47903	10910	6.3	13.9	29.2	24.7	25.9	100845	102314	97	98	7108	0.6	0.8	15.9	64.1	18.6	266234
78751	AUSTIN	29092	8199	32.7	28.6	26.1	8.5	4.2	40347	42807	34	44	1914	1.0	7.8	32.5	49.7	9.0	201389
78752	AUSTIN	17112	7604	31.4	32.3	29.1	5.8	1.4	38555	41116	28	36	1829	5.7	13.3	71.8	9.1	0.0	121704
78753	AUSTIN	23660	19052	18.5	26.5	39.0	12.5	3.5	55824	58881	72	79	7321	5.0	6.8	70.5	17.2	0.6	136943
78754	AUSTIN	32088	4263	9.3	23.5	45.0	17.0	5.2	65765	71018	84	88	2508	5.1	11.9	51.1	29.6	2.3	146176
78756	AUSTIN	34679	4770	26.2	28.3	28.5	11.6	5.4	45627	47463	50	60	1579	0.0	2.7	24.9	56.7	15.8	239983
78757	AUSTIN	31980	11315	13.7	28.0	39.8	13.8	4.7	59342	60812	77	83	5637	0.3	4.1	47.5	47.1	1.0	171767
78758	AUSTIN	27032	20896	15.7	29.0	39.5	12.2	3.7	55807	57318	72	79	5699	2.8	6.1	74.0	16.5	0.6	136195
78759	AUSTIN	50291	19744	8.5	18.3	35.6	21.0	16.6	76564	80359	90	93	8559	0.7	1.1	19.1	61.6	17.5	262267
78801	UVALDE	14411	7509	39.6	29.2	24.7	4.7	1.8	32157	34103	12	15	5270	36.2	29.4	22.5	10.7	1.2	65218
78827	ASHERTON	11225	529	46.9	32.7	17.6	2.1	0.8	26811	27373	4	6	402	71.6	18.4	7.5	2.2	0.2	28226
78828	BARKSDALE	21808	144	33.3	27.1	30.6	6.9	2.1	40000	45248	33	42	117	29.9	25.6	17.1	17.1	10.3	69444
78829	BATESVILLE	9326	411	55.2	27.7	13.1	3.9	0.0	22603	22928	2	3	320	69.4	11.6	19.1	0.0	0.0	26600
78830	BIG WELLS	8620	289	66.1	27.7	4.8	0.7	0.7	18568	18836	1	1	234	85.0	9.4	4.3	0.4	0.9	26000
78832	BRACKETTVILLE	18384	1287	35.7	31.3	25.6	4.3	3.2	35566	36991	19	25	985	44.5	26.0	21.2	6.9	1.4	55737
78833	CAMP WOOD	14501	521	43.2	32.4	20.7	2.9	0.8	28999	29454	7	8	398	39.9	23.1	23.1	8.8	5.0	63600
78834	CARRIZO SPRINGS	12221	2477	44.5	28.5	24.4	2.4	0.3	29485	31570	7	9	1753	56.4	25.7	15.2	2.1	0.6	44765
78837	COMSTOCK	16614	268	38.4	36.2	22.8	1.9	0.7	29167	30738	7	9	213	39.0	29.1	21.1	7.5	3.3	66071
	TEXAS	24551		22.3	25.0	34.3	11.1	7.3	52382	54495				16.5	22.7	36.5	19.7	4.6	109784
	UNITED STATES	27277		20.9	24.4	35.3	11.7	7.6	54719	56938				9.3	13.1	31.6	32.6	13.5	162279

ZIP CODE #	POST OFFICE NAME	FINANCIAL SERVICES: Auto Loan	Home Loan	Investments	Retirement Plans	THE HOME: Home Improvements: Home Repair	Lawn & Garden	Furnishings: Computers & Hardware-Personal	Major Appliances	TV, Radio, Sound Equipment	Furniture	ENTERTAINMENT: Dine out/ Carry out	Sports Equipment	Fees & Tickets	Toys & Games	Travel	Cable TV	PERSONAL: Apparel & Services	Auto Repairs	Health Insurance	Pets & Supplies
78621	ELGIN	96	92	80	88	89	93	88	91	90	90	90	67	85	93	85	92	62	90	93	107
78623	FISCHER	114	103	100	100	102	109	98	106	102	101	102	77	92	105	95	105	69	102	106	126
78624	FREDERICKSBURG	90	76	107	76	82	97	76	92	80	72	79	67	69	77	80	85	53	86	94	107
78626	GEORGETOWN	110	110	93	107	104	99	107	104	104	111	106	81	105	109	103	102	74	104	99	121
78628	GEORGETOWN	138	150	154	151	153	148	137	144	136	146	136	105	146	135	146	135	95	139	143	166
78629	GONZALES	79	60	74	56	61	76	62	74	67	60	66	54	51	67	59	72	44	70	76	86
78631	HARPER	101	85	133	84	94	110	83	105	87	81	86	75	75	82	91	93	58	97	105	121
78632	HARWOOD	85	61	87	59	63	86	62	79	69	58	68	60	50	69	62	76	45	73	83	94
78633	GEORGETOWN	156	168	195	166	181	176	149	167	151	167	150	114	162	145	164	153	104	158	172	189
78634	HUTTO	134	148	122	146	140	129	131	132	125	139	127	105	136	133	132	120	89	125	119	152
78635	HYE	104	84	135	82	92	110	84	106	87	78	86	78	72	83	91	93	57	98	105	123
78636	JOHNSON CITY	94	80	102	79	84	95	78	92	82	77	81	67	71	81	80	86	55	87	91	108
78638	KINGSBURY	103	84	98	82	85	104	84	98	89	80	88	74	73	90	82	96	59	92	101	116
78639	KINGSLAND	73	72	93	67	80	85	67	80	71	73	69	52	68	65	75	75	47	76	88	91
78640	KYLE	110	112	93	105	106	96	105	104	101	113	103	80	103	106	102	97	72	102	94	119
78641	LEANDER	137	145	120	140	137	124	130	130	124	140	126	102	131	133	127	119	88	124	116	149
78642	LIBERTY HILL	116	113	100	111	110	113	105	110	106	108	107	82	103	111	103	108	73	106	109	130
78643	LLANO	90	74	100	73	79	96	76	90	81	74	79	65	68	78	78	87	53	85	95	105
78644	LOCKHART	82	75	66	72	72	75	75	76	77	76	77	56	71	79	71	78	53	76	77	90
78645	LEANDER	109	108	123	108	113	121	103	114	107	104	106	81	104	103	109	111	73	110	122	132
78648	LULING	79	58	71	56	58	77	62	73	68	59	67	54	51	69	58	74	45	70	77	86
78650	MC DADE	98	75	96	72	76	98	75	91	82	72	81	68	63	82	73	89	54	85	94	108
78652	MANCHACA	145	170	148	173	165	161	148	153	144	151	146	120	162	149	158	143	103	147	148	179
78653	MANOR	118	119	102	115	114	112	109	112	108	114	109	85	108	113	107	108	75	108	107	131
78654	MARBLE FALLS	91	78	92	78	81	93	79	88	84	78	83	64	73	82	79	88	56	86	93	104
78655	MARTINDALE	85	79	69	76	77	79	75	79	77	78	78	58	71	81	71	79	53	77	78	93
78656	MAXWELL	88	82	70	78	78	79	80	80	81	83	81	61	75	84	75	81	56	80	79	96
78657	HORSESHOE BAY	118	119	143	117	130	134	109	124	114	120	113	82	114	108	118	119	77	119	134	143
78659	PAIGE	97	87	79	85	86	91	83	89	87	86	86	65	78	90	79	89	59	86	89	106
78660	PFLUGERVILLE	148	162	133	158	153	134	143	142	134	155	137	113	148	145	141	127	97	134	123	162
78662	RED ROCK	100	92	81	89	89	93	87	92	90	91	90	67	83	94	83	92	62	89	92	109
78663	ROUND MOUNTAIN	116	93	149	91	102	122	93	118	97	87	96	86	80	92	100	103	64	109	116	136
78664	ROUND ROCK	145	146	122	145	138	123	142	134	134	150	137	109	141	143	135	127	97	133	120	155
78665	ROUND ROCK	163	170	142	169	160	141	159	152	150	170	153	124	161	161	154	141	108	148	134	175
78666	SAN MARCOS	78	61	56	63	58	61	87	67	80	76	81	58	71	81	69	78	57	76	68	83
78669	SPICEWOOD	140	154	179	157	161	160	137	152	134	141	135	113	146	132	152	135	95	143	146	175
78671	STONEWALL	92	74	120	73	81	98	74	94	78	69	77	69	64	74	80	83	51	87	93	109
78672	TOW	57	54	69	50	60	64	51	61	54	55	53	40	51	50	56	57	35	58	67	69
78675	WILLOW CITY	113	78	125	78	82	120	87	108	90	70	89	89	63	88	86	98	58	100	114	132
78676	WIMBERLEY	117	108	148	108	116	129	102	123	105	101	105	89	99	101	112	110	71	115	123	142
78677	WRIGHTSBORO	54	37	59	37	39	57	41	51	43	33	42	42	30	42	41	46	27	48	54	63
78681	ROUND ROCK	171	191	164	192	184	162	170	168	160	184	164	136	181	171	173	151	117	161	148	192
78701	AUSTIN	116	92	96	101	91	95	131	102	127	119	130	88	116	125	113	126	92	120	113	128
78702	AUSTIN	56	44	38	41	42	45	50	49	55	51	54	34	45	54	44	57	38	52	53	57
78703	AUSTIN	142	147	168	159	155	135	163	144	152	163	155	121	168	150	165	145	114	152	135	170
78704	AUSTIN	90	69	66	74	66	66	93	75	91	90	93	65	83	92	81	88	65	87	77	94
78705	AUSTIN	50	25	25	30	23	27	67	36	55	48	56	38	43	54	40	51	40	49	37	49
78712	AUSTIN	0	0	0	0	0	0	0	0	0	0	0	0	0	0	0	0	0	0	0	0
78717	AUSTIN	203	247	215	254	241	203	205	208	190	230	193	173	233	205	217	174	142	190	171	232
78719	AUSTIN	85	85	73	75	84	70	84	83	79	91	81	62	80	81	81	75	57	83	72	91
78721	AUSTIN	64	55	46	54	52	57	58	57	63	61	63	40	55	63	54	66	44	61	63	69
78722	AUSTIN	84	67	67	72	66	69	91	75	89	83	89	63	80	88	78	88	63	84	79	92
78723	AUSTIN	77	63	54	65	59	63	78	68	78	75	79	55	71	79	69	78	55	76	71	83
78724	AUSTIN	81	79	68	72	77	69	78	77	76	84	77	58	75	78	75	73	54	78	71	88
78725	AUSTIN	116	121	100	116	113	107	110	110	108	117	110	82	110	113	107	106	76	107	104	129
78726	AUSTIN	238	289	250	297	281	237	240	243	221	270	225	202	272	239	253	202	166	222	198	271
78727	AUSTIN	135	120	104	125	113	107	132	117	128	135	131	97	125	134	121	123	92	125	111	141
78728	AUSTIN	125	99	85	105	91	89	121	101	118	122	120	87	109	124	105	113	84	113	97	124
78729	AUSTIN	144	133	112	135	124	116	140	127	135	145	138	104	134	143	129	129	96	132	118	151
78730	AUSTIN	252	331	336	347	341	294	271	282	253	296	256	223	325	260	306	240	192	261	243	317
78731	AUSTIN	149	148	160	158	154	140	161	146	153	164	155	119	165	153	161	148	112	153	141	173
78732	AUSTIN	268	325	280	335	316	266	270	273	249	303	253	228	306	270	284	228	186	249	223	305
78733	AUSTIN	215	267	238	271	261	227	223	227	207	242	211	183	254	219	239	195	154	211	195	256
78734	AUSTIN	143	162	157	164	163	153	144	149	140	152	141	112	155	142	153	138	100	143	142	172
78735	AUSTIN	187	202	200	209	204	174	198	187	183	210	185	154	206	187	202	171	134	186	164	216
78736	AUSTIN	136	144	121	141	137	129	130	132	127	138	129	100	133	133	129	124	89	127	123	153
78737	AUSTIN	160	202	199	208	205	184	169	177	161	181	163	136	196	163	189	156	118	167	161	202
78738	AUSTIN	204	264	280	272	278	238	222	233	206	245	207	178	261	207	252	196	153	216	207	260
78739	AUSTIN	252	307	268	316	300	254	255	259	236	286	240	214	290	254	270	217	176	237	214	290
78741	AUSTIN	65	37	32	41	34	37	68	47	64	60	65	42	50	65	48	61	45	59	48	60
78742	AUSTIN	77	72	61	68	68	69	71	71	71	74	72	54	67	74	67	71	49	71	69	84
78744	AUSTIN	85	76	65	71	74	66	83	77	79	87	81	60	76	82	76	76	57	81	70	88
78745	AUSTIN	97	87	76	87	82	80	95	87	93	96	95	69	89	96	87	91	66	92	85	104
78746	AUSTIN	197	229	253	243	242	211	216	209	203	228	205	167	244	204	232	194	153	207	190	240
78747	AUSTIN	148	160	157	156	161	155	142	152	142	154	142	110	150	143	149	141	99	144	150	173
78748	AUSTIN	130	135	117	132	128	120	126	125	121	132	123	97	126	127	124	118	86	122	115	145
78749	AUSTIN	158	160	138	164	153	137	156	147	149	166	152	121	158	158	150	140	108	146	131	171
78750	AUSTIN	173	198	186	203	196	176	177	176	169	189	171	140	194	175	185	161	124	170	159	203
78751	AUSTIN	77	57	57	63	55	58	87	65	82	77	83	58	73	82	70	80	59	77	68	82
78752	AUSTIN	68	47	44	50	45	45	74	56	70	68	72	49	60	71	59	67	51	68	56	69
78753	AUSTIN	97	79	69	81	74	72	96	82	94	96	96	68	87	97	84	91	67	92	81	100
78754	AUSTIN	114	107	94	107	102	98	112	103	109	115	111	83	108	114	105	107	77	108	100	123
78756	AUSTIN	87	70	69	76	68	70	91	76	91	88	92	63	84	90	81	91	65	87	83	95
78757	AUSTIN	95	91	86	93	89	88	99	91	98	98	100	72	98	98	95	98	70	97	94	109
78758	AUSTIN	99	73	64	78	68	68	97	79	96	96	98	67	85	99	82	92	68	91	79	98
78759	AUSTIN	149	137	126	145	131	125	152	134	147	153	150	112	148	152	142	142	106	143	129	162
78801	UVALDE	70	60	56	54	59	60	60	65	62	63	63	45	53	63	56	64	43	64	63	73
78827	ASHERTON	57	46	34	38	44	43	46	49	50	51	50	30	40	50	41	51	35	50	48	54
78828	BARKSDALE	73	69	89	64	77	83	66	78	70	71	68	51	65	64	72	74	46	75	86	89
78829	BATESVILLE	53	42	32	35	40	40	42	45	46	47	46	28	37	46	38	47	32	46	44	50
78830	BIG WELLS	40	32	24	27	31	30	32	34	35	36	35	21	28	35	29	36	24	35	33	38
78832	BRACKETTVILLE	74	63	74	58	67	75	63	73	68	66	66	49	57	65	64	72	45	71	79	83
78833	CAMP WOOD	65	47	72	45	49	66	49	61	53	46	52	46	39	53	49	58	35	57	63	73
78834	CARRIZO SPRINGS	58	51	41	45	49	47	51	52	52	55	53	36	46	54	47	53	37	53	50	59
78837	COMSTOCK	69	49	70	48	51	70	50	64	56	47	55	48	40	56	50	61	36	59	67	76
	TEXAS	104	96	90	94	93	94	99	97	99	101	100	75	94	101	94	99	70	99	96	114
	UNITED STATES	100	100	100	100	100	100	100	100	100	100	100	100	100	100	100	100	100	100	100	100

ZIP CODE #	POST OFFICE NAME	COUNTY FIPS CODE	POPULATION 2000	POPULATION 2009	POPULATION 2014	2000-2009 ANNUAL RATE % Rate	2000-2009 ANNUAL RATE State Centile	HOUSEHOLDS 2000	HOUSEHOLDS 2009	HOUSEHOLDS 2014	HOUSEHOLDS % Annual Rate 2000-2009	HOUSEHOLDS 2009 Average HH Size	FAMILIES 2000	FAMILIES 2009	FAMILIES % Annual Rate 2000-2009
78838	CONCAN	463	132	138	141	0.5	42	50	53	54	0.6	2.55	36	38	0.6
78839	CRYSTAL CITY	507	8474	8765	8910	0.4	37	2487	2643	2714	0.7	3.18	2032	2138	0.6
78840	DEL RIO	465	44247	47804	49567	0.8	52	13895	15167	15785	1.0	3.10	11139	12033	0.8
78843	LAUGHLIN A F B	465	44	43	42	-0.2	19	15	15	15	0.0	2.87	12	12	0.0
78850	D HANIS	325	1024	1225	1335	2.0	78	353	424	462	2.0	2.89	277	328	1.8
78851	DRYDEN	443	1084	982	930	-1.1	3	444	416	399	-0.7	2.36	296	272	-0.9
78852	EAGLE PASS	323	46100	52502	55124	1.4	67	12700	14562	15334	1.5	3.60	10927	12436	1.4
78861	HONDO	325	11764	12482	12887	0.6	46	3665	3900	4051	0.7	2.80	2822	2965	0.5
78870	KNIPPA	463	786	834	856	0.6	46	267	285	294	0.7	2.93	198	208	0.5
78872	LA PRYOR	507	1729	1728	1720	0.0	25	540	555	557	0.3	3.11	431	439	0.2
78873	LEAKEY	385	1390	1423	1454	0.3	34	607	644	663	0.6	2.19	413	431	0.5
78877	QUEMADO	323	1197	1253	1271	0.5	42	389	416	424	0.7	3.01	304	319	0.5
78879	RIO FRIO	385	353	365	374	0.4	37	154	166	172	0.8	2.17	109	116	0.7
78880	ROCKSPRINGS	137	1809	1635	1548	-1.1	3	647	596	568	-0.9	2.70	476	432	-1.0
78881	SABINAL	463	2202	2263	2266	0.3	34	807	839	843	0.4	2.68	602	619	0.3
78883	TARPLEY	019	153	182	200	1.9	76	68	80	88	1.8	2.28	49	57	1.6
78884	UTOPIA	463	745	777	793	0.5	42	315	333	341	0.6	2.29	227	236	0.4
78885	VANDERPOOL	019	297	359	396	2.1	79	135	162	178	2.0	2.21	96	113	1.8
78886	YANCEY	325	518	598	644	1.6	71	177	206	222	1.7	2.86	138	159	1.5
78931	BLEIBLERVILLE	015	346	393	420	1.4	67	148	166	177	1.2	2.37	108	119	1.1
78932	CARMINE	149	436	453	466	0.4	37	181	188	193	0.4	2.39	122	124	0.2
78933	CAT SPRING	089	1306	1662	1812	2.6	83	524	670	731	2.7	2.48	396	498	2.5
78934	COLUMBUS	089	6249	6631	6794	0.6	46	2387	2505	2569	0.5	2.41	1621	1671	0.3
78935	ALLEYTON	089	402	477	504	1.9	76	158	187	199	1.8	2.45	119	138	1.6
78938	ELLINGER	149	190	213	224	1.2	63	90	101	106	1.3	2.11	61	68	1.2
78940	FAYETTEVILLE	149	2028	2208	2294	0.9	55	835	906	942	0.9	2.43	585	625	0.7
78941	FLATONIA	149	2475	2559	2623	0.4	37	954	984	1010	0.3	2.54	669	680	0.2
78942	GIDDINGS	287	8236	8933	9237	0.9	55	2763	2953	3051	0.7	2.79	1998	2104	0.6
78944	INDUSTRY	015	525	622	682	1.8	75	205	242	264	1.8	2.57	151	176	1.7
78945	LA GRANGE	149	9949	10704	11083	0.8	52	3941	4203	4346	0.7	2.49	2778	2919	0.5
78946	LEDBETTER	287	964	1059	1109	1.0	58	406	444	465	1.0	2.39	283	305	0.8
78947	LEXINGTON	287	3832	4138	4291	0.8	52	1488	1600	1656	0.8	2.59	1116	1184	0.6
78948	LINCOLN	287	1458	1560	1616	0.7	49	566	601	621	0.7	2.60	411	430	0.5
78949	MULDOON	149	375	396	409	0.6	46	152	159	164	0.5	2.49	109	113	0.4
78950	NEW ULM	015	1870	2446	2701	2.9	86	764	991	1092	2.9	2.47	571	728	2.7
78953	ROSANKY	021	735	956	1060	2.9	86	314	397	439	2.6	2.41	233	290	2.4
78954	ROUND TOP	149	1030	1096	1134	0.7	49	464	492	510	0.6	2.21	309	321	0.4
78956	SCHULENBURG	149	5055	5274	5426	0.5	42	2009	2099	2162	0.5	2.39	1358	1395	0.3
78957	SMITHVILLE	021	8444	10247	11176	2.1	79	3230	3841	4182	1.9	2.63	2247	2632	1.7
78959	WAELDER	177	1466	1597	1640	0.9	55	554	595	609	0.8	2.68	382	403	0.6
78962	WEIMAR	089	5468	5576	5635	0.2	30	2004	2023	2045	0.1	2.63	1415	1407	-0.1
78963	WEST POINT	149	642	788	851	2.2	80	235	287	310	2.2	2.74	175	211	2.0
79001	ADRIAN	359	257	257	255	0.0	25	106	108	108	0.2	2.29	82	83	0.1
79005	BOOKER	295	1507	1572	1598	0.5	42	522	546	556	0.5	2.78	389	401	0.3
79007	BORGER	233	15857	15264	14943	-0.4	13	6123	5922	5818	-0.4	2.53	4445	4241	-0.5
79009	BOVINA	369	2998	2771	2657	-0.8	6	952	874	839	-0.9	3.17	791	720	-1.0
79011	BRISCOE	483	425	387	375	-1.0	4	165	151	147	-1.0	2.56	123	111	-1.1
79014	CANADIAN	211	3351	3404	3436	0.2	30	1280	1341	1368	0.5	2.43	948	980	0.4
79015	CANYON	381	17197	18648	19492	0.9	55	6452	7062	7420	1.0	2.47	4240	4609	0.9
79016	CANYON	381	213	207	210	-0.3	16	1	1	1	0.0	3.00	0	0	0.0
79018	CHANNING	205	651	634	630	-0.3	16	237	232	231	-0.2	2.73	189	183	-0.3
79019	CLAUDE	011	2015	2051	2060	0.2	30	748	754	756	0.1	2.63	572	571	0.0
79022	DALHART	111	8054	8013	8056	-0.1	21	3071	3018	3023	-0.2	2.62	2178	2109	-0.3
79027	DIMMITT	069	6363	5755	5403	-1.1	3	2147	1969	1856	-0.9	2.89	1661	1506	-1.1
79029	DUMAS	341	17839	17897	17814	0.0	25	5962	5929	5885	-0.1	2.99	4696	4619	-0.2
79031	EARTH	279	1453	1351	1301	-0.8	6	521	486	468	-0.7	2.78	395	364	-0.9
79034	FOLLETT	295	880	892	900	0.1	27	382	389	394	0.2	2.29	262	263	0.0
79035	FRIONA	369	4755	4811	4759	0.1	27	1574	1602	1587	0.2	2.96	1232	1241	0.1
79036	FRITCH	233	5147	4785	4635	-0.8	6	2041	1922	1869	-0.6	2.47	1576	1466	-0.8
79039	GROOM	065	817	799	779	-0.2	19	322	318	312	-0.1	2.51	245	239	-0.3
79040	GRUVER	195	1861	1754	1727	-0.6	9	677	645	638	-0.5	2.72	529	499	-0.6
79041	HALE CENTER	189	3241	3092	2995	-0.5	11	1142	1093	1060	-0.5	2.78	855	807	-0.6
79042	HAPPY	437	846	797	779	-0.6	9	347	329	323	-0.6	2.42	241	225	-0.7
79043	HART	069	1354	1145	1049	-1.8	0	420	362	334	-1.6	3.16	345	295	-1.7
79044	HARTLEY	205	2291	2255	2244	-0.2	19	334	325	323	-0.3	2.86	273	263	-0.4
79045	HEREFORD	117	18468	18693	18818	0.1	27	6147	6281	6345	0.2	2.94	4808	4858	0.1
79046	HIGGINS	295	626	649	663	0.4	37	276	288	294	0.5	2.25	178	183	0.3
79052	KRESS	437	1545	1436	1398	-0.8	6	543	507	495	-0.7	2.83	431	398	-0.9
79056	LIPSCOMB	295	44	46	47	0.5	42	25	26	27	0.4	1.77	16	17	0.7
79057	MCLEAN	179	1122	1046	1046	-0.8	6	456	427	428	-0.7	2.21	280	256	-1.0
79058	MASTERSON	375	185	205	211	1.1	61	76	83	85	1.0	2.47	61	66	0.9
79059	MIAMI	393	887	879	880	-0.1	21	362	367	370	0.1	2.40	275	275	0.0
79061	MOBEETIE	483	320	287	278	-1.2	3	138	125	121	-1.1	2.30	100	89	-1.3
79062	MORSE	195	177	165	162	-0.8	6	64	60	60	-0.7	2.75	48	45	-0.7
79063	NAZARETH	069	460	391	359	-1.7	1	159	137	127	-1.6	2.85	125	107	-1.7
79064	OLTON	279	2903	2774	2691	-0.5	11	973	926	897	-0.5	2.91	760	714	-0.7
79065	PAMPA	179	21631	21070	21409	-0.3	16	8342	8206	8385	-0.2	2.37	5776	5591	-0.4
79068	PANHANDLE	065	3786	3769	3716	0.0	25	1395	1404	1389	0.1	2.62	1069	1063	-0.1
79070	PERRYTON	357	9006	9656	10017	0.8	52	3261	3477	3604	0.7	2.76	2487	2619	0.6
79072	PLAINVIEW	189	28971	28073	27377	-0.3	16	9303	8998	8762	-0.4	2.86	7042	6724	-0.5
79079	SHAMROCK	483	2579	2388	2329	-0.8	6	1098	1022	999	-0.8	2.30	727	665	-1.0
79080	SKELLYTOWN	065	682	661	643	-0.3	16	264	259	253	-0.2	2.55	208	202	-0.3
79081	SPEARMAN	195	3331	3362	3374	0.1	27	1264	1287	1295	0.2	2.55	912	916	0.0
79082	SPRINGLAKE	279	338	311	298	-0.9	5	137	126	121	-0.9	2.47	112	102	-1.0
79083	STINNETT	233	2853	2545	2437	-1.2	3	1119	1009	970	-1.1	2.48	848	754	-1.3
79084	STRATFORD	421	2815	2870	2854	0.2	30	986	990	979	0.0	2.83	751	744	-0.1
79085	SUMMERFIELD	069	108	91	84	-1.8	0	35	30	27	-1.7	3.03	28	24	-1.7
79086	SUNRAY	341	2136	2030	1988	-0.5	11	752	708	691	-0.6	2.87	584	543	-0.8
79087	TEXLINE	111	763	754	756	-0.1	21	279	269	268	-0.4	2.80	210	200	-0.5
79088	TULIA	437	5987	5731	5638	-0.5	11	2035	1930	1896	-0.6	2.62	1482	1387	-0.7
79092	VEGA	359	1636	1643	1640	0.0	25	526	539	541	0.3	2.58	404	408	0.1
79094	WAYSIDE	011	116	119	120	0.3	34	48	49	49	0.2	2.20	36	36	0.0
79095	WELLINGTON	087	2996	2892	2880	-0.4	13	1204	1153	1146	-0.5	2.46	846	798	-0.6
79096	WHEELER	483	1960	1794	1747	-1.0	4	751	695	677	-0.8	2.48	536	489	-1.0
79097	WHITE DEER	065	1220	1193	1164	-0.2	19	483	479	469	-0.1	2.49	358	350	-0.2
	TEXAS					1.9					1.8	2.78			1.7
	UNITED STATES					1.0					1.1	2.59			0.9

ZIP CODE #	POST OFFICE NAME	RACE (%) White 2000	White 2009	Black 2000	Black 2009	Asian/Pacific 2000	Asian/Pacific 2009	% Hispanic Origin 2000	% Hispanic Origin 2009	2009 AGE DISTRIBUTION (%) 0-4	5-9	10-14	15-19	20-24	25-44	45-64	65-84	85+	18+	MEDIAN AGE 2009	% 2009 Males	% 2009 Females
78838	CONCAN	90.9	87.7	0.0	0.0	0.0	0.0	19.7	28.3	4.3	4.3	5.8	6.5	3.6	18.8	31.9	21.7	2.9	81.2	49.1	51.4	48.6
78839	CRYSTAL CITY	69.1	67.6	0.6	0.6	0.2	0.1	93.3	93.0	9.0	8.9	8.5	9.0	7.6	23.2	21.4	10.7	1.8	68.3	29.9	49.7	50.3
78840	DEL RIO	76.2	74.6	1.6	1.4	0.6	0.6	76.0	81.7	9.2	8.5	8.0	8.1	7.6	25.7	21.4	10.2	1.3	69.2	31.1	49.4	50.6
78843	LAUGHLIN A F B	95.3	90.7	2.3	2.3	0.0	2.3	4.7	9.3	20.9	9.3	4.7	0.0	14.0	51.2	0.0	0.0	0.0	65.1	25.3	51.2	48.8
78850	D HANIS	86.8	83.5	0.3	0.3	0.4	0.4	37.3	47.6	6.2	6.4	6.7	6.6	4.7	21.2	30.0	16.1	2.1	76.6	43.6	50.6	49.4
78851	DRYDEN	88.4	86.3	0.0	0.0	0.6	0.8	48.5	56.8	5.7	6.2	6.3	6.9	6.3	19.0	29.7	17.6	2.1	77.8	44.5	49.7	50.3
78852	EAGLE PASS	70.9	70.3	0.3	0.3	0.4	0.4	95.5	95.8	10.1	9.6	9.1	9.4	7.3	23.9	20.4	8.8	1.2	65.3	28.3	48.3	51.7
78861	HONDO	78.3	75.6	5.7	5.7	0.3	0.3	49.3	57.5	6.7	6.7	6.6	6.6	8.1	29.0	22.9	11.2	2.2	75.7	34.4	54.6	45.4
78870	KNIPPA	76.6	71.0	0.3	0.2	0.3	0.4	46.8	59.0	6.7	7.0	7.3	8.4	5.3	24.9	27.5	11.8	1.2	73.9	36.7	51.0	49.0
78872	LA PRYOR	55.0	53.6	0.1	0.1	0.1	0.1	84.1	83.6	9.6	9.3	9.2	9.7	6.7	25.5	20.2	8.7	1.2	65.6	29.2	48.4	51.6
78873	LEAKEY	92.8	92.4	0.1	0.1	0.2	0.2	16.0	17.5	4.6	4.6	5.0	5.8	4.5	19.0	32.0	21.6	2.7	82.1	49.3	48.3	51.7
78877	QUEMADO	70.0	68.8	0.5	0.5	0.0	0.1	76.0	77.1	7.3	8.1	7.2	8.1	5.7	20.9	27.8	13.5	1.4	72.2	38.7	51.3	48.7
78879	RIO FRIO	91.5	91.2	0.0	0.0	0.3	0.3	15.0	16.4	3.8	4.1	4.4	5.5	3.8	17.8	34.5	23.3	2.7	84.4	51.9	49.6	50.4
78880	ROCKSPRINGS	81.1	77.4	0.9	1.0	0.2	0.2	52.3	62.4	6.8	6.7	7.2	8.3	7.0	21.1	27.3	14.0	1.5	73.8	38.2	50.9	49.1
78881	SABINAL	82.5	78.9	0.0	0.0	0.1	0.1	53.0	63.3	6.8	6.7	7.0	7.8	5.9	22.9	26.6	14.2	2.0	74.4	39.6	50.2	49.8
78883	TARPLEY	96.1	95.1	0.0	0.0	0.0	0.0	7.8	11.0	5.5	5.5	6.0	4.9	4.4	17.6	35.2	18.7	2.2	80.2	48.9	48.9	51.1
78884	UTOPIA	91.7	88.2	0.0	0.0	0.1	0.3	17.9	26.3	4.4	4.6	5.5	6.6	3.6	18.5	33.2	21.0	2.6	81.5	49.5	52.0	48.0
78885	VANDERPOOL	95.9	94.7	0.0	0.0	0.3	0.3	8.1	11.1	4.5	4.7	5.0	4.7	3.9	15.0	35.7	24.0	2.5	82.7	52.4	51.0	49.0
78886	YANCEY	85.5	81.4	0.8	0.8	0.8	1.0	32.5	42.1	5.9	5.9	6.2	6.9	5.2	22.2	30.1	14.7	3.0	76.6	43.5	46.8	53.2
78931	BLEIBLERVILLE	93.4	91.9	2.9	3.3	0.0	0.0	5.2	7.6	5.6	5.9	6.1	5.9	4.3	22.4	32.1	15.0	2.8	78.6	44.9	49.4	50.6
78932	CARMINE	91.5	89.2	5.3	6.2	0.0	0.0	4.6	6.8	4.2	4.6	5.1	5.7	4.4	18.1	34.7	19.6	3.5	82.3	50.3	49.2	50.8
78933	CAT SPRING	86.5	83.5	7.4	7.8	0.2	0.2	10.0	14.5	6.0	6.3	7.0	7.2	4.1	22.5	31.1	14.1	1.7	76.0	42.7	50.2	49.8
78934	COLUMBUS	73.3	67.6	14.7	16.0	0.3	0.4	15.7	21.8	5.6	6.1	6.0	8.1	6.7	21.7	25.2	16.2	4.4	78.0	41.4	48.4	51.6
78935	ALLEYTON	87.1	83.9	4.5	4.8	0.2	0.2	9.9	14.0	4.8	5.5	6.9	9.9	4.4	20.8	31.9	14.5	1.5	77.1	43.4	50.1	49.9
78938	ELLINGER	93.7	91.5	1.6	1.4	0.0	0.5	6.3	9.4	4.7	5.2	5.6	5.6	5.2	21.1	33.3	16.4	2.8	81.2	46.4	49.8	50.2
78940	FAYETTEVILLE	92.5	90.0	3.2	3.8	0.3	0.5	5.0	7.6	4.9	5.3	5.7	6.2	4.6	21.1	31.6	17.4	3.2	80.5	46.4	50.3	49.7
78941	FLATONIA	80.3	76.3	5.5	5.6	0.2	0.2	26.5	33.7	6.3	6.6	6.7	6.6	4.8	21.3	29.2	15.0	3.5	76.3	43.2	50.4	49.6
78942	GIDDINGS	72.0	67.2	11.3	11.5	0.4	0.6	26.6	34.1	7.9	7.6	7.1	11.1	6.6	24.6	22.0	10.3	2.7	70.8	32.0	51.5	48.5
78944	INDUSTRY	89.0	86.2	6.3	7.6	0.2	0.3	7.4	10.8	5.8	6.1	6.6	6.4	4.0	22.8	30.9	14.6	2.7	77.3	43.6	51.3	48.7
78945	LA GRANGE	82.9	78.9	7.7	8.4	0.4	0.5	13.0	17.7	5.9	6.0	6.2	6.2	5.2	22.2	29.1	15.2	3.8	78.0	43.5	48.7	51.3
78946	LEDBETTER	72.9	68.9	20.0	21.4	0.2	0.3	9.5	13.3	5.9	5.9	6.1	6.9	5.7	21.9	28.9	16.2	2.5	78.1	43.2	49.3	50.7
78947	LEXINGTON	89.5	86.5	5.1	5.8	0.1	0.2	8.2	11.9	6.6	6.8	6.8	6.5	5.7	23.7	30.4	11.9	1.5	75.7	40.0	49.5	50.5
78948	LINCOLN	79.1	76.1	18.2	20.1	0.0	0.0	6.3	9.1	6.0	6.3	6.5	6.5	5.1	22.6	30.0	15.0	1.9	77.2	42.7	48.7	51.3
78949	MULDOON	89.0	85.4	2.9	3.3	0.3	0.3	12.8	17.9	5.1	5.6	6.1	6.6	4.8	18.4	33.3	17.4	2.8	79.0	47.2	50.5	49.5
78950	NEW ULM	90.7	87.9	4.6	5.5	0.2	0.2	6.3	9.4	5.1	5.5	6.1	6.3	4.1	21.1	33.0	16.3	2.3	79.2	46.0	51.0	49.0
78953	ROSANKY	87.2	82.8	6.3	7.7	0.3	0.5	10.1	14.9	6.4	6.6	6.9	6.5	4.9	23.7	31.2	12.4	1.4	76.0	41.6	50.3	49.7
78954	ROUND TOP	92.7	90.5	3.8	4.5	0.2	0.2	4.9	7.3	4.3	4.7	5.1	5.7	4.5	18.7	34.1	19.3	3.6	82.4	49.7	49.3	50.7
78956	SCHULENBURG	84.1	80.7	9.3	10.2	0.2	0.3	10.8	15.1	5.3	5.7	6.0	6.1	4.6	19.8	29.3	17.1	6.0	79.2	46.7	48.1	51.9
78957	SMITHVILLE	84.0	81.1	9.2	9.7	0.3	0.4	12.9	17.9	6.7	6.7	6.9	7.0	5.3	23.4	28.7	12.9	2.4	75.3	40.7	49.1	50.9
78959	WAELDER	57.6	54.8	18.3	17.1	0.2	0.2	49.3	57.7	6.6	7.1	7.0	6.8	5.6	23.0	28.7	13.3	2.1	75.3	40.1	50.0	50.0
78962	WEIMAR	78.4	73.0	12.1	13.4	0.4	0.5	14.2	20.6	5.5	5.8	6.0	8.0	6.6	19.5	29.4	16.0	3.2	78.5	43.8	48.7	51.3
78963	WEST POINT	87.1	83.6	6.2	6.9	0.0	0.1	12.5	17.5	5.6	5.8	6.1	6.5	4.9	22.6	32.9	13.5	2.2	78.7	43.8	50.0	50.0
79001	ADRIAN	86.8	86.4	1.6	1.6	0.8	0.8	14.3	16.0	7.4	7.8	8.6	6.2	3.9	24.1	29.2	12.1	0.8	71.6	38.4	49.8	50.2
79005	BOOKER	73.9	66.7	0.5	0.4	0.1	0.1	35.4	45.5	7.6	8.2	8.0	8.0	5.7	24.7	21.7	12.8	3.3	70.9	36.0	48.4	51.6
79007	BORGER	83.3	79.3	3.4	3.7	0.5	0.6	19.2	25.3	7.3	7.2	7.0	7.6	6.4	23.2	26.0	12.7	2.5	74.1	36.8	48.7	51.3
79009	BOVINA	61.5	55.4	1.0	1.2	0.2	0.2	55.1	63.5	9.2	8.9	9.1	9.2	5.4	25.0	21.9	9.8	1.4	67.2	31.5	50.1	49.9
79011	BRISCOE	96.7	95.1	0.0	0.0	0.2	0.5	3.8	5.4	6.2	7.2	7.8	7.0	3.9	22.7	31.3	12.1	1.8	74.2	41.0	50.6	49.4
79014	CANADIAN	87.6	87.0	1.6	1.6	0.3	0.3	15.6	16.8	5.6	6.0	6.5	8.8	4.9	21.6	30.7	13.5	2.6	75.7	42.1	51.2	48.8
79015	CANYON	89.9	87.3	1.5	1.5	1.6	1.9	9.6	13.1	6.6	6.2	6.2	10.1	12.7	24.3	22.8	9.3	1.6	76.9	30.8	49.1	50.9
79016	CANYON	81.1	76.8	4.7	4.8	4.2	5.3	14.2	18.8	4.3	3.4	2.9	22.7	29.0	18.4	12.1	6.3	1.0	87.0	22.9	47.8	52.2
79018	CHANNING	94.0	93.7	0.8	0.8	0.2	0.2	7.4	8.0	7.6	8.0	7.9	7.3	4.9	24.3	28.1	10.9	1.1	71.3	37.6	50.3	49.7
79019	CLAUDE	95.5	95.2	0.3	0.3	0.0	0.0	5.3	5.9	5.7	5.9	6.3	6.5	4.7	22.4	28.7	15.9	3.9	77.9	43.8	49.5	50.5
79022	DALHART	85.8	85.2	1.4	1.4	0.3	0.3	22.2	23.8	8.3	8.0	7.9	7.7	5.9	25.8	23.8	10.6	2.0	70.6	35.2	49.7	50.3
79027	DIMMITT	77.4	72.9	2.2	2.6	0.0	0.0	50.1	59.3	8.6	8.4	8.3	8.3	6.4	22.3	24.5	11.3	1.8	69.2	33.6	50.1	49.9
79029	DUMAS	62.7	61.6	0.7	0.7	1.0	1.0	49.2	51.3	9.7	9.2	8.3	8.1	7.0	26.2	21.3	8.8	1.4	67.7	30.4	50.5	49.5
79031	EARTH	76.6	71.7	2.3	2.4	0.0	0.0	46.2	56.6	7.3	7.6	7.5	9.4	5.0	21.7	25.8	13.9	1.8	71.3	37.3	48.5	51.5
79034	FOLLETT	91.0	87.4	0.6	0.6	0.0	0.0	8.9	13.1	5.7	6.4	6.7	6.6	4.3	17.9	33.0	16.5	2.9	77.2	46.3	49.8	50.2
79035	FRIONA	63.7	57.4	1.2	1.4	0.4	0.4	53.7	62.8	9.1	8.2	8.3	8.4	6.1	24.3	23.3	9.8	2.5	69.1	32.9	49.7	50.3
79036	FRITCH	95.5	94.2	0.4	0.5	0.2	0.3	4.7	7.0	5.5	6.4	7.1	6.6	4.8	22.1	32.3	13.6	1.6	76.8	43.0	49.5	50.5
79039	GROOM	95.5	95.2	0.0	0.0	0.1	0.1	5.8	6.1	5.3	5.8	6.3	7.6	4.1	24.3	28.7	15.8	2.3	78.1	41.9	51.6	48.4
79040	GRUVER	77.4	76.3	0.0	0.0	0.1	0.1	32.5	34.5	6.8	8.2	7.4	7.7	4.9	24.6	27.8	11.1	1.5	72.6	38.0	50.6	49.4
79041	HALE CENTER	80.3	77.1	3.9	3.8	0.0	0.0	50.1	60.2	8.7	8.5	7.9	7.8	6.3	23.3	22.4	12.3	2.7	70.3	34.4	49.2	50.8
79042	HAPPY	89.5	85.2	0.4	0.5	0.0	0.0	16.3	23.5	6.4	6.8	6.8	5.8	4.3	25.7	27.5	14.7	2.1	76.4	40.5	47.9	52.1
79043	HART	60.2	55.1	3.2	3.4	0.1	0.1	70.2	78.3	10.0	10.2	9.4	8.7	6.6	23.8	21.2	9.3	0.8	64.6	28.5	51.0	49.0
79044	HARTLEY	61.2	59.5	19.1	19.6	0.1	0.1	22.9	24.3	3.2	3.4	3.4	2.8	2.7	47.1	31.7	5.4	0.4	88.0	40.7	80.3	19.7
79045	HEREFORD	72.2	68.1	1.5	1.5	0.4	0.4	57.6	66.0	9.1	9.0	8.8	8.3	6.5	23.8	22.1	10.3	2.0	67.9	31.5	49.0	51.0
79046	HIGGINS	92.3	90.3	0.6	0.6	0.0	0.0	3.2	4.9	4.3	5.2	5.7	5.4	3.7	19.6	32.0	20.8	3.2	80.3	49.4	49.9	50.1
79052	KRESS	69.4	62.3	3.2	3.6	0.5	0.7	43.5	53.5	7.2	7.4	7.8	8.4	5.2	23.0	25.8	13.6	1.7	72.0	37.6	51.2	48.8
79056	LIPSCOMB	93.2	89.1	0.0	0.0	0.0	0.0	2.3	4.3	4.3	4.3	4.3	4.3	4.3	17.4	34.8	21.7	4.3	82.6	51.3	52.2	47.8
79057	MCLEAN	96.1	94.6	0.3	0.4	0.2	0.4	3.7	5.4	5.7	5.6	3.8	5.6	3.9	16.7	25.6	24.0	8.9	81.4	52.3	46.5	53.5
79058	MASTERSON	85.9	84.4	0.5	1.0	0.5	0.5	17.3	20.0	6.3	6.3	6.8	6.8	5.9	25.9	29.3	11.7	1.0	75.6	39.0	50.2	49.8
79059	MIAMI	96.5	96.4	0.3	0.3	0.1	0.1	3.2	3.4	5.0	5.3	6.0	6.5	3.9	20.5	36.7	14.2	1.8	79.4	46.3	52.0	48.0
79061	MOBEETIE	95.0	93.0	0.0	0.0	0.3	0.3	8.8	12.5	3.5	4.9	5.6	7.0	3.8	17.4	34.5	21.3	2.1	81.2	48.9	49.8	50.2
79062	MORSE	90.3	89.7	0.0	0.0	1.1	1.2	23.9	24.8	5.5	6.1	6.1	7.3	4.8	21.2	31.5	15.2	2.4	77.6	44.1	52.1	47.9
79063	NAZARETH	91.1	87.2	0.4	0.5	0.0	0.0	17.6	26.1	5.9	7.4	8.7	9.2	3.3	25.1	26.6	13.0	0.8	71.1	38.3	51.7	48.3
79064	OLTON	70.8	66.2	1.9	1.9	0.1	0.2	55.9	64.9	8.3	8.1	7.9	7.6	5.3	22.1	22.5	14.3	3.8	70.4	36.6	49.6	50.4
79065	PAMPA	81.4	77.0	6.1	6.6	0.4	0.5	13.5	18.2	5.9	5.9	5.9	6.9	6.5	25.0	26.3	14.7	3.0	78.3	40.4	51.4	48.6
79068	PANHANDLE	92.7	92.4	0.9	0.9	0.2	0.2	8.2	8.9	6.7	6.6	7.9	8.2	5.0	21.6	28.2	13.1	2.7	73.3	40.6	48.7	51.3
79070	PERRYTON	86.2	82.7	0.1	0.1	0.4	0.5	31.8	40.2	8.2	8.2	7.9	7.4	5.8	25.9	25.2	9.9	1.5	71.1	34.6	50.2	49.8
79072	PLAINVIEW	64.1	59.1	6.6	6.2	0.4	0.5	48.0	56.5	8.6	8.1	7.4	8.9	8.5	25.5	20.9	10.1	2.0	71.2	31.1	51.1	48.9
79079	SHAMROCK	86.2	82.8	4.7	5.2	1.1	1.4	12.0	16.2	5.7	6.1	6.0	6.4	5.6	19.9	27.3	19.4	3.5	78.4	45.2	46.9	53.1
79080	SKELLYTOWN	93.8	93.5	0.4	0.5	0.1	0.2	5.7	6.2	5.1	5.6	5.9	5.6	5.1	21.8	33.0	15.6	2.3	80.0	45.6	48.0	52.0
79081	SPEARMAN	80.7	79.8	0.1	0.1	0.3	0.3	31.3	33.4	7.0	7.1	7.3	7.2	5.3	22.7	27.1	13.1	3.2	73.8	39.7	48.7	51.3
79082	SPRINGLAKE	83.7	78.5	0.9	1.0	0.0	0.0	29.0	38.9	6.8	7.4	7.4	5.8	2.9	24.8	26.7	17.0	1.3	74.6	40.4	50.8	49.2
79083	STINNETT	91.9	88.9	0.2	0.2	0.1	0.2	7.5	11.1	5.5	6.0	6.9	7.9	4.9	23.1	29.1	14.7	1.9	76.3	41.9	50.1	49.9
79084	STRATFORD	82.6	81.8	0.5	0.5	0.0	0.0	28.0	29.8	7.1	7.2	7.6	8.0	4.7	24.6	26.4	12.0	2.3	72.5	38.3	51.0	49.0
79085	SUMMERFIELD	78.7	73.6	0.0	0.0	0.0	0.0	52.8	64.8	7.7	7.7	7.7	8.8	6.6	25.3	25.3	11.0	0.0	71.4	33.5	51.6	48.4
79086	SUNRAY	72.6	70.5	0.9	0.9	0.2	0.2	35.0	38.0	7.5	8.7	8.3	10.3	5.1	25.7	23.9	9.3	1.2	67.7	32.9	49.9	50.1
79087	TEXLINE	92.3	91.9	0.0	0.0	0.0	0.0	21.6	23.6	8.6	8.8	8.9	7.6	3.4	24.5	26.7	10.2	1.3	68.8	37.3	49.2	50.8
79088	TULIA	69.9	63.5	7.3	8.4	0.1	0.1	35.8	44.1	7.7	6.8	7.0	7.9	9.1	23.4	22.8	12.9	2.4	73.9	34.0	53.4	46.6
79092	VEGA	91.8	91.5	2.0	2.1	0.2	0.2	9.9	10.8	5.7	7.5	13.3	13.9	3.0	19.4	25.9	9.9	1.3	63.1	32.8	54.2	45.8
79094	WAYSIDE	94.8	95.0	0.0	0.0	0.0	0.0	6.9	7.6	5.9	5.9	6.7	5.9	4.2	22.7	27.7	16.0	5.0	77.3	43.9	49.6	50.4
79095	WELLINGTON	79.0	74.7	5.7	5.9	0.2	0.2	21.2	27.7	6.4	6.5	6.6	7.2	5.3	20.6	26.7	16.5	4.2	76.0	42.6	48.9	51.1
79096	WHEELER	87.0	82.6	1.3	1.4	0.2	0.3	15.9	21.5	6.4	6.9	6.9	6.2	4.6	21.6	28.6	14.9	4.1	75.9	42.7	48.8	51.2
79097	WHITE DEER	96.1	95.9	0.1	0.1	0.0	0.0	4.9	5.4	6.0	6.5	6.7	7.0	5.2	23.6	29.8	13.4	1.9	76.6	41.5	48.3	51.7
	TEXAS	71.0	67.6	11.5	11.4	2.8	3.5	32.0	37.4	7.9	7.5	7.2	7.5	7.4	28.3	24.0	8.8	1.4	73.0	33.6	49.7	50.3
	UNITED STATES	75.1	72.0	12.3	12.7	3.8	4.6	12.5	15.7	6.8	6.7	6.6	7.1	6.9	27.0	26.0	10.9	1.9	75.7	36.9	49.2	50.8

ZIP CODE #	POST OFFICE NAME	2009 Per Capita Income	2009 HH Income Base	2009 HOUSEHOLD INCOME DISTRIBUTION (%) Less than $25,000	$25,000 to $49,999	$50,000 to $99,999	$100,000 to $149,999	$150,000 or More	MEDIAN HOUSEHOLD INCOME 2009	2014	2009 National Centile	2009 State Centile	2009 Home Value Base	2009 HOME VALUE DISTRIBUTION (%) Less than $50,000	$50,000 to $89,999	$90,000 to $174,999	$175,000 to $399,999	$400,000 or More	2009 Median Home Value
78838	CONCAN	14702	53	35.8	32.1	30.2	1.9	0.0	35750	35000	20	26	41	24.4	19.5	26.8	22.0	7.3	103125
78839	CRYSTAL CITY	8943	2643	58.2	26.7	12.7	1.6	0.8	18869	19175	1	2	1807	62.3	23.7	11.6	2.1	0.3	40612
78840	DEL RIO	14041	15167	37.6	29.8	25.8	5.0	1.7	34425	35706	16	21	9873	27.7	27.3	34.7	9.6	0.8	81919
78843	LAUGHLIN A F B	24179	15	6.7	13.3	66.7	13.3	0.0	64354	61260	83	87	0	0.0	0.0	0.0	0.0	0.0	0
78850	D HANIS	17995	424	26.4	34.4	30.2	6.4	2.6	39568	43947	31	41	339	27.7	25.4	27.1	13.9	5.9	83824
78851	DRYDEN	15932	416	43.3	32.0	19.0	4.8	1.0	28731	29483	6	8	315	68.6	19.0	8.9	0.6	2.9	33661
78852	EAGLE PASS	9900	14562	48.7	28.2	18.9	2.7	1.5	25779	26854	4	5	9927	29.6	33.5	31.0	5.4	0.5	72591
78861	HONDO	16910	3900	31.5	30.7	30.4	5.7	1.6	40662	45475	35	45	2950	25.5	24.6	32.6	14.8	2.5	89759
78870	KNIPPA	16116	285	27.7	37.5	27.7	6.3	0.7	37746	39485	26	33	204	41.2	27.0	21.6	4.4	5.9	58182
78872	LA PRYOR	11639	555	49.7	28.5	18.9	1.4	1.4	25108	25992	3	4	458	74.2	15.9	9.4	0.4	0.0	25217
78873	LEAKEY	18239	644	38.4	32.6	24.4	3.7	0.9	31866	32970	11	14	491	17.5	23.4	32.4	17.7	9.0	110045
78877	QUEMADO	10107	416	58.9	19.2	18.8	3.1	0.0	19395	20661	1	2	319	34.5	27.9	28.8	8.8	0.0	80366
78879	RIO FRIO	19019	166	37.3	31.9	26.5	3.0	1.2	33492	35764	14	18	128	14.1	21.9	33.6	19.5	10.9	123214
78880	ROCKSPRINGS	14244	596	43.3	28.9	23.5	3.4	1.0	30000	30632	8	10	464	48.7	23.5	14.2	7.8	5.8	51463
78881	SABINAL	16425	839	37.3	30.4	25.1	5.5	1.7	35756	38840	20	26	654	47.6	24.8	19.7	6.3	1.7	52963
78883	TARPLEY	22692	80	25.0	30.0	33.8	10.0	1.3	45000	50000	48	59	66	16.7	16.7	30.3	28.8	7.6	134375
78884	UTOPIA	18698	333	36.3	32.1	27.6	2.4	1.5	34851	39331	17	22	260	23.8	18.8	29.2	21.9	6.2	105556
78885	VANDERPOOL	26183	162	24.7	29.0	34.6	9.3	2.5	46863	50000	54	64	131	15.3	17.6	33.6	24.4	9.2	131250
78886	YANCEY	21355	206	23.8	27.7	36.9	7.8	3.9	49153	50654	59	68	174	18.4	16.7	44.8	17.8	2.3	115517
78931	BLEIBLERVILLE	22119	166	31.3	28.9	31.9	4.8	3.0	43625	46444	44	55	138	13.8	28.3	31.2	12.3	14.5	106250
78932	CARMINE	23991	188	26.6	28.7	34.6	5.9	4.3	46047	45844	51	62	161	13.0	14.9	35.4	24.2	12.4	141912
78933	CAT SPRING	23861	670	21.6	28.5	39.4	6.7	3.7	49864	50194	61	70	535	12.7	18.9	30.8	30.1	7.5	127679
78934	COLUMBUS	21569	2505	33.4	22.4	34.3	6.5	3.4	43742	44019	45	55	1766	22.7	20.9	35.7	17.2	3.6	103306
78935	ALLEYTON	26195	187	17.6	24.6	44.9	7.5	5.3	56848	54509	74	81	154	15.6	14.9	26.6	35.7	7.1	141667
78938	ELLINGER	20178	101	37.6	29.7	25.7	5.0	2.0	32342	36295	12	15	85	12.9	27.1	34.1	16.5	9.4	115278
78940	FAYETTEVILLE	20367	906	32.8	28.7	30.8	5.1	2.6	39464	41964	31	40	752	16.0	24.5	31.3	21.3	7.0	112975
78941	FLATONIA	17228	984	35.2	30.7	26.7	6.0	1.4	36004	38865	21	27	781	25.2	23.7	29.8	15.7	5.5	92073
78942	GIDDINGS	18804	2953	25.5	32.7	31.7	7.3	2.8	42369	44632	41	51	2137	21.1	24.0	35.0	16.8	3.2	99682
78944	INDUSTRY	21029	242	28.1	26.9	36.0	7.0	2.1	45910	48435	51	61	194	12.9	25.3	31.4	19.6	10.8	117857
78945	LA GRANGE	21309	4203	27.5	26.9	34.9	7.4	3.2	45698	45181	50	61	3172	14.2	22.8	35.7	21.2	6.1	115702
78946	LEDBETTER	18904	444	35.8	28.2	29.7	4.5	1.8	36466	41226	22	29	372	26.3	20.7	30.1	16.7	6.2	96875
78947	LEXINGTON	22177	1600	22.4	29.3	38.5	6.4	3.4	48723	47412	58	68	1328	21.5	15.9	37.9	22.2	2.6	114005
78948	LINCOLN	18763	601	28.5	31.6	32.9	5.8	1.2	39696	43624	32	41	528	22.2	13.6	41.7	20.5	2.1	115141
78949	MULDOON	18632	159	32.1	29.6	29.6	8.2	0.6	38834	42117	29	37	136	15.4	18.4	35.3	20.6	10.3	125000
78950	NEW ULM	25780	991	24.7	26.4	36.7	8.0	4.1	48883	49442	59	68	821	13.9	17.9	26.8	30.6	10.8	136653
78953	ROSANKY	23594	397	25.2	28.2	34.0	9.3	3.3	47049	50462	54	64	328	14.9	22.9	31.7	23.2	7.3	124219
78954	ROUND TOP	24857	492	29.5	29.1	31.7	5.7	4.1	42998	44282	42	53	421	13.5	17.8	34.7	22.6	11.4	133232
78956	SCHULENBURG	22122	2099	30.9	30.7	29.8	5.0	3.5	38623	40675	29	36	1543	14.7	28.5	36.5	17.6	2.7	98294
78957	SMITHVILLE	20183	3841	30.2	25.6	32.5	8.3	3.3	45305	48738	49	59	2883	19.1	24.5	34.6	18.9	3.0	108058
78959	WAELDER	15672	595	43.0	29.9	21.8	2.9	2.4	28599	31858	6	8	430	51.2	18.1	17.0	10.0	3.7	48649
78962	WEIMAR	20507	2023	32.0	26.3	31.4	6.2	4.0	41349	42087	37	48	1645	21.6	27.7	30.6	16.5	3.6	91045
78963	WEST POINT	19720	287	13.2	30.7	49.5	6.3	0.3	51609	50000	65	73	238	14.7	16.4	45.8	18.9	4.2	116500
79001	ADRIAN	21290	108	26.9	36.1	27.8	5.6	3.7	38165	40000	27	34	72	38.9	20.8	27.8	6.9	5.6	70000
79005	BOOKER	16353	546	29.3	30.6	34.2	4.8	1.1	40944	43955	36	46	416	42.8	32.2	22.6	2.2	0.2	56818
79007	BORGER	21386	5922	25.0	30.1	34.1	7.9	2.8	45156	48228	49	59	4440	42.1	27.8	21.3	7.8	0.9	58329
79009	BOVINA	13626	874	31.0	40.3	23.2	3.5	1.9	34290	35141	16	21	598	50.8	23.2	16.1	9.2	0.7	49194
79011	BRISCOE	18138	151	25.8	37.7	30.5	2.6	3.3	38623	39651	29	36	106	46.2	19.8	20.8	6.6	6.6	56667
79014	CANADIAN	20444	1341	26.5	32.8	32.4	6.0	2.2	41851	42301	39	49	1025	27.3	28.2	29.5	11.6	3.4	82153
79015	CANYON	23383	7062	23.6	26.8	36.2	8.8	4.6	49274	52706	59	68	4323	13.1	24.2	44.4	16.1	2.2	109939
79016	CANYON	4207	0	0.0	0.0	0.0	0.0	0.0	0	0	0	0	0	0.0	0.0	0.0	0.0	0.0	0
79018	CHANNING	18880	232	21.6	28.9	41.4	6.9	1.3	49503	50750	60	69	150	38.0	26.0	30.0	3.3	2.7	65455
79019	CLAUDE	19736	754	24.7	29.4	36.3	7.4	2.1	46363	48408	52	63	592	30.1	26.9	32.4	9.6	1.0	78056
79022	DALHART	19383	3018	28.1	31.2	32.8	4.4	3.5	40540	45710	34	44	2082	27.5	32.6	26.9	12.3	0.7	74679
79027	DIMMITT	16132	1969	32.7	33.6	25.9	5.1	2.7	35672	36328	20	26	1377	38.3	32.1	20.7	7.9	0.9	61232
79029	DUMAS	17350	5929	25.5	33.8	32.8	6.1	1.8	43116	45753	43	54	4095	32.6	29.6	31.6	5.9	0.3	69923
79031	EARTH	16457	486	37.4	33.3	23.3	2.9	3.1	32241	34611	12	15	385	59.2	23.6	14.0	3.1	0.0	38167
79034	FOLLETT	20776	389	29.0	34.2	28.3	5.9	2.6	38728	39247	29	37	303	44.6	27.4	20.8	6.6	0.7	56600
79035	FRIONA	16709	1602	31.0	31.8	29.8	3.6	3.8	39198	42677	30	39	1133	35.7	31.5	26.3	5.1	1.4	64511
79036	FRITCH	21381	1922	24.0	29.3	38.2	7.0	1.5	47547	49670	56	66	1624	36.5	30.2	28.6	4.1	0.6	65882
79039	GROOM	19784	318	24.8	33.0	35.2	5.7	1.3	43494	46807	44	54	263	36.9	34.6	24.7	3.0	0.8	68167
79040	GRUVER	19466	645	24.7	36.7	31.2	4.8	2.6	42075	44606	40	50	462	33.3	22.5	34.0	8.2	1.9	81290
79041	HALE CENTER	17457	1093	35.8	31.2	25.6	4.6	2.8	35337	37355	19	24	719	46.2	23.5	23.8	6.3	0.3	55500
79042	HAPPY	17470	329	25.8	42.6	28.0	2.7	0.9	35589	37946	19	25	247	57.5	20.6	17.8	4.0	0.0	44219
79043	HART	12953	362	30.1	40.1	27.1	2.2	0.6	34030	33792	16	20	257	57.2	23.3	17.9	1.6	0.0	39722
79044	HARTLEY	17587	325	16.6	28.6	39.4	10.5	4.9	52151	52767	66	74	219	24.7	28.8	27.9	18.3	0.5	84643
79045	HEREFORD	15248	6281	33.5	34.8	25.6	4.4	1.8	35228	36083	18	24	4199	34.3	30.6	28.0	5.9	1.2	68166
79046	HIGGINS	22209	288	35.4	30.9	25.0	4.2	4.5	35521	36703	19	25	220	53.6	17.7	22.7	4.5	1.4	45789
79052	KRESS	16809	507	24.3	40.6	28.8	4.7	1.6	39391	41903	31	40	363	50.7	22.3	19.8	5.5	1.7	49468
79056	LIPSCOMB	22989	26	38.5	30.8	23.1	7.7	0.0	35000	35712	18	23	20	65.0	15.0	20.0	0.0	0.0	40000
79057	MCLEAN	18593	427	39.1	27.9	26.5	5.9	0.7	33387	37376	14	17	338	61.2	20.7	13.6	3.8	0.6	40256
79058	MASTERSON	24688	83	21.7	28.9	36.1	9.6	3.6	49319	48813	60	69	63	19.0	15.9	54.0	11.1	0.0	108594
79059	MIAMI	24046	367	22.1	26.4	40.9	7.4	3.3	50710	50981	63	72	288	27.8	39.2	24.0	7.6	1.4	70000
79061	MOBEETIE	20720	125	22.4	38.4	34.4	2.4	2.4	41593	44603	38	48	100	36.0	20.0	30.0	10.0	4.0	80000
79062	MORSE	17871	60	28.3	36.7	23.3	10.0	1.7	39264	42260	31	40	42	38.1	26.2	33.3	2.4	0.0	70000
79063	NAZARETH	19757	137	24.1	30.7	33.6	6.6	5.1	46885	50448	54	64	103	28.2	31.1	20.4	14.6	5.8	76875
79064	OLTON	13878	926	33.0	38.4	24.2	2.9	1.4	33649	36180	15	19	680	54.0	24.4	13.5	7.8	0.3	46447
79065	PAMPA	20664	8206	30.2	30.7	30.1	6.2	2.9	40270	42627	34	43	6221	47.1	24.2	22.5	5.1	1.1	53271
79068	PANHANDLE	23903	1404	17.6	28.5	40.1	10.8	3.1	53117	53791	68	76	1160	32.3	31.6	28.1	7.3	0.7	70909
79070	PERRYTON	19286	3477	25.3	28.6	36.9	6.5	2.7	46293	47478	52	63	2504	32.9	27.1	28.2	10.5	1.4	70533
79072	PLAINVIEW	16573	8998	30.5	32.7	29.7	4.8	2.2	38628	41352	29	36	5657	28.3	30.3	31.3	9.2	0.8	77562
79079	SHAMROCK	17625	1022	37.0	32.3	25.0	4.7	1.0	35649	36401	20	26	785	57.5	25.4	14.5	2.2	0.5	42952
79080	SKELLYTOWN	18525	259	28.6	34.7	29.3	3.9	3.5	39592	42821	31	41	222	63.1	25.7	7.7	2.7	0.9	34211
79081	SPEARMAN	20070	1287	30.6	27.4	34.1	4.9	3.0	43374	44865	43	54	974	48.4	25.6	22.9	2.3	0.9	52540
79082	SPRINGLAKE	25319	126	32.5	34.1	19.8	7.1	6.3	38178	40456	27	34	92	41.3	26.1	26.1	6.5	0.0	63750
79083	STINNETT	20681	1009	28.4	29.6	33.7	5.8	2.4	42798	46729	42	53	811	47.8	28.4	19.1	3.6	1.1	53646
79084	STRATFORD	18342	990	25.9	36.9	30.1	4.1	3.0	39519	40581	31	40	734	37.1	34.3	21.9	6.0	0.7	64286
79085	SUMMERFIELD	14341	30	33.3	33.3	26.7	6.7	0.0	37333	36120	25	32	21	42.9	38.1	14.3	4.8	0.0	61000
79086	SUNRAY	18212	708	23.4	34.3	34.7	5.4	2.1	41372	44936	37	48	516	43.6	29.3	21.7	5.0	0.4	56471
79087	TEXLINE	17767	269	28.3	38.7	25.3	4.8	3.0	37201	41343	24	31	165	42.4	35.2	14.5	7.9	0.0	59615
79088	TULIA	16714	1930	31.7	34.9	26.7	5.0	1.7	35959	37784	20	27	1314	46.7	24.3	21.4	7.2	0.5	55366
79092	VEGA	18549	539	27.3	35.3	31.4	3.3	2.8	40402	41556	34	44	351	38.5	34.2	20.8	5.7	0.9	63621
79094	WAYSIDE	20154	49	34.7	22.4	38.8	4.1	0.0	41158	43655	37	46	37	37.8	24.3	27.0	8.1	2.7	62500
79095	WELLINGTON	17803	1153	37.8	33.0	21.9	4.8	2.6	31732	33150	11	14	889	53.8	28.1	15.0	2.7	0.4	46105
79096	WHEELER	19366	695	27.8	37.0	28.8	3.6	2.9	37855	38489	26	34	546	46.2	29.3	19.6	3.7	1.3	54200
79097	WHITE DEER	20602	479	22.1	38.8	33.4	3.1	2.5	44309	46851	46	57	393	36.6	38.4	21.6	3.3	0.0	62237
	TEXAS	24551		22.3	25.0	34.3	11.1	7.3	52382	54495				16.5	22.7	36.5	19.7	4.6	109784
	UNITED STATES	27277		20.9	24.4	35.3	11.7	7.6	54719	56938				9.3	13.1	31.6	32.6	13.5	162279

ZIP CODE		FINANCIAL SERVICES				THE HOME						ENTERTAINMENT						PERSONAL			
						Home Improvements		Furnishings													
#	POST OFFICE NAME	Auto Loan	Home Loan	Invest-ments	Retire-ment Plans	Home Repair	Lawn & Garden	Comput-ers & Hard-ware-Personal	Major Appli-ances	TV, Radio, Sound Equip-ment	Furni-ture	Dine out/ Carry out	Sports Equip-ment	Fees & Tickets	Toys & Games	Travel	Cable TV	Apparel & Services	Auto Repairs	Health Insur-ance	Pets & Supplies
78838	CONCAN	63	50	80	49	55	66	50	64	53	47	52	47	43	50	54	56	35	59	63	74
78839	CRYSTAL CITY	47	37	28	31	36	35	37	40	41	42	41	25	33	41	33	42	29	41	39	44
78840	DEL RIO	72	59	51	53	57	59	60	63	63	64	64	44	53	65	55	65	44	64	62	72
78843	LAUGHLIN A F B	122	63	47	73	57	54	115	79	108	107	113	79	87	129	83	99	80	101	72	97
78850	D HANIS	93	67	95	64	69	94	68	87	76	64	74	65	55	75	68	83	49	80	90	103
78851	DRYDEN	64	48	58	44	48	61	50	60	55	48	54	43	41	55	48	59	36	57	62	70
78852	EAGLE PASS	58	49	38	42	47	45	49	52	52	54	52	33	43	52	44	52	36	52	49	57
78861	HONDO	82	64	74	60	64	78	66	76	71	65	70	56	56	72	62	75	47	72	78	89
78870	KNIPPA	84	60	86	58	63	86	62	79	69	58	67	59	50	68	61	76	45	72	82	94
78872	LA PRYOR	61	49	37	41	47	46	49	52	53	55	54	32	42	54	44	55	37	53	51	57
78873	LEAKEY	67	52	81	51	57	71	53	67	57	49	56	50	45	55	56	61	37	62	68	78
78877	QUEMADO	55	38	48	35	37	51	40	48	45	40	45	36	31	46	37	50	30	46	50	58
78879	RIO FRIO	69	55	89	55	61	73	55	70	58	52	57	51	48	55	60	62	38	65	70	82
78880	ROCKSPRINGS	65	51	51	45	50	56	52	58	56	54	56	40	44	55	49	58	38	57	59	66
78881	SABINAL	80	55	82	52	56	80	58	73	65	54	64	56	44	65	55	72	42	68	76	88
78883	TARPLEY	85	71	100	69	75	88	70	85	73	67	72	62	62	71	73	77	48	79	84	99
78884	UTOPIA	72	57	93	56	63	76	57	73	60	54	59	53	50	57	62	64	39	67	72	85
78885	VANDERPOOL	97	77	125	76	85	102	77	98	81	73	80	72	67	77	84	86	53	91	97	114
78886	YANCEY	109	79	113	76	82	111	81	103	89	75	88	77	65	89	80	98	58	94	107	122
78931	BLEIBLERVILLE	94	67	96	65	70	95	69	87	76	64	75	66	55	76	68	84	49	80	91	104
78932	CARMINE	97	76	120	75	83	102	77	97	81	72	80	71	65	78	82	87	53	90	97	113
78933	CAT SPRING	101	80	108	78	83	102	79	97	85	76	84	71	68	84	81	91	56	90	98	114
78934	COLUMBUS	88	68	88	67	70	90	73	85	79	67	77	64	61	78	71	86	52	81	91	101
78935	ALLEYTON	111	87	137	85	94	116	87	111	92	82	91	81	74	88	93	99	60	102	111	129
78938	ELLINGER	76	54	78	53	56	77	56	71	62	52	61	53	45	62	55	68	40	65	74	85
78940	FAYETTEVILLE	88	63	93	62	66	90	66	83	72	60	71	63	52	71	66	79	47	77	86	99
78941	FLATONIA	80	55	79	52	56	79	57	72	65	54	64	55	45	66	55	72	42	67	76	87
78942	GIDDINGS	86	75	74	71	74	80	75	80	77	77	77	60	68	80	72	80	53	78	80	94
78944	INDUSTRY	97	68	103	67	71	100	72	91	78	63	77	72	55	77	72	85	50	84	95	110
78945	LA GRANGE	90	68	92	67	70	93	73	86	78	65	76	67	60	76	71	84	51	82	92	103
78946	LEDBETTER	82	57	79	54	57	81	59	74	67	56	65	57	46	67	56	74	43	69	77	89
78947	LEXINGTON	97	79	89	77	80	95	78	90	83	77	82	66	68	85	75	88	55	85	92	107
78948	LINCOLN	87	61	92	60	64	90	65	82	70	57	69	64	50	69	64	77	45	76	86	99
78949	MULDOON	83	59	85	57	62	84	61	78	68	57	66	58	49	67	60	74	44	71	81	92
78950	NEW ULM	111	82	125	80	87	115	85	107	91	77	90	82	68	89	87	99	59	99	110	127
78953	ROSANKY	97	78	91	75	78	95	76	90	82	75	82	67	66	84	74	88	55	84	92	107
78954	ROUND TOP	94	72	112	71	78	98	73	93	78	68	77	69	61	76	77	85	51	86	94	109
78956	SCHULENBURG	94	66	97	65	69	98	72	89	79	63	77	69	56	78	70	87	51	83	95	107
78957	SMITHVILLE	88	70	83	69	71	88	72	82	78	69	77	62	63	78	70	84	52	79	87	98
78959	WAELDER	78	51	76	48	51	77	55	69	63	52	61	54	41	64	51	70	41	65	73	84
78962	WEIMAR	95	70	103	68	73	98	72	91	79	67	78	68	59	78	73	87	51	84	95	108
78963	WEST POINT	97	69	99	67	72	98	71	90	79	66	77	68	57	78	70	87	51	83	94	107
79001	ADRIAN	88	61	97	61	64	93	68	84	70	55	69	69	49	69	67	77	45	78	89	103
79005	BOOKER	70	67	63	60	66	60	67	68	63	70	65	51	61	65	65	61	45	67	61	76
79007	BORGER	80	75	68	75	73	81	76	78	79	74	78	59	74	80	74	82	54	78	83	92
79009	BOVINA	75	56	60	50	56	65	58	67	62	58	63	47	48	62	55	66	42	65	67	77
79011	BRISCOE	83	57	91	57	60	88	63	79	66	51	65	65	46	65	63	72	42	74	83	97
79014	CANADIAN	86	65	87	65	67	90	68	83	73	60	72	64	56	73	67	79	48	77	87	99
79015	CANYON	89	75	72	78	73	79	92	81	88	83	88	67	80	89	80	88	61	86	83	99
79016	CANYON	0	0	0	0	0	0	0	0	0	0	0	0	0	0	0	0	0	0	0	0
79018	CHANNING	92	63	101	63	66	97	70	87	73	57	72	72	52	72	70	80	47	82	92	108
79019	CLAUDE	85	69	92	69	71	94	71	84	74	62	74	66	61	73	73	80	49	80	91	101
79022	DALHART	80	68	69	68	66	78	72	75	74	67	73	59	64	75	68	77	50	75	80	91
79027	DIMMITT	81	61	67	55	60	73	63	73	68	62	68	53	51	68	59	72	46	71	74	85
79029	DUMAS	80	73	62	69	71	72	74	75	75	75	75	55	69	76	70	75	52	75	74	86
79031	EARTH	78	61	55	52	59	64	62	69	67	65	67	46	52	67	57	69	46	68	68	77
79034	FOLLETT	85	59	94	58	61	90	65	81	68	53	67	67	48	66	65	74	43	76	85	100
79035	FRIONA	83	66	75	61	66	76	69	77	70	67	71	58	57	71	66	73	48	75	76	90
79036	FRITCH	87	71	89	70	75	92	71	86	76	68	75	63	62	75	72	82	50	79	90	100
79039	GROOM	88	62	96	61	64	93	68	84	71	55	70	69	50	69	68	77	45	79	89	103
79040	GRUVER	95	65	104	65	68	100	72	90	75	59	74	74	53	74	72	82	48	84	95	111
79041	HALE CENTER	84	62	75	57	62	80	65	78	71	62	70	57	53	71	62	77	47	74	81	91
79042	HAPPY	76	52	83	52	54	80	58	72	60	47	59	59	42	59	57	66	39	67	76	88
79043	HART	69	55	44	46	53	54	55	60	60	60	60	38	47	60	50	62	42	60	59	67
79044	HARTLEY	116	80	127	80	84	122	89	110	92	72	91	91	65	90	88	101	59	103	116	136
79045	HEREFORD	73	61	58	55	60	64	61	67	65	63	65	47	54	65	58	67	45	66	67	76
79046	HIGGINS	89	62	98	61	64	94	68	85	71	55	70	70	50	70	68	77	46	79	90	104
79052	KRESS	82	62	69	56	61	74	64	74	69	63	69	53	52	69	61	73	46	72	75	86
79056	LIPSCOMB	73	50	80	50	52	77	56	69	58	45	57	57	41	57	55	63	37	64	73	85
79057	MCLEAN	71	51	71	50	53	74	56	69	63	50	60	52	45	61	54	69	40	65	75	81
79058	MASTERSON	99	89	83	86	87	94	84	91	88	87	88	66	79	91	81	91	60	88	92	108
79059	MIAMI	103	71	113	71	74	109	79	98	82	64	81	81	58	80	78	89	52	91	103	120
79061	MOBEETIE	85	59	93	58	61	90	65	81	68	53	67	67	48	66	65	74	43	75	85	99
79062	MORSE	88	60	97	60	63	93	67	83	70	54	69	69	49	68	67	76	45	78	88	103
79063	NAZARETH	101	69	111	69	73	106	77	96	80	62	79	79	56	79	77	87	51	89	101	118
79064	OLTON	71	52	64	48	52	66	55	64	58	51	58	48	43	58	52	62	39	62	66	76
79065	PAMPA	77	66	73	66	67	81	69	76	74	65	72	57	63	73	68	78	49	74	83	90
79068	PANHANDLE	95	92	99	91	90	104	87	95	89	83	89	74	85	89	90	92	61	92	100	114
79070	PERRYTON	90	71	82	68	70	87	74	83	77	70	76	65	61	78	70	81	51	80	85	100
79072	PLAINVIEW	75	67	62	62	66	68	67	71	69	69	69	50	62	69	64	70	48	70	70	81
79079	SHAMROCK	69	50	71	48	52	73	54	67	60	48	58	51	43	59	53	66	38	63	73	79
79080	SKELLYTOWN	84	60	87	59	63	86	62	79	69	58	68	59	50	68	61	76	45	72	82	94
79081	SPEARMAN	91	63	96	62	65	95	69	86	75	59	73	68	52	74	67	82	48	80	92	104
79082	SPRINGLAKE	112	77	121	76	80	117	85	106	89	70	88	87	63	87	85	97	57	99	111	130
79083	STINNETT	84	69	80	69	68	87	71	80	75	65	74	63	62	75	70	79	49	77	86	97
79084	STRATFORD	93	64	102	64	67	98	71	88	74	58	73	73	52	73	71	81	48	83	93	109
79085	SUMMERFIELD	79	56	65	55	56	75	59	68	65	57	64	52	47	68	53	71	43	65	72	83
79086	SUNRAY	88	69	89	66	71	85	73	84	73	67	74	67	60	73	72	76	49	80	83	99
79087	TEXLINE	89	61	98	61	64	94	68	85	71	55	70	70	50	69	68	77	45	79	89	104
79088	TULIA	74	58	63	54	58	69	61	69	65	60	65	49	51	65	57	70	44	67	72	80
79092	VEGA	88	64	94	63	66	91	69	83	71	58	70	68	53	70	68	76	46	78	86	102
79094	WAYSIDE	82	56	90	56	59	87	63	78	65	51	64	64	46	64	62	71	42	73	82	96
79095	WELLINGTON	74	54	73	54	55	76	60	71	65	52	63	56	48	64	57	70	42	68	76	85
79096	WHEELER	87	62	91	60	64	89	64	81	70	58	69	63	50	70	64	77	45	75	85	98
79097	WHITE DEER	80	72	72	75	74	85	71	81	74	64	72	61	66	75	71	78	49	74	83	94
	TEXAS	104	96	90	94	93	94	99	97	99	101	100	75	94	101	94	99	70	99	96	114
	UNITED STATES	100	100	100	100	100	100	100	100	100	100	100	100	100	100	100	100	100	100	100	100

POPULATION CHANGE

79098-79501

ZIP CODE #	POST OFFICE NAME	COUNTY FIPS CODE	POPULATION 2000	POPULATION 2009	POPULATION 2014	2000-2009 ANNUAL RATE % Rate	2000-2009 ANNUAL RATE State Centile	HOUSEHOLDS 2000	HOUSEHOLDS 2009	HOUSEHOLDS 2014	HOUSEHOLDS % Annual Rate 2000-2009	HOUSEHOLDS 2009 Average HH Size	FAMILIES 2000	FAMILIES 2009	FAMILIES % Annual Rate 2000-2009
79098	WILDORADO	359	385	384	381	0.0	25	136	138	138	0.2	2.70	106	106	0.0
79101	AMARILLO	375	2852	2956	2993	0.4	37	1176	1154	1160	-0.2	2.14	537	507	-0.6
79102	AMARILLO	375	9672	9946	10054	0.3	34	4105	4083	4102	-0.1	2.39	2377	2299	-0.4
79103	AMARILLO	381	9975	10367	10649	0.4	37	3453	3537	3630	0.3	2.93	2715	2731	0.1
79104	AMARILLO	375	7565	7929	8060	0.5	42	2439	2482	2511	0.2	3.18	1820	1816	0.0
79106	AMARILLO	375	28618	30219	30926	0.6	46	12144	12540	12822	0.3	2.32	7266	7264	0.0
79107	AMARILLO	375	31876	34005	34848	0.7	49	10476	10841	11059	0.4	3.12	7802	7930	0.2
79108	AMARILLO	375	16181	18290	18966	1.3	65	4099	4511	4717	1.0	2.86	3166	3434	0.9
79109	AMARILLO	381	43885	43584	43987	-0.1	21	19108	19034	19317	0.0	2.28	12161	11740	-0.4
79110	AMARILLO	381	17935	17784	18012	-0.1	21	6786	6781	6919	0.0	2.61	5010	4879	-0.3
79111	AMARILLO	375	1780	1870	1886	0.5	42	549	561	564	0.2	3.21	464	470	0.1
79118	AMARILLO	381	12348	17008	19063	3.5	89	4358	6086	6882	3.7	2.74	3444	4677	3.4
79119	AMARILLO	381	4645	9289	11286	7.8	97	1670	3212	3903	7.3	2.88	1340	2500	7.0
79121	AMARILLO	381	7202	7171	7242	0.0	25	2936	2939	2988	0.0	2.42	2098	2042	-0.3
79124	AMARILLO	375	5903	8270	9328	3.7	90	2244	3067	3440	3.4	2.65	1808	2435	3.3
79201	CHILDRESS	075	7659	7689	7633	0.0	25	2465	2416	2391	-0.2	2.42	1644	1585	-0.4
79220	AFTON	125	123	116	113	-0.6	9	52	48	46	-0.9	1.69	36	33	-0.9
79225	CHILLICOTHE	197	1112	1018	971	-1.0	4	443	404	386	-1.0	2.52	308	277	-1.1
79226	CLARENDON	129	3031	3212	3243	0.6	46	1240	1273	1287	0.3	2.28	837	846	0.1
79227	CROWELL	155	1709	1598	1540	-0.7	7	702	655	631	-0.7	2.38	465	427	-0.9
79229	DICKENS	125	588	555	540	-0.6	9	244	225	216	-0.9	1.68	168	153	-1.0
79230	DODSON	075	171	152	147	-1.3	2	73	64	62	-1.4	2.05	57	49	-1.6
79234	FLOMOT	345	87	84	84	-0.4	13	33	32	32	-0.3	2.63	24	22	-0.9
79235	FLOYDADA	153	4720	4414	4240	-0.7	7	1688	1569	1505	-0.8	2.75	1284	1179	-0.9
79237	HEDLEY	129	694	698	710	0.1	27	292	295	300	0.1	2.37	189	187	-0.1
79239	LAKEVIEW	191	286	247	231	-1.6	1	109	92	85	-1.8	2.68	76	63	-2.0
79240	LELIA LAKE	129	94	95	96	0.1	27	41	41	42	0.0	2.32	27	26	-0.4
79241	LOCKNEY	153	3051	2705	2557	-1.3	2	1042	921	871	-1.3	2.89	827	724	-1.4
79243	MCADOO	125	103	97	95	-0.6	9	50	46	44	-0.9	1.67	34	31	-1.0
79244	MATADOR	345	1001	977	984	-0.3	16	428	416	419	-0.3	2.35	308	295	-0.5
79245	MEMPHIS	191	2805	2624	2520	-0.7	7	1147	1044	994	-1.0	2.47	749	670	-1.2
79247	ODELL	487	88	98	101	1.2	63	34	38	39	1.2	2.58	26	28	0.8
79248	PADUCAH	269	2260	1999	1881	-1.3	2	928	833	786	-1.2	2.29	639	566	-1.3
79250	PETERSBURG	189	1572	1480	1426	-0.6	9	548	520	502	-0.6	2.85	432	405	-0.7
79251	QUAIL	087	68	58	56	-1.7	1	26	22	21	-1.8	2.64	20	17	-1.7
79252	QUANAH	197	3612	3354	3232	-0.8	6	1500	1402	1352	-0.7	2.35	1011	930	-0.9
79255	QUITAQUE	045	568	527	504	-0.8	6	236	219	210	-0.8	2.41	157	143	-1.0
79256	ROARING SPRINGS	345	338	325	327	-0.4	13	145	139	140	-0.5	2.34	103	98	-0.5
79257	SILVERTON	045	1222	1143	1099	-0.7	7	488	456	438	-0.7	2.51	354	326	-0.9
79259	TELL	191	14	12	12	-1.7	1	7	6	6	-1.7	2.00	5	4	-2.4
79261	TURKEY	191	677	610	578	-1.1	3	285	250	235	-1.4	2.44	184	157	-1.7
79311	ABERNATHY	189	3558	3620	3638	0.2	30	1249	1285	1296	0.3	2.82	1020	1036	0.2
79312	AMHERST	279	1132	1043	1001	-0.9	5	406	372	357	-0.9	2.72	311	283	-1.0
79313	ANTON	219	1550	1490	1449	-0.4	13	544	535	524	-0.2	2.79	417	405	-0.3
79316	BROWNFIELD	445	11561	10989	10678	-0.5	11	3887	3744	3653	-0.4	2.67	2918	2773	-0.5
79320	BULA	017	63	55	51	-1.5	1	19	17	16	-1.2	3.24	15	13	-1.5
79322	CROSBYTON	107	2439	2393	2341	-0.2	19	909	901	884	-0.1	2.58	659	644	-0.2
79323	DENVER CITY	501	5286	5465	5556	0.4	37	1792	1883	1925	0.5	2.88	1468	1527	0.4
79324	ENOCHS	017	66	57	54	-1.6	1	24	21	20	-1.4	2.71	18	16	-1.3
79325	FARWELL	369	2263	2049	1959	-1.1	3	796	721	687	-1.1	2.74	593	530	-1.2
79326	FIELDTON	279	18	17	16	-0.6	9	9	8	8	-1.3	2.13	7	7	0.0
79329	IDALOU	303	3582	3543	3592	-0.1	21	1287	1316	1346	0.2	2.68	993	993	0.0
79331	LAMESA	115	13801	13054	12660	-0.6	9	4295	4064	3933	-0.6	2.65	3157	2948	-0.7
79336	LEVELLAND	219	19081	18562	18146	-0.3	16	6728	6700	6599	0.0	2.68	5093	5008	-0.2
79339	LITTLEFIELD	279	7627	7400	7209	-0.3	16	2831	2730	2659	-0.4	2.63	2055	1953	-0.5
79342	LOOP	165	386	377	370	-0.3	16	123	118	115	-0.4	3.19	104	98	-0.6
79343	LORENZO	107	1834	1525	1436	-2.0	0	633	533	504	-1.8	2.86	470	390	-2.0
79344	MAPLE	017	162	141	132	-1.5	1	58	51	48	-1.4	2.76	45	39	-1.5
79345	MEADOW	445	1180	1108	1068	-0.7	7	383	362	351	-0.6	3.06	321	302	-0.7
79346	MORTON	079	3434	3043	2854	-1.3	2	1224	1104	1041	-1.1	2.70	952	849	-1.2
79347	MULESHOE	017	6303	6150	5984	-0.3	16	2247	2207	2153	-0.2	2.76	1700	1649	-0.3
79351	ODONNELL	305	1266	1205	1169	-0.5	11	458	441	429	-0.4	2.73	344	327	-0.5
79353	PEP	219	32	30	29	-0.7	7	14	13	13	-0.8	2.31	10	10	0.0
79355	PLAINS	501	2036	1994	1976	-0.2	19	677	666	662	-0.2	2.99	540	526	-0.3
79356	POST	169	4872	6192	6073	2.6	83	1663	1602	1565	-0.4	2.61	1218	1156	-0.6
79357	RALLS	107	2799	2763	2708	-0.1	21	970	954	936	-0.2	2.87	737	716	-0.3
79358	ROPESVILLE	219	1300	1341	1342	0.3	34	445	469	473	0.6	2.86	352	366	0.4
79359	SEAGRAVES	165	3181	3186	3233	0.0	25	1082	1079	1094	0.0	2.95	841	831	-0.1
79360	SEMINOLE	165	10900	11711	12110	0.8	52	3476	3759	3899	0.8	3.09	2811	3005	0.7
79363	SHALLOWATER	303	5632	6170	6502	1.0	58	1945	2191	2329	1.3	2.81	1544	1705	1.1
79364	SLATON	303	7923	7802	7889	-0.2	19	2921	2966	3029	0.2	2.59	2125	2105	-0.1
79366	RANSOM CANYON	303	1016	1022	1048	0.1	27	407	424	439	0.4	2.41	307	312	0.2
79370	SPUR	125	1948	1890	1848	-0.3	16	634	623	610	-0.2	2.62	400	386	-0.4
79371	SUDAN	279	1238	1334	1346	0.8	52	483	518	523	0.8	2.57	352	372	0.6
79373	TAHOKA	305	4236	4025	3915	-0.6	9	1539	1464	1425	-0.5	2.72	1154	1084	-0.7
79376	TOKIO	445	20	18	17	-1.1	3	8	7	7	-1.4	2.57	7	6	-1.7
79377	WELCH	115	518	453	428	-1.4	2	180	159	151	-1.3	2.85	143	125	-1.4
79379	WHITEFACE	079	296	246	228	-2.0	0	85	72	67	-1.8	3.21	65	54	-2.0
79381	WILSON	305	1048	1005	975	-0.5	11	357	343	333	-0.4	2.93	280	265	-0.6
79382	WOLFFORTH	303	4310	4563	4946	0.6	46	1506	1655	1813	1.0	2.73	1228	1311	0.7
79401	LUBBOCK	303	9268	8645	8547	-0.7	7	3851	3579	3557	-0.8	2.14	1578	1398	-1.3
79403	LUBBOCK	303	17668	17932	18335	0.2	30	5710	5968	6161	0.5	2.94	4438	4550	0.3
79404	LUBBOCK	303	10920	11537	11942	0.6	46	3348	3636	3806	0.9	2.94	2496	2649	0.6
79407	LUBBOCK	219	16754	18592	19535	1.1	61	6784	7695	8150	1.4	2.33	4038	4463	1.1
79409	LUBBOCK	303	4470	4726	4734	0.6	46	41	57	64	3.6	1.28	8	10	2.4
79410	LUBBOCK	303	9760	9452	9444	-0.3	16	4266	4226	4257	-0.1	2.15	2229	2110	-0.6
79411	LUBBOCK	303	8234	8462	8703	0.3	34	3103	3236	3349	0.5	2.60	1838	1842	0.0
79412	LUBBOCK	303	15317	15269	15435	0.0	25	5841	5912	6013	0.1	2.55	3965	3892	-0.2
79413	LUBBOCK	303	20564	20267	20432	-0.2	19	8717	8797	8945	0.1	2.28	5653	5526	-0.2
79414	LUBBOCK	303	16968	16754	16948	-0.1	21	7514	7655	7818	0.2	2.17	4114	4008	-0.3
79415	LUBBOCK	303	15281	15668	16041	0.3	34	5672	5954	6150	0.5	2.53	3346	3438	0.3
79416	LUBBOCK	303	23539	28875	31465	2.2	80	9439	11776	12899	2.4	2.42	5820	6979	2.0
79423	LUBBOCK	303	23920	29241	31871	2.2	80	9194	11565	12709	2.5	2.51	6789	8360	2.3
79424	LUBBOCK	303	27515	37298	41055	3.3	88	10966	14670	16153	3.2	2.52	7589	10226	3.3
79501	ANSON	253	3622	3331	3166	-0.9	5	1343	1236	1175	-0.9	2.60	992	898	-1.1
	TEXAS					1.9					1.8	2.78			1.7
	UNITED STATES					1.0					1.1	2.59			0.9

# ZIP CODE	POST OFFICE NAME	RACE (%) White 2000	White 2009	Black 2000	Black 2009	Asian/Pacific 2000	Asian/Pacific 2009	% Hispanic Origin 2000	% Hispanic Origin 2009	2009 AGE DISTRIBUTION (%) 0-4	5-9	10-14	15-19	20-24	25-44	45-64	65-84	85+	18+	MEDIAN AGE 2009	% 2009 Males	% 2009 Females
79098	WILDORADO	88.3	86.7	1.3	1.3	0.5	0.5	15.1	18.5	7.0	7.8	8.1	6.8	4.7	23.7	29.2	11.7	1.0	72.7	38.3	50.3	49.7
79101	AMARILLO	74.6	66.8	7.3	8.2	0.7	1.0	23.4	33.4	7.7	6.8	6.0	6.0	6.8	29.7	23.1	8.6	5.3	76.7	35.8	50.3	49.7
79102	AMARILLO	77.4	72.0	3.6	4.0	0.4	0.6	31.4	39.1	8.4	7.5	6.9	6.6	6.9	27.4	23.1	10.3	3.0	73.3	34.3	48.5	51.5
79103	AMARILLO	76.1	70.0	1.9	1.9	0.2	0.2	41.8	52.8	9.0	8.6	7.7	7.9	6.7	26.5	22.9	9.6	1.1	69.8	32.0	47.5	52.5
79104	AMARILLO	57.6	50.9	2.1	1.9	1.3	1.6	61.5	72.0	10.6	10.2	9.0	7.9	7.6	27.1	19.1	7.3	1.2	65.3	28.1	50.0	50.0
79106	AMARILLO	84.0	78.9	4.7	5.3	0.9	1.3	15.2	21.7	7.2	6.6	6.0	6.2	7.2	26.1	23.1	13.8	3.8	76.7	37.0	47.5	52.5
79107	AMARILLO	45.3	39.0	20.5	19.8	7.1	8.4	38.8	47.3	10.3	9.7	8.7	8.5	7.6	26.0	20.2	7.9	1.0	66.0	28.4	48.7	51.3
79108	AMARILLO	74.1	68.5	13.3	13.9	0.5	0.7	14.4	20.7	4.9	4.9	4.9	7.8	7.9	35.7	25.0	8.1	0.9	82.0	36.4	63.1	36.9
79109	AMARILLO	90.8	87.8	1.9	2.2	0.9	1.3	9.2	13.3	6.5	6.3	6.2	6.3	6.6	27.2	26.7	12.2	2.0	77.3	37.7	48.1	51.9
79110	AMARILLO	87.9	84.2	1.8	2.1	0.5	0.7	14.2	19.6	8.2	8.0	7.8	7.4	5.9	29.2	24.0	8.4	1.1	71.5	33.9	49.0	51.0
79111	AMARILLO	83.8	77.8	4.5	5.3	1.5	2.2	15.1	22.5	12.3	9.7	8.0	8.8	12.9	30.6	14.9	2.7	0.1	65.0	24.3	49.7	50.3
79118	AMARILLO	89.0	84.6	1.6	1.9	0.3	0.6	11.5	16.8	8.0	7.4	7.2	7.2	7.2	28.1	26.1	8.1	0.6	73.0	33.6	50.6	49.4
79119	AMARILLO	92.6	90.5	1.2	1.5	1.2	2.2	7.7	9.1	8.5	8.3	8.0	7.1	4.8	29.6	25.2	7.8	0.8	70.8	34.8	48.5	51.5
79121	AMARILLO	92.5	90.3	1.2	1.4	3.1	4.0	6.2	8.9	4.4	4.9	5.7	6.9	5.5	23.0	33.2	14.4	2.0	81.0	44.7	48.3	51.7
79124	AMARILLO	93.3	90.5	1.6	2.1	1.1	1.8	5.4	8.7	6.1	6.6	7.0	6.0	4.4	23.1	31.8	13.2	1.8	76.5	42.7	48.3	51.7
79201	CHILDRESS	67.8	66.5	14.0	14.3	0.4	0.4	20.5	21.7	5.7	5.6	5.4	7.6	9.3	28.9	22.3	12.6	2.5	79.0	36.7	59.7	40.3
79220	AFTON	80.5	77.6	12.2	12.9	0.0	0.0	20.3	26.7	2.6	3.4	3.4	3.4	16.4	36.2	20.7	11.2	2.6	87.9	34.6	69.8	30.2
79225	CHILLICOTHE	87.6	84.4	4.4	4.9	0.2	0.2	11.2	15.4	6.2	5.8	6.1	7.3	6.9	23.4	25.3	16.4	2.7	77.5	40.7	48.2	51.8
79226	CLARENDON	91.0	89.0	4.8	5.3	0.1	0.2	5.8	8.1	4.7	4.6	5.0	9.3	7.6	18.7	26.8	19.6	3.7	81.0	45.1	49.2	50.8
79227	CROWELL	84.6	83.4	3.2	3.4	0.2	0.3	16.2	17.6	6.3	6.3	6.4	7.2	5.1	21.1	26.0	17.0	4.6	76.5	42.9	47.4	52.6
79229	DICKENS	80.3	77.7	12.2	12.8	0.2	0.2	20.2	26.3	2.9	3.2	3.6	4.0	12.8	36.2	22.2	12.6	2.5	87.4	36.4	67.4	32.6
79230	DODSON	83.6	80.3	5.8	6.6	0.0	0.0	11.7	15.1	3.3	3.9	4.6	5.9	6.6	25.0	30.9	17.8	2.0	84.2	45.4	57.9	42.1
79234	FLOMOT	90.8	89.3	1.1	1.2	0.0	0.0	11.5	13.1	6.0	6.0	6.0	6.0	2.4	21.4	28.6	20.2	3.6	77.4	46.7	52.4	47.6
79235	FLOYDADA	73.4	68.8	3.9	4.3	0.2	0.3	46.3	54.5	8.3	7.9	8.2	8.0	5.3	22.5	23.4	13.5	2.8	70.3	36.3	49.1	50.9
79237	HEDLEY	92.9	90.7	0.9	1.0	0.0	0.0	8.6	12.2	5.7	6.3	6.6	7.0	4.7	21.6	27.4	17.6	3.0	76.9	43.3	48.4	51.6
79239	LAKEVIEW	61.5	54.3	4.9	4.9	0.0	0.0	42.3	51.4	8.1	8.1	7.3	6.1	5.7	21.1	25.5	15.4	2.8	72.9	40.2	53.8	46.2
79240	LELIA LAKE	93.5	90.5	1.1	1.1	0.0	0.0	8.6	11.6	6.3	6.3	6.3	6.3	4.2	21.1	28.4	17.9	3.2	76.8	44.6	47.4	52.6
79241	LOCKNEY	75.3	69.9	2.5	3.0	0.2	0.2	45.4	55.5	8.6	8.5	8.7	8.4	5.2	22.3	22.7	12.7	3.0	68.8	35.2	47.9	52.1
79243	MCADOO	79.8	77.3	12.5	13.4	0.0	0.0	20.2	25.8	3.1	3.1	4.1	4.1	7.2	38.1	23.7	13.4	3.1	86.6	38.1	64.9	35.1
79244	MATADOR	86.0	85.4	4.5	4.6	0.4	0.4	12.5	13.4	6.0	6.6	6.9	6.6	4.2	20.2	28.2	18.3	3.1	76.5	44.6	51.4	48.6
79245	MEMPHIS	72.0	66.5	9.2	9.3	0.1	0.2	26.0	33.4	7.3	7.2	7.1	7.0	5.5	20.5	24.2	17.1	4.1	73.9	40.5	47.2	52.8
79247	ODELL	89.7	82.7	1.1	2.0	0.0	0.0	12.6	18.4	5.1	6.1	9.2	7.1	3.1	24.5	28.6	14.3	2.0	74.5	40.8	50.0	50.0
79248	PADUCAH	83.5	80.7	8.3	8.8	0.0	0.0	17.4	22.5	5.6	6.2	6.6	6.7	5.1	20.6	27.4	17.6	4.4	76.9	44.5	48.1	51.9
79250	PETERSBURG	65.9	59.7	2.1	2.0	0.0	0.0	54.8	65.1	8.0	7.4	7.5	7.4	7.2	22.2	25.5	12.5	2.4	72.8	35.5	49.4	50.6
79251	QUAIL	92.5	87.9	0.0	0.0	0.0	0.0	9.0	12.1	3.4	3.4	5.2	5.2	3.4	20.7	32.8	22.4	3.4	82.8	51.0	53.4	46.6
79252	QUANAH	84.7	80.9	5.0	5.3	0.3	0.4	15.5	20.9	7.0	6.6	6.3	6.2	5.1	22.0	26.8	15.8	4.2	75.8	42.2	48.1	51.9
79255	QUITAQUE	80.6	76.3	4.9	5.3	0.0	0.0	25.5	33.2	4.0	6.6	8.7	8.3	2.8	18.2	32.1	16.7	2.5	75.9	45.8	49.5	50.5
79256	ROARING SPRINGS	90.8	90.2	1.2	1.2	0.0	0.0	11.3	12.3	5.8	6.8	6.5	4.9	3.1	20.6	29.5	19.4	3.4	77.5	46.6	52.3	47.7
79257	SILVERTON	84.6	80.1	1.1	1.1	0.1	0.1	21.4	28.3	8.2	7.9	8.0	6.2	4.0	21.9	25.5	15.8	2.5	72.0	39.6	48.7	51.3
79259	TELL	85.7	83.3	7.1	8.3	0.0	0.0	35.7	41.7	8.3	0.0	0.0	0.0	25.0	0.0	50.0	16.7	0.0	91.7	52.5	41.7	58.3
79261	TURKEY	76.1	70.5	5.8	5.9	0.3	0.3	27.3	35.1	7.0	7.2	8.4	8.2	3.9	20.0	25.9	16.1	3.3	72.5	41.2	51.0	49.0
79311	ABERNATHY	78.5	72.6	2.2	2.3	0.1	0.2	39.0	49.6	7.9	8.1	7.8	7.3	5.3	24.0	25.2	12.6	1.7	71.5	36.8	49.3	50.7
79312	AMHERST	74.0	67.7	6.8	7.6	0.0	0.0	33.7	43.4	7.8	6.5	7.1	7.6	4.7	21.4	24.7	16.3	3.9	73.1	41.4	48.7	51.3
79313	ANTON	74.9	69.3	4.5	4.5	0.0	0.0	41.2	51.7	8.1	7.4	7.0	7.4	7.2	23.2	24.0	14.0	1.5	73.0	35.9	48.7	51.3
79316	BROWNFIELD	76.1	72.0	5.5	6.0	0.2	0.3	44.0	52.5	7.4	6.5	7.1	7.5	6.9	25.0	24.4	12.8	2.4	74.5	36.5	52.6	47.4
79320	BULA	70.3	61.8	1.6	1.8	0.0	0.0	35.9	47.3	5.5	5.5	5.5	5.5	5.5	21.8	34.5	14.5	1.8	78.2	45.4	56.4	43.6
79322	CROSBYTON	66.6	60.8	5.0	5.0	0.2	0.3	41.9	50.9	7.9	7.1	6.6	7.0	5.9	22.2	24.8	15.3	3.2	73.8	38.5	47.1	52.9
79323	DENVER CITY	69.3	63.4	1.7	1.7	0.2	0.2	45.4	54.7	8.1	7.8	7.8	8.5	6.3	23.8	25.3	10.8	1.6	70.8	35.4	48.3	51.7
79324	ENOCHS	71.2	61.4	1.5	1.8	0.0	0.0	36.4	49.1	5.3	5.3	5.3	5.3	5.3	21.1	36.8	14.0	1.8	78.9	46.1	56.1	43.9
79325	FARWELL	76.9	70.3	0.6	0.9	0.6	0.7	32.0	40.8	7.6	8.0	7.7	7.1	4.6	23.4	24.9	13.2	3.5	72.2	38.5	48.2	51.8
79326	FIELDTON	88.9	88.2	0.0	0.0	0.0	0.0	22.2	29.4	11.8	11.8	11.8	5.9	0.0	23.5	23.5	11.8	0.0	58.8	33.8	35.3	64.7
79329	IDALOU	74.0	65.8	0.7	0.8	0.3	0.4	36.6	48.1	7.0	6.6	7.1	8.4	6.9	23.0	26.2	12.5	2.2	73.8	37.9	49.8	50.2
79331	LAMESA	71.7	69.0	9.4	8.9	0.2	0.3	49.4	57.6	6.5	6.1	6.4	6.7	7.3	30.8	22.8	11.1	2.3	76.9	35.7	56.4	43.6
79336	LEVELLAND	73.4	68.2	3.9	3.9	0.2	0.2	37.3	45.7	7.6	7.3	7.0	8.2	7.5	25.5	24.1	10.9	1.9	73.8	33.2	48.9	51.1
79339	LITTLEFIELD	78.4	74.9	5.2	5.5	0.2	0.2	42.3	50.7	7.6	7.4	6.9	7.4	6.2	23.5	24.2	13.6	3.1	73.3	37.1	49.2	50.8
79342	LOOP	80.6	75.6	0.5	0.5	0.0	0.0	35.2	44.3	8.5	8.5	7.7	9.5	5.8	23.3	24.9	10.9	0.8	69.2	34.0	49.3	50.7
79343	LORENZO	67.1	62.8	5.3	5.0	0.1	0.1	51.0	59.5	8.0	8.2	8.6	7.6	6.5	23.5	25.1	11.5	1.0	70.2	34.5	49.4	50.6
79344	MAPLE	71.4	62.4	1.2	1.4	0.0	0.0	37.3	48.9	5.7	5.7	6.4	6.4	5.0	22.7	30.5	15.6	2.1	78.7	43.4	52.5	47.5
79345	MEADOW	81.0	76.1	0.4	0.5	0.2	0.2	45.3	56.9	7.9	8.4	7.9	7.0	4.6	26.3	25.7	11.2	1.0	71.3	35.8	51.9	48.1
79346	MORTON	63.1	56.1	4.7	5.4	0.3	0.3	45.6	54.4	7.3	7.6	8.3	9.0	5.3	24.1	23.5	13.0	1.8	70.9	36.0	48.8	51.2
79347	MULESHOE	66.5	60.3	1.3	1.3	0.1	0.2	47.8	56.8	8.4	8.1	7.8	7.4	5.9	23.3	24.3	12.6	2.3	71.0	35.6	49.0	51.0
79351	ODONNELL	68.3	63.2	1.1	1.3	0.5	0.5	55.1	64.1	7.8	7.6	7.3	7.4	7.3	22.4	24.0	14.4	1.7	72.9	36.5	50.1	49.9
79353	PEP	75.0	70.0	0.0	0.0	0.0	0.0	37.5	50.0	6.7	6.7	6.7	6.7	10.0	26.7	26.7	10.0	0.0	76.7	35.0	50.0	50.0
79355	PLAINS	73.9	69.3	0.5	0.5	0.1	0.1	47.4	56.3	6.8	7.9	8.1	8.7	4.5	24.2	27.9	10.6	1.2	71.3	36.8	49.7	50.3
79356	POST	74.8	70.1	4.8	4.8	0.1	0.1	37.2	45.7	4.9	4.9	5.3	7.5	9.4	35.7	21.0	9.4	1.8	79.9	34.5	64.0	36.0
79357	RALLS	59.1	52.6	1.9	1.8	0.0	0.0	53.7	63.1	8.4	7.4	7.3	9.4	6.6	22.5	23.1	12.7	2.7	70.3	34.6	47.7	52.3
79358	ROPESVILLE	84.7	80.7	1.0	1.0	0.2	0.2	34.7	44.6	8.3	8.4	8.5	7.5	4.3	24.8	25.8	11.4	1.1	70.1	36.7	52.4	47.6
79359	SEAGRAVES	69.4	65.5	4.7	4.4	0.0	0.0	51.7	60.1	7.6	7.9	8.9	9.2	5.2	23.1	24.9	11.0	2.2	69.8	35.1	48.6	51.4
79360	SEMINOLE	83.4	78.9	1.6	1.8	0.2	0.2	31.1	40.2	8.8	8.6	9.8	9.9	7.1	24.0	21.8	8.7	1.4	66.4	29.6	49.3	50.7
79363	SHALLOWATER	85.0	77.8	0.7	0.8	0.1	0.1	23.1	34.1	7.4	7.4	7.4	8.0	7.0	26.0	26.1	9.5	1.2	72.8	34.7	49.3	50.7
79364	SLATON	76.0	70.2	6.5	6.8	0.3	0.3	36.6	47.0	7.5	7.4	7.4	7.3	5.7	23.3	26.1	12.7	2.5	73.1	37.3	47.4	52.6
79366	RANSOM CANYON	89.5	83.9	1.4	1.9	0.2	0.3	16.1	25.1	5.0	5.1	6.2	7.9	4.2	21.6	36.9	12.1	1.0	78.1	45.0	49.7	50.3
79370	SPUR	76.5	71.4	6.5	6.7	0.4	0.5	25.4	32.6	5.0	5.0	5.1	5.3	8.3	25.1	25.5	16.5	4.3	81.4	41.5	53.2	46.8
79371	SUDAN	73.6	66.7	5.1	5.7	0.0	0.0	31.7	41.4	7.0	6.7	6.6	6.9	6.8	21.6	26.8	14.8	2.7	75.4	39.9	46.9	53.1
79373	TAHOKA	77.2	72.7	3.9	4.3	0.1	0.1	41.3	49.8	7.3	7.5	8.2	8.2	5.0	23.2	26.0	12.4	2.1	71.7	38.0	49.5	50.5
79376	TOKIO	80.0	72.2	0.0	0.0	0.0	0.0	35.0	50.0	11.1	11.1	11.1	11.1	0.0	38.9	16.7	0.0	0.0	55.6	30.0	50.0	50.0
79377	WELCH	87.8	83.9	0.0	0.0	0.6	0.7	37.1	48.3	7.1	7.5	7.7	7.7	4.2	23.0	27.4	14.1	1.3	72.8	39.5	50.3	49.7
79379	WHITEFACE	80.4	74.8	2.4	2.8	0.3	0.4	27.4	35.4	5.7	6.5	7.7	9.8	4.9	21.1	26.4	16.3	1.6	73.2	40.9	48.0	52.0
79381	WILSON	77.4	71.9	0.7	0.9	0.0	0.0	45.6	55.9	8.0	7.6	7.8	8.6	6.4	21.4	28.0	11.2	1.2	70.9	36.7	51.7	48.3
79382	WOLFFORTH	87.6	81.9	1.0	1.3	0.4	0.5	19.1	28.1	7.3	8.2	8.0	7.0	5.9	28.8	25.9	7.7	1.2	72.0	34.7	48.4	51.6
79401	LUBBOCK	50.4	45.4	15.8	16.5	6.4	6.0	46.8	55.1	7.7	6.1	4.6	7.2	17.6	35.5	16.1	4.3	1.0	78.3	27.4	57.3	42.7
79403	LUBBOCK	43.2	38.2	31.6	30.9	0.1	0.1	37.4	45.4	8.6	8.6	8.1	8.4	7.2	24.0	23.6	10.3	1.2	69.4	32.0	48.5	51.5
79404	LUBBOCK	43.6	40.1	25.5	24.5	0.2	0.3	49.9	56.6	8.6	8.6	7.9	8.2	7.0	27.9	22.2	8.6	1.0	69.7	31.6	52.2	47.8
79407	LUBBOCK	82.4	75.4	4.5	5.3	1.1	1.3	22.2	32.5	7.2	6.6	5.9	8.0	13.9	28.0	20.2	8.8	1.4	76.7	29.5	48.1	51.9
79409	LUBBOCK	88.6	83.5	4.3	5.9	2.6	3.8	7.9	12.7	0.1	0.0	0.0	66.2	30.6	3.0	0.1	0.0	0.0	99.7	18.8	51.6	48.4
79410	LUBBOCK	85.3	79.0	4.0	5.1	1.2	1.5	15.8	23.8	5.6	4.9	5.1	6.4	17.1	26.1	20.0	10.9	3.9	81.2	31.7	48.9	51.1
79411	LUBBOCK	57.7	50.6	8.7	8.9	0.6	0.6	52.5	62.4	9.3	8.5	7.6	7.3	9.9	30.9	19.3	5.8	1.3	70.4	28.9	50.3	49.7
79412	LUBBOCK	61.3	53.5	10.4	11.1	0.6	0.6	43.0	53.4	9.7	8.1	6.8	7.0	8.8	26.3	20.1	11.1	2.1	71.2	31.1	47.4	52.6
79413	LUBBOCK	87.4	82.5	3.6	4.5	0.8	1.1	15.6	22.9	5.9	5.5	5.4	6.0	7.6	24.8	24.5	16.9	3.5	79.9	40.3	46.8	53.2
79414	LUBBOCK	80.1	72.2	4.9	6.3	1.9	2.4	21.5	31.5	7.8	6.1	5.1	6.4	14.2	31.7	18.2	8.8	1.8	78.0	29.5	48.0	52.0
79415	LUBBOCK	53.0	47.7	4.9	5.2	1.2	1.3	64.2	70.9	8.4	7.5	7.0	8.5	15.3	25.8	18.7	7.7	1.2	72.6	27.0	50.4	49.6
79416	LUBBOCK	82.3	74.9	4.1	5.2	2.0	2.7	18.8	27.9	7.0	6.3	6.0	7.3	14.7	27.9	20.5	8.4	1.8	77.0	29.9	48.8	51.2
79423	LUBBOCK	86.4	79.8	3.4	4.3	0.9	1.2	15.8	25.0	7.3	7.0	6.8	6.5	6.1	30.2	26.4	8.7	1.0	74.9	35.4	49.0	51.0
79424	LUBBOCK	91.5	87.5	1.3	1.7	2.4	2.9	8.4	14.8	6.6	6.4	6.4	6.5	7.8	29.1	26.4	9.3	1.6	76.6	35.1	48.4	51.6
79501	ANSON	79.0	73.1	2.6	2.7	0.7	0.8	27.7	36.3	7.1	6.8	6.6	6.9	6.1	22.7	25.4	14.5	3.8	75.0	39.4	48.7	51.3
	TEXAS	71.0	67.6	11.5	11.4	2.8	3.5	32.0	37.4	7.9	7.5	7.2	7.5	7.4	28.3	24.0	8.8	1.4	73.0	33.6	49.7	50.3
	UNITED STATES	75.1	72.0	12.3	12.7	3.8	4.6	12.5	15.7	6.8	6.7	6.6	7.1	6.9	27.0	26.0	10.9	1.9	75.7	36.9	49.2	50.8

79098-79501

#	POST OFFICE NAME	2009 Per Capita Income	2009 HH Income Base	2009 Household Income Distribution (%) Less than $25,000	$25,000 to $49,999	$50,000 to $99,999	$100,000 to $149,999	$150,000 or More	Median Household Income 2009	2014	2009 National Centile	2009 State Centile	2009 Home Value Base	2009 Home Value Distribution (%) Less than $50,000	$50,000 to $89,999	$90,000 to $174,999	$175,000 to $399,999	$400,000 or More	2009 Median Home Value
79098	WILDORADO	17617	138	28.3	34.8	28.3	5.8	2.9	39124	40563	30	38	90	32.2	21.1	30.0	11.1	5.6	86250
79101	AMARILLO	17066	1154	41.5	33.4	20.9	2.0	2.2	28609	31058	6	8	349	38.7	46.4	13.2	1.7	0.0	57745
79102	AMARILLO	19603	4083	33.5	31.9	28.8	2.8	3.0	35085	38086	18	23	2063	23.3	39.4	29.0	7.2	1.1	76216
79103	AMARILLO	16124	3537	25.3	32.9	37.7	3.0	1.1	42822	46812	42	53	2670	21.3	64.9	13.0	0.8	0.0	67187
79104	AMARILLO	12612	2482	33.8	40.2	22.2	2.5	1.4	34252	37762	16	20	1573	54.2	41.2	4.4	0.2	0.0	47509
79106	AMARILLO	21157	12540	30.5	33.1	28.6	5.1	2.6	39007	42525	30	38	6740	16.8	34.6	39.5	8.0	1.1	88229
79107	AMARILLO	12509	10841	40.1	32.9	23.2	2.6	1.3	30369	32787	9	11	6719	54.8	41.9	2.5	0.8	0.0	47599
79108	AMARILLO	17037	4511	23.9	32.4	35.9	5.7	2.1	45534	47065	50	60	3500	26.3	30.3	38.0	5.3	0.1	82813
79109	AMARILLO	29265	19034	20.9	24.4	37.1	12.6	5.0	53984	56964	70	77	11304	2.2	18.9	62.7	14.5	1.7	118722
79110	AMARILLO	21919	6781	17.5	28.0	47.3	5.5	1.6	52487	55586	67	75	4963	12.5	44.3	40.0	3.0	0.1	82828
79111	AMARILLO	17113	561	15.5	25.8	52.9	4.6	1.1	53383	53421	69	76	18	77.8	11.1	11.1	0.0	0.0	34375
79118	AMARILLO	22721	6086	16.3	26.9	43.3	9.7	3.8	53992	56302	70	77	4860	28.5	22.6	36.2	10.9	1.8	87931
79119	AMARILLO	30836	3212	10.5	19.2	38.3	18.6	13.4	70237	68930	87	90	2872	19.4	9.8	30.2	36.9	3.6	157152
79121	AMARILLO	40423	2939	12.3	15.1	37.3	19.5	15.8	76019	71071	90	92	2067	0.0	1.1	57.4	35.8	5.7	162318
79124	AMARILLO	31865	3067	10.2	19.7	45.0	16.5	8.6	66885	65563	85	88	2547	9.1	10.7	42.8	33.3	4.1	149871
79201	CHILDRESS	16956	2416	35.7	29.5	30.5	2.8	1.4	35143	36062	18	23	1682	42.8	33.4	18.7	5.1	0.0	57707
79220	AFTON	19173	48	50.0	25.0	20.8	4.2	0.0	25000	32349	3	4	36	47.2	27.8	19.4	5.6	0.0	53333
79225	CHILLICOTHE	18103	404	34.7	34.7	23.3	5.0	2.5	36082	37608	21	27	301	67.8	19.9	9.3	2.7	0.3	36310
79226	CLARENDON	19311	1273	33.2	32.3	27.3	5.5	1.7	36160	37973	21	28	932	36.7	31.2	23.8	6.3	1.9	67000
79227	CROWELL	17421	655	40.3	33.6	21.5	2.7	1.8	31864	32602	11	14	487	65.1	22.2	11.9	0.2	0.6	34792
79229	DICKENS	21137	225	45.8	27.6	20.0	4.4	2.2	29716	30000	8	9	171	52.6	26.3	17.5	3.5	0.0	47188
79230	DODSON	22133	64	28.1	34.4	32.8	4.7	0.0	40000	45614	33	42	52	40.4	32.7	23.1	3.8	0.0	60000
79234	FLOMOT	15792	32	34.4	37.5	21.9	6.3	0.0	33141	33141	14	17	24	50.0	25.0	20.8	4.2	0.0	50000
79235	FLOYDADA	15879	1569	38.3	30.1	23.7	5.7	2.2	32177	33653	12	15	1146	56.3	26.5	14.9	2.3	0.0	43077
79237	HEDLEY	17255	295	39.7	30.8	25.4	2.7	1.4	35109	35795	18	23	227	53.7	24.7	16.7	4.8	0.0	45750
79239	LAKEVIEW	12527	92	44.6	37.0	16.3	2.2	0.0	30538	30306	9	11	71	67.6	16.9	5.6	4.2	5.6	29750
79240	LELIA LAKE	14947	41	43.9	29.3	24.4	2.4	0.0	31134	37357	10	12	32	53.1	25.0	18.8	3.1	0.0	46667
79241	LOCKNEY	16979	921	31.8	34.7	23.9	6.2	3.4	35559	38138	19	25	668	43.9	28.7	20.5	5.8	1.0	56029
79243	MCADOO	21064	46	50.0	26.1	19.6	4.3	0.0	25000	30000	3	4	35	51.4	25.7	17.1	5.7	0.0	48333
79244	MATADOR	18817	416	36.1	34.6	23.8	4.1	1.4	33566	35626	15	18	318	66.0	18.9	12.9	1.6	0.6	40192
79245	MEMPHIS	14134	1044	43.3	34.6	18.8	3.1	0.3	27890	28884	5	7	744	68.1	21.1	9.7	1.1	0.0	34872
79247	ODELL	18165	38	31.6	36.8	23.7	7.9	0.0	36507	43645	22	29	27	29.6	25.9	37.0	7.4	0.0	77500
79248	PADUCAH	17058	833	39.1	32.2	24.5	2.9	1.3	32603	33241	13	16	555	64.1	19.6	11.9	4.3	0.0	36833
79250	PETERSBURG	17547	520	30.6	36.5	24.8	4.2	3.8	37140	39192	24	31	390	52.8	26.9	14.4	5.1	0.8	47885
79251	QUAIL	18515	22	27.3	36.4	31.8	4.5	0.0	40000	42367	33	42	18	33.3	38.9	27.8	0.0	0.0	65000
79252	QUANAH	19839	1402	33.7	32.9	26.8	3.6	3.1	34936	35897	17	22	1002	62.1	22.8	13.1	1.8	0.3	40833
79255	QUITAQUE	16436	219	38.4	27.4	29.7	4.6	0.0	35976	38043	20	27	162	57.4	28.4	13.0	0.0	1.2	40769
79256	ROARING SPRINGS	17935	139	36.0	35.3	21.6	6.5	0.7	32505	34224	12	15	105	46.7	21.9	25.7	3.8	1.9	55000
79257	SILVERTON	16893	456	33.3	35.1	26.5	3.7	1.3	35808	36734	20	26	355	53.2	31.8	11.5	1.7	1.7	45208
79259	TELL	13333	6	66.7	16.7	16.7	0.0	0.0	20000	32500	1	2	5	80.0	20.0	0.0	0.0	0.0	27500
79261	TURKEY	13912	250	49.2	32.0	16.4	1.2	1.2	25365	27006	3	4	198	87.4	5.1	6.6	1.0	0.0	19839
79311	ABERNATHY	17672	1285	28.5	33.6	30.3	5.2	2.4	40237	43044	33	43	912	36.6	29.6	28.3	5.4	0.1	67458
79312	AMHERST	16634	372	38.2	30.6	23.4	5.6	2.2	34123	35883	16	20	284	60.2	19.4	15.1	4.2	1.1	37778
79313	ANTON	17234	535	35.1	26.5	32.0	3.2	3.2	39352	43084	31	40	392	52.8	30.6	13.3	3.3	0.0	47925
79316	BROWNFIELD	16288	3744	38.3	29.1	25.6	4.4	2.7	34757	36331	17	22	2631	43.9	31.5	19.8	4.5	0.2	56088
79320	BULA	13935	17	29.4	35.3	29.4	5.9	0.0	36079	35000	21	27	11	18.2	36.4	45.5	0.0	0.0	67500
79322	CROSBYTON	18397	901	39.1	33.5	19.5	3.8	4.1	31808	33372	11	14	619	54.8	30.5	13.2	1.5	0.0	44636
79323	DENVER CITY	17306	1883	33.4	29.2	29.1	4.5	3.8	38383	40334	28	35	1456	48.8	28.2	17.7	4.7	0.6	51104
79324	ENOCHS	16984	21	33.3	28.6	33.3	4.8	0.0	36100	40000	21	27	13	30.8	23.1	46.2	0.0	0.0	65000
79325	FARWELL	15529	721	30.5	39.9	24.8	3.6	1.1	35516	36861	19	25	557	32.7	30.5	25.3	11.0	0.5	71047
79326	FIELDTON	19559	8	12.5	62.5	25.0	0.0	0.0	32505	42500	33	42	6	0.0	0.0	66.7	33.3	0.0	143750
79329	IDALOU	19162	1316	24.5	36.8	30.0	6.0	2.7	42286	45877	40	51	942	34.0	29.1	32.4	4.1	0.4	70263
79331	LAMESA	16828	4064	36.1	32.9	24.4	3.6	2.9	34169	36627	16	20	2960	49.5	28.0	17.6	4.7	0.2	50517
79336	LEVELLAND	17782	6700	30.9	34.2	27.4	5.1	2.4	37846	40274	26	34	4897	39.1	29.9	26.1	4.6	0.3	63279
79339	LITTLEFIELD	18077	2730	37.3	32.5	23.4	4.7	2.2	33580	35179	15	18	1999	53.0	25.2	19.0	2.5	0.4	47153
79342	LOOP	15532	118	28.8	38.1	22.0	5.1	5.9	38622	42781	29	36	85	35.3	41.2	16.5	7.1	0.0	58333
79343	LORENZO	14893	533	42.8	25.9	25.3	3.9	2.1	32355	34314	12	15	360	53.6	23.1	21.7	1.7	0.0	47593
79344	MAPLE	16592	51	31.4	33.3	27.5	5.9	2.0	35428	36525	19	24	32	34.4	25.0	37.5	3.1	0.0	65000
79345	MEADOW	14708	362	33.4	30.7	30.7	4.1	1.1	33902	34428	15	19	261	49.4	25.7	16.9	7.3	0.8	50882
79346	MORTON	15810	1104	36.7	34.2	23.4	3.6	2.1	32564	32871	13	16	812	68.3	18.5	10.6	2.1	0.5	34125
79347	MULESHOE	15480	2207	35.5	33.2	25.6	3.9	1.8	34357	35219	16	21	1569	50.4	25.9	19.4	3.8	0.4	49604
79351	ODONNELL	16453	441	41.5	28.3	21.5	6.1	2.5	31159	31669	10	13	326	66.3	17.8	13.5	2.1	0.3	35435
79353	PEP	16750	13	30.8	38.5	30.8	0.0	0.0	32308	42330	12	15	9	44.4	33.3	22.2	0.0	0.0	65000
79355	PLAINS	16721	666	29.6	35.9	26.4	5.0	3.2	38333	39348	28	35	509	39.5	29.3	23.6	7.1	0.6	63875
79356	POST	15118	1602	37.1	35.0	21.6	4.4	1.9	33695	35023	15	19	1119	47.0	28.5	15.7	7.7	1.1	52839
79357	RALLS	14990	954	39.7	32.9	22.0	4.1	1.3	30845	32611	9	12	663	55.5	32.7	10.0	0.9	0.9	43917
79358	ROPESVILLE	18582	469	26.4	36.2	28.8	5.1	3.4	39774	43642	32	41	348	36.8	33.6	21.0	8.0	0.6	67333
79359	SEAGRAVES	15626	1079	35.5	34.8	24.2	3.1	2.5	35086	35578	18	23	795	51.8	23.5	21.5	3.1	0.0	48141
79360	SEMINOLE	14833	3759	32.1	32.4	28.8	4.6	2.0	36394	38564	22	28	2957	37.6	29.0	26.5	6.0	0.9	66745
79363	SHALLOWATER	19285	2191	22.0	32.0	37.7	5.8	2.4	46808	49307	54	64	1655	33.7	26.1	32.0	7.8	0.4	72816
79364	SLATON	19004	2966	34.8	31.0	25.3	5.9	3.0	36464	39694	22	29	2048	44.8	28.2	18.2	7.7	1.1	55408
79366	RANSOM CANYON	27074	424	21.7	26.4	36.8	9.7	5.4	51327	51624	64	73	339	20.4	27.1	30.7	19.5	2.4	100765
79370	SPUR	14908	623	38.5	32.9	25.4	2.2	1.0	33254	34341	14	17	479	68.7	25.3	5.6	0.4	0.0	29750
79371	SUDAN	21056	518	30.9	33.4	25.1	7.1	3.5	39157	41971	30	39	403	56.6	27.8	13.6	1.5	0.5	45431
79373	TAHOKA	16195	1464	40.2	27.1	25.0	5.2	2.5	31619	32269	11	13	1069	47.1	24.7	23.1	4.9	0.3	53119
79376	TOKIO	9583	7	57.1	28.6	14.3	0.0	0.0	22183	27208	2	3	5	0.0	0.0	100.0	0.0	0.0	112500
79377	WELCH	19651	159	22.6	39.0	32.7	4.4	1.3	42324	46721	40	51	116	48.3	27.6	20.7	3.4	0.0	53333
79379	WHITEFACE	15756	72	31.9	31.9	26.4	6.9	2.8	38633	42408	29	36	49	49.0	30.6	16.3	4.1	0.0	50714
79381	WILSON	16723	343	31.5	32.1	28.6	5.2	2.6	36324	38658	21	28	257	49.8	21.0	24.1	4.3	0.8	50250
79382	WOLFFORTH	21101	1655	22.0	33.4	33.7	7.3	3.6	46659	48587	53	64	1267	24.3	35.8	25.0	13.4	1.4	72134
79401	LUBBOCK	13028	3579	60.5	26.7	10.9	1.4	0.5	20659	20903	2	2	600	48.2	42.8	8.2	0.8	0.0	51222
79403	LUBBOCK	14362	5968	40.9	30.4	23.6	2.9	2.3	31683	35007	11	13	4124	62.2	25.3	8.8	2.9	0.8	42070
79404	LUBBOCK	13366	3636	39.6	34.8	21.8	2.7	1.1	31993	34981	11	14	2263	59.7	29.3	7.6	2.5	0.8	43754
79407	LUBBOCK	20935	7695	33.3	31.6	28.3	4.1	2.8	36945	41225	23	31	3812	28.5	36.9	25.6	6.6	2.4	69699
79409	LUBBOCK	14087	57	57.9	5.3	36.8	0.0	0.0	9500	48222	0	1	0	0.0	0.0	0.0	0.0	0.0	0
79410	LUBBOCK	23502	4226	32.8	29.1	29.6	6.1	2.5	37969	42019	27	34	2088	14.5	40.5	34.8	9.4	0.9	83355
79411	LUBBOCK	13955	3236	44.2	29.0	23.4	2.5	0.9	28588	31719	6	8	1329	59.1	31.1	9.8	0.0	0.0	44600
79412	LUBBOCK	16513	5912	35.0	34.7	26.2	2.6	1.5	33940	36666	15	19	3010	34.0	42.0	23.6	0.4	0.0	58842
79413	LUBBOCK	25403	8797	23.5	32.2	33.0	7.6	3.8	46344	48106	52	63	5595	8.6	35.2	49.2	7.0	0.1	97643
79414	LUBBOCK	19886	7655	36.8	29.5	28.0	4.3	1.5	34565	38132	17	21	3073	13.3	58.4	27.7	0.6	0.0	74174
79415	LUBBOCK	13131	5954	50.8	28.7	17.6	2.1	0.7	24488	26214	3	4	2656	66.5	23.3	7.8	2.2	0.2	40437
79416	LUBBOCK	23596	11776	28.2	26.8	34.1	6.9	3.9	45515	48606	50	60	6800	9.1	39.6	38.5	11.1	1.6	91368
79423	LUBBOCK	28289	11565	14.9	26.1	40.8	11.6	6.7	57814	56957	75	82	8470	11.1	28.1	47.6	12.0	1.2	101591
79424	LUBBOCK	31995	14670	16.4	22.1	37.2	14.2	10.2	63994	63149	82	87	10182	4.8	10.3	57.1	24.3	3.5	133369
79501	ANSON	17875	1236	35.9	31.7	26.0	3.8	2.6	34931	36538	17	22	926	61.0	20.4	14.0	2.2	2.4	39819
	TEXAS	24551		22.3	25.0	34.3	11.1	7.3	52382	54495				16.5	22.7	36.5	19.7	4.6	109784
	UNITED STATES	27277		20.9	24.4	35.3	11.7	7.6	54719	56938				9.3	13.1	31.6	32.6	13.5	162279

ZIP CODE #	POST OFFICE NAME	FINANCIAL SERVICES: Auto Loan	Home Loan	Invest-ments	Retire-ment Plans	THE HOME: Home Improvements: Home Repair	Lawn & Garden	Furnishings: Comput-ers & Hard-ware-Personal	Major Appli-ances	TV, Radio, Sound Equip-ment	Furni-ture	ENTERTAINMENT: Dine out/ Carry out	Sports Equip-ment	Fees & Tickets	Toys & Games	Travel	Cable TV	PERSONAL: Apparel & Services	Auto Repairs	Health Insur-ance	Pets & Supplies
79098	WILDORADO	86	59	94	59	62	90	65	81	68	53	67	67	48	67	65	74	44	76	86	100
79101	AMARILLO	54	45	43	45	44	49	54	51	57	51	56	38	49	56	48	60	39	55	57	61
79102	AMARILLO	69	61	55	60	60	62	67	64	69	67	69	47	63	69	62	71	48	68	69	76
79103	AMARILLO	71	66	53	64	62	67	67	66	69	67	68	50	64	70	63	70	47	68	70	78
79104	AMARILLO	64	53	42	47	51	51	56	57	59	59	59	38	49	60	50	60	41	58	56	64
79106	AMARILLO	71	63	58	65	61	67	73	67	74	68	73	52	68	74	66	75	51	71	73	81
79107	AMARILLO	60	52	43	48	49	51	55	55	57	57	57	39	50	58	50	59	40	56	56	63
79108	AMARILLO	82	74	73	72	72	82	73	79	76	71	75	59	67	77	71	79	51	76	81	93
79109	AMARILLO	96	91	85	93	90	91	96	92	96	96	97	71	94	97	93	96	67	95	95	109
79110	AMARILLO	83	83	69	83	79	83	82	81	82	81	82	63	81	85	79	83	57	81	84	96
79111	AMARILLO	84	73	62	74	68	66	83	73	80	84	82	60	76	84	74	78	57	79	71	88
79118	AMARILLO	98	94	80	90	90	90	89	91	90	93	90	69	86	94	86	90	62	89	88	107
79119	AMARILLO	129	147	123	147	141	127	128	129	121	137	123	104	137	129	131	115	87	121	114	147
79121	AMARILLO	135	146	140	151	144	138	139	135	136	144	138	106	149	139	144	134	99	137	133	159
79124	AMARILLO	119	132	125	135	132	128	119	123	117	124	118	94	127	119	126	117	83	119	121	144
79201	CHILDRESS	73	53	71	52	54	75	59	69	64	52	62	54	47	63	56	70	41	66	75	83
79220	AFTON	62	43	68	43	45	65	47	59	49	38	49	49	35	48	47	54	32	55	62	72
79225	CHILLICOTHE	78	56	79	54	58	81	61	75	67	54	65	57	48	66	59	74	43	70	82	89
79226	CLARENDON	76	57	85	56	61	80	60	75	66	55	64	56	50	64	61	72	43	70	79	88
79227	CROWELL	72	51	75	50	53	75	56	69	61	48	59	54	44	60	55	67	39	65	75	83
79229	DICKENS	72	50	79	49	52	76	55	68	57	45	57	56	40	56	55	62	37	64	72	84
79230	DODSON	86	59	94	59	62	91	66	81	68	53	67	67	48	67	65	74	44	76	86	100
79234	FLOMOT	74	51	81	51	53	78	57	70	59	46	58	58	41	58	56	64	38	66	74	87
79235	FLOYDADA	70	60	56	54	59	62	60	65	63	62	63	45	54	63	57	65	44	64	65	74
79237	HEDLEY	73	50	80	50	53	77	56	69	58	45	57	57	41	57	55	63	37	65	73	85
79239	LAKEVIEW	60	41	66	41	43	63	46	57	48	37	47	47	34	47	46	52	31	53	60	70
79240	LELIA LAKE	62	43	68	43	45	65	47	59	49	38	49	49	35	48	47	54	32	55	62	72
79241	LOCKNEY	85	62	78	58	63	82	66	79	72	61	71	59	53	71	63	78	47	75	83	93
79243	MCADOO	61	42	67	42	44	65	47	58	49	38	48	48	34	48	47	53	31	54	61	72
79244	MATADOR	79	54	87	54	57	83	60	75	63	49	62	62	44	62	60	68	40	70	79	92
79245	MEMPHIS	59	42	59	41	44	62	46	57	52	41	50	43	37	51	45	57	33	53	62	67
79247	ODELL	84	58	92	57	60	88	64	79	67	52	66	66	47	65	64	73	43	74	84	98
79248	PADUCAH	68	48	71	47	50	71	53	66	58	46	56	51	41	56	52	63	37	61	71	78
79250	PETERSBURG	80	67	75	62	68	76	70	78	72	69	71	58	61	72	67	74	49	75	77	89
79251	QUAIL	87	60	96	60	63	92	67	83	69	54	69	69	49	68	66	76	44	77	88	102
79252	QUANAH	79	57	76	57	58	80	64	75	69	56	67	58	51	69	61	76	45	71	81	89
79255	QUITAQUE	71	49	78	49	51	75	54	67	56	44	56	56	40	55	54	61	36	63	71	83
79256	ROARING SPRINGS	75	52	82	51	54	79	57	71	60	46	59	59	42	58	57	65	38	66	75	88
79257	SILVERTON	76	52	83	52	55	80	58	72	60	47	59	59	42	59	58	66	39	67	76	88
79259	TELL	45	32	45	32	34	47	35	44	40	32	38	33	28	39	34	44	25	41	48	51
79261	TURKEY	60	42	66	41	44	64	46	57	48	38	48	47	34	48	46	53	31	54	61	70
79311	ABERNATHY	87	64	81	60	65	83	67	80	72	63	71	60	53	71	65	77	48	76	83	95
79312	AMHERST	81	56	89	56	59	86	62	77	65	50	64	64	45	63	62	70	41	72	81	95
79313	ANTON	81	58	81	57	61	85	64	79	71	57	69	59	51	70	62	78	46	73	86	92
79316	BROWNFIELD	73	57	64	54	57	70	61	67	64	57	64	50	51	64	57	68	43	66	71	80
79320	BULA	81	55	89	55	58	85	62	76	64	50	63	63	45	63	61	70	41	71	81	94
79322	CROSBYTON	82	60	77	57	61	80	64	77	70	59	69	57	51	69	62	76	46	73	81	90
79323	DENVER CITY	83	68	68	63	67	75	69	76	72	70	72	56	60	74	65	75	49	73	75	88
79324	ENOCHS	82	57	91	57	59	87	63	78	65	51	65	65	46	64	63	71	42	73	83	96
79325	FARWELL	75	54	71	51	55	72	58	69	61	53	61	53	45	61	56	66	41	66	71	83
79326	FIELDTON	74	51	82	51	54	78	57	71	59	46	58	58	42	58	56	64	38	66	75	87
79329	IDALOU	83	68	73	65	68	79	71	78	74	69	74	58	62	74	68	78	50	77	81	92
79331	LAMESA	75	62	65	57	61	72	62	71	67	62	67	49	55	67	60	72	45	68	74	81
79336	LEVELLAND	77	65	64	62	65	71	67	71	70	67	69	52	60	70	63	72	48	70	73	83
79339	LITTLEFIELD	82	60	75	57	60	79	64	76	71	60	69	56	52	70	61	76	46	73	81	90
79342	LOOP	89	61	97	61	64	94	68	84	70	55	70	70	50	69	67	77	45	79	89	104
79343	LORENZO	78	52	79	50	52	79	56	70	63	51	62	56	42	63	53	70	41	66	74	87
79344	MAPLE	82	56	90	56	59	87	63	78	65	51	64	64	46	64	62	71	42	73	82	96
79345	MEADOW	81	55	88	55	58	85	61	76	64	50	63	63	45	63	61	70	41	71	81	94
79346	MORTON	76	54	75	52	55	75	58	70	61	52	61	55	45	61	56	66	40	66	73	84
79347	MULESHOE	74	54	68	51	55	72	57	69	63	54	62	51	46	62	55	68	41	65	72	81
79351	ODONNELL	77	59	56	52	58	64	61	68	65	63	66	46	51	66	56	68	45	67	67	77
79353	PEP	69	48	76	47	50	73	53	66	55	43	54	54	39	54	53	60	35	61	69	81
79355	PLAINS	89	61	98	61	64	94	68	85	71	55	70	70	50	70	68	77	46	79	90	104
79356	POST	70	52	61	48	52	65	55	65	60	53	59	46	45	59	52	64	40	62	67	75
79357	RALLS	73	54	68	51	55	72	58	69	63	53	62	51	46	62	55	68	41	66	73	81
79358	ROPESVILLE	94	66	102	66	69	99	73	89	76	60	75	74	54	74	72	82	49	84	94	110
79359	SEAGRAVES	80	60	67	54	60	72	62	72	67	61	67	51	51	67	59	71	45	70	73	84
79360	SEMINOLE	77	61	67	57	61	72	63	71	66	62	66	53	53	67	60	70	45	68	72	83
79363	SHALLOWATER	84	79	69	77	76	80	77	78	78	78	78	59	73	81	73	80	54	78	79	93
79364	SLATON	82	64	77	60	65	79	67	78	72	64	71	56	56	71	65	77	48	75	81	90
79366	RANSOM CANYON	109	87	141	86	96	115	87	111	91	82	90	81	76	87	94	97	60	102	109	128
79370	SPUR	67	48	68	47	50	70	53	65	58	46	56	49	42	57	51	64	37	61	71	77
79371	SUDAN	92	66	93	64	68	96	72	89	80	64	77	67	57	79	70	88	52	83	97	105
79373	TAHOKA	78	56	74	53	57	75	60	72	63	54	63	55	46	63	58	68	42	68	74	86
79376	TOKIO	44	30	48	30	32	47	34	42	35	27	35	35	25	34	33	38	22	39	44	51
79377	WELCH	100	69	110	69	72	106	76	95	80	62	79	79	56	78	76	87	51	89	100	117
79379	WHITEFACE	91	64	98	63	66	95	69	86	73	58	72	69	52	72	68	80	47	80	90	105
79381	WILSON	79	67	77	63	68	74	70	76	68	68	69	60	60	69	68	69	47	74	73	89
79382	WOLFFORTH	94	85	82	82	83	89	80	87	83	83	83	65	75	86	77	85	56	83	86	103
79401	LUBBOCK	41	27	26	29	26	28	44	33	42	40	43	29	35	43	34	41	30	40	35	42
79403	LUBBOCK	67	54	53	52	52	61	57	60	63	59	62	44	51	63	53	67	42	61	65	73
79404	LUBBOCK	62	52	45	48	50	52	54	56	57	57	57	39	49	58	50	59	40	57	56	64
79407	LUBBOCK	74	62	58	63	60	63	76	66	74	71	74	53	66	74	65	73	51	71	68	81
79409	LUBBOCK	39	17	16	20	15	19	55	27	44	37	44	29	32	43	29	40	31	38	27	37
79410	LUBBOCK	75	58	53	61	56	62	83	66	79	71	78	56	68	80	66	79	55	75	70	82
79411	LUBBOCK	55	43	36	42	41	43	53	47	54	52	55	36	47	55	45	55	38	52	49	57
79412	LUBBOCK	63	52	48	53	51	54	62	57	63	60	63	44	55	63	55	64	44	61	60	69
79413	LUBBOCK	82	78	76	79	78	84	82	81	84	80	84	61	81	83	81	87	58	83	89	96
79414	LUBBOCK	64	49	44	52	47	51	68	55	66	61	66	46	57	67	56	66	46	63	59	69
79415	LUBBOCK	53	38	32	36	36	37	53	44	51	49	51	34	41	51	41	50	36	49	43	52
79416	LUBBOCK	84	76	71	77	74	75	87	78	84	83	84	62	80	85	78	83	59	82	79	94
79423	LUBBOCK	106	109	96	107	105	99	103	102	100	108	101	79	103	104	101	98	71	100	96	119
79424	LUBBOCK	118	122	108	121	118	110	120	114	114	122	116	90	119	119	115	111	81	113	107	133
79501	ANSON	79	57	77	56	59	81	64	75	69	56	67	58	51	68	60	75	45	71	82	90
	TEXAS	104	96	90	94	93	94	99	97	99	101	100	75	94	101	94	99	70	99	96	114
	UNITED STATES	100	100	100	100	100	100	100	100	100	100	100	100	100	100	100	100	100	100	100	100

ZIP CODE #	POST OFFICE NAME	COUNTY FIPS CODE	POPULATION 2000	POPULATION 2009	POPULATION 2014	2000-2009 ANNUAL RATE % Rate	2000-2009 ANNUAL RATE State Centile	HOUSEHOLDS 2000	HOUSEHOLDS 2009	HOUSEHOLDS 2014	HOUSEHOLDS % Annual Rate 2000-2009	HOUSEHOLDS 2009 Average HH Size	FAMILIES 2000	FAMILIES 2009	FAMILIES % Annual Rate 2000-2009
79502	ASPERMONT	433	1404	1261	1183	-1.2	3	571	521	490	-1.0	2.34	396	357	-1.1
79503	AVOCA	253	257	222	208	-1.6	1	98	85	79	-1.5	2.61	69	58	-1.9
79504	BAIRD	059	2484	2594	2672	0.5	42	1020	1066	1099	0.5	2.38	682	700	0.3
79506	BLACKWELL	353	888	834	805	-0.7	7	403	386	374	-0.5	2.16	282	265	-0.7
79508	BUFFALO GAP	441	1055	1096	1173	0.4	37	412	433	463	0.5	2.52	326	338	0.4
79510	CLYDE	059	7530	8189	8535	0.9	55	2869	3134	3274	1.0	2.60	2215	2388	0.8
79511	COAHOMA	227	1476	1332	1270	-1.1	3	565	522	501	-0.9	2.55	426	388	-1.0
79512	COLORADO CITY	335	8161	7850	7654	-0.4	13	2234	2099	2025	-0.7	2.45	1574	1458	-0.8
79517	FLUVANNA	033	247	238	235	-0.4	13	107	106	106	-0.1	2.25	84	82	-0.3
79518	GIRARD	263	128	123	122	-0.4	13	54	53	53	-0.2	2.32	40	39	-0.3
79519	GOLDSBORO	083	47	51	52	0.9	55	19	21	21	1.1	2.43	14	15	0.7
79520	HAMLIN	253	2570	2281	2149	-1.3	2	1048	933	879	-1.2	2.40	718	627	-1.5
79521	HASKELL	207	3646	3369	3207	-0.9	5	1524	1415	1351	-0.8	2.30	1039	949	-1.0
79525	HAWLEY	253	2920	2903	2828	-0.1	21	1037	1036	1010	0.0	2.80	838	824	-0.2
79526	HERMLEIGH	415	1010	1039	1057	0.3	34	402	422	434	0.5	2.23	292	303	0.4
79527	IRA	415	304	292	288	-0.4	13	126	124	124	-0.2	2.35	98	96	-0.2
79528	JAYTON	263	591	522	506	-1.3	2	240	214	208	-1.2	2.26	164	143	-1.5
79529	KNOX CITY	275	1456	1408	1376	-0.4	13	583	574	562	-0.2	2.37	392	379	-0.4
79530	LAWN	441	657	712	728	0.9	55	260	286	294	1.0	2.49	200	217	0.9
79532	LORAINE	335	1144	1093	1060	-0.5	11	449	433	422	-0.4	2.45	315	299	-0.6
79533	LUEDERS	253	443	380	360	-1.6	1	189	162	154	-1.7	2.34	131	110	-1.9
79534	MC CAULLEY	151	226	218	213	-0.4	13	92	91	89	-0.1	2.40	65	63	-0.3
79535	MARYNEAL	353	138	130	125	-0.6	9	56	53	52	-0.6	2.45	44	41	-0.8
79536	MERKEL	441	5019	4955	4907	-0.1	21	1886	1893	1885	0.0	2.59	1410	1391	-0.1
79537	NOLAN	353	143	128	121	-1.2	3	51	46	44	-1.1	2.78	35	31	-1.3
79538	NOVICE	083	232	252	257	0.9	55	92	100	102	0.9	2.52	69	73	0.6
79539	O BRIEN	207	287	249	234	-1.5	1	111	98	92	-1.3	2.53	78	67	-1.6
79540	OLD GLORY	433	289	220	203	-2.9	0	142	111	103	-2.6	1.98	97	74	-2.9
79541	OVALO	441	696	785	817	1.3	65	256	291	304	1.4	2.69	201	225	1.2
79543	ROBY	151	1301	1213	1172	-0.8	6	523	494	480	-0.6	2.41	373	347	-0.8
79544	ROCHESTER	207	583	507	475	-1.5	1	247	217	204	-1.4	2.32	173	150	-1.5
79545	ROSCOE	353	1815	1603	1515	-1.3	2	678	606	575	-1.2	2.58	522	462	-1.3
79546	ROTAN	151	2128	1996	1921	-0.7	7	884	844	817	-0.5	2.31	596	560	-0.7
79547	RULE	207	862	746	696	-1.6	1	364	318	298	-1.4	2.35	253	217	-1.6
79548	RULE	207	296	254	236	-1.6	1	131	114	107	-1.5	2.23	92	78	-1.8
79549	SNYDER	263	15072	15000	15037	-0.1	21	5243	5271	5327	0.1	2.52	3779	3746	-0.1
79553	STAMFORD	207	4108	3683	3477	-1.2	3	1593	1415	1333	-1.3	2.49	1132	987	-1.5
79556	SWEETWATER	353	13577	12725	12265	-0.7	7	5318	5047	4883	-0.6	2.43	3653	3413	-0.7
79560	SYLVESTER	151	220	215	210	-0.2	19	101	100	99	-0.1	2.15	73	71	-0.3
79561	TRENT	441	511	515	515	0.1	27	199	205	205	0.3	2.51	143	144	0.1
79562	TUSCOLA	441	2356	2861	2987	2.1	79	896	1095	1145	2.2	2.61	715	861	2.0
79563	TYE	441	1127	1129	1123	0.0	25	412	424	424	0.3	2.65	311	315	0.1
79565	WESTBROOK	335	400	364	348	-1.0	4	157	145	139	-0.9	2.51	110	99	-1.1
79566	WINGATE	399	357	395	401	1.1	61	157	176	179	1.2	2.24	119	132	1.1
79567	WINTERS	399	3756	3631	3549	-0.4	13	1448	1402	1371	-0.3	2.56	1027	981	-0.5
79601	ABILENE	253	21398	21754	21756	0.2	30	6937	7171	7218	0.4	2.19	3977	4040	0.2
79602	ABILENE	441	19521	20947	21474	0.8	52	6960	7585	7803	0.9	2.59	4959	5372	0.9
79603	ABILENE	441	24131	23500	23208	-0.3	16	8748	8723	8669	0.0	2.65	6373	6248	-0.2
79605	ABILENE	441	30064	28845	28385	-0.4	13	11853	11744	11627	-0.1	2.38	8097	7825	-0.4
79606	ABILENE	441	20659	22338	22955	0.8	52	8485	9344	9633	1.0	2.37	5721	6272	1.0
79607	DYESS AFB	441	4969	3989	3773	-2.3	0	1123	886	832	-2.5	3.49	1096	863	-2.6
79697	ABILENE	441	0	209	207	0.0	25	0	0	0	0.0	0.00	0	0	0.0
79698	ABILENE	441	710	693	685	-0.3	16	16	15	15	-0.7	2.53	10	9	-1.1
79699	ABILENE	441	1956	2069	2109	0.6	46	198	231	242	1.7	4.43	62	71	1.5
79701	MIDLAND	329	24563	26019	27047	0.6	46	8377	8869	9241	0.6	2.85	5982	6227	0.4
79703	MIDLAND	329	18438	19361	20146	0.5	42	6746	7153	7459	0.6	2.70	4983	5201	0.5
79705	MIDLAND	329	29053	30966	32322	0.7	49	11178	12003	12564	0.8	2.55	8013	8452	0.6
79706	MIDLAND	329	15250	17641	18729	1.6	71	5131	5989	6376	1.7	2.95	4163	4797	1.5
79707	MIDLAND	329	26699	31408	33656	1.8	75	10612	12537	13460	1.8	2.47	7234	8445	1.7
79713	ACKERLY	115	663	603	576	-1.0	4	250	231	222	-0.9	2.61	202	185	-0.9
79714	ANDREWS	003	13004	13363	13554	0.3	34	4601	4825	4931	0.5	2.75	3519	3644	0.4
79718	BALMORHEA	389	1251	886	840	-3.7	0	460	337	323	-3.3	2.63	331	238	-3.5
79719	BARSTOW	475	499	477	468	-0.5	11	183	176	174	-0.4	2.04	130	122	-0.7
79720	BIG SPRING	227	32054	31669	30665	-0.1	21	10800	10198	9835	-0.6	2.50	7499	6973	-0.8
79730	COYANOSA	371	312	310	309	-0.1	21	100	101	101	0.1	3.07	82	82	0.0
79731	CRANE	103	3996	4032	4046	0.1	27	1360	1381	1391	0.2	2.88	1083	1087	0.0
79734	FORT DAVIS	243	1932	2217	2372	1.5	69	787	909	975	1.6	2.36	551	627	1.4
79735	FORT STOCKTON	371	13962	13609	13538	-0.3	16	4191	4156	4167	-0.1	2.78	3261	3194	-0.2
79738	GAIL	033	515	502	491	-0.3	16	192	193	191	0.1	2.60	143	141	-0.2
79739	GARDEN CITY	173	1299	1222	1195	-0.7	7	448	434	429	-0.3	2.82	330	315	-0.5
79741	GOLDSMITH	135	337	372	392	1.1	61	135	150	158	1.1	2.48	103	111	0.8
79742	GRANDFALLS	475	566	517	504	-1.0	4	211	199	196	-0.6	2.60	152	141	-0.8
79743	IMPERIAL	371	678	673	671	-0.1	21	239	242	242	0.1	2.78	196	196	0.0
79744	IRAAN	371	1527	1458	1438	-0.5	11	530	511	506	-0.4	2.76	417	397	-0.5
79745	KERMIT	495	6196	5997	5954	-0.4	13	2223	2198	2200	-0.1	2.68	1692	1651	-0.3
79748	KNOTT	227	279	260	250	-0.8	6	93	89	86	-0.5	2.92	71	67	-0.6
79749	LENORAH	317	464	451	448	-0.3	16	160	158	158	-0.1	2.85	122	119	-0.3
79752	MC CAMEY	461	2169	2024	1996	-0.7	7	808	785	785	-0.3	2.54	587	562	-0.5
79754	MENTONE	301	67	59	57	-1.4	2	31	29	28	-0.7	2.03	20	18	-1.1
79755	MIDKIFF	461	1235	1177	1162	-0.5	11	448	442	442	-0.1	2.65	347	338	-0.3
79756	MONAHANS	475	9321	9060	8977	-0.3	16	3451	3442	3442	0.0	2.59	2565	2523	-0.2
79758	GARDENDALE	135	1638	1762	1842	0.8	52	633	684	717	0.8	2.58	502	535	0.7
79761	ODESSA	135	29224	31469	32691	0.8	52	10849	11716	12221	0.8	2.61	7526	7966	0.6
79762	ODESSA	135	34227	36148	37374	0.6	46	13670	14483	15021	0.6	2.48	9399	9739	0.4
79763	ODESSA	135	30430	33945	35768	1.2	63	10012	11101	11702	1.1	3.02	7717	8491	1.0
79764	ODESSA	135	18089	19900	20908	1.0	58	6400	7059	7429	1.1	2.81	4761	5182	0.9
79765	ODESSA	135	4864	6606	7362	3.4	89	1719	2370	2654	3.5	2.70	1302	1775	3.4
79766	ODESSA	135	4171	5339	5821	2.7	84	1077	1387	1531	2.8	3.42	922	1178	2.7
79772	PECOS	389	11886	12995	12694	1.0	58	3631	3262	3184	-1.2	2.89	2799	2484	-1.3
79777	PYOTE	475	523	499	491	-0.5	11	119	114	113	-0.5	3.30	84	80	-0.5
79781	SHEFFIELD	371	332	321	317	-0.4	13	94	91	91	-0.4	3.33	74	71	-0.4
79782	STANTON	317	3919	3920	3965	0.0	25	1351	1369	1393	0.1	2.80	1047	1050	0.0
79783	TARZAN	317	515	510	512	-0.1	21	166	167	169	0.1	3.05	132	132	0.0
79789	WINK	495	977	866	841	-1.3	2	361	327	319	-1.1	2.55	278	249	-1.2
79821	ANTHONY	141	6284	6752	7008	0.8	52	1343	1504	1592	1.2	3.48	1155	1273	1.1
	TEXAS					1.9					1.8	2.78			1.7
	UNITED STATES					1.0					1.1	2.59			0.9

ZIP CODE #	POST OFFICE NAME	RACE (%) White 2000	White 2009	Black 2000	Black 2009	Asian/Pacific 2000	Asian/Pacific 2009	% Hispanic Origin 2000	% Hispanic Origin 2009	2009 AGE DISTRIBUTION (%) 0-4	5-9	10-14	15-19	20-24	25-44	45-64	65-84	85+	18+	MEDIAN AGE 2009	% 2009 Males	% 2009 Females
79502	ASPERMONT	87.0	83.5	3.3	3.7	0.4	0.6	12.3	16.8	5.5	5.4	5.6	7.7	4.5	21.1	28.9	16.3	5.1	78.6	45.2	47.1	52.9
79503	AVOCA	79.5	74.8	5.8	5.9	0.0	0.0	26.4	34.2	7.2	7.2	7.2	6.8	5.9	22.1	25.2	15.8	2.7	73.9	38.5	46.8	53.2
79504	BAIRD	92.4	89.7	0.1	0.1	0.6	0.8	10.5	14.7	4.8	4.9	5.4	6.8	5.2	22.5	29.8	17.4	3.3	80.6	45.3	49.7	50.3
79506	BLACKWELL	90.8	87.6	0.9	1.0	0.0	0.0	10.6	14.7	5.6	5.8	5.9	5.6	4.4	19.4	30.2	20.6	2.4	79.4	47.4	47.8	52.2
79508	BUFFALO GAP	95.4	93.1	0.5	0.7	0.3	0.4	4.7	7.6	5.2	5.8	6.7	7.8	5.0	22.1	34.1	12.0	1.2	76.8	43.3	49.6	50.4
79510	CLYDE	95.4	93.9	0.3	0.4	0.3	0.5	5.0	7.2	6.3	6.4	6.5	6.7	5.8	22.5	29.6	14.3	1.9	76.7	41.9	48.4	51.6
79511	COAHOMA	90.4	87.0	0.3	0.4	0.1	0.2	20.7	26.7	5.2	5.5	5.9	7.4	5.9	23.0	30.6	14.8	1.7	78.9	42.8	48.4	51.6
79512	COLORADO CITY	74.3	70.8	14.6	15.6	0.4	0.5	31.0	38.4	4.4	4.1	4.1	7.9	9.0	31.6	25.4	10.9	2.5	83.6	38.5	65.4	34.6
79517	FLUVANNA	93.5	93.3	0.0	0.0	0.4	0.4	13.4	14.7	4.6	4.6	5.5	5.9	4.2	22.3	33.6	17.2	2.1	81.5	46.8	49.6	50.4
79518	GIRARD	93.8	93.5	0.0	0.0	0.0	0.0	8.6	9.8	4.9	4.9	4.9	6.5	4.9	19.5	32.5	18.7	3.3	81.3	47.3	52.0	48.0
79519	GOLDSBORO	95.7	92.2	0.0	0.0	0.0	2.0	6.5	9.8	3.9	5.9	5.9	7.8	3.9	17.6	31.4	19.6	3.9	76.5	48.1	51.0	49.0
79520	HAMLIN	81.7	76.5	5.5	6.0	0.7	0.8	19.4	26.7	6.0	6.0	6.4	6.9	5.5	21.1	26.3	17.4	4.4	77.0	43.2	47.6	52.4
79521	HASKELL	82.4	77.6	3.3	3.8	0.1	0.1	20.4	26.7	5.6	5.7	6.2	6.2	5.0	19.8	27.4	18.8	5.4	78.2	46.1	46.2	53.8
79525	HAWLEY	94.6	92.4	0.5	0.6	0.4	0.6	6.2	9.1	7.1	6.9	7.1	7.5	6.1	25.5	27.0	11.6	1.0	74.2	37.6	50.5	49.5
79526	HERMLEIGH	91.3	90.7	2.4	2.4	0.4	0.4	17.3	19.2	5.7	6.1	5.6	8.3	7.1	22.8	29.1	13.6	1.8	79.4	38.8	52.0	48.0
79527	IRA	95.4	94.9	0.0	0.0	0.0	0.0	12.5	14.0	4.1	4.8	5.8	7.5	4.5	22.9	33.2	15.4	1.7	80.5	45.2	51.4	48.6
79528	JAYTON	96.4	96.2	0.2	0.2	0.0	0.0	9.2	10.2	3.4	3.8	4.2	5.6	5.4	14.2	30.3	25.7	7.5	85.6	53.4	46.2	53.8
79529	KNOX CITY	72.4	66.5	8.9	9.2	0.4	0.5	22.5	29.5	6.7	6.7	6.2	5.9	6.8	19.9	26.4	17.4	4.0	76.5	42.8	45.5	54.5
79530	LAWN	96.6	94.7	0.0	0.0	0.5	0.8	5.5	8.7	3.8	6.0	8.8	8.0	3.2	22.2	29.1	14.6	4.2	75.8	43.4	50.1	49.9
79532	LORAINE	69.3	62.4	4.2	4.3	0.1	0.1	38.6	48.1	6.4	5.9	5.9	6.8	5.9	20.1	26.1	18.8	4.1	77.8	44.3	47.3	52.7
79533	LUEDERS	93.2	90.8	1.1	1.3	0.0	0.0	6.8	10.0	6.3	6.6	7.4	7.1	5.0	22.9	29.2	13.9	1.6	75.3	41.0	50.8	49.2
79534	MC CAULLEY	89.4	85.8	1.3	1.8	0.4	0.5	13.2	18.8	4.1	5.0	5.5	6.4	4.1	19.3	33.9	18.3	3.2	80.7	48.2	51.8	48.2
79535	MARYNEAL	93.4	90.0	0.0	0.0	0.0	0.0	10.9	16.2	4.6	6.2	8.5	7.7	2.3	21.5	30.0	16.9	2.3	74.6	44.5	50.8	49.2
79536	MERKEL	91.8	88.6	0.8	1.0	0.3	0.4	11.1	16.5	6.0	6.2	6.5	7.1	5.8	24.3	29.1	12.8	2.3	76.9	40.7	48.8	51.2
79537	NOLAN	87.3	82.0	1.4	1.6	0.0	0.0	15.5	22.7	7.8	7.8	7.0	5.5	5.5	20.3	25.8	18.0	2.3	74.2	41.4	47.7	52.3
79538	NOVICE	93.9	91.3	0.0	0.0	0.9	1.2	6.1	9.5	5.6	6.0	6.3	6.0	4.0	18.7	29.0	22.2	2.4	77.8	47.5	50.8	49.2
79539	O BRIEN	76.3	68.7	2.4	2.8	0.7	0.8	27.2	35.7	4.8	5.6	5.6	6.0	4.0	23.7	29.3	17.3	3.6	79.9	45.1	49.4	50.6
79540	OLD GLORY	94.1	91.8	1.0	1.4	0.0	0.0	9.0	12.3	3.6	3.6	4.1	4.1	3.6	17.3	33.2	25.9	4.5	85.9	52.8	50.0	50.0
79541	OVALO	95.8	94.3	0.3	0.3	0.4	0.5	5.2	8.0	4.5	6.0	7.5	7.9	4.3	22.2	31.5	13.5	2.7	76.8	43.3	49.6	50.4
79543	ROBY	89.8	86.6	1.8	1.9	0.0	0.0	16.4	22.4	6.4	6.8	6.9	7.1	4.1	19.8	27.5	18.3	3.1	75.6	44.0	48.4	51.6
79544	ROCHESTER	76.3	69.2	2.6	3.0	0.5	0.8	27.1	35.5	4.9	5.5	5.7	6.1	3.9	23.5	29.6	17.4	3.4	79.7	45.2	49.5	50.5
79545	ROSCOE	79.6	73.7	0.9	0.9	0.1	0.1	30.6	39.7	5.7	6.2	7.5	7.8	5.1	22.6	25.8	15.6	3.6	75.2	40.9	48.2	51.8
79546	ROTAN	76.6	71.2	4.3	4.6	0.2	0.3	28.4	36.3	6.3	6.4	6.2	6.4	5.3	20.7	26.9	17.6	4.3	77.6	43.9	47.6	52.4
79547	RULE	87.8	83.8	1.9	2.1	0.0	0.0	18.0	24.7	5.4	5.4	5.4	6.0	6.4	18.9	29.2	19.6	3.8	80.6	46.6	50.3	49.7
79548	RULE	89.2	85.0	1.4	1.6	0.0	0.0	13.9	19.7	4.3	4.7	5.1	6.3	4.7	17.3	33.9	19.7	3.9	82.7	50.0	48.0	52.0
79549	SNYDER	80.3	79.6	6.4	6.5	0.2	0.2	28.7	30.6	6.4	6.3	6.1	8.2	7.1	25.0	25.5	12.9	2.6	76.9	37.7	52.6	47.4
79553	STAMFORD	76.5	71.5	7.2	7.4	0.1	0.1	24.1	31.6	6.4	6.3	6.3	7.1	6.0	20.9	26.4	16.5	4.1	76.6	42.6	48.2	51.8
79556	SWEETWATER	78.1	73.2	5.3	5.7	0.3	0.4	28.1	35.6	6.8	6.6	6.5	7.3	6.7	23.7	26.2	13.7	2.5	75.8	38.5	49.0	51.0
79560	SYLVESTER	90.9	87.4	1.8	1.9	0.0	0.0	11.4	15.8	4.7	5.6	6.0	6.0	4.2	21.4	29.3	19.5	3.3	79.5	46.4	50.2	49.8
79561	TRENT	92.0	88.0	1.4	1.6	0.2	0.4	11.8	18.1	4.3	6.2	8.3	9.7	4.3	23.5	27.4	13.6	2.7	74.6	40.9	47.8	52.2
79562	TUSCOLA	96.2	94.2	0.3	0.5	0.1	0.2	5.0	7.9	5.1	5.7	6.3	7.4	5.3	22.5	33.2	13.4	1.2	78.1	43.5	49.8	50.2
79563	TYE	92.4	89.0	1.2	1.4	0.6	0.8	10.3	15.9	6.8	7.3	7.7	7.1	6.5	24.6	29.8	9.4	0.9	73.5	38.5	48.4	51.6
79565	WESTBROOK	95.2	93.1	0.0	0.0	0.0	0.0	10.1	14.0	4.4	4.9	5.2	4.7	4.1	20.3	34.6	19.5	2.2	82.4	49.4	49.7	50.3
79566	WINGATE	93.0	90.4	0.6	0.5	0.0	0.3	9.8	13.2	5.1	5.8	6.1	6.6	4.8	20.8	32.9	15.7	2.3	78.7	45.6	50.1	49.9
79567	WINTERS	79.5	75.1	1.8	1.8	0.4	0.5	32.6	40.2	7.1	6.9	7.1	7.5	5.8	20.6	26.1	15.5	3.4	74.1	40.5	47.8	52.2
79601	ABILENE	75.9	72.6	14.8	13.0	1.1	1.9	19.7	24.5	4.7	4.1	4.2	12.1	18.0	25.5	19.2	10.0	2.1	83.7	29.2	53.7	46.3
79602	ABILENE	83.6	80.2	5.3	5.6	1.2	1.5	17.0	22.2	7.0	6.8	6.9	7.4	7.0	28.1	25.9	9.8	1.2	74.9	35.7	49.8	50.2
79603	ABILENE	68.4	62.5	9.8	10.2	0.7	0.8	35.3	44.3	8.7	7.7	7.4	7.6	7.3	24.8	22.4	12.0	2.0	71.4	33.4	47.5	52.5
79605	ABILENE	81.6	76.2	6.4	7.2	1.3	1.7	14.7	20.9	7.5	6.6	6.6	7.5	8.1	25.1	23.4	12.5	2.8	75.2	35.3	47.7	52.3
79606	ABILENE	87.3	83.6	4.8	5.5	2.1	2.8	8.2	12.0	6.5	6.2	6.3	7.4	9.2	27.3	26.3	9.4	1.5	76.8	35.5	49.2	50.8
79607	DYESS AFB	71.9	64.9	12.8	14.8	3.3	4.1	13.4	19.1	15.5	10.2	6.6	8.6	23.0	34.7	1.3	0.2	0.0	64.8	22.0	57.1	42.9
79697	ABILENE	0.0	77.5	0.0	5.3	0.0	1.9	0.0	23.4	6.2	5.7	5.3	18.7	16.3	25.4	15.3	5.7	1.4	79.9	24.3	51.2	48.8
79698	ABILENE	84.1	78.6	4.9	5.8	0.1	0.1	19.1	27.7	3.0	2.6	3.3	34.1	32.0	9.8	9.7	5.1	0.4	89.0	21.1	44.0	56.0
79699	ABILENE	89.1	85.5	4.8	5.9	2.3	3.1	5.3	8.1	1.3	1.3	1.9	35.0	34.4	10.0	6.0	5.2	4.9	93.4	21.5	43.5	56.5
79701	MIDLAND	59.5	55.0	12.3	11.9	0.4	0.4	49.9	57.5	8.9	8.7	8.2	8.1	7.0	24.7	21.8	10.3	2.3	69.1	31.8	48.4	51.6
79703	MIDLAND	78.5	71.8	4.6	5.5	0.9	1.0	32.1	43.6	8.7	8.3	8.0	7.9	7.1	28.4	21.9	8.7	1.1	69.9	31.3	48.4	51.6
79705	MIDLAND	77.4	73.7	10.9	11.1	0.8	0.9	23.3	30.0	7.0	6.8	6.9	7.6	7.0	22.8	26.9	13.0	2.1	74.8	37.7	47.7	52.3
79706	MIDLAND	85.2	79.8	0.7	0.8	0.3	0.3	31.7	43.3	7.6	7.4	7.3	7.8	7.3	25.6	27.7	8.5	0.7	72.9	33.9	49.6	50.4
79707	MIDLAND	87.5	83.4	3.6	4.3	1.9	2.3	13.6	19.7	6.7	6.4	6.6	7.5	7.9	26.6	28.1	8.8	1.4	75.8	35.7	48.3	51.7
79713	ACKERLY	76.0	67.8	0.5	0.5	0.5	0.5	31.5	42.5	5.1	6.6	7.8	8.8	3.5	20.4	35.3	12.3	0.2	75.0	43.5	50.4	49.6
79714	ANDREWS	77.1	72.5	1.6	1.6	0.7	0.9	40.0	48.8	7.7	7.5	7.6	7.9	6.7	24.3	25.5	11.3	1.5	72.2	35.4	49.3	50.7
79718	BALMORHEA	78.4	75.3	0.0	0.0	0.0	0.0	81.9	90.2	7.4	6.5	7.1	7.8	7.6	21.0	22.7	17.9	1.9	73.9	37.6	49.8	50.2
79719	BARSTOW	75.8	73.2	8.8	9.2	0.2	0.2	55.3	63.7	5.2	5.0	7.8	26.2	5.2	15.3	21.4	12.4	1.5	61.0	25.7	65.6	34.4
79720	BIG SPRING	79.7	76.0	4.3	4.5	0.6	0.7	38.2	46.7	5.8	5.5	5.5	6.3	7.6	31.4	23.9	11.9	2.1	79.5	36.7	56.8	43.2
79730	COYANOSA	87.2	84.8	0.3	0.3	0.6	0.6	52.2	61.3	7.4	7.4	7.4	7.4	5.8	21.6	28.7	13.2	1.0	72.9	38.7	50.0	50.0
79731	CRANE	73.7	72.9	2.9	2.9	0.4	0.3	43.9	46.2	7.8	7.8	7.8	7.9	6.7	23.2	26.5	10.6	1.7	71.4	35.8	48.8	51.2
79734	FORT DAVIS	90.6	89.0	1.0	0.9	0.1	0.1	33.4	41.7	4.4	4.6	6.0	7.4	4.5	19.7	35.5	15.9	2.0	79.6	47.0	51.0	49.0
79735	FORT STOCKTON	73.1	69.7	5.0	5.7	0.6	0.6	64.7	70.9	6.8	6.5	6.4	9.2	10.7	26.5	22.1	10.5	1.3	75.3	32.3	55.9	44.1
79738	GAIL	90.7	90.0	0.2	0.2	0.0	0.0	11.9	13.1	4.4	4.8	4.8	6.4	4.8	23.5	31.7	18.1	1.6	82.1	45.7	50.4	49.6
79739	GARDEN CITY	77.1	75.9	0.5	0.5	0.2	0.2	30.3	32.2	8.3	8.9	8.3	7.8	4.6	23.1	28.2	10.1	0.7	69.4	36.8	52.5	47.5
79741	GOLDSMITH	82.2	76.9	0.3	0.3	0.0	0.0	37.7	49.5	8.1	8.3	8.1	7.0	5.1	23.4	26.9	12.1	1.1	71.2	36.1	52.2	47.8
79742	GRANDFALLS	73.3	67.1	0.2	0.2	0.0	0.0	45.9	56.7	7.7	7.7	7.4	9.9	3.9	24.6	24.0	13.0	1.9	70.2	37.7	46.8	53.2
79743	IMPERIAL	87.4	85.0	0.1	0.1	0.6	0.7	52.3	61.7	7.6	7.4	7.3	7.6	5.9	21.8	28.2	13.1	1.0	73.0	38.2	49.5	50.5
79744	IRAAN	90.5	88.1	1.5	2.0	0.0	0.0	37.9	47.0	7.1	6.9	7.1	7.5	8.4	26.1	27.5	8.0	1.4	74.1	35.2	53.8	46.2
79745	KERMIT	73.3	68.2	2.0	2.3	0.2	0.2	46.7	55.6	7.7	7.6	6.9	7.6	7.3	24.5	24.4	12.1	2.0	73.2	34.5	49.3	50.7
79748	KNOTT	82.8	77.3	0.7	0.8	0.0	0.0	28.0	36.9	5.4	5.4	6.2	6.9	3.8	24.2	26.2	19.6	2.3	78.5	43.5	50.4	49.6
79749	LENORAH	77.8	76.7	0.0	0.0	0.0	0.0	34.1	36.1	8.9	8.9	8.4	7.8	4.4	23.1	25.3	11.8	1.6	69.0	35.4	52.3	47.7
79752	MC CAMEY	74.3	69.9	1.5	1.5	0.0	0.0	48.8	57.5	6.4	5.8	6.1	8.1	6.8	21.6	28.5	13.9	2.8	76.9	40.7	48.4	51.6
79754	MENTONE	89.6	88.1	0.0	0.0	0.0	0.0	10.4	11.9	3.4	3.4	6.8	5.1	1.7	20.3	42.4	16.9	0.0	81.4	48.4	52.5	47.5
79755	MIDKIFF	84.0	79.7	1.9	2.0	0.2	0.2	31.6	41.0	5.2	5.8	7.4	8.2	5.0	22.9	31.4	12.7	1.4	76.0	42.1	48.9	51.1
79756	MONAHANS	80.6	76.9	4.4	4.8	0.3	0.4	40.3	49.0	6.8	6.9	7.5	8.2	5.9	23.2	27.5	12.2	1.9	73.7	38.3	48.8	51.2
79758	GARDENDALE	90.7	86.8	0.5	0.6	0.2	0.3	12.3	18.1	5.6	6.3	6.7	5.9	4.6	21.7	34.6	13.3	1.3	77.8	44.2	50.5	49.5
79761	ODESSA	68.4	65.6	8.7	8.5	0.7	0.9	46.6	52.8	8.3	7.4	7.0	7.7	7.5	25.2	23.4	11.5	1.9	72.8	33.4	48.9	51.1
79762	ODESSA	83.2	79.0	3.9	4.1	1.2	1.5	24.5	32.5	7.6	7.0	6.8	7.2	7.6	27.1	24.5	10.6	1.6	74.2	34.0	47.8	52.2
79763	ODESSA	67.0	62.5	4.1	3.7	0.3	0.3	57.6	66.9	8.8	8.2	7.7	8.8	8.2	26.1	22.6	8.3	1.3	70.0	30.0	48.6	51.4
79764	ODESSA	75.0	69.3	1.6	1.6	0.4	0.4	42.2	53.0	8.7	7.9	7.4	7.8	8.2	26.9	23.6	8.7	0.7	71.3	31.0	49.7	50.3
79765	ODESSA	80.6	75.6	1.5	1.6	2.0	2.7	24.8	32.3	6.9	6.6	7.5	8.1	6.2	25.3	27.4	10.4	1.6	73.7	37.7	49.7	50.3
79766	ODESSA	67.5	63.8	2.2	2.1	0.2	0.2	67.9	76.4	8.1	7.5	6.9	8.9	9.3	30.3	21.6	6.9	0.5	72.2	29.7	53.3	46.7
79772	PECOS	79.4	77.8	2.3	2.1	0.4	0.4	72.5	78.7	5.9	5.9	6.0	10.2	13.8	26.7	20.6	9.6	1.2	76.4	29.9	62.3	37.7
79777	PYOTE	75.7	73.1	9.0	9.2	0.2	0.2	55.3	63.9	5.4	4.8	7.8	26.1	5.0	15.4	21.0	12.8	1.6	60.9	26.2	65.1	34.9
79781	SHEFFIELD	89.7	86.6	2.7	3.4	0.0	0.0	40.2	49.2	6.9	6.9	6.9	7.8	9.0	26.2	27.4	7.8	1.2	75.1	34.3	54.8	45.2
79782	STANTON	78.7	77.9	1.9	1.9	0.2	0.2	42.8	45.3	8.5	8.7	8.7	7.8	5.0	24.0	24.0	11.1	2.2	68.6	34.4	48.7	51.3
79783	TARZAN	85.5	84.9	0.0	0.0	0.0	0.0	22.9	24.5	9.0	9.4	9.0	8.2	4.7	21.0	27.8	9.8	1.0	67.3	36.0	52.4	47.6
79789	WINK	84.3	79.4	0.8	1.0	0.0	0.0	26.8	35.1	5.8	6.0	6.2	7.9	7.3	25.3	30.1	10.2	1.3	77.3	38.0	48.5	51.5
79821	ANTHONY	80.9	81.1	2.6	2.1	0.2	0.2	86.4	90.5	7.4	7.1	6.7	7.8	9.4	35.2	20.4	5.3	0.6	74.1	30.3	61.0	39.0
	TEXAS	71.0	67.6	11.5	11.4	2.8	3.5	32.0	37.4	7.9	7.5	7.2	7.5	7.4	28.3	24.0	8.8	1.4	73.0	33.6	49.7	50.3
	UNITED STATES	75.1	72.0	12.3	12.7	3.8	4.6	12.5	15.7	6.8	6.7	6.6	7.1	6.9	27.0	26.0	10.9	1.9	75.7	36.9	49.2	50.8

C 79502-79821

ZIP CODE				2009 HOUSEHOLD INCOME DISTRIBUTION (%)					MEDIAN HOUSEHOLD INCOME					2009 HOME VALUE DISTRIBUTION (%)					
#	POST OFFICE NAME	2009 Per Capita Income	2009 HH Income Base	Less than $25,000	$25,000 to $49,999	$50,000 to $99,999	$100,000 to $149,999	$150,000 or More	2009	2014	2009 National Centile	2009 State Centile	2009 Home Value Base	Less than $50,000	$50,000 to $89,999	$90,000 to $174,999	$175,000 to $399,999	$400,000 or More	2009 Median Home Value
79502	ASPERMONT	17482	521	38.0	32.2	24.2	4.2	1.3	33502	34077	14	18	401	68.1	21.9	7.2	1.2	1.5	36474
79503	AVOCA	15750	85	35.3	35.3	23.5	4.7	1.2	33251	34700	14	17	60	50.0	25.0	21.7	3.3	0.0	50000
79504	BAIRD	17631	1066	37.8	30.1	26.5	4.1	1.4	33400	36171	14	17	813	41.7	29.5	21.8	6.2	0.9	58232
79506	BLACKWELL	20950	386	32.4	31.6	29.5	5.2	1.3	37797	40963	26	33	306	43.5	29.1	21.2	4.6	1.6	57143
79508	BUFFALO GAP	26266	433	14.8	30.3	42.5	8.5	3.9	56130	53371	73	80	358	21.8	17.6	37.7	20.4	2.5	111111
79510	CLYDE	17974	3134	26.5	36.4	30.8	4.8	1.5	41592	42665	38	48	2530	31.7	35.4	27.8	4.7	0.4	70000
79511	COAHOMA	19414	522	25.5	33.1	35.1	4.2	2.1	43455	45265	44	54	414	41.5	30.4	24.6	3.1	0.2	59211
79512	COLORADO CITY	15579	2099	40.8	31.2	23.9	2.7	1.4	31043	31317	10	12	1535	58.8	26.2	12.1	2.7	0.1	41837
79517	FLUVANNA	21433	106	27.4	34.0	31.1	7.5	0.0	39202	45656	30	39	83	31.3	21.7	44.6	1.2	1.2	86429
79518	GIRARD	17467	53	37.7	39.6	17.0	3.8	1.9	29566	30743	7	9	41	48.8	31.7	12.2	7.3	0.0	51250
79519	GOLDSBORO	17941	21	28.6	33.3	33.3	4.8	0.0	42367	42367	41	51	17	47.1	23.5	29.4	0.0	0.0	55000
79520	HAMLIN	18378	933	38.4	28.3	27.1	3.9	2.4	34770	35970	17	22	726	57.6	25.6	15.8	1.0	0.0	39211
79521	HASKELL	17212	1415	44.3	29.8	19.1	5.1	1.8	29512	29860	7	9	1064	59.8	24.8	14.4	1.0	0.0	43459
79525	HAWLEY	16639	1036	26.4	36.3	31.9	3.8	1.7	41212	44889	37	47	865	45.0	29.1	19.7	5.2	1.0	55241
79526	HERMLEIGH	19734	422	32.7	28.9	31.0	6.2	1.2	37243	40000	24	31	332	36.1	29.8	27.4	6.6	0.0	67143
79527	IRA	22334	124	29.0	32.3	29.0	5.6	4.0	38913	42366	29	38	96	32.3	29.2	30.2	7.3	1.0	72000
79528	JAYTON	20651	214	24.8	36.4	30.8	7.0	0.9	40755	43913	35	45	168	68.5	23.8	4.8	3.0	0.0	33750
79529	KNOX CITY	17827	574	38.5	34.3	21.3	4.2	1.7	31960	32924	11	14	434	58.8	25.8	14.5	0.5	0.5	38250
79530	LAWN	20049	286	26.2	37.4	30.1	3.1	3.1	41916	45780	39	50	240	45.4	18.3	29.2	3.8	3.3	60000
79532	LORAINE	18266	433	40.0	32.8	19.9	4.6	2.8	29801	29651	8	9	346	61.6	18.8	16.2	2.9	0.6	33824
79533	LUEDERS	18180	162	29.6	40.7	24.7	3.7	1.2	36367	36551	22	28	132	57.6	22.0	15.9	4.5	0.0	42857
79534	MC CAULLEY	18860	91	31.9	33.0	28.6	4.4	2.2	38805	43002	29	37	72	50.0	18.1	23.6	6.9	1.4	50000
79535	MARYNEAL	18558	53	28.3	28.3	37.7	5.7	0.0	44085	47338	46	56	42	33.3	40.5	21.4	4.8	0.0	62500
79536	MERKEL	18685	1893	28.1	36.3	28.2	4.9	2.5	40018	44611	33	42	1430	50.4	25.2	20.0	4.0	0.3	49643
79537	NOLAN	15336	46	37.0	34.8	23.9	4.3	0.0	33593	38182	15	18	34	61.8	20.6	14.7	2.9	0.0	42000
79538	NOVICE	20000	100	30.0	33.0	30.0	4.0	3.0	40000	45000	33	42	82	45.1	23.2	20.7	6.1	4.9	55714
79539	O BRIEN	16031	98	48.0	29.6	17.3	3.1	2.0	26500	29180	4	5	79	64.6	25.3	7.6	2.5	0.0	35625
79540	OLD GLORY	27728	111	32.4	24.3	33.3	8.1	1.8	41765	46395	39	49	90	32.2	34.4	18.9	11.1	3.3	68462
79541	OVALO	21270	291	21.0	33.3	37.1	5.8	2.7	47327	48654	55	65	243	34.2	18.5	32.9	11.9	2.5	82778
79543	ROBY	19255	494	33.4	31.2	30.4	3.0	2.0	37846	41374	26	34	393	51.1	29.3	13.0	5.3	1.3	48636
79544	ROCHESTER	17513	217	47.0	29.0	18.0	3.2	2.8	27526	28587	5	7	174	61.5	25.3	8.0	4.0	1.1	38500
79545	ROSCOE	16375	606	38.9	29.2	27.1	3.3	1.5	32055	35452	12	14	457	53.6	28.0	16.0	2.2	0.2	46071
79546	ROTAN	16864	844	41.8	27.4	26.9	2.7	1.2	30237	32183	8	11	596	62.9	21.8	10.9	3.4	1.0	37857
79547	RULE	17490	318	39.9	29.2	26.1	2.5	2.2	31727	33638	11	14	258	67.8	19.8	11.2	1.2	0.0	30870
79548	RULE	19394	114	39.5	24.6	28.9	4.4	2.6	35000	34092	18	23	93	45.2	31.2	20.4	3.2	0.0	61250
79549	SNYDER	19083	5271	32.5	28.9	31.0	5.0	2.7	39153	41478	30	39	3816	45.2	23.0	25.7	5.6	0.5	58512
79553	STAMFORD	17429	1415	41.6	29.0	21.6	5.4	2.3	31758	33094	11	14	1062	55.5	26.8	15.3	2.0	0.5	43012
79556	SWEETWATER	17652	5047	39.3	28.6	25.9	4.0	2.2	33464	35868	14	17	3294	53.7	26.4	15.5	3.8	0.6	45788
79560	SYLVESTER	21858	100	32.0	38.0	22.0	5.0	3.0	34466	34457	16	21	82	48.8	23.2	19.5	8.5	0.0	51667
79561	TRENT	19457	205	25.9	34.6	33.7	4.4	1.5	43987	46751	45	56	164	56.7	25.0	17.7	0.6	0.0	44762
79562	TUSCOLA	23720	1095	17.4	30.6	40.7	7.9	3.3	51679	51380	65	74	910	25.6	18.2	37.3	16.8	2.1	100487
79563	TYE	21950	424	26.7	29.7	32.3	6.8	4.5	45000	47497	48	59	319	52.4	21.9	19.1	5.6	0.9	47917
79565	WESTBROOK	17516	145	29.7	33.1	32.4	4.8	0.0	39232	43022	30	39	118	44.9	26.3	22.0	5.9	0.8	55455
79566	WINGATE	23461	176	22.7	35.2	35.2	4.5	2.3	43999	47516	45	56	144	37.5	16.0	33.3	11.1	2.1	78571
79567	WINTERS	15595	1402	37.3	30.7	28.2	2.9	0.9	34418	35032	16	21	1063	58.3	20.3	17.4	3.0	0.9	43493
79601	ABILENE	18862	7171	37.1	28.9	26.6	5.2	2.3	33594	36827	15	18	3853	34.8	25.0	33.4	5.9	0.9	72959
79602	ABILENE	21337	7585	25.8	29.1	33.6	7.5	4.0	45279	49396	49	59	5177	31.2	25.1	30.4	11.9	1.5	76927
79603	ABILENE	17550	8723	31.4	34.8	27.3	4.3	2.1	37530	41500	25	33	5692	46.9	40.1	12.3	0.6	0.0	52096
79605	ABILENE	22897	11744	23.1	35.7	31.9	5.4	3.9	43042	46772	43	53	6968	23.7	39.5	29.4	6.3	1.2	75639
79606	ABILENE	28580	9344	16.6	25.3	42.3	10.3	5.5	55974	55825	73	80	5364	7.2	14.5	57.8	18.2	2.3	121618
79607	DYESS AFB	14273	886	8.5	52.5	35.3	3.6	0.1	44258	47047	46	57	13	61.5	38.5	0.0	0.0	0.0	48125
79697	ABILENE	3743	0	0.0	0.0	0.0	0.0	0.0	0	0	0	0	0	0.0	0.0	0.0	0.0	0.0	0
79698	ABILENE	8284	15	53.3	33.3	13.3	0.0	0.0	22278	22278	2	3	7	57.1	42.9	0.0	0.0	0.0	45000
79699	ABILENE	12548	231	43.3	19.5	24.2	6.9	6.1	29818	34445	8	10	70	14.3	5.7	52.9	27.1	0.0	138235
79701	MIDLAND	16872	8869	37.3	29.6	24.9	4.8	3.4	33649	36018	15	19	6130	35.9	31.3	23.8	8.0	1.1	63987
79703	MIDLAND	19929	7153	19.1	32.9	40.2	6.0	1.8	48351	51227	57	67	4874	8.7	49.6	39.6	1.7	0.4	83541
79705	MIDLAND	28516	12003	20.7	23.8	35.4	12.0	8.1	55345	56464	72	79	8227	10.3	14.3	39.2	31.3	5.0	148331
79706	MIDLAND	19054	5989	24.4	28.5	37.5	6.7	2.9	47290	50474	55	65	4994	27.8	25.4	31.1	15.0	0.7	83861
79707	MIDLAND	33628	12537	16.9	21.5	36.0	13.4	12.3	62267	62784	80	85	7407	1.6	3.6	52.8	34.5	7.4	160801
79713	ACKERLY	24450	231	19.9	35.1	29.4	7.8	7.8	46284	50251	52	62	163	21.5	41.1	31.9	5.5	0.0	78333
79714	ANDREWS	18433	4825	27.5	33.8	32.3	4.3	2.1	41829	45109	39	49	3776	40.0	30.1	23.2	6.3	0.5	57908
79718	BALMORHEA	9473	337	64.1	25.2	9.5	0.9	0.3	19412	20248	1	2	264	81.8	12.9	5.3	0.0	0.0	26600
79719	BARSTOW	14327	176	48.3	35.2	15.3	1.1	0.0	25703	27879	4	5	134	87.3	9.7	3.0	0.0	0.0	15588
79720	BIG SPRING	18252	10198	33.4	30.0	28.7	5.2	2.7	38204	40577	27	35	6921	47.4	26.3	21.1	4.7	0.5	52849
79730	COYANOSA	13954	101	41.6	24.8	26.7	4.0	3.0	29673	32049	8	9	84	69.0	9.5	13.1	4.8	3.6	32000
79731	CRANE	16350	1381	31.1	32.7	27.8	7.2	1.2	38982	39647	30	38	1168	49.5	34.0	13.4	2.3	0.8	50417
79734	FORT DAVIS	21889	909	30.8	31.7	29.2	5.4	3.0	38647	39625	29	36	643	17.0	16.3	33.0	22.2	11.5	126122
79735	FORT STOCKTON	15048	4156	33.9	31.7	28.9	4.4	1.1	34043	34707	16	20	3040	49.0	30.1	15.2	5.3	0.4	51080
79738	GAIL	19723	193	32.1	30.6	26.4	7.3	3.6	35201	37371	18	24	142	37.3	26.1	27.5	4.2	4.9	65833
79739	GARDEN CITY	20566	434	27.0	30.9	31.6	5.8	4.8	42012	43260	39	50	287	24.7	25.4	34.8	11.8	3.1	89000
79741	GOLDSMITH	21732	150	22.7	34.0	36.0	5.3	2.0	44529	46398	47	57	121	47.9	35.5	14.9	1.7	0.0	52083
79742	GRANDFALLS	13743	199	45.7	24.1	27.1	2.5	0.5	31438	35000	10	13	152	73.7	15.1	9.9	1.3	0.0	28333
79743	IMPERIAL	15362	242	41.7	24.8	26.4	3.7	3.3	29467	32340	7	9	200	70.5	9.5	11.5	5.0	3.5	31154
79744	IRAAN	18440	511	24.1	28.6	38.4	7.8	1.2	46356	50541	52	63	349	45.3	36.4	15.8	2.6	0.0	54714
79745	KERMIT	16058	2198	30.9	37.7	26.5	4.0	1.0	36663	38423	23	30	1811	69.1	23.5	6.7	0.3	0.3	35996
79748	KNOTT	18929	89	31.5	37.1	21.3	2.2	7.9	32606	36146	13	16	64	39.1	12.5	39.1	9.4	0.0	85000
79749	LENORAH	17086	158	39.2	23.4	27.2	7.0	3.2	38638	41013	29	36	118	22.9	30.5	39.8	6.8	0.0	86923
79752	MC CAMEY	16405	785	37.1	30.8	26.8	4.6	0.8	32350	33137	12	15	603	65.0	25.4	8.6	0.5	0.5	38750
79754	MENTONE	26314	29	34.5	20.7	31.0	13.8	0.0	34038	35000	16	20	24	66.7	20.8	0.0	12.5	0.0	17500
79755	MIDKIFF	18744	442	33.0	25.3	34.8	3.6	3.2	43123	45727	43	54	313	60.4	26.2	9.9	2.9	0.6	41667
79756	MONAHANS	18298	3442	34.0	28.6	30.0	5.3	2.1	37903	40679	26	34	2651	54.9	25.6	16.7	2.3	0.4	45749
79758	GARDENDALE	26513	684	16.7	23.5	43.7	12.4	3.7	60458	57946	78	84	598	17.1	22.9	37.8	18.2	4.0	114706
79761	ODESSA	18610	11716	34.2	31.1	25.9	5.3	3.5	36757	39902	23	30	7415	33.9	29.9	28.7	6.9	0.6	69574
79762	ODESSA	23160	14483	25.2	29.5	33.7	7.7	3.9	45737	48280	50	61	8904	14.8	35.5	37.4	11.2	1.1	89601
79763	ODESSA	13927	11101	34.1	35.3	26.0	3.3	1.4	34830	37834	17	22	7942	44.3	37.3	16.9	1.5	0.0	53879
79764	ODESSA	16443	7059	31.2	32.9	30.2	3.9	1.8	39160	43632	30	39	5263	47.0	30.3	19.6	3.0	0.1	52617
79765	ODESSA	28422	2370	20.3	25.0	35.3	11.3	8.1	54945	55529	71	78	1739	16.3	19.1	29.4	26.9	8.2	121613
79766	ODESSA	14181	1387	28.8	31.7	33.1	4.7	1.8	39950	44457	32	42	1169	42.2	29.1	21.3	7.4	0.1	56880
79772	PECOS	13320	3262	42.0	33.5	21.0	2.6	1.0	29039	30073	7	8	2508	76.5	17.3	5.1	1.0	0.2	28581
79777	PYOTE	10219	114	48.2	35.1	15.8	0.9	0.0	25774	28436	4	5	86	86.0	11.6	2.3	0.0	0.0	16364
79781	SHEFFIELD	14464	91	26.4	31.9	35.2	6.6	0.0	42764	47772	42	52	61	44.3	39.3	13.1	3.3	0.0	55833
79782	STANTON	17274	1369	31.0	34.6	26.8	4.7	2.8	38157	40224	27	34	1032	42.5	24.7	27.1	4.9	0.7	62381
79783	TARZAN	19037	167	26.9	35.9	26.3	5.4	5.4	39428	39828	31	40	105	24.8	24.8	42.9	7.6	0.0	90500
79789	WINK	18980	327	32.1	22.6	38.2	5.5	1.5	45400	50045	49	60	276	64.1	25.0	8.3	1.1	1.4	40714
79821	ANTHONY	12250	1504	39.8	34.1	21.4	3.3	1.4	30295	33358	9	11	1120	28.5	40.4	28.7	2.2	0.2	71887
	TEXAS	24551		22.3	25.0	34.3	11.1	7.3	52382	54495				16.5	22.7	36.5	19.7	4.6	109784
	UNITED STATES	27277		20.9	24.4	35.3	11.7	7.6	54719	56938				9.3	13.1	31.6	32.6	13.5	162279

ZIP CODE		FINANCIAL SERVICES				THE HOME						ENTERTAINMENT						PERSONAL			
						Home Improvements		Furnishings													
#	POST OFFICE NAME	Auto Loan	Home Loan	Invest-ments	Retire-ment Plans	Home Repair	Lawn & Garden	Comput-ers & Hard-ware-Personal	Major Appli-ances	TV, Radio, Sound Equip-ment	Furni-ture	Dine out/ Carry out	Sports Equip-ment	Fees & Tickets	Toys & Games	Travel	Cable TV	Apparel & Services	Auto Repairs	Health Insur-ance	Pets & Supplies
79502	ASPERMONT	72	50	75	50	53	75	56	69	60	47	58	54	43	59	54	66	38	64	74	83
79503	AVOCA	70	50	71	49	52	73	55	68	61	49	59	51	44	60	53	67	39	63	73	80
79504	BAIRD	74	53	75	51	55	76	56	70	62	51	60	52	45	61	55	68	40	65	74	83
79506	BLACKWELL	76	57	86	56	61	80	60	76	65	55	64	56	50	63	61	71	42	70	79	88
79508	BUFFALO GAP	92	104	90	107	101	102	93	97	91	93	92	76	99	94	98	92	64	93	96	114
79510	CLYDE	82	61	82	59	62	83	62	77	68	58	67	57	51	68	61	75	44	71	80	91
79511	COAHOMA	88	63	91	61	66	90	65	83	72	60	71	63	52	71	65	79	47	76	86	99
79512	COLORADO CITY	67	51	61	48	52	65	54	63	59	52	58	46	45	59	51	64	39	61	66	74
79517	FLUVANNA	86	59	94	59	62	91	66	82	68	53	68	68	48	67	65	75	44	76	86	101
79518	GIRARD	73	50	80	50	52	76	55	69	58	45	57	57	41	56	55	63	37	64	73	85
79519	GOLDSBORO	78	56	80	54	58	79	57	73	63	53	62	55	46	63	57	70	41	67	76	87
79520	HAMLIN	75	54	76	53	56	78	59	73	66	52	63	54	47	64	57	72	42	68	79	86
79521	HASKELL	66	49	66	49	51	68	54	64	59	49	57	48	44	58	52	64	38	61	69	75
79525	HAWLEY	75	68	63	66	67	71	65	69	67	67	67	51	60	70	62	70	46	67	70	83
79526	HERMLEIGH	79	59	79	59	61	81	60	75	66	56	65	56	50	66	60	72	43	69	78	88
79527	IRA	94	65	103	64	68	99	72	89	74	58	74	73	53	73	71	81	48	83	94	109
79528	JAYTON	82	58	84	57	61	86	64	79	70	56	68	61	50	69	62	77	45	74	86	94
79529	KNOX CITY	72	52	72	50	54	75	57	70	63	51	61	52	45	62	55	70	41	65	76	82
79530	LAWN	89	64	91	62	66	90	66	83	73	61	71	62	53	72	65	80	47	76	86	99
79532	LORAINE	76	55	76	53	57	80	60	74	67	53	64	55	48	66	58	74	43	69	81	87
79533	LUEDERS	76	54	78	53	56	77	56	71	62	52	61	53	45	62	55	68	40	65	74	84
79534	MC CAULLEY	81	56	89	55	58	85	62	77	64	50	63	63	45	63	61	70	41	72	81	94
79535	MARYNEAL	80	56	87	55	58	85	62	77	65	51	64	62	46	64	61	71	42	72	82	94
79536	MERKEL	82	64	77	61	64	82	65	77	71	63	70	57	55	72	62	77	47	73	81	91
79537	NOLAN	72	52	72	51	54	75	57	70	63	51	61	52	45	62	55	70	41	65	76	82
79538	NOVICE	90	64	92	62	67	91	66	84	73	62	72	63	53	73	65	81	48	77	88	100
79539	O BRIEN	73	50	80	50	52	77	55	69	58	45	57	57	41	56	55	63	37	64	73	85
79540	OLD GLORY	98	68	108	67	71	104	75	93	78	61	77	77	55	77	75	85	50	87	99	115
79541	OVALO	92	81	91	81	81	97	78	90	82	74	81	69	72	82	79	86	55	84	92	107
79543	ROBY	81	57	85	56	59	85	63	78	68	53	66	61	48	66	62	74	43	73	83	94
79544	ROCHESTER	73	50	80	50	52	77	56	69	58	45	57	57	41	57	55	63	37	65	73	85
79545	ROSCOE	75	53	73	52	54	76	57	69	62	51	61	54	45	62	55	68	40	65	74	84
79546	ROTAN	67	48	69	47	50	70	52	65	57	46	56	50	41	56	51	63	37	60	70	77
79547	RULE	71	50	73	49	52	74	55	68	60	48	58	52	43	59	54	66	39	63	73	81
79548	RULE	77	53	85	53	56	82	59	73	61	48	61	61	43	60	59	67	39	68	77	90
79549	SNYDER	81	65	71	64	65	80	68	76	73	65	72	56	59	73	65	78	49	74	81	90
79553	STAMFORD	73	54	71	53	55	75	59	70	65	53	63	53	48	64	56	71	42	67	76	83
79556	SWEETWATER	68	54	60	54	54	66	61	64	64	56	63	49	52	64	56	68	43	64	69	77
79560	SYLVESTER	83	58	91	57	60	88	64	79	67	52	66	65	47	66	63	73	43	74	84	97
79561	TRENT	87	63	90	61	65	89	64	82	71	60	70	61	51	71	64	78	46	75	85	97
79562	TUSCOLA	92	92	85	95	91	99	86	94	87	83	87	72	85	89	88	90	60	88	94	109
79563	TYE	91	85	72	81	81	82	84	83	84	87	84	63	79	88	79	84	58	84	82	99
79565	WESTBROOK	73	59	95	58	64	78	59	75	61	55	61	55	51	58	64	66	40	69	74	87
79566	WINGATE	84	73	88	74	73	91	73	83	74	66	73	67	65	74	74	77	49	79	86	101
79567	WINTERS	67	50	61	48	50	66	55	63	59	50	58	48	44	58	52	63	39	61	67	75
79601	ABILENE	69	55	53	56	54	61	69	62	68	63	68	49	58	69	59	70	47	66	66	76
79602	ABILENE	85	79	72	78	77	81	81	80	82	80	81	61	77	83	77	83	57	81	82	95
79603	ABILENE	70	61	55	59	59	66	66	66	69	64	68	48	61	69	61	72	47	68	70	77
79605	ABILENE	80	74	70	75	73	78	79	77	80	77	80	59	76	81	76	82	55	79	82	92
79606	ABILENE	100	94	87	97	92	90	99	93	97	100	98	73	97	99	95	96	69	96	92	111
79607	DYESS AFB	88	46	34	53	41	39	83	57	78	77	82	57	63	93	60	72	57	73	52	70
79697	ABILENE	0	0	0	0	0	0	0	0	0	0	0	0	0	0	0	0	0	0	0	0
79698	ABILENE	41	33	29	33	31	38	39	37	41	36	39	29	33	41	33	43	27	39	42	45
79699	ABILENE	73	47	46	52	46	51	87	59	78	69	78	54	64	79	61	76	55	73	62	76
79701	MIDLAND	73	66	58	61	65	65	67	69	70	71	70	47	63	70	64	71	49	70	69	78
79703	MIDLAND	79	78	65	75	74	71	79	75	77	80	78	59	76	79	75	75	54	77	73	88
79705	MIDLAND	104	103	97	103	102	101	103	102	104	107	105	76	104	104	103	104	73	104	104	119
79706	MIDLAND	89	81	69	77	79	81	78	82	81	82	81	59	74	84	74	83	56	81	81	96
79707	MIDLAND	122	117	107	120	113	108	123	114	119	125	121	92	120	123	117	116	85	118	110	135
79713	ACKERLY	114	79	125	78	82	120	87	108	91	71	90	90	64	89	87	99	58	101	114	133
79714	ANDREWS	80	70	65	67	68	76	70	75	74	70	73	54	64	75	67	77	51	74	78	87
79718	BALMORHEA	42	34	25	28	32	31	33	36	36	38	37	22	29	37	30	38	26	36	35	40
79719	BARSTOW	55	36	53	34	36	54	38	48	44	36	43	38	29	45	36	49	29	45	51	59
79720	BIG SPRING	73	64	64	63	63	72	67	70	70	65	70	52	62	70	64	74	48	70	75	83
79730	COYANOSA	76	55	79	53	57	78	56	72	62	52	61	54	45	62	56	69	40	66	74	85
79731	CRANE	76	66	61	61	64	70	64	71	68	66	68	49	59	69	62	71	47	69	71	80
79734	FORT DAVIS	91	68	104	67	73	94	69	88	75	65	74	65	58	73	72	81	49	81	89	103
79735	FORT STOCKTON	71	57	59	52	56	64	57	64	62	59	62	46	50	62	54	65	42	63	65	75
79738	GAIL	92	63	101	63	66	97	70	87	73	57	72	72	51	71	70	79	47	81	92	107
79739	GARDEN CITY	104	71	114	71	75	109	79	98	82	64	81	81	58	81	79	90	53	92	104	121
79741	GOLDSMITH	96	69	99	67	72	98	71	90	79	66	77	68	57	78	70	86	51	83	94	107
79742	GRANDFALLS	60	43	61	42	45	63	47	59	53	42	51	44	38	52	46	58	34	55	64	69
79743	IMPERIAL	76	55	78	53	57	77	56	71	62	52	61	54	45	62	56	68	40	65	74	85
79744	IRAAN	88	71	72	68	70	83	70	78	75	70	75	59	61	79	65	80	50	75	81	94
79745	KERMIT	70	57	57	54	56	65	60	65	64	59	63	48	52	64	55	67	43	64	68	76
79748	KNOTT	99	68	109	68	71	104	76	94	79	61	78	78	55	77	75	86	50	88	99	116
79749	LENORAH	87	60	96	60	63	92	67	83	69	54	68	68	49	68	66	76	44	77	87	102
79752	MC CAMEY	73	53	68	49	53	71	55	67	62	53	60	49	44	61	53	67	40	63	70	79
79754	MENTONE	89	71	115	70	79	94	72	91	75	67	74	66	62	71	78	80	49	84	90	105
79755	MIDKIFF	89	63	94	61	65	92	66	84	72	59	71	65	51	71	66	79	46	77	88	101
79756	MONAHANS	78	64	66	60	63	74	65	72	69	65	69	53	57	70	62	73	47	70	74	85
79758	GARDENDALE	101	101	94	105	101	110	95	104	96	91	96	80	94	98	98	99	66	97	105	121
79761	ODESSA	73	65	57	63	63	66	68	68	71	70	72	49	65	72	64	73	50	70	71	79
79762	ODESSA	84	79	70	79	76	77	83	79	83	83	84	61	80	84	79	83	58	82	81	94
79763	ODESSA	67	57	49	52	55	56	59	60	61	61	62	43	53	62	54	62	43	61	60	69
79764	ODESSA	72	64	56	61	62	63	67	66	67	68	67	50	61	70	62	67	47	67	65	78
79765	ODESSA	112	116	108	118	114	107	112	109	109	117	110	85	115	111	112	106	77	109	104	128
79766	ODESSA	80	68	62	62	65	69	67	72	71	71	71	51	60	72	63	73	49	71	71	83
79772	PECOS	62	52	44	45	50	50	52	56	54	56	55	37	46	55	48	55	38	55	53	62
79777	PYOTE	55	36	53	34	36	54	38	48	44	36	43	38	29	45	36	49	29	46	51	59
79781	SHEFFIELD	87	62	72	61	62	82	65	75	72	63	71	58	52	75	59	78	47	71	80	92
79782	STANTON	85	63	79	59	64	81	65	78	70	62	70	58	52	70	63	76	47	74	80	92
79783	TARZAN	104	72	114	71	75	110	79	99	83	64	82	82	58	81	79	90	53	92	104	121
79789	WINK	79	72	64	70	71	74	68	72	71	71	71	52	64	74	65	73	48	70	72	86
79821	ANTHONY	68	55	42	47	53	52	55	59	60	61	60	37	48	61	50	61	42	60	57	65
	TEXAS	104	96	90	94	93	94	99	97	99	101	100	75	94	101	94	99	70	99	96	114
	UNITED STATES	100	100	100	100	100	100	100	100	100	100	100	100	100	100	100	100	100	100	100	100

ZIP CODE #	POST OFFICE NAME	COUNTY FIPS CODE	POPULATION 2000	POPULATION 2009	POPULATION 2014	2000-2009 ANNUAL RATE % Rate	2000-2009 ANNUAL RATE State Centile	HOUSEHOLDS 2000	HOUSEHOLDS 2009	HOUSEHOLDS 2014	HOUSEHOLDS % Annual Rate 2000-2009	HOUSEHOLDS 2009 Average HH Size	FAMILIES 2000	FAMILIES 2009	FAMILIES % Annual Rate 2000-2009
79830	ALPINE	043	7954	8343	8487	0.5	42	3278	3456	3541	0.6	2.27	1971	2036	0.4
79832	ALPINE	043	52	53	53	0.2	30	4	4	4	0.0	2.50	2	2	0.0
79834	BIG BEND NATIONAL PA	043	231	231	232	0.0	25	112	113	115	0.1	1.99	68	68	0.0
79835	CANUTILLO	141	10785	11420	11967	0.6	46	2849	3139	3330	1.1	3.63	2477	2680	0.9
79836	CLINT	141	17043	19327	20644	1.4	67	4527	5322	5739	1.8	3.63	4017	4659	1.6
79837	DELL CITY	229	625	595	584	-0.5	11	241	228	223	-0.6	2.61	182	170	-0.7
79839	FORT HANCOCK	229	1863	2028	2094	0.9	55	537	581	599	0.9	3.49	440	470	0.7
79842	MARATHON	043	554	523	509	-0.6	9	237	228	224	-0.4	2.29	152	144	-0.6
79843	MARFA	377	7232	8029	8337	1.1	61	2506	2797	2912	1.2	2.84	1845	2031	1.0
79847	SALT FLAT	109	165	157	150	-0.5	11	79	78	75	-0.1	2.01	49	47	-0.4
79849	SAN ELIZARIO	141	11344	13752	15059	2.1	79	2691	3389	3749	2.5	4.06	2495	3117	2.4
79851	SIERRA BLANCA	229	764	752	747	-0.2	19	274	268	266	-0.2	2.69	188	180	-0.5
79852	TERLINGUA	043	75	74	75	-0.1	21	38	38	39	0.0	1.95	23	23	0.0
79854	VALENTINE	243	275	308	334	1.2	63	109	123	134	1.3	2.50	82	91	1.1
79855	VAN HORN	109	2827	2474	2299	-1.4	2	984	894	842	-1.0	2.76	756	680	-1.1
79901	EL PASO	141	14012	13295	13171	-0.6	9	4514	4404	4401	-0.3	2.77	2935	2741	-0.7
79902	EL PASO	141	22993	22839	23073	-0.1	21	9052	9354	9562	0.4	2.40	5178	5078	-0.2
79903	EL PASO	141	19246	18905	18988	-0.2	19	6618	6748	6849	0.2	2.78	4725	4660	-0.1
79904	EL PASO	141	33248	33938	34641	0.2	30	10805	11393	11742	0.6	2.97	8369	8596	0.3
79905	EL PASO	141	28357	27467	27500	-0.3	16	8514	8608	8716	0.1	3.17	6679	6584	-0.2
79906	EL PASO	141	6710	6761	6829	0.1	27	1350	1391	1429	0.3	2.99	1251	1277	0.2
79907	EL PASO	141	55178	57375	59046	0.4	37	15289	16549	17207	0.9	3.45	13378	14267	0.7
79908	EL PASO	141	1060	1232	1284	1.6	71	303	339	362	1.2	2.61	282	313	1.1
79912	EL PASO	141	64247	70659	74179	1.0	58	23891	26759	28262	1.2	2.63	16845	18469	1.0
79915	EL PASO	141	42408	41637	41923	-0.2	19	12759	13082	13319	0.3	3.15	10501	10551	0.1
79916	EL PASO	141	734	724	722	-0.1	21	16	18	19	1.3	2.56	12	14	1.7
79918	EL PASO	141	212	246	257	1.6	71	0	0	0	0.0	0.00	0	0	0.0
79922	EL PASO	141	8783	8740	8858	-0.1	21	2770	2873	2945	0.4	2.99	2315	2354	0.2
79924	EL PASO	141	56995	58269	59523	0.2	30	18865	19987	20643	0.6	2.91	14792	15305	0.4
79925	EL PASO	141	40723	39820	39828	-0.2	19	15060	15255	15424	0.1	2.56	10623	10399	-0.2
79927	EL PASO	141	33342	36846	38835	1.1	61	8292	9609	10253	1.6	3.83	7621	8755	1.5
79928	EL PASO	141	19847	37314	44250	7.1	97	5154	9655	11535	7.0	3.81	4655	8641	6.9
79930	EL PASO	141	28480	27879	27919	-0.2	19	9416	9546	9662	0.1	2.89	6985	6870	-0.2
79932	EL PASO	141	16748	22517	25149	3.3	88	5222	7341	8300	3.8	3.06	4267	5867	3.5
79934	EL PASO	141	10132	14001	15825	3.6	90	3011	4284	4896	3.9	3.27	2669	3745	3.7
79935	EL PASO	141	19390	19072	19118	-0.2	19	6623	6745	6833	0.2	2.78	5012	4955	-0.1
79936	EL PASO	141	92089	111480	120819	2.1	79	26900	32776	35623	2.2	3.39	23301	28086	2.0
79938	EL PASO	141	18810	41482	50343	8.9	98	4161	11039	13761	11.1	3.51	3665	9511	10.9
79968	EL PASO	141	482	482	478	0.0	25	52	50	49	-0.4	2.62	43	40	-0.8
	TEXAS					1.9					1.8	2.78			1.7
	UNITED STATES					1.0					1.1	2.59			0.9

ZIP CODE #	POST OFFICE NAME	RACE (%) White 2000	White 2009	Black 2000	Black 2009	Asian/Pacific 2000	Asian/Pacific 2009	% Hispanic Origin 2000	% Hispanic Origin 2009	2009 AGE DISTRIBUTION (%) 0-4	5-9	10-14	15-19	20-24	25-44	45-64	65-84	85+	18+	MEDIAN AGE 2009	% 2009 Males	% 2009 Females
79830	ALPINE	80.6	77.1	1.3	1.2	0.5	0.5	43.5	52.4	5.6	5.6	5.5	8.5	7.8	26.0	26.1	12.9	2.0	79.3	36.8	49.7	50.3
79832	ALPINE	86.3	81.1	2.0	1.9	0.0	1.9	29.4	35.8	3.8	3.8	3.8	7.5	11.3	20.8	30.2	15.1	3.8	84.9	43.8	49.1	50.9
79834	BIG BEND NATIONAL PA	85.3	82.3	0.9	0.9	0.4	0.4	37.9	48.1	4.8	5.2	5.6	6.1	5.2	23.4	31.6	16.5	1.7	81.8	44.8	51.9	48.1
79835	CANUTILLO	92.3	91.9	0.5	0.5	0.1	0.1	91.6	94.2	10.1	9.5	8.9	9.6	8.0	26.4	20.1	6.8	0.6	65.6	27.5	49.2	50.8
79836	CLINT	79.7	79.8	0.4	0.4	0.0	0.0	93.5	95.7	10.5	10.5	9.8	9.8	8.1	24.5	19.2	6.9	0.7	63.0	25.9	48.8	51.2
79837	DELL CITY	67.4	62.5	1.1	1.2	0.3	0.3	58.9	66.9	5.9	5.9	6.4	8.4	6.2	21.5	26.4	18.3	1.0	76.8	41.6	49.6	50.4
79839	FORT HANCOCK	93.4	93.0	0.2	0.2	0.2	0.1	85.3	89.0	10.1	9.8	8.9	9.5	7.6	25.8	19.7	7.7	0.7	65.3	27.5	52.7	47.3
79842	MARATHON	85.2	82.2	0.7	0.8	0.0	0.0	48.9	59.1	3.1	3.1	3.8	5.0	5.9	23.5	34.0	19.5	2.1	87.2	50.9	52.6	47.4
79843	MARFA	85.0	84.1	0.3	0.2	0.1	0.1	84.4	85.5	8.7	8.1	7.8	9.0	7.8	23.4	22.3	11.6	1.6	69.8	32.1	48.6	51.4
79847	SALT FLAT	90.2	87.9	0.6	0.6	0.6	0.6	34.1	43.3	3.2	4.5	6.4	7.0	4.5	23.6	34.4	15.3	1.3	80.9	45.6	56.7	43.3
79849	SAN ELIZARIO	91.9	92.3	0.2	0.1	0.0	0.0	97.4	98.2	10.6	10.9	10.3	10.7	8.3	25.9	17.6	5.1	0.5	61.3	24.5	49.6	50.4
79851	SIERRA BLANCA	87.7	86.4	0.0	0.0	0.1	0.1	62.2	69.7	8.0	7.0	6.6	7.2	6.9	26.3	25.8	9.4	2.7	74.5	36.0	49.3	50.7
79852	TERLINGUA	85.3	82.4	1.3	1.4	0.0	0.0	40.0	50.0	5.4	5.4	5.4	5.4	4.1	23.0	31.1	17.6	2.7	78.4	46.3	50.0	50.0
79854	VALENTINE	90.2	88.3	0.4	0.3	0.0	0.0	50.2	60.7	1.6	7.5	9.1	6.5	0.6	19.8	35.4	16.9	2.6	78.2	47.6	51.0	49.0
79855	VAN HORN	67.8	64.6	0.7	0.8	0.6	0.6	74.4	80.4	8.0	7.9	7.8	8.7	7.5	24.1	23.5	11.4	1.1	70.9	33.1	50.1	49.9
79901	EL PASO	79.0	79.4	0.8	0.7	0.2	0.2	95.8	97.0	8.0	8.1	7.8	9.3	8.6	21.5	20.0	14.1	2.6	70.8	31.7	47.6	52.4
79902	EL PASO	80.1	79.7	1.6	1.4	1.6	1.5	75.7	80.6	7.3	6.5	5.9	6.3	7.5	27.8	23.7	12.3	2.6	76.6	36.0	48.6	51.4
79903	EL PASO	78.1	78.2	1.3	1.0	0.3	0.3	89.6	92.6	7.3	7.2	7.1	7.2	6.1	24.6	23.4	14.2	2.8	73.9	37.1	46.6	53.4
79904	EL PASO	66.2	65.2	6.9	6.4	1.4	1.5	69.3	74.8	10.6	9.2	7.8	7.6	7.9	26.5	19.4	9.6	1.5	67.9	29.3	48.1	51.9
79905	EL PASO	76.3	76.6	1.0	0.8	0.3	0.3	95.8	96.9	8.6	8.5	8.1	7.8	6.6	23.3	21.3	13.9	2.1	70.1	33.3	46.9	53.1
79906	EL PASO	59.7	55.7	23.0	23.3	2.7	3.2	22.2	27.9	12.6	7.4	4.5	11.2	29.5	31.0	3.1	0.6	0.1	73.5	22.4	64.0	36.0
79907	EL PASO	70.2	70.4	0.7	0.6	0.2	0.2	94.5	96.2	8.6	8.6	8.0	8.7	7.8	26.8	21.8	8.7	0.9	69.5	30.0	47.4	52.6
79908	EL PASO	56.1	53.0	31.0	31.3	4.0	4.6	19.0	25.0	6.2	6.7	11.6	9.3	9.7	47.3	8.7	0.4	0.0	68.8	28.6	61.0	39.0
79912	EL PASO	81.0	79.4	2.0	1.8	2.8	3.1	55.0	64.0	8.3	7.8	7.5	7.1	6.7	29.3	24.1	8.0	1.3	71.8	33.5	48.0	52.0
79915	EL PASO	70.2	70.5	1.8	1.4	0.3	0.2	93.5	95.4	8.3	8.3	7.8	8.2	6.6	25.4	20.7	13.0	1.6	70.5	33.0	47.5	52.5
79916	EL PASO	55.1	51.2	25.5	25.6	2.7	3.2	25.6	32.5	13.7	8.7	6.2	8.4	26.1	32.6	3.9	0.4	0.0	68.5	22.5	60.8	39.2
79918	EL PASO	56.4	53.3	31.3	31.3	3.8	4.5	19.0	25.2	6.5	6.5	11.8	9.3	9.8	47.2	8.9	0.0	0.0	68.7	28.4	61.0	39.0
79922	EL PASO	84.9	83.4	0.7	0.6	1.1	1.2	53.4	61.9	6.8	7.4	8.2	7.9	4.7	22.5	30.2	11.0	1.3	72.4	39.5	48.6	51.4
79924	EL PASO	65.8	64.1	8.7	7.9	2.4	2.7	59.2	67.0	7.8	7.6	7.4	8.0	7.3	25.6	23.9	11.3	1.2	72.3	33.4	46.7	53.3
79925	EL PASO	78.0	77.2	3.6	3.1	1.2	1.2	68.9	76.5	7.0	6.2	6.2	6.7	8.0	26.7	24.0	13.2	1.9	76.7	35.8	48.9	51.1
79927	EL PASO	73.6	73.7	0.4	0.3	0.1	0.1	96.3	97.4	9.5	9.1	8.8	9.1	8.2	26.3	21.6	6.8	0.6	67.1	28.4	48.5	51.5
79928	EL PASO	75.7	75.0	1.2	1.1	0.3	0.4	86.4	90.2	10.8	10.8	9.8	9.4	7.8	29.0	17.5	4.5	0.5	62.8	25.9	49.4	50.6
79930	EL PASO	76.9	76.8	2.0	1.8	0.5	0.5	87.3	90.6	8.4	8.1	7.6	7.6	6.7	25.6	22.0	11.9	2.2	71.4	33.9	47.5	52.5
79932	EL PASO	82.9	83.1	1.0	0.8	0.5	0.5	69.0	74.5	8.0	8.3	8.5	8.5	5.9	24.7	26.2	9.0	0.9	69.8	34.3	48.3	51.7
79934	EL PASO	62.6	62.1	14.9	13.0	3.2	3.5	46.7	55.4	8.9	8.7	8.5	8.5	6.8	30.8	24.1	3.5	0.2	68.7	30.2	48.8	51.2
79935	EL PASO	74.6	73.9	3.8	3.3	1.1	1.1	72.9	79.6	8.4	7.5	6.9	8.1	8.3	28.3	21.9	9.6	1.0	72.5	31.1	47.1	52.9
79936	EL PASO	69.4	68.3	2.4	1.9	1.1	1.0	81.4	87.2	9.6	9.4	8.9	8.7	6.8	30.7	20.8	4.5	0.6	66.6	29.1	48.5	51.5
79938	EL PASO	67.7	59.5	2.9	2.1	0.5	0.8	84.1	88.2	9.4	9.1	8.5	9.7	10.1	28.2	18.9	5.6	0.6	67.7	27.1	53.2	46.8
79968	EL PASO	68.3	68.3	9.1	7.9	9.3	9.3	57.9	65.4	4.1	1.7	1.2	21.0	17.0	17.6	3.9	19.7	13.7	91.7	28.4	44.8	55.2
	TEXAS	71.0	67.6	11.5	11.4	2.8	3.5	32.0	37.4	7.9	7.5	7.2	7.5	7.4	28.3	24.0	8.8	1.4	73.0	33.6	49.7	50.3
	UNITED STATES	75.1	72.0	12.3	12.7	3.8	4.6	12.5	15.7	6.8	6.7	6.6	7.1	6.9	27.0	26.0	10.9	1.9	75.7	36.9	49.2	50.8

79830-79968

ZIP CODE				2009 HOUSEHOLD INCOME DISTRIBUTION (%)					MEDIAN HOUSEHOLD INCOME					2009 HOME VALUE DISTRIBUTION (%)					
#	POST OFFICE NAME	2009 Per Capita Income	2009 HH Income Base	Less than $25,000	$25,000 to $49,999	$50,000 to $99,999	$100,000 to $149,999	$150,000 or More	2009	2014	2009 National Centile	2009 State Centile	2009 Home Value Base	Less than $50,000	$50,000 to $89,999	$90,000 to $174,999	$175,000 to $399,999	$400,000 or More	2009 Median Home Value
79830	ALPINE	18790	3456	35.4	32.7	25.6	4.0	2.3	34066	35836	16	20	2020	27.3	20.9	32.4	15.1	4.3	92606
79832	ALPINE	1121	4	100.0	0.0	0.0	0.0	0.0	6667	30000	0	1	0	0.0	0.0	0.0	0.0	0.0	0
79834	BIG BEND NATIONAL PA	23103	113	30.1	34.5	28.3	6.2	0.9	38717	41147	29	37	69	23.2	13.0	27.5	24.6	11.6	139063
79835	CANUTILLO	9788	3139	45.1	34.0	16.9	3.6	0.4	27182	29023	5	6	2352	36.0	44.0	17.4	2.3	0.3	60712
79836	CLINT	9527	5322	47.3	33.4	15.7	2.6	1.1	26512	28698	4	5	3884	43.0	36.3	18.0	2.6	0.1	55133
79837	DELL CITY	12971	228	51.3	28.5	17.1	1.3	1.8	24435	25198	3	4	175	64.0	22.3	11.4	2.3	0.0	39583
79839	FORT HANCOCK	8561	581	58.5	24.4	14.1	1.5	1.4	22028	22495	2	3	500	74.2	17.8	8.0	0.0	0.0	33562
79842	MARATHON	21649	228	44.3	21.1	25.4	5.7	3.5	29590	31509	7	9	163	41.1	20.2	25.8	9.2	3.7	75500
79843	MARFA	11309	2797	51.5	30.0	15.3	2.4	0.8	23854	24647	3	3	1938	50.5	26.5	17.3	4.5	1.2	49606
79847	SALT FLAT	20397	78	28.2	37.2	34.6	0.0	0.0	38293	43669	28	35	39	38.5	20.5	5.1	30.8	5.1	65000
79849	SAN ELIZARIO	7742	3389	51.1	30.5	16.5	1.6	0.3	24544	25524	3	4	2747	35.5	46.5	17.0	0.7	0.3	59399
79851	SIERRA BLANCA	17671	268	27.6	38.1	29.1	2.2	3.0	38601	38672	28	36	190	46.8	32.6	18.4	1.6	0.5	54000
79852	TERLINGUA	23503	38	28.9	36.8	26.3	7.9	0.0	38586	39065	28	36	23	30.4	13.0	26.1	17.4	13.0	118750
79854	VALENTINE	19435	123	31.7	31.7	26.0	6.5	4.1	42660	43358	41	52	72	59.7	27.8	6.9	0.0	5.6	32500
79855	VAN HORN	13264	894	42.4	31.4	23.2	2.0	1.0	30077	30815	8	10	639	65.6	24.3	7.0	2.3	0.8	39063
79901	EL PASO	7122	4404	79.0	15.8	4.7	0.3	0.2	11940	12405	1	1	517	31.7	44.1	22.1	1.7	0.4	60373
79902	EL PASO	19923	9354	45.0	25.9	18.5	5.3	5.3	29141	31704	7	8	3246	2.2	20.4	52.5	20.8	4.1	131372
79903	EL PASO	13988	6748	43.7	30.1	21.2	3.7	1.3	28213	30718	6	7	3788	3.8	47.6	45.1	3.2	0.3	89313
79904	EL PASO	14357	11393	38.3	32.9	22.3	5.0	1.7	33217	35384	14	17	5249	6.7	49.9	33.6	9.4	0.5	85175
79905	EL PASO	9533	8608	57.3	27.1	13.1	1.6	0.8	21290	21858	2	2	4015	14.1	55.9	29.2	0.6	0.1	75485
79906	EL PASO	16536	1391	21.9	37.4	33.1	3.9	3.7	42493	46279	41	51	88	1.1	64.8	34.1	0.0	0.0	85758
79907	EL PASO	11265	16549	39.6	32.9	23.8	2.9	0.7	31756	34495	11	14	10489	12.1	50.1	36.2	1.6	0.1	83717
79908	EL PASO	20969	339	0.0	35.7	58.7	0.0	5.6	54713	54585	71	78	7	0.0	0.0	100.0	0.0	0.0	103125
79912	EL PASO	29788	26759	17.7	20.7	38.7	13.9	9.0	61767	60861	80	85	15305	0.7	3.8	58.9	32.0	4.6	149395
79915	EL PASO	11676	13082	44.4	30.9	21.2	2.6	0.9	28302	30837	6	7	7579	5.9	56.9	35.6	1.3	0.3	83398
79916	EL PASO	4990	18	44.4	38.9	11.1	5.6	0.0	27247	26070	5	6	16	56.3	25.0	18.8	0.0	0.0	45000
79918	EL PASO	3957	0	0.0	0.0	0.0	0.0	0.0	0	0	0	0	0	0.0	0.0	0.0	0.0	0.0	0
79922	EL PASO	36010	2873	17.3	18.0	29.2	14.4	21.1	69206	68119	86	89	2264	5.0	8.1	38.3	30.2	18.4	167523
79924	EL PASO	16993	19987	27.2	30.6	35.1	5.6	1.4	43373	46462	43	54	13481	7.4	41.3	49.9	1.3	0.1	91056
79925	EL PASO	20962	15255	24.4	30.7	34.8	7.7	2.4	46172	48364	52	62	8188	1.8	12.3	74.8	10.8	0.2	120759
79927	EL PASO	9344	9609	41.6	35.7	20.0	2.1	0.6	29358	31967	7	9	7543	23.5	42.6	30.5	3.0	0.4	75673
79928	EL PASO	12132	9655	32.7	33.4	26.3	5.7	1.8	36235	39632	21	28	8321	17.9	29.9	44.0	8.2	0.0	92854
79930	EL PASO	13473	9546	43.5	31.7	19.7	3.7	1.4	28501	30842	6	7	4922	6.3	47.3	42.9	3.2	0.4	87986
79932	EL PASO	24340	7341	25.3	26.4	28.1	10.7	9.5	48311	50867	57	67	5211	14.4	15.8	36.8	27.2	5.8	132486
79934	EL PASO	20686	4284	11.4	26.0	47.9	10.2	4.4	59005	57900	76	83	3205	3.7	11.4	71.3	13.6	0.0	117471
79935	EL PASO	20275	6745	27.6	25.9	33.2	10.2	3.1	46586	49639	53	63	3519	0.4	14.1	69.0	16.2	0.3	126680
79936	EL PASO	17797	32776	16.1	29.1	43.3	8.8	2.7	53479	54089	69	77	24718	2.0	13.3	75.2	8.6	0.9	115558
79938	EL PASO	13154	11039	22.0	42.0	31.6	3.7	0.7	39935	43666	32	42	9746	13.3	24.7	52.0	9.3	0.7	102146
79968	EL PASO	12428	50	80.0	12.0	0.0	8.0	0.0	12896	13208	1	1	2	0.0	0.0	0.0	0.0	100.0	450000
	TEXAS	24551		22.3	25.0	34.3	11.1	7.3	52382	54495				16.5	22.7	36.5	19.7	4.6	109784
	UNITED STATES	27277		20.9	24.4	35.3	11.7	7.6	54719	56938				9.3	13.1	31.6	32.6	13.5	162279

ZIP CODE #	POST OFFICE NAME	FINANCIAL SERVICES: Auto Loan	FINANCIAL SERVICES: Home Loan	FINANCIAL SERVICES: Investments	FINANCIAL SERVICES: Retirement Plans	THE HOME: Home Improvements: Home Repair	THE HOME: Home Improvements: Lawn & Garden	THE HOME: Furnishings: Computers & Hardware-Personal	THE HOME: Furnishings: Major Appliances	THE HOME: Furnishings: TV, Radio, Sound Equipment	THE HOME: Furnishings: Furniture	ENTERTAINMENT: Dine out/ Carry out	ENTERTAINMENT: Sports Equipment	ENTERTAINMENT: Fees & Tickets	ENTERTAINMENT: Toys & Games	ENTERTAINMENT: Travel	ENTERTAINMENT: Cable TV	PERSONAL: Apparel & Services	PERSONAL: Auto Repairs	PERSONAL: Health Insurance	PERSONAL: Pets & Supplies
79830	ALPINE	69	56	61	55	57	64	62	64	64	59	63	48	54	63	58	66	43	64	66	76
79832	ALPINE	10	8	9	9	9	10	10	10	10	9	10	7	9	10	9	10	7	10	10	12
79834	BIG BEND NATIONAL PA	83	60	87	58	62	84	61	78	68	57	66	58	49	67	61	74	44	71	81	92
79835	CANUTILLO	59	49	37	42	46	46	48	51	52	54	52	33	43	53	44	53	36	52	50	57
79836	CLINT	57	47	36	40	45	43	47	50	50	53	51	32	42	51	43	51	36	50	47	55
79837	DELL CITY	60	43	61	42	45	61	44	56	49	42	49	42	36	49	44	54	32	52	58	67
79839	FORT HANCOCK	50	40	30	34	39	38	40	43	44	45	44	27	35	44	36	45	31	44	42	47
79842	MARATHON	89	64	91	62	66	90	65	83	72	61	71	62	52	72	65	80	47	76	86	99
79843	MARFA	54	42	39	37	41	45	43	48	47	46	47	32	36	47	39	49	32	47	48	54
79847	SALT FLAT	72	53	73	51	55	73	54	68	60	51	59	51	44	60	53	65	39	63	70	80
79849	SAN ELIZARIO	53	42	32	35	40	40	42	45	46	47	46	28	37	47	38	47	32	46	44	50
79851	SIERRA BLANCA	75	70	59	66	66	67	69	68	69	72	69	52	65	72	65	69	48	69	67	81
79852	TERLINGUA	82	59	84	57	61	83	60	76	67	56	65	57	48	66	59	73	43	70	80	91
79854	VALENTINE	87	62	89	60	65	88	64	81	71	59	70	61	51	70	63	78	46	75	85	97
79855	VAN HORN	62	49	39	42	47	48	49	54	53	54	54	34	42	54	44	56	37	54	52	59
79901	EL PASO	25	20	17	19	19	19	26	23	27	25	28	16	22	26	22	28	20	25	24	27
79902	EL PASO	69	59	55	59	58	57	69	64	70	69	71	48	64	70	64	70	51	69	64	75
79903	EL PASO	60	52	45	47	51	53	53	55	57	56	57	37	49	56	50	59	39	56	58	63
79904	EL PASO	66	54	47	51	53	53	61	59	62	62	63	43	54	64	55	62	44	62	58	67
79905	EL PASO	50	39	30	34	38	37	41	43	44	45	45	27	36	44	37	46	31	44	42	47
79906	EL PASO	95	52	39	58	47	44	88	63	84	83	88	61	68	99	65	78	62	79	58	76
79907	EL PASO	62	52	41	45	50	47	54	55	56	59	57	37	48	57	49	56	40	57	52	61
79908	EL PASO	109	57	42	65	50	48	102	71	96	95	101	70	78	115	74	88	71	90	64	86
79912	EL PASO	114	113	101	115	109	103	114	108	111	118	112	86	114	115	110	107	79	110	102	126
79915	EL PASO	58	50	40	44	48	46	50	52	53	55	54	35	46	54	47	54	38	53	51	58
79916	EL PASO	54	43	32	36	41	40	43	46	47	48	47	28	37	47	38	48	33	47	45	51
79918	EL PASO	0	0	0	0	0	0	0	0	0	0	0	0	0	0	0	0	0	0	0	0
79922	EL PASO	145	174	170	175	177	163	149	157	146	161	148	116	170	148	164	145	107	150	149	178
79924	EL PASO	72	71	62	69	68	69	70	70	70	72	71	53	69	72	69	71	49	71	70	81
79925	EL PASO	78	72	67	72	71	74	76	74	78	76	79	56	74	78	74	80	55	77	79	87
79927	EL PASO	60	48	36	41	46	45	48	52	52	54	53	32	42	53	43	54	37	52	50	57
79928	EL PASO	74	66	53	58	64	59	65	67	66	71	67	45	60	68	60	66	47	67	62	74
79930	EL PASO	62	51	42	46	50	51	53	55	57	57	57	37	48	57	49	59	40	57	56	62
79932	EL PASO	111	113	101	107	112	104	104	108	104	113	105	77	105	105	105	103	74	106	102	122
79934	EL PASO	101	109	91	105	104	90	98	98	92	107	95	76	100	98	97	87	67	94	85	110
79935	EL PASO	82	78	70	77	76	72	82	77	81	84	82	60	80	82	79	79	57	81	76	91
79936	EL PASO	90	94	79	89	90	79	88	87	83	95	85	66	87	87	86	80	60	85	77	98
79938	EL PASO	70	68	57	60	66	58	67	67	64	72	66	49	63	66	64	62	46	67	60	74
79968	EL PASO	32	21	20	23	20	23	38	26	34	30	34	24	28	34	27	33	24	32	27	33
	TEXAS	104	96	90	94	93	94	99	97	99	101	100	75	94	101	94	99	70	99	96	114
	UNITED STATES	100	100	100	100	100	100	100	100	100	100	100	100	100	100	100	100	100	100	100	100

POPULATION CHANGE

84001-84119

ZIP CODE #	POST OFFICE NAME	COUNTY FIPS CODE	POPULATION 2000	POPULATION 2009	POPULATION 2014	2000-2009 ANNUAL RATE % Rate	2000-2009 ANNUAL RATE State Centile	HOUSEHOLDS 2000	HOUSEHOLDS 2009	HOUSEHOLDS 2014	HOUSEHOLDS % Annual Rate 2000-2009	HOUSEHOLDS 2009 Average HH Size	FAMILIES 2000	FAMILIES 2009	FAMILIES % Annual Rate 2000-2009
84001	ALTAMONT	013	142	162	177	1.4	45	44	52	58	1.8	3.12	36	42	1.7
84003	AMERICAN FORK	049	30939	41631	49764	3.3	81	7948	10733	12838	3.3	3.84	7027	9261	3.0
84004	ALPINE	049	7428	10485	12495	3.8	86	1744	2501	2995	4.0	4.19	1625	2284	3.7
84005	EAGLE MOUNTAIN	049	2417	17031	23244	23.5	100	578	4200	5760	23.9	4.06	543	3813	23.5
84006	BINGHAM CANYON	035	726	769	809	0.6	26	273	291	307	0.7	2.64	192	173	-1.1
84007	BLUEBELL	013	1370	1563	1706	1.4	45	440	523	578	1.9	2.99	360	417	1.6
84010	BOUNTIFUL	011	43652	47848	51676	1.0	37	14180	16128	17608	1.4	2.94	11365	12457	1.0
84013	CEDAR VALLEY	049	2365	2989	3469	2.6	73	642	826	965	2.8	3.57	541	667	2.3
84014	CENTERVILLE	011	14512	16803	18640	1.6	48	4120	4965	5575	2.0	3.38	3519	4124	1.7
84015	CLEARFIELD	011	46542	61345	70582	3.0	77	14091	18895	21853	3.2	3.19	11456	15224	3.1
84017	COALVILLE	043	3411	4677	5284	3.5	85	1132	1583	1799	3.7	2.93	920	1253	3.4
84018	CROYDON	029	134	204	235	4.6	90	36	57	66	5.1	3.58	32	50	4.9
84020	DRAPER	035	25290	40275	46723	5.2	95	6326	11008	13044	6.2	3.31	5443	9211	5.9
84021	DUCHESNE	013	2653	3050	3328	1.5	47	824	994	1104	2.0	2.91	641	752	1.7
84022	DUGWAY	045	2105	2434	2685	1.6	48	376	495	583	3.0	2.93	284	358	2.5
84023	DUTCH JOHN	009	210	216	220	0.3	16	86	92	94	0.7	2.15	61	62	0.2
84025	FARMINGTON	011	12276	17119	19903	3.7	86	3138	4638	5477	4.3	3.58	2827	4101	4.1
84026	FORT DUCHESNE	047	1736	2143	2347	2.3	67	497	637	707	2.7	3.32	408	510	2.4
84028	GARDEN CITY	033	503	599	640	1.9	55	190	235	255	2.3	2.54	152	184	2.1
84029	GRANTSVILLE	045	6470	9858	11960	4.7	91	1979	3071	3752	4.9	3.15	1628	2444	4.5
84031	HANNA	013	55	65	71	1.8	52	17	21	23	2.3	3.10	13	15	1.6
84032	HEBER CITY	051	11617	16605	19654	3.9	87	3587	5205	6180	4.1	3.17	2931	4160	3.9
84033	HENEFER	043	785	889	1004	1.4	45	251	291	331	1.6	3.05	205	231	1.3
84035	JENSEN	047	589	710	774	2.0	58	196	245	271	2.4	2.90	162	198	2.2
84036	KAMAS	043	4405	7023	8148	5.2	95	1430	2229	2590	4.9	3.15	1130	1715	4.6
84037	KAYSVILLE	011	25190	32378	36945	2.8	76	6776	8727	9969	2.8	3.70	5962	7583	2.6
84038	LAKETOWN	033	382	455	486	1.9	55	126	156	169	2.3	2.90	101	122	2.1
84039	LAPOINT	047	397	494	543	2.4	69	128	165	184	2.8	2.99	107	135	2.5
84040	LAYTON	011	23082	25661	28039	1.2	41	6402	7344	8101	1.5	3.48	5759	6472	1.3
84041	LAYTON	011	36191	44382	49962	2.2	63	12026	14977	16954	2.4	2.96	9221	11109	2.0
84042	LINDON	049	8366	10076	11368	2.0	58	1937	2378	2702	2.2	4.21	1790	2148	2.0
84043	LEHI	049	19899	44160	56301	9.0	98	5375	12013	15382	9.1	3.67	4819	10606	8.9
84044	MAGNA	035	22828	25800	27780	1.3	43	6577	7655	8307	1.7	3.37	5458	6113	1.2
84045	SARATOGA SPRINGS	049	1138	12748	17410	29.8	100	305	3447	4742	30.0	3.70	280	3149	29.9
84046	MANILA	009	711	732	743	0.3	16	254	270	279	0.7	2.49	179	184	0.3
84047	MIDVALE	035	28039	29847	31349	0.7	29	10680	11573	12207	0.9	2.56	6985	7004	0.0
84049	MIDWAY	051	2720	4292	5367	5.1	93	901	1500	1887	5.7	2.86	724	1177	5.4
84050	MORGAN	029	6995	9231	10586	3.0	77	2010	2675	3077	3.1	3.45	1750	2292	3.0
84051	MOUNTAIN HOME	013	451	537	581	1.9	55	190	236	259	2.4	2.28	141	169	2.0
84052	MYTON	013	1068	1243	1361	1.7	50	328	393	436	2.0	3.16	275	323	1.8
84053	NEOLA	013	775	825	914	0.7	29	240	271	305	1.3	2.99	202	224	1.1
84054	NORTH SALT LAKE	011	8715	13445	16167	4.8	92	2829	4700	5763	5.6	2.86	2239	3513	5.0
84056	HILL AFB	011	4785	4812	5038	0.1	10	1158	1226	1306	0.6	3.47	1140	1203	0.6
84057	OREM	049	35342	37981	40989	0.8	31	9903	10904	11859	1.0	3.44	8131	8486	0.5
84058	OREM	049	28132	32241	35791	1.5	47	8153	9593	10732	1.8	3.34	6272	6851	1.0
84060	PARK CITY	043	7468	9130	9901	2.2	63	2739	3323	3613	2.1	2.74	1709	1957	1.5
84061	PEOA	043	546	662	751	2.1	60	163	203	231	2.4	3.26	133	162	2.2
84062	PLEASANT GROVE	049	26560	42452	51344	5.2	95	6803	10961	13305	5.3	3.87	6051	9523	5.0
84063	RANDLETT	047	76	94	103	2.3	67	27	35	39	2.8	2.69	21	27	2.8
84064	RANDOLPH	033	715	800	853	1.2	41	217	248	267	1.5	3.17	175	195	1.2
84065	RIVERTON	035	27474	35719	39964	2.9	76	6835	9073	10205	3.1	3.92	6333	8266	2.9
84066	ROOSEVELT	013	7835	9595	10452	2.2	63	2458	3114	3434	2.6	3.07	2003	2480	2.3
84067	ROY	057	33877	38610	41620	1.4	45	10959	12743	13754	1.6	3.02	8866	10030	1.3
84069	RUSH VALLEY	045	445	739	902	5.6	95	148	252	308	5.9	2.93	113	183	5.4
84070	SANDY	035	22133	24328	25750	1.0	37	7141	8183	8750	1.5	2.92	5392	5808	0.8
84071	STOCKTON	045	726	1115	1358	4.7	91	249	387	474	4.9	2.88	191	281	4.3
84072	TABIONA	013	479	570	617	1.9	55	159	197	216	2.3	2.89	118	141	1.9
84073	TALMAGE	013	342	398	433	1.7	50	116	142	157	2.2	2.70	89	105	1.8
84074	TOOELE	045	28961	41367	49413	3.9	87	9327	13202	15720	3.8	3.12	7453	10328	3.6
84075	SYRACUSE	011	9662	20816	25960	8.7	98	2556	5669	7138	9.0	3.67	2308	5031	8.8
84076	TRIDELL	047	350	437	480	2.4	69	95	123	137	2.8	3.55	79	100	2.6
84078	VERNAL	047	20391	24104	26317	1.8	52	6724	8177	9023	2.1	2.92	5345	6336	1.9
84080	VERNON	045	288	383	467	3.1	79	94	128	157	3.4	2.99	74	96	2.9
84081	WEST JORDAN	035	18650	36491	43517	7.5	97	4752	9325	11125	7.6	3.90	4371	8389	7.3
84082	WALLSBURG	051	792	799	942	0.1	10	229	233	276	0.2	3.42	196	196	0.0
84083	WENDOVER	045	2008	2943	3540	4.2	88	586	863	1040	4.3	3.41	440	623	3.8
84084	WEST JORDAN	035	32312	38865	42396	2.0	58	8972	11221	12360	2.4	3.44	7667	9298	2.1
84085	WHITEROCKS	047	886	1119	1234	2.6	73	263	344	384	2.9	3.25	213	271	2.6
84086	WOODRUFF	033	361	402	429	1.2	41	112	129	140	1.5	3.12	94	106	1.3
84087	WOODS CROSS	011	9947	13714	16011	3.5	85	2792	3980	4694	3.9	3.45	2440	3398	3.6
84088	WEST JORDAN	035	33367	36927	39545	1.1	39	9357	10682	11521	1.4	3.44	8013	8825	1.0
84092	SANDY	035	30172	31814	33427	0.6	26	8127	8880	9408	1.0	3.56	7401	7908	0.7
84093	SANDY	035	25226	25504	26333	0.1	10	7193	7508	7808	0.5	3.40	6347	6437	0.2
84094	SANDY	035	28626	29850	31173	0.5	22	8487	9123	9592	0.8	3.27	7096	7357	0.4
84095	SOUTH JORDAN	035	30475	47247	54289	4.9	93	7930	12646	14653	5.2	3.73	7052	11158	5.1
84096	HERRIMAN	035	5747	30383	38946	19.7	99	1570	8524	11024	20.1	3.56	1424	7333	19.4
84097	OREM	049	21089	22378	24132	0.6	26	5397	5931	6442	1.0	3.76	4742	5029	0.6
84098	PARK CITY	043	13150	16119	17580	2.2	63	4626	5735	6265	2.4	2.81	3412	4071	1.9
84101	SALT LAKE CITY	035	3244	4907	5674	4.6	90	1203	1936	2286	5.3	2.14	416	574	3.5
84102	SALT LAKE CITY	035	16952	17178	17535	0.1	10	8251	8492	8711	0.3	1.97	2932	2596	-1.3
84103	SALT LAKE CITY	035	22621	22760	23307	0.1	10	10811	11069	11367	0.3	2.02	5002	4609	-0.9
84104	SALT LAKE CITY	035	22549	24537	25677	0.9	34	6572	6940	7230	0.6	3.49	4818	4785	-0.1
84105	SALT LAKE CITY	035	22398	21917	22214	-0.2	3	9718	9797	10007	0.1	2.20	5261	4778	-1.0
84106	SALT LAKE CITY	035	32865	32904	33693	0.0	6	13390	13750	14167	0.3	2.35	8153	7634	-0.7
84107	SALT LAKE CITY	035	30834	31779	33009	0.3	16	12666	13288	13849	0.5	2.38	7936	7642	-0.4
84108	SALT LAKE CITY	035	20911	21155	21776	0.1	10	7857	8147	8440	0.4	2.53	5657	5501	-0.3
84109	SALT LAKE CITY	035	23883	24112	24880	0.1	10	8603	8936	9281	0.4	2.68	6089	5918	-0.3
84111	SALT LAKE CITY	035	10864	11155	11465	0.3	16	5285	5487	5684	0.4	1.93	1904	1714	-1.1
84112	SALT LAKE CITY	035	1372	1363	1363	-0.1	5	42	43	43	0.3	2.56	33	32	-0.3
84113	SALT LAKE CITY	035	527	523	522	-0.1	5	226	223	224	-0.1	1.70	169	156	-0.9
84115	SALT LAKE CITY	035	24275	25579	26708	0.6	26	9766	10359	10845	0.6	2.41	5354	5106	-0.5
84116	SALT LAKE CITY	035	31760	34590	36256	0.9	34	9706	10431	10921	0.8	3.29	7033	7062	0.0
84117	SALT LAKE CITY	035	23905	24464	25342	0.3	16	9607	10128	10577	0.6	2.38	6164	5981	-0.3
84118	SALT LAKE CITY	035	64000	68381	72118	0.7	29	17798	19495	20666	1.0	3.51	15347	16335	0.7
84119	SALT LAKE CITY	035	48599	52293	54969	0.8	31	15795	17318	18316	1.0	2.88	11066	11336	0.3
	UTAH					2.3					2.3	3.11			2.1
	UNITED STATES					1.0					1.1	2.59			0.9

ZIP CODE #	POST OFFICE NAME	RACE (%) White 2000	White 2009	Black 2000	Black 2009	Asian/Pacific 2000	Asian/Pacific 2009	% Hispanic Origin 2000	% Hispanic Origin 2009	2009 AGE DISTRIBUTION (%) 0-4	5-9	10-14	15-19	20-24	25-44	45-64	65-84	85+	18+	MEDIAN AGE 2009	% 2009 Males	% 2009 Females
84001	ALTAMONT	97.2	96.9	0.0	0.0	0.0	0.0	1.4	1.2	8.0	8.6	8.0	8.6	5.6	22.2	24.7	12.3	1.9	69.1	35.5	51.9	48.1
84003	AMERICAN FORK	95.9	95.0	0.2	0.2	0.8	1.0	3.8	4.7	11.2	10.6	10.3	9.6	6.7	26.6	18.4	5.6	1.0	61.6	26.2	50.3	49.7
84004	ALPINE	97.5	96.9	0.2	0.2	0.5	0.6	1.8	2.3	8.5	10.2	12.7	13.1	7.2	20.0	21.9	5.7	0.7	59.4	23.8	50.5	49.5
84005	EAGLE MOUNTAIN	96.7	95.8	0.2	0.4	0.4	0.6	2.9	4.0	13.2	11.2	9.2	6.7	4.4	34.1	17.2	3.6	0.3	62.1	28.7	49.6	50.4
84006	BINGHAM CANYON	93.3	91.7	0.0	0.0	0.7	0.8	8.5	10.7	8.7	8.8	8.7	7.3	4.8	28.3	22.5	8.1	2.7	69.2	35.2	49.2	50.8
84007	BLUEBELL	95.4	95.0	0.0	0.1	0.2	0.3	1.5	1.8	9.0	9.0	8.4	7.8	6.0	22.5	24.4	11.6	1.1	68.6	33.2	51.1	48.9
84010	BOUNTIFUL	94.9	93.8	0.3	0.4	1.5	1.9	3.5	4.3	8.8	8.1	7.6	7.0	6.3	27.1	21.2	11.8	2.0	71.0	32.7	48.7	51.3
84013	CEDAR VALLEY	93.7	91.8	0.2	0.2	0.2	0.4	7.4	9.2	13.2	11.5	10.3	7.9	6.0	28.7	16.6	5.1	0.7	59.9	25.8	50.6	49.4
84014	CENTERVILLE	97.1	96.5	0.2	0.3	1.0	1.3	1.9	2.3	8.3	8.8	9.6	10.2	7.0	24.8	23.8	6.6	0.9	66.6	29.9	49.9	50.1
84015	CLEARFIELD	87.8	86.2	1.9	2.2	2.4	2.8	8.8	10.0	11.7	9.8	8.5	8.2	7.6	32.2	16.5	4.7	0.6	65.0	27.1	50.3	49.7
84017	COALVILLE	95.0	93.5	0.1	0.1	0.4	0.4	5.1	6.6	9.0	8.9	8.9	7.8	5.5	27.4	23.8	7.5	1.1	68.2	32.2	51.1	48.9
84018	CROYDON	97.7	97.5	0.0	0.0	0.0	0.0	2.3	2.5	8.3	8.8	10.3	11.8	5.9	22.1	26.0	6.4	0.5	65.2	31.3	51.5	48.5
84020	DRAPER	91.2	89.7	1.5	1.8	1.7	2.1	5.9	7.1	10.7	9.6	8.6	7.2	6.7	34.9	18.2	3.5	0.5	66.5	29.7	54.2	45.8
84021	DUCHESNE	93.3	92.6	0.3	0.4	0.5	0.5	4.1	4.8	8.9	8.9	8.4	8.5	7.3	24.8	23.0	9.2	0.9	68.3	30.7	53.3	46.7
84022	DUGWAY	63.5	57.5	14.4	19.0	3.2	3.7	6.0	7.1	6.0	5.9	5.5	30.6	14.9	21.0	13.6	2.3	0.1	66.9	20.6	34.8	65.2
84023	DUTCH JOHN	94.8	94.9	0.5	0.5	0.0	0.0	5.2	4.6	6.5	6.9	6.5	5.1	4.6	25.5	28.7	15.3	0.9	76.9	40.0	54.6	45.4
84025	FARMINGTON	95.7	94.2	0.4	0.6	1.0	1.3	2.9	4.1	7.8	8.7	9.8	11.1	7.1	24.8	24.4	5.5	0.8	66.4	29.7	51.7	48.3
84026	FORT DUCHESNE	37.3	38.4	0.1	0.1	0.2	0.2	3.6	3.7	8.1	8.0	10.7	11.7	8.7	23.8	22.1	6.4	0.5	65.2	27.4	49.7	50.3
84028	GARDEN CITY	97.0	96.5	0.0	0.0	0.8	1.0	2.2	2.7	7.0	7.2	6.7	6.2	4.3	19.5	30.9	16.0	2.2	75.3	43.9	50.1	49.9
84029	GRANTSVILLE	94.1	92.6	0.7	1.0	0.4	0.4	4.9	6.2	9.8	9.3	9.1	8.6	6.7	28.1	20.5	6.9	1.0	66.5	29.1	49.7	50.3
84031	HANNA	100.0	96.9	0.0	0.0	0.0	0.0	3.7	3.1	6.2	6.2	6.2	6.2	6.2	21.5	27.7	20.0	0.0	76.9	43.1	50.8	49.2
84032	HEBER CITY	95.2	94.1	0.2	0.2	0.4	0.4	5.5	6.7	10.3	9.3	8.5	8.2	7.0	29.7	20.3	5.8	1.0	66.8	29.0	51.1	48.9
84033	HENEFER	96.0	94.6	0.1	0.1	0.4	0.6	4.2	5.5	9.1	9.1	9.1	7.5	4.8	27.7	23.6	8.1	0.9	67.8	32.9	52.1	47.9
84035	JENSEN	97.3	97.0	0.2	0.1	0.0	0.3	1.9	2.0	7.9	7.6	7.7	8.2	7.0	26.8	26.6	7.5	0.7	72.0	32.1	51.7	48.3
84036	KAMAS	97.3	96.6	0.2	0.3	0.2	0.3	3.5	4.5	7.8	8.3	9.2	9.2	5.6	27.1	24.8	7.2	0.9	68.5	33.8	50.8	49.2
84037	KAYSVILLE	96.9	96.3	0.3	0.3	0.8	0.9	2.7	3.2	10.4	10.4	10.5	10.2	6.3	25.3	20.2	5.9	0.8	62.0	27.1	50.0	50.0
84038	LAKETOWN	96.9	96.5	0.0	0.0	0.8	0.9	2.1	2.6	6.8	7.0	6.8	6.2	4.6	19.8	31.2	15.4	2.2	75.6	43.5	50.8	49.2
84039	LAPOINT	80.9	80.6	0.0	0.0	0.0	0.2	3.3	4.0	11.1	10.3	9.3	7.9	6.9	25.1	21.1	7.5	0.8	64.6	27.4	49.6	50.4
84040	LAYTON	93.2	91.6	1.2	1.7	1.8	2.2	4.0	4.8	8.3	8.8	9.9	10.4	6.3	26.0	24.4	5.4	0.6	66.3	30.4	50.1	49.9
84041	LAYTON	87.7	85.2	1.8	2.4	2.7	3.2	9.2	10.8	12.2	9.8	8.2	7.3	7.9	32.3	16.2	5.4	0.6	65.4	27.3	49.9	50.1
84042	LINDON	95.7	94.3	0.2	0.2	0.9	1.1	3.3	4.6	11.7	10.7	10.6	11.1	8.1	25.0	17.5	4.7	0.6	59.9	23.6	50.5	49.5
84043	LEHI	95.6	94.0	0.2	0.3	0.9	1.4	3.0	4.5	13.9	11.5	9.4	7.5	6.4	31.3	15.3	4.2	0.6	60.5	25.8	49.7	50.3
84044	MAGNA	86.3	82.7	0.6	0.8	2.0	2.3	15.0	18.6	10.7	10.1	9.1	9.0	7.7	30.5	17.4	4.8	0.7	64.5	26.9	50.4	49.6
84045	SARATOGA SPRINGS	94.5	92.9	0.6	1.3	2.0	1.3	3.7	6.2	10.1	9.5	8.7	6.8	3.6	31.5	23.6	5.6	0.5	67.4	33.5	49.6	50.4
84046	MANILA	94.5	94.4	0.7	0.7	0.1	0.1	5.1	5.3	6.4	6.6	6.3	4.9	4.8	25.3	30.5	14.5	0.8	77.7	40.9	55.5	44.5
84047	MIDVALE	82.9	79.2	1.1	1.4	2.6	3.1	19.9	23.4	9.4	8.3	6.9	5.8	7.7	35.3	17.7	7.8	1.2	72.1	30.3	50.7	49.3
84049	MIDWAY	97.2	96.7	0.1	0.1	0.6	0.7	3.1	3.6	8.4	7.4	8.9	8.9	6.8	23.3	25.9	9.2	1.1	69.4	33.8	51.4	48.6
84050	MORGAN	98.1	97.9	0.0	0.0	0.2	0.2	1.4	1.7	8.3	8.6	10.3	11.1	5.9	22.5	23.9	8.3	1.1	65.6	30.5	50.9	49.1
84051	MOUNTAIN HOME	97.8	97.4	0.0	0.0	0.2	0.2	2.9	3.4	6.5	6.9	7.3	6.7	5.6	19.6	27.7	18.6	1.1	75.4	42.5	50.7	49.3
84052	MYTON	82.0	80.3	0.1	0.1	0.4	0.5	8.5	10.5	7.7	10.0	9.8	10.4	7.3	21.4	24.2	8.3	0.9	65.3	29.2	50.8	49.2
84053	NEOLA	85.4	85.0	0.0	0.1	0.3	0.4	2.2	2.5	9.0	8.4	8.2	9.5	7.0	24.5	23.2	9.3	1.0	67.5	30.5	49.6	50.4
84054	NORTH SALT LAKE	93.1	91.4	0.3	0.5	1.8	2.2	5.9	7.4	9.6	8.7	7.8	6.9	6.3	30.1	21.8	7.9	1.0	69.8	31.3	49.5	50.5
84056	HILL AFB	77.8	73.4	8.5	11.1	3.6	4.3	9.3	11.0	15.4	11.0	9.2	7.0	16.5	38.3	2.4	0.2	0.0	61.0	22.2	55.2	44.8
84057	OREM	89.2	86.4	0.4	0.4	2.5	3.0	10.7	13.7	11.6	9.8	9.3	9.4	10.4	28.5	15.0	4.9	1.2	63.7	24.8	49.9	50.1
84058	OREM	90.7	88.2	0.4	0.4	2.4	3.0	8.2	10.6	10.0	7.9	7.3	10.9	16.5	25.3	15.7	5.3	1.1	69.3	24.2	49.8	50.2
84060	PARK CITY	80.6	75.4	0.4	0.5	1.8	2.1	19.5	24.4	5.4	4.8	4.8	5.4	7.2	37.9	27.1	6.9	0.4	81.8	34.9	53.7	46.3
84061	PEOA	96.1	94.7	0.2	0.2	0.4	0.6	4.8	6.2	7.9	8.9	10.3	10.6	5.0	26.6	23.7	6.0	1.1	65.6	33.1	51.2	48.8
84062	PLEASANT GROVE	95.3	94.3	0.3	0.3	0.9	1.0	4.3	5.3	12.6	10.6	9.4	8.9	7.0	28.4	17.3	5.2	0.7	61.7	26.0	50.1	49.9
84063	RANDLETT	52.6	54.3	0.0	0.0	0.0	0.0	7.9	7.4	8.5	6.4	8.5	9.6	8.5	23.4	26.6	6.4	2.1	71.3	32.5	52.1	47.9
84064	RANDOLPH	99.2	99.1	0.0	0.0	0.1	0.1	2.0	2.1	7.8	8.9	12.0	12.1	4.0	22.5	21.3	10.1	1.4	62.6	31.2	52.1	47.9
84065	RIVERTON	96.6	95.6	0.2	0.3	0.9	1.1	3.1	4.0	11.5	10.6	10.4	9.7	6.2	29.3	18.2	3.7	0.4	61.0	26.0	50.1	49.9
84066	ROOSEVELT	88.4	87.8	0.2	0.2	0.3	0.4	3.1	3.7	10.7	9.0	8.1	9.0	9.6	25.1	20.3	7.2	0.9	66.6	26.9	49.9	50.1
84067	ROY	90.8	88.0	1.1	1.5	1.9	2.3	7.6	10.2	10.8	9.5	8.3	7.0	5.8	33.0	18.0	6.7	0.9	67.0	29.8	49.4	50.6
84069	RUSH VALLEY	90.5	88.1	0.0	0.1	0.5	0.5	7.2	9.3	7.4	7.4	7.8	7.4	4.9	24.4	27.9	11.4	1.4	72.7	37.2	51.2	48.8
84070	SANDY	90.9	88.4	0.7	1.0	2.5	3.3	7.4	9.5	9.5	8.7	7.7	7.6	7.1	31.1	19.3	7.0	2.0	69.5	30.5	49.8	50.2
84071	STOCKTON	95.0	93.5	0.0	0.0	0.3	0.4	5.8	7.5	8.1	8.1	7.7	6.4	5.7	27.1	26.5	9.3	1.2	72.2	34.4	50.6	49.4
84072	TABIONA	97.5	97.4	0.0	0.0	0.2	0.2	2.9	3.3	6.5	6.8	7.2	6.7	5.6	18.9	28.8	18.4	1.1	75.4	43.1	50.2	49.8
84073	TALMAGE	96.2	95.7	0.0	0.0	0.6	0.5	3.2	3.8	8.3	8.3	8.0	7.8	6.5	22.9	23.9	13.3	1.0	70.6	34.5	52.3	47.7
84074	TOOELE	92.2	90.4	0.5	0.8	0.7	0.9	9.0	10.7	12.1	9.9	8.6	7.0	6.7	30.6	18.2	6.1	0.8	65.1	28.0	49.9	50.1
84075	SYRACUSE	93.8	92.7	0.6	0.8	1.7	2.0	4.3	4.9	12.1	10.3	8.8	7.3	6.2	33.4	17.6	4.0	0.3	64.3	27.7	50.2	49.8
84076	TRIDELL	80.6	80.3	0.0	0.0	0.0	0.2	3.1	3.9	10.8	10.3	9.2	8.0	6.9	24.9	22.0	7.1	0.9	65.0	27.8	49.7	50.3
84078	VERNAL	94.3	94.0	0.1	0.1	0.3	0.3	3.7	4.3	9.0	8.2	7.9	8.2	7.8	26.0	22.8	8.8	1.3	70.0	30.3	49.9	50.1
84080	VERNON	94.4	91.9	0.0	0.3	0.3	0.5	5.9	8.1	6.8	7.0	7.6	7.3	4.7	24.3	28.7	12.0	1.6	73.9	38.6	50.9	49.1
84081	WEST JORDAN	89.0	86.8	0.6	0.7	2.8	3.3	10.1	11.7	13.8	12.1	10.1	7.7	5.1	34.2	14.8	2.0	0.2	59.0	25.8	49.8	50.2
84082	WALLSBURG	95.6	94.4	0.1	0.1	0.4	0.4	6.3	8.0	7.5	7.5	8.8	10.0	7.1	24.5	26.3	7.6	0.6	70.1	32.6	51.9	48.1
84083	WENDOVER	53.3	46.6	1.0	1.0	0.9	0.9	53.9	59.9	12.5	10.2	8.4	9.2	10.4	28.7	15.2	4.9	0.6	63.7	24.7	52.7	47.3
84084	WEST JORDAN	88.2	85.6	0.5	0.8	3.1	3.8	11.6	14.0	9.4	9.1	9.4	9.8	7.5	29.9	20.4	3.9	0.4	65.9	28.0	50.5	49.5
84085	WHITEROCKS	35.6	36.0	0.0	0.0	0.0	0.1	1.8	2.2	8.0	8.8	10.9	10.9	8.6	22.8	22.7	6.8	0.4	65.8	27.2	48.3	51.7
84086	WOODRUFF	99.2	99.0	0.0	0.0	0.0	0.0	0.8	1.0	8.2	9.5	13.4	9.7	3.5	20.6	21.6	10.0	3.5	60.9	29.6	52.7	47.3
84087	WOODS CROSS	96.3	95.5	0.2	0.3	1.0	1.2	2.7	3.4	10.4	9.7	9.4	9.7	7.4	29.4	19.1	4.5	0.5	64.5	27.4	49.3	50.7
84088	WEST JORDAN	89.0	86.2	0.8	1.0	2.9	3.7	9.0	11.4	12.2	10.4	9.4	8.5	7.1	31.9	17.0	3.2	0.4	62.8	26.4	49.5	50.5
84092	SANDY	95.4	94.3	0.4	0.6	1.9	2.5	2.5	3.1	6.5	8.3	10.0	10.9	6.0	23.3	29.7	4.8	0.5	68.5	33.7	51.2	48.8
84093	SANDY	95.1	93.8	0.4	0.5	2.3	3.0	2.7	3.3	6.4	6.9	8.3	9.9	6.4	24.1	30.3	7.2	0.6	72.6	35.2	50.9	49.1
84094	SANDY	92.9	91.1	0.5	0.7	2.4	3.1	5.3	6.6	9.2	9.0	9.0	8.3	5.9	31.1	21.1	5.8	0.6	67.4	30.6	49.9	50.1
84095	SOUTH JORDAN	95.3	94.2	0.3	0.3	1.6	1.7	3.4	4.5	8.9	9.3	10.3	10.5	6.1	28.0	21.7	4.7	0.6	64.6	28.9	50.1	49.9
84096	HERRIMAN	95.7	94.4	0.3	0.4	0.5	0.6	3.6	4.8	11.9	10.3	8.7	6.5	5.1	35.3	17.8	4.1	0.4	65.0	29.5	50.1	49.9
84097	OREM	93.7	92.1	0.2	0.2	1.8	2.3	5.5	7.1	8.1	8.2	9.7	12.7	11.6	20.1	20.4	8.1	1.2	66.4	24.9	49.7	50.3
84098	PARK CITY	95.1	93.9	0.2	0.2	1.0	1.3	4.3	5.3	6.8	7.1	7.9	7.8	5.6	27.7	32.3	4.5	0.2	73.3	36.5	50.6	49.4
84101	SALT LAKE CITY	68.9	62.6	5.4	6.6	3.5	4.1	29.9	35.5	6.3	5.5	4.3	4.1	9.0	41.9	21.6	6.3	1.2	82.0	33.0	58.3	41.7
84102	SALT LAKE CITY	81.1	76.9	1.9	2.4	5.9	7.4	12.1	14.8	5.0	3.5	2.8	5.3	18.7	39.3	16.2	6.6	2.6	86.7	29.2	52.1	47.9
84103	SALT LAKE CITY	90.3	88.1	0.9	1.2	2.9	3.7	7.8	9.5	5.6	4.6	4.1	4.6	9.8	35.5	22.9	10.5	2.4	83.4	34.5	49.2	50.8
84104	SALT LAKE CITY	56.1	50.0	2.8	3.3	11.9	12.5	40.6	46.2	11.1	9.9	8.6	8.0	8.3	30.3	16.7	6.2	0.9	65.8	27.3	52.4	47.6
84105	SALT LAKE CITY	91.0	88.9	0.9	1.1	2.6	3.3	6.1	7.7	6.6	5.5	5.0	5.4	8.5	37.6	23.5	6.4	1.6	80.2	33.8	49.1	50.9
84106	SALT LAKE CITY	90.0	87.5	1.3	1.7	2.6	3.2	7.1	9.0	8.2	7.3	6.6	5.6	6.6	31.4	20.8	9.9	3.7	74.6	34.4	48.4	51.6
84107	SALT LAKE CITY	89.3	86.6	1.1	1.5	2.9	3.7	9.2	11.4	8.2	7.1	6.3	5.9	7.8	32.0	20.2	10.5	2.0	75.1	32.7	49.2	50.8
84108	SALT LAKE CITY	92.4	90.7	0.6	0.7	4.2	5.4	2.8	3.4	7.5	6.5	6.3	6.9	7.2	28.9	23.4	10.7	2.7	76.3	34.7	49.3	50.7
84109	SALT LAKE CITY	95.0	93.7	0.4	0.5	2.2	2.9	2.5	3.1	6.6	6.2	6.4	6.7	6.9	26.4	24.4	13.0	3.3	76.7	37.4	48.9	51.1
84111	SALT LAKE CITY	74.9	70.3	3.1	3.8	3.7	4.4	23.5	27.4	6.9	5.6	4.3	5.0	9.2	37.5	20.2	8.9	2.3	80.7	32.8	51.8	48.2
84112	SALT LAKE CITY	80.9	76.7	1.1	1.4	12.8	16.1	3.3	4.0	11.3	3.6	2.3	26.1	25.5	22.3	6.3	2.3	0.4	81.0	21.3	51.6	48.4
84113	SALT LAKE CITY	79.4	75.0	1.1	1.5	13.8	17.2	3.4	4.4	12.0	3.4	1.9	27.5	25.6	23.3	4.2	1.5	0.4	80.9	21.0	51.2	48.8
84115	SALT LAKE CITY	75.6	70.7	2.5	3.2	4.1	4.9	23.3	27.9	9.6	7.7	6.2	5.9	9.2	32.8	19.3	7.4	2.0	73.3	30.7	50.5	49.5
84116	SALT LAKE CITY	65.1	59.7	3.3	3.9	7.9	8.6	39.2	43.8	10.5	8.9	7.6	7.6	9.4	30.2	17.8	7.0	0.9	68.4	28.0	52.0	48.0
84117	SALT LAKE CITY	93.5	91.8	0.8	1.1	2.5	3.2	3.7	4.6	6.4	6.1	6.0	5.5	6.0	28.5	23.9	14.3	3.4	78.2	38.1	47.4	52.6
84118	SALT LAKE CITY	83.3	79.2	0.7	0.9	4.5	5.3	16.4	20.1	10.1	9.3	9.0	9.3	7.5	30.3	19.3	4.8	0.4	65.9	28.0	50.5	49.5
84119	SALT LAKE CITY	75.4	70.3	1.6	2.0	6.7	7.7	21.1	25.6	9.6	8.4	7.2	7.1	8.2	33.1	18.5	7.2	0.7	70.7	29.5	52.2	47.8
	UTAH	89.2	87.6	0.8	0.9	2.3	2.6	9.0	10.5	9.7	8.7	8.1	8.6	8.6	28.5	19.6	7.1	1.2	68.6	28.8	50.1	49.9
	UNITED STATES	75.1	72.0	12.3	12.7	3.8	4.6	12.5	15.7	6.8	6.7	6.6	7.1	6.9	27.0	26.0	10.9	1.9	75.7	36.9	49.2	50.8

#	POST OFFICE NAME	2009 Per Capita Income	2009 HH Income Base	2009 Household Income Distribution (%): Less than $25,000	$25,000 to $49,999	$50,000 to $99,999	$100,000 to $149,999	$150,000 or More	Median Household Income: 2009	2014	2009 National Centile	2009 State Centile	2009 Home Value Base	2009 Home Value Distribution (%): Less than $50,000	$50,000 to $89,999	$90,000 to $174,999	$175,000 to $399,999	$400,000 or More	2009 Median Home Value
84001	ALTAMONT	13951	52	23.1	38.5	36.5	1.9	0.0	40000	45000	33	24	46	8.7	13.0	43.5	30.4	4.3	141667
84003	AMERICAN FORK	23753	10733	7.8	17.2	44.2	20.0	10.9	76348	78173	90	90	8680	1.5	0.7	10.0	69.2	18.6	265420
84004	ALPINE	30133	2501	5.2	10.2	38.1	22.3	24.2	94076	96980	96	98	2167	0.0	1.0	1.6	40.5	56.9	444395
84005	EAGLE MOUNTAIN	20491	4200	3.9	16.7	57.4	14.9	7.0	68355	69974	86	82	3874	0.1	0.0	7.8	74.2	17.8	245581
84006	BINGHAM CANYON	20927	291	32.3	20.6	34.4	7.6	5.2	46058	48657	51	42	225	0.0	0.0	52.9	43.1	4.0	172711
84007	BLUEBELL	14881	523	25.4	37.7	33.3	2.5	1.1	40057	41197	33	24	472	10.0	13.6	50.6	23.9	1.9	132673
84010	BOUNTIFUL	30199	16128	10.2	21.2	40.0	16.7	11.8	68746	72186	86	83	11839	0.9	0.5	13.3	65.9	19.4	260936
84013	CEDAR VALLEY	18397	826	12.7	24.3	50.0	9.7	3.3	58172	61597	75	65	708	6.6	1.8	32.2	52.1	7.2	193132
84014	CENTERVILLE	27291	4965	6.0	17.6	40.1	26.1	10.2	79261	82647	92	93	4358	2.5	0.9	10.3	71.0	15.2	270822
84015	CLEARFIELD	22535	18895	10.1	21.2	49.4	15.1	4.2	64019	67326	82	77	14290	2.1	2.3	41.1	52.3	2.2	182077
84017	COALVILLE	24477	1583	11.2	26.7	47.4	10.0	4.7	59368	59511	77	67	1276	10.8	2.7	36.4	37.9	12.1	175291
84018	CROYDON	26298	57	8.8	17.5	43.9	17.5	12.3	78081	79122	91	92	51	0.0	0.0	7.8	72.5	19.6	313889
84020	DRAPER	36287	11008	3.6	9.0	35.8	26.3	25.3	102302	103729	97	100	9207	1.0	0.6	1.3	56.5	40.6	367998
84021	DUCHESNE	15661	994	26.7	38.9	29.7	3.4	1.3	39798	40436	32	21	796	16.6	14.4	49.4	16.6	3.0	124000
84022	DUGWAY	20387	495	9.7	24.8	50.3	14.5	0.6	63600	67427	82	76	30	23.3	33.3	10.0	3.3	30.0	78333
84023	DUTCH JOHN	22179	92	28.3	32.6	31.5	6.5	1.1	38185	40000	27	16	66	19.7	22.7	33.3	16.7	7.6	98333
84025	FARMINGTON	32393	4638	3.7	12.8	35.3	27.0	21.2	96440	97680	96	99	4045	0.4	0.0	7.5	68.9	23.0	291754
84026	FORT DUCHESNE	10282	637	44.0	32.2	21.7	1.9	0.3	28113	30445	6	3	472	26.3	18.2	38.3	15.5	1.7	101736
84028	GARDEN CITY	27336	235	19.1	29.8	35.7	8.9	6.4	51571	51513	65	52	200	2.0	8.5	44.0	32.5	13.0	166667
84029	GRANTSVILLE	20770	3071	15.1	22.6	47.6	10.8	3.8	59344	62915	77	67	2405	5.9	2.2	25.4	61.2	5.2	200051
84031	HANNA	11507	21	42.9	33.3	23.8	0.0	0.0	28571	31099	6	4	19	5.3	15.8	42.1	26.3	10.5	140625
84032	HEBER CITY	24375	5205	10.7	22.0	51.6	9.4	6.3	65648	65584	84	79	4193	3.2	1.4	8.1	56.5	30.8	297558
84033	HENEFER	24108	291	10.0	20.6	52.9	11.7	4.8	61549	63030	79	71	246	3.7	3.3	32.9	42.3	17.9	206818
84035	JENSEN	19676	245	15.1	42.0	34.3	6.1	2.4	43854	46637	45	33	207	15.0	13.5	44.9	23.7	2.9	127734
84036	KAMAS	23354	2229	11.5	25.7	45.1	13.1	4.6	63129	63093	81	74	1837	4.4	3.2	17.0	50.6	24.8	252901
84037	KAYSVILLE	26644	8727	7.7	14.1	37.7	27.5	12.9	85151	88679	94	96	7515	0.6	1.5	13.4	68.1	16.4	259679
84038	LAKETOWN	23875	156	18.6	29.5	36.5	9.0	6.4	53008	50325	68	56	133	2.3	7.5	43.6	33.1	13.5	168750
84039	LAPOINT	15635	165	23.0	33.9	39.4	3.6	0.0	46040	48058	51	41	136	14.0	20.6	50.0	14.0	1.5	111364
84040	LAYTON	29906	7344	6.0	11.3	39.0	27.6	16.2	89481	90976	95	97	6517	2.5	1.9	7.9	70.1	17.5	268868
84041	LAYTON	23372	14977	13.0	23.6	45.8	13.5	4.0	60776	64281	79	70	10012	7.8	5.3	38.4	46.3	2.2	172846
84042	LINDON	22587	2378	4.4	18.7	44.3	20.3	12.3	78591	78085	91	93	1999	2.8	0.9	4.7	59.5	32.2	342101
84043	LEHI	22367	12013	7.8	15.6	50.2	19.6	6.9	71985	73045	88	87	9646	1.6	0.3	10.9	76.2	11.0	233655
84044	MAGNA	18769	7655	12.1	27.9	48.1	9.6	2.3	58233	59439	73	60	6336	1.3	3.6	53.5	41.0	0.6	166582
84045	SARATOGA SPRINGS	25524	3447	6.6	14.5	45.0	23.8	10.1	82073	83617	93	95	2839	0.0	0.0	5.0	79.4	15.6	243194
84046	MANILA	19503	270	26.7	31.9	33.7	5.9	1.9	38964	39477	30	19	192	17.2	21.9	36.5	17.7	6.8	103704
84047	MIDVALE	24122	11573	16.0	30.1	41.9	8.7	3.4	52644	55406	67	54	5798	2.1	1.4	26.3	66.6	3.6	206621
84049	MIDWAY	27793	1500	9.1	26.7	46.4	11.0	6.8	62320	62990	80	73	1215	1.6	0.0	4.4	51.4	42.6	361087
84050	MORGAN	21864	2675	11.0	24.1	47.4	11.3	6.2	64416	68376	83	78	2360	1.8	1.4	17.6	61.9	17.3	256456
84051	MOUNTAIN HOME	15567	236	38.6	37.7	22.0	1.3	0.4	30294	31731	9	6	210	12.9	13.3	40.0	24.8	9.0	138514
84052	MYTON	13590	393	35.4	33.1	26.2	3.3	2.0	32805	34401	13	8	329	25.2	17.0	38.9	15.8	3.0	108681
84053	NEOLA	17439	271	19.9	33.9	40.2	3.7	2.2	46594	46622	53	43	236	5.5	11.9	53.4	23.7	5.5	139904
84054	NORTH SALT LAKE	28977	4700	10.3	28.0	36.0	15.1	10.6	61192	64231	79	71	3325	7.3	6.6	15.1	46.3	24.7	221291
84056	HILL AFB	15247	1226	10.8	46.2	36.9	4.4	1.6	46479	47166	53	43	7	0.0	0.0	0.0	100.0	0.0	235000
84057	OREM	19729	10904	14.0	26.5	43.9	10.8	4.8	56953	60307	74	62	6840	4.8	3.4	22.0	67.1	2.8	201630
84058	OREM	20547	9593	13.6	27.9	43.0	10.1	5.5	56105	60011	73	60	5338	4.6	1.7	16.3	65.2	12.3	227355
84060	PARK CITY	46598	3323	11.1	17.7	34.7	12.5	24.0	82297	87538	93	95	2027	0.5	0.0	3.3	28.0	68.2	604120
84061	PEOA	25262	203	9.4	27.1	40.9	15.8	6.9	66295	68709	84	80	168	2.4	2.4	19.0	52.4	23.8	257895
84062	PLEASANT GROVE	21803	10961	8.1	20.1	45.6	17.3	8.8	71691	73881	88	86	8396	1.6	0.4	11.5	77.4	9.1	264901
84063	RANDLETT	13240	35	48.6	28.6	20.0	2.9	0.0	26114	28613	4	2	25	40.0	20.0	24.0	12.0	4.0	67500
84064	RANDOLPH	15614	248	22.2	32.7	40.7	2.4	2.0	44575	48153	47	35	204	13.7	27.9	53.4	4.9	0.0	100625
84065	RIVERTON	24959	9073	4.4	9.0	49.6	25.5	11.5	85107	86413	94	96	8314	0.1	0.9	5.2	75.9	17.8	280405
84066	ROOSEVELT	15648	3114	28.6	31.8	33.8	3.9	1.9	41265	42527	37	26	2439	10.5	11.6	52.8	21.0	4.1	128366
84067	ROY	24127	12743	8.8	19.8	55.4	11.6	4.4	66541	67955	85	80	10693	3.1	2.3	45.7	48.1	0.8	173787
84069	RUSH VALLEY	19158	252	15.5	28.6	48.0	6.7	1.2	52818	54842	68	55	199	7.5	10.1	25.1	41.2	16.1	195139
84070	SANDY	23581	8183	11.4	26.5	45.8	11.3	4.9	60364	63499	78	69	5518	7.1	6.0	18.5	64.9	3.5	203414
84071	STOCKTON	20631	387	20.9	23.5	45.2	8.0	2.3	52689	54127	67	55	337	4.5	11.9	37.7	37.7	8.3	163362
84072	TABIONA	12273	197	39.1	37.1	21.8	1.5	0.5	30089	31831	8	6	175	13.1	13.1	38.9	25.7	9.1	139583
84073	TALMAGE	15828	142	30.3	38.0	28.2	2.1	1.4	34307	37043	16	10	121	13.2	13.2	43.0	24.0	6.6	135326
84074	TOOELE	22832	13202	11.2	20.1	51.0	13.5	4.1	63638	67458	82	76	10945	3.2	2.1	23.9	65.3	5.4	207428
84075	SYRACUSE	22654	5669	5.5	14.9	51.8	22.1	5.7	74450	76575	89	88	5144	0.0	0.8	25.6	66.7	7.0	221726
84076	TRIDELL	13096	123	23.6	34.1	39.0	3.3	0.0	45919	48188	51	40	101	13.9	19.8	51.5	13.9	1.0	112500
84078	VERNAL	18495	8177	23.6	30.3	37.7	5.9	2.5	45986	48875	51	41	6231	7.5	11.5	50.5	27.7	2.8	137604
84080	VERNON	19164	128	14.1	28.1	50.8	6.3	0.8	53895	56806	69	57	108	5.6	7.4	26.9	46.3	13.9	200000
84081	WEST JORDAN	23365	9325	2.6	13.2	57.4	19.2	7.7	79411	80606	92	94	8617	0.8	0.6	9.9	81.1	7.6	233234
84082	WALLSBURG	23220	233	12.0	15.9	56.2	9.9	6.0	71008	73897	87	85	197	4.1	3.0	6.6	44.7	41.6	363333
84083	WENDOVER	15010	863	24.4	33.0	34.4	6.4	1.7	43498	45345	44	33	386	40.2	14.8	25.9	9.6	9.6	77619
84084	WEST JORDAN	22612	11221	6.5	19.4	52.9	15.7	5.5	71300	74469	87	86	9140	0.5	1.7	21.2	74.7	2.0	209245
84085	WHITEROCKS	9282	344	50.9	29.4	18.0	1.7	0.0	24456	24087	3	1	270	35.9	17.0	33.7	13.0	0.4	83846
84086	WOODRUFF	15599	129	17.1	39.5	38.0	5.4	0.0	44076	47850	46	34	106	13.2	17.9	65.1	1.9	1.9	110000
84087	WOODS CROSS	23107	3980	7.8	16.8	51.0	19.7	4.7	70920	74766	87	85	3507	1.4	2.2	18.1	74.2	4.2	220782
84088	WEST JORDAN	23593	10682	6.1	18.2	51.1	18.6	6.1	70623	74510	87	84	8080	5.0	1.7	14.8	74.0	4.5	229381
84092	SANDY	38943	8880	3.6	7.4	31.8	26.4	30.9	111968	112942	98	100	8238	0.2	0.0	1.5	58.9	39.4	362564
84093	SANDY	34202	7508	4.2	12.1	38.9	24.1	20.7	90653	93083	95	97	6840	0.8	0.4	4.0	65.9	28.9	311385
84094	SANDY	26044	9123	7.2	14.9	49.0	21.4	7.6	76817	78898	90	90	7478	0.5	0.3	12.8	82.4	4.0	230949
84095	SOUTH JORDAN	28953	12646	4.1	8.7	41.1	29.6	16.5	94175	94064	96	98	11040	0.2	0.4	6.8	72.2	20.4	311637
84096	HERRIMAN	25610	8524	4.0	8.9	57.5	21.5	8.2	79860	80340	92	94	7932	0.3	0.1	8.5	72.7	18.5	263371
84097	OREM	23037	5931	9.4	19.2	43.5	17.6	10.2	71300	72882	87	86	4572	0.8	0.2	8.6	75.7	14.7	257627
84098	PARK CITY	47873	5735	6.5	9.2	34.9	21.5	28.0	99085	111345	97	99	4583	0.5	0.0	2.5	32.0	65.0	496299
84101	SALT LAKE CITY	19807	1936	37.1	28.7	27.7	4.3	2.2	34096	35616	16	9	346	0.0	0.0	75.4	17.6	6.9	131122
84102	SALT LAKE CITY	26267	8492	30.3	31.0	29.7	5.4	3.6	39946	40842	32	22	2070	1.0	1.3	29.1	56.5	12.1	217102
84103	SALT LAKE CITY	37871	11069	23.0	25.8	30.5	9.1	11.6	51251	54499	64	51	4720	0.0	0.8	10.8	47.4	41.0	348854
84104	SALT LAKE CITY	13941	6940	26.5	34.3	32.4	5.0	1.8	40577	42060	35	25	4097	3.7	9.6	59.4	26.9	0.4	141393
84105	SALT LAKE CITY	33316	9797	15.8	22.4	41.4	13.9	6.5	61678	65459	80	71	5755	0.7	0.7	13.4	72.2	13.0	249604
84106	SALT LAKE CITY	27574	13750	16.7	28.0	41.7	8.9	4.7	54197	58116	70	58	8585	0.9	0.7	20.5	71.1	6.7	227878
84107	SALT LAKE CITY	26605	13288	18.4	29.2	40.0	7.6	4.8	51847	54464	66	53	6899	3.4	2.0	25.9	59.6	9.1	212608
84108	SALT LAKE CITY	37531	8147	11.3	20.0	35.4	16.5	16.7	72163	75841	88	88	5787	0.0	0.0	2.5	56.7	40.7	362992
84109	SALT LAKE CITY	32046	8936	12.3	22.3	39.3	15.5	10.6	67600	71727	85	81	6828	0.0	0.0	7.3	70.1	22.6	293608
84111	SALT LAKE CITY	21432	5487	42.8	28.1	23.7	3.3	2.2	29754	30013	8	5	1329	3.3	1.1	50.4	42.7	2.6	167881
84112	SALT LAKE CITY	11216	43	25.6	14.0	14.0	16.3	30.2	80389	70794	92	95	27	0.0	3.7	0.0	3.7	92.6	791667
84113	SALT LAKE CITY	26570	223	43.9	36.3	14.3	0.9	4.5	26696	26163	4	3	18	0.0	0.0	0.0	0.0	100.0	958333
84115	SALT LAKE CITY	19674	10359	30.4	32.1	30.9	4.2	2.4	38527	39343	28	18	3990	2.9	2.0	56.5	37.9	0.8	162144
84116	SALT LAKE CITY	16412	10431	24.2	29.9	36.7	7.0	2.3	45805	48179	51	40	6248	3.3	3.8	45.8	45.8	1.3	171403
84117	SALT LAKE CITY	34432	10128	12.5	24.8	39.3	13.4	9.9	62888	67698	81	73	6563	1.3	3.0	15.8	52.3	27.6	293106
84118	SALT LAKE CITY	20755	19495	7.6	23.1	52.8	12.5	4.0	63959	67046	82	76	16365	0.8	1.2	36.9	59.0	2.1	186812
84119	SALT LAKE CITY	19676	17318	19.2	29.8	41.0	7.5	2.4	50648	52310	63	50	9912	7.6	7.8	37.9	46.0	0.7	170366
	UTAH	23420		14.7	23.9	42.1	12.6	6.7	60286	62873				3.1	3.0	25.7	56.7	11.5	213546
	UNITED STATES	27277		20.9	24.4	35.3	11.7	7.6	54719	56938				9.3	13.1	31.6	32.6	13.5	162279

ZIP CODE #	POST OFFICE NAME	FINANCIAL SERVICES: Auto Loan	Home Loan	Invest-ments	Retire-ment Plans	THE HOME: Home Improvements: Home Repair	Lawn & Garden	Furnishings: Comput-ers & Hard-ware-Personal	Major Appli-ances	TV, Radio, Sound Equip-ment	Furni-ture	ENTERTAINMENT: Dine out/ Carry out	Sports Equip-ment	Fees & Tickets	Toys & Games	Travel	Cable TV	PERSONAL: Apparel & Services	Auto Repairs	Health Insur-ance	Pets & Supplies
84001	ALTAMONT	78	53	85	53	56	82	59	74	62	48	61	61	43	61	59	67	40	69	78	91
84003	AMERICAN FORK	128	147	130	146	142	129	131	130	124	138	127	103	141	130	135	120	90	126	119	150
84004	ALPINE	177	216	188	221	210	180	180	182	167	199	170	150	204	179	191	154	124	168	152	205
84005	EAGLE MOUNTAIN	125	139	114	136	131	113	121	121	113	133	115	97	127	122	121	106	82	113	103	136
84006	BINGHAM CANYON	71	88	79	88	85	87	75	78	76	76	77	59	86	77	83	78	54	77	83	91
84007	BLUEBELL	79	56	84	55	58	82	59	75	64	52	63	58	46	63	59	70	41	69	78	90
84010	BOUNTIFUL	122	134	127	135	133	125	127	125	123	131	125	97	134	125	131	121	89	125	121	145
84013	CEDAR VALLEY	100	104	88	102	100	95	94	96	92	99	93	74	95	97	92	90	64	92	89	111
84014	CENTERVILLE	127	146	132	148	142	133	132	131	126	136	128	103	142	130	138	123	91	128	123	153
84015	CLEARFIELD	109	108	89	107	101	97	105	101	102	109	104	80	103	108	100	99	72	101	96	119
84017	COALVILLE	107	109	95	110	106	109	101	105	101	103	102	80	102	105	101	102	70	102	104	124
84018	CROYDON	127	159	140	159	154	137	133	136	125	140	128	108	150	131	144	120	92	129	121	156
84020	DRAPER	181	216	188	219	209	179	182	184	169	201	172	150	202	181	190	157	125	170	154	207
84021	DUCHESNE	79	60	77	59	62	79	61	73	66	58	65	55	51	66	59	71	43	68	76	88
84022	DUGWAY	103	106	87	102	99	93	97	97	95	104	96	73	96	100	94	92	66	94	90	113
84023	DUTCH JOHN	82	65	105	64	72	86	65	83	68	61	68	61	57	65	71	73	45	77	82	96
84025	FARMINGTON	159	196	179	197	192	172	166	169	157	176	160	133	187	163	179	151	116	161	152	194
84026	FORT DUCHESNE	62	42	61	40	43	62	44	56	50	42	49	43	34	51	42	56	32	52	59	68
84028	GARDEN CITY	116	93	150	91	102	123	93	118	97	87	96	86	80	92	101	104	64	109	116	137
84029	GRANTSVILLE	98	102	87	98	97	92	94	94	92	98	93	72	94	97	92	91	65	92	89	110
84031	HANNA	64	46	65	44	47	65	47	60	52	44	51	45	37	52	46	57	34	55	62	71
84032	HEBER CITY	112	121	102	120	115	109	112	111	107	115	109	88	115	112	112	105	76	108	104	129
84033	HENEFER	102	115	99	119	112	113	103	107	101	103	102	84	110	104	109	102	71	103	106	126
84035	JENSEN	92	84	75	81	82	86	79	84	82	83	82	61	75	86	76	85	56	81	84	100
84036	KAMAS	107	113	98	115	110	113	103	108	103	104	103	82	106	106	105	104	72	104	107	127
84037	KAYSVILLE	137	159	145	159	156	140	141	141	134	149	136	111	153	139	148	129	97	136	128	162
84038	LAKETOWN	116	93	150	91	102	122	93	118	97	87	96	86	80	92	100	103	64	109	116	137
84039	LAPOINT	75	69	61	67	67	71	65	69	68	68	68	50	62	70	62	69	46	67	69	82
84040	LAYTON	146	173	153	172	167	151	148	151	140	158	143	118	162	147	157	135	102	144	136	173
84041	LAYTON	104	103	87	101	97	92	101	97	98	105	99	77	99	103	96	95	69	97	92	114
84042	LINDON	139	158	132	157	150	135	137	138	129	147	131	111	146	138	140	123	93	130	122	158
84043	LEHI	124	129	108	125	121	110	120	117	114	127	116	93	120	122	116	109	81	114	105	135
84044	MAGNA	95	97	80	93	91	87	91	90	89	95	90	68	90	93	88	87	62	89	86	105
84045	SARATOGA SPRINGS	133	157	136	162	153	137	134	137	126	145	128	112	149	134	141	120	93	127	120	156
84046	MANILA	82	66	106	65	72	87	66	84	69	62	68	61	57	65	71	73	45	77	82	97
84047	MIDVALE	90	80	72	82	76	75	91	81	90	90	91	66	86	92	84	88	64	88	81	97
84049	MIDWAY	111	125	107	128	121	122	111	116	110	112	110	91	119	112	118	110	77	111	115	136
84050	MORGAN	104	121	105	124	118	114	106	110	103	108	104	86	115	106	113	102	73	105	105	128
84051	MOUNTAIN HOME	63	45	65	44	47	64	46	59	52	43	51	44	37	51	46	57	33	54	62	70
84052	MYTON	77	53	83	53	56	80	58	73	61	49	61	59	43	60	58	67	40	68	77	89
84053	NEOLA	84	77	68	74	75	79	73	77	75	76	75	56	69	78	69	77	51	75	77	91
84054	NORTH SALT LAKE	120	125	112	124	121	115	119	117	116	124	117	91	121	120	118	114	82	116	112	137
84056	HILL AFB	92	48	36	55	43	41	87	60	81	81	86	60	66	98	63	75	60	76	54	73
84057	OREM	100	100	86	100	95	88	100	94	96	103	98	75	99	101	96	93	69	95	88	110
84058	OREM	103	94	83	96	89	85	102	91	99	104	101	75	98	103	94	96	71	97	88	109
84060	PARK CITY	177	185	186	194	186	163	189	174	176	195	180	145	195	180	190	166	130	178	157	203
84061	PEOA	118	127	110	130	124	126	115	120	115	116	115	93	120	118	119	115	80	116	119	142
84062	PLEASANT GROVE	122	136	116	134	130	118	121	121	116	129	117	96	127	122	123	111	83	116	109	139
84063	RANDLETT	66	43	64	41	43	65	46	58	53	44	52	45	35	54	43	59	34	55	61	71
84064	RANDOLPH	88	61	97	61	64	93	68	84	70	55	70	69	50	69	67	77	45	78	89	103
84065	RIVERTON	144	164	136	161	155	136	142	142	133	153	136	114	150	143	144	125	96	134	123	161
84066	ROOSEVELT	74	64	59	64	62	68	70	68	71	66	71	53	63	72	63	73	48	70	71	82
84067	ROY	106	115	98	111	109	101	105	105	101	110	103	81	107	106	104	99	72	102	98	120
84069	RUSH VALLEY	87	80	77	82	80	91	79	87	81	73	80	66	73	83	78	85	54	81	89	101
84070	SANDY	101	102	88	101	97	92	101	96	98	104	99	76	100	102	97	95	69	97	92	113
84071	STOCKTON	94	87	79	86	86	92	83	89	86	83	85	66	78	89	80	89	58	85	90	105
84072	TABIONA	63	45	65	44	47	64	47	59	52	43	51	45	37	51	46	57	34	54	62	71
84073	TALMAGE	74	57	72	55	58	74	57	69	62	54	61	51	48	62	56	67	41	64	71	82
84074	TOOELE	106	112	93	108	105	98	103	102	100	108	101	80	104	106	101	97	71	99	95	118
84075	SYRACUSE	127	136	110	130	127	113	121	120	115	131	117	94	123	123	118	109	82	115	106	138
84076	TRIDELL	75	69	61	66	67	70	65	69	67	67	67	50	61	70	62	69	46	66	69	82
84078	VERNAL	82	76	68	76	73	79	77	77	79	76	78	59	73	80	73	80	54	77	80	92
84080	VERNON	89	81	80	84	83	95	80	90	82	72	81	68	74	84	80	87	55	83	93	105
84081	WEST JORDAN	138	151	123	146	141	124	133	132	125	144	128	105	137	135	131	118	90	125	115	150
84082	WALLSBURG	111	125	108	129	121	123	112	116	110	112	110	91	119	113	118	110	77	112	115	136
84083	WENDOVER	76	58	50	57	55	51	76	65	74	76	78	53	66	77	66	71	56	75	60	76
84084	WEST JORDAN	114	125	106	122	118	108	113	112	107	119	109	88	116	113	113	103	77	108	101	129
84085	WHITEROCKS	54	38	52	37	38	53	40	49	45	38	44	37	32	45	38	49	29	46	51	59
84086	WOODRUFF	87	60	95	60	63	92	66	82	69	54	68	68	49	68	66	75	44	77	87	102
84087	WOODS CROSS	118	129	107	125	122	111	115	115	110	122	112	90	118	117	114	106	78	110	104	132
84088	WEST JORDAN	123	129	106	125	121	108	119	116	113	127	115	92	120	120	115	107	81	112	103	133
84092	SANDY	183	236	227	243	237	207	195	201	182	210	185	160	228	189	216	174	137	188	176	228
84093	SANDY	154	195	184	199	194	172	163	167	153	173	156	132	188	158	179	147	114	158	149	191
84094	SANDY	123	139	118	136	132	120	122	122	116	130	119	96	129	123	125	112	84	117	111	141
84095	SOUTH JORDAN	156	179	153	178	171	151	155	156	146	168	149	125	167	156	160	139	106	147	137	177
84096	HERRIMAN	139	152	122	145	141	123	134	133	125	145	128	106	136	136	131	118	90	125	114	150
84097	OREM	118	139	125	140	135	127	122	124	118	128	120	97	134	121	130	115	85	120	117	143
84098	PARK CITY	181	214	217	221	221	184	196	193	179	212	181	157	215	183	209	166	133	185	164	218
84101	SALT LAKE CITY	60	47	46	52	44	46	66	52	66	60	67	45	60	65	57	66	48	61	56	66
84102	SALT LAKE CITY	77	55	53	60	52	55	85	63	80	75	81	56	70	81	67	78	57	75	66	80
84103	SALT LAKE CITY	104	98	103	104	99	95	114	100	111	112	113	83	113	109	110	108	80	109	102	121
84104	SALT LAKE CITY	72	67	58	62	65	56	72	68	68	76	71	52	67	70	67	65	50	71	60	76
84105	SALT LAKE CITY	101	103	102	106	102	98	108	100	105	107	106	80	109	104	106	103	75	104	100	119
84106	SALT LAKE CITY	87	91	87	91	90	88	94	88	93	92	93	69	96	92	94	93	66	92	92	104
84107	SALT LAKE CITY	89	83	77	85	81	79	93	83	91	92	93	67	90	92	88	90	65	90	86	100
84108	SALT LAKE CITY	126	143	151	144	148	134	140	134	133	141	134	104	149	132	146	130	97	135	129	154
84109	SALT LAKE CITY	111	130	133	129	133	126	122	121	119	122	119	91	133	118	130	119	86	121	123	139
84111	SALT LAKE CITY	59	43	42	48	41	45	63	50	64	59	64	43	55	63	53	64	45	60	56	64
84112	SALT LAKE CITY	154	165	196	177	180	160	192	161	169	179	169	133	194	167	178	159	127	166	146	185
84113	SALT LAKE CITY	67	30	29	36	27	34	94	47	75	64	76	51	56	73	51	68	54	66	47	63
84115	SALT LAKE CITY	70	55	49	57	52	55	72	60	72	67	72	50	63	73	62	71	50	69	64	75
84116	SALT LAKE CITY	81	74	65	71	71	68	79	75	77	81	79	58	74	79	74	75	55	78	72	87
84117	SALT LAKE CITY	109	118	122	120	121	116	117	114	115	118	116	87	123	114	121	116	82	116	118	133
84118	SALT LAKE CITY	107	114	95	111	107	102	104	104	101	109	103	80	107	106	103	99	72	101	98	121
84119	SALT LAKE CITY	85	77	67	76	74	71	84	77	82	85	84	61	79	85	78	81	59	82	75	91
	UTAH	107	107	98	107	104	101	106	103	103	108	104	81	105	106	103	102	73	103	99	121
	UNITED STATES	100	100	100	100	100	100	100	100	100	100	100	100	100	100	100	100	100	100	100	100

POPULATION CHANGE

84120-84729

ZIP CODE #	POST OFFICE NAME	COUNTY FIPS CODE	POPULATION 2000	POPULATION 2009	POPULATION 2014	2000-2009 ANNUAL RATE % Rate	2000-2009 ANNUAL RATE State Centile	HOUSEHOLDS 2000	HOUSEHOLDS 2009	HOUSEHOLDS 2014	HOUSEHOLDS % Annual Rate 2000-2009	HOUSEHOLDS 2009 Average HH Size	FAMILIES 2000	FAMILIES 2009	FAMILIES % Annual Rate 2000-2009
84120	SALT LAKE CITY	035	45131	47563	49879	0.6	26	12537	13506	14230	0.8	3.51	10812	11283	0.5
84121	SALT LAKE CITY	035	43044	44281	46042	0.3	16	14972	15895	16650	0.6	2.77	11381	11406	0.0
84123	SALT LAKE CITY	035	35601	37122	38757	0.5	22	12877	13704	14376	0.7	2.70	8836	8799	0.0
84124	SALT LAKE CITY	035	21254	21538	22246	0.1	10	7727	8088	8418	0.5	2.63	5670	5567	-0.2
84128	SALT LAKE CITY	035	20635	26042	28917	2.5	71	5480	7233	8118	3.0	3.60	4867	6212	2.7
84302	BRIGHAM CITY	003	21118	23715	25285	1.3	43	6648	7580	8124	1.4	3.09	5370	5975	1.2
84305	CLARKSTON	005	698	858	940	2.3	67	211	269	298	2.7	3.19	178	220	2.3
84306	COLLINSTON	003	415	578	632	3.6	85	120	166	183	3.6	3.48	101	137	3.4
84307	CORINNE	003	1153	1428	1583	2.3	67	350	442	493	2.6	3.23	298	369	2.3
84308	CORNISH	005	272	313	342	1.5	47	71	84	93	1.8	3.73	61	70	1.5
84309	DEWEYVILLE	003	376	439	475	1.7	50	134	159	174	1.9	2.76	113	131	1.6
84310	EDEN	057	3212	3868	4296	2.0	58	978	1209	1350	2.3	3.19	801	959	2.0
84311	FIELDING	003	680	804	886	1.8	52	211	254	282	2.0	3.17	181	213	1.8
84312	GARLAND	003	3712	4561	5026	2.3	67	1079	1351	1496	2.5	3.38	905	1107	2.2
84313	GROUSE CREEK	003	137	168	184	2.2	63	49	62	68	2.6	2.71	35	43	2.3
84314	HONEYVILLE	003	1752	2033	2233	1.6	48	524	619	684	1.8	3.28	451	523	1.6
84315	HOOPER	057	4300	4893	5312	1.4	45	1258	1483	1620	1.8	3.30	1116	1285	1.5
84317	HUNTSVILLE	057	2468	3273	3637	3.1	79	764	1044	1167	3.4	3.12	646	857	3.1
84318	HYDE PARK	005	3020	3745	4183	2.4	69	781	1017	1143	2.9	3.68	686	871	2.6
84319	HYRUM	005	6914	8283	9099	2.0	58	1842	2280	2523	2.3	3.63	1641	1986	2.1
84320	LEWISTON	005	2332	2749	3036	1.8	52	652	793	882	2.1	3.47	548	645	1.8
84321	LOGAN	005	32175	38300	41839	1.9	55	10909	13043	14268	2.0	2.89	7567	8752	1.6
84322	LOGAN	005	1026	1041	1073	0.2	12	316	318	329	0.1	3.17	119	106	-1.2
84324	MANTUA	003	805	863	902	0.8	31	221	241	254	0.9	3.58	193	207	0.8
84325	MENDON	005	1513	1888	2094	2.4	69	431	564	630	3.0	3.35	384	492	2.7
84328	PARADISE	005	1173	1434	1571	2.2	63	326	412	455	2.6	3.48	279	342	2.2
84329	PARK VALLEY	003	284	349	382	2.3	67	91	114	126	2.5	3.06	66	80	2.1
84330	PLYMOUTH	003	346	438	485	2.6	73	111	143	159	2.8	3.06	94	119	2.6
84331	PORTAGE	003	332	420	466	2.6	73	90	116	129	2.8	3.62	77	96	2.4
84332	PROVIDENCE	005	6121	8055	8991	3.0	77	1696	2371	2672	3.7	3.39	1481	1994	3.3
84333	RICHMOND	005	2259	2598	2857	1.5	47	681	815	903	2.0	3.19	585	679	1.6
84335	SMITHFIELD	005	9528	11542	12727	2.1	60	2705	3400	3776	2.5	3.39	2336	2854	2.2
84336	SNOWVILLE	003	606	750	828	2.3	67	182	230	255	2.6	3.26	154	191	2.4
84337	TREMONTON	003	8820	10896	11962	2.3	67	2609	3258	3591	2.4	3.33	2189	2674	2.2
84338	TRENTON	005	514	576	627	1.2	41	155	180	197	1.6	3.20	132	149	1.3
84339	WELLSVILLE	005	3703	4089	4499	1.1	39	1034	1188	1317	1.5	3.44	913	1023	1.2
84340	WILLARD	003	2216	2301	2398	0.4	19	726	765	801	0.6	3.01	585	600	0.3
84341	LOGAN	005	20136	25393	27957	2.5	71	5732	7473	8362	2.9	3.11	4109	5152	2.5
84401	OGDEN	057	30756	35910	38287	1.7	50	10196	11710	12453	1.5	2.95	6779	7613	1.3
84403	OGDEN	057	34899	37276	39000	0.7	29	12195	13102	13736	0.8	2.79	8756	8967	0.3
84404	OGDEN	057	44946	54344	59561	2.1	60	15665	19220	21090	2.2	2.81	11575	13732	1.9
84405	OGDEN	057	25733	30403	33144	1.8	52	8775	10558	11536	2.0	2.83	6712	7826	1.7
84414	OGDEN	057	20782	25613	28124	2.3	67	6041	7703	8512	2.7	3.32	5335	6624	2.4
84501	PRICE	007	12547	12512	12533	0.0	6	4407	4471	4517	0.2	2.67	3198	3143	-0.2
84510	ANETH	037	4001	4204	4280	0.5	22	1016	1087	1115	0.7	3.87	846	886	0.5
84511	BLANDING	037	4644	4637	4665	0.0	6	1386	1424	1448	0.3	3.19	1075	1073	0.0
84520	EAST CARBON	007	1804	1812	1823	0.0	6	726	746	757	0.3	2.43	493	485	-0.2
84523	FERRON	015	2373	2317	2294	-0.3	1	779	797	799	0.2	2.84	627	626	0.0
84525	GREEN RIVER	015	1090	1110	1107	0.2	12	385	398	401	0.4	2.79	276	274	-0.1
84526	HELPER	007	4154	4019	3992	-0.4	1	1619	1607	1613	-0.1	2.48	1158	1100	-0.6
84528	HUNTINGTON	015	7499	7357	7268	-0.2	3	2349	2404	2409	0.3	3.04	1925	1925	0.0
84531	MEXICAN HAT	037	959	1008	1029	0.5	22	216	231	237	0.7	4.36	186	195	0.5
84532	MOAB	019	8321	9064	9458	0.9	34	3353	3773	3981	1.3	2.37	2122	2281	0.8
84533	HITE	037	126	128	129	0.2	12	59	62	63	0.5	2.06	36	36	0.0
84535	MONTICELLO	037	3008	3121	3206	0.4	19	964	1032	1069	0.7	2.88	723	749	0.4
84536	MONUMENT VALLEY	037	1516	1594	1627	0.5	22	383	410	421	0.7	3.89	320	336	0.5
84540	THOMPSON	019	219	231	239	0.6	26	100	110	115	1.0	2.10	64	67	0.5
84542	WELLINGTON	007	1919	1880	1875	-0.2	3	662	667	672	0.1	2.81	531	521	-0.2
84601	PROVO	049	27798	32435	36190	1.7	50	8583	9998	11172	1.7	3.19	6564	7193	1.0
84604	PROVO	049	48325	57862	63995	2.0	58	12148	14758	16722	2.1	3.36	8328	9268	1.2
84606	PROVO	049	29662	35323	39560	1.9	55	8664	10387	11697	2.0	3.32	5211	5769	1.1
84621	AXTELL	039	203	220	235	0.9	34	68	74	79	0.9	2.97	54	57	0.6
84622	CENTERFIELD	039	1250	1375	1468	1.0	37	380	416	444	1.0	3.31	305	327	0.8
84624	DELTA	027	6894	7255	7430	0.6	26	2071	2233	2304	0.8	3.23	1688	1778	0.6
84627	EPHRAIM	039	4680	5758	6228	2.3	67	1178	1451	1580	2.3	3.61	796	946	1.9
84628	EUREKA	023	794	1068	1215	3.3	81	286	380	431	3.1	2.81	202	258	2.7
84629	FAIRVIEW	039	3159	3507	3687	1.1	39	958	1067	1123	1.2	3.28	788	859	0.9
84630	FAYETTE	039	239	259	277	0.9	34	76	83	88	1.0	3.12	60	64	0.7
84631	FILLMORE	027	4452	4877	5078	1.0	37	1445	1613	1691	1.2	2.95	1138	1237	0.9
84634	GUNNISON	039	2447	2705	2825	1.1	39	521	570	608	1.0	3.16	418	448	0.8
84635	HINCKLEY	027	859	926	959	0.8	31	261	289	302	1.1	3.20	218	236	0.9
84642	MANTI	039	4151	4466	4640	0.8	31	1275	1375	1430	0.8	3.20	1014	1068	0.6
84645	MONA	023	1432	1972	2269	3.5	85	343	466	534	3.4	4.23	304	406	3.2
84647	MOUNT PLEASANT	039	6634	7076	7347	0.7	29	2091	2232	2318	0.7	3.13	1630	1697	0.4
84648	NEPHI	023	5744	6919	7644	2.0	58	1745	2077	2286	1.9	3.28	1419	1651	1.7
84651	PAYSON	049	16853	22589	26242	3.2	80	4663	6399	7486	3.5	3.52	3992	5294	3.1
84653	SALEM	049	5885	7942	9489	3.3	81	1496	2056	2471	3.5	3.86	1349	1801	3.2
84654	SALINA	041	4550	4707	4847	0.4	19	1466	1535	1587	0.5	3.07	1207	1237	0.3
84655	SANTAQUIN	049	6300	8059	9343	2.7	73	1661	2155	2515	2.9	3.69	1467	1854	2.6
84660	SPANISH FORK	049	23542	36327	43393	4.8	92	6445	9804	11683	4.6	3.66	5584	8344	4.4
84663	SPRINGVILLE	049	20644	28325	33068	3.5	85	6055	8312	9701	3.5	3.39	5099	6691	3.0
84664	MAPLETON	049	5960	7466	8797	2.5	71	1472	1923	2292	2.9	3.88	1347	1732	2.8
84701	RICHFIELD	041	9778	10837	11390	1.1	39	3106	3511	3715	1.3	2.97	2496	2752	1.1
84710	ALTON	025	264	350	392	3.1	79	87	118	135	3.3	2.94	55	72	3.0
84712	ANTIMONY	017	190	197	197	0.4	19	52	54	54	0.4	3.56	42	43	0.3
84713	BEAVER	001	3132	3286	3338	0.5	22	1099	1174	1199	0.7	2.68	854	888	0.4
84714	BERYL	021	692	930	1077	3.2	80	206	275	320	3.2	3.36	166	215	2.8
84716	BOULDER	017	253	269	277	0.7	29	91	98	102	0.8	2.74	64	66	0.3
84719	BRIAN HEAD	021	118	161	187	3.4	82	55	75	87	3.4	2.15	42	56	3.2
84720	CEDAR CITY	021	15149	19510	22152	2.8	76	4861	6254	7148	2.8	3.01	3401	4197	2.3
84721	CEDAR CITY	021	13897	20078	23563	4.1	88	4174	6155	7286	4.3	3.20	3441	4924	4.0
84722	CENTRAL	053	1969	3042	3813	4.8	92	621	996	1263	5.2	3.05	518	803	4.9
84726	ESCALANTE	017	1980	2055	2066	0.4	19	676	707	713	0.5	2.87	508	515	0.1
84728	GARRISON	027	200	207	210	0.4	19	63	66	67	0.5	3.14	49	50	0.2
84729	GLENDALE	025	359	455	508	2.6	73	118	155	176	3.0	2.94	90	115	2.7
	UTAH					2.3					2.3	3.11			2.1
	UNITED STATES					1.0					1.1	2.59			0.9

ZIP CODE #	POST OFFICE NAME	RACE (%) White 2000	White 2009	Black 2000	Black 2009	Asian/Pacific 2000	Asian/Pacific 2009	% Hispanic Origin 2000	% Hispanic Origin 2009	2009 AGE DISTRIBUTION (%) 0-4	5-9	10-14	15-19	20-24	25-44	45-64	65-84	85+	18+	MEDIAN AGE 2009	% 2009 Males	% 2009 Females
84120	SALT LAKE CITY	78.3	73.8	1.0	1.3	8.8	10.4	17.9	21.4	10.1	9.5	8.8	8.2	6.9	30.3	19.7	6.2	0.5	66.7	29.0	50.1	49.9
84121	SALT LAKE CITY	93.9	92.3	0.6	0.8	2.5	3.3	2.9	3.7	6.3	6.3	6.6	6.5	5.6	29.1	26.3	11.7	1.4	76.7	37.0	49.7	50.3
84123	SALT LAKE CITY	87.0	84.1	1.2	1.6	3.7	4.5	10.4	12.8	8.5	7.8	7.2	7.6	8.5	31.7	20.4	7.2	1.0	72.0	30.1	49.6	50.4
84124	SALT LAKE CITY	93.4	91.8	0.5	0.7	2.6	3.4	3.5	4.4	6.4	6.4	6.5	6.3	5.5	26.7	24.9	14.6	2.8	76.8	38.5	48.7	51.3
84128	SALT LAKE CITY	83.9	79.8	0.9	1.1	3.4	3.7	15.3	19.5	12.2	11.0	9.8	8.5	6.4	32.6	16.5	2.8	0.2	61.6	26.3	50.4	49.6
84302	BRIGHAM CITY	91.9	90.3	0.2	0.2	0.8	1.0	7.1	8.6	9.9	8.9	8.2	7.9	7.0	26.7	20.1	9.6	1.6	67.9	29.7	50.3	49.7
84305	CLARKSTON	95.8	95.3	0.0	0.0	0.0	0.0	2.1	2.7	9.0	9.2	9.9	9.8	7.2	21.3	22.1	8.7	2.7	66.4	28.6	52.3	47.7
84306	COLLINSTON	96.4	95.8	0.0	0.0	1.0	1.2	2.9	3.5	8.0	8.7	9.2	10.0	6.6	22.7	24.0	9.7	1.2	67.5	31.5	50.0	50.0
84307	CORINNE	92.3	90.5	0.1	0.1	1.8	2.1	6.3	8.1	8.8	8.9	8.9	10.9	7.1	23.6	22.9	7.8	1.2	67.0	29.4	51.6	48.4
84308	CORNISH	95.2	94.9	0.0	0.0	0.7	0.6	5.5	6.7	10.2	8.3	7.7	12.8	9.3	20.1	21.4	8.3	1.9	65.8	26.3	50.8	49.2
84309	DEWEYVILLE	96.5	95.4	0.0	0.0	0.8	1.1	3.5	4.3	7.7	8.0	8.2	8.9	6.4	23.9	25.5	10.0	1.4	70.4	33.2	50.1	49.9
84310	EDEN	97.1	96.6	0.2	0.3	0.9	1.1	2.1	2.7	6.6	7.4	7.8	8.4	5.3	24.9	30.2	8.7	0.8	72.8	36.8	51.5	48.5
84311	FIELDING	96.9	96.3	0.1	0.1	0.9	1.1	2.5	3.0	8.5	9.7	10.2	11.2	6.7	21.3	22.5	8.8	1.1	63.8	28.4	50.6	49.4
84312	GARLAND	92.7	90.8	0.0	0.0	1.8	2.2	5.7	7.3	10.8	10.8	10.5	9.6	5.9	24.2	20.0	7.2	1.0	61.6	27.1	50.3	49.7
84313	GROUSE CREEK	93.4	91.7	0.0	0.0	0.7	0.6	13.2	15.5	9.5	8.3	11.3	10.1	7.1	22.0	18.5	11.3	1.8	64.9	28.0	53.6	46.4
84314	HONEYVILLE	94.5	93.3	0.0	0.0	1.9	2.3	4.4	5.3	9.1	9.7	10.0	9.2	5.6	23.1	22.4	9.3	1.4	65.1	30.4	52.0	48.0
84315	HOOPER	97.2	96.3	0.2	0.3	0.7	0.8	2.6	3.5	8.2	8.2	8.1	7.7	5.8	27.8	26.5	7.1	0.8	70.9	33.4	50.2	49.8
84317	HUNTSVILLE	97.6	97.2	0.2	0.2	0.5	0.6	2.5	3.2	6.4	7.9	8.3	9.3	6.0	22.6	29.0	9.2	1.3	71.2	36.7	50.8	49.2
84318	HYDE PARK	97.5	97.1	0.2	0.2	0.8	0.9	1.9	2.2	9.8	8.7	10.6	12.5	7.9	22.7	21.4	4.9	1.5	63.0	25.6	50.8	49.2
84319	HYRUM	89.0	86.7	0.2	0.3	0.6	0.7	12.6	15.0	13.3	11.8	10.0	8.5	6.7	29.3	15.6	4.4	0.5	59.7	24.9	50.4	49.6
84320	LEWISTON	95.3	94.3	0.1	0.1	0.2	0.2	4.9	6.0	10.1	9.3	9.5	11.4	8.5	23.0	18.6	7.2	2.4	63.8	25.9	50.6	49.4
84321	LOGAN	90.0	87.9	0.4	0.5	2.4	2.9	9.1	11.0	10.2	7.6	6.4	8.0	17.7	28.0	14.0	6.3	1.9	72.0	25.1	49.1	50.9
84322	LOGAN	92.8	91.5	0.4	0.5	4.3	5.2	2.9	3.4	3.3	0.9	0.5	19.4	55.1	17.0	1.7	1.2	1.0	93.6	22.4	34.5	65.5
84324	MANTUA	96.5	95.9	0.6	0.8	0.2	0.3	1.0	1.2	6.4	8.1	10.9	14.8	6.6	20.0	24.4	7.9	0.8	63.7	31.5	52.5	47.5
84325	MENDON	97.1	96.7	0.0	0.0	0.1	0.1	1.9	2.2	9.7	8.7	10.1	9.5	8.6	22.0	23.9	6.2	1.2	64.4	27.6	50.9	49.1
84328	PARADISE	98.3	98.2	0.3	0.3	0.7	0.7	1.9	2.2	9.9	10.2	9.7	8.9	5.7	25.7	22.5	6.7	0.8	64.6	29.4	52.0	48.0
84329	PARK VALLEY	93.0	91.1	0.0	0.0	0.7	0.9	13.0	15.5	9.7	8.3	11.7	10.0	6.9	21.8	18.1	11.7	1.7	63.6	27.9	53.6	46.4
84330	PLYMOUTH	98.0	97.5	0.0	0.2	0.3	0.2	2.9	3.7	10.5	10.0	9.4	9.1	7.3	24.4	21.5	7.1	0.7	64.6	27.2	49.3	50.7
84331	PORTAGE	97.9	97.4	0.0	0.2	0.3	0.2	3.0	3.8	10.7	10.0	9.3	9.0	7.1	24.8	21.4	6.9	0.7	64.3	27.3	50.0	50.0
84332	PROVIDENCE	96.3	95.3	0.1	0.1	0.7	0.8	2.7	3.8	10.4	10.2	9.5	9.3	6.3	28.1	19.9	5.2	1.0	64.1	28.7	50.0	50.0
84333	RICHMOND	96.5	95.8	0.1	0.2	0.2	0.3	2.7	3.4	10.0	10.0	9.5	8.7	6.2	24.9	21.7	7.9	1.0	65.0	29.1	49.5	50.5
84335	SMITHFIELD	95.4	94.3	0.1	0.1	0.6	0.8	5.1	6.1	10.6	10.0	9.9	9.3	7.2	25.2	20.2	6.7	1.1	63.5	27.4	50.1	49.9
84336	SNOWVILLE	94.2	92.9	0.3	0.4	0.7	0.7	7.2	8.8	10.0	9.5	11.7	11.9	7.5	23.3	19.2	6.1	0.8	61.5	24.6	52.1	47.9
84337	TREMONTON	92.9	91.4	0.2	0.2	1.2	1.4	7.5	8.8	10.5	10.1	9.7	9.2	6.5	25.7	19.7	7.2	1.5	63.8	27.8	50.7	49.3
84338	TRENTON	94.7	93.4	0.0	0.0	0.4	0.5	7.4	9.0	11.1	10.4	9.4	10.2	6.3	23.6	20.8	6.9	1.2	62.3	27.0	49.5	50.5
84339	WELLSVILLE	96.6	96.0	0.0	0.0	0.3	0.4	3.8	4.4	10.6	10.4	10.0	9.1	6.1	27.6	19.1	6.1	1.1	63.1	27.7	50.5	49.5
84340	WILLARD	95.6	94.6	0.1	0.1	0.7	0.9	4.6	5.6	8.4	8.5	8.2	7.5	5.3	26.4	26.0	8.7	0.9	70.2	32.9	49.9	50.1
84341	LOGAN	90.8	88.8	0.8	1.0	4.8	5.7	4.0	5.1	9.2	6.8	6.1	13.6	21.2	26.3	11.6	4.3	0.9	74.4	23.4	48.3	51.7
84401	OGDEN	74.6	71.6	2.8	3.0	1.3	1.4	30.3	32.8	9.9	8.8	8.0	7.9	8.0	30.0	19.8	6.3	1.2	68.7	29.3	52.9	47.1
84403	OGDEN	85.1	81.5	1.5	1.9	2.0	2.4	15.3	18.5	8.5	7.8	7.1	7.5	8.1	27.2	21.7	10.0	2.0	72.6	32.0	50.0	50.0
84404	OGDEN	88.7	85.7	1.2	1.6	1.1	1.3	11.3	14.3	9.2	8.4	8.0	7.9	7.1	28.0	21.2	8.6	1.5	69.5	31.1	49.6	50.4
84405	OGDEN	91.8	89.8	1.4	1.8	1.4	1.7	6.4	8.0	8.4	8.0	7.7	7.8	6.3	28.3	21.6	10.0	1.8	71.0	32.5	49.4	50.6
84414	OGDEN	95.9	94.4	0.4	0.5	0.8	1.1	3.8	5.2	8.9	8.7	8.8	8.9	6.5	26.5	22.5	8.4	0.9	68.2	30.8	49.9	50.1
84501	PRICE	91.7	90.0	0.2	0.3	0.5	0.6	9.4	11.1	7.8	7.5	7.4	9.5	7.6	24.8	23.5	9.8	2.0	72.6	32.2	48.9	51.1
84510	ANETH	1.7	1.8	0.0	0.0	0.0	0.0	0.7	0.7	11.7	10.4	9.7	11.0	9.5	23.2	17.5	6.4	0.6	61.5	23.8	50.0	50.0
84511	BLANDING	65.0	65.8	0.2	0.3	0.2	0.2	3.5	4.3	10.0	9.2	9.7	9.8	7.6	22.4	21.5	8.0	1.8	64.7	27.7	49.3	50.7
84520	EAST CARBON	83.3	79.0	0.2	0.3	0.1	0.1	20.7	25.0	6.1	5.8	6.1	7.0	6.2	21.5	28.9	15.2	3.2	77.8	42.3	47.2	52.8
84523	FERRON	97.6	97.4	0.3	0.3	0.3	0.3	1.3	1.5	7.2	7.2	7.2	7.5	7.0	21.3	28.2	11.8	2.7	73.2	37.5	49.7	50.3
84525	GREEN RIVER	90.3	88.2	0.6	0.7	1.2	1.4	16.7	19.0	9.9	8.9	8.7	8.3	6.6	26.7	19.5	10.2	1.2	67.3	30.8	48.6	51.4
84526	HELPER	91.0	88.8	0.4	0.5	0.3	0.3	10.8	13.0	6.9	6.9	6.8	6.5	5.7	24.9	27.8	12.1	2.3	75.4	38.2	49.2	50.8
84528	HUNTINGTON	95.8	95.1	0.1	0.1	0.3	0.4	4.8	5.6	9.4	9.0	8.4	8.0	7.1	25.4	23.5	8.1	1.0	68.0	29.6	50.7	49.3
84531	MEXICAN HAT	3.1	3.4	0.1	0.1	0.0	0.0	0.4	0.4	10.9	12.2	11.2	11.4	8.4	24.1	16.0	5.1	0.7	58.4	22.5	50.0	50.0
84532	MOAB	92.4	91.8	0.3	0.3	0.3	0.3	5.5	6.3	7.0	6.6	6.6	6.8	6.8	24.9	29.0	10.9	1.5	75.5	38.2	49.0	51.0
84533	HITE	44.0	45.3	0.0	0.0	0.0	0.0	3.2	3.1	7.8	7.0	6.3	7.0	10.9	27.3	26.6	7.0	0.0	75.0	30.6	49.2	50.8
84535	MONTICELLO	83.7	82.3	0.2	0.2	0.7	0.9	10.9	12.9	8.7	8.7	8.4	8.8	7.0	24.4	22.8	9.8	1.3	68.2	31.0	51.3	48.7
84536	MONUMENT VALLEY	3.1	3.3	0.1	0.1	0.1	0.1	0.3	0.4	10.7	11.7	11.5	10.9	8.0	23.2	17.4	6.0	0.7	59.1	23.3	49.3	50.7
84540	THOMPSON	94.1	93.1	0.5	0.4	0.5	0.4	6.4	7.4	6.9	6.9	7.4	6.5	5.2	25.1	29.9	11.3	0.9	74.0	38.4	48.1	51.9
84542	WELLINGTON	94.5	93.2	0.3	0.4	0.2	0.2	4.8	5.9	8.5	8.4	8.1	7.1	5.9	29.1	24.3	7.8	0.9	70.7	31.8	49.1	50.9
84601	PROVO	83.4	79.2	0.5	0.6	2.4	2.8	18.5	23.1	13.2	9.7	7.5	7.2	13.7	32.9	11.1	3.8	0.9	65.6	24.5	50.4	49.6
84604	PROVO	91.8	89.7	0.5	0.6	2.8	3.5	5.2	6.7	5.5	3.8	4.4	21.2	26.2	18.8	12.3	6.5	1.2	82.0	22.9	48.4	51.6
84606	PROVO	88.1	84.6	0.4	0.4	2.6	3.6	11.4	14.7	7.8	5.3	4.1	8.7	40.8	23.8	6.4	2.6	0.6	80.6	23.0	46.8	53.2
84621	AXTELL	90.2	88.2	0.0	0.0	0.0	0.0	8.3	10.9	7.3	9.5	10.0	10.5	5.9	19.5	23.2	12.7	1.4	66.4	33.1	52.3	47.7
84622	CENTERFIELD	93.1	91.6	0.1	0.1	0.1	0.1	7.5	9.2	9.7	9.2	8.4	8.7	8.0	24.8	21.5	8.9	0.9	67.6	28.5	51.9	48.1
84624	DELTA	94.9	93.9	0.1	0.1	0.5	0.6	6.7	7.8	9.2	9.6	9.9	10.4	5.6	22.0	22.9	8.8	1.5	64.2	29.1	51.2	48.8
84627	EPHRAIM	89.5	87.2	0.4	0.5	1.8	2.0	9.5	11.6	7.1	5.9	6.2	26.9	18.3	13.1	15.5	5.5	1.4	75.8	21.1	45.7	54.3
84628	EUREKA	91.2	90.5	0.5	0.5	0.6	0.7	5.2	6.1	9.6	8.3	7.3	8.4	8.8	28.0	19.9	8.6	1.1	69.9	29.1	50.4	49.6
84629	FAIRVIEW	94.5	93.4	0.1	0.1	0.6	0.7	4.5	5.5	9.1	8.7	9.3	9.1	6.3	22.9	23.4	9.7	1.4	66.5	31.3	50.1	49.9
84630	FAYETTE	90.8	88.8	0.0	0.0	0.0	0.0	8.4	10.4	7.3	9.7	9.7	11.6	6.2	18.9	23.2	12.0	1.5	65.3	31.6	52.9	47.1
84631	FILLMORE	92.6	91.4	0.1	0.1	1.1	1.3	8.2	9.5	8.5	8.0	7.7	8.4	7.1	23.1	23.0	12.0	2.2	70.3	32.5	51.0	49.0
84634	GUNNISON	87.9	86.0	1.8	2.2	1.3	1.5	7.4	9.1	6.1	6.1	6.2	7.8	10.6	32.9	20.5	8.2	1.5	76.6	33.2	67.3	32.7
84635	HINCKLEY	96.2	95.4	0.2	0.3	0.1	0.1	4.2	5.1	7.7	7.9	8.1	9.1	6.7	21.3	26.9	11.4	1.0	70.5	33.8	52.9	47.1
84642	MANTI	96.6	96.3	0.0	0.0	0.4	0.4	2.8	3.2	11.5	9.9	8.9	8.1	7.5	23.1	18.5	10.7	1.9	64.5	27.6	49.7	50.3
84645	MONA	98.5	98.4	0.0	0.0	0.1	0.1	1.2	1.4	14.7	13.0	11.3	9.1	6.8	25.4	15.3	4.0	0.6	55.3	21.5	48.5	51.5
84647	MOUNT PLEASANT	92.5	91.0	0.1	0.1	0.5	0.6	7.5	9.1	9.3	8.9	8.7	10.0	6.3	23.0	21.8	10.2	1.8	66.2	29.8	49.8	50.2
84648	NEPHI	97.1	96.7	0.1	0.1	0.4	0.5	2.5	3.0	11.4	10.1	9.0	8.4	6.3	24.8	19.7	8.5	1.8	63.8	28.1	50.2	49.8
84651	PAYSON	94.4	92.6	0.1	0.1	0.6	0.8	5.9	7.8	12.1	10.8	9.8	8.7	7.0	28.1	17.0	5.6	1.0	61.7	26.0	50.8	49.2
84653	SALEM	97.1	96.2	0.1	0.1	0.4	0.5	2.8	3.7	9.0	10.3	10.9	11.9	6.9	21.1	21.4	7.8	0.7	62.0	26.0	50.6	49.4
84654	SALINA	97.4	97.1	0.1	0.1	0.4	0.4	2.2	2.5	9.5	9.7	9.1	8.2	6.4	24.6	22.0	9.2	1.3	66.5	30.0	49.7	50.3
84655	SANTAQUIN	90.7	88.0	0.1	0.1	0.3	0.3	10.5	13.4	13.4	10.7	9.7	8.5	7.5	28.1	16.3	5.2	0.6	60.6	25.1	51.7	48.3
84660	SPANISH FORK	95.5	94.0	0.2	0.2	0.6	0.8	4.1	5.9	12.7	10.6	9.5	8.6	7.3	29.1	16.0	5.4	0.8	61.9	25.8	50.3	49.7
84663	SPRINGVILLE	94.6	92.4	0.1	0.1	0.7	1.3	4.7	6.3	12.6	10.9	9.4	7.7	6.7	29.8	16.1	5.8	0.9	62.2	26.7	49.6	50.4
84664	MAPLETON	97.5	96.8	0.1	0.1	0.6	0.7	2.0	2.8	8.7	9.9	10.6	11.2	6.8	21.9	22.6	7.4	1.0	63.5	28.0	50.5	49.5
84701	RICHFIELD	95.3	94.9	0.3	0.4	0.3	0.4	2.2	2.6	9.2	8.5	8.1	9.5	6.9	22.9	21.8	10.9	2.1	67.8	30.7	49.5	50.5
84710	ALTON	92.8	92.6	0.0	0.0	0.0	0.3	1.9	2.0	7.4	6.6	8.6	5.7	5.4	25.1	32.3	8.9	0.0	72.9	38.4	52.0	48.0
84712	ANTIMONY	96.3	95.9	0.0	0.0	0.0	0.0	2.1	2.5	10.2	9.6	8.6	7.1	4.6	21.3	24.4	11.7	2.5	66.0	34.3	50.8	49.2
84713	BEAVER	94.1	93.0	0.4	0.5	0.4	0.5	5.3	6.4	8.5	8.6	8.4	7.5	5.4	24.8	23.4	11.6	1.9	69.6	34.0	52.1	47.9
84714	BERYL	90.0	87.8	0.7	0.8	0.0	0.0	8.4	10.6	10.3	9.6	9.6	8.4	6.9	24.4	22.0	8.1	0.8	64.9	28.6	51.8	48.2
84716	BOULDER	95.3	95.2	0.0	0.0	0.8	0.7	3.2	3.3	8.2	7.8	7.8	7.1	5.9	24.9	27.9	9.3	1.1	72.1	35.1	50.9	49.1
84719	BRIAN HEAD	96.6	95.7	0.0	0.6	0.0	0.0	4.2	5.6	6.2	6.8	9.3	7.5	5.6	19.9	30.4	12.4	1.9	72.7	40.8	54.7	45.3
84720	CEDAR CITY	93.6	92.9	0.4	0.4	1.6	1.8	3.3	4.0	8.0	6.4	6.0	12.2	17.9	24.3	16.2	7.7	1.2	75.5	24.8	48.6	51.4
84721	CEDAR CITY	91.7	90.9	0.3	0.3	0.7	0.9	4.8	5.5	12.5	10.3	8.6	7.8	9.2	30.2	15.7	4.9	0.6	63.8	25.7	50.3	49.7
84722	CENTRAL	95.8	95.1	0.1	0.0	0.3	0.4	2.0	2.6	8.3	7.7	10.7	10.7	5.4	18.8	24.0	13.1	1.3	65.9	34.6	50.4	49.6
84726	ESCALANTE	95.4	95.1	0.0	0.0	0.5	0.5	3.0	3.3	9.0	9.0	8.5	7.3	5.0	22.2	26.1	11.0	1.9	68.4	35.1	50.9	49.1
84728	GARRISON	82.0	77.8	0.0	0.0	1.0	1.0	16.5	20.8	6.8	9.7	11.6	13.5	3.4	21.3	19.8	13.0	1.0	61.4	30.2	50.2	49.8
84729	GLENDALE	98.3	97.8	0.0	0.0	0.0	0.0	2.5	2.9	7.9	7.5	7.9	8.6	6.6	21.5	25.9	12.5	1.5	71.4	35.7	51.2	48.8
	UTAH	89.2	87.6	0.8	0.9	2.3	2.6	9.0	10.5	9.7	8.7	8.1	8.6	8.6	28.5	19.6	7.1	1.2	68.6	28.8	50.1	49.9
	UNITED STATES	75.1	72.0	12.3	12.7	3.8	4.6	12.5	15.7	6.8	6.7	6.6	7.1	6.9	27.0	26.0	10.9	1.9	75.7	36.9	49.2	50.8

84120-84729

ZIP CODE #	POST OFFICE NAME	2009 Per Capita Income	2009 HH Income Base	2009 Household Income Distribution (%): Less than $25,000	$25,000 to $49,999	$50,000 to $99,999	$100,000 to $149,999	$150,000 or More	Median Household Income: 2009	2014	2009 National Centile	2009 State Centile	2009 Home Value Base	2009 Home Value Distribution (%): Less than $50,000	$50,000 to $89,999	$90,000 to $174,999	$175,000 to $399,999	$400,000 or More	2009 Median Home Value
84120	SALT LAKE CITY	20170	13506	8.9	23.1	52.2	12.1	3.6	64205	66856	83	77	10613	2.0	1.4	33.2	62.0	1.3	188401
84121	SALT LAKE CITY	36753	15895	8.1	18.2	38.7	18.5	16.4	77709	80100	91	91	11865	0.1	0.1	8.2	64.5	27.2	292813
84123	SALT LAKE CITY	24358	13704	15.0	26.0	43.8	10.9	4.2	56678	60556	74	62	8349	8.6	6.7	22.5	59.0	3.2	202346
84124	SALT LAKE CITY	34015	8088	11.2	18.9	41.1	16.0	12.7	68704	71957	86	83	6000	0.3	0.2	4.4	63.2	31.9	329838
84128	SALT LAKE CITY	20466	7233	6.2	18.7	58.5	14.0	2.7	67898	70849	86	81	6365	1.8	1.8	32.9	62.9	0.7	188246
84302	BRIGHAM CITY	20494	7580	14.6	24.8	48.6	9.1	2.9	57615	58596	75	64	5887	2.1	1.7	40.9	52.1	3.3	182932
84305	CLARKSTON	17017	269	13.4	37.5	45.0	3.3	0.7	49304	51383	60	48	245	3.3	8.2	60.4	27.8	0.4	142763
84306	COLLINSTON	18154	166	15.1	22.9	50.6	9.0	2.4	56321	56277	73	61	144	0.7	4.2	36.1	51.4	7.6	189773
84307	CORINNE	19296	442	14.9	26.0	50.7	6.1	2.3	58253	59202	75	66	378	1.1	2.9	52.1	40.7	3.2	163942
84308	CORNISH	16766	84	13.1	34.5	42.9	6.0	3.6	51672	52288	65	52	69	2.9	5.8	44.9	42.0	4.3	167188
84309	DEWEYVILLE	24232	159	13.2	23.9	49.7	10.1	3.1	57451	56862	75	63	141	0.0	1.4	32.6	56.7	9.2	200962
84310	EDEN	28757	1209	7.2	13.7	48.1	17.5	13.5	78101	79565	91	92	1048	0.6	0.3	9.3	65.6	24.3	293750
84311	FIELDING	18855	254	15.4	21.7	53.1	9.1	0.8	56436	56405	73	61	215	1.4	8.4	43.3	43.3	3.7	169922
84312	GARLAND	17527	1351	13.5	29.8	47.9	7.8	1.0	54409	55365	70	58	1127	2.5	5.7	48.9	41.3	1.6	164198
84313	GROUSE CREEK	15589	62	21.0	46.8	29.0	3.2	0.0	33375	38630	14	9	40	35.0	12.5	17.5	12.5	22.5	100000
84314	HONEYVILLE	19210	619	13.9	28.9	46.2	8.9	2.1	55879	56117	72	59	548	0.7	4.2	40.0	51.6	3.5	184091
84315	HOOPER	24939	1483	6.7	14.8	55.2	16.6	6.7	75919	75999	90	89	1375	0.0	1.4	27.2	65.8	5.6	213925
84317	HUNTSVILLE	28828	1044	7.1	15.2	48.5	16.9	12.4	77595	77993	91	91	915	0.4	1.1	11.3	62.7	24.5	287500
84318	HYDE PARK	20193	1017	7.9	25.5	47.6	13.5	5.6	62930	63305	81	74	888	2.0	0.6	24.8	66.9	5.7	205224
84319	HYRUM	19551	2280	9.9	29.1	47.2	9.1	4.6	57552	58468	75	63	1904	5.4	2.4	42.7	45.5	4.1	174564
84320	LEWISTON	15837	793	18.0	35.9	37.2	6.9	1.9	47256	49722	55	45	645	1.7	2.6	52.7	39.4	3.6	162500
84321	LOGAN	19613	13043	24.0	31.9	34.4	6.3	3.4	44588	48412	47	35	7075	3.8	3.8	40.1	47.1	5.2	178682
84322	LOGAN	9470	318	50.6	35.8	11.6	1.9	0.0	24697	24799	3	1	24	0.0	0.0	41.7	58.3	0.0	191667
84324	MANTUA	20862	241	7.9	19.1	56.8	12.9	3.3	71977	71146	88	87	223	0.0	1.8	24.7	63.7	9.9	218359
84325	MENDON	22928	564	6.2	21.3	56.2	11.0	5.3	67692	68427	85	81	471	1.9	1.1	14.6	68.8	13.6	237381
84328	PARADISE	19890	412	14.1	25.0	45.1	11.4	4.4	59020	60164	76	67	372	0.5	0.5	18.0	73.9	7.0	227679
84329	PARK VALLEY	13936	114	19.3	47.4	28.9	3.5	0.9	34546	37971	17	10	73	34.2	12.3	16.4	12.3	24.7	127083
84330	PLYMOUTH	20670	143	14.7	20.3	53.1	10.5	1.4	63280	62888	81	75	123	2.4	5.7	42.3	47.2	2.4	174107
84331	PORTAGE	17478	116	13.8	20.7	54.3	10.3	0.9	63212	63045	81	75	100	3.0	6.0	43.0	45.0	3.0	170455
84332	PROVIDENCE	23371	2371	10.2	18.2	53.3	13.0	5.2	68696	67863	86	82	2028	1.5	0.9	32.5	57.9	7.2	204036
84333	RICHMOND	18423	815	15.5	29.7	45.6	7.4	1.8	53703	54298	69	57	678	5.0	3.1	42.3	46.2	3.4	174219
84335	SMITHFIELD	18982	3400	15.0	23.9	49.6	8.3	3.2	59393	60470	77	68	2845	3.9	1.1	34.7	55.5	4.8	189764
84336	SNOWVILLE	17200	230	17.4	30.4	43.0	8.7	0.4	51689	53361	65	53	189	5.8	5.8	48.7	38.6	1.1	150625
84337	TREMONTON	19543	3258	14.9	24.1	47.2	10.0	3.8	58455	59069	76	66	2615	2.9	4.4	41.3	46.6	4.8	177224
84338	TRENTON	16980	180	24.4	31.7	36.1	4.4	3.3	45000	48364	48	36	142	1.4	5.6	39.4	49.3	4.2	181250
84339	WELLSVILLE	19728	1188	11.0	25.1	50.7	10.0	3.2	61703	62503	80	72	1004	0.8	1.0	34.4	59.7	4.2	193194
84340	WILLARD	21339	765	14.8	23.0	50.6	8.9	2.7	60484	60433	78	70	649	8.9	1.5	32.2	51.0	6.3	190833
84341	LOGAN	19063	7473	23.1	30.3	34.4	7.3	4.9	46612	49863	53	44	3762	6.7	0.5	28.8	56.0	8.0	198611
84401	OGDEN	18724	11710	26.5	27.7	35.3	7.5	3.0	45495	48705	50	39	6802	2.2	7.0	49.6	38.1	3.1	157143
84403	OGDEN	25439	13102	18.3	26.9	37.3	9.1	8.5	53950	56350	70	57	9056	0.3	3.1	42.6	44.8	9.2	183302
84404	OGDEN	20894	19220	18.0	29.7	42.6	7.3	2.4	51431	53303	65	52	14385	4.7	5.0	56.2	32.2	2.0	151653
84405	OGDEN	25289	10558	12.7	24.2	43.1	14.5	5.5	61838	63966	80	72	8057	4.1	2.7	37.2	51.6	4.5	186171
84414	OGDEN	26247	7703	4.7	17.1	52.8	16.7	8.6	76126	75871	90	89	6959	0.5	0.6	27.1	65.1	6.7	205764
84501	PRICE	19469	4471	26.9	27.0	36.5	7.9	1.8	46184	48470	52	43	3321	4.6	15.1	54.0	23.9	2.5	134567
84510	ANETH	9150	1087	57.5	15.1	23.2	2.9	1.3	19077	20267	1	0	965	69.9	13.5	12.0	3.7	0.8	22218
84511	BLANDING	15451	1424	29.6	29.4	34.1	5.4	1.6	42568	45073	41	30	1005	15.1	17.4	47.1	18.5	1.9	115929
84520	EAST CARBON	16658	746	36.3	34.0	24.7	4.3	0.7	32428	35766	12	8	634	19.1	50.8	28.2	1.9	0.0	74375
84523	FERRON	17820	797	25.1	29.7	37.3	6.8	1.1	43490	46460	44	32	649	10.9	24.0	50.8	12.6	1.5	107396
84525	GREEN RIVER	15359	398	29.4	35.7	32.2	2.0	0.8	38116	41082	27	16	299	21.4	23.1	45.2	8.0	2.3	96111
84526	HELPER	19465	1607	32.2	30.5	28.9	6.4	2.0	38075	41264	27	15	1301	7.6	16.4	56.5	18.1	1.3	118950
84528	HUNTINGTON	17663	2404	20.2	27.9	43.8	6.5	1.5	50774	50915	63	50	2006	14.7	16.3	54.5	14.0	0.6	115189
84531	MEXICAN HAT	9614	231	41.6	27.3	26.8	2.6	1.7	29852	33350	8	5	196	58.2	17.9	10.7	13.3	0.0	31667
84532	MOAB	21918	3773	28.3	31.1	32.5	5.0	3.1	41349	43585	37	27	2686	11.6	6.9	40.5	35.0	6.0	156134
84533	HITE	21313	62	41.9	19.4	32.3	4.8	1.6	35000	37397	18	11	36	33.3	27.8	22.2	8.3	8.3	76667
84535	MONTICELLO	17663	1032	26.5	32.9	33.6	4.8	2.1	41354	43544	37	28	818	12.5	11.7	46.3	26.7	2.8	138758
84536	MONUMENT VALLEY	9709	410	48.0	20.7	26.6	2.7	2.0	26503	30095	4	2	331	58.9	19.0	10.3	11.8	0.0	32361
84540	THOMPSON	20115	110	34.5	30.0	30.0	4.5	0.9	32336	33627	12	7	87	10.3	6.9	37.9	36.8	8.0	164773
84542	WELLINGTON	19513	667	23.5	28.2	38.8	7.9	1.5	47967	49747	57	47	539	7.1	14.8	50.5	25.0	2.6	131181
84601	PROVO	16513	9998	22.3	31.1	38.9	6.0	1.6	47324	48908	55	45	4962	8.2	4.5	28.7	58.1	0.5	184907
84604	PROVO	19378	14758	21.2	28.7	32.6	11.5	6.1	50129	51565	61	49	6963	0.8	0.1	10.2	65.9	23.1	285874
84606	PROVO	13620	10387	30.4	38.1	26.0	3.8	1.7	35804	36622	20	11	2689	1.0	1.7	25.2	66.6	5.4	199045
84621	AXTELL	14008	74	36.5	36.5	21.6	4.1	1.4	30000	34303	8	5	60	0.0	6.7	45.0	43.3	5.0	170000
84622	CENTERFIELD	14361	416	27.9	33.2	32.9	5.0	1.0	40194	41633	33	25	364	9.1	9.9	47.0	31.9	2.2	140079
84624	DELTA	17302	2233	21.9	28.3	41.9	5.9	2.0	49767	49965	60	48	1754	7.9	17.0	55.6	18.3	1.2	123926
84627	EPHRAIM	13631	1451	26.5	35.6	30.4	5.6	1.9	37858	39166	26	14	883	9.4	1.7	39.5	48.4	1.0	173750
84628	EUREKA	18204	380	26.3	27.6	38.9	6.3	0.8	45765	51019	51	39	274	19.7	15.7	50.4	12.4	1.8	98163
84629	FAIRVIEW	15639	1067	23.2	30.9	39.8	4.3	1.7	45419	50255	49	38	934	5.5	5.5	48.7	37.7	2.7	157000
84630	FAYETTE	13298	83	36.1	37.3	21.7	3.6	1.2	30440	33890	9	7	67	0.0	6.0	44.8	44.8	4.5	172917
84631	FILLMORE	16495	1613	24.9	35.3	33.2	5.0	1.6	41281	44976	37	27	1326	9.7	13.5	52.7	21.9	2.2	128378
84634	GUNNISON	17122	570	23.5	32.5	34.7	7.4	1.9	43647	48352	44	33	495	2.8	10.5	54.3	31.1	1.2	145424
84635	HINCKLEY	17148	289	20.4	32.2	41.5	3.8	2.1	47656	48722	56	46	248	6.9	20.2	50.0	21.0	2.0	126829
84642	MANTI	15943	1375	28.0	30.1	36.4	3.4	2.1	42292	44544	40	29	1098	2.3	8.8	45.6	38.5	4.7	159711
84645	MONA	15661	466	15.7	22.3	50.0	7.1	4.9	58027	60155	75	65	364	4.4	0.8	26.4	65.9	2.5	203750
84647	MOUNT PLEASANT	15861	2232	25.4	33.9	33.7	5.2	1.8	42295	44013	40	29	1855	5.6	8.5	44.3	38.5	3.1	156037
84648	NEPHI	16645	2077	22.9	30.0	38.5	6.7	1.8	47921	51277	56	47	1703	4.0	3.1	46.4	42.0	4.5	170170
84651	PAYSON	19142	6399	14.5	22.7	48.4	10.5	3.9	59518	62456	77	68	5142	3.8	2.8	24.3	59.9	9.3	204004
84653	SALEM	22115	2056	9.4	18.1	45.7	18.5	8.3	68953	70517	86	84	1747	0.1	0.1	15.9	62.4	21.5	274203
84654	SALINA	17798	1535	21.0	30.4	41.2	4.2	3.1	48711	48919	58	48	1291	3.6	8.1	58.6	24.5	5.3	141481
84655	SANTAQUIN	18205	2155	9.2	25.3	52.3	9.8	3.2	57866	60899	75	64	1807	4.5	5.1	22.2	58.6	9.6	201574
84660	SPANISH FORK	20350	9804	9.1	19.9	53.6	12.7	4.7	65101	68422	83	78	7857	1.1	1.7	19.8	67.7	9.7	225735
84663	SPRINGVILLE	20001	8312	12.8	25.5	45.7	12.3	3.7	59721	62297	77	69	5991	4.6	2.2	20.4	65.1	7.7	217538
84664	MAPLETON	22677	1923	7.2	16.6	48.0	19.0	9.3	76161	76995	90	90	1724	0.3	1.2	5.9	66.9	25.7	308913
84701	RICHFIELD	17817	3511	22.3	32.8	37.1	5.6	2.2	45087	46338	49	37	2770	4.4	7.0	58.2	26.4	4.0	143273
84710	ALTON	16367	118	24.6	28.0	42.4	5.1	0.0	46170	45985	52	42	66	6.1	6.1	25.8	45.5	16.7	215385
84712	ANTIMONY	14135	54	20.4	29.6	44.4	5.6	0.0	50000	48882	61	49	43	11.6	16.3	55.8	11.6	4.7	118750
84713	BEAVER	17913	1174	25.7	34.5	33.5	5.1	1.2	39920	41530	32	22	933	4.5	10.6	57.7	26.3	1.0	140466
84714	BERYL	12591	275	34.5	28.4	33.5	3.6	0.0	36204	38666	21	13	198	18.2	9.6	45.5	25.3	1.5	134884
84716	BOULDER	16945	98	30.6	32.7	30.6	6.1	0.0	40000	42041	33	24	73	12.3	12.3	39.7	28.8	6.8	146875
84719	BRIAN HEAD	23710	75	26.7	30.7	34.7	2.7	5.3	38791	41174	29	19	64	0.0	15.6	48.4	31.3	4.7	152500
84720	CEDAR CITY	18854	6254	24.1	28.4	35.9	8.1	3.4	47036	50261	54	44	3783	2.2	2.0	30.4	57.4	8.0	211727
84721	CEDAR CITY	16188	6155	21.8	34.5	36.5	5.2	2.0	45201	46816	45	34	4239	6.4	3.5	43.1	44.4	2.6	171107
84722	CENTRAL	18580	996	21.5	32.8	36.4	4.8	4.4	45202	50492	49	38	856	3.0	6.5	37.3	48.9	4.2	180400
84726	ESCALANTE	16290	707	27.0	31.4	35.9	5.4	0.3	42520	45291	41	30	542	11.3	13.5	51.8	18.3	5.2	130707
84728	GARRISON	9179	66	34.8	65.2	0.0	0.0	0.0	28973	29223	7	4	30	26.7	36.7	36.7	0.0	0.0	70000
84729	GLENDALE	15155	155	27.7	36.1	34.2	1.3	0.6	39294	41628	31	20	131	3.8	16.0	57.3	16.0	6.9	131048
	UTAH	23420		14.7	23.9	42.1	12.6	6.7	60286	62873				3.1	3.0	25.7	56.7	11.5	213546
	UNITED STATES	27277		20.9	24.4	35.3	11.7	7.6	54719	56938				9.3	13.1	31.6	32.6	13.5	162279

ZIP CODE		FINANCIAL SERVICES				THE HOME						ENTERTAINMENT						PERSONAL			
						Home Improvements		Furnishings													
#	POST OFFICE NAME	Auto Loan	Home Loan	Invest-ments	Retire-ment Plans	Home Repair	Lawn & Garden	Comput-ers & Hard-ware-Personal	Major Appli-ances	TV, Radio, Sound Equip-ment	Furni-ture	Dine out/ Carry out	Sports Equip-ment	Fees & Tickets	Toys & Games	Travel	Cable TV	Apparel & Services	Auto Repairs	Health Insur-ance	Pets & Supplies
84120	SALT LAKE CITY	104	110	92	106	104	98	102	101	99	107	101	77	103	103	100	97	70	99	95	117
84121	SALT LAKE CITY	137	159	155	162	159	149	143	145	139	150	141	111	158	140	154	137	101	142	140	167
84123	SALT LAKE CITY	98	88	78	89	84	82	97	88	95	97	97	71	92	98	90	93	67	94	87	105
84124	SALT LAKE CITY	119	138	139	138	141	132	127	128	123	131	124	96	138	123	136	123	89	126	127	147
84128	SALT LAKE CITY	112	120	97	115	112	100	107	107	102	115	104	83	108	109	104	97	72	102	95	122
84302	BRIGHAM CITY	91	94	82	94	90	94	90	91	90	89	90	70	91	92	90	91	62	90	93	107
84305	CLARKSTON	84	76	76	80	78	90	75	85	78	68	76	65	69	79	75	82	52	79	88	99
84306	COLLINSTON	97	90	88	94	91	104	88	99	90	80	89	75	82	92	88	95	61	91	101	115
84307	CORINNE	97	88	87	92	90	103	87	98	89	79	88	74	80	91	87	95	60	90	101	114
84308	CORNISH	110	78	118	78	82	116	86	105	89	70	88	86	65	88	85	97	57	98	111	129
84309	DEWEYVILLE	101	97	93	101	98	109	93	103	95	87	94	79	89	97	95	99	64	96	105	120
84310	EDEN	124	155	136	155	149	135	130	132	122	136	125	105	146	128	140	118	90	126	119	152
84311	FIELDING	93	85	83	87	86	98	83	93	86	77	84	70	77	88	82	90	58	86	95	108
84312	GARLAND	90	85	82	88	86	96	82	91	84	77	83	69	78	86	83	88	57	85	93	106
84313	GROUSE CREEK	76	52	83	52	54	80	58	72	60	47	59	59	42	59	57	65	38	67	76	88
84314	HONEYVILLE	98	89	88	93	91	105	88	99	91	79	89	75	81	92	88	96	61	91	102	115
84315	HOOPER	115	131	113	134	127	125	116	120	113	118	114	94	125	116	122	112	80	115	116	140
84317	HUNTSVILLE	123	149	130	150	144	134	127	130	121	132	123	103	141	126	136	118	88	124	121	151
84318	HYDE PARK	105	118	101	120	114	112	105	108	102	107	103	85	112	106	110	101	72	104	104	126
84319	HYRUM	107	112	93	105	107	93	104	103	98	112	100	79	103	103	102	93	70	100	91	116
84320	LEWISTON	88	76	83	78	77	94	76	88	79	67	77	68	67	80	76	84	52	81	91	103
84321	LOGAN	84	72	64	74	69	69	90	75	84	83	85	63	79	86	77	82	60	82	74	91
84322	LOGAN	45	19	19	23	17	22	63	31	50	43	51	34	37	49	34	46	36	44	31	42
84324	MANTUA	104	117	101	121	114	115	105	109	103	105	103	85	112	106	111	103	72	105	108	128
84325	MENDON	108	120	104	123	117	119	108	112	106	107	106	88	114	109	113	107	74	108	111	132
84328	PARADISE	96	109	94	112	105	107	97	101	95	97	96	79	103	98	102	96	67	97	100	119
84329	PARK VALLEY	76	52	84	52	55	81	58	72	61	47	60	60	43	59	58	66	39	68	76	89
84330	PLYMOUTH	102	93	83	90	91	95	88	93	91	92	91	68	83	95	84	94	62	90	94	111
84331	PORTAGE	102	93	83	90	91	95	88	93	91	92	91	68	83	95	84	94	62	90	94	111
84332	PROVIDENCE	114	129	108	128	123	116	113	115	109	118	110	91	120	114	117	106	77	110	107	133
84333	RICHMOND	91	83	82	86	85	98	82	92	84	74	83	70	75	86	82	89	56	85	95	107
84335	SMITHFIELD	95	98	89	99	95	100	90	96	90	89	90	74	90	92	92	91	62	91	95	113
84336	SNOWVILLE	90	82	74	80	81	85	78	83	81	81	81	61	73	84	74	83	55	80	83	99
84337	TREMONTON	98	98	87	97	95	98	92	96	92	92	92	72	90	95	91	94	64	92	95	113
84338	TRENTON	97	67	107	67	70	102	74	92	77	60	76	76	54	76	74	84	50	86	97	113
84339	WELLSVILLE	96	107	92	109	104	103	96	99	94	97	94	77	101	97	100	93	66	95	96	116
84340	WILLARD	97	98	85	97	95	98	90	94	91	92	91	71	90	94	90	92	63	91	94	111
84341	LOGAN	92	69	61	74	65	66	97	75	91	89	92	65	81	93	78	87	65	86	74	93
84401	OGDEN	79	74	65	74	70	71	80	75	80	79	81	59	77	82	75	80	57	79	76	89
84403	OGDEN	99	102	96	103	101	100	103	100	101	102	102	77	104	102	102	101	71	101	101	117
84404	OGDEN	86	84	73	83	81	83	84	83	84	84	85	63	82	86	81	85	59	83	85	98
84405	OGDEN	102	107	96	107	104	103	102	101	101	104	102	78	105	103	103	101	71	101	102	119
84414	OGDEN	120	142	124	140	136	127	123	125	119	128	121	97	135	123	130	116	85	120	118	144
84501	PRICE	79	73	69	73	72	80	73	76	76	71	75	58	70	77	71	79	51	75	81	91
84510	ANETH	60	48	36	40	46	45	48	51	52	53	52	32	41	52	43	53	36	52	50	56
84511	BLANDING	77	71	62	69	68	71	70	71	72	71	72	53	66	74	65	73	49	70	72	85
84520	EAST CARBON	68	49	69	48	51	71	54	66	60	48	58	50	43	59	52	66	39	62	72	78
84523	FERRON	84	68	82	69	70	88	69	82	73	63	72	62	59	74	68	79	48	76	85	96
84525	GREEN RIVER	76	56	63	55	56	72	58	67	64	57	63	51	48	66	53	69	42	63	70	81
84526	HELPER	78	64	73	64	66	81	66	76	70	61	69	57	58	71	64	75	46	72	81	90
84528	HUNTINGTON	89	75	74	74	75	86	74	82	79	74	78	61	66	81	70	83	53	78	84	98
84531	MEXICAN HAT	71	57	42	47	54	53	56	61	61	63	62	37	49	62	51	63	43	61	59	67
84532	MOAB	81	70	80	70	72	80	73	79	75	71	74	59	67	75	72	78	51	77	81	93
84533	HITE	68	64	54	61	61	61	63	63	63	66	64	48	60	66	59	63	44	63	62	75
84535	MONTICELLO	83	71	76	71	72	84	70	80	74	67	73	59	63	75	69	78	49	75	82	94
84536	MONUMENT VALLEY	64	51	38	43	49	48	51	55	55	57	56	34	44	56	45	57	39	55	53	60
84540	THOMPSON	67	62	55	60	60	63	58	62	60	61	60	45	55	63	56	62	41	60	62	73
84542	WELLINGTON	88	81	72	78	79	83	76	81	79	80	79	59	72	83	73	81	54	78	81	96
84601	PROVO	81	68	59	69	64	62	82	69	78	79	79	58	72	81	70	75	55	75	67	84
84604	PROVO	96	80	78	86	79	79	111	86	100	98	101	74	95	100	91	96	72	96	85	105
84606	PROVO	68	45	41	48	42	45	82	54	71	66	72	50	60	72	56	67	51	66	54	69
84621	AXTELL	74	51	82	51	54	79	57	71	59	46	58	58	42	58	57	65	38	66	75	87
84622	CENTERFIELD	86	61	73	60	61	82	64	75	71	61	69	58	51	73	59	77	46	71	79	91
84624	DELTA	93	76	90	76	77	96	77	89	80	70	79	69	66	81	76	85	53	84	92	107
84627	EPHRAIM	71	53	48	56	50	56	80	61	75	67	75	52	64	75	62	74	52	70	65	76
84628	EUREKA	80	75	63	71	71	71	74	73	74	77	74	56	69	77	69	74	51	73	72	87
84629	FAIRVIEW	89	67	96	65	70	91	69	85	74	64	73	65	56	73	69	80	48	79	87	101
84630	FAYETTE	74	51	81	51	53	78	57	70	59	46	58	58	42	58	56	64	38	66	74	87
84631	FILLMORE	81	64	80	63	65	82	68	77	70	61	69	60	56	70	66	74	46	74	81	93
84634	GUNNISON	85	73	78	73	75	85	78	82	81	74	79	61	70	80	75	84	54	81	88	97
84635	HINCKLEY	87	76	82	79	78	93	76	87	79	68	77	67	68	80	76	84	52	81	91	103
84642	MANTI	77	68	70	70	70	79	72	77	74	68	73	57	66	74	70	77	50	75	81	89
84645	MONA	106	98	87	95	95	100	92	98	96	96	96	71	87	100	88	98	65	95	98	116
84647	MOUNT PLEASANT	78	69	70	71	70	81	69	77	72	64	70	58	63	73	68	76	48	72	80	90
84648	NEPHI	82	79	66	79	75	82	77	78	79	77	79	59	75	81	74	81	54	78	82	94
84651	PAYSON	101	106	89	103	101	96	97	98	94	102	95	76	98	99	95	92	66	94	91	113
84653	SALEM	120	137	117	138	132	127	121	124	117	125	118	98	129	122	126	115	83	119	117	144
84654	SALINA	84	79	70	79	77	84	76	80	79	75	78	61	73	81	74	81	53	78	83	95
84655	SANTAQUIN	103	108	90	104	102	95	97	98	94	103	95	76	98	100	95	91	66	94	90	113
84660	SPANISH FORK	109	116	98	115	111	105	108	107	104	111	105	85	110	109	107	101	74	104	100	124
84663	SPRINGVILLE	97	106	92	104	102	96	97	97	94	101	96	75	101	99	98	92	67	95	92	112
84664	MAPLETON	121	147	127	147	141	129	125	127	118	131	120	101	138	123	133	114	86	121	115	146
84701	RICHFIELD	83	74	80	74	76	84	73	81	76	72	75	60	68	77	73	80	51	78	83	95
84710	ALTON	80	64	104	63	71	85	64	82	67	60	67	60	56	64	70	72	44	76	81	95
84712	ANTIMONY	84	67	108	66	73	88	67	85	70	63	69	62	58	66	72	75	46	78	84	99
84713	BEAVER	85	61	94	60	64	88	64	81	69	57	68	63	51	67	65	75	45	75	84	97
84714	BERYL	75	56	62	54	56	71	57	66	63	56	62	50	47	65	52	68	42	62	69	79
84716	BOULDER	75	69	61	66	67	70	65	69	67	67	67	50	61	70	62	69	46	66	69	81
84719	BRIAN HEAD	85	68	110	67	75	90	68	86	71	64	70	63	59	68	74	76	47	80	85	100
84720	CEDAR CITY	86	80	70	79	76	74	88	79	83	85	84	64	80	86	78	80	58	81	76	93
84721	CEDAR CITY	80	76	65	74	72	69	76	73	74	78	75	57	72	78	71	72	52	73	69	86
84722	CENTRAL	89	79	89	81	82	96	78	91	81	71	80	68	71	81	80	86	54	84	93	105
84726	ESCALANTE	78	64	85	62	67	79	63	76	67	61	66	56	55	66	65	71	44	71	76	89
84728	GARRISON	44	35	31	36	34	41	42	40	44	38	43	31	36	45	36	46	29	42	45	49
84729	GLENDALE	79	57	82	55	59	81	58	74	65	54	64	56	47	64	58	71	42	68	77	88
	UTAH	107	107	98	107	104	101	106	103	103	108	104	81	105	106	103	102	73	103	99	121
	UNITED STATES	100	100	100	100	100	100	100	100	100	100	100	100	100	100	100	100	100	100	100	100

POPULATION CHANGE

84731-84790

ZIP CODE #	POST OFFICE NAME	COUNTY FIPS CODE	POPULATION 2000	POPULATION 2009	POPULATION 2014	2000-2009 ANNUAL RATE % Rate	2000-2009 ANNUAL RATE State Centile	HOUSEHOLDS 2000	HOUSEHOLDS 2009	HOUSEHOLDS 2014	HOUSEHOLDS % Annual Rate 2000-2009	HOUSEHOLDS 2009 Average HH Size	FAMILIES 2000	FAMILIES 2009	FAMILIES % Annual Rate 2000-2009
84731	GREENVILLE	001	298	314	321	0.6	26	40	42	43	0.5	6.60	33	34	0.3
84734	HANKSVILLE	055	714	803	849	1.3	43	299	350	376	1.7	2.29	203	228	1.3
84737	HURRICANE	053	13508	20182	24817	4.4	89	4223	6665	8305	5.1	3.01	3335	5051	4.6
84738	IVINS	053	4474	7412	9234	5.6	95	1442	2544	3211	6.3	2.91	1236	2127	6.0
84739	JOSEPH	041	541	594	624	1.0	37	166	184	193	1.1	3.23	142	154	0.9
84741	KANAB	025	4578	4955	5191	0.9	34	1717	1938	2061	1.3	2.52	1258	1374	1.0
84743	KINGSTON	031	972	963	952	-0.1	5	332	331	329	0.0	2.89	252	244	-0.3
84745	LA VERKIN	053	4244	5210	5931	2.2	63	1314	1660	1913	2.6	3.12	1059	1287	2.1
84747	LOA	055	1155	1183	1199	0.3	16	368	389	399	0.6	3.02	295	304	0.3
84750	MARYSVALE	031	463	448	437	-0.4	1	177	174	170	-0.2	2.52	138	132	-0.5
84751	MILFORD	001	2575	2751	2799	0.7	29	843	893	908	0.6	3.06	644	664	0.3
84753	MODENA	021	32	33	38	0.3	16	16	17	20	0.7	1.88	13	13	0.0
84754	MONROE	041	3919	4395	4647	1.2	41	1323	1505	1598	1.4	2.91	1044	1158	1.1
84755	MOUNT CARMEL	025	17	22	24	2.8	76	8	10	12	2.4	2.20	6	8	3.2
84756	NEWCASTLE	021	365	380	443	0.4	19	102	111	130	0.9	3.41	81	86	0.6
84757	NEW HARMONY	053	229	295	345	2.8	76	81	107	126	3.1	2.76	71	91	2.7
84758	ORDERVILLE	025	631	813	907	2.8	76	207	276	312	3.2	2.95	156	203	2.9
84759	PANGUITCH	017	2185	2267	2308	0.4	19	696	734	752	0.6	2.95	542	556	0.3
84760	PARAGONAH	021	609	840	973	3.5	85	199	281	328	3.8	2.99	153	208	3.4
84761	PAROWAN	021	2642	3612	4176	3.4	82	912	1283	1501	3.8	2.78	698	948	3.4
84765	SANTA CLARA	053	4706	6963	8809	4.3	89	1282	1922	2457	4.5	3.62	1181	1754	4.4
84766	SEVIER	041	54	59	62	1.0	37	20	22	23	1.0	2.68	17	19	1.2
84770	SAINT GEORGE	053	30639	43911	52813	4.0	87	10785	16133	19688	4.4	2.67	7778	11183	4.0
84772	SUMMIT	021	275	378	438	3.5	85	102	143	167	3.7	2.63	78	106	3.4
84773	TEASDALE	055	217	222	224	0.2	12	92	97	99	0.6	2.29	66	67	0.2
84775	TORREY	055	747	764	772	0.2	12	292	307	314	0.5	2.49	211	214	0.2
84780	WASHINGTON	053	8140	17595	22672	8.7	98	2600	5698	7444	8.9	3.02	2107	4448	8.4
84781	PINE VALLEY	053	71	239	298	14.0	99	29	98	123	14.1	2.44	24	78	13.6
84782	VEYO	053	839	820	1005	-0.2	3	277	273	338	-0.2	3.00	235	222	-0.6
84783	DAMMERON VALLEY	053	255	443	533	6.2	96	86	160	195	6.9	2.77	74	132	6.5
84790	SAINT GEORGE	053	21280	37652	47862	6.4	96	7199	12953	16558	6.6	2.90	5812	10292	6.4
	UTAH					2.3					2.3	3.11			2.1
	UNITED STATES					1.0					1.1	2.59			0.9

ZIP CODE #	POST OFFICE NAME	RACE (%) White 2000	White 2009	Black 2000	Black 2009	Asian/Pacific 2000	Asian/Pacific 2009	% Hispanic Origin 2000	% Hispanic Origin 2009	2009 AGE DISTRIBUTION (%) 0-4	5-9	10-14	15-19	20-24	25-44	45-64	65-84	85+	18+	MEDIAN AGE 2009	% 2009 Males	% 2009 Females
84731	GREENVILLE	94.0	93.6	1.3	1.6	1.3	1.3	4.7	5.4	7.3	7.3	7.0	6.4	7.3	24.8	25.5	12.7	1.6	74.5	37.0	58.0	42.0
84734	HANKSVILLE	93.7	93.6	0.0	0.0	0.3	0.4	1.5	1.7	8.3	8.6	8.8	6.8	5.5	22.2	29.8	9.1	0.9	69.5	35.6	50.7	49.3
84737	HURRICANE	95.5	94.5	0.1	0.1	0.7	0.8	3.0	3.9	11.0	9.9	9.0	7.3	5.3	21.6	21.2	13.3	1.5	65.4	31.5	49.8	50.2
84738	IVINS	94.3	93.4	0.1	0.1	0.7	0.9	3.7	4.7	9.7	8.0	7.6	7.2	6.2	22.8	23.4	13.5	1.5	70.0	34.1	49.4	50.6
84739	JOSEPH	89.5	88.9	1.1	1.3	0.6	0.5	7.0	7.9	11.1	10.9	10.3	7.9	5.2	21.5	21.4	10.3	1.3	62.8	29.0	50.7	49.3
84741	KANAB	96.0	95.5	0.0	0.1	0.3	0.4	2.3	2.8	6.3	6.1	6.4	6.5	5.8	19.4	31.3	15.9	2.3	77.1	44.4	48.8	51.2
84743	KINGSTON	95.7	95.6	0.1	0.1	0.3	0.3	4.9	4.9	8.2	6.7	8.7	8.3	4.2	17.5	27.7	15.3	3.3	70.0	41.7	51.5	48.5
84745	LA VERKIN	94.4	93.2	0.1	0.1	0.3	0.3	4.4	5.7	9.7	9.0	9.3	8.7	6.3	24.5	21.3	9.7	1.6	66.6	30.2	49.9	50.1
84747	LOA	98.4	98.3	0.3	0.3	0.3	0.3	2.1	2.1	10.9	10.6	10.2	7.9	4.4	23.5	21.7	8.9	1.9	62.8	29.8	50.9	49.1
84750	MARYSVALE	95.5	95.3	0.2	0.2	0.2	0.2	3.5	3.8	7.6	7.8	8.0	7.6	3.6	21.4	25.4	16.3	2.2	71.2	39.6	53.1	46.9
84751	MILFORD	92.1	90.5	0.0	0.0	1.0	1.2	6.0	7.5	11.2	9.9	9.6	8.7	7.1	22.4	20.3	9.1	1.7	63.1	27.7	51.1	48.9
84753	MODENA	87.9	87.9	0.0	0.0	0.0	0.0	9.1	9.1	12.1	12.1	9.1	9.1	6.1	24.2	27.3	0.0	0.0	57.6	26.3	51.5	48.5
84754	MONROE	95.2	94.7	0.3	0.4	0.3	0.3	3.2	3.7	8.5	8.6	8.3	7.8	5.3	22.5	25.2	12.1	1.7	69.6	34.6	50.0	50.0
84755	MOUNT CARMEL	100.0	100.0	0.0	0.0	0.0	0.0	0.0	0.0	9.1	9.1	9.1	9.1	9.1	27.3	27.3	0.0	0.0	63.6	27.5	50.0	50.0
84756	NEWCASTLE	89.3	87.4	0.8	0.8	0.0	0.0	8.8	11.1	10.3	9.7	8.7	8.4	6.8	24.2	22.6	8.4	0.8	65.5	29.3	51.6	48.4
84757	NEW HARMONY	96.1	95.3	0.0	0.0	0.0	0.0	4.4	5.4	5.1	5.4	8.1	7.8	3.7	17.6	34.9	15.9	1.4	75.6	46.5	51.5	48.5
84758	ORDERVILLE	97.8	97.5	0.0	0.0	0.0	0.0	2.4	2.7	7.7	7.6	8.0	8.5	6.4	21.4	26.2	12.5	1.6	71.5	35.8	51.5	48.5
84759	PANGUITCH	94.4	93.5	0.4	0.5	0.4	0.5	2.8	3.5	8.1	8.5	8.3	6.8	5.1	24.8	25.2	11.7	1.4	70.5	34.8	51.5	48.5
84760	PARAGONAH	96.2	95.7	0.3	0.4	0.3	0.2	4.6	5.4	6.0	7.4	9.2	7.3	5.7	19.3	30.1	13.0	2.1	72.9	41.4	53.8	46.2
84761	PAROWAN	96.4	95.6	0.0	0.0	0.3	0.4	3.1	3.9	7.3	7.5	7.6	7.4	5.5	22.4	26.5	13.1	2.7	72.4	37.9	49.5	50.5
84765	SANTA CLARA	96.7	96.2	0.1	0.1	0.8	0.8	2.2	2.7	10.3	9.3	9.1	9.1	7.2	25.5	20.8	7.9	0.9	65.9	27.8	51.5	48.5
84766	SEVIER	88.9	88.1	1.9	1.7	0.0	0.0	7.4	6.8	10.2	10.2	10.2	6.8	5.1	23.7	22.0	11.9	0.0	62.7	30.6	49.2	50.8
84770	SAINT GEORGE	90.8	89.0	0.3	0.3	1.1	1.3	8.4	10.3	9.7	7.9	6.7	7.5	7.9	26.0	18.5	12.7	2.9	71.9	30.7	48.6	51.4
84772	SUMMIT	96.7	95.5	0.0	0.3	0.0	0.5	3.6	4.5	6.6	7.4	8.2	7.4	5.6	20.9	28.6	13.0	2.4	72.5	40.0	51.3	48.7
84773	TEASDALE	97.2	97.3	0.0	0.0	0.0	0.0	2.3	2.3	6.3	6.3	6.8	5.9	4.1	23.4	28.8	16.2	2.3	76.6	42.5	51.4	48.6
84775	TORREY	97.5	97.5	0.0	0.0	0.1	0.1	2.4	2.4	6.3	6.4	6.5	6.0	4.3	23.2	29.2	16.1	2.0	77.0	42.4	50.9	49.1
84780	WASHINGTON	94.2	93.7	0.4	0.4	0.4	0.5	4.8	5.6	9.4	8.3	7.4	6.6	6.1	27.3	21.1	11.9	1.9	70.9	33.0	49.7	50.3
84781	PINE VALLEY	97.2	97.1	0.0	0.0	0.0	0.4	1.4	2.1	5.9	5.9	6.3	6.3	4.2	20.9	32.6	17.2	0.8	77.8	45.4	51.0	49.0
84782	VEYO	91.9	91.8	0.0	0.1	0.6	0.7	2.6	2.8	6.8	6.5	8.7	7.0	4.0	20.7	30.6	14.5	1.2	73.4	42.1	50.5	49.5
84783	DAMMERON VALLEY	89.8	88.0	0.0	0.0	0.4	0.9	3.1	3.6	7.9	7.0	10.2	7.7	4.1	21.0	28.9	12.0	1.4	70.0	38.5	49.7	50.3
84790	SAINT GEORGE	95.0	94.4	0.1	0.1	1.1	1.3	3.8	4.4	7.7	6.9	6.9	7.2	6.1	21.3	25.1	16.6	2.2	74.3	39.5	48.6	51.4
	UTAH	89.2	87.6	0.8	0.9	2.3	2.6	9.0	10.5	9.7	8.7	8.1	8.6	8.6	28.5	19.6	7.1	1.2	68.6	28.8	50.1	49.9
	UNITED STATES	75.1	72.0	12.3	12.7	3.8	4.6	12.5	15.7	6.8	6.7	6.6	7.1	6.9	27.0	26.0	10.9	1.9	75.7	36.9	49.2	50.8

ZIP CODE #	POST OFFICE NAME	2009 Per Capita Income	2009 HH Income Base	2009 HOUSEHOLD INCOME DISTRIBUTION (%) Less than $25,000	$25,000 to $49,999	$50,000 to $99,999	$100,000 to $149,999	$150,000 or More	MEDIAN HOUSEHOLD INCOME 2009	2014	2009 National Centile	2009 State Centile	2009 Home Value Base	2009 HOME VALUE DISTRIBUTION (%) Less than $50,000	$50,000 to $89,999	$90,000 to $174,999	$175,000 to $399,999	$400,000 or More	2009 Median Home Value
84731	GREENVILLE	10549	42	28.6	31.0	33.3	2.4	4.8	40000	47347	33	24	36	5.6	11.1	58.3	13.9	11.1	133333
84734	HANKSVILLE	19377	350	31.4	28.9	35.1	4.6	0.0	38506	41211	28	17	223	9.4	13.9	38.1	29.6	9.0	147917
84737	HURRICANE	16544	6665	24.6	34.7	34.5	4.3	1.9	40905	45114	36	26	4871	9.2	6.4	28.9	43.2	12.2	185603
84738	IVINS	20711	2544	14.5	33.5	41.8	6.3	3.9	51072	53342	64	51	2235	1.8	1.3	31.4	55.6	9.9	192344
84739	JOSEPH	13976	184	28.3	36.4	31.0	3.8	0.5	41908	43880	39	28	154	9.1	8.4	42.9	37.7	1.9	148077
84741	KANAB	20161	1938	21.3	36.0	35.7	5.4	1.7	42828	44899	42	31	1552	8.1	9.0	42.3	38.1	2.5	153012
84743	KINGSTON	15004	331	32.0	34.1	29.0	3.6	1.2	36704	38731	23	13	283	13.8	21.9	45.2	17.3	1.8	111436
84745	LA VERKIN	15517	1660	24.0	34.0	37.0	3.7	1.3	43058	46948	43	32	1316	6.8	6.2	36.6	44.7	5.7	175486
84747	LOA	17275	389	32.6	27.2	31.6	6.2	2.3	42630	44566	41	31	320	3.1	8.8	60.0	26.3	1.9	136885
84750	MARYSVALE	17534	174	31.0	31.6	32.8	2.3	2.3	36744	37011	23	14	154	11.0	23.4	48.1	11.7	5.8	109483
84751	MILFORD	17246	893	26.0	29.0	38.2	5.4	1.5	45415	46777	49	38	704	10.2	16.9	60.2	10.5	2.1	114265
84753	MODENA	19564	17	35.3	35.3	29.4	0.0	0.0	36079	37292	21	12	12	8.3	0.0	58.3	33.3	0.0	145000
84754	MONROE	16403	1505	28.0	37.3	30.4	2.6	1.7	38738	41317	29	19	1303	7.5	10.4	51.3	28.3	2.5	140348
84755	MOUNT CARMEL	18182	10	30.0	40.0	30.0	0.0	0.0	35000	40000	18	11	8	0.0	12.5	75.0	12.5	0.0	133333
84756	NEWCASTLE	12321	111	35.1	27.9	33.3	3.6	0.0	36105	37827	21	12	79	20.3	8.9	46.8	22.8	1.3	131250
84757	NEW HARMONY	22046	107	25.2	20.6	41.1	7.5	5.6	53626	54416	69	56	94	3.2	4.3	10.6	59.6	22.3	295000
84758	ORDERVILLE	15147	276	27.9	35.5	33.7	1.8	1.1	39729	42124	32	21	229	4.4	15.3	54.6	18.3	7.4	133088
84759	PANGUITCH	16478	734	24.0	32.4	37.6	5.4	0.5	44667	46082	47	36	615	5.4	20.5	54.6	17.2	2.3	122185
84760	PARAGONAH	17026	281	27.4	32.0	32.7	3.2	4.6	38304	41348	28	17	241	0.8	17.0	47.3	30.3	4.6	150338
84761	PAROWAN	16940	1283	27.0	37.3	29.3	4.8	1.6	37549	39630	25	14	1027	2.2	3.0	48.4	42.6	3.7	169581
84765	SANTA CLARA	20369	1922	8.1	19.4	54.0	14.2	4.4	65461	65949	84	79	1698	0.1	0.4	10.1	78.3	11.2	243473
84766	SEVIER	16952	22	31.8	36.4	27.3	4.5	0.0	40000	40703	33	24	18	5.6	5.6	50.0	38.9	0.0	150000
84770	SAINT GEORGE	19615	16133	24.9	33.1	34.0	4.8	3.3	42393	46716	41	29	9694	5.2	3.9	33.7	49.6	7.5	187582
84772	SUMMIT	18573	143	27.3	35.0	31.5	3.5	2.8	37868	39828	26	15	118	0.0	9.3	49.2	37.3	4.2	161842
84773	TEASDALE	20658	97	23.7	37.1	32.0	6.2	1.0	39140	39211	30	20	77	3.9	6.5	44.2	32.5	13.0	160417
84775	TORREY	19052	307	24.1	37.1	32.2	5.5	1.0	38672	39827	29	18	243	5.3	6.6	41.6	32.9	13.6	164375
84780	WASHINGTON	17795	5698	20.7	34.1	37.3	4.9	3.0	45189	50159	49	37	4702	3.4	5.1	39.2	45.3	7.0	178356
84781	PINE VALLEY	29057	98	21.4	18.4	40.8	11.2	8.2	56658	56719	74	62	89	0.0	2.2	19.1	69.7	9.0	238636
84782	VEYO	20494	273	21.6	25.3	38.5	9.2	5.5	51967	53504	66	54	239	2.9	4.6	20.9	56.1	15.5	245370
84783	DAMMERON VALLEY	19747	160	20.6	31.3	36.9	7.5	3.8	47387	51417	55	46	137	5.1	6.6	20.4	46.0	21.9	261667
84790	SAINT GEORGE	23391	12953	14.7	29.5	42.4	8.1	5.2	54638	57714	71	59	10673	2.1	1.0	14.7	65.9	16.4	240872
	UTAH	23420		14.7	23.9	42.1	12.6	6.7	60286	62873				3.1	3.0	25.7	56.7	11.5	213546
	UNITED STATES	27277		20.9	24.4	35.3	11.7	7.6	54719	56938				9.3	13.1	31.6	32.6	13.5	162279

ZIP CODE		FINANCIAL SERVICES				THE HOME						ENTERTAINMENT						PERSONAL			
						Home Improvements		Furnishings													
#	POST OFFICE NAME	Auto Loan	Home Loan	Invest-ments	Retire-ment Plans	Home Repair	Lawn & Garden	Comput-ers & Hard-ware-Personal	Major Appli-ances	TV, Radio, Sound Equip-ment	Furni-ture	Dine out/ Carry out	Sports Equip-ment	Fees & Tickets	Toys & Games	Travel	Cable TV	Apparel & Services	Auto Repairs	Health Insur-ance	Pets & Supplies
84731	GREENVILLE	114	80	128	80	85	120	88	109	91	73	90	89	66	89	88	99	59	102	114	133
84734	HANKSVILLE	76	59	83	58	62	77	59	73	63	57	63	54	51	63	61	68	42	68	74	86
84737	HURRICANE	80	70	82	67	73	81	67	78	71	69	70	55	63	70	69	75	47	74	81	91
84738	IVINS	92	86	86	85	88	92	84	89	86	86	86	65	81	87	83	89	59	87	93	105
84739	JOSEPH	70	64	63	66	65	75	63	71	65	57	64	54	58	66	63	69	43	65	73	82
84741	KANAB	81	70	93	68	74	84	70	81	72	69	71	59	63	70	73	76	48	77	83	95
84743	KINGSTON	78	53	85	53	56	82	59	74	62	48	61	61	43	60	59	67	40	69	78	91
84745	LA VERKIN	78	70	72	68	70	76	67	74	69	68	69	54	62	71	65	72	47	71	74	87
84747	LOA	93	64	103	64	67	99	71	89	74	58	73	73	52	73	71	81	48	83	94	109
84750	MARYSVALE	79	54	87	54	57	83	60	75	63	49	62	62	44	62	60	68	40	70	79	92
84751	MILFORD	87	69	87	69	69	92	73	83	75	63	75	68	61	75	72	80	50	80	90	102
84753	MODENA	67	50	55	48	49	64	51	59	56	50	55	45	42	59	47	61	37	56	62	71
84754	MONROE	84	62	85	60	64	85	63	79	69	59	68	59	52	69	62	76	45	73	82	94
84755	MOUNT CARMEL	71	51	75	50	54	72	53	67	58	49	57	50	42	57	53	64	38	61	69	79
84756	NEWCASTLE	75	55	62	53	55	71	57	65	63	55	61	50	46	65	52	68	41	62	69	79
84757	NEW HARMONY	101	81	131	80	89	107	81	103	85	76	84	75	70	81	88	91	56	95	102	120
84758	ORDERVILLE	79	57	83	55	60	81	59	75	65	55	64	56	47	64	58	71	42	68	77	89
84759	PANGUITCH	82	64	103	63	70	87	65	83	68	59	68	62	55	65	70	73	45	76	83	97
84760	PARAGONAH	85	68	110	67	75	90	68	86	71	64	70	63	59	68	74	76	47	80	85	100
84761	PAROWAN	84	60	87	58	63	85	62	79	69	58	67	59	50	68	61	75	45	72	82	94
84765	SANTA CLARA	108	119	99	117	113	106	106	107	102	111	103	85	110	107	107	99	72	103	100	124
84766	SEVIER	70	64	63	67	65	76	63	71	65	57	64	54	58	66	63	69	44	66	74	83
84770	SAINT GEORGE	77	72	71	72	72	74	76	74	76	76	76	56	72	76	73	76	52	76	77	88
84772	SUMMIT	85	64	97	62	68	87	65	82	70	60	69	61	54	68	67	76	46	76	83	97
84773	TEASDALE	79	63	102	62	69	83	63	80	66	59	65	59	55	63	68	70	43	74	79	93
84775	TORREY	79	63	102	62	70	84	63	81	66	59	65	59	55	63	69	71	44	74	79	93
84780	WASHINGTON	81	79	81	76	80	82	75	81	76	79	76	58	73	76	76	78	52	78	83	93
84781	PINE VALLEY	118	95	153	93	104	125	95	120	99	89	98	88	82	94	103	106	65	111	119	139
84782	VEYO	102	82	132	81	90	108	82	104	86	77	85	76	71	82	89	92	57	96	103	121
84783	DAMMERON VALLEY	91	74	116	72	80	95	73	92	76	69	76	68	64	73	79	81	50	85	91	107
84790	SAINT GEORGE	95	102	108	102	106	105	94	100	94	99	94	72	99	92	100	95	65	97	102	115
	UTAH	107	107	98	107	104	101	106	103	103	108	104	81	105	106	103	102	73	103	99	121
	UNITED STATES	100	100	100	100	100	100	100	100	100	100	100	100	100	100	100	100	100	100	100	100

05001-05440

ZIP CODE #	POST OFFICE NAME	COUNTY FIPS CODE	POPULATION 2000	POPULATION 2009	POPULATION 2014	2000-2009 ANNUAL RATE % Rate	2000-2009 ANNUAL RATE State Centile	HOUSEHOLDS 2000	HOUSEHOLDS 2009	HOUSEHOLDS 2014	HOUSEHOLDS % Annual Rate 2000-2009	HOUSEHOLDS 2009 Average HH Size	FAMILIES 2000	FAMILIES 2009	FAMILIES % Annual Rate 2000-2009
05001	WHITE RIVER JUNCTION	027	10481	10635	10506	0.2	37	4552	4795	4787	0.6	2.20	2829	2908	0.3
05032	BETHEL	027	2558	2386	2307	-0.7	2	1057	1025	1001	-0.3	2.33	712	674	-0.6
05033	BRADFORD	017	2792	3022	3122	0.9	81	1096	1239	1296	1.3	2.38	742	819	1.1
05034	BRIDGEWATER	027	118	119	117	0.1	32	49	51	51	0.4	2.33	31	32	0.3
05035	BRIDGEWATER CORNERS	027	481	486	480	0.1	32	194	203	202	0.5	2.39	124	127	0.3
05036	BROOKFIELD	017	940	883	862	-0.7	2	377	370	366	-0.2	2.37	278	269	-0.4
05037	BROWNSVILLE	027	566	589	585	0.4	52	232	250	251	0.8	2.33	166	176	0.6
05038	CHELSEA	017	1223	1198	1191	-0.2	15	481	498	501	0.4	2.32	317	320	0.1
05039	CORINTH	017	1147	1228	1264	0.7	70	423	475	496	1.3	2.59	325	359	1.1
05040	EAST CORINTH	017	464	493	504	0.7	70	169	187	194	1.1	2.64	128	140	1.0
05041	EAST RANDOLPH	017	220	229	233	0.4	52	86	95	99	1.1	1.72	61	66	0.9
05042	EAST RYEGATE	005	592	568	555	-0.4	8	228	230	226	0.1	2.46	169	167	-0.1
05043	EAST THETFORD	017	672	718	733	0.7	70	268	294	304	1.0	2.44	187	201	0.8
05045	FAIRLEE	017	1646	1768	1818	0.8	75	665	741	772	1.2	2.37	457	498	0.9
05046	GROTON	005	1033	1296	1397	2.5	100	402	529	576	3.0	2.45	298	383	2.8
05048	HARTLAND	027	1972	2026	2006	0.3	44	779	829	829	0.7	2.44	560	585	0.5
05051	NEWBURY	017	731	731	721	0.0	25	302	308	307	0.2	2.34	190	188	-0.1
05052	NORTH HARTLAND	027	314	335	335	0.7	70	113	125	126	1.1	2.68	80	87	0.9
05053	NORTH POMFRET	027	274	263	256	-0.4	8	100	99	97	-0.1	2.66	71	70	-0.2
05055	NORWICH	027	3507	3774	3775	0.8	75	1351	1487	1500	1.0	2.54	933	1007	0.8
05056	PLYMOUTH	027	306	323	321	0.6	64	140	152	153	0.9	2.13	94	100	0.7
05058	POST MILLS	017	333	361	373	0.9	81	128	143	149	1.2	2.52	91	100	1.0
05060	RANDOLPH	017	4618	4644	4639	0.1	32	1874	1965	1990	0.5	2.34	1209	1233	0.2
05061	RANDOLPH CENTER	017	1570	1624	1648	0.4	52	425	463	478	0.9	2.65	300	320	0.7
05062	READING	027	704	667	646	-0.6	3	288	280	273	-0.3	2.38	206	196	-0.5
05065	SHARON	027	955	971	958	0.2	37	375	393	393	0.5	2.47	257	265	0.3
05067	SOUTH POMFRET	027	170	163	159	-0.5	5	69	68	67	-0.2	2.40	49	48	-0.2
05068	SOUTH ROYALTON	027	3192	3310	3294	0.4	52	1396	1501	1507	0.8	2.20	799	831	0.4
05069	SOUTH RYEGATE	017	832	806	791	-0.3	11	315	320	318	0.2	2.52	235	234	0.0
05070	SOUTH STRAFFORD	017	401	435	449	0.9	81	162	184	192	1.4	2.36	114	127	1.2
05071	SOUTH WOODSTOCK	027	359	364	361	0.1	32	156	165	165	0.6	2.18	105	108	0.3
05072	STRAFFORD	017	579	633	658	1.0	84	238	273	287	1.5	2.32	168	189	1.3
05073	TAFTSVILLE	027	38	38	38	0.0	25	15	16	16	0.7	2.31	9	10	1.1
05075	THETFORD CENTER	017	1499	1624	1674	0.9	81	582	649	676	1.2	2.50	415	454	1.0
05076	TOPSHAM	017	524	522	519	0.0	25	193	200	201	0.4	2.61	149	151	0.1
05077	TUNBRIDGE	017	1174	1236	1263	0.6	64	462	508	527	1.0	2.43	325	350	0.8
05079	VERSHIRE	017	582	558	547	-0.5	5	241	241	239	0.0	2.31	161	157	-0.3
05081	WELLS RIVER	017	773	755	748	-0.3	11	335	343	344	0.3	2.20	230	231	0.0
05083	WEST FAIRLEE	017	258	274	281	0.7	70	101	111	115	1.0	2.47	71	76	0.7
05084	WEST HARTFORD	027	164	157	153	-0.5	5	60	60	58	0.0	2.62	43	42	-0.3
05086	WEST TOPSHAM	017	835	865	878	0.4	52	308	334	342	0.9	2.59	236	251	0.7
05089	WINDSOR	027	5193	5122	5032	-0.1	19	2147	2192	2173	0.2	2.21	1380	1377	0.0
05091	WOODSTOCK	027	4196	4127	4052	-0.2	15	1767	1801	1784	0.2	2.23	1139	1134	0.0
05101	BELLOWS FALLS	025	5005	5098	5046	0.2	37	2063	2188	2193	0.6	2.31	1287	1326	0.3
05141	CAMBRIDGEPORT	025	101	100	96	-0.1	19	39	40	39	0.3	2.50	28	28	0.0
05142	CAVENDISH	027	801	817	808	0.2	37	335	356	355	0.7	2.28	233	243	0.5
05143	CHESTER	027	4699	4667	4593	-0.1	19	1995	2067	2056	0.4	2.25	1327	1344	0.1
05146	GRAFTON	025	540	566	571	0.5	57	238	261	267	1.0	2.17	153	163	0.7
05148	LONDONDERRY	003	1298	1270	1247	-0.2	15	520	521	516	0.0	2.44	350	343	-0.2
05149	LUDLOW	027	2685	2996	3030	1.2	91	1167	1359	1390	1.7	2.16	730	830	1.4
05150	NORTH SPRINGFIELD	027	805	825	817	0.3	44	352	376	377	0.7	2.10	229	238	0.4
05151	PERKINSVILLE	027	1469	1457	1434	-0.1	19	611	630	625	0.3	2.31	432	437	0.1
05152	PERU	003	163	160	156	-0.2	15	60	59	58	-0.2	2.71	44	42	-0.5
05153	PROCTORSVILLE	027	749	747	734	0.0	25	314	324	322	0.3	2.30	220	223	0.1
05154	SAXTONS RIVER	025	343	340	327	-0.1	19	133	136	133	0.2	2.50	97	97	0.0
05155	SOUTH LONDONDERRY	025	885	853	839	-0.4	8	404	405	403	0.0	2.11	258	253	-0.2
05156	SPRINGFIELD	027	8990	8812	8627	-0.2	15	3820	3879	3835	0.2	2.26	2487	2470	-0.1
05158	WESTMINSTER	025	849	865	866	0.2	37	326	347	351	0.7	2.49	221	230	0.4
05161	WESTON	027	571	542	526	-0.6	3	248	245	241	-0.1	2.17	160	153	-0.5
05201	BENNINGTON	003	15325	14938	14555	-0.3	11	6140	6242	6140	0.2	2.27	3884	3855	-0.1
05250	ARLINGTON	003	3277	3550	3594	0.9	81	1374	1547	1582	1.3	2.29	936	1030	1.0
05251	DORSET	003	1448	1592	1630	1.0	84	626	706	729	1.3	2.25	440	485	1.1
05252	EAST ARLINGTON	003	332	375	385	1.3	92	138	161	167	1.7	2.33	96	110	1.5
05253	EAST DORSET	003	588	646	662	1.0	84	230	260	268	1.3	2.48	161	178	1.1
05255	MANCHESTER CENTER	003	4184	4425	4457	0.6	64	1822	1989	2025	1.0	2.19	1159	1230	0.6
05257	NORTH BENNINGTON	003	2721	2816	2816	0.4	52	927	1003	1014	0.9	2.42	639	676	0.6
05260	NORTH POWNAL	003	380	389	389	0.3	44	124	132	134	0.7	2.95	87	91	0.5
05261	POWNAL	003	2480	2514	2499	0.1	32	971	1016	1019	0.5	2.47	717	735	0.3
05262	SHAFTSBURY	003	2588	2710	2710	0.5	57	1001	1088	1099	0.9	2.49	743	791	0.7
05301	BRATTLEBORO	025	16620	16235	15956	-0.3	11	7152	7261	7207	0.2	2.15	4115	4068	-0.1
05340	BONDVILLE	003	592	657	672	1.1	89	261	296	305	1.4	2.22	173	191	1.1
05341	EAST DOVER	025	358	377	381	0.6	64	141	156	160	1.1	2.42	86	93	0.8
05342	JACKSONVILLE	025	710	719	707	0.1	32	288	303	302	0.6	2.37	205	212	0.4
05343	JAMAICA	025	914	868	854	-0.6	3	405	401	400	-0.1	2.16	242	234	-0.4
05345	NEWFANE	025	1532	1603	1616	0.5	57	628	683	697	0.9	2.35	420	446	0.7
05346	PUTNEY	025	5276	5442	5455	0.3	44	2030	2180	2210	0.8	2.36	1328	1388	0.5
05350	READSBORO	003	809	825	800	0.2	37	321	337	330	0.5	2.38	225	231	0.3
05351	SOUTH NEWFANE	025	301	303	302	0.1	32	129	136	137	0.6	2.03	86	89	0.4
05352	STAMFORD	003	813	849	852	0.5	57	313	338	343	0.8	2.51	235	249	0.6
05353	TOWNSHEND	025	1040	1006	966	-0.4	8	420	422	410	0.1	2.32	286	280	-0.2
05354	VERNON	025	2141	2198	2201	0.3	44	741	785	794	0.6	2.68	574	598	0.4
05355	WARDSBORO	025	703	733	740	0.5	57	296	322	329	0.9	2.28	195	206	0.6
05356	WEST DOVER	025	1057	1116	1131	0.6	64	472	523	537	1.1	2.13	287	309	0.8
05358	WEST HALIFAX	025	246	247	240	0.0	25	94	97	96	0.3	2.55	63	64	0.2
05359	WEST TOWNSHEND	025	492	483	476	-0.2	15	213	220	219	0.4	2.18	137	138	0.1
05360	WEST WARDSBORO	025	228	235	236	0.3	44	98	106	107	0.9	2.22	61	64	0.5
05361	WHITINGHAM	025	755	772	766	0.2	37	300	320	322	0.7	2.41	216	226	0.5
05362	WILLIAMSVILLE	025	292	295	294	0.1	32	117	124	125	0.6	2.38	80	82	0.3
05363	WILMINGTON	025	2302	2437	2469	0.6	64	1025	1132	1160	1.1	2.14	621	666	0.8
05401	BURLINGTON	007	27976	29000	29162	0.4	52	11828	12682	12890	0.8	2.00	4289	4410	0.3
05403	SOUTH BURLINGTON	007	15742	17498	18366	1.1	89	6294	7159	7538	1.4	2.31	3763	4191	1.2
05404	WINOOSKI	007	6561	6586	6571	0.0	25	2944	3036	3056	0.3	2.15	1467	1451	-0.1
05405	BURLINGTON	007	515	534	541	0.4	52	9	10	11	1.1	2.60	3	3	0.0
05408	BURLINGTON	007	10513	10343	10237	-0.2	15	4097	4162	4159	0.2	2.41	2791	2758	-0.1
05440	ALBURGH	013	1952	2318	2498	1.9	99	791	979	1065	2.3	2.37	529	641	2.1
	VERMONT					0.4					0.8	2.36			0.5
	UNITED STATES					1.0					1.1	2.59			0.9

ZIP CODE		RACE (%)						% Hispanic Origin		2009 AGE DISTRIBUTION (%)										MEDIAN AGE		
#	POST OFFICE NAME	White 2000	White 2009	Black 2000	Black 2009	Asian/Pacific 2000	Asian/Pacific 2009	2000	2009	0-4	5-9	10-14	15-19	20-24	25-44	45-64	65-84	85+	18+	2009	% 2009 Males	% 2009 Females
05001	WHITE RIVER JUNCTION	97.0	96.4	0.5	0.7	0.9	1.3	0.8	1.1	5.3	5.1	5.4	6.3	6.5	24.5	31.2	13.5	2.1	80.8	42.8	47.6	52.4
05032	BETHEL	98.1	97.8	0.2	0.3	0.4	0.5	1.1	1.4	5.5	6.1	6.4	5.8	5.9	23.9	32.5	12.2	1.8	78.4	42.5	49.0	51.0
05033	BRADFORD	97.7	97.4	0.5	0.6	0.4	0.5	0.6	0.7	5.7	6.4	7.1	6.6	5.3	22.8	30.2	13.1	2.8	76.0	42.1	47.7	52.3
05034	BRIDGEWATER	98.3	98.3	0.0	0.0	0.8	0.8	0.0	0.0	4.2	5.0	6.7	6.7	3.4	25.2	36.1	10.9	1.7	79.0	44.3	52.1	47.9
05035	BRIDGEWATER CORNERS	98.8	98.4	0.0	0.0	0.4	0.8	0.0	0.0	4.3	5.1	6.2	6.2	4.1	25.1	34.0	12.8	2.3	79.6	44.4	51.0	49.0
05036	BROOKFIELD	97.6	97.1	0.2	0.2	1.0	1.5	0.1	0.1	5.0	5.9	6.7	6.8	4.4	23.9	33.9	12.3	1.1	78.3	43.1	49.8	50.2
05037	BROWNSVILLE	98.2	98.3	0.4	0.3	0.2	0.2	1.4	1.7	4.4	5.1	5.1	6.8	3.2	20.0	39.6	14.6	1.2	80.5	47.1	50.4	49.6
05038	CHELSEA	98.1	97.8	0.2	0.3	0.1	0.2	0.4	0.5	4.9	5.3	6.1	6.3	4.4	20.8	34.9	13.6	3.6	83.1	46.3	50.7	49.3
05039	CORINTH	98.8	98.6	0.2	0.2	0.0	0.0	1.0	1.3	5.5	5.9	6.4	7.3	5.6	22.6	31.8	13.5	1.5	77.8	42.7	49.7	50.3
05040	EAST CORINTH	98.5	98.2	0.2	0.4	0.4	0.4	0.6	0.8	5.3	6.5	7.1	7.3	4.9	23.5	31.6	12.4	1.4	76.3	42.0	49.5	50.5
05041	EAST RANDOLPH	96.8	96.5	0.5	0.4	0.9	1.3	0.5	0.4	3.9	5.2	5.2	17.9	16.6	18.8	23.6	7.4	1.3	81.7	26.4	57.6	42.4
05042	EAST RYEGATE	98.3	98.1	0.2	0.2	0.3	0.5	0.2	0.4	4.0	6.5	7.6	7.2	4.8	21.5	33.1	13.6	1.8	77.1	43.9	51.6	48.4
05043	EAST THETFORD	97.9	97.6	0.4	0.6	0.4	0.6	0.6	0.7	5.7	6.4	7.4	7.1	4.5	24.9	33.7	8.9	1.4	76.5	41.1	49.4	50.6
05045	FAIRLEE	97.6	97.3	0.2	0.3	0.5	0.7	0.5	0.6	5.8	6.5	6.8	6.6	4.8	25.6	29.9	12.6	1.5	76.9	41.8	49.3	50.7
05046	GROTON	96.8	96.6	0.0	0.1	0.1	0.1	0.4	0.5	5.7	6.3	7.0	7.3	5.1	22.5	30.6	13.9	1.6	76.5	42.3	47.7	52.3
05048	HARTLAND	98.6	98.3	0.1	0.1	0.4	0.7	0.7	0.9	4.7	5.7	7.1	7.4	5.0	23.7	34.1	11.2	1.1	77.5	42.9	50.0	50.0
05051	NEWBURY	97.7	97.4	0.1	0.1	0.1	0.1	0.1	0.1	4.8	6.3	7.0	8.1	4.1	21.1	31.1	16.1	1.5	80.4	44.2	48.8	51.2
05052	NORTH HARTLAND	99.0	97.9	0.0	0.3	0.3	0.9	0.6	0.6	5.1	5.7	6.3	8.1	6.3	24.2	33.1	9.9	1.5	77.9	41.7	48.7	51.3
05053	NORTH POMFRET	98.5	97.7	0.0	0.0	0.7	1.1	1.5	1.5	4.9	6.1	7.6	6.1	2.7	21.3	36.9	13.7	0.8	81.4	45.6	48.7	51.3
05055	NORWICH	96.0	94.8	0.5	0.7	1.6	2.4	0.8	1.1	4.5	4.8	5.9	7.3	6.5	20.6	36.2	12.6	1.6	80.4	45.2	48.9	51.1
05056	PLYMOUTH	99.3	99.1	0.3	0.6	0.0	0.0	0.0	0.0	4.0	4.0	4.6	4.6	3.1	19.5	35.9	21.7	2.5	84.8	50.6	52.3	47.7
05058	POST MILLS	97.6	97.2	0.3	0.6	0.6	0.8	0.3	0.3	6.1	6.6	7.5	6.4	4.4	24.4	33.2	10.5	0.8	75.9	41.4	48.5	51.5
05060	RANDOLPH	98.0	97.6	0.1	0.2	0.6	0.8	0.5	0.8	5.7	5.7	6.6	6.9	6.1	23.4	30.2	12.6	2.7	77.4	41.7	47.9	52.1
05061	RANDOLPH CENTER	97.5	97.0	0.3	0.5	0.8	1.0	0.6	0.7	4.1	5.0	5.5	16.2	15.3	19.8	24.3	8.4	1.4	81.7	29.5	56.2	43.8
05062	READING	98.4	98.4	0.4	0.4	0.1	0.1	1.0	1.3	5.2	6.4	6.9	5.5	2.7	23.8	34.5	13.6	1.2	78.3	44.6	48.1	51.9
05065	SHARON	97.3	96.8	0.5	0.7	0.6	0.9	0.9	1.3	5.9	6.4	7.1	7.0	5.9	23.6	34.3	9.2	0.7	76.3	41.2	50.3	49.7
05067	SOUTH POMFRET	97.7	97.5	0.0	0.0	1.2	1.2	1.2	1.8	5.5	6.1	8.0	6.1	2.5	20.9	35.6	14.1	1.2	80.4	45.4	49.1	50.9
05068	SOUTH ROYALTON	97.2	96.7	0.7	0.9	0.8	1.1	0.9	1.1	5.1	5.3	5.5	5.8	8.5	30.4	28.5	9.4	1.5	80.6	37.6	50.8	49.2
05069	SOUTH RYEGATE	97.7	97.4	0.4	0.4	0.4	0.6	0.1	0.1	4.7	6.5	7.2	6.7	4.2	22.6	32.9	13.9	1.4	77.2	43.9	51.1	48.9
05070	SOUTH STRAFFORD	98.5	98.4	0.3	0.2	0.3	0.5	0.5	0.7	5.5	7.8	7.4	6.9	2.1	24.1	34.5	11.0	0.7	74.5	42.8	50.1	49.9
05071	SOUTH WOODSTOCK	97.8	97.3	0.8	1.1	0.6	0.8	1.1	1.4	3.6	4.1	6.9	7.4	2.7	20.1	38.7	14.3	2.2	79.9	47.4	49.7	50.3
05072	STRAFFORD	98.3	98.1	0.2	0.3	0.3	0.5	0.5	0.6	5.4	8.1	7.4	7.0	1.6	24.2	34.4	11.4	0.6	74.1	43.0	50.2	49.8
05073	TAFTSVILLE	100.0	100.0	0.0	0.0	0.0	0.0	0.0	0.0	5.3	5.3	5.3	5.3	5.3	21.1	31.6	18.4	2.6	78.9	46.3	50.0	50.0
05075	THETFORD CENTER	97.6	97.1	0.4	0.6	0.6	1.0	0.5	0.6	5.8	6.8	7.5	6.5	4.2	23.5	34.7	10.0	0.9	75.9	42.0	48.6	51.4
05076	TOPSHAM	98.9	98.3	0.4	0.6	0.6	1.0	0.6	0.6	5.9	6.3	6.9	7.7	5.0	25.3	31.0	10.5	1.3	75.9	39.8	48.3	51.7
05077	TUNBRIDGE	99.0	98.9	0.3	0.3	0.2	0.2	0.9	1.2	5.7	7.4	7.4	4.4	3.9	27.6	29.8	11.7	2.0	76.5	40.3	49.8	50.2
05079	VERSHIRE	98.1	97.7	0.3	0.5	0.3	0.5	0.3	0.4	5.9	6.3	6.3	5.7	6.3	24.6	34.4	9.5	1.1	77.8	42.0	49.6	50.4
05081	WELLS RIVER	97.8	97.5	0.3	0.3	0.1	0.3	0.4	0.4	4.9	5.2	5.6	6.8	5.2	21.1	32.6	16.4	2.4	80.3	45.8	48.7	51.3
05083	WEST FAIRLEE	98.8	98.2	0.0	0.4	0.4	0.7	0.0	0.0	6.6	6.6	6.9	6.6	5.8	28.1	29.2	9.1	1.1	75.5	39.3	50.0	50.0
05084	WEST HARTFORD	98.2	97.5	0.0	0.0	1.2	1.3	1.2	1.9	5.1	6.4	7.6	6.4	2.5	20.4	35.7	14.6	1.3	80.9	45.8	50.3	49.7
05086	WEST TOPSHAM	98.4	98.3	0.2	0.3	0.5	0.6	0.8	1.0	5.9	6.5	6.8	6.8	5.1	24.3	31.9	11.4	1.3	76.5	41.1	48.8	51.2
05089	WINDSOR	98.0	97.8	0.2	0.2	0.3	0.4	1.0	1.2	4.8	5.0	5.3	6.3	5.7	22.4	30.6	16.0	3.9	80.7	45.3	48.4	51.6
05091	WOODSTOCK	98.2	97.7	0.3	0.4	0.6	0.9	0.7	0.9	3.7	4.3	6.0	6.2	3.5	20.9	36.8	15.5	3.3	81.9	47.9	49.0	51.0
05101	BELLOWS FALLS	97.3	96.6	0.3	0.5	0.6	0.9	1.1	1.5	5.9	5.7	6.0	6.5	6.5	23.8	30.5	12.5	2.6	78.3	41.6	48.8	51.2
05141	CAMBRIDGEPORT	99.0	98.0	0.0	0.0	0.0	1.0	1.0	1.0	5.0	5.0	5.0	6.0	4.0	18.0	40.0	15.0	2.0	82.0	48.2	48.0	52.0
05142	CAVENDISH	97.8	97.4	0.1	0.1	0.9	1.2	1.0	1.3	4.5	5.1	5.6	5.9	3.2	21.7	36.6	15.2	2.2	80.5	47.0	50.1	49.9
05143	CHESTER	98.5	98.2	0.3	0.4	0.3	0.5	0.8	1.0	4.6	5.5	6.1	6.8	4.3	21.9	33.8	14.9	2.1	79.3	45.4	49.3	50.7
05146	GRAFTON	98.0	97.7	0.2	0.2	0.4	0.5	0.9	1.2	4.8	5.5	5.5	4.4	3.2	19.8	36.2	18.7	1.9	81.4	49.1	52.5	47.5
05148	LONDONDERRY	98.5	98.2	0.1	0.1	0.5	0.7	0.5	0.6	5.1	6.6	5.9	6.2	3.1	23.4	33.1	14.8	1.8	78.3	44.8	50.6	49.4
05149	LUDLOW	98.5	98.2	0.2	0.3	0.4	0.6	0.2	0.3	4.4	5.0	5.5	5.7	4.7	21.9	34.0	16.0	2.7	81.3	46.6	49.7	50.3
05150	NORTH SPRINGFIELD	98.8	98.7	0.0	0.0	0.4	0.5	0.6	0.8	4.5	4.6	4.8	5.0	5.1	22.4	28.6	19.8	5.2	82.9	47.5	47.6	52.4
05151	PERKINSVILLE	98.4	98.2	0.1	0.2	0.2	0.3	0.8	1.0	4.7	5.7	5.9	5.4	3.2	23.1	35.9	13.6	2.5	80.1	46.0	49.1	50.9
05152	PERU	98.2	98.1	0.0	0.0	0.6	0.6	0.6	0.6	5.0	7.5	5.6	7.5	1.9	22.5	36.3	12.5	1.3	76.9	45.0	50.6	49.4
05153	PROCTORSVILLE	98.0	97.7	0.1	0.1	0.7	0.9	0.8	1.1	5.0	5.5	6.2	6.0	3.1	22.6	34.9	14.7	2.0	79.3	45.9	50.2	49.8
05154	SAXTONS RIVER	98.8	98.2	0.0	0.0	0.3	0.6	0.9	1.2	4.7	5.3	5.6	5.9	4.4	20.3	37.6	14.4	1.8	80.9	47.5	50.3	49.7
05155	SOUTH LONDONDERRY	98.5	98.1	0.1	0.2	0.5	0.7	0.5	0.6	5.0	6.0	6.0	5.4	3.6	24.0	32.4	15.5	2.1	79.4	45.0	51.3	48.7
05156	SPRINGFIELD	97.6	97.1	0.2	0.3	0.8	1.2	0.7	0.9	5.6	5.8	5.9	5.8	5.6	23.0	29.7	15.3	3.2	79.0	43.7	47.7	52.3
05158	WESTMINSTER	97.5	97.1	0.4	0.5	0.2	0.3	0.7	0.9	5.5	6.5	7.2	6.5	4.5	25.7	32.9	9.6	1.6	76.4	41.4	48.2	51.8
05161	WESTON	97.5	96.9	0.2	0.4	0.5	0.9	1.2	1.5	3.9	4.1	4.8	4.8	3.5	16.8	36.0	24.2	2.0	83.9	52.2	51.1	48.9
05201	BENNINGTON	97.3	96.5	0.6	0.8	0.8	1.2	0.9	1.2	5.7	5.7	5.9	7.1	6.9	23.5	27.4	14.4	3.5	78.5	41.4	47.0	53.0
05250	ARLINGTON	98.4	97.9	0.2	0.3	0.5	0.8	0.5	0.6	4.8	5.0	5.5	5.8	4.7	20.6	35.2	16.3	2.1	81.1	47.2	48.6	51.4
05251	DORSET	99.0	98.7	0.4	0.6	0.1	0.3	0.4	0.4	3.5	4.0	4.6	5.7	4.0	18.4	39.3	18.3	2.1	84.3	50.7	50.3	49.7
05252	EAST ARLINGTON	98.5	98.1	0.3	0.3	0.9	1.3	0.6	0.8	5.1	5.6	6.1	5.3	4.3	21.3	34.1	16.5	1.6	79.7	46.3	48.5	51.5
05253	EAST DORSET	98.8	98.8	0.5	0.5	0.2	0.3	0.3	0.6	3.6	3.9	4.6	5.7	4.0	18.3	39.6	18.3	2.0	84.4	50.7	50.2	49.8
05255	MANCHESTER CENTER	97.9	97.4	0.4	0.6	0.3	0.5	1.7	2.3	4.3	5.7	6.7	5.7	3.3	20.8	33.4	16.6	3.5	79.8	47.2	46.4	53.6
05257	NORTH BENNINGTON	96.6	95.6	0.5	0.6	1.4	2.1	1.0	1.3	4.9	4.9	5.5	10.8	12.4	20.0	26.3	12.7	2.6	80.5	37.8	45.2	54.8
05260	NORTH POWNAL	98.7	98.7	0.0	0.0	0.3	0.3	0.5	0.8	4.9	5.4	6.2	6.9	4.9	24.2	32.4	13.9	1.3	78.9	43.1	49.9	50.1
05261	POWNAL	97.5	96.8	0.3	0.5	0.7	1.1	0.4	0.5	5.5	6.0	6.5	6.8	4.8	23.9	32.7	12.6	1.2	77.7	42.3	51.3	48.7
05262	SHAFTSBURY	98.8	98.5	0.2	0.4	0.3	0.4	0.9	1.1	5.0	5.6	6.5	6.8	4.6	22.8	34.2	13.1	1.4	78.8	44.2	49.0	51.0
05301	BRATTLEBORO	95.0	93.7	0.8	1.1	1.4	2.1	1.4	1.8	4.8	4.9	5.4	6.9	6.6	23.7	31.7	12.9	3.1	80.7	43.3	47.2	52.8
05340	BONDVILLE	98.1	98.0	0.5	0.5	0.2	0.3	2.7	3.5	4.0	4.4	4.9	4.0	3.0	22.5	37.6	17.8	1.8	84.0	49.8	49.2	50.8
05341	EAST DOVER	98.0	97.3	0.0	0.0	0.8	1.3	1.1	1.6	5.6	4.2	5.6	6.4	5.6	25.2	33.7	13.0	0.8	80.4	43.2	52.5	47.5
05342	JACKSONVILLE	98.9	98.6	0.0	0.0	0.0	0.1	0.8	1.0	5.6	5.8	7.6	6.1	4.2	23.4	33.4	12.4	1.5	76.9	43.1	49.5	50.5
05343	JAMAICA	98.5	98.2	0.0	0.1	0.4	0.7	0.5	0.8	6.5	6.1	5.4	3.5	4.7	27.9	31.2	12.9	1.8	79.6	41.6	52.8	47.2
05345	NEWFANE	98.0	97.6	0.1	0.2	0.3	0.4	1.0	1.2	6.1	5.6	6.8	6.2	3.2	24.3	36.4	10.2	1.2	77.2	43.6	48.5	51.5
05346	PUTNEY	96.9	96.0	0.7	1.0	0.6	0.9	1.1	1.4	4.9	5.4	5.8	7.9	9.3	23.3	32.5	9.6	1.4	79.6	40.2	49.9	50.1
05350	READSBORO	98.8	98.5	0.0	0.0	0.2	0.4	1.1	1.3	5.2	4.7	5.0	6.7	8.2	20.5	30.3	16.8	2.5	84.8	44.7	49.8	50.2
05351	SOUTH NEWFANE	98.0	97.4	0.0	0.3	1.0	1.3	1.0	1.0	3.6	5.0	5.6	10.9	6.9	20.8	36.3	9.2	1.7	80.5	43.4	48.8	51.2
05352	STAMFORD	98.5	98.4	0.0	0.0	0.4	0.6	0.2	0.4	4.7	5.7	6.7	7.7	4.6	18.4	36.7	14.4	1.2	78.3	46.1	50.4	49.6
05353	TOWNSHEND	97.8	97.4	0.3	0.4	0.3	0.4	0.7	0.9	6.4	5.6	6.4	6.1	2.6	25.4	31.3	13.2	3.1	77.4	43.6	47.4	52.6
05354	VERNON	98.6	98.2	0.3	0.4	0.2	0.3	0.8	1.1	5.7	6.4	7.1	7.1	4.4	22.3	31.9	11.3	3.6	75.7	43.0	50.2	49.8
05355	WARDSBORO	98.4	98.0	0.4	0.5	0.1	0.3	0.6	0.7	5.5	6.3	6.4	5.7	4.4	24.7	35.5	11.2	0.4	78.2	43.3	52.4	47.6
05356	WEST DOVER	97.5	96.7	0.1	0.2	1.1	1.7	1.2	1.5	5.1	3.9	5.0	5.9	6.7	24.9	34.5	13.1	0.8	82.3	43.7	51.6	48.4
05358	WEST HALIFAX	97.2	96.8	0.0	0.0	0.4	0.4	1.2	1.2	5.3	4.9	7.7	6.9	3.6	23.1	34.0	13.0	1.6	76.5	44.2	49.4	50.6
05359	WEST TOWNSHEND	98.2	97.9	0.2	0.2	0.2	0.4	0.8	1.0	5.4	5.4	5.8	4.8	3.3	21.9	35.0	16.1	2.3	80.3	46.9	50.9	49.1
05360	WEST WARDSBORO	98.7	97.9	0.0	0.4	0.0	0.0	1.8	2.1	5.5	6.8	6.0	4.7	3.8	26.8	33.2	12.8	0.4	78.3	43.2	52.3	47.7
05361	WHITINGHAM	99.3	99.4	0.0	0.0	0.0	0.0	0.7	0.9	5.4	5.7	8.0	5.7	4.0	23.3	33.9	12.0	1.8	77.3	43.3	49.9	50.1
05362	WILLIAMSVILLE	99.7	99.3	0.0	0.0	0.0	0.3	1.0	1.4	3.7	5.8	6.1	7.5	3.1	23.4	39.0	9.5	2.0	79.0	45.2	47.1	52.9
05363	WILMINGTON	97.8	97.3	0.2	0.3	0.6	0.8	0.9	1.1	4.3	4.4	6.3	6.9	4.1	23.4	35.2	13.3	1.9	80.5	45.2	50.2	49.8
05401	BURLINGTON	91.5	89.3	2.0	2.7	3.0	4.3	1.5	1.8	4.0	3.3	3.1	10.5	23.6	29.2	17.5	7.0	1.8	87.5	27.5	49.1	50.9
05403	SOUTH BURLINGTON	93.8	91.8	0.8	1.1	3.4	5.1	1.2	1.5	5.1	5.2	5.4	9.5	7.0	26.8	27.2	11.2	2.5	80.2	38.5	47.5	52.5
05404	WINOOSKI	90.6	87.6	1.2	1.7	5.4	7.8	1.1	1.4	6.4	5.7	5.4	6.0	8.9	31.8	22.2	11.2	2.3	79.2	35.3	48.7	51.3
05405	BURLINGTON	94.4	92.9	1.2	1.7	1.9	2.8	2.5	3.2	0.9	0.6	0.6	44.6	40.4	5.8	4.9	1.5	0.7	97.2	20.4	48.1	51.9
05408	BURLINGTON	94.4	92.8	1.3	1.8	1.9	2.8	1.1	1.4	5.7	6.4	6.5	6.4	5.3	25.3	28.2	12.9	3.4	77.1	41.3	46.9	53.1
05440	ALBURGH	96.7	96.9	0.0	0.0	0.2	0.2	0.2	0.3	6.4	6.7	6.7	5.9	4.9	23.4	31.2	13.3	1.6	76.5	42.2	50.7	49.3
	VERMONT	96.8	96.1	0.5	0.7	0.9	1.3	0.9	1.1	5.4	5.8	6.2	7.4	7.0	24.6	29.9	11.6	2.0	78.6	40.4	49.1	50.9
	UNITED STATES	75.1	72.0	12.3	12.7	3.8	4.6	12.5	15.7	6.8	6.7	6.6	7.1	6.9	27.0	26.0	10.9	1.9	75.7	36.9	49.2	50.8

INCOME

05001-05440

ZIP CODE #	POST OFFICE NAME	2009 Per Capita Income	2009 HH Income Base	2009 HOUSEHOLD INCOME DISTRIBUTION (%) Less than $25,000	$25,000 to $49,999	$50,000 to $99,999	$100,000 to $149,999	$150,000 or More	MEDIAN HOUSEHOLD INCOME 2009	2014	2009 National Centile	2009 State Centile	2009 Home Value Base	2009 HOME VALUE DISTRIBUTION (%) Less than $50,000	$50,000 to $89,999	$90,000 to $174,999	$175,000 to $399,999	$400,000 or More	2009 Median Home Value
05001	WHITE RIVER JUNCTION	30806	4795	18.7	24.5	40.3	10.8	5.8	57880	58597	75	75	3215	4.5	5.3	18.0	56.9	15.2	235321
05032	BETHEL	25905	1025	22.0	31.0	35.8	6.5	4.7	47437	50487	55	35	753	3.9	6.4	25.6	50.3	13.8	215144
05033	BRADFORD	25299	1239	23.1	26.0	38.3	9.0	3.6	50779	52378	63	48	885	3.6	2.6	35.9	50.4	7.5	194971
05034	BRIDGEWATER	25899	51	19.6	29.4	41.2	7.8	2.0	50836	52248	63	49	37	0.0	0.0	27.0	54.1	18.9	225000
05035	BRIDGEWATER CORNERS	25352	203	20.2	30.0	38.4	7.9	3.4	49786	50936	61	43	151	4.0	2.6	24.5	45.7	23.2	228125
05036	BROOKFIELD	29466	370	12.2	27.3	44.6	11.1	4.9	59415	60909	77	79	308	2.9	1.9	23.7	58.1	13.3	232143
05037	BROWNSVILLE	32146	250	14.8	19.6	46.0	13.6	6.0	64546	63727	83	92	205	1.5	0.5	8.8	46.3	42.9	360811
05038	CHELSEA	21130	498	28.3	31.3	32.7	6.2	1.4	41721	44655	38	15	379	3.4	5.8	30.9	51.2	8.7	193750
05039	CORINTH	18725	475	23.6	41.1	29.3	4.0	2.1	40358	42613	34	9	404	5.0	6.9	38.4	39.9	9.9	174643
05040	EAST CORINTH	22158	187	19.8	32.6	38.0	7.0	2.7	48130	50975	57	37	160	5.0	5.6	37.5	43.8	8.1	180769
05041	EAST RANDOLPH	33442	95	11.6	22.1	55.8	8.4	2.1	62921	63204	81	89	78	1.3	0.0	34.6	55.1	9.0	213333
05042	EAST RYEGATE	24208	230	19.6	36.1	35.2	5.7	3.5	46736	47660	53	31	194	1.5	10.8	41.2	37.1	9.3	166667
05043	EAST THETFORD	27243	294	13.6	23.1	50.3	9.5	3.4	60000	60000	77	81	235	3.8	2.6	8.5	61.3	23.8	273718
05045	FAIRLEE	24201	741	16.7	28.5	45.9	7.2	1.8	52968	53327	68	60	536	3.2	4.3	17.9	58.8	15.9	241892
05046	GROTON	19861	529	24.0	34.4	35.3	5.7	0.6	43556	43836	44	20	430	2.6	10.9	37.2	41.6	7.7	173585
05048	HARTLAND	29149	829	12.7	25.9	47.3	8.8	5.3	61197	61167	79	83	677	2.5	5.9	13.9	56.4	21.3	264189
05051	NEWBURY	19813	308	28.6	35.1	30.5	4.5	1.3	36170	37441	21	4	228	5.3	6.6	30.7	48.7	8.8	193478
05052	NORTH HARTLAND	23528	125	12.0	30.4	48.8	5.6	3.2	56336	56312	73	71	98	1.0	11.2	23.5	50.0	14.3	221429
05053	NORTH POMFRET	30742	99	15.2	20.2	45.5	9.1	10.1	63422	62932	82	90	75	0.0	0.0	10.7	40.0	49.3	395000
05055	NORWICH	46182	1487	8.5	12.3	37.0	17.7	24.5	85014	89895	94	99	1125	0.0	0.7	4.3	30.7	64.4	499080
05056	PLYMOUTH	29599	152	22.4	24.3	39.5	10.5	3.3	53433	54204	69	62	127	6.3	4.7	11.0	41.7	36.2	312500
05058	POST MILLS	27233	143	13.3	27.3	42.0	12.6	4.9	57589	57254	75	75	113	2.7	4.4	15.0	56.6	21.2	259722
05060	RANDOLPH	26053	1965	21.2	28.7	36.1	10.8	3.2	50108	51766	61	46	1405	7.8	3.7	33.0	49.9	5.6	187341
05061	RANDOLPH CENTER	23531	463	13.4	21.0	53.1	9.3	3.2	63857	64279	82	91	382	2.4	0.3	30.6	58.1	8.6	217442
05062	READING	27483	280	17.9	25.0	45.0	8.2	3.9	55984	56168	73	70	227	2.6	5.3	17.6	48.0	26.4	265972
05065	SHARON	25789	393	19.3	30.5	36.1	8.4	5.6	50092	52421	61	45	294	6.5	5.1	20.1	52.0	16.3	214912
05067	SOUTH POMFRET	34225	68	13.2	20.6	47.1	8.8	10.3	64276	63491	83	92	52	0.0	0.0	9.6	38.5	51.9	412500
05068	SOUTH ROYALTON	23580	1501	28.8	30.7	31.6	5.7	3.2	41044	44041	36	13	940	6.5	4.9	24.3	46.9	17.4	215891
05069	SOUTH RYEGATE	24938	320	19.4	31.6	37.8	6.9	4.4	49276	51446	59	40	269	2.2	9.7	35.7	41.6	10.8	182065
05070	SOUTH STRAFFORD	29461	184	17.4	26.1	40.2	10.3	6.0	54931	55188	71	67	151	1.3	2.6	13.9	55.0	27.2	289286
05071	SOUTH WOODSTOCK	36871	165	12.1	25.5	43.0	11.5	7.9	59709	58457	77	80	124	8.1	0.0	8.9	37.9	45.2	360000
05072	STRAFFORD	30560	273	16.1	25.3	41.8	10.6	6.2	56929	56158	74	72	227	2.2	3.1	13.2	52.0	29.5	295968
05073	TAFTSVILLE	36622	16	6.3	25.0	43.8	18.8	6.3	75000	68989	89	96	12	0.0	0.0	0.0	58.3	41.7	350000
05075	THETFORD CENTER	28902	649	12.0	25.1	43.5	13.7	5.7	61243	60000	79	84	525	2.7	2.5	11.0	59.2	24.6	279722
05076	TOPSHAM	20206	200	19.0	35.5	39.5	5.0	1.0	46848	49177	54	32	172	5.8	7.6	45.3	35.5	5.8	161111
05077	TUNBRIDGE	24237	508	22.8	25.8	42.9	4.3	4.1	50905	51903	63	50	408	5.1	5.1	25.2	52.0	12.5	220946
05079	VERSHIRE	21544	241	21.2	35.7	36.5	5.4	1.2	46400	48123	53	30	192	2.1	9.9	52.1	27.6	8.3	147500
05081	WELLS RIVER	24416	343	22.2	33.8	36.7	4.7	2.6	43159	46760	43	19	247	2.4	4.9	34.8	47.4	10.5	195313
05083	WEST FAIRLEE	21889	111	17.1	35.1	40.5	5.4	1.8	48302	50765	57	38	82	6.1	9.8	36.6	37.8	9.8	170000
05084	WEST HARTFORD	30898	60	15.0	21.7	45.0	8.3	10.0	62891	63623	81	88	46	0.0	0.0	10.9	41.3	47.8	383333
05086	WEST TOPSHAM	20539	334	18.9	33.2	41.3	5.4	1.2	48204	50132	57	38	290	4.5	6.6	42.4	42.1	4.5	169565
05089	WINDSOR	27005	2192	20.1	28.5	38.4	8.4	4.5	51145	52946	64	50	1480	5.9	4.7	31.9	44.7	12.8	191134
05091	WOODSTOCK	36132	1801	14.1	22.8	40.4	13.3	9.5	62593	62598	81	88	1288	2.7	1.0	9.1	43.4	43.8	363303
05101	BELLOWS FALLS	22945	2188	27.6	27.4	37.3	5.5	2.2	43663	46101	44	21	1243	3.1	5.2	46.3	40.2	5.2	170061
05141	CAMBRIDGEPORT	22725	40	17.5	32.5	37.5	10.0	2.5	50000	52135	61	45	31	0.0	9.7	29.0	51.6	9.7	192500
05142	CAVENDISH	23853	356	21.9	34.6	35.7	5.1	2.8	45356	47664	49	27	288	4.5	7.3	33.0	45.8	9.4	185714
05143	CHESTER	27054	2067	20.5	27.9	40.3	7.5	3.8	51437	52869	65	51	1560	3.3	3.3	27.0	49.2	17.2	219960
05146	GRAFTON	27704	261	18.4	27.6	44.4	5.0	4.6	52160	52467	66	55	202	3.5	5.4	29.2	42.6	19.3	214583
05148	LONDONDERRY	28041	521	20.2	25.0	39.2	9.0	6.7	53750	54668	69	63	385	2.3	3.1	12.2	47.5	34.8	290865
05149	LUDLOW	27536	1359	23.4	29.9	37.6	5.2	3.9	47048	50134	54	33	981	3.9	4.8	11.1	58.4	21.8	248897
05150	NORTH SPRINGFIELD	30686	376	10.9	28.5	49.5	7.2	4.0	59428	60526	77	80	293	1.4	6.5	46.8	42.3	3.1	168864
05151	PERKINSVILLE	26632	630	20.8	25.6	43.5	5.4	4.8	51912	52982	66	54	530	5.5	12.6	24.2	47.5	10.2	190299
05152	PERU	29072	59	18.6	23.7	33.9	13.6	10.2	58836	60000	76	78	46	2.2	6.5	4.3	30.4	56.5	442857
05153	PROCTORSVILLE	24121	324	21.6	32.7	37.0	6.2	2.5	46537	49176	53	31	259	3.9	6.9	32.4	47.1	9.7	190086
05154	SAXTONS RIVER	27863	136	18.4	30.9	35.3	10.3	5.1	50473	51326	62	47	107	0.9	6.5	34.6	50.5	7.5	187500
05155	SOUTH LONDONDERRY	30174	405	19.3	25.9	42.2	7.2	5.4	53099	53771	68	61	290	0.7	2.1	16.2	56.2	24.8	257778
05156	SPRINGFIELD	25841	3879	21.7	30.7	35.7	9.0	3.0	47873	51177	56	35	2649	2.1	4.9	47.1	40.3	5.6	168368
05158	WESTMINSTER	24578	347	22.5	22.2	45.0	6.9	3.5	55331	55302	72	68	273	5.1	5.1	34.8	46.9	8.1	186250
05161	WESTON	34188	245	20.0	24.5	37.6	9.0	9.0	54700	55149	71	65	189	1.6	0.0	12.2	47.6	38.6	352222
05201	BENNINGTON	24053	6242	26.8	27.8	34.8	7.1	3.6	45627	48868	50	28	3938	6.4	5.4	33.2	48.0	7.0	185195
05250	ARLINGTON	29617	1547	20.4	26.3	38.6	8.3	6.3	52474	54296	67	57	1202	2.7	2.0	18.2	54.0	23.0	267935
05251	DORSET	40821	706	16.6	22.2	35.0	12.0	14.2	62629	64144	81	88	569	0.7	1.1	6.5	38.0	53.8	439815
05252	EAST ARLINGTON	24700	161	22.4	28.0	39.8	6.8	3.1	49332	52135	60	41	128	1.6	5.5	25.8	53.9	13.3	231579
05253	EAST DORSET	36961	260	16.5	21.5	35.4	11.9	14.6	63631	64626	82	90	210	1.0	1.0	6.2	38.1	53.8	440000
05255	MANCHESTER CENTER	37577	1989	17.7	20.1	39.5	11.9	10.9	62488	63089	81	87	1401	5.1	2.1	7.9	40.5	44.4	371661
05257	NORTH BENNINGTON	25831	1003	21.0	22.7	39.5	11.3	5.5	57100	58625	74	72	723	0.1	1.1	30.0	57.8	10.9	214890
05260	NORTH POWNAL	19616	132	25.0	20.5	43.2	9.8	1.5	52354	53370	67	56	99	4.0	1.0	37.4	45.5	12.1	186719
05261	POWNAL	21874	1016	20.1	34.0	39.4	4.7	1.9	47039	49883	54	33	807	17.2	8.8	26.6	40.6	6.7	169220
05262	SHAFTSBURY	30097	1088	14.5	24.6	40.2	15.0	5.7	62060	62815	80	85	913	0.0	1.9	16.2	62.1	19.8	244038
05301	BRATTLEBORO	27131	7261	24.7	27.5	34.8	8.8	4.2	47325	49893	55	34	4362	4.1	4.2	22.2	58.9	10.6	217369
05340	BONDVILLE	38855	296	13.9	20.3	38.9	11.8	15.2	66021	66390	84	94	235	0.0	2.1	8.5	44.3	45.1	371951
05341	EAST DOVER	28725	156	16.0	25.0	44.9	8.3	5.8	59212	60646	76	79	115	2.6	3.5	14.8	60.0	19.1	264474
05342	JACKSONVILLE	25318	303	16.5	36.3	38.6	4.6	4.0	47829	48514	56	35	248	0.4	6.9	27.8	54.4	10.5	206977
05343	JAMAICA	28988	401	23.9	30.7	30.7	7.2	7.5	45119	47817	49	26	302	1.0	2.0	22.2	53.0	21.9	246591
05345	NEWFANE	26696	683	18.7	26.5	41.7	9.4	3.7	53565	53974	69	63	551	3.3	6.2	23.2	54.8	12.5	217857
05346	PUTNEY	27608	2180	18.4	23.9	44.5	8.1	5.1	57492	58002	75	73	1628	6.2	5.5	26.2	49.1	13.0	209533
05350	READSBORO	26014	337	22.3	25.2	39.5	8.3	4.7	52905	54515	68	60	241	0.0	2.9	62.7	29.9	4.6	149364
05351	SOUTH NEWFANE	33214	136	18.4	25.0	39.0	11.0	6.6	54755	57208	71	66	112	0.9	0.9	19.6	58.0	20.5	261111
05352	STAMFORD	25898	338	16.3	22.8	51.2	7.7	2.1	61714	62570	80	84	293	0.0	5.1	30.0	57.3	7.5	223718
05353	TOWNSHEND	24590	422	22.7	28.7	38.6	5.9	4.0	48992	49194	59	40	330	0.9	3.3	18.5	67.3	10.0	230405
05354	VERNON	25563	785	12.9	21.5	50.1	11.2	4.3	63798	64064	82	91	640	1.6	2.7	15.3	69.2	11.3	248507
05355	WARDSBORO	23091	322	22.0	35.7	33.9	4.7	3.7	44035	46426	45	23	264	4.5	3.8	37.5	41.3	12.9	192188
05356	WEST DOVER	32866	523	17.6	24.5	42.8	8.6	6.5	58858	60152	76	78	381	2.6	2.6	14.2	58.8	21.8	270082
05358	WEST HALIFAX	22805	97	23.7	34.0	34.0	4.1	4.1	45274	46701	49	27	82	4.9	7.3	31.7	50.0	6.1	188889
05359	WEST TOWNSHEND	27055	220	19.5	28.2	42.7	5.5	4.1	51307	51439	64	51	169	1.2	4.1	24.3	53.3	17.2	228448
05360	WEST WARDSBORO	31029	106	12.3	38.7	33.0	6.6	9.4	49375	48821	60	41	88	2.3	4.5	25.0	47.7	20.5	225000
05361	WHITINGHAM	26260	320	15.0	35.0	40.6	4.7	4.7	50000	50000	61	45	261	0.4	6.5	24.9	55.9	12.3	216860
05362	WILLIAMSVILLE	30419	124	20.2	21.0	42.7	11.3	4.8	57505	61091	75	74	104	0.0	1.9	19.2	61.5	17.3	252941
05363	WILMINGTON	29682	1132	24.6	29.1	34.2	6.6	5.5	46334	48304	52	30	783	1.4	1.8	23.0	57.7	16.1	232031
05401	BURLINGTON	27299	12682	27.4	30.4	27.9	9.3	5.1	41468	45672	38	14	4248	0.4	0.4	21.6	61.6	15.9	241743
05403	SOUTH BURLINGTON	36783	7159	9.8	21.4	37.3	21.1	10.4	71005	78350	87	95	4963	0.2	0.0	15.9	69.5	14.4	245607
05404	WINOOSKI	22748	3036	28.9	30.5	32.9	5.9	1.8	39856	43736	32	8	1273	0.4	0.7	24.7	72.2	2.0	206844
05405	BURLINGTON	11027	10	40.0	20.0	30.0	10.0	0.0	30000	27273	8	1	4	0.0	0.0	0.0	50.0	50.0	400000
05408	BURLINGTON	29467	4162	12.3	25.7	43.2	13.5	5.3	63170	70079	81	89	2982	1.8	0.4	18.0	73.5	6.3	220925
05440	ALBURGH	21209	979	26.1	33.1	32.9	6.1	1.7	42380	45942	41	17	785	5.1	6.5	34.3	45.6	8.5	186607
	VERMONT	27546		19.3	26.3	38.8	10.3	5.3	54205	56824				3.4	4.6	25.9	52.9	13.2	216547
	UNITED STATES	27277		20.9	24.4	35.3	11.7	7.6	54719	56938				9.3	13.1	31.6	32.6	13.5	162279

ZIP CODE		FINANCIAL SERVICES				THE HOME						ENTERTAINMENT						PERSONAL			
						Home Improvements		Furnishings													
#	POST OFFICE NAME	Auto Loan	Home Loan	Invest-ments	Retire-ment Plans	Home Repair	Lawn & Garden	Comput-ers & Hard-ware-Personal	Major Appli-ances	TV, Radio, Sound Equip-ment	Furni-ture	Dine out/ Carry out	Sports Equip-ment	Fees & Tickets	Toys & Games	Travel	Cable TV	Apparel & Services	Auto Repairs	Health Insur-ance	Pets & Supplies
05001	WHITE RIVER JUNCTION	100	94	103	95	95	102	96	100	97	93	97	76	93	96	96	99	67	99	102	118
05032	BETHEL	94	81	97	83	85	98	84	94	86	78	85	70	76	85	84	91	58	90	98	110
05033	BRADFORD	93	84	100	84	87	98	84	94	87	81	86	69	79	85	86	91	58	91	97	110
05034	BRIDGEWATER	101	81	130	79	89	107	81	103	85	76	83	75	70	80	87	90	55	95	101	119
05035	BRIDGEWATER CORNERS	101	81	131	80	89	107	81	103	85	76	84	75	70	81	88	90	56	95	102	119
05036	BROOKFIELD	98	109	96	112	107	108	98	103	97	98	97	80	104	99	104	97	68	99	102	121
05037	BROWNSVILLE	126	101	163	99	111	133	101	128	105	94	104	93	87	100	109	112	69	118	126	148
05038	CHELSEA	83	66	106	65	73	87	66	84	69	62	69	61	58	66	72	74	46	78	83	97
05039	CORINTH	75	68	68	71	70	81	67	76	69	61	68	58	62	71	67	74	47	70	78	88
05040	EAST CORINTH	88	84	87	86	85	97	80	91	83	75	82	68	77	84	83	87	56	85	94	106
05041	EAST RANDOLPH	119	95	154	94	104	126	95	121	100	89	98	88	82	95	103	106	65	112	119	140
05042	EAST RYEGATE	99	80	128	78	87	105	80	101	83	75	82	74	69	79	86	89	55	93	100	117
05043	EAST THETFORD	93	104	90	107	101	102	93	97	92	94	92	76	99	94	98	92	64	93	96	114
05045	FAIRLEE	95	79	111	77	84	98	78	94	81	75	80	69	69	79	82	86	54	88	93	110
05046	GROTON	76	68	72	71	70	81	67	77	70	61	68	58	62	70	68	74	47	71	79	89
05048	HARTLAND	105	108	98	108	107	110	99	104	100	101	100	78	101	103	101	102	69	101	106	123
05051	NEWBURY	78	61	97	60	67	82	62	79	66	58	65	58	53	63	66	70	43	73	79	91
05052	NORTH HARTLAND	101	93	82	90	91	95	88	93	91	91	91	68	83	95	84	94	62	90	93	110
05053	NORTH POMFRET	136	109	176	107	120	144	109	139	114	102	113	101	95	108	118	122	75	128	137	161
05055	NORWICH	151	188	203	193	198	172	167	172	155	179	156	132	187	152	187	148	113	164	155	195
05056	PLYMOUTH	105	84	136	83	92	111	84	107	88	79	87	78	73	84	91	94	58	99	105	124
05058	POST MILLS	103	103	104	104	103	109	95	104	96	95	96	79	95	97	99	98	66	99	103	122
05060	RANDOLPH	92	85	92	85	86	99	84	93	88	81	87	69	80	88	85	92	59	89	98	109
05061	RANDOLPH CENTER	112	99	141	98	105	122	95	116	99	91	98	85	89	95	104	104	66	108	116	134
05062	READING	109	87	141	86	96	115	87	111	92	82	90	81	76	87	95	98	60	103	110	129
05065	SHARON	102	94	84	91	92	96	89	94	92	92	92	68	85	95	85	94	63	91	94	111
05067	SOUTH POMFRET	137	110	177	108	120	145	110	139	115	103	113	102	95	109	119	122	75	129	138	161
05068	SOUTH ROYALTON	78	66	74	67	66	74	75	74	76	70	75	57	68	75	71	77	52	76	77	89
05069	SOUTH RYEGATE	105	84	135	83	92	111	84	107	88	79	87	78	73	83	91	94	58	98	105	124
05070	SOUTH STRAFFORD	116	94	143	92	102	121	94	116	98	89	97	85	82	94	100	104	64	108	115	135
05071	SOUTH WOODSTOCK	129	111	165	110	121	141	108	134	113	104	112	97	99	108	118	120	75	124	134	155
05072	STRAFFORD	118	95	153	93	104	125	95	120	99	89	98	88	82	94	103	106	65	111	119	139
05073	TAFTSVILLE	112	132	136	132	137	139	115	126	118	120	118	87	129	114	129	122	82	121	136	143
05075	THETFORD CENTER	105	110	110	112	109	115	100	109	100	99	100	84	103	101	107	102	69	104	108	128
05076	TOPSHAM	82	74	74	77	76	88	73	83	76	66	74	63	68	77	73	80	51	76	85	96
05077	TUNBRIDGE	98	79	127	77	86	104	79	100	82	74	81	73	68	78	85	88	54	92	99	116
05079	VERSHIRE	80	73	66	71	72	76	69	74	72	72	72	54	65	75	66	74	49	71	74	88
05081	WELLS RIVER	90	67	98	66	71	95	71	89	78	65	76	66	59	76	71	86	51	83	94	104
05083	WEST FAIRLEE	87	80	71	77	78	81	75	80	78	78	78	58	71	81	72	80	53	77	80	95
05084	WEST HARTFORD	135	108	174	106	119	143	108	137	113	101	112	100	94	107	117	121	74	127	136	159
05086	WEST TOPSHAM	82	75	74	78	77	88	74	84	76	67	75	63	68	78	74	81	51	77	86	97
05089	WINDSOR	95	82	98	82	86	98	85	95	88	81	87	69	78	87	85	93	59	91	99	110
05091	WOODSTOCK	122	117	155	117	127	139	109	130	113	110	113	91	109	108	121	119	77	122	135	149
05101	BELLOWS FALLS	80	68	75	69	68	80	75	78	78	69	77	59	68	77	72	82	53	78	84	93
05141	CAMBRIDGEPORT	95	76	122	75	83	100	76	96	79	71	78	70	66	75	82	85	52	89	95	112
05142	CAVENDISH	89	74	109	73	80	95	73	91	77	68	76	67	65	74	78	82	51	84	91	106
05143	CHESTER	97	82	106	83	87	102	84	98	87	78	86	72	75	85	86	92	58	92	100	114
05146	GRAFTON	100	80	130	79	88	106	80	102	84	75	83	74	70	80	87	90	55	94	101	118
05148	LONDONDERRY	114	91	147	90	100	121	91	116	96	86	94	85	79	91	99	102	63	107	115	135
05149	LUDLOW	97	79	113	78	84	99	83	96	86	77	85	72	73	83	85	90	57	92	97	113
05150	NORTH SPRINGFIELD	92	94	94	93	95	105	89	97	94	87	93	69	92	93	93	99	64	94	108	112
05151	PERKINSVILLE	104	82	125	80	88	109	82	104	87	77	86	76	70	84	87	94	57	96	104	121
05152	PERU	131	105	170	104	116	139	105	134	110	99	109	98	91	105	114	118	72	124	132	155
05153	PROCTORSVILLE	90	76	103	76	81	96	75	91	78	70	77	68	67	77	79	83	52	84	92	106
05154	SAXTONS RIVER	116	93	150	92	102	123	93	118	97	87	96	86	81	92	101	104	64	109	117	137
05155	SOUTH LONDONDERRY	106	85	137	84	93	112	85	108	89	80	88	79	74	84	92	95	58	100	107	125
05156	SPRINGFIELD	86	79	83	80	81	91	81	87	85	77	83	64	77	84	81	89	57	85	94	101
05158	WESTMINSTER	90	91	84	94	91	98	86	93	86	82	86	71	85	88	88	89	59	87	94	108
05161	WESTON	125	100	162	99	110	132	100	128	105	94	104	93	87	100	109	112	69	118	126	148
05201	BENNINGTON	83	75	79	76	76	86	78	83	81	74	80	62	73	80	77	85	55	81	88	97
05250	ARLINGTON	110	90	129	90	97	114	93	111	96	87	95	81	82	93	97	102	64	104	112	128
05251	DORSET	154	123	198	121	135	162	123	156	129	115	127	114	107	122	133	137	84	144	154	181
05252	EAST ARLINGTON	94	77	115	76	83	98	78	95	81	73	80	70	68	78	82	86	54	89	95	110
05253	EAST DORSET	153	123	198	121	135	162	123	156	128	115	127	114	106	122	133	137	84	144	154	181
05255	MANCHESTER CENTER	131	113	166	112	124	142	111	135	116	110	115	96	103	110	120	123	77	127	139	156
05257	NORTH BENNINGTON	94	97	95	98	97	103	93	98	95	92	95	72	96	95	96	98	66	96	103	114
05260	NORTH POWNAL	90	81	81	85	83	96	80	91	83	73	81	69	74	85	80	88	56	84	94	106
05261	POWNAL	90	73	86	74	75	94	73	87	78	67	77	66	64	79	73	84	52	81	91	103
05262	SHAFTSBURY	101	119	109	122	117	116	104	109	102	106	103	83	115	104	113	102	73	104	108	127
05301	BRATTLEBORO	84	82	84	83	82	85	84	84	85	82	85	65	83	84	85	86	59	85	88	100
05340	BONDVILLE	144	115	186	113	126	152	115	146	121	108	119	107	100	115	125	129	79	135	145	170
05341	EAST DOVER	108	95	128	95	99	112	96	109	98	92	97	82	88	95	100	101	66	104	109	128
05342	JACKSONVILLE	97	82	109	83	87	103	82	99	85	75	84	73	73	83	85	90	56	91	99	114
05343	JAMAICA	105	84	135	82	92	111	84	107	88	79	87	78	73	83	91	94	58	98	105	123
05345	NEWFANE	104	84	135	82	92	111	84	106	88	78	87	78	73	83	91	93	58	98	105	123
05346	PUTNEY	99	95	99	97	96	103	94	100	95	92	94	76	92	95	95	97	65	97	102	117
05350	READSBORO	94	83	86	84	85	95	89	93	92	85	90	68	82	91	86	95	62	92	99	109
05351	SOUTH NEWFANE	119	95	154	94	105	126	95	121	100	89	99	88	83	95	103	106	65	112	120	140
05352	STAMFORD	91	102	88	105	99	100	91	95	90	91	90	74	97	92	96	90	63	91	94	112
05353	TOWNSHEND	96	77	125	76	85	102	77	98	81	72	80	72	67	77	84	86	53	91	97	114
05354	VERNON	97	110	95	113	107	108	98	102	96	98	97	80	105	99	104	97	68	98	101	120
05355	WARDSBORO	88	70	113	69	77	93	70	89	74	66	73	65	61	70	76	78	48	82	88	103
05356	WEST DOVER	107	96	123	96	100	110	97	107	99	95	99	81	92	96	101	102	67	104	107	126
05358	WEST HALIFAX	97	78	125	76	85	102	78	99	81	73	80	72	67	77	84	87	53	91	97	114
05359	WEST TOWNSHEND	99	79	128	78	87	104	79	100	83	74	82	73	69	79	86	88	54	93	99	116
05360	WEST WARDSBORO	115	92	148	90	101	121	92	117	96	86	95	85	80	91	100	103	63	108	115	135
05361	WHITINGHAM	102	87	115	88	92	109	86	104	90	79	88	77	77	88	90	95	59	96	105	121
05362	WILLIAMSVILLE	121	97	156	95	106	128	97	123	101	91	100	90	84	96	105	108	66	113	121	142
05363	WILMINGTON	106	85	137	84	94	113	85	108	89	80	88	79	74	85	92	95	59	100	107	126
05401	BURLINGTON	85	64	63	69	62	64	95	72	89	84	90	63	79	89	77	87	64	85	75	91
05403	SOUTH BURLINGTON	121	127	119	131	124	118	127	120	123	129	125	96	132	126	127	121	89	123	118	142
05404	WINOOSKI	65	62	59	63	61	62	73	64	72	67	72	51	70	71	68	73	51	70	69	77
05405	BURLINGTON	63	41	39	45	40	44	75	51	67	60	67	47	55	68	53	66	47	62	54	65
05408	BURLINGTON	96	105	100	105	104	104	102	101	101	100	102	77	107	101	105	102	72	102	105	118
05440	ALBURGH	90	64	92	62	67	91	66	84	73	61	72	63	53	73	65	80	47	77	87	100
	VERMONT	98	92	100	93	93	101	93	98	94	90	94	75	89	94	93	97	65	96	101	116
	UNITED STATES	100	100	100	100	100	100	100	100	100	100	100	100	100	100	100	100	100	100	100	100

VERMONT

POPULATION CHANGE

05441-05764

ZIP CODE #	POST OFFICE NAME	COUNTY FIPS CODE	POPULATION 2000	POPULATION 2009	POPULATION 2014	2000-2009 ANNUAL RATE % Rate	2000-2009 ANNUAL RATE State Centile	HOUSEHOLDS 2000	HOUSEHOLDS 2009	HOUSEHOLDS 2014	HOUSEHOLDS % Annual Rate 2000-2009	HOUSEHOLDS 2009 Average HH Size	FAMILIES 2000	FAMILIES 2009	FAMILIES % Annual Rate 2000-2009
05441	BAKERSFIELD	011	351	382	398	0.9	81	130	146	154	1.3	2.62	97	106	1.0
05442	BELVIDERE CENTER	015	257	263	262	0.2	37	95	100	100	0.6	2.59	66	67	0.2
05443	BRISTOL	001	6123	6430	6531	0.5	57	2331	2528	2592	0.9	2.54	1669	1774	0.7
05444	CAMBRIDGE	011	1604	1881	1987	1.7	98	597	724	771	2.1	2.60	429	510	1.9
05445	CHARLOTTE	007	3609	3846	3947	0.7	70	1302	1430	1481	1.0	2.69	1003	1081	0.8
05446	COLCHESTER	007	17224	17446	17539	0.1	32	6227	6521	6613	0.5	2.43	4241	4308	0.2
05447	EAST BERKSHIRE	011	90	92	92	0.2	37	31	33	33	0.7	2.79	24	24	0.0
05448	EAST FAIRFIELD	011	1006	1128	1184	1.2	91	366	426	450	1.7	2.65	281	320	1.4
05450	ENOSBURG FALLS	011	5091	5609	5835	1.1	89	1884	2131	2232	1.3	2.61	1359	1501	1.1
05452	ESSEX JUNCTION	007	18437	19553	19974	0.6	64	6952	7633	7878	1.0	2.53	4981	5334	0.7
05454	FAIRFAX	011	4391	4932	5286	1.3	92	1446	1768	1910	2.2	2.79	1147	1377	2.0
05455	FAIRFIELD	011	1131	1294	1363	1.5	97	377	451	478	2.0	2.86	296	347	1.7
05456	FERRISBURGH	001	1259	1325	1354	0.6	64	466	512	529	1.0	2.59	345	371	0.8
05457	FRANKLIN	011	1420	1637	1729	1.5	97	481	574	612	1.9	2.82	386	453	1.7
05458	GRAND ISLE	013	1955	2306	2455	1.8	98	772	932	1002	2.1	2.47	572	679	1.9
05459	HIGHGATE CENTER	011	1811	2068	2186	1.4	95	635	754	804	1.9	2.74	488	567	1.6
05461	HINESBURG	007	4439	4714	4819	0.7	70	1627	1774	1829	0.9	2.66	1198	1278	0.7
05462	HUNTINGTON	007	1804	1947	2005	0.8	75	668	746	775	1.2	2.60	494	539	0.9
05463	ISLE LA MOTTE	013	488	528	544	0.9	81	202	229	238	1.4	2.31	143	159	1.2
05464	JEFFERSONVILLE	015	2402	2730	2876	1.4	95	955	1132	1204	1.9	2.41	677	786	1.6
05465	JERICHO	007	5346	5455	5492	0.2	37	1876	1974	2003	0.6	2.76	1491	1539	0.3
05468	MILTON	007	11718	12571	12903	0.8	75	4076	4532	4697	1.2	2.77	3227	3525	1.0
05471	MONTGOMERY CENTER	011	828	940	986	1.4	95	342	398	422	1.7	2.36	240	272	1.4
05472	NEW HAVEN	001	1848	2053	2134	1.1	89	684	781	819	1.4	2.63	517	578	1.2
05473	NORTH FERRISBURG	001	1256	1358	1400	0.8	75	489	549	571	1.3	2.47	370	408	1.1
05474	NORTH HERO	013	810	1009	1101	2.4	100	333	434	479	2.9	2.32	237	304	2.7
05476	RICHFORD	011	2867	2942	2948	0.3	44	1092	1155	1168	0.6	2.51	757	779	0.3
05477	RICHMOND	007	4588	4899	5021	0.7	70	1697	1861	1922	1.0	2.62	1239	1328	0.8
05478	SAINT ALBANS	011	14480	15402	15620	0.7	70	5645	6049	6168	0.8	2.50	3835	4032	0.5
05482	SHELBURNE	007	6992	7244	7332	0.4	52	2652	2817	2874	0.7	2.52	1862	1925	0.4
05483	SHELDON	011	1461	1662	1748	1.4	95	495	581	617	1.7	2.85	398	459	1.6
05486	SOUTH HERO	013	1695	1690	1683	0.0	25	662	682	686	0.3	2.48	472	477	0.1
05487	STARKSBORO	001	1610	1627	1623	0.1	32	563	577	579	0.3	2.82	410	410	0.0
05488	SWANTON	011	7410	7842	8024	0.6	64	2803	3077	3178	1.0	2.49	2045	2190	0.7
05489	UNDERHILL	007	3481	3739	3847	0.8	75	1236	1370	1422	1.1	2.73	995	1084	0.9
05491	VERGENNES	001	5879	6313	6472	0.8	75	2117	2352	2438	1.1	2.55	1520	1652	0.9
05492	WATERVILLE	015	822	856	861	0.4	52	305	327	332	0.8	2.58	212	222	0.5
05494	WESTFORD	007	1435	1517	1552	0.6	64	491	532	548	0.9	2.85	381	405	0.7
05495	WILLISTON	007	8275	9199	9542	1.2	91	3155	3618	3795	1.5	2.52	2318	2596	1.2
05602	MONTPELIER	023	11752	11717	11553	0.0	25	5224	5416	5406	0.4	2.12	3014	3035	0.1
05640	ADAMANT	023	197	206	210	0.5	57	81	89	92	1.0	2.31	54	58	0.8
05641	BARRE	023	16582	16607	16490	0.0	25	6993	7276	7290	0.4	2.23	4351	4430	0.2
05647	CABOT	023	885	1006	1047	1.4	95	329	390	411	1.9	2.58	232	269	1.6
05648	CALAIS	023	354	370	377	0.5	57	145	160	165	1.1	2.31	97	104	0.8
05649	EAST BARRE	017	605	625	633	0.4	52	240	260	266	0.9	2.39	170	181	0.7
05650	EAST CALAIS	023	906	939	954	0.4	52	379	413	424	0.9	2.27	252	268	0.7
05651	EAST MONTPELIER	023	1435	1516	1538	0.6	64	550	605	621	1.0	2.50	391	419	0.8
05652	EDEN	015	716	788	820	1.0	84	254	289	303	1.4	2.72	193	215	1.2
05653	EDEN MILLS	015	451	498	519	1.1	89	166	190	200	1.5	2.62	127	142	1.2
05654	GRANITEVILLE	023	1692	1724	1716	0.2	37	667	711	716	0.7	2.42	472	491	0.4
05655	HYDE PARK	015	2784	2939	3006	0.6	64	1111	1225	1265	1.1	2.39	757	817	0.8
05656	JOHNSON	015	3321	3543	3639	0.7	70	1191	1332	1387	1.2	2.34	689	749	0.9
05658	MARSHFIELD	023	1368	1411	1410	0.3	44	525	565	570	0.8	2.50	375	394	0.5
05660	MORETOWN	023	2040	2254	2329	1.1	89	781	892	932	1.4	2.52	520	578	1.1
05661	MORRISVILLE	015	5344	5632	5733	0.6	64	2173	2361	2423	0.9	2.33	1370	1451	0.6
05663	NORTHFIELD	023	6534	6723	6764	0.3	44	2096	2258	2302	0.8	2.40	1420	1492	0.5
05666	NORTH MONTPELIER	023	62	64	65	0.3	44	22	24	25	0.9	2.67	15	16	0.7
05667	PLAINFIELD	023	2364	2477	2508	0.5	57	918	1006	1031	1.0	2.36	628	671	0.7
05669	ROXBURY	023	407	381	370	-0.7	2	160	156	154	-0.3	2.44	116	111	-0.5
05672	STOWE	015	4351	4943	5177	1.4	95	1912	2210	2330	1.6	2.23	1135	1275	1.3
05673	WAITSFIELD	023	2347	2608	2705	1.1	89	1044	1212	1271	1.6	2.15	686	775	1.3
05674	WARREN	023	1681	1888	1951	1.3	92	742	854	892	1.5	2.21	437	487	1.2
05675	WASHINGTON	017	1033	1127	1170	0.9	81	397	454	476	1.5	2.48	283	318	1.3
05676	WATERBURY	023	4057	4373	4462	0.8	75	1707	1899	1958	1.2	2.26	1061	1151	0.9
05677	WATERBURY CENTER	023	2335	2398	2387	0.3	44	893	953	962	0.7	2.52	661	688	0.4
05679	WILLIAMSTOWN	017	3086	3442	3585	1.2	91	1196	1390	1466	1.6	2.48	854	973	1.4
05680	WOLCOTT	015	2168	2400	2502	1.1	89	812	932	981	1.5	2.57	592	667	1.3
05681	WOODBURY	023	316	327	332	0.4	52	122	133	136	0.9	2.46	78	82	0.5
05682	WORCESTER	023	1240	1248	1228	0.1	32	467	491	489	0.5	2.54	340	349	0.3
05701	RUTLAND	021	21206	20588	20287	-0.3	11	9031	9082	9041	0.1	2.18	5330	5212	-0.2
05730	BELMONT	021	334	326	322	-0.3	11	133	135	135	0.2	2.41	92	91	-0.1
05732	BOMOSEEN	021	1154	1162	1167	0.1	32	480	505	513	0.6	2.13	319	328	0.3
05733	BRANDON	021	5683	5999	6110	0.6	64	2288	2515	2588	1.0	2.38	1585	1703	0.8
05734	BRIDPORT	001	1314	1274	1253	-0.3	11	493	499	496	0.1	2.55	372	370	-0.1
05735	CASTLETON	021	3568	3619	3628	0.2	37	1204	1270	1286	0.6	2.50	782	802	0.3
05736	CENTER RUTLAND	021	629	649	655	0.3	44	290	314	320	0.9	2.05	197	209	0.6
05737	CHITTENDEN	021	641	619	607	-0.4	8	251	251	249	0.0	2.47	192	189	-0.2
05738	CUTTINGSVILLE	021	1130	1157	1162	0.3	44	438	469	477	0.7	2.40	331	348	0.5
05739	DANBY	021	1306	1306	1303	0.0	25	523	543	548	0.4	2.41	368	374	0.2
05742	EAST WALLINGFORD	021	649	665	668	0.3	44	261	279	284	0.7	2.37	190	199	0.5
05743	FAIR HAVEN	021	4487	4722	4791	0.6	64	1767	1936	1987	1.0	2.40	1203	1285	0.7
05744	FLORENCE	021	646	664	669	0.3	44	255	271	276	0.7	2.45	168	174	0.4
05746	GAYSVILLE	027	25	25	25	0.0	25	10	10	10	0.0	2.50	7	7	0.0
05747	GRANVILLE	001	303	328	338	0.9	81	127	143	149	1.3	2.29	85	93	1.0
05748	HANCOCK	001	342	370	382	0.9	81	148	166	173	1.2	2.23	99	108	0.9
05751	KILLINGTON	021	1101	1020	987	-0.8	0	502	481	470	-0.5	2.12	283	260	-0.9
05753	MIDDLEBURY	001	10226	10313	10352	0.1	32	3434	3599	3649	0.5	2.25	2100	2147	0.2
05757	MIDDLETOWN SPRINGS	021	904	966	989	0.7	70	361	406	420	1.3	2.38	260	286	1.0
05758	MOUNT HOLLY	021	720	704	695	-0.2	15	283	287	287	0.2	2.45	196	194	-0.1
05759	NORTH CLARENDON	021	2533	2459	2432	-0.3	11	1066	1086	1087	0.2	2.24	722	717	-0.1
05760	ORWELL	001	1304	1402	1447	0.8	75	484	544	568	1.3	2.57	368	407	1.1
05761	PAWLET	021	979	1045	1064	0.7	70	405	449	462	1.1	2.33	286	309	0.8
05762	PITTSFIELD	021	522	515	511	-0.1	19	215	220	221	0.2	2.34	146	146	0.0
05763	PITTSFORD	021	2784	2762	2741	-0.1	19	1127	1157	1162	0.3	2.38	788	792	0.1
05764	POULTNEY	021	3586	3614	3617	0.1	32	1264	1317	1328	0.4	2.32	830	843	0.2
	VERMONT					0.4					0.8	2.36			0.5
	UNITED STATES					1.0					1.1	2.59			0.9

ZIP CODE #	POST OFFICE NAME	RACE (%) White 2000	White 2009	Black 2000	Black 2009	Asian/Pacific 2000	Asian/Pacific 2009	% Hispanic Origin 2000	% Hispanic Origin 2009	2009 AGE DISTRIBUTION (%) 0-4	5-9	10-14	15-19	20-24	25-44	45-64	65-84	85+	18+	MEDIAN AGE 2009	% 2009 Males	% 2009 Females
05441	BAKERSFIELD	97.7	97.6	0.3	0.3	0.0	0.3	0.0	0.0	7.1	7.9	8.9	7.6	3.9	26.2	29.3	8.4	0.8	71.5	37.6	48.4	51.6
05442	BELVIDERE CENTER	97.7	97.7	0.0	0.0	0.4	0.4	0.0	0.0	6.5	6.5	7.2	8.0	4.9	27.0	28.9	9.9	1.1	73.8	37.9	52.9	47.1
05443	BRISTOL	98.2	97.8	0.2	0.3	0.5	0.7	0.6	0.8	5.9	6.4	7.2	7.4	5.0	24.7	32.9	9.1	1.3	75.7	40.5	49.5	50.5
05444	CAMBRIDGE	96.9	96.7	0.2	0.2	0.2	0.3	0.7	0.9	6.5	7.3	7.7	6.8	3.7	30.1	29.5	7.5	0.8	74.0	38.3	52.0	48.0
05445	CHARLOTTE	97.9	97.5	0.2	0.3	0.6	0.9	0.7	0.9	5.2	6.9	8.0	8.0	3.5	23.5	34.7	9.4	0.7	74.4	42.1	49.7	50.3
05446	COLCHESTER	96.5	95.1	0.6	0.9	1.6	2.6	1.1	1.5	5.7	5.6	5.6	9.4	10.9	26.9	27.3	8.0	0.8	79.8	35.0	48.5	51.5
05447	EAST BERKSHIRE	97.8	96.7	1.1	1.1	0.0	0.0	0.0	1.1	6.5	6.5	7.6	7.6	4.3	26.1	32.6	8.7	0.0	73.9	39.3	48.9	51.1
05448	EAST FAIRFIELD	97.1	96.9	0.1	0.1	0.3	0.4	0.6	0.8	7.1	7.9	8.2	7.3	3.9	26.8	30.5	7.5	0.8	72.0	38.0	50.5	49.5
05450	ENOSBURG FALLS	96.5	96.0	0.2	0.3	0.2	0.3	0.6	0.7	6.4	6.6	7.4	7.8	5.1	25.5	28.8	10.6	1.8	74.7	39.0	49.3	50.7
05452	ESSEX JUNCTION	95.4	93.9	0.9	1.2	2.3	3.3	0.9	1.1	5.9	6.2	6.6	7.4	6.8	25.7	31.0	9.2	1.1	76.2	38.7	48.9	51.1
05454	FAIRFAX	97.7	97.4	0.5	0.6	0.3	0.4	0.7	0.8	6.7	7.7	8.0	11.8	4.5	31.7	24.1	5.0	0.5	74.5	33.4	49.1	50.9
05455	FAIRFIELD	97.1	96.7	0.0	0.1	0.3	0.5	1.1	1.5	7.0	7.8	7.7	7.3	4.3	27.6	30.0	7.5	0.9	72.7	37.7	49.5	50.5
05456	FERRISBURGH	97.8	97.4	0.2	0.3	0.5	0.7	0.6	0.7	6.1	6.6	6.4	6.4	4.0	25.6	32.5	11.0	1.4	76.8	41.9	49.5	50.5
05457	FRANKLIN	96.6	96.2	0.3	0.3	0.2	0.4	0.1	0.1	6.4	7.1	7.7	7.4	5.1	24.9	29.6	10.6	1.3	74.2	39.5	49.6	50.4
05458	GRAND ISLE	97.5	97.4	0.2	0.3	0.4	0.5	0.6	0.7	5.6	5.6	7.5	5.9	3.9	23.7	35.5	11.4	0.8	77.4	43.7	49.9	50.1
05459	HIGHGATE CENTER	93.1	92.5	0.1	0.0	0.2	0.2	0.1	0.1	6.8	8.4	8.6	6.9	5.5	27.6	25.4	10.3	0.6	71.8	36.3	49.4	50.6
05461	HINESBURG	97.9	97.6	0.1	0.2	0.5	0.8	0.8	1.0	6.7	7.2	8.3	7.1	4.6	30.3	29.1	6.1	0.7	73.1	36.6	48.7	51.3
05462	HUNTINGTON	97.5	97.0	0.4	0.6	0.5	0.7	0.4	0.5	7.0	7.6	7.4	6.5	3.4	33.0	29.2	5.0	1.0	73.1	37.3	49.8	50.2
05463	ISLE LA MOTTE	97.7	97.9	0.0	0.0	0.2	0.4	0.0	0.0	5.5	5.7	7.0	7.0	2.1	22.5	32.4	15.5	2.3	76.7	45.1	47.9	52.1
05464	JEFFERSONVILLE	96.5	96.2	0.2	0.3	0.1	0.2	0.7	0.8	5.9	6.4	6.9	6.3	3.5	30.6	30.6	8.8	1.0	76.5	39.7	51.3	48.7
05465	JERICHO	97.5	96.8	0.6	0.9	0.6	0.9	1.1	1.3	6.3	7.1	7.9	8.0	4.7	23.9	33.4	7.9	0.8	73.7	40.1	49.6	50.4
05468	MILTON	98.1	97.8	0.2	0.3	0.3	0.5	0.6	0.8	7.0	7.6	7.9	7.2	4.6	28.7	29.6	6.8	0.6	72.9	37.5	50.2	49.8
05471	MONTGOMERY CENTER	96.9	96.7	0.2	0.3	0.0	0.0	0.5	0.6	5.6	6.1	6.5	5.1	3.5	21.1	36.2	14.8	1.2	78.6	46.4	51.5	48.5
05472	NEW HAVEN	98.3	98.1	0.2	0.3	0.1	0.1	0.8	1.1	5.8	6.5	7.2	7.1	4.0	25.7	33.6	9.2	0.9	76.0	41.4	51.1	48.9
05473	NORTH FERRISBURG	98.0	97.6	0.2	0.3	0.5	0.7	0.6	0.7	6.3	7.1	7.3	6.6	4.1	24.3	33.9	9.4	1.2	75.2	41.7	49.9	50.1
05474	NORTH HERO	97.5	97.3	0.2	0.3	0.4	0.6	0.6	0.7	4.4	4.8	6.1	6.5	3.3	22.7	39.9	11.2	1.1	79.8	46.1	50.2	49.8
05476	RICHFORD	97.6	97.2	0.3	0.5	0.0	0.1	0.6	0.8	6.8	7.0	7.3	6.8	4.6	23.9	28.2	13.0	2.4	74.6	40.4	49.3	50.7
05477	RICHMOND	98.3	98.0	0.1	0.1	0.5	0.7	0.8	1.0	6.7	8.2	7.8	6.5	4.7	28.6	29.8	6.8	0.9	72.5	38.0	49.2	50.8
05478	SAINT ALBANS	96.5	96.0	0.3	0.5	0.4	0.5	0.7	0.9	7.1	7.4	7.2	6.8	5.6	26.7	26.1	11.2	2.0	74.1	37.7	48.9	51.1
05482	SHELBURNE	97.6	96.9	0.2	0.3	1.0	1.5	0.9	1.1	6.0	6.8	7.4	6.8	4.3	20.7	32.6	12.3	3.1	75.0	43.7	47.9	52.1
05483	SHELDON	94.7	94.2	0.1	0.1	0.2	0.2	0.6	0.9	7.1	7.4	9.4	7.6	4.4	28.0	27.9	7.3	1.0	70.8	35.8	49.6	50.4
05486	SOUTH HERO	97.9	97.8	0.2	0.3	0.3	0.4	0.5	0.7	4.6	7.0	7.0	6.7	3.8	25.3	34.4	10.2	0.9	76.6	42.4	49.9	50.1
05487	STARKSBORO	96.6	96.2	0.2	0.3	0.7	1.0	0.2	0.3	7.2	8.4	8.6	7.1	5.1	27.4	29.4	6.1	0.8	71.1	35.9	48.5	51.5
05488	SWANTON	92.9	92.1	0.4	0.6	0.4	0.6	0.5	0.6	6.8	6.9	7.0	8.0	5.6	25.7	28.0	10.5	1.5	74.9	38.1	49.5	50.5
05489	UNDERHILL	98.4	98.1	0.3	0.4	0.2	0.4	0.7	1.0	5.5	6.4	7.8	8.0	4.1	25.9	34.0	7.7	0.6	74.9	41.1	50.3	49.7
05491	VERGENNES	95.9	95.2	1.0	1.4	0.4	0.6	1.6	2.0	6.0	6.3	6.6	10.2	6.4	24.1	28.5	10.2	1.7	75.1	38.2	50.1	49.9
05492	WATERVILLE	97.7	97.7	0.0	0.0	0.2	0.2	0.1	0.1	6.2	6.5	7.1	7.8	4.7	27.5	29.3	9.7	1.2	74.5	38.5	52.3	47.7
05494	WESTFORD	98.2	97.7	0.3	0.5	0.4	0.7	1.0	1.3	6.5	7.4	8.2	8.0	4.6	24.4	32.5	7.6	0.7	72.7	40.3	49.9	50.1
05495	WILLISTON	97.5	96.5	0.5	0.7	1.1	1.7	1.0	1.3	6.2	6.9	7.2	7.7	5.2	23.4	31.4	10.6	1.4	74.4	40.9	48.6	51.4
05602	MONTPELIER	96.7	96.1	0.6	0.8	0.7	1.1	1.2	1.5	4.7	4.9	5.2	6.0	7.0	24.8	33.1	11.7	2.7	81.6	43.2	47.0	53.0
05640	ADAMANT	97.0	97.1	0.0	0.0	0.5	0.5	0.5	0.0	4.9	4.9	7.3	5.8	3.4	22.8	40.3	9.7	1.0	78.2	45.3	49.5	50.5
05641	BARRE	97.8	97.4	0.3	0.5	0.4	0.6	1.5	1.9	5.8	5.5	5.8	6.3	6.5	24.0	29.1	13.7	3.3	79.0	42.2	47.5	52.5
05647	CABOT	95.9	95.8	0.1	0.1	0.3	0.5	0.7	0.8	5.1	5.7	6.3	7.4	5.6	25.5	33.3	10.1	1.1	78.4	41.5	49.1	50.9
05648	CALAIS	96.9	96.8	0.0	0.0	0.3	0.5	0.3	0.3	4.9	5.4	7.6	5.9	3.2	22.4	40.5	9.2	0.8	77.3	45.2	49.7	50.3
05649	EAST BARRE	99.3	99.0	0.2	0.3	0.2	0.3	1.3	1.6	4.8	4.6	5.3	7.4	6.2	24.5	30.7	14.6	1.9	80.2	43.1	49.3	50.7
05650	EAST CALAIS	94.1	93.6	0.4	0.5	0.3	0.6	0.8	1.0	4.3	4.8	6.1	6.7	4.8	24.6	37.9	10.0	0.9	80.6	44.2	50.7	49.3
05651	EAST MONTPELIER	96.7	96.4	0.6	0.9	0.3	0.5	1.3	1.4	5.4	6.1	6.8	6.1	3.9	26.2	32.9	11.2	1.4	77.9	42.1	49.5	50.5
05652	EDEN	95.7	95.6	0.1	0.3	0.6	0.5	1.1	1.4	6.9	6.9	7.1	7.6	6.6	27.7	28.4	8.1	0.8	74.5	36.6	50.8	49.2
05653	EDEN MILLS	95.6	95.4	0.2	0.2	0.4	0.6	1.1	1.4	6.8	6.8	7.0	7.4	6.6	28.1	28.3	8.0	0.8	74.7	36.8	50.2	49.8
05654	GRANITEVILLE	97.5	97.0	0.2	0.3	0.4	0.6	2.3	3.2	7.0	6.6	6.6	6.0	6.0	24.4	27.7	13.9	1.9	76.2	40.7	48.6	51.4
05655	HYDE PARK	97.7	97.3	0.5	0.7	0.4	0.5	0.8	1.0	6.0	5.9	6.3	6.2	5.6	26.2	29.1	13.0	1.7	78.0	40.5	49.1	50.9
05656	JOHNSON	96.6	96.0	0.6	0.8	0.7	1.0	0.8	0.9	6.3	5.6	5.2	12.1	11.9	28.1	21.3	8.3	1.2	79.4	30.5	50.7	49.3
05658	MARSHFIELD	96.3	95.8	0.6	0.8	0.4	0.6	0.7	0.9	5.8	6.6	7.2	7.1	5.0	23.8	32.5	10.9	1.1	76.0	41.5	50.2	49.8
05660	MORETOWN	98.2	97.8	0.1	0.2	0.6	0.9	0.7	1.0	5.7	6.1	6.5	6.3	5.1	24.7	34.3	10.2	1.1	77.8	42.3	50.1	49.9
05661	MORRISVILLE	97.5	97.1	0.3	0.5	0.5	0.7	0.8	1.0	5.0	5.5	6.0	6.6	6.1	25.4	29.9	12.8	2.9	79.4	41.9	48.4	51.6
05663	NORTHFIELD	95.5	94.6	0.9	1.3	1.2	1.8	2.0	2.6	4.2	4.7	4.9	12.1	14.9	21.1	25.0	10.5	2.5	82.2	33.5	54.3	45.7
05666	NORTH MONTPELIER	96.7	95.3	0.0	1.6	0.0	0.0	0.0	0.0	3.1	3.1	6.3	7.8	4.7	25.0	40.6	9.4	0.0	82.8	45.0	46.9	53.1
05667	PLAINFIELD	96.4	95.9	0.7	1.0	0.3	0.6	1.1	1.3	5.5	5.6	6.2	7.4	7.7	23.4	32.6	10.4	1.3	78.5	41.0	48.7	51.3
05669	ROXBURY	94.1	93.7	0.5	0.8	0.0	0.0	1.2	1.6	5.5	5.8	6.6	6.0	3.7	22.8	36.7	12.1	0.8	78.2	44.7	50.7	49.3
05672	STOWE	97.5	97.1	0.3	0.4	0.4	0.7	1.1	1.3	4.1	4.1	4.6	6.2	5.8	25.4	32.9	15.0	2.0	83.5	44.9	49.9	50.1
05673	WAITSFIELD	97.5	97.0	0.9	1.2	0.4	0.6	1.1	1.4	5.1	5.7	5.8	5.3	5.0	26.8	33.4	11.9	1.0	80.1	42.8	49.0	51.0
05674	WARREN	98.0	97.8	0.2	0.3	0.2	0.4	1.0	1.3	4.2	5.2	5.6	6.0	4.8	26.7	35.6	10.8	1.0	80.5	43.2	50.9	49.1
05675	WASHINGTON	97.2	97.1	0.5	0.6	0.2	0.3	0.7	0.8	3.5	6.1	8.1	8.2	3.7	25.9	34.2	9.3	1.0	76.8	41.6	51.4	48.6
05676	WATERBURY	97.7	97.3	0.2	0.3	0.7	1.1	0.6	0.7	6.2	6.1	6.3	6.3	6.3	26.6	31.0	9.7	1.6	77.2	40.3	50.0	50.0
05677	WATERBURY CENTER	98.1	97.7	0.3	0.4	0.5	0.8	0.7	0.9	5.6	6.5	7.5	7.0	3.9	23.5	35.0	9.8	1.0	75.9	42.7	49.8	50.2
05679	WILLIAMSTOWN	98.3	98.2	0.1	0.1	0.2	0.2	0.7	0.9	6.2	6.6	7.0	6.4	4.9	27.1	30.1	10.8	1.0	76.3	40.3	51.4	48.6
05680	WOLCOTT	98.6	98.4	0.0	0.1	0.3	0.4	0.4	0.5	6.4	6.6	7.0	7.5	5.9	28.1	29.5	8.3	0.8	74.9	38.2	50.8	49.2
05681	WOODBURY	91.5	90.8	0.3	0.6	0.9	1.2	1.3	1.2	4.0	4.9	5.8	5.8	5.2	25.7	37.6	10.1	0.9	82.0	44.2	52.0	48.0
05682	WORCESTER	97.7	97.6	0.1	0.2	0.1	0.1	0.7	1.0	4.6	6.5	8.1	6.7	4.6	24.8	37.4	6.3	0.9	76.4	41.6	50.2	49.8
05701	RUTLAND	97.9	97.5	0.4	0.6	0.5	0.7	0.9	1.1	5.3	5.3	5.5	6.2	6.9	22.8	29.7	14.5	3.7	80.3	43.5	47.8	52.2
05730	BELMONT	97.3	97.2	0.3	0.3	0.3	0.3	0.3	0.3	5.2	6.4	7.7	6.7	3.1	27.3	31.0	11.0	1.5	75.5	41.3	50.9	49.1
05732	BOMOSEEN	98.1	97.6	0.1	0.1	0.5	0.9	1.1	1.5	3.7	5.2	6.0	10.2	11.2	20.4	31.4	10.6	1.4	81.1	39.6	49.6	50.4
05733	BRANDON	98.8	98.6	0.2	0.2	0.2	0.3	0.3	0.4	5.2	5.9	6.0	6.4	5.5	24.1	32.9	12.5	1.6	78.9	43.0	49.0	51.0
05734	BRIDPORT	98.3	98.1	0.1	0.1	0.4	0.5	0.1	0.1	6.4	6.9	7.5	7.0	3.8	24.9	30.9	11.0	1.6	74.7	40.5	52.2	47.8
05735	CASTLETON	97.7	97.2	0.3	0.3	0.6	0.9	1.1	1.5	3.7	5.2	5.7	12.6	13.9	20.4	27.6	9.5	1.3	81.4	34.8	49.7	50.3
05736	CENTER RUTLAND	99.0	99.1	0.2	0.2	0.3	0.3	0.5	0.8	3.5	4.0	4.8	5.9	4.6	19.0	38.1	17.9	2.3	84.1	50.2	49.3	50.7
05737	CHITTENDEN	98.4	98.1	0.2	0.3	0.3	0.5	0.3	0.3	5.8	7.1	7.3	5.3	4.5	21.0	37.0	11.1	0.8	76.4	44.3	49.6	50.4
05738	CUTTINGSVILLE	98.3	98.0	0.2	0.3	0.3	0.3	1.2	1.6	4.4	5.0	5.8	6.7	4.9	21.4	36.4	14.1	1.2	79.9	46.0	51.5	48.5
05739	DANBY	98.6	98.5	0.0	0.0	0.2	0.3	0.5	0.7	6.0	6.1	6.4	6.4	4.7	25.6	29.9	13.3	1.5	77.4	41.7	51.2	48.8
05742	EAST WALLINGFORD	98.6	98.3	0.2	0.3	0.2	0.3	0.3	0.5	5.1	5.9	6.3	5.3	4.1	24.2	34.7	13.1	1.4	78.6	44.5	50.2	49.8
05743	FAIR HAVEN	97.7	97.2	0.5	0.7	0.3	0.5	0.8	1.1	6.2	6.2	6.7	6.7	6.7	24.8	29.0	11.6	2.0	76.3	39.3	49.1	50.9
05744	FLORENCE	98.8	98.6	0.3	0.3	0.3	0.5	0.3	0.5	4.8	5.0	5.6	6.3	6.3	23.0	32.4	14.3	2.3	80.9	44.2	49.2	50.8
05746	GAYSVILLE	100.0	100.0	0.0	0.0	0.0	0.0	0.0	0.0	8.0	8.0	8.0	8.0	0.0	28.0	32.0	8.0	0.0	68.0	38.8	52.0	48.0
05747	GRANVILLE	97.0	96.6	0.0	0.3	0.3	0.6	1.0	0.3	4.9	6.1	6.7	6.4	4.0	27.1	30.8	13.4	0.6	78.7	41.6	52.1	47.9
05748	HANCOCK	97.4	97.0	0.0	0.3	0.3	0.5	0.9	0.3	4.6	5.9	6.5	6.2	3.8	26.8	32.7	13.0	0.5	79.5	42.5	53.5	46.5
05751	KILLINGTON	97.6	97.1	0.4	0.5	0.6	1.0	0.9	1.2	3.7	3.7	4.6	6.1	5.4	25.3	34.8	15.5	0.9	84.2	45.7	52.5	47.5
05753	MIDDLEBURY	95.1	94.0	0.9	1.3	1.6	2.1	1.9	2.3	4.2	4.5	4.8	13.2	16.0	18.3	24.5	11.9	2.6	83.4	33.0	48.2	51.8
05757	MIDDLETOWN SPRINGS	97.8	97.5	0.4	0.6	0.3	0.5	0.4	0.5	5.8	6.9	5.7	6.2	3.6	24.4	34.5	11.0	1.9	76.9	43.4	48.1	51.9
05758	MOUNT HOLLY	98.1	97.7	0.1	0.3	0.1	0.3	0.1	0.3	5.1	6.4	7.5	6.8	3.0	27.4	31.5	10.8	1.4	75.9	41.4	51.0	49.0
05759	NORTH CLARENDON	98.1	97.6	0.3	0.4	0.6	0.9	0.5	0.7	3.8	4.4	5.1	6.1	5.0	21.5	37.1	14.9	2.2	82.9	47.5	47.7	52.3
05760	ORWELL	99.0	98.8	0.2	0.2	0.4	0.6	0.8	1.1	5.7	6.4	7.1	7.3	4.1	22.0	33.8	12.1	1.5	76.1	43.2	48.7	51.3
05761	PAWLET	98.9	98.9	0.2	0.3	0.1	0.1	0.5	0.5	5.3	5.8	6.3	6.3	4.1	23.3	32.3	15.0	1.5	78.7	44.4	51.6	48.4
05762	PITTSFIELD	98.5	98.1	0.0	0.2	0.2	0.4	0.4	0.6	5.2	5.6	6.2	5.0	3.7	21.7	38.3	13.0	1.2	79.6	46.2	49.5	50.5
05763	PITTSFORD	99.1	98.9	0.2	0.3	0.2	0.3	0.4	0.5	5.2	5.7	6.2	5.8	5.2	23.2	34.2	12.7	1.8	79.0	44.1	50.7	49.3
05764	POULTNEY	97.1	96.4	0.7	1.0	0.9	1.3	0.6	0.7	4.5	4.6	5.0	10.9	11.7	21.0	26.3	13.4	2.6	81.6	38.9	49.8	50.2
	VERMONT	96.8	96.1	0.5	0.7	0.9	1.3	0.9	1.1	5.4	5.8	6.2	7.4	7.0	24.6	29.9	11.6	2.0	78.6	40.4	49.1	50.9
	UNITED STATES	75.1	72.0	12.3	12.7	3.8	4.6	12.5	15.7	6.8	6.7	6.6	7.1	6.9	27.0	26.0	10.9	1.9	75.7	36.9	49.2	50.8

05441-05764

#	POST OFFICE NAME	2009 Per Capita Income	2009 HH Income Base	2009 HOUSEHOLD INCOME DISTRIBUTION (%) Less than $25,000	$25,000 to $49,999	$50,000 to $99,999	$100,000 to $149,999	$150,000 or More	MEDIAN HOUSEHOLD INCOME 2009	2014	2009 National Centile	2009 State Centile	2009 Home Value Base	2009 HOME VALUE DISTRIBUTION (%) Less than $50,000	$50,000 to $89,999	$90,000 to $174,999	$175,000 to $399,999	$400,000 or More	2009 Median Home Value
05441	BAKERSFIELD	21374	146	15.1	32.2	45.9	5.5	1.4	51860	54567	66	53	123	0.8	5.7	38.2	49.6	5.7	187500
05442	BELVIDERE CENTER	22576	100	19.0	31.0	39.0	7.0	4.0	50000	50000	61	45	79	11.4	10.1	21.5	44.3	12.7	187500
05443	BRISTOL	26050	2528	16.4	24.1	46.3	8.8	4.3	57588	57649	75	74	1904	3.6	4.8	21.8	61.6	8.1	218170
05444	CAMBRIDGE	25502	724	12.3	26.7	47.9	9.8	3.3	60443	61108	78	82	558	0.2	2.0	19.4	67.6	10.9	238043
05445	CHARLOTTE	43499	1430	6.7	11.4	40.3	20.2	21.3	85408	89174	94	100	1168	0.0	0.0	6.0	36.4	57.6	472358
05446	COLCHESTER	32114	6521	9.1	21.4	42.2	19.4	8.0	69760	76138	87	94	4518	5.6	3.2	14.9	63.0	13.4	237110
05447	EAST BERKSHIRE	19758	33	24.2	27.3	36.4	9.1	3.0	48642	46145	58	39	27	0.0	11.1	44.4	40.7	3.7	169643
05448	EAST FAIRFIELD	23590	426	16.9	27.2	44.6	8.7	2.6	55492	58152	72	69	357	1.1	4.5	33.3	54.6	6.4	201506
05450	ENOSBURG FALLS	20652	2131	24.1	31.3	36.4	5.8	2.4	45791	49662	51	29	1609	4.4	8.5	41.0	39.8	6.3	169809
05452	ESSEX JUNCTION	36396	7633	6.0	16.6	43.5	23.3	10.6	77279	81859	91	98	5777	0.2	0.1	13.1	74.5	12.1	253028
05454	FAIRFAX	26045	1768	9.2	20.2	54.4	13.0	3.3	67456	67900	85	94	1492	1.1	1.4	19.0	69.8	8.7	239861
05455	FAIRFIELD	22162	451	19.3	24.8	43.7	8.9	3.3	57763	60265	75	75	370	1.9	3.8	35.4	53.5	5.4	196154
05456	FERRISBURGH	28945	512	12.3	20.7	44.5	17.0	5.5	64558	63989	83	93	415	0.2	2.4	20.2	52.3	24.8	271364
05457	FRANKLIN	21790	574	15.9	32.4	39.9	9.1	2.8	51580	54533	65	52	481	3.7	4.0	38.9	46.2	7.3	182366
05458	GRAND ISLE	29358	932	11.9	24.9	48.8	9.1	5.3	61977	62972	80	85	761	2.0	3.2	9.9	57.7	27.3	279107
05459	HIGHGATE CENTER	20683	754	16.7	30.6	44.0	6.9	1.7	51490	53815	65	52	601	7.2	6.0	44.3	37.9	4.7	167432
05461	HINESBURG	27702	1774	9.1	26.6	43.3	15.7	5.2	62435	67810	81	86	1415	5.4	4.6	14.3	62.4	13.3	242949
05462	HUNTINGTON	25911	746	12.6	24.4	49.1	11.1	2.8	62389	66987	80	85	638	1.7	0.6	26.3	62.5	8.8	213272
05463	ISLE LA MOTTE	24579	229	22.7	31.9	34.9	7.0	3.5	45878	50000	51	29	189	8.5	1.6	25.9	39.7	24.3	221774
05464	JEFFERSONVILLE	26733	1132	12.6	29.3	46.1	9.0	2.9	58353	58902	76	76	832	0.7	2.0	14.7	66.3	16.2	250342
05465	JERICHO	31904	1974	5.9	14.1	44.8	27.2	8.1	77178	80984	91	98	1673	1.0	0.5	12.1	71.7	14.7	255789
05468	MILTON	25699	4532	10.1	22.8	51.2	12.3	3.6	64351	68954	83	92	3826	4.0	3.0	16.2	71.0	5.8	225685
05471	MONTGOMERY CENTER	21385	398	28.9	28.9	33.7	6.0	2.5	43812	46554	45	21	325	1.2	11.1	43.4	39.4	4.9	168664
05472	NEW HAVEN	26873	781	12.9	22.9	50.3	9.0	4.9	60630	61752	78	83	633	0.9	1.4	20.4	56.7	20.5	246681
05473	NORTH FERRISBURG	30499	549	11.7	20.6	45.9	15.7	6.2	65227	64847	83	93	460	0.9	2.2	18.5	58.0	20.4	254762
05474	NORTH HERO	31982	434	13.8	29.7	41.7	8.3	6.5	57982	60895	75	76	366	0.0	0.8	10.4	60.1	28.7	296923
05476	RICHFORD	17977	1155	32.7	31.3	30.2	4.2	1.6	36772	39327	23	5	855	10.5	19.6	48.4	20.1	1.3	126736
05477	RICHMOND	33634	1861	8.5	15.4	44.8	21.4	9.8	75315	79531	90	97	1472	5.3	2.4	11.1	69.0	12.1	236575
05478	SAINT ALBANS	24289	6049	17.8	26.1	45.3	8.3	2.5	55406	57619	72	69	3992	3.2	2.1	30.0	58.2	6.6	204449
05482	SHELBURNE	46805	2817	6.8	13.0	36.0	21.4	22.9	88433	94373	95	100	2203	1.0	1.9	4.3	57.2	35.6	334742
05483	SHELDON	20313	581	18.2	27.9	46.1	6.2	1.5	52715	55047	67	58	480	4.6	4.6	36.9	49.2	4.8	183482
05486	SOUTH HERO	35931	682	12.2	17.3	42.1	17.9	10.6	72619	73786	88	96	546	1.5	0.7	6.6	56.6	34.6	339130
05487	STARKSBORO	21818	577	14.6	27.0	48.4	7.1	2.9	54907	54717	71	67	476	10.5	9.7	22.3	50.0	7.6	197500
05488	SWANTON	25281	3077	18.1	27.4	41.1	9.0	4.3	54876	57997	71	66	2303	2.9	4.2	30.7	51.1	11.2	199956
05489	UNDERHILL	34803	1370	5.1	14.1	41.8	28.9	10.1	82204	86167	93	99	1200	0.9	0.2	8.3	71.2	19.4	280350
05491	VERGENNES	23925	2352	17.8	25.4	45.6	8.6	2.6	57125	57830	74	73	1751	3.2	4.2	23.9	57.0	11.8	212539
05492	WATERVILLE	22985	327	18.3	31.5	39.8	7.3	3.1	50124	51300	61	46	257	6.2	8.6	19.8	52.1	13.2	208523
05494	WESTFORD	29589	532	6.0	15.6	46.6	25.8	6.0	76335	80596	90	97	460	2.2	2.0	17.4	67.4	11.1	238679
05495	WILLISTON	40787	3618	5.4	15.5	41.9	21.6	15.6	79806	84139	92	98	2967	1.9	1.1	10.2	63.4	23.5	285819
05602	MONTPELIER	31049	5416	20.3	24.5	39.5	10.2	5.5	55213	57160	72	68	3434	3.1	2.7	30.1	57.1	7.0	209554
05640	ADAMANT	28686	89	11.2	30.3	47.2	7.9	3.4	55716	58452	72	69	74	0.0	4.1	16.2	60.8	18.9	262500
05641	BARRE	26911	7276	23.4	26.9	36.3	9.4	4.0	49727	52923	60	42	4505	1.7	2.6	42.2	49.4	4.1	181360
05647	CABOT	24077	390	19.2	27.4	42.1	6.9	4.4	53096	55136	68	61	321	1.6	5.9	37.4	46.7	8.4	185577
05648	CALAIS	28955	160	10.0	30.6	46.9	8.1	4.4	56681	58457	74	71	134	0.0	2.2	15.7	64.2	17.9	257143
05649	EAST BARRE	32017	260	12.7	25.0	43.5	10.0	8.8	60604	61529	78	82	198	3.0	7.6	42.9	41.9	4.5	170395
05650	EAST CALAIS	25833	413	16.0	31.5	43.1	6.5	2.9	51984	54585	66	54	340	2.9	8.2	32.6	47.6	8.5	197826
05651	EAST MONTPELIER	26631	605	13.9	28.4	45.0	7.9	4.8	58388	59748	76	77	455	4.4	7.5	18.7	58.7	10.8	220066
05652	EDEN	17322	289	23.9	36.7	35.6	3.1	0.7	43151	46069	43	19	233	6.0	12.9	42.5	35.6	3.0	160598
05653	EDEN MILLS	17708	190	24.2	37.4	34.7	3.2	0.5	42128	45832	40	15	153	7.2	13.7	41.8	34.6	2.6	157589
05654	GRANITEVILLE	25932	711	17.2	29.7	38.4	11.0	3.8	52480	54613	67	58	511	1.8	6.8	49.9	39.3	2.2	165543
05655	HYDE PARK	27901	1225	15.2	27.8	41.7	10.5	4.7	54976	55050	71	67	961	5.2	7.8	28.5	49.0	9.5	200812
05656	JOHNSON	20858	1332	27.7	30.0	34.2	5.9	2.3	41693	45226	38	14	849	11.5	8.5	30.9	40.4	8.7	173295
05658	MARSHFIELD	23765	565	20.2	29.0	39.8	7.3	3.7	50564	52770	63	48	453	2.9	9.1	37.7	41.9	8.4	175938
05660	MORETOWN	28945	892	12.9	24.8	45.7	10.8	5.8	63673	64289	82	90	690	3.0	4.5	18.7	57.1	16.7	246903
05661	MORRISVILLE	24235	2361	21.5	31.5	36.8	6.5	3.8	47173	49401	55	33	1532	2.3	3.2	24.0	60.1	10.4	224843
05663	NORTHFIELD	24233	2258	16.8	24.8	45.5	9.9	2.9	59031	60377	76	79	1593	5.3	8.0	31.3	52.0	3.5	186817
05666	NORTH MONTPELIER	20234	24	16.7	29.2	50.0	4.2	0.0	52860	55657	68	59	20	0.0	5.0	30.0	55.0	10.0	216667
05667	PLAINFIELD	25963	1006	16.7	27.4	43.3	9.4	3.1	54665	56355	71	65	768	2.6	8.9	29.9	49.6	9.0	195370
05669	ROXBURY	23957	156	19.9	28.2	44.2	3.2	4.5	51228	53600	64	50	133	0.0	9.0	51.1	36.1	3.8	164453
05672	STOWE	41714	2210	12.7	21.7	36.5	15.8	13.3	72282	72724	88	95	1503	0.6	0.4	5.4	35.7	58.0	444925
05673	WAITSFIELD	35076	1212	14.3	24.5	41.5	12.4	7.3	62417	63485	81	86	885	4.2	1.8	10.2	54.0	29.8	303514
05674	WARREN	34138	854	17.9	22.7	42.9	8.3	8.2	61028	61935	79	83	629	1.1	3.0	13.8	52.0	30.0	298214
05675	WASHINGTON	23610	454	18.5	27.8	44.9	6.6	2.2	52436	53195	67	57	389	5.1	9.3	35.5	38.8	11.3	175338
05676	WATERBURY	29130	1899	16.5	28.6	38.8	11.7	4.3	54163	56397	70	64	1264	6.6	2.8	23.3	56.7	10.5	216878
05677	WATERBURY CENTER	36707	953	7.9	19.6	39.7	21.1	11.8	73054	73020	88	96	791	4.2	2.4	14.7	54.7	24.0	275568
05679	WILLIAMSTOWN	22820	1390	18.7	33.5	39.5	5.4	2.9	48125	50159	57	36	1137	7.0	10.0	34.1	43.7	5.1	172500
05680	WOLCOTT	21370	932	19.4	34.4	38.7	4.8	2.6	46657	48557	53	31	762	3.5	6.6	30.8	48.2	10.9	197697
05681	WOODBURY	21696	133	19.5	36.1	36.1	5.3	3.0	43398	48672	44	19	109	1.8	10.1	44.0	37.6	6.4	166875
05682	WORCESTER	24925	491	14.7	31.2	41.1	9.8	3.3	54694	57440	71	65	399	3.8	5.3	28.1	56.6	6.3	204276
05701	RUTLAND	25490	9082	26.7	26.9	36.1	6.8	3.4	45923	50186	51	29	5303	1.2	3.2	38.7	50.5	6.5	191981
05730	BELMONT	25259	135	18.5	31.1	40.0	6.7	3.7	50251	53458	62	47	114	2.6	11.4	27.2	43.0	15.8	205263
05732	BOMOSEEN	30913	505	18.4	25.0	41.8	9.1	5.7	55733	56980	72	70	373	4.8	4.3	26.3	55.5	9.1	198904
05733	BRANDON	24786	2515	20.2	31.7	39.0	5.3	3.8	48079	51202	57	36	1934	4.3	6.0	39.2	43.0	7.4	175905
05734	BRIDPORT	25355	499	18.6	27.1	39.3	11.0	4.0	53509	53351	69	62	382	0.0	1.3	22.5	62.6	13.6	221053
05735	CASTLETON	24078	1270	20.9	26.6	39.1	8.7	4.7	52129	54658	66	55	928	7.2	6.6	26.0	54.0	6.3	192336
05736	CENTER RUTLAND	36164	314	19.1	25.8	36.0	11.1	8.0	58737	61380	76	77	251	2.8	4.0	22.7	49.0	21.5	249286
05737	CHITTENDEN	27989	251	12.0	26.7	44.6	10.8	6.0	58686	59239	76	77	202	3.0	1.5	22.3	52.5	20.8	252941
05738	CUTTINGSVILLE	28684	469	13.4	29.4	40.7	11.3	5.1	59828	61259	77	81	392	1.0	6.4	18.6	59.2	14.8	250781
05739	DANBY	21463	543	23.8	33.1	35.9	4.8	2.4	45567	47479	50	28	420	11.7	9.0	30.0	36.9	12.4	172973
05742	EAST WALLINGFORD	26910	279	14.0	27.6	44.8	9.7	3.9	56023	57434	73	71	233	2.1	5.6	20.2	57.9	14.2	234239
05743	FAIR HAVEN	24079	1936	20.7	29.4	40.8	6.6	2.5	49882	52642	61	43	1316	8.1	6.6	46.0	35.0	4.3	156675
05744	FLORENCE	26278	271	17.3	29.9	39.9	8.5	4.4	52881	56423	68	60	192	4.2	1.0	40.6	47.4	6.8	183696
05746	GAYSVILLE	20400	10	10.0	40.0	50.0	0.0	0.0	50000	50000	61	45	9	0.0	0.0	22.2	66.7	11.1	225000
05747	GRANVILLE	20531	143	25.9	32.9	35.7	4.2	1.4	40982	46139	36	12	108	7.4	9.3	39.8	38.0	5.6	163333
05748	HANCOCK	21210	166	26.5	32.5	35.5	4.2	1.2	40568	45942	35	10	125	9.6	10.4	40.0	34.4	5.6	156618
05751	KILLINGTON	42100	481	14.1	25.8	32.0	12.3	15.8	62440	65698	81	87	352	0.6	0.0	13.4	40.1	46.0	383133
05753	MIDDLEBURY	25881	3599	22.3	25.1	37.1	9.4	6.0	51864	52832	66	54	2366	2.6	2.1	17.6	57.7	19.9	245690
05757	MIDDLETOWN SPRINGS	23160	406	23.6	34.7	30.8	8.6	2.2	43910	46148	45	22	331	3.3	5.7	23.9	48.3	18.7	231604
05758	MOUNT HOLLY	24888	287	18.1	30.7	40.8	7.0	3.5	50842	53515	63	49	243	4.9	10.3	28.0	40.7	16.0	200714
05759	NORTH CLARENDON	26728	1086	19.2	28.6	40.1	8.7	3.4	51770	54260	65	53	845	7.9	5.3	26.7	51.6	8.4	203711
05760	ORWELL	23182	544	17.5	32.0	38.4	8.3	3.9	50240	51475	62	46	454	0.7	2.9	25.8	58.4	12.3	220879
05761	PAWLET	25833	449	20.7	33.2	33.4	7.1	5.6	47028	50399	54	32	335	4.5	6.3	23.6	48.4	17.3	233140
05762	PITTSFIELD	27946	220	16.8	26.8	44.1	6.8	5.5	54651	55946	71	64	168	0.6	3.0	20.2	61.3	14.9	256522
05763	PITTSFORD	26322	1157	15.6	30.0	41.5	9.4	3.5	53710	55884	69	63	884	1.9	3.1	30.5	56.3	8.1	208239
05764	POULTNEY	20435	1317	27.5	29.6	35.0	5.6	2.3	42766	46817	42	18	950	2.5	9.1	46.9	35.9	5.6	163559
	VERMONT	27546		19.3	26.3	38.8	10.3	5.3	54205	56824				3.4	4.6	25.9	52.9	13.2	216547
	UNITED STATES	27277		20.9	24.4	35.3	11.7	7.6	54719	56938				9.3	13.1	31.6	32.6	13.5	162279

ZIP CODE #	POST OFFICE NAME	FINANCIAL SERVICES: Auto Loan	Home Loan	Investments	Retirement Plans	THE HOME: Home Improvements: Home Repair	Lawn & Garden	Furnishings: Computers & Hardware-Personal	Major Appliances	TV, Radio, Sound Equipment	Furniture	ENTERTAINMENT: Dine out/Carry out	Sports Equipment	Fees & Tickets	Toys & Games	Travel	Cable TV	PERSONAL: Apparel & Services	Auto Repairs	Health Insurance	Pets & Supplies
05441	BAKERSFIELD	78	88	76	90	85	86	78	81	77	79	78	64	84	79	83	77	54	78	81	96
05442	BELVIDERE CENTER	94	87	77	84	85	89	82	87	85	85	85	63	77	88	78	87	58	84	87	103
05443	BRISTOL	93	100	91	102	98	102	93	97	92	90	92	75	95	94	96	94	65	94	98	114
05444	CAMBRIDGE	92	104	90	107	101	102	93	97	91	93	92	75	99	94	98	91	64	93	96	114
05445	CHARLOTTE	149	194	208	200	204	180	163	172	153	176	154	130	192	152	186	148	113	161	157	194
05446	COLCHESTER	114	122	115	124	120	114	118	114	115	120	117	90	123	117	120	114	83	115	112	135
05447	EAST BERKSHIRE	99	68	108	68	71	104	75	93	78	61	77	77	55	77	75	85	50	87	99	115
05448	EAST FAIRFIELD	89	96	85	99	94	98	87	93	87	86	87	72	90	89	91	88	60	88	93	109
05450	ENOSBURG FALLS	89	73	86	72	74	91	74	86	78	69	77	66	64	78	73	83	52	81	89	102
05452	ESSEX JUNCTION	124	143	133	144	140	131	132	130	127	134	129	102	143	130	138	125	92	129	126	152
05454	FAIRFAX	101	114	98	118	111	112	102	106	100	102	101	83	109	103	108	100	70	102	104	124
05455	FAIRFIELD	94	94	87	97	94	102	89	97	90	84	89	74	87	92	91	93	61	91	98	113
05456	FERRISBURGH	116	108	135	109	112	125	102	119	104	99	104	89	98	102	110	108	70	112	118	139
05457	FRANKLIN	102	83	101	85	85	108	85	100	88	74	87	79	72	89	85	95	58	93	104	119
05458	GRAND ISLE	110	106	125	107	109	119	100	114	101	97	101	86	97	100	106	104	69	107	113	133
05459	HIGHGATE CENTER	95	77	82	77	77	96	78	89	83	73	82	68	67	86	74	89	55	83	93	106
05461	HINESBURG	110	115	102	113	112	110	103	107	103	108	104	81	106	107	104	103	72	103	103	126
05462	HUNTINGTON	94	106	91	109	103	104	95	98	93	95	94	77	101	96	100	93	65	95	97	116
05463	ISLE LA MOTTE	95	76	122	74	83	100	76	96	79	71	78	70	66	75	82	84	52	89	95	112
05464	JEFFERSONVILLE	90	101	87	104	98	99	90	94	89	91	89	73	96	91	95	89	62	90	93	110
05465	JERICHO	120	148	130	147	143	129	125	127	118	131	120	101	139	123	134	114	86	121	115	146
05468	MILTON	101	111	97	111	108	107	100	103	99	101	100	80	105	102	104	99	70	100	101	121
05471	MONTGOMERY CENTER	84	67	109	66	74	89	67	86	71	63	70	63	58	67	73	75	46	79	85	99
05472	NEW HAVEN	98	111	95	114	108	109	99	103	97	99	98	80	106	100	105	98	68	99	102	121
05473	NORTH FERRISBURG	112	113	121	115	114	122	104	116	104	102	104	88	105	105	111	107	72	110	114	135
05474	NORTH HERO	124	99	160	98	109	131	99	126	104	93	103	92	86	99	108	111	68	117	125	146
05476	RICHFORD	79	57	81	56	59	81	60	75	66	55	64	57	48	65	59	72	43	69	79	89
05477	RICHMOND	122	140	128	141	137	128	125	126	121	130	122	98	135	124	131	118	87	123	119	146
05478	SAINT ALBANS	85	87	81	88	86	89	87	87	87	83	87	68	88	88	87	89	61	87	89	102
05482	SHELBURNE	158	189	190	193	192	181	166	172	162	175	163	129	186	161	182	160	117	166	167	198
05483	SHELDON	90	81	81	84	83	96	80	91	83	73	82	69	74	85	80	88	56	84	94	106
05486	SOUTH HERO	130	134	166	136	141	146	122	139	121	124	121	103	125	118	135	123	84	130	134	160
05487	STARKSBORO	92	93	82	94	91	94	86	90	87	87	87	68	86	90	86	88	60	87	90	107
05488	SWANTON	95	90	84	93	89	101	89	95	92	83	90	73	85	93	88	95	62	92	100	112
05489	UNDERHILL	127	159	147	160	156	141	134	138	126	141	129	107	151	130	146	122	92	131	125	158
05491	VERGENNES	88	93	92	93	92	95	87	92	87	85	87	71	89	88	91	88	61	89	92	108
05492	WATERVILLE	94	89	78	87	87	90	83	88	86	86	86	65	80	89	81	88	59	85	88	104
05494	WESTFORD	114	143	125	142	138	123	120	121	112	126	115	97	135	117	129	108	82	116	109	139
05495	WILLISTON	141	158	153	161	158	149	146	146	142	151	144	112	157	144	153	140	102	144	142	171
05602	MONTPELIER	92	93	91	95	92	95	95	93	95	93	95	72	95	94	95	95	66	94	97	110
05640	ADAMANT	111	89	143	87	97	117	89	113	93	83	92	82	77	88	96	99	61	104	111	131
05641	BARRE	85	81	78	83	80	87	86	85	88	82	87	65	83	87	84	91	61	87	93	101
05647	CABOT	87	97	84	100	94	96	87	91	86	87	86	71	93	88	92	86	60	87	90	107
05648	CALAIS	111	90	143	89	99	118	90	113	93	84	92	83	78	89	97	99	62	105	112	131
05649	EAST BARRE	112	105	106	107	107	117	108	113	111	104	109	84	103	110	107	115	75	111	121	132
05650	EAST CALAIS	88	86	88	88	87	96	81	91	83	77	82	69	79	83	84	86	56	85	92	106
05651	EAST MONTPELIER	92	105	93	108	103	103	93	97	92	94	92	75	100	93	99	91	65	93	96	114
05652	EDEN	76	70	62	67	68	71	66	70	68	68	68	51	62	71	63	70	46	67	70	83
05653	EDEN MILLS	74	68	61	66	67	70	65	68	67	67	67	50	61	70	62	69	46	66	69	81
05654	GRANITEVILLE	96	85	86	86	87	97	89	94	91	85	90	69	82	91	86	95	62	92	99	110
05655	HYDE PARK	98	93	91	95	94	101	95	98	96	92	95	74	91	96	94	99	65	97	103	115
05656	JOHNSON	75	65	61	67	64	71	75	71	76	70	75	55	69	76	68	78	52	74	76	85
05658	MARSHFIELD	90	86	82	89	87	97	83	92	84	77	83	70	79	86	84	88	57	85	93	107
05660	MORETOWN	101	113	102	115	110	108	103	104	101	104	102	81	110	103	108	100	72	102	103	123
05661	MORRISVILLE	88	79	77	79	79	86	80	84	83	79	82	62	75	84	77	86	56	83	88	99
05663	NORTHFIELD	93	91	87	93	91	100	90	94	92	86	91	71	88	93	90	95	63	92	100	111
05666	NORTH MONTPELIER	75	85	73	87	82	83	76	79	74	76	75	61	81	76	80	75	52	76	78	93
05667	PLAINFIELD	93	88	86	91	89	97	88	93	89	85	88	70	85	90	88	92	61	90	97	109
05669	ROXBURY	91	83	82	86	84	97	81	92	84	74	82	70	75	86	81	89	56	85	95	107
05672	STOWE	126	141	135	143	139	131	133	130	129	136	130	101	141	130	138	127	93	130	127	153
05673	WAITSFIELD	114	106	131	107	110	117	105	115	106	103	106	87	101	103	109	108	73	111	114	135
05674	WARREN	117	103	138	103	108	121	104	118	106	101	106	89	97	103	108	110	72	113	117	138
05675	WASHINGTON	91	82	85	85	84	98	81	93	84	74	82	70	74	85	82	89	56	85	95	107
05676	WATERBURY	92	94	87	98	93	93	95	92	94	94	95	72	97	94	95	94	66	94	94	110
05677	WATERBURY CENTER	125	148	139	152	148	142	129	135	125	133	126	103	142	126	140	124	89	129	131	157
05679	WILLIAMSTOWN	89	82	77	82	81	90	79	86	81	76	81	64	74	84	77	85	55	81	88	101
05680	WOLCOTT	88	81	72	78	79	83	76	81	79	80	79	59	72	83	73	82	54	79	81	96
05681	WOODBURY	83	75	74	78	77	89	74	84	77	67	75	63	68	78	74	81	51	77	86	97
05682	WORCESTER	89	99	87	102	96	98	89	93	87	89	88	72	94	89	94	88	61	89	92	109
05701	RUTLAND	81	74	77	75	75	83	80	81	83	76	82	60	76	81	78	86	57	82	88	95
05730	BELMONT	102	81	131	80	89	108	82	104	85	76	84	76	71	81	88	91	56	96	102	120
05732	BOMOSEEN	110	91	125	91	98	114	94	110	98	89	97	81	84	95	97	103	65	105	112	128
05733	BRANDON	95	79	99	79	82	99	81	94	85	76	84	70	72	84	82	90	56	89	97	110
05734	BRIDPORT	116	80	127	79	83	122	88	110	92	72	91	91	65	90	88	100	59	103	116	135
05735	CASTLETON	99	85	105	85	89	102	89	99	92	84	90	73	80	90	89	96	61	96	103	116
05736	CENTER RUTLAND	123	99	155	98	109	130	100	125	105	94	103	91	88	100	107	111	69	116	124	145
05737	CHITTENDEN	96	108	93	112	105	106	97	101	95	97	96	79	103	98	102	95	67	97	100	118
05738	CUTTINGSVILLE	98	109	95	112	106	108	98	102	96	98	97	80	104	99	103	97	68	98	101	120
05739	DANBY	92	66	95	64	69	94	68	86	75	63	74	65	54	75	67	83	49	79	90	103
05742	EAST WALLINGFORD	94	97	99	99	97	102	89	97	88	87	89	74	90	89	94	90	61	92	96	114
05743	FAIR HAVEN	88	80	80	81	80	90	82	86	84	79	83	65	77	84	80	87	57	85	91	102
05744	FLORENCE	96	86	87	87	87	97	91	94	94	87	92	70	85	93	88	97	63	94	102	111
05746	GAYSVILLE	85	68	110	67	75	90	68	87	71	64	70	63	59	68	74	76	47	80	85	100
05747	GRANVILLE	79	63	102	62	69	83	63	80	66	59	65	58	55	63	68	70	43	74	79	93
05748	HANCOCK	79	63	102	62	69	83	63	80	66	59	65	59	55	63	68	70	43	74	79	93
05751	KILLINGTON	121	135	130	137	134	126	127	125	123	130	125	97	135	124	132	121	89	125	121	146
05753	MIDDLEBURY	97	88	105	88	91	106	90	98	93	84	93	75	85	90	93	98	63	97	108	117
05757	MIDDLETOWN SPRINGS	92	73	118	72	80	97	74	93	77	69	76	68	63	74	79	83	51	86	93	109
05758	MOUNT HOLLY	102	82	132	80	90	108	82	104	85	76	84	76	71	81	88	91	56	96	102	120
05759	NORTH CLARENDON	92	84	84	87	86	98	84	93	87	77	85	70	78	88	83	91	58	88	97	109
05760	ORWELL	106	75	115	74	78	111	82	100	85	68	84	82	61	83	81	92	55	94	105	123
05761	PAWLET	107	75	117	74	78	112	81	102	86	68	85	82	61	84	81	94	55	95	107	124
05762	PITTSFIELD	103	93	123	93	97	110	89	106	91	85	90	79	83	89	95	95	61	99	104	123
05763	PITTSFORD	95	87	87	90	89	100	88	96	90	82	89	72	82	91	87	94	61	91	100	112
05764	POULTNEY	81	67	78	67	69	83	69	79	73	65	72	59	61	73	68	78	49	75	83	93
	VERMONT	98	92	100	93	93	101	93	98	94	90	94	75	89	94	93	97	65	96	101	116
	UNITED STATES	100	100	100	100	100	100	100	100	100	100	100	100	100	100	100	100	100	100	100	100

05765-05907

ZIP CODE #	POST OFFICE NAME	COUNTY FIPS CODE	POPULATION 2000	POPULATION 2009	POPULATION 2014	2000-2009 ANNUAL RATE % Rate	2000-2009 ANNUAL RATE State Centile	HOUSEHOLDS 2000	HOUSEHOLDS 2009	HOUSEHOLDS 2014	HOUSEHOLDS % Annual Rate 2000-2009	HOUSEHOLDS 2009 Average HH Size	FAMILIES 2000	FAMILIES 2009	FAMILIES % Annual Rate 2000-2009
05765	PROCTOR	021	1906	1850	1815	-0.3	11	776	779	774	0.0	2.37	543	532	-0.2
05766	RIPTON	001	542	585	603	0.8	75	202	225	235	1.2	2.53	144	157	0.9
05767	ROCHESTER	027	1323	1280	1254	-0.4	8	579	587	581	0.1	2.16	374	370	-0.1
05769	SALISBURY	001	1207	1343	1402	1.2	91	476	556	586	1.7	2.39	339	386	1.4
05770	SHOREHAM	001	970	1044	1080	0.8	75	353	396	414	1.3	2.64	267	294	1.0
05772	STOCKBRIDGE	027	649	652	643	0.0	25	271	283	282	0.5	2.30	186	190	0.2
05773	WALLINGFORD	021	2219	2227	2231	0.0	25	885	929	941	0.5	2.38	634	651	0.3
05774	WELLS	021	1187	1259	1280	0.6	64	493	541	555	1.0	2.33	352	376	0.7
05775	WEST PAWLET	021	580	632	644	0.9	81	236	263	271	1.2	2.40	159	173	0.9
05776	WEST RUPERT	003	690	725	728	0.5	57	289	314	319	0.9	2.31	198	210	0.6
05777	WEST RUTLAND	021	3689	3798	3831	0.3	44	1443	1547	1576	0.8	2.46	990	1036	0.5
05778	WHITING	001	733	780	804	0.7	70	279	310	323	1.1	2.52	204	222	0.9
05819	SAINT JOHNSBURY	005	9207	9141	9104	-0.1	19	3824	3934	3956	0.3	2.22	2398	2416	0.1
05820	ALBANY	019	488	541	566	1.1	89	194	228	242	1.8	2.37	137	157	1.5
05821	BARNET	005	1411	1399	1385	-0.1	19	536	554	555	0.4	2.45	372	374	0.1
05822	BARTON	019	1788	1954	2031	1.0	84	761	880	929	1.6	2.21	496	558	1.3
05824	CONCORD	009	1179	1264	1290	0.8	75	460	508	526	1.1	2.45	315	340	0.8
05825	COVENTRY	019	145	155	160	0.7	70	51	57	60	1.2	2.72	39	42	0.8
05826	CRAFTSBURY	019	827	856	877	0.4	52	311	342	356	1.0	2.30	220	235	0.7
05827	CRAFTSBURY COMMON	019	393	412	424	0.5	57	151	168	176	1.2	2.29	107	116	0.9
05828	DANVILLE	005	1731	1872	1929	0.9	81	672	755	786	1.3	2.47	484	531	1.0
05829	DERBY	019	1698	1683	1672	-0.1	19	708	735	740	0.4	2.26	503	511	0.2
05830	DERBY LINE	019	1552	1698	1755	1.0	84	617	700	734	1.4	2.42	445	493	1.1
05832	EAST BURKE	005	671	715	733	0.7	70	290	325	338	1.2	2.20	203	221	0.9
05833	EAST CHARLESTON	019	113	132	140	1.7	98	47	58	62	2.3	2.28	34	41	2.0
05836	EAST HARDWICK	005	983	999	1000	0.2	37	370	389	393	0.5	2.57	262	269	0.3
05837	EAST HAVEN	009	360	377	386	0.5	57	142	155	160	1.0	2.43	103	110	0.7
05839	GLOVER	019	674	743	774	1.1	89	260	303	321	1.7	2.35	182	207	1.4
05841	GREENSBORO	019	369	347	339	-0.7	2	157	155	153	-0.1	2.15	108	104	-0.4
05842	GREENSBORO BEND	005	588	587	588	0.0	25	230	241	244	0.5	2.39	163	167	0.3
05843	HARDWICK	005	2701	2803	2816	0.4	52	1038	1103	1118	0.7	2.54	732	759	0.4
05845	IRASBURG	019	1104	1224	1279	1.1	89	413	485	514	1.8	2.52	318	367	1.6
05846	ISLAND POND	009	1392	1328	1306	-0.5	5	593	591	588	0.0	2.25	401	391	-0.3
05847	LOWELL	019	755	812	840	0.8	75	278	314	330	1.3	2.59	210	233	1.1
05850	LYNDON CENTER	005	166	168	166	0.1	32	70	73	73	0.5	2.22	38	38	0.0
05851	LYNDONVILLE	005	5899	6215	6329	0.6	64	2195	2408	2483	1.0	2.37	1458	1558	0.7
05853	MORGAN	019	639	726	762	1.4	95	237	279	296	1.8	2.60	176	203	1.6
05855	NEWPORT	019	7810	7831	7823	0.0	25	3144	3307	3350	0.5	2.24	1975	2024	0.3
05857	NEWPORT CENTER	019	1399	1412	1410	0.1	32	540	580	588	0.8	2.43	403	425	0.6
05858	NORTH CONCORD	009	304	316	322	0.4	52	121	131	134	0.9	2.39	86	91	0.6
05859	NORTH TROY	019	1941	2234	2360	1.5	97	751	917	982	2.2	2.43	528	632	2.0
05860	ORLEANS	019	2303	2386	2412	0.4	52	900	973	998	0.8	2.36	617	652	0.6
05862	PEACHAM	005	190	182	177	-0.5	5	83	83	82	0.0	2.19	58	57	-0.2
05866	SHEFFIELD	005	756	825	853	0.9	81	286	328	343	1.5	2.52	214	240	1.2
05867	SUTTON	005	842	963	1013	1.5	97	300	360	382	2.0	2.67	215	252	1.7
05868	TROY	019	5	5	5	0.0	25	3	3	3	0.0	1.67	2	0	-100.0
05871	WEST BURKE	005	1509	1656	1715	1.0	84	596	683	716	1.5	2.42	437	490	1.2
05872	WEST CHARLESTON	019	738	858	909	1.6	97	293	359	385	2.2	2.39	211	253	2.0
05873	WEST DANVILLE	005	925	970	987	0.5	57	365	400	412	1.0	2.42	263	281	0.7
05874	WESTFIELD	019	498	595	645	1.9	99	199	253	278	2.6	2.33	142	178	2.5
05875	WEST GLOVER	019	518	570	594	1.0	84	213	248	263	1.7	2.25	148	168	1.4
05901	AVERILL	009	8	9	9	1.3	92	3	3	4	0.0	3.00	2	2	0.0
05902	BEECHER FALLS	009	226	233	237	0.3	44	85	91	94	0.7	2.56	59	62	0.5
05903	CANAAN	009	852	879	895	0.3	44	356	383	393	0.8	2.30	248	261	0.6
05904	GILMAN	009	9	9	10	0.0	25	4	4	5	0.0	2.25	3	3	0.0
05905	GUILDHALL	009	878	941	967	0.8	75	351	392	407	1.2	2.40	246	268	0.9
05906	LUNENBURG	009	1479	1539	1569	0.4	52	578	625	642	0.8	2.46	410	434	0.6
05907	NORTON	009	224	245	253	1.0	84	95	108	113	1.4	2.27	65	73	1.3
	VERMONT					0.4					0.8	2.36			0.5
	UNITED STATES					1.0					1.1	2.59			0.9

ZIP CODE #	POST OFFICE NAME	RACE (%) White 2000	White 2009	Black 2000	Black 2009	Asian/Pacific 2000	Asian/Pacific 2009	% Hispanic Origin 2000	% Hispanic Origin 2009	2009 AGE DISTRIBUTION (%) 0-4	5-9	10-14	15-19	20-24	25-44	45-64	65-84	85+	18+	MEDIAN AGE 2009	% 2009 Males	% 2009 Females
05765	PROCTOR	99.1	99.0	0.2	0.2	0.1	0.1	0.6	0.8	5.8	6.1	6.4	7.0	5.9	23.4	30.4	12.4	2.6	77.5	42.1	47.0	53.0
05766	RIPTON	97.4	97.1	0.2	0.3	0.6	0.7	0.6	0.9	6.0	5.5	8.0	5.8	4.6	24.4	36.6	7.5	1.5	75.7	42.1	53.0	47.0
05767	ROCHESTER	98.5	98.3	0.2	0.2	0.2	0.3	1.1	1.5	4.1	5.4	5.5	5.3	5.4	20.9	34.8	15.9	2.7	81.2	47.0	47.7	52.3
05769	SALISBURY	98.3	98.0	0.0	0.1	0.2	0.4	0.3	0.4	5.8	6.1	7.2	6.3	4.3	25.5	32.3	10.8	1.6	76.4	41.5	50.3	49.7
05770	SHOREHAM	98.7	98.2	0.6	0.9	0.3	0.5	0.5	0.7	5.0	6.9	8.0	8.0	4.0	24.6	30.7	11.4	1.3	74.2	40.9	49.3	50.7
05772	STOCKBRIDGE	98.3	97.5	0.6	0.9	0.6	1.1	0.5	0.6	5.2	6.3	6.6	5.2	3.2	20.1	37.1	14.9	1.4	78.5	46.7	51.1	48.9
05773	WALLINGFORD	98.4	98.2	0.1	0.1	0.3	0.4	0.5	0.7	4.8	5.2	5.7	5.7	4.9	22.9	34.5	14.5	1.8	80.6	45.5	48.6	51.4
05774	WELLS	98.7	98.5	0.3	0.5	0.0	0.0	1.0	1.3	3.9	5.5	6.8	6.9	3.7	21.6	33.0	16.5	2.1	79.1	46.1	48.9	51.1
05775	WEST PAWLET	98.6	98.4	0.3	0.6	0.0	0.0	1.2	1.6	6.0	6.3	6.8	7.4	4.3	21.0	31.6	13.9	2.5	76.1	43.5	52.7	47.3
05776	WEST RUPERT	98.8	98.6	0.3	0.4	0.4	0.6	0.7	1.0	3.9	4.1	4.7	6.1	4.1	19.7	36.3	18.8	2.3	83.4	49.3	49.0	51.0
05777	WEST RUTLAND	98.2	97.8	0.3	0.4	0.6	0.9	0.4	0.5	4.8	5.4	5.9	6.2	5.5	24.8	32.6	12.9	1.8	80.1	43.2	49.1	50.9
05778	WHITING	98.2	98.1	0.3	0.4	0.4	0.5	0.5	0.8	5.3	6.5	6.7	6.4	4.2	24.1	32.8	12.6	1.4	77.1	42.7	50.3	49.7
05819	SAINT JOHNSBURY	96.7	96.1	0.5	0.7	0.6	0.9	1.0	1.3	5.3	5.3	5.5	6.2	6.9	24.8	29.1	13.5	3.3	80.2	41.7	49.4	50.6
05820	ALBANY	97.3	97.4	0.2	0.4	0.2	0.2	0.2	0.4	7.0	7.4	7.2	5.7	4.1	22.7	32.5	11.8	1.5	74.7	42.0	50.5	49.5
05821	BARNET	97.3	96.7	0.6	0.8	0.4	0.7	0.5	0.6	4.7	5.6	7.4	7.5	4.6	22.2	32.7	13.6	1.7	77.4	43.5	50.5	49.5
05822	BARTON	97.4	97.3	0.4	0.6	0.1	0.1	0.3	0.3	4.8	5.1	5.7	7.0	5.3	24.4	32.2	13.6	2.0	80.1	43.5	50.2	49.8
05824	CONCORD	97.0	96.8	0.1	0.2	0.3	0.3	1.2	1.5	7.4	7.0	7.1	6.5	5.3	24.8	28.7	11.9	1.3	77.3	39.3	50.4	49.6
05825	COVENTRY	98.6	97.4	0.0	0.6	0.0	0.0	0.7	1.3	7.1	7.1	7.1	5.8	5.8	28.4	28.4	9.7	0.6	75.5	37.3	51.0	49.0
05826	CRAFTSBURY	96.6	96.4	0.4	0.5	0.5	0.7	1.1	1.5	4.8	5.3	6.0	6.8	5.8	21.4	29.2	16.4	4.4	80.5	45.0	48.0	52.0
05827	CRAFTSBURY COMMON	96.9	96.6	0.3	0.5	0.3	0.5	1.0	1.2	5.1	5.6	6.1	6.6	5.6	21.6	29.9	15.5	4.1	79.9	44.6	48.5	51.5
05828	DANVILLE	99.1	98.9	0.2	0.3	0.1	0.2	0.5	0.6	5.3	6.9	7.1	5.8	3.3	21.0	34.9	13.5	2.2	76.3	45.3	48.6	51.4
05829	DERBY	97.6	97.4	0.2	0.2	0.3	0.4	0.8	1.0	5.9	6.7	7.0	6.8	4.9	22.0	30.7	13.5	2.3	75.7	42.4	50.3	49.7
05830	DERBY LINE	97.6	97.2	0.3	0.5	0.4	0.6	0.3	0.4	6.2	6.5	7.1	7.0	5.5	23.5	29.1	12.9	2.1	75.3	40.8	49.0	51.0
05832	EAST BURKE	96.7	96.4	0.4	0.6	0.1	0.3	0.7	1.1	6.0	5.7	6.0	5.7	4.9	25.5	33.7	10.9	1.5	78.5	42.6	50.2	49.8
05833	EAST CHARLESTON	96.5	95.5	0.0	0.0	0.0	0.8	0.9	0.8	5.3	5.3	5.3	6.8	4.5	25.0	32.6	13.6	1.5	80.3	43.1	50.0	50.0
05836	EAST HARDWICK	98.0	97.9	0.1	0.2	0.1	0.1	0.3	0.3	6.1	6.5	7.0	7.1	4.8	23.8	32.6	10.6	1.4	76.1	41.3	49.7	50.3
05837	EAST HAVEN	97.5	96.8	0.3	0.5	0.3	0.5	0.6	0.5	5.6	5.8	6.4	6.4	4.8	23.3	32.4	13.5	1.9	78.0	43.5	48.3	51.7
05839	GLOVER	96.6	96.1	0.1	0.3	0.1	0.3	0.6	0.8	5.2	4.0	6.9	6.3	3.9	20.2	39.0	11.4	3.0	79.8	46.7	50.1	49.9
05841	GREENSBORO	96.5	96.3	0.0	0.0	0.0	0.0	0.5	0.6	4.9	4.9	5.2	4.6	4.3	22.5	34.0	14.7	4.9	81.6	47.3	47.6	52.4
05842	GREENSBORO BEND	96.8	96.8	0.2	0.2	0.0	0.0	0.7	0.9	5.1	5.5	6.5	5.3	4.3	24.0	33.6	12.8	3.1	79.0	44.6	49.1	50.9
05843	HARDWICK	97.9	97.5	0.1	0.2	0.1	0.1	0.4	0.5	6.6	6.7	7.2	7.7	5.4	23.8	30.6	10.6	1.4	74.8	40.1	49.1	50.9
05845	IRASBURG	98.4	98.2	0.1	0.1	0.2	0.2	0.3	0.4	6.4	6.7	7.1	7.0	4.2	24.4	31.2	11.7	1.3	75.4	41.1	49.4	50.6
05846	ISLAND POND	95.3	95.0	0.1	0.2	0.4	0.7	0.3	0.4	4.7	5.0	5.5	7.3	5.7	22.7	30.9	15.8	2.3	80.3	44.3	48.6	51.4
05847	LOWELL	98.0	97.5	1.2	1.7	0.0	0.0	1.2	1.6	6.2	6.4	9.0	7.4	5.2	26.4	28.2	10.5	0.9	72.7	37.3	50.4	49.6
05850	LYNDON CENTER	98.2	97.6	0.0	0.0	0.6	1.2	1.2	1.2	5.4	4.8	7.7	8.9	14.3	24.4	21.4	10.1	3.0	77.4	31.7	51.2	48.8
05851	LYNDONVILLE	97.7	97.2	0.2	0.3	0.6	0.9	0.5	0.6	5.0	4.9	5.4	9.2	10.2	23.4	27.2	12.3	2.3	80.8	37.4	50.3	49.7
05853	MORGAN	97.5	97.4	0.5	0.6	0.2	0.3	0.6	1.0	6.1	7.6	9.1	7.3	3.7	25.2	30.7	9.8	0.6	71.2	39.0	50.0	50.0
05855	NEWPORT	96.6	96.2	0.6	0.9	0.5	0.7	1.1	1.4	5.7	5.9	6.3	6.4	5.7	24.3	28.4	14.4	2.8	78.0	41.7	49.8	50.2
05857	NEWPORT CENTER	97.2	97.1	0.3	0.4	0.4	0.5	0.5	0.7	5.2	5.7	6.8	5.8	4.7	25.1	32.7	12.9	1.1	78.4	42.9	50.9	49.1
05858	NORTH CONCORD	97.0	97.2	0.3	0.3	0.3	0.3	0.7	0.9	6.3	6.3	6.6	6.3	5.4	23.7	30.4	13.3	1.6	78.8	41.9	48.7	51.3
05859	NORTH TROY	98.0	97.6	0.1	0.2	0.3	0.4	0.5	0.7	5.7	5.8	6.1	6.1	5.9	26.1	31.0	11.9	1.5	78.6	41.3	50.7	49.3
05860	ORLEANS	97.4	97.1	0.2	0.3	0.3	0.5	0.3	0.4	5.2	5.5	5.9	6.5	4.8	22.6	31.5	14.8	3.2	79.2	44.6	49.4	50.6
05862	PEACHAM	98.4	98.4	0.5	0.5	0.5	0.5	1.1	1.6	3.8	6.6	9.9	6.6	2.7	17.6	36.8	13.7	2.2	75.3	46.3	49.5	50.5
05866	SHEFFIELD	97.9	97.8	0.0	0.1	0.0	0.1	0.8	1.1	5.7	6.5	8.4	6.4	3.8	27.0	32.4	9.5	0.4	74.4	40.5	51.2	48.8
05867	SUTTON	97.9	97.9	0.1	0.1	0.2	0.3	0.4	0.6	6.0	6.5	7.2	7.2	4.9	24.0	32.3	10.8	1.1	74.8	40.5	50.5	49.5
05868	TROY	100.0	100.0	0.0	0.0	0.0	0.0	0.0	0.0	0.0	0.0	0.0	0.0	0.0	20.0	80.0	0.0	0.0	100.0	48.8	80.0	20.0
05871	WEST BURKE	97.5	97.2	0.1	0.2	0.2	0.3	1.1	1.4	6.3	6.5	7.1	6.9	5.2	26.4	29.8	10.6	1.1	75.4	38.8	52.2	47.8
05872	WEST CHARLESTON	96.5	96.4	0.0	0.0	0.3	0.5	0.4	0.6	4.7	4.8	5.7	6.6	4.5	24.4	34.5	13.4	1.4	80.7	44.4	48.6	51.4
05873	WEST DANVILLE	98.7	98.5	0.3	0.5	0.1	0.2	0.5	0.5	5.1	6.6	7.5	6.4	3.7	21.5	34.9	12.3	2.0	76.4	44.4	49.3	50.7
05874	WESTFIELD	96.8	96.5	0.2	0.3	0.4	0.5	1.2	1.7	5.4	5.7	6.2	6.1	6.1	22.5	34.8	11.8	1.5	78.3	43.7	50.1	49.9
05875	WEST GLOVER	96.5	96.7	0.4	0.4	0.2	0.2	0.4	0.7	5.6	5.3	6.8	6.3	4.2	21.6	36.1	11.6	2.5	78.1	45.1	50.4	49.6
05901	AVERILL	100.0	100.0	0.0	0.0	0.0	0.0	0.0	0.0	0.0	0.0	0.0	0.0	0.0	0.0	100.0	0.0	0.0	100.0	51.9	55.6	44.4
05902	BEECHER FALLS	96.0	95.7	0.0	0.4	0.0	0.0	0.4	0.4	4.7	4.7	5.6	7.7	7.3	22.3	33.9	11.6	2.1	80.7	43.3	49.8	50.2
05903	CANAAN	95.8	95.7	0.2	0.2	0.1	0.2	0.2	0.3	5.2	5.2	5.7	7.5	6.9	22.5	33.0	12.2	1.7	79.5	42.8	50.4	49.6
05904	GILMAN	100.0	100.0	0.0	0.0	0.0	0.0	0.0	0.0	0.0	0.0	0.0	0.0	0.0	33.3	66.7	0.0	0.0	100.0	48.8	55.6	44.4
05905	GUILDHALL	96.7	96.5	0.3	0.4	0.2	0.4	0.1	0.2	4.5	4.7	5.4	7.0	5.5	20.5	33.4	17.3	1.7	81.2	46.4	50.5	49.5
05906	LUNENBURG	97.4	97.3	0.1	0.1	0.2	0.3	0.5	0.7	5.9	6.0	6.2	6.5	6.1	25.1	29.2	13.3	1.6	78.3	41.3	51.7	48.3
05907	NORTON	96.0	96.3	0.4	0.4	0.4	0.4	0.0	0.0	3.7	4.5	4.9	7.3	5.7	19.6	33.5	19.2	1.6	82.9	47.5	51.8	48.2
	VERMONT	96.8	96.1	0.5	0.7	0.9	1.3	0.9	1.1	5.4	5.8	6.2	7.4	7.0	24.6	29.9	11.6	2.0	78.6	40.4	49.1	50.9
	UNITED STATES	75.1	72.0	12.3	12.7	3.8	4.6	12.5	15.7	6.8	6.7	6.6	7.1	6.9	27.0	26.0	10.9	1.9	75.7	36.9	49.2	50.8

ZIP CODE #	POST OFFICE NAME	2009 Per Capita Income	2009 HH Income Base	2009 HOUSEHOLD INCOME DISTRIBUTION (%) Less than $25,000	$25,000 to $49,999	$50,000 to $99,999	$100,000 to $149,999	$150,000 or More	MEDIAN HOUSEHOLD INCOME 2009	2014	2009 National Centile	2009 State Centile	2009 Home Value Base	2009 HOME VALUE DISTRIBUTION (%) Less than $50,000	$50,000 to $89,999	$90,000 to $174,999	$175,000 to $399,999	$400,000 or More	2009 Median Home Value
05765	PROCTOR	26896	779	17.5	25.4	44.9	9.1	3.1	57376	59112	74	73	575	0.5	3.1	47.0	45.4	4.0	174252
05766	RIPTON	22390	225	21.3	29.8	37.8	9.8	1.3	48658	51027	58	39	173	1.7	2.9	26.6	56.1	12.7	216429
05767	ROCHESTER	27824	587	16.4	34.4	39.0	6.5	3.7	49543	51226	60	42	424	2.4	6.6	26.2	50.9	13.9	207547
05769	SALISBURY	25654	556	18.7	31.7	39.2	6.1	4.3	49654	51062	60	42	452	3.1	3.5	21.7	53.5	18.1	229710
05770	SHOREHAM	22739	396	16.9	33.8	36.9	9.3	3.0	49284	50734	59	40	308	1.9	4.2	29.9	46.1	17.9	214286
05772	STOCKBRIDGE	25040	283	20.8	32.5	37.5	6.0	3.2	47216	50201	55	34	245	4.9	5.3	32.2	46.1	11.4	200610
05773	WALLINGFORD	24567	929	18.6	27.6	42.6	8.2	3.0	52719	54704	67	59	738	2.6	6.8	29.7	51.2	9.8	197253
05774	WELLS	21668	541	28.7	26.6	38.4	4.4	1.8	41764	46958	39	15	451	4.2	8.0	34.8	44.1	8.9	182849
05775	WEST PAWLET	23242	263	23.6	31.6	35.7	5.7	3.4	44317	49728	46	23	192	1.6	10.9	27.1	47.9	12.5	212121
05776	WEST RUPERT	26173	314	21.0	30.3	38.2	5.1	5.4	48471	51294	58	38	257	3.1	3.5	21.4	47.9	24.1	245000
05777	WEST RUTLAND	23600	1547	20.0	26.8	43.9	6.8	2.5	52422	54376	67	56	1157	2.5	4.2	41.8	46.8	4.6	177661
05778	WHITING	28071	310	17.4	30.0	35.5	10.0	7.1	52397	53273	67	56	250	1.6	4.4	21.6	50.0	22.4	243902
05819	SAINT JOHNSBURY	23990	3934	29.0	26.2	34.7	6.9	3.3	44453	45863	47	24	2458	3.6	6.8	39.8	43.3	6.5	174590
05820	ALBANY	20402	228	32.0	29.4	32.9	3.9	1.8	38603	40921	28	6	186	14.0	14.5	29.6	33.9	8.1	151563
05821	BARNET	22562	554	23.5	32.5	33.0	7.9	3.1	45255	47821	49	26	459	2.2	4.4	33.8	47.9	11.8	197704
05822	BARTON	19054	880	35.2	34.3	25.3	3.8	1.4	36957	37351	23	6	631	7.1	12.8	34.5	37.2	8.2	163125
05824	CONCORD	19951	508	25.4	32.7	36.4	4.3	1.2	44507	47391	47	25	414	9.7	14.7	39.9	30.9	4.8	144340
05825	COVENTRY	16267	57	31.6	31.6	33.3	3.5	0.0	40757	43211	35	11	45	15.6	15.6	28.9	33.3	6.7	146875
05826	CRAFTSBURY	22167	342	29.8	24.6	36.3	5.8	3.5	43565	47228	44	20	281	8.9	8.9	26.0	40.6	15.7	201596
05827	CRAFTSBURY COMMON	22113	168	30.4	25.6	35.7	5.4	3.0	42367	46335	41	16	138	9.4	10.9	26.8	38.4	14.5	187500
05828	DANVILLE	24032	755	19.2	26.6	43.3	7.8	3.0	52675	54708	67	58	623	1.9	7.7	29.7	53.5	7.2	205637
05829	DERBY	22669	735	29.3	30.3	32.9	5.0	2.4	40983	43884	36	12	590	10.2	16.1	25.4	42.0	6.3	170192
05830	DERBY LINE	20975	700	22.9	35.7	33.9	6.1	1.4	44875	48319	48	25	523	2.5	9.8	47.2	35.0	5.5	159335
05832	EAST BURKE	25831	325	22.2	29.8	38.5	6.8	2.8	48163	50171	57	37	252	5.2	6.7	31.0	44.0	13.1	188636
05833	EAST CHARLESTON	19551	58	39.7	31.0	22.4	3.4	3.4	31526	36824	11	2	46	13.0	10.9	32.6	39.1	4.3	156250
05836	EAST HARDWICK	19668	389	26.5	31.4	33.7	6.9	1.5	44621	45293	47	25	304	4.6	11.8	36.2	42.8	4.6	169118
05837	EAST HAVEN	19437	155	29.7	36.1	27.7	4.5	1.9	38625	38363	29	7	132	9.1	15.2	40.9	30.3	4.5	139706
05839	GLOVER	20023	303	27.1	33.0	34.7	4.0	1.3	42727	43959	42	17	260	3.5	14.2	36.2	35.8	10.4	165000
05841	GREENSBORO	25932	155	25.2	32.3	31.6	5.8	5.2	43633	43682	44	21	122	6.6	5.7	22.1	30.3	35.2	250000
05842	GREENSBORO BEND	21787	241	25.7	31.5	35.7	4.6	2.5	42895	42104	42	18	196	7.7	10.2	28.6	33.7	19.9	186667
05843	HARDWICK	18872	1103	30.0	31.9	31.1	4.7	2.3	41397	42184	37	13	802	7.2	15.7	44.5	30.4	2.1	140051
05845	IRASBURG	21265	485	22.7	34.8	34.8	4.5	3.1	43959	47824	45	22	391	6.6	13.3	34.3	40.2	5.6	166912
05846	ISLAND POND	17978	591	36.7	33.2	25.4	4.1	0.7	33210	34521	14	2	418	6.0	23.7	40.0	26.3	4.1	122984
05847	LOWELL	16705	314	36.0	34.4	26.4	0.6	2.5	33982	35000	15	3	261	9.6	16.5	43.7	27.2	3.1	131071
05850	LYNDON CENTER	16943	73	39.7	27.4	31.5	1.4	0.0	36113	37331	21	4	29	0.0	3.4	44.8	51.7	0.0	181250
05851	LYNDONVILLE	22525	2408	24.5	30.6	37.0	4.4	3.4	45308	46891	49	27	1703	8.0	13.9	33.6	40.6	3.9	163696
05853	MORGAN	17382	279	30.5	33.3	29.0	6.1	1.1	39225	40323	30	8	231	6.5	16.5	29.0	35.9	12.1	169886
05855	NEWPORT	22034	3307	33.4	25.8	32.9	5.4	2.4	39183	42279	30	8	2094	3.4	8.7	38.0	40.3	9.6	174691
05857	NEWPORT CENTER	23334	580	22.4	34.3	32.9	6.4	4.0	44074	48681	46	23	475	4.4	10.3	30.9	42.1	12.2	187500
05858	NORTH CONCORD	19363	131	29.8	35.9	29.0	3.8	1.5	38963	41004	30	7	111	9.0	17.1	42.3	27.9	3.6	135156
05859	NORTH TROY	18831	917	31.0	32.6	31.3	4.0	1.1	40366	41451	34	10	682	3.1	13.6	37.4	38.7	7.2	163889
05860	ORLEANS	18734	973	32.5	33.0	29.3	4.2	1.0	36825	38245	23	5	734	5.7	14.4	41.1	31.1	7.6	147895
05862	PEACHAM	27576	83	24.1	24.1	39.8	10.8	1.2	51597	55058	65	52	68	0.0	4.4	25.0	57.4	13.2	254545
05866	SHEFFIELD	18436	328	27.1	31.4	38.1	3.4	0.0	40264	41826	34	9	278	10.4	17.3	39.6	30.6	2.2	139865
05867	SUTTON	19014	360	23.3	32.2	38.3	4.7	1.4	44447	46565	47	24	300	6.0	11.7	46.7	34.0	1.7	152604
05868	TROY	0	0	0.0	0.0	0.0	0.0	0.0	0	81250	0	0	2	0.0	0.0	0.0	100.0	0.0	225000
05871	WEST BURKE	24107	683	28.6	29.9	31.5	5.6	4.5	42291	44059	40	16	540	4.8	11.5	42.2	38.9	2.6	160443
05872	WEST CHARLESTON	18804	359	35.7	32.9	24.8	4.2	2.5	35083	36483	18	4	283	11.0	12.0	33.2	39.2	4.6	156771
05873	WEST DANVILLE	24297	400	20.5	28.5	39.0	9.0	3.0	50591	52303	63	48	334	2.4	7.5	30.5	51.8	7.8	201961
05874	WESTFIELD	21593	253	25.7	32.8	34.0	5.1	2.4	42749	45000	42	17	207	6.8	7.2	30.9	44.0	11.1	190441
05875	WEST GLOVER	20624	248	30.6	31.9	32.7	3.6	1.2	40492	41767	34	10	204	8.3	15.2	34.3	33.3	8.8	153947
05901	AVERILL	0	0	0.0	0.0	0.0	0.0	0.0	0	0	0	0	0	0.0	0.0	0.0	0.0	0.0	0
05902	BEECHER FALLS	16942	91	31.9	34.1	33.0	1.1	0.0	40827	41980	35	11	69	5.8	18.8	40.6	29.0	5.8	145313
05903	CANAAN	18808	383	31.6	33.2	33.2	1.6	0.5	41435	42168	37	13	291	4.5	18.9	41.2	30.2	5.2	146382
05904	GILMAN	27222	4	0.0	0.0	100.0	0.0	0.0	60000	66333	77	81	3	0.0	0.0	100.0	0.0	0.0	137500
05905	GUILDHALL	18546	392	36.0	33.2	24.7	4.6	1.5	33652	34722	15	3	334	5.7	19.5	38.6	30.8	5.4	138462
05906	LUNENBURG	17470	625	30.7	35.4	30.7	2.6	0.6	38555	39814	28	6	501	11.4	26.7	38.5	21.8	1.6	115042
05907	NORTON	19334	108	37.0	32.4	23.1	5.6	1.9	32683	33276	13	2	92	5.4	20.7	34.8	33.7	5.4	139583
	VERMONT	27546		19.3	26.3	38.8	10.3	5.3	54205	56824				3.4	4.6	25.9	52.9	13.2	216547
	UNITED STATES	27277		20.9	24.4	35.3	11.7	7.6	54719	56938				9.3	13.1	31.6	32.6	13.5	162279

ZIP CODE #	POST OFFICE NAME	FINANCIAL SERVICES: Auto Loan	Home Loan	Invest-ments	Retire-ment Plans	THE HOME — Home Improvements: Home Repair	Lawn & Garden	Furnishings: Comput-ers & Hard-ware-Personal	Major Appli-ances	TV, Radio, Sound Equip-ment	Furni-ture	ENTERTAINMENT: Dine out/ Carry out	Sports Equip-ment	Fees & Tickets	Toys & Games	Travel	Cable TV	PERSONAL: Apparel & Services	Auto Repairs	Health Insur-ance	Pets & Supplies
05765	PROCTOR	86	97	85	97	92	99	88	90	90	87	90	69	95	91	93	92	63	90	97	107
05766	RIPTON	96	76	124	75	84	101	77	97	80	72	79	71	66	76	83	85	53	90	96	113
05767	ROCHESTER	95	80	105	80	85	98	83	95	86	79	85	70	75	84	85	91	57	91	98	111
05769	SALISBURY	103	82	132	81	90	109	82	105	86	77	85	77	71	82	89	92	57	97	104	122
05770	SHOREHAM	107	74	118	74	77	113	82	102	85	66	84	84	60	84	81	93	55	95	107	125
05772	STOCKBRIDGE	96	77	124	76	85	102	77	98	81	72	80	72	67	77	84	86	53	90	97	114
05773	WALLINGFORD	84	86	87	86	86	96	79	88	83	78	82	65	81	83	84	87	57	84	94	103
05774	WELLS	84	67	108	66	73	89	67	86	71	63	70	63	58	67	73	75	46	79	85	99
05775	WEST PAWLET	100	69	110	69	72	105	76	95	79	62	78	78	56	78	76	87	51	89	100	117
05776	WEST RUPERT	101	81	130	79	89	107	81	103	85	76	83	75	70	80	87	90	55	95	101	119
05777	WEST RUTLAND	88	81	80	83	82	92	81	88	83	76	82	66	76	84	81	87	56	84	92	103
05778	WHITING	125	88	140	87	92	132	96	120	100	79	99	98	72	98	97	109	64	112	126	146
05819	SAINT JOHNSBURY	78	71	71	74	72	81	77	78	79	72	78	59	72	78	74	83	54	78	86	93
05820	ALBANY	87	60	95	59	62	91	66	82	69	54	68	68	48	67	66	75	44	77	87	101
05821	BARNET	91	76	104	77	81	96	76	92	79	70	78	68	68	77	80	84	52	85	92	107
05822	BARTON	71	56	70	56	58	74	57	69	61	52	60	52	49	61	57	66	40	63	71	81
05824	CONCORD	87	64	80	63	65	85	66	78	72	64	71	59	54	74	63	78	48	74	81	94
05825	COVENTRY	71	65	58	63	64	67	62	65	64	64	64	47	58	66	59	66	43	63	65	77
05826	CRAFTSBURY	94	65	104	65	68	99	72	89	75	58	74	74	53	73	72	82	48	83	94	110
05827	CRAFTSBURY COMMON	93	64	102	64	67	98	71	88	74	57	73	73	52	72	71	80	47	82	93	108
05828	DANVILLE	99	79	127	78	87	105	79	101	83	74	82	74	69	79	86	89	55	93	100	117
05829	DERBY	88	68	87	68	70	91	69	84	75	64	73	63	58	75	68	81	49	78	88	100
05830	DERBY LINE	81	66	78	66	69	82	70	78	74	67	73	58	62	73	68	79	49	76	83	92
05832	EAST BURKE	94	77	115	76	83	99	76	95	80	72	79	70	67	77	82	85	53	88	94	110
05833	EAST CHARLESTON	79	57	82	55	59	81	58	74	65	54	64	56	47	64	58	71	42	68	77	88
05836	EAST HARDWICK	90	64	95	62	67	93	67	85	73	60	72	66	52	72	67	80	47	78	89	102
05837	EAST HAVEN	82	62	83	61	64	84	63	78	69	58	67	59	52	69	62	75	45	72	81	93
05839	GLOVER	80	64	103	63	70	84	64	81	67	60	66	59	55	63	69	71	44	75	80	94
05841	GREENSBORO	95	76	123	75	83	100	76	97	80	71	79	71	66	76	82	85	52	89	95	112
05842	GREENSBORO BEND	90	69	106	67	74	93	69	88	75	65	73	65	58	72	72	81	49	81	89	103
05843	HARDWICK	86	61	88	59	64	87	63	80	70	58	69	61	50	69	63	77	45	74	84	96
05845	IRASBURG	95	67	103	66	70	100	73	90	76	60	75	74	55	75	73	83	49	85	95	111
05846	ISLAND POND	69	49	69	48	51	72	54	66	60	48	58	50	43	59	52	66	38	62	72	78
05847	LOWELL	77	55	79	54	57	78	57	72	63	53	62	54	46	63	56	69	41	66	75	86
05850	LYNDON CENTER	52	45	44	47	44	45	56	48	56	54	56	39	53	55	52	55	39	54	52	59
05851	LYNDONVILLE	83	71	76	71	72	82	78	81	81	73	80	60	70	80	74	86	55	81	87	96
05853	MORGAN	81	58	83	56	60	82	59	76	66	55	65	57	47	65	59	72	43	69	79	90
05855	NEWPORT	79	65	78	64	67	80	70	78	74	65	72	58	61	73	68	79	49	75	83	91
05857	NEWPORT CENTER	102	70	112	70	73	107	78	96	81	63	80	80	57	79	77	88	52	90	102	119
05858	NORTH CONCORD	83	60	79	58	61	83	62	76	68	58	67	57	49	69	59	75	45	70	79	91
05859	NORTH TROY	78	61	74	61	63	78	62	73	67	59	65	55	53	67	61	72	44	68	76	87
05860	ORLEANS	78	56	79	55	58	80	59	74	66	54	64	56	48	65	58	72	42	68	78	88
05862	PEACHAM	101	81	130	79	89	107	81	103	85	76	84	75	70	80	88	90	56	95	101	119
05866	SHEFFIELD	83	59	85	57	62	84	61	77	68	57	66	58	49	67	60	74	44	71	81	92
05867	SUTTON	79	72	71	75	73	85	71	80	73	64	72	60	65	74	71	77	49	74	82	93
05868	TROY	0	0	0	0	0	0	0	0	0	0	0	0	0	0	0	0	0	0	0	0
05871	WEST BURKE	93	84	81	84	84	92	81	89	84	80	83	66	76	86	79	88	57	84	90	105
05872	WEST CHARLESTON	80	58	82	56	60	81	59	75	65	55	64	56	47	65	58	72	42	69	78	89
05873	WEST DANVILLE	100	77	122	76	83	106	79	100	83	71	82	76	66	79	84	89	54	92	100	118
05874	WESTFIELD	84	68	106	67	74	89	68	85	71	63	70	62	59	68	73	75	46	79	84	99
05875	WEST GLOVER	80	61	96	60	65	84	63	79	66	56	65	60	51	64	66	71	43	73	80	94
05901	AVERILL	0	0	0	0	0	0	0	0	0	0	0	0	0	0	0	0	0	0	0	0
05902	BEECHER FALLS	78	56	65	55	56	74	58	68	65	57	64	52	47	68	53	71	43	64	72	83
05903	CANAAN	78	56	64	54	56	74	58	68	65	57	63	52	47	67	53	70	43	64	71	82
05904	GILMAN	111	79	91	77	79	105	83	96	92	80	90	74	66	95	75	100	60	91	101	117
05905	GUILDHALL	80	57	81	55	59	81	58	74	65	54	64	56	47	65	58	71	42	68	77	88
05906	LUNENBURG	77	55	68	54	56	75	57	69	64	55	63	52	46	66	53	70	42	64	72	83
05907	NORTON	78	56	80	54	58	80	58	73	64	54	63	55	46	63	57	70	41	67	76	87
	VERMONT	98	92	100	93	93	101	93	98	94	90	94	75	89	94	93	97	65	96	101	116
	UNITED STATES	100	100	100	100	100	100	100	100	100	100	100	100	100	100	100	100	100	100	100	100

ZIP CODE			POPULATION			2000-2009 ANNUAL RATE		HOUSEHOLDS					FAMILIES		
#	POST OFFICE NAME	COUNTY FIPS CODE	2000	2009	2014	% Rate	State Centile	2000	2009	2014	% Annual Rate 2000-2009	2009 Average HH Size	2000	2009	% Annual Rate 2000-2009
20105	ALDIE	107	1445	9014	12278	21.9	100	558	3066	4152	20.2	2.94	406	2221	20.2
20106	AMISSVILLE	157	4023	5051	5745	2.5	89	1426	1817	2075	2.7	2.78	1149	1443	2.5
20107	ARCOLA	107	21	143	200	23.0	100	7	38	53	20.1	3.76	5	29	20.9
20109	MANASSAS	153	29346	36814	39688	2.5	89	10982	13809	14928	2.5	2.66	7084	8547	2.1
20110	MANASSAS	683	39460	42151	43078	0.7	54	13022	13823	14086	0.6	2.98	9540	9854	0.4
20111	MANASSAS	153	24209	31455	34870	2.9	92	7776	10110	11229	2.9	3.09	6213	7896	2.6
20112	MANASSAS	153	17796	22618	24624	2.6	90	5621	7143	7786	2.6	3.16	4950	6182	2.4
20115	MARSHALL	061	5436	6455	6810	1.9	83	2033	2378	2523	1.7	2.70	1530	1740	1.4
20117	MIDDLEBURG	107	3137	3506	3721	1.2	69	1375	1500	1589	0.9	2.32	881	906	0.3
20119	CATLETT	061	4062	4540	4637	1.2	69	1431	1577	1619	1.1	2.87	1130	1228	0.9
20120	CENTREVILLE	059	34482	38819	40292	1.3	72	11670	13110	13607	1.3	2.96	8880	9880	1.2
20121	CENTREVILLE	059	26043	27164	27521	0.5	45	9579	9648	9734	0.1	2.82	6509	6317	-0.3
20124	CLIFTON	059	14750	15323	15299	0.4	42	4626	4686	4674	0.1	3.27	3926	3916	0.0
20129	PAEONIAN SPRINGS	107	231	271	292	1.7	79	84	96	103	1.5	2.80	68	76	1.2
20130	PARIS	043	353	412	433	1.7	79	142	168	178	1.8	2.45	105	120	1.5
20132	PURCELLVILLE	107	8836	14100	17340	5.2	97	3097	4806	5896	4.9	2.93	2469	3702	4.5
20135	BLUEMONT	043	2355	2834	3078	2.0	85	940	1142	1251	2.1	2.48	667	780	1.7
20136	BRISTOW	153	7720	20253	25794	11.0	99	2464	6608	8444	11.3	3.05	2103	5505	11.0
20137	BROAD RUN	061	2172	2565	2805	1.8	81	753	856	935	1.4	3.00	603	672	1.2
20141	ROUND HILL	107	3205	5201	6201	5.4	98	1113	1753	2083	5.0	2.97	898	1373	4.7
20143	CATHARPIN	153	752	962	1099	2.7	90	251	322	370	2.7	2.98	211	269	2.7
20144	DELAPLANE	061	937	1135	1214	2.1	86	384	460	496	2.0	2.44	270	315	1.7
20147	ASHBURN	107	29479	55692	71331	7.1	98	10075	17613	22343	6.2	3.16	7613	12671	5.7
20148	ASHBURN	107	3808	25308	34894	22.7	100	1224	8281	11415	23.0	3.05	1035	6726	22.4
20151	CHANTILLY	059	17162	19787	20962	1.6	78	5281	6168	6545	1.7	3.20	4415	5079	1.5
20152	CHANTILLY	107	6492	19288	26751	12.5	99	2408	7167	9906	12.5	2.69	1833	5253	12.1
20155	GAINESVILLE	153	7722	21012	27009	11.4	99	2810	7975	10309	11.9	2.63	2252	6097	11.4
20158	HAMILTON	107	3220	4096	4654	2.6	90	1162	1428	1615	2.3	2.86	907	1082	1.9
20164	STERLING	107	35102	38525	40921	1.0	64	11954	12764	13523	0.7	3.02	8815	8998	0.2
20165	STERLING	107	26832	34389	38002	2.7	90	9522	11929	13177	2.5	2.87	7313	8815	2.0
20166	STERLING	107	4041	9411	11936	9.6	99	1533	3359	4226	8.9	2.80	1125	2457	8.8
20169	HAYMARKET	153	5910	17897	22172	12.7	99	2036	6455	8063	13.3	2.76	1661	5106	12.9
20170	HERNDON	059	37105	40044	41035	0.8	58	11569	12386	12667	0.7	3.23	8927	9305	0.4
20171	HERNDON	059	33918	43041	46723	2.6	90	11011	14343	15674	2.9	3.00	9105	11595	2.6
20175	LEESBURG	107	16915	26313	31569	4.9	97	6342	9420	11203	4.4	2.76	4450	6273	3.8
20176	LEESBURG	107	19449	42210	53549	8.7	99	6858	15278	19445	9.0	2.74	5129	11338	9.0
20180	LOVETTSVILLE	107	4299	6383	7491	4.4	96	1506	2182	2559	4.1	2.92	1215	1707	3.7
20181	NOKESVILLE	153	7559	14792	17680	7.5	99	2534	4998	6007	7.6	2.96	2124	4071	7.3
20184	UPPERVILLE	107	910	1111	1220	2.2	87	414	499	549	2.0	2.23	283	327	1.6
20186	WARRENTON	061	11323	14902	16391	3.0	92	4365	5634	6239	2.8	2.59	3048	3795	2.4
20187	WARRENTON	061	12054	15732	18091	2.9	92	4005	5204	6008	2.9	3.00	3279	4175	2.6
20190	RESTON	059	14258	16757	17698	1.8	81	6338	7762	8291	2.2	2.09	3334	3826	1.5
20191	RESTON	059	28881	28623	28396	-0.1	18	11373	11330	11250	0.0	2.53	7580	7297	-0.4
20194	RESTON	059	13674	13860	13871	0.1	28	5763	5839	5829	0.1	2.37	3689	3594	-0.3
20197	WATERFORD	107	1196	1832	2229	4.7	97	408	612	744	4.5	2.96	343	500	4.2
20198	THE PLAINS	061	2134	2518	2619	1.8	81	895	1038	1084	1.6	2.43	594	665	1.2
22003	ANNANDALE	059	53549	53408	53031	0.0	23	19285	18994	18811	-0.2	2.79	13845	13256	-0.5
22015	BURKE	059	43627	42731	42333	-0.2	14	14623	14462	14349	-0.1	2.94	11769	11415	-0.3
22025	DUMFRIES	153	12396	17622	20183	3.9	95	4050	5930	6856	4.2	2.97	3383	4803	3.9
22026	DUMFRIES	153	10115	14643	17090	4.1	96	3436	5034	5903	4.2	2.91	2495	3511	3.8
22027	DUNN LORING	059	1643	1830	1911	1.2	69	533	607	636	1.4	2.99	386	427	1.1
22030	FAIRFAX	059	39406	48425	52194	2.3	88	13165	16957	18543	2.8	2.60	9081	11105	2.2
22031	FAIRFAX	059	26878	30190	31158	1.3	72	9988	11235	11596	1.3	2.65	6567	7054	0.8
22032	FAIRFAX	059	29165	29108	28975	0.0	23	9703	9727	9681	0.0	2.97	8137	8019	-0.2
22033	FAIRFAX	059	31251	34687	35959	1.1	66	12971	14335	14822	1.1	2.41	7841	8267	0.6
22039	FAIRFAX STATION	059	18288	19254	19514	0.6	49	5617	5854	5931	0.4	3.29	5277	5464	0.4
22041	FALLS CHURCH	059	25937	26877	27022	0.4	42	9516	9622	9633	0.1	2.78	5679	5535	-0.3
22042	FALLS CHURCH	059	30246	30509	30485	0.1	28	11056	11088	11059	0.0	2.75	7210	6984	-0.3
22043	FALLS CHURCH	059	23224	23801	23998	0.3	38	9131	9471	9582	0.4	2.50	5733	5683	-0.1
22044	FALLS CHURCH	059	11733	11637	11595	-0.1	18	4677	4599	4578	-0.2	2.52	2909	2753	-0.6
22046	FALLS CHURCH	610	13893	14630	14978	0.6	49	5662	5977	6119	0.6	2.44	3513	3548	0.1
22060	FORT BELVOIR	059	8210	9088	9169	1.1	66	2454	2831	2895	1.6	3.09	2171	2350	0.9
22066	GREAT FALLS	059	16713	17751	18225	0.7	54	5306	5663	5811	0.7	3.13	4787	5054	0.6
22067	GREENWAY	059	225	227	227	0.1	28	77	79	79	0.3	2.72	64	64	0.0
22079	LORTON	059	22151	27232	29531	2.3	88	7171	10107	10979	3.8	2.68	5053	6877	3.4
22101	MC LEAN	059	28037	28014	28026	0.0	23	10423	10542	10573	0.1	2.65	7968	7847	-0.2
22102	MC LEAN	059	18751	19718	20151	0.5	45	8539	9048	9273	0.6	2.18	4795	4876	0.2
22124	OAKTON	059	15618	16305	16416	0.5	45	5790	6098	6156	0.6	2.67	4350	4498	0.4
22134	QUANTICO	153	7132	6573	6431	-0.9	3	1684	1558	1524	-0.8	3.20	1459	1312	-1.1
22150	SPRINGFIELD	059	22464	26274	27733	1.7	79	7470	8665	9125	1.6	3.02	5503	6226	1.3
22151	SPRINGFIELD	059	16619	16603	16534	0.0	23	5767	5754	5729	0.0	2.88	4396	4275	-0.3
22152	SPRINGFIELD	059	27291	26929	26757	-0.1	18	9849	9796	9747	-0.1	2.75	7499	7280	-0.3
22153	SPRINGFIELD	059	31247	31020	30887	-0.1	18	10219	10243	10213	0.0	3.03	8587	8458	-0.2
22172	TRIANGLE	153	6035	7955	8989	3.0	92	2403	3153	3564	3.0	2.52	1551	1921	2.3
22180	VIENNA	059	22088	22258	22620	0.1	28	8246	8458	8649	0.3	2.62	5968	5912	-0.1
22181	VIENNA	059	13814	14524	14704	0.5	45	4908	5232	5316	0.7	2.76	3902	4062	0.4
22182	VIENNA	059	23310	23970	24250	0.3	38	8024	8366	8488	0.5	2.86	6539	6693	0.3
22191	WOODBRIDGE	153	39351	53301	61187	3.3	94	13172	18101	20921	3.5	2.93	9684	12822	3.1
22192	WOODBRIDGE	153	49460	56202	58434	1.4	73	17970	20736	21672	1.6	2.70	13167	14702	1.2
22193	WOODBRIDGE	153	61631	71404	76144	1.6	78	19422	22771	24351	1.7	3.13	15906	18257	1.5
22201	ARLINGTON	013	25973	30778	33040	1.9	83	14087	16249	17346	1.6	1.85	4540	4951	0.9
22202	ARLINGTON	013	18215	22068	23908	2.1	86	10214	12175	13078	1.9	1.79	3472	3911	1.3
22203	ARLINGTON	013	18659	20401	21881	1.0	64	8859	9785	10490	1.1	2.06	3597	3661	0.2
22204	ARLINGTON	013	49495	50801	51505	0.3	38	19784	19393	19541	-0.2	2.60	10359	9785	-0.6
22205	ARLINGTON	013	15879	16109	16251	0.2	33	6410	6362	6377	-0.1	2.53	3970	3822	-0.4
22206	ARLINGTON	013	16629	19471	20765	1.7	79	8168	8868	9294	0.9	2.20	3303	3595	0.9
22207	ARLINGTON	013	28991	29275	29549	0.1	28	11178	11048	11081	-0.1	2.57	7471	7191	-0.4
22209	ARLINGTON	013	11375	12688	13596	1.2	69	6719	7164	7560	0.7	1.76	1838	1859	0.1
22211	FT MYER	013	2171	2146	2136	-0.1	18	183	171	167	-0.7	2.89	175	163	-0.8
22213	ARLINGTON	013	2538	2634	2676	0.4	42	1039	1066	1080	0.3	2.46	700	696	-0.1
22301	ALEXANDRIA	510	11261	11044	10881	-0.2	14	5133	4964	4867	-0.4	2.16	2632	2416	-0.9
22302	ALEXANDRIA	510	17517	17887	17893	0.2	33	9106	9193	9178	0.1	1.92	3931	3724	-0.6
22303	ALEXANDRIA	059	14042	15393	15537	1.0	64	6717	7447	7541	1.1	2.07	3083	3178	0.3
22304	ALEXANDRIA	510	41217	45004	45983	1.0	64	19978	21328	21669	0.7	2.10	8836	8937	0.1
22305	ALEXANDRIA	510	15738	18217	19390	1.6	78	6089	6641	6956	0.9	2.74	3392	3557	0.5
	VIRGINIA					1.2					1.3	2.52			1.0
	UNITED STATES					1.0					1.1	2.59			0.9

ZIP CODE #	POST OFFICE NAME	RACE (%) White 2000	White 2009	Black 2000	Black 2009	Asian/Pacific 2000	Asian/Pacific 2009	% Hispanic Origin 2000	% Hispanic Origin 2009	2009 AGE DISTRIBUTION (%) 0-4	5-9	10-14	15-19	20-24	25-44	45-64	65-84	85+	18+	MEDIAN AGE 2009	% 2009 Males	% 2009 Females
20105	ALDIE	86.0	81.0	8.4	6.5	2.5	6.5	3.4	9.0	11.0	10.7	9.2	4.9	2.3	37.1	19.9	4.4	0.4	65.7	35.2	49.2	50.8
20106	AMISSVILLE	93.0	91.2	4.6	5.2	0.3	0.5	1.6	2.7	5.9	6.7	7.6	7.0	3.4	22.5	32.9	12.7	1.2	75.2	43.1	50.6	49.4
20107	ARCOLA	90.5	87.4	4.8	4.9	4.8	2.1	4.8	4.2	7.0	8.4	8.4	7.0	2.8	25.9	33.6	6.3	0.7	71.3	40.2	49.7	50.3
20109	MANASSAS	65.3	56.7	16.4	17.0	4.6	6.3	16.5	25.1	9.3	8.2	7.2	6.5	7.4	34.7	20.8	5.4	0.6	71.4	31.2	50.1	49.9
20110	MANASSAS	73.4	67.4	12.3	12.3	3.5	4.7	14.2	21.3	8.5	8.1	7.8	7.2	6.4	31.5	23.7	5.9	0.8	71.1	32.8	50.8	49.2
20111	MANASSAS	77.7	71.6	8.8	9.0	3.1	4.3	13.5	20.3	9.1	8.9	8.4	6.8	5.0	30.7	24.3	6.2	0.6	69.3	34.4	50.4	49.6
20112	MANASSAS	86.7	79.9	6.8	8.9	2.2	3.7	4.2	8.4	7.3	8.1	8.6	7.6	3.9	28.6	29.9	5.7	0.4	70.9	37.0	50.5	49.5
20115	MARSHALL	89.6	87.6	7.8	8.6	0.4	0.6	2.1	3.6	4.6	5.2	6.0	6.1	4.2	22.5	35.2	14.6	1.6	80.3	45.8	49.5	50.5
20117	MIDDLEBURG	83.9	79.5	13.2	15.5	0.5	0.8	3.5	6.6	5.1	4.9	5.4	5.5	6.0	23.6	32.7	14.7	2.2	81.1	44.7	47.0	53.0
20119	CATLETT	89.2	87.3	8.4	9.2	0.5	0.7	1.3	2.2	5.7	6.4	7.1	6.9	3.9	24.3	31.7	12.8	1.2	76.4	42.4	51.0	49.0
20120	CENTREVILLE	75.8	68.1	7.1	7.1	11.8	17.3	6.6	10.3	8.1	8.7	8.8	7.1	4.6	31.6	26.5	4.3	0.4	69.9	35.1	49.7	50.3
20121	CENTREVILLE	65.9	58.1	10.2	10.0	16.0	20.8	10.1	15.4	9.6	8.4	7.4	5.8	6.6	39.0	20.2	2.8	0.2	71.0	31.8	49.7	50.3
20124	CLIFTON	84.3	78.4	2.9	3.1	9.6	13.6	3.4	5.9	5.9	7.6	9.6	8.8	4.2	23.9	33.8	5.7	0.5	70.7	39.1	49.8	50.2
20129	PAEONIAN SPRINGS	94.8	92.6	3.5	4.1	0.4	1.1	1.3	2.2	5.2	6.6	8.1	8.1	3.7	17.3	35.8	13.3	1.8	74.2	45.5	47.6	52.4
20130	PARIS	95.8	94.4	2.3	2.7	0.3	0.5	1.4	2.4	4.9	6.8	6.8	6.1	3.4	28.4	31.8	11.2	0.7	77.2	41.8	51.5	48.5
20132	PURCELLVILLE	92.8	90.1	4.1	5.0	0.9	1.4	1.8	3.4	6.5	7.2	8.0	7.7	4.5	22.8	32.6	9.3	1.3	73.0	40.8	49.3	50.7
20135	BLUEMONT	95.0	93.0	2.3	2.7	0.3	0.5	1.4	2.6	5.7	6.6	6.9	5.6	4.1	23.6	35.3	11.4	0.9	77.3	43.7	49.1	50.9
20136	BRISTOW	88.1	81.5	6.5	9.2	2.5	4.2	3.9	7.7	11.5	11.1	9.9	6.3	3.1	33.1	21.0	3.6	0.3	62.9	32.6	49.5	50.5
20137	BROAD RUN	92.9	90.9	4.8	5.7	0.9	1.4	1.5	2.5	5.8	6.8	7.8	6.6	3.4	22.8	35.6	10.1	1.1	75.0	43.0	48.8	51.2
20141	ROUND HILL	94.2	92.7	3.2	3.6	0.6	0.9	1.6	3.2	6.2	7.2	8.2	7.2	3.9	21.2	34.2	10.6	1.2	73.7	42.5	49.5	50.5
20143	CATHARPIN	92.6	88.5	2.9	3.8	1.5	2.6	1.7	3.6	5.7	6.4	7.2	6.0	3.2	19.9	31.7	18.6	1.2	76.9	46.0	49.1	50.9
20144	DELAPLANE	85.7	83.6	11.5	12.4	0.3	0.5	3.5	5.8	5.5	5.6	5.9	5.6	5.1	24.0	32.8	13.7	2.0	79.4	44.0	48.7	51.3
20147	ASHBURN	83.4	77.5	6.6	7.3	5.9	9.0	4.5	7.6	11.2	10.7	9.5	6.3	3.1	34.4	21.3	3.1	0.3	64.4	32.8	49.3	50.7
20148	ASHBURN	85.4	81.4	5.7	6.2	5.6	7.2	3.5	6.1	10.3	10.7	10.2	7.0	3.0	30.0	24.9	3.7	0.3	64.2	34.4	49.4	50.6
20151	CHANTILLY	72.4	64.0	5.3	5.6	15.0	19.7	10.4	16.7	7.6	8.0	8.6	7.7	4.9	27.6	29.2	6.1	0.4	71.0	36.1	50.7	49.3
20152	CHANTILLY	86.5	80.9	4.9	5.7	4.7	7.1	5.2	9.6	11.7	11.3	9.6	4.7	2.0	39.1	18.2	3.3	0.3	64.3	34.5	49.1	50.9
20155	GAINESVILLE	90.3	86.0	5.3	6.7	1.6	2.4	3.1	6.1	7.7	7.9	7.9	6.2	3.4	27.0	28.1	10.9	0.9	72.4	39.0	49.3	50.7
20158	HAMILTON	95.5	93.5	2.3	2.7	0.7	1.2	1.7	3.4	5.8	7.0	8.0	7.0	3.5	20.4	35.9	11.1	1.3	74.6	44.0	49.4	50.6
20164	STERLING	72.1	63.3	9.2	9.5	9.7	13.4	11.6	19.4	8.0	7.8	7.7	7.2	6.0	32.3	25.1	5.5	0.5	72.0	34.2	50.4	49.6
20165	STERLING	83.6	76.9	5.4	6.0	6.9	10.5	4.8	8.7	9.5	10.0	9.7	6.5	3.1	30.2	25.8	4.5	0.7	66.5	35.8	48.8	51.2
20166	STERLING	72.5	65.3	10.0	9.8	9.7	13.3	10.8	19.1	8.8	7.3	6.6	5.8	7.9	36.1	21.9	5.2	0.4	73.9	31.7	50.0	50.0
20169	HAYMARKET	92.7	87.8	4.0	5.6	1.3	2.7	1.5	4.1	6.4	7.2	7.9	7.2	4.0	25.2	32.3	8.9	0.8	73.9	40.4	49.6	50.4
20170	HERNDON	64.4	56.9	8.5	8.0	12.8	15.5	19.1	27.2	7.6	7.7	7.9	7.2	6.5	31.0	27.3	4.5	0.4	72.4	33.6	51.4	48.6
20171	HERNDON	74.9	64.8	5.3	6.1	14.9	20.8	5.6	10.6	8.1	8.2	8.6	7.5	6.0	28.2	28.6	4.5	0.3	70.4	34.5	49.9	50.1
20175	LEESBURG	88.4	84.8	6.5	7.0	2.0	3.2	4.0	7.2	8.8	8.9	8.8	6.7	4.5	28.7	26.5	6.4	0.8	68.9	35.8	49.5	50.5
20176	LEESBURG	82.2	75.9	9.1	9.5	3.3	6.4	6.4	9.8	10.3	10.0	9.3	6.7	3.8	31.3	22.9	5.0	0.8	66.0	33.7	49.2	50.8
20180	LOVETTSVILLE	96.9	95.3	0.8	1.0	0.7	1.2	1.3	2.4	5.7	6.7	8.1	7.8	3.7	22.9	34.5	9.5	1.3	74.3	42.4	50.0	50.0
20181	NOKESVILLE	93.6	88.5	3.2	4.7	0.9	2.1	2.3	6.2	7.9	8.1	7.9	6.0	3.7	29.5	27.9	8.3	0.7	72.1	37.8	49.8	50.2
20184	UPPERVILLE	87.9	84.9	8.4	9.5	0.5	0.8	3.4	5.9	5.3	5.7	6.3	5.5	4.5	23.1	34.7	13.4	1.4	79.4	44.7	48.8	51.2
20186	WARRENTON	84.3	81.5	12.6	14.0	0.9	1.3	2.3	3.8	6.1	6.2	6.5	6.5	5.4	24.7	29.9	12.4	2.2	77.0	41.2	48.5	51.5
20187	WARRENTON	91.0	88.8	6.1	6.9	0.8	1.2	1.7	2.8	6.3	7.0	7.8	7.4	4.3	23.4	32.4	10.0	1.3	74.0	41.0	49.8	50.2
20190	RESTON	71.2	66.2	10.0	9.4	9.7	12.5	12.1	16.7	5.9	5.1	4.9	4.7	7.3	33.0	25.3	11.0	2.8	81.1	38.4	48.3	51.7
20191	RESTON	70.0	64.7	10.4	10.0	10.7	13.2	12.0	17.4	6.4	6.5	6.6	5.6	5.2	28.9	29.5	10.4	0.8	77.1	39.5	49.2	50.8
20194	RESTON	83.2	77.6	5.4	5.8	7.8	11.2	4.3	7.4	7.1	7.0	7.6	5.9	5.0	29.3	31.9	5.9	0.4	74.6	39.0	48.7	51.3
20197	WATERFORD	95.6	93.9	2.2	2.7	0.8	1.3	1.8	3.9	6.1	7.2	8.2	7.4	3.4	21.4	36.7	8.5	1.0	72.9	42.9	50.1	49.9
20198	THE PLAINS	90.8	89.0	6.5	7.1	0.1	0.2	3.5	5.9	5.2	5.2	5.7	5.9	5.0	24.7	32.2	14.2	1.9	80.3	43.9	47.0	53.0
22003	ANNANDALE	65.6	58.2	5.7	5.3	19.0	23.5	13.4	19.6	6.1	6.2	6.4	5.8	5.2	26.9	29.5	12.3	1.7	77.7	40.7	48.6	51.4
22015	BURKE	73.0	65.3	5.0	5.0	15.5	20.4	8.4	13.2	5.5	6.3	7.2	6.9	4.4	26.5	33.4	8.6	0.9	76.4	40.4	48.8	51.2
22025	DUMFRIES	74.9	66.6	17.5	21.4	3.3	5.1	4.4	7.9	7.5	7.8	8.1	7.3	4.9	28.3	29.4	6.1	0.5	72.0	36.3	48.8	51.2
22026	DUMFRIES	51.4	44.6	36.2	37.1	2.9	4.5	11.4	17.3	10.4	9.1	8.1	7.2	7.5	33.5	20.2	3.7	0.3	68.0	29.3	49.0	51.0
22027	DUNN LORING	68.4	58.7	3.3	3.2	20.3	27.2	7.5	10.8	7.7	8.4	8.3	5.0	2.6	30.8	28.2	8.2	0.9	72.3	39.3	49.3	50.7
22030	FAIRFAX	71.1	63.2	7.5	7.3	13.6	19.4	10.0	14.0	6.0	5.8	5.9	8.1	8.4	30.5	25.2	8.8	1.3	78.9	35.9	50.4	49.6
22031	FAIRFAX	63.3	55.2	5.4	5.1	21.6	26.9	13.5	19.2	6.3	5.8	5.7	5.4	6.2	32.7	26.4	9.3	2.3	79.0	37.2	49.7	50.3
22032	FAIRFAX	77.4	70.1	4.1	4.3	14.0	19.3	5.6	9.2	5.4	6.1	7.1	6.7	4.2	24.1	32.9	12.4	1.0	77.1	42.5	49.5	50.5
22033	FAIRFAX	74.3	66.5	5.3	5.4	16.0	21.7	5.7	9.1	6.4	6.0	6.0	5.2	6.4	37.1	25.7	6.6	0.7	78.5	35.7	49.2	50.8
22039	FAIRFAX STATION	84.2	78.5	3.7	4.1	9.4	13.5	3.0	5.2	5.0	6.9	8.7	8.6	3.9	17.5	38.9	9.9	0.6	73.8	44.5	50.2	49.8
22041	FALLS CHURCH	50.4	45.0	9.8	8.5	13.1	14.3	37.1	46.3	7.4	6.7	6.1	5.7	6.9	34.0	23.9	7.6	1.7	76.5	34.9	51.2	48.8
22042	FALLS CHURCH	61.5	53.7	4.8	4.3	19.2	22.8	22.4	30.9	6.7	6.3	6.2	5.7	5.7	32.5	26.6	9.1	1.2	77.3	37.5	49.9	50.1
22043	FALLS CHURCH	69.9	62.7	5.0	4.6	15.8	19.9	13.8	20.2	5.8	5.4	5.5	5.2	6.9	33.5	26.8	9.5	1.3	80.0	37.6	50.0	50.0
22044	FALLS CHURCH	63.4	59.3	4.8	3.9	15.7	17.2	28.2	35.7	6.5	6.5	6.3	5.7	5.3	31.3	27.5	9.3	1.6	77.3	38.0	51.3	48.7
22046	FALLS CHURCH	81.2	76.3	3.5	3.4	8.3	10.9	10.9	16.1	5.8	5.4	5.9	6.0	6.0	26.8	31.9	10.0	2.2	78.9	41.0	49.6	50.4
22060	FORT BELVOIR	55.5	50.3	31.5	30.5	3.3	5.1	10.3	16.4	13.2	12.0	9.2	6.3	8.6	35.7	9.7	3.5	1.9	61.5	25.4	50.1	49.9
22066	GREAT FALLS	86.1	80.6	1.9	2.2	9.1	13.2	2.5	4.4	6.0	7.7	10.1	8.6	3.5	16.5	36.0	10.9	0.8	70.6	43.3	50.4	49.6
22067	GREENWAY	83.5	76.7	2.2	2.6	10.3	14.5	2.2	4.4	4.4	6.2	7.9	7.0	3.1	21.1	32.2	16.7	1.3	77.5	45.2	48.0	52.0
22079	LORTON	54.9	50.4	29.7	27.4	7.4	10.4	8.9	14.4	7.4	7.2	7.3	6.8	6.4	29.5	27.5	6.8	1.2	73.9	35.5	49.0	51.0
22101	MC LEAN	84.0	78.0	1.7	1.8	10.9	15.4	3.9	6.8	5.4	6.5	8.1	6.9	3.6	17.8	33.9	14.9	2.9	75.4	46.0	48.1	51.9
22102	MC LEAN	75.9	68.5	2.8	2.8	15.8	21.2	5.5	8.9	4.4	4.4	5.2	5.2	6.1	30.5	29.6	12.9	1.7	82.8	40.7	48.1	51.9
22124	OAKTON	86.9	82.1	3.0	3.2	7.0	10.1	4.2	7.2	5.6	6.4	8.1	7.0	4.4	23.1	34.4	10.2	0.7	75.4	42.0	48.4	51.6
22134	QUANTICO	72.4	63.6	16.4	18.5	2.9	4.3	9.0	15.7	13.7	8.8	5.4	6.6	27.1	32.6	4.8	0.9	0.1	69.6	22.9	61.3	38.7
22150	SPRINGFIELD	57.7	49.0	7.4	6.8	21.8	27.6	18.5	24.2	6.7	6.7	6.8	6.4	5.6	28.2	27.7	10.0	1.9	75.8	38.4	49.8	50.2
22151	SPRINGFIELD	71.4	63.0	4.6	4.5	16.6	21.9	9.6	14.9	6.5	6.8	7.4	6.7	4.6	25.0	29.6	11.9	1.5	75.0	40.8	49.8	50.2
22152	SPRINGFIELD	74.0	66.5	5.6	5.7	14.3	19.1	7.9	12.7	5.5	6.1	7.0	6.8	4.3	25.2	32.8	11.4	0.9	77.0	41.9	48.4	51.6
22153	SPRINGFIELD	72.2	64.8	9.3	9.6	12.0	16.3	6.9	11.3	6.3	7.1	8.0	7.7	4.4	25.2	33.6	7.4	0.4	73.7	39.8	49.0	51.0
22172	TRIANGLE	60.6	53.3	28.8	30.4	3.0	4.4	7.7	13.0	9.1	8.0	7.2	6.6	8.1	29.8	23.2	7.3	0.7	71.8	31.5	49.9	50.1
22180	VIENNA	76.9	69.0	3.5	3.6	13.0	17.8	8.9	14.2	6.1	6.5	7.0	5.6	4.0	28.1	29.1	12.1	1.6	76.8	41.0	50.2	49.8
22181	VIENNA	82.5	76.2	2.8	3.0	10.4	14.7	6.1	9.8	5.8	6.6	7.7	6.2	3.5	24.8	32.6	11.7	1.1	75.8	42.4	50.0	50.0
22182	VIENNA	79.7	72.7	2.8	3.0	12.6	17.6	3.5	5.9	6.8	7.8	9.2	6.6	3.3	21.4	32.5	11.4	0.9	71.8	41.9	49.4	50.6
22191	WOODBRIDGE	55.2	49.0	26.0	25.5	5.0	6.6	17.4	24.8	8.7	7.9	7.4	7.4	7.8	30.1	22.8	7.1	0.9	71.5	31.8	49.8	50.2
22192	WOODBRIDGE	72.8	64.1	16.5	19.5	4.5	6.5	7.1	12.4	7.2	7.1	7.2	6.9	6.0	30.6	28.3	6.0	0.8	74.2	35.7	48.4	51.6
22193	WOODBRIDGE	58.8	50.1	27.4	29.5	5.1	7.1	9.4	15.4	8.0	8.0	8.2	8.0	5.7	31.3	25.2	5.3	0.3	70.7	33.2	49.1	50.9
22201	ARLINGTON	77.8	71.2	5.1	5.1	8.6	11.6	11.3	17.8	3.8	2.7	2.4	2.7	10.7	47.3	22.9	6.5	1.1	89.5	34.4	51.5	48.5
22202	ARLINGTON	70.8	62.2	8.1	10.5	12.5	16.2	11.9	16.6	3.3	2.8	2.5	2.4	7.3	41.4	26.7	11.5	2.1	90.0	38.8	50.9	49.1
22203	ARLINGTON	68.2	61.8	4.6	4.2	11.2	14.0	26.3	33.5	4.7	4.0	3.6	3.6	7.5	40.6	23.8	9.0	3.2	85.6	36.9	52.0	48.0
22204	ARLINGTON	49.6	43.6	17.4	15.2	10.1	11.5	32.8	44.0	6.9	6.2	5.5	5.4	7.9	36.6	23.7	6.7	1.1	78.3	34.3	50.8	49.2
22205	ARLINGTON	86.1	80.0	2.8	3.1	5.7	8.3	7.7	13.4	6.1	6.1	6.4	4.9	4.8	31.5	29.4	9.0	1.8	78.1	39.8	49.4	50.6
22206	ARLINGTON	64.9	55.7	14.5	13.4	5.9	7.7	19.7	32.9	5.8	4.4	3.9	4.4	8.6	41.1	25.5	5.6	0.7	83.2	34.5	47.8	52.2
22207	ARLINGTON	85.3	80.4	4.8	4.9	4.6	6.7	7.4	12.4	5.6	6.1	7.0	6.7	5.0	24.4	30.6	11.8	2.8	77.5	42.1	49.1	50.9
22209	ARLINGTON	68.2	59.3	5.6	5.7	13.2	16.5	18.2	29.2	3.2	2.1	1.7	2.5	13.6	48.8	22.2	5.2	0.7	91.6	32.6	53.8	46.2
22211	FT MYER	63.4	54.8	25.6	28.0	1.3	1.9	7.7	13.5	4.0	1.4	1.4	9.7	45.9	30.5	7.1	0.0	0.0	92.4	23.7	80.8	19.2
22213	ARLINGTON	89.0	83.4	1.5	1.7	5.7	8.6	5.9	10.8	6.0	6.2	6.9	5.6	3.5	27.3	30.4	11.4	2.8	76.9	41.8	49.1	50.9
22301	ALEXANDRIA	80.4	75.7	13.4	14.6	2.0	3.1	6.0	10.2	6.0	4.7	4.8	3.8	4.6	35.5	28.4	9.8	2.4	81.9	40.0	47.7	52.3
22302	ALEXANDRIA	74.4	67.9	11.1	11.7	5.5	7.7	8.2	12.9	5.5	4.9	4.8	3.6	5.3	35.2	28.5	9.9	2.4	82.6	39.9	46.5	53.5
22303	ALEXANDRIA	65.9	56.1	15.1	14.7	7.0	9.9	16.3	26.5	5.5	5.0	4.7	4.6	7.3	34.8	27.0	9.8	1.3	82.1	38.0	50.3	49.7
22304	ALEXANDRIA	54.4	49.5	24.4	22.3	8.8	11.4	15.0	21.8	6.0	4.7	4.2	4.3	8.2	38.3	24.4	8.4	1.4	82.5	35.6	48.3	51.7
22305	ALEXANDRIA	42.4	36.0	25.9	23.1	3.1	3.6	36.6	48.2	7.9	6.5	5.6	6.6	10.3	35.3	21.8	5.4	0.6	76.2	31.3	53.2	46.8
	VIRGINIA	72.3	68.8	19.6	20.1	3.7	5.1	4.7	7.0	6.5	6.4	6.5	6.9	6.9	27.5	27.2	10.5	1.6	76.7	37.7	49.2	50.8
	UNITED STATES	75.1	72.0	12.3	12.7	3.8	4.6	12.5	15.7	6.8	6.7	6.6	7.1	6.9	27.0	26.0	10.9	1.9	75.7	36.9	49.2	50.8

20105-22305

#	POST OFFICE NAME	2009 Per Capita Income	2009 HH Income Base	2009 HOUSEHOLD INCOME DISTRIBUTION (%) Less than $25,000	$25,000 to $49,999	$50,000 to $99,999	$100,000 to $149,999	$150,000 or More	MEDIAN HOUSEHOLD INCOME 2009	2014	2009 National Centile	2009 State Centile	2009 Home Value Base	2009 HOME VALUE DISTRIBUTION (%) Less than $50,000	$50,000 to $89,999	$90,000 to $174,999	$175,000 to $399,999	$400,000 or More	2009 Median Home Value
20105	ALDIE	49983	3066	3.1	7.1	26.7	26.9	36.2	125362	129978	99	98	2598	0.0	0.0	4.3	44.8	50.9	407667
20106	AMISSVILLE	31312	1817	10.8	16.1	38.6	25.6	9.0	72603	73776	88	84	1559	1.7	1.1	12.6	44.8	39.8	347517
20107	ARCOLA	55081	38	2.6	5.3	23.7	18.4	50.0	150000	152712	100	99	34	0.0	0.0	0.0	44.1	55.9	450000
20109	MANASSAS	29201	13809	9.4	22.7	41.7	20.4	5.8	67951	71676	86	81	6421	0.5	1.7	30.6	60.7	6.5	219783
20110	MANASSAS	31702	13823	6.7	15.2	38.1	29.0	11.0	82952	88357	93	89	9855	1.6	0.9	25.9	59.2	12.4	258203
20111	MANASSAS	31899	10110	6.9	15.1	37.8	28.4	11.8	84624	89158	94	89	7917	2.3	1.6	12.2	63.1	20.8	250720
20112	MANASSAS	41962	7143	3.4	4.3	24.1	39.8	28.4	122718	124140	99	97	6737	6.0	0.3	3.8	48.6	41.4	369714
20115	MARSHALL	40074	2378	11.7	13.8	29.7	28.5	16.2	88929	96649	95	90	1806	0.4	0.4	14.0	37.7	47.5	383929
20117	MIDDLEBURG	61293	1500	12.7	14.3	28.1	17.9	27.0	87592	90136	95	90	799	0.0	2.5	3.0	25.4	69.1	641725
20119	CATLETT	32521	1577	11.0	18.3	33.5	24.1	13.2	77439	83445	91	86	1246	0.6	1.4	13.7	53.0	31.3	321812
20120	CENTREVILLE	47669	13110	2.7	7.3	25.2	33.2	31.6	124282	129716	99	97	9994	1.0	0.7	6.6	54.6	37.2	348656
20121	CENTREVILLE	38122	9648	3.3	8.7	40.0	34.3	13.7	96946	100430	96	93	6342	1.6	1.2	13.6	62.6	20.9	261741
20124	CLIFTON	56356	4686	3.0	5.7	17.3	21.4	52.6	153953	158901	100	99	4066	0.5	1.6	2.9	12.5	82.4	614627
20129	PAEONIAN SPRINGS	63274	96	6.3	3.1	15.6	18.8	56.3	156075	156860	100	99	80	0.0	3.8	12.5	22.5	61.3	569444
20130	PARIS	36349	168	11.9	17.9	31.0	30.4	8.9	79956	80664	92	87	141	0.0	0.7	22.7	41.8	34.8	294643
20132	PURCELLVILLE	44697	4806	6.6	10.6	31.0	26.3	25.5	102725	105337	97	94	3918	0.4	0.6	2.0	37.4	59.4	470076
20135	BLUEMONT	39981	1142	7.4	15.7	42.3	21.5	13.2	75305	77290	90	85	916	2.1	2.4	20.4	40.2	34.9	283333
20136	BRISTOW	40155	6608	3.8	6.1	27.0	42.6	20.5	114619	117524	98	96	6147	0.7	0.5	2.5	60.0	36.4	352061
20137	BROAD RUN	43987	856	6.3	8.2	30.3	27.1	28.2	109509	112689	98	95	739	0.1	0.1	2.3	42.6	54.8	452985
20141	ROUND HILL	46397	1753	4.3	7.2	30.2	27.6	30.6	114197	121890	98	96	1512	0.1	0.4	5.4	38.3	55.8	442512
20143	CATHARPIN	45444	322	1.2	2.5	35.7	35.4	25.2	112329	114084	98	96	307	3.6	3.6	4.9	30.9	57.0	437719
20144	DELAPLANE	38430	460	13.9	18.0	32.6	25.0	10.4	72572	78949	88	84	310	0.3	0.3	18.4	39.0	41.9	328571
20147	ASHBURN	47536	17613	1.9	6.6	25.5	29.9	36.1	126605	131136	99	98	14144	0.0	0.2	4.2	47.5	48.1	392671
20148	ASHBURN	63519	8281	2.0	4.4	16.2	25.8	51.5	152606	156482	100	99	7243	0.0	0.0	0.0	39.8	60.2	480866
20151	CHANTILLY	43671	6168	3.0	7.1	25.0	35.8	29.1	124029	127717	99	97	5333	6.0	2.6	13.9	42.6	34.9	341092
20152	CHANTILLY	53569	7167	2.0	7.0	26.8	28.1	36.1	125850	130325	99	98	6232	0.0	0.0	4.8	46.9	48.3	394108
20155	GAINESVILLE	45340	7975	3.4	9.5	32.7	31.7	22.7	105488	106212	97	94	7433	2.5	0.6	7.1	46.0	43.7	372360
20158	HAMILTON	52245	1428	5.3	8.8	23.2	29.7	33.0	127006	129712	99	98	1185	1.3	1.4	3.4	40.8	53.2	430000
20164	STERLING	35993	12764	4.0	10.1	41.1	28.5	16.3	90640	90291	95	91	9333	0.6	0.4	8.8	76.1	14.1	310246
20165	STERLING	57242	11929	1.9	4.7	23.1	28.4	41.9	133098	138109	99	99	9375	0.1	1.5	0.7	41.4	56.4	436152
20166	STERLING	40262	3359	3.0	10.0	35.5	35.8	15.7	101205	102786	97	93	2486	1.4	0.8	4.2	69.0	24.6	342598
20169	HAYMARKET	45100	6455	3.1	6.6	32.1	31.9	26.2	111170	112295	98	95	6047	0.4	0.1	4.9	55.5	39.0	359567
20170	HERNDON	41593	12386	4.5	10.1	26.7	33.2	25.4	112496	120939	98	96	8855	0.3	0.3	13.9	55.6	29.8	333832
20171	HERNDON	55903	14343	1.9	5.6	21.4	31.2	39.8	131837	136602	99	98	10908	1.2	0.4	1.3	40.3	56.8	433171
20175	LEESBURG	49084	9420	7.0	11.6	29.4	24.3	27.7	103929	110666	97	94	6993	1.6	0.3	8.0	45.1	45.1	373372
20176	LEESBURG	49377	15278	4.6	10.6	29.0	28.6	27.2	108437	115453	98	95	11784	1.5	0.6	5.6	41.7	50.6	404738
20180	LOVETTSVILLE	44803	2182	6.3	7.4	32.4	25.9	28.0	106166	109753	97	94	1855	0.3	0.3	4.2	41.5	53.6	435904
20181	NOKESVILLE	41061	4998	3.4	7.2	29.1	40.2	20.0	112840	116733	98	96	4567	0.2	0.0	2.3	62.3	35.2	354333
20184	UPPERVILLE	50736	499	9.0	13.2	35.3	23.8	18.6	84500	88645	94	89	315	1.6	1.0	8.9	33.0	55.6	470000
20186	WARRENTON	35096	5634	11.4	14.7	36.5	25.6	11.7	80174	84907	92	87	3958	0.5	0.6	14.9	53.4	30.7	309894
20187	WARRENTON	38547	5204	5.0	9.7	33.3	30.1	21.9	102378	105135	97	93	4446	0.0	0.2	5.5	61.8	32.5	341327
20190	RESTON	52320	7762	10.3	14.1	28.4	28.1	19.1	93902	101477	96	92	4141	0.0	0.2	21.2	54.7	23.9	281311
20191	RESTON	52020	11330	6.6	10.3	28.9	28.8	25.3	105930	111459	97	94	8123	0.5	1.4	21.4	39.6	37.1	306401
20194	RESTON	71879	5839	2.9	5.5	24.3	28.1	39.2	130152	137387	99	98	4211	0.0	0.4	4.2	34.6	60.8	476338
20197	WATERFORD	64427	612	4.1	6.4	23.2	15.7	50.7	151056	153765	100	99	510	1.8	0.8	2.9	16.9	77.6	680970
20198	THE PLAINS	45684	1038	16.9	17.6	29.2	16.6	19.7	75129	80777	89	85	595	1.7	0.7	7.1	39.0	51.6	414394
22003	ANNANDALE	42147	18994	7.0	10.9	30.9	30.2	21.1	101622	106503	97	93	13221	1.6	1.6	11.3	44.4	41.2	368349
22015	BURKE	47747	14462	3.2	5.6	26.1	35.5	29.5	120121	127003	98	97	11780	1.1	0.3	6.3	58.1	34.3	341693
22025	DUMFRIES	39526	5930	3.2	7.0	33.6	36.2	20.1	106790	108415	98	95	5000	0.3	0.3	11.4	67.7	20.2	293099
22026	DUMFRIES	26938	5034	10.6	22.8	35.8	25.8	4.9	70078	75868	87	83	2990	4.3	2.0	22.2	63.7	7.7	215240
22027	DUNN LORING	53808	607	1.6	4.9	24.2	32.3	36.9	128252	135505	99	98	469	4.9	0.0	0.0	26.0	69.1	550176
22030	FAIRFAX	46854	16957	5.0	10.0	30.3	29.8	24.8	106727	111878	98	95	11732	2.6	1.0	4.8	51.6	40.0	365773
22031	FAIRFAX	42855	11235	7.1	12.1	33.4	29.0	18.5	94902	100893	96	92	6133	0.8	0.6	10.3	44.2	44.1	369482
22032	FAIRFAX	46284	9727	2.5	5.1	25.7	35.4	31.4	123259	129590	99	97	8531	1.0	0.1	1.5	58.7	38.8	371926
22033	FAIRFAX	53181	14335	3.5	8.6	31.7	33.1	23.1	107872	114408	98	95	8662	0.6	0.2	6.0	63.0	30.1	341525
22039	FAIRFAX STATION	67719	5854	1.1	2.7	8.1	24.2	64.0	177164	184385	100	100	5601	0.8	0.7	0.8	3.8	93.8	686525
22041	FALLS CHURCH	34383	9622	11.4	20.0	36.6	18.5	13.6	74105	75142	89	85	4170	1.3	3.2	25.1	40.0	30.3	284339
22042	FALLS CHURCH	36693	11088	7.3	15.3	34.1	29.3	14.0	87149	88960	94	90	7195	0.7	1.4	11.2	66.8	19.9	310158
22043	FALLS CHURCH	48392	9471	5.1	10.1	35.7	28.9	20.1	98072	103303	96	93	5487	1.4	0.2	9.7	51.6	37.1	348249
22044	FALLS CHURCH	46543	4599	14.2	14.0	28.8	18.9	24.1	86341	89852	94	89	2176	0.5	3.4	15.5	21.3	59.2	456620
22046	FALLS CHURCH	53847	5977	6.5	10.6	32.5	24.3	26.1	100626	106090	97	93	4038	0.2	1.0	12.2	40.0	46.6	387679
22060	FORT BELVOIR	22974	2831	10.0	30.7	39.1	15.0	5.1	60453	62503	78	75	508	0.0	3.0	12.4	83.3	1.4	235032
22066	GREAT FALLS	80225	5663	2.0	4.1	9.0	15.5	69.4	211458	220258	100	100	5350	0.2	0.6	0.9	3.7	94.6	873719
22067	GREENWAY	86783	79	0.0	3.8	16.5	10.1	69.6	205349	215293	100	100	72	0.0	5.6	4.2	4.2	86.1	1000001
22079	LORTON	41631	10107	5.2	12.1	37.4	23.9	21.4	91653	92933	95	91	6898	0.3	1.0	18.3	50.1	30.3	276915
22101	MC LEAN	79494	10542	4.0	5.8	14.5	22.0	53.7	159200	169165	100	100	8765	0.0	0.4	0.9	9.4	89.3	687755
22102	MC LEAN	77017	9048	6.0	8.2	27.8	24.1	33.9	115247	126386	98	96	4966	0.0	0.9	17.5	23.4	58.2	577855
22124	OAKTON	76331	6098	2.6	5.0	18.6	20.6	53.2	159869	167921	100	100	5033	0.0	0.0	5.5	23.1	71.4	617097
22134	QUANTICO	17779	1558	15.1	37.1	35.8	10.7	1.3	48426	49078	58	54	94	30.9	10.6	44.7	12.8	1.1	125758
22150	SPRINGFIELD	35445	8665	5.5	10.4	36.3	33.3	14.5	96182	101160	96	92	6007	0.9	0.0	2.2	80.7	16.2	319616
22151	SPRINGFIELD	40131	5754	3.1	10.3	31.9	35.2	19.4	104690	109453	97	94	4759	1.6	0.7	1.5	85.4	10.8	329176
22152	SPRINGFIELD	46589	9796	3.0	6.9	31.9	34.3	23.9	110622	118708	98	95	7888	0.9	0.5	10.8	65.5	22.4	328186
22153	SPRINGFIELD	47835	10243	2.3	4.6	25.9	35.5	31.7	122216	128528	99	97	8529	0.5	0.5	4.7	62.1	32.3	347241
22172	TRIANGLE	25398	3153	13.4	37.3	33.7	11.2	4.4	49326	51087	60	56	1236	4.3	1.1	22.0	63.0	9.6	230800
22180	VIENNA	50372	8458	3.7	8.1	28.4	33.6	26.2	114268	123128	98	96	6362	0.7	0.1	4.0	52.1	43.1	382163
22181	VIENNA	66816	5232	2.6	5.4	17.6	26.2	48.2	146087	153021	100	99	4241	0.0	0.0	1.9	24.9	73.2	565625
22182	VIENNA	68391	8366	5.5	4.9	14.3	22.6	52.7	156201	165505	100	99	7054	0.6	0.1	0.4	11.0	87.9	639763
22191	WOODBRIDGE	25904	18101	7.8	26.9	40.8	18.5	6.0	64998	68015	83	80	9888	4.4	0.8	23.1	67.3	4.4	210637
22192	WOODBRIDGE	39661	20736	4.4	13.5	36.2	28.6	17.3	92205	94846	95	91	14020	2.1	0.8	14.0	65.0	18.1	265444
22193	WOODBRIDGE	30680	22771	4.3	13.2	40.5	31.8	10.1	86778	90711	94	90	17061	0.7	0.6	13.6	77.8	7.3	245345
22201	ARLINGTON	60562	16249	8.0	12.5	34.6	26.2	18.7	90968	97697	95	91	5699	0.4	1.5	14.3	38.5	45.3	376421
22202	ARLINGTON	57699	12175	11.3	11.0	35.1	27.8	14.8	87765	94106	95	90	3179	0.0	1.6	11.7	35.1	51.6	409167
22203	ARLINGTON	48325	9785	12.4	13.9	35.9	22.5	15.3	81201	85435	93	88	3219	0.7	3.6	11.2	46.9	37.5	349813
22204	ARLINGTON	29903	19393	12.6	22.8	39.3	18.3	7.0	64871	68371	83	80	6890	1.1	4.6	24.2	50.7	19.4	264616
22205	ARLINGTON	53624	6362	5.4	8.8	26.0	29.0	30.8	116645	119812	98	97	4683	0.2	0.0	1.0	39.9	58.9	438049
22206	ARLINGTON	45538	8868	6.5	13.5	41.1	26.6	12.4	83096	86700	93	89	4124	0.4	1.2	19.4	72.3	6.8	243838
22207	ARLINGTON	59792	11048	4.9	7.1	23.0	27.9	37.1	126548	126900	99	98	8680	0.1	0.5	3.8	16.7	79.0	603497
22209	ARLINGTON	54313	7164	11.5	20.6	35.8	20.2	11.9	73681	79162	89	84	1591	1.0	7.5	23.4	29.3	38.8	260539
22211	FT MYER	20410	171	17.5	19.9	21.1	27.5	14.0	70145	82618	87	83	2	0.0	0.0	0.0	100.0	0.0	350000
22213	ARLINGTON	56993	1066	2.1	4.1	27.2	35.0	31.6	123610	125525	99	97	895	0.6	0.0	0.0	40.8	58.7	430512
22301	ALEXANDRIA	53187	4964	6.4	13.2	32.0	28.1	20.3	96628	102307	96	93	3086	0.9	0.6	7.3	45.6	45.5	376728
22302	ALEXANDRIA	53478	9193	7.1	13.4	39.6	25.1	14.8	83216	87245	93	89	4483	0.0	2.3	33.6	29.2	34.8	225487
22303	ALEXANDRIA	43475	7447	8.1	19.2	40.2	24.0	8.5	75060	74836	89	85	3297	1.8	2.9	23.5	60.7	11.2	233238
22304	ALEXANDRIA	39679	21328	11.8	19.7	39.7	20.2	8.5	68489	74049	86	82	7643	0.7	1.6	32.7	42.3	22.7	228289
22305	ALEXANDRIA	30036	6641	10.6	23.5	38.5	17.7	9.7	65538	68586	84	80	2268	0.4	2.9	25.5	33.3	38.0	280928
	VIRGINIA	30912		17.0	22.6	35.9	15.0	9.5	61855	64957				5.3	6.3	30.4	41.5	16.5	203135
	UNITED STATES	27277		20.9	24.4	35.3	11.7	7.6	54719	56938				9.3	13.1	31.6	32.6	13.5	162279

ZIP CODE #	POST OFFICE NAME	FINANCIAL SERVICES: Auto Loan	Home Loan	Invest-ments	Retire-ment Plans	THE HOME: Home Improvements: Home Repair	Lawn & Garden	Furnishings: Comput-ers & Hard-ware-Personal	Major Appli-ances	TV, Radio, Sound Equip-ment	Furni-ture	ENTERTAINMENT: Dine out/ Carry out	Sports Equip-ment	Fees & Tickets	Toys & Games	Travel	Cable TV	PERSONAL: Apparel & Services	Auto Repairs	Health Insur-ance	Pets & Supplies
20105	ALDIE	206	251	224	258	247	207	211	213	193	236	197	177	239	207	224	177	145	196	175	238
20106	AMISSVILLE	114	142	145	146	146	134	121	128	116	129	117	95	138	115	135	114	84	121	121	146
20107	ARCOLA	269	352	356	369	361	312	288	299	269	315	273	238	345	277	325	255	204	277	258	337
20109	MANASSAS	113	109	99	112	105	97	115	104	110	117	113	85	113	115	109	107	80	109	99	124
20110	MANASSAS	138	143	128	144	138	126	139	132	133	145	135	106	142	138	137	127	96	133	121	154
20111	MANASSAS	137	158	144	158	156	137	142	141	134	151	136	112	153	139	147	127	98	136	125	160
20112	MANASSAS	179	226	213	234	226	194	187	192	174	206	177	155	218	183	204	163	131	177	163	215
20115	MARSHALL	143	174	177	179	178	164	152	158	145	161	147	119	170	145	168	143	105	151	149	181
20117	MIDDLEBURG	178	224	262	228	246	192	213	211	186	228	187	168	233	180	238	171	139	203	177	234
20119	CATLETT	126	150	141	154	150	144	130	137	126	135	127	104	144	128	142	125	90	130	132	158
20120	CENTREVILLE	198	227	209	235	223	195	203	199	190	219	194	163	223	200	210	178	141	190	172	227
20121	CENTREVILLE	159	160	138	165	152	136	158	146	150	167	153	122	160	160	152	141	109	147	131	171
20124	CLIFTON	237	297	322	313	313	272	258	262	243	279	244	205	304	246	287	232	183	249	232	296
20129	PAEONIAN SPRINGS	213	297	359	305	332	276	250	267	228	279	226	197	305	219	300	217	170	246	239	292
20130	PARIS	117	143	146	147	147	135	124	130	119	132	120	97	140	119	138	117	86	124	123	149
20132	PURCELLVILLE	170	214	219	218	220	196	184	190	174	196	175	145	211	174	205	168	127	181	175	216
20135	BLUEMONT	133	157	152	162	159	148	141	145	134	145	135	113	154	135	153	131	96	139	136	167
20136	BRISTOW	172	211	186	216	207	174	175	178	162	195	165	147	199	175	186	150	121	163	147	198
20137	BROAD RUN	171	216	221	219	222	202	183	193	175	193	177	143	209	175	206	173	127	183	182	219
20141	ROUND HILL	179	224	234	231	233	209	193	202	182	206	184	152	220	181	217	177	133	191	186	230
20143	CATHARPIN	177	221	245	229	235	213	185	199	179	203	179	148	218	176	211	175	131	186	187	225
20144	DELAPLANE	126	147	146	151	148	138	133	135	128	138	130	103	146	129	143	126	92	131	129	156
20147	ASHBURN	215	253	219	261	246	209	216	215	200	240	204	180	241	216	224	184	149	200	178	242
20148	ASHBURN	269	333	301	344	329	279	276	281	255	307	259	231	317	272	296	235	191	257	233	314
20151	CHANTILLY	193	225	211	231	223	199	199	199	188	213	191	159	220	196	210	180	139	191	177	228
20152	CHANTILLY	205	248	214	256	242	203	206	209	190	232	194	174	234	206	217	174	142	190	170	233
20155	GAINESVILLE	169	193	185	194	194	179	167	175	162	181	163	133	182	166	177	157	116	165	163	200
20158	HAMILTON	191	246	266	253	259	231	208	221	197	226	198	164	243	194	239	191	144	208	205	249
20164	STERLING	151	169	153	170	164	147	157	151	149	163	152	122	167	156	160	143	109	150	138	175
20165	STERLING	229	278	249	285	273	235	235	237	219	258	222	194	265	232	249	204	163	220	202	267
20166	STERLING	167	160	141	167	152	141	166	150	159	171	163	126	165	168	158	152	116	156	139	179
20169	HAYMARKET	167	208	198	211	207	186	175	181	166	187	168	140	199	170	192	160	122	171	164	207
20170	HERNDON	183	207	200	213	207	183	193	186	183	201	186	150	210	189	200	175	136	184	169	215
20171	HERNDON	231	256	253	270	257	230	240	232	228	254	232	188	261	236	249	218	169	229	209	269
20175	LEESBURG	190	218	201	226	215	190	196	192	184	210	187	157	214	193	203	174	136	185	171	221
20176	LEESBURG	192	227	202	229	223	190	195	196	182	214	185	159	216	194	204	170	134	183	167	220
20180	LOVETTSVILLE	169	218	225	227	225	200	181	190	172	196	173	146	214	173	205	166	128	178	172	216
20181	NOKESVILLE	161	206	198	208	207	179	171	176	160	184	162	139	197	167	188	153	119	164	155	197
20184	UPPERVILLE	145	181	197	185	191	164	162	166	149	173	150	127	181	146	181	142	109	158	149	188
20186	WARRENTON	123	143	137	145	142	132	130	130	125	134	127	101	142	127	138	123	91	128	124	151
20187	WARRENTON	155	191	181	193	190	174	163	168	155	172	158	130	183	158	178	151	113	160	156	193
20190	RESTON	158	150	150	158	150	133	168	148	157	170	161	125	164	161	162	149	115	158	137	176
20191	RESTON	174	198	203	203	202	179	189	184	179	197	181	145	204	180	199	172	132	183	170	211
20194	RESTON	232	257	268	268	265	228	248	238	231	263	234	193	267	236	259	218	171	236	211	273
20197	WATERFORD	229	320	388	329	358	297	269	288	246	301	243	213	329	237	324	234	183	266	257	315
20198	THE PLAINS	136	178	198	176	191	156	161	162	145	168	146	125	181	143	181	138	108	156	143	179
22003	ANNANDALE	150	181	195	183	189	165	169	166	159	173	161	129	188	159	183	155	118	164	155	188
22015	BURKE	184	233	230	240	236	208	198	202	186	210	189	159	229	191	218	178	139	191	180	230
22025	DUMFRIES	162	194	176	196	190	168	167	168	157	178	160	134	185	165	177	150	116	160	150	192
22026	DUMFRIES	115	116	101	119	111	101	115	107	110	120	112	89	116	116	111	104	79	108	98	126
22027	DUNN LORING	204	274	286	283	285	247	224	233	210	240	212	182	271	214	256	202	159	218	206	262
22030	FAIRFAX	174	192	194	197	194	173	187	177	178	191	181	142	199	182	192	172	131	179	165	205
22031	FAIRFAX	152	168	175	171	172	153	165	158	158	168	160	124	175	159	171	154	116	159	149	182
22032	FAIRFAX	172	234	246	236	244	211	192	200	180	203	182	153	230	183	220	175	135	188	181	223
22033	FAIRFAX	182	183	175	192	179	166	187	172	180	191	184	142	192	186	184	173	132	178	162	204
22039	FAIRFAX STATION	271	376	433	393	409	347	306	325	286	338	285	248	384	286	361	273	218	299	285	358
22041	FALLS CHURCH	127	128	127	131	128	117	140	126	135	138	139	101	141	136	137	133	100	134	123	148
22042	FALLS CHURCH	128	153	157	150	157	137	144	139	138	143	140	108	157	140	152	136	103	140	133	158
22043	FALLS CHURCH	164	179	182	183	182	162	176	167	167	180	170	133	186	170	181	162	123	169	157	193
22044	FALLS CHURCH	147	165	178	168	172	146	173	160	160	174	165	129	182	158	179	153	122	165	146	182
22046	FALLS CHURCH	167	202	220	204	212	183	190	186	177	196	178	146	209	175	207	170	131	184	172	212
22060	FORT BELVOIR	115	74	64	81	70	70	112	86	109	106	113	77	93	121	90	104	79	103	88	104
22066	GREAT FALLS	299	424	514	444	473	397	342	367	321	381	318	276	442	320	409	307	248	336	322	399
22067	GREENWAY	291	416	511	436	466	392	334	360	314	373	311	270	435	313	403	301	243	329	317	392
22079	LORTON	159	168	158	172	165	151	161	155	155	170	157	124	169	160	162	149	112	154	144	180
22101	MC LEAN	251	348	419	358	387	326	292	310	272	320	270	231	361	266	346	262	205	288	281	339
22102	MC LEAN	222	224	246	240	232	215	243	219	236	246	239	179	254	235	243	230	174	232	218	260
22124	OAKTON	260	323	365	338	346	302	284	289	270	306	271	223	337	273	317	260	203	277	263	325
22134	QUANTICO	97	55	45	63	51	49	93	67	88	87	92	64	73	102	70	82	65	83	63	82
22150	SPRINGFIELD	135	172	180	165	179	149	154	154	143	158	145	118	172	144	169	138	106	150	139	170
22151	SPRINGFIELD	139	189	200	183	197	170	161	165	153	162	155	124	189	155	183	152	115	160	155	182
22152	SPRINGFIELD	164	212	214	214	217	192	179	184	169	187	171	142	208	173	200	165	126	175	169	208
22153	SPRINGFIELD	192	241	232	247	242	214	204	208	192	218	195	164	234	198	223	184	142	197	185	237
22172	TRIANGLE	86	87	81	87	85	80	93	85	91	91	93	69	94	92	91	90	66	90	85	101
22180	VIENNA	163	217	234	213	228	197	185	189	175	190	177	142	217	178	209	173	131	182	177	209
22181	VIENNA	228	306	352	319	333	279	259	270	239	284	239	208	314	238	300	226	181	252	236	299
22182	VIENNA	236	324	385	335	358	296	274	287	252	301	251	219	335	248	322	239	191	267	251	316
22191	WOODBRIDGE	107	109	98	109	105	98	111	103	107	111	109	83	112	111	108	105	77	107	100	121
22192	WOODBRIDGE	152	168	152	171	163	147	155	151	147	163	150	121	164	154	158	141	107	148	136	175
22193	WOODBRIDGE	138	158	136	156	151	134	138	138	130	148	133	110	148	138	142	124	95	132	122	158
22201	ARLINGTON	158	129	138	145	128	122	174	138	167	165	172	123	161	168	157	161	124	159	139	173
22202	ARLINGTON	143	121	130	135	121	114	159	128	151	152	156	112	149	152	145	146	112	146	128	158
22203	ARLINGTON	134	121	127	130	121	117	150	126	145	143	149	106	144	144	141	142	106	141	131	154
22204	ARLINGTON	101	99	102	102	99	89	117	100	111	111	114	84	114	110	112	108	83	110	98	118
22205	ARLINGTON	164	211	242	213	228	190	195	193	179	200	181	151	222	177	218	172	135	189	175	215
22206	ARLINGTON	136	121	120	129	118	113	150	125	145	142	150	106	142	146	138	142	107	140	127	153
22207	ARLINGTON	190	246	291	253	270	224	225	226	205	239	207	175	261	201	256	195	155	218	202	251
22209	ARLINGTON	133	104	111	119	102	99	148	114	141	138	147	104	134	142	131	136	105	134	115	144
22211	FT MYER	157	82	61	94	73	69	148	102	139	137	146	102	112	167	106	127	102	130	92	124
22213	ARLINGTON	168	232	267	230	252	210	198	206	183	209	183	155	235	180	231	177	137	195	187	226
22301	ALEXANDRIA	154	165	179	173	171	149	174	159	161	176	164	132	180	160	178	153	120	164	147	186
22302	ALEXANDRIA	139	129	138	138	131	125	153	132	149	149	152	109	151	148	146	146	109	145	136	159
22303	ALEXANDRIA	125	119	118	124	117	111	132	117	128	130	131	96	130	131	126	126	93	126	117	141
22304	ALEXANDRIA	119	102	101	110	100	96	125	105	121	122	124	89	118	123	115	118	88	117	105	129
22305	ALEXANDRIA	114	96	98	101	97	88	124	104	118	122	123	87	115	119	114	113	88	118	100	124
	VIRGINIA	115	112	112	114	111	114	112	112	112	112	112	88	111	114	111	113	79	112	112	132
	UNITED STATES	100	100	100	100	100	100	100	100	100	100	100	100	100	100	100	100	100	100	100	100

POPULATION CHANGE

ZIP CODE #	POST OFFICE NAME	COUNTY FIPS CODE	POPULATION 2000	POPULATION 2009	POPULATION 2014	2000-2009 ANNUAL RATE % Rate	2000-2009 ANNUAL RATE State Centile	HOUSEHOLDS 2000	HOUSEHOLDS 2009	HOUSEHOLDS 2014	HOUSEHOLDS % Annual Rate 2000-2009	HOUSEHOLDS 2009 Average HH Size	FAMILIES 2000	FAMILIES 2009	FAMILIES % Annual Rate 2000-2009
22306	ALEXANDRIA	059	26040	27184	27474	0.5	45	9914	10303	10399	0.4	2.62	6435	6439	0.0
22307	ALEXANDRIA	059	9662	9411	9317	-0.3	11	4556	4476	4430	-0.2	2.10	2547	2402	-0.6
22308	ALEXANDRIA	059	12554	12228	12086	-0.3	11	4769	4687	4641	-0.2	2.58	3736	3591	-0.4
22309	ALEXANDRIA	059	28582	29264	29421	0.3	38	10575	10826	10878	0.3	2.70	7488	7419	-0.1
22310	ALEXANDRIA	059	23370	24637	25035	0.6	49	9188	9716	9868	0.6	2.53	6067	6220	0.3
22311	ALEXANDRIA	510	15360	15866	15890	0.4	42	7208	7251	7218	0.1	2.12	3106	2972	-0.5
22312	ALEXANDRIA	059	27727	30114	30875	0.9	61	10046	10545	10777	0.5	2.84	6589	6700	0.2
22314	ALEXANDRIA	510	24585	29267	32684	1.9	83	13407	15954	17897	1.9	1.79	5329	5956	1.2
22315	ALEXANDRIA	059	26935	27983	28245	0.4	42	11000	11511	11635	0.5	2.43	7097	7144	0.1
22401	FREDERICKSBURG	630	19277	22168	23666	1.5	76	8101	9597	10429	1.8	2.04	3924	4402	1.3
22405	FREDERICKSBURG	179	23249	29856	32423	2.7	90	8105	10403	11294	2.7	2.84	6323	8014	2.6
22406	FREDERICKSBURG	179	11183	19365	23569	6.1	98	3996	7094	8653	6.4	2.73	3050	5200	5.9
22407	FREDERICKSBURG	177	40424	55282	62077	3.4	94	13853	19101	21518	3.5	2.87	10825	14637	3.3
22408	FREDERICKSBURG	177	18505	25899	29330	3.7	95	6701	9568	10902	3.9	2.70	5063	7014	3.6
22427	BOWLING GREEN	033	2903	3497	3869	2.0	85	1118	1393	1560	2.4	2.45	786	945	2.0
22432	BURGESS	133	590	673	717	1.4	73	249	290	310	1.7	2.32	175	198	1.3
22433	BURR HILL	137	105	103	121	-0.2	14	38	38	45	0.0	2.71	31	30	-0.4
22435	CALLAO	133	2297	2461	2507	0.7	54	991	1085	1115	1.0	2.24	685	726	0.6
22436	CARET	057	402	444	473	1.1	66	159	181	195	1.4	2.45	116	129	1.2
22437	CENTER CROSS	057	414	533	589	2.8	91	178	236	263	3.1	2.26	125	160	2.7
22438	CHAMPLAIN	057	616	683	727	1.1	66	244	279	300	1.5	2.44	178	199	1.2
22443	COLONIAL BEACH	193	7528	8120	8372	0.8	58	3110	3414	3539	1.0	2.35	2076	2199	0.6
22448	DAHLGREN	099	958	1364	1621	3.9	95	198	314	387	5.1	3.64	196	310	5.1
22454	DUNNSVILLE	057	2150	2341	2460	0.9	61	870	972	1029	1.2	2.41	619	671	0.9
22460	FARNHAM	159	1619	1720	1744	0.7	54	654	711	730	0.9	2.05	463	488	0.6
22469	HAGUE	193	2253	2351	2399	0.5	45	912	981	1010	0.8	2.40	635	661	0.4
22473	HEATHSVILLE	133	4886	5435	5660	1.2	69	2140	2430	2546	1.4	2.23	1486	1633	1.0
22476	HUSTLE	057	390	431	459	1.1	66	136	155	167	1.4	2.78	99	110	1.1
22480	IRVINGTON	103	770	1046	1132	3.4	94	247	367	404	4.4	2.29	176	252	4.0
22482	KILMARNOCK	133	2545	2635	2677	0.4	42	1183	1250	1279	0.6	2.06	802	820	0.2
22485	KING GEORGE	099	15847	22433	26655	3.8	95	5894	8493	10152	4.0	2.63	4329	6051	3.7
22488	KINSALE	193	1439	1472	1493	0.2	33	592	622	638	0.5	2.37	415	424	0.2
22503	LANCASTER	103	4547	4528	4481	0.0	23	1980	2033	2034	0.3	2.21	1353	1342	-0.1
22504	LANEVIEW	057	242	314	348	2.9	92	90	120	134	3.2	2.62	63	81	2.8
22508	LOCUST GROVE	137	7520	11117	13157	4.3	96	3090	4663	5559	4.5	2.38	2391	3513	4.2
22509	LORETTO	057	5	6	6	2.0	85	3	3	3	0.0	2.00	2	2	0.0
22511	LOTTSBURG	133	1283	1377	1399	0.8	58	591	645	658	0.9	2.13	410	433	0.6
22514	MILFORD	033	2224	2478	2729	1.2	69	838	956	1060	1.4	2.59	626	693	1.1
22520	MONTROSS	193	5279	5425	5465	0.3	38	2129	2240	2275	0.6	2.41	1489	1518	0.2
22534	PARTLOW	177	2067	2550	2736	2.3	88	699	878	950	2.5	2.90	558	683	2.2
22535	PORT ROYAL	033	814	963	1042	1.8	81	208	282	318	3.3	2.41	148	194	3.0
22538	RAPPAHANNOCK ACADEMY	033	297	356	398	2.0	85	112	137	155	2.2	2.57	81	96	1.9
22539	REEDVILLE	133	2291	2579	2701	1.3	72	1069	1229	1295	1.5	2.10	730	812	1.2
22542	RHOADESVILLE	137	1510	1888	2147	2.4	88	552	702	802	2.6	2.69	432	537	2.4
22546	RUTHER GLEN	033	9721	14117	16552	4.1	96	3531	5275	6248	4.4	2.66	2720	3955	4.1
22551	SPOTSYLVANIA	177	15024	19091	20771	2.6	90	5154	6670	7308	2.8	2.86	4127	5211	2.6
22553	SPOTSYLVANIA	177	11248	16956	19182	4.5	97	3707	5685	6481	4.7	2.98	3133	4692	4.5
22554	STAFFORD	179	37676	51479	57072	3.4	94	11993	16231	17974	3.3	3.15	10019	13366	3.2
22556	STAFFORD	179	20232	26202	28442	2.8	91	6129	7968	8685	2.9	3.19	5130	6567	2.7
22560	TAPPAHANNOCK	057	6022	6695	7078	1.2	69	2417	2766	2955	1.5	2.36	1611	1776	1.1
22567	UNIONVILLE	137	2421	2989	3305	2.3	88	891	1128	1258	2.6	2.64	684	841	2.3
22572	WARSAW	159	7119	7562	7645	0.7	54	2257	2445	2509	0.9	2.40	1518	1587	0.5
22576	WEEMS	103	2081	2057	2036	-0.1	18	880	888	885	0.1	2.22	596	580	-0.3
22578	WHITE STONE	103	2719	2773	2782	0.2	33	1227	1269	1281	0.4	2.16	843	842	0.0
22579	WICOMICO CHURCH	133	105	113	115	0.8	58	45	50	51	1.1	2.26	32	34	0.7
22580	WOODFORD	033	5137	5939	6591	1.6	78	1876	2238	2508	1.9	2.63	1397	1617	1.6
22601	WINCHESTER	840	24186	26551	27471	1.0	64	10225	11332	11765	1.1	2.26	5796	6136	0.6
22602	WINCHESTER	069	21151	27492	31038	2.9	92	7879	10375	11778	3.0	2.64	6001	7690	2.7
22603	WINCHESTER	069	11356	14284	15775	2.5	89	4374	5638	6300	2.8	2.43	3203	3999	2.4
22610	BENTONVILLE	187	1628	1865	1964	1.5	76	660	769	815	1.7	2.43	482	544	1.3
22611	BERRYVILLE	043	7609	8809	9423	1.6	78	2948	3570	3873	2.1	2.43	2098	2464	1.8
22620	BOYCE	043	2317	2621	2772	1.3	72	939	1100	1178	1.7	2.37	672	764	1.4
22624	CLEAR BROOK	069	2448	2987	3306	2.2	87	896	1119	1249	2.4	2.67	712	870	2.2
22625	CROSS JUNCTION	069	2739	3768	4319	3.5	94	957	1354	1571	3.8	2.73	757	1047	3.6
22627	FLINT HILL	157	483	504	509	0.5	45	218	232	235	0.7	2.17	159	164	0.3
22630	FRONT ROYAL	187	25946	29895	31654	1.5	76	9887	11460	12177	1.6	2.55	6917	7767	1.3
22637	GORE	069	1986	2162	2312	0.9	61	749	833	900	1.2	2.55	589	641	0.9
22639	HUME	061	537	673	736	2.5	89	218	271	297	2.4	2.47	166	202	2.1
22640	HUNTLY	157	538	542	537	0.1	28	213	217	217	0.2	2.50	152	150	-0.1
22641	STRASBURG	171	380	423	442	1.2	69	147	167	176	1.4	2.53	113	125	1.1
22642	LINDEN	061	3312	4389	4920	3.1	93	1226	1640	1847	3.2	2.67	879	1139	2.8
22643	MARKHAM	061	479	577	602	2.0	85	197	234	246	1.9	2.41	142	165	1.6
22644	MAURERTOWN	171	1990	2282	2435	1.5	76	752	880	946	1.7	2.56	574	657	1.5
22645	MIDDLETOWN	069	2970	3550	3899	1.9	83	1193	1454	1609	2.2	2.44	870	1027	1.8
22649	MIDDLETOWN	187	32	36	39	1.3	72	15	17	18	1.4	2.12	11	13	1.8
22650	RILEYVILLE	139	1019	1095	1132	0.8	58	406	451	472	1.1	2.42	295	318	0.8
22652	FORT VALLEY	171	1139	1273	1339	1.2	69	468	531	560	1.4	2.40	343	378	1.1
22654	STAR TANNERY	069	458	529	615	1.6	78	188	216	252	1.5	2.45	139	155	1.2
22655	STEPHENS CITY	069	13790	18680	21292	3.3	94	5075	7026	8067	3.6	2.65	3859	5222	3.3
22656	STEPHENSON	069	1751	2136	2370	2.2	87	654	811	907	2.4	2.63	505	610	2.1
22657	STRASBURG	171	7850	10179	11332	2.8	91	3298	4338	4848	3.0	2.35	2236	2838	2.6
22660	TOMS BROOK	171	1469	1679	1784	1.5	76	578	675	722	1.7	2.47	437	498	1.4
22663	WHITE POST	043	1767	2105	2446	1.9	83	578	711	828	2.3	2.78	431	519	2.0
22664	WOODSTOCK	171	7350	8652	9304	1.8	81	2970	3530	3814	1.9	2.36	2035	2344	1.5
22701	CULPEPER	047	22262	32397	37940	4.1	96	8470	12563	14824	4.4	2.54	6063	8730	4.0
22709	ARODA	113	563	645	684	1.5	76	189	224	241	1.9	2.85	145	167	1.5
22712	BEALETON	061	6425	8697	9507	3.3	94	2169	2939	3233	3.3	2.95	1717	2270	3.1
22713	BOSTON	047	1259	1504	1696	1.9	83	466	564	640	2.1	2.67	365	435	1.9
22714	BRANDY STATION	047	580	681	741	1.8	81	208	249	272	2.0	2.73	151	174	1.5
22715	BRIGHTWOOD	113	1213	1403	1492	1.6	78	455	545	587	2.0	2.54	361	423	1.7
22716	CASTLETON	157	801	880	910	1.0	64	314	355	371	1.3	2.48	229	252	1.0
22718	ELKWOOD	047	631	760	840	2.0	85	224	276	307	2.3	2.71	174	208	1.9
22719	ETLAN	113	694	789	834	1.4	73	271	321	344	1.8	2.46	198	227	1.5
22720	GOLDVEIN	061	1059	1186	1207	1.2	69	363	400	409	1.1	2.96	294	318	0.9
22722	HAYWOOD	113	306	350	371	1.5	76	114	135	145	1.8	2.59	85	99	1.7
	VIRGINIA					1.2					1.3	2.52			1.0
	UNITED STATES					1.0					1.1	2.59			0.9

ZIP CODE #	POST OFFICE NAME	RACE (%) White 2000	White 2009	Black 2000	Black 2009	Asian/Pacific 2000	Asian/Pacific 2009	% Hispanic Origin 2000	% Hispanic Origin 2009	2009 AGE DISTRIBUTION (%) 0-4	5-9	10-14	15-19	20-24	25-44	45-64	65-84	85+	18+	MEDIAN AGE 2009	% 2009 Males	% 2009 Females
22306	ALEXANDRIA	50.3	44.9	27.2	25.0	8.1	10.2	19.5	27.8	7.6	7.1	6.8	6.4	6.9	30.4	25.7	8.1	1.0	74.6	35.4	49.2	50.8
22307	ALEXANDRIA	84.7	80.5	6.7	6.8	2.8	4.0	7.3	12.1	4.7	5.2	5.7	5.0	5.1	23.2	33.3	14.6	3.3	81.3	45.6	47.6	52.4
22308	ALEXANDRIA	89.0	85.8	5.4	5.8	3.1	4.5	2.8	5.0	5.7	6.8	8.4	7.2	3.5	15.0	33.6	16.5	3.1	74.2	46.8	47.9	52.1
22309	ALEXANDRIA	54.4	50.3	27.7	25.8	6.5	8.1	14.5	21.1	7.1	6.7	6.6	6.6	6.7	27.3	27.8	10.1	1.2	75.6	37.0	48.4	51.6
22310	ALEXANDRIA	69.8	63.0	11.6	11.4	9.6	12.5	11.2	17.5	6.3	6.1	6.2	5.6	5.4	29.4	29.8	10.0	1.2	78.0	39.9	48.7	51.3
22311	ALEXANDRIA	50.0	43.9	24.9	23.1	9.4	11.8	17.0	24.7	6.1	4.8	4.3	4.5	10.2	36.5	21.1	7.6	4.9	82.2	34.5	49.0	51.0
22312	ALEXANDRIA	47.8	42.6	22.1	19.4	13.2	16.1	21.7	29.6	7.5	7.0	6.5	6.2	6.9	31.1	25.9	8.0	1.0	75.4	35.6	49.5	50.5
22314	ALEXANDRIA	71.7	65.8	22.6	25.0	2.2	3.5	5.1	8.9	4.3	3.6	3.2	2.9	5.8	39.0	29.1	10.4	1.7	87.2	39.4	47.8	52.2
22315	ALEXANDRIA	70.2	63.5	13.2	13.7	10.6	14.3	7.1	11.4	6.9	6.8	6.5	5.2	5.1	33.8	29.5	5.9	0.4	76.5	38.0	48.3	51.7
22401	FREDERICKSBURG	73.2	68.9	20.4	21.7	1.6	2.2	4.9	7.7	6.0	4.5	4.0	10.8	14.6	27.0	20.0	11.0	2.1	83.0	30.8	45.5	54.5
22405	FREDERICKSBURG	88.5	86.0	7.5	8.2	1.2	1.7	2.3	3.7	6.7	6.9	7.3	7.5	5.0	26.5	28.2	10.2	1.6	74.1	38.5	49.2	50.8
22406	FREDERICKSBURG	85.5	81.4	9.4	10.6	1.5	2.4	2.5	4.4	8.2	7.5	7.1	6.6	6.6	32.0	24.6	6.7	0.7	73.2	33.1	49.7	50.3
22407	FREDERICKSBURG	81.8	78.3	12.9	14.0	1.8	2.5	3.5	5.6	8.0	7.5	7.4	7.2	6.1	29.7	25.6	7.4	1.2	72.7	34.2	48.9	51.1
22408	FREDERICKSBURG	82.7	79.1	12.4	13.9	1.4	2.0	3.1	5.0	8.7	8.1	7.6	6.6	5.2	31.0	23.4	8.4	0.9	71.4	33.9	48.5	51.5
22427	BOWLING GREEN	63.4	58.5	31.9	35.1	0.7	0.9	2.3	3.6	5.8	5.8	6.1	6.3	5.0	23.4	28.5	15.9	3.2	78.1	43.3	47.2	52.8
22432	BURGESS	65.8	62.7	33.1	35.7	0.0	0.0	1.7	2.7	4.0	4.3	4.9	5.3	3.6	18.7	32.8	24.2	2.1	83.4	50.7	47.5	52.5
22433	BURR HILL	89.5	88.3	8.6	9.7	0.0	0.0	1.9	1.9	5.8	7.8	7.8	6.8	3.9	24.3	32.0	10.7	1.0	73.8	40.9	51.5	48.5
22435	CALLAO	76.6	73.8	22.1	24.3	0.1	0.1	1.0	1.8	5.0	5.5	5.8	5.7	4.1	21.9	31.5	17.6	3.0	80.1	46.3	47.7	52.3
22436	CARET	33.6	30.2	62.9	65.8	0.5	0.7	0.2	0.5	5.0	5.0	5.9	7.0	4.5	24.8	31.1	14.9	2.0	79.7	43.7	47.1	52.9
22437	CENTER CROSS	73.5	70.7	25.1	27.8	0.2	0.2	1.0	1.5	4.3	4.7	4.9	5.3	3.8	20.5	37.3	17.1	2.3	82.7	49.4	48.2	51.8
22438	CHAMPLAIN	40.3	36.5	56.2	59.0	0.5	0.7	0.6	0.9	5.1	5.1	5.9	6.6	4.5	24.0	32.4	14.3	2.0	79.8	44.2	47.9	52.1
22443	COLONIAL BEACH	78.2	73.8	17.0	19.1	0.4	0.6	4.6	7.3	5.4	5.5	5.9	6.1	4.3	20.9	31.4	17.7	2.6	79.1	46.1	48.1	51.9
22448	DAHLGREN	76.9	73.3	15.9	16.7	1.7	2.4	6.9	11.0	16.1	13.2	7.3	5.7	14.4	40.2	2.9	0.3	0.0	62.4	22.7	57.8	42.2
22454	DUNNSVILLE	71.9	68.3	25.3	27.8	0.5	0.7	0.7	1.0	4.8	5.0	6.0	6.2	3.8	23.2	34.4	14.7	1.9	79.9	45.6	49.2	50.8
22460	FARNHAM	66.8	63.8	31.4	33.6	0.4	0.6	1.1	1.7	3.7	4.0	4.5	5.5	5.3	27.9	29.7	15.6	3.7	84.2	44.3	54.2	45.8
22469	HAGUE	50.7	46.9	47.6	50.7	0.3	0.3	1.5	2.4	5.1	5.4	5.7	5.6	4.9	20.5	32.5	18.6	1.9	80.6	46.9	47.3	52.7
22473	HEATHSVILLE	64.8	61.2	33.9	37.0	0.2	0.3	0.9	1.4	4.7	5.1	5.4	5.1	3.6	17.8	32.8	22.8	2.7	81.6	50.3	48.4	51.6
22476	HUSTLE	33.6	30.2	62.8	65.7	0.5	0.7	0.3	0.5	4.9	4.9	5.6	7.0	4.4	24.8	31.8	14.6	2.1	80.0	44.0	47.6	52.4
22480	IRVINGTON	88.7	86.1	11.2	13.7	0.1	0.2	0.0	0.0	2.1	2.3	2.6	3.3	2.5	10.2	31.1	34.2	11.8	90.7	63.0	44.6	55.4
22482	KILMARNOCK	69.4	65.8	29.0	31.8	0.4	0.5	0.7	1.1	3.7	3.8	4.3	4.6	3.2	14.4	30.1	30.4	5.5	85.2	56.9	45.9	54.1
22485	KING GEORGE	77.7	74.5	18.9	20.7	1.0	1.5	1.5	2.4	7.0	7.0	7.2	6.8	5.2	26.7	28.4	10.3	1.4	74.4	38.4	49.2	50.8
22488	KINSALE	41.4	37.0	57.0	60.9	0.1	0.1	0.9	1.5	4.3	4.5	5.2	6.0	5.0	20.6	32.3	19.8	2.3	82.4	48.3	47.4	52.6
22503	LANCASTER	60.3	56.1	38.4	42.2	0.4	0.5	0.8	1.3	4.1	4.4	4.9	5.6	4.4	18.4	32.8	22.3	3.0	83.1	50.5	46.9	53.1
22504	LANEVIEW	74.0	70.7	25.2	27.7	0.0	0.3	0.8	1.6	4.5	4.5	4.8	5.1	3.8	20.7	37.3	17.2	2.2	83.1	49.4	47.8	52.2
22508	LOCUST GROVE	92.3	90.3	5.3	6.3	0.7	1.0	1.5	2.6	5.0	5.1	5.5	5.3	3.7	17.9	31.8	23.7	2.1	81.2	50.0	48.2	51.8
22509	LORETTO	40.0	33.3	60.0	66.7	0.0	0.0	0.0	0.0	0.0	0.0	0.0	0.0	0.0	50.0	50.0	0.0	0.0	100.0	47.5	50.0	50.0
22511	LOTTSBURG	80.2	77.6	18.9	21.0	0.5	0.7	0.8	1.4	4.2	4.2	4.8	5.1	3.3	16.8	32.6	25.9	3.1	83.5	53.1	47.3	52.7
22514	MILFORD	59.8	54.6	35.3	39.1	0.4	0.6	1.1	1.6	6.1	6.3	6.7	6.6	4.7	23.9	30.3	13.6	1.8	76.7	42.0	48.7	51.3
22520	MONTROSS	60.6	56.6	35.6	38.0	0.4	0.6	3.5	5.4	4.7	4.8	5.3	5.8	4.4	20.5	32.0	19.9	2.5	81.4	48.0	48.1	51.9
22534	PARTLOW	85.5	82.6	10.7	12.0	0.9	1.3	0.9	1.4	6.9	7.1	7.4	7.3	5.1	26.7	29.1	9.4	0.9	74.0	38.2	50.4	49.6
22535	PORT ROYAL	55.6	55.7	42.0	40.7	0.1	0.2	3.1	4.6	5.0	5.2	5.1	6.1	9.8	35.5	22.5	9.4	1.3	82.0	35.0	62.2	37.8
22538	RAPPAHANNOCK ACADEMY	75.5	71.9	20.8	23.0	0.3	0.3	2.7	4.5	7.0	7.3	7.6	6.2	3.9	24.7	28.7	12.9	1.7	74.2	40.2	50.6	49.4
22539	REEDVILLE	82.8	80.2	16.4	18.7	0.1	0.1	0.8	1.1	2.9	3.2	3.5	3.8	2.6	13.6	33.2	33.5	3.6	87.9	59.2	48.7	51.3
22542	RHOADESVILLE	87.0	84.9	11.2	12.5	0.3	0.4	1.3	2.2	6.9	7.2	7.4	6.8	5.1	25.3	29.2	11.1	1.1	74.3	39.4	49.5	50.5
22546	RUTHER GLEN	63.0	59.8	34.5	36.6	0.4	0.5	1.2	1.8	6.5	6.7	7.0	6.8	5.1	26.5	29.5	10.8	1.2	75.5	39.4	50.1	49.9
22551	SPOTSYLVANIA	84.4	81.9	11.9	13.0	0.9	1.4	1.5	2.4	7.0	7.2	7.5	7.6	5.3	26.8	28.9	8.8	0.9	73.6	37.6	50.2	49.8
22553	SPOTSYLVANIA	84.0	80.9	12.0	13.1	1.1	1.8	2.5	4.2	7.6	7.7	8.1	7.9	5.2	27.9	27.8	7.1	0.6	71.7	35.6	49.7	50.3
22554	STAFFORD	77.5	73.4	15.6	16.9	2.1	2.9	4.7	7.4	8.4	8.0	8.1	7.8	6.2	29.7	26.3	5.1	0.5	70.6	32.9	49.5	50.5
22556	STAFFORD	81.1	77.7	12.6	13.4	1.8	2.6	3.7	6.0	7.9	8.2	8.3	8.2	7.4	29.4	25.5	4.7	0.4	70.3	32.1	51.3	48.7
22560	TAPPAHANNOCK	56.2	51.8	40.7	43.9	1.1	1.6	0.8	1.1	5.4	5.4	5.9	6.4	5.2	24.3	28.9	15.4	3.1	79.4	43.2	46.6	53.4
22567	UNIONVILLE	83.3	80.3	15.2	17.5	0.2	0.3	1.0	1.6	6.2	6.5	6.8	6.5	4.9	25.0	30.2	12.5	1.4	76.4	41.2	50.1	49.9
22572	WARSAW	63.1	59.3	34.8	37.6	0.4	0.5	2.3	3.8	4.1	4.2	4.4	4.8	6.5	30.9	27.2	14.7	3.2	84.1	41.8	57.3	42.7
22576	WEEMS	68.3	63.8	30.4	34.2	0.4	0.6	0.9	1.3	4.9	5.1	5.2	4.7	3.6	16.2	31.8	23.3	5.1	81.9	52.7	46.7	53.3
22578	WHITE STONE	82.9	79.7	15.9	18.3	0.6	0.8	0.2	0.4	3.5	3.9	4.3	4.3	3.4	14.8	34.3	27.8	3.8	85.5	55.5	49.1	50.9
22579	WICOMICO CHURCH	71.4	69.0	26.7	29.2	0.0	0.0	1.0	0.9	4.4	5.3	5.3	4.4	2.7	17.7	31.9	25.7	2.7	81.4	51.3	49.6	50.4
22580	WOODFORD	67.5	62.9	29.8	33.3	0.4	0.6	1.0	1.5	6.3	6.7	6.9	6.7	4.7	24.4	29.1	13.3	1.9	75.9	40.9	49.4	50.6
22601	WINCHESTER	82.2	78.0	10.4	11.1	1.6	2.3	6.4	10.2	6.2	5.6	5.5	7.2	8.5	28.4	24.8	11.7	2.1	79.3	36.1	49.0	51.0
22602	WINCHESTER	94.5	92.7	2.8	3.2	0.8	1.1	1.8	3.0	6.8	6.8	7.0	6.9	5.1	27.5	28.2	10.6	1.1	75.0	38.4	49.8	50.2
22603	WINCHESTER	95.1	93.8	2.8	3.2	0.5	0.8	1.1	1.9	5.8	6.0	6.4	6.8	5.0	26.1	29.6	12.0	2.4	77.5	41.3	50.3	49.7
22610	BENTONVILLE	97.1	96.2	1.8	2.3	0.0	0.1	0.6	1.0	5.3	5.7	6.3	6.4	4.5	22.1	33.3	14.3	2.1	78.8	44.8	49.5	50.5
22611	BERRYVILLE	90.8	88.8	7.0	7.9	0.6	0.9	1.5	2.6	5.3	5.9	6.5	6.8	4.4	22.0	31.9	14.6	2.6	77.8	44.4	48.2	51.8
22620	BOYCE	90.5	88.5	7.2	8.2	0.5	0.7	1.5	2.6	4.1	5.8	6.1	6.1	3.9	22.9	35.4	14.2	1.7	79.8	45.6	51.1	48.9
22624	CLEAR BROOK	96.2	94.9	2.1	2.4	0.3	0.5	1.2	2.2	5.1	6.4	7.0	7.2	4.3	25.4	33.0	10.6	1.0	76.8	41.8	51.7	48.3
22625	CROSS JUNCTION	97.7	97.0	0.7	0.8	0.4	0.6	0.5	0.8	5.9	6.5	7.4	7.0	3.8	25.0	31.0	12.2	1.4	75.7	41.8	50.6	49.4
22627	FLINT HILL	94.6	93.1	3.7	4.4	0.2	0.4	1.2	2.2	5.4	6.2	6.9	6.7	3.8	21.4	32.9	15.1	1.6	77.2	44.7	50.6	49.4
22630	FRONT ROYAL	91.8	89.9	5.5	6.2	0.5	0.8	1.7	2.8	6.6	6.6	6.8	6.9	6.0	25.3	28.1	12.0	1.8	75.9	39.4	49.1	50.9
22637	GORE	97.3	96.6	0.9	1.0	0.7	0.9	0.5	0.8	5.7	6.2	6.8	6.3	4.3	23.8	32.0	13.0	1.9	77.3	43.0	49.8	50.2
22639	HUME	90.1	88.6	7.3	7.7	0.6	0.9	1.7	3.1	4.5	5.1	5.9	6.4	4.6	21.0	35.5	15.3	1.8	80.4	46.5	49.0	51.0
22640	HUNTLY	96.8	95.9	2.4	2.8	0.2	0.4	0.4	0.7	5.9	6.5	7.4	7.0	4.2	20.3	32.3	15.1	1.3	76.2	44.1	49.3	50.7
22641	STRASBURG	98.4	97.6	0.5	0.7	0.3	0.7	0.8	1.4	5.7	6.1	6.6	6.4	4.3	22.5	31.2	15.6	1.7	77.5	44.0	49.4	50.6
22642	LINDEN	94.0	92.5	3.6	4.1	0.4	0.5	1.7	2.8	7.4	7.6	7.8	6.7	4.6	28.0	29.9	7.3	0.7	72.9	37.9	50.7	49.3
22643	MARKHAM	83.9	81.8	13.4	14.4	0.2	0.3	3.1	5.0	5.5	5.2	5.2	5.7	6.6	24.8	31.2	13.3	2.4	80.1	42.7	48.5	51.5
22644	MAURERTOWN	98.1	97.2	0.4	0.4	0.2	0.4	1.1	2.0	5.3	5.8	6.3	5.9	4.3	23.9	31.2	15.6	1.8	79.0	44.1	50.2	49.8
22645	MIDDLETOWN	96.8	95.7	2.0	2.4	0.3	0.5	0.9	1.6	5.2	5.5	6.2	6.8	4.5	24.3	32.7	13.0	1.8	78.8	43.4	50.2	49.8
22649	MIDDLETOWN	100.0	100.0	0.0	0.0	0.0	0.0	0.0	0.0	5.6	5.6	5.6	5.6	5.6	22.2	30.6	19.4	0.0	77.8	45.0	50.0	50.0
22650	RILEYVILLE	97.2	96.2	1.4	1.6	0.6	0.7	0.5	0.9	4.7	4.8	5.4	5.8	4.5	24.3	32.7	16.3	1.6	80.8	45.3	51.5	48.5
22652	FORT VALLEY	97.7	96.2	0.1	0.3	0.3	0.5	1.1	2.0	4.6	5.2	6.5	5.1	3.5	19.6	38.0	15.9	1.5	81.3	48.1	51.6	48.4
22654	STAR TANNERY	98.7	98.1	0.2	0.2	0.2	0.4	0.7	0.9	5.7	6.4	7.2	7.2	4.3	23.3	33.3	11.5	1.1	76.2	42.4	51.2	48.8
22655	STEPHENS CITY	94.7	93.1	2.9	3.2	0.9	1.4	1.9	3.1	7.3	7.1	7.1	7.0	5.8	29.6	26.8	8.5	1.0	74.3	35.9	49.0	51.0
22656	STEPHENSON	97.5	96.4	1.2	1.5	0.2	0.3	0.9	1.5	5.5	5.9	7.3	7.7	4.3	25.3	31.0	11.7	1.2	76.5	41.3	50.9	49.1
22657	STRASBURG	95.5	94.2	2.6	2.9	0.4	0.6	1.1	2.0	5.9	5.9	6.3	6.8	5.6	25.1	29.0	13.6	1.8	77.9	41.4	48.9	51.1
22660	TOMS BROOK	97.3	96.2	0.5	0.6	0.3	0.4	1.2	2.0	5.6	6.0	6.4	6.1	4.2	24.2	30.6	15.2	1.7	78.4	43.4	50.3	49.7
22663	WHITE POST	86.1	82.9	8.7	9.2	0.2	0.3	9.2	15.4	5.7	6.2	6.4	7.3	6.4	27.5	29.1	9.8	1.6	77.2	38.3	56.5	43.5
22664	WOODSTOCK	94.2	91.5	1.7	1.8	0.3	0.4	5.0	8.6	5.5	5.5	5.8	6.0	5.4	23.2	27.2	17.1	4.3	81.3	43.9	47.3	52.7
22701	CULPEPER	77.0	73.0	18.9	21.1	0.8	1.2	3.0	4.7	6.6	6.4	6.5	6.9	6.1	26.6	27.1	12.0	1.8	76.1	38.6	48.9	51.1
22709	ARODA	84.9	82.5	13.1	14.9	0.0	0.0	0.4	0.5	5.7	6.0	6.7	6.8	4.8	23.4	31.5	12.9	2.2	77.4	42.2	49.5	50.5
22712	BEALETON	86.8	84.6	10.1	11.0	0.5	0.7	2.2	3.4	8.1	8.0	7.9	7.4	5.1	29.4	26.3	7.0	0.9	71.1	34.9	49.2	50.8
22713	BOSTON	86.8	83.8	10.7	12.4	0.2	0.3	1.2	2.1	5.3	5.5	6.7	6.6	4.1	25.4	33.5	11.6	1.2	78.1	42.8	49.1	50.9
22714	BRANDY STATION	81.0	76.7	14.7	16.2	0.0	0.0	4.8	8.2	6.3	6.6	7.0	7.2	4.6	27.9	28.5	10.3	1.6	75.5	38.6	50.7	49.3
22715	BRIGHTWOOD	92.2	90.8	6.7	7.6	0.3	0.4	0.7	1.2	5.7	6.2	6.5	5.9	4.4	24.2	30.4	14.6	2.1	77.5	42.9	48.8	51.2
22716	CASTLETON	94.1	92.3	4.0	4.5	0.0	0.1	1.6	2.6	4.9	4.1	6.5	5.7	3.5	23.1	39.0	11.9	1.4	80.3	46.1	49.8	50.2
22718	ELKWOOD	78.4	73.7	16.6	18.7	0.8	1.2	3.5	5.8	5.9	6.7	7.5	7.2	4.6	27.1	28.6	10.9	1.4	75.4	39.2	49.9	50.1
22719	ETLAN	91.8	90.0	6.5	7.5	0.4	0.6	0.7	1.0	4.9	5.6	6.2	6.1	4.4	23.4	33.2	14.3	1.8	79.5	44.5	49.0	51.0
22720	GOLDVEIN	91.8	90.3	6.2	6.7	0.5	0.7	1.0	1.7	6.0	6.7	7.3	7.5	4.5	25.8	31.7	9.6	1.0	75.3	40.5	50.4	49.6
22722	HAYWOOD	92.1	90.6	6.6	7.4	0.3	0.6	0.7	1.1	5.1	5.7	6.3	6.0	4.6	23.4	33.1	14.0	1.7	79.1	44.2	48.6	51.4
	VIRGINIA	72.3	68.8	19.6	20.1	3.7	5.1	4.7	7.0	6.5	6.4	6.5	6.9	6.9	27.5	27.2	10.5	1.6	76.7	37.7	49.2	50.8
	UNITED STATES	75.1	72.0	12.3	12.7	3.8	4.6	12.5	15.7	6.8	6.7	6.6	7.1	6.9	27.0	26.0	10.9	1.9	75.7	36.9	49.2	50.8

# ZIP CODE	POST OFFICE NAME	2009 Per Capita Income	2009 HH Income Base	2009 Household Income Distribution (%): Less than $25,000	$25,000 to $49,999	$50,000 to $99,999	$100,000 to $149,999	$150,000 or More	Median Household Income: 2009	2014	2009 National Centile	2009 State Centile	2009 Home Value Base	2009 Home Value Distribution (%): Less than $50,000	$50,000 to $89,999	$90,000 to $174,999	$175,000 to $399,999	$400,000 or More	2009 Median Home Value
22306	ALEXANDRIA	31330	10303	14.2	23.3	33.2	19.1	10.2	65742	66840	84	80	5084	16.6	2.2	7.6	54.5	19.2	269973
22307	ALEXANDRIA	66818	4476	7.4	11.6	29.3	25.4	26.4	102618	108397	97	94	3320	0.3	0.8	23.3	24.9	50.8	406906
22308	ALEXANDRIA	59279	4687	5.5	6.3	20.4	32.0	35.8	128680	135092	99	98	4162	0.4	0.0	1.1	36.4	62.1	451959
22309	ALEXANDRIA	37699	10826	8.4	18.0	34.7	23.6	15.3	80618	80123	92	87	6865	3.6	3.9	19.7	44.2	28.7	286495
22310	ALEXANDRIA	46387	9716	4.3	8.7	34.6	31.9	20.5	102880	108674	97	94	7330	1.4	0.3	6.0	66.6	25.7	309909
22311	ALEXANDRIA	34545	7251	12.1	26.8	40.5	14.6	5.9	61157	63572	79	76	1093	0.0	1.6	7.5	61.1	29.8	347122
22312	ALEXANDRIA	33841	10545	9.9	18.5	35.2	24.3	12.1	76693	78248	90	86	5407	1.1	2.7	15.5	52.0	28.7	330333
22314	ALEXANDRIA	66233	15954	11.4	10.4	30.6	25.6	22.0	94601	101464	96	92	7647	0.1	0.1	11.5	33.7	54.6	444943
22315	ALEXANDRIA	50681	11511	2.5	6.1	33.1	36.7	21.6	108970	115326	98	95	8043	0.3	1.1	6.5	71.3	20.9	318345
22401	FREDERICKSBURG	28555	9597	24.9	28.2	33.6	7.8	5.6	46269	49913	52	47	3345	1.5	3.7	29.2	48.7	16.9	224727
22405	FREDERICKSBURG	32581	10403	7.0	18.2	36.0	27.8	10.9	81164	85328	92	88	8491	1.4	0.6	17.6	68.2	12.2	242953
22406	FREDERICKSBURG	34245	7094	6.9	17.4	37.6	28.1	10.1	80869	84798	92	88	5254	1.7	1.4	14.3	58.0	24.6	295982
22407	FREDERICKSBURG	29920	19101	6.9	17.6	46.6	20.4	8.4	76735	81033	90	86	14930	2.2	1.4	14.7	71.8	9.9	237694
22408	FREDERICKSBURG	30128	9568	8.9	21.3	45.7	16.9	7.2	71739	76600	88	83	7693	9.6	3.8	16.9	58.3	11.3	226085
22427	BOWLING GREEN	22959	1393	23.7	30.9	34.0	8.4	3.1	45646	48416	50	45	1023	8.2	6.5	38.5	40.4	6.5	168891
22432	BURGESS	27833	290	23.8	22.1	38.6	7.6	7.9	53406	55393	69	66	240	6.3	8.3	39.2	22.5	23.8	163750
22433	BURR HILL	22931	38	13.2	28.9	47.4	7.9	2.6	54378	57433	70	67	32	0.0	0.0	28.1	56.3	15.6	212500
22435	CALLAO	21600	1085	27.6	30.6	35.3	4.9	1.7	41654	43597	38	35	915	11.7	15.7	50.3	16.4	5.9	117388
22436	CARET	21150	181	23.2	29.8	38.7	6.6	1.7	46460	50194	53	48	151	7.3	25.8	34.4	29.1	3.3	124306
22437	CENTER CROSS	24200	236	19.5	34.7	34.7	7.6	3.4	47203	48557	55	50	200	9.5	8.5	36.0	36.0	10.0	147561
22438	CHAMPLAIN	22188	279	22.6	28.7	38.7	7.5	2.5	48308	50804	57	53	233	9.9	19.3	34.3	29.6	6.9	137019
22443	COLONIAL BEACH	23322	3414	29.8	24.6	35.7	6.6	3.2	44564	45708	47	42	2511	5.9	3.5	49.0	34.2	7.3	162759
22448	DAHLGREN	16517	314	7.6	33.1	51.9	5.4	1.9	55454	58379	72	69	4	0.0	0.0	0.0	50.0	50.0	325000
22454	DUNNSVILLE	20580	972	25.7	28.7	36.7	8.7	0.1	45999	47729	51	46	773	1.6	8.5	44.9	39.6	5.4	162167
22460	FARNHAM	22721	711	35.0	25.2	32.5	5.2	2.1	39327	40000	31	27	579	5.4	15.4	50.1	21.4	7.8	136932
22469	HAGUE	20645	981	34.7	23.2	34.8	5.7	1.6	41555	42523	38	35	811	10.2	15.5	41.1	29.6	3.6	129844
22473	HEATHSVILLE	26462	2430	30.6	22.6	33.9	7.2	5.7	44499	48331	47	42	2104	9.0	13.3	28.5	28.9	20.3	172047
22476	HUSTLE	18636	155	22.6	29.0	40.0	6.5	1.9	47805	50226	56	52	129	6.2	25.6	34.9	29.5	3.9	127206
22480	IRVINGTON	31154	367	16.3	28.3	34.3	10.4	10.6	54645	59083	71	68	313	1.3	10.2	32.6	29.1	26.8	211806
22482	KILMARNOCK	29009	1250	26.6	28.1	29.2	9.6	6.5	44339	46319	46	41	1013	5.0	11.5	27.1	26.4	30.0	222170
22485	KING GEORGE	27792	8493	12.0	23.9	43.7	14.3	6.2	63156	64086	81	78	6266	7.2	4.7	16.8	53.7	17.7	241642
22488	KINSALE	21470	622	34.7	27.3	26.0	8.5	3.4	35477	36446	19	16	518	12.9	14.9	35.9	28.2	8.1	154598
22503	LANCASTER	21681	2033	34.8	28.7	27.1	7.4	2.0	34795	36628	17	15	1727	13.6	17.4	30.2	23.6	15.2	140051
22504	LANEVIEW	20982	120	20.8	35.0	33.3	7.5	3.3	46358	48301	52	48	102	7.8	9.8	35.3	36.3	10.8	148810
22508	LOCUST GROVE	31148	4663	7.7	26.5	47.6	13.1	5.1	62695	64053	81	77	4106	1.9	2.7	12.4	64.0	19.0	267339
22509	LORETTO	29532	3	0.0	0.0	100.0	0.0	0.0	63750	63750	82	79	0	0.0	0.0	0.0	0.0	0.0	0
22511	LOTTSBURG	30812	645	20.5	22.9	43.7	7.4	5.4	55991	57289	73	70	573	8.2	12.7	33.3	29.0	16.8	158446
22514	MILFORD	21043	956	20.5	34.7	34.9	8.2	1.7	45484	48524	50	45	776	9.3	6.1	42.5	38.0	4.1	156627
22520	MONTROSS	22101	2240	24.2	28.3	38.5	7.0	2.0	47512	47853	55	51	1841	10.5	8.2	33.9	36.7	10.7	170071
22534	PARTLOW	21394	878	16.2	25.6	48.2	8.7	1.4	60670	62625	78	75	763	3.9	6.6	29.0	56.2	4.3	193463
22535	PORT ROYAL	20782	282	24.8	37.6	27.7	6.4	3.5	40898	42804	36	32	220	20.5	9.1	28.6	26.8	15.0	154545
22538	RAPPAHANNOCK ACADEMY	21258	137	23.4	39.4	27.0	6.6	3.6	41128	43977	36	33	110	20.9	9.1	28.2	25.5	16.4	154545
22539	REEDVILLE	28856	1229	18.6	28.1	39.5	8.3	5.5	51998	52911	66	63	1070	1.7	9.9	32.5	32.1	23.7	199231
22542	RHOADESVILLE	20985	702	19.2	29.5	42.2	7.0	2.1	50723	52079	63	60	602	4.0	6.1	23.6	53.5	12.8	211739
22546	RUTHER GLEN	22265	5275	17.3	30.7	39.9	9.6	2.5	51607	55983	65	62	4429	4.3	5.4	54.6	31.5	4.3	154786
22551	SPOTSYLVANIA	24422	6670	12.8	22.6	49.1	11.4	4.1	64550	67338	83	79	5726	2.4	3.5	29.9	54.0	10.2	202038
22553	SPOTSYLVANIA	29907	5685	5.6	15.3	48.5	21.3	9.2	79521	84459	92	87	4882	1.4	1.9	15.3	64.7	16.7	249662
22554	STAFFORD	33358	16231	4.0	11.6	35.4	34.1	14.9	98104	101867	96	93	12934	4.4	1.5	6.6	69.4	18.1	312558
22556	STAFFORD	30122	7968	7.9	11.7	38.7	28.9	12.8	86717	90927	94	89	6607	6.6	2.3	9.8	66.9	14.4	276502
22560	TAPPAHANNOCK	22637	2766	24.7	28.7	37.0	7.3	2.2	46750	48390	53	49	2018	11.1	6.1	40.6	32.4	9.8	160019
22567	UNIONVILLE	20330	1128	22.1	32.2	35.8	7.8	2.1	46852	48261	54	49	946	6.7	5.8	29.3	47.6	10.7	194307
22572	WARSAW	20296	2445	29.3	27.4	34.0	7.5	1.8	43581	44749	44	40	1830	9.0	10.5	44.2	28.8	7.4	154070
22576	WEEMS	25714	888	24.5	37.6	25.2	6.4	6.2	39830	41282	32	29	694	8.2	15.3	31.6	23.6	21.3	156383
22578	WHITE STONE	33468	1269	24.1	24.0	33.0	9.9	9.1	52192	57239	66	63	1065	3.9	13.0	25.6	25.6	31.8	238603
22579	WICOMICO CHURCH	25560	50	28.0	22.0	36.0	8.0	6.0	50000	46165	61	58	42	2.4	9.5	28.6	33.3	26.2	233333
22580	WOODFORD	21130	2238	19.7	31.5	40.1	7.0	1.7	49151	51736	59	56	1785	10.0	7.6	44.2	30.9	7.3	156470
22601	WINCHESTER	25259	11332	24.2	31.3	33.2	7.2	4.2	44395	47519	47	41	5229	3.5	4.0	53.1	32.8	6.7	157080
22602	WINCHESTER	25403	10375	12.5	28.2	43.5	11.4	4.4	58323	61628	76	72	8254	6.1	6.1	40.2	41.0	6.5	170944
22603	WINCHESTER	26213	5638	15.4	28.1	41.9	10.2	4.4	55913	60438	73	70	4506	10.7	6.2	35.7	39.7	7.6	169510
22610	BENTONVILLE	24430	769	17.0	31.6	38.9	10.7	1.8	50742	51974	63	60	629	5.6	6.0	29.6	47.4	11.4	203481
22611	BERRYVILLE	28522	3570	13.4	23.0	46.7	12.4	4.5	62834	65892	81	77	2596	0.6	2.1	26.0	51.5	19.8	255903
22620	BOYCE	33352	1100	15.2	21.3	39.0	15.9	8.6	65069	68988	83	80	842	0.8	3.6	26.1	36.1	33.4	270313
22624	CLEAR BROOK	23069	1119	16.8	30.0	40.2	8.8	4.1	53876	60302	69	66	975	4.2	4.4	36.8	46.5	8.1	189833
22625	CROSS JUNCTION	24101	1354	10.1	26.4	49.8	10.7	3.0	60523	62406	78	75	1157	4.1	4.9	37.6	48.0	5.4	182315
22627	FLINT HILL	33276	232	14.2	23.7	43.1	12.9	6.0	62351	62062	80	77	180	1.7	3.9	30.0	37.2	27.2	233333
22630	FRONT ROYAL	23534	11460	18.6	29.1	38.8	10.6	2.9	52101	55869	66	63	8070	2.5	3.7	37.8	49.3	6.7	189345
22637	GORE	21377	833	21.0	25.3	45.4	7.3	1.0	53282	59180	68	66	691	3.2	8.2	43.8	37.8	6.9	164747
22639	HUME	41365	271	14.8	15.5	28.0	26.2	15.5	81988	86502	93	88	220	0.0	0.0	16.8	30.9	52.3	416129
22640	HUNTLY	26668	217	13.4	26.7	48.4	8.3	3.2	59728	59348	77	74	164	0.0	5.5	36.6	31.7	26.2	203571
22641	STRASBURG	25103	167	9.0	33.5	44.3	9.6	3.6	54622	57339	71	68	143	2.1	2.8	33.6	57.3	4.2	193750
22642	LINDEN	28611	1640	7.9	19.6	51.0	17.9	3.6	68299	70653	86	81	1419	0.8	1.1	29.7	62.3	6.2	203255
22643	MARKHAM	35376	234	17.1	19.7	31.2	23.5	8.5	66667	70800	85	81	164	0.6	0.6	23.2	35.4	40.2	292857
22644	MAURERTOWN	22380	880	19.1	29.8	41.8	6.9	2.4	50665	52057	63	60	744	6.9	2.7	36.2	45.0	9.3	182143
22645	MIDDLETOWN	23616	1454	15.3	34.1	42.2	6.2	2.2	50447	53640	62	59	1104	1.7	3.9	48.5	39.0	6.9	167021
22649	MIDDLETOWN	26319	17	17.6	29.4	47.1	5.9	0.0	52117	54495	66	63	14	0.0	0.0	42.9	50.0	7.1	200000
22650	RILEYVILLE	22218	451	15.5	40.4	36.6	5.3	2.2	46370	46760	52	48	376	0.0	12.2	40.7	37.0	10.1	166912
22652	FORT VALLEY	27843	531	20.9	20.9	39.9	13.7	4.5	57116	60080	74	72	460	3.7	4.3	22.2	51.5	18.3	237500
22654	STAR TANNERY	26908	216	8.8	28.2	48.1	9.7	5.1	56413	58768	73	71	189	7.4	7.9	33.9	41.8	9.0	177500
22655	STEPHENS CITY	25827	7026	14.1	19.6	49.6	13.6	3.2	62483	64105	81	77	5406	2.5	5.7	44.7	44.7	2.5	170550
22656	STEPHENSON	23160	811	14.8	34.4	37.6	10.4	2.8	50686	54165	63	60	704	24.7	4.8	23.4	42.0	5.0	168092
22657	STRASBURG	23813	4338	19.9	30.7	40.4	6.0	3.0	49327	51166	60	56	2900	3.0	1.6	40.9	50.0	4.6	181781
22660	TOMS BROOK	23902	675	15.0	30.1	46.7	5.8	2.5	52661	54440	67	64	562	5.5	2.5	30.2	50.7	11.0	192935
22663	WHITE POST	23939	711	18.6	28.0	40.9	8.0	4.5	52756	56022	67	65	505	12.5	3.8	24.8	42.4	16.6	214041
22664	WOODSTOCK	23396	3530	19.9	32.7	38.1	6.9	2.3	48315	49776	57	53	2357	2.9	2.0	34.1	52.4	8.7	199210
22701	CULPEPER	23836	12563	20.3	25.0	42.9	8.5	3.3	54355	59749	70	67	8112	4.4	2.7	16.1	61.6	15.1	241162
22709	ARODA	18935	224	20.5	30.4	39.3	8.0	1.8	48921	50603	59	55	178	7.3	3.4	34.3	43.8	11.2	193750
22712	BEALETON	26662	2939	10.7	17.8	48.4	16.8	6.3	69247	72844	86	82	2163	6.8	4.1	14.2	60.5	14.3	235060
22713	BOSTON	26015	564	16.3	24.5	40.1	13.7	5.5	59353	61344	77	73	469	2.6	0.4	14.1	65.0	17.9	270221
22714	BRANDY STATION	23727	249	16.1	31.3	40.6	7.2	4.8	51330	53511	64	61	156	4.5	2.6	9.0	59.6	24.4	277500
22715	BRIGHTWOOD	21890	545	23.5	32.7	33.4	7.0	3.5	44154	46878	46	41	451	3.3	4.9	39.2	42.1	10.4	181250
22716	CASTLETON	28186	355	17.5	20.3	42.5	14.6	5.1	58032	57655	75	72	276	1.4	0.4	33.7	39.9	24.6	242000
22718	ELKWOOD	22027	276	14.9	33.0	41.3	8.3	2.5	51513	54201	65	62	206	4.4	4.9	12.6	58.3	19.9	243421
22719	ETLAN	21514	321	19.9	35.5	34.3	9.0	1.2	44860	47129	48	43	255	6.7	8.6	33.3	41.6	9.8	179167
22720	GOLDVEIN	33301	400	9.8	8.8	38.3	31.3	12.0	88824	96647	95	90	350	0.6	2.0	10.6	68.9	18.0	285965
22722	HAYWOOD	20889	135	20.7	34.8	34.1	8.9	1.5	44688	47357	47	42	108	5.6	7.4	35.2	41.7	10.2	180000
	VIRGINIA	30912		17.0	22.6	35.9	15.0	9.5	61855	64957				5.3	6.3	30.4	41.5	16.5	203135
	UNITED STATES	27277		20.9	24.4	35.3	11.7	7.6	54719	56938				9.3	13.1	31.6	32.6	13.5	162279

ZIP CODE		FINANCIAL SERVICES				THE HOME						ENTERTAINMENT						PERSONAL			
						Home Improvements		Furnishings													
#	POST OFFICE NAME	Auto Loan	Home Loan	Invest-ments	Retire-ment Plans	Home Repair	Lawn & Garden	Comput-ers & Hard-ware-Personal	Major Appli-ances	TV, Radio, Sound Equip-ment	Furni-ture	Dine out/ Carry out	Sports Equip-ment	Fees & Tickets	Toys & Games	Travel	Cable TV	Apparel & Services	Auto Repairs	Health Insur-ance	Pets & Supplies
22306	ALEXANDRIA	113	116	112	117	115	107	120	112	116	120	118	89	121	118	118	114	84	116	108	131
22307	ALEXANDRIA	179	205	227	212	216	194	202	195	192	208	194	152	220	189	216	187	141	196	188	224
22308	ALEXANDRIA	182	256	293	256	278	236	213	225	201	225	201	166	260	198	251	197	151	211	208	247
22309	ALEXANDRIA	138	150	151	150	152	136	148	141	141	151	143	110	155	143	151	137	103	143	133	162
22310	ALEXANDRIA	156	180	182	180	183	163	168	163	161	171	163	127	183	165	176	158	118	163	154	186
22311	ALEXANDRIA	113	82	78	90	79	79	113	91	111	110	114	77	100	114	96	108	80	106	93	113
22312	ALEXANDRIA	129	134	132	135	134	121	141	129	135	139	138	103	143	137	139	131	100	135	123	150
22314	ALEXANDRIA	157	158	176	171	163	149	177	156	170	175	174	130	182	168	176	165	127	166	153	186
22315	ALEXANDRIA	175	189	172	195	183	164	178	170	169	188	173	140	188	178	179	161	124	168	152	197
22401	FREDERICKSBURG	90	71	67	76	68	70	91	76	91	89	92	64	83	92	81	90	64	87	81	95
22405	FREDERICKSBURG	127	150	137	149	146	137	131	134	126	137	128	102	143	130	139	124	91	129	127	154
22406	FREDERICKSBURG	136	143	125	144	137	123	136	129	129	142	132	105	140	137	134	124	94	129	117	151
22407	FREDERICKSBURG	125	138	119	136	132	120	124	123	118	132	121	97	130	125	126	114	85	119	112	142
22408	FREDERICKSBURG	121	129	110	125	123	113	118	117	113	124	115	92	120	119	117	109	80	113	107	135
22427	BOWLING GREEN	89	77	87	76	78	94	76	87	82	74	81	64	71	82	76	88	55	83	93	102
22432	BURGESS	108	86	139	85	95	114	86	110	90	81	89	80	75	86	94	96	59	101	108	127
22433	BURR HILL	87	98	84	100	95	96	87	91	86	87	86	71	93	88	92	86	60	87	90	107
22435	CALLAO	85	63	94	61	67	87	64	82	70	60	69	61	53	68	65	76	45	75	83	96
22436	CARET	93	66	95	64	69	94	68	87	76	63	74	65	54	75	67	83	49	79	90	103
22437	CENTER CROSS	91	73	118	72	80	96	73	93	76	68	76	68	63	73	79	81	50	86	92	108
22438	CHAMPLAIN	95	70	105	69	74	98	72	91	78	67	77	68	59	76	73	85	51	84	93	107
22443	COLONIAL BEACH	85	73	98	73	78	90	75	87	79	71	77	63	68	76	78	83	52	83	90	101
22448	DAHLGREN	105	55	41	63	49	46	99	68	93	92	98	68	75	111	71	85	68	87	62	83
22454	DUNNSVILLE	83	66	107	65	73	87	66	84	69	62	68	61	57	66	72	74	45	78	83	98
22460	FARNHAM	85	63	95	62	67	87	64	82	70	60	69	61	53	68	66	76	45	75	83	96
22469	HAGUE	86	64	95	61	66	88	65	82	72	62	70	61	54	71	66	78	47	76	84	97
22473	HEATHSVILLE	99	79	125	77	86	105	79	100	83	74	82	73	68	79	85	89	54	92	100	116
22476	HUSTLE	93	66	95	64	69	94	68	87	75	63	74	65	54	75	67	83	49	79	90	103
22480	IRVINGTON	109	114	155	113	132	135	103	122	109	116	107	76	113	98	119	114	73	116	135	137
22482	KILMARNOCK	85	85	115	84	97	103	79	93	84	86	82	60	83	77	89	88	56	89	104	106
22485	KING GEORGE	105	110	102	109	109	107	103	105	103	105	103	80	106	105	105	103	72	103	104	123
22488	KINSALE	80	70	93	68	73	88	67	81	72	64	71	59	63	70	71	78	48	76	85	95
22503	LANCASTER	77	65	89	63	69	83	64	78	68	62	67	56	58	66	67	73	45	73	82	90
22504	LANEVIEW	92	73	118	72	81	97	73	93	77	69	76	68	64	73	79	82	50	86	92	108
22508	LOCUST GROVE	106	109	131	107	119	122	99	113	103	109	102	74	104	97	108	107	70	108	122	129
22509	LORETTO	105	76	108	73	78	107	77	99	86	72	85	74	62	86	77	95	56	91	103	117
22511	LOTTSBURG	110	88	142	86	96	116	88	112	92	82	91	82	76	87	95	98	60	103	110	129
22514	MILFORD	90	75	87	73	76	92	73	86	79	71	78	64	65	80	73	84	52	81	90	102
22520	MONTROSS	87	71	100	70	76	94	71	87	76	68	75	63	63	74	74	82	50	81	92	102
22534	PARTLOW	96	93	82	92	91	94	86	91	88	89	89	68	85	92	85	90	61	88	91	108
22535	PORT ROYAL	95	67	97	65	70	96	69	88	77	65	76	66	55	77	68	85	50	81	92	105
22538	RAPPAHANNOCK ACADEMY	97	70	100	67	72	99	71	91	79	66	78	68	57	79	71	87	51	83	94	108
22539	REEDVILLE	88	86	122	85	98	104	79	96	84	86	82	63	82	76	90	88	56	90	103	109
22542	RHOADESVILLE	86	85	75	84	83	86	79	83	80	81	80	62	78	83	78	82	55	80	83	98
22546	RUTHER GLEN	94	86	83	86	85	93	83	91	85	81	85	68	77	87	81	88	58	85	91	106
22551	SPOTSYLVANIA	103	108	96	106	105	104	98	102	98	101	98	78	100	101	100	98	68	99	99	120
22553	SPOTSYLVANIA	126	148	127	146	142	128	127	129	121	135	123	102	138	127	133	116	87	123	116	148
22554	STAFFORD	151	172	149	172	165	146	152	151	143	163	146	121	163	152	155	135	104	144	132	172
22556	STAFFORD	137	157	137	157	151	135	140	138	132	148	135	111	150	139	144	126	96	134	123	159
22560	TAPPAHANNOCK	81	74	84	73	76	85	74	82	77	72	76	59	70	76	75	81	52	79	87	95
22567	UNIONVILLE	83	79	72	80	78	84	75	81	77	74	76	60	72	79	74	79	52	77	81	95
22572	WARSAW	84	66	84	66	69	85	69	81	74	66	73	60	60	73	68	79	49	77	84	95
22576	WEEMS	91	78	116	77	87	101	77	95	81	76	80	66	71	76	83	87	54	88	99	109
22578	WHITE STONE	110	101	149	100	114	126	96	117	101	100	99	79	95	93	107	106	67	110	123	134
22579	WICOMICO CHURCH	96	77	125	76	85	102	77	98	81	72	80	72	67	77	84	86	53	91	97	114
22580	WOODFORD	91	77	84	77	78	93	76	88	81	72	79	66	68	82	75	86	54	82	91	103
22601	WINCHESTER	78	76	73	78	75	74	84	77	83	82	84	61	83	83	81	83	59	82	80	92
22602	WINCHESTER	97	103	97	102	101	99	95	98	93	96	94	76	98	96	97	93	66	95	95	114
22603	WINCHESTER	93	97	89	97	95	98	90	94	91	91	91	72	92	92	92	92	63	91	95	110
22610	BENTONVILLE	89	87	82	90	87	96	83	91	84	77	83	69	80	86	84	87	57	85	93	106
22611	BERRYVILLE	98	103	102	105	104	108	97	103	97	96	97	77	100	97	102	99	68	100	105	120
22620	BOYCE	125	111	162	111	120	136	107	130	109	104	109	95	100	105	117	115	74	121	127	150
22624	CLEAR BROOK	89	93	89	96	93	98	86	93	86	84	85	71	88	87	90	88	59	87	92	108
22625	CROSS JUNCTION	92	104	89	107	101	102	93	96	91	93	92	75	99	94	98	91	64	93	95	113
22627	FLINT HILL	98	116	109	119	115	111	101	106	98	104	99	81	111	99	110	97	70	101	102	123
22630	FRONT ROYAL	84	88	83	87	87	88	85	86	86	84	86	66	87	86	86	87	60	86	89	101
22637	GORE	83	79	76	82	80	89	76	84	78	71	77	64	73	79	77	81	53	79	86	98
22639	HUME	136	164	166	168	167	155	143	149	138	151	139	112	160	137	158	135	100	142	141	171
22640	HUNTLY	93	104	90	108	101	103	93	97	92	94	92	76	100	94	99	92	65	93	96	114
22641	STRASBURG	98	90	89	93	92	106	88	100	91	80	90	76	82	93	88	97	61	92	103	116
22642	LINDEN	112	122	103	120	116	110	109	111	106	114	107	87	113	111	110	103	75	106	104	129
22643	MARKHAM	117	130	125	133	129	122	123	120	119	126	121	94	131	120	128	117	86	120	117	141
22644	MAURERTOWN	89	81	82	84	83	96	80	91	82	72	81	68	74	84	80	87	55	84	93	105
22645	MIDDLETOWN	89	82	80	85	83	95	80	90	82	73	81	68	75	84	80	87	55	83	93	105
22649	MIDDLETOWN	86	79	78	82	80	93	78	88	80	70	79	66	72	82	77	85	54	81	90	102
22650	RILEYVILLE	86	74	92	76	78	92	74	87	76	68	75	65	66	76	76	81	51	81	88	101
22652	FORT VALLEY	111	89	144	88	98	118	89	113	93	84	92	83	77	89	97	99	61	105	112	131
22654	STAR TANNERY	93	102	89	105	100	103	92	97	91	91	92	76	96	94	97	92	64	93	97	114
22655	STEPHENS CITY	98	108	95	107	104	97	98	98	95	102	96	77	102	99	100	92	68	95	92	114
22656	STEPHENSON	97	87	86	88	87	99	85	95	88	81	87	72	78	91	83	92	59	88	96	110
22657	STRASBURG	84	77	76	79	77	87	79	83	81	73	80	63	74	82	77	84	55	81	88	98
22660	TOMS BROOK	91	83	82	87	85	98	82	93	85	74	83	70	76	86	82	90	57	86	96	108
22663	WHITE POST	108	97	113	96	100	110	93	106	96	92	95	78	87	96	96	99	65	100	105	124
22664	WOODSTOCK	82	75	80	77	78	87	78	83	81	74	79	61	74	80	77	85	55	81	89	97
22701	CULPEPER	83	89	83	89	88	87	87	86	85	85	86	67	89	86	88	85	60	86	86	100
22709	ARODA	84	76	75	79	78	90	75	85	77	68	76	64	69	79	75	82	52	78	87	99
22712	BEALETON	116	128	109	125	122	113	112	114	108	119	110	89	117	114	114	105	77	109	104	132
22713	BOSTON	99	107	110	109	108	110	96	104	95	97	95	79	101	95	104	96	66	99	102	121
22714	BRANDY STATION	88	100	88	102	98	97	91	93	90	91	90	73	98	91	96	90	64	91	92	109
22715	BRIGHTWOOD	86	79	78	82	80	93	78	88	80	70	79	66	72	82	78	85	54	81	90	102
22716	CASTLETON	112	97	145	96	105	121	94	116	97	90	96	85	86	93	102	102	65	107	114	134
22718	ELKWOOD	83	93	81	96	91	91	84	87	83	84	83	68	90	85	89	83	58	84	86	102
22719	ETLAN	82	75	74	78	76	88	74	83	76	66	75	63	68	77	73	80	51	77	86	96
22720	GOLDVEIN	132	165	151	166	162	146	139	143	131	147	133	111	157	135	152	127	96	136	130	164
22722	HAYWOOD	84	76	75	79	78	90	75	85	77	68	76	64	69	79	75	82	52	78	87	99
	VIRGINIA	115	112	112	114	111	114	112	112	112	112	112	88	111	114	111	113	79	112	112	132
	UNITED STATES	100	100	100	100	100	100	100	100	100	100	100	100	100	100	100	100	100	100	100	100

POPULATION CHANGE

22724-23024

ZIP CODE #	POST OFFICE NAME	COUNTY FIPS CODE	POPULATION 2000	POPULATION 2009	POPULATION 2014	2000-2009 ANNUAL RATE % Rate	2000-2009 ANNUAL RATE State Centile	HOUSEHOLDS 2000	HOUSEHOLDS 2009	HOUSEHOLDS 2014	HOUSEHOLDS % Annual Rate 2000-2009	HOUSEHOLDS 2009 Average HH Size	FAMILIES 2000	FAMILIES 2009	FAMILIES % Annual Rate 2000-2009
22724	JEFFERSONTON	047	1794	2939	3431	5.5	98	596	1008	1186	5.8	2.92	500	831	5.6
22725	LEON	113	314	363	386	1.6	78	119	143	153	2.0	2.51	94	111	1.8
22726	LIGNUM	047	481	583	650	2.1	86	160	201	226	2.5	2.84	129	158	2.2
22727	MADISON	113	5130	5524	5710	0.8	58	2016	2260	2367	1.2	2.41	1438	1562	0.9
22728	MIDLAND	061	3078	3504	3781	1.4	73	1069	1178	1276	1.1	2.96	839	907	0.8
22729	MITCHELLS	047	121	132	141	0.9	61	47	53	62	1.3	1.70	34	37	0.9
22730	OAKPARK	113	310	360	382	1.6	78	103	124	134	2.0	2.79	79	92	1.7
22731	PRATTS	113	59	58	57	-0.2	14	27	27	27	0.0	2.07	19	18	-0.6
22732	RADIANT	113	1724	1987	2109	1.5	76	597	715	769	2.0	2.70	453	528	1.7
22733	RAPIDAN	047	2333	2635	2862	1.3	72	342	447	515	2.9	3.46	256	324	2.6
22734	REMINGTON	061	2517	2987	3143	1.9	83	881	1028	1089	1.7	2.90	699	801	1.5
22735	REVA	047	974	1572	1865	5.3	97	348	588	706	5.8	2.67	274	454	5.6
22736	RICHARDSVILLE	047	429	619	690	4.0	95	136	202	227	4.4	3.00	110	159	4.1
22737	RIXEYVILLE	047	2463	3119	3675	2.6	90	861	1117	1325	2.9	2.79	721	918	2.6
22738	ROCHELLE	113	576	660	700	1.5	76	234	278	298	1.9	2.35	179	207	1.6
22740	SPERRYVILLE	157	1295	1336	1351	0.3	38	546	581	593	0.7	2.29	383	395	0.3
22741	STEVENSBURG	047	191	231	254	2.1	86	66	81	90	2.2	2.81	47	56	1.9
22742	SUMERDUCK	061	1696	1941	1992	1.5	76	571	643	663	1.3	3.02	467	516	1.1
22743	SYRIA	113	223	254	268	1.4	73	108	128	137	1.9	1.98	79	90	1.4
22747	WASHINGTON	157	1287	1328	1333	0.3	38	520	552	559	0.6	2.39	366	376	0.3
22749	WOODVILLE	157	309	319	322	0.3	38	134	143	145	0.7	2.23	94	97	0.3
22801	HARRISONBURG	165	32693	32701	34735	0.0	23	9828	11132	11860	1.4	2.65	5143	5623	1.0
22802	HARRISONBURG	165	23286	26224	27909	1.3	72	9004	10164	10825	1.3	2.48	5638	6110	0.9
22807	HARRISONBURG	660	144	4118	4187	43.7	100	38	35	34	-0.9	1.46	19	16	-1.8
22810	BASYE	171	918	1074	1193	1.7	79	430	515	576	2.0	2.09	303	353	1.7
22811	BERGTON	165	397	419	435	0.6	49	168	184	192	1.0	2.28	128	136	0.7
22812	BRIDGEWATER	165	8249	8694	8948	0.6	49	2848	3066	3191	0.8	2.46	2048	2141	0.5
22815	BROADWAY	165	7483	8801	9508	1.8	81	2840	3438	3737	2.1	2.54	2117	2495	1.8
22820	CRIDERS	165	259	274	286	0.6	49	105	115	121	1.0	2.38	80	86	0.8
22821	DAYTON	165	5577	6204	6580	1.2	69	1984	2248	2397	1.4	2.76	1512	1670	1.1
22824	EDINBURG	171	5448	6226	6612	1.5	76	2190	2549	2723	1.7	2.44	1594	1803	1.3
22827	ELKTON	165	10471	11317	11887	0.8	58	4096	4566	4829	1.2	2.47	2980	3228	0.9
22830	FULKS RUN	165	1605	1738	1827	0.9	61	599	670	709	1.2	2.59	459	501	1.0
22831	HINTON	165	448	513	552	1.5	76	180	212	229	1.8	2.42	139	159	1.5
22832	KEEZLETOWN	165	1153	1236	1329	0.8	58	447	488	527	1.0	2.53	322	340	0.6
22834	LINVILLE	165	1644	1828	1967	1.2	69	604	689	746	1.4	2.65	470	523	1.2
22835	LURAY	139	11522	12220	12561	0.6	49	4658	5089	5290	1.0	2.35	3255	3442	0.6
22840	MC GAHEYSVILLE	165	3321	4094	4497	2.3	88	1264	1603	1772	2.6	2.55	969	1193	2.3
22841	MOUNT CRAWFORD	165	2775	3133	3329	1.3	72	1029	1187	1270	1.6	2.63	792	892	1.3
22842	MOUNT JACKSON	171	4500	5235	5573	1.6	78	1805	2129	2277	1.8	2.46	1283	1470	1.5
22843	MOUNT SOLON	015	2628	2703	2684	0.3	38	961	1004	1003	0.5	2.69	759	775	0.2
22844	NEW MARKET	171	3818	4576	4993	2.0	85	1579	1938	2131	2.2	2.28	1080	1283	1.9
22845	ORKNEY SPRINGS	171	38	44	49	1.6	78	20	24	27	2.0	1.83	14	16	1.5
22846	PENN LAIRD	165	677	934	1034	3.5	94	247	359	399	4.1	2.60	194	273	3.8
22847	QUICKSBURG	171	736	859	917	1.7	79	281	334	358	1.9	2.57	220	255	1.6
22849	SHENANDOAH	139	4933	5034	5134	0.2	33	1986	2111	2178	0.7	2.38	1440	1485	0.3
22851	STANLEY	139	5415	6043	6344	1.2	69	2134	2459	2611	1.5	2.46	1560	1746	1.2
22853	TIMBERVILLE	165	4318	4853	5173	1.3	72	1708	1980	2129	1.6	2.40	1246	1398	1.3
22901	CHARLOTTESVILLE	003	30394	31995	32710	0.6	49	13278	14413	14859	0.9	2.18	7883	8127	0.3
22902	CHARLOTTESVILLE	003	18622	19475	19870	0.5	45	8110	8793	9059	0.9	2.15	4497	4659	0.4
22903	CHARLOTTESVILLE	003	37944	37550	38886	-0.1	18	13452	15066	15744	1.2	2.26	5985	6545	1.0
22904	CHARLOTTESVILLE	003	116	3680	3693	45.3	100	42	51	52	2.1	2.55	10	11	1.0
22911	CHARLOTTESVILLE	003	12147	16050	17820	3.1	93	4345	5995	6753	3.5	2.63	3304	4372	3.1
22920	AFTON	125	3655	3971	4188	0.9	61	1459	1637	1743	1.3	2.41	1045	1133	0.9
22922	ARRINGTON	125	1532	1574	1611	0.3	38	622	659	682	0.6	2.35	453	468	0.4
22923	BARBOURSVILLE	003	3576	4422	4861	2.3	88	1343	1691	1873	2.5	2.61	1028	1257	2.2
22931	COVESVILLE	003	322	362	379	1.3	72	126	148	157	1.8	2.43	93	105	1.3
22932	CROZET	003	5464	6580	7131	2.0	85	2024	2530	2776	2.4	2.48	1467	1762	2.0
22935	DYKE	079	996	1180	1278	1.8	81	380	461	503	2.1	2.56	296	350	1.8
22936	EARLYSVILLE	003	4494	4935	5153	1.0	64	1646	1873	1977	1.4	2.63	1309	1444	1.1
22937	ESMONT	003	1038	1175	1243	1.3	72	403	474	507	1.8	2.48	281	315	1.2
22938	FABER	125	1442	1545	1603	0.7	54	558	620	651	1.1	2.43	387	415	0.8
22939	FISHERSVILLE	015	3166	4183	4600	3.1	93	1095	1520	1688	3.6	2.65	870	1181	3.4
22940	FREE UNION	003	879	1055	1111	2.0	85	271	333	353	2.3	3.07	203	242	1.9
22942	GORDONSVILLE	109	7250	9243	10490	2.7	90	2887	3795	4354	3.0	2.41	2066	2629	2.6
22943	GREENWOOD	003	614	672	714	1.0	64	247	283	303	1.5	2.37	176	194	1.1
22946	KEENE	003	51	50	50	-0.2	14	23	24	24	0.5	2.08	16	15	-0.7
22947	KESWICK	003	3373	3810	4018	1.3	72	1362	1593	1695	1.7	2.37	1018	1151	1.3
22948	LOCUST DALE	113	421	488	519	1.6	78	134	162	175	2.1	2.90	101	119	1.8
22949	LOVINGSTON	125	1396	1486	1539	0.7	54	575	636	668	1.1	2.29	383	409	0.7
22952	LYNDHURST	015	2523	2806	2923	1.2	69	991	1135	1192	1.5	2.46	753	840	1.2
22958	NELLYSFORD	125	1474	1862	2018	2.6	90	660	865	949	3.0	2.15	472	601	2.6
22959	NORTH GARDEN	003	2011	2182	2271	0.9	61	763	863	908	1.3	2.49	553	600	0.9
22960	ORANGE	137	9011	11209	12404	2.4	88	3483	4456	5009	2.7	2.39	2420	2984	2.3
22963	PALMYRA	065	10844	15236	17398	3.7	95	4223	6047	6966	4.0	2.48	3325	4652	3.7
22964	PINEY RIVER	125	203	208	212	0.3	38	87	92	95	0.6	2.20	62	64	0.3
22967	ROSELAND	125	2185	2307	2386	0.6	49	888	974	1021	1.0	2.34	630	671	0.7
22968	RUCKERSVILLE	079	8042	9567	10384	1.9	83	2892	3456	3762	1.9	2.75	2277	2663	1.7
22969	SCHUYLER	125	1167	1436	1539	2.3	88	462	591	640	2.7	2.42	330	406	2.3
22971	SHIPMAN	125	1543	1651	1712	0.7	54	614	676	708	1.0	2.33	423	451	0.7
22972	SOMERSET	137	272	331	378	2.1	86	116	145	168	2.4	2.27	84	102	2.1
22973	STANARDSVILLE	079	5463	6692	7320	2.2	87	2076	2587	2839	2.4	2.56	1551	1881	2.1
22974	TROY	065	4113	4702	4927	1.5	76	1237	1406	1498	1.4	2.74	951	1052	1.1
22976	TYRO	125	433	446	457	0.3	38	170	182	188	0.7	2.45	116	120	0.4
22980	WAYNESBORO	015	29638	32575	34025	1.0	64	12228	13709	14414	1.2	2.35	8453	9189	0.9
23002	AMELIA COURT HOUSE	007	9025	10489	11219	1.6	78	3330	3963	4271	1.9	2.62	2496	2892	1.6
23004	ARVONIA	029	1271	1322	1336	0.4	42	475	512	524	0.8	2.58	348	365	0.5
23005	ASHLAND	085	14554	16339	17109	1.3	72	5279	6018	6340	1.4	2.50	3834	4237	1.1
23009	AYLETT	101	4851	6347	7157	2.9	92	1768	2373	2700	3.2	2.67	1405	1844	3.0
23011	BARHAMSVILLE	127	803	883	931	1.0	64	300	342	366	1.4	2.13	227	252	1.1
23015	BEAVERDAM	085	3724	4535	4928	2.2	87	1327	1636	1790	2.3	2.76	1070	1286	2.0
23021	BOHANNON	115	419	432	439	0.3	38	178	184	188	0.4	2.30	131	132	0.1
23022	BREMO BLUFF	065	1309	1545	1685	1.8	81	463	555	613	2.0	2.65	335	389	1.6
23023	BRUINGTON	097	177	190	197	0.8	58	78	87	91	1.2	2.18	55	60	0.9
23024	BUMPASS	109	6475	8458	9548	2.9	92	2517	3369	3834	3.2	2.50	1897	2469	2.9
	VIRGINIA					1.2					1.3	2.52			1.0
	UNITED STATES					1.0					1.1	2.59			0.9

ZIP CODE #	POST OFFICE NAME	RACE (%) White 2000	White 2009	Black 2000	Black 2009	Asian/Pacific 2000	Asian/Pacific 2009	% Hispanic Origin 2000	% Hispanic Origin 2009	2009 AGE DISTRIBUTION (%) 0-4	5-9	10-14	15-19	20-24	25-44	45-64	65-84	85+	18+	MEDIAN AGE 2009	% 2009 Males	% 2009 Females
22724	JEFFERSONTON	85.8	84.7	12.3	12.5	0.3	0.4	1.2	2.1	6.5	7.2	8.0	7.2	4.0	23.3	31.5	11.3	0.9	73.6	41.2	50.1	49.9
22725	LEON	92.4	90.6	6.7	7.7	0.3	0.3	0.6	1.1	5.8	6.1	6.6	6.1	4.4	24.5	29.8	14.6	2.2	77.4	42.6	48.2	51.8
22726	LIGNUM	78.0	73.2	17.0	19.2	1.2	1.7	2.5	4.3	5.7	6.7	7.9	7.2	4.6	26.6	28.5	11.5	1.4	75.5	39.6	49.1	50.9
22727	MADISON	86.7	84.7	11.6	12.9	0.5	0.7	0.5	0.9	5.4	5.8	6.4	6.2	4.1	24.1	31.3	14.3	2.4	78.5	43.7	48.4	51.6
22728	MIDLAND	88.6	86.8	9.1	10.0	0.4	0.6	1.3	2.1	6.2	6.6	7.2	7.2	4.6	25.9	30.7	10.5	1.0	75.3	40.3	50.3	49.7
22729	MITCHELLS	52.5	47.7	46.7	50.8	0.0	0.8	0.8	1.5	1.5	2.3	3.0	9.1	8.3	47.7	22.7	5.3	0.0	87.9	35.3	81.1	18.9
22730	OAKPARK	80.9	77.5	16.2	17.8	1.3	1.9	1.9	2.8	6.4	6.9	7.2	6.7	5.0	24.4	28.3	13.1	1.9	75.0	40.6	47.8	52.2
22731	PRATTS	84.5	82.8	15.5	17.2	0.0	0.0	0.0	0.0	6.9	6.9	6.9	6.9	3.4	22.4	31.0	13.8	1.7	72.4	42.5	46.6	53.4
22732	RADIANT	81.7	78.5	15.6	17.5	0.8	1.3	1.3	2.1	6.0	6.6	6.9	6.7	5.0	23.9	30.0	12.7	2.1	76.1	41.3	48.6	51.4
22733	RAPIDAN	59.5	56.1	39.0	41.6	0.3	0.5	1.1	1.8	3.1	3.3	3.9	8.4	7.4	40.8	24.1	8.0	0.9	84.5	36.9	70.8	29.2
22734	REMINGTON	84.2	81.5	12.2	13.3	0.6	0.7	2.7	4.4	9.2	8.5	8.0	7.2	5.5	31.8	23.5	5.6	0.6	69.6	32.2	48.3	51.7
22735	REVA	85.8	82.3	12.4	14.9	0.1	0.2	1.2	2.2	6.1	6.4	6.8	6.0	4.4	27.5	30.9	10.6	1.2	76.7	40.7	49.4	50.6
22736	RICHARDSVILLE	77.9	73.5	17.0	19.1	1.2	1.8	2.6	4.4	5.7	6.6	7.8	7.3	4.7	26.7	28.9	11.1	1.3	75.6	39.7	49.4	50.6
22737	RIXEYVILLE	91.0	89.2	7.0	7.9	0.2	0.4	1.1	1.9	6.6	7.3	8.0	7.1	3.9	24.9	30.4	10.8	1.0	73.6	40.5	49.6	50.4
22738	ROCHELLE	84.9	82.6	13.2	14.8	0.0	0.0	0.3	0.5	5.6	6.2	6.7	6.7	5.0	23.3	31.5	12.9	2.1	77.4	42.2	49.1	50.9
22740	SPERRYVILLE	90.4	88.6	7.4	8.3	0.3	0.4	0.9	1.6	4.5	4.5	6.1	4.8	3.8	21.6	39.1	13.5	2.1	81.6	47.6	49.6	50.4
22741	STEVENSBURG	69.1	63.6	25.1	27.7	0.5	0.9	4.2	6.5	6.9	7.4	7.4	6.5	5.6	27.7	26.8	10.4	1.3	74.9	37.0	50.6	49.4
22742	SUMERDUCK	93.4	91.9	4.5	5.0	0.6	0.8	1.0	1.6	6.1	6.8	7.3	7.4	4.8	27.0	31.2	8.4	1.0	75.2	39.4	50.3	49.7
22743	SYRIA	92.3	90.2	6.3	7.5	0.5	0.4	0.9	0.8	5.1	5.5	6.3	6.3	4.3	23.6	32.7	14.2	2.0	78.3	44.2	48.8	51.2
22747	WASHINGTON	90.0	88.0	8.0	9.0	0.3	0.5	1.1	1.9	4.1	4.5	5.4	5.0	3.5	20.7	39.6	14.9	2.2	82.5	48.9	49.4	50.6
22749	WOODVILLE	91.6	90.0	6.1	6.9	0.3	0.3	1.0	1.6	5.0	4.4	6.9	5.0	4.1	21.9	37.9	12.9	1.9	79.9	46.4	50.5	49.5
22801	HARRISONBURG	87.9	81.8	4.2	6.4	3.0	4.0	6.6	11.9	5.1	4.7	4.6	10.2	25.9	21.1	17.8	8.4	2.2	82.4	24.9	48.5	51.5
22802	HARRISONBURG	87.8	84.4	5.1	5.4	1.5	2.2	10.8	16.2	6.2	5.9	5.7	7.1	8.8	28.4	24.0	11.7	2.2	78.6	35.6	49.4	50.6
22807	HARRISONBURG	91.0	63.8	5.6	23.4	1.4	7.2	2.1	6.3	3.1	3.2	2.8	21.6	33.0	20.7	10.0	4.8	1.0	88.9	22.9	50.8	49.2
22810	BASYE	97.1	95.9	0.9	0.9	0.4	0.7	1.3	2.2	4.3	4.7	5.2	4.9	3.1	19.5	36.3	20.2	1.8	82.7	50.3	50.8	49.2
22811	BERGTON	98.7	98.3	0.0	0.0	0.3	0.2	0.8	1.4	4.5	5.0	5.5	5.3	3.8	22.2	35.6	16.0	2.1	81.6	46.9	51.8	48.2
22812	BRIDGEWATER	96.4	95.1	1.8	2.0	0.4	0.5	2.3	4.1	5.3	5.5	5.7	10.7	10.5	21.7	25.1	11.7	3.8	80.4	37.3	47.1	52.9
22815	BROADWAY	98.0	97.1	0.4	0.5	0.4	0.6	1.9	3.3	6.1	6.4	6.9	6.4	4.6	25.6	30.1	12.3	1.6	76.7	41.0	49.2	50.8
22820	CRIDERS	99.2	98.2	0.0	0.0	0.0	0.4	0.8	1.5	4.7	5.5	5.8	5.8	4.0	23.0	34.3	15.0	1.8	79.6	45.6	51.8	48.2
22821	DAYTON	97.0	95.5	0.6	0.6	0.2	0.2	3.4	6.0	7.5	7.8	7.7	6.9	5.2	26.6	25.8	10.8	1.7	72.7	36.7	50.4	49.6
22824	EDINBURG	96.5	89.6	0.2	5.7	0.2	0.3	3.9	5.9	5.6	5.9	6.3	5.9	4.4	23.8	30.4	15.8	1.9	79.1	43.7	48.9	51.1
22827	ELKTON	96.4	95.4	2.3	2.7	0.2	0.4	1.1	2.0	6.3	6.5	6.6	6.1	5.0	26.5	28.9	12.7	1.5	77.0	40.4	49.2	50.8
22830	FULKS RUN	98.8	98.2	0.2	0.3	0.1	0.2	0.4	0.9	6.1	6.4	6.7	6.4	4.9	27.2	29.2	11.9	1.2	76.9	39.5	53.1	46.9
22831	HINTON	98.2	98.1	0.4	0.4	0.2	0.4	0.7	1.4	6.4	6.6	6.6	6.0	5.3	27.3	28.7	11.7	1.4	76.4	39.1	51.1	48.9
22832	KEEZLETOWN	97.1	96.2	1.4	1.6	0.1	0.2	3.6	6.2	5.1	5.7	6.2	6.0	4.7	25.3	33.1	12.5	1.4	79.4	43.1	51.0	49.0
22834	LINVILLE	98.3	97.4	0.2	0.2	0.5	0.9	0.9	1.6	5.6	6.1	6.6	6.7	4.4	25.7	31.1	12.3	1.5	77.5	41.5	49.7	50.3
22835	LURAY	94.6	93.2	3.6	4.2	0.4	0.5	1.2	2.0	5.3	5.5	5.7	6.1	4.7	24.7	28.8	16.4	2.9	79.7	43.6	48.8	51.2
22840	MC GAHEYSVILLE	94.1	92.7	3.8	4.2	0.3	0.5	2.1	3.9	5.7	6.3	6.9	6.7	4.3	25.6	31.6	11.7	1.1	76.8	41.7	50.4	49.6
22841	MOUNT CRAWFORD	97.2	95.9	0.8	0.7	0.4	0.6	3.4	6.3	5.8	6.3	6.7	6.0	4.8	25.5	31.4	11.9	1.6	78.0	41.6	49.6	50.4
22842	MOUNT JACKSON	94.1	91.2	0.5	0.6	0.3	0.4	6.6	10.3	5.4	5.8	6.3	6.1	4.1	23.7	31.3	15.5	1.8	78.8	44.0	50.7	49.3
22843	MOUNT SOLON	97.1	95.9	1.1	1.3	0.2	0.2	2.7	4.6	7.1	7.6	7.6	6.2	3.8	26.0	28.7	11.5	1.4	73.7	39.4	50.8	49.2
22844	NEW MARKET	95.8	85.4	0.7	9.4	0.8	1.0	3.7	6.2	4.9	5.0	5.4	6.0	4.9	21.7	32.2	17.1	2.9	83.4	46.3	48.3	51.7
22845	ORKNEY SPRINGS	100.0	97.7	0.0	0.0	0.0	0.0	0.0	2.3	4.5	4.5	4.5	4.5	4.5	22.7	36.4	18.2	0.0	81.8	47.5	52.3	47.7
22846	PENN LAIRD	95.6	93.8	1.9	2.0	0.1	0.3	4.3	7.3	5.8	6.3	7.1	7.3	4.5	26.1	30.7	10.8	1.4	76.2	40.5	50.6	49.4
22847	QUICKSBURG	98.0	96.9	0.3	0.2	0.3	0.5	2.2	3.7	4.8	5.1	5.8	6.8	4.7	23.6	33.2	14.3	1.7	80.1	44.5	50.3	49.7
22849	SHENANDOAH	97.3	96.4	1.3	1.6	0.2	0.3	0.9	1.5	5.6	5.8	6.1	6.2	5.0	26.4	29.9	13.3	1.7	78.6	41.5	49.2	50.8
22851	STANLEY	98.4	97.5	0.1	0.1	0.1	0.2	1.3	2.1	6.5	6.5	6.7	6.3	5.0	27.0	28.4	12.2	1.4	76.5	39.6	49.5	50.5
22853	TIMBERVILLE	97.9	96.8	0.4	0.5	0.1	0.2	3.6	6.6	5.3	5.6	6.1	6.7	4.7	25.8	29.8	13.6	2.5	78.9	42.3	49.6	50.4
22901	CHARLOTTESVILLE	81.7	77.3	11.7	12.6	3.6	5.6	3.1	5.2	5.8	5.7	5.9	6.2	7.2	26.1	26.6	13.5	3.1	78.8	39.8	46.7	53.3
22902	CHARLOTTESVILLE	75.9	72.4	19.8	21.1	1.1	1.7	3.1	4.9	6.5	5.9	5.9	5.8	7.0	30.0	27.1	10.1	1.7	78.5	38.0	48.3	51.7
22903	CHARLOTTESVILLE	70.9	66.3	18.8	20.9	7.3	8.8	2.4	3.8	4.5	4.3	4.3	9.8	23.8	24.5	18.7	8.2	1.8	84.1	26.8	47.8	52.2
22904	CHARLOTTESVILLE	58.1	54.9	19.7	27.3	18.8	12.0	3.4	6.7	4.0	3.8	3.2	20.6	23.6	28.4	10.9	4.5	1.1	87.2	23.9	53.3	46.7
22911	CHARLOTTESVILLE	88.0	83.6	7.6	9.6	2.5	4.0	1.6	2.9	7.5	7.4	7.8	7.0	5.5	27.4	26.8	9.2	1.5	72.6	36.6	48.3	51.7
22920	AFTON	90.8	88.8	7.3	8.5	0.4	0.6	2.1	3.6	4.9	5.5	6.1	5.6	4.0	24.0	35.1	13.4	1.3	79.9	44.9	49.2	50.8
22922	ARRINGTON	71.5	67.5	25.8	28.7	0.1	0.1	2.5	3.9	5.0	5.4	5.8	6.3	4.8	22.9	32.1	15.4	2.2	79.5	44.8	49.4	50.6
22923	BARBOURSVILLE	88.0	85.4	9.8	11.3	0.5	0.7	1.4	2.2	6.6	7.1	7.6	6.7	4.6	25.5	30.6	10.3	1.0	74.4	39.9	50.0	50.0
22931	COVESVILLE	84.8	82.0	12.4	13.8	0.3	0.3	4.0	6.9	5.8	6.4	6.6	6.4	4.7	22.9	32.3	13.5	1.4	77.3	43.0	49.7	50.3
22932	CROZET	91.9	89.8	5.5	6.1	0.8	1.2	2.0	3.5	5.7	6.2	7.1	7.1	5.0	22.6	30.8	13.7	1.9	76.4	42.6	47.5	52.5
22935	DYKE	97.3	96.4	1.0	1.2	0.4	0.6	0.8	1.4	5.6	6.0	6.6	6.8	4.9	25.1	32.4	11.6	1.0	77.4	41.7	49.9	50.1
22936	EARLYSVILLE	95.8	94.5	2.6	3.0	0.6	1.0	1.0	1.9	5.3	6.2	7.3	7.4	4.4	20.8	34.5	12.8	1.3	76.4	44.1	48.8	51.2
22937	ESMONT	66.3	61.4	31.5	35.0	0.1	0.2	1.4	2.6	5.4	5.7	6.1	6.2	4.6	23.0	32.9	14.6	1.6	79.2	44.3	48.1	51.9
22938	FABER	84.4	81.6	13.1	15.0	0.4	0.4	2.4	4.3	5.3	5.8	6.0	5.0	4.4	21.3	34.8	15.2	2.3	79.6	46.4	48.9	51.1
22939	FISHERSVILLE	95.1	93.6	3.2	3.8	0.5	0.8	0.9	1.5	5.8	6.3	6.9	6.4	3.9	24.0	30.7	13.4	2.6	76.8	42.9	48.4	51.6
22940	FREE UNION	96.4	95.1	1.8	1.9	0.5	0.8	1.1	1.9	5.0	5.6	6.7	7.1	5.1	23.3	33.3	12.6	1.2	78.0	42.9	49.1	50.9
22942	GORDONSVILLE	78.1	74.8	19.7	22.0	0.3	0.5	1.0	1.6	6.0	6.4	6.8	6.1	4.3	25.3	30.9	12.5	1.7	76.9	41.8	48.4	51.6
22943	GREENWOOD	89.6	87.2	8.1	9.2	0.7	1.0	2.6	4.8	5.5	6.3	7.3	7.6	4.5	22.9	33.0	11.6	1.3	76.2	42.4	48.4	51.6
22946	KEENE	66.7	62.0	31.4	36.0	0.0	0.0	0.0	2.0	4.0	4.0	4.0	6.0	4.0	20.0	44.0	12.0	2.0	82.0	50.0	44.0	56.0
22947	KESWICK	84.7	82.2	13.5	15.1	0.7	1.1	1.2	2.2	4.5	5.3	6.3	6.3	3.6	20.3	35.7	16.6	1.5	79.9	47.0	49.0	51.0
22948	LOCUST DALE	79.3	75.6	17.3	19.3	1.4	2.0	1.9	3.1	6.1	7.0	7.2	6.8	4.9	24.4	29.1	12.5	2.0	75.4	40.8	48.2	51.8
22949	LOVINGSTON	81.5	78.1	15.4	17.3	0.5	0.5	3.3	5.7	5.5	5.4	5.9	5.2	5.4	20.7	33.3	15.9	2.7	79.9	46.2	49.2	50.8
22952	LYNDHURST	94.8	93.1	3.1	3.6	0.4	0.6	1.7	3.0	6.1	6.5	6.9	6.3	4.4	25.6	30.2	12.4	1.5	76.3	41.1	49.1	50.9
22958	NELLYSFORD	92.7	91.5	5.3	5.9	0.4	0.4	1.0	1.6	3.7	4.7	4.4	4.6	3.3	18.6	41.1	18.6	1.0	84.0	51.3	49.2	50.8
22959	NORTH GARDEN	84.3	80.9	13.0	14.7	0.4	0.6	5.0	8.7	5.6	6.4	6.8	6.4	4.7	22.9	33.0	12.8	1.5	77.1	43.1	48.4	51.6
22960	ORANGE	78.9	75.5	19.4	22.0	0.2	0.4	1.3	2.0	6.1	6.1	6.2	5.9	5.1	25.1	27.7	14.6	3.1	77.9	41.8	48.1	51.9
22963	PALMYRA	85.4	83.4	12.3	13.3	0.4	0.6	1.3	2.2	6.0	6.4	7.0	6.3	3.9	23.7	28.6	16.5	1.6	76.5	42.9	47.4	52.6
22964	PINEY RIVER	66.2	62.0	30.4	33.2	0.0	0.0	4.9	7.7	4.3	4.8	4.8	5.8	5.3	22.1	35.6	15.4	1.9	81.7	46.4	51.4	48.6
22967	ROSELAND	80.5	78.1	17.3	18.9	0.2	0.2	2.7	4.3	4.5	4.9	5.5	5.4	4.7	21.8	35.0	16.2	2.0	81.4	46.9	49.7	50.3
22968	RUCKERSVILLE	90.2	88.2	7.1	7.9	0.5	0.8	1.6	2.7	8.4	8.1	7.9	6.8	5.2	30.3	24.6	7.8	1.0	71.2	35.2	49.6	50.4
22969	SCHUYLER	82.3	78.2	15.1	17.9	0.2	0.2	1.8	3.0	6.2	6.6	6.8	5.7	4.5	22.6	32.2	13.6	1.7	76.9	43.3	49.3	50.7
22971	SHIPMAN	79.2	75.9	17.0	18.7	0.2	0.2	2.7	4.4	5.8	6.1	6.3	5.1	3.9	21.6	32.5	15.6	3.1	78.4	45.8	49.1	50.9
22972	SOMERSET	83.4	79.8	15.1	17.5	0.4	0.6	1.1	1.8	5.7	6.3	6.3	5.7	4.5	24.5	32.0	13.0	1.8	77.9	42.9	48.3	51.7
22973	STANARDSVILLE	91.9	90.1	5.8	6.6	0.4	0.7	0.9	1.6	5.9	6.1	6.5	6.3	4.7	26.1	30.7	11.9	1.8	77.5	41.5	49.2	50.8
22974	TROY	75.9	71.5	22.0	25.5	0.6	0.9	1.0	1.6	5.5	5.9	6.2	5.2	5.4	34.7	27.3	9.0	0.7	79.0	38.5	40.5	59.5
22976	TYRO	91.0	89.2	7.1	8.1	0.5	0.4	3.0	5.4	4.7	5.4	5.4	5.2	4.9	24.7	32.5	15.7	1.6	81.2	44.8	49.8	50.2
22980	WAYNESBORO	89.5	87.4	7.7	8.5	0.5	0.8	2.5	4.1	6.3	6.1	6.2	6.4	5.9	24.3	27.9	14.5	2.4	77.5	41.3	48.1	51.9
23002	AMELIA COURT HOUSE	70.9	67.6	27.7	30.5	0.2	0.2	0.7	1.1	6.2	6.5	6.7	6.3	4.7	24.8	29.7	13.0	2.0	76.5	41.3	49.1	50.9
23004	ARVONIA	57.8	53.8	40.6	43.9	0.2	0.2	0.3	0.6	6.0	6.1	6.4	7.3	5.9	23.5	30.3	12.8	1.6	77.0	41.2	47.5	52.5
23005	ASHLAND	82.5	80.1	15.0	16.4	0.7	1.0	1.4	2.2	5.5	5.8	6.0	9.3	8.7	22.5	28.4	11.7	2.0	78.3	39.3	48.9	51.1
23009	AYLETT	77.8	74.5	19.4	21.8	0.2	0.3	0.8	1.1	7.6	7.8	7.7	6.0	4.1	30.1	27.6	8.3	0.8	73.0	37.4	49.9	50.1
23011	BARHAMSVILLE	67.3	61.8	30.5	35.1	0.4	0.7	1.5	1.8	3.5	4.0	6.0	8.0	6.9	29.2	30.2	10.6	1.5	82.2	40.4	54.2	45.8
23015	BEAVERDAM	86.1	83.7	12.1	13.7	0.4	0.6	0.6	1.0	6.2	6.7	7.4	6.9	4.2	24.1	32.0	11.1	1.3	75.1	41.4	49.5	50.5
23021	BOHANNON	85.2	82.9	13.9	15.5	0.0	0.0	0.7	1.2	4.6	4.9	5.1	4.9	3.5	19.2	35.6	18.5	3.7	81.7	50.0	48.1	51.9
23022	BREMO BLUFF	62.2	56.6	36.3	41.2	0.9	1.3	0.7	0.8	5.2	5.4	5.6	6.1	5.4	22.3	28.7	17.0	4.3	79.8	45.0	46.9	53.1
23023	BRUINGTON	55.6	52.1	40.4	43.7	0.6	0.5	0.6	1.1	5.3	5.3	6.3	5.8	4.7	23.2	32.6	15.3	1.6	79.5	44.6	49.5	50.5
23024	BUMPASS	84.8	82.6	13.4	14.9	0.3	0.4	0.7	1.1	5.8	6.3	6.7	6.5	4.6	26.3	32.4	10.6	0.8	77.0	41.2	49.8	50.2
	VIRGINIA	72.3	68.8	19.6	20.1	3.7	5.1	4.7	7.0	6.5	6.4	6.5	6.9	6.9	27.5	27.2	10.5	1.6	76.7	37.7	49.2	50.8
	UNITED STATES	75.1	72.0	12.3	12.7	3.8	4.6	12.5	15.7	6.8	6.7	6.6	7.1	6.9	27.0	26.0	10.9	1.9	75.7	36.9	49.2	50.8

#	POST OFFICE NAME	2009 Per Capita Income	2009 HH Income Base	2009 Household Income Distribution (%): Less than $25,000	$25,000 to $49,999	$50,000 to $99,999	$100,000 to $149,999	$150,000 or More	Median Household Income: 2009	2014	2009 National Centile	2009 State Centile	2009 Home Value Base	2009 Home Value Distribution (%): Less than $50,000	$50,000 to $89,999	$90,000 to $174,999	$175,000 to $399,999	$400,000 or More	2009 Median Home Value
22724	JEFFERSONTON	28293	1008	9.5	15.3	43.8	25.6	5.9	73396	74256	89	84	885	0.9	0.0	12.1	51.1	35.9	341274
22725	LEON	22125	143	23.1	32.2	34.3	7.0	3.5	44689	46278	47	42	118	3.4	5.1	39.0	42.4	10.2	181250
22726	LIGNUM	20289	201	13.9	34.8	41.3	8.5	1.5	51111	56282	64	61	165	4.2	6.7	15.2	56.4	17.6	232500
22727	MADISON	23039	2260	20.7	30.9	38.5	7.5	2.4	48013	50933	57	52	1716	5.0	7.6	32.1	44.5	10.8	191486
22728	MIDLAND	29849	1178	8.8	17.5	42.8	20.5	10.4	76011	78411	90	86	892	0.4	1.1	11.5	58.2	28.7	309524
22729	MITCHELLS	41895	53	5.7	24.5	45.3	15.1	9.4	64239	65616	83	79	38	13.2	10.5	2.6	60.5	13.2	275000
22730	OAKPARK	22250	124	16.1	30.6	44.4	6.5	2.4	52449	55704	67	64	87	2.3	11.5	29.9	49.4	6.9	192188
22731	PRATTS	24797	27	22.2	33.3	33.3	11.1	0.0	43624	43624	44	40	19	0.0	5.3	31.6	57.9	5.3	212500
22732	RADIANT	21929	715	16.9	30.3	43.4	7.0	2.4	51696	53653	65	62	520	4.4	7.5	30.8	48.3	9.0	198750
22733	RAPIDAN	19040	447	11.9	30.0	40.0	12.1	6.0	59248	61916	76	73	321	8.1	5.6	14.0	55.5	16.8	250893
22734	REMINGTON	25469	1028	13.1	19.6	47.4	13.7	6.1	64978	67416	83	80	744	14.5	6.3	16.8	55.2	7.1	204286
22735	REVA	20837	588	19.9	34.9	34.7	9.9	0.7	47510	48331	55	51	493	0.6	1.0	12.2	69.8	16.4	246591
22736	RICHARDSVILLE	19225	202	13.9	34.7	41.6	8.4	1.5	51265	55991	64	61	165	4.2	6.7	15.2	56.4	17.6	232500
22737	RIXEYVILLE	28251	1117	10.7	19.0	43.5	20.2	6.5	68445	69557	86	82	977	6.4	1.9	10.0	54.2	27.3	314808
22738	ROCHELLE	22872	278	20.1	30.6	39.2	8.6	1.4	49165	50385	59	56	221	7.2	4.1	33.0	43.9	11.8	195833
22740	SPERRYVILLE	28134	581	18.4	25.0	43.2	9.5	4.0	54441	54840	70	67	421	1.0	1.4	24.5	43.0	30.2	249638
22741	STEVENSBURG	20090	81	21.0	30.9	38.3	8.6	1.2	48005	50000	57	52	47	2.1	2.1	12.8	68.1	14.9	275000
22742	SUMERDUCK	32529	643	8.4	9.2	40.1	32.0	10.3	88056	95451	95	90	572	0.0	1.4	8.2	76.6	13.8	280189
22743	SYRIA	26572	128	19.5	35.9	35.2	8.6	0.8	45000	47914	48	44	102	6.9	8.8	33.3	41.2	9.8	177778
22747	WASHINGTON	28428	552	17.8	25.9	41.7	8.9	5.8	54693	55464	71	68	394	2.0	3.0	20.6	36.0	38.3	288095
22749	WOODVILLE	28276	143	18.2	23.1	44.1	11.2	3.5	56069	55424	73	70	106	0.0	0.0	29.2	47.2	23.6	238889
22801	HARRISONBURG	21411	11132	28.2	26.2	31.6	9.3	4.6	45195	48181	49	44	5449	4.4	2.4	21.5	58.0	13.6	233374
22802	HARRISONBURG	20895	10164	27.6	30.3	34.3	4.9	2.9	42801	45710	42	38	5462	8.4	3.9	45.7	34.0	8.0	164376
22807	HARRISONBURG	14736	35	0.0	0.0	51.4	40.0	8.6	96130	100000	96	92	26	0.0	0.0	0.0	100.0	0.0	246429
22810	BASYE	29677	515	17.5	29.1	40.4	9.5	3.5	53224	57055	68	66	447	2.7	6.3	37.4	39.4	14.3	188750
22811	BERGTON	20732	184	21.2	42.4	32.6	2.2	1.6	40633	41982	35	31	152	8.6	9.9	66.4	11.8	3.3	132692
22812	BRIDGEWATER	24302	3066	14.9	29.5	43.7	8.5	3.4	53984	57408	70	67	2155	2.5	2.1	34.3	51.9	9.2	201854
22815	BROADWAY	20365	3438	21.9	33.1	37.8	5.8	1.5	46260	48311	52	47	2643	7.1	6.8	50.1	30.3	5.7	155081
22820	CRIDERS	20114	115	20.9	44.3	30.4	2.6	1.7	40216	42075	33	30	95	8.4	14.7	57.9	15.8	3.2	129861
22821	DAYTON	19283	2248	20.6	33.4	39.2	5.1	1.8	46995	49274	54	49	1663	5.0	6.7	39.6	39.9	8.7	172586
22824	EDINBURG	23063	2549	18.1	33.1	38.6	8.1	2.2	49035	50796	59	56	1935	5.7	3.4	33.3	46.9	10.7	192693
22827	ELKTON	19930	4566	25.0	34.2	34.4	5.0	1.4	43321	45880	43	39	3566	11.2	7.9	43.1	33.7	4.1	153366
22830	FULKS RUN	17623	670	24.2	43.3	27.9	3.7	0.9	39135	40236	30	27	543	8.8	18.6	42.2	25.2	5.2	125750
22831	HINTON	18952	212	30.2	32.5	34.0	1.4	1.9	41143	43425	36	33	162	3.7	12.3	57.4	25.9	0.6	132895
22832	KEEZLETOWN	24374	488	17.2	26.8	43.6	9.8	2.5	55204	60271	72	69	391	6.6	5.9	34.8	43.0	9.7	181402
22834	LINVILLE	20851	689	19.6	29.0	43.7	5.4	2.3	50800	53625	63	60	553	4.9	3.8	49.9	34.7	6.7	164491
22835	LURAY	21427	5089	26.0	30.2	36.4	5.9	1.5	45284	45792	49	45	3637	4.8	6.2	45.6	37.8	5.6	165451
22840	MC GAHEYSVILLE	25676	1603	12.9	28.5	43.4	11.1	4.2	56090	59877	73	71	1341	5.0	4.0	33.0	50.2	7.8	198575
22841	MOUNT CRAWFORD	24867	1187	13.1	29.8	45.7	8.1	3.4	55930	60458	73	70	965	5.3	7.2	27.9	44.7	15.0	200676
22842	MOUNT JACKSON	22362	2129	20.5	33.1	37.5	6.5	2.3	46947	49177	54	49	1613	7.6	5.0	38.1	39.7	9.5	173733
22843	MOUNT SOLON	22160	1004	19.2	26.5	44.4	5.5	4.4	52153	53303	66	63	832	7.8	9.0	33.2	42.5	7.5	175000
22844	NEW MARKET	24522	1938	24.2	27.9	38.6	6.9	2.4	48219	49945	57	53	1392	5.2	4.4	32.2	47.6	10.6	194426
22845	ORKNEY SPRINGS	29261	24	20.8	29.2	41.7	8.3	0.0	50000	57183	61	58	21	0.0	4.8	42.9	38.1	14.3	187500
22846	PENN LAIRD	23992	359	14.2	30.9	42.1	9.5	3.3	53293	55932	69	66	281	3.6	4.6	45.2	32.4	14.2	170759
22847	QUICKSBURG	19323	334	21.9	37.7	34.1	5.1	1.2	43464	45831	44	40	261	6.5	7.3	31.8	45.6	8.8	186058
22849	SHENANDOAH	20945	2111	27.8	32.5	31.1	6.1	2.5	41239	42253	37	34	1667	7.3	10.0	52.8	27.0	2.9	145998
22851	STANLEY	17238	2459	31.6	36.4	27.7	3.6	0.8	36758	37343	23	20	1750	14.4	7.2	45.0	28.7	4.7	143474
22853	TIMBERVILLE	21005	1980	22.0	34.2	36.9	5.6	1.3	45705	47625	50	46	1474	5.6	6.5	58.1	26.1	3.7	147406
22901	CHARLOTTESVILLE	36365	14413	15.1	22.4	38.7	13.2	10.6	63439	66202	82	78	7939	2.0	1.9	16.4	51.2	28.6	279674
22902	CHARLOTTESVILLE	27774	8793	22.8	27.6	35.5	10.4	3.7	49608	53543	60	57	4864	7.5	3.7	36.1	43.9	8.8	184375
22903	CHARLOTTESVILLE	26256	15066	30.1	25.1	29.3	9.2	6.3	44505	47572	47	42	5833	2.0	3.3	24.2	42.2	28.3	252198
22904	CHARLOTTESVILLE	14787	51	45.1	39.2	15.7	0.0	0.0	26832	27773	5	4	0	0.0	0.0	0.0	0.0	0.0	0
22911	CHARLOTTESVILLE	34630	5995	9.8	16.7	39.3	22.5	11.7	77920	79904	91	86	4286	6.3	1.2	10.0	55.5	27.0	304369
22920	AFTON	26797	1637	14.2	26.3	46.2	10.5	2.8	58515	60549	76	73	1270	2.9	8.4	33.1	39.1	16.4	195349
22922	ARRINGTON	20618	659	31.1	31.6	30.7	3.8	2.9	37641	39228	26	22	544	10.7	14.9	48.2	22.1	4.2	128090
22923	BARBOURSVILLE	25164	1691	13.4	29.3	43.3	9.9	4.1	57781	60254	75	72	1370	8.5	3.4	28.8	43.9	15.3	199423
22931	COVESVILLE	23139	148	20.3	31.1	35.8	10.8	2.0	48649	52838	58	54	114	0.0	13.2	32.5	36.0	18.4	192857
22932	CROZET	26956	2530	15.3	22.5	46.3	11.1	4.7	60796	63338	79	75	1987	7.9	2.9	32.0	38.7	18.6	199409
22935	DYKE	26987	461	18.2	27.8	36.7	10.2	7.2	56262	60582	73	71	365	3.6	3.6	30.7	40.8	21.4	217614
22936	EARLYSVILLE	36222	1873	8.8	15.1	38.3	26.1	11.8	81949	83833	93	88	1647	2.2	1.2	9.5	48.1	39.0	342880
22937	ESMONT	23575	474	28.9	21.7	37.8	10.5	1.1	49604	52005	60	57	382	8.1	7.9	44.2	24.3	15.4	159524
22938	FABER	23188	620	20.6	30.3	38.4	7.7	2.9	48714	50678	58	55	472	4.0	11.7	36.2	36.7	11.4	171875
22939	FISHERSVILLE	25072	1520	14.3	23.9	44.4	13.9	3.5	59671	61053	77	74	1330	5.9	3.5	18.5	63.1	9.0	232900
22940	FREE UNION	25938	333	14.1	29.1	34.2	11.4	11.1	60278	62128	78	74	252	2.8	3.2	22.6	34.9	36.5	297619
22942	GORDONSVILLE	23546	3795	21.4	30.0	36.7	9.7	2.2	48664	50638	58	54	2812	7.0	5.9	39.3	36.2	11.6	171036
22943	GREENWOOD	27416	283	11.3	21.2	55.8	11.0	0.7	62942	65272	81	78	207	0.0	2.4	35.3	44.0	18.4	227381
22946	KEENE	29417	24	20.8	29.2	33.3	16.7	0.0	50000	60000	61	58	19	0.0	0.0	47.4	31.6	21.1	187500
22947	KESWICK	40932	1593	9.4	20.3	35.9	18.7	15.6	76125	79432	90	86	1294	0.7	0.8	17.7	33.0	47.8	377778
22948	LOCUST DALE	21809	162	14.2	29.6	48.1	5.6	2.5	54743	57625	71	68	110	2.7	10.0	27.3	52.7	7.3	205556
22949	LOVINGSTON	24465	636	23.6	31.8	32.4	8.5	3.8	45474	47190	50	45	454	3.1	14.3	39.2	34.1	9.3	160000
22952	LYNDHURST	24026	1135	16.2	25.8	47.5	8.6	1.9	55969	59096	73	70	980	8.6	5.4	37.9	41.8	6.3	171617
22958	NELLYSFORD	38539	865	19.3	23.4	33.2	15.3	8.9	60247	61318	78	74	736	6.1	3.0	23.1	35.2	32.6	295556
22959	NORTH GARDEN	24876	863	19.4	25.1	41.3	11.4	2.9	54790	60079	71	68	634	0.6	7.6	27.0	41.6	23.2	238406
22960	ORANGE	22467	4456	26.1	29.0	33.6	8.1	3.1	44975	46980	48	43	2876	6.7	4.2	37.0	41.9	10.2	180000
22963	PALMYRA	28184	6047	11.2	21.3	49.3	13.7	4.4	62437	64324	81	77	5247	1.3	3.0	22.0	62.2	11.5	228370
22964	PINEY RIVER	22259	92	35.9	22.8	32.6	5.4	3.3	38185	41758	27	24	76	14.5	7.9	42.1	31.6	3.9	138889
22967	ROSELAND	24986	974	27.5	25.9	34.4	8.0	4.2	45902	48500	51	46	793	10.8	10.6	34.4	32.4	11.7	157649
22968	RUCKERSVILLE	24950	3456	9.5	28.4	46.5	12.1	3.5	62384	63258	80	77	2897	6.9	3.0	27.8	55.5	6.8	199619
22969	SCHUYLER	20884	591	28.8	33.5	28.3	7.6	1.9	41275	42991	37	34	492	14.2	16.1	37.2	24.8	7.7	135377
22971	SHIPMAN	23342	676	21.6	33.6	34.9	6.7	3.3	44063	46339	46	41	534	8.4	16.1	43.3	26.4	5.8	140909
22972	SOMERSET	25534	145	19.3	27.6	43.4	6.9	2.8	52413	55164	67	64	106	7.5	4.7	37.7	35.8	14.2	175000
22973	STANARDSVILLE	22939	2587	17.2	31.7	40.7	7.7	2.7	51543	54761	65	62	2030	3.0	5.2	35.9	47.2	8.7	187983
22974	TROY	21740	1406	17.6	24.3	46.9	6.9	4.3	55385	59113	72	69	1171	3.1	7.7	29.4	42.7	17.2	201752
22976	TYRO	19958	182	25.3	37.4	28.6	7.7	1.1	36761	38187	23	20	142	18.3	16.9	38.7	22.5	3.5	115278
22980	WAYNESBORO	23656	13709	23.4	28.2	37.8	8.1	2.5	48408	50670	58	54	9374	6.0	5.8	41.9	39.7	6.6	169211
23002	AMELIA COURT HOUSE	21995	3963	17.9	33.4	37.5	8.6	2.6	49015	52190	59	56	3200	6.9	11.6	44.4	33.7	3.4	152856
23004	ARVONIA	16633	512	38.7	31.8	24.4	3.3	1.8	35000	36826	18	15	415	18.6	27.0	37.6	13.0	3.9	101411
23005	ASHLAND	30615	6018	15.3	22.3	36.1	18.0	8.3	64749	68113	83	79	4398	9.3	3.4	21.7	49.3	16.3	228319
23009	AYLETT	26201	2373	11.7	21.9	48.0	15.1	3.3	64421	68073	83	79	2092	3.8	3.1	36.3	51.4	5.4	188202
23011	BARHAMSVILLE	30465	342	19.9	29.8	34.8	9.1	6.4	50410	56406	62	59	299	5.0	6.7	30.4	45.8	12.0	202841
23015	BEAVERDAM	27802	1636	10.3	23.0	43.0	17.2	6.5	67239	71174	85	81	1390	1.3	8.2	26.7	46.3	17.5	224877
23021	BOHANNON	26225	184	16.8	30.4	41.3	8.7	2.7	51645	55215	65	62	155	5.2	7.7	34.2	32.3	20.6	183036
23022	BREMO BLUFF	20788	555	21.6	32.8	38.0	3.6	4.0	46182	48572	52	47	426	9.4	14.1	45.5	24.6	6.3	133642
23023	BRUINGTON	23965	87	29.9	27.6	33.3	6.9	2.3	43376	45372	43	39	72	13.9	11.1	47.2	22.2	5.6	136538
23024	BUMPASS	24508	3369	19.6	27.0	42.1	7.9	3.4	52186	55460	66	63	2933	3.5	8.7	40.2	38.0	9.5	171403
	VIRGINIA	30912		17.0	22.6	35.9	15.0	9.5	61855	64957				5.3	6.3	30.4	41.5	16.5	203135
	UNITED STATES	27277		20.9	24.4	35.3	11.7	7.6	54719	56938				9.3	13.1	31.6	32.6	13.5	162279

ZIP CODE #	POST OFFICE NAME	FINANCIAL SERVICES: Auto Loan	Home Loan	Investments	Retirement Plans	THE HOME: Home Improvements: Home Repair	Lawn & Garden	Furnishings: Computers & Hardware Personal	Major Appliances	TV, Radio, Sound Equipment	Furniture	ENTERTAINMENT: Dine out/ Carry out	Sports Equipment	Fees & Tickets	Toys & Games	Travel	Cable TV	PERSONAL: Apparel & Services	Auto Repairs	Health Insurance	Pets & Supplies
22724	JEFFERSONTON	112	132	125	136	132	127	115	121	112	119	113	92	127	113	125	111	80	115	117	140
22725	LEON	86	78	78	82	80	93	77	87	80	70	78	66	71	81	77	84	54	81	90	102
22726	LIGNUM	80	91	78	93	88	89	81	84	80	81	80	66	86	82	85	80	56	81	83	99
22727	MADISON	84	80	79	83	82	92	77	86	79	72	78	65	74	80	79	83	54	80	89	100
22728	MIDLAND	128	140	127	139	137	133	124	129	122	129	123	98	130	126	128	122	86	124	124	151
22729	MITCHELLS	104	123	127	123	128	129	107	118	110	112	110	81	120	106	120	113	76	113	127	133
22730	OAKPARK	89	97	85	100	95	98	88	92	87	87	87	72	92	89	92	88	61	88	92	109
22731	PRATTS	81	74	73	77	75	87	73	82	75	66	74	62	67	77	73	79	50	76	85	95
22732	RADIANT	87	90	82	93	89	95	83	90	84	80	83	69	84	86	86	86	58	85	90	105
22733	RAPIDAN	93	107	102	108	108	107	97	101	97	98	97	75	106	96	105	98	68	98	104	117
22734	REMINGTON	109	122	101	119	115	102	107	107	101	115	103	85	112	108	108	96	72	102	95	122
22735	REVA	79	86	76	88	84	87	78	82	77	77	77	64	81	79	81	78	54	78	82	96
22736	RICHARDSVILLE	80	91	78	93	88	89	81	84	80	81	80	66	86	82	85	80	56	81	83	99
22737	RIXEYVILLE	107	126	118	130	125	122	110	115	107	114	108	88	121	108	119	106	76	110	112	134
22738	ROCHELLE	83	76	75	79	78	90	75	85	77	68	76	64	69	79	75	82	52	78	87	98
22740	SPERRYVILLE	107	87	137	85	95	113	86	109	90	81	89	80	75	86	93	96	59	101	108	127
22741	STEVENSBURG	74	86	78	86	84	81	81	80	79	79	79	63	86	80	84	79	57	79	79	93
22742	SUMERDUCK	132	166	146	166	160	143	139	141	131	146	133	113	157	136	150	126	96	134	126	162
22743	SYRIA	82	74	74	77	76	88	73	83	76	66	74	63	67	77	73	80	51	76	85	96
22747	WASHINGTON	110	94	141	94	102	118	92	113	95	88	94	83	84	91	100	100	63	105	111	131
22749	WOODVILLE	105	84	136	83	93	111	84	107	88	79	87	78	73	84	91	94	58	99	106	124
22801	HARRISONBURG	85	70	66	73	68	71	94	75	87	83	88	64	80	87	77	85	62	83	76	92
22802	HARRISONBURG	79	67	65	69	65	72	77	73	77	72	77	58	69	78	70	78	53	75	75	88
22807	HARRISONBURG	155	157	150	161	153	151	161	152	159	162	160	120	164	159	159	157	112	157	154	182
22810	BASYE	103	83	133	81	91	109	83	105	87	78	85	77	72	82	90	92	57	97	104	122
22811	BERGTON	74	66	66	69	68	79	66	74	68	59	67	56	60	69	65	72	45	69	77	86
22812	BRIDGEWATER	90	90	87	91	90	98	87	93	89	84	88	69	86	89	89	92	61	90	97	108
22815	BROADWAY	84	71	74	73	72	87	71	81	75	66	74	62	63	77	70	80	50	76	84	96
22820	CRIDERS	77	66	68	68	67	80	66	75	70	61	68	57	59	71	65	74	46	70	78	88
22821	DAYTON	83	74	81	75	75	88	74	83	76	67	75	64	67	77	74	80	51	78	86	98
22824	EDINBURG	89	77	83	78	79	92	78	88	81	73	80	66	70	82	77	86	54	83	91	103
22827	ELKTON	83	66	71	66	66	82	68	76	72	65	71	58	59	74	64	77	48	72	80	91
22830	FULKS RUN	82	59	68	58	59	78	62	72	68	60	67	55	50	71	56	74	45	68	76	87
22831	HINTON	81	60	69	59	60	79	62	72	68	59	67	56	50	71	57	74	45	68	76	88
22832	KEEZLETOWN	96	87	86	91	89	103	86	97	89	78	87	73	79	90	86	94	59	90	100	113
22834	LINVILLE	86	78	80	81	79	93	77	87	79	69	78	67	70	80	77	83	53	81	90	102
22835	LURAY	80	68	77	68	69	85	69	79	73	64	72	59	62	73	68	78	49	75	84	93
22840	MC GAHEYSVILLE	95	99	90	102	98	104	92	98	92	88	91	76	93	94	95	94	63	93	99	115
22841	MOUNT CRAWFORD	97	100	87	101	97	100	91	96	92	93	92	73	93	95	93	93	64	92	95	113
22842	MOUNT JACKSON	91	75	89	75	77	94	75	88	79	70	78	66	66	80	75	85	53	82	90	104
22843	MOUNT SOLON	90	86	84	89	87	97	83	92	85	77	84	70	79	86	84	88	57	86	94	107
22844	NEW MARKET	89	76	95	77	80	93	78	89	81	73	80	66	70	79	79	85	54	85	92	104
22845	ORKNEY SPRINGS	89	72	116	71	79	95	72	91	75	67	74	66	62	71	78	80	49	84	90	106
22846	PENN LAIRD	91	94	85	97	93	99	87	94	87	84	87	72	88	89	90	90	60	89	94	110
22847	QUICKSBURG	77	70	69	73	71	83	69	78	71	63	70	59	64	73	69	76	48	72	81	91
22849	SHENANDOAH	82	67	74	67	67	84	68	77	73	64	72	59	60	74	66	78	48	74	82	93
22851	STANLEY	76	55	65	53	55	73	57	67	63	55	62	51	46	65	53	69	41	63	71	81
22853	TIMBERVILLE	80	70	72	72	72	84	70	79	73	64	72	60	63	75	69	78	49	74	82	93
22901	CHARLOTTESVILLE	111	111	111	115	111	107	115	108	113	117	114	85	117	113	114	112	81	113	109	128
22902	CHARLOTTESVILLE	87	79	74	81	77	80	87	81	88	86	88	64	83	89	81	89	62	86	86	98
22903	CHARLOTTESVILLE	89	68	66	73	66	69	104	76	94	89	95	67	85	94	81	91	67	88	77	95
22904	CHARLOTTESVILLE	44	19	19	23	17	22	62	31	50	42	51	33	37	49	33	45	36	44	31	42
22911	CHARLOTTESVILLE	133	146	128	148	141	127	132	131	126	141	128	105	140	133	134	120	91	126	117	151
22920	AFTON	92	99	91	102	98	102	90	96	90	89	90	73	94	91	95	91	62	92	97	112
22922	ARRINGTON	86	63	88	61	65	87	64	81	71	60	69	61	52	70	64	77	46	74	84	96
22923	BARBOURSVILLE	100	98	90	99	97	103	92	99	93	91	93	75	90	96	92	96	64	94	99	116
22931	COVESVILLE	85	82	78	85	82	92	79	87	80	73	79	66	76	82	80	83	54	81	88	101
22932	CROZET	94	103	105	104	103	107	93	100	94	93	94	75	99	93	101	96	66	97	103	117
22935	DYKE	101	106	92	107	103	105	96	101	97	98	97	77	99	100	98	98	67	97	100	119
22936	EARLYSVILLE	130	155	144	158	154	145	134	139	129	139	130	107	148	131	145	126	92	132	131	161
22937	ESMONT	99	77	98	77	80	103	78	95	85	72	83	72	66	85	78	92	56	88	99	113
22938	FABER	90	78	95	79	81	95	78	91	81	72	80	67	71	80	80	86	54	85	93	105
22939	FISHERSVILLE	96	104	90	106	101	103	94	98	94	95	94	76	98	96	98	94	65	95	97	116
22940	FREE UNION	115	124	138	124	130	127	112	122	110	117	109	91	118	109	121	110	77	115	117	140
22942	GORDONSVILLE	89	80	84	82	82	94	79	90	82	73	80	67	73	83	79	86	55	83	92	104
22943	GREENWOOD	91	102	88	105	99	100	91	95	90	92	90	74	97	92	96	90	63	91	94	112
22946	KEENE	95	86	86	90	88	102	85	96	88	77	86	73	79	90	85	93	59	89	99	112
22947	KESWICK	135	150	195	152	164	158	134	153	130	140	129	113	145	126	154	130	92	141	143	172
22948	LOCUST DALE	89	100	86	103	97	98	89	93	88	89	88	72	95	90	94	88	62	89	92	109
22949	LOVINGSTON	89	75	96	75	79	92	78	89	81	74	79	65	70	79	79	85	54	85	91	103
22952	LYNDHURST	84	91	81	91	89	91	81	85	83	83	83	64	87	85	85	84	58	83	87	100
22958	NELLYSFORD	116	119	156	119	135	140	109	127	115	120	113	82	117	105	123	120	77	121	141	145
22959	NORTH GARDEN	89	95	85	98	94	97	87	92	87	85	87	72	90	89	91	88	60	88	92	108
22960	ORANGE	80	77	76	77	78	86	75	81	78	72	77	60	73	78	76	82	53	78	86	95
22963	PALMYRA	98	107	107	106	109	112	95	104	98	99	98	74	102	97	102	101	68	100	109	120
22964	PINEY RIVER	88	63	90	61	66	89	65	82	72	60	71	62	52	71	64	79	47	76	86	98
22967	ROSELAND	98	78	114	76	84	104	78	97	84	75	82	70	68	81	81	90	55	90	100	113
22968	RUCKERSVILLE	105	110	91	106	104	97	99	100	96	105	97	78	99	102	97	93	67	96	92	116
22969	SCHUYLER	88	66	88	65	69	90	67	83	74	62	72	63	56	73	67	80	48	77	87	99
22971	SHIPMAN	91	74	101	74	78	96	74	91	78	69	77	68	65	77	77	84	52	84	92	106
22972	SOMERSET	90	81	81	85	83	96	81	91	83	73	82	68	74	85	80	88	56	84	94	105
22973	STANARDSVILLE	87	89	80	91	88	91	83	88	83	82	83	67	83	85	84	84	57	83	87	103
22974	TROY	91	95	88	96	94	96	87	92	87	89	87	69	89	89	89	88	61	88	91	108
22976	TYRO	87	63	90	61	65	89	64	82	71	60	70	61	51	71	64	78	46	75	85	97
22980	WAYNESBORO	80	77	73	78	76	83	79	79	81	76	80	60	77	81	77	83	55	80	85	94
23002	AMELIA COURT HOUSE	95	80	87	80	81	97	79	91	84	75	82	68	70	85	78	89	56	85	94	107
23004	ARVONIA	80	52	77	49	52	78	56	70	64	53	63	55	42	65	52	72	42	66	74	86
23005	ASHLAND	109	119	116	120	119	114	113	113	110	115	111	87	118	111	117	109	79	112	111	131
23009	AYLETT	102	113	94	112	107	102	100	102	96	104	98	80	105	101	102	94	68	97	95	118
23011	BARHAMSVILLE	91	113	101	112	108	111	96	100	97	97	98	75	110	98	106	99	69	98	106	117
23015	BEAVERDAM	110	119	108	122	117	119	107	113	106	108	107	87	112	109	112	107	74	108	112	133
23021	BOHANNON	102	81	131	80	89	107	81	103	85	76	84	75	70	81	88	91	56	95	102	120
23022	BREMO BLUFF	93	70	90	68	72	95	74	89	82	68	79	66	62	81	72	89	53	84	96	105
23023	BRUINGTON	93	67	96	65	69	95	69	87	76	64	75	66	55	76	68	84	49	80	91	104
23024	BUMPASS	98	89	93	87	89	97	85	94	88	86	87	69	79	89	84	91	59	90	94	111
	VIRGINIA	115	112	112	114	111	114	112	112	112	112	112	88	111	114	111	113	79	112	112	132
	UNITED STATES	100	100	100	100	100	100	100	100	100	100	100	100	100	100	100	100	100	100	100	100

ZIP CODE			POPULATION			2000-2009 ANNUAL RATE		HOUSEHOLDS					FAMILIES		
#	POST OFFICE NAME	COUNTY FIPS CODE	2000	2009	2014	% Rate	State Centile	2000	2009	2014	% Annual Rate 2000-2009	2009 Average HH Size	2000	2009	% Annual Rate 2000-2009
23025	CARDINAL	115	430	443	450	0.3	38	178	184	188	0.4	2.36	131	132	0.1
23027	CARTERSVILLE	049	1239	1302	1335	0.5	45	471	511	530	0.9	2.55	334	351	0.5
23030	CHARLES CITY	036	5137	5411	5513	0.6	49	1999	2186	2257	1.0	2.48	1471	1564	0.7
23032	CHURCH VIEW	119	489	530	544	0.9	61	207	230	239	1.1	2.30	145	156	0.8
23035	COBBS CREEK	115	1449	1503	1518	0.4	42	641	670	678	0.5	2.24	471	477	0.1
23038	COLUMBIA	075	1726	2084	2281	2.1	86	682	846	935	2.4	2.46	490	589	2.0
23039	CROZIER	075	950	1101	1193	1.6	78	402	481	526	2.0	2.28	308	359	1.7
23040	CUMBERLAND	049	4294	4565	4705	0.7	54	1570	1721	1792	1.0	2.62	1161	1239	0.7
23043	DELTAVILLE	119	1470	1614	1662	1.0	64	711	799	828	1.3	2.02	455	492	0.8
23045	DIGGS	115	131	135	137	0.3	38	54	56	57	0.4	2.38	40	40	0.0
23047	DOSWELL	085	1861	2128	2264	1.5	76	671	775	827	1.6	2.73	525	590	1.3
23050	DUTTON	115	315	337	348	0.7	54	125	136	140	0.9	2.48	96	102	0.7
23055	FORK UNION	065	673	1050	1211	4.9	97	261	418	486	5.2	2.51	195	302	4.8
23056	FOSTER	115	297	306	311	0.3	38	119	123	125	0.4	2.45	87	88	0.1
23059	GLEN ALLEN	085	15411	26653	31124	6.1	98	5892	10574	12446	6.5	2.52	4320	7609	6.3
23060	GLEN ALLEN	087	26682	31732	34163	1.9	83	10459	12393	13347	1.9	2.54	7307	8279	1.4
23061	GLOUCESTER	073	18911	21537	22833	1.4	73	6892	7993	8525	1.6	2.65	5308	6001	1.3
23062	GLOUCESTER POINT	073	2523	2569	2599	0.2	33	1090	1133	1155	0.4	2.27	742	742	0.0
23063	GOOCHLAND	075	3789	4827	5467	2.7	90	1447	1908	2191	3.0	2.46	1053	1345	2.7
23065	GUM SPRING	075	1379	1976	2254	4.0	95	535	780	898	4.2	2.53	405	575	3.9
23066	GWYNN	115	685	697	702	0.2	33	333	341	345	0.3	2.04	211	208	-0.2
23069	HANOVER	085	3432	3836	4099	1.2	69	959	1120	1215	1.7	2.93	767	875	1.4
23070	HARDYVILLE	119	708	816	868	1.5	76	324	384	410	1.9	2.13	223	255	1.5
23071	HARTFIELD	119	925	996	1030	0.8	58	415	458	478	1.1	2.17	298	319	0.7
23072	HAYES	073	11870	12868	13360	0.9	61	4597	5075	5303	1.1	2.53	3398	3643	0.8
23075	HIGHLAND SPRINGS	087	10328	10606	10852	0.3	38	4003	4162	4273	0.4	2.52	2834	2821	0.0
23079	JAMAICA	119	470	512	530	0.9	61	199	223	233	1.2	2.30	142	155	1.0
23083	JETERSVILLE	007	1910	2028	2092	0.7	54	719	781	811	0.9	2.60	540	570	0.6
23084	KENTS STORE	065	1204	2050	2373	5.9	98	483	822	959	5.9	2.49	368	611	5.6
23085	KING AND QUEEN COURT	097	539	575	592	0.7	54	204	225	234	1.1	2.56	147	157	0.7
23086	KING WILLIAM	101	2498	2821	3070	1.3	72	952	1099	1204	1.6	2.57	749	845	1.3
23089	LANEXA	127	4526	5552	6234	2.2	87	1682	2125	2411	2.6	2.55	1259	1544	2.2
23091	LITTLE PLYMOUTH	097	396	425	438	0.8	58	154	170	177	1.1	2.50	116	125	0.8
23092	LOCUST HILL	119	229	261	275	1.4	73	95	109	116	1.5	2.39	64	71	1.1
23093	LOUISA	109	9744	12520	14156	2.7	90	3783	4998	5707	3.1	2.48	2677	3423	2.7
23102	MAIDENS	075	2549	2990	3239	1.7	79	831	1004	1116	2.1	2.44	630	742	1.8
23103	MANAKIN SABOT	075	3190	4266	4840	3.2	93	1253	1730	1990	3.5	2.42	1000	1353	3.3
23106	MANQUIN	101	1002	1178	1285	1.8	81	352	422	463	2.0	2.79	289	341	1.8
23109	MATHEWS	115	1482	1530	1552	0.3	38	612	636	646	0.4	2.38	449	454	0.1
23110	MATTAPONI	097	796	836	860	0.5	45	347	377	392	0.9	2.22	231	243	0.5
23111	MECHANICSVILLE	085	30870	36242	38504	1.7	79	11700	13761	14625	1.8	2.62	8970	10307	1.5
23112	MIDLOTHIAN	041	39053	47287	51028	2.1	86	13879	17020	18461	2.2	2.78	10919	12933	1.8
23113	MIDLOTHIAN	041	19327	23990	26374	2.4	88	6796	8530	9407	2.5	2.78	5626	6996	2.4
23114	MIDLOTHIAN	041	11566	16821	19094	4.1	96	3818	5754	6600	4.5	2.90	3252	4731	4.1
23116	MECHANICSVILLE	085	23150	27254	29007	1.8	81	7843	9226	9824	1.8	2.94	6655	7691	1.6
23117	MINERAL	109	7071	9224	10413	2.9	92	2775	3704	4211	3.2	2.48	2068	2684	2.9
23119	MOON	115	273	283	286	0.4	42	121	126	128	0.4	2.23	89	90	0.1
23120	MOSELEY	041	3177	4834	5591	4.6	97	1062	1635	1901	4.8	2.96	900	1363	4.6
23123	NEW CANTON	029	1587	1653	1667	0.4	42	637	688	702	0.8	2.40	458	480	0.5
23124	NEW KENT	127	2210	2917	3334	3.0	92	784	1063	1226	3.3	2.72	639	850	3.1
23125	NEW POINT	115	112	115	116	0.3	38	53	55	55	0.4	2.09	36	36	0.0
23126	NEWTOWN	097	511	550	572	0.8	58	204	227	239	1.2	2.42	144	155	0.8
23128	NORTH	115	2201	2325	2379	0.6	49	869	924	947	0.7	2.51	653	677	0.4
23129	OILVILLE	075	336	419	466	2.4	88	135	173	195	2.7	2.42	105	132	2.5
23130	ONEMO	115	356	366	371	0.3	38	148	153	155	0.4	2.37	105	105	0.0
23138	PORT HAYWOOD	115	1234	1266	1285	0.3	38	540	557	566	0.3	2.26	380	380	0.0
23139	POWHATAN	145	20495	26329	29459	2.7	90	6588	8836	10052	3.2	2.69	5351	7034	3.0
23140	PROVIDENCE FORGE	127	3012	4368	5021	4.1	96	1140	1719	2001	4.5	2.54	878	1294	4.3
23141	QUINTON	127	5506	7160	8180	2.9	92	2031	2684	3083	3.1	2.67	1641	2128	2.8
23146	ROCKVILLE	085	3006	3504	3744	1.7	79	1108	1309	1407	1.8	2.66	893	1029	1.5
23148	SAINT STEPHENS CHURC	097	1391	1496	1555	0.8	58	538	599	630	1.2	2.50	380	410	0.8
23149	SALUDA	119	2540	2837	2949	1.2	69	903	1023	1075	1.4	2.54	657	722	1.0
23150	SANDSTON	087	11131	12234	12938	1.0	64	4499	5007	5312	1.2	2.44	3269	3491	0.7
23153	SANDY HOOK	075	1074	1451	1657	3.3	94	409	571	658	3.7	2.54	313	425	3.4
23156	SHACKLEFORDS	097	1736	1871	1940	0.8	58	707	787	826	1.2	2.38	508	549	0.8
23160	STATE FARM	075	770	893	899	1.6	78	27	31	33	1.5	2.61	19	21	1.1
23161	STEVENSVILLE	097	132	141	144	0.7	54	50	55	57	1.0	2.56	36	39	0.9
23163	SUSAN	115	458	469	476	0.3	38	198	204	207	0.3	2.30	136	135	-0.1
23168	TOANO	095	4017	5736	6394	3.9	95	1480	2200	2476	4.4	2.61	1174	1702	4.1
23169	TOPPING	119	1597	1783	1863	1.2	69	675	764	804	1.3	2.33	455	498	1.0
23173	UNIVERSITY OF RICHMO	760	1671	1937	1937	1.6	78	1	1	1	0.0	3.00	1	1	0.0
23175	URBANNA	119	1720	1870	1905	0.9	61	792	875	899	1.1	2.04	539	575	0.7
23176	WAKE	119	390	407	414	0.5	45	151	161	165	0.7	2.53	110	113	0.3
23177	WALKERTON	097	876	949	989	0.9	61	351	392	412	1.2	2.42	253	274	0.9
23180	WATER VIEW	119	235	257	268	1.0	64	92	104	109	1.3	2.47	67	73	0.9
23181	WEST POINT	101	4538	5718	6402	2.5	89	1749	2245	2530	2.7	2.47	1315	1644	2.4
23185	WILLIAMSBURG	095	38737	45373	49329	1.7	79	14785	17846	19647	2.1	2.32	10101	11851	1.7
23186	WILLIAMSBURG	830	1489	1580	1607	0.6	49	15	21	23	3.7	2.57	6	8	3.2
23188	WILLIAMSBURG	095	23744	35091	41244	4.3	96	9221	14222	16916	4.8	2.43	6755	10134	4.5
23192	MONTPELIER	085	5779	6923	7486	2.0	85	2066	2510	2723	2.1	2.76	1691	2007	1.9
23219	RICHMOND	760	1983	2705	2979	3.4	94	987	1443	1632	4.2	1.60	226	274	2.1
23220	RICHMOND	760	29497	30866	31387	0.5	45	13218	13574	13831	0.3	1.96	4496	4405	-0.2
23221	RICHMOND	760	14319	13786	13683	-0.4	8	7858	7555	7492	-0.4	1.80	2764	2527	-1.0
23222	RICHMOND	087	28428	27252	27132	-0.5	6	10796	10341	10307	-0.5	2.59	7038	6513	-0.8
23223	RICHMOND	087	43092	45897	47467	0.7	54	16725	18009	18739	0.8	2.40	10413	10574	0.2
23224	RICHMOND	760	31810	31533	31657	-0.1	18	12367	12141	12189	-0.2	2.57	8032	7605	-0.6
23225	RICHMOND	760	38283	37497	37403	-0.2	14	18105	17633	17585	-0.3	2.09	9264	8607	-0.8
23226	RICHMOND	760	16408	16857	17132	0.3	38	7035	7142	7257	0.2	2.14	3846	3714	-0.4
23227	RICHMOND	087	21621	22155	22687	0.3	38	10074	10233	10470	0.2	2.08	5320	5176	-0.3
23228	RICHMOND	087	32038	33938	35082	0.6	49	14635	15598	16181	0.7	2.09	7854	7848	0.0
23229	RICHMOND	087	31827	32434	33081	0.2	33	13305	13734	14069	0.3	2.34	8825	8683	-0.2
23230	RICHMOND	087	6542	6309	6268	-0.4	8	3008	2908	2897	-0.4	2.09	1526	1374	-1.1
23231	RICHMOND	087	27116	32480	35135	2.0	85	10416	12553	13613	2.0	2.58	7488	8749	1.7
23233	RICHMOND	087	26415	29328	30869	1.1	66	9770	10684	11242	1.0	2.71	7086	7449	0.5
23234	RICHMOND	041	36712	39332	40825	0.7	54	13949	15021	15634	0.8	2.61	9722	10092	0.4
	VIRGINIA					1.2					1.3	2.52			1.0
	UNITED STATES					1.0					1.1	2.59			0.9

ZIP CODE #	POST OFFICE NAME	RACE (%) White 2000	White 2009	Black 2000	Black 2009	Asian/Pacific 2000	Asian/Pacific 2009	% Hispanic Origin 2000	% Hispanic Origin 2009	2009 AGE DISTRIBUTION (%) 0-4	5-9	10-14	15-19	20-24	25-44	45-64	65-84	85+	18+	MEDIAN AGE 2009	% 2009 Males	% 2009 Females
23025	CARDINAL	85.1	82.8	14.0	15.6	0.0	0.0	0.7	1.1	4.7	5.0	5.2	5.0	3.6	19.6	35.0	18.3	3.6	81.5	49.2	49.2	50.8
23027	CARTERSVILLE	67.2	63.4	30.5	33.2	0.1	0.2	1.5	2.3	7.8	7.9	7.8	6.8	4.4	26.2	25.3	12.4	1.5	72.2	38.0	48.9	51.1
23030	CHARLES CITY	37.0	40.4	56.2	51.9	0.1	0.1	0.6	0.9	5.2	6.1	6.2	5.8	4.6	23.5	33.7	13.4	1.4	78.9	43.9	49.8	50.2
23032	CHURCH VIEW	65.8	62.1	32.3	35.7	0.2	0.4	0.4	0.6	4.0	4.3	5.3	6.4	4.5	20.2	34.3	18.7	2.3	82.3	47.9	48.5	51.5
23035	COBBS CREEK	87.1	85.0	11.2	12.6	0.1	0.3	0.8	1.4	4.3	4.7	5.1	5.2	3.2	20.8	34.8	19.5	2.3	82.3	49.4	48.3	51.7
23038	COLUMBIA	64.3	59.8	32.6	35.7	0.6	0.9	1.4	2.2	5.6	5.9	6.8	6.6	4.8	24.9	31.3	12.7	1.4	77.6	42.1	48.5	51.5
23039	CROZIER	78.5	74.8	20.1	23.1	0.6	1.2	0.7	1.4	4.5	5.4	6.5	5.8	3.4	22.1	36.4	14.4	1.5	79.8	46.2	51.1	48.9
23040	CUMBERLAND	58.4	54.9	39.6	42.4	0.1	0.2	1.9	2.8	6.2	6.2	6.9	7.4	5.2	24.6	29.2	12.6	1.6	75.6	40.5	47.8	52.2
23043	DELTAVILLE	95.4	94.3	3.4	4.0	0.2	0.3	0.3	0.7	2.3	2.5	3.2	4.1	2.5	13.6	37.4	29.8	4.5	89.4	58.9	48.1	51.9
23045	DIGGS	85.4	83.0	13.8	15.6	0.0	0.0	0.8	0.7	4.4	5.2	5.2	5.2	3.0	19.3	37.0	17.8	3.0	80.7	50.3	48.1	51.9
23047	DOSWELL	76.2	73.0	21.6	23.8	0.1	0.2	0.9	1.5	5.1	5.5	6.3	6.0	4.8	22.4	34.5	13.8	1.7	79.3	45.0	49.5	50.5
23050	DUTTON	86.6	84.0	11.1	12.5	0.3	0.6	1.3	1.8	5.3	5.6	5.9	6.2	3.9	22.6	32.9	15.7	1.8	79.2	45.3	49.0	51.0
23055	FORK UNION	57.9	52.5	40.3	44.9	0.3	0.5	0.7	1.0	5.4	5.5	6.7	6.4	5.2	22.2	30.5	15.8	2.3	78.4	43.8	47.4	52.6
23056	FOSTER	85.1	83.0	13.9	15.7	0.0	0.0	0.7	1.3	4.9	4.9	5.2	5.2	3.6	19.6	35.0	18.0	3.6	81.4	49.2	48.7	51.3
23059	GLEN ALLEN	85.3	81.2	9.4	10.8	3.4	5.0	1.7	2.7	8.4	7.4	6.7	5.4	4.9	31.8	26.6	8.1	0.8	74.0	36.8	49.6	50.4
23060	GLEN ALLEN	75.9	70.3	16.5	18.5	5.3	7.9	1.7	2.8	7.9	7.7	7.4	6.2	5.7	31.2	26.3	6.7	1.0	73.2	35.9	48.0	52.0
23061	GLOUCESTER	85.1	82.6	12.0	13.4	0.5	0.7	1.6	2.7	5.8	6.2	6.6	7.2	5.2	24.4	31.5	11.2	1.9	76.8	41.4	49.0	51.0
23062	GLOUCESTER POINT	90.4	88.3	5.7	6.3	1.3	1.8	1.5	2.8	5.3	5.3	5.3	5.5	6.5	27.1	29.6	13.6	1.9	80.8	41.1	49.3	50.7
23063	GOOCHLAND	60.3	55.3	37.7	41.9	0.2	0.3	1.0	1.4	5.4	5.9	6.6	6.4	4.3	23.0	32.6	13.6	2.2	77.7	44.0	48.9	51.1
23065	GUM SPRING	78.4	74.8	19.7	22.5	0.4	0.6	0.8	1.3	5.9	6.6	7.1	6.2	3.9	24.8	33.2	10.9	1.2	76.3	42.3	49.5	50.5
23066	GWYNN	97.4	96.1	0.4	0.6	0.7	1.1	0.3	0.6	3.7	4.3	4.2	3.4	2.6	17.8	33.1	26.8	4.0	85.7	55.7	50.8	49.2
23069	HANOVER	69.5	66.2	29.0	31.7	0.3	0.4	1.0	1.7	3.8	4.4	5.2	12.3	4.9	24.5	31.5	12.1	1.2	77.2	41.4	55.9	44.1
23070	HARDYVILLE	92.8	91.1	5.4	6.3	0.3	0.4	0.3	0.4	3.6	3.9	4.5	5.3	2.9	16.8	33.5	26.8	2.7	84.6	53.8	48.4	51.6
23071	HARTFIELD	78.6	75.8	19.8	21.9	0.1	0.2	0.4	0.7	4.3	5.2	6.2	6.4	3.3	20.0	33.6	18.6	2.3	79.9	47.8	48.8	51.2
23072	HAYES	88.5	86.4	8.4	9.2	1.0	1.3	1.6	2.6	5.9	6.2	6.4	6.4	5.1	25.4	30.4	12.8	1.4	77.6	41.2	49.4	50.6
23075	HIGHLAND SPRINGS	48.9	43.5	47.0	51.0	0.6	0.8	1.6	2.5	7.8	7.4	7.3	7.1	6.5	28.3	25.1	8.8	1.7	73.1	34.8	46.2	53.8
23079	JAMAICA	64.5	60.7	33.3	36.7	0.2	0.2	0.6	1.0	3.9	4.7	5.7	6.4	4.3	21.7	35.0	16.2	2.1	81.6	46.6	49.2	50.8
23083	JETERSVILLE	71.0	67.8	27.4	30.0	0.4	0.5	1.2	1.9	6.2	6.4	6.7	7.0	5.6	25.3	28.8	12.7	1.3	76.4	40.1	51.1	48.9
23084	KENTS STORE	63.8	57.2	33.3	39.2	0.3	0.3	1.2	1.5	6.0	6.3	7.6	7.1	4.5	24.0	30.8	12.1	1.6	75.4	41.2	48.4	51.6
23085	KING AND QUEEN COURT	57.9	53.9	39.5	42.8	0.2	0.2	0.7	1.4	5.0	5.7	6.3	5.7	4.5	21.9	33.7	15.3	1.7	79.5	45.5	49.0	51.0
23086	KING WILLIAM	69.1	65.3	26.5	29.1	0.2	0.3	0.6	0.8	7.1	7.3	7.4	5.9	4.2	27.6	28.7	10.5	1.2	74.5	39.2	50.5	49.5
23089	LANEXA	81.8	78.5	15.2	17.5	0.3	0.5	1.3	2.2	5.2	5.5	6.3	6.7	4.3	25.5	32.6	12.6	1.3	78.6	42.9	51.1	48.9
23091	LITTLE PLYMOUTH	76.8	74.1	20.2	22.4	0.0	0.0	0.5	0.5	4.5	5.2	5.9	6.6	4.0	24.7	32.2	15.1	1.9	80.2	44.5	49.9	50.1
23092	LOCUST HILL	73.2	69.0	25.4	28.4	0.0	0.0	0.9	1.1	4.2	5.0	5.7	5.4	3.8	19.9	36.0	18.0	1.9	81.2	48.9	49.8	50.2
23093	LOUISA	70.5	67.3	27.5	30.0	0.3	0.4	0.8	1.1	6.0	6.2	6.6	6.4	5.3	23.9	30.2	13.3	2.1	77.2	41.8	48.8	51.2
23102	MAIDENS	69.7	66.3	29.3	32.2	0.2	0.4	0.5	0.8	4.2	5.0	5.7	5.1	4.8	32.4	32.1	9.6	1.2	81.9	41.3	52.7	47.3
23103	MANAKIN SABOT	83.2	80.0	15.3	17.8	0.8	1.1	1.1	1.7	4.6	5.5	7.1	6.7	2.9	19.5	35.2	17.2	1.4	78.2	47.2	49.6	50.4
23106	MANQUIN	68.5	64.1	29.1	32.7	0.1	0.2	0.7	1.0	6.5	7.2	7.5	6.4	3.9	26.9	30.8	9.9	0.9	74.8	39.9	50.8	49.2
23109	MATHEWS	85.9	83.7	12.8	14.4	0.1	0.1	0.8	1.4	4.5	4.8	5.2	5.0	3.4	20.0	35.1	19.0	3.1	82.1	49.5	48.6	51.4
23110	MATTAPONI	62.6	59.0	35.9	38.9	0.0	0.0	0.4	0.6	5.5	5.6	5.6	5.3	4.8	22.4	29.5	17.6	3.7	80.1	45.5	48.1	51.9
23111	MECHANICSVILLE	91.1	89.1	6.4	7.2	0.8	1.3	1.1	1.8	7.0	7.0	7.0	6.5	5.0	27.9	27.9	10.4	1.4	74.7	38.5	48.6	51.4
23112	MIDLOTHIAN	87.3	83.2	8.8	11.1	1.9	2.7	1.9	3.4	7.5	7.9	8.2	7.6	5.0	28.0	28.4	6.6	0.8	71.3	36.6	48.8	51.2
23113	MIDLOTHIAN	90.8	88.0	5.0	5.6	2.7	4.3	1.4	2.3	4.9	6.3	7.8	8.2	4.5	19.1	36.6	11.0	1.6	75.4	44.4	48.7	51.3
23114	MIDLOTHIAN	89.7	86.0	5.4	6.6	3.6	5.4	1.3	2.3	6.3	7.5	8.6	8.1	4.4	25.2	32.6	6.4	0.9	72.2	38.8	49.3	50.7
23116	MECHANICSVILLE	91.1	89.0	6.5	7.4	1.1	1.7	0.9	1.5	6.9	7.6	7.6	7.5	4.0	24.8	30.7	9.8	1.0	72.8	39.8	49.9	50.1
23117	MINERAL	78.1	75.6	20.1	21.8	0.3	0.5	0.8	1.2	5.0	5.7	6.1	5.6	4.0	23.0	35.5	13.8	1.3	79.7	45.3	50.4	49.6
23119	MOON	86.8	84.5	11.7	13.1	0.0	0.4	0.7	1.8	4.6	4.6	5.3	4.9	3.2	20.8	34.3	19.4	2.8	81.6	49.4	49.1	50.9
23120	MOSELEY	93.5	92.0	4.8	5.5	0.8	1.3	0.8	1.5	6.4	7.5	8.3	6.9	3.5	25.1	32.6	8.8	1.0	73.0	40.6	49.2	50.8
23123	NEW CANTON	54.5	50.5	43.6	46.8	0.1	0.1	1.7	2.6	5.5	5.5	5.9	7.0	5.3	24.0	29.8	15.2	1.8	78.8	43.0	47.8	52.2
23124	NEW KENT	77.1	72.7	20.2	23.9	0.5	0.6	0.8	1.2	6.0	6.7	7.4	7.0	4.1	25.3	33.3	9.3	1.0	75.3	41.2	50.2	49.8
23125	NEW POINT	88.4	87.0	10.7	12.2	0.0	0.0	0.9	1.7	4.3	5.2	5.2	5.2	3.5	19.1	33.9	20.9	2.6	82.6	49.3	47.8	52.2
23126	NEWTOWN	54.8	50.7	40.9	44.0	0.4	0.7	0.8	1.1	5.1	5.5	6.0	6.0	4.5	23.5	32.5	14.9	2.0	79.6	44.6	49.3	50.7
23128	NORTH	86.3	84.1	11.7	13.0	0.3	0.5	1.0	1.8	4.9	5.3	5.8	5.8	3.7	21.6	34.0	16.9	2.1	80.2	46.7	49.2	50.8
23129	OILVILLE	81.3	78.3	18.2	21.0	0.0	0.0	0.6	1.2	4.3	5.5	6.9	6.9	3.6	19.6	37.9	13.8	1.4	79.0	46.7	49.2	50.8
23130	ONEMO	86.3	84.4	12.3	13.9	0.3	0.3	0.8	1.6	4.4	4.9	4.9	4.9	3.8	18.6	35.5	19.7	3.3	82.2	50.0	48.6	51.4
23138	PORT HAYWOOD	87.2	85.0	11.8	13.3	0.2	0.3	1.0	1.6	4.3	4.7	5.1	4.8	3.7	18.4	35.9	20.1	3.0	82.7	50.3	48.8	51.2
23139	POWHATAN	80.4	77.8	18.1	20.0	0.2	0.3	0.8	1.4	5.8	6.1	6.6	7.5	5.0	29.2	29.4	9.5	0.9	76.8	39.4	54.6	45.4
23140	PROVIDENCE FORGE	51.3	58.9	35.7	28.3	0.2	0.3	1.3	2.3	5.3	6.0	6.6	6.7	4.4	25.1	32.3	12.3	1.3	78.0	42.5	49.3	50.7
23141	QUINTON	86.6	83.7	10.1	11.9	0.8	1.2	1.2	2.0	5.7	6.4	7.2	6.7	4.2	23.6	35.0	10.5	0.8	76.5	42.8	49.5	50.5
23146	ROCKVILLE	87.6	85.3	11.1	12.8	0.6	0.8	0.4	0.7	5.7	6.5	7.7	6.8	3.3	21.0	34.8	12.8	1.4	75.4	44.4	48.4	51.6
23148	SAINT STEPHENS CHURC	54.7	50.7	40.9	44.1	0.5	0.7	0.8	1.1	5.2	5.6	6.1	6.0	4.6	23.2	32.5	14.8	1.9	79.5	44.5	49.3	50.7
23149	SALUDA	72.9	69.6	25.3	27.8	0.1	0.1	1.0	1.7	4.1	4.7	5.5	6.4	5.2	22.2	32.3	16.2	3.3	81.7	46.2	49.9	50.1
23150	SANDSTON	83.5	80.4	13.2	14.7	0.4	0.6	1.7	3.0	6.1	6.1	6.2	6.4	5.6	26.1	29.2	12.5	1.7	77.4	40.4	48.1	51.9
23153	SANDY HOOK	75.8	71.6	21.7	24.8	0.6	0.8	1.0	1.4	6.5	7.2	7.6	6.3	4.0	25.3	32.0	9.9	1.1	74.5	41.3	49.0	51.0
23156	SHACKLEFORDS	68.4	65.0	29.0	31.4	0.2	0.3	1.3	2.1	5.0	5.5	5.9	6.5	4.3	24.1	32.4	14.2	2.2	79.6	44.1	48.3	51.7
23160	STATE FARM	34.9	30.8	64.7	68.9	0.1	0.1	0.4	0.7	0.3	0.3	0.4	1.1	9.7	73.0	13.5	1.3	0.1	98.7	35.2	60.8	39.2
23161	STEVENSVILLE	58.3	54.6	39.4	42.6	0.0	0.0	0.8	0.7	5.0	5.7	6.4	5.7	4.3	21.3	35.5	14.9	1.4	79.4	46.1	47.5	52.5
23163	SUSAN	88.4	86.1	10.5	11.9	0.2	0.4	1.1	1.7	4.3	4.7	4.9	4.7	3.8	17.9	35.8	21.1	2.8	83.2	50.6	49.0	51.0
23168	TOANO	76.1	73.0	21.6	23.7	0.7	1.0	1.0	1.7	6.0	6.7	7.3	7.0	4.3	23.8	33.4	10.4	1.0	75.6	41.8	49.3	50.7
23169	TOPPING	78.0	74.9	21.0	23.6	0.1	0.1	0.8	1.3	4.5	4.8	5.2	5.2	4.0	21.1	34.7	18.5	2.1	82.1	48.4	48.8	51.2
23173	UNIVERSITY OF RICHMO	89.0	84.1	5.6	7.3	1.4	2.1	2.3	4.3	0.1	0.1	0.1	43.0	54.7	0.9	0.8	0.4	0.0	99.5	20.6	48.6	51.4
23175	URBANNA	80.5	77.8	18.6	20.8	0.1	0.1	0.5	0.7	3.4	3.6	4.2	5.0	4.5	18.4	36.3	21.4	3.2	85.6	51.6	46.2	53.8
23176	WAKE	80.3	77.6	19.2	21.6	0.3	0.2	0.3	0.5	5.4	5.7	5.9	5.7	4.2	20.9	32.4	17.7	2.2	79.4	46.4	47.7	52.3
23177	WALKERTON	54.3	50.3	42.0	45.3	0.1	0.2	0.8	1.2	5.3	5.9	6.3	5.9	4.5	21.9	33.4	14.9	1.9	78.9	45.1	49.3	50.7
23180	WATER VIEW	63.7	59.1	34.2	37.7	0.0	0.4	0.9	1.2	3.9	5.1	6.2	6.6	3.9	22.2	36.6	13.6	1.9	80.2	45.8	48.6	51.4
23181	WEST POINT	75.3	71.8	21.0	23.4	0.7	1.1	1.4	2.1	5.4	5.5	6.3	7.1	5.1	23.7	29.3	14.9	2.5	77.6	42.9	48.1	51.9
23185	WILLIAMSBURG	81.1	78.2	14.0	14.8	2.5	3.7	1.9	3.0	4.5	4.6	4.8	8.2	10.1	20.9	28.1	16.2	2.6	82.9	42.3	47.5	52.5
23186	WILLIAMSBURG	84.5	80.1	6.9	7.5	6.5	9.6	3.0	4.4	0.8	0.3	0.4	36.8	48.7	4.2	3.3	3.6	2.0	98.2	21.2	45.1	54.9
23188	WILLIAMSBURG	80.1	77.2	16.0	17.4	1.6	2.3	1.9	2.9	5.6	5.6	6.0	6.0	5.1	23.9	29.9	16.2	1.8	79.1	43.5	48.0	52.0
23192	MONTPELIER	82.5	79.7	16.0	18.2	0.3	0.5	0.5	0.8	6.2	6.9	7.7	7.4	4.4	23.0	32.5	10.9	1.1	74.5	41.6	49.2	50.8
23219	RICHMOND	23.9	25.7	71.2	67.3	1.7	2.8	1.0	1.8	4.7	5.4	5.0	5.8	10.4	35.9	20.9	10.5	1.5	82.5	34.2	52.0	48.0
23220	RICHMOND	48.4	42.4	45.5	48.9	3.2	4.4	1.9	3.0	3.9	3.7	3.2	11.8	17.8	29.6	20.5	8.0	1.6	87.1	29.3	48.6	51.4
23221	RICHMOND	83.3	78.7	12.9	15.5	1.6	2.3	1.6	2.8	4.1	3.6	3.4	3.4	10.0	39.1	24.2	9.9	2.3	87.1	36.9	49.3	50.7
23222	RICHMOND	8.5	7.3	89.5	90.3	0.3	0.4	1.0	1.3	6.5	6.9	7.1	7.8	6.5	22.7	27.3	13.1	2.0	74.6	39.0	45.1	54.9
23223	RICHMOND	13.7	13.0	84.3	84.4	0.3	0.5	1.0	1.4	7.3	6.9	6.5	7.2	7.6	27.9	24.3	10.4	1.8	74.8	34.9	46.8	53.2
23224	RICHMOND	17.8	14.5	74.9	75.5	1.2	1.5	6.0	8.6	8.2	7.7	6.8	7.5	8.5	27.3	24.0	8.9	1.2	73.0	32.6	46.6	53.4
23225	RICHMOND	46.6	39.9	46.9	51.1	2.0	2.6	3.7	5.7	6.4	5.7	5.3	5.7	8.5	29.6	25.5	10.7	2.6	79.4	37.1	46.2	53.8
23226	RICHMOND	88.4	83.2	5.9	7.4	2.5	4.0	3.2	6.2	5.4	4.9	4.8	7.6	9.4	27.8	23.7	12.7	3.6	82.2	38.2	47.4	52.6
23227	RICHMOND	49.3	44.4	47.1	50.6	1.3	1.8	1.5	2.3	6.0	5.3	4.9	4.6	6.5	27.2	26.0	13.8	5.7	81.2	41.6	44.6	55.4
23228	RICHMOND	68.7	63.3	23.2	25.1	3.9	5.5	3.4	5.4	5.8	5.2	5.1	5.6	7.9	30.6	24.0	12.6	3.1	80.6	38.2	47.0	53.0
23229	RICHMOND	90.1	86.8	5.0	5.8	3.2	4.8	1.9	3.2	5.2	5.5	6.3	6.4	5.2	23.1	29.3	15.6	3.4	79.0	43.7	47.2	52.8
23230	RICHMOND	66.5	61.4	17.3	17.9	9.3	11.8	8.3	11.3	6.1	4.9	4.8	5.8	7.1	31.8	23.6	12.4	3.4	80.7	37.9	48.8	51.2
23231	RICHMOND	47.6	43.8	49.5	52.4	0.5	0.7	1.1	1.6	6.8	7.0	6.9	7.1	6.2	26.1	28.7	9.9	1.3	74.9	37.6	47.1	52.9
23233	RICHMOND	90.3	86.3	3.2	3.8	5.1	7.7	1.7	3.0	8.1	8.8	8.4	6.3	4.7	28.9	27.5	5.7	1.6	70.5	36.6	48.6	51.4
23234	RICHMOND	44.6	39.3	45.9	47.3	2.7	3.6	7.6	11.4	7.4	7.3	6.9	7.1	7.1	28.4	25.4	9.4	1.1	74.2	34.9	48.5	51.5
	VIRGINIA	72.3	68.8	19.6	20.1	3.7	5.1	4.7	7.0	6.5	6.4	6.5	6.9	6.9	27.5	27.2	10.5	1.6	76.7	37.7	49.2	50.8
	UNITED STATES	75.1	72.0	12.3	12.7	3.8	4.6	12.5	15.7	6.8	6.7	6.6	7.1	6.9	27.0	26.0	10.9	1.9	75.7	36.9	49.2	50.8

INCOME

ZIP CODE #	POST OFFICE NAME	2009 Per Capita Income	2009 HH Income Base	2009 HOUSEHOLD INCOME DISTRIBUTION (%) Less than $25,000	$25,000 to $49,999	$50,000 to $99,999	$100,000 to $149,999	$150,000 or More	MEDIAN HOUSEHOLD INCOME 2009	2014	2009 National Centile	2009 State Centile	2009 Home Value Base	2009 HOME VALUE DISTRIBUTION (%) Less than $50,000	$50,000 to $89,999	$90,000 to $174,999	$175,000 to $399,999	$400,000 or More	2009 Median Home Value
23025	CARDINAL	25582	184	16.8	30.4	41.3	8.7	2.7	51645	55215	65	62	155	5.2	7.7	34.2	32.3	20.6	183036
23027	CARTERSVILLE	21169	511	21.5	21.5	49.7	7.2	0.0	54142	58267	70	67	393	6.6	13.7	43.0	33.8	2.8	141944
23030	CHARLES CITY	23037	2186	22.9	26.4	39.8	8.7	2.2	50511	53358	62	59	1828	7.4	20.2	43.9	21.3	7.2	134221
23032	CHURCH VIEW	20511	230	28.3	33.0	31.7	6.1	0.9	41997	43239	39	36	190	6.3	14.2	53.2	24.2	2.1	134524
23035	COBBS CREEK	28476	670	16.3	27.3	42.1	10.1	4.2	54452	58527	70	67	554	3.2	5.8	26.7	44.4	19.9	219355
23038	COLUMBIA	21627	846	35.0	22.6	30.6	9.2	2.6	43089	45104	43	38	682	6.9	15.0	41.1	27.9	9.2	146552
23039	CROZIER	34472	481	10.8	17.9	48.9	17.5	5.0	68117	72423	86	81	410	0.0	0.0	21.0	53.2	25.9	260811
23040	CUMBERLAND	17772	1721	28.2	32.2	33.0	6.4	0.2	41276	44163	37	34	1405	12.2	14.7	44.8	22.9	5.3	124287
23043	DELTAVILLE	29039	799	21.0	31.0	37.3	6.3	4.4	48039	49018	57	52	668	7.2	8.4	20.1	41.5	22.9	244286
23045	DIGGS	25468	56	16.1	32.1	41.1	8.9	1.8	51001	55932	64	60	47	0.0	8.5	36.2	31.9	23.4	190625
23047	DOSWELL	33223	775	9.9	18.5	35.0	23.9	12.8	80111	84336	92	87	631	2.7	2.4	23.1	51.2	20.6	266333
23050	DUTTON	26333	136	11.0	27.2	49.3	9.6	2.9	59288	60674	77	73	118	0.8	5.9	24.6	56.8	11.9	218750
23055	FORK UNION	22952	418	21.8	30.9	36.6	5.5	5.3	48134	49438	57	53	314	6.7	10.2	37.9	34.7	10.5	162069
23056	FOSTER	24768	123	17.1	30.1	42.3	8.1	2.4	51692	55583	65	62	103	6.8	7.8	31.1	33.0	21.4	186250
23059	GLEN ALLEN	43890	10574	5.5	14.4	36.6	21.9	21.6	89961	92147	95	91	8018	2.3	0.6	11.6	52.6	33.0	334647
23060	GLEN ALLEN	32739	12393	7.6	18.3	47.4	20.1	6.6	75891	77419	90	85	9942	0.2	0.5	33.5	64.0	1.8	206737
23061	GLOUCESTER	23454	7993	14.2	30.4	43.7	8.4	3.3	55485	58552	72	69	6666	4.8	6.5	30.4	49.1	9.1	194277
23062	GLOUCESTER POINT	29378	1133	14.3	27.8	43.8	10.6	3.5	58673	60307	76	73	793	4.4	0.0	20.2	57.9	17.5	226528
23063	GOOCHLAND	23300	1908	23.8	23.1	42.4	8.8	1.9	52385	54346	67	64	1570	6.1	12.0	32.2	40.4	9.2	174204
23065	GUM SPRING	26057	780	15.8	25.5	43.5	12.8	2.4	58497	62467	76	73	671	5.4	5.2	35.9	45.2	8.3	182730
23066	GWYNN	27745	341	19.4	32.0	38.4	8.2	2.1	49074	52928	59	56	295	2.0	3.4	49.5	40.7	4.4	166159
23069	HANOVER	25590	1120	14.2	20.4	34.5	24.3	6.7	68341	71666	86	82	964	5.2	2.9	31.0	50.0	10.9	205090
23070	HARDYVILLE	28145	384	15.4	32.3	42.4	8.1	1.8	52305	53962	66	64	339	14.7	2.7	20.9	47.2	14.5	208929
23071	HARTFIELD	27365	458	24.0	27.5	33.6	10.0	4.8	48140	49543	57	53	381	8.1	2.4	33.9	35.2	20.5	189527
23072	HAYES	24112	5075	18.6	25.9	42.0	10.6	2.9	55555	58485	72	69	3953	7.3	5.7	29.0	47.1	10.9	193780
23075	HIGHLAND SPRINGS	22248	4162	20.9	28.4	43.4	5.6	1.7	50609	55042	63	59	2457	0.2	10.9	78.5	9.7	0.7	125377
23079	JAMAICA	20489	223	27.4	33.6	31.4	6.3	1.3	41369	42469	37	34	183	3.3	9.8	56.8	26.2	3.8	140160
23083	JETERSVILLE	19744	781	23.4	32.1	37.8	4.6	2.0	46132	49271	52	47	647	8.8	14.8	35.1	36.5	4.8	147962
23084	KENTS STORE	24388	822	22.6	26.0	38.4	8.9	4.0	51082	53971	64	61	700	4.0	8.7	43.9	34.7	8.7	164048
23085	KING AND QUEEN COURT	21931	225	27.6	24.4	37.3	6.2	4.4	48266	49670	57	53	190	17.9	6.3	44.2	22.1	9.5	141447
23086	KING WILLIAM	24766	1099	12.6	22.7	53.0	10.6	1.0	62389	65174	80	77	938	4.4	5.0	43.8	43.4	3.4	171250
23089	LANEXA	26095	2125	16.1	25.5	44.8	9.3	4.3	60588	64737	78	75	1787	5.8	8.2	30.4	39.6	16.1	196848
23091	LITTLE PLYMOUTH	21174	170	21.2	33.5	36.5	7.1	1.8	45912	47730	51	46	147	17.0	6.1	41.5	27.9	7.5	142262
23092	LOCUST HILL	21069	109	24.8	36.7	30.3	5.5	2.8	41391	44088	37	34	90	11.1	4.4	41.1	30.0	13.3	156250
23093	LOUISA	22009	4998	25.0	28.4	36.7	7.2	2.7	46609	49553	53	49	3728	8.0	6.5	44.9	34.0	6.5	159408
23102	MAIDENS	27360	1004	13.5	19.4	45.7	17.2	4.1	66143	70593	84	81	870	2.4	1.6	23.3	57.1	15.5	226224
23103	MANAKIN SABOT	57456	1730	4.3	10.8	34.5	23.9	26.5	100483	104232	97	93	1525	0.5	0.0	15.1	40.2	44.2	360667
23106	MANQUIN	23162	422	12.1	27.0	47.9	11.1	1.9	60917	63943	79	76	370	5.7	2.4	41.4	47.6	3.0	175962
23109	MATHEWS	25952	636	16.5	28.6	42.8	9.1	3.0	53132	56210	68	65	531	4.0	7.0	31.6	37.3	20.2	194750
23110	MATTAPONI	21160	377	28.6	36.3	25.5	7.7	1.9	38790	40989	29	26	292	12.0	6.8	65.4	11.6	4.1	121382
23111	MECHANICSVILLE	31259	13761	7.9	18.8	47.7	19.7	6.0	74014	77588	89	85	11361	0.7	0.5	20.5	70.7	7.6	219497
23112	MIDLOTHIAN	33650	17020	5.0	13.7	47.6	23.8	10.0	81758	85904	93	88	13922	0.6	0.5	35.6	57.2	6.2	201655
23113	MIDLOTHIAN	48509	8530	5.1	9.5	30.3	24.7	30.4	108907	113085	98	95	7544	0.5	0.1	12.0	42.0	45.3	381191
23114	MIDLOTHIAN	36678	5754	4.0	7.2	44.8	27.1	16.9	92741	98477	96	92	5234	0.7	0.0	14.4	80.4	4.4	251494
23116	MECHANICSVILLE	36438	9226	4.7	11.1	39.5	28.6	16.1	92025	100122	95	91	8323	0.8	0.7	10.1	67.6	20.9	286266
23117	MINERAL	23318	3704	20.7	29.2	37.6	9.2	3.3	50072	52378	61	58	3093	7.8	9.2	37.7	32.5	12.8	165593
23119	MOON	28309	126	15.9	27.0	43.7	9.5	4.0	55086	57511	71	69	104	1.9	6.7	27.9	43.3	20.2	216667
23120	MOSELEY	32787	1635	7.4	13.3	37.5	30.8	10.9	86726	90698	94	89	1494	2.4	2.1	17.0	55.8	22.7	262698
23123	NEW CANTON	18389	688	35.2	25.9	33.3	4.9	0.7	41017	42293	36	33	524	9.0	20.4	51.7	15.3	3.6	117188
23124	NEW KENT	27395	1063	7.7	24.9	48.1	14.5	4.8	66035	68788	84	81	949	2.7	3.2	23.8	63.9	6.4	226337
23125	NEW POINT	25304	55	20.0	30.9	43.6	5.5	0.0	48665	48665	58	55	47	0.0	2.1	36.2	42.6	19.1	188750
23126	NEWTOWN	20982	227	30.4	30.0	31.3	6.6	1.8	40873	43024	36	32	184	13.0	13.6	45.7	22.3	5.4	131522
23128	NORTH	25553	924	13.5	27.9	45.8	9.5	3.2	56268	60024	73	71	785	2.8	6.9	26.6	47.6	16.1	210746
23129	OILVILLE	38609	173	10.4	8.1	50.9	19.1	11.6	80634	82660	92	87	150	0.0	0.0	15.3	48.0	36.7	300000
23130	ONEMO	23960	153	19.0	30.7	41.8	7.2	1.3	50275	54563	62	59	129	1.6	5.4	38.0	34.9	20.2	184028
23138	PORT HAYWOOD	24783	557	19.6	31.4	40.4	6.8	1.8	48898	53424	59	55	471	2.3	5.1	36.3	36.3	20.0	185387
23139	POWHATAN	27465	8836	10.8	21.2	45.8	16.2	6.0	65832	69665	84	81	7758	1.9	1.6	28.0	55.3	13.3	226963
23140	PROVIDENCE FORGE	24663	1719	20.7	21.3	44.0	11.4	2.6	60166	63236	78	74	1517	5.3	11.7	37.0	35.7	10.2	165738
23141	QUINTON	30181	2684	7.1	17.3	50.2	20.2	5.2	72511	76763	88	84	2383	2.7	2.4	28.7	62.2	3.9	215494
23146	ROCKVILLE	37223	1309	7.0	13.0	39.3	30.3	10.5	87761	94139	95	90	1174	0.3	1.3	16.6	50.7	31.1	300448
23148	SAINT STEPHENS CHURC	20333	599	30.6	29.9	30.6	6.8	2.2	40842	43110	35	32	487	12.9	13.3	46.4	22.0	5.3	130943
23149	SALUDA	23468	1023	23.6	25.8	39.7	6.4	4.6	50546	52946	62	59	847	6.3	9.3	40.5	31.3	12.6	156607
23150	SANDSTON	26926	5007	12.7	27.4	47.7	9.3	2.9	59683	63155	77	74	3838	6.2	4.4	54.3	33.5	1.7	154444
23153	SANDY HOOK	26441	571	14.0	24.9	42.4	17.2	1.6	63059	67245	81	78	504	4.4	5.8	33.1	48.0	8.7	192347
23156	SHACKLEFORDS	20032	787	22.5	39.0	32.7	5.3	0.5	42585	45099	41	37	637	11.8	7.5	51.0	26.2	3.5	134441
23160	STATE FARM	19103	31	6.5	16.1	32.3	22.6	22.6	90857	87588	95	91	21	28.6	0.0	0.0	33.3	38.1	364286
23161	STEVENSVILLE	22332	55	27.3	21.8	40.0	5.5	5.5	50842	51080	63	60	47	19.1	4.3	42.6	23.4	10.6	143750
23163	SUSAN	23179	204	21.6	32.8	38.7	5.9	1.0	44537	51328	47	42	173	1.2	3.5	37.0	39.3	19.1	185985
23168	TOANO	26806	2200	14.0	23.1	47.7	11.0	4.0	63985	69418	82	79	1857	9.4	3.7	17.9	55.9	13.1	221845
23169	TOPPING	21034	764	27.4	35.2	30.5	5.1	1.8	41431	42966	37	34	618	11.3	9.2	33.3	34.6	11.5	162500
23173	UNIVERSITY OF RICHMO	17027	0	0.0	0.0	0.0	0.0	0.0	0	0	0	0	0	0.0	0.0	0.0	0.0	0.0	0
23175	URBANNA	30450	875	21.9	27.9	37.0	8.8	4.3	50140	50898	61	58	694	4.6	7.9	37.5	36.9	13.1	175000
23176	WAKE	21494	161	28.0	29.2	30.4	8.7	3.7	45183	45471	49	44	132	9.8	7.6	27.3	35.6	19.7	189583
23177	WALKERTON	22729	392	26.8	24.0	39.0	6.4	3.8	49183	51194	59	56	330	16.4	7.6	42.4	25.8	7.9	143333
23180	WATER VIEW	18918	104	26.9	34.6	30.8	5.8	1.9	40552	42323	35	31	85	2.4	8.2	56.5	28.2	4.7	142614
23181	WEST POINT	27712	2245	16.9	24.1	40.4	13.1	5.5	61068	63823	79	76	1772	3.9	8.9	40.2	39.6	7.4	169923
23185	WILLIAMSBURG	36614	17846	13.3	20.4	37.3	16.3	12.7	68497	72640	86	82	12771	4.9	3.0	17.7	38.3	36.1	313678
23186	WILLIAMSBURG	15688	21	33.3	23.8	23.8	4.8	14.3	37357	37362	25	21	8	0.0	0.0	0.0	25.0	75.0	500000
23188	WILLIAMSBURG	33463	14222	13.5	17.3	43.7	16.9	8.6	70098	74940	87	83	10353	3.5	1.6	16.0	48.4	30.4	291775
23192	MONTPELIER	28482	2510	9.8	21.8	43.8	18.8	5.8	69664	74723	87	83	2203	1.5	3.9	20.4	47.7	26.5	268435
23219	RICHMOND	19015	1443	58.8	26.5	11.7	1.9	1.2	19309	20975	1	1	273	2.9	1.1	80.6	13.9	1.5	149416
23220	RICHMOND	24767	13574	39.3	25.0	24.8	6.4	4.4	34854	36829	17	15	4211	1.6	12.5	47.8	25.1	12.9	144521
23221	RICHMOND	42579	7555	16.4	28.5	33.5	11.3	10.4	55605	60386	72	70	3381	0.0	3.9	33.9	38.4	23.8	230577
23222	RICHMOND	18394	10341	30.1	32.7	30.2	4.9	2.0	38349	40648	28	25	5664	1.3	20.0	72.1	5.6	1.0	109645
23223	RICHMOND	19481	18009	33.5	29.9	29.4	5.3	1.9	37759	40729	26	23	8310	2.7	14.7	64.1	17.7	0.8	124687
23224	RICHMOND	17405	12141	31.9	34.2	28.4	4.4	1.1	36674	38682	23	19	5509	6.0	25.0	64.1	4.7	0.3	104332
23225	RICHMOND	26824	17633	22.5	31.8	35.0	7.5	3.2	46324	48543	52	48	7595	2.2	8.8	59.0	27.4	2.7	142098
23226	RICHMOND	39232	7142	12.0	26.4	36.3	12.3	13.0	62111	65359	80	76	4975	0.6	1.8	38.9	35.1	23.5	206694
23227	RICHMOND	27976	10233	23.2	26.6	38.9	7.9	3.4	50155	53318	62	59	5319	0.6	1.4	56.1	38.8	3.1	165835
23228	RICHMOND	26904	15598	17.6	32.6	40.9	6.7	2.2	49812	52543	61	57	7961	1.2	2.4	70.7	25.1	0.5	144724
23229	RICHMOND	37796	13734	10.5	21.2	42.1	14.3	11.8	69590	72469	87	83	9638	0.2	0.2	28.2	48.5	22.8	236940
23230	RICHMOND	27416	2908	20.6	32.8	36.9	6.7	3.1	47077	49634	54	50	1491	0.2	1.3	65.9	30.4	2.3	147855
23231	RICHMOND	25495	12553	18.1	24.6	42.9	10.7	3.8	58921	63078	76	73	8918	0.5	7.8	53.2	35.3	3.2	156038
23233	RICHMOND	41095	10684	4.9	10.6	40.4	24.9	19.2	91829	91936	95	91	8274	0.2	0.0	13.8	63.6	22.3	285729
23234	RICHMOND	22433	15021	18.3	29.4	42.1	7.8	2.3	51788	54378	65	63	8940	3.5	11.1	62.0	22.9	0.5	137494
	VIRGINIA	30912		17.0	22.6	35.9	15.0	9.5	61855	64957				5.3	6.3	30.4	41.5	16.5	203135
	UNITED STATES	27277		20.9	24.4	35.3	11.7	7.6	54719	56938				9.3	13.1	31.6	32.6	13.5	162279

ZIP CODE #	POST OFFICE NAME	FINANCIAL SERVICES: Auto Loan	Home Loan	Invest-ments	Retire-ment Plans	THE HOME: Home Improvements: Home Repair	Lawn & Garden	Furnishings: Computers & Hardware-Personal	Major Appliances	TV, Radio, Sound Equipment	Furniture	ENTERTAINMENT: Dine out/ Carry out	Sports Equip-ment	Fees & Tickets	Toys & Games	Travel	Cable TV	PERSONAL: Apparel & Services	Auto Repairs	Health Insur-ance	Pets & Supplies
23025	CARDINAL	102	81	131	80	89	107	81	103	85	76	84	75	70	81	88	91	56	95	102	120
23027	CARTERSVILLE	87	79	72	76	77	82	75	80	78	78	78	58	70	81	71	81	53	77	80	95
23030	CHARLES CITY	91	78	91	78	79	96	77	90	82	73	81	67	70	82	78	88	55	84	94	106
23032	CHURCH VIEW	82	62	93	60	65	85	62	79	68	58	67	59	52	66	64	74	44	73	81	94
23035	COBBS CREEK	106	85	138	84	94	113	85	108	89	80	88	79	74	85	92	95	59	100	107	126
23038	COLUMBIA	90	73	86	70	73	88	72	84	77	71	76	62	63	78	70	82	51	79	85	100
23039	CROZIER	107	125	115	129	124	121	110	115	107	113	108	88	120	109	119	107	76	110	112	134
23040	CUMBERLAND	81	62	77	60	63	80	62	75	68	60	67	56	52	69	60	73	45	70	77	89
23043	DELTAVILLE	85	83	118	82	95	101	77	93	81	83	80	61	80	74	87	85	54	88	100	106
23045	DIGGS	101	81	131	80	89	107	81	103	85	76	84	75	70	81	88	90	56	95	102	119
23047	DOSWELL	128	138	139	141	141	139	127	134	126	131	126	99	133	126	134	127	88	129	133	155
23050	DUTTON	101	94	118	94	97	109	89	104	91	86	90	78	85	89	95	94	61	98	103	121
23055	FORK UNION	97	72	105	70	76	102	77	96	84	69	82	71	63	82	77	92	54	89	101	112
23056	FOSTER	102	81	131	80	89	107	81	103	85	76	84	75	71	81	88	91	56	95	102	120
23059	GLEN ALLEN	159	166	150	172	161	149	160	154	153	167	156	125	165	160	159	147	111	153	142	180
23060	GLEN ALLEN	122	127	110	127	121	110	122	116	116	127	119	94	124	122	119	112	84	116	106	135
23061	GLOUCESTER	93	94	88	94	93	97	86	92	88	88	88	68	88	90	88	90	61	89	93	108
23062	GLOUCESTER POINT	87	99	94	99	98	92	95	92	92	95	94	72	102	93	99	91	67	93	91	107
23063	GOOCHLAND	92	81	94	82	84	96	79	92	82	75	81	68	73	82	81	86	55	86	93	107
23065	GUM SPRING	95	102	89	104	99	102	92	97	92	93	92	75	96	94	96	93	64	93	96	114
23066	GWYNN	95	76	122	75	83	100	76	96	79	71	78	70	66	75	82	85	52	89	95	112
23069	HANOVER	115	121	127	123	122	127	108	119	109	111	109	90	113	110	116	111	76	113	117	139
23070	HARDYVILLE	100	80	129	79	88	105	80	102	84	75	83	74	69	79	87	89	55	94	100	118
23071	HARTFIELD	99	79	128	78	87	105	80	101	83	75	82	74	69	79	86	89	55	93	100	117
23072	HAYES	89	91	89	90	91	94	85	90	86	85	86	67	86	87	87	88	60	87	92	106
23075	HIGHLAND SPRINGS	80	80	66	81	74	78	81	77	81	79	81	61	81	83	78	81	56	79	81	92
23079	JAMAICA	80	62	98	61	67	84	63	80	66	59	66	58	53	64	66	71	43	73	80	93
23083	JETERSVILLE	85	73	69	71	72	80	71	77	75	73	74	57	65	78	67	78	50	74	78	92
23084	KENTS STORE	98	86	95	85	88	98	83	95	87	82	86	70	77	88	83	91	58	89	95	111
23085	KING AND QUEEN COURT	100	72	103	69	74	102	74	94	82	68	80	70	59	81	73	90	53	86	97	111
23086	KING WILLIAM	93	98	86	100	96	97	90	95	88	90	89	74	91	92	92	89	62	90	92	110
23089	LANEXA	99	101	106	103	101	108	93	102	93	91	93	78	94	93	99	95	64	97	101	120
23091	LITTLE PLYMOUTH	85	73	79	75	75	90	73	84	76	66	75	64	65	77	73	81	51	78	87	98
23092	LOCUST HILL	84	67	108	66	74	89	67	85	70	63	69	62	58	67	73	75	46	79	84	99
23093	LOUISA	85	75	85	75	77	89	75	85	78	71	77	64	69	78	76	83	53	81	88	99
23102	MAIDENS	102	112	103	115	110	112	101	107	100	101	100	83	106	101	107	100	70	102	105	125
23103	MANAKIN SABOT	185	230	236	236	236	218	195	207	187	209	189	154	223	186	220	184	136	196	195	237
23106	MANQUIN	90	101	87	104	98	100	91	94	89	91	90	74	97	91	96	89	63	91	93	111
23109	MATHEWS	103	83	134	81	91	109	83	105	87	78	86	77	72	82	90	92	57	97	104	122
23110	MATTAPONI	79	59	78	58	61	82	63	77	69	56	67	57	51	68	61	76	45	71	83	90
23111	MECHANICSVILLE	116	130	115	129	125	116	117	117	113	123	115	92	124	117	121	110	81	114	110	135
23112	MIDLOTHIAN	133	151	136	151	147	133	133	135	127	143	129	105	143	132	138	122	92	129	123	155
23113	MIDLOTHIAN	174	222	228	232	229	204	189	194	179	202	181	152	222	181	211	173	134	184	178	222
23114	MIDLOTHIAN	145	180	166	184	178	157	150	154	141	163	144	123	173	148	163	134	105	144	135	174
23116	MECHANICSVILLE	145	177	165	181	176	159	151	155	143	161	145	122	170	148	164	138	105	147	141	177
23117	MINERAL	95	79	107	79	84	99	79	95	82	74	81	70	70	81	82	87	54	88	95	111
23119	MOON	106	85	137	83	93	112	85	108	89	79	88	79	73	84	92	95	58	99	106	125
23120	MOSELEY	131	157	153	160	158	147	135	142	130	143	132	107	151	132	148	128	94	135	134	163
23123	NEW CANTON	80	55	80	53	57	80	58	73	65	54	64	56	45	65	56	72	42	68	77	88
23124	NEW KENT	104	117	101	121	114	115	105	109	103	105	104	85	112	106	111	103	72	105	108	128
23125	NEW POINT	88	71	114	70	78	93	71	90	74	66	73	66	61	70	77	79	49	83	89	104
23126	NEWTOWN	91	65	93	63	67	92	67	85	74	62	73	64	53	74	66	81	48	78	88	101
23128	NORTH	103	89	126	89	95	110	87	105	89	83	89	78	79	86	93	94	60	98	104	122
23129	OILVILLE	124	152	153	156	155	144	130	137	125	138	126	102	147	125	145	123	90	130	130	157
23130	ONEMO	95	76	123	75	84	100	76	97	80	71	79	71	66	76	82	85	52	89	95	112
23138	PORT HAYWOOD	94	75	121	74	82	99	75	95	78	70	77	70	65	74	81	84	51	88	94	110
23139	POWHATAN	108	121	108	123	118	117	108	113	106	110	106	87	114	109	113	105	74	108	110	131
23140	PROVIDENCE FORGE	92	93	87	96	93	100	87	95	88	84	88	72	87	90	90	91	60	89	96	111
23141	QUINTON	112	128	117	130	126	122	113	118	110	117	111	90	122	112	120	109	78	112	113	137
23146	ROCKVILLE	132	161	162	166	165	153	138	146	133	146	134	109	156	133	154	131	96	138	139	167
23148	SAINT STEPHENS CHURC	91	65	93	63	67	92	67	85	74	62	73	64	53	74	66	81	48	78	88	101
23149	SALUDA	100	84	113	83	89	102	83	99	86	81	86	72	74	85	86	91	57	93	98	116
23150	SANDSTON	90	99	88	98	96	96	92	92	92	92	93	71	97	94	95	93	65	92	95	108
23153	SANDY HOOK	96	104	90	106	101	103	94	98	93	95	94	76	98	96	97	94	65	95	97	116
23156	SHACKLEFORDS	80	64	77	64	66	83	64	77	69	59	68	58	55	69	64	75	45	71	80	91
23160	STATE FARM	128	159	163	164	163	151	135	143	130	145	131	107	154	129	152	127	94	136	135	164
23161	STEVENSVILLE	102	73	105	71	76	104	75	96	83	70	82	72	60	83	74	92	54	88	99	114
23163	SUSAN	89	71	115	70	78	94	71	91	75	67	74	66	62	71	77	79	49	84	89	105
23168	TOANO	97	110	102	113	108	108	98	103	96	99	96	79	105	97	104	96	67	98	101	120
23169	TOPPING	82	65	106	64	72	86	65	83	69	61	68	61	57	65	71	73	45	77	82	96
23173	UNIVERSITY OF RICHMO	0	0	0	0	0	0	0	0	0	0	0	0	0	0	0	0	0	0	0	0
23175	URBANNA	108	84	132	82	91	113	84	107	90	79	88	79	72	86	90	96	59	99	107	125
23176	WAKE	91	73	117	71	80	96	73	92	76	68	75	67	63	72	79	81	50	85	91	107
23177	WALKERTON	96	72	96	71	74	98	73	91	80	68	79	68	60	80	72	87	52	83	94	108
23180	WATER VIEW	78	62	101	61	69	82	62	79	65	59	65	58	54	62	68	70	43	73	78	92
23181	WEST POINT	94	105	98	106	104	111	94	101	97	92	97	75	101	97	101	101	67	97	108	117
23185	WILLIAMSBURG	125	128	135	129	131	132	126	127	126	130	126	93	129	123	129	127	88	127	132	149
23186	WILLIAMSBURG	105	68	65	74	66	73	125	85	112	99	112	77	91	112	87	109	79	104	89	108
23188	WILLIAMSBURG	114	122	125	123	124	121	115	118	113	120	114	88	121	113	120	113	80	116	118	137
23192	MONTPELIER	109	126	109	128	122	119	110	114	107	112	108	89	119	111	117	106	76	109	110	133
23219	RICHMOND	45	28	29	32	27	31	48	36	48	44	48	31	39	47	38	48	34	45	41	46
23220	RICHMOND	74	52	52	57	51	56	83	62	79	71	79	54	67	78	64	79	56	73	67	78
23221	RICHMOND	107	95	97	102	94	93	117	99	113	111	115	83	110	112	107	110	81	109	101	121
23222	RICHMOND	67	62	56	64	59	68	65	64	70	65	70	47	65	69	62	74	48	67	73	78
23223	RICHMOND	68	57	52	59	54	60	67	61	70	66	70	47	63	70	61	72	49	67	67	75
23224	RICHMOND	66	54	48	56	51	57	65	58	68	62	67	46	59	68	57	69	47	64	64	72
23225	RICHMOND	80	67	65	71	65	69	82	72	83	80	84	58	77	82	75	84	58	81	79	89
23226	RICHMOND	120	126	127	129	127	122	127	122	125	129	125	95	133	124	129	123	89	125	123	143
23227	RICHMOND	82	78	78	79	79	81	84	80	85	85	85	60	84	84	83	86	59	84	87	95
23228	RICHMOND	82	74	67	77	71	74	83	76	83	82	84	60	80	84	78	83	58	81	79	92
23229	RICHMOND	115	133	138	134	137	131	124	125	122	127	123	93	137	121	134	123	88	124	128	144
23230	RICHMOND	82	72	68	75	70	73	84	75	85	83	86	60	80	85	78	85	60	83	82	92
23231	RICHMOND	93	96	82	97	91	94	93	91	94	94	94	70	95	96	92	95	66	92	94	109
23233	RICHMOND	158	178	163	184	175	154	161	158	152	173	155	129	175	160	166	144	112	152	139	181
23234	RICHMOND	84	80	69	80	76	79	84	79	85	83	85	62	82	86	79	86	59	83	83	95
	VIRGINIA	115	112	112	114	111	114	112	112	112	112	112	88	111	114	111	113	79	112	112	132
	UNITED STATES	100	100	100	100	100	100	100	100	100	100	100	100	100	100	100	100	100	100	100	100

POPULATION CHANGE

ZIP CODE #	POST OFFICE NAME	COUNTY FIPS CODE	POPULATION 2000	POPULATION 2009	POPULATION 2014	2000-2009 ANNUAL RATE % Rate	2000-2009 ANNUAL RATE State Centile	HOUSEHOLDS 2000	HOUSEHOLDS 2009	HOUSEHOLDS 2014	HOUSEHOLDS % Annual Rate 2000-2009	HOUSEHOLDS 2009 Average HH Size	FAMILIES 2000	FAMILIES 2009	FAMILIES % Annual Rate 2000-2009
23235	RICHMOND	041	29463	31126	32087	0.6	49	11876	12787	13271	0.8	2.38	8261	8570	0.4
23236	RICHMOND	041	24589	27033	28392	1.0	64	8961	10111	10708	1.3	2.67	7077	7779	1.0
23237	RICHMOND	041	19860	21707	22700	1.0	64	7200	7999	8413	1.1	2.70	5432	5856	0.8
23238	RICHMOND	075	23519	25433	26624	0.8	58	9688	10588	11119	1.0	2.33	6260	6549	0.5
23294	RICHMOND	087	15563	16695	17366	0.8	58	7497	8055	8391	0.8	2.06	3746	3819	0.2
23298	RICHMOND	760	427	496	496	1.6	78	0	0	0	0.0	0.00	0	0	0.0
23301	ACCOMAC	001	2155	2161	2139	0.0	23	764	765	756	0.0	2.63	518	501	-0.4
23302	ASSAWOMAN	001	129	130	129	0.1	28	41	42	41	0.3	3.05	29	28	-0.4
23303	ATLANTIC	001	605	610	604	0.1	28	242	246	244	0.2	2.47	168	165	-0.2
23306	BELLE HAVEN	001	1045	1048	1035	0.0	23	448	454	450	0.1	2.29	312	306	-0.2
23307	BIRDSNEST	131	933	1001	1036	0.8	58	365	400	416	1.0	2.46	256	271	0.6
23308	BLOXOM	001	2599	2645	2620	0.2	33	946	961	952	0.2	2.63	661	650	-0.2
23310	CAPE CHARLES	131	6086	6429	6563	0.6	49	2446	2629	2701	0.8	2.37	1565	1619	0.4
23314	CARROLLTON	093	4401	6951	8278	5.1	97	1668	2705	3249	5.4	2.57	1363	2152	5.1
23315	CARRSVILLE	093	1527	1609	1671	0.6	49	595	644	675	0.9	2.47	422	440	0.5
23320	CHESAPEAKE	550	44422	50745	53505	1.4	73	17061	19816	21042	1.6	2.52	11978	13427	1.2
23321	CHESAPEAKE	550	30211	33506	34879	1.1	66	10745	12145	12710	1.3	2.76	8693	9621	1.1
23322	CHESAPEAKE	550	54309	61983	65167	1.4	73	16797	19329	20393	1.5	3.07	14561	16495	1.4
23323	CHESAPEAKE	550	31645	35668	37274	1.3	72	10547	11978	12550	1.4	2.95	8551	9546	1.2
23324	CHESAPEAKE	550	21721	23627	24422	0.9	61	8356	9216	9565	1.1	2.55	5644	6000	0.7
23325	CHESAPEAKE	550	16971	18161	18546	0.7	54	6449	7064	7261	1.0	2.56	4775	5066	0.6
23336	CHINCOTEAGUE ISLAND	001	4317	4301	4233	0.0	23	2063	2069	2040	0.0	2.07	1241	1189	-0.5
23337	WALLOPS ISLAND	001	435	473	477	0.9	61	183	200	201	1.0	2.36	128	135	0.6
23350	EXMORE	131	3882	4181	4299	0.8	58	1643	1808	1872	1.0	2.29	1128	1200	0.7
23354	FRANKTOWN	131	983	1042	1054	0.6	49	349	379	387	0.9	2.48	238	250	0.5
23356	GREENBACKVILLE	001	607	716	735	1.8	81	296	350	360	1.8	2.04	212	243	1.5
23357	GREENBUSH	001	864	873	865	0.1	28	307	313	310	0.2	2.63	206	203	-0.2
23359	HALLWOOD	001	855	859	849	0.1	28	305	306	302	0.0	2.70	222	216	-0.3
23395	HORNTOWN	001	406	479	492	1.8	81	134	159	163	1.9	3.01	96	110	1.5
23404	LOCUSTVILLE	001	29	28	28	-0.4	8	14	14	14	0.0	2.00	9	9	0.0
23405	MACHIPONGO	131	924	990	1022	0.7	54	393	430	446	1.0	2.23	274	290	0.6
23409	MEARS	001	170	170	167	0.0	23	67	67	66	0.0	2.52	48	46	-0.5
23410	MELFA	001	2904	2966	2941	0.2	33	1216	1253	1244	0.3	2.35	845	843	0.0
23413	NASSAWADOX	131	288	313	326	0.9	61	126	140	147	1.1	2.24	86	92	0.7
23415	NEW CHURCH	001	5853	6661	6782	1.4	73	2162	2467	2514	1.4	2.69	1527	1686	1.1
23416	OAK HALL	001	255	256	253	0.0	23	105	106	105	0.1	2.41	73	71	-0.3
23417	ONANCOCK	001	4179	4184	4130	0.0	23	1779	1794	1774	0.1	2.24	1164	1130	-0.3
23418	ONLEY	001	923	922	907	0.0	23	379	383	379	0.1	2.41	252	245	-0.3
23420	PAINTER	001	3422	3454	3422	0.1	28	1311	1340	1330	0.2	2.49	907	896	-0.1
23421	PARKSLEY	001	4072	4125	4086	0.1	28	1540	1564	1550	0.2	2.54	1052	1032	-0.2
23426	SANFORD	001	607	594	581	-0.2	14	270	266	261	-0.2	2.23	188	179	-0.5
23430	SMITHFIELD	093	15075	17773	19276	1.8	81	5688	6862	7494	2.0	2.57	4402	5161	1.7
23432	SUFFOLK	800	1448	1583	1628	1.0	64	542	615	640	1.4	2.57	424	463	1.0
23433	SUFFOLK	800	1230	1345	1383	1.0	64	496	563	586	1.4	2.39	388	424	1.0
23434	SUFFOLK	800	39663	48290	52259	2.2	87	14682	18258	19919	2.4	2.59	10810	13024	2.0
23435	SUFFOLK	800	15082	26451	31888	6.3	98	5190	9284	11287	6.5	2.83	4294	7437	6.1
23436	SUFFOLK	800	782	855	879	1.0	64	296	336	349	1.4	2.54	232	253	0.9
23437	SUFFOLK	800	3986	4593	4834	1.5	76	1509	1804	1921	1.9	2.55	1156	1325	1.5
23438	SUFFOLK	800	1448	1723	1843	1.9	83	556	682	738	2.2	2.53	417	490	1.8
23440	TANGIER	001	693	675	662	-0.3	11	281	277	272	-0.2	2.44	210	201	-0.5
23442	TEMPERANCEVILLE	001	1178	1186	1172	0.1	28	445	450	446	0.1	2.61	318	311	-0.2
23451	VIRGINIA BEACH	810	41050	41206	40600	0.0	23	18914	19473	19344	0.3	2.04	9848	9510	-0.4
23452	VIRGINIA BEACH	810	61107	59398	58004	-0.3	11	22319	22316	21996	0.0	2.64	16307	15741	-0.4
23453	VIRGINIA BEACH	810	34327	35936	36029	0.5	45	11428	12264	12395	0.8	2.93	8822	9133	0.4
23454	VIRGINIA BEACH	810	60513	60658	59962	0.0	23	22306	22851	22732	0.3	2.63	15913	15810	-0.1
23455	VIRGINIA BEACH	810	44881	44559	43714	-0.1	18	18194	18601	18412	0.2	2.39	12227	11986	-0.2
23456	VIRGINIA BEACH	810	43578	51767	53874	1.9	83	13337	15953	16677	2.0	3.18	11561	13589	1.8
23457	VIRGINIA BEACH	810	3785	3975	3964	0.5	45	1371	1470	1477	0.8	2.70	1082	1128	0.5
23459	VIRGINIA BEACH	810	1035	1033	1021	0.0	23	178	178	176	0.0	3.46	169	168	-0.1
23460	VIRGINIA BEACH	810	1561	1594	1585	0.2	33	86	83	81	-0.4	3.59	83	80	-0.4
23461	VIRGINIA BEACH	810	843	857	844	0.2	33	21	22	22	0.5	2.55	19	19	0.0
23462	VIRGINIA BEACH	810	57550	60194	60256	0.5	45	21827	23295	23478	0.7	2.58	15123	15546	0.3
23463	VIRGINIA BEACH	810	26	94	114	14.9	99	9	36	44	16.2	2.61	5	21	16.8
23464	VIRGINIA BEACH	810	71078	72450	72065	0.2	33	23967	25131	25222	0.5	2.87	19310	19818	0.3
23487	WINDSOR	093	5754	6374	6727	1.1	66	2200	2496	2660	1.4	2.55	1654	1817	1.0
23502	NORFOLK	710	21433	21174	20999	-0.1	18	7793	7841	7823	0.1	2.55	5381	5224	-0.3
23503	NORFOLK	710	30588	31085	31062	0.2	33	13329	13794	13888	0.4	2.22	7452	7393	-0.1
23504	NORFOLK	710	23541	23106	22877	-0.2	14	8106	8036	7986	-0.1	2.64	5250	4995	-0.5
23505	NORFOLK	710	27083	26694	26497	-0.2	14	11586	11555	11541	0.0	2.17	6630	6315	-0.5
23507	NORFOLK	710	6612	6329	6253	-0.5	6	3471	3414	3399	-0.2	1.78	1264	1157	-1.0
23508	NORFOLK	710	17770	17359	17206	-0.3	11	6454	6355	6320	-0.2	2.48	3443	3219	-0.7
23509	NORFOLK	710	12583	12480	12387	-0.1	18	4921	4949	4938	0.1	2.49	3125	3014	-0.4
23510	NORFOLK	710	5303	6021	6250	1.4	73	1932	2433	2598	2.5	1.83	925	1050	1.4
23511	NORFOLK	710	18871	22624	22983	2.0	85	660	877	942	3.1	5.95	644	853	3.1
23513	NORFOLK	710	29436	29127	28915	-0.1	18	11220	11354	11349	0.1	2.57	7396	7193	-0.3
23517	NORFOLK	710	4162	4037	3993	-0.3	11	2142	2136	2126	0.0	1.82	775	725	-0.7
23518	NORFOLK	710	29566	28365	27917	-0.4	8	11944	11745	11639	-0.2	2.41	7790	7384	-0.6
23521	NORFOLK	810	3938	3946	3865	0.0	23	502	505	491	0.1	4.21	487	488	0.0
23523	NORFOLK	710	7454	7270	7194	-0.3	11	2651	2658	2652	0.0	2.73	1839	1780	-0.4
23601	NEWPORT NEWS	700	24759	24721	24602	0.0	23	10197	10463	10475	0.3	2.34	6496	6401	-0.2
23602	NEWPORT NEWS	700	40925	41359	41386	0.1	28	15937	16721	16852	0.5	2.44	10935	11120	0.2
23603	NEWPORT NEWS	700	3718	3489	3440	-0.7	4	1325	1336	1327	0.1	2.45	885	860	-0.3
23604	FORT EUSTIS	700	5738	5115	5202	-1.2	1	965	1054	1079	1.0	3.65	946	1031	0.9
23605	NEWPORT NEWS	700	14499	14281	14151	-0.2	14	6188	6263	6245	0.1	2.27	3798	3687	-0.3
23606	NEWPORT NEWS	700	26285	26756	26901	0.2	33	11273	12038	12220	0.7	2.18	6794	6868	0.1
23607	NEWPORT NEWS	700	26206	24740	24236	-0.6	4	10134	9947	9802	-0.2	2.43	6275	5899	-0.7
23608	NEWPORT NEWS	700	41548	43747	44066	0.6	49	15154	16358	16575	0.8	2.67	11141	11680	0.5
23651	FORT MONROE	650	1253	1138	1104	-1.0	2	363	331	321	-1.0	3.21	338	306	-1.1
23661	HAMPTON	650	14400	14326	14314	-0.1	18	5751	5773	5786	0.0	2.43	3792	3672	-0.3
23662	POQUOSON	735	11566	12165	12416	0.5	45	4166	4482	4608	0.8	2.69	3370	3552	0.6
23663	HAMPTON	650	14551	14452	14411	-0.1	18	5265	5256	5254	0.0	2.68	3696	3585	-0.3
23664	HAMPTON	650	10214	10111	10074	-0.1	18	4321	4307	4304	0.0	2.34	2801	2711	-0.4
23665	HAMPTON	650	14145	14541	14690	0.3	38	1608	1762	1811	1.0	3.70	1572	1724	1.0
23666	HAMPTON	650	48704	50503	51191	0.4	42	19732	20651	21019	0.5	2.42	12901	12946	0.0
23668	HAMPTON	650	80	77	76	-0.4	8	2	2	2	0.0	7.00	0	0	0.0
	VIRGINIA					1.2					1.3	2.52			1.0
	UNITED STATES					1.0					1.1	2.59			0.9

ZIP CODE #	POST OFFICE NAME	RACE (%) White 2000	White 2009	Black 2000	Black 2009	Asian/Pacific 2000	Asian/Pacific 2009	% Hispanic Origin 2000	% Hispanic Origin 2009	2009 AGE DISTRIBUTION (%) 0-4	5-9	10-14	15-19	20-24	25-44	45-64	65-84	85+	18+	MEDIAN AGE 2009	% 2009 Males	% 2009 Females
23235	RICHMOND	80.4	75.6	14.8	17.2	2.2	3.3	2.1	3.7	5.1	5.5	6.3	7.6	4.8	22.7	30.9	14.9	2.3	77.9	43.6	47.8	52.2
23236	RICHMOND	78.6	73.7	15.8	18.1	3.1	4.6	1.7	2.9	5.7	6.1	6.7	6.7	5.2	25.6	32.1	11.0	1.0	77.2	40.9	48.3	51.7
23237	RICHMOND	75.9	69.3	17.3	20.3	1.8	2.6	4.9	8.2	7.2	7.4	7.1	7.1	5.9	28.4	27.2	8.7	0.9	73.9	35.9	48.7	51.3
23238	RICHMOND	88.2	84.3	6.3	7.3	3.6	5.5	2.0	3.3	4.9	5.0	5.8	6.3	5.8	23.5	31.1	13.8	3.8	80.3	44.0	46.2	53.8
23294	RICHMOND	70.5	62.8	14.2	15.7	10.9	15.3	3.6	5.7	5.6	4.8	4.6	5.1	10.6	37.2	21.4	9.4	1.2	82.0	33.6	47.4	52.6
23298	RICHMOND	30.5	23.6	51.9	54.8	12.9	15.5	3.1	4.0	0.0	0.0	0.0	28.2	42.9	26.2	2.4	0.2	0.0	99.6	22.5	33.7	66.3
23301	ACCOMAC	47.4	41.3	40.4	40.4	1.5	1.9	12.2	19.0	6.4	6.2	6.0	5.6	6.1	26.3	26.6	14.4	2.4	78.3	39.9	53.2	46.8
23302	ASSAWOMAN	49.6	44.6	45.0	47.7	0.0	0.0	5.4	8.5	6.2	6.2	6.2	6.9	5.4	24.6	30.0	13.1	1.5	76.9	40.6	48.5	51.5
23303	ATLANTIC	53.1	48.2	44.1	47.5	0.0	0.0	2.6	4.4	5.2	5.7	6.2	6.6	4.4	24.4	30.8	14.8	1.8	78.4	42.9	48.9	51.1
23306	BELLE HAVEN	53.5	49.2	44.9	48.8	0.3	0.4	1.1	2.1	5.2	5.2	6.0	6.5	5.0	19.8	31.8	18.4	2.1	79.4	46.5	45.4	54.6
23307	BIRDSNEST	39.2	35.5	56.6	58.6	0.1	0.1	3.8	5.6	6.1	6.5	6.5	5.8	5.1	20.5	29.2	17.4	3.0	77.2	44.6	46.5	53.5
23308	BLOXOM	52.9	47.8	35.9	35.8	0.1	0.2	13.5	20.4	7.7	7.2	6.7	6.5	6.7	24.7	26.0	12.2	2.3	74.8	37.3	49.0	51.0
23310	CAPE CHARLES	53.4	49.2	42.3	44.6	0.3	0.2	4.4	6.8	5.7	5.6	5.8	6.7	6.4	21.2	29.8	16.2	2.8	78.8	43.8	47.6	52.4
23314	CARROLLTON	84.6	81.8	13.7	15.9	0.5	0.7	1.1	1.8	5.5	6.4	6.9	6.4	4.0	24.7	32.0	12.9	1.1	77.0	42.6	49.9	50.1
23315	CARRSVILLE	74.2	70.2	24.9	28.6	0.3	0.4	0.3	0.4	4.9	5.4	6.2	7.1	4.8	23.4	32.0	14.2	1.9	78.9	43.7	47.9	52.1
23320	CHESAPEAKE	63.8	58.3	29.2	31.8	3.4	4.9	2.9	4.5	7.5	6.7	6.5	6.3	6.8	30.7	25.8	8.5	1.2	75.6	35.4	47.1	52.9
23321	CHESAPEAKE	68.6	65.3	26.6	27.9	2.5	3.6	1.7	2.5	6.5	6.7	6.9	7.3	6.0	25.1	29.8	10.5	1.3	75.4	38.5	48.2	51.8
23322	CHESAPEAKE	85.1	81.6	11.3	13.2	1.3	2.0	1.9	3.1	6.4	7.1	7.6	8.4	6.3	27.1	29.6	6.8	0.7	73.7	36.7	51.2	48.8
23323	CHESAPEAKE	59.1	54.6	37.0	39.8	1.1	1.6	2.0	3.2	8.1	7.6	7.4	7.2	5.3	29.9	24.7	8.6	1.1	72.1	34.7	48.6	51.4
23324	CHESAPEAKE	42.6	38.3	54.0	57.1	1.0	1.3	1.4	2.0	8.1	7.8	7.2	7.2	7.4	24.7	23.4	12.5	1.7	72.4	34.3	45.5	54.5
23325	CHESAPEAKE	58.4	54.5	37.5	40.0	1.2	1.6	1.9	2.8	7.1	6.7	6.3	6.4	6.8	27.4	25.7	12.0	1.6	76.0	36.8	47.6	52.4
23336	CHINCOTEAGUE ISLAND	96.9	95.8	0.9	1.1	0.3	0.4	0.5	1.0	4.0	4.4	4.6	4.2	3.5	20.5	36.0	20.5	2.3	84.4	50.6	49.6	50.4
23337	WALLOPS ISLAND	59.2	54.8	37.6	40.2	0.0	0.2	3.2	5.3	6.1	6.6	7.2	7.4	4.9	24.1	29.0	13.5	1.3	75.5	39.9	49.7	50.3
23350	EXMORE	59.3	55.6	37.5	39.8	0.3	0.2	2.6	4.0	5.0	5.3	5.7	6.0	5.0	21.7	30.3	18.2	2.8	80.0	46.0	48.0	52.0
23354	FRANKTOWN	49.2	45.3	49.2	52.6	0.1	0.1	1.0	1.4	4.9	5.4	5.9	5.9	4.5	20.0	25.5	21.8	6.2	80.1	48.2	46.6	53.4
23356	GREENBACKVILLE	64.6	59.6	31.4	34.2	0.2	0.4	3.8	6.4	7.3	7.5	8.2	8.5	4.9	24.0	26.3	12.3	1.0	71.5	36.5	49.7	50.3
23357	GREENBUSH	38.4	34.5	51.3	50.4	0.2	0.2	13.1	19.7	6.1	6.0	6.0	6.9	6.6	26.1	26.5	12.9	3.0	77.7	38.8	50.9	49.1
23359	HALLWOOD	54.2	49.5	33.3	32.5	0.1	0.1	13.3	19.9	7.2	6.5	6.2	6.9	7.6	25.6	27.0	11.5	1.5	76.1	36.7	48.7	51.3
23395	HORNTOWN	64.6	59.9	31.4	34.2	0.2	0.2	3.7	6.5	7.3	7.7	8.4	8.6	5.0	24.0	25.9	12.3	0.8	71.4	36.2	50.1	49.9
23404	LOCUSTVILLE	57.1	53.6	42.9	42.9	0.0	0.0	3.6	3.6	7.1	7.1	7.1	7.1	7.1	28.6	28.6	7.1	0.0	71.4	35.0	50.0	50.0
23405	MACHIPONGO	40.8	37.0	55.4	57.7	0.1	0.1	3.5	5.2	5.9	6.4	6.4	5.8	5.1	20.4	28.8	18.0	3.4	77.8	45.1	46.5	53.5
23409	MEARS	73.5	67.6	16.5	17.1	0.0	0.6	11.8	20.0	6.5	6.5	6.5	6.5	5.3	25.3	28.8	12.9	1.8	77.1	40.0	50.0	50.0
23410	MELFA	58.0	53.5	39.2	42.3	0.1	0.2	3.1	4.9	5.8	6.0	6.3	6.5	5.2	23.4	30.1	14.6	2.2	78.0	42.5	47.7	52.3
23413	NASSAWADOX	68.1	65.2	28.1	29.7	0.3	0.3	3.1	4.5	5.8	6.4	6.1	5.1	4.8	21.1	33.9	14.4	2.6	78.9	45.5	46.6	53.4
23415	NEW CHURCH	59.3	55.0	37.0	39.3	0.3	0.4	3.3	5.7	7.2	7.6	8.2	8.3	5.0	24.7	25.7	12.2	1.1	71.8	36.4	49.6	50.4
23416	OAK HALL	57.3	52.7	40.0	43.0	0.0	0.0	2.4	4.3	5.1	5.5	5.9	6.6	4.3	24.2	31.6	14.8	2.0	78.9	43.8	49.2	50.8
23417	ONANCOCK	73.6	69.7	24.3	27.1	0.3	0.4	1.8	3.0	4.6	4.5	5.4	5.8	4.3	19.1	31.2	20.8	4.2	81.8	49.2	46.1	53.9
23418	ONLEY	61.1	56.3	35.1	38.1	0.3	0.4	3.5	5.5	5.2	5.2	5.6	6.0	5.6	21.9	31.3	16.5	2.6	80.4	45.3	46.9	53.1
23420	PAINTER	51.2	46.0	43.3	45.6	0.1	0.1	6.0	9.5	5.5	5.7	6.3	6.9	5.6	22.5	30.2	15.4	1.9	78.4	42.9	48.6	51.4
23421	PARKSLEY	56.6	52.4	36.1	36.6	0.3	0.5	10.4	16.3	6.2	6.3	6.4	6.9	6.0	23.9	26.5	14.3	3.4	76.8	40.5	47.9	52.1
23426	SANFORD	83.0	79.5	14.9	16.8	0.0	0.0	1.2	2.0	3.9	4.5	4.9	6.1	3.9	22.4	35.2	16.7	2.5	83.2	47.8	49.5	50.5
23430	SMITHFIELD	65.5	61.3	32.5	35.9	0.4	0.6	0.8	1.3	6.0	6.7	7.2	6.8	4.4	23.1	31.8	12.5	1.6	75.7	42.3	48.8	51.2
23432	SUFFOLK	73.8	67.0	23.9	30.3	1.2	1.5	0.3	0.4	4.1	5.0	6.1	6.4	3.7	20.0	35.8	16.7	2.1	80.7	47.5	49.4	50.6
23433	SUFFOLK	73.9	66.9	23.9	30.3	1.1	1.6	0.3	0.4	4.1	5.0	6.2	6.4	3.7	20.0	35.7	16.8	2.2	80.8	47.5	49.4	50.6
23434	SUFFOLK	47.9	45.2	50.0	52.0	0.5	0.7	1.1	1.6	7.2	7.2	7.2	7.2	5.9	26.4	26.1	11.1	1.8	74.0	37.3	47.4	52.6
23435	SUFFOLK	59.2	53.5	36.2	40.8	1.7	2.1	2.0	2.7	8.8	8.6	8.4	7.1	4.9	30.0	24.8	6.6	0.9	69.8	35.0	48.9	51.1
23436	SUFFOLK	73.8	66.9	23.9	30.3	1.3	1.5	0.3	0.4	4.1	4.9	6.1	6.3	3.7	20.1	35.8	16.8	2.1	80.8	47.6	49.4	50.6
23437	SUFFOLK	71.0	63.9	27.3	34.1	0.2	0.3	0.9	1.2	5.2	5.6	6.3	6.6	4.8	23.4	32.5	13.8	1.8	78.8	43.7	48.4	51.6
23438	SUFFOLK	63.8	56.0	34.6	42.1	0.2	0.2	0.8	1.0	4.6	5.3	6.0	6.8	4.4	23.0	34.8	13.5	1.5	79.8	44.9	50.3	49.7
23440	TANGIER	99.1	99.0	0.9	1.0	0.0	0.0	0.0	0.0	5.0	5.6	5.9	5.2	3.9	22.8	32.9	16.7	1.9	80.3	45.9	52.6	47.4
23442	TEMPERANCEVILLE	60.5	55.2	34.2	36.5	0.1	0.2	5.4	8.7	5.5	5.8	6.2	6.7	5.1	25.0	30.4	13.7	1.8	78.3	41.7	48.1	51.9
23451	VIRGINIA BEACH	84.6	81.5	10.1	10.9	1.6	2.3	3.1	5.0	5.9	5.2	4.8	5.2	7.6	31.2	25.2	11.5	3.3	81.4	38.0	50.3	49.7
23452	VIRGINIA BEACH	73.9	69.3	17.9	19.2	3.4	4.8	4.3	6.6	7.0	6.8	6.9	7.1	7.1	28.8	25.3	9.9	1.1	75.0	35.5	48.7	51.3
23453	VIRGINIA BEACH	59.6	53.2	25.9	26.6	8.3	11.6	5.4	8.1	8.9	7.8	7.2	7.6	9.1	33.0	21.6	4.6	0.3	71.6	29.7	49.2	50.8
23454	VIRGINIA BEACH	80.1	76.0	13.1	14.2	2.4	3.4	4.7	7.3	7.4	6.9	6.9	7.2	7.7	30.2	24.7	7.6	1.4	74.5	33.6	49.0	51.0
23455	VIRGINIA BEACH	77.0	72.7	14.8	15.5	4.0	5.9	3.6	5.6	6.4	6.3	6.2	5.9	6.5	27.7	26.6	12.5	2.0	77.5	38.8	49.1	50.9
23456	VIRGINIA BEACH	72.0	67.5	16.2	16.6	7.7	10.1	4.0	6.2	8.1	8.2	8.3	7.6	5.3	31.2	26.3	4.6	0.4	70.6	34.6	50.1	49.9
23457	VIRGINIA BEACH	90.0	87.5	7.9	9.4	0.2	0.4	0.8	1.4	4.7	5.6	6.6	6.7	4.3	24.6	34.0	11.9	1.5	78.8	43.6	49.7	50.3
23459	VIRGINIA BEACH	43.7	38.6	43.2	43.3	1.7	2.1	13.1	18.9	12.0	8.5	4.2	7.6	32.7	33.1	1.6	0.3	0.0	73.9	22.7	58.5	41.5
23460	VIRGINIA BEACH	67.5	61.3	20.1	21.3	2.4	3.3	9.9	15.0	2.7	3.6	1.8	22.0	40.5	27.9	1.5	0.0	0.0	91.2	22.5	80.2	19.8
23461	VIRGINIA BEACH	66.5	60.3	21.5	22.8	2.4	3.4	8.2	12.4	13.7	12.8	7.8	11.1	13.3	35.1	5.3	0.9	0.0	62.5	21.7	57.2	42.8
23462	VIRGINIA BEACH	60.3	54.9	30.5	32.1	4.1	5.9	4.5	6.7	8.0	7.0	6.6	7.2	9.4	31.4	21.8	7.9	0.8	74.1	31.8	49.0	51.0
23463	VIRGINIA BEACH	69.2	63.8	19.2	18.1	3.8	7.4	7.7	11.7	6.4	2.1	2.1	7.4	44.7	29.8	7.4	0.0	0.0	89.4	23.6	53.2	46.8
23464	VIRGINIA BEACH	65.1	59.1	21.3	22.1	9.2	12.8	3.6	5.5	6.4	6.6	6.9	7.7	7.4	28.1	27.6	8.2	0.9	75.3	35.7	48.9	51.1
23487	WINDSOR	74.9	70.6	23.3	26.8	0.2	0.3	1.1	1.7	5.3	5.7	6.3	7.0	5.4	26.0	30.9	11.9	1.3	78.2	41.1	49.4	50.6
23502	NORFOLK	45.3	40.4	47.7	50.0	3.2	4.4	3.2	4.5	6.8	6.3	6.2	7.8	8.0	27.1	23.8	11.5	2.6	76.8	35.5	48.3	51.7
23503	NORFOLK	71.8	66.0	19.1	21.1	2.8	4.1	5.2	7.8	7.6	6.5	5.9	6.6	9.5	31.1	23.5	7.9	1.4	76.4	32.6	51.2	48.8
23504	NORFOLK	4.8	4.2	93.2	93.3	0.3	0.4	1.2	1.4	9.0	9.0	8.1	11.3	10.4	20.9	19.8	9.4	2.1	69.0	26.8	42.6	57.4
23505	NORFOLK	58.2	53.2	31.6	33.0	4.0	5.5	5.2	7.4	7.9	6.7	5.6	6.4	12.7	31.1	18.9	8.6	2.1	76.8	30.0	51.3	48.7
23507	NORFOLK	87.3	83.3	7.0	8.2	3.1	4.7	2.2	3.6	4.1	2.8	2.5	3.0	10.4	38.5	26.6	9.5	2.5	88.8	36.6	48.5	51.5
23508	NORFOLK	51.7	47.4	41.4	43.7	3.7	4.7	2.0	2.9	5.3	5.5	5.4	13.0	16.2	24.9	20.1	8.2	1.4	80.4	28.0	49.7	50.3
23509	NORFOLK	44.2	40.3	51.5	54.0	1.2	1.7	2.2	3.1	6.6	6.7	6.9	7.0	6.2	24.7	27.4	12.1	2.4	75.5	38.7	47.5	52.5
23510	NORFOLK	31.5	32.2	65.7	63.6	1.2	1.9	1.4	2.0	7.1	5.8	4.3	5.3	11.4	37.0	19.0	8.6	1.4	80.7	32.7	54.6	45.4
23511	NORFOLK	54.2	47.8	33.8	35.7	2.9	4.0	10.0	14.2	4.1	4.2	2.7	13.9	46.5	26.9	1.6	0.1	0.0	88.2	22.7	79.9	20.1
23513	NORFOLK	34.8	30.7	57.5	58.9	3.7	5.1	2.7	3.8	7.7	7.2	7.0	7.7	9.3	27.6	23.4	8.7	1.5	73.6	32.1	47.8	52.2
23517	NORFOLK	59.5	55.9	35.1	36.3	2.1	3.1	2.8	4.2	3.9	3.7	3.7	5.1	9.9	37.2	24.1	10.1	2.3	85.9	36.3	50.7	49.3
23518	NORFOLK	66.2	60.3	23.9	25.7	4.4	6.3	4.1	6.2	7.7	6.7	6.3	6.6	8.0	27.8	24.2	10.9	1.7	75.4	35.1	49.9	50.1
23521	NORFOLK	62.4	56.6	26.3	27.6	2.8	3.8	8.4	12.9	8.9	9.1	6.3	14.6	24.5	33.0	3.2	0.3	0.0	73.0	22.3	66.3	33.7
23523	NORFOLK	1.5	1.3	96.9	96.7	0.1	0.1	1.0	1.2	8.1	9.7	9.8	8.9	7.2	21.4	22.1	10.9	1.9	66.6	30.4	42.0	58.0
23601	NEWPORT NEWS	69.6	68.7	25.1	25.9	1.5	1.5	2.9	3.0	7.4	6.8	6.6	6.7	7.2	27.1	25.1	10.6	2.4	75.1	36.4	48.3	51.7
23602	NEWPORT NEWS	59.4	58.2	31.2	32.1	3.8	4.0	4.6	4.7	7.6	6.9	6.8	6.9	7.2	28.7	24.6	9.9	1.4	74.7	35.3	47.9	52.1
23603	NEWPORT NEWS	62.5	60.5	28.9	30.8	1.9	2.0	6.8	7.0	10.3	7.0	5.4	7.9	14.6	31.2	18.3	4.8	0.5	73.8	26.9	50.8	49.2
23604	FORT EUSTIS	54.2	52.4	29.9	31.4	2.3	2.3	15.0	15.4	15.3	11.5	6.2	9.3	20.0	35.6	2.0	0.1	0.0	65.6	21.9	57.3	42.7
23605	NEWPORT NEWS	47.5	45.3	47.8	49.3	1.1	1.3	2.3	2.7	7.4	6.2	5.8	6.7	9.9	29.0	24.0	9.6	1.4	76.6	33.2	49.1	50.9
23606	NEWPORT NEWS	74.6	72.3	19.4	21.4	2.0	2.1	3.3	3.6	6.7	6.0	5.8	7.5	8.8	28.0	23.4	11.5	2.3	77.9	35.0	47.8	52.2
23607	NEWPORT NEWS	10.4	10.0	86.7	87.1	0.3	0.3	1.4	1.4	8.0	7.9	7.3	8.0	7.5	23.5	24.7	11.3	1.8	72.0	34.3	46.7	53.3
23608	NEWPORT NEWS	52.3	50.3	37.5	39.3	3.8	3.9	5.9	6.0	8.9	7.7	6.9	7.3	9.8	30.6	22.1	6.2	0.5	72.6	29.8	48.8	51.2
23651	FORT MONROE	63.1	57.4	24.7	25.7	1.8	2.5	10.7	15.9	14.5	12.3	7.6	4.8	12.4	37.3	10.8	0.4	0.0	62.7	24.4	52.1	47.9
23661	HAMPTON	31.9	29.5	65.1	66.6	0.7	0.9	1.3	1.8	5.3	5.6	6.1	7.2	6.1	23.3	29.9	13.9	2.6	78.6	42.3	47.3	52.7
23662	POQUOSON	96.3	94.7	0.7	0.8	1.6	2.4	1.1	1.8	4.9	5.8	6.9	7.4	5.6	21.9	33.0	12.7	1.7	77.5	43.2	50.4	49.6
23663	HAMPTON	44.9	40.6	48.9	51.0	1.6	2.1	2.9	4.1	7.3	7.1	6.9	9.0	8.4	25.5	25.3	9.4	1.0	73.7	33.1	48.0	52.0
23664	HAMPTON	78.4	74.9	17.2	18.7	1.3	1.9	2.2	3.6	5.4	5.5	6.1	6.4	5.2	25.0	31.9	13.1	1.5	79.1	42.5	49.8	50.2
23665	HAMPTON	67.5	62.2	24.8	26.8	2.3	3.2	5.3	8.3	6.6	6.8	5.5	5.0	14.9	55.9	5.1	0.1	0.0	78.6	29.0	65.0	35.0
23666	HAMPTON	49.4	44.9	43.9	45.9	2.7	3.8	3.0	4.5	6.9	6.3	6.1	6.1	8.2	29.8	24.5	10.3	1.8	77.0	34.9	48.0	52.0
23668	HAMPTON	6.3	5.2	91.1	90.9	0.0	0.0	2.5	2.6	0.0	0.0	0.0	48.1	39.0	5.2	3.9	3.9	0.0	100.0	20.3	40.3	59.7
	VIRGINIA	72.3	68.8	19.6	20.1	3.7	5.1	4.7	7.0	6.5	6.4	6.5	6.9	6.9	27.5	27.2	10.5	1.6	76.7	37.7	49.2	50.8
	UNITED STATES	75.1	72.0	12.3	12.7	3.8	4.6	12.5	15.7	6.8	6.7	6.6	7.1	6.9	27.0	26.0	10.9	1.9	75.7	36.9	49.2	50.8

ZIP CODE #	POST OFFICE NAME	2009 Per Capita Income	2009 HH Income Base	2009 HOUSEHOLD INCOME DISTRIBUTION (%) Less than $25,000	$25,000 to $49,999	$50,000 to $99,999	$100,000 to $149,999	$150,000 or More	MEDIAN HOUSEHOLD INCOME 2009	2014	2009 National Centile	2009 State Centile	2009 Home Value Base	2009 HOME VALUE DISTRIBUTION (%) Less than $50,000	$50,000 to $89,999	$90,000 to $174,999	$175,000 to $399,999	$400,000 or More	2009 Median Home Value
23235	RICHMOND	34061	12787	8.4	18.5	47.7	19.4	6.0	74212	77731	89	85	10306	2.5	0.9	36.4	56.7	3.5	192797
23236	RICHMOND	34803	10111	5.8	14.4	47.8	20.9	11.1	80119	84024	92	87	8879	0.3	0.7	37.3	53.1	8.5	197202
23237	RICHMOND	24723	7999	13.2	23.5	48.3	11.9	3.1	62382	64655	80	77	5868	4.9	5.1	59.9	29.7	0.4	146296
23238	RICHMOND	40525	10588	7.6	21.3	40.6	17.8	12.8	75107	76927	89	85	6891	0.3	0.6	23.9	54.1	21.0	257729
23294	RICHMOND	30189	8055	12.2	30.7	46.2	8.7	2.3	56094	60852	73	71	2965	0.5	0.5	62.1	35.9	1.0	164563
23298	RICHMOND	17108	0	0.0	0.0	0.0	0.0	0.0	0	0	0	0	0	0.0	0.0	0.0	0.0	0.0	0
23301	ACCOMAC	18986	765	29.5	34.2	27.5	6.4	2.4	40458	41708	34	31	518	15.1	12.0	37.6	25.7	9.7	134375
23302	ASSAWOMAN	13177	42	28.6	38.1	31.0	2.4	0.0	38596	36684	28	25	32	18.8	28.1	40.6	12.5	0.0	100000
23303	ATLANTIC	16983	246	25.6	41.9	30.5	2.0	0.0	39333	40998	31	28	187	17.6	24.1	40.1	16.6	1.6	116964
23306	BELLE HAVEN	20845	454	33.7	27.5	31.7	5.7	1.3	42261	44573	40	37	338	12.1	16.3	32.5	25.1	13.9	143548
23307	BIRDSNEST	17536	400	40.8	30.0	20.8	6.0	2.5	29696	30508	8	7	293	13.3	12.6	42.0	17.4	14.7	140549
23308	BLOXOM	14147	961	44.1	31.0	20.9	3.2	0.7	28720	29537	6	5	693	24.8	33.2	26.6	12.7	2.7	81190
23310	CAPE CHARLES	18791	2629	37.5	32.3	24.0	3.9	2.3	33988	35519	15	13	1722	15.0	18.4	33.7	25.4	7.5	125862
23314	CARROLLTON	29674	2705	14.1	15.8	46.0	17.6	6.5	68899	70143	86	82	2273	10.3	1.4	15.8	51.7	20.9	271512
23315	CARRSVILLE	22616	644	22.4	27.5	41.6	7.3	1.2	50122	53464	61	58	493	13.8	8.5	38.3	31.6	7.7	144643
23320	CHESAPEAKE	29212	19816	10.6	23.3	46.6	14.2	5.3	64312	68342	83	79	13520	4.1	1.3	32.5	53.0	9.2	201810
23321	CHESAPEAKE	29308	12145	8.8	19.5	45.6	19.4	6.6	72146	76395	88	84	9252	1.3	1.7	25.1	61.8	10.0	232720
23322	CHESAPEAKE	29834	19329	4.8	13.5	45.8	26.7	9.2	82725	84318	93	88	16971	0.6	0.6	10.6	72.5	15.7	289444
23323	CHESAPEAKE	24134	11978	12.8	20.8	48.5	12.9	5.0	64773	68983	83	80	9681	5.5	2.6	35.0	52.7	4.1	188650
23324	CHESAPEAKE	17668	9216	34.9	30.5	28.1	4.5	2.0	35575	37245	19	16	4614	11.4	11.1	66.0	10.4	1.1	129684
23325	CHESAPEAKE	23977	7064	17.0	28.3	42.8	9.1	2.8	54784	60892	71	68	4593	0.4	2.3	53.3	41.8	2.2	167665
23336	CHINCOTEAGUE ISLAND	22553	2069	31.1	36.8	23.4	7.2	1.4	35631	36777	20	17	1632	5.8	12.2	37.2	37.3	7.5	165841
23337	WALLOPS ISLAND	16957	200	30.5	40.0	27.0	2.5	0.0	36327	37167	22	18	152	16.4	18.4	48.0	15.1	2.0	115625
23350	EXMORE	21471	1808	35.0	29.1	28.2	4.9	2.8	37801	40000	26	23	1244	11.2	19.6	39.1	21.1	9.1	130378
23354	FRANKTOWN	23437	379	30.6	25.1	31.7	8.4	4.2	42145	45952	40	36	273	9.2	17.9	31.1	20.5	21.2	143750
23356	GREENBACKVILLE	18625	350	34.9	38.6	23.1	3.4	0.0	33320	34064	14	12	265	17.0	12.8	52.1	15.1	3.0	114619
23357	GREENBUSH	15684	313	33.9	33.5	28.1	2.9	1.6	33549	36701	14	13	207	19.8	31.4	34.8	13.0	1.0	85833
23359	HALLWOOD	14228	306	40.5	33.3	20.3	5.2	0.7	29134	29593	7	6	225	26.2	37.3	25.8	8.0	2.7	75526
23395	HORNTOWN	12617	159	35.2	38.4	22.6	3.8	0.0	33179	33819	14	12	121	16.5	13.2	52.9	14.9	2.5	113839
23404	LOCUSTVILLE	23303	14	35.7	21.4	42.9	0.0	0.0	45000	45000	48	44	9	0.0	33.3	44.4	22.2	0.0	112500
23405	MACHIPONGO	20758	430	39.1	28.6	23.0	6.7	2.6	31338	32421	10	9	313	12.8	13.1	39.0	18.5	16.6	142560
23409	MEARS	15326	67	35.8	32.8	26.9	4.5	0.0	31097	31482	10	8	52	26.9	34.6	26.9	11.5	0.0	75000
23410	MELFA	20156	1253	31.5	31.2	30.0	5.5	1.8	40468	43583	34	31	936	11.6	21.3	41.3	21.0	4.7	121729
23413	NASSAWADOX	20750	140	35.7	32.9	25.0	3.6	2.9	35892	38481	20	17	105	11.4	6.7	60.0	21.9	0.0	133152
23415	NEW CHURCH	14608	2467	35.9	36.0	24.0	3.7	0.4	33806	34692	15	13	1838	20.7	13.9	49.0	13.7	2.7	112463
23416	OAK HALL	17419	106	27.4	39.6	30.2	2.8	0.0	38869	40836	29	26	82	17.1	26.8	40.2	14.6	1.2	112500
23417	ONANCOCK	25702	1794	26.2	26.4	34.9	7.9	4.6	47419	50000	55	51	1318	6.3	11.2	37.9	32.3	12.3	160685
23418	ONLEY	21545	383	30.0	29.0	32.4	5.7	2.9	43071	45938	43	38	273	4.0	13.6	46.9	32.6	2.9	145479
23420	PAINTER	18198	1340	35.6	28.1	29.8	5.1	1.3	37320	40540	25	21	1021	17.2	18.7	32.6	22.5	8.9	118875
23421	PARKSLEY	17394	1564	30.6	32.0	32.9	2.9	1.5	38572	41660	28	25	1094	22.1	23.2	36.0	16.7	1.9	102679
23426	SANFORD	18402	266	41.7	27.1	24.1	4.9	2.3	29299	31279	7	6	219	16.0	46.1	24.7	8.7	4.6	75313
23430	SMITHFIELD	24353	6862	21.0	22.0	41.4	11.6	4.0	56498	60612	73	71	5437	10.9	5.8	25.0	43.7	14.7	212125
23432	SUFFOLK	35235	615	13.3	20.0	30.1	24.6	12.0	72830	76316	88	84	515	4.1	7.2	19.6	36.3	32.8	313235
23433	SUFFOLK	37950	563	13.3	20.1	29.8	24.7	12.1	72907	75753	88	84	472	4.2	7.0	19.5	36.4	32.8	314737
23434	SUFFOLK	21476	18258	26.8	27.5	34.6	7.4	3.7	46400	48771	53	48	11832	7.2	10.6	35.6	38.8	7.8	167505
23435	SUFFOLK	25664	9284	12.5	18.3	50.4	13.6	5.2	64884	65717	83	80	7650	2.6	4.8	15.2	64.8	12.6	259323
23436	SUFFOLK	35627	336	13.7	20.2	30.1	23.8	12.2	71787	75777	88	83	281	4.3	7.1	19.9	35.9	32.7	310185
23437	SUFFOLK	22935	1804	18.7	29.7	41.5	7.1	2.9	52156	58147	66	63	1408	6.3	9.5	42.1	38.5	3.6	153150
23438	SUFFOLK	19850	682	23.6	34.2	34.8	6.2	1.3	44692	46629	47	43	533	8.1	6.4	41.7	39.8	4.1	156534
23440	TANGIER	21822	277	34.3	28.9	30.0	1.1	5.8	32791	35831	13	11	255	19.6	22.0	48.6	7.1	2.7	96935
23442	TEMPERANCEVILLE	15982	450	30.4	38.2	26.9	4.0	0.4	36418	37327	22	19	343	20.1	26.2	37.6	14.0	2.0	97353
23451	VIRGINIA BEACH	36769	19473	15.5	26.7	36.9	11.8	9.1	57897	62498	75	72	9628	3.1	1.6	13.2	39.6	42.5	355934
23452	VIRGINIA BEACH	26972	22316	11.8	27.0	44.7	10.2	6.3	60126	63423	77	74	13701	0.3	1.0	35.6	48.3	14.8	197423
23453	VIRGINIA BEACH	22332	12264	12.7	27.4	46.5	10.1	3.2	59552	63142	77	74	8129	0.7	4.0	38.5	53.5	3.3	186921
23454	VIRGINIA BEACH	29601	22851	10.2	24.8	44.2	12.9	7.8	63749	67535	82	78	14537	3.0	1.1	22.5	52.7	20.7	241006
23455	VIRGINIA BEACH	31897	18601	11.7	25.3	41.8	14.1	7.1	63364	66830	82	78	11467	1.6	0.8	24.6	54.1	18.8	252443
23456	VIRGINIA BEACH	28173	15953	4.1	11.3	55.4	21.1	8.2	80057	81203	92	87	14032	0.2	0.3	11.3	73.3	14.9	275165
23457	VIRGINIA BEACH	28557	1470	11.3	16.0	50.9	16.4	5.4	68966	73145	86	82	1228	10.1	1.1	13.4	48.5	26.9	293793
23459	VIRGINIA BEACH	15231	178	15.7	44.9	37.1	2.2	0.0	42005	44248	39	36	0	0.0	0.0	0.0	0.0	0.0	0
23460	VIRGINIA BEACH	16976	83	0.0	45.8	54.2	0.0	0.0	52213	52205	66	64	62	51.6	21.0	12.9	3.2	11.3	46667
23461	VIRGINIA BEACH	5250	22	4.5	40.9	40.9	9.1	4.5	52835	54545	68	65	6	0.0	0.0	0.0	100.0	0.0	325000
23462	VIRGINIA BEACH	23363	23295	13.6	30.6	46.2	7.7	1.9	54506	60133	70	68	13110	5.9	2.0	48.8	41.8	1.5	167256
23463	VIRGINIA BEACH	15179	36	30.6	36.1	33.3	0.0	0.0	40000	40000	33	30	14	0.0	0.0	50.0	50.0	0.0	175000
23464	VIRGINIA BEACH	26795	25131	8.3	18.4	52.6	15.5	5.2	69316	72101	86	83	18870	0.2	0.5	24.2	71.9	3.2	217610
23487	WINDSOR	23038	2496	18.2	27.6	44.0	8.5	1.7	53148	56672	68	65	2045	24.0	7.9	28.7	33.0	6.5	144059
23502	NORFOLK	22194	7841	19.1	31.0	41.1	6.0	2.8	49931	53350	61	57	4565	2.8	0.9	53.5	39.8	2.8	167822
23503	NORFOLK	22979	13794	21.0	36.9	35.0	5.4	1.8	44400	46805	47	41	5886	0.5	1.8	53.1	40.7	3.9	169631
23504	NORFOLK	12846	8036	56.3	22.7	17.3	2.2	1.5	20205	20714	1	1	2286	3.8	18.2	57.8	19.6	0.6	133393
23505	NORFOLK	24337	11555	26.4	33.9	30.1	6.0	3.6	40120	43375	33	30	4497	3.0	3.8	44.3	36.3	12.6	173043
23507	NORFOLK	43921	3414	16.7	24.8	35.6	11.4	11.6	60418	63603	78	75	1263	0.0	0.6	14.7	46.5	38.2	339960
23508	NORFOLK	24381	6355	29.4	26.5	26.8	10.4	6.9	43274	46234	43	39	3016	2.0	4.9	25.9	51.6	15.6	228704
23509	NORFOLK	22302	4949	25.4	29.6	33.8	8.1	3.1	46002	48206	51	46	3153	1.0	4.2	65.2	21.3	8.3	149310
23510	NORFOLK	28357	2433	33.5	22.4	29.4	8.9	5.8	43568	46913	44	40	535	0.6	0.7	10.3	44.3	44.1	370833
23511	NORFOLK	15405	877	9.2	48.7	35.0	5.5	1.6	46608	47731	53	48	26	0.0	0.0	50.0	50.0	0.0	175000
23513	NORFOLK	18386	11354	27.8	33.3	33.7	3.9	1.3	40422	43739	34	30	5755	2.0	7.0	76.1	14.6	0.2	139504
23517	NORFOLK	29158	2136	26.4	33.3	29.2	7.0	4.1	41662	45028	38	35	690	0.4	5.9	34.1	50.0	9.6	212385
23518	NORFOLK	23140	11745	20.6	32.9	37.5	6.3	2.7	47353	49836	55	51	6529	5.1	0.4	45.0	44.2	5.3	174474
23521	NORFOLK	15358	505	10.9	41.8	38.8	6.7	1.8	48644	49660	58	54	30	0.0	0.0	33.3	66.7	0.0	190625
23523	NORFOLK	11372	2658	53.8	27.4	15.9	2.3	0.5	22218	22799	2	1	926	4.1	23.7	63.6	6.8	1.8	120833
23601	NEWPORT NEWS	23067	10463	23.0	30.6	38.3	6.2	1.9	47272	50611	55	51	5857	0.4	0.9	51.6	44.9	2.2	172576
23602	NEWPORT NEWS	25676	16721	16.0	27.0	43.8	9.8	3.4	56467	61158	73	71	9670	3.5	1.9	33.7	57.8	3.1	191746
23603	NEWPORT NEWS	21354	1336	18.9	33.6	41.6	4.8	1.1	48370	51914	57	54	538	1.3	3.0	50.6	44.2	0.9	168750
23604	FORT EUSTIS	14353	1054	17.1	45.7	33.6	2.2	1.4	42138	43509	40	36	61	14.8	27.9	57.4	0.0	0.0	100658
23605	NEWPORT NEWS	20070	6263	28.0	33.8	33.2	4.5	0.5	39439	42198	31	28	3066	8.3	2.9	74.5	14.2	0.1	134675
23606	NEWPORT NEWS	28215	12038	18.8	30.1	37.1	9.6	4.4	50929	54898	63	60	5833	7.1	1.4	21.5	59.2	10.8	218530
23607	NEWPORT NEWS	14939	9947	51.1	24.2	20.2	3.1	1.5	24196	24572	3	2	3695	5.1	22.6	56.5	14.7	1.1	115728
23608	NEWPORT NEWS	21827	16358	16.1	29.3	44.0	8.7	1.8	53922	59996	70	66	9139	4.8	3.7	37.8	52.7	1.1	180279
23651	FORT MONROE	20360	331	12.4	37.8	31.1	13.0	5.7	49773	54369	60	57	6	0.0	0.0	100.0	0.0	0.0	137500
23661	HAMPTON	23391	5773	24.4	28.5	35.8	8.2	3.2	47659	49705	56	52	3944	1.1	8.5	61.8	26.4	2.2	145667
23662	POQUOSON	34626	4482	8.3	16.8	37.3	26.0	11.5	81366	85949	93	88	3726	5.0	1.6	14.2	59.2	19.9	279153
23663	HAMPTON	20117	5256	23.4	28.7	40.9	4.8	2.1	47932	51955	56	52	3120	1.6	7.4	71.9	18.1	1.0	138772
23664	HAMPTON	30687	4307	18.2	24.3	35.3	15.8	6.5	60437	64522	78	75	2830	3.0	1.2	43.0	44.8	8.0	181154
23665	HAMPTON	16861	1762	5.3	44.8	38.8	7.9	3.2	49855	50333	61	57	25	0.0	0.0	60.0	40.0	0.0	169318
23666	HAMPTON	25885	20651	14.3	29.6	43.4	9.9	2.7	55680	60446	72	70	11832	3.1	2.2	44.7	48.3	1.7	174960
23668	HAMPTON	14085	0	0.0	0.0	0.0	0.0	0.0	0	0	0	0	0	0.0	0.0	0.0	0.0	0.0	0
	VIRGINIA	30912		17.0	22.6	35.9	15.0	9.5	61855	64957				5.3	6.3	30.4	41.5	16.5	203135
	UNITED STATES	27277		20.9	24.4	35.3	11.7	7.6	54719	56938				9.3	13.1	31.6	32.6	13.5	162279

ZIP CODE		FINANCIAL SERVICES				THE HOME						ENTERTAINMENT						PERSONAL			
						Home Improvements		Furnishings													
#	POST OFFICE NAME	Auto Loan	Home Loan	Invest-ments	Retire-ment Plans	Home Repair	Lawn & Garden	Comput-ers & Hard-ware-Personal	Major Appli-ances	TV, Radio, Sound Equip-ment	Furni-ture	Dine out/ Carry out	Sports Equip-ment	Fees & Tickets	Toys & Games	Travel	Cable TV	Apparel & Services	Auto Repairs	Health Insur-ance	Pets & Supplies
23235	RICHMOND	111	123	119	124	123	121	114	116	114	118	115	86	122	113	120	115	80	115	120	135
23236	RICHMOND	129	150	135	148	145	136	130	134	127	138	129	101	142	131	137	125	91	129	127	154
23237	RICHMOND	98	98	84	98	93	92	96	94	95	97	96	73	95	98	93	94	67	94	92	111
23238	RICHMOND	129	141	141	144	143	135	136	133	133	141	134	103	145	132	141	131	95	134	133	155
23294	RICHMOND	92	75	68	80	71	72	93	79	92	91	94	66	86	94	83	90	66	88	81	97
23298	RICHMOND	0	0	0	0	0	0	0	0	0	0	0	0	0	0	0	0	0	0	0	0
23301	ACCOMAC	86	62	86	60	63	89	67	82	75	61	72	62	53	74	64	82	48	77	89	97
23302	ASSAWOMAN	72	51	73	49	52	72	52	66	58	49	57	50	41	58	51	64	38	61	69	79
23303	ATLANTIC	75	54	77	52	56	76	55	70	61	51	60	52	44	61	54	67	40	64	73	83
23306	BELLE HAVEN	80	61	91	59	65	84	64	80	69	58	67	59	53	67	65	75	45	74	83	93
23307	BIRDSNEST	75	56	76	53	56	77	56	70	63	53	62	53	47	63	56	69	41	65	74	84
23308	BLOXOM	68	45	66	42	45	67	48	60	55	45	54	47	36	56	45	61	36	57	64	74
23310	CAPE CHARLES	76	54	74	52	55	76	60	71	67	55	65	54	48	66	56	73	43	68	76	85
23314	CARROLLTON	109	116	117	120	119	122	106	116	105	105	105	87	110	106	113	107	73	108	114	133
23315	CARRSVILLE	88	79	81	81	79	93	77	87	80	72	79	67	71	82	77	85	54	82	90	103
23320	CHESAPEAKE	109	106	94	107	101	97	108	101	105	111	107	81	106	109	103	103	75	104	98	120
23321	CHESAPEAKE	112	124	115	124	121	119	113	115	112	117	113	88	121	114	118	112	79	113	114	134
23322	CHESAPEAKE	129	153	137	153	148	133	133	134	126	141	128	106	145	131	140	121	92	128	121	154
23323	CHESAPEAKE	104	112	95	110	106	99	102	101	99	107	101	79	105	104	102	97	70	99	95	118
23324	CHESAPEAKE	63	56	51	58	54	59	64	59	67	62	67	46	61	66	59	68	46	64	66	72
23325	CHESAPEAKE	85	87	79	88	84	85	87	84	87	86	88	65	89	89	87	88	62	87	87	100
23336	CHINCOTEAGUE ISLAND	78	62	101	61	68	82	62	79	65	58	64	58	54	62	68	70	43	73	78	92
23337	WALLOPS ISLAND	73	50	73	48	51	73	52	66	59	49	58	50	41	59	50	65	38	61	69	80
23350	EXMORE	83	63	92	62	67	87	65	82	71	60	70	60	55	69	67	78	46	76	86	96
23354	FRANKTOWN	84	87	90	85	87	99	79	90	85	77	84	64	82	84	85	91	58	86	100	103
23356	GREENBACKVILLE	71	46	68	43	46	69	49	62	57	47	56	48	37	58	46	63	37	58	66	76
23357	GREENBUSH	76	50	74	47	50	75	53	67	61	51	60	52	40	62	50	68	40	63	71	82
23359	HALLWOOD	70	47	69	44	47	69	50	63	57	47	56	48	38	58	47	63	37	59	66	77
23395	HORNTOWN	70	46	68	43	46	69	49	62	57	47	55	48	37	58	46	63	37	58	65	76
23404	LOCUSTVILLE	83	60	85	58	62	84	61	78	68	57	67	58	49	67	61	75	44	71	81	93
23405	MACHIPONGO	78	62	79	59	63	82	61	74	68	58	67	56	53	68	61	74	45	70	80	88
23409	MEARS	72	47	69	44	47	70	50	63	58	48	56	49	37	59	47	64	37	59	67	78
23410	MELFA	79	62	76	61	62	81	64	75	69	60	68	57	55	69	62	74	46	71	79	90
23413	NASSAWADOX	80	60	94	58	64	83	61	78	66	58	65	58	51	65	63	72	43	72	79	92
23415	NEW CHURCH	71	49	67	47	49	69	52	63	58	50	57	49	41	60	49	64	38	60	66	77
23416	OAK HALL	75	54	77	52	56	76	55	70	61	51	60	52	44	61	54	67	40	64	73	83
23417	ONANCOCK	88	81	97	81	85	95	80	90	83	78	82	65	77	81	83	87	56	86	94	104
23418	ONLEY	82	68	78	68	70	83	72	79	75	69	74	59	64	75	70	80	50	77	84	93
23420	PAINTER	80	58	86	56	61	82	60	76	66	56	65	57	49	65	60	72	43	70	78	90
23421	PARKSLEY	79	54	79	52	55	80	58	73	66	54	64	56	45	66	55	73	42	68	77	88
23426	SANFORD	73	53	75	51	55	75	54	69	60	50	59	52	43	59	53	66	39	63	71	82
23430	SMITHFIELD	92	92	90	94	92	99	86	93	89	86	88	70	87	90	89	92	61	89	95	109
23432	SUFFOLK	119	148	151	152	152	140	126	133	121	134	122	99	143	120	141	118	87	126	126	152
23433	SUFFOLK	119	148	151	152	152	140	126	133	121	134	122	99	143	120	141	118	87	126	126	152
23434	SUFFOLK	81	81	74	81	78	80	78	79	80	80	80	60	79	81	77	81	55	79	80	93
23435	SUFFOLK	106	120	103	118	115	103	104	106	99	111	101	83	111	105	107	95	71	100	95	121
23436	SUFFOLK	119	148	151	152	152	140	126	133	121	134	122	99	143	120	141	118	87	126	126	152
23437	SUFFOLK	83	87	82	89	87	95	80	88	82	77	82	66	82	83	84	86	57	83	91	102
23438	SUFFOLK	79	70	78	72	72	84	69	80	72	63	70	60	63	72	70	76	48	74	82	93
23440	TANGIER	95	65	104	65	68	100	73	90	76	59	75	75	53	74	72	82	48	84	95	111
23442	TEMPERANCEVILLE	76	52	76	50	53	76	54	69	61	51	60	53	42	61	53	68	40	64	72	83
23451	VIRGINIA BEACH	110	99	103	104	100	97	112	102	110	114	111	81	109	110	107	108	78	109	102	122
23452	VIRGINIA BEACH	101	102	94	104	99	96	103	97	101	105	102	76	105	103	102	99	72	100	97	115
23453	VIRGINIA BEACH	100	90	76	91	84	80	97	88	94	100	96	71	91	99	89	91	67	92	83	105
23454	VIRGINIA BEACH	112	113	105	114	110	102	114	107	110	118	111	85	115	113	111	106	79	109	102	126
23455	VIRGINIA BEACH	107	108	106	110	108	106	108	105	108	111	109	81	112	108	110	107	76	108	107	124
23456	VIRGINIA BEACH	128	151	131	151	146	128	129	130	121	139	124	104	142	128	135	115	89	123	114	148
23457	VIRGINIA BEACH	106	122	111	126	120	119	108	113	105	110	106	87	117	107	116	105	75	108	110	132
23459	VIRGINIA BEACH	84	44	33	51	39	37	79	55	74	73	78	54	60	89	57	68	55	70	49	67
23460	VIRGINIA BEACH	98	51	38	59	46	44	93	64	87	86	92	64	70	105	67	80	64	82	58	78
23461	VIRGINIA BEACH	108	56	42	65	50	48	101	70	95	94	100	70	77	114	73	87	70	89	63	85
23462	VIRGINIA BEACH	89	79	70	81	75	75	88	80	87	89	89	64	84	90	82	86	62	86	80	96
23463	VIRGINIA BEACH	61	26	25	32	24	30	85	42	68	58	69	46	50	66	46	62	49	60	42	57
23464	VIRGINIA BEACH	108	118	105	118	113	107	111	108	107	114	109	85	116	110	112	104	77	107	102	126
23487	WINDSOR	89	88	79	87	86	91	81	87	84	83	84	64	81	86	81	86	57	83	88	102
23502	NORFOLK	80	79	72	79	76	79	81	78	83	80	83	61	82	83	80	84	58	81	83	93
23503	NORFOLK	73	64	58	66	61	62	76	66	75	73	76	54	71	76	69	75	53	73	70	81
23504	NORFOLK	47	36	33	38	34	41	46	41	51	45	50	31	42	49	40	54	35	46	49	52
23505	NORFOLK	77	64	62	68	63	64	80	69	79	77	80	56	74	79	72	79	56	77	73	84
23507	NORFOLK	111	97	100	106	95	93	120	100	116	116	120	86	115	117	111	114	85	112	101	124
23508	NORFOLK	87	77	76	81	76	79	95	81	92	89	92	66	88	91	84	92	65	89	84	99
23509	NORFOLK	77	77	70	78	74	81	77	77	81	77	80	57	79	80	76	83	56	79	84	92
23510	NORFOLK	84	62	65	70	61	66	87	71	90	83	90	59	78	88	75	91	64	83	79	91
23511	NORFOLK	95	50	37	57	44	42	90	62	84	83	89	62	68	101	65	78	62	79	56	76
23513	NORFOLK	68	60	52	62	57	61	68	62	70	66	70	49	65	70	62	70	48	67	67	76
23517	NORFOLK	75	60	62	66	59	64	78	66	80	75	81	55	73	79	71	81	57	76	75	83
23518	NORFOLK	78	75	68	76	73	74	80	75	80	79	81	59	79	81	77	80	57	79	78	90
23521	NORFOLK	101	53	39	61	47	45	95	66	90	89	94	66	72	108	69	82	66	84	60	80
23523	NORFOLK	44	36	34	37	34	41	42	40	48	42	47	29	40	46	38	51	32	44	47	50
23601	NEWPORT NEWS	75	72	67	74	70	73	77	73	78	76	78	57	76	78	75	78	55	77	78	87
23602	NEWPORT NEWS	89	86	80	89	84	82	91	85	90	91	91	67	91	91	88	89	64	89	85	101
23603	NEWPORT NEWS	85	62	51	65	57	55	83	67	79	81	82	59	71	87	68	75	57	76	63	81
23604	FORT EUSTIS	86	45	33	52	40	38	81	56	76	75	80	56	61	91	58	70	56	71	50	68
23605	NEWPORT NEWS	66	57	49	59	54	59	67	60	68	63	68	48	62	69	60	69	47	65	65	73
23606	NEWPORT NEWS	87	79	77	82	78	78	90	81	90	90	91	64	88	90	86	89	64	88	84	98
23607	NEWPORT NEWS	52	41	38	43	39	46	50	46	55	50	55	35	47	54	45	58	38	51	54	58
23608	NEWPORT NEWS	86	76	68	78	72	70	86	76	84	87	86	62	81	87	79	82	60	83	75	92
23651	FORT MONROE	116	60	45	70	54	51	109	75	103	101	108	75	83	123	79	94	76	96	68	92
23661	HAMPTON	79	81	73	81	78	85	79	79	82	79	82	58	81	81	79	85	57	80	87	95
23662	POQUOSON	128	146	140	148	146	138	131	134	128	137	129	101	142	129	140	126	91	131	130	156
23663	HAMPTON	77	74	62	76	69	78	77	74	79	74	79	58	76	80	73	81	54	77	81	90
23664	HAMPTON	98	105	102	107	104	106	100	102	101	101	101	77	106	101	104	102	71	101	106	119
23665	HAMPTON	106	55	41	64	49	47	100	69	94	93	99	69	76	113	72	86	69	88	62	84
23666	HAMPTON	92	86	76	87	82	81	91	84	91	92	92	67	89	93	86	89	64	89	85	101
23668	HAMPTON	0	0	0	0	0	0	0	0	0	0	0	0	0	0	0	0	0	0	0	0
	VIRGINIA	115	112	112	114	111	114	112	112	112	112	112	88	111	114	111	113	79	112	112	132
	UNITED STATES	100	100	100	100	100	100	100	100	100	100	100	100	100	100	100	100	100	100	100	100

ZIP CODE #	POST OFFICE NAME	COUNTY FIPS CODE	POPULATION 2000	POPULATION 2009	POPULATION 2014	2000-2009 ANNUAL RATE % Rate	2000-2009 ANNUAL RATE State Centile	HOUSEHOLDS 2000	HOUSEHOLDS 2009	HOUSEHOLDS 2014	HOUSEHOLDS % Annual Rate 2000-2009	HOUSEHOLDS 2009 Average HH Size	FAMILIES 2000	FAMILIES 2009	FAMILIES % Annual Rate 2000-2009
23669	HAMPTON	650	44511	44722	44838	0.1	28	16595	16724	16801	0.1	2.50	11129	10885	-0.2
23690	YORKTOWN	199	2727	2907	2977	0.7	54	929	1017	1050	1.0	2.52	663	704	0.7
23692	YORKTOWN	199	16630	18444	19166	1.1	66	6405	7296	7643	1.4	2.51	4932	5469	1.1
23693	YORKTOWN	199	19045	22704	24326	1.9	83	6590	7929	8526	2.0	2.86	5305	6242	1.8
23696	SEAFORD	199	3441	3800	3853	1.1	66	1290	1441	1469	1.2	2.58	1007	1100	1.0
23701	PORTSMOUTH	740	27101	26394	26005	-0.3	11	10325	10173	10081	-0.2	2.47	7178	6831	-0.5
23702	PORTSMOUTH	740	11510	11397	11319	-0.1	18	4450	4431	4412	0.0	2.57	3011	2893	-0.4
23703	PORTSMOUTH	740	27517	28556	28703	0.4	42	9616	10023	10145	0.4	2.56	6977	7072	0.1
23704	PORTSMOUTH	740	19344	19926	20026	0.3	38	7488	7717	7782	0.3	2.44	4490	4434	-0.1
23707	PORTSMOUTH	740	14786	14308	14128	-0.4	8	6228	6104	6063	-0.2	2.30	3776	3530	-0.7
23708	PORTSMOUTH	740	179	212	212	1.8	81	0	0	0	0.0	0.00	0	0	0.0
23709	PORTSMOUTH	740	20	20	20	0.0	23	6	6	6	0.0	3.33	6	6	0.0
23801	FORT LEE	149	7269	6181	5913	-1.7	1	1401	1082	1008	-2.8	3.20	1224	935	-2.9
23803	PETERSBURG	041	39459	39395	39940	0.0	23	15281	15568	15864	0.2	2.43	10095	10003	-0.1
23805	PETERSBURG	149	18364	18380	18370	0.0	23	7391	7509	7547	0.2	2.39	4939	4858	-0.2
23806	PETERSBURG	041	1695	1795	1792	0.6	49	11	11	11	0.0	2.55	6	6	0.0
23821	ALBERTA	025	1591	1548	1498	-0.3	11	643	649	634	0.1	2.31	439	428	-0.3
23824	BLACKSTONE	135	6929	7043	7012	0.2	33	2715	2796	2796	0.3	2.43	1823	1812	-0.1
23827	BOYKINS	175	1578	1732	1810	1.0	64	639	721	759	1.3	2.40	444	484	0.9
23828	BRANCHVILLE	175	415	454	475	1.0	64	164	185	194	1.3	2.45	114	124	0.9
23829	CAPRON	175	2608	2479	2517	-0.5	6	495	524	544	0.6	2.43	349	358	0.3
23830	CARSON	053	1069	1159	1195	0.9	61	425	469	487	1.1	2.47	315	340	0.8
23831	CHESTER	041	25895	32020	35055	2.3	88	9595	12125	13369	2.6	2.64	7384	9039	2.2
23832	CHESTERFIELD	041	26687	34979	39105	3.0	92	9034	12202	13779	3.3	2.78	7190	9498	3.1
23833	CHURCH ROAD	053	1933	2127	2234	1.0	64	715	823	876	1.5	2.50	545	611	1.2
23834	COLONIAL HEIGHTS	041	23850	25655	26745	0.8	58	9533	10447	10942	1.0	2.43	6719	7147	0.7
23836	CHESTER	041	8264	11033	12269	3.2	93	3015	4079	4562	3.3	2.70	2348	3065	2.9
23837	COURTLAND	175	3732	3960	4097	0.6	49	1497	1643	1718	1.0	2.30	1047	1112	0.7
23838	CHESTERFIELD	041	9925	13937	15753	3.7	95	3432	4884	5545	3.9	2.85	2963	4141	3.7
23839	DENDRON	181	805	956	1022	1.9	83	280	337	362	2.0	2.84	210	245	1.7
23840	DEWITT	053	1457	1578	1629	0.9	61	549	622	650	1.4	2.51	408	448	1.0
23841	DINWIDDIE	053	3326	3562	3651	0.7	54	1274	1418	1468	1.2	2.51	976	1058	0.9
23842	DISPUTANTA	149	5274	5929	6050	1.3	72	1911	2194	2259	1.5	2.60	1501	1693	1.3
23843	DOLPHIN	025	558	516	491	-0.8	3	237	227	219	-0.5	2.26	165	154	-0.7
23844	DREWRYVILLE	175	824	870	903	0.6	49	308	332	348	0.8	2.62	221	231	0.5
23845	EBONY	025	488	474	458	-0.3	11	217	219	214	0.1	2.16	146	142	-0.3
23846	ELBERON	181	760	857	902	1.3	72	274	314	333	1.5	2.73	206	229	1.2
23847	EMPORIA	081	16561	17239	17297	0.4	42	5317	5616	5694	0.6	2.52	3609	3693	0.2
23850	FORD	053	1225	1369	1446	1.2	69	471	545	581	1.6	2.51	334	376	1.3
23851	FRANKLIN	175	13304	13775	14075	0.4	42	5305	5670	5855	0.7	2.38	3625	3742	0.3
23856	FREEMAN	025	1275	1238	1194	-0.3	11	485	484	472	0.0	2.49	343	332	-0.4
23857	GASBURG	025	577	579	565	0.0	23	256	268	264	0.5	2.16	180	183	0.2
23860	HOPEWELL	149	26852	31968	32479	1.9	83	10696	11286	11566	0.6	2.43	7399	7565	0.2
23866	IVOR	175	2173	2508	2666	1.6	78	834	986	1057	1.8	2.54	625	718	1.5
23867	JARRATT	183	2194	2297	2323	0.5	45	909	986	1012	0.9	1.76	619	649	0.5
23868	LAWRENCEVILLE	025	7952	7994	7813	0.1	28	2035	2015	1960	-0.1	2.47	1381	1322	-0.5
23872	MC KENNEY	053	2167	2457	2585	1.4	73	830	976	1038	1.8	2.50	611	696	1.4
23874	NEWSOMS	175	1042	1089	1127	0.5	45	422	454	473	0.8	2.40	306	319	0.5
23875	PRINCE GEORGE	149	9355	11149	11537	1.9	83	3511	4225	4397	2.0	2.62	2703	3199	1.8
23876	RAWLINGS	025	538	519	501	-0.4	8	211	211	206	0.0	2.46	148	144	-0.3
23878	SEDLEY	175	1060	1170	1222	1.1	66	399	451	475	1.3	2.55	297	327	1.0
23879	SKIPPERS	081	518	557	582	0.8	58	205	229	242	1.2	2.43	147	160	0.9
23881	SPRING GROVE	181	4620	2593	2636	-6.1	0	998	1059	1081	0.6	2.45	715	739	0.4
23882	STONY CREEK	183	2368	2409	2461	0.2	33	977	1032	1066	0.6	2.31	676	692	0.3
23883	SURRY	181	2302	2422	2461	0.6	49	885	948	970	0.7	2.55	648	672	0.4
23885	SUTHERLAND	053	2609	2885	3024	1.1	66	981	1124	1192	1.5	2.55	774	867	1.2
23887	VALENTINES	025	608	628	617	0.4	42	270	290	288	0.8	2.17	194	202	0.4
23888	WAKEFIELD	183	2510	2433	2427	-0.3	11	1031	1027	1033	0.0	2.34	716	693	-0.4
23889	WARFIELD	025	576	534	508	-0.8	3	235	227	218	-0.4	2.35	164	154	-0.7
23890	WAVERLY	183	6830	6956	6996	0.2	33	1722	1778	1813	0.3	2.55	1187	1188	0.0
23893	WHITE PLAINS	025	573	556	538	-0.3	11	243	245	240	0.1	2.27	168	164	-0.3
23894	WILSONS	053	371	409	428	1.1	66	157	179	189	1.4	2.28	112	124	1.1
23897	YALE	183	577	619	639	0.8	58	233	260	272	1.2	2.38	169	183	0.9
23898	ZUNI	093	1838	2009	2110	1.0	64	681	766	813	1.3	2.58	524	573	1.0
23901	FARMVILLE	049	15715	17676	18373	1.3	72	5079	5796	6152	1.4	2.33	3218	3541	1.0
23915	BASKERVILLE	117	1341	1382	1381	0.3	38	337	362	368	0.8	2.78	238	248	0.4
23917	BOYDTON	117	3732	3937	4006	0.6	49	1203	1314	1352	1.0	2.45	840	888	0.6
23919	BRACEY	117	1916	2033	2060	0.6	49	894	973	994	0.9	2.09	642	677	0.6
23920	BRODNAX	025	3233	3301	3261	0.2	33	1259	1325	1321	0.6	2.49	864	880	0.2
23921	BUCKINGHAM	029	2120	2205	2227	0.4	42	883	948	968	0.8	2.30	581	601	0.4
23922	BURKEVILLE	135	3701	3906	3940	0.6	49	923	1003	1026	0.9	2.71	638	670	0.5
23923	CHARLOTTE COURT HOUS	037	2202	2228	2214	0.1	28	873	910	915	0.4	2.39	605	609	0.1
23924	CHASE CITY	117	6436	6551	6553	0.2	33	2712	2831	2858	0.5	2.27	1801	1814	0.1
23927	CLARKSVILLE	117	4311	4349	4331	0.1	28	1924	1994	2003	0.4	2.18	1314	1318	0.0
23930	CREWE	135	5898	5874	5809	0.0	23	2355	2379	2368	0.1	2.33	1649	1614	-0.2
23934	CULLEN	037	562	599	614	0.7	54	224	246	254	1.0	2.42	152	161	0.6
23936	DILLWYN	029	6800	7092	7178	0.5	45	1854	1994	2048	0.8	2.45	1311	1368	0.5
23937	DRAKES BRANCH	037	1935	1994	1995	0.3	38	782	831	841	0.7	2.34	535	551	0.3
23938	DUNDAS	025	668	683	683	0.2	33	265	280	283	0.6	2.43	185	189	0.2
23942	GREEN BAY	147	983	1092	1150	1.1	66	419	482	513	1.5	2.07	288	320	1.1
23944	KENBRIDGE	111	4049	4090	4109	0.1	28	1656	1727	1755	0.5	2.35	1113	1121	0.1
23947	KEYSVILLE	111	4357	4438	4401	0.2	33	1812	1895	1897	0.5	2.28	1233	1246	0.1
23950	LA CROSSE	117	3242	3326	3335	0.3	38	1305	1373	1387	0.6	2.41	921	937	0.2
23952	LUNENBURG	111	258	256	254	-0.1	18	105	108	108	0.3	2.37	72	71	-0.2
23954	MEHERRIN	147	1801	1910	1971	0.6	49	685	750	780	1.0	2.53	486	515	0.6
23958	PAMPLIN	147	2745	2958	3066	0.8	58	1084	1193	1250	1.0	2.38	791	845	0.7
23959	PHENIX	037	1037	1052	1049	0.2	33	404	421	424	0.4	2.48	296	299	0.1
23960	PROSPECT	147	1989	1986	1991	0.0	23	750	761	770	0.2	2.46	517	508	-0.2
23962	RANDOLPH	037	906	898	879	-0.1	18	361	369	365	0.2	2.37	253	250	-0.1
23963	RED HOUSE	037	699	680	669	-0.3	11	260	261	259	0.0	2.58	190	185	-0.3
23964	RED OAK	037	1172	1213	1222	0.4	42	460	491	499	0.7	2.45	325	335	0.3
23966	RICE	147	2062	2327	2463	1.3	72	815	946	1013	1.6	2.42	556	621	1.2
23967	SAXE	037	1154	1178	1182	0.2	33	436	461	469	0.6	2.53	319	328	0.3
23968	SKIPWITH	117	1121	1138	1133	0.2	33	440	457	458	0.4	2.49	320	323	0.1
23970	SOUTH HILL	117	7820	7927	7936	0.1	28	3142	3250	3278	0.4	2.33	2160	2160	0.0
	VIRGINIA					1.2					1.3	2.52			1.0
	UNITED STATES					1.0					1.1	2.59			0.9

ZIP CODE		RACE (%)								2009 AGE DISTRIBUTION (%)										MEDIAN AGE		
#	POST OFFICE NAME	White		Black		Asian/Pacific		% Hispanic Origin													%	%
		2000	2009	2000	2009	2000	2009	2000	2009	0-4	5-9	10-14	15-19	20-24	25-44	45-64	65-84	85+	18+	2009	2009 Males	2009 Females
23669	HAMPTON	46.6	42.9	47.9	49.6	1.7	2.4	2.7	3.9	6.5	6.2	6.2	10.5	9.7	24.7	25.0	10.2	1.2	76.7	33.7	47.6	52.4
23690	YORKTOWN	43.2	38.4	50.6	52.9	1.0	1.3	4.2	6.4	8.4	8.1	7.3	9.6	12.0	23.7	20.8	9.0	1.1	72.1	28.2	51.6	48.4
23692	YORKTOWN	89.7	86.9	5.7	6.5	2.5	3.6	1.9	3.1	4.9	5.3	6.0	6.6	4.8	22.1	33.5	15.1	1.7	79.4	45.1	48.7	51.3
23693	YORKTOWN	80.4	75.3	10.4	11.7	5.7	8.1	2.8	4.4	6.2	6.4	7.0	7.8	5.7	28.3	31.7	6.4	0.5	75.5	36.9	48.9	51.1
23696	SEAFORD	94.2	92.2	3.5	4.2	0.8	1.4	1.6	2.8	5.4	6.3	7.2	6.8	3.3	20.9	32.8	15.6	1.6	76.8	45.0	50.0	50.0
23701	PORTSMOUTH	44.0	41.4	53.4	55.1	0.5	0.7	1.0	1.4	5.9	6.1	6.0	6.3	6.5	25.9	25.5	15.2	2.5	78.2	40.1	47.9	52.1
23702	PORTSMOUTH	54.8	48.9	40.8	45.1	0.7	0.9	2.1	3.0	8.7	7.9	7.0	7.2	8.7	28.4	22.7	8.0	1.4	72.0	31.4	48.1	51.9
23703	PORTSMOUTH	56.0	50.4	39.1	42.7	1.6	2.2	2.9	4.3	6.7	6.3	6.0	8.7	11.6	27.5	22.5	8.9	1.7	77.1	32.3	52.2	47.8
23704	PORTSMOUTH	20.5	18.2	77.1	78.6	0.5	0.6	1.3	1.7	7.4	7.2	7.0	8.1	7.1	24.6	23.9	11.8	2.8	73.2	35.7	47.1	52.9
23707	PORTSMOUTH	56.9	54.6	39.9	40.9	0.5	0.8	1.2	1.8	7.9	7.2	6.7	6.5	6.9	26.0	25.2	10.7	2.8	74.4	36.6	46.7	53.3
23708	PORTSMOUTH	48.6	42.0	33.5	34.9	7.8	9.4	14.5	20.3	0.0	0.0	0.0	10.8	51.4	37.3	0.5	0.0	0.0	100.0	23.8	70.8	29.2
23709	PORTSMOUTH	90.0	85.0	10.0	15.0	0.0	0.0	0.0	0.0	0.0	10.0	10.0	10.0	5.0	15.0	40.0	10.0	0.0	70.0	45.0	50.0	50.0
23801	FORT LEE	39.7	33.9	46.9	46.4	2.8	3.3	11.4	18.1	9.2	7.8	5.5	17.9	23.5	33.5	2.3	0.2	0.1	74.6	22.0	58.3	41.7
23803	PETERSBURG	33.1	32.0	64.5	64.7	0.4	0.6	1.4	2.1	6.5	6.5	6.5	7.4	6.9	25.7	27.1	11.7	1.7	76.3	38.2	47.4	52.6
23805	PETERSBURG	42.3	39.3	54.5	56.4	1.2	1.6	1.3	2.0	5.4	5.4	5.9	6.4	6.2	24.4	29.0	14.5	2.7	79.3	42.3	46.8	53.2
23806	PETERSBURG	4.5	3.6	92.5	92.4	0.1	0.1	2.4	3.1	0.6	1.0	0.9	49.6	38.7	4.5	2.6	1.3	0.7	96.3	19.8	39.6	60.4
23821	ALBERTA	44.7	41.5	53.8	56.6	0.7	1.0	1.5	2.3	4.9	5.2	5.6	7.0	5.9	22.5	31.9	15.1	1.9	80.4	44.2	47.2	52.8
23824	BLACKSTONE	55.6	51.8	41.3	43.4	0.6	0.9	2.4	3.8	6.0	6.1	6.1	6.1	5.5	22.5	28.0	15.9	3.7	77.9	43.1	47.4	52.6
23827	BOYKINS	47.2	42.4	51.5	55.9	0.1	0.1	1.0	1.4	5.6	5.9	6.1	6.3	5.4	21.4	31.4	15.4	2.4	78.5	44.4	48.8	51.2
23828	BRANCHVILLE	46.0	41.2	52.8	57.0	0.0	0.2	1.0	1.5	5.7	5.9	5.9	6.4	5.5	21.1	31.7	15.2	2.4	78.4	44.5	48.7	51.3
23829	CAPRON	39.2	35.5	59.9	63.2	0.4	0.5	0.6	0.8	2.7	2.9	3.0	6.6	17.3	30.5	25.7	10.3	1.1	88.8	35.2	74.1	25.9
23830	CARSON	67.4	64.2	30.8	33.6	0.3	0.4	0.8	1.5	5.3	5.6	6.1	6.4	5.1	25.1	32.6	12.3	1.4	79.0	42.4	49.3	50.7
23831	CHESTER	81.8	77.1	13.2	15.5	2.3	3.3	2.7	4.5	6.6	6.9	7.1	7.1	5.4	26.1	30.2	9.6	1.0	74.9	38.9	48.7	51.3
23832	CHESTERFIELD	73.5	69.1	21.9	23.9	1.8	2.8	2.3	3.7	7.4	7.5	7.5	7.1	5.9	29.3	27.6	6.9	0.8	73.0	35.6	48.5	51.5
23833	CHURCH ROAD	77.4	74.2	21.1	23.7	0.1	0.1	0.6	0.9	6.1	6.5	6.8	5.8	4.4	27.1	30.6	11.3	1.5	76.6	41.4	52.2	47.8
23834	COLONIAL HEIGHTS	82.6	78.5	12.9	14.8	2.4	3.6	1.8	3.0	6.4	6.2	6.3	6.6	6.1	25.7	27.3	13.2	2.3	77.0	39.5	47.6	52.4
23836	CHESTER	82.8	76.8	10.9	12.8	3.8	6.2	2.3	4.2	6.7	7.2	7.5	7.2	5.1	24.6	31.2	9.6	0.8	74.0	39.6	49.4	50.6
23837	COURTLAND	64.1	59.9	34.8	38.6	0.3	0.5	0.4	0.6	5.0	5.2	5.6	6.2	5.8	24.1	30.9	14.3	2.8	80.1	43.5	50.4	49.6
23838	CHESTERFIELD	87.5	83.8	10.2	12.5	1.1	1.7	0.8	1.6	5.3	6.3	7.4	7.3	4.3	21.2	37.1	10.4	0.9	76.5	43.9	50.2	49.8
23839	DENDRON	48.4	44.9	50.2	53.5	0.1	0.1	0.6	0.9	6.2	6.5	6.8	6.8	5.3	22.0	31.2	13.2	2.1	76.6	42.3	47.9	52.1
23840	DEWITT	63.0	58.7	35.8	39.6	0.1	0.2	0.3	0.6	4.6	5.0	5.7	6.8	4.8	22.2	34.5	14.6	1.9	79.9	45.6	51.1	48.9
23841	DINWIDDIE	55.2	51.2	43.5	47.1	0.2	0.3	0.6	0.8	5.0	5.5	6.1	6.1	4.4	23.8	32.1	15.4	1.6	79.5	44.3	49.1	50.9
23842	DISPUTANTA	68.4	64.2	29.1	32.3	0.8	0.9	1.6	2.8	5.2	5.9	6.7	6.8	5.1	29.0	30.0	10.3	1.0	78.0	39.8	53.5	46.5
23843	DOLPHIN	39.1	35.3	59.7	63.0	0.0	0.0	0.7	1.0	4.7	5.0	5.8	6.4	4.8	23.4	31.4	16.1	2.3	80.8	44.8	48.4	51.6
23844	DREWRYVILLE	44.5	39.8	54.5	58.9	0.0	0.0	0.7	0.9	6.7	6.6	6.7	7.2	5.7	21.3	30.1	13.7	2.1	75.7	42.0	47.5	52.5
23845	EBONY	58.9	54.9	39.9	43.5	0.0	0.0	0.6	0.8	4.2	4.9	5.1	5.5	3.8	23.6	31.2	20.0	1.7	82.5	47.9	46.2	53.8
23846	ELBERON	49.5	45.9	48.6	51.6	0.0	0.0	0.8	1.2	5.7	6.2	6.7	7.1	5.3	22.3	31.6	13.3	1.9	77.0	42.7	47.6	52.4
23847	EMPORIA	39.8	37.2	58.8	61.1	0.5	0.6	1.2	1.5	4.8	4.7	5.0	5.7	6.6	30.2	27.2	13.1	2.6	82.0	40.6	55.5	44.5
23850	FORD	66.0	62.2	32.6	35.9	0.1	0.1	0.4	0.6	4.7	5.0	5.8	6.9	4.6	22.6	33.6	15.0	1.8	80.1	45.2	49.8	50.2
23851	FRANKLIN	50.1	46.5	48.3	51.4	0.5	0.8	0.5	0.7	5.6	6.0	6.1	6.8	5.9	23.4	28.9	14.3	2.9	78.1	42.0	45.9	54.1
23856	FREEMAN	31.1	27.9	67.7	70.4	0.1	0.1	2.0	2.8	5.9	6.1	6.7	7.5	5.7	23.3	28.3	14.0	2.5	76.6	41.1	46.1	53.9
23857	GASBURG	66.5	63.4	33.0	35.8	0.0	0.2	0.7	1.0	5.2	5.7	5.9	4.8	3.3	20.2	32.5	20.6	1.9	80.3	48.4	50.1	49.9
23860	HOPEWELL	63.8	59.1	31.8	33.6	1.1	2.2	2.9	5.0	6.2	6.0	5.8	6.5	7.3	31.8	24.1	10.6	1.7	78.2	35.8	53.9	46.1
23866	IVOR	64.2	59.5	34.3	38.4	0.1	0.2	0.7	0.9	5.4	5.9	6.3	6.5	5.3	22.7	31.8	14.2	2.0	78.4	43.5	49.8	50.2
23867	JARRATT	33.0	31.1	65.8	67.6	0.3	0.3	0.6	0.8	4.4	4.3	4.9	5.1	6.6	34.0	26.9	11.9	1.9	83.1	39.6	60.1	39.9
23868	LAWRENCEVILLE	35.9	32.4	62.8	65.7	0.2	0.3	1.3	1.9	4.0	4.0	4.1	6.6	9.6	38.1	22.2	10.0	1.6	85.1	35.7	61.4	38.6
23872	MC KENNEY	62.5	58.5	36.2	39.8	0.3	0.4	1.1	1.4	4.9	5.3	5.9	6.8	4.7	22.8	32.2	15.1	2.3	79.4	44.7	49.6	50.4
23874	NEWSOMS	57.0	52.2	41.7	46.1	0.1	0.1	0.9	1.2	5.4	6.0	6.5	6.2	4.3	23.3	33.1	13.0	2.1	78.2	43.6	47.6	52.4
23875	PRINCE GEORGE	67.1	60.7	27.4	31.0	2.1	2.9	3.1	5.5	6.2	6.6	6.9	7.4	6.1	27.4	29.0	9.6	0.8	75.7	37.5	48.9	51.1
23876	RAWLINGS	42.2	39.5	56.9	59.2	0.6	0.6	2.0	3.1	5.4	6.0	6.6	6.6	5.2	22.5	30.8	15.0	1.9	77.8	43.3	48.0	52.0
23878	SEDLEY	69.5	65.3	29.1	32.7	0.2	0.3	0.8	1.1	5.7	6.0	6.2	6.5	5.1	23.9	31.0	13.2	2.3	77.9	42.7	49.7	50.3
23879	SKIPPERS	45.7	42.0	53.2	56.6	0.0	0.0	1.0	1.3	5.0	5.6	5.9	5.7	5.0	22.8	33.2	14.9	1.8	79.7	44.9	49.6	50.4
23881	SPRING GROVE	44.3	48.7	51.0	48.8	1.0	0.4	5.3	1.6	5.2	5.7	5.9	6.1	4.7	24.2	32.1	14.2	1.8	79.4	43.7	50.3	49.7
23882	STONY CREEK	42.3	40.8	56.3	57.7	0.1	0.1	0.5	0.6	5.1	5.2	6.2	6.1	5.0	23.6	32.6	13.9	2.4	79.8	44.2	48.5	51.5
23883	SURRY	45.2	41.7	53.4	56.5	0.2	0.2	0.7	1.0	5.2	5.9	6.9	6.9	5.6	24.4	32.0	11.6	1.4	77.5	41.8	48.7	51.3
23885	SUTHERLAND	74.9	71.8	24.0	26.8	0.3	0.4	0.5	0.9	4.9	5.5	6.1	6.4	4.2	24.4	32.8	14.1	1.5	79.3	44.0	50.7	49.3
23887	VALENTINES	76.0	73.2	23.5	26.3	0.2	0.2	0.5	0.6	5.1	5.7	5.6	3.8	2.7	17.0	35.2	22.9	1.9	81.1	51.4	51.9	48.1
23888	WAKEFIELD	48.0	46.5	50.6	51.9	0.1	0.1	0.6	0.7	5.9	6.2	6.5	6.7	5.2	23.2	30.4	13.6	2.2	77.2	42.2	48.1	51.9
23889	WARFIELD	40.8	37.1	58.0	61.0	0.2	0.2	1.0	1.7	4.9	5.2	5.8	6.2	4.5	23.4	31.8	15.7	2.4	80.3	45.0	48.5	51.5
23890	WAVERLY	32.3	31.5	66.2	67.0	0.1	0.1	1.1	1.1	3.6	4.1	4.4	4.8	9.4	36.5	25.0	10.3	2.0	84.9	37.4	65.0	35.0
23893	WHITE PLAINS	53.8	50.0	45.9	49.3	0.0	0.0	0.9	1.4	5.6	5.8	6.3	6.3	4.5	24.3	29.5	16.2	1.6	78.2	43.0	48.9	51.1
23894	WILSONS	66.3	62.6	32.1	35.5	0.3	0.2	0.5	0.5	4.6	5.1	5.9	6.8	4.6	22.0	34.0	15.2	1.7	80.0	45.4	49.4	50.6
23897	YALE	50.3	48.3	48.9	50.9	0.2	0.2	0.5	0.3	5.8	6.5	7.3	7.3	4.2	22.3	28.6	16.0	2.1	75.9	42.8	50.1	49.9
23898	ZUNI	77.4	73.2	21.3	24.9	0.3	0.4	0.8	1.1	5.3	5.9	6.4	6.7	5.0	25.4	32.1	11.8	1.3	77.9	41.9	49.9	50.1
23901	FARMVILLE	66.8	63.1	30.8	33.5	0.9	1.2	1.1	1.6	4.5	4.5	4.7	14.6	15.1	19.5	22.2	12.1	2.9	83.2	32.0	48.5	51.5
23915	BASKERVILLE	53.4	49.5	45.3	48.8	0.1	0.1	1.6	2.2	3.7	3.8	4.1	5.0	6.6	36.5	26.8	12.1	1.4	85.3	39.4	63.3	36.7
23917	BOYDTON	51.4	47.3	47.3	50.9	0.2	0.3	0.5	0.8	3.7	3.8	4.2	5.3	6.5	29.9	29.5	15.2	1.8	85.0	42.6	56.9	43.1
23919	BRACEY	79.6	77.2	18.9	20.7	0.1	0.2	1.1	1.8	4.7	4.9	4.9	4.3	3.4	18.5	33.2	24.2	2.0	82.8	51.3	49.0	51.0
23920	BRODNAX	48.8	45.4	50.0	53.0	0.3	0.4	0.9	1.4	6.0	6.4	6.7	6.1	5.2	24.0	30.2	13.8	1.6	77.0	41.5	48.3	51.7
23921	BUCKINGHAM	67.0	63.2	30.8	33.7	0.3	0.5	0.6	0.9	5.4	5.6	5.9	5.7	4.9	23.0	32.0	15.3	2.0	79.5	44.5	48.7	51.3
23922	BURKEVILLE	47.4	43.7	51.0	54.0	0.5	0.6	1.0	1.5	3.8	4.0	4.3	4.9	8.8	34.5	24.7	13.2	1.7	85.0	38.5	62.5	37.5
23923	CHARLOTTE COURT HOUS	62.7	59.1	35.2	38.2	0.1	0.1	1.5	2.3	5.6	5.9	6.1	6.4	5.3	23.2	29.6	15.8	2.2	79.4	42.9	50.3	49.7
23924	CHASE CITY	53.7	49.7	44.5	47.8	0.2	0.4	1.2	1.8	6.1	6.0	6.4	6.6	5.5	23.0	28.9	15.0	2.5	77.5	42.1	47.7	52.3
23927	CLARKSVILLE	66.2	62.5	32.3	35.4	0.1	0.2	0.8	1.2	5.0	5.2	5.4	5.3	4.3	21.5	31.5	19.3	2.5	81.1	47.4	47.9	52.1
23930	CREWE	65.2	61.4	33.2	36.4	0.2	0.3	0.9	1.4	6.0	5.9	6.2	6.6	6.6	25.3	27.4	13.7	2.2	77.8	40.0	50.6	49.4
23934	CULLEN	59.4	55.8	39.1	42.4	0.0	0.0	0.7	1.2	5.7	5.8	6.3	6.2	5.2	22.5	31.6	14.7	2.0	80.1	43.5	50.1	49.9
23936	DILLWYN	54.7	51.1	43.7	46.8	0.2	0.3	0.8	1.1	4.3	4.3	4.9	5.8	7.2	35.7	26.2	10.0	1.7	82.8	38.6	63.4	36.6
23937	DRAKES BRANCH	67.0	63.8	31.6	34.2	0.1	0.1	1.8	3.0	4.9	6.2	6.6	6.9	5.0	23.4	28.7	15.3	3.1	78.0	42.6	47.4	52.6
23938	DUNDAS	61.9	58.4	36.3	39.1	0.4	0.6	1.8	2.9	5.7	6.0	6.3	5.7	5.4	22.1	32.8	14.1	1.9	78.2	44.0	50.1	49.9
23942	GREEN BAY	63.1	59.1	34.8	38.3	0.2	0.3	0.7	1.1	4.6	4.8	5.4	6.8	5.7	27.8	30.1	13.0	1.8	81.1	41.9	54.3	45.7
23944	KENBRIDGE	56.9	53.0	40.5	43.1	0.3	0.4	2.6	4.2	5.7	5.7	6.0	6.0	5.2	22.8	30.0	16.2	2.5	78.9	43.9	49.7	50.3
23947	KEYSVILLE	66.8	63.1	31.5	34.4	0.1	0.1	1.7	2.8	5.1	5.4	5.9	6.7	5.2	22.2	30.5	16.3	2.7	79.2	44.6	48.4	51.6
23950	LA CROSSE	59.1	56.2	39.2	41.5	0.2	0.2	1.8	2.7	5.4	5.7	6.1	5.4	4.8	23.5	30.5	17.0	1.7	79.5	44.3	48.6	51.4
23952	LUNENBURG	59.7	55.9	38.4	41.4	0.0	0.0	1.2	1.6	4.3	4.7	5.1	5.5	4.7	21.1	34.0	19.1	1.6	82.4	48.3	48.4	51.6
23954	MEHERRIN	54.1	49.4	44.5	48.5	0.1	0.1	0.6	0.9	5.5	5.8	6.2	6.7	5.8	22.4	32.5	13.6	1.7	78.4	43.2	49.3	50.7
23958	PAMPLIN	65.2	62.4	33.8	36.2	0.1	0.1	0.9	1.4	5.9	6.2	6.6	8.2	7.0	22.0	28.9	13.4	1.7	77.1	40.5	51.7	48.3
23959	PHENIX	73.5	70.5	25.3	27.7	0.0	0.0	1.4	2.2	5.6	5.9	5.7	5.8	5.2	23.4	29.8	16.1	2.5	79.2	43.9	48.4	51.6
23960	PROSPECT	54.6	50.5	44.2	48.0	0.3	0.3	0.6	0.9	6.1	6.3	6.5	8.9	7.9	22.1	27.3	13.0	1.9	76.8	39.1	51.3	48.7
23962	RANDOLPH	58.0	54.2	40.7	43.8	0.0	0.1	1.1	1.7	5.8	5.9	6.0	6.9	5.7	22.6	28.0	16.6	2.6	78.2	42.8	49.9	50.1
23963	RED HOUSE	67.4	64.0	30.6	32.9	0.1	0.1	1.7	2.6	6.0	6.3	6.5	6.8	4.9	24.0	29.3	14.6	1.8	76.8	41.7	49.9	50.1
23964	RED OAK	60.7	56.9	37.2	40.0	0.9	1.4	1.5	2.4	5.9	6.3	6.9	7.1	4.9	23.3	29.5	13.8	2.2	76.4	41.6	49.2	50.8
23966	RICE	59.0	54.9	39.2	42.6	0.5	0.7	1.0	1.3	5.7	5.8	6.1	6.1	5.2	25.1	29.4	14.1	2.6	78.7	42.0	47.3	52.7
23967	SAXE	62.7	59.5	36.0	38.7	0.1	0.1	1.9	3.2	6.0	6.7	7.0	7.0	5.5	24.6	27.8	13.3	1.9	76.0	39.7	47.3	52.7
23968	SKIPWITH	67.1	63.3	31.3	34.4	0.2	0.3	0.9	1.4	5.4	5.9	6.2	5.7	4.1	21.9	30.3	18.5	1.8	78.9	45.4	49.0	51.0
23970	SOUTH HILL	55.5	51.8	42.3	45.1	0.8	1.1	1.5	2.3	6.0	5.9	5.8	6.1	5.6	24.7	28.2	14.6	3.1	78.5	41.7	47.8	52.2
	VIRGINIA	72.3	68.8	19.6	20.1	3.7	5.1	4.7	7.0	6.5	6.4	6.5	6.9	6.9	27.5	27.2	10.5	1.6	76.7	37.7	49.2	50.8
	UNITED STATES	75.1	72.0	12.3	12.7	3.8	4.6	12.5	15.7	6.8	6.7	6.6	7.1	6.9	27.0	26.0	10.9	1.9	75.7	36.9	49.2	50.8

ZIP CODE #	POST OFFICE NAME	2009 Per Capita Income	2009 HH Income Base	2009 HOUSEHOLD INCOME DISTRIBUTION (%) Less than $25,000	$25,000 to $49,999	$50,000 to $99,999	$100,000 to $149,999	$150,000 or More	MEDIAN HOUSEHOLD INCOME 2009	2014	2009 National Centile	2009 State Centile	2009 Home Value Base	2009 HOME VALUE DISTRIBUTION (%) Less than $50,000	$50,000 to $89,999	$90,000 to $174,999	$175,000 to $399,999	$400,000 or More	2009 Median Home Value
23669	HAMPTON	23570	16724	22.8	27.3	36.3	9.8	3.7	49876	53322	61	57	9436	0.6	3.2	46.7	45.2	4.4	174385
23690	YORKTOWN	18341	1017	37.3	31.9	22.0	6.4	2.5	34435	34486	16	14	441	7.5	10.4	45.8	26.3	10.0	149464
23692	YORKTOWN	37936	7296	5.7	17.3	37.0	28.7	11.3	82687	87944	93	88	6117	3.2	0.9	13.5	64.8	17.7	273492
23693	YORKTOWN	35605	7929	4.7	13.6	35.3	31.8	14.6	93135	98776	96	92	6196	2.5	0.3	15.8	58.5	22.9	308587
23696	SEAFORD	39399	1441	3.9	14.2	34.6	34.3	13.1	94763	100204	96	92	1307	0.3	1.8	11.7	61.1	25.0	299084
23701	PORTSMOUTH	21855	10173	20.7	31.2	39.3	6.9	1.9	47967	51132	57	52	6738	0.7	3.5	72.4	21.7	1.7	148052
23702	PORTSMOUTH	16487	4431	33.2	35.1	28.3	2.8	0.7	37877	39737	26	23	2118	4.5	6.3	82.0	7.2	0.0	125075
23703	PORTSMOUTH	24412	10023	13.1	28.9	44.7	10.5	2.9	58604	62001	76	73	6814	0.5	2.3	36.2	57.1	4.0	191349
23704	PORTSMOUTH	17593	7717	38.7	28.8	26.4	4.4	1.6	33075	35105	13	12	3305	3.0	15.3	64.7	14.1	2.9	129145
23707	PORTSMOUTH	20192	6104	32.7	28.5	32.2	5.1	1.5	39054	41739	30	27	3222	0.5	6.1	67.4	24.1	1.8	149253
23708	PORTSMOUTH	17288	0	0.0	0.0	0.0	0.0	0.0	0	0	0	0	0	0.0	0.0	0.0	0.0	0.0	0
23709	PORTSMOUTH	36250	6	0.0	0.0	0.0	100.0	0.0	115118	115118	98	96	0	0.0	0.0	0.0	0.0	0.0	0
23801	FORT LEE	17170	1082	15.2	37.2	39.8	7.6	0.2	48172	49640	57	53	29	13.8	34.5	34.5	17.2	0.0	95000
23803	PETERSBURG	20017	15568	30.0	29.4	33.2	5.5	1.9	41125	44195	36	33	9100	7.4	18.5	56.4	16.0	1.8	122200
23805	PETERSBURG	26448	7509	16.4	27.0	42.7	10.2	3.8	56018	60659	73	70	5089	4.0	6.6	59.8	26.0	3.6	146099
23806	PETERSBURG	15256	11	45.5	36.4	18.2	0.0	0.0	25998	22247	4	3	4	0.0	0.0	75.0	25.0	0.0	137500
23821	ALBERTA	19735	649	34.5	31.1	28.4	4.5	1.5	34233	36154	16	14	508	13.2	19.1	48.4	16.1	3.1	113492
23824	BLACKSTONE	19001	2796	36.1	25.0	32.5	4.6	1.9	35517	38025	19	16	1910	16.6	18.3	38.7	22.8	3.6	120513
23827	BOYKINS	17688	721	35.6	30.9	29.3	3.2	1.0	35282	36178	19	16	487	9.7	20.3	46.8	21.1	2.1	119196
23828	BRANCHVILLE	17005	185	37.3	30.3	28.6	3.2	0.5	34346	35772	16	14	125	9.6	20.0	47.2	21.6	1.6	119022
23829	CAPRON	18478	524	29.8	30.3	33.2	5.9	0.8	40673	41702	35	32	392	12.0	15.3	45.4	25.5	1.8	119578
23830	CARSON	22595	469	19.8	28.4	43.1	6.0	2.8	51366	55256	65	61	364	20.3	9.9	32.1	34.6	3.0	150000
23831	CHESTER	30849	12125	10.3	17.8	45.3	19.9	6.7	74874	78473	89	85	9434	8.2	2.0	31.4	54.1	4.3	197740
23832	CHESTERFIELD	31138	12202	3.4	15.9	51.3	22.4	6.9	78195	83089	91	86	10503	0.2	0.6	44.0	48.5	6.7	185769
23833	CHURCH ROAD	23697	823	18.2	28.6	40.7	11.1	1.5	52987	56409	68	65	698	3.9	8.7	41.7	41.8	3.9	168802
23834	COLONIAL HEIGHTS	28296	10447	12.8	27.1	42.2	13.5	4.3	60560	63767	78	75	7472	1.6	3.8	55.8	37.0	1.8	156755
23836	CHESTER	31737	4079	9.1	19.7	41.0	21.8	8.4	76504	81311	90	86	3524	14.2	1.6	31.4	43.1	9.7	184690
23837	COURTLAND	23909	1643	26.1	25.7	37.2	8.4	2.6	48420	48579	58	54	1195	7.2	10.9	44.9	33.4	3.7	157282
23838	CHESTERFIELD	36762	4884	6.5	10.6	40.0	28.1	14.7	89926	100572	95	90	4601	2.4	2.4	21.1	49.6	24.4	282559
23839	DENDRON	16918	337	26.1	28.5	40.1	4.2	1.2	46029	47985	51	47	269	14.1	14.5	36.4	25.3	9.7	126630
23840	DEWITT	24410	622	17.5	25.4	46.8	8.0	2.3	57097	60608	74	72	520	7.3	15.6	46.5	26.9	3.7	146364
23841	DINWIDDIE	25137	1418	20.2	24.4	41.4	10.8	3.2	56125	60267	73	71	1146	4.5	15.6	45.1	31.5	3.2	149675
23842	DISPUTANTA	26861	2194	15.1	22.2	42.5	15.4	4.8	63490	67097	82	78	1833	8.8	7.1	32.3	47.0	4.9	180107
23843	DOLPHIN	21709	227	30.4	30.8	32.2	4.8	1.8	42495	44015	41	37	182	7.1	15.9	47.3	20.9	8.8	130208
23844	DREWRYVILLE	14744	332	35.8	38.0	24.7	1.2	0.3	33370	35459	14	12	247	23.9	12.6	42.1	20.6	0.8	111824
23845	EBONY	17740	219	33.8	39.7	21.9	4.6	0.0	28917	29028	7	5	175	32.6	9.1	33.1	18.3	6.9	128906
23846	ELBERON	18044	314	23.6	31.8	40.4	3.2	1.0	45677	48086	50	46	252	14.7	10.7	44.8	25.0	4.8	132692
23847	EMPORIA	18042	5616	32.6	31.3	30.3	4.3	1.5	37568	39429	25	22	3782	12.5	20.7	47.8	17.4	1.7	117061
23850	FORD	21709	545	22.8	29.2	38.7	7.7	1.7	47386	50795	55	51	436	5.3	18.1	37.2	32.6	6.9	152885
23851	FRANKLIN	21176	5670	33.7	26.5	29.2	7.7	2.9	39727	41261	32	29	3405	7.7	12.2	44.1	30.2	5.8	151452
23856	FREEMAN	17419	484	33.7	30.8	30.6	3.9	1.0	40390	41173	34	30	364	13.7	19.0	44.2	17.6	5.5	107258
23857	GASBURG	23710	268	22.4	34.0	35.4	5.6	2.6	46019	47213	51	46	227	12.3	9.7	34.4	35.2	8.4	161574
23860	HOPEWELL	21887	11286	23.0	30.1	36.5	7.8	2.5	47152	49814	54	50	6708	2.6	9.5	61.2	23.2	3.4	139388
23866	IVOR	18929	986	28.3	31.1	33.5	5.1	2.0	41714	43653	38	35	771	8.0	9.9	40.6	36.1	5.4	157763
23867	JARRATT	23976	986	31.0	33.5	29.2	4.6	1.7	35659	37437	20	17	726	17.9	17.5	44.8	16.9	2.9	115657
23868	LAWRENCEVILLE	17943	2015	33.5	28.7	32.3	3.5	1.9	39308	40956	31	27	1509	11.8	23.0	46.1	16.3	2.8	110119
23872	MC KENNEY	22042	976	20.5	30.4	38.9	8.3	1.8	48792	53612	58	55	755	9.8	16.8	48.6	22.3	2.5	122077
23874	NEWSOMS	21159	454	22.7	35.2	37.0	4.0	1.1	43528	44655	44	40	350	6.6	16.0	51.4	21.1	4.9	124342
23875	PRINCE GEORGE	26813	4225	13.9	23.6	45.8	11.9	4.9	63798	68581	82	79	3177	17.8	2.9	35.4	40.2	3.7	165036
23876	RAWLINGS	18418	211	37.9	26.1	29.9	4.3	1.9	31548	33877	11	9	158	15.8	20.9	44.9	15.8	2.5	108824
23878	SEDLEY	19489	451	28.6	26.6	37.3	6.2	1.3	42609	45966	52	47	343	9.3	8.5	39.1	40.2	2.9	162760
23879	SKIPPERS	18207	229	31.9	31.9	31.0	4.4	0.9	37687	38523	26	23	185	16.2	27.0	40.5	15.7	0.5	99615
23881	SPRING GROVE	21769	1059	28.3	25.4	38.1	5.9	2.4	44817	48815	48	43	761	8.0	8.9	36.9	40.3	5.8	166220
23882	STONY CREEK	21119	1032	31.2	28.2	33.4	4.8	2.3	40580	42705	35	31	782	13.9	21.0	49.1	15.9	0.1	108740
23883	SURRY	20189	948	21.9	33.8	37.4	6.5	0.3	45309	47610	49	45	752	20.6	9.7	33.1	29.4	7.2	143458
23885	SUTHERLAND	27468	1124	13.4	25.2	41.4	15.8	4.2	61438	62709	79	76	974	1.5	6.1	43.0	40.1	9.2	173855
23887	VALENTINES	27208	290	16.6	29.3	43.4	6.6	4.1	52862	55751	68	65	254	3.5	7.1	28.7	50.8	9.8	210870
23888	WAKEFIELD	18247	1027	33.4	32.3	28.6	4.6	1.1	34787	36461	17	15	709	16.6	16.4	43.3	21.2	2.5	119401
23889	WARFIELD	20028	227	33.0	29.1	30.8	4.8	2.2	39610	40344	32	28	175	7.4	21.1	46.9	17.7	6.9	123125
23890	WAVERLY	18461	1778	30.0	28.3	33.8	6.1	1.8	41475	44050	38	35	1213	14.9	18.4	44.8	19.5	2.3	120139
23893	WHITE PLAINS	18259	245	28.6	40.4	26.9	3.3	0.8	37148	38821	24	20	198	21.7	15.7	46.5	10.1	6.1	107500
23894	WILSONS	23531	179	22.9	29.6	39.1	7.3	1.1	46681	49659	53	49	141	6.4	17.7	36.9	31.9	7.1	150781
23897	YALE	18309	260	28.5	33.1	33.1	5.4	0.0	40665	41371	35	32	199	7.5	16.1	53.8	22.6	0.0	122348
23898	ZUNI	22371	766	18.9	25.6	46.1	7.7	1.7	53199	55511	68	66	640	16.3	6.6	34.4	39.1	3.8	157308
23901	FARMVILLE	19901	5796	32.8	28.6	31.0	5.0	2.6	38300	39971	28	24	3767	7.8	14.1	40.7	32.1	5.2	143636
23915	BASKERVILLE	17174	362	26.8	41.2	25.4	3.6	3.0	37942	38563	26	23	262	9.5	16.8	54.2	17.9	1.5	128448
23917	BOYDTON	19815	1314	28.8	36.5	27.0	4.6	3.2	40466	42169	34	31	1048	11.3	14.3	43.7	24.5	6.2	129369
23919	BRACEY	24228	973	25.3	34.5	29.5	7.6	3.1	42706	44526	42	38	834	11.8	14.0	36.2	29.1	8.9	144737
23920	BRODNAX	17370	1325	33.8	34.4	26.7	3.8	1.2	36108	37620	21	18	976	19.0	17.2	46.8	15.2	1.8	108639
23921	BUCKINGHAM	19175	948	31.3	34.2	28.4	5.0	1.2	37099	38469	24	20	714	11.2	6.4	48.2	30.0	4.2	154965
23922	BURKEVILLE	16413	1003	33.6	27.4	33.8	4.0	1.2	39735	40896	32	29	766	11.1	16.3	46.9	23.4	2.3	131473
23923	CHARLOTTE COURT HOUS	18560	910	32.4	35.4	27.6	2.4	2.2	35983	36652	21	18	730	9.7	18.1	41.9	24.2	6.0	133967
23924	CHASE CITY	17142	2831	43.8	29.8	21.1	4.2	1.1	29887	30761	8	7	1998	19.1	21.4	45.0	12.0	2.6	100262
23927	CLARKSVILLE	24794	1994	23.1	32.2	34.8	7.5	2.4	45042	47509	48	44	1571	7.1	11.8	44.4	29.7	6.9	154117
23930	CREWE	19828	2379	32.2	28.1	32.7	5.6	1.3	41098	42568	36	33	1693	8.1	17.4	52.9	20.0	1.7	128016
23934	CULLEN	18148	246	31.7	38.6	25.2	2.0	2.4	34219	35341	16	14	192	7.8	19.3	41.7	26.6	4.7	130000
23936	DILLWYN	17721	1994	36.4	29.4	27.0	6.2	1.1	34469	35929	16	14	1495	15.9	15.8	38.7	25.8	3.9	128037
23937	DRAKES BRANCH	17771	831	36.3	34.5	24.3	3.5	1.3	31964	33819	11	10	629	18.4	17.2	42.8	18.9	2.7	112064
23938	DUNDAS	17717	280	32.5	36.8	26.8	3.2	0.7	32717	34849	13	11	224	16.1	24.1	42.4	15.2	2.2	107407
23942	GREEN BAY	21707	482	36.3	22.6	35.3	2.7	3.1	39093	39375	30	27	386	15.3	18.7	37.8	16.3	11.9	136310
23944	KENBRIDGE	18904	1727	36.8	27.9	29.9	4.1	1.3	35604	37581	20	17	1321	12.6	21.3	41.7	21.7	2.6	113791
23947	KEYSVILLE	18696	1895	36.6	32.3	26.1	2.9	2.1	33359	34710	14	12	1406	12.5	17.3	44.0	23.2	3.1	128073
23950	LA CROSSE	18955	1373	31.0	35.5	27.2	4.2	2.0	37556	38878	25	22	1064	15.5	18.5	39.6	21.9	4.5	125143
23952	LUNENBURG	22491	108	28.7	35.2	26.9	5.6	3.7	37301	40000	24	21	89	14.6	19.1	44.9	20.2	1.1	113281
23954	MEHERRIN	17286	750	38.1	27.5	28.0	4.7	1.7	34111	35000	16	14	596	16.1	17.6	35.9	23.7	6.7	121591
23958	PAMPLIN	20054	1193	29.5	34.8	29.8	3.8	2.2	38366	39675	28	25	944	14.1	18.6	38.2	24.7	4.3	119213
23959	PHENIX	17699	421	38.7	24.5	31.8	4.3	0.7	33023	37612	13	12	346	9.0	26.0	46.5	17.1	1.4	116204
23960	PROSPECT	19496	761	29.8	31.9	28.8	8.7	0.8	42379	43530	41	37	575	7.7	18.8	33.6	30.3	9.7	146272
23962	RANDOLPH	16859	369	40.1	31.2	24.4	3.0	1.4	29919	32022	8	7	304	17.4	17.1	47.0	17.4	1.0	114623
23963	RED HOUSE	18164	261	32.2	28.7	34.1	3.8	1.1	38852	41753	29	26	213	11.3	22.1	37.6	21.6	7.5	131250
23964	RED OAK	14638	491	41.5	31.6	23.4	3.5	0.0	28827	29691	6	5	379	30.1	11.3	41.7	14.8	2.1	106419
23966	RICE	20891	946	28.1	31.2	32.5	5.2	3.1	43396	45220	44	39	643	12.1	11.2	29.4	40.1	7.2	165885
23967	SAXE	15940	461	38.2	30.6	27.3	3.5	0.4	35112	35688	18	15	359	23.4	17.5	34.5	18.1	6.4	105163
23968	SKIPWITH	18513	457	33.7	30.0	28.4	7.4	0.4	37442	39117	25	22	360	15.6	17.2	39.4	22.8	5.0	130114
23970	SOUTH HILL	20939	3250	30.8	32.6	29.0	5.5	2.0	40731	42593	35	32	2086	10.2	16.2	39.9	27.9	5.8	138447
	VIRGINIA	30912		17.0	22.6	35.9	15.0	9.5	61855	64957				5.3	6.3	30.4	41.5	16.5	203135
	UNITED STATES	27277		20.9	24.4	35.3	11.7	7.6	54719	56938				9.3	13.1	31.6	32.6	13.5	162279

ZIP CODE #	POST OFFICE NAME	FINANCIAL SERVICES: Auto Loan	Home Loan	Investments	Retirement Plans	THE HOME: Home Improvements: Home Repair	Lawn & Garden	Furnishings: Computers & Hardware-Personal	Major Appliances	TV, Radio, Sound Equipment	Furniture	ENTERTAINMENT: Dine out/Carry out	Sports Equipment	Fees & Tickets	Toys & Games	Travel	Cable TV	PERSONAL: Apparel & Services	Auto Repairs	Health Insurance	Pets & Supplies
23669	HAMPTON	83	80	75	82	78	81	87	81	87	84	87	63	85	87	83	88	61	85	86	97
23690	YORKTOWN	66	54	50	57	52	60	65	59	71	63	70	45	62	70	59	74	49	66	69	73
23692	YORKTOWN	126	151	149	153	153	143	134	137	129	139	131	104	149	130	146	128	93	133	133	158
23693	YORKTOWN	144	170	148	173	165	143	146	146	136	160	139	120	162	145	152	127	101	137	124	165
23696	SEAFORD	136	168	171	173	172	159	143	151	137	153	138	113	163	136	160	134	99	143	142	173
23701	PORTSMOUTH	77	75	68	76	72	79	76	75	79	76	79	56	77	79	75	81	55	77	82	90
23702	PORTSMOUTH	61	54	45	56	50	55	62	55	63	59	63	45	58	64	56	64	44	60	60	68
23703	PORTSMOUTH	89	93	85	92	90	87	93	89	91	94	92	69	95	93	92	90	65	91	90	104
23704	PORTSMOUTH	61	53	48	55	50	58	60	56	64	59	64	42	57	63	55	67	44	61	65	70
23707	PORTSMOUTH	66	59	52	61	56	63	66	61	69	64	69	48	63	69	61	72	48	66	69	76
23708	PORTSMOUTH	0	0	0	0	0	0	0	0	0	0	0	0	0	0	0	0	0	0	0	0
23709	PORTSMOUTH	171	208	180	214	203	170	173	175	159	194	162	146	196	173	182	146	119	160	143	195
23801	FORT LEE	96	50	37	58	45	42	90	63	85	84	89	62	69	102	65	78	63	80	56	76
23803	PETERSBURG	70	64	58	65	61	69	68	66	73	67	72	50	66	72	64	76	49	69	75	81
23805	PETERSBURG	90	88	87	88	87	95	88	90	92	87	91	67	88	90	89	95	63	91	99	107
23806	PETERSBURG	40	33	36	33	34	39	41	40	44	37	42	29	36	42	37	46	29	42	46	47
23821	ALBERTA	82	59	82	57	60	82	60	75	67	57	66	57	48	67	59	73	44	70	78	90
23824	BLACKSTONE	74	59	71	59	60	76	63	71	68	59	66	53	55	67	61	73	45	68	77	84
23827	BOYKINS	77	53	74	51	53	76	56	69	63	53	62	54	43	64	53	70	41	65	73	84
23828	BRANCHVILLE	76	51	73	49	51	75	55	68	62	52	61	53	42	63	51	69	40	64	72	83
23829	CAPRON	78	64	72	64	65	81	64	75	69	59	67	57	56	70	63	74	46	70	78	89
23830	CARSON	96	75	91	72	76	95	75	89	81	73	80	66	64	83	72	88	54	83	91	106
23831	CHESTER	113	127	114	127	123	117	115	115	112	119	114	89	123	115	119	110	80	113	111	135
23832	CHESTERFIELD	128	142	119	139	134	122	126	126	121	134	123	99	132	127	127	116	86	121	114	145
23833	CHURCH ROAD	89	89	86	91	88	96	83	91	84	80	84	70	82	86	85	87	58	86	92	107
23834	COLONIAL HEIGHTS	97	101	91	102	98	99	98	97	98	98	98	75	101	99	98	98	68	97	100	115
23836	CHESTER	124	135	118	132	130	128	119	124	119	124	121	93	125	124	123	120	84	120	122	145
23837	COURTLAND	85	76	78	78	78	88	78	85	81	73	79	63	72	81	77	85	54	81	89	99
23838	CHESTERFIELD	142	169	160	173	169	160	146	154	141	152	143	118	162	144	159	140	101	146	146	177
23839	DENDRON	86	61	88	59	64	87	63	80	70	59	69	60	50	69	62	77	45	74	83	95
23840	DEWITT	99	83	93	85	86	105	84	98	89	76	87	74	74	90	83	95	59	91	102	115
23841	DINWIDDIE	99	88	91	91	90	106	87	100	91	79	89	75	79	92	87	96	61	92	103	116
23842	DISPUTANTA	100	108	100	109	106	112	97	104	99	97	99	79	103	101	103	101	69	100	107	122
23843	DOLPHIN	84	65	83	64	67	86	65	80	71	61	70	60	55	71	65	77	47	74	83	95
23844	DREWRYVILLE	72	47	69	44	47	70	50	63	58	48	56	49	38	59	47	65	37	59	67	78
23845	EBONY	69	49	70	48	51	70	50	64	56	47	55	48	40	56	50	62	36	59	67	76
23846	ELBERON	82	66	79	67	68	86	67	80	71	61	70	60	58	72	66	77	47	73	83	94
23847	EMPORIA	75	58	72	57	58	77	61	70	68	59	66	53	53	68	59	73	45	68	76	85
23850	FORD	96	71	97	69	73	98	72	91	79	67	78	68	59	79	71	87	52	83	94	107
23851	FRANKLIN	75	67	69	68	66	76	70	72	74	68	73	55	66	74	67	78	51	73	78	87
23856	FREEMAN	75	56	72	55	57	77	58	70	64	54	63	54	48	65	56	70	42	65	73	84
23857	GASBURG	88	67	104	66	72	91	68	86	73	64	72	64	57	71	71	79	48	80	87	101
23860	HOPEWELL	77	75	65	76	71	78	78	75	80	75	80	58	77	81	75	83	56	78	82	91
23866	IVOR	75	68	67	71	69	80	67	76	69	61	68	57	62	70	67	73	46	70	78	88
23867	JARRATT	82	56	81	53	57	83	60	75	69	56	67	58	47	69	57	76	44	71	81	91
23868	LAWRENCEVILLE	76	60	71	59	60	77	61	71	66	58	65	54	52	67	59	71	44	67	75	85
23872	MC KENNEY	89	73	85	74	75	94	75	88	80	68	78	66	65	80	74	86	53	82	93	103
23874	NEWSOMS	80	71	73	73	72	85	70	80	73	64	72	61	64	75	70	78	49	74	83	93
23875	PRINCE GEORGE	104	108	94	106	103	104	99	101	99	102	100	78	101	103	99	99	69	99	100	119
23876	RAWLINGS	82	57	83	55	59	82	59	75	66	55	65	57	47	66	58	73	43	69	79	90
23878	SEDLEY	77	69	69	72	71	81	70	77	72	64	71	58	64	73	69	76	48	72	80	90
23879	SKIPPERS	80	56	81	54	57	80	58	74	65	54	64	56	46	65	56	72	42	68	77	88
23881	SPRING GROVE	90	71	88	71	73	93	72	87	77	66	76	65	61	77	71	83	51	80	90	102
23882	STONY CREEK	90	60	89	57	61	89	64	81	73	60	71	62	49	73	61	81	47	75	85	98
23883	SURRY	89	67	90	67	70	92	69	85	75	63	74	64	57	75	68	82	49	78	88	101
23885	SUTHERLAND	100	106	100	109	106	112	97	105	98	95	98	79	100	99	102	101	68	100	108	122
23887	VALENTINES	98	79	127	77	86	104	79	100	82	74	81	73	68	78	85	88	54	92	99	116
23888	WAKEFIELD	76	54	75	53	55	77	56	70	63	53	61	53	45	63	54	69	41	65	73	84
23889	WARFIELD	84	60	86	58	63	85	62	79	69	58	67	59	49	68	61	76	45	72	82	94
23890	WAVERLY	85	62	81	60	63	85	65	78	72	61	70	60	53	72	62	78	47	74	82	94
23893	WHITE PLAINS	74	53	76	51	55	75	54	69	60	51	59	52	43	60	54	66	39	63	72	82
23894	WILSONS	95	70	96	68	72	97	71	89	78	66	77	67	58	78	70	86	51	82	93	106
23897	YALE	79	53	82	52	55	81	58	73	63	51	62	59	43	63	56	70	41	68	77	89
23898	ZUNI	88	86	78	87	85	91	81	87	82	79	82	66	79	85	81	85	56	83	88	102
23901	FARMVILLE	76	62	74	62	64	78	66	74	71	63	69	55	59	69	64	75	47	72	80	87
23915	BASKERVILLE	87	60	87	57	61	87	62	79	70	58	69	60	49	70	60	78	45	73	83	95
23917	BOYDTON	88	64	96	62	67	90	66	83	72	62	71	63	53	71	66	79	47	77	86	99
23919	BRACEY	80	69	98	66	76	87	67	83	71	68	70	58	62	67	73	76	47	78	87	95
23920	BRODNAX	78	54	77	51	55	78	57	71	64	53	62	54	44	64	54	71	41	66	75	86
23921	BUCKINGHAM	79	56	81	55	59	80	58	74	64	54	63	55	46	64	57	71	42	68	77	88
23922	BURKEVILLE	79	55	79	53	56	79	57	72	64	53	63	55	45	64	55	71	41	67	75	87
23923	CHARLOTTE COURT HOUS	79	56	80	55	59	80	58	74	65	54	64	56	47	64	58	72	42	68	78	88
23924	CHASE CITY	69	47	67	45	48	68	51	62	58	48	57	48	40	58	48	64	38	59	66	76
23927	CLARKSVILLE	85	73	93	73	77	91	73	86	77	69	76	63	67	76	75	82	51	81	90	100
23930	CREWE	76	61	73	61	62	78	63	73	68	59	67	55	55	68	62	73	45	70	78	87
23934	CULLEN	79	56	81	54	58	80	58	73	64	54	63	55	46	64	57	70	42	67	76	87
23936	DILLWYN	79	56	77	54	57	79	58	72	65	55	64	55	46	66	55	71	42	67	75	87
23937	DRAKES BRANCH	75	52	73	50	53	75	55	68	61	51	60	52	43	62	52	68	40	63	72	82
23938	DUNDAS	77	55	79	53	56	78	56	72	63	53	62	54	45	63	55	69	41	66	75	86
23942	GREEN BAY	81	58	83	56	60	83	60	76	67	56	66	57	48	66	59	74	43	70	80	91
23944	KENBRIDGE	77	55	78	54	57	79	59	73	65	53	63	55	47	64	57	72	42	68	78	87
23947	KEYSVILLE	77	54	78	52	55	77	56	71	63	52	61	54	44	62	55	69	41	65	74	85
23950	LA CROSSE	80	59	85	56	62	82	60	75	66	57	65	56	49	65	60	73	43	70	79	90
23952	LUNENBURG	95	68	98	66	71	97	70	89	78	65	76	67	56	77	69	85	50	82	93	106
23954	MEHERRIN	78	56	80	54	58	79	57	73	64	54	63	55	46	63	57	70	41	67	76	87
23958	PAMPLIN	84	62	82	61	64	84	64	78	70	60	69	59	53	70	62	77	46	73	82	93
23959	PHENIX	79	56	81	54	58	80	58	73	64	54	63	55	46	64	57	70	42	67	76	87
23960	PROSPECT	83	62	81	60	63	83	65	77	71	61	69	58	53	71	63	77	46	73	82	92
23962	RANDOLPH	71	49	70	48	51	71	53	65	59	49	58	50	41	59	50	65	38	61	70	78
23963	RED HOUSE	84	60	82	58	62	84	62	77	69	58	68	58	50	69	60	76	45	71	81	92
23964	RED OAK	66	44	63	42	44	65	47	58	54	45	52	45	36	55	44	59	35	55	62	71
23966	RICE	86	66	84	65	68	86	68	81	74	65	73	61	58	74	67	80	49	76	85	96
23967	SAXE	72	52	64	50	52	70	54	64	60	52	59	49	43	62	50	65	39	61	68	78
23968	SKIPWITH	78	61	77	61	63	81	62	75	67	57	66	57	52	67	61	72	44	69	78	89
23970	SOUTH HILL	80	66	79	64	67	80	67	76	71	65	70	58	60	72	66	76	48	73	79	90
	VIRGINIA	115	112	112	114	111	114	112	112	112	112	112	88	111	114	111	113	79	112	112	132
	UNITED STATES	100	100	100	100	100	100	100	100	100	100	100	100	100	100	100	100	100	100	100	100

ZIP CODE			POPULATION			2000-2009 ANNUAL RATE		HOUSEHOLDS					FAMILIES		
#	POST OFFICE NAME	COUNTY FIPS CODE	2000	2009	2014	% Rate	State Centile	2000	2009	2014	% Annual Rate 2000-2009	2009 Average HH Size	2000	2009	% Annual Rate 2000-2009
23974	VICTORIA	111	5181	5356	5411	0.4	42	1728	1838	1881	0.7	2.32	1143	1172	0.3
23976	WYLLIESBURG	037	349	371	376	0.7	54	152	168	172	1.1	2.20	105	112	0.7
24011	ROANOKE	770	52	55	56	0.6	49	17	18	18	0.6	2.56	3	3	0.0
24012	ROANOKE	770	26788	27338	27800	0.2	33	12020	12394	12641	0.3	2.16	7326	7275	-0.1
24013	ROANOKE	770	8094	7748	7659	-0.5	6	3191	3117	3102	-0.3	2.43	1980	1846	-0.8
24014	ROANOKE	161	16107	16560	16800	0.3	38	7209	7563	7731	0.5	2.16	4558	4581	0.1
24015	ROANOKE	770	15129	14820	14748	-0.2	14	7265	7211	7215	-0.1	2.03	3806	3571	-0.7
24016	ROANOKE	770	9988	9045	8788	-1.1	2	4178	3765	3664	-1.1	2.03	1830	1551	-1.8
24017	ROANOKE	770	23233	23126	23187	0.0	23	9487	9696	9808	0.2	2.34	6160	6038	-0.2
24018	ROANOKE	161	35515	37419	38413	0.6	49	15380	16310	16807	0.6	2.29	10195	10430	0.2
24019	ROANOKE	161	25413	27776	28890	1.0	64	9775	10815	11303	1.1	2.48	7179	7722	0.8
24020	ROANOKE	161	216	215	215	-0.1	18	59	59	59	0.0	1.51	31	30	-0.4
24053	ARARAT	141	2857	2905	2907	0.2	33	1180	1232	1246	0.5	2.36	872	885	0.2
24054	AXTON	089	6634	6723	6670	0.1	28	2548	2664	2672	0.5	2.52	1934	1968	0.2
24055	BASSETT	089	14922	14650	14417	-0.2	14	6085	6161	6126	0.1	2.36	4366	4282	-0.2
24059	BENT MOUNTAIN	161	897	1004	1058	1.2	69	352	397	421	1.3	2.53	258	281	0.9
24060	BLACKSBURG	121	48312	51188	52582	0.6	49	16808	17815	18448	0.6	2.36	7143	7027	-0.2
24064	BLUE RIDGE	019	4721	5064	5234	0.8	58	1777	1962	2050	1.1	2.57	1431	1542	0.8
24065	BOONES MILL	067	5381	6065	6376	1.3	72	2190	2530	2679	1.6	2.39	1637	1834	1.2
24066	BUCHANAN	023	4619	4899	5035	0.6	49	1889	2046	2119	0.9	2.38	1386	1454	0.5
24067	CALLAWAY	067	2165	2414	2531	1.2	69	823	942	997	1.5	2.50	624	695	1.2
24069	CASCADE	143	1967	2035	2055	0.4	42	752	803	820	0.7	2.51	569	592	0.4
24070	CATAWBA	045	1857	1884	1897	0.2	33	716	739	750	0.3	2.44	542	544	0.0
24072	CHECK	063	1356	1577	1679	1.6	78	559	665	713	1.9	2.37	419	484	1.6
24073	CHRISTIANSBURG	121	24424	27475	29044	1.3	72	9959	11298	11983	1.4	2.39	6899	7496	0.9
24076	CLAUDVILLE	141	935	954	956	0.2	33	403	423	427	0.5	2.26	290	295	0.2
24077	CLOVERDALE	023	551	587	606	0.7	54	221	236	244	0.7	2.48	166	172	0.4
24078	COLLINSVILLE	089	7176	6481	6176	-1.1	2	3199	2956	2843	-0.9	2.15	2038	1810	-1.3
24079	COPPER HILL	063	1708	1924	2043	1.3	72	697	803	859	1.5	2.40	509	568	1.2
24082	CRITZ	141	330	340	344	0.3	38	128	136	139	0.7	2.50	96	99	0.3
24083	DALEVILLE	023	2184	2913	3157	3.2	93	854	1165	1272	3.4	2.50	710	952	3.2
24084	DUBLIN	155	11065	11529	11722	0.4	42	4327	4626	4763	0.7	2.28	3040	3144	0.4
24085	EAGLE ROCK	023	2296	2349	2374	0.2	33	931	975	992	0.5	2.38	672	681	0.1
24086	EGGLESTON	071	156	172	178	1.1	66	57	65	68	1.4	2.65	42	47	1.2
24087	ELLISTON	121	3912	4244	4449	0.9	61	1541	1689	1778	1.0	2.51	1126	1188	0.6
24088	FERRUM	067	4418	4727	4829	0.7	54	1561	1690	1747	0.9	2.40	1122	1175	0.5
24089	FIELDALE	089	2625	2480	2406	-0.6	4	1152	1122	1100	-0.3	2.18	812	768	-0.6
24090	FINCASTLE	023	4154	4663	4891	1.3	72	1605	1835	1941	1.5	2.45	1248	1387	1.1
24091	FLOYD	063	6268	6973	7335	1.2	69	2673	3035	3213	1.4	2.28	1864	2049	1.0
24092	GLADE HILL	067	2516	2709	2865	0.8	58	1023	1128	1204	1.1	2.40	756	807	0.7
24093	GLEN LYN	071	154	150	148	-0.3	11	58	58	57	0.0	2.52	42	41	-0.3
24095	GOODVIEW	019	3934	4330	4543	1.0	64	1518	1727	1828	1.4	2.51	1190	1321	1.1
24101	HARDY	067	4631	5611	6068	2.1	86	1811	2254	2460	2.4	2.49	1440	1748	2.1
24102	HENRY	067	1490	1612	1670	0.9	61	598	665	696	1.2	2.39	438	471	0.8
24104	HUDDLESTON	019	2955	3388	3602	1.5	76	1265	1501	1613	1.9	2.26	953	1100	1.6
24105	INDIAN VALLEY	063	576	622	647	0.8	58	234	257	269	1.0	2.42	178	191	0.8
24112	MARTINSVILLE	089	35757	33908	32867	-0.6	4	14793	14352	14011	-0.3	2.30	9961	9346	-0.7
24120	MEADOWS OF DAN	141	2009	2048	2045	0.2	33	905	946	953	0.5	2.16	633	641	0.1
24121	MONETA	019	8507	9587	10114	1.3	72	3633	4185	4447	1.5	2.27	2794	3136	1.3
24122	MONTVALE	019	1680	1898	2017	1.3	72	679	792	851	1.7	2.37	499	565	1.4
24124	NARROWS	071	5401	5389	5369	0.0	23	2235	2285	2295	0.2	2.34	1592	1579	-0.1
24127	NEW CASTLE	045	4040	4133	4167	0.2	33	1630	1710	1738	0.5	2.40	1193	1216	0.2
24128	NEWPORT	071	1347	1370	1368	0.2	33	583	611	616	0.5	2.24	406	412	0.2
24131	PAINT BANK	045	143	145	146	0.2	33	52	54	55	0.4	2.65	39	40	0.3
24133	PATRICK SPRINGS	141	2988	2997	3001	0.0	23	1225	1261	1273	0.3	2.38	913	915	0.0
24134	PEARISBURG	071	5832	6202	6326	0.7	54	2487	2715	2792	1.0	2.28	1731	1830	0.6
24136	PEMBROKE	071	3011	3024	2989	0.0	23	1257	1298	1295	0.3	2.33	861	859	0.0
24137	PENHOOK	067	2394	2792	2920	1.7	79	1019	1234	1305	2.1	2.26	750	885	1.8
24138	PILOT	121	1434	1540	1598	0.8	58	552	603	630	1.0	2.51	426	450	0.6
24139	PITTSVILLE	143	541	578	581	0.7	54	221	245	249	1.1	2.36	159	170	0.7
24141	RADFORD	155	20021	20311	20757	0.2	33	8783	9168	9461	0.5	2.06	4743	4742	0.0
24142	RADFORD	750	2755	2547	2501	-0.8	3	8	7	7	-1.4	2.57	1	1	0.0
24147	RICH CREEK	071	819	843	846	0.3	38	349	369	374	0.6	2.20	244	251	0.3
24148	RIDGEWAY	089	8483	8273	8080	-0.3	11	3505	3535	3491	0.1	2.34	2550	2492	-0.2
24149	RINER	121	2760	3068	3227	1.2	69	1087	1224	1294	1.3	2.51	839	914	0.9
24150	RIPPLEMEAD	071	456	462	458	0.1	28	193	202	202	0.5	2.29	138	139	0.1
24151	ROCKY MOUNT	067	17846	19407	20118	0.9	61	7162	7975	8349	1.2	2.37	5026	5419	0.8
24153	SALEM	161	35559	37165	37821	0.5	45	14082	14766	15093	0.5	2.35	9692	9845	0.2
24161	SANDY LEVEL	143	391	416	424	0.7	54	164	181	186	1.1	2.30	117	124	0.6
24162	SHAWSVILLE	121	2314	2515	2609	0.9	61	889	980	1022	1.1	2.42	655	693	0.6
24165	SPENCER	141	1446	1398	1368	-0.4	8	638	638	631	0.0	2.19	456	441	-0.4
24167	STAFFORDSVILLE	071	297	321	329	0.8	58	118	130	135	1.1	2.47	88	95	0.8
24168	STANLEYTOWN	089	216	212	208	-0.2	14	86	86	86	0.0	2.29	57	55	-0.4
24171	STUART	141	8801	8875	8869	0.1	28	3693	3823	3852	0.4	2.26	2569	2575	0.0
24174	THAXTON	019	2236	2531	2689	1.3	72	916	1070	1149	1.7	2.36	658	745	1.4
24175	TROUTVILLE	023	7378	8051	8401	0.9	61	2747	3040	3194	1.1	2.54	2198	2372	0.8
24176	UNION HALL	067	1191	1539	1682	2.8	91	502	666	735	3.1	2.31	383	494	2.8
24179	VINTON	019	18933	19947	20490	0.6	49	7730	8250	8523	0.7	2.40	5662	5876	0.4
24184	WIRTZ	067	2984	3614	3916	2.1	86	1193	1480	1619	2.4	2.44	909	1096	2.0
24185	WOOLWINE	141	889	889	881	0.0	23	380	389	388	0.3	2.29	267	264	-0.1
24201	BRISTOL	520	16632	16809	16857	0.1	28	7335	7577	7671	0.4	2.12	4570	4535	-0.1
24202	BRISTOL	191	11578	12050	12274	0.4	42	4740	5089	5242	0.8	2.36	3569	3725	0.5
24210	ABINGDON	191	15136	16095	16524	0.7	54	6588	7176	7444	0.9	2.15	4280	4503	0.6
24211	ABINGDON	191	8935	9585	9885	0.8	58	3700	4096	4278	1.1	2.30	2708	2906	0.8
24216	APPALACHIA	195	3308	3058	2938	-0.8	3	1384	1336	1300	-0.4	2.29	945	881	-0.8
24217	BEE	051	371	356	346	-0.4	8	155	155	153	0.0	2.30	114	110	-0.4
24219	BIG STONE GAP	195	10941	11738	11492	0.8	58	4419	4452	4402	0.1	2.35	3164	3096	-0.2
24220	BIRCHLEAF	051	1050	1022	1004	-0.3	11	394	399	397	0.1	2.56	311	309	-0.1
24221	BLACKWATER	105	1008	1012	1008	0.0	23	425	434	437	0.2	2.33	305	303	-0.1
24224	CASTLEWOOD	167	8385	8439	8386	0.1	28	3392	3538	3560	0.5	2.37	2533	2573	0.2
24225	CLEVELAND	167	1958	1948	1929	-0.1	18	811	838	838	0.4	2.32	587	588	0.0
24226	CLINCHCO	051	1734	1694	1658	-0.3	11	714	724	718	0.2	2.34	528	521	-0.1
24228	CLINTWOOD	051	7748	7717	7570	0.0	23	3231	3296	3274	0.2	2.27	2300	2275	-0.1
24230	COEBURN	195	9345	9420	9279	0.1	28	3654	3822	3813	0.5	2.40	2713	2760	0.2
24236	DAMASCUS	191	3284	3310	3338	0.1	28	1445	1507	1539	0.5	2.19	972	975	0.0
	VIRGINIA					1.2					1.3	2.52			1.0
	UNITED STATES					1.0					1.1	2.59			0.9

#	POST OFFICE NAME	White 2000	White 2009	Black 2000	Black 2009	Asian/Pacific 2000	Asian/Pacific 2009	% Hispanic Origin 2000	% Hispanic Origin 2009	0-4	5-9	10-14	15-19	20-24	25-44	45-64	65-84	85+	18+	MEDIAN AGE 2009	% 2009 Males	% 2009 Females
23974	VICTORIA	57.3	53.6	40.5	43.2	0.3	0.4	1.6	2.4	4.3	4.3	4.6	5.8	6.2	31.9	26.9	13.9	2.1	83.4	40.5	58.9	41.1
23976	WYLLIESBURG	66.2	62.8	33.0	35.8	0.3	0.5	0.6	0.8	6.7	6.7	7.0	6.7	4.6	25.6	27.0	13.5	2.2	75.2	40.1	51.5	48.5
24011	ROANOKE	45.1	38.2	52.9	58.2	0.0	1.8	0.0	0.0	0.0	0.0	0.0	5.5	23.6	54.5	16.4	0.0	0.0	100.0	31.6	80.0	20.0
24012	ROANOKE	83.0	78.9	12.5	14.5	1.7	2.5	1.8	2.9	6.3	6.0	5.9	5.6	5.6	26.1	27.4	14.0	3.1	78.4	41.1	47.4	52.6
24013	ROANOKE	90.9	87.5	5.3	6.7	0.9	1.4	1.3	2.4	7.2	6.8	6.5	7.2	7.2	26.6	26.1	10.7	1.8	75.3	37.1	50.1	49.9
24014	ROANOKE	93.6	91.1	3.9	4.9	1.1	1.7	0.9	1.6	5.3	5.2	5.6	5.8	5.3	25.1	30.5	14.3	2.9	80.4	43.3	47.5	52.5
24015	ROANOKE	92.7	90.0	4.5	5.7	1.0	1.5	1.1	2.0	6.4	5.9	5.6	5.1	6.8	29.3	27.4	10.5	3.0	79.1	39.1	47.0	53.0
24016	ROANOKE	47.1	41.1	47.6	51.7	0.8	1.1	2.4	3.5	5.8	5.9	5.0	6.5	9.4	31.4	23.7	9.3	3.1	79.8	35.7	51.0	49.0
24017	ROANOKE	29.7	25.5	66.6	69.5	0.9	1.2	1.2	1.7	7.1	6.9	6.7	7.3	6.4	23.7	26.3	13.2	2.3	74.8	38.2	45.7	54.3
24018	ROANOKE	93.7	91.3	2.3	2.7	2.6	3.9	1.3	2.2	5.0	5.2	5.8	6.1	5.2	22.6	31.8	15.2	3.0	80.2	45.1	47.3	52.7
24019	ROANOKE	90.5	88.3	6.5	7.3	1.4	2.1	0.9	1.4	5.4	5.7	6.3	7.0	5.4	23.2	30.1	14.5	2.4	78.6	42.9	47.1	52.9
24020	ROANOKE	81.5	77.7	13.0	14.0	2.8	3.7	2.8	4.7	1.9	2.3	1.9	29.8	23.3	16.3	16.3	7.4	0.9	92.1	23.1	25.6	74.4
24053	ARARAT	92.2	89.7	4.7	5.2	0.3	0.5	2.6	4.3	6.2	6.2	6.5	5.9	4.7	27.0	27.7	14.2	1.7	77.4	40.7	51.8	48.2
24054	AXTON	64.3	61.0	33.1	35.3	0.2	0.3	3.5	5.5	6.3	6.4	6.7	6.3	5.4	26.1	29.1	12.4	1.2	76.6	40.0	48.6	51.4
24055	BASSETT	83.5	80.6	13.1	14.3	0.2	0.3	4.9	8.0	5.6	5.7	5.9	5.6	4.9	25.7	28.8	15.8	2.0	79.4	42.7	49.6	50.4
24059	BENT MOUNTAIN	94.4	93.0	2.9	3.4	0.7	1.0	1.2	2.1	4.3	4.8	6.2	7.5	4.1	22.3	38.0	11.6	1.3	80.1	45.4	50.3	49.7
24060	BLACKSBURG	86.3	81.2	4.0	4.3	6.7	10.1	2.1	3.4	3.3	2.9	2.9	17.2	33.2	20.2	13.6	5.8	1.1	89.1	23.6	55.1	44.9
24064	BLUE RIDGE	96.1	95.0	2.2	2.5	0.6	1.0	0.5	0.8	5.3	6.0	6.6	6.2	4.3	23.3	34.5	12.8	1.2	78.2	44.0	49.1	50.9
24065	BOONES MILL	94.3	92.9	4.1	4.7	0.4	0.6	1.1	1.8	5.2	5.7	6.2	6.2	4.3	24.2	32.6	14.0	1.7	79.0	44.0	49.2	50.8
24066	BUCHANAN	95.2	94.2	3.6	4.1	0.2	0.3	0.4	0.7	5.2	5.6	6.1	6.0	4.2	24.1	32.3	14.7	1.8	79.1	44.2	49.1	50.9
24067	CALLAWAY	95.2	94.0	3.4	4.1	0.4	0.6	0.6	1.0	5.6	6.1	6.6	7.0	5.1	24.7	31.2	12.2	1.6	78.0	41.7	49.6	50.4
24069	CASCADE	57.6	54.0	41.1	44.0	0.2	0.2	1.2	2.0	5.7	5.9	6.3	6.3	5.4	24.8	31.0	13.0	1.6	77.9	41.9	48.9	51.1
24070	CATAWBA	96.8	96.0	1.7	2.0	0.1	0.1	0.3	0.4	5.1	5.8	6.5	6.4	4.1	23.4	32.5	14.3	1.9	78.5	44.1	50.7	49.3
24072	CHECK	97.3	96.8	1.7	1.9	0.1	0.2	0.7	1.3	6.3	6.8	7.2	6.2	4.1	24.8	30.3	12.8	1.6	75.8	41.6	50.0	50.0
24073	CHRISTIANSBURG	94.3	92.8	3.9	4.4	0.4	0.6	0.9	1.6	6.9	6.7	6.6	6.1	5.6	29.6	26.4	10.7	1.4	76.0	37.8	48.9	51.1
24076	CLAUDVILLE	91.9	90.0	5.8	6.4	0.2	0.3	1.9	3.4	5.7	6.1	6.5	6.1	4.4	25.4	30.0	14.0	1.9	78.0	41.6	50.4	49.6
24077	CLOVERDALE	92.4	90.6	4.9	5.5	1.1	1.5	0.7	1.2	5.6	6.6	7.3	7.0	4.3	21.5	34.8	11.8	1.2	76.1	43.4	49.1	50.9
24078	COLLINSVILLE	84.0	80.6	12.1	13.3	0.8	1.2	3.8	6.3	5.9	5.5	5.6	5.8	6.2	26.5	26.6	15.0	2.9	79.5	41.2	47.7	52.3
24079	COPPER HILL	95.9	95.0	2.8	3.1	0.2	0.2	0.8	1.2	5.6	6.2	6.4	5.7	4.1	24.8	31.4	14.1	1.7	78.3	43.1	49.9	50.1
24082	CRITZ	83.0	80.6	15.8	17.6	0.0	0.3	0.3	0.6	6.2	6.5	6.5	6.8	5.6	26.8	29.1	11.2	1.5	76.5	39.8	49.4	50.6
24083	DALEVILLE	97.0	96.3	2.1	2.3	0.4	0.6	0.9	1.5	5.5	6.3	7.3	6.4	3.4	20.0	34.5	15.2	1.4	76.8	45.6	50.3	49.7
24084	DUBLIN	92.9	91.2	5.5	6.5	0.3	0.4	0.5	0.9	5.1	5.0	5.2	5.2	5.5	29.2	30.2	12.6	1.9	81.4	41.6	51.5	48.5
24085	EAGLE ROCK	94.7	93.5	3.9	4.5	0.0	0.1	0.7	1.1	5.2	5.7	6.0	5.4	4.1	21.7	34.1	15.6	2.1	79.7	46.1	50.2	49.8
24086	EGGLESTON	97.4	96.5	1.9	2.3	0.0	0.0	0.6	0.6	5.2	5.8	5.8	5.8	4.1	25.0	34.3	12.2	1.7	79.7	43.9	54.7	45.3
24087	ELLISTON	95.3	93.9	2.4	2.7	0.3	0.4	1.2	2.0	6.6	6.7	6.7	6.6	5.9	26.7	29.6	10.2	1.0	75.7	38.9	50.8	49.2
24088	FERRUM	93.1	91.5	5.4	6.4	0.2	0.2	1.3	2.2	5.2	5.2	5.4	12.0	11.0	23.1	26.4	10.5	1.3	80.6	35.3	50.6	49.4
24089	FIELDALE	76.7	73.3	20.7	22.7	0.3	0.4	4.6	7.8	5.6	5.6	5.7	5.8	5.4	25.6	27.6	16.2	2.4	79.5	42.4	49.4	50.6
24090	FINCASTLE	94.8	93.5	3.9	4.5	0.3	0.4	0.6	1.0	4.6	5.0	5.9	5.9	4.3	24.0	34.6	13.9	1.8	80.6	45.2	50.7	49.3
24091	FLOYD	95.9	94.9	2.8	3.1	0.1	0.2	1.6	2.8	5.3	5.6	6.0	5.9	4.1	24.4	30.7	15.2	2.8	79.4	44.1	48.7	51.3
24092	GLADE HILL	89.5	87.3	8.8	10.1	0.1	0.1	1.8	3.1	5.5	5.8	6.1	5.8	4.2	23.9	32.9	14.5	1.4	79.1	44.1	49.8	50.2
24093	GLEN LYN	98.7	98.7	0.6	0.7	0.0	0.0	0.6	1.3	5.3	5.3	6.0	5.3	4.7	22.7	28.7	18.0	4.0	80.7	45.5	50.7	49.3
24095	GOODVIEW	95.6	94.6	3.2	3.6	0.2	0.2	0.7	1.2	5.5	5.9	6.6	6.7	4.3	25.2	33.0	11.8	1.0	77.7	42.5	50.6	49.4
24101	HARDY	94.9	93.5	4.1	4.9	0.2	0.3	0.8	1.4	5.0	5.8	6.4	6.0	3.7	23.8	35.5	12.8	1.2	79.1	44.7	51.0	49.0
24102	HENRY	93.5	92.6	5.2	5.5	0.6	0.9	1.1	1.9	5.5	5.8	6.1	6.0	4.7	24.3	30.9	14.8	2.0	78.6	43.4	48.8	51.2
24104	HUDDLESTON	92.1	90.6	6.3	7.0	0.3	0.5	0.7	1.1	4.4	4.8	5.1	4.7	3.8	19.0	33.0	23.3	1.9	82.8	50.5	49.9	50.1
24105	INDIAN VALLEY	98.3	97.6	0.9	1.0	0.0	0.0	0.9	1.6	6.1	6.4	6.8	6.1	4.8	25.6	30.4	12.2	1.6	76.8	41.3	51.3	48.7
24112	MARTINSVILLE	61.3	58.0	36.3	38.6	0.5	0.7	2.6	4.0	5.4	5.6	5.7	6.0	5.5	24.3	29.6	15.4	2.6	79.7	43.3	47.8	52.2
24120	MEADOWS OF DAN	96.9	95.8	1.3	1.5	0.2	0.3	2.1	3.4	4.9	5.2	5.5	5.5	4.1	23.3	29.9	19.0	2.5	80.9	46.0	50.1	49.9
24121	MONETA	93.6	92.4	5.1	5.9	0.2	0.2	0.9	1.6	4.3	4.6	5.2	4.6	3.9	20.9	35.7	19.4	1.4	83.0	49.2	50.8	49.2
24122	MONTVALE	96.2	95.1	2.3	2.6	0.2	0.4	0.2	0.4	5.6	5.7	5.9	5.7	5.5	25.1	32.7	12.2	1.6	79.1	42.6	51.8	48.2
24124	NARROWS	97.9	97.3	1.3	1.5	0.1	0.2	0.6	1.1	5.9	6.0	6.0	5.5	4.7	24.0	28.8	16.2	2.7	78.6	43.3	49.0	51.0
24127	NEW CASTLE	98.9	98.6	0.2	0.2	0.1	0.2	0.3	0.6	5.4	5.8	6.5	6.3	4.7	24.5	31.6	13.5	1.6	78.0	42.9	51.3	48.7
24128	NEWPORT	98.2	97.7	0.2	0.2	0.1	0.2	0.5	0.9	4.0	4.5	5.0	5.3	3.9	26.7	35.4	13.6	1.6	83.3	45.4	50.7	49.3
24131	PAINT BANK	99.3	98.6	0.0	0.0	0.0	0.7	0.7	0.7	5.5	5.5	6.2	6.9	5.5	25.5	31.7	11.7	1.4	78.6	41.3	51.7	48.3
24133	PATRICK SPRINGS	92.6	91.2	5.9	6.7	0.1	0.2	0.9	1.6	5.9	6.0	6.4	6.3	5.1	26.1	30.1	12.7	1.4	77.8	41.2	48.8	51.2
24134	PEARISBURG	96.8	96.0	2.0	2.2	0.3	0.4	0.6	1.0	5.8	5.8	6.0	5.9	4.9	23.9	29.4	15.8	2.5	78.6	43.4	49.6	50.4
24136	PEMBROKE	96.3	95.6	2.9	3.2	0.1	0.2	0.6	1.0	5.0	5.2	5.6	5.8	4.7	26.1	31.7	14.1	1.8	80.7	43.5	49.8	50.2
24137	PENHOOK	81.7	79.7	17.0	18.6	0.1	0.2	0.8	1.3	5.1	5.2	5.7	5.5	4.4	22.2	33.6	16.8	1.4	80.5	46.1	49.9	50.1
24138	PILOT	98.7	98.4	0.6	0.6	0.2	0.3	0.8	1.4	5.6	6.0	6.5	6.2	4.5	25.6	31.8	12.4	1.5	78.0	42.2	49.8	50.2
24139	PITTSVILLE	78.6	75.8	19.6	21.6	0.0	0.0	0.7	1.2	5.0	4.7	5.4	5.7	5.4	22.1	35.3	15.1	1.4	81.1	46.0	49.1	50.9
24141	RADFORD	90.3	88.2	6.9	7.7	1.0	1.5	0.9	1.5	4.6	4.4	4.6	9.7	18.1	22.6	22.6	11.5	1.9	83.5	32.3	47.6	52.4
24142	RADFORD	88.2	85.2	7.5	8.4	1.6	2.4	1.9	3.1	0.4	0.3	0.4	42.0	48.6	5.0	2.1	0.9	0.2	98.4	20.7	41.2	58.8
24147	RICH CREEK	98.9	98.6	0.6	0.7	0.2	0.4	1.0	1.8	6.3	6.3	5.9	5.2	4.6	22.8	26.8	17.9	4.2	78.2	44.0	48.4	51.6
24148	RIDGEWAY	80.0	76.9	18.2	20.4	0.5	0.7	1.2	2.0	5.3	5.6	6.0	6.0	4.7	24.8	31.4	14.6	1.5	79.4	43.4	49.5	50.5
24149	RINER	99.1	98.7	0.3	0.3	0.1	0.2	1.0	1.7	5.6	5.9	6.3	6.7	4.9	26.1	31.4	12.0	1.2	78.2	41.5	48.3	51.7
24150	RIPPLEMEAD	95.6	94.6	4.0	4.5	0.0	0.0	0.7	1.1	5.4	5.8	6.1	5.6	4.1	25.3	30.7	14.9	1.9	78.8	43.5	49.8	50.2
24151	ROCKY MOUNT	82.1	79.3	15.6	17.4	0.6	0.8	1.5	2.4	5.8	6.1	6.4	6.4	5.4	25.2	29.1	13.4	2.2	77.7	41.3	48.7	51.3
24153	SALEM	93.4	92.0	4.6	5.2	0.8	1.3	0.8	1.3	4.6	4.7	5.2	7.6	6.7	22.8	29.6	15.7	3.2	81.8	43.8	47.4	52.6
24161	SANDY LEVEL	80.8	77.4	16.4	18.5	0.0	0.0	0.8	1.2	4.6	3.4	4.6	4.6	5.0	20.0	38.5	17.8	1.7	84.1	50.2	49.3	50.7
24162	SHAWSVILLE	96.2	95.2	2.7	3.3	0.2	0.2	0.7	1.3	4.7	5.0	5.5	5.5	4.3	27.0	31.1	14.4	2.5	81.2	43.7	49.3	50.7
24165	SPENCER	80.3	77.4	18.4	20.6	0.1	0.1	0.8	1.4	5.4	5.5	5.9	5.6	4.5	26.0	30.2	15.3	1.7	79.8	43.3	48.6	51.4
24167	STAFFORDSVILLE	98.0	97.2	1.3	1.9	0.3	0.3	0.7	1.2	6.9	6.9	6.5	5.6	5.0	25.2	29.9	12.5	1.6	76.6	40.9	51.7	48.3
24168	STANLEYTOWN	84.3	80.7	10.6	11.3	0.5	0.5	7.4	12.3	3.8	3.8	3.8	4.2	5.2	24.1	28.8	21.7	4.7	86.3	48.2	47.6	52.4
24171	STUART	91.1	89.3	6.9	7.7	0.2	0.3	2.0	3.2	5.5	5.8	5.9	5.4	4.6	24.0	29.4	16.2	3.1	79.4	44.1	48.8	51.2
24174	THAXTON	97.6	96.9	1.3	1.5	0.2	0.2	0.8	1.4	5.3	5.5	6.0	6.4	4.9	26.1	31.6	12.8	1.4	79.3	42.3	50.8	49.2
24175	TROUTVILLE	95.0	93.6	3.4	4.0	0.5	0.8	0.5	0.9	5.2	5.7	6.5	6.0	4.1	23.7	33.4	14.0	1.4	78.6	44.2	51.6	48.4
24176	UNION HALL	89.3	87.5	9.5	10.6	0.2	0.3	0.9	1.5	4.2	4.6	4.9	4.6	3.2	21.0	35.6	20.5	1.3	83.3	49.9	50.2	49.8
24179	VINTON	96.3	95.1	2.0	2.3	0.5	0.8	0.8	1.4	5.8	6.0	6.3	6.0	5.1	24.7	30.3	13.7	2.2	78.2	42.3	48.5	51.5
24184	WIRTZ	94.8	93.5	3.4	3.9	0.3	0.3	1.0	1.6	5.0	5.9	6.6	6.1	4.2	25.3	32.8	12.8	1.2	78.6	42.9	50.3	49.7
24185	WOOLWINE	95.2	93.6	2.6	2.9	0.1	0.1	2.4	4.0	5.2	5.4	5.6	5.3	4.6	23.8	30.5	17.5	2.0	80.5	45.0	51.2	48.8
24201	BRISTOL	92.3	90.6	5.8	6.5	0.4	0.6	1.0	1.6	5.3	5.2	5.3	6.3	6.4	23.4	27.2	17.2	3.6	80.7	43.4	46.0	54.0
24202	BRISTOL	98.6	98.0	0.5	0.5	0.2	0.2	0.6	1.1	5.0	5.4	6.0	6.2	4.4	25.2	31.4	15.0	1.5	79.7	43.6	49.5	50.5
24210	ABINGDON	96.7	95.8	1.9	2.1	0.4	0.5	0.8	1.3	4.9	4.9	5.1	5.1	5.3	24.8	29.9	16.6	3.3	82.0	44.9	47.0	53.0
24211	ABINGDON	98.4	97.8	0.6	0.6	0.3	0.5	0.5	1.0	4.8	5.0	5.5	5.9	5.2	23.8	32.9	15.3	1.6	81.1	44.9	49.1	50.9
24216	APPALACHIA	95.6	94.6	3.3	3.8	0.2	0.3	0.8	1.3	5.8	6.0	6.2	6.2	5.0	25.8	28.6	13.9	2.5	78.2	41.3	47.5	52.5
24217	BEE	99.5	98.9	0.0	0.0	0.0	0.0	1.1	2.0	5.1	5.9	7.0	7.6	4.2	26.4	30.1	12.6	1.1	76.7	41.3	52.2	47.8
24219	BIG STONE GAP	96.2	91.7	2.3	5.0	0.4	1.3	0.5	1.3	5.7	5.8	5.9	7.8	6.5	25.8	27.3	12.9	2.3	79.5	39.0	49.0	51.0
24220	BIRCHLEAF	99.6	99.6	0.0	0.0	0.0	0.0	0.2	0.4	5.5	6.9	6.9	7.7	5.7	27.0	29.2	10.1	1.0	75.4	38.6	50.3	49.7
24221	BLACKWATER	98.9	98.3	0.0	0.0	0.0	0.0	0.4	0.6	5.0	5.4	5.4	5.0	4.2	24.4	32.2	15.8	2.5	80.9	45.3	50.1	49.9
24224	CASTLEWOOD	98.5	98.0	0.8	0.9	0.1	0.1	0.5	0.8	5.1	5.4	5.7	5.8	4.5	25.9	31.5	14.3	1.7	80.2	43.3	48.9	51.1
24225	CLEVELAND	99.0	98.6	0.4	0.5	0.1	0.1	0.6	1.0	5.2	5.4	5.7	5.6	4.6	25.4	31.5	14.7	1.8	80.2	43.5	50.1	49.9
24226	CLINCHCO	98.4	98.0	0.7	0.9	0.1	0.1	0.3	0.6	5.1	5.5	5.7	5.8	4.8	25.0	32.3	14.0	1.7	80.0	43.7	48.9	51.1
24228	CLINTWOOD	98.7	98.2	0.5	0.5	0.1	0.2	0.4	0.6	5.1	5.5	5.6	5.1	4.5	24.5	31.6	15.6	2.5	80.7	44.7	48.4	51.6
24230	COEBURN	96.2	95.1	2.5	2.9	0.1	0.2	1.0	1.5	5.4	5.9	6.1	7.6	5.4	25.9	30.1	12.0	1.6	78.6	40.7	50.4	49.6
24236	DAMASCUS	98.7	98.4	0.6	0.7	0.2	0.2	0.6	1.0	4.9	5.0	5.5	6.3	4.8	25.3	29.5	16.4	2.2	80.8	43.7	47.9	52.1
	VIRGINIA	72.3	68.8	19.6	20.1	3.7	5.1	4.7	7.0	6.5	6.4	6.5	6.9	6.9	27.5	27.2	10.5	1.6	76.7	37.7	49.2	50.8
	UNITED STATES	75.1	72.0	12.3	12.7	3.8	4.6	12.5	15.7	6.8	6.7	6.6	7.1	6.9	27.0	26.0	10.9	1.9	75.7	36.9	49.2	50.8

ZIP CODE #	POST OFFICE NAME	2009 Per Capita Income	2009 HH Income Base	2009 HOUSEHOLD INCOME DISTRIBUTION (%) Less than $25,000	$25,000 to $49,999	$50,000 to $99,999	$100,000 to $149,999	$150,000 or More	MEDIAN HOUSEHOLD INCOME 2009	2014	2009 National Centile	2009 State Centile	2009 Home Value Base	2009 HOME VALUE DISTRIBUTION (%) Less than $50,000	$50,000 to $89,999	$90,000 to $174,999	$175,000 to $399,999	$400,000 or More	2009 Median Home Value
23974	VICTORIA	17028	1838	39.1	31.0	25.5	3.4	1.0	31707	34384	11	10	1366	13.0	30.2	38.2	17.7	0.9	97881
23976	WYLLIESBURG	17092	168	35.7	34.5	26.2	3.6	0.0	31157	32346	10	8	121	21.5	12.4	49.6	12.4	4.1	106250
24011	ROANOKE	22438	18	66.7	16.7	11.1	5.6	0.0	16330	17981	1	1	1	0.0	0.0	100.0	0.0	0.0	112500
24012	ROANOKE	23002	12394	25.9	32.0	34.4	6.9	0.9	43064	46160	43	38	7395	2.0	10.9	66.7	19.5	0.9	134196
24013	ROANOKE	14922	3117	40.2	37.1	20.1	1.9	0.7	30641	32006	9	8	1690	12.0	47.9	39.6	0.5	0.0	81765
24014	ROANOKE	32506	7563	18.1	27.4	38.3	9.3	6.8	54273	59664	70	67	5025	5.8	10.1	42.0	30.0	12.0	151049
24015	ROANOKE	28187	7211	18.3	34.0	38.4	6.8	2.5	48126	50669	57	53	4241	1.2	4.1	64.6	29.1	1.0	150900
24016	ROANOKE	16432	3765	51.6	28.8	16.2	2.9	0.5	23450	24136	2	2	1079	23.2	31.0	38.9	6.3	0.6	82018
24017	ROANOKE	18441	9696	34.6	31.1	29.9	3.5	0.9	35563	36997	19	16	5494	4.2	24.7	67.0	3.8	0.3	109641
24018	ROANOKE	36637	16310	11.0	20.6	42.1	16.2	10.0	68780	72987	86	82	11606	0.6	2.1	29.5	55.3	12.5	214555
24019	ROANOKE	27915	10815	11.9	23.1	49.0	12.4	3.6	63575	65978	82	78	8847	2.9	2.7	49.1	42.8	2.6	169217
24020	ROANOKE	20330	59	45.8	33.9	20.3	0.0	0.0	31333	30429	10	9	28	21.4	32.1	25.0	21.4	0.0	88000
24053	ARARAT	17493	1232	36.2	35.2	25.0	2.8	0.8	29009	29930	7	5	965	15.4	14.4	46.0	22.1	2.1	128125
24054	AXTON	18029	2664	29.7	31.1	34.5	3.5	1.2	41915	43305	39	35	2207	17.4	22.4	45.6	12.2	2.3	103945
24055	BASSETT	18471	6161	34.3	32.5	27.9	4.0	1.3	34087	35504	16	13	4841	14.6	17.6	50.7	16.1	1.0	115601
24059	BENT MOUNTAIN	29307	397	12.3	24.2	47.6	8.6	7.3	58859	64337	76	73	338	8.6	3.0	28.1	46.7	13.6	200769
24060	BLACKSBURG	20086	17815	41.0	24.7	23.7	6.3	4.3	32704	34277	13	11	6743	12.8	5.7	27.1	44.4	10.0	188789
24064	BLUE RIDGE	24765	1962	16.0	27.4	43.0	10.3	3.4	55236	57442	72	69	1745	9.1	7.0	38.9	43.2	1.8	164432
24065	BOONES MILL	23376	2530	23.5	27.5	39.2	7.5	2.3	48988	50616	59	56	2094	10.4	13.5	43.5	28.5	4.2	143557
24066	BUCHANAN	21295	2046	22.2	31.5	40.3	4.9	1.1	47225	49261	55	50	1681	9.9	16.4	45.3	25.4	3.0	127531
24067	CALLAWAY	22726	942	18.3	33.4	38.9	6.7	2.8	48574	50130	58	54	789	9.0	14.2	39.3	31.6	6.0	148750
24069	CASCADE	17997	803	30.1	27.4	39.5	1.5	1.5	43127	45363	43	38	645	14.4	26.5	50.2	8.4	0.5	97405
24070	CATAWBA	21853	739	22.2	32.1	36.8	7.7	1.2	47249	48218	55	51	603	5.3	8.8	43.8	33.7	8.5	148558
24072	CHECK	19977	665	23.3	35.2	37.1	3.8	0.6	42628	45652	41	37	556	10.6	11.5	36.7	37.2	4.0	152727
24073	CHRISTIANSBURG	23948	11298	20.7	27.3	41.1	8.9	2.0	51671	55491	65	62	7852	13.0	11.6	47.7	25.2	2.6	135620
24076	CLAUDVILLE	18722	423	30.5	38.1	28.1	2.6	0.7	35329	37166	19	16	341	11.7	21.7	46.6	18.5	1.5	99741
24077	CLOVERDALE	28367	236	14.8	22.0	46.6	11.0	5.5	62168	63600	80	76	198	6.1	6.6	24.7	54.0	8.6	218182
24078	COLLINSVILLE	22459	2956	26.4	33.1	34.3	4.8	1.3	41164	43459	37	33	1804	9.8	14.9	49.4	24.0	1.9	134754
24079	COPPER HILL	20233	803	26.8	30.8	36.5	5.6	0.4	45652	46944	50	46	666	11.9	14.6	33.9	35.4	4.2	147222
24082	CRITZ	14448	136	36.8	40.4	20.6	2.2	0.0	28319	28770	6	5	111	17.1	24.3	29.7	27.9	0.9	112500
24083	DALEVILLE	35822	1165	10.3	14.2	48.2	15.2	12.2	70911	73751	87	83	1061	2.4	1.0	20.2	56.1	20.4	249049
24084	DUBLIN	22826	4626	22.6	28.7	41.2	6.1	1.4	48820	51546	58	55	3464	10.9	13.7	55.6	17.7	2.2	122187
24085	EAGLE ROCK	20633	975	26.9	29.9	38.2	4.0	1.0	44657	47100	47	42	861	19.6	19.5	40.2	17.5	3.1	106209
24086	EGGLESTON	18096	65	30.8	30.8	32.3	6.2	0.0	38013	39057	27	24	57	21.1	21.1	45.6	8.8	3.5	105357
24087	ELLISTON	21583	1689	23.0	30.0	39.3	4.4	3.4	47604	49774	56	51	1388	36.6	11.7	33.6	14.0	4.0	96053
24088	FERRUM	20373	1690	24.6	35.8	33.7	3.7	2.2	41444	43552	37	34	1349	16.8	17.1	46.3	18.7	1.1	119386
24089	FIELDALE	17872	1122	36.5	35.9	23.3	3.8	0.5	31653	32165	11	10	873	13.7	26.7	48.2	10.5	0.8	102854
24090	FINCASTLE	25124	1835	17.9	25.7	42.5	11.2	2.8	55263	58715	72	69	1582	5.1	7.8	33.9	42.3	10.9	186062
24091	FLOYD	19723	3035	31.0	33.4	30.9	3.1	1.5	35653	37144	20	17	2356	11.9	11.2	43.1	27.4	6.4	144609
24092	GLADE HILL	22157	1128	28.2	28.1	34.9	5.8	3.0	43419	45473	44	40	890	10.6	14.3	44.3	22.4	8.5	135857
24093	GLEN LYN	20047	58	25.9	31.0	39.7	3.4	0.0	45000	47980	48	44	46	17.4	21.7	45.7	15.2	0.0	104545
24095	GOODVIEW	23529	1727	11.8	32.3	47.4	6.6	1.9	52717	53857	67	65	1500	6.1	13.0	42.1	31.9	6.9	155282
24101	HARDY	25541	2254	17.9	21.8	47.6	9.3	3.4	56777	59260	74	72	1992	6.1	5.6	38.4	42.1	7.9	174908
24102	HENRY	18658	665	30.1	37.3	28.7	2.6	1.4	39641	40957	32	28	550	21.3	12.4	45.5	17.6	3.3	125000
24104	HUDDLESTON	24203	1501	17.5	32.2	43.9	4.7	1.7	50147	51803	61	59	1282	4.2	9.1	28.2	40.1	18.4	212299
24105	INDIAN VALLEY	17968	257	27.6	37.0	31.5	3.5	0.4	37496	39405	25	22	228	14.9	18.4	40.4	18.0	8.3	120588
24112	MARTINSVILLE	20763	14352	32.2	30.1	30.5	5.0	2.2	38004	40138	27	23	9925	9.3	17.6	51.8	17.9	3.3	123846
24120	MEADOWS OF DAN	18116	946	38.5	35.9	21.9	2.7	1.0	30226	30929	8	8	775	11.9	15.7	44.4	23.6	4.4	132770
24121	MONETA	28013	4185	16.7	31.2	40.4	7.2	4.5	51697	54383	65	63	3646	7.8	8.0	30.9	31.8	21.6	193789
24122	MONTVALE	20579	792	22.0	36.6	36.4	2.5	2.5	42124	45416	40	36	664	24.2	10.2	45.0	19.1	1.4	111990
24124	NARROWS	20823	2285	27.7	31.5	35.4	3.9	1.6	39986	43438	32	29	1799	13.5	29.1	46.6	10.1	0.7	98042
24127	NEW CASTLE	20444	1710	24.3	35.0	34.4	4.6	1.7	43365	45125	43	39	1379	10.9	14.1	43.5	24.7	6.8	133225
24128	NEWPORT	25567	611	25.4	28.8	34.7	7.5	3.6	45551	47526	50	45	494	15.6	19.2	36.2	21.7	7.3	113021
24131	PAINT BANK	16179	54	22.2	46.3	29.6	1.9	0.0	38685	39515	29	26	44	11.4	18.2	47.7	22.7	0.0	112500
24133	PATRICK SPRINGS	18932	1261	30.3	32.8	31.6	4.0	1.2	38050	40263	27	24	1006	11.6	19.6	44.8	20.1	3.9	127825
24134	PEARISBURG	23028	2715	25.1	30.7	36.5	5.8	1.8	44971	46484	48	43	2116	10.2	23.1	52.0	12.8	1.9	111974
24136	PEMBROKE	22692	1298	26.3	29.8	36.2	5.1	2.5	43234	45895	43	39	1016	16.1	21.7	46.7	13.2	2.4	101964
24137	PENHOOK	25163	1234	24.1	28.8	36.1	7.2	3.9	46813	48816	54	49	1036	13.5	17.2	35.6	21.9	11.8	131858
24138	PILOT	20621	603	16.3	40.0	38.3	4.5	1.0	45278	47179	49	44	511	12.9	12.7	46.0	27.4	1.0	128977
24139	PITTSVILLE	19410	245	30.2	31.0	32.7	4.9	1.2	39177	41480	30	27	201	21.4	18.4	45.8	11.9	2.5	99762
24141	RADFORD	23192	9168	33.8	25.7	32.5	5.4	2.6	39232	42617	30	27	5001	8.3	10.8	54.7	22.8	3.5	130812
24142	RADFORD	9973	7	85.7	14.3	0.0	0.0	0.0	7000	8750	0	1	0	0.0	0.0	0.0	0.0	0.0	0
24147	RICH CREEK	23714	369	22.2	34.7	36.3	5.1	1.6	43883	45538	45	41	264	14.8	29.2	49.2	6.1	0.8	95517
24148	RIDGEWAY	20538	3535	27.5	33.6	32.1	4.8	2.0	41774	42758	39	35	2855	17.9	16.3	40.2	23.7	1.9	124035
24149	RINER	21921	1224	19.1	34.6	38.5	6.1	1.6	46301	49390	52	47	1031	12.1	11.3	38.4	33.0	5.2	148004
24150	RIPPLEMEAD	21190	202	26.2	31.2	37.1	4.5	1.0	42389	45344	41	37	166	15.1	21.1	53.0	10.8	0.0	103125
24151	ROCKY MOUNT	19997	7975	31.0	29.4	32.4	5.4	1.8	40504	42319	34	31	5960	12.6	18.0	42.5	24.3	2.6	126539
24153	SALEM	26488	14766	17.5	28.8	39.4	9.7	4.6	53381	58102	69	66	10696	5.5	6.5	48.4	33.9	5.8	157115
24161	SANDY LEVEL	21973	181	23.8	34.3	33.7	6.6	1.7	40991	43005	36	33	151	29.1	7.9	41.7	15.2	6.0	110795
24162	SHAWSVILLE	22503	980	19.2	35.2	39.5	4.4	1.7	47012	48902	54	49	742	11.1	15.5	53.4	18.2	1.9	118462
24165	SPENCER	22103	638	27.1	34.5	31.5	6.1	0.8	42115	43833	40	36	532	15.6	21.1	39.3	20.9	3.2	109247
24167	STAFFORDSVILLE	20178	130	23.1	33.8	38.5	3.1	1.5	45443	46884	50	45	114	9.6	28.1	53.5	7.9	0.9	101471
24168	STANLEYTOWN	23771	86	33.7	30.2	24.4	8.1	3.5	35000	40000	18	15	63	11.1	17.5	41.3	20.6	9.5	134375
24171	STUART	18911	3823	32.7	35.1	27.2	3.9	1.0	36404	37926	22	19	3004	13.6	16.8	45.1	21.8	2.7	122141
24174	THAXTON	20085	1070	20.4	39.9	34.9	4.0	0.8	43270	45664	43	39	906	19.6	12.8	44.9	20.3	2.3	120614
24175	TROUTVILLE	28449	3040	14.2	20.9	44.8	14.4	5.7	63318	65742	82	78	2668	2.5	5.7	30.9	50.1	10.8	206452
24176	UNION HALL	31181	666	22.1	24.2	34.2	11.0	8.6	53288	55391	68	66	547	6.4	11.7	27.6	25.2	29.1	218103
24179	VINTON	23371	8250	18.5	31.4	41.2	7.0	1.8	50009	52529	61	58	6376	7.3	7.5	50.8	33.1	1.2	150986
24184	WIRTZ	25707	1480	21.2	33.2	31.6	7.9	6.0	47128	48128	54	50	1229	9.3	7.9	36.2	32.1	14.5	166766
24185	WOOLWINE	17275	389	36.5	38.8	20.3	3.1	1.3	30110	31523	8	7	320	13.1	11.6	50.3	21.6	3.4	131780
24201	BRISTOL	21516	7577	34.1	33.3	26.3	4.2	2.1	35974	37814	20	18	4817	8.0	24.1	53.7	12.9	1.3	110802
24202	BRISTOL	21080	5089	27.6	32.7	32.6	5.6	1.6	42224	45031	40	37	4135	12.3	16.9	48.1	20.7	2.0	121804
24210	ABINGDON	23442	7176	29.9	30.6	31.7	4.8	3.0	39644	42667	32	29	4865	13.1	11.4	49.5	20.9	5.1	129756
24211	ABINGDON	27125	4096	18.6	29.5	37.7	10.4	3.8	52217	57857	66	64	3409	9.1	8.1	37.4	37.2	8.2	165457
24216	APPALACHIA	15394	1336	47.5	31.1	17.4	2.8	1.1	26076	26218	4	3	954	30.3	44.3	23.2	2.1	0.1	63182
24217	BEE	13880	155	50.3	25.8	23.2	0.6	0.0	24637	26107	3	3	133	15.8	33.1	42.1	9.0	0.0	90789
24219	BIG STONE GAP	18937	4452	40.4	23.7	29.4	4.7	1.8	33403	35805	14	12	3207	13.6	21.2	44.9	16.7	3.6	118227
24220	BIRCHLEAF	12868	399	50.1	28.3	18.0	3.5	0.0	24933	24820	3	3	346	22.0	29.5	39.6	9.0	0.0	87727
24221	BLACKWATER	16590	434	35.9	36.4	23.3	4.4	0.0	31442	33986	10	9	357	35.0	25.8	27.2	10.4	1.7	73393
24224	CASTLEWOOD	17374	3538	37.3	33.6	23.7	4.0	1.3	32551	33646	12	11	2835	21.9	21.0	39.6	15.3	2.1	100689
24225	CLEVELAND	16419	838	39.4	32.8	24.3	3.0	0.5	29681	30594	8	6	687	23.1	25.3	40.0	10.2	1.3	91981
24226	CLINCHCO	15428	724	44.3	34.5	18.1	1.9	1.1	28978	29457	7	5	604	25.3	31.5	36.3	6.8	0.2	78448
24228	CLINTWOOD	15991	3296	45.2	31.4	20.1	2.2	1.1	28783	29663	6	5	2604	22.9	24.1	37.8	13.3	1.9	94756
24230	COEBURN	15955	3822	40.5	34.2	21.5	2.7	1.1	30171	31042	8	7	2992	20.3	25.5	38.9	14.7	0.6	95727
24236	DAMASCUS	18237	1507	36.6	35.5	24.4	2.3	1.3	34100	35292	16	13	1062	23.9	19.4	45.0	10.5	1.1	97320
	VIRGINIA	30912		17.0	22.6	35.9	15.0	9.5	61855	64957				5.3	6.3	30.4	41.5	16.5	203135
	UNITED STATES	27277		20.9	24.4	35.3	11.7	7.6	54719	56938				9.3	13.1	31.6	32.6	13.5	162279

ZIP CODE #	POST OFFICE NAME	FINANCIAL SERVICES: Auto Loan	FINANCIAL SERVICES: Home Loan	FINANCIAL SERVICES: Invest-ments	FINANCIAL SERVICES: Retire-ment Plans	THE HOME: Home Improvements: Home Repair	THE HOME: Home Improvements: Lawn & Garden	THE HOME: Furnishings: Comput-ers & Hard-ware-Personal	THE HOME: Furnishings: Major Appli-ances	THE HOME: Furnishings: TV, Radio, Sound Equip-ment	THE HOME: Furnishings: Furni-ture	ENTERTAINMENT: Dine out/ Carry out	ENTERTAINMENT: Sports Equip-ment	ENTERTAINMENT: Fees & Tickets	ENTERTAINMENT: Toys & Games	ENTERTAINMENT: Travel	ENTERTAINMENT: Cable TV	PERSONAL: Apparel & Services	PERSONAL: Auto Repairs	PERSONAL: Health Insur-ance	PERSONAL: Pets & Supplies
23974	VICTORIA	69	48	69	47	50	70	52	65	58	47	56	49	41	58	50	64	37	60	69	77
23976	WYLLIESBURG	68	48	58	47	48	65	51	59	56	49	55	46	40	59	46	62	37	56	63	72
24011	ROANOKE	32	24	29	27	25	30	39	31	42	35	42	24	35	36	34	45	29	39	44	41
24012	ROANOKE	71	66	62	67	65	71	71	69	73	68	72	53	69	73	68	75	50	71	76	83
24013	ROANOKE	55	43	42	44	42	51	52	51	55	48	54	39	45	55	45	59	37	53	57	61
24014	ROANOKE	97	102	102	103	102	105	100	101	99	99	99	78	102	99	102	101	70	100	105	119
24015	ROANOKE	80	76	71	78	74	78	84	78	84	80	84	61	81	83	79	84	58	82	83	94
24016	ROANOKE	46	36	34	38	34	39	49	41	51	45	51	33	43	50	41	53	36	47	47	52
24017	ROANOKE	62	56	48	57	52	60	60	57	64	59	64	44	58	64	56	67	44	61	66	71
24018	ROANOKE	112	121	123	124	124	123	117	118	117	119	117	88	124	115	123	118	83	118	124	137
24019	ROANOKE	97	106	100	106	105	107	97	101	98	98	98	76	103	98	102	100	68	99	105	118
24020	ROANOKE	47	38	42	38	39	45	47	46	50	43	49	34	41	48	43	53	34	48	53	54
24053	ARARAT	74	53	61	52	53	71	56	65	62	54	60	50	45	64	51	67	41	61	68	79
24054	AXTON	82	58	70	56	58	79	61	72	68	59	67	55	48	71	56	74	45	68	76	87
24055	BASSETT	77	56	69	55	56	76	58	70	65	55	63	53	47	66	55	71	42	65	74	84
24059	BENT MOUNTAIN	103	116	101	120	113	114	104	108	102	104	103	84	111	105	110	102	72	104	107	127
24060	BLACKSBURG	72	51	49	55	50	53	86	60	76	70	77	54	66	76	63	73	54	71	61	76
24064	BLUE RIDGE	95	96	94	97	96	101	88	96	89	88	89	73	89	91	91	92	62	91	96	113
24065	BOONES MILL	88	79	85	79	80	94	76	87	80	72	79	65	71	81	77	85	54	82	92	102
24066	BUCHANAN	83	69	76	70	71	86	69	81	74	64	72	61	61	75	68	79	49	75	84	95
24067	CALLAWAY	89	80	82	83	82	96	79	90	82	72	81	68	72	84	79	87	55	83	93	105
24069	CASCADE	82	59	67	57	58	78	61	71	68	59	66	54	49	70	55	74	45	67	75	86
24070	CATAWBA	81	79	75	82	79	87	75	82	76	72	76	63	73	78	76	79	52	77	83	96
24072	CHECK	76	65	71	67	67	80	65	75	68	59	67	57	58	69	65	73	45	70	78	88
24073	CHRISTIANSBURG	87	84	77	83	81	85	82	84	82	81	82	64	79	85	80	83	57	82	84	99
24076	CLAUDVILLE	76	55	63	53	54	72	57	66	63	55	62	51	46	66	52	69	42	63	70	81
24077	CLOVERDALE	105	106	103	108	104	113	97	106	98	96	98	82	98	100	101	101	68	101	106	125
24078	COLLINSVILLE	73	64	65	65	65	72	69	71	71	66	70	53	63	71	66	74	48	71	76	84
24079	COPPER HILL	82	65	80	65	67	85	65	79	70	60	69	59	56	70	65	76	46	73	82	93
24082	CRITZ	65	47	54	45	47	62	49	57	54	47	53	44	39	56	44	59	36	54	60	69
24083	DALEVILLE	120	144	141	148	146	138	125	131	120	131	122	99	139	121	137	119	86	125	126	151
24084	DUBLIN	82	74	76	74	74	84	74	80	77	70	76	61	69	77	73	80	52	78	84	95
24085	EAGLE ROCK	87	64	88	62	66	88	65	82	72	60	70	61	53	71	64	78	47	75	85	97
24086	EGGLESTON	86	61	88	59	64	87	63	80	70	59	69	60	50	69	62	77	45	73	83	95
24087	ELLISTON	82	80	72	78	78	80	77	80	77	78	77	60	74	80	75	78	53	78	79	94
24088	FERRUM	88	66	81	65	67	88	67	81	74	63	72	61	56	75	65	80	48	75	84	97
24089	FIELDALE	69	49	61	48	50	68	52	62	58	49	57	47	42	59	48	64	38	59	66	75
24090	FINCASTLE	94	92	94	94	93	102	86	96	87	83	87	73	85	88	89	91	60	90	96	112
24091	FLOYD	77	59	77	59	61	80	60	74	65	55	64	56	50	65	60	71	43	68	77	87
24092	GLADE HILL	93	70	93	68	72	93	71	87	77	68	76	65	59	78	70	84	51	81	89	103
24093	GLEN LYN	89	64	91	62	66	91	67	84	74	61	72	63	53	73	65	81	48	77	89	99
24095	GOODVIEW	91	87	79	87	86	92	82	88	84	82	84	66	80	87	81	87	57	84	89	104
24101	HARDY	98	92	112	93	95	105	87	101	88	84	88	76	84	87	93	92	60	95	100	117
24102	HENRY	80	57	75	55	58	79	59	72	66	56	65	55	47	67	56	72	43	67	76	87
24104	HUDDLESTON	87	75	95	74	80	94	72	86	78	74	77	60	68	76	75	84	52	81	92	101
24105	INDIAN VALLEY	78	56	77	54	57	78	57	72	64	54	62	54	46	64	56	70	41	66	75	86
24112	MARTINSVILLE	75	63	67	64	64	76	66	72	70	63	69	54	60	71	63	75	47	70	77	86
24120	MEADOWS OF DAN	70	50	70	48	52	70	51	65	57	48	56	49	41	57	50	63	37	60	67	77
24121	MONETA	95	92	109	90	99	105	85	97	90	92	89	66	86	86	91	94	60	93	104	113
24122	MONTVALE	76	70	65	70	70	76	69	74	70	67	70	55	64	73	67	73	48	71	74	87
24124	NARROWS	82	62	82	61	64	86	65	79	72	60	70	59	54	71	64	78	47	74	85	93
24127	NEW CASTLE	81	67	70	68	68	83	67	77	72	63	70	59	59	74	65	77	48	72	80	91
24128	NEWPORT	96	77	94	77	79	100	77	93	83	71	81	70	66	83	77	90	55	86	97	110
24131	PAINT BANK	78	56	64	54	55	74	58	67	64	56	63	52	46	67	53	70	42	64	71	82
24133	PATRICK SPRINGS	81	58	67	57	58	77	61	71	67	59	66	54	49	70	55	73	44	67	74	86
24134	PEARISBURG	84	69	82	68	71	88	71	82	77	67	75	61	63	76	70	83	51	78	89	96
24136	PEMBROKE	88	69	87	69	71	90	72	85	77	67	76	63	61	77	70	83	51	79	89	100
24137	PENHOOK	98	75	100	73	79	98	76	92	83	74	81	68	65	82	76	89	54	86	95	109
24138	PILOT	82	75	70	75	75	82	72	79	75	71	74	58	68	77	70	78	51	75	80	92
24139	PITTSVILLE	77	61	74	58	63	78	61	72	67	62	66	53	53	67	60	72	44	69	78	86
24141	RADFORD	73	58	59	60	58	65	77	67	74	67	73	54	64	73	65	74	51	71	70	81
24142	RADFORD	15	7	6	8	6	8	22	11	17	15	17	12	13	17	12	16	12	15	11	14
24147	RICH CREEK	89	64	89	62	66	93	70	86	78	62	75	64	56	77	68	86	50	81	94	101
24148	RIDGEWAY	83	64	75	63	65	82	65	76	71	62	69	58	55	72	62	76	47	72	80	91
24149	RINER	87	81	73	80	80	85	76	82	79	77	79	60	73	82	74	81	54	79	83	97
24150	RIPPLEMEAD	84	62	84	61	65	85	65	79	71	61	69	59	53	70	64	77	46	74	83	94
24151	ROCKY MOUNT	79	64	71	63	64	79	65	74	70	62	69	56	57	71	62	75	46	70	77	88
24153	SALEM	88	92	87	93	92	97	89	91	90	88	90	68	92	90	91	93	63	90	98	107
24161	SANDY LEVEL	76	70	88	65	77	85	67	79	72	72	70	53	65	67	72	76	47	76	88	92
24162	SHAWSVILLE	87	79	75	80	79	88	77	85	79	73	78	63	71	82	75	83	53	80	86	99
24165	SPENCER	87	63	80	61	63	85	65	78	71	61	70	59	52	73	61	78	47	73	82	94
24167	STAFFORDSVILLE	90	65	74	63	64	85	67	78	74	65	73	60	54	78	61	81	49	74	82	95
24168	STANLEYTOWN	94	68	94	66	70	98	74	91	82	66	80	68	59	81	71	91	53	85	100	107
24171	STUART	75	55	69	53	55	74	57	68	64	55	62	52	46	64	54	69	42	64	72	82
24174	THAXTON	81	65	70	63	65	78	65	73	69	64	69	55	56	72	61	74	46	70	75	88
24175	TROUTVILLE	108	112	115	113	113	117	102	112	102	102	102	85	103	103	107	103	71	105	109	129
24176	UNION HALL	121	96	149	94	104	127	96	121	102	91	100	89	83	98	102	109	67	112	121	141
24179	VINTON	81	81	74	81	79	86	78	81	80	76	80	62	78	81	78	83	55	80	85	96
24184	WIRTZ	102	89	106	87	91	102	86	99	89	86	89	72	79	89	87	93	60	93	98	116
24185	WOOLWINE	71	51	64	49	52	69	53	64	58	50	57	48	42	60	50	64	38	59	67	77
24201	BRISTOL	68	60	66	60	61	73	63	68	68	59	66	50	59	66	62	72	45	67	76	80
24202	BRISTOL	84	67	73	67	67	85	68	78	73	64	72	60	58	75	65	79	48	73	82	93
24210	ABINGDON	79	65	74	65	67	80	70	76	75	67	74	56	63	74	67	80	50	75	83	90
24211	ABINGDON	95	90	88	90	91	98	87	94	90	86	89	69	84	91	86	94	61	90	98	110
24216	APPALACHIA	63	43	62	41	43	63	46	58	52	43	51	44	36	53	44	58	34	54	62	69
24217	BEE	59	39	57	36	39	58	41	52	48	39	47	41	31	49	39	53	31	49	55	64
24219	BIG STONE GAP	73	60	67	59	60	73	62	70	66	59	64	52	54	66	59	70	44	67	73	82
24220	BIRCHLEAF	61	40	59	38	40	60	43	54	49	41	48	42	32	50	40	55	32	51	57	66
24221	BLACKWATER	69	49	71	48	51	70	51	65	56	47	55	48	41	56	50	62	37	59	67	77
24224	CASTLEWOOD	72	53	68	51	54	72	55	67	61	51	59	51	44	61	52	66	40	62	70	80
24225	CLEVELAND	68	47	68	45	48	69	50	63	56	46	55	48	39	56	48	62	36	59	67	75
24226	CLINCHCO	66	44	65	42	45	66	47	59	54	44	52	46	36	54	45	60	35	55	62	72
24228	CLINTWOOD	66	44	65	42	44	66	47	59	54	44	53	46	36	54	44	60	35	56	63	72
24230	COEBURN	70	48	69	46	49	69	50	63	57	47	55	48	39	57	48	62	37	59	66	76
24236	DAMASCUS	70	50	63	49	51	69	53	64	60	50	58	48	43	60	50	65	39	60	69	77
	VIRGINIA	115	112	112	114	111	114	112	112	112	112	112	88	111	114	111	113	79	112	112	132
	UNITED STATES	100	100	100	100	100	100	100	100	100	100	100	100	100	100	100	100	100	100	100	100

ZIP CODE #	POST OFFICE NAME	COUNTY FIPS CODE	POPULATION 2000	POPULATION 2009	POPULATION 2014	2000-2009 ANNUAL RATE % Rate	2000-2009 ANNUAL RATE State Centile	HOUSEHOLDS 2000	HOUSEHOLDS 2009	HOUSEHOLDS 2014	HOUSEHOLDS % Annual Rate 2000-2009	HOUSEHOLDS 2009 Average HH Size	FAMILIES 2000	FAMILIES 2009	FAMILIES % Annual Rate 2000-2009
24237	DANTE	051	987	960	939	-0.3	11	411	416	413	0.1	2.31	301	297	-0.1
24239	DAVENPORT	027	26	23	22	-1.3	1	8	8	7	0.0	2.88	6	6	0.0
24243	DRYDEN	105	2321	2427	2462	0.5	45	854	931	958	0.9	2.52	633	670	0.6
24244	DUFFIELD	169	5588	5648	5579	0.1	28	2197	2221	2214	0.1	2.36	1607	1583	-0.2
24245	DUNGANNON	169	1154	1130	1114	-0.2	14	493	496	494	0.1	2.27	362	356	-0.2
24248	EWING	105	2413	2427	2427	0.1	28	1005	1050	1063	0.5	2.31	712	720	0.1
24250	FORT BLACKMORE	169	1306	1261	1237	-0.4	8	533	534	530	0.0	2.36	403	395	-0.2
24251	GATE CITY	169	8105	8716	8932	0.8	58	3478	3859	4004	1.1	2.23	2439	2615	0.8
24256	HAYSI	051	3207	3071	2982	-0.5	6	1327	1323	1303	0.0	2.32	973	942	-0.3
24258	HILTONS	169	2602	2543	2518	-0.2	14	1085	1101	1104	0.2	2.31	786	777	-0.1
24260	HONAKER	167	5761	5672	5600	-0.2	14	2302	2362	2362	0.3	2.40	1755	1755	0.0
24263	JONESVILLE	105	6285	6312	6297	0.0	23	2662	2777	2807	0.5	2.26	1824	1836	0.1
24265	KEOKEE	105	1519	1493	1483	-0.2	14	596	611	614	0.3	2.43	428	425	-0.1
24266	LEBANON	167	7175	6864	6756	-0.5	6	2880	2847	2829	-0.1	2.30	2059	1971	-0.5
24269	MC CLURE	051	78	76	75	-0.3	11	34	34	34	0.0	2.24	26	26	0.0
24270	MENDOTA	191	506	527	538	0.4	42	206	222	229	0.8	2.37	157	165	0.5
24271	NICKELSVILLE	169	2903	2777	2733	-0.5	6	1187	1174	1170	-0.1	2.35	859	827	-0.4
24272	NORA	051	587	592	583	0.1	28	231	242	242	0.5	2.45	170	173	0.2
24273	NORTON	195	5822	5552	5399	-0.5	6	2515	2509	2472	0.0	2.19	1656	1591	-0.4
24277	PENNINGTON GAP	105	5499	7052	7020	2.7	90	2342	2407	2423	0.3	2.23	1610	1603	0.0
24279	POUND	195	4969	6039	5953	2.1	86	1967	2042	2033	0.4	2.45	1492	1508	0.1
24280	ROSEDALE	167	3660	2749	2776	-3.0	0	1048	1144	1170	1.0	2.39	829	881	0.7
24281	ROSE HILL	105	2335	2359	2362	0.1	28	975	1023	1037	0.5	2.31	688	698	0.2
24282	SAINT CHARLES	105	395	391	391	-0.1	18	158	163	165	0.3	2.36	114	114	0.0
24283	SAINT PAUL	195	2445	2408	2359	-0.2	14	1033	1061	1054	0.3	2.27	728	725	0.0
24290	WEBER CITY	169	1990	2011	1996	0.1	28	881	899	902	0.2	2.11	619	613	-0.1
24292	WHITETOP	077	619	562	532	-1.0	2	267	251	241	-0.7	2.24	184	167	-1.0
24293	WISE	195	10736	10753	10583	0.0	23	4165	4340	4321	0.4	2.31	2944	2972	0.1
24301	PULASKI	155	15329	14797	14649	-0.4	8	6562	6505	6510	-0.1	2.24	4427	4234	-0.5
24311	ATKINS	173	1393	1414	1400	0.2	33	591	620	620	0.5	2.28	416	423	0.2
24312	AUSTINVILLE	035	2043	2123	2148	0.4	42	867	930	949	0.8	2.26	653	682	0.5
24313	BARREN SPRINGS	197	953	1090	1151	1.5	76	382	454	485	1.9	2.40	291	336	1.6
24314	BASTIAN	021	1650	1668	1654	0.1	28	659	694	697	0.6	2.37	504	517	0.3
24315	BLAND	021	3610	3722	3739	0.3	38	1230	1311	1334	0.7	2.38	899	931	0.4
24316	BROADFORD	173	22	22	21	0.0	23	9	9	9	0.0	2.44	6	6	0.0
24317	CANA	035	3495	3543	3523	0.1	28	1442	1507	1514	0.5	2.34	1053	1069	0.2
24318	CERES	021	703	708	699	0.1	28	295	309	309	0.5	2.29	214	218	0.2
24319	CHILHOWIE	173	7079	6999	6896	-0.1	18	2774	2826	2813	0.2	2.38	2050	2029	-0.1
24322	CRIPPLE CREEK	197	91	91	91	0.0	23	45	47	47	0.5	1.94	32	32	0.0
24323	CROCKETT	197	501	537	555	0.8	58	195	216	226	1.1	2.49	143	154	0.8
24324	DRAPER	155	1856	1923	1958	0.4	42	766	819	843	0.7	2.35	568	590	0.4
24325	DUGSPUR	035	1351	1399	1400	0.4	42	576	608	613	0.6	2.28	420	429	0.2
24326	ELK CREEK	077	1202	1145	1104	-0.5	6	536	528	515	-0.2	2.17	386	369	-0.5
24328	FANCY GAP	035	2140	2128	2101	-0.1	18	907	930	926	0.3	2.28	685	684	0.0
24330	FRIES	077	4119	3991	3887	-0.3	11	1765	1761	1733	0.0	2.27	1243	1204	-0.3
24333	GALAX	077	17718	17758	17640	0.0	23	7566	7744	7744	0.3	2.28	5182	5131	-0.1
24340	GLADE SPRING	191	4765	5123	5281	0.8	58	1957	2159	2254	1.1	2.25	1426	1527	0.7
24343	HILLSVILLE	035	8904	9095	9089	0.2	33	3713	3901	3932	0.5	2.25	2595	2641	0.2
24347	HIWASSEE	155	1638	1743	1795	0.7	54	668	737	767	1.1	2.36	505	542	0.8
24348	INDEPENDENCE	077	3924	3940	3882	0.0	23	1677	1730	1720	0.3	2.21	1136	1132	0.0
24350	IVANHOE	197	1238	1396	1456	1.3	72	507	594	627	1.7	2.35	364	413	1.4
24351	LAMBSBURG	035	752	763	755	0.2	33	292	303	303	0.4	2.52	215	217	0.1
24352	LAUREL FORK	035	891	906	900	0.2	33	345	360	361	0.5	2.44	248	251	0.1
24354	MARION	173	16110	15484	15100	-0.4	8	6597	6517	6410	-0.1	2.25	4568	4367	-0.5
24360	MAX MEADOWS	197	5567	5891	6060	0.6	49	2181	2393	2491	1.0	2.45	1687	1799	0.7
24361	MEADOWVIEW	191	5987	6413	6562	0.7	54	2106	2290	2375	0.9	2.54	1565	1654	0.6
24363	MOUTH OF WILSON	077	1549	1447	1387	-0.7	4	695	671	650	-0.4	2.14	477	445	-0.7
24366	ROCKY GAP	021	502	514	518	0.3	38	209	223	228	0.7	2.18	162	169	0.5
24368	RURAL RETREAT	197	5030	5343	5469	0.7	54	2029	2227	2305	1.0	2.40	1480	1573	0.7
24370	SALTVILLE	173	6939	6894	6815	-0.1	18	2854	2933	2928	0.3	2.35	2097	2091	0.0
24374	SPEEDWELL	197	627	656	671	0.5	45	253	274	284	0.9	2.39	183	192	0.5
24375	SUGAR GROVE	173	1853	1839	1809	-0.1	18	761	777	771	0.2	2.37	548	542	-0.1
24377	TANNERSVILLE	185	291	290	285	0.0	23	112	116	115	0.4	2.50	92	93	0.1
24378	TROUTDALE	077	2388	1275	1226	-6.6	0	593	579	563	-0.3	2.20	425	402	-0.6
24380	WILLIS	063	2681	2875	2976	0.8	58	1076	1181	1233	1.0	2.43	784	836	0.7
24381	WOODLAWN	035	3323	3373	3358	0.2	33	1360	1415	1418	0.4	2.31	984	994	0.1
24382	WYTHEVILLE	197	14081	14273	14395	0.1	28	6092	6382	6510	0.5	2.18	4034	4068	0.1
24401	STAUNTON	015	34674	35703	36818	0.3	38	14020	15268	15887	0.9	2.22	8928	9384	0.5
24413	BLUE GRASS	091	176	175	173	-0.1	18	74	76	76	0.3	2.30	50	50	0.0
24416	BUENA VISTA	163	8665	8913	8953	0.3	38	3457	3549	3595	0.3	2.36	2427	2417	0.0
24421	CHURCHVILLE	015	3182	3327	3366	0.5	45	1220	1309	1338	0.8	2.53	954	1000	0.5
24422	CLIFTON FORGE	005	7321	6970	6836	-0.5	6	3099	3016	2976	-0.3	2.23	2041	1911	-0.7
24426	COVINGTON	005	15823	15483	15256	-0.2	14	6594	6574	6525	0.0	2.31	4604	4452	-0.4
24430	CRAIGSVILLE	015	2527	1859	1872	-3.3	0	709	769	780	0.9	2.03	499	524	0.5
24431	CRIMORA	015	2491	2678	2781	0.8	58	978	1079	1128	1.1	2.48	730	784	0.8
24432	DEERFIELD	015	334	328	320	-0.2	14	151	152	149	0.1	2.16	103	99	-0.4
24433	DOE HILL	091	282	280	278	-0.1	18	118	122	122	0.4	2.30	78	78	0.0
24435	FAIRFIELD	163	1658	1775	1836	0.7	54	670	731	760	0.9	2.43	499	532	0.7
24437	FORT DEFIANCE	015	852	851	860	0.0	23	320	325	331	0.2	2.62	261	260	0.0
24439	GOSHEN	163	1355	2571	2603	7.2	98	559	611	628	1.0	2.88	394	417	0.6
24440	GREENVILLE	015	2761	2752	2929	0.0	23	820	994	1070	2.1	2.57	627	740	1.8
24441	GROTTOES	015	5523	6409	6846	1.6	78	2164	2593	2792	2.0	2.47	1589	1847	1.6
24442	HEAD WATERS	091	101	100	100	-0.1	18	43	44	44	0.2	2.27	29	28	-0.4
24445	HOT SPRINGS	017	2704	2806	2822	0.4	42	1113	1185	1201	0.7	2.31	793	821	0.4
24450	LEXINGTON	163	15301	16689	17250	0.9	61	5667	6305	6593	1.2	2.25	3516	3786	0.8
24458	MC DOWELL	091	335	333	330	-0.1	18	155	160	160	0.3	2.08	103	103	0.0
24459	MIDDLEBROOK	015	662	644	643	-0.3	11	251	252	253	0.0	2.56	190	185	-0.3
24460	MILLBORO	017	1848	1799	1779	-0.3	11	706	708	705	0.0	2.33	513	500	-0.3
24464	MONTEBELLO	125	156	161	165	0.3	38	68	73	75	0.8	2.21	46	48	0.5
24465	MONTEREY	091	1422	1391	1374	-0.2	14	647	655	654	0.1	2.12	440	429	-0.3
24467	MOUNT SIDNEY	015	2028	2211	2259	0.9	61	783	869	894	1.1	2.54	619	672	0.9
24468	MUSTOE	091	220	218	217	-0.1	18	94	97	97	0.3	2.25	64	64	0.0
24471	PORT REPUBLIC	165	1226	1461	1566	1.9	83	492	596	644	2.1	2.45	384	455	1.9
24472	RAPHINE	015	2639	2849	2942	0.8	58	1091	1206	1253	1.1	2.36	794	853	0.8
24473	ROCKBRIDGE BATHS	163	848	913	942	0.8	58	355	389	403	1.0	2.34	256	272	0.7
	VIRGINIA					1.2					1.3	2.52			1.0
	UNITED STATES					1.0					1.1	2.59			0.9

ZIP CODE #	POST OFFICE NAME	RACE (%) White 2000	White 2009	Black 2000	Black 2009	Asian/Pacific 2000	Asian/Pacific 2009	% Hispanic Origin 2000	% Hispanic Origin 2009	2009 AGE DISTRIBUTION (%) 0-4	5-9	10-14	15-19	20-24	25-44	45-64	65-84	85+	18+	MEDIAN AGE 2009	% 2009 Males	% 2009 Females
24237	DANTE	97.9	97.4	1.5	1.8	0.0	0.0	0.3	0.6	5.1	5.2	5.4	5.6	5.0	25.2	31.3	15.3	1.9	80.8	43.9	51.1	48.9
24239	DAVENPORT	100.0	100.0	0.0	0.0	0.0	0.0	0.0	0.0	4.3	8.7	8.7	4.3	8.7	34.8	30.4	0.0	0.0	73.9	33.8	47.8	52.2
24243	DRYDEN	98.8	98.4	0.3	0.4	0.1	0.1	0.1	0.2	6.1	6.4	6.6	6.3	4.8	25.2	29.5	12.8	2.2	76.9	41.2	48.6	51.4
24244	DUFFIELD	98.7	98.4	0.4	0.4	0.1	0.1	0.3	0.6	5.0	5.1	5.1	6.1	5.2	25.6	29.2	15.7	3.0	81.0	43.5	50.2	49.8
24245	DUNGANNON	99.2	99.0	0.3	0.3	0.0	0.0	0.2	0.4	5.5	5.8	6.0	6.0	5.0	24.8	31.1	14.0	1.9	79.1	42.9	48.1	51.9
24248	EWING	99.2	99.0	0.2	0.2	0.0	0.0	0.8	1.3	5.2	5.6	6.1	5.9	4.4	23.9	31.5	15.6	1.9	79.5	44.3	47.8	52.2
24250	FORT BLACKMORE	99.2	98.8	0.1	0.2	0.0	0.0	0.5	0.7	4.8	5.1	5.4	5.4	4.7	24.7	31.8	16.2	2.0	81.5	45.0	50.0	50.0
24251	GATE CITY	97.9	97.4	1.1	1.3	0.1	0.2	0.5	0.8	5.1	5.3	5.6	5.5	4.6	24.4	29.7	17.2	2.7	80.5	44.7	48.7	51.3
24256	HAYSI	99.4	99.2	0.2	0.2	0.0	0.0	0.5	1.0	5.4	5.8	5.9	5.6	4.8	24.6	33.1	13.4	1.3	79.4	43.5	48.2	51.8
24258	HILTONS	99.2	98.8	0.1	0.1	0.0	0.0	0.3	0.4	5.0	5.3	5.8	6.0	4.6	26.2	30.8	14.4	1.8	80.1	43.2	49.8	50.2
24260	HONAKER	99.3	99.0	0.1	0.1	0.0	0.1	0.9	1.4	5.2	6.0	6.1	5.9	4.8	25.8	31.9	12.7	1.6	79.0	42.3	49.2	50.8
24263	JONESVILLE	98.3	97.7	0.4	0.6	0.2	0.3	0.5	0.9	5.8	5.8	5.8	5.4	5.1	24.2	29.8	15.6	2.4	79.3	43.4	49.4	50.6
24265	KEOKEE	98.4	97.9	0.3	0.3	0.1	0.1	0.5	0.8	5.4	6.0	7.1	6.4	5.4	26.6	30.1	11.5	1.6	77.2	40.3	50.6	49.4
24266	LEBANON	97.1	96.5	2.1	2.4	0.0	0.1	0.3	0.6	5.5	5.7	6.1	5.4	5.8	26.3	28.7	14.1	2.5	79.3	41.5	48.4	51.6
24269	MC CLURE	100.0	100.0	0.0	0.0	0.0	0.0	0.0	0.0	5.3	5.3	5.3	5.3	3.9	30.3	31.6	11.8	1.3	78.9	41.7	50.0	50.0
24270	MENDOTA	97.6	96.2	0.0	0.0	0.2	0.4	1.2	2.1	4.9	5.3	5.7	6.6	4.7	24.7	32.1	14.4	1.5	80.1	43.8	49.1	50.9
24271	NICKELSVILLE	98.7	98.1	0.2	0.2	0.1	0.1	0.8	1.3	5.6	5.8	6.1	5.3	3.7	24.9	30.5	15.7	2.4	79.3	44.0	48.9	51.1
24272	NORA	99.5	99.5	0.2	0.2	0.0	0.0	0.5	1.0	5.2	5.4	5.7	5.7	5.1	28.0	31.1	12.2	1.5	80.4	41.5	50.8	49.2
24273	NORTON	94.1	92.7	4.2	4.8	0.8	1.2	0.8	1.3	5.1	5.6	5.6	5.8	5.8	26.5	29.4	14.2	2.1	80.2	41.8	46.8	53.2
24277	PENNINGTON GAP	97.6	96.9	0.9	0.9	0.3	0.6	0.6	1.1	4.2	4.3	4.4	5.9	8.1	33.2	26.1	11.8	2.0	83.6	38.8	59.3	40.7
24279	POUND	99.3	91.5	0.0	5.2	0.1	1.6	0.5	1.8	5.2	5.5	5.6	9.1	7.2	25.8	28.6	11.4	1.6	81.1	38.9	50.5	49.5
24280	ROSEDALE	79.8	79.2	18.7	14.3	0.0	3.6	2.3	2.4	4.1	3.5	3.8	11.1	9.4	32.9	27.0	7.9	0.4	85.9	35.5	57.7	42.3
24281	ROSE HILL	99.0	98.6	0.2	0.3	0.1	0.2	0.6	1.0	5.6	5.7	6.0	6.0	4.4	24.8	29.7	15.8	2.0	79.0	43.3	48.6	51.4
24282	SAINT CHARLES	99.2	99.2	0.5	0.5	0.0	0.0	0.3	0.5	5.9	5.9	6.4	6.9	5.6	26.6	29.4	11.3	2.0	78.0	40.4	50.4	49.6
24283	SAINT PAUL	97.9	97.1	0.7	0.9	0.3	0.5	0.4	0.6	5.6	5.8	6.0	5.9	5.0	25.2	31.1	13.5	1.8	78.9	42.4	47.6	52.4
24290	WEBER CITY	98.0	97.3	0.7	0.8	0.1	0.1	0.3	0.5	4.4	4.6	4.7	4.8	4.0	21.6	29.6	21.0	5.2	83.3	49.0	45.7	54.3
24292	WHITETOP	78.5	66.5	20.6	29.9	0.2	1.8	0.3	1.8	4.1	4.1	3.9	7.8	8.4	32.0	26.2	11.9	1.6	85.4	37.7	60.0	40.0
24293	WISE	97.5	96.4	1.0	1.3	0.5	0.8	0.8	1.4	5.3	5.6	5.6	7.5	6.6	27.4	28.7	11.8	1.5	79.9	39.2	49.5	50.5
24301	PULASKI	91.3	89.5	6.3	7.0	0.5	0.7	1.5	2.6	5.4	5.6	5.8	5.6	4.8	24.7	29.3	16.1	2.7	79.6	43.6	48.5	51.5
24311	ATKINS	99.1	98.7	0.1	0.1	0.1	0.1	0.9	1.6	6.1	6.0	5.9	5.7	5.4	26.4	29.6	13.4	1.6	78.6	41.2	49.4	50.6
24312	AUSTINVILLE	98.8	98.3	0.5	0.7	0.0	0.1	0.8	1.3	5.1	5.4	6.0	6.0	5.0	25.7	29.5	14.7	2.6	79.2	42.8	50.4	49.6
24313	BARREN SPRINGS	99.3	99.3	0.3	0.3	0.0	0.0	0.1	0.3	5.3	5.3	6.1	6.1	4.6	28.6	28.8	13.6	1.6	79.4	41.6	51.7	48.3
24314	BASTIAN	98.8	98.6	0.4	0.5	0.1	0.1	0.2	0.2	4.2	4.6	5.1	5.8	4.1	25.1	33.0	16.1	2.1	82.4	45.7	50.3	49.7
24315	BLAND	92.2	90.8	6.6	7.5	0.2	0.2	0.6	1.0	4.0	4.3	4.8	4.7	5.7	31.9	30.2	13.0	1.5	84.1	42.0	58.9	41.1
24316	BROADFORD	100.0	100.0	0.0	0.0	0.0	0.0	0.0	0.0	9.1	9.1	9.1	9.1	4.5	36.4	22.7	0.0	0.0	63.6	30.0	50.0	50.0
24317	CANA	98.1	97.1	0.1	0.2	0.1	0.1	1.4	2.5	6.0	6.1	6.3	5.7	4.7	26.6	28.3	14.9	1.4	78.1	41.6	50.6	49.4
24318	CERES	99.3	98.9	0.0	0.0	0.0	0.0	0.3	0.4	6.5	6.8	6.9	5.5	4.1	24.3	29.9	14.3	1.7	76.3	42.4	49.9	50.1
24319	CHILHOWIE	97.0	95.9	1.5	1.8	0.2	0.3	1.0	1.8	5.1	5.3	5.9	6.3	4.3	25.3	30.1	14.7	3.0	79.7	43.6	49.0	51.0
24322	CRIPPLE CREEK	98.9	97.8	1.1	1.1	0.0	0.0	1.1	2.2	4.4	5.5	4.4	5.5	4.4	22.0	35.2	16.5	2.2	81.3	47.2	53.8	46.2
24323	CROCKETT	98.2	97.4	0.2	0.4	0.2	0.2	0.8	1.3	6.5	6.5	6.7	6.7	4.3	28.3	27.4	12.1	1.5	76.4	39.0	48.6	51.4
24324	DRAPER	95.2	94.2	3.3	3.5	0.5	0.7	0.6	0.9	5.1	5.6	6.1	5.5	4.1	24.5	32.9	14.8	1.2	79.7	44.3	51.3	48.7
24325	DUGSPUR	98.4	97.5	0.0	0.0	0.3	0.4	1.0	1.7	5.3	5.4	5.9	5.6	4.1	24.2	29.9	16.6	2.9	79.4	44.6	48.2	51.8
24326	ELK CREEK	97.3	96.1	1.5	2.0	0.2	0.3	0.8	1.4	4.4	4.7	5.3	5.8	4.5	22.2	33.2	17.9	2.1	82.2	47.0	49.8	50.2
24328	FANCY GAP	98.0	96.8	0.1	0.2	0.0	0.1	2.0	3.5	5.5	6.8	6.3	5.3	4.1	26.2	29.8	14.0	1.9	77.9	41.8	51.0	49.0
24330	FRIES	97.6	96.3	0.8	1.1	0.0	0.0	1.6	2.7	5.3	6.0	6.6	5.3	4.7	24.7	29.4	15.6	2.3	78.8	42.8	49.4	50.6
24333	GALAX	92.2	91.1	3.8	4.2	0.3	0.4	5.5	6.6	5.9	6.0	6.2	6.0	4.9	25.1	28.6	15.0	2.3	78.2	42.2	49.0	51.0
24340	GLADE SPRING	96.7	96.0	2.5	2.8	0.2	0.3	0.5	0.8	4.8	4.9	5.3	7.7	7.3	23.5	30.5	14.3	1.7	81.5	42.5	49.2	50.8
24343	HILLSVILLE	98.1	97.2	0.2	0.3	0.1	0.2	1.6	2.7	5.3	5.3	5.5	5.2	4.8	25.0	30.0	15.9	3.0	80.6	44.2	49.2	50.8
24347	HIWASSEE	97.4	96.8	2.0	2.3	0.1	0.1	0.4	0.7	5.3	5.6	6.1	5.7	4.6	24.4	32.0	14.7	1.5	79.6	43.9	51.7	48.3
24348	INDEPENDENCE	95.1	93.3	3.0	3.8	0.1	0.1	2.0	3.5	4.8	5.1	5.2	5.1	4.6	22.9	31.5	17.4	3.4	81.9	46.4	49.6	50.4
24350	IVANHOE	96.9	96.1	1.9	2.3	0.2	0.3	0.7	1.3	5.2	5.7	6.2	5.7	4.5	25.6	31.2	14.0	1.9	79.2	42.8	50.6	49.4
24351	LAMBSBURG	98.1	97.2	0.3	0.4	0.0	0.1	1.6	2.8	5.9	6.0	6.3	5.8	5.2	26.6	29.0	13.8	1.4	78.1	41.3	50.6	49.4
24352	LAUREL FORK	98.0	96.9	0.3	0.3	0.0	0.0	2.0	3.5	4.5	4.7	5.2	5.4	3.9	21.4	31.2	20.1	3.5	82.0	47.9	47.9	52.1
24354	MARION	95.7	94.5	2.9	3.3	0.3	0.5	1.0	1.6	5.4	5.3	5.5	6.3	5.5	25.4	28.3	15.8	2.5	80.1	42.5	48.7	51.3
24360	MAX MEADOWS	97.3	96.4	1.4	1.7	0.3	0.4	0.5	0.9	5.5	5.8	6.2	6.1	4.7	28.0	29.7	12.7	1.4	78.7	41.1	49.8	50.2
24361	MEADOWVIEW	96.5	95.5	2.2	2.6	0.5	0.7	0.5	0.9	4.8	4.8	5.0	9.2	9.5	23.7	29.2	12.1	1.6	81.9	39.7	49.8	50.2
24363	MOUTH OF WILSON	95.0	92.3	4.4	6.1	0.1	0.4	0.7	1.5	4.2	4.8	5.1	5.2	4.2	24.0	32.4	17.5	2.6	83.1	46.6	52.1	47.9
24366	ROCKY GAP	98.0	97.5	0.8	1.0	0.0	0.0	0.4	0.6	3.3	3.5	4.3	5.4	4.3	25.7	31.9	17.7	3.9	84.8	47.0	49.0	51.0
24368	RURAL RETREAT	98.2	97.5	0.6	0.8	0.3	0.4	0.6	1.0	6.0	6.2	6.5	6.3	4.7	26.9	29.1	12.7	1.6	77.4	40.5	49.5	50.5
24370	SALTVILLE	98.9	98.5	0.3	0.4	0.0	0.0	0.5	0.8	5.0	5.3	5.7	6.2	4.7	25.2	30.0	16.1	1.8	80.1	43.5	49.6	50.4
24374	SPEEDWELL	98.4	97.9	0.6	0.6	0.2	0.3	1.0	1.5	5.6	5.8	6.1	6.6	4.9	25.5	30.5	13.4	1.7	78.5	42.0	50.3	49.7
24375	SUGAR GROVE	96.9	96.1	1.9	2.2	0.0	0.0	0.6	1.0	5.4	5.4	6.0	6.6	5.3	27.0	29.6	13.0	1.6	79.2	41.3	51.0	49.0
24377	TANNERSVILLE	99.0	99.0	0.0	0.0	0.0	0.0	0.3	0.7	4.1	4.5	5.2	5.9	4.5	25.2	36.2	13.1	1.4	82.4	45.4	50.0	50.0
24378	TROUTDALE	71.3	84.9	27.6	12.6	0.2	0.9	0.5	1.4	4.0	4.3	4.8	6.4	5.9	26.1	30.6	15.9	2.0	83.8	43.9	53.8	46.2
24380	WILLIS	97.8	96.9	0.7	0.8	0.0	0.0	1.4	2.4	5.3	5.5	5.9	5.9	4.6	25.0	31.2	14.4	2.2	79.7	43.5	51.5	48.5
24381	WOODLAWN	97.5	96.4	0.9	1.1	0.1	0.1	1.8	3.1	5.7	5.9	6.3	5.8	5.2	26.3	29.4	13.8	1.6	78.6	41.4	50.7	49.3
24382	WYTHEVILLE	93.8	92.4	4.6	5.2	0.5	0.8	0.6	1.0	5.2	5.2	5.4	5.4	5.2	25.2	28.8	16.3	3.3	80.9	43.9	46.7	53.3
24401	STAUNTON	86.8	84.7	10.8	11.8	0.5	0.7	1.1	1.8	5.3	5.1	5.4	6.2	6.1	24.6	28.8	15.6	2.9	80.6	42.9	47.4	52.6
24413	BLUE GRASS	99.4	99.4	0.0	0.0	0.6	0.6	0.0	0.0	4.0	4.6	5.1	6.3	3.4	19.4	35.4	18.9	2.9	82.3	49.2	49.1	50.9
24416	BUENA VISTA	94.5	93.2	4.0	4.5	0.4	0.6	1.0	1.6	5.7	5.5	5.7	8.6	6.9	23.7	27.0	14.7	2.2	79.2	40.7	47.4	52.6
24421	CHURCHVILLE	98.3	97.7	0.7	0.8	0.2	0.3	1.0	1.8	5.2	5.7	6.5	6.6	4.5	23.9	33.1	13.0	1.5	78.4	43.4	49.6	50.4
24422	CLIFTON FORGE	88.3	86.0	9.7	11.1	0.1	0.1	0.7	1.1	5.3	5.4	5.6	5.9	5.1	22.2	28.7	17.9	3.9	80.0	45.4	46.8	53.2
24426	COVINGTON	91.5	89.9	6.7	7.5	0.4	0.6	0.4	0.8	5.7	5.9	6.2	6.1	4.5	23.9	29.2	15.8	2.6	78.3	43.3	49.4	50.6
24430	CRAIGSVILLE	81.0	86.0	17.7	11.4	0.1	0.5	0.3	0.9	5.4	5.4	5.4	6.5	6.7	28.9	27.4	12.5	1.7	80.7	39.6	53.1	46.9
24431	CRIMORA	97.4	96.4	1.1	1.3	0.2	0.3	1.0	1.8	6.0	5.9	6.0	7.2	7.0	26.0	29.5	11.5	1.0	77.8	39.5	49.3	50.7
24432	DEERFIELD	98.5	98.2	0.3	0.3	0.3	0.3	0.3	0.6	3.4	6.4	5.8	4.9	2.4	22.0	38.7	13.4	3.0	81.4	47.5	53.4	46.6
24433	DOE HILL	99.3	99.3	0.0	0.0	0.0	0.0	0.7	0.7	3.6	3.9	4.6	6.4	3.9	20.4	33.6	20.7	2.9	83.6	48.7	51.4	48.6
24435	FAIRFIELD	96.9	96.2	2.0	2.3	0.4	0.5	0.4	0.7	5.9	6.3	6.6	6.0	4.5	24.7	31.0	13.7	1.4	77.5	42.4	50.9	49.1
24437	FORT DEFIANCE	98.0	97.5	1.2	1.3	0.2	0.2	0.6	0.9	5.3	5.9	6.6	6.8	4.6	22.9	33.7	12.6	1.6	77.9	43.6	51.0	49.0
24439	GOSHEN	91.7	77.3	7.5	20.2	0.1	1.1	0.4	1.1	3.9	4.1	4.2	6.7	8.1	32.3	28.2	11.2	1.2	85.8	39.2	60.4	39.6
24440	GREENVILLE	87.5	82.4	11.1	9.4	0.4	5.4	0.7	2.3	4.3	5.1	5.7	2.8	4.2	34.2	31.5	11.0	1.1	83.6	41.3	59.7	40.3
24441	GROTTOES	95.9	94.8	2.9	3.4	0.1	0.2	1.6	3.0	7.2	7.1	6.9	6.2	4.9	28.4	27.6	10.7	1.0	74.8	38.1	49.5	50.5
24442	HEAD WATERS	100.0	100.0	0.0	0.0	0.0	0.0	1.0	0.0	4.0	4.0	4.0	6.0	4.0	21.0	34.0	20.0	3.0	84.0	48.5	50.0	50.0
24445	HOT SPRINGS	95.1	94.7	3.7	3.8	0.5	0.7	0.4	0.5	4.7	5.5	6.2	5.9	4.0	22.5	32.0	16.6	2.5	79.6	45.6	48.5	51.5
24450	LEXINGTON	91.8	90.1	5.8	6.4	1.2	1.8	1.0	1.7	4.0	3.9	4.2	11.9	14.1	19.7	25.2	14.6	2.4	84.8	37.1	52.7	47.3
24458	MC DOWELL	99.4	99.4	0.0	0.0	0.0	0.0	0.6	0.6	3.6	4.2	4.5	6.6	3.9	20.7	33.9	20.1	2.4	83.5	48.4	51.1	48.9
24459	MIDDLEBROOK	97.7	97.4	1.2	1.4	0.2	0.2	0.2	0.3	5.1	5.6	6.2	6.2	4.7	21.6	35.1	13.7	1.9	79.3	45.3	51.4	48.6
24460	MILLBORO	89.0	88.4	9.5	9.9	0.5	0.6	0.5	0.6	4.0	5.0	5.6	6.0	4.3	26.8	33.1	13.8	1.3	81.2	43.8	52.5	47.5
24464	MONTEBELLO	91.0	88.8	7.1	8.1	0.6	0.6	3.2	5.6	5.0	5.0	5.6	5.6	5.0	24.2	32.9	14.9	1.9	80.7	44.8	50.3	49.7
24465	MONTEREY	99.1	99.1	0.1	0.1	0.1	0.1	0.6	0.6	3.8	4.4	4.9	5.1	3.5	18.3	38.2	18.8	2.9	83.8	50.9	49.0	51.0
24467	MOUNT SIDNEY	99.0	98.6	0.2	0.2	0.2	0.2	0.5	0.9	4.4	5.0	5.8	6.3	4.7	22.3	36.3	13.2	1.9	80.9	45.7	49.7	50.3
24468	MUSTOE	99.5	99.5	0.0	0.0	0.5	0.5	0.0	0.0	3.7	4.1	5.0	6.0	3.2	19.3	37.2	18.8	2.8	83.0	50.2	50.0	50.0
24471	PORT REPUBLIC	97.9	96.7	0.7	0.9	0.4	0.5	1.7	3.6	5.7	6.2	6.6	6.1	4.7	25.9	32.3	11.0	1.4	77.6	41.5	50.1	49.9
24472	RAPHINE	97.7	97.1	1.4	1.6	0.4	0.5	0.3	0.5	5.2	5.5	5.9	5.8	4.3	24.5	32.5	14.7	1.6	79.8	44.2	50.4	49.6
24473	ROCKBRIDGE BATHS	97.6	97.0	1.2	1.4	0.2	0.3	0.7	1.0	4.8	4.9	5.4	5.7	5.3	21.4	34.1	16.6	1.9	81.3	46.5	49.8	50.2
	VIRGINIA	72.3	68.8	19.6	20.1	3.7	5.1	4.7	7.0	6.5	6.4	6.5	6.9	6.9	27.5	27.2	10.5	1.6	76.7	37.7	49.2	50.8
	UNITED STATES	75.1	72.0	12.3	12.7	3.8	4.6	12.5	15.7	6.8	6.7	6.6	7.1	6.9	27.0	26.0	10.9	1.9	75.7	36.9	49.2	50.8

INCOME

ZIP CODE				2009 HOUSEHOLD INCOME DISTRIBUTION (%)					MEDIAN HOUSEHOLD INCOME					2009 HOME VALUE DISTRIBUTION (%)					
#	POST OFFICE NAME	2009 Per Capita Income	2009 HH Income Base	Less than $25,000	$25,000 to $49,999	$50,000 to $99,999	$100,000 to $149,999	$150,000 or More	2009	2014	2009 National Centile	2009 State Centile	2009 Home Value Base	Less than $50,000	$50,000 to $89,999	$90,000 to $174,999	$175,000 to $399,999	$400,000 or More	2009 Median Home Value
24237	DANTE	15207	416	46.9	36.1	14.4	1.4	1.2	26465	26606	4	3	360	37.2	29.4	27.2	6.1	0.0	61538
24239	DAVENPORT	7283	8	75.0	12.5	12.5	0.0	0.0	15000	12071	1	1	7	0.0	28.6	42.9	28.6	0.0	137500
24243	DRYDEN	15741	931	45.8	26.2	21.2	5.4	1.5	28827	29742	6	5	690	18.6	21.7	39.9	18.7	1.2	105000
24244	DUFFIELD	15531	2221	40.3	32.2	25.8	1.5	0.2	29165	30598	7	6	1766	26.4	20.0	43.0	9.4	1.2	94809
24245	DUNGANNON	14953	496	50.6	26.0	20.6	2.6	0.2	24667	24705	3	3	390	31.8	26.4	35.1	6.4	0.3	80000
24248	EWING	17323	1050	45.3	28.7	20.9	3.8	1.3	31205	32163	10	8	827	19.7	24.9	37.4	15.5	2.5	102530
24250	FORT BLACKMORE	14342	534	46.4	30.0	20.8	2.8	0.0	26511	26898	4	4	451	32.8	22.2	35.3	8.2	1.6	81667
24251	GATE CITY	20058	3859	32.5	31.7	29.3	5.2	1.4	36983	38071	24	20	2935	17.7	18.6	48.2	13.9	1.6	107147
24256	HAYSI	14229	1323	48.3	33.4	16.3	1.6	0.4	25876	25449	4	3	1049	25.8	29.7	36.7	7.2	0.5	80085
24258	HILTONS	18231	1101	36.0	28.2	30.5	4.5	0.7	33115	35619	14	12	884	19.7	20.9	39.5	17.8	2.1	103788
24260	HONAKER	15510	2362	43.9	29.8	22.7	2.8	0.8	28466	29424	6	5	1939	28.6	22.2	35.4	12.7	1.1	88628
24263	JONESVILLE	17001	2777	46.8	27.4	19.4	4.9	1.5	27250	27927	5	4	1950	16.5	17.7	47.4	15.8	2.6	113942
24265	KEOKEE	13258	611	54.3	27.8	15.5	1.0	1.3	23346	23422	2	2	490	46.3	22.2	21.6	9.6	0.2	56207
24266	LEBANON	20002	2847	31.2	33.3	28.4	5.2	2.0	38010	39915	27	24	2101	18.9	13.8	40.7	23.1	3.4	126726
24269	MC CLURE	16529	34	47.1	23.5	23.5	5.9	0.0	30000	23529	8	7	28	28.6	28.6	35.7	7.1	0.0	76667
24270	MENDOTA	17376	222	35.1	36.9	26.6	0.9	0.5	32325	34396	12	10	175	21.1	22.3	42.3	11.4	2.9	96053
24271	NICKELSVILLE	16388	1174	38.5	30.7	27.0	3.6	0.3	31953	33069	11	10	904	20.6	20.1	43.9	13.7	1.7	100906
24272	NORA	16019	242	43.0	31.8	22.3	2.1	0.8	30483	31599	9	8	211	31.8	18.5	34.1	15.6	0.0	89500
24273	NORTON	18526	2509	44.7	25.8	23.4	4.7	1.5	29620	30824	7	6	1604	21.5	21.7	42.6	12.2	1.9	97569
24277	PENNINGTON GAP	16492	2407	48.7	27.9	19.4	3.0	1.0	26169	26875	4	3	1640	22.1	23.5	37.5	15.5	1.5	97019
24279	POUND	16077	2042	38.4	33.5	25.0	2.5	0.6	32337	33285	12	10	1623	24.0	22.8	38.7	13.6	1.0	94907
24280	ROSEDALE	19722	1144	25.5	34.7	32.3	6.7	0.7	41773	44397	39	35	969	11.2	11.2	46.1	28.4	3.0	138880
24281	ROSE HILL	14781	1023	53.4	24.8	18.2	2.2	1.4	23233	23459	2	2	781	19.5	28.8	38.5	11.1	2.0	92647
24282	SAINT CHARLES	11470	163	62.0	28.2	9.2	0.6	0.0	21002	21421	2	1	125	56.8	18.4	17.6	7.2	0.0	42273
24283	SAINT PAUL	17941	1061	40.4	28.7	26.5	3.3	1.0	31179	32499	10	8	758	23.2	25.5	37.5	13.2	0.7	92174
24290	WEBER CITY	20698	899	29.4	36.7	29.1	3.9	0.9	38841	39433	29	26	637	12.1	18.2	58.1	11.5	0.2	115819
24292	WHITETOP	17054	251	37.5	32.7	26.3	3.2	0.4	30169	30558	8	7	215	15.8	21.9	34.0	25.6	2.8	110081
24293	WISE	18619	4340	35.2	33.8	25.5	4.0	1.6	35163	36764	18	15	3274	19.8	20.3	37.8	20.3	1.8	110824
24301	PULASKI	21649	6505	34.1	26.6	32.5	4.6	2.2	38565	40868	28	25	4384	16.3	25.7	41.2	14.8	1.9	100345
24311	ATKINS	18860	620	31.9	34.4	30.0	3.2	0.5	34628	35000	17	14	468	26.7	19.9	32.1	18.8	2.6	98889
24312	AUSTINVILLE	20373	930	32.4	31.1	32.7	2.5	1.4	40685	41847	35	32	750	13.1	21.5	48.7	15.2	1.6	106852
24313	BARREN SPRINGS	18294	454	28.9	33.7	33.9	3.5	0.0	38768	39265	29	26	390	16.4	27.7	39.0	16.9	0.0	95610
24314	BASTIAN	20609	694	24.1	41.6	25.4	7.9	1.0	37492	37961	25	22	597	15.7	21.4	48.6	9.9	4.4	107008
24315	BLAND	18700	1311	33.4	27.5	33.2	4.9	1.0	35898	38095	20	17	1096	14.2	20.4	42.9	20.3	2.1	119298
24316	BROADFORD	14091	9	44.4	22.2	33.3	0.0	0.0	27247	22222	5	4	7	0.0	28.6	71.4	0.0	0.0	112500
24317	CANA	16654	1507	38.8	35.2	22.1	2.9	1.1	31127	32361	10	8	1283	13.3	25.9	43.4	14.4	3.0	101267
24318	CERES	18653	309	37.9	33.7	21.0	5.5	1.9	33981	33845	15	13	266	18.4	18.0	41.7	15.4	6.4	113953
24319	CHILHOWIE	19053	2826	30.1	34.3	30.6	3.5	1.4	37975	39673	27	23	2144	16.9	14.7	47.7	18.8	1.8	119363
24322	CRIPPLE CREEK	23716	47	34.0	34.0	25.5	4.3	2.1	35544	39290	19	16	37	18.9	21.6	43.2	10.8	5.4	103125
24323	CROCKETT	18833	216	30.1	36.1	27.8	3.7	2.3	37301	37755	24	21	176	11.4	15.9	50.0	19.3	3.4	118382
24324	DRAPER	20478	819	29.4	34.9	28.0	6.8	0.9	38164	40059	27	24	703	16.6	16.9	40.7	24.0	1.7	120536
24325	DUGSPUR	21514	608	32.1	27.5	34.7	3.1	2.6	39696	43039	32	29	518	5.6	20.1	43.6	23.6	7.1	126119
24326	ELK CREEK	22578	528	26.1	37.3	32.4	2.5	1.7	37180	40309	24	21	455	7.7	23.1	50.8	16.3	2.2	119250
24328	FANCY GAP	19766	930	31.8	36.2	26.2	3.5	2.2	35693	37061	20	17	784	11.1	20.4	50.1	16.2	2.2	111993
24330	FRIES	16635	1761	40.7	33.9	23.2	1.2	1.1	29676	30834	8	6	1408	20.0	31.9	38.8	8.5	0.9	87679
24333	GALAX	19926	7744	32.9	33.7	28.4	3.3	1.6	36139	37399	21	18	5890	17.1	20.9	43.3	16.0	2.6	108581
24340	GLADE SPRING	20276	2159	31.8	31.1	31.1	4.7	1.3	39364	41476	31	28	1700	16.1	20.6	46.3	13.7	3.3	104746
24343	HILLSVILLE	20717	3901	33.3	30.3	30.3	4.4	1.7	37527	39693	25	22	2900	10.4	13.3	48.6	24.8	2.9	132943
24347	HIWASSEE	20246	737	28.9	30.1	36.0	3.7	1.4	42240	45233	40	37	630	16.8	18.7	43.0	20.3	1.1	111392
24348	INDEPENDENCE	19171	1730	35.6	35.0	23.4	4.7	1.3	32315	34079	12	10	1288	15.0	13.8	43.0	24.1	4.0	128616
24350	IVANHOE	15922	594	35.5	37.0	25.1	2.4	0.0	31282	33167	10	9	508	17.5	28.5	42.5	10.2	1.2	92740
24351	LAMBSBURG	15676	303	36.3	37.0	23.8	2.3	0.7	34553	34850	17	14	259	15.4	24.3	42.1	14.3	3.9	103041
24352	LAUREL FORK	20298	360	26.1	31.9	36.9	2.8	2.2	41453	44817	38	34	311	3.9	19.9	51.4	18.0	6.8	130398
24354	MARION	20424	6517	31.0	34.0	28.4	4.6	2.1	36326	37648	22	18	4511	13.6	20.0	45.2	19.3	1.9	118841
24360	MAX MEADOWS	21110	2393	24.3	31.7	36.1	5.4	2.5	45250	46120	49	44	2033	14.1	18.9	39.8	26.0	1.2	123578
24361	MEADOWVIEW	18193	2290	30.5	32.6	30.7	4.9	1.4	39429	41817	31	28	1807	17.0	19.5	44.7	16.0	2.9	107651
24363	MOUTH OF WILSON	19571	671	35.3	32.3	26.5	5.1	0.7	36278	37609	21	18	560	10.4	18.9	42.5	25.2	3.0	123462
24366	ROCKY GAP	25124	223	13.5	40.4	37.2	7.2	1.8	47339	48304	55	51	191	13.1	15.7	49.2	15.7	6.3	128017
24368	RURAL RETREAT	20811	2227	28.2	33.2	32.6	3.1	2.7	39320	40508	31	27	1841	12.3	15.6	50.2	19.0	2.9	121014
24370	SALTVILLE	18048	2933	34.8	31.6	29.2	3.8	0.7	36102	37406	21	18	2352	18.6	25.9	44.2	10.5	0.9	96037
24374	SPEEDWELL	19444	274	31.8	36.9	26.3	2.2	2.9	35803	36535	20	17	227	10.1	18.1	53.7	12.8	5.3	115988
24375	SUGAR GROVE	18770	777	32.9	33.8	28.6	2.8	1.8	37268	38208	24	21	604	24.2	21.4	36.4	17.1	1.0	103354
24377	TANNERSVILLE	18835	116	18.1	39.7	36.2	6.0	0.0	44376	44685	46	41	101	22.8	19.8	41.6	14.9	1.0	110417
24378	TROUTDALE	20752	579	29.9	35.4	30.4	2.9	1.4	35592	37267	20	17	490	11.2	19.4	48.4	18.0	3.1	119841
24380	WILLIS	18070	1181	31.6	34.7	27.8	4.1	1.9	35179	36241	18	15	1008	10.7	14.6	42.4	25.4	6.9	128636
24381	WOODLAWN	18546	1415	31.8	34.4	30.0	2.8	1.0	38068	39357	27	24	1124	12.8	17.6	50.0	16.9	2.7	115367
24382	WYTHEVILLE	21473	6382	34.5	28.7	30.2	4.4	2.2	37405	38999	25	22	4424	11.9	15.3	43.1	26.8	3.0	133632
24401	STAUNTON	24574	15268	25.2	28.4	36.4	7.0	3.0	46356	48976	52	48	9945	2.7	5.9	45.0	39.0	7.4	169041
24413	BLUE GRASS	16557	76	34.2	42.1	21.1	1.3	1.3	33576	35000	15	13	64	4.7	9.4	45.3	31.3	9.4	150000
24416	BUENA VISTA	20236	3549	26.6	33.7	33.5	4.7	1.5	42171	44254	40	36	2551	9.8	13.2	53.1	20.6	3.3	130784
24421	CHURCHVILLE	23983	1309	15.7	31.3	39.2	11.6	2.2	52260	53544	66	64	1136	4.2	4.7	34.2	44.0	12.9	190800
24422	CLIFTON FORGE	20456	3016	32.5	31.2	30.7	3.8	1.7	38645	40495	29	26	2170	15.6	27.0	43.5	12.1	1.7	100242
24426	COVINGTON	22223	6574	25.2	30.4	37.0	5.8	1.6	44831	46709	48	43	5050	10.6	22.8	47.9	17.4	1.2	112050
24430	CRAIGSVILLE	19944	769	35.0	35.1	26.8	1.6	1.6	36593	37906	22	19	552	22.1	21.7	43.7	12.5	0.0	97727
24431	CRIMORA	22107	1079	23.3	30.7	36.5	5.7	3.9	47017	48213	54	50	967	38.7	8.9	24.5	24.0	3.9	104688
24432	DEERFIELD	22059	152	17.1	40.8	34.9	7.2	0.0	43785	45553	45	40	127	6.3	11.8	47.2	25.2	9.4	140972
24433	DOE HILL	16468	122	37.7	36.9	22.1	3.3	0.0	31568	31932	11	9	106	0.9	15.1	49.1	21.7	13.2	141667
24435	FAIRFIELD	22504	731	18.1	32.8	41.9	6.0	1.2	49330	50768	60	57	574	8.0	5.9	39.4	28.4	18.3	167460
24437	FORT DEFIANCE	24618	325	17.5	24.6	44.0	10.2	3.7	57946	60059	75	72	280	3.9	1.4	20.0	58.2	16.4	241667
24439	GOSHEN	16714	611	28.6	32.7	31.4	6.1	1.1	40436	42804	34	30	466	15.7	13.1	33.9	24.5	12.9	146739
24440	GREENVILLE	22411	994	15.2	32.4	42.8	6.6	3.0	51061	51758	64	61	859	14.4	12.1	35.4	31.9	6.2	153098
24441	GROTTOES	21277	2593	21.8	32.0	38.1	7.3	0.8	47225	48925	55	50	2114	11.4	8.6	46.2	30.6	3.1	151243
24442	HEAD WATERS	16803	44	34.1	38.6	22.7	4.5	0.0	32770	32233	13	11	38	0.0	15.8	47.4	23.7	13.2	150000
24445	HOT SPRINGS	25757	1185	20.3	29.6	40.6	6.8	2.8	50104	51183	61	58	949	5.9	13.6	50.4	25.4	4.7	134889
24450	LEXINGTON	23442	6305	29.0	26.9	32.3	8.3	3.6	44236	46779	46	41	4182	4.8	5.1	36.7	37.7	15.8	188139
24458	MC DOWELL	18415	160	35.6	38.1	22.5	3.8	0.0	32387	32248	12	11	138	2.2	15.2	46.4	22.5	13.8	145455
24459	MIDDLEBROOK	22553	252	23.8	23.8	42.5	5.2	4.8	53173	57391	68	65	205	2.9	6.3	22.9	46.8	21.0	260938
24460	MILLBORO	24357	708	19.2	38.8	31.4	7.2	3.4	43241	45044	43	39	573	8.4	12.4	32.1	39.6	7.5	164688
24464	MONTEBELLO	22115	73	24.7	41.1	27.4	6.8	0.0	34742	38358	17	15	57	19.3	15.8	38.6	22.8	3.5	116071
24465	MONTEREY	21710	655	29.3	36.2	29.8	2.6	2.1	40475	41224	34	31	530	10.6	9.6	44.9	28.5	6.4	140714
24467	MOUNT SIDNEY	25210	869	19.1	24.2	42.2	10.6	3.9	54625	56165	71	68	727	1.0	3.4	30.1	54.5	11.0	224769
24468	MUSTOE	19347	97	30.9	41.2	21.6	3.1	3.1	35448	34730	19	16	81	6.2	9.9	40.7	30.9	12.3	157813
24471	PORT REPUBLIC	24610	596	13.9	29.9	45.6	9.1	1.5	54931	59805	71	68	495	7.5	3.4	38.8	35.8	14.5	175833
24472	RAPHINE	23169	1206	22.2	30.3	38.6	6.2	2.7	47751	49772	56	52	970	10.7	6.8	33.1	37.3	12.1	173485
24473	ROCKBRIDGE BATHS	22569	389	24.4	30.8	35.7	6.9	2.1	45107	47581	49	44	315	10.5	6.7	30.5	34.6	17.8	183929
	VIRGINIA	30912		17.0	22.6	35.9	15.0	9.5	61855	64957				5.3	6.3	30.4	41.5	16.5	203135
	UNITED STATES	27277		20.9	24.4	35.3	11.7	7.6	54719	56938				9.3	13.1	31.6	32.6	13.5	162279

ZIP CODE		FINANCIAL SERVICES				THE HOME						ENTERTAINMENT						PERSONAL			
						Home Improvements		Furnishings													
#	POST OFFICE NAME	Auto Loan	Home Loan	Investments	Retirement Plans	Home Repair	Lawn & Garden	Computers & Hardware-Personal	Major Appliances	TV, Radio, Sound Equipment	Furniture	Dine out/ Carry out	Sports Equipment	Fees & Tickets	Toys & Games	Travel	Cable TV	Apparel & Services	Auto Repairs	Health Insurance	Pets & Supplies
24237	DANTE	65	43	63	41	43	64	46	58	52	43	51	45	35	53	43	58	34	54	61	70
24239	DAVENPORT	39	25	38	24	25	38	27	34	31	26	31	27	20	32	25	35	20	32	36	42
24243	DRYDEN	72	50	67	48	50	70	52	63	59	50	58	49	41	60	49	65	38	60	66	78
24244	DUFFIELD	66	45	64	43	46	66	48	60	54	45	53	46	37	54	45	60	35	56	63	72
24245	DUNGANNON	62	42	61	40	42	62	44	56	50	42	49	43	34	51	42	56	33	52	59	68
24248	EWING	72	51	73	50	53	73	53	67	58	49	57	50	42	58	52	64	38	61	70	80
24250	FORT BLACKMORE	62	42	57	40	42	60	45	54	51	43	50	42	34	52	41	56	33	51	58	67
24251	GATE CITY	73	59	74	57	60	78	60	72	66	55	64	53	52	65	59	72	43	67	78	84
24256	HAYSI	61	40	59	38	41	60	43	54	49	41	48	42	33	50	41	55	32	51	57	66
24258	HILTONS	76	54	68	53	55	74	56	68	62	54	61	52	45	64	53	68	41	63	71	82
24260	HONAKER	68	46	65	44	46	67	49	61	55	46	54	47	37	56	46	62	36	57	64	74
24263	JONESVILLE	65	47	65	46	49	66	51	62	57	47	55	46	42	56	49	62	37	58	66	73
24265	KEOKEE	58	39	56	37	40	58	42	53	48	39	47	40	32	48	40	53	31	49	56	64
24266	LEBANON	79	59	75	58	60	79	62	74	68	58	67	56	51	69	60	74	45	70	79	88
24269	MC CLURE	69	45	66	42	45	67	48	60	55	46	54	47	36	56	45	62	36	57	64	74
24270	MENDOTA	74	53	61	52	53	71	56	65	62	54	60	50	45	64	51	67	41	61	68	79
24271	NICKELSVILLE	69	49	71	48	51	70	51	64	56	47	55	48	40	56	50	62	36	59	67	76
24272	NORA	71	50	72	48	51	71	51	65	57	48	56	49	41	57	50	63	37	60	68	78
24273	NORTON	67	51	65	50	52	67	55	63	60	52	59	48	46	60	52	65	39	61	67	75
24277	PENNINGTON GAP	63	44	62	43	46	63	48	58	54	44	52	44	38	53	46	59	35	55	63	70
24279	POUND	70	48	70	46	49	70	51	64	57	48	56	49	39	57	49	63	37	59	67	77
24280	ROSEDALE	80	65	73	63	65	78	64	74	69	63	68	55	56	70	62	73	46	70	76	88
24281	ROSE HILL	61	43	62	42	45	62	45	57	50	42	49	43	35	50	44	55	32	52	59	68
24282	SAINT CHARLES	50	32	48	30	32	49	35	44	40	33	39	34	26	41	32	45	26	41	46	54
24283	SAINT PAUL	71	51	66	49	52	71	54	66	61	50	59	50	43	61	51	67	39	62	71	78
24290	WEBER CITY	76	54	76	53	56	78	58	73	65	53	63	54	47	64	57	72	42	67	78	86
24292	WHITETOP	68	49	65	48	50	68	51	62	56	48	55	47	41	57	49	62	37	58	65	75
24293	WISE	74	58	70	56	58	72	59	69	63	57	62	51	50	64	57	67	42	65	70	82
24301	PULASKI	76	63	71	63	64	79	67	75	72	62	70	56	59	71	65	77	47	72	81	88
24311	ATKINS	70	60	62	59	59	69	60	66	62	58	62	50	54	64	58	65	42	63	67	78
24312	AUSTINVILLE	78	60	70	60	61	79	63	73	68	58	66	56	52	69	60	74	45	69	78	87
24313	BARREN SPRINGS	79	57	65	55	57	75	59	69	66	58	64	53	47	68	54	72	43	65	73	84
24314	BASTIAN	85	64	84	63	66	87	65	80	71	61	70	61	54	72	64	78	47	74	84	95
24315	BLAND	76	60	74	60	62	79	61	73	65	56	64	55	52	66	60	71	43	67	76	86
24316	BROADFORD	62	45	51	43	44	59	46	54	51	45	50	42	37	54	42	56	34	51	57	66
24317	CANA	70	50	58	49	50	67	53	61	58	51	57	47	42	61	48	64	38	58	64	74
24318	CERES	76	55	75	53	56	77	56	71	63	53	61	53	45	63	55	69	41	65	74	84
24319	CHILHOWIE	80	59	76	57	60	80	61	74	67	57	66	56	49	68	58	73	44	69	78	88
24322	CRIPPLE CREEK	82	59	84	57	61	83	60	77	67	56	66	58	48	66	60	74	43	70	80	91
24323	CROCKETT	78	63	69	64	64	79	64	74	68	60	67	56	55	70	62	74	45	69	77	88
24324	DRAPER	78	65	71	67	66	82	66	76	70	60	68	58	58	71	65	75	46	71	79	90
24325	DUGSPUR	82	67	71	67	67	83	67	77	72	63	71	59	58	74	64	77	48	72	81	92
24326	ELK CREEK	88	63	85	61	64	87	65	80	72	61	71	61	52	73	62	79	47	74	84	96
24328	FANCY GAP	81	58	76	56	59	80	60	73	66	57	65	56	48	67	57	73	43	68	77	88
24330	FRIES	68	48	60	46	48	66	50	60	56	48	55	46	40	58	46	62	37	57	64	73
24333	GALAX	77	59	68	58	59	76	62	71	67	58	66	54	51	69	58	73	44	67	75	85
24340	GLADE SPRING	81	59	76	58	61	80	62	74	68	58	66	56	50	68	59	74	44	69	78	89
24343	HILLSVILLE	75	60	72	61	62	76	65	73	69	60	67	54	56	68	62	74	46	70	77	86
24347	HIWASSEE	80	65	70	65	65	81	66	75	70	61	69	57	57	72	63	75	47	70	78	89
24348	INDEPENDENCE	71	54	69	53	55	71	57	67	62	53	61	50	48	62	55	68	41	64	72	80
24350	IVANHOE	67	48	58	47	48	65	50	59	56	49	55	45	40	58	46	61	37	56	62	72
24351	LAMBSBURG	71	51	59	50	51	68	53	62	59	52	58	48	43	62	48	64	39	59	65	75
24352	LAUREL FORK	84	67	82	67	69	87	67	81	72	62	71	61	57	72	67	78	47	75	84	96
24354	MARION	75	61	65	61	61	75	64	70	68	61	67	53	56	70	60	73	46	68	75	84
24360	MAX MEADOWS	89	69	77	69	70	88	70	82	76	67	75	62	60	79	67	82	50	76	85	98
24361	MEADOWVIEW	80	60	72	59	61	79	63	73	69	60	67	55	52	70	59	74	45	69	77	88
24363	MOUTH OF WILSON	74	54	74	53	56	75	56	69	61	52	60	52	45	61	55	67	40	64	72	82
24366	ROCKY GAP	87	78	79	81	80	93	77	88	80	70	79	66	71	82	77	85	54	81	91	102
24368	RURAL RETREAT	87	66	80	65	67	87	67	80	73	63	72	61	56	75	64	80	48	75	84	96
24370	SALTVILLE	72	55	66	55	56	73	57	68	62	53	61	51	48	63	55	68	41	63	72	80
24374	SPEEDWELL	84	60	77	58	61	82	62	75	69	59	67	57	50	70	59	75	45	70	79	91
24375	SUGAR GROVE	78	59	65	58	59	76	60	70	66	58	65	53	50	68	56	71	44	66	73	84
24377	TANNERSVILLE	73	66	66	69	68	78	66	74	68	59	66	56	60	69	65	72	45	68	76	86
24378	TROUTDALE	82	59	79	57	60	81	60	75	67	57	66	57	48	68	58	74	44	69	78	90
24380	WILLIS	76	58	72	57	59	77	59	71	64	55	63	54	49	65	57	70	42	66	74	85
24381	WOODLAWN	77	55	63	54	55	73	58	67	64	56	63	51	47	67	53	70	42	64	71	81
24382	WYTHEVILLE	73	62	68	62	63	74	64	70	69	62	68	52	59	69	62	73	46	69	76	83
24401	STAUNTON	78	75	73	76	75	81	78	78	80	75	79	59	76	79	77	83	55	79	85	92
24413	BLUE GRASS	68	47	75	47	49	72	52	65	54	42	54	53	38	53	52	59	35	60	68	80
24416	BUENA VISTA	72	66	65	67	66	75	68	72	70	63	69	54	63	70	66	74	47	70	77	85
24421	CHURCHVILLE	91	88	84	92	89	99	85	93	86	79	85	71	82	88	86	90	58	87	95	109
24422	CLIFTON FORGE	73	59	69	59	60	75	63	71	68	58	66	53	55	67	61	72	45	68	77	84
24426	COVINGTON	79	70	73	71	70	84	71	79	75	66	74	59	65	75	70	80	50	75	85	93
24430	CRAIGSVILLE	73	51	69	50	52	73	55	67	62	51	60	51	43	62	52	68	40	63	72	81
24431	CRIMORA	85	80	71	77	77	81	78	80	79	79	79	61	73	82	74	80	54	79	80	95
24432	DEERFIELD	79	64	102	63	70	84	64	81	67	60	66	59	55	63	69	71	44	75	80	94
24433	DOE HILL	68	46	74	46	49	71	52	64	54	42	53	53	38	53	51	59	34	60	68	79
24435	FAIRFIELD	88	75	78	77	76	92	75	86	79	70	78	65	67	81	73	85	53	80	89	101
24437	FORT DEFIANCE	90	101	87	104	98	99	90	94	89	91	89	73	96	91	95	89	62	90	93	111
24439	GOSHEN	83	61	92	59	64	85	63	79	68	59	67	59	51	67	64	74	44	73	81	94
24440	GREENVILLE	98	79	97	79	81	102	79	95	84	73	83	72	68	85	79	91	56	88	98	112
24441	GROTTOES	88	71	76	72	72	89	72	82	77	68	76	63	62	79	69	83	51	77	86	98
24442	HEAD WATERS	68	47	75	47	49	72	52	65	54	42	54	54	38	53	52	59	35	61	68	80
24445	HOT SPRINGS	87	87	92	85	87	100	79	91	85	78	84	66	81	84	85	91	58	86	99	105
24450	LEXINGTON	82	71	86	73	74	84	78	82	80	73	79	61	71	77	77	83	54	81	87	96
24458	MC DOWELL	69	47	75	47	49	72	52	65	54	42	54	54	38	53	52	59	35	61	69	80
24459	MIDDLEBROOK	89	81	82	85	83	96	80	91	83	73	81	68	74	84	80	87	55	84	93	105
24460	MILLBORO	97	78	124	77	86	103	78	99	82	73	81	72	68	78	84	87	54	91	98	114
24464	MONTEBELLO	87	62	89	60	65	88	64	81	71	60	70	61	51	71	63	78	46	75	85	97
24465	MONTEREY	79	59	96	59	64	84	62	78	65	55	64	60	50	63	65	70	42	73	80	93
24467	MOUNT SIDNEY	89	101	87	104	98	99	90	93	88	90	89	73	96	91	95	89	62	90	92	110
24468	MUSTOE	78	53	85	53	56	82	59	74	62	48	61	61	43	61	59	67	40	69	78	91
24471	PORT REPUBLIC	92	89	84	91	88	96	84	90	85	82	85	70	82	88	85	88	59	86	92	107
24472	RAPHINE	89	76	85	77	77	92	75	87	79	70	77	66	67	80	75	84	53	81	89	102
24473	ROCKBRIDGE BATHS	89	70	110	69	77	93	71	89	74	66	73	66	61	71	76	80	49	82	89	104
	VIRGINIA	115	112	112	114	111	114	112	112	112	112	112	88	111	114	111	113	79	112	112	132
	UNITED STATES	100	100	100	100	100	100	100	100	100	100	100	100	100	100	100	100	100	100	100	100

24477-24657

#	POST OFFICE NAME	COUNTY FIPS CODE	POPULATION 2000	POPULATION 2009	POPULATION 2014	2000-2009 ANNUAL RATE % Rate	2000-2009 ANNUAL RATE State Centile	HOUSEHOLDS 2000	HOUSEHOLDS 2009	HOUSEHOLDS 2014	HOUSEHOLDS % Annual Rate 2000-2009	HOUSEHOLDS 2009 Average HH Size	FAMILIES 2000	FAMILIES 2009	FAMILIES % Annual Rate 2000-2009
24477	STUARTS DRAFT	015	8298	8849	9072	0.7	54	3088	3385	3498	1.0	2.59	2450	2626	0.8
24479	SWOOPE	015	1811	1894	1905	0.5	45	690	740	749	0.8	2.56	542	567	0.5
24482	VERONA	015	4765	4866	4843	0.2	33	1967	2069	2077	0.5	2.35	1395	1422	0.2
24483	VESUVIUS	163	589	611	622	0.4	42	256	272	279	0.7	2.25	190	197	0.4
24484	WARM SPRINGS	017	939	893	874	-0.5	6	393	386	381	-0.2	2.28	276	263	-0.5
24485	WEST AUGUSTA	015	372	369	361	-0.1	18	163	165	162	0.1	2.24	112	109	-0.3
24486	WEYERS CAVE	015	2127	2957	3291	3.6	94	788	1109	1240	3.8	2.67	628	862	3.5
24487	WILLIAMSVILLE	017	150	137	133	-1.0	2	62	58	57	-0.7	2.36	46	42	-1.0
24501	LYNCHBURG	680	22249	23477	23841	0.6	49	9179	9459	9660	0.3	2.24	5334	5212	-0.2
24502	LYNCHBURG	680	35585	40810	42526	1.5	76	13745	15456	16259	1.3	2.33	9161	9975	0.9
24503	LYNCHBURG	019	18188	19380	19859	0.7	54	7463	7764	7973	0.4	2.30	4873	4868	0.0
24504	LYNCHBURG	031	9821	10360	10611	0.6	49	3611	3733	3861	0.4	2.44	2238	2207	-0.2
24517	ALTAVISTA	031	5133	5026	4993	-0.2	14	2196	2204	2209	0.0	2.24	1461	1420	-0.3
24520	ALTON	083	2513	2567	2550	0.2	33	978	1037	1043	0.6	2.48	731	753	0.3
24521	AMHERST	009	10724	11271	11528	0.5	45	3887	4252	4402	1.0	2.38	2740	2901	0.6
24522	APPOMATTOX	011	10061	10841	11275	0.8	58	3903	4301	4508	1.1	2.49	2942	3159	0.8
24523	BEDFORD	019	18895	19910	20479	0.6	49	7546	8139	8437	0.8	2.34	5294	5551	0.5
24526	BIG ISLAND	019	1399	1560	1639	1.2	69	569	654	693	1.5	2.38	434	485	1.2
24527	BLAIRS	143	2787	2769	2754	-0.1	18	1055	1082	1088	0.3	2.56	821	822	0.0
24528	BROOKNEAL	031	3575	3632	3623	0.2	33	1395	1451	1461	0.4	2.45	979	986	0.1
24529	BUFFALO JUNCTION	117	1745	1755	1743	0.1	28	727	754	756	0.4	2.33	520	521	0.0
24530	CALLANDS	143	1253	1303	1305	0.4	42	520	559	567	0.8	2.33	371	387	0.5
24531	CHATHAM	143	8577	8805	8794	0.3	38	3511	3718	3753	0.6	2.29	2420	2476	0.2
24534	CLOVER	083	1759	1682	1644	-0.5	6	697	686	676	-0.2	2.45	499	476	-0.5
24536	COLEMAN FALLS	019	255	260	263	0.2	33	99	103	105	0.4	2.51	74	74	0.0
24538	CONCORD	031	4294	5322	5646	2.3	88	1628	2086	2234	2.7	2.54	1252	1557	2.4
24539	CRYSTAL HILL	083	156	156	155	0.0	23	77	80	80	0.4	1.95	51	51	0.0
24540	DANVILLE	143	34323	32925	32077	-0.4	8	14140	13847	13583	-0.2	2.31	9597	9119	-0.6
24541	DANVILLE	143	30905	28881	27919	-0.7	4	13124	12519	12174	-0.5	2.25	8423	7758	-0.9
24549	DRY FORK	143	4268	4415	4427	0.4	42	1673	1782	1808	0.7	2.48	1299	1353	0.4
24550	EVINGTON	031	5874	6083	6138	0.4	42	2336	2496	2546	0.7	2.44	1724	1790	0.4
24551	FOREST	019	16974	20207	21694	1.9	83	6452	7783	8388	2.0	2.59	4912	5809	1.8
24553	GLADSTONE	125	1991	2136	2207	0.8	58	758	834	870	1.0	2.56	572	613	0.8
24554	GLADYS	031	3831	3975	4042	0.4	42	1513	1620	1663	0.7	2.45	1121	1165	0.4
24555	GLASGOW	163	1675	1723	1745	0.3	38	719	751	764	0.5	2.27	496	502	0.1
24556	GOODE	019	2402	2811	3038	1.7	79	901	1067	1159	1.8	2.63	745	866	1.6
24557	GRETNA	143	8462	8454	8319	0.0	23	3464	3576	3557	0.3	2.34	2441	2444	0.0
24558	HALIFAX	083	6494	6448	6377	-0.1	18	2550	2625	2624	0.3	2.37	1833	1826	0.0
24562	HOWARDSVILLE	125	78	129	140	5.6	98	29	51	56	6.3	2.53	20	35	6.2
24563	HURT	143	5232	5324	5295	0.2	33	2200	2317	2327	0.6	2.30	1580	1614	0.2
24565	JAVA	143	1461	1400	1362	-0.5	6	554	550	541	-0.1	2.55	420	406	-0.4
24566	KEELING	143	1287	1337	1345	0.4	42	508	545	556	0.8	2.45	377	393	0.5
24569	LONG ISLAND	143	996	962	953	-0.4	8	376	377	377	0.0	2.55	281	274	-0.3
24570	LOWRY	019	84	90	94	0.7	54	34	38	40	1.2	2.37	24	26	0.9
24571	LYNCH STATION	031	1886	1966	1990	0.5	45	758	815	833	0.8	2.41	556	580	0.5
24572	MADISON HEIGHTS	009	16233	16473	16573	0.2	33	6216	6491	6589	0.5	2.43	4543	4613	0.2
24574	MONROE	009	4153	4268	4323	0.3	38	1515	1605	1642	0.6	2.61	1125	1162	0.4
24577	NATHALIE	083	5511	5285	5162	-0.5	6	2186	2166	2140	-0.1	2.44	1588	1527	-0.4
24578	NATURAL BRIDGE	163	1210	1270	1297	0.5	45	482	516	530	0.7	2.40	349	363	0.4
24579	NATURAL BRIDGE STATI	163	1734	1850	1902	0.7	54	687	744	767	0.9	2.42	479	502	0.5
24580	NELSON	117	659	640	629	-0.3	11	271	272	270	0.0	2.35	193	186	-0.4
24586	RINGGOLD	143	5005	5009	4966	0.0	23	1939	2010	2016	0.4	2.49	1451	1463	0.1
24588	RUSTBURG	031	8972	9199	9294	0.3	38	3456	3642	3718	0.6	2.47	2524	2580	0.2
24589	SCOTTSBURG	083	2593	2450	2385	-0.6	4	1036	1011	994	-0.3	2.42	757	716	-0.6
24590	SCOTTSVILLE	029	7221	7750	8187	0.8	58	2786	3100	3303	1.2	2.50	1992	2148	0.8
24592	SOUTH BOSTON	083	14065	13519	13234	-0.4	8	5761	5704	5631	-0.1	2.26	3803	3636	-0.5
24593	SPOUT SPRING	011	834	889	923	0.7	54	324	354	370	1.0	2.50	243	259	0.7
24594	SUTHERLIN	083	1501	1507	1482	0.0	23	595	619	616	0.4	2.43	449	455	0.1
24597	VERNON HILL	083	1337	1347	1335	0.1	28	532	558	559	0.5	2.41	388	394	0.2
24598	VIRGILINA	083	2192	2140	2103	-0.3	11	899	909	904	0.1	2.35	644	630	-0.2
24599	WINGINA	029	721	812	847	1.3	72	295	340	358	1.5	2.39	212	236	1.2
24602	BANDY	185	2143	2052	2001	-0.5	6	871	869	857	0.0	2.36	643	625	-0.3
24603	BIG ROCK	027	1031	932	881	-1.1	2	420	397	380	-0.6	2.35	326	301	-0.9
24605	BLUEFIELD	185	10457	10256	10023	-0.2	14	4344	4400	4350	0.1	2.26	3053	2992	-0.2
24609	CEDAR BLUFF	185	2978	2972	2928	0.0	23	1254	1299	1295	0.4	2.27	928	935	0.1
24613	FALLS MILLS	185	1143	1123	1098	-0.2	14	457	466	461	0.2	2.41	319	314	-0.2
24614	GRUNDY	027	8484	7693	7261	-1.1	2	3374	3173	3030	-0.7	2.34	2480	2267	-1.0
24620	HURLEY	027	4503	4069	3841	-1.1	2	1794	1693	1618	-0.6	2.39	1379	1269	-0.9
24622	JEWELL RIDGE	027	862	780	737	-1.1	2	349	330	316	-0.6	2.36	262	242	-0.9
24627	MAVISDALE	027	141	127	120	-1.1	2	58	55	52	-0.6	2.29	42	39	-0.8
24630	NORTH TAZEWELL	185	6728	6717	6621	0.0	23	2796	2902	2897	0.4	2.31	2071	2087	0.1
24631	OAKWOOD	027	3254	3007	2874	-0.8	3	983	905	859	-0.9	2.30	728	652	-1.2
24634	PILGRIMS KNOB	027	576	519	489	-1.1	2	225	212	202	-0.6	2.45	173	159	-0.9
24637	POUNDING MILL	185	4526	4461	4375	-0.2	14	1764	1801	1787	0.2	2.48	1418	1420	0.0
24639	RAVEN	027	4112	3919	3800	-0.5	6	1674	1663	1633	-0.1	2.35	1255	1214	-0.4
24641	RICHLANDS	185	6629	6683	6585	0.1	28	2865	3016	3011	0.6	2.22	1945	1977	0.2
24646	ROWE	027	1162	1051	992	-1.1	2	464	438	420	-0.6	2.40	369	342	-0.8
24649	SWORDS CREEK	167	2697	2683	2662	-0.1	18	1073	1111	1117	0.4	2.41	842	851	0.1
24651	TAZEWELL	185	7042	6811	6629	-0.4	8	2728	2711	2666	-0.1	2.33	1955	1888	-0.4
24656	VANSANT	027	3903	3502	3298	-1.2	1	1584	1486	1418	-0.7	2.35	1198	1094	-1.0
24657	WHITEWOOD	027	585	525	494	-1.2	1	234	219	209	-0.7	2.40	185	169	-1.0
	VIRGINIA					1.2					1.3	2.52			1.0
	UNITED STATES					1.0					1.1	2.59			0.9

# ZIP CODE	POST OFFICE NAME	RACE (%) White 2000	White 2009	Black 2000	Black 2009	Asian/Pacific 2000	Asian/Pacific 2009	% Hispanic Origin 2000	% Hispanic Origin 2009	2009 AGE DISTRIBUTION (%) 0-4	5-9	10-14	15-19	20-24	25-44	45-64	65-84	85+	18+	MEDIAN AGE 2009	% 2009 Males	% 2009 Females
24477	STUARTS DRAFT	96.2	94.8	2.5	3.0	0.2	0.6	1.0	1.8	5.9	6.4	6.7	6.3	4.8	25.8	30.2	12.4	1.6	77.1	41.2	49.1	50.9
24479	SWOOPE	96.6	95.9	2.4	2.7	0.3	0.5	0.8	1.3	4.8	5.4	6.5	6.4	4.9	23.0	33.6	14.2	1.2	79.4	44.3	49.3	50.7
24482	VERONA	95.7	94.3	2.6	3.1	0.5	0.8	0.6	1.0	5.5	5.8	6.1	6.0	5.2	25.3	31.0	13.8	1.4	79.0	42.2	49.5	50.5
24483	VESUVIUS	92.9	91.2	5.9	6.9	0.2	0.3	0.7	1.1	5.2	5.9	6.4	6.2	4.3	24.7	32.1	13.9	1.3	78.7	43.2	50.1	49.9
24484	WARM SPRINGS	93.4	93.1	4.9	5.0	0.3	0.3	0.2	0.2	4.1	5.3	5.6	5.8	3.7	22.5	34.8	16.1	2.0	81.1	46.8	50.5	49.5
24485	WEST AUGUSTA	98.1	98.1	0.5	0.5	0.3	0.3	0.3	0.5	3.5	6.2	6.0	5.1	3.0	22.0	37.9	13.6	2.7	81.0	47.1	53.4	46.6
24486	WEYERS CAVE	98.1	97.2	0.5	0.6	0.0	0.1	0.6	1.0	6.2	6.9	7.5	7.2	4.3	24.2	31.7	10.6	1.4	74.9	40.8	51.1	48.9
24487	WILLIAMSVILLE	95.3	94.9	3.4	3.6	0.0	0.0	0.0	0.0	4.4	5.8	5.8	6.6	2.9	22.6	37.2	13.1	1.5	78.8	46.3	51.8	48.2
24501	LYNCHBURG	58.3	52.9	37.8	41.8	1.4	1.9	1.1	1.7	6.5	6.0	5.9	9.8	10.0	25.3	22.4	11.4	2.7	77.6	33.7	46.8	53.2
24502	LYNCHBURG	83.4	79.3	12.5	14.7	1.8	2.6	1.6	2.7	5.5	5.4	5.6	10.4	10.5	24.7	23.3	12.4	2.2	80.2	35.0	47.4	52.6
24503	LYNCHBURG	83.8	81.0	13.8	15.6	0.8	1.2	0.8	1.3	5.2	5.7	5.9	8.0	7.8	20.7	28.1	14.6	4.1	79.3	42.3	45.0	55.0
24504	LYNCHBURG	38.9	35.1	58.9	62.0	0.2	0.3	1.0	1.3	5.4	5.7	5.7	6.7	7.1	26.4	27.7	12.7	2.7	79.4	39.9	50.1	49.9
24517	ALTAVISTA	75.6	72.9	23.2	25.4	0.2	0.3	0.8	1.2	5.5	5.3	5.7	6.2	5.8	22.6	29.0	16.6	3.3	79.8	44.1	46.7	53.3
24520	ALTON	59.0	55.0	39.4	42.7	0.2	0.3	1.0	1.6	5.8	6.2	6.7	6.9	4.6	23.6	30.2	14.1	1.9	77.1	42.2	49.6	50.4
24521	AMHERST	75.4	72.1	22.3	24.7	0.4	0.6	1.2	1.8	5.4	5.6	6.1	10.4	8.8	21.5	26.7	13.2	2.4	78.4	38.6	45.6	54.4
24522	APPOMATTOX	75.7	72.7	23.2	25.7	0.2	0.3	0.5	0.7	6.1	6.4	6.7	6.5	4.9	24.2	29.0	14.3	2.0	76.8	41.6	48.5	51.5
24523	BEDFORD	83.6	81.5	14.8	16.3	0.4	0.5	0.7	1.0	5.3	5.4	5.8	6.2	5.2	23.3	29.8	15.9	3.0	79.6	44.1	49.1	50.9
24526	BIG ISLAND	86.1	83.8	12.4	14.0	0.1	0.2	1.0	1.6	4.8	5.3	5.9	6.2	4.1	23.8	33.3	14.8	1.8	80.1	44.9	50.2	49.8
24527	BLAIRS	68.0	64.2	30.1	33.0	0.4	0.6	1.5	2.4	5.4	5.7	6.1	5.7	5.5	25.4	32.5	12.3	1.3	79.3	42.1	49.8	50.2
24528	BROOKNEAL	67.9	64.7	31.1	33.9	0.0	0.0	1.4	2.2	6.1	6.2	6.6	7.1	6.1	22.2	28.2	14.4	2.9	76.3	41.7	47.2	52.8
24529	BUFFALO JUNCTION	66.4	62.6	31.8	34.6	0.2	0.3	1.5	2.4	5.3	5.6	6.0	6.4	4.7	20.6	32.3	17.2	2.1	79.2	45.9	49.0	51.0
24530	CALLANDS	74.1	70.8	24.6	27.6	0.1	0.1	1.1	1.8	5.4	5.7	6.0	5.9	5.1	24.3	32.8	13.0	1.8	79.2	43.4	49.0	51.0
24531	CHATHAM	68.5	64.8	30.1	33.2	0.2	0.2	1.0	1.5	5.0	5.2	5.6	5.6	5.1	23.4	32.0	15.4	2.5	80.6	45.0	49.3	50.7
24534	CLOVER	50.3	46.4	48.6	52.0	0.1	0.2	1.1	1.5	6.2	6.7	6.8	7.1	5.2	21.3	30.0	14.3	2.3	76.0	42.5	48.4	51.6
24536	COLEMAN FALLS	90.6	89.2	8.2	9.2	0.0	0.0	1.2	1.5	5.8	6.5	6.9	6.2	3.8	24.2	32.7	12.3	1.5	76.2	42.8	50.4	49.6
24538	CONCORD	80.6	78.2	17.6	19.1	0.1	0.3	0.7	1.2	6.3	6.5	6.7	6.2	5.3	26.4	29.7	11.7	1.2	76.6	39.7	49.8	50.2
24539	CRYSTAL HILL	66.7	62.8	32.1	35.3	0.0	0.0	0.6	0.6	6.4	6.4	6.4	6.4	5.1	21.8	31.4	13.5	2.6	76.9	43.2	50.0	50.0
24540	DANVILLE	60.8	57.4	37.2	39.8	0.5	0.7	1.4	2.2	6.1	6.4	6.4	6.1	5.2	24.1	28.0	14.6	3.1	77.3	41.7	46.7	53.3
24541	DANVILLE	61.1	58.5	37.1	38.8	0.6	0.8	1.4	2.2	5.7	6.0	6.1	6.6	5.9	23.2	28.6	15.3	2.7	78.4	42.5	47.4	52.6
24549	DRY FORK	82.9	80.2	15.7	17.8	0.3	0.4	1.0	1.6	5.7	6.1	6.6	6.1	4.6	25.3	31.8	12.3	1.4	77.8	41.9	50.3	49.7
24550	EVINGTON	84.7	82.0	13.5	15.4	0.3	0.5	0.8	1.3	6.0	6.2	6.7	6.6	5.1	25.2	30.8	12.2	1.2	77.0	40.9	49.3	50.7
24551	FOREST	92.0	90.2	5.7	6.5	1.1	1.6	0.8	1.4	6.3	6.6	7.0	7.1	5.6	25.1	30.8	10.5	1.0	75.7	40.0	49.0	51.0
24553	GLADSTONE	72.9	69.3	25.4	28.3	0.1	0.2	0.6	0.8	5.3	6.0	6.9	6.8	4.6	23.5	31.1	14.1	1.7	77.6	42.6	48.5	51.5
24554	GLADYS	75.0	72.2	23.9	26.3	0.0	0.0	0.8	1.2	4.9	5.7	6.2	6.7	5.6	24.8	30.3	14.0	1.9	78.9	42.4	49.4	50.6
24555	GLASGOW	87.1	84.7	10.3	11.6	0.4	0.5	0.5	0.9	4.9	5.2	5.6	6.2	4.9	23.2	30.8	16.9	2.4	80.4	45.0	49.3	50.7
24556	GOODE	89.6	87.8	8.6	9.7	0.2	0.4	1.2	2.1	5.7	6.3	6.9	7.0	4.4	22.5	32.9	13.0	1.3	76.7	43.3	49.1	50.9
24557	GRETNA	73.1	70.1	26.0	28.5	0.1	0.2	0.8	1.2	5.0	5.3	5.7	6.0	5.1	22.8	31.4	16.4	2.4	80.3	45.1	48.5	51.5
24558	HALIFAX	62.2	58.3	36.4	39.7	0.2	0.3	1.1	1.8	5.4	5.8	6.3	6.5	4.8	24.4	30.4	14.6	1.9	78.9	42.6	49.4	50.6
24562	HOWARDSVILLE	78.2	72.1	19.2	24.8	0.0	0.0	1.3	2.3	6.2	6.2	6.2	6.2	4.7	23.3	31.8	14.0	1.6	77.5	43.3	48.8	51.2
24563	HURT	77.3	74.2	21.7	24.4	0.2	0.2	0.6	1.0	5.3	5.5	5.9	6.2	4.7	26.3	29.1	15.1	1.8	79.4	42.4	48.0	52.0
24565	JAVA	48.7	44.6	49.1	52.1	0.2	0.3	2.4	3.6	5.6	6.0	6.4	6.4	5.3	22.4	33.1	13.3	1.7	78.2	43.4	48.0	52.0
24566	KEELING	81.4	79.0	17.2	19.1	0.0	0.0	1.6	2.6	6.0	6.4	6.8	5.8	4.9	26.0	32.0	10.8	1.3	77.1	40.6	49.2	50.8
24569	LONG ISLAND	61.5	58.0	37.0	39.8	0.0	0.0	1.8	2.5	5.8	5.9	6.2	6.3	5.7	24.2	29.7	14.0	2.0	78.2	41.7	49.8	50.2
24570	LOWRY	73.5	67.8	26.5	30.0	0.0	1.1	0.0	1.1	5.6	5.6	5.6	6.7	5.6	26.7	31.1	12.2	1.1	78.9	40.8	52.2	47.8
24571	LYNCH STATION	82.6	79.9	15.9	17.9	0.1	0.2	0.4	0.7	5.7	5.9	6.2	6.0	5.1	23.6	31.7	14.0	1.8	78.5	43.2	49.1	50.9
24572	MADISON HEIGHTS	78.4	75.6	18.9	20.8	0.4	0.6	0.9	1.3	5.9	6.0	6.3	6.1	4.9	26.4	29.4	13.4	1.6	78.1	41.4	48.8	51.2
24574	MONROE	80.1	77.5	17.3	19.1	0.3	0.4	0.9	1.4	5.6	6.0	6.5	7.9	4.8	24.9	29.9	13.0	1.4	77.1	40.9	49.9	50.1
24577	NATHALIE	57.4	53.5	41.4	44.7	0.0	0.1	1.0	1.5	5.8	6.1	6.5	6.5	4.4	23.1	30.5	14.8	2.2	77.7	43.2	49.4	50.6
24578	NATURAL BRIDGE	92.9	91.7	5.3	5.8	0.5	0.7	0.2	0.2	4.5	4.9	5.3	5.0	4.2	22.6	32.6	18.8	2.1	82.0	47.3	51.6	48.4
24579	NATURAL BRIDGE STATI	92.2	90.1	4.3	4.9	0.3	0.4	0.9	1.5	7.2	7.4	7.3	8.3	4.5	24.1	26.5	13.4	1.4	72.3	38.7	51.9	48.1
24580	NELSON	72.7	69.5	26.9	29.8	0.0	0.0	0.8	1.3	4.8	5.5	5.8	6.3	4.4	23.6	32.7	15.3	1.7	80.2	44.8	51.3	48.7
24586	RINGGOLD	77.0	74.1	21.9	24.3	0.1	0.2	1.1	1.7	5.6	5.9	6.2	5.7	5.1	25.2	31.9	12.9	1.5	78.8	42.4	49.5	50.5
24588	RUSTBURG	84.9	82.3	13.6	15.6	0.2	0.3	0.5	0.9	5.9	6.2	6.6	6.8	5.1	27.8	29.1	11.4	1.1	77.0	39.7	50.5	49.5
24589	SCOTTSBURG	69.7	66.1	28.7	31.6	0.1	0.1	1.4	2.2	6.2	6.5	6.7	6.3	4.6	23.0	30.6	14.1	2.1	76.7	42.6	49.8	50.2
24590	SCOTTSVILLE	77.2	74.3	20.9	23.0	0.2	0.3	0.9	1.5	6.0	6.2	6.5	6.5	5.2	25.0	30.9	12.2	1.4	77.3	41.3	49.1	50.9
24592	SOUTH BOSTON	58.9	55.4	39.0	41.6	0.4	0.7	1.5	2.3	5.9	5.8	6.1	6.2	5.3	22.7	28.0	16.5	3.5	78.2	43.4	46.7	53.3
24593	SPOUT SPRING	77.2	74.0	21.2	23.6	0.5	0.7	0.6	0.9	5.5	5.8	6.4	6.4	4.5	25.5	29.0	15.1	1.7	78.3	42.1	51.4	48.6
24594	SUTHERLIN	75.0	71.9	24.2	26.9	0.1	0.1	1.3	2.0	6.2	6.4	6.7	6.2	5.3	25.1	31.0	11.8	1.3	76.8	40.7	50.4	49.6
24597	VERNON HILL	48.5	45.0	49.6	52.3	0.0	0.1	1.9	2.8	5.1	5.5	6.0	6.7	5.0	24.3	31.6	13.7	2.1	79.0	43.1	48.4	51.6
24598	VIRGILINA	78.7	76.0	20.2	22.5	0.1	0.2	0.7	1.0	4.8	5.1	5.7	5.7	4.3	23.3	32.3	16.4	2.4	80.9	45.7	49.2	50.8
24599	WINGINA	76.3	73.3	21.5	23.4	0.0	0.0	1.1	2.0	5.5	6.0	6.3	6.2	5.0	21.2	33.6	14.3	1.8	78.4	44.8	49.5	50.5
24602	BANDY	97.9	97.3	1.2	1.4	0.1	0.2	0.3	0.6	4.9	5.5	5.7	5.9	4.6	23.6	32.6	15.3	1.9	80.3	44.8	49.0	51.0
24603	BIG ROCK	99.8	99.6	0.0	0.0	0.0	0.0	0.1	0.1	4.9	5.5	5.9	5.8	3.4	24.6	33.9	14.4	1.6	80.0	44.9	48.8	51.2
24605	BLUEFIELD	94.0	92.5	3.8	4.3	0.9	1.4	0.7	1.1	4.7	5.0	5.4	6.4	5.4	23.0	30.8	16.5	3.0	81.7	45.2	47.9	52.1
24609	CEDAR BLUFF	99.1	98.7	0.1	0.2	0.1	0.2	0.7	1.2	5.5	5.8	5.9	5.3	4.6	26.4	31.6	13.5	1.3	79.5	42.5	48.0	52.0
24613	FALLS MILLS	87.7	85.8	10.6	11.8	0.1	0.2	1.5	2.0	6.0	6.1	6.0	5.8	5.4	24.4	30.2	14.2	2.0	78.4	41.9	48.3	51.7
24614	GRUNDY	96.6	95.8	2.4	2.7	0.3	0.5	0.6	1.0	4.6	5.6	6.4	6.8	4.8	24.6	32.1	13.3	1.7	78.8	43.0	48.5	51.5
24620	HURLEY	99.5	99.3	0.1	0.1	0.0	0.1	0.5	0.8	5.1	5.3	5.8	7.7	5.4	27.4	32.8	9.6	1.0	78.9	40.6	49.4	50.6
24622	JEWELL RIDGE	99.3	98.8	0.0	0.0	0.0	0.1	0.1	0.3	4.7	5.1	5.4	6.5	5.4	24.4	33.3	13.5	1.7	80.8	43.8	50.6	49.4
24627	MAVISDALE	100.0	100.0	0.0	0.0	0.0	0.0	0.0	0.0	3.9	4.7	4.7	10.2	7.1	26.0	32.3	9.4	1.6	79.5	40.8	51.2	48.8
24630	NORTH TAZEWELL	96.7	95.7	1.9	2.3	0.4	0.7	0.4	0.6	4.9	5.6	5.9	6.0	4.5	24.4	32.3	14.6	1.8	79.9	44.0	48.9	51.1
24631	OAKWOOD	84.3	82.0	15.0	16.9	0.2	0.3	0.7	1.3	2.8	3.9	3.5	6.1	8.6	38.2	28.2	7.7	0.9	86.2	38.1	64.4	35.6
24634	PILGRIMS KNOB	99.0	98.3	0.0	0.0	0.2	0.2	0.5	1.0	5.4	5.6	5.2	7.9	6.6	25.6	33.9	8.3	1.5	79.0	40.7	49.5	50.5
24637	POUNDING MILL	99.0	98.6	0.2	0.2	0.2	0.4	0.5	0.8	4.9	5.5	6.1	6.2	4.3	25.0	34.0	12.9	1.3	79.7	43.6	48.7	51.3
24639	RAVEN	98.2	97.2	0.3	0.3	1.0	1.6	0.5	0.9	5.3	5.8	5.8	6.0	4.6	26.0	31.6	13.7	1.2	79.5	42.6	49.5	50.5
24641	RICHLANDS	98.4	97.7	0.1	0.1	0.8	1.3	0.4	0.7	5.3	5.6	5.7	5.4	4.6	24.4	32.0	14.8	2.1	80.0	44.1	46.8	53.2
24646	ROWE	99.7	99.7	0.0	0.0	0.0	0.0	0.2	0.3	4.5	4.9	5.4	6.9	6.7	26.6	32.3	11.3	1.4	80.8	41.8	50.4	49.6
24649	SWORDS CREEK	98.9	98.3	0.0	0.0	0.0	0.1	0.8	1.3	5.3	5.4	5.7	5.6	4.5	27.9	31.8	12.5	1.3	80.1	42.2	48.2	51.8
24651	TAZEWELL	93.9	92.4	4.6	5.3	0.4	0.7	0.4	0.6	4.9	5.1	5.4	5.5	5.3	25.0	30.3	15.5	3.0	81.2	44.0	48.8	51.2
24656	VANSANT	99.6	99.5	0.1	0.1	0.0	0.0	0.4	0.6	4.8	5.4	5.5	6.4	5.7	25.1	33.2	12.6	1.4	80.1	43.1	49.5	50.5
24657	WHITEWOOD	99.1	98.5	0.0	0.0	0.0	0.2	0.3	0.6	5.1	5.9	5.3	7.4	5.7	25.1	33.7	10.1	1.5	79.2	41.8	50.7	49.3
	VIRGINIA	72.3	68.8	19.6	20.1	3.7	5.1	4.7	7.0	6.5	6.4	6.5	6.9	6.9	27.5	27.2	10.5	1.6	76.7	37.7	49.2	50.8
	UNITED STATES	75.1	72.0	12.3	12.7	3.8	4.6	12.5	15.7	6.8	6.7	6.6	7.1	6.9	27.0	26.0	10.9	1.9	75.7	36.9	49.2	50.8

C 24477-24657

ZIP CODE #	POST OFFICE NAME	2009 Per Capita Income	2009 HH Income Base	2009 HOUSEHOLD INCOME DISTRIBUTION (%) Less than $25,000	$25,000 to $49,999	$50,000 to $99,999	$100,000 to $149,999	$150,000 or More	MEDIAN HOUSEHOLD INCOME 2009	2014	2009 National Centile	2009 State Centile	2009 Home Value Base	2009 HOME VALUE DISTRIBUTION (%) Less than $50,000	$50,000 to $89,999	$90,000 to $174,999	$175,000 to $399,999	$400,000 or More	2009 Median Home Value
24477	STUARTS DRAFT	23601	3385	13.1	27.1	47.7	10.8	1.3	56451	58367	73	71	2826	3.0	5.0	40.0	49.8	2.2	178125
24479	SWOOPE	22128	740	21.8	26.5	41.8	7.8	2.2	51189	52162	64	61	635	5.2	8.5	39.7	37.8	8.8	161218
24482	VERONA	23819	2069	13.2	38.9	37.8	8.7	1.3	48598	49590	58	54	1602	8.7	2.1	42.6	40.7	6.0	169636
24483	VESUVIUS	23075	272	21.7	36.0	34.9	5.1	2.2	45199	47223	49	44	220	11.8	20.0	45.9	20.9	1.4	127703
24484	WARM SPRINGS	23047	386	22.3	33.4	37.0	4.9	2.3	43625	44902	44	40	303	6.6	13.5	41.6	30.4	7.9	142402
24485	WEST AUGUSTA	20935	165	18.8	40.6	33.3	7.3	0.0	42802	44444	42	38	137	8.0	12.4	46.0	24.8	8.8	138194
24486	WEYERS CAVE	22692	1109	19.7	22.9	44.5	10.6	2.3	54068	55357	70	67	924	1.0	5.3	29.1	50.9	13.7	214634
24487	WILLIAMSVILLE	21469	58	25.9	32.8	32.8	6.9	1.7	40000	44303	33	30	47	4.3	17.0	36.2	34.0	8.5	148438
24501	LYNCHBURG	18505	9459	39.8	30.3	25.5	2.8	1.7	32523	33880	12	11	4421	17.5	29.7	44.0	7.6	1.3	92144
24502	LYNCHBURG	23905	15456	20.0	28.8	40.1	8.9	2.2	51039	54664	64	61	10574	5.1	6.7	59.2	27.6	1.4	147536
24503	LYNCHBURG	32721	7764	18.5	22.0	35.6	14.9	9.1	61356	63903	79	76	5377	3.3	6.3	29.4	46.7	14.2	209116
24504	LYNCHBURG	16076	3733	40.5	30.5	24.6	3.8	0.5	31625	33516	11	9	2151	22.6	24.2	37.4	14.3	1.5	93516
24517	ALTAVISTA	22351	2204	29.6	29.5	31.1	7.5	2.3	41210	44384	37	34	1546	10.4	22.0	45.5	19.8	2.3	112785
24520	ALTON	17358	1037	37.2	27.3	29.9	5.2	0.4	36485	37835	22	19	837	9.6	20.8	52.4	13.7	3.5	122032
24521	AMHERST	22166	4252	25.3	28.4	36.7	7.2	2.4	46785	49581	53	49	3291	10.1	12.2	47.3	25.3	5.2	138739
24522	APPOMATTOX	20675	4301	26.7	29.4	35.9	6.0	2.0	44691	45798	47	42	3398	11.9	17.3	45.0	22.1	3.8	127221
24523	BEDFORD	21514	8139	26.1	31.0	35.0	6.1	1.8	43414	46252	44	39	6202	11.3	13.2	44.5	26.1	5.0	136870
24526	BIG ISLAND	24761	654	23.7	24.6	40.4	8.3	3.1	51024	52560	64	61	555	14.2	18.6	31.9	25.0	10.3	119792
24527	BLAIRS	18711	1082	24.9	36.7	32.3	5.0	1.2	39861	42096	32	29	902	16.3	20.4	51.6	10.8	1.0	104706
24528	BROOKNEAL	18448	1451	35.3	28.5	29.6	5.2	1.4	37174	39111	24	21	1056	18.6	30.4	39.1	11.0	0.9	91250
24529	BUFFALO JUNCTION	21311	754	30.5	31.7	28.8	7.3	1.7	36830	39191	23	20	595	16.8	10.4	38.3	28.1	6.4	139375
24530	CALLANDS	20176	559	29.0	38.3	25.0	5.5	2.1	37717	38797	26	23	460	19.3	25.0	50.7	3.9	1.1	95098
24531	CHATHAM	21256	3718	29.6	32.6	29.7	5.9	2.1	39406	41094	31	28	2843	19.0	23.2	45.4	10.9	1.5	97141
24534	CLOVER	15066	686	45.0	33.8	17.6	1.9	1.6	27664	28077	5	4	543	16.8	21.7	42.4	17.7	1.5	107923
24536	COLEMAN FALLS	26221	103	19.4	20.4	43.7	11.7	4.9	61516	60329	79	76	86	8.1	15.1	20.9	31.4	24.4	200000
24538	CONCORD	20125	2086	20.7	33.1	39.3	6.6	0.3	47212	48802	55	50	1751	12.5	13.8	45.0	27.1	1.5	134991
24539	CRYSTAL HILL	20008	80	37.5	33.8	23.8	5.0	0.0	32279	33120	12	10	60	10.0	23.3	48.3	16.7	1.7	116667
24540	DANVILLE	20208	13847	31.0	29.9	32.6	5.1	1.4	39604	42453	32	28	9054	14.8	24.9	50.8	8.7	0.7	99142
24541	DANVILLE	21926	12519	35.0	27.8	28.8	5.3	3.1	36663	39316	23	19	7584	15.1	24.9	45.9	12.1	2.0	98873
24549	DRY FORK	21265	1782	23.0	31.0	37.4	6.7	1.9	46320	47690	52	47	1483	15.2	15.6	47.5	18.4	3.2	113118
24550	EVINGTON	21512	2496	27.5	29.0	33.7	7.9	1.9	43962	46769	45	41	2060	17.2	14.5	39.0	25.8	3.4	130216
24551	FOREST	29565	7783	10.1	23.6	43.5	16.8	6.1	65338	66529	84	80	6433	2.9	2.1	33.9	51.1	10.1	206554
24553	GLADSTONE	18808	834	28.4	33.8	31.3	4.9	1.6	38613	40997	28	25	710	12.4	16.6	52.5	16.1	2.4	121654
24554	GLADYS	18430	1620	32.0	30.5	32.5	4.0	1.0	39144	40978	30	27	1313	21.5	22.7	41.0	12.8	2.1	97650
24555	GLASGOW	20254	751	29.0	31.6	34.8	3.7	0.9	40409	42460	34	30	570	14.4	14.7	40.9	25.1	4.9	129514
24556	GOODE	25723	1067	17.2	23.4	45.8	10.0	3.6	61200	62027	79	76	952	4.9	5.3	21.6	53.5	14.7	226902
24557	GRETNA	18413	3576	32.2	32.3	31.2	3.7	0.7	37192	38700	24	21	2761	17.4	27.7	47.7	6.7	0.4	93865
24558	HALIFAX	20245	2625	29.6	31.2	32.0	5.9	1.3	40777	42540	35	32	2084	13.0	16.3	47.3	20.2	3.3	124669
24562	HOWARDSVILLE	20612	51	31.4	25.5	37.3	5.9	0.0	45555	45724	50	45	43	14.0	11.6	46.5	20.9	7.0	146875
24563	HURT	19273	2317	29.7	31.2	35.3	3.4	0.5	40911	42761	36	33	1848	18.5	30.1	47.7	3.4	0.3	91150
24565	JAVA	17321	550	33.8	30.5	28.9	5.1	1.6	38722	39335	29	26	433	22.6	31.4	35.1	9.9	0.9	85000
24566	KEELING	17428	545	30.1	34.3	31.4	3.9	0.4	36722	38819	23	20	448	15.8	26.6	51.6	6.0	0.0	95862
24569	LONG ISLAND	16919	377	33.2	32.4	29.4	4.2	0.8	36760	38811	23	20	301	19.6	25.6	45.2	9.6	0.0	94677
24570	LOWRY	19750	38	23.7	39.5	34.2	2.6	0.0	40000	45000	33	30	33	3.0	24.2	39.4	24.2	9.1	137500
24571	LYNCH STATION	20982	815	26.3	35.6	27.6	8.7	1.8	40820	42761	35	32	702	14.7	18.8	32.9	30.5	3.1	127817
24572	MADISON HEIGHTS	20894	6491	24.0	30.8	37.8	5.8	1.6	45776	48560	51	46	4901	8.0	12.9	58.0	20.0	1.1	134830
24574	MONROE	21780	1605	19.9	29.6	41.1	6.7	2.7	50462	54934	62	59	1336	8.5	10.8	50.2	27.5	3.0	147707
24577	NATHALIE	16618	2166	39.0	33.5	23.0	3.5	1.1	29452	30436	7	6	1718	15.3	13.4	51.6	18.5	1.2	120419
24578	NATURAL BRIDGE	20411	516	25.4	35.7	33.1	3.7	2.1	42082	44266	40	36	416	4.3	9.9	37.0	38.0	10.8	172768
24579	NATURAL BRIDGE STATI	18476	744	32.9	29.3	32.9	4.2	0.7	38244	40314	27	24	623	26.6	24.7	35.5	10.8	2.4	86852
24580	NELSON	22026	272	32.0	25.4	30.1	8.5	4.0	36763	40000	23	20	226	18.1	10.6	53.5	15.5	2.2	126667
24586	RINGGOLD	19410	2010	26.4	30.1	38.2	4.5	0.7	45255	46442	49	44	1627	20.9	26.1	40.9	12.0	0.0	93345
24588	RUSTBURG	21727	3642	22.8	28.9	39.9	6.9	1.5	48714	51389	58	55	3032	21.4	14.4	36.5	25.5	2.2	120424
24589	SCOTTSBURG	18327	1011	32.6	31.8	30.9	3.9	0.8	39793	40947	32	29	789	18.1	18.1	40.4	20.7	2.7	115625
24590	SCOTTSVILLE	21698	3100	22.7	28.7	40.0	7.0	1.5	48711	50862	58	55	2417	6.5	10.5	42.7	32.2	8.1	157808
24592	SOUTH BOSTON	20337	5704	34.2	30.1	28.9	4.9	1.9	36527	37837	22	19	3887	7.9	18.6	51.9	19.0	2.6	128229
24593	SPOUT SPRING	21372	354	25.4	29.1	37.9	5.1	2.5	46398	47080	53	48	286	10.8	11.2	42.7	31.8	3.5	140625
24594	SUTHERLIN	19519	619	25.4	39.6	29.7	4.0	1.3	42701	43580	41	37	499	22.8	20.4	39.5	16.0	1.2	102534
24597	VERNON HILL	19407	558	34.6	28.3	31.0	4.3	1.8	37461	39448	25	22	448	10.0	18.1	46.9	20.5	4.5	116033
24598	VIRGILINA	21792	909	28.4	29.7	32.3	7.6	2.0	42838	45000	42	38	756	11.5	14.4	56.5	15.6	2.0	126181
24599	WINGINA	18860	340	34.4	37.6	20.0	6.5	1.5	36388	37429	22	19	284	24.6	18.3	34.2	21.1	1.8	114423
24602	BANDY	15531	869	40.7	36.5	19.3	2.8	0.7	31353	31523	10	9	715	36.9	27.3	29.8	5.5	0.6	62900
24603	BIG ROCK	15769	397	42.8	32.0	20.2	5.0	0.0	31737	31794	11	10	329	33.4	22.5	35.9	8.2	0.0	77000
24605	BLUEFIELD	22434	4400	30.9	33.0	26.9	5.6	3.6	38014	39439	27	24	3446	17.6	21.9	38.5	18.1	3.9	107805
24609	CEDAR BLUFF	18386	1299	36.6	34.2	24.6	3.5	1.1	33147	33760	14	12	996	19.8	19.2	41.9	17.8	1.4	104098
24613	FALLS MILLS	14597	466	40.1	37.1	19.7	2.6	0.4	30000	30526	8	7	334	27.8	30.8	31.7	8.7	0.9	80333
24614	GRUNDY	16311	3173	45.0	27.5	23.1	3.2	1.1	29083	29928	7	6	2487	27.2	20.7	38.9	11.8	1.4	94008
24620	HURLEY	13158	1693	54.5	28.0	14.6	2.7	0.1	22794	22656	2	2	1417	36.1	27.5	29.4	5.9	1.1	67000
24622	JEWELL RIDGE	14943	330	50.6	22.4	22.7	3.0	1.2	24528	24778	3	2	266	30.5	25.2	31.6	8.6	4.1	82857
24627	MAVISDALE	15533	55	47.3	30.9	18.2	3.6	0.0	27318	30000	5	4	47	29.8	25.5	40.4	4.3	0.0	83750
24630	NORTH TAZEWELL	17978	2902	37.3	31.3	27.6	2.1	1.7	32752	33695	13	11	2298	21.3	22.2	42.9	12.5	1.1	98142
24631	OAKWOOD	17640	905	42.3	27.6	24.8	3.6	1.7	33570	34303	15	13	703	30.2	23.8	34.6	11.0	0.6	82568
24634	PILGRIMS KNOB	14178	212	52.4	20.8	22.2	2.8	1.9	23552	24183	2	2	171	30.4	18.1	32.2	17.0	2.3	92778
24637	POUNDING MILL	18407	1801	29.2	34.1	31.4	4.1	1.1	38406	39500	28	25	1525	14.7	16.5	46.8	19.9	2.1	126488
24639	RAVEN	14166	1663	54.8	25.3	16.6	2.3	1.0	22970	23006	2	2	1267	33.5	26.2	27.9	11.4	0.9	75511
24641	RICHLANDS	18025	3016	45.8	27.9	20.0	4.3	2.1	27966	28408	6	4	2121	25.6	22.3	39.4	11.2	1.6	92987
24646	ROWE	13819	438	52.3	24.0	21.7	2.1	0.0	24114	23931	3	2	384	25.8	26.0	39.3	7.3	1.6	87308
24649	SWORDS CREEK	13826	1111	44.7	33.9	18.6	2.0	0.7	26782	26971	4	4	947	38.3	29.8	22.5	9.4	0.0	65608
24651	TAZEWELL	19668	2711	30.8	30.5	31.8	4.6	2.3	38639	40615	29	25	1965	12.4	16.6	45.1	22.1	3.8	121074
24656	VANSANT	14931	1486	44.5	32.4	20.5	2.3	0.3	30030	30468	8	7	1253	31.7	21.4	38.4	8.3	0.2	86468
24657	WHITEWOOD	12352	219	58.9	21.5	18.7	0.0	0.9	19877	20101	1	1	184	33.2	21.7	28.8	14.1	2.2	82500
	VIRGINIA	30912		17.0	22.6	35.9	15.0	9.5	61855	64957				5.3	6.3	30.4	41.5	16.5	203135
	UNITED STATES	27277		20.9	24.4	35.3	11.7	7.6	54719	56938				9.3	13.1	31.6	32.6	13.5	162279

ZIP CODE		FINANCIAL SERVICES				THE HOME						ENTERTAINMENT						PERSONAL			
						Home Improvements		Furnishings													
#	POST OFFICE NAME	Auto Loan	Home Loan	Invest-ments	Retire-ment Plans	Home Repair	Lawn & Garden	Comput-ers & Hard-ware-Personal	Major Appli-ances	TV, Radio, Sound Equip-ment	Furni-ture	Dine out/ Carry out	Sports Equip-ment	Fees & Tickets	Toys & Games	Travel	Cable TV	Apparel & Services	Auto Repairs	Health Insur-ance	Pets & Supplies
24477	STUARTS DRAFT	87	92	85	93	91	96	85	91	86	83	86	69	87	87	88	88	60	87	93	106
24479	SWOOPE	88	80	79	83	82	94	79	88	81	72	80	67	73	83	79	86	55	82	91	103
24482	VERONA	83	79	74	82	79	88	79	83	80	74	79	64	76	81	78	83	55	81	88	98
24483	VESUVIUS	82	72	73	75	74	86	72	81	75	65	73	62	65	76	71	79	50	75	84	95
24484	WARM SPRINGS	83	73	100	71	77	91	70	86	74	67	74	62	65	72	75	80	49	80	89	99
24485	WEST AUGUSTA	78	62	98	61	68	82	63	79	66	59	65	58	54	63	67	70	43	73	78	92
24486	WEYERS CAVE	84	95	82	98	92	93	85	88	83	85	84	69	90	86	90	84	59	85	87	104
24487	WILLIAMSVILLE	85	68	109	67	74	89	68	86	71	64	70	63	59	67	73	76	47	79	85	100
24501	LYNCHBURG	64	49	49	51	48	57	60	57	63	56	62	45	52	63	53	66	43	61	64	70
24502	LYNCHBURG	83	80	79	80	80	87	80	83	83	79	82	62	79	83	80	86	57	83	89	98
24503	LYNCHBURG	108	112	109	114	112	114	111	110	111	111	111	83	114	110	112	113	78	111	116	129
24504	LYNCHBURG	59	48	47	48	47	57	52	54	59	53	57	39	48	57	48	63	39	56	62	66
24517	ALTAVISTA	80	65	75	63	65	82	68	77	74	64	73	57	60	74	65	81	49	74	84	91
24520	ALTON	73	57	68	57	58	75	58	69	63	54	62	52	49	64	56	68	41	64	72	82
24521	AMHERST	85	75	77	76	75	87	75	83	78	71	77	63	69	79	73	82	53	79	86	98
24522	APPOMATTOX	85	69	78	70	70	88	70	82	75	65	74	62	61	76	68	81	50	76	86	97
24523	BEDFORD	80	68	73	69	69	82	70	77	74	66	73	58	64	75	68	79	50	74	82	91
24526	BIG ISLAND	91	84	82	87	85	98	82	93	85	75	83	70	76	86	82	89	57	86	95	107
24527	BLAIRS	85	64	70	62	63	80	65	74	71	64	70	56	54	74	60	77	47	71	78	90
24528	BROOKNEAL	78	57	69	56	58	77	61	71	68	58	66	54	50	69	57	74	44	68	76	86
24529	BUFFALO JUNCTION	87	63	89	60	64	89	65	80	73	62	71	61	53	73	64	80	48	76	85	97
24530	CALLANDS	85	61	76	59	61	82	63	76	70	60	68	58	50	71	59	76	46	71	79	91
24531	CHATHAM	86	63	85	61	64	87	65	81	72	60	70	61	52	72	63	79	47	75	85	96
24534	CLOVER	69	45	66	42	45	67	48	60	55	46	54	47	36	56	45	62	36	57	64	74
24536	COLEMAN FALLS	92	104	89	107	101	102	93	96	91	93	92	75	99	93	98	91	64	93	95	113
24538	CONCORD	85	73	70	71	71	81	70	77	75	71	74	57	64	78	67	78	50	74	79	92
24539	CRYSTAL HILL	73	47	70	45	47	71	51	64	58	48	57	50	38	59	47	65	38	60	67	78
24540	DANVILLE	73	62	65	62	62	74	64	70	69	62	68	52	58	69	62	74	46	68	76	83
24541	DANVILLE	74	64	67	64	63	75	68	71	73	65	72	53	63	72	65	78	49	72	80	86
24549	DRY FORK	84	75	75	76	75	86	73	80	76	70	75	62	68	78	72	79	51	76	83	96
24550	EVINGTON	91	71	76	69	70	87	71	81	77	70	76	62	60	80	66	83	51	77	85	98
24551	FOREST	106	120	109	120	117	110	109	109	105	112	107	85	116	108	113	104	76	107	104	127
24553	GLADSTONE	82	64	80	64	66	85	65	79	70	60	69	59	55	70	64	76	46	72	81	93
24554	GLADYS	81	58	73	56	59	79	60	72	67	58	66	55	49	68	56	73	44	68	76	87
24555	GLASGOW	78	58	77	57	60	81	62	75	68	56	66	56	51	67	60	74	44	70	81	89
24556	GOODE	98	104	92	106	102	105	95	100	94	94	95	77	98	97	98	96	66	96	100	118
24557	GRETNA	77	55	69	54	56	75	58	69	64	55	63	53	46	66	54	70	42	65	73	83
24558	HALIFAX	82	63	76	63	64	84	65	78	71	60	69	59	55	72	63	77	47	72	81	92
24562	HOWARDSVILLE	93	67	96	65	69	95	68	87	76	64	75	65	55	75	68	84	49	80	91	104
24563	HURT	80	57	66	56	57	76	60	69	66	58	65	53	48	69	54	72	44	66	73	85
24565	JAVA	79	57	73	55	58	78	59	71	65	56	64	54	47	66	56	71	43	66	75	86
24566	KEELING	77	55	64	54	55	73	58	67	64	56	63	52	46	67	52	70	42	64	71	82
24569	LONG ISLAND	78	55	69	54	56	76	58	69	64	55	63	53	46	66	54	70	42	65	73	84
24570	LOWRY	84	61	70	59	60	80	63	73	70	61	69	56	51	73	57	76	46	69	77	89
24571	LYNCH STATION	91	65	88	63	67	90	67	83	74	63	73	63	54	75	65	81	48	77	87	99
24572	MADISON HEIGHTS	79	71	72	71	71	83	71	78	74	66	73	59	66	75	70	78	50	74	82	92
24574	MONROE	82	84	74	87	82	89	80	84	81	77	80	65	80	82	81	83	55	81	87	99
24577	NATHALIE	74	50	72	48	51	73	53	66	60	50	59	51	41	61	50	67	39	62	70	81
24578	NATURAL BRIDGE	83	65	81	65	67	86	66	80	71	61	70	60	56	71	66	77	47	74	83	94
24579	NATURAL BRIDGE STATI	78	59	66	59	59	76	61	70	66	58	65	54	51	69	57	72	44	66	74	84
24580	NELSON	93	66	95	63	68	94	68	86	76	63	74	65	54	76	67	84	49	79	90	103
24586	RINGGOLD	82	65	70	65	65	82	66	76	71	62	70	58	56	74	62	77	47	71	79	91
24588	RUSTBURG	86	78	74	77	77	84	75	81	78	75	77	60	70	80	72	80	53	78	82	96
24589	SCOTTSBURG	79	57	75	55	58	79	59	72	65	55	64	55	47	66	56	72	43	67	75	87
24590	SCOTTSVILLE	87	75	80	75	75	87	75	83	78	73	77	62	68	79	73	82	53	79	86	98
24592	SOUTH BOSTON	72	60	67	60	61	75	63	71	68	59	67	53	56	68	61	73	45	68	77	83
24593	SPOUT SPRING	87	74	76	75	75	90	74	84	78	68	76	64	65	80	72	83	52	78	87	99
24594	SUTHERLIN	83	63	70	62	63	81	65	75	70	62	69	57	54	73	60	76	46	70	78	90
24597	VERNON HILL	84	60	80	58	61	83	62	76	69	59	68	58	50	70	59	75	45	71	80	91
24598	VIRGILINA	86	69	81	69	71	89	70	83	74	64	73	62	60	75	68	80	49	76	86	97
24599	WINGINA	80	58	82	56	60	82	59	75	65	55	64	56	47	65	58	72	42	69	78	89
24602	BANDY	67	46	67	44	47	67	48	61	54	45	53	46	37	54	46	60	35	56	64	73
24603	BIG ROCK	69	45	66	42	45	68	48	60	55	46	54	47	36	56	45	62	36	57	64	74
24605	BLUEFIELD	81	68	83	67	70	87	68	80	74	65	72	59	62	73	69	80	49	76	86	94
24609	CEDAR BLUFF	75	53	73	51	54	75	55	69	62	52	60	52	44	62	53	68	40	64	72	82
24613	FALLS MILLS	59	44	55	43	45	59	48	55	52	44	51	42	39	52	45	57	34	53	59	66
24614	GRUNDY	68	47	66	45	47	68	50	61	57	47	55	47	40	57	48	63	37	58	65	74
24620	HURLEY	58	38	56	36	38	57	41	51	47	39	46	40	30	48	38	52	30	48	54	63
24622	JEWELL RIDGE	64	44	64	42	45	64	46	58	52	43	51	45	36	52	45	58	34	54	61	70
24627	MAVISDALE	66	43	63	40	43	64	46	58	53	44	52	45	34	54	43	59	34	54	61	71
24630	NORTH TAZEWELL	73	54	70	52	55	73	55	68	61	52	60	51	45	62	53	67	40	63	71	81
24631	OAKWOOD	76	50	73	47	49	74	53	67	61	50	60	52	40	62	50	68	40	63	70	82
24634	PILGRIMS KNOB	65	42	62	40	42	63	45	57	52	43	51	44	34	53	42	58	34	53	60	70
24637	POUNDING MILL	76	62	72	62	63	78	62	72	66	59	65	55	54	67	61	71	44	67	74	86
24639	RAVEN	62	40	60	38	40	61	43	54	50	41	49	42	32	50	40	55	32	51	57	67
24641	RICHLANDS	71	49	70	46	49	72	52	65	59	48	58	50	41	59	50	66	38	61	70	79
24646	ROWE	61	41	60	39	41	60	43	55	49	41	48	42	33	50	41	55	32	51	57	66
24649	SWORDS CREEK	61	42	56	40	41	59	44	54	50	42	49	42	34	51	41	55	33	51	57	66
24651	TAZEWELL	77	60	72	60	62	77	63	73	68	59	66	55	54	68	61	73	45	69	77	86
24656	VANSANT	65	43	63	40	43	64	46	57	52	43	51	45	34	53	43	58	34	54	61	70
24657	WHITEWOOD	55	36	53	34	36	54	38	48	44	36	43	38	29	45	36	49	29	46	51	60
	VIRGINIA	115	112	112	114	111	114	112	112	112	112	112	88	111	114	111	113	79	112	112	132
	UNITED STATES	100	100	100	100	100	100	100	100	100	100	100	100	100	100	100	100	100	100	100	100

POPULATION CHANGE

ZIP CODE			POPULATION			2000-2009 ANNUAL RATE		HOUSEHOLDS					FAMILIES		
#	POST OFFICE NAME	COUNTY FIPS CODE	2000	2009	2014	% Rate	State Centile	2000	2009	2014	% Annual Rate 2000-2009	2009 Average HH Size	2000	2009	% Annual Rate 2000-2009
98001	AUBURN	033	25408	30114	32523	1.9	81	8836	10619	11491	2.0	2.83	6839	8165	1.9
98002	AUBURN	033	30786	31626	32581	0.3	16	12549	13005	13438	0.4	2.39	7562	7618	0.1
98003	FEDERAL WAY	033	41720	43767	45054	0.5	28	16621	17392	17906	0.5	2.48	10461	10675	0.2
98004	BELLEVUE	033	22265	25765	27440	1.6	73	10316	12542	13591	2.1	2.01	5806	6405	1.1
98005	BELLEVUE	033	16824	17656	18203	0.5	28	7460	7874	8119	0.6	2.21	4400	4543	0.3
98006	BELLEVUE	033	35018	36790	38117	0.5	28	12942	13824	14382	0.7	2.66	9983	10489	0.5
98007	BELLEVUE	033	23182	23959	24500	0.4	23	10284	10706	10980	0.4	2.22	5676	5711	0.1
98008	BELLEVUE	033	23651	24059	24474	0.2	12	9135	9388	9589	0.3	2.53	6480	6521	0.1
98010	BLACK DIAMOND	033	4317	4693	5171	0.9	45	1582	1758	1937	1.1	2.67	1230	1339	0.9
98011	BOTHELL	033	26177	30081	32126	1.5	69	10371	12139	13007	1.7	2.47	6881	7862	1.5
98012	BOTHELL	061	39203	51238	57222	2.9	93	14643	19554	21913	3.2	2.62	10646	13978	3.0
98014	CARNATION	033	6792	7470	7862	1.0	49	2341	2599	2744	1.1	2.87	1854	2029	1.0
98019	DUVALL	033	8188	9795	10603	2.0	83	2829	3429	3723	2.1	2.85	2290	2743	2.0
98020	EDMONDS	061	17621	18948	19826	0.8	40	7838	8662	9136	1.1	2.16	4941	5335	0.8
98021	BOTHELL	061	21541	26638	29184	2.3	87	7914	10029	11056	2.6	2.65	5905	7352	2.4
98022	ENUMCLAW	033	21902	22831	23507	0.5	28	8068	8459	8728	0.5	2.67	5822	5993	0.3
98023	FEDERAL WAY	033	48398	50695	52173	0.5	28	17336	18254	18806	0.6	2.78	12692	13124	0.4
98024	FALL CITY	033	4334	5581	6174	2.8	92	1626	2053	2264	2.6	2.71	1226	1530	2.4
98026	EDMONDS	061	35657	36885	38057	0.4	23	13846	14744	15302	0.7	2.48	9757	10212	0.5
98027	ISSAQUAH	033	25539	28976	30808	1.4	66	9914	11430	12170	1.6	2.51	6978	7871	1.3
98028	KENMORE	033	18718	20846	22045	1.2	57	7334	8310	8835	1.4	2.49	5000	5472	1.0
98029	ISSAQUAH	033	14155	20620	23129	4.2	98	5288	7775	8745	4.3	2.63	3912	5649	4.1
98030	KENT	033	31096	33514	35102	0.8	40	11445	12350	12937	0.8	2.69	7734	8161	0.6
98031	KENT	033	34301	37255	39021	0.9	45	12187	13370	14030	1.0	2.78	8943	9650	0.8
98032	KENT	033	27538	30960	32284	1.3	61	11771	13116	13681	1.2	2.33	6418	7108	1.1
98033	KIRKLAND	033	31142	32261	33270	0.4	23	14052	14870	15403	0.6	2.15	7889	8141	0.3
98034	KIRKLAND	033	40264	41971	43369	0.4	23	16275	17333	17975	0.7	2.39	10194	10605	0.4
98036	LYNNWOOD	061	31762	35794	38110	1.3	61	11957	13761	14716	1.5	2.58	7903	8941	1.3
98037	LYNNWOOD	061	23025	26620	28574	1.6	73	8701	10310	11133	1.9	2.56	5920	6868	1.6
98038	MAPLE VALLEY	033	22522	28477	31270	2.6	90	7680	9787	10749	2.7	2.91	6279	7944	2.6
98039	MEDINA	033	3011	2985	3007	-0.1	4	1111	1108	1115	0.0	2.69	904	889	-0.2
98040	MERCER ISLAND	033	22036	22950	23659	0.4	23	8437	9024	9369	0.7	2.52	6273	6555	0.5
98042	KENT	033	36945	43131	46284	1.7	75	12444	14675	15774	1.8	2.93	10171	11880	1.7
98043	MOUNTLAKE TERRACE	061	20400	21302	22016	0.5	28	7969	8551	8891	0.8	2.48	5045	5283	0.5
98045	NORTH BEND	033	13755	15043	15789	1.0	49	5078	5633	5934	1.1	2.65	3796	4141	0.9
98047	PACIFIC	033	4920	5163	5341	0.5	28	1740	1836	1899	0.6	2.81	1265	1310	0.4
98051	RAVENSDALE	033	2878	4676	5349	5.4	99	1024	1658	1895	5.3	2.82	771	1223	5.1
98052	REDMOND	033	49713	55726	59016	1.2	57	20456	23299	24751	1.4	2.36	12583	14020	1.2
98053	REDMOND	033	11801	20391	23871	6.1	99	3812	6497	7606	5.9	3.14	3280	5639	6.0
98055	RENTON	033	18396	22506	24451	2.2	86	7661	9491	10329	2.3	2.36	4488	5432	2.1
98056	RENTON	033	27143	30818	32807	1.4	66	11718	13592	14539	1.6	2.26	6967	7823	1.3
98057	RENTON	033	9156	10265	10856	1.2	57	4373	4988	5309	1.4	2.03	2096	2277	0.9
98058	RENTON	033	37299	42376	45023	1.4	66	13448	15472	16468	1.5	2.74	10156	11564	1.4
98059	RENTON	033	22286	28270	31221	2.6	90	8362	10635	11731	2.6	2.66	6109	7641	2.4
98065	SNOQUALMIE	033	4413	12469	14996	11.9	100	1582	4494	5443	11.9	2.74	1168	3380	12.2
98070	VASHON	033	10123	10839	11299	0.7	35	4193	4581	4797	1.0	2.36	2839	3034	0.7
98072	WOODINVILLE	033	21751	23419	24422	0.8	40	7706	8434	8821	1.0	2.77	5868	6296	0.8
98074	SAMMAMISH	033	20626	24062	25904	1.7	75	6852	8121	8772	1.9	2.96	5845	6865	1.8
98075	SAMMAMISH	033	13882	19206	21656	3.6	96	4406	5939	6661	3.3	3.21	3820	5118	3.2
98077	WOODINVILLE	033	13896	14344	15059	0.3	16	4378	4548	4769	0.4	3.15	3890	4004	0.3
98087	LYNNWOOD	061	19992	28762	33093	4.0	97	8068	11743	13544	4.1	2.44	5039	7040	3.7
98092	AUBURN	033	26720	40105	45023	4.5	98	9132	13933	15727	4.7	2.85	7208	10974	4.6
98101	SEATTLE	033	8955	10233	11028	1.5	69	5918	7000	7610	1.8	1.28	1007	1113	1.1
98102	SEATTLE	033	20456	21229	21887	0.4	23	13179	13876	14340	0.6	1.52	2579	2573	0.0
98103	SEATTLE	033	41948	43798	45228	0.5	28	21138	22448	23258	0.7	1.93	7778	7908	0.2
98104	SEATTLE	033	13119	14123	14668	0.8	40	5414	6066	6414	1.2	1.53	1170	1263	0.8
98105	SEATTLE	033	37310	39029	40378	0.5	28	14967	16187	16884	0.9	2.11	5472	5619	0.3
98106	SEATTLE	033	23343	25054	26204	0.8	40	8474	9143	9566	0.8	2.73	5368	5639	0.5
98107	SEATTLE	033	19155	20205	20936	0.6	31	10180	11008	11481	0.8	1.81	3723	3825	0.3
98108	SEATTLE	033	22018	24251	25507	1.0	49	7371	8008	8391	0.9	2.98	4883	5226	0.7
98109	SEATTLE	033	14856	16754	17900	1.3	61	8597	9951	10775	1.6	1.60	2412	2575	0.7
98110	BAINBRIDGE ISLAND	035	20308	22920	24106	1.3	61	7979	9169	9681	1.5	2.48	5785	6522	1.3
98112	SEATTLE	033	19674	20043	20502	0.2	12	9378	9765	10039	0.4	2.03	4235	4236	0.0
98115	SEATTLE	033	42892	45046	46486	0.5	28	19223	20510	21254	0.7	2.17	10186	10457	0.3
98116	SEATTLE	033	20380	21030	21599	0.3	16	10338	10907	11253	0.6	1.91	4828	4901	0.2
98117	SEATTLE	033	29505	29940	30575	0.2	12	13059	13406	13716	0.3	2.21	7245	7223	0.0
98118	SEATTLE	033	40556	44330	46344	1.0	49	13864	15037	15683	0.9	2.90	9228	9826	0.7
98119	SEATTLE	033	20801	22183	22773	0.7	35	10922	11718	12137	0.8	1.66	3393	3399	0.0
98121	SEATTLE	033	8748	11987	13628	3.5	95	6012	8486	9772	3.8	1.29	910	1240	3.4
98122	SEATTLE	033	28057	31517	32886	1.3	61	13589	15058	15867	1.1	1.84	4144	4305	0.4
98125	SEATTLE	033	34994	37885	39577	0.9	45	15967	17369	18141	0.9	2.16	7983	8420	0.6
98126	SEATTLE	033	19296	20598	21438	0.7	35	8603	9332	9749	0.9	2.16	4611	4846	0.5
98133	SEATTLE	033	42798	44455	45704	0.4	23	19059	20021	20645	0.5	2.17	9902	10056	0.2
98134	SEATTLE	033	1350	1339	1352	-0.1	4	432	435	442	0.1	2.01	157	151	-0.4
98136	SEATTLE	033	14015	14360	14725	0.3	16	6731	7023	7225	0.5	2.03	3454	3486	0.1
98144	SEATTLE	033	24809	27447	28882	1.1	52	9686	10773	11337	1.2	2.47	5398	5782	0.7
98146	SEATTLE	033	25724	26610	27237	0.4	23	9782	10056	10281	0.3	2.62	6406	6439	0.1
98148	SEATTLE	033	8640	8790	8950	0.2	12	3801	3889	3965	0.2	2.26	2120	2116	0.0
98155	SEATTLE	033	33684	34658	35498	0.3	16	13009	13516	13877	0.4	2.49	8634	8771	0.2
98166	SEATTLE	033	21139	21330	21983	0.1	8	8984	9160	9477	0.2	2.32	5848	5832	0.0
98168	SEATTLE	033	33044	34429	35268	0.4	23	12764	13117	13397	0.3	2.62	7682	7688	0.0
98177	SEATTLE	033	18403	18957	19402	0.3	16	7305	7591	7792	0.4	2.43	5089	5180	0.2
98178	SEATTLE	033	20878	21988	22733	0.6	31	7965	8448	8751	0.6	2.59	5317	5488	0.3
98188	SEATTLE	033	19526	20375	20880	0.5	28	8188	8379	8555	0.2	2.43	4760	4756	0.0
98195	SEATTLE	033	2180	7479	7479	14.3	100	0	1	1	0.0	6.00	0	1	0.0
98198	SEATTLE	033	35073	36178	37151	0.3	16	13276	13689	14083	0.3	2.48	8464	8519	0.1
98199	SEATTLE	033	19156	19568	19972	0.2	12	9077	9399	9622	0.4	2.07	4782	4772	0.0
98201	EVERETT	061	30286	31533	33432	0.4	23	11812	12747	13635	0.8	2.22	6169	6442	0.5
98203	EVERETT	061	32060	34576	36128	0.8	40	12377	13575	14243	1.0	2.51	8389	9050	0.8
98204	EVERETT	061	30851	37002	40109	2.0	83	12639	15229	16521	2.0	2.42	7304	8511	1.7
98205	EVERETT	061	12282	14788	16317	2.0	83	4191	5088	5618	2.1	2.90	3307	3983	2.0
98208	EVERETT	061	45603	52378	56351	1.5	69	16807	19607	21176	1.7	2.65	12158	14100	1.6
98220	ACME	073	521	563	591	0.8	40	185	204	214	1.1	2.76	135	147	0.9
98221	ANACORTES	057	18827	21724	23282	1.6	73	7915	9106	9737	1.5	2.36	5475	6241	1.4
98223	ARLINGTON	061	34003	41309	45241	2.1	85	11997	14901	16403	2.4	2.76	9121	11149	2.2
	WASHINGTON					1.4					1.4	2.53			1.2
	UNITED STATES					1.0					1.1	2.59			0.9

ZIP CODE #	POST OFFICE NAME	RACE (%) White 2000	White 2009	Black 2000	Black 2009	Asian/Pacific 2000	Asian/Pacific 2009	% Hispanic Origin 2000	% Hispanic Origin 2009	2009 AGE DISTRIBUTION (%) 0-4	5-9	10-14	15-19	20-24	25-44	45-64	65-84	85+	18+	MEDIAN AGE 2009	% 2009 Males	% 2009 Females
98001	AUBURN	84.3	80.7	2.7	3.1	6.3	8.0	4.2	5.8	6.4	6.9	7.3	7.7	5.1	26.6	30.2	9.0	0.8	74.6	38.3	49.9	50.1
98002	AUBURN	82.6	79.2	2.4	2.7	3.7	4.6	8.2	11.1	7.9	7.0	6.5	6.7	7.5	28.4	23.5	10.5	2.0	74.6	34.6	49.4	50.6
98003	FEDERAL WAY	68.2	63.0	8.6	9.3	12.1	14.1	8.5	11.2	8.0	6.8	6.2	6.6	9.1	29.1	23.0	9.6	1.5	75.1	33.0	48.9	51.1
98004	BELLEVUE	85.2	81.3	1.3	1.4	9.6	12.7	3.2	4.4	4.4	4.4	4.8	4.9	5.7	27.4	28.2	16.0	4.3	83.5	43.9	48.5	51.5
98005	BELLEVUE	74.8	70.7	2.0	2.2	17.0	20.0	5.3	6.8	5.3	5.0	5.0	4.6	5.6	32.6	26.8	12.7	2.4	82.0	39.6	49.8	50.2
98006	BELLEVUE	75.1	70.3	1.6	1.8	19.0	22.9	2.7	3.7	5.7	6.4	7.2	6.8	4.8	24.7	32.2	11.1	1.2	76.4	41.5	49.6	50.4
98007	BELLEVUE	65.0	59.6	2.8	3.0	22.7	26.2	9.6	12.2	6.2	5.2	4.7	4.9	8.8	37.7	21.5	9.3	1.7	81.1	34.2	51.5	48.5
98008	BELLEVUE	77.6	73.0	1.9	2.1	14.2	17.0	5.9	8.1	5.8	5.8	6.2	5.9	5.0	25.6	29.3	14.4	2.2	78.7	42.5	49.9	50.1
98010	BLACK DIAMOND	93.8	92.5	0.1	0.1	0.9	1.2	2.2	3.1	6.5	6.9	7.4	6.8	4.7	27.0	30.8	8.9	1.0	74.7	39.2	51.1	48.9
98011	BOTHELL	87.0	83.9	1.3	1.5	5.9	7.5	4.8	6.4	6.4	6.5	6.6	6.5	6.0	30.3	28.3	8.1	1.3	76.6	37.0	49.1	50.9
98012	BOTHELL	84.9	82.8	1.3	1.4	8.6	9.8	4.0	5.3	7.0	7.0	7.2	6.9	6.0	29.9	27.4	7.4	1.0	74.4	36.2	49.2	50.8
98014	CARNATION	93.4	91.8	0.2	0.2	2.0	2.7	3.0	4.3	7.1	8.1	8.4	8.2	4.4	25.5	32.0	5.6	0.7	71.0	38.3	50.8	49.2
98019	DUVALL	93.8	92.1	0.4	0.5	1.7	2.2	3.8	5.5	8.1	8.6	8.6	7.1	3.9	30.7	28.3	4.4	0.3	70.0	36.2	49.8	50.2
98020	EDMONDS	91.4	89.6	0.9	1.0	4.1	5.0	2.3	3.2	4.2	4.4	4.9	5.1	4.4	21.3	30.7	20.6	4.3	83.3	48.9	46.4	53.6
98021	BOTHELL	87.6	85.0	1.0	1.1	6.6	8.2	3.3	4.7	6.1	6.7	7.2	7.2	4.8	28.0	30.0	8.7	1.4	75.3	39.2	49.1	50.9
98022	ENUMCLAW	92.9	91.5	0.3	0.3	0.8	1.0	3.8	5.3	6.4	6.7	7.1	7.6	6.1	25.4	28.8	10.0	1.9	74.9	38.3	49.3	50.7
98023	FEDERAL WAY	71.0	66.4	7.0	7.5	13.7	16.4	6.1	8.0	7.6	7.2	7.1	7.2	7.5	29.3	26.1	7.2	0.8	73.7	33.7	49.4	50.6
98024	FALL CITY	93.4	90.7	0.6	0.8	1.3	2.8	2.9	4.0	5.7	6.6	7.7	7.7	4.1	24.1	34.4	8.6	1.1	75.0	41.6	50.8	49.2
98026	EDMONDS	84.7	81.7	1.5	1.7	8.1	9.8	3.6	4.9	5.7	6.0	6.5	6.6	5.7	24.7	31.6	11.6	1.6	77.7	41.4	48.6	51.4
98027	ISSAQUAH	89.3	86.3	1.0	1.1	5.4	7.3	3.3	4.5	5.9	6.5	7.2	6.7	4.5	27.0	32.2	8.8	1.3	76.1	40.5	49.7	50.3
98028	KENMORE	86.5	83.6	1.4	1.6	7.5	9.1	3.5	5.1	5.6	5.8	6.4	6.5	5.7	27.5	30.9	10.0	1.5	78.0	40.2	49.5	50.5
98029	ISSAQUAH	81.5	80.9	0.8	0.8	13.6	13.7	2.7	3.5	8.5	8.9	8.8	6.9	3.5	28.5	25.6	7.4	2.0	69.3	36.9	48.4	51.6
98030	KENT	70.4	65.5	8.9	9.7	10.3	12.6	7.1	9.4	9.1	8.0	7.5	7.2	7.2	30.9	22.7	6.2	1.1	71.0	31.7	49.2	50.8
98031	KENT	70.3	65.4	6.0	6.5	15.2	18.1	5.3	7.1	7.7	7.5	7.4	7.7	7.3	28.9	25.7	7.0	0.8	72.8	33.7	49.7	50.3
98032	KENT	69.4	65.2	9.0	9.7	9.1	10.6	10.7	13.4	7.7	6.6	5.7	5.9	8.3	32.2	23.8	8.6	1.2	76.7	33.6	49.7	50.3
98033	KIRKLAND	87.5	84.5	1.2	1.3	6.9	8.7	3.2	4.5	5.1	4.9	5.1	5.3	5.8	31.3	31.1	9.9	1.4	81.9	40.6	49.4	50.6
98034	KIRKLAND	82.5	78.7	1.8	2.1	9.7	11.8	5.1	7.0	6.3	6.1	6.1	6.0	6.3	31.9	27.9	8.2	1.3	77.9	37.4	49.3	50.7
98036	LYNNWOOD	77.8	74.1	2.7	2.9	11.5	13.5	6.5	8.7	7.1	6.9	6.8	6.9	6.8	29.0	26.6	8.2	1.7	75.1	35.7	49.5	50.5
98037	LYNNWOOD	76.8	72.8	2.4	2.6	14.6	17.4	4.5	5.9	6.8	6.5	6.4	6.2	6.5	28.7	26.6	10.4	1.8	76.5	37.0	49.1	50.9
98038	MAPLE VALLEY	92.1	90.0	1.0	1.1	2.2	2.9	2.9	4.3	8.2	8.4	8.7	7.7	4.7	29.0	27.0	5.8	0.6	69.7	35.5	50.1	49.9
98039	MEDINA	92.6	90.8	0.2	0.2	5.0	6.4	1.4	1.9	6.7	8.1	9.8	7.8	2.9	16.8	32.0	13.6	2.3	70.2	43.6	49.8	50.2
98040	MERCER ISLAND	84.1	80.3	1.1	1.3	11.9	14.9	1.9	2.6	4.3	5.3	6.9	7.5	4.5	17.0	34.3	16.4	3.8	78.5	47.8	47.9	52.1
98042	KENT	87.7	84.9	2.2	2.6	4.5	5.7	3.6	5.0	6.7	7.3	7.7	7.8	5.3	27.3	29.9	7.4	0.7	73.4	37.2	50.2	49.8
98043	MOUNTLAKE TERRACE	77.8	73.9	2.5	2.7	11.2	13.3	5.7	7.6	6.6	6.2	6.0	6.6	7.4	31.6	25.7	8.6	1.4	77.4	35.5	49.4	50.6
98045	NORTH BEND	93.5	92.0	0.5	0.6	1.8	2.3	2.7	3.8	7.8	8.1	8.5	6.8	3.9	30.6	27.0	6.1	1.2	71.1	36.3	51.3	48.7
98047	PACIFIC	85.2	82.0	1.5	1.7	5.1	6.4	6.3	8.7	8.4	7.7	7.3	7.6	8.0	28.9	25.0	6.4	0.6	72.2	31.9	49.4	50.6
98051	RAVENSDALE	95.0	93.9	0.6	0.5	0.6	0.9	1.8	2.9	5.6	7.5	8.3	7.9	4.1	28.5	31.1	6.3	0.6	73.7	38.9	51.9	48.1
98052	REDMOND	80.0	76.0	1.4	1.6	12.6	15.0	5.5	7.7	6.2	5.9	6.0	5.7	6.6	33.5	26.1	7.9	2.1	78.4	36.5	50.3	49.7
98053	REDMOND	91.1	88.8	0.7	1.0	4.5	5.6	2.8	4.0	7.0	8.5	9.5	7.9	3.6	23.6	33.7	5.5	0.5	69.7	39.5	50.7	49.3
98055	RENTON	63.0	57.7	9.4	9.9	18.4	21.7	6.1	7.7	7.0	6.2	5.8	5.9	8.1	31.1	25.7	8.7	1.4	77.6	35.4	49.3	50.7
98056	RENTON	74.8	70.5	4.9	5.3	11.6	13.4	7.4	10.2	6.9	6.2	5.9	5.5	5.9	31.4	26.0	10.2	2.0	77.7	37.7	49.4	50.6
98057	RENTON	61.9	58.5	15.9	16.3	12.7	14.3	7.3	9.6	5.9	5.1	4.8	5.2	7.4	30.7	25.8	11.6	3.6	81.3	38.8	49.4	50.6
98058	RENTON	76.1	71.6	5.0	5.6	12.5	15.4	3.6	4.7	6.5	7.0	7.3	7.1	5.5	27.1	30.0	8.8	0.7	74.7	38.2	49.7	50.3
98059	RENTON	81.0	77.7	2.5	2.6	10.4	12.7	4.6	5.9	6.6	6.8	7.0	6.5	5.7	29.0	29.6	8.1	0.7	75.7	37.7	50.2	49.8
98065	SNOQUALMIE	91.0	81.0	0.9	3.6	1.9	3.0	3.3	6.9	7.2	8.1	9.0	7.4	4.0	25.4	31.8	6.4	0.7	70.2	38.6	50.4	49.6
98070	VASHON	93.6	92.1	0.5	0.6	1.6	2.0	2.6	3.7	4.2	5.2	6.3	6.2	4.0	19.8	38.5	13.7	2.0	80.1	47.2	48.6	51.4
98072	WOODINVILLE	88.7	86.2	0.8	0.9	4.7	5.9	4.9	6.4	5.8	6.5	7.6	7.6	5.1	25.7	32.4	8.0	1.4	75.3	39.7	50.1	49.9
98074	SAMMAMISH	87.7	84.4	0.9	1.1	7.9	10.2	2.6	3.7	7.9	8.6	9.4	7.4	4.0	28.4	29.3	4.6	0.4	69.1	36.4	50.7	49.3
98075	SAMMAMISH	88.5	85.2	0.7	0.9	7.7	10.0	2.3	3.1	7.9	9.3	9.8	7.9	3.7	22.8	30.3	7.2	1.0	67.8	38.0	50.0	50.0
98077	WOODINVILLE	91.8	89.7	0.7	0.8	3.9	4.9	2.7	3.8	6.3	8.2	10.1	8.7	3.4	23.3	34.5	4.9	0.4	69.3	39.6	50.8	49.2
98087	LYNNWOOD	78.4	74.5	2.4	2.6	10.9	13.0	5.9	7.9	7.7	6.8	6.4	6.1	7.7	33.7	23.6	7.1	1.0	75.7	33.1	49.8	50.2
98092	AUBURN	86.1	85.1	1.7	2.0	3.5	4.2	4.1	5.2	6.6	7.1	7.6	7.9	5.4	26.1	30.1	8.3	0.8	73.7	37.9	50.0	50.0
98101	SEATTLE	72.6	68.6	10.5	11.5	8.2	9.7	5.3	8.1	1.7	1.2	1.0	2.4	9.6	37.7	25.8	14.6	6.1	95.5	42.6	52.7	47.3
98102	SEATTLE	85.0	81.8	3.3	3.8	6.2	7.8	3.9	5.4	1.8	1.2	1.1	1.8	10.7	53.0	22.8	6.6	1.1	95.3	34.1	53.9	46.1
98103	SEATTLE	85.3	82.1	2.3	2.7	6.4	8.0	4.0	5.5	4.2	3.0	2.7	3.1	9.3	45.3	24.4	6.4	1.7	88.3	34.9	49.7	50.3
98104	SEATTLE	49.4	44.8	20.1	21.0	20.5	23.2	7.5	9.5	2.4	1.8	1.5	3.1	7.8	45.0	25.4	10.8	2.0	93.1	38.8	65.1	34.9
98105	SEATTLE	79.1	74.4	2.0	2.8	13.0	15.8	3.6	4.9	3.8	3.1	3.3	9.7	24.5	29.6	18.0	6.4	1.5	87.6	27.4	50.9	49.1
98106	SEATTLE	47.6	42.2	11.8	12.4	24.4	27.1	10.9	13.7	7.5	6.6	6.3	7.0	7.6	32.0	24.8	7.1	1.1	75.4	33.6	49.5	50.5
98107	SEATTLE	87.2	84.4	2.0	2.2	4.0	5.0	4.7	6.5	3.9	3.3	3.3	3.4	6.9	40.0	27.3	9.3	2.8	87.7	39.1	48.7	51.3
98108	SEATTLE	26.4	22.1	14.9	15.5	44.0	46.3	12.6	14.7	7.1	6.7	6.3	6.9	7.5	29.6	24.4	9.7	1.8	75.9	35.2	50.6	49.4
98109	SEATTLE	86.5	82.3	3.1	4.5	5.7	7.2	3.3	4.8	3.0	2.2	2.0	2.2	8.4	46.2	24.8	8.6	2.5	91.7	37.0	49.9	50.1
98110	BAINBRIDGE ISLAND	92.9	91.2	0.3	0.3	2.5	3.2	2.2	3.0	4.5	5.5	6.9	7.5	4.7	17.3	37.6	13.5	2.5	78.2	47.1	48.5	51.5
98112	SEATTLE	83.0	80.2	8.9	9.9	3.9	4.8	2.7	3.7	4.4	4.2	4.5	4.0	6.2	33.5	29.5	10.9	2.8	84.2	41.0	48.0	52.0
98115	SEATTLE	84.3	80.9	1.8	2.1	8.6	10.7	3.0	4.1	5.1	4.5	4.7	4.2	6.2	33.8	28.5	10.1	2.9	83.2	40.0	48.4	51.6
98116	SEATTLE	88.7	86.2	1.7	2.0	3.9	4.9	3.4	4.8	4.5	4.3	4.4	4.1	4.9	30.0	33.1	11.5	3.2	84.4	43.8	48.2	51.8
98117	SEATTLE	87.8	85.3	1.5	1.7	4.9	6.0	3.7	5.2	5.0	4.7	4.8	4.7	5.4	31.6	31.9	9.3	2.6	82.6	41.6	48.3	51.7
98118	SEATTLE	27.2	23.3	26.0	25.8	35.7	39.0	6.9	8.3	6.7	6.3	6.3	6.6	7.0	28.3	26.3	10.3	2.0	76.7	36.9	49.2	50.8
98119	SEATTLE	88.3	85.7	2.0	2.4	4.8	5.9	3.2	4.5	2.6	2.2	1.9	7.6	13.2	39.6	23.5	7.6	1.9	92.0	34.0	47.4	52.6
98121	SEATTLE	75.4	71.0	8.5	9.6	8.4	10.0	5.2	7.8	1.5	1.0	0.8	4.9	10.0	42.6	26.2	10.8	2.3	96.3	38.5	56.4	43.6
98122	SEATTLE	57.7	53.8	25.0	25.5	7.7	9.8	7.1	9.2	3.5	2.9	2.8	7.8	13.2	39.4	21.7	7.1	1.6	88.7	33.1	51.9	48.1
98125	SEATTLE	70.7	65.7	5.0	5.5	15.3	18.3	5.8	7.7	4.9	4.5	4.3	4.4	7.4	33.3	27.1	10.9	3.2	83.8	39.0	49.0	51.0
98126	SEATTLE	71.1	65.9	7.8	8.8	11.7	14.0	6.4	8.5	6.4	6.1	5.8	5.3	6.1	30.2	28.0	9.3	2.8	78.6	39.3	47.8	52.2
98133	SEATTLE	73.1	68.4	4.2	4.6	14.7	17.5	5.2	6.9	4.8	4.5	4.4	5.1	7.3	30.4	27.7	12.1	3.7	83.4	40.5	48.4	51.6
98134	SEATTLE	47.8	43.6	17.4	18.1	22.1	24.6	9.0	11.5	2.7	2.2	1.6	2.4	8.0	34.4	35.5	10.5	2.8	92.4	44.0	62.9	37.1
98136	SEATTLE	88.0	85.3	2.3	2.7	4.1	5.1	3.8	5.3	4.8	4.7	5.0	4.4	4.9	28.5	33.4	11.0	3.4	82.8	43.7	47.5	52.5
98144	SEATTLE	35.3	31.1	22.2	23.4	31.2	32.5	8.6	11.2	5.7	5.5	5.5	5.9	6.5	31.2	26.7	10.7	2.3	79.6	38.5	49.2	50.8
98146	SEATTLE	64.7	59.8	5.6	5.9	17.0	19.2	11.2	14.3	6.6	6.6	6.6	6.5	5.7	27.1	28.0	10.8	2.1	76.2	38.8	49.3	50.7
98148	SEATTLE	73.2	69.1	6.0	6.5	9.0	10.5	10.3	13.3	6.3	5.6	5.4	6.5	8.0	28.6	27.8	10.2	1.5	79.0	37.4	49.7	50.3
98155	SEATTLE	78.6	74.4	2.7	3.1	12.1	14.7	3.5	4.8	5.1	5.3	5.8	6.2	5.6	26.4	31.9	11.5	2.2	79.9	42.1	48.7	51.3
98166	SEATTLE	84.1	81.0	3.4	3.8	4.6	5.6	7.6	10.1	5.2	5.2	5.6	6.2	6.3	22.4	31.5	14.7	3.0	80.3	44.3	48.3	51.7
98168	SEATTLE	62.2	56.9	8.7	9.1	13.7	15.7	13.5	17.3	7.4	6.5	6.1	6.4	8.0	30.2	25.5	8.6	1.3	76.3	34.9	51.3	48.7
98177	SEATTLE	87.4	84.6	1.3	1.5	6.9	8.6	2.6	3.6	4.3	4.8	5.9	6.0	4.8	20.6	34.0	15.6	4.0	81.2	47.2	47.9	52.1
98178	SEATTLE	40.7	36.2	26.5	27.2	24.3	27.1	4.4	5.6	5.9	5.9	6.1	6.6	6.0	27.4	28.4	11.6	2.2	78.1	39.7	48.9	51.1
98188	SEATTLE	62.4	57.7	9.8	10.3	13.9	15.7	11.2	14.3	6.9	6.2	5.8	6.2	6.8	30.0	26.4	10.2	1.4	77.5	36.9	51.7	48.3
98195	SEATTLE	57.2	54.1	2.8	3.2	30.9	32.5	3.2	4.6	0.8	0.7	0.7	45.1	35.1	14.3	2.1	1.0	0.2	92.8	20.4	53.2	46.8
98198	SEATTLE	71.2	67.2	8.2	8.8	10.2	11.8	8.7	11.3	6.7	6.2	5.9	6.3	7.3	28.6	25.2	10.8	3.1	77.5	37.1	49.4	50.6
98199	SEATTLE	87.3	84.4	1.7	2.0	6.1	7.7	3.4	4.8	5.1	5.0	5.2	4.2	5.3	28.8	31.4	12.1	2.9	82.2	42.8	48.3	51.7
98201	EVERETT	83.0	80.3	3.5	3.7	4.0	4.8	6.6	8.9	6.7	5.9	5.3	6.9	10.7	29.2	23.4	9.3	2.6	78.6	34.0	52.8	47.2
98203	EVERETT	85.8	82.9	2.0	2.2	6.0	7.4	5.0	6.8	7.1	6.8	6.7	6.7	6.0	27.9	27.2	9.6	1.9	75.1	37.3	49.3	50.7
98204	EVERETT	74.8	71.1	4.1	4.4	9.1	10.5	10.8	13.7	9.2	7.3	6.1	6.9	10.9	32.9	19.7	6.1	0.9	73.6	29.4	50.5	49.5
98205	EVERETT	90.9	88.6	1.0	1.1	2.5	3.3	4.3	6.1	9.3	9.0	8.9	7.2	4.8	32.1	22.7	5.4	0.7	68.1	33.3	50.9	49.1
98208	EVERETT	82.0	78.8	2.7	3.0	8.4	10.1	4.9	6.5	8.2	7.8	7.5	6.7	6.2	30.6	24.9	7.0	1.1	72.4	34.3	49.6	50.4
98220	ACME	88.9	86.9	0.2	0.2	0.6	0.7	5.0	6.7	4.4	6.2	9.6	8.7	5.7	23.3	32.5	8.5	1.1	73.7	39.3	50.3	49.7
98221	ANACORTES	93.4	92.0	0.3	0.3	1.6	2.0	2.7	4.0	4.8	5.3	6.0	6.1	4.5	19.7	33.1	17.4	3.2	80.1	47.2	48.7	51.3
98223	ARLINGTON	92.6	90.9	0.6	0.6	1.6	2.0	3.6	5.1	7.3	7.1	7.2	7.2	5.9	27.2	28.2	8.8	1.2	74.0	36.7	49.8	50.2
	WASHINGTON	81.8	79.0	3.2	3.4	5.9	6.9	7.5	9.7	6.7	6.5	6.5	7.0	7.0	27.4	27.0	10.1	1.8	76.3	36.9	49.8	50.2
	UNITED STATES	75.1	72.0	12.3	12.7	3.8	4.6	12.5	15.7	6.8	6.7	6.6	7.1	6.9	27.0	26.0	10.9	1.9	75.7	36.9	49.2	50.8

ZIP CODE #	POST OFFICE NAME	2009 Per Capita Income	2009 HH Income Base	2009 HOUSEHOLD INCOME DISTRIBUTION (%) Less than $25,000	$25,000 to $49,999	$50,000 to $99,999	$100,000 to $149,999	$150,000 or More	MEDIAN HOUSEHOLD INCOME 2009	2014	2009 National Centile	2009 State Centile	2009 Home Value Base	2009 HOME VALUE DISTRIBUTION (%) Less than $50,000	$50,000 to $89,999	$90,000 to $174,999	$175,000 to $399,999	$400,000 or More	2009 Median Home Value
98001	AUBURN	31429	10619	10.1	13.1	44.1	24.3	8.5	80022	85787	92	92	8507	0.9	0.9	9.1	74.7	14.4	265303
98002	AUBURN	24226	13005	23.9	26.9	37.6	9.1	2.6	49112	50605	59	47	6342	11.9	11.1	23.1	51.8	2.1	183201
98003	FEDERAL WAY	27896	17392	16.6	24.5	41.7	10.8	6.5	57948	60301	75	65	9122	7.2	6.4	18.1	58.3	9.9	227405
98004	BELLEVUE	60098	12542	11.0	15.3	34.3	16.3	23.1	82425	89923	93	94	7105	0.0	0.0	2.1	21.4	76.4	634906
98005	BELLEVUE	47873	7874	9.6	15.5	37.2	19.4	18.3	81056	88890	92	93	4397	0.4	0.2	4.0	22.3	73.2	554767
98006	BELLEVUE	53666	13824	4.7	8.7	32.2	22.4	32.0	107283	113455	98	99	10671	0.9	1.4	3.0	21.9	72.9	566637
98007	BELLEVUE	38110	10706	14.0	19.1	40.7	16.2	10.0	68470	73770	86	83	4596	2.7	1.6	10.2	44.6	40.9	361240
98008	BELLEVUE	43673	9388	8.4	12.4	39.8	19.7	19.7	84973	92217	94	96	6771	1.4	0.6	2.3	41.9	53.9	418826
98010	BLACK DIAMOND	36334	1758	9.8	14.4	40.0	25.4	10.3	70488	75477	87	85	1522	4.3	4.1	4.5	56.1	30.9	306752
98011	BOTHELL	37533	12139	9.2	16.5	41.9	19.8	12.6	79529	84568	92	92	8037	5.2	0.4	5.9	52.1	36.4	356920
98012	BOTHELL	37406	19554	6.8	15.2	39.4	26.6	12.0	82231	84719	93	94	13693	2.7	2.4	2.6	46.4	46.0	386510
98014	CARNATION	41210	2599	6.2	13.3	39.5	21.5	19.5	87515	95279	94	97	2159	1.4	1.3	2.2	41.7	53.4	424020
98019	DUVALL	41908	3429	4.9	9.8	36.9	26.0	22.4	97353	105417	96	98	2919	2.4	5.7	1.3	38.3	52.3	413776
98020	EDMONDS	43869	8662	11.2	19.4	37.3	18.6	13.6	70143	75247	87	85	6138	0.9	0.2	2.7	41.0	55.3	433716
98021	BOTHELL	35592	10029	7.8	14.6	38.0	28.9	10.6	83207	84941	93	95	8028	4.2	3.7	6.5	47.9	37.6	359960
98022	ENUMCLAW	30059	8459	15.2	16.7	42.4	17.0	8.7	73380	76838	89	88	6156	5.2	2.6	9.1	55.3	27.8	291526
98023	FEDERAL WAY	31989	18254	9.4	16.6	44.5	19.1	10.4	77341	81092	91	90	11379	1.2	0.5	6.4	72.0	19.8	290821
98024	FALL CITY	40521	2053	10.2	13.4	34.6	24.5	17.3	86409	98680	94	96	1695	4.2	0.1	3.6	36.8	55.3	443720
98026	EDMONDS	37253	14744	9.2	19.1	37.2	23.0	11.5	74259	78335	89	88	10477	1.1	0.4	3.5	51.5	43.5	380067
98027	ISSAQUAH	48142	11430	7.7	11.7	34.5	20.5	25.6	93183	102674	96	98	8457	1.2	1.2	4.1	26.2	67.3	527996
98028	KENMORE	41032	8310	9.4	14.7	41.2	18.4	16.2	81168	86167	92	93	5828	5.9	1.1	2.4	43.8	46.7	388817
98029	ISSAQUAH	54619	7775	5.5	9.9	29.1	23.1	32.4	109469	116141	98	99	6134	0.8	0.7	1.0	23.7	73.8	538207
98030	KENT	26469	12350	16.5	23.5	41.1	12.6	6.4	62038	64846	80	73	6046	4.4	1.4	11.0	67.7	15.4	283607
98031	KENT	29782	13370	10.5	19.0	40.6	21.7	8.2	75483	79123	90	88	8460	1.6	3.8	10.6	70.0	14.0	287426
98032	KENT	29325	13116	18.6	22.0	41.7	12.1	5.5	60526	62800	78	70	6062	8.6	0.7	13.7	69.4	7.6	241238
98033	KIRKLAND	57467	14870	6.7	10.0	38.7	22.5	22.1	91604	101456	95	98	9554	0.3	0.2	3.1	27.5	69.0	516149
98034	KIRKLAND	39369	17333	8.1	15.7	43.5	20.4	12.4	79968	84689	92	92	10739	0.4	0.9	8.6	50.6	39.5	367193
98036	LYNNWOOD	29252	13761	12.4	23.0	39.7	18.4	6.5	65642	69367	84	80	8194	4.1	1.0	7.4	63.2	24.3	322024
98037	LYNNWOOD	29554	10310	11.8	23.3	39.8	19.1	6.0	67220	72707	85	81	6533	5.9	2.7	7.7	55.5	28.1	338500
98038	MAPLE VALLEY	37394	9787	4.9	9.0	42.0	28.2	15.9	91942	100948	95	98	8302	0.5	0.2	3.9	62.5	32.9	349413
98039	MEDINA	79572	1108	5.3	6.3	15.4	11.6	61.4	192929	201721	100	100	967	0.0	0.0	0.0	0.6	99.4	1000001
98040	MERCER ISLAND	65450	9024	7.0	9.0	26.0	17.8	40.2	121025	127335	99	99	6908	0.3	0.5	1.0	8.1	90.1	857536
98042	KENT	34707	14675	4.7	10.4	47.2	24.1	13.6	85937	92485	94	96	12448	1.9	2.4	5.1	60.7	29.9	313784
98043	MOUNTLAKE TERRACE	29007	8551	10.6	23.3	48.9	12.9	4.3	64085	67965	82	76	5174	1.4	1.9	6.3	81.6	8.8	285294
98045	NORTH BEND	38401	5633	9.1	11.7	39.6	23.8	15.7	86601	93727	94	97	4263	2.9	1.5	6.4	45.1	44.0	375049
98047	PACIFIC	25564	1836	12.3	22.8	45.9	13.9	5.2	65387	69415	84	79	1091	2.8	0.5	15.4	80.7	0.6	222776
98051	RAVENSDALE	31237	1658	7.8	15.8	48.8	20.9	6.7	79019	82748	92	91	1433	7.7	1.7	6.8	52.8	30.9	321633
98052	REDMOND	49125	23299	7.3	13.1	37.0	21.0	21.5	89000	97694	95	97	13259	3.2	2.2	4.4	31.2	59.0	448893
98053	REDMOND	60691	6497	3.4	6.2	23.2	20.5	46.7	139166	150000	99	100	5839	0.9	0.4	1.4	13.5	83.7	692848
98055	RENTON	32192	9491	13.9	22.3	40.2	15.5	8.2	64343	68411	83	77	5246	3.0	4.8	18.4	60.0	13.8	271585
98056	RENTON	35985	13592	14.2	19.5	41.8	15.0	9.5	69705	73709	87	84	8116	2.5	5.1	13.2	51.5	27.7	298793
98057	RENTON	29317	4988	24.8	26.3	36.2	8.3	4.4	48406	50754	58	44	1810	2.4	0.3	18.0	64.0	15.3	243593
98058	RENTON	35658	15472	7.0	14.8	41.2	23.8	13.1	83599	90478	93	95	11503	2.8	1.3	8.2	64.8	22.9	318049
98059	RENTON	38390	10635	7.5	11.9	43.3	22.5	14.9	84642	91702	94	95	7998	1.9	1.6	6.8	54.0	35.6	349025
98065	SNOQUALMIE	38834	4494	9.3	9.5	39.1	22.4	19.8	89094	99041	95	97	3818	2.0	0.2	2.1	35.2	60.5	475849
98070	VASHON	42818	4581	11.5	16.4	38.9	18.1	15.2	78934	83810	92	91	3546	0.0	0.0	5.2	37.3	57.6	456513
98072	WOODINVILLE	46209	8434	6.0	10.4	33.1	25.4	25.0	100622	106019	97	98	6528	0.6	1.0	2.5	30.1	65.8	512692
98074	SAMMAMISH	55092	8121	2.7	5.9	24.3	24.4	42.7	132591	136165	99	99	6929	0.4	0.6	0.6	13.7	84.8	597160
98075	SAMMAMISH	60834	5939	2.8	6.2	19.8	22.1	49.1	147443	154425	100	100	5196	0.4	0.2	0.3	8.0	91.1	706533
98077	WOODINVILLE	49519	4548	4.5	8.6	25.9	23.6	37.4	121741	127429	99	99	4084	0.3	0.3	1.7	15.3	82.4	646511
98087	LYNNWOOD	27589	11743	13.3	25.4	44.1	13.6	3.6	61950	65503	80	72	6059	12.1	6.4	5.1	56.6	19.8	305259
98092	AUBURN	35619	13933	7.6	12.2	41.1	25.0	14.1	86256	91571	94	96	11523	2.9	3.6	7.2	54.2	32.2	336233
98101	SEATTLE	54779	7000	30.8	24.7	24.7	9.2	10.6	41424	45362	37	20	1428	1.3	1.2	6.0	34.7	56.8	449744
98102	SEATTLE	60541	13876	13.6	21.8	39.1	13.1	12.4	61493	69633	83	78	3663	0.7	0.0	7.6	32.2	59.4	517246
98103	SEATTLE	46082	22448	12.2	19.4	39.5	16.4	12.5	71624	76544	88	87	10129	0.4	0.2	2.8	35.6	61.1	458634
98104	SEATTLE	23574	6066	54.2	20.8	18.1	3.4	3.4	21782	21961	2	1	342	1.8	0.6	9.4	28.7	59.6	500000
98105	SEATTLE	38437	16187	25.9	19.7	27.9	11.5	15.0	56082	58895	73	61	5990	0.0	0.4	3.7	20.3	75.6	588102
98106	SEATTLE	23946	9143	21.4	21.3	40.9	11.2	5.2	57222	60073	74	64	5003	1.6	0.4	12.7	76.6	8.8	247581
98107	SEATTLE	40880	11008	15.3	24.3	38.9	14.1	7.5	62018	65296	80	72	4033	1.8	1.1	3.3	43.3	50.4	402132
98108	SEATTLE	22869	8008	20.7	24.6	37.6	11.1	5.9	55784	58664	72	61	4401	4.4	0.9	13.7	65.5	15.5	272496
98109	SEATTLE	61610	9951	11.4	23.2	32.6	15.7	17.2	75519	78629	90	89	3380	1.8	0.2	4.9	27.9	65.3	550713
98110	BAINBRIDGE ISLAND	42610	9169	11.1	17.0	31.2	21.0	19.7	82065	84545	93	93	7068	0.4	0.5	1.0	21.8	76.3	602478
98112	SEATTLE	67733	9765	12.7	15.0	28.4	15.6	28.2	87589	98063	95	97	5530	0.1	0.4	1.0	13.1	85.5	729885
98115	SEATTLE	46882	20510	10.6	15.4	36.7	20.3	17.0	81481	88460	93	93	13289	0.9	0.2	3.6	31.3	63.9	473784
98116	SEATTLE	52942	10907	10.4	17.8	36.1	19.5	16.2	79009	85050	92	91	6311	0.1	0.3	1.5	31.8	66.3	487841
98117	SEATTLE	42558	13406	8.9	16.6	42.0	18.9	13.7	78618	83304	91	90	9365	0.6	0.1	1.5	41.9	55.8	425911
98118	SEATTLE	26309	15037	18.8	20.3	38.8	13.2	8.8	63016	66412	81	75	9109	1.7	0.6	10.2	61.2	26.4	302954
98119	SEATTLE	57279	11718	11.2	19.6	35.3	16.9	17.0	74565	79943	89	88	4554	0.9	1.0	4.0	21.5	72.6	596012
98121	SEATTLE	61327	8486	27.7	20.8	28.8	10.3	12.4	51792	55764	65	53	2543	0.0	1.7	4.2	46.0	48.0	389981
98122	SEATTLE	36973	15058	26.6	23.2	31.3	9.9	9.0	50138	52017	61	48	4899	0.6	0.4	7.2	38.5	53.4	422351
98125	SEATTLE	34014	17369	19.4	23.4	35.8	13.1	8.4	59050	62649	76	68	8752	0.8	0.6	4.1	59.3	35.1	357997
98126	SEATTLE	36099	9332	19.4	18.2	38.1	14.3	10.1	64680	68463	83	77	5333	0.7	0.1	7.9	57.7	33.6	336913
98133	SEATTLE	31458	20021	18.8	23.8	39.6	11.9	5.9	57123	59797	74	64	10663	3.8	0.8	7.3	65.8	22.3	326536
98134	SEATTLE	31578	435	19.1	28.5	26.2	18.9	7.4	58616	65500	76	67	129	8.5	0.0	10.1	62.8	18.6	268125
98136	SEATTLE	51609	7023	10.2	18.8	36.4	18.1	16.5	79301	84972	92	92	4459	0.4	0.1	1.5	37.2	60.9	470260
98144	SEATTLE	32418	10773	23.9	19.2	33.7	12.1	11.2	58214	61319	75	66	5735	2.4	1.1	6.4	50.5	39.7	357435
98146	SEATTLE	28598	10056	16.6	20.5	41.1	14.7	7.2	62967	66023	81	74	6224	1.2	0.8	10.1	63.8	24.1	285607
98148	SEATTLE	29181	3889	17.0	29.1	39.2	9.8	4.9	53163	54956	68	56	1846	0.8	2.9	17.9	69.8	8.7	243684
98155	SEATTLE	35408	13516	9.8	18.4	41.2	18.6	12.0	76114	80157	90	89	9415	1.5	0.8	3.5	61.8	32.4	345378
98166	SEATTLE	36816	9160	15.9	22.7	32.3	17.3	11.8	66147	71057	84	80	5918	0.5	0.3	6.3	46.5	46.5	382857
98168	SEATTLE	25115	13117	17.6	25.2	41.5	11.6	4.2	56314	58912	73	62	7145	3.0	1.8	20.3	70.1	4.8	220012
98177	SEATTLE	43874	7591	9.6	15.9	36.9	19.1	18.5	82487	88963	93	94	5832	0.4	0.1	1.9	32.0	65.7	506345
98178	SEATTLE	30194	8448	12.8	21.2	42.9	15.4	7.8	67270	72032	85	81	5865	4.3	0.7	12.1	66.6	16.3	272626
98188	SEATTLE	27813	8379	17.8	27.3	39.6	10.1	5.2	55183	57988	71	60	4428	9.6	2.7	16.5	62.3	8.9	233008
98195	SEATTLE	17455	0	0.0	0.0	0.0	0.0	0.0	0	0	0	0	0	0.0	0.0	0.0	0.0	0.0	0
98198	SEATTLE	29564	13689	13.2	24.3	41.7	14.3	6.5	63400	67301	82	76	7886	6.5	1.3	11.9	65.2	15.0	263033
98199	SEATTLE	52131	9399	9.4	15.7	36.4	19.4	19.1	82129	89441	93	94	5870	0.2	0.1	2.6	21.9	75.2	594438
98201	EVERETT	24745	12747	27.0	27.9	33.9	7.8	3.4	44858	47773	48	31	5200	1.5	0.4	9.1	75.4	13.6	246893
98203	EVERETT	32367	13575	11.5	20.5	41.8	18.2	8.1	68162	73286	86	82	8931	0.9	2.6	8.0	67.9	20.6	296767
98204	EVERETT	23134	15229	19.9	31.4	39.0	7.8	1.9	48906	52144	59	46	5211	7.9	8.4	21.1	57.7	4.9	211727
98205	EVERETT	31270	5088	5.4	13.7	46.7	25.3	8.9	78905	82410	92	91	4191	2.6	2.3	12.0	67.2	15.9	289365
98208	EVERETT	32585	19607	9.3	17.7	41.0	23.6	8.4	72858	77424	88	87	13330	1.7	3.9	6.1	61.4	26.8	339478
98220	ACME	21801	204	18.6	25.5	44.6	8.8	2.5	55542	59380	72	61	154	0.0	0.0	24.7	59.1	16.2	264706
98221	ANACORTES	28848	9106	15.7	28.5	38.0	12.3	5.5	54787	58184	71	59	6575	1.3	0.3	4.7	58.4	35.3	334696
98223	ARLINGTON	27968	14901	10.6	18.5	48.0	18.0	4.9	68272	72571	86	83	11557	2.8	2.9	10.7	59.5	24.0	298383
	WASHINGTON	29418		17.0	23.3	38.4	13.6	7.7	60852	63758				3.4	2.9	16.8	52.3	24.6	272173
	UNITED STATES	27277		20.9	24.4	35.3	11.7	7.6	54719	56938				9.3	13.1	31.6	32.6	13.5	162279

ZIP CODE #	POST OFFICE NAME	FINANCIAL SERVICES: Auto Loan	Home Loan	Investments	Retirement Plans	THE HOME: Home Improvements: Home Repair	Lawn & Garden	Furnishings: Computers & Hardware Personal	Major Appliances	TV, Radio, Sound Equipment	Furniture	ENTERTAINMENT: Dine out/ Carry out	Sports Equipment	Fees & Tickets	Toys & Games	Travel	Cable TV	PERSONAL: Apparel & Services	Auto Repairs	Health Insurance	Pets & Supplies
98001	AUBURN	123	143	126	142	138	130	126	128	122	130	123	99	136	126	132	120	87	124	121	148
98002	AUBURN	82	76	73	76	75	74	85	78	84	83	85	62	81	84	81	84	60	83	80	93
98003	FEDERAL WAY	100	91	84	94	88	87	102	92	100	102	102	74	98	102	96	99	71	98	94	110
98004	BELLEVUE	158	174	192	181	183	161	179	168	168	182	171	134	189	166	186	162	124	172	160	194
98005	BELLEVUE	144	153	161	159	157	142	155	146	148	159	150	116	163	149	159	143	108	149	139	170
98006	BELLEVUE	182	229	245	234	240	207	201	204	189	213	191	158	232	191	224	183	141	196	185	229
98007	BELLEVUE	119	106	107	111	105	96	128	108	122	124	125	92	122	124	119	118	90	121	105	130
98008	BELLEVUE	137	177	190	173	186	162	156	158	149	158	150	119	179	149	174	148	110	155	151	177
98010	BLACK DIAMOND	139	156	135	154	150	144	137	141	133	142	135	109	145	139	141	132	95	135	134	163
98011	BOTHELL	125	140	134	142	138	127	133	129	128	136	130	102	141	130	138	125	93	129	123	150
98012	BOTHELL	138	149	136	153	145	134	141	136	135	146	137	109	148	140	143	131	98	136	127	159
98014	CARNATION	156	195	180	196	192	173	167	170	158	174	161	133	188	163	181	154	116	163	156	195
98019	DUVALL	167	204	179	208	199	171	171	173	158	188	161	142	193	169	181	147	118	160	146	195
98020	EDMONDS	123	141	147	142	146	141	132	134	132	136	132	99	145	128	142	133	94	133	142	154
98021	BOTHELL	132	150	141	150	148	137	134	136	128	141	130	106	144	132	140	125	92	131	127	157
98022	ENUMCLAW	113	123	114	123	121	117	114	116	112	116	113	89	119	114	118	111	79	113	113	135
98023	FEDERAL WAY	126	130	119	133	126	117	129	122	124	133	126	98	132	128	128	120	89	124	115	143
98024	FALL CITY	150	179	161	184	176	167	154	160	148	161	150	126	171	153	166	145	107	152	150	185
98026	EDMONDS	123	141	140	142	142	129	132	129	127	135	129	100	143	129	139	125	93	129	124	149
98027	ISSAQUAH	163	191	187	199	192	174	172	172	164	182	166	136	191	167	183	158	121	166	158	198
98028	KENMORE	136	156	155	158	157	144	147	143	140	151	142	112	159	141	154	137	102	143	137	166
98029	ISSAQUAH	196	241	233	245	246	212	204	212	191	228	192	166	233	197	223	179	140	196	187	235
98030	KENT	104	98	87	100	94	88	105	95	102	107	104	78	102	105	99	98	73	101	91	113
98031	KENT	119	119	108	120	116	108	121	113	116	123	118	91	121	120	118	113	84	116	107	133
98032	KENT	98	87	82	90	84	83	101	89	100	99	101	72	96	101	93	99	71	97	91	108
98033	KIRKLAND	162	185	198	191	192	166	181	172	168	187	171	139	195	169	191	161	125	172	157	198
98034	KIRKLAND	130	138	133	142	137	127	137	129	132	139	134	103	143	134	138	129	96	132	125	152
98036	LYNNWOOD	106	108	99	109	105	99	110	103	107	111	108	82	111	109	108	104	77	106	100	121
98037	LYNNWOOD	104	109	104	111	108	102	109	104	106	110	108	82	113	108	110	105	76	106	103	123
98038	MAPLE VALLEY	154	181	158	180	175	155	156	158	146	167	149	125	169	155	162	139	107	149	139	179
98039	MEDINA	253	361	444	378	405	340	291	313	273	324	270	235	378	271	350	262	211	286	275	340
98040	MERCER ISLAND	200	261	309	269	287	246	232	240	218	250	217	180	275	211	267	211	162	229	225	266
98042	KENT	142	167	150	167	162	148	145	147	138	153	140	115	158	143	153	133	100	140	134	169
98043	MOUNTLAKE TERRACE	99	104	97	103	102	95	105	98	101	104	103	78	107	104	104	100	73	101	96	115
98045	NORTH BEND	142	165	148	168	161	146	146	146	138	154	141	117	159	144	152	133	101	140	132	168
98047	PACIFIC	98	104	94	102	101	94	104	98	101	103	103	78	107	103	104	100	73	101	96	115
98051	RAVENSDALE	129	138	121	138	134	132	124	129	122	128	123	98	128	127	126	122	86	123	124	151
98052	REDMOND	165	166	164	173	165	152	170	158	163	175	166	128	174	168	169	158	119	163	149	186
98053	REDMOND	247	322	329	338	332	286	265	275	247	290	250	218	317	254	299	234	187	255	237	310
98055	RENTON	108	100	94	103	97	94	112	100	110	111	111	81	108	111	106	108	78	108	101	120
98056	RENTON	112	111	110	114	111	107	118	110	116	117	117	87	118	116	116	115	83	115	112	130
98057	RENTON	83	76	72	78	74	74	88	78	87	85	88	63	84	87	82	87	62	85	83	95
98058	RENTON	132	152	143	154	150	138	139	137	133	143	135	108	151	137	146	130	97	135	129	159
98059	RENTON	143	156	143	159	152	141	147	142	141	152	143	114	155	146	149	136	102	141	133	166
98065	SNOQUALMIE	141	178	173	181	180	158	150	154	142	160	144	121	173	146	165	137	105	146	138	175
98070	VASHON	138	158	172	162	164	155	142	151	136	148	137	115	154	135	157	134	97	144	142	173
98072	WOODINVILLE	170	206	200	213	207	186	180	181	172	191	174	144	204	176	195	166	127	174	166	208
98074	SAMMAMISH	220	270	260	280	271	236	231	233	216	251	219	188	264	225	250	204	161	220	203	265
98075	SAMMAMISH	259	332	334	343	341	293	275	286	256	304	259	226	324	265	306	242	192	264	247	319
98077	WOODINVILLE	201	265	271	276	273	236	217	226	203	236	205	178	261	208	246	193	153	210	197	254
98087	LYNNWOOD	99	92	82	95	88	85	99	90	97	100	98	74	96	100	93	94	69	95	87	108
98092	AUBURN	142	163	152	165	161	149	144	147	138	152	140	114	156	143	152	135	100	141	137	170
98101	SEATTLE	108	79	82	91	76	77	118	89	115	109	119	81	104	115	101	113	85	108	95	115
98102	SEATTLE	128	102	110	116	101	97	142	110	136	133	141	100	130	137	126	131	101	129	112	139
98103	SEATTLE	121	111	117	120	111	102	136	114	128	132	132	99	130	127	129	122	94	126	110	138
98104	SEATTLE	51	38	44	44	39	43	60	47	62	54	63	39	53	57	53	64	44	58	60	61
98105	SEATTLE	121	96	106	106	98	93	152	108	131	129	134	99	126	129	121	123	97	126	103	133
98106	SEATTLE	92	90	81	90	87	81	96	88	93	96	95	71	94	95	92	91	67	93	85	104
98107	SEATTLE	99	94	101	100	96	86	113	96	105	110	108	83	110	104	109	100	78	106	93	116
98108	SEATTLE	88	97	100	96	101	82	103	95	94	103	96	76	104	92	104	89	70	98	85	108
98109	SEATTLE	138	121	133	134	123	112	156	127	147	150	152	112	148	147	145	141	110	143	124	156
98110	BAINBRIDGE ISLAND	132	170	186	175	180	160	147	153	140	158	141	116	172	137	167	137	103	146	146	173
98112	SEATTLE	177	196	224	208	208	179	204	189	189	209	192	154	217	186	214	180	141	193	174	218
98115	SEATTLE	133	149	160	153	154	138	149	141	141	151	142	112	158	140	155	136	103	143	135	164
98116	SEATTLE	130	147	161	150	154	131	151	141	138	152	141	114	158	137	158	132	103	144	129	162
98117	SEATTLE	122	141	150	142	146	128	138	133	129	141	130	105	147	128	146	124	94	133	124	152
98118	SEATTLE	95	110	111	108	112	98	111	105	106	109	108	82	117	105	115	104	79	107	100	119
98119	SEATTLE	140	124	136	138	125	115	159	129	150	152	155	114	152	150	148	144	112	145	126	158
98121	SEATTLE	120	88	91	101	84	85	130	98	127	121	131	90	115	127	111	123	93	118	103	126
98122	SEATTLE	100	85	90	93	85	80	113	90	106	106	109	80	104	106	102	102	79	103	89	111
98125	SEATTLE	99	98	100	100	98	94	107	97	105	106	106	77	107	104	105	105	76	104	101	116
98126	SEATTLE	105	106	109	109	108	101	115	106	112	113	113	85	116	111	114	111	81	111	106	125
98133	SEATTLE	91	92	93	93	92	88	99	91	98	97	99	72	101	97	98	98	71	97	95	108
98134	SEATTLE	110	84	87	96	81	81	121	92	117	112	121	84	108	118	105	113	86	110	95	118
98136	SEATTLE	134	153	169	157	162	137	156	147	142	159	145	119	164	139	165	135	105	149	134	169
98144	SEATTLE	100	108	115	110	112	98	119	108	114	114	117	86	121	111	119	113	86	113	105	125
98146	SEATTLE	97	111	109	108	112	103	107	104	104	107	106	80	114	104	112	104	76	106	103	119
98148	SEATTLE	89	86	86	87	86	84	96	87	95	93	96	69	94	94	93	95	68	94	91	104
98155	SEATTLE	115	138	141	137	141	127	127	126	122	129	123	96	140	122	137	120	89	125	122	144
98166	SEATTLE	108	126	131	125	129	121	121	119	118	120	119	90	131	117	128	119	86	120	121	136
98168	SEATTLE	89	89	83	89	87	83	96	87	94	94	95	70	96	95	93	93	68	93	88	104
98177	SEATTLE	133	171	190	170	182	161	151	156	145	157	145	115	175	142	171	143	106	151	151	174
98178	SEATTLE	101	118	116	115	118	111	111	110	109	109	110	84	119	109	117	109	79	110	110	126
98188	SEATTLE	94	91	84	92	88	87	98	90	97	97	98	71	97	98	95	96	69	96	93	107
98195	SEATTLE	0	0	0	0	0	0	0	0	0	0	0	0	0	0	0	0	0	0	0	0
98198	SEATTLE	104	103	98	105	101	98	109	101	107	109	109	80	109	108	107	106	77	106	102	120
98199	SEATTLE	138	154	172	160	163	141	160	149	148	162	150	121	169	145	167	141	110	152	138	172
98201	EVERETT	76	72	70	74	71	71	82	75	82	80	83	59	80	81	79	82	58	81	79	89
98203	EVERETT	113	122	113	121	120	112	118	115	114	119	115	90	122	116	119	112	82	115	111	134
98204	EVERETT	85	65	58	69	61	61	85	70	83	84	85	59	75	86	73	81	59	80	70	87
98205	EVERETT	137	145	128	141	139	130	130	134	125	137	127	105	132	132	131	122	89	127	122	154
98208	EVERETT	123	128	115	129	123	114	126	119	121	130	123	96	129	125	124	117	87	121	112	139
98220	ACME	102	79	109	80	81	108	83	98	85	71	84	80	68	84	84	91	56	93	103	120
98221	ANACORTES	97	99	112	99	103	108	94	102	95	95	95	74	96	93	100	98	66	99	107	119
98223	ARLINGTON	112	118	104	118	114	110	111	111	108	113	109	87	113	112	111	106	76	109	107	130
	WASHINGTON	106	107	105	108	106	104	108	105	106	108	107	82	108	107	107	105	75	106	104	124
	UNITED STATES	100	100	100	100	100	100	100	100	100	100	100	100	100	100	100	100	100	100	100	100

ZIP CODE #	POST OFFICE NAME	COUNTY FIPS CODE	POPULATION 2000	POPULATION 2009	POPULATION 2014	2000-2009 ANNUAL RATE % Rate	2000-2009 ANNUAL RATE State Centile	HOUSEHOLDS 2000	HOUSEHOLDS 2009	HOUSEHOLDS 2014	HOUSEHOLDS % Annual Rate 2000-2009	HOUSEHOLDS 2009 Average HH Size	FAMILIES 2000	FAMILIES 2009	FAMILIES % Annual Rate 2000-2009
98224	BARING	033	77	85	90	1.1	52	33	37	39	1.2	2.27	18	20	1.1
98225	BELLINGHAM	073	42321	45528	47448	0.8	40	17786	19647	20684	1.1	2.08	7829	8236	0.5
98226	BELLINGHAM	073	30917	39716	44296	2.7	91	11597	15517	17485	3.2	2.53	8201	10604	2.8
98229	BELLINGHAM	073	25481	29714	32076	1.7	75	10388	12282	13277	1.8	2.41	6724	7774	1.6
98230	BLAINE	073	10890	15182	17231	3.7	96	4408	6253	7123	3.9	2.42	3095	4316	3.7
98232	BOW	057	3660	4087	4310	1.2	57	1380	1542	1624	1.2	2.64	1038	1144	1.1
98233	BURLINGTON	057	12281	14837	16129	2.1	85	4499	5331	5776	1.9	2.73	3232	3753	1.6
98236	CLINTON	029	5343	6241	6681	1.7	75	2165	2518	2707	1.6	2.48	1584	1819	1.5
98237	CONCRETE	057	4026	4987	5526	2.3	87	1527	1892	2091	2.3	2.63	1085	1321	2.2
98239	COUPEVILLE	029	5959	6836	7232	1.5	69	2572	2934	3117	1.4	2.28	1787	2009	1.3
98240	CUSTER	073	2890	3174	3397	1.0	49	995	1118	1200	1.3	2.84	780	862	1.1
98241	DARRINGTON	061	1934	2420	2682	2.5	89	776	999	1112	2.8	2.42	513	648	2.6
98244	DEMING	073	2378	2866	3130	2.0	83	872	1097	1210	2.5	2.61	629	761	2.1
98245	EASTSOUND	055	3534	4052	4283	1.5	69	1648	1934	2057	1.7	2.09	987	1135	1.5
98247	EVERSON	073	7977	9035	9665	1.4	66	2656	3068	3289	1.6	2.94	2101	2396	1.4
98248	FERNDALE	073	18568	21877	23811	1.8	78	6625	7939	8660	2.0	2.75	5005	5895	1.8
98249	FREELAND	029	3590	4401	4764	2.2	86	1561	1903	2068	2.2	2.31	1065	1281	2.0
98250	FRIDAY HARBOR	055	6894	7853	8235	1.4	66	3059	3524	3713	1.5	2.20	1924	2176	1.3
98251	GOLD BAR	061	4491	5290	5720	1.8	78	1678	1984	2148	1.8	2.66	1160	1347	1.6
98252	GRANITE FALLS	061	6502	8270	9220	2.6	90	2319	2977	3324	2.7	2.77	1709	2163	2.6
98253	GREENBANK	029	1503	1707	1822	1.4	66	700	792	848	1.3	2.16	494	551	1.2
98257	LA CONNER	057	3589	4262	4609	1.9	81	1555	1826	1979	1.8	2.30	1088	1254	1.5
98258	LAKE STEVENS	061	21042	24908	27260	1.8	78	7216	8692	9547	2.0	2.86	5556	6603	1.9
98260	LANGLEY	029	5206	5873	6199	1.3	61	2217	2488	2634	1.3	2.36	1493	1648	1.1
98261	LOPEZ ISLAND	055	2414	2685	2795	1.2	57	1131	1290	1353	1.4	2.07	715	801	1.2
98262	LUMMI ISLAND	073	822	987	1086	2.0	83	387	477	527	2.3	2.07	228	273	2.0
98264	LYNDEN	073	16207	18907	20439	1.7	75	5683	6849	7448	2.0	2.74	4349	5132	1.8
98266	MAPLE FALLS	073	2829	3219	3432	1.4	66	919	1042	1110	1.4	3.09	674	760	1.3
98267	MARBLEMOUNT	057	403	474	519	1.8	78	162	192	209	1.9	2.43	107	124	1.6
98270	MARYSVILLE	061	34935	43047	47175	2.3	87	12595	15499	16955	2.3	2.76	9237	11388	2.3
98271	MARYSVILLE	061	23243	25342	26868	0.9	45	8114	9107	9713	1.3	2.78	6311	6985	1.1
98272	MONROE	061	23466	28087	29959	2.0	83	7439	8826	9490	1.9	2.90	5656	6654	1.8
98273	MOUNT VERNON	057	25523	29274	31216	1.5	69	9159	10328	10979	1.3	2.79	6224	6899	1.1
98274	MOUNT VERNON	057	13316	16131	17512	2.1	85	4892	5865	6358	2.0	2.69	3541	4193	1.8
98275	MUKILTEO	061	17999	20328	21616	1.3	61	6748	7747	8269	1.5	2.62	4977	5584	1.3
98277	OAK HARBOR	029	34592	38519	40272	1.2	57	12932	14305	15014	1.1	2.67	9526	10402	1.0
98278	OAK HARBOR	029	2044	1560	1567	-2.9	0	293	304	307	0.4	3.02	270	279	0.4
98279	OLGA	055	1059	1199	1257	1.4	66	522	605	640	1.6	1.98	324	368	1.4
98281	POINT ROBERTS	073	1308	1699	1897	2.9	93	607	797	892	3.0	2.13	373	477	2.7
98282	CAMANO ISLAND	029	13358	16316	17606	2.2	86	5360	6385	6888	1.9	2.56	4033	4749	1.8
98283	ROCKPORT	057	261	303	336	1.6	73	105	122	134	1.6	2.48	72	82	1.4
98284	SEDRO WOOLLEY	057	22609	26018	27940	1.5	69	8292	9593	10309	1.6	2.64	5922	6739	1.4
98288	SKYKOMISH	033	347	382	403	1.0	49	163	183	194	1.3	2.08	91	98	0.8
98290	SNOHOMISH	061	30473	33568	35639	1.1	52	10740	12138	12941	1.3	2.73	8140	9103	1.2
98292	STANWOOD	061	18234	21296	22957	1.7	75	6514	7731	8368	1.9	2.72	4882	5675	1.6
98294	SULTAN	061	5987	7584	8426	2.6	90	2232	2846	3164	2.7	2.66	1582	1985	2.5
98295	SUMAS	073	2050	2493	2739	2.1	85	708	868	953	2.2	2.86	525	633	2.0
98296	SNOHOMISH	061	19581	25676	28482	3.0	94	6419	8631	9617	3.3	2.97	5397	7164	3.1
98303	ANDERSON ISLAND	053	900	1072	1175	1.9	81	421	506	556	2.0	2.12	288	336	1.7
98304	ASHFORD	053	813	896	948	1.1	52	368	410	436	1.2	2.19	238	257	0.8
98305	BEAVER	009	407	456	484	1.2	57	168	194	207	1.6	2.35	116	132	1.4
98310	BREMERTON	035	18730	18838	18952	0.1	8	8181	8376	8457	0.3	2.22	4760	4752	0.0
98311	BREMERTON	035	23564	24643	25277	0.5	28	8386	8996	9283	0.8	2.73	6432	6806	0.6
98312	BREMERTON	035	31726	32409	32831	0.2	12	12445	12896	13095	0.4	2.49	8343	8499	0.2
98315	SILVERDALE	035	6436	6917	6895	0.8	40	1079	1093	1095	0.1	3.66	1072	1087	0.2
98320	BRINNON	031	1234	1277	1279	0.4	23	592	627	635	0.6	2.04	382	395	0.4
98321	BUCKLEY	053	15260	17393	18711	1.4	66	5140	5982	6475	1.7	2.84	3993	4558	1.4
98323	CARBONADO	053	744	901	990	2.1	85	237	291	321	2.2	3.10	182	218	2.0
98325	CHIMACUM	031	1462	1695	1797	1.6	73	563	662	705	1.8	2.56	402	462	1.5
98326	CLALLAM BAY	009	1605	1901	1966	1.8	78	320	382	412	1.9	2.54	205	239	1.7
98327	DUPONT	053	2174	6182	7913	12.0	100	877	2524	3245	12.1	2.44	605	1689	11.7
98328	EATONVILLE	053	8528	10379	11351	2.1	85	3041	3735	4099	2.2	2.76	2338	2815	2.0
98329	GIG HARBOR	053	9550	10912	11701	1.5	69	3369	3898	4197	1.6	2.79	2639	2993	1.4
98330	ELBE	053	385	429	455	1.2	57	163	183	195	1.3	2.33	107	116	0.9
98331	FORKS	009	6762	6991	7323	0.4	23	2371	2666	2809	1.3	2.58	1673	1843	1.1
98332	GIG HARBOR	053	13103	15520	17038	1.8	78	4742	5725	6344	2.1	2.56	3694	4377	1.9
98333	FOX ISLAND	053	2803	3393	3732	2.1	85	1048	1276	1407	2.2	2.66	848	1014	2.0
98335	GIG HARBOR	053	22980	25425	26830	1.1	52	8808	9813	10386	1.2	2.55	6605	7217	1.0
98336	GLENOMA	041	1139	1236	1292	0.9	45	444	481	503	0.9	2.57	325	346	0.7
98337	BREMERTON	035	8359	8658	8740	0.4	23	2883	3035	3084	0.6	2.18	1355	1375	0.2
98338	GRAHAM	053	21069	24622	26836	1.7	75	7093	8378	9159	1.8	2.92	5766	6709	1.7
98339	PORT HADLOCK	031	3091	3454	3623	1.2	57	1245	1436	1515	1.6	2.40	843	953	1.3
98340	HANSVILLE	035	1980	2468	2668	2.4	88	861	1090	1182	2.6	2.26	633	788	2.4
98342	INDIANOLA	035	1794	2043	2155	1.4	66	699	805	851	1.5	2.54	523	592	1.3
98345	KEYPORT	035	403	410	414	0.2	12	151	157	159	0.4	2.57	110	112	0.2
98346	KINGSTON	035	8086	9206	9729	1.4	66	3068	3562	3783	1.6	2.58	2262	2582	1.4
98349	LAKEBAY	053	5543	6344	6822	1.5	69	1554	1873	2055	2.0	2.62	1123	1318	1.7
98351	LONGBRANCH	053	908	1247	1400	3.5	95	390	528	592	3.3	2.36	284	375	3.1
98354	MILTON	053	5289	5944	6296	1.3	61	2182	2496	2660	1.5	2.35	1407	1556	1.1
98355	MINERAL	041	557	632	674	1.4	66	232	263	280	1.4	2.40	155	173	1.2
98356	MORTON	041	1986	2149	2232	0.9	45	826	892	928	0.8	2.38	560	595	0.7
98358	NORDLAND	031	837	888	901	0.6	31	395	427	435	0.8	2.08	268	284	0.6
98359	OLALLA	035	4533	4944	5115	0.9	45	1583	1768	1843	1.2	2.77	1274	1404	1.1
98360	ORTING	053	7159	10946	12828	4.7	98	2471	3788	4449	4.7	2.84	1906	2854	4.5
98361	PACKWOOD	041	847	984	1059	1.6	73	401	465	500	1.6	2.12	270	307	1.4
98362	PORT ANGELES	009	21023	22635	23374	0.8	40	9171	10031	10416	1.0	2.22	5786	6247	0.8
98363	PORT ANGELES	009	12258	13279	13736	0.9	45	4940	5446	5668	1.1	2.42	3408	3691	0.9
98365	PORT LUDLOW	031	3666	4385	4696	2.0	83	1726	2100	2262	2.1	2.08	1281	1533	2.0
98366	PORT ORCHARD	035	31716	33288	34216	0.5	28	11785	12823	13246	0.9	2.55	8290	8876	0.7
98367	PORT ORCHARD	035	23687	25891	26984	1.0	49	8303	9262	9708	1.2	2.79	6645	7320	1.1
98368	PORT TOWNSEND	031	13002	14586	15295	1.3	61	6036	6925	7303	1.5	2.10	3660	4130	1.3
98370	POULSBO	035	24836	27714	29083	1.2	57	9525	10814	11399	1.4	2.54	6958	7779	1.2
98371	PUYALLUP	053	19352	21325	22525	1.1	52	7662	8488	9001	1.1	2.48	5231	5646	0.8
98372	PUYALLUP	053	21386	23188	24256	0.9	45	8473	9247	9722	0.9	2.45	5611	5931	0.6
98373	PUYALLUP	053	16273	20184	22464	2.4	88	6243	7781	8693	2.4	2.59	4529	5532	2.2
	WASHINGTON					1.4					1.4	2.53			1.2
	UNITED STATES					1.0					1.1	2.59			0.9

ZIP CODE #	POST OFFICE NAME	RACE (%) White 2000	White 2009	Black 2000	Black 2009	Asian/Pacific 2000	Asian/Pacific 2009	% Hispanic Origin 2000	% Hispanic Origin 2009	2009 AGE DISTRIBUTION (%) 0-4	5-9	10-14	15-19	20-24	25-44	45-64	65-84	85+	18+	MEDIAN AGE 2009	% 2009 Males	% 2009 Females
98224	BARING	93.4	90.6	0.0	0.0	1.3	1.2	2.6	2.4	3.5	4.7	4.7	4.7	3.5	30.6	35.3	12.9	0.0	83.5	44.3	54.1	45.9
98225	BELLINGHAM	88.4	86.0	0.9	1.0	3.9	4.7	4.3	5.9	4.2	3.7	3.7	10.7	19.4	25.7	21.0	8.6	2.9	86.0	29.7	48.2	51.8
98226	BELLINGHAM	84.0	82.6	0.7	0.9	3.8	4.8	4.6	6.4	6.5	6.4	6.5	7.1	7.2	25.7	27.6	11.1	1.8	76.4	37.8	49.6	50.4
98229	BELLINGHAM	90.2	88.4	0.8	0.8	3.3	3.9	3.8	5.0	5.8	5.4	5.5	5.8	7.4	28.9	27.9	11.6	1.8	79.9	38.0	49.1	50.9
98230	BLAINE	91.1	89.6	1.0	1.0	2.6	2.9	4.3	5.8	6.0	6.1	6.4	6.6	5.4	23.4	30.8	13.8	1.5	77.3	42.1	49.8	50.2
98232	BOW	92.9	90.8	0.1	0.0	1.8	2.2	6.1	8.6	4.6	5.8	6.9	6.4	3.9	22.2	37.5	11.1	1.7	78.6	45.2	50.2	49.8
98233	BURLINGTON	82.8	77.8	0.5	0.5	1.9	2.3	16.9	23.3	7.8	7.3	6.9	6.9	6.5	28.0	23.9	10.7	2.0	73.8	34.8	50.1	49.9
98236	CLINTON	94.4	93.0	0.5	0.7	1.2	1.6	2.2	3.2	4.6	5.9	6.8	6.6	3.5	20.3	36.4	14.3	1.7	78.3	46.2	49.6	50.4
98237	CONCRETE	93.5	92.3	0.2	0.2	0.6	0.7	2.0	2.9	6.8	7.5	8.0	7.0	4.6	23.5	29.7	11.9	1.0	73.2	39.7	50.2	49.8
98239	COUPEVILLE	92.3	90.3	1.1	1.4	1.7	2.2	3.2	4.6	4.4	5.2	5.5	4.9	3.3	19.5	34.3	19.6	3.4	81.5	49.3	48.5	51.5
98240	CUSTER	92.5	90.8	0.6	0.6	1.3	1.5	5.7	7.8	6.0	6.9	7.5	7.8	4.8	24.2	32.7	9.3	0.8	74.5	40.1	51.1	48.9
98241	DARRINGTON	93.5	92.4	0.2	0.2	0.5	0.7	1.3	1.9	5.7	5.8	6.2	6.7	6.0	23.4	29.9	14.3	2.1	77.9	41.9	48.9	51.1
98244	DEMING	89.8	88.8	0.3	0.3	0.5	0.6	2.9	3.9	6.0	7.8	8.4	7.5	4.4	25.3	30.4	9.3	0.8	72.7	38.7	51.4	48.6
98245	EASTSOUND	94.5	93.4	0.3	0.3	1.2	1.4	1.8	2.5	3.6	4.1	5.2	5.0	2.8	18.4	43.0	15.8	2.0	83.5	50.9	49.7	50.3
98247	EVERSON	86.4	83.6	0.3	0.4	1.2	1.5	10.6	14.2	7.8	7.5	7.9	8.4	6.3	26.4	26.5	8.2	1.1	72.6	34.5	49.7	50.3
98248	FERNDALE	86.9	84.3	0.6	0.7	1.8	2.1	7.6	10.2	7.3	7.5	7.8	7.4	5.3	25.8	28.5	9.2	1.2	72.6	37.1	49.7	50.3
98249	FREELAND	95.0	93.8	0.3	0.4	1.3	1.7	1.7	2.6	3.5	4.0	4.7	5.2	3.4	17.2	39.4	20.1	2.7	84.6	52.3	48.6	51.4
98250	FRIDAY HARBOR	95.1	94.2	0.3	0.3	1.0	1.2	2.8	3.8	3.6	4.7	5.7	5.2	3.3	18.5	38.2	17.9	2.9	83.2	49.9	48.7	51.3
98251	GOLD BAR	92.9	91.4	0.4	0.4	1.2	1.5	2.8	4.0	7.5	7.3	7.4	7.1	5.2	29.6	28.0	7.4	0.6	73.4	36.7	51.9	48.1
98252	GRANITE FALLS	93.4	91.8	0.3	0.4	1.0	1.3	3.7	5.1	7.7	7.6	7.8	8.0	5.8	28.5	27.4	6.4	0.7	71.8	35.4	50.1	49.9
98253	GREENBANK	94.0	92.5	0.3	0.4	1.3	1.8	1.7	2.6	3.4	3.7	4.5	3.9	2.8	13.6	39.6	25.8	2.8	86.0	56.5	48.9	51.1
98257	LA CONNER	78.0	76.8	0.2	0.3	0.5	0.6	4.0	5.7	4.3	4.4	4.7	4.6	4.0	17.7	32.7	23.8	3.7	83.6	52.9	48.5	51.5
98258	LAKE STEVENS	93.1	91.6	0.6	0.8	1.2	1.5	3.2	4.4	7.6	8.1	8.3	8.0	5.0	30.2	25.6	6.4	0.8	70.8	34.8	50.4	49.6
98260	LANGLEY	94.9	93.6	0.3	0.4	1.6	2.0	1.8	2.7	4.2	5.0	6.1	6.2	3.6	19.2	38.6	14.9	2.1	80.7	47.9	48.2	51.8
98261	LOPEZ ISLAND	95.2	94.5	0.1	0.1	0.8	1.0	2.3	3.2	2.8	3.7	4.3	4.1	3.2	15.6	43.4	20.6	2.3	86.3	53.8	49.4	50.6
98262	LUMMI ISLAND	95.9	95.1	0.5	0.5	0.5	0.6	0.7	1.0	3.7	3.4	6.3	5.4	1.6	19.1	44.6	14.4	1.4	83.1	49.1	48.9	51.1
98264	LYNDEN	91.9	90.0	0.3	0.3	1.9	2.3	7.0	9.2	7.3	7.2	7.5	7.8	6.2	24.4	24.9	11.9	2.8	73.0	36.8	48.9	51.1
98266	MAPLE FALLS	91.8	90.1	0.3	0.3	0.5	0.7	3.7	4.9	9.5	8.2	7.9	9.2	9.3	25.8	24.0	5.8	0.5	69.0	29.0	51.0	49.0
98267	MARBLEMOUNT	93.8	92.4	0.2	0.4	0.5	0.6	1.7	2.3	5.3	7.2	7.6	8.9	3.2	22.2	34.2	10.3	1.3	74.3	42.4	51.9	48.1
98270	MARYSVILLE	88.6	86.3	1.0	1.2	4.1	5.1	4.6	6.0	8.5	8.0	7.6	7.4	5.9	29.8	23.2	7.8	1.8	71.3	34.0	48.9	51.1
98271	MARYSVILLE	83.1	81.4	0.6	0.6	2.3	2.7	4.3	5.8	6.8	6.9	7.1	7.6	5.5	26.6	29.3	9.4	0.9	74.4	37.8	50.3	49.7
98272	MONROE	89.5	87.3	1.8	2.2	1.9	2.2	7.2	9.6	8.1	7.9	7.5	6.7	5.9	32.0	24.1	6.5	1.2	72.3	34.7	53.8	46.2
98273	MOUNT VERNON	77.9	73.6	0.6	0.7	2.5	2.7	22.5	28.3	7.9	7.0	6.7	7.6	8.3	27.5	24.2	9.1	1.6	74.0	32.9	50.1	49.9
98274	MOUNT VERNON	86.4	83.0	0.5	0.5	1.8	2.1	11.8	15.7	6.6	6.5	6.8	7.0	5.8	25.3	27.7	11.3	2.9	75.7	39.3	48.8	51.2
98275	MUKILTEO	82.3	78.7	1.7	2.0	10.6	12.8	3.0	4.2	5.9	6.4	7.1	7.5	6.2	27.5	30.8	7.9	0.8	75.9	37.7	49.4	50.6
98277	OAK HARBOR	80.8	77.0	3.8	4.4	7.6	9.4	5.4	7.3	8.6	7.4	6.7	6.3	7.9	29.1	22.5	9.9	1.6	73.3	33.1	50.3	49.7
98278	OAK HARBOR	66.8	60.6	10.0	11.2	11.5	13.8	11.0	14.7	11.7	3.9	1.6	9.4	40.4	29.0	3.0	0.5	0.3	81.9	22.9	61.9	38.1
98279	OLGA	95.1	94.3	0.2	0.2	0.8	0.9	2.0	2.8	3.2	3.8	4.3	4.4	2.3	17.5	43.4	18.9	2.2	85.9	52.2	47.0	53.0
98281	POINT ROBERTS	94.9	94.1	0.6	0.6	2.1	2.4	1.3	1.8	5.7	6.0	5.1	4.5	2.2	22.9	35.7	16.2	1.8	80.3	47.1	50.7	49.3
98282	CAMANO ISLAND	95.6	94.5	0.2	0.3	0.9	1.2	2.1	3.0	5.1	5.7	6.4	6.5	3.9	20.1	33.6	16.7	1.9	78.5	46.3	50.0	50.0
98283	ROCKPORT	93.8	92.7	0.4	0.3	0.0	0.0	1.5	2.0	5.6	6.9	6.9	8.3	4.0	21.5	33.0	12.5	1.3	75.2	42.8	51.5	48.5
98284	SEDRO WOOLLEY	92.0	90.3	0.4	0.5	0.9	1.1	5.4	7.6	6.7	6.7	6.9	7.6	5.9	26.5	27.0	10.6	2.1	75.0	37.5	49.7	50.3
98288	SKYKOMISH	91.7	90.3	0.6	0.5	1.1	1.3	2.3	2.9	3.9	5.0	4.5	5.5	3.1	27.7	35.3	13.9	1.0	82.5	45.1	52.9	47.1
98290	SNOHOMISH	94.6	93.4	0.4	0.4	1.2	1.4	3.0	4.1	6.2	7.0	7.6	7.5	5.0	26.3	30.9	8.1	1.3	74.3	38.7	50.4	49.6
98292	STANWOOD	94.2	92.9	0.4	0.5	1.0	1.3	3.2	4.4	6.3	7.1	7.6	7.0	4.9	25.3	29.8	9.7	2.3	74.5	39.6	49.9	50.1
98294	SULTAN	92.0	90.3	0.3	0.3	1.3	1.7	3.8	5.4	7.5	7.2	7.4	7.3	5.6	29.4	26.4	8.0	1.1	73.4	35.9	51.1	48.9
98295	SUMAS	88.9	86.2	0.1	0.1	2.4	2.9	8.1	11.1	7.7	7.4	7.5	8.0	6.9	26.5	26.2	8.8	1.2	71.9	34.1	50.0	50.0
98296	SNOHOMISH	91.3	89.4	0.5	0.7	3.8	4.5	2.9	4.0	7.3	8.2	8.3	7.4	4.1	27.6	30.5	6.0	0.6	71.4	37.4	50.0	50.0
98303	ANDERSON ISLAND	96.0	95.1	0.4	0.6	1.2	1.6	2.1	3.2	3.5	3.9	4.4	4.7	3.0	11.0	35.1	31.7	2.8	85.4	57.7	50.6	49.4
98304	ASHFORD	93.1	91.4	0.4	0.3	0.7	0.9	2.6	3.7	4.1	5.4	7.6	6.8	3.6	24.8	33.8	12.8	1.1	78.1	43.8	51.0	49.0
98305	BEAVER	93.3	92.5	0.2	0.2	0.5	0.7	0.7	0.9	5.3	4.2	6.4	7.9	4.4	20.0	39.3	11.2	1.5	78.1	45.9	51.5	48.5
98310	BREMERTON	78.4	74.8	5.2	5.9	7.1	8.4	4.5	6.0	7.0	6.1	5.8	6.0	7.4	26.3	23.5	13.8	4.0	77.5	38.1	47.6	52.4
98311	BREMERTON	78.6	74.9	3.7	4.2	10.0	11.9	3.7	5.0	6.8	6.7	6.7	7.3	7.3	26.9	27.4	9.7	1.2	75.3	35.6	49.4	50.6
98312	BREMERTON	80.9	78.1	4.9	5.3	5.2	6.1	5.1	6.7	8.0	7.1	6.4	6.4	7.8	27.6	25.8	9.3	1.6	74.7	34.6	50.2	49.8
98315	SILVERDALE	76.8	73.0	8.0	8.8	5.5	6.5	10.2	13.6	11.6	6.8	4.7	5.9	21.2	47.4	2.2	0.1	0.1	74.8	24.9	68.6	31.4
98320	BRINNON	90.9	89.1	0.2	0.2	0.7	0.9	1.9	2.6	2.1	2.7	2.8	3.8	4.1	11.9	39.2	30.1	3.3	90.4	57.7	51.4	48.6
98321	BUCKLEY	94.0	92.7	0.6	0.7	1.0	1.3	2.4	3.5	7.9	7.6	7.5	7.1	5.6	29.1	27.6	6.9	0.8	72.5	35.8	50.3	49.7
98323	CARBONADO	95.6	94.2	0.4	0.6	0.5	0.8	2.0	2.9	9.0	8.1	7.9	7.1	4.0	31.1	26.7	5.4	0.7	70.3	35.1	51.9	48.1
98325	CHIMACUM	91.6	89.7	0.5	0.6	1.1	1.4	2.2	3.1	5.4	6.7	7.8	7.3	4.1	22.8	33.3	11.4	1.1	74.9	42.4	51.3	48.7
98326	CLALLAM BAY	73.7	71.6	14.0	14.7	2.9	3.2	8.9	12.0	2.9	2.8	3.5	14.1	12.4	36.2	21.6	5.7	0.8	83.9	32.2	75.7	24.3
98327	DUPONT	78.4	73.9	5.8	6.7	8.1	10.2	4.8	6.6	9.3	8.6	7.9	6.0	4.8	34.4	22.5	5.9	0.6	69.8	33.8	49.1	50.9
98328	EATONVILLE	92.1	90.2	0.5	0.6	1.4	1.8	3.0	4.4	5.9	6.4	7.2	7.3	5.5	24.4	31.7	10.5	1.0	75.8	40.4	50.8	49.2
98329	GIG HARBOR	92.2	90.3	0.6	0.8	1.4	1.9	2.2	3.2	6.1	6.7	7.3	7.5	5.4	25.7	31.5	8.8	0.9	75.1	38.9	51.0	49.0
98330	ELBE	93.8	92.1	0.3	0.5	1.0	1.2	2.3	3.5	4.0	5.1	7.5	6.8	3.5	24.9	33.6	13.3	1.4	78.6	44.0	50.6	49.4
98331	FORKS	77.3	74.5	1.4	1.2	1.3	3.4	12.1	16.0	7.0	7.0	7.4	7.5	6.5	27.3	28.3	8.1	0.9	74.6	35.3	54.8	45.2
98332	GIG HARBOR	91.7	89.8	1.9	2.2	1.9	2.5	2.8	4.0	4.7	5.4	6.4	6.8	4.5	23.7	33.1	13.5	1.8	79.2	43.9	46.4	53.6
98333	FOX ISLAND	94.1	92.5	0.6	0.8	1.8	2.3	1.9	2.7	4.7	5.8	7.3	7.8	4.2	17.1	37.0	14.6	1.4	77.2	46.5	49.7	50.3
98335	GIG HARBOR	93.0	91.1	0.9	1.1	2.2	2.9	2.7	4.0	5.5	6.0	6.8	6.7	4.8	21.7	32.6	13.4	2.6	77.4	43.9	48.2	51.8
98336	GLENOMA	95.7	94.8	0.3	0.4	0.2	0.2	2.3	3.4	5.7	5.7	6.2	7.0	6.0	21.0	31.6	15.0	1.5	78.2	43.6	49.8	50.2
98337	BREMERTON	71.6	67.6	9.8	10.7	5.7	6.7	9.9	13.0	6.1	5.0	4.4	9.0	21.2	30.0	18.5	4.9	0.8	81.9	26.9	60.1	39.9
98338	GRAHAM	89.5	87.0	1.6	1.9	2.4	3.1	3.2	4.6	7.2	7.8	7.9	7.7	5.4	28.2	28.1	7.0	0.7	72.1	36.1	50.4	49.6
98339	PORT HADLOCK	90.7	88.8	0.3	0.3	1.5	1.9	2.5	3.5	5.2	5.6	6.0	6.6	5.6	23.6	33.6	12.1	1.6	79.1	43.0	49.0	51.0
98340	HANSVILLE	93.9	92.6	0.2	0.2	1.6	1.9	2.0	2.8	5.2	5.4	4.6	4.4	3.0	20.4	36.7	18.0	2.3	81.5	49.2	49.4	50.6
98342	INDIANOLA	88.1	86.5	0.5	0.6	1.7	2.1	2.7	3.7	6.6	6.7	7.0	7.2	5.5	27.6	30.8	7.8	0.8	75.3	38.8	49.5	50.5
98345	KEYPORT	89.6	87.8	1.0	1.0	3.5	4.4	2.7	3.7	5.1	5.1	5.1	6.1	6.6	23.2	32.2	14.4	2.2	80.5	43.9	50.5	49.5
98346	KINGSTON	86.0	84.3	0.4	0.5	1.7	2.1	2.8	3.8	6.2	6.4	6.6	6.8	6.1	23.3	32.7	10.7	1.2	76.7	41.2	49.9	50.1
98349	LAKEBAY	87.8	86.9	6.5	6.4	0.8	1.1	5.3	6.9	4.4	4.6	5.1	5.6	6.4	31.6	30.8	10.8	0.7	82.8	40.6	60.8	39.2
98351	LONGBRANCH	93.7	91.9	0.4	0.6	0.7	1.0	3.3	4.8	5.9	6.2	6.7	6.9	5.1	22.1	32.3	13.9	1.0	77.0	43.1	49.0	51.0
98354	MILTON	89.6	87.1	1.2	1.4	3.5	4.5	3.5	5.0	5.8	5.7	6.0	6.7	7.2	28.1	27.5	10.3	2.7	78.2	38.3	48.6	51.4
98355	MINERAL	96.6	96.0	0.2	0.3	0.5	0.6	1.6	2.2	2.7	4.9	7.0	6.3	2.5	22.6	36.6	15.3	2.1	80.5	46.5	51.6	48.4
98356	MORTON	95.5	94.5	0.3	0.3	0.8	0.9	1.5	2.3	5.3	5.5	6.0	6.7	5.7	20.9	29.9	16.5	3.5	78.5	44.9	48.7	51.3
98358	NORDLAND	96.4	95.4	0.0	0.0	1.1	1.2	1.8	2.7	2.7	3.4	5.0	4.1	2.3	15.9	40.5	23.9	2.4	85.9	53.7	49.4	50.6
98359	OLALLA	91.0	89.4	0.6	0.7	1.7	2.0	3.2	4.3	5.7	6.3	7.0	7.5	5.5	24.1	33.2	9.8	0.9	76.1	40.7	50.6	49.4
98360	ORTING	92.8	87.0	0.5	1.7	1.2	4.6	3.1	4.6	8.0	7.8	7.7	7.8	5.5	28.9	25.3	8.1	1.0	72.4	35.3	50.9	49.1
98361	PACKWOOD	97.9	97.4	0.0	0.0	0.2	0.3	1.3	1.6	3.7	4.6	6.0	5.9	2.3	18.6	37.8	19.7	1.4	81.8	50.5	50.9	49.1
98362	PORT ANGELES	93.2	92.3	0.5	0.5	1.1	1.4	2.0	2.7	4.8	4.9	5.4	6.3	5.6	21.3	31.7	16.9	3.2	81.2	46.2	48.8	51.2
98363	PORT ANGELES	88.7	87.6	0.5	0.6	1.2	1.5	2.2	3.0	6.2	6.4	6.7	6.9	5.6	22.8	31.4	12.2	2.0	76.4	41.6	49.1	50.9
98365	PORT LUDLOW	94.9	93.8	0.4	0.5	1.3	1.7	1.7	2.4	2.3	2.9	3.5	3.6	2.0	11.5	36.9	34.2	3.2	88.9	59.8	49.6	50.4
98366	PORT ORCHARD	86.2	83.9	2.2	2.5	4.3	5.1	4.1	5.7	6.8	6.4	6.5	7.1	7.1	26.1	27.5	10.6	1.8	76.1	37.5	49.8	50.2
98367	PORT ORCHARD	89.5	87.4	1.1	1.2	3.4	4.1	3.1	4.3	6.0	6.7	7.5	7.5	4.8	25.0	32.2	9.4	0.9	74.9	40.1	50.7	49.3
98368	PORT TOWNSEND	93.8	92.3	0.4	0.5	1.5	1.9	1.9	2.7	3.9	4.3	4.9	5.1	3.6	18.5	37.1	19.4	3.2	83.5	51.0	47.4	52.6
98370	POULSBO	90.1	88.1	0.8	0.9	2.9	3.6	3.4	4.7	5.7	6.1	6.8	7.0	5.1	22.9	31.9	12.2	2.4	77.0	42.5	49.1	50.9
98371	PUYALLUP	89.4	86.7	1.3	1.6	2.8	3.5	4.4	6.3	5.9	6.1	6.4	6.6	5.5	25.0	29.8	12.5	2.2	77.4	41.2	49.0	51.0
98372	PUYALLUP	89.6	86.5	1.2	1.5	3.1	4.1	4.2	6.2	6.5	6.2	6.1	6.7	7.3	27.7	27.1	10.3	2.1	77.3	36.9	48.8	51.2
98373	PUYALLUP	87.3	84.1	2.5	3.0	3.6	4.5	3.7	5.4	7.1	6.8	6.7	6.8	6.4	30.3	26.0	9.0	0.9	75.2	35.7	49.3	50.7
	WASHINGTON	81.8	79.0	3.2	3.4	5.9	6.9	7.5	9.7	6.7	6.5	6.5	7.0	7.0	27.4	27.0	10.1	1.8	76.3	36.9	49.8	50.2
	UNITED STATES	75.1	72.0	12.3	12.7	3.8	4.6	12.5	15.7	6.8	6.7	6.6	7.1	6.9	27.0	26.0	10.9	1.9	75.7	36.9	49.2	50.8

ZIP CODE #	POST OFFICE NAME	2009 Per Capita Income	2009 HH Income Base	2009 HOUSEHOLD INCOME DISTRIBUTION (%) Less than $25,000	$25,000 to $49,999	$50,000 to $99,999	$100,000 to $149,999	$150,000 or More	MEDIAN HOUSEHOLD INCOME 2009	2014	2009 National Centile	2009 State Centile	2009 Home Value Base	2009 HOME VALUE DISTRIBUTION (%) Less than $50,000	$50,000 to $89,999	$90,000 to $174,999	$175,000 to $399,999	$400,000 or More	2009 Median Home Value
98224	BARING	26502	37	18.9	24.3	43.2	10.8	2.7	54435	56532	70	58	27	0.0	7.4	59.3	29.6	3.7	137500
98225	BELLINGHAM	23115	19647	35.6	27.3	27.9	6.1	3.2	36764	38694	23	8	8114	1.9	1.3	10.7	63.7	22.3	275368
98226	BELLINGHAM	26158	15517	16.3	26.4	40.7	11.9	4.8	56529	60576	73	63	10725	2.7	2.1	11.1	57.2	26.9	325008
98229	BELLINGHAM	28044	12282	18.6	25.7	36.5	13.7	5.5	56328	60554	73	62	8341	5.2	3.6	7.0	52.3	31.9	326041
98230	BLAINE	27141	6253	18.2	25.2	42.4	10.3	4.0	55008	58829	71	59	4431	4.9	2.7	17.7	48.6	26.1	261387
98232	BOW	29381	1542	12.1	20.8	44.5	16.5	6.0	64583	65741	83	77	1269	3.8	1.0	5.6	55.9	33.6	336738
98233	BURLINGTON	22998	5331	17.7	25.8	42.6	11.8	2.1	55349	58913	72	60	3382	1.3	2.5	16.8	67.6	11.9	245529
98236	CLINTON	28270	2518	17.6	23.5	41.7	11.0	6.2	58338	60649	76	66	1994	1.4	0.5	5.1	46.7	46.3	384454
98237	CONCRETE	18924	1892	30.3	29.0	31.4	7.3	2.0	41910	45112	39	22	1384	6.1	9.1	28.3	48.6	8.0	191978
98239	COUPEVILLE	27950	2934	14.9	25.2	47.0	9.4	3.5	59757	61231	77	69	2243	4.5	2.0	5.5	61.3	26.8	303432
98240	CUSTER	24830	1118	14.7	24.9	45.3	11.5	3.7	61444	63297	79	71	892	2.9	0.0	11.7	60.8	24.7	314717
98241	DARRINGTON	22617	999	25.9	29.4	35.5	5.7	3.4	42196	47213	40	22	747	4.1	4.7	41.6	46.6	2.9	174361
98244	DEMING	22638	1097	24.9	25.4	38.0	8.4	3.3	49673	51741	60	47	854	3.0	2.9	19.4	54.0	20.6	252574
98245	EASTSOUND	35094	1934	23.5	25.7	35.1	7.2	8.4	50820	52629	63	50	1375	0.0	0.0	10.5	33.3	56.1	482843
98247	EVERSON	20655	3068	15.6	28.7	44.6	8.8	2.3	54677	58745	71	59	2242	3.4	3.8	12.1	62.5	18.1	259273
98248	FERNDALE	22698	7939	16.8	28.4	40.9	11.0	2.9	54519	59275	70	59	5825	5.8	2.4	9.7	62.1	20.0	285750
98249	FREELAND	28454	1903	14.4	31.1	40.0	9.4	5.2	53595	55965	69	57	1550	2.1	0.3	4.8	50.0	42.8	372457
98250	FRIDAY HARBOR	33532	3524	17.7	25.0	42.1	8.3	6.9	56330	57470	73	62	2607	3.6	1.8	4.5	32.8	57.3	509673
98251	GOLD BAR	25608	1984	11.9	25.3	47.0	11.8	4.0	61345	65160	79	71	1607	8.3	4.5	22.0	58.9	6.3	209708
98252	GRANITE FALLS	27256	2977	11.2	17.3	49.6	16.5	5.3	67052	70738	85	81	2304	2.6	2.3	14.6	66.4	14.1	257045
98253	GREENBANK	32962	792	13.5	19.6	49.6	12.2	5.1	63358	64434	82	75	654	1.2	1.2	5.0	53.1	39.4	359884
98257	LA CONNER	30377	1826	18.4	23.5	38.5	12.0	7.5	56597	60209	73	63	1340	2.2	2.2	9.0	51.0	35.7	336634
98258	LAKE STEVENS	31202	8692	8.5	13.6	45.7	23.4	8.8	76032	79670	90	89	6747	1.2	1.8	5.0	66.3	25.7	329332
98260	LANGLEY	28398	2488	18.8	25.7	39.4	9.6	6.4	54191	56746	70	57	1898	0.6	0.9	8.4	47.6	42.5	368293
98261	LOPEZ ISLAND	30957	1290	17.4	33.0	36.0	8.8	4.8	49782	49984	61	48	993	1.9	0.8	14.5	25.2	57.6	486782
98262	LUMMI ISLAND	32976	477	25.8	21.6	36.3	10.3	6.1	51701	53992	65	53	369	0.0	0.0	4.9	43.9	51.2	418750
98264	LYNDEN	24459	6849	16.1	26.2	42.8	10.9	4.0	56379	60330	73	63	4791	2.1	1.0	5.3	69.0	22.6	324914
98266	MAPLE FALLS	17595	1042	23.4	30.3	36.5	6.0	3.8	47615	49547	56	42	798	11.4	19.2	34.7	23.6	11.2	129706
98267	MARBLEMOUNT	28333	192	25.0	24.0	31.3	13.5	6.3	51144	53936	64	51	136	7.4	12.5	32.4	37.5	10.3	168750
98270	MARYSVILLE	28621	15499	11.2	18.9	42.8	20.9	6.1	69234	75128	86	84	10982	2.2	2.7	7.4	72.3	15.3	293952
98271	MARYSVILLE	27336	9107	10.9	19.9	46.4	18.4	4.5	68517	73243	86	83	7476	8.7	6.0	11.2	61.0	13.1	248065
98272	MONROE	28718	8826	10.1	14.4	45.1	22.4	8.0	72944	76976	88	87	6525	0.6	1.1	3.8	65.0	29.3	343924
98273	MOUNT VERNON	22288	10328	20.4	29.1	36.6	9.2	4.7	50433	53685	62	50	6345	5.0	3.3	11.7	62.1	18.0	255368
98274	MOUNT VERNON	27364	5865	13.5	24.9	39.9	15.8	6.0	62336	64354	80	73	4403	2.9	2.7	10.7	58.5	25.2	279726
98275	MUKILTEO	39265	7747	6.2	15.1	37.7	25.2	15.8	84324	85949	94	95	5071	0.2	0.7	4.0	34.1	61.2	459029
98277	OAK HARBOR	23211	14305	16.3	29.1	43.0	8.3	3.3	53991	57728	70	57	8257	5.6	2.5	9.1	67.8	15.0	272762
98278	OAK HARBOR	14177	304	37.2	47.0	11.8	3.9	0.0	29191	29766	7	2	18	0.0	0.0	0.0	100.0	0.0	237500
98279	OLGA	39460	605	17.7	25.1	36.2	13.9	7.1	61657	62238	80	71	460	0.0	0.0	4.8	24.1	71.1	598276
98281	POINT ROBERTS	27019	797	26.7	29.7	28.5	12.4	2.6	44265	45859	46	30	566	1.9	3.9	28.4	40.3	25.4	231098
98282	CAMANO ISLAND	29049	6385	13.0	22.9	44.0	14.4	5.7	64802	65294	83	78	5513	0.5	0.8	7.3	52.9	38.4	349324
98283	ROCKPORT	22437	122	31.1	27.0	28.7	9.8	3.3	40645	44216	35	18	95	7.4	11.6	31.6	43.2	6.3	173438
98284	SEDRO WOOLLEY	23727	9593	18.8	27.4	38.7	11.7	3.4	53171	56505	68	56	7052	6.5	2.9	20.7	56.8	13.0	225276
98288	SKYKOMISH	29123	183	16.4	23.0	49.2	8.7	2.7	57054	58560	74	64	133	5.3	6.8	53.4	28.6	6.0	138021
98290	SNOHOMISH	33713	12138	8.9	16.1	39.3	25.0	10.7	78156	81566	91	90	9359	1.9	0.8	5.5	51.9	39.9	361810
98292	STANWOOD	30633	7731	11.6	17.3	46.1	17.7	7.3	70298	75618	87	85	5924	1.4	1.0	9.5	60.0	28.1	319778
98294	SULTAN	27171	2846	13.1	19.4	49.2	13.6	4.6	64714	69226	83	78	2196	6.3	3.6	9.7	61.9	18.4	262245
98295	SUMAS	19750	868	22.6	29.3	38.2	7.0	2.9	48524	50680	58	44	556	4.1	2.9	18.2	51.8	23.0	247980
98296	SNOHOMISH	38342	8631	4.8	9.0	32.9	35.9	17.3	103983	105043	97	98	7754	1.6	0.9	1.9	39.1	56.5	435228
98303	ANDERSON ISLAND	28263	506	29.6	22.7	37.7	4.9	4.9	48397	49879	58	44	435	2.5	0.5	21.4	45.7	29.9	310714
98304	ASHFORD	24562	410	22.9	29.8	38.8	5.1	3.4	46830	50550	54	40	308	5.5	3.9	27.9	47.7	14.9	203333
98305	BEAVER	21126	194	21.1	37.6	36.6	4.6	0.0	43923	45158	45	29	148	12.8	5.4	10.8	56.1	14.9	208065
98310	BREMERTON	24029	8376	24.9	29.9	35.4	7.3	2.4	46040	48329	51	37	4287	1.4	2.1	35.0	55.2	6.3	195756
98311	BREMERTON	26981	8996	10.1	22.1	46.8	16.4	4.6	65446	67563	84	79	6552	4.6	3.9	12.9	72.4	6.1	225258
98312	BREMERTON	24872	12896	20.4	27.1	37.9	9.9	4.7	52313	56687	67	54	7593	3.0	2.9	32.7	49.5	11.9	206646
98315	SILVERDALE	14581	1093	13.7	54.1	30.3	1.3	0.6	42662	44029	41	25	14	0.0	0.0	42.9	21.4	35.7	250000
98320	BRINNON	21463	627	35.1	33.7	24.4	5.6	1.3	36195	37025	21	7	543	4.4	10.9	36.6	28.9	19.2	165948
98321	BUCKLEY	26184	5982	10.7	20.1	49.0	15.2	4.9	67414	68282	85	82	4845	3.2	4.3	12.2	64.4	15.9	268697
98323	CARBONADO	25092	291	9.6	18.2	52.2	15.1	4.8	71600	71797	88	86	244	2.5	2.9	17.2	62.7	14.8	255000
98325	CHIMACUM	21547	662	25.8	23.6	40.6	6.9	3.0	50310	51472	62	49	496	8.5	13.1	19.0	44.6	14.9	200735
98326	CLALLAM BAY	17805	382	30.1	37.2	28.8	2.1	1.8	38663	40136	29	13	237	12.2	13.5	38.0	32.5	3.8	149609
98327	DUPONT	34813	2524	5.2	12.4	52.7	24.1	5.6	76291	78173	90	89	1793	0.0	0.4	13.7	71.4	14.5	275322
98328	EATONVILLE	24782	3735	12.4	26.1	43.9	13.1	4.6	59930	61675	77	69	2982	4.0	2.3	15.7	55.6	22.5	266118
98329	GIG HARBOR	26148	3898	10.3	22.3	48.2	14.9	4.4	64493	65770	83	77	3208	0.7	2.2	19.9	59.5	17.6	236149
98330	ELBE	22158	183	24.6	30.6	37.7	4.9	2.2	44305	48131	46	30	137	6.6	4.4	32.1	45.3	11.7	189844
98331	FORKS	19067	2666	26.2	29.5	38.8	4.5	1.0	45304	48501	49	34	1840	17.2	8.2	37.0	33.3	4.3	152907
98332	GIG HARBOR	33207	5725	9.9	16.2	44.6	19.6	9.7	71641	72597	88	87	4684	2.8	2.2	4.4	48.9	41.8	361623
98333	FOX ISLAND	39417	1276	2.7	9.6	52.0	21.0	14.7	82487	83116	93	94	1129	1.1	1.0	1.2	36.7	60.1	485338
98335	GIG HARBOR	34083	9813	9.3	21.0	41.0	17.7	11.0	69866	71412	87	84	7135	1.5	0.7	1.2	52.3	44.3	378355
98336	GLENOMA	18332	481	31.2	28.1	33.9	5.4	1.5	40916	43287	36	19	354	12.7	10.2	28.5	44.9	3.7	172283
98337	BREMERTON	18714	3035	35.2	36.5	23.5	3.3	1.6	33858	35291	15	4	1118	0.0	8.1	65.2	25.4	1.3	147335
98338	GRAHAM	24939	8378	11.2	20.3	48.9	16.1	3.6	65910	66689	84	80	7166	3.3	6.6	14.4	59.8	15.9	255150
98339	PORT HADLOCK	20564	1436	28.8	31.8	31.5	5.5	2.4	41392	43631	37	20	1052	7.5	6.7	28.1	46.1	11.5	194231
98340	HANSVILLE	35482	1090	13.0	21.3	38.8	18.6	8.3	69040	71173	86	84	941	0.9	0.7	6.8	56.7	34.9	332464
98342	INDIANOLA	29806	805	10.9	19.9	48.0	16.9	4.3	68203	70045	86	82	669	0.6	1.5	16.4	63.5	17.9	239482
98345	KEYPORT	30453	157	11.5	17.8	47.1	19.7	3.8	68035	71686	86	82	121	5.0	1.7	6.6	45.5	41.3	341667
98346	KINGSTON	27587	3562	12.2	26.3	41.6	14.5	5.3	61504	64412	79	71	2769	3.6	2.2	12.5	53.3	28.4	286696
98349	LAKEBAY	23529	1873	22.2	24.0	36.1	11.4	6.3	53429	56451	69	57	1542	2.4	2.1	18.1	49.5	27.9	266667
98351	LONGBRANCH	28098	528	25.6	22.0	34.5	11.9	6.1	52737	56453	67	55	438	3.0	2.3	18.9	50.5	25.3	249315
98354	MILTON	27625	2496	14.9	23.4	47.3	11.7	2.7	58876	61105	76	68	1398	0.1	0.6	11.4	77.5	10.4	280866
98355	MINERAL	18924	263	31.9	31.2	31.9	3.8	1.1	38294	40649	28	11	206	6.3	7.3	40.8	39.8	5.8	164286
98356	MORTON	21301	892	25.0	31.3	37.4	4.0	2.2	43405	47375	44	27	633	4.1	8.4	38.5	42.2	6.8	173065
98358	NORDLAND	30210	427	9.8	42.6	36.3	8.2	3.0	48576	49822	58	45	351	2.6	2.3	1.4	30.5	63.2	522246
98359	OLALLA	24739	1768	14.4	23.8	48.4	10.0	3.4	60684	63337	78	70	1492	4.3	1.2	25.3	53.4	15.8	229644
98360	ORTING	26714	3788	10.7	19.7	47.3	18.1	4.1	69909	70848	87	85	3131	1.0	1.8	19.8	66.6	10.7	243741
98361	PACKWOOD	23112	465	28.4	34.8	29.9	4.3	2.6	40943	41593	36	19	363	6.6	6.9	35.3	44.4	6.9	178516
98362	PORT ANGELES	24554	10031	27.4	26.5	35.9	7.3	2.8	45887	48864	51	36	6841	2.2	2.9	25.4	55.6	13.9	220190
98363	PORT ANGELES	22839	5446	21.4	30.6	39.0	6.7	2.3	48304	51050	57	43	3924	3.2	3.3	23.8	56.9	12.8	215028
98365	PORT LUDLOW	35580	2100	9.2	26.9	47.9	10.6	5.4	62394	63609	80	73	1832	1.5	3.0	7.9	40.8	46.8	385013
98366	PORT ORCHARD	25092	12823	17.0	25.3	42.6	11.6	3.5	58457	61707	76	67	8231	2.0	1.8	21.6	63.4	11.2	225559
98367	PORT ORCHARD	26395	9262	11.1	21.1	49.0	14.2	4.6	66379	68238	84	81	7908	2.8	2.5	18.1	63.0	13.5	245739
98368	PORT TOWNSEND	28042	6925	24.9	27.6	34.7	8.8	4.0	47247	49940	55	40	4983	4.4	2.6	13.5	50.8	28.8	288737
98370	POULSBO	28878	10814	12.5	22.2	42.1	18.2	5.0	64472	66811	83	77	8148	2.2	2.2	11.5	58.2	25.9	299182
98371	PUYALLUP	27162	8488	15.8	27.5	38.6	12.7	5.4	57007	60397	74	63	6006	10.3	3.5	5.7	66.9	13.7	270861
98372	PUYALLUP	27430	9247	15.8	26.3	39.9	13.1	4.8	57958	60767	75	65	5268	6.5	3.0	7.9	62.0	20.6	280030
98373	PUYALLUP	28353	7781	9.7	23.6	46.4	15.7	4.5	64569	65493	83	77	4776	2.4	1.2	5.1	81.1	10.3	292678
	WASHINGTON	29418		17.0	23.3	38.4	13.6	7.7	60852	63758				3.4	2.9	16.8	52.3	24.6	272173
	UNITED STATES	27277		20.9	24.4	35.3	11.7	7.6	54719	56938				9.3	13.1	31.6	32.6	13.5	162279

ZIP CODE		FINANCIAL SERVICES				THE HOME						ENTERTAINMENT						PERSONAL			
						Home Improvements		Furnishings													
#	POST OFFICE NAME	Auto Loan	Home Loan	Invest-ments	Retire-ment Plans	Home Repair	Lawn & Garden	Comput-ers & Hard-ware-Personal	Major Appli-ances	TV, Radio, Sound Equip-ment	Furni-ture	Dine out/ Carry out	Sports Equip-ment	Fees & Tickets	Toys & Games	Travel	Cable TV	Apparel & Services	Auto Repairs	Health Insur-ance	Pets & Supplies
98224	BARING	101	81	131	80	89	107	81	103	85	76	84	75	70	81	88	91	56	95	102	120
98225	BELLINGHAM	68	58	58	61	58	59	79	63	74	70	75	53	69	73	67	73	53	71	66	77
98226	BELLINGHAM	94	94	88	96	92	91	96	92	94	96	95	72	96	95	95	93	67	94	92	110
98229	BELLINGHAM	94	97	95	99	97	93	97	94	95	99	96	73	99	96	98	94	68	96	93	111
98230	BLAINE	99	95	105	94	96	102	91	100	92	90	92	75	89	92	94	95	63	96	99	117
98232	BOW	114	117	135	118	120	126	107	120	106	107	107	90	109	105	116	109	74	113	117	139
98233	BURLINGTON	88	92	85	92	91	89	90	89	89	90	90	68	92	90	90	89	63	89	89	104
98236	CLINTON	113	97	140	96	103	120	95	116	98	90	97	85	86	94	102	103	65	107	114	134
98237	CONCRETE	83	67	81	66	69	83	68	79	72	66	71	58	59	72	66	77	48	74	81	93
98239	COUPEVILLE	95	88	124	87	97	108	85	101	90	86	89	70	83	83	94	95	60	96	108	116
98240	CUSTER	101	108	98	111	107	111	98	105	98	97	98	81	102	100	103	100	68	100	105	123
98241	DARRINGTON	92	70	90	68	71	94	73	88	81	68	78	66	61	80	71	88	52	83	94	104
98244	DEMING	89	89	86	89	88	92	82	88	83	83	83	67	82	85	84	84	57	85	88	104
98245	EASTSOUND	122	98	158	97	108	129	98	124	103	93	101	90	86	97	107	109	67	115	123	144
98247	EVERSON	87	91	85	91	89	92	85	88	85	85	86	68	87	87	88	86	60	86	88	104
98248	FERNDALE	92	93	88	93	91	94	87	91	88	88	88	70	88	90	89	89	61	89	91	108
98249	FREELAND	110	88	142	86	97	116	88	112	92	82	91	82	76	87	95	98	60	103	110	129
98250	FRIDAY HARBOR	109	104	136	104	114	120	100	114	103	106	102	79	101	98	109	107	70	110	119	131
98251	GOLD BAR	108	103	101	99	101	103	96	103	96	99	97	77	91	100	94	97	66	98	99	120
98252	GRANITE FALLS	112	117	102	114	113	110	107	110	106	111	107	84	108	111	107	106	74	106	106	128
98253	GREENBANK	106	99	145	98	112	123	93	114	98	98	97	76	94	90	105	104	66	107	121	130
98257	LA CONNER	104	97	130	97	108	118	94	110	98	98	97	75	93	92	102	103	66	105	118	126
98258	LAKE STEVENS	126	145	124	143	139	127	128	129	122	134	124	102	136	128	132	118	88	124	118	148
98260	LANGLEY	112	90	144	88	98	118	90	114	94	84	93	83	78	89	97	100	62	105	112	132
98261	LOPEZ ISLAND	99	89	133	88	100	112	85	105	89	86	88	72	82	83	95	94	59	98	109	120
98262	LUMMI ISLAND	114	91	147	90	100	120	91	116	95	85	94	85	79	91	99	102	63	107	114	134
98264	LYNDEN	93	98	98	98	99	100	95	97	94	92	94	75	97	94	98	95	66	96	98	113
98266	MAPLE FALLS	84	80	68	77	76	77	78	78	78	81	78	59	74	81	74	78	54	78	76	93
98267	MARBLEMOUNT	115	94	142	92	101	120	93	116	97	89	96	85	82	94	99	103	64	107	114	134
98270	MARYSVILLE	116	118	105	118	114	108	114	112	111	118	112	89	114	115	112	109	79	111	107	130
98271	MARYSVILLE	116	115	111	113	113	115	106	114	107	110	107	85	105	109	108	107	73	109	111	132
98272	MONROE	123	135	118	135	130	122	124	124	120	128	121	98	129	124	126	117	85	121	116	144
98273	MOUNT VERNON	89	85	84	87	84	85	90	86	89	89	90	68	88	90	88	89	63	89	87	103
98274	MOUNT VERNON	100	111	115	110	112	109	104	107	102	103	103	82	110	102	111	103	73	105	106	124
98275	MUKILTEO	143	159	151	164	158	144	147	144	141	155	143	115	158	145	153	136	103	142	134	168
98277	OAK HARBOR	94	84	80	85	82	83	90	86	89	90	91	68	85	93	85	89	63	89	85	102
98278	OAK HARBOR	63	33	25	38	29	28	59	41	56	55	59	41	45	67	43	51	41	52	37	50
98279	OLGA	114	110	158	109	126	135	102	124	108	110	106	81	105	99	116	114	72	117	133	141
98281	POINT ROBERTS	96	77	124	76	84	102	77	98	81	72	80	71	67	76	83	86	53	90	97	113
98282	CAMANO ISLAND	116	105	145	104	113	126	100	120	103	99	102	87	95	99	108	108	69	112	120	139
98283	ROCKPORT	96	73	111	71	78	100	74	94	80	69	78	69	61	77	76	86	52	86	95	110
98284	SEDRO WOOLLEY	94	92	88	91	91	94	89	92	90	89	90	69	87	91	88	91	62	90	93	109
98288	SKYKOMISH	101	81	131	80	89	107	81	103	85	76	84	75	70	81	88	90	56	95	102	119
98290	SNOHOMISH	126	145	133	146	142	133	131	131	126	135	128	103	142	129	138	124	91	129	125	153
98292	STANWOOD	116	129	123	130	128	124	118	121	115	121	116	94	125	117	124	114	82	118	118	141
98294	SULTAN	107	110	103	108	107	107	103	107	101	103	102	83	103	105	104	102	71	103	103	124
98295	SUMAS	89	83	76	82	82	86	79	84	81	80	81	62	75	84	76	83	55	81	84	100
98296	SNOHOMISH	156	193	170	195	187	166	162	165	151	173	154	132	183	159	174	144	112	155	144	188
98303	ANDERSON ISLAND	82	87	118	86	100	102	78	92	82	88	81	57	86	74	90	86	55	88	102	104
98304	ASHFORD	87	72	111	70	80	94	72	90	75	69	74	64	64	71	78	80	49	83	91	104
98305	BEAVER	83	66	107	65	73	88	66	84	69	62	69	62	58	66	72	74	46	78	83	98
98310	BREMERTON	74	70	68	71	69	71	77	73	78	74	78	56	74	77	74	79	54	76	77	87
98311	BREMERTON	105	111	97	110	106	102	106	103	103	109	105	81	108	106	106	101	73	103	100	121
98312	BREMERTON	90	84	76	85	81	83	91	85	90	88	90	67	87	92	85	90	63	88	87	101
98315	SILVERDALE	80	42	31	48	37	36	75	52	71	70	74	52	57	85	54	65	52	66	47	64
98320	BRINNON	64	61	78	56	68	73	58	69	62	63	60	45	57	56	64	65	40	66	76	79
98321	BUCKLEY	112	115	100	112	111	108	106	108	105	110	106	83	107	110	105	105	74	105	104	127
98323	CARBONADO	117	128	104	124	120	107	113	113	107	122	109	90	116	115	112	101	76	107	100	129
98325	CHIMACUM	91	75	110	73	80	94	75	91	78	71	77	67	66	75	79	82	51	85	90	106
98326	CLALLAM BAY	70	64	86	60	71	78	61	74	65	64	63	50	59	60	67	69	43	70	80	85
98327	DUPONT	130	141	113	135	131	115	125	124	117	136	120	99	127	127	122	110	84	117	107	140
98328	EATONVILLE	102	104	99	104	102	107	95	102	96	96	96	78	96	98	98	98	66	98	102	121
98329	GIG HARBOR	108	115	100	114	111	108	103	107	102	107	103	82	106	106	104	101	72	102	102	125
98330	ELBE	82	71	100	68	78	88	69	84	73	70	72	59	64	69	75	77	48	79	87	97
98331	FORKS	82	67	81	65	68	80	67	77	71	66	70	58	59	71	66	75	47	74	78	92
98332	GIG HARBOR	116	140	138	143	142	136	121	128	118	127	119	95	136	118	134	117	84	122	125	147
98333	FOX ISLAND	138	171	175	176	175	162	145	154	139	155	141	114	166	139	163	137	101	146	145	176
98335	GIG HARBOR	118	137	133	139	138	130	123	126	119	128	120	95	134	120	131	118	85	122	122	145
98336	GLENOMA	84	60	86	58	63	85	62	79	69	58	67	59	50	68	61	75	45	72	82	93
98337	BREMERTON	61	47	42	50	45	48	63	52	63	59	63	44	56	64	54	63	44	60	56	65
98338	GRAHAM	109	113	97	112	109	108	103	107	102	107	103	81	105	107	103	102	71	103	103	125
98339	PORT HADLOCK	77	72	70	70	73	75	68	73	71	72	70	52	66	72	67	72	48	71	74	86
98340	HANSVILLE	110	117	154	116	133	135	105	122	110	118	109	78	116	100	121	115	75	117	135	139
98342	INDIANOLA	111	122	101	121	116	108	109	110	104	114	106	87	113	110	110	101	74	105	101	127
98345	KEYPORT	107	119	114	121	118	111	112	110	109	115	110	86	119	110	116	107	78	110	107	129
98346	KINGSTON	101	108	104	109	108	105	100	103	99	104	100	77	104	100	103	99	70	100	101	120
98349	LAKEBAY	108	92	119	90	96	109	90	106	94	88	93	77	81	93	93	98	63	100	105	124
98351	LONGBRANCH	108	96	101	93	96	104	91	101	95	93	95	74	85	97	90	99	64	97	101	120
98354	MILTON	88	92	85	93	89	88	93	88	92	92	94	69	96	93	93	92	66	92	91	105
98355	MINERAL	67	63	81	59	70	76	60	72	64	65	63	47	59	59	66	68	42	69	80	82
98356	MORTON	84	65	85	64	68	86	69	81	74	64	72	60	59	73	68	80	48	77	86	95
98358	NORDLAND	86	91	123	90	105	107	82	97	86	93	85	60	90	78	94	90	58	92	108	109
98359	OLALLA	98	107	92	109	103	104	97	100	95	98	96	78	101	98	100	95	67	97	98	118
98360	ORTING	113	121	103	119	116	109	110	111	106	115	107	87	112	112	110	103	75	106	104	128
98361	PACKWOOD	75	67	93	63	75	83	65	79	69	67	67	54	62	64	71	73	45	75	84	91
98362	PORT ANGELES	80	74	87	74	78	86	76	82	78	74	77	60	73	76	77	82	53	81	88	96
98363	PORT ANGELES	85	77	87	77	79	87	77	84	79	74	78	63	72	79	77	82	53	82	87	99
98365	PORT LUDLOW	103	107	146	106	123	127	97	114	102	109	100	72	105	92	111	107	69	109	127	130
98366	PORT ORCHARD	91	92	88	92	90	89	92	90	91	92	92	70	92	92	92	91	64	91	90	106
98367	PORT ORCHARD	105	117	102	117	113	111	104	107	102	106	102	83	109	105	108	101	72	103	104	126
98368	PORT TOWNSEND	86	82	108	81	89	97	79	91	82	80	81	64	78	77	86	87	56	87	97	105
98370	POULSBO	104	111	105	112	109	109	103	106	102	105	103	81	107	103	107	103	72	104	106	124
98371	PUYALLUP	92	101	101	100	101	101	95	98	94	94	95	75	99	94	100	95	66	96	99	114
98372	PUYALLUP	95	95	90	96	93	90	98	93	96	99	97	73	98	97	96	95	68	96	92	110
98373	PUYALLUP	105	109	96	111	105	101	106	102	103	108	104	81	109	106	106	101	73	103	99	121
	WASHINGTON	106	107	105	108	106	104	108	105	106	108	107	82	108	107	107	105	75	106	104	124
	UNITED STATES	100	100	100	100	100	100	100	100	100	100	100	100	100	100	100	100	100	100	100	100

ZIP CODE #	POST OFFICE NAME	COUNTY FIPS CODE	POPULATION 2000	POPULATION 2009	POPULATION 2014	2000-2009 ANNUAL RATE % Rate	2000-2009 ANNUAL RATE State Centile	HOUSEHOLDS 2000	HOUSEHOLDS 2009	HOUSEHOLDS 2014	HOUSEHOLDS % Annual Rate 2000-2009	HOUSEHOLDS 2009 Average HH Size	FAMILIES 2000	FAMILIES 2009	FAMILIES % Annual Rate 2000-2009
98374	PUYALLUP	053	30004	39015	43571	2.9	93	10546	13971	15678	3.1	2.79	8157	10569	2.8
98375	PUYALLUP	053	14170	25111	29712	6.4	99	4707	8547	10162	6.7	2.93	3844	6850	6.4
98376	QUILCENE	031	1746	2034	2158	1.7	75	755	906	970	2.0	2.24	496	581	1.7
98377	RANDLE	041	2474	2770	2931	1.2	57	1033	1154	1223	1.2	2.40	708	777	1.0
98380	SEABECK	035	3419	4140	4448	2.1	85	1252	1546	1667	2.3	2.68	964	1176	2.2
98381	SEKIU	009	1794	2090	2222	1.7	75	656	773	828	1.8	2.54	442	509	1.5
98382	SEQUIM	009	21547	25180	26893	1.7	75	9848	11677	12556	1.9	2.13	6666	7753	1.6
98383	SILVERDALE	035	19736	21018	21530	0.7	35	7184	7664	7870	0.7	2.67	5223	5489	0.5
98387	SPANAWAY	053	34179	41619	45894	2.2	86	11491	13965	15411	2.1	2.97	9056	10819	1.9
98388	STEILACOOM	053	5952	6208	6408	0.5	28	2528	2674	2771	0.6	2.32	1735	1782	0.3
98390	SUMNER	053	9438	10004	10469	0.6	31	3891	4147	4356	0.7	2.39	2505	2578	0.3
98391	BONNEY LAKE	053	35358	44128	48679	2.4	88	11919	15091	16731	2.6	2.92	9623	11999	2.4
98392	SUQUAMISH	035	2443	2527	2570	0.4	23	990	1051	1077	0.6	2.40	662	688	0.4
98394	VAUGHN	053	742	846	909	1.4	66	299	346	373	1.6	2.43	219	247	1.3
98402	TACOMA	053	4422	5127	5371	1.6	73	2033	2476	2684	2.2	1.46	375	498	3.1
98403	TACOMA	053	7637	7532	7562	-0.1	4	4167	4134	4179	-0.1	1.78	1623	1519	-0.7
98404	TACOMA	053	30825	32796	34184	0.7	35	10218	10861	11325	0.7	2.99	7308	7564	0.4
98405	TACOMA	053	23346	24778	25740	0.6	31	9478	10077	10480	0.7	2.35	5003	5129	0.3
98406	TACOMA	053	21920	22833	23423	0.4	23	9242	9672	9966	0.5	2.20	5301	5340	0.1
98407	TACOMA	053	20197	20462	20898	0.1	8	8656	8893	9125	0.3	2.28	5311	5264	-0.1
98408	TACOMA	053	19172	19541	19953	0.2	12	7218	7405	7578	0.3	2.60	4762	4735	-0.1
98409	TACOMA	053	22596	24124	25135	0.7	35	8880	9484	9905	0.7	2.51	5491	5667	0.3
98416	TACOMA	053	953	1128	1130	1.8	78	13	13	13	0.0	2.54	7	6	-1.7
98418	TACOMA	053	10352	10647	10886	0.3	16	3865	3997	4100	0.4	2.62	2477	2475	0.0
98421	TACOMA	053	610	1162	1296	7.2	99	34	62	78	6.7	2.55	17	30	6.3
98422	TACOMA	053	19529	21328	22496	1.0	49	7301	7993	8469	1.0	2.65	5520	5919	0.8
98424	TACOMA	053	5272	7416	8417	3.8	97	2307	3292	3756	3.9	2.24	1270	1770	3.7
98433	TACOMA	053	19666	23621	24287	2.0	83	3573	3994	4219	1.2	3.63	3489	3818	1.0
98438	MCCHORD AFB	053	513	462	455	-1.1	1	52	48	48	-0.9	2.54	51	47	-0.9
98439	LAKEWOOD	053	2707	2690	2723	-0.1	4	1089	1098	1116	0.1	2.45	652	635	-0.3
98443	TACOMA	053	5496	5582	5692	0.2	12	2027	2078	2127	0.3	2.68	1546	1551	0.0
98444	TACOMA	053	31095	32661	33679	0.5	28	11565	12129	12541	0.5	2.54	7438	7566	0.2
98445	TACOMA	053	23835	27592	29921	1.6	73	8662	10147	11039	1.7	2.71	6450	7337	1.4
98446	TACOMA	053	8764	11242	12355	2.7	91	3243	4150	4568	2.7	2.70	2469	3142	2.6
98447	TACOMA	053	81	80	82	-0.1	4	36	36	37	0.0	2.22	20	20	0.0
98465	TACOMA	053	7247	7566	7823	0.5	28	3339	3519	3650	0.6	2.12	1721	1735	0.1
98466	TACOMA	053	25370	27230	28270	0.8	40	10882	11690	12159	0.8	2.33	6926	7242	0.5
98467	UNIVERSITY PLACE	053	13768	15135	16066	1.0	49	5265	5896	6274	1.2	2.54	3755	4076	0.9
98498	LAKEWOOD	053	28993	29074	29566	0.0	6	11467	11702	11944	0.2	2.39	7710	7643	-0.1
98499	LAKEWOOD	053	32777	33308	34089	0.2	12	13218	13653	14045	0.4	2.39	8372	8345	0.0
98501	OLYMPIA	067	33347	38757	42135	1.6	73	13954	16065	17417	1.5	2.39	8604	9800	1.4
98502	OLYMPIA	067	25557	30190	32876	1.8	78	10693	12579	13738	1.8	2.31	6384	7311	1.5
98503	LACEY	067	33300	36846	39191	1.1	52	13199	14552	15522	1.1	2.49	8926	9582	0.8
98505	OLYMPIA	067	651	575	676	-1.3	1	4	9	11	9.2	2.56	3	6	7.8
98506	OLYMPIA	067	16992	18453	19498	0.9	45	7247	7910	8388	1.0	2.26	4220	4439	0.5
98512	OLYMPIA	067	23929	26987	29219	1.3	61	9564	10824	11771	1.3	2.44	6433	7106	1.1
98513	OLYMPIA	067	24164	31330	35286	2.8	92	8786	11602	13162	3.1	2.70	6839	8811	2.8
98516	OLYMPIA	067	13953	20450	23844	4.2	98	5318	7803	9127	4.2	2.62	3900	5673	4.1
98520	ABERDEEN	027	21520	23328	23412	0.9	45	8526	8513	8535	0.0	2.51	5601	5505	-0.2
98524	ALLYN	045	1597	2245	2613	3.8	97	686	979	1139	3.9	2.29	505	709	3.7
98526	AMANDA PARK	027	453	485	503	0.7	35	167	180	187	0.8	2.69	124	133	0.8
98528	BELFAIR	045	7839	9535	10470	2.1	85	3031	3684	4051	2.1	2.56	2147	2569	2.0
98531	CENTRALIA	041	21887	23834	24859	0.9	45	8514	9224	9637	0.9	2.52	5541	5896	0.7
98532	CHEHALIS	041	21169	23157	24210	1.0	49	7832	8510	8908	0.9	2.65	5728	6147	0.8
98533	CINEBAR	041	588	689	743	1.7	75	225	263	284	1.7	2.62	164	189	1.5
98535	COPALIS BEACH	027	323	322	326	0.0	6	138	139	141	0.1	2.32	86	85	-0.1
98536	COPALIS CROSSING	027	493	526	547	0.7	35	228	245	254	0.8	2.15	144	151	0.5
98537	COSMOPOLIS	027	2041	2211	2296	0.9	45	810	880	913	0.9	2.51	577	616	0.7
98538	CURTIS	041	330	349	360	0.6	31	124	131	135	0.6	2.66	97	102	0.5
98541	ELMA	027	9301	9985	10369	0.8	40	3492	3767	3909	0.8	2.64	2474	2627	0.7
98542	ETHEL	041	478	540	576	1.3	61	175	198	211	1.3	2.73	135	150	1.1
98546	GRAPEVIEW	045	1875	2365	2619	2.5	89	808	1015	1124	2.5	2.33	597	738	2.3
98547	GRAYLAND	027	1741	1974	2045	1.4	66	834	915	953	1.0	2.06	486	520	0.7
98548	HOODSPORT	045	1809	2175	2380	2.0	83	883	1068	1171	2.1	2.04	581	690	1.9
98550	HOQUIAM	027	11535	11449	11483	-0.1	4	4539	4535	4544	0.0	2.51	2934	2879	-0.2
98552	HUMPTULIPS	027	281	295	304	0.5	28	106	112	116	0.6	2.63	80	84	0.5
98555	LILLIWAUP	045	430	511	556	1.9	81	223	266	290	1.9	1.92	142	167	1.8
98557	MCCLEARY	027	2643	2929	3068	1.1	52	1027	1156	1212	1.3	2.48	737	817	1.1
98560	MATLOCK	045	152	171	182	1.3	61	56	63	68	1.3	2.71	39	43	1.1
98562	MOCLIPS	027	598	691	736	1.6	73	265	310	330	1.7	2.23	142	161	1.4
98563	MONTESANO	031	7421	8127	8300	1.0	49	2927	3117	3195	0.7	2.52	2085	2185	0.5
98564	MOSSYROCK	041	2257	2678	2895	1.9	81	862	1019	1102	1.8	2.63	633	737	1.7
98568	OAKVILLE	027	2334	2685	2843	1.5	69	796	914	968	1.5	2.94	591	669	1.3
98569	OCEAN SHORES	027	4180	4974	5333	1.9	81	1969	2363	2535	2.0	2.10	1308	1540	1.8
98570	ONALASKA	041	3720	4307	4625	1.6	73	1367	1581	1701	1.6	2.72	1035	1180	1.4
98571	PACIFIC BEACH	027	125	135	141	0.8	40	46	50	52	0.9	2.70	28	30	0.7
98572	PE ELL	041	879	982	1041	1.2	57	334	369	390	1.1	2.66	243	263	0.9
98575	QUINAULT	027	499	525	541	0.6	31	190	202	209	0.7	2.60	135	141	0.5
98576	RAINIER	067	3623	4543	5100	2.5	89	1339	1685	1897	2.5	2.70	999	1224	2.2
98577	RAYMOND	049	6511	6457	6457	-0.1	4	2634	2654	2664	0.1	2.41	1785	1774	-0.1
98579	ROCHESTER	067	9652	12535	14234	2.9	93	3494	4571	5201	2.9	2.73	2686	3434	2.7
98580	ROY	053	9374	11359	12496	2.1	85	3216	3937	4350	2.2	2.87	2544	3053	2.0
98581	RYDERWOOD	015	422	473	503	1.2	57	242	274	292	1.4	1.73	164	183	1.2
98582	SALKUM	041	337	381	406	1.3	61	142	160	171	1.3	2.38	109	121	1.1
98584	SHELTON	045	31577	36597	39449	1.6	73	11468	13419	14559	1.7	2.55	8151	9412	1.6
98585	SILVER CREEK	041	608	700	750	1.5	69	244	281	301	1.5	2.49	181	205	1.4
98586	SOUTH BEND	049	2385	2474	2485	0.4	23	932	969	975	0.4	2.48	632	647	0.3
98587	TAHOLAH	027	909	985	1027	0.9	45	266	292	304	1.0	3.37	206	223	0.9
98588	TAHUYA	045	1604	1990	2210	2.4	88	679	847	941	2.4	2.35	462	566	2.2
98589	TENINO	067	6865	8194	9046	1.9	81	2529	3029	3353	2.0	2.71	1920	2245	1.7
98590	TOKELAND	049	450	475	488	0.6	31	196	208	214	0.6	2.28	127	133	0.5
98591	TOLEDO	041	3335	3606	3763	0.8	40	1243	1340	1400	0.8	2.69	939	999	0.7
98592	UNION	045	1309	1628	1827	2.4	88	601	753	845	2.5	2.16	432	532	2.3
98593	VADER	041	1062	1208	1285	1.4	66	374	419	446	1.2	2.88	284	314	1.1
98595	WESTPORT	027	2793	3005	3126	0.8	40	1312	1428	1486	0.9	2.10	732	775	0.6
	WASHINGTON					1.4					1.4	2.53			1.2
	UNITED STATES					1.0					1.1	2.59			0.9

ZIP CODE #	POST OFFICE NAME	RACE (%) White 2000	White 2009	Black 2000	Black 2009	Asian/Pacific 2000	Asian/Pacific 2009	% Hispanic Origin 2000	% Hispanic Origin 2009	2009 AGE DISTRIBUTION (%) 0-4	5-9	10-14	15-19	20-24	25-44	45-64	65-84	85+	18+	MEDIAN AGE 2009	% 2009 Males	% 2009 Females
98374	PUYALLUP	88.1	85.1	1.9	2.4	3.6	4.5	4.1	5.9	7.9	7.5	7.4	7.5	6.8	28.1	26.0	7.4	1.2	72.6	34.4	48.6	51.4
98375	PUYALLUP	86.7	84.3	2.4	2.6	4.1	5.0	4.4	5.8	7.8	7.6	7.7	7.8	6.0	28.6	26.9	6.8	0.7	71.9	34.8	49.6	50.4
98376	QUILCENE	89.6	87.6	0.8	0.9	0.9	1.1	1.6	2.3	3.4	6.3	6.4	6.2	3.2	19.6	38.9	14.0	2.0	79.8	47.3	50.6	49.4
98377	RANDLE	96.0	95.3	0.3	0.4	0.3	0.4	2.0	2.8	4.6	5.7	6.7	7.2	3.4	20.4	33.7	16.5	1.8	78.6	46.2	51.0	49.0
98380	SEABECK	92.6	90.9	0.3	0.3	1.6	2.0	2.7	3.8	4.4	5.0	5.9	6.8	5.2	22.7	36.8	12.0	1.2	80.4	45.0	51.2	48.8
98381	SEKIU	29.4	27.8	1.6	1.7	0.5	0.6	6.0	7.4	8.9	7.9	7.6	9.1	9.3	26.7	23.0	6.9	0.6	70.2	29.1	55.0	45.0
98382	SEQUIM	94.3	93.2	0.2	0.2	1.4	1.8	2.3	3.2	3.7	3.8	4.1	4.3	3.5	13.4	32.5	29.1	5.6	85.8	57.4	46.9	53.1
98383	SILVERDALE	79.5	75.7	3.1	3.5	10.4	12.4	4.3	5.9	7.0	6.5	6.6	7.2	9.8	29.3	24.3	7.9	1.4	75.4	32.6	50.5	49.5
98387	SPANAWAY	76.5	71.9	7.0	8.2	6.7	8.1	5.2	7.1	8.4	7.9	7.6	7.5	6.3	30.3	24.5	6.9	0.6	71.5	33.2	49.3	50.7
98388	STEILACOOM	78.2	74.0	6.5	7.5	7.1	8.7	5.3	7.2	5.5	5.4	5.6	5.6	5.1	26.6	28.1	16.3	1.8	80.0	42.1	48.5	51.5
98390	SUMNER	90.4	87.9	0.9	1.1	2.0	2.5	5.7	8.2	7.4	6.8	6.4	6.6	7.4	27.2	25.1	10.9	2.1	75.2	35.6	48.7	51.3
98391	BONNEY LAKE	93.8	91.8	0.5	0.6	1.4	2.0	3.0	4.3	7.1	7.3	7.6	7.8	5.5	29.2	28.5	6.3	0.5	73.0	35.9	50.3	49.7
98392	SUQUAMISH	80.5	78.4	0.4	0.5	2.7	3.4	3.1	4.2	6.1	6.1	7.2	6.6	5.2	25.2	32.0	10.0	1.5	76.4	40.9	49.7	50.3
98394	VAUGHN	94.6	93.3	0.1	0.2	1.1	1.4	2.0	3.2	5.0	5.6	6.7	6.5	3.5	21.5	37.4	13.1	0.7	78.6	45.6	51.2	48.8
98402	TACOMA	68.8	66.0	16.2	17.3	5.7	6.3	5.1	6.5	3.2	2.7	2.3	3.9	9.0	37.7	24.6	11.8	4.8	90.7	40.0	60.2	39.8
98403	TACOMA	86.7	83.6	4.0	4.7	2.6	3.3	3.8	5.4	4.8	3.8	3.6	4.7	8.0	36.0	27.6	9.6	1.9	85.2	37.6	47.9	52.1
98404	TACOMA	53.4	48.1	12.8	13.9	14.4	16.0	13.1	16.8	8.5	8.2	8.0	8.2	7.4	27.0	22.9	8.3	1.4	70.3	31.6	49.4	50.6
98405	TACOMA	59.6	54.1	21.3	23.7	7.9	9.4	6.0	8.0	7.4	6.6	6.4	7.1	8.1	28.5	23.1	9.4	3.3	75.3	34.5	48.5	51.5
98406	TACOMA	85.1	81.6	4.7	5.6	3.9	5.0	3.4	4.8	5.0	4.6	5.1	8.1	9.5	24.4	26.2	12.8	4.3	81.6	39.6	47.0	53.0
98407	TACOMA	86.1	83.1	4.4	5.1	3.2	4.1	3.3	4.7	5.2	5.0	5.3	5.9	6.5	25.2	30.2	13.4	3.3	81.0	42.7	47.6	52.4
98408	TACOMA	68.4	63.2	10.3	11.6	9.9	11.7	6.8	9.0	7.0	6.5	6.4	7.2	6.9	27.1	26.1	10.7	2.0	75.6	36.9	48.8	51.2
98409	TACOMA	62.6	57.1	15.7	17.5	7.9	9.2	9.4	12.6	9.0	7.5	6.7	7.4	9.7	30.1	20.9	7.2	1.5	72.5	30.0	49.5	50.5
98416	TACOMA	83.5	79.4	1.1	1.3	8.4	10.5	2.0	2.8	1.4	0.8	1.5	47.5	35.5	5.7	5.1	2.2	0.4	94.6	19.9	38.7	61.3
98418	TACOMA	68.2	62.9	10.2	11.6	8.3	9.7	8.0	10.9	8.2	7.3	6.8	6.9	8.2	29.2	24.1	8.0	1.4	73.6	33.3	50.1	49.9
98421	TACOMA	90.2	88.4	2.1	2.6	2.0	2.2	1.8	2.5	1.9	2.9	4.0	8.5	13.3	38.4	22.5	7.7	0.8	89.1	32.5	68.6	31.4
98422	TACOMA	79.5	75.0	5.1	6.0	8.5	10.7	3.9	5.4	7.7	7.3	7.1	6.4	5.4	29.9	28.4	7.3	0.6	73.9	36.6	49.7	50.3
98424	TACOMA	71.2	67.4	6.2	6.6	7.2	8.3	12.3	15.2	8.7	7.1	6.3	6.5	9.2	32.4	21.6	7.3	0.9	74.3	31.3	50.6	49.4
98433	TACOMA	60.5	55.2	20.3	22.1	5.2	6.1	13.1	17.0	11.5	8.9	5.7	9.5	24.8	36.3	2.7	0.5	0.1	71.4	22.9	65.6	34.4
98438	MCCHORD AFB	76.4	71.6	8.6	9.7	4.7	5.6	8.2	11.7	13.9	11.9	8.0	6.7	18.6	38.5	2.4	0.0	0.0	63.4	22.6	55.4	44.6
98439	LAKEWOOD	63.4	58.3	17.0	19.0	5.1	5.8	12.5	16.3	13.6	10.2	7.5	8.1	11.7	32.1	13.6	2.8	0.4	64.2	24.5	48.1	51.9
98443	TACOMA	89.5	87.2	2.1	2.5	2.0	2.6	3.1	4.4	5.3	5.8	6.3	6.6	5.0	23.8	32.8	12.9	1.5	78.6	43.1	49.7	50.3
98444	TACOMA	64.4	59.3	12.6	13.7	11.3	13.3	7.2	9.4	8.4	7.2	6.2	8.7	11.6	28.2	20.3	8.2	1.3	74.6	29.5	48.5	51.5
98445	TACOMA	73.0	67.7	8.3	9.7	8.5	10.2	5.1	7.0	7.3	6.8	6.7	7.0	6.9	27.5	26.2	10.3	1.3	74.8	35.9	49.0	51.0
98446	TACOMA	85.2	80.6	3.2	4.2	4.3	6.3	3.6	5.1	6.3	6.4	6.8	6.8	4.9	26.7	29.3	11.4	1.3	76.2	40.1	49.8	50.2
98447	TACOMA	79.3	75.0	0.0	0.0	11.0	13.8	1.2	2.5	2.5	2.5	1.3	6.3	22.5	21.3	27.5	16.3	0.0	90.0	37.5	42.5	57.5
98465	TACOMA	76.1	71.5	9.2	10.7	6.7	8.2	5.0	7.0	5.6	5.1	4.8	5.9	8.1	26.7	27.1	13.4	3.4	81.3	40.1	47.8	52.2
98466	TACOMA	79.7	75.9	8.0	9.2	5.6	7.0	3.6	5.0	5.6	5.4	5.8	6.6	6.8	25.5	28.2	14.0	2.0	79.3	40.5	47.2	52.8
98467	UNIVERSITY PLACE	70.4	65.2	10.5	11.7	10.6	13.3	4.7	6.2	7.4	7.3	7.1	7.2	6.3	27.0	27.8	8.7	1.1	73.7	35.1	48.1	51.9
98498	LAKEWOOD	69.8	64.6	11.0	12.5	9.5	11.4	6.0	8.2	6.0	5.6	5.7	6.0	6.4	26.1	27.8	14.5	1.9	79.3	40.6	48.8	51.2
98499	LAKEWOOD	61.4	56.2	12.9	14.1	12.0	13.9	10.1	12.9	8.7	7.3	6.2	6.3	9.4	29.4	20.9	10.1	1.6	74.4	31.8	49.5	50.5
98501	OLYMPIA	88.8	86.7	1.2	1.3	4.0	4.9	3.8	5.1	5.7	5.7	6.1	6.6	6.7	26.5	30.1	10.7	1.9	78.5	39.7	48.6	51.4
98502	OLYMPIA	86.4	84.1	1.6	1.7	6.1	7.3	3.9	5.1	5.1	5.0	5.2	6.6	8.3	29.1	28.2	10.7	1.8	81.5	37.6	48.6	51.4
98503	LACEY	79.9	76.7	4.3	4.6	7.3	8.6	6.2	8.3	7.3	6.7	6.5	6.7	6.9	27.4	24.3	11.3	3.0	75.7	36.0	48.0	52.0
98505	OLYMPIA	86.9	84.7	1.7	1.7	5.2	6.4	2.5	3.5	5.0	6.1	6.3	13.0	18.1	23.0	24.3	4.0	0.2	80.0	26.3	50.3	49.7
98506	OLYMPIA	88.5	86.6	1.6	1.7	4.0	4.8	3.5	4.8	5.4	5.1	5.3	5.6	7.1	26.7	29.5	12.4	2.9	80.9	41.2	48.3	51.7
98512	OLYMPIA	90.3	88.7	1.4	1.5	3.0	3.5	3.2	4.4	5.5	5.3	5.5	6.2	7.0	27.8	30.0	10.8	1.9	80.0	39.3	49.7	50.3
98513	OLYMPIA	78.0	75.4	4.6	5.2	7.5	8.6	5.3	7.0	6.7	6.8	7.1	6.7	5.1	28.5	28.9	9.1	1.0	75.3	37.7	48.9	51.1
98516	OLYMPIA	80.1	77.5	4.1	4.3	8.4	9.8	4.8	6.3	6.3	6.7	7.2	6.9	5.0	26.0	30.6	9.9	1.2	75.4	39.3	49.5	50.5
98520	ABERDEEN	87.0	85.1	0.4	0.5	1.9	2.2	7.4	9.4	6.4	6.2	6.1	6.8	7.4	27.8	26.2	11.1	2.0	77.0	37.1	53.2	46.8
98524	ALLYN	92.9	91.6	0.4	0.6	1.0	1.2	2.0	3.0	3.6	4.2	4.7	5.0	3.5	15.4	36.0	24.8	2.7	84.4	53.5	50.3	49.7
98526	AMANDA PARK	47.9	45.8	0.0	0.0	0.4	0.6	6.8	9.7	7.0	7.6	8.2	8.2	5.4	23.9	29.7	9.1	0.8	71.5	36.0	53.8	46.2
98528	BELFAIR	90.2	88.2	0.7	0.8	2.4	2.9	3.7	5.1	5.6	5.9	6.6	7.7	5.0	23.4	31.7	12.8	1.4	76.9	42.3	50.6	49.4
98531	CENTRALIA	90.2	88.1	0.5	0.6	1.2	1.5	8.8	11.8	7.2	6.5	6.2	6.9	6.7	24.3	25.0	13.6	3.7	75.8	38.2	48.4	51.6
98532	CHEHALIS	92.9	91.3	0.6	0.7	1.0	1.2	5.0	6.9	6.7	6.5	6.7	7.7	6.2	24.9	27.1	12.2	2.1	75.3	38.0	50.4	49.6
98533	CINEBAR	95.7	94.9	0.2	0.1	0.5	0.7	1.9	2.8	4.1	7.1	7.3	7.1	4.1	20.8	33.1	15.2	1.3	76.5	44.7	50.8	49.2
98535	COPALIS BEACH	90.1	89.1	0.3	0.3	1.5	1.9	1.5	2.2	3.7	4.3	5.9	6.2	3.4	17.1	38.5	18.9	1.9	82.0	51.0	49.4	50.6
98536	COPALIS CROSSING	90.1	88.4	0.2	0.2	2.0	2.7	1.8	2.7	3.4	4.2	6.5	7.6	3.6	16.7	38.4	17.9	1.7	81.0	49.8	49.4	50.6
98537	COSMOPOLIS	91.4	89.6	0.1	0.1	1.8	2.3	3.3	4.7	5.8	5.9	6.4	6.9	5.7	24.0	30.2	13.4	1.7	77.7	41.7	49.6	50.4
98538	CURTIS	93.0	91.4	0.0	0.0	0.3	0.3	4.3	5.7	5.4	6.3	6.6	7.2	5.7	20.6	33.0	12.9	2.3	77.1	43.2	50.4	49.6
98541	ELMA	91.7	90.0	0.5	0.5	1.2	1.4	3.7	5.3	6.5	6.4	6.7	7.0	6.6	24.7	27.7	12.5	1.8	76.1	39.0	49.9	50.1
98542	ETHEL	94.8	93.9	0.0	0.0	0.6	0.7	3.6	5.2	6.1	6.5	6.9	6.5	5.2	21.7	31.1	14.4	1.7	76.7	42.7	50.9	49.1
98546	GRAPEVIEW	93.7	92.6	0.6	0.7	0.9	1.0	1.9	2.8	3.5	4.1	4.9	5.1	3.3	17.3	37.0	22.6	2.2	84.3	52.2	49.8	50.2
98547	GRAYLAND	92.4	91.3	0.3	0.3	1.1	1.5	2.3	3.2	2.9	3.3	3.5	4.3	4.2	19.5	37.4	22.2	2.6	87.6	52.9	53.6	46.4
98548	HOODSPORT	92.3	90.9	0.3	0.4	1.0	1.2	1.7	2.5	2.7	3.5	3.8	4.3	3.7	14.0	36.1	30.0	2.0	87.4	57.0	49.7	50.3
98550	HOQUIAM	90.1	88.4	0.3	0.4	1.1	1.4	5.1	7.3	6.6	6.4	6.5	7.1	6.7	24.5	27.7	12.0	2.5	76.2	38.5	49.4	50.6
98552	HUMPTULIPS	89.7	87.5	0.4	0.3	0.4	0.3	6.0	8.8	5.1	5.8	6.4	7.1	5.4	21.4	34.9	12.9	1.0	78.3	44.0	50.5	49.5
98555	LILLIWAUP	92.1	90.4	0.2	0.4	1.2	1.4	1.9	2.7	2.5	2.5	2.5	3.3	4.3	11.9	37.2	32.9	2.7	90.6	59.7	49.5	50.5
98557	MCCLEARY	94.1	93.0	0.2	0.2	0.4	0.5	2.0	3.0	6.1	6.5	6.8	6.4	5.4	24.7	28.9	12.3	2.9	77.8	40.8	48.4	51.6
98560	MATLOCK	93.4	91.8	0.0	0.0	1.3	1.8	0.0	0.0	2.3	2.9	5.8	7.6	4.7	19.3	42.1	15.2	0.0	84.8	48.7	50.9	49.1
98562	MOCLIPS	64.7	62.4	0.2	0.1	1.3	1.6	7.2	9.7	4.6	5.2	5.6	5.2	3.5	20.4	38.4	15.3	1.7	81.3	48.5	50.8	49.2
98563	MONTESANO	94.4	92.2	0.1	0.2	0.9	1.3	1.9	2.9	5.6	5.9	6.2	6.3	5.4	23.8	31.7	12.9	2.2	78.6	42.5	50.0	50.0
98564	MOSSYROCK	94.1	93.0	0.3	0.3	0.4	0.4	3.7	5.2	5.6	5.8	6.6	7.1	4.4	21.4	32.8	14.6	1.6	77.3	44.3	50.2	49.8
98568	OAKVILLE	74.9	72.7	0.4	0.4	0.6	0.9	5.1	7.3	7.7	8.0	7.8	7.1	5.5	23.5	27.7	11.7	1.0	72.0	37.4	49.5	50.5
98569	OCEAN SHORES	92.3	91.2	0.6	0.6	1.3	1.6	1.7	2.5	3.9	4.1	4.4	4.1	3.1	15.9	34.6	27.3	2.6	85.1	55.7	48.6	51.4
98570	ONALASKA	95.3	94.2	0.1	0.2	0.4	0.4	3.2	4.6	5.6	6.0	6.4	6.5	5.4	23.5	31.3	13.7	1.7	78.0	42.1	50.9	49.1
98571	PACIFIC BEACH	86.4	84.4	0.0	0.0	1.6	2.2	2.4	3.7	3.7	4.4	6.7	7.4	3.7	17.0	37.0	17.8	2.2	79.3	49.3	48.9	51.1
98572	PE ELL	94.2	93.2	0.3	0.4	1.1	1.2	1.8	2.5	6.9	7.3	7.7	7.6	5.4	22.8	28.4	12.0	1.7	73.1	39.2	50.6	49.4
98575	QUINAULT	85.8	82.9	0.0	0.0	0.2	0.4	9.6	14.1	4.2	4.8	5.7	7.2	5.7	22.7	34.5	13.7	1.5	81.0	44.7	52.2	47.8
98576	RAINIER	93.1	91.8	0.7	0.7	0.9	1.1	2.8	3.9	5.6	5.9	7.2	7.8	5.3	26.1	31.1	10.2	0.8	76.2	40.0	49.0	51.0
98577	RAYMOND	88.7	86.8	0.2	0.2	4.0	4.8	6.1	8.0	5.8	5.6	6.0	6.4	5.6	21.4	30.2	16.2	2.9	78.7	44.4	49.6	50.4
98579	ROCHESTER	90.9	89.2	0.6	0.6	0.8	0.9	6.6	8.9	7.3	7.4	7.5	7.3	5.1	27.1	27.5	9.8	1.0	73.2	37.0	50.3	49.7
98580	ROY	90.1	87.8	1.1	1.3	1.8	2.2	3.8	5.4	6.2	6.6	7.5	7.6	5.5	26.2	30.8	8.7	0.8	74.9	38.8	50.6	49.4
98581	RYDERWOOD	95.2	93.9	1.0	1.1	0.5	0.6	1.9	2.7	3.6	4.0	3.8	3.0	3.0	14.8	27.9	35.5	4.4	86.5	60.3	48.8	51.2
98582	SALKUM	95.2	94.5	0.0	0.0	0.6	0.8	3.9	5.2	6.0	6.6	6.8	6.3	5.2	22.0	30.4	14.7	1.8	76.6	42.7	51.4	48.6
98584	SHELTON	86.7	84.9	1.6	1.7	1.4	1.6	5.9	8.0	5.7	5.8	6.1	6.8	6.3	24.4	28.2	14.4	2.4	78.5	41.1	52.0	48.0
98585	SILVER CREEK	95.1	93.9	0.2	0.3	0.3	0.4	3.5	4.7	4.7	5.7	7.1	7.4	4.1	20.7	34.3	14.3	1.6	77.1	45.1	50.4	49.6
98586	SOUTH BEND	84.1	81.6	0.1	0.2	3.4	4.2	7.8	10.5	5.8	6.0	6.2	7.1	5.4	22.0	27.6	16.9	3.0	77.4	42.7	49.8	50.2
98587	TAHOLAH	18.9	18.1	0.0	0.0	0.7	0.9	4.7	6.7	9.0	9.7	10.3	8.9	5.2	25.3	25.8	5.4	0.4	64.5	29.9	54.6	45.4
98588	TAHUYA	91.8	90.3	0.2	0.4	1.7	2.1	3.0	4.4	4.1	4.6	5.4	6.3	4.6	21.4	36.2	15.8	1.6	82.1	46.9	51.9	48.1
98589	TENINO	92.5	91.1	0.5	0.6	1.4	1.7	3.2	4.4	5.6	6.2	6.5	7.0	5.6	25.9	31.4	10.7	1.1	77.6	40.4	50.5	49.5
98590	TOKELAND	85.1	83.4	0.2	0.2	2.4	2.9	6.0	8.2	5.5	5.7	5.9	6.1	4.8	20.0	30.5	19.2	2.3	79.2	46.5	50.9	49.1
98591	TOLEDO	94.9	93.9	0.3	0.3	0.4	0.5	3.0	4.4	6.2	6.5	6.7	6.6	5.4	22.8	30.1	13.9	1.7	76.5	41.8	49.9	50.1
98592	UNION	93.4	92.0	0.2	0.3	0.9	1.2	2.4	3.3	3.9	4.5	5.2	5.0	3.4	16.9	38.5	20.6	2.1	83.3	51.9	49.9	50.1
98593	VADER	93.4	92.1	0.0	0.0	0.2	0.2	4.5	6.5	7.4	7.5	7.6	7.4	5.5	22.6	28.9	11.8	1.3	72.8	38.6	48.7	51.3
98595	WESTPORT	93.2	92.2	0.3	0.3	0.8	1.0	2.5	3.7	4.1	4.9	5.8	5.3	3.7	20.3	35.2	18.3	2.4	81.9	48.6	49.8	50.2
	WASHINGTON	81.8	79.0	3.2	3.4	5.9	6.9	7.5	9.7	6.7	6.5	6.5	7.0	7.0	27.4	27.0	10.1	1.8	76.3	36.9	49.8	50.2
	UNITED STATES	75.1	72.0	12.3	12.7	3.8	4.6	12.5	15.7	6.8	6.7	6.6	7.1	6.9	27.0	26.0	10.9	1.9	75.7	36.9	49.2	50.8

ZIP CODE #	POST OFFICE NAME	2009 Per Capita Income	2009 HH Income Base	2009 HOUSEHOLD INCOME DISTRIBUTION (%) Less than $25,000	$25,000 to $49,999	$50,000 to $99,999	$100,000 to $149,999	$150,000 or More	MEDIAN HOUSEHOLD INCOME 2009	2014	2009 National Centile	2009 State Centile	2009 Home Value Base	2009 HOME VALUE DISTRIBUTION (%) Less than $50,000	$50,000 to $89,999	$90,000 to $174,999	$175,000 to $399,999	$400,000 or More	2009 Median Home Value
98374	PUYALLUP	28410	13971	9.7	19.5	47.5	16.7	6.6	69695	71100	87	84	9880	4.6	3.3	5.9	72.4	13.9	290798
98375	PUYALLUP	27813	8547	7.3	19.4	46.2	20.3	6.8	71493	70111	88	86	7107	4.5	4.0	13.3	68.2	10.1	256330
98376	QUILCENE	24731	906	24.2	28.0	37.7	7.1	3.0	47788	50000	56	42	724	2.8	8.6	21.5	46.8	20.3	241477
98377	RANDLE	18479	1154	30.2	37.0	28.0	3.8	1.0	38715	39842	29	13	875	13.1	10.6	38.2	35.5	2.5	155931
98380	SEABECK	28308	1546	12.2	18.0	48.8	16.8	4.2	68869	69999	86	83	1329	0.7	1.4	15.3	57.4	25.1	267571
98381	SEKIU	17196	773	37.1	28.7	29.1	3.9	1.2	36812	38599	23	8	504	10.9	9.1	39.9	38.1	2.0	156618
98382	SEQUIM	27048	11677	22.2	30.7	37.0	6.9	3.1	47604	49994	56	41	9190	4.4	3.7	16.5	53.2	22.2	262333
98383	SILVERDALE	27272	7664	11.3	26.5	41.8	15.5	4.9	63124	65552	81	75	4258	1.9	1.8	6.3	71.4	18.6	286024
98387	SPANAWAY	23832	13965	12.1	21.9	47.8	14.4	3.7	64311	66149	83	76	10556	6.4	4.4	17.3	67.3	4.6	220937
98388	STEILACOOM	33295	2674	12.6	30.7	33.2	13.6	9.8	58063	61262	75	66	1651	0.4	0.5	6.8	54.3	38.0	339787
98390	SUMNER	24704	4147	17.5	30.6	40.1	9.9	2.0	51409	53833	65	52	2230	8.1	1.3	12.1	71.1	7.5	239898
98391	BONNEY LAKE	29922	15091	7.4	15.6	45.6	23.0	8.4	76187	77904	90	89	12936	0.9	3.3	13.4	59.3	23.2	289229
98392	SUQUAMISH	27329	1051	14.5	29.1	39.6	13.1	3.7	57161	61700	74	64	794	2.5	3.1	28.3	50.5	15.5	210227
98394	VAUGHN	27586	346	16.2	24.3	42.8	11.0	5.8	57711	60380	75	65	287	1.4	2.4	19.5	50.2	26.5	282407
98402	TACOMA	21197	2476	55.3	24.2	17.4	1.6	1.5	21331	22276	2	1	248	8.9	11.3	19.8	40.3	19.8	203333
98403	TACOMA	36660	4134	21.7	29.4	31.6	10.0	7.2	48884	50914	59	46	1343	0.7	1.0	9.0	41.0	48.3	390779
98404	TACOMA	16866	10861	26.6	30.2	35.7	5.9	1.6	43804	46238	45	28	6408	2.4	3.7	47.5	45.1	1.2	170710
98405	TACOMA	19515	10077	34.3	28.6	30.1	5.4	1.6	38907	40807	29	14	4178	0.7	2.8	42.3	52.1	2.1	181462
98406	TACOMA	28719	9672	20.5	24.0	39.7	11.1	4.7	54453	56850	70	58	6121	0.9	0.4	9.5	77.8	11.4	262092
98407	TACOMA	30355	8893	16.8	23.2	41.3	13.0	5.7	58869	61288	76	68	5916	1.0	0.5	10.5	68.6	19.3	262782
98408	TACOMA	21994	7405	19.6	29.1	41.2	7.8	2.4	50889	52775	63	50	4989	0.7	2.1	41.7	54.9	0.6	182788
98409	TACOMA	19146	9484	26.2	34.4	33.3	4.5	1.6	41579	43257	38	21	3861	1.3	1.3	56.2	40.4	0.8	166893
98416	TACOMA	12853	13	23.1	23.1	46.2	7.7	0.0	63023	37321	81	75	7	0.0	0.0	0.0	85.7	14.3	337500
98418	TACOMA	19853	3997	22.4	31.6	39.4	5.3	1.3	46718	48799	53	40	2320	1.0	1.6	54.0	42.8	0.6	169362
98421	TACOMA	13474	62	16.1	16.1	58.1	3.2	6.5	56119	56842	73	61	33	15.2	12.1	24.2	24.2	24.2	168750
98422	TACOMA	35386	7993	7.0	12.9	46.0	22.5	11.7	77845	79742	91	90	6078	1.3	0.9	2.9	58.0	36.9	350063
98424	TACOMA	22694	3292	22.6	36.9	32.0	6.4	2.0	42921	45737	42	26	1424	8.7	2.5	12.0	57.5	19.2	277833
98433	TACOMA	15669	3994	8.8	50.4	34.8	4.9	1.1	44469	46980	47	30	246	8.1	3.3	19.1	58.5	11.0	245455
98438	MCCHORD AFB	7834	48	10.4	45.8	41.7	2.1	0.0	45000	47330	48	33	0	0.0	0.0	0.0	0.0	0.0	0
98439	LAKEWOOD	12337	1098	49.3	37.2	11.7	1.0	0.9	25308	24776	3	1	168	65.5	11.3	4.8	7.1	11.3	29167
98443	TACOMA	27268	2078	13.1	21.0	44.9	15.9	5.1	64936	65138	83	78	1704	3.2	3.7	6.6	71.9	14.7	270141
98444	TACOMA	19296	12129	27.2	32.4	33.2	5.6	1.5	41547	44129	38	21	5245	5.7	2.4	31.8	57.1	2.9	191598
98445	TACOMA	24190	10147	16.4	24.3	44.9	10.7	3.7	57953	60567	75	65	6934	4.4	3.1	14.4	72.5	5.7	224823
98446	TACOMA	28611	4150	10.6	23.9	42.4	16.2	6.9	65833	66591	84	80	3368	3.0	1.9	8.6	70.6	15.9	279426
98447	TACOMA	41742	36	0.0	38.9	22.2	27.8	11.1	78919	81081	92	91	19	0.0	0.0	31.6	42.1	26.3	237500
98465	TACOMA	24170	3519	30.2	27.6	30.9	8.8	2.4	40620	43392	35	18	1473	0.6	2.2	19.6	56.2	21.5	248221
98466	TACOMA	30119	11690	14.6	26.3	40.8	12.5	5.7	58409	61212	76	67	6468	0.3	0.2	7.0	74.8	17.8	293362
98467	UNIVERSITY PLACE	29021	5896	13.6	29.5	32.9	17.1	6.8	58427	61905	76	67	3332	2.0	0.9	4.1	67.3	25.6	342857
98498	LAKEWOOD	27470	11702	19.5	26.9	35.4	12.7	5.4	53305	56252	69	56	6852	0.9	0.5	12.6	72.6	13.4	258276
98499	LAKEWOOD	21735	13653	26.8	32.4	30.9	7.4	2.6	42291	45064	40	23	5211	14.3	2.6	16.0	53.2	14.0	215577
98501	OLYMPIA	28666	16065	18.2	25.0	37.8	13.0	6.0	59879	63000	77	69	9802	3.8	1.8	8.9	66.7	18.9	282970
98502	OLYMPIA	31178	12579	18.7	23.4	35.1	14.6	8.2	60234	63011	78	70	7231	1.4	2.2	8.2	53.1	35.1	333075
98503	LACEY	25551	14552	16.4	26.3	42.7	12.0	2.7	58753	61933	76	68	8408	4.6	2.3	13.8	74.1	5.2	229924
98505	OLYMPIA	4048	9	0.0	33.3	22.2	22.2	22.2	85912	117343	94	96	5	0.0	0.0	0.0	60.0	40.0	350000
98506	OLYMPIA	28250	7910	17.5	26.6	41.0	10.9	4.0	57060	61372	74	64	4745	3.0	2.3	13.5	61.6	19.5	257637
98512	OLYMPIA	29081	10824	12.9	25.8	41.5	14.5	5.3	62293	64875	80	73	7346	8.5	3.8	10.9	61.2	15.7	266286
98513	OLYMPIA	28518	11602	8.8	20.0	49.9	15.8	5.5	68139	69649	86	82	9082	3.7	4.3	15.0	66.8	10.1	237482
98516	OLYMPIA	31251	7803	12.0	18.9	41.2	18.9	8.9	70159	74189	87	85	5994	3.9	2.0	10.2	54.5	29.4	304923
98520	ABERDEEN	20468	8513	28.5	28.4	34.6	5.8	2.7	43012	46207	42	26	5560	5.9	9.3	43.0	36.9	4.8	160941
98524	ALLYN	29003	979	20.0	23.0	39.5	12.3	5.2	59750	60322	77	69	841	3.2	5.4	12.2	52.4	26.8	311136
98526	AMANDA PARK	17277	180	31.1	31.7	30.0	6.1	1.1	38623	40224	29	12	124	14.5	12.9	42.7	24.2	5.6	131250
98528	BELFAIR	24422	3684	18.3	27.8	40.0	10.0	3.9	55258	56077	72	60	2970	3.4	3.3	19.8	52.5	21.1	246667
98531	CENTRALIA	20673	9224	28.1	29.7	34.2	5.3	2.7	42656	45289	41	25	5835	6.4	4.9	33.0	50.6	5.1	188274
98532	CHEHALIS	21826	8510	21.0	28.8	39.9	7.5	2.8	50194	53016	62	48	6082	2.4	2.9	24.6	56.9	13.2	230160
98533	CINEBAR	18801	263	38.0	21.3	33.1	4.9	2.7	40523	44095	34	17	216	5.1	10.6	28.2	42.1	13.9	189130
98535	COPALIS BEACH	17563	139	39.6	30.2	26.6	2.9	0.7	34599	35197	17	5	101	4.0	6.9	41.6	40.6	6.9	168750
98536	COPALIS CROSSING	20764	245	38.4	24.1	32.7	3.7	1.2	38126	39668	27	11	173	8.1	4.6	45.1	31.8	10.4	158125
98537	COSMOPOLIS	22107	880	21.4	26.6	43.2	6.8	2.0	51424	54408	65	52	718	5.2	8.2	40.0	43.2	3.5	169643
98538	CURTIS	20192	131	26.7	29.0	36.6	6.1	1.5	41957	47388	39	22	103	2.9	6.8	28.2	49.5	12.6	229545
98541	ELMA	19367	3767	25.2	29.7	38.4	5.2	1.5	45647	48326	50	35	2711	7.4	8.0	32.2	44.4	8.0	180921
98542	ETHEL	17308	198	21.7	40.4	34.8	2.0	1.0	43069	45325	43	26	153	1.3	2.6	22.9	58.8	14.4	236458
98546	GRAPEVIEW	26088	1015	17.5	31.4	37.9	9.7	3.4	50700	51107	63	50	856	2.7	3.7	14.0	39.6	40.0	331746
98547	GRAYLAND	24074	915	32.6	30.9	27.8	6.1	2.6	39923	42159	32	15	691	8.7	8.0	53.3	28.7	1.4	141108
98548	HOODSPORT	24186	1068	21.3	35.8	37.7	4.2	1.0	43666	46674	44	27	904	2.7	6.0	28.8	52.8	9.8	204000
98550	HOQUIAM	19105	4535	28.6	31.9	33.3	4.8	1.3	40916	43022	36	19	2826	5.3	10.3	51.8	28.6	4.1	147115
98552	HUMPTULIPS	19158	112	27.7	34.8	29.5	6.3	1.8	40000	45000	33	16	84	7.1	7.1	42.9	35.7	7.1	161364
98555	LILLIWAUP	24071	266	22.9	35.0	38.7	2.6	0.8	44159	46975	46	29	223	3.6	6.3	25.1	52.0	13.0	212500
98557	MCCLEARY	20348	1156	21.7	35.9	36.2	4.5	1.6	44781	46801	48	31	844	3.2	7.0	35.3	45.3	9.2	181690
98560	MATLOCK	20160	63	19.0	31.7	42.9	6.3	0.0	49096	51029	59	47	54	5.6	0.0	24.1	55.6	14.8	216667
98562	MOCLIPS	19302	310	32.3	34.5	26.5	6.1	0.6	36200	38454	21	7	192	8.3	15.1	32.3	34.4	9.9	163542
98563	MONTESANO	22790	3117	21.1	26.5	40.9	9.8	1.8	51802	54663	66	53	2391	5.3	4.6	26.6	51.2	12.3	204602
98564	MOSSYROCK	17746	1019	27.4	30.7	38.2	2.9	0.8	42746	45330	42	25	775	9.5	3.9	25.2	45.2	16.3	208409
98568	OAKVILLE	16698	914	25.3	33.5	35.3	5.1	0.8	43082	45803	43	26	686	3.4	10.2	33.8	38.3	14.3	182143
98569	OCEAN SHORES	24297	2363	31.1	27.8	32.2	6.0	2.9	42851	45693	42	25	1773	0.0	5.4	25.4	55.1	14.2	225179
98570	ONALASKA	18281	1581	24.7	35.3	32.8	5.4	1.8	44259	46154	46	29	1240	5.7	8.0	24.9	47.2	14.2	212258
98571	PACIFIC BEACH	16485	50	38.0	28.0	28.0	4.0	2.0	36115	38613	21	6	34	8.8	5.9	38.2	35.3	11.8	168750
98572	PE ELL	16599	369	31.4	34.1	30.1	3.8	0.5	37043	38893	24	9	300	5.3	8.7	46.7	34.0	5.3	157609
98575	QUINAULT	20407	202	25.2	30.7	34.2	7.4	2.5	43912	47827	45	28	137	8.0	16.1	34.3	35.0	6.6	146591
98576	RAINIER	21847	1685	18.2	29.7	41.2	9.1	1.7	51863	55374	66	54	1333	1.1	4.2	22.5	54.5	17.6	225526
98577	RAYMOND	19438	2654	29.8	31.7	32.0	5.5	1.1	40078	42147	33	16	2002	5.7	11.5	44.1	33.8	4.8	154059
98579	ROCHESTER	22629	4571	15.8	30.9	40.1	10.5	2.7	52695	56332	67	55	3634	7.0	3.3	21.4	61.6	6.7	218503
98580	ROY	23190	3937	14.4	25.6	44.5	11.4	4.1	58866	61147	76	68	3216	3.3	4.9	20.3	53.8	17.8	237411
98581	RYDERWOOD	28446	274	35.4	32.1	24.5	5.5	2.6	35728	37523	20	6	244	9.4	12.7	45.1	25.4	7.4	128571
98582	SALKUM	20485	160	20.6	40.0	35.6	1.9	1.9	43623	45686	44	27	123	2.4	4.1	20.3	57.7	15.4	227381
98584	SHELTON	21257	13419	22.2	29.8	39.2	6.8	2.0	48385	49644	58	43	10159	2.6	4.7	30.7	49.6	12.4	199969
98585	SILVER CREEK	20372	281	28.5	27.8	37.0	3.9	2.8	44788	47476	48	31	225	6.2	7.1	22.2	48.4	16.0	211310
98586	SOUTH BEND	19504	969	29.6	31.9	31.5	4.7	2.3	39873	41838	32	15	706	6.5	11.9	44.1	33.4	4.1	152320
98587	TAHOLAH	12007	292	36.6	33.9	24.7	4.5	0.3	34749	35667	17	5	203	21.7	10.8	46.8	15.8	4.9	126136
98588	TAHUYA	25530	847	16.8	31.5	41.8	7.0	3.0	51387	51979	65	52	733	7.2	5.5	26.3	41.3	19.6	205841
98589	TENINO	22870	3029	15.7	28.9	43.9	9.1	2.3	56128	60960	73	62	2381	6.3	9.6	19.8	53.8	10.5	221078
98590	TOKELAND	21941	208	30.3	27.9	33.2	5.3	3.4	42541	44538	41	24	155	7.1	7.7	49.0	31.0	5.2	152604
98591	TOLEDO	19778	1340	20.9	35.4	37.6	4.3	1.9	45862	47722	51	36	1024	2.6	3.1	28.3	56.2	9.8	217123
98592	UNION	29410	753	19.5	27.8	39.0	8.2	5.4	52327	52813	67	54	640	2.0	1.1	18.6	56.9	21.4	282051
98593	VADER	18495	419	22.0	30.5	40.3	5.3	1.9	47250	51030	55	40	334	3.3	8.4	36.5	37.1	14.7	180769
98595	WESTPORT	22910	1428	31.4	31.5	30.0	4.6	2.5	38308	40992	28	12	988	10.3	9.3	33.6	40.5	6.3	167000
	WASHINGTON	29418		17.0	23.3	38.4	13.6	7.7	60852	63758				3.4	2.9	16.8	52.3	24.6	272173
	UNITED STATES	27277		20.9	24.4	35.3	11.7	7.6	54719	56938				9.3	13.1	31.6	32.6	13.5	162279

ZIP CODE #	POST OFFICE NAME	FINANCIAL SERVICES: Auto Loan	FINANCIAL SERVICES: Home Loan	FINANCIAL SERVICES: Invest-ments	FINANCIAL SERVICES: Retire-ment Plans	THE HOME: Home Improvements: Home Repair	THE HOME: Home Improvements: Lawn & Garden	THE HOME: Furnishings: Comput-ers & Hard-ware-Personal	THE HOME: Furnishings: Major Appli-ances	THE HOME: Furnishings: TV, Radio, Sound Equip-ment	THE HOME: Furnishings: Furni-ture	ENTERTAINMENT: Dine out/ Carry out	ENTERTAINMENT: Sports Equip-ment	ENTERTAINMENT: Fees & Tickets	ENTERTAINMENT: Toys & Games	ENTERTAINMENT: Travel	ENTERTAINMENT: Cable TV	PERSONAL: Apparel & Services	PERSONAL: Auto Repairs	PERSONAL: Health Insur-ance	PERSONAL: Pets & Supplies
98374	PUYALLUP	114	118	106	118	114	107	115	111	111	119	112	88	117	114	114	108	79	111	105	130
98375	PUYALLUP	124	128	109	124	123	117	116	119	114	122	116	90	117	120	114	113	80	114	112	138
98376	QUILCENE	92	74	120	73	82	98	74	94	78	70	77	69	64	74	80	83	51	87	93	109
98377	RANDLE	70	60	83	57	66	77	59	72	63	60	62	50	54	59	63	67	41	68	77	83
98380	SEABECK	104	119	107	121	117	118	105	111	104	107	105	84	113	106	113	105	73	106	111	129
98381	SEKIU	68	63	64	59	63	63	62	65	62	65	62	48	58	62	61	62	43	64	63	75
98382	SEQUIM	83	80	108	77	89	97	77	90	81	81	79	60	77	74	85	86	54	86	100	103
98383	SILVERDALE	108	100	90	104	96	93	108	98	105	109	107	80	105	108	102	102	75	103	96	117
98387	SPANAWAY	104	111	94	108	106	98	102	102	99	107	100	79	104	104	101	96	70	99	94	118
98388	STEILACOOM	103	118	116	118	119	116	107	110	106	111	107	82	117	106	115	107	76	108	113	127
98390	SUMNER	85	82	77	82	81	80	86	82	85	85	85	64	83	86	83	84	59	84	83	97
98391	BONNEY LAKE	128	143	122	140	136	125	125	127	120	133	122	99	131	127	127	116	86	121	115	146
98392	SUQUAMISH	107	93	111	91	96	106	90	103	93	90	93	75	83	93	91	97	63	98	102	121
98394	VAUGHN	108	93	132	93	99	115	91	110	94	87	93	82	83	91	98	98	62	103	109	128
98402	TACOMA	42	32	39	35	33	39	47	41	50	42	50	32	42	45	43	53	35	48	53	52
98403	TACOMA	92	82	83	87	81	78	99	85	96	96	97	71	94	95	92	93	69	93	86	104
98404	TACOMA	72	68	59	67	65	65	73	69	73	73	73	54	70	74	69	73	51	72	70	81
98405	TACOMA	63	57	53	59	55	58	67	59	68	63	68	48	64	68	62	69	48	65	65	73
98406	TACOMA	87	90	88	91	90	92	91	89	92	91	93	67	95	91	93	94	65	92	96	105
98407	TACOMA	91	100	100	100	101	98	98	96	97	99	98	73	103	96	102	98	69	98	100	112
98408	TACOMA	80	81	68	82	76	81	82	78	83	79	83	62	83	84	80	83	57	81	84	94
98409	TACOMA	70	59	52	61	56	59	72	62	71	68	72	51	66	73	64	71	50	69	66	77
98416	TACOMA	86	56	53	61	54	60	102	70	92	81	92	63	75	92	72	89	65	85	73	89
98418	TACOMA	72	71	61	72	68	72	76	70	76	71	76	56	75	77	72	77	53	74	76	85
98421	TACOMA	126	86	137	86	90	132	96	119	100	78	99	98	71	98	96	109	64	112	126	147
98422	TACOMA	134	146	135	147	142	130	136	133	129	143	131	106	142	134	139	124	93	131	122	155
98424	TACOMA	78	61	58	64	58	59	76	66	75	75	76	55	67	77	67	73	53	74	66	81
98433	TACOMA	92	51	38	57	45	43	87	61	81	81	86	60	67	97	64	75	60	77	55	74
98438	MCCHORD AFB	93	48	36	56	43	41	87	60	82	81	86	60	66	98	63	75	60	77	54	73
98439	LAKEWOOD	46	29	28	33	28	28	46	36	46	45	47	31	38	47	38	44	33	44	36	45
98443	TACOMA	100	114	101	115	111	114	101	106	101	101	102	81	109	103	108	103	71	102	109	124
98444	TACOMA	71	61	55	63	58	59	74	64	73	70	73	52	68	74	66	72	51	71	66	78
98445	TACOMA	91	98	86	97	93	92	94	91	92	95	93	71	97	95	94	92	65	92	91	107
98446	TACOMA	110	120	105	120	116	117	108	112	108	110	108	86	114	111	112	108	75	108	112	131
98447	TACOMA	122	138	131	135	138	151	123	135	131	121	130	94	135	128	134	140	90	130	154	154
98465	TACOMA	70	65	62	67	64	65	74	67	75	73	75	53	72	74	71	75	53	73	72	81
98466	TACOMA	94	98	96	99	98	96	100	96	99	100	100	74	103	98	101	99	71	99	99	113
98467	UNIVERSITY PLACE	104	104	101	107	103	98	107	101	104	109	106	79	108	105	106	101	75	104	98	119
98498	LAKEWOOD	91	93	90	94	92	92	94	91	94	95	95	70	97	94	95	95	67	94	95	107
98499	LAKEWOOD	76	63	61	66	62	63	77	68	77	75	78	55	71	78	70	76	54	75	70	82
98501	OLYMPIA	95	98	94	100	97	94	99	94	97	99	98	74	101	97	99	96	69	97	95	112
98502	OLYMPIA	101	104	104	107	104	101	105	102	103	106	104	80	108	103	106	101	73	103	101	120
98503	LACEY	90	92	83	92	89	88	92	88	90	93	91	68	93	92	91	90	64	90	90	104
98505	OLYMPIA	134	149	143	151	148	139	141	137	136	144	138	107	149	137	146	134	98	137	134	161
98506	OLYMPIA	88	89	89	91	90	90	93	89	92	92	93	68	94	91	93	92	65	92	93	105
98512	OLYMPIA	103	105	99	106	104	100	102	100	100	105	102	78	104	102	102	100	71	101	99	118
98513	OLYMPIA	114	120	105	119	116	111	109	111	107	115	108	85	112	111	110	106	75	108	106	130
98516	OLYMPIA	113	129	119	129	126	118	116	117	112	120	114	90	125	115	121	110	81	114	111	135
98520	ABERDEEN	74	70	69	71	70	77	74	74	76	70	75	56	71	75	72	78	52	75	80	88
98524	ALLYN	96	96	127	95	106	113	88	104	92	92	91	70	92	86	99	96	62	98	111	119
98526	AMANDA PARK	83	60	85	58	62	84	61	78	68	57	67	58	49	67	60	75	44	71	81	92
98528	BELFAIR	99	89	110	88	93	103	86	99	88	85	88	72	81	87	89	92	59	94	99	115
98531	CENTRALIA	75	70	69	71	70	75	74	74	76	71	75	56	71	75	72	78	52	75	80	88
98532	CHEHALIS	86	83	82	83	82	88	82	85	83	80	83	65	79	84	81	85	57	84	88	101
98533	CINEBAR	76	68	89	63	74	84	65	79	70	69	68	53	62	65	70	75	46	75	86	91
98535	COPALIS BEACH	63	56	79	53	62	70	54	66	57	56	56	45	51	53	59	61	37	62	70	76
98536	COPALIS CROSSING	65	62	80	57	69	75	59	70	63	64	61	46	59	57	65	66	41	67	78	80
98537	COSMOPOLIS	84	79	73	81	77	89	78	84	80	72	79	64	74	81	77	84	54	80	88	99
98538	CURTIS	95	69	102	67	73	97	71	90	78	66	76	67	58	77	71	85	51	83	93	107
98541	ELMA	82	69	73	68	69	81	71	78	75	68	74	58	63	76	68	79	50	75	81	92
98542	ETHEL	84	60	87	58	63	86	62	79	69	58	68	59	50	68	61	76	45	72	82	94
98546	GRAPEVIEW	92	84	120	83	94	104	81	97	85	83	83	66	79	79	89	89	56	92	102	111
98547	GRAYLAND	78	69	96	66	76	86	67	81	71	69	69	56	63	66	73	75	46	77	86	94
98548	HOODSPORT	73	69	89	64	76	83	66	78	69	70	68	51	64	64	72	73	45	75	86	89
98550	HOQUIAM	73	63	64	64	62	74	67	70	70	63	69	54	61	70	64	74	47	70	77	84
98552	HUMPTULIPS	90	65	93	63	67	92	66	84	74	62	72	63	53	73	66	81	48	77	88	100
98555	LILLIWAUP	68	65	83	60	72	77	62	73	65	67	64	48	61	60	67	69	43	70	81	83
98557	MCCLEARY	82	69	75	68	69	84	69	80	74	65	72	59	61	74	67	79	49	75	83	93
98560	MATLOCK	91	73	118	72	80	97	73	93	77	69	76	68	63	73	79	82	50	86	92	108
98562	MOCLIPS	72	57	93	57	63	76	57	73	60	54	59	53	50	57	62	64	39	67	72	85
98563	MONTESANO	83	85	87	85	84	92	79	86	81	78	81	65	81	81	83	84	56	83	89	101
98564	MOSSYROCK	80	61	95	60	66	83	62	79	66	58	65	58	52	64	65	71	43	73	79	92
98568	OAKVILLE	86	64	87	62	66	88	65	81	71	60	70	61	53	71	64	78	46	75	84	96
98569	OCEAN SHORES	77	71	100	68	80	87	68	82	71	71	70	55	67	66	75	75	47	77	88	94
98570	ONALASKA	86	66	84	64	68	86	66	80	72	64	71	60	56	72	65	78	47	75	83	95
98571	PACIFIC BEACH	67	62	83	58	68	75	59	71	63	62	61	48	57	58	65	66	41	68	77	82
98572	PE ELL	79	57	81	55	59	80	58	74	64	54	63	55	46	64	57	71	42	68	77	88
98575	QUINAULT	95	68	97	66	70	96	70	89	77	65	76	66	56	77	69	85	50	81	92	105
98576	RAINIER	94	85	87	84	84	94	81	90	84	81	84	67	76	86	80	88	57	85	91	106
98577	RAYMOND	73	62	71	63	64	78	64	73	68	59	67	54	58	68	63	74	45	69	79	85
98579	ROCHESTER	99	91	83	88	89	94	86	92	89	89	89	67	81	92	83	91	61	89	92	109
98580	ROY	104	101	88	99	98	99	93	98	95	97	95	73	91	99	91	96	65	94	96	115
98581	RYDERWOOD	72	69	88	63	76	82	65	77	69	71	67	51	65	63	71	73	45	74	86	88
98582	SALKUM	87	62	89	60	65	88	64	81	71	60	70	61	51	71	63	78	46	75	85	97
98584	SHELTON	84	75	89	74	78	88	75	84	78	74	77	61	71	77	77	82	53	81	88	98
98585	SILVER CREEK	84	68	100	65	73	89	67	84	72	65	71	60	59	69	71	77	47	78	87	98
98586	SOUTH BEND	84	61	86	59	63	87	64	80	71	58	69	60	51	70	63	78	46	74	85	95
98587	TAHOLAH	72	52	74	50	54	73	53	68	59	49	58	51	43	59	53	65	38	62	70	80
98588	TAHUYA	98	84	107	82	87	99	82	96	85	80	85	70	74	84	84	89	57	90	95	112
98589	TENINO	98	91	85	90	90	96	86	92	89	88	88	68	82	91	84	91	60	89	93	109
98590	TOKELAND	84	63	93	62	67	88	67	83	73	61	71	62	55	71	67	79	47	77	88	97
98591	TOLEDO	94	69	96	67	71	95	70	88	77	66	76	66	57	77	69	85	50	81	92	105
98592	UNION	106	85	137	84	93	112	85	108	89	80	88	79	74	84	92	95	58	99	106	125
98593	VADER	86	77	80	75	77	83	74	81	76	75	76	59	68	78	72	79	52	78	81	96
98595	WESTPORT	75	66	95	63	73	83	64	79	68	65	66	54	60	63	70	72	44	74	82	90
	WASHINGTON	106	107	105	108	106	104	108	105	106	108	107	82	108	107	107	105	75	106	104	124
	UNITED STATES	100	100	100	100	100	100	100	100	100	100	100	100	100	100	100	100	100	100	100	100

ZIP CODE			POPULATION			2000-2009 ANNUAL RATE		HOUSEHOLDS					FAMILIES		
#	POST OFFICE NAME	COUNTY FIPS CODE	2000	2009	2014	% Rate	State Centile	2000	2009	2014	% Annual Rate 2000-2009	2009 Average HH Size	2000	2009	% Annual Rate 2000-2009
98596	WINLOCK	041	5912	6591	6933	1.2	57	2142	2364	2488	1.1	2.79	1628	1772	0.9
98597	YELM	067	14014	18955	21665	3.3	95	5132	6994	8029	3.4	2.70	3758	4992	3.1
98601	AMBOY	011	2266	2792	3085	2.3	87	746	911	1006	2.2	3.06	602	724	2.0
98602	APPLETON	039	249	252	254	0.1	8	92	94	95	0.2	2.66	71	72	0.2
98603	ARIEL	015	938	1068	1154	1.4	66	331	381	412	1.5	2.80	254	288	1.4
98604	BATTLE GROUND	011	23457	33215	38154	3.8	97	7664	10769	12360	3.7	3.06	6281	8664	3.5
98605	BINGEN	059	666	662	663	-0.1	4	235	237	239	0.1	2.79	172	171	-0.1
98606	BRUSH PRAIRIE	011	8343	9561	10287	1.5	69	2667	3047	3279	1.5	3.14	2240	2533	1.3
98607	CAMAS	011	18288	26442	30717	4.1	97	6435	9049	10455	3.8	2.91	5022	7047	3.7
98610	CARSON	059	2433	2745	2892	1.3	61	920	1043	1101	1.4	2.63	668	746	1.2
98611	CASTLE ROCK	015	8824	9604	10094	0.9	45	3339	3677	3874	1.0	2.60	2530	2741	0.9
98612	CATHLAMET	069	2583	2875	3028	1.2	57	1060	1191	1259	1.3	2.36	737	817	1.1
98613	CENTERVILLE	039	596	631	651	0.6	31	218	235	244	0.8	2.69	157	167	0.7
98616	COUGAR	015	103	119	128	1.6	73	43	50	54	1.6	2.38	33	38	1.5
98617	DALLESPORT	039	63	66	68	0.5	28	21	22	23	0.5	3.00	15	16	0.7
98619	GLENWOOD	039	534	545	552	0.2	12	208	216	220	0.4	2.52	156	159	0.2
98620	GOLDENDALE	039	7234	8189	8686	1.3	61	2841	3272	3491	1.5	2.46	1979	2247	1.4
98621	GRAYS RIVER	069	206	214	220	0.4	23	80	84	87	0.5	2.55	61	64	0.5
98624	ILWACO	049	1283	1345	1375	0.5	28	534	571	588	0.7	2.32	335	352	0.5
98625	KALAMA	015	4509	5373	5798	1.9	81	1741	2094	2267	2.0	2.57	1312	1552	1.8
98626	KELSO	015	22566	24265	25261	0.8	40	8484	9111	9489	0.8	2.64	6046	6409	0.6
98628	KLICKITAT	039	392	394	394	0.1	8	126	128	129	0.2	2.96	93	93	0.0
98629	LA CENTER	011	6795	8613	9677	2.6	90	2262	2867	3224	2.6	3.00	1853	2316	2.4
98631	LONG BEACH	049	4078	4348	4443	0.7	35	1929	2059	2114	0.7	2.06	1131	1184	0.5
98632	LONGVIEW	015	46791	49570	51305	0.6	31	18536	19711	20428	0.7	2.46	12330	12865	0.5
98635	LYLE	039	2791	2882	2932	0.3	16	1094	1142	1167	0.5	2.51	803	828	0.3
98638	NASELLE	049	2011	2220	2278	1.1	52	806	871	901	0.8	2.30	575	612	0.7
98640	OCEAN PARK	049	3762	3923	3966	0.5	28	1822	1924	1954	0.6	2.04	1162	1204	0.4
98642	RIDGEFIELD	011	11797	15009	16878	2.6	90	4226	5378	6057	2.6	2.78	3362	4200	2.4
98643	ROSBURG	069	395	410	422	0.4	23	164	172	178	0.5	2.38	126	131	0.4
98645	SILVERLAKE	015	1112	1165	1201	0.5	28	421	446	461	0.6	2.61	336	351	0.5
98647	SKAMOKAWA	069	402	420	429	0.5	28	154	162	166	0.5	2.59	112	116	0.4
98648	STEVENSON	059	3753	4270	4523	1.4	66	1469	1699	1810	1.6	2.48	1033	1178	1.4
98649	TOUTLE	015	745	784	811	0.6	31	261	278	288	0.7	2.82	205	215	0.5
98650	TROUT LAKE	039	792	812	828	0.3	16	316	330	338	0.5	2.46	226	233	0.3
98651	UNDERWOOD	059	728	715	714	-0.2	2	287	285	286	-0.1	2.51	215	211	-0.2
98660	VANCOUVER	011	10483	12578	13716	2.0	83	4309	5356	5947	2.4	2.15	2202	2505	1.4
98661	VANCOUVER	011	36101	43321	47253	2.0	83	14550	17167	18734	1.8	2.50	8803	10116	1.5
98662	VANCOUVER	011	24534	31915	35908	2.9	93	8953	11606	13076	2.8	2.72	6370	8123	2.7
98663	VANCOUVER	011	14153	14916	15473	0.6	31	5755	6008	6225	0.5	2.44	3580	3655	0.2
98664	VANCOUVER	011	20538	23424	25168	1.4	66	8263	9442	10174	1.5	2.46	5454	6047	1.1
98665	VANCOUVER	011	20738	25072	27565	2.1	85	8145	9680	10594	1.9	2.58	5479	6417	1.7
98671	WASHOUGAL	059	14843	20009	22663	3.3	95	5550	7503	8501	3.3	2.67	4126	5513	3.2
98672	WHITE SALMON	039	5839	6047	6168	0.4	23	2333	2451	2514	0.5	2.46	1639	1697	0.4
98674	WOODLAND	015	9208	11431	12508	2.4	88	3268	4093	4495	2.5	2.75	2489	3063	2.3
98675	YACOLT	011	5855	6987	7662	1.9	81	1651	1991	2189	2.0	3.38	1355	1611	1.9
98682	VANCOUVER	011	42425	52919	58847	2.4	88	14223	17609	19556	2.3	3.00	11029	13414	2.1
98683	VANCOUVER	011	28148	33454	36523	1.9	81	11375	13271	14437	1.7	2.50	7695	8801	1.5
98684	VANCOUVER	011	21551	29682	33962	3.5	95	7696	10443	11918	3.4	2.84	5699	7647	3.2
98685	VANCOUVER	011	21272	27602	31020	2.9	93	7803	9937	11119	2.6	2.77	5906	7403	2.5
98686	VANCOUVER	011	13615	17735	19995	2.9	93	4933	6399	7215	2.9	2.77	3901	4973	2.7
98801	WENATCHEE	007	36657	40218	41810	1.0	49	13847	14696	15178	0.6	2.67	9360	9792	0.5
98802	EAST WENATCHEE	017	23260	26903	29005	1.6	73	8517	9757	10486	1.5	2.73	6417	7273	1.4
98812	BREWSTER	047	3927	4050	4038	0.3	16	1222	1220	1210	0.0	3.26	942	931	-0.1
98813	BRIDGEPORT	017	3319	3773	4065	1.4	66	1086	1203	1287	1.1	3.13	842	919	1.0
98814	CARLTON	047	522	537	542	0.3	16	223	231	234	0.4	2.31	161	165	0.3
98815	CASHMERE	007	8340	8714	8955	0.5	28	2943	3024	3084	0.3	2.84	2134	2162	0.1
98816	CHELAN	007	6260	6955	7336	1.1	52	2470	2707	2836	1.0	2.53	1696	1827	0.8
98822	ENTIAT	007	2094	2285	2369	0.9	45	777	835	862	0.8	2.73	562	595	0.6
98823	EPHRATA	025	9742	10520	11064	0.8	40	3494	3803	3989	0.9	2.70	2549	2748	0.8
98826	LEAVENWORTH	007	6052	6990	7469	1.6	73	2499	2844	3016	1.4	2.45	1737	1943	1.2
98827	LOOMIS	047	523	520	516	-0.1	4	189	188	187	-0.1	2.68	141	139	-0.2
98828	MALAGA	007	1991	2210	2329	1.1	52	682	746	783	1.0	2.96	542	586	0.8
98830	MANSFIELD	017	612	704	764	1.5	69	271	309	334	1.4	2.27	179	200	1.2
98831	MANSON	007	3248	3764	4039	1.6	73	1114	1270	1354	1.4	2.93	830	932	1.3
98832	MARLIN	025	660	700	731	0.6	31	221	241	253	0.9	2.64	162	174	0.8
98833	MAZAMA	047	170	310	365	6.7	99	84	154	182	6.8	2.01	56	100	6.5
98834	METHOW	047	713	726	731	0.2	12	258	264	265	0.2	2.69	196	199	0.2
98837	MOSES LAKE	025	32216	36326	38745	1.3	61	11321	12965	13869	1.5	2.75	8145	9167	1.3
98840	OKANOGAN	047	5354	5384	5378	0.1	8	1999	2012	2006	0.1	2.57	1423	1415	-0.1
98841	OMAK	047	8696	8915	8937	0.3	16	3241	3314	3327	0.2	2.62	2310	2330	0.1
98843	ORONDO	017	1535	2054	2322	3.2	94	487	648	731	3.1	3.13	393	514	2.9
98844	OROVILLE	047	4163	4334	4382	0.4	23	1656	1728	1746	0.5	2.47	1127	1160	0.3
98845	PALISADES	017	97	114	124	1.8	78	37	43	47	1.6	2.65	29	33	1.4
98846	PATEROS	047	735	744	745	0.1	8	264	263	262	0.0	2.70	184	181	-0.2
98847	PESHASTIN	007	1874	1982	2044	0.6	31	652	678	693	0.4	2.91	478	489	0.2
98848	QUINCY	025	9883	11171	11881	1.3	61	3062	3436	3646	1.3	3.23	2456	2725	1.1
98849	RIVERSIDE	047	1231	1257	1254	0.2	12	491	506	507	0.3	2.44	348	354	0.2
98850	ROCK ISLAND	017	1698	1809	1884	0.7	35	533	555	574	0.4	3.26	420	431	0.3
98851	SOAP LAKE	025	3868	4409	4719	1.4	66	1588	1805	1927	1.4	2.41	1026	1143	1.2
98852	STEHEKIN	007	106	126	136	1.9	81	39	46	50	1.8	2.65	18	20	1.1
98855	TONASKET	047	5667	5757	5763	0.2	12	2168	2209	2212	0.2	2.52	1509	1516	0.1
98856	TWISP	047	2510	2598	2619	0.4	23	1132	1179	1190	0.4	2.20	735	754	0.3
98857	WARDEN	025	3820	4307	4599	1.3	61	1149	1301	1387	1.4	3.31	936	1049	1.2
98858	WATERVILLE	017	1850	2104	2274	1.4	66	698	791	853	1.4	2.64	521	581	1.2
98859	WAUCONDA	047	338	372	384	1.0	49	148	164	169	1.1	2.26	103	113	1.0
98862	WINTHROP	047	1543	1697	1750	1.0	49	702	775	799	1.1	2.18	453	493	0.9
98901	YAKIMA	077	28340	30153	30959	0.7	35	9049	9343	9564	0.3	3.04	6344	6441	0.2
98902	YAKIMA	077	43506	44114	44526	0.2	12	16756	16628	16687	-0.1	2.60	10500	10163	-0.4
98903	YAKIMA	077	12527	13444	14018	0.8	40	4525	4834	5011	0.7	2.74	3325	3501	0.6
98908	YAKIMA	077	31430	34921	36687	1.1	52	12111	13238	13795	1.0	2.62	8947	9669	0.8
98922	CLE ELUM	037	7398	9303	10323	2.5	89	3196	4062	4528	2.6	2.29	2094	2576	2.3
98923	COWICHE	077	1436	1529	1576	0.7	35	438	458	468	0.5	3.30	370	383	0.4
98926	ELLENSBURG	037	25261	29770	31657	1.8	78	9928	11198	11975	1.3	2.34	5486	6055	1.1
98930	GRANDVIEW	077	12634	13507	13967	0.7	35	3721	3929	4043	0.6	3.41	3044	3175	0.5
	WASHINGTON					1.4					1.4	2.53			1.2
	UNITED STATES					1.0					1.1	2.59			0.9

ZIP CODE #	POST OFFICE NAME	RACE (%) White 2000	White 2009	Black 2000	Black 2009	Asian/Pacific 2000	Asian/Pacific 2009	% Hispanic Origin 2000	% Hispanic Origin 2009	2009 AGE DISTRIBUTION (%) 0-4	5-9	10-14	15-19	20-24	25-44	45-64	65-84	85+	18+	MEDIAN AGE 2009	% 2009 Males	% 2009 Females
98596	WINLOCK	92.5	90.8	0.2	0.2	0.6	0.8	5.2	7.1	6.9	7.0	7.3	7.3	5.6	23.4	28.9	12.3	1.3	74.1	38.9	49.0	51.0
98597	YELM	89.4	87.4	1.2	1.3	1.9	2.2	4.4	6.0	7.1	7.1	7.3	7.4	6.1	26.8	27.0	10.1	1.2	73.9	36.7	48.8	51.2
98601	AMBOY	95.2	94.3	0.4	0.5	0.7	0.9	1.9	2.7	7.7	7.9	8.3	8.4	6.3	24.2	28.9	7.4	0.8	70.8	34.3	50.9	49.1
98602	APPLETON	94.0	93.3	0.0	0.0	1.2	1.6	2.8	4.0	5.2	5.6	6.7	6.7	3.6	23.0	34.9	12.3	2.0	77.8	44.5	51.6	48.4
98603	ARIEL	95.8	95.3	0.1	0.1	0.6	0.7	1.6	2.2	6.1	6.3	7.2	8.0	5.2	23.0	32.7	10.7	0.8	75.6	41.1	50.9	49.1
98604	BATTLE GROUND	94.7	93.1	0.5	0.6	0.9	1.0	3.0	4.9	8.8	8.4	8.2	7.5	5.9	27.5	25.3	7.3	1.0	69.8	33.0	49.7	50.3
98605	BINGEN	89.9	87.5	0.2	0.2	0.3	0.5	9.5	13.1	7.3	7.3	7.6	5.6	3.6	26.3	31.7	9.5	1.2	74.3	39.9	52.0	48.0
98606	BRUSH PRAIRIE	95.5	94.6	0.3	0.3	1.0	1.3	1.7	2.5	5.9	6.8	8.3	8.7	5.2	21.6	34.0	8.8	0.8	73.6	39.9	50.4	49.6
98607	CAMAS	92.6	90.2	0.6	0.8	3.3	4.7	2.6	3.7	8.3	8.4	8.5	7.5	5.2	26.3	26.8	7.8	1.0	70.0	35.9	49.2	50.8
98610	CARSON	89.5	88.1	0.4	0.5	0.9	0.9	5.3	7.1	6.7	7.4	7.5	6.8	5.4	25.8	29.1	9.7	1.6	73.7	38.6	49.5	50.5
98611	CASTLE ROCK	94.4	93.2	0.2	0.3	0.7	0.8	2.3	3.2	5.7	5.9	6.3	6.7	5.3	22.9	31.2	14.4	1.7	78.0	42.8	49.2	50.8
98612	CATHLAMET	94.1	93.1	0.3	0.3	0.4	0.4	2.0	2.7	5.5	5.6	6.1	5.3	4.2	18.6	32.9	18.5	3.2	79.3	48.1	49.9	50.1
98613	CENTERVILLE	85.6	84.3	0.2	0.2	0.7	0.8	3.9	5.2	5.9	6.3	6.8	6.0	5.4	20.1	32.2	15.7	1.6	77.2	44.5	51.3	48.7
98616	COUGAR	97.1	97.5	0.0	0.0	0.0	0.0	1.0	0.8	5.9	5.9	7.6	8.4	5.0	23.5	30.3	11.8	1.7	75.6	40.8	49.6	50.4
98617	DALLESPORT	87.1	84.8	0.0	0.0	1.6	1.5	4.8	6.1	6.1	6.1	6.1	6.1	6.1	21.2	31.8	15.2	1.5	75.8	43.8	50.0	50.0
98619	GLENWOOD	81.1	79.6	0.7	0.7	0.2	0.2	3.0	4.0	6.1	5.9	6.2	8.8	4.6	22.6	33.0	11.7	1.1	75.4	42.3	50.1	49.9
98620	GOLDENDALE	88.1	86.5	0.3	0.4	0.8	1.0	5.0	6.8	6.3	6.4	6.9	6.6	5.5	21.4	30.8	14.0	2.1	76.2	42.5	49.3	50.7
98621	GRAYS RIVER	91.3	89.3	0.0	0.0	1.0	1.4	4.4	6.5	4.7	4.7	5.6	5.6	3.7	20.6	36.9	16.8	1.4	81.3	48.4	51.4	48.6
98624	ILWACO	93.6	92.0	0.2	0.2	0.7	0.9	4.7	6.7	3.9	4.3	4.9	5.2	4.1	19.0	36.4	19.5	2.7	83.6	50.6	49.1	50.9
98625	KALAMA	95.9	95.1	0.4	0.5	0.5	0.6	1.7	2.4	5.3	5.7	6.5	7.3	5.0	22.9	32.6	13.6	1.2	78.1	43.1	50.4	49.6
98626	KELSO	92.1	90.6	0.5	0.6	0.9	1.1	4.7	6.2	7.1	6.8	6.7	7.2	6.7	26.5	26.5	10.9	1.7	75.1	36.7	49.9	50.1
98628	KLICKITAT	93.1	92.4	0.3	0.3	0.8	1.0	2.3	3.0	8.4	7.6	8.4	9.1	6.1	21.3	28.9	8.6	1.5	68.3	34.0	48.5	51.5
98629	LA CENTER	94.0	92.4	0.3	0.3	1.0	1.2	3.4	4.9	7.0	7.3	8.3	7.5	5.0	25.2	30.8	8.1	0.8	72.3	38.2	50.6	49.4
98631	LONG BEACH	93.2	91.7	0.1	0.1	1.1	1.4	4.1	5.7	3.7	3.9	4.2	4.9	4.1	16.8	34.9	23.3	4.2	85.4	53.4	47.3	52.7
98632	LONGVIEW	90.4	88.5	0.6	0.7	2.1	2.6	5.0	6.7	6.8	6.4	6.3	7.1	6.5	24.6	27.2	12.3	2.7	76.3	38.7	48.8	51.2
98635	LYLE	89.6	87.8	0.2	0.2	1.6	2.0	4.3	5.9	5.8	6.2	6.7	6.4	4.4	21.1	33.7	13.6	2.0	77.0	44.5	49.5	50.5
98638	NASELLE	90.6	88.7	0.7	0.8	0.8	1.0	3.1	4.4	4.0	4.2	6.0	14.4	3.4	18.1	31.8	16.4	1.7	75.0	45.0	55.3	44.7
98640	OCEAN PARK	94.8	93.7	0.1	0.2	0.5	0.7	4.0	5.6	2.8	3.1	3.3	3.8	3.5	13.6	32.8	33.7	3.4	88.5	59.0	49.4	50.6
98642	RIDGEFIELD	94.5	93.3	0.4	0.5	1.4	1.7	2.2	3.1	5.4	5.9	6.7	7.0	5.0	22.5	33.5	12.5	1.5	77.5	43.2	49.2	50.8
98643	ROSBURG	91.1	89.5	0.0	0.0	1.0	1.0	4.6	6.1	4.6	4.9	5.4	5.4	3.9	21.0	36.1	17.1	1.7	81.7	48.2	50.5	49.5
98645	SILVERLAKE	94.7	93.4	0.2	0.3	0.7	0.9	2.3	3.2	5.3	5.8	6.3	7.2	5.5	24.2	32.5	12.1	1.1	78.2	41.7	50.0	50.0
98647	SKAMOKAWA	94.5	93.6	0.2	0.2	0.2	0.2	2.2	3.3	4.5	6.0	8.8	7.1	3.8	23.1	36.4	9.5	0.7	75.5	42.9	51.4	48.6
98648	STEVENSON	92.4	91.3	0.2	0.3	0.9	1.1	2.9	4.0	5.4	5.6	6.4	7.2	5.4	24.0	31.7	12.7	1.7	77.9	42.1	48.7	51.3
98649	TOUTLE	93.0	91.1	0.1	0.1	0.5	0.8	3.5	5.0	4.6	5.1	5.9	6.9	5.5	23.2	34.9	12.8	1.1	80.5	44.0	50.0	50.0
98650	TROUT LAKE	93.3	92.0	0.0	0.0	0.9	0.9	4.5	6.3	4.3	5.3	8.4	8.4	4.7	21.6	35.3	10.5	1.6	76.5	43.4	51.2	48.8
98651	UNDERWOOD	92.0	90.1	0.1	0.1	0.3	0.4	7.5	10.6	7.0	7.1	7.4	5.2	3.2	26.6	32.3	9.8	1.4	75.1	40.6	53.1	46.9
98660	VANCOUVER	88.5	86.0	2.4	2.7	1.6	2.0	6.4	8.9	6.3	5.6	5.3	6.4	8.1	30.1	25.8	10.4	2.2	79.3	37.0	52.0	48.0
98661	VANCOUVER	81.8	78.5	3.2	3.5	4.0	4.7	9.8	12.7	8.3	7.2	6.4	6.7	7.8	28.5	23.6	9.8	1.8	74.4	33.8	49.2	50.8
98662	VANCOUVER	88.1	86.2	1.9	2.1	4.5	5.0	4.2	5.8	7.3	7.1	7.0	6.7	6.0	28.1	26.4	9.6	1.9	74.5	36.3	49.2	50.8
98663	VANCOUVER	88.2	85.6	2.0	2.3	2.3	2.7	6.4	8.9	6.8	6.2	6.0	6.1	7.0	27.1	26.9	11.1	2.7	77.3	38.2	49.6	50.4
98664	VANCOUVER	87.5	85.0	2.3	2.7	4.1	4.9	4.8	6.6	6.9	6.4	6.3	6.2	6.3	27.9	26.3	11.5	2.1	76.6	37.6	47.9	52.1
98665	VANCOUVER	87.5	84.8	2.5	2.7	2.4	2.9	7.1	9.7	7.5	7.1	7.0	6.6	6.4	25.9	26.7	10.9	1.8	74.4	37.0	49.3	50.7
98671	WASHOUGAL	94.4	93.4	0.3	0.4	0.9	1.2	2.3	3.2	6.9	7.1	7.4	7.0	5.7	25.0	30.2	9.5	1.3	74.2	38.3	50.2	49.8
98672	WHITE SALMON	86.8	83.4	0.1	0.1	0.7	0.8	12.5	16.8	6.4	6.5	7.8	7.0	4.5	23.7	30.9	11.3	1.8	74.5	40.8	50.1	49.9
98674	WOODLAND	93.1	91.3	0.2	0.3	0.7	0.9	6.5	8.8	7.4	7.4	7.5	7.2	5.5	25.9	27.1	10.6	1.5	73.1	37.0	51.1	48.9
98675	YACOLT	94.2	92.9	1.2	1.5	0.8	1.0	2.2	3.1	8.5	8.4	8.7	8.8	6.7	24.7	26.3	7.2	0.7	68.8	32.3	52.9	47.1
98682	VANCOUVER	87.3	84.6	1.8	2.0	4.8	5.9	4.2	5.8	10.2	9.0	8.2	7.4	6.5	32.3	20.9	5.0	0.5	68.1	30.1	49.5	50.5
98683	VANCOUVER	82.7	79.2	2.3	2.6	9.1	11.0	4.5	6.1	8.0	7.3	6.8	6.4	6.4	29.1	23.8	10.3	2.0	74.0	35.3	48.5	51.5
98684	VANCOUVER	87.2	84.7	2.0	2.2	5.2	6.2	4.3	5.8	8.8	8.1	7.7	7.2	6.7	31.2	23.6	6.0	0.7	70.9	32.1	49.6	50.4
98685	VANCOUVER	91.8	90.3	1.2	1.3	2.8	3.3	3.1	4.3	6.0	6.4	7.1	7.7	5.8	23.9	31.9	10.0	1.2	75.6	40.5	49.1	50.9
98686	VANCOUVER	92.8	91.3	1.0	1.2	2.4	2.9	4.7	6.4	6.4	6.7	7.3	7.3	5.3	25.3	31.0	9.7	1.0	75.0	39.0	49.2	50.8
98801	WENATCHEE	82.2	78.5	0.3	0.4	1.0	1.2	19.9	25.1	7.5	7.0	7.0	7.3	6.2	25.6	25.1	11.4	2.7	74.1	36.7	49.5	50.5
98802	EAST WENATCHEE	88.5	85.6	0.3	0.3	0.7	0.8	14.0	18.8	7.1	6.9	7.2	7.3	6.2	24.2	27.7	11.5	1.9	74.4	38.1	48.9	51.1
98812	BREWSTER	61.0	55.3	0.9	1.1	0.5	0.4	48.3	57.2	9.7	9.3	8.3	8.8	7.3	26.3	20.3	8.2	1.9	67.4	29.3	51.9	48.1
98813	BRIDGEPORT	68.7	64.4	0.4	0.5	0.3	0.3	49.7	58.9	10.1	9.9	9.2	8.5	5.7	25.1	21.4	9.0	1.1	65.5	30.0	51.4	48.6
98814	CARLTON	94.6	93.7	0.2	0.2	0.4	0.4	5.7	8.0	4.8	5.4	6.5	6.7	3.2	19.9	39.9	11.5	2.0	79.0	46.7	51.0	49.0
98815	CASHMERE	87.3	83.8	0.2	0.2	0.5	0.6	19.1	25.8	6.9	7.0	7.3	7.4	6.5	24.5	27.1	11.1	2.1	74.1	37.6	49.9	50.1
98816	CHELAN	80.7	75.6	0.1	0.1	0.5	0.5	22.3	29.5	6.2	5.6	6.4	7.2	6.2	21.9	29.4	14.6	2.6	77.3	42.1	50.2	49.8
98822	ENTIAT	81.5	76.1	0.5	0.5	0.6	0.7	18.5	24.9	7.5	7.9	8.0	7.8	6.3	23.8	28.5	9.4	0.8	71.6	36.4	50.1	49.9
98823	EPHRATA	90.0	87.2	0.3	0.3	0.7	0.8	11.4	16.1	7.1	6.7	7.6	8.2	6.5	24.2	25.8	11.6	2.3	73.0	37.1	49.8	50.2
98826	LEAVENWORTH	94.6	93.2	0.1	0.2	0.4	0.4	4.9	7.0	5.2	5.4	5.9	6.0	4.8	20.6	34.1	16.0	2.0	79.7	46.4	49.6	50.4
98827	LOOMIS	82.4	78.1	0.2	0.2	0.6	0.6	18.9	25.4	6.9	6.9	7.1	6.7	4.4	23.3	29.8	13.3	1.5	74.8	40.9	51.5	48.5
98828	MALAGA	89.8	86.5	0.1	0.1	0.9	1.0	12.5	17.6	6.3	6.4	7.2	8.3	6.6	24.8	31.4	8.3	0.7	75.0	38.1	51.0	49.0
98830	MANSFIELD	91.3	89.1	0.0	0.0	0.3	0.4	6.2	9.1	6.1	7.2	7.4	6.0	3.8	19.3	32.0	14.9	3.3	75.0	45.1	47.9	52.1
98831	MANSON	72.7	67.1	0.1	0.1	0.3	0.3	36.8	45.7	7.8	8.2	8.7	8.0	4.7	23.8	26.0	10.9	2.0	69.8	36.2	50.6	49.4
98832	MARLIN	90.7	88.0	0.8	1.1	1.4	1.7	7.0	10.1	6.1	6.3	7.3	7.9	4.3	22.0	31.4	12.9	1.9	75.0	42.2	51.0	49.0
98833	MAZAMA	98.2	97.4	0.0	0.0	1.8	2.6	0.6	0.6	2.9	3.5	4.5	5.2	2.6	18.7	44.5	16.8	1.3	85.2	50.8	48.1	51.9
98834	METHOW	88.7	86.2	0.3	0.3	1.0	1.1	19.0	26.0	6.6	7.3	7.0	7.3	5.1	22.0	32.5	10.5	1.7	74.7	40.9	50.4	49.6
98837	MOSES LAKE	79.5	75.3	1.9	2.0	1.2	1.4	21.1	27.3	8.8	8.2	7.7	7.7	6.9	26.1	23.3	9.6	1.6	70.7	32.7	50.0	50.0
98840	OKANOGAN	78.9	75.3	0.3	0.3	0.3	0.3	12.3	16.7	6.0	6.1	6.7	7.7	6.1	23.2	27.9	13.7	2.5	75.9	40.5	50.0	50.0
98841	OMAK	68.5	65.3	0.2	0.2	0.8	1.0	11.1	15.1	6.9	6.4	6.3	7.6	8.0	25.3	25.7	11.9	1.9	75.6	36.4	49.0	51.0
98843	ORONDO	66.9	59.1	0.5	0.6	0.5	0.5	46.1	56.9	9.4	9.5	9.2	8.4	6.7	26.4	22.3	7.3	0.7	66.5	30.2	52.7	47.3
98844	OROVILLE	84.9	81.5	0.3	0.3	0.6	0.6	14.0	19.1	6.6	6.5	6.9	7.1	5.9	21.0	29.7	14.6	1.8	75.2	42.1	50.7	49.3
98845	PALISADES	89.8	87.7	0.0	0.0	1.0	0.9	7.1	10.5	4.4	6.1	8.8	7.9	2.6	22.8	33.3	12.3	1.8	76.3	43.5	51.8	48.2
98846	PATEROS	76.9	71.4	0.0	0.0	0.4	0.4	31.4	40.6	7.8	8.5	7.9	7.4	4.8	25.4	24.2	11.6	2.4	72.8	36.3	49.3	50.7
98847	PESHASTIN	82.6	77.5	0.3	0.4	0.6	0.6	22.3	29.9	6.7	6.7	6.9	7.8	6.4	26.2	28.8	9.5	1.1	74.8	37.1	50.0	50.0
98848	QUINCY	72.4	69.0	0.2	0.2	0.8	0.8	48.7	56.5	10.0	9.5	8.6	8.2	6.6	25.6	21.8	8.6	1.2	66.8	29.9	52.3	47.7
98849	RIVERSIDE	88.5	86.0	0.1	0.2	0.3	0.3	7.8	10.7	4.9	5.2	5.6	6.0	5.2	20.5	35.9	15.0	1.6	80.0	46.6	50.7	49.3
98850	ROCK ISLAND	69.7	63.0	0.5	0.7	0.6	0.6	34.3	43.3	10.1	8.8	7.7	9.0	6.0	25.6	23.2	9.0	0.7	67.9	31.8	50.4	49.6
98851	SOAP LAKE	89.6	86.9	0.8	1.0	0.3	0.3	9.5	13.6	7.3	7.1	7.0	7.0	5.8	19.6	26.2	17.0	3.1	74.3	41.7	48.7	51.3
98852	STEHEKIN	96.2	96.0	0.0	0.0	1.9	2.4	2.8	4.8	3.2	10.3	7.1	5.6	7.1	33.3	30.2	2.4	0.8	77.0	37.2	53.2	46.8
98855	TONASKET	85.3	81.3	0.2	0.2	0.5	0.6	13.0	17.6	5.6	6.1	7.1	7.1	5.0	19.9	32.8	14.0	2.3	76.3	44.3	49.5	50.5
98856	TWISP	96.4	95.7	0.0	0.0	0.4	0.5	1.7	2.5	4.3	4.4	5.7	5.9	4.3	20.9	38.0	14.1	2.3	81.4	47.2	49.3	50.7
98857	WARDEN	55.4	49.2	0.2	0.2	0.7	0.8	53.7	62.2	10.9	9.9	9.1	8.1	6.2	25.4	21.0	8.3	1.2	65.1	29.1	51.5	48.5
98858	WATERVILLE	90.8	87.8	0.6	0.8	0.4	0.6	7.7	11.1	5.7	6.6	8.1	7.4	3.8	20.8	32.4	12.9	2.4	74.8	43.3	50.2	49.8
98859	WAUCONDA	92.3	90.6	0.0	0.0	0.3	0.3	3.9	5.6	3.5	4.0	8.1	7.8	4.0	17.7	41.9	12.6	0.3	79.3	47.0	50.3	49.7
98862	WINTHROP	97.3	96.5	0.3	0.4	0.5	0.6	1.7	2.5	3.7	3.8	6.3	5.2	3.1	19.6	42.1	14.8	1.4	82.5	48.7	50.7	49.3
98901	YAKIMA	59.6	54.3	2.6	2.4	0.8	0.8	43.3	51.0	9.5	8.6	7.8	8.5	7.7	26.8	21.2	8.5	1.4	69.1	30.4	51.5	48.5
98902	YAKIMA	74.2	67.9	1.6	1.7	1.3	1.5	28.3	37.1	8.9	8.0	7.0	6.7	7.2	27.1	21.3	10.3	3.3	72.1	33.0	48.3	51.7
98903	YAKIMA	81.0	75.5	0.4	0.5	0.6	0.7	18.8	26.2	6.7	6.6	6.8	7.0	6.1	24.5	28.3	12.1	2.0	75.5	39.0	50.4	49.6
98908	YAKIMA	89.7	86.2	0.8	0.9	1.7	2.0	9.9	14.8	6.1	6.3	6.7	6.9	5.4	23.6	29.7	13.0	2.4	76.6	41.1	48.5	51.5
98922	CLE ELUM	95.9	95.2	0.3	0.3	0.6	0.8	2.3	3.0	4.8	4.9	5.8	6.0	3.9	20.4	35.9	16.5	1.8	80.5	47.6	50.2	49.8
98923	COWICHE	83.6	78.2	0.1	0.1	0.3	0.3	32.0	43.6	9.0	8.7	8.4	8.7	6.0	26.3	23.9	8.2	0.7	68.6	31.9	49.4	50.6
98926	ELLENSBURG	90.5	88.4	0.8	0.9	2.9	3.5	5.8	8.0	4.9	4.4	4.7	12.9	19.4	22.1	20.6	8.9	2.0	82.6	27.6	49.0	51.0
98930	GRANDVIEW	56.0	50.0	0.6	0.6	0.9	0.8	60.9	70.4	10.5	9.6	8.8	8.6	7.2	27.3	18.9	7.7	1.4	65.6	28.3	50.0	50.0
	WASHINGTON	81.8	79.0	3.2	3.4	5.9	6.9	7.5	9.7	6.7	6.5	6.5	7.0	7.0	27.4	27.0	10.1	1.8	76.3	36.9	49.8	50.2
	UNITED STATES	75.1	72.0	12.3	12.7	3.8	4.6	12.5	15.7	6.8	6.7	6.6	7.1	6.9	27.0	26.0	10.9	1.9	75.7	36.9	49.2	50.8

ZIP CODE				2009 HOUSEHOLD INCOME DISTRIBUTION (%)					MEDIAN HOUSEHOLD INCOME					2009 HOME VALUE DISTRIBUTION (%)					
#	POST OFFICE NAME	2009 Per Capita Income	2009 HH Income Base	Less than $25,000	$25,000 to $49,999	$50,000 to $99,999	$100,000 to $149,999	$150,000 or More	2009	2014	2009 National Centile	2009 State Centile	2009 Home Value Base	Less than $50,000	$50,000 to $89,999	$90,000 to $174,999	$175,000 to $399,999	$400,000 or More	2009 Median Home Value
98596	WINLOCK	19394	2364	22.8	28.8	40.1	6.8	1.4	48532	50958	58	45	1867	3.1	4.5	29.2	51.6	11.6	213628
98597	YELM	21937	6994	19.7	27.2	41.9	8.9	2.3	53221	58823	68	56	5197	2.4	5.0	24.5	58.0	10.1	216745
98601	AMBOY	21073	911	14.2	25.1	49.0	8.6	3.2	58739	62716	76	67	774	7.1	0.8	11.0	58.3	22.9	287500
98602	APPLETON	18787	94	26.6	31.9	34.0	6.4	1.1	45000	46770	48	33	73	2.7	6.8	28.8	41.1	20.5	206818
98603	ARIEL	18968	381	21.5	26.8	45.1	5.8	0.8	51135	54414	64	51	299	7.0	4.7	22.7	59.2	6.4	218846
98604	BATTLE GROUND	26578	10769	10.1	15.9	45.8	21.3	6.9	71296	74683	87	86	8899	3.1	2.6	5.9	63.5	24.9	291785
98605	BINGEN	21560	237	25.3	26.6	33.8	10.1	4.2	48471	51009	58	44	171	2.3	1.8	23.4	50.3	22.2	253571
98606	BRUSH PRAIRIE	31928	3047	5.8	12.0	44.5	24.1	13.7	80012	82180	92	92	2716	3.9	3.1	3.7	38.0	51.3	408159
98607	CAMAS	35321	9049	8.0	14.9	37.1	24.6	15.3	82921	85395	93	94	7345	1.4	1.1	8.2	54.4	34.9	341367
98610	CARSON	18522	1043	25.4	31.4	37.6	4.2	1.4	44501	47826	47	30	777	13.8	2.7	25.5	52.0	6.0	189335
98611	CASTLE ROCK	23425	3677	17.4	26.1	45.0	9.3	2.2	55387	59777	72	60	2949	3.1	4.1	31.8	52.2	8.8	202449
98612	CATHLAMET	25252	1191	16.9	31.3	41.7	7.8	2.3	51262	52161	64	52	936	3.3	7.3	20.0	51.1	18.4	242727
98613	CENTERVILLE	17835	235	30.6	29.8	34.0	3.8	1.7	41235	43745	37	19	173	9.8	9.2	34.1	33.5	13.3	166912
98616	COUGAR	19187	50	26.0	26.0	44.0	4.0	0.0	40000	47500	33	16	39	7.7	5.1	23.1	61.5	2.6	219444
98617	DALLESPORT	17120	22	27.3	27.3	40.9	4.5	0.0	45000	42372	48	33	16	0.0	12.5	56.3	31.3	0.0	160000
98619	GLENWOOD	21547	216	23.6	25.9	43.5	4.2	2.8	50262	51784	62	48	151	6.0	6.0	31.1	43.7	13.2	188125
98620	GOLDENDALE	19116	3272	31.8	29.1	32.4	5.6	1.1	39159	41612	30	14	2248	4.8	6.8	37.4	40.6	10.4	177051
98621	GRAYS RIVER	20814	84	17.9	35.7	39.3	6.0	1.2	46866	46634	54	40	68	2.9	5.9	30.9	47.1	13.2	207143
98624	ILWACO	21210	571	31.3	32.2	28.9	5.1	2.5	39907	41803	32	15	412	5.6	2.4	31.1	51.5	9.5	195833
98625	KALAMA	23442	2094	21.3	24.7	41.4	8.9	3.8	54229	59357	70	58	1649	2.9	3.6	28.6	48.8	16.1	216961
98626	KELSO	21286	9111	24.5	26.3	38.8	7.7	2.8	49245	52873	59	47	6140	6.8	5.8	35.0	46.3	6.1	180441
98628	KLICKITAT	15463	128	34.4	22.7	35.9	6.3	0.8	45442	46705	50	34	78	1.3	14.1	43.6	30.8	10.3	142857
98629	LA CENTER	25537	2867	9.3	19.8	45.2	21.4	4.4	68300	70457	86	83	2477	2.8	2.1	8.6	58.9	27.6	317582
98631	LONG BEACH	22473	2059	32.3	32.2	29.2	5.0	1.4	37667	39633	26	10	1410	3.4	5.0	32.5	47.1	12.1	195031
98632	LONGVIEW	23418	19711	23.9	27.2	36.7	8.8	3.4	48943	51757	59	46	12360	4.0	4.1	32.3	53.2	6.5	195169
98635	LYLE	20736	1142	25.6	29.9	36.7	6.6	1.3	45397	46839	49	34	840	5.8	7.6	33.0	42.1	11.4	184036
98638	NASELLE	22961	871	23.3	34.0	33.5	6.2	3.0	44844	46781	48	31	679	4.3	2.8	30.9	51.8	10.2	197639
98640	OCEAN PARK	20589	1924	34.5	35.8	25.4	3.7	0.6	34456	35559	16	4	1568	3.4	10.1	34.1	43.4	8.9	179768
98642	RIDGEFIELD	31811	5378	10.2	20.2	37.4	21.7	10.4	73065	76124	88	87	4285	2.3	0.8	5.6	47.3	44.0	372655
98643	ROSBURG	22404	172	19.2	36.6	37.2	6.4	0.6	45000	47152	48	33	139	3.6	5.8	29.5	47.5	13.7	208929
98645	SILVERLAKE	23555	446	13.0	23.5	55.2	7.0	1.3	56277	60036	73	62	370	1.1	4.6	30.5	56.2	7.6	204167
98647	SKAMOKAWA	18625	162	20.4	38.9	38.3	2.5	0.0	45000	46754	48	33	133	2.3	9.0	40.6	42.9	5.3	164583
98648	STEVENSON	22038	1699	23.8	30.6	36.4	6.9	2.3	46026	49274	51	37	1168	4.2	3.5	19.9	56.1	16.4	229911
98649	TOUTLE	19386	278	22.7	24.8	44.6	6.8	1.1	51419	54738	65	52	229	0.0	6.1	35.4	51.1	7.4	193750
98650	TROUT LAKE	21743	330	21.8	33.3	36.4	6.4	2.1	46461	48058	53	39	229	1.3	2.6	11.8	53.3	31.0	293421
98651	UNDERWOOD	25929	285	22.8	25.3	34.7	11.9	5.3	51990	57191	66	54	214	3.3	1.9	19.6	51.9	23.4	260000
98660	VANCOUVER	22170	5356	36.3	24.3	30.8	6.2	2.4	37844	38617	26	10	2507	4.5	2.4	27.4	59.6	6.1	204776
98661	VANCOUVER	21950	17167	25.7	30.8	32.0	8.9	2.6	43771	46296	45	28	7341	3.3	1.2	25.0	61.8	8.7	216390
98662	VANCOUVER	26816	11606	12.1	22.9	45.8	13.6	5.6	62703	65618	81	74	7757	2.7	1.2	12.1	73.1	10.9	234182
98663	VANCOUVER	24876	6008	21.0	25.1	38.6	12.4	2.9	52932	56714	68	55	3484	2.4	1.7	25.4	66.9	3.6	215590
98664	VANCOUVER	29088	9442	13.6	26.1	40.2	14.9	5.2	60139	63580	78	69	5538	0.6	0.4	12.9	72.6	13.6	242038
98665	VANCOUVER	28141	9680	16.1	24.8	39.0	14.1	6.1	59946	63211	77	69	6134	4.7	3.2	12.3	67.6	12.2	254789
98671	WASHOUGAL	27003	7503	12.8	23.4	45.0	14.9	3.9	63010	66064	81	74	5684	4.4	2.3	13.0	59.4	20.9	265478
98672	WHITE SALMON	21853	2451	24.6	31.0	35.3	6.7	2.3	45936	47579	51	37	1653	2.0	2.2	26.7	47.1	22.0	238358
98674	WOODLAND	23390	4093	17.4	23.5	45.3	10.3	3.4	58193	61270	75	66	3032	3.9	3.3	18.5	56.4	18.0	233333
98675	YACOLT	21093	1991	11.2	17.9	51.4	15.6	3.9	64703	66969	83	78	1685	2.1	1.1	12.4	54.9	29.6	314728
98682	VANCOUVER	24717	17609	8.9	20.5	51.1	15.4	4.2	65475	68385	84	79	12615	2.7	4.0	9.3	77.9	6.1	228783
98683	VANCOUVER	31509	13271	11.0	20.8	44.2	16.8	7.2	65172	68897	83	79	8175	2.6	0.8	6.2	73.7	16.7	289187
98684	VANCOUVER	26368	10443	10.3	20.7	45.5	19.5	4.1	66171	69322	84	81	6369	3.6	1.6	8.9	77.8	8.0	234179
98685	VANCOUVER	32364	9937	10.4	15.5	39.3	24.3	10.5	76635	79156	90	90	7880	3.8	1.4	6.5	67.4	21.0	290367
98686	VANCOUVER	31439	6399	10.5	18.2	38.7	22.8	9.8	74086	78277	89	88	4799	2.3	0.7	6.2	66.3	24.6	308577
98801	WENATCHEE	22898	14696	21.9	31.2	34.1	8.2	4.6	47390	49984	55	41	9183	2.8	3.0	19.7	58.5	15.9	235420
98802	EAST WENATCHEE	21857	9757	18.8	27.5	41.6	9.5	2.6	53629	58399	69	57	7086	4.8	3.0	14.0	67.2	11.0	243057
98812	BREWSTER	13206	1220	40.2	32.6	20.7	4.8	1.7	31642	32626	11	3	689	7.5	6.2	37.2	43.8	5.2	173407
98813	BRIDGEPORT	13361	1203	31.1	39.2	25.8	3.2	0.7	35671	36735	20	6	739	18.4	15.2	47.0	15.6	3.9	104297
98814	CARLTON	23477	231	25.5	26.4	37.7	8.2	2.2	47833	50000	56	42	177	1.1	0.6	20.9	55.4	22.0	245690
98815	CASHMERE	20206	3024	21.7	30.2	36.9	8.4	2.8	47874	51217	56	42	2042	4.9	4.6	15.6	55.9	19.0	248182
98816	CHELAN	22298	2707	26.8	31.2	30.4	7.2	4.4	42598	45576	41	25	1728	4.5	1.3	16.6	47.2	30.4	285185
98822	ENTIAT	19679	835	24.7	30.5	36.5	4.4	3.8	44950	48868	48	32	554	3.4	4.9	20.9	56.5	14.3	215385
98823	EPHRATA	21353	3803	20.6	32.4	35.3	7.9	3.8	47491	50581	55	41	2786	6.9	3.9	38.2	44.8	6.2	176841
98826	LEAVENWORTH	25634	2844	17.9	31.6	36.4	8.3	5.8	50578	54606	63	50	2075	1.2	1.0	8.7	63.4	25.7	301081
98827	LOOMIS	14352	188	38.8	37.2	19.1	3.2	1.6	29477	30550	7	2	129	1.6	6.2	40.3	35.7	16.3	180208
98828	MALAGA	23233	746	14.6	21.0	51.2	7.9	5.2	62190	63646	80	73	565	3.9	0.4	15.8	61.2	18.8	242699
98830	MANSFIELD	21703	309	33.7	21.0	36.6	7.4	1.3	46082	47495	52	38	212	9.9	20.8	45.8	18.9	4.7	110294
98831	MANSON	17577	1270	24.8	35.3	32.4	5.0	2.6	43301	45985	43	27	846	9.8	2.8	13.9	45.0	28.4	268229
98832	MARLIN	18266	241	20.7	42.7	29.0	7.1	0.4	39322	41284	31	15	180	7.8	12.2	33.9	34.4	11.7	162500
98833	MAZAMA	49132	154	24.7	13.6	32.5	15.6	13.6	65565	65985	84	79	122	0.0	0.0	15.6	50.8	33.6	328571
98834	METHOW	22119	264	21.2	26.5	41.3	8.3	2.7	51618	54889	65	52	179	1.1	2.2	23.5	55.9	17.3	225735
98837	MOSES LAKE	20638	12965	21.2	30.7	37.5	7.2	3.3	48422	50780	58	44	8630	6.2	6.5	34.0	43.2	10.1	182532
98840	OKANOGAN	17289	2012	33.8	33.4	26.7	4.4	1.7	36680	38076	23	8	1363	5.1	7.2	48.3	33.1	6.4	156881
98841	OMAK	17560	3314	30.4	33.2	30.9	4.6	0.9	39930	41827	32	16	2269	7.3	9.2	48.7	29.8	5.1	152401
98843	ORONDO	18693	648	24.5	35.2	27.2	7.6	5.6	41807	44801	39	22	351	7.7	6.8	12.0	38.2	35.3	316935
98844	OROVILLE	16165	1728	37.3	35.9	21.6	4.1	1.2	33567	34748	15	4	1141	5.5	10.6	43.7	32.3	7.9	154011
98845	PALISADES	22060	43	20.9	30.2	39.5	7.0	2.3	48656	56578	58	45	33	0.0	12.1	42.4	39.4	6.1	168750
98846	PATEROS	16762	263	28.1	38.4	27.4	5.3	0.8	37632	38299	26	10	174	8.6	4.0	33.3	48.3	5.7	182000
98847	PESHASTIN	23874	678	16.8	26.5	43.5	7.4	5.8	57297	59381	74	65	446	6.7	1.1	17.7	59.0	15.5	302532
98848	QUINCY	15787	3436	21.6	38.0	33.4	4.8	2.2	43372	45561	43	27	2275	7.3	5.1	30.2	46.9	10.5	187959
98849	RIVERSIDE	17807	506	32.6	37.2	25.9	3.0	1.4	35306	37449	19	5	387	7.2	8.3	45.7	30.0	8.8	154087
98850	ROCK ISLAND	15558	555	24.5	37.1	31.5	5.4	1.4	40209	43151	33	17	411	7.8	12.2	31.6	38.7	9.7	171543
98851	SOAP LAKE	16434	1805	40.0	32.2	23.8	2.9	1.1	30520	31692	9	3	1228	6.4	9.6	41.7	37.9	4.4	155208
98852	STEHEKIN	13207	46	43.5	41.3	10.9	0.0	4.3	37308	37317	24	9	13	0.0	0.0	23.1	53.8	23.1	237500
98855	TONASKET	16629	2209	36.4	34.1	25.0	3.3	1.3	33396	34600	14	3	1570	9.6	12.1	41.4	29.0	7.8	150935
98856	TWISP	21421	1179	28.8	35.5	29.5	4.5	1.8	40061	41224	33	16	840	5.7	3.3	24.4	48.1	18.5	222973
98857	WARDEN	16372	1301	22.9	32.7	35.0	7.1	2.4	45997	48230	51	37	878	7.3	5.6	46.0	34.7	6.4	158043
98858	WATERVILLE	21712	791	19.6	31.4	39.7	6.3	3.0	49050	51547	59	46	600	4.0	8.2	45.2	36.8	5.8	162640
98859	WAUCONDA	18868	164	39.0	25.0	30.5	4.9	0.6	34210	35322	16	4	135	9.6	15.6	37.0	26.7	11.1	153289
98862	WINTHROP	26364	775	24.5	32.3	33.4	5.7	4.1	45042	46862	48	33	593	2.5	3.5	17.9	44.7	31.4	272984
98901	YAKIMA	15697	9343	33.8	30.9	28.1	4.4	2.7	36130	37797	21	6	5301	9.7	11.8	37.6	36.6	4.4	156548
98902	YAKIMA	18790	16628	29.5	33.5	30.0	4.7	2.2	38843	40932	29	13	9106	5.2	7.0	51.9	33.1	2.8	153254
98903	YAKIMA	20236	4834	22.3	29.0	39.9	6.5	2.3	48805	51630	58	45	3554	9.9	10.4	38.5	34.9	6.3	154884
98908	YAKIMA	27544	13238	14.3	25.2	42.6	11.3	6.6	60352	63020	78	70	9726	4.3	3.0	20.6	58.3	13.8	227077
98922	CLE ELUM	26986	4062	23.0	26.5	36.2	9.7	4.7	50417	52575	62	49	3066	2.4	2.3	20.8	47.7	26.8	245979
98923	COWICHE	18869	458	17.0	31.7	38.9	9.2	3.3	51043	54427	64	51	291	3.1	12.0	35.7	40.9	8.2	173670
98926	ELLENSBURG	20398	11198	37.2	26.2	28.1	6.0	2.5	37489	39081	25	10	5759	5.7	1.9	18.1	57.9	16.4	235137
98930	GRANDVIEW	15928	3929	22.4	33.3	35.9	6.2	2.1	43880	47175	45	28	2703	6.2	11.2	53.2	26.4	3.0	139014
	WASHINGTON	29418		17.0	23.3	38.4	13.6	7.7	60852	63758				3.4	2.9	16.8	52.3	24.6	272173
	UNITED STATES	27277		20.9	24.4	35.3	11.7	7.6	54719	56938				9.3	13.1	31.6	32.6	13.5	162279

ZIP CODE		FINANCIAL SERVICES				THE HOME						ENTERTAINMENT						PERSONAL			
						Home Improvements		Furnishings													
#	POST OFFICE NAME	Auto Loan	Home Loan	Invest-ments	Retire-ment Plans	Home Repair	Lawn & Garden	Comput-ers & Hard-ware-Personal	Major Appli-ances	TV, Radio, Sound Equip-ment	Furni-ture	Dine out/ Carry out	Sports Equip-ment	Fees & Tickets	Toys & Games	Travel	Cable TV	Apparel & Services	Auto Repairs	Health Insur-ance	Pets & Supplies
98596	WINLOCK	88	77	81	76	77	86	74	83	78	74	77	61	68	79	73	81	52	79	84	98
98597	YELM	91	87	79	85	86	88	83	86	85	85	85	64	80	88	81	87	59	84	87	102
98601	AMBOY	102	96	85	94	94	98	90	95	93	93	93	70	87	96	87	95	63	92	95	113
98602	APPLETON	84	65	102	64	71	88	67	84	71	62	70	62	56	68	70	76	46	78	85	98
98603	ARIEL	82	80	70	78	78	81	74	78	76	76	76	58	72	79	73	77	52	76	78	93
98604	BATTLE GROUND	116	132	114	130	126	116	117	118	111	123	113	92	124	117	120	108	80	113	108	135
98605	BINGEN	99	82	118	81	88	103	81	99	85	78	84	72	72	82	85	90	56	92	98	115
98606	BRUSH PRAIRIE	136	166	149	167	162	150	141	145	134	147	136	114	157	139	152	131	97	138	134	167
98607	CAMAS	143	163	151	165	161	148	147	148	140	153	142	118	158	146	153	136	102	142	136	169
98610	CARSON	77	71	65	68	69	71	69	71	70	71	70	53	65	73	66	71	48	70	70	85
98611	CASTLE ROCK	89	89	83	91	88	96	85	91	87	82	86	69	84	88	86	90	59	87	94	107
98612	CATHLAMET	98	80	116	79	86	102	81	98	85	77	84	72	71	82	85	91	56	92	100	115
98613	CENTERVILLE	85	62	90	60	65	87	63	80	69	59	68	60	51	69	63	76	45	74	83	95
98616	COUGAR	73	67	60	65	66	69	64	67	66	66	66	49	60	69	61	68	45	65	67	80
98617	DALLESPORT	92	66	94	64	68	93	67	86	75	63	73	64	54	74	67	82	49	79	89	102
98619	GLENWOOD	91	73	117	71	80	96	73	92	76	68	75	67	63	72	79	81	50	85	91	107
98620	GOLDENDALE	75	61	77	61	63	75	65	73	68	61	67	55	57	67	64	72	46	71	76	86
98621	GRAYS RIVER	89	71	113	69	77	94	71	90	74	66	73	66	61	71	76	79	49	83	89	104
98624	ILWACO	82	66	106	65	72	87	66	84	69	62	68	61	57	66	72	74	45	77	83	97
98625	KALAMA	92	88	91	89	89	96	83	92	85	81	84	69	80	86	85	88	58	87	92	108
98626	KELSO	81	80	73	80	78	82	80	80	81	79	80	62	79	82	79	82	56	80	83	95
98628	KLICKITAT	77	55	77	54	57	80	60	75	68	54	65	56	48	66	58	74	43	70	82	88
98629	LA CENTER	111	122	103	122	117	113	109	112	106	113	107	87	114	111	111	104	75	107	105	130
98631	LONG BEACH	72	64	89	60	71	79	62	75	65	64	64	51	59	61	68	69	43	71	80	87
98632	LONGVIEW	81	80	74	81	78	82	82	80	83	80	83	62	82	83	81	85	58	82	85	96
98635	LYLE	90	68	103	66	73	93	69	88	74	64	73	65	57	72	71	81	49	81	89	103
98638	NASELLE	90	72	117	71	80	96	72	92	76	68	75	67	63	72	79	81	50	85	91	107
98640	OCEAN PARK	62	59	75	54	65	70	56	66	59	60	58	43	55	54	61	63	39	63	73	75
98642	RIDGEFIELD	119	139	131	142	138	132	124	127	121	127	122	98	136	122	134	120	87	123	124	148
98643	ROSBURG	89	71	115	70	78	94	71	91	75	67	74	66	62	71	77	80	49	84	90	105
98645	SILVERLAKE	94	92	82	91	90	94	86	91	87	87	87	68	84	90	85	89	60	87	91	107
98647	SKAMOKAWA	86	62	89	60	64	88	63	81	70	59	69	61	51	70	63	77	46	74	84	96
98648	STEVENSON	84	75	97	74	79	88	76	86	77	72	77	64	70	75	79	81	52	82	87	100
98649	TOUTLE	85	78	76	80	79	90	76	85	79	70	77	64	70	80	75	83	53	79	87	99
98650	TROUT LAKE	89	71	115	70	78	94	71	91	75	67	74	66	62	71	77	80	49	84	90	105
98651	UNDERWOOD	108	87	140	85	95	115	87	110	91	81	90	81	75	86	94	97	60	102	109	128
98660	VANCOUVER	65	60	59	61	59	62	70	63	71	66	71	50	67	69	66	73	50	69	71	77
98661	VANCOUVER	76	71	66	72	69	68	80	72	79	79	81	58	78	79	76	78	57	78	74	86
98662	VANCOUVER	102	108	98	109	105	102	105	102	103	106	104	80	108	104	106	102	73	103	102	120
98663	VANCOUVER	82	84	78	85	82	83	88	83	88	85	88	65	89	87	86	88	62	86	87	99
98664	VANCOUVER	98	106	99	105	104	100	102	100	101	103	101	77	106	102	104	100	72	101	100	117
98665	VANCOUVER	101	105	99	105	103	102	104	102	103	103	103	79	106	104	104	103	73	103	103	119
98671	WASHOUGAL	100	109	97	109	106	106	102	103	101	101	101	80	106	103	105	101	71	101	103	121
98672	WHITE SALMON	86	75	87	74	76	88	74	84	77	72	76	63	68	77	74	81	52	80	86	99
98674	WOODLAND	94	96	84	97	94	96	91	93	92	91	92	71	92	94	91	93	64	91	93	110
98675	YACOLT	110	109	96	107	106	108	100	105	102	104	102	78	99	106	99	103	70	102	104	124
98682	VANCOUVER	112	115	96	112	108	99	109	106	104	115	106	83	108	110	104	100	74	104	96	122
98683	VANCOUVER	113	114	104	114	111	105	114	109	112	118	113	85	114	114	112	110	79	111	107	128
98684	VANCOUVER	113	113	95	111	107	99	110	105	105	115	107	83	108	111	105	102	75	105	97	123
98685	VANCOUVER	121	142	133	145	140	130	127	127	122	132	124	100	140	124	135	119	89	124	120	148
98686	VANCOUVER	120	135	127	137	133	126	123	124	119	128	121	96	132	121	129	118	86	122	119	144
98801	WENATCHEE	86	87	86	87	87	88	87	88	87	86	87	66	87	86	88	88	61	88	90	102
98802	EAST WENATCHEE	87	86	82	86	85	88	84	86	85	84	85	65	84	86	84	86	59	85	87	101
98812	BREWSTER	68	57	64	53	58	61	61	66	60	60	61	52	53	60	60	59	42	65	61	75
98813	BRIDGEPORT	70	57	54	52	56	60	58	63	61	61	61	45	50	62	54	62	42	61	61	72
98814	CARLTON	91	73	117	71	80	96	73	92	76	68	75	67	63	72	79	81	50	85	91	107
98815	CASHMERE	89	80	80	80	79	88	81	85	83	78	82	65	75	84	79	85	56	84	88	102
98816	CHELAN	86	76	86	75	78	86	79	85	82	76	81	63	73	81	78	85	55	84	88	99
98822	ENTIAT	85	78	70	76	76	80	75	78	78	74	78	57	71	80	71	80	53	77	79	93
98823	EPHRATA	91	82	79	81	82	88	81	86	84	81	83	63	76	86	78	87	57	84	88	102
98826	LEAVENWORTH	101	84	118	84	90	105	86	102	89	81	88	75	76	86	89	94	59	96	103	118
98827	LOOMIS	65	50	79	49	54	68	51	64	54	47	53	47	43	52	54	58	35	59	65	75
98828	MALAGA	107	103	91	102	101	104	96	101	98	99	98	75	94	102	94	100	67	98	101	120
98830	MANSFIELD	88	61	97	61	63	93	67	84	70	55	69	69	49	69	67	76	45	78	88	103
98831	MANSON	81	72	89	68	75	77	72	81	71	73	72	60	65	71	74	72	49	78	76	92
98832	MARLIN	87	60	95	59	62	91	66	82	69	54	68	68	48	67	66	75	44	77	87	101
98833	MAZAMA	165	132	213	130	145	174	132	168	138	124	137	123	115	131	143	147	91	155	166	195
98834	METHOW	101	79	126	78	86	106	80	101	84	75	83	74	68	80	85	90	55	93	101	118
98837	MOSES LAKE	83	81	73	81	79	83	81	81	81	80	82	63	79	83	79	83	57	81	83	96
98840	OKANOGAN	72	57	72	57	59	72	62	69	64	57	63	52	53	64	60	68	43	67	72	82
98841	OMAK	71	61	62	61	61	69	65	68	67	63	66	50	59	68	61	70	45	67	71	80
98843	ORONDO	93	82	88	75	82	84	84	90	81	84	83	70	74	82	82	81	57	87	84	103
98844	OROVILLE	64	50	67	50	52	65	55	62	59	51	57	47	47	57	54	63	39	60	66	74
98845	PALISADES	104	73	113	72	76	109	80	99	83	66	82	81	59	82	79	90	54	92	104	121
98846	PATEROS	81	58	83	56	60	82	59	75	66	55	65	57	48	65	59	72	43	69	78	90
98847	PESHASTIN	104	106	92	105	103	106	97	102	98	99	98	77	97	101	97	100	68	98	101	120
98848	QUINCY	82	69	78	66	70	77	72	79	72	70	72	61	63	73	70	73	50	76	76	91
98849	RIVERSIDE	76	57	84	55	60	78	57	73	63	54	62	54	47	61	59	68	41	67	75	86
98850	ROCK ISLAND	81	72	71	69	69	76	72	75	73	72	73	59	65	75	69	74	50	74	75	90
98851	SOAP LAKE	64	48	63	48	50	64	54	61	59	50	57	45	45	57	51	64	39	59	66	72
98852	STEHEKIN	47	41	40	43	40	41	51	44	51	49	51	36	48	50	47	51	36	49	48	54
98855	TONASKET	73	54	80	53	57	75	55	70	60	51	59	52	45	59	56	66	39	64	72	83
98856	TWISP	76	63	87	62	67	79	64	76	67	61	66	56	57	65	67	71	44	72	77	88
98857	WARDEN	86	76	81	70	76	78	78	83	75	78	77	64	69	76	76	75	53	81	78	95
98858	WATERVILLE	103	71	113	70	74	108	78	97	82	64	81	81	57	80	78	89	52	91	103	120
98859	WAUCONDA	71	57	92	56	63	75	57	72	60	53	59	53	49	57	62	64	39	67	71	84
98862	WINTHROP	96	77	124	76	84	101	77	98	80	72	79	71	67	76	83	86	53	90	96	113
98901	YAKIMA	71	62	57	61	61	63	67	66	69	67	70	49	62	69	63	70	49	68	67	77
98902	YAKIMA	68	64	60	64	63	65	70	66	71	67	71	51	68	71	67	73	50	70	71	79
98903	YAKIMA	84	80	75	80	79	85	78	82	79	77	79	63	75	81	77	81	54	80	83	97
98908	YAKIMA	101	107	101	109	107	107	102	104	101	103	101	79	106	102	105	102	71	102	105	122
98922	CLE ELUM	102	82	127	81	89	108	83	103	87	78	86	76	72	83	88	93	57	96	104	120
98923	COWICHE	97	93	82	91	91	94	87	92	89	90	89	68	84	93	85	91	61	89	92	109
98926	ELLENSBURG	71	58	62	60	58	64	77	66	73	67	73	54	65	72	66	72	51	71	68	80
98930	GRANDVIEW	85	79	76	73	78	75	78	81	76	81	77	61	72	78	76	75	53	79	75	92
	WASHINGTON	106	107	105	108	106	104	108	105	106	108	107	82	108	107	107	105	75	106	104	124
	UNITED STATES	100	100	100	100	100	100	100	100	100	100	100	100	100	100	100	100	100	100	100	100

POPULATION CHANGE

98932-99179

ZIP CODE #	POST OFFICE NAME	COUNTY FIPS CODE	POPULATION 2000	POPULATION 2009	POPULATION 2014	2000-2009 ANNUAL RATE % Rate	2000-2009 ANNUAL RATE State Centile	HOUSEHOLDS 2000	HOUSEHOLDS 2009	HOUSEHOLDS 2014	HOUSEHOLDS % Annual Rate 2000-2009	HOUSEHOLDS 2009 Average HH Size	FAMILIES 2000	FAMILIES 2009	FAMILIES % Annual Rate 2000-2009
98932	GRANGER	077	4252	4710	4925	1.1	52	1050	1132	1178	0.8	4.15	899	960	0.7
98933	HARRAH	077	1184	1278	1335	0.8	40	344	367	381	0.7	3.48	282	297	0.6
98935	MABTON	077	3916	4236	4414	0.9	45	989	1052	1089	0.7	3.99	845	890	0.6
98936	MOXEE	077	3797	5065	5581	3.2	94	1292	1705	1872	3.0	2.96	1017	1313	2.8
98937	NACHES	077	4112	4580	4826	1.2	57	1561	1728	1814	1.1	2.64	1180	1285	0.9
98938	OUTLOOK	077	1793	2017	2133	1.3	61	518	572	600	1.1	3.52	432	473	1.0
98942	SELAH	077	15620	17228	18085	1.1	52	5463	5983	6254	1.0	2.85	4310	4654	0.8
98944	SUNNYSIDE	077	19849	21425	22237	0.8	40	5522	5808	5982	0.5	3.65	4426	4593	0.4
98946	THORP	037	643	754	823	1.7	75	238	282	309	1.9	2.67	191	223	1.7
98947	TIETON	077	2765	3061	3213	1.1	52	873	942	982	0.8	3.25	690	734	0.7
98948	TOPPENISH	077	13243	13769	14044	0.4	23	3527	3588	3636	0.2	3.78	2861	2872	0.0
98951	WAPATO	077	13548	13970	14190	0.3	16	3682	3714	3748	0.1	3.73	3025	3016	0.0
98952	WHITE SWAN	077	2760	2996	3125	0.9	45	653	699	726	0.7	4.11	554	587	0.6
98953	ZILLAH	077	6136	7238	7775	1.8	78	1997	2319	2474	1.6	3.10	1602	1835	1.5
99001	AIRWAY HEIGHTS	063	4369	4903	5167	1.3	61	910	1121	1228	2.3	2.61	620	741	1.9
99003	CHATTAROY	063	4545	5087	5447	1.2	57	1621	1881	2027	1.6	2.69	1327	1515	1.4
99004	CHENEY	063	14484	18546	19825	2.7	91	5213	6297	6842	2.1	2.42	3158	3772	1.9
99005	COLBERT	063	6561	8542	9499	2.9	93	2135	2825	3159	3.1	3.01	1853	2422	2.9
99006	DEER PARK	063	9121	10868	11754	1.9	81	3293	3987	4329	2.1	2.71	2487	2956	1.9
99008	EDWALL	043	601	655	679	0.9	45	218	239	248	1.0	2.74	160	174	0.9
99009	ELK	063	3177	3599	3832	1.4	66	1128	1309	1401	1.6	2.75	882	1004	1.4
99011	FAIRCHILD AIR FORCE	063	4361	3632	3533	-2.0	1	1072	983	959	-0.9	3.27	1050	961	-1.0
99012	FAIRFIELD	063	1022	1105	1165	0.8	40	376	418	443	1.2	2.56	282	306	0.9
99013	FORD	065	1221	1408	1505	1.6	73	437	513	552	1.7	2.74	331	383	1.6
99016	GREENACRES	063	8674	12371	14100	3.9	97	3284	4821	5542	4.2	2.53	2330	3307	3.9
99017	LAMONT	075	259	252	253	-0.3	2	98	96	96	-0.2	2.63	74	73	-0.1
99018	LATAH	063	221	240	254	0.9	45	87	97	104	1.2	2.37	65	71	1.0
99019	LIBERTY LAKE	063	5069	7470	8554	4.3	98	1928	2832	3253	4.2	2.61	1485	2135	4.0
99021	MEAD	063	8635	9683	10296	1.2	57	3076	3519	3757	1.5	2.74	2391	2685	1.3
99022	MEDICAL LAKE	063	7567	9691	10480	2.7	91	2462	3049	3357	2.3	2.63	1846	2228	2.1
99023	MICA	063	129	185	203	4.0	97	48	68	74	3.8	2.72	40	56	3.7
99025	NEWMAN LAKE	063	4313	4584	4769	0.7	35	1427	1564	1641	1.0	2.91	1181	1272	0.8
99026	NINE MILE FALLS	063	7630	8865	9541	1.6	73	2600	3096	3354	1.9	2.84	2175	2558	1.8
99027	OTIS ORCHARDS	063	5628	5816	5980	0.4	23	2107	2232	2307	0.6	2.60	1606	1665	0.4
99029	REARDAN	043	1201	1253	1270	0.5	28	435	458	464	0.6	2.72	341	355	0.4
99030	ROCKFORD	063	834	891	939	0.7	35	301	330	349	1.0	2.67	233	251	0.8
99031	SPANGLE	063	1048	1188	1272	1.4	66	392	453	486	1.6	2.62	299	339	1.4
99032	SPRAGUE	043	765	804	816	0.5	28	318	334	340	0.5	2.40	221	228	0.3
99033	TEKOA	075	995	1015	1017	0.2	12	390	398	400	0.2	2.40	273	277	0.2
99034	TUMTUM	065	306	366	397	2.0	83	123	150	163	2.2	2.44	90	109	2.1
99036	VALLEYFORD	063	1365	1532	1652	1.3	61	472	543	589	1.5	2.82	383	433	1.3
99037	VERADALE	063	10471	12097	12982	1.6	73	3685	4368	4722	1.9	2.73	2877	3334	1.6
99040	WELLPINIT	065	909	995	1040	1.0	49	280	313	329	1.2	3.18	214	236	1.1
99101	ADDY	065	1702	1812	1870	0.7	35	631	683	709	0.9	2.65	479	511	0.7
99103	ALMIRA	043	602	651	671	0.8	40	234	255	263	0.9	2.55	166	178	0.8
99105	BENGE	001	30	31	32	0.4	23	13	13	14	0.0	2.38	10	10	0.0
99107	BOYDS	019	156	168	174	0.8	40	67	74	77	1.1	2.27	50	55	1.0
99109	CHEWELAH	065	4458	4949	5198	1.1	52	1726	1948	2061	1.3	2.51	1210	1335	1.1
99110	CLAYTON	065	1489	1783	1929	2.0	83	525	636	691	2.1	2.80	401	477	1.9
99111	COLFAX	075	4138	4089	4112	-0.1	4	1683	1683	1696	0.0	2.32	1109	1103	-0.1
99113	COLTON	075	846	864	863	0.2	12	317	324	324	0.2	2.67	231	235	0.2
99114	COLVILLE	065	12071	12510	12757	0.4	23	4677	4917	5040	0.5	2.49	3249	3370	0.4
99115	COULEE CITY	025	994	1080	1153	0.9	45	454	505	541	1.2	2.14	293	318	0.9
99116	COULEE DAM	047	3551	3498	3465	-0.2	2	1287	1269	1258	-0.2	2.73	922	897	-0.3
99117	CRESTON	043	401	414	419	0.3	16	189	196	199	0.4	2.11	134	137	0.2
99118	CURLEW	019	1005	1006	1008	0.0	6	337	345	348	0.3	2.64	233	235	0.1
99119	CUSICK	051	1091	1191	1250	1.0	49	435	478	503	1.0	2.49	319	346	0.9
99121	DANVILLE	019	127	124	122	-0.3	2	55	55	55	0.0	2.25	38	37	-0.3
99122	DAVENPORT	043	3249	3405	3442	0.5	28	1327	1393	1408	0.5	2.39	916	950	0.4
99123	ELECTRIC CITY	025	1134	1266	1371	1.2	57	470	537	582	1.5	2.36	354	398	1.3
99125	ENDICOTT	075	956	680	682	-3.6	0	270	272	273	0.1	2.50	193	193	0.0
99126	EVANS	065	543	587	608	0.8	40	187	206	215	1.1	2.85	143	155	0.9
99128	FARMINGTON	075	358	362	362	0.1	8	151	152	152	0.1	2.36	103	103	0.0
99129	FRUITLAND	065	696	704	705	0.1	8	250	257	258	0.3	2.74	190	192	0.1
99130	GARFIELD	075	883	887	886	0.0	6	347	352	352	0.2	2.52	245	247	0.1
99131	GIFFORD	065	203	210	214	0.4	23	90	94	96	0.5	2.23	67	69	0.3
99133	GRAND COULEE	017	1331	1410	1478	0.6	31	601	648	680	0.8	2.14	382	404	0.6
99134	HARRINGTON	043	692	690	690	0.0	6	291	291	291	0.0	2.36	205	202	-0.2
99135	HARTLINE	025	321	322	330	0.0	6	129	133	136	0.3	2.42	93	94	0.1
99136	HAY	075	16	16	16	0.0	6	8	8	8	0.0	1.88	6	6	0.0
99137	HUNTERS	065	389	402	410	0.4	23	134	140	142	0.5	2.87	100	103	0.3
99138	INCHELIUM	019	1196	1220	1199	0.2	12	450	472	468	0.5	2.58	311	321	0.3
99139	IONE	051	1185	1304	1372	1.0	49	479	539	570	1.3	2.41	330	366	1.1
99140	KELLER	019	453	451	438	0.0	6	166	170	166	0.3	2.65	112	113	0.1
99141	KETTLE FALLS	065	5376	5901	6179	1.0	49	2126	2382	2512	1.2	2.47	1535	1691	1.1
99143	LACROSSE	075	848	842	843	-0.1	4	353	354	356	0.0	2.37	247	246	0.0
99147	LINCOLN	043	133	137	139	0.3	16	58	60	61	0.4	2.28	41	42	0.3
99148	LOON LAKE	065	2181	2564	2755	1.8	78	873	1029	1109	1.8	2.49	647	751	1.6
99150	MALO	019	471	487	494	0.4	23	179	191	197	0.7	2.12	127	134	0.6
99153	METALINE FALLS	051	663	718	749	0.9	45	301	332	348	1.1	2.16	173	186	0.8
99156	NEWPORT	051	7681	8621	9145	1.3	61	2998	3438	3668	1.5	2.49	2117	2391	1.3
99157	NORTHPORT	065	442	481	501	0.9	45	190	210	220	1.1	2.29	131	142	0.9
99158	OAKESDALE	075	596	633	654	0.7	35	235	250	258	0.7	2.53	171	181	0.6
99159	ODESSA	043	1396	1402	1402	0.0	6	569	569	570	0.0	2.38	391	385	-0.2
99161	PALOUSE	075	1346	1397	1439	0.4	23	572	602	621	0.6	2.32	401	419	0.5
99163	PULLMAN	075	26082	27930	28926	0.7	35	9699	10683	11188	1.1	2.20	4190	4516	0.8
99164	PULLMAN	075	716	999	1001	3.7	96	27	28	28	0.4	6.18	22	23	0.5
99166	REPUBLIC	019	2869	3035	3070	0.6	31	1176	1275	1301	0.9	2.35	820	877	0.7
99167	RICE	065	641	688	714	0.8	40	243	266	278	1.0	2.56	186	201	0.8
99169	RITZVILLE	001	2743	2709	2718	-0.1	4	1103	1077	1076	-0.3	2.35	726	689	-0.6
99170	ROSALIA	075	1373	1419	1430	0.4	23	532	547	551	0.3	2.59	385	394	0.3
99171	SAINT JOHN	075	1055	1061	1062	0.1	8	457	464	465	0.2	2.29	320	323	0.1
99173	SPRINGDALE	065	952	1023	1059	0.8	40	344	375	389	0.9	2.72	263	283	0.8
99176	THORNTON	075	165	177	184	0.8	40	66	71	74	0.8	2.49	49	52	0.6
99179	UNIONTOWN	075	389	397	396	0.2	12	156	159	159	0.2	2.50	114	116	0.2
	WASHINGTON					1.4					1.4	2.53			1.2
	UNITED STATES					1.0					1.1	2.59			0.9

#	POST OFFICE NAME	RACE (%) White 2000	White 2009	Black 2000	Black 2009	Asian/Pacific 2000	Asian/Pacific 2009	% Hispanic Origin 2000	% Hispanic Origin 2009	2009 AGE DISTRIBUTION (%) 0-4	5-9	10-14	15-19	20-24	25-44	45-64	65-84	85+	18+	MEDIAN AGE 2009	% 2009 Males	% 2009 Females
98932	GRANGER	37.0	30.1	0.0	0.0	0.2	0.2	66.7	75.1	11.7	11.1	9.6	9.2	7.3	26.6	17.9	5.9	0.7	61.8	25.7	52.1	47.9
98933	HARRAH	40.7	34.9	0.3	0.2	1.8	1.8	35.9	45.9	9.2	10.2	8.5	8.0	6.3	25.5	24.0	7.6	0.8	66.7	31.3	51.3	48.7
98935	MABTON	37.3	31.6	0.2	0.1	0.6	0.5	68.4	76.1	10.2	9.3	8.9	9.8	8.3	26.3	19.4	6.9	0.9	65.5	27.1	51.6	48.4
98936	MOXEE	76.8	68.1	0.7	0.7	0.4	0.4	25.4	36.0	7.4	8.1	7.8	7.3	5.6	26.8	26.2	9.8	1.1	71.8	35.5	51.0	49.0
98937	NACHES	90.6	86.9	0.2	0.2	0.5	0.5	10.0	15.1	5.9	6.2	6.8	7.3	5.1	23.8	31.1	12.4	1.4	76.6	41.5	51.4	48.6
98938	OUTLOOK	58.9	49.7	0.2	0.1	0.4	0.4	47.9	59.8	9.1	8.6	9.2	8.7	7.2	23.8	24.4	7.9	1.0	67.8	31.0	51.5	48.5
98942	SELAH	89.8	85.7	0.5	0.7	0.7	0.9	9.8	15.2	7.2	7.5	7.7	7.5	5.8	26.0	27.4	9.7	1.2	72.8	36.8	49.6	50.4
98944	SUNNYSIDE	47.0	40.8	0.4	0.4	0.6	0.6	67.4	76.1	11.6	10.4	9.2	8.4	7.9	25.7	17.6	7.5	1.8	63.6	26.6	50.5	49.5
98946	THORP	95.0	94.2	0.2	0.1	0.5	0.5	3.6	4.6	4.8	5.6	6.6	7.8	4.8	20.8	34.7	13.7	1.2	78.2	44.7	49.5	50.5
98947	TIETON	71.4	64.0	0.4	0.4	0.4	0.4	39.5	51.1	9.5	9.4	8.9	8.5	6.6	26.9	21.6	7.7	1.0	67.0	29.8	50.9	49.1
98948	TOPPENISH	32.2	28.5	0.5	0.5	0.7	0.7	62.7	70.7	11.1	10.1	9.2	9.5	7.9	26.2	18.3	6.7	1.1	63.9	26.4	51.2	48.8
98951	WAPATO	34.1	30.1	0.3	0.3	2.3	2.2	51.1	59.6	10.3	9.7	8.7	8.9	7.7	26.4	19.6	7.5	1.2	65.9	28.0	51.4	48.6
98952	WHITE SWAN	25.9	23.6	0.4	0.5	0.4	0.5	13.8	18.5	10.6	9.8	8.9	11.5	9.2	25.0	18.8	5.6	0.4	64.2	25.0	52.4	47.6
98953	ZILLAH	70.1	62.3	0.6	0.7	0.8	0.8	33.0	43.8	8.8	8.6	8.1	7.9	6.9	25.6	24.0	8.7	1.3	69.6	32.3	49.8	50.2
99001	AIRWAY HEIGHTS	79.5	77.1	10.2	11.0	2.3	2.8	9.8	12.9	5.6	4.6	4.8	5.1	9.1	42.7	22.9	4.9	0.3	82.2	34.2	70.1	29.9
99003	CHATTAROY	96.5	95.8	0.1	0.1	0.4	0.5	1.3	1.9	5.3	5.8	6.4	7.3	5.9	22.7	35.1	10.5	1.0	77.8	42.4	50.2	49.8
99004	CHENEY	88.9	86.1	1.5	1.7	4.4	5.9	3.5	4.9	4.7	4.7	5.0	15.5	20.0	20.3	21.2	7.5	1.1	82.1	25.0	48.0	52.0
99005	COLBERT	96.6	95.9	0.2	0.2	0.7	0.8	1.6	2.3	5.8	7.0	8.0	7.9	5.0	22.7	33.2	9.4	1.0	73.7	40.7	48.7	51.3
99006	DEER PARK	94.9	94.0	0.2	0.3	0.4	0.5	2.0	2.8	6.5	6.6	6.9	7.6	6.6	23.1	29.1	12.0	1.6	75.0	39.4	49.5	50.5
99008	EDWALL	95.2	94.4	0.3	0.3	0.3	0.5	2.0	2.7	5.2	6.0	6.6	7.0	4.9	21.7	34.0	13.1	1.5	77.9	43.9	50.4	49.6
99009	ELK	95.8	95.1	0.2	0.2	0.5	0.6	1.0	1.5	5.6	6.1	7.1	7.8	5.9	24.4	32.6	9.6	0.9	76.2	40.3	50.2	49.8
99011	FAIRCHILD AIR FORCE	78.2	74.5	7.9	8.8	3.9	4.4	8.5	11.4	15.6	10.6	7.5	6.9	18.9	37.9	2.1	0.3	0.1	65.5	22.5	54.7	45.3
99012	FAIRFIELD	96.7	96.2	0.4	0.4	0.2	0.3	2.1	2.9	5.1	5.3	5.9	6.3	5.7	22.3	32.9	13.5	3.1	79.0	44.5	50.6	49.4
99013	FORD	59.0	58.6	0.4	0.4	0.8	1.0	2.8	3.3	8.0	8.2	8.0	8.2	6.7	23.2	27.8	9.3	0.7	70.7	35.1	50.4	49.6
99016	GREENACRES	95.3	94.1	0.5	0.6	1.0	1.3	2.1	2.9	6.2	6.5	7.3	7.3	5.3	24.9	28.7	11.4	2.5	75.4	39.9	49.2	50.8
99017	LAMONT	96.9	96.8	0.0	0.0	0.4	0.4	1.9	2.8	6.3	7.1	7.1	6.7	4.0	20.2	30.6	15.5	2.4	75.4	43.7	50.4	49.6
99018	LATAH	95.9	95.4	0.5	0.4	0.5	0.4	2.3	3.3	5.0	5.0	5.4	6.3	5.8	22.9	32.5	13.3	3.8	79.6	44.7	50.4	49.6
99019	LIBERTY LAKE	94.0	92.0	0.7	0.9	2.6	3.5	2.1	3.1	8.7	8.4	8.2	6.5	4.6	27.0	26.4	9.3	1.0	69.9	36.4	50.3	49.7
99021	MEAD	95.7	94.9	0.4	0.4	0.8	0.9	1.7	2.5	6.5	6.5	7.7	8.2	5.4	24.8	31.1	8.5	1.2	73.9	38.7	49.8	50.2
99022	MEDICAL LAKE	91.4	89.1	2.6	3.6	1.5	1.9	3.3	4.9	4.6	4.9	5.6	7.5	7.0	29.1	29.4	10.6	1.2	80.8	39.5	51.5	48.5
99023	MICA	98.4	97.8	0.0	0.0	0.0	0.5	0.8	0.5	4.3	7.0	9.2	9.2	4.9	21.1	37.8	5.9	0.5	73.0	41.7	50.3	49.7
99025	NEWMAN LAKE	95.1	94.1	0.3	0.4	1.0	1.2	1.7	2.4	6.5	7.0	8.0	8.8	5.8	25.9	31.0	6.3	0.7	72.3	37.4	50.6	49.4
99026	NINE MILE FALLS	95.1	94.2	0.5	0.5	1.0	1.3	1.4	2.0	6.0	6.7	8.0	8.2	5.0	24.8	31.9	8.6	0.9	73.9	39.8	50.1	49.9
99027	OTIS ORCHARDS	95.2	94.3	0.2	0.2	1.1	1.4	1.7	2.4	5.5	6.3	7.1	7.4	5.0	24.9	31.8	10.8	1.2	76.2	41.0	49.8	50.2
99029	REARDAN	94.2	93.3	0.2	0.3	0.7	0.9	1.9	2.7	5.8	6.5	7.2	7.0	4.0	23.1	32.4	12.8	1.2	75.9	42.4	52.7	47.3
99030	ROCKFORD	98.0	97.4	0.1	0.1	0.1	0.1	0.6	0.9	4.9	5.7	6.8	7.1	5.2	21.9	35.5	10.8	2.1	77.4	43.8	48.9	51.1
99031	SPANGLE	96.9	96.4	0.2	0.3	0.5	0.6	1.4	2.0	5.6	6.3	6.8	6.8	4.6	22.4	34.0	12.0	1.4	77.0	43.1	51.4	48.6
99032	SPRAGUE	95.7	94.9	0.0	0.0	0.1	0.1	2.6	3.7	5.7	6.5	7.1	6.8	4.4	20.3	33.1	14.3	1.9	76.5	44.4	50.4	49.6
99033	TEKOA	94.1	93.4	0.3	0.3	1.2	1.4	1.4	1.9	6.4	6.2	6.7	7.6	7.0	17.9	26.6	16.9	4.6	75.5	43.4	45.9	54.1
99034	TUMTUM	93.8	92.6	0.3	0.5	1.3	1.4	1.3	1.6	6.0	6.3	7.1	7.4	5.5	23.2	32.5	11.2	0.8	75.7	41.0	51.1	48.9
99036	VALLEYFORD	97.5	97.1	0.1	0.1	0.4	0.4	0.7	1.1	4.6	7.4	8.2	9.1	3.2	22.6	35.5	8.5	0.8	73.5	42.2	50.8	49.2
99037	VERADALE	93.7	92.4	0.9	1.0	2.5	3.0	2.0	2.9	6.3	6.4	6.9	7.9	6.5	24.6	29.7	9.9	1.8	75.2	38.1	49.0	51.0
99040	WELLPINIT	18.2	17.4	0.3	0.3	0.7	0.8	4.4	4.9	10.5	9.8	8.6	8.9	9.5	24.3	20.8	6.9	0.5	65.3	26.6	48.4	51.6
99101	ADDY	93.9	93.0	0.2	0.2	1.0	1.2	1.3	1.8	5.5	6.8	8.1	7.4	3.8	21.2	34.1	11.9	1.3	74.3	42.9	50.6	49.4
99103	ALMIRA	95.5	95.2	0.2	0.2	0.7	0.8	1.0	1.2	5.7	6.3	6.6	6.1	4.1	21.5	32.1	15.8	1.7	77.4	44.7	49.6	50.4
99105	BENGE	100.0	96.8	0.0	0.0	0.0	0.0	3.4	6.5	6.5	6.5	6.5	6.5	6.5	19.4	29.0	19.4	0.0	74.2	43.8	51.6	48.4
99107	BOYDS	92.3	89.9	0.0	0.0	0.0	0.6	2.6	3.6	4.8	5.4	6.0	6.0	4.2	19.0	33.9	19.6	1.2	80.4	48.3	51.2	48.8
99109	CHEWELAH	94.0	92.9	0.1	0.1	0.6	0.7	1.7	2.5	5.6	6.0	6.7	7.7	5.9	20.0	30.8	14.5	2.8	76.5	43.4	49.9	50.1
99110	CLAYTON	94.0	93.0	0.2	0.2	0.5	0.6	1.4	1.9	5.8	6.7	7.2	7.2	5.3	22.2	32.2	12.2	1.2	75.8	41.9	50.1	49.9
99111	COLFAX	95.2	94.4	0.2	0.2	1.5	1.9	1.6	2.2	5.9	5.9	6.4	6.4	5.1	21.7	28.5	15.4	4.6	77.2	43.9	49.9	50.1
99113	COLTON	96.8	96.2	0.0	0.0	0.9	1.0	2.2	3.1	6.9	7.5	8.0	8.0	3.7	21.1	30.9	12.0	1.9	72.3	41.7	49.4	50.6
99114	COLVILLE	93.9	92.9	0.2	0.2	0.6	0.7	1.8	2.5	6.1	6.3	6.7	6.9	5.5	21.4	31.0	13.1	2.9	76.3	42.6	48.3	51.7
99115	COULEE CITY	95.8	94.9	0.6	0.7	0.7	0.7	2.5	3.5	4.4	4.4	4.2	4.6	5.4	19.1	35.2	20.5	2.4	84.4	50.6	50.7	49.3
99116	COULEE DAM	37.4	36.0	0.2	0.2	0.3	0.3	5.0	6.7	7.0	7.3	7.2	8.2	6.9	23.0	27.0	11.7	1.7	73.2	36.7	50.0	50.0
99117	CRESTON	91.7	90.3	0.5	0.5	0.3	0.5	1.3	1.4	4.3	4.8	5.3	6.0	4.3	15.9	37.2	19.8	2.2	81.6	50.8	51.2	48.8
99118	CURLEW	84.5	82.5	0.3	0.3	0.6	0.7	3.5	4.9	3.9	5.8	7.4	14.4	5.2	17.3	35.5	9.3	1.3	73.6	41.9	55.4	44.6
99119	CUSICK	81.6	80.4	0.3	0.3	0.4	0.4	1.3	1.5	5.6	6.6	6.8	6.0	3.6	20.5	32.6	17.0	1.3	77.1	45.6	51.1	48.9
99121	DANVILLE	85.7	83.9	0.0	0.0	0.0	0.0	1.6	2.4	4.0	5.6	7.3	8.1	3.2	16.9	41.9	11.3	1.6	76.6	47.0	51.6	48.4
99122	DAVENPORT	95.8	95.4	0.3	0.3	0.2	0.3	2.1	2.8	5.8	6.0	6.4	6.3	5.2	18.6	30.9	17.0	3.6	77.6	46.1	48.8	51.2
99123	ELECTRIC CITY	90.7	90.0	0.2	0.2	0.9	1.0	2.0	3.0	4.4	5.7	7.1	5.7	3.6	16.7	39.4	15.4	2.0	79.1	48.1	49.5	50.5
99125	ENDICOTT	93.6	92.8	0.5	2.5	2.7	1.8	2.5	2.8	5.4	6.0	6.3	6.3	3.8	24.9	29.9	14.7	2.6	78.2	42.3	51.3	48.7
99126	EVANS	91.3	89.8	0.4	0.3	0.6	0.9	1.8	2.4	5.3	7.2	7.8	9.2	4.4	19.9	35.6	9.4	1.2	73.4	42.3	51.1	48.9
99128	FARMINGTON	96.6	96.4	0.0	0.0	0.6	0.6	2.2	2.8	5.2	6.1	6.6	7.7	5.0	18.5	32.3	15.5	3.0	76.8	45.5	50.0	50.0
99129	FRUITLAND	43.0	42.6	0.3	0.3	0.4	0.6	3.2	3.6	8.9	7.7	7.2	8.0	8.7	22.6	25.7	10.2	1.0	70.0	31.4	46.2	53.8
99130	GARFIELD	96.9	96.3	0.0	0.0	0.1	0.1	1.1	1.6	5.4	6.9	7.2	9.0	3.0	22.3	30.9	13.2	2.0	74.0	42.8	49.5	50.5
99131	GIFFORD	92.6	91.9	0.5	0.5	0.0	0.0	1.0	1.4	6.2	6.7	7.1	6.7	3.8	16.7	34.3	17.1	1.4	74.3	47.0	48.1	51.9
99133	GRAND COULEE	85.0	83.8	0.8	0.9	1.1	1.3	4.5	6.5	5.2	5.7	6.0	5.2	5.2	19.1	31.1	18.9	3.5	79.8	47.4	47.4	52.6
99134	HARRINGTON	96.5	95.8	0.1	0.1	0.1	0.1	2.6	3.8	5.5	6.1	6.4	6.7	5.1	20.0	33.0	14.9	2.3	77.1	45.2	51.4	48.6
99135	HARTLINE	96.0	95.0	0.0	0.0	0.6	0.6	3.1	4.7	3.7	4.0	5.0	5.6	4.3	18.9	39.8	17.4	1.2	83.9	50.4	52.2	47.8
99136	HAY	100.0	100.0	0.0	0.0	0.0	0.0	0.0	0.0	0.0	6.3	6.3	6.3	0.0	12.5	68.8	0.0	0.0	81.3	50.0	62.5	37.5
99137	HUNTERS	92.5	91.3	0.5	0.5	0.3	0.2	1.0	1.5	6.2	6.7	7.2	7.0	4.0	16.9	34.3	16.4	1.2	74.4	46.5	48.0	52.0
99138	INCHELIUM	26.6	24.8	0.0	0.0	0.1	0.2	2.2	2.3	6.6	6.6	6.8	7.0	6.1	24.8	28.9	12.3	0.9	75.7	38.2	49.2	50.8
99139	IONE	94.0	93.4	0.2	0.2	0.7	0.8	1.9	2.6	5.1	7.1	7.1	6.7	3.2	19.2	35.4	14.9	1.5	76.4	45.8	50.4	49.6
99140	KELLER	24.9	23.5	0.2	0.2	0.0	0.0	3.3	3.8	8.0	8.9	8.4	7.8	4.7	23.1	26.6	11.3	1.3	69.8	36.3	53.0	47.0
99141	KETTLE FALLS	92.2	90.9	0.3	0.3	0.5	0.6	2.2	3.0	5.9	6.5	6.8	7.2	5.2	21.0	31.7	14.2	1.6	76.1	42.9	50.3	49.7
99143	LACROSSE	95.8	95.2	0.0	0.0	0.7	0.8	0.7	1.0	5.8	6.8	7.2	7.2	4.0	18.4	32.7	15.2	2.6	75.3	45.2	52.4	47.6
99147	LINCOLN	91.7	89.8	0.8	0.7	0.0	0.7	1.5	1.5	4.4	4.4	5.1	6.6	4.4	16.1	37.2	19.7	2.2	81.8	51.0	51.1	48.9
99148	LOON LAKE	93.9	93.0	0.4	0.4	0.6	0.7	1.5	2.0	4.6	6.9	7.5	8.4	3.5	20.6	34.3	12.9	1.2	75.1	44.0	50.6	49.4
99150	MALO	84.9	83.0	0.4	0.4	0.8	1.0	4.9	6.6	4.3	6.6	6.8	19.5	7.0	17.5	29.2	7.8	1.4	69.6	33.9	56.7	43.3
99153	METALINE FALLS	95.2	94.4	0.0	0.0	0.8	1.0	1.4	1.8	5.3	6.0	5.8	5.8	5.2	18.0	33.8	17.7	2.4	79.5	47.5	50.0	50.0
99156	NEWPORT	94.9	94.1	0.1	0.1	0.9	1.1	2.3	3.2	5.5	6.1	7.8	7.2	3.5	20.8	34.6	13.1	1.4	75.4	44.3	50.4	49.6
99157	NORTHPORT	92.7	91.7	0.7	0.8	0.5	0.4	3.2	4.4	4.6	5.4	5.8	5.8	4.0	17.9	39.1	15.8	1.7	80.2	49.0	50.7	49.3
99158	OAKESDALE	98.2	97.6	0.0	0.0	0.2	0.2	1.8	2.5	5.2	5.7	6.3	7.1	4.6	20.5	33.6	14.8	2.1	78.4	45.3	50.9	49.1
99159	ODESSA	97.2	96.6	0.1	0.1	0.1	0.1	1.7	2.4	5.1	5.4	5.8	6.5	5.6	18.8	28.8	19.0	5.0	79.0	46.9	48.4	51.6
99161	PALOUSE	96.7	96.3	0.0	0.0	0.2	0.3	1.0	1.4	4.4	5.4	5.7	6.7	6.4	22.8	33.4	13.2	2.1	80.2	44.1	48.4	51.6
99163	PULLMAN	84.3	81.6	2.2	2.4	8.0	9.5	3.7	4.9	4.6	3.4	2.9	13.4	32.8	24.3	13.3	4.5	0.8	87.1	23.9	51.0	49.0
99164	PULLMAN	75.2	72.3	2.7	3.2	16.9	17.6	4.6	6.2	4.0	2.5	2.7	34.7	26.2	23.4	4.2	1.9	0.3	86.9	21.2	59.3	40.7
99166	REPUBLIC	92.3	90.9	0.3	0.3	0.3	0.4	2.6	3.4	5.2	5.2	6.0	8.0	4.5	20.0	35.3	14.1	1.6	78.1	45.6	50.4	49.6
99167	RICE	93.0	91.9	0.3	0.3	0.6	0.7	1.3	1.6	5.5	6.1	6.5	6.8	4.9	18.9	33.9	15.7	1.6	76.7	45.9	49.0	51.0
99169	RITZVILLE	95.6	94.4	0.2	0.3	0.5	0.7	3.5	5.3	5.2	5.6	5.9	6.4	5.4	20.4	30.5	16.6	3.9	79.0	45.7	50.3	49.7
99170	ROSALIA	97.1	96.9	0.3	0.3	0.1	0.1	1.0	1.5	7.0	7.5	7.7	6.7	4.6	21.1	29.6	14.0	1.8	73.6	41.6	50.5	49.5
99171	SAINT JOHN	93.4	91.5	0.7	3.3	2.8	2.2	2.6	2.7	5.0	5.7	6.0	6.2	3.8	26.7	28.9	14.7	2.9	79.5	41.4	51.5	48.5
99173	SPRINGDALE	89.6	88.4	0.4	0.5	0.5	0.6	2.4	3.1	6.1	6.5	7.1	7.9	5.6	20.9	31.7	13.1	1.2	74.9	41.5	51.8	48.2
99176	THORNTON	97.6	97.2	0.0	0.6	0.6	0.0	1.8	2.3	5.1	5.6	6.2	6.8	4.5	21.5	33.9	14.7	1.7	78.5	45.2	51.4	48.6
99179	UNIONTOWN	97.2	96.5	0.0	0.0	0.8	1.0	2.3	3.0	7.1	7.6	8.1	7.8	3.5	20.9	31.5	11.8	1.8	72.3	42.0	49.1	50.9
	WASHINGTON	81.8	79.0	3.2	3.4	5.9	6.9	7.5	9.7	6.7	6.5	6.5	7.0	7.0	27.4	27.0	10.1	1.8	76.3	36.9	49.8	50.2
	UNITED STATES	75.1	72.0	12.3	12.7	3.8	4.6	12.5	15.7	6.8	6.7	6.6	7.1	6.9	27.0	26.0	10.9	1.9	75.7	36.9	49.2	50.8

ZIP CODE #	POST OFFICE NAME	2009 Per Capita Income	2009 HH Income Base	2009 HOUSEHOLD INCOME DISTRIBUTION (%) Less than $25,000	$25,000 to $49,999	$50,000 to $99,999	$100,000 to $149,999	$150,000 or More	MEDIAN HOUSEHOLD INCOME 2009	2014	2009 National Centile	2009 State Centile	2009 Home Value Base	2009 HOME VALUE DISTRIBUTION (%) Less than $50,000	$50,000 to $89,999	$90,000 to $174,999	$175,000 to $399,999	$400,000 or More	2009 Median Home Value
98932	GRANGER	11032	1132	28.3	36.6	29.0	4.8	1.4	38347	40959	28	12	759	8.6	5.5	51.1	28.3	6.5	149021
98933	HARRAH	16349	367	22.3	26.2	40.6	8.4	2.5	51251	54543	64	51	243	4.5	7.0	44.9	34.6	9.1	163929
98935	MABTON	11594	1052	27.4	37.8	29.6	3.9	1.3	38403	40669	28	12	697	8.8	14.6	53.4	21.7	1.6	127229
98936	MOXEE	19493	1705	17.1	32.5	39.7	8.3	2.5	50374	53521	62	49	1230	8.2	4.3	42.1	39.6	5.8	166094
98937	NACHES	21609	1728	20.3	30.0	41.5	6.4	1.9	49731	53157	60	48	1295	5.9	9.3	37.8	39.2	7.9	170265
98938	OUTLOOK	15123	572	23.6	32.7	35.0	5.9	2.8	45896	47975	51	36	399	7.5	5.8	35.8	45.4	5.5	176750
98942	SELAH	21950	5983	15.4	27.1	46.5	8.3	2.7	56798	60744	74	63	4337	3.7	3.1	27.8	60.5	4.9	207473
98944	SUNNYSIDE	13031	5808	30.1	32.4	30.4	5.1	2.0	38173	40251	27	11	3586	11.2	9.3	50.5	25.1	3.9	142271
98946	THORP	27090	282	9.6	28.0	45.0	12.4	5.0	61817	63778	80	72	220	2.7	2.3	10.9	53.6	30.5	318868
98947	TIETON	16223	942	25.2	30.4	37.4	5.2	1.9	45788	48023	51	36	632	2.1	8.2	46.7	35.3	7.8	165090
98948	TOPPENISH	11456	3588	31.4	36.9	27.0	3.3	1.3	35362	36908	19	5	2200	9.1	9.1	57.4	23.1	1.3	137707
98951	WAPATO	12710	3714	30.8	35.4	27.4	4.2	2.3	38032	39812	27	11	2268	7.1	11.9	50.1	26.8	4.1	138154
98952	WHITE SWAN	12133	699	32.9	25.2	33.8	6.6	1.6	40366	43742	34	17	417	9.1	9.8	50.1	24.5	6.5	139527
98953	ZILLAH	17806	2319	22.1	33.5	35.7	6.2	2.5	46693	48345	53	39	1542	5.1	6.2	36.4	44.7	7.7	181207
99001	AIRWAY HEIGHTS	18058	1121	26.1	36.5	32.6	3.6	1.2	41350	43721	37	20	616	26.0	7.8	39.0	24.4	2.9	142279
99003	CHATTAROY	22428	1881	19.1	27.3	41.5	10.0	2.2	53266	56821	68	56	1633	3.7	3.2	18.9	58.4	15.8	244715
99004	CHENEY	20032	6297	30.9	27.5	33.4	6.7	1.5	41584	45608	38	21	3602	4.9	3.8	25.3	55.7	10.3	208900
99005	COLBERT	26808	2825	10.6	17.5	45.5	18.4	8.1	70442	72101	87	85	2556	1.6	1.3	10.1	61.9	25.2	289870
99006	DEER PARK	20731	3987	22.5	27.5	41.6	5.9	2.6	50028	52284	61	48	3106	3.6	3.8	32.2	53.3	7.0	191615
99008	EDWALL	20501	239	17.2	37.2	35.1	8.4	2.1	46380	49028	52	39	182	3.3	9.9	35.2	45.6	6.0	178409
99009	ELK	19954	1309	22.7	32.3	36.7	6.3	2.0	47430	48725	55	41	1126	5.1	4.9	24.0	51.7	14.4	218548
99011	FAIRCHILD AIR FORCE	14831	983	12.1	56.1	28.7	2.2	0.9	42457	44390	41	24	18	0.0	16.7	83.3	0.0	0.0	95455
99012	FAIRFIELD	19806	418	23.0	31.1	39.2	4.8	1.9	46602	48460	53	39	312	7.4	7.4	43.3	35.6	6.4	162245
99013	FORD	17940	513	28.8	30.8	33.7	5.3	1.4	42346	44124	40	23	399	8.0	7.3	39.1	35.3	10.3	165278
99016	GREENACRES	23449	4821	17.2	29.2	43.0	7.2	3.4	52494	55522	67	55	3950	2.5	5.2	34.3	48.9	9.1	191970
99017	LAMONT	18693	96	26.0	37.5	30.2	4.2	2.1	39363	41296	31	15	68	10.3	23.5	36.8	23.5	5.9	118182
99018	LATAH	21188	97	23.7	30.9	38.1	5.2	2.1	45454	47362	50	35	71	8.5	8.5	45.1	33.8	4.2	153750
99019	LIBERTY LAKE	35235	2832	6.4	14.3	49.5	20.4	9.4	76903	78202	91	90	2241	1.2	0.5	5.1	69.5	23.7	296625
99021	MEAD	25400	3519	14.7	24.6	42.3	13.7	4.8	62034	64246	80	72	3107	9.0	7.1	21.2	53.4	9.2	208298
99022	MEDICAL LAKE	22966	3049	15.5	25.5	47.9	8.7	2.5	60767	62313	78	71	2219	5.9	2.7	26.1	57.5	7.8	201188
99023	MICA	30122	68	5.9	22.1	48.5	13.2	10.3	71360	73423	88	86	62	0.0	3.2	9.7	43.5	43.5	366667
99025	NEWMAN LAKE	23170	1564	11.9	23.6	52.3	9.6	2.6	63149	64432	81	75	1392	1.4	2.4	31.9	53.8	10.5	198804
99026	NINE MILE FALLS	25509	3096	9.8	19.5	53.5	13.7	3.5	65829	66508	84	80	2767	1.8	1.4	11.5	71.6	13.6	264347
99027	OTIS ORCHARDS	22430	2232	15.5	32.0	43.5	7.3	1.7	51859	54088	66	53	1974	12.3	5.5	29.7	47.8	4.7	179237
99029	REARDAN	23493	458	13.5	30.8	43.0	9.6	3.1	55918	59412	73	61	358	7.5	3.1	27.7	53.9	7.8	198864
99030	ROCKFORD	21628	330	17.3	31.5	40.9	7.6	2.7	50920	54536	63	51	271	1.5	4.4	33.2	43.5	17.3	199583
99031	SPANGLE	23173	453	13.7	29.6	46.1	9.5	1.1	54268	56770	70	58	362	5.2	3.9	24.3	51.9	14.6	216935
99032	SPRAGUE	21822	334	21.9	39.2	29.6	7.2	2.1	42314	44247	40	23	249	5.6	16.9	43.0	28.9	5.6	141927
99033	TEKOA	19672	398	27.6	33.9	31.2	5.8	1.5	40914	44392	36	18	285	11.6	17.5	48.8	18.6	3.5	125219
99034	TUMTUM	21007	150	26.7	29.3	39.3	4.0	0.7	46127	46990	52	38	127	7.1	3.1	36.2	41.7	11.8	183654
99036	VALLEYFORD	27407	543	9.6	23.2	45.1	15.1	7.0	67131	68232	85	81	480	0.0	2.3	12.9	48.5	36.3	313158
99037	VERADALE	27596	4368	12.5	23.9	45.7	10.6	7.3	62597	64703	81	74	3232	1.5	0.6	13.2	69.1	15.5	249921
99040	WELLPINIT	13224	313	34.5	34.5	25.6	4.5	1.0	36223	36910	21	7	220	10.0	13.2	52.7	20.5	3.6	126515
99101	ADDY	17867	683	28.4	38.1	26.5	5.3	1.8	38706	40543	29	13	548	9.3	8.9	27.7	40.1	13.9	190278
99103	ALMIRA	20445	255	23.1	41.2	25.1	8.6	2.0	41337	42989	37	20	193	15.0	18.7	29.5	29.5	7.3	138971
99105	BENGE	18790	13	23.1	46.2	23.1	7.7	0.0	37321	45000	25	9	8	0.0	12.5	50.0	37.5	0.0	150000
99107	BOYDS	22357	74	27.0	31.1	36.5	5.4	0.0	44068	46925	46	29	62	3.2	4.8	35.5	46.8	9.7	187500
99109	CHEWELAH	19736	1948	29.0	31.0	33.5	4.6	2.0	39396	42424	31	15	1379	2.2	7.1	32.4	47.6	10.6	194303
99110	CLAYTON	18240	636	26.4	24.5	42.1	4.9	2.0	48846	50290	59	46	529	4.2	1.9	35.0	46.5	12.5	198750
99111	COLFAX	23843	1683	19.8	32.3	38.4	7.5	1.9	48080	50892	57	43	1126	4.8	7.1	42.6	37.1	8.3	167130
99113	COLTON	23894	324	11.4	32.7	43.8	8.6	3.4	55103	60683	71	60	247	9.7	4.9	35.2	45.3	4.9	175521
99114	COLVILLE	20116	4917	28.6	29.9	34.2	5.1	2.3	40954	43394	36	19	3566	4.5	6.1	34.5	46.8	8.1	186447
99115	COULEE CITY	21055	505	33.7	29.7	31.9	3.2	1.6	40231	43739	33	17	375	4.0	15.5	44.0	31.2	5.3	146382
99116	COULEE DAM	17629	1269	25.3	37.8	29.9	6.0	0.9	40830	42883	35	18	876	10.6	16.8	45.8	22.4	4.5	134766
99117	CRESTON	21323	196	29.1	34.2	31.6	2.6	2.6	40514	42029	34	17	150	7.3	19.3	34.0	26.0	13.3	145000
99118	CURLEW	17108	345	32.5	31.0	30.4	4.6	1.4	36670	38288	23	8	266	10.5	12.0	32.3	38.0	7.1	158750
99119	CUSICK	18327	478	36.8	26.2	30.8	4.8	1.5	36339	38586	22	7	391	13.6	7.2	29.2	39.9	10.2	175481
99121	DANVILLE	21293	55	27.3	30.9	36.4	5.5	0.0	40756	40756	35	18	44	6.8	13.6	31.8	38.6	9.1	166667
99122	DAVENPORT	23492	1393	22.3	30.9	36.9	7.3	2.5	47570	48960	56	41	1074	5.9	7.7	38.6	42.3	5.5	170714
99123	ELECTRIC CITY	23176	537	28.5	22.3	37.1	10.8	1.3	48795	53057	58	45	411	6.3	11.2	41.4	37.7	3.4	152188
99125	ENDICOTT	20318	272	22.1	36.4	34.6	5.5	1.5	43431	45831	44	27	203	8.4	17.7	41.4	26.1	6.4	130729
99126	EVANS	15316	206	33.0	33.0	29.6	3.4	1.0	37832	39811	26	10	169	3.0	5.3	42.0	43.2	6.5	174609
99128	FARMINGTON	22372	152	18.4	38.8	32.9	8.6	1.3	45367	48313	49	34	112	5.4	14.3	50.0	20.5	9.8	133824
99129	FRUITLAND	16279	257	31.1	34.6	28.4	4.7	1.2	38800	40000	29	13	201	7.5	11.9	36.3	33.3	10.9	161932
99130	GARFIELD	20063	352	22.7	35.8	34.1	5.7	1.7	45727	47417	50	35	260	5.0	15.4	55.4	18.8	5.4	138265
99131	GIFFORD	19481	94	34.0	34.0	26.6	4.3	1.1	36523	39075	22	7	76	7.9	7.9	26.3	36.8	21.1	193750
99133	GRAND COULEE	20173	648	36.4	29.2	28.7	4.9	0.8	35731	38096	20	6	428	11.9	20.8	35.7	29.0	2.6	127500
99134	HARRINGTON	22254	291	23.7	35.4	30.2	8.2	2.4	42428	44181	41	24	215	6.5	15.8	43.7	27.0	7.0	134375
99135	HARTLINE	23412	133	18.8	30.8	41.4	6.0	3.0	50292	53735	62	49	104	3.8	11.5	22.1	47.1	15.4	210714
99136	HAY	26321	8	12.5	37.5	37.5	12.5	0.0	45000	63351	48	33	5	0.0	0.0	40.0	60.0	0.0	187500
99137	HUNTERS	15152	140	32.1	35.7	26.4	4.3	1.4	37327	39378	25	10	113	8.0	8.0	26.5	37.2	20.4	194318
99138	INCHELIUM	15334	472	41.7	28.8	24.8	4.0	0.6	28912	29849	7	2	323	9.9	14.9	39.9	22.9	12.4	143056
99139	IONE	18290	539	36.9	28.6	29.1	5.0	0.4	37184	38511	24	9	414	11.1	13.5	39.1	23.4	12.8	144872
99140	KELLER	12499	170	47.1	29.4	22.4	1.2	0.0	27599	28433	5	1	113	15.9	15.0	46.9	18.6	3.5	119375
99141	KETTLE FALLS	19031	2382	29.0	32.0	33.9	4.2	0.8	41392	43045	37	20	1827	4.5	6.3	40.9	39.7	8.6	172389
99143	LACROSSE	20628	354	21.5	36.7	35.9	4.8	1.1	42895	46251	42	26	247	16.6	13.8	42.5	23.5	3.6	128017
99147	LINCOLN	19774	60	28.3	33.3	35.0	1.7	1.7	41830	42324	39	22	46	2.2	17.4	41.3	26.1	13.0	146875
99148	LOON LAKE	20751	1029	25.6	30.6	34.8	6.9	2.1	45103	46400	49	33	858	3.3	10.6	28.7	44.6	12.8	193605
99150	MALO	19131	191	36.1	31.9	26.7	4.2	1.0	35610	36460	20	6	141	12.8	12.8	31.2	37.6	5.7	155208
99153	METALINE FALLS	18490	332	40.1	30.1	24.7	4.5	0.6	29221	29820	7	2	223	6.3	9.4	43.9	30.0	10.3	149375
99156	NEWPORT	19902	3438	30.2	30.2	31.4	6.2	2.1	41736	43608	38	21	2645	5.0	7.2	32.4	43.6	11.8	188755
99157	NORTHPORT	17831	210	36.2	32.9	27.1	3.3	0.5	33311	35591	14	3	163	6.7	9.8	42.9	31.9	8.6	150781
99158	OAKESDALE	21644	250	22.0	33.2	37.6	6.4	0.8	45603	48099	50	35	191	8.4	12.6	50.3	22.0	6.8	135547
99159	ODESSA	21194	569	23.4	34.3	34.8	5.8	1.8	43708	45777	44	28	442	6.1	13.8	51.4	26.5	2.3	131522
99161	PALOUSE	23339	602	17.6	34.2	40.2	5.6	2.3	48161	52042	57	43	451	4.7	7.1	48.1	34.8	5.3	162358
99163	PULLMAN	19989	10683	45.6	22.3	22.6	6.1	3.5	29258	31087	7	2	3737	6.6	2.3	17.3	62.1	11.7	237968
99164	PULLMAN	15164	28	53.6	42.9	3.6	0.0	0.0	20000	23086	1	0	0	0.0	0.0	0.0	0.0	0.0	0
99166	REPUBLIC	20135	1275	32.0	31.2	30.6	4.2	2.0	38967	41127	30	14	900	8.6	10.6	40.7	33.0	7.2	152551
99167	RICE	18998	266	24.4	37.2	33.8	4.1	0.4	41225	42698	37	19	218	4.1	6.9	31.2	39.0	18.8	197368
99169	RITZVILLE	22054	1077	25.1	29.4	36.9	5.9	2.7	46054	47659	51	38	774	5.3	9.6	51.3	32.4	1.4	150394
99170	ROSALIA	18677	547	23.0	35.5	37.1	2.9	1.5	44235	46831	46	29	406	11.6	15.0	43.1	23.6	6.7	135662
99171	SAINT JOHN	22511	464	21.3	36.0	35.3	6.0	1.3	44686	47340	47	31	352	7.4	15.6	44.3	26.7	6.0	133523
99173	SPRINGDALE	16450	375	34.7	27.7	32.8	3.2	1.6	36938	38688	23	9	307	8.1	7.5	30.6	43.0	10.7	183456
99176	THORNTON	22200	71	22.5	31.0	40.8	5.6	0.0	46748	48649	53	40	55	9.1	10.9	52.7	21.8	5.5	131944
99179	UNIONTOWN	25540	159	11.3	32.7	45.3	8.2	2.5	55098	60560	71	60	122	9.0	5.7	35.2	45.1	4.9	175000
	WASHINGTON	29418		17.0	23.3	38.4	13.6	7.7	60852	63758				3.4	2.9	16.8	52.3	24.6	272173
	UNITED STATES	27277		20.9	24.4	35.3	11.7	7.6	54719	56938				9.3	13.1	31.6	32.6	13.5	162279

ZIP CODE #	POST OFFICE NAME	FINANCIAL SERVICES: Auto Loan	Home Loan	Invest-ments	Retire-ment Plans	THE HOME: Home Improvements: Home Repair	Lawn & Garden	Furnishings: Comput-ers & Hard-ware-Personal	Major Appli-ances	TV, Radio, Sound Equip-ment	Furni-ture	ENTERTAINMENT: Dine out/ Carry out	Sports Equip-ment	Fees & Tickets	Toys & Games	Travel	Cable TV	PERSONAL: Apparel & Services	Auto Repairs	Health Insur-ance	Pets & Supplies
98932	GRANGER	69	68	59	61	67	58	67	67	63	72	65	50	63	65	65	61	46	66	59	74
98933	HARRAH	84	86	74	80	84	77	82	83	79	86	80	63	80	81	82	76	56	82	76	94
98935	MABTON	74	65	55	56	63	59	64	68	66	70	67	46	58	67	60	66	47	67	63	75
98936	MOXEE	91	85	75	81	83	82	82	85	82	86	83	62	77	85	78	83	57	83	82	99
98937	NACHES	93	81	86	80	81	93	78	89	82	77	81	65	71	83	77	86	55	84	90	104
98938	OUTLOOK	83	78	71	73	77	74	76	78	75	80	76	58	71	77	73	74	53	77	74	90
98942	SELAH	90	94	83	95	91	92	89	90	88	89	88	70	91	90	90	88	62	88	89	106
98944	SUNNYSIDE	71	67	57	60	65	56	69	67	66	74	68	50	65	68	66	63	49	69	60	74
98946	THORP	102	112	110	115	112	114	101	108	99	102	100	83	106	100	108	100	70	103	106	126
98947	TIETON	79	78	69	73	77	73	76	78	74	78	75	59	72	76	74	73	52	76	73	88
98948	TOPPENISH	66	62	51	55	60	54	61	62	61	67	62	44	57	62	58	59	43	62	57	69
98951	WAPATO	74	67	58	60	65	62	67	70	67	70	68	50	61	68	63	67	47	69	65	78
98952	WHITE SWAN	73	73	63	67	72	64	71	71	68	76	69	53	69	70	69	66	49	71	64	80
98953	ZILLAH	84	76	84	74	76	83	78	83	78	74	78	66	72	78	78	79	54	82	82	98
99001	AIRWAY HEIGHTS	74	67	63	66	66	70	69	70	70	69	69	52	64	71	66	72	48	70	72	83
99003	CHATTAROY	89	93	81	93	90	92	85	89	85	86	85	67	86	88	86	86	59	85	88	105
99004	CHENEY	75	59	57	61	57	62	82	66	76	71	76	56	66	76	65	75	53	73	67	81
99005	COLBERT	110	132	116	134	128	121	114	117	109	117	111	92	125	113	122	107	79	112	110	136
99006	DEER PARK	85	80	78	81	81	86	79	84	81	78	80	62	76	82	78	83	55	81	86	98
99008	EDWALL	97	73	99	72	75	99	77	91	80	68	80	73	62	80	76	86	52	86	95	111
99009	ELK	89	79	84	77	79	86	75	84	79	77	78	61	70	80	74	81	53	80	84	99
99011	FAIRCHILD AIR FORCE	83	43	32	50	39	37	78	54	74	73	78	54	60	89	57	68	54	69	49	66
99012	FAIRFIELD	89	65	92	65	68	92	68	85	73	61	72	65	54	73	68	80	48	78	88	101
99013	FORD	77	68	65	68	65	73	68	71	72	69	71	53	65	73	65	74	49	71	74	86
99016	GREENACRES	86	87	79	88	85	90	83	86	85	83	84	65	84	86	84	86	58	85	89	102
99017	LAMONT	88	60	96	60	63	93	67	83	70	54	69	69	49	68	67	76	45	78	88	102
99018	LATAH	90	64	94	63	67	93	67	85	73	61	72	65	53	73	66	81	47	78	88	102
99019	LIBERTY LAKE	135	152	132	148	146	131	133	135	126	143	129	104	140	133	136	121	90	128	122	153
99021	MEAD	105	108	99	107	106	104	98	102	97	103	98	78	100	101	99	97	68	98	98	119
99022	MEDICAL LAKE	86	94	89	94	93	93	90	90	89	89	89	69	94	89	93	90	63	90	92	105
99023	MICA	108	134	137	138	137	126	114	120	109	122	110	90	130	108	128	107	79	114	113	137
99025	NEWMAN LAKE	98	107	93	106	102	99	96	98	93	99	94	76	99	97	98	92	66	95	93	115
99026	NINE MILE FALLS	105	116	100	116	112	108	103	106	100	106	101	82	108	104	106	99	71	101	100	123
99027	OTIS ORCHARDS	88	87	87	88	87	93	80	88	82	81	82	67	80	83	83	84	56	84	89	104
99029	REARDAN	107	85	122	85	89	115	87	106	90	77	89	84	73	88	90	96	59	99	108	127
99030	ROCKFORD	86	85	85	88	87	95	80	89	82	76	81	67	79	83	83	85	56	83	90	104
99031	SPANGLE	98	83	105	85	85	106	84	97	85	75	85	78	74	85	86	90	57	92	100	117
99032	SPRAGUE	94	64	103	64	67	99	71	89	74	58	73	73	52	73	71	81	48	83	94	109
99033	TEKOA	81	58	81	57	60	84	63	78	70	56	68	59	51	69	61	78	45	73	85	92
99034	TUMTUM	82	76	67	73	74	77	71	76	74	74	74	55	67	77	68	76	50	73	76	90
99036	VALLEYFORD	103	125	129	128	128	120	107	114	103	113	104	85	121	103	120	102	74	108	108	131
99037	VERADALE	105	115	105	116	112	106	108	106	105	111	106	84	114	107	110	103	75	105	102	125
99040	WELLPINIT	64	56	46	56	51	58	59	56	63	60	62	43	56	64	54	64	43	59	61	70
99101	ADDY	83	62	92	60	65	85	63	79	68	58	67	59	52	67	64	74	44	73	81	94
99103	ALMIRA	93	64	103	64	67	98	71	89	74	58	73	73	52	73	71	81	48	83	93	109
99105	BENGE	80	55	88	55	58	85	61	76	64	50	63	63	45	62	61	69	41	71	80	94
99107	BOYDS	85	68	109	67	74	90	68	86	71	64	70	63	59	67	73	76	47	80	85	100
99109	CHEWELAH	77	65	81	65	67	79	68	77	72	64	70	57	61	70	68	76	48	74	81	90
99110	CLAYTON	83	73	79	72	74	81	70	79	73	70	73	58	65	74	70	76	49	75	79	93
99111	COLFAX	83	77	85	78	80	89	78	84	80	75	79	62	74	79	79	84	54	82	90	98
99113	COLTON	113	79	124	79	82	120	87	108	90	71	89	89	64	89	87	98	58	101	114	132
99114	COLVILLE	78	66	84	66	69	81	69	78	72	65	71	58	62	70	70	76	48	75	81	91
99115	COULEE CITY	68	62	84	58	69	76	60	72	63	63	62	49	58	58	65	67	41	69	78	83
99116	COULEE DAM	74	65	70	65	65	77	65	72	70	63	69	54	62	70	65	74	47	70	78	86
99117	CRESTON	75	60	97	59	66	79	60	76	63	56	62	56	52	60	65	67	41	71	76	89
99118	CURLEW	77	59	92	58	64	80	60	76	64	56	63	56	50	62	63	69	42	70	77	89
99119	CUSICK	77	60	94	59	65	81	61	77	64	57	64	57	51	62	64	69	42	71	77	90
99121	DANVILLE	80	64	103	63	70	85	64	82	67	60	66	60	56	64	70	72	44	75	80	94
99122	DAVENPORT	90	75	98	75	79	92	78	89	81	73	80	66	69	79	79	85	54	85	92	104
99123	ELECTRIC CITY	91	73	118	72	80	96	73	93	76	68	75	68	63	73	79	81	50	86	92	108
99125	ENDICOTT	91	62	100	62	65	96	69	86	72	56	71	71	51	71	69	79	46	81	91	106
99126	EVANS	77	56	83	55	59	79	57	73	63	54	62	55	47	62	58	69	41	67	75	87
99128	FARMINGTON	94	65	102	65	68	99	72	89	76	59	74	73	53	74	71	83	49	83	95	109
99129	FRUITLAND	71	63	69	61	63	68	62	68	64	63	63	51	57	64	62	65	43	66	67	80
99130	GARFIELD	90	62	99	62	65	95	69	86	72	56	71	71	51	70	69	78	46	80	90	105
99131	GIFFORD	73	58	94	57	64	77	58	74	61	55	60	54	50	58	63	65	40	68	73	86
99133	GRAND COULEE	74	53	78	52	56	77	58	72	63	51	61	54	46	62	57	69	41	67	77	85
99134	HARRINGTON	94	65	103	65	68	99	72	89	75	58	74	74	53	73	71	81	48	83	94	110
99135	HARTLINE	95	76	122	74	83	100	76	96	79	71	78	70	66	75	82	84	52	89	95	112
99136	HAY	94	65	103	64	68	99	72	89	74	58	74	74	52	73	71	81	48	83	94	110
99137	HUNTERS	73	58	94	57	64	77	58	74	61	54	60	54	50	58	63	65	40	68	73	86
99138	INCHELIUM	71	51	73	49	53	72	52	66	58	48	57	50	42	57	51	64	37	61	69	79
99139	IONE	76	58	89	56	62	79	58	74	63	55	62	55	49	61	61	68	41	68	75	87
99140	KELLER	56	40	56	39	42	59	44	54	49	39	47	41	35	48	43	54	32	51	59	64
99141	KETTLE FALLS	77	62	82	62	66	79	64	75	68	61	66	56	56	66	65	72	45	71	77	88
99143	LACROSSE	87	60	96	60	63	92	67	83	70	54	69	69	49	68	67	76	45	78	88	102
99147	LINCOLN	75	60	97	59	66	80	60	77	63	57	62	56	52	60	65	67	41	71	76	89
99148	LOON LAKE	87	69	107	67	74	92	69	87	73	65	72	64	59	70	73	78	48	81	87	102
99150	MALO	73	53	78	52	56	75	54	69	60	51	59	52	44	59	55	66	39	64	72	82
99153	METALINE FALLS	68	50	71	48	52	71	53	66	59	48	57	49	43	57	52	64	38	61	70	77
99156	NEWPORT	81	65	100	64	70	85	67	82	71	62	69	60	58	67	70	75	46	77	83	96
99157	NORTHPORT	68	55	88	54	60	72	55	69	57	51	56	51	47	54	59	61	37	64	68	80
99158	OAKESDALE	98	67	108	67	71	103	75	93	78	61	77	77	55	76	74	85	50	87	98	114
99159	ODESSA	72	73	79	71	73	86	68	77	72	64	71	56	68	70	72	77	49	74	86	90
99161	PALOUSE	86	70	84	71	73	88	76	83	78	70	77	64	66	77	74	83	52	81	89	99
99163	PULLMAN	66	46	44	50	44	47	81	55	71	65	72	50	61	70	58	67	51	66	55	69
99164	PULLMAN	40	17	16	21	15	19	56	27	44	38	45	30	33	43	30	40	32	39	27	37
99166	REPUBLIC	79	62	92	62	67	82	64	78	67	60	66	58	55	65	66	72	44	73	79	91
99167	RICE	79	67	82	67	70	83	66	79	70	61	68	59	59	69	68	74	46	73	80	92
99169	RITZVILLE	83	69	86	68	71	90	71	83	76	65	75	63	63	75	72	82	50	79	90	98
99170	ROSALIA	86	60	95	60	63	91	66	82	69	54	68	68	49	68	66	75	44	77	87	101
99171	SAINT JOHN	92	63	101	63	66	97	70	87	73	57	72	72	51	72	70	80	47	82	92	108
99173	SPRINGDALE	78	58	82	56	60	80	59	74	65	55	64	55	48	64	59	71	42	68	76	88
99176	THORNTON	99	68	109	68	71	104	76	94	79	61	78	78	55	77	75	86	50	88	99	116
99179	UNIONTOWN	114	78	125	78	82	120	87	108	91	71	90	89	64	89	87	99	58	101	114	133
	WASHINGTON	106	107	105	108	106	104	108	105	106	108	107	82	108	107	107	105	75	106	104	124
	UNITED STATES	100	100	100	100	100	100	100	100	100	100	100	100	100	100	100	100	100	100	100	100

ZIP CODE #	POST OFFICE NAME	COUNTY FIPS CODE	POPULATION 2000	POPULATION 2009	POPULATION 2014	2000-2009 ANNUAL RATE % Rate	2000-2009 ANNUAL RATE State Centile	HOUSEHOLDS 2000	HOUSEHOLDS 2009	HOUSEHOLDS 2014	HOUSEHOLDS % Annual Rate 2000-2009	HOUSEHOLDS 2009 Average HH Size	FAMILIES 2000	FAMILIES 2009	FAMILIES % Annual Rate 2000-2009
99180	USK	051	682	709	725	0.4	23	270	285	294	0.6	2.48	201	210	0.5
99181	VALLEY	065	1968	2159	2259	1.0	49	730	811	851	1.1	2.66	539	588	0.9
99185	WILBUR	043	1447	1479	1485	0.2	12	592	606	607	0.3	2.43	411	413	0.1
99201	SPOKANE	063	14052	14123	14370	0.1	8	6946	7081	7206	0.2	1.83	2324	2269	-0.3
99202	SPOKANE	063	19280	20691	21283	0.8	40	7267	7682	7934	0.6	2.34	3867	3935	0.2
99203	SPOKANE	063	20265	20861	21396	0.3	16	8754	9163	9439	0.5	2.26	5653	5728	0.1
99204	SPOKANE	063	7013	6737	6757	-0.4	1	3740	3699	3712	-0.1	1.76	1218	1138	-0.7
99205	SPOKANE	063	43020	44151	45143	0.3	16	17689	18428	18900	0.4	2.36	11056	11146	0.1
99206	SPOKANE	063	31383	34214	35781	0.9	45	12321	13552	14230	1.0	2.47	8304	8931	0.8
99207	SPOKANE	063	29925	30914	31612	0.4	23	12085	12514	12814	0.4	2.43	6978	6958	0.0
99208	SPOKANE	063	40692	46854	50265	1.5	69	15835	18195	19565	1.5	2.52	10985	12629	1.5
99212	SPOKANE	063	17816	18530	19204	0.4	23	7813	8270	8602	0.6	2.22	4784	4903	0.3
99216	SPOKANE	063	21717	23805	24921	1.0	49	8773	9802	10334	1.2	2.37	5684	6116	0.8
99217	SPOKANE	063	15949	18900	20062	1.9	81	6039	7570	8143	2.5	2.47	4077	4813	1.8
99218	SPOKANE	063	11944	13325	13942	1.2	57	4669	5290	5574	1.4	2.35	3222	3520	1.0
99223	SPOKANE	063	26828	31560	33916	1.8	78	10524	12483	13456	1.9	2.49	7194	8392	1.7
99224	SPOKANE	063	13294	17533	19448	3.0	94	5311	7192	8037	3.3	2.34	3577	4803	3.2
99251	SPOKANE	063	845	1028	1062	2.1	85	14	16	17	1.5	2.56	10	11	1.0
99301	PASCO	021	41093	65956	81075	5.2	98	12617	20062	24585	5.1	3.26	9769	15436	5.1
99320	BENTON CITY	005	8219	9693	10654	1.8	78	2763	3241	3560	1.7	2.99	2189	2529	1.6
99321	BEVERLY	025	182	199	207	1.0	49	53	56	58	0.6	3.52	43	45	0.5
99322	BICKLETON	039	323	367	388	1.4	66	113	127	134	1.3	2.86	86	95	1.1
99323	BURBANK	071	3629	3779	3834	0.4	23	1197	1236	1252	0.3	3.06	990	1013	0.2
99324	COLLEGE PLACE	071	8188	8958	9326	1.0	49	3047	3372	3529	1.1	2.32	2003	2169	0.9
99326	CONNELL	021	3716	4347	4921	1.7	75	1013	1191	1369	1.8	3.12	804	921	1.5
99328	DAYTON	013	3869	3894	3883	0.1	8	1615	1646	1649	0.2	2.32	1086	1089	0.0
99330	ELTOPIA	021	896	1071	1228	1.9	81	279	338	386	2.1	3.17	229	270	1.8
99336	KENNEWICK	005	38797	43477	45710	1.2	57	15146	16712	17593	1.1	2.55	9662	10331	0.7
99337	KENNEWICK	005	25868	29111	30790	1.3	61	9076	10111	10680	1.2	2.86	7204	7908	1.0
99338	KENNEWICK	005	7681	9645	10935	2.5	89	2508	3104	3503	2.3	3.11	2150	2651	2.3
99341	LIND	001	882	900	916	0.2	12	337	340	345	0.1	2.65	253	250	-0.1
99343	MESA	021	2979	3295	3670	1.1	52	753	843	936	1.2	3.88	648	712	1.0
99344	OTHELLO	001	13901	15578	16482	1.2	57	4075	4507	4749	1.1	3.44	3367	3681	1.0
99347	POMEROY	023	2378	2329	2287	-0.2	2	980	960	943	-0.2	2.39	665	640	-0.4
99348	PRESCOTT	071	1601	1857	1966	1.6	73	455	509	537	1.2	3.61	371	410	1.1
99349	MATTAWA	025	5707	7854	8859	3.5	95	1352	1804	2018	3.2	4.35	1148	1518	3.1
99350	PROSSER	005	12121	13767	14647	1.4	66	3865	4338	4606	1.3	3.16	3076	3407	1.1
99352	RICHLAND	005	19766	26726	29736	3.3	95	7729	10143	11227	3.0	2.63	5554	7274	3.0
99353	WEST RICHLAND	005	9523	12478	13777	3.0	94	3365	4310	4743	2.7	2.89	2666	3366	2.6
99354	RICHLAND	005	20441	22124	23030	0.9	45	8393	8992	9362	0.7	2.45	5547	5812	0.5
99356	ROOSEVELT	039	233	265	280	1.4	66	96	108	114	1.3	2.43	73	81	1.1
99357	ROYAL CITY	025	4070	4810	5199	1.8	78	1073	1245	1338	1.6	3.86	887	1019	1.5
99360	TOUCHET	071	1441	1673	1779	1.6	73	487	564	600	1.6	2.96	404	462	1.5
99361	WAITSBURG	071	2179	2315	2376	0.7	35	839	891	914	0.7	2.60	590	613	0.4
99362	WALLA WALLA	071	38297	40608	41638	0.6	31	13679	14525	14891	0.7	2.52	8921	9321	0.5
99371	WASHTUCNA	001	481	497	510	0.4	23	197	202	207	0.3	2.46	146	146	0.0
99401	ANATONE	003	222	242	252	0.9	45	81	89	93	1.0	2.72	63	68	0.8
99402	ASOTIN	003	1445	1571	1635	0.9	45	553	608	635	1.0	2.58	427	462	0.9
99403	CLARKSTON	003	18941	19674	20107	0.4	23	7751	8155	8365	0.6	2.38	5176	5357	0.4
	WASHINGTON					1.4					1.4	2.53			1.2
	UNITED STATES					1.0					1.1	2.59			0.9

POPULATION COMPOSITION

ZIP CODE #	POST OFFICE NAME	RACE (%) White 2000	White 2009	Black 2000	Black 2009	Asian/Pacific 2000	Asian/Pacific 2009	% Hispanic Origin 2000	% Hispanic Origin 2009	2009 AGE DISTRIBUTION (%) 0-4	5-9	10-14	15-19	20-24	25-44	45-64	65-84	85+	18+	MEDIAN AGE 2009	% 2009 Males	% 2009 Females
99180	USK	92.5	92.0	0.3	0.3	1.2	1.3	1.8	2.7	4.9	6.2	7.8	7.3	3.0	19.9	36.2	13.7	1.0	76.3	45.5	50.9	49.1
99181	VALLEY	94.8	94.1	0.2	0.2	0.6	0.6	2.1	2.8	5.9	7.4	7.7	8.0	4.3	20.9	33.2	11.4	1.2	73.1	42.1	51.2	48.8
99185	WILBUR	95.4	94.7	0.1	0.1	0.4	0.5	1.5	2.0	5.3	5.7	5.8	5.3	4.0	18.2	34.3	18.3	3.1	79.4	49.0	49.0	51.0
99201	SPOKANE	85.2	83.1	3.2	3.6	2.1	2.5	4.2	5.7	5.5	4.5	4.2	6.0	10.0	31.4	25.5	11.0	2.0	82.8	36.3	53.1	46.9
99202	SPOKANE	82.5	79.8	4.6	5.0	3.7	4.4	4.3	5.9	6.8	6.1	5.5	11.1	12.8	24.4	20.7	9.0	3.6	78.0	30.2	48.6	51.4
99203	SPOKANE	93.6	92.3	1.0	1.2	1.8	2.1	2.3	3.2	6.0	6.2	6.4	6.0	5.4	24.2	29.5	13.0	3.3	77.4	42.0	47.0	53.0
99204	SPOKANE	88.3	86.2	2.7	3.1	2.1	2.4	2.9	4.1	6.0	4.3	3.7	4.6	10.9	34.2	23.2	10.0	3.0	83.9	34.5	46.8	53.2
99205	SPOKANE	91.6	90.1	1.4	1.6	1.9	2.2	2.7	3.8	7.1	6.7	6.6	6.8	6.6	28.3	24.8	10.8	2.3	75.7	36.5	48.1	51.9
99206	SPOKANE	93.6	92.4	0.9	1.1	1.3	1.6	2.6	3.7	6.7	6.4	6.4	6.9	6.7	26.2	27.2	11.2	2.2	76.0	37.6	48.9	51.1
99207	SPOKANE	86.8	84.5	2.6	3.0	2.6	3.1	3.7	5.1	8.4	7.1	6.3	7.0	9.8	29.4	21.2	8.2	2.6	74.2	31.6	48.6	51.4
99208	SPOKANE	92.4	91.2	1.3	1.5	2.2	2.7	2.3	3.1	6.1	5.9	6.5	7.5	6.9	23.3	28.7	12.6	2.4	77.0	40.1	48.7	51.3
99212	SPOKANE	92.6	91.2	1.0	1.2	1.6	2.0	2.3	3.2	6.2	6.0	6.0	6.2	6.3	26.1	29.0	12.1	2.0	78.1	40.0	50.1	49.9
99216	SPOKANE	93.4	92.1	0.9	1.1	1.8	2.2	2.5	3.6	7.0	6.5	6.2	6.6	7.6	27.2	24.6	11.4	2.9	76.3	36.1	48.4	51.6
99217	SPOKANE	90.9	89.1	0.9	1.0	2.5	3.0	2.6	3.7	7.0	6.7	6.7	7.0	6.4	28.1	26.4	10.0	1.7	75.5	36.2	49.8	50.2
99218	SPOKANE	92.9	91.4	1.0	1.2	2.1	2.6	2.4	3.3	5.8	5.4	5.9	9.6	9.1	23.9	26.0	11.4	2.7	78.4	35.8	47.1	52.9
99223	SPOKANE	92.5	91.2	1.4	1.6	2.4	2.9	2.0	2.7	6.0	6.1	6.6	6.9	5.8	23.8	29.8	12.1	3.0	76.9	40.9	48.0	52.0
99224	SPOKANE	91.5	90.1	1.5	1.6	2.1	2.4	2.8	3.7	5.5	5.6	5.9	6.5	6.3	26.9	30.1	11.5	1.8	79.6	40.4	50.2	49.8
99251	SPOKANE	92.1	90.5	0.9	1.1	2.6	3.1	2.3	3.1	3.0	3.1	3.5	26.2	19.3	13.8	18.3	11.1	1.8	86.9	23.7	42.9	57.1
99301	PASCO	60.1	56.5	2.7	2.5	1.7	1.8	47.9	54.2	9.6	8.7	8.0	7.8	6.9	26.9	22.5	8.4	1.3	68.9	31.3	51.1	48.9
99320	BENTON CITY	88.5	84.7	0.3	0.3	0.9	1.1	13.8	19.2	8.0	8.0	8.1	8.0	6.1	26.3	27.2	7.6	0.7	70.9	34.2	50.7	49.3
99321	BEVERLY	59.7	55.3	0.0	0.0	0.0	0.0	60.8	69.3	12.6	11.6	9.5	9.0	7.5	31.7	14.6	3.5	0.0	60.3	24.8	52.8	47.2
99322	BICKLETON	78.0	73.3	1.2	1.6	1.9	1.6	24.8	31.9	6.8	7.4	7.9	7.9	4.4	24.5	28.9	10.6	1.6	73.3	38.4	52.3	47.7
99323	BURBANK	90.2	87.4	0.2	0.3	0.5	0.7	10.4	14.4	6.9	7.7	8.0	7.7	5.1	25.5	29.3	8.8	1.0	72.5	37.2	49.9	50.1
99324	COLLEGE PLACE	86.0	82.3	1.5	1.9	2.1	2.5	14.1	19.1	6.6	5.8	6.0	8.8	12.6	23.1	20.2	13.4	3.6	78.4	32.8	48.4	51.6
99326	CONNELL	67.1	57.5	3.2	3.4	3.7	3.1	39.0	54.7	9.2	8.6	7.9	9.1	8.3	32.3	18.7	5.3	0.6	68.5	28.5	57.5	42.5
99328	DAYTON	93.7	93.6	0.2	0.2	0.5	0.5	6.5	6.7	5.3	5.8	6.0	6.7	5.0	21.3	30.6	16.5	2.8	78.6	44.9	48.2	51.8
99330	ELTOPIA	79.2	67.7	0.2	0.3	0.9	1.1	31.3	48.9	9.5	9.2	8.5	7.5	5.9	29.4	22.6	6.7	0.7	68.3	31.0	52.9	47.1
99336	KENNEWICK	79.9	75.4	1.2	1.3	2.1	2.3	19.1	24.9	9.2	7.6	6.8	7.2	8.3	29.1	21.5	8.7	1.6	72.1	30.9	49.8	50.2
99337	KENNEWICK	90.3	87.6	0.6	0.7	1.5	1.8	8.5	12.0	6.7	6.9	7.4	7.6	6.1	24.3	29.5	10.2	1.4	74.2	37.9	49.6	50.4
99338	KENNEWICK	92.6	90.7	0.5	0.6	1.5	1.8	6.0	8.3	5.9	6.7	8.0	8.9	5.5	23.2	33.3	7.7	0.7	73.7	39.4	50.1	49.9
99341	LIND	89.5	85.9	0.1	0.1	0.3	0.4	11.6	16.7	6.6	7.2	8.3	8.7	4.6	20.3	31.0	11.6	1.8	72.2	41.1	52.4	47.6
99343	MESA	71.0	60.9	0.2	0.2	0.7	0.6	47.3	63.6	12.4	11.0	9.3	9.0	8.6	27.3	17.4	4.6	0.5	61.6	24.9	52.8	47.2
99344	OTHELLO	57.7	52.5	0.3	0.3	0.7	0.7	59.0	67.6	11.2	10.4	9.2	8.5	7.7	27.2	18.4	6.7	0.8	64.0	26.8	51.2	48.8
99347	POMEROY	96.4	96.4	0.0	0.0	0.7	0.7	1.9	2.0	4.9	5.0	5.5	7.2	5.7	19.8	32.1	16.3	3.6	80.1	46.1	49.7	50.3
99348	PRESCOTT	52.3	45.1	0.5	0.5	0.4	0.4	53.1	62.1	12.7	10.9	8.5	8.5	7.3	29.8	16.6	5.3	0.5	62.4	26.3	53.7	46.3
99349	MATTAWA	45.0	40.7	0.1	0.2	0.9	0.8	71.4	78.6	11.7	10.8	9.4	8.9	7.4	31.8	14.5	4.9	0.5	62.6	26.0	54.2	45.8
99350	PROSSER	75.5	69.3	0.3	0.3	0.9	0.9	34.5	44.4	8.6	8.2	8.2	8.2	6.8	25.4	24.1	9.0	1.4	69.8	32.2	49.7	50.3
99352	RICHLAND	90.5	88.5	1.4	1.5	3.5	4.2	4.8	7.1	6.6	6.9	7.2	7.3	5.5	24.4	30.1	10.5	1.4	74.7	39.5	49.0	51.0
99353	WEST RICHLAND	93.5	91.5	0.4	0.5	1.8	2.2	4.7	7.0	8.6	8.2	8.1	7.2	5.7	27.8	26.5	7.4	0.6	70.4	33.9	49.6	50.4
99354	RICHLAND	88.8	86.2	1.3	1.5	4.6	5.5	4.7	6.9	6.5	6.1	6.3	6.9	6.3	23.5	28.3	13.6	2.5	76.8	40.5	48.6	51.4
99356	ROOSEVELT	77.7	72.8	1.3	1.9	1.7	1.9	24.9	32.5	7.2	7.2	7.9	7.9	4.2	24.5	28.7	10.9	1.5	72.8	38.4	52.1	47.9
99357	ROYAL CITY	68.4	65.8	0.2	0.2	0.5	0.5	62.9	70.7	12.1	10.7	9.0	9.2	8.7	29.2	15.4	5.1	0.5	62.4	25.1	53.8	46.2
99360	TOUCHET	90.6	88.0	0.1	0.1	0.3	0.4	15.1	20.6	7.8	7.8	8.7	7.5	3.6	25.6	26.4	10.9	1.8	70.2	37.2	52.4	47.6
99361	WAITSBURG	93.7	92.1	0.4	0.5	0.6	0.7	4.8	6.9	5.8	6.6	7.4	7.5	5.2	21.3	30.4	13.9	1.9	75.5	42.5	50.0	50.0
99362	WALLA WALLA	85.5	82.7	2.0	2.1	1.4	1.5	15.5	20.1	6.0	5.8	5.7	8.1	9.4	24.5	25.1	12.2	3.2	78.8	36.7	51.0	49.0
99371	WASHTUCNA	96.5	95.6	0.0	0.0	0.0	0.0	3.5	5.4	4.6	5.0	5.8	6.6	4.2	20.1	34.2	17.9	1.4	80.9	47.1	51.7	48.3
99401	ANATONE	97.3	97.1	0.0	0.0	0.5	0.4	1.4	1.2	5.4	6.2	7.9	9.1	3.7	21.9	31.4	12.4	2.1	74.0	42.4	49.2	50.8
99402	ASOTIN	97.4	97.0	0.1	0.2	0.3	0.4	1.0	1.5	5.0	6.0	7.8	9.0	3.4	21.8	32.3	12.9	1.8	74.9	43.1	49.3	50.7
99403	CLARKSTON	95.5	94.7	0.2	0.2	0.5	0.7	2.0	2.8	6.9	6.4	6.3	6.8	5.7	23.2	27.3	14.2	3.0	76.1	40.5	47.9	52.1
	WASHINGTON	81.8	79.0	3.2	3.4	5.9	6.9	7.5	9.7	6.7	6.5	6.5	7.0	7.0	27.4	27.0	10.1	1.8	76.3	36.9	49.8	50.2
	UNITED STATES	75.1	72.0	12.3	12.7	3.8	4.6	12.5	15.7	6.8	6.7	6.6	7.1	6.9	27.0	26.0	10.9	1.9	75.7	36.9	49.2	50.8

#	POST OFFICE NAME	2009 Per Capita Income	2009 HH Income Base	2009 Household Income Distribution (%): Less than $25,000	$25,000 to $49,999	$50,000 to $99,999	$100,000 to $149,999	$150,000 or More	Median Household Income: 2009	2014	2009 National Centile	2009 State Centile	2009 Home Value Base	2009 Home Value Distribution (%): Less than $50,000	$50,000 to $89,999	$90,000 to $174,999	$175,000 to $399,999	$400,000 or More	2009 Median Home Value
99180	USK	20109	285	29.5	29.8	33.3	5.6	1.8	42361	44607	41	23	229	10.0	7.4	27.5	44.5	10.5	188068
99181	VALLEY	17161	811	32.1	32.4	28.9	5.4	1.2	39078	41193	30	14	656	7.2	11.3	32.0	38.7	10.8	173810
99185	WILBUR	19427	606	27.9	32.8	34.2	4.0	1.2	41578	43590	38	21	475	7.6	16.0	51.2	21.7	3.6	136618
99201	SPOKANE	16690	7081	55.3	27.1	15.6	1.3	0.6	21538	22246	2	1	1612	9.8	14.9	53.3	20.2	1.8	127188
99202	SPOKANE	18127	7682	37.0	32.2	26.4	3.1	1.3	34315	36079	16	4	3801	1.6	5.7	65.7	23.8	3.2	147613
99203	SPOKANE	32072	9163	16.0	27.1	37.9	11.7	7.2	58067	61283	75	66	6741	0.1	0.3	23.2	61.7	14.7	230536
99204	SPOKANE	22763	3699	42.0	34.6	17.2	4.0	2.2	30216	30777	8	2	891	0.8	2.0	26.8	61.2	9.2	210139
99205	SPOKANE	21583	18428	22.1	34.0	38.2	4.6	1.2	46153	47967	52	38	12928	0.5	1.2	68.6	28.8	0.9	158496
99206	SPOKANE	23501	13552	19.4	30.2	39.6	8.2	2.6	50319	53221	62	49	8507	2.9	2.0	27.3	63.9	4.0	199429
99207	SPOKANE	16619	12514	34.7	36.2	26.1	2.3	0.8	35040	36310	18	5	6650	0.4	5.1	81.2	13.1	0.2	136506
99208	SPOKANE	26801	18195	17.2	25.9	39.5	11.8	5.6	57241	61178	74	65	12815	1.6	0.9	25.7	63.1	8.7	220815
99212	SPOKANE	24353	8270	23.9	31.4	35.9	6.0	2.9	45263	48287	49	34	5670	5.1	5.5	45.9	38.9	4.6	166993
99216	SPOKANE	22585	9802	19.2	33.7	40.2	5.4	1.5	47672	49723	56	42	5590	1.5	2.1	34.6	59.7	2.1	188098
99217	SPOKANE	22835	7570	21.7	32.8	35.5	6.5	3.5	46285	48681	52	38	4755	6.6	4.2	43.1	36.8	9.3	169244
99218	SPOKANE	27308	5290	17.9	29.1	35.6	12.6	4.8	52891	55761	68	55	3283	1.4	0.6	13.4	76.2	8.4	239368
99223	SPOKANE	30360	12483	15.3	23.6	38.9	14.7	7.6	62531	64880	81	73	8828	0.6	0.7	15.4	68.2	15.1	259420
99224	SPOKANE	27463	7192	17.6	29.0	39.1	9.1	5.2	53154	57493	68	56	5042	8.1	4.1	18.2	53.5	16.0	236997
99251	SPOKANE	8035	16	6.3	25.0	56.3	6.3	6.3	64018	63223	82	76	12	0.0	0.0	16.7	83.3	0.0	225000
99301	PASCO	18820	20062	22.5	25.1	38.7	9.5	4.2	52024	55229	66	54	13342	5.7	5.8	45.7	37.2	5.6	162697
99320	BENTON CITY	22658	3241	14.9	25.5	42.0	13.5	4.1	60246	63597	78	70	2662	7.1	10.0	49.3	30.8	2.8	147250
99321	BEVERLY	10163	56	37.5	39.3	21.4	1.8	0.0	31464	32275	10	3	24	4.2	0.0	41.7	16.7	37.5	250000
99322	BICKLETON	20928	127	20.5	22.0	47.2	6.3	3.9	54399	56762	70	58	90	0.0	10.0	44.4	24.4	21.1	166667
99323	BURBANK	21596	1236	10.3	26.7	50.6	8.7	3.8	61868	63369	80	72	1043	1.6	6.6	36.2	49.3	6.2	188188
99324	COLLEGE PLACE	20057	3372	31.4	29.1	33.0	4.7	1.8	38532	41878	28	12	2018	5.3	6.5	30.0	51.9	6.3	194186
99326	CONNELL	16437	1191	26.5	34.8	33.0	3.5	2.2	42335	43601	40	23	706	23.8	12.7	54.4	8.1	1.0	105250
99328	DAYTON	22693	1646	25.6	30.3	34.6	7.4	2.1	44920	46801	48	31	1146	3.3	9.9	47.4	35.2	4.3	156211
99330	ELTOPIA	15757	338	28.7	32.0	32.5	4.7	2.1	36850	37468	23	8	203	9.9	9.4	51.7	20.7	8.4	139205
99336	KENNEWICK	21507	16712	22.3	33.3	33.4	9.0	1.9	45926	47860	51	37	8620	7.5	7.8	56.1	28.1	0.6	142266
99337	KENNEWICK	25618	10111	11.6	24.2	42.4	16.5	5.3	63702	65976	82	76	8166	5.0	5.8	42.1	42.6	4.5	171465
99338	KENNEWICK	30561	3104	5.2	13.4	42.7	28.0	10.7	83038	85023	93	95	2717	4.3	4.2	17.2	65.7	8.6	224068
99341	LIND	19747	340	20.6	31.8	42.1	4.1	1.5	47960	48578	56	43	240	12.1	15.8	45.0	26.3	0.8	128472
99343	MESA	13309	843	26.1	38.0	28.5	4.4	3.1	38964	39825	30	14	472	23.1	12.5	43.0	12.5	8.9	113793
99344	OTHELLO	14799	4507	20.3	38.4	35.8	4.1	1.4	42287	44733	40	23	3007	13.2	7.3	40.9	32.8	5.7	157242
99347	POMEROY	20986	960	28.3	28.2	35.8	6.4	1.3	42475	44473	41	24	711	7.6	17.4	45.4	25.9	3.7	129367
99348	PRESCOTT	14005	509	24.6	34.4	35.4	3.5	2.2	45683	47330	50	35	178	13.5	14.6	32.6	25.3	14.0	148684
99349	MATTAWA	12018	1804	19.6	40.5	31.9	6.0	2.0	45000	46545	48	33	1023	6.5	11.2	34.3	45.9	2.0	171781
99350	PROSSER	17789	4338	21.0	31.3	37.7	7.6	2.4	48470	50468	58	44	3097	7.5	8.0	47.2	33.6	3.7	155296
99352	RICHLAND	31927	10143	12.8	20.2	36.9	20.0	10.1	70021	73976	87	85	7355	1.5	4.3	33.3	53.4	7.6	204622
99353	WEST RICHLAND	27413	4310	10.7	21.2	41.2	20.9	5.9	70765	73312	87	86	3707	7.8	7.1	38.0	43.4	3.7	170503
99354	RICHLAND	29799	8992	16.4	21.4	40.8	14.7	6.7	62929	65254	81	74	5509	5.1	4.4	41.4	45.7	3.5	173688
99356	ROOSEVELT	24591	108	19.4	22.2	48.1	5.6	4.6	55034	57635	71	59	77	0.0	9.1	46.8	23.4	20.8	163750
99357	ROYAL CITY	11941	1245	29.6	34.7	29.6	5.2	1.0	37938	40471	26	11	695	19.7	5.2	35.7	30.1	9.4	147361
99360	TOUCHET	19768	564	17.2	30.5	41.3	9.0	2.0	51740	54600	65	53	401	3.0	5.0	31.9	45.4	14.7	210500
99361	WAITSBURG	20720	891	25.8	29.0	37.3	5.9	2.0	45758	48757	51	35	682	4.5	7.8	42.2	34.0	11.4	169038
99362	WALLA WALLA	21592	14525	26.7	28.0	34.1	8.3	2.9	45867	48449	51	36	9372	2.9	4.7	34.9	47.8	9.8	192406
99371	WASHTUCNA	22266	202	16.3	34.2	39.6	7.4	2.5	49573	50897	60	47	132	7.6	21.2	41.7	25.8	3.8	129688
99401	ANATONE	19592	89	25.8	31.5	36.0	4.5	2.2	44534	48639	47	30	65	9.2	1.5	27.7	43.1	18.5	203571
99402	ASOTIN	20868	608	23.0	31.6	37.8	5.1	2.5	46605	49465	53	39	448	8.9	2.2	27.7	44.9	16.3	195833
99403	CLARKSTON	21856	8155	25.4	33.5	32.3	6.4	2.5	42487	45402	41	24	5398	5.7	4.3	38.1	43.8	8.1	178331
	WASHINGTON	29418		17.0	23.3	38.4	13.6	7.7	60852	63758				3.4	2.9	16.8	52.3	24.6	272173
	UNITED STATES	27277		20.9	24.4	35.3	11.7	7.6	54719	56938				9.3	13.1	31.6	32.6	13.5	162279

ZIP CODE	FINANCIAL SERVICES				THE HOME						ENTERTAINMENT						PERSONAL			
					Home Improvements		Furnishings													
# POST OFFICE NAME	Auto Loan	Home Loan	Investments	Retirement Plans	Home Repair	Lawn & Garden	Computers & Hardware-Personal	Major Appliances	TV, Radio, Sound Equipment	Furniture	Dine out/ Carry out	Sports Equipment	Fees & Tickets	Toys & Games	Travel	Cable TV	Apparel & Services	Auto Repairs	Health Insurance	Pets & Supplies
99180 USK	85	66	102	64	71	89	66	84	71	62	70	62	56	68	70	76	46	78	85	98
99181 VALLEY	79	60	90	58	64	82	60	77	65	56	64	57	50	63	63	71	43	71	78	90
99185 WILBUR	79	62	101	61	68	84	63	80	66	58	65	59	54	63	68	71	43	74	80	93
99201 SPOKANE	42	32	32	34	31	35	45	37	46	41	46	30	40	44	39	48	32	44	44	47
99202 SPOKANE	61	50	46	52	48	53	64	55	64	59	64	44	57	64	55	65	45	61	61	68
99203 SPOKANE	97	107	105	108	107	106	101	102	101	103	102	76	108	100	107	102	72	102	107	119
99204 SPOKANE	55	42	44	46	42	45	61	49	61	56	61	41	54	59	53	61	43	58	56	62
99205 SPOKANE	71	70	62	71	68	75	73	71	74	69	74	55	72	74	70	77	51	73	79	85
99206 SPOKANE	83	81	77	82	80	81	83	81	83	83	84	62	83	84	82	84	58	83	84	96
99207 SPOKANE	58	50	43	51	47	53	60	53	61	54	60	43	54	61	53	62	42	58	59	65
99208 SPOKANE	94	99	92	100	97	96	98	95	96	98	97	73	100	97	98	96	68	96	96	111
99212 SPOKANE	74	75	68	76	73	78	78	75	78	74	78	58	78	78	76	80	54	77	81	89
99216 SPOKANE	76	74	68	75	71	74	77	73	77	76	78	57	76	78	75	78	54	76	77	88
99217 SPOKANE	81	78	71	80	76	78	82	78	81	80	81	61	80	82	79	81	57	80	80	93
99218 SPOKANE	91	91	92	94	92	93	93	92	93	94	94	70	95	92	94	93	66	94	95	108
99223 SPOKANE	102	115	112	116	115	112	106	108	105	109	106	81	115	104	112	105	75	106	110	125
99224 SPOKANE	94	93	99	94	94	96	93	95	92	92	92	73	91	91	94	93	64	94	95	111
99251 SPOKANE	94	111	115	111	115	117	96	106	99	101	99	73	109	96	109	102	69	102	115	121
99301 PASCO	87	89	83	86	88	81	88	87	85	91	87	67	88	87	88	83	62	87	80	98
99320 BENTON CITY	102	105	90	103	101	99	96	99	95	100	96	76	96	100	95	95	66	95	95	116
99321 BEVERLY	53	53	45	47	52	43	52	52	49	57	50	38	50	50	51	46	36	52	45	57
99322 BICKLETON	107	74	118	74	77	113	82	102	85	66	84	84	60	84	81	93	55	95	107	125
99323 BURBANK	102	99	87	98	97	100	92	97	94	95	94	72	90	98	90	96	65	94	97	115
99324 COLLEGE PLACE	70	56	58	58	57	63	70	65	71	65	70	50	62	70	63	72	49	69	70	78
99326 CONNELL	77	75	65	68	74	65	74	74	71	79	72	55	70	73	71	68	51	73	66	82
99328 DAYTON	78	73	78	73	74	85	73	79	76	69	75	59	70	75	74	80	51	77	86	93
99330 ELTOPIA	80	74	65	71	72	75	69	74	72	72	72	54	66	75	66	74	49	71	74	87
99336 KENNEWICK	81	72	65	73	69	69	81	74	80	80	81	59	76	81	75	79	56	79	75	88
99337 KENNEWICK	109	111	100	109	108	109	103	107	104	106	104	80	104	106	103	105	72	104	106	125
99338 KENNEWICK	131	153	141	154	150	141	134	138	129	140	130	107	146	132	142	126	93	132	129	159
99341 LIND	93	66	98	65	69	96	69	88	76	62	74	68	54	75	69	83	49	81	92	105
99343 MESA	80	75	70	69	74	70	74	77	72	78	73	58	69	74	72	71	51	75	71	87
99344 OTHELLO	79	72	67	66	70	69	73	75	72	76	73	57	67	73	70	71	51	75	70	86
99347 POMEROY	86	61	90	60	64	91	67	83	73	58	71	64	53	72	66	81	47	78	90	99
99348 PRESCOTT	75	75	64	66	74	61	74	73	69	80	71	54	70	71	72	66	50	73	63	80
99349 MATTAWA	78	78	67	69	77	64	77	76	72	83	74	57	73	74	74	68	52	76	66	83
99350 PROSSER	90	79	78	76	78	86	78	84	81	79	81	63	72	83	75	84	55	82	85	99
99352 RICHLAND	117	129	119	130	126	121	119	119	116	123	117	92	126	119	123	114	83	117	116	139
99353 WEST RICHLAND	120	127	108	124	121	112	114	115	110	122	112	90	116	117	113	107	78	110	105	133
99354 RICHLAND	101	104	98	106	102	103	104	101	104	104	104	78	106	104	104	104	73	103	104	120
99356 ROOSEVELT	107	74	118	74	77	113	82	102	85	66	84	84	60	83	81	93	55	95	107	125
99357 ROYAL CITY	68	65	55	59	63	55	68	65	64	71	66	51	64	66	65	60	47	67	57	72
99360 TOUCHET	102	75	110	74	78	106	80	97	83	69	83	78	63	82	80	90	54	91	101	118
99361 WAITSBURG	94	69	103	68	73	97	71	90	77	66	76	68	58	76	72	84	50	83	93	107
99362 WALLA WALLA	79	75	79	76	76	80	79	79	80	76	79	59	77	78	78	82	55	80	83	93
99371 WASHTUCNA	98	67	108	67	71	103	75	93	78	61	77	77	55	76	74	85	50	87	98	114
99401 ANATONE	89	71	115	70	78	94	71	90	74	67	74	66	62	71	77	79	49	83	89	105
99402 ASOTIN	90	72	116	71	79	95	72	92	75	68	74	67	62	72	78	80	49	84	90	106
99403 CLARKSTON	77	69	69	70	70	77	74	75	76	70	75	57	69	76	71	79	52	76	81	89
WASHINGTON	106	107	105	108	106	104	108	105	106	108	107	82	108	107	107	105	75	106	104	124
UNITED STATES	100	100	100	100	100	100	100	100	100	100	100	100	100	100	100	100	100	100	100	100

24701-25064

ZIP CODE #	POST OFFICE NAME	COUNTY FIPS CODE	POPULATION 2000	POPULATION 2009	POPULATION 2014	2000-2009 ANNUAL RATE % Rate	2000-2009 ANNUAL RATE State Centile	HOUSEHOLDS 2000	HOUSEHOLDS 2009	HOUSEHOLDS 2014	HOUSEHOLDS % Annual Rate 2000-2009	HOUSEHOLDS 2009 Average HH Size	FAMILIES 2000	FAMILIES 2009	FAMILIES % Annual Rate 2000-2009
24701	BLUEFIELD	055	20902	20438	20256	-0.2	48	9040	9214	9249	0.2	2.20	5874	5757	-0.2
24712	ATHENS	055	2037	1838	1806	-1.1	6	623	612	605	-0.2	2.13	427	405	-0.6
24714	BEESON	055	343	354	358	0.3	81	141	153	157	0.9	2.31	104	110	0.6
24715	BRAMWELL	055	487	432	416	-1.3	2	217	204	198	-0.7	2.12	139	125	-1.1
24726	HERNDON	109	1819	1678	1599	-0.9	10	730	715	691	-0.2	2.35	529	504	-0.5
24731	KEGLEY	055	101	111	114	1.0	91	31	36	37	1.6	3.08	23	26	1.3
24733	LASHMEET	055	788	743	728	-0.6	25	303	300	298	-0.1	2.47	229	220	-0.4
24736	MATOAKA	055	1110	1024	989	-0.9	10	448	436	427	-0.3	2.34	338	320	-0.6
24740	PRINCETON	055	29702	28497	28039	-0.4	35	12743	12770	12723	0.0	2.21	8563	8283	-0.4
24747	ROCK	055	4912	4922	4914	0.0	65	1964	2071	2098	0.6	2.38	1485	1523	0.3
24801	WELCH	047	8420	7458	6979	-1.3	2	3491	3247	3070	-0.8	2.21	2313	2072	-1.2
24815	BERWIND	047	2268	1995	1853	-1.4	1	921	856	807	-0.8	2.33	636	573	-1.1
24818	BRENTON	109	2729	2549	2450	-0.7	19	1063	1055	1027	-0.1	2.42	779	750	-0.4
24822	CLEAR FORK	109	667	633	617	-0.6	25	263	265	262	0.1	2.39	206	203	-0.2
24823	COAL MOUNTAIN	109	115	109	107	-0.6	25	44	44	44	0.0	2.48	35	34	-0.3
24827	CYCLONE	109	2017	1899	1838	-0.6	25	790	792	776	0.0	2.40	618	605	-0.2
24828	DAVY	047	2293	2009	1869	-1.4	1	896	834	787	-0.8	2.41	664	601	-1.1
24834	FANROCK	109	114	106	103	-0.8	14	47	47	46	0.0	2.26	35	34	-0.3
24839	HANOVER	109	1424	1339	1284	-0.7	19	584	582	567	0.0	2.30	420	406	-0.4
24844	IAEGER	047	4532	4036	3791	-1.2	3	1850	1758	1673	-0.5	2.29	1361	1257	-0.9
24849	JESSE	109	381	353	338	-0.8	14	157	156	151	-0.1	2.26	115	111	-0.4
24850	JOLO	047	2572	2290	2147	-1.2	3	1073	1023	972	-0.5	2.24	789	731	-0.8
24859	MARIANNA	109	833	769	734	-0.9	10	333	328	318	-0.2	2.34	235	225	-0.5
24860	MATHENY	109	651	611	585	-0.7	19	281	279	271	-0.1	2.19	214	207	-0.4
24862	MOHAWK	047	1361	1195	1112	-1.4	1	545	511	483	-0.7	2.34	418	382	-1.0
24868	NORTHFORK	047	3194	2822	2624	-1.3	2	1316	1227	1156	-0.8	2.29	889	799	-1.1
24869	NORTH SPRING	109	131	122	119	-0.8	14	54	54	53	0.0	2.26	40	38	-0.6
24870	OCEANA	109	3568	3335	3197	-0.7	19	1450	1433	1391	-0.1	2.33	1124	1084	-0.4
24873	PAYNESVILLE	047	1229	1086	1012	-1.3	2	502	470	444	-0.7	2.31	359	325	-1.1
24874	PINEVILLE	109	3426	3171	3039	-0.8	14	1470	1453	1411	-0.1	2.14	1032	988	-0.5
24879	RAYSAL	047	1405	1267	1202	-1.1	6	537	514	494	-0.5	2.46	397	369	-0.8
24882	SIMON	109	647	612	596	-0.6	25	246	248	244	0.1	2.47	191	187	-0.2
24884	SQUIRE	047	804	706	656	-1.4	1	333	309	292	-0.8	2.28	240	216	-1.1
24901	LEWISBURG	025	7824	8024	8044	0.3	81	3550	3773	3827	0.7	2.08	2242	2294	0.2
24910	ALDERSON	089	4941	4984	4938	0.1	72	1493	1559	1561	0.5	2.59	1015	1022	0.1
24915	ARBOVALE	075	544	499	477	-0.9	10	224	214	207	-0.5	2.32	141	129	-1.0
24916	ASBURY	025	407	424	428	0.4	83	170	184	188	0.9	2.30	128	134	0.5
24918	BALLARD	063	1275	1310	1324	0.3	81	506	543	555	0.8	2.41	379	395	0.4
24920	BARTOW	075	589	528	500	-1.2	3	244	225	215	-0.9	2.35	174	157	-1.1
24925	CALDWELL	025	211	217	218	0.3	81	99	106	108	0.7	2.05	74	78	0.6
24927	CASS	075	823	755	720	-0.9	10	356	339	327	-0.5	2.19	226	207	-0.9
24931	CRAWLEY	025	1445	1545	1572	0.7	89	581	647	666	1.2	2.39	443	480	0.9
24934	DUNMORE	075	249	228	218	-0.9	10	116	110	106	-0.6	2.05	81	75	-0.8
24935	FOREST HILL	089	295	275	265	-0.8	14	128	125	123	-0.3	2.13	92	87	-0.6
24938	FRANKFORD	025	1184	1216	1219	0.3	81	467	499	507	0.7	2.43	361	376	0.4
24941	GAP MILLS	063	769	787	792	0.3	81	317	337	343	0.7	2.34	225	232	0.3
24943	GRASSY MEADOWS	025	200	212	214	0.6	88	79	87	89	1.0	2.44	60	64	0.7
24944	GREEN BANK	075	437	399	381	-1.0	7	169	160	155	-0.6	2.49	121	111	-0.9
24945	GREENVILLE	063	1361	1400	1414	0.3	81	542	581	595	0.8	2.37	387	402	0.4
24946	HILLSBORO	075	1542	1415	1356	-0.9	10	565	533	513	-0.6	2.31	390	356	-1.0
24951	LINDSIDE	063	808	818	824	0.1	72	343	363	371	0.6	2.13	239	244	0.2
24954	MARLINTON	075	4175	3953	3824	-0.6	25	1828	1784	1740	-0.3	2.16	1169	1098	-0.7
24957	MAXWELTON	025	108	113	114	0.5	86	47	51	53	0.9	2.22	36	38	0.6
24962	PENCE SPRINGS	089	294	295	293	0.0	65	121	125	124	0.4	1.70	87	87	0.0
24963	PETERSTOWN	063	4121	4181	4211	0.2	76	1740	1848	1882	0.7	2.26	1244	1281	0.3
24966	RENICK	025	1659	1751	1764	0.6	88	662	716	731	0.9	2.37	485	509	0.5
24970	RONCEVERTE	025	5785	5855	5856	0.1	72	2295	2420	2448	0.6	2.36	1600	1630	0.2
24974	SECONDCREEK	063	452	462	467	0.2	76	185	195	199	0.6	2.36	139	143	0.3
24976	SINKS GROVE	063	1052	1071	1079	0.2	76	409	430	437	0.5	2.48	302	308	0.2
24977	SMOOT	025	887	916	914	0.3	81	349	374	378	0.8	2.45	257	267	0.4
24981	TALCOTT	089	748	738	727	-0.1	57	321	329	327	0.3	1.78	223	220	-0.1
24983	UNION	063	1822	1828	1826	0.0	65	783	815	824	0.4	2.24	535	539	0.1
24984	WAITEVILLE	063	447	453	455	0.1	72	184	194	197	0.6	2.34	128	130	0.2
24985	WAYSIDE	063	533	539	537	0.1	72	222	231	232	0.4	1.69	158	159	0.1
24986	WHITE SULPHUR SPRING	025	5068	5279	5259	0.4	83	2218	2326	2341	0.5	2.12	1440	1450	0.1
24991	WILLIAMSBURG	025	779	817	825	0.5	86	305	333	340	1.0	2.45	231	245	0.6
24993	WOLFCREEK	063	224	225	224	0.0	65	89	92	93	0.4	2.45	62	62	0.0
25003	ALUM CREEK	039	2706	2620	2569	-0.3	40	1077	1074	1063	0.0	2.44	807	781	-0.4
25005	AMMA	087	317	310	304	-0.2	48	119	121	120	0.2	2.55	92	91	-0.1
25007	ARNETT	081	318	317	317	0.0	65	114	118	119	0.4	2.69	85	85	0.0
25008	ARTIE	081	540	522	513	-0.4	35	205	205	204	0.0	2.55	157	152	-0.3
25009	ASHFORD	005	588	586	578	0.0	65	222	232	232	0.5	2.53	168	171	0.2
25015	BELLE	039	7292	6585	6376	-1.1	6	3089	2827	2752	-1.0	2.33	2113	1865	-1.3
25019	BICKMORE	015	375	371	366	-0.1	57	150	156	156	0.4	2.38	115	116	0.1
25021	BIM	005	670	636	621	-0.6	25	279	280	277	0.0	2.27	200	195	-0.3
25024	BLOOMINGROSE	005	693	688	677	-0.1	57	275	284	284	0.3	2.42	196	197	0.1
25025	BLOUNT	039	682	656	645	-0.4	35	265	259	255	-0.2	2.53	211	200	-0.6
25028	BOB WHITE	005	488	477	469	-0.2	48	196	202	201	0.3	2.36	141	141	0.0
25030	BOMONT	015	134	132	130	-0.2	48	55	57	57	0.4	2.32	42	43	0.3
25033	BUFFALO	079	2273	2456	2567	0.8	90	916	1031	1089	1.3	2.37	668	731	1.0
25035	CABIN CREEK	039	1063	953	916	-1.2	3	435	396	383	-1.0	2.41	298	261	-1.4
25039	CEDAR GROVE	039	2589	2346	2263	-1.1	6	1103	1013	982	-0.9	2.30	768	677	-1.4
25043	CLAY	015	2382	2373	2335	0.0	65	952	988	985	0.4	2.38	659	662	0.0
25044	CLEAR CREEK	081	39	38	37	-0.3	40	16	16	16	0.0	2.38	12	12	0.0
25045	CLENDENIN	039	6021	5851	5754	-0.3	40	2404	2379	2356	-0.1	2.45	1766	1692	-0.5
25047	CLOTHIER	045	1180	1122	1090	-0.5	30	485	485	477	0.0	2.27	355	344	-0.3
25048	COLCORD	081	66	64	63	-0.3	40	28	28	28	0.0	2.29	21	21	0.0
25049	COMFORT	005	389	387	381	-0.1	57	152	157	157	0.4	2.46	109	110	0.1
25051	COSTA	005	470	462	455	-0.2	48	187	193	192	0.3	2.39	143	144	0.1
25053	DANVILLE	005	3993	3976	3924	0.0	65	1567	1631	1631	0.4	2.41	1139	1152	0.1
25059	DIXIE	067	668	625	610	-0.7	19	249	246	243	-0.1	2.53	192	185	-0.4
25060	DOROTHY	081	240	232	228	-0.4	35	100	100	100	0.0	2.32	77	75	-0.3
25062	DRY CREEK	081	1181	1207	1223	0.2	76	463	490	501	0.6	2.46	341	351	0.3
25063	DUCK	015	1393	1362	1344	-0.2	48	552	564	564	0.2	2.37	390	385	-0.1
25064	DUNBAR	039	10557	10108	9901	-0.5	30	4732	4558	4485	-0.4	2.09	2780	2547	-0.9
	WEST VIRGINIA					0.2					0.5	2.33			0.1
	UNITED STATES					1.0					1.1	2.59			0.9

ZIP CODE #	POST OFFICE NAME	RACE (%) White 2000	White 2009	Black 2000	Black 2009	Asian/Pacific 2000	Asian/Pacific 2009	% Hispanic Origin 2000	% Hispanic Origin 2009	2009 AGE DISTRIBUTION (%) 0-4	5-9	10-14	15-19	20-24	25-44	45-64	65-84	85+	18+	MEDIAN AGE 2009	% 2009 Males	% 2009 Females
24701	BLUEFIELD	85.6	84.6	12.8	13.4	0.3	0.5	0.5	0.6	5.6	5.8	5.9	5.7	4.7	24.5	29.1	15.8	3.0	79.2	43.2	47.6	52.4
24712	ATHENS	93.6	93.1	3.9	3.6	1.4	2.1	0.7	0.9	2.9	3.2	3.7	17.0	20.0	18.6	22.5	10.7	1.4	87.3	27.8	55.4	44.6
24714	BEESON	99.7	99.4	0.0	0.0	0.0	0.3	0.0	0.0	5.6	5.9	5.9	5.4	4.5	28.8	29.1	12.7	2.0	79.1	40.4	48.6	51.4
24715	BRAMWELL	90.3	90.0	7.4	7.4	0.0	0.0	0.2	0.2	4.9	4.9	5.1	6.0	5.1	22.9	30.1	18.3	2.8	81.9	46.0	49.1	50.9
24726	HERNDON	97.0	96.5	1.4	1.7	0.1	0.1	0.7	0.8	4.6	5.1	5.4	5.7	4.5	25.6	30.9	16.4	1.8	81.5	44.3	50.2	49.8
24731	KEGLEY	99.0	99.1	0.0	0.0	0.0	0.0	0.0	0.0	5.4	5.4	7.2	6.3	4.5	25.2	29.7	14.4	1.8	77.5	42.2	52.3	47.7
24733	LASHMEET	98.9	98.5	0.1	0.1	0.1	0.3	0.3	0.3	6.1	6.2	6.3	6.2	4.8	26.6	28.7	13.1	2.0	77.4	40.5	48.5	51.5
24736	MATOAKA	98.3	97.9	0.5	0.5	0.3	0.5	0.3	0.3	5.3	5.3	5.7	6.6	5.1	26.2	29.7	14.4	1.9	79.6	42.0	49.5	50.5
24740	PRINCETON	95.4	95.1	2.8	2.7	0.6	0.9	0.4	0.5	5.7	5.7	5.7	5.3	5.0	25.6	28.7	15.4	2.8	79.6	42.6	47.3	52.7
24747	ROCK	98.2	98.1	0.9	0.8	0.1	0.2	0.5	0.7	5.5	5.9	6.2	5.8	4.5	24.6	31.8	13.9	1.8	78.7	43.1	50.5	49.5
24801	WELCH	78.1	77.2	20.4	20.9	0.1	0.2	0.7	0.8	4.9	5.0	5.1	5.7	5.8	22.3	30.5	17.1	3.7	81.5	46.0	46.5	53.5
24815	BERWIND	95.0	94.7	4.1	4.3	0.0	0.1	0.3	0.3	5.6	6.2	6.6	6.8	5.6	22.9	30.9	13.2	2.4	77.4	42.4	47.8	52.2
24818	BRENTON	99.0	98.9	0.1	0.1	0.1	0.1	0.6	0.8	5.5	6.2	6.3	5.4	4.8	24.2	34.8	11.7	1.2	78.7	42.9	49.5	50.5
24822	CLEAR FORK	99.3	99.2	0.1	0.2	0.0	0.0	0.7	0.9	5.4	5.7	5.7	5.5	4.6	27.5	31.3	13.1	1.3	79.6	42.1	50.1	49.9
24823	COAL MOUNTAIN	99.1	99.1	0.0	0.0	0.0	0.0	0.9	0.9	5.5	5.5	5.5	5.5	4.6	26.6	32.1	13.8	0.9	79.8	42.8	51.4	48.6
24827	CYCLONE	99.6	99.6	0.0	0.0	0.0	0.1	0.6	0.7	5.4	5.5	5.7	5.4	4.7	26.9	32.4	12.7	1.3	80.0	42.5	49.7	50.3
24828	DAVY	97.4	97.2	2.0	2.0	0.1	0.1	0.3	0.4	5.1	5.6	6.2	6.2	5.5	25.4	32.3	11.9	1.8	79.7	42.0	49.3	50.7
24834	FANROCK	99.1	99.1	0.0	0.0	0.0	0.0	0.0	0.0	5.7	5.7	5.7	5.7	4.7	22.6	35.8	12.3	1.9	80.2	45.0	50.0	50.0
24839	HANOVER	99.6	99.6	0.1	0.1	0.0	0.0	1.0	1.2	5.9	6.1	6.3	5.7	4.9	25.8	32.7	11.6	1.0	78.3	41.8	49.3	50.7
24844	IAEGER	98.3	98.1	0.9	1.0	0.0	0.0	0.6	0.7	4.9	5.7	6.4	6.2	5.1	25.8	32.7	11.7	1.4	79.0	42.0	48.6	51.4
24849	JESSE	99.5	99.2	0.0	0.0	0.0	0.3	0.5	0.6	4.5	4.8	5.4	5.7	4.8	21.5	36.0	15.3	2.0	81.9	47.2	49.9	50.1
24850	JOLO	99.5	99.4	0.2	0.2	0.0	0.0	0.2	0.2	5.4	6.6	7.3	7.0	5.1	24.5	31.7	10.8	1.4	76.2	40.9	47.9	52.1
24859	MARIANNA	99.2	99.1	0.1	0.1	0.1	0.1	0.7	0.9	4.9	5.3	5.5	5.3	4.9	23.3	34.9	14.2	1.7	80.9	45.5	49.4	50.6
24860	MATHENY	99.4	99.3	0.0	0.0	0.0	0.0	0.5	0.5	4.3	5.1	5.6	5.4	4.4	22.1	37.8	13.7	1.6	81.7	47.1	50.9	49.1
24862	MOHAWK	99.7	99.7	0.0	0.0	0.0	0.0	0.1	0.2	4.7	5.9	6.9	6.7	5.6	27.4	32.6	9.5	0.8	78.1	40.4	51.5	48.5
24868	NORTHFORK	61.4	60.4	37.1	37.9	0.0	0.0	0.6	0.7	5.6	6.0	6.3	6.7	5.7	22.8	29.5	14.4	3.2	77.8	42.3	47.2	52.8
24869	NORTH SPRING	99.2	99.2	0.0	0.0	0.0	0.0	0.0	0.0	4.9	5.7	6.6	4.9	4.1	23.8	36.1	12.3	1.6	80.3	45.0	49.2	50.8
24870	OCEANA	99.4	99.4	0.0	0.0	0.0	0.0	0.4	0.4	5.1	5.7	6.2	5.8	4.5	25.1	33.9	12.4	1.3	79.3	43.2	49.6	50.4
24873	PAYNESVILLE	92.4	91.9	6.7	7.0	0.1	0.2	0.4	0.4	4.5	5.0	6.3	6.1	6.3	23.9	32.3	13.6	2.0	80.3	43.6	48.7	51.3
24874	PINEVILLE	98.9	98.6	0.3	0.3	0.1	0.2	0.4	0.5	5.3	5.7	5.8	5.0	4.6	22.5	33.1	15.5	2.4	80.0	45.7	47.7	52.3
24879	RAYSAL	96.9	96.7	2.5	2.6	0.0	0.0	0.2	0.3	6.2	6.7	7.1	6.0	5.3	25.2	31.0	11.0	1.5	76.2	40.2	47.7	52.3
24882	SIMON	99.2	99.2	0.2	0.2	0.0	0.0	0.8	0.8	5.4	5.7	5.7	5.4	4.7	27.3	31.9	12.7	1.1	80.2	42.2	51.0	49.0
24884	SQUIRE	92.7	92.2	6.1	6.4	0.0	0.0	0.1	0.1	4.4	4.5	5.0	6.5	5.0	22.5	35.7	14.2	2.3	82.2	46.4	51.4	48.6
24901	LEWISBURG	94.3	93.8	3.8	4.0	0.4	0.6	0.8	0.9	5.0	5.3	5.7	5.5	4.5	23.4	30.8	16.3	3.6	80.7	45.4	46.8	53.2
24910	ALDERSON	82.8	84.7	15.7	12.9	0.3	0.8	1.1	1.2	4.0	4.1	4.5	14.5	10.2	24.0	24.5	12.3	2.0	85.4	36.1	45.2	54.8
24915	ARBOVALE	98.7	98.4	0.2	0.2	0.2	0.4	0.7	1.0	4.8	4.4	6.0	4.4	5.4	26.5	33.1	14.0	1.4	82.0	44.0	53.1	46.9
24916	ASBURY	98.0	97.4	0.2	0.2	0.0	0.5	0.2	0.2	5.0	5.4	5.7	5.9	4.2	22.4	35.8	13.9	1.7	80.0	45.9	47.6	52.4
24918	BALLARD	98.5	98.3	0.4	0.5	0.1	0.1	0.2	0.2	6.0	6.0	6.3	6.0	4.9	26.6	28.3	13.9	2.0	78.3	41.0	50.2	49.8
24920	BARTOW	99.0	98.9	0.8	0.9	0.2	0.2	0.3	0.4	4.7	4.9	5.5	7.6	5.3	23.5	30.9	15.3	2.3	80.3	44.0	50.9	49.1
24925	CALDWELL	99.0	99.1	0.0	0.0	0.0	0.0	0.0	0.5	6.0	6.5	6.5	6.0	4.1	24.9	30.0	14.7	1.4	77.4	42.0	49.3	50.7
24927	CASS	98.7	98.4	0.5	0.5	0.1	0.3	0.6	0.7	4.9	4.8	5.7	5.0	5.0	24.9	32.1	15.2	2.4	81.5	44.8	52.2	47.8
24931	CRAWLEY	99.0	98.8	0.1	0.1	0.1	0.2	0.4	0.5	5.1	5.6	6.0	5.6	4.4	22.8	34.4	14.4	1.7	79.6	45.2	49.8	50.2
24934	DUNMORE	98.8	98.7	0.4	0.4	0.4	0.4	0.4	0.4	4.8	4.8	7.0	6.1	3.9	21.1	31.6	18.4	2.2	79.4	46.4	50.9	49.1
24935	FOREST HILL	98.3	97.8	0.7	0.7	0.0	0.4	0.3	0.4	4.7	4.7	5.5	6.2	4.4	21.5	30.5	18.9	3.6	81.1	47.1	51.3	48.7
24938	FRANKFORD	98.0	97.7	0.8	0.8	0.1	0.2	0.6	0.7	5.2	5.6	6.2	5.3	4.3	23.1	34.0	14.9	1.6	79.8	45.3	50.0	50.0
24941	GAP MILLS	97.4	97.2	1.4	1.5	0.0	0.0	0.1	0.1	5.5	5.7	6.4	6.2	4.1	23.9	31.6	15.4	1.3	78.5	43.5	49.9	50.1
24943	GRASSY MEADOWS	99.0	99.1	0.0	0.0	0.0	0.0	1.0	0.9	6.1	6.6	7.1	7.1	3.3	24.5	30.2	13.7	1.4	75.0	41.7	49.5	50.5
24944	GREEN BANK	98.9	98.5	0.2	0.3	0.2	0.5	0.5	0.5	4.5	4.5	7.5	6.5	4.3	22.1	31.3	18.0	1.3	79.2	45.4	51.9	48.1
24945	GREENVILLE	97.1	96.2	1.3	1.8	0.1	0.3	0.2	0.3	4.6	4.5	4.9	6.3	5.6	23.4	32.4	15.6	2.9	82.1	45.5	49.1	50.9
24946	HILLSBORO	97.3	97.1	1.7	1.8	0.0	0.0	0.5	0.6	3.3	3.7	4.3	4.7	5.2	29.2	32.2	15.5	1.8	85.2	44.7	56.1	43.9
24951	LINDSIDE	97.5	97.1	1.1	1.2	0.0	0.0	0.4	0.5	5.4	4.5	4.8	5.1	5.6	19.2	34.6	15.6	5.1	82.2	48.5	48.8	51.2
24954	MARLINTON	98.3	98.1	0.8	0.9	0.2	0.3	0.3	0.4	5.1	5.3	5.7	5.7	4.5	22.7	30.8	16.9	3.3	80.3	45.6	49.3	50.7
24957	MAXWELTON	98.1	97.3	0.9	0.9	0.0	0.9	0.9	0.9	5.3	5.3	5.3	6.2	5.3	23.0	33.6	14.2	1.8	78.8	44.6	49.6	50.4
24962	PENCE SPRINGS	98.0	89.8	1.4	8.1	0.0	1.0	0.3	1.0	3.1	3.1	3.1	25.1	18.0	19.7	17.6	9.2	1.4	90.8	24.4	44.4	55.6
24963	PETERSTOWN	98.5	98.3	0.4	0.5	0.0	0.1	0.4	0.4	5.8	5.8	6.1	5.8	4.6	25.8	28.5	15.2	2.4	78.8	42.2	49.6	50.4
24966	RENICK	97.7	97.5	0.8	0.8	0.2	0.3	0.4	0.5	5.2	5.5	6.0	6.6	6.4	20.2	33.2	14.8	2.1	79.3	45.1	50.6	49.4
24970	RONCEVERTE	94.6	94.2	3.7	3.7	0.2	0.4	0.8	1.0	5.8	6.1	6.6	6.2	4.2	24.1	29.9	14.6	2.5	77.6	42.8	48.9	51.1
24974	SECONDCREEK	98.7	98.3	0.0	0.0	0.2	0.6	0.2	0.2	5.6	6.1	6.3	7.4	4.3	27.7	30.3	11.5	0.9	77.5	40.9	49.4	50.6
24976	SINKS GROVE	97.0	95.7	1.5	2.4	0.4	0.6	0.3	0.4	5.4	5.8	6.0	7.5	4.8	27.0	30.1	12.3	1.2	78.6	41.0	48.5	51.5
24977	SMOOT	98.9	98.8	0.1	0.1	0.0	0.0	0.6	0.7	5.7	6.2	6.4	6.0	3.9	23.5	31.7	14.7	1.9	77.8	43.6	51.0	49.0
24981	TALCOTT	93.1	89.6	5.6	8.4	0.1	0.5	0.4	0.7	3.9	4.2	4.5	13.3	9.8	22.5	26.2	13.7	2.0	84.8	38.5	48.2	51.8
24983	UNION	96.8	96.2	1.8	2.0	0.2	0.3	0.2	0.2	5.1	5.2	5.8	6.3	5.0	23.0	29.5	17.5	2.6	80.0	44.6	49.0	51.0
24984	WAITEVILLE	97.5	97.4	1.3	1.3	0.0	0.0	0.0	0.0	5.5	5.7	6.2	6.4	4.2	23.2	30.9	16.3	1.5	78.6	43.9	49.4	50.6
24985	WAYSIDE	91.8	81.8	6.9	15.4	0.2	1.1	0.6	1.1	2.8	2.8	3.3	20.0	13.9	23.6	21.5	10.6	1.5	90.0	31.7	43.4	56.6
24986	WHITE SULPHUR SPRING	91.0	90.9	7.3	7.2	0.2	0.2	0.7	0.9	4.8	4.4	4.8	6.7	8.0	21.0	30.0	17.6	2.8	82.3	45.2	49.1	50.9
24991	WILLIAMSBURG	97.1	96.8	0.8	0.7	0.3	0.4	0.4	0.5	5.4	5.9	6.2	6.2	4.9	21.9	33.4	14.2	1.8	78.3	44.6	50.2	49.8
24993	WOLFCREEK	75.9	58.2	22.3	38.2	0.4	1.3	1.3	1.8	2.7	2.7	3.1	13.8	9.8	32.9	24.0	9.8	1.3	90.7	36.1	37.3	62.7
25003	ALUM CREEK	98.4	98.2	0.1	0.2	0.2	0.3	0.3	0.4	5.6	6.0	6.3	5.8	3.9	25.7	32.8	12.5	1.4	78.5	42.5	49.6	50.4
25005	AMMA	98.4	98.4	0.0	0.0	0.3	0.3	0.3	0.3	5.2	5.5	7.1	7.1	5.5	25.5	32.6	11.0	0.6	78.1	41.9	50.0	50.0
25007	ARNETT	100.0	100.0	0.0	0.0	0.0	0.0	0.3	0.3	5.4	5.4	6.0	6.6	4.7	24.6	32.8	12.9	1.6	79.2	42.9	51.4	48.6
25008	ARTIE	99.8	99.8	0.0	0.0	0.0	0.0	0.0	0.0	4.8	4.8	5.4	7.5	6.3	24.5	31.6	13.2	1.9	80.5	43.0	49.2	50.8
25009	ASHFORD	98.5	98.3	0.0	0.0	0.0	0.2	0.5	0.5	6.3	6.7	6.7	6.1	4.8	24.2	31.6	12.3	1.4	76.5	40.9	50.3	49.7
25015	BELLE	97.5	97.2	0.5	0.6	0.0	0.1	0.6	0.7	5.5	5.7	5.9	5.8	4.6	25.4	29.5	14.9	2.6	79.3	42.7	48.1	51.9
25019	BICKMORE	97.6	97.6	0.0	0.0	0.0	0.0	0.0	0.0	5.7	5.7	6.7	7.3	5.4	24.5	30.2	13.2	1.3	77.4	40.9	51.2	48.8
25021	BIM	99.7	99.7	0.0	0.0	0.0	0.0	0.4	0.5	4.4	4.7	5.5	5.8	4.4	23.3	35.1	15.1	1.7	81.8	46.5	48.9	51.1
25024	BLOOMINGROSE	98.6	98.4	0.3	0.3	0.1	0.1	0.4	0.6	7.1	7.3	7.8	7.0	4.2	27.5	26.0	11.3	1.7	73.3	38.0	49.4	50.6
25025	BLOUNT	98.7	98.5	0.3	0.3	0.1	0.2	0.0	0.0	5.8	6.3	6.4	5.9	4.4	27.0	30.6	12.3	1.2	77.7	40.9	50.9	49.1
25028	BOB WHITE	98.8	98.5	0.8	1.0	0.0	0.0	0.6	0.6	3.8	4.2	4.8	5.9	4.8	24.1	35.8	14.5	2.1	83.4	46.7	49.7	50.3
25030	BOMONT	98.5	98.5	0.0	0.0	0.0	0.0	0.0	0.0	5.3	5.3	7.6	9.1	6.1	24.2	28.0	13.6	0.8	75.8	40.0	50.0	50.0
25033	BUFFALO	98.2	98.0	0.1	0.1	0.1	0.2	0.7	0.9	5.5	5.6	6.0	6.0	5.2	25.7	31.5	13.0	1.6	79.2	42.2	50.0	50.0
25035	CABIN CREEK	98.8	98.6	0.5	0.5	0.0	0.0	0.3	0.3	4.8	5.0	5.4	5.8	4.6	23.9	31.9	16.5	2.1	81.2	45.3	50.4	49.6
25039	CEDAR GROVE	94.2	93.8	4.3	4.6	0.2	0.2	0.5	0.5	5.2	5.5	5.9	5.5	4.5	24.3	30.5	16.1	2.5	79.7	44.2	48.8	51.2
25043	CLAY	98.4	98.4	0.1	0.1	0.0	0.0	0.3	0.3	6.4	6.4	6.3	6.7	6.2	25.3	27.3	13.5	1.9	76.6	39.1	48.8	51.2
25044	CLEAR CREEK	100.0	100.0	0.0	0.0	0.0	0.0	0.0	0.0	5.3	5.3	5.3	7.9	5.3	26.3	31.6	13.2	0.0	78.9	42.5	47.4	52.6
25045	CLENDENIN	98.6	98.3	0.0	0.1	0.1	0.1	0.2	0.3	5.6	6.0	6.2	5.6	4.6	24.4	31.5	14.1	1.9	78.7	43.3	49.7	50.3
25047	CLOTHIER	96.3	95.9	2.9	3.1	0.2	0.2	0.9	1.2	6.0	6.1	6.2	6.1	4.5	26.1	29.3	13.5	2.0	77.7	41.1	46.5	53.5
25048	COLCORD	100.0	100.0	0.0	0.0	0.0	0.0	0.0	0.0	6.3	6.3	6.3	6.3	6.3	25.0	28.1	14.1	1.6	78.1	40.0	46.9	53.1
25049	COMFORT	98.7	98.2	0.3	0.3	0.0	0.3	0.5	0.5	7.0	7.2	7.2	6.7	4.4	26.9	27.1	11.6	1.8	74.2	38.6	49.4	50.6
25051	COSTA	98.7	98.5	0.2	0.2	0.0	0.0	0.6	0.9	4.8	5.4	5.6	5.8	4.8	25.3	34.4	11.7	2.2	80.5	43.6	50.9	49.1
25053	DANVILLE	98.7	98.6	0.4	0.4	0.2	0.3	0.4	0.4	5.8	6.3	6.5	5.9	4.6	25.7	31.7	11.7	1.8	77.5	41.3	49.2	50.8
25059	DIXIE	99.0	98.6	0.0	0.0	0.0	0.0	0.1	0.2	5.4	5.8	5.8	5.9	5.1	25.6	30.2	14.7	1.4	79.7	41.9	49.6	50.4
25060	DOROTHY	100.0	100.0	0.0	0.0	0.0	0.0	0.0	0.0	4.7	4.7	5.6	7.3	6.5	24.1	31.9	13.4	1.7	81.0	43.2	49.1	50.9
25062	DRY CREEK	99.2	98.9	0.0	0.0	0.1	0.2	0.3	0.4	5.6	5.8	6.2	6.0	4.6	24.0	32.4	13.9	1.5	78.6	43.2	49.4	50.6
25063	DUCK	98.7	98.5	0.1	0.1	0.1	0.1	0.3	0.3	5.8	5.9	6.2	6.4	4.8	24.1	29.1	15.1	2.6	78.0	42.6	50.0	50.0
25064	DUNBAR	78.8	77.1	17.8	18.6	1.4	2.1	0.6	0.7	5.2	5.1	5.0	6.4	7.1	24.1	27.8	15.8	3.6	81.6	42.6	47.1	52.9
	WEST VIRGINIA	95.0	94.5	3.2	3.3	0.5	0.8	0.7	0.8	5.5	5.6	5.9	6.5	6.1	25.2	29.3	13.8	2.2	79.3	41.5	49.0	51.0
	UNITED STATES	75.1	72.0	12.3	12.7	3.8	4.6	12.5	15.7	6.8	6.7	6.6	7.1	6.9	27.0	26.0	10.9	1.9	75.7	36.9	49.2	50.8

# ZIP CODE	POST OFFICE NAME	2009 Per Capita Income	2009 HH Income Base	2009 HOUSEHOLD INCOME DISTRIBUTION (%) Less than $25,000	$25,000 to $49,999	$50,000 to $99,999	$100,000 to $149,999	$150,000 or More	MEDIAN HOUSEHOLD INCOME 2009	2014	2009 National Centile	2009 State Centile	2009 Home Value Base	2009 HOME VALUE DISTRIBUTION (%) Less than $50,000	$50,000 to $89,999	$90,000 to $174,999	$175,000 to $399,999	$400,000 or More	2009 Median Home Value
24701	BLUEFIELD	20159	9214	38.1	31.8	23.2	4.4	2.5	33244	33324	14	54	6721	26.2	27.1	35.2	9.8	1.7	86100
24712	ATHENS	16784	612	36.3	30.4	27.0	4.6	1.8	35948	36388	20	71	485	22.9	20.2	37.3	17.3	2.3	99853
24714	BEESON	20829	153	52.3	20.9	20.3	5.2	1.3	23783	25419	3	10	132	26.5	28.8	22.7	15.2	6.8	86500
24715	BRAMWELL	15550	204	49.0	29.9	19.1	1.5	0.5	25470	26302	4	15	173	47.4	22.5	24.3	4.6	1.2	54500
24726	HERNDON	19617	715	45.3	25.9	21.3	4.5	3.1	28099	28239	6	26	615	51.5	29.6	16.1	2.8	0.0	47564
24731	KEGLEY	12895	36	36.1	38.9	22.2	2.8	0.0	35000	35733	18	66	31	29.0	29.0	32.3	6.5	3.2	77500
24733	LASHMEET	14090	300	49.3	30.0	18.3	2.0	0.3	25276	26091	3	14	248	53.2	26.2	14.5	4.4	1.6	45789
24736	MATOAKA	15656	436	46.6	35.3	15.1	1.1	1.8	26288	26625	4	17	369	68.6	15.2	16.0	0.3	0.0	32900
24740	PRINCETON	20657	12770	37.5	29.7	26.2	4.3	2.4	34237	34310	16	61	9697	23.7	24.1	36.1	13.9	2.2	93472
24747	ROCK	15466	2071	40.1	36.2	20.8	2.5	0.4	31043	31277	10	44	1768	36.3	27.4	27.5	7.7	1.1	67234
24801	WELCH	15238	3247	52.7	26.7	17.6	1.6	1.4	23046	23549	2	7	2438	65.9	20.2	11.9	2.0	0.0	35641
24815	BERWIND	11415	856	60.7	27.6	9.7	1.8	0.2	19223	19292	1	2	665	72.3	17.7	8.4	1.5	0.0	33185
24818	BRENTON	15642	1055	48.2	24.5	23.5	2.9	0.8	26250	27196	4	17	828	33.3	34.4	24.3	7.9	0.1	67612
24822	CLEAR FORK	14734	265	46.0	29.4	21.1	3.0	0.4	27417	27774	5	23	225	44.9	25.3	26.2	3.6	0.0	57188
24823	COAL MOUNTAIN	14332	44	43.2	31.8	20.5	4.5	0.0	30000	26083	8	35	38	47.4	26.3	23.7	2.6	0.0	53333
24827	CYCLONE	15737	792	43.1	31.2	22.3	2.7	0.8	30000	30077	8	35	672	44.6	27.4	24.9	3.1	0.0	55902
24828	DAVY	11168	834	59.7	28.8	9.7	1.3	0.5	18833	18751	1	2	667	69.9	18.4	10.5	1.2	0.0	29202
24834	FANROCK	17016	47	48.9	25.5	21.3	4.3	0.0	25729	28579	4	15	40	35.0	32.5	25.0	7.5	0.0	62500
24839	HANOVER	15478	582	51.2	22.7	22.2	2.6	1.4	24055	25388	3	10	493	45.8	28.8	17.8	7.5	0.0	52412
24844	IAEGER	12629	1758	56.7	30.0	11.2	1.3	0.9	19783	19804	1	3	1470	53.5	23.1	20.9	2.4	0.1	45234
24849	JESSE	17134	156	46.2	30.8	17.9	2.6	2.6	26651	27410	4	20	129	40.3	31.8	24.8	3.1	0.0	62917
24850	JOLO	11799	1023	63.9	24.2	9.6	0.2	2.1	16905	16848	1	1	831	57.5	23.5	15.8	3.0	0.2	43557
24859	MARIANNA	17454	328	46.0	26.8	20.7	4.6	1.8	27287	28250	5	22	268	38.8	31.0	24.6	4.1	1.5	63810
24860	MATHENY	21968	279	48.4	22.9	19.4	3.6	5.7	26456	28110	4	19	233	33.5	36.1	25.8	4.7	0.0	69737
24862	MOHAWK	10160	511	60.1	35.2	3.1	1.0	0.6	18729	18819	1	2	431	57.3	26.5	13.2	3.0	0.0	43571
24868	NORTHFORK	10650	1227	63.8	26.2	9.0	0.7	0.2	17661	17416	1	2	965	76.5	16.7	6.0	0.8	0.0	27540
24869	NORTH SPRING	16987	54	44.4	31.5	20.4	3.7	0.0	28592	27928	6	28	46	34.8	32.6	23.9	8.7	0.0	65000
24870	OCEANA	18133	1433	42.3	29.7	22.7	3.1	2.2	30835	31033	9	43	1202	36.3	31.8	27.7	4.2	0.0	67701
24873	PAYNESVILLE	11695	470	53.6	36.0	9.6	0.6	0.2	22271	22276	2	6	401	73.1	19.0	7.2	0.7	0.0	27188
24874	PINEVILLE	19049	1453	40.1	32.1	21.3	4.6	1.8	30660	30918	9	41	1161	33.9	33.5	25.5	6.1	1.0	67598
24879	RAYSAL	10452	514	65.4	23.3	8.8	1.2	1.4	16944	16936	1	1	409	70.4	21.3	7.6	0.7	0.0	30603
24882	SIMON	14205	248	47.2	27.8	21.8	3.2	0.0	26650	27685	4	19	208	39.4	26.4	27.9	6.3	0.0	64375
24884	SQUIRE	12216	309	56.6	32.0	10.0	1.3	0.0	21258	21577	2	4	263	75.3	19.8	3.4	1.5	0.0	32125
24901	LEWISBURG	25349	3773	36.3	26.0	27.7	5.4	4.6	36546	37287	22	74	2730	14.7	11.5	31.8	34.2	7.8	151206
24910	ALDERSON	13671	1559	44.8	30.7	19.4	3.2	1.9	27675	28306	5	24	1226	23.0	25.9	37.1	12.0	2.0	91944
24915	ARBOVALE	20279	214	27.1	32.2	34.1	5.6	0.9	41049	42360	36	86	168	17.9	26.8	26.2	23.8	5.4	99000
24916	ASBURY	19316	184	40.2	28.3	25.5	2.7	3.3	35953	37081	20	71	154	24.0	22.7	33.1	14.3	5.8	98333
24918	BALLARD	19179	543	38.9	29.1	26.5	3.1	2.4	32726	33186	13	52	455	20.2	24.6	44.2	10.8	0.2	98103
24920	BARTOW	14007	225	49.8	32.9	12.9	2.7	1.8	25081	25847	3	13	181	30.4	30.9	32.6	6.1	0.0	75769
24925	CALDWELL	25750	106	23.6	46.2	20.8	4.7	4.7	38962	39296	30	82	91	13.2	12.1	52.7	16.5	5.5	125625
24927	CASS	19407	339	33.3	32.4	28.9	4.4	0.9	34668	34306	17	62	266	18.8	28.6	30.1	18.0	4.5	93684
24931	CRAWLEY	20641	647	32.8	33.5	24.9	5.1	3.7	38038	39795	27	80	545	14.5	18.7	47.7	17.4	1.7	118364
24934	DUNMORE	20343	110	36.4	36.4	21.8	4.5	0.9	37326	36864	25	77	93	21.5	19.4	38.7	18.3	2.2	114773
24935	FOREST HILL	16665	125	46.4	31.2	18.4	4.0	0.0	28043	29640	6	25	100	19.0	27.0	45.0	7.0	2.0	95000
24938	FRANKFORD	20504	499	31.1	33.7	30.3	2.6	2.4	35828	35923	20	70	422	16.6	15.4	41.9	21.6	4.5	126408
24941	GAP MILLS	20779	337	33.5	35.0	24.6	3.9	3.0	36903	37831	23	75	287	27.5	29.6	28.6	11.1	3.1	84744
24943	GRASSY MEADOWS	16563	87	43.7	28.7	21.8	4.6	1.1	28238	28415	6	26	74	25.7	16.2	36.5	16.2	5.4	107500
24944	GREEN BANK	17113	160	35.0	36.9	21.3	5.0	1.9	39066	40401	30	82	138	22.5	18.8	35.5	21.0	2.2	117857
24945	GREENVILLE	18427	581	41.5	29.4	24.6	2.6	1.9	30213	30931	8	36	498	23.5	25.9	37.3	11.0	2.2	91034
24946	HILLSBORO	15891	533	38.3	33.0	24.6	3.4	0.8	35354	34905	19	67	443	24.2	29.8	29.8	12.0	4.3	85000
24951	LINDSIDE	20162	363	43.5	27.0	25.1	2.5	1.9	31191	31556	10	46	319	25.1	28.8	39.2	6.9	0.0	85690
24954	MARLINTON	18421	1784	38.7	35.1	21.2	3.5	1.5	30834	31066	9	43	1406	22.5	26.7	35.0	12.1	3.7	91122
24957	MAXWELTON	25639	51	33.3	35.3	19.6	5.9	5.9	36706	39079	23	74	42	11.9	14.3	33.3	38.1	2.4	141667
24962	PENCE SPRINGS	17754	125	56.8	22.4	20.0	0.0	0.8	20633	20957	2	4	108	29.6	23.1	32.4	10.2	4.6	82500
24963	PETERSTOWN	20562	1848	36.2	30.6	26.9	3.3	3.0	34150	34260	16	60	1520	20.1	20.5	43.2	15.7	0.5	106829
24966	RENICK	17053	716	42.0	33.5	20.0	2.1	2.4	30482	31082	9	38	590	23.6	20.5	33.9	20.2	1.9	102410
24970	RONCEVERTE	19316	2420	34.6	35.4	23.2	4.2	2.6	35256	35038	19	66	1839	17.2	21.6	41.2	16.2	3.8	108899
24974	SECONDCREEK	20609	195	28.7	34.9	28.2	3.6	4.6	42424	43608	41	89	174	22.4	19.0	38.5	16.7	3.4	102778
24976	SINKS GROVE	18925	430	30.2	34.9	27.4	3.7	3.7	41079	41993	36	86	377	21.2	19.6	38.2	17.8	3.2	103602
24977	SMOOT	17336	374	37.4	33.7	23.8	3.5	1.6	34439	33560	16	61	317	24.3	17.0	42.3	13.9	2.5	107552
24981	TALCOTT	16814	329	52.6	28.0	17.0	1.2	1.2	22938	24277	2	7	270	34.1	27.0	27.0	7.8	4.1	70500
24983	UNION	18736	815	36.0	33.3	25.2	4.9	0.7	32332	32374	12	51	671	17.7	20.3	37.4	21.5	3.1	107403
24984	WAITEVILLE	20060	194	35.6	33.5	24.7	4.1	2.1	35000	34391	18	66	162	22.8	27.8	30.9	14.8	3.7	89524
24985	WAYSIDE	17898	231	50.2	28.1	19.5	0.9	1.3	24850	26183	3	12	198	26.8	24.7	32.3	11.6	4.5	86250
24986	WHITE SULPHUR SPRING	17765	2326	37.4	35.7	22.5	3.4	0.9	33287	33253	14	55	1732	18.2	23.8	47.0	9.6	1.4	99789
24991	WILLIAMSBURG	20537	333	32.7	38.4	20.7	4.2	3.9	35524	34793	19	68	274	20.8	17.2	33.9	25.5	2.6	117361
24993	WOLFCREEK	16530	92	37.0	39.1	18.5	3.3	2.2	29133	29803	7	31	76	17.1	27.6	39.5	15.8	0.0	98000
25003	ALUM CREEK	21119	1074	35.0	27.7	29.1	4.4	3.7	37946	40051	27	80	901	30.0	22.4	34.0	11.8	1.9	86161
25005	AMMA	15127	121	40.5	32.2	22.3	4.1	0.8	28364	28944	6	27	104	19.2	27.9	32.7	20.2	0.0	95000
25007	ARNETT	15217	118	42.4	30.5	22.0	2.5	2.5	28950	29752	7	30	94	38.3	26.6	23.4	8.5	3.2	65000
25008	ARTIE	13086	205	54.1	22.4	20.0	3.4	0.0	22716	23107	2	6	167	34.7	32.3	28.1	4.8	0.0	68333
25009	ASHFORD	15168	232	45.3	27.2	22.0	4.7	0.9	27683	29046	5	24	190	31.1	31.1	34.7	3.2	0.0	76667
25015	BELLE	19951	2827	30.9	32.8	30.7	4.3	1.3	37845	39529	26	79	2065	29.5	33.8	34.1	2.5	0.1	74898
25019	BICKMORE	12806	156	49.4	31.4	16.0	1.9	1.3	25390	26483	3	14	130	53.8	17.7	25.4	3.1	0.0	37000
25021	BIM	17042	280	42.9	23.9	30.0	3.2	0.0	32770	35172	13	53	225	42.7	36.0	20.0	0.0	1.3	56875
25024	BLOOMINGROSE	21440	284	39.8	26.4	27.5	2.1	4.2	36559	37656	22	74	215	54.0	20.9	20.5	4.7	0.0	42273
25025	BLOUNT	17081	259	33.6	25.9	37.1	2.7	0.8	38289	39611	28	81	215	47.9	31.2	17.2	3.7	0.0	54500
25028	BOB WHITE	16155	202	43.1	28.7	23.8	4.5	0.0	29279	31115	7	31	163	41.7	31.3	24.5	0.0	2.5	59643
25030	BOMONT	14442	57	43.9	36.8	19.3	0.0	0.0	28309	29417	6	26	46	43.5	30.4	21.7	4.3	0.0	55000
25033	BUFFALO	18215	1031	37.9	31.0	25.6	4.4	1.1	32767	32750	13	53	872	36.0	23.3	31.1	8.5	1.1	75000
25035	CABIN CREEK	17019	396	35.9	40.4	22.0	1.0	0.8	30336	31362	9	37	301	45.8	37.2	16.9	0.0	0.0	54167
25039	CEDAR GROVE	19382	1013	36.5	27.0	30.8	3.9	1.7	36392	38224	22	72	773	40.4	35.6	22.6	1.4	0.0	60844
25043	CLAY	13998	988	53.9	25.8	16.0	2.4	1.8	22351	23794	2	6	711	39.2	29.8	25.5	5.1	0.4	70066
25044	CLEAR CREEK	14031	16	56.3	25.0	18.8	0.0	0.0	22205	20000	2	5	13	38.5	30.8	30.8	0.0	0.0	65000
25045	CLENDENIN	16941	2379	39.4	29.1	26.1	4.6	0.8	31467	32437	10	47	1954	31.6	32.8	27.3	7.7	0.6	71635
25047	CLOTHIER	20268	485	37.7	30.9	23.3	5.6	2.5	33486	33645	14	56	360	24.7	31.9	37.8	5.3	0.3	77857
25048	COLCORD	12852	28	53.6	28.6	17.9	0.0	0.0	23086	27297	2	8	23	39.1	34.8	21.7	4.3	0.0	62500
25049	COMFORT	19891	157	43.3	25.5	25.5	2.5	3.2	29736	35457	8	33	121	45.5	25.6	24.0	5.0	0.0	56875
25051	COSTA	12955	193	50.3	31.1	17.1	1.6	0.0	24860	26799	3	12	170	45.9	28.8	18.8	5.9	0.6	55000
25053	DANVILLE	16939	1631	40.6	29.3	24.9	4.0	1.2	32386	33688	12	51	1262	28.8	28.8	32.2	9.9	0.4	77453
25059	DIXIE	17478	246	41.1	31.3	23.6	1.6	2.4	30000	30135	8	35	207	31.9	22.7	43.5	1.9	0.0	85000
25060	DOROTHY	14366	100	57.0	20.0	20.0	3.0	0.0	21283	22528	2	4	80	36.3	31.3	27.5	5.0	0.0	67143
25062	DRY CREEK	18041	490	41.2	23.7	29.6	4.5	1.0	32957	33323	13	54	414	27.8	36.2	30.0	5.8	0.2	66216
25063	DUCK	13037	564	50.9	31.4	15.2	2.3	0.2	24332	25819	3	11	459	37.5	32.7	22.0	7.6	0.2	71121
25064	DUNBAR	23979	4558	29.8	26.6	34.7	5.9	2.9	45569	46623	50	93	2870	13.6	34.1	47.2	4.8	0.3	92672
	WEST VIRGINIA	20563		34.3	29.3	28.3	5.4	2.7	37099	38541				22.0	23.9	36.4	15.5	2.2	98135
	UNITED STATES	27277		20.9	24.4	35.3	11.7	7.6	54719	56938				9.3	13.1	31.6	32.6	13.5	162279

#	POST OFFICE NAME	FINANCIAL SERVICES: Auto Loan	FINANCIAL SERVICES: Home Loan	FINANCIAL SERVICES: Invest-ments	FINANCIAL SERVICES: Retire-ment Plans	THE HOME: Home Improvements: Home Repair	THE HOME: Home Improvements: Lawn & Garden	THE HOME: Furnishings: Comput-ers & Hard-ware-Personal	THE HOME: Furnishings: Major Appli-ances	THE HOME: Furnishings: TV, Radio, Sound Equip-ment	THE HOME: Furnishings: Furni-ture	ENTERTAINMENT: Dine out/ Carry out	ENTERTAINMENT: Sports Equip-ment	ENTERTAINMENT: Fees & Tickets	ENTERTAINMENT: Toys & Games	ENTERTAINMENT: Travel	ENTERTAINMENT: Cable TV	PERSONAL: Apparel & Services	PERSONAL: Auto Repairs	PERSONAL: Health Insur-ance	PERSONAL: Pets & Supplies
24701	BLUEFIELD	73	57	72	55	58	75	60	70	66	56	64	52	51	65	58	71	43	67	76	83
24712	ATHENS	75	56	74	55	58	76	59	71	65	55	63	53	49	64	58	70	42	67	76	84
24714	BEESON	86	62	88	60	64	87	63	81	70	59	69	60	51	70	63	77	46	74	84	96
24715	BRAMWELL	56	40	56	39	42	58	44	54	49	39	47	40	35	48	42	54	31	50	59	63
24726	HERNDON	83	56	81	53	56	83	60	75	69	56	67	58	46	69	57	76	44	71	80	91
24731	KEGLEY	71	50	73	49	52	72	52	66	58	49	57	50	41	58	51	64	38	61	69	79
24733	LASHMEET	64	43	63	41	43	63	45	57	52	43	51	44	34	52	43	58	34	54	60	70
24736	MATOAKA	68	45	66	42	44	67	48	60	55	45	54	47	36	56	44	61	36	57	63	74
24740	PRINCETON	74	60	72	58	61	76	62	72	67	59	66	53	54	67	61	72	44	69	77	84
24747	ROCK	67	46	66	43	46	67	48	60	54	45	53	46	37	55	46	60	35	56	63	73
24801	WELCH	59	41	56	40	42	59	46	54	52	42	50	41	37	51	43	57	34	52	59	65
24815	BERWIND	49	32	47	31	32	48	35	43	40	33	39	34	26	40	33	44	26	41	46	53
24818	BRENTON	70	46	68	43	46	69	49	62	57	47	55	48	37	58	46	63	37	58	65	76
24822	CLEAR FORK	65	43	63	40	43	64	46	57	53	43	51	45	34	54	43	59	34	54	61	71
24823	COAL MOUNTAIN	66	43	64	41	43	65	46	58	53	44	52	45	34	54	43	59	34	55	61	71
24827	CYCLONE	70	46	68	43	46	69	49	62	56	47	55	48	37	57	46	63	37	58	65	76
24828	DAVY	50	33	48	31	33	49	35	44	40	33	39	34	26	41	33	45	26	41	46	54
24834	FANROCK	71	47	69	44	46	70	50	63	57	47	56	49	37	58	46	64	37	59	66	77
24839	HANOVER	66	43	64	41	43	65	46	58	53	44	52	45	35	54	43	59	34	55	62	72
24844	IAEGER	54	35	52	33	35	53	38	47	43	36	42	37	28	44	35	48	28	45	50	58
24849	JESSE	68	47	67	45	48	69	51	64	58	47	56	48	40	58	48	64	37	59	68	76
24850	JOLO	49	32	47	30	32	48	34	43	40	33	39	34	26	40	32	44	26	41	46	53
24859	MARIANNA	72	50	71	48	51	73	54	67	61	49	59	51	42	61	51	67	39	63	72	80
24860	MATHENY	88	60	87	57	61	87	63	79	71	59	70	61	49	71	60	79	46	74	83	96
24862	MOHAWK	44	29	43	27	29	43	31	39	36	29	35	30	23	36	29	40	23	37	41	48
24868	NORTHFORK	40	29	35	28	28	39	32	36	37	32	36	26	27	37	29	41	24	36	41	44
24869	NORTH SPRING	71	47	69	44	46	70	50	63	57	47	56	49	37	58	46	64	37	59	66	77
24870	OCEANA	77	52	76	50	53	77	55	70	62	52	61	53	42	63	53	69	40	65	73	84
24873	PAYNESVILLE	50	33	48	31	33	49	35	44	40	33	39	34	26	41	33	45	26	42	47	54
24874	PINEVILLE	71	50	71	48	52	73	55	68	61	49	59	51	43	61	52	68	39	63	73	80
24879	RAYSAL	48	31	46	29	31	47	33	42	38	32	38	33	25	39	31	43	25	40	44	52
24882	SIMON	65	43	63	40	42	64	45	57	52	43	51	45	34	53	42	59	34	54	61	70
24884	SQUIRE	52	34	50	32	34	51	36	46	42	34	41	36	27	42	34	47	27	43	48	56
24901	LEWISBURG	83	74	82	73	75	87	73	82	77	72	76	60	69	77	73	81	52	79	87	96
24910	ALDERSON	69	49	70	48	51	71	52	65	58	48	56	49	41	57	51	64	37	60	69	77
24915	ARBOVALE	79	63	102	62	69	83	63	80	66	59	65	59	55	63	68	70	43	74	79	93
24916	ASBURY	79	57	82	55	59	81	58	74	65	54	64	56	47	64	58	71	42	68	77	88
24918	BALLARD	83	60	75	58	60	81	62	74	68	59	67	57	49	70	58	75	45	69	78	90
24920	BARTOW	61	40	59	38	40	60	43	54	49	41	48	42	32	50	40	55	32	51	57	66
24925	CALDWELL	94	67	97	65	70	96	69	88	77	64	75	66	55	76	68	84	50	81	92	105
24927	CASS	73	55	85	54	59	76	57	72	62	53	60	53	47	60	59	67	40	67	74	84
24931	CRAWLEY	88	63	90	61	65	89	65	82	72	60	71	62	52	71	64	79	47	76	86	98
24934	DUNMORE	70	55	87	54	60	74	56	71	59	52	58	52	48	57	60	64	39	66	71	82
24935	FOREST HILL	65	46	66	45	48	66	47	60	53	44	52	45	38	52	47	58	34	55	63	72
24938	FRANKFORD	89	64	92	62	66	91	66	83	73	61	71	63	52	72	65	80	47	77	87	99
24941	GAP MILLS	87	62	89	60	64	88	64	81	71	59	69	61	51	70	63	78	46	74	84	96
24943	GRASSY MEADOWS	72	52	74	50	54	73	53	67	59	49	58	51	42	58	52	65	38	62	70	80
24944	GREEN BANK	71	57	92	56	63	75	57	72	60	53	59	53	49	57	62	64	39	67	72	84
24945	GREENVILLE	79	57	76	55	58	79	58	72	65	55	64	55	47	65	56	71	42	67	76	87
24946	HILLSBORO	71	51	73	49	53	72	52	66	58	49	57	50	42	58	52	64	38	61	69	79
24951	LINDSIDE	80	57	82	55	59	81	58	74	65	54	64	56	47	65	58	71	42	68	77	89
24954	MARLINTON	70	50	71	49	52	72	53	67	59	49	58	50	43	59	52	65	38	62	71	79
24957	MAXWELTON	101	73	104	70	75	103	75	95	83	69	81	71	60	82	74	91	54	87	99	113
24962	PENCE SPRINGS	59	42	60	41	44	60	43	55	48	40	47	41	35	48	43	53	31	50	57	65
24963	PETERSTOWN	82	59	80	57	61	83	62	76	68	58	67	57	49	69	59	75	45	71	80	91
24966	RENICK	74	53	75	51	55	75	54	69	60	50	59	52	43	60	53	66	39	63	71	82
24970	RONCEVERTE	81	59	82	57	61	83	61	77	68	56	66	57	49	67	60	75	44	71	81	91
24974	SECONDCREEK	87	62	89	60	65	88	64	81	71	60	70	61	51	71	63	78	46	75	85	97
24976	SINKS GROVE	84	60	86	58	62	85	62	79	69	57	67	59	49	68	61	76	45	72	82	93
24977	SMOOT	76	54	78	53	56	77	56	71	62	52	61	53	45	61	55	68	40	65	74	84
24981	TALCOTT	63	43	63	41	44	63	45	57	51	42	50	43	35	51	43	56	33	53	60	69
24983	UNION	73	53	75	51	55	75	55	70	62	51	60	52	44	61	54	68	40	64	74	82
24984	WAITEVILLE	83	59	84	57	61	84	62	78	69	57	67	58	49	68	61	75	44	72	82	92
24985	WAYSIDE	65	46	67	45	48	66	48	61	53	44	52	46	38	53	47	58	34	56	63	72
24986	WHITE SULPHUR SPRING	67	49	67	48	50	68	52	63	58	48	56	47	43	57	51	63	38	60	68	75
24991	WILLIAMSBURG	91	63	92	61	65	91	66	84	74	62	72	63	52	74	64	82	48	77	87	100
24993	WOLFCREEK	72	52	74	50	54	73	53	68	59	49	58	51	42	59	53	65	38	62	70	80
25003	ALUM CREEK	93	65	94	62	66	94	67	85	76	63	74	65	53	76	66	84	49	79	89	103
25005	AMMA	69	50	71	48	51	70	51	65	56	47	55	49	41	56	50	62	37	59	67	77
25007	ARNETT	76	50	73	47	50	75	53	67	61	50	60	52	40	62	50	68	40	63	71	82
25008	ARTIE	62	40	60	38	40	61	43	54	50	41	49	42	32	51	40	56	32	51	58	67
25009	ASHFORD	71	46	69	44	46	70	50	63	57	47	56	49	37	58	46	64	37	59	66	77
25015	BELLE	75	60	76	58	61	81	61	74	68	57	66	55	53	67	61	75	45	70	81	87
25019	BICKMORE	56	37	55	35	37	56	40	50	45	38	44	39	30	46	37	51	29	47	53	61
25021	BIM	72	47	69	44	47	71	50	63	58	48	57	49	38	59	47	65	37	60	67	78
25024	BLOOMINGROSE	97	63	93	59	63	95	67	85	78	64	76	66	50	79	63	87	50	80	90	104
25025	BLOUNT	79	54	72	52	54	77	57	69	65	55	63	54	44	66	53	71	42	66	73	85
25028	BOB WHITE	71	46	68	44	46	70	49	62	57	47	56	49	37	58	46	64	37	59	66	77
25030	BOMONT	62	41	60	39	41	61	44	55	50	41	49	42	33	50	41	55	32	51	58	67
25033	BUFFALO	80	54	75	51	54	78	57	70	65	54	63	54	43	66	53	72	42	66	74	86
25035	CABIN CREEK	73	50	72	48	50	74	54	67	61	50	59	51	42	61	51	68	39	63	72	81
25039	CEDAR GROVE	78	54	77	53	56	80	59	73	67	54	64	55	47	66	57	74	43	69	79	87
25043	CLAY	57	40	54	38	40	56	45	52	50	42	49	40	35	50	41	55	33	51	56	63
25044	CLEAR CREEK	62	40	60	38	40	61	43	54	50	41	49	42	32	51	40	56	32	51	58	67
25045	CLENDENIN	74	52	74	50	53	75	55	69	61	51	60	52	43	61	53	68	40	64	72	82
25047	CLOTHIER	80	57	80	55	58	82	62	76	69	55	67	57	49	68	59	76	44	71	83	90
25048	COLCORD	55	36	53	34	35	54	38	48	44	36	43	37	29	45	36	49	28	45	51	59
25049	COMFORT	91	59	88	56	59	89	64	80	73	60	72	62	48	75	59	82	47	75	85	99
25051	COSTA	58	38	56	35	37	57	40	51	46	38	45	40	30	47	38	52	30	48	54	62
25053	DANVILLE	76	50	74	48	51	75	53	67	61	51	60	52	41	62	51	68	40	63	71	82
25059	DIXIE	83	54	80	51	54	81	58	72	66	55	65	57	43	68	54	74	43	68	77	89
25060	DOROTHY	62	40	60	38	40	61	43	54	50	41	49	42	32	51	40	56	32	51	58	67
25062	DRY CREEK	83	54	80	51	54	81	58	73	67	55	65	57	43	68	54	74	43	68	77	89
25063	DUCK	57	38	56	36	39	57	41	51	46	38	45	40	31	47	39	51	30	48	54	62
25064	DUNBAR	76	67	71	67	68	75	74	74	77	71	76	56	69	75	71	80	52	76	82	88
	WEST VIRGINIA	79	63	76	62	64	80	66	75	71	63	70	57	58	71	64	77	47	72	80	90
	UNITED STATES	100	100	100	100	100	100	100	100	100	100	100	100	100	100	100	100	100	100	100	100

POPULATION CHANGE

ZIP CODE #	POST OFFICE NAME	COUNTY FIPS CODE	POPULATION 2000	POPULATION 2009	POPULATION 2014	2000-2009 ANNUAL RATE % Rate	2000-2009 ANNUAL RATE State Centile	HOUSEHOLDS 2000	HOUSEHOLDS 2009	HOUSEHOLDS 2014	HOUSEHOLDS % Annual Rate 2000-2009	HOUSEHOLDS 2009 Average HH Size	FAMILIES 2000	FAMILIES 2009	FAMILIES % Annual Rate 2000-2009
25071	ELKVIEW	039	11260	11420	11426	0.2	76	4582	4718	4744	0.3	2.42	3377	3369	0.0
25075	ESKDALE	039	2183	1954	1878	-1.2	3	876	796	770	-1.0	2.45	621	544	-1.4
25079	FALLING ROCK	039	27	29	29	0.8	90	11	12	12	0.9	2.33	8	8	0.0
25081	FOSTER	005	2372	2401	2377	0.1	72	929	983	987	0.6	2.43	707	727	0.3
25082	FRAZIERS BOTTOM	079	1466	1661	1761	1.4	93	566	665	713	1.8	2.50	443	508	1.5
25083	GALLAGHER	039	2070	1887	1820	-1.0	7	860	796	773	-0.8	2.37	585	520	-1.3
25085	GAULEY BRIDGE	019	1253	1229	1211	-0.2	48	531	542	540	0.2	2.23	373	368	-0.1
25088	GLEN	015	160	157	155	-0.2	48	63	65	65	0.3	2.42	49	50	0.2
25093	GORDON	005	198	192	188	-0.3	40	82	83	83	0.1	2.31	52	51	-0.2
25103	HANSFORD	039	155	138	133	-1.2	3	70	63	61	-1.1	2.19	49	43	-1.4
25106	HENDERSON	053	492	468	456	-0.5	30	202	199	196	-0.2	2.35	149	143	-0.4
25107	HERNSHAW	039	629	603	590	-0.5	30	262	255	251	-0.3	2.36	196	185	-0.6
25108	HEWETT	005	1852	1828	1794	-0.1	57	706	728	725	0.3	2.51	535	536	0.0
25111	INDORE	015	1437	1416	1391	-0.2	48	541	558	556	0.3	2.54	423	426	0.1
25113	IVYDALE	015	173	172	168	-0.1	57	69	71	71	0.3	2.42	48	48	0.0
25114	JEFFREY	005	464	456	448	-0.2	48	174	179	179	0.3	2.55	129	129	0.0
25115	KANAWHA FALLS	019	97	97	96	0.0	65	38	40	40	0.6	2.40	29	30	0.4
25118	KIMBERLY	019	166	166	164	0.0	65	66	67	67	0.2	1.67	47	45	-0.5
25119	KINCAID	019	437	423	414	-0.4	35	173	174	173	0.1	2.43	122	117	-0.5
25121	LAKE	045	964	907	881	-0.7	19	376	375	370	0.0	2.42	295	287	-0.3
25123	LEON	053	2964	3003	3010	0.1	72	1178	1244	1264	0.6	2.41	872	893	0.3
25124	LIBERTY	079	1100	1247	1330	1.4	93	432	513	552	1.9	2.43	335	388	1.6
25125	LIZEMORES	015	369	363	356	-0.2	48	131	135	135	0.3	2.69	102	103	0.1
25130	MADISON	005	4244	4105	4013	-0.4	35	1832	1854	1838	0.1	2.21	1274	1249	-0.2
25132	MAMMOTH	039	346	330	323	-0.5	30	132	127	125	-0.4	2.58	102	96	-0.7
25133	MAYSEL	015	541	545	542	0.1	72	216	227	228	0.5	2.40	160	163	0.2
25136	MONTGOMERY	019	9553	9270	9105	-0.3	40	3532	3497	3455	-0.1	2.23	2294	2189	-0.5
25140	NAOMA	081	1134	1117	1109	-0.2	48	442	451	453	0.2	2.48	328	325	-0.1
25141	NEBO	015	285	290	290	0.2	76	118	126	127	0.7	2.24	82	84	0.3
25142	NELLIS	005	560	561	553	0.0	65	212	222	222	0.5	2.53	165	169	0.3
25143	NITRO	039	9843	9666	9601	-0.2	48	4257	4249	4244	0.0	2.27	2779	2666	-0.4
25148	ORGAS	005	732	696	676	-0.5	30	300	297	292	-0.1	2.34	213	204	-0.5
25154	PEYTONA	005	588	582	574	-0.1	57	233	242	242	0.4	2.40	177	179	0.1
25159	POCA	079	6707	7230	7538	0.8	90	2635	2961	3124	1.3	2.44	1989	2172	1.0
25160	POND GAP	039	636	602	588	-0.6	25	238	228	224	-0.5	2.61	184	171	-0.8
25161	POWELLTON	019	768	752	739	-0.2	48	286	292	290	0.2	2.58	223	218	-0.2
25164	PROCIOUS	015	1804	1811	1798	0.0	65	683	713	716	0.5	2.54	508	515	0.1
25165	RACINE	005	630	629	621	0.0	65	258	270	270	0.5	2.33	194	198	0.2
25168	RED HOUSE	079	3956	4434	4693	1.2	92	1612	1882	2014	1.7	2.36	1211	1373	1.4
25169	RIDGEVIEW	005	281	288	285	0.3	81	102	108	109	0.6	2.64	79	81	0.3
25173	ROBSON	019	372	360	353	-0.4	35	143	144	143	0.1	2.50	101	97	-0.4
25174	ROCK CREEK	081	135	136	136	0.1	72	46	48	49	0.5	2.83	34	34	0.0
25177	SAINT ALBANS	039	25289	24189	23708	-0.5	30	10541	10193	10038	-0.4	2.35	7306	6812	-0.8
25180	SAXON	081	161	162	162	0.1	72	54	56	57	0.4	2.89	41	41	0.0
25181	SETH	005	1994	1970	1939	-0.1	57	776	803	801	0.4	2.45	546	545	0.0
25187	SOUTHSIDE	053	667	700	708	0.5	86	271	298	305	1.0	2.35	200	214	0.7
25193	SYLVESTER	005	1542	1511	1482	-0.2	48	686	703	699	0.3	2.15	478	474	-0.1
25202	TORNADO	039	1381	1389	1381	0.1	72	525	536	536	0.2	2.59	404	400	-0.1
25204	TWILIGHT	005	476	454	444	-0.5	30	205	207	205	0.1	2.19	148	145	-0.2
25208	WHARTON	005	686	651	635	-0.6	25	294	295	292	0.0	2.21	212	206	-0.3
25209	WHITESVILLE	081	912	878	863	-0.4	35	357	356	353	0.0	2.47	270	262	-0.3
25213	WINFIELD	079	4981	6020	6477	2.1	97	1995	2449	2668	2.2	2.43	1511	1812	2.0
25214	WINIFREDE	039	14	12	12	-1.7	0	6	5	5	-2.0	2.40	5	4	-2.4
25231	ADVENT	035	129	127	126	-0.2	48	46	48	48	0.5	2.65	36	36	0.0
25234	ARNOLDSBURG	013	1757	1717	1682	-0.2	48	720	732	727	0.2	2.34	525	518	-0.1
25235	CHLOE	013	931	933	944	0.0	65	377	396	406	0.5	2.34	273	278	0.2
25239	COTTAGEVILLE	035	1420	1386	1359	-0.3	40	558	568	564	0.2	2.44	437	433	-0.1
25241	EVANS	035	1498	1457	1548	-0.3	40	574	601	647	0.5	2.42	444	451	0.2
25243	GANDEEVILLE	087	1207	1215	1209	0.1	72	483	505	508	0.5	2.41	372	378	0.2
25244	GAY	035	1147	1136	1130	-0.1	57	430	445	447	0.4	2.55	340	343	0.1
25245	GIVEN	035	1544	1964	2023	2.6	97	574	724	753	2.5	2.71	464	568	2.2
25248	KENNA	035	2984	3005	2998	0.1	72	1140	1199	1212	0.5	2.51	891	914	0.3
25251	LEFT HAND	087	388	383	379	-0.1	57	149	153	152	0.3	2.50	112	112	0.0
25252	LE ROY	035	691	925	987	3.2	98	262	365	394	3.6	2.53	209	284	3.4
25253	LETART	053	4555	4506	4457	-0.1	57	1865	1928	1932	0.4	2.33	1382	1386	0.0
25259	LOONEYVILLE	087	715	766	781	0.7	89	278	309	319	1.1	2.48	209	226	0.8
25260	MASON	053	2672	2670	2655	0.0	65	1089	1132	1140	0.4	2.28	753	755	0.0
25261	MILLSTONE	013	767	749	734	-0.3	40	302	307	305	0.2	2.43	218	214	-0.2
25262	MILLWOOD	035	1429	1408	1386	-0.2	48	553	566	563	0.3	2.49	436	435	0.0
25264	MOUNT ALTO	035	345	332	325	-0.4	35	132	133	132	0.1	2.50	104	102	-0.2
25266	NEWTON	087	919	935	939	0.2	76	357	377	383	0.6	2.48	252	258	0.3
25267	NORMANTOWN	021	708	670	653	-0.6	25	289	282	278	-0.3	2.34	214	204	-0.5
25268	ORMA	013	645	642	648	-0.1	57	259	270	276	0.5	2.37	189	192	0.2
25270	REEDY	087	1946	1971	1984	0.1	72	778	821	833	0.6	2.40	575	589	0.3
25271	RIPLEY	035	7388	7870	7980	0.7	89	2991	3312	3394	1.1	2.32	2106	2273	0.8
25275	SANDYVILLE	035	1737	1615	1557	-0.8	14	687	664	649	-0.4	2.43	522	487	-0.7
25276	SPENCER	087	7566	7537	7486	0.0	65	3065	3146	3154	0.3	2.36	2140	2125	-0.1
25285	WALLBACK	015	964	978	976	0.2	76	359	379	383	0.6	2.57	264	270	0.2
25286	WALTON	087	1621	1665	1676	0.3	81	619	658	670	0.7	2.53	480	497	0.4
25287	WEST COLUMBIA	053	1035	1072	1079	0.4	83	336	365	373	0.9	2.88	262	278	0.6
25301	CHARLESTON	039	3272	3092	3016	-0.6	25	1867	1735	1690	-0.8	1.46	476	406	-1.7
25302	CHARLESTON	039	16501	15694	15350	-0.5	30	7748	7449	7324	-0.4	2.11	4460	4102	-0.9
25303	CHARLESTON	039	7390	6894	6715	-0.7	19	3368	3188	3122	-0.6	2.16	2095	1895	-1.1
25304	CHARLESTON	039	8857	8568	8415	-0.4	35	3972	3842	3786	-0.4	2.06	2265	2084	-0.9
25306	CHARLESTON	039	7499	6955	6751	-0.8	14	3189	2994	2923	-0.7	2.30	2215	2004	-1.1
25309	CHARLESTON	039	12553	11909	11643	-0.6	25	5422	5157	5057	-0.5	2.22	3459	3166	-1.0
25311	CHARLESTON	039	10957	10225	9952	-0.7	19	5067	4748	4638	-0.7	2.07	2656	2367	-1.2
25312	CHARLESTON	039	15727	14922	14622	-0.6	25	6583	6326	6235	-0.4	2.36	4514	4185	-0.8
25313	CHARLESTON	039	11861	11924	11910	0.1	72	4796	4886	4910	0.2	2.44	3466	3414	-0.2
25314	CHARLESTON	039	14647	14247	14035	-0.3	40	6195	6093	6036	-0.2	2.31	4206	3981	-0.6
25315	CHARLESTON	039	3959	3706	3602	-0.7	19	1760	1670	1634	-0.6	2.18	1131	1025	-1.1
25320	CHARLESTON	039	6129	5997	5916	-0.2	48	2364	2344	2328	-0.1	2.51	1812	1745	-0.4
25401	MARTINSBURG	003	13644	16067	17607	1.8	95	5874	7009	7712	1.9	2.23	3299	3733	1.3
25403	MARTINSBURG	003	7039	10859	12946	4.8	99	2622	4135	4969	5.0	2.62	2018	3080	4.7
25404	MARTINSBURG	003	15610	22503	26291	4.0	99	6277	9179	10779	4.2	2.43	4274	6013	3.8
	WEST VIRGINIA					0.2					0.5	2.33			0.1
	UNITED STATES					1.0					1.1	2.59			0.9

ZIP CODE #	POST OFFICE NAME	RACE (%) White 2000	White 2009	Black 2000	Black 2009	Asian/Pacific 2000	Asian/Pacific 2009	% Hispanic Origin 2000	% Hispanic Origin 2009	2009 AGE DISTRIBUTION (%) 0-4	5-9	10-14	15-19	20-24	25-44	45-64	65-84	85+	18+	MEDIAN AGE 2009	% 2009 Males	% 2009 Females
25071	ELKVIEW	98.7	98.4	0.3	0.3	0.2	0.3	0.4	0.6	5.5	5.8	6.2	5.8	4.3	25.0	31.9	14.0	1.6	78.9	43.2	49.5	50.5
25075	ESKDALE	98.1	97.8	1.1	1.2	0.1	0.2	0.5	0.6	5.3	5.5	5.7	5.9	4.9	25.0	31.2	14.6	1.9	79.9	43.1	49.7	50.3
25079	FALLING ROCK	96.3	96.6	0.0	0.0	0.0	0.0	0.0	0.0	6.9	6.9	6.9	6.9	6.9	27.6	27.6	10.3	0.0	75.9	36.3	48.3	51.7
25081	FOSTER	98.6	98.5	0.6	0.6	0.1	0.1	0.4	0.5	6.0	6.5	6.7	5.4	4.2	25.1	32.4	12.2	1.6	77.3	41.8	49.0	51.0
25082	FRAZIERS BOTTOM	98.6	98.5	0.4	0.4	0.1	0.1	0.4	0.4	5.1	5.7	5.8	5.5	4.5	25.7	33.4	13.1	1.3	80.0	43.5	50.2	49.8
25083	GALLAGHER	90.2	89.3	8.0	8.4	0.5	0.7	0.4	0.4	4.8	4.9	5.1	5.7	5.0	26.1	29.4	16.5	2.5	82.0	43.6	47.6	52.4
25085	GAULEY BRIDGE	95.8	95.4	2.8	2.8	0.2	0.4	0.9	1.1	5.9	6.0	5.9	5.4	4.1	26.4	28.2	14.9	3.3	79.1	41.9	48.3	51.7
25088	GLEN	98.8	98.7	0.0	0.0	0.0	0.0	0.0	0.0	4.5	5.1	7.6	8.9	6.4	24.2	29.9	12.7	0.6	77.1	40.6	52.2	47.8
25093	GORDON	99.0	99.0	0.5	0.5	0.0	0.0	0.5	0.5	5.2	5.2	6.3	6.3	4.2	23.4	34.9	12.5	2.1	79.2	44.6	50.5	49.5
25103	HANSFORD	96.8	96.4	1.9	2.2	0.0	0.0	0.6	0.7	5.8	5.8	5.8	5.8	4.3	24.6	29.7	15.9	2.2	79.0	43.3	49.3	50.7
25106	HENDERSON	98.4	98.3	0.0	0.0	0.0	0.0	0.2	0.2	6.0	6.0	6.2	6.2	5.1	24.6	30.3	14.3	1.3	78.0	41.6	48.1	51.9
25107	HERNSHAW	98.1	97.7	0.0	0.0	0.0	0.2	0.5	0.7	5.6	6.1	6.6	6.8	4.1	26.4	30.0	12.8	1.5	77.3	41.0	49.9	50.1
25108	HEWETT	99.1	99.1	0.2	0.2	0.0	0.0	0.2	0.3	5.6	6.5	6.3	6.8	5.3	26.1	29.5	11.9	2.0	77.4	40.2	49.1	50.9
25111	INDORE	96.5	96.5	0.1	0.1	0.0	0.0	0.2	0.2	5.6	5.7	7.2	8.2	5.6	24.2	29.8	11.9	1.7	76.8	39.6	51.3	48.7
25113	IVYDALE	98.8	98.8	0.0	0.0	0.0	0.0	0.6	0.6	6.4	7.0	6.4	6.4	5.8	27.3	27.3	12.2	1.2	76.2	37.7	49.4	50.6
25114	JEFFREY	97.2	97.1	2.2	2.2	0.0	0.0	0.9	1.1	6.8	7.7	7.2	5.9	4.8	25.0	30.3	10.7	1.5	74.3	38.9	48.9	51.1
25115	KANAWHA FALLS	96.9	96.9	1.0	1.0	0.0	0.0	1.0	1.0	5.2	5.2	6.2	6.2	4.1	24.7	34.0	12.4	2.1	79.4	43.8	53.6	46.4
25118	KIMBERLY	84.3	83.1	13.3	13.3	1.2	1.8	0.0	0.0	3.6	3.6	3.6	15.1	23.5	19.3	18.7	11.4	1.2	86.7	25.5	58.4	41.6
25119	KINCAID	86.3	85.8	11.6	12.1	0.2	0.2	0.5	0.5	6.1	6.1	6.4	5.7	5.0	25.1	30.7	13.0	1.9	77.5	41.7	49.2	50.8
25121	LAKE	98.1	98.0	1.5	1.5	0.1	0.1	0.4	0.4	6.2	6.7	6.6	5.1	3.9	25.9	32.2	11.8	1.7	77.3	41.6	48.8	51.2
25123	LEON	99.6	99.5	0.1	0.1	0.0	0.1	0.4	0.5	5.2	5.8	6.3	6.4	4.7	25.1	31.7	13.5	1.4	78.9	42.7	51.1	48.9
25124	LIBERTY	99.1	98.9	0.4	0.4	0.2	0.3	0.4	0.4	6.7	7.1	7.1	5.2	3.8	26.9	28.9	13.0	1.3	75.9	40.6	50.9	49.1
25125	LIZEMORES	97.8	97.8	0.0	0.0	0.0	0.0	0.0	0.0	5.0	5.2	7.4	9.1	5.8	23.7	29.5	12.9	1.4	76.9	40.5	51.2	48.8
25130	MADISON	97.3	97.1	2.0	2.1	0.2	0.2	0.6	0.7	5.7	6.2	6.4	5.5	4.3	24.6	32.6	12.9	1.8	78.1	42.7	48.1	51.9
25132	MAMMOTH	98.0	97.6	0.9	0.9	0.0	0.0	0.3	0.3	4.8	5.5	5.8	6.1	4.5	26.1	31.8	13.9	1.5	80.0	43.1	51.8	48.2
25133	MAYSEL	98.9	98.9	0.0	0.0	0.0	0.0	0.7	0.7	6.2	6.4	6.8	6.8	5.1	25.9	29.5	11.9	1.3	76.1	40.1	48.8	51.2
25136	MONTGOMERY	87.7	86.8	9.7	10.0	0.9	1.3	0.4	0.5	4.6	4.8	4.8	5.7	7.0	28.6	27.6	14.0	2.8	83.1	40.7	55.1	44.9
25140	NAOMA	99.3	99.3	0.1	0.1	0.0	0.0	0.2	0.3	4.8	5.3	5.6	6.3	4.7	24.3	33.0	14.1	1.9	80.3	44.2	50.5	49.5
25141	NEBO	98.9	99.0	0.0	0.0	0.0	0.0	0.4	0.0	5.5	5.5	5.9	6.2	4.8	24.5	29.0	15.5	3.1	79.0	43.3	51.0	49.0
25142	NELLIS	99.5	99.5	0.0	0.0	0.0	0.0	0.5	0.5	7.0	7.0	7.0	6.1	4.8	28.9	27.3	10.9	1.2	75.4	37.9	50.1	49.9
25143	NITRO	96.0	95.3	2.1	2.2	0.5	0.7	0.6	0.7	5.7	5.7	5.8	5.3	5.2	26.8	28.6	14.4	2.4	79.5	41.4	48.0	52.0
25148	ORGAS	99.5	99.4	0.1	0.1	0.0	0.0	0.3	0.4	6.8	7.3	6.3	4.6	4.6	22.6	30.3	15.4	2.2	76.7	43.2	46.3	53.7
25154	PEYTONA	98.8	98.6	0.0	0.0	0.0	0.0	0.5	0.7	5.5	6.0	6.2	5.8	4.6	24.6	33.3	12.2	1.7	78.5	42.6	50.5	49.5
25159	POCA	98.4	98.2	0.7	0.7	0.1	0.2	0.3	0.4	6.3	6.6	6.7	5.8	5.0	26.7	30.3	11.4	1.2	76.8	40.1	49.9	50.1
25160	POND GAP	98.4	98.3	0.3	0.3	0.0	0.0	0.2	0.2	5.1	5.6	5.8	6.1	4.5	25.9	31.2	14.1	1.5	79.1	42.7	51.3	48.7
25161	POWELLTON	90.0	89.2	7.6	7.8	0.4	0.5	0.4	0.4	5.7	6.3	6.4	5.5	4.4	25.0	33.9	11.6	1.3	78.1	42.1	48.7	51.3
25164	PROCIOUS	98.7	98.7	0.1	0.1	0.0	0.0	0.8	0.8	6.2	6.4	6.8	6.8	5.2	25.7	30.0	11.6	1.2	76.4	40.1	49.0	51.0
25165	RACINE	98.6	98.3	0.2	0.2	0.0	0.2	0.5	0.5	6.4	6.7	6.8	6.0	4.5	24.8	30.7	12.6	1.6	76.3	40.7	49.1	50.9
25168	RED HOUSE	99.1	98.8	0.1	0.0	0.2	0.3	0.7	0.8	5.4	5.6	5.9	5.9	5.0	25.8	29.9	14.9	1.6	79.5	42.6	49.6	50.4
25169	RIDGEVIEW	98.6	97.9	0.0	0.0	0.0	0.7	0.4	0.7	6.9	7.3	6.9	5.9	4.2	26.0	30.6	10.8	1.4	74.7	39.8	50.3	49.7
25173	ROBSON	85.0	84.4	12.9	13.3	0.3	0.3	0.3	0.6	6.1	6.4	6.4	5.6	5.0	25.3	30.0	13.3	1.9	77.8	41.5	48.9	51.1
25174	ROCK CREEK	100.0	100.0	0.0	0.0	0.0	0.0	0.0	0.0	5.1	5.9	5.9	5.9	4.4	24.3	33.8	13.2	1.5	78.7	43.8	51.5	48.5
25177	SAINT ALBANS	94.7	94.1	3.2	3.4	0.4	0.6	0.6	0.8	6.0	5.6	5.9	5.7	5.1	24.9	29.3	14.9	2.6	79.0	42.5	47.8	52.2
25180	SAXON	100.0	100.0	0.0	0.0	0.0	0.0	0.6	0.6	4.9	5.6	6.2	6.2	4.9	25.3	31.5	13.6	1.9	79.6	42.5	50.6	49.4
25181	SETH	98.7	98.7	0.6	0.7	0.1	0.1	0.6	0.8	5.4	5.9	6.1	5.7	4.4	24.9	32.5	13.1	1.9	79.0	43.1	48.9	51.1
25187	SOUTHSIDE	99.3	99.1	0.1	0.1	0.0	0.0	0.6	0.6	5.3	5.4	5.9	5.9	5.3	23.9	32.6	14.1	1.7	79.7	43.8	50.3	49.7
25193	SYLVESTER	98.4	98.1	0.8	0.8	0.0	0.1	0.6	0.7	5.0	5.4	5.6	5.4	4.4	25.3	34.0	13.0	2.0	80.8	44.2	50.0	50.0
25202	TORNADO	97.7	97.4	0.7	0.6	0.4	0.5	0.4	0.4	6.1	6.6	6.8	5.7	4.6	26.7	31.6	10.7	1.2	76.7	40.2	50.2	49.8
25204	TWILIGHT	99.0	98.9	0.2	0.2	0.0	0.0	0.2	0.2	4.2	4.6	5.3	5.7	4.0	24.7	35.2	14.8	1.5	82.4	46.1	48.0	52.0
25208	WHARTON	99.3	99.2	0.1	0.2	0.0	0.0	0.3	0.3	4.6	4.9	5.5	5.8	3.8	24.0	34.6	15.1	1.7	81.3	46.0	47.9	52.1
25209	WHITESVILLE	99.5	99.4	0.0	0.0	0.0	0.0	0.1	0.1	5.0	5.1	5.6	7.1	5.5	24.5	31.7	13.6	2.1	80.0	43.1	49.3	50.7
25213	WINFIELD	98.8	98.4	0.2	0.2	0.3	0.6	0.3	0.4	5.9	6.4	6.8	6.1	4.2	26.0	31.4	11.6	1.5	77.0	41.7	48.9	51.1
25214	WINIFREDE	100.0	100.0	0.0	0.0	0.0	0.0	0.0	0.0	0.0	0.0	0.0	0.0	0.0	0.0	100.0	0.0	0.0	100.0	55.0	75.0	25.0
25231	ADVENT	100.0	100.0	0.0	0.0	0.0	0.0	0.0	0.0	6.3	6.3	6.3	5.5	4.7	23.6	33.9	11.8	1.6	77.2	42.8	51.2	48.8
25234	ARNOLDSBURG	98.7	98.7	0.2	0.2	0.0	0.0	0.9	1.0	5.0	5.5	5.6	6.0	5.2	23.0	31.6	15.7	2.3	80.2	44.7	49.2	50.8
25235	CHLOE	99.1	98.9	0.1	0.1	0.1	0.2	0.2	0.2	5.9	6.1	6.2	5.1	4.1	24.3	31.3	15.0	1.9	78.2	43.7	50.9	49.1
25239	COTTAGEVILLE	99.0	98.9	0.1	0.1	0.1	0.3	0.1	0.1	5.4	5.6	6.7	6.6	4.8	27.4	28.9	13.1	1.4	77.6	40.5	50.0	50.0
25241	EVANS	98.8	98.5	0.1	0.1	0.6	0.9	0.4	0.5	6.5	6.6	7.0	6.9	5.3	27.4	28.2	10.9	1.2	75.6	38.4	48.5	51.5
25243	GANDEEVILLE	98.5	98.5	0.4	0.4	0.2	0.2	0.4	0.4	4.6	4.5	5.2	7.2	5.1	24.4	33.0	14.2	1.6	81.2	44.1	50.9	49.1
25244	GAY	99.5	99.5	0.0	0.0	0.0	0.0	0.0	0.0	5.6	6.0	6.6	6.4	4.5	24.2	32.0	13.4	1.2	77.7	42.4	52.9	47.1
25245	GIVEN	98.3	98.1	0.1	0.1	0.3	0.6	0.1	0.3	6.3	6.6	6.8	6.4	5.0	26.8	29.9	11.1	1.0	76.3	39.8	49.7	50.3
25248	KENNA	99.3	99.3	0.0	0.0	0.1	0.2	0.2	0.3	6.0	6.4	6.6	5.6	4.4	25.8	31.9	12.0	1.3	77.4	41.6	49.6	50.4
25251	LEFT HAND	98.7	98.7	0.0	0.0	0.3	0.3	0.3	0.3	5.5	5.7	6.8	6.8	5.2	24.8	32.6	11.2	1.3	77.8	42.1	50.1	49.9
25252	LE ROY	99.1	99.0	0.1	0.2	0.0	0.0	0.0	0.0	5.2	5.2	5.6	7.0	6.7	25.7	30.9	12.2	1.4	79.8	41.6	50.8	49.2
25253	LETART	99.0	98.8	0.2	0.2	0.1	0.2	0.3	0.4	5.6	5.9	6.2	5.8	4.7	24.6	30.4	14.9	1.9	78.7	42.9	49.7	50.3
25259	LOONEYVILLE	99.0	99.1	0.3	0.3	0.1	0.1	1.3	1.2	5.5	5.7	6.3	6.4	5.2	24.9	31.5	12.9	1.6	78.7	41.9	50.4	49.6
25260	MASON	97.9	97.5	0.3	0.3	0.1	0.2	0.3	0.4	5.8	6.1	6.3	5.8	4.3	23.2	28.8	17.2	2.4	78.3	43.8	49.8	50.2
25261	MILLSTONE	99.0	98.8	0.1	0.1	0.1	0.1	1.0	1.3	4.9	5.2	5.3	5.5	5.2	23.0	33.9	14.6	2.4	81.0	45.5	49.1	50.9
25262	MILLWOOD	99.2	99.0	0.1	0.1	0.1	0.2	0.1	0.1	7.1	7.2	7.5	6.6	4.2	28.3	25.4	12.6	1.0	73.8	37.9	48.7	51.3
25264	MOUNT ALTO	98.8	98.5	0.0	0.0	0.3	0.6	0.0	0.0	4.2	4.5	6.0	6.6	5.1	25.6	31.9	14.5	1.5	80.4	43.5	51.2	48.8
25266	NEWTON	99.3	99.4	0.0	0.0	0.1	0.1	0.4	0.4	6.6	6.7	6.8	6.0	4.3	23.6	31.2	12.8	1.8	75.9	41.8	49.9	50.1
25267	NORMANTOWN	98.2	97.9	0.4	0.6	0.0	0.1	0.8	0.9	4.3	4.6	4.9	5.5	5.2	24.5	34.0	14.9	1.9	82.7	45.5	51.3	48.7
25268	ORMA	99.1	98.9	0.2	0.2	0.2	0.2	0.3	0.3	5.8	6.2	6.2	5.3	4.2	24.3	31.0	15.1	1.9	78.2	43.5	50.3	49.7
25270	REEDY	99.4	99.4	0.1	0.1	0.0	0.0	0.4	0.4	6.0	6.3	6.5	5.4	4.2	24.0	31.1	14.9	1.6	77.6	43.2	49.5	50.5
25271	RIPLEY	98.6	98.4	0.0	0.0	0.2	0.3	0.4	0.5	6.3	6.3	6.5	6.1	5.0	25.3	26.6	15.3	2.6	77.3	40.7	47.1	52.9
25275	SANDYVILLE	98.9	98.8	0.1	0.1	0.1	0.1	0.1	0.1	5.9	6.2	6.4	6.4	4.7	26.2	29.3	13.5	1.3	77.5	41.2	49.6	50.4
25276	SPENCER	98.3	98.3	0.3	0.3	0.3	0.3	0.8	0.8	5.9	6.1	6.1	5.9	5.0	24.7	28.7	15.0	2.7	78.3	42.1	49.3	50.7
25285	WALLBACK	98.1	98.2	0.0	0.0	0.0	0.0	0.5	0.5	6.1	6.2	6.5	6.5	5.3	25.6	29.8	12.3	1.6	77.0	40.8	49.1	50.9
25286	WALTON	98.5	98.6	0.1	0.1	0.2	0.2	0.8	0.8	5.0	5.2	5.4	5.7	5.3	27.4	32.2	12.3	1.5	81.1	42.1	50.9	49.1
25287	WEST COLUMBIA	97.9	97.1	0.5	0.6	0.4	0.6	0.8	1.0	5.1	5.5	6.1	6.7	4.5	24.1	32.0	14.6	1.5	79.2	43.5	48.7	51.3
25301	CHARLESTON	63.5	61.4	31.0	31.8	1.5	2.3	0.9	1.2	4.3	3.8	2.8	3.6	5.9	24.6	27.3	20.5	7.1	87.1	48.4	43.8	56.2
25302	CHARLESTON	84.2	83.5	13.2	13.3	0.5	0.8	0.5	0.6	5.3	5.3	5.5	5.5	5.6	24.3	30.1	15.2	3.2	80.6	43.9	46.7	53.3
25303	CHARLESTON	91.3	90.3	6.0	6.3	1.1	1.7	0.4	0.5	5.1	5.1	5.0	5.4	5.1	24.1	32.0	15.2	3.0	81.4	45.1	46.3	53.7
25304	CHARLESTON	89.3	87.2	6.3	6.7	2.7	4.1	0.9	1.1	3.8	3.9	4.3	6.0	8.0	23.1	28.7	17.4	4.9	85.2	45.8	46.1	53.9
25306	CHARLESTON	87.0	86.0	10.4	11.0	0.2	0.3	0.6	0.7	5.4	5.7	5.9	5.8	4.8	24.7	30.6	14.9	2.3	79.5	43.2	46.9	53.1
25309	CHARLESTON	91.9	91.0	5.8	6.1	0.7	1.1	0.6	0.7	5.3	5.4	5.6	5.3	5.1	25.0	29.0	16.0	3.3	80.3	43.6	47.7	52.3
25311	CHARLESTON	75.6	74.6	19.8	20.0	1.3	1.9	1.1	1.2	5.6	5.6	5.5	7.3	6.0	26.6	28.1	12.9	2.5	79.2	40.4	47.7	52.3
25312	CHARLESTON	88.8	88.3	9.5	9.7	0.3	0.4	0.5	0.6	5.6	6.0	6.1	6.0	5.1	25.9	30.8	12.9	1.6	78.7	41.8	48.7	51.3
25313	CHARLESTON	94.1	93.0	3.3	3.5	1.3	1.9	0.6	0.7	5.7	5.7	6.0	6.2	5.7	27.3	30.3	11.6	1.4	78.7	40.3	48.4	51.6
25314	CHARLESTON	91.6	89.6	3.6	3.8	3.3	5.0	0.7	0.8	5.0	5.4	6.2	6.1	4.8	22.4	33.2	14.5	2.3	79.6	45.0	47.8	52.2
25315	CHARLESTON	94.3	93.8	4.5	4.7	0.1	0.2	0.5	0.5	5.0	5.3	5.7	5.5	4.4	23.9	29.8	17.1	3.4	80.5	45.2	47.1	52.9
25320	CHARLESTON	98.7	98.5	0.3	0.3	0.1	0.2	0.4	0.5	5.5	5.9	6.1	5.6	4.5	25.4	32.0	13.2	1.8	79.0	42.7	49.2	50.8
25401	MARTINSBURG	86.2	84.3	9.6	10.4	0.7	1.1	2.6	3.2	7.1	6.4	6.1	6.0	6.9	26.3	24.9	13.6	2.7	76.8	37.8	48.3	51.7
25403	MARTINSBURG	95.5	94.8	2.3	2.4	0.8	1.3	1.2	1.5	7.3	6.6	7.1	7.1	5.0	27.0	30.0	9.9	0.9	75.2	39.2	50.1	49.9
25404	MARTINSBURG	89.3	88.9	7.9	7.7	0.4	0.6	1.7	2.1	7.3	6.9	6.7	6.4	6.0	28.8	26.3	10.2	1.3	75.2	36.7	49.0	51.0
	WEST VIRGINIA	95.0	94.5	3.2	3.3	0.5	0.8	0.7	0.8	5.5	5.6	5.9	6.5	6.1	25.2	29.3	13.8	2.2	79.3	41.5	49.0	51.0
	UNITED STATES	75.1	72.0	12.3	12.7	3.8	4.6	12.5	15.7	6.8	6.7	6.6	7.1	6.9	27.0	26.0	10.9	1.9	75.7	36.9	49.2	50.8

#	POST OFFICE NAME	2009 Per Capita Income	2009 HH Income Base	2009 HOUSEHOLD INCOME DISTRIBUTION (%) Less than $25,000	$25,000 to $49,999	$50,000 to $99,999	$100,000 to $149,999	$150,000 or More	MEDIAN HOUSEHOLD INCOME 2009	2014	2009 National Centile	2009 State Centile	2009 Home Value Base	2009 HOME VALUE DISTRIBUTION (%) Less than $50,000	$50,000 to $89,999	$90,000 to $174,999	$175,000 to $399,999	$400,000 or More	2009 Median Home Value
25071	ELKVIEW	20825	4718	30.3	27.7	33.7	6.4	1.9	41853	45140	39	88	3768	24.5	22.7	40.0	12.3	0.5	95333
25075	ESKDALE	15446	796	50.9	24.0	22.2	2.1	0.8	24496	25714	3	11	655	46.3	39.4	12.2	2.1	0.0	56447
25079	FALLING ROCK	17639	12	41.7	25.0	25.0	8.3	0.0	30000	40000	8	35	10	30.0	50.0	20.0	0.0	0.0	60000
25081	FOSTER	17417	983	36.0	32.9	25.5	4.6	1.0	32262	33070	12	50	802	33.9	25.6	29.8	10.2	0.5	77111
25082	FRAZIERS BOTTOM	25269	665	22.7	28.1	35.5	8.1	5.6	49226	51285	59	96	577	18.0	21.7	31.0	28.6	0.7	111569
25083	GALLAGHER	18698	796	36.8	28.6	28.0	5.7	0.9	36274	36900	21	72	588	37.6	36.6	22.4	3.4	0.0	66604
25085	GAULEY BRIDGE	20867	542	34.9	30.8	27.9	4.4	2.0	36395	36651	22	73	397	28.0	30.7	31.7	9.1	0.5	77857
25088	GLEN	12914	65	44.6	35.4	20.0	0.0	0.0	27252	27983	5	22	52	48.1	32.7	17.3	1.9	0.0	51250
25093	GORDON	16605	83	48.2	21.7	26.5	3.6	0.0	26100	26886	4	17	62	51.6	24.2	22.6	1.6	0.0	48333
25103	HANSFORD	14428	63	52.4	28.6	17.5	1.6	0.0	23295	25739	2	8	53	62.3	24.5	13.2	0.0	0.0	39375
25106	HENDERSON	16062	199	45.2	35.7	14.6	1.5	3.0	26817	27736	4	20	157	50.3	18.5	24.8	5.7	0.6	49762
25107	HERNSHAW	17313	255	42.4	28.6	25.5	2.0	1.6	31677	32453	11	47	211	46.0	32.7	18.5	1.4	1.4	55313
25108	HEWETT	13743	728	46.3	30.6	21.3	0.5	1.2	27202	28692	5	21	601	22.1	25.8	44.6	6.7	0.8	92976
25111	INDORE	12681	558	46.4	32.4	19.9	0.4	0.9	26569	27538	4	19	464	49.6	27.2	20.5	2.8	0.0	50476
25113	IVYDALE	12886	71	56.3	23.9	16.9	1.4	1.4	21914	21549	2	5	52	34.6	36.5	21.2	7.7	0.0	70000
25114	JEFFREY	15148	179	41.3	33.5	21.2	2.2	1.7	31026	31869	10	44	136	30.1	29.4	34.6	5.9	0.0	80000
25115	KANAWHA FALLS	19341	40	35.0	27.5	32.5	5.0	0.0	36511	35000	22	73	34	23.5	23.5	29.4	20.6	2.9	100000
25118	KIMBERLY	16669	67	50.7	28.4	17.9	3.0	0.0	24568	25350	3	12	54	24.1	40.7	31.5	3.7	0.0	75000
25119	KINCAID	14742	174	43.7	36.2	19.5	0.6	0.0	27228	28096	5	22	142	41.5	31.0	21.8	4.2	1.4	60000
25121	LAKE	15996	375	40.5	29.9	25.3	4.3	0.0	28572	28981	6	28	319	24.1	27.9	39.2	8.8	0.0	86750
25123	LEON	15738	1244	41.7	29.9	25.1	2.8	0.5	30305	30682	9	37	1083	31.6	23.4	26.3	17.5	1.2	82465
25124	LIBERTY	19687	513	34.1	23.8	33.5	8.0	0.6	37493	39228	25	78	464	22.0	23.9	37.3	16.4	0.4	101500
25125	LIZEMORES	11852	135	46.7	33.3	20.0	0.0	0.0	26398	28284	4	18	110	49.1	30.9	18.2	1.8	0.0	50714
25130	MADISON	20999	1854	35.1	30.5	27.8	4.2	2.4	34789	35763	17	63	1352	28.7	24.5	36.7	8.8	1.3	84028
25132	MAMMOTH	15775	127	39.4	26.0	30.7	2.4	1.6	31770	32057	11	48	103	58.3	28.2	11.7	1.9	0.0	43929
25133	MAYSEL	17478	227	39.6	33.0	22.0	4.0	1.3	32999	33245	13	54	182	29.7	28.0	31.9	9.3	1.1	79286
25136	MONTGOMERY	17011	3497	41.5	28.7	24.0	4.1	1.7	30930	31094	10	43	2461	26.9	33.9	31.7	6.5	1.0	76345
25140	NAOMA	16940	451	42.1	28.8	23.5	2.9	2.7	30317	30954	9	37	358	38.0	29.1	22.9	7.5	2.5	64667
25141	NEBO	12986	126	53.2	31.0	13.5	2.4	0.0	22769	24634	2	7	101	40.6	35.6	20.8	3.0	0.0	69000
25142	NELLIS	12906	222	38.3	40.1	21.6	0.0	0.0	32116	34140	12	49	191	56.0	13.1	23.6	7.3	0.0	33021
25143	NITRO	24601	4249	25.7	28.4	35.9	6.2	3.8	45583	47154	50	93	2974	12.9	36.8	42.8	6.8	0.7	90472
25148	ORGAS	19965	297	42.8	22.9	27.6	5.1	1.7	30563	32344	9	39	247	39.3	19.4	40.1	1.2	0.0	80227
25154	PEYTONA	14560	242	47.5	28.9	19.8	3.3	0.4	26321	27573	4	18	207	37.7	30.0	27.1	4.8	0.5	69545
25159	POCA	22488	2961	26.5	27.1	37.1	6.9	2.3	45447	47876	50	93	2555	27.8	19.3	41.3	10.6	0.9	96869
25160	POND GAP	15293	228	40.8	26.8	28.9	1.8	1.8	30888	32006	10	43	185	57.8	25.4	13.5	3.2	0.0	44200
25161	POWELLTON	17112	292	37.0	30.8	26.7	3.4	2.1	36439	36655	22	73	238	25.2	29.8	37.4	5.5	2.1	81429
25164	PROCIOUS	16323	713	39.0	33.8	21.9	3.6	1.7	34135	34058	16	60	576	28.3	27.8	31.6	10.9	1.4	81463
25165	RACINE	17571	270	43.0	27.0	23.7	5.2	1.1	29213	30736	7	31	219	30.6	31.1	34.2	4.1	0.0	77400
25168	RED HOUSE	22459	1882	26.7	29.5	35.8	5.9	2.1	44025	46159	45	92	1561	19.8	20.8	47.9	11.0	0.6	105581
25169	RIDGEVIEW	14422	108	38.0	35.2	23.1	3.7	0.0	30347	30812	9	37	88	42.0	20.5	20.5	17.0	0.0	68000
25173	ROBSON	14528	144	41.0	38.9	19.4	0.7	0.0	27985	28328	6	25	117	41.0	31.6	23.1	3.4	0.9	60417
25174	ROCK CREEK	12923	48	43.8	27.1	25.0	4.2	0.0	28583	29277	6	28	39	35.9	28.2	28.2	5.1	2.6	65000
25177	SAINT ALBANS	22773	10193	25.5	28.7	36.8	6.6	2.5	46727	47509	53	94	7806	16.8	34.9	41.1	7.0	0.2	88493
25180	SAXON	15104	56	41.1	30.4	23.2	3.6	1.8	30000	32294	8	35	45	35.6	26.7	24.4	8.9	4.4	71667
25181	SETH	16564	803	43.7	25.3	25.5	4.4	1.1	29017	30934	7	30	631	37.2	28.1	30.3	4.3	0.2	71250
25187	SOUTHSIDE	15615	298	49.3	21.8	26.8	1.3	0.7	25817	26953	4	16	257	30.0	21.4	32.7	16.0	0.0	88333
25193	SYLVESTER	16757	703	52.6	21.5	21.6	3.6	0.7	23039	24803	2	7	554	41.3	31.8	24.7	2.2	0.0	59796
25202	TORNADO	21937	536	22.2	31.0	37.7	5.8	3.4	47282	47878	55	95	448	19.6	26.6	40.8	11.6	1.3	95862
25204	TWILIGHT	17597	207	46.4	17.4	35.3	1.0	0.0	33833	35558	15	58	171	51.5	36.3	9.4	2.9	0.0	48611
25208	WHARTON	17748	295	46.1	17.3	34.9	1.7	0.0	33644	35977	15	56	241	49.0	37.3	11.2	2.5	0.0	50926
25209	WHITESVILLE	14474	356	49.4	25.8	21.3	2.8	0.6	25461	27196	4	15	291	35.7	34.0	26.1	4.1	0.0	66500
25213	WINFIELD	28845	2449	14.1	24.0	44.4	12.0	5.5	61325	63168	79	99	2143	14.1	9.3	44.9	28.4	3.3	140248
25214	WINIFREDE	6042	5	80.0	20.0	0.0	0.0	0.0	12000	22111	1	1	4	75.0	0.0	25.0	0.0	0.0	15000
25231	ADVENT	15344	48	35.4	31.3	29.2	4.2	0.0	35000	33107	18	66	42	16.7	19.0	33.3	26.2	4.8	116667
25234	ARNOLDSBURG	14458	732	47.8	31.1	18.7	2.0	0.3	26032	26737	4	16	583	25.7	32.6	33.1	5.3	3.3	77717
25235	CHLOE	12626	396	52.0	32.6	12.9	2.5	0.0	23479	23772	2	9	314	32.8	32.5	30.3	4.5	0.0	72903
25239	COTTAGEVILLE	18551	568	31.5	28.0	37.3	2.8	0.4	40525	41757	34	85	484	20.2	14.5	46.7	15.3	3.3	117917
25241	EVANS	20985	601	31.4	30.6	28.1	5.7	4.2	41564	42278	38	87	503	12.3	15.1	45.9	21.3	5.4	119622
25243	GANDEEVILLE	16730	505	38.4	37.4	18.6	4.0	1.6	31340	31848	10	46	434	17.7	26.5	41.2	11.5	3.0	98065
25244	GAY	16771	445	35.7	33.3	27.2	2.9	0.9	37341	38881	25	77	388	32.2	19.8	34.5	10.1	3.4	86364
25245	GIVEN	20622	724	22.8	27.3	40.2	8.3	1.4	49886	48843	61	96	639	9.2	18.9	34.3	33.5	4.1	130990
25248	KENNA	17554	1199	32.8	30.5	31.1	5.6	0.0	37686	38062	26	79	1045	15.4	18.9	36.2	24.4	5.2	124038
25251	LEFT HAND	15229	153	43.1	30.7	21.6	3.9	0.7	27661	28704	5	23	131	22.1	29.8	29.8	18.3	0.0	87727
25252	LE ROY	15672	365	27.9	44.9	26.0	1.1	0.0	36760	36938	23	75	326	19.9	23.9	50.0	6.1	0.0	94878
25253	LETART	18763	1928	37.6	29.0	27.6	4.5	1.3	34223	33949	16	60	1642	23.1	25.6	42.0	6.9	2.4	91774
25259	LOONEYVILLE	13311	309	51.5	26.5	18.8	3.2	0.0	24226	25473	3	10	263	32.7	25.5	29.3	12.2	0.4	77188
25260	MASON	17391	1132	36.7	33.0	26.3	3.6	0.4	32955	32872	13	53	915	36.5	25.7	28.9	8.9	0.1	68409
25261	MILLSTONE	15524	307	42.7	31.3	22.5	2.9	0.7	29419	30210	7	32	240	25.0	31.3	32.9	6.3	4.6	78571
25262	MILLWOOD	21299	566	21.4	31.4	41.5	3.5	2.1	47202	46833	55	95	478	18.4	16.7	45.6	18.4	0.8	114844
25264	MOUNT ALTO	16645	133	38.3	27.1	30.8	3.8	0.0	37313	38770	25	77	114	20.2	11.4	50.0	14.0	4.4	125833
25266	NEWTON	14336	377	48.0	26.8	21.2	4.0	0.0	25983	26561	4	16	313	29.4	33.5	24.9	12.1	0.0	75690
25267	NORMANTOWN	15279	282	49.3	25.9	21.6	0.0	3.2	25407	26870	3	15	236	21.6	35.2	32.2	11.0	0.0	83846
25268	ORMA	12552	270	52.2	32.6	13.0	2.2	0.0	23374	23848	2	8	214	30.4	32.2	33.2	4.2	0.0	75000
25270	REEDY	17940	821	33.7	35.7	25.0	3.4	2.2	33540	33040	14	56	727	18.3	24.3	35.6	19.5	2.2	105804
25271	RIPLEY	19704	3312	35.4	29.5	28.8	4.1	2.1	36211	36866	21	71	2443	16.2	13.5	47.6	20.8	1.9	117902
25275	SANDYVILLE	19712	664	31.3	33.4	28.6	5.0	1.7	41316	41848	37	87	537	22.9	21.0	40.8	13.8	1.5	98125
25276	SPENCER	16378	3146	42.7	32.5	18.7	4.6	1.5	28902	29504	7	30	2283	24.2	25.8	35.6	13.1	1.4	90035
25285	WALLBACK	16096	379	42.0	31.1	21.4	4.0	1.6	30524	30998	9	39	301	31.9	28.2	33.2	6.6	0.0	76458
25286	WALTON	16514	658	37.5	35.6	21.3	5.0	0.6	32926	32862	13	53	558	26.3	31.5	28.5	13.4	0.2	81020
25287	WEST COLUMBIA	19054	365	27.1	30.1	31.8	7.1	3.8	43717	45556	44	91	326	17.8	18.1	46.3	16.6	1.2	110776
25301	CHARLESTON	19860	1735	61.0	19.3	15.1	2.1	2.5	16330	16786	1	1	247	8.5	30.4	41.3	18.2	1.6	113214
25302	CHARLESTON	25542	7449	30.9	28.0	31.0	6.2	3.9	40745	44064	35	86	4694	14.4	32.0	41.9	10.9	0.8	96789
25303	CHARLESTON	32251	3188	22.5	23.4	35.4	12.4	6.4	54585	55590	71	98	2209	4.5	19.6	58.7	16.6	0.6	118671
25304	CHARLESTON	35835	3842	20.1	25.1	36.2	9.4	9.3	54341	54855	70	98	2497	6.6	12.1	47.1	26.8	7.4	137028
25306	CHARLESTON	18306	2994	37.1	30.9	27.8	3.1	1.0	33714	33876	15	57	2211	33.7	36.6	27.7	1.7	0.3	70893
25309	CHARLESTON	25773	5157	28.9	27.5	31.4	8.1	4.1	42556	45611	41	89	3597	18.2	30.1	41.6	9.1	1.0	93125
25311	CHARLESTON	25560	4748	37.5	27.7	24.0	4.8	6.0	32539	32786	12	52	2462	19.4	27.6	31.6	16.9	4.5	99146
25312	CHARLESTON	19566	6326	36.7	28.6	27.9	4.9	2.0	34678	34883	17	63	4575	28.7	30.6	32.8	7.8	0.1	78696
25313	CHARLESTON	27491	4886	17.4	26.5	40.6	10.2	5.2	57322	57430	74	98	3752	13.0	20.0	53.8	12.8	0.4	112929
25314	CHARLESTON	46056	6093	11.9	17.0	32.9	17.7	20.4	77367	78914	91	100	4757	5.7	8.9	39.2	38.2	8.0	166152
25315	CHARLESTON	20110	1670	34.2	33.4	27.8	3.6	1.1	36409	37824	22	73	1115	35.2	37.0	25.0	2.1	0.7	67000
25320	CHARLESTON	20449	2344	29.1	27.9	35.2	5.9	1.9	42942	45738	42	90	1914	29.1	26.3	33.4	10.9	0.4	81557
25401	MARTINSBURG	21240	7009	31.5	31.6	29.8	5.2	2.0	38672	39851	29	82	3528	10.5	13.6	47.4	26.5	2.0	137430
25403	MARTINSBURG	25664	4135	17.5	25.4	40.3	11.5	5.2	56362	56804	73	98	3457	19.3	4.0	13.8	50.0	13.0	214419
25404	MARTINSBURG	21837	9179	22.9	32.4	37.1	5.5	2.1	46349	48492	52	94	6159	12.3	7.8	33.4	41.6	5.0	168801
	WEST VIRGINIA	20563		34.3	29.3	28.3	5.4	2.7	37099	38541				22.0	23.9	36.4	15.5	2.2	98135
	UNITED STATES	27277		20.9	24.4	35.3	11.7	7.6	54719	56938				9.3	13.1	31.6	32.6	13.5	162279

ZIP CODE #	POST OFFICE NAME	FINANCIAL SERVICES: Auto Loan	Home Loan	Invest-ments	Retire-ment Plans	THE HOME: Home Improvements: Home Repair	Lawn & Garden	Furnishings: Comput-ers & Hard-ware-Personal	Major Appli-ances	TV, Radio, Sound Equip-ment	Furni-ture	ENTERTAINMENT: Dine out/ Carry out	Sports Equip-ment	Fees & Tickets	Toys & Games	Travel	Cable TV	PERSONAL: Apparel & Services	Auto Repairs	Health Insur-ance	Pets & Supplies
25071	ELKVIEW	84	66	81	66	68	86	68	80	74	64	72	60	59	74	67	79	48	75	85	95
25075	ESKDALE	67	48	66	45	47	68	49	61	56	47	55	47	40	57	47	62	37	58	65	74
25079	FALLING ROCK	72	52	72	50	54	75	56	70	63	50	61	52	45	62	54	69	40	65	76	82
25081	FOSTER	78	52	77	50	53	77	55	70	63	52	62	54	42	64	52	70	41	65	73	85
25082	FRAZIERS BOTTOM	105	85	100	86	87	109	86	102	91	79	90	77	74	92	85	98	60	94	105	120
25083	GALLAGHER	66	58	66	57	59	71	60	66	65	57	64	48	56	64	59	70	44	65	74	78
25085	GAULEY BRIDGE	81	57	80	55	59	83	62	77	70	56	67	58	49	69	60	77	45	72	84	91
25088	GLEN	58	38	56	36	38	57	40	51	47	38	46	40	30	47	38	52	30	48	54	63
25093	GORDON	71	47	69	44	46	70	50	63	57	47	56	49	37	58	46	64	37	59	66	77
25103	HANSFORD	59	38	57	36	38	58	41	52	47	39	46	40	31	48	38	53	31	49	55	64
25106	HENDERSON	70	46	66	44	46	68	49	61	57	47	55	48	37	58	46	63	37	58	65	75
25107	HERNSHAW	76	50	73	47	49	75	53	67	61	50	60	52	40	62	50	68	40	63	71	82
25108	HEWETT	61	42	61	41	43	62	45	57	51	42	50	43	35	51	43	57	33	53	60	68
25111	INDORE	60	39	58	37	39	59	42	53	48	40	47	41	31	49	39	54	31	49	56	65
25113	IVYDALE	58	38	56	36	38	57	40	51	47	38	46	40	30	48	38	52	30	48	54	63
25114	JEFFREY	71	47	69	44	47	70	50	63	58	47	56	49	38	58	47	64	37	59	67	77
25115	KANAWHA FALLS	83	60	86	58	62	85	61	78	68	57	67	59	49	68	61	75	44	72	81	93
25118	KIMBERLY	59	42	59	41	44	61	46	57	52	41	50	43	37	51	45	57	33	53	62	67
25119	KINCAID	67	43	64	41	43	65	46	59	54	44	52	46	35	55	43	60	35	55	62	72
25121	LAKE	71	48	70	46	48	70	50	64	57	47	56	49	39	58	48	64	37	59	67	77
25123	LEON	69	47	69	45	48	69	50	63	56	47	55	48	38	57	47	62	36	58	66	76
25124	LIBERTY	86	62	76	60	62	83	64	76	71	62	70	58	51	73	60	78	47	72	80	92
25125	LIZEMORES	59	39	57	36	39	58	41	52	48	39	47	41	31	48	39	53	31	49	55	64
25130	MADISON	84	57	83	55	58	84	61	76	69	57	67	58	47	69	58	76	45	71	81	92
25132	MAMMOTH	76	50	73	47	49	74	53	67	61	50	60	52	40	62	50	68	40	63	71	82
25133	MAYSEL	77	52	76	50	53	76	55	69	62	52	61	53	42	63	52	69	40	64	73	84
25136	MONTGOMERY	70	52	68	50	53	71	56	66	62	52	61	50	47	62	54	68	41	63	72	79
25140	NAOMA	76	51	74	48	51	76	55	69	63	51	61	53	42	63	52	70	40	64	73	83
25141	NEBO	55	36	53	34	36	54	38	48	44	36	43	38	29	45	36	49	28	45	51	59
25142	NELLIS	61	40	58	37	39	59	42	53	49	40	48	42	32	50	39	54	32	50	56	66
25143	NITRO	85	75	86	74	76	91	76	85	81	72	79	63	71	80	76	86	54	82	92	100
25148	ORGAS	87	57	84	53	57	85	61	76	70	58	68	60	45	71	57	78	45	72	81	94
25154	PEYTONA	65	43	63	40	43	64	45	57	52	43	51	45	34	53	43	58	34	54	61	70
25159	POCA	90	77	79	75	77	89	75	84	80	75	79	62	68	82	72	85	54	80	87	99
25160	POND GAP	75	49	72	46	49	73	52	66	60	50	59	51	39	61	49	67	39	62	69	81
25161	POWELLTON	79	56	81	55	59	80	58	74	64	54	63	55	46	64	57	71	42	68	77	88
25164	PROCIOUS	75	52	75	50	53	75	54	69	61	51	60	52	42	61	52	68	40	64	72	83
25165	RACINE	76	50	74	47	50	75	53	67	61	50	60	52	40	62	50	68	40	63	71	82
25168	RED HOUSE	85	72	84	70	73	91	70	83	77	68	76	61	64	77	71	83	51	78	89	97
25169	RIDGEVIEW	71	46	69	44	46	70	50	63	57	47	56	49	37	58	46	64	37	59	66	77
25173	ROBSON	67	44	65	42	44	66	47	59	54	45	53	46	35	55	44	60	35	56	63	73
25174	ROCK CREEK	68	44	66	42	44	67	48	60	55	45	53	47	36	56	44	61	35	56	63	74
25177	SAINT ALBANS	79	74	76	74	74	85	74	80	78	71	77	58	71	78	74	82	53	78	87	93
25180	SAXON	81	54	79	51	54	80	57	72	65	54	64	56	43	66	54	72	42	67	76	88
25181	SETH	75	49	73	47	49	74	53	66	61	50	59	52	40	62	49	68	39	62	70	82
25187	SOUTHSIDE	66	47	55	46	47	63	49	58	55	48	54	44	40	57	45	60	36	55	61	70
25193	SYLVESTER	67	44	65	41	44	66	47	59	54	44	53	46	35	55	44	60	35	55	62	72
25202	TORNADO	96	79	83	77	78	92	78	88	83	77	82	66	69	85	74	88	55	83	89	104
25204	TWILIGHT	72	47	69	44	47	70	50	63	58	48	56	49	37	59	47	64	37	59	67	78
25208	WHARTON	73	47	70	45	47	71	51	64	59	48	57	50	38	60	47	65	38	60	68	79
25209	WHITESVILLE	65	43	63	41	44	65	47	58	53	44	52	45	35	54	44	59	34	55	62	71
25213	WINFIELD	98	110	97	111	107	109	98	102	98	99	99	78	105	100	103	99	69	99	104	120
25214	WINIFREDE	27	18	26	17	17	26	19	24	22	18	21	18	14	22	18	24	14	22	25	29
25231	ADVENT	73	52	74	50	54	74	53	68	59	50	58	51	43	59	53	65	38	62	71	81
25234	ARNOLDSBURG	62	42	61	40	42	61	44	56	50	41	49	43	34	51	42	56	33	52	59	68
25235	CHLOE	53	38	54	36	39	54	39	49	43	36	43	37	31	43	38	48	28	45	51	59
25239	COTTAGEVILLE	78	61	74	59	62	77	61	72	66	59	65	54	52	66	59	70	43	68	74	86
25241	EVANS	82	74	68	72	73	78	71	76	73	73	73	55	66	76	67	76	50	73	76	90
25243	GANDEEVILLE	73	50	73	48	51	73	53	67	59	49	58	51	41	60	51	66	38	62	70	80
25244	GAY	76	55	78	53	57	78	56	71	62	52	61	54	45	62	56	69	40	66	74	85
25245	GIVEN	91	82	75	79	80	86	77	83	81	80	81	61	72	84	74	83	55	80	84	99
25248	KENNA	76	59	73	57	60	76	59	71	64	57	63	53	50	65	57	69	42	66	73	84
25251	LEFT HAND	69	48	69	46	49	69	50	63	56	47	55	48	39	56	49	62	36	58	66	76
25252	LE ROY	72	51	60	50	51	68	53	62	59	52	58	48	43	62	49	65	39	59	66	76
25253	LETART	74	57	73	55	58	77	58	71	64	54	63	53	49	64	57	70	42	66	76	84
25259	LOONEYVILLE	61	40	59	38	40	60	43	54	49	41	48	42	32	50	40	55	32	51	57	66
25260	MASON	72	49	71	47	50	73	53	66	60	49	58	50	41	60	51	67	39	62	71	80
25261	MILLSTONE	67	47	68	46	49	68	50	63	56	46	54	47	39	55	48	61	36	58	66	75
25262	MILLWOOD	85	77	72	76	76	83	73	80	76	73	76	59	68	79	71	80	52	76	81	95
25264	MOUNT ALTO	74	53	76	51	55	75	55	69	61	51	59	52	44	60	54	67	39	64	72	83
25266	NEWTON	66	43	64	41	44	65	46	58	53	44	52	45	35	54	43	59	34	55	61	71
25267	NORMANTOWN	66	45	65	43	46	66	47	60	53	44	52	46	37	53	45	59	34	55	63	72
25268	ORMA	54	38	54	36	39	54	39	50	44	36	43	37	31	43	38	48	28	46	52	59
25270	REEDY	74	57	73	57	59	76	58	70	62	53	61	53	48	63	57	68	41	65	73	83
25271	RIPLEY	74	64	70	62	64	76	63	72	68	61	66	52	57	68	62	72	45	68	76	84
25275	SANDYVILLE	86	61	88	59	64	87	63	80	70	59	69	60	50	69	62	77	45	73	83	95
25276	SPENCER	68	48	68	47	50	70	52	64	57	47	56	48	41	57	50	63	37	60	69	76
25285	WALLBACK	77	51	75	48	51	76	54	68	62	51	60	53	41	63	51	69	40	64	72	83
25286	WALTON	75	54	68	52	54	73	56	67	62	53	61	51	44	63	52	68	41	63	70	81
25287	WEST COLUMBIA	90	76	83	78	77	94	76	88	80	70	79	67	68	82	75	86	53	82	91	104
25301	CHARLESTON	39	31	37	35	32	37	47	39	50	42	50	30	42	44	42	54	35	47	53	50
25302	CHARLESTON	77	70	72	70	71	80	75	77	79	71	78	57	71	77	73	83	54	78	86	91
25303	CHARLESTON	95	97	98	98	99	105	97	100	100	95	99	73	99	98	99	103	69	99	109	116
25304	CHARLESTON	107	108	113	109	111	116	109	112	112	108	111	82	111	109	112	116	78	112	122	130
25306	CHARLESTON	73	52	71	50	53	74	56	68	63	52	61	51	45	62	53	70	41	64	74	82
25309	CHARLESTON	89	78	83	78	79	92	82	87	86	78	85	65	76	85	79	91	58	86	95	103
25311	CHARLESTON	80	70	78	71	71	80	77	78	79	73	78	60	71	78	74	82	54	79	83	93
25312	CHARLESTON	76	59	68	59	59	76	63	71	68	59	67	53	54	69	59	74	45	68	76	85
25313	CHARLESTON	98	97	98	97	97	101	94	97	95	94	95	74	94	95	95	96	66	96	99	115
25314	CHARLESTON	141	166	178	168	174	163	150	157	146	157	146	117	166	143	165	145	104	151	154	179
25315	CHARLESTON	75	54	73	52	55	77	59	71	66	54	64	53	48	65	56	73	43	67	78	84
25320	CHARLESTON	91	68	85	66	69	90	69	83	76	66	75	63	57	77	66	83	50	78	87	100
25401	MARTINSBURG	67	61	58	61	60	65	69	65	71	65	71	50	65	70	65	74	49	69	73	78
25403	MARTINSBURG	103	100	91	100	97	104	94	99	96	95	96	75	92	99	93	98	66	96	100	118
25404	MARTINSBURG	81	75	71	74	73	77	76	77	77	75	77	59	72	79	72	79	53	76	78	91
	WEST VIRGINIA	79	63	76	62	64	80	66	75	71	63	70	57	58	71	64	77	47	72	80	90
	UNITED STATES	100	100	100	100	100	100	100	100	100	100	100	100	100	100	100	100	100	100	100	100

#	POST OFFICE NAME	COUNTY FIPS CODE	POPULATION 2000	POPULATION 2009	POPULATION 2014	2000-2009 ANNUAL RATE % Rate	2000-2009 ANNUAL RATE State Centile	HOUSEHOLDS 2000	HOUSEHOLDS 2009	HOUSEHOLDS 2014	HOUSEHOLDS % Annual Rate 2000-2009	2009 Average HH Size	FAMILIES 2000	FAMILIES 2009	FAMILIES % Annual Rate 2000-2009
25405	MARTINSBURG	003	7453	12062	14592	5.3	99	2751	4652	5706	5.8	2.50	2016	3267	5.4
25411	BERKELEY SPRINGS	065	10949	12396	13042	1.4	93	4535	5304	5631	1.7	2.31	3186	3616	1.4
25413	BUNKER HILL	003	5784	7080	8169	2.2	97	2137	2671	3103	2.4	2.65	1646	1991	2.1
25414	CHARLES TOWN	037	12865	16803	19133	2.9	98	5164	7008	8072	3.4	2.38	3525	4610	2.9
25419	FALLING WATERS	003	7145	9853	11841	3.5	98	2747	3879	4701	3.8	2.54	2054	2792	3.4
25420	GERRARDSTOWN	003	3292	3920	4553	1.9	96	1199	1448	1692	2.1	2.71	924	1080	1.7
25422	GREAT CACAPON	065	1408	1894	2117	3.3	98	603	851	961	3.8	2.23	406	552	3.4
25425	HARPERS FERRY	037	11066	13727	15181	2.4	97	4330	5520	6156	2.7	2.48	3095	3825	2.3
25427	HEDGESVILLE	003	10559	14597	16768	3.6	99	3942	5595	6480	3.9	2.61	2968	4054	3.4
25428	INWOOD	003	6226	9533	11454	4.7	99	2335	3645	4406	4.9	2.61	1773	2663	4.5
25430	KEARNEYSVILLE	037	6329	7633	8505	2.0	96	2304	2939	3333	2.7	2.54	1744	2156	2.3
25431	LEVELS	027	147	171	185	1.6	94	58	71	77	2.2	2.41	40	47	1.8
25434	PAW PAW	027	1878	2290	2511	2.2	97	754	955	1060	2.6	2.39	537	659	2.2
25437	POINTS	027	123	144	156	1.7	95	50	61	67	2.2	2.33	36	43	1.9
25438	RANSON	037	3802	5543	6319	4.2	99	1519	2279	2620	4.5	2.43	1008	1479	4.2
25442	SHENANDOAH JUNCTION	037	2138	2873	3268	3.2	98	746	1036	1188	3.6	2.76	539	738	3.5
25443	SHEPHERDSTOWN	037	5697	6804	7371	1.9	96	1986	2547	2826	2.7	2.29	1291	1602	2.4
25444	SLANESVILLE	027	769	917	1000	1.9	96	280	350	387	2.4	2.61	205	249	2.1
25446	SUMMIT POINT	037	1185	1400	1527	1.8	95	453	549	606	2.1	2.55	357	423	1.9
25501	ALKOL	043	1516	1523	1511	0.0	65	609	646	649	0.6	2.36	446	459	0.3
25502	APPLE GROVE	053	1506	1551	1557	0.3	81	606	651	662	0.8	2.38	450	468	0.4
25503	ASHTON	053	876	904	906	0.3	81	348	374	380	0.8	2.42	261	272	0.4
25504	BARBOURSVILLE	011	11204	11737	11831	0.5	86	4494	4827	4907	0.8	2.39	3267	3393	0.4
25505	BIG CREEK	045	301	303	298	0.1	72	106	112	111	0.6	2.71	87	90	0.4
25506	BRANCHLAND	043	2797	2952	2975	0.6	88	1109	1227	1252	1.1	2.41	824	885	0.8
25508	CHAPMANVILLE	045	11724	11681	11482	0.0	65	4558	4788	4772	0.5	2.41	3393	3463	0.2
25510	CULLODEN	011	4769	4708	4706	-0.1	57	1842	1870	1888	0.2	2.45	1416	1397	-0.1
25511	DUNLOW	099	694	671	655	-0.4	35	262	266	262	0.2	2.52	200	197	-0.2
25512	EAST LYNN	099	1633	1557	1511	-0.5	30	660	659	649	0.0	2.36	478	462	-0.4
25514	FORT GAY	099	3930	3673	3532	-0.7	19	1493	1449	1409	-0.3	2.53	1146	1082	-0.6
25515	GALLIPOLIS FERRY	053	2291	2296	2284	0.0	65	915	955	961	0.5	2.40	682	691	0.1
25517	GENOA	099	2501	2463	2411	-0.2	48	925	949	941	0.3	2.60	702	700	0.0
25520	GLENWOOD	011	2306	2364	2370	0.3	81	894	945	958	0.6	2.49	679	696	0.3
25521	GRIFFITHSVILLE	043	617	625	618	0.1	72	230	242	242	0.6	2.58	173	177	0.2
25523	HAMLIN	043	3123	2996	2907	-0.4	35	1278	1279	1259	0.0	2.29	932	905	-0.3
25524	HARTS	043	2109	2120	2107	0.1	72	774	823	828	0.7	2.58	627	652	0.4
25526	HURRICANE	079	19280	20723	21520	0.8	90	7341	8172	8562	1.2	2.52	5673	6163	0.9
25529	JULIAN	005	1312	1299	1281	-0.1	57	517	535	534	0.4	2.36	377	378	0.0
25530	KENOVA	099	7791	7323	7058	-0.7	19	3400	3318	3236	-0.3	2.20	2281	2157	-0.6
25534	KIAHSVILLE	099	337	322	313	-0.5	30	124	124	122	0.0	2.60	90	87	-0.4
25535	LAVALETTE	099	3647	3811	3780	0.5	86	1466	1600	1607	1.0	2.36	1132	1202	0.7
25537	LESAGE	011	1696	1624	1602	-0.5	30	662	650	647	-0.2	2.47	494	467	-0.6
25540	MIDKIFF	043	128	139	140	0.9	90	43	49	50	1.4	2.84	32	35	1.0
25541	MILTON	011	7471	7278	7212	-0.3	40	3048	3047	3044	0.0	2.37	2214	2138	-0.4
25544	MYRA	043	234	236	233	0.1	72	86	90	90	0.5	2.61	62	63	0.2
25545	ONA	011	5391	5582	5615	0.4	83	2016	2131	2159	0.6	2.59	1580	1622	0.3
25547	PECKS MILL	045	912	842	811	-0.9	10	371	363	355	-0.2	2.32	286	273	-0.5
25550	POINT PLEASANT	053	7941	7653	7504	-0.4	35	3404	3400	3372	0.0	2.20	2279	2202	-0.4
25555	PRICHARD	099	1386	1426	1408	0.3	81	533	573	573	0.8	2.49	407	426	0.5
25557	RANGER	043	4595	4465	4383	-0.3	40	1746	1793	1784	0.3	2.49	1323	1322	0.0
25559	SALT ROCK	011	1644	1755	1774	0.7	89	629	692	706	1.0	2.54	502	538	0.8
25560	SCOTT DEPOT	079	7654	8113	8395	0.6	88	2927	3228	3380	1.1	2.50	2277	2450	0.8
25564	SOD	043	2227	2289	2287	0.3	81	902	974	986	0.8	2.35	691	728	0.6
25565	SPURLOCKVILLE	043	675	683	681	0.1	72	255	274	276	0.8	2.49	198	207	0.5
25567	SUMERCO	043	703	699	686	-0.1	57	280	290	289	0.4	2.41	218	221	0.1
25570	WAYNE	099	5524	5415	5291	-0.2	48	2205	2253	2230	0.2	2.38	1625	1607	-0.1
25571	WEST HAMLIN	043	1887	1931	1920	0.2	76	718	764	769	0.7	2.52	547	566	0.4
25573	YAWKEY	043	733	723	712	-0.1	57	309	320	319	0.4	2.26	224	225	0.0
25601	LOGAN	045	10954	10155	9775	-0.8	14	4455	4328	4214	-0.3	2.27	3086	2903	-0.7
25607	AMHERSTDALE	045	2531	2356	2279	-0.8	14	956	947	930	-0.1	2.48	738	713	-0.4
25608	BAISDEN	059	855	809	787	-0.6	25	343	350	345	0.2	2.31	256	253	-0.1
25617	DAVIN	045	2371	2210	2135	-0.8	14	911	902	884	-0.1	2.45	714	689	-0.4
25621	GILBERT	059	3097	2919	2836	-0.6	25	1279	1293	1273	0.1	2.26	953	933	-0.2
25632	LYBURN	045	504	468	452	-0.8	14	192	189	185	-0.2	2.43	136	130	-0.5
25635	MAN	045	3103	2912	2824	-0.7	19	1240	1237	1216	0.0	2.35	915	885	-0.4
25638	OMAR	045	3760	3490	3371	-0.8	14	1448	1427	1397	-0.2	2.44	1114	1069	-0.4
25650	VERNER	059	1161	1092	1062	-0.7	19	463	468	461	0.1	2.33	342	335	-0.2
25651	WHARNCLIFFE	059	379	359	350	-0.6	25	142	145	143	0.2	2.48	108	107	-0.1
25654	YOLYN	045	1086	993	951	-1.0	7	424	410	399	-0.4	2.42	318	299	-0.7
25661	WILLIAMSON	059	6850	6419	6196	-0.7	19	2931	2905	2840	-0.1	2.17	1921	1835	-0.5
25666	BREEDEN	059	625	605	590	-0.4	35	242	251	249	0.4	2.41	187	188	0.1
25669	CRUM	099	754	716	697	-0.6	25	283	282	278	0.0	2.54	210	203	-0.4
25670	DELBARTON	059	5220	5160	5066	-0.1	57	2004	2110	2100	0.6	2.44	1504	1541	0.3
25671	DINGESS	059	1867	1793	1751	-0.4	35	689	711	704	0.3	2.52	531	532	0.0
25674	KERMIT	059	2928	2748	2662	-0.7	19	1123	1120	1101	0.0	2.45	847	821	-0.3
25676	LENORE	059	1592	1502	1462	-0.6	25	609	617	609	0.1	2.43	469	462	-0.2
25678	MATEWAN	059	3252	3091	3000	-0.5	30	1302	1319	1299	0.1	2.34	954	935	-0.2
25699	WILSONDALE	099	923	878	852	-0.5	30	359	359	354	0.0	2.44	273	265	-0.3
25701	HUNTINGTON	011	23911	22731	22381	-0.5	30	11262	10893	10797	-0.4	1.99	5627	5157	-0.9
25702	HUNTINGTON	011	7795	7202	7036	-0.9	10	3470	3269	3216	-0.6	2.18	2114	1894	-1.2
25703	HUNTINGTON	011	5569	5505	5472	-0.1	57	2447	2435	2430	-0.1	2.17	1003	893	-1.2
25704	HUNTINGTON	099	17386	16609	16196	-0.5	30	7286	7178	7070	-0.2	2.30	4959	4728	-0.5
25705	HUNTINGTON	011	21103	19915	19573	-0.6	25	9083	8787	8705	-0.4	2.25	6053	5602	-0.8
25755	HUNTINGTON	011	1491	1599	1598	0.8	90	0	0	0	0.0	0.00	0	0	0.0
25801	BECKLEY	081	36891	37067	37105	0.1	72	15785	16306	16486	0.4	2.23	10340	10300	0.0
25811	AMIGO	109	500	462	442	-0.9	10	225	221	213	-0.2	2.09	157	149	-0.6
25812	ANSTED	019	162	160	158	-0.1	57	65	67	67	0.3	2.39	45	45	0.0
25813	BEAVER	081	5751	5970	6019	0.4	83	1315	1384	1408	0.6	3.51	982	999	0.2
25817	BOLT	081	358	371	376	0.4	83	134	144	148	0.8	2.58	106	111	0.5
25820	CAMP CREEK	055	37	36	36	-0.3	40	14	14	15	0.0	2.57	11	11	0.0
25823	COAL CITY	081	1978	2067	2108	0.5	86	803	869	895	0.9	2.38	600	630	0.5
25825	COOL RIDGE	081	1490	1558	1588	0.5	86	559	605	622	0.9	2.58	439	463	0.6
25827	CRAB ORCHARD	081	5451	5585	5652	0.3	81	2301	2442	2500	0.6	2.29	1622	1661	0.3
25831	DANESE	019	1407	1397	1383	-0.1	57	562	583	583	0.4	2.40	398	398	0.0
25832	DANIELS	081	4436	4572	4612	0.3	81	1894	2013	2058	0.7	1.91	1285	1314	0.2
	WEST VIRGINIA					0.2					0.5	2.33			0.1
	UNITED STATES					1.0					1.1	2.59			0.9

ZIP CODE #	POST OFFICE NAME	RACE (%) White 2000	White 2009	Black 2000	Black 2009	Asian/Pacific 2000	Asian/Pacific 2009	% Hispanic Origin 2000	% Hispanic Origin 2009	2009 AGE DISTRIBUTION (%) 0-4	5-9	10-14	15-19	20-24	25-44	45-64	65-84	85+	18+	MEDIAN AGE 2009	% 2009 Males	% 2009 Females
25405	MARTINSBURG	92.5	91.0	5.2	5.8	0.5	0.8	1.4	1.8	6.7	7.1	7.5	7.0	5.0	27.7	27.2	10.7	1.1	73.9	37.7	50.9	49.1
25411	BERKELEY SPRINGS	98.7	98.5	0.3	0.3	0.1	0.2	0.6	0.8	5.7	5.9	6.3	5.9	4.4	23.2	30.1	16.1	2.4	78.4	43.9	48.7	51.3
25413	BUNKER HILL	96.9	96.4	1.2	1.3	0.3	0.4	1.1	1.4	6.2	6.4	6.8	7.1	5.4	27.8	30.0	9.3	0.9	76.2	39.0	49.3	50.7
25414	CHARLES TOWN	88.7	88.2	8.4	8.2	0.7	1.1	2.0	2.3	6.7	6.5	6.3	6.3	5.9	26.4	27.8	12.2	1.9	76.6	39.7	48.3	51.7
25419	FALLING WATERS	97.3	96.8	0.9	1.0	0.4	0.6	1.1	1.4	5.9	6.0	6.2	6.8	6.0	27.5	30.5	10.3	0.8	77.5	39.5	50.3	49.7
25420	GERRARDSTOWN	96.9	96.4	1.0	1.1	0.2	0.3	1.3	1.7	6.7	6.7	7.0	7.3	5.5	29.6	29.2	7.6	0.5	75.2	37.6	49.6	50.4
25422	GREAT CACAPON	98.6	98.4	0.4	0.4	0.0	0.0	0.6	0.7	4.5	5.1	5.6	5.8	4.4	20.9	34.3	17.5	2.0	81.2	47.6	49.6	50.4
25425	HARPERS FERRY	95.9	95.1	1.7	1.8	0.5	0.8	1.3	1.6	6.3	6.8	7.2	6.2	4.5	26.6	31.6	9.8	1.1	75.7	40.6	50.3	49.7
25427	HEDGESVILLE	97.6	97.1	0.9	1.0	0.2	0.3	0.9	1.1	5.8	6.3	7.2	6.9	5.0	26.3	31.5	10.2	0.7	76.2	40.2	50.4	49.6
25428	INWOOD	95.9	95.2	2.0	2.1	0.4	0.7	1.2	1.4	6.6	6.7	7.0	6.9	5.2	29.1	28.1	9.4	0.9	75.3	38.0	49.7	50.3
25430	KEARNEYSVILLE	91.9	90.6	5.1	5.6	0.4	0.7	2.1	2.6	5.9	6.3	6.8	6.9	5.4	26.2	30.7	10.7	1.0	76.5	39.9	50.5	49.5
25431	LEVELS	99.3	98.8	0.7	0.6	0.0	0.0	0.7	0.6	7.6	7.6	7.6	6.4	4.7	23.4	28.1	12.9	1.8	73.1	39.4	49.7	50.3
25434	PAW PAW	95.5	95.1	3.0	3.1	0.1	0.2	1.5	2.0	6.0	6.2	6.6	6.3	5.4	24.4	28.4	14.9	1.8	77.5	41.3	49.8	50.2
25437	POINTS	99.2	98.6	0.0	0.0	0.0	0.0	0.8	1.4	4.2	4.9	5.6	6.9	4.9	23.6	30.6	17.4	2.1	81.3	45.0	50.0	50.0
25438	RANSON	84.1	83.1	12.3	12.8	0.3	0.5	2.9	3.5	7.2	6.7	6.3	6.6	7.3	28.1	25.7	10.7	1.3	75.9	36.1	48.7	51.3
25442	SHENANDOAH JUNCTION	92.0	91.6	5.3	4.9	0.7	1.2	0.9	1.1	6.2	6.3	6.3	6.3	5.8	26.6	29.8	11.1	1.6	77.2	39.4	49.3	50.7
25443	SHEPHERDSTOWN	89.3	88.3	7.2	7.3	1.4	2.0	1.5	1.7	4.0	3.9	4.1	10.6	12.6	25.2	26.0	11.9	1.8	86.8	34.8	49.1	50.9
25444	SLANESVILLE	98.2	98.1	0.6	0.7	0.0	0.0	0.9	1.1	6.1	6.3	6.8	6.5	5.6	23.6	30.3	13.5	1.3	76.9	41.4	50.6	49.4
25446	SUMMIT POINT	92.8	92.1	5.7	6.0	0.4	0.8	1.2	1.4	6.6	7.1	7.9	6.5	3.8	26.2	32.5	8.6	0.8	74.2	40.6	49.7	50.3
25501	ALKOL	98.5	98.6	0.0	0.0	0.1	0.1	0.5	0.5	5.6	6.0	6.2	6.4	4.5	27.0	30.8	12.0	1.6	78.1	41.1	50.6	49.4
25502	APPLE GROVE	99.1	99.0	0.1	0.1	0.2	0.3	0.7	0.7	5.5	5.7	6.0	6.2	5.0	26.6	31.5	12.4	1.2	79.0	41.4	50.9	49.1
25503	ASHTON	99.2	99.0	0.1	0.1	0.1	0.2	0.7	0.8	5.9	6.3	6.5	6.0	4.3	27.0	31.2	11.6	1.2	77.4	40.6	50.4	49.6
25504	BARBOURSVILLE	98.6	98.2	0.3	0.3	0.4	0.6	0.5	0.6	5.7	5.9	6.1	5.7	5.0	26.3	29.6	13.9	1.8	78.8	41.5	48.2	51.8
25505	BIG CREEK	99.0	99.0	0.0	0.0	0.7	0.7	0.3	0.7	6.6	6.9	7.3	6.6	4.0	31.7	27.4	8.6	1.0	75.2	37.0	50.2	49.8
25506	BRANCHLAND	99.1	99.0	0.0	0.0	0.2	0.3	0.9	0.9	6.1	6.5	6.5	6.7	5.4	26.1	29.0	12.2	1.5	76.8	40.0	49.8	50.2
25508	CHAPMANVILLE	98.3	97.9	0.6	0.6	0.4	0.7	0.5	0.6	5.4	5.9	6.1	6.2	5.3	25.8	31.4	12.3	1.7	78.8	41.4	49.2	50.8
25510	CULLODEN	98.8	98.5	0.3	0.3	0.3	0.4	0.3	0.4	5.6	5.9	6.1	5.6	4.3	26.6	29.6	14.1	2.1	79.0	42.3	49.7	50.3
25511	DUNLOW	98.8	98.7	0.0	0.0	0.0	0.1	0.3	0.4	5.7	7.5	7.9	6.9	4.2	26.4	29.2	11.3	1.0	75.0	38.8	53.2	46.8
25512	EAST LYNN	99.1	99.0	0.1	0.1	0.1	0.1	0.4	0.4	5.7	6.2	6.4	6.3	4.9	25.0	30.1	14.0	1.5	77.8	41.5	51.0	49.0
25514	FORT GAY	98.8	98.6	0.1	0.1	0.1	0.2	0.6	0.7	6.7	6.9	6.9	6.7	5.3	26.8	28.2	11.0	1.6	75.5	38.4	49.7	50.3
25515	GALLIPOLIS FERRY	98.8	98.7	0.0	0.0	0.1	0.1	0.5	0.7	5.7	6.0	5.9	6.4	5.1	26.8	30.7	12.0	1.3	78.3	40.8	49.5	50.5
25517	GENOA	99.0	98.8	0.1	0.1	0.1	0.2	0.3	0.3	6.6	7.3	7.5	7.6	5.6	25.7	27.3	11.3	1.1	73.9	37.5	51.3	48.7
25520	GLENWOOD	99.1	98.9	0.2	0.2	0.1	0.2	0.6	0.8	6.0	6.5	6.8	6.1	4.2	26.6	30.6	11.9	1.3	76.8	40.7	49.9	50.1
25521	GRIFFITHSVILLE	98.9	98.9	0.2	0.2	0.2	0.2	0.2	0.2	7.0	7.5	7.2	5.9	4.3	26.4	28.6	11.4	1.6	74.6	38.5	47.8	52.2
25523	HAMLIN	99.1	99.1	0.1	0.1	0.0	0.0	0.7	0.7	5.3	5.6	6.1	6.3	4.8	25.2	29.2	14.5	3.0	79.4	42.4	47.5	52.5
25524	HARTS	99.1	99.2	0.0	0.0	0.1	0.1	0.2	0.2	5.7	5.9	6.1	8.1	7.3	26.3	29.3	10.0	1.2	77.1	38.5	51.2	48.8
25526	HURRICANE	97.2	96.4	0.8	0.8	1.1	1.7	0.6	0.8	6.8	7.0	7.2	6.5	4.9	26.4	29.3	10.5	1.5	74.8	39.0	48.9	51.1
25529	JULIAN	98.8	98.7	0.1	0.1	0.2	0.2	0.4	0.5	5.8	6.2	6.3	5.5	4.2	25.7	30.7	13.2	2.4	78.1	42.6	49.4	50.6
25530	KENOVA	98.7	98.5	0.1	0.2	0.3	0.4	0.4	0.5	5.2	5.4	5.5	6.1	5.0	24.9	28.6	16.9	2.6	80.0	43.5	46.8	53.2
25534	KIAHSVILLE	98.8	98.8	0.0	0.0	0.0	0.0	0.3	0.3	4.7	7.1	7.8	6.8	3.4	25.8	29.2	14.3	0.9	76.4	40.9	52.2	47.8
25535	LAVALETTE	99.0	98.8	0.1	0.1	0.2	0.4	0.3	0.3	5.8	6.1	6.4	5.6	4.3	26.4	28.9	14.7	1.8	78.1	41.9	50.0	50.0
25537	LESAGE	99.4	99.3	0.1	0.1	0.1	0.1	0.6	0.8	6.1	6.5	6.7	5.8	4.4	26.2	29.2	13.9	1.4	77.0	41.3	49.4	50.6
25540	MIDKIFF	99.2	99.3	0.0	0.0	0.0	0.0	1.6	2.2	7.2	7.2	7.2	6.5	3.6	25.9	27.3	13.7	1.4	74.1	40.2	53.2	46.8
25541	MILTON	99.0	98.8	0.2	0.2	0.2	0.3	0.5	0.6	5.6	5.8	6.1	5.9	4.3	26.6	29.0	14.8	2.0	78.9	42.1	48.6	51.4
25544	MYRA	99.6	99.6	0.0	0.0	0.0	0.0	0.4	0.4	5.1	5.1	6.8	8.5	5.9	24.6	28.4	13.1	2.5	77.5	41.1	51.3	48.7
25545	ONA	98.6	98.4	0.2	0.2	0.4	0.6	0.5	0.6	5.8	6.3	6.6	6.4	4.5	26.2	29.7	13.0	1.5	77.2	41.2	48.8	51.2
25547	PECKS MILL	98.9	98.8	0.0	0.0	0.2	0.2	0.1	0.1	4.6	5.0	4.6	3.7	5.1	24.3	32.9	17.3	2.4	83.5	47.2	48.8	51.2
25550	POINT PLEASANT	97.2	96.6	1.3	1.4	0.6	1.0	0.5	0.6	5.6	5.7	5.8	5.8	5.0	23.7	28.5	17.0	3.0	79.4	43.6	46.9	53.1
25555	PRICHARD	99.1	99.0	0.1	0.1	0.1	0.1	0.2	0.2	6.3	6.3	6.9	6.7	4.6	28.3	27.7	11.7	1.5	76.3	38.8	51.3	48.7
25557	RANGER	99.2	99.1	0.0	0.0	0.0	0.0	0.5	0.5	6.0	6.2	6.7	7.3	5.7	25.9	29.6	11.3	1.2	76.7	39.2	50.3	49.7
25559	SALT ROCK	98.8	98.5	0.2	0.2	0.3	0.5	0.6	0.9	6.0	6.7	6.7	6.6	5.3	27.7	29.9	10.0	1.2	76.6	39.0	49.7	50.3
25560	SCOTT DEPOT	97.8	97.2	0.5	0.5	0.7	1.1	0.6	0.7	5.8	6.2	7.0	7.0	4.6	24.5	31.3	11.7	1.8	76.5	41.4	49.4	50.6
25564	SOD	98.9	99.0	0.2	0.2	0.1	0.1	0.5	0.5	5.2	5.7	5.7	4.9	4.2	26.6	32.7	13.4	1.5	80.4	43.5	49.0	51.0
25565	SPURLOCKVILLE	99.4	99.4	0.0	0.0	0.0	0.0	0.1	0.1	5.6	6.0	6.1	7.5	5.9	26.1	30.0	11.6	1.3	77.6	40.2	51.0	49.0
25567	SUMERCO	97.9	97.9	0.1	0.1	0.4	0.4	0.6	0.4	6.6	7.4	7.3	5.2	3.4	26.2	29.2	13.3	1.4	75.5	40.6	49.8	50.2
25570	WAYNE	98.6	98.4	0.1	0.1	0.2	0.3	0.5	0.6	6.0	6.4	6.4	6.4	4.6	26.1	29.0	13.2	1.9	77.4	40.9	49.0	51.0
25571	WEST HAMLIN	99.3	99.3	0.0	0.0	0.1	0.1	0.7	0.7	6.2	7.5	7.1	6.8	5.5	26.5	27.3	10.7	2.3	75.4	38.0	48.2	51.8
25573	YAWKEY	98.6	98.6	0.0	0.0	0.3	0.3	0.8	1.0	6.4	6.6	6.5	5.8	4.6	26.4	28.6	13.4	1.7	76.8	40.8	48.5	51.5
25601	LOGAN	93.6	93.0	5.1	5.3	0.3	0.4	0.5	0.5	5.1	5.3	5.5	5.8	5.3	25.4	30.3	15.0	2.3	80.6	43.1	48.4	51.6
25607	AMHERSTDALE	97.1	96.9	2.3	2.4	0.0	0.0	0.8	0.9	5.3	6.1	6.2	5.3	4.4	24.9	34.6	11.9	1.2	79.1	43.1	50.0	50.0
25608	BAISDEN	98.8	98.8	0.6	0.6	0.0	0.0	0.0	0.0	5.6	5.2	6.4	7.7	8.4	27.6	29.8	8.7	0.7	78.2	38.3	50.7	49.3
25617	DAVIN	96.9	96.7	2.3	2.4	0.2	0.3	0.4	0.4	5.2	5.6	5.7	5.6	4.8	26.0	31.7	14.1	1.3	80.0	42.8	49.2	50.8
25621	GILBERT	99.1	98.9	0.0	0.0	0.2	0.3	0.5	0.6	6.1	5.9	5.7	6.6	6.2	28.6	29.0	11.1	1.0	78.5	39.4	49.5	50.5
25632	LYBURN	94.8	94.4	4.2	4.5	0.2	0.2	0.6	0.4	5.8	6.2	5.8	4.9	4.1	25.4	31.8	14.1	1.9	79.1	43.3	49.4	50.6
25635	MAN	95.0	94.3	3.3	3.4	0.9	1.4	0.5	0.5	5.8	6.1	6.1	5.3	4.4	26.3	30.8	13.7	1.5	78.7	42.1	49.5	50.5
25638	OMAR	97.6	97.4	1.8	1.9	0.0	0.1	1.0	1.2	5.9	6.1	6.5	6.6	4.7	26.2	30.8	11.9	1.4	77.1	40.6	48.2	51.8
25650	VERNER	99.5	99.5	0.1	0.1	0.1	0.1	0.7	0.8	5.8	5.8	6.6	6.8	5.2	27.2	29.2	12.3	1.2	78.3	40.5	50.3	49.7
25651	WHARNCLIFFE	99.2	99.2	0.3	0.3	0.0	0.0	0.3	0.3	6.1	6.1	6.4	6.7	7.0	27.0	29.8	10.0	0.8	77.2	39.1	51.0	49.0
25654	YOLYN	97.6	97.4	1.9	2.1	0.0	0.0	0.5	0.6	4.9	5.3	5.5	5.4	4.1	24.1	33.2	15.5	1.8	80.8	45.4	50.1	49.9
25661	WILLIAMSON	90.8	90.2	7.3	7.5	0.5	0.8	0.6	0.6	5.1	5.3	5.2	5.8	6.3	23.6	30.9	15.3	2.5	81.0	44.0	47.1	52.9
25666	BREEDEN	98.2	98.2	0.0	0.0	0.2	0.2	0.3	0.3	6.3	7.9	6.9	7.4	7.3	27.1	27.6	8.3	1.2	73.9	34.6	50.7	49.3
25669	CRUM	99.5	99.4	0.3	0.3	0.1	0.1	0.4	0.4	4.1	7.7	8.5	7.0	5.6	28.4	27.4	10.5	1.0	75.7	37.3	51.4	48.6
25670	DELBARTON	97.9	97.8	0.7	0.7	0.1	0.2	0.5	0.6	6.0	6.2	6.3	7.2	5.8	25.9	30.5	10.9	1.4	77.1	40.1	48.8	51.2
25671	DINGESS	98.7	98.4	0.1	0.1	0.2	0.3	0.4	0.4	5.9	7.5	6.9	7.6	6.9	26.8	29.1	8.3	1.1	74.8	35.9	50.0	50.0
25674	KERMIT	98.9	98.7	0.3	0.3	0.2	0.3	0.4	0.5	5.5	6.0	6.5	7.1	6.0	27.2	29.1	11.2	1.3	77.5	39.0	49.2	50.8
25676	LENORE	99.3	99.2	0.1	0.1	0.1	0.1	0.5	0.6	5.3	6.5	6.9	7.9	6.7	27.0	30.0	8.8	0.9	76.6	37.8	49.4	50.6
25678	MATEWAN	95.8	95.4	2.8	3.0	0.1	0.1	0.4	0.5	6.0	6.3	6.4	7.4	6.0	25.9	30.0	10.5	1.5	76.7	39.5	47.8	52.2
25699	WILSONDALE	98.8	98.7	0.5	0.6	0.1	0.1	0.2	0.3	5.0	6.0	6.5	6.6	5.5	26.5	30.0	12.6	1.3	78.4	40.4	49.3	50.7
25701	HUNTINGTON	87.7	86.5	8.9	9.2	1.2	1.8	1.0	1.2	4.4	4.3	4.5	5.8	10.4	25.6	25.6	15.8	3.7	83.8	41.0	48.6	51.4
25702	HUNTINGTON	96.9	96.4	1.3	1.3	0.3	0.5	0.5	0.6	5.4	5.2	5.1	5.7	5.3	26.1	27.7	16.4	3.1	81.0	42.7	46.6	53.4
25703	HUNTINGTON	79.3	78.4	17.3	17.4	0.9	1.5	1.2	1.5	4.1	4.0	3.5	12.2	28.9	20.5	17.2	7.9	1.6	86.1	24.5	47.3	52.7
25704	HUNTINGTON	97.7	97.3	0.6	0.7	0.4	0.6	0.7	0.8	5.8	5.7	5.7	5.7	5.2	26.1	27.6	15.7	2.5	79.4	41.8	47.7	52.3
25705	HUNTINGTON	94.1	93.0	2.8	3.0	1.3	2.1	0.5	0.6	5.9	5.8	5.7	5.4	5.3	26.3	27.5	15.7	2.3	79.4	41.4	47.4	52.6
25755	HUNTINGTON	85.0	83.4	12.5	13.4	0.8	1.2	0.9	1.1	0.0	0.0	0.0	58.8	39.3	1.6	0.3	0.1	0.0	99.7	19.3	44.5	55.5
25801	BECKLEY	84.4	83.4	13.1	13.2	1.2	1.8	0.7	0.8	5.4	5.3	5.6	5.9	5.4	23.9	30.1	15.5	2.9	80.0	43.8	47.0	53.0
25811	AMIGO	95.6	94.8	2.8	3.2	0.4	0.6	0.8	0.9	4.5	5.0	5.4	5.6	4.3	22.9	32.5	17.3	2.4	81.6	46.6	47.8	52.2
25812	ANSTED	97.5	97.5	1.9	1.9	0.0	0.0	1.2	1.3	6.3	6.3	6.3	6.3	4.4	24.4	26.3	17.5	2.5	77.5	42.0	49.4	50.6
25813	BEAVER	87.2	85.9	11.3	12.0	0.8	1.2	2.4	2.9	4.4	4.8	5.1	5.0	6.4	32.5	29.1	11.2	1.4	82.5	39.3	57.7	42.3
25817	BOLT	99.4	99.5	0.0	0.0	0.0	0.0	0.8	0.8	5.4	5.9	5.9	5.9	4.6	25.6	32.9	12.4	1.3	79.0	42.2	49.9	50.1
25820	CAMP CREEK	100.0	100.0	0.0	0.0	0.0	0.0	0.0	0.0	5.6	5.6	5.6	5.6	5.6	22.2	38.9	11.1	0.0	77.8	45.0	47.2	52.8
25823	COAL CITY	98.2	97.9	0.7	0.7	0.1	0.1	0.8	0.9	4.9	5.4	6.1	6.0	4.4	25.0	31.3	14.9	1.9	79.8	43.5	49.1	50.9
25825	COOL RIDGE	98.7	98.5	0.5	0.5	0.2	0.3	0.5	0.5	5.2	5.3	6.5	6.6	5.7	25.6	32.6	10.9	1.5	78.6	41.7	49.4	50.6
25827	CRAB ORCHARD	97.8	97.5	1.0	1.1	0.1	0.3	0.3	0.4	5.2	5.5	6.0	5.9	4.2	26.6	30.4	14.3	1.8	79.5	42.6	47.7	52.3
25831	DANESE	98.7	98.5	0.2	0.2	0.3	0.4	0.5	0.7	6.0	6.0	6.1	5.9	5.2	25.1	30.0	13.9	1.8	78.3	41.9	50.0	50.0
25832	DANIELS	90.8	89.7	7.9	8.5	0.7	1.0	2.0	2.3	4.9	5.1	5.1	4.6	6.4	30.8	26.5	13.8	2.8	82.0	40.1	54.8	45.2
	WEST VIRGINIA	95.0	94.5	3.2	3.3	0.5	0.8	0.7	0.8	5.5	5.6	5.9	6.5	6.1	25.2	29.3	13.8	2.2	79.3	41.5	49.0	51.0
	UNITED STATES	75.1	72.0	12.3	12.7	3.8	4.6	12.5	15.7	6.8	6.7	6.6	7.1	6.9	27.0	26.0	10.9	1.9	75.7	36.9	49.2	50.8

ZIP CODE #	POST OFFICE NAME	2009 Per Capita Income	2009 HH Income Base	2009 HOUSEHOLD INCOME DISTRIBUTION (%) Less than $25,000	$25,000 to $49,999	$50,000 to $99,999	$100,000 to $149,999	$150,000 or More	MEDIAN HOUSEHOLD INCOME 2009	2014	2009 National Centile	2009 State Centile	2009 Home Value Base	2009 HOME VALUE DISTRIBUTION (%) Less than $50,000	$50,000 to $89,999	$90,000 to $174,999	$175,000 to $399,999	$400,000 or More	2009 Median Home Value
25405	MARTINSBURG	22931	4652	18.6	31.1	38.8	8.6	3.0	50221	52299	62	96	3855	13.7	5.0	27.7	50.8	2.8	180522
25411	BERKELEY SPRINGS	22743	5304	23.8	34.1	33.2	6.2	2.6	42733	45063	42	90	4347	11.5	10.4	38.0	35.2	4.8	156020
25413	BUNKER HILL	22793	2671	18.0	28.9	39.1	11.3	2.8	52656	53689	67	97	2215	12.5	6.1	28.7	48.7	4.0	179528
25414	CHARLES TOWN	27180	7008	22.8	22.7	40.3	9.0	5.3	56509	60705	73	98	4921	5.9	5.5	21.8	56.1	10.7	212129
25419	FALLING WATERS	22563	3879	22.2	25.1	42.6	8.2	1.9	52239	53354	66	97	3248	20.7	10.6	18.0	45.6	5.1	176768
25420	GERRARDSTOWN	20351	1448	18.7	33.4	39.2	6.7	2.0	48677	50561	58	96	1183	15.3	11.1	36.9	29.0	7.8	150237
25422	GREAT CACAPON	20183	851	32.8	37.6	27.4	1.4	0.8	37028	37376	24	76	736	15.1	16.7	44.3	21.6	2.3	119444
25425	HARPERS FERRY	28866	5520	16.2	23.6	42.1	11.4	6.6	62231	64846	80	99	4570	4.2	7.0	26.7	50.5	11.6	194765
25427	HEDGESVILLE	22479	5595	20.6	29.3	39.1	8.3	2.7	50042	51420	61	96	4672	13.6	9.1	29.7	38.9	8.8	168649
25428	INWOOD	21585	3645	20.4	31.8	37.2	8.1	2.5	48132	50443	57	95	3014	14.2	3.8	30.8	46.6	4.6	177122
25430	KEARNEYSVILLE	23507	2939	20.1	26.9	40.7	10.0	2.2	52909	54808	68	97	2485	12.9	12.3	28.9	39.6	6.2	165474
25431	LEVELS	17082	71	29.6	38.0	31.0	1.4	0.0	35559	37368	19	68	60	21.7	23.3	46.7	5.0	3.3	97500
25434	PAW PAW	19946	955	28.4	32.7	34.1	2.6	2.2	41866	43389	39	88	770	20.3	29.2	34.7	14.0	1.8	91379
25437	POINTS	21639	61	31.1	34.4	23.0	3.3	8.2	36721	39087	23	75	52	11.5	19.2	53.8	13.5	1.9	111667
25438	RANSON	18927	2279	35.5	26.2	31.7	4.7	1.8	40534	41259	34	85	1461	13.4	10.3	39.8	32.6	3.8	145979
25442	SHENANDOAH JUNCTION	29784	1036	13.2	19.6	39.4	17.4	10.4	70975	75334	87	100	826	5.2	4.4	19.1	51.0	20.3	251235
25443	SHEPHERDSTOWN	31684	2547	17.8	17.5	40.0	13.6	11.1	66993	70695	85	100	1877	1.9	3.0	20.1	51.5	23.5	264409
25444	SLANESVILLE	18169	350	26.3	35.7	32.0	2.9	3.1	41800	42750	39	88	301	17.3	23.6	39.2	17.6	2.3	109115
25446	SUMMIT POINT	27409	549	12.9	24.2	46.8	13.1	2.9	65056	71306	83	99	455	3.5	11.0	20.0	54.9	10.5	227652
25501	ALKOL	11222	646	60.1	25.9	12.5	1.4	0.2	20288	20650	1	3	522	38.9	32.2	21.3	7.5	0.2	62391
25502	APPLE GROVE	18766	651	42.1	25.3	28.0	2.8	1.8	32468	32852	12	52	549	30.4	19.5	35.5	10.6	4.0	90119
25503	ASHTON	17856	374	41.7	26.2	27.0	4.5	0.5	31071	31884	10	44	317	30.3	19.6	31.9	15.1	3.2	90294
25504	BARBOURSVILLE	23866	4827	25.6	28.1	35.4	7.7	3.2	45825	47367	51	93	3749	14.3	21.7	50.7	12.3	1.0	110242
25505	BIG CREEK	17649	112	35.7	24.1	34.8	2.7	2.7	42875	44452	42	90	85	28.2	16.5	31.8	15.3	8.2	103125
25506	BRANCHLAND	14566	1227	46.4	30.3	19.8	2.8	0.7	27450	28633	5	23	950	34.6	28.2	30.2	6.5	0.4	70800
25508	CHAPMANVILLE	18088	4788	42.4	26.7	24.4	4.3	2.2	30682	31283	9	41	3758	22.4	20.8	39.5	15.3	2.0	100643
25510	CULLODEN	21759	1870	23.4	33.0	33.6	7.5	2.5	44209	46198	46	92	1563	19.1	20.2	47.5	11.8	1.3	106830
25511	DUNLOW	13622	266	53.0	26.7	17.3	1.1	1.9	23234	23738	2	8	222	49.5	26.1	21.6	2.7	0.0	51000
25512	EAST LYNN	13755	659	50.7	27.2	19.6	2.4	0.2	24449	25098	3	11	517	38.7	27.5	32.3	1.5	0.0	72556
25514	FORT GAY	14384	1449	42.4	31.3	23.9	2.3	0.2	30633	32618	9	40	1116	34.1	28.7	31.3	5.7	0.3	73021
25515	GALLIPOLIS FERRY	17207	955	40.7	31.1	23.1	2.7	2.3	32264	32706	12	50	802	33.8	16.6	39.8	7.9	2.0	89250
25517	GENOA	14747	949	50.8	26.2	18.7	1.7	2.6	24380	25617	3	11	801	36.5	26.2	32.5	4.9	0.0	72438
25520	GLENWOOD	17424	945	37.9	29.0	27.3	4.9	1.0	33174	33772	14	54	803	27.3	22.9	33.6	13.0	3.2	89531
25521	GRIFFITHSVILLE	15342	242	45.5	25.6	24.8	2.1	2.1	26417	27128	4	18	189	32.3	33.3	29.6	4.8	0.0	74200
25523	HAMLIN	18693	1279	40.7	29.4	23.7	3.2	3.0	31755	32306	11	47	939	18.5	32.5	37.3	10.9	0.9	88516
25524	HARTS	12822	823	49.7	29.0	17.1	4.1	0.0	25122	26311	3	13	669	43.5	32.4	20.2	3.7	0.1	62321
25526	HURRICANE	28627	8172	18.7	21.7	38.2	14.0	7.4	60736	62683	78	99	6634	9.3	12.4	43.2	31.1	4.1	137976
25529	JULIAN	15157	535	42.4	33.1	21.5	2.8	0.2	28728	30134	6	29	412	39.3	25.7	24.0	10.9	0.0	69200
25530	KENOVA	20814	3318	36.0	30.4	26.6	5.1	1.9	34577	36242	17	62	2353	18.4	26.7	44.4	9.8	0.6	97882
25534	KIAHSVILLE	11929	124	54.0	24.2	21.8	0.0	0.0	22953	23647	2	7	100	45.0	28.0	27.0	0.0	0.0	64000
25535	LAVALETTE	19515	1600	32.7	27.9	33.3	5.1	1.0	39935	41305	32	84	1353	19.6	23.9	41.8	13.5	1.2	103409
25537	LESAGE	16497	650	36.0	36.8	22.2	4.8	0.3	33910	34167	15	59	547	28.3	30.7	30.5	8.0	2.4	78716
25540	MIDKIFF	9801	49	55.1	32.7	12.2	0.0	0.0	22630	23825	2	6	41	36.6	14.6	41.5	7.3	0.0	75000
25541	MILTON	20308	3047	28.6	33.6	31.2	4.6	1.9	40328	41932	34	84	2385	23.0	23.6	40.2	11.9	1.3	97837
25544	MYRA	14624	90	38.9	33.3	25.6	2.2	0.0	30537	31169	9	39	69	31.9	29.0	30.4	8.7	0.0	76250
25545	ONA	21417	2131	25.5	27.9	36.5	7.0	3.1	46471	47662	53	94	1803	19.6	19.8	42.3	15.1	3.2	110391
25547	PECKS MILL	16731	363	41.9	23.1	34.2	0.8	0.0	30615	30862	9	40	294	24.5	30.6	37.8	7.1	0.0	84000
25550	POINT PLEASANT	20358	3400	36.9	30.8	24.5	4.7	3.1	34486	34463	16	61	2426	15.0	26.2	42.5	14.8	1.5	103632
25555	PRICHARD	17158	573	31.2	38.0	26.7	2.4	1.6	35937	37532	20	70	470	19.6	36.0	30.9	13.2	0.4	81875
25557	RANGER	12589	1793	51.6	28.5	17.5	1.8	0.5	23485	25378	2	9	1435	45.2	29.5	22.6	2.4	0.3	56150
25559	SALT ROCK	19927	692	25.3	31.9	33.7	8.1	1.0	42953	44870	42	90	599	25.4	24.4	36.9	13.4	0.0	90556
25560	SCOTT DEPOT	29845	3228	14.0	23.2	45.1	11.5	6.1	62149	63723	80	99	2753	8.8	8.5	49.4	30.4	3.0	145636
25564	SOD	18240	974	43.7	23.3	26.0	5.2	1.7	30756	32447	9	42	828	25.5	22.6	38.9	12.6	0.5	95161
25565	SPURLOCKVILLE	12590	274	55.1	25.5	16.1	3.3	0.0	20761	21267	2	4	217	48.4	22.6	23.0	6.0	0.0	52500
25567	SUMERCO	16272	290	41.4	29.0	25.9	3.1	0.7	30409	31685	9	38	238	33.6	30.7	31.9	3.8	0.0	72727
25570	WAYNE	16382	2253	41.9	28.1	25.5	3.5	0.9	30664	32801	9	41	1732	29.3	25.9	36.3	8.1	0.4	83130
25571	WEST HAMLIN	15631	764	43.8	28.7	22.9	3.1	1.4	29168	30850	7	31	559	21.8	39.2	33.8	4.8	0.4	79124
25573	YAWKEY	15189	320	44.7	31.6	21.9	1.6	0.3	26498	27425	4	19	255	32.9	31.4	31.0	4.3	0.4	76786
25601	LOGAN	18881	4328	41.2	29.2	22.4	4.8	2.4	30439	30878	9	38	3090	27.0	28.0	36.1	8.5	0.3	83529
25607	AMHERSTDALE	17581	947	42.0	23.7	29.1	3.4	1.8	31363	32288	10	46	789	33.7	27.0	32.1	7.2	0.0	75189
25608	BAISDEN	14014	350	60.9	20.3	15.4	2.6	0.9	17132	18181	1	1	302	37.1	19.2	38.1	5.6	0.0	80952
25617	DAVIN	14902	902	42.6	32.4	21.5	3.5	0.0	27883	28168	5	25	733	38.7	30.8	24.0	6.0	0.4	65833
25621	GILBERT	16092	1293	43.9	32.6	19.6	2.6	1.3	28349	29164	6	26	1086	39.6	24.1	24.7	11.4	0.2	68246
25632	LYBURN	15632	189	46.6	27.5	21.2	3.2	1.6	26412	27351	4	18	138	29.7	23.9	39.1	6.5	0.7	82857
25635	MAN	17044	1237	45.6	26.6	22.3	3.4	2.1	27350	28181	5	22	935	33.4	27.6	30.7	7.7	0.6	72583
25638	OMAR	13529	1427	50.3	29.4	16.7	3.3	0.3	24817	25733	3	12	1125	33.0	29.3	32.4	4.8	0.5	73702
25650	VERNER	14262	468	52.1	26.3	17.9	1.7	1.9	23560	24752	2	9	373	42.6	25.7	21.7	8.8	1.1	57857
25651	WHARNCLIFFE	12097	145	55.9	27.6	13.1	2.8	0.7	20234	21387	1	3	124	33.9	14.5	41.1	10.5	0.0	92500
25654	YOLYN	19146	410	34.9	29.3	28.5	5.9	1.5	39746	42149	32	83	334	27.2	23.7	36.8	12.3	0.0	88500
25661	WILLIAMSON	18005	2905	47.6	24.8	21.7	3.6	2.2	26848	27832	5	20	2015	27.4	19.8	39.0	13.3	0.6	94492
25666	BREEDEN	13738	251	50.6	26.7	19.1	2.0	1.6	24381	24776	3	11	208	41.3	26.0	26.9	5.8	0.0	62500
25669	CRUM	17681	282	55.3	28.7	9.9	2.8	3.2	20503	21804	2	4	241	40.2	14.1	39.8	5.8	0.0	76538
25670	DELBARTON	15111	2110	45.9	31.8	18.1	2.9	1.3	27298	28164	5	22	1671	27.8	29.7	32.3	9.6	0.7	79790
25671	DINGESS	13762	711	50.1	27.6	18.3	3.1	1.0	24937	25901	3	13	582	38.5	21.8	31.3	8.4	0.0	71351
25674	KERMIT	13192	1120	53.1	25.3	20.0	0.9	0.7	22248	23835	2	5	879	36.5	28.6	29.9	4.8	0.2	71250
25676	LENORE	14918	617	48.8	29.2	17.5	3.6	1.0	25822	26905	4	16	501	33.7	18.4	35.9	12.0	0.0	86818
25678	MATEWAN	14786	1319	52.7	25.8	18.7	1.7	1.1	23139	24604	2	8	968	29.6	30.1	33.4	6.6	0.3	76579
25699	WILSONDALE	13587	359	52.9	25.6	19.5	1.4	0.6	22900	23577	2	7	289	43.9	27.3	27.0	1.7	0.0	60313
25701	HUNTINGTON	23856	10893	41.7	24.6	24.5	5.4	3.8	32934	33630	13	53	5697	10.6	26.9	43.4	16.9	2.3	110054
25702	HUNTINGTON	17370	3269	43.1	31.6	22.9	1.7	1.2	29109	29785	7	31	2038	26.2	39.6	27.8	6.1	0.2	73561
25703	HUNTINGTON	13970	2435	61.2	21.3	13.9	2.3	1.3	18075	17993	1	2	839	31.0	42.9	24.0	1.5	0.6	66238
25704	HUNTINGTON	19614	7178	36.6	29.5	27.6	4.2	2.2	34770	35968	17	63	4976	17.9	32.3	41.7	7.0	1.1	89810
25705	HUNTINGTON	27041	8787	28.4	26.4	30.8	7.8	6.6	44033	46322	45	92	6097	10.0	28.0	46.5	13.4	2.1	109102
25755	HUNTINGTON	6957	0	0.0	0.0	0.0	0.0	0.0	0	0	0	0	0	0.0	0.0	0.0	0.0	0.0	0
25801	BECKLEY	21944	16306	35.4	28.4	27.2	5.6	3.3	37031	38120	24	76	11650	16.6	22.3	41.2	17.6	2.3	107674
25811	AMIGO	22207	221	40.7	28.1	22.2	5.9	3.2	30126	30317	8	35	184	45.1	29.9	22.8	1.6	0.5	55625
25812	ANSTED	18362	67	40.3	34.3	17.9	4.5	3.0	32311	31882	12	50	53	41.5	32.1	24.5	1.9	0.0	61000
25813	BEAVER	13697	1384	24.7	29.6	37.6	6.1	2.0	44461	45892	47	92	1145	13.1	13.7	37.7	31.9	3.6	138579
25817	BOLT	21699	144	27.1	31.9	31.9	6.3	2.8	41742	45000	38	87	122	18.0	23.8	38.5	17.2	2.5	105882
25820	CAMP CREEK	14028	14	42.9	21.4	35.7	0.0	0.0	35000	42343	18	66	12	8.3	16.7	58.3	16.7	0.0	116667
25823	COAL CITY	16959	869	40.5	29.3	24.9	5.3	0.0	31107	32333	10	45	728	34.3	27.5	33.0	4.8	0.4	72931
25825	COOL RIDGE	16076	605	39.3	32.4	23.0	4.0	1.3	31982	32630	11	49	518	28.8	20.1	31.5	15.1	4.6	91875
25827	CRAB ORCHARD	19215	2442	39.5	28.4	27.8	2.8	1.4	31753	31613	11	47	1913	28.4	30.8	35.0	5.0	0.7	77363
25831	DANESE	13136	583	47.3	32.8	18.9	1.0	0.0	26251	26980	4	17	498	38.6	28.7	25.1	7.4	0.2	63235
25832	DANIELS	24780	2013	32.0	31.7	28.4	4.2	3.7	36874	37729	23	75	1582	22.6	16.8	38.7	18.3	3.5	109255
	WEST VIRGINIA	20563		34.3	29.3	28.3	5.4	2.7	37099	38541				22.0	23.9	36.4	15.5	2.2	98135
	UNITED STATES	27277		20.9	24.4	35.3	11.7	7.6	54719	56938				9.3	13.1	31.6	32.6	13.5	162279

ZIP CODE #	POST OFFICE NAME	FINANCIAL SERVICES: Auto Loan	Home Loan	Invest-ments	Retire-ment Plans	THE HOME: Home Improvements: Home Repair	Lawn & Garden	Furnishings: Comput-ers & Hard-ware-Personal	Major Appli-ances	TV, Radio, Sound Equip-ment	Furni-ture	ENTERTAINMENT: Dine out/ Carry out	Sports Equip-ment	Fees & Tickets	Toys & Games	Travel	Cable TV	PERSONAL: Apparel & Services	Auto Repairs	Health Insur-ance	Pets & Supplies
25405	MARTINSBURG	92	87	78	85	85	89	82	86	84	84	84	63	79	87	79	87	58	84	87	102
25411	BERKELEY SPRINGS	88	69	85	68	71	91	71	84	77	66	76	63	61	78	69	84	51	79	90	100
25413	BUNKER HILL	94	91	80	89	88	92	84	89	86	87	86	66	82	89	83	88	59	86	89	105
25414	CHARLES TOWN	88	94	89	95	93	92	93	91	92	92	92	70	96	92	94	92	65	92	92	107
25419	FALLING WATERS	92	84	75	81	81	86	80	84	83	83	83	62	75	86	76	85	56	82	84	100
25420	GERRARDSTOWN	88	81	73	79	79	84	76	81	79	79	79	60	72	83	73	82	54	79	82	97
25422	GREAT CACAPON	79	56	80	55	59	81	59	75	66	54	64	56	47	65	58	73	43	69	79	88
25425	HARPERS FERRY	104	108	103	110	107	110	100	106	100	101	100	81	102	102	103	102	70	102	105	124
25427	HEDGESVILLE	94	84	89	83	85	94	81	90	84	80	83	67	75	85	80	87	57	86	91	106
25428	INWOOD	90	83	74	81	81	85	79	83	81	82	81	61	75	85	75	84	55	81	83	99
25430	KEARNEYSVILLE	99	86	83	85	85	96	84	92	88	84	87	68	76	91	80	92	59	88	94	109
25431	LEVELS	73	53	75	51	55	75	54	69	60	50	59	52	43	60	53	66	39	63	71	82
25434	PAW PAW	84	60	79	58	61	84	64	77	71	59	69	58	51	71	60	78	46	72	83	92
25437	POINTS	91	65	93	63	68	92	67	85	74	62	73	64	53	74	66	82	48	78	88	101
25438	RANSON	68	61	55	61	59	64	67	64	68	64	67	50	62	69	61	70	47	66	68	77
25442	SHENANDOAH JUNCTION	113	127	119	128	125	118	117	116	114	121	115	91	125	116	122	112	82	115	112	136
25443	SHEPHERDSTOWN	111	122	117	125	121	115	117	114	114	119	115	89	124	115	120	112	82	114	112	134
25444	SLANESVILLE	85	61	77	60	62	83	63	76	70	61	69	58	51	72	60	77	46	71	80	92
25446	SUMMIT POINT	98	109	95	112	106	108	98	102	96	98	97	80	104	99	103	97	68	98	101	120
25501	ALKOL	49	32	47	30	32	48	34	43	40	33	39	34	26	40	32	44	26	41	46	53
25502	APPLE GROVE	82	56	75	53	55	80	59	72	67	56	65	56	45	69	54	74	44	68	76	88
25503	ASHTON	78	55	74	53	55	77	57	70	64	54	63	54	45	65	54	70	42	66	74	85
25504	BARBOURSVILLE	87	82	84	81	82	93	79	87	83	77	82	64	76	83	79	87	56	83	93	102
25505	BIG CREEK	77	69	64	67	68	73	66	71	69	68	69	52	62	72	63	71	47	69	72	85
25506	BRANCHLAND	65	43	63	40	42	64	45	57	52	43	51	45	34	53	42	58	34	54	60	70
25508	CHAPMANVILLE	76	55	75	53	56	77	58	71	65	55	63	53	47	65	56	71	42	67	75	85
25510	CULLODEN	95	72	93	70	73	95	72	88	79	69	78	66	60	79	71	86	52	82	91	105
25511	DUNLOW	64	42	62	39	42	63	45	56	51	42	50	44	33	52	42	57	33	53	59	69
25512	EAST LYNN	60	40	56	38	40	59	42	53	49	41	48	41	32	50	39	54	32	50	56	65
25514	FORT GAY	67	45	63	43	45	66	48	59	55	46	53	46	36	56	44	61	35	56	62	73
25515	GALLIPOLIS FERRY	76	52	68	49	52	73	55	66	62	53	61	51	42	64	50	68	40	63	70	81
25517	GENOA	71	46	69	44	46	70	50	63	57	47	56	49	37	58	46	64	37	59	66	77
25520	GLENWOOD	77	56	70	55	57	76	58	70	64	55	63	53	47	66	55	70	42	65	73	84
25521	GRIFFITHSVILLE	74	48	71	45	48	72	51	65	59	49	58	51	38	60	48	66	38	61	68	80
25523	HAMLIN	77	54	77	51	55	78	57	72	64	53	63	54	45	64	55	71	42	67	76	86
25524	HARTS	61	40	59	38	40	60	43	54	49	41	48	42	32	50	40	55	32	51	57	66
25526	HURRICANE	108	108	103	107	106	111	101	107	102	102	102	81	101	104	102	104	71	103	108	126
25529	JULIAN	67	44	65	41	44	66	47	59	54	45	53	46	35	55	44	61	35	56	63	73
25530	KENOVA	74	58	70	58	59	76	63	72	68	57	66	54	53	67	60	73	44	68	78	84
25534	KIAHSVILLE	58	38	56	35	37	56	40	51	46	38	45	39	30	47	37	52	30	48	54	62
25535	LAVALETTE	81	61	78	59	62	80	62	75	68	59	67	56	51	68	60	74	44	70	78	89
25537	LESAGE	74	52	69	50	53	73	54	67	61	52	59	51	43	62	51	67	40	62	70	80
25540	MIDKIFF	52	34	50	32	34	51	36	45	42	34	41	35	27	42	34	46	27	43	48	56
25541	MILTON	80	64	80	62	65	83	65	78	70	61	69	58	56	70	64	76	46	73	82	92
25544	MYRA	71	46	69	44	46	70	50	63	57	47	56	49	37	58	46	64	37	59	66	77
25545	ONA	86	81	83	80	80	90	77	84	80	76	79	64	74	81	78	83	55	80	86	99
25547	PECKS MILL	66	47	66	46	49	68	52	64	58	46	55	48	41	57	50	63	37	59	69	75
25550	POINT PLEASANT	67	60	64	60	60	72	62	67	67	58	65	50	58	65	61	71	45	66	75	79
25555	PRICHARD	77	55	66	54	55	74	57	68	64	56	62	52	46	66	53	69	42	64	71	82
25557	RANGER	58	38	56	36	38	57	41	51	47	39	46	40	30	48	38	52	30	48	54	63
25559	SALT ROCK	86	69	77	67	69	83	68	78	74	69	73	58	60	76	65	78	49	74	80	94
25560	SCOTT DEPOT	103	118	104	118	113	116	103	108	104	105	104	82	112	106	110	105	73	105	110	126
25564	SOD	78	53	78	51	54	78	56	71	63	53	62	54	43	64	54	70	41	66	74	86
25565	SPURLOCKVILLE	58	38	56	36	38	57	41	51	47	39	46	40	30	48	38	52	30	48	54	63
25567	SUMERCO	72	48	71	46	48	71	51	64	58	48	57	50	39	59	48	65	38	60	68	79
25570	WAYNE	72	49	69	47	49	71	51	64	58	49	57	49	40	59	49	64	38	60	68	78
25571	WEST HAMLIN	73	48	71	45	48	72	51	64	59	49	58	50	38	60	48	66	38	61	68	79
25573	YAWKEY	64	42	62	39	41	63	45	56	51	42	50	44	33	52	42	57	33	53	59	69
25601	LOGAN	73	55	72	53	56	75	58	69	65	54	63	52	49	64	56	71	42	66	75	82
25607	AMHERSTDALE	81	53	78	50	53	80	57	71	65	54	64	56	43	66	53	73	42	67	75	88
25608	BAISDEN	60	39	58	37	39	59	42	53	48	40	47	41	31	49	39	54	31	50	56	65
25617	DAVIN	68	44	65	42	44	67	47	60	55	45	53	47	35	56	44	61	35	56	63	73
25621	GILBERT	68	44	65	41	44	66	47	59	54	45	53	46	35	55	44	61	35	56	63	73
25632	LYBURN	70	47	69	45	48	70	50	63	57	47	56	48	39	57	48	63	37	59	67	76
25635	MAN	73	50	73	48	51	73	52	66	59	49	58	51	40	60	50	66	38	62	69	80
25638	OMAR	60	41	58	39	41	59	43	53	49	41	48	41	34	50	41	54	32	50	56	65
25650	VERNER	62	40	60	38	40	61	43	54	50	41	49	42	32	51	40	56	32	51	57	67
25651	WHARNCLIFFE	56	36	54	34	36	55	39	49	45	37	44	38	29	46	36	50	29	46	52	60
25654	YOLYN	82	58	83	57	61	84	61	77	68	56	66	58	49	67	60	75	44	71	81	92
25661	WILLIAMSON	64	48	61	47	48	63	54	60	59	50	58	45	45	58	50	64	39	59	66	72
25666	BREEDEN	62	40	59	38	40	60	43	54	50	41	48	42	32	50	40	55	32	51	57	67
25669	CRUM	84	54	81	51	54	82	58	73	67	55	66	57	44	68	54	75	43	69	78	90
25670	DELBARTON	69	45	66	42	45	67	48	60	55	46	54	47	36	56	45	62	36	57	64	74
25671	DINGESS	65	42	62	40	42	63	45	57	52	43	51	44	34	53	42	58	34	53	60	70
25674	KERMIT	60	39	58	37	39	59	42	53	48	40	47	41	31	49	39	54	31	50	56	65
25676	LENORE	68	44	65	41	44	66	47	59	54	45	53	46	35	55	44	61	35	56	63	73
25678	MATEWAN	64	42	62	40	42	63	45	57	52	43	51	44	34	53	42	58	34	53	60	70
25699	WILSONDALE	62	40	60	38	40	61	43	54	50	41	48	42	32	51	40	55	32	51	57	67
25701	HUNTINGTON	72	58	63	60	59	68	74	68	74	66	73	53	64	72	65	76	51	72	74	82
25702	HUNTINGTON	59	46	55	46	47	60	53	58	57	47	55	43	45	56	49	61	38	57	64	68
25703	HUNTINGTON	46	29	28	32	28	33	55	37	50	43	50	34	40	49	38	49	35	46	40	48
25704	HUNTINGTON	70	59	67	58	60	72	62	69	66	58	65	51	56	66	60	71	44	67	75	81
25705	HUNTINGTON	90	82	86	83	84	94	85	90	89	82	87	66	81	88	84	93	60	89	98	105
25755	HUNTINGTON	0	0	0	0	0	0	0	0	0	0	0	0	0	0	0	0	0	0	0	0
25801	BECKLEY	76	64	74	64	66	80	67	75	73	64	71	55	61	71	66	78	48	73	83	88
25811	AMIGO	78	57	79	55	59	82	62	76	69	55	66	57	49	68	60	76	44	71	83	89
25812	ANSTED	74	53	74	52	55	77	58	72	65	52	63	54	47	64	56	72	42	67	78	84
25813	BEAVER	85	73	84	73	74	90	72	84	77	68	75	64	66	77	73	81	51	79	87	99
25817	BOLT	100	72	102	69	74	101	73	93	82	68	80	70	59	81	72	90	53	86	97	111
25820	CAMP CREEK	65	46	64	45	48	65	48	60	53	45	52	45	38	53	46	58	34	55	62	71
25823	COAL CITY	71	50	72	48	52	72	53	67	59	49	58	50	42	59	52	66	38	62	71	79
25825	COOL RIDGE	74	53	76	51	55	73	55	68	61	52	59	52	44	61	54	66	40	63	70	81
25827	CRAB ORCHARD	76	55	76	54	57	78	58	72	65	53	63	54	47	64	57	71	42	67	77	86
25831	DANESE	58	38	57	36	39	57	41	52	47	39	46	40	31	48	39	52	30	48	54	63
25832	DANIELS	93	67	94	65	69	96	71	89	79	64	77	66	57	78	69	87	51	82	95	105
	WEST VIRGINIA	79	63	76	62	64	80	66	75	71	63	70	57	58	71	64	77	47	72	80	90
	UNITED STATES	100	100	100	100	100	100	100	100	100	100	100	100	100	100	100	100	100	100	100	100

25837-26180

ZIP CODE #	POST OFFICE NAME	COUNTY FIPS CODE	POPULATION 2000	POPULATION 2009	POPULATION 2014	2000-2009 ANNUAL RATE % Rate	2000-2009 ANNUAL RATE State Centile	HOUSEHOLDS 2000	HOUSEHOLDS 2009	HOUSEHOLDS 2014	HOUSEHOLDS % Annual Rate 2000-2009	HOUSEHOLDS 2009 Average HH Size	FAMILIES 2000	FAMILIES 2009	FAMILIES % Annual Rate 2000-2009
25837	EDMOND	019	104	103	102	-0.1	57	36	37	37	0.3	2.78	27	27	0.0
25839	FAIRDALE	081	326	338	343	0.4	83	126	135	139	0.7	2.50	100	105	0.5
25840	FAYETTEVILLE	019	7725	7800	7737	0.1	72	3110	3271	3283	0.5	2.36	2214	2253	0.2
25841	FLAT TOP	055	722	709	703	-0.2	48	290	298	299	0.3	2.37	223	223	0.0
25843	GHENT	081	970	1015	1035	0.5	86	408	442	455	0.9	2.30	321	339	0.6
25844	GLEN DANIEL	081	2301	2372	2405	0.3	81	881	941	965	0.7	2.52	678	703	0.4
25845	GLEN FORK	109	304	282	270	-0.8	14	129	128	124	-0.1	2.20	91	87	-0.5
25848	GLEN ROGERS	109	400	371	354	-0.8	14	144	141	137	-0.2	2.63	113	108	-0.5
25854	HICO	019	703	683	673	-0.3	40	286	290	289	0.2	2.36	215	211	-0.2
25857	JOSEPHINE	081	376	382	385	0.2	76	144	151	154	0.5	2.53	109	111	0.2
25862	LANSING	019	91	89	88	-0.2	48	38	39	39	0.3	2.28	26	26	0.0
25864	LAYLAND	081	83	84	84	0.1	72	31	32	33	0.3	2.63	23	23	0.0
25865	LESTER	081	1019	1044	1058	0.3	81	422	448	458	0.6	2.33	310	318	0.3
25868	LOOKOUT	019	290	282	278	-0.3	40	116	118	117	0.2	2.39	86	85	-0.1
25870	MABEN	109	368	342	328	-0.8	14	145	143	138	-0.2	2.38	104	99	-0.5
25876	SAULSVILLE	109	623	573	546	-0.9	10	250	244	235	-0.3	2.34	193	183	-0.6
25880	MOUNT HOPE	019	8901	8837	8798	-0.1	57	3488	3582	3605	0.3	2.37	2464	2450	-0.1
25882	MULLENS	109	2432	2344	2280	-0.4	35	1051	1063	1047	0.1	2.16	711	695	-0.2
25901	OAK HILL	019	15278	15090	14861	-0.1	57	6311	6427	6395	0.2	2.30	4298	4232	-0.2
25902	ODD	081	553	562	565	0.2	76	207	217	221	0.5	2.59	156	159	0.2
25908	PRINCEWICK	081	355	362	365	0.2	76	150	159	162	0.6	2.28	108	111	0.3
25913	RAVENCLIFF	109	1278	1197	1145	-0.7	19	481	476	462	-0.1	2.51	375	363	-0.4
25915	RHODELL	081	1128	1134	1134	0.1	72	426	443	447	0.4	2.56	315	317	0.1
25917	SCARBRO	019	1293	1298	1287	0.0	65	526	548	549	0.4	2.37	373	376	0.1
25918	SHADY SPRING	081	4897	5110	5158	0.5	86	2008	2161	2216	0.8	1.92	1474	1535	0.4
25920	SLAB FORK	081	850	876	889	0.3	81	339	362	371	0.7	2.42	267	278	0.4
25922	SPANISHBURG	055	1025	1006	998	-0.2	48	385	394	396	0.3	2.55	289	288	0.0
25928	STEPHENSON	109	264	242	231	-0.9	10	106	103	100	-0.3	2.35	77	73	-0.6
25932	SURVEYOR	081	295	300	302	0.2	76	128	134	137	0.5	2.24	93	94	0.1
25936	THURMOND	019	14	14	14	0.0	65	9	9	9	0.0	1.56	6	5	-2.0
25938	VICTOR	019	2372	2367	2342	0.0	65	925	959	959	0.4	2.42	680	684	0.1
25951	HINTON	089	5856	5581	5414	-0.5	30	2552	2537	2493	-0.1	2.16	1621	1546	-0.5
25958	CHARMCO	025	638	637	618	0.0	65	263	275	270	0.5	2.24	182	184	0.1
25962	RAINELLE	025	3778	3538	3420	-0.7	19	1613	1566	1529	-0.3	2.22	1089	1018	-0.7
25965	ELTON	089	207	206	203	-0.1	57	81	85	85	0.5	2.42	57	58	0.2
25966	GREEN SULPHUR SPRING	089	680	674	663	-0.1	57	292	305	304	0.5	2.21	205	206	0.1
25969	JUMPING BRANCH	089	1144	1145	1128	0.0	65	466	489	488	0.5	2.32	354	362	0.2
25971	LERONA	055	1048	1012	998	-0.4	35	411	416	416	0.1	2.41	313	308	-0.2
25976	MEADOW BRIDGE	019	1655	1729	1733	0.5	86	678	739	749	0.9	2.34	498	527	0.6
25977	MEADOW CREEK	089	192	191	188	-0.1	57	84	88	88	0.5	2.17	59	60	0.2
25978	NIMITZ	089	603	604	595	0.0	65	241	253	253	0.5	2.36	184	188	0.2
25979	PIPESTEM	089	592	588	579	-0.1	57	244	255	254	0.5	2.31	183	186	0.2
25981	QUINWOOD	025	1708	1701	1653	0.0	65	699	726	714	0.4	2.34	528	531	0.1
25984	RUPERT	025	1500	1521	1518	0.2	76	609	644	650	0.6	2.35	410	417	0.2
25985	SANDSTONE	089	428	420	411	-0.2	48	194	200	199	0.3	2.10	132	132	0.0
25986	SPRING DALE	019	97	104	105	0.8	90	42	47	48	1.2	2.21	31	33	0.7
25989	WHITE OAK	081	462	491	501	0.7	89	184	201	208	1.0	2.24	143	152	0.7
26003	WHEELING	069	47020	43963	42389	-0.7	19	19541	18809	18231	-0.4	2.21	12091	11186	-0.8
26031	BENWOOD	051	2395	2324	2259	-0.3	40	1007	1005	986	0.0	2.31	664	641	-0.4
26032	BETHANY	009	1092	1048	1018	-0.4	35	225	218	210	-0.3	2.82	150	139	-0.8
26033	CAMERON	051	2640	2465	2370	-0.7	19	1047	1005	977	-0.4	2.39	732	680	-0.8
26034	CHESTER	029	6050	5670	5460	-0.7	19	2469	2409	2347	-0.3	2.32	1740	1645	-0.6
26035	COLLIERS	009	2288	2087	1985	-1.0	7	889	855	824	-0.4	2.44	686	644	-0.7
26036	DALLAS	051	819	741	705	-1.1	6	310	291	280	-0.7	2.55	241	220	-1.0
26037	FOLLANSBEE	009	7434	6811	6481	-0.9	10	3051	2922	2815	-0.5	2.28	2142	1990	-0.8
26038	GLEN DALE	051	3271	3117	3012	-0.5	30	1366	1353	1322	-0.1	2.30	999	960	-0.4
26039	GLEN EASTON	051	1963	1824	1751	-0.8	14	705	682	662	-0.4	2.66	554	524	-0.6
26040	MCMECHEN	051	1937	1764	1682	-1.0	7	865	819	790	-0.6	2.14	560	509	-1.0
26041	MOUNDSVILLE	051	17703	16685	16092	-0.6	25	7076	6876	6692	-0.3	2.32	4931	4636	-0.7
26047	NEW CUMBERLAND	029	6518	5869	5578	-1.1	6	2662	2516	2422	-0.6	2.33	1946	1787	-0.9
26050	NEWELL	029	2502	2222	2098	-1.3	2	1029	947	904	-0.9	2.35	698	619	-1.3
26055	PROCTOR	103	1720	1563	1492	-1.0	7	645	612	590	-0.6	2.55	500	462	-0.9
26059	TRIADELPHIA	069	2607	2418	2318	-0.8	14	1047	1011	978	-0.4	2.38	767	715	-0.8
26060	VALLEY GROVE	069	1736	1605	1540	-0.8	14	665	643	622	-0.4	2.30	468	435	-0.8
26062	WEIRTON	029	21526	20393	19675	-0.6	25	9393	9252	9038	-0.2	2.18	6227	5914	-0.6
26070	WELLSBURG	009	10704	9967	9550	-0.8	14	4356	4220	4089	-0.3	2.29	3074	2887	-0.7
26101	PARKERSBURG	107	31120	29538	28853	-0.6	25	13131	12742	12544	-0.3	2.27	8404	7825	-0.8
26104	PARKERSBURG	107	17497	17946	18031	0.3	81	7489	7885	7988	0.6	2.22	4872	4944	0.2
26105	VIENNA	107	12299	12296	12181	0.0	65	5297	5446	5445	0.3	2.22	3559	3506	-0.2
26133	BELLEVILLE	107	1205	1293	1322	0.8	90	441	491	506	1.2	2.63	355	386	0.9
26134	BELMONT	073	1567	1205	1121	-2.8	0	601	469	439	-2.6	2.44	451	344	-2.9
26136	BIG BEND	013	837	808	788	-0.4	35	337	341	336	0.1	2.37	243	238	-0.2
26137	BIG SPRINGS	021	681	647	631	-0.6	25	269	267	263	-0.1	2.42	195	187	-0.5
26138	BROHARD	105	6	6	5	0.0	65	3	3	3	0.0	2.00	2	2	0.0
26141	CRESTON	105	358	342	336	-0.5	30	142	140	139	-0.2	2.42	101	97	-0.4
26142	DAVISVILLE	107	2428	2517	2535	0.4	83	903	964	981	0.7	2.61	705	735	0.5
26143	ELIZABETH	105	3382	3167	3071	-0.7	19	1325	1277	1249	-0.4	2.46	978	915	-0.7
26146	FRIENDLY	095	932	913	894	-0.2	48	365	373	370	0.2	2.45	279	277	-0.1
26147	GRANTSVILLE	013	1739	1691	1667	-0.3	40	722	730	729	0.1	2.30	502	491	-0.2
26148	MACFARLAN	085	468	460	452	-0.2	48	193	197	195	0.2	2.34	142	141	-0.1
26149	MIDDLEBOURNE	095	2762	2637	2561	-0.5	30	1097	1093	1073	0.0	2.40	810	784	-0.4
26150	MINERAL WELLS	107	5767	5839	5852	0.1	72	2199	2299	2325	0.5	2.54	1720	1748	0.2
26151	MOUNT ZION	013	227	222	220	-0.2	48	101	103	103	0.2	2.14	70	69	-0.2
26152	MUNDAY	105	157	146	141	-0.8	14	61	59	57	-0.4	2.47	45	42	-0.7
26155	NEW MARTINSVILLE	103	6961	6679	6490	-0.4	35	2871	2860	2808	0.0	2.28	1974	1900	-0.4
26159	PADEN CITY	103	3368	3200	3079	-0.6	25	1380	1354	1318	-0.2	2.35	1012	965	-0.5
26160	PALESTINE	105	933	862	832	-0.9	10	359	343	334	-0.5	2.51	268	249	-0.8
26161	PETROLEUM	085	469	461	453	-0.2	48	183	186	185	0.2	2.48	134	132	-0.2
26164	RAVENSWOOD	035	7818	7333	7139	-0.7	19	3165	3086	3039	-0.3	2.33	2257	2126	-0.6
26167	READER	103	2199	2012	1917	-1.0	7	855	814	785	-0.5	2.47	639	593	-0.8
26169	ROCKPORT	107	1108	1125	1125	0.2	76	404	420	424	0.4	2.68	326	331	0.2
26170	SAINT MARYS	073	5423	5631	5563	0.4	83	2092	2237	2224	0.7	2.43	1533	1595	0.4
26175	SISTERSVILLE	095	3560	3399	3301	-0.5	30	1436	1418	1391	-0.1	2.35	1029	987	-0.4
26178	SMITHVILLE	085	562	553	544	-0.2	48	224	228	227	0.2	2.43	165	164	-0.1
26180	WALKER	107	3565	3942	4040	1.1	91	1338	1530	1584	1.5	2.54	1025	1140	1.2
	WEST VIRGINIA					0.2					0.5	2.33			0.1
	UNITED STATES					1.0					1.1	2.59			0.9

ZIP CODE #	POST OFFICE NAME	RACE (%) White 2000	White 2009	Black 2000	Black 2009	Asian/Pacific 2000	Asian/Pacific 2009	% Hispanic Origin 2000	% Hispanic Origin 2009	2009 AGE DISTRIBUTION (%) 0-4	5-9	10-14	15-19	20-24	25-44	45-64	65-84	85+	18+	MEDIAN AGE 2009	% 2009 Males	% 2009 Females
25837	EDMOND	100.0	100.0	0.0	0.0	0.0	0.0	0.0	0.0	5.8	5.8	5.8	4.9	4.9	24.3	35.0	11.7	1.9	78.6	43.8	49.5	50.5
25839	FAIRDALE	99.7	99.4	0.0	0.0	0.0	0.0	0.9	0.9	5.3	5.9	5.9	5.9	4.7	25.4	33.4	11.8	1.5	79.3	42.3	48.8	51.2
25840	FAYETTEVILLE	96.4	96.0	2.6	2.8	0.1	0.2	0.6	0.7	5.3	5.5	5.8	5.9	4.9	24.3	31.5	14.5	2.2	79.7	43.6	49.1	50.9
25841	FLAT TOP	99.6	99.4	0.0	0.0	0.1	0.1	0.3	0.3	5.6	6.5	6.6	4.9	3.5	25.8	31.2	14.0	1.8	77.9	42.8	48.7	51.3
25843	GHENT	99.3	98.9	0.1	0.2	0.3	0.5	0.4	0.4	5.2	5.0	5.5	6.1	5.3	24.5	35.1	11.6	1.6	80.2	43.8	49.8	50.2
25844	GLEN DANIEL	96.7	96.5	2.6	2.7	0.0	0.0	0.5	0.6	5.5	5.9	6.2	5.8	4.7	26.0	32.5	11.9	1.5	78.8	41.7	49.9	50.1
25845	GLEN FORK	99.0	98.6	0.0	0.0	0.3	0.4	0.3	0.7	5.0	5.7	5.7	5.0	4.6	21.3	34.8	16.3	1.8	80.1	46.9	48.6	51.4
25848	GLEN ROGERS	98.7	98.7	1.0	1.1	0.0	0.0	0.3	0.3	5.9	6.5	6.5	7.0	6.5	25.3	31.3	10.0	1.1	76.8	40.4	50.4	49.6
25854	HICO	99.3	99.3	0.1	0.1	0.0	0.0	0.9	1.0	5.0	5.7	6.0	5.6	3.8	25.0	32.7	14.2	2.0	79.9	44.1	49.9	50.1
25857	JOSEPHINE	95.7	95.3	2.7	2.9	0.0	0.0	0.8	1.0	6.0	6.3	7.6	7.1	5.8	26.2	29.3	10.5	1.3	75.4	38.9	49.5	50.5
25862	LANSING	98.9	98.9	0.0	0.0	0.0	0.0	0.0	0.0	5.6	5.6	5.6	6.7	6.7	24.7	28.1	14.6	2.2	78.7	40.5	51.7	48.3
25864	LAYLAND	94.0	94.0	4.8	4.8	0.0	0.0	1.2	1.2	4.8	6.0	6.0	4.8	4.8	23.8	34.5	14.3	1.2	78.6	45.0	47.6	52.4
25865	LESTER	92.9	92.4	6.1	6.4	0.0	0.1	0.0	0.0	5.7	6.0	6.1	5.7	4.9	25.8	32.3	11.9	1.6	78.7	41.7	49.8	50.2
25868	LOOKOUT	99.7	99.3	0.0	0.0	0.0	0.4	0.7	0.7	5.3	5.7	6.0	5.3	4.3	24.1	33.3	13.8	2.1	79.4	44.4	50.0	50.0
25870	MABEN	97.0	96.2	2.2	2.6	0.3	0.6	0.3	0.3	5.0	5.3	5.8	6.4	5.6	23.7	31.0	15.2	2.0	79.8	43.8	48.5	51.5
25876	SAULSVILLE	98.6	98.1	1.4	1.7	0.0	0.0	0.2	0.2	5.4	5.9	6.5	7.5	7.2	25.0	31.4	9.9	1.2	77.5	40.8	50.6	49.4
25880	MOUNT HOPE	91.0	90.5	6.8	6.8	0.4	0.7	0.8	0.9	5.9	6.3	6.4	6.8	6.2	25.7	28.7	11.9	2.0	77.4	39.3	48.2	51.8
25882	MULLENS	96.3	95.6	2.6	3.1	0.2	0.3	0.4	0.5	5.2	5.4	5.6	5.2	4.8	24.6	29.3	17.2	2.7	80.6	44.3	49.4	50.6
25901	OAK HILL	92.2	91.5	5.8	6.1	0.3	0.5	0.9	1.1	5.6	5.6	5.9	6.0	5.1	24.7	29.8	14.7	2.7	79.2	42.8	48.3	51.7
25902	ODD	96.7	96.1	2.0	2.1	0.0	0.0	0.7	0.7	6.0	6.2	7.1	6.4	5.2	26.2	29.4	11.7	1.8	76.3	40.5	50.0	50.0
25908	PRINCEWICK	96.3	96.1	2.3	2.5	0.0	0.0	1.1	1.4	6.1	6.4	6.9	5.8	3.6	24.3	31.2	14.4	1.4	76.8	42.4	49.4	50.6
25913	RAVENCLIFF	98.5	98.3	0.5	0.6	0.1	0.1	0.3	0.3	6.3	6.7	6.6	6.2	5.5	24.5	32.2	10.9	1.2	76.5	40.6	49.0	51.0
25915	RHODELL	94.4	93.9	3.9	4.1	0.0	0.0	0.8	1.1	7.1	7.3	7.4	6.5	4.6	25.0	28.7	12.0	1.4	74.1	39.2	50.0	50.0
25917	SCARBRO	96.1	95.6	2.6	2.7	0.1	0.2	0.6	0.8	6.1	6.3	6.5	5.8	4.5	24.5	30.4	13.9	2.1	77.6	42.4	49.1	50.9
25918	SHADY SPRING	88.3	87.2	10.4	11.0	0.5	0.7	2.6	3.0	4.2	4.6	4.9	4.7	6.6	32.6	29.1	11.9	1.5	83.4	39.8	58.4	41.6
25920	SLAB FORK	97.6	97.3	1.4	1.5	0.1	0.1	0.2	0.3	5.4	5.6	5.9	5.6	5.4	27.2	31.4	12.2	1.4	79.7	41.4	49.5	50.5
25922	SPANISHBURG	98.9	98.8	0.2	0.2	0.1	0.1	0.2	0.3	6.5	6.7	6.7	5.9	4.7	29.1	28.2	10.9	1.4	76.5	38.7	50.1	49.9
25928	STEPHENSON	95.8	95.5	3.0	3.3	0.0	0.0	1.5	1.7	4.1	4.5	5.0	5.0	5.0	24.8	33.1	16.5	2.1	83.1	46.3	49.2	50.8
25932	SURVEYOR	92.9	92.7	6.1	6.3	0.0	0.0	0.3	0.3	5.7	6.0	6.3	5.7	4.3	26.0	32.3	12.3	1.3	78.0	42.0	50.3	49.7
25936	THURMOND	100.0	100.0	0.0	0.0	0.0	0.0	0.0	0.0	7.1	7.1	7.1	0.0	14.3	35.7	28.6	0.0	0.0	78.6	30.0	71.4	28.6
25938	VICTOR	98.0	97.8	1.4	1.5	0.0	0.1	0.5	0.6	5.4	5.6	5.8	6.0	4.6	25.3	30.2	14.2	3.0	79.4	42.9	49.0	51.0
25951	HINTON	95.8	95.5	2.7	2.7	0.2	0.3	0.5	0.7	4.5	4.9	5.1	5.6	5.0	22.5	29.8	18.7	3.9	82.1	46.7	48.3	51.7
25958	CHARMCO	96.6	96.4	1.6	1.6	0.2	0.2	0.5	0.6	5.2	5.5	5.7	5.8	4.9	23.5	29.7	16.2	3.6	80.5	44.5	50.4	49.6
25962	RAINELLE	97.6	97.4	0.8	0.8	0.1	0.1	0.7	0.8	5.0	5.3	5.6	5.6	4.4	22.6	30.1	18.5	3.1	80.9	46.3	48.4	51.6
25965	ELTON	99.0	99.0	0.0	0.0	0.0	0.0	1.0	1.0	3.9	3.9	4.4	5.3	4.4	23.8	32.0	19.9	2.4	84.5	48.2	51.9	48.1
25966	GREEN SULPHUR SPRING	98.5	98.4	0.1	0.1	0.1	0.1	0.9	1.0	3.7	4.0	4.5	5.2	4.6	22.8	34.3	18.7	2.2	84.7	48.6	51.8	48.2
25969	JUMPING BRANCH	99.1	99.1	0.1	0.1	0.0	0.0	0.2	0.2	4.5	5.0	5.6	5.2	3.6	24.8	33.3	15.5	2.6	81.3	45.9	49.6	50.4
25971	LERONA	99.3	99.2	0.2	0.2	0.1	0.2	0.5	0.6	5.1	5.9	6.2	5.7	3.6	24.6	32.0	14.9	1.9	78.8	44.2	49.0	51.0
25976	MEADOW BRIDGE	99.1	98.9	0.2	0.2	0.2	0.4	0.2	0.2	4.9	5.1	5.4	5.7	5.1	25.0	31.9	15.0	1.9	81.1	44.1	48.4	51.6
25977	MEADOW CREEK	99.0	99.0	0.0	0.0	0.0	0.0	0.5	1.0	3.7	4.2	4.7	5.2	4.7	23.6	31.4	19.9	2.6	84.3	47.7	50.8	49.2
25978	NIMITZ	99.3	99.3	0.0	0.0	0.0	0.0	0.2	0.0	4.5	5.1	5.6	5.1	3.3	24.7	33.3	15.7	2.6	81.3	46.2	49.7	50.3
25979	PIPESTEM	98.8	98.8	0.2	0.2	0.2	0.2	1.2	1.4	4.8	5.4	6.0	6.0	4.1	23.5	33.3	15.1	1.9	80.3	45.2	49.8	50.2
25981	QUINWOOD	95.4	95.2	2.5	2.5	0.1	0.1	0.6	0.8	6.0	6.1	6.1	5.3	4.6	22.3	31.2	16.3	2.0	78.5	44.6	49.7	50.3
25984	RUPERT	97.0	96.8	1.0	1.0	0.0	0.0	0.7	0.8	5.9	6.2	6.2	6.2	4.7	23.3	29.8	15.0	2.6	78.0	43.0	49.4	50.6
25985	SANDSTONE	97.7	97.6	0.5	0.5	0.0	0.0	1.2	1.2	3.8	4.5	5.0	4.5	4.5	21.0	38.3	16.4	1.9	83.6	49.0	51.9	48.1
25986	SPRING DALE	100.0	100.0	0.0	0.0	0.0	0.0	0.0	0.0	4.8	4.8	5.8	5.8	4.8	25.0	33.7	14.4	1.0	79.8	44.3	47.1	52.9
25989	WHITE OAK	94.4	94.3	4.8	4.9	0.2	0.2	1.1	1.2	5.3	5.7	6.1	5.7	5.9	28.3	30.3	11.4	1.2	79.2	40.1	53.4	46.6
26003	WHEELING	94.5	93.6	3.6	3.8	0.8	1.3	0.5	0.6	4.9	5.1	5.6	7.2	6.7	22.1	29.1	16.0	3.3	80.7	43.7	46.8	53.2
26031	BENWOOD	98.5	98.3	0.8	0.9	0.1	0.1	0.3	0.3	6.2	6.0	6.1	6.3	5.3	25.0	28.6	13.6	2.8	77.9	41.0	46.5	53.5
26032	BETHANY	96.0	94.7	2.1	2.8	1.2	1.8	0.5	0.6	3.5	3.2	3.2	18.7	27.7	16.5	16.6	9.4	1.1	87.7	23.8	50.7	49.3
26033	CAMERON	98.0	97.8	0.3	0.4	0.0	0.0	0.3	0.4	5.4	5.6	5.8	6.3	5.4	22.0	29.9	16.1	3.4	79.4	44.5	48.6	51.4
26034	CHESTER	98.9	98.7	0.1	0.1	0.3	0.5	0.9	1.0	5.5	5.7	6.0	5.8	4.6	24.3	30.4	14.9	2.9	79.4	43.7	47.9	52.1
26035	COLLIERS	98.5	98.0	0.4	0.6	0.3	0.4	0.6	0.8	4.5	4.8	5.4	5.8	4.3	24.7	34.4	14.8	1.4	81.8	45.3	50.4	49.6
26036	DALLAS	98.3	98.0	0.6	0.8	0.1	0.1	0.2	0.3	5.8	6.2	6.5	5.8	4.5	24.6	31.8	13.6	1.2	77.9	42.3	50.3	49.7
26037	FOLLANSBEE	98.8	98.5	0.3	0.4	0.2	0.3	0.4	0.5	5.0	5.2	5.6	5.7	4.8	23.5	30.4	16.5	3.3	80.6	45.2	47.1	52.9
26038	GLEN DALE	98.7	98.3	0.0	0.0	0.6	0.9	0.6	0.6	4.0	4.4	5.2	6.1	4.5	21.7	33.4	17.9	2.8	82.6	47.8	47.7	52.3
26039	GLEN EASTON	98.7	98.5	0.2	0.2	0.3	0.4	0.5	0.5	5.8	5.9	6.5	7.1	5.0	26.5	31.3	10.9	1.0	77.4	40.5	50.3	49.7
26040	MCMECHEN	98.6	98.3	0.4	0.5	0.1	0.2	0.4	0.5	4.2	4.4	4.9	6.0	5.2	23.2	31.0	17.9	3.3	82.6	46.6	47.6	52.4
26041	MOUNDSVILLE	98.3	98.0	0.5	0.6	0.3	0.4	0.9	1.1	5.2	5.4	5.6	5.9	5.5	25.0	29.8	14.9	2.7	80.2	43.1	49.0	51.0
26047	NEW CUMBERLAND	98.6	98.4	0.3	0.3	0.3	0.4	0.6	0.8	4.9	5.3	5.9	5.9	4.4	24.6	32.8	14.7	1.5	80.3	44.3	49.9	50.1
26050	NEWELL	98.8	98.6	0.2	0.2	0.0	0.1	0.6	0.8	6.4	6.5	6.5	6.1	5.0	25.8	28.5	13.4	1.7	76.8	39.6	49.7	50.3
26055	PROCTOR	98.8	98.6	0.2	0.2	0.1	0.1	0.3	0.4	5.1	6.3	6.7	6.6	4.9	24.6	32.1	12.4	1.4	77.6	42.4	51.9	48.1
26059	TRIADELPHIA	98.5	98.2	0.7	0.8	0.2	0.2	0.3	0.3	5.7	6.0	6.6	6.5	4.3	25.2	31.7	12.6	1.4	77.5	42.0	50.6	49.4
26060	VALLEY GROVE	98.4	98.1	0.8	1.0	0.2	0.2	0.4	0.4	5.2	5.6	5.9	8.8	8.2	24.0	29.3	11.7	1.2	79.6	39.0	51.0	49.0
26062	WEIRTON	94.7	94.1	3.7	3.8	0.6	0.9	0.7	0.8	4.8	5.0	5.2	5.3	4.7	22.9	30.5	18.0	3.6	81.7	46.4	47.4	52.6
26070	WELLSBURG	98.0	97.6	0.9	1.1	0.1	0.2	0.3	0.4	4.8	5.1	5.6	6.6	5.5	23.4	30.6	15.8	2.7	80.7	44.2	48.4	51.6
26101	PARKERSBURG	96.6	96.1	1.5	1.6	0.4	0.6	0.7	0.8	6.1	5.8	5.8	5.9	6.0	25.7	27.4	14.6	2.6	78.8	41.0	47.9	52.1
26104	PARKERSBURG	97.3	96.7	1.1	1.2	0.7	1.0	0.6	0.7	5.3	5.4	5.8	5.8	4.9	24.3	29.0	15.9	3.6	80.0	43.9	47.2	52.8
26105	VIENNA	96.7	95.7	0.9	1.0	1.4	2.2	0.5	0.7	4.8	5.1	5.7	6.6	4.8	22.6	30.3	17.0	3.0	80.3	45.2	47.2	52.8
26133	BELLEVILLE	98.7	98.6	0.0	0.0	0.1	0.1	0.8	0.9	5.1	5.5	5.6	7.3	5.3	26.1	31.9	12.3	0.9	79.4	42.1	50.9	49.1
26134	BELMONT	98.5	98.3	0.3	0.2	0.2	0.3	0.4	0.5	6.1	6.3	6.4	5.8	4.7	24.3	30.0	13.5	2.9	77.9	42.1	47.6	52.4
26136	BIG BEND	98.7	98.4	0.0	0.0	0.1	0.2	0.4	0.4	4.7	4.1	5.9	8.5	5.4	22.8	32.7	13.9	2.0	79.5	43.9	48.9	51.1
26137	BIG SPRINGS	99.0	98.8	0.0	0.0	0.3	0.5	0.3	0.3	5.6	6.0	5.7	4.8	4.0	25.0	30.4	16.4	2.0	79.6	44.2	49.6	50.4
26138	BROHARD	100.0	100.0	0.0	0.0	0.0	0.0	0.0	0.0	0.0	0.0	0.0	0.0	0.0	66.7	33.3	0.0	0.0	100.0	40.0	50.0	50.0
26141	CRESTON	98.9	98.8	0.0	0.0	0.3	0.3	0.3	0.3	4.7	4.7	5.3	6.7	5.3	22.5	32.5	15.5	2.9	80.7	45.6	49.1	50.9
26142	DAVISVILLE	98.7	98.5	0.5	0.5	0.1	0.2	0.7	0.9	6.4	7.5	7.2	6.8	5.4	28.7	26.9	10.3	0.9	74.3	37.5	50.2	49.8
26143	ELIZABETH	98.7	98.7	0.2	0.2	0.0	0.0	0.1	0.1	5.9	6.2	6.5	6.6	5.0	24.9	30.4	12.8	1.6	77.1	41.4	50.6	49.4
26146	FRIENDLY	99.0	98.9	0.0	0.0	0.1	0.1	0.4	0.4	5.8	6.2	6.5	5.7	4.4	24.3	31.0	14.6	1.5	78.0	43.0	47.4	52.6
26147	GRANTSVILLE	98.9	98.7	0.1	0.1	0.2	0.3	0.4	0.5	4.7	4.9	5.0	5.7	5.4	23.1	32.2	16.0	3.0	81.9	45.8	49.4	50.6
26148	MACFARLAN	98.9	98.9	0.2	0.2	0.0	0.0	0.2	0.2	4.3	4.6	5.0	6.3	5.2	22.4	35.0	15.4	1.7	82.2	46.1	50.7	49.3
26149	MIDDLEBOURNE	99.4	99.3	0.0	0.0	0.0	0.0	0.4	0.4	4.6	5.6	5.8	6.1	4.7	25.0	32.2	14.1	1.8	80.1	43.7	49.3	50.7
26150	MINERAL WELLS	98.7	98.5	0.3	0.3	0.2	0.3	0.3	0.4	6.3	6.6	6.9	6.6	5.0	26.0	30.8	10.9	1.0	76.2	40.0	49.3	50.7
26151	MOUNT ZION	99.1	99.1	0.0	0.0	0.0	0.0	0.4	0.5	5.0	5.0	5.0	5.4	5.4	22.5	33.3	15.3	3.2	82.0	46.2	47.7	52.3
26152	MUNDAY	98.7	99.3	0.6	0.0	0.0	0.0	0.6	0.7	5.5	5.5	6.2	6.2	4.8	26.0	29.5	15.1	1.4	79.5	42.0	54.1	45.9
26155	NEW MARTINSVILLE	98.6	98.1	0.1	0.1	0.7	1.1	0.4	0.6	5.6	5.7	5.8	5.9	5.2	22.2	30.1	16.3	3.1	79.3	44.6	47.9	52.1
26159	PADEN CITY	99.2	99.0	0.1	0.2	0.2	0.3	0.5	0.7	5.6	6.6	6.0	5.6	5.1	22.1	28.8	18.1	2.1	78.0	44.2	48.2	51.8
26160	PALESTINE	98.6	98.6	0.1	0.1	0.3	0.3	0.2	0.3	4.5	4.8	5.6	7.4	5.2	23.2	32.5	14.4	2.4	79.8	44.5	49.5	50.5
26161	PETROLEUM	99.1	99.1	0.2	0.2	0.0	0.0	0.4	0.4	4.8	5.0	5.2	6.1	5.0	22.8	33.8	15.6	1.7	81.3	45.7	50.3	49.7
26164	RAVENSWOOD	98.5	98.1	0.2	0.2	0.4	0.6	0.4	0.5	5.7	5.8	5.9	6.1	5.4	23.3	27.4	17.4	2.9	78.8	43.2	47.7	52.3
26167	READER	99.3	99.1	0.0	0.0	0.1	0.2	0.4	0.5	6.3	6.4	7.0	6.9	5.0	24.2	28.9	13.9	1.5	75.9	41.0	50.4	49.6
26169	ROCKPORT	98.6	98.3	0.0	0.1	0.1	0.1	0.3	0.3	4.6	6.7	9.9	7.3	4.3	24.8	31.1	9.2	2.1	74.3	39.2	52.0	48.0
26170	SAINT MARYS	98.2	97.9	0.6	0.6	0.2	0.3	0.3	0.3	5.5	5.8	6.3	6.3	5.0	25.8	29.7	13.7	2.0	78.4	41.9	51.4	48.6
26175	SISTERSVILLE	99.4	99.3	0.0	0.0	0.1	0.1	0.5	0.5	5.3	5.9	5.9	5.6	5.2	22.4	30.3	16.4	3.0	79.3	44.8	48.2	51.8
26178	SMITHVILLE	98.9	98.9	0.4	0.4	0.0	0.0	0.4	0.4	4.3	4.7	4.9	6.5	5.6	22.4	33.6	15.9	2.0	82.3	45.8	50.3	49.7
26180	WALKER	98.3	98.1	0.3	0.3	0.2	0.3	0.6	0.6	5.6	5.9	7.1	7.5	5.3	26.3	30.2	10.9	1.3	76.3	40.1	51.6	48.4
	WEST VIRGINIA	95.0	94.5	3.2	3.3	0.5	0.8	0.7	0.8	5.5	5.6	5.9	6.5	6.1	25.2	29.3	13.8	2.2	79.3	41.5	49.0	51.0
	UNITED STATES	75.1	72.0	12.3	12.7	3.8	4.6	12.5	15.7	6.8	6.7	6.6	7.1	6.9	27.0	26.0	10.9	1.9	75.7	36.9	49.2	50.8

#	POST OFFICE NAME	2009 Per Capita Income	2009 HH Income Base	2009 HOUSEHOLD INCOME DISTRIBUTION (%) Less than $25,000	$25,000 to $49,999	$50,000 to $99,999	$100,000 to $149,999	$150,000 or More	MEDIAN HOUSEHOLD INCOME 2009	2014	2009 National Centile	2009 State Centile	2009 Home Value Base	2009 HOME VALUE DISTRIBUTION (%) Less than $50,000	$50,000 to $89,999	$90,000 to $174,999	$175,000 to $399,999	$400,000 or More	2009 Median Home Value
25837	EDMOND	12712	37	45.9	32.4	18.9	2.7	0.0	26644	27889	4	19	32	28.1	34.4	31.3	6.3	0.0	70000
25839	FAIRDALE	22511	135	26.7	31.9	31.9	6.7	3.0	42043	44606	39	89	114	17.5	23.7	38.6	17.5	2.6	106250
25840	FAYETTEVILLE	19445	3271	36.9	29.0	27.2	4.9	2.0	34573	34342	17	62	2635	21.7	26.9	33.7	15.7	2.0	91995
25841	FLAT TOP	18987	298	39.6	21.8	33.2	4.7	0.7	35413	35997	19	67	259	20.8	13.5	37.1	26.6	1.9	121181
25843	GHENT	23528	442	30.8	26.9	33.7	4.8	3.8	43712	46062	44	91	388	19.3	11.6	37.1	27.1	4.9	136806
25844	GLEN DANIEL	19951	941	33.3	29.6	29.5	5.1	2.4	38159	40048	27	81	781	25.1	24.3	35.9	12.8	1.9	91000
25845	GLEN FORK	18684	128	32.8	38.3	24.2	3.1	1.6	32287	32420	12	50	104	35.6	27.9	29.8	6.7	0.0	72000
25848	GLEN ROGERS	14410	141	45.4	26.2	26.2	2.1	0.0	27749	28467	5	24	121	39.7	27.3	26.4	5.0	1.7	59615
25854	HICO	17863	290	36.2	30.7	29.0	4.1	0.0	32318	31972	12	51	246	32.9	22.0	37.8	7.3	0.0	80000
25857	JOSEPHINE	11088	151	54.3	33.1	11.3	1.3	0.0	22424	24542	2	6	124	58.9	18.5	17.7	3.2	1.6	36667
25862	LANSING	16573	39	38.5	35.9	25.6	0.0	0.0	30729	31287	9	42	32	25.0	28.1	25.0	21.9	0.0	85000
25864	LAYLAND	13424	32	40.6	37.5	21.9	0.0	0.0	30000	29255	8	35	27	29.6	40.7	29.6	0.0	0.0	67500
25865	LESTER	17902	448	42.0	25.0	28.8	3.1	1.1	30641	31525	9	40	361	32.4	25.5	35.2	6.6	0.3	82297
25868	LOOKOUT	16063	118	43.2	29.7	23.7	3.4	0.0	28116	28633	6	26	100	36.0	24.0	31.0	8.0	1.0	70000
25870	MABEN	18348	143	40.6	28.0	26.6	2.8	2.1	31115	32295	10	45	120	40.8	30.8	25.8	1.7	0.8	60000
25876	SAULSVILLE	16230	244	47.5	23.0	27.9	1.2	0.4	26962	28833	5	21	210	39.5	27.1	26.2	4.3	2.9	59565
25880	MOUNT HOPE	17445	3582	40.2	30.3	24.9	3.5	1.1	31776	32076	11	48	2632	29.0	31.4	31.3	7.0	1.3	76124
25882	MULLENS	21098	1063	38.7	27.9	25.9	4.7	2.8	33163	34237	14	54	834	36.9	39.6	21.2	1.9	0.4	62353
25901	OAK HILL	17094	6427	42.4	30.2	22.5	3.5	1.4	30339	30966	9	37	4766	23.9	33.7	33.7	7.7	1.0	79286
25902	ODD	11147	217	53.9	31.8	12.0	2.3	0.0	22624	23564	2	6	179	60.3	20.7	11.7	6.1	1.1	40750
25908	PRINCEWICK	16069	159	49.7	22.6	22.0	5.7	0.0	25162	26158	3	13	131	48.1	23.7	26.0	2.3	0.0	53125
25913	RAVENCLIFF	15334	476	41.8	31.9	22.9	2.3	1.1	28641	28765	6	29	402	37.3	27.4	29.1	5.5	0.7	65926
25915	RHODELL	9560	443	61.9	29.1	7.9	1.1	0.0	19941	20309	1	3	362	76.0	16.3	4.7	3.0	0.0	25833
25917	SCARBRO	14407	548	45.8	31.6	19.5	2.6	0.5	26860	26940	5	20	447	34.5	34.9	24.2	4.9	1.6	63750
25918	SHADY SPRING	20934	2161	37.4	30.1	24.3	5.4	2.8	31927	31971	11	48	1818	21.5	17.5	36.6	18.9	5.6	111123
25920	SLAB FORK	16691	362	41.7	27.3	27.1	3.9	0.0	31139	32604	10	45	287	27.9	26.1	37.6	7.7	0.7	86406
25922	SPANISHBURG	14720	394	41.9	31.2	23.1	3.8	0.0	30143	31033	8	36	340	30.6	25.0	33.2	9.7	1.5	84412
25928	STEPHENSON	19827	103	47.6	23.3	18.4	7.8	2.9	26214	26588	4	17	87	49.4	26.4	19.5	4.6	0.0	50455
25932	SURVEYOR	18161	134	42.5	27.6	26.1	3.0	0.7	30751	32340	9	42	109	33.9	22.0	35.8	8.3	0.0	81875
25936	THURMOND	18308	9	55.6	22.2	22.2	0.0	0.0	22222	22222	2	5	8	37.5	62.5	0.0	0.0	0.0	60000
25938	VICTOR	17728	959	37.4	32.5	24.2	4.4	1.5	33890	33482	15	59	801	31.5	27.8	33.2	7.2	0.2	75761
25951	HINTON	16726	2537	47.5	30.3	17.9	3.0	1.2	26353	27293	4	18	1870	25.0	27.4	35.6	11.1	1.0	85644
25958	CHARMCO	19224	275	40.0	29.5	26.5	1.8	2.2	35875	37380	20	70	213	30.5	24.4	37.6	6.6	0.9	83438
25962	RAINELLE	18163	1566	44.4	31.1	20.1	2.9	1.5	29315	30019	7	32	1201	30.5	32.1	30.3	6.6	0.5	71364
25965	ELTON	14136	85	42.4	34.1	20.0	2.4	1.2	29583	30709	7	33	70	31.4	34.3	25.7	8.6	0.0	72000
25966	GREEN SULPHUR SPRING	14722	305	46.2	33.1	18.4	1.6	0.7	27185	28131	5	21	253	32.8	32.8	25.7	8.7	0.0	71842
25969	JUMPING BRANCH	18187	489	39.7	28.6	23.9	6.1	1.6	31047	31242	10	44	408	24.0	18.1	43.9	10.3	3.7	102381
25971	LERONA	18022	416	37.5	25.5	32.0	4.3	0.7	36621	37186	22	74	362	22.9	12.4	37.0	26.8	0.8	115455
25976	MEADOW BRIDGE	14919	739	41.9	35.2	20.7	2.2	0.0	30175	30464	8	36	632	39.6	19.1	26.4	14.9	0.0	70811
25977	MEADOW CREEK	15905	88	40.9	35.2	20.5	2.3	1.1	30000	30000	8	35	72	30.6	33.3	27.8	8.3	0.0	74000
25978	NIMITZ	18050	253	41.1	26.9	24.1	6.7	1.2	30514	30810	9	39	210	25.7	17.1	43.3	10.0	3.8	103448
25979	PIPESTEM	15543	255	43.9	32.9	21.6	1.6	0.0	28519	29753	6	28	205	21.5	27.8	39.0	11.7	0.0	91250
25981	QUINWOOD	12686	726	51.2	33.3	13.9	1.1	0.4	24171	25643	3	10	589	46.5	28.7	21.4	3.2	0.2	54020
25984	RUPERT	15312	644	43.6	35.6	18.6	1.6	0.6	28633	29077	6	29	499	34.3	30.5	30.1	4.4	0.8	70139
25985	SANDSTONE	12990	200	58.0	29.0	12.0	1.0	0.0	20000	19872	1	3	169	34.9	28.4	21.9	14.8	0.0	76786
25986	SPRING DALE	15991	47	44.7	31.9	21.3	2.1	0.0	29056	27282	7	30	40	40.0	20.0	22.5	17.5	0.0	70000
25989	WHITE OAK	17915	201	38.3	31.8	22.4	6.0	1.5	30434	30770	9	38	172	22.1	23.8	33.1	14.0	7.0	97778
26003	WHEELING	22984	18809	33.1	26.5	30.8	6.1	3.5	39394	41043	31	83	12988	17.8	30.2	38.4	12.1	1.5	94187
26031	BENWOOD	18487	1005	38.5	29.1	28.5	3.3	0.7	32607	32537	13	52	697	28.6	39.6	29.0	2.6	0.3	67593
26032	BETHANY	14743	218	24.3	30.7	35.8	6.0	3.2	44601	47941	47	93	166	12.7	26.5	57.8	3.0	0.0	102679
26033	CAMERON	17455	1005	38.2	28.4	28.5	4.3	0.7	35657	36153	20	68	778	43.1	30.1	23.4	2.8	0.6	58710
26034	CHESTER	19988	2409	30.1	33.5	31.4	3.3	1.7	37567	38151	25	78	1878	28.3	38.0	28.8	4.5	0.3	73487
26035	COLLIERS	20124	855	24.1	37.7	31.2	5.5	1.5	40830	41978	35	86	731	26.4	26.9	41.0	5.3	0.3	86048
26036	DALLAS	18808	291	25.4	38.5	29.2	5.2	1.7	39656	40898	32	83	233	19.7	21.0	52.4	6.0	0.9	104750
26037	FOLLANSBEE	21117	2922	27.1	33.4	32.9	4.6	2.0	41875	43262	39	88	2263	25.8	34.3	34.1	5.4	0.4	81284
26038	GLEN DALE	28295	1353	20.3	28.0	34.6	11.8	5.3	51773	52895	65	97	1141	8.8	19.5	55.0	15.6	1.1	117243
26039	GLEN EASTON	19629	682	27.9	25.8	40.0	5.0	1.3	46324	47399	52	94	568	24.3	28.2	37.9	8.6	1.1	86818
26040	MCMECHEN	20449	819	36.9	30.2	27.6	4.4	1.0	34403	34206	16	61	597	33.7	49.9	15.7	0.7	0.0	59198
26041	MOUNDSVILLE	19750	6876	35.5	28.0	28.9	5.3	2.3	35803	36371	20	69	5141	24.3	36.6	33.8	5.0	0.3	78073
26047	NEW CUMBERLAND	21630	2516	24.6	34.6	33.9	4.5	2.4	42203	43580	40	89	2075	25.3	30.4	37.0	6.3	1.1	83629
26050	NEWELL	17221	947	35.4	32.5	29.4	1.9	0.8	34963	34653	17	64	714	50.4	30.8	17.1	1.7	0.0	49589
26055	PROCTOR	21256	612	30.9	26.0	33.3	6.9	2.9	44590	46029	47	92	528	19.9	28.8	42.0	8.3	0.9	91458
26059	TRIADELPHIA	21466	1011	28.4	30.3	33.7	4.5	3.1	41497	43174	38	87	817	25.3	28.9	32.7	12.1	1.0	81977
26060	VALLEY GROVE	20039	643	29.7	31.9	31.4	4.5	2.5	39931	41586	32	84	497	24.7	30.6	33.0	10.7	1.0	80862
26062	WEIRTON	25031	9252	25.9	28.6	35.6	6.9	3.0	45512	47129	50	93	6781	13.5	40.7	38.4	7.0	0.4	86360
26070	WELLSBURG	22286	4220	29.0	33.6	28.8	5.7	2.8	39816	41222	32	83	3310	28.4	34.9	32.5	4.0	0.1	74127
26101	PARKERSBURG	19479	12742	36.9	29.6	26.8	4.9	1.7	34708	34737	17	63	8103	18.9	38.5	35.7	6.7	0.2	81801
26104	PARKERSBURG	23515	7885	28.5	30.4	30.3	7.7	3.1	41878	43437	39	88	5649	13.3	30.0	41.4	14.6	0.7	101871
26105	VIENNA	30217	5446	22.5	27.2	33.5	9.2	7.6	50235	50742	62	97	4125	6.8	27.5	45.7	16.2	3.8	111574
26133	BELLEVILLE	17036	491	28.1	39.5	25.7	6.1	0.6	37071	37889	24	76	440	19.8	28.2	37.3	14.8	0.0	94091
26134	BELMONT	19888	469	33.5	29.0	28.6	6.4	2.6	39348	42130	31	83	363	22.6	23.1	47.1	6.9	0.3	100116
26136	BIG BEND	14059	341	51.3	27.0	19.9	1.8	0.0	23995	25000	3	10	263	31.9	45.6	19.0	3.4	0.0	63654
26137	BIG SPRINGS	15424	267	40.1	34.8	21.7	3.4	0.0	29889	30080	8	34	214	28.0	25.2	38.8	7.9	0.0	82222
26138	BROHARD	0	0	0.0	0.0	0.0	0.0	0.0	0	0	0	0	0	0.0	0.0	0.0	0.0	0.0	0
26141	CRESTON	15722	140	42.9	29.3	24.3	3.6	0.0	31127	30838	10	45	114	28.9	36.8	26.3	6.1	1.8	73636
26142	DAVISVILLE	18154	964	23.9	39.3	31.2	4.7	0.9	40268	41784	34	84	785	17.3	45.6	28.5	8.0	0.5	73205
26143	ELIZABETH	17300	1277	34.8	35.3	25.4	2.7	1.8	35258	36086	19	66	1004	30.3	28.1	35.1	6.6	0.0	78700
26146	FRIENDLY	19037	373	30.6	33.5	29.5	5.4	1.1	37346	38093	25	77	323	31.6	24.1	34.7	9.3	0.3	81957
26147	GRANTSVILLE	16025	730	47.1	25.3	23.7	3.2	0.7	27443	27914	5	23	570	36.8	30.7	26.1	5.1	1.2	64318
26148	MACFARLAN	17516	197	42.1	30.5	23.4	2.0	2.0	31789	32643	11	48	162	37.0	22.8	23.5	13.6	3.1	74286
26149	MIDDLEBOURNE	18360	1093	31.1	36.6	25.6	6.0	0.6	33687	33628	15	57	898	22.6	22.0	43.7	11.0	0.7	95517
26150	MINERAL WELLS	21050	2299	21.4	36.4	33.3	7.2	1.7	44009	45878	45	91	1944	18.9	20.8	37.9	20.2	2.1	105596
26151	MOUNT ZION	17864	103	44.7	25.2	25.2	3.9	1.0	29524	30236	7	32	79	32.9	31.6	25.3	6.3	3.8	66429
26152	MUNDAY	14777	59	37.3	37.3	22.0	3.4	0.0	33761	34512	15	57	49	30.6	28.6	36.7	4.1	0.0	76250
26155	NEW MARTINSVILLE	22939	2860	33.0	24.4	32.5	6.0	4.0	41658	42904	38	87	2103	18.4	21.3	44.5	15.4	0.5	105962
26159	PADEN CITY	20930	1354	29.8	31.6	32.6	4.7	1.4	40993	42052	36	86	1123	20.7	30.7	43.1	5.5	0.0	88760
26160	PALESTINE	16237	343	33.5	37.6	24.5	4.1	0.3	37224	38946	24	76	298	22.8	36.6	30.9	6.7	3.0	82222
26161	PETROLEUM	16798	186	40.3	30.6	24.7	2.7	1.6	32902	32981	13	53	154	36.4	22.7	25.3	12.3	3.2	76250
26164	RAVENSWOOD	20953	3086	30.4	32.0	29.0	5.6	3.0	40737	41733	35	85	2315	14.8	19.2	45.4	18.7	1.9	108548
26167	READER	17689	814	36.5	30.0	29.1	3.7	0.7	35999	36692	21	71	681	29.5	27.8	38.0	4.7	0.0	84244
26169	ROCKPORT	15853	420	34.8	35.5	24.5	4.0	1.2	35524	35000	19	68	361	21.3	24.7	45.4	7.8	0.8	96042
26170	SAINT MARYS	19554	2237	29.6	34.2	28.3	6.3	1.6	39740	41389	32	83	1796	28.3	24.3	38.6	7.0	1.7	86116
26175	SISTERSVILLE	20675	1418	31.5	32.0	27.6	6.1	2.7	38106	39828	27	81	1157	26.6	25.2	37.6	9.9	0.6	87529
26178	SMITHVILLE	15630	228	43.0	32.9	21.1	1.8	1.3	30238	30718	8	36	188	36.2	23.4	23.9	13.8	2.7	77778
26180	WALKER	17681	1530	33.3	36.8	23.5	4.7	1.8	37642	39490	26	79	1339	31.4	29.8	31.0	7.5	0.4	76261
	WEST VIRGINIA	20563		34.3	29.3	28.3	5.4	2.7	37099	38541				22.0	23.9	36.4	15.5	2.2	98135
	UNITED STATES	27277		20.9	24.4	35.3	11.7	7.6	54719	56938				9.3	13.1	31.6	32.6	13.5	162279

ZIP CODE	FINANCIAL SERVICES				THE HOME						ENTERTAINMENT						PERSONAL			
					Home Improvements		Furnishings													
# POST OFFICE NAME	Auto Loan	Home Loan	Invest-ments	Retire-ment Plans	Home Repair	Lawn & Garden	Comput-ers & Hard-ware-Personal	Major Appli-ances	TV, Radio, Sound Equip-ment	Furni-ture	Dine out/ Carry out	Sports Equip-ment	Fees & Tickets	Toys & Games	Travel	Cable TV	Apparel & Services	Auto Repairs	Health Insur-ance	Pets & Supplies
25837 EDMOND	63	45	65	44	47	64	46	59	52	43	51	44	37	51	46	57	33	54	61	70
25839 FAIRDALE	101	72	103	70	75	102	74	94	82	69	81	71	59	82	73	90	53	86	98	112
25840 FAYETTEVILLE	73	61	75	60	63	79	61	72	67	58	66	53	55	66	62	73	44	68	79	85
25841 FLAT TOP	81	58	83	56	60	82	59	75	66	55	65	57	47	65	59	72	43	69	78	90
25843 GHENT	91	72	115	70	78	96	72	91	76	68	75	67	62	73	77	81	50	85	91	106
25844 GLEN DANIEL	91	63	91	61	64	91	66	83	74	62	73	63	51	74	64	82	48	77	87	100
25845 GLEN FORK	70	50	70	49	52	73	55	68	61	49	59	50	44	60	53	67	39	63	74	79
25848 GLEN ROGERS	71	46	68	43	46	69	49	62	57	47	55	48	37	58	46	63	37	58	65	76
25854 HICO	75	54	77	52	56	76	55	70	61	51	60	53	44	61	55	67	40	64	73	84
25857 JOSEPHINE	52	34	50	32	34	51	36	46	42	35	41	36	27	43	34	47	27	43	48	56
25862 LANSING	64	46	64	45	48	67	50	62	56	45	54	46	40	55	49	62	36	58	68	73
25864 LAYLAND	66	43	63	40	43	64	46	58	53	43	51	45	34	54	43	59	34	54	61	71
25865 LESTER	77	51	73	48	51	75	54	68	62	52	61	53	41	64	51	69	40	64	72	83
25868 LOOKOUT	69	49	70	48	51	70	50	64	56	47	55	48	40	56	50	62	36	59	67	76
25870 MABEN	76	53	76	51	54	78	58	72	65	53	63	54	45	65	55	72	42	67	77	86
25876 SAULSVILLE	71	46	68	44	46	69	49	62	57	47	56	49	37	58	46	64	37	59	66	77
25880 MOUNT HOPE	72	53	69	52	54	73	56	67	63	53	61	50	46	62	54	69	41	64	72	80
25882 MULLENS	78	56	78	55	58	81	61	76	68	55	66	57	49	67	59	76	44	71	83	89
25901 OAK HILL	68	48	67	47	49	69	53	64	59	48	58	48	42	59	50	65	38	61	69	76
25902 ODD	53	35	52	33	35	53	37	47	43	36	42	37	28	44	35	48	28	44	50	58
25908 PRINCEWICK	66	46	67	44	47	66	48	61	54	45	53	46	37	54	46	60	35	56	63	73
25913 RAVENCLIFF	70	47	68	44	47	70	50	63	58	47	56	49	38	58	47	64	37	59	67	77
25915 RHODELL	46	30	44	28	30	45	32	40	37	30	36	31	24	37	30	41	24	38	42	49
25917 SCARBRO	62	41	60	39	42	62	45	56	51	42	50	43	34	51	42	57	33	52	60	68
25918 SHADY SPRING	83	59	83	57	61	84	61	77	68	57	67	58	49	68	60	75	44	71	80	92
25920 SLAB FORK	74	51	64	50	51	70	54	64	60	52	59	49	42	63	49	66	40	61	68	78
25922 SPANISHBURG	68	48	60	47	48	66	50	60	56	48	55	46	40	58	47	61	37	56	63	73
25928 STEPHENSON	79	57	79	55	59	82	62	76	69	55	67	57	50	68	60	76	44	71	83	90
25932 SURVEYOR	75	50	73	48	51	74	53	67	60	50	59	52	40	61	50	67	39	62	70	81
25936 THURMOND	53	35	51	33	34	52	37	47	43	35	42	36	28	43	34	48	28	44	49	57
25938 VICTOR	78	54	77	51	55	78	57	71	64	53	63	54	44	64	55	71	41	67	76	86
25951 HINTON	59	46	59	45	47	61	49	57	54	45	52	43	42	53	48	59	35	55	62	68
25958 CHARMCO	74	54	75	52	56	78	58	72	65	52	63	54	47	64	57	72	42	67	79	85
25962 RAINELLE	70	51	71	49	52	73	54	67	60	49	58	50	43	59	53	66	39	62	72	79
25965 ELTON	58	42	58	41	43	60	45	56	51	41	49	42	36	50	44	56	33	52	61	66
25966 GREEN SULPHUR SPRING	56	40	56	39	42	58	43	54	48	39	47	40	35	47	42	53	31	50	58	63
25969 JUMPING BRANCH	76	54	78	53	56	77	56	71	62	52	61	53	45	61	55	68	40	65	74	84
25971 LERONA	78	56	80	54	58	79	57	73	64	53	63	55	46	63	57	70	41	67	76	87
25976 MEADOW BRIDGE	63	44	63	42	45	63	46	58	51	43	50	44	36	51	44	57	33	54	60	70
25977 MEADOW CREEK	58	42	59	41	44	61	46	57	51	41	49	42	37	50	44	56	33	53	62	66
25978 NIMITZ	77	55	79	53	57	78	56	72	62	52	61	54	45	62	56	69	41	66	75	85
25979 PIPESTEM	64	46	66	44	48	65	47	60	52	44	51	45	38	52	47	57	34	55	62	71
25981 QUINWOOD	54	37	54	35	38	54	39	49	44	36	43	38	30	44	37	49	28	46	51	59
25984 RUPERT	63	44	62	43	45	64	48	59	54	43	52	45	38	53	46	59	35	55	64	70
25985 SANDSTONE	49	35	50	34	36	49	36	46	40	33	39	34	29	40	35	44	26	42	48	54
25986 SPRING DALE	63	45	65	44	47	64	46	59	52	43	51	44	37	51	46	57	33	54	61	70
25989 WHITE OAK	76	55	68	53	55	74	57	68	63	54	62	52	45	64	53	69	41	64	71	82
26003 WHEELING	77	70	76	70	71	83	72	78	77	69	75	57	69	75	72	82	52	77	86	91
26031 BENWOOD	66	53	62	54	55	68	59	65	63	53	61	49	51	62	56	68	42	63	71	77
26032 BETHANY	85	75	78	76	77	86	80	84	83	77	81	62	74	82	77	86	56	83	90	98
26033 CAMERON	72	52	73	51	54	75	56	70	63	50	61	52	45	62	54	69	40	65	75	82
26034 CHESTER	82	59	80	57	60	83	62	77	69	57	67	58	50	69	60	76	45	71	82	91
26035 COLLIERS	85	64	86	63	66	87	65	81	71	61	70	61	54	71	65	78	47	74	84	96
26036 DALLAS	86	61	88	59	64	87	63	80	70	59	69	60	50	69	62	77	45	73	83	95
26037 FOLLANSBEE	80	61	78	60	63	83	66	78	72	59	70	58	55	71	64	79	47	74	84	91
26038 GLEN DALE	91	96	92	96	96	106	88	97	92	85	92	71	92	92	93	97	63	92	106	112
26039 GLEN EASTON	88	71	83	70	72	89	71	83	76	68	75	62	61	77	69	81	50	78	86	99
26040 MCMECHEN	74	54	75	52	55	78	58	72	65	52	63	54	47	64	56	72	42	67	79	85
26041 MOUNDSVILLE	74	60	72	60	61	78	64	73	69	59	68	54	56	68	62	75	46	70	80	86
26047 NEW CUMBERLAND	83	67	78	67	68	86	68	80	74	63	72	61	59	74	67	79	49	75	85	95
26050 NEWELL	70	50	62	49	49	68	55	63	61	51	59	49	44	61	50	66	40	61	67	76
26055 PROCTOR	90	73	88	73	75	94	73	88	78	67	77	66	63	79	73	85	52	81	91	103
26059 TRIADELPHIA	86	68	86	68	70	90	69	83	74	64	73	63	59	74	68	80	49	77	87	98
26060 VALLEY GROVE	84	63	84	62	65	86	65	80	71	59	69	60	53	71	64	77	46	74	84	95
26062 WEIRTON	76	78	76	77	78	87	74	80	79	72	78	57	77	78	77	84	54	78	90	93
26070 WELLSBURG	86	68	83	67	69	90	70	83	76	64	75	62	60	76	68	83	50	78	90	98
26101 PARKERSBURG	70	57	64	56	57	71	62	68	67	57	65	51	54	66	59	71	44	66	74	80
26104 PARKERSBURG	81	71	79	70	72	85	73	81	77	69	76	59	67	76	72	82	52	78	87	94
26105 VIENNA	95	98	100	98	100	108	93	101	96	92	95	73	95	95	97	100	66	97	108	116
26133 BELLEVILLE	81	58	75	56	59	79	60	73	66	57	65	55	48	67	57	72	43	68	76	88
26134 BELMONT	90	64	87	62	66	90	66	82	74	63	72	62	53	74	64	81	48	76	86	99
26136 BIG BEND	62	40	60	38	40	61	43	54	50	41	49	42	32	51	40	56	32	51	58	67
26137 BIG SPRINGS	65	47	66	45	48	67	49	62	55	45	53	46	40	54	48	61	35	57	66	73
26138 BROHARD	0	0	0	0	0	0	0	0	0	0	0	0	0	0	0	0	0	0	0	0
26141 CRESTON	67	48	68	46	49	69	50	63	56	46	55	48	40	56	49	62	36	59	67	75
26142 DAVISVILLE	80	66	77	64	66	78	64	75	68	64	68	56	57	69	63	71	45	70	75	88
26143 ELIZABETH	76	55	78	53	57	77	56	71	62	52	61	54	45	62	55	69	40	65	74	85
26146 FRIENDLY	83	60	85	58	62	85	61	78	68	57	67	58	49	67	61	75	44	71	81	93
26147 GRANTSVILLE	63	45	63	44	47	65	49	61	55	44	53	45	39	54	47	61	35	57	66	71
26148 MACFARLAN	73	52	75	51	54	74	54	68	60	50	59	51	43	59	53	66	39	63	71	81
26149 MIDDLEBOURNE	79	57	81	55	59	80	58	74	64	54	63	55	46	64	57	71	42	68	77	88
26150 MINERAL WELLS	87	76	73	75	75	85	74	81	78	74	77	60	67	80	71	81	52	77	83	96
26151 MOUNT ZION	66	47	67	46	49	68	51	63	57	46	55	47	41	56	49	62	36	59	68	75
26152 MUNDAY	65	47	67	45	49	66	48	61	53	45	52	46	38	53	48	59	35	56	64	73
26155 NEW MARTINSVILLE	87	69	85	68	70	91	71	83	78	67	76	63	62	78	70	84	51	79	90	99
26159 PADEN CITY	83	60	84	58	62	87	66	81	73	58	71	60	53	72	63	81	47	75	88	95
26160 PALESTINE	73	52	75	51	54	74	54	68	59	50	58	51	43	59	53	65	39	63	71	81
26161 PETROLEUM	74	53	76	52	55	75	55	70	61	51	60	52	44	60	54	67	39	64	72	83
26164 RAVENSWOOD	79	65	74	65	66	82	67	77	72	62	71	57	59	72	65	78	48	73	83	90
26167 READER	75	57	68	56	58	75	59	69	64	56	63	53	49	66	56	70	42	65	74	83
26169 ROCKPORT	75	56	62	55	56	72	57	66	63	56	62	51	47	66	53	68	42	63	69	80
26170 SAINT MARYS	83	62	80	61	64	85	65	79	71	60	70	59	54	71	63	78	47	73	84	93
26175 SISTERSVILLE	81	64	82	62	66	86	65	78	72	61	70	58	57	71	65	79	47	74	85	93
26178 SMITHVILLE	68	48	69	46	49	69	50	63	56	46	55	48	39	56	48	61	36	58	66	75
26180 WALKER	81	58	76	57	59	80	60	74	67	57	65	56	48	68	57	73	44	68	77	88
WEST VIRGINIA	79	63	76	62	64	80	66	75	71	63	70	57	58	71	64	77	47	72	80	90
UNITED STATES	100	100	100	100	100	100	100	100	100	100	100	100	100	100	100	100	100	100	100	100

ZIP CODE #	POST OFFICE NAME	COUNTY FIPS CODE	POPULATION 2000	POPULATION 2009	POPULATION 2014	2000-2009 ANNUAL RATE % Rate	2000-2009 ANNUAL RATE State Centile	HOUSEHOLDS 2000	HOUSEHOLDS 2009	HOUSEHOLDS 2014	HOUSEHOLDS % Annual Rate 2000-2009	HOUSEHOLDS 2009 Average HH Size	FAMILIES 2000	FAMILIES 2009	FAMILIES % Annual Rate 2000-2009
26181	WASHINGTON	107	6029	6094	6105	0.1	72	2296	2401	2427	0.5	2.53	1869	1907	0.2
26184	WAVERLY	107	2327	2275	2246	-0.2	48	865	877	876	0.1	2.55	673	665	-0.1
26187	WILLIAMSTOWN	107	6154	6252	6261	0.2	76	2475	2578	2604	0.4	2.42	1821	1834	0.1
26201	BUCKHANNON	097	17256	17638	17840	0.2	76	6604	7076	7238	0.7	2.32	4574	4745	0.4
26202	FENWICK	067	396	382	375	-0.4	35	149	151	150	0.1	2.53	117	115	-0.2
26203	ERBACON	101	234	267	271	1.4	93	98	118	122	2.0	2.22	72	84	1.7
26205	CRAIGSVILLE	067	3769	3727	3704	-0.1	57	1533	1577	1588	0.3	2.36	1121	1122	0.0
26206	COWEN	101	3034	3055	3022	0.1	72	1219	1293	1296	0.6	2.32	894	919	0.3
26208	CAMDEN ON GAULEY	101	1109	1095	1080	-0.1	57	429	447	446	0.4	2.45	312	314	0.1
26210	ADRIAN	097	933	918	911	-0.2	48	364	375	377	0.3	2.45	272	272	0.0
26215	CLEVELAND	097	423	406	398	-0.4	35	166	167	166	0.1	2.43	124	121	-0.3
26217	DIANA	101	881	869	855	-0.1	57	367	384	383	0.5	2.26	258	261	0.1
26218	FRENCH CREEK	097	2349	2280	2250	-0.3	40	904	918	918	0.2	2.48	675	666	-0.1
26222	HACKER VALLEY	101	618	601	588	-0.3	40	248	256	254	0.3	2.35	185	184	-0.1
26224	HELVETIA	083	203	193	189	-0.5	30	84	83	82	-0.1	2.33	59	57	-0.4
26228	KANAWHA HEAD	097	176	170	168	-0.4	35	64	65	65	0.2	2.62	46	45	-0.2
26230	PICKENS	083	226	216	211	-0.5	30	95	94	93	-0.1	2.13	67	64	-0.5
26234	ROCK CAVE	097	636	616	606	-0.3	40	260	263	263	0.1	2.34	185	181	-0.2
26236	SELBYVILLE	097	28	27	27	-0.4	35	13	13	13	0.0	2.08	9	9	0.0
26237	TALLMANSVILLE	097	489	476	469	-0.3	40	184	186	185	0.1	2.56	148	147	-0.1
26238	VOLGA	001	1318	1314	1309	0.0	65	504	522	526	0.4	2.52	381	384	0.1
26241	ELKINS	083	13686	13901	13945	0.2	76	5680	5940	6010	0.5	2.23	3637	3677	0.1
26250	BELINGTON	001	5257	5517	5614	0.5	86	2074	2256	2320	0.9	2.43	1511	1595	0.6
26253	BEVERLY	083	3682	3623	3565	-0.2	48	1427	1454	1448	0.2	2.44	1070	1057	-0.1
26254	BOWDEN	083	150	147	143	-0.2	48	65	67	66	0.3	2.19	48	47	-0.2
26257	COALTON	083	1423	1403	1376	-0.2	48	551	562	558	0.2	2.50	420	416	-0.1
26260	DAVIS	093	1233	1104	1046	-1.2	3	548	512	490	-0.7	2.08	358	321	-1.2
26261	RICHWOOD	067	3629	3527	3477	-0.3	40	1501	1512	1509	0.1	2.25	1018	992	-0.3
26263	DRYFORK	083	267	261	254	-0.2	48	114	117	114	0.3	2.23	84	83	-0.1
26264	DURBIN	075	119	107	101	-1.1	6	45	42	40	-0.7	2.55	32	29	-1.1
26266	UPPERGLADE	101	393	400	397	0.2	76	147	159	160	0.9	2.52	104	108	0.4
26267	ELLAMORE	097	448	439	433	-0.2	48	163	166	165	0.2	2.64	130	129	-0.1
26268	GLADY	083	671	653	635	-0.3	40	269	273	268	0.2	2.33	200	196	-0.2
26269	HAMBLETON	093	809	759	727	-0.7	19	308	300	291	-0.3	2.53	231	219	-0.6
26270	HARMAN	083	593	581	566	-0.2	48	247	254	249	0.3	2.29	182	180	-0.1
26271	HENDRICKS	093	328	300	285	-1.0	7	129	122	118	-0.6	2.46	98	91	-0.8
26273	HUTTONSVILLE	083	1381	1364	1334	-0.1	57	220	222	217	0.1	4.18	164	160	-0.3
26276	KERENS	083	606	603	597	-0.1	57	224	231	231	0.3	2.61	164	164	0.0
26278	MABIE	083	418	414	409	-0.1	57	146	149	149	0.2	2.78	112	111	-0.1
26280	MILL CREEK	083	1984	1963	1933	-0.1	57	761	773	764	0.2	2.01	578	569	-0.2
26282	MONTERVILLE	083	70	67	66	-0.5	30	27	27	27	0.0	2.48	18	17	-0.6
26283	MONTROSE	083	1105	1136	1142	0.3	81	432	461	468	0.7	2.46	323	334	0.4
26287	PARSONS	093	3391	3190	3074	-0.7	19	1415	1380	1345	-0.3	2.31	1019	961	-0.6
26288	WEBSTER SPRINGS	101	3430	3324	3257	-0.3	40	1495	1527	1517	0.2	2.17	986	971	-0.2
26289	RED CREEK	093	278	253	240	-1.0	7	118	113	108	-0.5	2.24	83	77	-0.8
26291	SLATYFORK	075	553	520	499	-0.7	19	252	245	237	-0.3	2.12	166	156	-0.7
26292	THOMAS	093	823	744	709	-1.1	6	347	325	312	-0.7	2.00	203	181	-1.2
26293	VALLEY BEND	083	973	979	974	0.1	72	379	392	395	0.4	2.49	290	292	0.1
26294	VALLEY HEAD	083	963	934	908	-0.3	40	405	408	400	0.1	2.29	277	269	-0.3
26296	WHITMER	083	364	354	343	-0.3	40	151	154	151	0.2	2.30	110	109	-0.1
26301	CLARKSBURG	033	32318	32431	32442	0.0	65	13759	14049	14132	0.2	2.27	8806	8649	-0.2
26320	ALMA	095	1273	1205	1166	-0.6	25	519	511	499	-0.2	2.36	397	381	-0.4
26321	ALUM BRIDGE	041	785	753	740	-0.4	35	314	313	312	0.0	2.41	227	221	-0.3
26325	AUBURN	085	291	287	283	-0.1	57	110	112	111	0.2	2.56	81	80	-0.1
26327	BEREA	085	123	122	119	-0.1	57	48	49	49	0.2	2.49	35	35	0.0
26330	BRIDGEPORT	033	13065	13361	13460	0.2	76	5211	5462	5545	0.5	2.43	3720	3767	0.1
26335	BURNSVILLE	007	1460	1425	1403	-0.3	40	592	598	596	0.1	2.37	412	403	-0.2
26337	CAIRO	085	1416	1395	1375	-0.2	48	574	582	578	0.1	2.40	413	406	-0.2
26338	CAMDEN	041	621	615	613	-0.1	57	237	245	247	0.4	2.51	166	166	0.0
26339	CENTER POINT	017	176	181	180	0.3	81	72	76	76	0.6	2.38	50	51	0.2
26342	COXS MILLS	021	705	791	777	1.3	92	291	287	284	-0.1	2.29	203	194	-0.5
26343	CRAWFORD	041	637	636	635	0.0	65	245	256	259	0.5	2.48	182	184	0.1
26346	ELLENBORO	085	848	859	852	0.1	72	334	347	347	0.4	2.48	257	261	0.2
26347	FLEMINGTON	091	2574	2601	2613	0.1	72	974	1014	1027	0.4	2.57	740	749	0.1
26348	FOLSOM	103	351	316	299	-1.1	6	130	121	116	-0.8	2.61	95	86	-1.1
26351	GLENVILLE	021	2533	4356	4350	6.0	100	938	997	1006	0.7	2.18	519	528	0.2
26354	GRAFTON	091	10203	10172	10116	0.0	65	4059	4145	4156	0.2	2.33	2796	2757	-0.2
26362	HARRISVILLE	085	3290	3258	3213	-0.1	57	1360	1394	1388	0.3	2.28	954	947	-0.1
26372	HORNER	041	267	289	297	0.9	90	110	124	129	1.3	2.33	85	94	1.1
26374	INDEPENDENCE	077	1267	1328	1358	0.5	86	488	533	552	1.0	2.38	370	392	0.6
26376	IRELAND	007	488	482	481	-0.1	57	188	194	196	0.3	2.48	137	137	0.0
26377	JACKSONBURG	103	624	568	542	-1.0	7	246	233	225	-0.6	2.44	188	174	-0.8
26378	JANE LEW	041	4717	4747	4754	0.1	72	1906	1985	2008	0.4	2.35	1374	1384	0.1
26384	LINN	021	732	686	668	-0.7	19	282	275	271	-0.3	2.49	215	205	-0.5
26385	LOST CREEK	033	3542	3555	3567	0.0	65	1329	1370	1386	0.3	2.59	1046	1052	0.1
26386	LUMBERPORT	033	2392	2370	2357	-0.1	57	904	920	924	0.2	2.55	682	674	-0.1
26404	MEADOWBROOK	033	1076	1090	1095	0.1	72	432	449	456	0.4	2.43	311	312	0.0
26405	MOATSVILLE	001	1340	1324	1315	-0.1	57	529	544	546	0.3	2.43	401	402	0.0
26408	MOUNT CLARE	033	1616	1758	1810	0.9	90	630	705	733	1.2	2.49	479	521	0.9
26410	NEWBURG	077	1367	1402	1427	0.3	81	475	509	526	0.8	2.63	355	370	0.4
26411	NEW MILTON	017	851	865	866	0.2	76	325	341	344	0.5	2.54	242	247	0.2
26412	ORLANDO	041	203	226	235	1.2	92	76	88	92	1.6	2.57	58	65	1.2
26415	PENNSBORO	085	3032	3148	3139	0.4	83	1221	1308	1317	0.7	2.41	865	898	0.4
26416	PHILIPPI	001	7863	7852	7838	0.0	65	3085	3183	3204	0.3	2.36	2134	2128	0.0
26419	PINE GROVE	103	705	634	601	-1.1	6	287	269	258	-0.7	2.36	215	196	-1.0
26421	PULLMAN	085	268	262	258	-0.2	48	103	104	103	0.1	2.52	78	77	-0.1
26425	ROWLESBURG	077	671	688	701	0.3	81	264	283	292	0.8	2.43	177	183	0.4
26426	SALEM	017	8209	7879	7767	-0.4	35	3046	2983	2959	-0.2	2.44	2154	2053	-0.5
26430	SAND FORK	021	664	618	602	-0.8	14	257	250	246	-0.3	2.47	193	184	-0.5
26431	SHINNSTON	033	5774	5834	5851	0.1	72	2326	2407	2433	0.4	2.42	1674	1679	0.0
26437	SMITHFIELD	103	678	608	575	-1.2	3	275	255	244	-0.8	2.38	204	184	-1.1
26440	THORNTON	091	1127	1148	1158	0.2	76	454	480	490	0.6	2.37	326	334	0.3
26443	TROY	021	105	99	98	-0.6	25	45	44	44	-0.2	2.25	32	30	-0.7
26444	TUNNELTON	077	3084	3178	3242	0.3	81	1221	1313	1357	0.8	2.42	894	932	0.5
26447	WALKERSVILLE	041	1476	1544	1568	0.5	86	584	635	651	0.9	2.43	430	455	0.6
	WEST VIRGINIA					0.2					0.5	2.33			0.1
	UNITED STATES					1.0					1.1	2.59			0.9

ZIP CODE #	POST OFFICE NAME	RACE (%) White 2000	White 2009	Black 2000	Black 2009	Asian/Pacific 2000	Asian/Pacific 2009	% Hispanic Origin 2000	% Hispanic Origin 2009	2009 AGE DISTRIBUTION (%) 0-4	5-9	10-14	15-19	20-24	25-44	45-64	65-84	85+	18+	MEDIAN AGE 2009	% 2009 Males	% 2009 Females
26181	WASHINGTON	98.5	98.1	0.4	0.4	0.3	0.4	0.5	0.7	5.5	6.0	6.4	6.6	4.2	24.2	31.2	14.6	1.2	77.8	43.0	50.7	49.3
26184	WAVERLY	97.7	97.4	0.7	0.8	0.5	0.7	0.4	0.4	6.1	6.2	6.6	7.6	5.7	25.8	30.4	10.7	1.1	77.2	39.9	49.5	50.5
26187	WILLIAMSTOWN	98.3	97.9	0.4	0.5	0.3	0.5	0.5	0.6	5.5	5.7	6.1	6.3	5.1	24.7	30.2	14.3	2.0	78.7	42.7	48.0	52.0
26201	BUCKHANNON	97.9	97.5	0.8	0.8	0.4	0.5	0.6	0.8	5.3	5.6	5.8	8.7	8.2	23.0	27.8	13.3	2.4	79.6	39.5	48.1	51.9
26202	FENWICK	99.0	98.7	0.0	0.0	0.5	0.8	0.8	0.8	5.5	6.0	6.5	6.3	4.7	24.3	31.7	13.4	1.6	77.7	42.8	48.2	51.8
26203	ERBACON	99.6	99.6	0.0	0.0	0.0	0.0	0.9	0.7	5.2	5.6	6.0	6.7	5.2	24.3	31.1	13.5	2.2	78.7	42.6	49.4	50.6
26205	CRAIGSVILLE	98.8	98.5	0.1	0.1	0.1	0.2	0.2	0.2	5.9	6.1	6.4	6.1	4.9	25.1	30.6	13.3	1.6	77.8	41.4	49.3	50.7
26206	COWEN	99.1	99.1	0.0	0.0	0.1	0.1	0.3	0.3	5.7	5.9	6.2	6.7	5.0	24.5	30.6	12.9	2.4	77.9	42.0	50.2	49.8
26208	CAMDEN ON GAULEY	99.4	99.4	0.0	0.0	0.1	0.1	0.3	0.3	4.7	5.1	5.4	6.4	4.9	24.3	33.0	14.2	2.0	80.8	44.3	49.2	50.8
26210	ADRIAN	99.5	99.5	0.0	0.0	0.1	0.1	0.4	0.5	5.4	5.9	6.2	6.8	4.1	25.7	32.0	12.4	1.4	78.2	41.8	49.7	50.3
26215	CLEVELAND	99.1	99.0	0.5	0.5	0.0	0.0	0.7	0.7	5.9	5.9	6.4	6.2	4.4	22.9	30.8	15.3	2.2	77.8	43.8	50.5	49.5
26217	DIANA	99.7	99.7	0.0	0.0	0.0	0.0	0.2	0.2	4.9	5.3	5.5	5.9	5.6	21.7	32.9	16.1	2.0	80.7	45.7	47.5	52.5
26218	FRENCH CREEK	98.9	98.6	0.1	0.1	0.4	0.6	0.3	0.4	5.6	5.8	6.1	6.1	4.9	25.2	31.4	13.3	1.7	78.9	42.5	51.1	48.9
26222	HACKER VALLEY	99.4	99.3	0.0	0.0	0.0	0.0	0.6	0.7	4.3	4.5	4.8	6.5	5.8	25.0	30.1	16.8	2.2	82.7	44.4	50.4	49.6
26224	HELVETIA	100.0	100.0	0.0	0.0	0.0	0.0	0.0	0.0	4.1	4.7	5.2	6.2	4.7	22.3	35.2	15.5	2.1	82.4	46.6	53.9	46.1
26228	KANAWHA HEAD	100.0	100.0	0.0	0.0	0.0	0.0	0.6	0.6	4.7	4.7	5.3	7.1	4.1	24.7	32.4	15.9	1.2	81.2	44.7	53.5	46.5
26230	PICKENS	98.7	98.6	1.3	1.4	0.0	0.0	0.4	0.5	3.7	4.2	4.6	5.6	6.0	25.5	34.7	14.4	1.4	84.3	45.3	58.3	41.7
26234	ROCK CAVE	99.7	99.7	0.0	0.0	0.2	0.2	0.5	0.5	4.4	4.5	5.4	7.1	4.5	25.2	31.5	16.2	1.1	81.3	44.4	53.6	46.4
26236	SELBYVILLE	100.0	100.0	0.0	0.0	0.0	0.0	0.0	0.0	3.7	3.7	7.4	7.4	7.4	29.6	29.6	11.1	0.0	77.8	38.8	51.9	48.1
26237	TALLMANSVILLE	98.4	98.1	0.0	0.0	0.4	0.6	0.2	0.2	5.7	5.7	6.1	5.7	5.3	27.1	30.3	12.0	2.3	79.0	41.5	51.9	48.1
26238	VOLGA	99.3	99.2	0.2	0.2	0.0	0.1	0.4	0.5	5.0	5.3	5.9	6.3	4.6	25.4	32.5	13.3	1.6	79.8	43.2	50.2	49.8
26241	ELKINS	97.7	97.7	0.6	0.6	0.7	0.7	0.8	0.7	5.1	5.2	5.5	7.1	6.0	23.6	29.0	15.4	3.2	80.2	43.1	48.4	51.6
26250	BELINGTON	98.8	98.6	0.1	0.1	0.1	0.2	0.4	0.5	5.7	5.9	6.2	6.5	5.0	23.8	29.3	15.2	2.4	78.2	42.6	50.0	50.0
26253	BEVERLY	99.0	99.0	0.2	0.2	0.2	0.2	0.6	0.6	6.2	6.4	6.8	6.8	5.0	26.0	28.3	12.1	2.3	75.9	40.2	48.5	51.5
26254	BOWDEN	98.7	98.6	0.7	0.7	0.0	0.0	0.7	0.0	4.8	4.8	6.1	4.8	4.1	25.2	32.0	16.3	2.0	81.0	45.2	51.0	49.0
26257	COALTON	98.5	98.4	1.0	1.0	0.1	0.1	0.4	0.4	5.9	6.4	6.9	7.7	4.7	24.9	28.9	12.9	1.6	75.8	40.7	49.8	50.2
26260	DAVIS	98.1	97.9	0.2	0.2	0.0	0.0	0.3	0.4	3.7	3.6	4.4	10.0	4.5	21.1	35.8	14.4	2.4	81.1	46.5	50.1	49.9
26261	RICHWOOD	98.8	98.4	0.1	0.1	0.3	0.5	0.5	0.6	4.8	4.8	5.0	5.4	5.3	22.4	30.0	18.3	4.0	82.1	46.8	47.6	52.4
26263	DRYFORK	98.9	98.9	0.4	0.4	0.0	0.0	0.4	0.4	4.6	5.0	5.4	5.4	3.8	24.5	33.3	16.1	1.9	81.2	45.8	51.7	48.3
26264	DURBIN	99.2	99.1	0.8	0.9	0.0	0.0	0.0	0.0	4.7	4.7	5.6	7.5	5.6	23.4	30.8	15.9	1.9	80.4	44.1	52.3	47.7
26266	UPPERGLADE	99.7	99.8	0.0	0.0	0.0	0.0	0.5	0.5	6.8	6.8	7.3	6.5	4.8	25.8	29.3	11.8	1.3	75.3	39.6	51.8	48.2
26267	ELLAMORE	99.1	99.1	0.4	0.5	0.0	0.0	0.7	0.7	5.9	6.2	6.6	6.8	4.8	25.1	30.3	13.0	1.4	76.8	41.1	49.7	50.3
26268	GLADY	98.8	98.8	0.1	0.2	0.0	0.0	0.3	0.3	5.4	5.8	6.1	5.8	3.8	22.8	32.8	14.7	2.8	79.0	45.1	48.1	51.9
26269	HAMBLETON	99.8	99.7	0.0	0.0	0.0	0.0	0.0	0.0	5.5	5.8	6.1	6.5	3.8	26.6	29.1	15.4	1.2	78.8	42.6	50.5	49.5
26270	HARMAN	98.7	98.6	0.5	0.5	0.0	0.0	0.5	0.5	4.6	5.2	5.7	5.2	4.0	24.6	33.4	15.7	1.7	81.1	45.5	52.0	48.0
26271	HENDRICKS	99.7	99.3	0.0	0.0	0.0	0.3	0.0	0.0	5.7	5.7	5.7	6.3	5.7	23.3	28.7	16.3	2.7	79.3	43.1	47.3	52.7
26273	HUTTONSVILLE	92.5	92.4	6.9	7.0	0.1	0.1	0.6	0.7	3.2	3.7	4.3	5.2	9.5	37.4	25.3	9.9	1.6	85.9	38.2	65.8	34.2
26276	KERENS	98.0	98.0	0.0	0.0	0.5	0.5	0.7	0.7	5.6	6.3	6.1	6.0	5.1	24.5	30.0	14.6	1.7	77.8	42.5	50.4	49.6
26278	MABIE	99.0	99.0	0.0	0.0	0.0	0.0	0.7	0.7	4.3	6.3	7.0	7.0	4.8	25.1	30.2	13.3	1.9	77.5	41.7	51.0	49.0
26280	MILL CREEK	94.7	94.6	4.3	4.4	0.2	0.2	0.5	0.4	5.1	5.1	5.2	5.3	8.2	34.3	26.1	9.2	1.3	81.2	37.2	59.6	40.4
26282	MONTERVILLE	100.0	100.0	0.0	0.0	0.0	0.0	0.0	0.0	3.0	3.0	6.0	6.0	4.5	23.9	34.3	16.4	3.0	82.1	47.5	50.7	49.3
26283	MONTROSE	98.0	98.1	0.0	0.0	0.5	0.4	0.9	0.8	5.5	6.7	6.0	6.4	5.9	24.9	30.8	12.5	1.3	77.3	41.2	51.6	48.4
26287	PARSONS	99.0	98.8	0.1	0.1	0.2	0.2	0.3	0.3	5.0	5.7	6.1	6.0	4.5	23.8	30.1	16.7	2.3	79.5	44.4	49.0	51.0
26288	WEBSTER SPRINGS	99.0	99.0	0.0	0.0	0.1	0.1	0.4	0.5	4.5	4.9	5.2	5.9	4.9	23.5	33.4	15.5	2.2	81.7	45.7	48.0	52.0
26289	RED CREEK	98.9	98.4	0.0	0.0	0.0	0.0	0.4	0.4	3.6	3.6	4.7	6.3	2.8	20.6	42.7	15.4	0.4	83.8	49.5	49.8	50.2
26291	SLATYFORK	99.1	99.0	0.0	0.0	0.0	0.0	0.5	0.8	5.8	6.3	6.7	5.4	4.6	25.0	32.3	12.5	1.3	77.9	42.7	52.5	47.5
26292	THOMAS	99.1	99.1	0.0	0.0	0.0	0.0	0.0	0.0	4.4	4.4	4.8	4.3	3.4	20.3	27.4	22.4	8.5	83.5	52.5	44.6	55.4
26293	VALLEY BEND	99.3	99.3	0.1	0.1	0.1	0.1	1.4	1.4	4.8	7.8	8.4	6.0	4.3	26.6	28.2	12.3	1.7	75.0	39.3	47.5	52.5
26294	VALLEY HEAD	99.3	99.3	0.0	0.0	0.0	0.0	0.6	0.6	4.2	5.0	5.9	6.4	4.7	23.1	32.8	15.5	2.4	80.8	45.4	50.1	49.9
26296	WHITMER	98.4	98.3	0.0	0.0	0.0	0.0	0.3	0.3	5.4	5.9	6.2	5.6	3.7	23.7	33.1	15.0	1.4	79.1	44.6	48.0	52.0
26301	CLARKSBURG	95.6	95.1	2.6	2.7	0.3	0.6	1.0	1.2	5.8	5.8	5.9	5.9	5.2	24.8	28.2	15.0	3.3	78.8	42.3	47.5	52.5
26320	ALMA	99.2	98.9	0.0	0.0	0.2	0.2	0.3	0.3	5.7	5.9	6.3	6.4	4.1	23.2	31.2	15.4	1.7	78.2	43.7	49.3	50.7
26321	ALUM BRIDGE	98.9	98.8	0.1	0.1	0.0	0.0	0.3	0.3	5.3	5.8	6.1	6.6	4.6	24.6	31.2	13.8	1.9	78.8	42.7	49.3	50.7
26325	AUBURN	98.3	98.3	0.0	0.0	0.3	0.3	0.3	0.3	5.2	5.6	6.6	7.3	5.2	22.3	31.0	14.6	2.1	78.0	43.1	49.8	50.2
26327	BEREA	98.4	98.4	0.0	0.0	0.0	0.0	0.0	0.0	5.7	5.7	6.6	7.4	4.9	22.1	31.1	13.9	2.5	77.9	42.9	49.2	50.8
26330	BRIDGEPORT	97.3	96.6	1.1	1.2	0.8	1.2	1.2	1.4	5.4	5.6	6.2	6.5	4.9	23.5	31.3	14.1	2.5	78.7	43.5	47.9	52.1
26335	BURNSVILLE	98.8	98.7	0.3	0.4	0.1	0.1	0.5	0.6	6.0	6.4	6.7	6.6	4.4	25.0	29.0	13.5	2.3	76.6	41.3	51.2	48.8
26337	CAIRO	99.4	99.4	0.1	0.1	0.1	0.1	0.5	0.5	5.9	6.2	6.3	5.6	4.2	24.9	30.9	14.4	1.6	78.1	42.9	49.0	51.0
26338	CAMDEN	98.7	98.5	0.2	0.2	0.0	0.0	0.6	0.8	5.5	6.0	6.3	6.8	4.9	24.1	30.4	14.3	1.6	77.9	42.7	51.2	48.8
26339	CENTER POINT	98.9	98.9	0.0	0.0	0.0	0.0	0.6	0.6	6.1	6.6	6.6	6.1	5.0	23.2	30.9	13.8	1.7	76.8	42.5	51.9	48.1
26342	COXS MILLS	98.6	98.2	0.3	0.4	0.1	0.4	0.1	0.4	4.8	5.2	5.1	5.4	6.8	30.6	27.1	13.1	1.9	82.3	39.8	56.0	44.0
26343	CRAWFORD	98.9	98.7	0.2	0.2	0.2	0.2	0.5	0.5	5.8	6.9	6.4	6.0	4.9	24.4	30.8	13.1	1.7	77.2	42.0	52.4	47.6
26346	ELLENBORO	98.5	98.5	0.1	0.1	0.2	0.2	0.4	0.3	6.1	6.8	6.5	5.4	4.7	27.8	30.6	10.9	1.3	77.3	40.3	49.7	50.3
26347	FLEMINGTON	98.9	98.8	0.3	0.3	0.1	0.2	0.8	1.0	5.3	5.6	6.0	6.1	4.8	26.6	30.9	13.0	1.7	79.4	42.1	50.7	49.3
26348	FOLSOM	99.4	99.4	0.0	0.0	0.0	0.0	0.3	0.3	6.6	6.6	6.6	6.0	4.1	24.7	29.4	14.2	1.6	76.6	41.3	47.8	52.2
26351	GLENVILLE	94.9	95.2	2.1	1.6	1.5	1.6	1.0	1.1	2.3	2.2	2.5	9.5	18.3	37.6	18.3	7.3	1.9	90.3	32.1	69.2	30.8
26354	GRAFTON	98.1	97.9	0.9	0.9	0.1	0.2	0.5	0.6	5.1	5.1	5.3	5.7	5.6	26.0	29.2	14.9	3.1	80.9	43.0	48.7	51.3
26362	HARRISVILLE	98.5	98.5	0.1	0.1	0.2	0.2	0.5	0.6	5.3	5.6	5.7	5.9	4.4	24.6	30.4	15.0	3.0	79.9	43.9	48.4	51.6
26372	HORNER	98.5	98.6	0.0	0.0	0.0	0.0	0.7	0.7	5.9	5.9	6.6	6.2	4.5	25.3	32.5	12.1	1.0	77.5	42.0	50.5	49.5
26374	INDEPENDENCE	98.6	98.3	0.2	0.3	0.1	0.2	0.6	0.8	5.2	5.6	5.9	5.3	4.1	24.2	32.2	15.4	2.0	79.8	44.7	49.8	50.2
26376	IRELAND	99.0	98.8	0.0	0.0	0.2	0.2	0.2	0.4	5.6	7.1	6.2	5.4	5.4	24.3	31.7	12.2	2.1	78.0	42.0	52.9	47.1
26377	JACKSONBURG	99.4	99.3	0.0	0.0	0.0	0.0	0.6	0.7	5.6	5.8	6.3	6.0	4.2	23.6	31.2	15.1	2.1	78.5	43.8	48.9	51.1
26378	JANE LEW	99.0	98.9	0.0	0.0	0.1	0.1	0.4	0.5	5.4	5.7	6.1	6.3	4.3	24.9	30.4	14.1	2.8	78.6	43.1	48.6	51.4
26384	LINN	99.2	99.0	0.0	0.0	0.0	0.0	0.7	0.9	6.7	6.7	6.4	5.8	5.4	26.1	25.9	14.9	2.0	76.4	40.5	51.0	49.0
26385	LOST CREEK	98.7	98.3	0.1	0.1	0.1	0.2	0.7	0.9	6.0	6.2	6.6	7.1	4.8	27.5	29.6	10.9	1.3	76.7	39.8	49.8	50.2
26386	LUMBERPORT	99.2	98.9	0.1	0.1	0.1	0.2	0.8	1.0	5.6	6.3	6.6	7.0	4.6	25.2	29.6	12.9	2.2	77.0	41.5	50.0	50.0
26404	MEADOWBROOK	98.1	97.7	0.7	0.8	0.1	0.3	1.5	1.7	7.0	6.8	6.9	7.0	5.4	24.8	26.2	13.8	2.2	75.2	39.6	47.8	52.2
26405	MOATSVILLE	97.0	96.8	0.3	0.3	0.1	0.2	0.5	0.7	3.9	5.1	5.7	7.1	4.9	24.1	33.3	13.7	2.1	80.6	44.4	51.5	48.5
26408	MOUNT CLARE	98.1	97.7	0.6	0.6	0.4	0.7	1.0	1.2	5.3	5.9	6.8	6.5	4.1	24.1	33.6	12.2	1.6	78.0	43.3	47.4	52.6
26410	NEWBURG	98.7	98.6	0.2	0.2	0.0	0.0	0.6	0.7	5.0	5.3	5.6	6.0	4.9	23.8	31.8	15.8	1.9	80.5	44.6	50.4	49.6
26411	NEW MILTON	98.4	98.4	0.0	0.0	0.2	0.2	0.8	0.8	5.4	5.8	6.4	6.5	4.4	23.0	32.1	14.6	1.8	78.3	43.9	51.6	48.4
26412	ORLANDO	98.5	98.7	0.0	0.0	0.0	0.0	0.5	0.9	6.2	6.6	6.6	5.8	4.4	26.1	31.4	11.5	1.3	76.5	41.4	49.6	50.4
26415	PENNSBORO	98.5	98.6	0.2	0.2	0.1	0.1	0.5	0.5	5.6	5.8	6.1	6.3	5.0	24.5	30.6	14.3	2.0	78.8	42.6	48.3	51.7
26416	PHILIPPI	96.3	95.9	0.8	0.8	0.4	0.7	0.5	0.6	5.3	5.7	5.8	7.8	6.7	24.7	27.9	13.5	2.5	79.3	40.2	48.5	51.5
26419	PINE GROVE	99.6	99.5	0.0	0.0	0.0	0.0	0.6	0.6	5.4	6.0	6.8	6.6	4.6	24.9	30.6	12.9	2.2	77.6	41.8	48.6	51.4
26421	PULLMAN	97.4	97.3	0.0	0.0	0.4	0.4	0.4	0.4	5.0	5.0	5.7	6.1	6.1	23.7	32.8	13.4	2.3	81.3	43.8	47.7	52.3
26425	ROWLESBURG	99.0	98.5	0.0	0.0	0.1	0.3	0.1	0.1	5.2	5.4	5.5	6.1	5.7	23.8	29.1	16.9	2.3	80.1	43.7	48.3	51.7
26426	SALEM	94.7	93.7	1.2	1.1	2.5	3.5	0.8	0.9	5.2	5.3	5.9	9.0	8.1	23.3	27.6	13.2	2.4	78.4	39.3	50.0	50.0
26430	SAND FORK	99.1	99.0	0.0	0.0	0.2	0.2	0.6	0.6	5.2	4.5	7.1	8.6	5.5	25.1	28.2	13.3	2.6	77.3	40.8	49.2	50.8
26431	SHINNSTON	98.4	98.2	0.5	0.6	0.2	0.2	0.8	0.9	5.5	6.0	6.4	5.9	4.6	25.5	29.6	14.2	2.3	78.4	42.2	48.6	51.4
26437	SMITHFIELD	99.4	99.3	0.0	0.0	0.0	0.0	0.6	0.7	6.3	6.6	6.6	6.1	4.1	24.8	29.8	14.1	1.6	76.6	41.6	48.5	51.5
26440	THORNTON	98.5	98.3	0.2	0.2	0.4	0.5	0.6	0.7	4.6	4.9	5.3	6.3	5.2	24.5	32.1	14.5	2.6	81.0	44.5	50.6	49.4
26443	TROY	99.0	99.0	0.0	0.0	0.0	0.0	0.0	0.0	5.1	6.1	7.1	6.1	4.0	23.2	31.3	15.2	2.0	76.8	43.8	48.5	51.5
26444	TUNNELTON	99.2	99.0	0.1	0.1	0.0	0.1	0.6	0.7	5.2	5.5	6.0	6.6	5.1	24.5	31.5	14.0	1.7	79.3	43.1	50.1	49.9
26447	WALKERSVILLE	98.5	98.4	0.1	0.1	0.1	0.1	0.5	0.6	5.7	6.4	6.3	5.9	4.7	25.3	31.7	12.3	1.6	77.9	42.1	51.2	48.8
	WEST VIRGINIA	95.0	94.5	3.2	3.3	0.5	0.8	0.7	0.8	5.5	5.6	5.9	6.5	6.1	25.2	29.3	13.8	2.2	79.3	41.5	49.0	51.0
	UNITED STATES	75.1	72.0	12.3	12.7	3.8	4.6	12.5	15.7	6.8	6.7	6.6	7.1	6.9	27.0	26.0	10.9	1.9	75.7	36.9	49.2	50.8

26181-26447

ZIP CODE #	POST OFFICE NAME	2009 Per Capita Income	2009 HH Income Base	2009 HOUSEHOLD INCOME DISTRIBUTION (%) Less than $25,000	$25,000 to $49,999	$50,000 to $99,999	$100,000 to $149,999	$150,000 or More	MEDIAN HOUSEHOLD INCOME 2009	2014	2009 National Centile	2009 State Centile	2009 Home Value Base	2009 HOME VALUE DISTRIBUTION (%) Less than $50,000	$50,000 to $89,999	$90,000 to $174,999	$175,000 to $399,999	$400,000 or More	2009 Median Home Value
26181	WASHINGTON	25761	2401	15.5	26.3	42.7	11.3	4.2	58014	58067	75	99	2162	11.1	16.9	54.5	17.3	0.2	117736
26184	WAVERLY	21185	877	28.2	27.8	33.6	7.5	2.9	42966	45567	42	91	763	26.0	21.1	40.0	12.1	0.9	99000
26187	WILLIAMSTOWN	24254	2578	22.8	29.4	36.2	8.2	3.5	47617	49361	56	95	2060	12.1	22.6	54.5	10.1	0.7	109961
26201	BUCKHANNON	18049	7076	35.6	31.7	27.0	4.2	1.6	35301	35763	19	67	5233	14.9	20.2	45.3	17.0	2.5	110081
26202	FENWICK	14633	151	44.4	32.5	17.9	5.3	0.0	28066	29605	6	26	133	46.6	15.0	34.6	3.8	0.0	55625
26203	ERBACON	13412	118	54.2	24.6	18.6	0.8	1.7	19391	23611	1	2	90	41.1	31.1	26.7	1.1	0.0	63333
26205	CRAIGSVILLE	17564	1577	38.6	33.9	23.5	2.3	1.8	31392	31593	10	46	1307	30.8	25.7	37.1	5.7	0.6	79713
26206	COWEN	13929	1293	49.8	30.6	17.4	1.2	0.9	25097	25684	3	13	1024	33.4	32.6	27.1	6.2	0.8	66238
26208	CAMDEN ON GAULEY	14298	447	48.5	30.4	16.8	3.1	1.1	25804	26314	4	15	354	33.9	34.5	24.0	5.9	1.7	64138
26210	ADRIAN	16997	375	33.9	36.5	25.9	2.7	1.1	33930	34259	15	59	311	14.5	28.0	44.4	8.7	4.5	102455
26215	CLEVELAND	13505	167	46.7	32.3	17.4	3.6	0.0	27882	27817	5	25	143	21.0	30.1	37.1	11.9	0.0	88846
26217	DIANA	11404	384	61.7	25.5	11.5	1.0	0.3	20000	19939	1	3	313	34.5	40.6	22.7	1.3	1.0	65000
26218	FRENCH CREEK	15382	918	43.1	31.7	20.8	3.4	1.0	28677	29374	6	29	771	24.9	27.1	34.2	10.4	3.4	87877
26222	HACKER VALLEY	16228	256	33.2	45.7	18.4	1.2	1.6	33255	32524	14	55	221	35.7	28.1	33.5	2.7	0.0	74167
26224	HELVETIA	14647	83	47.0	31.3	19.3	2.4	0.0	25851	26797	4	16	71	28.2	28.2	33.8	5.6	4.2	79000
26228	KANAWHA HEAD	12464	65	49.2	33.8	15.4	0.0	1.5	25294	25294	3	14	55	25.5	32.7	36.4	3.6	1.8	83571
26230	PICKENS	15181	94	44.7	33.0	19.1	3.2	0.0	26654	27212	4	20	80	28.8	26.3	36.3	5.0	3.8	80000
26234	ROCK CAVE	13801	263	51.3	32.7	14.4	0.0	1.5	24400	25220	3	11	223	24.2	33.6	36.3	4.0	1.8	84167
26236	SELBYVILLE	13981	13	53.8	30.8	15.4	0.0	0.0	23495	27290	2	9	11	9.1	45.5	45.5	0.0	0.0	87500
26237	TALLMANSVILLE	15106	186	44.6	27.4	25.3	0.5	2.2	27127	27351	5	21	158	41.1	29.1	28.5	1.3	0.0	63636
26238	VOLGA	15281	522	36.6	37.0	23.2	3.3	0.0	34203	33964	16	60	445	15.7	33.3	37.1	13.9	0.0	91552
26241	ELKINS	20456	5940	33.1	33.6	26.2	5.2	1.9	36957	38110	23	75	4144	12.9	20.9	45.0	19.2	2.0	114684
26250	BELINGTON	15368	2256	44.7	30.7	21.9	1.7	1.1	28544	28821	6	28	1803	25.2	32.2	33.8	8.0	0.8	77963
26253	BEVERLY	17109	1454	35.4	35.4	24.7	3.4	1.1	34837	35041	17	64	1121	23.9	17.6	38.8	16.7	3.0	101320
26254	BOWDEN	18469	67	35.8	35.8	23.9	4.5	0.0	32713	33382	13	52	55	29.1	16.4	34.5	20.0	0.0	101786
26257	COALTON	13470	562	47.9	27.8	23.8	0.5	0.0	26064	27126	4	17	503	28.8	28.4	30.4	9.5	2.8	77424
26260	DAVIS	23561	512	38.3	26.0	27.5	3.9	4.3	33881	33895	15	58	402	20.4	25.4	28.6	24.6	1.0	101630
26261	RICHWOOD	16028	1512	43.8	32.0	19.4	3.4	1.3	27830	28387	5	25	1169	49.7	24.4	22.4	3.5	0.0	50402
26263	DRYFORK	20669	117	35.9	34.2	23.9	4.3	1.7	33063	33128	13	54	96	28.1	14.6	33.3	22.9	1.0	110000
26264	DURBIN	12554	42	52.4	31.0	11.9	2.4	2.4	23984	26743	3	10	34	35.3	29.4	32.4	2.9	0.0	70000
26266	UPPERGLADE	13007	159	50.3	33.3	15.7	0.0	0.6	24638	25259	3	12	130	31.5	33.8	26.2	8.5	0.0	65833
26267	ELLAMORE	14385	166	42.8	30.7	24.1	1.8	0.6	30000	31078	8	35	144	27.1	20.8	37.5	9.7	4.9	92727
26268	GLADY	19093	273	35.2	33.0	25.3	3.7	2.9	35925	35889	20	70	231	19.0	16.5	40.7	21.2	2.6	116369
26269	HAMBLETON	17513	300	32.0	44.3	16.7	4.7	2.3	35808	35553	20	70	257	26.5	23.3	38.5	10.1	1.6	90333
26270	HARMAN	19973	254	34.3	35.8	23.2	4.7	2.0	33717	33526	15	57	208	29.8	14.4	32.7	22.6	0.5	105435
26271	HENDRICKS	20682	122	36.9	33.6	22.1	4.1	3.3	32037	32298	11	49	106	29.2	36.8	29.2	4.7	0.0	70000
26273	HUTTONSVILLE	8202	222	45.0	32.9	18.9	2.7	0.5	27149	27352	5	21	188	28.7	31.4	31.4	5.9	2.7	74615
26276	KERENS	15749	231	36.4	33.8	26.4	2.6	0.9	34566	34877	17	62	189	19.6	23.3	38.1	18.0	1.1	101563
26278	MABIE	13296	149	38.3	36.9	23.5	1.3	0.0	29831	30178	8	33	130	17.7	30.8	34.6	14.6	2.3	92222
26280	MILL CREEK	16709	773	40.4	34.9	22.4	1.3	1.0	30970	31704	10	44	610	32.0	28.5	30.3	6.9	2.3	70233
26282	MONTERVILLE	18688	27	44.4	33.3	14.8	3.7	3.7	27247	27247	5	22	22	36.4	18.2	40.9	4.5	0.0	80000
26283	MONTROSE	16127	461	35.1	36.2	26.2	2.0	0.4	34129	34276	16	59	393	21.1	22.1	38.4	18.3	0.0	99138
26287	PARSONS	18489	1380	39.2	32.5	24.1	2.2	2.0	33423	33783	14	56	1150	28.5	27.6	34.6	9.0	0.3	80541
26288	WEBSTER SPRINGS	16285	1527	49.6	29.9	16.9	2.1	1.5	25231	26086	3	14	1161	35.5	32.0	28.3	3.2	0.9	65781
26289	RED CREEK	24923	113	37.2	19.5	31.0	5.3	7.1	37361	40000	25	78	93	14.0	17.2	22.6	45.2	1.1	165278
26291	SLATYFORK	19931	245	40.4	26.5	26.9	5.7	0.4	31810	33273	11	48	197	23.4	22.3	27.4	23.9	3.0	98500
26292	THOMAS	16614	325	44.6	30.8	22.2	1.5	0.9	26767	27358	4	20	254	30.3	30.7	33.9	5.1	0.0	78095
26293	VALLEY BEND	16031	392	32.1	40.6	24.7	2.6	0.0	34165	35117	16	60	317	23.7	16.4	49.2	10.7	0.0	101982
26294	VALLEY HEAD	19931	408	43.4	30.9	18.1	3.4	4.2	27686	28639	5	24	341	29.9	22.6	36.4	9.7	1.5	85278
26296	WHITMER	19172	154	38.3	31.8	23.4	3.2	3.2	35000	34449	18	66	132	19.7	18.2	40.9	19.7	1.5	110714
26301	CLARKSBURG	20209	14049	36.9	29.3	26.5	5.1	2.1	35030	34989	18	66	9749	22.0	29.0	36.9	10.6	1.6	88393
26320	ALMA	16289	511	38.0	37.8	21.1	2.5	0.6	31929	31683	11	48	442	30.1	23.5	32.8	11.8	1.8	83600
26321	ALUM BRIDGE	15934	313	40.9	31.3	24.0	2.2	1.6	29524	30000	7	32	244	26.6	21.7	38.9	11.1	1.6	92857
26325	AUBURN	15492	112	52.7	28.6	14.3	1.8	2.7	23539	24725	2	9	94	29.8	28.7	25.5	11.7	4.3	76000
26327	BEREA	14201	49	57.1	24.5	14.3	2.0	2.0	21802	22234	2	5	41	31.7	29.3	22.0	12.2	4.9	69000
26330	BRIDGEPORT	25512	5462	21.2	26.0	38.9	10.3	3.6	52480	52734	67	97	4360	8.6	12.4	37.5	36.0	5.5	150844
26335	BURNSVILLE	15072	598	42.6	37.1	16.4	2.8	1.0	29515	29362	7	32	459	30.1	28.3	34.9	6.1	0.7	80128
26337	CAIRO	18248	582	33.5	33.2	29.0	3.3	1.0	35680	35412	20	69	493	33.1	23.1	31.0	8.7	4.1	80469
26338	CAMDEN	13753	245	43.3	35.5	20.0	0.4	0.8	28577	28990	6	28	193	34.7	25.4	27.5	12.4	0.0	77083
26339	CENTER POINT	14876	76	43.4	35.5	19.7	0.0	1.3	30613	30528	9	40	62	24.2	32.3	35.5	8.1	0.0	75000
26342	COXS MILLS	15012	287	37.3	36.9	20.9	4.2	0.7	30309	30759	9	37	218	18.3	25.7	43.1	11.5	1.4	107895
26343	CRAWFORD	14141	256	45.7	31.6	19.1	2.3	1.2	27692	28014	5	24	206	22.8	30.6	35.0	10.2	1.5	85882
26346	ELLENBORO	17686	347	30.3	34.3	31.7	2.6	1.2	37370	39101	25	78	295	32.2	24.4	29.2	11.5	2.7	81136
26347	FLEMINGTON	15671	1014	38.9	32.9	24.2	2.7	1.4	30610	31288	9	40	835	32.0	24.4	29.9	11.5	2.2	77941
26348	FOLSOM	16354	121	44.6	31.4	19.0	4.1	0.8	28442	29417	6	27	97	53.6	24.7	15.5	6.2	0.0	47083
26351	GLENVILLE	12922	997	45.7	28.8	19.4	4.3	1.8	27668	28712	5	24	589	21.9	26.0	33.6	16.3	2.2	93571
26354	GRAFTON	16390	4145	38.8	34.3	22.6	3.4	0.9	31513	32041	11	47	3218	28.1	23.7	35.8	10.4	2.0	87062
26362	HARRISVILLE	18280	1394	38.5	29.2	27.5	3.8	1.0	34512	34190	17	61	1085	24.6	25.3	36.2	11.9	1.9	90057
26372	HORNER	18504	124	37.9	33.9	21.8	4.0	2.4	35000	36426	18	66	99	23.2	18.2	38.4	17.2	3.0	103409
26374	INDEPENDENCE	19243	533	31.1	31.3	31.0	5.1	1.5	38911	40130	29	82	466	23.6	19.3	43.1	13.1	0.9	105460
26376	IRELAND	14783	194	42.8	34.0	20.1	2.1	1.0	28497	28681	6	27	150	21.3	31.3	36.7	10.0	0.7	85000
26377	JACKSONBURG	16654	233	37.8	34.3	24.0	3.0	0.9	32022	32038	11	49	189	37.6	31.2	25.9	5.3	0.0	63000
26378	JANE LEW	18028	1985	35.3	32.3	27.3	4.0	1.1	35776	35964	20	69	1509	17.8	22.2	41.3	16.0	2.8	104967
26384	LINN	14738	275	50.9	26.2	17.1	3.6	2.2	24571	25821	3	12	214	30.8	22.9	40.7	5.1	0.5	81111
26385	LOST CREEK	20741	1370	27.4	31.5	31.2	6.4	3.4	41897	43735	39	88	1136	15.1	18.8	44.2	19.5	2.5	116286
26386	LUMBERPORT	19066	920	34.7	27.9	28.4	7.1	2.0	36185	36467	21	71	752	31.4	23.3	35.2	8.0	2.1	81463
26404	MEADOWBROOK	16035	449	36.7	36.1	25.6	0.9	0.7	32346	32390	12	51	348	31.6	35.9	26.1	6.0	0.3	65625
26405	MOATSVILLE	15842	544	34.2	45.2	15.4	4.0	1.1	29857	29810	8	33	478	24.7	28.5	31.4	14.9	0.6	85714
26408	MOUNT CLARE	26233	705	16.9	25.7	44.0	9.9	3.5	57784	58561	75	98	606	8.4	10.6	35.0	40.3	5.8	164091
26410	NEWBURG	14561	509	42.2	28.3	25.1	2.8	1.6	32093	33911	12	49	445	28.3	31.0	34.2	6.5	0.0	75147
26411	NEW MILTON	18047	341	33.7	36.7	23.8	5.0	0.9	35530	36227	19	68	278	19.4	31.3	30.9	15.8	2.5	89429
26412	ORLANDO	16125	88	37.5	36.4	18.2	4.5	3.4	35000	34065	18	66	70	25.7	20.0	35.7	14.3	4.3	96000
26415	PENNSBORO	17843	1308	36.8	31.4	26.0	4.0	1.8	35000	35331	18	66	1059	32.5	26.9	28.6	10.8	1.2	73904
26416	PHILIPPI	15836	3183	41.6	33.0	20.8	3.6	0.9	30619	31235	9	40	2385	23.9	24.6	37.1	13.7	0.6	92537
26419	PINE GROVE	19466	269	34.6	33.8	26.0	3.0	2.6	35700	35375	20	69	205	33.2	36.1	26.3	4.4	0.0	66176
26421	PULLMAN	17214	104	40.4	23.1	28.8	7.7	0.0	32332	33046	12	51	88	26.1	22.7	28.4	19.3	3.4	91667
26425	ROWLESBURG	17974	283	35.0	33.6	27.6	2.5	1.4	36347	37716	22	72	229	37.1	34.9	24.9	3.1	0.0	60263
26426	SALEM	17286	2983	37.5	32.8	23.6	3.8	2.3	33983	34024	15	59	2308	23.4	24.3	36.3	14.6	1.4	93557
26430	SAND FORK	14073	250	50.0	30.0	18.0	0.4	1.6	25000	25269	3	13	197	34.5	17.8	36.0	10.7	1.0	83571
26431	SHINNSTON	19518	2407	35.6	28.5	28.2	5.4	2.3	35354	35331	19	67	1882	23.5	26.6	35.5	13.0	1.4	89919
26437	SMITHFIELD	18031	255	40.4	32.5	22.4	3.5	1.2	30810	30993	9	42	206	47.6	26.2	18.9	7.3	0.0	52381
26440	THORNTON	15765	480	43.8	33.8	17.9	2.9	1.7	29182	30499	7	31	402	32.8	29.1	29.1	8.7	0.2	72973
26443	TROY	17275	44	40.9	34.1	20.5	4.5	0.0	28832	30000	6	30	34	17.6	29.4	35.3	14.7	2.9	105000
26444	TUNNELTON	14505	1313	43.4	36.2	17.5	2.1	0.8	28665	30442	6	29	1141	42.6	27.8	24.5	4.8	0.4	60422
26447	WALKERSVILLE	16104	635	39.7	36.1	19.5	3.0	1.7	30948	30700	10	44	497	25.2	24.3	36.0	11.9	2.6	90735
	WEST VIRGINIA	20563		34.3	29.3	28.3	5.4	2.7	37099	38541				22.0	23.9	36.4	15.5	2.2	98135
	UNITED STATES	27277		20.9	24.4	35.3	11.7	7.6	54719	56938				9.3	13.1	31.6	32.6	13.5	162279

ZIP CODE		FINANCIAL SERVICES				THE HOME						ENTERTAINMENT						PERSONAL			
						Home Improvements		Furnishings													
#	POST OFFICE NAME	Auto Loan	Home Loan	Invest-ments	Retire-ment Plans	Home Repair	Lawn & Garden	Comput-ers & Hard-ware-Personal	Major Appli-ances	TV, Radio, Sound Equip-ment	Furni-ture	Dine out/ Carry out	Sports Equip-ment	Fees & Tickets	Toys & Games	Travel	Cable TV	Apparel & Services	Auto Repairs	Health Insur-ance	Pets & Supplies
26181	WASHINGTON	99	96	98	96	95	107	89	100	92	87	92	76	88	94	92	96	63	94	102	117
26184	WAVERLY	89	77	78	77	77	89	75	84	79	73	78	63	68	81	73	83	53	79	87	100
26187	WILLIAMSTOWN	83	86	82	86	86	94	80	87	84	78	83	63	82	84	84	88	57	84	94	101
26201	BUCKHANNON	72	56	69	55	57	73	60	69	64	55	63	52	50	64	57	70	42	66	73	82
26202	FENWICK	66	47	68	46	49	67	49	62	54	45	53	46	39	54	48	59	35	57	64	74
26203	ERBACON	56	36	54	34	36	55	39	49	45	37	44	38	29	46	36	50	29	46	52	60
26205	CRAIGSVILLE	74	51	71	49	52	74	55	68	62	51	60	52	43	62	52	68	40	63	72	82
26206	COWEN	61	40	59	37	39	60	42	53	49	40	48	42	32	50	39	54	32	50	56	66
26208	CAMDEN ON GAULEY	65	42	63	40	42	64	45	57	52	43	51	45	34	53	42	58	34	54	60	70
26210	ADRIAN	74	53	76	52	55	75	55	70	61	51	60	52	44	60	54	67	39	64	72	83
26215	CLEVELAND	59	42	60	41	44	60	43	55	48	40	47	41	34	48	43	53	31	50	57	65
26217	DIANA	48	31	46	30	31	47	34	42	39	32	38	33	25	39	31	43	25	40	44	52
26218	FRENCH CREEK	68	49	70	47	51	69	50	64	56	47	55	48	40	55	49	61	36	59	66	76
26222	HACKER VALLEY	69	49	59	47	49	66	51	60	57	50	56	46	41	59	47	62	37	57	63	73
26224	HELVETIA	61	43	62	42	45	62	45	57	50	42	49	43	35	50	44	55	32	52	59	68
26228	KANAWHA HEAD	58	42	59	40	43	59	43	54	48	40	47	41	34	47	42	52	31	50	57	65
26230	PICKENS	61	43	61	41	44	61	44	56	49	41	48	42	35	49	43	54	32	52	58	67
26234	ROCK CAVE	58	41	59	40	43	59	42	54	47	39	46	41	34	47	42	52	31	50	56	64
26236	SELBYVILLE	52	37	53	36	39	53	38	49	42	35	42	36	30	42	38	47	27	44	50	58
26237	TALLMANSVILLE	72	47	69	44	47	70	50	63	58	48	56	49	38	59	47	64	37	59	67	78
26238	VOLGA	69	49	71	48	51	70	50	64	56	47	55	48	40	56	50	62	36	59	67	76
26241	ELKINS	73	62	73	61	64	77	64	72	69	60	67	53	58	68	63	74	46	69	79	85
26250	BELINGTON	66	47	66	45	48	67	49	62	55	45	54	47	39	55	48	61	36	57	66	74
26253	BEVERLY	74	56	63	55	56	72	57	67	63	55	61	51	47	65	53	68	41	63	70	80
26254	BOWDEN	72	52	74	50	54	73	53	68	59	50	58	51	43	59	53	65	38	62	70	80
26257	COALTON	62	41	61	39	42	61	44	55	50	41	49	43	33	50	42	56	32	52	58	67
26260	DAVIS	84	64	96	62	68	89	67	84	73	61	71	62	56	70	68	79	47	78	87	98
26261	RICHWOOD	64	45	64	44	47	65	49	61	55	44	53	45	39	54	47	60	35	56	65	72
26263	DRYFORK	82	59	85	57	62	83	61	77	67	56	66	58	49	66	60	74	43	71	80	92
26264	DURBIN	59	39	57	37	39	58	41	52	48	39	47	41	31	49	39	53	31	49	55	64
26266	UPPERGLADE	61	40	59	37	40	60	42	53	49	40	48	42	32	50	40	55	32	50	57	66
26267	ELLAMORE	69	48	69	46	49	69	50	63	56	47	55	48	39	56	48	62	36	58	66	76
26268	GLADY	78	59	79	58	61	81	60	75	66	56	65	56	50	66	60	72	43	69	77	88
26269	HAMBLETON	78	56	80	55	58	80	58	74	65	54	63	55	47	64	57	71	42	68	77	88
26270	HARMAN	82	58	84	57	61	83	60	76	67	56	65	57	48	66	59	73	43	70	79	91
26271	HENDRICKS	86	62	86	60	64	90	68	83	75	60	73	62	54	74	65	83	48	78	91	98
26273	HUTTONSVILLE	66	46	66	44	47	66	48	60	54	44	52	46	37	54	46	59	35	56	63	72
26276	KERENS	71	52	71	51	54	73	55	68	60	50	59	51	45	60	54	66	39	62	72	80
26278	MABIE	66	47	68	46	49	67	48	62	54	45	53	46	39	53	48	59	35	57	64	73
26280	MILL CREEK	71	49	63	47	48	68	51	62	58	49	57	48	40	60	47	64	38	58	65	76
26282	MONTERVILLE	80	57	80	56	59	82	61	76	68	55	66	57	49	67	60	75	44	71	82	90
26283	MONTROSE	70	50	72	49	52	72	52	66	58	48	57	50	42	58	51	64	38	61	69	78
26287	PARSONS	74	53	75	51	54	76	56	70	63	51	61	53	45	63	55	70	41	65	76	83
26288	WEBSTER SPRINGS	63	43	62	41	44	64	46	58	53	43	51	44	36	53	44	59	34	54	62	70
26289	RED CREEK	93	75	120	73	82	98	75	95	78	70	77	69	65	74	81	83	51	87	94	110
26291	SLATYFORK	74	55	82	53	58	76	56	71	61	52	60	53	46	59	57	66	40	65	73	84
26292	THOMAS	61	44	61	43	45	63	48	59	53	43	51	44	38	52	46	59	34	55	64	69
26293	VALLEY BEND	72	51	72	50	53	72	53	66	58	49	57	50	42	58	52	64	38	61	69	79
26294	VALLEY HEAD	79	57	80	55	59	81	60	75	67	55	65	56	48	66	59	74	43	70	81	89
26296	WHITMER	79	56	81	55	59	80	58	74	64	54	63	55	46	64	57	71	42	68	77	87
26301	CLARKSBURG	74	58	72	58	60	76	63	72	68	58	67	54	54	67	61	74	45	69	79	85
26320	ALMA	69	49	70	48	51	70	50	64	56	47	55	48	40	56	50	62	36	59	67	76
26321	ALUM BRIDGE	69	49	70	47	51	70	50	64	56	47	55	48	40	56	50	62	36	59	67	76
26325	AUBURN	72	50	72	48	52	72	52	66	58	49	57	50	41	58	51	64	38	61	69	79
26327	BEREA	63	45	65	44	47	64	46	59	52	43	51	44	37	51	46	57	33	54	61	70
26330	BRIDGEPORT	96	88	93	88	90	101	85	95	89	84	88	70	81	89	86	94	60	90	100	111
26335	BURNSVILLE	64	46	64	44	47	64	47	59	52	44	52	45	38	53	46	58	34	55	62	71
26337	CAIRO	78	56	78	54	58	79	58	72	64	54	63	55	46	64	56	70	42	67	76	86
26338	CAMDEN	63	43	62	41	43	63	45	57	51	42	50	44	35	52	43	57	33	53	60	69
26339	CENTER POINT	63	45	65	44	47	64	46	59	52	43	51	44	37	51	46	57	33	54	62	70
26342	COXS MILLS	67	48	68	47	50	67	51	63	56	47	55	47	41	55	49	61	36	58	65	74
26343	CRAWFORD	64	44	64	42	45	64	46	58	52	43	51	44	36	52	45	57	33	54	61	70
26346	ELLENBORO	79	57	65	55	56	75	59	69	65	57	64	53	47	68	54	71	43	65	72	84
26347	FLEMINGTON	71	52	72	50	53	72	53	67	59	49	58	50	43	59	52	64	38	61	69	79
26348	FOLSOM	79	52	77	49	52	78	55	70	64	53	62	54	41	65	52	71	41	66	74	86
26351	GLENVILLE	65	48	57	49	49	61	61	60	62	53	60	47	49	61	53	64	41	61	64	72
26354	GRAFTON	67	49	65	48	50	68	53	63	58	48	57	48	43	58	50	64	38	60	68	75
26362	HARRISVILLE	74	53	74	51	54	76	56	70	62	51	61	53	44	62	54	69	40	65	75	83
26372	HORNER	77	55	79	53	57	78	57	72	63	53	62	54	45	62	56	69	41	66	75	86
26374	INDEPENDENCE	81	62	79	62	64	83	63	77	68	59	67	58	53	69	62	74	45	71	79	91
26376	IRELAND	67	46	66	43	46	67	48	61	54	45	53	46	37	55	46	60	35	56	64	73
26377	JACKSONBURG	72	51	73	49	53	73	53	67	60	49	58	51	43	59	52	66	39	62	71	80
26378	JANE LEW	75	55	75	54	57	77	57	71	62	52	61	53	46	62	56	68	41	65	74	84
26384	LINN	68	45	66	42	45	67	48	60	55	45	54	47	36	56	45	61	35	57	64	74
26385	LOST CREEK	90	72	88	72	74	94	73	87	78	67	76	66	62	78	72	84	51	80	91	103
26386	LUMBERPORT	88	62	89	60	64	89	64	82	71	60	70	61	51	71	63	79	46	75	85	97
26404	MEADOWBROOK	66	48	67	46	49	69	52	64	58	46	56	48	41	57	50	64	37	60	69	75
26405	MOATSVILLE	69	49	71	48	51	70	51	64	56	47	55	48	40	56	50	62	36	59	67	77
26408	MOUNT CLARE	96	97	93	100	96	104	91	98	92	88	91	76	91	93	94	94	63	94	100	116
26410	NEWBURG	72	49	71	46	49	71	51	65	58	48	57	50	39	58	49	64	38	60	68	78
26411	NEW MILTON	82	59	84	57	61	83	60	76	67	56	66	57	48	66	59	73	43	70	80	91
26412	ORLANDO	74	53	76	51	55	75	54	69	60	51	59	52	43	60	54	66	39	63	72	82
26415	PENNSBORO	74	53	73	51	54	76	57	70	64	52	62	53	45	63	55	70	41	66	76	83
26416	PHILIPPI	66	47	66	46	49	67	51	62	56	47	55	47	41	56	49	62	37	58	66	74
26419	PINE GROVE	79	57	80	55	59	82	61	76	68	55	66	57	49	67	59	74	44	70	81	89
26421	PULLMAN	77	55	80	54	58	79	57	72	63	53	62	54	46	63	56	69	41	66	75	86
26425	ROWLESBURG	74	53	75	52	55	77	58	72	65	52	62	54	46	64	56	71	42	67	78	84
26426	SALEM	72	56	70	56	58	73	60	70	65	55	64	52	51	64	58	70	43	66	74	82
26430	SAND FORK	65	42	62	40	42	63	45	57	52	43	51	44	34	53	42	58	34	54	60	70
26431	SHINNSTON	78	63	79	61	64	82	63	76	69	59	67	56	55	68	63	75	45	71	81	89
26437	SMITHFIELD	79	53	78	50	53	78	56	71	64	53	62	55	43	65	53	71	41	66	74	86
26440	THORNTON	69	46	67	44	46	68	49	62	56	46	55	48	37	56	46	62	36	58	65	75
26443	TROY	69	50	71	48	52	70	51	65	57	47	56	49	41	56	50	62	37	60	68	77
26444	TUNNELTON	64	43	63	41	44	64	46	58	52	43	51	44	35	52	44	58	34	54	61	70
26447	WALKERSVILLE	70	50	72	48	51	71	51	65	57	48	56	49	41	57	50	63	37	60	68	78
	WEST VIRGINIA	79	63	76	62	64	80	66	75	71	63	70	57	58	71	64	77	47	72	80	90
	UNITED STATES	100	100	100	100	100	100	100	100	100	100	100	100	100	100	100	100	100	100	100	100

POPULATION CHANGE

ZIP CODE #	POST OFFICE NAME	COUNTY FIPS CODE	POPULATION 2000	POPULATION 2009	POPULATION 2014	2000-2009 ANNUAL RATE % Rate	2000-2009 ANNUAL RATE State Centile	HOUSEHOLDS 2000	HOUSEHOLDS 2009	HOUSEHOLDS 2014	HOUSEHOLDS % Annual Rate 2000-2009	HOUSEHOLDS 2009 Average HH Size	FAMILIES 2000	FAMILIES 2009	FAMILIES % Annual Rate 2000-2009
26448	WALLACE	033	1325	1310	1299	-0.1	57	501	509	510	0.2	2.57	373	367	-0.2
26451	WEST MILFORD	033	1628	1625	1627	0.0	65	588	603	609	0.3	2.68	464	464	0.0
26452	WESTON	041	9723	9829	9834	0.1	72	4067	4252	4299	0.5	2.28	2731	2754	0.1
26456	WEST UNION	017	3244	3253	3227	0.0	65	1286	1322	1320	0.3	2.46	929	927	0.0
26501	MORGANTOWN	061	21542	21259	21257	-0.1	57	9278	9184	9226	-0.1	2.25	5635	5315	-0.6
26505	MORGANTOWN	061	30492	33924	34911	1.2	92	12814	13990	14559	1.0	2.01	4854	4957	0.2
26506	MORGANTOWN	061	496	469	458	-0.6	25	283	269	264	-0.5	1.69	41	35	-1.7
26508	MORGANTOWN	061	23705	25903	27000	1.0	91	9288	10218	10686	1.0	2.52	6601	7047	0.7
26519	ALBRIGHT	077	1244	1686	1725	3.3	98	489	507	530	0.4	2.45	359	361	0.1
26521	BLACKSVILLE	061	337	305	294	-1.1	6	141	129	125	-1.0	2.33	109	97	-1.3
26525	BRUCETON MILLS	077	4077	6660	6880	5.4	100	1628	1960	2081	2.0	2.39	1186	1386	1.7
26537	KINGWOOD	077	6501	6498	6513	0.0	65	2558	2653	2693	0.4	2.37	1809	1820	0.1
26541	MAIDSVILLE	061	841	851	876	0.1	72	311	319	330	0.3	2.67	231	229	-0.1
26542	MASONTOWN	077	680	707	721	0.4	83	252	273	283	0.9	2.59	187	197	0.6
26546	PURSGLOVE	061	225	217	214	-0.4	35	91	89	88	-0.2	2.44	69	65	-0.6
26547	REEDSVILLE	077	3610	3810	3919	0.6	88	1496	1657	1726	1.1	2.30	1068	1147	0.8
26554	FAIRMONT	049	41646	41363	41516	-0.1	57	17658	18028	18278	0.2	2.21	11142	10944	-0.2
26560	BAXTER	049	430	435	442	0.1	72	174	184	189	0.6	2.36	124	127	0.3
26561	BIG RUN	103	545	486	459	-1.2	3	206	190	182	-0.9	2.56	157	141	-1.2
26562	BURTON	061	762	699	673	-0.9	10	310	293	284	-0.6	2.39	212	194	-1.0
26568	ENTERPRISE	033	1803	1781	1765	-0.1	57	684	693	692	0.1	2.57	523	515	-0.2
26570	FAIRVIEW	061	3973	4019	3978	0.1	72	1175	1146	1144	-0.3	2.84	894	846	-0.6
26571	FARMINGTON	049	3442	3371	3390	-0.2	48	1409	1439	1465	0.2	2.34	1022	1008	-0.1
26575	HUNDRED	103	1080	972	921	-1.1	6	463	433	415	-0.7	2.24	289	260	-1.1
26581	LITTLETON	103	750	679	643	-1.1	6	280	264	253	-0.6	2.57	213	196	-0.9
26582	MANNINGTON	049	5337	5573	5714	0.5	86	2151	2329	2413	0.9	2.39	1578	1648	0.5
26585	METZ	049	890	895	902	0.1	72	343	357	363	0.4	2.51	250	251	0.0
26587	RACHEL	049	307	301	301	-0.2	48	115	117	118	0.2	2.57	85	83	-0.3
26588	RIVESVILLE	049	3174	3285	3340	0.4	83	1270	1351	1391	0.7	2.36	918	942	0.3
26590	WANA	061	690	640	623	-0.8	14	247	232	227	-0.7	2.76	194	178	-0.9
26591	WORTHINGTON	049	1362	1356	1371	0.0	65	506	525	536	0.4	2.55	375	376	0.0
26601	SUTTON	007	5151	5096	5040	-0.1	57	1876	1922	1919	0.3	2.50	1330	1321	-0.1
26610	BIRCH RIVER	067	1496	1466	1452	-0.2	48	582	594	596	0.2	2.47	430	427	-0.1
26611	CEDARVILLE	021	387	368	361	-0.5	30	146	145	144	-0.1	2.54	112	109	-0.3
26615	COPEN	007	194	191	189	-0.2	48	69	71	71	0.3	2.69	52	52	0.0
26617	DILLE	015	399	402	397	0.1	72	162	169	169	0.5	2.36	124	126	0.2
26619	EXCHANGE	007	314	311	309	-0.1	57	121	125	126	0.4	2.49	91	92	0.1
26621	FLATWOODS	007	849	842	836	-0.1	57	348	360	362	0.4	1.89	245	246	0.0
26623	FRAMETOWN	007	1865	1757	1713	-0.6	25	742	727	717	-0.2	2.42	546	521	-0.5
26624	GASSAWAY	007	2977	3051	3048	0.3	81	1252	1324	1338	0.6	2.30	867	887	0.2
26627	HEATERS	007	247	245	243	-0.1	57	101	104	105	0.3	1.68	71	71	0.0
26629	LITTLE BIRCH	007	519	540	544	0.4	83	203	220	224	0.9	2.45	154	162	0.5
26631	NAPIER	007	187	186	185	-0.1	57	78	81	82	0.4	2.26	55	55	0.0
26636	ROSEDALE	021	505	479	471	-0.6	25	204	202	201	-0.1	2.37	149	144	-0.4
26638	SHOCK	021	182	169	165	-0.8	14	68	66	65	-0.3	2.56	49	46	-0.7
26651	SUMMERSVILLE	067	7027	7331	7432	0.5	86	2953	3231	3322	1.0	2.25	2000	2110	0.6
26656	BELVA	067	374	356	349	-0.5	30	156	156	155	0.0	2.26	118	115	-0.3
26660	CALVIN	067	757	754	752	0.0	65	285	295	298	0.4	2.56	224	227	0.1
26662	CANVAS	067	1370	1341	1329	-0.2	48	520	535	538	0.3	2.50	397	398	0.0
26667	DRENNEN	067	199	192	190	-0.4	35	86	87	87	0.1	2.21	63	62	-0.2
26675	KESLERS CROSS LANES	067	782	762	754	-0.3	40	304	311	312	0.2	2.45	222	222	0.0
26676	LEIVASY	067	971	955	945	-0.2	48	411	424	426	0.3	2.25	315	317	0.1
26678	MOUNT LOOKOUT	067	1189	1189	1189	0.0	65	450	471	477	0.5	2.52	357	365	0.2
26679	MOUNT NEBO	067	1885	1874	1869	-0.1	57	752	784	792	0.5	2.39	583	594	0.2
26680	NALLEN	019	65	61	60	-0.7	19	29	29	28	0.0	2.10	21	20	-0.5
26681	NETTIE	067	1199	1172	1160	-0.2	48	471	484	486	0.3	2.42	361	361	0.0
26684	POOL	067	153	153	153	0.0	65	60	63	64	0.5	2.43	47	49	0.5
26690	SWISS	067	560	530	521	-0.6	25	219	219	218	0.0	2.42	165	160	-0.3
26691	TIOGA	067	318	300	293	-0.6	25	114	112	111	-0.2	2.67	86	82	-0.5
26704	AUGUSTA	027	3493	4557	5020	2.9	98	1358	1841	2056	3.3	2.44	1012	1326	3.0
26705	AURORA	077	909	936	956	0.3	81	357	384	397	0.8	2.44	273	286	0.5
26710	BURLINGTON	057	3763	3764	3716	0.0	65	1418	1470	1466	0.4	2.54	1122	1138	0.2
26711	CAPON BRIDGE	027	1321	1564	1699	1.8	95	556	685	754	2.3	2.27	400	477	1.9
26714	DELRAY	027	834	809	887	-0.3	40	309	319	354	0.3	2.53	227	227	0.0
26716	EGLON	077	647	671	684	0.4	83	244	264	273	0.9	2.54	182	192	0.6
26717	ELK GARDEN	057	1022	983	963	-0.4	35	394	391	387	-0.1	2.51	301	291	-0.4
26719	FORT ASHBY	057	2358	2366	2359	0.0	65	927	972	979	0.5	2.40	662	675	0.2
26720	GORMANIA	023	714	741	755	0.4	83	301	330	341	1.0	2.25	216	228	0.6
26722	GREEN SPRING	027	761	874	942	1.5	94	313	376	411	2.0	2.32	216	248	1.5
26726	KEYSER	057	9520	10209	10399	0.8	90	3854	4297	4433	1.2	2.28	2564	2760	0.8
26731	LAHMANSVILLE	023	543	580	599	0.7	89	228	256	269	1.3	2.27	165	180	0.9
26739	MOUNT STORM	023	834	878	900	0.6	88	344	380	395	1.1	2.31	252	270	0.7
26743	NEW CREEK	057	1576	1588	1582	0.1	72	607	636	640	0.5	2.49	449	455	0.1
26750	PIEDMONT	057	1050	984	956	-0.7	19	435	418	409	-0.4	2.35	281	261	-0.8
26753	RIDGELEY	057	6369	6369	6312	0.0	65	2554	2658	2663	0.4	2.39	1920	1950	0.2
26755	RIO	027	416	474	513	1.4	93	158	187	206	1.8	2.53	122	141	1.6
26757	ROMNEY	027	5497	5818	6051	0.6	88	2236	2445	2564	1.0	2.26	1455	1534	0.6
26761	SHANKS	027	1221	1386	1483	1.4	93	423	498	539	1.8	2.76	323	370	1.5
26763	SPRINGFIELD	027	1445	1612	1711	1.2	92	591	690	742	1.7	2.31	420	470	1.2
26764	TERRA ALTA	077	5145	5087	5077	-0.1	57	2024	2089	2112	0.3	2.38	1454	1454	0.0
26767	WILEY FORD	057	1095	1076	1054	-0.2	48	463	470	465	0.2	2.29	309	303	-0.2
26801	BAKER	031	1435	1659	1764	1.6	94	584	707	760	2.1	2.30	393	458	1.7
26802	BRANDYWINE	071	506	498	486	-0.2	48	212	219	216	0.4	2.26	142	141	-0.1
26804	CIRCLEVILLE	071	607	567	545	-0.7	19	250	245	239	-0.2	2.29	179	170	-0.6
26807	FRANKLIN	071	2841	2722	2635	-0.5	30	1160	1155	1132	0.0	2.27	807	778	-0.4
26808	HIGH VIEW	027	1280	1491	1606	1.7	95	500	600	653	2.0	2.46	363	421	1.6
26810	LOST CITY	031	578	694	740	2.0	96	265	327	353	2.3	2.12	182	216	1.9
26812	MATHIAS	031	1391	1581	1668	1.4	93	571	677	722	1.9	2.34	408	465	1.4
26814	RIVERTON	071	306	286	275	-0.7	19	120	118	115	-0.2	2.40	86	81	-0.6
26815	SUGAR GROVE	071	1318	1303	1277	-0.1	57	499	514	509	0.3	2.44	354	353	0.0
26817	BLOOMERY	027	1050	1263	1381	2.0	96	400	501	554	2.5	2.52	299	363	2.1
26818	FISHER	031	241	254	261	0.6	88	86	92	96	0.7	2.76	62	65	0.5
26833	MAYSVILLE	023	3117	3433	3581	1.0	91	1189	1367	1446	1.5	2.51	936	1049	1.2
26836	MOOREFIELD	031	7341	7508	7634	0.2	76	3006	3177	3258	0.6	2.36	2054	2103	0.3
26838	MILAM	071	503	494	482	-0.2	48	216	222	219	0.3	2.20	146	145	-0.1
	WEST VIRGINIA					0.2					0.5	2.33			0.1
	UNITED STATES					1.0					1.1	2.59			0.9

ZIP CODE #	POST OFFICE NAME	RACE (%) White 2000	White 2009	Black 2000	Black 2009	Asian/Pacific 2000	Asian/Pacific 2009	% Hispanic Origin 2000	% Hispanic Origin 2009	2009 AGE DISTRIBUTION (%) 0-4	5-9	10-14	15-19	20-24	25-44	45-64	65-84	85+	18+	MEDIAN AGE 2009	% 2009 Males	% 2009 Females
26448	WALLACE	98.6	98.2	0.1	0.1	0.2	0.2	0.8	0.8	4.5	6.1	6.9	7.3	5.6	26.9	30.4	10.8	1.6	77.7	40.0	51.3	48.7
26451	WEST MILFORD	98.7	98.3	0.2	0.2	0.1	0.1	0.8	0.9	6.2	6.6	6.7	6.8	4.8	25.4	31.0	11.3	1.4	76.1	40.5	49.7	50.3
26452	WESTON	98.4	98.3	0.2	0.2	0.5	0.4	0.6	0.7	4.9	5.1	5.4	5.9	5.1	24.7	30.4	15.9	2.6	81.1	44.2	48.2	51.8
26456	WEST UNION	98.4	98.4	0.0	0.0	0.1	0.1	0.4	0.4	6.1	6.4	6.4	5.8	4.7	23.5	29.6	15.3	2.2	77.5	42.6	48.2	51.8
26501	MORGANTOWN	92.7	91.7	4.2	4.4	1.0	1.6	0.8	1.0	5.3	5.2	5.3	5.9	8.4	28.9	27.4	11.7	1.9	81.0	38.5	49.8	50.2
26505	MORGANTOWN	89.2	85.5	3.8	5.0	4.7	6.9	1.4	1.7	3.2	2.6	2.8	14.5	28.6	22.3	15.9	7.9	2.2	89.6	24.7	49.9	50.1
26506	MORGANTOWN	72.2	65.2	5.4	4.9	17.9	25.6	3.0	3.4	2.6	1.5	1.7	10.7	46.7	25.4	3.4	3.6	4.5	91.9	23.6	56.3	43.7
26508	MORGANTOWN	96.2	95.4	1.2	1.1	1.2	1.9	0.7	0.9	6.3	6.5	6.7	6.3	5.4	28.1	29.7	9.8	1.2	76.6	38.8	49.2	50.8
26519	ALBRIGHT	98.8	98.6	0.2	0.2	0.1	0.2	0.3	0.5	3.8	4.2	4.4	6.0	7.9	36.1	26.9	9.4	1.2	84.0	38.2	62.8	37.2
26521	BLACKSVILLE	98.8	98.7	0.6	0.7	0.0	0.0	0.0	0.0	4.6	5.2	5.9	5.9	3.9	25.6	32.5	14.8	1.6	80.7	44.2	50.8	49.2
26525	BRUCETON MILLS	98.9	98.9	0.0	0.0	0.2	0.2	0.5	0.6	3.8	4.1	4.2	5.8	8.6	37.8	25.6	8.9	1.2	84.4	37.4	63.6	36.4
26537	KINGWOOD	98.0	97.6	0.9	1.1	0.3	0.5	0.5	0.6	5.4	5.7	6.2	7.0	5.0	24.9	28.8	13.8	3.1	77.9	42.0	48.3	51.7
26541	MAIDSVILLE	97.1	97.1	1.3	1.3	0.1	0.2	0.4	0.5	5.8	6.0	6.7	7.9	5.4	24.8	32.3	10.2	0.9	76.7	40.3	49.5	50.5
26542	MASONTOWN	99.4	99.3	0.0	0.0	0.3	0.4	0.3	0.4	6.1	6.2	6.4	5.9	5.2	24.8	31.5	12.3	1.6	77.7	41.8	52.5	47.5
26546	PURSGLOVE	98.2	98.2	0.4	0.5	0.4	0.5	0.4	0.5	6.0	6.5	6.9	6.5	4.6	30.4	28.6	9.2	1.4	76.0	38.6	47.9	52.1
26547	REEDSVILLE	99.4	99.3	0.0	0.0	0.1	0.2	1.0	1.2	6.3	6.6	6.7	5.4	4.6	26.9	28.9	13.0	1.7	77.0	40.5	48.4	51.6
26554	FAIRMONT	94.1	93.5	4.0	4.1	0.5	0.8	0.7	0.9	5.0	5.1	5.3	6.4	6.7	25.3	27.8	15.2	3.3	81.4	42.1	47.6	52.4
26560	BAXTER	94.9	94.9	3.5	3.4	0.2	0.2	0.5	0.7	4.8	4.8	5.1	6.2	4.8	25.1	30.3	16.3	2.5	81.4	44.5	47.6	52.4
26561	BIG RUN	99.8	99.8	0.0	0.0	0.0	0.0	0.6	0.6	4.9	6.0	7.4	6.4	4.3	24.1	31.7	13.2	2.1	77.2	42.7	52.9	47.1
26562	BURTON	98.6	98.4	0.5	0.6	0.0	0.0	0.3	0.3	4.6	5.0	5.3	5.9	5.0	24.3	30.9	16.6	2.4	81.5	44.9	49.1	50.9
26568	ENTERPRISE	98.9	98.8	0.4	0.4	0.0	0.0	0.7	0.8	6.6	7.2	7.4	6.2	5.2	26.6	26.9	12.8	1.2	75.0	38.8	49.5	50.5
26570	FAIRVIEW	90.8	89.6	8.3	9.2	0.1	0.2	0.6	0.7	4.6	4.9	5.2	5.0	5.5	32.9	28.6	12.1	1.3	82.4	40.2	59.4	40.6
26571	FARMINGTON	96.5	96.2	2.3	2.5	0.1	0.1	0.5	0.6	5.2	5.3	5.5	5.9	5.3	24.7	30.1	15.5	2.5	80.5	43.6	48.7	51.3
26575	HUNDRED	98.4	98.3	0.1	0.1	0.0	0.0	0.1	0.1	4.6	4.5	4.9	6.8	6.4	22.5	30.8	17.2	2.3	81.8	45.1	48.8	51.2
26581	LITTLETON	98.7	98.5	0.1	0.1	0.0	0.0	0.0	0.0	5.7	6.0	6.3	6.2	4.0	26.7	29.3	13.7	2.1	77.9	41.7	48.3	51.7
26582	MANNINGTON	98.4	98.2	0.4	0.4	0.1	0.2	0.7	0.8	5.8	5.8	6.0	6.1	4.8	24.4	29.1	15.5	2.4	78.5	42.8	47.8	52.2
26585	METZ	98.8	98.5	0.0	0.0	0.1	0.1	0.8	1.0	5.1	5.4	6.3	6.7	5.0	23.2	31.1	15.0	2.2	78.9	43.6	48.5	51.5
26587	RACHEL	98.4	98.3	1.0	1.0	0.0	0.0	0.3	0.7	5.6	5.6	6.0	6.0	4.7	24.6	28.9	15.9	2.7	78.7	43.0	47.2	52.8
26588	RIVESVILLE	97.0	96.7	2.2	2.3	0.2	0.3	0.5	0.6	4.9	5.0	5.3	5.6	5.1	26.3	30.4	14.7	2.6	81.4	43.4	50.2	49.8
26590	WANA	98.5	98.4	0.6	0.6	0.0	0.0	0.3	0.5	5.5	6.1	6.3	6.1	3.9	25.9	30.8	13.8	1.7	78.1	42.3	50.0	50.0
26591	WORTHINGTON	98.4	98.3	0.9	0.9	0.1	0.2	0.5	0.6	4.2	4.4	5.0	6.3	5.1	25.6	33.6	13.6	2.1	82.7	44.6	49.2	50.8
26601	SUTTON	97.1	96.8	1.1	1.1	0.1	0.2	0.4	0.5	5.0	5.4	5.7	5.6	6.1	26.6	30.1	13.2	2.4	80.4	42.0	51.8	48.2
26610	BIRCH RIVER	98.4	98.0	0.0	0.0	0.4	0.6	0.3	0.4	4.7	6.3	7.3	7.8	5.9	25.4	29.4	11.1	2.2	76.9	39.2	51.2	48.8
26611	CEDARVILLE	98.2	97.6	0.8	1.1	0.0	0.3	0.8	0.8	5.2	5.7	5.7	6.3	5.2	24.7	30.4	14.9	1.9	79.3	42.8	51.1	48.9
26615	COPEN	98.4	97.9	0.5	0.5	0.0	0.5	0.5	0.5	6.3	7.3	7.3	5.8	4.7	26.2	29.3	11.5	1.6	75.4	39.0	50.3	49.7
26617	DILLE	99.2	99.3	0.0	0.0	0.0	0.0	0.0	0.0	5.7	6.0	6.5	6.5	4.7	25.9	30.1	13.2	1.5	77.6	41.5	50.7	49.3
26619	EXCHANGE	98.4	98.1	0.3	0.3	0.3	0.3	0.6	0.6	6.4	7.1	7.1	5.8	4.8	26.0	29.9	11.3	1.6	75.6	39.4	49.8	50.2
26621	FLATWOODS	97.1	97.0	1.8	1.8	0.4	0.4	0.1	0.1	3.4	3.8	4.2	4.5	7.4	31.1	30.8	12.4	2.5	85.6	42.4	57.4	42.6
26623	FRAMETOWN	98.4	98.0	0.2	0.2	0.3	0.5	0.4	0.5	6.3	6.3	6.7	6.4	4.6	24.5	29.6	14.0	1.8	76.7	41.7	48.9	51.1
26624	GASSAWAY	99.1	98.9	0.2	0.3	0.1	0.2	0.5	0.6	4.9	5.0	5.7	6.3	4.9	22.9	31.5	16.0	2.8	80.5	45.1	48.7	51.3
26627	HEATERS	96.4	95.9	2.8	2.9	0.4	0.4	0.0	0.0	3.3	3.3	3.7	4.1	9.0	35.5	26.9	11.4	2.9	86.9	40.1	60.4	39.6
26629	LITTLE BIRCH	97.5	97.0	0.6	0.6	0.2	0.2	1.0	1.1	5.7	6.9	7.6	7.2	5.6	25.4	28.5	10.9	2.2	75.4	39.0	51.1	48.9
26631	NAPIER	98.9	98.4	0.5	0.5	0.0	0.0	0.5	0.5	3.8	4.3	4.8	5.4	4.8	24.2	37.1	13.4	2.2	83.9	46.7	52.7	47.3
26636	ROSEDALE	98.4	98.3	0.2	0.4	0.0	0.0	0.8	0.8	4.6	5.0	5.2	5.2	4.8	24.4	34.0	14.8	1.9	81.6	45.4	51.1	48.9
26638	SHOCK	98.4	98.2	0.0	0.0	0.0	0.0	1.1	1.2	4.7	4.7	4.7	4.7	4.7	24.3	34.9	15.4	1.8	82.8	46.3	50.9	49.1
26651	SUMMERSVILLE	98.5	98.1	0.0	0.0	0.3	0.5	0.9	1.0	5.2	5.5	5.7	5.9	5.3	24.3	31.1	14.4	2.5	79.9	43.4	48.1	51.9
26656	BELVA	98.4	98.3	0.5	0.6	0.0	0.0	0.3	0.3	5.1	5.6	5.6	5.9	5.1	25.6	30.1	14.9	2.2	80.1	42.6	49.7	50.3
26660	CALVIN	98.8	98.4	0.0	0.0	0.4	0.5	0.1	0.1	5.4	5.7	6.0	6.0	4.8	25.5	32.4	12.7	1.6	79.0	42.5	49.6	50.4
26662	CANVAS	99.1	99.0	0.1	0.1	0.1	0.1	0.3	0.3	5.1	5.3	5.8	6.0	4.8	24.9	33.3	13.3	1.6	80.2	43.7	49.7	50.3
26667	DRENNEN	99.0	99.0	0.0	0.0	0.0	0.0	1.0	1.0	5.2	5.2	5.2	5.2	5.2	27.6	30.2	14.1	2.1	81.3	42.1	50.0	50.0
26675	KESLERS CROSS LANES	99.6	99.5	0.0	0.0	0.0	0.0	0.9	0.9	7.2	6.3	5.8	6.0	7.7	26.8	29.4	9.1	1.7	77.0	36.1	50.7	49.3
26676	LEIVASY	99.4	99.2	0.0	0.0	0.1	0.2	0.2	0.2	5.3	5.8	6.1	6.0	4.6	24.5	32.1	13.9	1.7	79.2	43.5	50.6	49.4
26678	MOUNT LOOKOUT	99.5	99.5	0.1	0.1	0.0	0.0	0.3	0.4	4.7	5.2	5.8	6.1	4.8	24.6	35.9	11.2	1.7	80.5	44.1	49.1	50.9
26679	MOUNT NEBO	99.4	99.2	0.0	0.0	0.1	0.2	0.2	0.2	5.2	6.2	5.9	6.6	5.3	25.8	32.2	11.1	1.7	78.5	41.4	50.6	49.4
26680	NALLEN	100.0	100.0	0.0	0.0	0.0	0.0	1.5	1.6	4.9	4.9	4.9	4.9	3.3	26.2	32.8	16.4	1.6	80.3	45.8	52.5	47.5
26681	NETTIE	99.1	99.0	0.1	0.1	0.2	0.2	0.3	0.3	5.0	5.4	5.8	6.1	4.8	24.9	32.9	13.5	1.6	80.1	43.7	49.3	50.7
26684	POOL	99.3	99.3	0.0	0.0	0.0	0.0	0.0	0.0	5.2	5.9	5.9	6.5	5.2	25.5	32.7	11.8	1.3	79.1	41.8	48.4	51.6
26690	SWISS	98.8	98.7	0.0	0.0	0.0	0.0	0.5	0.8	4.9	5.3	5.3	5.1	4.7	26.4	30.4	16.2	1.7	81.3	43.7	49.6	50.4
26691	TIOGA	98.7	98.3	0.0	0.0	0.0	0.3	0.3	0.3	5.3	6.3	6.7	6.3	5.3	25.0	31.7	11.7	1.7	78.0	41.1	51.0	49.0
26704	AUGUSTA	98.3	98.2	0.5	0.5	0.1	0.2	0.5	0.6	6.5	6.6	6.8	6.5	5.5	25.2	28.4	13.0	1.5	75.8	40.2	50.8	49.2
26705	AURORA	99.3	99.1	0.1	0.2	0.1	0.2	0.7	0.7	4.8	5.1	5.7	6.7	5.3	22.9	32.1	15.4	2.0	80.3	44.6	50.6	49.4
26710	BURLINGTON	98.7	98.5	0.5	0.5	0.1	0.2	0.5	0.6	5.2	6.0	7.1	6.9	4.7	26.4	30.2	12.3	1.2	77.3	40.9	51.1	48.9
26711	CAPON BRIDGE	97.8	97.5	1.4	1.6	0.2	0.2	0.4	0.4	5.0	5.4	6.1	7.2	4.7	23.3	33.4	13.4	1.5	78.8	43.9	51.2	48.8
26714	DELRAY	98.0	97.9	0.6	0.6	0.1	0.2	0.2	0.4	7.2	7.2	7.3	6.9	5.3	25.3	26.7	13.0	1.1	73.8	38.3	51.8	48.2
26716	EGLON	99.5	99.6	0.3	0.3	0.0	0.0	0.3	0.4	5.1	5.4	5.8	6.6	4.9	21.9	32.3	16.4	1.6	79.6	45.2	52.3	47.7
26717	ELK GARDEN	96.3	96.2	2.8	2.7	0.0	0.0	0.9	1.1	4.3	5.4	5.9	6.4	5.1	25.0	32.3	13.8	1.7	80.7	43.4	51.8	48.2
26719	FORT ASHBY	98.8	98.6	0.3	0.3	0.2	0.3	0.4	0.5	5.5	5.7	6.0	6.2	4.6	24.8	29.5	15.3	2.3	78.8	43.0	49.2	50.8
26720	GORMANIA	97.5	97.3	0.7	0.8	0.1	0.1	0.4	0.4	4.6	5.1	5.7	4.7	4.0	24.8	33.6	15.5	1.9	81.9	45.8	48.4	51.6
26722	GREEN SPRING	98.9	98.7	0.5	0.6	0.1	0.2	0.4	0.6	6.8	6.9	7.2	6.3	4.7	23.6	28.7	14.3	1.6	75.3	40.6	49.2	50.8
26726	KEYSER	93.4	92.9	4.7	4.9	0.3	0.5	0.5	0.7	5.5	5.7	5.8	7.4	6.2	23.8	27.3	15.2	3.0	79.7	41.3	48.4	51.6
26731	LAHMANSVILLE	99.1	98.8	0.4	0.5	0.0	0.0	0.6	0.5	5.9	6.2	6.6	5.0	4.3	24.7	31.0	14.8	1.6	78.3	43.2	51.9	48.1
26739	MOUNT STORM	98.7	98.6	0.2	0.2	0.1	0.1	0.2	0.3	5.2	5.8	6.0	5.1	4.2	24.7	31.7	15.6	1.6	79.6	44.2	51.3	48.7
26743	NEW CREEK	97.5	97.3	0.8	0.8	0.4	0.5	0.5	0.6	5.4	6.0	6.4	6.2	4.6	24.5	32.2	13.4	1.4	78.1	42.7	50.1	49.9
26750	PIEDMONT	81.2	80.7	15.4	15.3	0.0	0.0	1.6	2.1	6.7	7.7	7.2	6.7	6.1	26.1	26.3	11.7	1.4	74.6	36.8	48.7	51.3
26753	RIDGELEY	99.2	99.1	0.2	0.2	0.1	0.2	0.7	0.8	5.7	6.0	6.4	6.2	4.6	24.9	30.8	13.7	1.6	78.0	42.4	48.8	51.2
26755	RIO	98.3	98.1	0.7	0.6	0.0	0.2	0.2	0.2	6.8	6.8	7.0	7.2	6.1	25.3	27.8	12.0	1.1	75.1	38.7	49.4	50.6
26757	ROMNEY	97.3	97.0	1.4	1.4	0.3	0.6	0.7	0.8	5.6	6.0	6.9	6.7	5.6	23.4	28.2	14.9	2.8	77.2	41.8	48.1	51.9
26761	SHANKS	98.1	98.1	0.7	0.7	0.2	0.3	0.4	0.4	6.6	6.6	6.7	6.9	5.9	25.3	28.5	12.2	1.3	76.0	39.6	49.3	50.7
26763	SPRINGFIELD	99.1	99.0	0.3	0.3	0.1	0.2	0.4	0.5	5.6	5.8	6.1	6.3	4.8	23.5	30.5	15.6	1.9	78.5	43.3	50.1	49.9
26764	TERRA ALTA	99.0	98.9	0.2	0.2	0.1	0.2	0.5	0.6	5.8	5.9	6.1	7.6	4.9	24.0	30.2	13.9	1.7	77.3	41.9	50.3	49.7
26767	WILEY FORD	99.1	99.0	0.3	0.3	0.1	0.2	0.2	0.2	4.1	4.0	4.7	6.9	6.1	22.6	30.0	19.4	2.1	83.1	46.0	47.1	52.9
26801	BAKER	98.5	98.4	0.6	0.7	0.1	0.1	0.3	0.5	5.4	5.8	5.9	5.2	4.2	24.1	31.8	15.1	2.5	79.7	44.6	49.6	50.4
26802	BRANDYWINE	96.6	96.4	1.4	1.4	0.6	0.8	0.6	0.6	7.0	7.0	7.2	6.2	4.6	25.7	28.9	11.6	1.6	74.7	39.2	50.0	50.0
26804	CIRCLEVILLE	99.5	99.5	0.0	0.0	0.0	0.0	0.0	0.0	4.9	4.8	5.5	6.3	5.6	26.6	27.3	16.8	2.1	80.8	42.4	52.6	47.4
26807	FRANKLIN	94.9	94.5	3.2	3.3	0.1	0.2	0.7	0.8	4.7	5.1	5.6	5.7	4.6	21.4	32.1	16.8	4.0	81.1	46.9	48.3	51.7
26808	HIGH VIEW	98.6	98.3	0.8	0.9	0.2	0.3	0.7	0.9	6.1	6.4	7.0	6.8	4.2	25.1	30.1	12.8	1.5	75.5	41.5	49.8	50.2
26810	LOST CITY	99.0	98.7	0.3	0.4	0.0	0.0	0.5	0.7	5.0	5.5	6.2	6.2	3.9	22.8	33.7	14.7	2.0	79.4	45.3	49.9	50.1
26812	MATHIAS	98.6	98.5	0.4	0.4	0.1	0.1	0.4	0.4	4.9	5.5	6.0	6.3	4.0	22.5	34.6	14.2	2.0	79.6	45.5	48.4	51.6
26814	RIVERTON	99.3	99.3	0.0	0.0	0.0	0.0	0.0	0.0	4.9	4.9	5.2	6.3	5.9	26.9	27.3	16.4	2.1	80.8	42.3	52.4	47.6
26815	SUGAR GROVE	92.6	92.1	5.0	5.1	0.4	0.6	2.6	2.9	7.1	7.1	7.3	7.1	6.3	26.2	25.7	11.8	1.3	73.9	37.2	50.6	49.4
26817	BLOOMERY	98.0	97.9	0.7	0.7	0.1	0.1	0.5	0.4	6.2	6.7	7.0	6.3	4.4	23.7	31.7	12.7	1.3	76.2	42.2	49.6	50.4
26818	FISHER	96.3	96.9	3.3	2.8	0.0	0.0	0.8	1.6	6.3	6.3	7.1	7.1	5.1	30.3	25.6	11.0	1.2	76.0	38.6	51.6	48.4
26833	MAYSVILLE	98.8	98.7	0.3	0.3	0.1	0.2	0.4	0.5	6.6	6.8	7.2	6.3	5.0	26.3	28.8	11.7	1.3	75.5	39.4	50.4	49.6
26836	MOOREFIELD	95.8	95.5	2.8	2.9	0.2	0.2	0.8	1.0	6.2	6.2	6.5	6.6	5.3	25.8	28.6	13.2	1.6	77.1	40.7	49.6	50.4
26838	MILAM	96.8	96.6	1.6	1.6	0.4	0.6	0.6	0.8	7.1	7.1	7.1	6.3	4.9	25.7	28.7	11.5	1.6	74.7	39.1	49.8	50.2
	WEST VIRGINIA	95.0	94.5	3.2	3.3	0.5	0.8	0.7	0.8	5.5	5.6	5.9	6.5	6.1	25.2	29.3	13.8	2.2	79.3	41.5	49.0	51.0
	UNITED STATES	75.1	72.0	12.3	12.7	3.8	4.6	12.5	15.7	6.8	6.7	6.6	7.1	6.9	27.0	26.0	10.9	1.9	75.7	36.9	49.2	50.8

ZIP CODE #	POST OFFICE NAME	2009 Per Capita Income	2009 HH Income Base	2009 HOUSEHOLD INCOME DISTRIBUTION (%) Less than $25,000	$25,000 to $49,999	$50,000 to $99,999	$100,000 to $149,999	$150,000 or More	MEDIAN HOUSEHOLD INCOME 2009	2014	2009 National Centile	2009 State Centile	2009 Home Value Base	2009 HOME VALUE DISTRIBUTION (%) Less than $50,000	$50,000 to $89,999	$90,000 to $174,999	$175,000 to $399,999	$400,000 or More	2009 Median Home Value
26448	WALLACE	16336	509	41.3	31.2	22.4	3.1	2.0	30530	30528	9	39	427	39.1	16.6	32.3	10.5	1.4	67188
26451	WEST MILFORD	17019	603	30.7	36.5	27.9	4.0	1.0	37898	39565	26	80	504	20.4	29.8	37.7	10.9	1.2	89630
26452	WESTON	18352	4252	37.2	31.6	26.6	3.0	1.6	34703	34697	17	63	3033	20.5	25.8	39.8	12.1	1.8	95284
26456	WEST UNION	15856	1322	40.2	33.4	22.8	3.0	0.7	30741	31104	9	42	1039	31.4	22.6	36.1	9.7	0.2	84679
26501	MORGANTOWN	19985	9184	36.1	27.9	28.7	5.5	1.8	35764	37150	20	69	6101	20.7	21.7	43.6	13.0	1.1	103630
26505	MORGANTOWN	19736	13990	49.2	21.2	19.6	6.2	3.8	25842	27094	4	16	5779	15.0	10.6	41.0	30.0	3.4	139739
26506	MORGANTOWN	16424	269	68.8	20.1	8.2	1.5	1.5	15635	16163	1	1	12	50.0	0.0	33.3	0.0	16.7	70000
26508	MORGANTOWN	25652	10218	23.3	27.5	33.2	10.3	5.7	49040	50075	59	96	8089	22.3	11.7	34.3	26.6	5.0	126793
26519	ALBRIGHT	14410	507	35.3	35.5	25.8	2.2	1.2	33582	35000	15	56	428	16.6	29.0	43.7	8.6	2.1	100000
26521	BLACKSVILLE	21480	129	28.7	33.3	32.6	2.3	3.1	40377	43648	34	85	106	25.5	26.4	41.5	6.6	0.0	86000
26525	BRUCETON MILLS	15778	1960	32.6	32.6	28.7	3.5	2.6	37823	39381	26	79	1645	15.9	21.1	43.1	17.3	2.6	112913
26537	KINGWOOD	18221	2653	37.2	30.7	25.3	4.8	2.0	34236	35906	16	60	2055	18.6	26.3	42.1	12.6	0.4	101972
26541	MAIDSVILLE	15978	319	31.3	36.7	27.6	3.1	1.3	34531	34160	17	62	258	34.9	17.1	31.8	16.3	0.0	86154
26542	MASONTOWN	14074	273	38.5	37.0	23.4	1.1	0.0	30650	32694	9	41	241	16.6	35.3	41.5	6.6	0.0	86786
26546	PURSGLOVE	16380	89	37.1	29.2	31.5	2.2	0.0	31983	32556	11	49	74	43.2	21.6	32.4	2.7	0.0	66000
26547	REEDSVILLE	18812	1657	34.6	29.7	32.3	2.7	0.7	36128	37757	21	71	1338	21.3	22.3	46.0	9.4	1.0	103198
26554	FAIRMONT	21748	18028	34.2	27.9	29.2	5.6	3.0	37888	39626	26	79	12993	16.4	23.9	42.2	15.9	1.7	105022
26560	BAXTER	17553	184	43.5	24.5	26.1	5.4	0.5	30897	31712	10	43	154	22.1	33.1	39.0	5.2	0.6	84667
26561	BIG RUN	17195	190	28.9	38.9	27.9	4.2	0.0	38052	40000	27	81	159	35.2	26.4	34.0	4.4	0.0	71500
26562	BURTON	18713	293	39.6	24.6	27.3	6.1	2.4	33685	33928	15	57	232	28.0	28.9	32.8	7.8	2.6	81579
26568	ENTERPRISE	17054	693	36.7	31.6	27.3	3.0	1.4	34797	34747	17	63	564	33.3	28.5	28.2	9.9	0.0	72340
26570	FAIRVIEW	14476	1146	29.6	35.6	30.2	3.1	1.6	37295	38080	24	76	966	29.2	28.5	36.4	5.7	0.2	76719
26571	FARMINGTON	19581	1439	32.3	33.2	29.3	4.3	0.9	35906	35909	20	70	1178	26.2	39.8	28.9	4.6	0.5	73594
26575	HUNDRED	16859	433	46.4	26.3	22.6	3.7	0.9	28372	30271	6	27	335	48.1	25.4	20.9	4.2	1.5	51970
26581	LITTLETON	15295	264	37.5	28.0	32.6	1.9	0.0	34535	34798	17	62	226	31.0	19.0	41.6	8.4	0.0	90000
26582	MANNINGTON	18557	2329	37.4	29.9	28.1	3.9	0.8	34474	34551	16	61	1862	29.9	37.3	27.6	5.2	0.0	67956
26585	METZ	17626	357	32.2	36.4	27.5	3.1	0.8	35252	34486	19	66	286	28.3	32.2	33.9	5.2	0.3	70667
26587	RACHEL	18594	117	25.6	34.2	37.6	1.7	0.9	42352	45000	40	89	95	18.9	51.6	27.4	2.1	0.0	76071
26588	RIVESVILLE	19048	1351	34.7	26.6	32.3	5.8	0.6	36904	37887	23	75	1120	20.3	30.5	37.4	11.4	0.4	88977
26590	WANA	17587	232	31.9	27.2	34.5	3.4	3.0	39083	41684	30	82	196	27.6	24.0	42.3	5.1	1.0	87500
26591	WORTHINGTON	16029	525	42.9	28.2	23.8	3.8	1.3	30871	31557	9	43	427	30.7	28.8	27.9	11.7	0.9	71774
26601	SUTTON	15506	1922	44.2	30.0	20.5	3.7	1.7	28803	29440	6	29	1474	29.5	25.0	31.7	11.6	2.2	81728
26610	BIRCH RIVER	16409	594	40.6	36.2	18.9	2.0	2.4	29698	29741	8	33	497	37.8	25.2	31.2	5.8	0.0	67750
26611	CEDARVILLE	10953	145	55.9	29.0	15.2	0.0	0.0	21507	22494	2	4	119	31.1	38.7	21.0	8.4	0.8	74231
26615	COPEN	12928	71	43.7	32.4	22.5	1.4	0.0	30301	30695	9	36	56	35.7	30.4	23.2	8.9	1.8	80000
26617	DILLE	13287	169	52.7	32.0	13.6	0.6	1.2	23053	25370	2	8	141	45.4	36.9	17.0	0.7	0.0	57222
26619	EXCHANGE	14109	125	44.0	32.0	23.2	0.8	0.0	30487	30846	9	39	100	35.0	29.0	21.0	11.0	4.0	80000
26621	FLATWOODS	21634	360	35.0	37.2	20.0	3.6	4.2	33791	32970	15	58	279	20.4	21.5	35.1	20.4	2.5	105313
26623	FRAMETOWN	14681	727	45.7	31.8	19.5	2.1	1.0	27772	28585	5	25	605	27.4	30.9	23.0	16.9	1.8	78061
26624	GASSAWAY	18539	1324	42.8	27.6	24.5	3.3	1.8	30465	30962	9	38	1009	27.6	27.9	30.3	9.2	5.0	83063
26627	HEATERS	24291	104	30.8	36.5	24.0	3.8	4.8	37803	37765	26	79	79	20.3	20.3	30.4	26.6	2.5	116071
26629	LITTLE BIRCH	14464	220	48.6	28.2	19.5	2.7	0.9	25717	26918	4	15	187	38.5	28.9	23.0	7.0	2.7	60357
26631	NAPIER	17436	81	39.5	40.7	14.8	2.5	2.5	29109	28997	7	31	66	21.2	24.2	39.4	13.6	1.5	96000
26636	ROSEDALE	16146	202	46.5	26.7	22.8	0.5	3.5	26979	27413	5	21	167	21.0	33.5	34.7	10.8	0.0	85833
26638	SHOCK	18035	66	37.9	25.8	30.3	0.0	6.1	36543	38657	22	74	56	16.1	30.4	39.3	14.3	0.0	96667
26651	SUMMERSVILLE	23083	3231	33.3	30.7	28.0	4.3	3.7	37567	38984	25	78	2502	22.5	19.5	36.3	17.1	4.6	104839
26656	BELVA	19712	156	41.7	31.4	22.4	2.6	1.9	30438	31301	9	38	131	33.6	23.7	37.4	5.3	0.0	81364
26660	CALVIN	16254	295	37.6	37.3	21.0	1.7	2.4	31136	31613	10	45	261	25.7	31.8	32.2	9.2	1.1	80250
26662	CANVAS	16444	535	38.1	34.4	22.1	4.1	1.3	32453	32425	12	51	476	30.3	20.6	39.9	8.0	1.3	88667
26667	DRENNEN	19989	87	42.5	31.0	21.8	2.3	2.3	29584	28919	7	33	73	27.4	34.2	26.0	11.0	1.4	75000
26675	KESLERS CROSS LANES	14912	311	42.1	26.7	29.6	1.6	0.0	30655	31432	9	41	263	15.6	47.9	28.9	3.8	3.8	76852
26676	LEIVASY	18824	424	39.9	32.3	22.9	3.1	1.9	33267	33674	14	55	373	32.7	18.5	34.0	12.3	2.4	87955
26678	MOUNT LOOKOUT	17240	471	32.7	39.7	20.0	6.4	1.3	33851	33300	15	58	415	19.3	22.4	42.2	13.7	2.4	98415
26679	MOUNT NEBO	19016	784	33.4	36.5	23.9	4.0	2.3	36538	37229	22	73	683	27.5	21.4	32.9	16.1	2.0	91415
26680	NALLEN	20079	29	34.5	31.0	31.0	3.4	0.0	33610	30000	15	56	24	41.7	20.8	33.3	4.2	0.0	60000
26681	NETTIE	16823	484	38.2	34.3	21.5	4.5	1.4	32242	32054	12	50	430	31.9	20.2	39.3	7.7	0.9	86400
26684	POOL	16029	63	33.3	41.3	20.6	4.8	0.0	33333	34045	14	55	55	21.8	21.8	38.2	16.4	1.8	97000
26690	SWISS	19066	219	43.4	32.0	20.1	1.8	2.7	28440	28985	6	27	183	34.4	22.4	34.4	8.7	0.0	81071
26691	TIOGA	16198	112	35.7	37.5	20.5	3.6	2.7	35000	33625	18	66	94	29.8	22.3	37.2	9.6	1.1	87143
26704	AUGUSTA	16587	1841	34.0	31.5	32.5	1.7	0.3	35742	36272	20	69	1541	16.6	19.1	44.9	17.5	1.9	117124
26705	AURORA	14173	384	45.3	34.4	17.7	1.3	1.3	27423	29306	5	23	335	27.2	28.4	38.8	5.1	0.6	81957
26710	BURLINGTON	19729	1470	26.3	36.2	30.6	4.5	2.4	40578	42974	35	85	1284	12.8	22.9	41.9	18.7	3.7	117952
26711	CAPON BRIDGE	25068	685	20.0	32.3	41.2	3.8	2.8	48180	48804	57	95	573	11.7	15.0	50.4	21.1	1.7	131250
26714	DELRAY	16537	319	35.4	25.7	37.0	1.9	0.0	37972	40000	27	80	260	19.6	28.5	35.0	14.2	2.7	96250
26716	EGLON	12727	264	45.8	36.7	14.8	1.5	1.1	26599	27955	4	19	229	22.7	29.3	45.4	2.6	0.0	88043
26717	ELK GARDEN	14534	391	40.2	37.9	19.7	1.8	0.5	30799	30765	9	42	330	35.8	32.1	26.7	5.5	0.0	69667
26719	FORT ASHBY	18210	972	30.2	35.1	29.3	5.0	0.3	36549	37398	22	74	787	13.9	19.2	41.2	24.9	0.9	133635
26720	GORMANIA	19472	330	43.0	30.0	20.0	3.6	3.3	31287	32023	10	46	272	29.8	21.7	37.5	9.9	1.1	88095
26722	GREEN SPRING	17603	376	32.7	35.4	29.0	2.9	0.0	36305	36785	21	72	315	22.2	18.4	47.3	8.9	3.2	105388
26726	KEYSER	18634	4297	37.0	30.1	27.5	4.0	1.3	35025	35463	18	66	2990	14.2	21.2	50.7	13.0	0.8	111909
26731	LAHMANSVILLE	18599	256	35.9	30.9	28.5	3.9	0.8	33662	34007	15	57	215	19.1	19.1	38.6	17.7	5.6	109722
26739	MOUNT STORM	20896	380	32.1	31.8	27.4	5.8	2.9	38511	40142	28	81	321	19.0	21.8	35.8	17.1	6.2	106641
26743	NEW CREEK	20982	636	26.1	29.7	35.1	6.1	3.0	44290	45949	46	92	545	15.0	19.8	24.8	38.0	2.4	130469
26750	PIEDMONT	14084	418	49.5	29.4	18.7	1.9	0.5	25295	26167	3	14	228	39.5	31.6	26.3	2.6	0.0	65000
26753	RIDGELEY	21145	2658	26.2	32.5	33.8	5.7	1.8	42920	45210	42	90	2240	11.3	15.3	49.0	22.0	2.5	133849
26755	RIO	16705	187	30.5	35.3	31.0	3.2	0.0	36348	36529	22	72	154	20.8	24.0	37.7	15.6	1.9	102381
26757	ROMNEY	18513	2445	37.7	31.5	25.6	3.3	1.9	32537	33039	12	52	1750	13.5	21.3	44.7	18.5	2.1	114487
26761	SHANKS	15662	498	30.3	36.5	29.5	3.2	0.4	36231	36503	21	72	405	19.0	22.2	39.3	17.3	2.2	108263
26763	SPRINGFIELD	17397	690	33.0	36.4	27.4	3.0	0.1	33830	34121	15	58	583	16.0	21.4	46.7	13.0	2.9	112132
26764	TERRA ALTA	16339	2089	40.1	33.2	23.0	2.9	0.8	31190	32784	10	46	1704	27.3	30.6	33.2	8.3	0.6	79023
26767	WILEY FORD	20613	470	28.3	36.0	30.2	3.0	2.6	41918	43384	39	89	382	12.0	24.9	46.6	13.9	2.6	112342
26801	BAKER	19816	707	30.4	31.1	33.9	4.1	0.4	40278	41580	34	84	597	11.6	22.8	32.0	22.3	11.4	126509
26802	BRANDYWINE	18753	219	32.0	41.6	21.0	4.1	1.4	37504	38531	25	78	168	24.4	21.4	36.3	14.9	3.0	103125
26804	CIRCLEVILLE	15145	245	40.4	40.0	15.9	3.7	0.0	29876	30211	8	34	210	29.5	20.0	43.3	7.1	0.0	90714
26807	FRANKLIN	20650	1155	29.5	38.9	26.4	2.3	2.9	37905	38942	26	80	892	11.7	22.3	48.4	15.5	2.1	112184
26808	HIGH VIEW	22123	600	19.3	35.8	37.8	3.3	3.7	46852	47471	54	94	501	9.0	16.0	49.5	21.6	4.0	131830
26810	LOST CITY	23868	327	31.5	28.7	31.5	4.0	4.3	42918	45059	42	90	286	16.1	19.6	39.9	20.6	3.8	127000
26812	MATHIAS	19319	677	33.5	31.6	27.8	4.9	2.2	40362	42109	34	84	581	17.4	19.4	41.8	18.4	2.9	117188
26814	RIVERTON	14435	118	40.7	39.8	15.3	4.2	0.0	30000	30158	8	35	101	29.7	19.8	42.6	7.9	0.0	90833
26815	SUGAR GROVE	17091	514	27.0	37.9	33.5	1.6	0.0	37892	38701	26	80	360	15.6	21.9	47.2	12.5	2.8	110000
26817	BLOOMERY	20328	501	28.9	32.7	30.7	4.6	3.0	41229	42541	37	87	426	13.1	14.6	37.8	29.6	4.9	145667
26818	FISHER	16017	92	23.9	39.1	33.7	3.3	0.0	40633	42695	35	85	74	27.0	24.3	35.1	10.8	2.7	80000
26833	MAYSVILLE	17361	1367	34.9	34.9	25.7	2.8	1.7	34843	34897	17	64	1201	16.1	16.3	46.5	18.6	2.6	117202
26836	MOOREFIELD	18532	3177	33.7	34.4	26.8	3.5	1.6	35462	35425	19	67	2453	23.2	18.1	39.6	15.5	3.6	105858
26838	MILAM	19255	222	32.0	40.5	22.5	4.1	0.9	37293	38249	24	76	170	23.5	21.2	37.6	15.3	2.4	103906
	WEST VIRGINIA	20563		34.3	29.3	28.3	5.4	2.7	37099	38541				22.0	23.9	36.4	15.5	2.2	98135
	UNITED STATES	27277		20.9	24.4	35.3	11.7	7.6	54719	56938				9.3	13.1	31.6	32.6	13.5	162279

ZIP CODE		FINANCIAL SERVICES				THE HOME						ENTERTAINMENT						PERSONAL			
						Home Improvements		Furnishings													
#	POST OFFICE NAME	Auto Loan	Home Loan	Invest-ments	Retire-ment Plans	Home Repair	Lawn & Garden	Comput-ers & Hard-ware-Personal	Major Appli-ances	TV, Radio, Sound Equip-ment	Furni-ture	Dine out/ Carry out	Sports Equip-ment	Fees & Tickets	Toys & Games	Travel	Cable TV	Apparel & Services	Auto Repairs	Health Insur-ance	Pets & Supplies
26448	WALLACE	78	51	75	48	51	77	55	69	63	52	61	54	41	64	51	70	41	65	73	84
26451	WEST MILFORD	82	59	84	57	61	83	60	76	67	56	65	57	48	66	60	73	43	70	79	91
26452	WESTON	70	52	70	51	54	72	56	68	62	51	61	50	47	61	55	68	41	64	73	80
26456	WEST UNION	68	48	68	47	50	70	51	64	58	47	56	48	41	57	50	63	37	60	69	76
26501	MORGANTOWN	71	60	63	60	60	68	65	66	67	62	67	51	59	68	61	70	46	67	70	80
26505	MORGANTOWN	66	45	44	49	43	48	79	55	71	64	71	50	60	70	57	68	50	66	57	69
26506	MORGANTOWN	43	18	18	23	17	21	61	30	48	41	49	33	36	47	33	44	35	43	30	41
26508	MORGANTOWN	100	93	91	93	92	99	91	96	93	91	93	72	87	95	89	96	64	93	97	113
26519	ALBRIGHT	74	53	76	52	55	76	55	70	61	51	60	52	44	60	54	67	39	64	72	83
26521	BLACKSVILLE	90	65	93	63	67	92	66	84	74	62	72	63	53	73	66	81	48	77	88	100
26525	BRUCETON MILLS	83	59	85	57	62	84	61	78	68	57	66	58	49	67	60	74	44	71	81	92
26537	KINGWOOD	75	57	73	55	58	77	58	71	65	55	63	53	49	65	57	71	42	66	76	84
26541	MAIDSVILLE	77	55	64	53	55	73	57	67	64	56	62	51	46	66	52	70	42	63	71	82
26542	MASONTOWN	65	47	65	45	48	66	48	60	53	45	52	45	38	53	47	59	35	56	63	72
26546	PURSGLOVE	64	59	52	57	58	60	56	59	58	58	58	43	53	60	53	59	39	57	59	70
26547	REEDSVILLE	72	57	66	57	58	74	59	69	63	54	62	52	50	64	57	69	42	64	73	81
26554	FAIRMONT	76	64	74	64	65	79	68	75	72	63	71	56	61	71	66	77	48	73	81	88
26560	BAXTER	70	51	70	49	52	73	55	68	62	49	59	51	44	60	53	68	40	63	74	80
26561	BIG RUN	79	56	81	54	58	80	58	73	64	54	63	55	46	64	57	70	42	67	76	87
26562	BURTON	77	55	78	54	58	80	59	74	66	54	64	55	47	65	58	72	42	68	79	87
26568	ENTERPRISE	80	55	80	53	56	80	57	73	65	54	63	55	45	65	55	71	42	67	76	87
26570	FAIRVIEW	82	59	84	57	61	83	60	77	67	56	66	58	48	67	60	74	44	71	80	91
26571	FARMINGTON	78	56	78	54	58	81	61	75	68	54	66	56	49	67	59	75	44	70	82	88
26575	HUNDRED	68	46	66	44	47	68	50	62	56	46	55	47	38	57	47	63	36	58	66	75
26581	LITTLETON	70	50	71	49	52	71	52	65	57	48	56	49	41	57	51	63	37	60	68	78
26582	MANNINGTON	77	54	77	52	56	79	59	73	66	53	64	55	46	65	56	73	42	68	79	87
26585	METZ	77	55	79	54	58	79	58	73	65	53	63	55	47	64	57	71	42	68	78	87
26587	RACHEL	81	58	81	57	60	84	64	79	71	57	68	59	51	70	61	78	46	73	86	92
26588	RIVESVILLE	78	57	78	56	59	81	61	75	67	55	66	56	49	67	59	74	44	70	80	89
26590	WANA	87	62	89	60	64	88	64	81	71	59	69	61	51	70	63	78	46	74	84	96
26591	WORTHINGTON	75	51	74	49	52	75	54	68	61	50	59	52	42	61	52	67	39	63	72	82
26601	SUTTON	71	49	70	47	50	72	53	66	59	49	58	50	41	59	50	66	38	61	70	79
26610	BIRCH RIVER	75	49	73	46	49	74	53	66	61	50	59	52	39	62	49	68	39	62	70	81
26611	CEDARVILLE	51	34	47	33	34	50	37	45	42	35	41	35	28	43	34	46	27	42	47	55
26615	COPEN	63	45	53	44	45	60	47	55	52	45	51	42	37	54	43	57	34	52	58	67
26617	DILLE	59	38	56	36	38	57	41	51	47	39	46	40	31	48	38	53	30	48	54	63
26619	EXCHANGE	63	45	53	44	45	60	47	55	52	46	51	42	38	54	43	57	35	52	58	67
26621	FLATWOODS	85	61	87	59	63	86	62	79	69	58	68	59	50	69	62	76	45	73	82	94
26623	FRAMETOWN	63	45	65	44	47	64	47	59	52	43	51	44	37	51	46	57	34	54	62	70
26624	GASSAWAY	75	54	77	52	56	77	56	71	62	52	61	53	45	62	55	69	40	65	75	84
26627	HEATERS	93	67	95	65	69	94	68	87	76	64	75	65	55	75	68	83	49	80	91	103
26629	LITTLE BIRCH	66	43	64	41	43	65	46	58	53	44	52	45	34	54	43	59	34	55	61	71
26631	NAPIER	71	51	73	49	53	72	52	66	58	49	57	50	42	58	52	64	38	61	69	79
26636	ROSEDALE	69	49	70	47	50	69	50	64	56	47	55	48	40	56	49	62	36	59	66	76
26638	SHOCK	82	59	85	57	61	84	61	77	67	56	66	58	48	67	60	74	44	71	80	92
26651	SUMMERSVILLE	87	67	91	65	70	91	69	83	76	65	75	62	59	74	69	83	50	78	90	99
26656	BELVA	83	55	81	52	55	82	58	73	67	55	65	57	44	68	55	74	43	69	77	90
26660	CALVIN	75	52	76	51	54	75	54	69	61	51	60	52	43	61	53	67	39	64	72	83
26662	CANVAS	74	53	76	51	55	75	54	69	60	50	59	52	43	60	54	66	39	63	72	82
26667	DRENNEN	80	55	80	53	57	80	58	73	65	54	64	56	45	65	56	72	42	68	76	88
26675	KESLERS CROSS LANES	68	44	66	42	44	67	47	60	55	45	53	47	35	56	44	61	35	56	63	73
26676	LEIVASY	77	53	77	51	55	77	55	70	62	52	61	53	43	62	54	69	40	65	74	85
26678	MOUNT LOOKOUT	78	56	80	54	58	79	57	73	63	53	62	55	46	63	57	70	41	67	76	86
26679	MOUNT NEBO	82	58	83	56	60	82	60	76	66	56	65	57	47	66	58	73	43	70	79	90
26680	NALLEN	75	54	77	52	56	77	55	71	62	52	60	53	44	61	55	68	40	65	73	84
26681	NETTIE	73	52	75	50	54	74	53	68	59	50	58	51	43	59	53	65	38	62	71	81
26684	POOL	70	50	71	48	52	71	51	65	57	48	56	49	41	56	51	62	37	60	68	77
26690	SWISS	84	57	84	55	58	84	60	76	68	57	67	58	47	69	58	76	44	71	80	92
26691	TIOGA	79	54	78	51	55	79	57	71	64	53	63	55	44	65	54	71	42	67	75	87
26704	AUGUSTA	73	53	65	51	53	71	55	65	60	52	59	50	44	62	51	66	40	61	69	79
26705	AURORA	62	44	63	43	46	63	45	58	50	42	49	43	36	50	45	55	33	53	60	69
26710	BURLINGTON	89	65	85	64	67	89	67	82	74	63	73	62	54	75	65	81	48	76	86	98
26711	CAPON BRIDGE	92	79	86	81	81	97	78	91	82	71	81	69	70	83	78	88	55	84	94	106
26714	DELRAY	76	54	62	53	54	72	56	66	63	55	61	50	45	65	51	68	41	62	69	80
26716	EGLON	58	41	59	40	43	59	42	54	47	40	46	41	34	47	42	52	31	50	56	64
26717	ELK GARDEN	67	45	65	42	45	66	48	60	55	45	53	46	36	56	45	61	35	56	63	73
26719	FORT ASHBY	78	57	80	55	59	80	58	73	64	54	63	55	47	64	57	70	42	67	76	87
26720	GORMANIA	78	56	80	54	58	79	57	73	64	53	63	55	46	63	57	70	41	67	76	87
26722	GREEN SPRING	73	52	75	51	54	74	54	68	60	50	59	51	43	59	53	66	39	63	71	81
26726	KEYSER	72	53	67	53	54	72	60	68	65	54	63	51	49	65	56	71	43	66	74	81
26731	LAHMANSVILLE	76	54	69	53	55	74	56	68	62	54	61	52	45	64	53	68	41	63	71	82
26739	MOUNT STORM	86	62	86	60	64	87	64	80	71	60	69	60	51	71	62	78	46	74	83	95
26743	NEW CREEK	81	74	74	76	75	87	73	82	75	66	74	62	67	77	73	80	50	76	85	96
26750	PIEDMONT	55	41	45	40	39	52	46	49	50	43	49	38	38	51	41	54	33	49	54	60
26753	RIDGELEY	85	68	82	67	69	87	68	81	74	64	72	61	59	74	67	79	48	76	84	96
26755	RIO	76	55	63	53	55	73	57	66	63	56	62	51	46	66	52	69	42	63	70	81
26757	ROMNEY	74	54	70	53	55	73	58	69	64	54	63	52	47	64	55	70	42	65	73	82
26761	SHANKS	78	56	68	55	56	75	58	69	65	56	63	53	47	67	54	71	42	65	73	84
26763	SPRINGFIELD	72	52	74	50	54	73	53	68	59	50	58	51	43	59	53	65	38	62	70	80
26764	TERRA ALTA	69	50	67	49	51	69	53	64	58	49	57	48	43	58	51	63	38	60	67	76
26767	WILEY FORD	80	57	80	56	60	83	63	77	70	56	67	58	50	69	61	77	45	72	84	91
26801	BAKER	80	60	87	59	64	82	61	77	67	58	65	57	51	66	62	72	44	71	78	91
26802	BRANDYWINE	76	55	75	53	56	76	56	70	62	53	61	53	45	62	55	68	40	65	73	84
26804	CIRCLEVILLE	63	45	52	44	45	60	47	55	52	46	51	42	38	54	43	57	34	52	58	67
26807	FRANKLIN	85	61	86	59	63	86	63	80	70	58	69	60	51	70	62	77	46	74	84	95
26808	HIGH VIEW	85	77	77	81	79	91	76	86	79	69	77	65	70	80	76	83	53	79	89	100
26810	LOST CITY	90	65	95	63	68	92	67	85	73	62	72	63	54	73	67	80	48	78	88	100
26812	MATHIAS	81	58	83	56	60	82	59	75	66	55	65	57	47	65	59	72	43	69	78	90
26814	RIVERTON	63	45	53	44	45	60	47	55	52	45	51	42	38	54	43	57	34	52	58	67
26815	SUGAR GROVE	77	55	63	54	55	73	57	67	64	56	62	51	46	66	52	69	42	63	71	81
26817	BLOOMERY	92	66	92	64	68	92	67	85	75	63	74	64	54	75	66	82	49	78	89	101
26818	FISHER	80	57	66	56	57	76	60	69	66	58	65	53	48	69	54	72	44	66	73	84
26833	MAYSVILLE	79	56	65	55	56	75	59	68	65	57	64	53	47	68	53	71	43	65	72	83
26836	MOOREFIELD	76	56	67	54	56	74	59	68	65	56	64	52	48	67	55	71	43	65	73	82
26838	MILAM	77	55	74	53	56	76	57	70	63	53	62	53	45	63	54	69	41	65	73	84
	WEST VIRGINIA	79	63	76	62	64	80	66	75	71	63	70	57	58	71	64	77	47	72	80	90
	UNITED STATES	100	100	100	100	100	100	100	100	100	100	100	100	100	100	100	100	100	100	100	100

ZIP CODE #	POST OFFICE NAME	COUNTY FIPS CODE	POPULATION 2000	POPULATION 2009	POPULATION 2014	2000-2009 ANNUAL RATE % Rate	2000-2009 ANNUAL RATE State Centile	HOUSEHOLDS 2000	HOUSEHOLDS 2009	HOUSEHOLDS 2014	HOUSEHOLDS % Annual Rate 2000-2009	HOUSEHOLDS 2009 Average HH Size	FAMILIES 2000	FAMILIES 2009	FAMILIES % Annual Rate 2000-2009
26845	OLD FIELDS	031	177	323	345	6.7	100	68	123	133	6.6	2.63	49	87	6.4
26847	PETERSBURG	023	5593	5858	6003	0.5	86	2333	2548	2645	1.0	2.24	1556	1639	0.6
26851	WARDENSVILLE	031	1874	2219	2363	1.8	95	766	940	1013	2.2	2.31	522	620	1.9
26852	PURGITSVILLE	027	947	1082	1166	1.5	94	380	454	496	1.9	2.37	275	313	1.4
26855	CABINS	023	87	97	102	1.2	92	37	43	46	1.6	2.26	29	32	1.1
26865	YELLOW SPRING	027	187	217	234	1.6	94	74	88	96	1.9	2.44	54	62	1.5
26866	UPPER TRACT	071	1097	1045	1009	-0.5	30	462	461	452	0.0	2.27	337	326	-0.4
26884	SENECA ROCKS	071	1066	1015	984	-0.5	30	450	446	437	-0.1	2.28	318	305	-0.5
	WEST VIRGINIA					0.2					0.5	2.33			0.1
	UNITED STATES					1.0					1.1	2.59			0.9

ZIP CODE		RACE (%)						% Hispanic Origin		2009 AGE DISTRIBUTION (%)										MEDIAN AGE		
#	POST OFFICE NAME	White		Black		Asian/Pacific																
		2000	2009	2000	2009	2000	2009	2000	2009	0-4	5-9	10-14	15-19	20-24	25-44	45-64	65-84	85+	18+	2009	% 2009 Males	% 2009 Females
26845	OLD FIELDS	98.3	97.8	1.1	1.2	0.0	0.0	0.6	0.3	5.6	5.6	6.2	6.8	6.2	25.1	31.3	12.1	1.2	78.3	41.4	50.8	49.2
26847	PETERSBURG	98.0	97.8	1.0	1.0	0.2	0.3	0.7	0.8	6.0	6.0	6.4	5.8	4.7	25.2	27.4	15.6	3.0	78.1	42.2	49.1	50.9
26851	WARDENSVILLE	98.1	98.0	1.0	1.1	0.1	0.1	0.5	0.6	5.5	5.9	6.1	6.1	4.6	23.6	30.4	15.6	2.2	78.6	43.8	49.8	50.2
26852	PURGITSVILLE	97.7	97.4	0.1	0.1	0.3	0.5	0.1	0.1	5.0	5.5	6.3	6.9	4.1	24.3	30.3	15.8	1.8	79.9	43.6	50.7	49.3
26855	CABINS	100.0	99.0	0.0	0.0	0.0	0.0	1.2	1.0	6.2	6.2	6.2	6.2	5.2	27.8	28.9	12.4	1.0	75.3	40.3	49.5	50.5
26865	YELLOW SPRING	99.5	99.1	0.5	0.5	0.0	0.5	1.1	0.9	6.5	6.9	6.9	6.5	3.7	26.3	29.0	12.9	1.4	74.7	40.7	48.8	51.2
26866	UPPER TRACT	99.4	99.3	0.1	0.1	0.1	0.1	0.8	1.0	3.8	4.1	4.8	5.8	3.9	23.6	35.2	16.4	2.3	83.6	47.3	52.4	47.6
26884	SENECA ROCKS	98.7	98.5	0.0	0.0	0.3	0.3	0.4	0.4	4.3	4.7	5.2	5.0	3.8	23.7	33.1	17.2	2.8	82.6	46.8	50.8	49.2
	WEST VIRGINIA	95.0	94.5	3.2	3.3	0.5	0.8	0.7	0.8	5.5	5.6	5.9	6.5	6.1	25.2	29.3	13.8	2.2	79.3	41.5	49.0	51.0
	UNITED STATES	75.1	72.0	12.3	12.7	3.8	4.6	12.5	15.7	6.8	6.7	6.6	7.1	6.9	27.0	26.0	10.9	1.9	75.7	36.9	49.2	50.8

ZIP CODE				2009 HOUSEHOLD INCOME DISTRIBUTION (%)					MEDIAN HOUSEHOLD INCOME					2009 HOME VALUE DISTRIBUTION (%)					
#	POST OFFICE NAME	2009 Per Capita Income	2009 HH Income Base	Less than $25,000	$25,000 to $49,999	$50,000 to $99,999	$100,000 to $149,999	$150,000 or More	2009	2014	2009 National Centile	2009 State Centile	2009 Home Value Base	Less than $50,000	$50,000 to $89,999	$90,000 to $174,999	$175,000 to $399,999	$400,000 or More	2009 Median Home Value
26845	OLD FIELDS	16379	123	34.1	39.0	21.1	4.9	0.8	33359	32599	14	55	109	19.3	16.5	29.4	23.9	11.0	124038
26847	PETERSBURG	19510	2548	35.7	32.7	27.7	2.4	1.6	33887	34129	15	58	1912	17.3	16.7	46.7	16.7	2.7	116494
26851	WARDENSVILLE	21068	940	25.2	33.7	33.4	6.2	1.5	43049	45071	43	91	757	8.5	17.2	51.5	18.9	4.0	125295
26852	PURGITSVILLE	16304	454	36.8	35.0	27.3	0.9	0.0	37345	40000	25	77	397	24.7	24.4	40.1	9.1	1.8	98750
26855	CABINS	17964	43	34.9	34.9	27.9	2.3	0.0	35540	35000	19	68	38	15.8	13.2	50.0	15.8	5.3	125000
26865	YELLOW SPRING	22170	88	19.3	36.4	37.5	3.4	3.4	46708	47066	53	94	73	8.2	16.4	49.3	21.9	4.1	131250
26866	UPPER TRACT	24636	461	29.3	35.1	26.7	2.6	6.3	38500	40318	28	81	407	21.1	22.9	36.4	13.8	5.9	100205
26884	SENECA ROCKS	17366	446	38.1	36.3	21.5	2.5	1.6	31563	31521	11	47	380	20.8	15.0	40.8	19.5	3.9	120588
	WEST VIRGINIA	20563		34.3	29.3	28.3	5.4	2.7	37099	38541				22.0	23.9	36.4	15.5	2.2	98135
	UNITED STATES	27277		20.9	24.4	35.3	11.7	7.6	54719	56938				9.3	13.1	31.6	32.6	13.5	162279

ZIP CODE	FINANCIAL SERVICES				THE HOME						ENTERTAINMENT						PERSONAL			
					Home Improvements		Furnishings													
# POST OFFICE NAME	Auto Loan	Home Loan	Invest-ments	Retire-ment Plans	Home Repair	Lawn & Garden	Comput-ers & Hard-ware-Personal	Major Appli-ances	TV, Radio, Sound Equip-ment	Furni-ture	Dine out/ Carry out	Sports Equip-ment	Fees & Tickets	Toys & Games	Travel	Cable TV	Apparel & Services	Auto Repairs	Health Insur-ance	Pets & Supplies
26845 OLD FIELDS	78	56	64	54	55	74	58	67	64	56	63	52	47	67	53	70	42	64	71	82
26847 PETERSBURG	78	56	70	55	57	77	60	71	66	56	64	54	48	67	56	73	43	67	76	85
26851 WARDENSVILLE	88	63	91	61	66	90	65	83	72	60	71	62	52	71	64	79	47	76	86	98
26852 PURGITSVILLE	69	50	71	48	51	70	51	65	56	47	55	49	41	56	50	62	37	59	67	77
26855 CABINS	73	52	60	51	52	69	55	64	61	53	59	49	44	63	50	66	40	60	67	77
26865 YELLOW SPRING	84	77	76	80	78	91	76	86	78	69	77	65	70	80	76	83	52	79	88	99
26866 UPPER TRACT	100	71	102	69	74	101	73	93	81	68	80	70	59	81	73	89	53	86	97	111
26884 SENECA ROCKS	71	51	72	49	52	72	52	66	58	48	57	50	42	57	51	63	37	61	69	78
WEST VIRGINIA	79	63	76	62	64	80	66	75	71	63	70	57	58	71	64	77	47	72	80	90
UNITED STATES	100	100	100	100	100	100	100	100	100	100	100	100	100	100	100	100	100	100	100	100

53001-53147

ZIP CODE #	POST OFFICE NAME	COUNTY FIPS CODE	POPULATION 2000	POPULATION 2009	POPULATION 2014	2000-2009 ANNUAL RATE % Rate	2000-2009 ANNUAL RATE State Centile	HOUSEHOLDS 2000	HOUSEHOLDS 2009	HOUSEHOLDS 2014	HOUSEHOLDS % Annual Rate 2000-2009	HOUSEHOLDS 2009 Average HH Size	FAMILIES 2000	FAMILIES 2009	FAMILIES % Annual Rate 2000-2009
53001	ADELL	117	1888	1913	1935	0.1	20	687	731	747	0.7	2.57	537	565	0.6
53002	ALLENTON	131	2236	2407	2506	0.8	61	796	911	965	1.5	2.63	628	711	1.4
53004	BELGIUM	089	3030	3324	3533	1.0	72	1077	1211	1296	1.3	2.73	830	925	1.2
53005	BROOKFIELD	133	20027	20085	20009	0.0	16	7345	7577	7623	0.3	2.62	5938	6060	0.2
53006	BROWNSVILLE	027	1994	2003	1997	0.0	16	738	773	780	0.5	2.59	574	596	0.4
53007	BUTLER	133	1850	1775	1751	-0.4	2	903	897	895	-0.1	1.97	453	437	-0.4
53010	CAMPBELLSPORT	039	7108	7625	7871	0.8	61	2618	2910	3039	1.1	2.58	1966	2154	1.0
53011	CASCADE	117	2027	2431	2566	2.0	95	787	988	1053	2.5	2.39	609	752	2.3
53012	CEDARBURG	089	17780	18846	19316	0.6	51	6728	7268	7502	0.8	2.56	5042	5390	0.7
53013	CEDAR GROVE	117	3119	3612	3744	1.6	91	1127	1350	1412	2.0	2.67	900	1060	1.8
53014	CHILTON	015	8268	8337	8373	0.1	20	3152	3352	3414	0.7	2.44	2229	2323	0.4
53015	CLEVELAND	071	2618	2855	2939	0.9	68	954	1094	1140	1.5	2.60	728	825	1.4
53017	COLGATE	131	5513	6319	6620	1.5	88	1905	2287	2429	2.0	2.76	1608	1925	2.0
53018	DELAFIELD	133	7324	8011	8279	1.0	72	2462	2775	2897	1.3	2.76	2006	2242	1.2
53019	EDEN	039	1910	2048	2111	0.8	61	679	755	787	1.2	2.71	514	563	1.0
53020	ELKHART LAKE	117	3635	3689	3720	0.2	24	1363	1450	1477	0.7	2.51	1036	1086	0.5
53021	FREDONIA	089	4128	4591	4802	1.2	81	1467	1686	1783	1.5	2.71	1154	1317	1.4
53022	GERMANTOWN	131	17204	19518	20497	1.4	86	6534	7649	8120	1.7	2.54	4861	5598	1.5
53023	GLENBEULAH	117	2650	2655	2648	0.0	16	518	535	536	0.3	3.35	417	426	0.2
53024	GRAFTON	089	14548	16245	16832	1.2	81	5645	6461	6754	1.5	2.51	4156	4740	1.4
53027	HARTFORD	131	18960	22048	23374	1.6	91	7114	8664	9337	2.2	2.53	5243	6339	2.1
53029	HARTLAND	133	17648	19151	19777	0.9	68	6330	7046	7343	1.2	2.72	4963	5475	1.1
53032	HORICON	027	4746	4763	4742	0.0	16	1841	1923	1939	0.5	2.47	1332	1376	0.4
53033	HUBERTUS	131	4495	4634	4809	0.3	32	1589	1741	1834	1.0	2.66	1354	1472	0.9
53034	HUSTISFORD	027	1539	1621	1665	0.6	51	631	701	728	1.1	2.31	422	460	0.9
53035	IRON RIDGE	027	2554	2970	3127	1.6	91	902	1092	1164	2.1	2.72	692	829	2.0
53036	IXONIA	055	2066	2498	2713	2.1	96	743	914	1004	2.3	2.73	608	741	2.2
53037	JACKSON	131	6966	8892	9737	2.7	97	2644	3542	3935	3.2	2.51	2004	2670	3.2
53038	JOHNSON CREEK	055	2853	3363	3532	1.8	93	1086	1306	1382	2.0	2.57	787	939	1.9
53039	JUNEAU	027	4984	5271	5362	0.6	51	1759	1935	1994	1.0	2.46	1273	1380	0.9
53040	KEWASKUM	131	7096	8180	8671	1.5	88	2551	3086	3324	2.1	2.63	2017	2413	2.0
53042	KIEL	071	6897	7094	7138	0.3	32	2693	2871	2919	0.7	2.47	1945	2044	0.5
53044	KOHLER	117	2368	2567	2614	0.9	68	917	1046	1079	1.4	2.45	711	805	1.4
53045	BROOKFIELD	133	21589	22517	22817	0.5	44	7852	8476	8693	0.8	2.61	6085	6478	0.7
53046	LANNON	133	1041	1032	1023	-0.1	11	438	449	450	0.3	2.30	328	331	0.1
53048	LOMIRA	027	2843	3094	3195	0.9	68	1030	1174	1228	1.4	2.59	752	846	1.3
53049	MALONE	039	2498	2673	2755	0.7	56	896	994	1038	1.1	2.56	718	789	1.0
53050	MAYVILLE	027	7015	7198	7272	0.3	32	2715	2931	3002	0.8	2.42	1915	2041	0.7
53051	MENOMONEE FALLS	133	32610	35562	36653	0.9	68	12831	14302	14853	1.2	2.47	9248	10230	1.1
53057	MOUNT CALVARY	039	2003	2064	2086	0.3	32	546	583	597	0.7	2.74	420	443	0.6
53058	NASHOTAH	133	3211	3320	3331	0.4	39	1248	1317	1333	0.6	2.52	926	962	0.4
53059	NEOSHO	027	1837	2013	2095	1.0	72	645	745	784	1.6	2.70	514	588	1.5
53061	NEW HOLSTEIN	015	5003	4875	4843	-0.3	4	1969	2037	2054	0.4	2.31	1396	1412	0.1
53063	NEWTON	071	1665	1728	1749	0.4	39	580	637	653	1.0	2.62	465	506	0.9
53065	OAKFIELD	039	2006	2114	2179	0.6	51	698	762	793	1.0	2.77	554	597	0.8
53066	OCONOMOWOC	133	29089	32891	34492	1.3	84	10929	12706	13466	1.6	2.54	8119	9301	1.5
53069	OKAUCHEE	133	845	880	885	0.4	39	374	401	408	0.8	2.19	235	244	0.4
53070	OOSTBURG	117	4520	4856	5000	0.8	61	1624	1823	1898	1.3	2.65	1282	1420	1.1
53072	PEWAUKEE	133	21530	23408	24211	0.9	68	8733	9821	10281	1.3	2.36	5982	6602	1.1
53073	PLYMOUTH	117	13967	14465	14680	0.4	39	5322	5736	5885	0.8	2.36	3721	3941	0.6
53074	PORT WASHINGTON	089	12136	12717	12930	0.5	44	4723	5087	5219	0.8	2.42	3215	3420	0.7
53075	RANDOM LAKE	117	3945	3276	3352	-2.0	0	1161	1272	1316	1.0	2.57	862	931	0.8
53076	RICHFIELD	131	3559	4140	4386	1.6	91	1214	1487	1600	2.2	2.78	1036	1253	2.1
53078	RUBICON	027	1660	1864	1948	1.3	84	548	645	682	1.8	2.89	448	523	1.7
53079	SAINT CLOUD	039	1597	1761	1835	1.1	76	576	659	694	1.5	2.62	433	488	1.3
53080	SAUKVILLE	089	5979	6159	6206	0.3	32	2248	2383	2423	0.6	2.58	1657	1738	0.5
53081	SHEBOYGAN	117	43952	43552	43217	-0.1	11	17810	18201	18243	0.2	2.33	11044	11081	0.0
53083	SHEBOYGAN	117	19230	20834	21484	0.9	68	7554	8414	8745	1.2	2.46	5395	5974	1.1
53085	SHEBOYGAN FALLS	117	10071	11121	11528	1.1	76	3928	4538	4754	1.6	2.39	2816	3200	1.4
53086	SLINGER	131	7361	8236	8721	1.2	81	2698	3154	3380	1.7	2.59	1997	2302	1.5
53089	SUSSEX	133	15867	17889	18691	1.3	84	5806	6712	7074	1.6	2.66	4585	5287	1.6
53090	WEST BEND	131	20244	22029	23011	0.9	68	7386	8496	9009	1.5	2.57	5576	6344	1.4
53091	THERESA	027	2128	2246	2303	0.6	51	787	873	906	1.1	2.57	614	675	1.0
53092	THIENSVILLE	089	20314	20966	21175	0.3	32	7685	8131	8289	0.6	2.55	5947	6241	0.5
53093	WALDO	117	1764	1889	1977	0.7	56	635	716	759	1.3	2.56	508	568	1.2
53094	WATERTOWN	055	16868	18405	19110	0.9	68	6183	6914	7228	1.2	2.55	4407	4890	1.1
53095	WEST BEND	131	24643	26315	27137	0.7	56	9684	10828	11319	1.2	2.36	6670	7412	1.1
53097	MEQUON	089	4866	5897	5934	2.1	96	1716	1829	1860	0.7	2.77	1386	1465	0.6
53098	WATERTOWN	027	11569	12037	12205	0.4	39	4298	4674	4794	0.9	2.49	3125	3376	0.8
53103	BIG BEND	133	3922	4131	4222	0.6	51	1336	1458	1509	0.9	2.83	1138	1232	0.9
53104	BRISTOL	059	5470	6044	6388	1.1	76	2053	2307	2451	1.3	2.61	1506	1671	1.1
53105	BURLINGTON	101	28453	30987	31985	0.9	68	10490	11691	12138	1.2	2.62	7721	8515	1.1
53108	CALEDONIA	101	3100	3223	3280	0.4	39	1190	1286	1321	0.8	2.50	925	989	0.7
53110	CUDAHY	079	18429	18311	18452	-0.1	11	7888	8081	8195	0.3	2.25	4894	4972	0.2
53114	DARIEN	127	2836	3170	3280	1.2	81	971	1114	1157	1.5	2.79	750	850	1.4
53115	DELAVAN	127	14597	15286	15167	0.5	44	5482	5819	5778	0.6	2.60	3797	3962	0.5
53118	DOUSMAN	133	6526	7158	7418	1.0	72	2392	2732	2868	1.4	2.56	1864	2108	1.3
53119	EAGLE	133	4660	5401	5712	1.6	91	1568	1864	1992	1.9	2.90	1315	1549	1.8
53120	EAST TROY	127	8796	10059	10391	1.5	88	3269	3849	3990	1.8	2.59	2495	2905	1.7
53121	ELKHORN	127	15643	19114	20268	2.2	96	5763	7246	7715	2.5	2.54	4135	5121	2.3
53122	ELM GROVE	133	6369	6273	6199	-0.2	8	2494	2525	2519	0.1	2.42	1815	1811	0.0
53125	FONTANA	127	1856	1962	2002	0.6	51	814	877	897	0.8	2.12	564	597	0.6
53126	FRANKSVILLE	101	6026	6442	6706	0.7	56	2129	2354	2472	1.1	2.73	1752	1919	1.0
53128	GENOA CITY	127	6767	8033	8638	1.9	94	2430	2926	3150	2.0	2.72	1761	2087	1.9
53129	GREENDALE	079	14221	13835	13980	-0.3	4	5938	5984	6095	0.1	2.29	4156	4150	0.0
53130	HALES CORNERS	079	7715	7534	7607	-0.3	4	3247	3273	3330	0.1	2.27	2116	2110	0.0
53132	FRANKLIN	079	29524	34232	36273	1.6	91	10613	12747	13630	2.0	2.53	7706	9185	1.9
53137	HELENVILLE	055	1439	1473	1540	0.3	32	510	542	573	0.7	2.70	395	414	0.5
53139	KANSASVILLE	101	2612	2762	2828	0.6	51	960	1046	1080	0.9	2.61	722	777	0.8
53140	KENOSHA	059	29532	30803	31323	0.5	44	11424	12031	12315	0.6	2.42	6824	7004	0.3
53142	KENOSHA	059	28159	31656	33224	1.3	84	10774	12168	12797	1.3	2.58	7718	8603	1.2
53143	KENOSHA	059	24234	24300	24335	0.0	16	9221	9340	9397	0.1	2.53	6036	6019	0.0
53144	KENOSHA	059	22253	25982	27599	1.7	91	8176	9721	10406	1.9	2.52	5447	6355	1.7
53146	NEW BERLIN	133	7547	7832	7932	0.4	39	2803	3014	3087	0.8	2.59	2219	2357	0.7
53147	LAKE GENEVA	127	15024	16515	18364	1.0	72	6199	6922	7768	1.2	2.37	3995	4382	1.0
	WISCONSIN					0.7					1.0	2.43			0.9
	UNITED STATES					1.0					1.1	2.59			0.9

ZIP CODE #	POST OFFICE NAME	RACE (%) White 2000	White 2009	Black 2000	Black 2009	Asian/Pacific 2000	Asian/Pacific 2009	% Hispanic Origin 2000	% Hispanic Origin 2009	2009 AGE DISTRIBUTION (%) 0-4	5-9	10-14	15-19	20-24	25-44	45-64	65-84	85+	18+	MEDIAN AGE 2009	% 2009 Males	% 2009 Females
53001	ADELL	98.1	97.2	0.1	0.3	0.4	0.5	1.4	2.1	5.3	6.8	6.8	8.0	5.5	24.9	30.8	10.6	1.3	77.0	40.0	51.4	48.6
53002	ALLENTON	99.2	99.1	0.0	0.0	0.1	0.1	0.8	1.1	6.1	6.4	6.6	6.9	5.5	27.7	30.1	9.6	1.0	76.3	39.6	50.8	49.2
53004	BELGIUM	97.1	95.9	0.3	0.6	0.4	0.6	2.6	3.7	7.7	8.1	8.5	7.4	5.4	26.1	27.2	8.4	1.3	70.9	37.4	50.5	49.5
53005	BROOKFIELD	94.4	92.3	0.9	1.1	3.6	5.3	1.3	2.0	4.9	5.7	6.8	7.2	4.3	18.0	32.9	17.1	3.0	77.6	46.8	48.3	51.7
53006	BROWNSVILLE	98.2	97.7	0.2	0.2	0.6	0.8	1.2	1.7	6.9	7.2	7.3	6.4	4.7	28.3	27.9	10.1	1.2	74.5	38.6	51.3	48.7
53007	BUTLER	97.4	96.8	0.3	0.3	0.6	0.9	0.9	1.3	4.5	4.5	4.4	5.4	5.5	28.1	24.1	19.1	4.6	83.3	43.5	47.7	52.3
53010	CAMPBELLSPORT	98.2	97.8	0.1	0.1	0.2	0.3	0.9	1.3	5.5	5.8	6.4	6.5	5.3	26.9	29.2	11.9	2.5	78.0	40.9	50.0	50.0
53011	CASCADE	98.5	97.6	0.0	0.4	0.2	0.4	1.0	1.7	5.4	6.0	6.3	7.2	5.1	23.5	33.2	11.8	1.4	79.6	42.5	51.3	48.7
53012	CEDARBURG	98.3	97.8	0.2	0.3	0.6	0.9	0.8	1.2	6.2	6.5	7.0	7.3	6.0	20.6	31.3	12.6	2.6	75.6	42.4	48.4	51.6
53013	CEDAR GROVE	98.3	97.6	0.2	0.2	0.2	0.3	2.1	3.3	7.6	8.4	8.5	6.7	4.7	24.2	28.4	10.1	1.4	70.9	38.1	50.1	49.9
53014	CHILTON	98.5	98.0	0.3	0.3	0.2	0.3	0.8	1.2	5.9	6.4	6.8	6.8	5.3	26.7	28.3	11.4	2.3	76.4	39.6	51.3	48.7
53015	CLEVELAND	98.3	97.7	0.2	0.2	0.2	0.2	1.3	2.1	6.2	6.7	6.9	6.1	4.8	25.6	31.2	10.9	1.7	76.4	41.2	51.7	48.3
53017	COLGATE	98.4	98.0	0.3	0.3	0.4	0.5	0.9	1.3	5.5	6.3	7.2	7.2	4.6	21.9	35.4	11.2	0.8	76.5	43.2	50.0	50.0
53018	DELAFIELD	94.1	92.9	3.1	3.6	0.6	0.9	1.7	2.4	5.8	6.6	8.0	11.2	4.8	20.7	33.7	8.1	1.2	71.1	40.2	51.6	48.4
53019	EDEN	98.3	97.8	0.1	0.0	0.2	0.3	2.5	3.7	5.7	6.3	6.9	8.0	5.5	26.4	29.8	10.4	1.0	76.1	39.3	52.5	47.5
53020	ELKHART LAKE	98.9	98.5	0.1	0.1	0.2	0.2	0.8	1.4	5.3	5.9	6.3	5.4	4.1	24.6	34.5	11.9	1.9	79.0	43.9	50.6	49.4
53021	FREDONIA	97.5	95.4	0.6	1.7	0.4	0.9	1.2	2.1	6.6	6.5	6.9	6.6	10.4	25.3	28.5	7.9	1.2	76.1	36.1	48.9	51.1
53022	GERMANTOWN	95.7	94.3	1.4	1.8	1.7	2.5	1.1	1.5	7.5	7.5	6.8	6.4	4.9	28.7	27.9	9.0	1.1	74.0	37.7	49.5	50.5
53023	GLENBEULAH	78.7	74.8	19.0	23.0	0.2	0.2	3.4	4.5	4.1	4.7	4.7	4.6	17.8	36.3	21.4	5.9	0.5	85.4	32.8	63.7	36.3
53024	GRAFTON	97.9	97.2	0.3	0.4	0.7	1.0	1.4	2.0	5.8	6.1	6.6	6.9	5.7	24.1	31.3	12.0	1.5	77.1	41.4	49.6	50.4
53027	HARTFORD	97.6	96.9	0.2	0.3	0.4	0.6	1.9	2.7	7.0	6.9	7.0	6.8	6.2	26.7	27.8	10.0	1.6	74.7	38.0	49.8	50.2
53029	HARTLAND	98.2	97.6	0.2	0.3	0.5	0.8	1.2	1.8	6.5	6.8	7.3	7.8	6.0	25.3	30.7	8.6	0.9	74.5	38.2	49.1	50.9
53032	HORICON	98.1	97.5	0.3	0.4	0.2	0.3	1.6	2.3	5.9	6.0	6.3	6.5	5.9	27.0	29.7	11.0	1.7	77.9	39.7	49.3	50.7
53033	HUBERTUS	98.6	98.2	0.2	0.3	0.6	0.8	0.6	0.8	5.0	5.7	6.7	6.7	4.2	22.2	36.4	12.3	0.9	78.4	44.6	51.1	48.9
53034	HUSTISFORD	99.3	99.1	0.1	0.1	0.1	0.1	1.2	1.7	7.2	6.8	6.6	6.2	6.5	25.5	27.1	12.3	2.0	75.7	38.4	49.6	50.4
53035	IRON RIDGE	98.9	98.8	0.1	0.1	0.1	0.1	0.6	0.9	7.0	7.0	7.6	7.8	6.1	26.2	27.7	9.6	1.1	73.6	37.3	51.3	48.7
53036	IXONIA	98.5	98.0	0.0	0.1	0.4	0.6	0.9	1.4	5.8	6.4	7.0	6.8	4.3	25.0	32.1	11.4	1.2	76.5	41.6	51.1	48.9
53037	JACKSON	98.8	98.5	0.1	0.1	0.2	0.3	0.9	1.3	8.1	7.7	7.3	6.2	4.9	31.4	24.8	8.4	1.0	72.7	35.7	49.9	50.1
53038	JOHNSON CREEK	96.5	95.5	0.2	0.3	0.2	0.2	3.1	4.4	6.7	7.0	7.2	6.7	4.4	30.2	27.6	9.3	1.1	74.9	37.7	50.9	49.1
53039	JUNEAU	97.8	97.1	0.2	0.3	0.2	0.3	2.4	3.5	6.0	6.3	6.5	5.9	4.9	27.0	27.4	12.7	3.3	77.6	40.6	51.4	48.6
53040	KEWASKUM	98.6	98.2	0.2	0.2	0.3	0.4	0.8	1.1	6.4	6.6	6.6	7.1	5.8	28.0	27.5	10.2	1.7	75.9	38.1	50.0	50.0
53042	KIEL	98.4	97.8	0.1	0.1	0.3	0.5	0.9	1.4	6.7	6.8	7.0	7.0	5.5	25.3	28.4	11.4	1.9	75.3	39.4	49.5	50.5
53044	KOHLER	97.4	95.7	0.1	0.2	1.6	2.8	0.9	1.4	6.2	7.1	8.1	7.4	4.5	21.6	32.1	11.4	1.6	73.9	42.0	47.9	52.1
53045	BROOKFIELD	93.9	91.7	0.8	1.0	4.0	5.8	1.0	1.5	5.1	6.0	7.4	7.5	4.5	17.6	32.9	15.8	3.1	76.0	46.0	47.5	52.5
53046	LANNON	98.1	97.6	0.7	0.9	0.4	0.6	1.0	1.5	5.4	5.9	6.5	5.7	4.4	24.2	32.4	14.1	1.5	78.6	43.7	51.5	48.5
53048	LOMIRA	98.5	98.0	0.2	0.3	0.2	0.2	1.8	2.7	7.3	7.4	7.3	6.8	5.6	29.2	24.9	9.2	2.4	73.6	36.7	50.6	49.4
53049	MALONE	97.6	96.9	0.8	1.0	0.4	0.5	1.1	1.6	4.5	5.0	5.7	7.2	5.2	24.5	32.1	14.0	1.8	80.0	43.6	50.5	49.5
53050	MAYVILLE	98.4	97.8	0.1	0.1	0.4	0.5	1.3	1.9	6.0	6.0	6.1	6.6	6.2	25.3	29.0	11.8	3.0	77.8	40.9	50.5	49.5
53051	MENOMONEE FALLS	96.5	95.3	1.5	2.0	0.9	1.3	1.2	1.7	6.7	6.5	6.4	6.1	4.6	25.1	28.1	14.1	2.4	76.5	41.6	48.5	51.5
53057	MOUNT CALVARY	92.6	89.8	0.4	0.5	2.8	4.1	3.7	5.3	4.3	4.7	6.1	13.9	4.3	20.4	25.9	15.2	5.1	74.0	42.0	55.4	44.6
53058	NASHOTAH	98.7	98.3	0.1	0.2	0.3	0.5	1.2	1.9	6.0	6.5	7.1	6.4	4.7	22.0	31.7	13.6	2.0	76.3	43.1	49.3	50.7
53059	NEOSHO	98.9	98.6	0.0	0.0	0.2	0.3	0.5	0.7	6.4	7.1	7.9	6.9	4.6	25.1	31.2	9.9	0.9	74.2	39.9	51.3	48.7
53061	NEW HOLSTEIN	98.7	98.2	0.0	0.0	0.2	0.4	0.6	1.0	5.2	5.4	5.7	6.3	5.1	25.0	29.4	14.4	3.6	79.7	43.3	49.3	50.7
53063	NEWTON	98.4	97.9	0.1	0.1	0.2	0.4	1.3	1.9	5.7	5.9	6.8	8.0	4.5	24.4	30.4	11.9	2.3	76.4	41.6	50.4	49.6
53065	OAKFIELD	98.7	98.3	0.1	0.1	0.2	0.4	1.6	2.4	6.5	6.8	7.0	7.4	5.3	26.1	29.8	9.9	1.2	75.1	39.2	51.3	48.7
53066	OCONOMOWOC	97.9	97.3	0.4	0.5	0.5	0.7	1.3	1.9	5.9	6.3	7.1	7.0	4.8	23.9	30.9	11.8	2.4	76.1	41.8	49.1	50.9
53069	OKAUCHEE	98.2	97.7	0.1	0.1	0.2	0.5	0.5	0.7	4.4	4.4	4.5	5.2	5.6	29.8	32.4	11.5	2.2	83.2	42.4	51.6	48.4
53070	OOSTBURG	98.7	98.2	0.1	0.2	0.4	0.6	1.1	1.7	6.8	7.2	7.5	7.0	4.7	24.9	28.7	11.4	1.8	73.7	39.4	51.1	48.9
53072	PEWAUKEE	97.0	96.0	0.3	0.5	1.3	2.0	1.1	1.7	6.4	6.2	6.3	5.8	5.3	27.2	30.1	11.3	1.5	77.4	40.4	49.1	50.9
53073	PLYMOUTH	96.9	95.8	1.5	2.0	0.6	0.9	1.0	1.6	5.7	5.8	6.0	7.5	7.8	24.5	29.1	11.0	2.6	78.6	39.5	50.2	49.8
53074	PORT WASHINGTON	97.0	96.2	0.7	1.0	0.5	0.7	1.5	2.1	6.6	6.6	6.7	6.7	6.4	26.5	27.1	11.2	2.2	75.7	38.3	49.4	50.6
53075	RANDOM LAKE	97.6	96.9	0.4	0.3	0.3	0.4	1.3	2.2	5.7	6.0	6.2	7.1	7.6	25.6	29.5	10.8	1.4	77.9	39.1	49.9	50.1
53076	RICHFIELD	97.8	97.1	0.3	0.4	1.2	1.6	1.0	1.4	6.7	7.3	7.6	6.8	4.5	24.5	31.5	10.2	0.9	74.1	40.2	50.9	49.1
53078	RUBICON	98.5	98.1	0.1	0.2	0.2	0.3	0.9	1.3	6.1	6.4	7.0	7.1	5.1	25.9	32.2	9.2	1.0	76.0	40.3	51.2	48.8
53079	SAINT CLOUD	98.8	98.5	0.1	0.1	0.3	0.3	0.8	1.1	5.4	5.7	6.5	8.1	4.8	25.3	30.2	12.2	1.9	77.2	41.3	51.3	48.7
53080	SAUKVILLE	97.7	97.1	0.5	0.6	0.5	0.7	1.9	2.7	6.8	7.0	7.5	7.2	5.4	28.4	28.1	8.4	1.1	74.1	37.3	51.2	48.8
53081	SHEBOYGAN	87.1	82.3	0.9	1.2	6.7	9.6	6.4	9.1	7.2	6.5	6.2	6.7	7.3	27.5	24.3	11.3	3.0	76.0	36.4	49.5	50.5
53083	SHEBOYGAN	95.0	92.9	0.3	0.3	2.9	4.4	2.0	2.8	6.3	6.7	7.1	6.8	5.2	25.1	29.6	11.1	2.1	75.7	40.2	49.3	50.7
53085	SHEBOYGAN FALLS	98.2	97.5	0.3	0.3	0.4	0.7	0.8	1.3	5.8	5.9	6.1	6.4	5.9	25.5	29.5	12.0	2.9	78.1	41.1	48.9	51.1
53086	SLINGER	98.3	97.8	0.2	0.3	0.3	0.4	1.1	1.7	6.2	6.5	6.9	7.1	5.7	25.4	30.6	9.9	1.6	75.7	40.0	49.5	50.5
53089	SUSSEX	97.7	97.1	0.5	0.7	0.6	0.9	1.2	1.8	7.3	7.4	7.7	7.0	5.1	25.7	29.0	9.7	1.1	73.0	38.1	49.3	50.7
53090	WEST BEND	97.8	97.2	0.2	0.3	0.4	0.5	1.6	2.3	7.1	7.1	7.0	6.5	5.4	28.9	27.6	9.0	1.3	74.7	37.2	50.4	49.6
53091	THERESA	98.4	97.9	0.1	0.1	0.2	0.4	0.9	1.3	6.5	6.9	7.1	7.1	4.8	26.4	28.9	11.3	1.2	75.2	40.2	51.0	49.0
53092	THIENSVILLE	94.3	92.4	2.1	2.7	2.3	3.3	1.2	1.6	4.8	5.9	7.3	7.3	4.8	17.1	35.0	15.3	2.5	77.2	46.6	48.7	51.3
53093	WALDO	98.2	97.5	0.2	0.3	0.4	0.7	0.9	1.2	6.1	6.8	6.9	6.6	4.8	23.8	31.7	11.7	1.7	76.1	41.6	51.3	48.7
53094	WATERTOWN	95.7	94.6	0.3	0.3	0.6	0.8	4.9	6.6	7.0	6.8	6.7	7.4	7.2	27.4	25.8	10.2	1.6	75.3	36.3	49.2	50.8
53095	WEST BEND	97.9	97.3	0.3	0.3	0.5	0.7	1.4	2.0	6.3	6.3	6.3	6.1	5.2	25.6	27.3	12.9	4.0	77.3	40.8	48.6	51.4
53097	MEQUON	95.4	92.7	1.7	3.1	2.1	3.0	1.2	2.0	4.2	5.4	6.7	13.2	7.0	17.1	32.9	12.0	1.4	78.8	42.1	49.7	50.3
53098	WATERTOWN	97.6	96.9	0.2	0.3	0.6	0.7	2.9	4.2	6.1	6.0	6.3	6.6	5.8	26.7	25.4	12.9	4.2	77.4	39.8	49.0	51.0
53103	BIG BEND	98.3	97.8	0.2	0.3	0.3	0.5	1.2	1.7	4.9	5.7	6.7	7.2	4.7	24.0	35.2	10.6	1.1	78.3	42.7	52.0	48.0
53104	BRISTOL	97.4	96.3	0.3	0.5	0.9	1.2	2.4	3.8	5.6	6.1	6.7	7.2	4.6	25.6	31.6	11.1	1.5	76.7	41.5	49.9	50.1
53105	BURLINGTON	97.1	95.6	0.4	0.6	0.4	0.6	2.9	4.8	6.3	6.6	6.9	7.1	5.6	26.0	29.1	10.6	1.8	75.5	39.2	49.8	50.2
53108	CALEDONIA	97.7	96.8	0.6	1.0	0.1	0.1	1.6	2.7	4.8	5.5	5.9	5.7	4.2	23.3	32.5	16.8	1.4	80.2	45.4	51.6	48.4
53110	CUDAHY	93.9	90.8	0.9	1.8	0.9	1.4	4.7	7.7	6.3	6.1	6.0	5.8	5.9	26.9	27.1	13.5	2.3	78.1	40.1	48.7	51.3
53114	DARIEN	94.3	92.0	0.4	0.5	0.1	0.2	10.5	15.4	7.6	7.9	7.6	6.8	5.7	27.0	27.3	8.7	1.3	72.4	34.8	51.6	48.4
53115	DELAVAN	88.9	85.3	0.9	1.1	0.7	1.0	14.7	20.1	7.1	6.8	7.0	7.1	6.7	26.6	26.4	10.5	1.9	74.6	36.4	49.6	50.4
53118	DOUSMAN	97.4	96.4	0.6	0.9	0.4	0.6	1.4	2.2	5.8	6.3	7.1	7.9	5.6	22.6	31.9	10.5	2.4	75.4	41.5	49.9	50.1
53119	EAGLE	97.3	96.3	0.4	0.5	0.3	0.5	1.5	2.4	7.4	8.1	8.7	7.8	4.0	26.1	29.6	7.4	0.8	70.8	38.1	48.4	51.6
53120	EAST TROY	97.8	96.9	0.2	0.3	0.4	0.6	1.9	2.9	6.4	6.8	7.2	6.8	4.7	25.3	30.4	10.8	1.6	75.3	40.4	50.0	50.0
53121	ELKHORN	96.1	94.6	0.5	0.6	0.6	0.8	4.3	6.3	6.6	6.6	6.6	7.1	6.2	26.1	27.3	11.0	2.4	75.5	38.6	49.8	50.2
53122	ELM GROVE	97.2	96.1	0.4	0.5	1.6	2.3	1.2	1.8	4.7	5.5	6.7	7.1	4.6	14.8	32.7	19.7	4.1	78.2	49.1	46.9	53.1
53125	FONTANA	98.2	97.5	0.2	0.2	0.8	1.2	2.0	3.2	5.0	5.4	6.0	5.9	3.9	18.7	29.7	20.1	5.4	79.8	48.3	48.3	51.7
53126	FRANKSVILLE	96.8	95.4	0.8	1.3	0.9	1.4	1.8	3.0	6.1	7.0	7.6	6.8	3.9	24.1	32.0	11.5	1.1	74.8	41.9	50.8	49.2
53128	GENOA CITY	96.9	96.0	0.7	0.9	0.4	0.5	2.9	4.3	8.3	7.9	7.6	7.4	6.1	28.2	25.0	8.1	1.4	71.3	34.7	50.2	49.8
53129	GREENDALE	96.2	93.9	0.3	0.5	2.1	3.4	2.4	4.0	5.0	5.2	5.6	5.7	5.1	20.8	29.5	19.8	3.3	80.4	46.8	46.9	53.1
53130	HALES CORNERS	97.1	95.5	0.2	0.4	1.0	1.7	2.1	3.5	4.7	4.6	4.9	5.9	6.5	25.3	29.9	14.6	3.6	82.1	43.5	47.8	52.2
53132	FRANKLIN	90.8	87.2	5.1	6.4	2.1	3.6	2.6	4.4	5.4	5.9	6.3	6.8	5.9	27.1	31.0	10.4	1.2	78.3	40.3	51.6	48.4
53137	HELENVILLE	98.3	98.0	0.1	0.1	0.1	0.1	1.9	2.9	5.7	6.3	6.8	7.1	4.3	25.6	32.6	10.6	1.0	76.4	41.5	50.8	49.2
53139	KANSASVILLE	96.4	94.6	0.5	0.8	0.7	1.0	4.0	6.6	5.6	7.5	7.6	7.7	5.0	27.9	28.7	8.9	1.0	73.9	38.3	50.5	49.5
53140	KENOSHA	80.8	76.3	9.3	11.2	0.8	1.0	12.3	16.4	7.5	6.7	6.1	8.1	9.9	27.3	21.7	10.2	2.4	75.8	32.8	49.6	50.4
53142	KENOSHA	92.4	88.6	2.4	3.8	1.5	2.3	4.9	7.7	7.2	7.0	7.1	6.8	5.3	27.3	26.9	10.4	2.0	74.2	38.0	48.5	51.5
53143	KENOSHA	83.2	78.8	8.1	9.9	0.7	0.8	10.7	14.8	7.4	7.2	6.9	7.3	6.8	26.8	24.7	10.2	2.5	74.0	35.8	48.7	51.3
53144	KENOSHA	82.5	78.4	8.7	10.3	1.3	1.7	8.6	11.7	7.2	6.9	6.4	8.3	8.9	28.0	24.4	8.4	1.5	75.2	33.8	50.1	49.9
53146	NEW BERLIN	96.3	94.9	0.2	0.2	2.0	3.0	1.7	2.6	5.9	6.5	7.1	6.5	4.4	24.8	31.0	12.8	1.2	76.3	42.0	49.7	50.3
53147	LAKE GENEVA	93.2	90.8	1.0	1.3	0.8	1.2	9.6	13.4	5.6	5.6	5.9	6.2	5.7	25.7	29.6	13.7	2.1	79.0	41.8	49.8	50.2
	WISCONSIN	88.9	86.9	5.7	6.3	1.7	2.3	3.6	4.8	6.4	6.4	6.5	7.2	7.2	26.0	27.1	11.1	2.2	76.6	38.0	49.5	50.5
	UNITED STATES	75.1	72.0	12.3	12.7	3.8	4.6	12.5	15.7	6.8	6.7	6.6	7.1	6.9	27.0	26.0	10.9	1.9	75.7	36.9	49.2	50.8

ZIP CODE #	POST OFFICE NAME	2009 Per Capita Income	2009 HH Income Base	2009 HOUSEHOLD INCOME DISTRIBUTION (%) Less than $25,000	$25,000 to $49,999	$50,000 to $99,999	$100,000 to $149,999	$150,000 or More	MEDIAN HOUSEHOLD INCOME 2009	2014	2009 National Centile	2009 State Centile	2009 Home Value Base	2009 HOME VALUE DISTRIBUTION (%) Less than $50,000	$50,000 to $89,999	$90,000 to $174,999	$175,000 to $399,999	$400,000 or More	2009 Median Home Value
53001	ADELL	26174	731	12.3	24.8	49.4	10.1	3.4	60285	62532	78	73	604	1.2	4.0	44.9	46.4	3.6	175000
53002	ALLENTON	28293	911	10.4	18.7	45.4	22.8	2.6	70417	76604	87	90	734	0.8	3.4	27.0	61.9	6.9	216346
53004	BELGIUM	27751	1211	10.3	25.3	43.8	16.5	4.1	63929	65715	82	83	937	1.0	1.5	30.3	56.9	10.4	198611
53005	BROOKFIELD	44118	7577	6.3	13.4	34.6	26.8	18.8	92482	100360	96	98	6974	0.4	0.5	9.3	77.1	12.6	248149
53006	BROWNSVILLE	26530	773	11.9	24.3	50.8	9.4	3.5	62183	63255	80	78	596	3.0	6.0	42.8	43.6	4.5	171429
53007	BUTLER	28385	897	23.4	30.8	35.8	7.6	2.5	47297	48334	55	41	439	0.0	1.8	63.1	35.1	0.0	162404
53010	CAMPBELLSPORT	25514	2910	13.2	25.1	48.7	10.2	2.9	60798	62361	79	75	2349	3.9	5.4	47.3	41.0	2.5	164221
53011	CASCADE	27638	988	11.2	26.6	48.5	10.4	3.2	60715	62748	78	75	864	2.4	5.9	49.2	37.6	4.9	161570
53012	CEDARBURG	39161	7268	8.6	17.3	35.1	23.5	15.5	83635	89699	93	97	5503	0.1	0.0	11.5	73.1	15.3	263390
53013	CEDAR GROVE	26253	1350	9.3	26.8	49.7	9.3	4.9	61359	63091	79	76	1100	0.3	1.6	54.1	40.0	4.0	167105
53014	CHILTON	24718	3352	16.3	29.4	45.0	7.1	2.2	54520	57763	70	61	2582	3.5	16.2	53.4	25.4	1.5	133712
53015	CLEVELAND	25140	1094	14.3	22.9	51.5	9.1	2.3	61943	62829	80	78	933	7.2	5.7	56.5	28.1	2.6	145148
53017	COLGATE	42937	2287	5.7	10.9	34.7	30.2	18.5	97504	104462	96	99	2153	1.2	2.8	6.9	66.7	22.4	292302
53018	DELAFIELD	46166	2775	8.4	9.5	27.6	24.0	30.5	108360	113053	98	100	2370	1.1	0.1	8.6	56.4	33.7	328860
53019	EDEN	23489	755	13.6	28.3	46.8	7.8	3.4	55512	57696	72	64	644	17.4	6.7	46.4	26.4	3.1	138274
53020	ELKHART LAKE	29727	1450	7.9	24.3	51.1	11.1	5.5	65978	68499	84	86	1230	1.8	4.7	45.0	40.1	8.4	172238
53021	FREDONIA	27319	1686	8.8	20.6	50.6	16.6	3.4	68220	70372	86	88	1327	0.0	0.8	26.0	65.8	7.4	211838
53022	GERMANTOWN	35711	7649	7.2	17.0	37.5	28.2	10.0	81764	90748	93	96	5975	1.3	3.0	19.4	70.0	6.4	245039
53023	GLENBEULAH	18406	535	10.3	26.2	50.5	8.8	4.3	60507	62514	78	74	475	2.9	7.4	45.3	38.9	5.5	162260
53024	GRAFTON	36055	6461	9.1	20.1	38.6	21.3	11.0	76853	80830	90	94	4780	1.1	1.3	18.2	68.2	11.1	220208
53027	HARTFORD	32449	8664	12.7	18.5	40.9	20.4	7.6	71577	76514	88	91	6366	1.1	0.8	24.4	64.6	9.1	223086
53029	HARTLAND	42824	7046	7.2	12.5	34.6	26.2	19.5	92544	100313	96	99	5280	0.3	1.1	10.1	59.3	29.2	294737
53032	HORICON	29214	1923	11.8	23.5	46.6	13.6	4.4	64959	65792	83	85	1470	3.3	8.9	57.3	28.6	1.9	142914
53033	HUBERTUS	41136	1741	3.4	8.6	37.4	37.1	13.5	100442	104726	97	99	1643	0.1	0.2	9.3	75.5	15.0	267368
53034	HUSTISFORD	30151	701	15.0	21.8	48.9	9.6	4.7	63352	64475	82	83	462	0.6	3.7	50.9	42.6	2.2	166176
53035	IRON RIDGE	22891	1092	14.9	26.6	45.8	10.3	2.4	55943	57072	73	65	903	12.5	3.3	39.8	41.7	2.7	165717
53036	IXONIA	26726	914	8.3	23.4	51.3	12.9	4.0	64355	65091	83	84	752	2.0	3.2	26.2	59.4	9.2	212368
53037	JACKSON	34325	3542	8.2	14.9	47.2	21.4	8.4	75613	80168	90	93	2690	8.4	6.4	13.9	66.1	5.2	220732
53038	JOHNSON CREEK	24434	1306	15.8	28.9	42.7	9.1	3.4	54327	56390	70	61	983	19.3	7.0	26.3	41.4	5.9	169239
53039	JUNEAU	23862	1935	16.5	26.7	46.1	8.1	2.5	55726	57377	72	64	1427	2.3	6.7	54.9	33.3	2.7	150431
53040	KEWASKUM	29461	3086	9.6	19.4	46.3	20.1	4.6	69697	75027	87	90	2324	0.7	1.5	32.3	58.4	7.0	206371
53042	KIEL	26706	2871	16.2	25.1	47.4	7.9	3.4	59976	61078	77	73	2298	5.1	8.0	55.2	28.9	2.8	142401
53044	KOHLER	40147	1046	8.7	13.1	40.6	26.5	11.1	81682	82846	93	96	928	0.0	0.8	49.0	45.3	5.0	175467
53045	BROOKFIELD	50678	8476	6.3	12.7	29.7	24.1	27.2	101932	106690	97	99	7092	0.5	0.5	6.3	65.6	27.1	295547
53046	LANNON	33484	449	11.6	23.8	39.2	18.5	6.9	67519	70804	85	88	396	8.1	9.8	27.0	51.5	3.5	183197
53048	LOMIRA	24111	1174	17.1	24.5	48.3	7.8	2.3	56964	58548	74	67	814	10.0	8.5	44.7	35.0	1.8	153252
53049	MALONE	25261	994	12.8	27.9	46.8	8.5	4.1	58554	61028	76	70	878	2.6	5.4	49.5	39.0	3.5	162956
53050	MAYVILLE	25330	2931	16.9	24.7	46.4	9.4	2.7	56464	57736	73	66	2130	2.3	6.2	59.8	30.0	1.7	148211
53051	MENOMONEE FALLS	36311	14302	10.3	18.8	38.0	22.4	10.5	76607	80500	90	94	11012	1.5	1.2	19.0	70.2	8.1	219299
53057	MOUNT CALVARY	21217	583	14.9	24.9	48.0	9.3	2.9	59517	61243	77	72	503	2.4	8.9	55.3	30.8	2.6	145516
53058	NASHOTAH	44129	1317	8.2	18.4	34.2	20.0	19.3	82826	87948	93	96	936	0.3	0.2	10.7	50.7	38.0	344279
53059	NEOSHO	25930	745	10.5	23.5	51.8	10.2	4.0	63727	64750	82	83	606	0.7	3.1	38.9	52.3	5.0	186957
53061	NEW HOLSTEIN	25342	2037	15.2	28.5	48.1	6.6	1.7	54810	57214	71	62	1583	6.0	12.0	64.3	17.1	0.6	121635
53063	NEWTON	25713	637	13.0	22.9	50.2	10.4	3.5	62810	63455	81	81	569	3.7	8.8	49.0	34.3	4.2	155735
53065	OAKFIELD	24758	762	10.4	24.3	51.7	10.1	3.5	61326	62630	79	76	629	3.8	4.0	54.4	37.0	0.8	153267
53066	OCONOMOWOC	37806	12706	9.4	17.3	38.2	22.2	12.8	78581	82241	91	94	9568	1.1	1.9	18.1	58.5	20.4	246429
53069	OKAUCHEE	37290	401	12.2	22.7	43.6	12.0	9.5	63075	63472	81	82	236	0.0	0.0	13.6	51.7	34.7	323404
53070	OOSTBURG	26156	1823	11.0	27.5	47.7	9.2	4.6	61257	63551	79	76	1465	0.0	1.9	57.1	37.5	3.4	160079
53072	PEWAUKEE	45051	9821	5.7	17.1	36.1	23.8	17.3	85648	91923	94	98	7220	0.6	1.3	20.4	56.0	21.7	257827
53073	PLYMOUTH	28454	5736	15.2	24.2	45.5	9.8	5.3	59728	62043	77	72	4141	3.5	3.9	53.0	36.2	3.4	157837
53074	PORT WASHINGTON	32481	5087	11.3	19.7	43.9	19.2	5.9	75248	77470	89	93	3256	0.6	1.1	34.7	58.9	4.7	192371
53075	RANDOM LAKE	27180	1272	12.9	23.7	48.3	10.1	5.0	62025	64232	80	78	969	0.1	2.5	44.9	49.1	3.4	179003
53076	RICHFIELD	37465	1487	6.9	10.9	37.6	29.7	15.0	91193	101267	95	98	1322	2.3	1.8	9.8	67.5	18.5	278392
53078	RUBICON	23678	645	9.0	25.0	51.8	11.6	2.6	62538	63179	81	80	554	0.7	1.3	32.3	56.7	9.0	206356
53079	SAINT CLOUD	24334	659	15.2	25.0	47.5	9.6	2.7	60276	62107	78	73	565	3.4	10.3	57.0	26.0	3.4	137015
53080	SAUKVILLE	31192	2383	12.2	18.9	38.8	24.1	6.0	75571	79093	90	93	1601	0.0	1.2	30.4	62.5	5.9	201676
53081	SHEBOYGAN	25345	18201	19.7	27.6	42.6	7.6	2.5	52264	54926	66	56	11023	4.0	14.2	66.3	14.6	0.8	118342
53083	SHEBOYGAN	29791	8414	13.6	21.6	47.7	11.8	5.3	64138	66536	82	84	6361	0.6	5.5	59.7	30.8	3.4	148911
53085	SHEBOYGAN FALLS	28457	4538	11.6	24.1	50.4	10.4	3.5	61721	63343	80	77	3495	8.3	7.6	53.1	29.5	1.5	144113
53086	SLINGER	31009	3154	12.5	18.1	40.8	21.2	7.4	68424	73932	86	89	2442	9.2	3.6	18.8	53.7	14.7	231504
53089	SUSSEX	34774	6712	8.4	12.9	40.9	28.2	9.6	83651	88848	93	97	5367	5.3	1.5	9.2	76.6	7.3	244321
53090	WEST BEND	29533	8496	10.1	19.1	47.2	19.2	4.4	69118	73134	86	89	6378	1.7	1.2	29.1	64.0	4.0	203016
53091	THERESA	23938	873	13.9	24.9	52.2	7.0	2.1	59362	60173	77	71	721	5.5	13.3	47.3	30.9	2.9	148958
53092	THIENSVILLE	60621	8131	5.6	12.4	26.1	22.6	33.4	110551	115214	98	100	7011	0.6	1.0	8.7	53.8	35.8	326767
53093	WALDO	26430	716	10.3	27.0	50.0	9.8	2.9	59364	61370	77	71	600	1.8	7.0	51.0	38.0	2.2	159794
53094	WATERTOWN	24336	6914	16.1	27.2	45.8	7.9	3.1	56060	58025	73	65	4561	2.5	4.8	49.6	39.4	3.6	165885
53095	WEST BEND	33879	10828	11.5	23.8	38.6	17.9	8.3	66553	71527	85	87	7307	0.5	0.9	26.3	59.5	12.9	223136
53097	MEQUON	42512	1829	4.7	12.0	26.9	29.0	27.4	109385	113170	98	100	1625	0.0	0.0	4.6	65.7	29.7	315296
53098	WATERTOWN	25717	4674	15.5	23.3	48.8	9.4	3.0	60518	61246	78	74	3405	0.9	6.4	53.8	35.1	3.9	159916
53103	BIG BEND	31303	1458	4.3	13.4	49.8	26.7	5.7	80837	84442	92	96	1333	0.0	2.0	16.4	74.6	7.0	232168
53104	BRISTOL	27562	2307	11.7	24.9	45.4	13.6	4.5	62938	65959	81	81	1911	12.3	4.5	22.0	52.9	8.3	197917
53105	BURLINGTON	27680	11691	12.4	22.5	47.7	12.0	5.4	64727	68018	83	84	8765	3.9	4.6	39.6	45.6	6.4	179236
53108	CALEDONIA	32526	1286	7.9	23.4	39.6	22.6	6.5	74161	77636	89	92	1169	0.0	5.4	43.5	44.1	6.9	178034
53110	CUDAHY	25963	8081	18.8	27.7	43.9	7.7	1.9	52763	54888	67	58	4827	2.1	4.5	74.8	18.3	0.4	141960
53114	DARIEN	24238	1114	14.0	21.6	48.6	12.5	3.3	62813	63500	81	81	821	4.3	5.0	48.2	37.4	5.1	161630
53115	DELAVAN	25247	5819	16.9	25.7	43.6	9.9	3.9	57126	58663	74	68	3824	2.2	9.1	47.0	38.1	3.6	160324
53118	DOUSMAN	37600	2732	7.7	16.4	36.6	26.9	12.4	83461	88053	93	97	2190	2.5	3.1	15.9	66.1	12.5	255690
53119	EAGLE	33029	1864	6.5	9.8	46.2	27.0	10.4	84675	89437	94	97	1699	1.0	1.6	17.2	68.8	11.4	233765
53120	EAST TROY	28443	3849	10.4	21.8	51.3	12.5	3.9	64988	65753	83	85	3143	5.8	4.9	25.0	55.0	9.3	195211
53121	ELKHORN	26392	7246	15.9	24.5	44.4	10.8	4.4	59293	60378	77	71	5093	4.5	3.2	35.9	48.0	8.4	186510
53122	ELM GROVE	57731	2525	10.8	11.4	27.4	17.5	32.8	100677	107815	97	99	2234	0.7	0.6	5.5	56.8	36.4	350891
53125	FONTANA	41562	877	11.3	18.7	40.9	16.9	12.2	70419	71221	87	91	723	0.3	1.2	17.3	63.9	17.3	249444
53126	FRANKSVILLE	30614	2354	8.1	19.2	48.7	18.2	5.9	73433	76551	89	92	2045	0.5	1.9	34.2	53.8	9.6	208356
53128	GENOA CITY	24657	2926	12.6	24.2	47.4	12.5	3.2	62067	63035	80	78	2379	2.7	9.2	52.3	33.1	2.6	155679
53129	GREENDALE	34678	5984	12.1	20.4	44.8	15.4	7.4	70032	71469	87	90	4123	0.2	0.5	30.7	65.5	3.2	196705
53130	HALES CORNERS	32136	3273	12.1	19.0	48.0	17.2	3.7	69200	70197	86	89	2010	0.9	1.8	25.4	69.5	2.4	196956
53132	FRANKLIN	35956	12747	7.7	16.1	41.9	21.5	12.8	79875	80814	92	95	9851	1.8	1.5	27.2	66.8	2.7	204823
53137	HELENVILLE	24670	542	12.4	24.7	51.1	8.7	3.1	61127	61746	79	75	464	6.3	6.0	26.1	53.9	7.8	202907
53139	KANSASVILLE	28203	1046	11.4	27.4	42.9	12.0	6.3	61446	65367	79	76	889	4.9	7.1	34.6	42.4	10.9	184335
53140	KENOSHA	21639	12031	27.3	28.2	34.2	8.3	2.0	43668	46209	44	26	6063	2.3	9.5	69.0	18.2	1.0	141832
53142	KENOSHA	30673	12168	11.4	18.7	43.4	19.8	6.6	71360	75854	88	91	9385	3.0	2.9	44.8	47.8	1.4	173957
53143	KENOSHA	25395	9340	19.1	25.7	42.0	9.0	4.1	55825	60132	72	65	5989	6.4	8.9	62.4	21.4	0.9	142322
53144	KENOSHA	26971	9721	16.3	24.6	39.5	13.8	5.8	59900	62932	77	73	5838	3.8	3.7	45.3	43.0	4.2	170336
53146	NEW BERLIN	37406	3014	5.7	15.4	38.1	29.2	11.7	85214	92076	94	97	2597	1.2	1.1	21.1	70.5	6.1	216781
53147	LAKE GENEVA	29071	6922	18.1	25.0	40.1	10.6	6.1	57072	60113	74	68	4597	4.1	6.6	38.5	38.7	12.2	177197
	WISCONSIN	27384		18.4	25.3	40.0	11.0	5.2	56363	58927				5.6	11.9	43.5	34.2	4.7	150766
	UNITED STATES	27277		20.9	24.4	35.3	11.7	7.6	54719	56938				9.3	13.1	31.6	32.6	13.5	162279

ZIP CODE #	POST OFFICE NAME	FINANCIAL SERVICES: Auto Loan	FINANCIAL SERVICES: Home Loan	FINANCIAL SERVICES: Invest-ments	FINANCIAL SERVICES: Retire-ment Plans	THE HOME: Home Improvements: Home Repair	THE HOME: Home Improvements: Lawn & Garden	THE HOME: Furnishings: Comput-ers & Hard-ware-Personal	THE HOME: Furnishings: Major Appli-ances	THE HOME: Furnishings: TV, Radio, Sound Equip-ment	THE HOME: Furnishings: Furni-ture	ENTERTAINMENT: Dine out/ Carry out	ENTERTAINMENT: Sports Equip-ment	ENTERTAINMENT: Fees & Tickets	ENTERTAINMENT: Toys & Games	ENTERTAINMENT: Travel	ENTERTAINMENT: Cable TV	PERSONAL: Apparel & Services	PERSONAL: Auto Repairs	PERSONAL: Health Insur-ance	PERSONAL: Pets & Supplies
53001	ADELL	98	103	93	107	102	107	95	101	95	92	95	78	97	97	99	97	66	96	102	119
53002	ALLENTON	99	114	102	115	111	108	106	106	103	104	104	83	113	105	111	103	74	105	105	124
53004	BELGIUM	106	119	103	123	116	117	106	111	105	107	105	87	114	107	112	105	74	106	110	130
53005	BROOKFIELD	152	187	188	190	190	181	160	169	157	168	158	125	182	156	179	157	113	162	168	194
53006	BROWNSVILLE	98	106	93	108	103	107	96	101	96	95	96	78	100	98	100	97	67	97	101	119
53007	BUTLER	73	76	79	76	78	81	77	78	80	76	79	57	80	76	80	83	55	79	89	91
53010	CAMPBELLSPORT	95	98	91	100	98	103	93	99	93	89	93	76	94	95	96	96	65	94	100	115
53011	CASCADE	100	98	93	102	98	109	93	103	95	88	94	79	91	97	95	99	65	96	105	120
53012	CEDARBURG	136	157	150	160	156	145	143	143	138	148	140	111	156	140	151	135	100	140	136	166
53013	CEDAR GROVE	98	110	95	113	107	108	98	102	97	99	97	80	105	99	104	97	68	98	101	120
53014	CHILTON	93	86	82	89	86	100	85	94	87	78	86	72	80	89	85	92	59	88	98	110
53015	CLEVELAND	96	98	90	102	97	104	91	99	92	88	91	76	92	94	94	94	63	93	99	115
53017	COLGATE	159	198	180	198	194	177	167	172	158	175	161	134	188	163	182	154	115	163	158	197
53018	DELAFIELD	173	213	214	220	217	195	184	188	175	195	177	146	211	177	202	170	129	180	173	216
53019	EDEN	106	87	92	87	87	107	87	99	93	83	92	76	76	96	83	100	62	93	103	118
53020	ELKHART LAKE	106	117	102	120	114	117	105	110	104	105	104	86	111	107	111	105	73	106	110	130
53021	FREDONIA	100	114	101	116	111	110	105	106	103	104	104	83	112	105	110	103	73	104	105	124
53022	GERMANTOWN	127	142	128	145	139	127	130	128	124	137	126	102	140	129	134	120	90	125	118	148
53023	GLENBEULAH	102	104	96	107	103	111	97	105	98	93	97	81	97	100	100	101	67	99	106	123
53024	GRAFTON	121	138	132	141	137	132	128	128	125	130	126	99	138	125	135	124	89	126	126	149
53027	HARTFORD	107	126	118	126	124	117	117	116	113	117	115	90	127	115	123	112	82	115	113	134
53029	HARTLAND	159	187	174	190	184	165	166	165	157	176	159	132	183	163	175	150	115	160	149	190
53032	HORICON	102	106	91	109	101	112	102	103	103	97	102	81	104	105	102	106	71	102	111	123
53033	HUBERTUS	146	183	170	184	180	163	154	159	146	163	148	123	174	149	169	141	106	151	145	182
53034	HUSTISFORD	89	104	97	102	102	96	100	96	97	97	98	76	107	98	104	97	70	98	96	112
53035	IRON RIDGE	95	93	83	93	91	96	87	92	89	88	89	69	85	92	86	91	61	89	92	109
53036	IXONIA	102	114	99	117	111	113	102	107	101	102	101	83	108	103	108	101	71	102	106	126
53037	JACKSON	132	139	115	134	131	120	124	126	120	133	122	98	125	128	122	115	85	119	113	144
53038	JOHNSON CREEK	96	95	83	94	93	96	88	92	89	90	89	69	87	92	87	91	61	89	92	109
53039	JUNEAU	90	90	81	93	88	97	86	91	87	82	86	71	85	89	87	90	60	88	94	108
53040	KEWASKUM	105	118	105	118	115	112	110	109	108	110	109	85	117	110	115	108	77	109	109	128
53042	KIEL	97	96	89	99	96	104	93	99	93	88	93	76	91	95	94	96	64	94	101	116
53044	KOHLER	131	157	151	160	158	150	138	143	133	142	135	109	152	134	150	132	96	137	138	165
53045	BROOKFIELD	172	215	227	221	224	203	187	195	178	199	179	146	213	176	209	174	130	185	185	221
53046	LANNON	104	121	106	124	117	119	106	111	106	107	107	85	117	108	115	107	75	107	112	130
53048	LOMIRA	99	93	83	92	91	96	88	93	90	90	90	69	84	93	85	92	62	90	93	110
53049	MALONE	99	97	92	100	97	108	92	102	94	86	93	78	89	96	94	98	64	95	104	119
53050	MAYVILLE	90	88	84	90	88	96	87	92	88	82	87	70	84	89	87	91	60	89	96	108
53051	MENOMONEE FALLS	119	139	128	140	137	131	126	127	124	129	125	98	138	125	133	123	89	124	127	147
53057	MOUNT CALVARY	100	91	90	95	93	107	90	101	92	81	91	76	83	94	89	98	62	93	104	117
53058	NASHOTAH	146	175	180	179	180	164	157	160	150	165	151	121	174	149	171	146	109	155	152	184
53059	NEOSHO	98	109	95	113	106	108	98	103	97	98	97	80	104	99	103	97	68	98	102	121
53061	NEW HOLSTEIN	90	84	80	88	84	97	83	91	86	76	84	70	79	87	83	90	58	86	95	107
53063	NEWTON	99	104	94	107	102	109	96	103	96	93	96	79	97	98	99	98	66	97	103	120
53065	OAKFIELD	96	108	93	111	105	106	96	100	95	97	95	78	103	97	102	95	67	96	99	118
53066	OCONOMOWOC	128	153	150	155	154	145	136	140	132	141	133	107	151	132	148	130	95	135	135	161
53069	OKAUCHEE	111	124	119	126	122	115	117	114	113	119	114	89	124	114	121	111	81	114	111	134
53070	OOSTBURG	103	103	96	107	103	112	97	106	98	92	97	81	96	100	100	101	67	99	107	123
53072	PEWAUKEE	151	163	152	167	160	147	154	149	147	161	150	119	162	152	157	142	107	148	139	174
53073	PLYMOUTH	101	99	91	102	98	106	99	101	100	95	99	78	97	101	98	102	68	100	106	120
53074	PORT WASHINGTON	107	119	109	118	116	113	114	112	112	114	113	87	120	114	117	112	80	113	113	130
53075	RANDOM LAKE	93	106	96	106	104	101	99	99	97	97	98	78	105	99	104	98	69	98	99	116
53076	RICHFIELD	144	173	150	173	166	153	148	151	140	155	143	120	163	147	157	136	102	144	138	174
53078	RUBICON	95	107	92	111	104	105	96	100	94	96	95	78	102	97	101	94	66	96	99	117
53079	SAINT CLOUD	100	91	90	95	93	107	90	101	92	81	91	76	83	94	89	98	62	93	104	117
53080	SAUKVILLE	112	123	109	124	119	112	116	113	111	118	113	90	121	115	118	109	80	112	107	132
53081	SHEBOYGAN	81	80	71	82	77	83	86	81	87	81	87	63	85	87	82	89	61	84	88	97
53083	SHEBOYGAN	101	111	98	113	108	112	103	105	103	102	103	81	109	105	107	104	72	103	109	124
53085	SHEBOYGAN FALLS	97	101	97	100	99	102	97	99	97	94	98	77	98	99	99	99	69	98	100	117
53086	SLINGER	107	125	113	125	122	117	114	114	111	114	112	90	124	113	121	110	80	113	112	133
53089	SUSSEX	133	148	127	146	141	131	133	132	127	139	130	104	139	134	135	124	91	128	122	153
53090	WEST BEND	105	118	105	117	115	110	108	109	106	110	107	85	114	108	112	105	75	107	107	127
53091	THERESA	94	89	85	92	90	101	86	95	88	79	87	73	81	90	87	92	59	89	98	111
53092	THIENSVILLE	201	249	268	256	261	236	216	225	208	231	209	170	250	207	241	203	153	214	212	255
53093	WALDO	106	97	96	101	99	114	96	108	98	87	97	82	89	100	96	104	66	99	111	125
53094	WATERTOWN	88	93	81	94	89	94	90	90	90	87	90	70	92	91	90	91	63	89	93	106
53095	WEST BEND	107	122	117	122	122	119	114	115	113	115	114	87	123	112	120	114	80	114	118	133
53097	MEQUON	169	217	225	226	225	201	181	191	172	196	173	146	213	173	206	166	127	179	173	216
53098	WATERTOWN	91	97	88	97	95	97	92	94	91	90	92	72	94	93	93	93	64	92	96	109
53103	BIG BEND	121	145	126	147	140	133	125	128	120	129	122	101	137	124	134	118	86	123	121	149
53104	BRISTOL	108	108	106	110	106	116	100	109	101	98	101	84	100	103	103	104	69	103	109	129
53105	BURLINGTON	101	111	99	112	107	107	103	104	102	103	102	81	108	104	106	101	72	102	103	122
53108	CALEDONIA	109	127	116	129	124	126	113	117	112	115	113	88	124	113	121	114	79	114	121	136
53110	CUDAHY	79	82	75	82	80	85	82	81	84	80	84	61	84	84	82	87	58	83	90	96
53114	DARIEN	104	106	90	103	101	98	97	100	96	101	97	75	96	100	95	95	67	96	95	116
53115	DELAVAN	96	92	86	93	90	96	94	94	95	90	95	74	91	96	92	96	66	95	98	112
53118	DOUSMAN	129	153	149	153	153	142	138	139	133	141	135	107	151	134	147	132	97	136	133	160
53119	EAGLE	129	161	143	161	156	141	135	138	127	142	130	109	152	132	146	123	93	131	124	159
53120	EAST TROY	101	116	101	118	113	113	103	107	102	104	103	83	112	104	110	102	72	103	107	125
53121	ELKHORN	95	101	90	102	98	96	98	96	96	98	97	76	101	98	99	95	68	96	95	113
53122	ELM GROVE	175	231	267	233	252	215	201	211	186	217	186	157	235	181	233	180	137	199	194	233
53125	FONTANA	119	143	145	144	147	142	125	133	124	131	125	96	141	122	139	125	88	128	135	152
53126	FRANKSVILLE	115	132	120	136	130	129	117	122	114	119	115	94	127	116	125	115	81	117	121	142
53128	GENOA CITY	97	102	87	101	96	99	96	96	95	96	96	76	97	99	95	95	66	95	97	114
53129	GREENDALE	106	118	119	119	120	122	110	114	111	112	111	84	119	109	118	114	78	112	122	132
53130	HALES CORNERS	97	110	103	110	107	108	102	102	103	103	104	77	111	102	108	104	73	103	108	120
53132	FRANKLIN	126	149	139	149	146	135	134	133	129	138	131	104	146	131	142	126	93	131	127	155
53137	HELENVILLE	95	104	90	106	101	102	93	97	93	94	93	75	98	95	97	93	65	94	97	115
53139	KANSASVILLE	103	117	101	120	114	114	104	108	102	105	103	84	112	105	110	102	72	104	106	127
53140	KENOSHA	72	69	63	70	67	70	77	70	79	73	78	55	75	78	73	80	55	76	78	85
53142	KENOSHA	108	124	109	123	120	118	111	113	110	114	111	87	120	113	117	110	78	111	114	131
53143	KENOSHA	90	92	81	92	88	93	92	90	94	90	94	69	93	94	90	96	65	92	96	107
53144	KENOSHA	101	97	87	99	93	93	102	95	100	101	101	76	100	103	97	99	71	99	95	114
53146	NEW BERLIN	127	155	146	156	153	145	135	139	132	140	133	106	152	134	147	130	95	134	135	159
53147	LAKE GENEVA	105	95	106	96	96	107	97	104	99	93	98	79	91	98	97	102	67	101	107	122
	WISCONSIN	98	94	92	96	93	99	96	96	96	93	96	75	94	97	95	98	67	96	99	114
	UNITED STATES	100	100	100	100	100	100	100	100	100	100	100	100	100	100	100	100	100	100	100	100

#	POST OFFICE NAME	COUNTY FIPS CODE	POPULATION 2000	POPULATION 2009	POPULATION 2014	2000-2009 ANNUAL RATE % Rate	2000-2009 ANNUAL RATE State Centile	HOUSEHOLDS 2000	HOUSEHOLDS 2009	HOUSEHOLDS 2014	HOUSEHOLDS % Annual Rate 2000-2009	HOUSEHOLDS 2009 Average HH Size	FAMILIES 2000	FAMILIES 2009	FAMILIES % Annual Rate 2000-2009
53149	MUKWONAGO	133	16684	18616	19485	1.2	81	5850	6770	7171	1.6	2.73	4724	5407	1.5
53150	MUSKEGO	133	21964	24580	25505	1.2	81	7738	8901	9333	1.5	2.73	6275	7154	1.4
53151	NEW BERLIN	133	30642	31810	32231	0.4	39	11680	12487	12788	0.7	2.53	8787	9307	0.6
53153	NORTH PRAIRIE	133	1985	2206	2307	1.1	76	680	783	829	1.5	2.82	579	660	1.4
53154	OAK CREEK	079	28456	32440	34180	1.4	86	11239	13206	14022	1.8	2.45	7525	8778	1.7
53156	PALMYRA	055	3045	3445	3649	1.3	84	1169	1355	1446	1.6	2.54	838	963	1.5
53158	PLEASANT PRAIRIE	059	11689	15628	17343	3.2	98	4072	5518	6154	3.3	2.82	3215	4314	3.2
53168	SALEM	059	8106	9048	9603	1.2	81	2904	3271	3483	1.3	2.76	2194	2444	1.2
53170	SILVER LAKE	059	2100	2318	2426	1.1	76	754	838	881	1.1	2.76	534	586	1.0
53172	SOUTH MILWAUKEE	079	21256	21206	21469	0.0	16	8694	8944	9118	0.3	2.33	5620	5731	0.2
53177	STURTEVANT	101	7680	8392	8835	1.0	72	2431	2817	3021	1.6	2.48	1744	1988	1.4
53178	SULLIVAN	055	2837	3015	3095	0.7	56	1128	1233	1277	1.0	2.45	838	904	0.8
53179	TREVOR	059	4583	5930	6376	2.8	97	1628	2103	2265	2.8	2.81	1225	1562	2.7
53181	TWIN LAKES	059	6589	7162	7442	0.9	68	2479	2727	2846	1.0	2.61	1826	1983	0.9
53182	UNION GROVE	101	8759	9179	9404	0.5	44	2990	3263	3379	0.9	2.54	2226	2401	0.8
53183	WALES	133	2635	2385	2463	-1.1	1	881	842	882	-0.5	2.83	776	738	-0.5
53184	WALWORTH	127	3979	4569	4780	1.5	88	1367	1605	1685	1.8	2.77	979	1133	1.6
53185	WATERFORD	101	16487	18231	18974	1.1	76	5901	6700	7027	1.4	2.72	4656	5234	1.3
53186	WAUKESHA	133	33470	33521	33423	0.0	16	13518	13922	14028	0.3	2.33	8424	8538	0.1
53188	WAUKESHA	133	33704	35695	36310	0.6	51	12897	13984	14335	0.9	2.46	8670	9367	0.8
53189	WAUKESHA	133	22021	25009	26303	1.4	86	7721	9006	9560	1.7	2.77	6250	7221	1.6
53190	WHITEWATER	127	18030	19504	20003	0.9	68	5822	6576	6795	1.3	2.42	3020	3436	1.4
53191	WILLIAMS BAY	127	2411	2736	2819	1.4	86	1026	1187	1224	1.6	2.22	676	769	1.4
53202	MILWAUKEE	079	20967	22517	23328	0.8	61	13637	15237	15919	1.2	1.37	2234	2432	0.9
53203	MILWAUKEE	079	331	712	869	8.6	100	219	500	617	9.3	1.37	45	101	9.1
53204	MILWAUKEE	079	42719	43977	44400	0.3	32	12551	12796	12897	0.2	3.39	8489	8475	0.0
53205	MILWAUKEE	079	10441	9874	9781	-0.6	1	3545	3461	3452	-0.3	2.78	2244	2170	-0.4
53206	MILWAUKEE	079	33259	30351	29551	-1.0	1	10764	10134	9932	-0.6	2.98	7629	7120	-0.7
53207	MILWAUKEE	079	36569	35495	35477	-0.3	4	16203	16214	16315	0.0	2.18	9183	9075	-0.1
53208	MILWAUKEE	079	35005	33130	32653	-0.6	1	12837	12392	12283	-0.4	2.63	7126	6772	-0.5
53209	MILWAUKEE	079	48773	47789	47825	-0.2	8	19183	19159	19272	0.0	2.47	12483	12325	-0.1
53210	MILWAUKEE	079	30181	28993	28702	-0.4	2	10280	9985	9911	-0.3	2.87	7048	6771	-0.4
53211	MILWAUKEE	079	35013	34340	34678	-0.2	8	15791	15958	16223	0.1	2.02	6596	6560	-0.1
53212	MILWAUKEE	079	31144	30181	30125	-0.3	4	12220	12279	12367	0.1	2.42	6469	6377	-0.2
53213	MILWAUKEE	079	26155	25815	26031	-0.1	11	11296	11465	11638	0.2	2.22	6649	6663	0.0
53214	MILWAUKEE	079	35932	35080	35298	-0.3	4	16071	16183	16395	0.1	2.12	8663	8617	-0.1
53215	MILWAUKEE	079	54427	55795	56887	0.3	32	19195	19322	19677	0.1	2.87	12388	12356	0.0
53216	MILWAUKEE	079	34104	33589	33557	-0.2	8	13164	13090	13109	-0.1	2.56	8723	8583	-0.2
53217	MILWAUKEE	079	29637	29056	29265	-0.2	8	11816	11897	12051	0.1	2.39	8311	8295	0.0
53218	MILWAUKEE	079	41287	41261	41597	0.0	16	14601	14622	14756	0.0	2.81	10421	10348	-0.1
53219	MILWAUKEE	079	33934	33163	33412	-0.2	8	15685	15778	15992	0.1	2.09	8940	8882	-0.1
53220	MILWAUKEE	079	25179	24834	25189	-0.1	11	11163	11380	11629	0.2	2.12	6613	6670	0.1
53221	MILWAUKEE	079	35088	34949	35450	0.0	16	15159	15582	15917	0.3	2.21	9380	9524	0.2
53222	MILWAUKEE	079	24500	23992	24196	-0.2	8	11067	11122	11279	0.1	2.12	6266	6214	-0.1
53223	MILWAUKEE	079	29836	29195	29332	-0.2	8	12441	12451	12567	0.0	2.27	7623	7559	-0.1
53224	MILWAUKEE	079	19855	20425	20848	0.3	32	7194	7516	7707	0.5	2.68	4859	5041	0.4
53225	MILWAUKEE	079	25499	25326	25521	-0.1	11	9959	9998	10101	0.0	2.48	6630	6591	-0.1
53226	MILWAUKEE	079	18771	18537	18764	-0.1	11	8202	8358	8521	0.2	2.12	4902	4931	0.1
53227	MILWAUKEE	079	23785	23159	23209	-0.3	4	10908	10960	11077	0.1	2.07	6059	6010	-0.1
53228	MILWAUKEE	079	13827	14178	14487	0.3	32	5735	6153	6360	0.8	2.27	3610	3813	0.6
53233	MILWAUKEE	079	15541	15517	15749	0.0	16	5076	5377	5533	0.6	1.87	1228	1264	0.3
53235	MILWAUKEE	079	8912	9270	9562	0.4	39	4148	4479	4655	0.8	2.04	2217	2352	0.6
53402	RACINE	101	33246	34288	34755	0.3	32	12818	13558	13837	0.6	2.50	9163	9618	0.5
53403	RACINE	101	27174	27458	27536	0.1	20	10376	10756	10874	0.4	2.47	6556	6675	0.2
53404	RACINE	101	17029	16561	16362	-0.3	4	5795	5756	5724	-0.1	2.75	4023	3933	-0.2
53405	RACINE	101	25764	25568	25453	-0.1	11	10178	10372	10407	0.2	2.46	6992	7020	0.0
53406	RACINE	101	22310	25533	26885	1.5	88	9183	10882	11566	1.9	2.29	6117	7202	1.8
53502	ALBANY	045	2175	2573	2718	1.8	93	826	1008	1073	2.2	2.55	601	729	2.1
53503	ARENA	049	1753	2005	2105	1.5	88	657	784	831	1.9	2.56	494	583	1.8
53504	ARGYLE	065	2114	2190	2192	0.4	39	815	863	871	0.6	2.53	583	611	0.5
53505	AVALON	105	368	383	390	0.4	39	143	154	158	0.8	2.49	106	112	0.6
53506	AVOCA	049	1023	1122	1168	1.0	72	398	453	477	1.4	2.48	274	308	1.3
53507	BARNEVELD	049	1897	1975	1968	0.4	39	698	751	755	0.8	2.61	535	571	0.7
53508	BELLEVILLE	025	4256	5111	5516	2.0	95	1613	1990	2164	2.3	2.56	1217	1481	2.1
53510	BELMONT	065	1379	1358	1334	-0.2	8	551	570	566	0.4	2.38	380	389	0.3
53511	BELOIT	105	47154	48569	49324	0.3	32	17828	18715	19126	0.5	2.52	12256	12716	0.4
53515	BLACK EARTH	025	2232	2423	2533	0.9	68	839	936	987	1.2	2.55	613	670	1.0
53516	BLANCHARDVILLE	065	1921	2005	2018	0.5	44	753	806	819	0.7	2.46	526	559	0.7
53517	BLUE MOUNDS	025	1644	1686	1710	0.3	32	622	653	668	0.5	2.58	482	497	0.3
53518	BLUE RIVER	103	1440	1472	1478	0.2	24	567	608	619	0.8	2.42	416	439	0.6
53520	BRODHEAD	105	6609	7031	7258	0.7	56	2480	2707	2812	1.0	2.59	1841	1986	0.8
53521	BROOKLYN	045	2986	3565	3779	1.9	94	1092	1338	1429	2.2	2.66	873	1053	2.0
53522	BROWNTOWN	045	1278	1354	1390	0.6	51	480	530	548	1.1	2.55	370	404	1.0
53523	CAMBRIDGE	025	4709	4981	5156	0.6	51	1850	1998	2079	0.8	2.48	1324	1405	0.6
53525	CLINTON	105	3903	4314	4521	1.1	76	1390	1570	1655	1.3	2.70	1034	1152	1.2
53526	COBB	049	531	567	587	0.7	56	223	246	257	1.1	2.30	160	175	1.0
53527	COTTAGE GROVE	025	7749	9858	10824	2.6	97	2724	3546	3927	2.9	2.77	2174	2784	2.7
53528	CROSS PLAINS	025	4845	5376	5680	1.1	76	1838	2100	2237	1.5	2.55	1362	1523	1.2
53529	DANE	025	1721	1973	2117	1.5	88	594	698	753	1.8	2.83	461	533	1.6
53530	DARLINGTON	065	4348	4374	4346	0.1	20	1670	1724	1727	0.3	2.47	1168	1194	0.2
53531	DEERFIELD	025	3730	4251	4532	1.4	86	1307	1533	1652	1.7	2.71	1004	1154	1.5
53532	DE FOREST	025	12011	14261	15524	1.9	94	4277	5194	5701	2.1	2.73	3360	4007	1.9
53533	DODGEVILLE	049	6441	6778	6837	0.6	51	2540	2777	2832	1.0	2.39	1724	1862	0.8
53534	EDGERTON	105	10528	11514	11998	1.0	72	4202	4693	4921	1.2	2.44	2885	3176	1.0
53536	EVANSVILLE	105	7222	8043	8485	1.2	81	2736	3109	3297	1.4	2.55	1952	2180	1.2
53538	FORT ATKINSON	055	17435	18329	18797	0.5	44	6933	7468	7719	0.8	2.42	4698	4996	0.7
53541	GRATIOT	065	1038	1080	1096	0.4	39	385	420	430	0.9	2.56	290	314	0.9
53543	HIGHLAND	049	1720	1848	1917	0.8	61	643	721	755	1.2	2.55	465	517	1.2
53544	HOLLANDALE	049	773	841	874	0.9	68	301	341	358	1.4	2.45	221	247	1.2
53545	JANESVILLE	105	23649	24011	24463	0.2	24	9520	9964	10209	0.5	2.35	6081	6274	0.3
53546	JANESVILLE	105	27986	30978	32422	1.1	76	10774	12199	12856	1.4	2.51	7626	8477	1.2
53548	JANESVILLE	105	19012	19722	20119	0.4	39	7492	7952	8172	0.6	2.41	4986	5250	0.6
53549	JEFFERSON	055	10111	10584	10832	0.5	44	3768	4067	4205	0.8	2.42	2549	2716	0.7
53550	JUDA	045	1328	1541	1638	1.6	91	463	558	598	2.0	2.76	382	456	1.9
53551	LAKE MILLS	055	7097	7916	8316	1.2	81	2773	3160	3344	1.4	2.48	1962	2206	1.3
	WISCONSIN					0.7					1.0	2.43			0.9
	UNITED STATES					1.0					1.1	2.59			0.9

ZIP CODE #	POST OFFICE NAME	RACE (%) White 2000	White 2009	Black 2000	Black 2009	Asian/Pacific 2000	Asian/Pacific 2009	% Hispanic Origin 2000	% Hispanic Origin 2009	2009 AGE DISTRIBUTION (%) 0-4	5-9	10-14	15-19	20-24	25-44	45-64	65-84	85+	18+	MEDIAN AGE 2009	% 2009 Males	% 2009 Females
53149	MUKWONAGO	98.1	97.5	0.2	0.3	0.3	0.5	1.6	2.4	6.4	6.6	7.0	7.3	5.3	26.9	31.0	8.4	1.1	75.4	38.5	49.5	50.5
53150	MUSKEGO	98.1	97.4	0.2	0.2	0.5	0.8	1.3	2.1	6.4	6.8	7.3	7.0	4.8	25.0	31.3	9.8	1.7	75.0	40.4	49.4	50.6
53151	NEW BERLIN	95.7	94.0	0.5	0.7	2.5	3.6	1.5	2.3	5.6	6.2	6.7	6.3	5.1	23.6	31.9	12.7	1.9	77.4	42.6	48.6	51.4
53153	NORTH PRAIRIE	98.4	98.0	0.1	0.0	0.2	0.3	1.3	2.0	5.6	6.2	7.1	7.7	4.8	25.0	33.5	9.4	0.7	76.2	40.5	49.5	50.5
53154	OAK CREEK	92.0	87.0	1.8	3.6	2.4	3.8	4.5	7.1	6.8	6.4	6.2	6.1	7.1	30.9	26.7	8.8	1.1	76.9	36.1	49.6	50.4
53156	PALMYRA	95.8	94.2	0.2	0.2	0.1	0.2	5.2	7.7	6.3	6.9	6.9	6.1	4.4	26.9	29.2	11.8	1.5	76.0	40.4	48.9	51.1
53158	PLEASANT PRAIRIE	93.9	91.7	1.4	2.0	1.5	2.0	3.5	5.4	6.3	6.6	7.0	7.4	5.4	27.2	30.4	8.9	0.9	75.2	38.7	50.4	49.6
53168	SALEM	97.1	96.0	0.4	0.6	0.5	0.6	3.0	4.7	6.5	6.6	7.3	7.7	5.9	28.0	29.2	7.7	1.0	74.7	37.5	50.8	49.2
53170	SILVER LAKE	97.0	95.7	0.3	0.5	0.2	0.3	3.3	5.3	6.6	6.6	7.0	8.3	6.3	25.6	29.7	8.6	1.3	74.3	38.1	50.9	49.1
53172	SOUTH MILWAUKEE	94.8	92.0	1.0	1.9	0.7	1.2	4.0	6.6	6.2	5.9	5.8	6.2	6.6	26.0	27.4	12.9	3.0	78.3	40.2	48.6	51.4
53177	STURTEVANT	85.4	79.6	11.0	15.7	0.5	0.7	4.7	7.3	5.4	5.4	5.4	6.0	7.9	32.4	25.6	10.6	1.3	80.4	37.2	58.5	41.5
53178	SULLIVAN	98.3	97.7	0.1	0.2	0.2	0.3	0.9	1.4	5.9	6.3	6.8	6.1	3.6	27.3	31.0	11.7	1.3	77.1	41.7	50.3	49.7
53179	TREVOR	97.4	96.2	0.5	0.7	0.3	0.4	2.7	4.2	7.2	7.3	7.9	7.7	5.2	28.2	27.9	7.7	0.9	72.8	37.5	51.3	48.7
53181	TWIN LAKES	97.5	96.6	0.3	0.5	0.5	0.7	2.4	3.9	6.3	6.4	6.7	7.1	5.7	25.7	29.1	11.4	1.5	76.0	39.6	49.6	50.4
53182	UNION GROVE	95.2	93.4	2.1	2.9	0.5	0.7	2.3	3.8	5.9	6.1	6.2	7.3	5.7	29.1	28.4	9.7	1.5	76.8	38.9	47.7	52.3
53183	WALES	98.5	97.9	0.1	0.2	0.3	0.4	1.2	1.8	5.5	6.5	7.6	7.9	5.0	21.8	36.3	8.9	0.5	75.5	42.0	49.9	50.1
53184	WALWORTH	97.6	96.7	0.5	0.6	0.5	0.7	5.0	7.4	5.8	5.8	6.1	7.4	6.3	24.6	28.6	12.6	2.7	77.5	40.3	50.1	49.9
53185	WATERFORD	98.3	97.5	0.3	0.5	0.3	0.4	1.7	2.9	7.0	7.3	7.6	7.2	5.2	25.5	30.0	9.1	1.0	73.4	39.1	50.2	49.8
53186	WAUKESHA	90.6	87.4	1.0	1.2	2.3	3.3	9.7	13.7	6.5	6.3	6.1	7.3	7.5	28.0	25.4	10.7	2.2	77.4	36.4	48.6	51.4
53188	WAUKESHA	93.5	91.6	1.3	1.5	1.8	2.5	5.5	7.7	6.7	6.5	6.5	6.4	6.4	28.5	27.0	9.8	2.3	76.4	37.7	49.1	50.9
53189	WAUKESHA	95.4	93.7	0.7	0.9	1.3	2.1	4.1	5.7	7.2	7.7	7.5	7.4	5.5	27.1	29.9	7.2	0.6	72.7	37.0	49.8	50.2
53190	WHITEWATER	93.3	90.3	1.8	2.5	1.2	1.7	6.1	9.1	4.1	3.9	4.2	13.6	24.1	19.6	18.7	9.0	2.7	85.1	25.1	50.2	49.8
53191	WILLIAMS BAY	98.5	97.9	0.4	0.5	0.5	0.6	2.7	4.1	5.3	5.2	5.7	6.4	5.4	20.9	29.6	18.2	3.5	79.6	45.7	48.7	51.3
53202	MILWAUKEE	83.7	74.8	8.8	14.9	3.6	5.4	3.4	5.2	1.8	1.2	0.8	3.1	11.8	45.7	21.2	10.8	3.6	95.8	34.9	54.8	45.2
53203	MILWAUKEE	77.4	66.6	12.7	19.9	6.3	9.1	2.7	3.7	2.2	1.8	1.3	2.0	8.7	52.5	22.6	7.3	1.5	94.2	34.8	56.3	43.7
53204	MILWAUKEE	44.3	37.7	8.1	10.1	3.4	3.7	64.4	70.6	11.0	9.4	7.6	8.7	10.2	30.8	16.3	5.1	0.9	66.8	26.5	53.0	47.0
53205	MILWAUKEE	4.5	2.8	86.5	89.2	5.5	5.0	4.0	3.8	11.1	11.3	11.1	9.9	7.9	23.1	17.7	7.0	0.9	60.3	24.1	45.6	54.4
53206	MILWAUKEE	1.5	0.8	96.0	97.2	0.4	0.4	1.3	1.3	10.3	10.4	9.6	9.8	7.7	22.9	19.7	8.6	1.1	63.6	26.7	45.0	55.0
53207	MILWAUKEE	90.1	85.5	1.4	2.4	1.1	1.7	10.3	15.6	6.3	5.9	5.8	5.8	6.5	29.0	28.3	10.6	1.9	78.6	39.1	49.6	50.4
53208	MILWAUKEE	33.9	27.3	51.0	58.0	8.5	8.5	5.8	6.5	9.5	9.6	8.9	9.0	8.4	26.9	21.1	5.6	1.1	66.6	27.9	48.2	51.8
53209	MILWAUKEE	32.6	25.8	63.0	69.7	1.4	1.7	2.3	2.6	7.8	8.0	7.6	8.0	7.1	24.6	24.0	10.7	2.3	71.6	34.1	44.9	55.1
53210	MILWAUKEE	25.2	18.8	68.9	75.5	2.2	2.2	2.9	3.3	9.8	10.0	9.3	9.4	8.6	26.2	20.4	5.2	1.1	65.0	26.9	45.5	54.5
53211	MILWAUKEE	91.0	85.8	2.5	4.6	3.5	5.6	2.6	4.1	3.8	3.2	3.5	8.5	18.5	29.6	22.1	8.4	2.4	87.1	30.6	48.3	51.7
53212	MILWAUKEE	27.7	21.5	63.3	68.6	0.7	0.8	10.3	11.9	9.1	8.5	7.6	7.9	9.2	28.1	20.9	7.6	1.0	70.1	29.4	47.3	52.7
53213	MILWAUKEE	93.6	90.1	2.2	3.8	1.7	2.7	2.3	3.8	6.8	6.2	6.1	5.8	7.3	28.9	27.6	8.7	2.6	77.2	37.9	47.0	53.0
53214	MILWAUKEE	91.8	87.3	2.1	3.7	1.6	2.5	5.2	8.3	6.3	5.7	5.5	5.9	7.6	29.5	26.8	10.4	2.3	78.9	38.0	50.0	50.0
53215	MILWAUKEE	63.5	54.3	3.9	5.4	4.1	4.9	38.4	48.6	9.5	8.5	7.4	7.7	8.4	29.3	20.2	7.4	1.7	70.0	29.8	50.0	50.0
53216	MILWAUKEE	19.8	12.5	75.3	83.0	1.4	1.4	2.2	2.3	8.2	8.2	8.0	8.6	7.8	25.8	24.4	7.7	1.2	70.2	31.3	45.0	55.0
53217	MILWAUKEE	93.0	88.8	2.7	4.8	2.9	4.5	1.7	2.7	5.5	6.2	7.2	7.0	5.3	19.6	32.1	14.1	2.9	76.7	44.5	48.0	52.0
53218	MILWAUKEE	30.6	19.6	59.4	70.6	5.9	6.1	3.0	3.2	9.2	9.4	8.8	8.9	7.7	25.2	22.1	7.7	1.1	67.0	29.2	45.8	54.2
53219	MILWAUKEE	94.6	91.4	0.9	1.7	0.8	1.2	4.5	7.4	5.7	5.7	5.5	5.1	5.3	26.9	27.8	14.3	3.6	79.9	42.2	47.9	52.1
53220	MILWAUKEE	93.2	89.3	1.0	1.8	2.1	3.3	4.8	8.0	5.2	5.0	5.1	5.2	5.4	25.9	26.9	17.3	4.0	81.5	43.7	47.3	52.7
53221	MILWAUKEE	88.8	83.0	2.1	3.7	2.6	4.0	7.9	12.5	5.9	5.7	5.6	5.6	6.1	26.0	26.8	15.2	3.1	79.5	41.3	47.7	52.3
53222	MILWAUKEE	87.3	79.9	7.5	12.8	2.0	3.0	2.8	4.3	6.2	6.2	6.3	5.2	4.5	25.8	26.1	14.8	4.8	78.0	42.3	45.5	54.5
53223	MILWAUKEE	61.1	47.6	32.2	44.7	2.9	3.6	2.8	3.6	6.2	6.3	6.3	6.3	5.4	25.0	26.3	14.4	3.8	77.2	40.8	46.4	53.6
53224	MILWAUKEE	48.8	35.7	44.1	56.8	2.5	3.0	3.8	4.5	9.4	8.4	7.7	7.7	9.0	27.0	19.7	8.7	2.5	70.0	29.6	47.0	53.0
53225	MILWAUKEE	55.9	43.3	37.3	49.3	2.4	2.9	3.2	4.0	9.3	8.2	7.4	7.2	7.3	27.4	21.2	9.6	2.6	70.6	32.1	46.7	53.3
53226	MILWAUKEE	94.1	90.8	1.8	2.9	2.5	4.0	1.6	2.6	5.5	5.6	5.9	6.0	5.4	23.5	27.8	15.5	4.8	79.4	43.6	46.8	53.2
53227	MILWAUKEE	92.9	88.8	2.1	3.8	2.1	3.4	3.2	5.1	5.5	5.2	5.1	5.2	5.9	27.6	25.9	14.8	4.7	81.0	41.6	47.6	52.4
53228	MILWAUKEE	95.6	93.0	0.6	1.3	1.9	3.1	2.9	4.7	5.0	5.0	5.2	5.7	5.7	26.3	28.9	14.4	3.9	81.1	42.8	47.2	52.8
53233	MILWAUKEE	53.5	42.2	35.0	44.4	6.2	7.5	4.9	6.0	4.5	2.7	2.1	18.8	32.7	22.7	12.1	3.9	0.5	88.9	23.3	53.2	46.8
53235	MILWAUKEE	93.7	90.3	1.0	1.9	1.1	1.7	4.7	7.8	4.7	4.6	4.8	5.7	6.8	27.2	29.0	14.1	3.2	82.5	42.3	49.0	51.0
53402	RACINE	87.5	82.8	6.0	8.2	1.1	1.6	6.9	10.2	7.4	7.3	7.3	6.6	5.7	25.4	27.3	10.9	2.0	73.7	38.0	48.3	51.7
53403	RACINE	61.3	54.7	28.4	32.4	0.9	1.2	15.5	19.3	7.5	7.2	7.0	7.7	7.7	26.7	25.1	9.5	1.6	73.9	34.3	50.0	50.0
53404	RACINE	54.4	47.7	28.2	31.4	0.5	0.6	21.2	26.2	9.2	8.5	7.4	8.5	8.8	25.7	20.8	9.1	1.9	70.4	29.7	50.2	49.8
53405	RACINE	85.0	78.2	8.1	11.6	0.6	0.8	8.2	12.9	7.2	6.7	6.8	6.8	6.3	26.5	27.0	10.6	2.0	75.1	37.5	48.7	51.3
53406	RACINE	86.7	82.5	8.9	11.7	1.3	1.7	4.5	6.5	5.5	5.4	5.6	5.9	5.6	22.4	29.4	16.4	3.7	79.8	44.6	47.0	53.0
53502	ALBANY	98.3	97.7	0.1	0.1	0.3	0.5	1.1	1.5	6.1	6.3	6.5	6.7	5.9	26.6	29.3	11.2	1.5	76.7	39.8	50.9	49.1
53503	ARENA	98.7	98.3	0.0	0.0	0.9	1.3	0.8	1.1	6.4	6.5	7.2	7.2	4.8	28.2	30.1	8.9	0.7	75.0	38.4	51.4	48.6
53504	ARGYLE	98.9	98.7	0.2	0.3	0.1	0.1	0.8	1.2	6.3	7.0	7.4	7.1	4.4	23.2	29.7	13.0	1.9	74.2	41.4	52.4	47.6
53505	AVALON	100.0	100.0	0.0	0.0	0.0	0.0	1.9	2.9	5.7	6.5	7.3	6.8	3.9	24.0	33.4	10.7	1.6	76.0	42.2	52.0	48.0
53506	AVOCA	98.3	97.9	0.2	0.3	0.6	0.8	0.3	0.4	5.4	6.1	6.8	8.6	5.0	25.3	30.4	11.0	1.4	76.1	40.3	50.8	49.2
53507	BARNEVELD	98.8	98.5	0.3	0.4	0.1	0.1	0.2	0.3	6.5	7.0	7.5	7.2	4.7	27.7	30.5	7.8	1.0	74.3	39.4	51.8	48.2
53508	BELLEVILLE	98.5	98.1	0.2	0.2	0.3	0.4	0.5	0.8	6.7	7.5	8.1	6.8	3.9	26.3	30.7	8.8	1.3	73.2	39.9	50.7	49.3
53510	BELMONT	98.9	98.6	0.1	0.1	0.4	0.6	0.4	0.6	6.3	6.9	7.1	7.7	5.9	25.0	26.0	12.9	2.3	74.5	38.5	50.7	49.3
53511	BELOIT	79.8	74.7	12.7	15.8	1.0	1.4	7.4	9.9	7.0	6.7	6.7	7.7	7.4	25.1	25.8	11.5	2.1	75.4	36.5	48.6	51.4
53515	BLACK EARTH	97.3	96.2	0.2	0.2	0.4	0.7	1.4	2.4	5.7	6.3	7.0	7.3	4.8	24.2	30.8	11.3	2.5	76.1	41.9	50.4	49.6
53516	BLANCHARDVILLE	99.0	98.8	0.1	0.1	0.2	0.2	0.4	0.6	6.1	6.6	6.9	6.9	4.5	23.7	31.2	11.4	2.6	75.6	42.1	50.0	50.0
53517	BLUE MOUNDS	98.4	97.8	0.1	0.1	0.5	0.8	0.5	0.8	6.3	7.2	7.9	6.9	4.4	23.1	34.6	8.7	0.8	74.0	41.6	50.5	49.5
53518	BLUE RIVER	99.0	98.6	0.1	0.1	0.2	0.3	0.7	1.0	5.5	6.1	6.4	6.9	4.9	22.4	32.2	13.9	1.7	77.8	43.3	52.3	47.7
53520	BRODHEAD	97.9	97.3	0.3	0.4	0.2	0.3	1.0	1.5	6.6	6.7	7.0	7.4	5.7	25.3	27.9	11.4	1.9	75.1	38.9	49.2	50.8
53521	BROOKLYN	98.0	97.4	0.3	0.4	0.5	0.8	0.9	1.4	6.2	7.0	7.8	7.8	4.3	24.2	33.5	8.1	1.0	74.0	40.6	50.3	49.7
53522	BROWNTOWN	99.1	98.7	0.2	0.3	0.1	0.1	0.7	1.1	5.5	6.6	7.2	7.3	4.6	23.6	32.8	11.2	1.2	75.6	41.6	51.3	48.7
53523	CAMBRIDGE	97.6	96.7	0.3	0.5	0.6	1.0	1.5	2.3	5.8	6.5	7.2	6.6	4.8	23.8	32.2	11.1	1.9	76.0	42.0	50.7	49.3
53525	CLINTON	96.0	94.1	0.4	0.6	0.6	0.9	3.5	5.5	6.6	7.1	7.4	7.0	5.5	25.5	29.1	9.7	2.2	74.5	38.3	49.9	50.1
53526	COBB	98.7	98.4	0.0	0.0	0.2	0.4	0.2	0.4	6.5	6.9	7.4	7.1	4.1	24.2	30.0	12.0	1.9	74.6	40.8	52.7	47.3
53527	COTTAGE GROVE	96.7	95.0	1.2	1.7	0.6	1.1	1.4	2.3	8.3	8.3	8.2	7.0	5.1	29.7	26.8	5.8	0.8	70.3	35.1	50.3	49.7
53528	CROSS PLAINS	98.5	98.0	0.3	0.4	0.3	0.4	0.5	0.7	6.7	7.0	7.8	6.6	4.9	29.2	28.1	8.7	1.1	74.3	37.5	49.7	50.3
53529	DANE	97.4	96.0	0.2	0.4	1.0	1.8	1.0	1.6	7.8	8.1	8.4	7.0	4.4	26.9	27.8	8.7	0.9	71.3	37.4	51.1	48.9
53530	DARLINGTON	99.0	98.7	0.0	0.1	0.2	0.2	1.0	1.5	6.1	6.6	6.6	6.7	5.2	23.7	27.7	14.1	3.3	76.5	41.3	49.6	50.4
53531	DEERFIELD	94.8	92.8	2.0	2.7	0.9	1.4	2.1	3.2	6.7	7.2	7.7	7.2	4.8	26.5	30.6	8.4	1.1	73.5	39.0	52.3	47.7
53532	DE FOREST	96.1	94.5	1.0	1.5	0.8	1.3	1.8	2.7	7.5	7.3	7.5	7.4	5.8	28.1	27.8	7.5	1.1	72.6	36.3	48.3	51.7
53533	DODGEVILLE	98.3	97.8	0.3	0.4	0.5	0.7	0.3	0.5	6.9	6.9	6.9	6.7	5.7	25.1	27.1	12.2	2.6	74.7	39.9	48.6	51.4
53534	EDGERTON	97.5	96.6	0.2	0.3	0.3	0.5	2.4	3.6	5.8	6.2	6.8	6.7	5.1	25.6	30.0	11.8	2.0	76.9	40.9	50.4	49.6
53536	EVANSVILLE	97.7	96.8	0.2	0.3	0.4	0.5	1.4	2.2	7.3	7.6	7.7	7.3	5.1	25.4	28.1	9.5	2.1	72.8	38.2	49.1	50.9
53538	FORT ATKINSON	96.8	95.7	0.2	0.3	0.5	0.7	3.4	4.9	6.0	6.0	6.1	6.2	6.0	26.8	29.1	11.6	2.2	77.9	40.0	49.3	50.7
53541	GRATIOT	98.8	98.7	0.7	0.8	0.0	0.0	0.1	0.1	5.7	6.3	6.3	5.7	4.8	24.5	33.1	11.9	1.6	77.9	42.5	50.6	49.4
53543	HIGHLAND	99.6	99.5	0.1	0.1	0.1	0.2	0.2	0.3	6.1	6.5	6.8	7.0	4.1	25.8	30.0	11.8	1.8	75.7	40.3	50.3	49.7
53544	HOLLANDALE	99.2	99.2	0.1	0.1	0.0	0.0	0.3	0.4	5.0	5.5	6.2	6.8	4.6	25.2	33.3	11.5	1.9	78.7	43.2	51.8	48.2
53545	JANESVILLE	96.0	94.5	1.3	1.9	0.7	1.0	2.3	3.6	6.3	6.0	6.3	6.7	6.5	26.2	26.3	13.3	2.5	77.2	39.3	49.0	51.0
53546	JANESVILLE	95.8	94.1	1.3	1.8	0.8	1.3	2.4	3.6	7.3	7.2	7.0	6.6	5.8	28.4	26.1	10.1	1.6	74.3	36.9	49.3	50.7
53548	JANESVILLE	94.0	91.8	1.7	2.5	1.3	1.7	2.7	4.0	6.5	6.4	6.5	7.0	6.5	26.7	27.6	11.0	1.7	76.3	38.2	50.0	50.0
53549	JEFFERSON	95.4	93.8	0.4	0.5	0.4	0.6	5.3	7.6	5.7	5.8	5.9	5.9	5.7	27.9	26.9	13.1	3.1	79.2	40.2	49.5	50.5
53550	JUDA	98.1	97.4	0.1	0.1	0.9	1.3	0.5	0.6	6.3	6.8	7.0	7.1	4.5	23.9	31.4	11.6	1.4	75.5	41.2	50.0	50.0
53551	LAKE MILLS	97.6	96.7	0.2	0.2	0.8	1.1	2.3	3.4	6.7	6.6	6.7	6.6	6.1	25.2	28.6	11.2	2.3	75.6	39.5	49.1	50.9
	WISCONSIN	88.9	86.9	5.7	6.3	1.7	2.3	3.6	4.8	6.4	6.4	6.5	7.2	7.2	26.0	27.1	11.1	2.2	76.6	38.0	49.5	50.5
	UNITED STATES	75.1	72.0	12.3	12.7	3.8	4.6	12.5	15.7	6.8	6.7	6.6	7.1	6.9	27.0	26.0	10.9	1.9	75.7	36.9	49.2	50.8

#	POST OFFICE NAME	2009 Per Capita Income	2009 HH Income Base	2009 HOUSEHOLD INCOME DISTRIBUTION (%) Less than $25,000	$25,000 to $49,999	$50,000 to $99,999	$100,000 to $149,999	$150,000 or More	MEDIAN HOUSEHOLD INCOME 2009	2014	2009 National Centile	2009 State Centile	2009 Home Value Base	2009 HOME VALUE DISTRIBUTION (%) Less than $50,000	$50,000 to $89,999	$90,000 to $174,999	$175,000 to $399,999	$400,000 or More	2009 Median Home Value
53149	MUKWONAGO	35455	6770	7.4	14.0	40.6	26.8	11.2	84345	88761	94	97	5454	1.0	1.1	14.2	73.7	10.0	236940
53150	MUSKEGO	34407	8901	6.9	13.5	42.9	25.8	10.9	83141	87782	93	96	7301	0.7	0.3	16.4	74.9	7.7	235330
53151	NEW BERLIN	41988	12487	6.4	14.8	36.2	24.5	18.1	88329	94415	95	98	9900	0.5	0.9	13.9	75.9	8.7	230497
53153	NORTH PRAIRIE	35519	783	4.5	8.9	44.1	32.4	10.1	89075	95697	95	98	690	0.0	2.3	24.5	66.2	7.0	223512
53154	OAK CREEK	31509	13206	10.6	18.9	47.7	16.2	6.6	69269	70146	86	90	7871	2.9	2.0	38.1	56.4	0.6	184025
53156	PALMYRA	24658	1355	16.0	26.3	45.2	9.7	2.8	56143	57624	73	65	1013	7.3	4.8	38.7	43.0	6.1	173832
53158	PLEASANT PRAIRIE	33597	5518	7.1	18.7	41.2	20.1	12.9	79613	81616	92	95	4641	8.3	5.3	20.6	58.7	7.1	208324
53168	SALEM	28871	3271	9.6	22.2	43.0	19.1	6.1	71261	75632	87	91	2676	5.6	5.6	40.5	42.3	6.1	172511
53170	SILVER LAKE	25539	838	14.8	21.5	45.0	14.9	3.8	64880	68023	83	85	648	8.3	9.1	45.5	33.8	3.2	157051
53172	SOUTH MILWAUKEE	28010	8944	15.3	26.1	45.2	9.4	4.0	59158	60758	76	71	5531	0.9	4.8	65.8	28.3	0.3	149072
53177	STURTEVANT	26419	2817	11.8	21.3	51.4	11.9	3.6	67741	72071	85	88	2048	6.6	4.5	58.4	28.3	2.1	147640
53178	SULLIVAN	26514	1233	15.2	26.0	46.6	8.9	3.3	57921	59446	75	69	982	12.4	12.9	18.6	47.7	8.4	191954
53179	TREVOR	23609	2103	15.5	25.8	41.7	13.6	3.5	60428	63047	78	74	1752	2.2	7.9	39.8	46.1	3.9	175104
53181	TWIN LAKES	28010	2727	13.5	21.3	45.1	15.3	4.7	66370	71410	84	87	2064	0.0	1.8	38.1	50.0	10.0	200701
53182	UNION GROVE	26923	3263	11.5	20.3	51.4	12.5	4.3	66620	69893	85	87	2345	8.5	3.9	35.6	45.8	6.2	178599
53183	WALES	42324	842	3.0	9.3	32.5	33.1	22.1	105716	108865	97	100	760	0.0	0.5	5.8	77.8	15.9	286996
53184	WALWORTH	25471	1605	14.0	24.6	44.1	12.8	4.5	62167	63057	80	78	1120	1.3	3.0	44.3	45.1	6.3	177131
53185	WATERFORD	32267	6700	7.8	14.8	47.6	21.2	8.6	78589	80497	91	95	5493	0.8	2.7	29.5	60.9	6.1	213278
53186	WAUKESHA	31539	13922	15.8	23.0	38.0	16.2	7.0	62534	63867	81	80	8024	0.8	2.5	37.0	56.6	3.1	193964
53188	WAUKESHA	34713	13984	11.8	18.8	38.5	20.2	10.7	76026	79311	90	93	8988	1.7	0.8	26.8	65.1	5.6	218726
53189	WAUKESHA	36455	9006	6.0	15.0	38.5	26.5	14.0	86414	92380	94	98	7021	0.5	0.2	12.4	75.6	11.2	251787
53190	WHITEWATER	21809	6576	25.5	28.1	35.0	7.8	3.6	47044	49948	54	40	3401	9.9	4.4	35.6	44.4	5.6	175091
53191	WILLIAMS BAY	36387	1187	18.1	19.9	36.8	15.1	10.1	63057	64155	81	82	902	0.8	3.8	24.7	58.8	12.0	225000
53202	MILWAUKEE	42137	15237	28.8	27.1	30.0	8.4	5.7	43975	47661	45	28	2215	2.2	10.1	39.6	38.8	9.3	171088
53203	MILWAUKEE	61034	500	24.2	16.4	35.6	8.4	15.4	62684	63544	81	80	192	0.0	0.0	0.0	87.5	12.5	252273
53204	MILWAUKEE	12055	12796	38.9	31.7	24.8	3.2	1.3	32693	33659	13	2	3593	30.6	53.9	13.9	1.5	0.1	60504
53205	MILWAUKEE	10056	3461	61.5	22.9	13.7	1.2	0.5	18898	18914	1	1	853	38.8	43.6	14.0	1.9	1.8	56920
53206	MILWAUKEE	11506	10134	49.7	29.5	17.7	1.7	1.4	25143	25363	3	1	3957	56.0	36.5	6.2	1.1	0.3	47415
53207	MILWAUKEE	27031	16214	19.0	27.9	43.6	7.3	2.3	52612	54817	67	57	10036	2.0	14.6	70.3	12.7	0.4	123727
53208	MILWAUKEE	16745	12392	37.9	28.0	27.8	4.4	1.8	34583	35768	17	2	4176	15.2	30.7	43.3	10.5	0.3	95073
53209	MILWAUKEE	21447	19159	28.9	31.1	30.6	6.3	3.2	41245	43346	37	17	10349	10.1	45.3	28.8	15.3	0.5	83815
53210	MILWAUKEE	16952	9985	31.3	29.3	32.1	5.1	2.3	40301	42263	34	13	4608	9.9	40.7	41.3	7.9	0.2	89510
53211	MILWAUKEE	37162	15958	18.2	25.5	36.1	9.8	10.5	56323	58379	73	66	6483	0.8	2.8	20.1	62.5	14.0	235083
53212	MILWAUKEE	16285	12279	42.3	29.8	23.6	2.9	1.4	30316	31713	9	1	3819	28.9	44.3	21.8	4.2	0.8	65671
53213	MILWAUKEE	35177	11465	11.5	21.1	46.6	13.0	7.9	66683	67735	85	87	7463	0.5	4.5	46.8	45.7	2.5	172269
53214	MILWAUKEE	25973	16183	21.1	29.3	41.7	6.0	1.9	49522	52052	60	47	8745	3.0	11.7	77.7	7.5	0.1	122003
53215	MILWAUKEE	17377	19322	28.2	30.5	34.5	4.9	1.8	42262	44417	40	21	9246	5.6	38.5	50.5	5.2	0.2	94092
53216	MILWAUKEE	18683	13090	30.4	30.6	32.8	4.4	1.8	40245	42392	33	13	7048	8.0	47.9	41.7	2.4	0.0	86497
53217	MILWAUKEE	49402	11897	9.5	15.1	32.8	17.9	24.8	87096	88433	94	98	9417	0.3	1.3	17.0	59.8	21.6	252059
53218	MILWAUKEE	17032	14622	28.9	32.2	33.7	3.6	1.6	40763	42630	35	16	8498	6.4	60.3	32.1	1.1	0.1	80186
53219	MILWAUKEE	27790	15778	18.5	28.1	44.4	7.1	1.9	52653	54765	67	57	10202	0.4	6.1	78.2	15.0	0.3	135466
53220	MILWAUKEE	28564	11380	15.1	28.5	46.6	7.5	2.3	54830	56599	71	63	6672	0.6	3.1	68.0	28.0	0.3	152133
53221	MILWAUKEE	27830	15582	16.5	28.0	43.9	8.7	3.0	54913	57029	71	63	9814	4.0	7.4	63.6	24.7	0.3	143457
53222	MILWAUKEE	29120	11122	17.4	28.0	43.3	8.1	3.3	54412	56739	70	61	7814	0.3	11.7	71.5	15.8	0.7	125917
53223	MILWAUKEE	28067	12451	16.8	25.7	43.9	9.3	4.3	56937	58799	74	67	7327	1.8	21.3	60.2	16.2	0.5	122269
53224	MILWAUKEE	23257	7516	20.6	25.1	40.8	9.5	4.0	54041	56309	70	60	3640	5.0	17.4	58.4	18.4	0.8	129021
53225	MILWAUKEE	23163	9998	18.9	31.0	40.6	7.1	2.4	50133	52742	61	49	4632	1.2	14.9	69.2	14.1	0.5	124672
53226	MILWAUKEE	36741	8358	11.9	21.6	43.6	15.5	7.4	68714	70152	86	89	5596	0.4	0.8	39.8	57.8	1.2	188816
53227	MILWAUKEE	28159	10960	18.5	29.1	43.3	6.7	2.4	51936	54279	66	55	5909	4.6	3.1	65.3	26.7	0.3	149369
53228	MILWAUKEE	31582	6153	13.2	23.7	43.9	14.0	5.2	64207	65611	83	84	3644	0.1	7.4	37.9	53.2	1.4	182818
53233	MILWAUKEE	13811	5377	64.1	23.2	10.9	1.0	0.9	17213	17239	1	0	284	25.7	40.8	14.1	17.6	1.8	81455
53235	MILWAUKEE	27360	4479	22.0	30.3	39.1	6.1	2.5	47552	50780	56	42	2356	0.6	5.2	83.7	10.4	0.0	129962
53402	RACINE	31659	13558	13.0	21.6	42.4	15.3	7.7	68505	73233	86	89	10050	0.9	8.4	54.3	32.7	3.7	150182
53403	RACINE	23807	10756	25.6	25.4	36.2	8.6	4.2	48821	51800	58	45	6146	6.8	17.9	54.1	19.2	2.1	115380
53404	RACINE	20383	5756	28.4	26.5	33.4	7.6	4.1	43313	46631	43	26	3049	6.9	19.6	60.5	12.8	0.2	112162
53405	RACINE	27877	10372	15.2	25.2	44.5	10.6	4.5	61681	64446	80	77	7613	1.2	11.5	71.5	15.0	0.7	122947
53406	RACINE	31269	10882	18.0	21.8	38.8	14.5	6.9	62350	65980	80	79	7506	0.3	3.2	57.5	37.5	1.6	160366
53502	ALBANY	26496	1008	13.0	26.1	48.5	8.4	4.0	59891	61032	77	72	758	1.8	15.8	49.5	28.5	4.4	146303
53503	ARENA	23686	784	16.5	25.8	48.6	7.5	1.7	57967	60114	75	69	618	6.8	7.9	43.7	34.5	7.1	160227
53504	ARGYLE	20946	863	20.9	32.0	41.1	4.4	1.6	47547	50214	56	42	682	7.3	16.6	49.3	21.4	5.4	130200
53505	AVALON	29366	154	10.4	22.7	52.6	9.7	4.5	65883	67283	84	86	114	3.5	9.6	48.2	28.1	10.5	148611
53506	AVOCA	20883	453	30.2	29.1	32.9	4.9	2.9	41097	43650	36	16	356	23.0	24.7	27.5	19.4	5.3	93636
53507	BARNEVELD	25163	751	14.6	22.0	51.9	9.1	2.4	62792	63249	81	81	602	2.0	3.8	43.7	41.7	8.8	175904
53508	BELLEVILLE	26182	1990	10.2	27.4	48.5	10.9	3.1	61280	63496	79	76	1557	2.4	4.7	32.4	53.9	6.6	192695
53510	BELMONT	20396	570	25.8	32.8	36.1	3.9	1.4	41968	43841	39	20	417	11.3	16.8	59.2	9.8	2.9	113971
53511	BELOIT	23456	18715	21.5	27.5	39.9	7.8	3.3	51056	54102	64	52	12713	9.5	32.9	43.6	13.2	0.7	96785
53515	BLACK EARTH	27580	936	12.2	21.8	49.1	13.6	3.3	64212	67366	83	84	723	4.8	5.0	33.7	49.7	6.8	187917
53516	BLANCHARDVILLE	23627	806	19.4	27.0	43.7	7.6	2.4	52617	54249	67	57	648	7.4	13.0	41.7	31.2	6.8	138636
53517	BLUE MOUNDS	28218	653	12.1	25.6	43.2	14.1	5.1	61047	63295	79	75	561	17.5	12.5	14.8	41.0	14.3	194408
53518	BLUE RIVER	20605	608	26.5	30.8	36.5	4.6	1.6	43062	45514	43	25	495	14.3	22.0	42.4	19.4	1.8	110041
53520	BRODHEAD	22605	2707	19.2	26.9	43.1	9.0	1.8	53160	55286	68	59	2174	8.2	12.8	54.4	22.8	1.8	133353
53521	BROOKLYN	30151	1338	8.1	19.3	48.7	18.2	5.8	70610	73171	87	91	1147	2.0	4.4	27.0	56.7	9.9	214136
53522	BROWNTOWN	22869	530	17.2	31.5	41.1	7.2	3.0	50708	52034	63	51	428	10.0	12.1	42.5	29.7	5.6	141038
53523	CAMBRIDGE	28374	1998	13.8	22.5	45.4	14.5	3.8	63856	65961	82	83	1606	7.5	4.2	27.3	50.0	11.0	200704
53525	CLINTON	23170	1570	17.1	25.2	45.7	9.4	2.6	59275	61044	77	71	1116	7.9	7.3	56.5	26.3	2.0	141843
53526	COBB	22015	246	22.8	39.4	30.1	6.5	1.2	43185	45298	43	25	195	4.6	22.1	55.9	15.9	1.5	116768
53527	COTTAGE GROVE	36441	3546	5.8	8.2	39.4	36.0	10.6	94448	95633	96	99	2788	0.9	1.5	17.2	74.0	6.5	227088
53528	CROSS PLAINS	32946	2100	6.7	17.1	47.2	22.1	6.9	72623	76243	88	92	1503	0.8	0.7	22.6	63.6	12.2	225517
53529	DANE	25729	698	11.0	19.8	50.4	15.3	3.4	64120	66520	82	83	532	4.7	0.4	29.7	57.1	8.1	209091
53530	DARLINGTON	20559	1724	23.8	30.9	38.8	5.4	1.1	45790	48298	51	36	1300	7.8	26.4	49.2	14.3	2.3	106992
53531	DEERFIELD	25578	1533	11.4	23.9	46.2	14.8	3.7	63218	66204	81	82	1190	1.5	1.3	32.4	58.2	6.6	203571
53532	DE FOREST	31271	5194	6.7	14.0	47.5	25.1	6.6	76654	79647	90	94	3979	0.1	0.3	28.0	66.4	5.1	209569
53533	DODGEVILLE	27006	2777	16.4	27.9	41.2	10.0	4.4	56951	59911	74	67	1985	3.2	11.6	58.5	23.2	3.5	133063
53534	EDGERTON	27396	4693	15.5	23.0	47.4	10.5	3.6	61700	63308	80	77	3567	2.5	9.6	54.6	30.9	2.5	144261
53536	EVANSVILLE	26417	3109	14.1	25.2	47.4	9.4	3.9	62290	64912	80	78	2313	7.4	5.6	51.6	33.2	2.1	149918
53538	FORT ATKINSON	28025	7468	15.1	24.3	46.2	9.7	4.6	60680	61700	78	74	5266	2.8	5.2	47.1	41.5	3.4	167650
53541	GRATIOT	21322	420	18.6	31.4	40.7	7.9	1.4	50000	51689	61	48	327	12.2	22.6	45.0	13.5	6.7	105388
53543	HIGHLAND	20316	721	22.2	33.3	38.3	4.9	1.4	45800	48825	51	36	585	9.2	19.3	47.7	20.5	3.2	119875
53544	HOLLANDALE	22627	341	22.9	27.9	38.4	8.8	2.1	49344	52914	60	46	276	5.1	16.7	41.3	30.4	6.5	140441
53545	JANESVILLE	29097	9964	14.8	27.0	42.1	10.7	5.4	60145	62105	78	73	6672	0.3	7.4	70.9	19.7	1.7	134263
53546	JANESVILLE	29758	12199	10.4	24.1	45.4	13.7	6.3	66215	68969	84	87	9092	9.1	7.1	56.7	26.5	0.7	138577
53548	JANESVILLE	26883	7952	17.7	28.6	38.5	10.8	4.6	54592	58377	71	62	5481	3.4	15.7	54.7	24.2	2.0	131201
53549	JEFFERSON	25851	4067	16.1	25.9	45.3	9.4	3.3	56840	58580	74	67	2706	5.4	6.1	44.0	40.9	3.5	166573
53550	JUDA	22519	558	14.7	31.0	46.6	5.2	2.5	52305	53865	66	56	444	3.8	12.4	46.2	28.6	9.0	144063
53551	LAKE MILLS	26995	3160	15.9	23.9	45.4	10.9	3.8	59498	60529	77	71	2350	7.9	3.5	33.9	48.3	6.4	181532
	WISCONSIN	27384		18.4	25.3	40.0	11.0	5.2	56363	58927				5.6	11.9	43.5	34.2	4.7	150766
	UNITED STATES	27277		20.9	24.4	35.3	11.7	7.6	54719	56938				9.3	13.1	31.6	32.6	13.5	162279

ZIP CODE		FINANCIAL SERVICES				THE HOME						ENTERTAINMENT						PERSONAL			
						Home Improvements		Furnishings													
#	POST OFFICE NAME	Auto Loan	Home Loan	Invest-ments	Retire-ment Plans	Home Repair	Lawn & Garden	Comput-ers & Hard-ware-Personal	Major Appli-ances	TV, Radio, Sound Equip-ment	Furni-ture	Dine out/ Carry out	Sports Equip-ment	Fees & Tickets	Toys & Games	Travel	Cable TV	Apparel & Services	Auto Repairs	Health Insur-ance	Pets & Supplies
53149	MUKWONAGO	133	157	140	157	152	140	138	139	132	144	134	110	150	137	146	128	96	134	129	161
53150	MUSKEGO	130	153	137	154	149	140	133	136	128	139	130	106	146	132	142	126	92	131	129	157
53151	NEW BERLIN	143	165	158	168	164	154	151	151	146	157	148	117	164	147	159	143	105	148	146	175
53153	NORTH PRAIRIE	135	169	149	169	163	146	142	144	133	149	136	115	160	139	153	128	98	137	129	165
53154	OAK CREEK	108	109	99	112	105	101	112	104	109	113	111	84	113	112	110	107	78	108	103	124
53156	PALMYRA	95	90	87	93	91	103	87	97	89	81	88	74	83	91	88	94	60	90	99	113
53158	PLEASANT PRAIRIE	131	152	137	153	148	138	135	136	129	140	131	107	146	133	142	127	93	132	128	158
53168	SALEM	117	126	107	125	121	115	114	116	111	119	112	90	117	116	115	109	78	111	109	135
53170	SILVER LAKE	94	108	97	108	105	102	100	100	98	99	99	78	107	99	105	98	70	99	99	117
53172	SOUTH MILWAUKEE	88	93	85	93	91	93	94	91	94	90	94	70	96	94	94	95	66	93	96	107
53177	STURTEVANT	98	107	102	106	105	108	100	103	101	98	101	79	105	102	105	103	71	102	107	120
53178	SULLIVAN	94	98	89	101	97	103	91	97	91	87	90	75	92	93	94	93	63	92	98	114
53179	TREVOR	101	102	88	101	99	100	93	97	94	97	94	74	94	98	93	94	65	94	95	115
53181	TWIN LAKES	98	114	102	115	111	109	103	104	101	103	102	81	112	103	109	101	72	102	105	122
53182	UNION GROVE	98	110	100	110	108	105	102	103	100	102	101	80	108	101	106	100	71	101	102	120
53183	WALES	158	203	190	207	201	178	168	173	158	179	161	137	195	163	186	151	117	163	153	197
53184	WALWORTH	93	108	100	107	106	102	101	100	99	100	100	78	109	100	106	99	71	100	100	117
53185	WATERFORD	119	142	125	141	137	127	125	125	119	128	121	99	136	123	132	116	86	121	117	145
53186	WAUKESHA	101	105	100	106	104	102	107	102	106	107	107	79	110	105	108	106	75	105	106	120
53188	WAUKESHA	120	127	117	129	124	118	125	119	122	127	124	95	131	124	126	120	88	122	117	140
53189	WAUKESHA	140	161	145	162	157	142	145	144	137	153	140	114	157	143	151	132	100	140	131	165
53190	WHITEWATER	84	69	66	72	68	73	93	76	86	81	87	64	78	86	77	85	60	83	79	93
53191	WILLIAMS BAY	110	126	126	127	129	126	114	119	114	118	115	87	125	112	124	115	81	116	123	137
53202	MILWAUKEE	86	63	65	72	60	62	95	71	92	86	94	65	83	92	80	89	67	86	75	91
53203	MILWAUKEE	120	89	92	103	85	86	131	99	127	122	132	91	117	128	113	123	94	119	103	127
53204	MILWAUKEE	56	45	39	46	43	43	60	50	61	57	62	41	55	61	52	60	45	58	51	60
53205	MILWAUKEE	40	27	25	30	25	31	39	33	44	37	43	26	34	42	32	46	30	39	40	43
53206	MILWAUKEE	51	35	32	38	33	42	48	42	54	47	53	32	42	53	40	57	37	48	51	54
53207	MILWAUKEE	81	81	71	82	77	82	85	80	86	81	85	63	85	86	82	87	60	84	86	97
53208	MILWAUKEE	62	50	45	53	47	52	64	55	67	61	67	44	59	66	56	69	47	62	61	69
53209	MILWAUKEE	75	67	60	70	64	72	74	69	79	73	78	53	72	78	69	82	54	75	78	86
53210	MILWAUKEE	71	57	49	60	53	61	70	61	74	67	73	49	65	74	61	76	51	69	69	78
53211	MILWAUKEE	108	96	99	103	96	93	122	100	114	113	116	85	112	114	109	111	83	111	101	122
53212	MILWAUKEE	56	42	38	45	39	45	58	48	61	54	61	39	51	60	48	63	43	56	55	61
53213	MILWAUKEE	108	115	107	116	112	109	114	108	111	113	112	85	117	112	113	110	79	110	108	128
53214	MILWAUKEE	78	73	65	74	70	75	81	75	82	76	82	59	78	82	76	83	57	79	81	91
53215	MILWAUKEE	68	62	55	62	59	62	73	65	74	68	74	52	69	74	66	75	53	71	69	79
53216	MILWAUKEE	70	61	51	63	55	65	67	63	72	66	71	49	64	72	61	74	49	68	71	79
53217	MILWAUKEE	151	186	202	189	196	178	167	171	161	175	162	128	191	159	186	160	118	166	167	194
53218	MILWAUKEE	70	61	50	63	55	65	67	62	72	66	71	49	65	72	61	74	49	67	71	79
53219	MILWAUKEE	78	80	74	81	78	84	82	80	84	78	84	61	83	83	81	87	58	82	90	95
53220	MILWAUKEE	81	87	83	87	86	89	86	85	87	84	88	64	90	86	88	90	61	87	93	100
53221	MILWAUKEE	82	86	83	85	85	88	87	86	89	84	88	65	89	87	88	91	62	88	93	101
53222	MILWAUKEE	84	87	80	88	85	93	87	87	90	84	89	65	89	89	88	93	62	88	97	103
53223	MILWAUKEE	88	90	84	91	88	91	91	89	93	90	93	68	93	92	91	95	65	91	96	106
53224	MILWAUKEE	92	80	71	82	76	77	92	82	92	91	93	66	86	94	84	91	65	89	84	100
53225	MILWAUKEE	82	74	65	76	70	75	84	76	85	81	86	61	80	86	77	86	60	82	82	93
53226	MILWAUKEE	102	119	119	118	120	119	110	112	111	111	112	82	121	109	118	114	79	112	121	129
53227	MILWAUKEE	78	80	78	81	80	82	83	81	84	81	84	61	85	83	84	86	59	83	88	95
53228	MILWAUKEE	94	102	99	103	102	103	101	99	102	100	102	75	107	100	105	103	72	101	107	116
53233	MILWAUKEE	39	21	21	25	20	24	48	29	43	37	43	28	33	42	31	41	30	38	32	39
53235	MILWAUKEE	76	76	72	77	75	79	80	77	81	77	81	59	80	80	79	83	56	80	85	92
53402	RACINE	110	117	104	118	113	114	113	111	113	114	113	86	117	114	114	113	79	112	114	131
53403	RACINE	81	78	69	80	74	80	86	79	88	81	87	62	84	87	81	90	61	84	87	96
53404	RACINE	77	75	64	76	70	76	82	75	84	77	84	59	80	84	77	86	59	80	82	91
53405	RACINE	95	99	84	100	94	100	98	95	98	95	98	74	100	99	97	99	68	97	102	114
53406	RACINE	97	104	100	105	104	107	100	101	102	101	103	75	106	101	105	105	72	102	110	119
53502	ALBANY	94	101	83	104	95	102	96	95	96	93	96	75	99	98	96	97	66	95	101	114
53503	ARENA	93	86	85	90	88	100	84	95	87	77	85	72	79	88	85	91	58	88	97	110
53504	ARGYLE	88	71	88	72	73	94	73	86	76	63	75	68	61	76	73	81	50	80	90	103
53505	AVALON	102	115	99	118	111	112	102	106	101	103	101	83	109	103	108	101	71	102	105	125
53506	AVOCA	93	66	84	65	67	91	70	83	76	65	75	65	55	78	65	83	50	78	88	101
53507	BARNEVELD	92	103	90	106	100	102	92	96	91	92	91	75	98	93	97	91	64	93	95	113
53508	BELLEVILLE	93	105	91	108	102	103	94	98	92	94	93	76	100	95	99	93	65	94	97	115
53510	BELMONT	84	59	88	58	62	88	65	81	71	56	69	63	50	69	64	77	45	75	87	97
53511	BELOIT	84	83	73	84	79	88	85	83	87	80	86	64	84	88	82	90	60	85	91	100
53515	BLACK EARTH	93	113	100	113	109	111	97	101	97	98	98	77	110	99	106	99	69	98	105	118
53516	BLANCHARDVILLE	91	82	89	85	83	98	81	92	83	73	82	72	74	84	82	87	56	86	94	109
53517	BLUE MOUNDS	101	114	98	118	111	112	102	106	100	102	101	83	109	103	108	101	71	102	105	125
53518	BLUE RIVER	89	62	95	61	65	92	67	84	72	58	71	67	51	71	66	78	46	78	88	102
53520	BRODHEAD	88	84	77	85	81	92	82	86	84	79	83	66	79	86	80	87	57	84	91	103
53521	BROOKLYN	110	130	113	132	126	121	113	116	109	116	110	92	124	112	121	107	78	111	110	135
53522	BROWNTOWN	104	72	114	72	75	110	80	99	83	65	82	82	58	81	79	90	53	92	105	122
53523	CAMBRIDGE	98	109	97	112	107	111	98	103	98	97	98	79	104	100	104	99	68	99	105	121
53525	CLINTON	96	93	85	94	92	99	88	95	90	86	89	71	85	92	88	92	61	90	96	111
53526	COBB	91	62	100	62	65	96	69	86	72	56	71	71	51	71	69	79	46	80	91	106
53527	COTTAGE GROVE	150	167	138	162	158	140	147	147	138	158	141	116	152	148	147	131	99	139	130	168
53528	CROSS PLAINS	122	137	116	136	131	122	120	123	115	127	117	96	127	121	124	112	82	117	113	141
53529	DANE	101	114	98	118	111	112	102	106	100	102	101	83	109	103	108	100	70	102	105	125
53530	DARLINGTON	85	66	85	67	67	90	70	82	74	61	73	65	58	73	69	79	48	78	88	99
53531	DEERFIELD	97	110	95	113	107	108	98	102	96	99	97	80	105	99	104	96	68	98	100	120
53532	DE FOREST	117	138	120	135	132	120	123	122	117	127	119	97	132	122	128	114	85	119	113	140
53533	DODGEVILLE	98	89	91	90	88	102	92	96	94	86	93	75	86	94	90	98	63	95	104	116
53534	EDGERTON	100	96	95	98	95	106	94	101	96	89	95	77	91	96	95	99	65	97	104	118
53536	EVANSVILLE	92	103	94	104	101	102	95	97	94	94	95	75	101	96	100	95	67	95	98	114
53538	FORT ATKINSON	95	99	92	99	97	100	97	98	97	94	97	75	98	98	98	99	68	97	101	115
53541	GRATIOT	98	67	107	67	70	103	75	93	78	61	77	77	55	76	74	85	50	87	98	114
53543	HIGHLAND	93	64	102	64	67	98	71	88	74	57	73	73	52	72	70	80	47	82	93	108
53544	HOLLANDALE	98	70	106	70	73	103	76	93	79	63	78	77	58	78	76	85	51	87	98	114
53545	JANESVILLE	95	97	88	98	94	99	98	95	99	95	99	74	100	99	97	101	69	98	103	114
53546	JANESVILLE	111	112	96	112	107	108	108	107	106	108	107	84	107	110	106	106	74	106	107	127
53548	JANESVILLE	92	94	84	96	91	97	93	93	94	90	94	72	94	95	92	96	65	93	98	110
53549	JEFFERSON	93	92	89	92	91	95	91	93	92	89	92	71	91	93	92	94	64	93	96	109
53550	JUDA	109	79	118	79	81	115	85	104	88	71	87	85	65	87	85	95	57	97	109	128
53551	LAKE MILLS	96	99	92	99	98	101	95	97	95	94	95	74	96	97	96	97	66	96	100	114
	WISCONSIN	98	94	92	96	93	99	96	96	96	93	96	75	94	97	95	98	67	96	99	114
	UNITED STATES	100	100	100	100	100	100	100	100	100	100	100	100	100	100	100	100	100	100	100	100

WISCONSIN

POPULATION CHANGE

53553-53950

ZIP CODE #	POST OFFICE NAME	COUNTY FIPS CODE	POPULATION 2000	POPULATION 2009	POPULATION 2014	2000-2009 ANNUAL RATE % Rate	2000-2009 ANNUAL RATE State Centile	HOUSEHOLDS 2000	HOUSEHOLDS 2009	HOUSEHOLDS 2014	HOUSEHOLDS % Annual Rate 2000-2009	HOUSEHOLDS 2009 Average HH Size	FAMILIES 2000	FAMILIES 2009	FAMILIES % Annual Rate 2000-2009
53553	LINDEN	049	700	779	814	1.2	81	249	284	299	1.4	2.61	185	209	1.3
53554	LIVINGSTON	043	1044	1163	1202	1.2	81	407	468	490	1.5	2.49	279	316	1.4
53555	LODI	021	7763	8201	8354	0.6	51	2986	3255	3345	0.9	2.49	2172	2340	0.8
53556	LONE ROCK	103	2728	2841	2885	0.4	39	1093	1188	1221	0.9	2.37	756	812	0.8
53557	LOWELL	027	436	448	450	0.3	32	166	177	179	0.7	2.53	123	130	0.6
53558	MC FARLAND	025	9186	10694	11724	1.7	91	3439	4033	4425	1.7	2.65	2524	2888	1.5
53559	MARSHALL	025	5427	6086	6445	1.2	81	1994	2267	2416	1.4	2.67	1510	1684	1.2
53560	MAZOMANIE	025	3419	3699	3860	0.9	68	1301	1444	1520	1.1	2.56	996	1087	0.9
53561	MERRIMAC	111	1613	1735	1778	0.8	61	697	781	808	1.2	2.22	486	538	1.1
53562	MIDDLETON	025	19303	22345	23826	1.6	91	8338	9872	10625	1.8	2.25	5057	5816	1.5
53563	MILTON	105	9365	11180	11878	1.9	94	3522	4275	4559	2.1	2.61	2630	3182	2.1
53565	MINERAL POINT	049	4601	4777	4767	0.4	39	1788	1917	1932	0.8	2.45	1232	1306	0.6
53566	MONROE	045	14605	15465	15731	0.6	51	6012	6547	6715	0.9	2.31	3876	4159	0.8
53569	MONTFORT	043	1174	1226	1237	0.5	44	423	452	461	0.7	2.71	304	321	0.6
53570	MONTICELLO	045	2336	2572	2679	1.0	72	920	1053	1107	1.5	2.42	648	729	1.3
53572	MOUNT HOREB	025	8449	9395	9941	1.2	81	3174	3588	3822	1.3	2.58	2288	2529	1.1
53573	MUSCODA	043	3439	3551	3585	0.3	32	1371	1466	1499	0.7	2.37	942	993	0.6
53574	NEW GLARUS	045	3132	3458	3604	1.1	76	1218	1393	1465	1.5	2.44	869	980	1.3
53575	OREGON	025	13530	15515	16603	1.5	88	4715	5559	6001	1.8	2.65	3621	4191	1.6
53576	ORFORDVILLE	105	2218	2552	2693	1.5	88	791	937	997	1.8	2.70	618	724	1.7
53577	PLAIN	111	1357	1440	1468	0.6	51	536	592	609	1.1	2.43	398	436	1.0
53578	PRAIRIE DU SAC	111	4992	5624	5877	1.3	84	1947	2262	2385	1.6	2.45	1341	1541	1.5
53579	REESEVILLE	027	1919	1945	1945	0.1	20	733	778	786	0.6	2.50	528	553	0.5
53580	REWEY	049	616	691	723	1.2	81	215	247	261	1.5	2.80	160	181	1.3
53581	RICHLAND CENTER	103	9997	10060	10074	0.1	20	4071	4251	4301	0.5	2.31	2630	2713	0.3
53582	RIDGEWAY	049	1133	1108	1076	-0.2	8	443	450	441	0.2	2.44	324	326	0.1
53583	SAUK CITY	111	5240	5596	5756	0.7	56	2072	2286	2368	1.1	2.43	1442	1573	0.9
53585	SHARON	127	2291	2572	2679	1.3	84	847	981	1026	1.6	2.62	641	732	1.4
53586	SHULLSBURG	065	2098	2210	2229	0.6	51	833	914	934	1.0	2.40	572	619	0.9
53587	SOUTH WAYNE	065	1295	1374	1400	0.6	51	506	562	579	1.1	2.44	363	399	1.0
53588	SPRING GREEN	111	3938	4144	4204	0.6	51	1512	1656	1695	1.0	2.45	1055	1141	0.9
53589	STOUGHTON	025	19369	20424	21110	0.6	51	7356	7914	8232	0.8	2.53	5240	5528	0.6
53590	SUN PRAIRIE	025	25777	33757	37331	3.0	97	9753	12949	14392	3.1	2.59	6962	9281	3.2
53593	VERONA	025	12943	20223	23514	4.9	99	4619	7332	8586	5.1	2.73	3498	5513	5.0
53594	WATERLOO	055	5125	5388	5518	0.5	44	1902	2050	2116	0.8	2.59	1365	1452	0.7
53597	WAUNAKEE	025	13334	16158	17523	2.1	96	4898	6055	6614	2.3	2.64	3596	4360	2.1
53598	WINDSOR	025	1877	2275	2473	2.1	96	721	904	992	2.5	2.51	546	668	2.2
53703	MADISON	025	26697	29348	30804	1.0	72	12693	14489	15428	1.4	1.79	1587	1623	0.2
53704	MADISON	025	44065	46027	47323	0.5	44	20012	21278	22013	0.7	2.12	10202	10528	0.3
53705	MADISON	025	23513	23740	24097	0.1	20	11007	11343	11599	0.3	2.07	6093	6087	0.0
53706	MADISON	025	6692	5539	5540	-2.0	0	20	20	20	0.0	2.75	2	2	0.0
53711	MADISON	025	41594	44356	45892	0.7	56	16978	18384	19140	0.9	2.38	10557	11176	0.6
53713	MADISON	025	22558	24076	24828	0.7	56	9753	10390	10755	0.7	2.29	4749	4806	0.1
53714	MADISON	025	15597	15493	15690	-0.1	11	6607	6730	6869	0.2	2.27	3989	3943	-0.1
53715	MADISON	025	10430	11689	11872	1.2	81	4487	4610	4711	0.3	2.19	962	916	-0.5
53716	MADISON	025	19209	18881	18952	-0.2	8	8109	8164	8266	0.1	2.30	5179	5069	-0.2
53717	MADISON	025	10724	12612	13580	1.8	93	4852	5866	6367	2.1	2.14	2724	3158	1.6
53718	MADISON	025	3552	9005	11177	10.6	100	1553	4065	5097	11.0	2.20	1028	2550	10.3
53719	MADISON	025	19690	26877	30161	3.4	98	8674	12146	13745	3.7	2.19	4706	6465	3.5
53726	MADISON	025	5095	5284	5429	0.4	39	2207	2374	2472	0.8	2.12	756	772	0.2
53801	BAGLEY	043	837	882	902	0.6	51	358	398	412	1.2	2.22	263	289	1.0
53803	BENTON	065	1153	1139	1118	-0.1	11	463	478	475	0.3	2.38	314	321	0.2
53804	BLOOMINGTON	043	1730	1749	1756	0.1	20	666	707	720	0.6	2.47	474	497	0.5
53805	BOSCOBEL	043	5294	5317	5297	0.0	16	2004	2076	2092	0.4	2.44	1361	1396	0.3
53806	CASSVILLE	043	2025	2052	2047	0.1	20	848	898	908	0.6	2.28	579	606	0.5
53807	CUBA CITY	043	6009	5957	5928	-0.1	11	2227	2320	2340	0.4	2.48	1626	1679	0.3
53809	FENNIMORE	043	3876	3930	3938	0.1	20	1526	1611	1636	0.6	2.39	1032	1075	0.4
53810	GLEN HAVEN	043	495	514	522	0.4	39	185	202	208	1.0	2.54	141	153	0.9
53811	HAZEL GREEN	043	3254	3324	3357	0.2	24	1167	1257	1286	0.8	2.56	878	935	0.7
53813	LANCASTER	043	6352	6134	6034	-0.4	2	2413	2409	2397	0.0	2.43	1649	1631	-0.1
53816	MOUNT HOPE	043	628	646	654	0.3	32	261	283	291	0.9	2.28	187	200	0.7
53818	PLATTEVILLE	043	13365	13610	13594	0.2	24	4503	4702	4753	0.5	2.35	2632	2709	0.3
53820	POTOSI	043	2595	2608	2620	0.1	20	987	1047	1066	0.6	2.49	731	767	0.5
53821	PRAIRIE DU CHIEN	023	8367	8299	8149	-0.1	11	3273	3288	3260	0.0	2.29	2139	2119	-0.1
53825	STITZER	043	431	468	479	0.9	68	147	165	171	1.3	2.84	112	125	1.2
53826	WAUZEKA	023	1609	1737	1773	0.8	61	582	656	679	1.3	2.64	421	468	1.2
53827	WOODMAN	043	351	362	367	0.3	32	136	148	152	0.9	2.45	96	103	0.8
53901	PORTAGE	021	13437	13980	14156	0.4	39	5253	5675	5804	0.8	2.28	3347	3569	0.7
53910	ADAMS	001	3571	3760	3861	0.6	51	1453	1613	1671	1.1	2.30	924	1015	1.0
53911	ARLINGTON	021	1285	1409	1454	1.0	72	485	552	575	1.4	2.55	372	419	1.3
53913	BARABOO	111	18340	20192	20909	1.0	72	7455	8464	8851	1.4	2.34	4880	5467	1.2
53916	BEAVER DAM	027	20933	21660	21859	0.4	39	8555	9144	9325	0.7	2.34	5688	6010	0.6
53919	BRANDON	039	2790	2971	3053	0.7	56	983	1074	1115	1.0	2.77	792	856	0.8
53920	BRIGGSVILLE	077	498	524	528	0.6	51	213	230	234	0.8	2.26	160	172	0.8
53922	BURNETT	027	1030	1059	1061	0.3	32	373	398	404	0.7	2.66	298	316	0.6
53923	CAMBRIA	021	2595	2784	2837	0.8	61	900	993	1023	1.1	2.80	674	737	1.0
53924	CAZENOVIA	103	1615	1676	1697	0.4	39	589	629	643	0.7	2.66	435	460	0.6
53925	COLUMBUS	021	7281	7718	7885	0.6	51	2843	3118	3217	1.0	2.44	1971	2135	0.9
53926	DALTON	047	1433	1493	1502	0.4	39	475	510	518	0.8	2.92	357	381	0.7
53929	ELROY	057	2957	3509	3543	1.9	94	1154	1247	1274	0.8	2.39	791	844	0.7
53930	ENDEAVOR	077	1293	1401	1446	0.9	68	464	518	539	1.2	2.68	341	377	1.1
53932	FALL RIVER	021	2155	2561	2718	1.9	94	799	975	1044	2.2	2.62	594	718	2.1
53933	FOX LAKE	027	3911	4185	4256	0.7	56	1110	1233	1278	1.1	2.47	754	824	1.0
53934	FRIENDSHIP	001	4560	4997	5065	1.0	72	1954	2191	2244	1.2	2.20	1311	1455	1.1
53936	GRAND MARSH	001	1385	2985	3073	8.7	100	579	669	709	1.6	2.65	394	452	1.5
53937	HILLPOINT	111	995	1049	1073	0.6	51	329	360	372	1.0	2.91	266	289	0.9
53939	KINGSTON	047	169	174	174	0.3	32	77	82	82	0.7	2.12	58	61	0.5
53941	LA VALLE	111	2669	3050	3212	1.5	88	977	1143	1212	1.7	2.67	770	894	1.6
53943	LOGANVILLE	111	1035	1104	1129	0.7	56	378	418	431	1.1	2.64	291	320	1.0
53944	LYNDON STATION	057	1663	1877	1970	1.3	84	669	775	822	1.6	2.38	488	559	1.5
53946	MARKESAN	047	4299	4289	4239	0.0	16	1737	1796	1791	0.4	2.37	1252	1283	0.3
53947	MARQUETTE	047	121	125	125	0.4	39	51	55	55	0.8	2.27	36	38	0.6
53948	MAUSTON	057	7839	8863	9065	1.3	84	3160	3478	3594	1.0	2.36	2122	2310	0.9
53949	MONTELLO	077	7141	6214	6343	-1.5	0	2470	2712	2794	1.0	2.25	1676	1821	0.9
53950	NEW LISBON	057	4082	4441	4533	0.9	68	1686	1867	1925	1.1	2.33	1164	1275	1.0
	WISCONSIN					0.7					1.0	2.43			0.9
	UNITED STATES					1.0					1.1	2.59			0.9

ZIP CODE #	POST OFFICE NAME	RACE (%) White 2000	White 2009	Black 2000	Black 2009	Asian/Pacific 2000	Asian/Pacific 2009	% Hispanic Origin 2000	% Hispanic Origin 2009	2009 AGE DISTRIBUTION (%) 0-4	5-9	10-14	15-19	20-24	25-44	45-64	65-84	85+	18+	MEDIAN AGE 2009	% 2009 Males	% 2009 Females
53553	LINDEN	98.9	98.8	0.3	0.3	0.0	0.0	0.1	0.1	7.1	8.0	8.1	7.1	4.5	27.1	23.0	12.2	3.1	72.1	37.5	50.1	49.9
53554	LIVINGSTON	99.6	99.6	0.0	0.0	0.0	0.0	0.3	0.3	6.1	6.9	7.1	7.2	3.9	26.8	27.6	12.6	1.9	75.2	39.5	51.5	48.5
53555	LODI	98.4	97.9	0.2	0.3	0.3	0.5	0.7	1.1	6.7	6.7	7.1	6.5	4.9	24.7	30.1	11.2	2.1	75.3	40.8	50.2	49.8
53556	LONE ROCK	98.4	98.0	0.1	0.2	0.2	0.3	1.0	1.4	6.1	6.5	6.8	6.5	5.6	26.1	28.8	11.7	1.9	76.6	39.7	49.6	50.4
53557	LOWELL	97.5	97.3	0.2	0.2	0.5	0.4	2.1	2.9	7.8	7.8	7.8	6.0	4.2	26.1	28.1	10.9	1.1	72.5	39.2	51.3	48.7
53558	MC FARLAND	97.1	95.9	0.3	0.5	0.8	1.3	1.4	2.2	5.8	6.5	7.2	7.2	5.0	25.0	33.0	9.2	1.0	75.5	40.3	49.7	50.3
53559	MARSHALL	95.3	93.0	0.8	1.1	0.3	0.4	4.1	6.6	7.8	7.7	8.1	7.3	4.6	26.9	27.0	9.2	1.4	71.8	36.8	50.8	49.2
53560	MAZOMANIE	97.4	96.4	0.5	0.7	0.2	0.3	1.4	2.2	5.9	6.6	7.2	6.9	4.4	25.4	32.3	10.0	1.4	75.9	41.3	50.3	49.7
53561	MERRIMAC	98.6	98.4	0.2	0.3	0.2	0.2	0.6	0.9	4.5	4.7	5.4	6.5	4.0	22.1	36.7	14.8	1.4	81.4	46.7	50.8	49.2
53562	MIDDLETON	93.1	90.4	1.7	2.2	2.4	3.9	2.4	3.4	5.6	5.4	5.8	6.2	7.3	28.2	31.0	8.9	1.6	79.1	39.2	48.6	51.4
53563	MILTON	98.0	97.2	0.2	0.3	0.5	0.8	1.2	1.8	6.1	6.3	6.7	7.2	6.2	26.3	30.0	9.8	1.3	76.3	38.8	50.0	50.0
53565	MINERAL POINT	98.7	98.5	0.2	0.2	0.3	0.4	0.5	0.7	6.6	6.9	7.0	6.4	4.9	25.3	28.8	11.5	2.6	75.3	40.2	49.5	50.5
53566	MONROE	98.0	97.5	0.3	0.4	0.3	0.4	1.2	1.7	6.0	6.1	6.4	6.7	6.0	23.9	28.5	13.3	3.2	77.2	41.1	48.3	51.7
53569	MONTFORT	99.0	98.8	0.2	0.2	0.2	0.2	0.1	0.2	6.2	6.0	6.5	8.0	7.7	25.3	27.5	11.2	1.6	76.4	37.2	51.4	48.6
53570	MONTICELLO	98.5	98.1	0.2	0.2	0.1	0.2	0.6	1.0	6.4	6.9	7.2	6.0	4.4	24.8	30.9	11.3	2.1	75.5	41.3	50.5	49.5
53572	MOUNT HOREB	98.1	97.4	0.3	0.4	0.4	0.7	0.7	1.1	7.6	7.8	7.6	6.3	5.4	27.6	25.7	9.5	2.5	72.7	36.9	48.9	51.1
53573	MUSCODA	98.5	97.9	0.2	0.3	0.2	0.3	1.0	1.4	5.9	6.2	6.4	6.6	5.4	23.7	28.8	13.7	3.3	77.4	42.1	51.1	48.9
53574	NEW GLARUS	98.5	98.0	0.1	0.1	0.3	0.5	1.0	1.5	6.4	6.9	7.3	7.1	5.0	23.7	29.6	10.9	3.2	74.8	40.9	48.8	51.2
53575	OREGON	95.0	93.4	3.4	4.3	0.6	1.0	1.0	1.5	6.5	6.8	7.3	7.0	6.0	27.9	29.6	7.7	1.2	74.9	38.0	51.6	48.4
53576	ORFORDVILLE	97.8	97.1	0.3	0.4	0.1	0.2	1.4	2.2	6.3	6.5	7.1	7.8	5.1	24.7	30.6	10.5	1.5	75.0	40.2	50.0	50.0
53577	PLAIN	98.7	98.5	0.1	0.1	0.0	0.0	0.9	1.3	6.5	7.3	7.6	7.2	4.2	21.7	31.6	12.0	1.9	74.1	41.7	52.3	47.7
53578	PRAIRIE DU SAC	97.7	96.9	0.2	0.2	0.4	0.7	2.5	3.6	6.5	6.2	6.3	6.7	6.4	24.8	28.6	11.7	2.8	76.7	40.2	49.6	50.4
53579	REESEVILLE	97.4	96.7	0.6	0.8	0.2	0.2	2.1	3.1	6.4	7.0	7.2	6.8	4.4	26.5	29.9	10.5	1.2	75.0	39.7	52.6	47.4
53580	REWEY	98.5	98.4	0.2	0.1	0.0	0.0	0.3	0.4	7.8	9.3	9.7	8.0	3.5	26.2	25.6	9.6	0.4	67.9	35.4	49.6	50.4
53581	RICHLAND CENTER	98.3	97.9	0.2	0.2	0.3	0.4	1.0	1.3	5.6	5.7	5.8	7.1	6.8	23.2	27.6	14.5	3.5	78.7	41.5	48.6	51.4
53582	RIDGEWAY	98.8	98.6	0.1	0.1	0.6	0.8	0.1	0.1	6.4	7.0	7.6	6.1	4.5	27.5	30.1	9.5	1.2	75.1	39.6	50.5	49.5
53583	SAUK CITY	98.0	97.4	0.2	0.2	0.2	0.3	2.2	3.2	6.5	6.5	6.6	6.5	6.4	25.1	29.4	10.9	2.1	76.5	39.8	49.9	50.1
53585	SHARON	95.2	93.6	0.3	0.5	0.3	0.5	5.4	8.0	6.5	6.8	7.2	7.3	5.8	25.0	30.4	10.0	1.1	75.0	38.5	50.7	49.3
53586	SHULLSBURG	99.2	99.0	0.0	0.1	0.4	0.5	0.0	0.0	6.0	6.5	6.6	6.7	4.9	23.5	29.1	14.3	2.5	77.1	41.8	49.9	50.1
53587	SOUTH WAYNE	99.7	99.6	0.1	0.1	0.0	0.0	0.6	0.9	5.6	6.3	6.6	7.1	4.7	23.2	32.5	12.3	1.8	77.1	42.7	52.2	47.8
53588	SPRING GREEN	98.8	98.6	0.1	0.1	0.1	0.1	0.7	1.0	5.9	6.0	6.4	6.3	5.6	23.1	31.0	13.0	2.7	77.6	42.7	49.4	50.6
53589	STOUGHTON	97.2	96.1	0.7	1.0	0.7	1.1	1.1	1.8	6.8	7.0	7.0	6.8	5.5	25.5	28.4	10.3	2.6	74.6	39.4	48.4	51.6
53590	SUN PRAIRIE	93.7	91.3	2.6	3.4	1.2	2.0	2.4	3.5	7.8	7.6	7.5	6.8	6.1	29.0	26.3	7.5	1.3	72.7	35.4	49.0	51.0
53593	VERONA	97.0	95.7	0.7	1.1	1.0	1.6	0.9	1.4	6.2	6.7	7.6	7.7	5.6	25.2	32.1	7.7	1.2	73.9	39.2	49.4	50.6
53594	WATERLOO	95.0	93.1	0.8	1.0	0.3	0.4	5.6	8.3	6.8	6.5	6.5	7.0	6.7	27.1	28.0	9.7	1.7	75.7	37.6	50.6	49.4
53597	WAUNAKEE	97.8	96.9	0.4	0.6	0.6	1.0	1.0	1.5	7.0	7.3	7.3	7.5	5.7	26.1	27.4	9.9	1.9	73.6	38.0	49.2	50.8
53598	WINDSOR	95.6	94.0	0.6	0.9	1.3	1.9	1.4	2.2	7.6	7.1	6.9	5.9	5.4	29.8	26.5	10.0	0.7	74.7	37.0	49.5	50.5
53703	MADISON	86.6	81.1	4.7	6.3	5.0	7.8	3.6	5.3	1.3	0.7	0.8	9.0	47.3	28.9	8.8	2.1	0.9	96.5	24.0	53.5	46.5
53704	MADISON	84.5	79.7	7.0	9.1	3.3	4.8	4.6	6.7	6.0	5.3	5.1	5.2	7.6	33.7	26.6	9.0	1.5	80.7	36.6	48.8	51.2
53705	MADISON	81.0	75.1	2.3	3.0	13.1	17.5	3.3	4.6	5.6	4.5	4.4	4.6	7.3	30.6	26.5	13.3	3.2	82.7	39.5	47.3	52.7
53706	MADISON	90.0	85.7	1.5	2.1	5.3	8.2	2.1	3.0	0.0	0.0	0.0	73.6	25.7	0.4	0.2	0.0	0.0	99.7	18.4	44.2	55.8
53711	MADISON	85.5	81.6	6.3	7.6	4.1	5.8	3.5	5.0	6.0	5.9	6.1	6.6	8.8	26.1	28.5	9.9	2.1	78.1	38.3	48.6	51.4
53713	MADISON	63.1	55.2	17.1	20.2	7.1	9.2	14.9	19.0	8.1	5.9	4.9	6.5	13.3	36.7	18.7	5.3	0.6	77.9	29.0	51.1	48.9
53714	MADISON	88.3	84.3	5.8	7.7	2.1	3.1	3.4	5.0	5.7	5.7	5.8	5.9	6.3	29.2	28.8	10.6	2.0	79.4	39.5	48.7	51.3
53715	MADISON	82.7	77.0	3.9	4.7	9.5	13.5	3.6	5.0	1.6	1.2	1.4	14.5	43.2	19.5	11.6	5.1	1.9	94.6	23.6	52.9	47.1
53716	MADISON	93.3	90.6	2.6	3.7	1.2	2.0	2.4	3.6	4.9	5.0	5.5	6.1	6.2	25.0	31.5	13.7	2.1	81.0	43.2	48.4	51.6
53717	MADISON	86.4	82.2	3.9	4.7	6.0	8.7	3.6	4.8	5.9	5.3	5.6	6.0	7.4	30.8	28.4	9.4	1.2	79.3	36.9	48.1	51.9
53718	MADISON	95.3	93.1	1.8	2.7	1.0	1.6	1.6	2.4	5.9	5.7	5.8	5.7	5.7	30.0	29.8	10.3	1.2	78.9	39.3	49.3	50.7
53719	MADISON	85.6	80.9	5.1	6.2	5.0	7.5	5.0	6.9	7.7	6.2	5.2	4.9	10.5	38.7	20.5	5.0	1.2	77.9	31.2	49.6	50.4
53726	MADISON	85.5	78.8	1.5	2.0	10.1	15.4	2.5	3.7	2.4	2.3	2.7	7.9	37.7	22.1	18.6	5.4	0.8	90.8	24.6	52.0	48.0
53801	BAGLEY	98.1	97.5	0.0	0.0	0.2	0.5	0.7	1.1	4.8	5.4	5.9	6.6	4.9	21.1	31.3	18.0	2.0	79.9	45.8	51.4	48.6
53803	BENTON	99.0	98.7	0.1	0.1	0.7	1.0	0.0	0.0	6.4	6.3	6.7	6.8	5.3	22.7	29.6	14.3	1.8	76.6	41.6	49.8	50.2
53804	BLOOMINGTON	99.5	99.4	0.0	0.0	0.1	0.1	0.3	0.5	5.2	5.8	6.9	8.3	4.5	24.4	29.1	14.0	1.9	76.6	41.8	51.3	48.7
53805	BOSCOBEL	96.7	96.0	2.2	2.6	0.2	0.3	0.9	1.2	6.1	6.0	6.5	6.8	6.5	25.5	25.7	13.7	3.3	77.2	39.4	50.7	49.3
53806	CASSVILLE	99.2	99.1	0.0	0.0	0.0	0.1	0.3	0.5	5.0	5.0	5.6	7.1	6.1	21.3	30.2	17.2	2.5	79.6	44.9	50.4	49.6
53807	CUBA CITY	99.2	99.1	0.1	0.1	0.2	0.3	0.2	0.2	6.1	6.6	6.9	6.7	4.5	24.2	27.9	14.2	2.9	75.9	41.2	49.8	50.2
53809	FENNIMORE	99.0	98.8	0.1	0.1	0.3	0.4	0.8	1.1	6.1	6.2	6.5	6.6	5.7	24.8	27.1	13.6	3.4	77.3	40.2	49.9	50.1
53810	GLEN HAVEN	99.6	99.2	0.0	0.0	0.0	0.2	0.2	0.4	5.1	5.4	6.0	7.0	4.5	23.3	30.2	16.9	1.6	78.8	44.1	51.8	48.2
53811	HAZEL GREEN	99.2	99.0	0.1	0.2	0.2	0.2	0.3	0.5	6.2	6.2	6.4	6.6	5.5	23.8	28.2	14.5	2.6	77.1	41.2	48.0	52.0
53813	LANCASTER	99.3	99.1	0.1	0.1	0.2	0.3	0.3	0.5	5.8	6.2	6.5	7.2	6.1	24.1	27.4	13.3	3.4	76.9	40.4	49.5	50.5
53816	MOUNT HOPE	99.8	99.8	0.0	0.0	0.0	0.0	0.5	0.6	5.1	5.6	6.2	6.5	4.2	24.8	32.4	13.9	1.4	78.8	43.2	52.5	47.5
53818	PLATTEVILLE	96.6	95.5	0.9	1.2	1.3	1.9	0.7	1.0	3.9	4.1	4.4	14.9	22.0	18.8	19.9	9.8	2.2	84.0	25.6	54.0	46.0
53820	POTOSI	99.3	99.2	0.0	0.0	0.0	0.1	0.5	0.8	5.8	6.2	6.6	7.2	5.0	24.4	30.0	13.4	1.5	76.9	41.5	52.0	48.0
53821	PRAIRIE DU CHIEN	96.0	95.0	2.6	3.4	0.3	0.4	0.7	1.0	5.8	5.9	6.3	9.4	7.1	22.3	26.5	13.3	3.4	76.4	39.6	51.6	48.4
53825	STITZER	99.3	99.1	0.2	0.2	0.2	0.4	0.5	0.4	7.3	8.1	8.1	8.3	4.9	25.2	27.1	9.8	1.1	70.7	36.5	52.6	47.4
53826	WAUZEKA	99.2	98.9	0.0	0.0	0.3	0.5	0.6	0.8	7.8	8.0	8.0	7.3	5.2	26.2	26.7	9.5	1.3	71.2	35.4	51.3	48.7
53827	WOODMAN	99.7	99.7	0.0	0.0	0.0	0.0	0.6	0.6	5.2	5.8	5.8	5.2	3.6	24.9	32.9	14.6	1.9	79.8	44.5	52.2	47.8
53901	PORTAGE	94.4	93.0	2.9	3.6	0.6	0.8	2.7	3.7	5.7	5.4	5.4	6.2	7.8	27.3	27.1	12.1	2.8	79.7	39.3	51.2	48.8
53910	ADAMS	97.2	96.6	0.3	0.4	0.3	0.4	1.8	2.6	6.2	6.3	6.5	6.5	5.0	21.9	28.4	16.5	2.7	77.0	43.0	49.0	51.0
53911	ARLINGTON	98.9	98.7	0.1	0.1	0.1	0.1	0.9	1.4	6.5	7.1	7.3	6.2	4.3	24.2	32.2	10.9	1.4	75.2	41.3	52.5	47.5
53913	BARABOO	96.7	95.9	0.4	0.5	0.4	0.6	1.9	2.7	6.6	6.3	6.4	6.7	6.3	26.4	27.7	11.2	2.4	76.7	39.0	49.0	51.0
53916	BEAVER DAM	96.2	95.0	0.4	0.5	0.6	0.7	3.9	5.6	6.7	6.6	6.6	6.1	5.9	25.4	27.7	12.3	2.7	76.3	39.7	49.2	50.8
53919	BRANDON	99.1	98.9	0.1	0.1	0.1	0.1	0.7	1.1	7.4	7.9	7.8	7.2	4.9	24.5	28.2	10.5	1.4	72.4	38.3	50.6	49.4
53920	BRIGGSVILLE	97.6	95.8	0.6	1.3	0.0	0.2	1.2	1.7	5.3	5.7	7.4	4.6	2.9	23.5	31.1	18.3	1.1	77.9	45.3	50.6	49.4
53922	BURNETT	98.5	98.1	0.2	0.2	0.2	0.3	1.2	1.8	6.4	6.9	7.0	6.1	5.2	23.1	31.5	12.2	1.5	75.8	42.0	52.3	47.7
53923	CAMBRIA	97.0	96.1	0.1	0.1	0.1	0.2	2.8	3.9	7.8	7.7	7.6	7.2	5.5	24.2	27.2	11.0	1.8	72.4	37.1	50.8	49.2
53924	CAZENOVIA	98.6	98.4	0.1	0.1	0.2	0.3	0.5	0.7	6.3	6.9	7.0	7.0	4.5	23.2	30.1	13.4	1.7	75.5	41.0	52.5	47.5
53925	COLUMBUS	98.2	97.6	0.4	0.5	0.3	0.4	1.2	1.8	6.4	6.2	6.4	6.6	6.1	25.2	27.9	12.2	2.8	76.5	40.1	49.3	50.7
53926	DALTON	97.6	97.5	0.1	0.1	0.1	0.1	1.4	1.6	7.5	7.8	7.6	7.3	5.5	24.0	27.7	10.9	1.7	72.4	37.4	49.2	50.8
53929	ELROY	98.8	98.4	0.2	0.3	0.2	0.3	0.7	1.1	5.1	5.1	5.3	6.7	7.1	27.2	27.7	12.5	3.4	79.9	40.1	54.7	45.3
53930	ENDEAVOR	96.9	95.6	0.3	0.6	0.4	0.6	2.4	3.9	7.1	7.1	7.4	6.8	6.2	25.8	27.1	11.3	1.2	74.3	37.6	50.0	50.0
53932	FALL RIVER	98.4	97.8	0.4	0.5	0.2	0.3	1.1	1.6	7.1	7.3	7.4	6.4	5.2	27.9	28.0	9.4	1.3	74.1	38.4	50.4	49.6
53933	FOX LAKE	85.6	82.2	12.4	15.5	0.2	0.2	3.3	4.6	3.2	3.8	4.5	5.2	9.3	34.9	25.2	11.9	2.0	85.3	38.5	63.5	36.5
53934	FRIENDSHIP	97.6	97.1	0.2	0.3	0.4	0.6	1.5	2.1	4.4	4.6	4.9	5.6	4.3	19.3	31.8	21.6	3.4	82.5	49.4	50.7	49.3
53936	GRAND MARSH	97.6	92.8	0.4	3.4	0.1	1.2	2.0	3.0	2.8	3.1	3.4	3.6	6.6	40.0	27.7	11.8	1.1	89.0	40.1	71.2	28.8
53937	HILLPOINT	99.3	99.0	0.1	0.2	0.0	0.0	1.2	1.7	7.0	7.4	7.7	7.6	5.1	23.6	29.6	10.5	1.4	73.0	39.0	51.1	48.9
53939	KINGSTON	97.6	97.7	0.0	0.0	0.0	0.0	1.2	1.1	8.0	8.6	8.0	7.5	5.7	24.1	26.4	9.8	1.7	70.1	35.0	47.7	52.3
53941	LA VALLE	98.7	98.4	0.2	0.2	0.0	0.1	1.0	1.5	6.5	7.0	7.0	6.6	5.2	22.9	29.1	14.2	1.7	75.5	41.0	50.0	50.0
53943	LOGANVILLE	99.2	99.0	0.0	0.1	0.0	0.0	1.7	2.5	6.9	7.5	7.4	6.6	4.3	23.9	30.3	11.8	1.4	73.9	40.5	50.7	49.3
53944	LYNDON STATION	91.0	89.6	0.7	0.8	0.2	0.3	1.7	2.5	6.0	6.3	6.7	6.8	5.2	24.5	30.5	12.8	1.3	76.7	41.2	51.8	48.2
53946	MARKESAN	98.8	98.7	0.2	0.3	0.1	0.1	1.5	1.6	5.9	6.1	5.9	5.5	5.2	22.6	30.5	16.0	2.4	78.7	44.0	50.3	49.7
53947	MARQUETTE	98.3	98.4	0.0	0.0	0.0	0.0	0.8	1.6	4.8	5.6	5.6	4.8	3.2	16.8	38.4	18.4	2.4	80.0	48.8	52.8	47.2
53948	MAUSTON	97.0	96.1	0.5	0.6	0.8	1.2	1.5	2.0	5.5	5.5	5.8	6.6	6.5	25.6	27.5	14.3	2.7	79.1	40.9	51.7	48.3
53949	MONTELLO	88.6	86.6	7.2	8.3	0.4	0.6	4.1	5.4	4.6	4.7	4.8	6.7	5.7	24.1	29.0	18.0	2.6	82.8	44.6	53.3	46.7
53950	NEW LISBON	97.8	97.3	0.1	0.2	0.5	0.7	1.0	1.4	5.9	5.6	6.0	6.6	5.5	22.6	29.8	15.5	2.5	78.4	43.4	50.5	49.5
	WISCONSIN	88.9	86.9	5.7	6.3	1.7	2.3	3.6	4.8	6.4	6.4	6.5	7.2	7.2	26.0	27.1	11.1	2.2	76.6	38.0	49.5	50.5
	UNITED STATES	75.1	72.0	12.3	12.7	3.8	4.6	12.5	15.7	6.8	6.7	6.6	7.1	6.9	27.0	26.0	10.9	1.9	75.7	36.9	49.2	50.8

ZIP CODE #	POST OFFICE NAME	2009 Per Capita Income	2009 HH Income Base	2009 HOUSEHOLD INCOME DISTRIBUTION (%) Less than $25,000	$25,000 to $49,999	$50,000 to $99,999	$100,000 to $149,999	$150,000 or More	MEDIAN HOUSEHOLD INCOME 2009	2014	2009 National Centile	2009 State Centile	2009 Home Value Base	2009 HOME VALUE DISTRIBUTION (%) Less than $50,000	$50,000 to $89,999	$90,000 to $174,999	$175,000 to $399,999	$400,000 or More	2009 Median Home Value
53553	LINDEN	21069	284	21.1	30.6	38.0	7.4	2.8	48096	50940	57	43	224	12.5	19.6	38.4	23.2	6.3	126786
53554	LIVINGSTON	19846	468	27.1	31.6	34.6	5.1	1.5	43031	45334	42	24	365	13.2	24.4	46.8	12.1	3.6	103209
53555	LODI	29882	3255	12.3	21.9	47.3	13.4	5.0	65560	67222	84	85	2606	4.3	3.2	30.2	53.0	9.4	199245
53556	LONE ROCK	23541	1188	18.4	31.6	43.3	4.3	2.4	49909	51537	61	48	931	14.8	18.9	46.9	16.2	3.1	112807
53557	LOWELL	21909	177	19.8	25.4	48.0	5.1	1.7	52752	54021	67	58	136	6.6	6.6	44.9	38.2	3.7	158824
53558	MC FARLAND	34347	4033	6.4	18.2	39.6	28.0	7.8	78789	81521	91	95	3102	2.1	0.7	13.5	74.7	9.0	228468
53559	MARSHALL	25411	2267	11.5	25.8	47.9	11.6	3.2	61174	63641	79	75	1779	12.9	6.0	21.4	53.6	6.1	195514
53560	MAZOMANIE	28424	1444	10.2	24.3	46.1	15.7	3.6	63376	66478	82	83	1174	6.7	6.4	33.6	46.4	6.9	182738
53561	MERRIMAC	30016	781	17.0	24.8	43.3	10.1	4.7	56708	58348	74	66	649	6.2	6.5	32.0	43.9	11.4	192250
53562	MIDDLETON	42305	9872	10.4	20.8	34.0	20.3	14.5	72539	77744	88	92	5873	1.0	0.3	16.7	62.0	20.0	260233
53563	MILTON	29089	4275	9.4	24.9	44.5	16.3	5.1	68183	71641	86	88	3247	1.7	4.8	50.9	40.0	2.6	161698
53565	MINERAL POINT	23620	1917	19.4	29.3	41.6	7.4	2.3	51173	53968	64	53	1381	4.9	16.4	48.7	25.5	4.5	133496
53566	MONROE	26872	6547	21.0	27.6	40.5	6.8	4.0	51133	53489	64	53	4376	3.8	11.0	58.0	24.9	2.3	137951
53569	MONTFORT	19572	452	20.6	33.6	38.7	5.5	1.5	46696	49897	53	39	359	12.5	26.5	47.4	12.0	1.7	103827
53570	MONTICELLO	26145	1053	18.0	25.0	46.3	7.0	3.6	55472	57148	72	64	803	1.7	7.7	54.8	29.9	5.9	147393
53572	MOUNT HOREB	31180	3588	9.6	19.5	43.7	21.5	5.6	70761	75503	87	91	2480	1.7	2.1	18.8	66.0	11.4	224821
53573	MUSCODA	20157	1466	29.1	31.9	33.8	3.8	1.6	40432	42384	34	14	1128	17.5	30.5	37.1	12.8	2.2	92212
53574	NEW GLARUS	28293	1393	13.7	24.8	47.0	10.1	4.4	62942	63947	81	82	1096	5.4	3.6	41.4	42.5	7.0	174277
53575	OREGON	33670	5559	6.7	14.6	42.9	27.3	8.5	78899	81462	92	95	4299	2.6	2.6	17.4	70.1	7.4	225611
53576	ORFORDVILLE	23735	937	14.5	28.0	44.3	9.9	3.3	58141	60614	75	69	766	4.6	13.3	51.3	27.9	2.9	133486
53577	PLAIN	25483	592	19.6	28.2	39.2	9.1	3.9	51814	54265	66	55	468	2.6	8.1	44.4	35.7	9.2	159615
53578	PRAIRIE DU SAC	29752	2262	15.0	25.0	41.4	11.9	6.6	59542	61085	77	72	1590	3.1	3.6	34.3	53.6	5.3	188143
53579	REESEVILLE	22586	778	18.0	26.7	48.6	4.8	1.9	52992	54366	68	58	591	8.8	9.5	48.2	30.5	3.0	146379
53580	REWEY	19281	247	23.5	35.2	34.4	4.0	2.8	43799	46490	45	27	183	16.4	21.3	33.9	19.1	9.3	114205
53581	RICHLAND CENTER	21480	4251	29.2	30.3	33.5	5.2	1.9	40735	42294	35	15	2925	10.0	24.2	50.4	13.5	2.0	107104
53582	RIDGEWAY	24025	450	20.2	26.9	42.2	8.7	2.0	53222	56373	68	59	369	2.2	13.3	43.9	31.2	9.5	153963
53583	SAUK CITY	27282	2286	16.1	24.9	44.5	11.3	3.2	58956	60820	76	70	1629	2.0	2.2	47.8	41.6	6.3	172375
53585	SHARON	21796	981	16.8	31.8	42.1	7.5	1.7	51220	53135	64	52	724	0.8	9.0	54.1	29.6	6.5	153958
53586	SHULLSBURG	20227	914	28.0	32.2	33.7	4.7	1.4	41878	43391	39	20	724	11.0	31.4	46.1	9.7	1.8	97237
53587	SOUTH WAYNE	22344	562	23.7	29.5	37.5	6.8	2.5	47419	49462	55	42	431	10.7	22.3	48.7	14.4	3.9	110918
53588	SPRING GREEN	26810	1656	16.2	25.3	44.4	9.3	4.8	58183	59850	75	69	1301	5.7	9.9	43.4	35.8	5.2	155321
53589	STOUGHTON	30899	7914	10.9	21.7	42.4	18.9	6.1	67230	72139	85	88	5779	2.8	2.0	30.9	58.2	6.1	202282
53590	SUN PRAIRIE	33184	12949	8.5	18.8	40.8	23.8	8.1	74878	78659	89	93	8630	0.8	0.2	23.4	69.7	5.9	221794
53593	VERONA	41543	7332	7.6	12.3	34.0	27.0	19.1	92890	94016	96	99	5827	1.1	0.4	12.9	66.3	19.2	264893
53594	WATERLOO	28237	2050	10.9	25.4	46.5	12.1	5.1	64423	65872	83	84	1570	8.0	6.2	39.5	42.7	3.6	169528
53597	WAUNAKEE	34393	6055	6.2	18.9	42.0	23.6	9.3	73881	77748	89	92	4314	2.5	0.1	9.4	75.1	13.0	253975
53598	WINDSOR	39623	904	5.6	16.6	42.9	23.6	11.3	74773	78656	89	93	583	0.0	0.3	26.9	66.6	6.2	215062
53703	MADISON	19241	12489	49.9	29.1	15.7	3.5	1.7	25024	24351	3	1	1438	1.3	4.7	23.6	59.3	11.0	219970
53704	MADISON	31244	21278	15.8	28.3	39.2	12.2	4.5	56111	60435	73	65	11442	2.9	3.5	47.4	42.5	3.7	170602
53705	MADISON	40464	11343	18.0	21.3	32.5	15.9	12.2	62478	65628	81	79	5769	1.3	1.4	17.7	66.1	13.4	237228
53706	MADISON	13414	20	80.0	20.0	0.0	0.0	0.0	16233	16233	1	0	0	0.0	0.0	0.0	0.0	0.0	0
53711	MADISON	36556	18384	10.7	20.0	38.3	21.3	9.8	70630	74870	87	91	11570	0.9	1.0	17.3	70.4	10.4	226306
53713	MADISON	24731	10390	22.5	36.7	29.6	7.2	4.0	41957	43695	39	20	3145	15.7	6.6	31.8	34.6	11.3	165634
53714	MADISON	29782	6730	12.0	24.4	45.1	16.1	2.5	61628	64221	80	77	4322	2.4	0.5	57.1	39.1	0.8	165407
53715	MADISON	17451	4610	44.0	29.0	20.7	4.7	1.6	28932	29610	7	1	927	2.0	0.9	41.4	51.3	4.3	184795
53716	MADISON	31744	8164	11.0	20.4	47.1	17.6	3.8	65501	68675	84	85	5827	1.5	0.6	40.7	53.0	4.3	185278
53717	MADISON	47572	5866	9.8	18.0	34.2	21.7	16.3	77467	81392	91	94	3396	1.9	0.6	14.2	65.7	17.6	268117
53718	MADISON	40760	4065	5.3	17.4	39.6	29.1	8.6	79474	82317	92	95	2844	1.7	0.2	17.7	72.2	8.3	229340
53719	MADISON	37855	12146	8.0	20.1	43.5	20.6	7.9	70112	74875	87	90	5557	2.2	1.2	14.3	74.6	7.6	227072
53726	MADISON	29180	2374	43.6	16.2	19.0	13.3	8.0	32358	34347	12	2	809	0.0	0.0	3.7	63.7	32.6	330100
53801	BAGLEY	20186	398	32.2	35.9	26.6	3.3	2.0	35658	37241	20	3	329	18.2	28.6	28.3	20.7	4.3	96176
53803	BENTON	19189	478	32.2	33.1	28.7	4.8	1.3	36048	37933	21	4	377	9.5	30.0	51.7	7.2	1.6	98404
53804	BLOOMINGTON	19931	707	26.2	35.6	32.2	4.7	1.3	41664	43742	38	19	577	19.4	30.0	35.0	12.7	2.9	90875
53805	BOSCOBEL	19176	2076	27.5	32.2	36.3	2.7	1.3	42355	44789	40	22	1516	16.6	25.9	41.9	13.5	2.2	97808
53806	CASSVILLE	19097	898	33.7	34.3	27.5	3.2	1.2	36600	37965	22	4	697	20.2	29.6	37.4	11.3	1.4	90211
53807	CUBA CITY	21683	2320	20.1	32.2	40.0	5.8	1.9	48143	50819	57	43	1788	4.5	18.9	55.4	18.3	2.9	125368
53809	FENNIMORE	21479	1611	25.0	32.0	36.4	5.3	1.3	44260	47029	46	30	1167	13.4	25.2	43.0	15.6	2.8	106551
53810	GLEN HAVEN	17411	202	31.2	34.7	29.7	4.0	0.5	36877	38281	23	4	157	13.4	26.1	35.7	20.4	4.5	104861
53811	HAZEL GREEN	22953	1257	15.4	31.3	44.1	7.1	2.2	52395	54304	67	56	997	7.3	19.2	51.2	19.8	2.6	122656
53813	LANCASTER	21386	2409	24.0	31.2	36.6	5.8	2.5	45089	48479	49	33	1740	8.0	22.5	51.2	16.6	1.8	110401
53816	MOUNT HOPE	21569	283	24.7	35.3	33.2	5.3	1.4	42905	45374	42	24	228	23.7	25.4	32.9	14.0	3.9	91538
53818	PLATTEVILLE	21889	4702	24.6	27.8	37.1	7.5	3.1	47575	50779	56	42	2778	5.7	14.5	57.5	19.8	2.5	124683
53820	POTOSI	20613	1047	21.2	33.6	39.3	5.0	1.0	46017	48968	51	37	842	13.5	20.8	46.1	18.2	1.4	112500
53821	PRAIRIE DU CHIEN	23030	3288	25.7	28.1	37.5	5.8	2.9	46105	48165	52	37	2383	14.2	23.5	47.8	13.3	1.2	106815
53825	STITZER	18690	165	23.0	29.7	38.8	6.7	1.8	47610	50148	56	42	132	10.6	14.4	46.2	25.8	3.0	125000
53826	WAUZEKA	19288	656	25.0	27.7	41.6	4.7	0.9	46677	49068	53	39	517	18.6	26.5	40.8	11.6	2.5	95795
53827	WOODMAN	19692	148	23.6	34.5	36.5	4.7	0.7	43990	45501	45	28	119	25.2	26.9	31.1	13.4	3.4	86875
53901	PORTAGE	25295	5675	20.2	27.5	42.1	7.5	2.7	52047	54939	66	55	3814	6.8	10.3	53.4	26.5	3.1	139497
53910	ADAMS	18992	1613	33.4	33.7	27.9	3.8	1.2	36495	37644	22	4	1191	15.5	32.7	43.3	7.7	0.8	91807
53911	ARLINGTON	26607	552	11.4	26.1	48.2	10.9	3.4	61519	62936	79	76	419	1.0	3.3	36.5	52.7	6.4	190779
53913	BARABOO	25410	8464	18.7	28.1	43.3	6.8	3.1	52654	54840	67	57	5889	11.3	12.5	44.7	27.8	3.7	136668
53916	BEAVER DAM	25537	9144	18.4	27.4	43.7	7.5	2.9	53386	55544	69	60	6263	7.2	9.2	54.0	27.5	2.1	139786
53919	BRANDON	21526	1074	17.3	26.7	46.5	7.2	2.3	54202	56617	70	61	888	3.9	19.5	53.5	21.8	1.2	124273
53920	BRIGGSVILLE	24453	230	15.7	32.2	45.7	5.7	0.9	51546	53390	65	54	193	4.1	14.5	52.3	25.9	3.1	126786
53922	BURNETT	25623	398	13.8	21.9	49.5	12.6	2.3	62797	63157	81	81	343	4.1	7.9	42.0	40.2	5.8	166964
53923	CAMBRIA	20421	993	19.3	29.0	42.5	7.0	2.1	51099	53707	64	53	797	7.5	16.2	48.6	23.7	4.0	132372
53924	CAZENOVIA	20101	629	25.0	29.9	38.5	3.7	3.0	45073	47004	48	33	508	12.2	20.3	44.3	20.9	2.4	115805
53925	COLUMBUS	27371	3118	14.8	24.1	48.6	9.6	2.9	60852	62375	79	75	2208	3.9	4.3	46.6	40.0	5.3	167626
53926	DALTON	17653	510	18.8	36.7	39.0	4.1	1.4	45435	48096	50	35	423	6.1	20.3	47.5	23.2	2.8	126025
53929	ELROY	20903	1247	24.6	29.5	38.7	5.1	2.1	46217	48139	52	38	917	12.2	30.8	40.2	14.1	2.7	97414
53930	ENDEAVOR	19310	518	23.2	27.0	45.2	3.3	1.4	49803	51112	61	48	434	12.4	15.9	51.4	18.0	2.3	120930
53932	FALL RIVER	23888	975	16.6	25.4	44.5	11.4	2.1	57770	60397	75	68	752	7.2	8.2	40.6	41.5	2.5	164183
53933	FOX LAKE	22098	1233	17.2	27.5	44.8	7.1	3.3	54589	56674	71	62	966	3.7	12.5	44.4	34.2	5.2	146667
53934	FRIENDSHIP	21738	2191	28.7	34.0	30.9	4.6	1.9	38583	40313	28	8	1818	14.6	31.1	40.1	12.6	1.5	94783
53936	GRAND MARSH	15602	669	27.1	37.4	31.1	4.0	0.4	39306	41034	31	11	579	15.0	25.7	44.9	13.1	1.2	101894
53937	HILLPOINT	19168	360	23.1	27.2	40.3	8.3	1.1	49747	51740	60	47	302	5.0	10.9	42.4	30.5	11.3	155469
53939	KINGSTON	23850	82	19.5	39.0	36.6	3.7	1.2	43854	46864	45	27	67	6.0	25.4	49.3	16.4	3.0	117045
53941	LA VALLE	22086	1143	19.0	30.1	41.2	6.6	3.1	50649	52755	63	51	983	6.5	14.2	42.3	31.8	5.1	149121
53943	LOGANVILLE	21181	418	18.7	32.3	40.2	6.2	2.6	49155	51646	59	46	313	4.5	10.5	48.2	26.5	10.2	142448
53944	LYNDON STATION	22380	775	21.5	33.9	36.9	5.4	2.2	44939	46722	48	32	614	10.4	19.1	46.1	20.7	3.7	126176
53946	MARKESAN	26000	1796	18.8	27.8	42.4	7.9	3.1	52513	53859	67	56	1396	3.5	15.3	52.3	22.3	6.6	134624
53947	MARQUETTE	23288	55	23.6	30.9	40.0	5.5	0.0	45760	50574	51	36	47	2.1	12.8	44.7	34.0	6.4	156250
53948	MAUSTON	21779	3478	24.5	32.1	36.4	4.8	2.2	43918	46156	45	28	2541	13.5	31.4	38.7	14.5	1.8	95977
53949	MONTELLO	21454	2712	26.1	34.2	34.4	3.8	1.5	42459	44449	41	22	2229	10.0	17.7	48.6	21.5	2.2	123135
53950	NEW LISBON	22613	1867	24.8	32.0	36.5	4.5	2.2	43882	45781	45	27	1481	12.4	28.1	44.2	13.8	1.6	99895
	WISCONSIN	27384		18.4	25.3	40.0	11.0	5.2	56363	58927				5.6	11.9	43.5	34.2	4.7	150766
	UNITED STATES	27277		20.9	24.4	35.3	11.7	7.6	54719	56938				9.3	13.1	31.6	32.6	13.5	162279

ZIP CODE #	POST OFFICE NAME	FINANCIAL SERVICES: Auto Loan	Home Loan	Investments	Retirement Plans	THE HOME: Home Improvements: Home Repair	Lawn & Garden	Furnishings: Computers & Hardware Personal	Major Appliances	TV, Radio, Sound Equipment	Furniture	ENTERTAINMENT: Dine out/ Carry out	Sports Equipment	Fees & Tickets	Toys & Games	Travel	Cable TV	PERSONAL: Apparel & Services	Auto Repairs	Health Insurance	Pets & Supplies
53553	LINDEN	100	69	110	69	72	106	77	95	80	62	79	79	56	78	76	87	51	89	100	117
53554	LIVINGSTON	88	61	97	61	63	93	67	84	70	55	69	69	49	69	67	76	45	78	88	103
53555	LODI	104	112	112	112	111	112	105	109	104	103	104	85	109	104	111	105	73	107	109	128
53556	LONE ROCK	86	78	77	81	77	91	78	85	80	71	79	66	73	82	78	84	54	81	90	101
53557	LOWELL	85	79	77	82	80	92	77	87	79	70	78	66	72	81	77	84	53	80	89	101
53558	MC FARLAND	125	147	131	146	142	129	130	130	123	136	126	102	141	128	136	119	90	126	119	150
53559	MARSHALL	104	105	90	103	101	101	96	100	96	100	97	75	95	100	94	96	67	96	97	117
53560	MAZOMANIE	101	114	99	117	111	112	102	106	100	102	101	82	109	103	108	101	71	102	106	124
53561	MERRIMAC	108	92	134	91	98	115	90	110	93	85	92	81	81	90	97	98	62	102	109	128
53562	MIDDLETON	131	139	133	143	137	129	138	130	133	140	135	104	143	135	139	130	96	133	126	154
53563	MILTON	101	116	104	116	113	109	108	107	105	107	106	84	115	107	113	105	75	106	106	125
53565	MINERAL POINT	96	77	94	78	79	99	81	92	84	73	83	72	69	84	79	89	55	88	97	111
53566	MONROE	91	86	85	87	85	97	88	91	91	82	90	70	85	90	87	95	62	91	99	109
53569	MONTFORT	82	72	76	73	69	87	75	79	76	67	76	64	68	77	73	80	51	78	86	97
53570	MONTICELLO	99	90	95	93	91	107	88	100	90	80	89	78	81	91	89	95	61	93	102	118
53572	MOUNT HOREB	117	124	107	124	118	111	117	114	113	121	115	90	120	118	117	110	80	113	108	133
53573	MUSCODA	85	62	86	61	64	87	64	80	70	58	69	61	51	70	63	76	45	74	83	95
53574	NEW GLARUS	92	108	97	108	105	104	97	99	96	97	97	76	106	98	104	97	69	97	100	115
53575	OREGON	129	147	132	146	143	133	131	133	126	136	128	104	139	130	136	123	90	128	124	153
53576	ORFORDVILLE	99	91	90	95	93	107	90	101	92	81	91	76	83	94	89	98	62	93	104	117
53577	PLAIN	110	77	121	77	80	116	85	105	88	69	87	87	63	86	84	96	57	98	111	129
53578	PRAIRIE DU SAC	104	104	110	104	105	109	104	107	104	100	104	82	103	103	106	106	72	106	109	125
53579	REESEVILLE	85	82	78	85	82	92	79	87	80	73	79	66	75	82	80	84	54	81	89	102
53580	REWEY	96	66	106	66	69	102	74	92	77	60	76	76	54	75	73	84	49	85	97	113
53581	RICHLAND CENTER	79	62	77	63	64	81	70	77	73	62	72	60	59	72	67	78	48	75	84	92
53582	RIDGEWAY	102	75	111	75	78	108	81	98	83	68	83	80	63	82	81	90	54	92	103	120
53583	SAUK CITY	92	97	94	97	96	98	94	95	93	91	94	75	96	94	97	94	66	95	97	113
53585	SHARON	90	83	77	83	82	90	80	86	82	78	82	64	75	85	78	85	56	82	88	102
53586	SHULLSBURG	84	59	88	58	62	88	65	81	71	56	69	63	50	70	64	78	46	75	87	97
53587	SOUTH WAYNE	98	67	107	67	70	103	75	93	78	60	77	77	55	76	74	85	50	87	98	114
53588	SPRING GREEN	105	89	103	90	92	110	93	104	96	84	94	79	82	95	92	101	64	99	109	123
53589	STOUGHTON	106	122	112	122	120	114	112	112	109	113	110	87	120	111	117	108	78	110	110	130
53590	SUN PRAIRIE	119	131	118	133	127	118	124	120	119	127	121	96	131	123	126	116	86	120	114	140
53593	VERONA	155	183	170	187	180	162	163	161	154	171	157	129	179	159	172	148	113	157	147	187
53594	WATERLOO	97	112	101	111	109	104	105	103	102	103	103	81	112	104	109	102	73	103	102	120
53597	WAUNAKEE	129	142	125	142	136	127	132	129	126	136	128	103	138	131	134	123	91	127	121	150
53598	WINDSOR	141	156	140	155	151	138	143	141	137	150	139	111	150	142	146	133	99	138	132	163
53703	MADISON	54	28	28	33	26	31	71	40	59	52	60	40	47	58	43	55	43	53	40	53
53704	MADISON	96	88	82	91	86	85	98	89	97	98	98	71	95	98	93	96	69	95	91	107
53705	MADISON	114	114	118	120	115	111	123	112	119	122	121	90	125	119	122	118	87	118	113	134
53706	MADISON	29	12	12	15	11	14	40	20	32	27	33	21	24	31	22	29	23	28	20	27
53711	MADISON	120	127	124	130	127	122	125	121	123	128	124	94	131	123	127	121	88	123	121	142
53713	MADISON	89	60	54	66	56	58	87	68	86	85	88	59	74	89	71	84	61	82	70	87
53714	MADISON	94	97	86	98	93	94	98	93	97	96	98	74	99	99	96	97	69	96	96	111
53715	MADISON	59	36	35	40	34	39	74	46	64	57	64	44	52	63	49	60	46	58	47	60
53716	MADISON	97	109	102	109	107	107	102	102	102	103	103	77	110	102	107	103	73	102	107	119
53717	MADISON	147	145	136	151	141	132	149	137	144	153	146	112	150	149	145	139	104	142	130	163
53718	MADISON	125	137	127	138	134	125	129	126	125	133	127	99	136	128	132	122	90	125	121	148
53719	MADISON	126	113	100	118	107	101	124	110	120	126	123	92	119	126	114	115	86	117	104	132
53726	MADISON	92	59	61	67	57	61	122	74	101	93	103	72	87	99	81	94	74	93	72	95
53801	BAGLEY	80	55	88	55	58	84	61	76	64	50	63	63	45	62	61	69	41	71	80	93
53803	BENTON	78	56	80	55	58	82	61	76	67	53	65	58	48	66	60	74	43	71	82	90
53804	BLOOMINGTON	88	61	97	61	63	93	67	84	70	55	69	69	49	69	67	76	45	78	88	103
53805	BOSCOBEL	75	59	77	59	61	79	65	74	69	58	68	56	55	68	63	75	46	71	81	88
53806	CASSVILLE	75	53	78	52	55	79	58	72	64	51	62	56	45	63	57	70	41	67	78	86
53807	CUBA CITY	90	72	88	74	74	95	75	88	79	66	77	69	63	79	74	84	52	82	93	105
53809	FENNIMORE	87	65	89	65	68	90	71	84	75	62	73	66	57	74	70	81	49	79	89	101
53810	GLEN HAVEN	79	54	87	54	57	84	61	75	63	49	62	62	44	62	60	69	40	70	79	93
53811	HAZEL GREEN	91	83	81	85	81	97	84	90	86	76	85	71	78	87	82	90	58	87	96	107
53813	LANCASTER	83	70	83	70	71	89	72	82	76	66	75	63	65	75	72	82	51	79	89	98
53816	MOUNT HOPE	88	61	97	60	63	93	67	84	70	54	69	69	49	69	67	76	45	78	88	103
53818	PLATTEVILLE	86	66	71	68	67	77	87	79	84	76	83	64	71	84	74	86	57	83	83	96
53820	POTOSI	83	70	79	72	72	88	71	82	73	63	72	64	62	74	71	78	49	76	85	97
53821	PRAIRIE DU CHIEN	88	73	83	73	73	91	75	85	80	70	79	65	67	80	74	85	53	81	91	101
53825	STITZER	95	65	104	65	68	100	72	90	75	59	74	74	53	74	72	82	48	84	95	111
53826	WAUZEKA	86	70	81	68	70	85	70	80	73	67	73	62	60	74	68	77	49	76	82	96
53827	WOODMAN	86	59	95	59	62	91	66	82	68	53	68	68	48	67	65	75	44	76	86	101
53901	PORTAGE	84	83	79	83	82	87	85	85	86	82	86	64	84	86	83	88	60	86	90	100
53910	ADAMS	76	55	78	54	58	78	58	73	64	54	63	54	47	63	57	71	42	67	77	86
53911	ARLINGTON	94	106	92	109	103	103	95	98	94	95	94	77	102	96	101	94	66	95	98	116
53913	BARABOO	88	85	79	85	84	89	85	87	86	84	85	66	83	87	84	88	59	86	90	103
53916	BEAVER DAM	86	83	77	85	82	90	85	86	87	81	86	66	83	87	84	89	59	86	92	102
53919	BRANDON	92	85	83	88	86	99	83	93	85	75	84	71	77	87	83	90	57	86	96	108
53920	BRIGGSVILLE	93	74	120	73	81	98	74	94	78	70	77	69	64	74	80	83	51	87	93	109
53922	BURNETT	106	96	95	100	98	113	95	107	98	86	96	81	88	100	95	103	66	99	110	124
53923	CAMBRIA	93	75	93	76	75	99	80	90	82	69	81	73	67	82	78	87	54	87	97	110
53924	CAZENOVIA	95	66	104	66	69	100	73	91	76	60	75	75	54	75	73	83	49	84	96	111
53925	COLUMBUS	90	99	90	99	97	95	96	94	94	93	95	74	100	96	98	95	67	95	95	110
53926	DALTON	80	73	74	75	74	86	72	81	74	65	73	62	66	75	72	78	49	75	84	95
53929	ELROY	86	69	83	69	70	90	73	84	77	65	76	65	63	77	71	83	51	79	90	100
53930	ENDEAVOR	84	75	76	73	75	81	72	79	75	73	74	57	67	76	70	77	50	75	79	93
53932	FALL RIVER	97	94	83	93	92	96	87	92	89	89	89	69	85	93	86	91	61	89	93	109
53933	FOX LAKE	87	92	97	91	93	102	84	94	88	82	87	68	88	86	91	93	60	90	102	108
53934	FRIENDSHIP	76	65	87	61	70	83	64	78	69	65	68	54	59	66	68	75	45	74	85	90
53936	GRAND MARSH	80	58	86	57	61	82	60	76	65	56	64	57	49	64	60	71	42	70	78	90
53937	HILLPOINT	100	69	110	69	72	105	76	95	79	62	78	78	56	78	76	87	51	89	100	117
53939	KINGSTON	78	71	71	74	73	84	70	80	73	64	71	60	65	74	70	77	49	73	82	92
53941	LA VALLE	94	81	89	84	83	101	82	94	84	73	83	73	72	85	82	90	56	87	97	111
53943	LOGANVILLE	100	69	110	69	72	105	76	95	79	62	79	78	56	78	76	87	51	89	100	117
53944	LYNDON STATION	90	74	86	72	74	90	73	85	77	71	77	64	64	78	72	82	51	80	87	101
53946	MARKESAN	100	82	109	82	85	105	85	99	88	78	87	76	74	86	86	93	58	94	103	118
53947	MARQUETTE	88	71	114	70	78	93	71	90	74	66	73	66	61	70	77	79	49	83	89	104
53948	MAUSTON	87	68	84	67	69	88	72	83	77	67	76	63	62	77	70	83	51	79	88	99
53949	MONTELLO	78	65	81	64	69	83	65	78	70	63	68	56	58	68	67	75	46	73	83	91
53950	NEW LISBON	88	70	87	69	71	91	72	84	77	67	76	64	62	77	71	83	51	80	89	100
	WISCONSIN	98	94	92	96	93	99	96	96	96	93	96	75	94	97	95	98	67	96	99	114
	UNITED STATES	100	100	100	100	100	100	100	100	100	100	100	100	100	100	100	100	100	100	100	100

ZIP CODE #	POST OFFICE NAME	COUNTY FIPS CODE	POPULATION 2000	POPULATION 2009	POPULATION 2014	2000-2009 ANNUAL RATE % Rate	2000-2009 ANNUAL RATE State Centile	HOUSEHOLDS 2000	HOUSEHOLDS 2009	HOUSEHOLDS 2014	HOUSEHOLDS % Annual Rate 2000-2009	HOUSEHOLDS 2009 Average HH Size	FAMILIES 2000	FAMILIES 2009	FAMILIES % Annual Rate 2000-2009
53951	NORTH FREEDOM	111	1621	1720	1741	0.6	51	602	655	667	0.9	2.62	451	486	0.8
53952	OXFORD	077	2745	2983	3061	0.9	68	1144	1275	1324	1.2	2.17	796	879	1.1
53954	PARDEEVILLE	021	6658	7290	7577	1.0	72	2541	2903	3044	1.5	2.47	1837	2077	1.3
53955	POYNETTE	021	5548	6412	6749	1.6	91	2207	2638	2801	1.9	2.43	1554	1831	1.8
53956	RANDOLPH	021	3273	3348	3352	0.2	24	1207	1270	1287	0.6	2.36	873	908	0.4
53959	REEDSBURG	111	11938	13547	14226	1.4	86	4593	5334	5646	1.6	2.48	3163	3639	1.5
53960	RIO	021	3166	3602	3780	1.4	86	1216	1421	1503	1.7	2.51	904	1046	1.6
53961	ROCK SPRINGS	111	715	763	777	0.7	56	262	289	298	1.1	2.63	206	225	1.0
53963	WAUPUN	039	13673	13955	13938	0.2	24	4284	4426	4465	0.4	2.42	3008	3064	0.2
53964	WESTFIELD	077	3155	3403	3512	0.8	61	1307	1456	1517	1.2	2.32	889	978	1.0
53965	WISCONSIN DELLS	001	9362	10338	10760	1.1	76	3768	4304	4518	1.4	2.37	2548	2889	1.4
53968	WONEWOC	057	2550	2788	2831	1.0	72	1002	1090	1113	0.9	2.48	717	773	0.8
54001	AMERY	095	7850	8236	8267	0.5	44	3113	3371	3413	0.9	2.39	2177	2343	0.8
54002	BALDWIN	109	4741	6325	7157	3.2	98	1806	2476	2824	3.5	2.52	1288	1759	3.4
54003	BELDENVILLE	093	1023	1083	1130	0.6	51	361	397	419	1.0	2.73	282	307	0.9
54004	CLAYTON	005	2304	2522	2615	1.0	72	866	980	1028	1.3	2.57	637	713	1.2
54005	CLEAR LAKE	095	2863	3176	3308	1.1	76	1067	1221	1287	1.5	2.59	726	819	1.3
54006	CUSHING	095	1251	1364	1387	0.9	68	489	553	568	1.3	2.47	360	403	1.2
54007	DEER PARK	109	1296	1458	1521	1.3	84	456	533	563	1.7	2.74	356	412	1.6
54009	DRESSER	095	1914	2314	2508	2.1	96	744	932	1019	2.5	2.48	539	667	2.3
54011	ELLSWORTH	093	6138	6823	7223	1.2	81	2309	2681	2869	1.6	2.50	1645	1874	1.4
54013	GLENWOOD CITY	109	3305	3943	4237	1.9	94	1180	1460	1586	2.3	2.67	878	1076	2.2
54014	HAGER CITY	093	2043	2813	2981	3.5	98	767	1072	1148	3.7	2.62	587	810	3.5
54015	HAMMOND	109	1906	3011	3595	5.1	99	680	1102	1332	5.4	2.69	522	848	5.4
54016	HUDSON	109	22738	30643	34476	3.3	98	8352	11686	13289	3.7	2.60	6145	8492	3.6
54017	NEW RICHMOND	109	12111	16470	18615	3.4	98	4565	6462	7391	3.8	2.50	3099	4352	3.7
54020	OSCEOLA	095	6163	7131	7483	1.6	91	2286	2715	2868	1.9	2.61	1656	1949	1.8
54021	PRESCOTT	093	5563	6544	6980	1.8	93	2016	2459	2647	2.2	2.64	1508	1817	2.0
54022	RIVER FALLS	093	19011	21147	22327	1.2	81	6502	7573	8111	1.7	2.51	4139	4777	1.6
54023	ROBERTS	109	2512	3738	4324	4.4	99	902	1400	1639	4.9	2.67	679	1039	4.7
54024	SAINT CROIX FALLS	095	4027	4788	5075	1.9	94	1644	2031	2177	2.3	2.30	1068	1306	2.2
54025	SOMERSET	109	4680	6700	7705	4.0	99	1725	2562	2979	4.4	2.62	1286	1896	4.3
54026	STAR PRAIRIE	095	1682	1878	1962	1.2	81	605	701	741	1.6	2.68	464	533	1.5
54027	WILSON	109	831	977	1043	1.8	93	308	377	407	2.2	2.59	242	294	2.1
54028	WOODVILLE	109	2078	2376	2547	1.5	88	790	933	1009	1.8	2.50	575	671	1.7
54082	HOULTON	109	1339	1616	1768	2.1	96	500	623	689	2.4	2.59	388	482	2.4
54101	ABRAMS	083	2445	2719	2861	1.2	81	875	1016	1081	1.6	2.67	666	764	1.5
54102	AMBERG	075	934	921	903	-0.2	8	421	434	431	0.3	2.12	275	278	0.1
54103	ARMSTRONG CREEK	041	531	544	544	0.3	32	239	249	252	0.4	2.18	154	158	0.3
54104	ATHELSTANE	075	1043	1076	1077	0.3	32	459	497	505	0.9	2.16	317	338	0.7
54106	BLACK CREEK	087	4828	5181	5372	0.8	61	1761	2000	2105	1.4	2.59	1346	1498	1.2
54107	BONDUEL	115	3356	3644	3771	0.9	68	1286	1454	1519	1.3	2.50	951	1063	1.2
54110	BRILLION	015	5486	5879	6027	0.8	61	2035	2295	2384	1.3	2.55	1501	1661	1.1
54111	CECIL	115	2118	2344	2430	1.1	76	836	956	1001	1.5	2.45	630	713	1.3
54112	COLEMAN	075	2369	2399	2392	0.1	20	930	989	999	0.7	2.42	666	699	0.5
54113	COMBINED LOCKS	087	2412	2820	3089	1.7	91	880	1075	1193	2.2	2.62	728	870	1.9
54114	CRIVITZ	075	4983	5300	5392	0.7	56	2186	2432	2508	1.2	2.14	1491	1635	1.0
54115	DE PERE	009	30519	38587	41727	2.6	97	11060	14469	15794	2.9	2.55	7762	10234	3.0
54119	DUNBAR	075	1290	1339	1357	0.4	39	268	299	307	1.2	2.98	189	207	1.0
54120	FENCE	037	337	347	354	0.3	32	160	174	180	0.9	1.99	104	111	0.7
54121	FLORENCE	037	3189	3221	3226	0.1	20	1323	1403	1424	0.6	2.25	893	936	0.5
54124	GILLETT	083	3565	3847	3912	0.8	61	1401	1547	1586	1.1	2.47	988	1074	0.9
54125	GOODMAN	075	736	753	750	0.2	24	317	338	341	0.7	2.23	214	225	0.5
54126	GREENLEAF	009	3530	4002	4219	1.4	86	1177	1399	1495	1.9	2.85	954	1113	1.7
54128	GRESHAM	115	1957	2065	2112	0.6	51	697	757	783	0.9	2.70	515	554	0.8
54129	HILBERT	015	3986	4208	4328	0.6	51	1439	1598	1673	1.1	2.63	1071	1166	0.9
54130	KAUKAUNA	087	21584	24934	26349	1.6	91	7888	9530	10184	2.1	2.59	5732	6884	2.0
54135	KESHENA	078	4173	4278	4328	0.3	32	1248	1333	1365	0.7	3.17	984	1043	0.6
54136	KIMBERLY	087	6236	6378	6460	0.2	24	2545	2742	2811	0.8	2.32	1761	1855	0.6
54137	KRAKOW	115	1035	1244	1307	2.0	95	390	485	514	2.4	2.56	309	382	2.3
54138	LAKEWOOD	083	911	1004	1047	1.1	76	413	472	498	1.5	2.13	290	326	1.3
54139	LENA	083	3084	3403	3546	1.1	76	1202	1388	1462	1.6	2.45	859	977	1.4
54140	LITTLE CHUTE	087	8753	9399	9710	0.8	61	3259	3674	3845	1.3	2.54	2324	2568	1.1
54141	LITTLE SUAMICO	083	1938	2712	2987	3.7	99	738	1062	1182	4.0	2.55	574	821	3.9
54143	MARINETTE	075	16018	15401	15016	-0.4	2	6717	6723	6628	0.0	2.24	4259	4212	-0.1
54149	MOUNTAIN	083	1260	1383	1436	1.0	72	579	660	693	1.4	2.10	395	442	1.2
54150	NEOPIT	078	16	16	16	0.0	16	6	6	6	0.0	2.67	5	5	0.0
54151	NIAGARA	075	3985	4031	4036	0.1	20	1593	1690	1715	0.6	2.35	1096	1147	0.5
54153	OCONTO	083	7284	7489	7499	0.3	32	2862	3068	3109	0.8	2.40	1982	2091	0.6
54154	OCONTO FALLS	083	5236	5592	5717	0.7	56	2050	2270	2343	1.1	2.42	1395	1521	0.9
54155	ONEIDA	087	4377	5256	5578	2.0	95	1439	1771	1907	2.3	2.92	1206	1477	2.2
54156	PEMBINE	075	1823	1890	1903	0.4	39	764	837	854	1.0	2.10	524	566	0.8
54157	PESHTIGO	075	5597	5941	5976	0.6	51	2114	2332	2375	1.1	2.41	1511	1645	0.9
54159	PORTERFIELD	075	1501	1529	1538	0.2	24	598	641	653	0.8	2.39	459	487	0.6
54161	POUND	075	2768	2917	2958	0.6	51	1118	1233	1265	1.1	2.37	790	859	0.9
54162	PULASKI	115	7995	9038	9421	1.3	84	2843	3328	3506	1.7	2.70	2168	2507	1.6
54165	SEYMOUR	087	7162	7653	7886	0.7	56	2553	2863	2989	1.2	2.64	1926	2118	1.0
54166	SHAWANO	115	16087	16477	16564	0.3	32	6609	7014	7129	0.6	2.27	4353	4557	0.5
54169	SHERWOOD	015	1464	2349	2647	5.2	99	538	912	1046	5.9	2.57	438	726	5.6
54170	SHIOCTON	087	3777	4074	4218	0.8	61	1381	1570	1649	1.4	2.57	1055	1176	1.2
54171	SOBIESKI	083	2689	3003	3291	1.2	81	893	1035	1148	1.6	2.90	745	856	1.5
54173	SUAMICO	009	3398	4007	4269	1.8	93	1207	1480	1596	2.2	2.70	996	1199	2.0
54174	SURING	083	3010	3249	3313	0.8	61	1244	1391	1433	1.2	2.30	865	951	1.0
54175	TOWNSEND	083	984	1076	1115	1.0	72	451	512	538	1.4	2.10	318	355	1.2
54177	WAUSAUKEE	075	3302	3396	3416	0.3	32	1359	1459	1485	0.8	2.33	945	1001	0.6
54180	WRIGHTSTOWN	009	2020	2444	2644	2.1	96	726	927	1017	2.7	2.63	551	687	2.4
54201	ALGOMA	061	5650	5817	5848	0.3	32	2341	2511	2557	0.8	2.28	1556	1644	0.6
54202	BAILEYS HARBOR	029	1260	1233	1230	-0.2	8	603	623	630	0.4	1.98	389	395	0.2
54204	BRUSSELS	029	1707	1951	2053	1.5	88	642	770	823	2.0	2.53	492	584	1.9
54205	CASCO	061	2117	2271	2324	0.8	61	751	842	873	1.2	2.69	596	663	1.2
54208	DENMARK	009	5853	6606	6947	1.3	84	2124	2515	2680	1.8	2.62	1601	1854	1.6
54209	EGG HARBOR	029	1182	1432	1500	2.1	96	502	650	693	2.8	2.20	357	456	2.7
54210	ELLISON BAY	029	1028	1016	1007	-0.1	11	453	470	471	0.4	2.16	321	329	0.3
54212	FISH CREEK	029	1050	1124	1165	0.7	56	466	525	553	1.3	2.14	319	353	1.1
54213	FORESTVILLE	029	1287	1462	1536	1.4	86	488	580	618	1.9	2.52	370	435	1.8
	WISCONSIN					0.7					1.0	2.43			0.9
	UNITED STATES					1.0					1.1	2.59			0.9

ZIP CODE #	POST OFFICE NAME	RACE (%) White 2000	White 2009	Black 2000	Black 2009	Asian/Pacific 2000	Asian/Pacific 2009	% Hispanic Origin 2000	% Hispanic Origin 2009	2009 AGE DISTRIBUTION (%) 0-4	5-9	10-14	15-19	20-24	25-44	45-64	65-84	85+	18+	MEDIAN AGE 2009	% 2009 Males	% 2009 Females
53951	NORTH FREEDOM	97.0	96.2	0.1	0.1	0.2	0.3	3.1	4.4	6.9	7.3	7.6	7.0	5.3	25.5	29.1	9.8	1.5	73.9	38.8	51.4	48.6
53952	OXFORD	97.6	95.9	0.5	1.4	0.6	1.0	1.5	2.4	4.8	5.0	5.3	5.3	4.7	25.0	32.1	15.9	1.9	81.7	44.9	54.2	45.8
53954	PARDEEVILLE	98.2	97.7	0.2	0.2	0.4	0.5	1.5	2.2	6.4	6.6	6.9	6.5	5.0	24.3	28.6	13.5	2.2	75.9	41.1	50.9	49.1
53955	POYNETTE	97.7	97.0	0.1	0.2	0.2	0.3	1.0	1.5	6.1	6.4	6.7	6.8	5.2	25.9	31.0	10.5	1.4	76.3	40.6	52.1	47.9
53956	RANDOLPH	95.3	93.9	3.2	4.2	0.2	0.2	1.8	2.5	5.8	6.2	6.3	6.3	6.4	27.4	25.4	12.7	3.6	77.9	38.8	53.7	46.3
53959	REEDSBURG	97.5	96.9	0.1	0.2	0.2	0.3	1.2	1.8	6.9	6.5	6.6	6.7	6.4	25.7	26.4	12.0	2.8	75.8	38.7	49.2	50.8
53960	RIO	98.1	97.6	0.1	0.2	0.4	0.6	1.4	2.0	6.1	6.4	6.7	6.7	5.1	24.7	31.1	11.1	2.0	76.5	41.3	50.6	49.4
53961	ROCK SPRINGS	98.6	98.4	0.1	0.1	0.1	0.1	1.3	2.0	5.2	5.8	6.0	6.0	4.7	26.2	32.4	11.8	1.8	79.6	42.5	51.2	48.8
53963	WAUPUN	88.0	85.0	10.0	12.5	0.3	0.4	2.6	3.5	5.2	5.1	5.1	6.5	9.0	33.9	23.4	9.7	2.2	81.1	35.7	60.0	40.0
53964	WESTFIELD	97.8	96.9	0.3	0.5	0.3	0.4	2.0	3.2	5.9	5.9	6.1	5.7	4.6	22.7	31.1	15.8	2.3	78.2	44.3	51.5	48.5
53965	WISCONSIN DELLS	95.6	94.7	0.4	0.5	0.3	0.4	1.4	2.0	5.0	5.1	5.5	5.9	5.3	23.4	31.9	15.5	2.5	80.9	44.9	49.1	50.9
53968	WONEWOC	98.8	98.4	0.1	0.1	0.1	0.2	0.8	1.2	5.8	6.1	6.5	7.4	4.8	22.1	28.8	14.8	3.7	76.6	42.7	48.6	51.4
54001	AMERY	98.4	98.2	0.1	0.1	0.3	0.4	0.7	1.0	5.4	6.0	6.5	6.5	4.9	22.9	29.5	14.7	3.6	77.8	43.3	48.9	51.1
54002	BALDWIN	98.1	97.5	0.1	0.1	0.6	0.9	0.6	0.8	6.6	6.2	6.1	6.9	6.8	25.7	26.9	12.3	2.5	76.7	38.8	48.7	51.3
54003	BELDENVILLE	98.7	98.3	0.2	0.3	0.3	0.4	0.7	1.0	5.4	7.7	7.7	7.2	4.5	27.3	31.8	7.5	0.9	74.5	39.2	51.0	49.0
54004	CLAYTON	98.3	97.8	0.2	0.3	0.3	0.4	0.4	0.6	6.5	6.8	7.1	7.3	5.0	25.9	29.5	10.6	1.3	75.0	38.8	51.2	48.8
54005	CLEAR LAKE	98.3	98.0	0.1	0.2	0.1	0.2	1.6	2.1	6.5	6.6	7.1	7.7	5.6	26.2	28.1	10.3	2.0	75.1	38.1	51.3	48.7
54006	CUSHING	98.5	98.1	0.2	0.3	0.6	1.0	0.6	0.7	5.4	5.7	6.3	7.0	5.2	23.0	33.6	12.4	1.4	78.3	43.1	50.9	49.1
54007	DEER PARK	98.7	98.4	0.0	0.0	0.4	0.6	0.4	0.5	6.9	6.4	7.2	7.8	4.7	26.1	30.0	10.2	0.8	74.1	38.9	52.3	47.7
54009	DRESSER	98.5	98.3	0.2	0.2	0.1	0.1	0.8	1.2	7.0	7.3	7.6	6.7	4.3	26.8	28.6	10.1	1.4	73.6	38.9	50.4	49.6
54011	ELLSWORTH	98.4	97.9	0.1	0.1	0.2	0.3	0.9	1.2	6.6	6.9	7.0	6.6	5.2	27.2	28.5	10.0	1.9	75.4	38.4	50.5	49.5
54013	GLENWOOD CITY	98.2	97.6	0.1	0.1	0.8	1.2	0.5	0.7	6.0	7.0	7.9	8.1	5.0	25.6	26.2	11.9	2.2	73.5	38.4	50.7	49.3
54014	HAGER CITY	98.6	98.2	0.2	0.3	0.1	0.3	0.7	1.0	6.0	6.7	7.0	6.3	4.5	26.9	31.0	10.5	1.0	76.3	40.3	52.5	47.5
54015	HAMMOND	98.5	98.2	0.1	0.1	0.3	0.4	0.4	0.7	6.5	6.4	6.6	7.0	6.2	27.1	29.0	9.0	2.2	75.9	38.1	49.6	50.4
54016	HUDSON	97.7	97.1	0.3	0.3	0.7	1.0	0.9	1.3	7.2	7.3	7.4	7.2	5.7	28.3	28.4	7.5	1.1	73.5	36.9	50.1	49.9
54017	NEW RICHMOND	97.8	97.3	0.5	0.7	0.4	0.6	0.8	1.1	7.0	7.0	6.9	7.3	6.3	28.4	25.7	9.5	1.8	74.7	35.9	49.7	50.3
54020	OSCEOLA	98.0	97.6	0.3	0.3	0.3	0.4	0.8	1.2	7.2	7.7	7.9	7.6	5.6	27.7	26.9	8.0	1.4	72.2	36.3	50.1	49.9
54021	PRESCOTT	98.5	98.0	0.2	0.3	0.2	0.4	1.0	1.5	6.7	6.7	6.8	6.8	6.1	27.2	28.9	9.3	1.4	75.4	37.8	50.3	49.7
54022	RIVER FALLS	97.2	95.4	0.4	1.5	0.8	1.2	0.9	1.6	5.3	5.5	5.4	11.1	15.5	25.1	22.7	7.3	2.0	80.1	30.2	47.7	52.3
54023	ROBERTS	98.5	98.1	0.2	0.3	0.4	0.5	0.6	0.9	6.5	6.9	7.2	7.0	4.7	28.6	30.4	7.9	0.7	75.0	38.1	50.2	49.8
54024	SAINT CROIX FALLS	98.3	97.8	0.2	0.3	0.4	0.5	0.9	1.3	5.8	6.0	6.4	6.5	5.3	23.7	30.0	13.1	3.3	77.4	42.3	50.1	49.9
54025	SOMERSET	97.6	97.0	0.3	0.3	0.6	0.9	0.6	0.8	7.3	7.6	8.0	7.2	5.0	29.4	27.6	7.3	0.7	72.5	36.2	50.9	49.1
54026	STAR PRAIRIE	98.1	97.6	0.1	0.2	0.7	1.0	0.5	0.8	6.8	7.5	7.7	6.8	4.1	26.8	30.0	9.4	0.8	73.6	38.7	51.0	49.0
54027	WILSON	97.1	96.0	0.0	0.1	1.7	2.6	0.5	0.7	5.9	6.6	6.9	6.9	4.7	25.9	31.3	10.8	1.0	76.5	40.3	52.0	48.0
54028	WOODVILLE	97.7	97.0	0.0	0.0	1.0	1.4	0.9	1.2	7.0	7.2	7.4	7.0	4.6	27.5	27.4	9.7	2.2	74.2	37.8	50.4	49.6
54082	HOULTON	97.5	96.8	0.2	0.3	1.0	1.4	0.7	1.0	6.4	6.9	7.5	7.4	4.8	25.8	31.6	8.9	0.7	74.6	39.6	51.1	48.9
54101	ABRAMS	98.2	97.9	0.1	0.1	0.1	0.1	0.6	0.9	5.8	6.8	7.0	6.8	4.3	26.2	32.4	9.7	0.9	76.1	41.0	51.1	48.9
54102	AMBERG	96.6	96.1	1.1	1.4	0.2	0.2	1.2	1.5	4.7	4.7	5.8	6.7	3.5	18.0	37.1	18.0	1.5	80.8	48.8	51.7	48.3
54103	ARMSTRONG CREEK	95.9	95.0	0.6	0.9	0.4	0.4	1.1	1.7	5.9	5.9	6.3	6.4	5.3	21.5	28.5	17.1	3.1	77.8	43.9	49.4	50.6
54104	ATHELSTANE	98.1	97.8	0.2	0.3	0.1	0.3	0.6	0.8	3.5	4.2	4.4	4.7	3.5	15.3	37.9	24.9	1.5	84.9	55.0	52.6	47.4
54106	BLACK CREEK	97.7	96.9	0.0	0.1	0.3	0.5	1.1	1.7	6.7	7.4	7.5	6.9	4.9	27.7	28.2	9.4	1.2	73.8	37.9	51.6	48.4
54107	BONDUEL	97.4	96.7	0.1	0.1	0.2	0.2	1.0	1.4	7.3	7.6	7.5	6.6	4.5	26.4	25.7	12.5	1.9	73.3	38.8	51.2	48.8
54110	BRILLION	98.4	97.9	0.1	0.2	0.1	0.3	0.6	0.9	6.5	6.8	7.1	7.2	5.4	26.9	27.8	10.5	1.8	75.3	38.6	50.2	49.8
54111	CECIL	96.1	95.2	0.0	0.1	0.1	0.2	1.1	1.5	5.5	6.0	6.2	6.1	4.6	21.8	31.3	16.4	2.2	78.7	44.9	51.5	48.5
54112	COLEMAN	98.8	98.6	0.0	0.0	0.1	0.2	0.7	1.0	6.0	6.2	6.4	6.3	5.7	22.6	30.2	14.3	2.4	77.1	42.4	51.2	48.8
54113	COMBINED LOCKS	98.1	97.4	0.2	0.3	0.6	0.9	1.2	1.9	9.4	9.4	8.6	6.7	3.4	29.0	23.7	9.2	0.5	67.5	35.7	50.2	49.8
54114	CRIVITZ	98.0	97.5	0.2	0.2	0.2	0.3	0.8	1.2	4.4	4.7	5.1	5.7	4.5	18.5	32.3	21.5	3.2	82.1	49.6	50.8	49.2
54115	DE PERE	94.7	94.0	0.4	0.6	0.7	1.0	1.0	1.5	6.9	6.9	7.0	8.4	7.7	26.9	25.9	8.7	1.6	75.0	35.5	49.5	50.5
54119	DUNBAR	97.7	97.2	0.2	0.1	0.6	0.9	1.1	1.6	3.3	3.5	3.7	18.1	22.0	15.8	22.1	10.5	1.0	86.0	24.9	48.1	51.9
54120	FENCE	97.9	97.7	0.3	0.3	0.3	0.6	0.3	0.3	3.5	4.0	5.5	5.5	3.7	20.2	38.0	17.9	1.7	83.3	49.0	52.7	47.3
54121	FLORENCE	98.1	98.0	0.1	0.2	0.3	0.3	0.4	0.4	4.6	5.9	6.3	6.6	3.4	23.2	32.0	14.8	3.1	78.7	45.0	51.2	48.8
54124	GILLETT	96.9	96.4	0.1	0.2	0.1	0.2	0.5	0.8	6.1	6.2	6.6	6.9	5.3	23.3	29.7	13.3	2.7	77.9	42.0	50.3	49.7
54125	GOODMAN	97.4	96.9	0.4	0.5	0.4	0.5	0.8	1.3	4.2	5.0	5.2	5.6	3.7	19.1	36.1	19.1	1.9	82.2	50.0	51.4	48.6
54126	GREENLEAF	98.4	97.8	0.2	0.3	0.2	0.3	0.8	1.4	7.8	7.7	7.9	7.7	4.8	27.8	27.2	7.9	1.0	71.8	36.2	51.4	48.6
54128	GRESHAM	68.3	65.3	0.1	0.1	0.2	0.2	2.3	2.9	7.1	7.1	7.4	7.7	5.0	23.4	27.7	13.2	1.5	72.8	39.5	49.4	50.6
54129	HILBERT	98.1	97.4	0.0	0.0	0.6	1.0	0.7	1.2	6.4	7.2	7.7	7.3	5.1	25.5	28.5	10.9	1.4	76.3	38.7	50.7	49.3
54130	KAUKAUNA	96.4	95.5	0.2	0.3	1.5	2.1	0.7	1.1	7.0	7.0	7.0	7.1	6.2	27.2	27.2	9.4	1.8	74.5	37.1	49.9	50.1
54135	KESHENA	12.4	12.4	0.1	0.1	0.0	0.0	2.8	3.2	9.8	10.2	9.9	9.2	6.8	21.6	23.4	8.7	0.4	63.7	28.7	49.2	50.8
54136	KIMBERLY	97.7	96.9	0.2	0.3	0.8	1.3	0.7	1.2	7.0	6.7	6.6	6.8	5.7	29.1	25.0	11.2	1.8	75.3	37.5	49.1	50.9
54137	KRAKOW	98.3	97.8	0.1	0.2	0.4	0.5	0.4	0.6	7.2	7.6	7.8	7.2	4.5	26.2	27.9	10.2	1.4	72.8	39.0	50.5	49.5
54138	LAKEWOOD	97.6	97.3	0.0	0.0	0.1	0.1	0.7	0.9	2.3	2.6	2.8	4.2	3.9	13.1	36.5	32.4	2.3	89.8	58.4	51.2	48.8
54139	LENA	98.3	98.1	0.1	0.1	0.2	0.3	0.6	0.9	6.0	6.2	6.2	6.6	5.9	25.3	29.4	12.6	1.9	78.7	40.6	51.7	48.3
54140	LITTLE CHUTE	96.5	94.9	0.1	0.1	0.9	1.5	2.0	3.1	8.3	7.6	7.1	7.1	7.3	29.7	23.7	7.8	1.5	72.6	33.2	49.3	50.7
54141	LITTLE SUAMICO	97.6	97.1	0.7	0.9	0.3	0.4	0.8	1.0	6.5	7.0	7.2	7.4	5.3	28.2	30.2	7.3	0.8	74.8	38.3	51.5	48.5
54143	MARINETTE	97.8	97.4	0.3	0.4	0.3	0.5	0.8	1.2	5.6	5.6	5.7	6.3	6.3	24.7	29.2	13.3	3.4	79.3	41.8	48.3	51.7
54149	MOUNTAIN	97.7	97.3	0.0	0.0	0.2	0.4	0.6	0.9	2.6	3.6	3.8	5.0	3.5	15.6	37.5	25.9	2.4	86.8	55.1	51.1	48.9
54150	NEOPIT	0.0	0.0	0.0	0.0	0.0	0.0	0.0	0.0	12.5	12.5	12.5	12.5	12.5	25.0	12.5	0.0	0.0	56.3	20.0	56.3	43.7
54151	NIAGARA	98.9	98.7	0.1	0.2	0.2	0.2	0.9	1.2	5.1	6.2	7.7	7.6	4.5	25.4	27.4	13.5	2.6	76.0	40.9	49.6	50.4
54153	OCONTO	97.5	97.0	0.1	0.1	0.3	0.5	0.9	1.4	6.1	6.3	6.3	6.5	5.9	25.8	28.3	12.3	2.5	77.0	40.3	49.5	50.5
54154	OCONTO FALLS	98.4	98.1	0.1	0.1	0.2	0.3	0.4	0.6	6.4	6.3	6.4	6.8	6.2	24.4	28.2	12.2	3.1	76.6	40.7	48.7	51.3
54155	ONEIDA	71.3	69.3	0.2	0.4	0.4	0.6	1.7	2.2	6.7	7.1	8.0	9.0	4.9	22.5	33.5	7.5	0.8	74.2	39.4	49.0	51.0
54156	PEMBINE	97.3	96.7	0.5	0.6	0.4	0.6	1.2	1.7	3.7	4.7	5.8	9.7	7.5	20.1	30.9	15.9	1.6	81.2	44.0	50.7	49.3
54157	PESHTIGO	98.4	97.9	0.1	0.1	0.4	0.7	0.6	0.7	5.9	6.2	6.5	6.7	4.8	22.9	27.8	14.8	4.5	77.0	42.8	48.3	51.7
54159	PORTERFIELD	98.3	98.0	0.1	0.2	0.1	0.1	0.3	0.5	4.8	5.4	5.8	6.1	4.6	22.5	34.9	14.4	1.4	80.3	45.4	51.2	48.8
54161	POUND	98.7	98.3	0.1	0.1	0.1	0.3	0.8	1.2	5.1	5.6	6.4	6.8	4.3	21.3	30.6	17.5	2.4	78.6	45.3	51.5	48.5
54162	PULASKI	98.2	97.7	0.2	0.2	0.4	0.6	0.7	1.0	7.2	7.3	7.7	7.7	5.7	27.8	25.8	9.2	1.6	72.9	36.6	50.5	49.5
54165	SEYMOUR	92.9	91.4	0.1	0.1	0.2	0.2	1.0	1.6	7.3	7.4	7.5	7.3	6.0	27.1	26.5	9.0	1.9	73.2	36.5	50.3	49.7
54166	SHAWANO	91.1	89.8	0.2	0.3	0.4	0.6	1.3	1.9	6.0	5.9	5.9	6.0	5.8	23.5	27.7	15.7	3.5	78.3	42.7	49.3	50.7
54169	SHERWOOD	98.4	97.8	0.2	0.3	0.8	1.1	0.6	0.9	7.3	8.0	8.3	7.0	4.2	24.8	30.4	8.9	1.0	71.8	39.5	50.7	49.3
54170	SHIOCTON	97.1	95.9	0.1	0.1	0.1	0.2	3.1	4.7	7.0	7.1	7.6	6.6	5.4	28.0	27.1	10.3	0.9	74.1	37.9	52.6	47.4
54171	SOBIESKI	98.3	98.1	0.2	0.2	0.2	0.2	0.7	0.8	7.6	8.2	8.2	7.5	4.0	29.5	28.3	6.1	0.7	71.3	36.8	51.1	48.9
54173	SUAMICO	97.5	96.5	0.1	0.2	0.6	0.9	0.9	1.4	6.4	6.8	7.1	7.0	5.3	27.2	31.8	7.6	0.7	75.1	38.7	51.3	48.7
54174	SURING	96.6	96.0	0.1	0.1	0.2	0.3	0.5	0.6	5.1	5.4	5.7	6.6	4.9	21.9	29.9	17.6	2.9	79.3	45.2	50.2	49.8
54175	TOWNSEND	97.6	97.3	0.1	0.1	0.1	0.1	0.5	0.7	2.2	2.5	2.8	4.4	3.8	12.5	35.5	33.9	2.3	89.8	59.2	51.0	49.0
54177	WAUSAUKEE	98.0	97.5	0.3	0.4	0.2	0.4	0.4	0.7	4.8	4.9	5.5	6.4	4.9	19.1	33.7	18.7	2.0	80.7	47.6	50.5	49.5
54180	WRIGHTSTOWN	97.5	96.2	0.2	0.4	0.8	1.4	1.5	2.6	10.1	8.8	8.1	6.8	5.2	33.1	20.7	6.5	0.8	68.5	32.0	50.6	49.4
54201	ALGOMA	98.3	97.9	0.1	0.2	0.1	0.1	1.2	1.7	5.3	5.5	5.8	6.1	5.2	24.4	29.8	14.4	3.6	79.6	43.4	49.2	50.8
54202	BAILEYS HARBOR	98.3	97.9	0.1	0.1	0.2	0.3	1.4	2.1	3.2	4.0	4.5	4.9	3.2	20.0	37.6	20.7	2.1	85.4	51.2	49.6	50.4
54204	BRUSSELS	98.5	98.1	0.3	0.4	0.4	0.5	0.4	0.7	5.8	6.3	6.7	7.1	4.5	24.4	31.3	12.6	1.3	76.7	41.7	50.5	49.5
54205	CASCO	98.0	97.5	0.0	0.0	0.1	0.2	1.2	1.7	6.3	6.9	7.4	7.2	5.4	25.8	28.3	10.8	1.9	74.7	38.5	50.8	49.2
54208	DENMARK	98.4	97.8	0.2	0.3	0.3	0.5	0.5	0.8	6.7	7.2	7.5	7.2	5.2	26.2	28.8	9.5	1.6	74.1	38.2	51.1	48.9
54209	EGG HARBOR	97.9	97.3	0.2	0.3	0.4	0.6	0.8	1.2	3.1	4.3	4.7	5.2	3.4	18.9	38.8	19.9	1.7	84.7	51.1	50.1	49.9
54210	ELLISON BAY	99.2	99.0	0.0	0.0	0.1	0.2	0.7	1.1	3.5	3.9	4.6	5.0	3.4	15.2	36.6	24.9	2.8	84.9	54.1	48.3	51.7
54212	FISH CREEK	98.1	97.8	0.2	0.2	0.2	0.2	1.2	1.8	3.8	4.4	5.0	4.5	2.8	16.7	38.9	21.9	2.0	84.0	52.7	50.0	50.0
54213	FORESTVILLE	98.1	97.7	0.3	0.3	0.3	0.5	0.3	0.4	5.5	6.2	6.6	7.3	4.7	24.8	31.6	11.6	1.7	77.1	41.4	50.5	49.5
	WISCONSIN	88.9	86.9	5.7	6.3	1.7	2.3	3.6	4.8	6.4	6.4	6.5	7.2	7.2	26.0	27.1	11.1	2.2	76.6	38.0	49.5	50.5
	UNITED STATES	75.1	72.0	12.3	12.7	3.8	4.6	12.5	15.7	6.8	6.7	6.6	7.1	6.9	27.0	26.0	10.9	1.9	75.7	36.9	49.2	50.8

ZIP CODE #	POST OFFICE NAME	2009 Per Capita Income	2009 HH Income Base	2009 HOUSEHOLD INCOME DISTRIBUTION (%) Less than $25,000	$25,000 to $49,999	$50,000 to $99,999	$100,000 to $149,999	$150,000 or More	MEDIAN HOUSEHOLD INCOME 2009	2014	2009 National Centile	2009 State Centile	2009 Home Value Base	2009 HOME VALUE DISTRIBUTION (%) Less than $50,000	$50,000 to $89,999	$90,000 to $174,999	$175,000 to $399,999	$400,000 or More	2009 Median Home Value
53951	NORTH FREEDOM	22894	655	20.8	24.9	44.6	6.3	3.5	53221	54840	68	59	548	13.0	15.7	34.1	31.0	6.2	124713
53952	OXFORD	22101	1275	22.6	34.6	37.7	4.0	1.1	44689	46391	47	31	1071	9.0	21.8	48.0	19.0	2.3	116929
53954	PARDEEVILLE	25716	2903	17.6	26.5	44.1	8.4	3.4	54522	57188	70	61	2313	4.4	6.1	44.5	41.6	3.4	166223
53955	POYNETTE	27545	2638	15.0	24.0	46.6	11.0	3.3	61248	62877	79	75	2042	6.4	4.0	37.4	46.3	5.9	179229
53956	RANDOLPH	24693	1270	17.9	28.0	42.8	8.6	2.7	53844	56565	69	60	976	4.1	10.6	54.7	26.4	4.2	143324
53959	REEDSBURG	25227	5334	17.9	26.5	43.3	8.4	3.8	54710	56658	71	62	3873	10.4	11.0	48.2	26.8	3.6	136916
53960	RIO	25456	1421	12.9	29.0	45.3	10.3	2.5	60074	61924	77	73	1158	5.4	6.9	45.5	37.7	4.6	159694
53961	ROCK SPRINGS	24697	289	16.3	25.3	45.7	9.7	3.1	57867	59679	75	69	241	2.9	17.8	36.5	37.3	5.4	153125
53963	WAUPUN	23117	4426	15.8	25.7	47.5	8.1	2.9	57834	59944	75	68	3212	3.5	14.3	61.8	19.6	0.9	129348
53964	WESTFIELD	21458	1456	28.6	33.9	31.2	3.5	2.7	39193	41253	30	11	1114	9.3	19.8	48.6	19.6	2.7	117929
53965	WISCONSIN DELLS	24839	4304	19.7	30.9	39.2	6.9	3.4	49449	52050	60	47	3292	13.0	17.1	41.7	24.0	4.3	127643
53968	WONEWOC	20448	1090	23.9	36.4	33.4	3.9	2.4	41770	43727	39	19	845	12.3	22.8	43.0	19.2	2.7	109149
54001	AMERY	23845	3371	20.8	29.0	38.5	9.0	2.6	50128	51947	61	49	2711	8.8	12.7	43.6	30.3	4.5	145081
54002	BALDWIN	25633	2476	15.8	27.1	43.4	10.8	2.9	60292	63406	78	74	1764	7.4	6.0	29.3	49.0	8.4	189130
54003	BELDENVILLE	25402	397	12.8	22.7	51.9	9.8	2.8	63307	66964	82	82	347	2.9	7.2	31.7	47.6	10.7	198750
54004	CLAYTON	20414	980	22.6	30.1	40.8	4.8	1.7	47110	50056	54	41	802	13.2	18.1	44.5	22.3	1.9	119643
54005	CLEAR LAKE	19947	1221	24.3	29.6	39.2	5.3	1.5	46373	48965	52	38	963	15.3	18.0	42.5	22.5	1.8	119943
54006	CUSHING	21002	553	19.7	33.6	40.5	5.2	0.9	47059	50187	54	40	492	11.6	19.7	39.6	27.6	1.4	129231
54007	DEER PARK	22792	533	14.4	26.1	50.3	7.5	1.7	60422	61473	78	74	455	5.3	11.4	37.8	40.2	5.3	167115
54009	DRESSER	25046	932	14.5	32.0	43.0	7.3	3.2	53042	54890	68	58	725	8.1	9.2	44.7	33.8	4.1	149898
54011	ELLSWORTH	24775	2681	15.8	26.3	46.4	9.2	2.3	57743	60836	75	68	2041	8.8	10.6	41.8	34.0	4.9	153029
54013	GLENWOOD CITY	22236	1460	20.1	29.1	39.8	8.2	2.8	50949	54974	63	52	1183	11.3	15.0	34.3	32.3	7.1	147288
54014	HAGER CITY	26064	1072	12.6	23.9	49.6	10.9	3.0	62063	65319	80	78	917	7.3	8.7	38.6	37.6	7.7	165252
54015	HAMMOND	26596	1102	11.3	21.0	51.7	12.5	3.4	67962	72669	86	88	851	7.2	4.6	31.7	47.4	9.2	189453
54016	HUDSON	38095	11686	7.5	13.2	41.0	23.6	14.7	83406	86225	93	97	8881	0.9	2.3	11.8	63.6	21.4	283930
54017	NEW RICHMOND	26991	6462	14.3	23.2	46.9	12.1	3.6	62971	65861	81	82	4732	6.9	3.8	31.2	50.5	7.5	190103
54020	OSCEOLA	24434	2715	13.4	26.3	46.7	11.0	2.5	59408	59967	77	71	2073	6.4	6.5	40.2	41.5	5.4	169136
54021	PRESCOTT	29318	2459	8.4	18.3	54.8	13.6	4.8	75026	76655	89	93	1821	4.3	1.8	28.3	53.8	11.8	205779
54022	RIVER FALLS	27830	7573	15.8	20.7	43.3	14.2	6.0	65680	70931	84	86	4794	3.3	2.6	26.0	56.4	11.7	216152
54023	ROBERTS	28388	1400	11.8	21.8	45.8	14.0	6.6	67155	70616	85	87	1156	12.1	7.1	16.3	53.0	11.5	209777
54024	SAINT CROIX FALLS	24917	2031	22.6	27.3	39.4	7.7	2.9	50020	52069	61	48	1525	9.3	13.0	43.3	30.7	3.7	143557
54025	SOMERSET	28538	2562	10.0	21.4	49.7	14.2	4.8	66883	70356	85	87	2015	5.4	2.7	21.8	56.9	13.2	226643
54026	STAR PRAIRIE	25261	701	9.8	24.4	52.2	11.0	2.6	62992	63844	81	82	609	1.5	6.6	28.2	54.8	8.9	197940
54027	WILSON	25934	377	12.5	26.0	48.5	10.1	2.9	62508	64716	81	79	339	6.8	10.0	30.4	43.4	9.4	182917
54028	WOODVILLE	24416	933	16.4	31.5	40.3	9.5	2.3	53207	60042	68	59	722	17.9	6.9	28.9	39.2	7.1	165878
54082	HOULTON	38568	623	6.3	10.8	40.0	30.0	13.0	90864	92214	95	98	554	12.6	0.5	9.6	54.2	23.1	283684
54101	ABRAMS	24464	1016	11.8	26.2	50.8	9.1	2.2	60066	60933	77	73	826	5.5	13.0	47.2	31.0	3.3	141987
54102	AMBERG	23834	434	31.6	32.0	29.3	4.1	3.0	38527	40257	28	8	370	18.1	26.5	44.6	10.5	0.3	95882
54103	ARMSTRONG CREEK	20149	249	33.7	30.5	31.3	3.2	1.2	37565	40000	25	6	200	13.5	37.5	40.5	8.0	0.5	89091
54104	ATHELSTANE	24245	497	23.5	33.6	34.6	6.4	1.8	43513	46657	44	26	441	17.0	30.6	36.1	13.8	2.5	92442
54106	BLACK CREEK	23612	2000	15.0	28.3	47.4	7.3	2.1	56578	60172	73	66	1671	6.7	11.9	49.6	28.7	3.1	138923
54107	BONDUEL	22503	1454	18.8	33.0	39.8	6.1	2.3	48541	49100	58	44	1152	4.6	11.9	58.8	21.7	3.0	132309
54110	BRILLION	24927	2295	15.8	27.1	47.1	7.0	2.9	56765	59653	74	67	1819	10.4	13.5	57.3	17.5	1.3	120636
54111	CECIL	22623	956	21.1	29.9	40.2	6.9	1.9	48749	49317	58	45	807	7.9	17.8	45.0	25.0	4.2	123482
54112	COLEMAN	20875	989	27.3	29.9	36.1	5.4	1.3	44009	45908	45	28	798	10.2	26.2	49.2	13.3	1.1	108193
54113	COMBINED LOCKS	29635	1075	8.0	19.8	53.5	13.2	5.5	68525	73383	86	89	957	0.0	6.0	58.1	32.8	3.1	147847
54114	CRIVITZ	22531	2432	26.9	33.7	32.2	5.8	1.4	41441	43388	37	18	1994	10.7	25.5	43.9	17.1	2.8	107778
54115	DE PERE	30427	14469	11.0	21.7	46.6	13.7	7.0	67472	71702	85	88	10344	1.5	4.7	44.2	43.7	5.8	174112
54119	DUNBAR	15260	299	28.8	32.8	31.4	5.4	1.7	40110	42088	33	12	233	17.6	31.3	40.8	10.3	0.0	91136
54120	FENCE	23450	174	30.5	36.8	27.6	3.4	1.7	37330	37519	25	5	156	16.7	32.1	34.6	15.4	1.3	91053
54121	FLORENCE	21963	1403	27.6	31.1	35.0	4.9	1.4	43051	44128	43	24	1190	13.2	25.2	38.6	21.1	1.9	112500
54124	GILLETT	20608	1547	25.3	32.6	36.3	4.0	1.8	43284	45480	43	25	1231	15.2	32.8	39.7	10.6	1.6	91856
54125	GOODMAN	22448	338	26.6	32.8	32.8	5.3	2.4	41206	43644	37	17	289	21.5	29.8	39.4	9.0	0.3	88409
54126	GREENLEAF	24020	1399	9.5	25.5	53.1	8.2	3.6	62682	65715	81	80	1213	6.7	8.7	44.9	36.2	3.5	154250
54128	GRESHAM	18007	757	25.8	30.1	38.6	4.8	0.8	43869	45595	45	27	604	13.4	22.2	49.5	12.7	2.2	110714
54129	HILBERT	24257	1598	14.6	27.7	46.7	7.9	3.0	56913	59757	74	67	1334	10.3	11.8	50.7	23.9	3.3	129930
54130	KAUKAUNA	26208	9530	12.9	21.9	51.7	10.1	3.4	63786	66848	82	83	7392	0.8	7.2	63.8	26.4	1.8	140607
54135	KESHENA	12816	1333	34.7	30.8	30.6	3.5	0.4	35676	37080	20	3	980	26.6	28.2	32.0	12.0	1.1	83380
54136	KIMBERLY	30022	2742	13.6	21.8	49.5	11.7	3.4	64766	67981	83	85	2079	1.0	5.7	72.4	20.6	0.2	131115
54137	KRAKOW	23668	485	14.8	28.7	47.0	7.4	2.1	54809	54820	71	62	439	5.0	14.1	50.3	26.7	3.9	137351
54138	LAKEWOOD	25712	472	23.9	34.1	33.1	5.9	3.0	42682	45000	41	23	422	11.1	19.4	43.1	23.0	3.3	118952
54139	LENA	22605	1388	22.9	29.7	38.4	6.9	2.1	47300	50683	55	41	1118	12.2	25.5	44.3	16.1	2.0	103551
54140	LITTLE CHUTE	27213	3674	12.7	25.4	48.2	9.4	4.3	62389	65782	80	79	2494	7.9	7.6	63.4	20.9	0.2	135971
54141	LITTLE SUAMICO	27424	1062	7.9	21.1	57.5	11.1	2.4	65814	65886	84	86	964	8.9	9.5	50.7	29.0	1.8	140270
54143	MARINETTE	24181	6723	24.2	29.7	37.3	5.8	2.9	45670	49386	50	35	4982	14.7	33.9	39.1	11.6	0.8	91629
54149	MOUNTAIN	25449	660	21.8	35.2	36.1	5.0	2.0	45184	47189	49	33	578	14.2	24.2	41.7	17.0	2.9	104545
54150	NEOPIT	10781	6	33.3	50.0	16.7	0.0	0.0	30000	30000	8	1	4	25.0	50.0	25.0	0.0	0.0	75000
54151	NIAGARA	21462	1690	25.2	31.1	36.0	6.4	1.2	44122	46338	46	29	1388	15.3	33.9	40.5	9.9	0.5	91026
54153	OCONTO	22598	3068	25.0	30.0	37.5	5.1	2.4	45059	48281	48	33	2311	9.0	30.8	43.4	15.3	1.6	100428
54154	OCONTO FALLS	23067	2270	21.9	27.0	42.3	7.1	1.8	50953	52994	63	52	1663	8.2	22.3	49.4	18.5	1.6	110679
54155	ONEIDA	31669	1771	12.6	16.3	37.7	20.9	12.4	78880	81225	92	95	1546	1.7	6.2	36.9	45.7	9.4	188167
54156	PEMBINE	22464	837	29.4	32.9	30.6	5.4	1.8	40186	41765	33	13	703	17.9	27.3	44.2	10.1	0.4	94855
54157	PESHTIGO	21027	2332	22.9	32.1	37.0	6.9	1.1	45690	48195	50	36	1754	9.6	25.9	45.1	18.4	1.0	109622
54159	PORTERFIELD	21961	641	21.1	29.6	43.4	5.3	0.6	49432	51883	60	47	585	9.4	21.7	49.4	17.4	2.1	116005
54161	POUND	20274	1233	27.7	33.1	32.9	4.7	1.5	41149	42823	36	17	1010	11.5	25.2	42.1	18.9	2.3	106040
54162	PULASKI	24717	3328	16.7	20.9	48.2	11.0	3.2	63831	66059	82	83	2636	5.2	7.7	49.6	35.2	2.4	149886
54165	SEYMOUR	23608	2863	13.9	28.0	47.6	8.6	1.9	58419	61162	76	70	2209	3.2	8.2	54.6	31.9	2.0	143120
54166	SHAWANO	23533	7014	24.1	31.8	35.2	5.9	3.0	45402	46733	49	34	5091	6.1	19.2	53.4	19.3	2.0	120668
54169	SHERWOOD	30550	912	9.4	16.3	56.6	10.9	6.8	69480	73556	86	90	799	1.3	3.8	36.4	52.3	6.3	188275
54170	SHIOCTON	23791	1570	13.8	28.7	48.2	7.5	1.8	57852	60597	75	69	1332	7.7	15.0	48.4	26.3	2.6	133412
54171	SOBIESKI	27372	1035	9.9	13.4	55.4	15.3	6.1	75073	75684	89	93	970	5.1	7.3	42.4	43.1	2.2	165873
54173	SUAMICO	33847	1480	3.9	11.8	61.1	14.0	9.2	78091	79467	91	94	1302	0.0	3.5	35.3	51.8	9.4	197256
54174	SURING	21072	1391	27.7	33.5	33.1	4.3	1.4	40620	42210	35	15	1129	14.3	33.7	37.2	12.8	2.0	92765
54175	TOWNSEND	25464	512	25.6	34.6	30.9	6.1	2.9	40000	42184	33	12	461	11.3	18.4	43.6	23.4	3.3	121573
54177	WAUSAUKEE	19634	1459	29.9	33.6	32.0	3.8	0.7	40321	41959	34	14	1233	16.5	23.3	44.0	15.2	1.1	104273
54180	WRIGHTSTOWN	29847	927	10.1	22.2	46.2	15.2	6.3	68346	72288	86	88	688	1.5	7.1	54.5	34.7	2.2	151316
54201	ALGOMA	23145	2511	23.7	30.2	38.8	5.8	1.5	46891	49394	54	40	1959	8.9	27.8	47.6	14.0	1.6	103116
54202	BAILEYS HARBOR	29962	623	19.4	31.3	37.1	8.8	3.4	49504	50469	60	47	523	4.6	3.1	32.1	44.2	16.1	210197
54204	BRUSSELS	23266	770	19.9	28.4	40.1	9.4	2.2	51293	51969	64	53	669	7.2	12.3	45.1	27.1	8.4	141540
54205	CASCO	21619	842	19.6	26.8	44.5	6.4	2.6	52597	54562	67	56	695	4.5	14.2	54.8	24.3	2.2	132095
54208	DENMARK	24432	2515	15.6	26.8	45.8	8.7	3.1	57863	60891	75	69	1952	4.9	11.2	52.7	28.2	3.0	139081
54209	EGG HARBOR	30518	650	20.5	27.4	36.9	8.2	7.1	51872	52481	66	55	561	5.0	5.5	30.8	36.7	21.9	204044
54210	ELLISON BAY	30017	470	20.0	26.0	40.6	7.2	6.2	52412	52679	67	56	409	0.2	3.7	30.8	43.3	22.0	225980
54212	FISH CREEK	34997	525	18.3	26.1	37.5	9.5	8.6	54677	55135	71	62	448	1.3	2.5	23.4	49.6	23.2	261957
54213	FORESTVILLE	22707	580	20.0	28.8	42.1	7.2	1.9	51031	51602	64	52	495	7.9	15.8	49.3	25.1	2.0	123500
	WISCONSIN	27384		18.4	25.3	40.0	11.0	5.2	56363	58927				5.6	11.9	43.5	34.2	4.7	150766
	UNITED STATES	27277		20.9	24.4	35.3	11.7	7.6	54719	56938				9.3	13.1	31.6	32.6	13.5	162279

ZIP CODE		FINANCIAL SERVICES				THE HOME						ENTERTAINMENT						PERSONAL			
						Home Improvements		Furnishings													
#	POST OFFICE NAME	Auto Loan	Home Loan	Investments	Retirement Plans	Home Repair	Lawn & Garden	Computers & Hardware-Personal	Major Appliances	TV, Radio, Sound Equipment	Furniture	Dine out/ Carry out	Sports Equipment	Fees & Tickets	Toys & Games	Travel	Cable TV	Apparel & Services	Auto Repairs	Health Insurance	Pets & Supplies
53951	NORTH FREEDOM	90	88	81	90	87	94	84	90	85	81	85	69	82	87	85	88	58	86	91	106
53952	OXFORD	83	64	99	63	69	87	66	83	70	61	69	61	55	68	68	76	46	77	85	97
53954	PARDEEVILLE	89	95	90	96	95	99	89	94	90	86	90	71	92	90	93	92	63	91	97	109
53955	POYNETTE	95	102	90	102	100	100	94	97	94	95	94	74	98	96	97	94	66	94	96	114
53956	RANDOLPH	94	86	88	88	85	100	86	93	88	79	87	72	80	89	85	92	59	90	99	111
53959	REEDSBURG	92	87	84	89	86	95	90	92	91	85	90	71	86	92	88	94	62	91	97	109
53960	RIO	91	96	83	99	92	99	90	93	90	88	90	73	92	92	92	92	62	91	96	111
53961	ROCK SPRINGS	99	93	92	97	94	107	91	101	92	83	91	77	85	94	92	97	62	94	104	118
53963	WAUPUN	89	91	77	92	86	95	89	89	90	85	90	69	90	92	88	93	62	89	96	107
53964	WESTFIELD	84	64	95	63	68	88	67	83	72	61	70	62	55	70	68	78	47	77	87	97
53965	WISCONSIN DELLS	92	81	95	81	84	95	82	91	84	80	83	67	76	83	83	88	57	88	95	107
53968	WONEWOC	90	64	94	62	66	93	68	86	75	60	73	66	53	74	67	82	48	79	91	102
54001	AMERY	88	80	87	81	82	93	80	89	82	75	81	67	74	82	81	86	55	85	92	104
54002	BALDWIN	88	92	85	95	90	90	93	89	92	91	93	71	96	92	94	92	65	92	91	107
54003	BELDENVILLE	98	108	95	111	105	108	97	102	96	97	96	80	102	98	102	96	67	98	101	120
54004	CLAYTON	87	71	84	71	72	90	72	84	75	66	74	65	62	76	71	80	50	79	86	100
54005	CLEAR LAKE	88	70	78	69	70	87	71	80	76	68	75	62	61	78	67	81	50	76	83	97
54006	CUSHING	80	73	72	76	75	86	72	81	74	65	73	62	66	76	72	79	50	75	84	95
54007	DEER PARK	95	90	89	93	91	102	87	96	88	81	87	74	83	90	88	92	60	90	98	113
54009	DRESSER	94	94	82	93	92	95	87	91	88	89	88	68	86	91	86	90	61	88	91	108
54011	ELLSWORTH	88	92	88	94	92	96	88	92	87	84	87	72	89	89	91	89	61	89	93	108
54013	GLENWOOD CITY	93	84	91	87	85	100	83	94	84	75	84	73	76	85	84	89	57	88	96	111
54014	HAGER CITY	98	104	94	108	103	107	96	101	95	94	95	79	99	97	100	97	66	97	101	119
54015	HAMMOND	96	110	99	110	108	104	102	102	100	101	101	80	109	102	107	100	72	101	101	119
54016	HUDSON	138	154	137	155	148	136	144	139	137	147	140	112	152	142	146	133	100	138	129	162
54017	NEW RICHMOND	94	100	91	101	97	97	97	96	96	95	96	75	100	97	99	96	68	96	97	113
54020	OSCEOLA	91	96	83	99	93	93	91	91	89	92	90	72	94	92	93	89	63	90	90	108
54021	PRESCOTT	105	119	109	120	117	113	110	110	107	111	108	86	117	109	115	107	77	109	108	129
54022	RIVER FALLS	103	103	96	106	101	98	110	100	105	107	107	81	108	107	105	103	75	104	99	119
54023	ROBERTS	111	119	105	118	116	113	106	111	105	110	106	84	110	109	108	105	74	106	106	129
54024	SAINT CROIX FALLS	89	80	82	82	82	93	81	89	84	75	82	67	75	84	80	88	56	84	93	104
54025	SOMERSET	101	116	102	117	113	110	105	107	103	105	104	84	113	105	111	103	73	104	105	125
54026	STAR PRAIRIE	94	106	91	109	103	104	95	99	93	95	94	77	101	96	100	93	66	95	98	116
54027	WILSON	94	105	91	109	102	104	94	98	93	94	93	77	100	95	99	93	65	94	97	115
54028	WOODVILLE	93	93	82	93	91	94	86	90	87	88	87	68	86	90	86	88	60	87	90	107
54082	HOULTON	133	165	148	165	160	145	142	143	134	147	137	113	159	139	152	130	98	138	131	164
54101	ABRAMS	96	99	89	101	97	103	91	98	92	89	92	75	92	94	94	94	63	93	98	115
54102	AMBERG	81	68	91	64	74	87	67	82	72	68	71	57	61	68	70	78	47	77	88	95
54103	ARMSTRONG CREEK	73	55	78	53	58	77	59	72	64	54	62	53	48	63	58	71	42	67	78	85
54104	ATHELSTANE	78	73	94	67	81	88	70	83	74	75	72	55	68	68	76	78	48	79	92	95
54106	BLACK CREEK	93	88	85	91	89	100	85	95	87	79	86	72	81	89	86	91	59	88	97	110
54107	BONDUEL	87	79	80	82	81	94	78	89	81	71	79	67	72	82	78	85	54	82	91	103
54110	BRILLION	98	90	88	93	90	105	89	98	91	81	90	75	83	93	88	96	61	92	103	115
54111	CECIL	87	78	83	80	80	93	77	88	79	70	78	66	70	80	77	84	53	81	90	102
54112	COLEMAN	84	66	83	66	68	88	68	82	74	62	72	62	58	73	67	80	48	76	87	97
54113	COMBINED LOCKS	111	124	104	125	119	115	110	113	107	113	108	89	116	111	114	105	76	108	108	132
54114	CRIVITZ	78	65	82	62	68	84	65	78	70	63	68	56	58	68	66	76	46	73	84	91
54115	DE PERE	114	122	106	122	117	113	114	113	111	117	112	89	117	115	114	109	79	111	110	132
54119	DUNBAR	79	65	101	63	71	84	64	81	67	61	66	58	57	64	70	72	44	75	81	93
54120	FENCE	78	62	101	61	69	82	62	79	65	59	65	58	54	62	68	70	43	73	78	92
54121	FLORENCE	84	64	98	63	69	88	66	84	71	61	70	62	56	69	69	77	46	77	86	97
54124	GILLETT	86	66	85	66	68	90	69	83	74	62	72	64	57	74	68	81	48	77	88	99
54125	GOODMAN	77	69	97	65	76	86	67	81	70	68	69	56	63	65	73	75	46	77	86	93
54126	GREENLEAF	96	108	93	111	104	106	96	100	95	96	95	78	103	97	101	95	66	96	99	118
54128	GRESHAM	87	62	89	60	65	88	64	81	71	60	70	61	51	71	63	78	46	75	85	97
54129	HILBERT	107	86	99	87	87	110	88	101	92	80	91	79	75	94	85	99	61	95	105	121
54130	KAUKAUNA	98	101	87	102	97	101	97	97	97	95	97	75	98	99	96	98	67	96	100	115
54135	KESHENA	66	52	66	53	52	65	55	62	59	53	58	47	49	58	54	63	39	61	65	75
54136	KIMBERLY	98	105	88	104	100	104	98	99	99	98	99	76	102	101	99	100	69	98	105	116
54137	KRAKOW	91	89	84	92	89	98	85	93	86	79	85	71	82	88	86	89	59	87	95	108
54138	LAKEWOOD	80	77	98	71	85	91	73	86	77	79	75	56	72	70	80	82	50	83	96	98
54139	LENA	87	77	79	77	75	90	77	84	80	72	79	65	70	81	75	83	53	81	88	101
54140	LITTLE CHUTE	98	100	87	100	96	95	100	96	99	99	99	76	101	101	98	98	70	98	97	114
54141	LITTLE SUAMICO	111	104	93	102	102	106	98	104	100	101	100	77	93	105	95	102	69	100	103	122
54143	MARINETTE	79	75	75	75	74	85	76	80	79	72	78	60	74	78	76	83	53	79	88	95
54149	MOUNTAIN	78	75	95	69	83	89	71	84	75	77	73	55	70	69	78	79	49	81	93	96
54150	NEOPIT	43	36	29	38	32	39	40	37	43	40	43	29	38	44	36	45	29	40	42	48
54151	NIAGARA	81	69	75	70	69	85	70	79	73	65	72	60	63	74	69	78	49	75	83	93
54153	OCONTO	89	73	81	73	74	92	75	86	80	69	78	65	65	81	72	86	53	81	91	101
54154	OCONTO FALLS	88	76	79	77	77	89	79	85	82	76	81	64	72	83	76	86	55	82	89	100
54155	ONEIDA	128	150	140	153	149	143	130	136	127	136	128	104	143	129	141	125	90	130	130	158
54156	PEMBINE	83	64	95	62	68	86	64	81	70	61	68	59	55	67	67	75	45	75	83	95
54157	PESHTIGO	80	71	73	73	72	86	72	80	75	65	73	61	66	76	71	79	50	75	85	94
54159	PORTERFIELD	81	74	73	77	75	87	73	82	75	66	74	62	67	77	73	80	50	76	85	96
54161	POUND	83	63	90	61	66	86	64	80	69	59	68	59	53	68	65	75	45	74	82	94
54162	PULASKI	98	100	85	101	96	95	97	95	94	97	95	76	97	98	95	93	66	94	93	112
54165	SEYMOUR	93	92	82	93	90	95	88	92	89	86	89	70	87	92	87	91	61	89	93	109
54166	SHAWANO	83	72	80	73	74	87	75	83	79	70	77	62	68	78	74	83	52	80	88	97
54169	SHERWOOD	110	123	106	127	120	121	110	115	108	111	109	90	118	111	116	109	76	110	113	135
54170	SHIOCTON	95	87	86	90	88	102	85	96	88	77	87	73	79	90	85	93	59	89	99	112
54171	SOBIESKI	119	128	106	125	121	113	114	116	110	121	112	91	117	117	114	106	78	110	106	133
54173	SUAMICO	135	149	123	146	141	130	132	133	126	139	128	105	137	134	133	122	89	127	122	153
54174	SURING	86	63	90	60	65	88	64	81	71	60	69	61	52	70	64	78	46	75	85	97
54175	TOWNSEND	78	75	96	69	83	89	71	84	75	77	74	55	70	69	78	80	49	81	94	96
54177	WAUSAUKEE	79	60	80	58	62	81	61	75	66	57	65	56	51	66	61	72	43	69	79	89
54180	WRIGHTSTOWN	117	129	105	125	121	110	114	114	108	121	110	91	117	116	114	103	77	109	103	131
54201	ALGOMA	87	70	81	70	72	89	73	84	78	67	76	63	63	78	71	83	51	79	89	99
54202	BAILEYS HARBOR	99	79	128	78	87	104	79	101	83	74	82	73	69	79	86	88	54	93	99	116
54204	BRUSSELS	92	83	87	86	85	99	82	93	84	74	83	70	75	85	82	89	56	86	96	108
54205	CASCO	92	81	89	83	82	99	81	93	83	72	82	72	72	84	81	88	55	86	96	109
54208	DENMARK	94	93	86	96	91	102	90	95	91	85	90	74	89	92	91	94	62	92	99	113
54209	EGG HARBOR	112	90	145	88	99	119	90	114	94	84	93	83	78	89	97	100	62	105	113	132
54210	ELLISON BAY	108	87	140	85	95	114	87	110	91	81	90	80	75	86	94	97	60	102	109	128
54212	FISH CREEK	125	100	162	98	110	132	100	127	105	94	104	93	87	99	108	112	69	117	126	147
54213	FORESTVILLE	89	80	81	84	82	96	80	90	82	72	81	68	73	84	79	87	55	83	93	105
	WISCONSIN	98	94	92	96	93	99	96	96	96	93	96	75	94	97	95	98	67	96	99	114
	UNITED STATES	100	100	100	100	100	100	100	100	100	100	100	100	100	100	100	100	100	100	100	100

ZIP CODE			POPULATION			2000-2009 ANNUAL RATE		HOUSEHOLDS					FAMILIES		
#	POST OFFICE NAME	COUNTY FIPS CODE	2000	2009	2014	% Rate	State Centile	2000	2009	2014	% Annual Rate 2000-2009	2009 Average HH Size	2000	2009	% Annual Rate 2000-2009
54216	KEWAUNEE	061	6065	6072	6042	0.0	16	2310	2390	2403	0.4	2.49	1649	1687	0.2
54217	LUXEMBURG	061	6739	7531	7845	1.2	81	2370	2764	2914	1.7	2.70	1857	2142	1.6
54220	MANITOWOC	071	41115	40868	40672	-0.1	11	16745	17218	17296	0.3	2.31	10767	10928	0.2
54227	MARIBEL	071	1583	1665	1695	0.5	44	547	606	624	1.1	2.75	447	490	1.0
54228	MISHICOT	071	2805	2843	2848	0.1	20	1053	1118	1133	0.6	2.54	802	841	0.5
54229	NEW FRANKEN	009	3414	3954	4196	1.6	91	1119	1427	1535	2.7	2.75	911	1132	2.4
54230	REEDSVILLE	071	4503	4758	4880	0.6	51	1624	1802	1871	1.1	2.64	1236	1353	1.0
54234	SISTER BAY	029	1949	1985	1999	0.2	24	916	986	1009	0.8	1.92	560	592	0.6
54235	STURGEON BAY	029	17366	18281	18727	0.6	51	7290	8023	8336	1.0	2.24	4855	5275	0.9
54241	TWO RIVERS	071	15933	15289	14985	-0.4	2	6422	6395	6336	0.0	2.37	4357	4278	-0.2
54245	VALDERS	071	2284	2455	2517	0.8	61	840	946	981	1.3	2.59	638	710	1.2
54246	WASHINGTON ISLAND	029	660	708	727	0.8	61	293	324	337	1.1	2.19	199	217	0.9
54247	WHITELAW	071	2429	2443	2443	0.1	20	891	940	952	0.6	2.60	691	721	0.5
54301	GREEN BAY	009	25942	25547	25347	-0.2	8	9803	9963	9984	0.2	2.29	5888	5810	-0.1
54302	GREEN BAY	009	29947	30680	30877	0.3	32	12666	13345	13596	0.6	2.26	7299	7410	0.2
54303	GREEN BAY	009	27549	27211	27087	-0.1	11	12050	12356	12457	0.3	2.16	6493	6374	-0.2
54304	GREEN BAY	009	30070	29259	29013	-0.3	4	12737	12971	13027	0.2	2.22	8104	7987	-0.2
54311	GREEN BAY	009	27767	33468	36001	2.0	95	9745	12270	13381	2.5	2.59	6724	8274	2.3
54313	GREEN BAY	009	31154	35937	38014	1.6	91	10824	13030	13947	2.0	2.75	8715	10345	1.9
54401	WAUSAU	073	30235	31435	31885	0.4	39	11859	12827	13175	0.9	2.41	7961	8496	0.7
54403	WAUSAU	073	24369	24979	25280	0.3	32	9605	10258	10504	0.7	2.34	6125	6453	0.6
54405	ABBOTSFORD	073	2950	3049	3081	0.4	39	1143	1220	1243	0.7	2.44	788	832	0.6
54406	AMHERST	097	3199	3368	3467	0.6	51	1177	1303	1360	1.1	2.55	873	950	0.9
54407	AMHERST JUNCTION	097	1719	1820	1873	0.6	51	650	719	750	1.1	2.53	491	534	0.9
54408	ANIWA	073	1267	1353	1394	0.7	56	456	510	531	1.2	2.65	363	401	1.1
54409	ANTIGO	067	14083	14552	14813	0.4	39	5639	6004	6171	0.7	2.38	3799	4002	0.6
54410	ARPIN	141	2181	2235	2247	0.3	32	729	790	805	0.9	2.69	559	599	0.7
54411	ATHENS	073	5049	5464	5655	0.9	68	1673	1893	1988	1.3	2.89	1338	1494	1.2
54412	AUBURNDALE	141	1986	1980	1967	0.0	16	732	771	777	0.6	2.57	568	593	0.5
54413	BABCOCK	141	288	302	305	0.5	44	117	127	130	0.9	2.38	86	92	0.7
54414	BIRNAMWOOD	115	3289	3492	3581	0.6	51	1184	1308	1356	1.1	2.65	872	953	1.0
54416	BOWLER	078	1978	2065	2093	0.5	44	678	733	751	0.8	2.79	511	546	0.7
54418	BRYANT	067	1243	1358	1411	1.0	72	457	519	545	1.4	2.62	353	397	1.3
54420	CHILI	019	1196	1239	1239	0.4	39	385	401	402	0.4	3.09	317	329	0.4
54421	COLBY	073	3075	3420	3520	1.2	81	1089	1268	1322	1.7	2.61	805	922	1.5
54422	CURTISS	019	1151	1193	1196	0.4	39	343	361	362	0.6	3.30	274	286	0.5
54423	CUSTER	097	2190	2375	2467	0.9	68	771	878	924	1.4	2.71	611	685	1.2
54424	DEERBROOK	067	1597	1713	1768	0.8	61	648	723	755	1.2	2.37	484	534	1.1
54425	DORCHESTER	019	1933	2145	2190	1.1	76	697	801	824	1.5	2.68	509	578	1.4
54426	EDGAR	073	4109	4623	4871	1.3	84	1420	1696	1815	1.9	2.72	1101	1293	1.8
54427	ELAND	073	1099	1192	1242	0.9	68	417	477	503	1.5	2.48	301	340	1.3
54428	ELCHO	067	1211	1254	1281	0.4	39	563	608	628	0.8	2.06	381	405	0.7
54430	ELTON	067	112	125	132	1.2	81	44	52	55	1.8	2.40	35	41	1.7
54433	GILMAN	119	1882	1986	2011	0.6	51	692	761	782	1.0	2.56	505	549	0.9
54435	GLEASON	069	2035	2103	2119	0.4	39	817	883	901	0.8	2.37	595	633	0.7
54436	GRANTON	019	2225	2195	2165	-0.1	11	731	731	724	0.0	3.00	576	573	-0.1
54437	GREENWOOD	019	3042	3096	3085	0.2	24	1070	1113	1112	0.4	2.75	770	793	0.3
54440	HATLEY	073	2833	3084	3240	0.9	68	1054	1215	1293	1.5	2.54	834	948	1.4
54441	HEWITT	141	664	702	714	0.6	51	232	260	268	1.2	2.70	187	209	1.2
54442	IRMA	069	1450	1508	1522	0.4	39	440	479	491	0.9	2.62	327	351	0.8
54443	JUNCTION CITY	097	2328	2383	2426	0.3	32	859	928	958	0.8	2.56	653	696	0.7
54446	LOYAL	019	3228	3152	3100	-0.3	4	1093	1079	1062	-0.1	2.92	834	816	-0.2
54447	LUBLIN	119	543	558	559	0.3	32	207	220	223	0.7	2.53	150	158	0.6
54448	MARATHON	073	4517	4900	5095	0.9	68	1628	1862	1962	1.5	2.62	1273	1439	1.3
54449	MARSHFIELD	141	26193	26781	26876	0.2	24	10805	11567	11754	0.7	2.28	6964	7386	0.6
54451	MEDFORD	119	11074	11025	10975	0.0	16	4375	4568	4606	0.5	2.39	3036	3140	0.4
54452	MERRILL	069	19455	19910	19992	0.3	32	7588	8079	8194	0.7	2.41	5410	5709	0.6
54454	MILLADORE	141	1315	1331	1335	0.1	20	460	492	501	0.7	2.69	366	389	0.7
54455	MOSINEE	073	15284	16859	17676	1.1	76	5691	6615	7028	1.6	2.54	4380	5028	1.5
54456	NEILLSVILLE	019	6347	6220	6124	-0.2	8	2478	2478	2449	0.0	2.42	1652	1635	-0.1
54457	NEKOOSA	001	8707	8605	8466	-0.1	11	3446	3547	3531	0.3	2.40	2556	2606	0.2
54459	OGEMA	099	1420	1452	1440	0.2	24	569	607	609	0.7	2.39	405	426	0.5
54460	OWEN	019	2541	2644	2649	0.4	39	869	913	917	0.5	2.66	622	647	0.4
54462	PEARSON	067	377	378	382	0.0	16	167	175	179	0.5	2.16	118	122	0.4
54463	PELICAN LAKE	085	655	686	696	0.5	44	292	316	325	0.9	2.17	211	226	0.7
54465	PICKEREL	067	782	829	853	0.6	51	376	419	437	1.2	1.98	267	295	1.1
54466	PITTSVILLE	141	2790	3015	3081	0.8	61	1054	1182	1227	1.2	2.47	785	870	1.1
54467	PLOVER	097	11928	12924	13448	0.9	68	4502	5140	5423	1.4	2.51	3282	3682	1.3
54469	PORT EDWARDS	141	1920	1876	1830	-0.3	4	694	695	685	0.0	2.51	511	505	-0.1
54470	RIB LAKE	119	1950	2004	2006	0.3	32	758	815	828	0.8	2.38	536	569	0.6
54471	RINGLE	073	1515	1926	2073	2.6	97	533	734	801	3.5	2.62	452	614	3.4
54473	ROSHOLT	097	2711	2960	3080	1.0	72	971	1110	1171	1.5	2.67	740	833	1.3
54474	ROTHSCHILD	073	3864	3749	3717	-0.3	4	1510	1549	1555	0.3	2.40	1098	1107	0.1
54475	RUDOLPH	141	1722	1682	1643	-0.3	4	640	656	650	0.3	2.56	497	503	0.1
54476	SCHOFIELD	073	15176	17238	18083	1.4	86	5866	6881	7278	1.7	2.48	4017	4692	1.7
54479	SPENCER	019	3602	3703	3739	0.3	32	1335	1432	1463	0.8	2.59	958	1006	0.5
54480	STETSONVILLE	119	1202	1223	1229	0.2	24	434	463	472	0.7	2.64	339	358	0.6
54481	STEVENS POINT	097	37567	38915	39608	0.4	39	14033	15144	15618	0.8	2.35	8300	8859	0.7
54484	STRATFORD	073	4457	4948	5199	1.1	76	1633	1917	2037	1.7	2.57	1265	1462	1.6
54485	SUMMIT LAKE	067	289	315	327	0.9	68	134	152	160	1.4	2.07	90	101	1.3
54486	TIGERTON	115	2555	2609	2602	0.2	24	1007	1058	1063	0.5	2.43	699	727	0.4
54487	TOMAHAWK	069	9879	10166	10208	0.3	32	4092	4344	4405	0.6	2.30	2853	3002	0.6
54488	UNITY	073	1157	1190	1203	0.3	32	398	425	434	0.7	2.80	316	334	0.6
54489	VESPER	141	1530	1619	1646	0.6	51	585	655	676	1.2	2.47	432	478	1.1
54490	WESTBORO	119	917	930	930	0.2	24	344	366	371	0.7	2.46	237	248	0.5
54491	WHITE LAKE	067	1637	1838	1926	1.3	84	691	804	852	1.7	2.28	492	565	1.5
54493	WILLARD	019	829	830	824	0.0	16	336	346	344	0.3	2.40	247	252	0.2
54494	WISCONSIN RAPIDS	141	27712	27848	27669	0.1	20	10966	11492	11561	0.5	2.38	7674	7953	0.4
54495	WISCONSIN RAPIDS	141	7539	7315	7153	-0.3	4	3154	3186	3158	0.1	2.29	2013	2005	0.0
54498	WITHEE	119	2202	2304	2313	0.5	44	773	821	827	0.7	2.80	586	617	0.6
54499	WITTENBERG	115	3069	3212	3271	0.5	44	1115	1224	1263	1.0	2.47	790	854	0.8
54501	RHINELANDER	085	20234	20813	20929	0.3	32	8112	8604	8722	0.6	2.34	5421	5685	0.5
54511	ARGONNE	041	1526	1531	1532	0.0	16	612	642	651	0.5	2.37	418	433	0.4
54512	BOULDER JUNCTION	125	865	994	1077	1.5	88	400	476	519	1.9	2.09	287	339	1.8
54513	BRANTWOOD	099	502	495	487	-0.2	8	217	223	221	0.3	2.22	148	150	0.1
	WISCONSIN					0.7					1.0	2.43			0.9
	UNITED STATES					1.0					1.1	2.59			0.9

ZIP CODE		RACE (%)								2009 AGE DISTRIBUTION (%)										MEDIAN AGE		
#	POST OFFICE NAME	White		Black		Asian/Pacific		% Hispanic Origin														
		2000	2009	2000	2009	2000	2009	2000	2009	0-4	5-9	10-14	15-19	20-24	25-44	45-64	65-84	85+	18+	2009	% 2009 Males	% 2009 Females
54216	KEWAUNEE	98.5	98.2	0.3	0.3	0.2	0.3	0.5	0.7	5.6	5.8	6.1	6.3	5.2	24.0	30.2	13.5	3.2	78.4	42.7	51.0	49.0
54217	LUXEMBURG	98.9	98.6	0.1	0.2	0.1	0.2	0.5	0.7	6.8	7.2	7.5	7.0	5.1	27.0	27.5	10.2	1.8	74.0	38.0	50.8	49.2
54220	MANITOWOC	94.1	92.2	0.5	0.6	3.2	4.6	2.2	3.1	6.0	5.9	6.0	6.5	6.0	24.6	28.1	13.6	3.3	78.1	41.3	49.2	50.8
54227	MARIBEL	98.2	97.7	0.0	0.0	0.4	0.6	0.6	0.8	6.3	7.3	8.1	7.3	4.8	24.6	32.1	8.3	1.1	76.8	39.8	52.3	47.7
54228	MISHICOT	98.6	98.1	0.1	0.2	0.2	0.3	1.0	1.5	5.6	6.9	8.8	7.6	4.5	25.2	28.7	11.3	1.5	73.8	39.6	52.0	48.0
54229	NEW FRANKEN	96.8	94.7	1.5	1.8	0.4	1.7	0.6	1.0	6.1	6.4	7.3	6.0	7.1	26.8	30.1	9.4	0.9	76.9	39.0	49.9	50.1
54230	REEDSVILLE	98.6	98.2	0.0	0.0	0.2	0.3	1.0	1.5	5.9	6.4	6.7	7.0	5.1	26.3	30.1	10.9	1.6	76.7	39.9	51.6	48.4
54234	SISTER BAY	98.8	98.4	0.1	0.1	0.2	0.3	0.7	1.0	3.1	3.4	3.8	3.8	2.8	14.3	35.2	26.8	7.0	87.2	57.5	47.1	52.9
54235	STURGEON BAY	97.4	96.8	0.2	0.3	0.3	0.5	1.1	1.6	4.6	5.1	5.7	6.3	5.3	22.4	32.2	15.3	3.0	80.5	45.3	49.6	50.4
54241	TWO RIVERS	96.3	95.0	0.1	0.2	1.9	2.8	1.2	1.7	5.7	5.6	6.0	7.1	6.3	24.9	28.7	13.4	2.4	78.2	40.9	49.8	50.2
54245	VALDERS	98.5	98.0	0.0	0.0	0.2	0.2	1.1	1.7	6.4	6.8	7.0	7.1	4.8	25.1	29.5	11.6	1.6	75.4	40.4	50.9	49.1
54246	WASHINGTON ISLAND	98.8	98.6	0.0	0.0	0.3	0.4	0.2	0.3	3.5	4.1	4.8	6.9	4.2	14.1	39.0	20.8	2.5	83.3	52.9	48.7	51.3
54247	WHITELAW	98.7	98.2	0.0	0.1	0.3	0.5	0.7	1.2	5.9	6.6	7.0	7.2	5.1	25.8	30.7	10.0	1.6	75.8	39.9	51.5	48.5
54301	GREEN BAY	87.8	84.0	3.9	5.0	2.2	3.2	5.2	7.5	6.1	5.6	5.6	7.2	9.1	28.1	24.2	11.3	2.8	78.5	36.8	52.4	47.6
54302	GREEN BAY	82.0	76.2	1.4	1.7	4.3	5.9	14.0	19.7	7.5	6.5	5.9	6.9	9.5	30.5	22.6	8.8	1.8	76.4	32.3	50.2	49.8
54303	GREEN BAY	86.3	81.8	1.7	2.3	4.6	6.9	3.6	5.4	7.6	6.5	5.9	6.1	8.0	30.2	22.9	10.2	2.6	76.3	34.8	48.6	51.4
54304	GREEN BAY	90.4	87.3	0.8	1.1	2.7	4.1	2.5	3.8	6.4	6.1	6.1	6.4	7.0	27.1	26.0	12.4	2.7	77.7	38.5	48.2	51.8
54311	GREEN BAY	95.0	92.6	0.7	0.9	1.7	2.7	2.5	3.9	6.9	6.7	6.6	8.3	7.7	30.7	24.6	7.2	1.2	75.6	33.6	49.0	51.0
54313	GREEN BAY	95.3	94.2	0.3	0.5	0.9	1.4	0.9	1.4	6.9	6.9	7.4	7.5	5.6	27.6	30.3	7.1	0.6	73.8	37.1	49.8	50.2
54401	WAUSAU	88.7	84.7	0.3	0.4	9.3	13.1	0.8	1.1	6.2	6.4	6.6	7.3	6.0	26.0	27.4	11.9	2.3	76.4	38.8	49.1	50.9
54403	WAUSAU	89.8	85.9	0.6	0.7	7.8	11.3	0.9	1.3	6.0	5.7	6.2	6.8	6.4	24.9	27.6	12.9	3.4	77.7	40.3	49.4	50.6
54405	ABBOTSFORD	98.6	98.3	0.1	0.2	0.2	0.2	1.6	2.2	6.5	6.9	7.3	6.7	5.2	25.2	25.4	13.0	3.7	75.1	39.2	51.5	48.5
54406	AMHERST	98.8	98.4	0.3	0.4	0.2	0.4	0.9	1.3	6.4	7.0	7.3	6.7	4.7	25.8	30.2	9.7	2.2	75.0	40.0	51.4	48.6
54407	AMHERST JUNCTION	97.9	97.4	0.1	0.1	0.6	0.8	0.7	1.0	6.1	6.4	7.0	6.9	4.9	25.8	30.5	10.7	1.8	76.3	40.7	51.9	48.1
54408	ANIWA	96.4	95.4	0.1	0.1	0.9	1.5	0.6	0.9	6.7	6.7	7.5	7.5	5.2	26.2	28.2	10.7	1.3	74.4	38.7	52.9	47.1
54409	ANTIGO	97.6	97.1	0.2	0.2	0.3	0.4	1.0	1.4	6.2	6.0	6.2	6.9	6.0	24.2	27.2	13.7	3.6	77.2	40.7	49.3	50.7
54410	ARPIN	98.0	97.4	0.1	0.1	0.4	0.7	0.6	0.8	6.3	6.6	7.1	6.8	4.7	24.6	28.9	10.6	4.5	75.5	40.8	50.4	49.6
54411	ATHENS	98.8	98.4	0.1	0.2	0.1	0.2	1.1	1.7	8.3	8.5	8.3	7.6	4.8	26.2	25.1	9.8	1.4	70.0	35.4	50.7	49.3
54412	AUBURNDALE	99.3	99.2	0.1	0.1	0.1	0.1	0.2	0.3	5.9	7.1	7.1	7.1	4.3	28.0	27.0	12.1	1.4	75.2	38.6	52.5	47.5
54413	BABCOCK	97.2	96.0	0.7	1.0	0.0	0.3	0.7	1.3	6.0	6.3	6.3	7.3	5.3	22.8	29.5	14.6	2.0	76.5	42.4	51.0	49.0
54414	BIRNAMWOOD	96.0	95.1	0.2	0.2	0.7	1.1	0.4	0.6	6.7	6.9	7.1	7.3	5.3	25.9	27.6	11.4	1.8	74.3	38.8	51.7	48.3
54416	BOWLER	56.5	54.9	0.1	0.1	0.2	0.2	0.8	1.1	7.5	7.8	8.4	7.2	5.8	24.1	26.8	10.9	1.5	71.5	36.1	48.8	51.2
54418	BRYANT	98.7	98.3	0.1	0.1	0.2	0.3	0.4	0.5	5.5	6.0	6.2	6.7	5.0	19.8	33.3	15.9	1.6	78.2	45.4	51.4	48.6
54420	CHILI	98.1	97.3	0.0	0.0	0.8	1.3	1.1	1.6	9.2	9.5	9.0	7.3	4.8	25.7	24.9	8.5	1.0	67.6	32.6	51.2	48.8
54421	COLBY	97.5	96.6	0.1	0.2	0.3	0.5	2.3	3.4	7.2	7.2	7.0	7.2	6.2	24.2	25.7	11.9	3.4	74.0	38.0	49.5	50.5
54422	CURTISS	96.0	94.6	0.1	0.1	0.2	0.2	3.4	4.7	8.8	9.0	9.2	8.9	5.3	25.3	22.8	9.2	1.5	67.3	32.7	51.4	48.6
54423	CUSTER	98.7	98.3	0.0	0.0	0.1	0.2	0.9	1.3	5.7	6.2	6.7	6.7	4.5	26.8	31.9	10.1	1.3	77.1	40.4	52.2	47.8
54424	DEERBROOK	99.0	98.8	0.1	0.1	0.1	0.2	0.5	0.8	4.6	4.9	5.3	6.0	5.0	21.4	33.0	17.8	1.9	81.6	46.5	50.6	49.4
54425	DORCHESTER	97.8	97.0	0.1	0.0	0.1	0.1	1.9	2.8	8.3	8.5	8.6	6.9	5.8	25.7	24.7	9.9	1.7	70.3	34.9	51.6	48.4
54426	EDGAR	99.0	98.6	0.1	0.1	0.4	0.6	0.3	0.4	6.7	7.2	8.0	7.8	5.0	26.5	26.5	10.8	1.6	73.3	37.5	51.8	48.2
54427	ELAND	97.0	96.3	0.1	0.1	0.5	0.8	0.9	1.4	5.8	6.0	6.5	7.0	5.1	25.4	29.6	12.7	2.0	77.1	41.1	51.6	48.4
54428	ELCHO	98.0	97.5	0.1	0.1	0.7	1.2	0.2	0.2	3.8	3.9	4.2	5.1	4.1	18.7	32.5	25.0	2.6	85.0	52.2	51.4	48.6
54430	ELTON	99.1	97.6	0.0	0.0	0.0	0.8	0.0	0.0	5.6	6.4	6.4	7.2	6.4	20.8	31.2	14.4	1.6	77.6	42.8	50.4	49.6
54433	GILMAN	98.6	98.2	0.0	0.0	0.3	0.4	0.6	0.9	5.9	6.4	6.7	7.0	4.7	22.7	29.9	13.8	2.9	76.2	42.3	51.9	48.1
54435	GLEASON	98.4	98.1	0.1	0.1	0.3	0.4	0.6	0.8	4.7	5.6	6.3	6.9	4.4	23.7	32.1	14.4	1.9	78.8	43.9	52.6	47.4
54436	GRANTON	98.6	98.1	0.1	0.1	0.3	0.4	1.2	1.7	8.3	8.6	8.3	7.1	5.0	24.6	27.1	9.9	1.1	70.3	35.3	51.3	48.7
54437	GREENWOOD	98.6	98.2	0.1	0.1	0.3	0.4	0.8	1.1	8.0	8.1	7.9	7.4	5.3	22.8	27.0	11.5	2.1	71.3	37.3	50.5	49.5
54440	HATLEY	98.6	98.2	0.1	0.2	0.1	0.2	0.9	1.3	6.4	6.7	6.9	6.8	4.6	28.2	29.0	10.1	1.2	75.5	38.8	52.0	48.0
54441	HEWITT	99.5	99.4	0.0	0.0	0.2	0.3	0.5	0.6	5.7	6.6	7.1	7.1	5.1	24.6	34.0	8.1	1.6	76.1	41.3	49.4	50.6
54442	IRMA	90.1	88.0	4.8	6.0	0.6	0.9	2.3	3.1	4.0	4.6	6.8	19.0	4.0	19.3	28.4	12.9	1.0	67.9	38.1	59.5	40.5
54443	JUNCTION CITY	98.2	97.3	0.1	0.1	0.9	1.5	1.3	1.9	5.9	6.5	7.0	7.3	4.7	25.3	31.1	10.5	1.5	75.9	40.4	51.5	48.5
54446	LOYAL	98.9	98.7	0.2	0.3	0.1	0.1	0.9	1.3	9.7	9.3	9.1	7.8	5.5	24.3	22.1	10.5	1.7	66.9	32.1	50.7	49.3
54447	LUBLIN	99.1	98.9	0.0	0.0	0.2	0.2	0.7	0.9	5.9	6.3	7.2	6.8	4.3	23.5	30.1	13.8	2.2	76.3	42.0	53.8	46.2
54448	MARATHON	98.4	97.6	0.1	0.1	1.0	1.7	0.4	0.7	6.2	7.0	7.6	7.4	4.6	26.7	28.7	10.5	1.3	74.4	38.8	51.4	48.6
54449	MARSHFIELD	97.6	96.7	0.3	0.4	1.2	1.8	0.7	0.9	5.9	5.9	6.4	6.8	6.0	25.1	28.9	12.1	3.0	77.6	40.6	48.8	51.2
54451	MEDFORD	98.6	98.3	0.1	0.1	0.3	0.4	0.6	0.9	6.0	6.6	7.0	7.2	5.8	25.8	27.2	11.6	2.8	75.7	39.0	50.5	49.5
54452	MERRILL	98.0	97.5	0.2	0.3	0.4	0.6	0.8	1.2	6.2	6.4	6.4	7.0	5.6	25.5	27.4	12.4	3.0	76.5	39.9	49.6	50.4
54454	MILLADORE	98.5	98.0	0.0	0.0	0.5	0.8	0.5	0.7	6.4	7.0	7.0	6.5	5.0	26.6	30.1	10.3	1.2	75.7	39.1	52.9	47.1
54455	MOSINEE	98.5	97.8	0.1	0.2	0.6	1.0	0.5	0.8	6.5	6.7	7.1	6.8	5.0	27.1	29.4	9.9	1.4	75.3	39.3	50.6	49.4
54456	NEILLSVILLE	97.5	97.0	0.2	0.2	0.6	0.9	1.0	1.4	6.3	6.2	6.4	7.0	6.0	22.3	27.7	14.5	3.8	76.6	41.7	49.2	50.8
54457	NEKOOSA	95.9	94.9	0.1	0.1	0.6	0.9	1.8	2.6	5.5	6.4	6.8	6.5	4.4	22.5	29.4	16.7	1.8	77.1	43.3	50.5	49.5
54459	OGEMA	98.9	98.7	0.1	0.2	0.1	0.2	0.6	0.7	6.1	6.3	6.7	6.1	5.1	22.3	30.7	14.7	2.0	77.0	42.7	52.2	47.8
54460	OWEN	98.1	97.5	0.3	0.4	0.2	0.3	1.1	1.6	7.7	7.7	7.6	6.9	4.9	23.0	24.1	13.8	4.4	72.7	38.7	49.5	50.5
54462	PEARSON	98.9	98.9	0.0	0.0	0.3	0.3	0.3	0.3	2.6	2.6	3.2	4.2	3.7	15.3	36.5	29.6	2.1	89.4	56.9	52.6	47.4
54463	PELICAN LAKE	98.5	98.4	0.0	0.0	0.2	0.1	0.2	0.1	4.1	5.1	6.3	5.0	3.6	22.9	32.8	17.8	2.5	80.6	46.8	52.2	47.8
54465	PICKEREL	89.5	88.2	0.0	0.1	0.0	0.1	0.3	0.1	4.5	4.7	5.1	5.4	3.9	18.3	33.9	22.3	1.9	82.5	49.9	51.9	48.1
54466	PITTSVILLE	95.3	94.4	1.4	1.7	0.4	0.5	0.5	0.8	5.8	6.1	6.2	7.0	6.3	25.8	28.6	12.4	1.7	77.6	39.6	52.9	47.1
54467	PLOVER	96.9	95.9	0.4	0.5	1.1	1.6	1.2	1.8	7.1	7.0	7.0	6.8	6.3	29.0	28.1	7.9	0.8	74.4	35.8	49.9	50.1
54469	PORT EDWARDS	93.2	91.2	0.6	0.7	3.9	5.6	0.9	1.3	5.4	5.3	5.5	7.6	6.4	22.0	25.6	16.8	5.3	78.7	43.3	47.8	52.2
54470	RIB LAKE	98.9	98.6	0.1	0.1	0.4	0.6	0.6	0.8	5.4	5.5	6.2	7.2	5.6	24.1	28.5	14.0	3.4	78.0	41.9	51.4	48.6
54471	RINGLE	97.6	96.6	0.1	0.2	0.3	0.9	0.5	0.7	6.5	6.9	7.6	7.1	4.8	25.2	31.2	9.8	0.8	74.4	39.6	49.7	50.3
54473	ROSHOLT	98.4	97.9	0.2	0.2	0.1	0.2	1.7	2.5	6.4	6.6	6.6	6.6	5.7	26.7	29.0	10.8	1.6	76.4	39.1	51.8	48.2
54474	ROTHSCHILD	95.7	93.5	0.3	0.4	3.3	5.4	0.2	0.3	5.7	6.0	6.9	7.0	5.0	24.2	31.0	11.9	2.2	76.8	41.6	50.2	49.8
54475	RUDOLPH	96.9	95.8	0.2	0.3	2.0	3.0	0.7	1.0	6.2	6.5	6.8	6.2	4.8	24.5	29.8	13.4	1.8	76.5	41.4	50.2	49.8
54476	SCHOFIELD	93.8	91.2	0.3	0.4	4.2	6.5	0.8	1.1	7.8	7.1	6.7	6.6	7.1	30.4	24.0	8.9	1.4	74.3	34.2	49.4	50.6
54479	SPENCER	98.7	98.3	0.1	0.1	0.3	0.5	0.9	1.3	7.1	7.1	7.3	7.3	6.0	27.3	26.8	9.5	1.6	74.0	35.9	49.6	50.4
54480	STETSONVILLE	98.8	98.4	0.2	0.2	0.1	0.1	1.3	2.0	6.9	7.1	7.4	7.3	5.2	25.3	28.9	10.7	1.3	74.1	38.9	51.3	48.7
54481	STEVENS POINT	94.3	92.4	0.4	0.5	3.5	5.0	1.4	1.9	5.3	5.2	5.4	10.0	15.1	23.7	23.1	10.0	2.1	80.4	32.0	49.1	50.9
54484	STRATFORD	98.9	98.4	0.0	0.0	0.5	0.8	0.6	0.9	7.3	7.3	7.1	7.1	5.8	27.1	26.7	9.8	1.7	74.1	37.1	50.9	49.1
54485	SUMMIT LAKE	97.9	97.1	0.0	0.0	0.7	1.3	0.0	0.0	4.4	4.8	5.1	4.8	3.8	20.0	33.3	21.0	2.9	82.2	49.3	51.4	48.6
54486	TIGERTON	95.6	94.9	0.5	0.6	0.3	0.5	0.6	0.8	6.1	6.3	6.7	6.9	4.6	23.2	28.6	14.4	3.2	76.5	42.0	49.8	50.2
54487	TOMAHAWK	98.6	98.2	0.1	0.1	0.4	0.6	0.6	0.8	4.8	5.1	5.7	6.1	4.5	21.3	32.1	17.4	3.0	80.2	46.5	49.5	50.5
54488	UNITY	97.8	97.0	0.0	0.0	1.1	1.8	0.6	0.8	8.2	8.7	8.7	7.9	4.5	24.3	28.2	8.4	1.3	69.5	35.8	50.9	49.1
54489	VESPER	97.8	97.5	0.1	0.1	0.1	0.2	0.5	0.8	6.0	6.5	7.8	7.0	4.8	25.1	29.5	11.3	2.0	75.3	40.4	50.8	49.2
54490	WESTBORO	98.8	98.3	0.2	0.3	0.2	0.3	0.4	0.8	5.7	6.1	6.3	6.6	5.8	24.9	28.5	12.6	3.4	77.4	40.9	50.4	49.6
54491	WHITE LAKE	98.5	98.1	0.0	0.0	0.2	0.3	0.8	1.3	4.8	5.2	5.4	6.6	5.4	17.6	34.0	18.7	2.3	80.3	47.6	52.6	47.4
54493	WILLARD	97.5	97.1	0.1	0.2	0.0	0.0	0.8	1.1	6.5	7.0	7.2	6.9	4.8	21.6	31.6	12.5	1.9	74.9	41.7	51.2	48.8
54494	WISCONSIN RAPIDS	96.2	95.0	0.3	0.3	1.9	2.7	0.9	1.3	6.1	6.3	6.6	6.6	5.5	24.4	29.0	13.0	2.5	76.7	41.2	49.0	51.0
54495	WISCONSIN RAPIDS	93.5	91.6	0.2	0.3	3.1	4.5	1.6	2.3	6.8	6.9	6.9	6.7	6.0	25.8	25.7	12.7	2.4	75.2	37.9	49.0	51.0
54498	WITHEE	97.9	97.3	0.0	0.0	0.1	0.2	1.6	2.3	7.5	7.6	8.2	7.9	4.9	22.8	26.7	12.2	2.2	71.6	37.9	50.7	49.3
54499	WITTENBERG	95.1	94.2	0.9	1.1	0.2	0.3	0.7	1.1	6.4	6.5	7.3	7.5	5.2	22.9	26.4	13.8	4.1	74.7	40.4	51.4	48.6
54501	RHINELANDER	97.6	97.1	0.3	0.4	0.4	0.6	0.6	0.9	5.3	5.7	6.1	6.3	5.2	23.9	30.5	14.4	2.7	78.8	43.2	49.2	50.8
54511	ARGONNE	94.2	93.3	0.1	0.2	0.4	0.6	0.5	0.7	4.6	4.7	4.9	5.4	4.3	20.8	31.9	21.0	2.4	82.6	48.6	52.2	47.8
54512	BOULDER JUNCTION	93.1	92.7	0.0	0.1	0.1	0.1	0.6	0.7	3.5	4.1	4.7	4.8	3.3	17.0	36.5	23.2	2.7	84.5	52.6	50.7	49.3
54513	BRANTWOOD	98.8	98.8	0.2	0.2	0.2	0.2	1.2	1.8	4.0	4.2	4.4	6.1	5.9	22.8	33.3	16.8	2.4	83.6	46.4	51.5	48.5
	WISCONSIN	88.9	86.9	5.7	6.3	1.7	2.3	3.6	4.8	6.4	6.4	6.5	7.2	7.2	26.0	27.1	11.1	2.2	76.6	38.0	49.5	50.5
	UNITED STATES	75.1	72.0	12.3	12.7	3.8	4.6	12.5	15.7	6.8	6.7	6.6	7.1	6.9	27.0	26.0	10.9	1.9	75.7	36.9	49.2	50.8

#	POST OFFICE NAME	2009 Per Capita Income	2009 HH Income Base	2009 Household Income Distribution (%): Less than $25,000	$25,000 to $49,999	$50,000 to $99,999	$100,000 to $149,999	$150,000 or More	Median Household Income: 2009	2014	2009 National Centile	2009 State Centile	2009 Home Value Base	2009 Home Value Distribution (%): Less than $50,000	$50,000 to $89,999	$90,000 to $174,999	$175,000 to $399,999	$400,000 or More	2009 Median Home Value
54216	KEWAUNEE	22222	2390	21.8	26.4	42.5	7.4	1.9	51383	53916	65	53	1991	7.1	22.1	50.6	17.8	2.5	113078
54217	LUXEMBURG	23325	2764	15.5	25.5	47.2	9.1	2.7	57306	58976	74	68	2284	5.6	9.5	52.0	28.3	4.7	142564
54220	MANITOWOC	25627	17218	20.3	27.7	41.8	7.4	2.8	51737	54134	65	54	12182	5.6	17.6	55.8	19.2	1.8	122356
54227	MARIBEL	24624	606	12.9	22.3	52.8	9.4	2.6	62868	63451	81	81	534	3.6	11.2	43.3	39.5	2.4	158203
54228	MISHICOT	23912	1118	16.1	28.4	45.4	8.2	1.9	55454	57586	72	64	939	3.5	16.1	56.0	22.7	1.7	125815
54229	NEW FRANKEN	29978	1427	7.4	19.0	52.0	14.2	7.4	71754	75609	88	92	1274	0.8	3.2	37.4	52.7	5.8	191124
54230	REEDSVILLE	23893	1802	15.8	26.5	46.6	8.9	2.2	56114	57617	73	65	1516	5.3	15.1	50.7	26.2	2.6	135728
54234	SISTER BAY	33823	986	20.2	26.5	37.9	9.7	5.7	52816	53461	68	58	733	0.3	1.6	26.5	52.0	19.6	240509
54235	STURGEON BAY	25323	8023	23.2	31.0	35.4	6.9	3.5	45885	47978	51	37	6106	8.3	13.0	45.4	24.1	9.3	136223
54241	TWO RIVERS	26071	6395	18.8	25.7	44.4	7.8	3.2	54992	56897	71	63	4813	2.5	23.0	57.9	15.0	1.6	114484
54245	VALDERS	23972	946	16.2	24.7	48.3	8.2	2.5	57707	58957	75	68	798	7.1	10.9	47.6	31.2	3.1	146289
54246	WASHINGTON ISLAND	21303	324	34.0	26.5	34.0	4.0	1.5	37791	39580	26	6	270	1.5	9.6	37.4	40.4	11.1	179545
54247	WHITELAW	24765	940	15.1	25.9	46.7	9.8	2.6	58340	59796	76	70	815	4.5	14.1	49.7	29.1	2.6	139325
54301	GREEN BAY	27336	9963	22.1	25.5	36.0	10.6	5.7	52546	55676	67	56	6419	1.1	8.9	60.4	28.3	1.3	143917
54302	GREEN BAY	24565	13345	24.8	29.0	36.8	6.3	3.1	45989	48529	51	37	6779	12.2	12.5	55.7	18.3	1.3	119155
54303	GREEN BAY	22875	12356	26.4	31.3	37.0	3.9	1.3	43047	44546	43	24	5733	1.5	18.1	72.6	7.6	0.2	113478
54304	GREEN BAY	27866	12971	17.3	27.2	44.8	7.5	3.2	55981	60070	73	65	8066	1.2	8.7	72.8	17.1	0.2	133143
54311	GREEN BAY	28763	12270	9.5	22.6	49.0	13.2	5.7	68737	73618	86	89	8175	6.4	3.1	44.4	43.8	2.3	169194
54313	GREEN BAY	31925	13030	7.5	14.9	52.6	15.8	9.2	76897	78712	91	94	10508	0.8	1.6	42.9	51.2	3.5	182320
54401	WAUSAU	28264	12827	15.6	25.8	43.9	9.4	5.3	57775	60455	75	68	9014	4.3	12.3	52.1	28.0	3.2	135976
54403	WAUSAU	27829	10258	22.0	24.8	38.6	9.2	5.4	53016	56056	68	58	6885	2.7	9.5	61.7	23.5	2.7	136263
54405	ABBOTSFORD	20365	1220	25.4	32.0	37.3	3.8	1.5	44595	45900	47	31	931	17.1	28.9	43.8	9.0	1.2	94167
54406	AMHERST	22213	1303	19.1	27.9	44.6	6.2	2.2	52738	54863	67	57	1045	4.0	12.6	48.1	32.4	2.8	144468
54407	AMHERST JUNCTION	24277	719	17.8	28.8	42.8	6.3	4.3	53235	55337	68	59	610	5.1	11.6	50.0	29.0	4.3	140054
54408	ANIWA	21611	510	20.6	30.8	40.8	5.5	2.4	48770	51035	58	45	445	9.9	18.0	46.5	23.4	2.2	127331
54409	ANTIGO	21217	6004	29.0	29.4	35.2	4.3	2.1	41741	43992	38	19	4420	10.0	36.9	41.2	10.8	1.1	93038
54410	ARPIN	20151	790	19.7	31.8	40.4	6.2	1.9	48072	51382	57	42	662	10.9	21.1	43.1	23.3	1.7	117602
54411	ATHENS	19241	1893	21.0	25.7	45.9	5.9	1.6	52679	55611	67	57	1606	8.2	20.9	51.4	17.8	1.7	116134
54412	AUBURNDALE	22335	771	18.4	29.1	43.5	7.7	1.4	51670	53600	65	54	643	6.4	19.4	49.9	22.4	1.9	118706
54413	BABCOCK	22582	127	21.3	31.5	41.7	5.5	0.0	46962	50953	54	40	109	9.2	32.1	44.0	11.9	2.8	102717
54414	BIRNAMWOOD	20023	1308	22.0	31.0	39.7	5.5	1.8	46974	48630	54	40	1058	15.6	24.9	44.3	14.2	1.0	101752
54416	BOWLER	16504	733	27.7	32.5	36.0	2.6	1.2	41173	42513	37	17	570	18.4	26.3	41.2	12.8	1.2	95000
54418	BRYANT	20264	519	22.2	34.1	37.2	4.0	2.5	44924	48002	48	32	456	10.1	24.8	44.3	18.6	2.2	111184
54420	CHILI	15523	401	27.2	33.9	34.2	2.7	2.0	41565	42772	38	18	348	12.4	28.2	42.2	16.1	1.1	100862
54421	COLBY	20103	1268	22.3	32.6	37.9	5.4	1.8	46155	48037	52	37	1021	11.5	27.9	46.6	12.5	1.5	102655
54422	CURTISS	15158	361	25.2	32.7	35.5	4.7	1.9	44191	45328	46	29	319	16.0	28.2	36.7	17.2	1.9	99250
54423	CUSTER	23943	878	12.5	25.5	51.3	7.9	2.8	60161	60709	78	73	776	5.2	8.4	45.4	36.7	4.4	158879
54424	DEERBROOK	21845	723	24.5	32.8	36.5	4.4	1.8	44523	46935	47	31	659	6.4	23.7	47.0	20.0	2.9	117807
54425	DORCHESTER	19189	801	23.1	32.8	37.7	4.6	1.7	44825	46413	48	31	623	12.7	28.3	46.7	10.6	1.8	99912
54426	EDGAR	22785	1696	18.9	26.1	45.2	7.4	2.4	54205	56843	70	61	1414	9.2	14.2	52.2	23.1	1.3	131299
54427	ELAND	21080	477	24.7	29.8	38.6	5.0	1.9	45638	48546	50	35	396	13.4	24.0	47.2	13.6	1.8	107083
54428	ELCHO	23083	608	28.5	36.0	30.1	3.3	2.1	37572	38701	25	6	509	8.8	24.6	48.1	16.5	2.0	111699
54430	ELTON	22554	52	21.2	34.6	38.5	5.8	0.0	45000	49091	48	33	46	13.0	23.9	41.3	19.6	2.2	110714
54433	GILMAN	20402	761	29.2	27.7	35.9	4.5	2.8	42512	45000	41	22	653	16.7	27.9	39.5	13.8	2.1	97717
54435	GLEASON	21690	883	23.2	30.9	39.6	4.9	1.4	46497	49223	53	38	783	7.9	18.6	49.8	21.5	2.2	121188
54436	GRANTON	16296	731	26.4	34.5	33.2	4.2	1.6	41882	43042	39	20	638	14.7	28.5	38.4	16.0	2.4	98431
54437	GREENWOOD	17172	1113	29.0	31.5	34.7	3.2	1.5	39671	40514	32	11	891	12.0	32.2	39.8	13.7	2.2	96358
54440	HATLEY	25078	1215	17.0	24.3	47.7	8.2	2.8	56966	59528	74	67	1061	5.7	11.4	53.2	27.0	2.7	140338
54441	HEWITT	24976	260	12.7	24.6	50.4	8.1	4.2	59640	60594	77	72	232	1.7	12.1	52.6	32.3	1.3	139444
54442	IRMA	19771	479	18.8	29.9	44.1	6.1	1.3	51137	52484	64	53	427	8.4	14.8	50.6	24.4	1.9	124543
54443	JUNCTION CITY	24811	928	18.3	24.2	46.2	7.1	4.1	56704	58120	74	66	778	6.7	16.6	42.5	28.1	6.0	136207
54446	LOYAL	17685	1079	29.2	28.4	36.0	4.8	1.7	42318	44343	40	21	877	13.2	31.0	38.7	15.1	2.1	96645
54447	LUBLIN	18697	220	32.7	30.0	31.4	3.2	2.7	37348	39747	25	6	183	23.0	31.7	31.7	13.7	0.0	83462
54448	MARATHON	25256	1862	15.0	25.3	46.8	9.8	3.1	59804	61286	77	72	1602	8.6	9.4	45.6	34.0	2.3	145833
54449	MARSHFIELD	28116	11567	21.3	27.0	39.6	6.9	5.2	51515	53932	65	54	7862	7.6	17.2	53.6	20.0	1.6	121110
54451	MEDFORD	23357	4568	21.5	29.4	40.3	6.4	2.4	49024	50627	59	45	3515	9.6	21.6	51.3	16.3	1.2	113369
54452	MERRILL	23181	8079	21.6	26.4	42.7	7.4	1.9	51500	53275	65	54	6160	8.1	18.4	52.4	19.8	1.3	120721
54454	MILLADORE	22693	492	16.7	22.0	51.0	8.7	1.6	58341	59284	76	70	435	8.0	21.1	47.1	23.2	0.5	116713
54455	MOSINEE	27274	6615	12.8	20.1	52.9	11.1	3.1	62109	63113	80	78	5497	5.6	8.2	53.2	30.9	2.0	149503
54456	NEILLSVILLE	19848	2478	28.8	31.6	33.0	4.8	1.8	40265	41721	34	13	1917	13.3	31.6	42.5	11.9	0.7	95898
54457	NEKOOSA	24559	3547	17.5	29.3	43.1	8.2	1.9	52603	54623	67	57	3039	5.1	26.9	46.4	20.1	1.4	117082
54459	OGEMA	19985	607	29.3	33.9	31.8	3.1	1.8	38714	39351	29	9	517	20.1	27.3	37.5	12.8	2.3	93293
54460	OWEN	16860	913	31.0	31.9	32.2	3.6	1.3	39096	40457	30	10	723	21.7	32.1	32.9	11.9	1.4	84811
54462	PEARSON	23595	175	24.6	37.7	30.9	4.0	2.9	39781	41901	32	12	155	9.0	22.6	47.7	19.4	1.3	116447
54463	PELICAN LAKE	22322	316	20.3	45.6	31.0	2.5	0.6	40449	41791	34	14	274	6.6	22.3	43.1	26.6	1.5	120455
54465	PICKEREL	23664	419	28.9	36.3	29.4	3.6	1.9	37892	39232	26	7	347	8.1	21.6	48.1	20.5	1.7	119866
54466	PITTSVILLE	23146	1182	19.4	30.3	41.2	6.3	2.8	50266	52511	62	50	974	12.5	23.7	47.9	13.7	2.2	105634
54467	PLOVER	28994	5140	11.6	25.8	45.4	11.1	6.1	62381	63244	80	79	3640	9.4	5.8	48.4	34.1	2.3	154772
54469	PORT EDWARDS	28223	695	15.5	18.6	46.0	12.8	7.1	65760	66660	84	86	587	0.9	21.6	63.4	13.3	0.9	115341
54470	RIB LAKE	19704	815	28.3	31.0	35.6	4.2	0.9	42643	43669	41	23	651	13.5	27.2	49.6	9.4	0.3	97857
54471	RINGLE	27659	734	11.2	19.2	53.4	12.8	3.4	65786	66917	84	86	670	1.2	5.8	47.9	41.8	3.3	167826
54473	ROSHOLT	22289	1110	18.1	25.7	46.2	7.2	2.8	54745	56469	71	62	943	7.0	19.5	45.4	25.6	2.5	127047
54474	ROTHSCHILD	28321	1549	15.3	24.3	46.5	9.6	4.2	61803	63360	80	77	1246	0.6	11.5	63.3	24.1	0.6	129487
54475	RUDOLPH	24308	656	17.7	24.7	46.0	8.2	3.4	56303	57967	73	66	547	3.3	20.7	57.2	17.7	1.1	123144
54476	SCHOFIELD	27624	6881	14.2	23.0	46.6	12.7	3.5	61338	63165	79	76	4649	9.9	6.1	53.1	29.4	1.5	147627
54479	SPENCER	21168	1432	20.6	27.6	45.2	5.3	1.3	51091	53036	64	53	1125	12.1	26.0	48.1	12.8	1.1	103289
54480	STETSONVILLE	21842	463	17.3	32.2	41.9	5.6	3.0	50418	51788	62	50	387	11.1	18.9	54.8	13.2	2.1	113021
54481	STEVENS POINT	24597	15144	23.5	26.3	38.2	8.0	4.0	50171	52924	62	49	9634	5.9	13.6	53.0	25.5	2.0	132883
54484	STRATFORD	23437	1917	18.6	23.9	47.1	8.3	2.1	55313	57449	72	64	1597	9.6	20.9	48.2	20.0	1.3	117009
54485	SUMMIT LAKE	22927	152	30.9	32.2	32.2	3.3	1.3	38611	39488	28	8	130	5.4	21.5	49.2	19.2	4.6	120652
54486	TIGERTON	18899	1058	30.0	32.3	31.9	4.8	0.9	40660	42272	35	15	823	13.1	25.8	42.4	16.3	2.4	104457
54487	TOMAHAWK	22374	4344	24.8	30.8	36.7	6.1	1.5	44885	47293	48	32	3497	6.1	18.0	44.7	28.7	2.5	130632
54488	UNITY	18577	425	23.3	32.9	37.2	4.7	1.9	45082	46899	48	33	366	10.9	26.5	40.7	18.9	3.0	110484
54489	VESPER	21964	655	22.9	26.1	43.2	6.0	1.8	50566	52261	63	51	562	8.2	24.4	50.0	16.7	0.7	112500
54490	WESTBORO	19801	366	24.0	34.7	36.3	3.6	1.4	43412	44601	44	26	299	12.4	27.1	49.8	10.0	0.7	98077
54491	WHITE LAKE	20901	804	27.9	34.0	32.3	4.4	1.5	39238	40649	30	11	668	13.3	32.0	40.1	13.3	1.2	96327
54493	WILLARD	20401	346	26.3	33.8	34.1	4.0	1.7	40265	42058	34	13	305	10.8	23.3	47.5	17.0	1.3	114096
54494	WISCONSIN RAPIDS	27676	11492	18.5	21.7	45.0	10.1	4.7	59832	60797	77	72	9053	4.2	20.5	54.6	19.4	1.2	122027
54495	WISCONSIN RAPIDS	22086	3186	25.0	32.3	36.6	4.7	1.4	43220	45600	43	25	2049	9.3	34.4	44.2	11.8	0.4	96080
54498	WITHEE	17810	821	26.2	33.5	34.2	3.9	2.2	41165	42893	37	17	699	16.9	30.5	40.2	11.3	1.1	92937
54499	WITTENBERG	19778	1224	28.2	31.5	34.3	4.2	1.8	42675	44287	41	23	922	10.2	23.9	47.5	16.7	1.7	109516
54501	RHINELANDER	22399	8604	25.5	30.4	35.5	6.3	2.3	44441	45678	47	30	6470	7.5	19.2	47.1	23.2	3.0	125420
54511	ARGONNE	20572	642	32.4	29.1	31.0	4.8	2.6	39030	41042	30	10	560	14.1	26.1	40.5	16.6	2.7	103086
54512	BOULDER JUNCTION	25673	476	25.2	31.3	34.9	5.0	3.6	44324	46260	46	30	403	3.7	9.7	35.2	35.2	16.1	180288
54513	BRANTWOOD	22117	223	28.3	30.9	35.0	3.6	2.2	39125	39471	30	11	193	15.0	36.8	33.7	14.5	0.0	88600
	WISCONSIN	27384		18.4	25.3	40.0	11.0	5.2	56363	58927				5.6	11.9	43.5	34.2	4.7	150766
	UNITED STATES	27277		20.9	24.4	35.3	11.7	7.6	54719	56938				9.3	13.1	31.6	32.6	13.5	162279

ZIP CODE #	POST OFFICE NAME	FINANCIAL SERVICES				THE HOME						ENTERTAINMENT						PERSONAL			
						Home Improvements		Furnishings													
		Auto Loan	Home Loan	Invest-ments	Retire-ment Plans	Home Repair	Lawn & Garden	Comput-ers & Hard-ware-Personal	Major Appli-ances	TV, Radio, Sound Equip-ment	Furni-ture	Dine out/ Carry out	Sports Equip-ment	Fees & Tickets	Toys & Games	Travel	Cable TV	Apparel & Services	Auto Repairs	Health Insur-ance	Pets & Supplies
54216	KEWAUNEE	93	72	92	72	74	98	76	91	81	67	79	69	63	81	74	88	53	84	97	107
54217	LUXEMBURG	96	91	90	94	92	104	88	98	90	81	89	75	83	92	89	94	61	91	100	115
54220	MANITOWOC	85	84	77	85	82	90	84	85	87	81	86	65	83	87	83	90	59	85	92	101
54227	MARIBEL	97	103	92	107	102	106	95	101	94	93	94	78	97	97	99	96	65	96	101	118
54228	MISHICOT	94	86	85	89	88	101	85	96	87	76	86	72	78	89	84	92	58	88	98	111
54229	NEW FRANKEN	113	134	118	136	130	125	116	120	112	119	113	94	128	115	125	110	80	115	114	140
54230	REEDSVILLE	97	90	88	93	91	104	88	99	90	80	89	75	82	92	88	95	61	91	101	115
54234	SISTER BAY	100	94	136	93	106	116	88	107	92	92	91	72	88	85	99	97	62	101	113	122
54235	STURGEON BAY	88	78	90	79	80	92	79	88	82	75	81	66	74	81	80	86	55	85	92	103
54241	TWO RIVERS	88	88	77	90	85	95	87	89	89	83	89	68	87	90	86	92	61	88	97	105
54245	VALDERS	96	88	87	91	89	103	86	98	89	78	88	74	80	91	86	94	60	90	100	113
54246	WASHINGTON ISLAND	78	62	100	61	68	82	62	79	65	58	64	58	54	62	67	69	43	73	78	92
54247	WHITELAW	99	91	90	95	93	107	90	101	92	82	91	76	83	94	90	97	62	93	103	117
54301	GREEN BAY	91	91	85	93	89	92	95	90	95	93	96	70	96	95	93	96	67	94	96	108
54302	GREEN BAY	82	68	61	71	64	67	83	72	83	80	84	59	76	85	74	83	59	80	75	89
54303	GREEN BAY	70	62	56	64	59	63	73	65	74	69	74	52	69	73	67	74	51	71	71	80
54304	GREEN BAY	86	86	78	87	83	87	89	85	90	87	90	66	89	90	87	91	63	88	91	102
54311	GREEN BAY	113	115	98	115	109	103	112	107	108	116	110	85	111	113	108	104	76	107	101	126
54313	GREEN BAY	125	142	122	141	136	125	126	127	120	132	122	100	134	126	129	116	86	122	116	146
54401	WAUSAU	98	99	91	100	96	103	97	98	98	95	97	76	97	99	97	100	68	98	103	117
54403	WAUSAU	93	93	87	94	91	99	94	94	96	90	95	72	93	95	93	99	66	95	102	112
54405	ABBOTSFORD	85	64	82	64	66	88	68	81	73	61	71	63	55	73	66	80	48	76	86	97
54406	AMHERST	86	83	79	86	83	93	79	88	81	74	80	67	77	83	81	84	55	82	89	102
54407	AMHERST JUNCTION	94	87	86	91	89	102	86	96	88	78	86	73	80	90	86	93	59	89	99	112
54408	ANIWA	93	79	82	81	80	96	79	90	83	73	82	68	70	85	77	89	56	84	93	106
54409	ANTIGO	78	67	71	68	67	81	71	77	74	64	73	58	64	74	68	79	50	75	83	91
54410	ARPIN	89	75	86	77	77	95	76	89	79	67	78	69	66	80	76	84	52	82	92	105
54411	ATHENS	96	72	95	72	73	99	76	90	80	67	79	72	61	81	74	87	52	85	95	110
54412	AUBURNDALE	93	78	89	80	80	99	79	92	82	70	81	72	69	83	79	88	54	85	96	109
54413	BABCOCK	83	76	75	79	77	89	75	84	77	68	76	64	69	79	75	82	52	78	87	98
54414	BIRNAMWOOD	85	74	76	76	75	89	73	84	77	67	75	63	66	79	72	82	51	78	87	98
54416	BOWLER	81	59	80	58	60	81	61	75	67	57	66	56	50	67	60	74	44	70	79	90
54418	BRYANT	84	73	88	75	77	90	73	86	75	67	74	64	66	75	75	80	50	79	87	99
54420	CHILI	86	59	94	59	62	91	66	81	68	53	67	67	48	67	65	74	44	76	86	100
54421	COLBY	86	71	78	71	69	89	74	81	77	67	76	65	64	78	71	82	51	79	87	99
54422	CURTISS	89	62	98	62	65	94	68	85	71	56	70	70	50	70	68	78	46	79	90	104
54423	CUSTER	91	101	88	104	98	101	91	95	90	90	90	74	95	92	95	90	63	91	95	112
54424	DEERBROOK	82	71	86	73	75	88	71	84	74	65	72	62	64	73	73	78	49	77	85	97
54425	DORCHESTER	91	67	80	66	67	89	70	82	76	65	74	63	56	78	65	82	50	77	86	99
54426	EDGAR	100	83	99	85	85	105	86	98	89	77	88	77	75	89	86	94	59	93	103	117
54427	ELAND	82	74	74	76	75	87	73	82	75	66	74	62	67	77	72	80	51	76	85	96
54428	ELCHO	76	64	86	60	69	83	63	77	68	64	67	54	57	65	66	73	44	72	83	90
54430	ELTON	84	76	76	80	78	90	75	85	78	68	76	64	70	79	75	82	52	79	88	99
54433	GILMAN	94	65	103	65	68	99	72	89	75	58	74	74	53	73	71	81	48	83	94	110
54435	GLEASON	83	71	85	72	74	88	71	83	73	64	72	62	63	73	72	78	49	77	85	97
54436	GRANTON	88	61	90	60	63	90	66	81	70	57	69	66	50	70	65	77	45	76	86	100
54437	GREENWOOD	82	58	86	57	61	86	64	79	69	55	67	62	49	68	62	76	44	74	85	95
54440	HATLEY	97	91	88	95	92	105	89	99	91	81	89	75	83	93	89	96	61	92	102	115
54441	HEWITT	94	106	91	109	103	104	95	98	93	95	93	77	101	95	100	93	65	95	97	116
54442	IRMA	86	77	80	80	79	92	76	87	79	69	78	66	70	80	77	84	53	80	90	101
54443	JUNCTION CITY	94	94	88	97	94	103	89	97	90	84	89	74	87	92	91	93	61	91	98	113
54446	LOYAL	91	63	96	63	66	95	70	87	75	59	73	69	53	73	69	82	48	81	93	105
54447	LUBLIN	85	58	93	58	61	89	65	80	67	52	67	66	47	66	64	73	43	75	85	99
54448	MARATHON	100	97	95	100	97	108	92	102	93	87	93	79	89	95	95	97	64	96	103	120
54449	MARSHFIELD	92	88	84	91	87	95	92	92	93	87	93	71	89	94	90	96	64	92	98	109
54451	MEDFORD	89	75	84	75	76	91	77	86	81	72	80	66	69	81	76	86	54	83	91	103
54452	MERRILL	83	79	75	80	77	89	79	83	81	74	80	64	76	82	78	85	55	81	89	99
54454	MILLADORE	95	86	86	90	88	102	85	96	88	77	86	73	79	90	85	93	59	89	99	112
54455	MOSINEE	104	103	94	104	101	107	97	103	98	96	98	79	96	101	97	100	67	99	103	121
54456	NEILLSVILLE	82	60	82	58	62	84	65	79	72	59	70	59	53	71	63	79	47	74	85	93
54457	NEKOOSA	92	82	94	83	83	97	82	92	84	77	83	70	76	84	83	89	57	88	96	108
54459	OGEMA	85	61	82	59	62	85	63	78	70	59	69	59	51	71	61	77	46	73	83	93
54460	OWEN	80	56	84	55	58	83	62	76	66	52	65	60	47	65	60	73	43	71	82	92
54462	PEARSON	75	71	91	66	79	85	68	80	72	73	70	52	67	66	74	76	47	77	89	92
54463	PELICAN LAKE	81	64	103	63	71	86	65	82	68	61	67	60	56	65	70	73	45	76	81	95
54465	PICKEREL	75	63	96	61	70	81	62	78	66	61	65	55	56	62	68	70	43	73	79	90
54466	PITTSVILLE	88	81	78	84	80	94	81	87	84	75	82	68	76	85	80	88	56	84	93	104
54467	PLOVER	105	109	96	110	105	103	104	103	102	106	103	81	106	105	104	101	72	102	100	122
54469	PORT EDWARDS	99	108	96	108	105	116	100	105	105	97	104	77	107	104	105	110	72	104	119	123
54470	RIB LAKE	82	58	86	57	60	86	64	79	69	54	67	62	49	68	62	76	44	74	85	95
54471	RINGLE	105	112	99	114	109	112	102	108	101	101	101	84	105	104	105	102	70	102	106	126
54473	ROSHOLT	86	87	77	90	85	93	84	88	85	79	84	68	83	86	84	87	58	85	92	104
54474	ROTHSCHILD	93	102	88	103	98	106	94	97	97	92	96	74	100	97	98	100	67	96	106	115
54475	RUDOLPH	96	88	87	92	90	104	87	98	89	79	88	74	80	91	87	95	60	90	101	114
54476	SCHOFIELD	102	100	86	100	95	93	100	96	98	102	99	76	98	102	96	96	69	97	94	114
54479	SPENCER	86	76	78	76	74	89	77	82	79	71	78	65	70	80	75	82	53	80	87	100
54480	STETSONVILLE	90	81	81	85	83	96	80	91	83	72	81	69	74	84	80	88	55	84	94	106
54481	STEVENS POINT	87	79	73	81	77	83	91	83	89	83	88	66	83	89	82	89	61	86	87	100
54484	STRATFORD	98	82	90	83	82	102	84	94	87	76	86	74	73	88	82	93	58	89	99	113
54485	SUMMIT LAKE	82	62	96	61	67	85	63	80	68	59	67	59	53	65	66	73	44	74	81	94
54486	TIGERTON	76	61	74	61	62	80	63	75	67	56	65	57	54	67	62	72	44	69	79	88
54487	TOMAHAWK	83	68	90	68	72	87	71	83	75	65	73	62	62	73	72	79	49	78	86	97
54488	UNITY	93	64	102	64	67	98	71	88	74	58	73	73	52	72	71	81	47	82	93	109
54489	VESPER	87	74	84	76	76	93	75	87	78	66	76	67	66	78	75	83	52	81	90	103
54490	WESTBORO	81	64	80	64	66	86	67	80	72	59	70	61	56	71	66	78	47	74	85	94
54491	WHITE LAKE	82	63	89	61	66	85	63	79	68	59	67	59	53	67	65	74	45	73	81	93
54493	WILLARD	87	62	92	60	64	90	65	82	71	58	70	64	50	70	65	77	46	76	86	99
54494	WISCONSIN RAPIDS	93	98	88	99	95	103	93	96	94	90	94	73	95	95	95	97	65	94	102	113
54495	WISCONSIN RAPIDS	75	68	66	68	67	76	71	73	74	67	73	55	66	74	68	78	50	73	80	87
54498	WITHEE	87	62	91	61	64	91	67	83	72	57	71	66	52	71	66	79	46	78	89	100
54499	WITTENBERG	81	66	76	67	68	85	68	80	73	61	71	60	59	73	67	78	48	74	84	93
54501	RHINELANDER	82	71	82	72	73	84	74	82	77	69	75	61	68	76	73	80	51	79	84	96
54511	ARGONNE	79	65	96	63	71	85	65	81	69	63	68	57	58	66	69	74	45	75	84	93
54512	BOULDER JUNCTION	89	72	115	70	79	94	72	91	75	67	74	66	62	71	78	80	49	84	90	105
54513	BRANTWOOD	86	64	88	62	66	88	65	81	71	60	70	61	53	71	64	78	46	75	85	97
	WISCONSIN	98	94	92	96	93	99	96	96	96	93	96	75	94	97	95	98	67	96	99	114
	UNITED STATES	100	100	100	100	100	100	100	100	100	100	100	100	100	100	100	100	100	100	100	100

#	POST OFFICE NAME	COUNTY FIPS CODE	POPULATION 2000	POPULATION 2009	POPULATION 2014	2000-2009 ANNUAL RATE % Rate	2000-2009 ANNUAL RATE State Centile	HOUSEHOLDS 2000	HOUSEHOLDS 2009	HOUSEHOLDS 2014	HOUSEHOLDS % Annual Rate 2000-2009	HOUSEHOLDS 2009 Average HH Size	FAMILIES 2000	FAMILIES 2009	FAMILIES % Annual Rate 2000-2009
54514	BUTTERNUT	003	2223	2167	2136	-0.3	4	911	924	920	0.2	2.34	630	630	0.0
54515	CATAWBA	099	506	509	503	0.1	20	205	216	216	0.6	2.36	146	152	0.4
54517	CLAM LAKE	003	2	2	2	0.0	16	1	1	1	0.0	2.00	1	1	0.0
54519	CONOVER	125	1179	1212	1242	0.3	32	502	535	553	0.7	2.27	354	374	0.6
54520	CRANDON	041	4011	4144	4208	0.4	39	1619	1757	1806	0.9	2.30	1100	1179	0.8
54521	EAGLE RIVER	125	7930	8419	8670	0.6	51	3423	3730	3880	0.9	2.19	2320	2496	0.8
54524	FIFIELD	099	700	713	705	0.2	24	298	316	316	0.6	2.25	208	219	0.6
54526	GLEN FLORA	107	890	1008	1056	1.4	86	341	405	428	1.9	2.49	240	281	1.7
54527	GLIDDEN	003	981	1168	1211	1.9	94	415	517	541	2.4	2.26	286	351	2.2
54529	HARSHAW	085	1027	1058	1059	0.3	32	439	467	472	0.7	2.25	321	338	0.6
54530	HAWKINS	107	741	825	859	1.2	81	300	351	369	1.7	2.35	215	248	1.6
54531	HAZELHURST	085	1486	1662	1727	1.2	81	627	725	759	1.6	2.29	503	577	1.5
54534	HURLEY	051	2759	2722	2691	-0.1	11	1204	1226	1223	0.2	2.12	714	717	0.0
54536	IRON BELT	051	284	285	281	0.0	16	122	126	126	0.3	2.26	86	87	0.1
54537	KENNAN	099	648	640	629	-0.1	11	243	250	248	0.3	2.56	187	190	0.2
54538	LAC DU FLAMBEAU	125	2652	2807	2903	0.6	51	941	1018	1058	0.9	2.72	707	760	0.8
54539	LAKE TOMAHAWK	085	1744	1928	2000	1.1	76	742	856	898	1.6	2.14	524	596	1.4
54540	LAND O LAKES	125	975	971	978	0.0	16	449	464	472	0.4	2.09	304	312	0.3
54541	LAONA	041	1735	1811	1835	0.5	44	617	670	687	0.9	2.54	427	459	0.8
54542	LONG LAKE	041	628	618	615	-0.2	8	293	303	306	0.4	2.00	189	192	0.2
54545	MANITOWISH WATERS	125	815	1035	1146	2.6	97	382	502	561	3.0	2.06	263	343	2.9
54546	MELLEN	003	1768	1707	1682	-0.4	2	745	749	745	0.1	2.23	493	489	-0.1
54547	MERCER	051	1792	1883	1914	0.5	44	857	933	959	0.9	2.02	550	590	0.8
54548	MINOCQUA	085	5188	5648	5808	0.9	68	2330	2618	2716	1.3	2.14	1576	1746	1.1
54550	MONTREAL	051	1033	1025	1014	-0.1	11	461	476	476	0.3	2.15	293	297	0.1
54552	PARK FALLS	099	4814	4742	4669	-0.2	8	2059	2126	2120	0.3	2.17	1338	1364	0.2
54554	PHELPS	125	1217	1238	1260	0.2	24	505	530	545	0.5	2.25	354	368	0.4
54555	PHILLIPS	099	5541	5406	5295	-0.3	4	2307	2343	2323	0.2	2.26	1525	1531	0.0
54556	PRENTICE	099	1283	1276	1256	-0.1	11	539	559	557	0.4	2.28	357	366	0.3
54557	PRESQUE ISLE	125	877	1169	1287	3.2	98	414	575	638	3.6	2.03	293	401	3.5
54558	SAINT GERMAIN	125	2003	2215	2340	1.1	76	926	1059	1129	1.5	2.09	656	742	1.3
54559	SAXON	051	508	499	489	-0.2	8	208	213	211	0.3	2.34	155	157	0.1
54560	SAYNER	125	577	663	705	1.5	88	256	303	325	1.8	2.19	181	212	1.7
54562	THREE LAKES	085	1982	2164	2233	1.0	72	891	1000	1040	1.3	2.14	619	688	1.1
54563	TONY	107	788	850	874	0.8	61	293	329	343	1.3	2.58	216	240	1.1
54564	TRIPOLI	085	489	498	496	0.2	24	225	236	238	0.5	2.11	162	168	0.4
54565	UPSON	051	61	61	60	0.0	16	28	29	29	0.4	2.10	20	20	0.0
54566	WABENO	041	1640	1659	1665	0.1	20	655	690	703	0.6	2.22	458	477	0.4
54568	WOODRUFF	125	4705	5284	5553	1.3	84	2052	2382	2526	1.6	2.20	1351	1551	1.5
54601	LA CROSSE	063	48410	48706	49217	0.1	20	19130	20094	20542	0.5	2.19	9811	10033	0.2
54603	LA CROSSE	063	14848	14898	15051	0.0	16	6343	6628	6767	0.5	2.24	3715	3767	0.2
54610	ALMA	011	2317	2339	2319	0.1	20	933	982	987	0.6	2.37	649	674	0.4
54611	ALMA CENTER	053	1029	1072	1078	0.4	39	391	420	426	0.8	2.55	283	301	0.7
54612	ARCADIA	121	4423	4411	4401	0.0	16	1779	1838	1852	0.4	2.35	1137	1160	0.2
54613	ARKDALE	001	1592	1773	1814	1.2	81	723	842	871	1.7	2.11	506	583	1.5
54614	BANGOR	063	3162	3450	3598	0.9	68	1161	1325	1398	1.4	2.57	894	999	1.2
54615	BLACK RIVER FALLS	053	10114	10601	10778	0.5	44	3620	3949	4038	0.9	2.42	2353	2542	0.8
54616	BLAIR	121	2524	2594	2612	0.3	32	970	1031	1049	0.7	2.41	652	683	0.5
54618	CAMP DOUGLAS	057	2239	2567	2668	1.5	88	865	1006	1058	1.6	2.46	618	712	1.5
54619	CASHTON	081	3537	3841	4000	0.9	68	1148	1283	1348	1.2	2.99	864	950	1.0
54621	CHASEBURG	123	1031	1098	1129	0.7	56	391	429	445	1.0	2.56	301	327	0.9
54622	COCHRANE	011	2129	2212	2236	0.4	39	882	957	978	0.9	2.31	636	684	0.8
54623	COON VALLEY	063	1626	1716	1761	0.6	51	604	660	682	1.0	2.52	441	476	0.8
54624	DE SOTO	123	1202	1231	1245	0.3	32	512	546	557	0.7	2.25	357	377	0.6
54625	DODGE	121	247	265	273	0.8	61	99	111	116	1.2	2.39	73	82	1.3
54626	EASTMAN	023	1402	1464	1485	0.5	44	531	584	600	1.0	2.51	397	432	0.9
54627	ETTRICK	121	1843	1885	1891	0.2	24	749	797	808	0.7	2.37	523	551	0.6
54628	FERRYVILLE	023	1317	1323	1320	0.0	16	539	563	566	0.5	2.34	383	395	0.3
54629	FOUNTAIN CITY	011	2611	2683	2691	0.3	32	1067	1143	1156	0.7	2.31	717	759	0.6
54630	GALESVILLE	121	3652	3935	4052	0.8	61	1454	1622	1688	1.2	2.39	984	1087	1.1
54631	GAYS MILLS	023	2292	2315	2306	0.1	20	889	939	948	0.6	2.46	646	675	0.5
54632	GENOA	123	1229	1278	1302	0.4	39	485	522	536	0.8	2.45	346	369	0.7
54634	HILLSBORO	123	3771	4155	4307	1.1	76	1347	1487	1542	1.1	2.75	945	1033	1.0
54635	HIXTON	053	1781	1834	1839	0.3	32	694	743	752	0.7	2.44	506	535	0.6
54636	HOLMEN	063	9744	11495	12381	1.8	93	3405	4172	4541	2.2	2.75	2731	3277	2.0
54638	KENDALL	081	1628	1861	1969	1.5	88	585	682	729	1.7	2.71	450	517	1.5
54639	LA FARGE	123	2179	2428	2534	1.2	81	841	950	993	1.3	2.53	579	650	1.3
54641	MATHER	057	34	34	36	0.0	16	13	15	16	1.6	2.27	9	11	2.2
54642	MELROSE	053	1874	2046	2125	1.0	72	715	804	842	1.3	2.54	508	564	1.1
54644	MINDORO	063	1296	1410	1468	0.9	68	498	561	590	1.3	2.51	387	428	1.1
54646	NECEDAH	057	3658	4430	4612	2.1	96	1376	1643	1728	1.9	2.57	988	1166	1.8
54648	NORWALK	081	1794	1971	2067	1.0	72	579	654	691	1.3	3.01	447	500	1.2
54650	ONALASKA	063	20611	23206	24288	1.3	84	7918	9288	9810	1.7	2.49	5684	6576	1.6
54651	ONTARIO	123	1164	1262	1310	0.9	68	450	500	523	1.1	2.52	319	350	1.0
54652	READSTOWN	123	786	898	944	1.5	88	315	364	383	1.6	2.47	214	244	1.4
54653	ROCKLAND	081	741	830	871	1.2	81	250	293	311	1.7	2.79	188	216	1.5
54655	SOLDIERS GROVE	023	1789	1826	1828	0.2	24	669	703	711	0.5	2.48	478	497	0.4
54656	SPARTA	081	15545	16878	17595	0.9	68	6019	6761	7112	1.3	2.43	4139	4606	1.2
54657	STEUBEN	023	222	241	247	0.9	68	70	79	82	1.3	3.05	54	60	1.1
54658	STODDARD	123	2695	2866	2958	0.7	56	1048	1158	1205	1.1	2.47	765	834	0.9
54659	TAYLOR	053	1244	1388	1450	1.2	81	450	519	548	1.6	2.67	335	381	1.4
54660	TOMAH	081	14385	15340	15875	0.7	56	5585	6156	6426	1.1	2.42	3786	4125	0.9
54661	TREMPEALEAU	121	2746	3093	3242	1.3	84	1125	1321	1398	1.8	2.34	774	898	1.6
54664	VIOLA	103	1494	1620	1668	0.9	68	599	669	696	1.2	2.42	433	478	1.1
54665	VIROQUA	123	7922	8189	8322	0.4	39	3236	3452	3534	0.7	2.30	2055	2161	0.5
54666	WARRENS	053	2355	2564	2683	0.9	68	893	1005	1068	1.3	2.38	669	745	1.2
54667	WESTBY	123	4704	4796	4844	0.2	24	1741	1814	1838	0.4	2.60	1273	1314	0.3
54669	WEST SALEM	063	7319	7884	8227	0.8	61	2577	2861	3016	1.1	2.66	1949	2118	0.9
54670	WILTON	081	1728	1926	2027	1.2	81	533	608	645	1.4	3.17	395	445	1.3
54701	EAU CLAIRE	035	36376	38113	39058	0.5	44	13827	15373	15973	1.2	2.21	8265	9037	1.0
54703	EAU CLAIRE	035	39683	41863	42961	0.6	51	15478	17129	17784	1.1	2.40	9421	10314	1.0
54720	ALTOONA	035	6865	6844	6941	0.0	16	2891	3035	3113	0.5	2.21	1805	1851	0.3
54721	ARKANSAW	091	1428	1525	1566	0.7	56	543	597	617	1.0	2.55	396	433	1.0
54722	AUGUSTA	035	3829	4148	4285	0.9	68	1371	1539	1607	1.3	2.66	992	1094	1.1
54723	BAY CITY	093	1311	1438	1480	1.0	72	491	559	582	1.4	2.57	371	417	1.3
	WISCONSIN					0.7					1.0	2.43			0.9
	UNITED STATES					1.0					1.1	2.59			0.9

ZIP CODE #	POST OFFICE NAME	RACE (%) White 2000	White 2009	Black 2000	Black 2009	Asian/Pacific 2000	Asian/Pacific 2009	% Hispanic Origin 2000	% Hispanic Origin 2009	2009 AGE DISTRIBUTION (%) 0-4	5-9	10-14	15-19	20-24	25-44	45-64	65-84	85+	18+	MEDIAN AGE 2009	% 2009 Males	% 2009 Females
54514	BUTTERNUT	98.6	98.4	0.3	0.3	0.1	0.1	0.3	0.3	4.9	5.4	5.5	6.0	5.0	22.1	33.5	15.1	2.5	80.1	45.7	51.3	48.7
54515	CATAWBA	99.2	99.2	0.0	0.0	0.0	0.0	0.0	0.0	5.1	5.5	6.1	6.7	4.9	23.2	33.0	13.4	2.2	79.4	43.9	51.7	48.3
54517	CLAM LAKE	100.0	100.0	0.0	0.0	0.0	0.0	0.0	0.0	0.0	0.0	0.0	0.0	0.0	0.0	100.0	0.0	0.0	100.0	55.0	0.0	100.0
54519	CONOVER	98.6	98.3	0.2	0.2	0.1	0.2	0.6	0.8	3.2	4.9	5.8	5.9	2.6	20.4	34.7	20.5	2.1	81.9	49.4	51.1	48.9
54520	CRANDON	85.9	84.2	0.1	0.2	0.1	0.1	0.8	1.1	6.1	6.1	6.3	6.8	4.8	22.2	28.3	16.4	2.9	77.1	43.2	48.6	51.4
54521	EAGLE RIVER	97.9	97.4	0.4	0.5	0.2	0.3	0.7	1.0	3.9	4.4	4.9	5.5	4.5	20.0	32.9	20.5	3.4	83.0	49.2	50.0	50.0
54524	FIFIELD	97.7	97.1	0.1	0.3	0.0	0.1	0.4	0.7	3.2	5.0	6.3	6.7	2.1	22.3	37.3	15.4	1.5	80.9	47.2	52.6	47.4
54526	GLEN FLORA	98.1	97.8	0.1	0.1	0.4	0.5	0.9	1.2	5.0	5.6	6.2	6.3	4.4	24.4	31.9	14.1	2.2	79.5	43.4	51.5	48.5
54527	GLIDDEN	98.6	98.1	0.0	0.0	0.1	0.2	0.3	0.5	6.1	6.2	6.1	6.2	5.8	23.0	28.1	15.9	2.7	77.9	42.3	50.7	49.3
54529	HARSHAW	98.6	98.4	0.3	0.4	0.0	0.1	0.4	0.5	3.3	3.7	4.4	4.7	3.6	19.8	37.8	21.1	1.5	85.5	50.4	52.3	47.7
54530	HAWKINS	98.1	97.8	0.1	0.1	0.4	0.5	0.9	1.2	5.1	5.6	6.2	6.5	4.4	24.5	31.6	14.1	2.1	79.0	43.0	51.3	48.7
54531	HAZELHURST	98.1	97.7	0.1	0.2	0.3	0.5	0.7	1.0	3.5	3.9	4.6	5.3	3.6	17.1	38.9	21.2	1.9	84.8	51.8	51.7	48.3
54534	HURLEY	98.0	97.9	0.0	0.0	0.2	0.2	0.8	0.7	4.4	4.3	4.7	6.0	5.9	21.6	28.9	18.0	6.3	83.1	46.9	48.0	52.0
54536	IRON BELT	98.6	98.6	0.0	0.0	0.0	0.0	0.4	0.4	4.9	5.3	5.3	6.3	5.6	19.6	32.3	18.6	2.1	81.1	46.8	48.8	51.2
54537	KENNAN	99.1	98.8	0.0	0.0	0.0	0.2	0.8	1.1	5.9	6.6	7.0	7.3	5.0	23.8	28.9	13.4	2.0	75.9	40.7	50.2	49.8
54538	LAC DU FLAMBEAU	48.0	41.9	0.2	0.2	0.0	0.0	1.4	1.7	6.7	6.9	6.9	6.9	4.3	20.8	28.9	16.4	2.1	75.0	42.6	50.2	49.8
54539	LAKE TOMAHAWK	96.2	95.2	2.3	3.0	0.2	0.4	0.7	0.9	3.4	3.9	4.8	5.2	4.4	23.0	35.0	18.4	1.9	84.3	48.1	53.0	47.0
54540	LAND O LAKES	98.2	97.7	0.0	0.0	0.2	0.3	0.6	0.8	3.7	4.1	4.5	4.6	3.5	17.7	36.7	22.6	2.6	84.9	52.3	50.7	49.3
54541	LAONA	82.5	80.6	2.8	3.4	0.2	0.3	1.7	2.3	6.1	6.2	6.4	9.3	6.2	20.4	27.3	15.4	2.9	76.3	41.2	50.1	49.9
54542	LONG LAKE	97.3	97.1	0.2	0.2	0.6	0.8	0.3	0.2	3.7	4.0	4.7	5.3	4.0	19.9	33.2	21.5	3.6	84.1	49.9	52.1	47.9
54545	MANITOWISH WATERS	96.2	96.3	0.0	0.0	0.0	0.0	1.0	1.3	2.8	3.3	3.8	4.4	3.0	17.2	37.6	25.1	2.8	87.3	54.6	50.4	49.6
54546	MELLEN	94.6	94.0	0.1	0.1	0.3	0.4	0.8	1.0	6.2	6.3	6.0	5.6	5.2	22.6	29.0	16.1	3.2	77.7	43.7	51.0	49.0
54547	MERCER	98.8	98.8	0.1	0.1	0.2	0.2	0.6	0.6	3.3	3.7	4.0	4.2	3.1	17.0	36.7	25.4	2.7	86.5	53.7	50.8	49.2
54548	MINOCQUA	94.2	93.4	0.2	0.2	0.2	0.3	1.0	1.4	4.2	4.7	5.3	5.2	3.8	18.6	35.2	20.2	2.7	82.4	50.0	50.1	49.9
54550	MONTREAL	98.1	98.0	0.0	0.0	0.2	0.2	0.9	0.9	5.9	5.9	5.8	5.9	5.8	22.1	30.7	14.8	3.2	79.1	44.1	47.8	52.2
54552	PARK FALLS	98.1	97.6	0.1	0.2	0.6	0.9	0.7	1.0	4.4	4.8	5.1	6.3	5.1	20.8	31.8	17.3	4.5	81.7	47.1	49.1	50.9
54554	PHELPS	98.0	97.5	0.2	0.2	0.3	0.5	0.7	1.1	3.0	3.6	4.0	4.8	3.7	17.0	37.6	21.6	4.7	86.2	53.0	49.7	50.3
54555	PHILLIPS	98.0	97.7	0.0	0.0	0.3	0.4	0.7	1.0	4.9	5.5	5.8	6.3	5.0	22.6	31.9	14.8	3.2	79.8	44.9	50.2	49.8
54556	PRENTICE	98.4	98.3	0.2	0.2	0.1	0.1	1.2	1.6	5.7	5.6	6.1	6.7	5.6	23.0	29.5	15.1	2.5	78.5	42.9	50.8	49.2
54557	PRESQUE ISLE	99.7	99.3	0.0	0.1	0.0	0.1	0.8	1.2	2.7	3.1	3.6	4.2	3.1	16.8	36.7	27.0	2.9	88.0	55.3	50.6	49.4
54558	SAINT GERMAIN	98.2	97.6	0.1	0.1	0.3	0.5	1.0	1.4	4.4	4.7	5.1	4.8	3.4	17.7	33.9	23.7	2.2	82.8	51.4	50.1	49.9
54559	SAXON	97.1	97.0	0.6	0.6	0.0	0.0	0.0	0.0	4.8	4.8	5.0	5.6	4.8	20.6	37.1	15.2	2.0	81.8	47.1	52.1	47.9
54560	SAYNER	98.3	97.7	0.2	0.3	0.2	0.2	0.7	0.9	4.2	4.7	5.0	4.7	3.5	17.6	36.2	21.9	2.3	83.1	51.4	50.2	49.8
54562	THREE LAKES	98.3	97.9	0.1	0.1	0.5	0.6	0.8	1.1	3.6	4.3	4.8	6.1	4.3	18.4	36.0	20.0	2.5	83.1	50.0	51.6	48.4
54563	TONY	99.0	98.6	0.1	0.1	0.1	0.2	0.4	0.7	6.4	6.6	6.8	6.8	5.2	22.6	29.6	13.9	2.1	75.3	41.8	50.8	49.2
54564	TRIPOLI	99.0	98.8	0.0	0.0	0.0	0.0	0.2	0.2	3.8	4.4	4.4	4.6	3.8	18.9	37.1	21.5	1.4	84.1	50.3	51.8	48.2
54565	UPSON	98.4	98.4	0.0	0.0	0.0	0.0	0.0	0.0	4.9	4.9	4.9	6.6	6.6	19.7	31.1	19.7	1.6	78.7	46.5	45.9	54.1
54566	WABENO	79.0	76.9	3.4	4.3	0.2	0.4	1.7	2.3	6.7	7.0	6.7	10.5	6.9	20.2	24.7	14.8	2.6	73.9	38.3	50.8	49.2
54568	WOODRUFF	93.1	92.3	0.1	0.1	0.4	0.5	1.0	1.3	4.6	4.9	5.3	5.6	4.0	20.2	32.5	19.5	3.4	81.6	48.5	49.0	51.0
54601	LA CROSSE	93.5	91.4	1.2	1.5	3.4	4.9	1.1	1.5	4.6	4.5	4.8	10.3	17.2	22.2	21.4	11.8	3.2	83.0	31.9	47.2	52.8
54603	LA CROSSE	89.4	86.1	1.8	2.3	6.3	8.9	1.0	1.3	6.5	5.9	5.7	6.5	7.2	28.8	26.8	10.9	1.7	78.1	36.9	49.5	50.5
54610	ALMA	97.8	97.5	0.3	0.3	0.3	0.4	0.9	1.2	5.3	5.7	6.5	7.4	4.7	23.6	28.7	16.1	2.0	77.9	42.9	50.9	49.1
54611	ALMA CENTER	95.9	94.7	0.1	0.1	0.1	0.2	3.1	4.4	6.9	6.8	7.1	6.8	6.4	24.7	28.1	11.3	1.9	75.1	38.5	52.0	48.0
54612	ARCADIA	98.3	97.8	0.1	0.1	0.2	0.2	2.4	3.4	6.6	6.9	6.9	6.4	4.4	26.1	27.1	12.7	2.9	75.4	40.0	50.0	50.0
54613	ARKDALE	97.9	97.6	0.3	0.3	0.1	0.2	1.4	1.9	3.9	4.5	5.0	5.5	3.4	19.3	36.0	20.4	1.9	82.8	50.2	52.8	47.2
54614	BANGOR	98.4	97.9	0.2	0.3	0.4	0.7	0.5	0.7	7.1	7.3	7.5	7.2	5.0	25.4	28.1	10.6	1.9	73.5	39.2	51.4	48.6
54615	BLACK RIVER FALLS	86.0	83.9	3.1	4.0	0.2	0.2	1.5	2.1	5.5	5.6	5.8	6.2	7.3	27.3	26.3	13.0	3.0	79.3	39.6	52.8	47.2
54616	BLAIR	98.8	98.3	0.2	0.2	0.1	0.2	1.0	1.4	6.4	7.2	7.1	7.1	4.4	22.9	25.8	15.2	4.0	75.0	41.0	48.6	51.4
54618	CAMP DOUGLAS	97.3	96.6	0.3	0.3	0.4	0.5	1.3	1.9	5.9	6.5	6.9	6.9	4.5	23.3	28.0	14.5	3.4	75.7	41.6	51.0	49.0
54619	CASHTON	98.3	97.8	0.1	0.1	0.8	1.1	1.2	1.7	9.9	9.2	8.5	8.0	5.4	23.4	23.1	10.8	1.6	67.2	32.9	50.3	49.7
54621	CHASEBURG	99.0	98.6	0.0	0.0	0.3	0.4	0.3	0.5	7.3	7.5	7.9	7.7	5.1	22.8	29.9	10.7	1.3	72.4	39.9	52.6	47.4
54622	COCHRANE	98.7	98.3	0.1	0.1	0.4	0.6	0.7	1.0	5.7	6.5	6.5	5.3	4.2	22.9	31.1	15.6	2.2	77.7	44.2	50.5	49.5
54623	COON VALLEY	99.0	98.7	0.1	0.1	0.4	0.6	0.4	0.5	6.1	6.4	6.7	6.2	4.6	23.3	28.8	14.7	3.3	76.6	42.9	49.8	50.2
54624	DE SOTO	98.0	97.6	0.1	0.1	0.2	0.4	1.3	1.9	4.4	5.0	5.6	5.2	3.7	17.0	38.4	18.8	1.9	81.6	50.6	50.5	49.5
54625	DODGE	99.2	98.9	0.0	0.4	0.4	0.4	0.0	0.0	4.2	6.4	8.7	8.7	3.8	25.3	29.8	12.1	1.1	75.1	40.6	50.6	49.4
54626	EASTMAN	98.4	97.7	0.1	0.1	0.6	0.9	0.8	1.2	6.0	6.9	7.8	7.9	4.0	22.0	31.1	12.6	1.7	73.8	41.5	51.8	48.2
54627	ETTRICK	99.0	98.9	0.1	0.1	0.2	0.2	0.4	0.7	5.6	6.0	6.4	6.3	4.7	23.8	31.7	13.4	2.1	78.0	43.0	50.7	49.3
54628	FERRYVILLE	98.3	98.0	0.4	0.5	0.2	0.2	0.7	1.0	6.1	6.8	7.2	6.8	4.2	20.0	31.4	15.4	2.0	75.4	44.1	51.0	49.0
54629	FOUNTAIN CITY	99.4	99.3	0.0	0.0	0.0	0.1	0.5	0.7	5.6	6.1	6.6	6.1	4.7	25.7	29.9	12.8	2.4	77.7	41.6	51.3	48.7
54630	GALESVILLE	98.9	98.6	0.1	0.2	0.2	0.3	0.4	0.6	6.0	6.4	6.9	6.7	5.3	23.9	29.8	12.2	2.9	76.5	41.4	49.8	50.2
54631	GAYS MILLS	98.2	97.8	0.3	0.4	0.3	0.3	1.1	1.6	5.0	5.7	6.3	7.0	4.4	21.7	33.5	14.6	1.8	78.4	45.0	50.5	49.5
54632	GENOA	98.7	98.5	0.0	0.0	0.2	0.3	0.4	0.5	7.3	7.8	8.0	6.4	4.1	22.4	29.8	12.8	1.3	72.9	40.9	50.7	49.3
54634	HILLSBORO	98.8	98.5	0.2	0.2	0.1	0.1	0.6	0.9	6.2	7.1	7.8	8.2	5.3	21.3	28.1	12.9	3.1	73.7	40.6	49.2	50.8
54635	HIXTON	97.3	96.7	0.2	0.2	0.2	0.3	1.0	1.4	6.1	6.7	7.0	6.3	4.1	24.2	30.0	13.7	1.8	76.2	41.7	52.1	47.9
54636	HOLMEN	96.2	94.6	0.2	0.3	2.4	3.6	0.6	0.9	7.3	7.9	8.0	7.5	5.4	27.8	27.8	7.4	0.9	71.6	35.5	50.1	49.9
54638	KENDALL	99.1	98.8	0.1	0.1	0.2	0.3	0.6	0.8	8.0	8.4	8.6	7.6	4.8	22.4	27.6	11.0	1.7	70.1	36.3	51.9	48.1
54639	LA FARGE	98.1	97.8	0.1	0.2	0.1	0.2	0.6	0.9	6.5	6.8	6.9	7.5	5.6	20.8	30.4	13.3	2.1	75.0	41.2	49.7	50.3
54641	MATHER	94.1	94.1	0.0	0.0	0.0	0.0	5.9	8.8	5.9	5.9	5.9	5.9	5.9	23.5	29.4	17.6	0.0	79.4	42.5	52.9	47.1
54642	MELROSE	99.0	98.9	0.1	0.1	0.2	0.2	0.3	0.4	5.4	6.4	6.8	7.6	4.5	23.7	30.7	12.7	2.2	76.4	42.3	53.0	47.0
54644	MINDORO	98.2	97.8	0.2	0.1	0.3	0.5	0.5	0.8	5.9	6.5	7.2	7.0	4.7	24.6	32.6	10.3	1.2	76.0	41.3	52.9	47.1
54646	NECEDAH	96.9	96.1	0.2	0.3	0.2	0.4	1.8	2.7	6.2	6.3	6.7	6.7	5.0	22.8	29.4	15.2	1.6	76.4	42.5	52.2	47.8
54648	NORWALK	92.6	89.7	0.1	0.1	0.2	0.3	8.8	12.3	7.9	8.2	8.1	7.4	4.9	26.6	26.3	9.1	1.5	71.1	35.6	52.4	47.6
54650	ONALASKA	95.6	93.9	0.5	0.7	2.5	3.8	0.9	1.3	7.1	6.9	6.9	6.7	5.8	27.8	28.2	9.3	1.3	74.8	36.8	48.7	51.3
54651	ONTARIO	96.7	95.8	0.1	0.1	0.2	0.2	2.3	3.3	6.8	7.1	7.4	7.6	5.2	22.4	29.0	12.6	1.8	73.7	39.8	51.0	49.0
54652	READSTOWN	99.7	99.8	0.0	0.0	0.0	0.0	0.3	0.3	6.2	6.3	6.8	7.3	4.9	22.7	29.0	14.0	2.7	75.9	41.5	52.2	47.8
54653	ROCKLAND	98.5	97.8	0.3	0.2	0.8	1.3	0.7	0.8	7.5	7.6	7.7	7.0	4.9	27.2	26.9	9.6	1.6	72.8	37.8	51.0	49.0
54655	SOLDIERS GROVE	98.5	98.0	0.1	0.1	0.1	0.2	0.9	1.4	5.9	6.2	6.2	5.6	4.9	21.4	29.6	15.1	4.9	77.8	44.8	49.3	50.7
54656	SPARTA	97.5	96.8	0.5	0.6	0.5	0.8	1.5	2.1	6.4	6.3	6.3	6.8	6.1	25.4	28.4	11.9	2.5	76.7	39.5	49.7	50.3
54657	STEUBEN	99.5	99.2	0.0	0.0	0.0	0.4	0.5	0.4	6.6	7.1	7.5	8.7	4.1	22.8	29.9	12.4	0.8	73.0	39.8	52.7	47.3
54658	STODDARD	98.7	98.3	0.1	0.1	0.3	0.5	0.3	0.5	5.8	6.4	6.8	6.5	4.4	24.4	32.0	12.6	1.3	77.0	42.2	50.9	49.1
54659	TAYLOR	98.1	97.7	0.1	0.1	0.2	0.4	0.1	0.1	6.8	7.4	7.5	7.4	5.2	23.9	28.0	12.4	1.3	73.4	38.8	51.4	48.6
54660	TOMAH	95.2	94.1	0.7	0.9	0.5	0.8	1.5	2.2	6.5	6.7	7.0	7.2	6.0	24.0	28.6	11.9	2.2	75.2	39.5	50.7	49.3
54661	TREMPEALEAU	98.8	98.4	0.1	0.1	0.2	0.3	0.5	0.8	5.9	6.3	7.0	6.7	4.6	25.9	30.8	11.4	1.4	76.5	40.9	51.1	48.9
54664	VIOLA	98.5	98.2	0.2	0.2	0.3	0.4	1.1	1.5	5.1	5.6	6.1	6.7	5.2	21.5	33.5	14.1	2.2	79.1	44.8	50.6	49.4
54665	VIROQUA	98.9	98.7	0.1	0.1	0.3	0.5	0.6	0.9	5.8	5.8	6.1	6.5	5.6	21.3	28.7	16.0	4.2	77.9	44.1	48.8	51.2
54666	WARRENS	90.0	88.6	3.0	3.7	0.2	0.2	1.6	2.2	6.0	6.5	6.7	6.7	6.7	25.9	29.2	11.2	1.2	76.8	38.8	53.0	47.0
54667	WESTBY	99.0	98.8	0.0	0.0	0.2	0.3	0.7	1.0	7.2	7.1	7.1	7.1	5.5	22.3	27.5	13.4	2.9	74.1	40.2	49.3	50.7
54669	WEST SALEM	97.8	97.1	0.4	0.5	0.7	1.0	0.5	0.8	7.2	7.4	7.6	7.5	5.7	24.3	28.0	10.0	2.2	73.1	38.0	49.6	50.4
54670	WILTON	98.2	97.4	0.0	0.1	0.1	0.2	2.9	4.2	10.0	10.1	9.6	7.8	4.6	23.7	23.3	9.4	1.4	65.3	31.9	53.6	46.4
54701	EAU CLAIRE	95.5	93.1	0.6	1.7	1.9	2.8	1.0	1.8	5.4	4.9	4.9	11.2	13.4	23.4	23.2	10.8	2.7	81.3	32.6	47.0	53.0
54703	EAU CLAIRE	92.9	90.7	0.6	0.7	4.4	6.2	0.9	1.2	6.4	6.1	6.2	6.5	12.9	27.1	24.2	9.0	1.6	77.5	33.3	49.8	50.2
54720	ALTOONA	96.0	94.9	0.4	0.5	1.1	1.6	0.8	1.1	6.9	6.3	6.0	6.2	7.1	27.8	24.8	11.5	3.4	77.3	36.7	48.1	51.9
54721	ARKANSAW	99.0	98.6	0.1	0.1	0.2	0.3	0.7	1.0	6.2	6.8	6.6	6.0	4.4	24.3	31.3	12.7	1.7	76.8	42.1	54.6	45.4
54722	AUGUSTA	97.8	97.3	0.2	0.2	0.3	0.5	1.0	1.4	7.5	7.5	7.8	8.1	5.3	23.3	25.4	12.4	2.7	71.7	37.4	49.5	50.5
54723	BAY CITY	99.2	99.0	0.1	0.1	0.1	0.1	0.8	1.2	6.1	6.6	6.9	6.4	4.2	28.2	29.2	11.3	1.2	76.4	39.4	50.4	49.6
	WISCONSIN	88.9	86.9	5.7	6.3	1.7	2.3	3.6	4.8	6.4	6.4	6.5	7.2	7.2	26.0	27.1	11.1	2.2	76.6	38.0	49.5	50.5
	UNITED STATES	75.1	72.0	12.3	12.7	3.8	4.6	12.5	15.7	6.8	6.7	6.6	7.1	6.9	27.0	26.0	10.9	1.9	75.7	36.9	49.2	50.8

ZIP CODE				2009 HOUSEHOLD INCOME DISTRIBUTION (%)					MEDIAN HOUSEHOLD INCOME					2009 HOME VALUE DISTRIBUTION (%)					
#	POST OFFICE NAME	2009 Per Capita Income	2009 HH Income Base	Less than $25,000	$25,000 to $49,999	$50,000 to $99,999	$100,000 to $149,999	$150,000 or More	2009	2014	2009 National Centile	2009 State Centile	2009 Home Value Base	Less than $50,000	$50,000 to $89,999	$90,000 to $174,999	$175,000 to $399,999	$400,000 or More	2009 Median Home Value
54514	BUTTERNUT	22210	924	23.8	32.4	36.9	4.8	2.2	44139	46593	46	29	768	10.4	28.4	46.2	13.7	1.3	100577
54515	CATAWBA	19413	216	27.3	35.2	31.5	5.1	0.9	39598	41304	32	11	190	21.1	38.9	31.1	7.4	1.6	77895
54517	CLAM LAKE	0	0	0.0	0.0	0.0	0.0	0.0	0	0	0	0	0	0.0	0.0	0.0	0.0	0.0	0
54519	CONOVER	22352	535	29.0	31.6	32.7	4.3	2.4	40209	41462	33	13	467	4.7	13.1	42.6	31.0	8.6	147250
54520	CRANDON	19625	1757	32.3	33.5	28.7	3.7	1.8	37957	39138	27	7	1297	11.3	22.9	47.3	17.0	1.5	111663
54521	EAGLE RIVER	23218	3730	26.3	31.0	34.5	6.0	2.3	43154	45120	43	25	3001	5.1	14.1	43.8	29.5	7.5	144004
54524	FIFIELD	23344	316	25.6	28.2	38.9	5.7	1.6	46712	47575	53	39	270	7.4	25.6	45.2	19.3	2.6	114674
54526	GLEN FLORA	18064	405	30.6	34.6	30.4	3.5	1.0	38485	40443	28	8	348	26.1	29.6	36.5	6.9	0.9	81667
54527	GLIDDEN	16655	517	39.8	34.2	23.8	1.4	0.8	30450	31436	9	1	414	30.2	38.4	28.7	2.7	0.0	68462
54529	HARSHAW	26072	467	21.4	29.8	39.4	6.0	3.4	48851	49463	59	45	426	7.0	15.0	44.1	29.1	4.7	137097
54530	HAWKINS	19201	351	30.2	34.8	30.2	4.0	0.9	38808	40426	29	9	305	25.9	29.5	37.0	6.6	1.0	82143
54531	HAZELHURST	30199	725	17.8	33.7	32.0	9.7	6.9	48702	49638	58	45	648	2.2	5.6	37.0	39.4	15.9	188281
54534	HURLEY	18269	1226	38.3	37.4	20.0	3.1	1.1	32114	32571	12	2	886	34.2	39.3	21.4	4.7	0.3	62766
54536	IRON BELT	20018	126	29.4	37.3	27.0	4.0	2.4	38767	40000	29	9	113	25.7	39.8	27.4	6.2	0.9	74091
54537	KENNAN	18428	250	30.0	31.6	31.2	5.6	1.6	40000	41263	33	12	222	18.9	26.1	41.0	13.5	0.5	97857
54538	LAC DU FLAMBEAU	17588	1018	30.2	32.7	30.2	4.4	2.6	38701	39758	29	8	729	7.0	12.5	32.2	33.6	14.7	169877
54539	LAKE TOMAHAWK	27748	856	21.0	35.4	33.4	5.8	4.3	45687	46770	50	36	740	8.8	9.9	45.0	30.0	6.4	146951
54540	LAND O LAKES	23442	464	30.0	32.1	30.8	4.7	2.4	38424	39837	28	7	377	5.6	12.7	37.9	32.9	10.9	158681
54541	LAONA	19288	670	27.0	29.7	36.9	4.6	1.8	44015	46668	45	29	538	11.3	30.3	44.4	12.3	1.7	100000
54542	LONG LAKE	23894	303	31.7	33.3	28.4	4.0	2.6	38137	38326	27	7	262	19.1	30.2	36.3	12.2	2.3	90952
54545	MANITOWISH WATERS	25425	502	30.5	27.1	31.7	7.6	3.2	41549	43544	38	18	431	3.5	8.1	29.0	36.7	22.7	209500
54546	MELLEN	19347	749	33.0	31.1	31.2	3.9	0.8	38702	40639	29	9	585	32.5	28.7	30.8	7.5	0.5	73375
54547	MERCER	22916	933	28.3	35.9	29.6	4.5	1.7	38344	40366	28	7	759	7.5	19.0	41.5	26.7	5.3	124107
54548	MINOCQUA	28501	2618	24.2	27.3	36.9	7.2	4.3	48208	48941	57	43	2036	3.9	6.7	38.7	36.1	14.6	176963
54550	MONTREAL	19837	476	34.7	36.8	24.6	2.1	1.9	34382	35000	16	2	389	37.8	41.6	18.0	2.3	0.3	58333
54552	PARK FALLS	22978	2126	28.6	29.5	34.3	5.4	2.2	42488	44476	41	22	1656	15.5	27.5	41.8	13.4	1.8	98923
54554	PHELPS	20615	530	29.4	35.5	28.1	5.5	1.5	38459	39334	28	8	451	6.7	12.6	43.0	31.0	6.7	145047
54555	PHILLIPS	22097	2343	27.7	29.7	35.3	5.4	1.9	44043	45494	46	29	1826	12.2	24.8	47.1	14.8	1.1	107456
54556	PRENTICE	20098	559	35.1	25.8	34.5	3.0	1.6	37347	38715	25	5	451	16.9	35.9	38.4	8.9	0.0	87283
54557	PRESQUE ISLE	25976	575	29.4	28.0	33.0	6.4	3.1	41685	43696	38	19	504	4.2	6.7	31.2	37.3	20.6	198810
54558	SAINT GERMAIN	26568	1059	26.2	30.1	35.0	5.5	3.2	44009	46038	45	28	906	5.7	8.5	44.2	33.2	8.4	155808
54559	SAXON	21318	213	28.6	31.5	31.9	5.6	2.3	41749	42673	38	19	191	22.0	27.2	40.3	10.5	0.0	90882
54560	SAYNER	24043	303	24.8	31.0	36.3	4.6	3.3	45354	47463	49	34	260	1.5	11.2	42.7	31.2	13.5	159091
54562	THREE LAKES	23959	1000	28.5	29.3	34.5	5.4	2.3	41911	43572	39	20	861	5.3	10.6	40.3	36.8	7.0	159265
54563	TONY	19176	329	28.3	30.4	36.8	2.4	2.1	43227	45337	43	25	273	14.7	27.1	40.7	16.8	0.7	98333
54564	TRIPOLI	26218	236	21.2	32.2	39.0	5.5	2.1	46553	48085	53	38	215	7.9	18.6	47.4	23.7	2.3	123264
54565	UPSON	18975	29	31.0	41.4	24.1	3.4	0.0	36125	41132	21	4	26	30.8	38.5	26.9	3.8	0.0	65000
54566	WABENO	21678	690	27.1	30.6	35.4	5.4	1.6	44102	46525	46	29	539	14.5	33.8	39.7	11.3	0.7	91727
54568	WOODRUFF	24326	2382	24.1	32.1	36.2	5.2	2.4	45337	46588	49	34	1852	10.2	10.2	51.5	24.8	3.3	135256
54601	LA CROSSE	25783	20094	25.5	29.8	33.1	6.6	5.0	44672	47563	47	31	11273	7.1	11.9	55.5	22.9	2.6	132632
54603	LA CROSSE	23163	6628	26.2	33.7	32.3	5.5	2.3	41830	43578	39	20	3733	6.3	25.4	55.9	11.4	0.9	108937
54610	ALMA	23775	982	24.3	29.6	36.4	7.1	2.5	46012	47354	51	37	724	14.2	21.5	39.4	20.0	4.8	113725
54611	ALMA CENTER	19639	420	28.1	28.6	37.6	4.0	1.7	44403	46058	47	30	326	13.5	28.5	41.4	14.4	2.1	98387
54612	ARCADIA	22068	1838	25.3	28.8	38.7	4.7	2.5	45285	47556	49	34	1286	8.1	25.8	46.6	17.1	2.4	109716
54613	ARKDALE	24106	842	25.4	35.5	32.3	4.9	1.9	40551	42524	35	15	732	13.8	30.7	40.8	13.3	1.4	96667
54614	BANGOR	22648	1325	18.7	30.8	42.3	5.5	2.6	50334	52561	62	50	1044	8.4	13.9	54.9	20.4	2.4	130076
54615	BLACK RIVER FALLS	22291	3949	24.0	29.1	38.0	6.0	3.0	47163	49076	55	41	2787	11.8	23.2	47.5	16.0	1.5	108936
54616	BLAIR	19432	1031	28.7	32.7	33.6	3.4	1.6	41423	43394	37	18	775	14.5	24.9	44.8	13.3	2.6	103304
54618	CAMP DOUGLAS	21033	1006	21.8	30.3	42.7	4.1	1.1	48092	49747	57	43	823	10.4	26.5	45.2	16.4	1.5	106298
54619	CASHTON	15069	1283	34.1	30.2	29.0	4.8	1.9	37097	38718	24	5	1040	14.3	24.0	40.1	19.3	2.2	107764
54621	CHASEBURG	21715	429	21.0	26.1	45.7	5.6	1.6	51896	52670	66	55	364	9.9	14.6	43.4	28.3	3.8	138393
54622	COCHRANE	23148	957	18.4	33.2	42.6	4.3	1.5	48574	48941	58	44	812	7.1	22.4	52.7	14.9	2.8	117695
54623	COON VALLEY	21457	660	21.5	30.6	40.5	5.5	2.0	48163	49485	57	43	547	16.1	15.5	50.1	16.3	2.0	113411
54624	DE SOTO	23715	546	25.8	29.9	36.8	5.3	2.2	43991	45838	45	28	475	19.2	24.6	35.8	18.7	1.7	99833
54625	DODGE	22143	111	22.5	27.0	42.3	6.3	1.8	50226	51101	62	50	89	7.9	15.7	44.9	28.1	3.4	138542
54626	EASTMAN	19140	584	26.2	33.2	34.2	4.8	1.5	41867	43425	39	20	487	18.3	26.9	37.0	14.8	3.1	97121
54627	ETTRICK	22062	797	22.6	31.9	38.9	4.8	1.9	46741	48698	53	39	621	10.1	18.0	47.5	23.0	1.3	118340
54628	FERRYVILLE	21038	563	30.9	31.6	30.6	3.9	3.0	38552	40149	28	8	445	18.9	25.6	34.2	18.4	2.9	96622
54629	FOUNTAIN CITY	25314	1143	20.6	29.1	40.8	5.8	3.8	50195	50518	62	49	877	6.5	22.3	48.7	19.8	2.6	118494
54630	GALESVILLE	23202	1622	22.6	28.4	41.1	5.7	2.2	49077	50556	59	46	1232	10.0	13.8	50.2	23.1	2.8	131778
54631	GAYS MILLS	19090	939	31.3	33.8	29.1	3.4	2.4	38628	39472	29	8	765	21.0	22.4	35.9	17.3	3.4	98559
54632	GENOA	21677	522	22.2	27.6	43.7	5.7	0.8	50118	50895	61	49	449	17.4	16.7	41.4	22.5	2.0	115485
54634	HILLSBORO	17216	1487	30.9	30.5	32.6	4.4	1.6	40342	41367	34	14	1163	15.1	22.7	40.8	18.9	2.4	106747
54635	HIXTON	21025	743	25.4	29.5	38.6	4.3	2.2	45859	47203	51	37	594	13.1	23.4	43.6	17.2	2.7	108929
54636	HOLMEN	22502	4172	12.8	30.4	46.6	7.6	2.5	56217	58352	73	66	3515	12.6	9.0	41.7	34.4	2.2	151283
54638	KENDALL	18155	682	27.4	32.4	34.5	4.3	1.5	40837	42896	35	16	545	10.5	25.0	40.9	20.4	3.3	117370
54639	LA FARGE	16814	950	34.4	34.1	26.6	3.7	1.2	34914	36166	17	3	774	22.0	26.9	33.9	15.5	1.8	91731
54641	MATHER	19338	15	26.7	33.3	40.0	0.0	0.0	42343	45000	40	21	13	7.7	23.1	53.8	15.4	0.0	112500
54642	MELROSE	21168	804	23.1	32.2	37.2	5.6	1.9	45632	46969	50	35	647	12.2	17.8	44.8	23.2	2.0	121408
54644	MINDORO	22729	561	19.6	30.3	41.9	5.5	2.7	50066	52296	61	48	475	9.1	16.8	46.1	23.6	4.4	131681
54646	NECEDAH	18385	1643	27.2	35.5	32.0	3.2	2.0	39900	41893	32	12	1325	12.5	29.1	46.6	10.3	1.5	99370
54648	NORWALK	16818	654	28.3	30.1	34.4	5.2	2.0	43825	45317	45	27	509	11.0	20.4	39.5	24.8	4.3	119368
54650	ONALASKA	29155	9288	13.4	24.0	45.3	11.8	5.5	62354	63501	80	79	6760	10.1	4.1	47.3	35.9	2.6	155199
54651	ONTARIO	16740	500	31.4	35.2	29.6	3.0	0.8	36423	37354	22	4	391	26.1	20.5	29.9	19.9	3.6	97500
54652	READSTOWN	17658	364	37.6	32.1	23.6	4.9	1.6	32740	33851	13	2	279	26.2	26.9	29.7	15.1	2.2	84688
54653	ROCKLAND	20202	293	19.8	31.1	41.0	6.1	2.0	49366	51225	60	46	224	10.3	14.7	50.4	21.9	2.7	129375
54655	SOLDIERS GROVE	17225	703	32.6	35.7	26.7	3.6	1.4	36015	36915	21	3	536	25.6	25.7	33.2	14.0	1.5	87813
54656	SPARTA	22411	6761	22.6	30.9	38.5	5.4	2.7	46576	48821	53	38	4929	11.8	22.0	51.4	13.4	1.4	111363
54657	STEUBEN	16106	79	24.1	34.2	38.0	3.8	0.0	42347	43902	40	22	65	23.1	20.0	35.4	18.5	3.1	101563
54658	STODDARD	23889	1158	18.3	27.6	44.7	6.6	2.7	53180	54386	68	59	970	13.2	15.4	44.0	25.6	1.9	129032
54659	TAYLOR	18023	519	26.0	35.5	32.4	4.6	1.5	40763	42570	35	16	385	17.4	28.3	33.2	18.2	2.9	96111
54660	TOMAH	21858	6156	23.0	30.9	38.2	5.9	2.0	46636	48413	53	38	4299	12.5	18.8	50.1	17.4	1.2	113554
54661	TREMPEALEAU	22870	1321	20.7	28.3	44.0	5.5	1.4	50521	51589	62	50	1090	11.8	14.8	51.9	20.1	1.4	125371
54664	VIOLA	19823	669	28.8	32.9	34.1	2.1	2.1	40371	41379	34	14	533	18.6	27.4	35.3	17.1	1.7	94886
54665	VIROQUA	19789	3452	32.2	33.6	29.0	3.2	2.0	37155	37744	24	5	2487	18.1	23.1	41.7	14.6	2.5	101655
54666	WARRENS	21019	1005	22.4	32.7	39.5	4.4	1.0	45287	47321	49	34	805	14.3	21.2	42.1	20.5	1.9	116104
54667	WESTBY	19495	1814	25.1	32.6	35.3	5.1	1.9	42445	43875	41	22	1470	12.2	22.1	45.9	18.3	1.6	111621
54669	WEST SALEM	27019	2861	11.6	25.2	46.8	10.2	6.2	61940	62993	80	77	2218	12.2	11.3	42.7	31.1	2.8	145044
54670	WILTON	15230	608	31.4	32.2	29.6	4.3	2.5	40551	41899	35	15	459	12.4	27.5	38.1	18.3	3.7	104167
54701	EAU CLAIRE	29142	15373	20.7	26.6	35.4	10.7	6.6	52895	55598	68	58	9316	3.8	5.1	50.4	37.5	3.1	157265
54703	EAU CLAIRE	23103	17129	18.9	31.2	42.7	5.5	1.7	49914	52439	61	48	10822	5.4	15.0	60.5	18.2	0.9	127164
54720	ALTOONA	29102	3035	17.7	28.6	41.0	7.6	5.0	53146	55538	68	59	1913	17.8	12.1	42.9	24.0	3.1	125593
54721	ARKANSAW	20649	597	20.8	32.8	40.2	4.2	2.0	46712	47746	53	39	502	10.0	22.5	42.6	22.5	2.4	115672
54722	AUGUSTA	17385	1539	30.1	31.1	34.2	3.1	1.6	39906	42011	32	12	1245	12.0	27.1	47.5	12.0	1.4	101453
54723	BAY CITY	25682	559	13.2	23.1	52.1	9.8	1.8	62409	65104	81	79	472	11.4	9.1	47.2	29.2	3.0	143000
	WISCONSIN	27384		18.4	25.3	40.0	11.0	5.2	56363	58927				5.6	11.9	43.5	34.2	4.7	150766
	UNITED STATES	27277		20.9	24.4	35.3	11.7	7.6	54719	56938				9.3	13.1	31.6	32.6	13.5	162279

SPENDING POTENTIAL INDICES

ZIP CODE #	POST OFFICE NAME	FINANCIAL SERVICES: Auto Loan	FINANCIAL SERVICES: Home Loan	FINANCIAL SERVICES: Invest-ments	FINANCIAL SERVICES: Retire-ment Plans	THE HOME: Home Improvements: Home Repair	THE HOME: Home Improvements: Lawn & Garden	THE HOME: Furnishings: Comput-ers & Hard-ware-Personal	THE HOME: Furnishings: Major Appli-ances	THE HOME: Furnishings: TV, Radio, Sound Equip-ment	THE HOME: Furnishings: Furni-ture	ENTERTAINMENT: Dine out/ Carry out	ENTERTAINMENT: Sports Equip-ment	ENTERTAINMENT: Fees & Tickets	ENTERTAINMENT: Toys & Games	ENTERTAINMENT: Travel	ENTERTAINMENT: Cable TV	PERSONAL: Apparel & Services	PERSONAL: Auto Repairs	PERSONAL: Health Insur-ance	PERSONAL: Pets & Supplies
54514	BUTTERNUT	85	68	85	68	70	90	70	84	76	63	74	63	60	75	70	82	50	78	89	98
54515	CATAWBA	82	59	82	57	60	82	60	76	67	56	66	57	48	67	59	73	43	70	79	90
54517	CLAM LAKE	0	0	0	0	0	0	0	0	0	0	0	0	0	0	0	0	0	0	0	0
54519	CONOVER	84	68	109	67	74	89	68	86	71	63	70	63	59	67	73	75	46	79	85	100
54520	CRANDON	78	58	88	57	62	81	60	76	65	56	64	56	50	63	62	71	42	70	78	89
54521	EAGLE RIVER	82	70	98	69	75	87	70	83	73	66	72	61	63	70	74	77	48	79	85	97
54524	FIFIELD	88	70	114	69	77	93	70	89	74	66	73	65	61	70	76	78	48	83	88	104
54526	GLEN FLORA	80	57	84	56	59	82	60	75	65	54	64	58	47	65	59	72	42	69	79	90
54527	GLIDDEN	63	46	63	46	48	66	50	61	56	45	54	46	41	55	49	61	36	57	67	72
54529	HARSHAW	98	79	126	78	86	104	79	100	82	74	81	73	68	78	85	88	54	92	99	116
54530	HAWKINS	81	57	83	56	59	82	60	75	65	54	64	58	47	65	59	72	42	70	79	91
54531	HAZELHURST	114	93	146	92	102	121	93	116	97	87	96	85	82	92	100	103	64	108	115	135
54534	HURLEY	64	47	63	46	49	65	53	62	58	48	56	46	44	57	51	64	38	59	68	73
54536	IRON BELT	77	55	77	54	57	80	60	74	67	54	65	55	48	66	58	74	43	69	81	87
54537	KENNAN	83	62	80	60	63	82	63	76	69	61	68	57	52	70	61	75	45	71	78	91
54538	LAC DU FLAMBEAU	80	64	104	63	70	85	64	82	67	60	66	60	56	64	70	72	44	75	81	95
54539	LAKE TOMAHAWK	102	81	131	80	89	107	81	103	85	76	84	76	71	81	88	91	56	95	102	120
54540	LAND O LAKES	82	65	106	64	72	87	66	83	69	61	68	61	57	65	71	73	45	77	82	97
54541	LAONA	84	64	96	62	68	88	66	83	72	61	70	62	55	70	68	78	47	77	86	97
54542	LONG LAKE	77	64	90	61	69	83	64	79	69	63	67	56	57	65	67	74	45	74	84	91
54545	MANITOWISH WATERS	87	70	113	69	77	92	70	89	73	66	72	65	61	70	76	78	48	82	88	103
54546	MELLEN	76	55	69	54	56	76	58	70	65	54	63	53	47	65	55	71	42	66	75	83
54547	MERCER	77	62	100	61	68	82	62	79	65	58	64	57	54	61	67	69	42	72	78	91
54548	MINOCQUA	99	84	120	84	90	105	83	101	86	79	85	74	75	83	89	90	57	94	100	117
54550	MONTREAL	72	52	72	51	54	75	57	70	63	51	61	52	45	62	55	70	41	65	76	82
54552	PARK FALLS	82	65	88	65	69	85	68	81	73	63	71	60	59	71	69	78	48	77	85	95
54554	PHELPS	78	63	101	62	69	83	63	80	66	59	65	58	54	62	68	70	43	74	79	92
54555	PHILLIPS	81	67	84	67	69	84	69	80	73	63	71	60	60	72	69	78	48	76	83	94
54556	PRENTICE	78	57	78	56	59	81	61	75	68	55	66	56	50	67	59	74	44	70	81	89
54557	PRESQUE ISLE	88	71	114	69	77	93	71	90	74	66	73	65	61	70	76	79	48	83	89	104
54558	SAINT GERMAIN	90	75	115	73	83	97	74	93	78	72	77	66	66	73	81	83	51	86	94	107
54559	SAXON	89	64	92	62	66	91	66	83	73	61	71	63	52	72	65	80	47	77	87	99
54560	SAYNER	88	70	113	69	77	93	70	89	74	66	73	65	61	70	76	78	48	82	88	104
54562	THREE LAKES	86	69	111	68	76	91	69	88	72	65	71	64	60	68	75	77	47	81	86	101
54563	TONY	88	63	93	61	65	91	66	83	72	59	70	64	51	71	65	79	46	77	87	100
54564	TRIPOLI	93	74	118	72	81	98	74	94	78	69	77	69	64	74	80	83	51	87	93	109
54565	UPSON	68	49	68	47	51	71	53	66	59	47	57	49	42	58	51	65	38	61	71	77
54566	WABENO	88	64	92	62	66	90	65	83	72	61	71	62	52	71	65	79	47	76	86	98
54568	WOODRUFF	85	72	103	70	79	91	72	87	76	71	75	62	66	72	77	80	50	82	90	101
54601	LA CROSSE	86	74	71	77	73	79	91	80	88	83	88	64	81	88	80	89	61	86	85	97
54603	LA CROSSE	73	68	60	70	65	72	75	70	77	70	76	55	72	77	70	79	53	74	77	85
54610	ALMA	94	72	96	72	75	97	78	90	81	69	80	71	64	80	76	87	53	86	96	108
54611	ALMA CENTER	89	64	80	63	65	88	68	80	74	63	72	62	54	76	63	80	48	75	84	97
54612	ARCADIA	85	68	84	68	68	90	72	82	76	63	74	66	61	75	71	81	50	79	89	100
54613	ARKDALE	76	71	94	66	78	86	68	81	71	71	70	54	65	66	74	76	47	77	88	93
54614	BANGOR	91	85	79	86	85	93	81	89	84	79	83	66	77	86	80	87	57	84	90	104
54615	BLACK RIVER FALLS	88	75	84	75	77	91	77	87	82	72	80	64	70	81	76	87	55	83	93	102
54616	BLAIR	81	59	84	58	61	85	64	78	69	55	67	61	50	68	63	76	45	73	84	94
54618	CAMP DOUGLAS	87	68	91	67	71	92	70	86	76	64	74	64	59	75	70	83	50	80	90	101
54619	CASHTON	79	55	83	55	58	83	61	75	65	51	64	60	46	64	60	71	42	70	81	91
54621	CHASEBURG	87	78	79	81	80	93	77	88	80	70	78	67	71	81	77	84	53	81	90	102
54622	COCHRANE	82	75	80	76	76	90	73	84	76	66	75	63	68	76	75	81	51	78	89	98
54623	COON VALLEY	93	73	90	73	75	95	74	89	79	69	78	67	63	80	73	86	52	82	92	105
54624	DE SOTO	90	71	114	70	77	95	72	91	75	66	74	68	61	72	77	80	49	84	91	106
54625	DODGE	95	65	104	65	68	100	72	90	75	59	74	74	53	74	72	82	48	84	95	110
54626	EASTMAN	86	60	92	59	62	89	65	81	69	55	68	65	49	68	64	75	44	75	85	99
54627	ETTRICK	81	73	74	76	75	87	73	82	75	65	74	62	66	76	72	79	50	76	85	96
54628	FERRYVILLE	88	61	97	61	64	93	67	84	70	55	69	69	49	69	67	76	45	78	88	103
54629	FOUNTAIN CITY	92	79	88	81	81	97	82	92	85	75	84	70	73	85	81	90	57	87	97	108
54630	GALESVILLE	88	77	81	78	78	91	78	86	80	73	79	65	70	81	76	85	54	82	90	102
54631	GAYS MILLS	84	58	92	58	61	88	64	80	67	53	66	65	47	66	64	73	43	74	84	98
54632	GENOA	89	71	91	71	74	93	71	86	76	66	75	65	62	76	72	82	50	80	89	102
54634	HILLSBORO	83	58	87	57	61	87	64	79	69	54	67	63	49	68	63	76	44	74	85	96
54635	HIXTON	91	64	98	64	67	96	70	87	73	58	72	71	53	72	70	80	47	81	91	106
54636	HOLMEN	91	95	83	96	93	95	87	91	87	88	87	69	89	89	88	88	60	87	90	107
54638	KENDALL	88	61	96	61	64	93	67	84	70	55	69	69	50	69	67	76	45	78	88	103
54639	LA FARGE	75	52	79	52	55	78	57	71	62	49	60	56	44	61	56	68	40	66	76	86
54641	MATHER	78	56	80	54	58	80	58	73	64	54	63	55	46	63	57	70	41	67	76	87
54642	MELROSE	95	67	103	67	70	100	74	91	77	60	76	74	55	75	73	83	49	85	96	111
54644	MINDORO	88	81	80	84	82	95	79	90	82	72	80	68	73	83	79	87	55	83	92	104
54646	NECEDAH	86	62	82	60	63	85	63	78	70	60	69	59	51	71	61	77	46	73	82	94
54648	NORWALK	86	66	87	67	69	91	70	83	72	60	71	66	57	72	69	78	47	77	87	100
54650	ONALASKA	105	108	98	108	105	105	104	104	102	105	103	80	104	105	103	102	72	103	103	122
54651	ONTARIO	75	53	79	52	56	78	56	71	61	50	60	55	44	60	56	67	39	65	74	85
54652	READSTOWN	78	56	80	54	58	79	57	73	63	53	62	55	46	63	57	70	41	67	76	87
54653	ROCKLAND	91	82	81	81	81	90	79	86	81	78	81	65	73	83	77	84	55	82	87	102
54655	SOLDIERS GROVE	77	54	81	53	57	79	57	72	62	51	61	57	44	61	57	68	40	67	76	87
54656	SPARTA	84	76	73	77	75	84	78	81	80	74	79	62	73	81	75	83	54	80	85	96
54657	STEUBEN	88	61	95	60	64	92	67	83	70	55	69	68	50	69	66	77	45	77	88	102
54658	STODDARD	94	84	91	84	84	98	81	92	84	78	84	70	75	85	81	89	57	86	94	109
54659	TAYLOR	86	61	91	59	63	89	64	81	69	57	68	63	50	69	64	76	45	75	85	97
54660	TOMAH	82	74	70	74	73	81	76	79	78	73	77	60	70	79	72	81	53	77	82	93
54661	TREMPEALEAU	85	76	75	77	76	87	74	83	77	71	76	62	68	79	73	81	52	78	84	97
54664	VIOLA	86	61	89	59	63	88	63	80	70	58	68	61	50	69	63	76	45	74	84	96
54665	VIROQUA	77	56	77	56	58	79	63	74	67	55	66	57	50	66	60	73	44	70	80	88
54666	WARRENS	83	71	79	72	72	87	70	82	74	65	73	62	63	75	70	79	49	76	84	96
54667	WESTBY	85	65	86	65	66	90	70	82	74	61	72	65	57	73	68	79	48	78	88	99
54669	WEST SALEM	104	111	95	111	106	110	103	105	103	103	103	81	106	106	105	104	72	103	107	124
54670	WILTON	86	59	95	59	62	91	66	82	69	53	68	68	48	67	66	75	44	76	86	101
54701	EAU CLAIRE	95	90	86	93	89	91	102	92	100	97	100	74	98	100	96	100	70	98	96	111
54703	EAU CLAIRE	80	76	66	78	73	77	83	77	81	78	82	62	79	83	77	81	57	80	80	92
54720	ALTOONA	90	88	83	89	87	89	93	89	94	91	94	68	92	93	90	95	65	92	95	105
54721	ARKANSAW	94	65	103	65	68	99	72	89	75	58	74	74	53	73	72	82	48	84	94	110
54722	AUGUSTA	78	59	79	58	61	82	63	76	67	55	66	59	51	67	61	74	44	71	81	90
54723	BAY CITY	100	95	92	99	96	108	92	102	94	85	93	78	88	96	93	98	64	95	104	119
	WISCONSIN	98	94	92	96	93	99	96	96	96	93	96	75	94	97	95	98	67	96	99	114
	UNITED STATES	100	100	100	100	100	100	100	100	100	100	100	100	100	100	100	100	100	100	100	100

ZIP CODE			POPULATION			2000-2009 ANNUAL RATE		HOUSEHOLDS					FAMILIES		
#	POST OFFICE NAME	COUNTY FIPS CODE	2000	2009	2014	% Rate	State Centile	2000	2009	2014	% Annual Rate 2000-2009	2009 Average HH Size	2000	2009	% Annual Rate 2000-2009
54724	BLOOMER	017	6686	7094	7217	0.6	51	2601	2821	2900	0.9	2.46	1851	1980	0.7
54725	BOYCEVILLE	033	2926	3200	3326	1.0	72	1096	1237	1295	1.3	2.59	761	844	1.1
54726	BOYD	017	1959	2062	2083	0.6	51	703	773	790	1.0	2.67	536	582	0.9
54727	CADOTT	017	4552	4963	5166	0.9	68	1685	1920	2026	1.4	2.57	1282	1443	1.3
54728	CHETEK	005	6206	6845	7114	1.1	76	2513	2869	3012	1.4	2.35	1781	2009	1.3
54729	CHIPPEWA FALLS	017	27800	32187	33395	1.6	91	10961	12564	13191	1.5	2.38	7433	8457	1.4
54730	COLFAX	033	4464	5194	5502	1.7	91	1692	2019	2160	1.9	2.53	1243	1461	1.8
54731	CONRATH	107	655	675	682	0.3	32	240	255	260	0.7	2.65	177	186	0.5
54732	CORNELL	017	2754	3063	3170	1.2	81	1064	1215	1276	1.4	2.44	753	845	1.3
54733	DALLAS	005	1593	1707	1757	0.8	61	574	639	666	1.2	2.62	434	479	1.1
54734	DOWNING	033	690	750	781	0.9	68	261	294	310	1.3	2.55	193	215	1.2
54736	DURAND	091	4037	4184	4202	0.4	39	1513	1603	1620	0.6	2.56	1058	1109	0.5
54737	EAU GALLE	033	373	377	374	0.1	20	145	152	152	0.5	2.47	110	114	0.4
54738	ELEVA	035	2576	3279	3453	2.6	97	981	1266	1349	2.8	2.58	755	972	2.8
54739	ELK MOUND	033	3873	4486	4662	1.6	91	1348	1608	1686	1.9	2.78	1080	1278	1.8
54740	ELMWOOD	093	2152	2348	2420	0.9	68	805	912	950	1.4	2.52	578	644	1.2
54741	FAIRCHILD	053	1564	1767	1844	1.3	84	539	632	668	1.7	2.72	386	444	1.5
54742	FALL CREEK	035	4261	4705	4967	1.1	76	1524	1753	1871	1.5	2.65	1177	1337	1.4
54745	HOLCOMBE	017	2140	2311	2354	0.8	61	855	934	964	1.0	2.38	620	666	0.8
54746	HUMBIRD	019	739	764	769	0.4	39	289	309	313	0.7	2.45	205	217	0.6
54747	INDEPENDENCE	121	2457	2501	2522	0.2	24	1023	1087	1107	0.7	2.28	666	698	0.5
54748	JIM FALLS	017	1230	1330	1368	0.8	61	455	515	537	1.3	2.58	364	408	1.2
54749	KNAPP	033	1242	1492	1591	2.0	95	468	582	627	2.4	2.56	343	421	2.2
54750	MAIDEN ROCK	093	1196	1235	1242	0.3	32	428	458	465	0.7	2.69	322	341	0.6
54751	MENOMONIE	033	23304	24924	25568	0.7	56	8162	9123	9475	1.2	2.41	4712	5199	1.1
54754	MERRILLAN	053	1564	1745	1820	1.2	81	643	746	787	1.6	2.26	440	502	1.4
54755	MONDOVI	011	6768	7009	7027	0.4	39	2546	2722	2751	0.7	2.54	1767	1872	0.6
54756	NELSON	011	951	952	934	0.0	16	398	414	411	0.4	2.30	278	286	0.3
54757	NEW AUBURN	017	2880	3168	3299	1.0	72	1113	1270	1335	1.4	2.49	801	900	1.3
54758	OSSEO	121	4817	5004	5081	0.4	39	1842	1979	2028	0.8	2.48	1316	1396	0.6
54759	PEPIN	091	1452	1628	1695	1.2	81	608	704	741	1.6	2.23	403	462	1.5
54761	PLUM CITY	093	1138	1192	1203	0.5	44	423	460	469	0.9	2.51	313	336	0.8
54762	PRAIRIE FARM	005	1326	1383	1399	0.5	44	480	516	525	0.8	2.61	346	367	0.6
54763	RIDGELAND	033	1002	1041	1045	0.4	39	403	432	437	0.8	2.40	287	302	0.6
54765	SAND CREEK	033	112	113	112	0.1	20	46	48	48	0.5	2.35	34	35	0.3
54766	SHELDON	119	1592	1652	1671	0.4	39	552	592	605	0.8	2.79	409	434	0.6
54767	SPRING VALLEY	093	2915	3383	3546	1.6	91	1079	1297	1372	2.0	2.56	787	937	1.9
54768	STANLEY	017	4007	4213	4205	0.5	44	1529	1617	1629	0.6	2.49	1039	1082	0.4
54769	STOCKHOLM	091	348	361	356	0.4	39	156	169	168	0.9	2.13	108	116	0.8
54770	STRUM	121	2018	2143	2200	0.7	56	791	873	907	1.1	2.41	576	628	0.9
54771	THORP	019	3961	4171	4186	0.6	51	1450	1562	1575	0.8	2.63	980	1042	0.7
54772	WHEELER	033	1108	1152	1166	0.4	39	409	438	447	0.7	2.63	307	326	0.7
54773	WHITEHALL	121	3363	3463	3482	0.3	32	1258	1340	1361	0.7	2.40	841	887	0.6
54801	SPOONER	129	6573	6552	6461	0.0	16	2696	2766	2747	0.3	2.32	1801	1831	0.2
54805	ALMENA	005	1719	1766	1780	0.3	32	638	680	692	0.7	2.59	490	518	0.6
54806	ASHLAND	003	12457	12123	11971	-0.3	4	4866	4869	4841	0.0	2.34	3029	2996	-0.1
54810	BALSAM LAKE	095	2351	2592	2694	1.1	76	997	1138	1194	1.4	2.24	699	789	1.3
54812	BARRON	005	5257	5158	5116	-0.2	8	2040	2074	2075	0.2	2.39	1372	1377	0.0
54813	BARRONETT	013	658	664	664	0.1	20	256	268	271	0.5	2.48	196	203	0.4
54814	BAYFIELD	007	2438	2368	2381	-0.3	4	951	947	957	0.0	2.48	661	652	-0.1
54817	BIRCHWOOD	129	2318	2598	2705	1.2	81	976	1132	1189	1.6	2.29	711	817	1.5
54819	BRUCE	107	2451	2507	2527	0.2	24	1040	1099	1119	0.6	2.28	689	719	0.5
54820	BRULE	031	919	947	960	0.3	32	355	380	390	0.7	2.49	243	257	0.6
54821	CABLE	007	1353	1436	1474	0.6	51	631	690	716	1.0	2.08	417	451	0.9
54822	CAMERON	005	3880	4445	4682	1.5	88	1509	1798	1913	1.9	2.46	1096	1290	1.8
54824	CENTURIA	095	2184	2441	2587	1.2	81	819	934	999	1.4	2.59	562	634	1.3
54826	COMSTOCK	005	875	934	949	0.7	56	360	399	409	1.1	2.32	254	279	1.0
54827	CORNUCOPIA	007	223	237	244	0.7	56	108	121	126	1.2	1.96	76	83	1.0
54828	COUDERAY	113	754	753	741	0.0	16	298	308	306	0.4	2.42	205	210	0.3
54829	CUMBERLAND	005	5346	5580	5641	0.5	44	2187	2364	2416	0.8	2.33	1523	1626	0.7
54830	DANBURY	013	2797	2921	2933	0.5	44	1287	1395	1415	0.9	2.09	880	942	0.7
54832	DRUMMOND	007	465	496	509	0.7	56	204	223	231	1.0	2.22	135	146	0.9
54835	EXELAND	113	1069	1153	1180	0.8	61	439	486	502	1.1	2.34	307	337	1.0
54836	FOXBORO	031	1035	1070	1074	0.4	39	396	425	432	0.8	2.52	290	308	0.7
54837	FREDERIC	095	4091	4367	4401	0.7	56	1655	1829	1862	1.1	2.32	1111	1214	1.0
54838	GORDON	031	1074	1085	1089	0.1	20	468	490	497	0.5	2.14	330	340	0.3
54839	GRAND VIEW	007	305	313	316	0.3	32	137	145	148	0.6	2.16	95	99	0.4
54840	GRANTSBURG	013	4365	4814	5002	1.1	76	1731	1981	2083	1.5	2.40	1184	1339	1.3
54843	HAYWARD	113	10907	11930	12299	1.0	72	4407	4958	5155	1.3	2.36	3041	3381	1.2
54844	HERBSTER	007	241	307	333	2.7	97	116	150	164	2.8	2.05	74	95	2.7
54845	HERTEL	013	137	150	156	1.0	72	54	61	64	1.3	2.44	41	46	1.3
54846	HIGH BRIDGE	003	566	534	521	-0.6	1	217	212	209	-0.3	2.52	170	164	-0.4
54847	IRON RIVER	007	2016	2195	2262	0.9	68	872	983	1022	1.3	2.23	596	665	1.2
54848	LADYSMITH	107	6811	6683	6637	-0.2	8	2665	2718	2728	0.2	2.32	1751	1764	0.1
54849	LAKE NEBAGAMON	031	1894	2054	2113	0.9	68	750	847	881	1.3	2.35	542	603	1.2
54850	LA POINTE	003	246	252	251	0.3	32	125	132	132	0.6	1.90	89	92	0.4
54853	LUCK	095	3697	3908	3924	0.6	51	1475	1606	1627	0.9	2.38	1029	1112	0.8
54854	MAPLE	031	938	999	1024	0.7	56	383	423	438	1.1	2.36	268	291	0.9
54855	MARENGO	003	680	666	656	-0.2	8	238	239	237	0.0	2.79	181	180	-0.1
54856	MASON	007	1523	1514	1509	-0.1	11	589	604	608	0.3	2.51	427	434	0.2
54858	MILLTOWN	095	1536	1876	2028	2.2	96	678	870	951	2.7	2.16	431	544	2.5
54859	MINONG	129	1876	1941	2033	0.4	39	827	891	941	0.8	2.17	552	584	0.6
54862	OJIBWA	113	398	408	411	0.3	32	157	166	168	0.6	2.42	108	113	0.5
54864	POPLAR	031	1214	1333	1377	1.0	72	438	499	521	1.4	2.65	331	372	1.3
54865	PORT WING	007	503	580	627	1.6	91	235	282	308	2.0	2.06	150	179	1.9
54867	RADISSON	113	449	447	440	0.0	16	194	199	198	0.3	2.22	131	133	0.2
54868	RICE LAKE	005	15307	16360	16788	0.7	56	6208	6834	7067	1.0	2.36	4115	4484	0.9
54870	SARONA	129	1451	1582	1567	0.9	68	608	676	674	1.2	2.33	441	485	1.0
54871	SHELL LAKE	129	3161	3526	3689	1.2	81	1251	1464	1549	1.7	2.35	882	1018	1.6
54872	SIREN	013	2813	2957	2976	0.5	44	1169	1272	1295	0.9	2.21	756	812	0.8
54873	SOLON SPRINGS	031	2568	2645	2671	0.3	32	1103	1171	1193	0.6	2.23	740	775	0.5
54874	SOUTH RANGE	031	3469	3798	3926	1.0	72	1236	1400	1459	1.4	2.70	968	1086	1.3
54875	SPRINGBROOK	129	1171	1645	1739	3.7	99	473	692	738	4.2	2.37	337	484	4.0
54876	STONE LAKE	113	1517	1547	1526	0.2	24	647	677	672	0.5	2.28	464	480	0.4
54880	SUPERIOR	031	30678	30833	30670	0.1	20	12870	13351	13404	0.4	2.22	7688	7849	0.2
	WISCONSIN					0.7					1.0	2.43			0.9
	UNITED STATES					1.0					1.1	2.59			0.9

ZIP CODE #	POST OFFICE NAME	RACE (%) White		RACE (%) Black		RACE (%) Asian/Pacific		% Hispanic Origin		2009 AGE DISTRIBUTION (%)										MEDIAN AGE	% 2009 Males	% 2009 Females
		2000	2009	2000	2009	2000	2009	2000	2009	0-4	5-9	10-14	15-19	20-24	25-44	45-64	65-84	85+	18+	2009		
54724	BLOOMER	99.2	99.0	0.0	0.0	0.1	0.2	0.4	0.5	6.3	6.6	6.9	7.1	6.0	24.6	26.9	12.2	3.5	75.6	39.2	49.6	50.4
54725	BOYCEVILLE	98.7	98.5	0.0	0.0	0.1	0.1	0.8	1.1	7.0	7.1	7.3	7.2	5.8	25.9	27.5	10.5	1.7	74.1	37.7	50.0	50.0
54726	BOYD	98.9	98.7	0.1	0.0	0.1	0.2	0.3	0.5	6.2	6.8	9.1	8.8	4.3	23.9	26.2	12.7	2.0	71.8	38.6	51.7	48.3
54727	CADOTT	98.5	98.1	0.1	0.1	0.3	0.4	0.5	0.8	6.0	6.9	7.6	8.0	4.5	25.6	28.6	11.1	1.7	74.0	38.9	51.9	48.1
54728	CHETEK	98.8	98.4	0.1	0.1	0.2	0.3	0.7	1.0	5.4	5.8	5.9	6.0	5.0	21.8	31.3	15.8	3.1	79.1	45.1	50.2	49.8
54729	CHIPPEWA FALLS	97.8	97.1	0.2	0.3	0.8	1.3	0.6	0.8	6.0	6.0	6.2	6.5	6.3	26.8	28.2	11.5	2.5	77.7	39.7	51.0	49.0
54730	COLFAX	98.7	98.2	0.1	0.1	0.4	0.7	0.6	0.8	5.9	6.0	6.7	7.1	4.9	25.3	30.4	11.5	2.2	76.7	41.0	50.5	49.5
54731	CONRATH	98.2	98.1	0.2	0.3	0.3	0.3	0.5	0.7	6.7	6.7	7.3	7.3	5.0	21.2	30.1	13.8	2.1	75.0	42.0	50.7	49.3
54732	CORNELL	98.6	98.3	0.0	0.0	0.3	0.4	0.4	0.5	6.0	6.1	6.9	7.4	5.5	23.1	27.7	13.9	3.4	76.2	41.2	49.9	50.1
54733	DALLAS	98.4	98.0	0.1	0.1	0.1	0.2	0.8	1.2	6.2	6.6	6.9	7.1	4.5	23.9	29.8	11.9	3.2	76.1	41.5	49.9	50.1
54734	DOWNING	99.1	99.1	0.0	0.0	0.1	0.1	1.6	2.4	6.3	6.9	7.1	6.0	5.2	26.3	29.9	10.9	1.5	76.0	38.9	52.1	47.9
54736	DURAND	98.9	98.6	0.1	0.1	0.3	0.4	0.3	0.5	6.6	6.6	6.6	7.5	5.7	24.8	26.6	12.3	3.3	75.3	39.1	49.6	50.4
54737	EAU GALLE	99.5	99.2	0.0	0.0	0.3	0.5	0.8	0.8	6.9	6.9	7.4	7.2	4.0	24.9	27.9	13.3	1.6	74.0	40.3	51.7	48.3
54738	ELEVA	98.6	98.0	0.1	0.1	0.4	0.8	0.8	1.2	6.2	6.6	7.2	7.4	4.8	23.0	31.3	11.8	1.6	74.9	41.5	51.9	48.1
54739	ELK MOUND	97.1	96.3	0.0	0.0	1.5	2.1	0.6	0.8	7.0	7.3	7.5	6.5	4.8	29.3	29.1	7.5	0.9	73.9	37.6	50.7	49.3
54740	ELMWOOD	98.5	98.0	0.1	0.2	0.2	0.3	0.9	1.4	6.0	6.4	7.0	7.2	5.1	24.3	26.8	13.8	3.3	75.9	40.9	49.3	50.7
54741	FAIRCHILD	95.7	95.0	0.1	0.1	0.2	0.2	2.9	4.0	7.6	7.8	7.8	7.8	5.5	23.0	26.6	11.9	2.1	71.7	37.5	50.7	49.3
54742	FALL CREEK	98.2	97.7	0.3	0.3	0.6	0.8	0.4	0.7	6.3	6.4	7.2	7.1	5.1	25.0	30.2	10.6	2.1	75.6	40.1	50.3	49.7
54745	HOLCOMBE	98.8	98.4	0.0	0.0	0.2	0.4	0.5	0.7	5.1	5.7	6.4	6.4	4.1	21.2	32.2	16.4	2.5	78.5	45.7	50.3	49.7
54746	HUMBIRD	95.9	95.0	0.3	0.3	0.1	0.1	1.9	2.7	5.6	5.9	6.3	6.5	5.1	22.0	32.5	14.3	1.8	78.1	43.9	52.1	47.9
54747	INDEPENDENCE	99.0	98.6	0.1	0.2	0.1	0.2	0.9	1.4	6.1	6.5	6.5	6.5	5.0	25.9	28.3	12.6	2.5	76.5	40.2	52.5	47.5
54748	JIM FALLS	99.0	98.9	0.1	0.1	0.1	0.2	0.1	0.1	5.4	6.2	6.7	6.9	4.4	24.4	33.2	11.5	1.3	77.4	42.4	51.7	48.3
54749	KNAPP	98.2	97.5	0.2	0.3	0.6	1.0	1.0	1.5	6.6	7.4	7.4	6.3	4.3	25.3	30.3	11.1	1.3	74.5	40.0	51.9	48.1
54750	MAIDEN ROCK	98.7	98.4	0.1	0.1	0.1	0.2	0.8	1.3	4.9	5.8	6.8	7.6	4.8	24.0	32.7	11.4	1.9	77.5	42.2	51.5	48.5
54751	MENOMONIE	94.5	92.6	0.5	0.7	3.2	4.6	0.9	1.3	5.4	4.8	5.1	11.3	20.3	21.9	20.5	8.5	2.1	81.3	27.3	50.3	49.7
54754	MERRILLAN	92.1	89.9	0.7	0.9	0.1	0.2	4.4	6.1	5.7	5.9	6.4	6.2	5.7	24.6	30.1	13.5	1.8	78.3	41.5	53.0	47.0
54755	MONDOVI	98.5	98.1	0.1	0.1	0.5	0.8	0.4	0.6	6.4	6.6	7.2	7.5	5.1	24.4	27.6	12.6	2.5	74.8	39.7	49.8	50.2
54756	NELSON	98.7	98.4	0.1	0.2	0.6	0.8	0.7	1.1	4.4	6.0	6.6	8.5	4.8	23.2	31.4	13.0	2.0	77.0	42.6	51.9	48.1
54757	NEW AUBURN	98.8	98.5	0.1	0.1	0.1	0.2	0.3	0.5	6.4	6.7	7.0	6.7	5.0	23.5	30.6	12.6	1.6	75.9	41.1	52.2	47.8
54758	OSSEO	98.0	97.6	0.1	0.1	0.3	0.4	1.1	1.5	6.4	6.6	6.9	7.0	5.2	24.1	27.9	13.1	2.9	75.6	40.6	49.7	50.3
54759	PEPIN	98.8	98.6	0.1	0.1	0.3	0.5	0.1	0.2	4.2	4.4	5.2	5.3	4.5	21.6	31.6	17.6	5.5	82.9	48.5	50.1	49.9
54761	PLUM CITY	99.5	99.5	0.0	0.0	0.0	0.0	0.3	0.4	4.8	5.5	5.9	7.0	4.9	22.7	31.3	13.6	4.4	78.9	44.4	51.3	48.7
54762	PRAIRIE FARM	99.0	98.9	0.0	0.0	0.3	0.4	1.1	1.7	6.2	6.7	6.9	6.2	4.7	24.4	29.4	12.5	2.9	75.6	41.3	50.7	49.3
54763	RIDGELAND	98.6	98.3	0.0	0.0	0.2	0.2	0.6	1.0	6.1	6.8	6.9	6.6	4.3	23.7	31.0	12.2	2.3	75.9	41.6	50.2	49.8
54765	SAND CREEK	99.1	97.3	0.0	0.0	0.0	0.9	0.0	0.0	6.2	7.1	7.1	6.2	3.5	22.1	33.6	12.4	1.8	76.1	43.2	54.0	46.0
54766	SHELDON	97.7	97.6	0.1	0.1	0.0	0.0	0.5	0.5	7.3	7.6	7.9	8.1	4.7	22.5	28.3	11.7	1.9	72.2	39.8	50.1	49.9
54767	SPRING VALLEY	98.6	98.3	0.2	0.2	0.1	0.1	0.4	0.6	6.3	6.8	7.2	7.3	5.5	25.2	29.1	10.1	2.5	75.1	39.0	50.8	49.2
54768	STANLEY	98.7	98.3	0.1	0.1	0.3	0.5	0.8	1.1	6.8	7.1	7.5	6.9	5.3	24.2	25.9	12.9	3.4	74.1	38.8	51.1	48.9
54769	STOCKHOLM	99.1	98.9	0.0	0.0	0.0	0.0	0.6	0.8	4.2	4.4	7.2	6.1	4.7	19.9	36.3	15.2	1.9	79.8	47.6	51.8	48.2
54770	STRUM	98.4	97.9	0.1	0.2	0.4	0.6	0.9	1.4	6.6	7.0	7.2	6.5	4.7	23.8	29.6	12.0	2.6	74.8	40.8	51.6	48.4
54771	THORP	99.2	99.0	0.1	0.0	0.2	0.2	0.5	0.7	7.7	7.7	8.3	7.8	5.5	22.0	25.4	12.1	3.5	71.3	37.2	49.6	50.4
54772	WHEELER	98.7	98.5	0.1	0.2	0.4	0.5	0.4	0.3	6.4	6.3	7.8	8.2	4.8	25.3	30.0	9.9	1.3	74.0	39.3	51.8	48.2
54773	WHITEHALL	99.0	98.8	0.2	0.2	0.1	0.1	0.4	0.7	5.6	5.9	6.4	6.9	4.9	23.9	29.3	13.5	3.4	77.4	42.3	50.4	49.6
54801	SPOONER	96.1	95.5	0.3	0.4	0.2	0.3	0.9	1.3	5.1	5.3	6.4	6.6	4.6	21.3	30.8	16.5	3.4	78.6	45.4	49.7	50.3
54805	ALMENA	98.5	98.3	0.1	0.1	0.1	0.1	0.7	1.0	6.3	6.5	6.7	7.0	4.8	25.5	28.2	13.5	1.5	76.1	40.4	51.7	48.3
54806	ASHLAND	86.0	84.2	0.2	0.3	0.4	0.6	1.3	1.7	6.4	6.0	6.1	8.3	8.4	23.6	26.2	12.0	3.0	77.3	37.3	49.2	50.8
54810	BALSAM LAKE	96.2	95.6	0.1	0.1	0.4	0.6	0.6	0.8	5.6	6.3	6.6	5.7	4.0	21.0	33.8	15.3	1.8	77.5	45.5	52.3	47.7
54812	BARRON	97.3	96.5	0.5	0.6	0.3	0.5	1.5	2.1	6.0	5.6	6.1	8.0	6.3	24.4	26.0	13.4	4.2	77.4	40.2	49.0	51.0
54813	BARRONETT	92.7	91.7	0.2	0.2	0.2	0.2	0.2	0.2	5.0	6.5	7.8	7.7	3.6	22.1	33.9	12.2	1.2	75.3	43.1	51.5	48.5
54814	BAYFIELD	50.6	43.5	0.2	0.2	0.0	0.0	1.5	1.9	6.6	8.1	7.3	6.4	4.8	22.7	31.5	11.3	1.3	73.6	40.6	50.3	49.7
54817	BIRCHWOOD	97.7	97.2	0.0	0.0	0.2	0.2	1.0	1.5	4.4	5.0	5.7	6.0	4.3	18.8	35.3	18.4	2.1	81.3	48.4	51.2	48.8
54819	BRUCE	98.6	98.2	0.0	0.1	0.3	0.4	0.5	0.7	4.5	5.1	5.9	6.4	4.3	21.3	31.3	18.4	2.7	80.3	46.5	50.7	49.3
54820	BRULE	97.7	97.1	0.0	0.0	0.1	0.2	0.7	1.0	6.3	7.1	7.1	6.1	3.7	23.8	31.7	12.7	1.6	75.6	41.9	51.4	48.6
54821	CABLE	99.6	99.4	0.0	0.0	0.1	0.2	0.4	0.6	3.4	4.0	4.5	4.8	3.3	15.2	39.3	23.2	2.2	85.0	52.8	51.5	48.5
54822	CAMERON	98.2	97.8	0.1	0.1	0.4	0.5	1.1	1.7	6.4	6.5	6.6	6.7	5.7	26.7	29.0	11.0	1.4	76.1	38.7	49.9	50.1
54824	CENTURIA	97.6	97.0	0.3	0.3	0.5	0.7	0.9	1.2	5.8	6.4	6.7	6.3	4.8	23.3	32.0	12.8	1.9	76.9	42.6	51.4	48.6
54826	COMSTOCK	93.4	92.5	0.1	0.1	0.2	0.3	0.7	0.9	4.6	5.6	6.2	7.1	4.5	21.9	31.8	15.6	2.7	78.9	45.1	51.0	49.0
54827	CORNUCOPIA	86.5	84.0	0.0	0.0	0.0	0.0	0.5	0.4	4.2	4.6	5.1	5.1	3.8	19.4	39.7	16.9	1.3	82.7	50.1	50.6	49.4
54828	COUDERAY	65.7	61.0	0.1	0.1	0.0	0.0	1.2	1.5	5.7	6.0	6.5	6.9	4.6	21.9	30.0	16.3	2.0	77.7	43.8	50.9	49.1
54829	CUMBERLAND	95.9	95.3	0.1	0.1	0.3	0.4	0.6	0.8	4.8	5.4	6.2	6.9	4.8	22.7	30.9	15.1	2.9	78.8	44.3	49.9	50.1
54830	DANBURY	91.6	90.6	0.5	0.6	0.1	0.2	0.5	0.7	3.2	3.5	3.7	4.2	3.6	14.5	33.7	31.4	2.2	86.9	56.8	51.0	49.0
54832	DRUMMOND	97.8	97.4	0.0	0.0	0.4	0.6	0.2	0.2	5.0	5.8	6.3	5.8	3.8	17.9	35.3	17.9	2.0	79.0	48.1	51.0	49.0
54835	EXELAND	93.6	92.5	0.7	0.8	0.5	0.4	1.4	1.8	4.8	5.1	5.5	6.2	5.6	19.8	33.1	17.6	2.3	80.8	46.7	51.3	48.7
54836	FOXBORO	98.4	97.8	0.0	0.1	0.2	0.4	0.1	0.2	4.7	6.4	7.5	6.8	3.7	26.2	32.9	10.5	1.3	76.8	41.9	53.2	46.8
54837	FREDERIC	97.2	96.7	0.1	0.1	0.3	0.4	0.5	0.7	5.1	5.6	6.0	6.3	5.3	20.7	31.2	16.1	3.5	79.2	45.6	49.7	50.3
54838	GORDON	95.3	94.6	1.7	2.0	0.3	0.4	0.5	0.6	3.4	3.8	4.4	5.2	3.7	18.8	36.7	22.3	1.8	84.8	51.0	54.5	45.5
54839	GRAND VIEW	96.1	94.6	0.3	0.6	0.7	1.0	0.3	0.3	6.1	6.7	7.3	7.0	4.5	21.1	30.7	14.7	1.9	75.4	43.1	51.4	48.6
54840	GRANTSBURG	96.7	96.1	0.3	0.4	0.3	0.4	1.1	1.6	5.9	5.8	6.1	6.7	6.0	22.3	30.8	13.6	2.8	78.1	42.8	50.6	49.4
54843	HAYWARD	81.8	80.0	0.1	0.1	0.3	0.5	0.7	0.9	5.8	6.0	6.3	6.4	5.3	21.1	31.1	15.5	2.5	77.8	44.3	49.9	50.1
54844	HERBSTER	96.7	95.8	0.4	0.3	0.0	0.3	1.2	1.6	3.9	4.2	4.6	4.2	3.9	18.9	39.1	19.2	2.0	84.4	50.7	51.1	48.9
54845	HERTEL	83.9	82.7	0.0	0.0	0.7	0.7	0.7	0.7	5.3	6.7	7.3	6.7	4.0	20.0	33.3	15.3	1.3	76.7	45.0	50.0	50.0
54846	HIGH BRIDGE	89.6	88.0	0.0	0.0	0.5	0.6	0.5	0.7	6.2	6.6	7.1	7.1	4.9	25.1	30.1	11.2	1.7	75.8	39.8	50.4	49.6
54847	IRON RIVER	97.0	96.1	0.0	0.0	0.4	0.6	0.2	0.4	5.5	6.0	6.2	5.5	3.9	19.0	34.4	17.3	2.3	78.9	47.4	50.8	49.2
54848	LADYSMITH	97.0	96.2	1.0	1.3	0.5	0.7	0.8	1.0	6.0	6.1	6.3	7.7	7.1	23.6	25.8	13.8	3.7	77.2	39.9	49.1	50.9
54849	LAKE NEBAGAMON	97.7	97.3	0.4	0.5	0.1	0.2	0.7	1.0	5.8	6.6	6.9	6.8	4.0	21.6	32.3	13.6	2.4	75.7	43.8	51.0	49.0
54850	LA POINTE	41.6	38.5	0.0	0.0	0.0	0.0	2.4	3.2	8.7	8.7	8.7	8.7	6.0	22.2	25.8	10.3	0.8	67.1	34.2	51.2	48.8
54853	LUCK	95.7	95.1	0.1	0.1	0.3	0.5	0.7	0.9	5.0	5.4	6.0	7.2	5.6	21.1	32.0	14.4	3.4	79.1	44.8	50.1	49.9
54854	MAPLE	97.2	96.8	0.0	0.0	0.2	0.3	0.9	1.1	6.2	6.9	7.0	6.2	3.9	24.2	31.5	12.5	1.5	75.9	41.9	51.4	48.6
54855	MARENGO	78.6	76.4	0.0	0.0	0.1	0.3	1.0	1.2	7.7	7.7	8.1	8.0	5.7	23.4	27.8	10.4	1.4	71.3	36.8	50.5	49.5
54856	MASON	96.2	95.1	0.4	0.5	0.4	0.5	0.3	0.5	5.7	6.3	6.7	6.4	4.5	21.9	31.9	14.6	1.9	77.3	43.9	51.7	48.3
54858	MILLTOWN	97.9	97.4	0.1	0.1	0.0	0.0	0.7	1.0	5.2	5.4	5.8	6.6	4.5	22.8	30.6	16.4	2.8	79.7	44.8	48.1	51.9
54859	MINONG	96.9	96.6	0.2	0.3	0.2	0.3	0.7	1.0	5.2	5.5	5.7	5.3	4.0	20.1	32.0	20.2	2.1	80.5	48.0	51.3	48.7
54862	OJIBWA	84.4	82.1	0.5	0.7	0.3	0.2	1.5	1.7	5.1	5.1	5.4	6.4	5.6	21.1	31.4	17.4	2.5	80.1	45.7	50.7	49.3
54864	POPLAR	97.0	96.5	0.1	0.2	0.3	0.5	0.4	0.7	6.5	7.1	7.1	6.8	5.1	22.8	31.0	11.9	1.9	75.1	41.6	50.6	49.4
54865	PORT WING	96.8	95.9	0.2	0.2	0.2	0.2	1.2	1.7	4.0	4.3	4.7	4.1	3.8	19.1	38.6	19.1	2.2	84.7	50.6	50.7	49.3
54867	RADISSON	72.5	68.7	0.0	0.0	0.0	0.0	1.3	1.6	5.4	5.4	6.3	6.9	4.9	22.4	29.8	16.8	2.2	79.2	44.1	50.8	49.2
54868	RICE LAKE	97.7	97.1	0.1	0.2	0.6	0.8	1.2	1.6	6.0	6.0	6.2	6.8	6.2	25.0	27.5	13.3	2.9	77.7	40.4	48.7	51.3
54870	SARONA	98.5	98.2	0.1	0.1	0.2	0.3	0.7	0.9	4.0	4.6	5.2	5.6	4.0	17.5	38.1	18.8	2.0	82.2	49.9	50.6	49.4
54871	SHELL LAKE	95.7	95.2	0.2	0.2	0.2	0.3	0.7	0.9	5.2	5.8	6.1	6.2	4.6	21.4	31.4	16.0	3.3	79.0	45.5	48.9	51.1
54872	SIREN	95.7	95.0	0.3	0.4	0.4	0.4	0.6	0.9	5.0	5.2	5.4	5.6	4.4	20.8	30.9	18.7	4.0	80.4	47.2	50.3	49.7
54873	SOLON SPRINGS	96.8	96.1	0.6	0.7	0.5	0.8	0.5	0.7	5.3	5.6	6.0	5.9	4.3	20.6	32.4	17.7	2.1	79.2	46.3	51.2	48.8
54874	SOUTH RANGE	97.1	96.5	0.3	0.3	0.3	0.4	0.9	1.3	5.8	6.5	7.2	7.5	4.6	24.4	31.7	11.0	1.4	75.9	41.0	50.7	49.3
54875	SPRINGBROOK	96.2	95.8	0.2	0.2	0.3	0.4	1.3	1.8	5.1	5.5	6.3	7.5	3.5	22.8	31.4	16.8	1.0	77.8	44.5	52.3	47.7
54876	STONE LAKE	75.4	72.1	0.0	0.0	0.3	0.4	0.8	1.0	4.8	5.6	6.1	6.3	3.9	19.2	34.2	17.8	1.9	79.8	47.4	51.3	48.7
54880	SUPERIOR	94.7	93.6	0.6	0.8	0.8	1.2	0.8	1.1	6.0	5.6	5.6	6.9	8.0	26.2	27.2	11.6	2.8	79.2	38.0	48.5	51.5
	WISCONSIN	88.9	86.9	5.7	6.3	1.7	2.3	3.6	4.8	6.4	6.4	6.5	7.2	7.2	26.0	27.1	11.1	2.2	76.6	38.0	49.5	50.5
	UNITED STATES	75.1	72.0	12.3	12.7	3.8	4.6	12.5	15.7	6.8	6.7	6.6	7.1	6.9	27.0	26.0	10.9	1.9	75.7	36.9	49.2	50.8

ZIP CODE #	POST OFFICE NAME	2009 Per Capita Income	2009 HH Income Base	2009 HOUSEHOLD INCOME DISTRIBUTION (%) Less than $25,000	$25,000 to $49,999	$50,000 to $99,999	$100,000 to $149,999	$150,000 or More	MEDIAN HOUSEHOLD INCOME 2009	2014	2009 National Centile	2009 State Centile	2009 Home Value Base	2009 HOME VALUE DISTRIBUTION (%) Less than $50,000	$50,000 to $89,999	$90,000 to $174,999	$175,000 to $399,999	$400,000 or More	2009 Median Home Value
54724	BLOOMER	23629	2821	21.9	25.4	43.4	5.8	3.5	51896	53760	66	55	2194	7.0	15.8	55.2	19.7	2.4	126282
54725	BOYCEVILLE	18514	1237	29.1	31.1	33.9	4.3	1.6	41329	43405	37	18	958	21.5	21.3	38.9	16.1	2.2	98961
54726	BOYD	18631	773	25.9	30.4	38.6	3.5	1.7	44479	47496	47	30	653	12.1	25.7	44.4	15.3	2.5	107625
54727	CADOTT	19677	1920	24.0	30.8	39.7	4.0	1.5	45771	48588	51	36	1527	12.4	19.2	48.7	18.2	1.4	116550
54728	CHETEK	21363	2869	28.0	30.4	34.4	5.2	2.0	42723	44144	42	23	2265	7.8	21.3	48.2	20.2	2.5	119490
54729	CHIPPEWA FALLS	23313	12564	20.2	28.4	42.0	6.8	2.5	51063	53439	64	52	8963	4.5	10.9	55.3	26.6	2.6	137825
54730	COLFAX	22137	2019	19.3	28.9	42.9	7.0	1.9	51211	52650	64	53	1648	8.5	18.0	43.2	28.4	1.9	133730
54731	CONRATH	17369	255	29.0	31.4	35.3	2.7	1.6	41583	44215	38	18	224	14.3	29.5	47.3	8.0	0.9	96087
54732	CORNELL	18357	1215	30.7	32.8	32.1	3.0	1.4	39025	40472	30	10	948	16.8	31.4	40.1	11.0	0.7	92464
54733	DALLAS	19964	639	23.0	32.4	36.2	5.9	2.5	44489	46416	47	30	541	13.1	27.4	40.3	16.8	2.4	103201
54734	DOWNING	21376	294	23.5	28.2	40.8	5.1	2.4	48217	51040	57	43	246	12.2	20.7	43.5	20.7	2.8	120395
54736	DURAND	20435	1603	25.9	29.8	35.4	6.7	2.2	43441	44535	44	26	1210	8.0	22.1	53.5	14.8	1.7	114049
54737	EAU GALLE	21042	152	19.7	32.9	42.8	3.3	1.3	48186	49565	57	43	123	8.1	19.5	40.7	29.3	2.4	133654
54738	ELEVA	25025	1266	17.7	26.4	40.7	10.8	4.4	55246	56761	72	63	1059	7.0	13.8	41.4	34.9	2.9	148145
54739	ELK MOUND	21045	1608	14.7	29.4	47.3	6.8	1.7	54045	55407	70	61	1323	8.1	10.3	47.9	31.5	2.2	141647
54740	ELMWOOD	20652	912	23.7	33.2	37.0	4.8	1.3	45069	46640	48	33	710	8.0	23.7	44.1	19.6	4.6	113445
54741	FAIRCHILD	16053	632	32.3	32.9	30.2	3.2	1.4	35154	37364	18	3	526	19.8	24.7	39.0	14.1	2.5	100000
54742	FALL CREEK	23476	1753	17.3	28.5	42.4	7.9	3.9	53261	55292	68	60	1426	6.9	12.7	46.8	30.7	2.9	141477
54745	HOLCOMBE	19676	934	30.5	28.4	34.9	4.9	1.3	40711	42848	35	15	799	10.8	27.4	37.5	21.4	2.9	109926
54746	HUMBIRD	19913	309	25.9	33.0	35.6	4.2	1.3	41595	43811	38	18	265	12.5	24.5	45.3	16.2	1.5	107267
54747	INDEPENDENCE	22504	1087	25.4	28.9	38.6	4.9	2.2	45232	47850	49	34	791	8.7	31.2	44.1	13.4	2.5	100302
54748	JIM FALLS	22725	515	19.2	26.6	45.8	5.8	2.5	54026	56121	70	60	442	8.6	12.2	51.6	24.4	3.2	130903
54749	KNAPP	21863	582	24.1	26.1	41.8	6.0	2.1	49772	51824	60	47	484	10.1	21.1	43.2	21.9	3.7	126563
54750	MAIDEN ROCK	23179	458	20.7	24.0	44.3	7.4	3.5	55264	57940	72	63	387	5.9	14.0	39.8	32.6	7.8	151563
54751	MENOMONIE	22038	9123	24.4	28.6	37.0	7.2	2.8	46648	50022	53	39	5413	12.1	11.0	47.2	28.1	1.6	137672
54754	MERRILLAN	21357	746	28.8	30.4	35.3	4.3	1.2	41002	42990	36	16	613	16.6	27.6	40.0	14.4	1.5	95917
54755	MONDOVI	20428	2722	24.3	30.5	38.0	5.4	1.8	44864	46810	48	32	2062	7.9	22.6	46.4	19.8	3.2	119764
54756	NELSON	22653	414	24.4	29.7	38.6	5.6	1.7	45000	46211	48	33	321	15.6	22.7	41.1	16.5	4.0	106389
54757	NEW AUBURN	18474	1270	27.2	34.3	33.9	3.6	1.0	41258	42890	37	17	1075	18.8	20.3	38.2	19.5	3.2	110963
54758	OSSEO	21612	1979	21.6	30.1	40.7	5.6	2.0	48465	50361	58	44	1486	8.6	22.1	47.4	19.7	2.3	115392
54759	PEPIN	21596	704	23.6	33.2	38.1	3.8	1.3	45177	46014	49	33	555	7.7	21.6	51.4	17.1	2.2	112402
54761	PLUM CITY	21589	460	24.8	31.7	33.5	6.7	3.3	44733	46333	47	31	359	10.6	22.6	45.4	16.4	5.0	111229
54762	PRAIRIE FARM	21190	516	22.1	29.5	41.5	3.7	3.3	48782	50265	58	45	419	15.8	27.0	41.5	14.1	1.7	99839
54763	RIDGELAND	20936	432	25.7	29.6	38.4	4.9	1.4	45360	47264	49	34	343	16.3	26.2	36.4	18.1	2.9	101389
54765	SAND CREEK	20828	48	27.1	29.2	37.5	6.3	0.0	45000	50000	48	33	39	10.3	23.1	46.2	20.5	0.0	114583
54766	SHELDON	16621	592	29.9	30.6	35.0	3.2	1.4	41482	42506	38	18	496	18.1	27.2	37.9	14.7	2.0	94894
54767	SPRING VALLEY	23632	1297	16.6	27.3	46.9	7.1	2.2	55276	58600	72	63	1050	8.8	16.5	37.6	30.7	6.5	137972
54768	STANLEY	19524	1617	30.2	30.3	34.6	2.8	2.0	39913	41496	32	12	1249	15.2	32.0	40.0	11.5	1.2	93594
54769	STOCKHOLM	26430	169	21.9	26.0	44.4	4.7	3.0	51544	51580	65	54	138	8.0	12.3	37.0	32.6	10.1	154167
54770	STRUM	22399	873	21.3	30.5	40.8	5.4	2.1	48331	50574	57	44	676	7.5	17.0	52.1	20.7	2.7	122203
54771	THORP	17337	1562	31.4	33.8	29.1	3.8	1.9	37912	38735	26	7	1237	14.7	29.8	42.7	11.6	1.1	95672
54772	WHEELER	20333	438	23.7	30.8	37.9	5.7	1.8	46426	48636	53	38	352	10.2	20.2	41.8	25.0	2.8	126111
54773	WHITEHALL	20056	1340	27.0	30.4	37.2	3.8	1.6	42714	44964	42	23	952	11.3	28.0	46.1	12.9	1.6	99352
54801	SPOONER	20265	2766	29.8	32.4	31.1	5.0	1.7	39013	40534	30	10	2113	11.5	23.7	43.7	18.6	2.6	110871
54805	ALMENA	20366	680	23.7	31.2	37.6	5.9	1.6	45597	47242	50	35	567	13.4	23.6	38.8	21.3	2.8	109844
54806	ASHLAND	20648	4869	28.7	30.1	35.0	4.7	1.6	42000	44242	39	21	3280	13.0	31.6	42.7	11.8	0.9	95477
54810	BALSAM LAKE	25705	1138	21.4	28.4	40.1	7.6	2.6	50177	52025	62	49	981	10.8	16.4	36.3	30.2	6.3	140771
54812	BARRON	21366	2074	25.4	28.8	39.2	5.2	1.3	45465	47619	50	35	1428	11.3	24.9	50.4	12.5	0.9	103333
54813	BARRONETT	23580	268	20.1	29.5	41.4	5.6	3.4	50242	51332	62	50	233	11.6	17.2	41.2	24.9	5.2	132500
54814	BAYFIELD	18716	947	32.0	30.7	29.6	5.8	1.9	40226	41265	33	13	652	22.5	17.8	38.5	17.3	3.8	106061
54817	BIRCHWOOD	22060	1132	29.1	28.6	34.2	5.7	2.5	42198	44314	40	21	960	11.6	19.6	41.5	23.0	4.4	122368
54819	BRUCE	19804	1099	30.6	33.6	30.8	4.2	0.8	37390	39427	25	6	890	18.7	30.8	40.0	9.3	1.2	90676
54820	BRULE	18143	380	27.4	34.5	34.5	3.4	0.3	40824	42961	35	16	321	13.4	24.6	41.1	19.3	1.6	108750
54821	CABLE	20811	690	37.0	31.0	27.0	3.9	1.2	35592	36452	20	3	582	8.8	13.7	41.9	25.4	10.1	137109
54822	CAMERON	22822	1798	22.0	26.8	43.0	5.5	2.7	50810	52024	63	51	1383	8.4	21.3	51.1	17.2	2.0	119059
54824	CENTURIA	21939	934	22.5	28.3	39.3	7.3	2.7	49205	51502	59	46	761	10.0	14.6	41.1	28.6	5.7	140809
54826	COMSTOCK	21360	399	27.3	30.8	34.6	5.8	1.5	42973	44501	42	24	311	8.7	22.2	43.1	22.8	3.2	122866
54827	CORNUCOPIA	23964	121	27.3	29.8	37.2	5.8	0.0	43829	46319	45	27	110	10.9	18.2	48.2	20.9	1.8	118056
54828	COUDERAY	18939	308	33.8	30.8	30.2	3.6	1.6	37874	39439	26	7	229	18.3	29.7	29.7	18.3	3.9	95000
54829	CUMBERLAND	21968	2364	27.1	28.6	36.8	5.5	1.9	44414	46132	47	30	1841	10.7	21.8	43.3	20.6	3.5	117537
54830	DANBURY	25789	1395	22.2	34.0	35.3	6.6	1.9	45798	47991	51	36	1249	7.5	19.8	42.1	25.9	4.6	128653
54832	DRUMMOND	19733	223	35.0	30.9	28.3	4.0	1.8	37299	37542	24	5	183	10.4	23.0	42.6	20.8	3.3	112109
54835	EXELAND	18456	486	35.6	31.1	28.4	3.3	1.6	35364	36573	19	3	406	16.0	32.0	36.2	13.5	2.2	93478
54836	FOXBORO	21857	425	18.6	30.4	44.9	4.9	1.2	50735	53017	63	51	387	11.4	20.2	48.1	19.4	1.0	122588
54837	FREDERIC	20085	1829	31.2	31.3	31.9	4.2	1.5	39650	41364	32	11	1482	13.3	24.8	42.9	17.7	1.3	107732
54838	GORDON	24462	490	22.4	28.4	42.0	5.5	1.6	49129	51737	59	46	441	10.0	15.2	40.6	27.0	7.3	143371
54839	GRAND VIEW	20108	145	34.5	31.7	29.7	2.8	1.4	37119	38790	24	5	121	12.4	26.4	39.7	20.7	0.8	103472
54840	GRANTSBURG	22663	1981	20.2	32.9	38.2	5.9	2.7	47412	50434	55	41	1601	11.1	23.5	49.3	14.8	1.3	108724
54843	HAYWARD	22024	4958	29.7	29.9	32.0	5.8	2.6	41117	43373	36	16	3723	7.2	17.5	41.5	27.5	6.3	131546
54844	HERBSTER	22820	150	28.0	34.7	31.3	5.3	0.7	38928	38992	30	9	130	5.4	27.7	43.1	21.5	2.3	123438
54845	HERTEL	20123	61	27.9	37.7	27.9	3.3	3.3	37273	39053	24	5	51	11.8	19.6	45.1	21.6	2.0	120313
54846	HIGH BRIDGE	19070	212	27.8	35.4	31.6	3.3	1.9	39105	41151	30	10	176	14.2	33.5	42.0	9.7	0.6	91379
54847	IRON RIVER	20397	982	30.8	31.9	31.2	4.9	1.1	38741	39718	29	9	845	9.1	23.6	45.1	20.1	2.1	114628
54848	LADYSMITH	20385	2718	30.9	29.8	33.3	4.3	1.8	40467	42528	34	14	1918	12.8	33.2	43.6	9.7	0.6	93393
54849	LAKE NEBAGAMON	25028	847	19.0	28.0	42.0	8.9	2.1	52791	55390	68	58	725	9.8	15.4	43.4	27.0	4.3	139923
54850	LA POINTE	23916	132	34.1	33.3	26.5	3.8	2.3	36009	36493	21	3	89	22.5	27.0	36.0	12.4	2.2	90625
54853	LUCK	22059	1606	22.4	31.0	39.4	5.4	1.9	46494	49765	53	38	1298	9.6	19.6	43.1	24.7	2.9	124590
54854	MAPLE	20046	423	24.6	35.5	35.7	3.3	0.9	42794	45620	42	23	360	13.1	23.6	43.3	18.1	1.9	111574
54855	MARENGO	17578	239	24.7	35.1	35.1	3.3	1.7	41604	44769	38	19	195	14.9	29.7	42.1	12.8	0.5	94200
54856	MASON	18533	604	31.1	30.8	32.6	4.0	1.5	40240	41213	33	13	525	10.1	20.6	44.8	22.9	1.7	116523
54858	MILLTOWN	23590	870	30.9	25.3	36.8	5.3	1.7	42972	45467	42	24	650	17.1	19.7	43.5	16.6	3.1	111413
54859	MINONG	21382	891	31.0	33.1	30.8	3.1	2.0	40519	41765	34	14	733	15.0	27.1	35.7	16.6	5.5	103397
54862	OJIBWA	17946	166	34.9	30.7	29.5	3.0	1.8	36386	37109	22	4	133	16.5	33.1	34.6	14.3	1.5	90833
54864	POPLAR	21626	499	19.0	29.9	41.9	6.8	2.4	50919	53390	63	51	439	8.9	19.8	49.4	20.0	1.8	123654
54865	PORT WING	22701	282	27.7	34.4	32.3	5.0	0.7	39044	39457	30	10	245	6.5	28.2	41.2	22.4	1.6	119758
54867	RADISSON	20441	199	33.7	32.7	29.1	2.5	2.0	37473	39200	25	6	153	19.6	33.3	31.4	13.7	2.0	85000
54868	RICE LAKE	23572	6834	25.0	27.3	37.5	6.6	3.6	47645	49492	56	42	4895	9.9	22.5	48.2	17.0	2.4	111357
54870	SARONA	23575	676	25.6	32.0	33.4	6.2	2.8	43375	45645	43	26	591	7.8	17.1	39.8	30.3	5.1	137660
54871	SHELL LAKE	20652	1464	27.7	32.4	32.9	5.0	2.0	40805	42701	35	16	1135	11.5	24.8	40.2	20.8	2.6	109811
54872	SIREN	21364	1272	30.7	34.0	28.6	4.8	2.0	38796	40250	29	9	1010	14.5	22.5	43.7	16.8	2.6	108226
54873	SOLON SPRINGS	21699	1171	28.9	30.3	34.0	5.6	1.3	41244	43442	37	17	985	11.3	19.8	46.1	20.2	2.6	122719
54874	SOUTH RANGE	21431	1400	17.4	29.9	44.4	6.4	2.0	52082	54109	66	55	1290	10.7	19.5	50.9	17.6	1.4	118202
54875	SPRINGBROOK	20367	692	23.3	37.6	34.0	3.6	1.6	42638	44535	41	23	604	11.3	23.3	41.7	18.9	4.8	117059
54876	STONE LAKE	20333	677	30.4	31.2	30.6	6.4	1.5	39082	40913	30	10	550	11.1	20.9	32.2	26.7	9.1	128500
54880	SUPERIOR	23180	13351	27.7	29.3	33.8	6.9	2.3	43811	46332	45	27	8483	13.4	27.4	44.4	13.7	1.0	101739
	WISCONSIN	27384		18.4	25.3	40.0	11.0	5.2	56363	58927				5.6	11.9	43.5	34.2	4.7	150766
	UNITED STATES	27277		20.9	24.4	35.3	11.7	7.6	54719	56938				9.3	13.1	31.6	32.6	13.5	162279

ZIP CODE		FINANCIAL SERVICES				THE HOME						ENTERTAINMENT						PERSONAL			
						Home Improvements		Furnishings													
#	POST OFFICE NAME	Auto Loan	Home Loan	Investments	Retirement Plans	Home Repair	Lawn & Garden	Computers & Hardware Personal	Major Appliances	TV, Radio, Sound Equipment	Furniture	Dine out/ Carry out	Sports Equipment	Fees & Tickets	Toys & Games	Travel	Cable TV	Apparel & Services	Auto Repairs	Health Insurance	Pets & Supplies
54724	BLOOMER	90	80	82	81	79	94	82	88	85	76	84	69	75	85	80	89	57	86	94	106
54725	BOYCEVILLE	83	63	76	63	64	83	65	77	70	60	69	60	54	71	63	75	46	72	80	92
54726	BOYD	88	62	95	62	65	93	68	84	71	56	70	69	51	70	68	77	46	78	88	103
54727	CADOTT	83	67	82	68	69	88	69	82	73	61	71	64	59	73	69	78	48	76	86	97
54728	CHETEK	85	66	94	65	69	89	68	84	72	61	71	63	57	71	69	78	47	78	87	98
54729	CHIPPEWA FALLS	83	81	75	83	79	85	81	82	82	79	82	63	80	83	80	84	56	82	85	98
54730	COLFAX	88	79	87	79	79	93	77	87	80	73	79	67	71	81	78	84	54	83	90	104
54731	CONRATH	82	58	86	57	60	85	61	77	66	54	65	60	47	66	61	73	43	71	81	93
54732	CORNELL	78	56	76	56	58	80	61	74	66	54	65	57	48	66	58	73	43	69	79	88
54733	DALLAS	91	67	96	68	70	96	72	88	75	60	74	71	56	74	72	81	49	82	92	106
54734	DOWNING	86	76	80	79	77	92	76	86	78	68	77	66	68	79	76	83	52	80	89	101
54736	DURAND	85	68	83	68	69	90	72	83	77	64	75	64	62	76	70	83	50	79	90	99
54737	EAU GALLE	93	65	100	65	68	97	71	88	74	59	73	72	53	73	71	81	48	82	92	108
54738	ELEVA	102	93	101	94	94	107	89	101	91	85	91	78	84	93	90	96	62	94	101	118
54739	ELK MOUND	87	89	78	90	87	90	82	86	82	83	83	65	83	85	83	84	57	83	86	102
54740	ELMWOOD	91	64	96	63	67	96	71	88	76	60	74	69	54	74	69	83	49	82	94	106
54741	FAIRCHILD	75	58	75	57	59	78	59	72	63	53	62	55	49	63	59	69	41	66	75	85
54742	FALL CREEK	97	87	100	88	88	104	87	98	88	78	88	77	79	89	88	93	60	93	101	116
54745	HOLCOMBE	81	61	95	60	65	85	64	80	67	57	66	61	52	65	66	73	44	74	82	95
54746	HUMBIRD	86	63	88	62	65	88	65	81	71	60	70	61	52	71	64	78	46	75	85	97
54747	INDEPENDENCE	84	68	83	69	68	89	72	81	74	62	73	65	61	74	71	78	49	78	87	99
54748	JIM FALLS	97	78	97	80	80	103	81	95	84	70	82	76	68	84	81	90	55	89	99	114
54749	KNAPP	88	78	84	81	80	95	78	89	80	70	79	68	70	81	78	85	53	82	91	104
54750	MAIDEN ROCK	106	81	113	82	84	113	86	102	88	73	87	84	69	87	86	94	58	96	107	125
54751	MENOMONIE	85	70	69	72	69	75	85	77	83	78	83	62	74	84	74	83	57	81	80	94
54754	MERRILLAN	85	64	85	63	66	87	65	80	71	60	70	61	53	71	64	78	46	74	84	95
54755	MONDOVI	86	67	87	67	69	90	72	84	75	63	74	65	60	75	71	81	49	79	89	100
54756	NELSON	93	65	98	64	68	96	70	88	75	61	74	69	53	74	69	82	48	81	92	106
54757	NEW AUBURN	79	61	77	60	62	81	62	75	67	57	66	57	52	68	61	73	44	69	78	89
54758	OSSEO	90	69	91	69	71	93	74	87	78	66	77	67	61	77	73	84	51	82	92	104
54759	PEPIN	83	60	88	59	63	87	65	81	71	58	69	61	52	70	64	78	46	75	87	96
54761	PLUM CITY	98	67	108	67	71	103	75	93	78	61	77	77	55	76	74	85	50	87	98	114
54762	PRAIRIE FARM	91	75	89	77	77	97	77	90	80	67	79	71	66	80	77	85	53	84	94	107
54763	RIDGELAND	89	62	97	63	65	94	69	85	72	56	71	70	51	70	68	78	46	79	90	104
54765	SAND CREEK	88	60	96	60	63	93	67	83	70	54	69	69	49	68	67	76	45	78	88	102
54766	SHELDON	83	57	91	57	60	88	63	79	66	51	65	65	46	65	63	72	42	73	83	97
54767	SPRING VALLEY	89	89	84	91	86	96	86	90	86	82	86	71	85	87	87	88	59	88	93	108
54768	STANLEY	85	61	89	60	63	89	66	82	72	57	70	64	52	70	65	78	46	76	88	98
54769	STOCKHOLM	95	74	118	73	80	101	76	96	79	69	78	71	63	76	80	85	52	88	96	112
54770	STRUM	89	74	86	75	76	94	75	88	78	66	77	68	65	79	75	84	52	81	91	104
54771	THORP	79	56	83	55	58	83	61	76	66	52	65	60	47	65	60	73	43	71	82	91
54772	WHEELER	91	72	89	70	73	92	74	85	77	67	76	67	61	77	72	81	50	81	88	104
54773	WHITEHALL	87	62	91	60	64	90	66	82	72	58	70	64	51	71	65	79	46	76	87	99
54801	SPOONER	79	61	87	59	64	83	63	78	69	58	67	58	53	66	64	74	45	73	82	91
54805	ALMENA	88	70	89	71	72	94	73	86	75	62	74	68	60	75	73	81	49	80	90	103
54806	ASHLAND	74	64	65	65	64	73	70	71	73	66	72	54	64	72	66	76	49	72	78	85
54810	BALSAM LAKE	96	78	119	78	85	102	78	98	81	73	80	72	68	78	84	87	54	90	97	113
54812	BARRON	81	66	74	67	67	81	73	78	76	66	75	60	64	76	69	80	51	77	84	93
54813	BARRONETT	96	78	105	79	82	102	80	96	83	71	82	74	68	82	82	89	55	89	98	113
54814	BAYFIELD	75	65	76	63	66	72	65	72	66	65	66	54	59	66	65	68	45	69	71	84
54817	BIRCHWOOD	85	66	100	65	71	89	68	85	72	62	71	62	57	70	71	78	47	78	86	99
54819	BRUCE	77	57	84	56	60	80	60	75	66	55	64	56	49	64	60	72	43	70	79	88
54820	BRULE	77	60	80	60	63	80	61	74	65	56	64	56	51	65	61	70	43	68	77	88
54821	CABLE	72	58	93	57	63	76	58	74	61	54	60	54	50	58	63	65	40	68	73	85
54822	CAMERON	82	81	71	83	78	87	79	81	81	76	80	63	78	83	78	83	55	80	87	97
54824	CENTURIA	90	79	93	81	83	97	78	92	81	72	80	69	71	81	80	86	54	85	93	107
54826	COMSTOCK	83	64	92	63	68	88	67	82	72	60	70	62	56	70	68	77	47	76	86	97
54827	CORNUCOPIA	78	63	101	62	69	83	63	80	66	59	65	58	54	62	68	70	43	74	79	92
54828	COUDERAY	81	59	88	58	63	83	61	77	66	57	65	57	50	65	62	72	43	71	79	91
54829	CUMBERLAND	86	65	91	64	68	91	69	85	75	62	73	64	57	74	69	82	49	79	90	100
54830	DANBURY	80	75	99	70	83	91	72	86	76	76	74	57	70	70	78	80	50	82	94	98
54832	DRUMMOND	75	58	89	56	62	78	58	74	62	54	62	55	49	61	61	68	41	68	75	87
54835	EXELAND	77	56	80	54	58	79	57	73	63	53	62	54	46	62	57	69	41	67	75	86
54836	FOXBORO	84	79	77	82	80	91	77	86	79	70	77	65	72	80	77	83	53	80	88	100
54837	FREDERIC	79	61	79	61	63	82	63	77	68	58	67	58	53	68	62	74	45	71	81	90
54838	GORDON	88	72	109	71	78	93	71	89	75	67	74	65	63	72	76	79	49	82	89	103
54839	GRAND VIEW	78	55	82	54	57	80	58	73	63	51	62	57	45	62	57	69	40	67	76	88
54840	GRANTSBURG	85	75	83	76	77	89	76	85	78	71	77	63	69	78	76	83	53	81	88	99
54843	HAYWARD	84	70	92	69	74	86	72	83	75	68	74	61	64	73	73	79	50	79	85	97
54844	HERBSTER	78	62	101	61	68	82	62	79	65	58	65	58	54	62	68	70	43	73	78	92
54845	HERTEL	85	63	102	63	68	90	67	84	69	58	69	65	53	67	69	75	45	78	85	100
54846	HIGH BRIDGE	86	61	88	59	64	87	63	80	70	59	69	60	50	70	62	77	45	74	84	95
54847	IRON RIVER	75	61	92	61	67	79	61	76	64	57	63	56	54	62	65	68	42	70	76	88
54848	LADYSMITH	75	62	71	62	62	78	67	73	71	60	69	56	59	70	64	76	47	72	80	87
54849	LAKE NEBAGAMON	91	87	100	88	89	98	82	94	83	79	83	71	79	83	87	86	57	88	93	109
54850	LA POINTE	82	58	84	57	61	83	60	76	67	56	65	57	48	66	59	73	43	70	79	91
54853	LUCK	83	72	84	73	75	87	73	83	76	69	75	62	67	75	74	80	51	79	86	97
54854	MAPLE	80	63	78	64	65	83	64	77	68	59	67	58	55	69	63	74	45	71	80	91
54855	MARENGO	84	66	81	64	67	84	66	79	71	64	70	58	56	72	64	77	47	73	81	93
54856	MASON	79	61	81	61	63	83	63	76	67	55	66	60	52	66	63	72	44	71	80	91
54858	MILLTOWN	85	64	92	63	67	90	68	84	74	61	72	62	56	72	68	81	48	78	89	98
54859	MINONG	78	60	93	59	65	82	62	78	66	57	65	57	52	64	65	72	43	72	80	91
54862	OJIBWA	78	56	80	54	58	79	57	73	64	53	62	55	46	63	57	70	41	67	76	87
54864	POPLAR	89	83	81	85	83	94	80	89	82	75	81	67	75	84	80	86	55	83	91	104
54865	PORT WING	78	62	100	62	68	82	62	79	65	58	65	58	54	62	68	70	43	73	78	92
54867	RADISSON	81	58	83	56	60	83	60	76	66	56	65	57	48	66	59	73	43	70	79	90
54868	RICE LAKE	85	74	76	76	75	85	80	83	82	75	80	63	72	82	76	85	55	82	88	98
54870	SARONA	92	74	117	73	81	97	74	93	77	69	76	68	64	73	80	82	51	86	92	108
54871	SHELL LAKE	82	63	89	63	67	86	66	81	70	59	69	61	55	69	67	76	46	75	84	95
54872	SIREN	81	62	93	60	66	85	64	80	69	59	68	59	54	67	66	75	45	75	83	94
54873	SOLON SPRINGS	80	65	87	64	68	84	66	80	70	60	68	59	57	68	67	75	46	74	82	93
54874	SOUTH RANGE	90	83	81	84	83	94	80	89	83	76	82	67	75	85	80	87	56	84	92	104
54875	SPRINGBROOK	83	63	96	62	67	86	64	81	69	60	68	60	53	67	66	75	45	75	82	95
54876	STONE LAKE	77	62	100	61	68	82	62	79	65	58	64	58	54	62	67	69	43	73	78	91
54880	SUPERIOR	75	68	65	70	67	75	75	73	77	71	76	56	71	77	71	79	53	75	80	88
	WISCONSIN	98	94	92	96	93	99	96	96	96	93	96	75	94	97	95	98	67	96	99	114
	UNITED STATES	100	100	100	100	100	100	100	100	100	100	100	100	100	100	100	100	100	100	100	100

54888-54986

ZIP CODE #	POST OFFICE NAME	COUNTY FIPS CODE	POPULATION 2000	POPULATION 2009	POPULATION 2014	2000-2009 ANNUAL RATE % Rate	2000-2009 ANNUAL RATE State Centile	HOUSEHOLDS 2000	HOUSEHOLDS 2009	HOUSEHOLDS 2014	HOUSEHOLDS % Annual Rate 2000-2009	HOUSEHOLDS 2009 Average HH Size	FAMILIES 2000	FAMILIES 2009	FAMILIES % Annual Rate 2000-2009
54888	TREGO	129	1406	1553	1618	1.1	76	580	660	693	1.4	2.35	410	461	1.3
54889	TURTLE LAKE	095	2698	2899	2963	0.8	61	1113	1240	1282	1.2	2.33	743	818	1.0
54891	WASHBURN	007	3632	4087	4279	1.3	84	1452	1691	1787	1.7	2.36	991	1143	1.6
54893	WEBSTER	013	3660	3791	3796	0.4	39	1619	1733	1751	0.7	2.17	1091	1156	0.6
54895	WEYERHAEUSER	107	1090	1145	1167	0.5	44	459	504	520	1.0	2.27	325	353	0.9
54896	WINTER	113	1541	1815	1916	1.8	93	652	796	850	2.2	2.19	439	530	2.1
54901	OSHKOSH	139	37528	37987	38044	0.1	20	12977	13658	13841	0.6	2.25	6963	7123	0.2
54902	OSHKOSH	139	22613	22463	22419	-0.1	11	9842	10252	10342	0.4	2.15	5949	6074	0.2
54904	OSHKOSH	139	18114	20594	21643	1.4	86	6855	8238	8766	2.0	2.44	5203	6148	1.8
54909	ALMOND	097	2193	2167	2172	-0.1	11	838	871	884	0.4	2.48	614	628	0.2
54911	APPLETON	087	27639	27242	27085	-0.2	8	10905	11263	11357	0.3	2.24	6586	6595	0.0
54913	APPLETON	087	10046	17182	20026	6.0	100	3463	6101	7188	6.3	2.81	2829	4812	5.9
54914	APPLETON	087	31415	31555	31504	0.0	16	12730	13317	13466	0.5	2.34	7983	8107	0.2
54915	APPLETON	015	36953	40194	41756	0.9	68	13667	15398	16136	1.3	2.58	9680	10786	1.2
54921	BANCROFT	097	1196	1210	1223	0.1	20	447	477	488	0.7	2.54	323	338	0.5
54922	BEAR CREEK	087	1439	1523	1572	0.6	51	525	585	612	1.2	2.60	417	457	1.0
54923	BERLIN	047	8602	8476	8372	-0.2	8	3387	3429	3414	0.1	2.43	2358	2367	0.0
54928	CAROLINE	115	452	506	528	1.2	81	161	187	197	1.6	2.71	126	145	1.5
54929	CLINTONVILLE	135	9315	9307	9280	0.0	16	3736	3804	3817	0.2	2.39	2562	2580	0.1
54930	COLOMA	137	1696	1835	1891	0.9	68	612	695	723	1.4	2.50	457	513	1.3
54932	ELDORADO	039	903	1010	1067	1.2	81	327	379	405	1.6	2.66	269	309	1.5
54935	FOND DU LAC	039	42295	43288	43704	0.3	32	16670	17393	17682	0.5	2.37	10403	10692	0.3
54937	FOND DU LAC	039	15399	17036	17682	1.1	76	5796	6616	6948	1.4	2.49	4398	4959	1.3
54940	FREMONT	137	3701	3905	3998	0.6	51	1468	1617	1671	1.1	2.39	1090	1185	0.9
54941	GREEN LAKE	047	2824	2978	2984	0.6	51	1249	1370	1388	1.0	2.14	824	895	0.9
54942	GREENVILLE	087	4965	7417	8356	4.4	99	1645	2566	2931	4.9	2.89	1398	2148	4.8
54943	HANCOCK	137	1872	2020	2050	0.8	61	766	841	860	1.0	2.36	540	586	0.9
54944	HORTONVILLE	087	7783	9001	9563	1.6	91	2693	3269	3527	2.1	2.74	2143	2550	1.9
54945	IOLA	135	3315	3588	3712	0.9	68	1366	1525	1592	1.2	2.32	936	1028	1.0
54947	LARSEN	139	2469	2593	2686	0.5	44	933	1030	1078	1.1	2.52	732	797	0.9
54948	LEOPOLIS	115	370	390	395	0.6	51	146	159	163	0.9	2.44	109	117	0.8
54949	MANAWA	135	3196	3490	3625	1.0	72	1173	1323	1387	1.3	2.60	832	928	1.2
54950	MARION	135	2995	3242	3350	0.9	68	1185	1335	1394	1.3	2.43	830	924	1.2
54952	MENASHA	015	23351	24584	25144	0.6	51	9644	10629	10975	1.1	2.30	6225	6811	1.0
54956	NEENAH	139	37991	41357	42811	0.9	68	14829	16857	17594	1.4	2.43	10481	11824	1.3
54960	NESHKORO	077	2705	2904	2954	0.8	61	1170	1292	1325	1.1	2.23	846	926	1.0
54961	NEW LONDON	135	14016	14563	14847	0.4	39	5318	5724	5890	0.8	2.50	3800	4037	0.7
54962	OGDENSBURG	135	1214	1260	1286	0.4	39	487	524	539	0.8	2.40	363	386	0.7
54963	OMRO	139	6435	7041	7278	1.0	72	2453	2843	2976	1.6	2.44	1791	2034	1.4
54964	PICKETT	139	961	1029	1062	0.7	56	367	413	431	1.3	2.49	288	320	1.1
54965	PINE RIVER	137	1199	1255	1263	0.5	44	478	519	527	0.9	2.41	359	386	0.8
54966	PLAINFIELD	137	2081	2135	2106	0.3	32	781	813	807	0.4	2.59	558	573	0.3
54967	POY SIPPI	137	442	475	487	0.8	61	191	211	218	1.1	2.24	139	153	1.0
54968	PRINCETON	047	3181	3181	3141	0.0	16	1268	1304	1298	0.3	2.29	853	867	0.2
54970	REDGRANITE	137	2837	3187	3289	1.3	84	1174	1335	1390	1.4	2.32	808	909	1.3
54971	RIPON	039	10494	10530	10527	0.0	16	4067	4195	4235	0.3	2.30	2647	2685	0.2
54974	ROSENDALE	039	1561	1697	1776	0.9	68	556	625	661	1.3	2.72	440	490	1.2
54977	SCANDINAVIA	135	1316	1466	1533	1.2	81	495	569	600	1.5	2.56	365	415	1.4
54978	TILLEDA	115	49	51	51	0.4	39	18	19	20	0.6	2.68	13	14	0.8
54979	VAN DYNE	039	1466	1578	1624	0.8	61	536	600	625	1.2	2.63	415	456	1.0
54981	WAUPACA	135	15343	16246	16657	0.6	51	5817	6381	6607	1.0	2.37	3977	4320	0.9
54982	WAUTOMA	137	7060	7980	7969	1.3	84	2899	3094	3113	0.7	2.29	1959	2066	0.6
54983	WEYAUWEGA	135	4732	5046	5181	0.7	56	1736	1915	1986	1.1	2.56	1260	1372	0.9
54984	WILD ROSE	137	3037	3220	3182	0.6	51	1284	1330	1322	0.4	2.25	886	908	0.3
54986	WINNECONNE	139	4417	5097	5370	1.6	91	1745	2121	2260	2.1	2.40	1318	1571	1.9
	WISCONSIN					0.7					1.0	2.43			0.9
	UNITED STATES					1.0					1.1	2.59			0.9

ZIP CODE #	POST OFFICE NAME	RACE (%) White 2000	White 2009	Black 2000	Black 2009	Asian/Pacific 2000	Asian/Pacific 2009	% Hispanic Origin 2000	% Hispanic Origin 2009	2009 AGE DISTRIBUTION (%) 0-4	5-9	10-14	15-19	20-24	25-44	45-64	65-84	85+	18+	MEDIAN AGE 2009	% 2009 Males	% 2009 Females
54888	TREGO	97.2	96.8	0.2	0.3	0.3	0.3	0.4	0.6	4.2	4.9	6.5	7.3	3.1	19.3	37.4	15.6	1.7	79.3	47.4	51.3	48.7
54889	TURTLE LAKE	96.6	96.1	0.1	0.1	0.1	0.2	0.9	1.3	5.8	6.0	6.3	6.4	5.3	24.2	29.9	14.0	2.1	77.7	41.9	50.1	49.9
54891	WASHBURN	92.9	91.5	0.1	0.1	0.4	0.6	0.5	0.7	4.4	5.5	6.9	7.4	5.3	21.0	34.2	12.3	2.9	78.5	44.6	49.0	51.0
54893	WEBSTER	90.6	89.1	0.4	0.5	0.4	0.6	0.7	0.9	4.4	4.9	5.4	5.8	3.7	19.0	33.8	20.7	2.3	81.5	49.6	49.6	50.4
54895	WEYERHAEUSER	98.1	97.6	0.2	0.2	0.1	0.2	1.3	1.9	4.0	4.5	5.4	6.5	4.5	20.7	34.4	17.6	2.4	82.1	47.7	51.1	48.9
54896	WINTER	93.3	92.1	2.1	2.5	0.3	0.4	1.6	2.1	4.7	5.1	5.0	4.8	5.7	18.7	33.5	20.2	2.4	82.3	49.0	53.3	46.7
54901	OSHKOSH	90.9	87.9	3.2	4.1	3.6	5.1	1.8	2.6	5.0	4.7	4.6	10.9	17.2	26.7	20.6	8.4	1.9	82.6	29.8	52.0	48.0
54902	OSHKOSH	95.7	94.3	0.6	0.7	2.2	3.1	1.6	2.2	5.5	5.3	5.4	6.4	6.7	26.6	25.8	14.2	4.0	79.8	40.8	47.8	52.2
54904	OSHKOSH	96.8	95.8	0.8	1.0	1.2	1.9	0.8	1.2	6.8	7.0	7.0	6.9	5.4	27.3	28.7	9.6	1.3	74.7	37.9	49.9	50.1
54909	ALMOND	97.1	96.0	0.1	0.1	0.4	0.5	4.9	7.0	5.9	6.6	7.2	7.2	4.5	24.2	31.3	11.5	1.5	75.5	41.0	51.5	48.5
54911	APPLETON	91.5	88.1	1.1	1.4	4.6	7.1	2.0	2.9	6.0	5.6	5.8	8.0	8.9	26.1	25.0	11.7	2.9	78.5	37.0	49.1	50.9
54913	APPLETON	97.5	96.0	0.4	0.6	0.9	1.7	0.9	1.4	7.0	7.6	8.2	7.6	4.6	26.0	30.4	7.7	0.8	72.2	37.6	50.8	49.2
54914	APPLETON	92.1	89.1	1.0	1.2	3.5	5.2	3.8	5.5	6.5	6.1	5.9	6.6	8.0	30.4	25.3	9.5	1.7	77.5	35.4	49.7	50.3
54915	APPLETON	93.5	91.3	0.6	0.8	3.4	4.7	2.6	3.6	8.0	7.4	7.0	6.9	6.9	29.0	25.4	8.0	1.5	73.3	34.5	49.2	50.8
54921	BANCROFT	96.4	95.1	0.2	0.2	0.8	1.2	3.7	5.2	5.5	6.3	7.2	7.6	5.1	26.1	29.1	11.7	1.5	76.1	39.6	51.7	48.3
54922	BEAR CREEK	97.5	96.1	0.1	0.1	0.1	0.1	3.2	5.1	6.4	6.9	7.3	7.9	5.1	26.1	28.0	10.7	1.6	74.5	38.3	52.4	47.6
54923	BERLIN	96.6	96.2	0.1	0.1	0.7	0.8	3.3	3.7	5.9	6.2	6.4	6.5	5.1	25.2	29.2	12.4	3.1	77.2	41.3	49.7	50.3
54928	CAROLINE	96.9	96.0	0.0	0.0	1.6	2.2	0.4	0.6	5.7	6.1	6.5	7.3	4.2	25.1	29.4	13.8	1.8	77.1	41.4	52.2	47.8
54929	CLINTONVILLE	97.6	96.8	0.1	0.2	0.3	0.5	1.4	2.0	5.8	5.7	6.4	7.2	6.0	23.8	27.4	14.5	3.3	78.5	41.4	49.2	50.8
54930	COLOMA	97.5	92.3	0.3	5.1	0.2	0.3	2.5	3.5	4.1	5.1	6.3	6.0	3.2	18.2	34.1	19.3	3.7	83.0	49.5	50.7	49.3
54932	ELDORADO	99.0	98.9	0.1	0.1	0.2	0.3	0.8	1.0	4.9	5.4	6.0	5.9	4.6	27.1	33.5	11.4	1.2	79.9	42.6	51.4	48.6
54935	FOND DU LAC	94.3	92.5	1.4	1.8	1.5	2.1	2.8	3.9	6.6	6.1	6.1	6.7	6.9	27.3	25.8	11.4	3.1	77.3	37.5	47.8	52.2
54937	FOND DU LAC	96.6	95.7	1.4	1.7	0.6	0.8	1.6	2.4	5.6	6.2	6.6	7.0	5.4	27.0	29.6	11.1	1.6	77.3	40.1	48.9	51.1
54940	FREMONT	98.4	98.0	0.2	0.3	0.2	0.3	0.9	1.3	5.2	6.0	6.6	6.6	4.4	22.9	33.7	13.0	1.6	77.7	43.9	51.7	48.3
54941	GREEN LAKE	98.7	98.6	0.1	0.2	0.1	0.2	1.0	1.1	4.4	5.0	5.4	5.1	4.0	20.4	36.1	17.3	2.4	82.0	48.6	50.7	49.3
54942	GREENVILLE	98.7	98.2	0.2	0.2	0.3	0.6	0.8	1.1	9.9	8.7	7.6	6.2	4.5	33.9	23.4	5.5	0.4	69.3	32.9	51.2	48.8
54943	HANCOCK	95.9	93.3	0.2	1.7	0.3	0.4	4.6	6.4	4.2	4.7	5.5	6.5	4.4	19.0	33.6	19.6	2.6	82.2	48.8	50.2	49.8
54944	HORTONVILLE	97.8	96.8	0.1	0.2	1.2	1.8	1.0	1.5	7.0	7.4	7.9	7.5	4.8	25.9	30.2	8.5	0.9	72.9	38.6	50.5	49.5
54945	IOLA	98.4	98.0	0.1	0.1	0.2	0.3	1.1	1.6	5.5	5.7	6.2	7.0	5.3	21.5	30.1	15.2	3.5	77.8	44.2	48.9	51.1
54947	LARSEN	98.7	98.3	0.2	0.2	0.1	0.1	0.9	1.2	5.9	6.7	7.3	6.5	4.2	23.0	33.7	11.2	1.5	75.9	42.9	52.0	48.0
54948	LEOPOLIS	65.4	62.6	0.0	0.0	0.5	0.8	1.1	1.3	6.7	6.7	6.9	7.2	5.6	24.9	27.7	12.6	1.8	74.9	39.6	49.2	50.8
54949	MANAWA	98.7	98.4	0.1	0.1	0.2	0.3	1.1	1.6	6.4	7.0	7.5	7.5	5.4	26.0	26.3	11.5	2.4	74.1	38.4	50.5	49.5
54950	MARION	98.7	98.3	0.1	0.1	0.6	0.9	0.4	0.6	5.7	5.8	6.2	6.8	5.0	24.5	29.3	14.4	2.3	78.1	42.2	49.9	50.1
54952	MENASHA	95.2	93.8	0.5	0.6	1.5	2.1	3.3	4.5	7.0	6.6	6.4	6.5	6.7	29.0	26.1	9.9	1.7	76.1	36.6	49.4	50.6
54956	NEENAH	96.6	95.5	0.3	0.4	1.0	1.6	1.6	2.3	6.5	6.8	6.9	6.9	5.8	26.4	29.2	9.8	1.6	75.3	38.7	49.0	51.0
54960	NESHKORO	98.2	97.6	0.1	0.2	0.6	0.9	0.8	1.2	4.2	4.6	5.0	4.7	3.7	18.0	32.9	24.6	2.4	83.2	51.1	51.1	48.9
54961	NEW LONDON	97.5	96.6	0.2	0.3	0.4	0.5	1.9	2.8	6.6	7.0	7.1	7.0	5.6	26.0	28.1	10.3	2.2	75.1	38.4	50.8	49.2
54962	OGDENSBURG	99.0	98.7	0.1	0.1	0.2	0.2	0.8	1.3	6.1	6.7	7.1	6.0	4.3	22.5	31.3	14.2	1.7	76.3	43.0	51.3	48.7
54963	OMRO	98.2	97.7	0.2	0.2	0.2	0.3	1.7	2.6	6.2	6.6	6.8	6.7	5.3	24.6	29.5	12.0	2.3	76.0	40.7	50.4	49.6
54964	PICKETT	99.2	98.9	0.0	0.0	0.1	0.2	0.3	0.5	5.1	5.8	6.3	6.7	4.9	22.0	35.0	12.9	1.4	78.5	44.5	51.2	48.8
54965	PINE RIVER	98.8	98.5	0.0	0.0	0.1	0.1	0.9	1.4	4.7	5.4	5.7	5.3	3.7	19.9	36.8	16.7	1.7	80.9	48.1	51.6	48.4
54966	PLAINFIELD	94.4	92.5	0.1	0.1	0.7	1.0	11.6	16.0	5.8	6.3	7.0	7.3	5.8	24.6	29.1	12.2	2.0	75.9	39.6	51.8	48.2
54967	POY SIPPI	98.0	97.5	0.2	0.2	0.0	0.0	1.4	1.9	4.8	5.3	6.3	6.5	3.4	22.1	34.1	15.2	2.3	79.2	45.9	51.2	48.8
54968	PRINCETON	98.5	98.4	0.4	0.5	0.1	0.1	0.8	0.8	4.8	5.2	5.4	5.4	4.4	19.6	31.7	17.6	6.0	81.2	48.0	48.5	51.5
54970	REDGRANITE	97.0	96.4	0.3	0.3	0.0	0.1	2.3	3.4	5.0	5.0	7.0	7.0	4.6	20.6	30.7	16.9	3.1	78.5	45.5	48.7	51.3
54971	RIPON	97.7	95.8	0.3	1.5	0.5	0.7	2.0	2.9	5.7	5.7	6.0	8.7	7.9	22.9	26.8	12.8	3.4	79.7	39.5	48.0	52.0
54974	ROSENDALE	99.2	98.9	0.1	0.1	0.1	0.1	0.6	0.9	6.6	7.0	7.3	7.1	4.4	25.3	30.4	10.4	1.4	74.7	39.7	50.3	49.7
54977	SCANDINAVIA	98.5	98.0	0.1	0.1	0.2	0.3	0.3	0.5	5.9	6.2	7.0	7.1	4.6	23.0	29.8	14.3	2.0	76.4	42.3	51.6	48.4
54978	TILLEDA	57.1	54.9	0.0	0.0	0.0	0.0	0.0	0.0	7.8	7.8	7.8	7.8	7.8	25.5	21.6	11.8	2.0	68.6	33.1	52.9	47.1
54979	VAN DYNE	99.5	99.2	0.0	0.0	0.2	0.3	0.5	0.7	5.1	6.3	6.8	7.5	4.7	24.3	32.6	11.9	1.0	76.9	42.3	51.0	49.0
54981	WAUPACA	97.6	96.9	0.2	0.2	0.2	0.3	1.8	2.6	5.7	5.8	6.2	6.4	5.1	22.6	29.0	15.8	3.4	78.2	43.6	50.8	49.2
54982	WAUTOMA	95.9	94.4	0.4	0.6	0.6	0.8	4.7	6.7	4.8	4.8	5.4	6.2	6.0	23.8	29.0	16.5	3.6	81.0	44.3	53.8	46.2
54983	WEYAUWEGA	98.2	97.8	0.2	0.3	0.2	0.3	0.8	1.2	5.9	6.4	6.8	6.8	5.1	24.0	29.5	12.6	2.8	77.2	41.5	50.2	49.8
54984	WILD ROSE	98.3	97.7	0.3	0.4	0.1	0.2	1.4	2.0	4.0	4.3	4.6	5.6	5.3	19.9	32.0	21.1	3.3	83.4	49.1	52.5	47.5
54986	WINNECONNE	98.9	98.6	0.1	0.1	0.1	0.2	0.5	0.7	4.8	5.2	5.8	6.7	5.4	22.5	33.5	14.0	1.9	79.6	44.6	50.3	49.7
	WISCONSIN	88.9	86.9	5.7	6.3	1.7	2.3	3.6	4.8	6.4	6.4	6.5	7.2	7.2	26.0	27.1	11.1	2.2	76.6	38.0	49.5	50.5
	UNITED STATES	75.1	72.0	12.3	12.7	3.8	4.6	12.5	15.7	6.8	6.7	6.6	7.1	6.9	27.0	26.0	10.9	1.9	75.7	36.9	49.2	50.8

INCOME

54888-54986

ZIP CODE				2009 HOUSEHOLD INCOME DISTRIBUTION (%)					MEDIAN HOUSEHOLD INCOME					2009 HOME VALUE DISTRIBUTION (%)					
#	POST OFFICE NAME	2009 Per Capita Income	2009 HH Income Base	Less than $25,000	$25,000 to $49,999	$50,000 to $99,999	$100,000 to $149,999	$150,000 or More	2009	2014	2009 National Centile	2009 State Centile	2009 Home Value Base	Less than $50,000	$50,000 to $89,999	$90,000 to $174,999	$175,000 to $399,999	$400,000 or More	2009 Median Home Value
54888	TREGO	20991	660	25.9	34.2	33.3	4.8	1.7	42087	43573	40	21	586	9.0	17.9	45.1	24.2	3.8	128763
54889	TURTLE LAKE	20843	1240	28.5	29.9	35.7	4.4	1.5	42875	44587	42	24	917	8.9	25.5	44.6	18.5	2.4	111759
54891	WASHBURN	21893	1691	24.8	28.2	39.1	6.6	1.2	47155	48783	55	41	1355	6.2	18.5	51.5	20.9	2.9	125423
54893	WEBSTER	22762	1733	25.7	34.4	33.5	4.6	1.7	42272	44157	40	21	1467	9.6	22.8	42.9	21.1	3.5	115975
54895	WEYERHAEUSER	18345	504	31.3	39.3	24.6	3.8	1.0	33623	34059	15	2	421	17.3	27.8	38.5	14.0	2.4	98200
54896	WINTER	20986	796	33.5	30.0	30.4	4.8	1.3	37828	39090	26	6	659	14.0	29.7	38.7	15.3	2.3	99222
54901	OSHKOSH	23100	13658	22.3	30.6	36.8	7.3	3.0	46969	50196	54	40	7349	4.4	19.1	61.4	13.6	1.5	111564
54902	OSHKOSH	27783	10252	19.0	30.0	41.1	6.7	3.1	50990	54293	64	52	6554	2.6	18.3	64.9	12.4	1.8	113760
54904	OSHKOSH	32767	8238	8.6	20.4	45.6	18.7	6.7	73557	75801	89	92	6423	2.0	2.5	47.5	44.0	3.9	171607
54909	ALMOND	22480	871	21.7	29.3	41.8	4.7	2.5	49035	51568	59	46	738	12.2	20.2	44.0	21.8	1.8	115417
54911	APPLETON	27414	11263	18.8	27.2	41.1	9.2	3.8	55421	59784	72	64	6946	1.9	6.7	73.2	17.5	0.6	131733
54913	APPLETON	36526	6101	6.2	14.6	47.0	16.7	15.6	79929	83291	92	96	4929	2.9	2.5	34.1	52.5	8.0	198027
54914	APPLETON	30482	13317	13.3	24.6	44.8	11.5	5.8	62753	65654	81	81	8094	1.8	7.7	61.1	28.5	0.9	140699
54915	APPLETON	29942	15398	9.8	21.0	48.9	14.4	5.8	69700	74559	87	90	11113	0.9	3.8	63.0	30.7	1.6	148291
54921	BANCROFT	21541	477	21.2	30.4	40.3	5.9	2.3	48447	51485	58	44	390	13.6	20.8	40.5	22.6	2.6	117347
54922	BEAR CREEK	21211	585	18.8	30.3	43.8	6.2	1.0	50747	53158	63	51	498	8.0	18.9	47.6	23.5	2.0	121910
54923	BERLIN	22459	3429	19.6	30.6	42.7	5.0	2.2	49788	51347	61	48	2592	6.1	19.0	57.3	16.5	1.2	117252
54928	CAROLINE	19397	187	17.6	35.8	40.1	4.8	1.6	46911	47739	54	40	168	6.0	24.4	53.0	13.7	3.0	110606
54929	CLINTONVILLE	21475	3804	24.5	28.3	40.5	5.3	1.4	47396	50152	55	41	2891	7.5	26.8	46.4	18.0	1.3	108601
54930	COLOMA	20398	695	22.4	36.5	34.2	4.7	2.0	44020	45789	45	29	585	6.0	22.2	48.4	20.3	3.1	122690
54932	ELDORADO	28592	379	10.0	19.5	54.4	11.3	4.7	65025	66329	83	85	335	2.1	9.3	53.4	31.3	3.9	149440
54935	FOND DU LAC	25857	17393	19.6	25.0	43.4	8.1	3.9	54973	58075	71	63	10875	4.0	15.3	60.3	19.2	1.1	121607
54937	FOND DU LAC	28294	6616	12.5	22.8	48.8	10.8	5.0	62666	64018	81	80	5556	13.6	10.8	43.5	28.0	4.1	138454
54940	FREMONT	25389	1617	18.4	26.6	44.3	7.9	2.8	54000	55687	70	60	1409	4.2	10.6	46.3	34.8	4.1	153503
54941	GREEN LAKE	27013	1370	21.4	29.0	39.7	7.2	2.7	49523	51562	60	47	1069	6.1	8.0	48.0	29.5	8.5	150477
54942	GREENVILLE	31675	2566	5.3	6.6	57.6	23.3	7.3	81706	82368	93	96	2180	1.1	0.7	37.9	55.9	4.4	189621
54943	HANCOCK	21582	841	21.9	33.1	39.4	4.3	1.4	46659	48347	53	39	699	10.9	25.0	43.9	18.7	1.4	111425
54944	HORTONVILLE	25886	3269	11.9	21.3	53.4	10.1	3.4	64526	67330	83	84	2730	2.2	4.9	55.0	34.2	3.7	153067
54945	IOLA	24660	1525	21.2	28.5	39.3	8.7	2.3	50225	52657	62	50	1205	4.6	18.1	51.3	23.2	2.8	129234
54947	LARSEN	26434	1030	12.7	24.7	49.9	10.8	1.9	62661	64546	81	80	940	7.3	7.1	46.0	37.6	2.0	151887
54948	LEOPOLIS	20085	159	25.2	30.8	38.4	4.4	1.3	43319	45760	43	26	131	15.3	24.4	45.8	13.0	1.5	101875
54949	MANAWA	20606	1323	23.0	27.2	41.6	7.2	1.1	49794	52070	61	48	1082	7.1	22.7	47.0	22.4	0.7	115125
54950	MARION	20928	1335	25.7	30.9	37.0	4.9	1.5	43966	46440	45	28	1063	6.6	26.5	50.1	15.1	1.7	111574
54952	MENASHA	29641	10629	14.2	26.3	44.3	10.8	4.4	60356	62868	78	74	7145	4.3	11.8	62.4	19.5	2.0	125255
54956	NEENAH	31764	16857	10.9	21.7	47.8	12.9	6.6	66003	68559	84	86	12562	2.7	7.2	59.2	27.8	3.0	139881
54960	NESHKORO	23522	1292	21.7	35.0	37.2	4.1	2.1	44880	47093	48	32	1147	5.6	21.6	44.1	26.8	1.9	127984
54961	NEW LONDON	23820	5724	19.4	25.1	45.0	8.4	2.2	54836	57056	71	63	4296	5.7	14.5	53.4	24.4	2.0	131844
54962	OGDENSBURG	22726	524	22.1	31.7	38.4	5.7	2.1	45598	50275	50	35	462	6.9	18.4	48.9	23.6	2.2	126493
54963	OMRO	24705	2843	15.4	30.1	44.6	7.8	2.0	55391	59158	72	64	2304	6.3	12.4	57.9	21.6	1.8	126781
54964	PICKETT	25592	413	12.6	28.1	49.4	7.5	2.4	58764	60544	76	70	357	0.8	9.8	54.9	32.2	2.2	140848
54965	PINE RIVER	23674	519	20.6	29.1	41.2	6.7	2.3	50214	51536	62	49	466	3.4	19.1	48.1	24.9	4.5	135211
54966	PLAINFIELD	19704	813	25.5	31.2	36.9	4.3	2.1	43903	45929	45	28	639	9.9	30.2	42.4	15.3	2.2	99922
54967	POY SIPPI	24102	211	23.2	28.4	40.3	7.1	0.9	48135	50262	57	43	180	2.8	26.1	49.4	19.4	2.2	115909
54968	PRINCETON	20653	1304	26.8	32.0	36.6	3.7	1.0	42862	45059	42	23	1050	5.8	23.9	46.9	20.7	2.8	117857
54970	REDGRANITE	19940	1335	27.6	32.8	34.5	4.0	1.0	41737	43518	38	19	1119	14.0	28.7	42.3	14.3	0.7	98150
54971	RIPON	24590	4195	22.6	25.3	42.3	7.4	2.3	51722	54393	65	54	2927	4.0	16.0	60.8	17.9	1.3	124442
54974	ROSENDALE	23616	625	13.1	24.8	50.7	9.0	2.4	59039	60770	76	70	532	3.4	9.6	54.7	31.6	0.8	146154
54977	SCANDINAVIA	22195	569	20.2	22.8	46.6	9.0	1.4	53727	54776	69	60	482	4.1	14.3	49.0	26.1	6.4	142105
54978	TILLEDA	18291	19	26.3	31.6	36.8	5.3	0.0	42361	54523	41	22	15	13.3	26.7	46.7	13.3	0.0	97500
54979	VAN DYNE	25056	600	11.5	19.5	58.2	9.3	1.5	62703	63631	81	80	511	2.3	7.8	52.8	33.5	3.5	149306
54981	WAUPACA	24328	6381	22.7	29.0	36.9	7.9	3.5	48337	51606	57	44	4641	4.5	13.2	52.2	25.5	4.6	136170
54982	WAUTOMA	22390	3094	24.5	31.8	36.0	5.4	2.3	44594	46676	47	31	2462	8.1	21.6	45.5	21.4	3.4	120013
54983	WEYAUWEGA	21350	1915	21.5	30.0	39.5	7.2	1.9	48690	51308	58	44	1538	4.9	17.2	53.9	22.0	1.9	125450
54984	WILD ROSE	24099	1330	25.1	32.9	33.2	5.9	2.9	43207	45421	43	25	1109	10.8	23.9	39.0	23.2	3.1	116223
54986	WINNECONNE	28461	2121	16.8	23.1	45.9	10.4	3.8	61803	63396	80	77	1745	1.5	9.5	56.1	27.9	5.0	139515
	WISCONSIN	27384		18.4	25.3	40.0	11.0	5.2	56363	58927				5.6	11.9	43.5	34.2	4.7	150766
	UNITED STATES	27277		20.9	24.4	35.3	11.7	7.6	54719	56938				9.3	13.1	31.6	32.6	13.5	162279

#	POST OFFICE NAME	FINANCIAL SERVICES: Auto Loan	FINANCIAL SERVICES: Home Loan	FINANCIAL SERVICES: Investments	FINANCIAL SERVICES: Retirement Plans	THE HOME: Home Improvements: Home Repair	THE HOME: Home Improvements: Lawn & Garden	THE HOME: Furnishings: Computers & Hardware-Personal	THE HOME: Furnishings: Major Appliances	THE HOME: Furnishings: TV, Radio, Sound Equipment	THE HOME: Furnishings: Furniture	ENTERTAINMENT: Dine out/Carry out	ENTERTAINMENT: Sports Equipment	ENTERTAINMENT: Fees & Tickets	ENTERTAINMENT: Toys & Games	ENTERTAINMENT: Travel	ENTERTAINMENT: Cable TV	PERSONAL: Apparel & Services	PERSONAL: Auto Repairs	PERSONAL: Health Insurance	PERSONAL: Pets & Supplies
54888	TREGO	82	66	106	65	72	87	66	84	69	62	68	61	57	66	72	74	45	77	83	97
54889	TURTLE LAKE	79	64	76	65	66	84	66	78	71	59	69	59	57	71	65	77	46	73	83	92
54891	WASHBURN	82	71	88	72	74	87	72	83	74	67	73	62	65	73	73	79	50	78	85	97
54893	WEBSTER	80	67	103	65	74	86	66	83	69	64	68	59	59	65	72	74	46	77	84	96
54895	WEYERHAEUSER	74	54	79	52	56	75	55	70	60	51	59	52	45	59	55	66	39	64	72	83
54896	WINTER	77	62	85	59	66	82	62	76	67	61	66	54	54	65	63	73	44	71	81	89
54901	OSHKOSH	81	73	66	76	71	77	86	77	85	79	84	62	80	85	77	85	59	82	83	93
54902	OSHKOSH	82	83	74	85	80	87	85	83	87	82	87	64	86	87	84	89	60	85	92	100
54904	OSHKOSH	118	123	108	123	118	114	117	115	114	119	115	91	118	118	116	112	80	114	111	135
54909	ALMOND	92	76	88	77	78	96	76	90	81	69	79	68	66	81	76	87	53	83	93	106
54911	APPLETON	88	89	82	90	86	92	90	88	92	87	92	68	91	92	89	95	64	90	96	105
54913	APPLETON	144	167	144	171	162	153	145	149	139	152	141	119	158	146	153	135	100	141	138	172
54914	APPLETON	103	99	88	102	95	96	105	97	103	103	104	78	103	105	100	102	73	102	99	117
54915	APPLETON	115	115	97	114	109	106	113	109	110	115	112	86	111	115	108	108	77	109	106	128
54921	BANCROFT	89	74	87	75	76	92	75	87	79	69	77	66	66	79	75	84	52	81	89	102
54922	BEAR CREEK	87	77	80	80	79	93	77	87	79	69	78	67	69	80	77	84	53	81	90	102
54923	BERLIN	86	76	76	78	76	90	76	84	80	70	78	64	70	81	75	84	53	80	89	100
54928	CAROLINE	94	65	103	64	68	99	72	89	75	58	74	74	52	73	71	81	48	83	94	110
54929	CLINTONVILLE	78	70	67	72	70	80	73	77	76	68	74	59	68	76	70	79	51	75	82	91
54930	COLOMA	87	69	111	68	76	92	69	88	73	65	72	64	60	69	75	78	48	81	87	102
54932	ELDORADO	106	119	103	123	116	117	107	111	105	107	106	87	114	108	113	105	74	107	110	131
54935	FOND DU LAC	88	87	79	88	84	91	89	88	90	86	90	68	88	91	87	93	62	89	94	105
54937	FOND DU LAC	103	107	95	109	104	109	101	104	101	100	101	81	102	103	102	102	70	102	105	123
54940	FREMONT	93	88	95	90	90	100	84	95	86	80	85	72	81	86	87	90	58	89	96	111
54941	GREEN LAKE	95	79	110	80	85	101	79	96	82	73	81	71	70	80	83	88	54	89	97	112
54942	GREENVILLE	139	152	122	145	141	124	134	133	126	145	128	106	137	136	132	119	90	126	115	151
54943	HANCOCK	87	68	100	65	72	91	68	85	73	65	72	62	58	71	71	79	48	79	88	100
54944	HORTONVILLE	102	109	97	112	107	111	100	105	99	98	99	82	103	102	104	100	69	100	105	123
54945	IOLA	89	77	84	79	79	93	81	88	83	74	82	67	73	83	79	87	56	85	93	104
54947	LARSEN	96	102	99	104	101	105	93	100	92	92	92	77	96	93	98	93	64	95	98	117
54948	LEOPOLIS	87	63	91	61	65	89	65	82	71	59	70	63	51	71	64	78	46	76	86	98
54949	MANAWA	91	72	80	72	73	92	74	85	79	69	77	65	63	81	70	85	52	80	89	102
54950	MARION	84	66	83	67	68	89	69	82	74	61	72	64	58	73	68	79	48	77	87	98
54952	MENASHA	99	97	84	97	92	95	99	95	98	97	98	75	96	101	95	99	68	97	98	113
54956	NEENAH	108	116	103	118	112	113	111	109	109	110	109	86	115	111	112	109	77	109	110	129
54960	NESHKORO	87	71	110	69	77	92	70	89	74	66	73	65	61	70	76	79	48	82	88	103
54961	NEW LONDON	86	86	76	89	84	91	85	87	86	81	85	67	84	87	84	88	59	85	91	103
54962	OGDENSBURG	85	77	78	80	78	92	76	86	78	68	77	66	69	80	76	83	52	80	89	100
54963	OMRO	90	87	78	90	85	96	85	90	87	79	86	70	82	89	85	91	59	87	95	107
54964	PICKETT	99	90	89	94	92	106	89	100	92	80	90	76	82	93	89	97	61	92	103	116
54965	PINE RIVER	94	77	113	77	84	100	77	95	81	72	79	70	68	78	82	86	53	88	95	111
54966	PLAINFIELD	91	66	83	65	67	90	68	82	76	65	74	63	55	77	65	83	50	77	86	99
54967	POY SIPPI	86	75	90	76	78	92	74	87	77	68	76	65	67	76	76	82	51	81	89	101
54968	PRINCETON	81	63	87	63	67	85	65	80	70	60	68	59	55	69	66	76	46	74	83	93
54970	REDGRANITE	82	61	82	59	63	82	62	76	68	59	67	57	51	69	61	74	45	71	79	91
54971	RIPON	87	79	80	80	79	92	82	87	86	77	84	65	77	85	80	90	58	85	95	102
54974	ROSENDALE	99	91	89	95	93	106	89	100	92	81	90	76	83	94	89	97	62	93	103	117
54977	SCANDINAVIA	88	80	80	83	82	94	79	89	82	72	80	67	73	83	79	87	55	83	92	104
54978	TILLEDA	88	63	90	61	65	89	64	82	72	60	70	62	52	71	64	79	46	75	85	98
54979	VAN DYNE	101	94	92	97	95	109	92	103	94	83	93	78	85	96	92	99	63	95	106	120
54981	WAUPACA	94	80	95	80	83	97	82	94	86	77	84	69	74	85	82	91	57	89	97	109
54982	WAUTOMA	86	70	94	69	74	88	74	85	78	69	76	63	64	76	74	83	51	82	89	100
54983	WEYAUWEGA	88	75	83	76	77	93	76	88	80	69	78	66	68	81	75	86	53	82	92	102
54984	WILD ROSE	90	74	103	71	80	97	75	91	80	74	78	64	67	76	78	86	52	86	98	106
54986	WINNECONNE	100	101	94	104	100	107	96	102	96	92	96	78	95	98	98	99	66	98	104	120
	WISCONSIN	98	94	92	96	93	99	96	96	96	93	96	75	94	97	95	98	67	96	99	114
	UNITED STATES	100	100	100	100	100	100	100	100	100	100	100	100	100	100	100	100	100	100	100	100

ZIP CODE		COUNTY FIPS CODE	POPULATION			2000-2009 ANNUAL RATE		HOUSEHOLDS					FAMILIES		
#	POST OFFICE NAME		2000	2009	2014	% Rate	State Centile	2000	2009	2014	% Annual Rate 2000-2009	2009 Average HH Size	2000	2009	% Annual Rate 2000-2009
82001	CHEYENNE	021	33676	34449	34821	0.2	33	13833	14513	14799	0.5	2.22	8401	8423	0.0
82005	FT WARREN AFB	021	1055	1090	1110	0.4	39	148	164	171	1.1	3.60	146	161	1.1
82007	CHEYENNE	021	16050	18106	18991	1.3	71	6139	7129	7546	1.6	2.52	4208	4681	1.2
82009	CHEYENNE	021	27065	30707	32331	1.4	76	10391	12147	12892	1.7	2.50	7789	8801	1.3
82050	ALBIN	021	320	360	379	1.3	71	124	142	150	1.5	2.54	92	100	0.9
82051	BOSLER	001	165	167	164	0.1	25	67	70	70	0.5	2.39	47	47	0.0
82052	BUFORD	001	45	49	50	0.9	56	18	20	21	1.1	2.45	13	15	1.6
82053	BURNS	021	1063	1215	1303	1.5	79	393	451	486	1.5	2.69	300	328	1.0
82054	CARPENTER	021	769	976	1060	2.6	93	256	328	360	2.7	2.97	196	243	2.4
82055	CENTENNIAL	001	275	280	275	0.2	33	134	141	140	0.6	1.99	95	95	0.0
82058	GARRETT	001	101	102	100	0.1	25	42	44	44	0.5	2.32	30	30	0.0
82063	JELM	001	73	80	82	1.0	61	39	45	46	1.6	1.78	29	32	1.1
82070	LARAMIE	001	16498	16768	16669	0.2	33	6804	7191	7219	0.6	2.13	3741	3752	0.0
82072	LARAMIE	001	14496	14656	14529	0.1	25	6025	6332	6337	0.5	2.17	2946	2937	0.0
82081	MERIDEN	021	15	20	23	3.2	96	4	6	7	4.5	3.33	3	5	5.7
82082	PINE BLUFFS	021	1594	1756	1834	1.1	65	639	716	754	1.2	2.45	464	491	0.6
82083	ROCK RIVER	001	408	415	409	0.2	33	155	164	164	0.6	2.53	109	110	0.1
82084	TIE SIDING	001	36	40	40	1.1	65	16	18	19	1.3	2.22	12	13	0.9
82190	YELLOWSTONE NATIONAL	029	539	615	653	1.4	76	275	327	352	1.9	1.88	115	126	1.0
82201	WHEATLAND	031	6458	6451	6335	0.0	19	2616	2719	2698	0.4	2.34	1828	1834	0.0
82210	CHUGWATER	031	375	378	370	0.1	25	141	146	145	0.4	2.59	107	108	0.1
82212	FORT LARAMIE	015	341	331	322	-0.3	14	161	162	160	0.1	2.04	108	105	-0.3
82213	GLENDO	031	551	510	489	-0.8	3	251	240	233	-0.5	2.13	166	153	-0.9
82214	GUERNSEY	031	1292	1166	1111	-1.1	1	561	528	508	-0.7	2.21	357	323	-1.1
82215	HARTVILLE	031	145	134	129	-0.8	3	62	59	58	-0.5	2.27	41	38	-0.8
82217	HAWK SPRINGS	015	184	177	173	-0.4	9	68	68	67	0.0	2.41	51	49	-0.4
82219	JAY EM	015	446	433	422	-0.3	14	168	169	167	0.1	2.56	113	109	-0.4
82221	LAGRANGE	015	475	458	447	-0.4	9	146	146	144	0.0	2.90	108	106	-0.2
82222	LANCE CREEK	027	227	222	220	-0.2	16	90	91	90	0.1	2.44	67	66	-0.2
82223	LINGLE	015	766	749	731	-0.2	16	310	313	309	0.1	2.39	227	222	-0.2
82224	LOST SPRINGS	027	2	2	2	0.0	19	1	1	1	0.0	2.00	1	1	0.0
82225	LUSK	027	2002	1936	1907	-0.4	9	842	836	826	-0.1	2.21	553	529	-0.5
82227	MANVILLE	027	172	168	167	-0.3	14	76	76	76	0.0	2.21	57	55	-0.4
82229	SHAWNEE	009	120	132	139	1.0	61	47	54	57	1.5	2.44	39	44	1.3
82240	TORRINGTON	015	9444	9145	8936	-0.3	14	3864	3918	3871	0.2	2.24	2562	2502	-0.3
82242	VAN TASSELL	027	4	4	4	0.0	19	2	2	2	0.0	2.00	1	1	0.0
82243	VETERAN	015	159	155	151	-0.3	14	60	61	60	0.2	2.51	48	47	-0.2
82244	YODER	015	723	698	681	-0.4	9	284	285	281	0.0	2.28	211	206	-0.3
82301	RAWLINS	007	9436	9507	9582	0.1	25	3481	3698	3777	0.7	2.45	2348	2407	0.3
82310	JEFFREY CITY	013	170	180	186	0.6	45	72	79	83	1.0	2.28	53	57	0.8
82321	BAGGS	007	483	470	474	-0.3	14	197	223	230	1.3	1.62	128	139	0.9
82322	BAIROIL	037	122	138	142	1.3	71	50	59	63	1.8	2.34	38	43	1.3
82323	DIXON	007	253	246	248	-0.3	14	112	127	131	1.4	1.62	73	79	0.9
82325	ENCAMPMENT	007	880	911	920	0.4	39	406	450	462	1.1	2.02	282	302	0.7
82327	HANNA	007	1358	1385	1413	0.2	33	550	596	616	0.9	2.32	382	401	0.5
82329	MEDICINE BOW	007	293	285	293	-0.3	14	137	142	148	0.4	2.01	99	99	0.0
82331	SARATOGA	007	2302	2360	2379	0.3	36	995	1095	1119	1.0	2.13	647	684	0.6
82332	SAVERY	007	94	91	92	-0.4	9	38	43	44	1.3	1.63	25	27	0.8
82334	SINCLAIR	007	441	447	462	0.1	25	175	186	195	0.7	2.40	126	129	0.3
82336	WAMSUTTER	037	353	310	293	-1.4	1	138	128	123	-0.8	2.38	98	87	-1.3
82401	WORLAND	043	7519	7203	7102	-0.5	5	2944	2924	2913	-0.1	2.40	2072	1990	-0.4
82410	BASIN	003	1847	1883	1893	0.2	33	701	741	750	0.6	2.32	487	498	0.2
82411	BURLINGTON	003	610	624	626	0.2	33	176	182	183	0.4	3.42	140	141	0.1
82414	CODY	029	14045	14943	15456	0.7	53	5811	6460	6766	1.2	2.28	3988	4278	0.8
82421	DEAVER	003	607	636	646	0.5	41	230	250	256	0.9	2.54	175	185	0.6
82426	GREYBULL	003	2655	2601	2568	-0.2	16	1107	1100	1090	-0.1	2.36	745	713	-0.5
82428	HYATTVILLE	003	107	109	110	0.2	33	47	49	50	0.5	2.22	35	35	0.0
82431	LOVELL	003	4824	4777	4753	-0.1	17	1742	1767	1765	0.2	2.66	1277	1257	-0.2
82432	MANDERSON	003	432	441	445	0.2	33	164	172	174	0.5	2.56	121	123	0.2
82433	MEETEETSE	029	850	973	1032	1.5	79	353	425	456	2.0	2.29	240	279	1.6
82434	OTTO	003	116	119	119	0.3	36	32	33	33	0.3	3.61	26	26	0.0
82435	POWELL	029	10497	11412	11850	0.9	56	3980	4502	4736	1.3	2.39	2756	3016	1.0
82441	SHELL	003	296	301	302	0.2	33	128	134	135	0.5	2.25	94	95	0.1
82442	TEN SLEEP	043	772	779	775	0.1	25	335	353	355	0.6	2.21	240	244	0.2
82443	THERMOPOLIS	017	4882	4672	4599	-0.5	5	2108	2097	2086	-0.1	2.16	1353	1294	-0.5
82501	RIVERTON	013	18190	19217	19775	0.6	45	6747	7407	7709	1.0	2.53	4717	5018	0.7
82510	ARAPAHOE	013	342	366	380	0.7	53	85	93	98	1.0	3.94	72	78	0.9
82512	CROWHEART	013	250	261	271	0.5	41	96	104	109	0.9	2.51	66	69	0.5
82513	DUBOIS	013	1778	1875	1931	0.6	45	815	907	946	1.2	2.07	515	548	0.7
82514	FORT WASHAKIE	013	926	992	1034	0.7	53	287	315	332	1.0	3.06	224	240	0.7
82516	KINNEAR	013	277	295	306	0.7	53	106	116	122	1.0	2.54	79	85	0.8
82520	LANDER	013	12018	12929	13379	0.8	54	4593	5145	5394	1.2	2.44	3194	3452	0.8
82523	PAVILLION	013	784	837	871	0.7	53	321	358	377	1.2	2.34	248	268	0.8
82601	CASPER	025	23370	25684	26861	1.0	61	9673	10729	11288	1.1	2.30	5761	6142	0.7
82604	CASPER	025	25706	27600	28773	0.8	54	10069	10993	11529	1.0	2.46	7177	7552	0.6
82609	CASPER	025	13270	14861	15736	1.2	66	5496	6208	6601	1.3	2.38	3717	4079	1.0
82620	ALCOVA	025	28	36	38	2.8	94	14	18	19	2.8	1.89	10	13	2.9
82633	DOUGLAS	009	8158	8712	9070	0.7	53	3172	3534	3727	1.2	2.44	2282	2464	0.8
82636	EVANSVILLE	025	3573	4086	4349	1.5	79	1334	1550	1661	1.6	2.64	923	1018	1.1
82637	GLENROCK	009	3742	4337	4622	1.6	81	1464	1783	1925	2.2	2.43	1080	1274	1.8
82639	KAYCEE	019	794	938	1018	1.8	86	310	384	421	2.3	2.44	237	285	2.0
82642	LYSITE	013	101	107	111	0.6	45	45	49	52	0.9	2.18	33	35	0.6
82643	MIDWEST	025	602	645	678	0.7	53	237	259	274	1.0	2.49	164	170	0.4
82649	SHOSHONI	013	968	1030	1066	0.7	53	378	418	438	1.1	2.46	282	303	0.8
82701	NEWCASTLE	045	5069	5328	5434	0.5	41	1966	2173	2248	1.1	2.33	1380	1476	0.7
82710	ALADDIN	011	224	247	264	1.1	65	90	105	114	1.7	2.35	64	73	1.4
82712	BEULAH	011	165	188	197	1.4	76	77	93	99	2.1	1.98	58	68	1.7
82714	DEVILS TOWER	011	115	134	141	1.7	84	46	57	61	2.3	2.35	34	41	2.0
82715	FOUR CORNERS	045	35	37	38	0.6	45	21	24	25	1.5	1.42	16	10	-5.0
82716	GILLETTE	005	15062	18644	20696	2.3	91	5724	7363	8275	2.8	2.50	3859	4813	2.4
82718	GILLETTE	005	15964	19961	22254	2.4	92	5530	7257	8201	3.0	2.74	4367	5572	2.7
82720	HULETT	011	1080	1193	1275	1.1	65	421	492	533	1.7	2.42	300	340	1.4
82721	MOORCROFT	011	2432	2854	3055	1.7	84	927	1149	1248	2.3	2.48	675	812	2.0
82723	OSAGE	045	241	257	263	0.7	53	113	130	135	1.5	1.78	86	95	1.1
82725	RECLUSE	005	97	93	104	-0.5	5	45	45	51	0.0	2.07	35	34	-0.3
	WYOMING					0.9					1.3	2.40			0.9
	UNITED STATES					1.0					1.1	2.59			0.9

ZIP CODE #	POST OFFICE NAME	RACE (%) White 2000	White 2009	Black 2000	Black 2009	Asian/Pacific 2000	Asian/Pacific 2009	% Hispanic Origin 2000	% Hispanic Origin 2009	2009 AGE DISTRIBUTION (%) 0-4	5-9	10-14	15-19	20-24	25-44	45-64	65-84	85+	18+	MEDIAN AGE 2009	% 2009 Males	% 2009 Females
82001	CHEYENNE	87.9	86.1	3.4	3.7	1.2	1.6	10.8	12.6	7.1	6.2	5.8	6.3	8.4	30.2	23.6	10.3	2.0	77.3	34.8	50.8	49.2
82005	FT WARREN AFB	79.7	77.0	9.4	10.1	2.6	3.5	8.7	10.0	10.3	7.2	4.6	7.0	21.7	47.2	2.1	0.0	0.0	76.1	24.9	66.0	34.0
82007	CHEYENNE	82.9	81.0	3.0	3.4	0.6	0.8	20.4	22.8	7.9	7.5	7.2	8.0	7.2	28.4	24.6	8.4	0.9	72.8	33.1	49.8	50.2
82009	CHEYENNE	93.1	92.0	1.5	1.6	1.3	1.7	6.3	7.2	5.4	5.9	6.7	6.8	5.0	24.0	32.8	11.8	1.7	77.5	42.4	49.0	51.0
82050	ALBIN	95.9	95.3	0.0	0.0	0.3	0.6	4.4	5.3	5.3	6.1	8.9	8.6	3.9	25.3	29.2	10.8	1.9	73.3	40.0	51.7	48.3
82051	BOSLER	97.6	95.8	0.0	0.0	0.0	0.6	3.0	3.0	4.2	3.6	7.2	6.6	3.6	22.2	40.7	10.8	1.2	80.2	46.4	53.9	46.1
82052	BUFORD	95.6	95.9	0.0	0.0	0.0	0.0	2.2	2.0	4.1	4.1	4.1	6.1	4.1	22.4	46.9	8.2	0.0	81.6	47.1	53.1	46.9
82053	BURNS	96.3	95.7	0.0	0.0	0.4	0.6	4.3	5.0	5.6	6.4	8.7	8.1	4.2	25.2	29.7	10.4	1.6	73.4	39.9	51.1	48.9
82054	CARPENTER	96.5	95.9	0.3	0.2	0.3	0.5	5.1	5.6	5.9	6.5	7.1	7.3	4.7	24.6	31.3	11.2	1.5	75.7	41.0	49.8	50.2
82055	CENTENNIAL	96.4	96.4	0.0	0.0	0.4	0.4	2.9	3.2	3.6	3.6	7.5	6.4	3.2	21.4	42.1	11.4	0.7	80.7	47.2	55.0	45.0
82058	GARRETT	97.0	96.1	0.0	0.0	0.0	0.0	3.0	2.9	3.9	2.9	6.9	6.9	3.9	22.5	42.2	10.8	0.0	80.4	46.5	53.9	46.1
82063	JELM	95.9	96.3	0.0	0.0	0.0	0.0	1.4	1.3	3.8	5.0	5.0	6.3	2.5	22.5	45.0	10.0	0.0	81.3	47.2	51.3	48.7
82070	LARAMIE	91.9	90.5	1.0	1.2	1.5	2.1	6.6	7.7	5.1	4.6	4.3	10.0	14.6	28.6	23.2	8.1	1.5	83.1	31.1	50.6	49.4
82072	LARAMIE	90.3	88.7	1.3	1.4	2.2	3.0	8.8	10.0	5.2	4.1	4.3	11.6	25.1	23.7	19.0	6.2	0.8	83.5	24.9	52.8	47.2
82081	MERIDEN	100.0	100.0	0.0	0.0	0.0	0.0	7.1	5.0	0.0	5.0	10.0	10.0	0.0	25.0	45.0	5.0	0.0	80.0	45.0	50.0	50.0
82082	PINE BLUFFS	95.9	95.4	0.3	0.3	0.2	0.2	5.9	6.9	5.2	5.8	7.0	7.9	4.7	23.2	30.6	13.1	2.4	76.5	42.2	50.5	49.5
82083	ROCK RIVER	96.6	95.7	0.0	0.2	0.2	0.5	3.4	3.9	4.1	4.1	7.2	6.7	3.9	21.7	39.0	12.3	1.0	79.8	46.3	54.7	45.3
82084	TIE SIDING	97.1	95.0	0.0	0.0	0.0	0.0	2.9	2.5	5.0	5.0	5.0	5.0	2.5	25.0	45.0	7.5	0.0	80.0	46.3	50.0	50.0
82190	YELLOWSTONE NATIONAL	98.0	97.4	0.0	0.0	0.9	1.3	0.7	0.8	6.2	4.2	5.7	5.2	4.1	36.7	35.8	2.1	0.0	80.5	39.2	51.9	48.1
82201	WHEATLAND	97.0	96.4	0.2	0.3	0.2	0.2	5.0	5.9	5.2	5.5	5.9	6.9	5.2	22.7	30.6	15.2	2.8	78.9	43.9	49.1	50.9
82210	CHUGWATER	97.9	97.9	0.0	0.0	0.0	0.0	2.9	3.4	6.1	6.6	6.9	6.6	4.5	22.5	31.7	13.5	1.6	76.2	42.6	49.2	50.8
82212	FORT LARAMIE	97.4	97.0	0.0	0.0	0.0	0.0	2.9	3.6	4.8	5.1	5.4	5.4	4.5	19.9	35.6	17.2	1.8	81.6	48.2	51.1	48.9
82213	GLENDO	95.1	94.7	0.2	0.2	0.2	0.2	5.3	5.9	3.3	4.9	5.9	8.4	2.9	20.8	34.9	16.3	2.5	80.2	47.9	50.8	49.2
82214	GUERNSEY	92.4	91.4	0.2	0.2	0.2	0.2	7.4	8.5	5.9	6.3	6.5	6.1	5.1	21.0	32.1	15.0	2.0	77.4	44.2	51.3	48.7
82215	HARTVILLE	95.2	94.8	0.0	0.0	0.0	0.0	5.5	6.0	3.7	5.2	6.0	9.0	3.7	20.9	33.6	15.7	2.2	79.1	46.1	52.2	47.8
82217	HAWK SPRINGS	94.6	93.8	0.0	0.0	1.1	1.1	4.9	6.2	5.6	6.8	6.8	8.5	7.9	20.9	29.4	12.4	1.7	77.4	38.8	52.0	48.0
82219	JAY EM	97.1	96.5	0.0	0.0	0.2	0.2	2.9	3.7	4.6	5.1	5.3	5.5	4.2	19.9	36.3	17.3	1.8	81.5	48.8	51.3	48.7
82221	LAGRANGE	95.1	93.9	0.0	0.0	0.6	0.9	4.9	5.7	6.1	6.6	6.8	9.2	7.6	21.0	29.0	12.2	1.5	76.6	38.3	51.3	48.7
82222	LANCE CREEK	97.8	97.7	0.0	0.0	0.0	0.0	1.3	1.4	5.0	5.4	5.9	5.4	3.6	17.1	33.3	22.5	1.8	80.2	48.7	52.7	47.3
82223	LINGLE	96.7	96.4	0.0	0.0	0.1	0.1	3.3	4.0	5.1	5.3	5.9	6.8	4.4	23.5	31.8	15.2	2.0	79.3	44.3	49.9	50.1
82224	LOST SPRINGS	100.0	100.0	0.0	0.0	0.0	0.0	0.0	0.0	0.0	0.0	0.0	0.0	0.0	0.0	100.0	0.0	0.0	100.0	47.5	50.0	50.0
82225	LUSK	98.0	97.9	0.1	0.2	0.1	0.2	1.5	1.6	4.5	5.0	5.4	6.7	6.1	21.3	31.0	17.1	2.8	80.9	45.6	48.1	51.9
82227	MANVILLE	98.3	98.2	0.0	0.0	0.0	0.0	1.2	1.2	4.2	5.4	6.0	5.4	3.0	18.5	33.3	22.0	2.4	81.0	48.6	52.4	47.6
82229	SHAWNEE	95.0	94.7	0.0	0.0	0.8	0.8	3.3	4.5	3.8	6.8	9.1	8.3	4.5	23.5	34.1	9.1	0.8	73.5	41.4	50.8	49.2
82240	TORRINGTON	93.1	92.1	0.3	0.3	0.3	0.4	10.5	12.0	6.0	5.7	6.1	6.9	6.1	22.1	28.4	15.3	3.4	78.5	42.5	49.7	50.3
82242	VAN TASSELL	100.0	100.0	0.0	0.0	0.0	0.0	0.0	0.0	0.0	0.0	0.0	0.0	0.0	0.0	100.0	0.0	0.0	100.0	48.3	75.0	25.0
82243	VETERAN	98.1	97.4	0.0	0.0	0.0	0.0	3.1	3.9	5.2	5.8	5.2	6.5	5.2	21.9	32.3	16.1	1.9	78.7	45.2	52.3	47.7
82244	YODER	94.8	94.1	0.1	0.1	0.7	0.9	4.7	5.6	6.0	6.3	6.9	9.3	7.4	20.9	29.7	11.9	1.6	76.9	38.8	51.3	48.7
82301	RAWLINS	86.8	85.0	0.7	0.8	0.9	1.2	19.9	22.5	6.7	6.1	5.9	6.5	7.7	26.4	29.2	10.1	1.5	77.5	37.2	52.3	47.7
82310	JEFFREY CITY	94.7	93.3	0.0	0.0	1.2	1.7	2.9	3.3	4.4	5.0	7.2	8.9	3.3	20.6	35.6	13.3	1.7	76.1	45.3	50.6	49.4
82321	BAGGS	89.4	88.1	3.1	3.4	0.6	1.1	8.9	10.6	2.6	3.0	3.2	5.3	11.7	35.7	29.6	8.1	0.9	88.5	38.4	71.5	28.5
82322	BAIROIL	93.4	92.8	0.0	0.0	0.0	0.0	6.6	8.0	4.3	5.8	5.8	6.5	5.8	23.2	35.5	12.3	0.7	80.4	43.8	52.2	47.8
82323	DIXON	89.3	88.2	3.2	3.3	0.8	0.8	9.1	11.0	2.8	2.8	3.3	5.7	10.6	35.8	29.7	8.5	0.8	87.8	38.6	71.1	28.9
82325	ENCAMPMENT	97.8	97.5	0.0	0.0	0.6	0.8	1.5	1.8	4.4	4.7	4.9	3.7	3.2	20.7	39.0	17.9	1.4	83.4	50.4	53.8	46.2
82327	HANNA	94.9	94.2	0.4	0.5	0.1	0.1	5.3	6.4	5.1	5.3	6.1	7.1	5.2	21.0	33.9	14.8	1.5	78.6	45.2	51.8	48.2
82329	MEDICINE BOW	97.6	97.2	0.0	0.0	1.0	1.4	1.0	1.1	4.2	3.9	5.6	6.7	3.5	14.0	40.7	18.9	2.5	81.8	49.9	50.5	49.5
82331	SARATOGA	95.7	95.0	0.1	0.1	0.6	0.8	4.2	5.1	4.7	5.0	5.3	5.2	4.6	20.2	36.6	16.4	2.2	81.6	47.9	51.0	49.0
82332	SAVERY	89.4	87.9	3.2	3.3	1.1	1.1	8.5	9.9	2.2	3.3	3.3	5.5	13.2	35.2	29.7	7.7	0.0	89.0	37.8	72.5	27.5
82334	SINCLAIR	96.4	95.5	0.2	0.2	0.2	0.2	4.1	5.1	3.1	5.8	8.1	9.2	2.0	23.0	34.7	11.0	3.1	76.3	44.4	50.8	49.2
82336	WAMSUTTER	92.9	91.9	0.0	0.0	0.8	1.3	8.5	10.0	5.5	5.2	6.1	8.7	6.8	28.4	30.0	9.4	0.0	77.1	37.6	51.9	48.1
82401	WORLAND	90.0	88.4	0.1	0.1	0.8	1.1	11.9	13.7	6.0	6.4	7.0	7.6	5.5	22.4	29.0	13.4	2.7	75.5	40.8	49.4	50.6
82410	BASIN	97.2	97.2	0.1	0.1	0.2	0.2	2.2	2.2	5.1	5.4	6.3	6.6	4.2	19.5	28.0	19.9	5.0	78.8	47.3	48.4	51.6
82411	BURLINGTON	86.9	86.7	0.5	0.5	0.3	0.3	13.4	13.9	11.7	11.5	10.9	9.1	4.5	20.7	18.6	10.6	2.4	59.5	28.2	51.1	48.9
82414	CODY	96.9	96.4	0.1	0.1	0.5	0.7	2.2	2.6	5.4	5.8	6.6	6.8	4.9	22.3	33.3	12.7	2.1	77.6	43.6	48.9	51.1
82421	DEAVER	96.5	96.4	0.0	0.0	0.2	0.2	3.6	3.9	7.2	7.5	7.5	6.8	5.0	23.7	28.6	12.1	1.4	73.9	38.5	49.2	50.8
82426	GREYBULL	95.1	95.0	0.3	0.3	0.5	0.5	5.3	5.5	6.0	6.1	6.1	6.7	5.8	22.1	29.9	14.8	2.5	77.3	42.8	49.7	50.3
82428	HYATTVILLE	93.5	93.6	0.0	0.0	0.0	0.0	5.6	5.5	6.4	6.4	7.3	6.4	4.6	18.3	31.2	17.4	1.8	76.1	45.3	50.5	49.5
82431	LOVELL	93.1	93.0	0.0	0.0	0.2	0.2	7.4	7.6	7.6	7.5	7.5	7.8	5.3	21.3	26.1	13.7	3.1	72.4	38.6	49.8	50.2
82432	MANDERSON	93.5	93.4	0.0	0.0	0.5	0.5	5.3	5.2	5.9	6.6	7.0	6.1	3.9	19.5	32.0	17.5	1.6	76.4	45.7	49.2	50.8
82433	MEETEETSE	95.2	94.6	0.0	0.0	0.2	0.2	3.3	3.7	4.7	4.9	7.2	7.9	2.7	23.8	34.2	12.4	2.1	77.6	44.1	50.9	49.1
82434	OTTO	87.1	87.4	0.9	0.8	0.0	0.0	13.8	14.3	11.8	8.4	10.1	9.2	5.0	21.8	18.5	12.6	2.5	63.0	31.3	48.7	51.3
82435	POWELL	95.8	95.2	0.1	0.1	0.4	0.6	5.9	6.7	5.9	6.0	6.0	8.0	7.0	23.4	27.8	13.2	2.7	78.3	39.3	48.2	51.8
82441	SHELL	93.3	93.4	0.3	0.3	0.7	0.7	5.7	5.6	5.3	6.3	6.3	6.6	3.0	20.6	35.2	15.0	1.7	77.7	45.9	52.2	47.8
82442	TEN SLEEP	92.5	91.4	0.0	0.0	0.4	0.5	7.1	8.2	4.4	6.2	7.3	7.4	1.7	20.9	35.8	13.9	2.4	77.2	46.1	52.9	47.1
82443	THERMOPOLIS	96.0	95.5	0.3	0.4	0.2	0.3	2.4	2.8	4.7	4.8	5.0	5.4	5.7	19.2	32.1	19.6	3.4	81.9	48.5	47.5	52.5
82501	RIVERTON	76.7	74.5	0.1	0.1	0.3	0.4	5.8	6.3	7.2	7.3	7.2	7.3	6.2	24.5	27.0	11.6	1.8	74.0	36.6	49.1	50.9
82510	ARAPAHOE	25.8	23.8	0.0	0.0	0.0	0.0	4.7	3.8	9.6	10.1	10.1	10.9	7.1	21.3	23.5	6.3	1.1	64.5	27.1	51.1	48.9
82512	CROWHEART	57.6	53.3	0.0	0.0	0.4	0.4	2.0	2.3	5.4	5.4	7.7	8.8	4.2	19.5	35.6	10.7	2.7	75.9	44.5	56.7	43.3
82513	DUBOIS	95.7	95.2	0.1	0.1	0.2	0.2	1.2	1.4	3.6	3.8	4.4	4.8	3.7	18.8	39.7	19.6	1.6	85.3	51.0	50.6	49.4
82514	FORT WASHAKIE	9.5	8.1	0.1	0.1	0.0	0.0	2.8	2.5	9.6	9.6	9.1	9.4	7.4	24.8	21.5	7.7	1.1	66.0	28.4	49.3	50.7
82516	KINNEAR	75.1	72.5	0.0	0.0	0.0	0.0	2.5	3.1	4.4	5.1	6.4	7.5	3.7	18.6	36.3	15.9	2.0	79.7	47.5	50.8	49.2
82520	LANDER	77.9	76.5	0.1	0.1	0.4	0.5	3.2	3.5	5.9	6.1	6.5	7.0	6.1	22.7	30.3	13.4	2.0	77.1	41.8	49.2	50.8
82523	PAVILLION	89.2	87.8	0.1	0.1	0.1	0.1	2.5	2.9	5.7	6.8	7.2	6.9	3.9	21.4	34.3	12.4	1.3	76.0	43.3	52.7	47.3
82601	CASPER	92.4	91.4	1.3	1.4	0.5	0.7	6.4	7.3	6.8	6.4	6.2	7.2	7.4	27.0	25.8	10.9	2.3	76.7	35.8	49.2	50.8
82604	CASPER	95.7	95.2	0.4	0.4	0.3	0.4	3.4	4.0	6.3	6.4	6.7	7.0	5.9	25.7	28.5	11.7	1.7	76.3	39.0	49.7	50.3
82609	CASPER	94.6	93.9	0.7	0.7	0.8	1.1	4.9	5.5	6.0	6.3	6.5	7.1	7.3	24.5	29.1	12.0	1.3	77.1	38.7	48.7	51.3
82620	ALCOVA	100.0	94.4	0.0	0.0	0.0	0.0	3.7	0.0	5.6	5.6	5.6	5.6	5.6	27.8	36.1	8.3	0.0	77.8	42.5	55.6	44.4
82633	DOUGLAS	94.7	93.9	0.1	0.1	0.2	0.3	6.1	7.0	6.5	7.1	7.6	7.2	5.3	25.1	29.9	9.8	1.5	73.9	38.5	49.3	50.7
82636	EVANSVILLE	92.4	91.4	0.8	0.9	0.2	0.2	6.2	7.2	7.9	7.6	7.3	7.2	6.8	28.3	26.6	7.8	0.6	72.9	33.5	48.9	51.1
82637	GLENROCK	94.8	94.2	0.3	0.3	0.4	0.5	4.2	4.9	6.1	6.5	6.8	7.3	6.0	22.7	32.5	11.1	1.1	75.8	41.1	50.4	49.6
82639	KAYCEE	97.9	97.7	0.0	0.0	0.1	0.1	2.6	3.0	4.9	5.3	6.3	6.6	4.1	23.3	34.0	14.1	1.4	79.2	44.6	51.4	48.6
82642	LYSITE	94.1	93.5	0.0	0.0	1.0	0.9	2.9	3.7	4.7	5.6	7.5	8.4	3.7	20.6	34.6	13.1	1.9	76.6	44.7	50.5	49.5
82643	MIDWEST	95.5	95.2	0.3	0.3	0.2	0.2	2.2	2.3	5.7	6.2	6.7	6.7	5.9	24.7	34.1	9.3	0.8	77.4	41.3	51.2	48.8
82649	SHOSHONI	92.9	91.6	0.1	0.1	0.7	1.1	2.9	3.4	4.7	5.5	7.2	8.3	3.6	21.1	35.7	12.6	1.4	76.8	44.8	50.7	49.3
82701	NEWCASTLE	95.7	95.2	0.1	0.2	0.2	0.3	2.1	2.5	5.3	5.5	6.1	6.6	5.4	24.1	31.1	13.3	2.7	79.1	42.9	50.7	49.3
82710	ALADDIN	98.7	98.4	0.0	0.0	0.0	0.0	0.9	0.8	5.7	5.7	6.5	7.7	4.5	22.3	32.4	13.4	2.0	76.9	43.4	51.4	48.6
82712	BEULAH	98.2	97.9	0.0	0.0	0.0	0.0	0.6	0.5	5.3	5.9	6.4	6.4	4.3	21.3	30.9	18.1	1.6	77.1	45.4	51.1	48.9
82714	DEVILS TOWER	97.4	97.8	0.0	0.0	0.0	0.0	1.7	1.5	5.2	5.2	8.2	8.2	2.2	21.6	35.1	11.9	2.2	75.4	44.5	53.7	46.3
82715	FOUR CORNERS	97.1	97.3	0.0	0.0	0.0	0.0	2.9	2.7	5.4	5.4	5.4	8.1	2.7	27.0	37.8	8.1	0.0	81.1	43.1	59.5	40.5
82716	GILLETTE	95.6	95.1	0.2	0.2	0.5	0.6	3.9	4.5	7.4	7.1	6.9	6.9	6.8	29.1	27.3	7.5	1.0	74.4	34.1	51.2	48.8
82718	GILLETTE	96.3	95.7	0.1	0.1	0.4	0.5	3.3	3.8	7.4	7.4	7.7	7.9	7.2	28.1	29.0	4.9	0.3	72.4	33.2	50.9	49.1
82720	HULETT	98.4	98.3	0.2	0.2	0.1	0.2	0.9	1.1	5.4	5.9	6.7	7.9	4.4	22.5	32.1	13.3	1.8	76.5	43.0	51.6	48.4
82721	MOORCROFT	98.0	97.8	0.0	0.0	0.0	0.0	1.4	1.6	6.1	6.3	7.5	7.1	4.9	25.1	31.8	10.0	1.4	75.5	39.9	51.8	48.2
82723	OSAGE	96.3	96.5	0.4	0.4	0.0	0.0	2.5	2.3	3.9	4.3	6.2	8.2	4.7	25.3	35.4	10.9	1.2	80.9	43.6	56.0	44.0
82725	RECLUSE	100.0	98.9	0.0	0.0	0.0	0.0	1.0	2.2	4.3	5.4	6.5	6.5	4.3	26.9	35.5	10.8	0.0	79.6	42.1	48.4	51.6
	WYOMING	92.1	91.2	0.8	0.8	0.6	0.8	6.4	7.2	6.3	6.2	6.4	7.3	7.2	25.6	28.6	10.8	1.7	76.8	37.8	50.2	49.8
	UNITED STATES	75.1	72.0	12.3	12.7	3.8	4.6	12.5	15.7	6.8	6.7	6.6	7.1	6.9	27.0	26.0	10.9	1.9	75.7	36.9	49.2	50.8

ZIP CODE #	POST OFFICE NAME	2009 Per Capita Income	2009 HH Income Base	2009 Household Income Distribution (%): Less than $25,000	$25,000 to $49,999	$50,000 to $99,999	$100,000 to $149,999	$150,000 or More	Median Household Income: 2009	2014	2009 National Centile	2009 State Centile	2009 Home Value Base	2009 Home Value Distribution (%): Less than $50,000	$50,000 to $89,999	$90,000 to $174,999	$175,000 to $399,999	$400,000 or More	2009 Median Home Value
82001	CHEYENNE	23575	14513	23.1	30.8	38.2	5.8	2.1	46280	50036	52	66	8786	5.2	3.6	56.2	34.3	0.7	156335
82005	FT WARREN AFB	15435	164	4.3	59.1	32.3	1.2	3.0	43902	46141	45	49	0	0.0	0.0	0.0	0.0	0.0	0
82007	CHEYENNE	19809	7129	24.8	34.1	34.9	4.8	1.5	42009	45941	39	41	5036	23.1	14.6	47.7	14.0	0.7	109982
82009	CHEYENNE	32699	12147	11.1	19.6	45.0	16.4	7.8	71385	72730	88	97	9468	2.9	1.8	20.9	65.1	9.3	220594
82050	ALBIN	21268	142	19.0	32.4	42.3	4.2	2.1	48466	51325	58	71	104	16.3	16.3	33.7	23.1	10.6	117857
82051	BOSLER	21640	70	40.0	21.4	24.3	8.6	5.7	35000	40000	18	14	47	8.5	14.9	17.0	23.4	36.2	243750
82052	BUFORD	22602	20	25.0	30.0	35.0	5.0	5.0	45000	50947	48	57	15	0.0	0.0	6.7	66.7	26.7	287500
82053	BURNS	20266	451	18.2	32.6	42.6	4.9	1.8	49135	51755	59	74	343	13.1	15.5	31.2	31.5	8.7	135776
82054	CARPENTER	17804	328	22.3	32.9	37.2	5.2	2.4	44773	48858	48	55	263	10.3	11.8	36.1	38.8	3.0	150568
82055	CENTENNIAL	26265	141	38.3	22.7	26.2	7.8	5.0	37372	38659	25	19	95	7.4	11.6	16.8	25.3	38.9	259375
82058	GARRETT	22210	44	40.9	20.5	25.0	9.1	4.5	35000	40000	18	14	29	3.4	10.3	17.2	24.1	44.8	287500
82063	JELM	38617	45	20.0	26.7	42.2	4.4	6.7	52087	53262	66	81	34	0.0	0.0	11.8	58.8	29.4	283333
82070	LARAMIE	23619	7191	33.8	25.8	30.5	6.8	3.1	39538	42924	31	26	3957	7.2	3.7	22.4	58.8	7.9	205813
82072	LARAMIE	21807	6332	37.6	27.1	26.0	6.5	2.7	34858	35341	17	10	2870	13.6	3.4	27.0	47.7	8.3	191259
82081	MERIDEN	27838	6	0.0	0.0	66.7	33.3	0.0	75000	83887	89	98	5	0.0	0.0	0.0	100.0	0.0	275000
82082	PINE BLUFFS	20241	716	27.4	33.4	32.7	2.9	3.6	41715	44535	38	36	531	11.7	11.5	51.2	23.2	2.4	128472
82083	ROCK RIVER	19984	164	39.0	23.2	25.6	7.3	4.9	35000	40000	18	14	111	12.6	14.4	20.7	21.6	30.6	195833
82084	TIE SIDING	26313	18	22.2	27.8	38.9	5.6	5.6	50000	51328	61	76	13	0.0	0.0	7.7	61.5	30.8	275000
82190	YELLOWSTONE NATIONAL	37683	327	8.6	29.1	45.9	10.4	6.1	60475	57884	78	93	16	75.0	0.0	0.0	25.0	0.0	30000
82201	WHEATLAND	22789	2719	25.3	31.6	34.2	6.2	2.8	44095	45602	46	51	2084	12.4	13.1	37.0	30.3	7.1	154467
82210	CHUGWATER	19791	146	31.5	30.8	26.0	5.5	6.2	40811	41606	35	31	114	6.1	21.9	40.4	25.4	6.1	146250
82212	FORT LARAMIE	26875	162	32.7	23.5	36.4	4.3	3.1	43902	45000	45	49	120	10.0	20.0	27.5	29.2	13.3	133333
82213	GLENDO	19477	240	43.3	30.0	19.2	3.3	4.2	27496	28004	5	4	183	19.7	23.0	25.7	24.0	7.7	115833
82214	GUERNSEY	19887	528	33.1	30.1	32.6	3.0	1.1	35789	37323	20	16	380	18.7	21.8	40.0	15.3	4.2	108772
82215	HARTVILLE	18311	59	44.1	30.5	18.6	3.4	3.4	27238	27257	5	3	45	17.8	24.4	26.7	22.2	8.9	115625
82217	HAWK SPRINGS	17538	68	36.8	25.0	32.4	5.9	0.0	35000	35558	18	14	49	0.0	14.3	26.5	24.5	34.7	255000
82219	JAY EM	21425	169	32.0	23.7	37.3	4.1	3.0	44721	45613	47	54	125	9.6	20.0	28.0	28.8	13.6	133929
82221	LAGRANGE	14754	146	35.6	26.7	32.9	4.8	0.0	35646	36002	20	14	105	1.9	13.3	27.6	22.9	34.3	245000
82222	LANCE CREEK	18467	91	35.2	33.0	23.1	7.7	1.1	34590	34188	17	9	67	16.4	14.9	13.4	19.4	35.8	196875
82223	LINGLE	21789	313	23.6	34.2	35.8	2.9	3.5	43718	44122	44	48	224	7.1	9.4	41.5	38.4	3.6	156250
82224	LOST SPRINGS	0	0	0.0	0.0	0.0	0.0	0.0	0	0	0	0	0	0.0	0.0	0.0	0.0	0.0	0
82225	LUSK	21295	836	33.7	32.4	25.4	6.1	2.4	37644	38233	26	20	607	15.5	22.6	33.9	17.1	10.9	112946
82227	MANVILLE	20607	76	35.5	32.9	22.4	7.9	1.3	34056	35734	16	9	56	12.5	12.5	14.3	16.1	44.6	275000
82229	SHAWNEE	27131	54	13.0	27.8	44.4	13.0	1.9	60000	55932	77	92	46	6.5	4.3	32.6	34.8	21.7	200000
82240	TORRINGTON	21191	3918	35.8	24.7	32.3	5.0	2.2	39773	41474	32	26	2755	13.9	14.5	42.4	24.2	4.9	131635
82242	VAN TASSELL	0	0	0.0	0.0	0.0	0.0	0.0	0	0	0	0	0	0.0	0.0	0.0	0.0	0.0	0
82243	VETERAN	17486	61	34.4	29.5	31.1	4.9	0.0	38655	41134	29	22	42	0.0	31.0	23.8	26.2	19.0	166667
82244	YODER	18633	285	35.8	27.0	31.6	4.9	0.7	35752	36656	20	16	205	3.9	14.1	27.3	22.9	31.7	212500
82301	RAWLINS	22072	3698	27.0	27.6	35.8	7.1	2.5	45155	47146	49	58	2525	14.2	15.0	43.6	24.4	2.8	131312
82310	JEFFREY CITY	25149	79	13.9	38.0	36.7	8.9	2.5	48003	48631	57	70	62	16.1	11.3	22.6	32.3	17.7	175000
82321	BAGGS	29324	223	31.8	30.5	33.6	3.1	0.9	40805	43448	35	31	171	19.3	18.1	34.5	21.6	6.4	116848
82322	BAIROIL	24457	59	18.6	27.1	47.5	6.8	0.0	53096	58000	68	84	47	23.4	17.0	31.9	17.0	10.6	108929
82323	DIXON	31264	127	31.5	30.7	32.3	3.9	1.6	40846	43307	35	32	98	20.4	18.4	32.7	22.4	6.1	115909
82325	ENCAMPMENT	25681	450	28.4	26.4	37.6	6.0	1.6	44759	47110	48	54	332	12.7	3.0	36.4	37.0	10.8	171983
82327	HANNA	20916	596	33.4	27.9	29.4	5.9	3.5	37219	40677	24	19	432	22.5	28.5	34.5	11.8	2.8	88947
82329	MEDICINE BOW	21470	142	26.1	40.8	30.3	2.1	0.7	35000	36905	18	14	106	26.4	42.5	26.4	4.7	0.0	69000
82331	SARATOGA	24969	1095	26.9	31.0	34.6	4.7	2.8	43178	45416	43	45	797	9.5	7.8	35.9	36.0	10.8	170511
82332	SAVERY	29275	43	30.2	30.2	37.2	2.3	0.0	42339	43191	40	42	33	18.2	21.2	30.3	24.2	6.1	120833
82334	SINCLAIR	24668	186	21.5	23.7	44.1	8.1	2.7	52945	52873	68	83	154	11.7	20.8	51.9	14.9	0.6	119565
82336	WAMSUTTER	26662	128	19.5	25.8	44.5	5.5	4.7	56303	57402	73	89	79	21.5	7.6	34.2	20.3	16.5	153125
82401	WORLAND	23070	2924	27.9	29.0	32.0	6.4	4.7	44053	44522	46	50	2160	8.5	12.2	48.8	25.7	4.9	138071
82410	BASIN	20962	741	29.1	31.7	31.8	5.1	2.2	41643	43262	38	36	558	14.7	20.3	35.7	26.7	2.7	121875
82411	BURLINGTON	13238	182	34.1	34.1	25.3	3.8	2.7	33734	35508	15	7	132	18.9	18.2	34.8	19.7	8.3	122917
82414	CODY	24879	6460	24.3	30.4	35.0	7.1	3.2	46203	47679	52	66	4661	6.5	3.2	22.1	52.0	16.2	225962
82421	DEAVER	20143	250	24.4	34.8	34.0	4.8	2.0	42787	45000	42	44	201	16.9	13.9	37.3	26.9	5.0	133523
82426	GREYBULL	20213	1100	29.4	33.7	30.4	4.5	2.0	40000	41372	33	29	803	14.2	16.6	40.0	19.4	9.8	127652
82428	HYATTVILLE	18349	49	36.7	34.7	24.5	2.0	2.0	33637	35000	15	6	35	11.4	11.4	34.3	40.0	2.9	154167
82431	LOVELL	17811	1767	28.9	32.8	32.4	4.6	1.4	41542	43220	38	35	1336	12.7	19.5	38.7	25.9	3.1	123705
82432	MANDERSON	18442	172	33.7	34.9	23.8	3.5	4.1	35679	36964	20	15	124	14.5	12.1	29.0	38.7	5.6	157500
82433	MEETEETSE	20317	425	27.8	41.9	22.4	7.5	0.5	38137	40382	27	21	304	7.6	11.5	31.6	32.6	16.8	173529
82434	OTTO	12585	33	33.3	33.3	27.3	3.0	3.0	34047	34047	16	8	24	12.5	20.8	41.7	16.7	8.3	130000
82435	POWELL	21372	4502	28.0	30.5	33.7	5.3	2.6	42689	45283	41	44	3298	6.5	5.4	32.1	46.2	9.6	195293
82441	SHELL	21682	134	31.3	35.8	25.4	4.5	3.0	36648	37515	22	18	99	10.1	9.1	28.3	36.4	16.2	185417
82442	TEN SLEEP	23163	353	30.6	34.3	26.1	6.5	2.5	39415	40902	31	24	237	9.7	8.9	20.3	41.8	19.4	198661
82443	THERMOPOLIS	22230	2097	32.5	30.1	28.8	7.0	1.7	38232	38393	27	21	1436	12.3	13.1	42.8	22.4	9.5	135746
82501	RIVERTON	19856	7407	30.8	29.8	31.9	4.8	2.6	41099	43163	36	34	5363	13.4	8.9	36.3	33.5	8.0	160676
82510	ARAPAHOE	8695	93	45.2	33.3	18.3	3.2	0.0	28021	30000	6	4	71	26.8	16.9	32.4	18.3	5.6	101563
82512	CROWHEART	26064	104	32.7	21.2	28.8	9.6	7.7	45921	45974	51	64	75	4.0	12.0	17.3	22.7	44.0	248077
82513	DUBOIS	24893	907	26.7	35.6	30.5	3.4	3.7	40286	41633	34	29	634	5.5	7.9	24.3	34.7	27.6	248214
82514	FORT WASHAKIE	11291	315	48.3	31.1	16.8	3.2	0.6	25958	26639	4	2	211	23.2	13.7	36.0	21.3	5.7	121500
82516	KINNEAR	20185	116	37.1	28.4	25.0	5.2	4.3	36301	36304	21	17	92	15.2	9.8	22.8	35.9	16.3	178846
82520	LANDER	22050	5145	27.4	31.2	31.7	6.8	2.9	41885	44657	39	40	3739	9.1	8.1	30.5	40.8	11.5	180977
82523	PAVILLION	22349	358	30.2	33.0	28.8	4.7	3.4	40437	41612	34	30	290	10.7	13.4	21.0	33.4	21.4	192500
82601	CASPER	22665	10729	28.1	30.5	32.1	6.8	2.5	41866	45429	39	39	6611	7.6	11.6	43.0	33.6	4.3	155929
82604	CASPER	24738	10993	19.1	29.1	39.4	8.9	3.5	51494	53729	65	79	8636	6.9	7.4	40.8	39.2	5.7	167153
82609	CASPER	29846	6208	17.1	25.5	39.6	11.2	6.6	57947	60482	75	91	4215	2.4	3.1	31.3	55.0	8.2	200430
82620	ALCOVA	30542	18	16.7	27.8	50.0	5.6	0.0	54495	52140	70	86	15	0.0	0.0	20.0	40.0	40.0	350000
82633	DOUGLAS	22678	3534	26.9	23.5	39.1	8.5	2.0	49537	50417	60	75	2598	9.3	8.6	34.3	40.9	7.0	170965
82636	EVANSVILLE	18096	1550	30.4	33.0	30.3	4.5	1.8	39939	42560	32	27	1020	19.2	15.6	35.9	21.9	7.5	129676
82637	GLENROCK	21876	1783	27.0	26.4	37.6	7.3	1.7	46978	48483	54	68	1342	6.4	8.0	47.9	29.0	8.6	157851
82639	KAYCEE	23909	384	24.2	27.9	38.0	5.2	4.7	47770	48688	56	69	292	3.8	5.5	19.9	46.2	24.7	240196
82642	LYSITE	26442	49	16.3	38.8	34.7	8.2	2.0	45756	47338	51	61	38	15.8	13.2	23.7	28.9	18.4	166667
82643	MIDWEST	21198	259	23.9	27.8	40.2	6.6	1.5	48864	50490	59	73	212	30.2	19.8	15.1	29.2	5.7	90000
82649	SHOSHONI	22766	418	19.4	35.2	35.6	7.2	2.6	45621	47046	50	60	333	12.6	10.8	21.0	37.8	17.7	204630
82701	NEWCASTLE	20851	2173	29.5	32.7	29.6	6.4	1.8	39451	40167	31	25	1660	18.0	17.2	36.2	23.0	5.5	121585
82710	ALADDIN	17557	105	40.0	31.4	22.9	3.8	1.9	31371	31856	10	6	83	20.5	14.5	27.7	15.7	21.7	143056
82712	BEULAH	25253	93	28.0	26.9	35.5	7.5	2.2	42386	42363	41	43	74	5.4	1.4	17.6	55.4	20.3	260526
82714	DEVILS TOWER	22983	57	29.8	17.5	38.6	12.3	1.8	51531	49438	65	80	50	6.0	2.0	28.0	40.0	24.0	230000
82715	FOUR CORNERS	38099	24	25.0	29.2	33.3	8.3	4.2	45000	38610	48	57	20	5.0	15.0	25.0	40.0	15.0	200000
82716	GILLETTE	23957	7363	20.7	24.8	43.6	8.4	2.5	54184	55460	70	86	4894	14.8	7.8	20.1	50.2	7.1	186917
82718	GILLETTE	27592	7257	10.2	19.1	49.9	16.1	4.7	69260	69285	86	96	5776	4.7	4.1	20.7	57.6	13.1	227849
82720	HULETT	17113	492	41.5	30.3	23.2	3.0	2.0	30370	32466	9	5	389	20.3	13.1	27.5	16.7	22.4	148438
82721	MOORCROFT	21265	1149	27.0	25.4	37.4	8.4	1.8	47813	47170	56	69	942	12.0	8.3	29.3	37.4	13.1	176408
82723	OSAGE	29859	130	26.9	27.7	33.1	9.2	3.1	41884	42380	39	39	111	15.3	15.3	22.5	30.6	16.2	167045
82725	RECLUSE	31650	45	13.3	24.4	48.9	13.3	0.0	57433	58126	75	90	37	10.8	8.1	13.5	54.1	13.5	225000
	WYOMING	24721		23.6	27.4	36.9	8.4	3.8	48927	50551				9.1	7.6	32.0	40.7	10.5	178177
	UNITED STATES	27277		20.9	24.4	35.3	11.7	7.6	54719	56938				9.3	13.1	31.6	32.6	13.5	162279

ZIP CODE #	POST OFFICE NAME	FINANCIAL SERVICES: Auto Loan	FINANCIAL SERVICES: Home Loan	FINANCIAL SERVICES: Invest-ments	FINANCIAL SERVICES: Retire-ment Plans	THE HOME: Home Improvements: Home Repair	THE HOME: Home Improvements: Lawn & Garden	THE HOME: Furnishings: Comput-ers & Hard-ware-Personal	THE HOME: Furnishings: Major Appli-ances	THE HOME: Furnishings: TV, Radio, Sound Equip-ment	THE HOME: Furnishings: Furni-ture	ENTERTAINMENT: Dine out/ Carry out	ENTERTAINMENT: Sports Equip-ment	ENTERTAINMENT: Fees & Tickets	ENTERTAINMENT: Toys & Games	ENTERTAINMENT: Travel	ENTERTAINMENT: Cable TV	PERSONAL: Apparel & Services	PERSONAL: Auto Repairs	PERSONAL: Health Insur-ance	PERSONAL: Pets & Supplies
82001	CHEYENNE	78	72	65	73	70	72	78	74	78	76	78	58	74	79	73	78	54	76	76	88
82005	FT WARREN AFB	92	48	36	56	43	41	87	60	82	81	86	60	66	98	63	75	60	77	54	73
82007	CHEYENNE	76	71	62	69	68	71	72	71	72	72	72	54	68	75	67	73	50	72	72	85
82009	CHEYENNE	111	127	124	128	127	123	115	119	113	118	114	90	124	113	123	112	80	115	117	137
82050	ALBIN	96	66	106	66	69	102	74	91	77	60	76	76	54	75	73	84	49	85	97	113
82051	BOSLER	86	69	111	68	76	91	69	88	72	65	71	64	60	69	75	77	47	81	87	102
82052	BUFORD	92	75	115	73	81	96	74	93	78	70	77	68	65	74	80	82	51	86	92	108
82053	BURNS	92	72	99	72	74	98	75	89	77	65	76	73	61	76	76	82	51	84	93	109
82054	CARPENTER	83	75	86	76	75	90	73	83	74	67	74	67	67	74	75	77	50	79	85	100
82055	CENTENNIAL	87	70	112	69	76	92	70	89	73	65	72	65	60	69	76	78	48	82	87	103
82058	GARRETT	86	69	111	68	76	91	69	87	72	64	71	64	60	68	75	77	47	81	86	101
82063	JELM	114	92	148	90	101	121	92	117	96	86	95	85	80	91	99	102	63	108	115	135
82070	LARAMIE	77	66	64	68	65	67	80	70	76	74	77	57	71	77	70	76	54	75	71	85
82072	LARAMIE	70	52	50	56	51	54	84	60	74	69	75	53	65	74	62	72	53	70	61	75
82081	MERIDEN	122	151	155	156	155	143	129	136	123	137	125	101	147	123	144	121	89	129	129	156
82082	PINE BLUFFS	89	61	97	61	64	93	68	84	70	55	70	70	50	69	67	77	45	79	89	103
82083	ROCK RIVER	86	67	105	66	72	90	67	86	71	63	70	63	57	69	71	77	47	79	86	100
82084	TIE SIDING	98	78	126	77	86	103	78	99	82	73	81	73	68	78	85	87	54	92	98	115
82190	YELLOWSTONE NATIONAL	106	87	81	93	83	83	106	90	104	105	106	75	98	106	95	101	74	101	91	111
82201	WHEATLAND	88	70	87	70	72	92	73	86	78	66	76	66	62	77	72	84	51	80	91	102
82210	CHUGWATER	92	63	101	63	66	97	70	87	73	57	72	72	51	71	70	79	47	81	92	107
82212	FORT LARAMIE	92	73	118	72	81	97	73	93	77	69	76	68	64	73	80	82	50	86	92	108
82213	GLENDO	69	55	89	54	61	73	55	70	58	52	57	51	48	55	60	62	38	65	69	81
82214	GUERNSEY	78	56	81	55	59	79	58	73	64	54	63	55	46	63	57	70	41	67	76	87
82215	HARTVILLE	69	56	90	55	61	73	56	71	58	52	57	52	48	55	60	62	38	65	70	82
82217	HAWK SPRINGS	76	52	83	52	55	80	58	72	60	47	60	60	43	59	58	66	39	67	76	89
82219	JAY EM	92	73	118	72	80	97	73	93	77	69	76	68	63	73	79	82	50	86	92	108
82221	LAGRANGE	76	52	83	52	55	80	58	72	60	47	60	60	43	59	58	66	39	67	76	89
82222	LANCE CREEK	81	55	88	55	58	85	62	76	64	50	63	63	45	63	61	70	41	71	81	94
82223	LINGLE	93	64	102	64	67	98	71	88	74	58	73	73	52	73	71	81	48	83	93	109
82224	LOST SPRINGS	0	0	0	0	0	0	0	0	0	0	0	0	0	0	0	0	0	0	0	0
82225	LUSK	82	58	84	57	60	85	64	79	70	56	68	60	50	69	62	77	45	73	85	93
82227	MANVILLE	81	56	89	56	59	86	62	77	65	50	64	64	46	63	62	71	42	72	82	95
82229	SHAWNEE	110	88	109	90	91	117	92	108	95	79	93	85	77	95	91	102	62	100	113	129
82240	TORRINGTON	76	64	72	63	64	76	66	73	70	63	69	55	59	70	65	74	47	71	77	86
82242	VAN TASSELL	0	0	0	0	0	0	0	0	0	0	0	0	0	0	0	0	0	0	0	0
82243	VETERAN	79	54	87	54	57	83	60	75	63	49	62	62	44	61	60	68	40	70	79	92
82244	YODER	77	53	84	53	55	81	59	73	61	47	60	60	43	60	58	66	39	68	77	90
82301	RAWLINS	85	72	72	72	70	77	79	78	80	76	80	61	71	81	73	81	55	80	79	94
82310	JEFFREY CITY	96	77	124	75	84	101	77	97	80	72	79	71	66	76	83	85	53	90	96	113
82321	BAGGS	85	58	93	58	61	89	65	80	67	52	66	66	47	66	64	73	43	75	85	99
82322	BAIROIL	92	84	75	82	82	86	80	84	83	83	83	61	75	86	76	85	56	82	85	100
82323	DIXON	84	58	93	58	61	89	65	80	67	52	66	66	47	66	64	73	43	75	85	99
82325	ENCAMPMENT	87	69	112	68	76	92	69	88	73	65	72	64	60	69	75	77	48	81	87	102
82327	HANNA	86	62	89	60	65	88	64	81	71	60	69	60	52	70	64	77	46	74	84	96
82329	MEDICINE BOW	63	60	77	56	67	72	57	68	61	62	59	44	57	56	63	64	40	65	75	78
82331	SARATOGA	92	70	106	68	75	95	71	90	76	66	75	67	59	74	73	83	50	83	91	105
82332	SAVERY	85	58	93	58	61	89	65	80	67	52	66	66	47	66	64	73	43	75	85	99
82334	SINCLAIR	99	79	128	78	87	105	79	101	83	74	82	74	69	79	86	88	54	93	99	117
82336	WAMSUTTER	103	94	84	91	92	96	89	94	92	92	92	69	84	96	85	95	63	91	95	112
82401	WORLAND	86	76	83	75	77	91	76	85	81	72	79	63	70	80	76	86	54	82	91	100
82410	BASIN	74	70	79	68	71	84	66	76	71	63	70	55	64	70	69	76	48	72	84	89
82411	BURLINGTON	81	56	89	56	58	85	62	77	64	50	64	63	45	63	62	70	41	72	81	95
82414	CODY	89	78	92	78	81	92	78	88	81	76	80	65	72	81	79	85	55	84	91	103
82421	DEAVER	90	65	95	65	67	93	70	85	73	60	72	69	54	72	69	79	47	80	89	104
82426	GREYBULL	81	59	86	58	62	85	64	79	70	57	68	59	52	68	63	77	45	74	85	93
82428	HYATTVILLE	73	50	80	50	53	77	56	69	58	45	57	57	41	57	55	63	37	65	73	85
82431	LOVELL	80	61	80	61	63	84	64	78	69	57	67	59	53	68	63	75	45	72	82	92
82432	MANDERSON	84	58	92	58	61	89	64	80	67	52	66	66	47	66	64	73	43	75	85	98
82433	MEETEETSE	83	57	92	57	60	88	63	79	66	52	65	65	47	65	63	72	42	74	83	97
82434	OTTO	81	56	89	56	58	86	62	77	64	50	64	64	45	63	62	70	41	72	81	95
82435	POWELL	79	71	77	72	72	82	72	78	74	69	74	59	68	74	72	78	50	76	82	92
82441	SHELL	85	62	99	61	66	90	66	83	69	57	68	65	52	67	68	74	45	77	85	99
82442	TEN SLEEP	85	68	110	67	75	90	68	87	71	64	71	63	59	68	74	76	47	80	86	101
82443	THERMOPOLIS	76	64	81	64	68	78	67	75	69	64	68	56	60	68	67	73	46	73	78	88
82501	RIVERTON	77	70	72	70	69	78	71	75	73	69	72	57	66	73	69	75	49	73	78	89
82510	ARAPAHOE	63	42	62	40	42	62	45	56	51	42	50	44	34	51	42	56	33	53	59	69
82512	CROWHEART	117	80	128	80	84	123	89	111	93	72	92	92	65	91	89	101	60	104	117	137
82513	DUBOIS	86	69	111	68	75	91	69	87	72	64	71	64	60	68	74	77	47	81	86	101
82514	FORT WASHAKIE	51	43	36	45	39	47	47	45	51	47	51	35	45	52	43	53	35	48	50	57
82516	KINNEAR	92	64	98	63	67	95	69	87	74	59	73	69	52	73	68	81	48	80	91	105
82520	LANDER	87	71	89	71	74	88	74	84	78	71	77	63	66	77	74	83	52	81	88	100
82523	PAVILLION	93	64	102	64	67	98	71	89	74	58	73	73	52	73	71	81	48	83	94	109
82601	CASPER	75	69	65	70	67	73	76	72	77	73	77	56	72	77	71	79	53	75	78	87
82604	CASPER	91	90	87	89	88	93	86	90	87	86	87	68	85	88	86	89	60	88	91	106
82609	CASPER	99	103	95	104	101	102	101	99	101	101	101	76	104	101	102	101	71	100	102	117
82620	ALCOVA	100	80	129	79	88	105	80	101	84	75	83	74	69	79	86	89	55	94	100	118
82633	DOUGLAS	89	79	82	77	77	88	77	85	79	75	79	65	71	81	76	82	54	81	86	101
82636	EVANSVILLE	76	69	68	66	67	71	67	71	68	69	68	53	63	70	65	70	47	70	70	84
82637	GLENROCK	83	74	74	74	75	83	74	80	77	72	76	60	68	78	72	80	52	77	83	95
82639	KAYCEE	104	72	115	72	75	110	80	99	83	65	82	82	59	81	79	90	53	92	104	122
82642	LYSITE	96	77	124	76	85	102	77	98	81	72	80	72	67	77	84	86	53	90	97	114
82643	MIDWEST	85	78	69	75	76	80	73	78	76	76	76	57	70	79	70	78	52	75	78	92
82649	SHOSHONI	92	76	113	76	82	98	76	93	78	71	78	70	67	76	81	83	52	86	93	109
82701	NEWCASTLE	82	65	84	63	67	83	66	79	71	62	70	58	57	71	66	77	47	74	83	93
82710	ALADDIN	74	51	81	51	53	78	56	70	59	46	58	58	41	58	56	64	38	65	74	86
82712	BEULAH	90	62	99	62	65	95	69	86	72	56	71	71	50	70	69	78	46	80	90	105
82714	DEVILS TOWER	90	72	116	71	79	95	72	92	76	68	75	67	63	72	78	81	50	85	91	106
82715	FOUR CORNERS	94	75	121	74	83	99	75	96	79	70	78	70	65	75	81	84	52	88	94	111
82716	GILLETTE	91	87	76	86	83	84	86	85	86	88	87	65	83	89	82	86	60	85	85	101
82718	GILLETTE	113	117	100	115	112	106	109	108	106	114	107	84	110	111	107	103	75	106	101	126
82720	HULETT	74	51	81	51	53	78	57	70	59	46	58	58	42	58	56	64	38	66	74	86
82721	MOORCROFT	86	75	88	73	77	85	72	83	75	72	75	60	66	75	73	79	50	79	83	97
82723	OSAGE	93	75	121	73	82	99	75	95	78	70	77	69	65	74	81	83	51	88	94	110
82725	RECLUSE	91	103	88	106	100	101	92	95	90	92	91	74	98	93	97	90	63	92	94	112
	WYOMING	91	83	87	83	82	90	85	88	86	83	86	67	80	86	83	88	59	87	90	104
	UNITED STATES	100	100	100	100	100	100	100	100	100	100	100	100	100	100	100	100	100	100	100	100

82727-83414

ZIP CODE #	POST OFFICE NAME	COUNTY FIPS CODE	POPULATION 2000	POPULATION 2009	POPULATION 2014	2000-2009 ANNUAL RATE % Rate	2000-2009 ANNUAL RATE State Centile	HOUSEHOLDS 2000	HOUSEHOLDS 2009	HOUSEHOLDS 2014	HOUSEHOLDS % Annual Rate 2000-2009	HOUSEHOLDS 2009 Average HH Size	FAMILIES 2000	FAMILIES 2009	FAMILIES % Annual Rate 2000-2009
82727	ROZET	005	692	766	853	1.1	65	236	277	313	1.7	2.77	202	231	1.5
82729	SUNDANCE	011	2106	2366	2508	1.3	71	833	991	1067	1.9	2.29	583	670	1.5
82730	UPTON	045	1299	1315	1363	0.1	25	524	567	595	0.9	2.32	387	407	0.5
82731	WESTON	005	184	247	275	3.2	96	70	96	108	3.5	2.57	55	73	3.1
82732	WRIGHT	005	1441	1655	1857	1.5	79	506	612	695	2.1	2.70	410	481	1.7
82801	SHERIDAN	033	22333	23841	24706	0.7	53	9420	10426	10918	1.1	2.23	5856	6214	0.6
82831	ARVADA	033	120	137	147	1.4	76	54	65	70	2.0	2.11	38	44	1.6
82832	BANNER	033	1321	1528	1624	1.6	81	595	715	768	2.0	2.14	414	478	1.6
82834	BUFFALO	019	6253	7399	8061	1.8	86	2637	3252	3588	2.3	2.25	1759	2091	1.9
82835	CLEARMONT	033	401	451	476	1.3	71	169	199	212	1.8	2.27	117	132	1.3
82836	DAYTON	033	1045	1174	1244	1.3	71	416	492	527	1.8	2.36	286	323	1.3
82838	PARKMAN	033	291	327	346	1.3	71	109	129	138	1.8	2.50	75	85	1.4
82839	RANCHESTER	033	952	1053	1108	1.1	65	371	434	463	1.7	2.24	270	304	1.3
82842	STORY	033	134	153	162	1.4	76	51	61	65	2.0	2.51	37	42	1.4
82844	WOLF	033	31	35	37	1.3	71	12	14	15	1.7	2.43	8	9	1.3
82901	ROCK SPRINGS	037	23934	25973	27022	0.9	56	9240	10480	11056	1.4	2.43	6375	6997	1.0
82922	BONDURANT	035	204	269	311	3.0	94	99	135	158	3.4	1.94	70	92	3.0
82923	BOULDER	035	160	272	316	5.9	99	69	121	142	6.3	2.25	48	82	6.0
82925	CORA	035	82	162	187	7.6	100	41	81	95	7.6	1.95	29	55	7.2
82930	EVANSTON	041	13784	14310	14561	0.4	39	4770	5189	5350	0.9	2.69	3534	3737	0.6
82933	FORT BRIDGER	041	3224	3319	3384	0.3	36	1148	1267	1312	1.1	2.62	903	972	0.8
82935	GREEN RIVER	037	13019	13829	14322	0.7	53	4610	5145	5407	1.2	2.66	3530	3830	0.9
82936	LONETREE	041	35	36	37	0.3	36	11	12	13	0.9	3.00	8	9	1.3
82937	LYMAN	041	2699	2754	2804	0.2	33	894	978	1012	1.0	2.82	701	748	0.7
82938	MC KINNON	037	193	204	214	0.6	45	69	77	83	1.2	2.55	57	62	0.9
82941	PINEDALE	035	3113	4156	4818	3.2	96	1260	1756	2059	3.7	2.34	887	1195	3.3
83001	JACKSON	039	13940	15837	16898	1.4	76	5755	6710	7207	1.7	2.34	3125	3463	1.1
83011	KELLY	039	143	157	167	1.0	61	63	72	77	1.5	2.18	34	36	0.6
83012	MOOSE	039	267	293	312	1.0	61	129	148	158	1.5	1.98	67	72	0.8
83013	MORAN	039	298	327	348	1.0	61	147	168	180	1.5	1.95	76	82	0.8
83014	WILSON	039	3022	3548	3832	1.7	84	1329	1611	1752	2.1	2.19	754	872	1.6
83101	KEMMERER	023	3678	3787	3884	0.3	36	1465	1606	1671	1.0	2.33	981	1029	0.5
83110	AFTON	023	4086	4961	5421	2.1	89	1334	1708	1896	2.7	2.89	1051	1306	2.4
83111	AUBURN	023	409	508	559	2.4	92	127	165	184	2.9	3.08	107	136	2.6
83112	BEDFORD	023	394	481	530	2.2	90	126	167	187	3.1	2.86	99	127	2.7
83113	BIG PINEY	035	1920	2590	3025	3.3	97	719	1002	1182	3.7	2.58	544	739	3.4
83114	COKEVILLE	023	915	1082	1177	1.8	86	306	383	423	2.5	2.82	236	286	2.1
83115	DANIEL	035	441	616	713	3.7	99	183	267	313	4.2	2.25	129	182	3.8
83118	ETNA	023	1436	1727	1940	2.0	87	569	723	824	2.6	2.39	429	526	2.2
83120	FREEDOM	023	265	321	359	2.1	89	88	113	128	2.7	2.84	70	88	2.5
83122	GROVER	023	976	1159	1282	1.9	86	345	437	491	2.6	2.65	274	337	2.3
83123	LA BARGE	023	613	717	783	1.7	84	230	287	318	2.4	2.50	161	193	2.0
83126	SMOOT	023	318	384	421	2.1	89	104	131	146	2.5	2.93	86	106	2.3
83127	THAYNE	023	1477	2076	2308	3.7	99	571	865	977	4.6	2.39	452	666	4.3
83414	ALTA	039	400	461	494	1.5	79	141	169	183	2.0	2.72	98	114	1.6
	WYOMING					0.9					1.3	2.40			0.9
	UNITED STATES					1.0					1.1	2.59			0.9

#	POST OFFICE NAME	RACE (%) White 2000	White 2009	Black 2000	Black 2009	Asian/Pacific 2000	Asian/Pacific 2009	% Hispanic Origin 2000	% Hispanic Origin 2009	2009 AGE DISTRIBUTION (%) 0-4	5-9	10-14	15-19	20-24	25-44	45-64	65-84	85+	18+	MEDIAN AGE 2009	% 2009 Males	% 2009 Females
82727	ROZET	97.3	96.7	0.0	0.0	0.4	0.7	2.9	3.7	7.4	7.7	7.6	7.7	7.0	26.8	30.3	5.2	0.3	72.5	34.2	51.2	48.8
82729	SUNDANCE	97.1	96.9	0.0	0.0	0.1	0.2	0.6	0.6	4.8	5.3	5.9	6.9	4.5	20.5	31.4	17.2	3.5	78.7	46.3	49.5	50.5
82730	UPTON	96.8	96.5	0.0	0.0	0.2	0.3	1.7	1.8	5.6	6.3	6.2	5.2	5.7	20.0	35.1	13.7	2.1	78.7	45.6	49.8	50.2
82731	WESTON	97.3	96.4	0.0	0.0	0.0	0.0	2.7	3.6	7.7	7.7	7.7	7.7	5.7	27.1	28.7	6.9	0.8	72.1	35.4	51.0	49.0
82732	WRIGHT	97.5	97.2	0.0	0.0	0.1	0.2	2.7	3.2	5.5	5.9	6.3	7.6	7.7	26.8	34.3	5.7	0.3	77.9	37.9	52.2	47.8
82801	SHERIDAN	96.0	95.4	0.2	0.2	0.6	0.8	2.4	2.8	5.4	5.6	6.1	7.4	5.8	23.0	30.7	13.4	2.6	78.3	42.3	48.6	51.4
82831	ARVADA	96.7	96.4	0.0	0.0	0.0	0.7	1.7	1.5	3.6	5.1	5.1	5.8	3.6	22.6	39.4	13.1	1.5	81.8	47.5	49.6	50.4
82832	BANNER	98.5	98.4	0.1	0.1	0.2	0.2	1.5	1.8	3.5	4.1	4.6	5.2	3.7	18.4	40.2	18.6	1.7	84.7	51.4	52.4	47.6
82834	BUFFALO	96.9	96.6	0.1	0.1	0.1	0.1	2.0	2.3	4.9	5.3	5.7	6.3	4.4	20.4	33.0	17.2	2.9	80.1	47.3	49.1	50.9
82835	CLEARMONT	96.3	95.8	0.2	0.2	0.5	0.9	1.2	1.6	3.8	4.4	5.3	6.0	3.5	22.2	39.5	14.2	1.1	82.5	48.1	49.9	50.1
82836	DAYTON	94.8	94.3	0.1	0.1	0.3	0.4	3.1	3.5	4.4	5.7	8.1	10.0	2.4	22.3	34.0	11.6	1.5	74.5	43.3	49.7	50.3
82838	PARKMAN	94.8	94.2	0.0	0.0	0.3	0.3	3.1	3.4	4.6	5.8	8.0	10.1	2.4	22.3	33.6	11.6	1.5	74.6	43.1	49.8	50.2
82839	RANCHESTER	91.9	91.1	0.3	0.4	0.2	0.3	3.2	3.6	5.0	5.0	7.9	8.0	4.3	20.8	31.9	14.9	2.2	76.7	44.3	53.3	46.7
82842	STORY	97.8	98.0	0.0	0.0	0.0	0.0	1.5	2.0	3.9	4.6	5.2	6.5	3.3	19.6	39.2	15.7	2.0	82.4	48.8	51.0	49.0
82844	WOLF	96.7	91.4	0.0	0.0	0.0	0.0	3.3	2.9	5.7	5.7	5.7	11.4	2.9	22.9	34.3	11.4	0.0	71.4	41.3	51.4	48.6
82901	ROCK SPRINGS	91.6	90.5	1.0	1.0	0.9	1.2	9.0	10.2	6.8	6.6	6.6	7.5	7.2	27.1	28.3	8.6	1.3	75.6	35.2	50.0	50.0
82922	BONDURANT	98.0	97.8	0.0	0.4	0.0	0.0	2.0	2.2	4.5	4.8	5.6	5.2	3.7	19.3	39.0	15.6	2.2	81.0	48.9	49.1	50.9
82923	BOULDER	96.9	96.0	0.0	0.4	0.6	0.7	1.9	2.6	5.9	7.0	7.0	6.3	4.4	23.2	34.9	10.7	0.7	75.7	42.6	52.2	47.8
82925	CORA	97.6	98.1	0.0	0.0	0.0	0.0	1.2	1.9	4.3	4.9	5.6	4.9	3.7	19.1	40.1	15.4	1.9	81.5	49.3	50.6	49.4
82930	EVANSTON	92.9	91.8	0.1	0.2	0.4	0.6	6.6	7.7	8.8	8.0	7.8	8.0	8.0	27.5	24.7	6.3	0.8	70.2	30.4	50.3	49.7
82933	FORT BRIDGER	97.7	97.4	0.1	0.1	0.2	0.2	1.9	2.2	7.1	7.3	7.3	6.8	6.7	26.2	30.2	7.7	0.7	74.2	35.5	51.8	48.2
82935	GREEN RIVER	91.6	90.4	0.3	0.4	0.3	0.5	10.3	11.8	7.0	6.9	6.8	7.2	7.6	26.5	29.5	7.5	0.9	74.9	34.5	50.3	49.7
82936	LONETREE	100.0	100.0	0.0	0.0	0.0	0.0	2.9	0.0	5.6	5.6	5.6	5.6	5.6	22.2	41.7	8.3	0.0	80.6	45.0	50.0	50.0
82937	LYMAN	97.7	97.6	0.0	0.0	0.1	0.1	2.9	3.2	8.5	8.3	8.4	7.9	7.3	25.0	27.2	6.7	0.7	70.0	30.8	52.0	48.0
82938	MC KINNON	94.8	94.6	0.0	0.0	0.5	0.5	7.7	8.3	5.4	5.4	6.4	7.4	5.9	24.0	32.8	9.8	2.9	77.5	40.5	49.5	50.5
82941	PINEDALE	97.3	96.9	0.2	0.2	0.3	0.5	2.0	2.3	5.1	6.0	6.1	5.8	4.2	21.3	37.4	12.7	1.5	78.8	45.8	51.3	48.7
83001	JACKSON	92.4	91.2	0.2	0.2	0.6	0.8	8.1	9.3	5.3	4.7	5.2	5.2	8.2	36.8	27.2	6.6	1.0	81.7	35.5	53.2	46.8
83011	KELLY	97.2	96.8	0.0	0.0	0.7	1.3	1.4	1.9	4.5	4.5	4.5	4.5	7.0	28.7	34.4	10.8	1.3	83.4	42.3	49.7	50.3
83012	MOOSE	97.4	96.2	0.0	0.0	1.1	1.4	1.5	1.7	4.1	3.8	3.8	4.1	7.5	28.3	36.9	10.9	0.7	86.0	43.7	48.5	51.5
83013	MORAN	96.7	96.3	0.0	0.0	1.0	1.5	1.7	1.5	4.0	4.0	4.0	4.3	8.0	28.4	34.6	11.9	0.9	85.9	42.9	49.5	50.5
83014	WILSON	97.3	96.8	0.1	0.1	0.4	0.6	1.6	1.9	4.9	4.8	5.3	4.9	4.5	30.1	32.9	11.8	0.7	81.6	42.5	52.3	47.7
83101	KEMMERER	96.7	96.1	0.1	0.1	0.6	0.8	3.5	4.2	5.2	5.6	6.2	7.3	6.5	23.7	33.6	10.3	1.7	78.5	41.3	50.2	49.8
83110	AFTON	97.3	97.1	0.0	0.0	0.1	0.1	2.1	2.5	8.6	8.4	8.2	8.2	6.5	24.2	24.8	9.5	1.5	69.7	32.4	49.5	50.5
83111	AUBURN	97.1	96.7	0.0	0.0	0.2	0.2	2.0	2.4	8.3	8.3	7.9	7.7	7.5	25.8	25.2	8.3	1.2	70.9	31.1	51.4	48.6
83112	BEDFORD	97.2	97.1	0.0	0.0	0.3	0.2	1.3	1.2	6.7	8.5	8.7	9.8	5.0	21.2	26.2	12.7	1.2	69.2	37.9	51.4	48.6
83113	BIG PINEY	97.7	97.3	0.2	0.2	0.4	0.5	1.8	2.2	7.0	7.1	7.0	6.6	6.2	25.4	30.2	9.7	0.7	74.9	38.2	50.5	49.5
83114	COKEVILLE	97.3	97.0	0.3	0.4	0.2	0.3	1.6	1.9	8.5	7.9	9.2	10.4	4.0	18.5	28.9	10.1	2.6	67.2	38.0	50.6	49.4
83115	DANIEL	97.5	97.6	0.2	0.2	0.2	0.2	1.8	2.1	4.5	5.2	5.5	5.4	4.1	19.8	38.5	14.9	2.1	81.0	48.1	49.5	50.5
83118	ETNA	97.4	96.9	0.1	0.2	0.3	0.5	1.0	1.2	5.0	5.3	5.7	5.3	3.2	20.7	35.0	18.2	1.4	80.5	47.9	50.7	49.3
83120	FREEDOM	97.0	97.2	0.4	0.3	0.4	0.3	1.1	1.2	5.9	6.5	6.9	5.9	3.7	19.6	33.6	16.5	1.2	76.6	45.9	50.2	49.8
83122	GROVER	97.2	97.0	0.1	0.1	0.2	0.3	1.5	1.7	7.0	7.6	7.7	7.9	5.6	23.0	28.0	12.1	1.2	72.6	37.7	51.4	48.6
83123	LA BARGE	96.7	96.5	0.0	0.0	0.2	0.1	2.6	2.9	6.1	7.0	7.0	7.0	7.3	22.2	34.6	8.6	0.3	74.1	39.6	52.4	47.6
83126	SMOOT	97.5	97.1	0.0	0.0	0.0	0.0	2.2	2.3	9.4	8.6	8.6	9.6	8.1	23.4	24.2	7.3	0.8	67.2	28.4	49.0	51.0
83127	THAYNE	97.4	97.1	0.2	0.2	0.2	0.3	1.2	1.3	6.2	7.3	7.6	7.6	4.2	20.2	30.5	15.0	1.3	73.7	42.7	50.7	49.3
83414	ALTA	98.5	98.5	0.0	0.0	0.5	0.7	0.7	0.9	3.9	4.8	5.2	6.3	3.9	20.0	40.6	14.5	0.9	82.2	48.1	52.9	47.1
	WYOMING	92.1	91.2	0.8	0.8	0.6	0.8	6.4	7.2	6.3	6.2	6.4	7.3	7.2	25.6	28.6	10.8	1.7	76.8	37.8	50.2	49.8
	UNITED STATES	75.1	72.0	12.3	12.7	3.8	4.6	12.5	15.7	6.8	6.7	6.6	7.1	6.9	27.0	26.0	10.9	1.9	75.7	36.9	49.2	50.8

ZIP CODE				2009 HOUSEHOLD INCOME DISTRIBUTION (%)					MEDIAN HOUSEHOLD INCOME					2009 HOME VALUE DISTRIBUTION (%)					
#	POST OFFICE NAME	2009 Per Capita Income	2009 HH Income Base	Less than $25,000	$25,000 to $49,999	$50,000 to $99,999	$100,000 to $149,999	$150,000 or More	2009	2014	2009 National Centile	2009 State Centile	2009 Home Value Base	Less than $50,000	$50,000 to $89,999	$90,000 to $174,999	$175,000 to $399,999	$400,000 or More	2009 Median Home Value
82727	ROZET	26143	277	13.7	19.9	45.1	15.9	5.4	67875	68352	85	96	250	9.6	3.6	20.0	56.4	10.4	198864
82729	SUNDANCE	22990	991	25.1	28.7	36.0	8.1	2.1	45766	45229	51	61	776	7.0	6.1	29.0	45.0	13.0	193902
82730	UPTON	20659	567	30.0	30.5	32.5	5.1	1.9	39377	40077	31	23	458	17.9	13.8	34.5	30.8	3.1	132222
82731	WESTON	23188	96	19.8	28.1	42.7	7.3	2.1	51520	54096	65	79	81	19.8	8.6	17.3	40.7	13.6	183750
82732	WRIGHT	23139	612	12.6	25.8	53.3	6.2	2.1	61221	61012	79	94	452	11.9	7.5	29.2	42.5	8.8	177381
82801	SHERIDAN	25099	10426	28.6	29.1	31.4	7.3	3.6	43271	43979	43	46	7094	7.1	4.7	31.2	45.3	11.7	196478
82831	ARVADA	26933	65	23.1	27.7	38.5	10.8	0.0	49097	47327	59	74	50	2.0	6.0	22.0	48.0	22.0	250000
82832	BANNER	27195	715	32.2	25.3	29.5	6.3	6.7	39447	40000	31	24	557	3.2	9.9	13.5	44.9	28.5	272692
82834	BUFFALO	23731	3252	26.8	31.3	33.9	4.2	3.8	41851	43581	39	38	2403	7.4	3.5	21.1	56.3	11.8	231091
82835	CLEARMONT	24182	199	24.6	30.7	32.7	11.1	1.0	45204	45000	49	59	149	4.0	6.7	22.8	45.6	20.8	248438
82836	DAYTON	22273	492	24.4	35.0	32.3	6.3	2.0	41792	42592	39	37	340	4.7	4.7	32.4	45.0	13.2	193421
82838	PARKMAN	21041	129	24.0	34.9	34.1	6.2	0.8	42039	42336	39	41	89	4.5	4.5	32.6	43.8	14.6	193750
82839	RANCHESTER	24180	434	23.7	29.7	36.4	7.6	2.5	45769	45069	51	62	304	7.9	6.3	27.3	33.2	25.3	208333
82842	STORY	27452	61	24.6	26.2	32.8	8.2	8.2	48669	45766	58	72	48	0.0	6.3	10.4	47.9	35.4	322222
82844	WOLF	17371	14	28.6	35.7	35.7	0.0	0.0	40000	42343	33	29	10	0.0	0.0	30.0	60.0	10.0	216667
82901	ROCK SPRINGS	26025	10480	19.9	23.2	42.7	10.3	3.9	56922	57351	74	89	7798	12.8	8.3	28.5	44.5	5.8	175816
82922	BONDURANT	29242	135	23.7	28.9	37.8	5.2	4.4	46407	45820	53	67	101	0.0	3.0	9.9	49.5	37.6	340476
82923	BOULDER	25057	121	25.6	29.8	34.7	5.8	4.1	45321	46275	49	59	88	2.3	2.3	5.7	53.4	36.4	307692
82925	CORA	29135	81	24.7	29.6	37.0	4.9	3.7	44444	45966	47	52	60	0.0	1.7	8.3	51.7	38.3	350000
82930	EVANSTON	21503	5189	21.9	23.9	44.3	7.7	2.2	53366	54568	69	85	3701	8.7	7.6	43.3	37.0	3.4	160365
82933	FORT BRIDGER	22854	1267	17.0	25.7	47.0	8.8	1.5	57519	57255	75	91	1042	11.3	9.0	34.5	39.3	5.9	166319
82935	GREEN RIVER	26458	5145	15.1	21.0	46.1	12.9	4.9	64008	64342	82	94	3902	10.2	4.8	25.2	54.3	5.5	187649
82936	LONETREE	19343	12	25.0	25.0	41.7	8.3	0.0	45000	54580	48	57	10	10.0	0.0	30.0	60.0	0.0	200000
82937	LYMAN	20457	978	20.4	22.8	49.3	6.4	1.0	56019	55741	73	88	800	12.8	8.3	44.9	32.0	2.1	155521
82938	MC KINNON	28574	77	9.1	24.7	48.1	13.0	5.2	65885	64738	84	95	58	0.0	0.0	13.8	69.0	17.2	263636
82941	PINEDALE	24200	1756	24.8	29.1	36.4	5.5	4.1	45820	46455	51	63	1296	3.1	2.9	7.9	50.0	36.2	318265
83001	JACKSON	43115	6710	8.7	18.9	39.5	20.5	12.4	76757	77343	90	99	3639	3.3	1.9	3.0	24.9	66.9	512849
83011	KELLY	32028	72	22.2	22.2	40.3	11.1	4.2	55251	56304	72	87	26	0.0	3.8	3.8	15.4	76.9	666667
83012	MOOSE	32440	148	23.6	23.6	38.5	9.5	4.7	52298	53109	66	81	47	0.0	2.1	4.3	12.8	80.9	712500
83013	MORAN	32768	168	23.8	24.4	38.1	9.5	4.2	51493	52935	65	78	53	0.0	3.8	3.8	15.1	77.4	670455
83014	WILSON	71670	1611	7.8	12.0	34.3	16.4	29.5	90713	90937	95	100	1055	2.4	0.1	0.2	9.0	88.3	1000001
83101	KEMMERER	24854	1606	21.1	26.2	42.5	7.7	2.6	51431	51401	65	77	1232	8.0	12.1	40.6	37.9	1.5	159624
83110	AFTON	17099	1708	22.7	34.9	36.3	5.0	1.1	44491	46485	47	53	1393	4.5	2.4	25.1	55.1	12.9	215833
83111	AUBURN	14601	165	24.8	38.2	32.7	3.6	0.6	40962	43061	36	33	142	4.2	0.7	28.2	52.8	14.1	205263
83112	BEDFORD	18091	167	24.6	35.9	32.3	4.8	2.4	41453	43352	38	34	135	8.1	6.7	11.1	53.3	20.7	248611
83113	BIG PINEY	20846	1002	21.3	33.2	36.9	6.6	2.0	45963	46609	51	64	740	8.9	6.2	23.2	52.6	9.1	200355
83114	COKEVILLE	17471	383	23.5	36.8	33.2	5.7	0.8	43560	45302	44	47	318	4.1	12.9	29.2	49.7	4.1	179412
83115	DANIEL	25202	267	24.0	29.2	37.1	5.2	4.5	46055	46493	51	65	199	1.5	2.5	9.5	49.2	37.2	331081
83118	ETNA	25674	723	14.2	31.0	43.7	8.4	2.6	52405	52448	67	82	600	4.3	2.5	12.2	56.0	25.0	307407
83120	FREEDOM	22851	113	12.4	31.0	44.2	8.0	4.4	53126	52800	68	84	96	3.1	2.1	17.7	45.8	31.3	305263
83122	GROVER	19383	437	22.0	35.7	35.7	5.3	1.4	43331	45979	43	46	362	5.5	3.6	17.1	55.0	18.8	246809
83123	LA BARGE	20672	287	24.0	27.5	41.1	5.2	2.1	48014	49175	57	71	220	19.1	16.4	25.5	34.5	4.5	142647
83126	SMOOT	15234	131	25.2	35.1	36.6	3.1	0.0	44232	46301	46	51	117	0.9	0.9	29.1	51.3	17.9	221591
83127	THAYNE	25368	865	16.6	32.1	39.9	7.3	4.0	50605	50910	63	76	722	5.1	4.4	15.4	47.6	27.4	280128
83414	ALTA	53570	169	12.4	20.7	29.6	11.8	25.4	76230	72241	90	99	121	0.8	0.8	1.7	4.1	92.6	1000001
	WYOMING	24721		23.6	27.4	36.9	8.4	3.8	48927	50551				9.1	7.6	32.0	40.7	10.5	178177
	UNITED STATES	27277		20.9	24.4	35.3	11.7	7.6	54719	56938				9.3	13.1	31.6	32.6	13.5	162279

#	POST OFFICE NAME	FINANCIAL SERVICES: Auto Loan	FINANCIAL SERVICES: Home Loan	FINANCIAL SERVICES: Invest-ments	FINANCIAL SERVICES: Retire-ment Plans	THE HOME: Home Improvements: Home Repair	THE HOME: Home Improvements: Lawn & Garden	THE HOME: Furnishings: Comput-ers & Hard-ware-Personal	THE HOME: Furnishings: Major Appli-ances	THE HOME: Furnishings: TV, Radio, Sound Equip-ment	THE HOME: Furnishings: Furni-ture	ENTERTAINMENT: Dine out/ Carry out	ENTERTAINMENT: Sports Equip-ment	ENTERTAINMENT: Fees & Tickets	ENTERTAINMENT: Toys & Games	ENTERTAINMENT: Travel	ENTERTAINMENT: Cable TV	PERSONAL: Apparel & Services	PERSONAL: Auto Repairs	PERSONAL: Health Insur-ance	PERSONAL: Pets & Supplies
82727	ROZET	113	110	94	106	106	104	102	105	103	108	104	78	99	108	98	103	71	102	101	124
82729	SUNDANCE	87	72	85	74	74	93	74	86	76	64	75	68	63	77	74	82	50	80	90	102
82730	UPTON	85	61	88	59	64	87	63	80	70	58	68	60	50	69	62	77	45	73	83	95
82731	WESTON	93	89	78	87	87	90	83	88	85	86	86	65	80	89	81	87	58	85	88	104
82732	WRIGHT	100	92	82	89	90	94	87	92	90	91	90	67	82	94	83	93	61	89	92	110
82801	SHERIDAN	83	77	83	77	78	86	79	83	81	76	80	62	75	80	78	85	55	82	88	98
82831	ARVADA	97	74	105	74	76	103	78	94	80	66	80	77	62	79	79	86	52	88	98	114
82832	BANNER	97	77	124	76	84	103	78	99	81	72	80	73	67	77	84	87	53	91	98	115
82834	BUFFALO	86	71	103	69	77	92	72	88	76	69	74	64	64	72	76	80	50	82	91	102
82835	CLEARMONT	98	67	108	67	71	103	75	93	78	61	77	77	55	76	74	85	50	87	98	114
82836	DAYTON	88	70	114	69	77	93	70	90	74	66	73	65	61	70	76	79	48	83	88	104
82838	PARKMAN	88	71	114	69	77	93	71	90	74	66	73	65	61	70	76	79	48	83	89	104
82839	RANCHESTER	93	74	120	73	82	98	74	95	78	70	77	69	64	74	81	83	51	87	93	110
82842	STORY	115	92	148	90	101	121	92	117	96	86	95	85	80	91	100	103	63	108	115	135
82844	WOLF	71	57	92	56	63	75	57	72	60	53	59	53	49	57	62	64	39	67	72	84
82901	ROCK SPRINGS	96	93	82	91	89	92	90	91	91	92	91	69	88	94	87	92	63	91	93	108
82922	BONDURANT	96	77	124	76	84	101	77	98	80	72	79	71	67	76	83	86	53	90	96	113
82923	BOULDER	94	75	121	74	83	99	75	96	79	71	78	70	65	75	82	84	52	88	94	111
82925	CORA	96	77	124	76	84	101	77	98	80	72	79	71	67	76	83	86	53	90	96	113
82930	EVANSTON	88	82	72	82	78	79	84	81	83	85	84	64	80	86	79	83	58	83	80	97
82933	FORT BRIDGER	96	88	78	85	86	90	83	88	86	87	86	64	79	90	79	89	59	85	88	105
82935	GREEN RIVER	106	105	92	104	101	102	101	102	100	103	101	78	99	104	98	100	70	100	100	120
82936	LONETREE	93	86	76	83	84	87	81	86	84	84	84	62	76	87	77	86	57	83	86	102
82937	LYMAN	92	85	75	82	83	87	80	85	83	83	83	62	76	87	76	85	57	82	85	101
82938	MC KINNON	103	116	100	120	113	114	104	108	102	104	103	84	111	105	110	102	72	104	107	127
82941	PINEDALE	95	76	123	75	83	100	76	97	79	71	79	70	66	75	82	85	52	89	95	112
83001	JACKSON	141	139	145	145	140	128	151	138	142	151	145	115	149	143	149	136	103	144	129	163
83011	KELLY	96	99	97	102	98	95	101	96	98	102	99	76	103	98	101	97	70	98	95	114
83012	MOOSE	89	90	86	92	88	87	93	87	91	93	92	69	94	91	91	90	65	90	89	105
83013	MORAN	88	90	85	92	88	87	92	87	91	92	91	69	93	91	91	90	64	89	88	104
83014	WILSON	203	243	294	247	268	219	233	236	207	246	207	186	250	199	259	193	152	226	201	263
83101	KEMMERER	94	83	81	80	82	91	80	88	84	81	84	64	74	87	77	88	57	84	90	104
83110	AFTON	78	71	68	72	71	80	69	76	71	66	70	57	64	73	68	74	48	71	78	89
83111	AUBURN	72	66	59	64	65	68	63	66	65	65	65	48	59	68	60	67	44	64	66	79
83112	BEDFORD	84	75	74	73	75	80	72	78	74	74	74	57	67	76	70	77	50	75	78	92
83113	BIG PINEY	87	79	75	76	78	83	75	81	78	77	77	59	70	80	72	80	53	78	81	96
83114	COKEVILLE	76	69	69	72	71	82	69	77	71	62	69	59	63	72	68	75	47	71	80	90
83115	DANIEL	96	77	124	75	84	101	77	97	80	72	79	71	66	76	83	85	53	90	96	113
83118	ETNA	102	82	132	81	90	108	82	104	86	77	85	76	71	81	89	91	56	96	103	121
83120	FREEDOM	108	87	137	86	95	113	87	109	91	82	90	80	76	87	93	97	60	101	108	127
83122	GROVER	83	73	81	71	74	81	70	79	73	71	73	58	65	74	70	76	49	75	79	93
83123	LA BARGE	83	76	67	74	74	78	72	76	75	75	75	55	68	78	68	77	51	74	76	90
83126	SMOOT	72	66	59	64	64	67	62	66	64	65	64	48	59	67	59	66	44	64	66	78
83127	THAYNE	100	84	115	82	89	102	82	99	86	80	85	72	73	84	86	90	57	93	98	115
83414	ALTA	243	195	315	192	214	257	195	248	204	183	202	181	169	194	211	218	134	229	245	287
	WYOMING	91	83	87	83	82	90	85	88	86	83	86	67	80	86	83	88	59	87	90	104
	UNITED STATES	100	100	100	100	100	100	100	100	100	100	100	100	100	100	100	100	100	100	100	100

State Summary Data

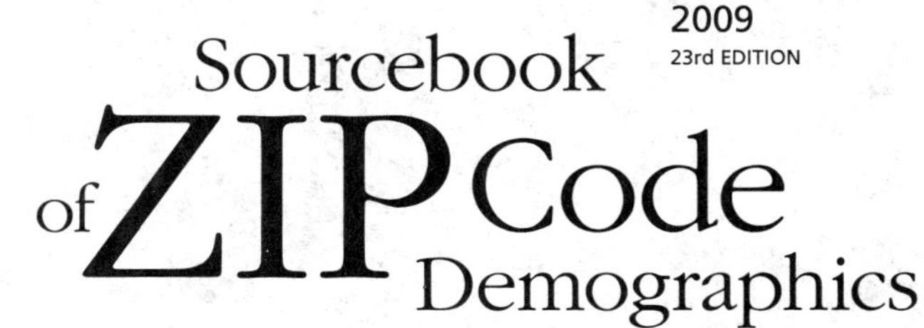

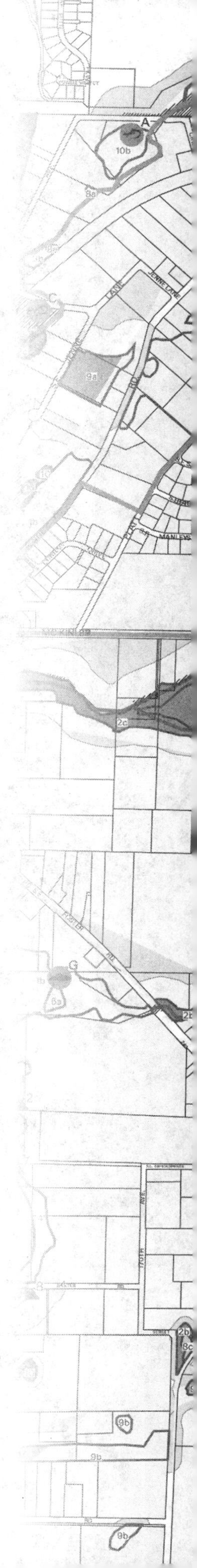

POPULATION CHANGE

STATE AND U.S. TOTALS

A

STATE	STATE FIPS CODE	POPULATION 2000	POPULATION 2009	POPULATION 2014	2000-2009 ANNUAL RATE % Rate	2000-2009 ANNUAL RATE National Rank	RACE (%) White 2000	White 2009	Black 2000	Black 2009	Asian/Pacific 2000	Asian/Pacific 2009
ALABAMA	01	4,447,100	4,705,127	4,839,658	0.6	34	71.1	69.3	26.0	26.7	0.7	1.0
ALASKA	02	626,932	693,413	726,990	1.1	18	69.3	66.7	3.5	3.2	4.5	5.0
ARIZONA	04	5,130,632	6,664,707	7,520,757	2.9	2	75.5	72.3	3.1	3.3	1.9	2.4
ARKANSAS	05	2,673,400	2,913,521	3,036,818	0.9	21	80.0	78.2	15.7	15.8	0.8	1.2
CALIFORNIA	06	33,871,648	37,933,734	39,882,752	1.2	16	59.5	54.5	6.7	6.2	11.3	12.5
COLORADO	08	4,301,261	5,026,916	5,416,283	1.7	9	82.8	80.7	3.8	3.8	2.3	2.9
CONNECTICUT	09	3,405,565	3,534,265	3,574,550	0.4	40	81.6	78.0	9.1	9.9	2.5	3.8
DELAWARE	10	783,600	885,393	936,227	1.3	13	74.6	70.5	19.2	21.1	2.1	3.3
DISTRICT OF COLUMBIA	11	572,059	590,484	600,706	0.3	44	30.8	33.9	60.0	55.4	2.7	3.3
FLORIDA	12	15,982,378	19,021,613	20,472,562	1.9	7	78.0	74.7	14.6	15.8	1.7	2.3
GEORGIA	13	8,186,453	9,932,949	10,860,806	2.1	5	65.1	61.1	28.7	30.1	2.2	2.9
HAWAII	15	1,211,537	1,309,261	1,355,862	0.8	25	24.3	25.5	1.8	2.3	51.0	48.8
IDAHO	16	1,293,953	1,562,163	1,712,315	2.1	5	91.0	89.5	0.4	0.5	1.0	1.3
ILLINOIS	17	12,419,293	13,114,513	13,412,757	0.6	34	73.5	70.6	15.1	15.3	3.4	4.4
INDIANA	18	6,080,485	6,461,343	6,646,788	0.7	29	87.5	85.6	8.4	8.9	1.0	1.5
IOWA	19	2,926,324	3,039,329	3,096,694	0.4	40	93.9	91.9	2.1	2.5	1.3	2.1
KANSAS	20	2,688,418	2,828,967	2,900,013	0.6	34	86.1	83.7	5.7	5.9	1.8	2.6
KENTUCKY	21	4,041,769	4,317,469	4,460,724	0.7	29	90.1	88.9	7.3	7.5	0.8	1.2
LOUISIANA	22	4,468,976	4,488,442	4,702,682	0.0	51	63.9	61.9	32.5	33.7	1.3	1.6
MAINE	23	1,274,923	1,343,984	1,368,079	0.6	34	96.9	96.3	0.5	0.7	0.7	1.1
MARYLAND	24	5,296,486	5,733,229	5,913,034	0.9	21	64.0	59.0	27.9	30.1	4.0	5.3
MASSACHUSETTS	25	6,349,097	6,499,354	6,543,317	0.3	44	84.5	81.0	5.4	6.0	3.8	5.4
MICHIGAN	26	9,938,444	10,194,648	10,227,800	0.3	44	80.2	78.3	14.2	14.5	1.8	2.8
MINNESOTA	27	4,919,479	5,332,824	5,504,188	0.9	21	89.4	86.8	3.5	4.3	2.9	3.9
MISSISSIPPI	28	2,844,658	2,977,504	3,043,108	0.5	38	61.4	59.6	36.3	37.4	0.7	0.9
MISSOURI	29	5,595,211	5,984,833	6,179,066	0.7	29	84.9	83.3	11.2	11.7	1.2	1.7
MONTANA	30	902,195	973,235	1,013,977	0.8	25	90.6	89.7	0.3	0.4	0.6	0.7
NEBRASKA	31	1,711,263	1,812,985	1,861,796	0.6	34	89.6	86.9	4.0	4.4	1.3	2.1
NEVADA	32	1,998,257	2,746,331	3,147,495	3.5	1	75.2	71.8	6.8	7.2	4.9	5.1
NEW HAMPSHIRE	33	1,235,786	1,337,493	1,373,929	0.9	21	96.0	94.8	0.7	0.9	1.3	2.1
NEW JERSEY	34	8,414,350	8,834,947	8,982,262	0.5	38	72.6	68.2	13.6	14.0	5.7	7.9
NEW MEXICO	35	1,819,046	2,058,296	2,187,927	1.3	13	66.8	65.0	1.9	2.0	1.1	1.4
NEW YORK	36	18,976,457	19,495,049	19,645,949	0.3	44	67.9	64.8	15.9	16.5	5.6	6.9
NORTH CAROLINA	37	8,049,313	9,370,242	10,132,240	1.7	9	72.1	69.8	21.6	21.5	1.5	2.1
NORTH DAKOTA	38	642,200	656,056	662,758	0.2	49	92.4	90.8	0.6	0.7	0.6	1.0
OHIO	39	11,353,140	11,577,283	11,649,385	0.2	49	85.0	83.1	11.5	12.2	1.2	1.9
OKLAHOMA	40	3,450,654	3,692,249	3,816,402	0.7	29	76.2	73.0	7.6	7.8	1.4	2.0
OREGON	41	3,421,399	3,841,859	4,064,906	1.3	13	86.6	83.7	1.6	1.7	3.2	4.0
PENNSYLVANIA	42	12,281,054	12,598,860	12,699,966	0.3	44	85.4	83.2	10.0	10.7	1.8	2.7
RHODE ISLAND	44	1,048,319	1,065,753	1,061,722	0.2	49	85.0	81.4	4.5	5.1	2.3	3.1
SOUTH CAROLINA	45	4,012,012	4,524,760	4,800,919	1.3	13	67.2	65.9	29.5	29.4	0.9	1.4
SOUTH DAKOTA	46	754,844	816,249	851,265	0.8	25	88.7	87.0	0.6	0.8	0.6	1.0
TENNESSEE	47	5,689,283	6,297,249	6,622,138	1.1	18	80.2	78.4	16.4	16.9	1.0	1.5
TEXAS	48	20,851,820	24,896,267	27,199,920	1.9	7	71.0	67.6	11.5	11.4	2.8	3.5
UTAH	49	2,233,169	2,748,395	3,055,386	2.3	3	89.2	87.6	0.8	0.9	2.3	2.6
VERMONT	50	608,827	631,968	638,352	0.4	40	96.8	96.1	0.5	0.7	0.9	1.3
VIRGINIA	51	7,078,515	7,895,075	8,269,206	1.2	16	72.3	68.8	19.6	20.1	3.7	5.1
WASHINGTON	53	5,894,121	6,691,182	7,118,535	1.4	10	81.8	79.0	3.2	3.4	5.9	6.9
WEST VIRGINIA	54	1,808,344	1,838,109	1,850,811	0.2	49	95.0	94.5	3.2	3.3	0.5	0.8
WISCONSIN	55	5,363,675	5,706,220	5,863,394	0.7	29	88.9	86.9	5.7	6.3	1.7	2.3
WYOMING	56	493,782	535,411	557,508	0.9	21	92.1	91.2	0.8	0.8	0.6	0.8
UNITED STATES					1.0		75.1	72.0	12.3	12.7	3.8	4.6

POPULATION COMPOSITION

STATE AND U.S. TOTALS

B

STATE	% HISPANIC ORIGIN		2009 AGE DISTRIBUTION (%)										MEDIAN AGE	% 2009 Males	% 2009 Females
	2000	2009	0-4	5-9	10-14	15-19	20-24	25-44	45-64	65-84	85+	18+	2009		
ALABAMA	1.7	2.8	6.6	6.6	6.6	6.9	6.6	26.4	26.7	11.7	1.8	76.1	37.8	48.6	51.4
ALASKA	4.1	5.7	7.6	7.3	7.4	7.8	7.4	28.4	26.9	6.5	0.6	72.9	33.6	51.3	48.7
ARIZONA	25.3	30.8	7.6	7.1	6.8	6.9	6.8	26.9	24.0	12.0	1.8	74.5	35.8	49.7	50.3
ARKANSAS	3.2	5.1	6.8	6.6	6.5	6.9	6.6	26.0	26.1	12.4	2.0	76.1	37.8	49.1	50.9
CALIFORNIA	32.4	38.3	7.5	7.1	6.9	7.5	7.4	28.5	24.2	9.3	1.6	74.1	34.3	49.9	50.1
COLORADO	17.1	20.2	6.9	6.7	6.7	6.9	7.0	29.0	26.5	8.8	1.4	75.7	35.9	50.2	49.8
CONNECTICUT	9.4	12.0	6.3	6.4	6.7	7.2	6.5	24.9	27.9	11.7	2.5	76.3	39.6	48.6	51.4
DELAWARE	4.8	6.6	6.5	6.4	6.4	7.1	6.8	26.1	26.7	12.1	1.8	76.7	38.3	48.6	51.4
DISTRICT OF COLUMBIA	7.9	9.0	5.7	5.6	5.2	7.1	8.9	29.9	25.2	10.3	2.0	80.2	35.8	47.2	52.8
FLORIDA	16.8	21.5	6.0	5.9	5.9	6.3	6.2	25.0	26.8	15.3	2.8	78.6	41.1	48.8	51.2
GEORGIA	5.3	7.7	7.3	7.0	6.9	7.1	7.1	29.3	25.1	8.9	1.3	74.7	35.0	49.4	50.6
HAWAII	7.2	8.2	6.6	6.2	6.1	6.6	7.1	27.5	26.3	11.4	2.0	77.1	37.5	50.0	50.0
IDAHO	7.9	9.5	7.7	7.4	7.3	7.7	7.0	26.7	25.0	9.6	1.6	73.1	34.4	50.1	49.9
ILLINOIS	12.3	15.7	7.1	6.9	6.8	7.1	6.9	27.5	25.4	10.3	1.9	75.0	36.1	49.1	50.9
INDIANA	3.5	5.0	6.9	6.8	6.8	7.2	6.9	26.5	26.2	10.8	1.9	75.4	36.8	49.3	50.7
IOWA	2.8	4.1	6.5	6.4	6.5	7.3	7.1	25.2	26.5	11.9	2.6	76.5	38.1	49.3	50.7
KANSAS	7.0	9.4	7.1	6.9	6.9	7.3	7.3	25.9	25.7	10.7	2.2	75.0	36.3	49.6	50.4
KENTUCKY	1.5	2.4	6.5	6.5	6.5	6.8	6.5	27.0	27.1	11.3	1.8	76.6	37.9	49.1	50.9
LOUISIANA	2.4	2.8	7.2	7.0	6.9	7.3	7.1	26.8	25.7	10.4	1.6	74.6	35.6	48.6	51.4
MAINE	0.7	1.1	5.4	5.6	6.1	6.9	6.2	24.7	30.2	12.7	2.3	78.8	41.6	48.8	51.2
MARYLAND	4.3	6.4	6.5	6.6	6.7	7.1	6.4	26.9	27.4	10.7	1.7	76.0	38.1	48.4	51.6
MASSACHUSETTS	6.8	8.7	6.1	6.2	6.3	7.1	7.1	26.5	27.1	11.3	2.3	77.4	38.6	48.4	51.6
MICHIGAN	3.3	4.1	6.7	6.7	6.8	7.2	6.6	26.3	26.9	10.9	1.9	75.6	37.6	49.2	50.8
MINNESOTA	2.9	4.1	6.8	6.7	6.7	7.2	6.8	27.2	26.3	10.2	2.1	75.6	36.9	49.6	50.4
MISSISSIPPI	1.4	2.0	7.2	7.1	7.0	7.5	7.1	26.4	25.3	10.6	1.7	74.3	35.6	48.6	51.4
MISSOURI	2.1	2.8	6.6	6.6	6.6	7.0	6.7	26.1	26.5	11.7	2.1	76.1	37.7	48.8	51.2
MONTANA	2.0	2.6	6.0	6.1	6.5	7.3	7.0	24.2	29.0	11.8	2.1	77.1	39.4	49.8	50.2
NEBRASKA	5.5	7.9	6.9	6.8	6.8	7.3	6.9	26.3	25.7	11.0	2.3	75.3	36.5	49.4	50.6
NEVADA	19.7	24.9	7.3	6.8	6.5	6.6	6.4	28.1	26.0	11.1	1.3	75.4	36.8	50.3	49.7
NEW HAMPSHIRE	1.7	2.4	5.9	6.1	6.5	7.4	6.6	25.3	29.3	10.9	1.9	77.1	39.8	49.2	50.8
NEW JERSEY	13.3	16.9	6.6	6.6	6.7	6.8	6.2	26.4	27.0	11.5	2.2	76.0	38.7	48.7	51.3
NEW MEXICO	42.1	44.2	7.3	7.1	7.0	7.5	7.2	26.0	25.9	10.5	1.6	74.2	35.5	49.3	50.7
NEW YORK	15.1	16.7	6.5	6.4	6.4	7.1	7.0	27.0	26.3	11.2	2.1	76.6	37.5	48.4	51.6
NORTH CAROLINA	4.7	6.9	6.6	6.5	6.5	6.8	6.9	27.7	26.5	10.9	1.6	76.5	37.4	49.3	50.7
NORTH DAKOTA	1.2	1.8	6.3	6.1	6.2	7.7	8.3	25.2	26.0	11.6	2.7	77.3	36.9	50.0	50.0
OHIO	1.9	2.4	6.6	6.5	6.6	7.1	6.7	25.9	26.9	11.7	2.1	76.2	38.2	48.7	51.3
OKLAHOMA	5.2	7.0	6.9	6.6	6.5	7.1	7.2	26.2	25.9	11.6	2.0	75.9	36.8	49.3	50.7
OREGON	8.0	11.2	6.5	6.2	6.3	6.8	6.8	26.7	27.5	11.1	2.1	77.0	38.0	49.6	50.4
PENNSYLVANIA	3.2	4.2	5.8	6.0	6.3	7.1	6.5	24.8	27.8	13.1	2.6	77.8	40.4	48.5	51.5
RHODE ISLAND	8.7	12.0	6.1	6.0	6.1	7.6	7.5	25.6	26.8	11.8	2.6	77.9	38.6	48.3	51.7
SOUTH CAROLINA	2.4	3.6	6.5	6.5	6.5	7.2	6.9	26.6	26.8	11.3	1.6	76.4	37.6	48.9	51.1
SOUTH DAKOTA	1.4	2.0	6.9	6.7	6.9	7.6	7.3	25.0	25.9	11.3	2.4	75.3	36.7	49.7	50.3
TENNESSEE	2.2	3.4	6.5	6.4	6.5	6.8	6.5	27.2	27.0	11.4	1.7	76.6	38.0	49.0	51.0
TEXAS	32.0	37.4	7.9	7.5	7.2	7.5	7.4	28.3	24.0	8.8	1.4	73.0	33.6	49.7	50.3
UTAH	9.0	10.5	9.7	8.7	8.1	8.6	8.6	28.5	19.6	7.1	1.2	68.6	28.8	50.1	49.9
VERMONT	0.9	1.1	5.4	5.8	6.2	7.4	7.0	24.6	29.9	11.6	2.0	78.6	40.4	49.1	50.9
VIRGINIA	4.7	7.0	6.5	6.4	6.5	6.9	6.9	27.5	27.2	10.5	1.6	76.7	37.7	49.2	50.8
WASHINGTON	7.5	9.7	6.7	6.5	6.5	7.0	7.0	27.4	27.0	10.1	1.8	76.3	36.9	49.8	50.2
WEST VIRGINIA	0.7	0.8	5.5	5.6	5.9	6.5	6.1	25.2	29.3	13.8	2.2	79.3	41.5	49.0	51.0
WISCONSIN	3.6	4.8	6.4	6.4	6.5	7.2	7.2	26.0	27.1	11.1	2.2	76.6	38.0	49.5	50.5
WYOMING	6.4	7.2	6.3	6.2	6.4	7.3	7.2	25.6	28.6	10.8	1.7	76.8	37.8	50.2	49.8
UNITED STATES	12.5	15.7	6.8	6.7	6.6	7.1	6.9	27.0	26.0	10.9	1.9	75.7	36.9	49.2	50.8

HOUSEHOLDS

STATE AND U.S. TOTALS

C

STATE	HOUSEHOLDS					FAMILIES			MEDIAN HOUSEHOLD INCOME		
	2000	2009	2014	% Annual Rate 2000-2009	2009 Average HH Size	2000	2009	% Annual Rate 2000-2009	2009	2014	2009 National Rank
ALABAMA	1,737,080	1,880,089	1,948,384	0.9	2.44	1,215,968	1,289,389	0.6	40,822	42,202	48
ALASKA	221,600	245,284	257,953	1.1	2.74	152,337	165,278	0.9	65,464	68,018	5
ARIZONA	1,901,327	2,435,778	2,744,881	2.7	2.69	1,287,367	1,621,606	2.5	55,275	58,294	21
ARKANSAS	1,042,696	1,149,616	1,203,457	1.1	2.46	732,261	778,744	0.7	42,685	44,760	46
CALIFORNIA	11,502,870	12,664,993	13,259,348	1.0	2.93	7,920,049	8,751,674	1.1	61,614	64,088	11
COLORADO	1,658,238	1,928,601	2,074,506	1.6	2.55	1,084,461	1,246,129	1.5	62,597	65,813	8
CONNECTICUT	1,301,670	1,353,024	1,371,527	0.4	2.53	881,170	907,599	0.3	70,949	74,487	2
DELAWARE	298,736	339,622	360,897	1.4	2.53	204,590	226,262	1.1	61,789	65,095	10
DISTRICT OF COLUMBIA	248,338	261,188	267,532	0.5	2.13	114,166	115,349	0.1	51,491	53,880	30
FLORIDA	6,337,929	7,543,036	8,134,518	1.9	2.47	4,210,760	4,920,180	1.7	50,413	52,516	34
GEORGIA	3,006,369	3,648,492	3,993,863	2.1	2.65	2,111,647	2,491,513	1.8	56,761	58,593	18
HAWAII	403,240	446,176	465,394	1.1	2.85	287,068	308,495	0.8	61,537	63,474	12
IDAHO	469,645	576,911	635,022	2.2	2.65	335,588	406,678	2.1	50,374	53,004	35
ILLINOIS	4,591,779	4,843,591	4,950,673	0.6	2.64	3,105,513	3,228,013	0.4	60,823	63,631	14
INDIANA	2,336,306	2,522,193	2,607,210	0.8	2.49	1,602,501	1,667,802	0.4	54,105	56,493	24
IOWA	1,149,276	1,224,377	1,254,785	0.7	2.40	769,684	799,802	0.4	50,616	52,941	33
KANSAS	1,037,891	1,101,084	1,131,209	0.6	2.49	701,547	736,798	0.5	52,748	54,940	27
KENTUCKY	1,590,647	1,739,883	1,810,922	1.0	2.41	1,104,398	1,162,337	0.6	44,205	46,476	44
LOUISIANA	1,656,053	1,678,332	1,768,086	0.1	2.60	1,156,438	1,163,714	0.1	37,868	38,644	49
MAINE	518,200	562,245	578,087	0.9	2.32	340,685	362,301	0.7	46,650	48,581	41
MARYLAND	1,980,859	2,146,767	2,219,100	0.9	2.60	1,359,318	1,424,385	0.5	67,267	70,086	4
MASSACHUSETTS	2,443,580	2,516,974	2,541,353	0.3	2.50	1,576,696	1,617,967	0.3	68,225	71,891	3
MICHIGAN	3,785,661	3,939,172	3,972,480	0.4	2.52	2,575,699	2,653,003	0.3	55,536	56,866	20
MINNESOTA	1,895,127	2,088,579	2,164,342	1.1	2.48	1,255,141	1,341,985	0.7	62,767	65,994	7
MISSISSIPPI	1,046,434	1,125,135	1,159,185	0.8	2.56	747,159	784,864	0.5	36,311	37,046	51
MISSOURI	2,194,594	2,369,595	2,455,513	0.8	2.45	1,476,516	1,538,383	0.4	49,522	52,035	36
MONTANA	358,667	390,009	408,126	0.9	2.43	237,407	249,407	0.5	40,864	42,494	47
NEBRASKA	666,184	714,873	736,989	0.8	2.46	443,411	473,287	0.7	50,953	53,316	32
NEVADA	751,165	1,033,339	1,183,165	3.5	2.63	498,333	678,533	3.4	58,128	60,817	17
NEW HAMPSHIRE	474,606	517,193	533,848	0.9	2.51	323,651	349,437	0.8	63,279	65,972	6
NEW JERSEY	3,064,645	3,216,258	3,272,634	0.5	2.69	2,154,539	2,247,758	0.5	72,809	76,895	1
NEW MEXICO	677,971	785,869	841,800	1.6	2.56	466,515	519,050	1.2	44,681	46,845	43
NEW YORK	7,056,860	7,245,427	7,309,487	0.3	2.61	4,639,387	4,681,519	0.1	58,747	62,337	16
NORTH CAROLINA	3,132,013	3,702,580	4,023,364	1.8	2.46	2,158,869	2,471,158	1.5	51,418	53,634	31
NORTH DAKOTA	257,152	276,831	283,364	0.8	2.27	166,150	169,313	0.2	45,981	48,456	42
OHIO	4,445,773	4,610,674	4,662,894	0.4	2.44	2,993,023	3,030,098	0.1	52,400	54,553	28
OKLAHOMA	1,342,293	1,451,122	1,505,258	0.8	2.46	921,750	972,243	0.6	43,746	45,901	45
OREGON	1,333,723	1,495,911	1,584,044	1.2	2.51	877,671	973,427	1.1	53,483	55,628	25
PENNSYLVANIA	4,777,003	4,958,883	5,020,042	0.4	2.45	3,208,388	3,242,236	0.1	53,225	55,819	26
RHODE ISLAND	408,424	413,947	413,296	0.1	2.48	265,398	263,928	-0.1	54,939	57,605	22
SOUTH CAROLINA	1,533,854	1,786,632	1,916,490	1.7	2.45	1,072,822	1,199,186	1.2	48,210	50,493	38
SOUTH DAKOTA	290,245	322,832	339,103	1.2	2.43	194,330	219,628	1.3	46,883	49,493	40
TENNESSEE	2,232,905	2,518,117	2,663,123	1.3	2.44	1,547,835	1,702,673	1.0	47,751	50,104	39
TEXAS	7,393,354	8,737,608	9,534,648	1.8	2.78	5,247,794	6,129,919	1.7	52,382	54,495	29
UTAH	701,281	869,228	968,159	2.3	3.11	535,294	646,709	2.1	60,286	62,873	15
VERMONT	240,634	258,698	263,783	0.8	2.36	157,763	165,856	0.5	54,205	56,824	23
VIRGINIA	2,699,173	3,032,884	3,186,794	1.3	2.52	1,847,796	2,025,539	1.0	61,855	64,957	9
WASHINGTON	2,271,398	2,584,164	2,752,996	1.4	2.53	1,499,127	1,680,249	1.2	60,852	63,758	13
WEST VIRGINIA	736,481	768,367	780,298	0.5	2.33	504,055	509,106	0.1	37,099	38,541	50
WISCONSIN	2,084,544	2,283,572	2,366,910	1.0	2.43	1,386,815	1,503,929	0.9	56,363	58,927	19
WYOMING	193,608	217,401	228,606	1.3	2.40	130,497	141,679	0.9	48,927	50,551	37
UNITED STATES				1.1	2.59			0.9	54,719	56,938	

INCOME

STATE AND U.S. TOTALS

STATE	2009 Per Capita Income	2009 HH Income Base	2009 HOUSEHOLD INCOME DISTRIBUTION (%)					2009 Home Value Base	2009 HOME VALUE DISTRIBUTION (%)					2009 Median Home Value
			Less than $25,000	$25,000 to $49,999	$50,000 to $99,999	$100,000 to $149,999	$150,000 or More		Less than $50,000	$50,000 to $89,999	$90,000 to $174,999	$175,000 to $399,999	$400,000 or More	
ALABAMA	21,187	1,880,087	31.4	27.9	30.6	6.9	3.2	1,355,687	18.1	22.4	35.8	19.6	4.0	107,730
ALASKA	28,744	245,284	15.0	21.0	38.1	16.8	9.1	153,199	7.3	5.5	18.9	55.0	13.4	236,447
ARIZONA	26,377	2,435,753	19.0	25.8	34.8	13.4	7.1	1,652,149	9.3	12.3	42.2	29.4	6.9	143,619
ARKANSAS	21,917	1,149,615	28.7	29.0	32.0	6.7	3.7	797,587	21.5	25.6	34.9	15.2	2.9	95,077
CALIFORNIA	28,199	12,664,802	18.5	22.2	33.9	14.0	11.5	7,167,439	3.3	2.6	13.6	41.0	39.5	321,752
COLORADO	30,807	1,928,584	15.5	22.5	37.5	15.8	8.6	1,295,895	4.4	4.3	23.6	52.9	14.8	220,998
CONNECTICUT	36,066	1,353,018	15.8	19.0	36.4	15.2	13.5	904,133	1.1	1.8	16.1	53.4	27.5	273,826
DELAWARE	29,883	339,622	16.0	22.6	38.7	14.2	8.5	244,854	5.8	4.2	23.8	53.6	12.6	217,670
DISTRICT OF COLUMBIA	34,644	261,179	25.5	23.1	29.2	11.1	11.1	112,332	0.4	0.5	4.5	45.8	48.9	393,913
FLORIDA	27,128	7,543,002	21.9	27.6	33.8	9.8	6.8	5,284,073	8.0	14.3	38.7	30.4	8.6	144,752
GEORGIA	26,980	3,648,481	20.7	23.1	36.8	11.7	7.7	2,460,554	13.2	17.9	39.1	24.2	5.5	121,444
HAWAII	27,398	446,166	17.4	22.5	35.8	14.8	9.4	253,215	0.8	0.9	3.3	23.8	71.3	581,441
IDAHO	23,160	576,907	20.9	28.6	37.9	8.3	4.4	417,964	6.9	7.8	39.2	38.3	7.9	167,282
ILLINOIS	28,587	4,843,507	18.2	22.2	39.3	12.1	8.2	3,256,132	6.3	10.0	30.9	40.6	12.3	185,324
INDIANA	26,003	2,522,143	19.5	26.3	38.6	10.5	5.1	1,801,056	12.2	24.1	44.1	17.2	2.4	108,938
IOWA	25,379	1,224,377	21.1	28.2	37.9	8.6	4.3	885,422	14.7	22.5	41.6	18.6	2.6	110,128
KANSAS	26,028	1,101,075	20.3	26.8	37.6	9.9	5.4	759,427	18.1	21.6	35.7	21.6	3.0	107,692
KENTUCKY	23,409	1,739,871	28.5	27.2	32.3	7.7	4.3	1,235,533	19.8	20.7	38.3	18.6	2.6	103,937
LOUISIANA	19,176	1,678,284	34.0	28.2	28.2	6.6	3.0	1,151,079	16.9	18.7	37.2	22.8	4.3	118,738
MAINE	24,559	562,241	25.0	28.4	35.2	7.5	3.8	402,099	6.4	9.4	36.7	38.7	8.8	170,226
MARYLAND	32,538	2,146,720	15.1	20.5	36.5	16.4	11.5	1,449,863	1.9	2.6	14.3	53.1	28.2	289,711
MASSACHUSETTS	34,904	2,516,954	17.4	19.0	33.1	18.1	12.4	1,564,744	0.7	1.2	13.3	53.8	31.0	297,007
MICHIGAN	26,713	3,939,133	20.1	24.2	38.5	11.3	5.9	2,900,591	13.2	21.9	40.3	21.5	3.2	115,137
MINNESOTA	31,285	2,088,578	15.9	22.3	36.8	16.4	8.6	1,546,350	6.5	9.7	37.4	39.4	7.0	167,369
MISSISSIPPI	18,363	1,125,133	35.3	29.0	27.5	5.7	2.5	813,748	25.4	28.2	31.6	12.7	2.1	84,642
MISSOURI	25,286	2,369,570	22.8	27.7	35.3	9.1	5.2	1,665,886	12.8	19.4	39.1	24.2	4.6	122,064
MONTANA	21,013	389,999	28.7	31.3	31.1	5.8	3.0	269,953	10.4	9.4	31.4	38.6	10.1	171,793
NEBRASKA	24,998	714,871	20.5	28.3	37.5	9.0	4.6	481,967	15.1	21.8	43.3	17.4	2.4	109,174
NEVADA	27,428	1,033,324	16.9	25.3	38.5	12.4	6.9	628,253	6.3	7.5	45.8	34.1	6.2	157,802
NEW HAMPSHIRE	30,567	517,193	15.4	22.0	39.7	14.4	8.5	364,152	4.2	5.0	30.0	49.8	11.0	202,897
NEW JERSEY	34,433	3,216,209	15.4	18.6	34.9	16.8	14.2	2,102,743	1.0	1.6	9.9	50.1	37.4	336,585
NEW MEXICO	22,470	785,849	27.2	27.7	32.6	8.1	4.5	549,638	12.7	11.8	31.3	35.2	9.1	159,744
NEW YORK	29,893	7,245,253	21.9	21.3	32.7	14.0	9.9	3,839,176	3.4	5.7	23.0	38.7	29.1	269,816
NORTH CAROLINA	25,989	3,702,577	22.3	26.1	36.6	9.4	5.6	2,562,572	12.2	15.1	38.7	27.9	6.1	132,724
NORTH DAKOTA	23,967	276,827	25.3	28.6	36.2	6.6	3.3	184,786	20.2	18.2	39.7	19.8	2.2	112,133
OHIO	26,577	4,610,653	21.4	25.9	36.7	10.4	5.7	3,171,863	10.3	22.0	45.6	19.3	2.8	114,865
OKLAHOMA	22,515	1,451,118	27.2	29.2	32.3	7.2	4.0	987,719	20.4	25.6	36.1	15.4	2.4	96,076
OREGON	26,362	1,495,910	20.3	25.9	37.7	10.2	5.9	957,176	4.6	3.5	17.3	54.4	20.2	249,991
PENNSYLVANIA	26,913	4,958,859	21.5	25.3	36.9	10.2	6.1	3,535,926	7.5	12.2	35.6	36.1	8.5	161,438
RHODE ISLAND	27,186	413,947	22.7	22.9	35.9	11.7	6.7	249,981	0.8	1.0	14.8	67.1	16.3	247,721
SOUTH CAROLINA	24,352	1,786,619	25.1	26.4	35.2	8.4	4.8	1,291,786	16.4	20.9	37.4	20.6	4.8	112,284
SOUTH DAKOTA	22,885	322,828	24.5	28.5	37.1	6.5	3.5	219,593	19.9	18.0	38.6	20.2	3.3	113,473
TENNESSEE	24,986	2,518,110	24.9	27.0	34.7	8.2	5.2	1,760,745	12.0	19.9	40.9	22.7	4.6	120,455
TEXAS	24,551	8,737,512	22.3	25.0	34.3	11.1	7.3	5,567,902	16.5	22.7	36.5	19.7	4.6	109,784
UTAH	23,420	869,224	14.7	23.9	42.1	12.6	6.7	624,062	3.1	3.0	25.7	56.7	11.5	213,546
VERMONT	27,546	258,698	19.3	26.3	38.8	10.3	5.3	182,303	3.4	4.6	25.9	52.9	13.2	216,547
VIRGINIA	30,912	3,032,869	17.0	22.6	35.9	15.0	9.5	2,061,923	5.3	6.3	30.4	41.5	16.5	203,135
WASHINGTON	29,418	2,584,148	17.0	23.3	38.4	13.6	7.7	1,667,157	3.4	2.9	16.8	52.3	24.6	272,173
WEST VIRGINIA	20,563	768,367	34.3	29.3	28.3	5.4	2.7	576,834	22.0	23.9	36.4	15.5	2.2	98,135
WISCONSIN	27,384	2,283,563	18.4	25.3	40.0	11.0	5.2	1,561,233	5.6	11.9	43.5	34.2	4.7	150,766
WYOMING	24,721	217,398	23.6	27.4	36.9	8.4	3.8	152,123	9.1	7.6	32.0	40.7	10.5	178,177
UNITED STATES	27,277		20.9	24.4	35.3	11.7	7.6		9.3	13.1	31.6	32.6	13.5	162,279

SPENDING POTENTIAL INDICES

STATE AND U.S. TOTALS

E

STATE	FINANCIAL SERVICES				THE HOME						ENTERTAINMENT						PERSONAL			
					Home Improvements		Furnishings													
	Auto Loan	Home Loan	Investments	Retirement Plans	Home Repair	Lawn & Garden	Computers & Hardware-Personal	Major Appliances	TV, Radio, Sound Equipment	Furniture	Dine out/ Carry out	Sports Equipment	Fees & Tickets	Toys & Games	Travel	Cable TV	Apparel & Services	Auto Repairs	Health Insurance	Pets & Supplies
ALABAMA	83	70	73	70	69	80	73	77	76	71	76	59	66	77	69	80	52	76	80	92
ALASKA	116	114	108	115	111	108	115	111	112	116	113	88	114	115	112	110	80	112	107	131
ARIZONA	104	101	100	99	102	100	101	102	101	105	102	76	100	101	101	100	71	102	102	118
ARKANSAS	88	73	79	72	73	85	76	82	80	74	79	62	68	81	72	84	54	80	86	98
CALIFORNIA	112	119	122	118	122	107	121	116	114	124	116	92	124	114	124	110	84	118	107	132
COLORADO	114	114	111	115	112	109	114	111	111	116	113	88	114	113	113	110	80	112	108	130
CONNECTICUT	120	136	136	137	137	129	132	128	129	132	130	99	141	128	137	129	94	130	128	149
DELAWARE	109	111	110	110	111	112	108	110	109	109	109	83	110	109	109	110	76	109	111	128
DISTRICT OF COLUMBIA	98	91	96	97	91	89	111	94	112	103	114	76	109	109	104	114	83	105	101	116
FLORIDA	96	94	97	93	96	98	95	97	96	97	96	71	95	94	96	97	67	97	101	113
GEORGIA	110	101	97	102	98	103	103	103	104	104	104	80	99	107	99	105	73	103	103	122
HAWAII	105	115	122	114	119	103	115	112	107	117	109	88	119	107	120	103	78	112	103	127
IDAHO	94	87	87	87	86	92	88	90	88	86	88	70	83	90	85	90	61	89	91	107
ILLINOIS	106	108	105	108	107	106	109	106	108	107	109	83	110	108	108	108	77	108	107	125
INDIANA	97	91	86	93	89	96	93	94	95	91	94	73	90	96	90	97	65	94	97	112
IOWA	93	84	87	85	83	95	87	91	89	82	88	71	81	90	85	92	61	90	96	108
KANSAS	98	90	91	91	89	97	94	95	94	90	94	74	88	96	90	96	65	95	98	113
KENTUCKY	90	77	81	77	76	88	80	85	83	78	83	65	73	85	76	87	57	83	88	101
LOUISIANA	78	67	68	67	66	75	70	72	73	70	73	55	65	74	67	76	50	73	76	87
MAINE	87	79	87	80	81	89	81	86	83	78	82	65	76	83	81	86	57	84	89	102
MARYLAND	116	125	123	126	125	119	122	119	120	123	121	92	127	121	124	119	86	120	118	139
MASSACHUSETTS	113	129	133	129	131	121	127	122	123	125	125	94	135	122	132	123	90	124	121	141
MICHIGAN	98	97	93	98	95	100	96	97	97	95	97	74	96	98	96	99	68	97	100	115
MINNESOTA	113	113	112	114	112	114	112	113	111	111	112	88	112	113	112	112	78	112	113	133
MISSISSIPPI	77	63	67	62	62	74	66	70	70	65	69	54	59	71	62	74	47	70	74	85
MISSOURI	94	86	87	87	85	93	89	91	91	87	90	70	84	92	86	93	62	90	94	108
MONTANA	80	69	77	69	70	79	73	77	75	69	74	59	67	74	71	77	51	76	80	92
NEBRASKA	95	85	88	86	84	94	89	91	90	85	90	72	83	91	86	92	62	91	94	109
NEVADA	104	102	99	102	101	98	103	101	102	106	103	78	103	103	102	100	72	102	99	118
NEW HAMPSHIRE	110	114	114	115	113	113	110	111	109	110	110	86	113	110	113	109	77	111	111	131
NEW JERSEY	119	138	141	137	141	129	132	129	129	132	131	98	143	128	139	129	95	130	128	148
NEW MEXICO	88	81	80	79	80	83	82	84	83	83	83	63	78	84	80	84	58	84	84	98
NEW YORK	100	106	110	108	107	104	112	106	113	106	114	81	115	110	112	116	83	110	110	124
NORTH CAROLINA	100	89	90	89	88	96	91	94	94	91	93	73	85	95	88	96	64	93	96	112
NORTH DAKOTA	87	73	80	73	72	84	80	82	81	74	81	65	71	81	75	84	55	82	85	99
OHIO	94	92	87	93	90	96	93	93	94	91	94	72	92	95	91	96	66	93	98	110
OKLAHOMA	87	75	78	75	74	84	79	82	82	77	81	63	73	83	75	85	56	82	86	98
OREGON	96	93	95	94	93	95	95	95	95	94	95	74	93	95	95	95	66	96	96	112
PENNSYLVANIA	94	95	95	95	95	100	94	96	96	91	95	73	94	96	94	99	67	95	101	113
RHODE ISLAND	90	98	97	98	98	94	98	94	96	96	98	73	103	96	100	97	70	97	96	110
SOUTH CAROLINA	95	83	86	82	82	92	85	89	88	84	88	68	79	90	81	91	60	88	92	106
SOUTH DAKOTA	88	76	83	76	75	87	80	84	82	76	82	66	72	82	77	85	56	83	88	101
TENNESSEE	95	84	85	84	82	93	87	90	90	85	89	69	80	91	83	93	61	89	93	107
TEXAS	104	96	90	94	93	94	99	97	99	101	100	75	94	101	94	99	70	99	96	114
UTAH	107	107	98	107	104	101	106	103	103	108	104	81	105	106	103	102	73	103	99	121
VERMONT	98	92	100	93	93	101	93	98	94	90	94	75	89	94	93	97	65	96	101	116
VIRGINIA	115	112	112	114	111	114	112	112	112	112	112	88	111	114	111	113	79	112	112	132
WASHINGTON	106	107	105	108	106	104	108	105	106	108	107	82	108	107	107	105	75	106	104	124
WEST VIRGINIA	79	63	76	62	64	80	66	75	71	63	70	57	58	71	64	77	47	72	80	90
WISCONSIN	98	94	92	96	93	99	96	96	96	93	96	75	94	97	95	98	67	96	99	114
WYOMING	91	83	87	83	82	90	85	88	86	83	86	67	80	86	83	88	59	87	90	104
UNITED STATES	100	100	100	100	100	100	100	100	100	100	100	100	100	100	100	100	100	100	100	100

Tapestry Data by ZIP Code

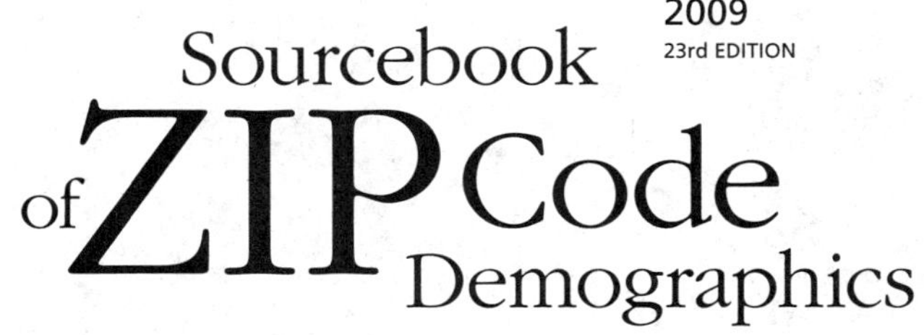

ZIP CODE	TOP TAPESTRY CONSUMER TYPE	% 2009 HOUSE-HOLDS	ZIP CODE	TOP TAPESTRY CONSUMER TYPE	% 2009 HOUSE-HOLDS	ZIP CODE	TOP TAPESTRY CONSUMER TYPE	% 2009 HOUSE-HOLDS
01001	24 Main Street, USA	33.1	01270	17 Green Acres	100.0	01588	24 Main Street, USA	51.2
01002	55 College Towns	35.4	01301	36 Old And Newcomers	14.9	01590	06 Sophisticated Squires	35.9
01003	63 Dorms To Diplomas	100.0	01330	13 In Style	55.3	01602	24 Main Street, USA	27.2
01005	24 Main Street, USA	39.7	01331	24 Main Street, USA	25.4	01603	24 Main Street, USA	53.3
01007	06 Sophisticated Squires	52.8	01337	17 Green Acres	66.3	01604	24 Main Street, USA	33.5
01008	18 Cozy And Comfortable	92.6	01338	17 Green Acres	100.0	01605	60 City Dimensions	25.8
01010	17 Green Acres	100.0	01339	18 Cozy And Comfortable	44.9	01606	24 Main Street, USA	53.9
01011	17 Green Acres	78.6	01340	17 Green Acres	100.0	01607	35 International Marketplace	27.1
01012	17 Green Acres	100.0	01341	07 Exurbanites	100.0	01608	64 City Commons	39.9
01013	60 City Dimensions	39.6	01342	18 Cozy And Comfortable	51.0	01609	52 Inner City Tenants	10.8
01020	29 Rustbelt Retirees	29.1	01343	25 Salt Of The Earth	100.0	01610	60 City Dimensions	43.8
01022	32 Rustbelt Traditions	45.9	01344	24 Main Street, USA	83.8	01611	24 Main Street, USA	65.4
01026	31 Rural Resort Dwellers	75.3	01346	17 Green Acres	100.0	01612	14 Prosperous Empty Nesters	46.8
01027	24 Main Street, USA	24.5	01349	24 Main Street, USA	99.2	01701	05 Wealthy Seaboard Suburbs	34.8
01028	07 Exurbanites	56.1	01350	18 Cozy And Comfortable	100.0	01702	35 International Marketplace	22.9
01030	07 Exurbanites	26.1	01351	13 In Style	72.1	01718	13 In Style	100.0
01031	17 Green Acres	82.0	01354	18 Cozy And Comfortable	100.0	01719	02 Suburban Splendor	50.0
01032	17 Green Acres	100.0	01355	17 Green Acres	99.7	01720	02 Suburban Splendor	46.4
01033	18 Cozy And Comfortable	78.0	01360	17 Green Acres	51.7	01721	13 In Style	43.8
01034	17 Green Acres	98.3	01364	25 Salt Of The Earth	23.9	01730	03 Connoisseurs	56.8
01035	14 Prosperous Empty Nesters	36.2	01366	14 Prosperous Empty Nesters	100.0	01731	40 Military Proximity	93.5
01036	07 Exurbanites	70.8	01367	18 Cozy And Comfortable	78.1	01740	02 Suburban Splendor	97.8
01038	14 Prosperous Empty Nesters	40.4	01368	17 Green Acres	97.3	01741	01 Top Rung	99.9
01039	22 Metropolitans	74.8	01370	17 Green Acres	36.1	01742	03 Connoisseurs	57.8
01040	58 NeWest Residents	24.3	01373	07 Exurbanites	57.8	01745	03 Connoisseurs	99.2
01050	17 Green Acres	58.1	01375	55 College Towns	61.3	01746	05 Wealthy Seaboard Suburbs	40.3
01053	13 In Style	60.0	01376	33 Midlife Junction	35.6	01747	06 Sophisticated Squires	38.6
01054	07 Exurbanites	99.7	01378	17 Green Acres	96.1	01748	02 Suburban Splendor	83.9
01056	18 Cozy And Comfortable	48.4	01379	17 Green Acres	98.7	01749	20 City Lights	30.0
01057	17 Green Acres	44.1	01420	24 Main Street, USA	40.0	01752	13 In Style	32.9
01060	27 Metro Renters	44.6	01430	06 Sophisticated Squires	46.2	01754	20 City Lights	49.2
01062	18 Cozy And Comfortable	27.5	01431	17 Green Acres	56.2	01756	02 Suburban Splendor	46.2
01063	27 Metro Renters	100.0	01432	24 Main Street, USA	54.5	01757	10 Pleasant-Ville	24.5
01068	06 Sophisticated Squires	100.0	01434	24 Main Street, USA	100.0	01760	05 Wealthy Seaboard Suburbs	33.7
01069	24 Main Street, USA	40.4	01436	24 Main Street, USA	69.4	01770	01 Top Rung	78.7
01070	31 Rural Resort Dwellers	100.0	01440	24 Main Street, USA	39.5	01772	02 Suburban Splendor	40.8
01071	18 Cozy And Comfortable	100.0	01450	02 Suburban Splendor	62.7	01773	01 Top Rung	46.3
01072	06 Sophisticated Squires	98.3	01451	01 Top Rung	64.4	01775	02 Suburban Splendor	80.7
01073	07 Exurbanites	73.7	01452	06 Sophisticated Squires	99.9	01776	01 Top Rung	45.0
01075	13 In Style	22.8	01453	24 Main Street, USA	45.7	01778	01 Top Rung	47.3
01077	17 Green Acres	46.1	01460	10 Pleasant-Ville	36.5	01801	20 City Lights	33.1
01080	24 Main Street, USA	100.0	01462	07 Exurbanites	42.0	01803	05 Wealthy Seaboard Suburbs	64.6
01081	17 Green Acres	100.0	01463	06 Sophisticated Squires	39.7	01810	02 Suburban Splendor	33.6
01082	24 Main Street, USA	37.8	01464	24 Main Street, USA	40.3	01821	10 Pleasant-Ville	51.1
01084	17 Green Acres	100.0	01468	17 Green Acres	75.2	01824	05 Wealthy Seaboard Suburbs	46.9
01085	07 Exurbanites	23.5	01469	06 Sophisticated Squires	82.8	01826	24 Main Street, USA	35.1
01088	13 In Style	100.0	01473	06 Sophisticated Squires	47.6	01827	02 Suburban Splendor	99.2
01089	36 Old And Newcomers	22.5	01474	06 Sophisticated Squires	100.0	01830	10 Pleasant-Ville	25.6
01092	24 Main Street, USA	82.4	01475	24 Main Street, USA	56.8	01832	24 Main Street, USA	35.0
01095	07 Exurbanites	59.8	01501	18 Cozy And Comfortable	36.8	01833	02 Suburban Splendor	50.1
01096	17 Green Acres	80.1	01503	05 Wealthy Seaboard Suburbs	56.2	01834	06 Sophisticated Squires	37.9
01098	17 Green Acres	100.0	01504	06 Sophisticated Squires	48.7	01835	13 In Style	37.4
01103	61 High Rise Renters	73.4	01505	13 In Style	46.4	01840	65 Social Security Set	49.6
01104	32 Rustbelt Traditions	20.3	01506	49 Senior Sun Seekers	37.6	01841	35 International Marketplace	36.1
01105	52 Inner City Tenants	27.5	01507	06 Sophisticated Squires	81.3	01843	35 International Marketplace	45.9
01106	03 Connoisseurs	35.9	01510	24 Main Street, USA	35.5	01844	10 Pleasant-Ville	28.4
01107	58 NeWest Residents	29.6	01515	18 Cozy And Comfortable	65.0	01845	02 Suburban Splendor	20.0
01108	60 City Dimensions	24.2	01516	06 Sophisticated Squires	61.9	01850	24 Main Street, USA	41.7
01109	45 City Strivers	28.2	01518	24 Main Street, USA	49.1	01851	35 International Marketplace	36.2
01118	18 Cozy And Comfortable	51.7	01519	13 In Style	48.5	01852	24 Main Street, USA	18.4
01119	32 Rustbelt Traditions	22.8	01520	10 Pleasant-Ville	26.0	01854	24 Main Street, USA	30.6
01128	18 Cozy And Comfortable	82.2	01521	17 Green Acres	100.0	01860	10 Pleasant-Ville	65.6
01129	18 Cozy And Comfortable	66.5	01522	06 Sophisticated Squires	53.9	01862	10 Pleasant-Ville	69.6
01151	60 City Dimensions	61.8	01523	13 In Style	30.7	01863	13 In Style	56.3
01201	18 Cozy And Comfortable	19.0	01524	06 Sophisticated Squires	46.1	01864	05 Wealthy Seaboard Suburbs	32.8
01220	29 Rustbelt Retirees	27.9	01527	24 Main Street, USA	41.2	01867	05 Wealthy Seaboard Suburbs	50.2
01222	17 Green Acres	88.9	01529	24 Main Street, USA	58.4	01876	10 Pleasant-Ville	54.7
01223	31 Rural Resort Dwellers	74.9	01531	17 Green Acres	74.3	01879	06 Sophisticated Squires	35.9
01224	07 Exurbanites	100.0	01532	02 Suburban Splendor	53.7	01880	05 Wealthy Seaboard Suburbs	41.5
01225	18 Cozy And Comfortable	99.0	01534	06 Sophisticated Squires	48.0	01886	02 Suburban Splendor	64.1
01226	24 Main Street, USA	38.2	01535	24 Main Street, USA	55.3	01887	10 Pleasant-Ville	53.3
01230	31 Rural Resort Dwellers	27.3	01536	10 Pleasant-Ville	33.1	01890	01 Top Rung	30.7
01235	17 Green Acres	83.1	01537	24 Main Street, USA	71.4	01901	65 Social Security Set	63.7
01236	07 Exurbanites	37.5	01540	18 Cozy And Comfortable	42.3	01902	35 International Marketplace	35.1
01237	07 Exurbanites	51.1	01541	02 Suburban Splendor	99.4	01904	10 Pleasant-Ville	64.5
01238	18 Cozy And Comfortable	35.3	01542	24 Main Street, USA	74.5	01905	24 Main Street, USA	32.3
01240	30 Retirement Communities	47.6	01543	06 Sophisticated Squires	47.8	01906	10 Pleasant-Ville	60.5
01243	17 Green Acres	100.0	01545	13 In Style	21.5	01907	03 Connoisseurs	21.3
01245	31 Rural Resort Dwellers	96.5	01550	24 Main Street, USA	36.1	01908	09 Urban Chic	41.2
01247	33 Midlife Junction	32.3	01560	24 Main Street, USA	100.0	01913	24 Main Street, USA	24.7
01253	31 Rural Resort Dwellers	100.0	01562	24 Main Street, USA	27.4	01915	20 City Lights	18.4
01254	07 Exurbanites	99.7	01564	17 Green Acres	43.1	01921	03 Connoisseurs	61.7
01255	31 Rural Resort Dwellers	100.0	01566	10 Pleasant-Ville	33.4	01922	02 Suburban Splendor	100.0
01256	25 Salt Of The Earth	98.0	01568	02 Suburban Splendor	51.5	01923	05 Wealthy Seaboard Suburbs	37.1
01257	31 Rural Resort Dwellers	68.7	01569	06 Sophisticated Squires	56.6	01929	09 Urban Chic	55.3
01258	15 Silver And Gold	100.0	01570	24 Main Street, USA	37.0	01930	24 Main Street, USA	23.1
01259	17 Green Acres	84.2	01571	24 Main Street, USA	36.4	01938	09 Urban Chic	19.8
01262	30 Retirement Communities	56.3	01581	02 Suburban Splendor	42.0	01940	03 Connoisseurs	43.0
01266	14 Prosperous Empty Nesters	40.0	01583	14 Prosperous Empty Nesters	55.9	01944	09 Urban Chic	51.9
01267	14 Prosperous Empty Nesters	26.3	01585	24 Main Street, USA	42.9	01945	09 Urban Chic	36.1

CONSUMER TYPE

ZIP CODE	TOP TAPESTRY CONSUMER TYPE	% 2009 HOUSE-HOLDS	ZIP CODE	TOP TAPESTRY CONSUMER TYPE	% 2009 HOUSE-HOLDS	ZIP CODE	TOP TAPESTRY CONSUMER TYPE	% 2009 HOUSE-HOLDS
01949	06 Sophisticated Squires	49.1	02210	27 Metro Renters	55.4	02659	31 Rural Resort Dwellers	65.9
01950	22 Metropolitans	18.3	02215	27 Metro Renters	74.0	02660	15 Silver And Gold	56.2
01951	09 Urban Chic	62.0	02301	35 International Marketplace	24.6	02664	49 Senior Sun Seekers	25.0
01952	24 Main Street, USA	65.7	02302	18 Cozy And Comfortable	40.4	02666	31 Rural Resort Dwellers	100.0
01960	10 Pleasant-Ville	32.9	02322	10 Pleasant-Ville	70.8	02667	31 Rural Resort Dwellers	100.0
01966	09 Urban Chic	29.6	02324	06 Sophisticated Squires	28.1	02668	07 Exurbanites	79.2
01969	05 Wealthy Seaboard Suburbs	50.4	02330	06 Sophisticated Squires	42.6	02670	15 Silver And Gold	100.0
01970	20 City Lights	28.2	02332	02 Suburban Splendor	38.7	02671	31 Rural Resort Dwellers	67.2
01982	05 Wealthy Seaboard Suburbs	36.7	02333	10 Pleasant-Ville	43.0	02673	33 Midlife Junction	43.3
01983	03 Connoisseurs	69.6	02338	06 Sophisticated Squires	36.7	02675	15 Silver And Gold	71.5
01984	03 Connoisseurs	46.4	02339	05 Wealthy Seaboard Suburbs	54.3	02702	10 Pleasant-Ville	48.1
01985	02 Suburban Splendor	100.0	02341	10 Pleasant-Ville	65.1	02703	24 Main Street, USA	28.4
02019	06 Sophisticated Squires	54.6	02343	10 Pleasant-Ville	36.6	02713	31 Rural Resort Dwellers	100.0
02021	05 Wealthy Seaboard Suburbs	52.7	02346	24 Main Street, USA	30.4	02715	10 Pleasant-Ville	89.4
02025	03 Connoisseurs	59.1	02347	10 Pleasant-Ville	51.1	02717	10 Pleasant-Ville	64.1
02026	05 Wealthy Seaboard Suburbs	33.6	02351	10 Pleasant-Ville	71.8	02718	06 Sophisticated Squires	35.8
02030	01 Top Rung	100.0	02356	02 Suburban Splendor	62.8	02719	24 Main Street, USA	31.9
02032	05 Wealthy Seaboard Suburbs	60.3	02357	55 College Towns	100.0	02720	35 International Marketplace	17.1
02035	02 Suburban Splendor	26.5	02359	06 Sophisticated Squires	41.2	02721	35 International Marketplace	23.3
02038	04 Boomburbs	48.3	02360	06 Sophisticated Squires	26.6	02723	35 International Marketplace	35.6
02043	03 Connoisseurs	54.6	02364	24 Main Street, USA	31.7	02724	57 Simple Living	27.7
02045	10 Pleasant-Ville	33.3	02367	06 Sophisticated Squires	100.0	02725	10 Pleasant-Ville	46.8
02048	04 Boomburbs	28.0	02368	10 Pleasant-Ville	62.0	02726	10 Pleasant-Ville	71.7
02050	10 Pleasant-Ville	44.5	02370	10 Pleasant-Ville	47.0	02738	07 Exurbanites	29.5
02052	09 Urban Chic	36.2	02375	13 In Style	62.5	02739	07 Exurbanites	36.6
02053	02 Suburban Splendor	24.4	02379	10 Pleasant-Ville	72.3	02740	60 City Dimensions	29.4
02054	13 In Style	51.7	02382	24 Main Street, USA	46.1	02743	10 Pleasant-Ville	57.0
02056	02 Suburban Splendor	78.5	02420	03 Connoisseurs	84.7	02744	60 City Dimensions	43.0
02061	02 Suburban Splendor	36.1	02421	03 Connoisseurs	64.1	02745	24 Main Street, USA	24.5
02062	20 City Lights	47.2	02445	08 Laptops And Lattes	59.9	02746	60 City Dimensions	49.7
02066	05 Wealthy Seaboard Suburbs	47.4	02446	08 Laptops And Lattes	93.7	02747	24 Main Street, USA	18.7
02067	02 Suburban Splendor	38.3	02451	05 Wealthy Seaboard Suburbs	21.3	02748	07 Exurbanites	26.2
02071	05 Wealthy Seaboard Suburbs	100.0	02452	09 Urban Chic	34.7	02760	24 Main Street, USA	27.1
02072	10 Pleasant-Ville	38.1	02453	23 Trendsetters	49.6	02762	10 Pleasant-Ville	45.0
02081	05 Wealthy Seaboard Suburbs	55.4	02458	08 Laptops And Lattes	30.8	02763	02 Suburban Splendor	64.5
02090	03 Connoisseurs	75.7	02459	01 Top Rung	31.2	02764	10 Pleasant-Ville	79.1
02093	10 Pleasant-Ville	40.1	02460	09 Urban Chic	52.9	02766	06 Sophisticated Squires	48.5
02108	08 Laptops And Lattes	74.9	02461	09 Urban Chic	64.7	02767	10 Pleasant-Ville	41.8
02109	27 Metro Renters	60.7	02462	09 Urban Chic	87.6	02769	07 Exurbanites	43.9
02110	08 Laptops And Lattes	86.6	02464	09 Urban Chic	97.7	02770	10 Pleasant-Ville	43.2
02111	65 Social Security Set	44.5	02465	09 Urban Chic	48.2	02771	10 Pleasant-Ville	68.6
02113	27 Metro Renters	95.9	02466	09 Urban Chic	87.3	02777	10 Pleasant-Ville	50.6
02114	08 Laptops And Lattes	49.8	02467	01 Top Rung	30.4	02779	06 Sophisticated Squires	98.4
02115	27 Metro Renters	54.3	02468	01 Top Rung	66.8	02780	24 Main Street, USA	49.0
02116	08 Laptops And Lattes	68.4	02472	23 Trendsetters	50.5	02790	10 Pleasant-Ville	65.8
02118	08 Laptops And Lattes	31.0	02474	23 Trendsetters	39.7	02804	10 Pleasant-Ville	43.0
02119	45 City Strivers	68.9	02476	05 Wealthy Seaboard Suburbs	27.4	02806	05 Wealthy Seaboard Suburbs	29.6
02120	55 College Towns	39.7	02478	09 Urban Chic	32.8	02807	09 Urban Chic	87.2
02121	45 City Strivers	84.6	02481	01 Top Rung	56.6	02808	24 Main Street, USA	68.4
02122	20 City Lights	40.6	02482	03 Connoisseurs	33.8	02809	10 Pleasant-Ville	29.6
02124	45 City Strivers	51.1	02492	03 Connoisseurs	41.0	02812	06 Sophisticated Squires	77.8
02125	35 International Marketplace	41.5	02493	01 Top Rung	91.9	02813	13 In Style	32.3
02126	45 City Strivers	88.2	02494	09 Urban Chic	82.7	02814	10 Pleasant-Ville	45.0
02127	23 Trendsetters	37.2	02532	13 In Style	22.3	02815	06 Sophisticated Squires	68.2
02128	35 International Marketplace	60.1	02535	31 Rural Resort Dwellers	66.9	02816	18 Cozy And Comfortable	29.6
02129	08 Laptops And Lattes	60.9	02536	10 Pleasant-Ville	42.0	02817	06 Sophisticated Squires	73.5
02130	23 Trendsetters	49.7	02537	07 Exurbanites	44.1	02818	02 Suburban Splendor	31.7
02131	20 City Lights	57.8	02538	24 Main Street, USA	68.9	02822	06 Sophisticated Squires	78.9
02132	05 Wealthy Seaboard Suburbs	31.0	02539	13 In Style	49.0	02825	10 Pleasant-Ville	45.8
02134	63 Dorms To Diplomas	41.7	02540	15 Silver And Gold	41.6	02827	06 Sophisticated Squires	100.0
02135	27 Metro Renters	41.4	02542	40 Military Proximity	100.0	02828	10 Pleasant-Ville	36.5
02136	20 City Lights	38.3	02543	15 Silver And Gold	100.0	02830	10 Pleasant-Ville	36.8
02138	27 Metro Renters	35.9	02554	09 Urban Chic	68.6	02831	06 Sophisticated Squires	55.2
02139	23 Trendsetters	46.9	02556	07 Exurbanites	31.1	02832	25 Salt Of The Earth	41.0
02140	08 Laptops And Lattes	43.9	02559	15 Silver And Gold	39.6	02833	10 Pleasant-Ville	94.4
02141	23 Trendsetters	57.0	02562	13 In Style	51.5	02835	09 Urban Chic	49.2
02142	27 Metro Renters	46.1	02563	06 Sophisticated Squires	51.8	02836	06 Sophisticated Squires	100.0
02143	23 Trendsetters	51.8	02568	09 Urban Chic	47.3	02837	07 Exurbanites	76.0
02144	23 Trendsetters	53.0	02571	24 Main Street, USA	57.1	02838	24 Main Street, USA	73.2
02145	23 Trendsetters	37.3	02575	09 Urban Chic	100.0	02839	17 Green Acres	67.1
02148	20 City Lights	50.1	02576	49 Senior Sun Seekers	47.5	02840	23 Trendsetters	29.1
02149	20 City Lights	83.1	02601	24 Main Street, USA	23.7	02841	40 Military Proximity	91.1
02150	35 International Marketplace	60.1	02630	15 Silver And Gold	70.5	02842	24 Main Street, USA	34.0
02151	20 City Lights	44.4	02631	31 Rural Resort Dwellers	31.0	02852	13 In Style	20.3
02152	20 City Lights	47.4	02632	14 Prosperous Empty Nesters	34.2	02857	07 Exurbanites	45.5
02153	23 Trendsetters	100.0	02633	15 Silver And Gold	83.2	02858	10 Pleasant-Ville	66.8
02155	20 City Lights	52.7	02635	15 Silver And Gold	65.9	02859	24 Main Street, USA	50.7
02163	27 Metro Renters	100.0	02638	15 Silver And Gold	95.2	02860	60 City Dimensions	27.0
02169	20 City Lights	22.0	02639	30 Retirement Communities	37.0	02861	24 Main Street, USA	53.8
02170	20 City Lights	43.0	02642	31 Rural Resort Dwellers	86.4	02863	58 NeWest Residents	67.4
02171	20 City Lights	50.4	02644	06 Sophisticated Squires	100.0	02864	07 Exurbanites	15.3
02176	05 Wealthy Seaboard Suburbs	41.5	02645	31 Rural Resort Dwellers	82.0	02865	05 Wealthy Seaboard Suburbs	21.4
02180	10 Pleasant-Ville	34.4	02646	15 Silver And Gold	52.4	02871	07 Exurbanites	59.2
02184	05 Wealthy Seaboard Suburbs	39.8	02648	10 Pleasant-Ville	45.5	02872	15 Silver And Gold	100.0
02186	05 Wealthy Seaboard Suburbs	50.4	02649	13 In Style	47.5	02873	10 Pleasant-Ville	100.0
02188	10 Pleasant-Ville	36.7	02650	15 Silver And Gold	100.0	02874	06 Sophisticated Squires	34.1
02189	10 Pleasant-Ville	27.3	02652	31 Rural Resort Dwellers	100.0	02877	06 Sophisticated Squires	100.0
02190	10 Pleasant-Ville	41.4	02653	15 Silver And Gold	63.3	02878	10 Pleasant-Ville	49.0
02191	10 Pleasant-Ville	68.0	02655	15 Silver And Gold	87.1	02879	24 Main Street, USA	15.4
02199	27 Metro Renters	100.0	02657	09 Urban Chic	60.3	02881	02 Suburban Splendor	65.8

ZIP CODE	TOP TAPESTRY CONSUMER TYPE	% 2009 HOUSE-HOLDS
02882	13 In Style	19.5
02885	30 Retirement Communities	20.7
02886	18 Cozy And Comfortable	31.4
02888	24 Main Street, USA	32.5
02889	24 Main Street, USA	46.7
02891	24 Main Street, USA	18.3
02892	06 Sophisticated Squires	96.7
02893	24 Main Street, USA	53.5
02894	17 Green Acres	93.8
02895	24 Main Street, USA	38.0
02896	10 Pleasant-Ville	72.8
02898	06 Sophisticated Squires	83.0
02903	65 Social Security Set	33.1
02904	24 Main Street, USA	26.2
02905	24 Main Street, USA	21.6
02906	08 Laptops And Lattes	26.7
02907	58 NeWest Residents	35.6
02908	60 City Dimensions	32.6
02909	58 NeWest Residents	27.2
02910	24 Main Street, USA	71.9
02911	36 Old And Newcomers	38.4
02912	63 Dorms To Diplomas	0.0
02914	24 Main Street, USA	47.2
02915	29 Rustbelt Retirees	24.7
02916	24 Main Street, USA	37.9
02917	13 In Style	20.0
02918	55 College Towns	96.3
02919	10 Pleasant-Ville	28.1
02920	24 Main Street, USA	29.1
02921	02 Suburban Splendor	66.4
03031	02 Suburban Splendor	70.6
03032	06 Sophisticated Squires	65.2
03033	06 Sophisticated Squires	59.7
03034	06 Sophisticated Squires	71.8
03036	06 Sophisticated Squires	97.4
03037	06 Sophisticated Squires	60.7
03038	06 Sophisticated Squires	41.2
03042	19 Milk And Cookies	36.9
03043	07 Exurbanites	100.0
03044	06 Sophisticated Squires	99.9
03045	06 Sophisticated Squires	38.9
03046	06 Sophisticated Squires	94.1
03047	17 Green Acres	100.0
03048	41 Crossroads	36.7
03049	02 Suburban Splendor	83.5
03051	06 Sophisticated Squires	63.9
03052	06 Sophisticated Squires	100.0
03053	06 Sophisticated Squires	80.9
03054	06 Sophisticated Squires	67.8
03055	06 Sophisticated Squires	40.1
03057	07 Exurbanites	95.3
03060	24 Main Street, USA	30.3
03062	06 Sophisticated Squires	30.5
03063	16 Enterprising Professionals	45.9
03064	07 Exurbanites	18.5
03070	06 Sophisticated Squires	98.0
03071	17 Green Acres	98.5
03076	06 Sophisticated Squires	100.0
03077	26 Midland Crowd	59.1
03079	10 Pleasant-Ville	32.5
03082	17 Green Acres	97.9
03084	06 Sophisticated Squires	100.0
03086	17 Green Acres	61.0
03087	02 Suburban Splendor	85.5
03101	65 Social Security Set	49.0
03102	24 Main Street, USA	36.5
03103	24 Main Street, USA	28.6
03104	24 Main Street, USA	21.7
03106	06 Sophisticated Squires	36.1
03109	18 Cozy And Comfortable	39.6
03110	02 Suburban Splendor	65.4
03216	17 Green Acres	66.4
03217	33 Midlife Junction	54.4
03218	25 Salt Of The Earth	53.8
03220	26 Midland Crowd	71.3
03221	31 Rural Resort Dwellers	97.3
03222	24 Main Street, USA	37.1
03223	33 Midlife Junction	59.2
03224	07 Exurbanites	99.7
03225	17 Green Acres	74.3
03226	31 Rural Resort Dwellers	95.6
03227	31 Rural Resort Dwellers	100.0
03229	07 Exurbanites	62.3
03230	25 Salt Of The Earth	96.4
03234	17 Green Acres	64.8
03235	57 Simple Living	30.1
03237	17 Green Acres	88.7
03240	26 Midland Crowd	57.3
03241	31 Rural Resort Dwellers	100.0
03242	22 Metropolitans	68.0
03243	17 Green Acres	98.3
03244	17 Green Acres	49.6
03245	31 Rural Resort Dwellers	97.8
03246	24 Main Street, USA	27.1
03249	18 Cozy And Comfortable	30.8
03251	33 Midlife Junction	50.4
03253	31 Rural Resort Dwellers	68.2
03254	31 Rural Resort Dwellers	68.8
03255	31 Rural Resort Dwellers	100.0
03256	17 Green Acres	85.6
03257	15 Silver And Gold	77.8
03258	17 Green Acres	99.5
03259	31 Rural Resort Dwellers	100.0
03261	17 Green Acres	96.4
03262	33 Midlife Junction	57.5
03263	24 Main Street, USA	59.1
03264	33 Midlife Junction	55.9
03266	31 Rural Resort Dwellers	100.0
03268	17 Green Acres	99.1
03269	17 Green Acres	64.0
03275	24 Main Street, USA	43.0
03276	26 Midland Crowd	35.3
03278	31 Rural Resort Dwellers	62.2
03279	46 Rooted Rural	100.0
03280	31 Rural Resort Dwellers	100.0
03281	06 Sophisticated Squires	58.0
03282	31 Rural Resort Dwellers	100.0
03284	31 Rural Resort Dwellers	100.0
03285	31 Rural Resort Dwellers	100.0
03287	07 Exurbanites	96.3
03290	06 Sophisticated Squires	97.5
03291	06 Sophisticated Squires	100.0
03301	36 Old And Newcomers	17.1
03303	28 Aspiring Young Families	39.3
03304	02 Suburban Splendor	88.5
03307	17 Green Acres	99.0
03431	55 College Towns	13.8
03440	24 Main Street, USA	54.4
03441	33 Midlife Junction	59.1
03442	24 Main Street, USA	97.8
03443	17 Green Acres	100.0
03444	07 Exurbanites	100.0
03445	17 Green Acres	99.7
03446	17 Green Acres	30.2
03447	17 Green Acres	66.1
03448	17 Green Acres	100.0
03449	14 Prosperous Empty Nesters	100.0
03450	31 Rural Resort Dwellers	97.3
03451	26 Midland Crowd	52.3
03452	24 Main Street, USA	57.9
03455	25 Salt Of The Earth	50.1
03456	25 Salt Of The Earth	94.3
03457	17 Green Acres	89.7
03458	13 In Style	48.9
03461	17 Green Acres	99.9
03462	17 Green Acres	53.0
03464	31 Rural Resort Dwellers	100.0
03465	25 Salt Of The Earth	57.8
03466	17 Green Acres	100.0
03467	07 Exurbanites	99.4
03470	33 Midlife Junction	24.1
03561	48 Great Expectations	43.6
03570	50 Heartland Communities	29.4
03574	33 Midlife Junction	53.7
03576	46 Rooted Rural	42.5
03579	31 Rural Resort Dwellers	100.0
03580	31 Rural Resort Dwellers	100.0
03581	33 Midlife Junction	68.3
03582	50 Heartland Communities	49.4
03583	31 Rural Resort Dwellers	99.5
03584	33 Midlife Junction	32.3
03585	31 Rural Resort Dwellers	39.4
03586	31 Rural Resort Dwellers	98.7
03588	25 Salt Of The Earth	80.6
03590	46 Rooted Rural	97.3
03592	31 Rural Resort Dwellers	100.0
03593	31 Rural Resort Dwellers	100.0
03598	31 Rural Resort Dwellers	49.7
03602	25 Salt Of The Earth	60.0
03603	25 Salt Of The Earth	58.3
03605	25 Salt Of The Earth	76.3
03607	31 Rural Resort Dwellers	91.5
03608	33 Midlife Junction	53.4
03609	32 Rustbelt Traditions	100.0
03740	31 Rural Resort Dwellers	100.0
03741	26 Midland Crowd	66.7
03743	57 Simple Living	26.6
03745	17 Green Acres	100.0
03748	13 In Style	41.5
03750	02 Suburban Splendor	55.0
03752	25 Salt Of The Earth	100.0
03753	14 Prosperous Empty Nesters	88.8
03755	08 Laptops And Lattes	48.4
03765	31 Rural Resort Dwellers	100.0
03766	36 Old And Newcomers	58.1
03768	03 Connoisseurs	51.1
03770	17 Green Acres	100.0
03771	31 Rural Resort Dwellers	100.0
03773	25 Salt Of The Earth	44.1
03774	33 Midlife Junction	59.5
03777	31 Rural Resort Dwellers	99.4
03779	31 Rural Resort Dwellers	100.0
03780	31 Rural Resort Dwellers	98.3
03781	17 Green Acres	100.0
03782	31 Rural Resort Dwellers	70.7
03784	36 Old And Newcomers	64.0
03785	33 Midlife Junction	94.1
03801	13 In Style	14.6
03809	31 Rural Resort Dwellers	64.4
03810	31 Rural Resort Dwellers	100.0
03811	07 Exurbanites	78.4
03812	31 Rural Resort Dwellers	100.0
03813	31 Rural Resort Dwellers	56.2
03814	31 Rural Resort Dwellers	59.1
03816	31 Rural Resort Dwellers	87.1
03817	31 Rural Resort Dwellers	100.0
03818	31 Rural Resort Dwellers	47.9
03819	12 Up And Coming Families	99.3
03820	36 Old And Newcomers	45.0
03823	13 In Style	93.1
03824	55 College Towns	46.8
03825	17 Green Acres	58.4
03826	13 In Style	90.8
03827	06 Sophisticated Squires	70.9
03830	31 Rural Resort Dwellers	100.0
03833	06 Sophisticated Squires	22.7
03835	32 Rustbelt Traditions	23.0
03836	31 Rural Resort Dwellers	100.0
03837	31 Rural Resort Dwellers	72.0
03838	31 Rural Resort Dwellers	100.0
03839	26 Midland Crowd	74.9
03840	07 Exurbanites	51.3
03841	07 Exurbanites	80.0
03842	13 In Style	41.4
03844	07 Exurbanites	100.0
03845	31 Rural Resort Dwellers	84.1
03846	31 Rural Resort Dwellers	100.0
03848	18 Cozy And Comfortable	37.8
03849	31 Rural Resort Dwellers	100.0
03851	26 Midland Crowd	88.7
03852	25 Salt Of The Earth	100.0
03853	31 Rural Resort Dwellers	55.8
03854	03 Connoisseurs	100.0
03855	17 Green Acres	94.8
03856	06 Sophisticated Squires	99.0
03857	16 Enterprising Professionals	41.8
03858	06 Sophisticated Squires	38.1
03860	31 Rural Resort Dwellers	33.8
03861	13 In Style	63.4
03862	31 Rural Resort Dwellers	41.2
03864	31 Rural Resort Dwellers	98.1
03865	13 In Style	45.6
03867	24 Main Street, USA	25.7
03868	33 Midlife Junction	50.6
03869	24 Main Street, USA	64.8
03870	09 Urban Chic	64.4
03871	15 Silver And Gold	99.2
03872	31 Rural Resort Dwellers	58.0
03873	06 Sophisticated Squires	99.7
03874	24 Main Street, USA	36.0
03875	31 Rural Resort Dwellers	100.0
03878	48 Great Expectations	23.4
03882	31 Rural Resort Dwellers	100.0
03883	31 Rural Resort Dwellers	100.0
03884	17 Green Acres	54.7
03885	07 Exurbanites	55.7
03886	31 Rural Resort Dwellers	100.0
03887	25 Salt Of The Earth	99.4
03890	31 Rural Resort Dwellers	100.0
03894	31 Rural Resort Dwellers	58.3
03901	17 Green Acres	42.4
03902	15 Silver And Gold	62.0
03903	17 Green Acres	40.7
03904	28 Aspiring Young Families	27.9
03905	14 Prosperous Empty Nesters	83.7
03906	17 Green Acres	72.3
03907	15 Silver And Gold	100.0
03908	17 Green Acres	32.2
03909	07 Exurbanites	47.4
04001	31 Rural Resort Dwellers	51.9

CONSUMER TYPE

ZIP CODE	TOP TAPESTRY CONSUMER TYPE	% 2009 HOUSE-HOLDS	ZIP CODE	TOP TAPESTRY CONSUMER TYPE	% 2009 HOUSE-HOLDS	ZIP CODE	TOP TAPESTRY CONSUMER TYPE	% 2009 HOUSE-HOLDS
04002	17 Green Acres	39.8	04258	17 Green Acres	96.0	04475	42 Southern Satellites	100.0
04003	31 Rural Resort Dwellers	100.0	04259	26 Midland Crowd	84.8	04476	31 Rural Resort Dwellers	99.7
04005	17 Green Acres	19.3	04260	17 Green Acres	69.3	04478	31 Rural Resort Dwellers	100.0
04006	15 Silver And Gold	100.0	04261	31 Rural Resort Dwellers	100.0	04479	50 Heartland Communities	55.8
04008	26 Midland Crowd	54.8	04263	25 Salt Of The Earth	100.0	04481	31 Rural Resort Dwellers	88.8
04009	25 Salt Of The Earth	37.5	04265	25 Salt Of The Earth	96.5	04487	46 Rooted Rural	100.0
04010	31 Rural Resort Dwellers	100.0	04266	26 Midland Crowd	100.0	04488	46 Rooted Rural	100.0
04011	41 Crossroads	10.4	04268	31 Rural Resort Dwellers	42.7	04490	31 Rural Resort Dwellers	91.3
04015	26 Midland Crowd	41.1	04270	31 Rural Resort Dwellers	42.1	04491	46 Rooted Rural	100.0
04017	07 Exurbanites	100.0	04274	17 Green Acres	41.4	04492	46 Rooted Rural	66.7
04019	31 Rural Resort Dwellers	100.0	04275	29 Rustbelt Retirees	100.0	04493	42 Southern Satellites	63.4
04020	25 Salt Of The Earth	100.0	04276	57 Simple Living	45.0	04495	46 Rooted Rural	100.0
04021	06 Sophisticated Squires	60.9	04280	26 Midland Crowd	100.0	04496	26 Midland Crowd	96.4
04022	31 Rural Resort Dwellers	100.0	04281	33 Midlife Junction	78.9	04497	46 Rooted Rural	100.0
04024	25 Salt Of The Earth	91.8	04282	17 Green Acres	56.6	04530	48 Great Expectations	37.4
04027	26 Midland Crowd	67.5	04284	31 Rural Resort Dwellers	100.0	04535	17 Green Acres	92.3
04029	31 Rural Resort Dwellers	94.4	04285	25 Salt Of The Earth	100.0	04537	31 Rural Resort Dwellers	100.0
04030	17 Green Acres	100.0	04287	26 Midland Crowd	99.6	04538	31 Rural Resort Dwellers	86.2
04032	26 Midland Crowd	18.9	04289	46 Rooted Rural	94.0	04539	31 Rural Resort Dwellers	100.0
04037	31 Rural Resort Dwellers	83.6	04290	25 Salt Of The Earth	100.0	04541	31 Rural Resort Dwellers	100.0
04038	06 Sophisticated Squires	27.2	04292	25 Salt Of The Earth	100.0	04543	31 Rural Resort Dwellers	50.1
04039	17 Green Acres	58.2	04294	33 Midlife Junction	40.2	04544	15 Silver And Gold	100.0
04040	31 Rural Resort Dwellers	54.1	04330	57 Simple Living	26.6	04547	31 Rural Resort Dwellers	55.2
04041	25 Salt Of The Earth	100.0	04341	31 Rural Resort Dwellers	100.0	04548	31 Rural Resort Dwellers	100.0
04042	17 Green Acres	66.5	04342	26 Midland Crowd	100.0	04549	31 Rural Resort Dwellers	100.0
04043	13 In Style	19.6	04344	33 Midlife Junction	80.4	04551	31 Rural Resort Dwellers	100.0
04046	15 Silver And Gold	30.0	04345	25 Salt Of The Earth	41.4	04553	31 Rural Resort Dwellers	100.0
04047	31 Rural Resort Dwellers	100.0	04346	33 Midlife Junction	90.7	04554	15 Silver And Gold	87.9
04048	25 Salt Of The Earth	56.5	04347	36 Old And Newcomers	44.8	04555	31 Rural Resort Dwellers	100.0
04049	26 Midland Crowd	58.0	04348	17 Green Acres	56.2	04556	31 Rural Resort Dwellers	100.0
04050	31 Rural Resort Dwellers	100.0	04349	31 Rural Resort Dwellers	99.8	04558	31 Rural Resort Dwellers	64.5
04051	31 Rural Resort Dwellers	100.0	04350	31 Rural Resort Dwellers	56.5	04562	31 Rural Resort Dwellers	57.3
04055	31 Rural Resort Dwellers	96.2	04351	17 Green Acres	59.4	04563	31 Rural Resort Dwellers	100.0
04061	12 Up And Coming Families	70.7	04352	31 Rural Resort Dwellers	100.0	04564	31 Rural Resort Dwellers	99.4
04062	24 Main Street, USA	35.6	04353	26 Midland Crowd	98.4	04568	31 Rural Resort Dwellers	100.0
04064	33 Midlife Junction	31.3	04354	31 Rural Resort Dwellers	100.0	04570	15 Silver And Gold	100.0
04066	31 Rural Resort Dwellers	100.0	04355	17 Green Acres	50.8	04571	31 Rural Resort Dwellers	100.0
04068	25 Salt Of The Earth	100.0	04357	26 Midland Crowd	66.9	04572	26 Midland Crowd	40.6
04069	17 Green Acres	97.5	04358	26 Midland Crowd	67.0	04573	31 Rural Resort Dwellers	100.0
04071	17 Green Acres	66.5	04360	31 Rural Resort Dwellers	100.0	04574	31 Rural Resort Dwellers	100.0
04072	24 Main Street, USA	29.0	04363	26 Midland Crowd	100.0	04576	15 Silver And Gold	100.0
04073	24 Main Street, USA	26.3	04364	31 Rural Resort Dwellers	29.8	04578	26 Midland Crowd	35.5
04074	13 In Style	40.8	04401	36 Old And Newcomers	18.1	04579	17 Green Acres	51.7
04076	17 Green Acres	56.5	04406	31 Rural Resort Dwellers	98.3	04605	31 Rural Resort Dwellers	62.1
04079	31 Rural Resort Dwellers	100.0	04408	46 Rooted Rural	98.8	04606	46 Rooted Rural	100.0
04083	24 Main Street, USA	70.0	04410	26 Midland Crowd	100.0	04607	31 Rural Resort Dwellers	73.4
04084	26 Midland Crowd	55.0	04411	26 Midland Crowd	100.0	04609	22 Metropolitans	34.9
04085	17 Green Acres	100.0	04412	48 Great Expectations	32.8	04611	37 Prairie Living	100.0
04086	17 Green Acres	45.0	04413	46 Rooted Rural	100.0	04612	31 Rural Resort Dwellers	100.0
04087	26 Midland Crowd	75.8	04414	50 Heartland Communities	94.1	04613	31 Rural Resort Dwellers	100.0
04088	31 Rural Resort Dwellers	100.0	04416	33 Midlife Junction	61.7	04614	31 Rural Resort Dwellers	100.0
04090	17 Green Acres	46.2	04417	42 Southern Satellites	100.0	04616	31 Rural Resort Dwellers	100.0
04091	25 Salt Of The Earth	100.0	04418	42 Southern Satellites	91.6	04617	31 Rural Resort Dwellers	100.0
04092	48 Great Expectations	24.9	04419	26 Midland Crowd	100.0	04619	33 Midlife Junction	38.2
04093	17 Green Acres	100.0	04421	15 Silver And Gold	100.0	04622	46 Rooted Rural	82.7
04095	31 Rural Resort Dwellers	99.4	04422	46 Rooted Rural	94.8	04623	46 Rooted Rural	94.1
04096	03 Connoisseurs	26.4	04424	50 Heartland Communities	63.6	04624	31 Rural Resort Dwellers	100.0
04097	07 Exurbanites	54.0	04426	50 Heartland Communities	41.6	04625	31 Rural Resort Dwellers	100.0
04101	27 Metro Renters	21.5	04427	26 Midland Crowd	60.2	04626	37 Prairie Living	100.0
04102	24 Main Street, USA	24.9	04428	33 Midlife Junction	41.3	04627	31 Rural Resort Dwellers	100.0
04103	22 Metropolitans	29.6	04429	31 Rural Resort Dwellers	55.5	04628	46 Rooted Rural	100.0
04105	02 Suburban Splendor	42.1	04430	50 Heartland Communities	71.8	04630	46 Rooted Rural	100.0
04106	24 Main Street, USA	30.8	04434	26 Midland Crowd	100.0	04631	50 Heartland Communities	100.0
04107	07 Exurbanites	40.5	04435	46 Rooted Rural	100.0	04634	46 Rooted Rural	88.2
04108	22 Metropolitans	90.6	04438	26 Midland Crowd	100.0	04635	37 Prairie Living	100.0
04109	15 Silver And Gold	100.0	04441	33 Midlife Junction	91.2	04640	31 Rural Resort Dwellers	100.0
04110	07 Exurbanites	100.0	04442	31 Rural Resort Dwellers	100.0	04642	31 Rural Resort Dwellers	100.0
04210	14 Prosperous Empty Nesters	15.7	04443	46 Rooted Rural	52.9	04643	46 Rooted Rural	100.0
04216	31 Rural Resort Dwellers	100.0	04444	17 Green Acres	44.0	04645	37 Prairie Living	100.0
04217	33 Midlife Junction	41.6	04448	50 Heartland Communities	78.2	04646	31 Rural Resort Dwellers	100.0
04219	31 Rural Resort Dwellers	90.1	04449	26 Midland Crowd	100.0	04648	31 Rural Resort Dwellers	100.0
04220	25 Salt Of The Earth	98.9	04450	46 Rooted Rural	100.0	04649	37 Prairie Living	100.0
04221	46 Rooted Rural	65.2	04451	46 Rooted Rural	100.0	04650	31 Rural Resort Dwellers	100.0
04222	17 Green Acres	100.0	04453	42 Southern Satellites	81.4	04652	46 Rooted Rural	64.7
04224	25 Salt Of The Earth	79.4	04454	46 Rooted Rural	100.0	04653	31 Rural Resort Dwellers	100.0
04226	31 Rural Resort Dwellers	100.0	04455	46 Rooted Rural	94.9	04654	57 Simple Living	33.2
04228	46 Rooted Rural	100.0	04456	26 Midland Crowd	100.0	04655	46 Rooted Rural	100.0
04231	31 Rural Resort Dwellers	100.0	04457	50 Heartland Communities	41.2	04657	46 Rooted Rural	100.0
04236	17 Green Acres	100.0	04459	46 Rooted Rural	100.0	04658	46 Rooted Rural	97.3
04237	31 Rural Resort Dwellers	100.0	04460	42 Southern Satellites	89.8	04660	31 Rural Resort Dwellers	91.6
04238	17 Green Acres	100.0	04461	26 Midland Crowd	100.0	04666	46 Rooted Rural	100.0
04239	26 Midland Crowd	34.6	04462	50 Heartland Communities	55.1	04667	46 Rooted Rural	52.0
04240	33 Midlife Junction	16.3	04463	50 Heartland Communities	86.8	04668	42 Southern Satellites	52.6
04250	33 Midlife Junction	56.5	04464	50 Heartland Communities	84.9	04669	31 Rural Resort Dwellers	100.0
04252	32 Rustbelt Traditions	71.9	04468	33 Midlife Junction	21.8	04671	46 Rooted Rural	100.0
04253	25 Salt Of The Earth	100.0	04469	63 Dorms To Diplomas	100.0	04673	31 Rural Resort Dwellers	100.0
04254	48 Great Expectations	39.6	04471	46 Rooted Rural	100.0	04674	31 Rural Resort Dwellers	100.0
04255	31 Rural Resort Dwellers	100.0	04472	25 Salt Of The Earth	67.7	04676	31 Rural Resort Dwellers	100.0
04256	26 Midland Crowd	53.2	04473	55 College Towns	59.5	04677	31 Rural Resort Dwellers	100.0
04257	50 Heartland Communities	55.4	04474	17 Green Acres	60.0	04679	31 Rural Resort Dwellers	100.0

ZIP CODE	TOP TAPESTRY CONSUMER TYPE	% 2009 HOUSE-HOLDS
04680	37 Prairie Living	100.0
04681	37 Prairie Living	100.0
04683	31 Rural Resort Dwellers	100.0
04684	31 Rural Resort Dwellers	100.0
04685	37 Prairie Living	100.0
04691	46 Rooted Rural	100.0
04693	33 Midlife Junction	100.0
04694	46 Rooted Rural	66.9
04730	50 Heartland Communities	36.1
04732	46 Rooted Rural	100.0
04733	46 Rooted Rural	100.0
04734	46 Rooted Rural	100.0
04735	46 Rooted Rural	96.6
04736	46 Rooted Rural	42.7
04737	37 Prairie Living	100.0
04740	46 Rooted Rural	92.5
04741	37 Prairie Living	100.0
04742	57 Simple Living	36.4
04743	57 Simple Living	31.8
04745	46 Rooted Rural	97.6
04746	50 Heartland Communities	97.3
04747	50 Heartland Communities	85.2
04750	32 Rustbelt Traditions	50.3
04751	32 Rustbelt Traditions	98.4
04756	50 Heartland Communities	37.3
04757	25 Salt Of The Earth	63.4
04758	50 Heartland Communities	100.0
04760	46 Rooted Rural	100.0
04761	31 Rural Resort Dwellers	95.7
04762	31 Rural Resort Dwellers	95.5
04763	50 Heartland Communities	76.0
04764	31 Rural Resort Dwellers	100.0
04765	46 Rooted Rural	80.4
04766	46 Rooted Rural	100.0
04768	46 Rooted Rural	100.0
04769	48 Great Expectations	29.2
04772	46 Rooted Rural	88.7
04773	25 Salt Of The Earth	95.9
04774	46 Rooted Rural	63.0
04776	46 Rooted Rural	100.0
04777	46 Rooted Rural	99.4
04779	31 Rural Resort Dwellers	100.0
04780	46 Rooted Rural	100.0
04781	25 Salt Of The Earth	100.0
04783	31 Rural Resort Dwellers	61.1
04785	50 Heartland Communities	63.9
04786	46 Rooted Rural	53.7
04787	46 Rooted Rural	95.9
04841	33 Midlife Junction	26.4
04843	31 Rural Resort Dwellers	35.4
04847	31 Rural Resort Dwellers	98.3
04848	31 Rural Resort Dwellers	100.0
04849	31 Rural Resort Dwellers	94.1
04851	37 Prairie Living	100.0
04852	37 Prairie Living	100.0
04853	37 Prairie Living	100.0
04854	31 Rural Resort Dwellers	98.8
04856	31 Rural Resort Dwellers	41.9
04858	25 Salt Of The Earth	51.6
04859	31 Rural Resort Dwellers	100.0
04860	31 Rural Resort Dwellers	100.0
04861	33 Midlife Junction	100.0
04862	31 Rural Resort Dwellers	67.6
04863	37 Prairie Living	100.0
04864	26 Midland Crowd	50.0
04901	57 Simple Living	20.6
04910	46 Rooted Rural	51.3
04911	46 Rooted Rural	77.0
04912	46 Rooted Rural	99.1
04915	46 Rooted Rural	48.3
04917	31 Rural Resort Dwellers	65.6
04920	50 Heartland Communities	50.2
04921	46 Rooted Rural	100.0
04922	42 Southern Satellites	100.0
04923	46 Rooted Rural	100.0
04924	26 Midland Crowd	93.3
04925	31 Rural Resort Dwellers	100.0
04927	26 Midland Crowd	60.8
04928	46 Rooted Rural	98.1
04929	42 Southern Satellites	100.0
04930	50 Heartland Communities	46.5
04932	26 Midland Crowd	100.0
04936	33 Midlife Junction	100.0
04937	26 Midland Crowd	42.4
04938	33 Midlife Junction	43.1
04939	42 Southern Satellites	100.0
04941	46 Rooted Rural	98.0
04942	46 Rooted Rural	100.0
04943	42 Southern Satellites	89.9
04945	46 Rooted Rural	94.3
04947	31 Rural Resort Dwellers	100.0
04949	31 Rural Resort Dwellers	100.0
04950	50 Heartland Communities	62.8
04951	46 Rooted Rural	100.0
04952	26 Midland Crowd	52.4
04953	33 Midlife Junction	42.7
04954	31 Rural Resort Dwellers	100.0
04955	25 Salt Of The Earth	99.2
04956	25 Salt Of The Earth	99.7
04957	25 Salt Of The Earth	79.1
04958	42 Southern Satellites	55.2
04961	31 Rural Resort Dwellers	78.3
04963	31 Rural Resort Dwellers	28.7
04965	46 Rooted Rural	93.3
04966	31 Rural Resort Dwellers	71.7
04967	46 Rooted Rural	26.2
04969	26 Midland Crowd	98.3
04970	31 Rural Resort Dwellers	98.9
04971	42 Southern Satellites	52.8
04973	25 Salt Of The Earth	100.0
04974	31 Rural Resort Dwellers	62.6
04976	25 Salt Of The Earth	25.9
04978	25 Salt Of The Earth	100.0
04979	46 Rooted Rural	80.3
04981	25 Salt Of The Earth	56.7
04982	33 Midlife Junction	68.4
04983	46 Rooted Rural	74.4
04984	46 Rooted Rural	100.0
04985	46 Rooted Rural	58.8
04986	46 Rooted Rural	100.0
04987	46 Rooted Rural	100.0
04988	57 Simple Living	54.5
04989	26 Midland Crowd	53.5
05001	33 Midlife Junction	25.2
05032	33 Midlife Junction	37.8
05033	33 Midlife Junction	46.0
05034	31 Rural Resort Dwellers	100.0
05035	31 Rural Resort Dwellers	100.0
05036	17 Green Acres	96.8
05037	31 Rural Resort Dwellers	100.0
05038	31 Rural Resort Dwellers	98.0
05039	25 Salt Of The Earth	100.0
05040	25 Salt Of The Earth	67.4
05041	31 Rural Resort Dwellers	100.0
05042	31 Rural Resort Dwellers	100.0
05043	17 Green Acres	100.0
05045	31 Rural Resort Dwellers	73.7
05046	25 Salt Of The Earth	88.8
05048	26 Midland Crowd	44.5
05051	31 Rural Resort Dwellers	84.7
05052	26 Midland Crowd	100.0
05053	31 Rural Resort Dwellers	100.0
05055	07 Exurbanites	60.3
05056	31 Rural Resort Dwellers	100.0
05058	17 Green Acres	57.3
05060	33 Midlife Junction	39.3
05061	31 Rural Resort Dwellers	77.5
05062	31 Rural Resort Dwellers	100.0
05065	26 Midland Crowd	96.4
05067	31 Rural Resort Dwellers	100.0
05068	48 Great Expectations	30.6
05069	31 Rural Resort Dwellers	100.0
05070	31 Rural Resort Dwellers	88.0
05071	31 Rural Resort Dwellers	80.0
05072	31 Rural Resort Dwellers	100.0
05073	14 Prosperous Empty Nesters	100.0
05075	17 Green Acres	78.9
05076	25 Salt Of The Earth	100.0
05077	31 Rural Resort Dwellers	100.0
05079	26 Midland Crowd	97.1
05081	50 Heartland Communities	71.7
05083	26 Midland Crowd	100.0
05084	31 Rural Resort Dwellers	100.0
05086	25 Salt Of The Earth	100.0
05089	33 Midlife Junction	59.6
05091	31 Rural Resort Dwellers	46.5
05101	57 Simple Living	31.1
05141	31 Rural Resort Dwellers	100.0
05142	31 Rural Resort Dwellers	78.4
05143	31 Rural Resort Dwellers	44.4
05146	31 Rural Resort Dwellers	100.0
05148	31 Rural Resort Dwellers	100.0
05149	31 Rural Resort Dwellers	74.2
05150	29 Rustbelt Retirees	61.2
05151	31 Rural Resort Dwellers	69.0
05152	31 Rural Resort Dwellers	100.0
05153	31 Rural Resort Dwellers	59.9
05154	31 Rural Resort Dwellers	100.0
05155	31 Rural Resort Dwellers	100.0
05156	33 Midlife Junction	44.8
05158	25 Salt Of The Earth	50.1
05161	31 Rural Resort Dwellers	100.0
05201	25 Salt Of The Earth	18.2
05250	31 Rural Resort Dwellers	67.7
05251	31 Rural Resort Dwellers	100.0
05252	31 Rural Resort Dwellers	78.9
05253	31 Rural Resort Dwellers	100.0
05255	31 Rural Resort Dwellers	61.5
05257	33 Midlife Junction	54.0
05260	25 Salt Of The Earth	99.2
05261	25 Salt Of The Earth	54.3
05262	17 Green Acres	47.7
05301	17 Green Acres	17.3
05340	31 Rural Resort Dwellers	100.0
05341	31 Rural Resort Dwellers	62.2
05342	31 Rural Resort Dwellers	55.1
05343	31 Rural Resort Dwellers	100.0
05345	31 Rural Resort Dwellers	100.0
05346	17 Green Acres	31.7
05350	33 Midlife Junction	100.0
05351	31 Rural Resort Dwellers	100.0
05352	17 Green Acres	100.0
05353	31 Rural Resort Dwellers	100.0
05354	17 Green Acres	100.0
05355	31 Rural Resort Dwellers	100.0
05356	31 Rural Resort Dwellers	51.2
05358	31 Rural Resort Dwellers	100.0
05359	31 Rural Resort Dwellers	100.0
05360	31 Rural Resort Dwellers	100.0
05361	31 Rural Resort Dwellers	55.9
05362	31 Rural Resort Dwellers	100.0
05363	31 Rural Resort Dwellers	99.9
05401	55 College Towns	36.1
05403	13 In Style	24.2
05404	24 Main Street, USA	35.5
05405	55 College Towns	100.0
05408	18 Cozy And Comfortable	30.8
05440	46 Rooted Rural	100.0
05441	17 Green Acres	99.3
05442	26 Midland Crowd	100.0
05443	17 Green Acres	50.2
05444	17 Green Acres	100.0
05445	07 Exurbanites	45.7
05446	13 In Style	58.2
05447	37 Prairie Living	100.0
05448	17 Green Acres	76.1
05450	50 Heartland Communities	29.4
05452	13 In Style	30.8
05454	17 Green Acres	97.2
05455	25 Salt Of The Earth	55.4
05456	31 Rural Resort Dwellers	55.3
05457	25 Salt Of The Earth	59.2
05458	17 Green Acres	53.6
05459	25 Salt Of The Earth	50.0
05461	26 Midland Crowd	56.3
05462	17 Green Acres	100.0
05463	31 Rural Resort Dwellers	100.0
05464	17 Green Acres	100.0
05465	06 Sophisticated Squires	92.7
05468	17 Green Acres	53.0
05471	31 Rural Resort Dwellers	100.0
05472	17 Green Acres	100.0
05473	17 Green Acres	68.5
05474	31 Rural Resort Dwellers	100.0
05476	46 Rooted Rural	47.1
05477	13 In Style	46.5
05478	24 Main Street, USA	33.8
05482	13 In Style	34.4
05483	25 Salt Of The Earth	95.0
05486	07 Exurbanites	58.9
05487	17 Green Acres	49.0
05488	25 Salt Of The Earth	48.9
05489	06 Sophisticated Squires	67.8
05491	17 Green Acres	48.2
05492	26 Midland Crowd	83.8
05494	06 Sophisticated Squires	100.0
05495	13 In Style	73.5
05602	22 Metropolitans	29.4
05640	31 Rural Resort Dwellers	100.0
05641	33 Midlife Junction	20.8
05647	17 Green Acres	99.5
05648	31 Rural Resort Dwellers	96.9
05649	33 Midlife Junction	77.3
05650	25 Salt Of The Earth	43.6
05651	17 Green Acres	83.5
05652	26 Midland Crowd	100.0
05653	26 Midland Crowd	100.0
05654	33 Midlife Junction	71.0
05655	33 Midlife Junction	65.6
05656	48 Great Expectations	55.7

CONSUMER TYPE

ZIP CODE	TOP TAPESTRY CONSUMER TYPE	% 2009 HOUSE-HOLDS	ZIP CODE	TOP TAPESTRY CONSUMER TYPE	% 2009 HOUSE-HOLDS	ZIP CODE	TOP TAPESTRY CONSUMER TYPE	% 2009 HOUSE-HOLDS
05658	25 Salt Of The Earth	73.6	05872	46 Rooted Rural	98.6	06247	17 Green Acres	100.0
05660	17 Green Acres	53.5	05873	31 Rural Resort Dwellers	66.5	06248	06 Sophisticated Squires	60.4
05661	33 Midlife Junction	61.8	05874	31 Rural Resort Dwellers	92.5	06249	06 Sophisticated Squires	59.1
05663	33 Midlife Junction	43.4	05875	31 Rural Resort Dwellers	58.5	06250	22 Metropolitans	49.4
05666	17 Green Acres	100.0	05901	46 Rooted Rural	100.0	06254	18 Cozy And Comfortable	60.9
05667	33 Midlife Junction	49.1	05902	42 Southern Satellites	100.0	06255	24 Main Street, USA	39.2
05669	25 Salt Of The Earth	100.0	05903	42 Southern Satellites	100.0	06256	41 Crossroads	63.7
05672	13 In Style	99.6	05904	42 Southern Satellites	100.0	06259	17 Green Acres	38.4
05673	31 Rural Resort Dwellers	45.2	05905	46 Rooted Rural	98.0	06260	24 Main Street, USA	57.4
05674	31 Rural Resort Dwellers	59.3	05906	42 Southern Satellites	72.2	06262	29 Rustbelt Retirees	100.0
05675	25 Salt Of The Earth	91.6	05907	46 Rooted Rural	100.0	06264	17 Green Acres	100.0
05676	17 Green Acres	44.0	06001	02 Suburban Splendor	43.6	06266	18 Cozy And Comfortable	100.0
05677	17 Green Acres	50.1	06002	30 Retirement Communities	31.6	06268	22 Metropolitans	25.0
05679	25 Salt Of The Earth	52.2	06010	24 Main Street, USA	39.6	06269	55 College Towns	100.0
05680	26 Midland Crowd	99.7	06013	07 Exurbanites	51.1	06277	18 Cozy And Comfortable	65.7
05681	25 Salt Of The Earth	100.0	06016	24 Main Street, USA	47.9	06278	13 In Style	63.3
05682	17 Green Acres	96.3	06018	33 Midlife Junction	52.8	06279	22 Metropolitans	42.8
05701	33 Midlife Junction	31.9	06019	13 In Style	49.1	06280	14 Prosperous Empty Nesters	28.4
05730	31 Rural Resort Dwellers	100.0	06021	07 Exurbanites	100.0	06281	17 Green Acres	30.7
05732	31 Rural Resort Dwellers	56.0	06023	10 Pleasant-Ville	83.4	06282	06 Sophisticated Squires	92.6
05733	31 Rural Resort Dwellers	29.5	06024	24 Main Street, USA	52.8	06320	52 Inner City Tenants	20.2
05734	37 Prairie Living	100.0	06026	07 Exurbanites	54.9	06330	18 Cozy And Comfortable	47.2
05735	33 Midlife Junction	63.9	06027	07 Exurbanites	100.0	06331	17 Green Acres	44.7
05736	31 Rural Resort Dwellers	89.5	06029	13 In Style	36.5	06333	02 Suburban Splendor	66.8
05737	17 Green Acres	100.0	06031	10 Pleasant-Ville	65.9	06334	18 Cozy And Comfortable	60.8
05738	17 Green Acres	98.1	06032	09 Urban Chic	52.4	06335	06 Sophisticated Squires	57.2
05739	46 Rooted Rural	100.0	06033	02 Suburban Splendor	32.4	06336	18 Cozy And Comfortable	100.0
05742	17 Green Acres	74.9	06035	07 Exurbanites	61.0	06339	07 Exurbanites	39.6
05743	33 Midlife Junction	39.8	06037	07 Exurbanites	39.3	06340	36 Old And Newcomers	29.4
05744	33 Midlife Junction	89.7	06039	09 Urban Chic	53.3	06349	40 Military Proximity	0.0
05746	31 Rural Resort Dwellers	100.0	06040	48 Great Expectations	18.7	06351	06 Sophisticated Squires	25.5
05747	31 Rural Resort Dwellers	100.0	06042	24 Main Street, USA	30.2	06353	33 Midlife Junction	79.2
05748	31 Rural Resort Dwellers	100.0	06043	13 In Style	31.8	06354	18 Cozy And Comfortable	35.2
05751	13 In Style	99.6	06051	60 City Dimensions	35.9	06355	18 Cozy And Comfortable	33.7
05753	37 Prairie Living	34.1	06052	14 Prosperous Empty Nesters	24.7	06357	13 In Style	78.1
05757	31 Rural Resort Dwellers	92.9	06053	24 Main Street, USA	30.1	06359	18 Cozy And Comfortable	56.6
05758	31 Rural Resort Dwellers	100.0	06057	07 Exurbanites	82.1	06360	24 Main Street, USA	20.4
05759	25 Salt Of The Earth	77.1	06058	07 Exurbanites	51.5	06365	10 Pleasant-Ville	33.7
05760	37 Prairie Living	89.0	06060	02 Suburban Splendor	78.6	06370	18 Cozy And Comfortable	70.8
05761	37 Prairie Living	79.3	06062	18 Cozy And Comfortable	38.3	06371	14 Prosperous Empty Nesters	34.2
05762	31 Rural Resort Dwellers	65.0	06063	07 Exurbanites	76.5	06374	18 Cozy And Comfortable	40.2
05763	25 Salt Of The Earth	52.0	06065	07 Exurbanites	68.4	06375	14 Prosperous Empty Nesters	28.3
05764	33 Midlife Junction	39.6	06066	36 Old And Newcomers	26.6	06377	17 Green Acres	98.5
05765	18 Cozy And Comfortable	52.4	06067	13 In Style	33.2	06378	07 Exurbanites	40.8
05766	31 Rural Resort Dwellers	100.0	06068	15 Silver And Gold	58.2	06379	33 Midlife Junction	28.4
05767	33 Midlife Junction	52.3	06069	14 Prosperous Empty Nesters	71.2	06380	48 Great Expectations	60.0
05769	31 Rural Resort Dwellers	94.2	06070	02 Suburban Splendor	51.9	06382	18 Cozy And Comfortable	37.6
05770	37 Prairie Living	100.0	06071	10 Pleasant-Ville	44.0	06384	17 Green Acres	100.0
05772	31 Rural Resort Dwellers	100.0	06073	02 Suburban Splendor	90.2	06385	18 Cozy And Comfortable	42.7
05773	29 Rustbelt Retirees	43.6	06074	13 In Style	31.8	06390	09 Urban Chic	100.0
05774	31 Rural Resort Dwellers	93.7	06076	17 Green Acres	37.1	06401	24 Main Street, USA	47.7
05775	37 Prairie Living	100.0	06078	07 Exurbanites	38.7	06403	18 Cozy And Comfortable	34.1
05776	31 Rural Resort Dwellers	100.0	06081	13 In Style	100.0	06405	13 In Style	22.7
05777	25 Salt Of The Earth	51.1	06082	18 Cozy And Comfortable	55.4	06409	10 Pleasant-Ville	84.5
05778	37 Prairie Living	87.7	06084	06 Sophisticated Squires	41.0	06410	02 Suburban Splendor	24.2
05819	25 Salt Of The Earth	23.3	06085	05 Wealthy Seaboard Suburbs	34.3	06412	10 Pleasant-Ville	39.9
05820	37 Prairie Living	100.0	06088	24 Main Street, USA	87.2	06413	06 Sophisticated Squires	22.4
05821	31 Rural Resort Dwellers	60.5	06089	07 Exurbanites	49.9	06415	06 Sophisticated Squires	38.4
05822	46 Rooted Rural	51.5	06090	02 Suburban Splendor	70.5	06416	13 In Style	20.8
05824	42 Southern Satellites	75.2	06091	07 Exurbanites	100.0	06417	14 Prosperous Empty Nesters	29.2
05825	26 Midland Crowd	100.0	06092	02 Suburban Splendor	78.0	06418	24 Main Street, USA	51.3
05826	37 Prairie Living	98.0	06093	07 Exurbanites	67.7	06419	02 Suburban Splendor	72.3
05827	37 Prairie Living	100.0	06095	18 Cozy And Comfortable	32.5	06420	06 Sophisticated Squires	99.9
05828	31 Rural Resort Dwellers	96.8	06096	18 Cozy And Comfortable	66.2	06422	06 Sophisticated Squires	42.9
05829	46 Rooted Rural	67.8	06098	24 Main Street, USA	46.4	06423	06 Sophisticated Squires	45.8
05830	33 Midlife Junction	66.0	06103	27 Metro Renters	87.4	06424	13 In Style	43.4
05832	31 Rural Resort Dwellers	84.0	06105	61 High Rise Renters	33.3	06426	03 Connoisseurs	42.2
05833	46 Rooted Rural	100.0	06106	60 City Dimensions	26.1	06437	07 Exurbanites	34.0
05836	46 Rooted Rural	67.1	06107	05 Wealthy Seaboard Suburbs	40.8	06438	07 Exurbanites	88.0
05837	46 Rooted Rural	81.9	06108	48 Great Expectations	21.3	06441	07 Exurbanites	71.4
05839	31 Rural Resort Dwellers	100.0	06109	14 Prosperous Empty Nesters	41.7	06442	10 Pleasant-Ville	45.0
05841	31 Rural Resort Dwellers	100.0	06110	24 Main Street, USA	33.8	06443	02 Suburban Splendor	48.5
05842	31 Rural Resort Dwellers	56.4	06111	13 In Style	26.2	06447	06 Sophisticated Squires	42.8
05843	46 Rooted Rural	91.9	06112	45 City Strivers	52.9	06450	18 Cozy And Comfortable	29.2
05845	37 Prairie Living	94.2	06114	58 NeWest Residents	32.7	06451	24 Main Street, USA	27.7
05846	50 Heartland Communities	87.3	06117	05 Wealthy Seaboard Suburbs	39.8	06455	10 Pleasant-Ville	53.4
05847	46 Rooted Rural	97.1	06118	18 Cozy And Comfortable	35.1	06457	24 Main Street, USA	28.7
05850	36 Old And Newcomers	100.0	06119	22 Metropolitans	20.2	06459	55 College Towns	100.0
05851	57 Simple Living	33.4	06120	64 City Commons	62.4	06460	10 Pleasant-Ville	27.5
05853	46 Rooted Rural	100.0	06226	60 City Dimensions	21.2	06461	10 Pleasant-Ville	30.3
05855	57 Simple Living	24.0	06231	06 Sophisticated Squires	65.3	06468	05 Wealthy Seaboard Suburbs	45.4
05857	37 Prairie Living	100.0	06232	06 Sophisticated Squires	66.0	06469	13 In Style	75.5
05858	46 Rooted Rural	64.1	06234	57 Simple Living	23.7	06470	02 Suburban Splendor	73.3
05859	42 Southern Satellites	45.5	06235	24 Main Street, USA	56.2	06471	10 Pleasant-Ville	69.7
05860	46 Rooted Rural	48.6	06237	10 Pleasant-Ville	45.1	06472	07 Exurbanites	31.7
05862	31 Rural Resort Dwellers	100.0	06238	06 Sophisticated Squires	53.7	06473	10 Pleasant-Ville	52.5
05866	46 Rooted Rural	100.0	06239	24 Main Street, USA	28.6	06475	14 Prosperous Empty Nesters	51.0
05867	25 Salt Of The Earth	99.7	06241	24 Main Street, USA	55.6	06477	05 Wealthy Seaboard Suburbs	66.4
05868	25 Salt Of The Earth	66.7	06242	17 Green Acres	99.5	06478	07 Exurbanites	33.1
05871	26 Midland Crowd	56.2	06243	18 Cozy And Comfortable	100.0	06479	24 Main Street, USA	58.6

ZIP CODE	TOP TAPESTRY CONSUMER TYPE	% 2009 HOUSE-HOLDS	ZIP CODE	TOP TAPESTRY CONSUMER TYPE	% 2009 HOUSE-HOLDS	ZIP CODE	TOP TAPESTRY CONSUMER TYPE	% 2009 HOUSE-HOLDS
06480	24 Main Street, USA	27.3	06890	09 Urban Chic	62.8	07104	35 International Marketplace	34.7
06481	14 Prosperous Empty Nesters	78.0	06896	03 Connoisseurs	82.0	07105	35 International Marketplace	82.8
06482	06 Sophisticated Squires	40.7	06897	01 Top Rung	79.3	07106	45 City Strivers	65.9
06483	24 Main Street, USA	38.1	06901	27 Metro Renters	61.2	07107	35 International Marketplace	38.9
06484	05 Wealthy Seaboard Suburbs	30.4	06902	35 International Marketplace	31.3	07108	45 City Strivers	55.5
06488	02 Suburban Splendor	30.4	06903	03 Connoisseurs	53.0	07109	20 City Lights	44.3
06489	07 Exurbanites	31.8	06905	05 Wealthy Seaboard Suburbs	32.5	07110	20 City Lights	44.4
06492	24 Main Street, USA	19.1	06906	23 Trendsetters	47.1	07111	45 City Strivers	77.4
06498	07 Exurbanites	35.6	06907	05 Wealthy Seaboard Suburbs	30.5	07112	45 City Strivers	80.5
06510	27 Metro Renters	92.5	07001	16 Enterprising Professionals	42.9	07114	61 High Rise Renters	41.4
06511	45 City Strivers	27.8	07002	20 City Lights	73.0	07201	35 International Marketplace	51.1
06512	24 Main Street, USA	40.0	07003	20 City Lights	33.6	07202	35 International Marketplace	78.6
06513	60 City Dimensions	18.5	07004	05 Wealthy Seaboard Suburbs	100.0	07203	10 Pleasant-Ville	33.5
06514	24 Main Street, USA	29.2	07005	20 City Lights	45.1	07204	20 City Lights	52.7
06515	36 Old And Newcomers	22.5	07006	05 Wealthy Seaboard Suburbs	23.7	07205	10 Pleasant-Ville	36.1
06516	24 Main Street, USA	32.8	07008	10 Pleasant-Ville	29.5	07206	47 Las Casas	59.1
06517	22 Metropolitans	28.6	07009	05 Wealthy Seaboard Suburbs	54.3	07208	35 International Marketplace	66.4
06518	16 Enterprising Professionals	22.7	07010	20 City Lights	35.7	07302	23 Trendsetters	43.9
06519	60 City Dimensions	49.6	07011	20 City Lights	56.1	07304	45 City Strivers	45.7
06524	05 Wealthy Seaboard Suburbs	55.3	07012	20 City Lights	23.8	07305	45 City Strivers	52.4
06525	03 Connoisseurs	50.7	07013	20 City Lights	33.4	07306	44 Urban Melting Pot	35.0
06604	35 International Marketplace	20.5	07014	20 City Lights	52.4	07307	35 International Marketplace	87.3
06605	58 NeWest Residents	19.9	07016	05 Wealthy Seaboard Suburbs	46.6	07310	27 Metro Renters	85.8
06606	24 Main Street, USA	32.4	07017	45 City Strivers	74.6	07401	03 Connoisseurs	100.0
06607	45 City Strivers	57.9	07018	45 City Strivers	61.1	07403	10 Pleasant-Ville	49.9
06608	58 NeWest Residents	48.0	07020	08 Laptops And Lattes	57.2	07405	02 Suburban Splendor	40.2
06610	35 International Marketplace	20.1	07021	01 Top Rung	73.0	07407	20 City Lights	68.2
06611	05 Wealthy Seaboard Suburbs	53.5	07022	20 City Lights	45.6	07410	05 Wealthy Seaboard Suburbs	50.1
06612	03 Connoisseurs	56.1	07023	05 Wealthy Seaboard Suburbs	99.8	07416	24 Main Street, USA	63.4
06614	10 Pleasant-Ville	44.6	07024	30 Retirement Communities	21.0	07417	01 Top Rung	72.9
06615	24 Main Street, USA	42.9	07026	20 City Lights	57.9	07418	06 Sophisticated Squires	77.0
06702	65 Social Security Set	80.8	07027	20 City Lights	84.2	07419	13 In Style	59.2
06704	60 City Dimensions	32.3	07028	05 Wealthy Seaboard Suburbs	27.9	07420	10 Pleasant-Ville	92.7
06705	24 Main Street, USA	35.2	07029	35 International Marketplace	98.6	07421	06 Sophisticated Squires	84.4
06706	24 Main Street, USA	35.2	07030	27 Metro Renters	49.0	07422	06 Sophisticated Squires	78.2
06708	24 Main Street, USA	30.1	07031	20 City Lights	76.2	07423	01 Top Rung	78.5
06710	60 City Dimensions	45.4	07032	20 City Lights	55.0	07424	20 City Lights	59.3
06712	07 Exurbanites	47.9	07033	10 Pleasant-Ville	76.8	07430	03 Connoisseurs	25.3
06716	10 Pleasant-Ville	46.0	07034	16 Enterprising Professionals	51.7	07432	05 Wealthy Seaboard Suburbs	66.6
06750	33 Midlife Junction	75.3	07035	13 In Style	31.6	07435	05 Wealthy Seaboard Suburbs	58.8
06751	07 Exurbanites	100.0	07036	10 Pleasant-Ville	25.6	07436	05 Wealthy Seaboard Suburbs	64.8
06752	07 Exurbanites	63.1	07039	05 Wealthy Seaboard Suburbs	51.1	07438	06 Sophisticated Squires	67.7
06754	07 Exurbanites	65.3	07040	10 Pleasant-Ville	15.5	07439	10 Pleasant-Ville	100.0
06755	06 Sophisticated Squires	98.4	07041	09 Urban Chic	36.6	07440	10 Pleasant-Ville	54.1
06756	07 Exurbanites	67.7	07042	45 City Strivers	17.4	07442	10 Pleasant-Ville	43.2
06757	13 In Style	56.5	07043	01 Top Rung	37.1	07444	05 Wealthy Seaboard Suburbs	60.9
06758	07 Exurbanites	100.0	07044	05 Wealthy Seaboard Suburbs	40.2	07446	03 Connoisseurs	25.5
06759	07 Exurbanites	45.2	07045	03 Connoisseurs	66.8	07450	03 Connoisseurs	39.5
06762	05 Wealthy Seaboard Suburbs	45.0	07046	01 Top Rung	65.8	07452	03 Connoisseurs	58.2
06763	07 Exurbanites	53.2	07047	35 International Marketplace	43.6	07456	05 Wealthy Seaboard Suburbs	37.6
06770	24 Main Street, USA	59.5	07050	45 City Strivers	56.1	07457	10 Pleasant-Ville	100.0
06776	24 Main Street, USA	32.0	07052	05 Wealthy Seaboard Suburbs	41.7	07458	01 Top Rung	100.0
06777	31 Rural Resort Dwellers	69.0	07054	23 Trendsetters	29.9	07460	06 Sophisticated Squires	50.4
06778	07 Exurbanites	98.6	07055	35 International Marketplace	40.1	07461	06 Sophisticated Squires	55.8
06779	24 Main Street, USA	63.8	07057	20 City Lights	76.9	07462	28 Aspiring Young Families	53.3
06782	18 Cozy And Comfortable	100.0	07058	03 Connoisseurs	48.4	07463	05 Wealthy Seaboard Suburbs	74.9
06783	03 Connoisseurs	100.0	07059	01 Top Rung	50.6	07465	10 Pleasant-Ville	38.9
06784	07 Exurbanites	66.9	07060	35 International Marketplace	37.5	07470	05 Wealthy Seaboard Suburbs	48.9
06785	10 Pleasant-Ville	73.1	07062	10 Pleasant-Ville	33.1	07480	06 Sophisticated Squires	41.6
06786	24 Main Street, USA	51.1	07063	24 Main Street, USA	35.1	07481	03 Connoisseurs	43.6
06787	24 Main Street, USA	52.3	07064	10 Pleasant-Ville	63.1	07501	47 Las Casas	23.9
06790	24 Main Street, USA	27.0	07065	24 Main Street, USA	44.4	07502	35 International Marketplace	62.1
06791	07 Exurbanites	37.3	07066	05 Wealthy Seaboard Suburbs	46.6	07503	35 International Marketplace	54.4
06793	09 Urban Chic	49.3	07067	10 Pleasant-Ville	76.5	07504	45 City Strivers	42.3
06794	03 Connoisseurs	48.5	07068	05 Wealthy Seaboard Suburbs	62.9	07505	61 High Rise Renters	75.7
06795	10 Pleasant-Ville	46.9	07069	01 Top Rung	41.0	07506	20 City Lights	71.4
06796	31 Rural Resort Dwellers	87.2	07070	05 Wealthy Seaboard Suburbs	44.3	07508	20 City Lights	28.0
06798	09 Urban Chic	32.3	07071	20 City Lights	88.0	07512	10 Pleasant-Ville	31.3
06801	13 In Style	25.5	07072	20 City Lights	99.9	07513	47 Las Casas	45.4
06804	02 Suburban Splendor	27.7	07073	20 City Lights	74.2	07514	35 International Marketplace	42.0
06807	01 Top Rung	33.4	07074	10 Pleasant-Ville	59.4	07522	35 International Marketplace	43.3
06810	35 International Marketplace	37.5	07075	10 Pleasant-Ville	71.8	07524	47 Las Casas	52.2
06811	10 Pleasant-Ville	26.1	07076	05 Wealthy Seaboard Suburbs	33.2	07601	35 International Marketplace	23.9
06812	02 Suburban Splendor	48.9	07077	10 Pleasant-Ville	70.4	07603	20 City Lights	59.5
06820	01 Top Rung	71.3	07078	01 Top Rung	96.0	07604	20 City Lights	47.1
06824	09 Urban Chic	28.2	07079	05 Wealthy Seaboard Suburbs	22.4	07605	05 Wealthy Seaboard Suburbs	28.0
06825	05 Wealthy Seaboard Suburbs	46.6	07080	10 Pleasant-Ville	68.5	07606	20 City Lights	97.5
06830	01 Top Rung	30.1	07081	05 Wealthy Seaboard Suburbs	29.2	07607	10 Pleasant-Ville	42.4
06831	01 Top Rung	47.2	07082	02 Suburban Splendor	41.5	07608	20 City Lights	58.3
06840	01 Top Rung	62.8	07083	10 Pleasant-Ville	57.9	07620	01 Top Rung	98.9
06850	03 Connoisseurs	17.6	07086	23 Trendsetters	54.1	07621	10 Pleasant-Ville	44.1
06851	05 Wealthy Seaboard Suburbs	30.9	07087	35 International Marketplace	55.0	07624	05 Wealthy Seaboard Suburbs	45.9
06853	01 Top Rung	36.8	07088	20 City Lights	53.0	07626	05 Wealthy Seaboard Suburbs	76.6
06854	35 International Marketplace	46.9	07090	01 Top Rung	21.9	07627	01 Top Rung	40.6
06855	20 City Lights	41.2	07092	03 Connoisseurs	72.6	07628	10 Pleasant-Ville	39.3
06870	01 Top Rung	63.7	07093	35 International Marketplace	38.4	07630	05 Wealthy Seaboard Suburbs	82.3
06877	01 Top Rung	38.7	07094	20 City Lights	38.8	07631	10 Pleasant-Ville	18.0
06878	01 Top Rung	55.7	07095	10 Pleasant-Ville	40.7	07632	03 Connoisseurs	46.4
06880	01 Top Rung	58.2	07102	65 Social Security Set	61.2	07640	05 Wealthy Seaboard Suburbs	44.9
06883	01 Top Rung	99.8	07103	45 City Strivers	43.7	07641	03 Connoisseurs	63.0

CONSUMER TYPE

ZIP CODE	TOP TAPESTRY CONSUMER TYPE	% 2009 HOUSE-HOLDS	ZIP CODE	TOP TAPESTRY CONSUMER TYPE	% 2009 HOUSE-HOLDS	ZIP CODE	TOP TAPESTRY CONSUMER TYPE	% 2009 HOUSE-HOLDS
07642	05 Wealthy Seaboard Suburbs	65.1	07866	02 Suburban Splendor	25.2	08083	18 Cozy And Comfortable	40.9
07643	20 City Lights	68.5	07869	02 Suburban Splendor	53.4	08084	18 Cozy And Comfortable	57.7
07644	20 City Lights	72.3	07871	02 Suburban Splendor	53.5	08085	04 Boomburbs	46.7
07645	05 Wealthy Seaboard Suburbs	33.5	07874	06 Sophisticated Squires	54.9	08086	36 Old And Newcomers	39.7
07646	05 Wealthy Seaboard Suburbs	50.2	07876	05 Wealthy Seaboard Suburbs	68.8	08087	18 Cozy And Comfortable	18.5
07647	05 Wealthy Seaboard Suburbs	59.3	07882	24 Main Street, USA	32.9	08088	07 Exurbanites	34.6
07648	05 Wealthy Seaboard Suburbs	42.2	07885	10 Pleasant-Ville	39.2	08089	18 Cozy And Comfortable	77.9
07649	03 Connoisseurs	69.5	07901	09 Urban Chic	35.6	08090	18 Cozy And Comfortable	44.0
07650	11 Pacific Heights	50.4	07920	01 Top Rung	42.9	08091	18 Cozy And Comfortable	72.7
07652	05 Wealthy Seaboard Suburbs	76.1	07921	16 Enterprising Professionals	77.7	08092	25 Salt Of The Earth	54.0
07656	05 Wealthy Seaboard Suburbs	46.6	07922	03 Connoisseurs	52.4	08093	28 Aspiring Young Families	31.0
07657	20 City Lights	52.8	07924	01 Top Rung	61.3	08094	18 Cozy And Comfortable	30.0
07660	20 City Lights	87.1	07927	05 Wealthy Seaboard Suburbs	100.0	08096	18 Cozy And Comfortable	29.7
07661	05 Wealthy Seaboard Suburbs	67.9	07928	09 Urban Chic	49.1	08097	18 Cozy And Comfortable	97.7
07662	20 City Lights	48.5	07930	01 Top Rung	69.2	08098	07 Exurbanites	33.7
07663	10 Pleasant-Ville	62.5	07931	03 Connoisseurs	59.9	08102	54 Urban Rows	30.4
07666	05 Wealthy Seaboard Suburbs	31.9	07932	09 Urban Chic	66.8	08103	54 Urban Rows	78.6
07670	03 Connoisseurs	35.6	07933	05 Wealthy Seaboard Suburbs	67.0	08104	54 Urban Rows	59.1
07675	05 Wealthy Seaboard Suburbs	32.8	07934	09 Urban Chic	53.9	08105	60 City Dimensions	48.6
07676	05 Wealthy Seaboard Suburbs	62.6	07935	09 Urban Chic	55.3	08106	24 Main Street, USA	45.9
07677	01 Top Rung	61.6	07936	05 Wealthy Seaboard Suburbs	49.7	08107	30 Retirement Communities	23.0
07701	22 Metropolitans	19.9	07940	09 Urban Chic	36.5	08108	24 Main Street, USA	33.2
07702	05 Wealthy Seaboard Suburbs	71.7	07945	03 Connoisseurs	54.7	08109	18 Cozy And Comfortable	39.8
07703	04 Boomburbs	86.4	07946	02 Suburban Splendor	49.2	08110	38 Industrious Urban Fringe	36.1
07704	05 Wealthy Seaboard Suburbs	42.6	07950	05 Wealthy Seaboard Suburbs	29.5	08201	24 Main Street, USA	34.4
07711	09 Urban Chic	50.8	07960	03 Connoisseurs	32.9	08202	15 Silver And Gold	95.9
07712	36 Old And Newcomers	14.5	07974	05 Wealthy Seaboard Suburbs	44.2	08203	13 In Style	32.9
07716	10 Pleasant-Ville	30.2	07976	03 Connoisseurs	100.0	08204	18 Cozy And Comfortable	18.0
07717	09 Urban Chic	100.0	07980	20 City Lights	50.3	08205	13 In Style	30.0
07718	10 Pleasant-Ville	87.6	07981	05 Wealthy Seaboard Suburbs	100.0	08210	18 Cozy And Comfortable	19.7
07719	10 Pleasant-Ville	25.8	08002	14 Prosperous Empty Nesters	26.0	08215	24 Main Street, USA	27.2
07720	36 Old And Newcomers	36.6	08003	02 Suburban Splendor	32.0	08221	07 Exurbanites	29.5
07721	13 In Style	34.2	08004	24 Main Street, USA	45.9	08223	07 Exurbanites	85.4
07722	01 Top Rung	47.3	08005	43 The Elders	26.5	08225	18 Cozy And Comfortable	60.7
07723	09 Urban Chic	39.9	08007	30 Retirement Communities	46.8	08226	15 Silver And Gold	50.5
07724	05 Wealthy Seaboard Suburbs	26.9	08008	15 Silver And Gold	89.0	08230	07 Exurbanites	58.8
07726	02 Suburban Splendor	53.2	08009	18 Cozy And Comfortable	31.0	08232	24 Main Street, USA	21.0
07727	10 Pleasant-Ville	31.3	08010	24 Main Street, USA	52.6	08234	06 Sophisticated Squires	32.7
07728	05 Wealthy Seaboard Suburbs	21.4	08012	18 Cozy And Comfortable	19.8	08241	13 In Style	100.0
07730	10 Pleasant-Ville	67.1	08014	32 Rustbelt Traditions	90.9	08242	50 Heartland Communities	46.9
07731	06 Sophisticated Squires	38.6	08015	18 Cozy And Comfortable	25.0	08243	15 Silver And Gold	71.6
07732	24 Main Street, USA	36.8	08016	12 Up And Coming Families	24.4	08244	24 Main Street, USA	68.7
07733	01 Top Rung	47.6	08019	17 Green Acres	90.4	08247	15 Silver And Gold	93.9
07734	24 Main Street, USA	52.5	08020	14 Prosperous Empty Nesters	36.2	08248	15 Silver And Gold	100.0
07735	10 Pleasant-Ville	27.6	08021	28 Aspiring Young Families	19.3	08251	29 Rustbelt Retirees	42.5
07737	10 Pleasant-Ville	66.4	08022	07 Exurbanites	49.6	08260	30 Retirement Communities	45.2
07738	02 Suburban Splendor	37.0	08026	18 Cozy And Comfortable	91.9	08270	06 Sophisticated Squires	35.4
07739	03 Connoisseurs	63.6	08027	18 Cozy And Comfortable	60.7	08302	18 Cozy And Comfortable	22.5
07740	24 Main Street, USA	24.3	08028	12 Up And Coming Families	20.2	08310	49 Senior Sun Seekers	37.6
07746	02 Suburban Splendor	69.0	08029	57 Simple Living	34.9	08311	25 Salt Of The Earth	96.7
07747	05 Wealthy Seaboard Suburbs	26.9	08030	32 Rustbelt Traditions	39.9	08312	32 Rustbelt Traditions	35.6
07748	10 Pleasant-Ville	28.8	08031	18 Cozy And Comfortable	39.8	08314	56 Rural Bypasses	54.7
07750	09 Urban Chic	35.0	08032	04 Boomburbs	78.8	08317	18 Cozy And Comfortable	100.0
07751	02 Suburban Splendor	32.3	08033	30 Retirement Communities	19.2	08318	17 Green Acres	25.2
07753	10 Pleasant-Ville	25.2	08034	05 Wealthy Seaboard Suburbs	46.2	08319	18 Cozy And Comfortable	100.0
07755	10 Pleasant-Ville	44.4	08035	14 Prosperous Empty Nesters	31.0	08322	18 Cozy And Comfortable	53.0
07756	36 Old And Newcomers	44.2	08036	06 Sophisticated Squires	68.5	08323	18 Cozy And Comfortable	99.0
07757	05 Wealthy Seaboard Suburbs	53.1	08037	24 Main Street, USA	39.9	08324	25 Salt Of The Earth	100.0
07758	10 Pleasant-Ville	57.2	08041	10 Pleasant-Ville	57.5	08326	24 Main Street, USA	61.6
07760	01 Top Rung	35.4	08043	02 Suburban Splendor	36.6	08327	25 Salt Of The Earth	100.0
07762	30 Retirement Communities	25.3	08045	34 Family Foundations	73.1	08328	24 Main Street, USA	74.1
07764	10 Pleasant-Ville	43.1	08046	18 Cozy And Comfortable	88.1	08330	28 Aspiring Young Families	45.7
07801	21 Urban Villages	39.5	08048	04 Boomburbs	34.7	08332	18 Cozy And Comfortable	14.8
07803	10 Pleasant-Ville	100.0	08049	24 Main Street, USA	70.1	08340	25 Salt Of The Earth	99.4
07821	06 Sophisticated Squires	21.7	08050	12 Up And Coming Families	28.0	08341	24 Main Street, USA	100.0
07822	07 Exurbanites	99.0	08051	13 In Style	25.8	08343	25 Salt Of The Earth	35.3
07823	30 Retirement Communities	30.6	08052	39 Young And Restless	25.5	08344	18 Cozy And Comfortable	56.1
07825	07 Exurbanites	55.1	08053	06 Sophisticated Squires	32.8	08345	50 Heartland Communities	75.7
07826	10 Pleasant-Ville	45.6	08054	07 Exurbanites	19.9	08346	34 Family Foundations	100.0
07827	24 Main Street, USA	50.2	08055	02 Suburban Splendor	34.5	08349	34 Family Foundations	52.7
07828	28 Aspiring Young Families	41.6	08056	06 Sophisticated Squires	54.0	08350	25 Salt Of The Earth	54.7
07830	01 Top Rung	31.3	08057	01 Top Rung	26.0	08353	17 Green Acres	100.0
07832	06 Sophisticated Squires	39.3	08059	29 Rustbelt Retirees	47.9	08360	60 City Dimensions	14.0
07834	05 Wealthy Seaboard Suburbs	46.6	08060	06 Sophisticated Squires	26.6	08361	24 Main Street, USA	21.0
07836	02 Suburban Splendor	40.2	08061	18 Cozy And Comfortable	87.6	08401	35 International Marketplace	23.8
07838	06 Sophisticated Squires	87.2	08062	07 Exurbanites	33.4	08402	14 Prosperous Empty Nesters	34.6
07840	13 In Style	51.8	08063	18 Cozy And Comfortable	67.4	08403	15 Silver And Gold	92.9
07843	06 Sophisticated Squires	44.9	08065	13 In Style	42.3	08406	44 Urban Melting Pot	18.6
07847	10 Pleasant-Ville	100.0	08066	32 Rustbelt Traditions	42.4	08501	02 Suburban Splendor	39.5
07848	07 Exurbanites	50.4	08067	18 Cozy And Comfortable	100.0	08502	04 Boomburbs	69.8
07849	10 Pleasant-Ville	65.6	08068	18 Cozy And Comfortable	36.4	08505	06 Sophisticated Squires	30.1
07850	10 Pleasant-Ville	67.8	08069	24 Main Street, USA	17.4	08510	02 Suburban Splendor	100.0
07851	10 Pleasant-Ville	100.0	08070	24 Main Street, USA	35.8	08511	06 Sophisticated Squires	100.0
07852	05 Wealthy Seaboard Suburbs	40.5	08071	24 Main Street, USA	30.5	08512	02 Suburban Splendor	36.2
07853	02 Suburban Splendor	69.0	08075	24 Main Street, USA	29.1	08514	07 Exurbanites	46.4
07856	13 In Style	64.8	08077	14 Prosperous Empty Nesters	33.5	08515	07 Exurbanites	100.0
07857	24 Main Street, USA	81.0	08078	18 Cozy And Comfortable	43.0	08518	24 Main Street, USA	53.4
07860	06 Sophisticated Squires	23.7	08079	18 Cozy And Comfortable	29.7	08520	13 In Style	40.8
07863	17 Green Acres	43.9	08080	06 Sophisticated Squires	44.3	08525	03 Connoisseurs	48.9
07865	10 Pleasant-Ville	31.2	08081	06 Sophisticated Squires	25.3	08527	06 Sophisticated Squires	39.1

ZIP CODE	TOP TAPESTRY CONSUMER TYPE	% 2009 HOUSE-HOLDS
08528	04 Boomburbs	100.0
08530	05 Wealthy Seaboard Suburbs	35.0
08533	06 Sophisticated Squires	37.8
08534	04 Boomburbs	49.1
08535	02 Suburban Splendor	100.0
08536	16 Enterprising Professionals	36.6
08540	09 Urban Chic	20.6
08542	08 Laptops And Lattes	49.6
08544	08 Laptops And Lattes	0.0
08550	02 Suburban Splendor	47.5
08551	02 Suburban Splendor	55.3
08553	09 Urban Chic	100.0
08554	24 Main Street, USA	76.8
08555	07 Exurbanites	100.0
08556	07 Exurbanites	100.0
08558	02 Suburban Splendor	95.6
08559	07 Exurbanites	69.0
08560	05 Wealthy Seaboard Suburbs	93.5
08562	17 Green Acres	41.3
08608	65 Social Security Set	63.6
08609	54 Urban Rows	28.6
08610	24 Main Street, USA	48.5
08611	48 Great Expectations	21.1
08618	45 City Strivers	23.1
08619	10 Pleasant-Ville	25.6
08620	24 Main Street, USA	48.2
08628	13 In Style	58.9
08629	24 Main Street, USA	46.1
08638	54 Urban Rows	23.5
08640	40 Military Proximity	97.2
08641	40 Military Proximity	100.0
08648	16 Enterprising Professionals	25.6
08690	10 Pleasant-Ville	34.6
08691	13 In Style	54.3
08701	43 The Elders	29.5
08721	18 Cozy And Comfortable	48.7
08722	18 Cozy And Comfortable	39.0
08723	10 Pleasant-Ville	28.2
08724	10 Pleasant-Ville	22.8
08730	05 Wealthy Seaboard Suburbs	43.1
08731	18 Cozy And Comfortable	38.2
08732	10 Pleasant-Ville	100.0
08733	24 Main Street, USA	48.4
08734	18 Cozy And Comfortable	47.1
08735	15 Silver And Gold	100.0
08736	09 Urban Chic	36.2
08738	15 Silver And Gold	89.8
08740	24 Main Street, USA	100.0
08741	10 Pleasant-Ville	82.5
08742	10 Pleasant-Ville	39.1
08750	03 Connoisseurs	56.8
08751	36 Old And Newcomers	40.2
08752	15 Silver And Gold	83.9
08753	10 Pleasant-Ville	21.7
08755	49 Senior Sun Seekers	26.9
08757	43 The Elders	78.4
08758	18 Cozy And Comfortable	51.4
08759	43 The Elders	82.9
08801	02 Suburban Splendor	66.6
08802	02 Suburban Splendor	72.2
08804	10 Pleasant-Ville	43.5
08805	35 International Marketplace	41.6
08807	04 Boomburbs	26.0
08809	09 Urban Chic	36.0
08810	06 Sophisticated Squires	50.3
08812	10 Pleasant-Ville	44.0
08816	05 Wealthy Seaboard Suburbs	26.8
08817	10 Pleasant-Ville	41.1
08820	05 Wealthy Seaboard Suburbs	31.7
08822	02 Suburban Splendor	54.2
08823	16 Enterprising Professionals	76.4
08824	04 Boomburbs	57.2
08825	13 In Style	32.8
08826	02 Suburban Splendor	39.0
08827	02 Suburban Splendor	62.4
08828	12 Up And Coming Families	73.6
08829	10 Pleasant-Ville	54.6
08830	10 Pleasant-Ville	54.2
08831	43 The Elders	45.5
08832	35 International Marketplace	40.6
08833	02 Suburban Splendor	30.9
08835	10 Pleasant-Ville	50.0
08836	01 Top Rung	70.8
08837	36 Old And Newcomers	23.4
08840	10 Pleasant-Ville	38.0
08844	02 Suburban Splendor	24.9
08846	10 Pleasant-Ville	58.1
08848	10 Pleasant-Ville	35.4
08850	10 Pleasant-Ville	47.3
08852	16 Enterprising Professionals	47.1
08853	02 Suburban Splendor	95.0
08854	10 Pleasant-Ville	20.6
08857	10 Pleasant-Ville	24.1
08859	10 Pleasant-Ville	42.9
08861	47 Las Casas	31.6
08863	10 Pleasant-Ville	38.7
08865	18 Cozy And Comfortable	19.1
08867	02 Suburban Splendor	56.3
08869	20 City Lights	36.7
08872	10 Pleasant-Ville	43.7
08873	13 In Style	28.5
08876	02 Suburban Splendor	28.3
08879	10 Pleasant-Ville	39.5
08880	24 Main Street, USA	81.9
08882	10 Pleasant-Ville	49.0
08884	10 Pleasant-Ville	55.9
08886	04 Boomburbs	59.2
08887	16 Enterprising Professionals	97.1
08889	02 Suburban Splendor	42.0
08901	35 International Marketplace	28.1
08902	16 Enterprising Professionals	18.5
08904	23 Trendsetters	24.7
10001	27 Metro Renters	36.6
10002	44 Urban Melting Pot	50.2
10003	08 Laptops And Lattes	50.2
10004	27 Metro Renters	69.7
10005	27 Metro Renters	100.0
10006	27 Metro Renters	100.0
10007	08 Laptops And Lattes	93.5
10009	27 Metro Renters	35.3
10010	08 Laptops And Lattes	55.2
10011	08 Laptops And Lattes	65.9
10012	08 Laptops And Lattes	53.8
10013	08 Laptops And Lattes	43.1
10014	08 Laptops And Lattes	94.5
10016	27 Metro Renters	54.8
10017	27 Metro Renters	52.5
10018	27 Metro Renters	50.3
10019	27 Metro Renters	43.1
10021	08 Laptops And Lattes	70.5
10022	08 Laptops And Lattes	83.3
10023	08 Laptops And Lattes	93.5
10024	08 Laptops And Lattes	85.9
10025	08 Laptops And Lattes	57.9
10026	61 High Rise Renters	83.8
10027	61 High Rise Renters	55.9
10028	08 Laptops And Lattes	60.9
10029	61 High Rise Renters	75.4
10030	61 High Rise Renters	70.0
10031	61 High Rise Renters	91.0
10032	61 High Rise Renters	86.7
10033	61 High Rise Renters	76.7
10034	61 High Rise Renters	68.9
10035	61 High Rise Renters	80.1
10036	27 Metro Renters	55.2
10037	65 Social Security Set	51.5
10038	30 Retirement Communities	31.1
10039	61 High Rise Renters	78.9
10040	61 High Rise Renters	86.9
10044	23 Trendsetters	100.0
10065	08 Laptops And Lattes	81.1
10075	08 Laptops And Lattes	66.5
10128	08 Laptops And Lattes	37.6
10280	08 Laptops And Lattes	100.0
10301	20 City Lights	33.8
10302	45 City Strivers	33.9
10303	45 City Strivers	45.4
10304	45 City Strivers	42.1
10305	20 City Lights	72.7
10306	20 City Lights	62.8
10307	20 City Lights	33.7
10308	10 Pleasant-Ville	57.8
10309	20 City Lights	31.1
10310	20 City Lights	37.1
10312	10 Pleasant-Ville	27.0
10314	20 City Lights	49.9
10451	61 High Rise Renters	80.8
10452	61 High Rise Renters	100.0
10453	61 High Rise Renters	97.6
10454	61 High Rise Renters	97.1
10455	61 High Rise Renters	98.2
10456	61 High Rise Renters	94.3
10457	61 High Rise Renters	99.2
10458	61 High Rise Renters	93.3
10459	61 High Rise Renters	83.7
10460	61 High Rise Renters	85.9
10461	20 City Lights	61.5
10462	45 City Strivers	30.1
10463	61 High Rise Renters	37.4
10464	20 City Lights	45.9
10465	20 City Lights	79.9
10466	45 City Strivers	41.4
10467	61 High Rise Renters	62.3
10468	61 High Rise Renters	90.7
10469	20 City Lights	50.0
10470	45 City Strivers	43.0
10471	30 Retirement Communities	38.5
10472	61 High Rise Renters	66.2
10473	61 High Rise Renters	42.8
10474	61 High Rise Renters	98.5
10475	34 Family Foundations	89.1
10501	01 Top Rung	55.8
10502	03 Connoisseurs	58.3
10504	01 Top Rung	75.2
10505	02 Suburban Splendor	81.3
10506	01 Top Rung	82.1
10507	09 Urban Chic	29.8
10509	02 Suburban Splendor	24.1
10510	01 Top Rung	57.6
10511	10 Pleasant-Ville	71.4
10512	10 Pleasant-Ville	54.9
10514	01 Top Rung	83.9
10516	05 Wealthy Seaboard Suburbs	49.3
10518	01 Top Rung	100.0
10520	09 Urban Chic	29.5
10522	09 Urban Chic	31.5
10523	20 City Lights	35.0
10524	03 Connoisseurs	41.0
10526	01 Top Rung	67.9
10527	01 Top Rung	52.4
10528	09 Urban Chic	34.4
10530	09 Urban Chic	35.6
10532	05 Wealthy Seaboard Suburbs	98.6
10533	01 Top Rung	54.1
10535	05 Wealthy Seaboard Suburbs	100.0
10536	01 Top Rung	53.7
10537	10 Pleasant-Ville	96.8
10538	01 Top Rung	50.6
10541	05 Wealthy Seaboard Suburbs	61.5
10543	20 City Lights	35.6
10546	01 Top Rung	100.0
10547	13 In Style	33.0
10548	10 Pleasant-Ville	95.6
10549	01 Top Rung	31.3
10550	45 City Strivers	43.5
10552	30 Retirement Communities	32.4
10553	45 City Strivers	52.8
10560	03 Connoisseurs	52.5
10562	35 International Marketplace	19.0
10566	13 In Style	28.3
10567	10 Pleasant-Ville	43.7
10570	03 Connoisseurs	37.2
10573	20 City Lights	27.7
10576	01 Top Rung	99.0
10577	01 Top Rung	100.0
10578	05 Wealthy Seaboard Suburbs	100.0
10579	05 Wealthy Seaboard Suburbs	45.2
10580	01 Top Rung	48.8
10583	01 Top Rung	57.4
10588	05 Wealthy Seaboard Suburbs	49.5
10589	15 Silver And Gold	63.4
10590	03 Connoisseurs	60.8
10591	09 Urban Chic	31.5
10594	05 Wealthy Seaboard Suburbs	79.0
10595	05 Wealthy Seaboard Suburbs	54.4
10597	01 Top Rung	59.7
10598	05 Wealthy Seaboard Suburbs	79.5
10601	36 Old And Newcomers	60.6
10603	20 City Lights	30.5
10604	20 City Lights	34.3
10605	03 Connoisseurs	28.0
10606	20 City Lights	33.5
10607	05 Wealthy Seaboard Suburbs	32.8
10701	61 High Rise Renters	27.2
10703	20 City Lights	37.5
10704	20 City Lights	86.3
10705	35 International Marketplace	38.0
10706	03 Connoisseurs	31.2
10707	05 Wealthy Seaboard Suburbs	26.3
10708	30 Retirement Communities	54.8
10709	03 Connoisseurs	34.6
10710	05 Wealthy Seaboard Suburbs	40.3
10801	20 City Lights	33.0
10803	01 Top Rung	32.0
10804	01 Top Rung	55.4
10805	23 Trendsetters	40.6
10901	05 Wealthy Seaboard Suburbs	23.6
10913	05 Wealthy Seaboard Suburbs	85.2
10916	06 Sophisticated Squires	47.1
10917	13 In Style	53.6

CONSUMER TYPE

ZIP CODE	TOP TAPESTRY CONSUMER TYPE	% 2009 HOUSE-HOLDS	ZIP CODE	TOP TAPESTRY CONSUMER TYPE	% 2009 HOUSE-HOLDS	ZIP CODE	TOP TAPESTRY CONSUMER TYPE	% 2009 HOUSE-HOLDS
10918	13 In Style	20.4	11226	61 High Rise Renters	62.1	11575	10 Pleasant-Ville	42.9
10919	10 Pleasant-Ville	86.5	11228	20 City Lights	65.6	11576	01 Top Rung	62.2
10920	05 Wealthy Seaboard Suburbs	56.9	11229	44 Urban Melting Pot	52.3	11577	01 Top Rung	40.2
10921	06 Sophisticated Squires	56.3	11230	44 Urban Melting Pot	81.7	11579	09 Urban Chic	55.4
10923	10 Pleasant-Ville	36.6	11231	08 Laptops And Lattes	37.5	11580	10 Pleasant-Ville	48.8
10924	07 Exurbanites	25.5	11232	35 International Marketplace	71.5	11581	05 Wealthy Seaboard Suburbs	35.2
10925	24 Main Street, USA	65.6	11233	45 City Strivers	57.8	11590	05 Wealthy Seaboard Suburbs	35.1
10926	13 In Style	87.9	11234	20 City Lights	54.4	11596	05 Wealthy Seaboard Suburbs	72.0
10927	35 International Marketplace	34.4	11235	44 Urban Melting Pot	51.4	11598	03 Connoisseurs	55.5
10928	24 Main Street, USA	48.4	11236	45 City Strivers	57.3	11691	45 City Strivers	27.6
10930	06 Sophisticated Squires	52.5	11237	58 NeWest Residents	58.0	11692	45 City Strivers	42.9
10931	10 Pleasant-Ville	100.0	11238	23 Trendsetters	50.3	11693	34 Family Foundations	27.8
10940	24 Main Street, USA	40.1	11239	61 High Rise Renters	100.0	11694	20 City Lights	23.1
10941	06 Sophisticated Squires	29.3	11354	44 Urban Melting Pot	56.9	11697	14 Prosperous Empty Nesters	42.5
10950	06 Sophisticated Squires	24.1	11355	44 Urban Melting Pot	77.1	11701	10 Pleasant-Ville	31.7
10952	05 Wealthy Seaboard Suburbs	41.4	11356	20 City Lights	68.1	11702	05 Wealthy Seaboard Suburbs	34.6
10954	05 Wealthy Seaboard Suburbs	39.0	11357	20 City Lights	51.0	11703	10 Pleasant-Ville	91.1
10956	05 Wealthy Seaboard Suburbs	45.7	11358	11 Pacific Heights	37.4	11704	10 Pleasant-Ville	79.2
10958	10 Pleasant-Ville	91.7	11359	14 Prosperous Empty Nesters	100.0	11705	05 Wealthy Seaboard Suburbs	43.7
10960	23 Trendsetters	39.0	11360	30 Retirement Communities	53.4	11706	10 Pleasant-Ville	32.5
10962	30 Retirement Communities	30.3	11361	20 City Lights	41.1	11709	05 Wealthy Seaboard Suburbs	60.2
10963	24 Main Street, USA	60.6	11362	11 Pacific Heights	27.3	11710	05 Wealthy Seaboard Suburbs	50.8
10964	03 Connoisseurs	55.5	11363	11 Pacific Heights	39.3	11713	10 Pleasant-Ville	36.2
10965	05 Wealthy Seaboard Suburbs	64.2	11364	11 Pacific Heights	46.1	11714	10 Pleasant-Ville	50.0
10968	09 Urban Chic	62.8	11365	20 City Lights	56.1	11715	10 Pleasant-Ville	52.3
10969	10 Pleasant-Ville	74.0	11366	11 Pacific Heights	41.2	11716	10 Pleasant-Ville	59.8
10970	13 In Style	33.0	11367	44 Urban Melting Pot	33.6	11717	21 Urban Villages	90.3
10973	10 Pleasant-Ville	95.0	11368	35 International Marketplace	41.6	11718	05 Wealthy Seaboard Suburbs	75.7
10974	10 Pleasant-Ville	68.0	11369	35 International Marketplace	38.2	11719	10 Pleasant-Ville	94.1
10975	13 In Style	100.0	11370	44 Urban Melting Pot	40.2	11720	10 Pleasant-Ville	98.7
10976	05 Wealthy Seaboard Suburbs	73.6	11372	44 Urban Melting Pot	73.3	11721	05 Wealthy Seaboard Suburbs	56.9
10977	05 Wealthy Seaboard Suburbs	25.7	11373	44 Urban Melting Pot	91.5	11722	21 Urban Villages	55.1
10980	10 Pleasant-Ville	47.2	11374	44 Urban Melting Pot	72.2	11724	01 Top Rung	96.3
10983	05 Wealthy Seaboard Suburbs	97.0	11375	22 Metropolitans	22.7	11725	05 Wealthy Seaboard Suburbs	79.8
10984	10 Pleasant-Ville	59.3	11377	44 Urban Melting Pot	74.7	11726	10 Pleasant-Ville	41.3
10985	06 Sophisticated Squires	100.0	11378	20 City Lights	83.5	11727	06 Sophisticated Squires	27.3
10986	05 Wealthy Seaboard Suburbs	93.4	11379	20 City Lights	79.7	11729	10 Pleasant-Ville	76.7
10987	13 In Style	67.7	11385	35 International Marketplace	37.0	11730	10 Pleasant-Ville	49.6
10989	05 Wealthy Seaboard Suburbs	64.8	11411	10 Pleasant-Ville	78.4	11731	05 Wealthy Seaboard Suburbs	63.0
10990	06 Sophisticated Squires	44.0	11412	34 Family Foundations	59.8	11732	05 Wealthy Seaboard Suburbs	61.4
10992	13 In Style	30.0	11413	10 Pleasant-Ville	40.0	11733	02 Suburban Splendor	32.3
10993	20 City Lights	59.0	11414	30 Retirement Communities	32.0	11735	10 Pleasant-Ville	58.7
10994	05 Wealthy Seaboard Suburbs	47.4	11415	44 Urban Melting Pot	67.7	11738	10 Pleasant-Ville	63.6
10996	40 Military Proximity	100.0	11416	35 International Marketplace	71.2	11740	05 Wealthy Seaboard Suburbs	42.9
10998	06 Sophisticated Squires	33.8	11417	20 City Lights	55.8	11741	10 Pleasant-Ville	44.6
11001	05 Wealthy Seaboard Suburbs	62.4	11418	35 International Marketplace	55.1	11742	10 Pleasant-Ville	39.7
11003	10 Pleasant-Ville	47.8	11419	35 International Marketplace	51.8	11743	05 Wealthy Seaboard Suburbs	22.3
11004	20 City Lights	55.1	11420	20 City Lights	40.6	11746	05 Wealthy Seaboard Suburbs	24.9
11005	43 The Elders	96.0	11421	35 International Marketplace	54.1	11747	05 Wealthy Seaboard Suburbs	41.3
11010	05 Wealthy Seaboard Suburbs	48.1	11422	20 City Lights	56.5	11749	13 In Style	39.4
11020	01 Top Rung	54.4	11423	21 Urban Villages	20.0	11751	10 Pleasant-Ville	60.6
11021	09 Urban Chic	21.4	11426	05 Wealthy Seaboard Suburbs	36.1	11752	10 Pleasant-Ville	100.0
11023	09 Urban Chic	38.3	11427	20 City Lights	29.0	11753	03 Connoisseurs	55.3
11024	01 Top Rung	57.8	11428	10 Pleasant-Ville	37.8	11754	10 Pleasant-Ville	41.0
11030	01 Top Rung	68.0	11429	10 Pleasant-Ville	28.7	11755	10 Pleasant-Ville	52.6
11040	05 Wealthy Seaboard Suburbs	73.4	11430	29 Rustbelt Retirees	100.0	11756	10 Pleasant-Ville	92.8
11042	01 Top Rung	0.0	11432	44 Urban Melting Pot	24.3	11757	10 Pleasant-Ville	85.9
11050	20 City Lights	27.5	11433	45 City Strivers	59.0	11758	05 Wealthy Seaboard Suburbs	60.5
11096	45 City Strivers	27.5	11434	34 Family Foundations	51.1	11762	05 Wealthy Seaboard Suburbs	87.8
11101	44 Urban Melting Pot	34.2	11435	44 Urban Melting Pot	28.0	11763	06 Sophisticated Squires	54.2
11102	44 Urban Melting Pot	45.5	11436	45 City Strivers	76.4	11764	06 Sophisticated Squires	50.0
11103	44 Urban Melting Pot	85.5	11439	05 Wealthy Seaboard Suburbs	100.0	11765	01 Top Rung	84.3
11104	44 Urban Melting Pot	96.7	11501	05 Wealthy Seaboard Suburbs	38.5	11766	02 Suburban Splendor	30.6
11105	44 Urban Melting Pot	53.2	11507	05 Wealthy Seaboard Suburbs	62.4	11767	02 Suburban Splendor	36.4
11106	44 Urban Melting Pot	60.9	11509	03 Connoisseurs	65.0	11768	03 Connoisseurs	52.6
11109	27 Metro Renters	100.0	11510	05 Wealthy Seaboard Suburbs	44.4	11769	10 Pleasant-Ville	48.3
11201	08 Laptops And Lattes	64.0	11514	05 Wealthy Seaboard Suburbs	50.3	11770	09 Urban Chic	100.0
11203	45 City Strivers	79.6	11516	09 Urban Chic	28.3	11771	20 City Lights	25.0
11204	44 Urban Melting Pot	89.5	11518	20 City Lights	37.9	11772	10 Pleasant-Ville	47.0
11205	61 High Rise Renters	29.1	11520	10 Pleasant-Ville	39.7	11776	10 Pleasant-Ville	58.1
11206	61 High Rise Renters	54.4	11530	03 Connoisseurs	31.0	11777	09 Urban Chic	35.0
11207	45 City Strivers	54.0	11542	20 City Lights	50.1	11778	24 Main Street, USA	31.0
11208	45 City Strivers	37.5	11545	05 Wealthy Seaboard Suburbs	61.1	11779	10 Pleasant-Ville	70.6
11209	44 Urban Melting Pot	51.1	11548	20 City Lights	59.3	11780	05 Wealthy Seaboard Suburbs	51.1
11210	45 City Strivers	41.6	11549	40 Military Proximity	0.0	11782	10 Pleasant-Ville	49.2
11211	61 High Rise Renters	38.2	11550	10 Pleasant-Ville	26.9	11783	05 Wealthy Seaboard Suburbs	63.9
11212	45 City Strivers	44.2	11552	05 Wealthy Seaboard Suburbs	50.7	11784	10 Pleasant-Ville	73.2
11213	45 City Strivers	51.9	11553	10 Pleasant-Ville	77.8	11786	06 Sophisticated Squires	36.4
11214	44 Urban Melting Pot	91.4	11554	05 Wealthy Seaboard Suburbs	49.6	11787	05 Wealthy Seaboard Suburbs	76.8
11215	08 Laptops And Lattes	43.5	11557	05 Wealthy Seaboard Suburbs	46.8	11788	05 Wealthy Seaboard Suburbs	75.7
11216	45 City Strivers	91.7	11558	05 Wealthy Seaboard Suburbs	44.3	11789	10 Pleasant-Ville	69.3
11217	08 Laptops And Lattes	38.4	11559	01 Top Rung	42.0	11790	05 Wealthy Seaboard Suburbs	76.8
11218	44 Urban Melting Pot	73.5	11560	01 Top Rung	32.6	11791	05 Wealthy Seaboard Suburbs	41.4
11219	44 Urban Melting Pot	91.9	11561	20 City Lights	25.4	11792	10 Pleasant-Ville	57.6
11220	44 Urban Melting Pot	58.3	11563	20 City Lights	27.9	11793	05 Wealthy Seaboard Suburbs	77.2
11221	45 City Strivers	55.0	11565	05 Wealthy Seaboard Suburbs	85.1	11794	05 Wealthy Seaboard Suburbs	100.0
11222	44 Urban Melting Pot	73.6	11566	05 Wealthy Seaboard Suburbs	64.9	11795	10 Pleasant-Ville	64.7
11223	44 Urban Melting Pot	73.7	11568	01 Top Rung	99.9	11796	10 Pleasant-Ville	95.0
11224	30 Retirement Communities	33.6	11570	03 Connoisseurs	16.3	11797	01 Top Rung	57.4
11225	45 City Strivers	52.8	11572	05 Wealthy Seaboard Suburbs	75.0	11798	10 Pleasant-Ville	32.5

ZIP CODE	TOP TAPESTRY CONSUMER TYPE	% 2009 HOUSE-HOLDS	ZIP CODE	TOP TAPESTRY CONSUMER TYPE	% 2009 HOUSE-HOLDS	ZIP CODE	TOP TAPESTRY CONSUMER TYPE	% 2009 HOUSE-HOLDS
11801	10 Pleasant-Ville	61.0	12090	25 Salt Of The Earth	38.9	12411	24 Main Street, USA	100.0
11803	05 Wealthy Seaboard Suburbs	68.6	12092	25 Salt Of The Earth	43.7	12412	18 Cozy And Comfortable	53.2
11804	05 Wealthy Seaboard Suburbs	76.0	12093	31 Rural Resort Dwellers	95.5	12413	33 Midlife Junction	57.6
11901	24 Main Street, USA	41.6	12094	26 Midland Crowd	51.9	12414	46 Rooted Rural	23.3
11933	33 Midlife Junction	44.8	12095	32 Rustbelt Traditions	23.1	12416	31 Rural Resort Dwellers	100.0
11934	10 Pleasant-Ville	73.0	12106	14 Prosperous Empty Nesters	55.2	12418	31 Rural Resort Dwellers	100.0
11935	14 Prosperous Empty Nesters	43.6	12108	31 Rural Resort Dwellers	100.0	12419	13 In Style	44.7
11937	31 Rural Resort Dwellers	27.3	12110	13 In Style	28.8	12421	31 Rural Resort Dwellers	100.0
11939	31 Rural Resort Dwellers	93.0	12115	07 Exurbanites	100.0	12422	31 Rural Resort Dwellers	100.0
11940	10 Pleasant-Ville	77.5	12116	31 Rural Resort Dwellers	52.7	12423	31 Rural Resort Dwellers	100.0
11941	03 Connoisseurs	30.0	12117	31 Rural Resort Dwellers	39.6	12424	31 Rural Resort Dwellers	100.0
11942	10 Pleasant-Ville	35.2	12118	18 Cozy And Comfortable	30.1	12427	31 Rural Resort Dwellers	100.0
11944	15 Silver And Gold	32.9	12120	31 Rural Resort Dwellers	100.0	12428	60 City Dimensions	48.2
11946	31 Rural Resort Dwellers	49.9	12121	18 Cozy And Comfortable	83.4	12430	31 Rural Resort Dwellers	60.6
11948	10 Pleasant-Ville	95.8	12122	33 Midlife Junction	25.1	12431	31 Rural Resort Dwellers	100.0
11949	04 Boomburbs	35.4	12123	18 Cozy And Comfortable	36.0	12433	14 Prosperous Empty Nesters	100.0
11950	19 Milk And Cookies	72.4	12125	31 Rural Resort Dwellers	51.9	12435	31 Rural Resort Dwellers	100.0
11951	24 Main Street, USA	40.4	12130	18 Cozy And Comfortable	97.0	12439	31 Rural Resort Dwellers	100.0
11952	14 Prosperous Empty Nesters	51.1	12131	31 Rural Resort Dwellers	100.0	12440	31 Rural Resort Dwellers	69.5
11953	28 Aspiring Young Families	29.6	12134	31 Rural Resort Dwellers	79.9	12442	31 Rural Resort Dwellers	100.0
11954	31 Rural Resort Dwellers	44.3	12136	31 Rural Resort Dwellers	69.3	12443	14 Prosperous Empty Nesters	47.7
11955	23 Trendsetters	49.0	12137	17 Green Acres	76.5	12444	31 Rural Resort Dwellers	100.0
11957	15 Silver And Gold	100.0	12138	25 Salt Of The Earth	76.6	12446	24 Main Street, USA	45.4
11958	31 Rural Resort Dwellers	100.0	12139	31 Rural Resort Dwellers	100.0	12448	09 Urban Chic	100.0
11961	43 The Elders	48.2	12140	17 Green Acres	70.9	12449	33 Midlife Junction	43.3
11963	31 Rural Resort Dwellers	37.6	12143	24 Main Street, USA	92.0	12450	31 Rural Resort Dwellers	100.0
11964	31 Rural Resort Dwellers	96.2	12144	18 Cozy And Comfortable	26.8	12451	31 Rural Resort Dwellers	54.5
11965	15 Silver And Gold	91.0	12147	31 Rural Resort Dwellers	94.3	12454	31 Rural Resort Dwellers	100.0
11967	06 Sophisticated Squires	37.1	12148	07 Exurbanites	72.4	12455	31 Rural Resort Dwellers	66.0
11968	09 Urban Chic	37.5	12149	42 Southern Satellites	30.3	12456	29 Rustbelt Retirees	100.0
11971	15 Silver And Gold	23.1	12150	33 Midlife Junction	100.0	12457	31 Rural Resort Dwellers	46.5
11976	03 Connoisseurs	69.6	12151	26 Midland Crowd	80.9	12458	18 Cozy And Comfortable	43.0
11977	09 Urban Chic	44.4	12153	18 Cozy And Comfortable	83.1	12460	31 Rural Resort Dwellers	100.0
11978	09 Urban Chic	44.0	12154	17 Green Acres	50.3	12461	31 Rural Resort Dwellers	99.9
11980	10 Pleasant-Ville	79.9	12155	33 Midlife Junction	34.3	12463	24 Main Street, USA	74.2
12007	18 Cozy And Comfortable	100.0	12156	17 Green Acres	68.0	12464	31 Rural Resort Dwellers	100.0
12008	18 Cozy And Comfortable	100.0	12157	33 Midlife Junction	46.6	12465	31 Rural Resort Dwellers	100.0
12009	13 In Style	37.7	12158	13 In Style	33.2	12466	24 Main Street, USA	53.2
12010	57 Simple Living	24.9	12159	30 Retirement Communities	23.7	12468	31 Rural Resort Dwellers	56.3
12015	31 Rural Resort Dwellers	39.7	12160	25 Salt Of The Earth	66.0	12469	31 Rural Resort Dwellers	100.0
12017	31 Rural Resort Dwellers	100.0	12164	31 Rural Resort Dwellers	100.0	12470	33 Midlife Junction	100.0
12018	17 Green Acres	55.9	12165	31 Rural Resort Dwellers	100.0	12472	22 Metropolitans	36.3
12019	07 Exurbanites	56.8	12166	46 Rooted Rural	45.2	12473	33 Midlife Junction	100.0
12020	12 Up And Coming Families	33.6	12167	31 Rural Resort Dwellers	53.5	12474	31 Rural Resort Dwellers	100.0
12022	25 Salt Of The Earth	100.0	12168	26 Midland Crowd	98.1	12477	18 Cozy And Comfortable	32.7
12023	18 Cozy And Comfortable	53.0	12169	26 Midland Crowd	90.8	12480	31 Rural Resort Dwellers	100.0
12024	07 Exurbanites	84.8	12170	26 Midland Crowd	43.2	12481	31 Rural Resort Dwellers	68.2
12025	25 Salt Of The Earth	48.5	12173	24 Main Street, USA	37.0	12482	31 Rural Resort Dwellers	59.7
12027	18 Cozy And Comfortable	45.4	12175	31 Rural Resort Dwellers	100.0	12484	07 Exurbanites	68.3
12028	31 Rural Resort Dwellers	48.2	12176	31 Rural Resort Dwellers	95.8	12485	31 Rural Resort Dwellers	100.0
12029	31 Rural Resort Dwellers	55.4	12180	55 College Towns	13.6	12486	24 Main Street, USA	56.3
12031	25 Salt Of The Earth	100.0	12182	48 Great Expectations	37.4	12487	18 Cozy And Comfortable	37.8
12032	29 Rustbelt Retirees	56.4	12183	32 Rustbelt Traditions	40.0	12491	14 Prosperous Empty Nesters	73.5
12033	07 Exurbanites	34.4	12184	13 In Style	48.9	12492	31 Rural Resort Dwellers	100.0
12035	26 Midland Crowd	69.1	12185	17 Green Acres	52.6	12494	31 Rural Resort Dwellers	100.0
12036	31 Rural Resort Dwellers	93.1	12186	07 Exurbanites	56.1	12495	09 Urban Chic	100.0
12037	24 Main Street, USA	39.0	12187	25 Salt Of The Earth	43.0	12496	31 Rural Resort Dwellers	100.0
12041	18 Cozy And Comfortable	100.0	12188	13 In Style	39.0	12498	14 Prosperous Empty Nesters	30.9
12042	18 Cozy And Comfortable	81.6	12189	36 Old And Newcomers	29.2	12501	24 Main Street, USA	71.9
12043	30 Retirement Communities	25.1	12190	31 Rural Resort Dwellers	100.0	12502	31 Rural Resort Dwellers	100.0
12046	18 Cozy And Comfortable	95.4	12192	17 Green Acres	39.3	12503	31 Rural Resort Dwellers	100.0
12047	48 Great Expectations	16.3	12193	25 Salt Of The Earth	81.5	12507	14 Prosperous Empty Nesters	62.2
12051	24 Main Street, USA	50.7	12194	31 Rural Resort Dwellers	100.0	12508	24 Main Street, USA	52.8
12052	18 Cozy And Comfortable	86.6	12196	18 Cozy And Comfortable	49.2	12513	29 Rustbelt Retirees	71.8
12053	17 Green Acres	45.4	12197	46 Rooted Rural	47.9	12514	07 Exurbanites	90.4
12054	14 Prosperous Empty Nesters	39.6	12198	18 Cozy And Comfortable	52.3	12515	24 Main Street, USA	49.2
12056	18 Cozy And Comfortable	56.7	12202	52 Inner City Tenants	27.9	12516	31 Rural Resort Dwellers	100.0
12057	25 Salt Of The Earth	100.0	12203	22 Metropolitans	21.4	12517	31 Rural Resort Dwellers	100.0
12058	26 Midland Crowd	53.5	12204	36 Old And Newcomers	39.9	12518	13 In Style	23.7
12059	18 Cozy And Comfortable	76.4	12205	18 Cozy And Comfortable	61.9	12520	10 Pleasant-Ville	83.7
12060	31 Rural Resort Dwellers	75.9	12206	45 City Strivers	35.2	12521	31 Rural Resort Dwellers	87.7
12061	13 In Style	32.9	12207	65 Social Security Set	57.6	12522	06 Sophisticated Squires	24.0
12062	18 Cozy And Comfortable	42.0	12208	22 Metropolitans	27.3	12523	31 Rural Resort Dwellers	73.6
12064	46 Rooted Rural	85.5	12209	48 Great Expectations	39.0	12524	13 In Style	43.7
12065	13 In Style	30.6	12210	27 Metro Renters	40.0	12525	26 Midland Crowd	56.4
12066	25 Salt Of The Earth	57.9	12211	14 Prosperous Empty Nesters	28.2	12526	31 Rural Resort Dwellers	79.0
12067	18 Cozy And Comfortable	35.6	12302	14 Prosperous Empty Nesters	41.3	12528	24 Main Street, USA	47.0
12068	33 Midlife Junction	35.0	12303	18 Cozy And Comfortable	19.0	12529	31 Rural Resort Dwellers	95.3
12070	18 Cozy And Comfortable	63.6	12304	18 Cozy And Comfortable	16.8	12531	10 Pleasant-Ville	48.3
12071	46 Rooted Rural	50.5	12305	36 Old And Newcomers	57.8	12533	02 Suburban Splendor	28.3
12072	46 Rooted Rural	64.3	12306	29 Rustbelt Retirees	20.9	12534	31 Rural Resort Dwellers	20.9
12074	18 Cozy And Comfortable	37.4	12307	60 City Dimensions	58.2	12538	24 Main Street, USA	27.0
12075	17 Green Acres	63.6	12308	48 Great Expectations	28.6	12540	06 Sophisticated Squires	51.0
12076	31 Rural Resort Dwellers	100.0	12309	07 Exurbanites	21.3	12542	10 Pleasant-Ville	28.1
12077	07 Exurbanites	41.6	12401	18 Cozy And Comfortable	15.4	12543	19 Milk And Cookies	55.1
12078	29 Rustbelt Retirees	17.7	12404	26 Midland Crowd	31.7	12545	10 Pleasant-Ville	38.8
12083	31 Rural Resort Dwellers	67.3	12405	31 Rural Resort Dwellers	81.8	12546	31 Rural Resort Dwellers	84.6
12084	16 Enterprising Professionals	42.9	12406	31 Rural Resort Dwellers	66.7	12547	17 Green Acres	56.9
12086	29 Rustbelt Retirees	52.0	12409	31 Rural Resort Dwellers	42.0	12548	26 Midland Crowd	79.1
12087	17 Green Acres	57.8	12410	31 Rural Resort Dwellers	100.0	12549	06 Sophisticated Squires	47.7

CONSUMER TYPE

ZIP CODE	TOP TAPESTRY CONSUMER TYPE	% 2009 HOUSE-HOLDS	ZIP CODE	TOP TAPESTRY CONSUMER TYPE	% 2009 HOUSE-HOLDS	ZIP CODE	TOP TAPESTRY CONSUMER TYPE	% 2009 HOUSE-HOLDS
12550	10 Pleasant-Ville	19.3	12822	25 Salt Of The Earth	25.6	12970	31 Rural Resort Dwellers	100.0
12553	10 Pleasant-Ville	18.4	12823	25 Salt Of The Earth	100.0	12972	26 Midland Crowd	37.9
12561	55 College Towns	23.6	12824	31 Rural Resort Dwellers	96.4	12973	31 Rural Resort Dwellers	100.0
12563	06 Sophisticated Squires	42.9	12827	25 Salt Of The Earth	42.2	12974	50 Heartland Communities	99.7
12564	07 Exurbanites	43.6	12828	32 Rustbelt Traditions	44.6	12978	25 Salt Of The Earth	100.0
12566	17 Green Acres	48.8	12831	26 Midland Crowd	54.8	12979	32 Rustbelt Traditions	38.0
12567	31 Rural Resort Dwellers	71.2	12832	25 Salt Of The Earth	59.9	12980	46 Rooted Rural	94.5
12569	13 In Style	31.3	12833	26 Midland Crowd	43.0	12981	33 Midlife Junction	24.3
12570	06 Sophisticated Squires	54.5	12834	33 Midlife Junction	45.6	12983	33 Midlife Junction	30.1
12571	13 In Style	35.3	12835	26 Midland Crowd	54.6	12985	17 Green Acres	61.2
12572	07 Exurbanites	33.0	12836	31 Rural Resort Dwellers	96.0	12986	33 Midlife Junction	62.3
12575	06 Sophisticated Squires	75.3	12837	25 Salt Of The Earth	100.0	12987	31 Rural Resort Dwellers	94.8
12577	06 Sophisticated Squires	80.5	12838	25 Salt Of The Earth	100.0	12989	31 Rural Resort Dwellers	92.5
12578	07 Exurbanites	55.6	12839	25 Salt Of The Earth	32.7	12992	25 Salt Of The Earth	45.5
12580	07 Exurbanites	65.4	12842	31 Rural Resort Dwellers	100.0	12993	31 Rural Resort Dwellers	81.1
12581	07 Exurbanites	92.9	12843	31 Rural Resort Dwellers	51.5	12996	31 Rural Resort Dwellers	59.9
12582	06 Sophisticated Squires	66.8	12844	31 Rural Resort Dwellers	71.9	12997	33 Midlife Junction	87.7
12583	22 Metropolitans	60.7	12845	31 Rural Resort Dwellers	45.9	13021	48 Great Expectations	21.6
12585	06 Sophisticated Squires	94.2	12846	31 Rural Resort Dwellers	64.5	13026	31 Rural Resort Dwellers	80.1
12586	10 Pleasant-Ville	35.9	12847	31 Rural Resort Dwellers	100.0	13027	33 Midlife Junction	20.7
12589	24 Main Street, USA	28.7	12849	25 Salt Of The Earth	100.0	13028	26 Midland Crowd	71.6
12590	10 Pleasant-Ville	25.0	12850	26 Midland Crowd	49.7	13029	19 Milk And Cookies	37.6
12592	24 Main Street, USA	95.6	12851	31 Rural Resort Dwellers	100.0	13030	18 Cozy And Comfortable	41.5
12594	24 Main Street, USA	35.7	12852	49 Senior Sun Seekers	100.0	13031	33 Midlife Junction	27.6
12601	36 Old And Newcomers	14.2	12853	31 Rural Resort Dwellers	100.0	13032	25 Salt Of The Earth	39.7
12603	10 Pleasant-Ville	28.7	12854	25 Salt Of The Earth	100.0	13033	25 Salt Of The Earth	68.9
12604	22 Metropolitans	100.0	12855	46 Rooted Rural	100.0	13034	25 Salt Of The Earth	93.4
12701	31 Rural Resort Dwellers	25.7	12857	31 Rural Resort Dwellers	100.0	13035	07 Exurbanites	35.8
12719	31 Rural Resort Dwellers	100.0	12858	31 Rural Resort Dwellers	100.0	13036	33 Midlife Junction	47.5
12720	31 Rural Resort Dwellers	100.0	12859	17 Green Acres	70.4	13037	19 Milk And Cookies	25.1
12721	19 Milk And Cookies	22.1	12860	31 Rural Resort Dwellers	100.0	13039	12 Up And Coming Families	30.6
12723	31 Rural Resort Dwellers	100.0	12861	25 Salt Of The Earth	98.8	13040	46 Rooted Rural	43.4
12725	31 Rural Resort Dwellers	100.0	12863	41 Crossroads	100.0	13041	19 Milk And Cookies	47.4
12726	31 Rural Resort Dwellers	100.0	12865	25 Salt Of The Earth	50.7	13042	25 Salt Of The Earth	61.1
12729	18 Cozy And Comfortable	36.3	12866	07 Exurbanites	17.6	13044	25 Salt Of The Earth	98.9
12732	31 Rural Resort Dwellers	100.0	12870	31 Rural Resort Dwellers	98.7	13045	48 Great Expectations	18.2
12733	57 Simple Living	56.4	12871	25 Salt Of The Earth	34.8	13052	25 Salt Of The Earth	46.4
12734	31 Rural Resort Dwellers	27.1	12872	31 Rural Resort Dwellers	100.0	13053	36 Old And Newcomers	35.1
12736	31 Rural Resort Dwellers	100.0	12873	31 Rural Resort Dwellers	100.0	13054	25 Salt Of The Earth	55.1
12737	31 Rural Resort Dwellers	100.0	12878	31 Rural Resort Dwellers	61.7	13057	29 Rustbelt Retirees	26.1
12738	31 Rural Resort Dwellers	100.0	12883	33 Midlife Junction	22.6	13060	18 Cozy And Comfortable	55.1
12740	25 Salt Of The Earth	51.5	12885	46 Rooted Rural	67.3	13061	17 Green Acres	83.8
12741	31 Rural Resort Dwellers	100.0	12886	46 Rooted Rural	100.0	13063	17 Green Acres	96.7
12742	31 Rural Resort Dwellers	100.0	12887	25 Salt Of The Earth	52.3	13066	22 Metropolitans	25.7
12743	31 Rural Resort Dwellers	100.0	12901	14 Prosperous Empty Nesters	18.3	13068	26 Midland Crowd	43.0
12745	31 Rural Resort Dwellers	100.0	12903	57 Simple Living	61.0	13069	26 Midland Crowd	33.2
12746	26 Midland Crowd	95.9	12910	25 Salt Of The Earth	44.5	13071	25 Salt Of The Earth	100.0
12747	41 Crossroads	39.9	12911	33 Midlife Junction	51.6	13072	25 Salt Of The Earth	40.4
12748	31 Rural Resort Dwellers	100.0	12912	33 Midlife Junction	33.2	13073	33 Midlife Junction	44.5
12750	31 Rural Resort Dwellers	100.0	12913	33 Midlife Junction	84.5	13074	42 Southern Satellites	91.2
12751	33 Midlife Junction	100.0	12914	46 Rooted Rural	99.4	13076	26 Midland Crowd	100.0
12752	31 Rural Resort Dwellers	100.0	12916	46 Rooted Rural	100.0	13077	17 Green Acres	19.6
12754	24 Main Street, USA	32.5	12917	37 Prairie Living	89.4	13078	03 Connoisseurs	17.0
12758	31 Rural Resort Dwellers	37.8	12918	18 Cozy And Comfortable	45.6	13080	25 Salt Of The Earth	49.3
12759	41 Crossroads	68.6	12919	50 Heartland Communities	35.4	13081	31 Rural Resort Dwellers	87.5
12760	46 Rooted Rural	55.2	12920	46 Rooted Rural	94.3	13082	26 Midland Crowd	52.0
12762	31 Rural Resort Dwellers	100.0	12921	25 Salt Of The Earth	45.7	13083	46 Rooted Rural	74.9
12763	31 Rural Resort Dwellers	69.2	12922	31 Rural Resort Dwellers	100.0	13084	18 Cozy And Comfortable	36.2
12764	31 Rural Resort Dwellers	100.0	12923	46 Rooted Rural	100.0	13088	29 Rustbelt Retirees	20.2
12765	17 Green Acres	51.7	12924	46 Rooted Rural	100.0	13090	19 Milk And Cookies	26.8
12766	31 Rural Resort Dwellers	100.0	12926	46 Rooted Rural	100.0	13092	26 Midland Crowd	45.6
12768	31 Rural Resort Dwellers	77.3	12928	46 Rooted Rural	67.6	13101	32 Rustbelt Traditions	43.9
12770	31 Rural Resort Dwellers	100.0	12930	46 Rooted Rural	96.7	13103	26 Midland Crowd	100.0
12771	24 Main Street, USA	31.5	12932	33 Midlife Junction	48.7	13104	07 Exurbanites	24.8
12775	31 Rural Resort Dwellers	100.0	12934	46 Rooted Rural	67.2	13108	18 Cozy And Comfortable	55.9
12776	31 Rural Resort Dwellers	53.4	12935	42 Southern Satellites	42.0	13110	25 Salt Of The Earth	49.4
12777	31 Rural Resort Dwellers	100.0	12936	31 Rural Resort Dwellers	100.0	13111	26 Midland Crowd	77.1
12779	24 Main Street, USA	79.0	12937	46 Rooted Rural	100.0	13112	18 Cozy And Comfortable	38.5
12780	26 Midland Crowd	91.0	12941	31 Rural Resort Dwellers	100.0	13114	26 Midland Crowd	87.2
12783	31 Rural Resort Dwellers	83.1	12942	31 Rural Resort Dwellers	100.0	13116	18 Cozy And Comfortable	51.6
12786	31 Rural Resort Dwellers	100.0	12943	31 Rural Resort Dwellers	100.0	13118	33 Midlife Junction	27.7
12787	31 Rural Resort Dwellers	100.0	12944	46 Rooted Rural	26.5	13120	32 Rustbelt Traditions	43.4
12788	31 Rural Resort Dwellers	61.0	12945	31 Rural Resort Dwellers	63.9	13122	07 Exurbanites	60.2
12789	33 Midlife Junction	89.2	12946	33 Midlife Junction	34.2	13124	42 Southern Satellites	79.6
12790	24 Main Street, USA	33.4	12950	46 Rooted Rural	100.0	13126	18 Cozy And Comfortable	20.1
12791	31 Rural Resort Dwellers	93.9	12952	29 Rustbelt Retirees	91.0	13131	26 Midland Crowd	100.0
12792	31 Rural Resort Dwellers	100.0	12953	57 Simple Living	24.8	13132	26 Midland Crowd	98.9
12801	48 Great Expectations	51.7	12955	46 Rooted Rural	93.2	13135	26 Midland Crowd	33.7
12803	18 Cozy And Comfortable	40.3	12956	46 Rooted Rural	46.5	13136	42 Southern Satellites	51.6
12804	14 Prosperous Empty Nesters	37.2	12957	46 Rooted Rural	100.0	13140	33 Midlife Junction	30.7
12808	31 Rural Resort Dwellers	100.0	12958	26 Midland Crowd	53.8	13141	17 Green Acres	85.6
12809	25 Salt Of The Earth	74.0	12959	42 Southern Satellites	69.6	13142	57 Simple Living	39.5
12810	46 Rooted Rural	72.0	12960	46 Rooted Rural	56.6	13143	42 Southern Satellites	52.8
12812	31 Rural Resort Dwellers	100.0	12961	46 Rooted Rural	100.0	13144	42 Southern Satellites	65.8
12814	31 Rural Resort Dwellers	100.0	12962	17 Green Acres	31.0	13145	50 Heartland Communities	89.2
12815	31 Rural Resort Dwellers	100.0	12964	29 Rustbelt Retirees	96.7	13146	42 Southern Satellites	84.9
12816	31 Rural Resort Dwellers	43.3	12965	46 Rooted Rural	100.0	13147	25 Salt Of The Earth	70.2
12817	31 Rural Resort Dwellers	91.3	12966	46 Rooted Rural	80.5	13148	33 Midlife Junction	30.1
12819	25 Salt Of The Earth	100.0	12967	46 Rooted Rural	100.0	13152	14 Prosperous Empty Nesters	51.4
12821	46 Rooted Rural	100.0	12969	31 Rural Resort Dwellers	100.0	13155	42 Southern Satellites	94.1

ZIP CODE	TOP TAPESTRY CONSUMER TYPE	% 2009 HOUSE-HOLDS	ZIP CODE	TOP TAPESTRY CONSUMER TYPE	% 2009 HOUSE-HOLDS	ZIP CODE	TOP TAPESTRY CONSUMER TYPE	% 2009 HOUSE-HOLDS
13156	31 Rural Resort Dwellers	45.9	13437	42 Southern Satellites	77.2	13680	33 Midlife Junction	48.4
13158	25 Salt Of The Earth	49.2	13438	32 Rustbelt Traditions	30.4	13681	46 Rooted Rural	65.2
13159	17 Green Acres	45.7	13439	50 Heartland Communities	36.1	13682	25 Salt Of The Earth	62.5
13160	18 Cozy And Comfortable	70.5	13440	29 Rustbelt Retirees	18.7	13684	46 Rooted Rural	86.5
13164	18 Cozy And Comfortable	97.8	13450	31 Rural Resort Dwellers	100.0	13685	33 Midlife Junction	64.9
13165	33 Midlife Junction	20.5	13452	50 Heartland Communities	56.3	13687	31 Rural Resort Dwellers	100.0
13166	25 Salt Of The Earth	44.6	13454	42 Southern Satellites	99.1	13690	29 Rustbelt Retirees	55.6
13167	26 Midland Crowd	79.7	13456	18 Cozy And Comfortable	61.9	13691	26 Midland Crowd	55.9
13202	64 City Commons	48.7	13459	25 Salt Of The Earth	52.2	13693	31 Rural Resort Dwellers	100.0
13203	60 City Dimensions	33.3	13460	46 Rooted Rural	49.2	13694	33 Midlife Junction	85.9
13204	60 City Dimensions	35.0	13461	18 Cozy And Comfortable	61.2	13695	49 Senior Sun Seekers	100.0
13205	51 Metro City Edge	28.9	13464	25 Salt Of The Earth	47.4	13696	46 Rooted Rural	100.0
13206	48 Great Expectations	36.6	13468	31 Rural Resort Dwellers	100.0	13697	46 Rooted Rural	66.3
13207	51 Metro City Edge	26.4	13469	25 Salt Of The Earth	43.1	13699	63 Dorms To Diplomas	100.0
13208	60 City Dimensions	37.5	13470	46 Rooted Rural	77.6	13730	46 Rooted Rural	73.5
13209	29 Rustbelt Retirees	27.9	13471	42 Southern Satellites	98.3	13731	31 Rural Resort Dwellers	100.0
13210	63 Dorms To Diplomas	25.9	13473	25 Salt Of The Earth	50.3	13732	18 Cozy And Comfortable	46.0
13211	32 Rustbelt Traditions	52.0	13475	42 Southern Satellites	100.0	13733	46 Rooted Rural	40.2
13212	29 Rustbelt Retirees	46.8	13476	25 Salt Of The Earth	49.1	13734	46 Rooted Rural	53.1
13214	14 Prosperous Empty Nesters	32.4	13477	25 Salt Of The Earth	99.0	13736	25 Salt Of The Earth	59.8
13215	18 Cozy And Comfortable	26.0	13478	25 Salt Of The Earth	73.4	13739	46 Rooted Rural	42.2
13219	29 Rustbelt Retirees	37.8	13480	33 Midlife Junction	48.2	13740	31 Rural Resort Dwellers	100.0
13224	14 Prosperous Empty Nesters	24.3	13482	25 Salt Of The Earth	100.0	13743	46 Rooted Rural	47.4
13244	63 Dorms To Diplomas	100.0	13483	42 Southern Satellites	72.0	13744	26 Midland Crowd	40.0
13301	50 Heartland Communities	92.0	13485	46 Rooted Rural	100.0	13746	26 Midland Crowd	46.9
13302	42 Southern Satellites	63.6	13486	46 Rooted Rural	55.9	13748	41 Crossroads	31.6
13303	46 Rooted Rural	41.4	13488	31 Rural Resort Dwellers	100.0	13750	46 Rooted Rural	97.2
13304	18 Cozy And Comfortable	82.8	13489	25 Salt Of The Earth	100.0	13751	46 Rooted Rural	100.0
13308	25 Salt Of The Earth	37.2	13490	17 Green Acres	90.0	13752	31 Rural Resort Dwellers	98.9
13309	50 Heartland Communities	24.4	13491	46 Rooted Rural	88.2	13753	33 Midlife Junction	68.9
13310	46 Rooted Rural	88.8	13492	14 Prosperous Empty Nesters	27.2	13754	50 Heartland Communities	73.2
13314	46 Rooted Rural	100.0	13493	42 Southern Satellites	86.2	13755	50 Heartland Communities	54.3
13315	25 Salt Of The Earth	68.6	13494	31 Rural Resort Dwellers	100.0	13756	46 Rooted Rural	97.2
13316	25 Salt Of The Earth	57.4	13495	32 Rustbelt Traditions	54.7	13757	31 Rural Resort Dwellers	65.3
13317	50 Heartland Communities	37.9	13501	60 City Dimensions	26.8	13760	29 Rustbelt Retirees	17.0
13318	41 Crossroads	74.8	13502	29 Rustbelt Retirees	26.1	13775	33 Midlife Junction	51.7
13319	14 Prosperous Empty Nesters	56.5	13601	48 Great Expectations	14.8	13776	31 Rural Resort Dwellers	55.0
13320	31 Rural Resort Dwellers	96.8	13602	40 Military Proximity	99.7	13777	26 Midland Crowd	100.0
13322	25 Salt Of The Earth	99.0	13603	40 Military Proximity	100.0	13778	33 Midlife Junction	54.5
13323	14 Prosperous Empty Nesters	29.9	13605	33 Midlife Junction	42.0	13780	46 Rooted Rural	62.2
13324	46 Rooted Rural	65.0	13606	26 Midland Crowd	69.8	13782	31 Rural Resort Dwellers	100.0
13325	46 Rooted Rural	81.1	13607	31 Rural Resort Dwellers	54.4	13783	50 Heartland Communities	60.3
13326	31 Rural Resort Dwellers	48.0	13608	46 Rooted Rural	72.2	13786	31 Rural Resort Dwellers	100.0
13327	25 Salt Of The Earth	98.4	13611	37 Prairie Living	100.0	13787	42 Southern Satellites	58.4
13328	32 Rustbelt Traditions	77.0	13612	26 Midland Crowd	59.4	13788	25 Salt Of The Earth	77.1
13329	50 Heartland Communities	53.9	13613	46 Rooted Rural	68.6	13790	50 Heartland Communities	15.3
13331	31 Rural Resort Dwellers	100.0	13614	31 Rural Resort Dwellers	91.7	13795	50 Heartland Communities	27.4
13332	46 Rooted Rural	95.9	13616	28 Aspiring Young Families	99.6	13796	25 Salt Of The Earth	60.0
13333	31 Rural Resort Dwellers	100.0	13617	33 Midlife Junction	37.6	13797	46 Rooted Rural	44.5
13334	33 Midlife Junction	56.5	13618	31 Rural Resort Dwellers	100.0	13801	46 Rooted Rural	100.0
13335	46 Rooted Rural	60.5	13619	33 Midlife Junction	21.1	13802	26 Midland Crowd	76.6
13337	31 Rural Resort Dwellers	71.3	13620	25 Salt Of The Earth	74.9	13803	32 Rustbelt Traditions	31.7
13338	31 Rural Resort Dwellers	95.0	13621	25 Salt Of The Earth	54.0	13804	46 Rooted Rural	100.0
13339	50 Heartland Communities	46.1	13622	31 Rural Resort Dwellers	75.8	13806	31 Rural Resort Dwellers	100.0
13340	29 Rustbelt Retirees	24.7	13624	33 Midlife Junction	41.6	13807	46 Rooted Rural	67.5
13342	31 Rural Resort Dwellers	76.5	13625	31 Rural Resort Dwellers	70.5	13808	46 Rooted Rural	83.7
13343	46 Rooted Rural	76.4	13626	26 Midland Crowd	81.0	13809	46 Rooted Rural	51.9
13345	46 Rooted Rural	100.0	13630	46 Rooted Rural	71.8	13810	31 Rural Resort Dwellers	51.1
13346	31 Rural Resort Dwellers	35.2	13633	37 Prairie Living	72.9	13811	26 Midland Crowd	60.0
13348	46 Rooted Rural	67.3	13634	25 Salt Of The Earth	55.6	13812	46 Rooted Rural	38.3
13350	57 Simple Living	38.6	13635	46 Rooted Rural	100.0	13813	46 Rooted Rural	92.8
13353	31 Rural Resort Dwellers	100.0	13636	37 Prairie Living	79.8	13815	46 Rooted Rural	23.3
13354	18 Cozy And Comfortable	75.0	13637	28 Aspiring Young Families	62.1	13820	55 College Towns	26.4
13355	31 Rural Resort Dwellers	57.5	13638	26 Midland Crowd	100.0	13825	46 Rooted Rural	54.3
13357	32 Rustbelt Traditions	28.7	13639	46 Rooted Rural	100.0	13826	46 Rooted Rural	100.0
13360	31 Rural Resort Dwellers	100.0	13640	31 Rural Resort Dwellers	65.9	13827	25 Salt Of The Earth	15.6
13361	42 Southern Satellites	46.1	13642	46 Rooted Rural	21.6	13830	46 Rooted Rural	40.7
13363	42 Southern Satellites	68.5	13646	46 Rooted Rural	78.5	13832	42 Southern Satellites	90.4
13365	53 Home Town	30.0	13648	46 Rooted Rural	73.7	13833	26 Midland Crowd	25.9
13367	33 Midlife Junction	27.5	13650	31 Rural Resort Dwellers	74.6	13834	31 Rural Resort Dwellers	100.0
13368	46 Rooted Rural	55.3	13652	46 Rooted Rural	87.0	13835	41 Crossroads	54.6
13402	46 Rooted Rural	82.9	13654	46 Rooted Rural	62.2	13838	29 Rustbelt Retirees	38.5
13403	17 Green Acres	47.7	13655	38 Industrious Urban Fringe	52.4	13839	46 Rooted Rural	75.0
13406	25 Salt Of The Earth	100.0	13656	26 Midland Crowd	76.5	13841	46 Rooted Rural	100.0
13407	46 Rooted Rural	31.7	13658	37 Prairie Living	52.9	13842	31 Rural Resort Dwellers	100.0
13408	33 Midlife Junction	48.3	13659	26 Midland Crowd	82.0	13843	31 Rural Resort Dwellers	28.9
13409	25 Salt Of The Earth	89.5	13660	46 Rooted Rural	91.7	13844	46 Rooted Rural	62.2
13411	46 Rooted Rural	52.4	13661	26 Midland Crowd	72.7	13846	31 Rural Resort Dwellers	100.0
13413	14 Prosperous Empty Nesters	29.7	13662	25 Salt Of The Earth	18.9	13849	26 Midland Crowd	52.5
13415	31 Rural Resort Dwellers	74.4	13665	46 Rooted Rural	100.0	13850	07 Exurbanites	20.1
13416	25 Salt Of The Earth	84.2	13666	50 Heartland Communities	89.2	13856	31 Rural Resort Dwellers	38.2
13417	30 Retirement Communities	45.9	13667	25 Salt Of The Earth	29.3	13859	26 Midland Crowd	100.0
13418	46 Rooted Rural	100.0	13668	33 Midlife Junction	70.6	13861	14 Prosperous Empty Nesters	74.2
13420	31 Rural Resort Dwellers	100.0	13669	33 Midlife Junction	16.0	13862	32 Rustbelt Traditions	49.5
13421	33 Midlife Junction	22.7	13670	46 Rooted Rural	54.2	13863	42 Southern Satellites	88.3
13424	29 Rustbelt Retirees	60.4	13672	46 Rooted Rural	61.4	13864	46 Rooted Rural	69.9
13425	32 Rustbelt Traditions	63.3	13673	28 Aspiring Young Families	52.7	13865	26 Midland Crowd	22.7
13428	46 Rooted Rural	99.9	13675	46 Rooted Rural	100.0	13901	33 Midlife Junction	16.9
13431	25 Salt Of The Earth	89.3	13676	55 College Towns	22.8	13903	32 Rustbelt Traditions	18.3
13433	46 Rooted Rural	56.7	13679	46 Rooted Rural	57.3	13904	50 Heartland Communities	29.1

ZIP CODE	TOP TAPESTRY CONSUMER TYPE	% 2009 HOUSE-HOLDS	ZIP CODE	TOP TAPESTRY CONSUMER TYPE	% 2009 HOUSE-HOLDS	ZIP CODE	TOP TAPESTRY CONSUMER TYPE	% 2009 HOUSE-HOLDS
13905	55 College Towns	25.3	14208	62 Modest Income Homes	61.9	14541	31 Rural Resort Dwellers	59.6
14001	25 Salt Of The Earth	40.2	14209	65 Social Security Set	40.6	14543	07 Exurbanites	39.2
14004	18 Cozy And Comfortable	64.1	14210	32 Rustbelt Traditions	31.8	14544	31 Rural Resort Dwellers	45.0
14005	18 Cozy And Comfortable	47.8	14211	62 Modest Income Homes	37.5	14545	25 Salt Of The Earth	100.0
14006	18 Cozy And Comfortable	53.2	14212	64 City Commons	27.7	14546	18 Cozy And Comfortable	59.4
14008	25 Salt Of The Earth	66.8	14213	60 City Dimensions	89.5	14548	32 Rustbelt Traditions	40.0
14009	25 Salt Of The Earth	38.4	14214	22 Metropolitans	29.3	14550	32 Rustbelt Traditions	48.8
14011	17 Green Acres	31.1	14215	51 Metro City Edge	41.5	14551	32 Rustbelt Traditions	57.4
14012	25 Salt Of The Earth	100.0	14216	48 Great Expectations	46.2	14555	25 Salt Of The Earth	99.8
14013	25 Salt Of The Earth	69.9	14217	32 Rustbelt Traditions	29.8	14559	18 Cozy And Comfortable	40.3
14020	48 Great Expectations	29.8	14218	29 Rustbelt Retirees	34.2	14560	31 Rural Resort Dwellers	47.7
14024	25 Salt Of The Earth	78.3	14219	32 Rustbelt Traditions	29.2	14561	25 Salt Of The Earth	61.0
14025	18 Cozy And Comfortable	52.1	14220	32 Rustbelt Traditions	40.9	14564	07 Exurbanites	51.9
14026	18 Cozy And Comfortable	100.0	14221	30 Retirement Communities	25.3	14568	12 Up And Coming Families	39.4
14028	29 Rustbelt Retirees	64.2	14222	22 Metropolitans	29.7	14569	25 Salt Of The Earth	31.3
14030	25 Salt Of The Earth	80.5	14223	29 Rustbelt Retirees	56.1	14571	25 Salt Of The Earth	56.6
14031	07 Exurbanites	39.3	14224	18 Cozy And Comfortable	50.3	14572	32 Rustbelt Traditions	37.1
14032	17 Green Acres	51.3	14225	29 Rustbelt Retirees	60.3	14580	06 Sophisticated Squires	20.7
14033	17 Green Acres	59.6	14226	18 Cozy And Comfortable	22.6	14586	13 In Style	78.3
14034	46 Rooted Rural	69.5	14227	29 Rustbelt Retirees	41.7	14589	32 Rustbelt Traditions	48.5
14036	24 Main Street, USA	33.2	14228	22 Metropolitans	25.5	14590	46 Rooted Rural	40.3
14037	17 Green Acres	72.1	14260	63 Dorms To Diplomas	0.0	14591	25 Salt Of The Earth	93.8
14039	25 Salt Of The Earth	100.0	14301	60 City Dimensions	31.2	14604	65 Social Security Set	82.4
14040	17 Green Acres	52.0	14303	57 Simple Living	39.1	14605	64 City Commons	77.0
14041	25 Salt Of The Earth	100.0	14304	29 Rustbelt Retirees	32.4	14606	60 City Dimensions	18.4
14042	41 Crossroads	24.4	14305	29 Rustbelt Retirees	30.8	14607	27 Metro Renters	64.8
14043	29 Rustbelt Retirees	34.9	14410	17 Green Acres	100.0	14608	64 City Commons	55.9
14047	18 Cozy And Comfortable	80.7	14411	53 Home Town	27.7	14609	32 Rustbelt Traditions	25.8
14048	32 Rustbelt Traditions	30.2	14414	26 Midland Crowd	49.4	14610	27 Metro Renters	19.4
14051	02 Suburban Splendor	47.7	14415	37 Prairie Living	100.0	14611	64 City Commons	28.4
14052	18 Cozy And Comfortable	37.8	14416	24 Main Street, USA	35.1	14612	06 Sophisticated Squires	30.1
14054	25 Salt Of The Earth	96.7	14418	31 Rural Resort Dwellers	79.3	14613	60 City Dimensions	34.7
14055	25 Salt Of The Earth	100.0	14420	19 Milk And Cookies	16.9	14614	65 Social Security Set	100.0
14057	18 Cozy And Comfortable	85.4	14422	25 Salt Of The Earth	34.7	14615	48 Great Expectations	26.1
14058	18 Cozy And Comfortable	51.6	14423	18 Cozy And Comfortable	33.2	14616	32 Rustbelt Traditions	45.8
14059	18 Cozy And Comfortable	40.2	14424	07 Exurbanites	13.1	14617	18 Cozy And Comfortable	37.1
14060	50 Heartland Communities	35.3	14425	41 Crossroads	31.2	14618	36 Old And Newcomers	22.1
14062	25 Salt Of The Earth	54.4	14427	25 Salt Of The Earth	50.5	14619	51 Metro City Edge	44.1
14063	24 Main Street, USA	29.5	14428	18 Cozy And Comfortable	41.3	14620	22 Metropolitans	18.4
14065	25 Salt Of The Earth	46.0	14432	57 Simple Living	23.2	14621	51 Metro City Edge	24.7
14066	25 Salt Of The Earth	75.5	14433	32 Rustbelt Traditions	33.0	14622	29 Rustbelt Retirees	57.4
14067	25 Salt Of The Earth	51.2	14435	17 Green Acres	56.1	14623	39 Young And Restless	20.6
14068	06 Sophisticated Squires	44.4	14437	32 Rustbelt Traditions	29.7	14624	18 Cozy And Comfortable	45.6
14069	25 Salt Of The Earth	67.3	14441	46 Rooted Rural	100.0	14625	07 Exurbanites	36.2
14070	48 Great Expectations	31.2	14445	32 Rustbelt Traditions	37.6	14626	18 Cozy And Comfortable	28.2
14072	07 Exurbanites	35.9	14450	14 Prosperous Empty Nesters	23.5	14627	63 Dorms To Diplomas	100.0
14075	18 Cozy And Comfortable	33.2	14454	55 College Towns	30.8	14642	55 College Towns	100.0
14080	17 Green Acres	66.6	14456	29 Rustbelt Retirees	14.8	14701	60 City Dimensions	21.5
14081	29 Rustbelt Retirees	46.0	14462	25 Salt Of The Earth	100.0	14706	26 Midland Crowd	33.5
14082	18 Cozy And Comfortable	42.9	14464	26 Midland Crowd	56.9	14708	31 Rural Resort Dwellers	56.5
14083	17 Green Acres	100.0	14466	17 Green Acres	80.3	14709	46 Rooted Rural	98.3
14085	18 Cozy And Comfortable	66.0	14467	18 Cozy And Comfortable	98.0	14710	31 Rural Resort Dwellers	52.2
14086	18 Cozy And Comfortable	36.9	14468	18 Cozy And Comfortable	43.0	14711	46 Rooted Rural	72.0
14091	25 Salt Of The Earth	45.2	14469	25 Salt Of The Earth	38.5	14712	31 Rural Resort Dwellers	34.1
14092	14 Prosperous Empty Nesters	40.8	14470	32 Rustbelt Traditions	65.7	14714	46 Rooted Rural	100.0
14094	18 Cozy And Comfortable	19.6	14471	25 Salt Of The Earth	45.9	14715	46 Rooted Rural	35.2
14098	25 Salt Of The Earth	97.0	14472	02 Suburban Splendor	42.2	14716	50 Heartland Communities	57.0
14101	46 Rooted Rural	60.5	14475	25 Salt Of The Earth	100.0	14717	50 Heartland Communities	51.7
14102	17 Green Acres	100.0	14476	18 Cozy And Comfortable	87.9	14718	29 Rustbelt Retirees	45.4
14103	32 Rustbelt Traditions	34.1	14477	25 Salt Of The Earth	97.4	14719	46 Rooted Rural	38.5
14105	25 Salt Of The Earth	55.2	14478	31 Rural Resort Dwellers	46.1	14721	25 Salt Of The Earth	100.0
14108	25 Salt Of The Earth	33.8	14480	18 Cozy And Comfortable	100.0	14723	46 Rooted Rural	79.3
14109	29 Rustbelt Retirees	0.0	14481	25 Salt Of The Earth	60.9	14724	25 Salt Of The Earth	45.6
14111	29 Rustbelt Retirees	39.9	14482	18 Cozy And Comfortable	35.4	14726	37 Prairie Living	54.5
14113	18 Cozy And Comfortable	79.7	14485	24 Main Street, USA	58.8	14727	46 Rooted Rural	45.5
14120	18 Cozy And Comfortable	26.9	14486	25 Salt Of The Earth	100.0	14728	46 Rooted Rural	43.9
14125	25 Salt Of The Earth	59.7	14487	18 Cozy And Comfortable	69.8	14729	25 Salt Of The Earth	64.3
14127	18 Cozy And Comfortable	27.7	14489	32 Rustbelt Traditions	41.7	14731	31 Rural Resort Dwellers	89.7
14129	25 Salt Of The Earth	59.7	14502	17 Green Acres	33.7	14733	50 Heartland Communities	40.5
14131	18 Cozy And Comfortable	56.5	14504	49 Senior Sun Seekers	54.6	14735	50 Heartland Communities	52.0
14132	29 Rustbelt Retirees	34.4	14505	17 Green Acres	52.7	14736	31 Rural Resort Dwellers	100.0
14134	25 Salt Of The Earth	100.0	14506	02 Suburban Splendor	54.7	14737	46 Rooted Rural	33.6
14136	29 Rustbelt Retirees	33.3	14507	31 Rural Resort Dwellers	76.8	14738	29 Rustbelt Retirees	47.5
14138	46 Rooted Rural	65.8	14510	48 Great Expectations	22.8	14739	46 Rooted Rural	52.9
14139	17 Green Acres	41.4	14512	17 Green Acres	23.9	14740	46 Rooted Rural	55.6
14141	33 Midlife Junction	55.0	14513	48 Great Expectations	23.3	14741	46 Rooted Rural	75.3
14143	18 Cozy And Comfortable	93.2	14514	33 Midlife Junction	59.4	14743	46 Rooted Rural	59.5
14145	17 Green Acres	98.7	14516	25 Salt Of The Earth	42.2	14744	33 Midlife Junction	96.4
14150	29 Rustbelt Retirees	53.5	14517	32 Rustbelt Traditions	59.9	14747	25 Salt Of The Earth	93.8
14167	25 Salt Of The Earth	56.5	14519	26 Midland Crowd	49.1	14748	25 Salt Of The Earth	62.9
14170	18 Cozy And Comfortable	82.5	14521	46 Rooted Rural	30.6	14750	14 Prosperous Empty Nesters	47.1
14171	25 Salt Of The Earth	54.3	14522	32 Rustbelt Traditions	30.4	14753	46 Rooted Rural	56.5
14172	18 Cozy And Comfortable	44.3	14525	25 Salt Of The Earth	37.4	14754	42 Southern Satellites	57.2
14174	18 Cozy And Comfortable	55.2	14526	07 Exurbanites	30.7	14755	25 Salt Of The Earth	41.1
14201	60 City Dimensions	37.4	14527	33 Midlife Junction	31.1	14757	46 Rooted Rural	34.1
14202	30 Retirement Communities	49.0	14530	29 Rustbelt Retirees	24.6	14760	48 Great Expectations	22.0
14203	65 Social Security Set	78.9	14532	32 Rustbelt Traditions	52.4	14767	25 Salt Of The Earth	75.7
14204	64 City Commons	34.0	14533	25 Salt Of The Earth	98.6	14769	50 Heartland Communities	78.3
14206	29 Rustbelt Retirees	26.6	14534	02 Suburban Splendor	34.3	14770	25 Salt Of The Earth	84.0
14207	60 City Dimensions	35.5	14536	25 Salt Of The Earth	77.6	14772	46 Rooted Rural	55.3

ZIP CODE	TOP TAPESTRY CONSUMER TYPE	% 2009 HOUSE-HOLDS	ZIP CODE	TOP TAPESTRY CONSUMER TYPE	% 2009 HOUSE-HOLDS	ZIP CODE	TOP TAPESTRY CONSUMER TYPE	% 2009 HOUSE-HOLDS
14775	25 Salt Of The Earth	60.6	15017	13 In Style	28.2	15217	22 Metropolitans	25.9
14777	50 Heartland Communities	100.0	15018	18 Cozy And Comfortable	72.2	15218	22 Metropolitans	26.3
14779	53 Home Town	63.9	15019	29 Rustbelt Retirees	52.1	15219	64 City Commons	31.7
14781	37 Prairie Living	61.7	15021	29 Rustbelt Retirees	45.0	15220	14 Prosperous Empty Nesters	32.6
14782	25 Salt Of The Earth	68.5	15022	29 Rustbelt Retirees	50.6	15221	57 Simple Living	13.0
14784	42 Southern Satellites	62.9	15024	29 Rustbelt Retirees	41.4	15222	65 Social Security Set	61.3
14787	33 Midlife Junction	40.4	15025	50 Heartland Communities	17.3	15223	29 Rustbelt Retirees	57.5
14801	42 Southern Satellites	49.7	15026	17 Green Acres	35.0	15224	57 Simple Living	45.4
14802	55 College Towns	60.7	15027	29 Rustbelt Retirees	99.6	15225	50 Heartland Communities	100.0
14803	33 Midlife Junction	59.5	15030	50 Heartland Communities	93.5	15226	29 Rustbelt Retirees	49.7
14804	33 Midlife Junction	66.9	15031	29 Rustbelt Retirees	89.6	15227	29 Rustbelt Retirees	38.5
14805	26 Midland Crowd	51.3	15033	50 Heartland Communities	47.5	15228	22 Metropolitans	21.7
14806	32 Rustbelt Traditions	47.1	15034	50 Heartland Communities	63.1	15229	32 Rustbelt Traditions	27.2
14807	46 Rooted Rural	45.5	15035	50 Heartland Communities	100.0	15232	27 Metro Renters	79.4
14808	46 Rooted Rural	100.0	15037	29 Rustbelt Retirees	66.8	15233	45 City Strivers	62.1
14809	46 Rooted Rural	98.9	15042	18 Cozy And Comfortable	36.8	15234	29 Rustbelt Retirees	37.0
14810	30 Retirement Communities	18.8	15043	26 Midland Crowd	95.1	15235	29 Rustbelt Retirees	60.5
14812	25 Salt Of The Earth	51.5	15044	06 Sophisticated Squires	29.8	15236	14 Prosperous Empty Nesters	28.5
14813	50 Heartland Communities	50.7	15045	29 Rustbelt Retirees	52.0	15237	14 Prosperous Empty Nesters	37.5
14814	14 Prosperous Empty Nesters	49.8	15049	29 Rustbelt Retirees	100.0	15238	01 Top Rung	24.0
14815	42 Southern Satellites	35.9	15050	26 Midland Crowd	72.8	15239	18 Cozy And Comfortable	41.5
14816	33 Midlife Junction	59.3	15051	07 Exurbanites	100.0	15241	03 Connoisseurs	44.8
14817	24 Main Street, USA	58.4	15052	29 Rustbelt Retirees	54.7	15243	18 Cozy And Comfortable	21.1
14818	31 Rural Resort Dwellers	66.8	15055	18 Cozy And Comfortable	100.0	15260	30 Retirement Communities	52.9
14819	42 Southern Satellites	83.3	15056	57 Simple Living	53.6	15275	16 Enterprising Professionals	90.3
14820	42 Southern Satellites	100.0	15057	18 Cozy And Comfortable	20.7	15282	63 Dorms To Diplomas	100.0
14821	18 Cozy And Comfortable	29.6	15059	62 Modest Income Homes	28.2	15301	29 Rustbelt Retirees	20.8
14822	46 Rooted Rural	96.2	15060	29 Rustbelt Retirees	94.0	15310	46 Rooted Rural	69.4
14823	46 Rooted Rural	26.1	15061	18 Cozy And Comfortable	32.1	15311	25 Salt Of The Earth	98.6
14824	46 Rooted Rural	70.8	15062	29 Rustbelt Retirees	58.2	15312	25 Salt Of The Earth	100.0
14825	26 Midland Crowd	51.5	15063	29 Rustbelt Retirees	78.1	15313	25 Salt Of The Earth	95.2
14826	25 Salt Of The Earth	43.4	15064	24 Main Street, USA	96.5	15314	50 Heartland Communities	38.8
14830	48 Great Expectations	29.0	15065	29 Rustbelt Retirees	52.5	15317	07 Exurbanites	25.0
14836	25 Salt Of The Earth	56.5	15066	25 Salt Of The Earth	23.3	15320	50 Heartland Communities	26.7
14837	46 Rooted Rural	31.0	15067	50 Heartland Communities	100.0	15321	17 Green Acres	95.1
14838	26 Midland Crowd	58.9	15068	29 Rustbelt Retirees	36.1	15322	50 Heartland Communities	79.2
14839	46 Rooted Rural	77.2	15071	16 Enterprising Professionals	33.5	15323	25 Salt Of The Earth	73.3
14840	31 Rural Resort Dwellers	92.7	15074	29 Rustbelt Retirees	30.6	15324	50 Heartland Communities	100.0
14841	31 Rural Resort Dwellers	94.3	15076	18 Cozy And Comfortable	70.0	15327	42 Southern Satellites	47.8
14842	25 Salt Of The Earth	79.7	15077	26 Midland Crowd	100.0	15329	25 Salt Of The Earth	75.3
14843	57 Simple Living	31.3	15078	29 Rustbelt Retirees	100.0	15330	07 Exurbanites	36.7
14845	18 Cozy And Comfortable	15.7	15083	29 Rustbelt Retirees	81.7	15331	50 Heartland Communities	100.0
14846	42 Southern Satellites	47.9	15084	29 Rustbelt Retirees	20.8	15332	29 Rustbelt Retirees	43.9
14847	33 Midlife Junction	30.6	15085	18 Cozy And Comfortable	29.0	15333	50 Heartland Communities	66.8
14850	22 Metropolitans	25.2	15086	07 Exurbanites	94.9	15337	46 Rooted Rural	56.7
14853	63 Dorms To Diplomas	100.0	15089	29 Rustbelt Retirees	36.2	15338	46 Rooted Rural	61.3
14855	42 Southern Satellites	99.3	15090	02 Suburban Splendor	66.6	15340	25 Salt Of The Earth	100.0
14858	42 Southern Satellites	55.3	15101	14 Prosperous Empty Nesters	27.5	15341	46 Rooted Rural	100.0
14859	26 Midland Crowd	67.6	15102	14 Prosperous Empty Nesters	33.6	15342	29 Rustbelt Retirees	70.4
14860	31 Rural Resort Dwellers	53.4	15104	62 Modest Income Homes	70.5	15344	46 Rooted Rural	51.5
14861	46 Rooted Rural	54.7	15106	29 Rustbelt Retirees	42.5	15345	50 Heartland Communities	46.6
14864	25 Salt Of The Earth	83.0	15108	18 Cozy And Comfortable	19.9	15346	50 Heartland Communities	96.4
14865	29 Rustbelt Retirees	33.0	15110	62 Modest Income Homes	50.1	15349	29 Rustbelt Retirees	54.4
14867	26 Midland Crowd	63.0	15112	33 Midlife Junction	31.0	15352	56 Rural Bypasses	90.2
14869	25 Salt Of The Earth	89.8	15116	18 Cozy And Comfortable	42.1	15353	42 Southern Satellites	100.0
14870	33 Midlife Junction	20.2	15120	29 Rustbelt Retirees	44.9	15357	50 Heartland Communities	51.5
14871	29 Rustbelt Retirees	30.0	15122	29 Rustbelt Retirees	67.9	15359	46 Rooted Rural	100.0
14872	42 Southern Satellites	68.5	15126	17 Green Acres	20.1	15360	25 Salt Of The Earth	83.2
14873	46 Rooted Rural	82.1	15129	13 In Style	25.3	15362	46 Rooted Rural	87.4
14874	31 Rural Resort Dwellers	100.0	15131	29 Rustbelt Retirees	89.6	15363	50 Heartland Communities	100.0
14877	37 Prairie Living	80.8	15132	50 Heartland Communities	37.8	15364	42 Southern Satellites	45.6
14878	46 Rooted Rural	56.7	15133	29 Rustbelt Retirees	69.7	15367	04 Boomburbs	57.5
14879	32 Rustbelt Traditions	36.6	15135	18 Cozy And Comfortable	29.1	15370	46 Rooted Rural	24.5
14880	46 Rooted Rural	81.6	15136	57 Simple Living	20.7	15376	25 Salt Of The Earth	51.1
14881	25 Salt Of The Earth	79.5	15137	29 Rustbelt Retirees	57.9	15377	25 Salt Of The Earth	77.3
14882	18 Cozy And Comfortable	40.8	15139	18 Cozy And Comfortable	32.0	15380	46 Rooted Rural	100.0
14883	26 Midland Crowd	91.8	15140	57 Simple Living	53.8	15401	50 Heartland Communities	22.5
14884	46 Rooted Rural	100.0	15142	14 Prosperous Empty Nesters	100.0	15410	50 Heartland Communities	100.0
14885	37 Prairie Living	100.0	15143	14 Prosperous Empty Nesters	23.2	15411	46 Rooted Rural	100.0
14886	26 Midland Crowd	28.2	15144	29 Rustbelt Retirees	66.5	15412	50 Heartland Communities	98.4
14889	42 Southern Satellites	61.2	15145	57 Simple Living	53.5	15413	50 Heartland Communities	100.0
14891	46 Rooted Rural	25.7	15146	29 Rustbelt Retirees	24.4	15417	50 Heartland Communities	58.0
14892	46 Rooted Rural	21.5	15147	29 Rustbelt Retirees	43.4	15419	55 College Towns	82.8
14894	26 Midland Crowd	48.1	15148	57 Simple Living	75.7	15423	29 Rustbelt Retirees	85.6
14895	33 Midlife Junction	28.9	15201	57 Simple Living	31.8	15424	46 Rooted Rural	57.9
14897	46 Rooted Rural	97.3	15202	48 Great Expectations	37.8	15425	50 Heartland Communities	19.7
14898	42 Southern Satellites	81.1	15203	57 Simple Living	31.6	15427	50 Heartland Communities	67.0
14901	32 Rustbelt Traditions	13.6	15204	32 Rustbelt Traditions	28.7	15428	46 Rooted Rural	58.3
14903	29 Rustbelt Retirees	17.2	15205	33 Midlife Junction	21.6	15431	56 Rural Bypasses	57.5
14904	50 Heartland Communities	20.3	15206	62 Modest Income Homes	15.9	15432	50 Heartland Communities	100.0
14905	29 Rustbelt Retirees	29.7	15207	29 Rustbelt Retirees	33.0	15433	50 Heartland Communities	100.0
15001	29 Rustbelt Retirees	31.9	15208	62 Modest Income Homes	46.1	15434	29 Rustbelt Retirees	100.0
15003	29 Rustbelt Retirees	33.9	15209	18 Cozy And Comfortable	32.6	15436	50 Heartland Communities	71.2
15005	29 Rustbelt Retirees	59.5	15210	53 Home Town	21.5	15437	42 Southern Satellites	38.3
15007	24 Main Street, USA	100.0	15211	48 Great Expectations	23.3	15438	29 Rustbelt Retirees	44.6
15009	14 Prosperous Empty Nesters	32.1	15212	57 Simple Living	20.7	15440	46 Rooted Rural	53.6
15010	18 Cozy And Comfortable	16.8	15213	55 College Towns	30.1	15442	50 Heartland Communities	72.7
15012	29 Rustbelt Retirees	47.7	15214	29 Rustbelt Retirees	27.2	15444	50 Heartland Communities	100.0
15014	29 Rustbelt Retirees	35.9	15215	22 Metropolitans	25.6	15445	29 Rustbelt Retirees	32.4
15015	03 Connoisseurs	94.3	15216	36 Old And Newcomers	20.8	15446	42 Southern Satellites	100.0

ZIP CODE	TOP TAPESTRY CONSUMER TYPE	% 2009 HOUSE-HOLDS	ZIP CODE	TOP TAPESTRY CONSUMER TYPE	% 2009 HOUSE-HOLDS	ZIP CODE	TOP TAPESTRY CONSUMER TYPE	% 2009 HOUSE-HOLDS
15450	50 Heartland Communities	100.0	15679	46 Rooted Rural	37.3	15931	33 Midlife Junction	29.0
15451	56 Rural Bypasses	89.1	15681	46 Rooted Rural	56.8	15935	29 Rustbelt Retirees	40.1
15456	29 Rustbelt Retirees	26.5	15683	29 Rustbelt Retirees	41.4	15936	50 Heartland Communities	59.5
15458	50 Heartland Communities	57.3	15684	46 Rooted Rural	66.5	15938	29 Rustbelt Retirees	42.8
15459	46 Rooted Rural	100.0	15686	42 Southern Satellites	38.1	15940	29 Rustbelt Retirees	57.9
15461	62 Modest Income Homes	33.2	15687	46 Rooted Rural	79.8	15942	29 Rustbelt Retirees	51.9
15462	42 Southern Satellites	96.1	15688	53 Home Town	52.5	15943	50 Heartland Communities	60.1
15463	50 Heartland Communities	94.6	15690	50 Heartland Communities	51.8	15944	46 Rooted Rural	59.4
15464	46 Rooted Rural	59.9	15692	32 Rustbelt Traditions	63.6	15945	29 Rustbelt Retirees	100.0
15468	50 Heartland Communities	84.2	15697	33 Midlife Junction	77.1	15946	50 Heartland Communities	54.7
15469	42 Southern Satellites	36.7	15698	50 Heartland Communities	100.0	15949	46 Rooted Rural	100.0
15470	25 Salt Of The Earth	52.9	15701	55 College Towns	26.1	15951	50 Heartland Communities	100.0
15473	29 Rustbelt Retirees	53.2	15705	63 Dorms To Diplomas	100.0	15952	25 Salt Of The Earth	96.5
15474	50 Heartland Communities	32.6	15711	46 Rooted Rural	100.0	15953	46 Rooted Rural	83.7
15475	50 Heartland Communities	100.0	15713	25 Salt Of The Earth	100.0	15954	46 Rooted Rural	45.4
15477	50 Heartland Communities	75.9	15714	50 Heartland Communities	71.9	15955	50 Heartland Communities	54.5
15478	46 Rooted Rural	51.5	15716	50 Heartland Communities	100.0	15956	50 Heartland Communities	46.8
15479	29 Rustbelt Retirees	71.7	15717	25 Salt Of The Earth	35.8	15957	46 Rooted Rural	99.1
15480	42 Southern Satellites	46.9	15720	46 Rooted Rural	100.0	15958	25 Salt Of The Earth	39.8
15482	50 Heartland Communities	85.7	15721	46 Rooted Rural	100.0	15960	46 Rooted Rural	100.0
15483	50 Heartland Communities	100.0	15722	29 Rustbelt Retirees	45.3	15961	50 Heartland Communities	34.4
15486	46 Rooted Rural	52.1	15724	46 Rooted Rural	92.8	15963	50 Heartland Communities	45.9
15488	46 Rooted Rural	100.0	15725	46 Rooted Rural	78.7	16001	18 Cozy And Comfortable	11.9
15490	25 Salt Of The Earth	56.5	15728	46 Rooted Rural	39.7	16002	25 Salt Of The Earth	29.6
15501	46 Rooted Rural	28.6	15729	46 Rooted Rural	97.8	16020	46 Rooted Rural	74.7
15521	42 Southern Satellites	80.9	15730	46 Rooted Rural	100.0	16022	42 Southern Satellites	100.0
15522	25 Salt Of The Earth	42.5	15732	46 Rooted Rural	99.2	16023	17 Green Acres	39.4
15530	25 Salt Of The Earth	49.5	15739	25 Salt Of The Earth	100.0	16025	25 Salt Of The Earth	61.3
15531	25 Salt Of The Earth	45.8	15742	46 Rooted Rural	100.0	16028	50 Heartland Communities	53.8
15533	42 Southern Satellites	56.6	15744	46 Rooted Rural	100.0	16030	46 Rooted Rural	100.0
15534	46 Rooted Rural	67.1	15747	46 Rooted Rural	47.4	16033	17 Green Acres	27.8
15535	46 Rooted Rural	92.9	15748	29 Rustbelt Retirees	38.4	16034	42 Southern Satellites	50.1
15536	46 Rooted Rural	100.0	15753	42 Southern Satellites	70.5	16036	46 Rooted Rural	100.0
15537	25 Salt Of The Earth	47.9	15757	46 Rooted Rural	94.6	16037	17 Green Acres	53.6
15538	46 Rooted Rural	100.0	15758	46 Rooted Rural	100.0	16038	46 Rooted Rural	99.2
15539	42 Southern Satellites	100.0	15759	46 Rooted Rural	82.9	16040	42 Southern Satellites	63.8
15540	46 Rooted Rural	72.7	15760	46 Rooted Rural	100.0	16041	25 Salt Of The Earth	40.2
15541	26 Midland Crowd	55.6	15762	25 Salt Of The Earth	61.9	16045	50 Heartland Communities	46.9
15542	42 Southern Satellites	53.5	15763	42 Southern Satellites	84.2	16046	04 Boomburbs	37.1
15545	46 Rooted Rural	68.1	15764	46 Rooted Rural	100.0	16049	46 Rooted Rural	73.4
15546	46 Rooted Rural	100.0	15765	25 Salt Of The Earth	66.3	16050	42 Southern Satellites	42.4
15550	46 Rooted Rural	59.3	15767	46 Rooted Rural	30.5	16051	41 Crossroads	42.7
15551	46 Rooted Rural	100.0	15770	46 Rooted Rural	100.0	16052	26 Midland Crowd	76.0
15552	46 Rooted Rural	40.0	15771	46 Rooted Rural	100.0	16053	17 Green Acres	31.4
15554	42 Southern Satellites	72.3	15772	50 Heartland Communities	67.7	16055	17 Green Acres	24.1
15557	46 Rooted Rural	51.2	15773	50 Heartland Communities	95.0	16056	33 Midlife Junction	36.3
15558	37 Prairie Living	48.1	15774	46 Rooted Rural	65.7	16057	55 College Towns	38.4
15559	25 Salt Of The Earth	92.8	15775	50 Heartland Communities	67.4	16059	17 Green Acres	39.6
15562	37 Prairie Living	100.0	15776	46 Rooted Rural	100.0	16061	26 Midland Crowd	74.0
15563	46 Rooted Rural	60.3	15777	46 Rooted Rural	100.0	16063	30 Retirement Communities	33.8
15601	33 Midlife Junction	13.8	15778	46 Rooted Rural	100.0	16066	04 Boomburbs	46.9
15610	26 Midland Crowd	35.6	15780	46 Rooted Rural	100.0	16101	29 Rustbelt Retirees	24.7
15611	17 Green Acres	100.0	15784	42 Southern Satellites	54.5	16102	25 Salt Of The Earth	35.9
15612	25 Salt Of The Earth	61.0	15801	17 Green Acres	29.1	16105	29 Rustbelt Retirees	38.6
15613	29 Rustbelt Retirees	28.3	15821	25 Salt Of The Earth	100.0	16110	42 Southern Satellites	82.1
15615	25 Salt Of The Earth	100.0	15823	42 Southern Satellites	80.7	16111	42 Southern Satellites	100.0
15617	18 Cozy And Comfortable	85.0	15824	25 Salt Of The Earth	52.1	16112	29 Rustbelt Retirees	51.1
15618	25 Salt Of The Earth	62.1	15825	25 Salt Of The Earth	29.7	16114	46 Rooted Rural	67.7
15620	50 Heartland Communities	56.0	15827	50 Heartland Communities	100.0	16115	46 Rooted Rural	51.9
15622	25 Salt Of The Earth	49.4	15828	46 Rooted Rural	56.0	16116	46 Rooted Rural	74.7
15623	29 Rustbelt Retirees	67.8	15829	46 Rooted Rural	87.2	16117	25 Salt Of The Earth	40.6
15625	29 Rustbelt Retirees	100.0	15832	46 Rooted Rural	98.1	16120	42 Southern Satellites	61.0
15626	18 Cozy And Comfortable	43.3	15834	25 Salt Of The Earth	48.1	16121	50 Heartland Communities	46.8
15627	25 Salt Of The Earth	34.4	15840	50 Heartland Communities	50.1	16123	25 Salt Of The Earth	100.0
15628	46 Rooted Rural	100.0	15845	50 Heartland Communities	88.8	16124	25 Salt Of The Earth	64.1
15631	50 Heartland Communities	100.0	15846	25 Salt Of The Earth	99.5	16125	29 Rustbelt Retirees	40.1
15632	07 Exurbanites	40.9	15848	46 Rooted Rural	98.5	16127	25 Salt Of The Earth	40.3
15634	29 Rustbelt Retirees	98.6	15849	46 Rooted Rural	96.1	16130	46 Rooted Rural	63.5
15636	17 Green Acres	47.4	15851	25 Salt Of The Earth	41.3	16131	42 Southern Satellites	79.6
15637	50 Heartland Communities	63.0	15853	25 Salt Of The Earth	31.5	16133	25 Salt Of The Earth	100.0
15639	18 Cozy And Comfortable	46.3	15856	25 Salt Of The Earth	99.5	16134	49 Senior Sun Seekers	46.4
15641	50 Heartland Communities	100.0	15857	29 Rustbelt Retirees	47.7	16137	25 Salt Of The Earth	39.8
15642	18 Cozy And Comfortable	33.9	15860	46 Rooted Rural	50.1	16141	42 Southern Satellites	39.1
15644	29 Rustbelt Retirees	32.4	15861	46 Rooted Rural	100.0	16142	25 Salt Of The Earth	37.1
15646	46 Rooted Rural	100.0	15864	46 Rooted Rural	43.8	16143	42 Southern Satellites	50.6
15647	25 Salt Of The Earth	56.8	15865	50 Heartland Communities	99.1	16145	25 Salt Of The Earth	40.1
15650	29 Rustbelt Retirees	42.7	15868	50 Heartland Communities	57.5	16146	53 Home Town	37.4
15655	31 Rural Resort Dwellers	98.4	15870	25 Salt Of The Earth	99.8	16148	29 Rustbelt Retirees	28.8
15656	29 Rustbelt Retirees	41.6	15901	65 Social Security Set	34.4	16150	29 Rustbelt Retirees	31.7
15658	31 Rural Resort Dwellers	55.1	15902	53 Home Town	31.3	16153	25 Salt Of The Earth	48.2
15661	29 Rustbelt Retirees	100.0	15904	29 Rustbelt Retirees	66.8	16154	42 Southern Satellites	46.8
15663	29 Rustbelt Retirees	100.0	15905	29 Rustbelt Retirees	42.7	16156	25 Salt Of The Earth	98.3
15665	32 Rustbelt Traditions	89.5	15906	50 Heartland Communities	48.4	16157	25 Salt Of The Earth	27.6
15666	29 Rustbelt Retirees	33.7	15909	29 Rustbelt Retirees	51.8	16159	29 Rustbelt Retirees	55.4
15668	07 Exurbanites	57.8	15920	46 Rooted Rural	100.0	16172	63 Dorms To Diplomas	100.0
15670	25 Salt Of The Earth	45.2	15923	46 Rooted Rural	70.2	16201	25 Salt Of The Earth	25.6
15672	33 Midlife Junction	50.1	15924	50 Heartland Communities	96.9	16210	46 Rooted Rural	100.0
15675	32 Rustbelt Traditions	52.1	15926	50 Heartland Communities	72.2	16212	29 Rustbelt Retirees	100.0
15677	31 Rural Resort Dwellers	82.5	15927	50 Heartland Communities	87.4	16213	46 Rooted Rural	100.0
15678	46 Rooted Rural	64.3	15928	50 Heartland Communities	51.0	16214	25 Salt Of The Earth	22.5

ZIP CODE	TOP TAPESTRY CONSUMER TYPE	% 2009 HOUSE-HOLDS	ZIP CODE	TOP TAPESTRY CONSUMER TYPE	% 2009 HOUSE-HOLDS	ZIP CODE	TOP TAPESTRY CONSUMER TYPE	% 2009 HOUSE-HOLDS
16217	50 Heartland Communities	100.0	16503	60 City Dimensions	69.9	16829	46 Rooted Rural	100.0
16218	46 Rooted Rural	100.0	16504	32 Rustbelt Traditions	33.3	16830	50 Heartland Communities	31.9
16222	46 Rooted Rural	62.2	16505	30 Retirement Communities	15.7	16832	25 Salt Of The Earth	100.0
16224	50 Heartland Communities	66.9	16506	07 Exurbanites	18.6	16833	25 Salt Of The Earth	36.3
16225	46 Rooted Rural	100.0	16507	60 City Dimensions	69.5	16836	46 Rooted Rural	53.4
16226	29 Rustbelt Retirees	29.4	16508	32 Rustbelt Traditions	43.8	16837	25 Salt Of The Earth	100.0
16229	25 Salt Of The Earth	44.3	16509	29 Rustbelt Retirees	19.6	16838	46 Rooted Rural	97.6
16232	25 Salt Of The Earth	38.8	16510	25 Salt Of The Earth	24.5	16839	32 Rustbelt Traditions	58.7
16233	46 Rooted Rural	57.1	16511	32 Rustbelt Traditions	26.0	16840	46 Rooted Rural	100.0
16234	25 Salt Of The Earth	100.0	16565	30 Retirement Communities	100.0	16841	25 Salt Of The Earth	48.4
16235	25 Salt Of The Earth	96.5	16601	29 Rustbelt Retirees	29.8	16844	25 Salt Of The Earth	56.6
16238	50 Heartland Communities	100.0	16602	29 Rustbelt Retirees	37.4	16845	46 Rooted Rural	100.0
16239	49 Senior Sun Seekers	50.7	16611	25 Salt Of The Earth	100.0	16852	37 Prairie Living	100.0
16240	46 Rooted Rural	59.7	16613	46 Rooted Rural	50.6	16854	32 Rustbelt Traditions	76.5
16242	50 Heartland Communities	60.2	16616	50 Heartland Communities	62.5	16858	46 Rooted Rural	61.3
16248	46 Rooted Rural	70.0	16617	25 Salt Of The Earth	59.5	16859	46 Rooted Rural	100.0
16249	46 Rooted Rural	57.1	16620	46 Rooted Rural	100.0	16860	46 Rooted Rural	83.6
16254	46 Rooted Rural	80.7	16621	42 Southern Satellites	100.0	16861	46 Rooted Rural	100.0
16255	50 Heartland Communities	55.2	16622	46 Rooted Rural	100.0	16863	46 Rooted Rural	93.0
16256	42 Southern Satellites	58.0	16623	46 Rooted Rural	100.0	16864	46 Rooted Rural	100.0
16258	53 Home Town	38.0	16625	46 Rooted Rural	49.2	16865	07 Exurbanites	83.9
16259	46 Rooted Rural	57.2	16627	42 Southern Satellites	35.8	16866	46 Rooted Rural	43.6
16260	46 Rooted Rural	71.1	16630	50 Heartland Communities	53.5	16870	06 Sophisticated Squires	52.3
16262	25 Salt Of The Earth	72.7	16634	42 Southern Satellites	100.0	16871	49 Senior Sun Seekers	58.8
16301	29 Rustbelt Retirees	27.8	16635	25 Salt Of The Earth	28.8	16872	37 Prairie Living	100.0
16311	25 Salt Of The Earth	99.0	16636	25 Salt Of The Earth	54.3	16874	25 Salt Of The Earth	56.1
16313	46 Rooted Rural	55.3	16637	42 Southern Satellites	39.4	16875	25 Salt Of The Earth	76.5
16314	25 Salt Of The Earth	85.2	16639	46 Rooted Rural	57.8	16877	25 Salt Of The Earth	70.4
16316	25 Salt Of The Earth	27.8	16640	46 Rooted Rural	88.0	16878	42 Southern Satellites	66.9
16317	25 Salt Of The Earth	75.8	16641	50 Heartland Communities	63.4	16879	32 Rustbelt Traditions	100.0
16319	29 Rustbelt Retirees	46.4	16645	50 Heartland Communities	100.0	16881	42 Southern Satellites	99.7
16321	46 Rooted Rural	100.0	16646	50 Heartland Communities	58.4	16882	25 Salt Of The Earth	100.0
16323	50 Heartland Communities	35.4	16647	25 Salt Of The Earth	100.0	16901	25 Salt Of The Earth	32.4
16326	42 Southern Satellites	58.5	16648	33 Midlife Junction	29.5	16912	50 Heartland Communities	92.3
16327	25 Salt Of The Earth	95.6	16650	42 Southern Satellites	57.6	16914	25 Salt Of The Earth	100.0
16329	50 Heartland Communities	86.0	16651	50 Heartland Communities	75.8	16915	33 Midlife Junction	33.7
16331	25 Salt Of The Earth	100.0	16652	25 Salt Of The Earth	33.9	16917	46 Rooted Rural	100.0
16332	25 Salt Of The Earth	98.6	16655	25 Salt Of The Earth	70.9	16920	50 Heartland Communities	99.3
16333	46 Rooted Rural	100.0	16656	42 Southern Satellites	60.8	16921	46 Rooted Rural	100.0
16334	25 Salt Of The Earth	100.0	16657	25 Salt Of The Earth	100.0	16922	50 Heartland Communities	55.0
16335	25 Salt Of The Earth	16.5	16659	25 Salt Of The Earth	100.0	16923	46 Rooted Rural	79.6
16340	42 Southern Satellites	58.6	16661	50 Heartland Communities	87.1	16925	46 Rooted Rural	53.4
16341	50 Heartland Communities	51.1	16662	25 Salt Of The Earth	54.1	16926	37 Prairie Living	100.0
16342	46 Rooted Rural	93.2	16664	25 Salt Of The Earth	99.8	16927	42 Southern Satellites	100.0
16345	25 Salt Of The Earth	100.0	16666	46 Rooted Rural	62.2	16928	50 Heartland Communities	71.9
16346	32 Rustbelt Traditions	43.4	16667	42 Southern Satellites	89.8	16929	42 Southern Satellites	100.0
16347	46 Rooted Rural	45.7	16668	50 Heartland Communities	54.2	16930	25 Salt Of The Earth	100.0
16350	42 Southern Satellites	66.6	16669	25 Salt Of The Earth	100.0	16932	25 Salt Of The Earth	99.0
16351	50 Heartland Communities	54.4	16671	50 Heartland Communities	100.0	16933	36 Old And Newcomers	23.6
16353	46 Rooted Rural	47.1	16673	25 Salt Of The Earth	49.5	16935	46 Rooted Rural	79.3
16354	46 Rooted Rural	37.4	16674	42 Southern Satellites	100.0	16936	25 Salt Of The Earth	100.0
16360	42 Southern Satellites	62.8	16678	46 Rooted Rural	58.7	16937	42 Southern Satellites	100.0
16362	25 Salt Of The Earth	79.4	16679	42 Southern Satellites	100.0	16938	46 Rooted Rural	82.5
16364	46 Rooted Rural	63.6	16680	50 Heartland Communities	100.0	16939	46 Rooted Rural	100.0
16365	25 Salt Of The Earth	24.9	16683	25 Salt Of The Earth	100.0	16940	46 Rooted Rural	88.6
16371	32 Rustbelt Traditions	43.9	16685	46 Rooted Rural	100.0	16941	42 Southern Satellites	100.0
16372	46 Rooted Rural	100.0	16686	25 Salt Of The Earth	43.0	16942	42 Southern Satellites	100.0
16373	46 Rooted Rural	52.6	16689	46 Rooted Rural	100.0	16943	46 Rooted Rural	100.0
16374	46 Rooted Rural	91.9	16691	46 Rooted Rural	100.0	16946	46 Rooted Rural	65.7
16401	42 Southern Satellites	40.3	16692	42 Southern Satellites	56.4	16947	46 Rooted Rural	38.7
16402	42 Southern Satellites	96.9	16693	25 Salt Of The Earth	32.8	16948	42 Southern Satellites	63.1
16403	25 Salt Of The Earth	57.4	16695	25 Salt Of The Earth	100.0	16950	46 Rooted Rural	44.8
16404	42 Southern Satellites	59.5	16701	29 Rustbelt Retirees	37.4	17002	42 Southern Satellites	56.1
16405	25 Salt Of The Earth	100.0	16720	42 Southern Satellites	63.2	17003	25 Salt Of The Earth	31.6
16406	42 Southern Satellites	45.8	16724	46 Rooted Rural	75.0	17004	46 Rooted Rural	55.8
16407	42 Southern Satellites	32.4	16726	46 Rooted Rural	80.6	17005	25 Salt Of The Earth	100.0
16410	25 Salt Of The Earth	55.3	16727	29 Rustbelt Retirees	80.9	17006	46 Rooted Rural	100.0
16411	42 Southern Satellites	66.3	16729	42 Southern Satellites	99.0	17007	17 Green Acres	77.4
16412	55 College Towns	22.9	16731	42 Southern Satellites	58.1	17009	50 Heartland Communities	55.4
16415	07 Exurbanites	34.7	16732	25 Salt Of The Earth	72.6	17011	29 Rustbelt Retirees	22.7
16417	25 Salt Of The Earth	36.9	16734	46 Rooted Rural	100.0	17013	18 Cozy And Comfortable	23.8
16420	42 Southern Satellites	100.0	16735	29 Rustbelt Retirees	30.6	17014	25 Salt Of The Earth	100.0
16421	33 Midlife Junction	36.0	16738	42 Southern Satellites	61.2	17015	25 Salt Of The Earth	26.2
16423	32 Rustbelt Traditions	64.7	16740	46 Rooted Rural	54.5	17017	25 Salt Of The Earth	100.0
16424	46 Rooted Rural	38.2	16743	32 Rustbelt Traditions	41.7	17018	18 Cozy And Comfortable	83.9
16426	17 Green Acres	77.5	16744	42 Southern Satellites	66.0	17019	17 Green Acres	58.9
16428	17 Green Acres	18.0	16745	42 Southern Satellites	82.1	17020	25 Salt Of The Earth	30.6
16430	42 Southern Satellites	100.0	16746	46 Rooted Rural	91.7	17021	46 Rooted Rural	76.5
16433	25 Salt Of The Earth	67.0	16748	46 Rooted Rural	50.8	17022	17 Green Acres	21.4
16434	42 Southern Satellites	93.8	16749	46 Rooted Rural	61.7	17023	25 Salt Of The Earth	68.4
16435	42 Southern Satellites	71.5	16750	42 Southern Satellites	85.5	17024	25 Salt Of The Earth	88.0
16436	25 Salt Of The Earth	100.0	16801	63 Dorms To Diplomas	35.6	17025	18 Cozy And Comfortable	38.3
16438	25 Salt Of The Earth	49.0	16802	63 Dorms To Diplomas	100.0	17026	25 Salt Of The Earth	87.0
16440	25 Salt Of The Earth	99.7	16803	16 Enterprising Professionals	21.9	17028	17 Green Acres	52.8
16441	25 Salt Of The Earth	34.1	16820	25 Salt Of The Earth	100.0	17029	42 Southern Satellites	100.0
16442	17 Green Acres	60.4	16821	46 Rooted Rural	100.0	17030	25 Salt Of The Earth	100.0
16443	42 Southern Satellites	77.1	16822	25 Salt Of The Earth	52.8	17032	25 Salt Of The Earth	83.6
16444	55 College Towns	100.0	16823	25 Salt Of The Earth	20.0	17033	14 Prosperous Empty Nesters	28.8
16501	65 Social Security Set	76.2	16827	07 Exurbanites	29.0	17034	33 Midlife Junction	47.8
16502	48 Great Expectations	40.3	16828	26 Midland Crowd	30.0	17035	42 Southern Satellites	100.0

CONSUMER TYPE

ZIP CODE	TOP TAPESTRY CONSUMER TYPE	% 2009 HOUSE-HOLDS
17036	16 Enterprising Professionals	18.7
17037	25 Salt Of The Earth	100.0
17038	25 Salt Of The Earth	98.8
17040	25 Salt Of The Earth	100.0
17042	17 Green Acres	15.5
17043	48 Great Expectations	54.7
17044	25 Salt Of The Earth	21.0
17045	25 Salt Of The Earth	71.3
17046	25 Salt Of The Earth	23.3
17047	37 Prairie Living	60.2
17048	50 Heartland Communities	51.5
17049	25 Salt Of The Earth	97.9
17050	07 Exurbanites	32.4
17051	25 Salt Of The Earth	44.6
17052	46 Rooted Rural	62.5
17053	17 Green Acres	41.3
17055	36 Old And Newcomers	17.5
17057	48 Great Expectations	13.3
17058	25 Salt Of The Earth	100.0
17059	25 Salt Of The Earth	72.2
17060	42 Southern Satellites	100.0
17061	25 Salt Of The Earth	58.3
17062	25 Salt Of The Earth	58.7
17063	42 Southern Satellites	72.4
17065	32 Rustbelt Traditions	71.3
17066	57 Simple Living	38.1
17067	25 Salt Of The Earth	41.7
17068	25 Salt Of The Earth	51.3
17070	14 Prosperous Empty Nesters	25.4
17071	46 Rooted Rural	100.0
17073	25 Salt Of The Earth	56.9
17074	25 Salt Of The Earth	60.2
17076	25 Salt Of The Earth	76.5
17078	29 Rustbelt Retirees	20.8
17080	25 Salt Of The Earth	100.0
17082	25 Salt Of The Earth	68.8
17084	25 Salt Of The Earth	89.6
17086	25 Salt Of The Earth	100.0
17087	25 Salt Of The Earth	97.8
17090	26 Midland Crowd	70.6
17094	25 Salt Of The Earth	68.6
17097	50 Heartland Communities	100.0
17098	25 Salt Of The Earth	59.3
17099	32 Rustbelt Traditions	69.9
17101	65 Social Security Set	53.9
17102	48 Great Expectations	32.0
17103	54 Urban Rows	33.7
17104	60 City Dimensions	21.3
17109	36 Old And Newcomers	35.0
17110	13 In Style	40.7
17111	29 Rustbelt Retirees	21.1
17112	18 Cozy And Comfortable	35.1
17113	32 Rustbelt Traditions	32.9
17201	48 Great Expectations	19.8
17202	25 Salt Of The Earth	24.3
17211	46 Rooted Rural	100.0
17212	42 Southern Satellites	67.1
17213	42 Southern Satellites	100.0
17214	33 Midlife Junction	100.0
17215	46 Rooted Rural	81.2
17217	25 Salt Of The Earth	100.0
17219	25 Salt Of The Earth	88.2
17220	25 Salt Of The Earth	56.6
17221	25 Salt Of The Earth	100.0
17222	29 Rustbelt Retirees	22.4
17223	46 Rooted Rural	100.0
17224	25 Salt Of The Earth	83.8
17225	17 Green Acres	32.6
17228	25 Salt Of The Earth	87.5
17229	46 Rooted Rural	100.0
17232	25 Salt Of The Earth	100.0
17233	42 Southern Satellites	62.1
17236	25 Salt Of The Earth	52.0
17237	25 Salt Of The Earth	100.0
17238	25 Salt Of The Earth	100.0
17239	25 Salt Of The Earth	97.1
17240	25 Salt Of The Earth	100.0
17241	25 Salt Of The Earth	65.0
17243	42 Southern Satellites	58.4
17244	25 Salt Of The Earth	100.0
17246	25 Salt Of The Earth	100.0
17252	25 Salt Of The Earth	48.8
17255	25 Salt Of The Earth	100.0
17257	26 Midland Crowd	31.1
17260	46 Rooted Rural	55.7
17262	42 Southern Satellites	53.9
17264	46 Rooted Rural	60.8
17265	25 Salt Of The Earth	100.0
17266	25 Salt Of The Earth	100.0
17267	42 Southern Satellites	78.8
17268	25 Salt Of The Earth	32.5
17271	25 Salt Of The Earth	100.0
17301	17 Green Acres	37.1
17302	25 Salt Of The Earth	64.4
17304	25 Salt Of The Earth	78.7
17307	25 Salt Of The Earth	83.6
17309	25 Salt Of The Earth	73.1
17313	32 Rustbelt Traditions	28.1
17314	26 Midland Crowd	44.0
17315	25 Salt Of The Earth	34.7
17316	17 Green Acres	68.8
17319	06 Sophisticated Squires	23.6
17320	12 Up And Coming Families	38.6
17321	17 Green Acres	98.4
17322	17 Green Acres	81.2
17324	25 Salt Of The Earth	88.2
17325	25 Salt Of The Earth	20.5
17327	17 Green Acres	31.5
17329	17 Green Acres	77.9
17331	17 Green Acres	31.3
17339	17 Green Acres	75.1
17340	17 Green Acres	49.6
17344	32 Rustbelt Traditions	50.3
17345	18 Cozy And Comfortable	23.6
17347	18 Cozy And Comfortable	49.4
17349	17 Green Acres	51.5
17350	26 Midland Crowd	29.4
17352	17 Green Acres	91.3
17353	25 Salt Of The Earth	79.6
17356	17 Green Acres	32.2
17360	25 Salt Of The Earth	52.1
17361	17 Green Acres	53.7
17362	25 Salt Of The Earth	37.2
17363	17 Green Acres	48.1
17364	25 Salt Of The Earth	84.2
17365	25 Salt Of The Earth	63.6
17366	26 Midland Crowd	39.3
17368	25 Salt Of The Earth	30.9
17370	26 Midland Crowd	50.1
17372	25 Salt Of The Earth	52.5
17401	60 City Dimensions	64.4
17402	14 Prosperous Empty Nesters	22.6
17403	60 City Dimensions	12.4
17404	32 Rustbelt Traditions	28.6
17406	17 Green Acres	15.5
17407	18 Cozy And Comfortable	61.2
17408	18 Cozy And Comfortable	25.7
17501	24 Main Street, USA	68.5
17502	25 Salt Of The Earth	99.1
17505	24 Main Street, USA	33.8
17509	17 Green Acres	64.6
17512	32 Rustbelt Traditions	24.6
17516	25 Salt Of The Earth	49.9
17517	17 Green Acres	66.6
17518	25 Salt Of The Earth	100.0
17519	25 Salt Of The Earth	72.2
17520	19 Milk And Cookies	43.6
17522	25 Salt Of The Earth	21.6
17527	17 Green Acres	43.9
17529	37 Prairie Living	66.7
17532	17 Green Acres	80.0
17535	17 Green Acres	45.5
17536	17 Green Acres	100.0
17538	17 Green Acres	28.9
17540	17 Green Acres	51.5
17543	17 Green Acres	30.2
17545	17 Green Acres	40.0
17547	32 Rustbelt Traditions	41.6
17551	24 Main Street, USA	27.2
17552	24 Main Street, USA	38.9
17554	24 Main Street, USA	35.6
17555	17 Green Acres	73.0
17557	25 Salt Of The Earth	36.6
17560	46 Rooted Rural	60.5
17562	25 Salt Of The Earth	75.1
17563	25 Salt Of The Earth	56.4
17565	17 Green Acres	90.6
17566	17 Green Acres	48.5
17569	17 Green Acres	70.2
17572	37 Prairie Living	30.4
17576	38 Industrious Urban Fringe	100.0
17578	17 Green Acres	52.0
17579	17 Green Acres	69.3
17581	25 Salt Of The Earth	100.0
17582	17 Green Acres	78.3
17584	30 Retirement Communities	44.6
17601	18 Cozy And Comfortable	15.9
17602	60 City Dimensions	22.9
17603	60 City Dimensions	16.6
17701	53 Home Town	17.2
17702	29 Rustbelt Retirees	47.1
17721	50 Heartland Communities	94.0
17723	31 Rural Resort Dwellers	100.0
17724	46 Rooted Rural	51.6
17728	42 Southern Satellites	42.2
17729	49 Senior Sun Seekers	62.3
17737	25 Salt Of The Earth	45.1
17740	25 Salt Of The Earth	51.5
17742	25 Salt Of The Earth	100.0
17744	25 Salt Of The Earth	49.2
17745	57 Simple Living	20.5
17747	25 Salt Of The Earth	100.0
17751	25 Salt Of The Earth	59.4
17752	25 Salt Of The Earth	63.4
17754	17 Green Acres	28.6
17756	25 Salt Of The Earth	46.3
17758	31 Rural Resort Dwellers	64.8
17763	46 Rooted Rural	100.0
17764	50 Heartland Communities	46.6
17765	25 Salt Of The Earth	74.5
17768	46 Rooted Rural	100.0
17771	25 Salt Of The Earth	73.3
17772	25 Salt Of The Earth	77.7
17774	46 Rooted Rural	63.7
17776	31 Rural Resort Dwellers	52.9
17777	42 Southern Satellites	39.7
17778	50 Heartland Communities	65.9
17779	42 Southern Satellites	52.4
17801	25 Salt Of The Earth	22.9
17810	25 Salt Of The Earth	53.8
17812	25 Salt Of The Earth	99.3
17813	25 Salt Of The Earth	100.0
17814	25 Salt Of The Earth	80.5
17815	25 Salt Of The Earth	33.4
17820	25 Salt Of The Earth	72.5
17821	25 Salt Of The Earth	26.9
17823	25 Salt Of The Earth	100.0
17824	14 Prosperous Empty Nesters	39.1
17827	29 Rustbelt Retirees	91.5
17830	25 Salt Of The Earth	100.0
17832	50 Heartland Communities	100.0
17834	50 Heartland Communities	64.5
17835	25 Salt Of The Earth	100.0
17836	25 Salt Of The Earth	100.0
17837	25 Salt Of The Earth	24.6
17841	42 Southern Satellites	43.3
17842	25 Salt Of The Earth	49.7
17844	25 Salt Of The Earth	34.6
17845	25 Salt Of The Earth	100.0
17846	25 Salt Of The Earth	74.0
17847	32 Rustbelt Traditions	33.4
17850	42 Southern Satellites	100.0
17851	50 Heartland Communities	79.2
17853	25 Salt Of The Earth	99.3
17855	32 Rustbelt Traditions	90.0
17856	25 Salt Of The Earth	100.0
17857	25 Salt Of The Earth	44.8
17859	25 Salt Of The Earth	39.9
17860	25 Salt Of The Earth	100.0
17864	25 Salt Of The Earth	53.9
17866	50 Heartland Communities	60.4
17867	25 Salt Of The Earth	100.0
17868	29 Rustbelt Retirees	100.0
17870	25 Salt Of The Earth	33.2
17872	57 Simple Living	50.2
17876	29 Rustbelt Retirees	56.6
17877	25 Salt Of The Earth	100.0
17878	25 Salt Of The Earth	100.0
17881	50 Heartland Communities	82.0
17888	50 Heartland Communities	100.0
17889	25 Salt Of The Earth	67.2
17901	29 Rustbelt Retirees	24.9
17921	50 Heartland Communities	49.9
17922	17 Green Acres	46.7
17923	50 Heartland Communities	100.0
17925	50 Heartland Communities	100.0
17929	32 Rustbelt Traditions	97.2
17931	29 Rustbelt Retirees	55.3
17935	50 Heartland Communities	85.3
17938	25 Salt Of The Earth	53.9
17941	25 Salt Of The Earth	92.5
17948	50 Heartland Communities	86.3
17954	50 Heartland Communities	56.3
17957	25 Salt Of The Earth	100.0
17959	50 Heartland Communities	100.0
17960	25 Salt Of The Earth	100.0
17961	17 Green Acres	38.1
17963	25 Salt Of The Earth	66.6
17964	37 Prairie Living	78.5
17965	50 Heartland Communities	90.7

ZIP CODE	TOP TAPESTRY CONSUMER TYPE	% 2009 HOUSE-HOLDS	ZIP CODE	TOP TAPESTRY CONSUMER TYPE	% 2009 HOUSE-HOLDS	ZIP CODE	TOP TAPESTRY CONSUMER TYPE	% 2009 HOUSE-HOLDS
17967	25 Salt Of The Earth	49.7	18327	36 Old And Newcomers	75.8	18623	46 Rooted Rural	50.8
17968	25 Salt Of The Earth	100.0	18328	19 Milk And Cookies	35.6	18624	31 Rural Resort Dwellers	95.9
17970	50 Heartland Communities	99.6	18330	17 Green Acres	87.0	18628	29 Rustbelt Retirees	100.0
17972	25 Salt Of The Earth	29.0	18331	25 Salt Of The Earth	100.0	18629	25 Salt Of The Earth	100.0
17976	57 Simple Living	38.6	18332	25 Salt Of The Earth	34.8	18630	25 Salt Of The Earth	55.1
17978	25 Salt Of The Earth	100.0	18333	17 Green Acres	90.1	18631	29 Rustbelt Retirees	85.2
17980	50 Heartland Communities	41.4	18334	26 Midland Crowd	61.4	18632	46 Rooted Rural	98.8
17981	50 Heartland Communities	62.5	18336	24 Main Street, USA	57.0	18634	29 Rustbelt Retirees	37.6
17983	29 Rustbelt Retirees	62.3	18337	06 Sophisticated Squires	68.8	18635	25 Salt Of The Earth	50.6
17985	25 Salt Of The Earth	93.0	18340	31 Rural Resort Dwellers	100.0	18636	50 Heartland Communities	56.7
18011	19 Milk And Cookies	38.6	18343	17 Green Acres	35.8	18640	29 Rustbelt Retirees	46.1
18013	17 Green Acres	29.4	18344	24 Main Street, USA	79.6	18641	29 Rustbelt Retirees	76.6
18014	17 Green Acres	33.9	18346	31 Rural Resort Dwellers	58.4	18642	29 Rustbelt Retirees	80.5
18015	60 City Dimensions	18.8	18347	31 Rural Resort Dwellers	42.7	18643	29 Rustbelt Retirees	26.5
18017	14 Prosperous Empty Nesters	28.3	18350	31 Rural Resort Dwellers	90.7	18644	29 Rustbelt Retirees	72.2
18018	29 Rustbelt Retirees	17.9	18352	17 Green Acres	100.0	18651	50 Heartland Communities	41.1
18020	18 Cozy And Comfortable	33.1	18353	17 Green Acres	85.9	18655	25 Salt Of The Earth	73.3
18031	49 Senior Sun Seekers	59.7	18354	25 Salt Of The Earth	66.0	18656	25 Salt Of The Earth	100.0
18032	24 Main Street, USA	27.4	18355	25 Salt Of The Earth	55.1	18657	25 Salt Of The Earth	77.3
18034	07 Exurbanites	82.9	18360	17 Green Acres	42.3	18660	46 Rooted Rural	69.3
18035	17 Green Acres	90.7	18370	25 Salt Of The Earth	82.1	18661	46 Rooted Rural	34.4
18036	07 Exurbanites	63.3	18371	12 Up And Coming Families	69.0	18701	65 Social Security Set	52.7
18037	17 Green Acres	19.0	18372	17 Green Acres	71.5	18702	50 Heartland Communities	22.9
18038	17 Green Acres	51.4	18403	29 Rustbelt Retirees	53.8	18704	29 Rustbelt Retirees	31.2
18040	06 Sophisticated Squires	66.9	18405	31 Rural Resort Dwellers	91.0	18705	29 Rustbelt Retirees	59.1
18041	24 Main Street, USA	53.4	18407	29 Rustbelt Retirees	27.5	18706	50 Heartland Communities	25.9
18042	32 Rustbelt Traditions	30.6	18411	07 Exurbanites	25.1	18707	17 Green Acres	28.2
18045	14 Prosperous Empty Nesters	23.8	18414	25 Salt Of The Earth	41.1	18708	18 Cozy And Comfortable	33.8
18049	13 In Style	25.2	18415	31 Rural Resort Dwellers	95.0	18709	32 Rustbelt Traditions	41.0
18051	17 Green Acres	51.7	18417	46 Rooted Rural	95.5	18801	25 Salt Of The Earth	57.3
18052	18 Cozy And Comfortable	23.7	18419	17 Green Acres	47.8	18810	25 Salt Of The Earth	39.7
18053	17 Green Acres	100.0	18421	31 Rural Resort Dwellers	26.8	18812	17 Green Acres	81.7
18054	07 Exurbanites	36.0	18424	31 Rural Resort Dwellers	41.9	18817	25 Salt Of The Earth	100.0
18055	14 Prosperous Empty Nesters	22.0	18425	31 Rural Resort Dwellers	100.0	18818	25 Salt Of The Earth	87.0
18056	42 Southern Satellites	100.0	18426	31 Rural Resort Dwellers	100.0	18821	50 Heartland Communities	55.6
18058	25 Salt Of The Earth	66.8	18427	31 Rural Resort Dwellers	100.0	18822	50 Heartland Communities	47.3
18059	06 Sophisticated Squires	92.0	18428	31 Rural Resort Dwellers	56.8	18823	25 Salt Of The Earth	68.9
18062	13 In Style	35.1	18430	31 Rural Resort Dwellers	100.0	18824	46 Rooted Rural	90.7
18064	18 Cozy And Comfortable	20.5	18431	31 Rural Resort Dwellers	33.3	18825	31 Rural Resort Dwellers	100.0
18066	17 Green Acres	97.5	18433	25 Salt Of The Earth	33.0	18826	25 Salt Of The Earth	99.8
18067	29 Rustbelt Retirees	21.5	18434	29 Rustbelt Retirees	80.3	18828	25 Salt Of The Earth	100.0
18069	02 Suburban Splendor	29.8	18435	31 Rural Resort Dwellers	100.0	18829	25 Salt Of The Earth	100.0
18070	17 Green Acres	65.6	18436	25 Salt Of The Earth	39.1	18830	25 Salt Of The Earth	100.0
18071	29 Rustbelt Retirees	27.5	18437	31 Rural Resort Dwellers	100.0	18831	25 Salt Of The Earth	100.0
18072	18 Cozy And Comfortable	29.2	18438	31 Rural Resort Dwellers	100.0	18832	42 Southern Satellites	70.5
18073	17 Green Acres	32.5	18439	31 Rural Resort Dwellers	100.0	18833	25 Salt Of The Earth	85.3
18074	17 Green Acres	68.5	18441	25 Salt Of The Earth	50.3	18834	25 Salt Of The Earth	67.3
18076	18 Cozy And Comfortable	37.6	18443	31 Rural Resort Dwellers	100.0	18837	25 Salt Of The Earth	53.1
18077	07 Exurbanites	61.6	18444	25 Salt Of The Earth	29.2	18840	33 Midlife Junction	28.5
18078	07 Exurbanites	53.3	18445	31 Rural Resort Dwellers	89.4	18842	31 Rural Resort Dwellers	100.0
18080	17 Green Acres	30.0	18446	46 Rooted Rural	52.2	18844	25 Salt Of The Earth	93.3
18087	02 Suburban Splendor	100.0	18447	29 Rustbelt Retirees	39.0	18845	46 Rooted Rural	100.0
18088	25 Salt Of The Earth	51.0	18451	31 Rural Resort Dwellers	100.0	18846	25 Salt Of The Earth	98.7
18091	17 Green Acres	28.0	18452	29 Rustbelt Retirees	41.7	18847	46 Rooted Rural	57.9
18092	07 Exurbanites	75.2	18453	31 Rural Resort Dwellers	100.0	18848	33 Midlife Junction	30.7
18101	60 City Dimensions	78.7	18455	31 Rural Resort Dwellers	100.0	18850	25 Salt Of The Earth	90.8
18102	60 City Dimensions	43.6	18456	31 Rural Resort Dwellers	68.2	18851	25 Salt Of The Earth	100.0
18103	48 Great Expectations	22.0	18458	31 Rural Resort Dwellers	71.4	18853	25 Salt Of The Earth	63.0
18104	14 Prosperous Empty Nesters	24.0	18460	31 Rural Resort Dwellers	100.0	18854	25 Salt Of The Earth	53.1
18106	13 In Style	52.7	18461	31 Rural Resort Dwellers	100.0	18901	07 Exurbanites	20.0
18109	32 Rustbelt Traditions	35.7	18462	31 Rural Resort Dwellers	100.0	18902	02 Suburban Splendor	55.6
18201	57 Simple Living	35.1	18463	25 Salt Of The Earth	100.0	18913	03 Connoisseurs	100.0
18202	50 Heartland Communities	30.5	18464	31 Rural Resort Dwellers	100.0	18914	07 Exurbanites	24.5
18210	31 Rural Resort Dwellers	80.7	18465	31 Rural Resort Dwellers	59.9	18915	10 Pleasant-Ville	99.1
18211	25 Salt Of The Earth	97.8	18466	19 Milk And Cookies	68.9	18917	28 Aspiring Young Families	100.0
18214	25 Salt Of The Earth	87.1	18469	31 Rural Resort Dwellers	100.0	18920	17 Green Acres	53.0
18216	29 Rustbelt Retirees	45.6	18470	46 Rooted Rural	54.4	18923	17 Green Acres	66.7
18218	50 Heartland Communities	72.5	18472	33 Midlife Junction	34.8	18925	07 Exurbanites	69.5
18219	14 Prosperous Empty Nesters	100.0	18503	65 Social Security Set	100.0	18927	10 Pleasant-Ville	100.0
18220	50 Heartland Communities	100.0	18504	57 Simple Living	23.6	18929	04 Boomburbs	55.5
18222	25 Salt Of The Earth	44.5	18505	29 Rustbelt Retirees	41.9	18930	17 Green Acres	57.9
18224	50 Heartland Communities	64.4	18507	29 Rustbelt Retirees	46.0	18932	07 Exurbanites	68.8
18229	31 Rural Resort Dwellers	32.0	18508	50 Heartland Communities	30.3	18933	03 Connoisseurs	100.0
18232	50 Heartland Communities	61.5	18509	57 Simple Living	29.4	18934	02 Suburban Splendor	54.0
18235	25 Salt Of The Earth	27.1	18510	33 Midlife Junction	21.6	18936	05 Wealthy Seaboard Suburbs	83.3
18237	50 Heartland Communities	59.6	18512	29 Rustbelt Retirees	81.8	18938	09 Urban Chic	25.6
18240	50 Heartland Communities	47.2	18517	29 Rustbelt Retirees	50.4	18940	02 Suburban Splendor	31.1
18246	29 Rustbelt Retirees	100.0	18518	29 Rustbelt Retirees	60.8	18942	17 Green Acres	70.7
18248	46 Rooted Rural	100.0	18519	29 Rustbelt Retirees	47.1	18944	17 Green Acres	20.6
18249	07 Exurbanites	32.1	18603	50 Heartland Communities	25.5	18947	02 Suburban Splendor	45.0
18250	29 Rustbelt Retirees	100.0	18610	26 Midland Crowd	91.6	18951	17 Green Acres	22.4
18252	50 Heartland Communities	26.4	18612	33 Midlife Junction	23.8	18954	02 Suburban Splendor	84.8
18255	29 Rustbelt Retirees	58.2	18614	46 Rooted Rural	57.7	18955	24 Main Street, USA	79.6
18301	06 Sophisticated Squires	26.1	18615	25 Salt Of The Earth	100.0	18960	24 Main Street, USA	36.9
18302	17 Green Acres	27.3	18616	31 Rural Resort Dwellers	99.8	18964	24 Main Street, USA	45.7
18321	17 Green Acres	100.0	18617	53 Home Town	49.9	18966	02 Suburban Splendor	18.2
18322	17 Green Acres	92.3	18618	33 Midlife Junction	50.7	18969	24 Main Street, USA	23.6
18324	18 Cozy And Comfortable	63.3	18619	46 Rooted Rural	100.0	18972	17 Green Acres	92.8
18325	31 Rural Resort Dwellers	97.7	18621	25 Salt Of The Earth	72.0	18974	10 Pleasant-Ville	31.5
18326	17 Green Acres	37.0	18622	25 Salt Of The Earth	100.0	18976	06 Sophisticated Squires	35.8

CONSUMER TYPE

ZIP CODE	TOP TAPESTRY CONSUMER TYPE	% 2009 HOUSE-HOLDS	ZIP CODE	TOP TAPESTRY CONSUMER TYPE	% 2009 HOUSE-HOLDS	ZIP CODE	TOP TAPESTRY CONSUMER TYPE	% 2009 HOUSE-HOLDS
18977	03 Connoisseurs	63.9	19134	54 Urban Rows	66.3	19533	17 Green Acres	72.8
19001	18 Cozy And Comfortable	35.5	19135	32 Rustbelt Traditions	45.8	19534	17 Green Acres	58.3
19002	03 Connoisseurs	30.0	19136	29 Rustbelt Retirees	29.0	19539	17 Green Acres	68.8
19003	22 Metropolitans	25.4	19137	54 Urban Rows	42.0	19540	17 Green Acres	44.3
19004	03 Connoisseurs	30.7	19138	54 Urban Rows	61.3	19541	17 Green Acres	88.4
19006	03 Connoisseurs	49.3	19139	54 Urban Rows	79.8	19543	17 Green Acres	65.0
19007	24 Main Street, USA	40.8	19140	54 Urban Rows	72.2	19547	17 Green Acres	63.0
19008	05 Wealthy Seaboard Suburbs	34.2	19141	54 Urban Rows	80.5	19549	25 Salt Of The Earth	100.0
19010	01 Top Rung	21.3	19142	54 Urban Rows	90.4	19551	25 Salt Of The Earth	31.9
19012	10 Pleasant-Ville	21.5	19143	54 Urban Rows	77.1	19555	25 Salt Of The Earth	48.5
19013	54 Urban Rows	63.6	19144	54 Urban Rows	51.3	19560	29 Rustbelt Retirees	58.5
19014	18 Cozy And Comfortable	33.3	19145	54 Urban Rows	51.8	19562	18 Cozy And Comfortable	79.6
19015	18 Cozy And Comfortable	26.0	19146	54 Urban Rows	61.9	19565	29 Rustbelt Retirees	49.2
19018	18 Cozy And Comfortable	30.6	19147	54 Urban Rows	28.6	19567	25 Salt Of The Earth	32.2
19020	06 Sophisticated Squires	21.3	19148	54 Urban Rows	80.1	19601	60 City Dimensions	44.6
19021	18 Cozy And Comfortable	61.5	19149	32 Rustbelt Traditions	50.6	19602	60 City Dimensions	57.1
19022	32 Rustbelt Traditions	62.1	19150	34 Family Foundations	82.8	19604	60 City Dimensions	39.3
19023	54 Urban Rows	49.9	19151	54 Urban Rows	57.4	19605	29 Rustbelt Retirees	36.6
19025	02 Suburban Splendor	43.1	19152	30 Retirement Communities	31.9	19606	06 Sophisticated Squires	15.2
19026	24 Main Street, USA	28.2	19153	34 Family Foundations	35.1	19607	29 Rustbelt Retirees	28.5
19027	52 Inner City Tenants	20.5	19154	18 Cozy And Comfortable	48.2	19608	13 In Style	22.3
19029	24 Main Street, USA	68.1	19301	30 Retirement Communities	25.5	19609	29 Rustbelt Retirees	45.8
19030	18 Cozy And Comfortable	35.7	19310	17 Green Acres	54.3	19610	14 Prosperous Empty Nesters	60.4
19031	05 Wealthy Seaboard Suburbs	56.3	19311	04 Boomburbs	57.5	19611	32 Rustbelt Traditions	32.1
19032	32 Rustbelt Traditions	33.0	19312	01 Top Rung	39.5	19701	16 Enterprising Professionals	24.6
19033	18 Cozy And Comfortable	62.9	19317	03 Connoisseurs	40.5	19702	12 Up And Coming Families	28.0
19034	09 Urban Chic	41.6	19319	02 Suburban Splendor	100.0	19703	36 Old And Newcomers	28.9
19035	01 Top Rung	99.8	19320	17 Green Acres	29.7	19706	33 Midlife Junction	63.6
19036	24 Main Street, USA	41.2	19330	17 Green Acres	99.6	19707	02 Suburban Splendor	52.8
19038	18 Cozy And Comfortable	20.9	19333	03 Connoisseurs	26.8	19709	04 Boomburbs	34.2
19040	18 Cozy And Comfortable	32.6	19335	06 Sophisticated Squires	26.2	19711	02 Suburban Splendor	16.6
19041	03 Connoisseurs	29.1	19341	16 Enterprising Professionals	33.2	19713	28 Aspiring Young Families	40.6
19043	18 Cozy And Comfortable	59.8	19342	05 Wealthy Seaboard Suburbs	44.1	19716	55 College Towns	80.0
19044	13 In Style	31.9	19343	02 Suburban Splendor	57.9	19720	18 Cozy And Comfortable	23.2
19046	30 Retirement Communities	25.6	19344	25 Salt Of The Earth	24.9	19734	17 Green Acres	62.9
19047	02 Suburban Splendor	22.7	19348	02 Suburban Splendor	25.6	19736	03 Connoisseurs	93.8
19050	24 Main Street, USA	21.0	19350	02 Suburban Splendor	93.7	19801	54 Urban Rows	26.2
19053	18 Cozy And Comfortable	27.2	19352	04 Boomburbs	51.0	19802	54 Urban Rows	42.8
19054	18 Cozy And Comfortable	65.6	19355	13 In Style	27.5	19803	14 Prosperous Empty Nesters	34.4
19055	18 Cozy And Comfortable	87.4	19362	17 Green Acres	48.7	19804	24 Main Street, USA	36.5
19056	18 Cozy And Comfortable	35.9	19363	17 Green Acres	38.1	19805	54 Urban Rows	25.4
19057	18 Cozy And Comfortable	66.9	19365	24 Main Street, USA	54.6	19806	27 Metro Renters	50.5
19061	32 Rustbelt Traditions	17.4	19372	06 Sophisticated Squires	56.5	19807	03 Connoisseurs	49.8
19063	13 In Style	23.7	19373	05 Wealthy Seaboard Suburbs	56.0	19808	13 In Style	22.0
19064	14 Prosperous Empty Nesters	35.5	19374	21 Urban Villages	72.5	19809	24 Main Street, USA	26.7
19066	03 Connoisseurs	44.8	19380	02 Suburban Splendor	28.9	19810	14 Prosperous Empty Nesters	41.3
19067	13 In Style	26.1	19382	02 Suburban Splendor	26.0	19901	41 Crossroads	28.3
19070	18 Cozy And Comfortable	41.1	19383	02 Suburban Splendor	100.0	19902	40 Military Proximity	100.0
19072	09 Urban Chic	30.6	19390	17 Green Acres	56.3	19904	26 Midland Crowd	15.5
19073	03 Connoisseurs	46.7	19401	60 City Dimensions	19.0	19930	15 Silver And Gold	100.0
19074	18 Cozy And Comfortable	56.6	19403	13 In Style	16.6	19931	56 Rural Bypasses	56.3
19075	14 Prosperous Empty Nesters	30.6	19405	24 Main Street, USA	64.6	19933	53 Home Town	29.6
19076	24 Main Street, USA	100.0	19406	27 Metro Renters	31.5	19934	18 Cozy And Comfortable	25.2
19078	18 Cozy And Comfortable	40.5	19422	03 Connoisseurs	40.5	19938	26 Midland Crowd	91.7
19079	54 Urban Rows	27.0	19425	02 Suburban Splendor	88.1	19939	31 Rural Resort Dwellers	29.5
19081	09 Urban Chic	19.3	19426	04 Boomburbs	54.9	19940	26 Midland Crowd	50.6
19082	54 Urban Rows	28.0	19428	24 Main Street, USA	26.5	19941	42 Southern Satellites	62.3
19083	10 Pleasant-Ville	43.9	19435	10 Pleasant-Ville	100.0	19943	26 Midland Crowd	63.5
19085	01 Top Rung	82.2	19436	03 Connoisseurs	100.0	19944	15 Silver And Gold	100.0
19086	14 Prosperous Empty Nesters	21.1	19438	13 In Style	26.9	19945	31 Rural Resort Dwellers	42.3
19087	03 Connoisseurs	34.5	19440	06 Sophisticated Squires	33.4	19946	41 Crossroads	40.9
19090	24 Main Street, USA	25.9	19444	04 Boomburbs	39.4	19947	26 Midland Crowd	24.0
19094	18 Cozy And Comfortable	30.8	19446	13 In Style	23.7	19950	25 Salt Of The Earth	85.4
19095	30 Retirement Communities	62.5	19453	13 In Style	70.9	19951	46 Rooted Rural	57.5
19096	03 Connoisseurs	40.7	19454	05 Wealthy Seaboard Suburbs	24.5	19952	26 Midland Crowd	33.3
19102	27 Metro Renters	99.9	19460	16 Enterprising Professionals	12.5	19953	26 Midland Crowd	96.5
19103	27 Metro Renters	65.5	19462	14 Prosperous Empty Nesters	34.9	19954	17 Green Acres	50.0
19104	63 Dorms To Diplomas	34.1	19464	29 Rustbelt Retirees	12.5	19956	26 Midland Crowd	52.8
19106	08 Laptops And Lattes	56.2	19465	07 Exurbanites	42.0	19958	31 Rural Resort Dwellers	45.3
19107	27 Metro Renters	71.5	19468	13 In Style	20.3	19960	26 Midland Crowd	61.0
19111	32 Rustbelt Traditions	21.0	19473	06 Sophisticated Squires	52.9	19962	41 Crossroads	30.1
19114	24 Main Street, USA	34.6	19475	24 Main Street, USA	50.9	19963	33 Midlife Junction	32.2
19115	30 Retirement Communities	47.8	19477	03 Connoisseurs	100.0	19964	26 Midland Crowd	72.8
19116	18 Cozy And Comfortable	29.0	19492	17 Green Acres	100.0	19966	49 Senior Sun Seekers	58.7
19118	22 Metropolitans	32.2	19501	24 Main Street, USA	100.0	19967	31 Rural Resort Dwellers	96.2
19119	22 Metropolitans	26.7	19503	18 Cozy And Comfortable	100.0	19968	31 Rural Resort Dwellers	31.5
19120	54 Urban Rows	77.2	19504	17 Green Acres	95.5	19970	15 Silver And Gold	54.4
19121	54 Urban Rows	63.5	19505	17 Green Acres	54.3	19971	49 Senior Sun Seekers	49.4
19122	54 Urban Rows	62.8	19506	25 Salt Of The Earth	52.1	19973	42 Southern Satellites	27.8
19123	54 Urban Rows	16.6	19507	25 Salt Of The Earth	84.5	19975	15 Silver And Gold	62.2
19124	54 Urban Rows	63.7	19508	17 Green Acres	29.9	19977	26 Midland Crowd	57.7
19125	54 Urban Rows	86.9	19510	12 Up And Coming Families	56.6	19979	46 Rooted Rural	88.7
19126	54 Urban Rows	38.3	19512	17 Green Acres	38.9	20001	45 City Strivers	40.8
19127	22 Metropolitans	46.6	19518	13 In Style	28.0	20002	45 City Strivers	36.3
19128	24 Main Street, USA	19.9	19520	17 Green Acres	39.4	20003	08 Laptops And Lattes	46.0
19129	27 Metro Renters	22.1	19522	17 Green Acres	44.0	20004	27 Metro Renters	100.0
19130	27 Metro Renters	36.6	19525	06 Sophisticated Squires	32.2	20005	27 Metro Renters	95.9
19131	54 Urban Rows	41.6	19526	25 Salt Of The Earth	29.8	20006	63 Dorms To Diplomas	98.3
19132	54 Urban Rows	88.7	19529	17 Green Acres	100.0	20007	08 Laptops And Lattes	66.6
19133	54 Urban Rows	65.5	19530	25 Salt Of The Earth	23.8	20008	27 Metro Renters	54.2

ZIP CODE	TOP TAPESTRY CONSUMER TYPE	% 2009 HOUSE-HOLDS	ZIP CODE	TOP TAPESTRY CONSUMER TYPE	% 2009 HOUSE-HOLDS	ZIP CODE	TOP TAPESTRY CONSUMER TYPE	% 2009 HOUSE-HOLDS
20009	27 Metro Renters	59.5	20640	24 Main Street, USA	33.5	20842	03 Connoisseurs	33.4
20010	61 High Rise Renters	28.9	20645	14 Prosperous Empty Nesters	100.0	20850	09 Urban Chic	16.6
20011	45 City Strivers	33.9	20646	07 Exurbanites	43.4	20851	10 Pleasant-Ville	60.2
20012	20 City Lights	25.3	20650	13 In Style	30.0	20852	27 Metro Renters	23.8
20015	08 Laptops And Lattes	33.1	20653	52 Inner City Tenants	24.9	20853	05 Wealthy Seaboard Suburbs	29.6
20016	08 Laptops And Lattes	32.0	20657	12 Up And Coming Families	71.1	20854	01 Top Rung	58.5
20017	34 Family Foundations	22.5	20658	18 Cozy And Comfortable	96.9	20855	02 Suburban Splendor	40.9
20018	34 Family Foundations	31.8	20659	06 Sophisticated Squires	48.6	20860	02 Suburban Splendor	61.0
20019	45 City Strivers	44.9	20662	10 Pleasant-Ville	58.9	20861	03 Connoisseurs	85.7
20020	45 City Strivers	49.8	20664	31 Rural Resort Dwellers	49.1	20862	02 Suburban Splendor	100.0
20024	27 Metro Renters	50.6	20667	24 Main Street, USA	93.8	20866	16 Enterprising Professionals	34.3
20032	45 City Strivers	50.1	20670	40 Military Proximity	100.0	20868	05 Wealthy Seaboard Suburbs	82.4
20036	27 Metro Renters	100.0	20674	31 Rural Resort Dwellers	65.0	20871	05 Wealthy Seaboard Suburbs	87.4
20037	27 Metro Renters	93.3	20675	07 Exurbanites	83.8	20872	10 Pleasant-Ville	28.3
20057	63 Dorms To Diplomas	100.0	20676	17 Green Acres	27.1	20874	16 Enterprising Professionals	36.9
20064	63 Dorms To Diplomas	100.0	20677	07 Exurbanites	72.2	20876	04 Boomburbs	51.1
20105	04 Boomburbs	87.9	20678	10 Pleasant-Ville	46.4	20877	35 International Marketplace	27.0
20106	07 Exurbanites	100.0	20680	31 Rural Resort Dwellers	82.2	20878	02 Suburban Splendor	31.4
20107	02 Suburban Splendor	86.8	20684	14 Prosperous Empty Nesters	60.4	20879	06 Sophisticated Squires	45.6
20109	16 Enterprising Professionals	38.6	20685	06 Sophisticated Squires	39.5	20882	02 Suburban Splendor	39.9
20110	28 Aspiring Young Families	18.0	20687	31 Rural Resort Dwellers	100.0	20886	13 In Style	26.3
20111	04 Boomburbs	25.4	20688	13 In Style	62.9	20895	05 Wealthy Seaboard Suburbs	33.1
20112	04 Boomburbs	46.1	20689	07 Exurbanites	69.4	20901	05 Wealthy Seaboard Suburbs	33.3
20115	07 Exurbanites	76.7	20690	31 Rural Resort Dwellers	100.0	20902	10 Pleasant-Ville	29.3
20117	09 Urban Chic	100.0	20692	14 Prosperous Empty Nesters	50.5	20903	35 International Marketplace	63.6
20119	07 Exurbanites	49.5	20693	10 Pleasant-Ville	70.0	20904	05 Wealthy Seaboard Suburbs	25.2
20120	04 Boomburbs	36.7	20695	12 Up And Coming Families	48.1	20905	05 Wealthy Seaboard Suburbs	38.9
20121	16 Enterprising Professionals	57.3	20701	41 Crossroads	86.7	20906	43 The Elders	18.8
20124	02 Suburban Splendor	50.8	20705	10 Pleasant-Ville	24.1	20910	27 Metro Renters	45.8
20129	03 Connoisseurs	99.0	20706	10 Pleasant-Ville	37.7	20912	23 Trendsetters	26.8
20130	07 Exurbanites	82.1	20707	13 In Style	27.8	21001	36 Old And Newcomers	16.4
20132	07 Exurbanites	27.6	20708	28 Aspiring Young Families	26.8	21005	40 Military Proximity	87.7
20135	17 Green Acres	58.2	20710	52 Inner City Tenants	61.2	21009	12 Up And Coming Families	47.3
20136	04 Boomburbs	91.2	20711	41 Crossroads	45.7	21010	40 Military Proximity	100.0
20137	07 Exurbanites	85.0	20712	52 Inner City Tenants	38.3	21012	02 Suburban Splendor	26.3
20141	07 Exurbanites	74.5	20714	12 Up And Coming Families	66.7	21013	02 Suburban Splendor	50.7
20143	02 Suburban Splendor	72.7	20715	10 Pleasant-Ville	70.1	21014	06 Sophisticated Squires	23.6
20144	13 In Style	56.3	20716	16 Enterprising Professionals	46.6	21015	13 In Style	21.1
20147	04 Boomburbs	90.3	20720	02 Suburban Splendor	53.9	21017	12 Up And Coming Families	87.2
20148	04 Boomburbs	75.4	20721	02 Suburban Splendor	26.2	21028	07 Exurbanites	62.1
20151	02 Suburban Splendor	42.4	20722	24 Main Street, USA	57.3	21029	04 Boomburbs	46.8
20152	04 Boomburbs	100.0	20723	02 Suburban Splendor	34.8	21030	39 Young And Restless	41.4
20155	04 Boomburbs	29.2	20724	16 Enterprising Professionals	57.4	21031	36 Old And Newcomers	100.0
20158	07 Exurbanites	67.2	20732	17 Green Acres	31.1	21032	07 Exurbanites	70.7
20164	06 Sophisticated Squires	27.2	20733	06 Sophisticated Squires	61.9	21034	25 Salt Of The Earth	50.8
20165	04 Boomburbs	66.7	20735	06 Sophisticated Squires	52.4	21035	07 Exurbanites	62.2
20166	16 Enterprising Professionals	74.9	20736	05 Wealthy Seaboard Suburbs	32.3	21036	02 Suburban Splendor	81.0
20169	06 Sophisticated Squires	38.0	20737	35 International Marketplace	33.6	21037	07 Exurbanites	32.2
20170	02 Suburban Splendor	34.6	20740	10 Pleasant-Ville	20.8	21040	28 Aspiring Young Families	24.2
20171	02 Suburban Splendor	50.3	20742	63 Dorms To Diplomas	71.0	21042	02 Suburban Splendor	61.0
20175	04 Boomburbs	46.3	20743	45 City Strivers	29.8	21043	04 Boomburbs	23.5
20176	04 Boomburbs	60.0	20744	10 Pleasant-Ville	32.7	21044	13 In Style	33.1
20180	02 Suburban Splendor	55.5	20745	52 Inner City Tenants	30.4	21045	16 Enterprising Professionals	20.8
20181	04 Boomburbs	45.4	20746	45 City Strivers	32.0	21046	16 Enterprising Professionals	66.0
20184	07 Exurbanites	54.3	20747	52 Inner City Tenants	19.8	21047	07 Exurbanites	76.0
20186	13 In Style	55.9	20748	10 Pleasant-Ville	29.9	21048	07 Exurbanites	41.2
20187	07 Exurbanites	44.1	20751	17 Green Acres	70.8	21050	13 In Style	46.7
20190	16 Enterprising Professionals	48.4	20754	07 Exurbanites	62.7	21051	07 Exurbanites	100.0
20191	13 In Style	33.5	20755	40 Military Proximity	99.5	21053	06 Sophisticated Squires	56.3
20194	16 Enterprising Professionals	40.0	20758	07 Exurbanites	84.9	21054	16 Enterprising Professionals	41.2
20197	03 Connoisseurs	100.0	20759	02 Suburban Splendor	100.0	21056	03 Connoisseurs	100.0
20198	09 Urban Chic	59.5	20762	40 Military Proximity	100.0	21057	14 Prosperous Empty Nesters	63.1
20601	06 Sophisticated Squires	34.3	20763	28 Aspiring Young Families	91.4	21060	18 Cozy And Comfortable	32.9
20602	28 Aspiring Young Families	25.4	20764	06 Sophisticated Squires	86.7	21061	18 Cozy And Comfortable	28.5
20603	06 Sophisticated Squires	39.6	20769	05 Wealthy Seaboard Suburbs	32.1	21071	07 Exurbanites	100.0
20606	18 Cozy And Comfortable	85.1	20770	39 Young And Restless	31.9	21074	12 Up And Coming Families	34.1
20607	10 Pleasant-Ville	56.5	20772	16 Enterprising Professionals	25.6	21075	28 Aspiring Young Families	33.7
20608	18 Cozy And Comfortable	64.2	20774	06 Sophisticated Squires	40.3	21076	06 Sophisticated Squires	51.8
20609	18 Cozy And Comfortable	36.1	20776	07 Exurbanites	72.8	21077	06 Sophisticated Squires	100.0
20611	07 Exurbanites	70.9	20777	02 Suburban Splendor	100.0	21078	12 Up And Coming Families	28.9
20613	10 Pleasant-Ville	63.2	20778	07 Exurbanites	86.8	21082	05 Wealthy Seaboard Suburbs	61.3
20615	10 Pleasant-Ville	100.0	20779	07 Exurbanites	97.3	21084	07 Exurbanites	86.9
20616	12 Up And Coming Families	46.5	20781	36 Old And Newcomers	20.8	21085	18 Cozy And Comfortable	42.0
20617	07 Exurbanites	67.8	20782	52 Inner City Tenants	22.0	21087	07 Exurbanites	57.6
20618	31 Rural Resort Dwellers	78.7	20783	58 NeWest Residents	21.2	21090	14 Prosperous Empty Nesters	52.1
20619	13 In Style	38.2	20784	10 Pleasant-Ville	38.3	21093	03 Connoisseurs	30.3
20620	13 In Style	59.8	20785	34 Family Foundations	15.3	21102	17 Green Acres	41.4
20621	12 Up And Coming Families	57.5	20794	13 In Style	32.4	21104	06 Sophisticated Squires	52.7
20622	06 Sophisticated Squires	78.3	20812	01 Top Rung	100.0	21108	02 Suburban Splendor	28.3
20623	04 Boomburbs	56.9	20814	27 Metro Renters	37.3	21111	07 Exurbanites	51.0
20624	17 Green Acres	81.5	20815	01 Top Rung	37.8	21113	16 Enterprising Professionals	38.3
20625	24 Main Street, USA	100.0	20816	03 Connoisseurs	44.8	21114	16 Enterprising Professionals	19.6
20626	29 Rustbelt Retirees	100.0	20817	03 Connoisseurs	53.3	21117	16 Enterprising Professionals	45.3
20628	31 Rural Resort Dwellers	50.8	20818	03 Connoisseurs	100.0	21120	07 Exurbanites	76.3
20630	14 Prosperous Empty Nesters	74.3	20832	02 Suburban Splendor	40.6	21122	12 Up And Coming Families	19.3
20632	10 Pleasant-Ville	58.8	20833	02 Suburban Splendor	74.4	21128	13 In Style	47.4
20634	12 Up And Coming Families	73.3	20837	02 Suburban Splendor	61.2	21131	03 Connoisseurs	45.5
20636	17 Green Acres	46.6	20838	03 Connoisseurs	100.0	21132	10 Pleasant-Ville	51.1
20637	05 Wealthy Seaboard Suburbs	41.9	20839	02 Suburban Splendor	58.9	21133	18 Cozy And Comfortable	23.2
20639	06 Sophisticated Squires	69.5	20841	05 Wealthy Seaboard Suburbs	72.8	21136	13 In Style	17.0

CONSUMER TYPE

ZIP CODE	TOP TAPESTRY CONSUMER TYPE	% 2009 HOUSE-HOLDS	ZIP CODE	TOP TAPESTRY CONSUMER TYPE	% 2009 HOUSE-HOLDS	ZIP CODE	TOP TAPESTRY CONSUMER TYPE	% 2009 HOUSE-HOLDS
21140	02 Suburban Splendor	53.7	21634	31 Rural Resort Dwellers	100.0	21817	46 Rooted Rural	47.3
21144	06 Sophisticated Squires	24.2	21635	31 Rural Resort Dwellers	57.9	21821	46 Rooted Rural	51.0
21146	02 Suburban Splendor	33.7	21636	17 Green Acres	59.7	21822	25 Salt Of The Earth	50.4
21152	13 In Style	58.8	21638	33 Midlife Junction	35.9	21824	37 Prairie Living	100.0
21153	03 Connoisseurs	100.0	21639	17 Green Acres	58.2	21826	13 In Style	27.2
21154	17 Green Acres	51.0	21640	42 Southern Satellites	77.7	21829	46 Rooted Rural	63.4
21155	07 Exurbanites	83.5	21643	17 Green Acres	30.5	21830	18 Cozy And Comfortable	36.0
21156	14 Prosperous Empty Nesters	85.2	21644	25 Salt Of The Earth	100.0	21835	25 Salt Of The Earth	100.0
21157	07 Exurbanites	21.6	21645	31 Rural Resort Dwellers	59.1	21837	25 Salt Of The Earth	99.6
21158	17 Green Acres	25.9	21647	31 Rural Resort Dwellers	100.0	21838	31 Rural Resort Dwellers	38.3
21160	18 Cozy And Comfortable	79.8	21648	31 Rural Resort Dwellers	100.0	21840	31 Rural Resort Dwellers	100.0
21161	07 Exurbanites	78.4	21649	42 Southern Satellites	76.2	21841	46 Rooted Rural	94.1
21162	18 Cozy And Comfortable	80.1	21650	25 Salt Of The Earth	100.0	21842	49 Senior Sun Seekers	28.8
21163	02 Suburban Splendor	48.9	21651	26 Midland Crowd	47.7	21849	26 Midland Crowd	40.7
21201	27 Metro Renters	39.7	21654	15 Silver And Gold	64.6	21850	26 Midland Crowd	67.0
21202	27 Metro Renters	35.0	21655	25 Salt Of The Earth	78.0	21851	46 Rooted Rural	39.3
21204	55 College Towns	29.2	21657	17 Green Acres	81.3	21853	46 Rooted Rural	32.3
21205	54 Urban Rows	65.5	21658	17 Green Acres	35.2	21856	31 Rural Resort Dwellers	88.4
21206	24 Main Street, USA	25.3	21659	46 Rooted Rural	79.9	21861	25 Salt Of The Earth	100.0
21207	24 Main Street, USA	34.5	21660	17 Green Acres	51.7	21863	50 Heartland Communities	25.7
21208	18 Cozy And Comfortable	17.8	21661	31 Rural Resort Dwellers	66.3	21864	46 Rooted Rural	100.0
21209	13 In Style	23.5	21662	31 Rural Resort Dwellers	100.0	21865	46 Rooted Rural	52.2
21210	22 Metropolitans	29.0	21663	15 Silver And Gold	66.6	21866	37 Prairie Living	100.0
21211	36 Old And Newcomers	27.3	21665	31 Rural Resort Dwellers	100.0	21869	46 Rooted Rural	63.7
21212	22 Metropolitans	24.3	21666	07 Exurbanites	30.5	21871	46 Rooted Rural	82.8
21213	54 Urban Rows	90.1	21667	31 Rural Resort Dwellers	100.0	21872	46 Rooted Rural	69.8
21214	24 Main Street, USA	62.3	21668	46 Rooted Rural	65.8	21874	26 Midland Crowd	80.8
21215	54 Urban Rows	41.2	21669	31 Rural Resort Dwellers	100.0	21875	26 Midland Crowd	29.4
21216	54 Urban Rows	63.5	21671	31 Rural Resort Dwellers	100.0	21901	17 Green Acres	25.5
21217	54 Urban Rows	36.3	21672	37 Prairie Living	100.0	21903	24 Main Street, USA	49.9
21218	54 Urban Rows	33.8	21673	24 Main Street, USA	38.6	21904	06 Sophisticated Squires	38.2
21219	18 Cozy And Comfortable	50.3	21675	37 Prairie Living	100.0	21911	24 Main Street, USA	31.6
21220	28 Aspiring Young Families	17.6	21676	31 Rural Resort Dwellers	100.0	21912	46 Rooted Rural	75.4
21221	52 Inner City Tenants	20.8	21677	31 Rural Resort Dwellers	100.0	21913	46 Rooted Rural	100.0
21222	29 Rustbelt Retirees	35.1	21678	31 Rural Resort Dwellers	43.5	21914	17 Green Acres	100.0
21223	54 Urban Rows	73.9	21679	17 Green Acres	100.0	21915	18 Cozy And Comfortable	40.8
21224	54 Urban Rows	32.7	21701	13 In Style	13.3	21917	06 Sophisticated Squires	47.6
21225	64 City Commons	18.8	21702	36 Old And Newcomers	18.7	21918	26 Midland Crowd	54.5
21226	12 Up And Coming Families	49.7	21703	28 Aspiring Young Families	36.5	21919	31 Rural Resort Dwellers	90.5
21227	18 Cozy And Comfortable	28.5	21704	10 Pleasant-Ville	66.7	21921	17 Green Acres	15.9
21228	13 In Style	17.2	21710	10 Pleasant-Ville	60.6	22003	05 Wealthy Seaboard Suburbs	28.2
21229	54 Urban Rows	42.0	21711	25 Salt Of The Earth	100.0	22015	02 Suburban Splendor	47.7
21230	54 Urban Rows	32.9	21713	17 Green Acres	42.2	22025	06 Sophisticated Squires	28.0
21231	27 Metro Renters	33.3	21716	24 Main Street, USA	68.7	22026	04 Boomburbs	35.0
21234	18 Cozy And Comfortable	22.4	21718	17 Green Acres	100.0	22027	02 Suburban Splendor	82.0
21236	06 Sophisticated Squires	18.5	21719	24 Main Street, USA	82.2	22030	16 Enterprising Professionals	34.2
21237	28 Aspiring Young Families	20.1	21722	25 Salt Of The Earth	57.0	22031	16 Enterprising Professionals	32.2
21239	34 Family Foundations	33.5	21723	02 Suburban Splendor	100.0	22032	02 Suburban Splendor	38.1
21244	24 Main Street, USA	30.3	21727	24 Main Street, USA	42.3	22033	16 Enterprising Professionals	46.4
21250	63 Dorms To Diplomas	100.0	21733	17 Green Acres	80.8	22039	01 Top Rung	49.3
21286	30 Retirement Communities	20.8	21737	02 Suburban Splendor	100.0	22041	16 Enterprising Professionals	24.2
21401	16 Enterprising Professionals	15.3	21738	02 Suburban Splendor	100.0	22042	10 Pleasant-Ville	27.2
21402	40 Military Proximity	83.7	21740	48 Great Expectations	14.1	22043	16 Enterprising Professionals	36.8
21403	13 In Style	23.1	21742	14 Prosperous Empty Nesters	23.9	22044	35 International Marketplace	43.7
21409	06 Sophisticated Squires	50.8	21750	50 Heartland Communities	56.0	22046	09 Urban Chic	33.6
21502	29 Rustbelt Retirees	40.0	21754	02 Suburban Splendor	68.3	22060	40 Military Proximity	65.4
21520	46 Rooted Rural	63.3	21755	12 Up And Coming Families	40.8	22066	01 Top Rung	95.7
21521	50 Heartland Communities	87.7	21756	17 Green Acres	60.5	22067	01 Top Rung	100.0
21522	25 Salt Of The Earth	100.0	21757	17 Green Acres	69.3	22079	16 Enterprising Professionals	40.5
21523	25 Salt Of The Earth	91.0	21758	17 Green Acres	56.9	22101	01 Top Rung	41.9
21530	46 Rooted Rural	100.0	21765	02 Suburban Splendor	100.0	22102	27 Metro Renters	40.0
21531	50 Heartland Communities	60.6	21766	46 Rooted Rural	97.4	22124	01 Top Rung	62.9
21532	33 Midlife Junction	30.2	21767	33 Midlife Junction	100.0	22134	40 Military Proximity	80.4
21536	46 Rooted Rural	52.3	21769	06 Sophisticated Squires	38.3	22150	05 Wealthy Seaboard Suburbs	30.1
21538	46 Rooted Rural	100.0	21770	06 Sophisticated Squires	56.3	22151	05 Wealthy Seaboard Suburbs	57.9
21539	50 Heartland Communities	84.8	21771	02 Suburban Splendor	41.4	22152	02 Suburban Splendor	28.0
21540	50 Heartland Communities	100.0	21773	06 Sophisticated Squires	50.7	22153	02 Suburban Splendor	50.8
21541	31 Rural Resort Dwellers	89.9	21774	04 Boomburbs	32.5	22172	24 Main Street, USA	69.7
21545	50 Heartland Communities	54.7	21776	17 Green Acres	41.2	22180	05 Wealthy Seaboard Suburbs	60.9
21550	46 Rooted Rural	40.9	21777	06 Sophisticated Squires	100.0	22181	01 Top Rung	34.3
21555	25 Salt Of The Earth	60.7	21778	18 Cozy And Comfortable	54.7	22182	01 Top Rung	47.1
21557	46 Rooted Rural	60.2	21779	17 Green Acres	100.0	22191	28 Aspiring Young Families	20.5
21561	31 Rural Resort Dwellers	53.9	21780	17 Green Acres	63.5	22192	06 Sophisticated Squires	19.1
21562	50 Heartland Communities	93.4	21782	17 Green Acres	85.0	22193	06 Sophisticated Squires	35.5
21601	31 Rural Resort Dwellers	16.6	21783	24 Main Street, USA	30.2	22201	27 Metro Renters	80.4
21607	25 Salt Of The Earth	99.5	21784	07 Exurbanites	23.6	22202	27 Metro Renters	75.6
21610	31 Rural Resort Dwellers	100.0	21787	24 Main Street, USA	61.8	22203	27 Metro Renters	39.4
21612	15 Silver And Gold	100.0	21788	24 Main Street, USA	43.4	22204	35 International Marketplace	29.9
21613	14 Prosperous Empty Nesters	14.4	21790	06 Sophisticated Squires	79.1	22205	05 Wealthy Seaboard Suburbs	40.2
21617	13 In Style	53.6	21791	17 Green Acres	33.9	22206	27 Metro Renters	46.7
21619	17 Green Acres	46.1	21793	06 Sophisticated Squires	52.3	22207	03 Connoisseurs	40.3
21620	31 Rural Resort Dwellers	25.7	21794	02 Suburban Splendor	100.0	22209	27 Metro Renters	80.7
21622	31 Rural Resort Dwellers	57.8	21795	18 Cozy And Comfortable	24.7	22211	40 Military Proximity	100.0
21623	17 Green Acres	95.7	21797	02 Suburban Splendor	58.2	22213	05 Wealthy Seaboard Suburbs	50.8
21625	17 Green Acres	100.0	21798	17 Green Acres	78.8	22301	22 Metropolitans	24.0
21626	37 Prairie Living	100.0	21801	17 Green Acres	13.7	22302	27 Metro Renters	42.4
21628	26 Midland Crowd	100.0	21804	33 Midlife Junction	21.7	22303	16 Enterprising Professionals	36.3
21629	17 Green Acres	50.6	21811	15 Silver And Gold	43.6	22304	27 Metro Renters	21.6
21631	25 Salt Of The Earth	84.3	21813	31 Rural Resort Dwellers	55.3	22305	58 NeWest Residents	28.0
21632	53 Home Town	33.0	21814	46 Rooted Rural	96.5	22306	28 Aspiring Young Families	19.8

ZIP CODE	TOP TAPESTRY CONSUMER TYPE	% 2009 HOUSE-HOLDS	ZIP CODE	TOP TAPESTRY CONSUMER TYPE	% 2009 HOUSE-HOLDS	ZIP CODE	TOP TAPESTRY CONSUMER TYPE	% 2009 HOUSE-HOLDS
22307	03 Connoisseurs	35.2	22718	17 Green Acres	89.1	23004	56 Rural Bypasses	100.0
22308	03 Connoisseurs	42.8	22719	25 Salt Of The Earth	100.0	23005	33 Midlife Junction	18.9
22309	28 Aspiring Young Families	24.3	22720	06 Sophisticated Squires	71.8	23009	17 Green Acres	56.3
22310	16 Enterprising Professionals	37.7	22722	25 Salt Of The Earth	100.0	23011	18 Cozy And Comfortable	100.0
22311	39 Young And Restless	53.2	22724	07 Exurbanites	52.3	23015	17 Green Acres	63.5
22312	35 International Marketplace	27.2	22725	25 Salt Of The Earth	100.0	23021	31 Rural Resort Dwellers	100.0
22314	08 Laptops And Lattes	41.8	22726	17 Green Acres	100.0	23022	50 Heartland Communities	81.8
22315	16 Enterprising Professionals	44.6	22727	25 Salt Of The Earth	79.6	23023	46 Rooted Rural	100.0
22401	39 Young And Restless	31.5	22728	26 Midland Crowd	40.0	23024	26 Midland Crowd	65.4
22405	07 Exurbanites	24.3	22729	14 Prosperous Empty Nesters	100.0	23025	31 Rural Resort Dwellers	100.0
22406	16 Enterprising Professionals	41.3	22730	17 Green Acres	86.3	23027	26 Midland Crowd	94.9
22407	12 Up And Coming Families	47.6	22731	25 Salt Of The Earth	100.0	23030	25 Salt Of The Earth	43.2
22408	12 Up And Coming Families	56.5	22732	17 Green Acres	58.3	23032	46 Rooted Rural	60.4
22427	29 Rustbelt Retirees	30.5	22733	14 Prosperous Empty Nesters	39.8	23035	31 Rural Resort Dwellers	100.0
22432	31 Rural Resort Dwellers	100.0	22734	12 Up And Coming Families	70.8	23038	26 Midland Crowd	46.0
22433	17 Green Acres	100.0	22735	17 Green Acres	82.3	23039	17 Green Acres	63.6
22435	46 Rooted Rural	68.8	22736	17 Green Acres	100.0	23040	46 Rooted Rural	61.7
22436	46 Rooted Rural	100.0	22737	17 Green Acres	55.7	23043	15 Silver And Gold	73.5
22437	31 Rural Resort Dwellers	100.0	22738	25 Salt Of The Earth	100.0	23045	31 Rural Resort Dwellers	100.0
22438	46 Rooted Rural	67.7	22740	31 Rural Resort Dwellers	95.9	23047	07 Exurbanites	53.9
22443	31 Rural Resort Dwellers	51.3	22741	24 Main Street, USA	63.0	23050	31 Rural Resort Dwellers	56.6
22448	40 Military Proximity	100.0	22742	06 Sophisticated Squires	100.0	23055	50 Heartland Communities	73.4
22454	31 Rural Resort Dwellers	100.0	22743	25 Salt Of The Earth	98.4	23056	31 Rural Resort Dwellers	100.0
22460	46 Rooted Rural	62.7	22747	31 Rural Resort Dwellers	83.3	23059	16 Enterprising Professionals	37.8
22469	56 Rural Bypasses	49.9	22749	31 Rural Resort Dwellers	100.0	23060	12 Up And Coming Families	32.6
22473	31 Rural Resort Dwellers	85.3	22801	63 Dorms To Diplomas	22.3	23061	26 Midland Crowd	45.7
22476	46 Rooted Rural	100.0	22802	28 Aspiring Young Families	20.7	23062	24 Main Street, USA	54.9
22480	15 Silver And Gold	100.0	22807	22 Metropolitans	100.0	23063	25 Salt Of The Earth	43.9
22482	15 Silver And Gold	81.0	22810	31 Rural Resort Dwellers	100.0	23065	17 Green Acres	76.9
22485	26 Midland Crowd	25.9	22811	25 Salt Of The Earth	96.2	23066	31 Rural Resort Dwellers	100.0
22488	31 Rural Resort Dwellers	46.3	22812	33 Midlife Junction	38.3	23069	07 Exurbanites	40.4
22503	46 Rooted Rural	32.0	22815	25 Salt Of The Earth	70.0	23070	31 Rural Resort Dwellers	100.0
22504	31 Rural Resort Dwellers	100.0	22820	25 Salt Of The Earth	73.9	23071	31 Rural Resort Dwellers	100.0
22508	15 Silver And Gold	70.3	22821	25 Salt Of The Earth	49.7	23072	26 Midland Crowd	25.3
22509	46 Rooted Rural	100.0	22824	25 Salt Of The Earth	49.6	23075	32 Rustbelt Traditions	40.4
22511	31 Rural Resort Dwellers	99.7	22827	42 Southern Satellites	56.7	23079	31 Rural Resort Dwellers	76.2
22514	46 Rooted Rural	49.9	22830	42 Southern Satellites	98.2	23083	26 Midland Crowd	76.1
22520	31 Rural Resort Dwellers	25.0	22831	42 Southern Satellites	84.4	23084	26 Midland Crowd	47.8
22534	26 Midland Crowd	72.7	22832	25 Salt Of The Earth	100.0	23085	46 Rooted Rural	100.0
22535	46 Rooted Rural	90.4	22834	25 Salt Of The Earth	80.4	23086	17 Green Acres	50.0
22538	46 Rooted Rural	99.3	22835	25 Salt Of The Earth	32.3	23089	17 Green Acres	68.5
22539	15 Silver And Gold	73.3	22840	17 Green Acres	62.1	23091	25 Salt Of The Earth	79.4
22542	26 Midland Crowd	65.8	22841	17 Green Acres	60.3	23092	31 Rural Resort Dwellers	100.0
22546	25 Salt Of The Earth	36.0	22842	25 Salt Of The Earth	46.7	23093	25 Salt Of The Earth	31.2
22551	26 Midland Crowd	35.1	22843	25 Salt Of The Earth	72.3	23102	17 Green Acres	88.8
22553	06 Sophisticated Squires	38.3	22844	33 Midlife Junction	42.1	23103	07 Exurbanites	98.6
22554	12 Up And Coming Families	29.6	22845	31 Rural Resort Dwellers	100.0	23106	17 Green Acres	100.0
22556	06 Sophisticated Squires	44.1	22846	17 Green Acres	61.3	23109	31 Rural Resort Dwellers	100.0
22560	30 Retirement Communities	23.1	22847	25 Salt Of The Earth	98.2	23110	50 Heartland Communities	78.5
22567	26 Midland Crowd	47.4	22849	42 Southern Satellites	27.9	23111	12 Up And Coming Families	30.4
22572	33 Midlife Junction	46.0	22851	42 Southern Satellites	81.0	23112	07 Exurbanites	30.9
22576	31 Rural Resort Dwellers	48.1	22853	25 Salt Of The Earth	80.8	23113	02 Suburban Splendor	67.2
22578	15 Silver And Gold	53.7	22901	13 In Style	17.4	23114	04 Boomburbs	35.0
22579	31 Rural Resort Dwellers	100.0	22902	16 Enterprising Professionals	17.8	23116	07 Exurbanites	28.5
22580	25 Salt Of The Earth	44.3	22903	63 Dorms To Diplomas	29.9	23117	31 Rural Resort Dwellers	57.8
22601	24 Main Street, USA	24.7	22904	63 Dorms To Diplomas	100.0	23119	31 Rural Resort Dwellers	100.0
22602	24 Main Street, USA	21.8	22911	12 Up And Coming Families	22.2	23120	07 Exurbanites	71.4
22603	17 Green Acres	36.7	22920	17 Green Acres	69.8	23123	46 Rooted Rural	63.5
22610	25 Salt Of The Earth	67.9	22922	46 Rooted Rural	87.9	23124	17 Green Acres	100.0
22611	17 Green Acres	42.5	22923	25 Salt Of The Earth	37.8	23125	31 Rural Resort Dwellers	100.0
22620	31 Rural Resort Dwellers	76.0	22931	25 Salt Of The Earth	70.3	23126	46 Rooted Rural	100.0
22624	17 Green Acres	40.1	22932	17 Green Acres	33.2	23128	31 Rural Resort Dwellers	77.2
22625	17 Green Acres	99.0	22935	17 Green Acres	64.2	23129	07 Exurbanites	89.6
22627	17 Green Acres	52.2	22936	07 Exurbanites	39.2	23130	31 Rural Resort Dwellers	100.0
22630	24 Main Street, USA	30.1	22937	46 Rooted Rural	65.2	23138	31 Rural Resort Dwellers	100.0
22637	25 Salt Of The Earth	73.9	22938	25 Salt Of The Earth	44.2	23139	17 Green Acres	54.2
22639	07 Exurbanites	75.3	22939	17 Green Acres	77.2	23140	17 Green Acres	47.2
22640	17 Green Acres	100.0	22940	03 Connoisseurs	36.0	23141	17 Green Acres	44.7
22641	25 Salt Of The Earth	100.0	22942	25 Salt Of The Earth	77.0	23146	07 Exurbanites	87.9
22642	12 Up And Coming Families	43.2	22943	17 Green Acres	100.0	23148	46 Rooted Rural	99.2
22643	13 In Style	100.0	22946	25 Salt Of The Earth	100.0	23149	31 Rural Resort Dwellers	65.1
22644	25 Salt Of The Earth	96.1	22947	03 Connoisseurs	53.9	23150	29 Rustbelt Retirees	20.5
22645	25 Salt Of The Earth	94.1	22948	17 Green Acres	100.0	23153	17 Green Acres	80.0
22649	25 Salt Of The Earth	100.0	22949	33 Midlife Junction	51.1	23156	46 Rooted Rural	49.9
22650	25 Salt Of The Earth	59.2	22952	18 Cozy And Comfortable	39.6	23160	07 Exurbanites	100.0
22652	31 Rural Resort Dwellers	100.0	22958	15 Silver And Gold	86.4	23161	46 Rooted Rural	100.0
22654	17 Green Acres	84.7	22959	17 Green Acres	72.1	23163	31 Rural Resort Dwellers	100.0
22655	12 Up And Coming Families	39.9	22960	33 Midlife Junction	32.5	23168	17 Green Acres	74.2
22656	25 Salt Of The Earth	63.5	22963	14 Prosperous Empty Nesters	60.2	23169	31 Rural Resort Dwellers	100.0
22657	25 Salt Of The Earth	47.1	22964	46 Rooted Rural	100.0	23173	15 Silver And Gold	100.0
22660	25 Salt Of The Earth	100.0	22967	46 Rooted Rural	49.3	23175	31 Rural Resort Dwellers	77.4
22663	31 Rural Resort Dwellers	41.6	22968	12 Up And Coming Families	60.5	23176	31 Rural Resort Dwellers	100.0
22664	33 Midlife Junction	41.1	22969	46 Rooted Rural	77.2	23177	46 Rooted Rural	81.6
22701	24 Main Street, USA	42.0	22971	31 Rural Resort Dwellers	42.8	23180	31 Rural Resort Dwellers	100.0
22709	25 Salt Of The Earth	100.0	22972	25 Salt Of The Earth	91.0	23181	18 Cozy And Comfortable	45.6
22712	06 Sophisticated Squires	39.8	22973	17 Green Acres	44.6	23185	15 Silver And Gold	27.7
22713	17 Green Acres	54.6	22974	17 Green Acres	50.9	23186	55 College Towns	100.0
22714	17 Green Acres	72.7	22976	46 Rooted Rural	100.0	23188	15 Silver And Gold	21.8
22715	25 Salt Of The Earth	100.0	22980	53 Home Town	18.9	23192	17 Green Acres	65.8
22716	31 Rural Resort Dwellers	82.5	23002	25 Salt Of The Earth	46.6	23219	39 Young And Restless	45.6

CONSUMER TYPE

ZIP CODE	TOP TAPESTRY CONSUMER TYPE	% 2009 HOUSE-HOLDS	ZIP CODE	TOP TAPESTRY CONSUMER TYPE	% 2009 HOUSE-HOLDS	ZIP CODE	TOP TAPESTRY CONSUMER TYPE	% 2009 HOUSE-HOLDS
23220	55 College Towns	35.4	23518	52 Inner City Tenants	25.6	23923	46 Rooted Rural	81.4
23221	27 Metro Renters	36.0	23521	40 Military Proximity	100.0	23924	56 Rural Bypasses	57.6
23222	34 Family Foundations	41.2	23523	62 Modest Income Homes	41.9	23927	31 Rural Resort Dwellers	31.1
23223	64 City Commons	19.0	23601	52 Inner City Tenants	21.7	23930	46 Rooted Rural	34.4
23224	64 City Commons	14.5	23602	13 In Style	22.3	23934	46 Rooted Rural	100.0
23225	36 Old And Newcomers	16.4	23603	28 Aspiring Young Families	62.7	23936	46 Rooted Rural	52.4
23226	22 Metropolitans	50.6	23604	40 Military Proximity	100.0	23937	46 Rooted Rural	50.8
23227	22 Metropolitans	19.5	23605	48 Great Expectations	29.8	23938	46 Rooted Rural	83.2
23228	28 Aspiring Young Families	18.5	23606	52 Inner City Tenants	24.9	23942	46 Rooted Rural	78.6
23229	14 Prosperous Empty Nesters	25.5	23607	64 City Commons	33.3	23944	50 Heartland Communities	57.4
23230	52 Inner City Tenants	30.9	23608	28 Aspiring Young Families	24.3	23947	46 Rooted Rural	74.5
23231	18 Cozy And Comfortable	19.4	23651	40 Military Proximity	100.0	23950	46 Rooted Rural	50.3
23233	04 Boomburbs	34.9	23661	34 Family Foundations	33.4	23952	46 Rooted Rural	100.0
23234	19 Milk And Cookies	20.8	23662	07 Exurbanites	46.3	23954	46 Rooted Rural	100.0
23235	14 Prosperous Empty Nesters	28.5	23663	32 Rustbelt Traditions	44.1	23958	46 Rooted Rural	57.1
23236	19 Milk And Cookies	29.8	23664	18 Cozy And Comfortable	31.3	23959	46 Rooted Rural	100.0
23237	19 Milk And Cookies	38.1	23665	40 Military Proximity	100.0	23960	46 Rooted Rural	45.7
23238	13 In Style	30.2	23666	39 Young And Restless	17.9	23962	50 Heartland Communities	37.4
23294	39 Young And Restless	30.7	23668	63 Dorms To Diplomas	100.0	23963	46 Rooted Rural	73.6
23298	63 Dorms To Diplomas	0.0	23669	18 Cozy And Comfortable	12.9	23964	56 Rural Bypasses	74.1
23301	50 Heartland Communities	74.1	23690	64 City Commons	52.9	23966	46 Rooted Rural	57.9
23302	46 Rooted Rural	85.7	23692	07 Exurbanites	43.9	23967	42 Southern Satellites	69.2
23303	46 Rooted Rural	100.0	23693	04 Boomburbs	67.4	23968	46 Rooted Rural	62.4
23306	50 Heartland Communities	53.7	23696	07 Exurbanites	96.3	23970	31 Rural Resort Dwellers	17.0
23307	46 Rooted Rural	47.5	23701	18 Cozy And Comfortable	21.7	23974	50 Heartland Communities	55.0
23308	56 Rural Bypasses	94.2	23702	32 Rustbelt Traditions	25.8	23976	42 Southern Satellites	86.9
23310	56 Rural Bypasses	41.1	23703	24 Main Street, USA	26.1	24011	65 Social Security Set	100.0
23314	07 Exurbanites	52.5	23704	62 Modest Income Homes	23.9	24012	48 Great Expectations	22.9
23315	25 Salt Of The Earth	65.2	23707	48 Great Expectations	24.9	24013	53 Home Town	65.2
23320	13 In Style	25.4	23708	40 Military Proximity	0.0	24014	32 Rustbelt Traditions	19.9
23321	06 Sophisticated Squires	15.2	23709	04 Boomburbs	100.0	24015	48 Great Expectations	24.0
23322	06 Sophisticated Squires	36.4	23801	40 Military Proximity	100.0	24016	60 City Dimensions	33.1
23323	19 Milk And Cookies	27.5	23803	62 Modest Income Homes	23.7	24017	32 Rustbelt Traditions	25.4
23324	52 Inner City Tenants	15.4	23805	33 Midlife Junction	22.7	24018	36 Old And Newcomers	19.2
23325	13 In Style	23.5	23806	57 Simple Living	100.0	24019	18 Cozy And Comfortable	28.1
23336	31 Rural Resort Dwellers	100.0	23821	46 Rooted Rural	75.5	24020	57 Simple Living	100.0
23337	46 Rooted Rural	49.5	23824	46 Rooted Rural	23.5	24053	42 Southern Satellites	99.9
23350	50 Heartland Communities	41.9	23827	56 Rural Bypasses	85.2	24054	42 Southern Satellites	85.7
23354	29 Rustbelt Retirees	79.9	23828	56 Rural Bypasses	89.7	24055	42 Southern Satellites	49.5
23356	56 Rural Bypasses	100.0	23829	25 Salt Of The Earth	67.7	24059	17 Green Acres	93.5
23357	56 Rural Bypasses	94.9	23830	46 Rooted Rural	44.6	24060	63 Dorms To Diplomas	39.1
23359	56 Rural Bypasses	82.7	23831	06 Sophisticated Squires	27.6	24064	17 Green Acres	33.4
23395	56 Rural Bypasses	100.0	23832	19 Milk And Cookies	28.7	24065	25 Salt Of The Earth	37.7
23404	46 Rooted Rural	100.0	23833	17 Green Acres	59.1	24066	25 Salt Of The Earth	63.1
23405	46 Rooted Rural	42.1	23834	32 Rustbelt Traditions	21.9	24067	25 Salt Of The Earth	92.9
23409	56 Rural Bypasses	100.0	23836	26 Midland Crowd	39.1	24069	42 Southern Satellites	100.0
23410	46 Rooted Rural	54.1	23837	33 Midlife Junction	53.3	24070	17 Green Acres	47.5
23413	31 Rural Resort Dwellers	66.4	23838	07 Exurbanites	44.0	24072	25 Salt Of The Earth	78.3
23415	56 Rural Bypasses	76.0	23839	46 Rooted Rural	100.0	24073	12 Up And Coming Families	16.8
23416	46 Rooted Rural	100.0	23840	25 Salt Of The Earth	67.5	24076	42 Southern Satellites	100.0
23417	33 Midlife Junction	39.9	23841	25 Salt Of The Earth	88.6	24077	17 Green Acres	77.1
23418	33 Midlife Junction	70.2	23842	17 Green Acres	38.0	24078	33 Midlife Junction	76.7
23420	46 Rooted Rural	51.6	23843	46 Rooted Rural	70.5	24079	46 Rooted Rural	57.4
23421	56 Rural Bypasses	50.5	23844	56 Rural Bypasses	100.0	24082	42 Southern Satellites	100.0
23426	46 Rooted Rural	100.0	23845	46 Rooted Rural	100.0	24083	07 Exurbanites	68.8
23430	25 Salt Of The Earth	26.9	23846	25 Salt Of The Earth	51.3	24084	25 Salt Of The Earth	29.3
23432	07 Exurbanites	100.0	23847	56 Rural Bypasses	44.4	24085	46 Rooted Rural	88.5
23433	07 Exurbanites	100.0	23850	46 Rooted Rural	89.2	24086	46 Rooted Rural	100.0
23434	12 Up And Coming Families	25.3	23851	25 Salt Of The Earth	18.4	24087	41 Crossroads	61.8
23435	12 Up And Coming Families	43.6	23856	56 Rural Bypasses	54.1	24088	46 Rooted Rural	42.4
23436	07 Exurbanites	100.0	23857	31 Rural Resort Dwellers	58.6	24089	42 Southern Satellites	60.0
23437	25 Salt Of The Earth	54.7	23860	32 Rustbelt Traditions	27.4	24090	25 Salt Of The Earth	34.7
23438	25 Salt Of The Earth	80.1	23866	25 Salt Of The Earth	99.2	24091	46 Rooted Rural	69.9
23440	37 Prairie Living	100.0	23867	56 Rural Bypasses	56.0	24092	46 Rooted Rural	40.8
23442	46 Rooted Rural	60.4	23868	56 Rural Bypasses	31.0	24093	46 Rooted Rural	70.7
23451	39 Young And Restless	20.9	23872	25 Salt Of The Earth	57.1	24095	26 Midland Crowd	51.1
23452	18 Cozy And Comfortable	25.0	23874	25 Salt Of The Earth	91.2	24101	31 Rural Resort Dwellers	50.1
23453	28 Aspiring Young Families	36.6	23875	19 Milk And Cookies	37.1	24102	46 Rooted Rural	47.1
23454	12 Up And Coming Families	19.9	23876	46 Rooted Rural	82.0	24104	15 Silver And Gold	43.1
23455	14 Prosperous Empty Nesters	16.1	23878	25 Salt Of The Earth	75.6	24105	46 Rooted Rural	84.8
23456	06 Sophisticated Squires	31.1	23879	46 Rooted Rural	71.6	24112	25 Salt Of The Earth	23.3
23457	17 Green Acres	74.1	23881	46 Rooted Rural	58.4	24120	46 Rooted Rural	87.4
23459	40 Military Proximity	100.0	23882	56 Rural Bypasses	71.6	24121	15 Silver And Gold	52.6
23460	40 Military Proximity	100.0	23883	46 Rooted Rural	77.7	24122	25 Salt Of The Earth	49.5
23461	40 Military Proximity	100.0	23885	17 Green Acres	45.6	24124	50 Heartland Communities	45.0
23462	28 Aspiring Young Families	28.8	23887	31 Rural Resort Dwellers	100.0	24127	25 Salt Of The Earth	62.8
23463	63 Dorms To Diplomas	100.0	23888	46 Rooted Rural	45.1	24128	46 Rooted Rural	56.5
23464	06 Sophisticated Squires	27.3	23889	46 Rooted Rural	100.0	24131	42 Southern Satellites	100.0
23487	26 Midland Crowd	56.5	23890	56 Rural Bypasses	52.6	24133	42 Southern Satellites	100.0
23502	24 Main Street, USA	25.0	23893	46 Rooted Rural	100.0	24134	50 Heartland Communities	31.5
23503	36 Old And Newcomers	28.1	23894	46 Rooted Rural	88.8	24136	46 Rooted Rural	57.6
23504	64 City Commons	43.8	23897	37 Prairie Living	54.6	24137	42 Southern Satellites	53.6
23505	36 Old And Newcomers	20.3	23898	26 Midland Crowd	35.5	24138	26 Midland Crowd	59.0
23507	27 Metro Renters	51.0	23901	33 Midlife Junction	42.4	24139	42 Southern Satellites	55.9
23508	22 Metropolitans	17.0	23915	46 Rooted Rural	59.9	24141	33 Midlife Junction	32.5
23509	51 Metro City Edge	27.5	23917	46 Rooted Rural	44.7	24142	63 Dorms To Diplomas	100.0
23510	27 Metro Renters	47.9	23919	49 Senior Sun Seekers	48.1	24147	50 Heartland Communities	100.0
23511	40 Military Proximity	100.0	23920	56 Rural Bypasses	47.0	24148	42 Southern Satellites	56.0
23513	32 Rustbelt Traditions	27.9	23921	46 Rooted Rural	100.0	24149	26 Midland Crowd	71.2
23517	27 Metro Renters	59.9	23922	46 Rooted Rural	69.7	24150	46 Rooted Rural	79.2

ZIP CODE	TOP TAPESTRY CONSUMER TYPE	% 2009 HOUSE-HOLDS	ZIP CODE	TOP TAPESTRY CONSUMER TYPE	% 2009 HOUSE-HOLDS	ZIP CODE	TOP TAPESTRY CONSUMER TYPE	% 2009 HOUSE-HOLDS
24151	25 Salt Of The Earth	24.9	24375	42 Southern Satellites	78.4	24593	25 Salt Of The Earth	71.5
24153	18 Cozy And Comfortable	16.5	24377	25 Salt Of The Earth	100.0	24594	42 Southern Satellites	70.4
24161	49 Senior Sun Seekers	86.2	24378	46 Rooted Rural	69.6	24597	46 Rooted Rural	62.0
24162	25 Salt Of The Earth	61.7	24380	46 Rooted Rural	52.4	24598	25 Salt Of The Earth	47.9
24165	42 Southern Satellites	51.4	24381	42 Southern Satellites	94.6	24599	46 Rooted Rural	100.0
24167	42 Southern Satellites	100.0	24382	42 Southern Satellites	24.4	24602	46 Rooted Rural	60.6
24168	50 Heartland Communities	100.0	24401	33 Midlife Junction	13.2	24603	56 Rural Bypasses	100.0
24171	42 Southern Satellites	49.0	24413	37 Prairie Living	100.0	24605	50 Heartland Communities	31.3
24174	26 Midland Crowd	44.8	24416	25 Salt Of The Earth	35.2	24609	46 Rooted Rural	54.1
24175	07 Exurbanites	40.0	24421	25 Salt Of The Earth	71.0	24613	46 Rooted Rural	50.2
24176	31 Rural Resort Dwellers	87.4	24422	33 Midlife Junction	26.3	24614	56 Rural Bypasses	74.8
24179	18 Cozy And Comfortable	22.2	24426	25 Salt Of The Earth	35.3	24620	56 Rural Bypasses	100.0
24184	26 Midland Crowd	54.5	24430	50 Heartland Communities	43.7	24622	46 Rooted Rural	59.1
24185	42 Southern Satellites	58.1	24431	41 Crossroads	66.5	24627	56 Rural Bypasses	100.0
24201	29 Rustbelt Retirees	26.2	24432	31 Rural Resort Dwellers	99.3	24630	46 Rooted Rural	34.1
24202	42 Southern Satellites	49.4	24433	37 Prairie Living	100.0	24631	56 Rural Bypasses	98.1
24210	33 Midlife Junction	41.0	24435	25 Salt Of The Earth	73.1	24634	56 Rural Bypasses	100.0
24211	26 Midland Crowd	33.2	24437	17 Green Acres	100.0	24637	46 Rooted Rural	36.9
24216	56 Rural Bypasses	53.1	24439	46 Rooted Rural	39.8	24639	56 Rural Bypasses	96.8
24217	56 Rural Bypasses	100.0	24440	46 Rooted Rural	61.6	24641	56 Rural Bypasses	50.7
24219	50 Heartland Communities	31.9	24441	42 Southern Satellites	54.2	24646	56 Rural Bypasses	72.8
24220	56 Rural Bypasses	100.0	24442	37 Prairie Living	100.0	24649	56 Rural Bypasses	60.0
24221	46 Rooted Rural	100.0	24445	29 Rustbelt Retirees	48.4	24651	33 Midlife Junction	32.5
24224	46 Rooted Rural	28.6	24450	31 Rural Resort Dwellers	24.3	24656	56 Rural Bypasses	93.9
24225	50 Heartland Communities	35.1	24458	37 Prairie Living	100.0	24657	56 Rural Bypasses	96.8
24226	56 Rural Bypasses	70.4	24459	25 Salt Of The Earth	94.0	24701	50 Heartland Communities	30.9
24228	56 Rural Bypasses	77.2	24460	31 Rural Resort Dwellers	96.5	24712	46 Rooted Rural	49.8
24230	56 Rural Bypasses	51.5	24464	46 Rooted Rural	100.0	24714	46 Rooted Rural	99.3
24236	42 Southern Satellites	54.5	24465	31 Rural Resort Dwellers	56.8	24715	50 Heartland Communities	99.0
24237	56 Rural Bypasses	76.2	24467	17 Green Acres	100.0	24726	56 Rural Bypasses	71.5
24239	56 Rural Bypasses	100.0	24468	37 Prairie Living	100.0	24731	46 Rooted Rural	83.3
24243	56 Rural Bypasses	75.9	24471	17 Green Acres	62.9	24733	56 Rural Bypasses	76.7
24244	56 Rural Bypasses	47.4	24472	25 Salt Of The Earth	44.2	24736	56 Rural Bypasses	100.0
24245	56 Rural Bypasses	73.8	24473	31 Rural Resort Dwellers	84.3	24740	50 Heartland Communities	27.8
24248	46 Rooted Rural	100.0	24477	17 Green Acres	46.7	24747	56 Rural Bypasses	65.5
24250	56 Rural Bypasses	62.7	24479	25 Salt Of The Earth	88.0	24801	56 Rural Bypasses	45.2
24251	50 Heartland Communities	41.7	24482	25 Salt Of The Earth	36.2	24815	56 Rural Bypasses	79.1
24256	56 Rural Bypasses	80.6	24483	25 Salt Of The Earth	89.7	24818	56 Rural Bypasses	100.0
24258	42 Southern Satellites	60.2	24484	31 Rural Resort Dwellers	57.8	24822	56 Rural Bypasses	100.0
24260	56 Rural Bypasses	71.8	24485	31 Rural Resort Dwellers	92.1	24823	56 Rural Bypasses	100.0
24263	46 Rooted Rural	44.4	24486	17 Green Acres	100.0	24827	56 Rural Bypasses	100.0
24265	56 Rural Bypasses	60.6	24487	31 Rural Resort Dwellers	100.0	24828	56 Rural Bypasses	99.8
24266	50 Heartland Communities	28.9	24501	53 Home Town	23.7	24834	56 Rural Bypasses	100.0
24269	56 Rural Bypasses	100.0	24502	33 Midlife Junction	30.5	24839	56 Rural Bypasses	100.0
24270	42 Southern Satellites	100.0	24503	14 Prosperous Empty Nesters	20.4	24844	56 Rural Bypasses	100.0
24271	46 Rooted Rural	100.0	24504	62 Modest Income Homes	61.3	24849	50 Heartland Communities	55.1
24272	46 Rooted Rural	80.6	24517	42 Southern Satellites	30.7	24850	56 Rural Bypasses	100.0
24273	33 Midlife Junction	29.2	24520	46 Rooted Rural	39.3	24859	50 Heartland Communities	62.2
24277	46 Rooted Rural	34.1	24521	25 Salt Of The Earth	29.4	24860	56 Rural Bypasses	50.5
24279	46 Rooted Rural	57.0	24522	25 Salt Of The Earth	49.9	24862	56 Rural Bypasses	100.0
24280	26 Midland Crowd	50.3	24523	25 Salt Of The Earth	30.9	24868	62 Modest Income Homes	56.4
24281	46 Rooted Rural	83.3	24526	25 Salt Of The Earth	96.3	24869	56 Rural Bypasses	100.0
24282	56 Rural Bypasses	100.0	24527	42 Southern Satellites	80.0	24870	56 Rural Bypasses	60.2
24283	50 Heartland Communities	58.2	24528	42 Southern Satellites	44.7	24873	56 Rural Bypasses	100.0
24290	50 Heartland Communities	74.1	24529	56 Rural Bypasses	65.9	24874	50 Heartland Communities	76.8
24292	46 Rooted Rural	61.0	24530	42 Southern Satellites	61.7	24879	56 Rural Bypasses	100.0
24293	46 Rooted Rural	53.0	24531	46 Rooted Rural	57.3	24882	56 Rural Bypasses	100.0
24301	50 Heartland Communities	28.4	24534	56 Rural Bypasses	99.4	24884	56 Rural Bypasses	100.0
24311	41 Crossroads	40.8	24536	17 Green Acres	100.0	24901	33 Midlife Junction	33.6
24312	42 Southern Satellites	42.4	24538	26 Midland Crowd	64.2	24910	46 Rooted Rural	55.9
24313	42 Southern Satellites	100.0	24539	56 Rural Bypasses	100.0	24915	31 Rural Resort Dwellers	100.0
24314	46 Rooted Rural	71.6	24540	62 Modest Income Homes	16.2	24916	46 Rooted Rural	100.0
24315	46 Rooted Rural	57.1	24541	29 Rustbelt Retirees	11.9	24918	42 Southern Satellites	62.8
24316	42 Southern Satellites	100.0	24549	17 Green Acres	37.2	24920	56 Rural Bypasses	96.9
24317	42 Southern Satellites	100.0	24550	42 Southern Satellites	64.1	24925	46 Rooted Rural	100.0
24318	46 Rooted Rural	79.9	24551	13 In Style	30.3	24927	31 Rural Resort Dwellers	57.8
24319	46 Rooted Rural	43.9	24553	46 Rooted Rural	60.9	24931	46 Rooted Rural	98.6
24322	46 Rooted Rural	100.0	24554	42 Southern Satellites	48.6	24934	31 Rural Resort Dwellers	83.6
24323	25 Salt Of The Earth	50.9	24555	50 Heartland Communities	59.7	24935	46 Rooted Rural	100.0
24324	25 Salt Of The Earth	70.6	24556	17 Green Acres	67.2	24938	46 Rooted Rural	100.0
24325	25 Salt Of The Earth	51.2	24557	42 Southern Satellites	63.5	24941	46 Rooted Rural	100.0
24326	46 Rooted Rural	69.1	24558	25 Salt Of The Earth	34.4	24943	46 Rooted Rural	100.0
24328	46 Rooted Rural	58.2	24562	46 Rooted Rural	100.0	24944	31 Rural Resort Dwellers	100.0
24330	42 Southern Satellites	58.1	24563	42 Southern Satellites	100.0	24945	46 Rooted Rural	70.2
24333	42 Southern Satellites	48.7	24565	42 Southern Satellites	54.2	24946	46 Rooted Rural	100.0
24340	46 Rooted Rural	52.3	24566	42 Southern Satellites	100.0	24951	46 Rooted Rural	100.0
24343	57 Simple Living	28.8	24569	42 Southern Satellites	65.8	24954	50 Heartland Communities	49.8
24347	25 Salt Of The Earth	49.1	24570	42 Southern Satellites	100.0	24957	46 Rooted Rural	100.0
24348	46 Rooted Rural	60.1	24571	46 Rooted Rural	73.1	24962	46 Rooted Rural	100.0
24350	42 Southern Satellites	82.3	24572	25 Salt Of The Earth	33.5	24963	46 Rooted Rural	52.7
24351	42 Southern Satellites	100.0	24574	17 Green Acres	40.4	24966	46 Rooted Rural	97.9
24352	46 Rooted Rural	57.5	24577	56 Rural Bypasses	70.8	24970	46 Rooted Rural	64.3
24354	42 Southern Satellites	44.1	24578	46 Rooted Rural	59.1	24974	46 Rooted Rural	100.0
24360	42 Southern Satellites	56.8	24579	42 Southern Satellites	72.0	24976	46 Rooted Rural	93.3
24361	42 Southern Satellites	52.1	24580	46 Rooted Rural	84.2	24977	46 Rooted Rural	100.0
24363	46 Rooted Rural	82.0	24586	42 Southern Satellites	60.4	24981	46 Rooted Rural	59.6
24366	25 Salt Of The Earth	96.4	24588	26 Midland Crowd	47.8	24983	46 Rooted Rural	60.1
24368	42 Southern Satellites	40.1	24589	46 Rooted Rural	39.8	24984	46 Rooted Rural	75.3
24370	50 Heartland Communities	34.7	24590	33 Midlife Junction	25.5	24985	46 Rooted Rural	100.0
24374	42 Southern Satellites	51.5	24592	25 Salt Of The Earth	29.1	24986	46 Rooted Rural	62.2

CONSUMER TYPE

ZIP CODE	TOP TAPESTRY CONSUMER TYPE	% 2009 HOUSE-HOLDS	ZIP CODE	TOP TAPESTRY CONSUMER TYPE	% 2009 HOUSE-HOLDS	ZIP CODE	TOP TAPESTRY CONSUMER TYPE	% 2009 HOUSE-HOLDS
24991	46 Rooted Rural	73.3	25245	26 Midland Crowd	92.1	25570	56 Rural Bypasses	52.4
24993	46 Rooted Rural	100.0	25248	46 Rooted Rural	66.6	25571	56 Rural Bypasses	100.0
25003	46 Rooted Rural	69.1	25251	46 Rooted Rural	72.5	25573	56 Rural Bypasses	100.0
25005	46 Rooted Rural	100.0	25252	42 Southern Satellites	96.4	25601	50 Heartland Communities	43.0
25007	56 Rural Bypasses	97.5	25253	46 Rooted Rural	39.0	25607	56 Rural Bypasses	93.6
25008	56 Rural Bypasses	100.0	25259	56 Rural Bypasses	86.1	25608	56 Rural Bypasses	100.0
25009	56 Rural Bypasses	100.0	25260	50 Heartland Communities	52.1	25617	56 Rural Bypasses	100.0
25015	50 Heartland Communities	55.6	25261	46 Rooted Rural	59.9	25621	56 Rural Bypasses	100.0
25019	56 Rural Bypasses	92.9	25262	26 Midland Crowd	66.4	25632	56 Rural Bypasses	56.1
25021	56 Rural Bypasses	100.0	25264	46 Rooted Rural	100.0	25635	56 Rural Bypasses	54.6
25024	56 Rural Bypasses	100.0	25266	56 Rural Bypasses	85.7	25638	56 Rural Bypasses	71.3
25025	56 Rural Bypasses	57.1	25267	46 Rooted Rural	55.7	25650	56 Rural Bypasses	100.0
25028	56 Rural Bypasses	100.0	25268	46 Rooted Rural	85.9	25651	56 Rural Bypasses	100.0
25030	56 Rural Bypasses	75.4	25270	46 Rooted Rural	64.4	25654	46 Rooted Rural	71.2
25033	56 Rural Bypasses	66.7	25271	50 Heartland Communities	40.4	25661	57 Simple Living	44.8
25035	56 Rural Bypasses	54.3	25275	46 Rooted Rural	99.4	25666	56 Rural Bypasses	100.0
25039	50 Heartland Communities	73.3	25276	50 Heartland Communities	55.2	25669	56 Rural Bypasses	100.0
25043	56 Rural Bypasses	67.8	25285	56 Rural Bypasses	86.8	25670	56 Rural Bypasses	100.0
25044	56 Rural Bypasses	100.0	25286	42 Southern Satellites	59.9	25671	56 Rural Bypasses	100.0
25045	46 Rooted Rural	45.4	25287	25 Salt Of The Earth	76.7	25674	56 Rural Bypasses	100.0
25047	50 Heartland Communities	86.8	25301	65 Social Security Set	86.1	25676	56 Rural Bypasses	100.0
25048	56 Rural Bypasses	100.0	25302	33 Midlife Junction	27.3	25678	56 Rural Bypasses	100.0
25049	56 Rural Bypasses	100.0	25303	14 Prosperous Empty Nesters	29.7	25699	56 Rural Bypasses	100.0
25051	56 Rural Bypasses	100.0	25304	22 Metropolitans	20.5	25701	55 College Towns	14.9
25053	56 Rural Bypasses	75.1	25306	50 Heartland Communities	62.9	25702	50 Heartland Communities	46.1
25059	56 Rural Bypasses	100.0	25309	33 Midlife Junction	37.2	25703	63 Dorms To Diplomas	46.3
25060	56 Rural Bypasses	100.0	25311	50 Heartland Communities	27.0	25704	50 Heartland Communities	30.8
25062	56 Rural Bypasses	99.6	25312	46 Rooted Rural	17.8	25705	33 Midlife Junction	50.4
25063	56 Rural Bypasses	70.2	25313	13 In Style	43.7	25755	63 Dorms To Diplomas	0.0
25064	28 Aspiring Young Families	21.4	25314	07 Exurbanites	24.5	25801	50 Heartland Communities	24.5
25071	46 Rooted Rural	34.9	25315	50 Heartland Communities	76.5	25811	50 Heartland Communities	100.0
25075	56 Rural Bypasses	84.4	25320	46 Rooted Rural	44.2	25812	50 Heartland Communities	100.0
25079	50 Heartland Communities	100.0	25401	48 Great Expectations	18.8	25813	17 Green Acres	41.0
25081	56 Rural Bypasses	73.1	25403	17 Green Acres	45.8	25817	46 Rooted Rural	95.8
25082	25 Salt Of The Earth	52.6	25404	26 Midland Crowd	28.2	25820	46 Rooted Rural	85.7
25083	29 Rustbelt Retirees	43.0	25405	26 Midland Crowd	70.1	25823	46 Rooted Rural	45.5
25085	50 Heartland Communities	82.5	25411	46 Rooted Rural	35.6	25825	56 Rural Bypasses	39.3
25088	56 Rural Bypasses	100.0	25413	26 Midland Crowd	74.3	25827	50 Heartland Communities	43.4
25093	56 Rural Bypasses	100.0	25414	13 In Style	31.2	25831	56 Rural Bypasses	85.6
25103	56 Rural Bypasses	100.0	25419	26 Midland Crowd	75.1	25832	50 Heartland Communities	57.4
25106	56 Rural Bypasses	83.4	25420	26 Midland Crowd	86.1	25837	46 Rooted Rural	100.0
25107	56 Rural Bypasses	100.0	25422	46 Rooted Rural	61.9	25839	46 Rooted Rural	97.8
25108	56 Rural Bypasses	38.2	25425	17 Green Acres	38.8	25840	29 Rustbelt Retirees	35.6
25111	56 Rural Bypasses	99.3	25427	26 Midland Crowd	53.4	25841	46 Rooted Rural	100.0
25113	56 Rural Bypasses	100.0	25428	26 Midland Crowd	97.5	25843	31 Rural Resort Dwellers	92.3
25114	56 Rural Bypasses	87.2	25430	26 Midland Crowd	52.2	25844	46 Rooted Rural	58.4
25115	46 Rooted Rural	100.0	25431	46 Rooted Rural	100.0	25845	50 Heartland Communities	100.0
25118	50 Heartland Communities	98.5	25434	50 Heartland Communities	43.0	25848	56 Rural Bypasses	100.0
25119	56 Rural Bypasses	100.0	25437	46 Rooted Rural	100.0	25854	46 Rooted Rural	100.0
25121	56 Rural Bypasses	61.6	25438	53 Home Town	31.0	25857	56 Rural Bypasses	100.0
25123	56 Rural Bypasses	54.9	25442	13 In Style	70.4	25862	50 Heartland Communities	100.0
25124	42 Southern Satellites	73.1	25443	13 In Style	83.0	25864	56 Rural Bypasses	100.0
25125	56 Rural Bypasses	100.0	25444	42 Southern Satellites	63.4	25865	56 Rural Bypasses	83.0
25130	56 Rural Bypasses	51.4	25446	17 Green Acres	96.0	25868	46 Rooted Rural	100.0
25132	56 Rural Bypasses	96.9	25501	56 Rural Bypasses	100.0	25870	50 Heartland Communities	66.4
25133	56 Rural Bypasses	56.8	25502	56 Rural Bypasses	61.4	25876	56 Rural Bypasses	98.0
25136	50 Heartland Communities	35.8	25503	46 Rooted Rural	41.7	25880	46 Rooted Rural	25.4
25140	56 Rural Bypasses	68.7	25504	29 Rustbelt Retirees	29.5	25882	50 Heartland Communities	100.0
25141	56 Rural Bypasses	100.0	25505	26 Midland Crowd	90.2	25901	50 Heartland Communities	52.0
25142	56 Rural Bypasses	100.0	25506	56 Rural Bypasses	99.4	25902	56 Rural Bypasses	92.2
25143	50 Heartland Communities	34.4	25508	46 Rooted Rural	36.1	25908	46 Rooted Rural	62.3
25148	56 Rural Bypasses	100.0	25510	46 Rooted Rural	77.6	25913	56 Rural Bypasses	74.8
25154	56 Rural Bypasses	93.0	25511	56 Rural Bypasses	100.0	25915	56 Rural Bypasses	100.0
25159	26 Midland Crowd	46.7	25512	56 Rural Bypasses	80.0	25917	56 Rural Bypasses	70.4
25160	56 Rural Bypasses	100.0	25514	56 Rural Bypasses	78.5	25918	46 Rooted Rural	83.0
25161	46 Rooted Rural	100.0	25515	56 Rural Bypasses	53.3	25920	42 Southern Satellites	72.4
25164	46 Rooted Rural	60.9	25517	56 Rural Bypasses	100.0	25922	42 Southern Satellites	70.3
25165	56 Rural Bypasses	90.4	25520	42 Southern Satellites	45.5	25928	50 Heartland Communities	100.0
25168	29 Rustbelt Retirees	38.2	25521	56 Rural Bypasses	100.0	25932	56 Rural Bypasses	70.1
25169	56 Rural Bypasses	100.0	25523	56 Rural Bypasses	35.8	25936	56 Rural Bypasses	100.0
25173	56 Rural Bypasses	92.4	25524	56 Rural Bypasses	100.0	25938	56 Rural Bypasses	39.8
25174	56 Rural Bypasses	100.0	25526	17 Green Acres	26.2	25951	46 Rooted Rural	39.8
25177	29 Rustbelt Retirees	33.7	25529	56 Rural Bypasses	100.0	25958	50 Heartland Communities	100.0
25180	56 Rural Bypasses	80.4	25530	50 Heartland Communities	51.3	25962	50 Heartland Communities	62.0
25181	56 Rural Bypasses	92.3	25534	56 Rural Bypasses	100.0	25965	50 Heartland Communities	97.6
25187	42 Southern Satellites	97.7	25535	46 Rooted Rural	57.6	25966	50 Heartland Communities	75.1
25193	56 Rural Bypasses	100.0	25537	46 Rooted Rural	43.2	25969	46 Rooted Rural	99.2
25202	26 Midland Crowd	35.3	25540	56 Rural Bypasses	100.0	25971	46 Rooted Rural	100.0
25204	56 Rural Bypasses	100.0	25541	46 Rooted Rural	40.5	25976	46 Rooted Rural	64.3
25208	56 Rural Bypasses	100.0	25544	56 Rural Bypasses	100.0	25977	50 Heartland Communities	100.0
25209	56 Rural Bypasses	79.5	25545	25 Salt Of The Earth	20.0	25978	46 Rooted Rural	100.0
25213	17 Green Acres	46.8	25547	50 Heartland Communities	99.7	25979	46 Rooted Rural	100.0
25214	56 Rural Bypasses	100.0	25550	29 Rustbelt Retirees	37.1	25981	56 Rural Bypasses	54.1
25231	46 Rooted Rural	100.0	25555	42 Southern Satellites	86.0	25984	50 Heartland Communities	67.7
25234	56 Rural Bypasses	62.4	25557	56 Rural Bypasses	100.0	25985	46 Rooted Rural	93.0
25235	46 Rooted Rural	83.6	25559	26 Midland Crowd	57.7	25986	46 Rooted Rural	100.0
25239	46 Rooted Rural	62.0	25560	18 Cozy And Comfortable	50.2	25989	42 Southern Satellites	65.7
25241	26 Midland Crowd	94.3	25564	56 Rural Bypasses	57.2	26003	50 Heartland Communities	20.8
25243	46 Rooted Rural	53.3	25565	56 Rural Bypasses	100.0	26031	57 Simple Living	35.8
25244	46 Rooted Rural	96.9	25567	56 Rural Bypasses	77.2	26032	33 Midlife Junction	100.0

ZIP CODE	TOP TAPESTRY CONSUMER TYPE	% 2009 HOUSE-HOLDS	ZIP CODE	TOP TAPESTRY CONSUMER TYPE	% 2009 HOUSE-HOLDS	ZIP CODE	TOP TAPESTRY CONSUMER TYPE	% 2009 HOUSE-HOLDS
26033	50 Heartland Communities	84.7	26291	46 Rooted Rural	63.3	26627	46 Rooted Rural	100.0
26034	50 Heartland Communities	46.7	26292	50 Heartland Communities	100.0	26629	56 Rural Bypasses	100.0
26035	46 Rooted Rural	78.9	26293	46 Rooted Rural	90.1	26631	46 Rooted Rural	100.0
26036	46 Rooted Rural	100.0	26294	50 Heartland Communities	61.0	26636	46 Rooted Rural	82.7
26037	50 Heartland Communities	58.3	26296	46 Rooted Rural	99.4	26638	46 Rooted Rural	100.0
26038	29 Rustbelt Retirees	50.9	26301	50 Heartland Communities	43.8	26651	46 Rooted Rural	70.7
26039	46 Rooted Rural	50.0	26320	46 Rooted Rural	100.0	26656	56 Rural Bypasses	85.3
26040	50 Heartland Communities	100.0	26321	46 Rooted Rural	95.2	26660	46 Rooted Rural	76.6
26041	50 Heartland Communities	40.6	26325	46 Rooted Rural	75.9	26662	46 Rooted Rural	100.0
26047	25 Salt Of The Earth	30.1	26327	46 Rooted Rural	100.0	26667	46 Rooted Rural	64.4
26050	56 Rural Bypasses	41.9	26330	14 Prosperous Empty Nesters	23.9	26675	56 Rural Bypasses	100.0
26055	46 Rooted Rural	50.8	26335	46 Rooted Rural	78.1	26676	46 Rooted Rural	65.8
26059	46 Rooted Rural	64.1	26337	46 Rooted Rural	85.9	26678	46 Rooted Rural	100.0
26060	46 Rooted Rural	64.5	26338	56 Rural Bypasses	60.4	26679	46 Rooted Rural	85.2
26062	29 Rustbelt Retirees	68.0	26339	46 Rooted Rural	100.0	26680	46 Rooted Rural	100.0
26070	50 Heartland Communities	46.7	26342	46 Rooted Rural	86.8	26681	46 Rooted Rural	100.0
26101	50 Heartland Communities	39.3	26343	46 Rooted Rural	66.4	26684	46 Rooted Rural	100.0
26104	33 Midlife Junction	18.1	26346	42 Southern Satellites	100.0	26690	56 Rural Bypasses	50.2
26105	29 Rustbelt Retirees	34.4	26347	46 Rooted Rural	79.1	26691	56 Rural Bypasses	58.9
26133	46 Rooted Rural	54.4	26348	56 Rural Bypasses	100.0	26704	42 Southern Satellites	69.0
26134	46 Rooted Rural	72.3	26351	55 College Towns	30.0	26705	46 Rooted Rural	100.0
26136	56 Rural Bypasses	95.0	26354	50 Heartland Communities	50.4	26710	46 Rooted Rural	61.3
26137	46 Rooted Rural	50.9	26362	50 Heartland Communities	49.6	26711	25 Salt Of The Earth	75.2
26138	46 Rooted Rural	100.0	26372	46 Rooted Rural	100.0	26714	42 Southern Satellites	100.0
26141	50 Heartland Communities	42.9	26374	46 Rooted Rural	59.8	26716	46 Rooted Rural	100.0
26142	46 Rooted Rural	61.4	26376	56 Rural Bypasses	57.7	26717	56 Rural Bypasses	95.7
26143	46 Rooted Rural	97.0	26377	46 Rooted Rural	65.2	26719	46 Rooted Rural	95.9
26146	46 Rooted Rural	100.0	26378	46 Rooted Rural	72.9	26720	46 Rooted Rural	100.0
26147	50 Heartland Communities	93.2	26384	56 Rural Bypasses	86.2	26722	46 Rooted Rural	100.0
26148	46 Rooted Rural	100.0	26385	46 Rooted Rural	53.1	26726	50 Heartland Communities	43.9
26149	46 Rooted Rural	100.0	26386	46 Rooted Rural	89.3	26731	42 Southern Satellites	56.3
26150	26 Midland Crowd	56.6	26404	50 Heartland Communities	88.0	26739	46 Rooted Rural	83.4
26151	50 Heartland Communities	66.0	26405	46 Rooted Rural	100.0	26743	25 Salt Of The Earth	96.5
26152	46 Rooted Rural	100.0	26408	17 Green Acres	67.8	26750	53 Home Town	63.6
26155	56 Rural Bypasses	31.9	26410	56 Rural Bypasses	56.2	26753	46 Rooted Rural	48.5
26159	50 Heartland Communities	100.0	26411	46 Rooted Rural	99.7	26755	42 Southern Satellites	100.0
26160	46 Rooted Rural	100.0	26412	46 Rooted Rural	100.0	26757	46 Rooted Rural	48.7
26161	46 Rooted Rural	100.0	26415	50 Heartland Communities	68.3	26761	42 Southern Satellites	80.5
26164	25 Salt Of The Earth	24.2	26416	46 Rooted Rural	54.3	26763	46 Rooted Rural	98.3
26167	42 Southern Satellites	50.1	26419	50 Heartland Communities	61.7	26764	46 Rooted Rural	78.4
26169	42 Southern Satellites	86.0	26421	46 Rooted Rural	100.0	26767	50 Heartland Communities	100.0
26170	50 Heartland Communities	42.9	26425	50 Heartland Communities	89.4	26801	31 Rural Resort Dwellers	43.1
26175	29 Rustbelt Retirees	28.1	26426	46 Rooted Rural	46.6	26802	46 Rooted Rural	81.3
26178	46 Rooted Rural	77.2	26430	56 Rural Bypasses	100.0	26804	42 Southern Satellites	97.1
26180	46 Rooted Rural	56.5	26431	46 Rooted Rural	51.7	26807	46 Rooted Rural	73.5
26181	17 Green Acres	37.6	26437	56 Rural Bypasses	72.2	26808	25 Salt Of The Earth	100.0
26184	25 Salt Of The Earth	42.1	26440	56 Rural Bypasses	71.7	26810	46 Rooted Rural	87.8
26187	29 Rustbelt Retirees	37.2	26443	46 Rooted Rural	100.0	26812	46 Rooted Rural	99.7
26201	46 Rooted Rural	46.6	26444	56 Rural Bypasses	57.9	26814	42 Southern Satellites	92.4
26202	46 Rooted Rural	100.0	26447	46 Rooted Rural	81.7	26815	42 Southern Satellites	100.0
26203	56 Rural Bypasses	100.0	26448	56 Rural Bypasses	98.4	26817	46 Rooted Rural	88.4
26205	56 Rural Bypasses	43.1	26451	46 Rooted Rural	97.2	26818	42 Southern Satellites	100.0
26206	56 Rural Bypasses	100.0	26452	50 Heartland Communities	50.3	26833	42 Southern Satellites	99.1
26208	56 Rural Bypasses	100.0	26456	50 Heartland Communities	56.0	26836	42 Southern Satellites	54.5
26210	46 Rooted Rural	100.0	26501	33 Midlife Junction	26.9	26838	46 Rooted Rural	68.9
26215	46 Rooted Rural	100.0	26505	63 Dorms To Diplomas	34.3	26845	42 Southern Satellites	100.0
26217	56 Rural Bypasses	94.0	26506	63 Dorms To Diplomas	100.0	26847	42 Southern Satellites	56.0
26218	46 Rooted Rural	95.3	26508	26 Midland Crowd	28.5	26851	46 Rooted Rural	99.8
26222	42 Southern Satellites	83.6	26519	46 Rooted Rural	100.0	26852	46 Rooted Rural	100.0
26224	46 Rooted Rural	88.0	26521	46 Rooted Rural	100.0	26855	42 Southern Satellites	100.0
26228	46 Rooted Rural	95.4	26525	46 Rooted Rural	100.0	26865	25 Salt Of The Earth	100.0
26230	46 Rooted Rural	80.9	26537	50 Heartland Communities	33.2	26866	46 Rooted Rural	100.0
26234	46 Rooted Rural	100.0	26541	42 Southern Satellites	95.9	26884	46 Rooted Rural	98.7
26236	46 Rooted Rural	100.0	26542	46 Rooted Rural	87.9	27006	25 Salt Of The Earth	30.3
26237	56 Rural Bypasses	96.8	26546	26 Midland Crowd	100.0	27007	42 Southern Satellites	70.9
26238	46 Rooted Rural	100.0	26547	25 Salt Of The Earth	43.7	27009	25 Salt Of The Earth	60.7
26241	50 Heartland Communities	35.4	26554	50 Heartland Communities	19.9	27011	42 Southern Satellites	84.8
26250	46 Rooted Rural	43.0	26560	50 Heartland Communities	100.0	27012	13 In Style	23.2
26253	42 Southern Satellites	75.0	26561	46 Rooted Rural	100.0	27013	26 Midland Crowd	68.1
26254	46 Rooted Rural	100.0	26562	50 Heartland Communities	58.4	27016	46 Rooted Rural	66.5
26257	56 Rural Bypasses	71.7	26568	46 Rooted Rural	59.9	27017	42 Southern Satellites	62.1
26260	50 Heartland Communities	53.1	26570	46 Rooted Rural	88.4	27018	42 Southern Satellites	53.2
26261	50 Heartland Communities	73.1	26571	50 Heartland Communities	97.6	27019	26 Midland Crowd	54.1
26263	46 Rooted Rural	94.9	26575	56 Rural Bypasses	57.0	27020	42 Southern Satellites	100.0
26264	56 Rural Bypasses	100.0	26581	46 Rooted Rural	93.6	27021	25 Salt Of The Earth	22.7
26266	56 Rural Bypasses	100.0	26582	50 Heartland Communities	66.6	27022	46 Rooted Rural	61.8
26267	46 Rooted Rural	66.9	26585	46 Rooted Rural	60.5	27023	17 Green Acres	51.9
26268	46 Rooted Rural	77.7	26587	50 Heartland Communities	100.0	27024	42 Southern Satellites	98.1
26269	46 Rooted Rural	84.7	26588	50 Heartland Communities	65.1	27025	42 Southern Satellites	57.3
26270	46 Rooted Rural	100.0	26590	46 Rooted Rural	100.0	27027	53 Home Town	46.8
26271	50 Heartland Communities	100.0	26591	56 Rural Bypasses	49.9	27028	42 Southern Satellites	46.0
26273	46 Rooted Rural	59.0	26601	56 Rural Bypasses	38.6	27030	42 Southern Satellites	36.9
26276	46 Rooted Rural	48.1	26610	56 Rural Bypasses	99.0	27040	17 Green Acres	28.8
26278	46 Rooted Rural	100.0	26611	56 Rural Bypasses	66.2	27041	42 Southern Satellites	61.2
26280	42 Southern Satellites	50.7	26615	42 Southern Satellites	90.1	27042	42 Southern Satellites	100.0
26282	50 Heartland Communities	74.1	26617	56 Rural Bypasses	100.0	27043	26 Midland Crowd	53.8
26283	46 Rooted Rural	80.7	26619	42 Southern Satellites	94.4	27045	25 Salt Of The Earth	34.1
26287	50 Heartland Communities	60.9	26621	46 Rooted Rural	100.0	27046	42 Southern Satellites	100.0
26288	56 Rural Bypasses	59.7	26623	46 Rooted Rural	98.9	27047	42 Southern Satellites	100.0
26289	31 Rural Resort Dwellers	100.0	26624	46 Rooted Rural	77.4	27048	42 Southern Satellites	62.2

CONSUMER TYPE

ZIP CODE	TOP TAPESTRY CONSUMER TYPE	% 2009 HOUSE-HOLDS	ZIP CODE	TOP TAPESTRY CONSUMER TYPE	% 2009 HOUSE-HOLDS	ZIP CODE	TOP TAPESTRY CONSUMER TYPE	% 2009 HOUSE-HOLDS
27050	26 Midland Crowd	28.0	27410	16 Enterprising Professionals	22.9	27803	26 Midland Crowd	14.4
27051	26 Midland Crowd	64.2	27411	55 College Towns	0.0	27804	28 Aspiring Young Families	16.1
27052	42 Southern Satellites	46.0	27413	63 Dorms To Diplomas	100.0	27805	56 Rural Bypasses	66.8
27053	42 Southern Satellites	95.7	27455	13 In Style	48.8	27806	56 Rural Bypasses	73.2
27054	42 Southern Satellites	87.2	27501	26 Midland Crowd	71.0	27807	42 Southern Satellites	87.0
27055	42 Southern Satellites	48.5	27502	12 Up And Coming Families	54.0	27808	46 Rooted Rural	84.7
27101	62 Modest Income Homes	21.7	27503	07 Exurbanites	51.8	27809	17 Green Acres	32.7
27103	36 Old And Newcomers	15.8	27504	26 Midland Crowd	30.4	27810	46 Rooted Rural	42.5
27104	13 In Style	18.7	27505	42 Southern Satellites	39.6	27812	56 Rural Bypasses	51.2
27105	34 Family Foundations	15.6	27507	42 Southern Satellites	81.5	27814	46 Rooted Rural	43.6
27106	52 Inner City Tenants	23.3	27508	56 Rural Bypasses	55.7	27816	56 Rural Bypasses	38.5
27107	17 Green Acres	15.6	27509	41 Crossroads	82.2	27817	42 Southern Satellites	31.3
27110	63 Dorms To Diplomas	0.0	27510	39 Young And Restless	40.9	27818	56 Rural Bypasses	100.0
27127	19 Milk And Cookies	19.1	27511	28 Aspiring Young Families	18.0	27820	56 Rural Bypasses	41.0
27203	42 Southern Satellites	26.7	27513	16 Enterprising Professionals	57.5	27821	46 Rooted Rural	100.0
27205	42 Southern Satellites	31.8	27514	08 Laptops And Lattes	37.3	27822	42 Southern Satellites	35.0
27207	42 Southern Satellites	51.1	27516	16 Enterprising Professionals	33.6	27823	56 Rural Bypasses	66.7
27208	46 Rooted Rural	53.7	27517	16 Enterprising Professionals	17.0	27824	56 Rural Bypasses	100.0
27209	42 Southern Satellites	78.5	27518	04 Boomburbs	91.7	27826	56 Rural Bypasses	100.0
27212	46 Rooted Rural	63.4	27519	04 Boomburbs	100.0	27828	56 Rural Bypasses	23.9
27214	28 Aspiring Young Families	30.4	27520	12 Up And Coming Families	56.1	27829	56 Rural Bypasses	64.9
27215	14 Prosperous Empty Nesters	15.9	27521	42 Southern Satellites	39.1	27830	42 Southern Satellites	22.7
27217	53 Home Town	22.5	27522	26 Midland Crowd	48.5	27831	56 Rural Bypasses	96.8
27229	42 Southern Satellites	77.7	27523	04 Boomburbs	66.2	27832	56 Rural Bypasses	51.5
27231	46 Rooted Rural	50.5	27524	42 Southern Satellites	44.3	27834	39 Young And Restless	21.5
27233	42 Southern Satellites	52.5	27525	12 Up And Coming Families	29.9	27837	26 Midland Crowd	41.0
27235	12 Up And Coming Families	51.8	27526	24 Main Street, USA	29.4	27839	56 Rural Bypasses	92.9
27239	42 Southern Satellites	99.9	27527	12 Up And Coming Families	86.9	27840	56 Rural Bypasses	100.0
27242	56 Rural Bypasses	52.2	27529	12 Up And Coming Families	31.3	27842	49 Senior Sun Seekers	93.9
27243	26 Midland Crowd	67.7	27530	26 Midland Crowd	25.0	27843	42 Southern Satellites	55.2
27244	25 Salt Of The Earth	22.1	27531	40 Military Proximity	100.0	27844	56 Rural Bypasses	100.0
27248	42 Southern Satellites	76.3	27534	26 Midland Crowd	18.6	27845	56 Rural Bypasses	52.7
27249	32 Rustbelt Traditions	29.3	27536	62 Modest Income Homes	26.2	27846	42 Southern Satellites	36.0
27252	46 Rooted Rural	74.3	27537	42 Southern Satellites	31.7	27847	56 Rural Bypasses	100.0
27253	26 Midland Crowd	46.9	27539	12 Up And Coming Families	42.6	27849	56 Rural Bypasses	100.0
27258	26 Midland Crowd	66.5	27540	12 Up And Coming Families	45.2	27850	56 Rural Bypasses	40.2
27260	53 Home Town	25.7	27541	26 Midland Crowd	50.9	27851	42 Southern Satellites	77.2
27262	32 Rustbelt Traditions	15.1	27542	46 Rooted Rural	59.0	27852	56 Rural Bypasses	31.2
27263	32 Rustbelt Traditions	22.2	27544	42 Southern Satellites	94.7	27853	56 Rural Bypasses	100.0
27265	28 Aspiring Young Families	17.1	27545	12 Up And Coming Families	65.7	27855	33 Midlife Junction	26.7
27278	17 Green Acres	18.5	27546	42 Southern Satellites	25.1	27856	42 Southern Satellites	27.6
27281	42 Southern Satellites	28.5	27549	46 Rooted Rural	31.6	27857	56 Rural Bypasses	100.0
27282	04 Boomburbs	44.2	27551	31 Rural Resort Dwellers	43.4	27858	16 Enterprising Professionals	23.9
27283	25 Salt Of The Earth	91.1	27553	56 Rural Bypasses	62.1	27860	46 Rooted Rural	99.8
27284	13 In Style	18.7	27557	42 Southern Satellites	41.9	27862	56 Rural Bypasses	89.4
27288	42 Southern Satellites	23.5	27559	42 Southern Satellites	49.3	27863	26 Midland Crowd	72.3
27291	42 Southern Satellites	38.7	27560	16 Enterprising Professionals	64.7	27864	56 Rural Bypasses	44.8
27292	42 Southern Satellites	27.9	27562	26 Midland Crowd	54.5	27865	46 Rooted Rural	94.5
27295	25 Salt Of The Earth	35.3	27563	56 Rural Bypasses	100.0	27866	56 Rural Bypasses	100.0
27298	42 Southern Satellites	52.0	27565	42 Southern Satellites	24.0	27869	56 Rural Bypasses	70.3
27299	42 Southern Satellites	98.6	27569	26 Midland Crowd	52.4	27870	56 Rural Bypasses	38.3
27301	26 Midland Crowd	35.4	27571	26 Midland Crowd	61.8	27871	56 Rural Bypasses	89.0
27302	26 Midland Crowd	37.1	27572	17 Green Acres	42.5	27872	56 Rural Bypasses	100.0
27305	42 Southern Satellites	85.2	27573	57 Simple Living	32.4	27874	56 Rural Bypasses	30.2
27306	56 Rural Bypasses	32.3	27574	25 Salt Of The Earth	33.4	27875	56 Rural Bypasses	100.0
27310	06 Sophisticated Squires	37.7	27576	42 Southern Satellites	24.5	27876	56 Rural Bypasses	100.0
27311	42 Southern Satellites	57.1	27577	26 Midland Crowd	29.4	27880	42 Southern Satellites	60.0
27312	17 Green Acres	34.6	27581	26 Midland Crowd	98.2	27882	56 Rural Bypasses	34.4
27313	17 Green Acres	47.5	27583	26 Midland Crowd	95.5	27883	42 Southern Satellites	67.5
27314	42 Southern Satellites	60.8	27587	12 Up And Coming Families	60.7	27884	42 Southern Satellites	100.0
27315	46 Rooted Rural	70.9	27589	56 Rural Bypasses	87.1	27885	46 Rooted Rural	86.1
27316	42 Southern Satellites	91.8	27591	26 Midland Crowd	37.3	27886	42 Southern Satellites	19.8
27317	42 Southern Satellites	62.0	27592	12 Up And Coming Families	64.2	27888	42 Southern Satellites	42.9
27320	42 Southern Satellites	22.5	27596	26 Midland Crowd	57.7	27889	14 Prosperous Empty Nesters	18.0
27325	42 Southern Satellites	72.6	27597	26 Midland Crowd	52.8	27890	51 Metro City Edge	41.2
27326	42 Southern Satellites	69.2	27601	64 City Commons	34.5	27891	56 Rural Bypasses	54.8
27330	26 Midland Crowd	25.5	27603	12 Up And Coming Families	25.9	27892	26 Midland Crowd	20.7
27332	26 Midland Crowd	28.9	27604	12 Up And Coming Families	28.7	27893	62 Modest Income Homes	14.1
27341	42 Southern Satellites	100.0	27605	27 Metro Renters	77.5	27896	07 Exurbanites	25.6
27343	46 Rooted Rural	61.2	27606	55 College Towns	57.8	27897	56 Rural Bypasses	100.0
27344	42 Southern Satellites	45.0	27607	22 Metropolitans	40.5	27909	26 Midland Crowd	31.9
27349	26 Midland Crowd	74.2	27608	09 Urban Chic	32.6	27910	56 Rural Bypasses	49.4
27350	42 Southern Satellites	57.6	27609	36 Old And Newcomers	19.7	27916	31 Rural Resort Dwellers	86.4
27355	42 Southern Satellites	81.2	27610	12 Up And Coming Families	19.4	27917	46 Rooted Rural	100.0
27356	42 Southern Satellites	98.1	27612	16 Enterprising Professionals	54.0	27919	46 Rooted Rural	100.0
27357	26 Midland Crowd	42.6	27613	16 Enterprising Professionals	46.2	27921	31 Rural Resort Dwellers	57.7
27358	17 Green Acres	32.2	27614	04 Boomburbs	39.8	27922	56 Rural Bypasses	100.0
27360	53 Home Town	17.8	27615	13 In Style	31.0	27923	31 Rural Resort Dwellers	83.3
27370	26 Midland Crowd	45.7	27616	12 Up And Coming Families	41.2	27924	56 Rural Bypasses	95.6
27371	42 Southern Satellites	39.9	27617	16 Enterprising Professionals	71.7	27925	56 Rural Bypasses	84.1
27376	15 Silver And Gold	47.5	27695	55 College Towns	100.0	27926	26 Midland Crowd	54.5
27377	25 Salt Of The Earth	55.8	27701	64 City Commons	27.1	27927	15 Silver And Gold	100.0
27379	56 Rural Bypasses	45.9	27703	12 Up And Coming Families	22.8	27928	56 Rural Bypasses	39.0
27401	64 City Commons	22.7	27704	48 Great Expectations	12.5	27929	17 Green Acres	78.0
27403	22 Metropolitans	24.8	27705	39 Young And Restless	21.1	27932	50 Heartland Communities	12.6
27405	48 Great Expectations	13.9	27707	39 Young And Restless	22.1	27935	46 Rooted Rural	80.2
27406	28 Aspiring Young Families	17.0	27709	33 Midlife Junction	62.5	27937	56 Rural Bypasses	67.2
27407	28 Aspiring Young Families	21.3	27712	07 Exurbanites	29.9	27938	46 Rooted Rural	81.8
27408	29 Rustbelt Retirees	19.1	27713	16 Enterprising Professionals	49.3	27939	46 Rooted Rural	100.0
27409	39 Young And Restless	41.1	27801	51 Metro City Edge	29.1	27941	31 Rural Resort Dwellers	76.3

ZIP CODE	TOP TAPESTRY CONSUMER TYPE	% 2009 HOUSE-HOLDS	ZIP CODE	TOP TAPESTRY CONSUMER TYPE	% 2009 HOUSE-HOLDS	ZIP CODE	TOP TAPESTRY CONSUMER TYPE	% 2009 HOUSE-HOLDS
27942	56 Rural Bypasses	100.0	28152	42 Southern Satellites	39.7	28387	30 Retirement Communities	21.9
27944	49 Senior Sun Seekers	37.7	28159	32 Rustbelt Traditions	73.4	28390	41 Crossroads	52.4
27946	46 Rooted Rural	83.4	28160	56 Rural Bypasses	57.9	28391	26 Midland Crowd	61.4
27947	46 Rooted Rural	43.4	28163	25 Salt Of The Earth	53.7	28392	42 Southern Satellites	66.6
27948	31 Rural Resort Dwellers	63.7	28164	26 Midland Crowd	49.2	28393	56 Rural Bypasses	61.0
27949	15 Silver And Gold	53.1	28166	25 Salt Of The Earth	39.2	28394	26 Midland Crowd	56.2
27950	26 Midland Crowd	77.9	28167	42 Southern Satellites	100.0	28395	46 Rooted Rural	77.2
27953	46 Rooted Rural	100.0	28168	42 Southern Satellites	76.9	28396	26 Midland Crowd	52.6
27954	26 Midland Crowd	75.1	28170	50 Heartland Communities	34.7	28398	56 Rural Bypasses	42.3
27956	46 Rooted Rural	100.0	28173	04 Boomburbs	44.4	28399	56 Rural Bypasses	96.0
27957	56 Rural Bypasses	50.5	28174	26 Midland Crowd	58.4	28401	62 Modest Income Homes	24.0
27958	26 Midland Crowd	62.6	28202	27 Metro Renters	56.0	28403	55 College Towns	42.3
27959	31 Rural Resort Dwellers	85.5	28203	08 Laptops And Lattes	29.6	28405	19 Milk And Cookies	23.2
27960	31 Rural Resort Dwellers	100.0	28204	27 Metro Renters	36.5	28409	07 Exurbanites	42.7
27962	46 Rooted Rural	27.1	28205	48 Great Expectations	25.3	28411	12 Up And Coming Families	39.6
27964	26 Midland Crowd	76.3	28206	52 Inner City Tenants	28.5	28412	17 Green Acres	28.3
27965	46 Rooted Rural	100.0	28207	09 Urban Chic	34.3	28420	41 Crossroads	37.3
27966	26 Midland Crowd	100.0	28208	51 Metro City Edge	43.6	28421	46 Rooted Rural	70.6
27970	56 Rural Bypasses	38.1	28209	36 Old And Newcomers	37.0	28422	41 Crossroads	44.2
27973	25 Salt Of The Earth	68.2	28210	39 Young And Restless	16.8	28423	42 Southern Satellites	88.4
27974	46 Rooted Rural	67.9	28211	08 Laptops And Lattes	18.1	28425	42 Southern Satellites	44.4
27976	25 Salt Of The Earth	76.8	28212	39 Young And Restless	36.8	28428	31 Rural Resort Dwellers	65.7
27978	46 Rooted Rural	100.0	28213	06 Sophisticated Squires	21.2	28429	26 Midland Crowd	80.9
27979	42 Southern Satellites	54.1	28214	19 Milk And Cookies	22.0	28430	56 Rural Bypasses	75.1
27980	46 Rooted Rural	54.7	28215	12 Up And Coming Families	16.9	28431	56 Rural Bypasses	56.9
27981	26 Midland Crowd	100.0	28216	12 Up And Coming Families	29.8	28432	46 Rooted Rural	61.2
27983	56 Rural Bypasses	74.2	28217	28 Aspiring Young Families	47.5	28433	56 Rural Bypasses	65.1
27986	56 Rural Bypasses	100.0	28226	02 Suburban Splendor	16.6	28434	56 Rural Bypasses	63.5
28001	25 Salt Of The Earth	32.2	28227	19 Milk And Cookies	38.2	28435	56 Rural Bypasses	74.0
28006	25 Salt Of The Earth	51.3	28262	16 Enterprising Professionals	68.4	28436	42 Southern Satellites	99.2
28012	32 Rustbelt Traditions	25.0	28269	16 Enterprising Professionals	40.2	28438	56 Rural Bypasses	100.0
28016	42 Southern Satellites	44.3	28270	04 Boomburbs	25.3	28439	56 Rural Bypasses	87.5
28018	42 Southern Satellites	100.0	28273	12 Up And Coming Families	50.6	28441	56 Rural Bypasses	92.7
28020	42 Southern Satellites	57.9	28274	09 Urban Chic	100.0	28442	56 Rural Bypasses	62.3
28021	42 Southern Satellites	43.0	28277	04 Boomburbs	48.8	28443	15 Silver And Gold	42.8
28023	26 Midland Crowd	38.0	28278	12 Up And Coming Families	44.0	28444	56 Rural Bypasses	83.5
28025	26 Midland Crowd	16.3	28301	62 Modest Income Homes	27.7	28445	31 Rural Resort Dwellers	48.7
28027	12 Up And Coming Families	44.6	28303	28 Aspiring Young Families	32.7	28447	56 Rural Bypasses	64.7
28031	16 Enterprising Professionals	33.3	28304	32 Rustbelt Traditions	24.4	28448	42 Southern Satellites	86.0
28032	53 Home Town	32.0	28305	36 Old And Newcomers	29.6	28449	31 Rural Resort Dwellers	100.0
28033	26 Midland Crowd	61.6	28306	41 Crossroads	26.4	28450	31 Rural Resort Dwellers	58.8
28034	25 Salt Of The Earth	23.3	28307	40 Military Proximity	96.8	28451	26 Midland Crowd	46.2
28036	04 Boomburbs	29.2	28308	40 Military Proximity	100.0	28452	46 Rooted Rural	83.9
28037	26 Midland Crowd	47.2	28310	40 Military Proximity	99.5	28453	42 Southern Satellites	84.0
28040	42 Southern Satellites	96.5	28311	19 Milk And Cookies	22.7	28454	56 Rural Bypasses	53.4
28043	42 Southern Satellites	45.2	28312	26 Midland Crowd	32.0	28455	42 Southern Satellites	54.7
28052	53 Home Town	23.6	28314	19 Milk And Cookies	22.5	28456	42 Southern Satellites	43.9
28054	36 Old And Newcomers	17.1	28315	33 Midlife Junction	38.7	28457	41 Crossroads	64.1
28056	06 Sophisticated Squires	18.9	28318	42 Southern Satellites	100.0	28458	42 Southern Satellites	43.2
28071	42 Southern Satellites	74.1	28320	42 Southern Satellites	48.6	28460	46 Rooted Rural	42.6
28073	42 Southern Satellites	96.5	28323	41 Crossroads	84.1	28461	33 Midlife Junction	28.7
28075	06 Sophisticated Squires	64.2	28326	41 Crossroads	67.0	28462	46 Rooted Rural	43.5
28078	04 Boomburbs	35.8	28327	26 Midland Crowd	29.6	28463	56 Rural Bypasses	65.5
28079	12 Up And Coming Families	84.5	28328	42 Southern Satellites	42.7	28464	56 Rural Bypasses	74.1
28080	42 Southern Satellites	48.5	28333	41 Crossroads	62.6	28465	31 Rural Resort Dwellers	72.1
28081	53 Home Town	28.4	28334	46 Rooted Rural	26.6	28466	42 Southern Satellites	27.2
28083	53 Home Town	23.9	28337	56 Rural Bypasses	39.3	28467	49 Senior Sun Seekers	71.9
28086	42 Southern Satellites	36.2	28338	56 Rural Bypasses	96.8	28468	15 Silver And Gold	51.4
28088	32 Rustbelt Traditions	67.1	28339	42 Southern Satellites	51.2	28469	15 Silver And Gold	36.4
28090	42 Southern Satellites	81.4	28340	56 Rural Bypasses	29.0	28470	46 Rooted Rural	50.8
28091	56 Rural Bypasses	100.0	28341	56 Rural Bypasses	56.7	28472	56 Rural Bypasses	29.8
28092	42 Southern Satellites	54.1	28343	56 Rural Bypasses	48.9	28478	42 Southern Satellites	62.6
28097	25 Salt Of The Earth	87.7	28344	42 Southern Satellites	64.3	28479	26 Midland Crowd	69.5
28098	32 Rustbelt Traditions	58.8	28345	42 Southern Satellites	38.6	28480	08 Laptops And Lattes	55.2
28103	25 Salt Of The Earth	36.5	28347	26 Midland Crowd	63.1	28501	62 Modest Income Homes	19.6
28104	12 Up And Coming Families	25.0	28348	26 Midland Crowd	47.1	28504	33 Midlife Junction	21.2
28105	06 Sophisticated Squires	19.3	28349	41 Crossroads	46.5	28508	41 Crossroads	85.3
28107	17 Green Acres	41.3	28351	42 Southern Satellites	56.6	28510	31 Rural Resort Dwellers	52.7
28110	12 Up And Coming Families	31.2	28352	26 Midland Crowd	16.1	28511	46 Rooted Rural	100.0
28112	25 Salt Of The Earth	38.0	28356	42 Southern Satellites	63.9	28512	31 Rural Resort Dwellers	64.0
28114	42 Southern Satellites	71.5	28357	56 Rural Bypasses	45.5	28513	26 Midland Crowd	31.8
28115	26 Midland Crowd	30.1	28358	41 Crossroads	20.7	28515	56 Rural Bypasses	95.8
28117	07 Exurbanites	34.4	28360	41 Crossroads	54.8	28516	31 Rural Resort Dwellers	27.0
28119	56 Rural Bypasses	88.1	28363	26 Midland Crowd	87.3	28518	46 Rooted Rural	47.3
28120	32 Rustbelt Traditions	23.3	28364	56 Rural Bypasses	44.8	28520	37 Prairie Living	100.0
28124	25 Salt Of The Earth	51.6	28365	42 Southern Satellites	63.8	28521	46 Rooted Rural	51.9
28125	26 Midland Crowd	89.2	28366	46 Rooted Rural	40.2	28523	46 Rooted Rural	47.1
28127	25 Salt Of The Earth	28.7	28369	46 Rooted Rural	57.0	28525	26 Midland Crowd	65.1
28128	25 Salt Of The Earth	31.0	28371	41 Crossroads	66.7	28526	56 Rural Bypasses	82.0
28129	25 Salt Of The Earth	47.8	28372	42 Southern Satellites	49.9	28527	46 Rooted Rural	43.9
28133	42 Southern Satellites	94.2	28373	26 Midland Crowd	74.4	28528	31 Rural Resort Dwellers	100.0
28134	12 Up And Coming Families	41.2	28374	15 Silver And Gold	67.0	28529	46 Rooted Rural	59.1
28135	56 Rural Bypasses	53.5	28376	41 Crossroads	50.6	28530	46 Rooted Rural	45.0
28137	26 Midland Crowd	50.2	28377	41 Crossroads	50.4	28531	31 Rural Resort Dwellers	100.0
28138	26 Midland Crowd	43.4	28379	56 Rural Bypasses	31.3	28532	40 Military Proximity	24.7
28139	42 Southern Satellites	53.3	28382	46 Rooted Rural	38.7	28537	37 Prairie Living	98.8
28144	48 Great Expectations	22.8	28383	56 Rural Bypasses	64.0	28538	56 Rural Bypasses	68.1
28146	26 Midland Crowd	36.9	28384	42 Southern Satellites	29.5	28539	12 Up And Coming Families	33.9
28147	26 Midland Crowd	51.2	28385	50 Heartland Communities	42.5	28540	41 Crossroads	29.4
28150	42 Southern Satellites	33.7	28386	41 Crossroads	90.7	28543	40 Military Proximity	100.0

CONSUMER TYPE

ZIP CODE	TOP TAPESTRY CONSUMER TYPE	% 2009 HOUSE-HOLDS
28544	40 Military Proximity	61.2
28546	28 Aspiring Young Families	24.1
28547	40 Military Proximity	100.0
28551	42 Southern Satellites	46.2
28552	37 Prairie Living	100.0
28553	31 Rural Resort Dwellers	100.0
28555	26 Midland Crowd	57.3
28556	49 Senior Sun Seekers	57.8
28557	26 Midland Crowd	20.6
28560	26 Midland Crowd	17.9
28562	14 Prosperous Empty Nesters	28.8
28570	26 Midland Crowd	28.8
28571	15 Silver And Gold	71.2
28572	42 Southern Satellites	91.4
28573	46 Rooted Rural	63.5
28574	26 Midland Crowd	36.1
28577	46 Rooted Rural	100.0
28578	41 Crossroads	59.2
28579	31 Rural Resort Dwellers	53.5
28580	42 Southern Satellites	53.3
28581	37 Prairie Living	100.0
28582	31 Rural Resort Dwellers	53.1
28584	31 Rural Resort Dwellers	38.2
28585	42 Southern Satellites	57.8
28586	42 Southern Satellites	85.8
28587	56 Rural Bypasses	100.0
28590	16 Enterprising Professionals	36.1
28594	15 Silver And Gold	61.4
28601	42 Southern Satellites	17.8
28602	42 Southern Satellites	20.6
28604	31 Rural Resort Dwellers	85.3
28605	31 Rural Resort Dwellers	79.9
28606	42 Southern Satellites	95.5
28607	55 College Towns	43.6
28608	63 Dorms To Diplomas	100.0
28609	42 Southern Satellites	70.7
28610	42 Southern Satellites	46.6
28611	42 Southern Satellites	91.7
28612	42 Southern Satellites	84.3
28613	42 Southern Satellites	26.0
28615	42 Southern Satellites	60.3
28617	46 Rooted Rural	98.5
28618	26 Midland Crowd	88.6
28621	42 Southern Satellites	34.9
28622	46 Rooted Rural	64.2
28623	46 Rooted Rural	62.2
28624	42 Southern Satellites	60.9
28625	26 Midland Crowd	27.3
28626	25 Salt Of The Earth	50.9
28627	31 Rural Resort Dwellers	51.3
28630	42 Southern Satellites	66.8
28631	46 Rooted Rural	98.5
28634	42 Southern Satellites	99.0
28635	42 Southern Satellites	100.0
28636	42 Southern Satellites	95.0
28637	42 Southern Satellites	86.8
28638	42 Southern Satellites	68.4
28640	46 Rooted Rural	57.6
28642	42 Southern Satellites	55.3
28643	46 Rooted Rural	100.0
28644	42 Southern Satellites	43.5
28645	42 Southern Satellites	56.4
28649	42 Southern Satellites	100.0
28650	42 Southern Satellites	41.0
28651	42 Southern Satellites	68.6
28654	42 Southern Satellites	45.1
28655	42 Southern Satellites	38.1
28657	46 Rooted Rural	69.9
28658	42 Southern Satellites	36.7
28659	42 Southern Satellites	46.9
28660	42 Southern Satellites	53.9
28663	37 Prairie Living	60.6
28665	42 Southern Satellites	75.5
28668	31 Rural Resort Dwellers	100.0
28669	42 Southern Satellites	100.0
28670	42 Southern Satellites	89.3
28672	42 Southern Satellites	100.0
28673	17 Green Acres	48.4
28675	50 Heartland Communities	40.6
28676	42 Southern Satellites	41.5
28677	26 Midland Crowd	16.5
28678	42 Southern Satellites	84.7
28679	46 Rooted Rural	84.2
28681	42 Southern Satellites	68.6
28682	31 Rural Resort Dwellers	100.0
28683	42 Southern Satellites	99.7
28684	46 Rooted Rural	49.6
28685	42 Southern Satellites	100.0
28689	42 Southern Satellites	74.2
28690	50 Heartland Communities	42.4
28692	46 Rooted Rural	75.9
28693	46 Rooted Rural	69.9
28694	46 Rooted Rural	36.9
28697	25 Salt Of The Earth	36.0
28698	46 Rooted Rural	95.5
28701	26 Midland Crowd	54.4
28702	46 Rooted Rural	95.6
28704	26 Midland Crowd	35.3
28705	46 Rooted Rural	55.3
28708	42 Southern Satellites	100.0
28709	42 Southern Satellites	55.3
28711	33 Midlife Junction	43.7
28712	46 Rooted Rural	17.8
28713	46 Rooted Rural	56.9
28714	46 Rooted Rural	57.1
28715	26 Midland Crowd	39.4
28716	46 Rooted Rural	44.7
28717	15 Silver And Gold	66.3
28718	31 Rural Resort Dwellers	100.0
28719	56 Rural Bypasses	47.3
28721	26 Midland Crowd	33.0
28722	30 Retirement Communities	31.7
28723	31 Rural Resort Dwellers	37.6
28726	42 Southern Satellites	44.7
28729	49 Senior Sun Seekers	97.8
28730	17 Green Acres	49.3
28731	15 Silver And Gold	34.6
28732	26 Midland Crowd	28.5
28733	46 Rooted Rural	100.0
28734	31 Rural Resort Dwellers	51.3
28735	31 Rural Resort Dwellers	84.5
28736	31 Rural Resort Dwellers	98.7
28739	31 Rural Resort Dwellers	19.1
28740	42 Southern Satellites	51.6
28741	31 Rural Resort Dwellers	81.4
28742	25 Salt Of The Earth	52.4
28743	56 Rural Bypasses	47.9
28745	15 Silver And Gold	100.0
28746	31 Rural Resort Dwellers	90.4
28747	42 Southern Satellites	43.0
28748	26 Midland Crowd	57.1
28751	31 Rural Resort Dwellers	99.0
28752	42 Southern Satellites	58.1
28753	46 Rooted Rural	48.9
28754	33 Midlife Junction	30.9
28756	42 Southern Satellites	90.7
28759	25 Salt Of The Earth	80.7
28761	42 Southern Satellites	91.6
28762	42 Southern Satellites	72.0
28763	31 Rural Resort Dwellers	100.0
28766	31 Rural Resort Dwellers	99.8
28768	42 Southern Satellites	33.5
28771	46 Rooted Rural	61.3
28772	42 Southern Satellites	47.6
28773	31 Rural Resort Dwellers	93.0
28774	31 Rural Resort Dwellers	91.3
28775	31 Rural Resort Dwellers	100.0
28777	46 Rooted Rural	56.7
28778	46 Rooted Rural	31.5
28779	33 Midlife Junction	43.6
28781	49 Senior Sun Seekers	98.5
28782	15 Silver And Gold	51.3
28783	46 Rooted Rural	54.7
28785	31 Rural Resort Dwellers	56.5
28786	31 Rural Resort Dwellers	30.6
28787	26 Midland Crowd	45.7
28789	46 Rooted Rural	70.4
28790	46 Rooted Rural	56.1
28791	33 Midlife Junction	23.7
28792	42 Southern Satellites	32.5
28801	55 College Towns	22.4
28803	33 Midlife Junction	17.9
28804	14 Prosperous Empty Nesters	38.9
28805	33 Midlife Junction	52.2
28806	33 Midlife Junction	24.6
28901	46 Rooted Rural	61.3
28902	31 Rural Resort Dwellers	100.0
28904	31 Rural Resort Dwellers	68.5
28905	46 Rooted Rural	64.5
28906	46 Rooted Rural	50.2
28909	31 Rural Resort Dwellers	100.0
29001	56 Rural Bypasses	60.7
29003	56 Rural Bypasses	41.9
29006	42 Southern Satellites	39.9
29009	46 Rooted Rural	53.8
29010	56 Rural Bypasses	62.4
29014	42 Southern Satellites	60.1
29015	56 Rural Bypasses	99.8
29016	26 Midland Crowd	51.5
29018	56 Rural Bypasses	84.8
29020	42 Southern Satellites	22.9
29030	46 Rooted Rural	51.0
29031	56 Rural Bypasses	83.2
29032	42 Southern Satellites	69.1
29033	48 Great Expectations	21.6
29036	07 Exurbanites	57.6
29037	42 Southern Satellites	93.3
29038	42 Southern Satellites	95.3
29039	41 Crossroads	77.8
29040	41 Crossroads	39.8
29042	56 Rural Bypasses	52.0
29044	56 Rural Bypasses	55.2
29045	26 Midland Crowd	48.5
29046	56 Rural Bypasses	100.0
29047	46 Rooted Rural	61.0
29048	56 Rural Bypasses	63.2
29051	56 Rural Bypasses	77.1
29052	34 Family Foundations	74.8
29053	41 Crossroads	93.3
29054	26 Midland Crowd	63.7
29055	42 Southern Satellites	51.5
29056	56 Rural Bypasses	100.0
29058	42 Southern Satellites	53.9
29059	56 Rural Bypasses	54.6
29061	26 Midland Crowd	24.5
29063	12 Up And Coming Families	60.5
29065	56 Rural Bypasses	100.0
29067	42 Southern Satellites	56.7
29069	56 Rural Bypasses	89.2
29070	41 Crossroads	34.1
29072	12 Up And Coming Families	36.6
29073	26 Midland Crowd	41.0
29075	25 Salt Of The Earth	54.6
29078	26 Midland Crowd	35.8
29080	56 Rural Bypasses	100.0
29081	46 Rooted Rural	98.7
29082	56 Rural Bypasses	99.2
29101	42 Southern Satellites	53.5
29102	56 Rural Bypasses	51.3
29104	56 Rural Bypasses	96.7
29105	42 Southern Satellites	90.8
29107	56 Rural Bypasses	40.2
29108	46 Rooted Rural	16.5
29111	56 Rural Bypasses	100.0
29112	56 Rural Bypasses	94.2
29113	56 Rural Bypasses	62.1
29114	56 Rural Bypasses	99.4
29115	62 Modest Income Homes	22.3
29117	55 College Towns	51.4
29118	07 Exurbanites	22.3
29123	41 Crossroads	100.0
29125	56 Rural Bypasses	54.7
29126	42 Southern Satellites	69.2
29127	31 Rural Resort Dwellers	41.8
29128	56 Rural Bypasses	81.0
29129	42 Southern Satellites	60.3
29130	56 Rural Bypasses	32.5
29133	56 Rural Bypasses	88.1
29135	56 Rural Bypasses	59.5
29137	56 Rural Bypasses	87.5
29138	42 Southern Satellites	39.9
29142	46 Rooted Rural	66.8
29145	42 Southern Satellites	70.6
29146	56 Rural Bypasses	100.0
29148	49 Senior Sun Seekers	35.0
29150	62 Modest Income Homes	17.9
29152	40 Military Proximity	100.0
29153	56 Rural Bypasses	33.8
29154	41 Crossroads	24.5
29160	26 Midland Crowd	31.0
29161	42 Southern Satellites	38.0
29162	46 Rooted Rural	54.1
29163	56 Rural Bypasses	96.7
29164	56 Rural Bypasses	50.5
29166	42 Southern Satellites	99.3
29168	41 Crossroads	52.1
29169	50 Heartland Communities	17.6
29170	19 Milk And Cookies	25.9
29172	41 Crossroads	49.7
29175	42 Southern Satellites	100.0
29178	53 Home Town	28.8
29180	56 Rural Bypasses	36.7
29201	48 Great Expectations	34.8
29203	34 Family Foundations	35.2
29204	30 Retirement Communities	17.6
29205	22 Metropolitans	32.2
29206	14 Prosperous Empty Nesters	51.4
29207	03 Connoisseurs	93.0
29208	63 Dorms To Diplomas	100.0
29209	14 Prosperous Empty Nesters	20.0

ZIP CODE	TOP TAPESTRY CONSUMER TYPE	% 2009 HOUSE-HOLDS	ZIP CODE	TOP TAPESTRY CONSUMER TYPE	% 2009 HOUSE-HOLDS	ZIP CODE	TOP TAPESTRY CONSUMER TYPE	% 2009 HOUSE-HOLDS
29210	39 Young And Restless	51.1	29511	46 Rooted Rural	33.6	29667	42 Southern Satellites	95.3
29212	12 Up And Coming Families	17.5	29512	56 Rural Bypasses	50.5	29669	42 Southern Satellites	49.5
29223	28 Aspiring Young Families	12.7	29516	56 Rural Bypasses	97.9	29670	50 Heartland Communities	23.1
29229	12 Up And Coming Families	81.1	29518	56 Rural Bypasses	100.0	29671	42 Southern Satellites	66.8
29301	56 Rural Bypasses	13.0	29520	50 Heartland Communities	16.8	29672	31 Rural Resort Dwellers	34.5
29302	32 Rustbelt Traditions	16.1	29525	56 Rural Bypasses	83.9	29673	26 Midland Crowd	30.8
29303	42 Southern Satellites	21.6	29526	26 Midland Crowd	39.3	29676	15 Silver And Gold	62.8
29306	62 Modest Income Homes	19.1	29527	41 Crossroads	37.2	29678	42 Southern Satellites	36.6
29307	14 Prosperous Empty Nesters	19.0	29530	56 Rural Bypasses	64.9	29680	12 Up And Coming Families	45.3
29316	12 Up And Coming Families	30.9	29532	42 Southern Satellites	18.4	29681	04 Boomburbs	36.5
29321	42 Southern Satellites	46.8	29536	56 Rural Bypasses	28.1	29682	42 Southern Satellites	56.4
29322	42 Southern Satellites	72.2	29540	56 Rural Bypasses	59.7	29684	42 Southern Satellites	91.9
29323	42 Southern Satellites	64.8	29541	26 Midland Crowd	41.7	29685	42 Southern Satellites	100.0
29325	56 Rural Bypasses	23.3	29543	46 Rooted Rural	90.1	29686	46 Rooted Rural	69.5
29330	42 Southern Satellites	52.6	29544	42 Southern Satellites	30.1	29687	26 Midland Crowd	22.8
29332	49 Senior Sun Seekers	56.8	29545	56 Rural Bypasses	89.3	29688	26 Midland Crowd	100.0
29334	26 Midland Crowd	20.9	29546	41 Crossroads	57.3	29689	46 Rooted Rural	54.1
29335	42 Southern Satellites	100.0	29547	56 Rural Bypasses	55.2	29690	25 Salt Of The Earth	31.8
29340	42 Southern Satellites	54.6	29550	42 Southern Satellites	31.7	29691	42 Southern Satellites	74.2
29341	26 Midland Crowd	31.7	29554	56 Rural Bypasses	92.1	29692	42 Southern Satellites	59.2
29349	42 Southern Satellites	23.2	29555	56 Rural Bypasses	80.2	29693	42 Southern Satellites	83.8
29351	42 Southern Satellites	37.8	29556	56 Rural Bypasses	54.9	29696	26 Midland Crowd	32.0
29353	56 Rural Bypasses	53.4	29560	56 Rural Bypasses	48.2	29697	42 Southern Satellites	26.9
29355	42 Southern Satellites	96.1	29563	56 Rural Bypasses	75.4	29702	42 Southern Satellites	59.9
29356	42 Southern Satellites	22.8	29564	56 Rural Bypasses	100.0	29704	26 Midland Crowd	91.6
29360	42 Southern Satellites	31.0	29565	56 Rural Bypasses	49.1	29706	42 Southern Satellites	44.5
29365	26 Midland Crowd	42.1	29566	31 Rural Resort Dwellers	61.9	29707	26 Midland Crowd	99.5
29369	26 Midland Crowd	36.6	29567	56 Rural Bypasses	93.5	29708	12 Up And Coming Families	51.6
29370	56 Rural Bypasses	58.1	29568	26 Midland Crowd	52.4	29709	42 Southern Satellites	81.5
29372	50 Heartland Communities	43.9	29569	56 Rural Bypasses	33.6	29710	26 Midland Crowd	44.1
29374	42 Southern Satellites	44.8	29570	56 Rural Bypasses	100.0	29712	26 Midland Crowd	81.7
29376	25 Salt Of The Earth	22.2	29571	56 Rural Bypasses	34.8	29714	42 Southern Satellites	100.0
29379	42 Southern Satellites	38.2	29572	15 Silver And Gold	33.8	29715	06 Sophisticated Squires	31.2
29384	42 Southern Satellites	45.4	29574	56 Rural Bypasses	70.8	29717	42 Southern Satellites	100.0
29385	26 Midland Crowd	39.1	29575	15 Silver And Gold	38.6	29718	56 Rural Bypasses	89.0
29388	42 Southern Satellites	44.0	29576	49 Senior Sun Seekers	39.4	29720	42 Southern Satellites	45.7
29401	08 Laptops And Lattes	32.7	29577	36 Old And Newcomers	20.0	29726	26 Midland Crowd	68.2
29403	62 Modest Income Homes	19.9	29579	39 Young And Restless	42.8	29727	56 Rural Bypasses	56.7
29404	40 Military Proximity	100.0	29580	56 Rural Bypasses	100.0	29728	42 Southern Satellites	41.0
29405	64 City Commons	20.2	29581	56 Rural Bypasses	76.3	29729	26 Midland Crowd	52.4
29406	28 Aspiring Young Families	46.7	29582	15 Silver And Gold	35.0	29730	26 Midland Crowd	24.9
29407	36 Old And Newcomers	16.6	29583	46 Rooted Rural	56.9	29732	17 Green Acres	28.4
29410	36 Old And Newcomers	31.1	29584	56 Rural Bypasses	85.7	29741	42 Southern Satellites	88.2
29412	33 Midlife Junction	19.5	29585	31 Rural Resort Dwellers	56.5	29742	42 Southern Satellites	90.6
29414	28 Aspiring Young Families	25.3	29588	26 Midland Crowd	38.5	29743	42 Southern Satellites	92.1
29418	52 Inner City Tenants	22.6	29590	56 Rural Bypasses	100.0	29745	26 Midland Crowd	54.1
29420	12 Up And Coming Families	58.3	29591	42 Southern Satellites	49.3	29801	62 Modest Income Homes	15.7
29426	56 Rural Bypasses	100.0	29592	56 Rural Bypasses	53.9	29803	07 Exurbanites	21.7
29429	42 Southern Satellites	37.8	29593	56 Rural Bypasses	74.8	29805	26 Midland Crowd	63.2
29431	46 Rooted Rural	38.0	29596	42 Southern Satellites	59.7	29808	41 Crossroads	100.0
29432	56 Rural Bypasses	100.0	29601	62 Modest Income Homes	34.8	29809	25 Salt Of The Earth	61.3
29434	56 Rural Bypasses	100.0	29605	22 Metropolitans	15.6	29810	56 Rural Bypasses	37.6
29435	42 Southern Satellites	46.1	29607	13 In Style	27.6	29812	56 Rural Bypasses	35.6
29436	56 Rural Bypasses	100.0	29609	22 Metropolitans	13.0	29817	56 Rural Bypasses	95.3
29437	42 Southern Satellites	79.7	29611	53 Home Town	27.9	29819	42 Southern Satellites	93.6
29438	56 Rural Bypasses	61.8	29613	18 Cozy And Comfortable	100.0	29821	46 Rooted Rural	61.2
29440	56 Rural Bypasses	38.4	29615	16 Enterprising Professionals	22.3	29824	46 Rooted Rural	31.2
29445	12 Up And Coming Families	28.0	29617	53 Home Town	26.0	29827	56 Rural Bypasses	70.1
29446	56 Rural Bypasses	100.0	29620	42 Southern Satellites	30.5	29828	56 Rural Bypasses	100.0
29448	56 Rural Bypasses	70.1	29621	06 Sophisticated Squires	16.5	29829	42 Southern Satellites	25.5
29449	56 Rural Bypasses	44.5	29624	62 Modest Income Homes	40.5	29831	41 Crossroads	38.1
29450	56 Rural Bypasses	94.6	29625	25 Salt Of The Earth	20.5	29832	56 Rural Bypasses	27.9
29451	03 Connoisseurs	74.5	29626	53 Home Town	18.8	29835	56 Rural Bypasses	50.1
29453	56 Rural Bypasses	100.0	29627	42 Southern Satellites	49.8	29836	56 Rural Bypasses	100.0
29455	56 Rural Bypasses	23.5	29628	42 Southern Satellites	39.3	29838	46 Rooted Rural	82.0
29456	19 Milk And Cookies	48.2	29630	55 College Towns	39.6	29840	15 Silver And Gold	100.0
29458	46 Rooted Rural	56.0	29631	55 College Towns	38.0	29841	33 Midlife Junction	20.6
29461	26 Midland Crowd	21.2	29632	33 Midlife Junction	85.0	29842	26 Midland Crowd	66.0
29464	13 In Style	48.4	29635	42 Southern Satellites	35.9	29843	56 Rural Bypasses	76.8
29466	04 Boomburbs	66.0	29638	42 Southern Satellites	57.9	29845	56 Rural Bypasses	74.6
29468	56 Rural Bypasses	100.0	29639	33 Midlife Junction	47.0	29847	42 Southern Satellites	83.6
29469	56 Rural Bypasses	48.3	29640	26 Midland Crowd	38.6	29848	42 Southern Satellites	82.9
29470	26 Midland Crowd	74.1	29642	17 Green Acres	27.6	29849	56 Rural Bypasses	100.0
29471	56 Rural Bypasses	100.0	29643	49 Senior Sun Seekers	45.9	29851	56 Rural Bypasses	67.5
29472	56 Rural Bypasses	62.1	29644	26 Midland Crowd	51.4	29853	56 Rural Bypasses	65.3
29474	46 Rooted Rural	42.2	29645	42 Southern Satellites	63.3	29856	41 Crossroads	97.5
29475	56 Rural Bypasses	58.2	29646	42 Southern Satellites	14.3	29860	06 Sophisticated Squires	33.2
29477	56 Rural Bypasses	99.3	29649	28 Aspiring Young Families	21.2	29902	33 Midlife Junction	38.1
29479	56 Rural Bypasses	87.1	29650	06 Sophisticated Squires	15.2	29906	41 Crossroads	43.7
29481	56 Rural Bypasses	88.8	29651	26 Midland Crowd	35.8	29907	12 Up And Coming Families	43.0
29482	09 Urban Chic	100.0	29653	42 Southern Satellites	50.6	29909	15 Silver And Gold	92.1
29483	26 Midland Crowd	24.7	29654	42 Southern Satellites	58.8	29910	15 Silver And Gold	38.7
29485	26 Midland Crowd	26.4	29655	42 Southern Satellites	43.1	29911	56 Rural Bypasses	100.0
29487	46 Rooted Rural	100.0	29657	42 Southern Satellites	68.1	29915	17 Green Acres	100.0
29488	41 Crossroads	26.6	29658	46 Rooted Rural	79.4	29916	56 Rural Bypasses	51.8
29492	12 Up And Coming Families	99.6	29659	42 Southern Satellites	100.0	29918	56 Rural Bypasses	84.3
29501	26 Midland Crowd	12.4	29661	42 Southern Satellites	88.2	29920	56 Rural Bypasses	60.5
29505	26 Midland Crowd	26.5	29662	13 In Style	30.3	29922	56 Rural Bypasses	100.0
29506	41 Crossroads	29.6	29664	31 Rural Resort Dwellers	56.8	29924	56 Rural Bypasses	51.0
29510	56 Rural Bypasses	66.5	29666	42 Southern Satellites	41.0	29926	15 Silver And Gold	66.0

CONSUMER TYPE

ZIP CODE	TOP TAPESTRY CONSUMER TYPE	% 2009 HOUSE-HOLDS
29927	41 Crossroads	53.5
29928	15 Silver And Gold	63.7
29929	56 Rural Bypasses	100.0
29932	56 Rural Bypasses	100.0
29934	56 Rural Bypasses	78.5
29935	48 Great Expectations	67.0
29936	56 Rural Bypasses	49.5
29940	56 Rural Bypasses	71.8
29941	56 Rural Bypasses	100.0
29943	42 Southern Satellites	53.4
29944	56 Rural Bypasses	62.4
29945	56 Rural Bypasses	98.4
30002	22 Metropolitans	48.5
30004	04 Boomburbs	37.8
30005	04 Boomburbs	75.1
30008	12 Up And Coming Families	31.1
30009	16 Enterprising Professionals	53.8
30011	12 Up And Coming Families	96.9
30012	28 Aspiring Young Families	16.8
30013	16 Enterprising Professionals	20.5
30014	26 Midland Crowd	26.0
30016	24 Main Street, USA	38.5
30017	12 Up And Coming Families	78.8
30019	12 Up And Coming Families	82.6
30021	52 Inner City Tenants	35.1
30022	04 Boomburbs	56.3
30024	04 Boomburbs	82.5
30025	26 Midland Crowd	70.6
30028	12 Up And Coming Families	90.1
30030	22 Metropolitans	49.6
30032	34 Family Foundations	33.0
30033	27 Metro Renters	33.7
30034	28 Aspiring Young Families	28.9
30035	28 Aspiring Young Families	40.4
30038	28 Aspiring Young Families	26.6
30039	06 Sophisticated Squires	65.9
30040	12 Up And Coming Families	38.0
30041	12 Up And Coming Families	38.0
30043	12 Up And Coming Families	51.0
30044	12 Up And Coming Families	46.5
30045	12 Up And Coming Families	59.4
30047	06 Sophisticated Squires	33.4
30052	12 Up And Coming Families	68.8
30054	17 Green Acres	47.3
30055	26 Midland Crowd	71.2
30056	42 Southern Satellites	53.6
30058	12 Up And Coming Families	49.9
30060	60 City Dimensions	15.2
30062	02 Suburban Splendor	32.0
30064	06 Sophisticated Squires	32.5
30066	06 Sophisticated Squires	40.0
30067	39 Young And Restless	60.1
30068	02 Suburban Splendor	39.9
30069	40 Military Proximity	100.0
30071	28 Aspiring Young Families	40.9
30075	02 Suburban Splendor	37.1
30076	39 Young And Restless	25.9
30078	06 Sophisticated Squires	33.8
30079	64 City Commons	34.6
30080	39 Young And Restless	39.1
30082	28 Aspiring Young Families	21.1
30083	19 Milk And Cookies	33.9
30084	13 In Style	31.2
30087	12 Up And Coming Families	28.7
30088	19 Milk And Cookies	49.6
30092	39 Young And Restless	36.0
30093	39 Young And Restless	43.2
30094	06 Sophisticated Squires	30.2
30096	16 Enterprising Professionals	40.7
30097	04 Boomburbs	83.2
30101	12 Up And Coming Families	54.7
30102	12 Up And Coming Families	43.7
30103	42 Southern Satellites	33.2
30104	42 Southern Satellites	76.4
30105	25 Salt Of The Earth	53.4
30106	12 Up And Coming Families	30.4
30107	17 Green Acres	48.8
30108	42 Southern Satellites	66.8
30110	42 Southern Satellites	80.9
30113	42 Southern Satellites	100.0
30114	19 Milk And Cookies	16.9
30115	17 Green Acres	51.6
30116	26 Midland Crowd	74.4
30117	26 Midland Crowd	22.7
30118	55 College Towns	100.0
30120	26 Midland Crowd	20.4
30121	26 Midland Crowd	35.3
30122	19 Milk And Cookies	23.8
30124	46 Rooted Rural	56.2
30125	42 Southern Satellites	52.5

ZIP CODE	TOP TAPESTRY CONSUMER TYPE	% 2009 HOUSE-HOLDS
30126	19 Milk And Cookies	25.6
30127	12 Up And Coming Families	34.7
30132	12 Up And Coming Families	40.7
30134	12 Up And Coming Families	32.8
30135	19 Milk And Cookies	44.7
30137	26 Midland Crowd	74.6
30139	42 Southern Satellites	85.4
30141	12 Up And Coming Families	54.2
30143	26 Midland Crowd	37.7
30144	12 Up And Coming Families	41.9
30145	12 Up And Coming Families	43.7
30147	32 Rustbelt Traditions	33.9
30148	42 Southern Satellites	58.2
30149	55 College Towns	100.0
30152	12 Up And Coming Families	66.3
30153	42 Southern Satellites	39.0
30157	12 Up And Coming Families	46.2
30161	53 Home Town	15.7
30165	33 Midlife Junction	33.2
30168	39 Young And Restless	24.7
30170	26 Midland Crowd	76.8
30171	26 Midland Crowd	92.8
30173	26 Midland Crowd	40.5
30175	26 Midland Crowd	55.2
30176	42 Southern Satellites	58.9
30177	42 Southern Satellites	98.7
30178	26 Midland Crowd	53.7
30179	26 Midland Crowd	76.0
30180	26 Midland Crowd	45.4
30182	42 Southern Satellites	87.2
30183	31 Rural Resort Dwellers	54.2
30184	26 Midland Crowd	91.7
30185	26 Midland Crowd	58.7
30187	17 Green Acres	76.4
30188	12 Up And Coming Families	32.7
30189	04 Boomburbs	48.3
30204	42 Southern Satellites	20.5
30205	17 Green Acres	46.5
30206	26 Midland Crowd	99.3
30213	18 Cozy And Comfortable	36.9
30214	07 Exurbanites	61.5
30215	06 Sophisticated Squires	40.5
30216	46 Rooted Rural	41.4
30217	42 Southern Satellites	74.0
30218	42 Southern Satellites	55.8
30220	42 Southern Satellites	66.9
30222	56 Rural Bypasses	86.6
30223	26 Midland Crowd	18.0
30224	48 Great Expectations	23.7
30228	12 Up And Coming Families	32.1
30230	42 Southern Satellites	56.3
30233	26 Midland Crowd	33.6
30234	42 Southern Satellites	96.0
30236	52 Inner City Tenants	25.0
30238	12 Up And Coming Families	48.6
30240	17 Green Acres	22.4
30241	28 Aspiring Young Families	15.3
30248	26 Midland Crowd	51.4
30251	42 Southern Satellites	74.5
30252	12 Up And Coming Families	36.1
30253	12 Up And Coming Families	43.8
30256	46 Rooted Rural	45.7
30257	26 Midland Crowd	61.5
30258	26 Midland Crowd	75.3
30259	17 Green Acres	94.7
30260	28 Aspiring Young Families	26.3
30263	26 Midland Crowd	23.5
30265	12 Up And Coming Families	63.4
30268	26 Midland Crowd	39.1
30269	04 Boomburbs	39.2
30273	19 Milk And Cookies	80.7
30274	28 Aspiring Young Families	58.3
30276	19 Milk And Cookies	48.2
30277	12 Up And Coming Families	61.7
30281	17 Green Acres	31.6
30285	42 Southern Satellites	75.5
30286	42 Southern Satellites	20.4
30288	32 Rustbelt Traditions	26.1
30290	17 Green Acres	44.3
30291	28 Aspiring Young Families	28.1
30292	26 Midland Crowd	59.9
30293	56 Rural Bypasses	62.3
30294	19 Milk And Cookies	41.8
30295	26 Midland Crowd	54.5
30296	28 Aspiring Young Families	46.5
30297	32 Rustbelt Traditions	33.2
30303	27 Metro Renters	68.4
30305	27 Metro Renters	31.4
30306	08 Laptops And Lattes	47.3
30307	08 Laptops And Lattes	34.5

ZIP CODE	TOP TAPESTRY CONSUMER TYPE	% 2009 HOUSE-HOLDS
30308	27 Metro Renters	87.2
30309	27 Metro Renters	76.6
30310	34 Family Foundations	28.2
30311	64 City Commons	36.1
30312	64 City Commons	23.0
30313	27 Metro Renters	46.7
30314	62 Modest Income Homes	44.0
30315	64 City Commons	35.8
30316	34 Family Foundations	25.4
30317	34 Family Foundations	40.1
30318	62 Modest Income Homes	21.5
30319	27 Metro Renters	16.8
30322	65 Social Security Set	100.0
30324	27 Metro Renters	44.3
30326	27 Metro Renters	53.1
30327	01 Top Rung	59.8
30328	16 Enterprising Professionals	30.1
30329	27 Metro Renters	62.3
30330	40 Military Proximity	100.0
30331	51 Metro City Edge	24.2
30334	27 Metro Renters	100.0
30336	06 Sophisticated Squires	47.4
30337	52 Inner City Tenants	44.9
30338	03 Connoisseurs	36.1
30339	27 Metro Renters	36.5
30340	39 Young And Restless	30.2
30341	36 Old And Newcomers	23.1
30342	27 Metro Renters	37.7
30344	52 Inner City Tenants	25.7
30345	05 Wealthy Seaboard Suburbs	24.3
30346	27 Metro Renters	100.0
30349	28 Aspiring Young Families	22.6
30350	39 Young And Restless	46.9
30354	51 Metro City Edge	23.9
30360	16 Enterprising Professionals	33.4
30363	08 Laptops And Lattes	100.0
30401	56 Rural Bypasses	32.4
30410	41 Crossroads	49.3
30411	42 Southern Satellites	47.0
30413	56 Rural Bypasses	100.0
30415	26 Midland Crowd	57.7
30417	56 Rural Bypasses	36.8
30420	46 Rooted Rural	53.3
30421	56 Rural Bypasses	59.5
30425	56 Rural Bypasses	56.0
30426	56 Rural Bypasses	100.0
30427	41 Crossroads	21.9
30428	56 Rural Bypasses	92.9
30434	56 Rural Bypasses	68.2
30436	41 Crossroads	32.5
30438	42 Southern Satellites	73.4
30439	56 Rural Bypasses	46.0
30441	56 Rural Bypasses	70.7
30442	56 Rural Bypasses	71.6
30445	56 Rural Bypasses	48.9
30446	56 Rural Bypasses	87.6
30450	56 Rural Bypasses	93.3
30452	41 Crossroads	65.7
30453	41 Crossroads	43.2
30454	56 Rural Bypasses	67.9
30455	42 Southern Satellites	98.7
30456	56 Rural Bypasses	100.0
30457	56 Rural Bypasses	100.0
30458	63 Dorms To Diplomas	21.9
30461	26 Midland Crowd	28.4
30467	56 Rural Bypasses	49.8
30470	42 Southern Satellites	57.5
30471	56 Rural Bypasses	92.4
30473	42 Southern Satellites	35.6
30474	41 Crossroads	26.5
30477	56 Rural Bypasses	75.5
30501	57 Simple Living	13.4
30504	52 Inner City Tenants	33.8
30506	17 Green Acres	47.0
30507	38 Industrious Urban Fringe	47.3
30510	42 Southern Satellites	90.4
30511	42 Southern Satellites	80.8
30512	31 Rural Resort Dwellers	66.3
30513	31 Rural Resort Dwellers	33.1
30516	42 Southern Satellites	76.3
30517	26 Midland Crowd	57.4
30518	12 Up And Coming Families	44.8
30519	12 Up And Coming Families	91.5
30520	42 Southern Satellites	42.7
30521	42 Southern Satellites	62.4
30522	31 Rural Resort Dwellers	80.5
30523	25 Salt Of The Earth	23.5
30525	31 Rural Resort Dwellers	29.9
30527	25 Salt Of The Earth	42.7
30528	26 Midland Crowd	63.2

ZIP CODE	TOP TAPESTRY CONSUMER TYPE	% 2009 HOUSE-HOLDS	ZIP CODE	TOP TAPESTRY CONSUMER TYPE	% 2009 HOUSE-HOLDS	ZIP CODE	TOP TAPESTRY CONSUMER TYPE	% 2009 HOUSE-HOLDS
30529	26 Midland Crowd	52.1	30730	42 Southern Satellites	100.0	31057	56 Rural Bypasses	100.0
30530	42 Southern Satellites	67.1	30731	46 Rooted Rural	50.2	31058	41 Crossroads	42.6
30531	42 Southern Satellites	36.0	30733	42 Southern Satellites	69.5	31060	56 Rural Bypasses	69.9
30533	26 Midland Crowd	74.7	30734	42 Southern Satellites	100.0	31061	26 Midland Crowd	21.2
30534	26 Midland Crowd	45.8	30735	42 Southern Satellites	77.7	31063	56 Rural Bypasses	43.7
30535	42 Southern Satellites	45.4	30736	26 Midland Crowd	35.3	31064	25 Salt Of The Earth	47.2
30536	42 Southern Satellites	37.4	30738	42 Southern Satellites	38.6	31065	56 Rural Bypasses	49.7
30537	31 Rural Resort Dwellers	61.0	30739	25 Salt Of The Earth	49.3	31066	46 Rooted Rural	57.7
30538	42 Southern Satellites	99.0	30740	26 Midland Crowd	24.8	31068	56 Rural Bypasses	82.8
30539	42 Southern Satellites	100.0	30741	50 Heartland Communities	26.3	31069	17 Green Acres	19.4
30540	42 Southern Satellites	69.4	30742	33 Midlife Junction	36.4	31070	56 Rural Bypasses	87.8
30541	25 Salt Of The Earth	64.7	30746	42 Southern Satellites	100.0	31071	56 Rural Bypasses	100.0
30542	12 Up And Coming Families	41.4	30747	42 Southern Satellites	61.6	31072	46 Rooted Rural	55.5
30543	42 Southern Satellites	43.4	30750	26 Midland Crowd	52.4	31075	42 Southern Satellites	100.0
30545	31 Rural Resort Dwellers	100.0	30751	42 Southern Satellites	100.0	31076	56 Rural Bypasses	92.4
30546	31 Rural Resort Dwellers	37.4	30752	42 Southern Satellites	93.1	31077	46 Rooted Rural	60.5
30547	42 Southern Satellites	100.0	30753	42 Southern Satellites	71.3	31078	56 Rural Bypasses	68.8
30548	26 Midland Crowd	69.6	30755	42 Southern Satellites	52.5	31079	56 Rural Bypasses	50.0
30549	26 Midland Crowd	79.7	30757	26 Midland Crowd	95.0	31081	46 Rooted Rural	100.0
30552	42 Southern Satellites	62.9	30802	26 Midland Crowd	72.3	31082	56 Rural Bypasses	31.2
30553	31 Rural Resort Dwellers	42.1	30803	42 Southern Satellites	92.6	31085	42 Southern Satellites	72.6
30554	42 Southern Satellites	50.2	30805	26 Midland Crowd	45.7	31087	56 Rural Bypasses	40.2
30555	50 Heartland Communities	55.5	30807	56 Rural Bypasses	100.0	31088	12 Up And Coming Families	40.5
30557	42 Southern Satellites	52.9	30808	41 Crossroads	51.3	31089	56 Rural Bypasses	93.5
30558	26 Midland Crowd	55.8	30809	04 Boomburbs	49.6	31090	56 Rural Bypasses	92.1
30559	46 Rooted Rural	100.0	30810	50 Heartland Communities	48.9	31091	56 Rural Bypasses	99.1
30560	46 Rooted Rural	51.1	30813	26 Midland Crowd	41.2	31092	56 Rural Bypasses	43.1
30563	25 Salt Of The Earth	42.3	30814	26 Midland Crowd	97.2	31093	32 Rustbelt Traditions	17.4
30564	26 Midland Crowd	65.9	30815	19 Milk And Cookies	29.0	31094	56 Rural Bypasses	82.6
30565	26 Midland Crowd	58.8	30816	56 Rural Bypasses	66.9	31096	56 Rural Bypasses	100.0
30566	28 Aspiring Young Families	44.0	30817	46 Rooted Rural	46.9	31097	42 Southern Satellites	87.6
30567	26 Midland Crowd	100.0	30818	26 Midland Crowd	63.3	31098	40 Military Proximity	87.6
30568	42 Southern Satellites	44.0	30820	46 Rooted Rural	74.7	31201	62 Modest Income Homes	30.8
30571	31 Rural Resort Dwellers	100.0	30821	56 Rural Bypasses	100.0	31204	62 Modest Income Homes	25.2
30572	31 Rural Resort Dwellers	100.0	30822	42 Southern Satellites	72.7	31206	51 Metro City Edge	21.2
30575	26 Midland Crowd	82.7	30823	56 Rural Bypasses	71.1	31210	13 In Style	20.5
30576	31 Rural Resort Dwellers	60.5	30824	42 Southern Satellites	19.1	31211	26 Midland Crowd	16.7
30577	25 Salt Of The Earth	23.9	30828	56 Rural Bypasses	77.6	31216	18 Cozy And Comfortable	38.1
30582	49 Senior Sun Seekers	87.7	30830	51 Metro City Edge	20.9	31217	62 Modest Income Homes	20.2
30597	26 Midland Crowd	0.0	30833	56 Rural Bypasses	29.6	31220	17 Green Acres	28.5
30601	64 City Commons	21.2	30901	62 Modest Income Homes	46.6	31301	41 Crossroads	99.5
30602	63 Dorms To Diplomas	100.0	30904	48 Great Expectations	26.4	31302	26 Midland Crowd	54.6
30605	55 College Towns	31.4	30905	40 Military Proximity	97.3	31303	26 Midland Crowd	84.6
30606	13 In Style	25.0	30906	34 Family Foundations	22.2	31304	56 Rural Bypasses	100.0
30607	28 Aspiring Young Families	38.5	30907	19 Milk And Cookies	14.9	31305	56 Rural Bypasses	45.4
30609	63 Dorms To Diplomas	100.0	30909	39 Young And Restless	20.5	31308	26 Midland Crowd	64.2
30619	56 Rural Bypasses	49.3	31001	56 Rural Bypasses	100.0	31309	41 Crossroads	100.0
30620	26 Midland Crowd	65.6	31002	56 Rural Bypasses	63.1	31312	26 Midland Crowd	85.7
30621	17 Green Acres	60.2	31003	46 Rooted Rural	100.0	31313	28 Aspiring Young Families	73.6
30622	07 Exurbanites	36.5	31005	06 Sophisticated Squires	31.9	31314	40 Military Proximity	94.4
30624	42 Southern Satellites	51.9	31006	56 Rural Bypasses	56.7	31315	40 Military Proximity	100.0
30625	25 Salt Of The Earth	87.7	31007	56 Rural Bypasses	100.0	31316	41 Crossroads	91.3
30627	42 Southern Satellites	76.7	31008	26 Midland Crowd	62.5	31319	56 Rural Bypasses	100.0
30628	26 Midland Crowd	98.3	31009	42 Southern Satellites	52.5	31320	41 Crossroads	47.5
30629	42 Southern Satellites	79.9	31011	56 Rural Bypasses	85.7	31321	41 Crossroads	51.5
30630	46 Rooted Rural	38.1	31012	56 Rural Bypasses	64.6	31322	26 Midland Crowd	37.3
30631	56 Rural Bypasses	93.6	31014	42 Southern Satellites	35.8	31323	56 Rural Bypasses	100.0
30633	42 Southern Satellites	65.0	31015	42 Southern Satellites	18.6	31324	06 Sophisticated Squires	54.1
30634	42 Southern Satellites	50.9	31016	46 Rooted Rural	53.2	31326	12 Up And Coming Families	55.4
30635	42 Southern Satellites	37.1	31017	56 Rural Bypasses	62.1	31328	31 Rural Resort Dwellers	100.0
30641	25 Salt Of The Earth	56.1	31018	56 Rural Bypasses	100.0	31329	26 Midland Crowd	91.7
30642	15 Silver And Gold	43.1	31019	42 Southern Satellites	58.2	31331	31 Rural Resort Dwellers	39.4
30643	31 Rural Resort Dwellers	27.9	31020	56 Rural Bypasses	43.4	31401	55 College Towns	28.3
30646	26 Midland Crowd	63.8	31021	26 Midland Crowd	23.0	31404	51 Metro City Edge	30.1
30648	42 Southern Satellites	60.4	31022	25 Salt Of The Earth	80.5	31405	34 Family Foundations	13.2
30650	26 Midland Crowd	42.2	31023	42 Southern Satellites	36.6	31406	19 Milk And Cookies	11.5
30655	56 Rural Bypasses	24.0	31024	31 Rural Resort Dwellers	51.1	31407	32 Rustbelt Traditions	52.3
30656	26 Midland Crowd	33.4	31025	42 Southern Satellites	56.5	31408	51 Metro City Edge	21.0
30660	56 Rural Bypasses	39.1	31027	56 Rural Bypasses	63.5	31409	40 Military Proximity	100.0
30662	42 Southern Satellites	49.8	31028	12 Up And Coming Families	36.6	31410	13 In Style	18.7
30663	26 Midland Crowd	58.3	31029	26 Midland Crowd	48.4	31411	15 Silver And Gold	100.0
30666	26 Midland Crowd	53.9	31030	56 Rural Bypasses	22.7	31415	62 Modest Income Homes	46.6
30667	46 Rooted Rural	100.0	31031	56 Rural Bypasses	39.3	31419	16 Enterprising Professionals	18.1
30668	56 Rural Bypasses	78.9	31032	26 Midland Crowd	42.6	31501	50 Heartland Communities	26.1
30669	56 Rural Bypasses	95.1	31033	26 Midland Crowd	65.2	31503	42 Southern Satellites	28.1
30673	56 Rural Bypasses	32.2	31035	56 Rural Bypasses	100.0	31510	42 Southern Satellites	53.5
30677	17 Green Acres	62.9	31036	46 Rooted Rural	25.6	31512	42 Southern Satellites	80.3
30678	31 Rural Resort Dwellers	71.0	31037	56 Rural Bypasses	87.6	31513	42 Southern Satellites	39.3
30680	26 Midland Crowd	42.8	31038	42 Southern Satellites	62.1	31516	41 Crossroads	31.4
30683	26 Midland Crowd	86.9	31041	56 Rural Bypasses	99.5	31518	46 Rooted Rural	59.8
30701	42 Southern Satellites	43.3	31042	56 Rural Bypasses	90.3	31519	42 Southern Satellites	76.1
30705	42 Southern Satellites	59.5	31044	56 Rural Bypasses	99.6	31520	62 Modest Income Homes	22.5
30707	42 Southern Satellites	62.6	31045	56 Rural Bypasses	100.0	31522	07 Exurbanites	22.8
30708	42 Southern Satellites	100.0	31046	26 Midland Crowd	55.2	31523	26 Midland Crowd	70.0
30710	17 Green Acres	47.7	31047	17 Green Acres	44.9	31525	26 Midland Crowd	38.4
30711	42 Southern Satellites	100.0	31049	56 Rural Bypasses	89.3	31527	15 Silver And Gold	100.0
30720	13 In Style	13.8	31050	26 Midland Crowd	97.5	31532	42 Southern Satellites	72.6
30721	42 Southern Satellites	30.7	31052	17 Green Acres	32.7	31533	42 Southern Satellites	50.2
30725	25 Salt Of The Earth	46.9	31054	46 Rooted Rural	67.8	31535	41 Crossroads	52.6
30728	42 Southern Satellites	52.2	31055	56 Rural Bypasses	60.8	31537	56 Rural Bypasses	67.5

CONSUMER TYPE

ZIP CODE	TOP TAPESTRY CONSUMER TYPE	% 2009 HOUSE-HOLDS	ZIP CODE	TOP TAPESTRY CONSUMER TYPE	% 2009 HOUSE-HOLDS	ZIP CODE	TOP TAPESTRY CONSUMER TYPE	% 2009 HOUSE-HOLDS
31539	42 Southern Satellites	35.5	31783	42 Southern Satellites	99.2	32112	49 Senior Sun Seekers	45.4
31542	46 Rooted Rural	70.4	31784	37 Prairie Living	51.4	32113	46 Rooted Rural	58.4
31543	42 Southern Satellites	53.1	31787	56 Rural Bypasses	86.9	32114	55 College Towns	19.9
31544	56 Rural Bypasses	100.0	31788	42 Southern Satellites	38.2	32117	32 Rustbelt Traditions	19.9
31545	41 Crossroads	31.5	31789	42 Southern Satellites	100.0	32118	36 Old And Newcomers	30.5
31546	46 Rooted Rural	34.4	31790	46 Rooted Rural	68.7	32119	15 Silver And Gold	19.8
31547	40 Military Proximity	100.0	31791	51 Metro City Edge	21.4	32124	17 Green Acres	100.0
31548	12 Up And Coming Families	36.4	31792	62 Modest Income Homes	20.3	32127	49 Senior Sun Seekers	23.3
31549	56 Rural Bypasses	100.0	31793	26 Midland Crowd	50.7	32128	15 Silver And Gold	93.5
31550	46 Rooted Rural	91.6	31794	26 Midland Crowd	15.2	32129	49 Senior Sun Seekers	34.2
31551	42 Southern Satellites	100.0	31795	42 Southern Satellites	72.8	32130	38 Industrious Urban Fringe	44.7
31552	42 Southern Satellites	98.1	31796	46 Rooted Rural	78.6	32131	31 Rural Resort Dwellers	33.6
31553	56 Rural Bypasses	53.5	31798	46 Rooted Rural	77.8	32132	29 Rustbelt Retirees	42.4
31554	41 Crossroads	38.2	31801	56 Rural Bypasses	52.5	32134	49 Senior Sun Seekers	57.1
31555	26 Midland Crowd	57.3	31803	56 Rural Bypasses	51.1	32136	15 Silver And Gold	70.5
31557	42 Southern Satellites	96.8	31804	17 Green Acres	99.4	32137	15 Silver And Gold	54.1
31558	12 Up And Coming Families	52.7	31805	41 Crossroads	89.9	32139	49 Senior Sun Seekers	79.2
31560	56 Rural Bypasses	52.7	31806	42 Southern Satellites	99.8	32140	42 Southern Satellites	87.3
31561	15 Silver And Gold	100.0	31807	17 Green Acres	100.0	32141	49 Senior Sun Seekers	40.9
31562	42 Southern Satellites	100.0	31808	17 Green Acres	74.0	32145	41 Crossroads	59.4
31563	56 Rural Bypasses	50.0	31811	26 Midland Crowd	33.5	32148	46 Rooted Rural	38.9
31565	46 Rooted Rural	96.8	31812	56 Rural Bypasses	100.0	32159	43 The Elders	65.5
31566	41 Crossroads	97.2	31815	56 Rural Bypasses	100.0	32162	49 Senior Sun Seekers	58.8
31567	42 Southern Satellites	85.3	31816	50 Heartland Communities	28.5	32164	31 Rural Resort Dwellers	43.1
31568	56 Rural Bypasses	80.8	31820	17 Green Acres	31.3	32168	57 Simple Living	20.0
31569	26 Midland Crowd	67.6	31821	56 Rural Bypasses	100.0	32169	15 Silver And Gold	83.5
31601	62 Modest Income Homes	24.4	31822	31 Rural Resort Dwellers	34.9	32174	49 Senior Sun Seekers	22.2
31602	28 Aspiring Young Families	27.2	31823	25 Salt Of The Earth	100.0	32176	15 Silver And Gold	46.6
31605	28 Aspiring Young Families	22.6	31824	56 Rural Bypasses	100.0	32177	57 Simple Living	23.6
31606	26 Midland Crowd	46.2	31825	56 Rural Bypasses	100.0	32179	49 Senior Sun Seekers	57.8
31620	42 Southern Satellites	35.4	31826	42 Southern Satellites	78.1	32180	46 Rooted Rural	100.0
31622	56 Rural Bypasses	63.5	31827	56 Rural Bypasses	100.0	32181	49 Senior Sun Seekers	98.2
31623	42 Southern Satellites	100.0	31829	06 Sophisticated Squires	100.0	32187	49 Senior Sun Seekers	74.6
31624	42 Southern Satellites	99.6	31830	56 Rural Bypasses	54.8	32189	49 Senior Sun Seekers	79.6
31625	56 Rural Bypasses	100.0	31831	56 Rural Bypasses	49.7	32190	46 Rooted Rural	100.0
31626	56 Rural Bypasses	86.2	31832	56 Rural Bypasses	100.0	32193	49 Senior Sun Seekers	100.0
31629	56 Rural Bypasses	100.0	31833	46 Rooted Rural	33.1	32195	26 Midland Crowd	41.5
31630	56 Rural Bypasses	99.6	31836	56 Rural Bypasses	100.0	32202	65 Social Security Set	87.5
31631	56 Rural Bypasses	100.0	31901	64 City Commons	26.2	32204	65 Social Security Set	28.9
31632	26 Midland Crowd	59.7	31903	51 Metro City Edge	28.7	32205	48 Great Expectations	20.0
31634	56 Rural Bypasses	85.8	31904	06 Sophisticated Squires	14.7	32206	62 Modest Income Homes	41.5
31635	56 Rural Bypasses	24.7	31905	40 Military Proximity	99.8	32207	48 Great Expectations	13.5
31636	26 Midland Crowd	47.2	31906	62 Modest Income Homes	22.4	32208	34 Family Foundations	52.3
31637	56 Rural Bypasses	53.3	31907	34 Family Foundations	26.4	32209	62 Modest Income Homes	56.7
31638	56 Rural Bypasses	87.1	31909	19 Milk And Cookies	29.9	32210	32 Rustbelt Traditions	22.6
31639	42 Southern Satellites	30.5	32003	06 Sophisticated Squires	100.0	32211	32 Rustbelt Traditions	25.3
31641	42 Southern Satellites	84.9	32008	46 Rooted Rural	71.8	32214	40 Military Proximity	100.0
31642	41 Crossroads	39.2	32009	26 Midland Crowd	100.0	32216	52 Inner City Tenants	30.7
31643	56 Rural Bypasses	47.7	32011	26 Midland Crowd	64.0	32217	13 In Style	31.0
31645	41 Crossroads	89.7	32013	46 Rooted Rural	68.8	32218	19 Milk And Cookies	30.7
31647	41 Crossroads	37.2	32024	26 Midland Crowd	34.5	32219	26 Midland Crowd	29.2
31648	41 Crossroads	100.0	32025	33 Midlife Junction	36.8	32220	26 Midland Crowd	80.8
31649	42 Southern Satellites	55.3	32033	29 Rustbelt Retirees	68.1	32221	26 Midland Crowd	32.2
31650	56 Rural Bypasses	65.8	32034	26 Midland Crowd	27.7	32222	41 Crossroads	47.6
31699	41 Crossroads	100.0	32038	46 Rooted Rural	66.1	32223	07 Exurbanites	36.6
31701	62 Modest Income Homes	39.8	32040	41 Crossroads	58.6	32224	16 Enterprising Professionals	66.0
31704	40 Military Proximity	100.0	32043	26 Midland Crowd	37.0	32225	12 Up And Coming Families	51.3
31705	64 City Commons	18.9	32044	41 Crossroads	93.3	32226	17 Green Acres	50.3
31707	14 Prosperous Empty Nesters	22.5	32046	42 Southern Satellites	56.2	32233	28 Aspiring Young Families	37.1
31709	48 Great Expectations	23.2	32052	56 Rural Bypasses	55.9	32234	26 Midland Crowd	66.7
31711	26 Midland Crowd	72.1	32053	42 Southern Satellites	46.5	32244	19 Milk And Cookies	36.2
31712	42 Southern Satellites	89.2	32054	41 Crossroads	45.4	32246	28 Aspiring Young Families	54.2
31714	46 Rooted Rural	37.9	32055	56 Rural Bypasses	31.1	32250	13 In Style	39.3
31716	26 Midland Crowd	48.9	32058	46 Rooted Rural	44.5	32254	51 Metro City Edge	46.0
31719	51 Metro City Edge	29.5	32059	46 Rooted Rural	100.0	32256	39 Young And Restless	42.6
31721	07 Exurbanites	32.0	32060	46 Rooted Rural	58.1	32257	28 Aspiring Young Families	60.8
31730	56 Rural Bypasses	36.1	32061	26 Midland Crowd	100.0	32258	06 Sophisticated Squires	41.0
31733	17 Green Acres	53.0	32062	46 Rooted Rural	100.0	32259	04 Boomburbs	60.2
31735	31 Rural Resort Dwellers	100.0	32063	26 Midland Crowd	48.5	32266	13 In Style	58.7
31738	56 Rural Bypasses	56.5	32064	46 Rooted Rural	21.8	32277	28 Aspiring Young Families	52.0
31743	56 Rural Bypasses	51.3	32065	19 Milk And Cookies	37.3	32301	55 College Towns	37.5
31744	42 Southern Satellites	47.8	32066	46 Rooted Rural	85.2	32303	55 College Towns	30.3
31749	41 Crossroads	49.8	32068	26 Midland Crowd	42.8	32304	63 Dorms To Diplomas	67.2
31750	56 Rural Bypasses	24.1	32071	46 Rooted Rural	100.0	32305	26 Midland Crowd	31.5
31756	42 Southern Satellites	100.0	32073	28 Aspiring Young Families	19.9	32306	63 Dorms To Diplomas	0.0
31757	26 Midland Crowd	51.7	32080	15 Silver And Gold	48.9	32307	63 Dorms To Diplomas	0.0
31760	42 Southern Satellites	100.0	32081	02 Suburban Splendor	94.1	32308	16 Enterprising Professionals	20.1
31763	26 Midland Crowd	77.5	32082	13 In Style	57.7	32309	07 Exurbanites	40.6
31764	42 Southern Satellites	45.1	32083	26 Midland Crowd	86.5	32310	41 Crossroads	28.6
31765	56 Rural Bypasses	60.0	32084	41 Crossroads	23.5	32311	17 Green Acres	25.8
31768	42 Southern Satellites	24.8	32086	33 Midlife Junction	30.1	32312	04 Boomburbs	34.5
31771	42 Southern Satellites	96.5	32087	41 Crossroads	83.1	32317	06 Sophisticated Squires	78.3
31772	42 Southern Satellites	99.5	32091	46 Rooted Rural	28.9	32320	46 Rooted Rural	39.9
31773	26 Midland Crowd	51.5	32092	17 Green Acres	54.8	32321	56 Rural Bypasses	39.3
31774	42 Southern Satellites	72.1	32094	46 Rooted Rural	63.2	32322	46 Rooted Rural	70.6
31775	56 Rural Bypasses	52.6	32095	26 Midland Crowd	81.1	32324	50 Heartland Communities	48.0
31778	46 Rooted Rural	42.4	32096	56 Rural Bypasses	69.2	32327	26 Midland Crowd	68.8
31779	46 Rooted Rural	29.1	32097	26 Midland Crowd	90.2	32328	46 Rooted Rural	68.0
31780	56 Rural Bypasses	44.8	32102	49 Senior Sun Seekers	68.6	32331	46 Rooted Rural	65.7
31781	42 Southern Satellites	91.2	32110	26 Midland Crowd	43.0	32332	56 Rural Bypasses	100.0

ZIP CODE	TOP TAPESTRY CONSUMER TYPE	% 2009 HOUSE-HOLDS	ZIP CODE	TOP TAPESTRY CONSUMER TYPE	% 2009 HOUSE-HOLDS	ZIP CODE	TOP TAPESTRY CONSUMER TYPE	% 2009 HOUSE-HOLDS
32333	56 Rural Bypasses	26.1	32580	14 Prosperous Empty Nesters	38.3	32820	41 Crossroads	72.6
32334	56 Rural Bypasses	53.1	32583	26 Midland Crowd	45.9	32821	27 Metro Renters	36.7
32336	56 Rural Bypasses	58.7	32601	63 Dorms To Diplomas	53.5	32822	39 Young And Restless	23.2
32340	46 Rooted Rural	31.6	32603	63 Dorms To Diplomas	69.3	32824	19 Milk And Cookies	76.5
32343	51 Metro City Edge	89.3	32605	14 Prosperous Empty Nesters	45.0	32825	12 Up And Coming Families	38.1
32344	46 Rooted Rural	48.2	32606	13 In Style	55.1	32826	28 Aspiring Young Families	34.0
32346	46 Rooted Rural	86.6	32607	63 Dorms To Diplomas	45.4	32827	07 Exurbanites	65.2
32347	26 Midland Crowd	30.0	32608	63 Dorms To Diplomas	47.5	32828	12 Up And Coming Families	100.0
32348	46 Rooted Rural	37.7	32609	51 Metro City Edge	17.4	32829	26 Midland Crowd	61.9
32350	46 Rooted Rural	100.0	32611	63 Dorms To Diplomas	100.0	32830	39 Young And Restless	88.9
32351	51 Metro City Edge	23.5	32615	26 Midland Crowd	55.5	32831	12 Up And Coming Families	100.0
32352	56 Rural Bypasses	52.5	32617	26 Midland Crowd	57.5	32832	07 Exurbanites	100.0
32355	46 Rooted Rural	100.0	32618	17 Green Acres	52.5	32833	13 In Style	80.0
32356	46 Rooted Rural	63.3	32619	46 Rooted Rural	61.3	32835	39 Young And Restless	51.0
32358	46 Rooted Rural	51.8	32621	41 Crossroads	39.6	32836	04 Boomburbs	38.0
32359	49 Senior Sun Seekers	80.4	32622	46 Rooted Rural	100.0	32837	16 Enterprising Professionals	39.0
32401	53 Home Town	18.6	32625	31 Rural Resort Dwellers	100.0	32839	52 Inner City Tenants	43.5
32403	40 Military Proximity	99.0	32626	49 Senior Sun Seekers	39.2	32901	30 Retirement Communities	20.2
32404	33 Midlife Junction	23.3	32628	56 Rural Bypasses	58.9	32903	14 Prosperous Empty Nesters	55.7
32405	33 Midlife Junction	17.7	32631	31 Rural Resort Dwellers	51.6	32904	33 Midlife Junction	22.6
32407	31 Rural Resort Dwellers	59.4	32640	49 Senior Sun Seekers	29.6	32905	29 Rustbelt Retirees	23.5
32408	13 In Style	52.0	32641	51 Metro City Edge	42.1	32907	19 Milk And Cookies	44.8
32409	26 Midland Crowd	69.0	32643	26 Midland Crowd	47.1	32908	19 Milk And Cookies	57.4
32413	31 Rural Resort Dwellers	80.5	32648	46 Rooted Rural	100.0	32909	19 Milk And Cookies	42.5
32420	46 Rooted Rural	61.2	32653	33 Midlife Junction	45.8	32920	36 Old And Newcomers	83.9
32421	46 Rooted Rural	69.9	32656	26 Midland Crowd	37.6	32922	60 City Dimensions	16.3
32423	46 Rooted Rural	80.5	32666	46 Rooted Rural	24.2	32925	40 Military Proximity	100.0
32424	56 Rural Bypasses	26.4	32667	31 Rural Resort Dwellers	41.7	32926	41 Crossroads	19.0
32425	46 Rooted Rural	79.8	32668	49 Senior Sun Seekers	68.1	32927	19 Milk And Cookies	52.8
32426	56 Rural Bypasses	95.7	32669	26 Midland Crowd	72.4	32931	15 Silver And Gold	37.6
32427	46 Rooted Rural	62.9	32680	49 Senior Sun Seekers	48.8	32934	13 In Style	24.4
32428	46 Rooted Rural	27.7	32686	46 Rooted Rural	48.0	32935	29 Rustbelt Retirees	21.4
32430	46 Rooted Rural	100.0	32693	46 Rooted Rural	40.5	32937	14 Prosperous Empty Nesters	38.7
32431	46 Rooted Rural	74.9	32694	46 Rooted Rural	34.9	32940	14 Prosperous Empty Nesters	46.6
32433	46 Rooted Rural	34.2	32696	49 Senior Sun Seekers	28.4	32948	38 Industrious Urban Fringe	57.9
32435	46 Rooted Rural	54.6	32701	36 Old And Newcomers	60.1	32949	43 The Elders	83.7
32437	46 Rooted Rural	100.0	32702	46 Rooted Rural	83.3	32950	07 Exurbanites	78.1
32438	41 Crossroads	68.0	32703	12 Up And Coming Families	16.3	32951	15 Silver And Gold	88.4
32439	26 Midland Crowd	44.2	32707	13 In Style	28.6	32952	14 Prosperous Empty Nesters	25.1
32440	46 Rooted Rural	54.6	32708	06 Sophisticated Squires	34.4	32953	33 Midlife Junction	28.7
32442	46 Rooted Rural	92.6	32709	26 Midland Crowd	96.1	32955	18 Cozy And Comfortable	36.8
32443	46 Rooted Rural	99.9	32712	14 Prosperous Empty Nesters	19.7	32958	49 Senior Sun Seekers	60.3
32444	07 Exurbanites	27.0	32713	15 Silver And Gold	24.7	32960	30 Retirement Communities	18.3
32445	56 Rural Bypasses	53.4	32714	28 Aspiring Young Families	42.2	32962	43 The Elders	18.7
32446	33 Midlife Junction	29.9	32720	31 Rural Resort Dwellers	19.0	32963	15 Silver And Gold	95.5
32448	46 Rooted Rural	32.2	32724	14 Prosperous Empty Nesters	21.8	32966	43 The Elders	42.0
32449	46 Rooted Rural	100.0	32725	29 Rustbelt Retirees	38.0	32967	15 Silver And Gold	20.6
32455	46 Rooted Rural	100.0	32726	49 Senior Sun Seekers	17.5	32968	17 Green Acres	79.5
32456	31 Rural Resort Dwellers	33.3	32730	24 Main Street, USA	44.8	32976	43 The Elders	64.8
32459	31 Rural Resort Dwellers	51.2	32732	17 Green Acres	100.0	33004	30 Retirement Communities	38.0
32460	46 Rooted Rural	89.4	32735	49 Senior Sun Seekers	100.0	33009	30 Retirement Communities	40.1
32462	46 Rooted Rural	76.0	32736	26 Midland Crowd	40.8	33010	58 NeWest Residents	43.8
32464	46 Rooted Rural	73.0	32738	19 Milk And Cookies	50.6	33012	59 Southwestern Families	25.2
32465	49 Senior Sun Seekers	51.3	32744	25 Salt Of The Earth	44.9	33013	59 Southwestern Families	39.4
32466	26 Midland Crowd	91.7	32746	16 Enterprising Professionals	30.6	33014	47 Las Casas	21.1
32501	62 Modest Income Homes	27.4	32750	06 Sophisticated Squires	32.8	33015	52 Inner City Tenants	35.8
32502	57 Simple Living	47.4	32751	36 Old And Newcomers	17.7	33016	38 Industrious Urban Fringe	58.8
32503	33 Midlife Junction	22.6	32754	46 Rooted Rural	35.1	33018	21 Urban Villages	50.2
32504	14 Prosperous Empty Nesters	26.3	32757	33 Midlife Junction	30.1	33019	30 Retirement Communities	54.9
32505	51 Metro City Edge	25.0	32759	49 Senior Sun Seekers	51.4	33020	36 Old And Newcomers	31.4
32506	12 Up And Coming Families	21.5	32763	43 The Elders	23.3	33021	43 The Elders	15.7
32507	12 Up And Coming Families	20.1	32764	31 Rural Resort Dwellers	57.1	33023	38 Industrious Urban Fringe	32.6
32508	40 Military Proximity	97.9	32765	04 Boomburbs	28.4	33024	38 Industrious Urban Fringe	23.2
32514	33 Midlife Junction	27.2	32766	12 Up And Coming Families	67.0	33025	16 Enterprising Professionals	25.6
32526	26 Midland Crowd	42.7	32767	26 Midland Crowd	39.3	33026	30 Retirement Communities	32.1
32531	26 Midland Crowd	54.8	32771	07 Exurbanites	23.7	33027	04 Boomburbs	42.9
32533	26 Midland Crowd	27.4	32773	28 Aspiring Young Families	21.1	33028	04 Boomburbs	100.0
32534	50 Heartland Communities	22.9	32776	26 Midland Crowd	52.1	33029	04 Boomburbs	83.5
32535	56 Rural Bypasses	53.2	32778	49 Senior Sun Seekers	47.8	33030	58 NeWest Residents	50.8
32536	12 Up And Coming Families	38.5	32779	07 Exurbanites	41.9	33031	07 Exurbanites	57.1
32539	12 Up And Coming Families	34.9	32780	30 Retirement Communities	27.5	33032	38 Industrious Urban Fringe	39.5
32541	13 In Style	76.4	32784	46 Rooted Rural	47.8	33033	38 Industrious Urban Fringe	51.6
32542	40 Military Proximity	99.8	32789	30 Retirement Communities	19.4	33034	38 Industrious Urban Fringe	24.5
32544	40 Military Proximity	100.0	32792	36 Old And Newcomers	31.9	33035	28 Aspiring Young Families	51.1
32547	28 Aspiring Young Families	27.6	32796	29 Rustbelt Retirees	30.3	33036	15 Silver And Gold	45.4
32548	33 Midlife Junction	15.5	32798	43 The Elders	80.7	33037	31 Rural Resort Dwellers	37.6
32550	15 Silver And Gold	100.0	32801	65 Social Security Set	38.2	33039	66 Unclassified	69.2
32561	14 Prosperous Empty Nesters	33.2	32803	22 Metropolitans	34.0	33040	23 Trendsetters	19.2
32563	07 Exurbanites	39.5	32804	22 Metropolitans	61.2	33042	31 Rural Resort Dwellers	57.5
32564	46 Rooted Rural	73.4	32805	64 City Commons	24.1	33043	31 Rural Resort Dwellers	79.3
32565	46 Rooted Rural	88.1	32806	22 Metropolitans	20.7	33050	31 Rural Resort Dwellers	44.3
32566	26 Midland Crowd	64.6	32807	28 Aspiring Young Families	23.5	33054	64 City Commons	28.6
32567	46 Rooted Rural	100.0	32808	28 Aspiring Young Families	27.8	33055	38 Industrious Urban Fringe	70.6
32568	46 Rooted Rural	99.1	32809	38 Industrious Urban Fringe	35.3	33056	34 Family Foundations	42.1
32569	28 Aspiring Young Families	66.4	32810	32 Rustbelt Traditions	20.5	33060	24 Main Street, USA	14.3
32570	18 Cozy And Comfortable	22.9	32811	52 Inner City Tenants	39.9	33062	30 Retirement Communities	42.0
32571	26 Midland Crowd	32.0	32812	52 Inner City Tenants	16.6	33063	36 Old And Newcomers	24.4
32577	25 Salt Of The Earth	62.7	32817	28 Aspiring Young Families	42.3	33064	38 Industrious Urban Fringe	12.6
32578	07 Exurbanites	36.8	32818	19 Milk And Cookies	32.4	33065	28 Aspiring Young Families	37.4
32579	14 Prosperous Empty Nesters	61.5	32819	02 Suburban Splendor	31.6	33066	43 The Elders	44.9

ZIP CODE	TOP TAPESTRY CONSUMER TYPE	% 2009 HOUSE-HOLDS
33067	04 Boomburbs	60.3
33068	19 Milk And Cookies	27.3
33069	30 Retirement Communities	49.2
33070	31 Rural Resort Dwellers	78.9
33071	02 Suburban Splendor	37.0
33073	12 Up And Coming Families	55.0
33076	04 Boomburbs	100.0
33109	65 Social Security Set	100.0
33125	58 NeWest Residents	45.3
33126	58 NeWest Residents	20.7
33127	58 NeWest Residents	24.5
33128	58 NeWest Residents	76.2
33129	08 Laptops And Lattes	61.6
33130	58 NeWest Residents	55.7
33131	08 Laptops And Lattes	37.8
33132	27 Metro Renters	59.1
33133	35 International Marketplace	17.6
33134	27 Metro Renters	18.0
33135	58 NeWest Residents	47.3
33136	64 City Commons	37.9
33137	27 Metro Renters	21.1
33138	58 NeWest Residents	11.4
33139	27 Metro Renters	52.1
33140	30 Retirement Communities	58.0
33141	36 Old And Newcomers	43.8
33142	62 Modest Income Homes	23.9
33143	36 Old And Newcomers	28.0
33144	30 Retirement Communities	37.4
33145	35 International Marketplace	42.2
33146	03 Connoisseurs	33.2
33147	62 Modest Income Homes	21.6
33149	09 Urban Chic	73.9
33150	64 City Commons	23.0
33154	30 Retirement Communities	54.8
33155	10 Pleasant-Ville	39.7
33156	01 Top Rung	43.1
33157	61 High Rise Renters	12.7
33158	05 Wealthy Seaboard Suburbs	50.6
33160	30 Retirement Communities	71.9
33161	52 Inner City Tenants	24.7
33162	38 Industrious Urban Fringe	34.6
33165	10 Pleasant-Ville	25.8
33166	24 Main Street, USA	26.2
33167	51 Metro City Edge	32.2
33168	34 Family Foundations	34.6
33169	52 Inner City Tenants	43.7
33170	34 Family Foundations	29.7
33172	28 Aspiring Young Families	35.7
33173	36 Old And Newcomers	33.8
33174	30 Retirement Communities	25.5
33175	10 Pleasant-Ville	24.0
33176	09 Urban Chic	14.9
33177	12 Up And Coming Families	46.8
33178	04 Boomburbs	58.1
33179	57 Simple Living	35.0
33180	15 Silver And Gold	37.9
33181	36 Old And Newcomers	37.4
33182	12 Up And Coming Families	96.0
33183	38 Industrious Urban Fringe	26.1
33184	38 Industrious Urban Fringe	25.8
33185	10 Pleasant-Ville	49.0
33186	06 Sophisticated Squires	38.6
33187	12 Up And Coming Families	44.8
33189	36 Old And Newcomers	19.8
33190	12 Up And Coming Families	47.5
33193	12 Up And Coming Families	32.0
33194	10 Pleasant-Ville	100.0
33196	12 Up And Coming Families	52.4
33199	63 Dorms To Diplomas	100.0
33301	09 Urban Chic	19.4
33304	30 Retirement Communities	18.8
33305	36 Old And Newcomers	33.5
33306	09 Urban Chic	40.4
33308	15 Silver And Gold	39.2
33309	36 Old And Newcomers	33.9
33311	34 Family Foundations	26.3
33312	34 Family Foundations	13.3
33313	51 Metro City Edge	26.2
33314	28 Aspiring Young Families	50.8
33315	24 Main Street, USA	29.6
33316	09 Urban Chic	27.1
33317	38 Industrious Urban Fringe	22.5
33319	30 Retirement Communities	25.5
33321	30 Retirement Communities	23.0
33322	43 The Elders	42.2
33323	06 Sophisticated Squires	49.2
33324	16 Enterprising Professionals	33.2
33325	41 Crossroads	41.7
33326	02 Suburban Splendor	39.6
33327	04 Boomburbs	100.0

ZIP CODE	TOP TAPESTRY CONSUMER TYPE	% 2009 HOUSE-HOLDS
33328	06 Sophisticated Squires	29.8
33330	02 Suburban Splendor	52.6
33331	04 Boomburbs	68.0
33332	04 Boomburbs	53.2
33334	52 Inner City Tenants	31.6
33351	28 Aspiring Young Families	29.5
33401	30 Retirement Communities	28.2
33403	24 Main Street, USA	27.0
33404	15 Silver And Gold	16.0
33405	38 Industrious Urban Fringe	40.2
33406	28 Aspiring Young Families	21.1
33407	24 Main Street, USA	13.7
33408	15 Silver And Gold	40.5
33409	13 In Style	23.6
33410	24 Main Street, USA	17.4
33411	06 Sophisticated Squires	31.6
33412	04 Boomburbs	94.5
33413	16 Enterprising Professionals	53.7
33414	06 Sophisticated Squires	30.6
33415	28 Aspiring Young Families	26.7
33417	43 The Elders	46.4
33418	15 Silver And Gold	60.7
33426	43 The Elders	31.4
33428	30 Retirement Communities	23.2
33430	38 Industrious Urban Fringe	27.5
33431	13 In Style	27.8
33432	30 Retirement Communities	35.3
33433	15 Silver And Gold	35.4
33434	43 The Elders	50.8
33435	30 Retirement Communities	11.8
33436	43 The Elders	24.6
33437	43 The Elders	46.3
33438	60 City Dimensions	95.0
33440	41 Crossroads	36.9
33441	39 Young And Restless	18.7
33442	30 Retirement Communities	44.4
33444	34 Family Foundations	13.9
33445	43 The Elders	20.7
33446	43 The Elders	50.2
33449	05 Wealthy Seaboard Suburbs	97.3
33455	49 Senior Sun Seekers	44.6
33458	04 Boomburbs	17.3
33460	60 City Dimensions	31.4
33461	38 Industrious Urban Fringe	22.2
33462	30 Retirement Communities	26.1
33463	19 Milk And Cookies	18.4
33467	07 Exurbanites	36.4
33469	15 Silver And Gold	55.5
33470	06 Sophisticated Squires	41.3
33471	49 Senior Sun Seekers	45.8
33472	05 Wealthy Seaboard Suburbs	31.1
33473	02 Suburban Splendor	100.0
33476	51 Metro City Edge	65.0
33477	15 Silver And Gold	83.8
33478	06 Sophisticated Squires	83.0
33480	43 The Elders	48.2
33483	15 Silver And Gold	57.1
33484	43 The Elders	80.2
33486	05 Wealthy Seaboard Suburbs	20.1
33487	15 Silver And Gold	66.1
33493	51 Metro City Edge	95.3
33496	01 Top Rung	24.4
33498	07 Exurbanites	71.9
33510	18 Cozy And Comfortable	34.0
33511	12 Up And Coming Families	28.2
33513	49 Senior Sun Seekers	51.3
33514	42 Southern Satellites	74.9
33523	49 Senior Sun Seekers	30.0
33525	33 Midlife Junction	20.7
33527	26 Midland Crowd	41.6
33534	41 Crossroads	90.1
33538	49 Senior Sun Seekers	96.9
33540	49 Senior Sun Seekers	43.9
33541	49 Senior Sun Seekers	96.8
33542	49 Senior Sun Seekers	53.3
33543	12 Up And Coming Families	80.6
33544	12 Up And Coming Families	81.6
33545	12 Up And Coming Families	95.9
33547	12 Up And Coming Families	59.2
33548	07 Exurbanites	54.3
33549	17 Green Acres	25.3
33556	04 Boomburbs	37.5
33558	16 Enterprising Professionals	49.2
33559	28 Aspiring Young Families	52.4
33563	32 Rustbelt Traditions	18.6
33565	26 Midland Crowd	54.2
33566	06 Sophisticated Squires	21.9
33567	26 Midland Crowd	41.0
33569	12 Up And Coming Families	37.0
33570	49 Senior Sun Seekers	50.2

ZIP CODE	TOP TAPESTRY CONSUMER TYPE	% 2009 HOUSE-HOLDS
33572	07 Exurbanites	62.1
33573	43 The Elders	97.4
33576	14 Prosperous Empty Nesters	58.9
33578	26 Midland Crowd	25.3
33579	12 Up And Coming Families	84.5
33584	18 Cozy And Comfortable	15.5
33585	46 Rooted Rural	91.7
33592	26 Midland Crowd	41.1
33594	12 Up And Coming Families	27.5
33596	04 Boomburbs	41.0
33597	46 Rooted Rural	90.4
33598	59 Southwestern Families	25.6
33602	27 Metro Renters	23.0
33603	48 Great Expectations	17.6
33604	32 Rustbelt Traditions	21.7
33605	62 Modest Income Homes	35.0
33606	27 Metro Renters	28.6
33607	29 Rustbelt Retirees	13.7
33609	36 Old And Newcomers	33.7
33610	34 Family Foundations	21.1
33611	33 Midlife Junction	20.9
33612	52 Inner City Tenants	36.5
33613	52 Inner City Tenants	35.2
33614	39 Young And Restless	19.7
33615	28 Aspiring Young Families	16.8
33616	32 Rustbelt Traditions	23.0
33617	52 Inner City Tenants	26.7
33618	13 In Style	37.1
33619	38 Industrious Urban Fringe	31.2
33620	63 Dorms To Diplomas	100.0
33621	40 Military Proximity	100.0
33624	28 Aspiring Young Families	26.6
33625	19 Milk And Cookies	51.3
33626	04 Boomburbs	74.7
33629	22 Metropolitans	20.0
33634	28 Aspiring Young Families	25.3
33635	12 Up And Coming Families	42.2
33637	28 Aspiring Young Families	44.5
33647	04 Boomburbs	48.6
33701	36 Old And Newcomers	30.0
33702	30 Retirement Communities	18.0
33703	32 Rustbelt Traditions	24.7
33704	22 Metropolitans	39.5
33705	36 Old And Newcomers	16.1
33706	15 Silver And Gold	66.5
33707	43 The Elders	30.6
33708	15 Silver And Gold	32.4
33709	49 Senior Sun Seekers	27.3
33710	29 Rustbelt Retirees	29.7
33711	15 Silver And Gold	21.9
33712	62 Modest Income Homes	27.0
33713	32 Rustbelt Traditions	32.6
33714	32 Rustbelt Traditions	26.1
33715	15 Silver And Gold	89.5
33716	39 Young And Restless	57.6
33755	48 Great Expectations	18.6
33756	30 Retirement Communities	17.7
33759	30 Retirement Communities	39.5
33760	33 Midlife Junction	30.5
33761	49 Senior Sun Seekers	28.7
33762	16 Enterprising Professionals	69.0
33763	43 The Elders	54.2
33764	49 Senior Sun Seekers	32.6
33765	36 Old And Newcomers	33.4
33767	15 Silver And Gold	87.7
33770	33 Midlife Junction	25.5
33771	49 Senior Sun Seekers	77.4
33772	33 Midlife Junction	21.8
33773	49 Senior Sun Seekers	40.1
33774	30 Retirement Communities	34.2
33776	07 Exurbanites	50.6
33777	33 Midlife Junction	37.6
33778	49 Senior Sun Seekers	43.3
33781	32 Rustbelt Traditions	31.9
33782	32 Rustbelt Traditions	33.3
33785	15 Silver And Gold	86.8
33786	15 Silver And Gold	100.0
33801	53 Home Town	21.3
33803	33 Midlife Junction	24.9
33805	51 Metro City Edge	32.5
33809	33 Midlife Junction	55.9
33810	26 Midland Crowd	46.0
33811	28 Aspiring Young Families	32.1
33812	06 Sophisticated Squires	65.4
33813	07 Exurbanites	36.4
33815	49 Senior Sun Seekers	54.9
33823	49 Senior Sun Seekers	31.4
33825	49 Senior Sun Seekers	41.6
33827	46 Rooted Rural	53.4
33830	29 Rustbelt Retirees	14.4

ZIP CODE	TOP TAPESTRY CONSUMER TYPE	% 2009 HOUSE-HOLDS	ZIP CODE	TOP TAPESTRY CONSUMER TYPE	% 2009 HOUSE-HOLDS	ZIP CODE	TOP TAPESTRY CONSUMER TYPE	% 2009 HOUSE-HOLDS
33834	49 Senior Sun Seekers	25.0	34140	15 Silver And Gold	100.0	34637	26 Midland Crowd	89.0
33837	31 Rural Resort Dwellers	59.4	34141	49 Senior Sun Seekers	99.9	34638	26 Midland Crowd	82.0
33838	46 Rooted Rural	82.5	34142	58 NeWest Residents	45.5	34639	12 Up And Coming Families	56.0
33839	46 Rooted Rural	51.1	34145	15 Silver And Gold	74.0	34652	49 Senior Sun Seekers	31.6
33841	26 Midland Crowd	23.6	34201	15 Silver And Gold	100.0	34653	33 Midlife Junction	37.0
33843	49 Senior Sun Seekers	33.3	34202	04 Boomburbs	50.4	34654	49 Senior Sun Seekers	35.9
33844	49 Senior Sun Seekers	28.5	34203	15 Silver And Gold	25.3	34655	07 Exurbanites	26.0
33849	49 Senior Sun Seekers	100.0	34205	57 Simple Living	24.7	34667	49 Senior Sun Seekers	88.3
33850	32 Rustbelt Traditions	37.8	34207	49 Senior Sun Seekers	27.6	34668	49 Senior Sun Seekers	52.3
33852	49 Senior Sun Seekers	60.7	34208	36 Old And Newcomers	15.7	34669	49 Senior Sun Seekers	72.4
33853	33 Midlife Junction	44.6	34209	43 The Elders	23.7	34677	13 In Style	38.6
33857	49 Senior Sun Seekers	100.0	34210	16 Enterprising Professionals	23.5	34683	07 Exurbanites	25.5
33859	49 Senior Sun Seekers	80.1	34211	15 Silver And Gold	68.2	34684	43 The Elders	23.8
33860	26 Midland Crowd	53.2	34212	31 Rural Resort Dwellers	56.2	34685	07 Exurbanites	33.3
33865	46 Rooted Rural	100.0	34215	15 Silver And Gold	100.0	34688	13 In Style	51.3
33868	49 Senior Sun Seekers	58.0	34217	15 Silver And Gold	70.1	34689	33 Midlife Junction	24.4
33870	49 Senior Sun Seekers	38.0	34219	31 Rural Resort Dwellers	33.5	34690	49 Senior Sun Seekers	75.1
33872	49 Senior Sun Seekers	41.9	34221	49 Senior Sun Seekers	44.0	34691	49 Senior Sun Seekers	65.5
33873	46 Rooted Rural	21.7	34222	43 The Elders	51.7	34695	13 In Style	28.4
33875	49 Senior Sun Seekers	76.5	34223	15 Silver And Gold	35.7	34698	49 Senior Sun Seekers	25.9
33876	49 Senior Sun Seekers	92.1	34224	49 Senior Sun Seekers	47.9	34705	46 Rooted Rural	79.1
33880	48 Great Expectations	20.4	34228	15 Silver And Gold	87.6	34711	12 Up And Coming Families	57.9
33881	43 The Elders	16.0	34229	15 Silver And Gold	52.3	34714	12 Up And Coming Families	50.9
33884	14 Prosperous Empty Nesters	28.1	34231	33 Midlife Junction	28.6	34715	12 Up And Coming Families	67.3
33890	42 Southern Satellites	98.8	34232	24 Main Street, USA	22.0	34731	49 Senior Sun Seekers	60.6
33896	31 Rural Resort Dwellers	43.8	34233	15 Silver And Gold	23.5	34734	28 Aspiring Young Families	86.9
33897	49 Senior Sun Seekers	100.0	34234	49 Senior Sun Seekers	23.9	34736	49 Senior Sun Seekers	50.0
33898	49 Senior Sun Seekers	40.3	34235	18 Cozy And Comfortable	36.8	34737	14 Prosperous Empty Nesters	58.5
33901	52 Inner City Tenants	20.9	34236	15 Silver And Gold	35.4	34739	49 Senior Sun Seekers	64.5
33903	43 The Elders	47.6	34237	36 Old And Newcomers	53.8	34741	52 Inner City Tenants	48.0
33904	15 Silver And Gold	30.4	34238	15 Silver And Gold	78.5	34743	38 Industrious Urban Fringe	79.8
33905	38 Industrious Urban Fringe	14.2	34239	33 Midlife Junction	19.6	34744	24 Main Street, USA	17.8
33907	39 Young And Restless	29.8	34240	07 Exurbanites	69.7	34746	17 Green Acres	34.7
33908	49 Senior Sun Seekers	41.0	34241	15 Silver And Gold	46.1	34747	09 Urban Chic	66.8
33909	19 Milk And Cookies	24.0	34242	15 Silver And Gold	74.5	34748	49 Senior Sun Seekers	34.0
33912	13 In Style	40.9	34243	15 Silver And Gold	31.9	34753	38 Industrious Urban Fringe	75.3
33913	05 Wealthy Seaboard Suburbs	75.8	34251	12 Up And Coming Families	60.0	34756	17 Green Acres	100.0
33914	24 Main Street, USA	20.2	34266	49 Senior Sun Seekers	30.2	34758	38 Industrious Urban Fringe	61.8
33916	39 Young And Restless	31.9	34269	49 Senior Sun Seekers	97.1	34759	38 Industrious Urban Fringe	51.9
33917	43 The Elders	32.9	34275	15 Silver And Gold	52.3	34761	12 Up And Coming Families	19.8
33919	15 Silver And Gold	27.8	34285	43 The Elders	70.6	34762	49 Senior Sun Seekers	69.0
33920	31 Rural Resort Dwellers	29.4	34286	12 Up And Coming Families	96.1	34769	32 Rustbelt Traditions	23.6
33921	15 Silver And Gold	65.6	34287	29 Rustbelt Retirees	38.7	34771	26 Midland Crowd	54.7
33922	49 Senior Sun Seekers	55.5	34288	12 Up And Coming Families	100.0	34772	26 Midland Crowd	57.4
33924	15 Silver And Gold	100.0	34289	12 Up And Coming Families	100.0	34773	41 Crossroads	79.9
33928	15 Silver And Gold	43.2	34291	12 Up And Coming Families	45.2	34785	49 Senior Sun Seekers	30.4
33931	15 Silver And Gold	46.2	34292	15 Silver And Gold	51.1	34786	02 Suburban Splendor	56.3
33935	59 Southwestern Families	18.5	34293	43 The Elders	37.5	34787	17 Green Acres	30.6
33936	49 Senior Sun Seekers	31.8	34420	49 Senior Sun Seekers	48.0	34788	49 Senior Sun Seekers	63.3
33946	15 Silver And Gold	58.9	34428	15 Silver And Gold	29.7	34797	49 Senior Sun Seekers	100.0
33947	15 Silver And Gold	63.4	34429	49 Senior Sun Seekers	46.5	34945	49 Senior Sun Seekers	91.3
33948	29 Rustbelt Retirees	31.7	34431	49 Senior Sun Seekers	87.8	34946	34 Family Foundations	43.0
33950	15 Silver And Gold	58.0	34432	15 Silver And Gold	40.9	34947	34 Family Foundations	19.1
33952	49 Senior Sun Seekers	42.9	34433	49 Senior Sun Seekers	75.9	34949	30 Retirement Communities	51.2
33953	43 The Elders	46.0	34434	49 Senior Sun Seekers	86.7	34950	62 Modest Income Homes	19.0
33954	14 Prosperous Empty Nesters	41.6	34436	49 Senior Sun Seekers	96.0	34951	49 Senior Sun Seekers	36.9
33955	15 Silver And Gold	45.7	34442	49 Senior Sun Seekers	49.7	34952	43 The Elders	17.5
33956	43 The Elders	45.9	34446	49 Senior Sun Seekers	53.5	34953	14 Prosperous Empty Nesters	33.6
33957	15 Silver And Gold	84.2	34448	49 Senior Sun Seekers	68.0	34956	49 Senior Sun Seekers	36.8
33960	49 Senior Sun Seekers	97.7	34449	49 Senior Sun Seekers	99.8	34957	49 Senior Sun Seekers	21.8
33966	13 In Style	100.0	34450	49 Senior Sun Seekers	92.1	34972	38 Industrious Urban Fringe	32.7
33967	12 Up And Coming Families	29.5	34452	49 Senior Sun Seekers	85.2	34974	49 Senior Sun Seekers	63.3
33971	12 Up And Coming Families	59.2	34453	49 Senior Sun Seekers	64.9	34981	25 Salt Of The Earth	34.2
33972	12 Up And Coming Families	26.0	34461	49 Senior Sun Seekers	41.6	34982	49 Senior Sun Seekers	26.5
33973	33 Midlife Junction	66.4	34465	43 The Elders	38.5	34983	18 Cozy And Comfortable	46.6
33974	49 Senior Sun Seekers	31.4	34470	49 Senior Sun Seekers	29.4	34984	18 Cozy And Comfortable	49.7
33976	19 Milk And Cookies	39.4	34471	33 Midlife Junction	33.1	34986	14 Prosperous Empty Nesters	100.0
33980	43 The Elders	45.2	34472	49 Senior Sun Seekers	27.9	34987	14 Prosperous Empty Nesters	86.7
33981	31 Rural Resort Dwellers	36.3	34473	49 Senior Sun Seekers	62.0	34988	17 Green Acres	100.0
33982	49 Senior Sun Seekers	52.0	34474	49 Senior Sun Seekers	69.4	34990	15 Silver And Gold	51.5
33983	14 Prosperous Empty Nesters	44.5	34475	62 Modest Income Homes	23.5	34994	57 Simple Living	29.9
33990	24 Main Street, USA	41.2	34476	15 Silver And Gold	40.3	34996	15 Silver And Gold	29.1
33991	19 Milk And Cookies	26.9	34479	25 Salt Of The Earth	36.6	34997	15 Silver And Gold	28.2
33993	12 Up And Coming Families	34.1	34480	33 Midlife Junction	44.7	35004	26 Midland Crowd	67.7
34102	15 Silver And Gold	47.5	34481	43 The Elders	81.6	35005	18 Cozy And Comfortable	38.3
34103	15 Silver And Gold	51.5	34482	49 Senior Sun Seekers	46.2	35006	42 Southern Satellites	57.5
34104	15 Silver And Gold	36.6	34484	46 Rooted Rural	57.6	35007	12 Up And Coming Families	76.3
34105	15 Silver And Gold	58.0	34488	49 Senior Sun Seekers	72.2	35010	42 Southern Satellites	37.4
34108	15 Silver And Gold	66.1	34491	49 Senior Sun Seekers	74.6	35014	56 Rural Bypasses	67.8
34109	15 Silver And Gold	59.1	34498	49 Senior Sun Seekers	100.0	35016	42 Southern Satellites	48.1
34110	15 Silver And Gold	86.6	34601	49 Senior Sun Seekers	26.0	35019	42 Southern Satellites	100.0
34112	15 Silver And Gold	28.8	34602	42 Southern Satellites	34.9	35020	62 Modest Income Homes	32.4
34113	15 Silver And Gold	55.0	34604	31 Rural Resort Dwellers	26.9	35022	29 Rustbelt Retirees	25.1
34114	49 Senior Sun Seekers	47.4	34606	49 Senior Sun Seekers	49.5	35023	17 Green Acres	22.8
34116	38 Industrious Urban Fringe	46.9	34607	15 Silver And Gold	79.7	35031	42 Southern Satellites	80.8
34117	12 Up And Coming Families	62.7	34608	49 Senior Sun Seekers	79.0	35033	42 Southern Satellites	70.1
34119	15 Silver And Gold	85.7	34609	29 Rustbelt Retirees	46.9	35034	56 Rural Bypasses	41.5
34120	12 Up And Coming Families	56.2	34610	26 Midland Crowd	64.7	35035	25 Salt Of The Earth	76.7
34134	15 Silver And Gold	82.8	34613	43 The Elders	60.0	35036	46 Rooted Rural	100.0
34135	15 Silver And Gold	42.5	34614	49 Senior Sun Seekers	72.6	35040	26 Midland Crowd	58.9

CONSUMER TYPE

ZIP CODE	TOP TAPESTRY CONSUMER TYPE	% 2009 HOUSE-HOLDS	ZIP CODE	TOP TAPESTRY CONSUMER TYPE	% 2009 HOUSE-HOLDS	ZIP CODE	TOP TAPESTRY CONSUMER TYPE	% 2009 HOUSE-HOLDS
35041	46 Rooted Rural	100.0	35224	50 Heartland Communities	35.8	35630	53 Home Town	16.9
35042	42 Southern Satellites	28.2	35226	22 Metropolitans	31.0	35633	17 Green Acres	26.0
35043	12 Up And Coming Families	48.0	35228	34 Family Foundations	45.4	35634	42 Southern Satellites	32.6
35044	42 Southern Satellites	43.8	35229	36 Old And Newcomers	100.0	35640	25 Salt Of The Earth	39.8
35045	42 Southern Satellites	32.0	35233	63 Dorms To Diplomas	42.2	35643	42 Southern Satellites	74.5
35046	42 Southern Satellites	63.5	35234	62 Modest Income Homes	58.4	35645	17 Green Acres	37.9
35049	42 Southern Satellites	85.3	35235	19 Milk And Cookies	39.0	35646	46 Rooted Rural	41.0
35051	26 Midland Crowd	73.8	35242	02 Suburban Splendor	34.8	35647	42 Southern Satellites	100.0
35053	31 Rural Resort Dwellers	82.9	35243	22 Metropolitans	35.4	35648	46 Rooted Rural	52.5
35054	31 Rural Resort Dwellers	63.6	35244	04 Boomburbs	35.3	35650	42 Southern Satellites	61.5
35055	57 Simple Living	32.3	35401	55 College Towns	36.6	35651	42 Southern Satellites	100.0
35057	42 Southern Satellites	51.5	35404	33 Midlife Junction	23.7	35652	42 Southern Satellites	44.8
35058	42 Southern Satellites	48.9	35405	52 Inner City Tenants	16.4	35653	56 Rural Bypasses	23.7
35061	50 Heartland Communities	74.9	35406	07 Exurbanites	16.6	35654	42 Southern Satellites	83.8
35062	26 Midland Crowd	33.3	35441	56 Rural Bypasses	76.3	35660	62 Modest Income Homes	19.6
35063	56 Rural Bypasses	73.5	35442	56 Rural Bypasses	74.2	35661	26 Midland Crowd	34.6
35064	34 Family Foundations	34.7	35443	62 Modest Income Homes	100.0	35670	42 Southern Satellites	96.1
35068	29 Rustbelt Retirees	51.6	35444	42 Southern Satellites	88.8	35671	26 Midland Crowd	68.0
35071	29 Rustbelt Retirees	42.7	35446	46 Rooted Rural	56.7	35672	42 Southern Satellites	64.0
35072	42 Southern Satellites	55.2	35447	56 Rural Bypasses	71.3	35673	42 Southern Satellites	54.9
35073	50 Heartland Communities	53.2	35452	26 Midland Crowd	61.9	35674	42 Southern Satellites	30.6
35077	42 Southern Satellites	59.4	35453	26 Midland Crowd	45.7	35677	46 Rooted Rural	55.4
35078	42 Southern Satellites	100.0	35456	41 Crossroads	50.5	35739	42 Southern Satellites	37.9
35079	42 Southern Satellites	51.4	35457	42 Southern Satellites	59.4	35740	42 Southern Satellites	71.0
35080	12 Up And Coming Families	85.3	35458	46 Rooted Rural	100.0	35741	17 Green Acres	59.6
35083	42 Southern Satellites	64.9	35459	56 Rural Bypasses	100.0	35744	42 Southern Satellites	100.0
35085	42 Southern Satellites	100.0	35460	56 Rural Bypasses	100.0	35745	42 Southern Satellites	100.0
35087	42 Southern Satellites	96.6	35461	42 Southern Satellites	94.4	35746	42 Southern Satellites	100.0
35089	56 Rural Bypasses	64.2	35462	56 Rural Bypasses	50.4	35747	42 Southern Satellites	42.3
35091	26 Midland Crowd	60.4	35463	46 Rooted Rural	100.0	35748	26 Midland Crowd	54.2
35094	33 Midlife Junction	26.6	35464	56 Rural Bypasses	100.0	35749	26 Midland Crowd	31.5
35096	31 Rural Resort Dwellers	32.8	35466	46 Rooted Rural	80.4	35750	42 Southern Satellites	49.6
35097	42 Southern Satellites	62.2	35469	56 Rural Bypasses	88.5	35751	42 Southern Satellites	100.0
35098	42 Southern Satellites	76.8	35470	56 Rural Bypasses	72.7	35752	42 Southern Satellites	85.7
35111	26 Midland Crowd	51.3	35473	26 Midland Crowd	22.8	35754	42 Southern Satellites	43.1
35114	12 Up And Coming Families	94.9	35474	56 Rural Bypasses	51.6	35755	31 Rural Resort Dwellers	51.0
35115	33 Midlife Junction	21.1	35475	17 Green Acres	32.7	35756	12 Up And Coming Families	60.0
35116	26 Midland Crowd	99.9	35476	33 Midlife Junction	20.0	35757	12 Up And Coming Families	49.4
35117	46 Rooted Rural	45.0	35480	46 Rooted Rural	98.2	35758	04 Boomburbs	25.8
35118	29 Rustbelt Retirees	58.6	35481	56 Rural Bypasses	69.5	35759	17 Green Acres	52.6
35120	26 Midland Crowd	54.3	35487	65 Social Security Set	67.7	35760	42 Southern Satellites	77.3
35121	42 Southern Satellites	73.5	35490	26 Midland Crowd	69.8	35761	42 Southern Satellites	50.4
35124	12 Up And Coming Families	24.9	35501	42 Southern Satellites	19.1	35763	04 Boomburbs	43.0
35125	42 Southern Satellites	58.1	35503	42 Southern Satellites	53.7	35764	42 Southern Satellites	100.0
35126	17 Green Acres	43.0	35504	42 Southern Satellites	38.4	35765	42 Southern Satellites	100.0
35127	18 Cozy And Comfortable	46.3	35540	42 Southern Satellites	99.8	35766	42 Southern Satellites	100.0
35128	42 Southern Satellites	45.7	35541	42 Southern Satellites	100.0	35768	42 Southern Satellites	48.4
35130	46 Rooted Rural	54.2	35542	42 Southern Satellites	100.0	35769	42 Southern Satellites	27.9
35131	42 Southern Satellites	42.0	35543	42 Southern Satellites	100.0	35771	42 Southern Satellites	100.0
35133	42 Southern Satellites	50.8	35544	42 Southern Satellites	100.0	35772	42 Southern Satellites	80.2
35135	26 Midland Crowd	74.2	35546	42 Southern Satellites	57.2	35773	26 Midland Crowd	75.2
35136	56 Rural Bypasses	49.5	35548	42 Southern Satellites	65.4	35774	42 Southern Satellites	100.0
35143	26 Midland Crowd	45.4	35549	56 Rural Bypasses	84.2	35775	42 Southern Satellites	100.0
35146	26 Midland Crowd	37.0	35550	56 Rural Bypasses	38.2	35776	42 Southern Satellites	96.6
35147	42 Southern Satellites	63.8	35552	42 Southern Satellites	100.0	35801	14 Prosperous Empty Nesters	26.7
35148	56 Rural Bypasses	50.6	35553	42 Southern Satellites	82.1	35802	14 Prosperous Empty Nesters	59.8
35150	53 Home Town	23.5	35554	42 Southern Satellites	85.1	35803	07 Exurbanites	35.7
35151	42 Southern Satellites	52.1	35555	42 Southern Satellites	45.0	35805	52 Inner City Tenants	30.1
35160	42 Southern Satellites	20.4	35563	42 Southern Satellites	62.8	35806	04 Boomburbs	30.5
35171	42 Southern Satellites	98.0	35564	42 Southern Satellites	61.9	35808	40 Military Proximity	100.0
35172	42 Southern Satellites	56.9	35565	42 Southern Satellites	72.7	35810	34 Family Foundations	24.5
35173	17 Green Acres	37.4	35570	42 Southern Satellites	88.9	35811	17 Green Acres	25.4
35175	26 Midland Crowd	49.2	35571	42 Southern Satellites	100.0	35816	52 Inner City Tenants	33.6
35176	26 Midland Crowd	81.6	35572	42 Southern Satellites	56.9	35824	16 Enterprising Professionals	100.0
35178	42 Southern Satellites	42.6	35574	42 Southern Satellites	96.3	35898	40 Military Proximity	100.0
35179	42 Southern Satellites	67.9	35575	42 Southern Satellites	100.0	35901	53 Home Town	12.8
35180	26 Midland Crowd	63.7	35576	56 Rural Bypasses	44.2	35903	25 Salt Of The Earth	21.2
35183	46 Rooted Rural	100.0	35578	42 Southern Satellites	52.0	35904	50 Heartland Communities	35.3
35184	42 Southern Satellites	52.1	35579	42 Southern Satellites	48.4	35905	25 Salt Of The Earth	52.7
35186	26 Midland Crowd	99.7	35580	56 Rural Bypasses	62.7	35906	17 Green Acres	53.3
35188	26 Midland Crowd	51.5	35581	42 Southern Satellites	72.6	35907	18 Cozy And Comfortable	51.2
35203	64 City Commons	55.0	35582	42 Southern Satellites	78.9	35950	42 Southern Satellites	38.1
35204	62 Modest Income Homes	60.4	35585	42 Southern Satellites	81.2	35951	42 Southern Satellites	64.1
35205	27 Metro Renters	45.5	35586	42 Southern Satellites	67.6	35952	42 Southern Satellites	80.9
35206	51 Metro City Edge	52.8	35587	56 Rural Bypasses	73.4	35953	42 Southern Satellites	78.1
35207	62 Modest Income Homes	66.9	35592	42 Southern Satellites	40.4	35954	42 Southern Satellites	47.9
35208	34 Family Foundations	50.4	35593	42 Southern Satellites	100.0	35956	42 Southern Satellites	58.9
35209	39 Young And Restless	46.6	35594	42 Southern Satellites	39.9	35957	42 Southern Satellites	45.7
35210	07 Exurbanites	20.8	35601	53 Home Town	19.6	35958	42 Southern Satellites	100.0
35211	34 Family Foundations	46.0	35603	13 In Style	35.5	35959	42 Southern Satellites	100.0
35212	64 City Commons	32.1	35610	42 Southern Satellites	100.0	35960	42 Southern Satellites	35.0
35213	22 Metropolitans	30.6	35611	42 Southern Satellites	17.4	35961	42 Southern Satellites	67.5
35214	18 Cozy And Comfortable	30.5	35613	26 Midland Crowd	39.6	35962	42 Southern Satellites	90.3
35215	19 Milk And Cookies	27.2	35614	42 Southern Satellites	69.0	35963	42 Southern Satellites	100.0
35216	13 In Style	30.3	35616	46 Rooted Rural	64.1	35966	42 Southern Satellites	100.0
35217	34 Family Foundations	22.0	35618	56 Rural Bypasses	78.9	35967	42 Southern Satellites	42.1
35218	51 Metro City Edge	44.6	35619	42 Southern Satellites	100.0	35968	42 Southern Satellites	88.8
35221	34 Family Foundations	65.6	35620	42 Southern Satellites	76.6	35971	42 Southern Satellites	77.3
35222	22 Metropolitans	27.0	35621	42 Southern Satellites	100.0	35972	42 Southern Satellites	84.7
35223	01 Top Rung	34.2	35622	42 Southern Satellites	90.5	35973	42 Southern Satellites	100.0

ZIP CODE	TOP TAPESTRY CONSUMER TYPE	% 2009 HOUSE-HOLDS	ZIP CODE	TOP TAPESTRY CONSUMER TYPE	% 2009 HOUSE-HOLDS	ZIP CODE	TOP TAPESTRY CONSUMER TYPE	% 2009 HOUSE-HOLDS
35974	42 Southern Satellites	100.0	36258	42 Southern Satellites	100.0	36524	56 Rural Bypasses	98.5
35975	42 Southern Satellites	89.8	36260	42 Southern Satellites	89.5	36525	56 Rural Bypasses	51.1
35976	33 Midlife Junction	29.8	36262	42 Southern Satellites	100.0	36526	06 Sophisticated Squires	23.5
35978	42 Southern Satellites	100.0	36263	42 Southern Satellites	100.0	36527	07 Exurbanites	82.8
35979	42 Southern Satellites	100.0	36264	42 Southern Satellites	69.9	36528	31 Rural Resort Dwellers	100.0
35980	42 Southern Satellites	100.0	36265	48 Great Expectations	17.5	36529	56 Rural Bypasses	63.6
35981	42 Southern Satellites	100.0	36266	42 Southern Satellites	38.3	36530	26 Midland Crowd	57.0
35983	42 Southern Satellites	100.0	36267	42 Southern Satellites	100.0	36532	14 Prosperous Empty Nesters	24.5
35984	46 Rooted Rural	51.4	36268	42 Southern Satellites	83.4	36535	26 Midland Crowd	29.7
35986	42 Southern Satellites	47.5	36269	42 Southern Satellites	100.0	36538	56 Rural Bypasses	82.7
35987	46 Rooted Rural	60.6	36271	42 Southern Satellites	63.7	36539	42 Southern Satellites	94.2
35988	42 Southern Satellites	100.0	36272	42 Southern Satellites	59.4	36540	62 Modest Income Homes	39.9
35989	42 Southern Satellites	97.4	36273	42 Southern Satellites	100.0	36541	42 Southern Satellites	60.9
36003	56 Rural Bypasses	65.0	36274	42 Southern Satellites	70.1	36542	31 Rural Resort Dwellers	78.0
36005	46 Rooted Rural	88.1	36276	42 Southern Satellites	59.6	36544	42 Southern Satellites	54.3
36006	42 Southern Satellites	80.8	36277	46 Rooted Rural	36.8	36545	56 Rural Bypasses	48.4
36009	56 Rural Bypasses	69.3	36278	42 Southern Satellites	41.5	36548	42 Southern Satellites	94.0
36010	56 Rural Bypasses	57.8	36279	42 Southern Satellites	41.1	36549	43 The Elders	72.8
36013	17 Green Acres	88.0	36280	42 Southern Satellites	77.6	36550	56 Rural Bypasses	56.8
36016	56 Rural Bypasses	81.8	36301	26 Midland Crowd	30.1	36551	56 Rural Bypasses	46.0
36017	56 Rural Bypasses	100.0	36303	62 Modest Income Homes	20.4	36553	42 Southern Satellites	52.9
36020	42 Southern Satellites	64.2	36305	12 Up And Coming Families	35.2	36555	31 Rural Resort Dwellers	81.9
36022	12 Up And Coming Families	29.7	36310	56 Rural Bypasses	55.7	36558	42 Southern Satellites	96.2
36024	42 Southern Satellites	46.8	36311	56 Rural Bypasses	58.7	36560	56 Rural Bypasses	90.6
36025	12 Up And Coming Families	46.7	36312	42 Southern Satellites	60.2	36561	31 Rural Resort Dwellers	49.3
36026	31 Rural Resort Dwellers	49.3	36314	42 Southern Satellites	100.0	36562	42 Southern Satellites	96.6
36027	42 Southern Satellites	45.0	36316	56 Rural Bypasses	51.2	36567	26 Midland Crowd	53.9
36028	56 Rural Bypasses	93.7	36317	56 Rural Bypasses	82.0	36569	42 Southern Satellites	69.6
36029	46 Rooted Rural	87.6	36318	46 Rooted Rural	87.8	36571	26 Midland Crowd	28.4
36030	56 Rural Bypasses	67.1	36319	46 Rooted Rural	53.5	36572	17 Green Acres	50.3
36031	56 Rural Bypasses	100.0	36320	42 Southern Satellites	66.5	36574	26 Midland Crowd	100.0
36032	46 Rooted Rural	35.9	36321	42 Southern Satellites	95.9	36575	26 Midland Crowd	59.7
36033	56 Rural Bypasses	65.1	36322	26 Midland Crowd	49.1	36576	26 Midland Crowd	90.0
36034	56 Rural Bypasses	48.9	36323	42 Southern Satellites	38.2	36578	42 Southern Satellites	82.3
36035	46 Rooted Rural	76.5	36330	28 Aspiring Young Families	24.1	36579	42 Southern Satellites	71.4
36036	46 Rooted Rural	67.5	36340	56 Rural Bypasses	29.8	36580	26 Midland Crowd	67.7
36037	56 Rural Bypasses	45.7	36343	42 Southern Satellites	61.1	36582	26 Midland Crowd	36.3
36038	46 Rooted Rural	42.9	36344	46 Rooted Rural	33.9	36583	42 Southern Satellites	100.0
36039	56 Rural Bypasses	80.9	36345	50 Heartland Communities	36.2	36584	56 Rural Bypasses	82.4
36040	56 Rural Bypasses	100.0	36346	46 Rooted Rural	41.3	36585	42 Southern Satellites	69.4
36041	56 Rural Bypasses	53.4	36349	42 Southern Satellites	60.4	36587	42 Southern Satellites	66.0
36042	56 Rural Bypasses	44.6	36350	46 Rooted Rural	30.5	36602	65 Social Security Set	65.9
36043	46 Rooted Rural	38.4	36351	46 Rooted Rural	86.4	36603	62 Modest Income Homes	42.8
36046	42 Southern Satellites	50.1	36352	26 Midland Crowd	54.6	36604	48 Great Expectations	28.1
36047	56 Rural Bypasses	45.9	36353	46 Rooted Rural	76.6	36605	51 Metro City Edge	19.8
36048	56 Rural Bypasses	100.0	36360	46 Rooted Rural	17.9	36606	48 Great Expectations	34.7
36049	50 Heartland Communities	65.6	36362	40 Military Proximity	100.0	36607	62 Modest Income Homes	21.6
36051	26 Midland Crowd	56.7	36370	56 Rural Bypasses	70.3	36608	36 Old And Newcomers	26.7
36052	56 Rural Bypasses	48.6	36373	56 Rural Bypasses	81.8	36609	13 In Style	28.5
36053	56 Rural Bypasses	95.9	36374	46 Rooted Rural	88.9	36610	62 Modest Income Homes	65.9
36054	26 Midland Crowd	58.2	36375	46 Rooted Rural	35.0	36611	50 Heartland Communities	36.2
36061	56 Rural Bypasses	99.0	36376	42 Southern Satellites	88.9	36612	62 Modest Income Homes	46.3
36064	07 Exurbanites	30.8	36401	56 Rural Bypasses	40.6	36613	26 Midland Crowd	34.1
36066	12 Up And Coming Families	50.2	36420	50 Heartland Communities	27.6	36615	51 Metro City Edge	100.0
36067	26 Midland Crowd	27.8	36421	50 Heartland Communities	37.4	36617	34 Family Foundations	47.0
36069	56 Rural Bypasses	56.4	36425	56 Rural Bypasses	100.0	36618	32 Rustbelt Traditions	38.9
36071	37 Prairie Living	41.3	36426	42 Southern Satellites	25.7	36619	32 Rustbelt Traditions	16.6
36075	56 Rural Bypasses	86.8	36432	56 Rural Bypasses	82.5	36688	63 Dorms To Diplomas	100.0
36078	42 Southern Satellites	28.6	36435	56 Rural Bypasses	100.0	36693	33 Midlife Junction	36.1
36079	28 Aspiring Young Families	45.1	36436	56 Rural Bypasses	99.2	36695	12 Up And Coming Families	37.9
36080	31 Rural Resort Dwellers	56.8	36441	42 Southern Satellites	86.1	36701	62 Modest Income Homes	17.5
36081	55 College Towns	20.2	36442	50 Heartland Communities	53.2	36703	62 Modest Income Homes	32.9
36082	63 Dorms To Diplomas	0.0	36444	56 Rural Bypasses	100.0	36720	56 Rural Bypasses	100.0
36083	51 Metro City Edge	36.2	36445	56 Rural Bypasses	56.7	36722	56 Rural Bypasses	100.0
36088	57 Simple Living	36.6	36446	56 Rural Bypasses	100.0	36726	56 Rural Bypasses	70.0
36089	56 Rural Bypasses	70.5	36451	56 Rural Bypasses	62.2	36727	56 Rural Bypasses	100.0
36091	42 Southern Satellites	67.9	36453	42 Southern Satellites	54.2	36728	56 Rural Bypasses	100.0
36092	42 Southern Satellites	29.9	36454	42 Southern Satellites	100.0	36732	62 Modest Income Homes	22.5
36093	17 Green Acres	75.2	36456	56 Rural Bypasses	98.7	36736	56 Rural Bypasses	100.0
36104	64 City Commons	40.9	36460	42 Southern Satellites	25.0	36738	56 Rural Bypasses	100.0
36105	62 Modest Income Homes	41.1	36467	46 Rooted Rural	21.5	36740	56 Rural Bypasses	100.0
36106	22 Metropolitans	26.7	36471	56 Rural Bypasses	94.5	36742	56 Rural Bypasses	55.2
36107	48 Great Expectations	55.4	36473	42 Southern Satellites	100.0	36744	56 Rural Bypasses	73.3
36108	34 Family Foundations	34.4	36474	42 Southern Satellites	95.4	36748	56 Rural Bypasses	65.1
36109	29 Rustbelt Retirees	26.1	36475	42 Southern Satellites	62.5	36749	56 Rural Bypasses	100.0
36110	53 Home Town	30.3	36477	46 Rooted Rural	46.0	36750	42 Southern Satellites	100.0
36111	36 Old And Newcomers	23.7	36480	42 Southern Satellites	100.0	36751	62 Modest Income Homes	100.0
36112	40 Military Proximity	100.0	36481	56 Rural Bypasses	100.0	36752	46 Rooted Rural	71.6
36115	40 Military Proximity	100.0	36482	56 Rural Bypasses	77.3	36754	56 Rural Bypasses	100.0
36116	51 Metro City Edge	22.9	36483	46 Rooted Rural	87.8	36756	56 Rural Bypasses	59.7
36117	13 In Style	26.9	36502	42 Southern Satellites	28.1	36758	56 Rural Bypasses	75.3
36201	62 Modest Income Homes	32.8	36505	26 Midland Crowd	100.0	36759	56 Rural Bypasses	71.0
36203	26 Midland Crowd	35.0	36507	42 Southern Satellites	43.9	36761	56 Rural Bypasses	100.0
36205	50 Heartland Communities	100.0	36509	56 Rural Bypasses	64.0	36765	56 Rural Bypasses	100.0
36206	50 Heartland Communities	33.1	36511	46 Rooted Rural	100.0	36767	56 Rural Bypasses	100.0
36207	14 Prosperous Empty Nesters	18.1	36515	42 Southern Satellites	100.0	36768	56 Rural Bypasses	100.0
36250	26 Midland Crowd	100.0	36518	42 Southern Satellites	65.4	36769	56 Rural Bypasses	70.8
36251	56 Rural Bypasses	45.7	36521	42 Southern Satellites	75.8	36773	56 Rural Bypasses	100.0
36255	42 Southern Satellites	99.5	36522	42 Southern Satellites	71.5	36775	56 Rural Bypasses	90.5
36256	42 Southern Satellites	100.0	36523	31 Rural Resort Dwellers	54.1	36776	56 Rural Bypasses	100.0

CONSUMER TYPE

ZIP CODE	TOP TAPESTRY CONSUMER TYPE	% 2009 HOUSE-HOLDS	ZIP CODE	TOP TAPESTRY CONSUMER TYPE	% 2009 HOUSE-HOLDS	ZIP CODE	TOP TAPESTRY CONSUMER TYPE	% 2009 HOUSE-HOLDS
36782	46 Rooted Rural	52.2	37073	26 Midland Crowd	79.5	37306	42 Southern Satellites	38.4
36783	56 Rural Bypasses	99.2	37074	42 Southern Satellites	45.8	37307	42 Southern Satellites	100.0
36784	42 Southern Satellites	48.3	37075	13 In Style	37.3	37308	25 Salt Of The Earth	50.6
36785	56 Rural Bypasses	75.1	37076	28 Aspiring Young Families	26.8	37309	42 Southern Satellites	100.0
36786	62 Modest Income Homes	62.3	37078	42 Southern Satellites	100.0	37310	25 Salt Of The Earth	61.7
36790	42 Southern Satellites	100.0	37079	42 Southern Satellites	81.8	37311	53 Home Town	22.7
36792	42 Southern Satellites	100.0	37080	26 Midland Crowd	42.3	37312	17 Green Acres	29.3
36793	42 Southern Satellites	75.3	37082	12 Up And Coming Families	46.6	37313	42 Southern Satellites	63.6
36801	62 Modest Income Homes	14.8	37083	42 Southern Satellites	68.5	37317	50 Heartland Communities	49.7
36804	26 Midland Crowd	50.7	37085	12 Up And Coming Families	68.4	37318	50 Heartland Communities	52.7
36830	55 College Towns	37.1	37086	12 Up And Coming Families	75.2	37321	42 Southern Satellites	88.4
36832	63 Dorms To Diplomas	68.9	37087	17 Green Acres	24.8	37322	42 Southern Satellites	100.0
36849	22 Metropolitans	100.0	37090	25 Salt Of The Earth	36.8	37323	42 Southern Satellites	61.0
36850	56 Rural Bypasses	69.6	37091	26 Midland Crowd	26.6	37324	50 Heartland Communities	35.8
36852	41 Crossroads	52.9	37095	42 Southern Satellites	93.7	37325	42 Southern Satellites	55.8
36853	31 Rural Resort Dwellers	50.4	37096	42 Southern Satellites	41.9	37327	42 Southern Satellites	100.0
36854	42 Southern Satellites	25.4	37097	46 Rooted Rural	72.9	37328	42 Southern Satellites	100.0
36855	42 Southern Satellites	69.9	37098	42 Southern Satellites	93.1	37329	42 Southern Satellites	74.7
36856	41 Crossroads	79.2	37101	42 Southern Satellites	96.0	37330	25 Salt Of The Earth	46.7
36858	56 Rural Bypasses	100.0	37110	25 Salt Of The Earth	27.6	37331	50 Heartland Communities	67.3
36860	56 Rural Bypasses	93.9	37115	48 Great Expectations	23.0	37332	42 Southern Satellites	100.0
36861	31 Rural Resort Dwellers	38.9	37118	17 Green Acres	68.2	37333	42 Southern Satellites	100.0
36862	56 Rural Bypasses	50.9	37122	17 Green Acres	60.2	37334	25 Salt Of The Earth	45.1
36863	42 Southern Satellites	32.9	37127	12 Up And Coming Families	35.0	37335	42 Southern Satellites	97.7
36866	56 Rural Bypasses	71.7	37128	12 Up And Coming Families	93.1	37336	17 Green Acres	40.1
36867	33 Midlife Junction	19.2	37129	26 Midland Crowd	17.8	37337	42 Southern Satellites	66.1
36869	42 Southern Satellites	31.5	37130	55 College Towns	33.3	37338	42 Southern Satellites	96.2
36870	12 Up And Coming Families	63.7	37132	55 College Towns	76.0	37339	42 Southern Satellites	91.3
36871	56 Rural Bypasses	71.0	37134	42 Southern Satellites	44.4	37340	56 Rural Bypasses	73.6
36874	26 Midland Crowd	78.5	37135	06 Sophisticated Squires	59.8	37341	17 Green Acres	34.8
36875	42 Southern Satellites	44.1	37137	46 Rooted Rural	59.5	37342	42 Southern Satellites	100.0
36877	26 Midland Crowd	66.8	37138	12 Up And Coming Families	21.8	37343	19 Milk And Cookies	16.1
36879	42 Southern Satellites	39.6	37140	46 Rooted Rural	100.0	37345	42 Southern Satellites	100.0
36904	56 Rural Bypasses	68.7	37141	25 Salt Of The Earth	83.0	37347	42 Southern Satellites	45.0
36907	56 Rural Bypasses	100.0	37142	25 Salt Of The Earth	50.7	37348	42 Southern Satellites	88.9
36908	46 Rooted Rural	49.6	37143	26 Midland Crowd	85.4	37350	03 Connoisseurs	100.0
36910	56 Rural Bypasses	100.0	37144	46 Rooted Rural	39.8	37352	46 Rooted Rural	45.6
36912	56 Rural Bypasses	100.0	37145	42 Southern Satellites	93.2	37353	42 Southern Satellites	58.0
36915	56 Rural Bypasses	100.0	37146	12 Up And Coming Families	42.9	37354	42 Southern Satellites	66.7
36916	56 Rural Bypasses	100.0	37148	26 Midland Crowd	35.1	37355	42 Southern Satellites	29.4
36919	56 Rural Bypasses	100.0	37149	42 Southern Satellites	58.6	37356	46 Rooted Rural	54.5
36921	42 Southern Satellites	57.3	37150	42 Southern Satellites	66.4	37357	42 Southern Satellites	50.6
36922	56 Rural Bypasses	100.0	37151	42 Southern Satellites	100.0	37359	46 Rooted Rural	88.8
36925	56 Rural Bypasses	57.5	37153	12 Up And Coming Families	63.5	37360	25 Salt Of The Earth	50.1
37010	17 Green Acres	54.3	37160	25 Salt Of The Earth	28.0	37361	42 Southern Satellites	100.0
37012	42 Southern Satellites	78.7	37166	42 Southern Satellites	49.2	37362	42 Southern Satellites	100.0
37013	39 Young And Restless	44.5	37167	28 Aspiring Young Families	44.6	37363	07 Exurbanites	23.8
37014	07 Exurbanites	56.6	37171	25 Salt Of The Earth	95.3	37365	56 Rural Bypasses	52.1
37015	26 Midland Crowd	63.2	37172	17 Green Acres	22.6	37366	42 Southern Satellites	94.1
37016	42 Southern Satellites	53.6	37174	12 Up And Coming Families	49.8	37367	42 Southern Satellites	85.2
37018	42 Southern Satellites	98.8	37175	49 Senior Sun Seekers	57.9	37369	42 Southern Satellites	60.4
37019	26 Midland Crowd	65.1	37178	42 Southern Satellites	59.6	37370	42 Southern Satellites	69.0
37020	26 Midland Crowd	69.6	37179	12 Up And Coming Families	78.7	37373	46 Rooted Rural	63.0
37022	25 Salt Of The Earth	52.9	37180	42 Southern Satellites	53.8	37374	42 Southern Satellites	100.0
37023	42 Southern Satellites	43.3	37181	42 Southern Satellites	100.0	37375	22 Metropolitans	36.9
37025	42 Southern Satellites	55.1	37183	25 Salt Of The Earth	60.9	37376	56 Rural Bypasses	97.9
37026	42 Southern Satellites	100.0	37184	25 Salt Of The Earth	52.1	37377	07 Exurbanites	41.2
37027	02 Suburban Splendor	41.8	37185	42 Southern Satellites	39.4	37379	25 Salt Of The Earth	27.4
37028	26 Midland Crowd	100.0	37186	42 Southern Satellites	82.1	37380	50 Heartland Communities	54.7
37029	26 Midland Crowd	60.6	37187	26 Midland Crowd	99.8	37381	46 Rooted Rural	34.4
37030	42 Southern Satellites	69.0	37188	12 Up And Coming Families	58.8	37385	42 Southern Satellites	83.7
37031	26 Midland Crowd	68.9	37189	18 Cozy And Comfortable	54.8	37387	56 Rural Bypasses	72.1
37032	26 Midland Crowd	58.9	37190	42 Southern Satellites	54.5	37388	53 Home Town	16.7
37033	50 Heartland Communities	55.5	37191	12 Up And Coming Families	70.5	37391	46 Rooted Rural	83.2
37034	26 Midland Crowd	50.8	37201	27 Metro Renters	83.5	37397	42 Southern Satellites	78.8
37035	26 Midland Crowd	100.0	37203	27 Metro Renters	30.9	37398	25 Salt Of The Earth	25.7
37036	42 Southern Satellites	54.0	37204	22 Metropolitans	38.5	37402	65 Social Security Set	86.9
37037	25 Salt Of The Earth	38.4	37205	16 Enterprising Professionals	19.4	37403	65 Social Security Set	49.6
37040	12 Up And Coming Families	28.7	37206	48 Great Expectations	19.1	37404	62 Modest Income Homes	44.1
37042	12 Up And Coming Families	26.3	37207	51 Metro City Edge	51.2	37405	48 Great Expectations	25.8
37043	17 Green Acres	24.6	37208	62 Modest Income Homes	37.1	37406	62 Modest Income Homes	31.8
37046	25 Salt Of The Earth	53.0	37209	22 Metropolitans	14.8	37407	53 Home Town	49.9
37047	42 Southern Satellites	54.0	37210	32 Rustbelt Traditions	22.5	37408	64 City Commons	91.2
37048	25 Salt Of The Earth	50.4	37211	16 Enterprising Professionals	20.0	37409	53 Home Town	42.2
37049	26 Midland Crowd	82.8	37212	22 Metropolitans	32.7	37410	64 City Commons	48.8
37050	46 Rooted Rural	64.4	37213	64 City Commons	100.0	37411	48 Great Expectations	28.1
37051	42 Southern Satellites	65.0	37214	28 Aspiring Young Families	30.6	37412	29 Rustbelt Retirees	20.0
37052	25 Salt Of The Earth	44.9	37215	22 Metropolitans	27.7	37415	29 Rustbelt Retirees	20.6
37055	26 Midland Crowd	39.6	37216	32 Rustbelt Traditions	39.8	37416	17 Green Acres	23.7
37057	42 Southern Satellites	70.0	37217	39 Young And Restless	24.7	37419	50 Heartland Communities	43.3
37058	46 Rooted Rural	71.3	37218	34 Family Foundations	31.6	37421	36 Old And Newcomers	16.4
37059	42 Southern Satellites	88.1	37219	27 Metro Renters	100.0	37601	33 Midlife Junction	20.7
37060	25 Salt Of The Earth	77.6	37220	03 Connoisseurs	43.3	37604	57 Simple Living	16.0
37061	42 Southern Satellites	45.7	37221	04 Boomburbs	21.0	37615	26 Midland Crowd	43.7
37062	17 Green Acres	38.4	37228	65 Social Security Set	86.2	37616	42 Southern Satellites	86.5
37064	04 Boomburbs	33.0	37240	63 Dorms To Diplomas	100.0	37617	26 Midland Crowd	26.4
37066	17 Green Acres	19.7	37301	42 Southern Satellites	91.7	37618	42 Southern Satellites	51.9
37067	04 Boomburbs	48.1	37302	17 Green Acres	64.6	37620	50 Heartland Communities	20.4
37069	02 Suburban Splendor	55.9	37303	53 Home Town	26.2	37640	46 Rooted Rural	65.0
37072	17 Green Acres	17.2	37305	56 Rural Bypasses	87.5	37641	42 Southern Satellites	96.5

ZIP CODE	TOP TAPESTRY CONSUMER TYPE	% 2009 HOUSE-HOLDS	ZIP CODE	TOP TAPESTRY CONSUMER TYPE	% 2009 HOUSE-HOLDS	ZIP CODE	TOP TAPESTRY CONSUMER TYPE	% 2009 HOUSE-HOLDS
37642	42 Southern Satellites	64.7	37848	42 Southern Satellites	100.0	38103	27 Metro Renters	88.9
37643	42 Southern Satellites	34.5	37849	33 Midlife Junction	23.8	38104	22 Metropolitans	26.6
37645	33 Midlife Junction	56.4	37852	56 Rural Bypasses	53.1	38105	64 City Commons	36.1
37650	50 Heartland Communities	49.7	37853	25 Salt Of The Earth	51.1	38106	62 Modest Income Homes	72.6
37656	46 Rooted Rural	43.3	37854	46 Rooted Rural	34.2	38107	62 Modest Income Homes	37.1
37657	42 Southern Satellites	100.0	37857	42 Southern Satellites	82.6	38108	62 Modest Income Homes	50.7
37658	56 Rural Bypasses	67.7	37860	42 Southern Satellites	60.8	38109	34 Family Foundations	59.6
37659	26 Midland Crowd	35.3	37861	42 Southern Satellites	62.4	38111	51 Metro City Edge	20.3
37660	50 Heartland Communities	29.3	37862	33 Midlife Junction	45.3	38112	62 Modest Income Homes	31.8
37663	25 Salt Of The Earth	36.6	37863	26 Midland Crowd	28.9	38114	62 Modest Income Homes	46.8
37664	50 Heartland Communities	24.5	37865	26 Midland Crowd	46.6	38115	39 Young And Restless	34.0
37665	50 Heartland Communities	88.0	37866	46 Rooted Rural	100.0	38116	34 Family Foundations	27.8
37680	46 Rooted Rural	100.0	37869	56 Rural Bypasses	78.6	38117	14 Prosperous Empty Nesters	22.0
37681	42 Southern Satellites	66.2	37870	46 Rooted Rural	66.3	38118	52 Inner City Tenants	38.3
37683	46 Rooted Rural	53.0	37871	42 Southern Satellites	56.9	38119	13 In Style	23.5
37686	25 Salt Of The Earth	47.5	37872	42 Southern Satellites	75.6	38120	09 Urban Chic	29.9
37687	46 Rooted Rural	85.0	37873	42 Southern Satellites	96.9	38122	32 Rustbelt Traditions	26.3
37688	46 Rooted Rural	100.0	37874	42 Southern Satellites	76.9	38125	12 Up And Coming Families	50.8
37690	42 Southern Satellites	70.2	37876	46 Rooted Rural	29.6	38126	64 City Commons	55.2
37691	42 Southern Satellites	100.0	37877	25 Salt Of The Earth	60.7	38127	51 Metro City Edge	68.0
37692	42 Southern Satellites	50.4	37878	46 Rooted Rural	59.2	38128	51 Metro City Edge	25.5
37694	46 Rooted Rural	81.6	37879	42 Southern Satellites	60.7	38131	49 Senior Sun Seekers	100.0
37701	50 Heartland Communities	30.5	37880	42 Southern Satellites	73.2	38132	49 Senior Sun Seekers	100.0
37705	42 Southern Satellites	28.8	37881	42 Southern Satellites	68.8	38133	12 Up And Coming Families	43.7
37708	42 Southern Satellites	78.9	37882	31 Rural Resort Dwellers	100.0	38134	39 Young And Restless	40.4
37709	42 Southern Satellites	100.0	37885	42 Southern Satellites	88.5	38135	06 Sophisticated Squires	47.1
37710	56 Rural Bypasses	100.0	37886	42 Southern Satellites	38.9	38138	07 Exurbanites	47.7
37711	42 Southern Satellites	100.0	37887	42 Southern Satellites	57.8	38139	02 Suburban Splendor	100.0
37713	42 Southern Satellites	63.6	37888	42 Southern Satellites	100.0	38141	19 Milk And Cookies	60.8
37714	42 Southern Satellites	69.2	37890	42 Southern Satellites	70.2	38152	55 College Towns	100.0
37715	56 Rural Bypasses	100.0	37891	42 Southern Satellites	80.9	38201	42 Southern Satellites	36.6
37716	26 Midland Crowd	17.5	37892	42 Southern Satellites	100.0	38220	42 Southern Satellites	52.2
37721	25 Salt Of The Earth	66.4	37902	65 Social Security Set	100.0	38221	46 Rooted Rural	49.7
37722	42 Southern Satellites	46.3	37909	55 College Towns	41.5	38222	49 Senior Sun Seekers	55.5
37723	42 Southern Satellites	71.8	37912	33 Midlife Junction	19.1	38224	46 Rooted Rural	50.4
37724	56 Rural Bypasses	37.2	37914	46 Rooted Rural	29.5	38225	42 Southern Satellites	63.3
37725	26 Midland Crowd	40.1	37915	64 City Commons	73.5	38226	42 Southern Satellites	100.0
37726	56 Rural Bypasses	64.2	37916	63 Dorms To Diplomas	100.0	38229	42 Southern Satellites	99.9
37727	42 Southern Satellites	54.2	37917	53 Home Town	23.4	38230	42 Southern Satellites	77.1
37729	56 Rural Bypasses	100.0	37918	33 Midlife Junction	31.0	38231	42 Southern Satellites	94.4
37731	42 Southern Satellites	97.1	37919	55 College Towns	18.3	38232	42 Southern Satellites	100.0
37737	26 Midland Crowd	48.8	37920	29 Rustbelt Retirees	20.7	38233	42 Southern Satellites	72.3
37738	31 Rural Resort Dwellers	66.9	37921	19 Milk And Cookies	21.3	38236	46 Rooted Rural	74.8
37742	25 Salt Of The Earth	59.2	37922	04 Boomburbs	41.7	38237	26 Midland Crowd	25.0
37743	42 Southern Satellites	34.5	37923	28 Aspiring Young Families	34.5	38238	55 College Towns	0.0
37745	42 Southern Satellites	30.0	37924	25 Salt Of The Earth	47.1	38240	42 Southern Satellites	87.4
37748	46 Rooted Rural	27.6	37931	26 Midland Crowd	34.3	38241	42 Southern Satellites	63.3
37752	42 Southern Satellites	36.7	37932	13 In Style	44.7	38242	50 Heartland Communities	27.6
37753	56 Rural Bypasses	99.4	37934	07 Exurbanites	49.3	38251	42 Southern Satellites	64.6
37754	26 Midland Crowd	52.0	37938	25 Salt Of The Earth	29.0	38253	42 Southern Satellites	84.2
37755	42 Southern Satellites	62.7	38001	50 Heartland Communities	39.5	38255	42 Southern Satellites	50.5
37756	56 Rural Bypasses	99.3	38002	12 Up And Coming Families	35.4	38256	49 Senior Sun Seekers	55.2
37757	42 Southern Satellites	60.5	38004	12 Up And Coming Families	67.1	38257	50 Heartland Communities	40.3
37760	33 Midlife Junction	22.2	38006	42 Southern Satellites	77.0	38258	42 Southern Satellites	100.0
37762	56 Rural Bypasses	79.1	38008	56 Rural Bypasses	24.3	38259	42 Southern Satellites	93.9
37763	26 Midland Crowd	22.6	38011	26 Midland Crowd	78.3	38260	42 Southern Satellites	84.8
37764	26 Midland Crowd	88.0	38012	51 Metro City Edge	23.8	38261	53 Home Town	30.5
37765	56 Rural Bypasses	100.0	38015	25 Salt Of The Earth	43.4	38301	62 Modest Income Homes	14.5
37766	46 Rooted Rural	23.4	38016	12 Up And Coming Families	33.9	38305	12 Up And Coming Families	16.8
37769	57 Simple Living	24.4	38017	04 Boomburbs	31.9	38310	42 Southern Satellites	47.9
37770	42 Southern Satellites	61.0	38018	12 Up And Coming Families	32.3	38311	42 Southern Satellites	100.0
37771	26 Midland Crowd	22.1	38019	42 Southern Satellites	23.1	38313	42 Southern Satellites	86.0
37772	25 Salt Of The Earth	39.9	38023	26 Midland Crowd	79.3	38315	42 Southern Satellites	97.9
37774	15 Silver And Gold	31.2	38024	42 Southern Satellites	30.2	38316	42 Southern Satellites	79.1
37777	26 Midland Crowd	21.3	38028	26 Midland Crowd	36.5	38317	50 Heartland Communities	60.9
37778	42 Southern Satellites	100.0	38030	42 Southern Satellites	100.0	38318	42 Southern Satellites	100.0
37779	42 Southern Satellites	68.7	38034	42 Southern Satellites	62.6	38320	46 Rooted Rural	40.4
37801	25 Salt Of The Earth	25.4	38037	56 Rural Bypasses	43.8	38321	42 Southern Satellites	63.8
37803	25 Salt Of The Earth	17.1	38039	56 Rural Bypasses	97.2	38326	31 Rural Resort Dwellers	55.1
37804	50 Heartland Communities	18.2	38040	42 Southern Satellites	50.9	38327	42 Southern Satellites	100.0
37806	42 Southern Satellites	100.0	38041	56 Rural Bypasses	92.3	38328	46 Rooted Rural	67.7
37807	42 Southern Satellites	65.3	38042	56 Rural Bypasses	100.0	38329	42 Southern Satellites	42.6
37809	42 Southern Satellites	100.0	38044	42 Southern Satellites	100.0	38330	42 Southern Satellites	65.2
37810	42 Southern Satellites	100.0	38049	42 Southern Satellites	60.0	38332	42 Southern Satellites	100.0
37811	42 Southern Satellites	99.3	38052	42 Southern Satellites	66.3	38333	46 Rooted Rural	100.0
37813	53 Home Town	29.2	38053	18 Cozy And Comfortable	20.4	38334	42 Southern Satellites	100.0
37814	53 Home Town	21.4	38057	26 Midland Crowd	41.3	38337	46 Rooted Rural	64.9
37818	42 Southern Satellites	91.4	38058	26 Midland Crowd	84.0	38339	42 Southern Satellites	100.0
37819	56 Rural Bypasses	100.0	38059	25 Salt Of The Earth	38.3	38340	42 Southern Satellites	42.7
37820	42 Southern Satellites	63.3	38060	26 Midland Crowd	58.0	38341	42 Southern Satellites	52.8
37821	42 Southern Satellites	35.7	38061	42 Southern Satellites	82.0	38342	42 Southern Satellites	88.1
37825	42 Southern Satellites	84.5	38063	42 Southern Satellites	49.7	38343	42 Southern Satellites	26.8
37826	42 Southern Satellites	73.2	38066	25 Salt Of The Earth	90.8	38344	42 Southern Satellites	65.6
37829	42 Southern Satellites	89.5	38067	56 Rural Bypasses	100.0	38345	42 Southern Satellites	100.0
37830	29 Rustbelt Retirees	20.2	38068	56 Rural Bypasses	34.7	38347	42 Southern Satellites	100.0
37840	42 Southern Satellites	32.7	38069	56 Rural Bypasses	72.9	38348	42 Southern Satellites	79.2
37841	42 Southern Satellites	64.6	38075	56 Rural Bypasses	70.5	38351	42 Southern Satellites	68.0
37843	42 Southern Satellites	80.9	38076	26 Midland Crowd	42.9	38352	42 Southern Satellites	100.0
37846	42 Southern Satellites	86.0	38079	57 Simple Living	43.8	38355	17 Green Acres	44.9
37847	56 Rural Bypasses	97.3	38080	56 Rural Bypasses	53.4	38356	26 Midland Crowd	59.9

CONSUMER TYPE

ZIP CODE	TOP TAPESTRY CONSUMER TYPE	% 2009 HOUSE-HOLDS	ZIP CODE	TOP TAPESTRY CONSUMER TYPE	% 2009 HOUSE-HOLDS	ZIP CODE	TOP TAPESTRY CONSUMER TYPE	% 2009 HOUSE-HOLDS
38357	42 Southern Satellites	89.7	38574	42 Southern Satellites	80.0	38801	53 Home Town	13.6
38358	42 Southern Satellites	26.6	38575	46 Rooted Rural	75.7	38804	42 Southern Satellites	22.2
38359	42 Southern Satellites	60.4	38577	46 Rooted Rural	99.0	38821	42 Southern Satellites	42.6
38361	46 Rooted Rural	74.5	38578	50 Heartland Communities	100.0	38824	42 Southern Satellites	54.9
38362	26 Midland Crowd	50.2	38579	46 Rooted Rural	89.5	38826	07 Exurbanites	41.1
38363	56 Rural Bypasses	37.9	38580	42 Southern Satellites	96.9	38827	42 Southern Satellites	100.0
38366	46 Rooted Rural	56.5	38581	42 Southern Satellites	98.3	38828	42 Southern Satellites	100.0
38367	42 Southern Satellites	74.4	38582	46 Rooted Rural	73.1	38829	42 Southern Satellites	60.0
38368	42 Southern Satellites	100.0	38583	42 Southern Satellites	63.0	38833	42 Southern Satellites	60.6
38369	50 Heartland Communities	55.4	38585	42 Southern Satellites	100.0	38834	42 Southern Satellites	30.6
38370	46 Rooted Rural	98.2	38587	42 Southern Satellites	78.7	38838	42 Southern Satellites	90.3
38371	42 Southern Satellites	71.6	38588	46 Rooted Rural	41.3	38841	42 Southern Satellites	100.0
38372	42 Southern Satellites	48.0	38589	56 Rural Bypasses	68.6	38843	42 Southern Satellites	71.7
38374	42 Southern Satellites	100.0	38601	56 Rural Bypasses	79.3	38844	42 Southern Satellites	100.0
38375	42 Southern Satellites	40.1	38603	56 Rural Bypasses	92.6	38846	42 Southern Satellites	98.9
38376	42 Southern Satellites	100.0	38606	56 Rural Bypasses	32.2	38847	42 Southern Satellites	100.0
38379	42 Southern Satellites	93.9	38610	56 Rural Bypasses	59.4	38848	42 Southern Satellites	100.0
38380	42 Southern Satellites	89.4	38611	56 Rural Bypasses	51.7	38849	42 Southern Satellites	93.6
38381	46 Rooted Rural	65.8	38614	62 Modest Income Homes	31.8	38850	56 Rural Bypasses	74.6
38382	42 Southern Satellites	29.6	38617	64 City Commons	74.8	38851	42 Southern Satellites	48.0
38387	42 Southern Satellites	100.0	38618	42 Southern Satellites	63.3	38852	46 Rooted Rural	35.6
38388	42 Southern Satellites	91.4	38619	56 Rural Bypasses	74.3	38855	42 Southern Satellites	100.0
38390	42 Southern Satellites	96.1	38620	56 Rural Bypasses	63.0	38856	42 Southern Satellites	100.0
38391	56 Rural Bypasses	90.6	38621	56 Rural Bypasses	71.0	38857	42 Southern Satellites	82.9
38392	56 Rural Bypasses	93.0	38625	42 Southern Satellites	100.0	38858	42 Southern Satellites	51.9
38401	26 Midland Crowd	20.2	38626	56 Rural Bypasses	71.8	38859	42 Southern Satellites	100.0
38425	50 Heartland Communities	59.9	38627	42 Southern Satellites	100.0	38860	56 Rural Bypasses	48.2
38449	42 Southern Satellites	55.7	38629	42 Southern Satellites	95.7	38862	42 Southern Satellites	55.9
38450	42 Southern Satellites	54.8	38631	62 Modest Income Homes	96.3	38863	42 Southern Satellites	68.9
38451	26 Midland Crowd	81.4	38632	26 Midland Crowd	38.3	38864	42 Southern Satellites	100.0
38452	42 Southern Satellites	100.0	38633	42 Southern Satellites	100.0	38865	42 Southern Satellites	81.9
38453	42 Southern Satellites	100.0	38635	56 Rural Bypasses	41.0	38866	42 Southern Satellites	48.7
38454	42 Southern Satellites	86.2	38637	32 Rustbelt Traditions	39.2	38868	42 Southern Satellites	98.0
38456	42 Southern Satellites	100.0	38641	26 Midland Crowd	83.0	38870	42 Southern Satellites	100.0
38457	42 Southern Satellites	100.0	38642	56 Rural Bypasses	100.0	38871	42 Southern Satellites	100.0
38459	42 Southern Satellites	100.0	38643	62 Modest Income Homes	62.9	38873	42 Southern Satellites	60.5
38460	42 Southern Satellites	100.0	38645	56 Rural Bypasses	71.5	38876	42 Southern Satellites	100.0
38461	26 Midland Crowd	62.4	38646	62 Modest Income Homes	44.1	38878	56 Rural Bypasses	54.3
38462	42 Southern Satellites	57.7	38647	56 Rural Bypasses	100.0	38901	42 Southern Satellites	27.4
38463	42 Southern Satellites	100.0	38650	42 Southern Satellites	100.0	38913	42 Southern Satellites	77.2
38464	42 Southern Satellites	36.4	38651	17 Green Acres	98.9	38914	42 Southern Satellites	83.9
38468	42 Southern Satellites	95.1	38652	42 Southern Satellites	59.8	38915	56 Rural Bypasses	43.2
38469	42 Southern Satellites	100.0	38654	12 Up And Coming Families	56.9	38916	56 Rural Bypasses	48.4
38471	42 Southern Satellites	100.0	38655	55 College Towns	41.7	38917	46 Rooted Rural	56.4
38472	46 Rooted Rural	50.1	38658	42 Southern Satellites	75.3	38920	56 Rural Bypasses	60.3
38473	42 Southern Satellites	100.0	38659	56 Rural Bypasses	96.7	38921	56 Rural Bypasses	86.6
38474	42 Southern Satellites	32.0	38661	42 Southern Satellites	74.2	38922	56 Rural Bypasses	89.0
38475	42 Southern Satellites	89.2	38663	42 Southern Satellites	73.9	38923	56 Rural Bypasses	53.6
38476	25 Salt Of The Earth	46.8	38664	41 Crossroads	100.0	38924	56 Rural Bypasses	100.0
38477	42 Southern Satellites	90.0	38665	42 Southern Satellites	72.1	38925	42 Southern Satellites	58.6
38478	42 Southern Satellites	39.8	38666	56 Rural Bypasses	59.9	38927	56 Rural Bypasses	86.3
38481	42 Southern Satellites	100.0	38668	26 Midland Crowd	24.3	38929	56 Rural Bypasses	86.8
38482	26 Midland Crowd	85.5	38670	51 Metro City Edge	63.2	38930	64 City Commons	22.3
38483	42 Southern Satellites	100.0	38671	28 Aspiring Young Families	33.6	38940	42 Southern Satellites	74.5
38485	56 Rural Bypasses	33.7	38672	17 Green Acres	70.4	38941	51 Metro City Edge	61.3
38486	42 Southern Satellites	99.5	38673	55 College Towns	67.6	38943	56 Rural Bypasses	100.0
38487	46 Rooted Rural	42.7	38674	42 Southern Satellites	100.0	38944	37 Prairie Living	92.8
38488	42 Southern Satellites	66.0	38676	51 Metro City Edge	51.9	38948	56 Rural Bypasses	52.4
38501	55 College Towns	27.6	38677	63 Dorms To Diplomas	100.0	38949	26 Midland Crowd	56.8
38504	46 Rooted Rural	98.1	38680	26 Midland Crowd	97.7	38950	56 Rural Bypasses	100.0
38505	63 Dorms To Diplomas	100.0	38683	42 Southern Satellites	67.0	38951	56 Rural Bypasses	70.8
38506	42 Southern Satellites	29.3	38685	56 Rural Bypasses	93.0	38952	56 Rural Bypasses	97.1
38541	46 Rooted Rural	62.6	38701	62 Modest Income Homes	35.2	38953	56 Rural Bypasses	58.7
38542	42 Southern Satellites	100.0	38703	51 Metro City Edge	27.8	38954	56 Rural Bypasses	57.7
38543	56 Rural Bypasses	82.8	38720	56 Rural Bypasses	95.1	38961	56 Rural Bypasses	100.0
38544	42 Southern Satellites	72.1	38721	56 Rural Bypasses	60.8	38963	62 Modest Income Homes	76.1
38545	42 Southern Satellites	66.6	38725	56 Rural Bypasses	100.0	38964	56 Rural Bypasses	100.0
38547	25 Salt Of The Earth	83.2	38726	56 Rural Bypasses	100.0	38965	42 Southern Satellites	34.9
38548	46 Rooted Rural	78.1	38730	26 Midland Crowd	79.9	38967	56 Rural Bypasses	39.6
38549	46 Rooted Rural	39.0	38731	56 Rural Bypasses	100.0	39038	51 Metro City Edge	31.5
38551	42 Southern Satellites	60.7	38732	62 Modest Income Homes	23.8	39039	56 Rural Bypasses	93.7
38552	42 Southern Satellites	99.6	38733	14 Prosperous Empty Nesters	100.0	39040	56 Rural Bypasses	71.0
38553	42 Southern Satellites	64.0	38736	46 Rooted Rural	52.9	39041	56 Rural Bypasses	39.5
38554	42 Southern Satellites	98.8	38737	62 Modest Income Homes	47.6	39042	26 Midland Crowd	17.1
38555	46 Rooted Rural	33.5	38740	56 Rural Bypasses	78.5	39044	42 Southern Satellites	67.1
38556	56 Rural Bypasses	32.8	38744	56 Rural Bypasses	100.0	39045	56 Rural Bypasses	96.6
38558	15 Silver And Gold	38.2	38746	62 Modest Income Homes	76.2	39046	56 Rural Bypasses	19.2
38559	42 Southern Satellites	84.8	38748	62 Modest Income Homes	43.9	39047	12 Up And Coming Families	28.7
38560	42 Southern Satellites	100.0	38751	51 Metro City Edge	55.6	39051	56 Rural Bypasses	38.2
38562	42 Southern Satellites	56.8	38753	56 Rural Bypasses	63.7	39056	28 Aspiring Young Families	14.2
38563	42 Southern Satellites	54.1	38754	56 Rural Bypasses	95.6	39057	42 Southern Satellites	94.6
38564	46 Rooted Rural	99.0	38756	51 Metro City Edge	28.0	39059	56 Rural Bypasses	26.5
38565	42 Southern Satellites	71.7	38759	56 Rural Bypasses	98.9	39063	62 Modest Income Homes	44.1
38567	42 Southern Satellites	87.4	38761	51 Metro City Edge	97.9	39066	51 Metro City Edge	37.3
38568	42 Southern Satellites	94.0	38762	62 Modest Income Homes	59.8	39067	56 Rural Bypasses	51.9
38569	42 Southern Satellites	100.0	38769	56 Rural Bypasses	58.3	39069	62 Modest Income Homes	56.1
38570	50 Heartland Communities	56.7	38771	51 Metro City Edge	71.2	39071	26 Midland Crowd	97.4
38571	46 Rooted Rural	54.8	38773	51 Metro City Edge	32.6	39073	26 Midland Crowd	65.8
38572	46 Rooted Rural	61.9	38774	62 Modest Income Homes	67.6	39074	56 Rural Bypasses	74.8
38573	42 Southern Satellites	56.2	38778	62 Modest Income Homes	53.9	39078	56 Rural Bypasses	77.8

ZIP CODE	TOP TAPESTRY CONSUMER TYPE	% 2009 HOUSE-HOLDS	ZIP CODE	TOP TAPESTRY CONSUMER TYPE	% 2009 HOUSE-HOLDS	ZIP CODE	TOP TAPESTRY CONSUMER TYPE	% 2009 HOUSE-HOLDS
39079	62 Modest Income Homes	70.1	39354	56 Rural Bypasses	95.5	39661	56 Rural Bypasses	99.5
39082	56 Rural Bypasses	100.0	39355	56 Rural Bypasses	44.7	39662	42 Southern Satellites	63.5
39083	56 Rural Bypasses	31.0	39356	56 Rural Bypasses	100.0	39663	56 Rural Bypasses	81.3
39086	56 Rural Bypasses	99.8	39358	56 Rural Bypasses	100.0	39664	42 Southern Satellites	43.5
39088	56 Rural Bypasses	100.0	39359	42 Southern Satellites	100.0	39665	56 Rural Bypasses	100.0
39090	56 Rural Bypasses	26.5	39360	56 Rural Bypasses	95.8	39666	56 Rural Bypasses	35.8
39092	56 Rural Bypasses	58.9	39361	56 Rural Bypasses	100.0	39667	56 Rural Bypasses	57.8
39094	56 Rural Bypasses	100.0	39362	56 Rural Bypasses	90.7	39668	56 Rural Bypasses	100.0
39095	56 Rural Bypasses	67.9	39363	56 Rural Bypasses	87.0	39669	56 Rural Bypasses	82.1
39096	56 Rural Bypasses	100.0	39364	56 Rural Bypasses	51.1	39701	62 Modest Income Homes	35.8
39097	56 Rural Bypasses	100.0	39365	56 Rural Bypasses	38.0	39702	26 Midland Crowd	25.4
39108	46 Rooted Rural	72.2	39366	56 Rural Bypasses	100.0	39705	17 Green Acres	23.9
39110	04 Boomburbs	44.6	39367	56 Rural Bypasses	58.5	39710	40 Military Proximity	100.0
39111	56 Rural Bypasses	42.2	39401	55 College Towns	22.4	39730	42 Southern Satellites	26.1
39113	62 Modest Income Homes	47.9	39402	28 Aspiring Young Families	22.2	39735	42 Southern Satellites	29.8
39114	56 Rural Bypasses	38.4	39406	63 Dorms To Diplomas	100.0	39739	56 Rural Bypasses	82.2
39116	42 Southern Satellites	72.4	39421	56 Rural Bypasses	99.4	39740	26 Midland Crowd	85.8
39117	42 Southern Satellites	58.6	39422	56 Rural Bypasses	74.2	39741	42 Southern Satellites	88.6
39119	56 Rural Bypasses	97.5	39423	42 Southern Satellites	51.4	39743	56 Rural Bypasses	100.0
39120	56 Rural Bypasses	26.7	39425	42 Southern Satellites	86.2	39744	56 Rural Bypasses	43.3
39140	56 Rural Bypasses	79.4	39426	26 Midland Crowd	47.6	39745	56 Rural Bypasses	63.1
39144	56 Rural Bypasses	100.0	39427	56 Rural Bypasses	100.0	39746	42 Southern Satellites	90.3
39145	42 Southern Satellites	62.5	39428	56 Rural Bypasses	43.7	39747	56 Rural Bypasses	98.0
39146	56 Rural Bypasses	97.0	39429	56 Rural Bypasses	33.4	39750	42 Southern Satellites	56.9
39149	56 Rural Bypasses	76.0	39437	42 Southern Satellites	40.5	39751	42 Southern Satellites	96.4
39150	56 Rural Bypasses	72.7	39439	56 Rural Bypasses	72.5	39752	42 Southern Satellites	63.2
39152	42 Southern Satellites	100.0	39440	33 Midlife Junction	22.2	39755	42 Southern Satellites	87.4
39153	42 Southern Satellites	69.7	39443	42 Southern Satellites	39.9	39756	56 Rural Bypasses	100.0
39154	26 Midland Crowd	43.6	39451	42 Southern Satellites	62.9	39759	55 College Towns	45.4
39156	46 Rooted Rural	41.3	39452	42 Southern Satellites	50.0	39762	63 Dorms To Diplomas	63.6
39157	39 Young And Restless	28.4	39455	56 Rural Bypasses	31.0	39766	25 Salt Of The Earth	77.6
39159	56 Rural Bypasses	44.8	39456	56 Rural Bypasses	51.1	39767	56 Rural Bypasses	100.0
39160	56 Rural Bypasses	93.1	39459	46 Rooted Rural	84.7	39769	46 Rooted Rural	73.6
39162	46 Rooted Rural	58.7	39461	42 Southern Satellites	92.7	39772	56 Rural Bypasses	100.0
39166	56 Rural Bypasses	100.0	39462	56 Rural Bypasses	76.6	39773	42 Southern Satellites	31.5
39168	56 Rural Bypasses	41.1	39464	42 Southern Satellites	97.1	39776	56 Rural Bypasses	64.1
39169	64 City Commons	39.6	39465	26 Midland Crowd	43.7	39813	56 Rural Bypasses	100.0
39170	17 Green Acres	56.3	39466	46 Rooted Rural	25.4	39815	56 Rural Bypasses	99.4
39175	56 Rural Bypasses	51.1	39470	46 Rooted Rural	48.1	39817	56 Rural Bypasses	31.3
39176	56 Rural Bypasses	76.0	39474	56 Rural Bypasses	90.5	39819	53 Home Town	24.6
39177	46 Rooted Rural	100.0	39475	26 Midland Crowd	45.4	39823	56 Rural Bypasses	85.1
39179	56 Rural Bypasses	100.0	39476	42 Southern Satellites	57.0	39824	56 Rural Bypasses	100.0
39180	33 Midlife Junction	16.5	39478	56 Rural Bypasses	100.0	39825	42 Southern Satellites	97.3
39183	17 Green Acres	30.3	39479	42 Southern Satellites	83.5	39826	56 Rural Bypasses	100.0
39189	56 Rural Bypasses	95.4	39480	56 Rural Bypasses	53.3	39827	26 Midland Crowd	59.7
39191	42 Southern Satellites	55.3	39481	42 Southern Satellites	52.6	39828	62 Modest Income Homes	24.8
39192	56 Rural Bypasses	52.2	39482	26 Midland Crowd	56.1	39834	42 Southern Satellites	70.7
39194	62 Modest Income Homes	27.9	39483	56 Rural Bypasses	54.5	39836	56 Rural Bypasses	100.0
39201	65 Social Security Set	97.6	39501	51 Metro City Edge	31.8	39837	46 Rooted Rural	48.5
39202	22 Metropolitans	30.1	39503	26 Midland Crowd	48.6	39840	56 Rural Bypasses	60.8
39203	62 Modest Income Homes	85.7	39507	36 Old And Newcomers	25.4	39841	56 Rural Bypasses	98.1
39204	51 Metro City Edge	30.9	39520	33 Midlife Junction	33.6	39842	56 Rural Bypasses	33.6
39206	51 Metro City Edge	32.2	39525	15 Silver And Gold	69.5	39845	56 Rural Bypasses	46.6
39208	26 Midland Crowd	19.1	39530	36 Old And Newcomers	21.5	39846	56 Rural Bypasses	100.0
39209	51 Metro City Edge	52.9	39531	36 Old And Newcomers	27.0	39851	56 Rural Bypasses	92.8
39210	64 City Commons	0.0	39532	26 Midland Crowd	58.3	39854	56 Rural Bypasses	100.0
39211	14 Prosperous Empty Nesters	30.4	39534	40 Military Proximity	100.0	39859	56 Rural Bypasses	87.4
39212	19 Milk And Cookies	34.0	39540	26 Midland Crowd	41.2	39861	56 Rural Bypasses	55.0
39213	62 Modest Income Homes	46.5	39553	41 Crossroads	36.5	39862	56 Rural Bypasses	100.0
39216	51 Metro City Edge	36.0	39556	41 Crossroads	72.7	39866	56 Rural Bypasses	100.0
39217	62 Modest Income Homes	0.0	39560	32 Rustbelt Traditions	24.2	39867	56 Rural Bypasses	100.0
39218	26 Midland Crowd	74.1	39561	26 Midland Crowd	80.2	39870	56 Rural Bypasses	80.3
39232	16 Enterprising Professionals	48.6	39562	42 Southern Satellites	49.2	39877	46 Rooted Rural	100.0
39272	19 Milk And Cookies	48.0	39563	34 Family Foundations	52.3	39886	56 Rural Bypasses	100.0
39301	62 Modest Income Homes	24.3	39564	26 Midland Crowd	20.6	39897	46 Rooted Rural	69.1
39305	22 Metropolitans	17.1	39565	26 Midland Crowd	87.1	40003	25 Salt Of The Earth	94.1
39307	62 Modest Income Homes	21.1	39567	57 Simple Living	21.0	40004	28 Aspiring Young Families	24.6
39309	26 Midland Crowd	73.3	39571	41 Crossroads	27.3	40006	42 Southern Satellites	74.5
39320	26 Midland Crowd	100.0	39572	56 Rural Bypasses	62.1	40007	42 Southern Satellites	100.0
39322	56 Rural Bypasses	62.4	39573	26 Midland Crowd	69.6	40008	42 Southern Satellites	82.8
39323	42 Southern Satellites	89.2	39574	26 Midland Crowd	61.6	40009	42 Southern Satellites	100.0
39325	26 Midland Crowd	68.0	39576	33 Midlife Junction	65.5	40010	06 Sophisticated Squires	100.0
39326	18 Cozy And Comfortable	83.8	39577	53 Home Town	20.3	40011	25 Salt Of The Earth	65.5
39327	46 Rooted Rural	55.5	39581	53 Home Town	17.6	40012	42 Southern Satellites	100.0
39328	56 Rural Bypasses	54.1	39601	42 Southern Satellites	31.7	40013	25 Salt Of The Earth	35.3
39330	56 Rural Bypasses	77.1	39629	42 Southern Satellites	52.4	40014	06 Sophisticated Squires	35.0
39332	42 Southern Satellites	62.4	39630	56 Rural Bypasses	100.0	40019	42 Southern Satellites	53.0
39335	26 Midland Crowd	54.4	39631	56 Rural Bypasses	79.4	40022	17 Green Acres	100.0
39336	42 Southern Satellites	99.4	39633	56 Rural Bypasses	100.0	40023	17 Green Acres	45.2
39337	46 Rooted Rural	90.3	39638	56 Rural Bypasses	89.3	40025	03 Connoisseurs	100.0
39338	56 Rural Bypasses	100.0	39641	46 Rooted Rural	62.2	40026	06 Sophisticated Squires	69.7
39339	56 Rural Bypasses	26.9	39643	56 Rural Bypasses	77.8	40031	26 Midland Crowd	35.5
39341	56 Rural Bypasses	72.3	39645	56 Rural Bypasses	53.6	40033	42 Southern Satellites	35.9
39342	60 City Dimensions	77.4	39647	46 Rooted Rural	48.9	40036	42 Southern Satellites	100.0
39345	56 Rural Bypasses	37.7	39648	56 Rural Bypasses	21.7	40037	42 Southern Satellites	92.0
39346	56 Rural Bypasses	93.4	39652	56 Rural Bypasses	84.0	40040	25 Salt Of The Earth	68.5
39347	56 Rural Bypasses	100.0	39653	56 Rural Bypasses	50.0	40045	42 Southern Satellites	64.7
39348	56 Rural Bypasses	100.0	39654	50 Heartland Communities	52.8	40046	26 Midland Crowd	83.6
39350	42 Southern Satellites	29.7	39656	42 Southern Satellites	100.0	40047	26 Midland Crowd	48.8
39352	56 Rural Bypasses	100.0	39657	56 Rural Bypasses	88.8	40050	50 Heartland Communities	70.0

CONSUMER TYPE

ZIP CODE	TOP TAPESTRY CONSUMER TYPE	% 2009 HOUSE-HOLDS	ZIP CODE	TOP TAPESTRY CONSUMER TYPE	% 2009 HOUSE-HOLDS	ZIP CODE	TOP TAPESTRY CONSUMER TYPE	% 2009 HOUSE-HOLDS
40051	42 Southern Satellites	85.1	40337	42 Southern Satellites	100.0	40840	56 Rural Bypasses	100.0
40052	42 Southern Satellites	100.0	40342	25 Salt Of The Earth	38.2	40843	56 Rural Bypasses	100.0
40055	26 Midland Crowd	81.3	40346	56 Rural Bypasses	84.2	40845	56 Rural Bypasses	100.0
40056	19 Milk And Cookies	51.5	40347	26 Midland Crowd	55.2	40847	56 Rural Bypasses	100.0
40057	42 Southern Satellites	78.7	40350	42 Southern Satellites	99.3	40855	56 Rural Bypasses	100.0
40059	02 Suburban Splendor	57.5	40351	26 Midland Crowd	25.9	40858	56 Rural Bypasses	100.0
40060	42 Southern Satellites	88.9	40353	25 Salt Of The Earth	26.4	40862	56 Rural Bypasses	100.0
40061	25 Salt Of The Earth	100.0	40355	25 Salt Of The Earth	48.6	40863	56 Rural Bypasses	100.0
40062	42 Southern Satellites	100.0	40356	28 Aspiring Young Families	31.5	40865	56 Rural Bypasses	100.0
40065	17 Green Acres	27.8	40358	42 Southern Satellites	100.0	40868	56 Rural Bypasses	100.0
40067	24 Main Street, USA	38.4	40359	50 Heartland Communities	33.6	40870	56 Rural Bypasses	100.0
40068	26 Midland Crowd	86.9	40360	42 Southern Satellites	47.2	40873	56 Rural Bypasses	99.7
40069	25 Salt Of The Earth	40.3	40361	48 Great Expectations	18.3	40902	56 Rural Bypasses	100.0
40070	26 Midland Crowd	100.0	40370	17 Green Acres	47.6	40903	56 Rural Bypasses	100.0
40071	17 Green Acres	58.3	40371	46 Rooted Rural	41.6	40906	56 Rural Bypasses	66.3
40075	25 Salt Of The Earth	51.8	40372	25 Salt Of The Earth	86.4	40913	56 Rural Bypasses	100.0
40076	17 Green Acres	49.8	40374	46 Rooted Rural	52.4	40914	56 Rural Bypasses	100.0
40077	17 Green Acres	99.4	40376	42 Southern Satellites	100.0	40915	26 Midland Crowd	62.7
40078	42 Southern Satellites	100.0	40379	42 Southern Satellites	77.9	40921	56 Rural Bypasses	100.0
40104	46 Rooted Rural	54.5	40380	42 Southern Satellites	55.1	40923	56 Rural Bypasses	100.0
40107	42 Southern Satellites	55.7	40383	17 Green Acres	34.4	40927	56 Rural Bypasses	100.0
40108	26 Midland Crowd	63.4	40385	42 Southern Satellites	61.2	40930	56 Rural Bypasses	100.0
40109	41 Crossroads	45.7	40387	42 Southern Satellites	100.0	40935	56 Rural Bypasses	100.0
40111	46 Rooted Rural	37.8	40390	28 Aspiring Young Families	41.2	40940	56 Rural Bypasses	100.0
40115	42 Southern Satellites	100.0	40391	26 Midland Crowd	23.1	40943	56 Rural Bypasses	100.0
40117	26 Midland Crowd	63.7	40402	42 Southern Satellites	81.9	40946	56 Rural Bypasses	99.7
40118	41 Crossroads	47.2	40403	26 Midland Crowd	26.9	40949	56 Rural Bypasses	56.6
40119	42 Southern Satellites	81.8	40409	42 Southern Satellites	59.2	40953	56 Rural Bypasses	100.0
40121	40 Military Proximity	100.0	40419	42 Southern Satellites	65.8	40958	56 Rural Bypasses	100.0
40140	42 Southern Satellites	100.0	40422	33 Midlife Junction	28.1	40962	56 Rural Bypasses	77.0
40142	26 Midland Crowd	76.3	40437	42 Southern Satellites	93.6	40964	56 Rural Bypasses	100.0
40143	50 Heartland Communities	51.6	40440	42 Southern Satellites	64.9	40965	56 Rural Bypasses	41.6
40144	46 Rooted Rural	50.9	40442	56 Rural Bypasses	53.1	40972	56 Rural Bypasses	100.0
40145	42 Southern Satellites	100.0	40444	25 Salt Of The Earth	17.3	40977	56 Rural Bypasses	66.2
40146	25 Salt Of The Earth	38.6	40445	56 Rural Bypasses	95.1	40979	56 Rural Bypasses	100.0
40150	25 Salt Of The Earth	42.4	40447	56 Rural Bypasses	79.9	40982	56 Rural Bypasses	100.0
40152	46 Rooted Rural	100.0	40456	56 Rural Bypasses	65.4	40983	56 Rural Bypasses	100.0
40155	41 Crossroads	60.9	40460	56 Rural Bypasses	100.0	40988	56 Rural Bypasses	100.0
40157	42 Southern Satellites	87.6	40461	42 Southern Satellites	31.6	40995	56 Rural Bypasses	100.0
40160	28 Aspiring Young Families	22.6	40464	42 Southern Satellites	70.6	40997	56 Rural Bypasses	100.0
40161	42 Southern Satellites	82.6	40468	25 Salt Of The Earth	52.2	41001	17 Green Acres	29.2
40162	26 Midland Crowd	59.3	40472	50 Heartland Communities	67.0	41002	42 Southern Satellites	61.8
40165	17 Green Acres	35.6	40475	26 Midland Crowd	16.2	41003	42 Southern Satellites	86.1
40170	46 Rooted Rural	100.0	40481	56 Rural Bypasses	100.0	41004	42 Southern Satellites	75.9
40171	46 Rooted Rural	100.0	40484	42 Southern Satellites	50.2	41005	12 Up And Coming Families	44.1
40175	26 Midland Crowd	41.3	40486	56 Rural Bypasses	60.2	41006	26 Midland Crowd	52.5
40176	42 Southern Satellites	63.2	40489	42 Southern Satellites	72.2	41007	25 Salt Of The Earth	50.5
40177	53 Home Town	61.2	40502	22 Metropolitans	48.9	41008	26 Midland Crowd	30.5
40178	46 Rooted Rural	100.0	40503	18 Cozy And Comfortable	34.6	41010	42 Southern Satellites	85.7
40202	65 Social Security Set	42.0	40504	48 Great Expectations	18.7	41011	60 City Dimensions	14.8
40203	64 City Commons	36.6	40505	32 Rustbelt Traditions	36.3	41014	48 Great Expectations	44.0
40204	22 Metropolitans	36.5	40507	36 Old And Newcomers	39.2	41015	32 Rustbelt Traditions	29.4
40205	22 Metropolitans	48.3	40508	63 Dorms To Diplomas	26.8	41016	32 Rustbelt Traditions	64.2
40206	48 Great Expectations	30.7	40509	16 Enterprising Professionals	23.6	41017	36 Old And Newcomers	15.0
40207	22 Metropolitans	40.4	40510	14 Prosperous Empty Nesters	92.0	41018	48 Great Expectations	17.1
40208	55 College Towns	33.1	40511	12 Up And Coming Families	30.8	41030	41 Crossroads	50.2
40209	53 Home Town	70.7	40513	13 In Style	79.5	41031	25 Salt Of The Earth	48.5
40210	62 Modest Income Homes	34.2	40514	12 Up And Coming Families	54.1	41033	42 Southern Satellites	88.8
40211	62 Modest Income Homes	46.0	40515	04 Boomburbs	25.9	41034	37 Prairie Living	78.1
40212	34 Family Foundations	31.6	40516	12 Up And Coming Families	62.7	41035	26 Midland Crowd	56.2
40213	32 Rustbelt Traditions	27.0	40517	28 Aspiring Young Families	46.5	41039	42 Southern Satellites	100.0
40214	48 Great Expectations	15.0	40601	33 Midlife Junction	10.3	41040	26 Midland Crowd	31.7
40215	53 Home Town	38.2	40701	56 Rural Bypasses	27.1	41041	42 Southern Satellites	56.1
40216	29 Rustbelt Retirees	28.6	40729	56 Rural Bypasses	82.1	41042	12 Up And Coming Families	25.8
40217	32 Rustbelt Traditions	34.7	40734	42 Southern Satellites	59.3	41043	42 Southern Satellites	76.0
40218	52 Inner City Tenants	16.5	40737	42 Southern Satellites	100.0	41044	42 Southern Satellites	61.7
40219	29 Rustbelt Retirees	19.6	40740	42 Southern Satellites	39.6	41045	26 Midland Crowd	82.1
40220	13 In Style	23.5	40741	42 Southern Satellites	23.6	41046	42 Southern Satellites	64.1
40222	36 Old And Newcomers	25.4	40744	42 Southern Satellites	56.8	41048	04 Boomburbs	46.2
40223	07 Exurbanites	21.0	40759	56 Rural Bypasses	66.7	41049	42 Southern Satellites	100.0
40228	18 Cozy And Comfortable	32.4	40763	56 Rural Bypasses	100.0	41051	12 Up And Coming Families	40.6
40229	32 Rustbelt Traditions	29.8	40769	56 Rural Bypasses	66.3	41052	26 Midland Crowd	59.0
40241	28 Aspiring Young Families	19.8	40771	56 Rural Bypasses	100.0	41055	37 Prairie Living	97.7
40242	18 Cozy And Comfortable	29.8	40801	56 Rural Bypasses	100.0	41056	50 Heartland Communities	17.2
40243	07 Exurbanites	36.3	40806	56 Rural Bypasses	72.7	41059	25 Salt Of The Earth	31.1
40245	04 Boomburbs	44.6	40807	50 Heartland Communities	100.0	41063	25 Salt Of The Earth	43.9
40258	32 Rustbelt Traditions	42.4	40808	56 Rural Bypasses	100.0	41064	46 Rooted Rural	99.9
40272	32 Rustbelt Traditions	41.5	40810	56 Rural Bypasses	100.0	41071	53 Home Town	21.3
40291	18 Cozy And Comfortable	26.8	40813	56 Rural Bypasses	87.3	41073	32 Rustbelt Traditions	37.1
40292	63 Dorms To Diplomas	0.0	40815	56 Rural Bypasses	100.0	41074	53 Home Town	43.2
40299	18 Cozy And Comfortable	18.6	40816	56 Rural Bypasses	100.0	41075	24 Main Street, USA	17.5
40311	42 Southern Satellites	44.6	40818	56 Rural Bypasses	100.0	41076	33 Midlife Junction	43.0
40312	42 Southern Satellites	57.4	40819	56 Rural Bypasses	100.0	41080	17 Green Acres	50.1
40313	41 Crossroads	43.2	40820	56 Rural Bypasses	100.0	41083	42 Southern Satellites	89.7
40316	42 Southern Satellites	100.0	40823	56 Rural Bypasses	46.8	41085	53 Home Town	100.0
40322	56 Rural Bypasses	67.3	40824	56 Rural Bypasses	100.0	41086	42 Southern Satellites	54.0
40324	12 Up And Coming Families	39.6	40826	56 Rural Bypasses	100.0	41091	04 Boomburbs	64.0
40328	42 Southern Satellites	72.1	40828	56 Rural Bypasses	100.0	41092	26 Midland Crowd	73.3
40330	25 Salt Of The Earth	24.0	40829	56 Rural Bypasses	100.0	41093	42 Southern Satellites	100.0
40336	42 Southern Satellites	51.3	40831	56 Rural Bypasses	48.3	41094	26 Midland Crowd	33.3

ZIP CODE	TOP TAPESTRY CONSUMER TYPE	% 2009 HOUSE-HOLDS	ZIP CODE	TOP TAPESTRY CONSUMER TYPE	% 2009 HOUSE-HOLDS	ZIP CODE	TOP TAPESTRY CONSUMER TYPE	% 2009 HOUSE-HOLDS
41095	26 Midland Crowd	54.1	41543	56 Rural Bypasses	98.9	41836	56 Rural Bypasses	100.0
41097	42 Southern Satellites	25.3	41544	56 Rural Bypasses	100.0	41837	56 Rural Bypasses	100.0
41098	42 Southern Satellites	100.0	41548	56 Rural Bypasses	100.0	41838	56 Rural Bypasses	100.0
41101	50 Heartland Communities	32.0	41553	56 Rural Bypasses	100.0	41839	56 Rural Bypasses	100.0
41102	46 Rooted Rural	32.0	41554	56 Rural Bypasses	97.4	41840	56 Rural Bypasses	100.0
41121	42 Southern Satellites	99.3	41555	56 Rural Bypasses	100.0	41843	56 Rural Bypasses	100.0
41124	56 Rural Bypasses	100.0	41557	42 Southern Satellites	58.4	41844	56 Rural Bypasses	100.0
41129	26 Midland Crowd	40.6	41558	56 Rural Bypasses	100.0	41845	56 Rural Bypasses	100.0
41132	56 Rural Bypasses	79.7	41559	46 Rooted Rural	53.5	41847	56 Rural Bypasses	100.0
41135	56 Rural Bypasses	99.5	41560	42 Southern Satellites	100.0	41848	56 Rural Bypasses	100.0
41139	50 Heartland Communities	49.4	41562	56 Rural Bypasses	78.5	41855	56 Rural Bypasses	100.0
41141	42 Southern Satellites	55.2	41563	56 Rural Bypasses	100.0	41858	56 Rural Bypasses	78.7
41143	42 Southern Satellites	37.1	41564	56 Rural Bypasses	100.0	41859	56 Rural Bypasses	100.0
41144	56 Rural Bypasses	31.6	41566	56 Rural Bypasses	100.0	41861	56 Rural Bypasses	100.0
41146	56 Rural Bypasses	100.0	41567	56 Rural Bypasses	64.2	41862	56 Rural Bypasses	100.0
41149	56 Rural Bypasses	100.0	41568	56 Rural Bypasses	100.0	42001	33 Midlife Junction	18.8
41159	56 Rural Bypasses	100.0	41571	56 Rural Bypasses	100.0	42003	33 Midlife Junction	19.4
41164	56 Rural Bypasses	49.5	41572	56 Rural Bypasses	100.0	42020	42 Southern Satellites	63.8
41166	42 Southern Satellites	100.0	41601	46 Rooted Rural	80.1	42021	42 Southern Satellites	54.7
41168	26 Midland Crowd	64.7	41602	56 Rural Bypasses	65.8	42023	42 Southern Satellites	61.6
41169	14 Prosperous Empty Nesters	31.3	41603	56 Rural Bypasses	83.7	42024	46 Rooted Rural	98.7
41171	56 Rural Bypasses	81.6	41604	56 Rural Bypasses	100.0	42025	25 Salt Of The Earth	36.6
41174	46 Rooted Rural	99.7	41605	46 Rooted Rural	75.1	42027	26 Midland Crowd	81.6
41175	50 Heartland Communities	42.4	41606	56 Rural Bypasses	100.0	42028	46 Rooted Rural	100.0
41179	56 Rural Bypasses	57.3	41607	26 Midland Crowd	59.0	42029	33 Midlife Junction	35.3
41180	56 Rural Bypasses	71.5	41615	56 Rural Bypasses	100.0	42031	46 Rooted Rural	39.8
41183	29 Rustbelt Retirees	55.4	41616	56 Rural Bypasses	97.6	42032	42 Southern Satellites	100.0
41189	42 Southern Satellites	51.5	41621	56 Rural Bypasses	100.0	42035	42 Southern Satellites	88.3
41201	56 Rural Bypasses	100.0	41622	56 Rural Bypasses	100.0	42036	42 Southern Satellites	100.0
41204	56 Rural Bypasses	100.0	41630	56 Rural Bypasses	100.0	42038	31 Rural Resort Dwellers	54.2
41214	56 Rural Bypasses	100.0	41631	56 Rural Bypasses	54.7	42039	42 Southern Satellites	99.2
41216	26 Midland Crowd	57.2	41632	56 Rural Bypasses	100.0	42040	46 Rooted Rural	64.0
41219	56 Rural Bypasses	66.2	41635	56 Rural Bypasses	75.0	42041	53 Home Town	38.9
41222	56 Rural Bypasses	62.5	41636	56 Rural Bypasses	100.0	42044	31 Rural Resort Dwellers	75.7
41224	56 Rural Bypasses	100.0	41640	56 Rural Bypasses	100.0	42045	46 Rooted Rural	74.8
41226	42 Southern Satellites	100.0	41642	56 Rural Bypasses	44.6	42047	46 Rooted Rural	100.0
41230	56 Rural Bypasses	32.1	41643	56 Rural Bypasses	100.0	42048	31 Rural Resort Dwellers	40.9
41231	56 Rural Bypasses	100.0	41645	56 Rural Bypasses	76.0	42049	46 Rooted Rural	90.3
41232	56 Rural Bypasses	89.7	41647	56 Rural Bypasses	100.0	42050	62 Modest Income Homes	30.1
41234	56 Rural Bypasses	79.0	41649	50 Heartland Communities	38.0	42051	42 Southern Satellites	59.1
41238	46 Rooted Rural	71.7	41650	56 Rural Bypasses	100.0	42053	46 Rooted Rural	42.7
41240	56 Rural Bypasses	54.4	41653	56 Rural Bypasses	54.0	42054	46 Rooted Rural	75.5
41250	56 Rural Bypasses	100.0	41655	56 Rural Bypasses	82.9	42055	46 Rooted Rural	69.0
41254	56 Rural Bypasses	100.0	41660	56 Rural Bypasses	100.0	42056	50 Heartland Communities	51.6
41255	56 Rural Bypasses	100.0	41666	56 Rural Bypasses	100.0	42058	46 Rooted Rural	100.0
41256	56 Rural Bypasses	71.1	41701	56 Rural Bypasses	56.6	42064	50 Heartland Communities	27.6
41257	56 Rural Bypasses	100.0	41712	56 Rural Bypasses	100.0	42066	42 Southern Satellites	22.8
41260	56 Rural Bypasses	63.0	41714	56 Rural Bypasses	100.0	42069	46 Rooted Rural	80.1
41262	56 Rural Bypasses	100.0	41719	56 Rural Bypasses	52.4	42071	55 College Towns	30.0
41263	56 Rural Bypasses	73.4	41721	56 Rural Bypasses	100.0	42076	49 Senior Sun Seekers	82.6
41265	46 Rooted Rural	39.1	41722	56 Rural Bypasses	100.0	42078	46 Rooted Rural	99.5
41267	56 Rural Bypasses	100.0	41723	56 Rural Bypasses	100.0	42079	46 Rooted Rural	99.2
41271	56 Rural Bypasses	100.0	41725	56 Rural Bypasses	100.0	42081	46 Rooted Rural	97.1
41274	56 Rural Bypasses	100.0	41727	42 Southern Satellites	89.8	42082	46 Rooted Rural	76.9
41301	56 Rural Bypasses	80.5	41729	46 Rooted Rural	99.3	42083	46 Rooted Rural	100.0
41311	56 Rural Bypasses	83.9	41731	56 Rural Bypasses	100.0	42085	46 Rooted Rural	92.6
41314	56 Rural Bypasses	74.2	41735	56 Rural Bypasses	100.0	42086	26 Midland Crowd	49.3
41317	56 Rural Bypasses	100.0	41736	56 Rural Bypasses	100.0	42087	46 Rooted Rural	97.1
41332	56 Rural Bypasses	59.9	41740	56 Rural Bypasses	100.0	42088	42 Southern Satellites	89.8
41338	56 Rural Bypasses	100.0	41745	56 Rural Bypasses	100.0	42101	26 Midland Crowd	15.5
41339	56 Rural Bypasses	79.0	41746	56 Rural Bypasses	100.0	42103	17 Green Acres	25.8
41348	56 Rural Bypasses	100.0	41749	56 Rural Bypasses	100.0	42104	13 In Style	21.8
41351	56 Rural Bypasses	100.0	41754	56 Rural Bypasses	100.0	42120	42 Southern Satellites	100.0
41360	56 Rural Bypasses	100.0	41759	56 Rural Bypasses	100.0	42122	17 Green Acres	89.2
41364	56 Rural Bypasses	100.0	41760	56 Rural Bypasses	100.0	42123	42 Southern Satellites	83.9
41365	56 Rural Bypasses	100.0	41763	56 Rural Bypasses	100.0	42124	42 Southern Satellites	100.0
41366	56 Rural Bypasses	100.0	41764	56 Rural Bypasses	100.0	42127	46 Rooted Rural	50.0
41367	56 Rural Bypasses	100.0	41766	56 Rural Bypasses	100.0	42129	42 Southern Satellites	82.3
41385	56 Rural Bypasses	100.0	41772	56 Rural Bypasses	100.0	42130	42 Southern Satellites	100.0
41386	56 Rural Bypasses	100.0	41773	56 Rural Bypasses	100.0	42131	42 Southern Satellites	61.4
41397	56 Rural Bypasses	100.0	41774	56 Rural Bypasses	100.0	42133	42 Southern Satellites	100.0
41425	42 Southern Satellites	66.2	41775	56 Rural Bypasses	100.0	42134	42 Southern Satellites	25.6
41464	56 Rural Bypasses	100.0	41776	56 Rural Bypasses	100.0	42140	42 Southern Satellites	100.0
41465	56 Rural Bypasses	92.6	41777	56 Rural Bypasses	100.0	42141	42 Southern Satellites	21.7
41472	56 Rural Bypasses	62.1	41804	56 Rural Bypasses	86.2	42151	42 Southern Satellites	100.0
41501	56 Rural Bypasses	38.6	41812	56 Rural Bypasses	100.0	42153	42 Southern Satellites	100.0
41503	29 Rustbelt Retirees	98.3	41815	56 Rural Bypasses	100.0	42154	42 Southern Satellites	62.4
41512	56 Rural Bypasses	100.0	41817	56 Rural Bypasses	100.0	42156	42 Southern Satellites	72.8
41513	46 Rooted Rural	97.3	41819	56 Rural Bypasses	100.0	42157	37 Prairie Living	93.2
41514	56 Rural Bypasses	72.6	41821	56 Rural Bypasses	100.0	42159	25 Salt Of The Earth	52.0
41519	56 Rural Bypasses	100.0	41822	56 Rural Bypasses	100.0	42160	42 Southern Satellites	49.1
41522	56 Rural Bypasses	88.5	41824	56 Rural Bypasses	100.0	42163	46 Rooted Rural	82.6
41524	56 Rural Bypasses	100.0	41825	56 Rural Bypasses	100.0	42164	42 Southern Satellites	58.1
41527	26 Midland Crowd	100.0	41826	46 Rooted Rural	59.1	42166	46 Rooted Rural	62.4
41528	56 Rural Bypasses	100.0	41828	56 Rural Bypasses	100.0	42167	42 Southern Satellites	42.8
41531	46 Rooted Rural	74.6	41831	56 Rural Bypasses	100.0	42170	25 Salt Of The Earth	74.0
41535	46 Rooted Rural	90.6	41832	46 Rooted Rural	95.0	42171	42 Southern Satellites	54.9
41537	56 Rural Bypasses	44.1	41833	56 Rural Bypasses	100.0	42202	42 Southern Satellites	80.2
41539	42 Southern Satellites	78.7	41834	56 Rural Bypasses	100.0	42204	37 Prairie Living	55.9
41540	56 Rural Bypasses	100.0	41835	56 Rural Bypasses	100.0	42206	42 Southern Satellites	89.9

CONSUMER TYPE

ZIP CODE	TOP TAPESTRY CONSUMER TYPE	% 2009 HOUSE-HOLDS	ZIP CODE	TOP TAPESTRY CONSUMER TYPE	% 2009 HOUSE-HOLDS	ZIP CODE	TOP TAPESTRY CONSUMER TYPE	% 2009 HOUSE-HOLDS
42207	46 Rooted Rural	80.9	42516	56 Rural Bypasses	99.3	43062	17 Green Acres	41.9
42210	42 Southern Satellites	51.1	42518	42 Southern Satellites	57.9	43064	17 Green Acres	35.9
42211	46 Rooted Rural	26.1	42519	42 Southern Satellites	40.6	43065	04 Boomburbs	31.4
42214	42 Southern Satellites	69.4	42528	42 Southern Satellites	92.4	43066	17 Green Acres	100.0
42215	42 Southern Satellites	44.6	42533	50 Heartland Communities	100.0	43067	17 Green Acres	89.2
42217	42 Southern Satellites	71.6	42539	56 Rural Bypasses	40.7	43068	12 Up And Coming Families	25.0
42220	42 Southern Satellites	92.7	42541	42 Southern Satellites	100.0	43071	25 Salt Of The Earth	80.9
42223	40 Military Proximity	99.3	42544	46 Rooted Rural	68.3	43072	25 Salt Of The Earth	92.1
42232	25 Salt Of The Earth	85.3	42553	42 Southern Satellites	49.0	43074	17 Green Acres	42.6
42234	42 Southern Satellites	82.0	42565	56 Rural Bypasses	62.1	43076	17 Green Acres	28.1
42236	26 Midland Crowd	86.2	42566	42 Southern Satellites	58.7	43078	17 Green Acres	29.6
42240	18 Cozy And Comfortable	15.9	42567	42 Southern Satellites	72.3	43080	25 Salt Of The Earth	36.8
42252	42 Southern Satellites	100.0	42602	56 Rural Bypasses	49.3	43081	16 Enterprising Professionals	28.7
42254	26 Midland Crowd	100.0	42603	42 Southern Satellites	90.3	43082	04 Boomburbs	66.6
42256	42 Southern Satellites	60.5	42629	46 Rooted Rural	94.8	43084	25 Salt Of The Earth	98.2
42259	46 Rooted Rural	100.0	42633	56 Rural Bypasses	44.0	43085	14 Prosperous Empty Nesters	22.6
42261	42 Southern Satellites	63.5	42634	56 Rural Bypasses	100.0	43102	25 Salt Of The Earth	69.0
42262	40 Military Proximity	89.9	42635	56 Rural Bypasses	100.0	43103	17 Green Acres	32.1
42265	25 Salt Of The Earth	58.8	42638	56 Rural Bypasses	100.0	43105	17 Green Acres	40.5
42266	46 Rooted Rural	75.9	42642	46 Rooted Rural	45.8	43106	42 Southern Satellites	72.0
42273	46 Rooted Rural	100.0	42647	56 Rural Bypasses	100.0	43107	25 Salt Of The Earth	93.4
42274	26 Midland Crowd	92.2	42649	56 Rural Bypasses	100.0	43110	28 Aspiring Young Families	51.6
42275	42 Southern Satellites	50.4	42653	56 Rural Bypasses	100.0	43112	07 Exurbanites	49.1
42276	42 Southern Satellites	37.9	42701	26 Midland Crowd	29.5	43113	17 Green Acres	23.8
42280	42 Southern Satellites	100.0	42712	42 Southern Satellites	94.0	43115	42 Southern Satellites	88.7
42285	42 Southern Satellites	100.0	42713	42 Southern Satellites	51.7	43116	17 Green Acres	100.0
42286	37 Prairie Living	82.1	42715	42 Southern Satellites	100.0	43119	28 Aspiring Young Families	63.2
42287	42 Southern Satellites	100.0	42716	25 Salt Of The Earth	78.9	43123	12 Up And Coming Families	23.5
42301	25 Salt Of The Earth	14.1	42717	46 Rooted Rural	53.7	43125	18 Cozy And Comfortable	21.9
42303	17 Green Acres	18.8	42718	25 Salt Of The Earth	34.3	43128	32 Rustbelt Traditions	58.8
42320	42 Southern Satellites	48.9	42721	42 Southern Satellites	53.1	43130	29 Rustbelt Retirees	13.0
42321	42 Southern Satellites	86.1	42722	37 Prairie Living	100.0	43135	42 Southern Satellites	31.9
42323	42 Southern Satellites	100.0	42724	25 Salt Of The Earth	54.5	43137	41 Crossroads	41.0
42324	42 Southern Satellites	69.1	42726	42 Southern Satellites	74.3	43138	25 Salt Of The Earth	26.3
42325	46 Rooted Rural	53.7	42728	42 Southern Satellites	38.5	43140	17 Green Acres	20.1
42326	42 Southern Satellites	100.0	42729	42 Southern Satellites	61.9	43143	32 Rustbelt Traditions	41.9
42327	46 Rooted Rural	46.7	42731	42 Southern Satellites	91.7	43145	46 Rooted Rural	61.7
42328	42 Southern Satellites	92.7	42732	42 Southern Satellites	56.9	43146	17 Green Acres	50.2
42330	42 Southern Satellites	40.5	42733	42 Southern Satellites	92.4	43147	12 Up And Coming Families	40.6
42333	42 Southern Satellites	77.6	42740	25 Salt Of The Earth	77.0	43148	17 Green Acres	58.6
42337	56 Rural Bypasses	68.0	42741	46 Rooted Rural	100.0	43149	25 Salt Of The Earth	92.3
42338	42 Southern Satellites	100.0	42742	42 Southern Satellites	100.0	43150	25 Salt Of The Earth	56.1
42339	42 Southern Satellites	51.9	42743	46 Rooted Rural	50.7	43152	42 Southern Satellites	55.5
42343	42 Southern Satellites	100.0	42746	42 Southern Satellites	55.9	43153	25 Salt Of The Earth	93.2
42344	56 Rural Bypasses	100.0	42748	26 Midland Crowd	26.0	43154	25 Salt Of The Earth	84.8
42345	46 Rooted Rural	31.4	42749	50 Heartland Communities	27.4	43155	25 Salt Of The Earth	94.2
42347	50 Heartland Communities	50.0	42753	42 Southern Satellites	100.0	43160	25 Salt Of The Earth	27.1
42348	42 Southern Satellites	92.2	42754	42 Southern Satellites	56.5	43162	32 Rustbelt Traditions	28.8
42349	46 Rooted Rural	88.7	42757	42 Southern Satellites	84.8	43164	25 Salt Of The Earth	66.7
42350	46 Rooted Rural	100.0	42762	42 Southern Satellites	100.0	43201	63 Dorms To Diplomas	51.8
42351	26 Midland Crowd	45.8	42764	46 Rooted Rural	45.8	43202	22 Metropolitans	36.2
42352	56 Rural Bypasses	86.1	42765	42 Southern Satellites	45.6	43203	64 City Commons	23.3
42354	42 Southern Satellites	100.0	42776	42 Southern Satellites	63.8	43204	51 Metro City Edge	14.5
42355	25 Salt Of The Earth	70.3	42782	42 Southern Satellites	70.5	43205	51 Metro City Edge	22.4
42361	46 Rooted Rural	61.3	42784	46 Rooted Rural	60.0	43206	51 Metro City Edge	35.1
42366	17 Green Acres	46.3	42788	25 Salt Of The Earth	100.0	43207	29 Rustbelt Retirees	13.9
42367	56 Rural Bypasses	100.0	43001	17 Green Acres	71.0	43209	14 Prosperous Empty Nesters	17.4
42368	42 Southern Satellites	100.0	43002	16 Enterprising Professionals	100.0	43210	55 College Towns	60.3
42369	46 Rooted Rural	100.0	43003	32 Rustbelt Traditions	57.5	43211	51 Metro City Edge	63.1
42371	46 Rooted Rural	50.2	43004	12 Up And Coming Families	50.8	43212	27 Metro Renters	32.2
42372	46 Rooted Rural	70.7	43006	42 Southern Satellites	68.3	43213	32 Rustbelt Traditions	18.9
42376	26 Midland Crowd	45.9	43008	50 Heartland Communities	85.8	43214	22 Metropolitans	24.4
42378	42 Southern Satellites	86.7	43009	17 Green Acres	51.4	43215	27 Metro Renters	60.8
42404	42 Southern Satellites	60.4	43011	17 Green Acres	32.6	43217	52 Inner City Tenants	100.0
42406	25 Salt Of The Earth	55.8	43013	17 Green Acres	100.0	43219	34 Family Foundations	31.1
42408	50 Heartland Communities	33.2	43014	25 Salt Of The Earth	64.0	43220	39 Young And Restless	25.7
42409	46 Rooted Rural	53.7	43015	12 Up And Coming Families	18.0	43221	14 Prosperous Empty Nesters	16.6
42410	53 Home Town	52.1	43016	16 Enterprising Professionals	57.1	43222	60 City Dimensions	52.1
42411	46 Rooted Rural	97.5	43017	02 Suburban Splendor	35.3	43223	32 Rustbelt Traditions	24.8
42413	25 Salt Of The Earth	53.8	43019	25 Salt Of The Earth	44.2	43224	32 Rustbelt Traditions	21.0
42420	53 Home Town	17.0	43021	07 Exurbanites	46.3	43227	29 Rustbelt Retirees	30.5
42431	50 Heartland Communities	17.0	43022	22 Metropolitans	43.9	43228	28 Aspiring Young Families	29.3
42436	26 Midland Crowd	85.3	43023	07 Exurbanites	30.1	43229	39 Young And Restless	27.3
42437	32 Rustbelt Traditions	26.9	43025	26 Midland Crowd	22.4	43230	16 Enterprising Professionals	24.1
42441	42 Southern Satellites	54.6	43026	16 Enterprising Professionals	35.7	43231	19 Milk And Cookies	27.9
42442	56 Rural Bypasses	62.3	43028	17 Green Acres	48.2	43232	52 Inner City Tenants	16.6
42445	50 Heartland Communities	43.3	43029	17 Green Acres	100.0	43235	16 Enterprising Professionals	38.2
42450	53 Home Town	39.5	43031	17 Green Acres	74.0	43240	16 Enterprising Professionals	100.0
42451	42 Southern Satellites	51.1	43035	04 Boomburbs	53.4	43302	32 Rustbelt Traditions	27.1
42452	25 Salt Of The Earth	62.0	43037	17 Green Acres	69.4	43310	32 Rustbelt Traditions	35.8
42453	56 Rural Bypasses	85.0	43040	12 Up And Coming Families	24.2	43311	48 Great Expectations	20.8
42455	42 Southern Satellites	86.2	43044	32 Rustbelt Traditions	38.9	43314	25 Salt Of The Earth	51.3
42456	25 Salt Of The Earth	73.0	43045	17 Green Acres	95.6	43315	25 Salt Of The Earth	40.9
42458	25 Salt Of The Earth	79.3	43046	25 Salt Of The Earth	41.3	43316	32 Rustbelt Traditions	39.5
42459	50 Heartland Communities	41.2	43050	33 Midlife Junction	16.2	43318	25 Salt Of The Earth	72.0
42461	42 Southern Satellites	98.2	43054	04 Boomburbs	36.0	43319	17 Green Acres	99.2
42462	26 Midland Crowd	58.8	43055	32 Rustbelt Traditions	18.6	43320	25 Salt Of The Earth	64.2
42464	42 Southern Satellites	53.5	43056	17 Green Acres	30.1	43321	42 Southern Satellites	100.0
42501	50 Heartland Communities	32.6	43060	26 Midland Crowd	71.5	43323	25 Salt Of The Earth	100.0
42503	26 Midland Crowd	27.2	43061	17 Green Acres	90.8	43324	25 Salt Of The Earth	59.7

ZIP CODE	TOP TAPESTRY CONSUMER TYPE	% 2009 HOUSE-HOLDS	ZIP CODE	TOP TAPESTRY CONSUMER TYPE	% 2009 HOUSE-HOLDS	ZIP CODE	TOP TAPESTRY CONSUMER TYPE	% 2009 HOUSE-HOLDS
43326	25 Salt Of The Earth	32.9	43566	06 Sophisticated Squires	38.0	43930	46 Rooted Rural	93.1
43331	49 Senior Sun Seekers	32.4	43567	25 Salt Of The Earth	35.5	43932	46 Rooted Rural	98.7
43332	50 Heartland Communities	42.6	43569	26 Midland Crowd	56.3	43933	46 Rooted Rural	72.1
43333	25 Salt Of The Earth	59.3	43570	42 Southern Satellites	51.1	43935	50 Heartland Communities	55.6
43334	25 Salt Of The Earth	47.7	43571	17 Green Acres	85.6	43938	50 Heartland Communities	50.5
43335	25 Salt Of The Earth	100.0	43604	65 Social Security Set	41.1	43942	50 Heartland Communities	59.0
43337	25 Salt Of The Earth	94.3	43605	53 Home Town	60.8	43943	46 Rooted Rural	44.5
43338	25 Salt Of The Earth	66.0	43606	48 Great Expectations	14.4	43944	46 Rooted Rural	62.5
43340	42 Southern Satellites	64.4	43607	62 Modest Income Homes	31.2	43945	42 Southern Satellites	49.0
43341	42 Southern Satellites	86.0	43608	51 Metro City Edge	53.0	43946	29 Rustbelt Retirees	51.3
43342	25 Salt Of The Earth	65.2	43609	60 City Dimensions	37.0	43947	29 Rustbelt Retirees	49.3
43343	25 Salt Of The Earth	100.0	43610	51 Metro City Edge	58.0	43950	29 Rustbelt Retirees	34.8
43344	32 Rustbelt Traditions	51.7	43611	32 Rustbelt Traditions	43.2	43952	29 Rustbelt Retirees	38.2
43345	25 Salt Of The Earth	99.7	43612	32 Rustbelt Traditions	57.2	43953	29 Rustbelt Retirees	48.8
43346	25 Salt Of The Earth	100.0	43613	32 Rustbelt Traditions	48.2	43963	50 Heartland Communities	100.0
43347	25 Salt Of The Earth	96.1	43614	36 Old And Newcomers	30.7	43964	25 Salt Of The Earth	26.2
43348	31 Rural Resort Dwellers	42.3	43615	33 Midlife Junction	15.7	43968	25 Salt Of The Earth	34.1
43351	32 Rustbelt Traditions	36.8	43616	18 Cozy And Comfortable	22.2	43971	50 Heartland Communities	94.0
43356	18 Cozy And Comfortable	75.5	43617	02 Suburban Splendor	40.5	43973	46 Rooted Rural	60.7
43357	17 Green Acres	47.4	43618	17 Green Acres	57.5	43976	50 Heartland Communities	58.7
43358	25 Salt Of The Earth	78.9	43619	32 Rustbelt Traditions	28.5	43977	46 Rooted Rural	79.2
43359	25 Salt Of The Earth	100.0	43620	64 City Commons	25.6	43983	46 Rooted Rural	100.0
43360	26 Midland Crowd	61.5	43623	18 Cozy And Comfortable	16.8	43986	50 Heartland Communities	40.7
43402	55 College Towns	22.7	43701	53 Home Town	14.5	43988	46 Rooted Rural	59.4
43403	63 Dorms To Diplomas	100.0	43713	50 Heartland Communities	73.9	44001	17 Green Acres	37.6
43406	32 Rustbelt Traditions	74.3	43716	46 Rooted Rural	70.8	44003	42 Southern Satellites	77.5
43407	18 Cozy And Comfortable	100.0	43718	46 Rooted Rural	45.0	44004	53 Home Town	22.9
43410	25 Salt Of The Earth	43.7	43719	50 Heartland Communities	70.9	44010	25 Salt Of The Earth	83.0
43412	17 Green Acres	59.8	43720	42 Southern Satellites	42.0	44011	07 Exurbanites	47.0
43413	25 Salt Of The Earth	97.3	43723	53 Home Town	41.9	44012	18 Cozy And Comfortable	30.1
43416	25 Salt Of The Earth	70.5	43724	25 Salt Of The Earth	35.9	44017	18 Cozy And Comfortable	40.9
43420	32 Rustbelt Traditions	25.0	43725	33 Midlife Junction	27.4	44021	17 Green Acres	45.6
43430	18 Cozy And Comfortable	41.7	43727	25 Salt Of The Earth	57.6	44022	03 Connoisseurs	33.8
43431	25 Salt Of The Earth	42.5	43728	42 Southern Satellites	74.0	44023	07 Exurbanites	48.1
43432	25 Salt Of The Earth	57.2	43730	42 Southern Satellites	88.9	44024	07 Exurbanites	27.4
43435	25 Salt Of The Earth	86.2	43731	42 Southern Satellites	61.8	44026	07 Exurbanites	100.0
43436	31 Rural Resort Dwellers	100.0	43732	25 Salt Of The Earth	76.8	44028	17 Green Acres	74.3
43438	31 Rural Resort Dwellers	100.0	43734	29 Rustbelt Retirees	65.1	44030	29 Rustbelt Retirees	20.4
43440	31 Rural Resort Dwellers	100.0	43739	17 Green Acres	49.4	44032	25 Salt Of The Earth	70.3
43442	25 Salt Of The Earth	91.7	43746	25 Salt Of The Earth	64.3	44035	32 Rustbelt Traditions	20.3
43443	29 Rustbelt Retirees	71.8	43747	46 Rooted Rural	78.5	44039	18 Cozy And Comfortable	55.6
43445	17 Green Acres	88.1	43748	42 Southern Satellites	91.9	44040	03 Connoisseurs	43.1
43447	18 Cozy And Comfortable	52.6	43749	46 Rooted Rural	99.4	44041	48 Great Expectations	21.9
43449	25 Salt Of The Earth	40.5	43754	46 Rooted Rural	63.1	44044	17 Green Acres	34.5
43450	17 Green Acres	58.5	43755	46 Rooted Rural	100.0	44046	17 Green Acres	84.2
43451	17 Green Acres	36.8	43756	50 Heartland Communities	42.2	44047	25 Salt Of The Earth	50.2
43452	31 Rural Resort Dwellers	41.8	43758	46 Rooted Rural	54.1	44048	25 Salt Of The Earth	63.1
43456	31 Rural Resort Dwellers	100.0	43760	26 Midland Crowd	49.3	44050	17 Green Acres	46.7
43457	25 Salt Of The Earth	55.1	43762	33 Midlife Junction	59.2	44052	32 Rustbelt Traditions	19.5
43460	18 Cozy And Comfortable	41.1	43764	32 Rustbelt Traditions	29.9	44053	24 Main Street, USA	62.2
43462	26 Midland Crowd	87.9	43766	56 Rural Bypasses	65.1	44054	17 Green Acres	23.7
43464	25 Salt Of The Earth	73.7	43767	25 Salt Of The Earth	86.1	44055	32 Rustbelt Traditions	39.8
43465	49 Senior Sun Seekers	39.1	43771	42 Southern Satellites	100.0	44056	17 Green Acres	46.6
43466	25 Salt Of The Earth	94.2	43772	50 Heartland Communities	62.4	44057	17 Green Acres	31.6
43469	17 Green Acres	40.0	43773	42 Southern Satellites	47.2	44060	18 Cozy And Comfortable	26.4
43501	25 Salt Of The Earth	100.0	43777	42 Southern Satellites	67.0	44062	38 Industrious Urban Fringe	21.6
43502	17 Green Acres	32.7	43778	46 Rooted Rural	57.0	44064	17 Green Acres	99.0
43504	17 Green Acres	100.0	43779	46 Rooted Rural	68.0	44065	07 Exurbanites	73.1
43506	42 Southern Satellites	22.3	43780	46 Rooted Rural	98.4	44067	13 In Style	20.6
43511	25 Salt Of The Earth	100.0	43782	42 Southern Satellites	100.0	44070	18 Cozy And Comfortable	44.0
43512	25 Salt Of The Earth	25.5	43783	25 Salt Of The Earth	40.4	44072	03 Connoisseurs	90.1
43515	25 Salt Of The Earth	35.6	43787	46 Rooted Rural	45.4	44074	17 Green Acres	24.0
43516	25 Salt Of The Earth	65.4	43788	42 Southern Satellites	78.0	44076	42 Southern Satellites	36.4
43517	25 Salt Of The Earth	63.1	43793	42 Southern Satellites	30.9	44077	17 Green Acres	17.1
43518	25 Salt Of The Earth	88.2	43802	42 Southern Satellites	82.8	44081	17 Green Acres	63.1
43521	53 Home Town	52.6	43804	42 Southern Satellites	60.9	44082	42 Southern Satellites	100.0
43522	17 Green Acres	63.1	43811	42 Southern Satellites	63.7	44084	17 Green Acres	64.0
43524	25 Salt Of The Earth	100.0	43812	53 Home Town	30.8	44085	17 Green Acres	53.5
43525	17 Green Acres	100.0	43821	25 Salt Of The Earth	49.5	44086	17 Green Acres	57.6
43526	25 Salt Of The Earth	54.2	43822	26 Midland Crowd	60.1	44087	13 In Style	37.2
43527	32 Rustbelt Traditions	53.1	43824	25 Salt Of The Earth	58.3	44089	18 Cozy And Comfortable	27.7
43528	02 Suburban Splendor	21.3	43830	17 Green Acres	29.4	44090	17 Green Acres	43.0
43532	25 Salt Of The Earth	93.4	43832	53 Home Town	26.0	44092	29 Rustbelt Retirees	69.5
43533	25 Salt Of The Earth	100.0	43837	25 Salt Of The Earth	62.0	44093	25 Salt Of The Earth	63.3
43534	25 Salt Of The Earth	81.6	43840	25 Salt Of The Earth	79.0	44094	30 Retirement Communities	31.5
43535	25 Salt Of The Earth	100.0	43843	26 Midland Crowd	51.3	44095	29 Rustbelt Retirees	30.9
43536	25 Salt Of The Earth	100.0	43844	42 Southern Satellites	52.0	44099	25 Salt Of The Earth	86.6
43537	13 In Style	26.1	43845	25 Salt Of The Earth	53.8	44102	60 City Dimensions	57.2
43540	25 Salt Of The Earth	100.0	43901	50 Heartland Communities	64.2	44103	62 Modest Income Homes	33.3
43542	06 Sophisticated Squires	62.6	43902	46 Rooted Rural	100.0	44104	62 Modest Income Homes	36.7
43543	25 Salt Of The Earth	35.4	43903	46 Rooted Rural	53.7	44105	53 Home Town	20.5
43545	25 Salt Of The Earth	26.7	43906	62 Modest Income Homes	25.4	44106	27 Metro Renters	19.3
43548	25 Salt Of The Earth	95.5	43907	50 Heartland Communities	66.0	44107	24 Main Street, USA	27.8
43549	25 Salt Of The Earth	100.0	43908	46 Rooted Rural	53.7	44108	62 Modest Income Homes	37.9
43551	13 In Style	14.1	43910	29 Rustbelt Retirees	33.4	44109	60 City Dimensions	30.6
43554	25 Salt Of The Earth	100.0	43912	50 Heartland Communities	80.5	44110	51 Metro City Edge	43.1
43556	25 Salt Of The Earth	56.1	43913	50 Heartland Communities	100.0	44111	32 Rustbelt Traditions	37.2
43557	25 Salt Of The Earth	67.3	43915	29 Rustbelt Retirees	49.6	44112	51 Metro City Edge	48.6
43558	17 Green Acres	36.3	43917	50 Heartland Communities	80.3	44113	60 City Dimensions	48.9
43560	13 In Style	21.9	43920	53 Home Town	30.5	44114	65 Social Security Set	65.6

CONSUMER TYPE

ZIP CODE	TOP TAPESTRY CONSUMER TYPE	% 2009 HOUSE-HOLDS	ZIP CODE	TOP TAPESTRY CONSUMER TYPE	% 2009 HOUSE-HOLDS	ZIP CODE	TOP TAPESTRY CONSUMER TYPE	% 2009 HOUSE-HOLDS
44115	64 City Commons	57.3	44401	17 Green Acres	93.9	44647	25 Salt Of The Earth	26.2
44116	30 Retirement Communities	33.5	44402	25 Salt Of The Earth	95.1	44651	25 Salt Of The Earth	51.1
44117	65 Social Security Set	44.3	44403	46 Rooted Rural	50.0	44654	25 Salt Of The Earth	28.3
44118	18 Cozy And Comfortable	16.0	44404	25 Salt Of The Earth	95.1	44656	42 Southern Satellites	59.9
44119	32 Rustbelt Traditions	40.3	44405	29 Rustbelt Retirees	48.7	44657	25 Salt Of The Earth	66.7
44120	51 Metro City Edge	25.1	44406	07 Exurbanites	35.3	44662	29 Rustbelt Retirees	43.4
44121	18 Cozy And Comfortable	25.6	44408	17 Green Acres	26.8	44663	25 Salt Of The Earth	26.7
44122	30 Retirement Communities	28.3	44410	25 Salt Of The Earth	33.6	44666	17 Green Acres	67.3
44123	32 Rustbelt Traditions	55.7	44411	26 Midland Crowd	100.0	44667	25 Salt Of The Earth	23.6
44124	30 Retirement Communities	27.4	44412	17 Green Acres	80.0	44669	25 Salt Of The Earth	100.0
44125	29 Rustbelt Retirees	45.1	44413	25 Salt Of The Earth	28.8	44672	32 Rustbelt Traditions	40.8
44126	14 Prosperous Empty Nesters	32.8	44417	25 Salt Of The Earth	94.5	44675	46 Rooted Rural	55.6
44127	60 City Dimensions	49.2	44418	17 Green Acres	51.8	44676	25 Salt Of The Earth	62.6
44128	34 Family Foundations	67.5	44420	29 Rustbelt Retirees	28.0	44677	24 Main Street, USA	50.1
44129	29 Rustbelt Retirees	32.0	44423	46 Rooted Rural	51.6	44680	33 Midlife Junction	48.2
44130	29 Rustbelt Retirees	32.2	44425	29 Rustbelt Retirees	18.4	44681	25 Salt Of The Earth	58.2
44131	14 Prosperous Empty Nesters	76.5	44427	25 Salt Of The Earth	81.6	44683	53 Home Town	45.4
44132	29 Rustbelt Retirees	34.6	44428	25 Salt Of The Earth	54.0	44685	06 Sophisticated Squires	22.5
44133	13 In Style	32.6	44429	32 Rustbelt Traditions	58.6	44688	46 Rooted Rural	34.2
44134	29 Rustbelt Retirees	40.2	44430	32 Rustbelt Traditions	29.7	44689	42 Southern Satellites	54.2
44135	32 Rustbelt Traditions	40.2	44431	25 Salt Of The Earth	68.4	44691	25 Salt Of The Earth	21.7
44136	06 Sophisticated Squires	24.7	44432	46 Rooted Rural	30.8	44695	46 Rooted Rural	98.9
44137	32 Rustbelt Traditions	50.0	44436	25 Salt Of The Earth	37.5	44699	46 Rooted Rural	71.9
44138	13 In Style	32.0	44437	18 Cozy And Comfortable	38.6	44702	65 Social Security Set	91.5
44139	02 Suburban Splendor	50.8	44438	50 Heartland Communities	45.1	44703	48 Great Expectations	58.6
44140	18 Cozy And Comfortable	30.1	44440	17 Green Acres	28.5	44704	62 Modest Income Homes	56.2
44141	07 Exurbanites	41.3	44441	42 Southern Satellites	43.8	44705	53 Home Town	54.4
44142	18 Cozy And Comfortable	45.7	44442	29 Rustbelt Retirees	100.0	44706	25 Salt Of The Earth	45.2
44143	14 Prosperous Empty Nesters	32.6	44443	46 Rooted Rural	70.6	44707	64 City Commons	28.2
44144	29 Rustbelt Retirees	33.9	44444	32 Rustbelt Traditions	27.6	44708	29 Rustbelt Retirees	28.9
44145	07 Exurbanites	22.9	44445	25 Salt Of The Earth	67.2	44709	48 Great Expectations	17.4
44146	57 Simple Living	23.7	44446	33 Midlife Junction	40.0	44710	53 Home Town	39.6
44147	13 In Style	67.0	44449	25 Salt Of The Earth	55.5	44714	32 Rustbelt Traditions	30.0
44149	07 Exurbanites	37.3	44450	25 Salt Of The Earth	86.3	44718	02 Suburban Splendor	37.0
44201	25 Salt Of The Earth	47.7	44451	25 Salt Of The Earth	56.9	44720	13 In Style	25.5
44202	04 Boomburbs	36.2	44452	17 Green Acres	73.4	44721	18 Cozy And Comfortable	41.6
44203	29 Rustbelt Retirees	18.0	44454	26 Midland Crowd	100.0	44730	25 Salt Of The Earth	95.3
44212	06 Sophisticated Squires	19.5	44455	42 Southern Satellites	45.5	44802	25 Salt Of The Earth	100.0
44214	25 Salt Of The Earth	86.2	44460	25 Salt Of The Earth	33.2	44804	25 Salt Of The Earth	61.3
44215	32 Rustbelt Traditions	76.0	44470	25 Salt Of The Earth	34.9	44805	25 Salt Of The Earth	22.8
44216	17 Green Acres	48.7	44471	29 Rustbelt Retirees	39.4	44807	25 Salt Of The Earth	98.6
44217	25 Salt Of The Earth	61.0	44473	46 Rooted Rural	42.4	44811	32 Rustbelt Traditions	41.7
44221	32 Rustbelt Traditions	23.9	44481	25 Salt Of The Earth	33.8	44813	25 Salt Of The Earth	82.2
44223	13 In Style	24.3	44483	29 Rustbelt Retirees	24.2	44814	17 Green Acres	96.1
44224	18 Cozy And Comfortable	16.4	44484	14 Prosperous Empty Nesters	16.4	44817	25 Salt Of The Earth	85.9
44230	17 Green Acres	35.6	44485	29 Rustbelt Retirees	22.8	44818	25 Salt Of The Earth	61.9
44231	42 Southern Satellites	33.9	44490	25 Salt Of The Earth	60.7	44820	25 Salt Of The Earth	25.3
44233	07 Exurbanites	77.5	44491	17 Green Acres	75.2	44822	25 Salt Of The Earth	87.6
44234	17 Green Acres	63.6	44502	53 Home Town	54.4	44824	18 Cozy And Comfortable	52.6
44235	17 Green Acres	100.0	44503	65 Social Security Set	100.0	44826	25 Salt Of The Earth	71.7
44236	02 Suburban Splendor	45.4	44504	30 Retirement Communities	24.5	44827	53 Home Town	25.8
44240	55 College Towns	25.7	44505	62 Modest Income Homes	40.4	44830	53 Home Town	27.6
44241	16 Enterprising Professionals	30.9	44506	62 Modest Income Homes	100.0	44833	25 Salt Of The Earth	24.3
44243	63 Dorms To Diplomas	100.0	44507	62 Modest Income Homes	47.5	44836	25 Salt Of The Earth	65.2
44253	17 Green Acres	93.3	44509	53 Home Town	33.5	44837	42 Southern Satellites	73.5
44254	17 Green Acres	35.6	44510	62 Modest Income Homes	83.9	44839	17 Green Acres	34.0
44255	17 Green Acres	64.9	44511	29 Rustbelt Retirees	47.6	44840	25 Salt Of The Earth	63.5
44256	07 Exurbanites	20.7	44512	18 Cozy And Comfortable	17.2	44841	25 Salt Of The Earth	92.8
44260	18 Cozy And Comfortable	40.2	44514	29 Rustbelt Retirees	34.3	44842	32 Rustbelt Traditions	22.4
44262	07 Exurbanites	65.6	44515	29 Rustbelt Retirees	26.1	44843	17 Green Acres	40.3
44264	07 Exurbanites	54.1	44555	62 Modest Income Homes	100.0	44844	25 Salt Of The Earth	78.7
44266	26 Midland Crowd	19.8	44601	53 Home Town	19.3	44846	17 Green Acres	51.6
44270	32 Rustbelt Traditions	45.5	44606	25 Salt Of The Earth	45.0	44847	25 Salt Of The Earth	58.5
44272	18 Cozy And Comfortable	51.0	44608	42 Southern Satellites	41.0	44849	25 Salt Of The Earth	60.8
44273	17 Green Acres	47.5	44609	25 Salt Of The Earth	74.6	44851	25 Salt Of The Earth	27.6
44275	17 Green Acres	100.0	44611	25 Salt Of The Earth	97.0	44853	25 Salt Of The Earth	100.0
44276	25 Salt Of The Earth	75.9	44612	17 Green Acres	48.1	44854	25 Salt Of The Earth	60.4
44278	29 Rustbelt Retirees	22.3	44613	25 Salt Of The Earth	94.3	44855	25 Salt Of The Earth	100.0
44280	07 Exurbanites	54.4	44614	18 Cozy And Comfortable	40.0	44857	32 Rustbelt Traditions	13.5
44281	07 Exurbanites	15.5	44615	25 Salt Of The Earth	43.4	44859	25 Salt Of The Earth	98.5
44286	07 Exurbanites	76.2	44618	26 Midland Crowd	36.9	44864	25 Salt Of The Earth	43.1
44287	25 Salt Of The Earth	59.5	44620	25 Salt Of The Earth	71.5	44865	42 Southern Satellites	68.3
44288	51 Metro City Edge	45.6	44621	50 Heartland Communities	31.5	44866	25 Salt Of The Earth	100.0
44301	32 Rustbelt Traditions	53.4	44622	25 Salt Of The Earth	23.0	44867	25 Salt Of The Earth	77.9
44302	48 Great Expectations	27.0	44624	47 Las Casas	37.4	44870	18 Cozy And Comfortable	17.2
44303	30 Retirement Communities	17.7	44625	25 Salt Of The Earth	100.0	44875	32 Rustbelt Traditions	22.7
44304	63 Dorms To Diplomas	33.9	44626	25 Salt Of The Earth	78.6	44878	42 Southern Satellites	50.0
44305	32 Rustbelt Traditions	77.7	44627	37 Prairie Living	39.2	44880	25 Salt Of The Earth	91.2
44306	53 Home Town	25.5	44628	42 Southern Satellites	58.4	44882	25 Salt Of The Earth	38.7
44307	51 Metro City Edge	33.6	44629	25 Salt Of The Earth	34.1	44883	25 Salt Of The Earth	26.5
44308	65 Social Security Set	97.1	44632	17 Green Acres	70.9	44887	25 Salt Of The Earth	100.0
44310	32 Rustbelt Traditions	34.6	44633	42 Southern Satellites	66.8	44889	17 Green Acres	58.2
44311	55 College Towns	20.7	44634	25 Salt Of The Earth	100.0	44890	25 Salt Of The Earth	39.7
44312	32 Rustbelt Traditions	34.9	44637	42 Southern Satellites	65.9	44902	53 Home Town	42.1
44313	18 Cozy And Comfortable	17.9	44638	25 Salt Of The Earth	55.0	44903	17 Green Acres	16.9
44314	32 Rustbelt Traditions	45.5	44641	18 Cozy And Comfortable	30.9	44904	07 Exurbanites	19.5
44319	18 Cozy And Comfortable	27.2	44643	29 Rustbelt Retirees	36.6	44905	32 Rustbelt Traditions	26.7
44320	34 Family Foundations	40.1	44644	42 Southern Satellites	28.5	44906	50 Heartland Communities	19.5
44321	18 Cozy And Comfortable	25.0	44645	25 Salt Of The Earth	63.4	44907	33 Midlife Junction	16.6
44333	03 Connoisseurs	25.2	44646	29 Rustbelt Retirees	15.1	45001	53 Home Town	59.3

ZIP CODE	TOP TAPESTRY CONSUMER TYPE	% 2009 HOUSE-HOLDS	ZIP CODE	TOP TAPESTRY CONSUMER TYPE	% 2009 HOUSE-HOLDS	ZIP CODE	TOP TAPESTRY CONSUMER TYPE	% 2009 HOUSE-HOLDS
45002	06 Sophisticated Squires	21.3	45237	57 Simple Living	24.1	45427	62 Modest Income Homes	35.4
45003	25 Salt Of The Earth	72.7	45238	18 Cozy And Comfortable	21.3	45429	14 Prosperous Empty Nesters	32.1
45005	18 Cozy And Comfortable	18.5	45239	32 Rustbelt Traditions	26.9	45430	07 Exurbanites	77.4
45011	12 Up And Coming Families	29.3	45240	19 Milk And Cookies	21.7	45431	07 Exurbanites	22.3
45013	32 Rustbelt Traditions	17.6	45241	13 In Style	21.5	45432	29 Rustbelt Retirees	32.3
45014	16 Enterprising Professionals	26.4	45242	02 Suburban Splendor	16.4	45433	40 Military Proximity	99.3
45015	32 Rustbelt Traditions	32.7	45243	01 Top Rung	26.0	45434	07 Exurbanites	42.7
45030	17 Green Acres	16.6	45244	02 Suburban Splendor	30.5	45439	48 Great Expectations	37.3
45034	12 Up And Coming Families	80.5	45245	16 Enterprising Professionals	17.9	45440	14 Prosperous Empty Nesters	21.6
45036	04 Boomburbs	17.6	45246	29 Rustbelt Retirees	19.4	45449	18 Cozy And Comfortable	23.6
45039	12 Up And Coming Families	43.0	45247	18 Cozy And Comfortable	32.0	45458	13 In Style	60.7
45040	04 Boomburbs	59.5	45248	07 Exurbanites	21.7	45459	13 In Style	33.1
45042	17 Green Acres	20.1	45249	02 Suburban Splendor	38.1	45469	63 Dorms To Diplomas	100.0
45044	48 Great Expectations	15.0	45251	19 Milk And Cookies	28.1	45502	18 Cozy And Comfortable	40.8
45050	12 Up And Coming Families	48.0	45252	13 In Style	56.0	45503	32 Rustbelt Traditions	21.6
45052	06 Sophisticated Squires	43.8	45255	06 Sophisticated Squires	20.7	45504	14 Prosperous Empty Nesters	14.7
45053	17 Green Acres	54.4	45275	41 Crossroads	100.0	45505	32 Rustbelt Traditions	20.3
45054	17 Green Acres	50.6	45302	25 Salt Of The Earth	55.8	45506	34 Family Foundations	29.2
45056	63 Dorms To Diplomas	36.7	45303	42 Southern Satellites	66.3	45601	42 Southern Satellites	18.6
45064	17 Green Acres	87.6	45304	25 Salt Of The Earth	42.7	45612	42 Southern Satellites	58.8
45065	42 Southern Satellites	72.2	45305	13 In Style	38.6	45613	42 Southern Satellites	100.0
45066	04 Boomburbs	36.0	45306	25 Salt Of The Earth	75.3	45614	46 Rooted Rural	64.4
45067	17 Green Acres	26.6	45308	25 Salt Of The Earth	52.3	45616	56 Rural Bypasses	49.3
45068	17 Green Acres	66.2	45309	18 Cozy And Comfortable	30.7	45619	50 Heartland Communities	33.4
45069	04 Boomburbs	30.4	45311	25 Salt Of The Earth	55.5	45620	46 Rooted Rural	89.8
45101	41 Crossroads	63.2	45312	17 Green Acres	77.4	45622	42 Southern Satellites	96.4
45102	12 Up And Coming Families	31.2	45314	17 Green Acres	66.1	45623	42 Southern Satellites	75.2
45103	12 Up And Coming Families	18.0	45315	17 Green Acres	52.1	45628	26 Midland Crowd	37.5
45106	25 Salt Of The Earth	22.7	45317	25 Salt Of The Earth	100.0	45629	46 Rooted Rural	74.0
45107	32 Rustbelt Traditions	24.0	45318	25 Salt Of The Earth	56.5	45631	26 Midland Crowd	22.2
45111	18 Cozy And Comfortable	100.0	45320	17 Green Acres	28.3	45634	42 Southern Satellites	55.9
45113	17 Green Acres	45.7	45321	25 Salt Of The Earth	100.0	45638	50 Heartland Communities	28.4
45118	26 Midland Crowd	84.7	45322	18 Cozy And Comfortable	33.9	45640	33 Midlife Junction	23.6
45120	26 Midland Crowd	63.9	45323	18 Cozy And Comfortable	30.4	45644	17 Green Acres	32.1
45121	26 Midland Crowd	32.1	45324	32 Rustbelt Traditions	15.7	45645	42 Southern Satellites	88.0
45122	25 Salt Of The Earth	57.0	45325	17 Green Acres	94.9	45646	56 Rural Bypasses	87.2
45123	25 Salt Of The Earth	41.8	45326	25 Salt Of The Earth	100.0	45647	42 Southern Satellites	77.0
45130	26 Midland Crowd	36.5	45327	25 Salt Of The Earth	38.3	45648	56 Rural Bypasses	31.9
45133	25 Salt Of The Earth	20.8	45331	25 Salt Of The Earth	34.2	45650	56 Rural Bypasses	100.0
45135	42 Southern Satellites	60.2	45332	25 Salt Of The Earth	100.0	45651	42 Southern Satellites	79.7
45140	04 Boomburbs	26.1	45333	25 Salt Of The Earth	65.0	45652	46 Rooted Rural	43.1
45142	25 Salt Of The Earth	48.6	45334	25 Salt Of The Earth	86.1	45653	46 Rooted Rural	55.1
45144	56 Rural Bypasses	40.4	45335	25 Salt Of The Earth	43.6	45654	42 Southern Satellites	96.4
45146	17 Green Acres	34.5	45337	25 Salt Of The Earth	79.3	45656	56 Rural Bypasses	38.9
45148	25 Salt Of The Earth	60.7	45338	25 Salt Of The Earth	90.1	45657	46 Rooted Rural	46.5
45150	06 Sophisticated Squires	21.7	45339	25 Salt Of The Earth	81.1	45658	42 Southern Satellites	86.5
45152	17 Green Acres	35.6	45340	25 Salt Of The Earth	53.2	45659	56 Rural Bypasses	82.8
45153	42 Southern Satellites	57.0	45341	29 Rustbelt Retirees	46.8	45660	42 Southern Satellites	56.1
45154	26 Midland Crowd	69.3	45342	16 Enterprising Professionals	38.5	45661	42 Southern Satellites	77.0
45157	26 Midland Crowd	30.5	45344	32 Rustbelt Traditions	45.1	45662	53 Home Town	18.1
45159	41 Crossroads	43.9	45345	25 Salt Of The Earth	59.4	45663	50 Heartland Communities	37.2
45160	33 Midlife Junction	74.3	45346	25 Salt Of The Earth	100.0	45669	29 Rustbelt Retirees	27.6
45162	17 Green Acres	73.9	45347	25 Salt Of The Earth	36.4	45671	42 Southern Satellites	99.0
45167	50 Heartland Communities	60.9	45348	37 Prairie Living	61.4	45672	42 Southern Satellites	100.0
45168	46 Rooted Rural	51.1	45356	32 Rustbelt Traditions	33.3	45673	42 Southern Satellites	100.0
45169	42 Southern Satellites	60.0	45359	25 Salt Of The Earth	64.1	45675	42 Southern Satellites	100.0
45171	25 Salt Of The Earth	56.0	45362	25 Salt Of The Earth	77.1	45678	46 Rooted Rural	63.4
45174	03 Connoisseurs	50.5	45363	17 Green Acres	85.4	45679	50 Heartland Communities	44.0
45176	26 Midland Crowd	34.6	45365	32 Rustbelt Traditions	25.3	45680	50 Heartland Communities	17.7
45177	17 Green Acres	20.4	45368	25 Salt Of The Earth	41.9	45681	25 Salt Of The Earth	51.1
45202	27 Metro Renters	31.2	45369	17 Green Acres	60.9	45682	42 Southern Satellites	50.7
45203	64 City Commons	47.9	45370	02 Suburban Splendor	44.3	45684	46 Rooted Rural	60.6
45204	60 City Dimensions	39.2	45371	13 In Style	15.5	45685	42 Southern Satellites	48.8
45205	48 Great Expectations	39.3	45373	32 Rustbelt Traditions	19.9	45686	42 Southern Satellites	56.7
45206	64 City Commons	19.5	45377	48 Great Expectations	27.5	45688	56 Rural Bypasses	96.9
45207	62 Modest Income Homes	28.8	45380	25 Salt Of The Earth	84.8	45690	42 Southern Satellites	18.9
45208	22 Metropolitans	28.5	45381	25 Salt Of The Earth	87.8	45692	42 Southern Satellites	38.7
45209	22 Metropolitans	47.9	45382	25 Salt Of The Earth	83.7	45693	46 Rooted Rural	35.5
45211	48 Great Expectations	33.1	45383	33 Midlife Junction	35.4	45694	33 Midlife Junction	27.8
45212	48 Great Expectations	45.9	45385	32 Rustbelt Traditions	17.0	45695	42 Southern Satellites	100.0
45213	48 Great Expectations	26.3	45387	22 Metropolitans	55.8	45696	56 Rural Bypasses	51.8
45214	64 City Commons	32.0	45388	25 Salt Of The Earth	94.1	45697	42 Southern Satellites	64.2
45215	36 Old And Newcomers	23.2	45390	53 Home Town	57.8	45701	63 Dorms To Diplomas	35.8
45216	32 Rustbelt Traditions	31.1	45402	62 Modest Income Homes	41.0	45710	26 Midland Crowd	36.9
45217	32 Rustbelt Traditions	38.6	45403	48 Great Expectations	31.8	45711	26 Midland Crowd	56.9
45218	48 Great Expectations	41.5	45404	53 Home Town	59.8	45714	33 Midlife Junction	21.7
45219	55 College Towns	46.0	45405	48 Great Expectations	37.0	45715	46 Rooted Rural	40.9
45220	27 Metro Renters	30.0	45406	51 Metro City Edge	32.3	45723	46 Rooted Rural	98.8
45223	48 Great Expectations	44.7	45408	62 Modest Income Homes	50.8	45724	42 Southern Satellites	63.9
45224	34 Family Foundations	25.3	45409	28 Aspiring Young Families	16.0	45727	42 Southern Satellites	49.5
45225	64 City Commons	62.4	45410	32 Rustbelt Traditions	39.6	45729	17 Green Acres	53.8
45226	22 Metropolitans	39.0	45414	32 Rustbelt Traditions	23.0	45732	56 Rural Bypasses	52.4
45227	32 Rustbelt Traditions	23.6	45415	07 Exurbanites	32.8	45734	46 Rooted Rural	98.4
45228	02 Suburban Splendor	100.0	45416	34 Family Foundations	37.1	45735	46 Rooted Rural	85.4
45229	64 City Commons	32.1	45417	62 Modest Income Homes	82.2	45741	46 Rooted Rural	52.8
45230	36 Old And Newcomers	32.0	45418	29 Rustbelt Retirees	29.3	45742	17 Green Acres	45.6
45231	18 Cozy And Comfortable	19.9	45419	55 College Towns	21.2	45743	46 Rooted Rural	56.1
45232	64 City Commons	67.2	45420	32 Rustbelt Traditions	59.7	45744	25 Salt Of The Earth	56.1
45233	07 Exurbanites	20.0	45424	19 Milk And Cookies	28.8	45745	46 Rooted Rural	38.9
45236	29 Rustbelt Retirees	23.0	45426	33 Midlife Junction	19.4	45746	56 Rural Bypasses	87.7

CONSUMER TYPE

ZIP CODE	TOP TAPESTRY CONSUMER TYPE	% 2009 HOUSE-HOLDS	ZIP CODE	TOP TAPESTRY CONSUMER TYPE	% 2009 HOUSE-HOLDS	ZIP CODE	TOP TAPESTRY CONSUMER TYPE	% 2009 HOUSE-HOLDS
45750	33 Midlife Junction	24.3	46034	17 Green Acres	74.3	46216	13 In Style	93.3
45760	56 Rural Bypasses	45.5	46035	42 Southern Satellites	88.0	46217	17 Green Acres	53.3
45761	26 Midland Crowd	41.9	46036	32 Rustbelt Traditions	46.0	46218	62 Modest Income Homes	29.1
45764	50 Heartland Communities	27.3	46037	04 Boomburbs	87.9	46219	32 Rustbelt Traditions	30.4
45766	26 Midland Crowd	92.7	46038	04 Boomburbs	41.6	46220	22 Metropolitans	52.8
45767	50 Heartland Communities	62.2	46039	25 Salt Of The Earth	100.0	46221	19 Milk And Cookies	39.0
45768	25 Salt Of The Earth	70.9	46040	32 Rustbelt Traditions	36.7	46222	53 Home Town	31.4
45769	46 Rooted Rural	53.6	46041	32 Rustbelt Traditions	22.6	46224	52 Inner City Tenants	43.4
45770	46 Rooted Rural	98.1	46044	25 Salt Of The Earth	45.5	46225	60 City Dimensions	27.2
45771	46 Rooted Rural	82.9	46048	26 Midland Crowd	100.0	46226	32 Rustbelt Traditions	21.1
45772	46 Rooted Rural	89.1	46049	25 Salt Of The Earth	100.0	46227	33 Midlife Junction	17.9
45773	25 Salt Of The Earth	54.5	46050	42 Southern Satellites	59.4	46228	12 Up And Coming Families	30.6
45775	56 Rural Bypasses	51.2	46051	32 Rustbelt Traditions	74.0	46229	48 Great Expectations	23.5
45776	41 Crossroads	47.3	46052	17 Green Acres	22.0	46231	19 Milk And Cookies	63.3
45778	46 Rooted Rural	50.3	46055	17 Green Acres	76.2	46234	28 Aspiring Young Families	21.5
45780	33 Midlife Junction	51.0	46056	25 Salt Of The Earth	95.7	46235	48 Great Expectations	27.9
45784	17 Green Acres	62.5	46057	25 Salt Of The Earth	83.8	46236	12 Up And Coming Families	41.6
45786	46 Rooted Rural	53.1	46058	32 Rustbelt Traditions	48.1	46237	12 Up And Coming Families	36.4
45788	25 Salt Of The Earth	70.1	46060	12 Up And Coming Families	17.9	46239	17 Green Acres	30.7
45789	42 Southern Satellites	77.8	46062	12 Up And Coming Families	65.2	46240	39 Young And Restless	26.8
45801	53 Home Town	35.0	46064	17 Green Acres	46.3	46241	53 Home Town	36.0
45804	53 Home Town	36.8	46065	25 Salt Of The Earth	97.0	46250	39 Young And Restless	32.9
45805	33 Midlife Junction	26.4	46068	17 Green Acres	45.7	46254	28 Aspiring Young Families	34.2
45806	17 Green Acres	26.9	46069	17 Green Acres	43.3	46256	06 Sophisticated Squires	35.8
45807	17 Green Acres	27.2	46070	42 Southern Satellites	55.5	46259	04 Boomburbs	41.3
45808	25 Salt Of The Earth	100.0	46071	25 Salt Of The Earth	63.2	46260	22 Metropolitans	27.4
45810	33 Midlife Junction	29.8	46072	25 Salt Of The Earth	37.7	46268	39 Young And Restless	21.7
45812	42 Southern Satellites	88.8	46074	12 Up And Coming Families	55.5	46278	04 Boomburbs	51.4
45813	25 Salt Of The Earth	99.9	46075	25 Salt Of The Earth	83.2	46280	18 Cozy And Comfortable	48.9
45814	25 Salt Of The Earth	82.5	46076	42 Southern Satellites	57.9	46290	14 Prosperous Empty Nesters	76.1
45817	25 Salt Of The Earth	24.1	46077	04 Boomburbs	31.5	46303	17 Green Acres	34.5
45821	42 Southern Satellites	61.7	46104	25 Salt Of The Earth	100.0	46304	17 Green Acres	25.7
45822	25 Salt Of The Earth	22.3	46105	42 Southern Satellites	47.4	46307	13 In Style	31.8
45827	42 Southern Satellites	44.1	46106	32 Rustbelt Traditions	28.5	46310	17 Green Acres	43.8
45828	25 Salt Of The Earth	44.3	46107	32 Rustbelt Traditions	38.1	46311	17 Green Acres	26.9
45830	25 Salt Of The Earth	60.7	46110	25 Salt Of The Earth	66.3	46312	60 City Dimensions	42.3
45831	42 Southern Satellites	50.9	46112	12 Up And Coming Families	23.6	46319	18 Cozy And Comfortable	39.7
45832	25 Salt Of The Earth	100.0	46113	17 Green Acres	42.7	46320	51 Metro City Edge	15.2
45833	25 Salt Of The Earth	34.9	46115	25 Salt Of The Earth	64.1	46321	14 Prosperous Empty Nesters	36.2
45835	25 Salt Of The Earth	96.9	46117	17 Green Acres	100.0	46322	24 Main Street, USA	30.9
45836	42 Southern Satellites	70.7	46118	25 Salt Of The Earth	65.7	46323	32 Rustbelt Traditions	56.5
45840	48 Great Expectations	15.5	46120	42 Southern Satellites	35.9	46324	32 Rustbelt Traditions	69.6
45841	25 Salt Of The Earth	83.9	46121	25 Salt Of The Earth	51.3	46327	53 Home Town	30.9
45843	42 Southern Satellites	60.5	46122	17 Green Acres	45.7	46340	25 Salt Of The Earth	100.0
45844	25 Salt Of The Earth	92.7	46123	12 Up And Coming Families	53.8	46341	24 Main Street, USA	26.8
45845	17 Green Acres	98.6	46124	32 Rustbelt Traditions	27.9	46342	18 Cozy And Comfortable	35.3
45846	25 Salt Of The Earth	83.3	46126	17 Green Acres	51.7	46347	32 Rustbelt Traditions	54.9
45849	42 Southern Satellites	85.5	46127	25 Salt Of The Earth	95.2	46348	25 Salt Of The Earth	99.3
45850	25 Salt Of The Earth	99.4	46128	25 Salt Of The Earth	83.1	46349	25 Salt Of The Earth	74.2
45851	25 Salt Of The Earth	73.3	46130	17 Green Acres	100.0	46350	17 Green Acres	31.5
45856	25 Salt Of The Earth	73.2	46131	28 Aspiring Young Families	22.2	46356	17 Green Acres	27.8
45858	25 Salt Of The Earth	47.3	46133	25 Salt Of The Earth	83.5	46360	32 Rustbelt Traditions	16.1
45860	17 Green Acres	100.0	46135	25 Salt Of The Earth	33.9	46365	17 Green Acres	54.8
45862	42 Southern Satellites	58.8	46140	17 Green Acres	43.1	46366	42 Southern Satellites	46.7
45863	25 Salt Of The Earth	100.0	46142	06 Sophisticated Squires	26.4	46368	41 Crossroads	34.2
45865	18 Cozy And Comfortable	46.6	46143	12 Up And Coming Families	29.0	46371	25 Salt Of The Earth	47.8
45867	25 Salt Of The Earth	98.7	46147	25 Salt Of The Earth	60.9	46373	06 Sophisticated Squires	53.4
45868	25 Salt Of The Earth	100.0	46148	32 Rustbelt Traditions	45.0	46374	25 Salt Of The Earth	92.1
45869	17 Green Acres	42.6	46149	26 Midland Crowd	55.4	46375	13 In Style	24.7
45871	32 Rustbelt Traditions	59.4	46150	25 Salt Of The Earth	86.9	46382	25 Salt Of The Earth	65.0
45872	32 Rustbelt Traditions	57.0	46151	17 Green Acres	41.0	46383	17 Green Acres	22.3
45873	42 Southern Satellites	74.4	46156	25 Salt Of The Earth	88.7	46385	07 Exurbanites	25.5
45874	25 Salt Of The Earth	50.6	46157	25 Salt Of The Earth	99.0	46390	25 Salt Of The Earth	100.0
45875	25 Salt Of The Earth	63.7	46158	17 Green Acres	32.6	46391	26 Midland Crowd	42.5
45877	25 Salt Of The Earth	97.9	46160	25 Salt Of The Earth	37.8	46392	25 Salt Of The Earth	35.5
45879	32 Rustbelt Traditions	45.7	46161	32 Rustbelt Traditions	44.2	46394	29 Rustbelt Retirees	43.7
45880	50 Heartland Communities	57.4	46162	25 Salt Of The Earth	54.9	46402	62 Modest Income Homes	42.7
45881	25 Salt Of The Earth	88.8	46163	06 Sophisticated Squires	38.6	46403	51 Metro City Edge	29.7
45882	25 Salt Of The Earth	67.6	46164	31 Rural Resort Dwellers	42.6	46404	34 Family Foundations	52.8
45883	25 Salt Of The Earth	50.8	46165	17 Green Acres	52.4	46405	32 Rustbelt Traditions	52.2
45885	32 Rustbelt Traditions	36.2	46166	25 Salt Of The Earth	56.7	46406	34 Family Foundations	35.8
45886	25 Salt Of The Earth	98.5	46167	17 Green Acres	58.3	46407	62 Modest Income Homes	44.6
45887	25 Salt Of The Earth	63.7	46168	18 Cozy And Comfortable	30.0	46408	34 Family Foundations	31.7
45889	17 Green Acres	100.0	46171	25 Salt Of The Earth	100.0	46409	51 Metro City Edge	86.2
45890	25 Salt Of The Earth	100.0	46172	25 Salt Of The Earth	64.2	46410	24 Main Street, USA	28.6
45891	32 Rustbelt Traditions	34.8	46173	25 Salt Of The Earth	21.5	46501	25 Salt Of The Earth	54.9
45894	25 Salt Of The Earth	100.0	46175	42 Southern Satellites	88.6	46504	32 Rustbelt Traditions	56.7
45895	17 Green Acres	29.4	46176	25 Salt Of The Earth	25.1	46506	25 Salt Of The Earth	37.5
45896	25 Salt Of The Earth	56.3	46180	25 Salt Of The Earth	100.0	46507	42 Southern Satellites	34.1
45898	32 Rustbelt Traditions	65.6	46181	17 Green Acres	58.4	46508	25 Salt Of The Earth	100.0
46001	32 Rustbelt Traditions	30.4	46182	25 Salt Of The Earth	98.8	46510	25 Salt Of The Earth	79.9
46011	18 Cozy And Comfortable	39.1	46184	12 Up And Coming Families	45.0	46511	50 Heartland Communities	31.2
46012	32 Rustbelt Traditions	16.2	46186	17 Green Acres	49.6	46514	32 Rustbelt Traditions	17.8
46013	50 Heartland Communities	32.2	46201	60 City Dimensions	31.1	46516	60 City Dimensions	21.9
46016	53 Home Town	55.5	46202	27 Metro Renters	27.9	46517	25 Salt Of The Earth	30.9
46017	32 Rustbelt Traditions	49.7	46203	53 Home Town	50.4	46524	42 Southern Satellites	99.2
46030	32 Rustbelt Traditions	46.7	46204	27 Metro Renters	69.2	46526	26 Midland Crowd	19.0
46031	25 Salt Of The Earth	49.9	46205	51 Metro City Edge	20.1	46528	17 Green Acres	36.4
46032	04 Boomburbs	30.2	46208	62 Modest Income Homes	52.5	46530	06 Sophisticated Squires	28.8
46033	04 Boomburbs	43.7	46214	39 Young And Restless	47.7	46531	26 Midland Crowd	51.1

ZIP CODE	TOP TAPESTRY CONSUMER TYPE	% 2009 HOUSE-HOLDS	ZIP CODE	TOP TAPESTRY CONSUMER TYPE	% 2009 HOUSE-HOLDS	ZIP CODE	TOP TAPESTRY CONSUMER TYPE	% 2009 HOUSE-HOLDS
46532	25 Salt Of The Earth	52.9	46795	25 Salt Of The Earth	93.1	47111	26 Midland Crowd	33.0
46534	25 Salt Of The Earth	35.5	46797	32 Rustbelt Traditions	48.4	47112	25 Salt Of The Earth	28.8
46536	25 Salt Of The Earth	29.1	46798	17 Green Acres	47.6	47114	26 Midland Crowd	100.0
46538	25 Salt Of The Earth	53.2	46802	60 City Dimensions	29.8	47115	46 Rooted Rural	59.8
46539	32 Rustbelt Traditions	50.6	46803	53 Home Town	19.6	47116	42 Southern Satellites	100.0
46540	17 Green Acres	61.9	46804	12 Up And Coming Families	25.9	47117	25 Salt Of The Earth	96.6
46542	25 Salt Of The Earth	43.7	46805	32 Rustbelt Traditions	40.7	47118	42 Southern Satellites	71.7
46543	17 Green Acres	58.1	46806	51 Metro City Edge	56.3	47119	17 Green Acres	57.2
46544	32 Rustbelt Traditions	38.9	46807	32 Rustbelt Traditions	36.8	47120	42 Southern Satellites	100.0
46545	36 Old And Newcomers	24.0	46808	32 Rustbelt Traditions	25.0	47122	17 Green Acres	51.8
46550	32 Rustbelt Traditions	24.8	46809	32 Rustbelt Traditions	44.9	47123	42 Southern Satellites	100.0
46552	25 Salt Of The Earth	34.2	46814	04 Boomburbs	57.0	47124	17 Green Acres	63.3
46553	32 Rustbelt Traditions	38.2	46815	18 Cozy And Comfortable	45.8	47125	42 Southern Satellites	99.9
46554	32 Rustbelt Traditions	36.0	46816	32 Rustbelt Traditions	34.4	47126	26 Midland Crowd	75.9
46555	25 Salt Of The Earth	67.1	46818	41 Crossroads	30.8	47129	57 Simple Living	25.5
46556	36 Old And Newcomers	100.0	46819	29 Rustbelt Retirees	27.6	47130	18 Cozy And Comfortable	20.1
46561	25 Salt Of The Earth	40.6	46825	32 Rustbelt Traditions	29.7	47135	25 Salt Of The Earth	98.7
46562	42 Southern Satellites	33.4	46835	32 Rustbelt Traditions	19.5	47136	17 Green Acres	59.8
46563	25 Salt Of The Earth	38.9	46845	06 Sophisticated Squires	37.2	47137	42 Southern Satellites	62.2
46565	38 Industrious Urban Fringe	34.5	46901	32 Rustbelt Traditions	19.9	47138	42 Southern Satellites	57.7
46567	25 Salt Of The Earth	34.0	46902	33 Midlife Junction	16.4	47140	56 Rural Bypasses	62.5
46570	25 Salt Of The Earth	97.3	46910	25 Salt Of The Earth	67.0	47141	25 Salt Of The Earth	89.7
46571	42 Southern Satellites	41.6	46911	25 Salt Of The Earth	100.0	47142	42 Southern Satellites	98.1
46573	25 Salt Of The Earth	35.2	46913	25 Salt Of The Earth	72.0	47143	25 Salt Of The Earth	66.6
46574	25 Salt Of The Earth	34.6	46914	42 Southern Satellites	53.4	47145	42 Southern Satellites	92.2
46580	32 Rustbelt Traditions	17.2	46917	25 Salt Of The Earth	100.0	47147	25 Salt Of The Earth	63.3
46582	26 Midland Crowd	49.2	46919	25 Salt Of The Earth	66.9	47150	33 Midlife Junction	17.6
46590	19 Milk And Cookies	62.9	46920	25 Salt Of The Earth	100.0	47160	25 Salt Of The Earth	100.0
46601	65 Social Security Set	33.6	46923	25 Salt Of The Earth	72.6	47161	26 Midland Crowd	100.0
46613	53 Home Town	70.5	46926	25 Salt Of The Earth	50.1	47162	25 Salt Of The Earth	57.4
46614	32 Rustbelt Traditions	21.5	46928	25 Salt Of The Earth	49.7	47163	25 Salt Of The Earth	52.5
46615	48 Great Expectations	33.8	46929	32 Rustbelt Traditions	55.1	47164	42 Southern Satellites	60.0
46616	48 Great Expectations	36.1	46932	25 Salt Of The Earth	96.1	47165	26 Midland Crowd	60.8
46617	36 Old And Newcomers	17.0	46933	32 Rustbelt Traditions	89.9	47166	26 Midland Crowd	68.1
46619	53 Home Town	28.2	46936	17 Green Acres	45.3	47167	42 Southern Satellites	44.7
46628	51 Metro City Edge	16.8	46938	25 Salt Of The Earth	50.4	47170	26 Midland Crowd	32.7
46635	07 Exurbanites	44.2	46939	25 Salt Of The Earth	34.5	47172	17 Green Acres	24.3
46637	33 Midlife Junction	28.7	46940	25 Salt Of The Earth	73.1	47174	42 Southern Satellites	100.0
46701	25 Salt Of The Earth	30.8	46941	42 Southern Satellites	65.9	47175	42 Southern Satellites	100.0
46702	25 Salt Of The Earth	55.0	46947	25 Salt Of The Earth	21.5	47177	25 Salt Of The Earth	54.9
46703	25 Salt Of The Earth	16.9	46950	37 Prairie Living	74.2	47201	25 Salt Of The Earth	19.9
46705	42 Southern Satellites	78.8	46951	25 Salt Of The Earth	44.7	47203	18 Cozy And Comfortable	13.0
46706	17 Green Acres	30.5	46952	14 Prosperous Empty Nesters	28.6	47220	46 Rooted Rural	45.0
46710	26 Midland Crowd	45.7	46953	53 Home Town	41.5	47223	42 Southern Satellites	100.0
46711	37 Prairie Living	24.6	46960	46 Rooted Rural	53.9	47224	26 Midland Crowd	63.1
46714	25 Salt Of The Earth	30.8	46962	25 Salt Of The Earth	28.0	47227	25 Salt Of The Earth	78.5
46721	25 Salt Of The Earth	41.4	46970	25 Salt Of The Earth	29.4	47229	42 Southern Satellites	81.8
46723	26 Midland Crowd	32.6	46974	42 Southern Satellites	76.9	47230	42 Southern Satellites	80.1
46725	25 Salt Of The Earth	32.8	46975	42 Southern Satellites	28.1	47231	42 Southern Satellites	75.7
46730	25 Salt Of The Earth	97.0	46978	32 Rustbelt Traditions	45.8	47232	25 Salt Of The Earth	57.6
46731	25 Salt Of The Earth	58.6	46979	17 Green Acres	63.3	47234	25 Salt Of The Earth	97.2
46732	42 Southern Satellites	48.7	46982	42 Southern Satellites	78.5	47235	42 Southern Satellites	52.5
46733	25 Salt Of The Earth	36.7	46985	25 Salt Of The Earth	71.9	47236	25 Salt Of The Earth	100.0
46737	31 Rural Resort Dwellers	40.3	46986	25 Salt Of The Earth	94.0	47240	25 Salt Of The Earth	34.7
46738	32 Rustbelt Traditions	44.7	46988	25 Salt Of The Earth	100.0	47243	33 Midlife Junction	27.0
46740	50 Heartland Communities	33.4	46989	17 Green Acres	33.1	47244	25 Salt Of The Earth	91.7
46741	26 Midland Crowd	38.6	46990	42 Southern Satellites	72.5	47246	25 Salt Of The Earth	29.6
46742	25 Salt Of The Earth	97.0	46991	32 Rustbelt Traditions	52.2	47250	33 Midlife Junction	38.1
46743	25 Salt Of The Earth	57.7	46992	25 Salt Of The Earth	28.8	47260	42 Southern Satellites	56.4
46745	25 Salt Of The Earth	55.9	46994	25 Salt Of The Earth	95.4	47264	42 Southern Satellites	81.4
46746	25 Salt Of The Earth	61.0	46996	25 Salt Of The Earth	34.9	47265	25 Salt Of The Earth	33.3
46747	25 Salt Of The Earth	50.0	47001	26 Midland Crowd	29.7	47270	25 Salt Of The Earth	93.9
46748	17 Green Acres	43.2	47003	26 Midland Crowd	73.7	47272	42 Southern Satellites	86.0
46750	32 Rustbelt Traditions	17.4	47006	17 Green Acres	60.0	47273	26 Midland Crowd	74.4
46755	32 Rustbelt Traditions	32.4	47010	25 Salt Of The Earth	100.0	47274	32 Rustbelt Traditions	25.6
46759	25 Salt Of The Earth	100.0	47011	42 Southern Satellites	42.1	47281	25 Salt Of The Earth	66.2
46760	25 Salt Of The Earth	53.6	47012	25 Salt Of The Earth	53.5	47282	25 Salt Of The Earth	100.0
46761	42 Southern Satellites	42.1	47016	26 Midland Crowd	54.7	47283	32 Rustbelt Traditions	52.4
46763	25 Salt Of The Earth	74.1	47017	25 Salt Of The Earth	98.3	47302	53 Home Town	51.8
46764	25 Salt Of The Earth	73.2	47018	25 Salt Of The Earth	60.0	47303	63 Dorms To Diplomas	24.0
46765	06 Sophisticated Squires	54.0	47020	42 Southern Satellites	100.0	47304	14 Prosperous Empty Nesters	19.1
46766	25 Salt Of The Earth	100.0	47022	17 Green Acres	84.7	47305	60 City Dimensions	46.7
46767	38 Industrious Urban Fringe	47.1	47023	25 Salt Of The Earth	82.6	47306	63 Dorms To Diplomas	100.0
46770	25 Salt Of The Earth	39.1	47024	42 Southern Satellites	82.8	47320	25 Salt Of The Earth	62.2
46772	32 Rustbelt Traditions	42.3	47025	17 Green Acres	30.2	47325	25 Salt Of The Earth	100.0
46773	25 Salt Of The Earth	70.7	47030	42 Southern Satellites	46.8	47326	25 Salt Of The Earth	55.8
46774	18 Cozy And Comfortable	37.9	47031	42 Southern Satellites	26.5	47327	25 Salt Of The Earth	50.2
46776	25 Salt Of The Earth	97.6	47032	26 Midland Crowd	49.7	47330	32 Rustbelt Traditions	57.3
46777	19 Milk And Cookies	26.9	47036	25 Salt Of The Earth	55.4	47331	25 Salt Of The Earth	22.4
46779	25 Salt Of The Earth	75.2	47037	25 Salt Of The Earth	49.2	47334	29 Rustbelt Retirees	68.1
46781	25 Salt Of The Earth	100.0	47038	42 Southern Satellites	85.5	47336	50 Heartland Communities	46.1
46783	25 Salt Of The Earth	37.6	47040	26 Midland Crowd	25.5	47338	32 Rustbelt Traditions	34.4
46784	42 Southern Satellites	48.0	47041	25 Salt Of The Earth	33.5	47339	25 Salt Of The Earth	100.0
46785	25 Salt Of The Earth	100.0	47042	33 Midlife Junction	36.2	47340	32 Rustbelt Traditions	51.3
46787	25 Salt Of The Earth	44.7	47043	46 Rooted Rural	54.1	47341	25 Salt Of The Earth	56.0
46788	17 Green Acres	49.0	47060	17 Green Acres	77.1	47342	25 Salt Of The Earth	46.4
46791	25 Salt Of The Earth	87.4	47102	53 Home Town	55.8	47345	25 Salt Of The Earth	100.0
46792	25 Salt Of The Earth	76.4	47106	17 Green Acres	36.3	47346	25 Salt Of The Earth	66.7
46793	25 Salt Of The Earth	30.5	47108	42 Southern Satellites	99.2	47348	25 Salt Of The Earth	33.5
46794	25 Salt Of The Earth	100.0	47110	42 Southern Satellites	100.0	47352	25 Salt Of The Earth	91.5

CONSUMER TYPE

ZIP CODE	TOP TAPESTRY CONSUMER TYPE	% 2009 HOUSE-HOLDS
47353	32 Rustbelt Traditions	23.1
47354	42 Southern Satellites	55.6
47355	50 Heartland Communities	30.7
47356	25 Salt Of The Earth	45.4
47357	42 Southern Satellites	49.3
47358	25 Salt Of The Earth	53.6
47359	42 Southern Satellites	39.9
47360	25 Salt Of The Earth	100.0
47362	53 Home Town	31.4
47368	25 Salt Of The Earth	61.1
47369	42 Southern Satellites	62.8
47371	25 Salt Of The Earth	30.2
47373	25 Salt Of The Earth	35.1
47374	33 Midlife Junction	21.0
47380	42 Southern Satellites	53.7
47381	42 Southern Satellites	100.0
47382	25 Salt Of The Earth	100.0
47383	25 Salt Of The Earth	52.9
47384	25 Salt Of The Earth	50.9
47385	25 Salt Of The Earth	73.8
47386	25 Salt Of The Earth	100.0
47387	25 Salt Of The Earth	100.0
47390	50 Heartland Communities	39.5
47392	25 Salt Of The Earth	100.0
47393	25 Salt Of The Earth	100.0
47394	50 Heartland Communities	44.0
47396	18 Cozy And Comfortable	26.9
47401	55 College Towns	13.9
47403	57 Simple Living	13.1
47404	17 Green Acres	20.1
47405	63 Dorms To Diplomas	100.0
47406	63 Dorms To Diplomas	100.0
47408	63 Dorms To Diplomas	43.4
47421	50 Heartland Communities	28.2
47424	26 Midland Crowd	26.0
47427	42 Southern Satellites	96.7
47429	17 Green Acres	31.1
47431	25 Salt Of The Earth	98.3
47432	46 Rooted Rural	39.2
47433	25 Salt Of The Earth	49.3
47436	25 Salt Of The Earth	51.4
47438	53 Home Town	54.6
47441	50 Heartland Communities	46.4
47443	46 Rooted Rural	56.6
47446	42 Southern Satellites	49.0
47448	31 Rural Resort Dwellers	44.1
47449	46 Rooted Rural	99.3
47451	50 Heartland Communities	83.0
47452	42 Southern Satellites	63.8
47453	46 Rooted Rural	61.5
47454	46 Rooted Rural	36.5
47456	25 Salt Of The Earth	70.0
47459	26 Midland Crowd	66.9
47460	26 Midland Crowd	45.3
47462	42 Southern Satellites	45.2
47465	46 Rooted Rural	65.7
47468	31 Rural Resort Dwellers	40.7
47469	42 Southern Satellites	45.7
47470	25 Salt Of The Earth	57.3
47471	50 Heartland Communities	65.3
47501	25 Salt Of The Earth	23.7
47512	50 Heartland Communities	32.0
47513	42 Southern Satellites	68.0
47514	42 Southern Satellites	98.3
47515	25 Salt Of The Earth	73.3
47516	50 Heartland Communities	55.7
47519	25 Salt Of The Earth	62.7
47520	42 Southern Satellites	94.3
47521	25 Salt Of The Earth	99.7
47522	46 Rooted Rural	100.0
47523	42 Southern Satellites	64.6
47524	37 Prairie Living	100.0
47525	46 Rooted Rural	68.5
47527	42 Southern Satellites	45.6
47528	46 Rooted Rural	99.0
47529	37 Prairie Living	46.6
47531	25 Salt Of The Earth	100.0
47532	25 Salt Of The Earth	49.8
47537	25 Salt Of The Earth	66.2
47541	25 Salt Of The Earth	83.7
47542	17 Green Acres	24.4
47546	17 Green Acres	23.1
47550	25 Salt Of The Earth	93.4
47551	46 Rooted Rural	63.3
47552	17 Green Acres	100.0
47553	50 Heartland Communities	45.0
47556	17 Green Acres	52.6
47557	46 Rooted Rural	60.0
47558	25 Salt Of The Earth	84.5
47561	50 Heartland Communities	38.9
47562	42 Southern Satellites	32.1
47564	42 Southern Satellites	89.5
47567	50 Heartland Communities	41.6
47568	25 Salt Of The Earth	98.4
47574	42 Southern Satellites	97.7
47575	25 Salt Of The Earth	57.1
47576	42 Southern Satellites	100.0
47577	25 Salt Of The Earth	89.0
47578	50 Heartland Communities	83.2
47579	17 Green Acres	92.0
47580	25 Salt Of The Earth	100.0
47581	42 Southern Satellites	54.3
47585	42 Southern Satellites	100.0
47586	50 Heartland Communities	34.0
47588	42 Southern Satellites	100.0
47590	42 Southern Satellites	93.5
47591	53 Home Town	16.8
47597	37 Prairie Living	52.7
47598	42 Southern Satellites	69.9
47601	25 Salt Of The Earth	33.8
47610	17 Green Acres	28.1
47611	25 Salt Of The Earth	79.2
47612	42 Southern Satellites	97.6
47613	25 Salt Of The Earth	72.2
47615	42 Southern Satellites	57.3
47616	46 Rooted Rural	100.0
47619	46 Rooted Rural	97.1
47620	17 Green Acres	24.8
47630	06 Sophisticated Squires	20.9
47631	25 Salt Of The Earth	44.4
47633	25 Salt Of The Earth	75.7
47634	25 Salt Of The Earth	72.9
47635	25 Salt Of The Earth	87.1
47637	42 Southern Satellites	69.4
47638	17 Green Acres	73.1
47639	17 Green Acres	63.2
47640	42 Southern Satellites	46.4
47647	25 Salt Of The Earth	100.0
47648	17 Green Acres	35.2
47649	25 Salt Of The Earth	100.0
47660	50 Heartland Communities	76.3
47665	42 Southern Satellites	44.1
47666	42 Southern Satellites	55.3
47670	25 Salt Of The Earth	25.2
47708	65 Social Security Set	100.0
47710	57 Simple Living	22.9
47711	32 Rustbelt Traditions	24.4
47712	32 Rustbelt Traditions	26.0
47713	62 Modest Income Homes	31.4
47714	32 Rustbelt Traditions	36.1
47715	52 Inner City Tenants	17.4
47720	17 Green Acres	45.9
47722	63 Dorms To Diplomas	100.0
47725	07 Exurbanites	45.1
47802	57 Simple Living	13.0
47803	32 Rustbelt Traditions	22.1
47804	53 Home Town	29.1
47805	32 Rustbelt Traditions	46.7
47807	55 College Towns	33.6
47809	55 College Towns	100.0
47832	42 Southern Satellites	91.0
47833	42 Southern Satellites	57.7
47834	25 Salt Of The Earth	43.9
47836	46 Rooted Rural	74.6
47837	42 Southern Satellites	61.4
47838	46 Rooted Rural	92.5
47840	25 Salt Of The Earth	99.4
47841	50 Heartland Communities	51.7
47842	50 Heartland Communities	30.2
47846	46 Rooted Rural	95.2
47847	42 Southern Satellites	57.4
47848	46 Rooted Rural	100.0
47849	25 Salt Of The Earth	100.0
47850	50 Heartland Communities	51.5
47854	25 Salt Of The Earth	61.1
47858	25 Salt Of The Earth	76.0
47859	25 Salt Of The Earth	93.0
47861	25 Salt Of The Earth	100.0
47862	42 Southern Satellites	51.9
47866	25 Salt Of The Earth	98.4
47868	26 Midland Crowd	50.9
47872	50 Heartland Communities	26.2
47874	46 Rooted Rural	35.8
47879	42 Southern Satellites	37.8
47882	46 Rooted Rural	27.8
47885	25 Salt Of The Earth	41.8
47901	55 College Towns	65.4
47904	32 Rustbelt Traditions	34.1
47905	36 Old And Newcomers	12.1
47906	63 Dorms To Diplomas	25.5
47907	63 Dorms To Diplomas	100.0
47909	32 Rustbelt Traditions	20.7
47917	37 Prairie Living	100.0
47918	25 Salt Of The Earth	38.8
47920	17 Green Acres	34.9
47921	50 Heartland Communities	87.8
47922	25 Salt Of The Earth	65.7
47923	25 Salt Of The Earth	40.2
47926	25 Salt Of The Earth	100.0
47928	42 Southern Satellites	33.4
47929	25 Salt Of The Earth	59.2
47930	42 Southern Satellites	56.6
47932	25 Salt Of The Earth	49.6
47933	25 Salt Of The Earth	24.8
47940	25 Salt Of The Earth	77.0
47942	37 Prairie Living	94.6
47943	25 Salt Of The Earth	98.5
47944	32 Rustbelt Traditions	69.2
47946	25 Salt Of The Earth	58.9
47948	42 Southern Satellites	48.1
47949	25 Salt Of The Earth	52.6
47950	42 Southern Satellites	67.1
47951	25 Salt Of The Earth	65.6
47952	42 Southern Satellites	96.2
47954	25 Salt Of The Earth	100.0
47955	32 Rustbelt Traditions	88.1
47957	42 Southern Satellites	93.3
47959	42 Southern Satellites	83.0
47960	25 Salt Of The Earth	25.6
47963	42 Southern Satellites	39.7
47967	25 Salt Of The Earth	94.1
47968	25 Salt Of The Earth	83.7
47970	32 Rustbelt Traditions	52.0
47971	25 Salt Of The Earth	93.6
47974	50 Heartland Communities	59.7
47975	25 Salt Of The Earth	100.0
47977	25 Salt Of The Earth	56.2
47978	25 Salt Of The Earth	29.7
47980	42 Southern Satellites	44.9
47981	17 Green Acres	77.2
47987	42 Southern Satellites	58.4
47989	25 Salt Of The Earth	99.5
47990	32 Rustbelt Traditions	71.8
47991	50 Heartland Communities	52.2
47992	18 Cozy And Comfortable	77.2
47993	25 Salt Of The Earth	36.8
47994	25 Salt Of The Earth	100.0
47995	25 Salt Of The Earth	51.0
48001	17 Green Acres	34.5
48002	17 Green Acres	100.0
48003	06 Sophisticated Squires	36.2
48005	17 Green Acres	49.2
48006	17 Green Acres	63.8
48009	22 Metropolitans	33.6
48014	17 Green Acres	51.2
48015	32 Rustbelt Traditions	48.9
48017	18 Cozy And Comfortable	51.5
48021	32 Rustbelt Traditions	54.4
48022	17 Green Acres	100.0
48023	41 Crossroads	45.1
48025	03 Connoisseurs	47.8
48026	18 Cozy And Comfortable	27.6
48027	17 Green Acres	100.0
48028	15 Silver And Gold	75.3
48030	32 Rustbelt Traditions	74.9
48032	17 Green Acres	43.9
48033	13 In Style	29.0
48034	36 Old And Newcomers	34.7
48035	24 Main Street, USA	29.5
48036	33 Midlife Junction	22.7
48038	39 Young And Restless	17.8
48039	32 Rustbelt Traditions	27.2
48040	18 Cozy And Comfortable	35.6
48041	17 Green Acres	61.4
48042	04 Boomburbs	64.3
48043	32 Rustbelt Traditions	23.7
48044	04 Boomburbs	41.7
48045	36 Old And Newcomers	25.6
48047	12 Up And Coming Families	30.7
48048	41 Crossroads	62.6
48049	17 Green Acres	70.9
48050	17 Green Acres	99.7
48051	41 Crossroads	42.3
48054	17 Green Acres	61.8
48059	18 Cozy And Comfortable	22.8
48060	48 Great Expectations	14.8
48062	24 Main Street, USA	47.2
48063	26 Midland Crowd	48.0
48064	17 Green Acres	71.1
48065	07 Exurbanites	22.8

ZIP CODE	TOP TAPESTRY CONSUMER TYPE	% 2009 HOUSE-HOLDS	ZIP CODE	TOP TAPESTRY CONSUMER TYPE	% 2009 HOUSE-HOLDS	ZIP CODE	TOP TAPESTRY CONSUMER TYPE	% 2009 HOUSE-HOLDS
48066	32 Rustbelt Traditions	42.1	48195	29 Rustbelt Retirees	26.6	48401	46 Rooted Rural	45.3
48067	22 Metropolitans	45.0	48197	39 Young And Restless	24.5	48412	17 Green Acres	100.0
48069	03 Connoisseurs	46.4	48198	32 Rustbelt Traditions	16.2	48413	25 Salt Of The Earth	37.2
48070	07 Exurbanites	37.0	48201	65 Social Security Set	41.6	48414	25 Salt Of The Earth	65.5
48071	32 Rustbelt Traditions	34.0	48202	62 Modest Income Homes	28.5	48415	17 Green Acres	27.6
48072	18 Cozy And Comfortable	33.0	48203	62 Modest Income Homes	37.1	48416	25 Salt Of The Earth	64.2
48073	22 Metropolitans	37.2	48204	62 Modest Income Homes	67.4	48417	25 Salt Of The Earth	100.0
48074	26 Midland Crowd	51.1	48205	51 Metro City Edge	70.6	48418	17 Green Acres	53.7
48075	18 Cozy And Comfortable	30.3	48206	62 Modest Income Homes	60.2	48419	31 Rural Resort Dwellers	42.7
48076	07 Exurbanites	20.7	48207	36 Old And Newcomers	21.2	48420	18 Cozy And Comfortable	42.6
48079	17 Green Acres	28.5	48208	62 Modest Income Homes	60.0	48421	17 Green Acres	55.5
48080	30 Retirement Communities	33.1	48209	60 City Dimensions	55.9	48422	42 Southern Satellites	43.1
48081	18 Cozy And Comfortable	45.6	48210	60 City Dimensions	50.6	48423	17 Green Acres	16.7
48082	18 Cozy And Comfortable	57.4	48211	62 Modest Income Homes	70.9	48426	25 Salt Of The Earth	100.0
48083	06 Sophisticated Squires	25.3	48212	60 City Dimensions	31.4	48427	50 Heartland Communities	35.9
48084	27 Metro Renters	33.7	48213	62 Modest Income Homes	43.9	48428	06 Sophisticated Squires	57.6
48085	07 Exurbanites	48.2	48214	62 Modest Income Homes	53.9	48429	17 Green Acres	27.6
48088	18 Cozy And Comfortable	63.9	48215	62 Modest Income Homes	36.4	48430	07 Exurbanites	29.6
48089	32 Rustbelt Traditions	40.3	48216	60 City Dimensions	66.9	48432	37 Prairie Living	58.6
48091	32 Rustbelt Traditions	22.0	48217	34 Family Foundations	70.0	48433	18 Cozy And Comfortable	27.3
48092	18 Cozy And Comfortable	34.4	48218	51 Metro City Edge	35.7	48435	25 Salt Of The Earth	81.0
48093	29 Rustbelt Retirees	25.3	48219	34 Family Foundations	43.4	48436	17 Green Acres	78.8
48094	26 Midland Crowd	29.4	48220	22 Metropolitans	27.6	48438	06 Sophisticated Squires	75.7
48095	17 Green Acres	42.5	48221	34 Family Foundations	72.5	48439	07 Exurbanites	25.5
48096	17 Green Acres	100.0	48223	51 Metro City Edge	33.3	48441	50 Heartland Communities	40.7
48097	17 Green Acres	47.3	48224	51 Metro City Edge	51.7	48442	17 Green Acres	35.5
48098	02 Suburban Splendor	88.1	48225	18 Cozy And Comfortable	34.7	48444	17 Green Acres	50.7
48101	18 Cozy And Comfortable	50.0	48226	65 Social Security Set	45.8	48445	53 Home Town	38.9
48103	22 Metropolitans	22.9	48227	51 Metro City Edge	61.9	48446	17 Green Acres	34.7
48104	63 Dorms To Diplomas	40.2	48228	51 Metro City Edge	61.6	48449	25 Salt Of The Earth	32.5
48105	09 Urban Chic	18.9	48229	53 Home Town	59.2	48450	29 Rustbelt Retirees	35.3
48108	39 Young And Restless	19.9	48230	09 Urban Chic	33.6	48451	17 Green Acres	20.1
48109	63 Dorms To Diplomas	100.0	48234	51 Metro City Edge	51.1	48453	37 Prairie Living	29.8
48111	41 Crossroads	22.5	48235	34 Family Foundations	75.9	48454	25 Salt Of The Earth	99.2
48114	02 Suburban Splendor	38.6	48236	03 Connoisseurs	31.9	48455	17 Green Acres	30.7
48116	06 Sophisticated Squires	16.3	48237	18 Cozy And Comfortable	30.6	48456	37 Prairie Living	100.0
48117	17 Green Acres	47.7	48238	62 Modest Income Homes	58.5	48457	25 Salt Of The Earth	64.2
48118	06 Sophisticated Squires	43.0	48239	18 Cozy And Comfortable	43.0	48458	41 Crossroads	25.0
48120	30 Retirement Communities	26.7	48240	32 Rustbelt Traditions	60.5	48460	25 Salt Of The Earth	60.2
48122	32 Rustbelt Traditions	46.1	48301	03 Connoisseurs	55.4	48461	17 Green Acres	46.2
48124	18 Cozy And Comfortable	47.3	48302	03 Connoisseurs	54.2	48462	06 Sophisticated Squires	81.9
48125	32 Rustbelt Traditions	62.8	48304	03 Connoisseurs	41.5	48463	17 Green Acres	44.1
48126	38 Industrious Urban Fringe	46.8	48306	02 Suburban Splendor	54.4	48464	25 Salt Of The Earth	91.1
48127	29 Rustbelt Retirees	35.8	48307	36 Old And Newcomers	16.3	48465	37 Prairie Living	91.9
48128	18 Cozy And Comfortable	65.5	48309	02 Suburban Splendor	28.0	48466	25 Salt Of The Earth	91.7
48130	07 Exurbanites	27.9	48310	06 Sophisticated Squires	35.6	48467	31 Rural Resort Dwellers	54.0
48131	24 Main Street, USA	56.5	48312	18 Cozy And Comfortable	28.2	48468	46 Rooted Rural	61.0
48133	18 Cozy And Comfortable	48.7	48313	06 Sophisticated Squires	44.1	48469	31 Rural Resort Dwellers	100.0
48134	41 Crossroads	20.5	48314	04 Boomburbs	31.8	48470	37 Prairie Living	100.0
48135	18 Cozy And Comfortable	68.7	48315	02 Suburban Splendor	34.7	48471	33 Midlife Junction	52.1
48137	17 Green Acres	63.0	48316	02 Suburban Splendor	22.5	48472	25 Salt Of The Earth	54.1
48138	07 Exurbanites	70.8	48317	24 Main Street, USA	26.7	48473	18 Cozy And Comfortable	33.0
48140	17 Green Acres	91.9	48320	24 Main Street, USA	40.7	48475	37 Prairie Living	44.9
48141	34 Family Foundations	28.0	48322	03 Connoisseurs	22.7	48502	65 Social Security Set	82.0
48144	17 Green Acres	58.3	48323	03 Connoisseurs	52.1	48503	32 Rustbelt Traditions	17.0
48145	17 Green Acres	49.7	48324	02 Suburban Splendor	39.3	48504	51 Metro City Edge	44.5
48146	32 Rustbelt Traditions	63.3	48326	16 Enterprising Professionals	47.8	48505	62 Modest Income Homes	51.2
48150	18 Cozy And Comfortable	75.6	48327	12 Up And Coming Families	22.8	48506	53 Home Town	29.0
48152	18 Cozy And Comfortable	23.3	48328	36 Old And Newcomers	26.6	48507	32 Rustbelt Traditions	25.6
48154	18 Cozy And Comfortable	37.2	48329	18 Cozy And Comfortable	44.6	48509	29 Rustbelt Retirees	30.3
48157	25 Salt Of The Earth	52.7	48331	02 Suburban Splendor	34.6	48519	18 Cozy And Comfortable	38.4
48158	17 Green Acres	46.8	48334	30 Retirement Communities	27.1	48529	53 Home Town	36.8
48159	17 Green Acres	65.9	48335	16 Enterprising Professionals	31.9	48532	18 Cozy And Comfortable	20.1
48160	17 Green Acres	39.4	48336	13 In Style	21.5	48601	62 Modest Income Homes	27.6
48161	41 Crossroads	20.2	48340	52 Inner City Tenants	29.4	48602	32 Rustbelt Traditions	30.0
48162	24 Main Street, USA	17.8	48341	51 Metro City Edge	24.6	48603	36 Old And Newcomers	20.6
48164	17 Green Acres	38.2	48342	34 Family Foundations	28.0	48604	32 Rustbelt Traditions	40.3
48165	06 Sophisticated Squires	89.7	48346	07 Exurbanites	18.1	48607	62 Modest Income Homes	62.3
48166	41 Crossroads	29.8	48348	02 Suburban Splendor	40.9	48609	18 Cozy And Comfortable	49.1
48167	13 In Style	27.5	48350	06 Sophisticated Squires	43.7	48610	46 Rooted Rural	50.2
48168	01 Top Rung	27.4	48353	07 Exurbanites	41.9	48611	33 Midlife Junction	42.2
48169	06 Sophisticated Squires	39.4	48356	17 Green Acres	33.4	48612	46 Rooted Rural	31.8
48170	02 Suburban Splendor	21.1	48357	41 Crossroads	42.9	48613	25 Salt Of The Earth	91.4
48173	18 Cozy And Comfortable	48.2	48359	16 Enterprising Professionals	42.5	48614	42 Southern Satellites	62.4
48174	41 Crossroads	22.1	48360	04 Boomburbs	62.8	48615	32 Rustbelt Traditions	49.8
48176	02 Suburban Splendor	31.4	48362	12 Up And Coming Families	36.4	48616	25 Salt Of The Earth	56.1
48178	12 Up And Coming Families	20.3	48363	02 Suburban Splendor	48.0	48617	57 Simple Living	25.3
48179	18 Cozy And Comfortable	40.8	48367	06 Sophisticated Squires	60.8	48618	25 Salt Of The Earth	43.2
48180	32 Rustbelt Traditions	34.5	48370	07 Exurbanites	54.5	48619	49 Senior Sun Seekers	100.0
48182	18 Cozy And Comfortable	36.1	48371	06 Sophisticated Squires	38.8	48621	50 Heartland Communities	46.6
48183	18 Cozy And Comfortable	27.7	48374	04 Boomburbs	100.0	48622	46 Rooted Rural	53.0
48184	32 Rustbelt Traditions	49.4	48375	13 In Style	67.1	48623	17 Green Acres	44.0
48185	36 Old And Newcomers	21.7	48377	13 In Style	42.8	48624	46 Rooted Rural	26.8
48186	18 Cozy And Comfortable	29.7	48380	02 Suburban Splendor	60.5	48625	49 Senior Sun Seekers	33.2
48187	13 In Style	30.1	48381	26 Midland Crowd	21.9	48626	17 Green Acres	32.7
48188	04 Boomburbs	48.9	48382	06 Sophisticated Squires	48.4	48628	25 Salt Of The Earth	65.9
48189	12 Up And Coming Families	22.3	48383	12 Up And Coming Families	51.2	48629	49 Senior Sun Seekers	49.1
48191	17 Green Acres	61.8	48386	06 Sophisticated Squires	35.7	48631	25 Salt Of The Earth	31.6
48192	32 Rustbelt Traditions	30.8	48390	06 Sophisticated Squires	29.0	48632	49 Senior Sun Seekers	65.2
48193	29 Rustbelt Retirees	14.9	48393	39 Young And Restless	34.2	48634	25 Salt Of The Earth	85.3

CONSUMER TYPE

ZIP CODE	TOP TAPESTRY CONSUMER TYPE	% 2009 HOUSE-HOLDS	ZIP CODE	TOP TAPESTRY CONSUMER TYPE	% 2009 HOUSE-HOLDS	ZIP CODE	TOP TAPESTRY CONSUMER TYPE	% 2009 HOUSE-HOLDS
48635	49 Senior Sun Seekers	62.6	48834	25 Salt Of The Earth	53.2	49047	25 Salt Of The Earth	43.2
48636	49 Senior Sun Seekers	100.0	48835	25 Salt Of The Earth	82.6	49048	32 Rustbelt Traditions	20.3
48637	25 Salt Of The Earth	95.6	48836	17 Green Acres	36.0	49050	25 Salt Of The Earth	88.1
48638	33 Midlife Junction	40.7	48837	07 Exurbanites	22.7	49051	25 Salt Of The Earth	64.9
48640	14 Prosperous Empty Nesters	13.5	48838	25 Salt Of The Earth	20.9	49052	25 Salt Of The Earth	100.0
48642	18 Cozy And Comfortable	13.7	48840	16 Enterprising Professionals	47.5	49053	17 Green Acres	29.4
48647	49 Senior Sun Seekers	41.6	48841	25 Salt Of The Earth	85.2	49055	25 Salt Of The Earth	44.0
48649	25 Salt Of The Earth	89.8	48842	18 Cozy And Comfortable	23.1	49056	42 Southern Satellites	88.7
48650	25 Salt Of The Earth	83.3	48843	06 Sophisticated Squires	21.2	49057	53 Home Town	48.8
48651	49 Senior Sun Seekers	75.2	48845	42 Southern Satellites	72.2	49058	25 Salt Of The Earth	36.4
48652	46 Rooted Rural	28.4	48846	25 Salt Of The Earth	30.5	49060	17 Green Acres	58.2
48653	49 Senior Sun Seekers	33.8	48847	25 Salt Of The Earth	44.9	49061	46 Rooted Rural	41.2
48654	31 Rural Resort Dwellers	41.4	48848	17 Green Acres	75.4	49064	42 Southern Satellites	54.7
48655	25 Salt Of The Earth	64.3	48849	17 Green Acres	26.8	49065	32 Rustbelt Traditions	26.0
48656	49 Senior Sun Seekers	53.5	48850	25 Salt Of The Earth	52.0	49066	25 Salt Of The Earth	100.0
48657	26 Midland Crowd	39.3	48851	25 Salt Of The Earth	72.6	49067	25 Salt Of The Earth	73.2
48658	46 Rooted Rural	38.4	48854	17 Green Acres	24.5	49068	25 Salt Of The Earth	24.1
48659	46 Rooted Rural	88.4	48855	17 Green Acres	45.6	49070	26 Midland Crowd	65.3
48661	31 Rural Resort Dwellers	28.8	48856	32 Rustbelt Traditions	44.2	49071	17 Green Acres	37.3
48662	25 Salt Of The Earth	83.7	48857	26 Midland Crowd	57.7	49072	25 Salt Of The Earth	83.5
48701	32 Rustbelt Traditions	52.3	48858	55 College Towns	30.2	49073	25 Salt Of The Earth	33.2
48703	31 Rural Resort Dwellers	58.2	48860	42 Southern Satellites	96.0	49076	25 Salt Of The Earth	51.6
48705	49 Senior Sun Seekers	68.8	48861	25 Salt Of The Earth	50.4	49078	25 Salt Of The Earth	44.0
48706	18 Cozy And Comfortable	17.6	48864	13 In Style	47.0	49079	25 Salt Of The Earth	23.1
48708	29 Rustbelt Retirees	21.8	48865	26 Midland Crowd	95.3	49080	17 Green Acres	31.0
48710	18 Cozy And Comfortable	100.0	48866	32 Rustbelt Traditions	45.9	49082	25 Salt Of The Earth	48.8
48720	46 Rooted Rural	88.8	48867	32 Rustbelt Traditions	21.2	49083	17 Green Acres	47.1
48721	31 Rural Resort Dwellers	100.0	48871	17 Green Acres	65.1	49085	36 Old And Newcomers	24.6
48722	18 Cozy And Comfortable	40.1	48872	17 Green Acres	30.7	49087	06 Sophisticated Squires	36.6
48723	25 Salt Of The Earth	39.4	48873	25 Salt Of The Earth	84.8	49088	17 Green Acres	63.2
48725	49 Senior Sun Seekers	93.7	48875	17 Green Acres	31.8	49089	42 Southern Satellites	89.9
48726	25 Salt Of The Earth	35.4	48876	41 Crossroads	43.9	49090	42 Southern Satellites	21.2
48727	25 Salt Of The Earth	100.0	48877	26 Midland Crowd	62.7	49091	25 Salt Of The Earth	32.0
48728	49 Senior Sun Seekers	92.7	48878	26 Midland Crowd	90.0	49092	25 Salt Of The Earth	100.0
48729	25 Salt Of The Earth	64.0	48879	17 Green Acres	44.5	49093	53 Home Town	32.0
48730	49 Senior Sun Seekers	36.0	48880	32 Rustbelt Traditions	32.4	49094	32 Rustbelt Traditions	49.6
48731	50 Heartland Communities	52.3	48881	26 Midland Crowd	46.0	49095	31 Rural Resort Dwellers	63.7
48732	33 Midlife Junction	44.7	48883	26 Midland Crowd	76.9	49096	25 Salt Of The Earth	99.0
48733	46 Rooted Rural	65.8	48884	42 Southern Satellites	62.9	49097	17 Green Acres	46.7
48734	13 In Style	34.9	48885	25 Salt Of The Earth	50.5	49098	25 Salt Of The Earth	28.7
48735	46 Rooted Rural	75.2	48886	50 Heartland Communities	37.4	49099	25 Salt Of The Earth	46.8
48737	49 Senior Sun Seekers	93.1	48888	25 Salt Of The Earth	56.6	49101	26 Midland Crowd	61.8
48738	31 Rural Resort Dwellers	82.7	48889	25 Salt Of The Earth	61.1	49102	42 Southern Satellites	67.6
48739	49 Senior Sun Seekers	76.9	48890	17 Green Acres	75.3	49103	17 Green Acres	27.8
48740	49 Senior Sun Seekers	56.6	48891	42 Southern Satellites	68.5	49106	25 Salt Of The Earth	85.4
48741	25 Salt Of The Earth	96.9	48892	26 Midland Crowd	63.1	49107	25 Salt Of The Earth	29.7
48742	46 Rooted Rural	59.3	48893	25 Salt Of The Earth	33.5	49111	25 Salt Of The Earth	64.6
48743	49 Senior Sun Seekers	100.0	48894	18 Cozy And Comfortable	89.5	49112	25 Salt Of The Earth	64.0
48744	25 Salt Of The Earth	48.0	48895	17 Green Acres	39.4	49113	25 Salt Of The Earth	61.5
48745	46 Rooted Rural	99.0	48897	25 Salt Of The Earth	100.0	49116	31 Rural Resort Dwellers	100.0
48746	25 Salt Of The Earth	46.5	48906	18 Cozy And Comfortable	15.5	49117	25 Salt Of The Earth	34.4
48747	25 Salt Of The Earth	97.1	48910	32 Rustbelt Traditions	36.5	49120	25 Salt Of The Earth	22.7
48748	49 Senior Sun Seekers	51.0	48911	48 Great Expectations	26.0	49125	31 Rural Resort Dwellers	43.5
48749	46 Rooted Rural	81.5	48912	48 Great Expectations	31.3	49126	46 Rooted Rural	60.9
48750	50 Heartland Communities	42.2	48915	51 Metro City Edge	27.3	49127	13 In Style	28.9
48754	46 Rooted Rural	50.0	48917	13 In Style	27.6	49128	31 Rural Resort Dwellers	32.5
48755	50 Heartland Communities	34.8	48933	65 Social Security Set	50.4	49129	31 Rural Resort Dwellers	58.6
48756	50 Heartland Communities	47.9	49001	48 Great Expectations	30.1	49130	17 Green Acres	57.1
48757	25 Salt Of The Earth	32.2	49002	17 Green Acres	26.0	49201	17 Green Acres	24.2
48759	29 Rustbelt Retirees	24.2	49004	32 Rustbelt Traditions	32.6	49202	32 Rustbelt Traditions	36.1
48760	25 Salt Of The Earth	100.0	49006	55 College Towns	42.9	49203	32 Rustbelt Traditions	18.7
48761	49 Senior Sun Seekers	100.0	49007	55 College Towns	36.3	49220	25 Salt Of The Earth	37.5
48762	31 Rural Resort Dwellers	48.5	49008	14 Prosperous Empty Nesters	16.3	49221	25 Salt Of The Earth	14.5
48763	31 Rural Resort Dwellers	33.4	49009	36 Old And Newcomers	18.0	49224	32 Rustbelt Traditions	18.9
48765	46 Rooted Rural	60.0	49010	26 Midland Crowd	34.2	49227	25 Salt Of The Earth	96.4
48766	46 Rooted Rural	96.9	49011	25 Salt Of The Earth	58.9	49228	25 Salt Of The Earth	37.4
48767	25 Salt Of The Earth	53.8	49012	17 Green Acres	47.8	49229	17 Green Acres	58.4
48768	25 Salt Of The Earth	36.3	49013	42 Southern Satellites	37.6	49230	17 Green Acres	36.1
48770	46 Rooted Rural	87.0	49014	53 Home Town	27.6	49232	25 Salt Of The Earth	61.7
48801	32 Rustbelt Traditions	17.3	49015	32 Rustbelt Traditions	16.6	49233	17 Green Acres	62.0
48806	25 Salt Of The Earth	56.1	49017	18 Cozy And Comfortable	22.0	49234	17 Green Acres	58.2
48807	25 Salt Of The Earth	65.9	49021	25 Salt Of The Earth	73.7	49235	25 Salt Of The Earth	98.8
48808	17 Green Acres	71.6	49022	51 Metro City Edge	23.1	49236	17 Green Acres	52.9
48809	32 Rustbelt Traditions	32.0	49024	36 Old And Newcomers	23.2	49237	25 Salt Of The Earth	81.7
48811	32 Rustbelt Traditions	35.9	49026	26 Midland Crowd	47.2	49238	25 Salt Of The Earth	81.2
48813	17 Green Acres	34.1	49028	25 Salt Of The Earth	52.9	49240	17 Green Acres	84.6
48815	25 Salt Of The Earth	57.3	49029	42 Southern Satellites	55.7	49241	25 Salt Of The Earth	76.3
48817	25 Salt Of The Earth	38.7	49030	25 Salt Of The Earth	51.2	49242	25 Salt Of The Earth	24.9
48818	31 Rural Resort Dwellers	46.1	49031	25 Salt Of The Earth	41.1	49245	25 Salt Of The Earth	40.0
48819	17 Green Acres	83.4	49032	26 Midland Crowd	38.4	49246	17 Green Acres	58.6
48820	06 Sophisticated Squires	30.1	49033	17 Green Acres	71.8	49247	25 Salt Of The Earth	52.8
48821	14 Prosperous Empty Nesters	47.9	49034	25 Salt Of The Earth	79.6	49248	25 Salt Of The Earth	99.5
48822	17 Green Acres	84.2	49036	25 Salt Of The Earth	29.5	49249	42 Southern Satellites	37.3
48823	63 Dorms To Diplomas	25.7	49037	32 Rustbelt Traditions	30.6	49250	25 Salt Of The Earth	36.7
48824	63 Dorms To Diplomas	100.0	49038	32 Rustbelt Traditions	50.7	49251	17 Green Acres	37.6
48825	39 Young And Restless	91.0	49040	42 Southern Satellites	39.7	49252	42 Southern Satellites	55.1
48827	17 Green Acres	45.9	49042	25 Salt Of The Earth	49.4	49253	25 Salt Of The Earth	32.8
48829	50 Heartland Communities	40.6	49043	56 Rural Bypasses	90.3	49254	25 Salt Of The Earth	46.8
48831	25 Salt Of The Earth	42.0	49045	25 Salt Of The Earth	34.0	49255	25 Salt Of The Earth	47.9
48832	26 Midland Crowd	86.1	49046	25 Salt Of The Earth	73.3	49256	25 Salt Of The Earth	54.7

ZIP CODE	TOP TAPESTRY CONSUMER TYPE	% 2009 HOUSE-HOLDS	ZIP CODE	TOP TAPESTRY CONSUMER TYPE	% 2009 HOUSE-HOLDS	ZIP CODE	TOP TAPESTRY CONSUMER TYPE	% 2009 HOUSE-HOLDS
49259	26 Midland Crowd	53.3	49448	26 Midland Crowd	40.3	49707	33 Midlife Junction	25.8
49262	25 Salt Of The Earth	100.0	49449	15 Silver And Gold	64.8	49709	31 Rural Resort Dwellers	37.4
49264	26 Midland Crowd	54.0	49450	41 Crossroads	37.6	49710	31 Rural Resort Dwellers	80.8
49265	17 Green Acres	88.2	49451	25 Salt Of The Earth	70.1	49712	31 Rural Resort Dwellers	28.6
49266	25 Salt Of The Earth	97.3	49452	42 Southern Satellites	83.1	49713	25 Salt Of The Earth	63.8
49267	17 Green Acres	72.3	49453	31 Rural Resort Dwellers	56.6	49715	26 Midland Crowd	61.6
49268	25 Salt Of The Earth	51.5	49454	25 Salt Of The Earth	53.6	49716	31 Rural Resort Dwellers	54.6
49269	25 Salt Of The Earth	48.5	49455	32 Rustbelt Traditions	24.5	49718	31 Rural Resort Dwellers	100.0
49270	17 Green Acres	71.3	49456	33 Midlife Junction	21.6	49719	31 Rural Resort Dwellers	92.5
49271	25 Salt Of The Earth	100.0	49457	17 Green Acres	31.3	49720	31 Rural Resort Dwellers	35.7
49272	17 Green Acres	76.5	49459	42 Southern Satellites	85.3	49721	31 Rural Resort Dwellers	43.3
49274	25 Salt Of The Earth	48.2	49460	17 Green Acres	37.3	49724	26 Midland Crowd	61.3
49276	17 Green Acres	58.3	49461	17 Green Acres	46.3	49725	31 Rural Resort Dwellers	100.0
49277	17 Green Acres	58.2	49464	17 Green Acres	30.7	49726	31 Rural Resort Dwellers	100.0
49279	25 Salt Of The Earth	80.7	49503	60 City Dimensions	14.6	49727	25 Salt Of The Earth	29.0
49283	30 Retirement Communities	56.9	49504	60 City Dimensions	29.3	49728	49 Senior Sun Seekers	92.7
49284	25 Salt Of The Earth	59.5	49505	32 Rustbelt Traditions	26.0	49729	31 Rural Resort Dwellers	54.6
49285	24 Main Street, USA	42.4	49506	22 Metropolitans	16.8	49730	46 Rooted Rural	58.2
49286	17 Green Acres	45.7	49507	51 Metro City Edge	23.4	49733	31 Rural Resort Dwellers	60.1
49287	17 Green Acres	100.0	49508	28 Aspiring Young Families	22.7	49735	33 Midlife Junction	26.1
49288	42 Southern Satellites	63.6	49509	32 Rustbelt Traditions	31.5	49736	31 Rural Resort Dwellers	100.0
49301	02 Suburban Splendor	35.2	49512	39 Young And Restless	56.0	49738	33 Midlife Junction	23.8
49302	06 Sophisticated Squires	58.8	49519	28 Aspiring Young Families	22.3	49740	31 Rural Resort Dwellers	52.4
49303	42 Southern Satellites	56.1	49525	06 Sophisticated Squires	19.3	49743	46 Rooted Rural	57.8
49304	49 Senior Sun Seekers	58.6	49534	17 Green Acres	37.5	49744	25 Salt Of The Earth	73.6
49305	46 Rooted Rural	72.7	49544	39 Young And Restless	45.2	49745	31 Rural Resort Dwellers	62.9
49306	06 Sophisticated Squires	53.6	49546	02 Suburban Splendor	24.1	49746	50 Heartland Communities	37.6
49307	26 Midland Crowd	22.9	49548	41 Crossroads	35.1	49747	46 Rooted Rural	42.2
49309	46 Rooted Rural	99.9	49601	25 Salt Of The Earth	19.1	49749	31 Rural Resort Dwellers	84.8
49310	25 Salt Of The Earth	42.7	49612	31 Rural Resort Dwellers	76.2	49751	31 Rural Resort Dwellers	51.4
49315	17 Green Acres	44.2	49613	31 Rural Resort Dwellers	100.0	49752	46 Rooted Rural	70.4
49316	17 Green Acres	34.4	49614	31 Rural Resort Dwellers	55.1	49753	31 Rural Resort Dwellers	55.7
49318	25 Salt Of The Earth	77.7	49615	31 Rural Resort Dwellers	97.5	49755	31 Rural Resort Dwellers	63.2
49319	26 Midland Crowd	38.3	49616	31 Rural Resort Dwellers	56.2	49756	49 Senior Sun Seekers	97.1
49321	39 Young And Restless	27.6	49617	31 Rural Resort Dwellers	40.9	49757	22 Metropolitans	100.0
49322	25 Salt Of The Earth	98.0	49618	46 Rooted Rural	84.8	49759	31 Rural Resort Dwellers	60.9
49323	12 Up And Coming Families	31.7	49619	31 Rural Resort Dwellers	98.6	49760	46 Rooted Rural	55.4
49325	17 Green Acres	66.9	49620	26 Midland Crowd	92.4	49762	49 Senior Sun Seekers	100.0
49326	26 Midland Crowd	45.4	49621	17 Green Acres	50.2	49765	46 Rooted Rural	47.5
49327	26 Midland Crowd	62.2	49622	31 Rural Resort Dwellers	63.0	49766	25 Salt Of The Earth	41.9
49328	25 Salt Of The Earth	52.2	49623	42 Southern Satellites	49.4	49768	49 Senior Sun Seekers	100.0
49329	26 Midland Crowd	91.6	49625	42 Southern Satellites	78.3	49769	26 Midland Crowd	83.3
49330	41 Crossroads	36.2	49629	31 Rural Resort Dwellers	73.7	49770	17 Green Acres	39.8
49331	17 Green Acres	49.5	49630	31 Rural Resort Dwellers	57.2	49774	31 Rural Resort Dwellers	69.0
49332	46 Rooted Rural	41.0	49631	46 Rooted Rural	36.0	49775	15 Silver And Gold	100.0
49333	17 Green Acres	37.9	49632	46 Rooted Rural	100.0	49776	46 Rooted Rural	74.6
49336	42 Southern Satellites	66.9	49633	26 Midland Crowd	45.4	49777	31 Rural Resort Dwellers	94.2
49337	26 Midland Crowd	36.2	49635	15 Silver And Gold	37.5	49779	50 Heartland Communities	61.3
49338	26 Midland Crowd	65.5	49636	15 Silver And Gold	100.0	49780	25 Salt Of The Earth	68.6
49339	25 Salt Of The Earth	57.2	49637	26 Midland Crowd	35.3	49781	33 Midlife Junction	53.2
49340	46 Rooted Rural	48.3	49638	46 Rooted Rural	92.7	49782	31 Rural Resort Dwellers	100.0
49341	06 Sophisticated Squires	33.4	49639	42 Southern Satellites	50.5	49783	32 Rustbelt Traditions	29.8
49342	46 Rooted Rural	44.6	49640	31 Rural Resort Dwellers	97.9	49788	48 Great Expectations	92.6
49343	26 Midland Crowd	75.5	49642	46 Rooted Rural	78.6	49792	46 Rooted Rural	100.0
49344	25 Salt Of The Earth	70.0	49643	26 Midland Crowd	76.8	49795	46 Rooted Rural	87.4
49345	17 Green Acres	30.4	49644	49 Senior Sun Seekers	98.1	49799	42 Southern Satellites	61.3
49346	15 Silver And Gold	46.7	49645	50 Heartland Communities	48.0	49801	29 Rustbelt Retirees	14.7
49347	25 Salt Of The Earth	100.0	49646	26 Midland Crowd	36.8	49802	32 Rustbelt Traditions	39.1
49348	26 Midland Crowd	29.3	49648	31 Rural Resort Dwellers	100.0	49806	31 Rural Resort Dwellers	100.0
49349	42 Southern Satellites	51.6	49649	26 Midland Crowd	91.2	49807	25 Salt Of The Earth	65.4
49401	12 Up And Coming Families	37.7	49650	12 Up And Coming Families	57.1	49812	46 Rooted Rural	59.4
49402	46 Rooted Rural	66.2	49651	46 Rooted Rural	46.3	49814	26 Midland Crowd	31.1
49403	17 Green Acres	64.7	49653	31 Rural Resort Dwellers	75.3	49815	46 Rooted Rural	100.0
49404	17 Green Acres	35.7	49654	15 Silver And Gold	100.0	49816	46 Rooted Rural	67.5
49405	46 Rooted Rural	75.3	49655	46 Rooted Rural	57.6	49817	31 Rural Resort Dwellers	100.0
49408	25 Salt Of The Earth	36.0	49656	46 Rooted Rural	62.3	49818	25 Salt Of The Earth	100.0
49410	46 Rooted Rural	56.3	49657	46 Rooted Rural	57.2	49820	49 Senior Sun Seekers	100.0
49411	46 Rooted Rural	69.2	49659	42 Southern Satellites	36.4	49821	46 Rooted Rural	97.4
49412	33 Midlife Junction	35.8	49660	50 Heartland Communities	22.7	49822	31 Rural Resort Dwellers	100.0
49415	17 Green Acres	70.1	49663	26 Midland Crowd	41.3	49825	31 Rural Resort Dwellers	95.9
49417	12 Up And Coming Families	20.4	49664	17 Green Acres	72.0	49826	31 Rural Resort Dwellers	100.0
49418	18 Cozy And Comfortable	22.4	49665	46 Rooted Rural	72.2	49827	49 Senior Sun Seekers	100.0
49419	12 Up And Coming Families	59.9	49667	46 Rooted Rural	100.0	49829	29 Rustbelt Retirees	20.2
49420	42 Southern Satellites	35.1	49668	46 Rooted Rural	57.3	49831	25 Salt Of The Earth	57.7
49421	46 Rooted Rural	55.6	49670	31 Rural Resort Dwellers	94.5	49833	46 Rooted Rural	98.3
49423	28 Aspiring Young Families	14.8	49675	31 Rural Resort Dwellers	91.6	49834	46 Rooted Rural	53.9
49424	12 Up And Coming Families	44.0	49676	31 Rural Resort Dwellers	89.4	49835	31 Rural Resort Dwellers	100.0
49425	42 Southern Satellites	77.8	49677	26 Midland Crowd	21.3	49836	46 Rooted Rural	79.8
49426	17 Green Acres	34.5	49679	42 Southern Satellites	75.3	49837	50 Heartland Communities	28.1
49428	17 Green Acres	17.3	49680	42 Southern Satellites	54.5	49838	49 Senior Sun Seekers	100.0
49431	31 Rural Resort Dwellers	21.5	49682	31 Rural Resort Dwellers	73.9	49839	31 Rural Resort Dwellers	100.0
49435	17 Green Acres	67.8	49683	46 Rooted Rural	61.3	49840	31 Rural Resort Dwellers	93.7
49436	31 Rural Resort Dwellers	100.0	49684	17 Green Acres	19.7	49841	52 Inner City Tenants	33.9
49437	25 Salt Of The Earth	38.7	49686	33 Midlife Junction	17.0	49847	46 Rooted Rural	71.6
49440	65 Social Security Set	53.3	49688	42 Southern Satellites	38.5	49848	50 Heartland Communities	100.0
49441	32 Rustbelt Traditions	14.5	49689	46 Rooted Rural	93.8	49849	50 Heartland Communities	18.1
49442	32 Rustbelt Traditions	27.3	49690	17 Green Acres	65.1	49853	31 Rural Resort Dwellers	69.7
49444	51 Metro City Edge	19.6	49701	31 Rural Resort Dwellers	100.0	49854	31 Rural Resort Dwellers	36.2
49445	18 Cozy And Comfortable	33.0	49705	46 Rooted Rural	100.0	49855	33 Midlife Junction	19.7
49446	25 Salt Of The Earth	82.9	49706	31 Rural Resort Dwellers	59.3	49858	42 Southern Satellites	13.3

CONSUMER TYPE

ZIP CODE	TOP TAPESTRY CONSUMER TYPE	% 2009 HOUSE-HOLDS	ZIP CODE	TOP TAPESTRY CONSUMER TYPE	% 2009 HOUSE-HOLDS	ZIP CODE	TOP TAPESTRY CONSUMER TYPE	% 2009 HOUSE-HOLDS
49861	31 Rural Resort Dwellers	54.3	50052	50 Heartland Communities	91.2	50206	37 Prairie Living	98.5
49862	31 Rural Resort Dwellers	38.1	50054	25 Salt Of The Earth	49.6	50207	37 Prairie Living	53.5
49866	32 Rustbelt Traditions	27.8	50055	37 Prairie Living	81.2	50208	32 Rustbelt Traditions	29.2
49868	50 Heartland Communities	58.8	50056	32 Rustbelt Traditions	69.6	50210	25 Salt Of The Earth	78.5
49870	50 Heartland Communities	96.1	50057	25 Salt Of The Earth	100.0	50211	19 Milk And Cookies	52.1
49873	46 Rooted Rural	100.0	50058	29 Rustbelt Retirees	38.9	50212	29 Rustbelt Retirees	38.8
49874	25 Salt Of The Earth	45.7	50059	37 Prairie Living	100.0	50213	33 Midlife Junction	42.0
49876	25 Salt Of The Earth	98.7	50060	50 Heartland Communities	69.1	50214	17 Green Acres	100.0
49878	31 Rural Resort Dwellers	75.0	50061	06 Sophisticated Squires	38.6	50216	50 Heartland Communities	51.2
49879	49 Senior Sun Seekers	100.0	50062	25 Salt Of The Earth	84.1	50217	37 Prairie Living	100.0
49880	46 Rooted Rural	84.6	50063	17 Green Acres	56.3	50218	17 Green Acres	100.0
49881	46 Rooted Rural	100.0	50064	37 Prairie Living	100.0	50219	17 Green Acres	32.5
49883	46 Rooted Rural	100.0	50065	37 Prairie Living	94.4	50220	32 Rustbelt Traditions	40.2
49884	25 Salt Of The Earth	74.9	50066	37 Prairie Living	100.0	50222	37 Prairie Living	93.4
49885	31 Rural Resort Dwellers	50.0	50067	37 Prairie Living	98.8	50223	37 Prairie Living	100.0
49886	46 Rooted Rural	66.7	50068	37 Prairie Living	95.0	50225	33 Midlife Junction	38.5
49887	46 Rooted Rural	45.1	50069	26 Midland Crowd	100.0	50226	17 Green Acres	37.9
49891	46 Rooted Rural	100.0	50070	32 Rustbelt Traditions	52.4	50227	37 Prairie Living	100.0
49892	25 Salt Of The Earth	67.8	50071	37 Prairie Living	100.0	50228	25 Salt Of The Earth	68.0
49893	25 Salt Of The Earth	76.2	50072	26 Midland Crowd	66.4	50229	17 Green Acres	100.0
49894	50 Heartland Communities	51.8	50073	17 Green Acres	100.0	50230	37 Prairie Living	100.0
49895	46 Rooted Rural	79.4	50074	31 Rural Resort Dwellers	89.7	50231	37 Prairie Living	100.0
49896	46 Rooted Rural	62.5	50075	37 Prairie Living	100.0	50232	25 Salt Of The Earth	60.8
49905	50 Heartland Communities	63.8	50076	37 Prairie Living	59.4	50233	50 Heartland Communities	76.9
49908	50 Heartland Communities	77.7	50101	37 Prairie Living	100.0	50234	25 Salt Of The Earth	100.0
49910	49 Senior Sun Seekers	61.8	50102	37 Prairie Living	100.0	50235	37 Prairie Living	99.5
49911	50 Heartland Communities	74.5	50103	37 Prairie Living	100.0	50236	17 Green Acres	97.5
49912	50 Heartland Communities	57.9	50104	37 Prairie Living	100.0	50237	17 Green Acres	80.4
49913	50 Heartland Communities	58.7	50105	26 Midland Crowd	100.0	50238	50 Heartland Communities	91.5
49916	33 Midlife Junction	46.6	50106	32 Rustbelt Traditions	56.8	50239	37 Prairie Living	96.5
49919	46 Rooted Rural	97.8	50107	50 Heartland Communities	80.8	50240	17 Green Acres	96.7
49920	49 Senior Sun Seekers	49.0	50108	37 Prairie Living	100.0	50242	37 Prairie Living	88.7
49921	33 Midlife Junction	100.0	50109	25 Salt Of The Earth	44.7	50244	18 Cozy And Comfortable	87.3
49925	50 Heartland Communities	88.9	50111	12 Up And Coming Families	69.1	50246	37 Prairie Living	100.0
49927	49 Senior Sun Seekers	81.9	50112	33 Midlife Junction	29.6	50247	25 Salt Of The Earth	88.8
49930	50 Heartland Communities	31.6	50115	50 Heartland Communities	67.5	50248	33 Midlife Junction	38.8
49931	55 College Towns	62.1	50116	42 Southern Satellites	83.0	50249	50 Heartland Communities	57.4
49935	50 Heartland Communities	57.2	50117	37 Prairie Living	100.0	50250	32 Rustbelt Traditions	50.7
49938	50 Heartland Communities	64.6	50118	25 Salt Of The Earth	100.0	50251	25 Salt Of The Earth	80.7
49945	50 Heartland Communities	61.8	50119	42 Southern Satellites	93.7	50252	17 Green Acres	100.0
49946	50 Heartland Communities	66.9	50120	25 Salt Of The Earth	83.6	50254	37 Prairie Living	95.2
49947	31 Rural Resort Dwellers	54.4	50122	50 Heartland Communities	63.4	50256	42 Southern Satellites	76.4
49948	46 Rooted Rural	55.3	50123	37 Prairie Living	100.0	50257	25 Salt Of The Earth	88.3
49950	50 Heartland Communities	74.4	50124	26 Midland Crowd	63.5	50258	37 Prairie Living	100.0
49952	50 Heartland Communities	67.4	50125	17 Green Acres	32.8	50261	26 Midland Crowd	74.0
49953	50 Heartland Communities	54.2	50126	29 Rustbelt Retirees	42.4	50262	37 Prairie Living	100.0
49958	46 Rooted Rural	72.3	50127	17 Green Acres	100.0	50263	12 Up And Coming Families	63.9
49962	49 Senior Sun Seekers	100.0	50128	37 Prairie Living	100.0	50264	37 Prairie Living	100.0
49965	50 Heartland Communities	77.5	50129	50 Heartland Communities	51.5	50265	16 Enterprising Professionals	26.7
49967	46 Rooted Rural	43.6	50130	32 Rustbelt Traditions	74.4	50266	16 Enterprising Professionals	64.8
49968	50 Heartland Communities	71.6	50131	04 Boomburbs	71.9	50268	50 Heartland Communities	73.6
49969	46 Rooted Rural	65.7	50132	37 Prairie Living	100.0	50271	37 Prairie Living	100.0
49970	46 Rooted Rural	100.0	50133	50 Heartland Communities	100.0	50272	46 Rooted Rural	67.6
50001	17 Green Acres	100.0	50134	19 Milk And Cookies	76.2	50273	33 Midlife Junction	41.1
50002	50 Heartland Communities	63.2	50135	25 Salt Of The Earth	100.0	50274	37 Prairie Living	100.0
50003	26 Midland Crowd	28.5	50136	37 Prairie Living	100.0	50275	37 Prairie Living	81.8
50005	25 Salt Of The Earth	86.2	50138	25 Salt Of The Earth	34.1	50276	32 Rustbelt Traditions	28.5
50006	37 Prairie Living	100.0	50139	37 Prairie Living	68.4	50277	31 Rural Resort Dwellers	76.4
50007	17 Green Acres	100.0	50140	55 College Towns	46.9	50278	32 Rustbelt Traditions	90.6
50008	50 Heartland Communities	76.5	50141	25 Salt Of The Earth	100.0	50309	65 Social Security Set	88.9
50009	19 Milk And Cookies	44.8	50142	32 Rustbelt Traditions	100.0	50310	32 Rustbelt Traditions	24.0
50010	07 Exurbanites	21.8	50143	37 Prairie Living	100.0	50311	22 Metropolitans	32.1
50011	63 Dorms To Diplomas	0.0	50144	50 Heartland Communities	85.3	50312	22 Metropolitans	17.7
50013	63 Dorms To Diplomas	0.0	50146	37 Prairie Living	96.9	50313	32 Rustbelt Traditions	57.8
50014	55 College Towns	41.2	50147	50 Heartland Communities	94.2	50314	51 Metro City Edge	26.1
50020	50 Heartland Communities	76.0	50148	37 Prairie Living	100.0	50315	32 Rustbelt Traditions	49.3
50021	16 Enterprising Professionals	27.5	50149	42 Southern Satellites	68.6	50316	60 City Dimensions	41.5
50022	50 Heartland Communities	28.1	50150	42 Southern Satellites	99.8	50317	32 Rustbelt Traditions	50.1
50023	28 Aspiring Young Families	30.7	50151	46 Rooted Rural	89.7	50320	28 Aspiring Young Families	40.1
50025	50 Heartland Communities	69.2	50152	17 Green Acres	100.0	50321	36 Old And Newcomers	43.8
50026	37 Prairie Living	100.0	50153	25 Salt Of The Earth	96.3	50322	06 Sophisticated Squires	23.7
50027	37 Prairie Living	100.0	50154	37 Prairie Living	100.0	50323	04 Boomburbs	100.0
50028	32 Rustbelt Traditions	63.4	50155	37 Prairie Living	100.0	50325	04 Suburban Splendor	37.1
50029	37 Prairie Living	100.0	50156	32 Rustbelt Traditions	31.4	50327	06 Sophisticated Squires	45.7
50033	17 Green Acres	100.0	50157	25 Salt Of The Earth	62.5	50401	32 Rustbelt Traditions	25.3
50034	37 Prairie Living	100.0	50158	29 Rustbelt Retirees	14.6	50420	37 Prairie Living	100.0
50035	19 Milk And Cookies	69.5	50161	25 Salt Of The Earth	72.1	50421	50 Heartland Communities	81.5
50036	33 Midlife Junction	48.8	50162	32 Rustbelt Traditions	68.3	50423	50 Heartland Communities	69.7
50038	26 Midland Crowd	100.0	50163	50 Heartland Communities	99.0	50424	50 Heartland Communities	80.0
50039	37 Prairie Living	100.0	50164	50 Heartland Communities	82.5	50428	33 Midlife Junction	52.8
50040	37 Prairie Living	100.0	50165	37 Prairie Living	100.0	50430	37 Prairie Living	99.6
50041	37 Prairie Living	100.0	50166	25 Salt Of The Earth	60.9	50432	37 Prairie Living	100.0
50042	37 Prairie Living	100.0	50167	25 Salt Of The Earth	58.0	50433	37 Prairie Living	100.0
50044	42 Southern Satellites	79.7	50168	17 Green Acres	66.5	50434	37 Prairie Living	98.3
50046	26 Midland Crowd	84.9	50169	32 Rustbelt Traditions	50.1	50435	25 Salt Of The Earth	80.7
50047	18 Cozy And Comfortable	37.4	50170	32 Rustbelt Traditions	40.7	50436	33 Midlife Junction	36.8
50048	37 Prairie Living	89.9	50171	33 Midlife Junction	31.4	50438	29 Rustbelt Retirees	32.7
50049	50 Heartland Communities	53.0	50173	42 Southern Satellites	71.8	50439	37 Prairie Living	100.0
50050	37 Prairie Living	100.0	50174	42 Southern Satellites	82.0	50440	37 Prairie Living	100.0
50051	37 Prairie Living	100.0	50201	33 Midlife Junction	44.0	50441	32 Rustbelt Traditions	33.4

ZIP CODE	TOP TAPESTRY CONSUMER TYPE	% 2009 HOUSE-HOLDS	ZIP CODE	TOP TAPESTRY CONSUMER TYPE	% 2009 HOUSE-HOLDS	ZIP CODE	TOP TAPESTRY CONSUMER TYPE	% 2009 HOUSE-HOLDS
50444	37 Prairie Living	94.6	50575	50 Heartland Communities	77.1	50837	37 Prairie Living	100.0
50446	37 Prairie Living	89.3	50576	37 Prairie Living	100.0	50840	50 Heartland Communities	97.2
50447	50 Heartland Communities	78.2	50577	37 Prairie Living	100.0	50841	50 Heartland Communities	42.8
50448	37 Prairie Living	78.6	50578	37 Prairie Living	100.0	50843	37 Prairie Living	100.0
50449	42 Southern Satellites	92.6	50579	50 Heartland Communities	75.6	50845	37 Prairie Living	100.0
50450	33 Midlife Junction	59.9	50581	50 Heartland Communities	78.3	50846	50 Heartland Communities	68.0
50451	37 Prairie Living	100.0	50582	37 Prairie Living	100.0	50847	37 Prairie Living	100.0
50452	37 Prairie Living	100.0	50583	50 Heartland Communities	83.0	50848	37 Prairie Living	98.1
50453	25 Salt Of The Earth	59.3	50585	50 Heartland Communities	71.0	50849	50 Heartland Communities	59.5
50454	37 Prairie Living	100.0	50586	37 Prairie Living	100.0	50851	50 Heartland Communities	65.3
50455	37 Prairie Living	100.0	50588	42 Southern Satellites	37.9	50853	37 Prairie Living	100.0
50456	32 Rustbelt Traditions	43.6	50590	50 Heartland Communities	63.5	50854	50 Heartland Communities	78.3
50457	37 Prairie Living	100.0	50591	37 Prairie Living	100.0	50857	37 Prairie Living	68.7
50458	25 Salt Of The Earth	57.8	50594	37 Prairie Living	100.0	50858	37 Prairie Living	100.0
50459	25 Salt Of The Earth	35.8	50595	32 Rustbelt Traditions	28.6	50859	37 Prairie Living	100.0
50460	37 Prairie Living	90.3	50597	50 Heartland Communities	61.8	50860	37 Prairie Living	100.0
50461	50 Heartland Communities	50.4	50598	37 Prairie Living	100.0	50861	37 Prairie Living	100.0
50464	25 Salt Of The Earth	74.3	50599	37 Prairie Living	100.0	50862	37 Prairie Living	100.0
50465	37 Prairie Living	100.0	50601	37 Prairie Living	53.4	50863	31 Rural Resort Dwellers	94.9
50466	37 Prairie Living	60.9	50602	50 Heartland Communities	70.9	50864	50 Heartland Communities	74.4
50467	25 Salt Of The Earth	100.0	50603	37 Prairie Living	100.0	51001	25 Salt Of The Earth	48.3
50468	50 Heartland Communities	60.8	50604	50 Heartland Communities	67.0	51002	32 Rustbelt Traditions	73.9
50469	32 Rustbelt Traditions	61.6	50605	37 Prairie Living	100.0	51003	25 Salt Of The Earth	78.1
50470	37 Prairie Living	100.0	50606	37 Prairie Living	100.0	51004	50 Heartland Communities	71.9
50471	37 Prairie Living	100.0	50607	37 Prairie Living	100.0	51005	50 Heartland Communities	70.9
50472	50 Heartland Communities	51.4	50608	37 Prairie Living	100.0	51006	50 Heartland Communities	70.0
50473	37 Prairie Living	100.0	50609	37 Prairie Living	100.0	51007	25 Salt Of The Earth	93.8
50475	50 Heartland Communities	61.2	50611	37 Prairie Living	100.0	51009	37 Prairie Living	100.0
50476	37 Prairie Living	100.0	50612	33 Midlife Junction	53.6	51010	37 Prairie Living	87.8
50477	37 Prairie Living	92.5	50613	22 Metropolitans	22.1	51011	37 Prairie Living	100.0
50478	37 Prairie Living	100.0	50614	22 Metropolitans	100.0	51012	50 Heartland Communities	45.4
50479	37 Prairie Living	96.5	50616	50 Heartland Communities	30.0	51014	37 Prairie Living	100.0
50480	37 Prairie Living	100.0	50619	50 Heartland Communities	59.1	51016	50 Heartland Communities	61.1
50482	31 Rural Resort Dwellers	86.4	50621	33 Midlife Junction	75.3	51018	37 Prairie Living	100.0
50483	37 Prairie Living	100.0	50622	25 Salt Of The Earth	51.5	51019	37 Prairie Living	98.8
50484	37 Prairie Living	100.0	50624	25 Salt Of The Earth	89.1	51020	37 Prairie Living	99.1
50501	53 Home Town	18.0	50625	50 Heartland Communities	63.6	51022	37 Prairie Living	100.0
50510	37 Prairie Living	100.0	50626	26 Midland Crowd	61.6	51023	50 Heartland Communities	44.2
50511	50 Heartland Communities	18.5	50627	50 Heartland Communities	57.1	51024	17 Green Acres	85.5
50514	50 Heartland Communities	68.4	50628	37 Prairie Living	98.4	51025	50 Heartland Communities	70.8
50515	37 Prairie Living	100.0	50629	42 Southern Satellites	61.9	51026	37 Prairie Living	100.0
50516	25 Salt Of The Earth	95.6	50630	50 Heartland Communities	52.5	51027	37 Prairie Living	100.0
50517	50 Heartland Communities	76.4	50632	32 Rustbelt Traditions	62.8	51028	29 Rustbelt Retirees	69.7
50518	37 Prairie Living	97.2	50633	37 Prairie Living	100.0	51029	37 Prairie Living	100.0
50519	37 Prairie Living	100.0	50634	25 Salt Of The Earth	100.0	51030	17 Green Acres	80.7
50520	37 Prairie Living	100.0	50635	50 Heartland Communities	74.1	51031	17 Green Acres	22.7
50521	37 Prairie Living	100.0	50636	37 Prairie Living	36.0	51033	37 Prairie Living	97.3
50522	50 Heartland Communities	67.8	50638	50 Heartland Communities	31.6	51034	50 Heartland Communities	94.9
50523	37 Prairie Living	100.0	50641	42 Southern Satellites	97.2	51035	50 Heartland Communities	66.6
50524	37 Prairie Living	100.0	50642	37 Prairie Living	100.0	51036	37 Prairie Living	100.0
50525	32 Rustbelt Traditions	38.6	50643	17 Green Acres	99.7	51037	37 Prairie Living	100.0
50527	37 Prairie Living	100.0	50644	25 Salt Of The Earth	28.5	51038	25 Salt Of The Earth	73.7
50528	37 Prairie Living	100.0	50645	37 Prairie Living	66.9	51039	26 Midland Crowd	70.3
50529	32 Rustbelt Traditions	91.6	50647	25 Salt Of The Earth	86.8	51040	50 Heartland Communities	61.0
50530	50 Heartland Communities	76.1	50648	25 Salt Of The Earth	49.6	51041	33 Midlife Junction	66.8
50531	37 Prairie Living	100.0	50649	37 Prairie Living	100.0	51044	37 Prairie Living	100.0
50532	42 Southern Satellites	85.9	50650	37 Prairie Living	100.0	51046	50 Heartland Communities	67.6
50533	50 Heartland Communities	29.5	50651	32 Rustbelt Traditions	37.4	51047	37 Prairie Living	100.0
50535	37 Prairie Living	100.0	50652	37 Prairie Living	100.0	51048	37 Prairie Living	93.5
50536	50 Heartland Communities	49.7	50653	37 Prairie Living	100.0	51049	37 Prairie Living	100.0
50538	50 Heartland Communities	94.2	50654	37 Prairie Living	91.6	51050	25 Salt Of The Earth	72.2
50539	37 Prairie Living	100.0	50655	37 Prairie Living	100.0	51051	37 Prairie Living	94.4
50540	50 Heartland Communities	55.8	50658	50 Heartland Communities	80.0	51052	25 Salt Of The Earth	86.5
50541	37 Prairie Living	85.2	50659	29 Rustbelt Retirees	38.1	51053	50 Heartland Communities	65.5
50542	50 Heartland Communities	86.4	50660	42 Southern Satellites	58.0	51054	26 Midland Crowd	84.8
50543	50 Heartland Communities	81.2	50662	50 Heartland Communities	42.8	51055	32 Rustbelt Traditions	82.6
50544	37 Prairie Living	100.0	50665	37 Prairie Living	34.0	51056	37 Prairie Living	100.0
50545	37 Prairie Living	100.0	50666	25 Salt Of The Earth	83.8	51058	50 Heartland Communities	65.8
50546	37 Prairie Living	100.0	50667	25 Salt Of The Earth	100.0	51060	50 Heartland Communities	87.0
50548	29 Rustbelt Retirees	36.6	50668	29 Rustbelt Retirees	58.5	51061	37 Prairie Living	100.0
50551	37 Prairie Living	93.9	50669	25 Salt Of The Earth	52.3	51062	17 Green Acres	96.9
50552	37 Prairie Living	100.0	50670	32 Rustbelt Traditions	44.5	51063	50 Heartland Communities	71.3
50554	50 Heartland Communities	51.1	50671	37 Prairie Living	98.3	51101	57 Simple Living	62.0
50556	37 Prairie Living	100.0	50672	50 Heartland Communities	92.5	51103	32 Rustbelt Traditions	31.1
50557	50 Heartland Communities	75.9	50674	37 Prairie Living	43.4	51104	32 Rustbelt Traditions	22.6
50558	37 Prairie Living	100.0	50675	29 Rustbelt Retirees	40.6	51105	60 City Dimensions	30.9
50559	37 Prairie Living	100.0	50676	50 Heartland Communities	46.3	51106	32 Rustbelt Traditions	40.3
50560	37 Prairie Living	100.0	50677	33 Midlife Junction	49.1	51108	32 Rustbelt Traditions	33.1
50561	50 Heartland Communities	56.8	50680	50 Heartland Communities	72.8	51109	53 Home Town	46.6
50562	37 Prairie Living	100.0	50681	37 Prairie Living	100.0	51111	28 Aspiring Young Families	89.8
50563	50 Heartland Communities	41.7	50682	37 Prairie Living	87.6	51201	25 Salt Of The Earth	25.0
50565	37 Prairie Living	100.0	50701	32 Rustbelt Traditions	17.5	51230	37 Prairie Living	100.0
50566	37 Prairie Living	100.0	50702	29 Rustbelt Retirees	24.9	51231	37 Prairie Living	100.0
50567	37 Prairie Living	100.0	50703	53 Home Town	39.0	51232	37 Prairie Living	100.0
50568	50 Heartland Communities	77.2	50707	32 Rustbelt Traditions	34.7	51234	37 Prairie Living	100.0
50569	32 Rustbelt Traditions	93.6	50801	32 Rustbelt Traditions	23.9	51235	37 Prairie Living	100.0
50570	37 Prairie Living	100.0	50830	50 Heartland Communities	61.9	51237	50 Heartland Communities	65.0
50571	37 Prairie Living	100.0	50833	50 Heartland Communities	73.9	51238	37 Prairie Living	100.0
50573	37 Prairie Living	100.0	50835	37 Prairie Living	100.0	51239	37 Prairie Living	61.4
50574	37 Prairie Living	58.6	50836	46 Rooted Rural	82.2	51240	37 Prairie Living	100.0

CONSUMER TYPE

ZIP CODE	TOP TAPESTRY CONSUMER TYPE	% 2009 HOUSE-HOLDS	ZIP CODE	TOP TAPESTRY CONSUMER TYPE	% 2009 HOUSE-HOLDS	ZIP CODE	TOP TAPESTRY CONSUMER TYPE	% 2009 HOUSE-HOLDS
51241	37 Prairie Living	50.9	51553	25 Salt Of The Earth	90.5	52141	50 Heartland Communities	59.2
51243	37 Prairie Living	100.0	51555	32 Rustbelt Traditions	26.9	52142	50 Heartland Communities	45.5
51245	50 Heartland Communities	68.7	51556	37 Prairie Living	99.6	52144	37 Prairie Living	100.0
51246	50 Heartland Communities	52.0	51557	25 Salt Of The Earth	88.2	52146	46 Rooted Rural	95.7
51247	25 Salt Of The Earth	47.2	51558	37 Prairie Living	100.0	52147	37 Prairie Living	100.0
51248	50 Heartland Communities	78.6	51559	25 Salt Of The Earth	92.7	52151	46 Rooted Rural	37.1
51249	50 Heartland Communities	31.2	51560	32 Rustbelt Traditions	55.5	52154	46 Rooted Rural	59.8
51250	17 Green Acres	28.4	51561	46 Rooted Rural	53.0	52155	37 Prairie Living	100.0
51301	50 Heartland Communities	17.0	51562	37 Prairie Living	100.0	52156	37 Prairie Living	100.0
51331	46 Rooted Rural	77.8	51563	25 Salt Of The Earth	99.7	52157	46 Rooted Rural	54.5
51333	37 Prairie Living	100.0	51564	50 Heartland Communities	73.0	52158	46 Rooted Rural	100.0
51334	50 Heartland Communities	27.7	51565	37 Prairie Living	100.0	52159	50 Heartland Communities	73.8
51338	37 Prairie Living	100.0	51566	53 Home Town	40.3	52160	46 Rooted Rural	88.0
51342	50 Heartland Communities	77.0	51570	37 Prairie Living	83.8	52161	37 Prairie Living	100.0
51343	37 Prairie Living	100.0	51571	17 Green Acres	84.3	52162	37 Prairie Living	69.3
51345	37 Prairie Living	100.0	51572	37 Prairie Living	99.6	52163	37 Prairie Living	100.0
51346	50 Heartland Communities	69.8	51573	25 Salt Of The Earth	69.6	52164	37 Prairie Living	97.1
51347	50 Heartland Communities	81.1	51575	18 Cozy And Comfortable	81.3	52165	37 Prairie Living	100.0
51350	37 Prairie Living	100.0	51576	25 Salt Of The Earth	55.7	52169	37 Prairie Living	100.0
51351	33 Midlife Junction	30.5	51577	37 Prairie Living	100.0	52170	37 Prairie Living	94.8
51354	37 Prairie Living	100.0	51578	37 Prairie Living	100.0	52171	37 Prairie Living	97.4
51355	31 Rural Resort Dwellers	97.1	51579	50 Heartland Communities	72.3	52172	50 Heartland Communities	72.7
51357	37 Prairie Living	100.0	51601	57 Simple Living	28.0	52175	50 Heartland Communities	29.6
51358	50 Heartland Communities	62.1	51630	37 Prairie Living	82.2	52201	37 Prairie Living	100.0
51360	31 Rural Resort Dwellers	30.0	51631	25 Salt Of The Earth	100.0	52202	17 Green Acres	97.2
51363	31 Rural Resort Dwellers	100.0	51632	33 Midlife Junction	27.4	52203	17 Green Acres	62.5
51364	37 Prairie Living	89.6	51636	37 Prairie Living	98.0	52205	32 Rustbelt Traditions	40.3
51365	37 Prairie Living	100.0	51637	25 Salt Of The Earth	100.0	52206	17 Green Acres	94.4
51366	37 Prairie Living	100.0	51638	25 Salt Of The Earth	58.6	52207	46 Rooted Rural	61.7
51401	33 Midlife Junction	22.0	51639	37 Prairie Living	100.0	52208	50 Heartland Communities	37.7
51430	37 Prairie Living	100.0	51640	25 Salt Of The Earth	57.4	52209	25 Salt Of The Earth	99.8
51431	37 Prairie Living	100.0	51645	37 Prairie Living	94.5	52210	25 Salt Of The Earth	97.4
51433	37 Prairie Living	100.0	51646	50 Heartland Communities	82.8	52211	25 Salt Of The Earth	66.3
51436	37 Prairie Living	100.0	51647	37 Prairie Living	100.0	52212	37 Prairie Living	95.5
51439	37 Prairie Living	100.0	51648	37 Prairie Living	95.5	52213	17 Green Acres	48.9
51440	37 Prairie Living	100.0	51649	37 Prairie Living	89.6	52214	32 Rustbelt Traditions	42.7
51441	37 Prairie Living	100.0	51650	37 Prairie Living	99.4	52215	37 Prairie Living	70.2
51442	50 Heartland Communities	31.3	51651	37 Prairie Living	100.0	52216	50 Heartland Communities	74.5
51443	50 Heartland Communities	59.5	51652	50 Heartland Communities	51.2	52217	37 Prairie Living	100.0
51444	37 Prairie Living	100.0	51653	33 Midlife Junction	77.1	52218	32 Rustbelt Traditions	43.4
51445	50 Heartland Communities	58.2	51654	37 Prairie Living	100.0	52219	25 Salt Of The Earth	100.0
51446	37 Prairie Living	100.0	51656	37 Prairie Living	100.0	52220	25 Salt Of The Earth	100.0
51447	37 Prairie Living	94.3	52001	32 Rustbelt Traditions	16.6	52221	37 Prairie Living	100.0
51448	37 Prairie Living	100.0	52002	25 Salt Of The Earth	25.3	52222	37 Prairie Living	99.1
51449	50 Heartland Communities	76.9	52003	17 Green Acres	20.8	52223	37 Prairie Living	70.7
51450	49 Senior Sun Seekers	43.1	52030	25 Salt Of The Earth	100.0	52224	29 Rustbelt Retirees	43.0
51451	37 Prairie Living	100.0	52031	25 Salt Of The Earth	66.2	52225	37 Prairie Living	87.7
51452	37 Prairie Living	100.0	52032	37 Prairie Living	62.3	52227	17 Green Acres	91.6
51453	37 Prairie Living	89.0	52033	25 Salt Of The Earth	40.8	52228	17 Green Acres	63.9
51454	50 Heartland Communities	65.9	52035	37 Prairie Living	100.0	52229	37 Prairie Living	100.0
51455	50 Heartland Communities	70.1	52036	37 Prairie Living	66.7	52231	37 Prairie Living	100.0
51458	37 Prairie Living	53.2	52037	37 Prairie Living	96.4	52232	25 Salt Of The Earth	83.5
51460	37 Prairie Living	100.0	52038	37 Prairie Living	100.0	52233	13 In Style	27.5
51461	50 Heartland Communities	79.9	52039	37 Prairie Living	37.3	52236	25 Salt Of The Earth	98.0
51462	37 Prairie Living	100.0	52040	32 Rustbelt Traditions	46.1	52237	42 Southern Satellites	55.3
51463	37 Prairie Living	100.0	52041	25 Salt Of The Earth	68.1	52240	28 Aspiring Young Families	26.6
51465	37 Prairie Living	100.0	52042	37 Prairie Living	100.0	52241	39 Young And Restless	49.8
51466	50 Heartland Communities	72.7	52043	29 Rustbelt Retirees	41.2	52242	63 Dorms To Diplomas	100.0
51467	37 Prairie Living	100.0	52044	37 Prairie Living	100.0	52245	22 Metropolitans	23.3
51501	32 Rustbelt Traditions	42.2	52045	25 Salt Of The Earth	69.2	52246	16 Enterprising Professionals	54.8
51503	07 Exurbanites	19.6	52046	25 Salt Of The Earth	71.3	52247	37 Prairie Living	38.4
51510	29 Rustbelt Retirees	32.2	52047	37 Prairie Living	100.0	52248	50 Heartland Communities	60.8
51520	37 Prairie Living	100.0	52048	37 Prairie Living	100.0	52249	29 Rustbelt Retirees	81.4
51521	50 Heartland Communities	52.7	52049	50 Heartland Communities	96.8	52251	37 Prairie Living	100.0
51523	37 Prairie Living	100.0	52050	37 Prairie Living	100.0	52253	26 Midland Crowd	75.2
51525	25 Salt Of The Earth	69.7	52052	50 Heartland Communities	40.2	52254	50 Heartland Communities	63.4
51526	17 Green Acres	78.0	52053	37 Prairie Living	88.8	52255	50 Heartland Communities	67.8
51527	37 Prairie Living	100.0	52054	25 Salt Of The Earth	80.2	52257	25 Salt Of The Earth	100.0
51528	46 Rooted Rural	66.2	52057	32 Rustbelt Traditions	26.1	52301	32 Rustbelt Traditions	61.1
51529	50 Heartland Communities	60.2	52060	25 Salt Of The Earth	33.6	52302	12 Up And Coming Families	31.5
51530	37 Prairie Living	100.0	52064	37 Prairie Living	98.7	52305	37 Prairie Living	90.6
51531	29 Rustbelt Retirees	90.1	52065	37 Prairie Living	100.0	52306	32 Rustbelt Traditions	58.9
51532	46 Rooted Rural	76.8	52068	17 Green Acres	89.8	52307	17 Green Acres	100.0
51533	50 Heartland Communities	60.1	52069	25 Salt Of The Earth	70.8	52308	37 Prairie Living	100.0
51534	33 Midlife Junction	30.9	52070	46 Rooted Rural	80.8	52309	46 Rooted Rural	61.0
51535	37 Prairie Living	61.6	52071	25 Salt Of The Earth	100.0	52310	25 Salt Of The Earth	31.5
51536	37 Prairie Living	68.8	52072	37 Prairie Living	95.3	52313	37 Prairie Living	100.0
51537	29 Rustbelt Retirees	38.0	52073	25 Salt Of The Earth	82.6	52314	18 Cozy And Comfortable	35.9
51540	37 Prairie Living	100.0	52074	37 Prairie Living	86.4	52315	25 Salt Of The Earth	95.5
51541	37 Prairie Living	93.9	52076	46 Rooted Rural	56.5	52316	50 Heartland Communities	62.9
51542	17 Green Acres	100.0	52077	37 Prairie Living	100.0	52317	28 Aspiring Young Families	91.4
51543	37 Prairie Living	100.0	52078	37 Prairie Living	86.8	52318	12 Up And Coming Families	98.6
51544	37 Prairie Living	100.0	52079	37 Prairie Living	90.9	52320	32 Rustbelt Traditions	74.4
51545	50 Heartland Communities	97.5	52101	17 Green Acres	24.8	52321	37 Prairie Living	90.6
51546	25 Salt Of The Earth	42.4	52132	37 Prairie Living	100.0	52322	26 Midland Crowd	36.0
51548	17 Green Acres	100.0	52133	37 Prairie Living	100.0	52323	50 Heartland Communities	91.0
51549	37 Prairie Living	91.0	52134	37 Prairie Living	100.0	52324	06 Sophisticated Squires	64.2
51550	25 Salt Of The Earth	64.3	52135	37 Prairie Living	100.0	52325	25 Salt Of The Earth	62.6
51551	50 Heartland Communities	69.8	52136	50 Heartland Communities	36.5	52326	25 Salt Of The Earth	100.0
51552	37 Prairie Living	97.2	52140	37 Prairie Living	86.2	52327	26 Midland Crowd	44.1

ZIP CODE	TOP TAPESTRY CONSUMER TYPE	% 2009 HOUSE-HOLDS	ZIP CODE	TOP TAPESTRY CONSUMER TYPE	% 2009 HOUSE-HOLDS	ZIP CODE	TOP TAPESTRY CONSUMER TYPE	% 2009 HOUSE-HOLDS
52328	06 Sophisticated Squires	58.3	52630	42 Southern Satellites	50.7	53033	06 Sophisticated Squires	62.8
52329	25 Salt Of The Earth	83.7	52631	37 Prairie Living	100.0	53034	24 Main Street, USA	91.3
52330	37 Prairie Living	94.7	52632	53 Home Town	21.5	53035	26 Midland Crowd	57.4
52332	25 Salt Of The Earth	100.0	52635	37 Prairie Living	94.0	53036	17 Green Acres	92.0
52333	07 Exurbanites	51.7	52637	25 Salt Of The Earth	53.7	53037	12 Up And Coming Families	68.4
52334	25 Salt Of The Earth	100.0	52638	42 Southern Satellites	52.4	53038	26 Midland Crowd	60.5
52335	37 Prairie Living	100.0	52639	46 Rooted Rural	59.2	53039	25 Salt Of The Earth	43.9
52336	32 Rustbelt Traditions	53.8	52640	42 Southern Satellites	76.4	53040	24 Main Street, USA	31.3
52337	25 Salt Of The Earth	86.0	52641	48 Great Expectations	18.0	53042	17 Green Acres	39.3
52338	17 Green Acres	42.0	52644	25 Salt Of The Earth	72.4	53044	07 Exurbanites	56.3
52339	41 Crossroads	30.6	52645	25 Salt Of The Earth	73.8	53045	07 Exurbanites	44.4
52340	28 Aspiring Young Families	86.4	52646	42 Southern Satellites	78.2	53046	17 Green Acres	63.3
52341	17 Green Acres	99.8	52647	37 Prairie Living	100.0	53048	26 Midland Crowd	76.0
52342	50 Heartland Communities	39.7	52649	25 Salt Of The Earth	82.2	53049	25 Salt Of The Earth	68.8
52345	26 Midland Crowd	98.8	52650	17 Green Acres	64.9	53050	25 Salt Of The Earth	41.6
52346	37 Prairie Living	87.2	52651	37 Prairie Living	100.0	53051	24 Main Street, USA	18.8
52347	25 Salt Of The Earth	80.2	52653	32 Rustbelt Traditions	56.3	53057	25 Salt Of The Earth	100.0
52348	37 Prairie Living	100.0	52654	37 Prairie Living	87.1	53058	13 In Style	49.5
52349	29 Rustbelt Retirees	28.4	52655	32 Rustbelt Traditions	30.6	53059	17 Green Acres	93.8
52352	25 Salt Of The Earth	80.2	52656	29 Rustbelt Retirees	50.3	53061	25 Salt Of The Earth	77.1
52353	32 Rustbelt Traditions	36.2	52657	37 Prairie Living	100.0	53063	17 Green Acres	63.1
52354	25 Salt Of The Earth	95.0	52658	25 Salt Of The Earth	99.6	53065	17 Green Acres	100.0
52355	37 Prairie Living	100.0	52659	50 Heartland Communities	70.9	53066	07 Exurbanites	27.4
52356	50 Heartland Communities	58.8	52660	37 Prairie Living	80.8	53069	13 In Style	100.0
52358	26 Midland Crowd	33.6	52701	37 Prairie Living	100.0	53070	25 Salt Of The Earth	53.4
52359	37 Prairie Living	100.0	52720	25 Salt Of The Earth	77.5	53072	16 Enterprising Professionals	29.1
52361	33 Midlife Junction	70.7	52721	37 Prairie Living	100.0	53073	17 Green Acres	35.1
52362	50 Heartland Communities	80.1	52722	07 Exurbanites	12.4	53074	24 Main Street, USA	42.1
52401	65 Social Security Set	39.9	52726	17 Green Acres	51.2	53075	24 Main Street, USA	55.8
52402	16 Enterprising Professionals	15.5	52727	25 Salt Of The Earth	75.4	53076	06 Sophisticated Squires	61.2
52403	29 Rustbelt Retirees	20.4	52728	17 Green Acres	96.7	53078	17 Green Acres	100.0
52404	41 Crossroads	24.5	52729	25 Salt Of The Earth	95.1	53079	25 Salt Of The Earth	100.0
52405	18 Cozy And Comfortable	26.9	52730	32 Rustbelt Traditions	29.4	53080	06 Sophisticated Squires	30.8
52411	07 Exurbanites	82.3	52731	37 Prairie Living	97.7	53081	32 Rustbelt Traditions	21.5
52501	50 Heartland Communities	21.8	52732	53 Home Town	36.0	53083	17 Green Acres	43.3
52530	25 Salt Of The Earth	82.3	52738	32 Rustbelt Traditions	36.3	53085	24 Main Street, USA	54.7
52531	50 Heartland Communities	53.2	52739	25 Salt Of The Earth	86.5	53086	24 Main Street, USA	45.0
52533	37 Prairie Living	78.9	52742	33 Midlife Junction	34.7	53089	06 Sophisticated Squires	43.2
52534	25 Salt Of The Earth	100.0	52745	17 Green Acres	63.7	53090	17 Green Acres	35.9
52535	46 Rooted Rural	75.2	52746	17 Green Acres	100.0	53091	25 Salt Of The Earth	81.1
52536	25 Salt Of The Earth	100.0	52747	25 Salt Of The Earth	51.0	53092	02 Suburban Splendor	31.4
52537	37 Prairie Living	36.7	52748	17 Green Acres	45.0	53093	25 Salt Of The Earth	97.1
52540	42 Southern Satellites	53.3	52749	26 Midland Crowd	57.1	53094	18 Cozy And Comfortable	24.9
52542	37 Prairie Living	98.6	52750	25 Salt Of The Earth	60.2	53095	24 Main Street, USA	29.7
52543	37 Prairie Living	81.4	52751	25 Salt Of The Earth	83.6	53097	07 Exurbanites	49.5
52544	50 Heartland Communities	38.0	52753	17 Green Acres	36.9	53098	25 Salt Of The Earth	22.4
52548	25 Salt Of The Earth	100.0	52754	25 Salt Of The Earth	90.1	53103	06 Sophisticated Squires	52.3
52549	46 Rooted Rural	86.3	52755	32 Rustbelt Traditions	53.3	53104	17 Green Acres	72.9
52550	50 Heartland Communities	80.9	52756	17 Green Acres	79.5	53105	17 Green Acres	42.1
52551	37 Prairie Living	51.2	52760	25 Salt Of The Earth	99.6	53108	07 Exurbanites	27.8
52552	37 Prairie Living	100.0	52761	32 Rustbelt Traditions	31.9	53110	32 Rustbelt Traditions	22.3
52553	42 Southern Satellites	54.5	52765	37 Prairie Living	100.0	53114	19 Milk And Cookies	71.1
52554	50 Heartland Communities	72.7	52766	25 Salt Of The Earth	81.2	53115	32 Rustbelt Traditions	22.4
52555	37 Prairie Living	100.0	52768	25 Salt Of The Earth	70.7	53118	24 Main Street, USA	44.0
52556	37 Prairie Living	15.7	52769	37 Prairie Living	100.0	53119	06 Sophisticated Squires	90.8
52557	22 Metropolitans	100.0	52772	25 Salt Of The Earth	22.6	53120	17 Green Acres	74.5
52560	46 Rooted Rural	63.5	52773	26 Midland Crowd	66.4	53121	17 Green Acres	43.9
52561	25 Salt Of The Earth	83.0	52774	25 Salt Of The Earth	100.0	53122	03 Connoisseurs	41.9
52563	37 Prairie Living	52.0	52776	32 Rustbelt Traditions	55.4	53125	14 Prosperous Empty Nesters	47.8
52565	50 Heartland Communities	61.8	52777	50 Heartland Communities	54.6	53126	17 Green Acres	70.7
52566	25 Salt Of The Earth	100.0	52778	32 Rustbelt Traditions	77.7	53128	32 Rustbelt Traditions	41.9
52567	25 Salt Of The Earth	89.4	52801	65 Social Security Set	95.3	53129	18 Cozy And Comfortable	22.4
52569	46 Rooted Rural	83.8	52802	53 Home Town	46.7	53130	18 Cozy And Comfortable	43.2
52570	37 Prairie Living	100.0	52803	32 Rustbelt Traditions	29.7	53132	06 Sophisticated Squires	39.3
52571	50 Heartland Communities	64.2	52804	32 Rustbelt Traditions	29.8	53137	17 Green Acres	82.3
52572	50 Heartland Communities	65.4	52806	33 Midlife Junction	20.2	53139	17 Green Acres	90.9
52573	37 Prairie Living	100.0	52807	16 Enterprising Professionals	23.9	53140	48 Great Expectations	21.4
52574	42 Southern Satellites	67.5	53001	17 Green Acres	69.1	53142	18 Cozy And Comfortable	28.9
52576	37 Prairie Living	100.0	53002	17 Green Acres	52.5	53143	18 Cozy And Comfortable	15.6
52577	33 Midlife Junction	30.1	53004	17 Green Acres	100.0	53144	28 Aspiring Young Families	23.9
52580	37 Prairie Living	100.0	53005	07 Exurbanites	47.2	53146	18 Cozy And Comfortable	34.3
52581	37 Prairie Living	100.0	53006	17 Green Acres	77.4	53147	31 Rural Resort Dwellers	24.7
52583	37 Prairie Living	97.5	53007	30 Retirement Communities	50.8	53149	06 Sophisticated Squires	40.3
52584	37 Prairie Living	100.0	53010	25 Salt Of The Earth	43.4	53150	06 Sophisticated Squires	21.3
52585	37 Prairie Living	100.0	53011	25 Salt Of The Earth	66.4	53151	07 Exurbanites	18.2
52586	37 Prairie Living	99.2	53012	13 In Style	46.6	53153	06 Sophisticated Squires	100.0
52588	37 Prairie Living	72.8	53013	17 Green Acres	100.0	53154	36 Old And Newcomers	20.5
52590	50 Heartland Communities	72.0	53014	25 Salt Of The Earth	81.3	53156	25 Salt Of The Earth	81.6
52591	50 Heartland Communities	75.4	53015	17 Green Acres	57.1	53158	13 In Style	27.7
52593	37 Prairie Living	100.0	53017	06 Sophisticated Squires	75.5	53168	17 Green Acres	32.4
52594	37 Prairie Living	83.1	53018	02 Suburban Splendor	47.1	53170	24 Main Street, USA	51.2
52601	32 Rustbelt Traditions	16.5	53019	42 Southern Satellites	56.4	53172	24 Main Street, USA	28.9
52619	25 Salt Of The Earth	91.0	53020	17 Green Acres	90.2	53177	24 Main Street, USA	42.4
52620	42 Southern Satellites	83.4	53021	17 Green Acres	65.6	53178	17 Green Acres	60.7
52621	37 Prairie Living	100.0	53022	06 Sophisticated Squires	32.1	53179	26 Midland Crowd	47.5
52623	25 Salt Of The Earth	99.9	53023	17 Green Acres	51.2	53181	17 Green Acres	38.0
52624	25 Salt Of The Earth	100.0	53024	07 Exurbanites	25.9	53182	17 Green Acres	41.1
52625	37 Prairie Living	36.3	53027	24 Main Street, USA	52.2	53183	06 Sophisticated Squires	61.4
52626	50 Heartland Communities	75.6	53029	06 Sophisticated Squires	35.9	53184	24 Main Street, USA	63.8
52627	50 Heartland Communities	36.5	53032	32 Rustbelt Traditions	51.6	53185	06 Sophisticated Squires	47.6

CONSUMER TYPE

ZIP CODE	TOP TAPESTRY CONSUMER TYPE	% 2009 HOUSE-HOLDS	ZIP CODE	TOP TAPESTRY CONSUMER TYPE	% 2009 HOUSE-HOLDS	ZIP CODE	TOP TAPESTRY CONSUMER TYPE	% 2009 HOUSE-HOLDS
53186	24 Main Street, USA	16.4	53569	32 Rustbelt Traditions	63.7	53963	32 Rustbelt Traditions	52.2
53188	06 Sophisticated Squires	27.0	53570	25 Salt Of The Earth	55.3	53964	50 Heartland Communities	42.9
53189	06 Sophisticated Squires	38.5	53572	28 Aspiring Young Families	32.0	53965	33 Midlife Junction	37.5
53190	63 Dorms To Diplomas	21.5	53573	46 Rooted Rural	57.8	53968	46 Rooted Rural	35.6
53191	14 Prosperous Empty Nesters	55.1	53574	17 Green Acres	38.5	54001	25 Salt Of The Earth	38.8
53202	27 Metro Renters	85.2	53575	06 Sophisticated Squires	37.8	54002	17 Green Acres	42.4
53203	27 Metro Renters	98.8	53576	25 Salt Of The Earth	98.6	54003	17 Green Acres	96.2
53204	60 City Dimensions	59.0	53577	37 Prairie Living	97.8	54004	37 Prairie Living	41.7
53205	64 City Commons	66.9	53578	24 Main Street, USA	42.6	54005	42 Southern Satellites	54.1
53206	64 City Commons	54.9	53579	25 Salt Of The Earth	76.2	54006	25 Salt Of The Earth	100.0
53207	32 Rustbelt Traditions	28.5	53580	37 Prairie Living	100.0	54007	25 Salt Of The Earth	55.2
53208	64 City Commons	24.3	53581	37 Prairie Living	33.3	54009	26 Midland Crowd	57.4
53209	51 Metro City Edge	38.8	53582	37 Prairie Living	86.4	54011	17 Green Acres	33.6
53210	51 Metro City Edge	31.2	53583	24 Main Street, USA	45.9	54013	25 Salt Of The Earth	47.0
53211	22 Metropolitans	26.0	53585	26 Midland Crowd	55.5	54014	17 Green Acres	69.4
53212	64 City Commons	30.0	53586	50 Heartland Communities	59.1	54015	24 Main Street, USA	51.6
53213	22 Metropolitans	49.0	53587	37 Prairie Living	100.0	54016	06 Sophisticated Squires	49.1
53214	48 Great Expectations	46.2	53588	33 Midlife Junction	41.7	54017	24 Main Street, USA	32.7
53215	60 City Dimensions	46.3	53589	24 Main Street, USA	27.7	54020	17 Green Acres	75.4
53216	51 Metro City Edge	59.7	53590	06 Sophisticated Squires	20.1	54021	13 In Style	45.2
53217	03 Connoisseurs	16.8	53593	06 Sophisticated Squires	42.3	54022	13 In Style	33.6
53218	51 Metro City Edge	53.4	53594	24 Main Street, USA	65.7	54023	26 Midland Crowd	43.3
53219	29 Rustbelt Retirees	26.6	53597	06 Sophisticated Squires	27.4	54024	25 Salt Of The Earth	58.9
53220	29 Rustbelt Retirees	27.0	53598	13 In Style	64.8	54025	17 Green Acres	64.3
53221	24 Main Street, USA	29.6	53703	63 Dorms To Diplomas	67.8	54026	17 Green Acres	99.3
53222	32 Rustbelt Traditions	27.8	53704	28 Aspiring Young Families	21.3	54027	17 Green Acres	100.0
53223	18 Cozy And Comfortable	20.1	53705	27 Metro Renters	33.4	54028	26 Midland Crowd	54.2
53224	52 Inner City Tenants	23.1	53706	63 Dorms To Diplomas	100.0	54082	06 Sophisticated Squires	77.7
53225	32 Rustbelt Traditions	18.7	53711	14 Prosperous Empty Nesters	20.3	54101	17 Green Acres	57.5
53226	30 Retirement Communities	26.9	53713	39 Young And Restless	44.8	54102	49 Senior Sun Seekers	59.4
53227	24 Main Street, USA	22.8	53714	24 Main Street, USA	17.3	54103	50 Heartland Communities	77.5
53228	30 Retirement Communities	26.1	53715	63 Dorms To Diplomas	46.2	54104	49 Senior Sun Seekers	94.8
53233	63 Dorms To Diplomas	44.7	53716	18 Cozy And Comfortable	26.8	54106	25 Salt Of The Earth	81.8
53235	30 Retirement Communities	18.3	53717	16 Enterprising Professionals	57.1	54107	25 Salt Of The Earth	96.0
53402	32 Rustbelt Traditions	25.4	53718	13 In Style	51.1	54110	25 Salt Of The Earth	71.6
53403	32 Rustbelt Traditions	30.2	53719	16 Enterprising Professionals	79.5	54111	25 Salt Of The Earth	86.3
53404	60 City Dimensions	32.2	53726	63 Dorms To Diplomas	67.0	54112	50 Heartland Communities	41.1
53405	32 Rustbelt Traditions	48.8	53801	37 Prairie Living	100.0	54113	17 Green Acres	71.5
53406	29 Rustbelt Retirees	19.7	53803	50 Heartland Communities	76.4	54114	49 Senior Sun Seekers	31.8
53502	32 Rustbelt Traditions	55.4	53804	37 Prairie Living	100.0	54115	17 Green Acres	30.0
53503	25 Salt Of The Earth	90.1	53805	37 Prairie Living	27.7	54119	31 Rural Resort Dwellers	86.0
53504	25 Salt Of The Earth	54.2	53806	50 Heartland Communities	66.4	54120	31 Rural Resort Dwellers	100.0
53505	17 Green Acres	100.0	53807	25 Salt Of The Earth	53.8	54121	31 Rural Resort Dwellers	57.6
53506	42 Southern Satellites	70.2	53809	37 Prairie Living	48.5	54124	50 Heartland Communities	29.2
53507	17 Green Acres	98.4	53810	37 Prairie Living	100.0	54125	49 Senior Sun Seekers	58.6
53508	17 Green Acres	99.1	53811	32 Rustbelt Traditions	44.3	54126	17 Green Acres	99.5
53510	50 Heartland Communities	53.9	53813	37 Prairie Living	27.8	54128	46 Rooted Rural	100.0
53511	32 Rustbelt Traditions	25.5	53816	37 Prairie Living	100.0	54129	42 Southern Satellites	35.0
53515	18 Cozy And Comfortable	71.2	53818	55 College Towns	39.3	54130	17 Green Acres	27.6
53516	25 Salt Of The Earth	50.9	53820	25 Salt Of The Earth	74.6	54135	31 Rural Resort Dwellers	45.0
53517	17 Green Acres	100.0	53821	46 Rooted Rural	30.9	54136	32 Rustbelt Traditions	42.9
53518	37 Prairie Living	57.7	53825	37 Prairie Living	100.0	54137	25 Salt Of The Earth	64.9
53520	32 Rustbelt Traditions	34.3	53826	26 Midland Crowd	57.5	54138	49 Senior Sun Seekers	100.0
53521	17 Green Acres	54.4	53827	37 Prairie Living	100.0	54139	32 Rustbelt Traditions	32.0
53522	37 Prairie Living	100.0	53901	33 Midlife Junction	19.5	54140	24 Main Street, USA	29.7
53523	17 Green Acres	52.4	53910	46 Rooted Rural	51.6	54141	26 Midland Crowd	70.9
53525	25 Salt Of The Earth	36.9	53911	17 Green Acres	91.1	54143	32 Rustbelt Traditions	25.0
53526	37 Prairie Living	100.0	53913	17 Green Acres	31.9	54149	49 Senior Sun Seekers	100.0
53527	12 Up And Coming Families	78.1	53916	25 Salt Of The Earth	18.4	54150	51 Metro City Edge	100.0
53528	12 Up And Coming Families	46.5	53919	25 Salt Of The Earth	94.4	54151	46 Rooted Rural	39.3
53529	17 Green Acres	98.6	53920	31 Rural Resort Dwellers	100.0	54153	25 Salt Of The Earth	34.0
53530	37 Prairie Living	41.1	53922	25 Salt Of The Earth	99.2	54154	33 Midlife Junction	53.0
53531	17 Green Acres	94.1	53923	37 Prairie Living	56.9	54155	07 Exurbanites	40.9
53532	24 Main Street, USA	34.0	53924	37 Prairie Living	94.9	54156	46 Rooted Rural	51.5
53533	32 Rustbelt Traditions	41.2	53925	24 Main Street, USA	55.4	54157	25 Salt Of The Earth	59.0
53534	25 Salt Of The Earth	27.4	53926	25 Salt Of The Earth	84.9	54159	25 Salt Of The Earth	100.0
53536	17 Green Acres	42.6	53929	50 Heartland Communities	37.5	54161	46 Rooted Rural	63.2
53538	24 Main Street, USA	35.3	53930	26 Midland Crowd	81.9	54162	17 Green Acres	25.6
53541	37 Prairie Living	100.0	53932	26 Midland Crowd	67.8	54165	17 Green Acres	38.6
53543	37 Prairie Living	99.3	53933	29 Rustbelt Retirees	63.3	54166	33 Midlife Junction	31.0
53544	37 Prairie Living	91.2	53934	49 Senior Sun Seekers	55.1	54169	17 Green Acres	100.0
53545	32 Rustbelt Traditions	22.9	53936	46 Rooted Rural	78.6	54170	25 Salt Of The Earth	98.1
53546	12 Up And Coming Families	19.4	53937	37 Prairie Living	100.0	54171	12 Up And Coming Families	60.8
53548	17 Green Acres	24.0	53939	25 Salt Of The Earth	100.0	54173	12 Up And Coming Families	59.5
53549	24 Main Street, USA	23.1	53941	25 Salt Of The Earth	74.2	54174	46 Rooted Rural	84.0
53550	37 Prairie Living	89.6	53943	37 Prairie Living	99.0	54175	49 Senior Sun Seekers	100.0
53551	33 Midlife Junction	26.9	53944	46 Rooted Rural	41.4	54177	46 Rooted Rural	76.6
53553	37 Prairie Living	100.0	53946	31 Rural Resort Dwellers	35.4	54180	12 Up And Coming Families	73.6
53554	37 Prairie Living	100.0	53947	31 Rural Resort Dwellers	100.0	54201	25 Salt Of The Earth	27.4
53555	24 Main Street, USA	42.5	53948	46 Rooted Rural	41.4	54202	31 Rural Resort Dwellers	98.7
53556	25 Salt Of The Earth	54.3	53949	49 Senior Sun Seekers	28.2	54204	25 Salt Of The Earth	89.5
53557	25 Salt Of The Earth	92.1	53950	46 Rooted Rural	46.9	54205	25 Salt Of The Earth	67.0
53558	06 Sophisticated Squires	54.0	53951	25 Salt Of The Earth	45.8	54208	17 Green Acres	35.6
53559	26 Midland Crowd	52.8	53952	31 Rural Resort Dwellers	62.0	54209	31 Rural Resort Dwellers	100.0
53560	17 Green Acres	86.3	53954	17 Green Acres	30.9	54210	31 Rural Resort Dwellers	100.0
53561	31 Rural Resort Dwellers	81.2	53955	17 Green Acres	51.1	54212	31 Rural Resort Dwellers	100.0
53562	13 In Style	31.4	53956	25 Salt Of The Earth	40.6	54213	25 Salt Of The Earth	96.4
53563	24 Main Street, USA	46.1	53959	33 Midlife Junction	36.3	54216	50 Heartland Communities	48.2
53565	37 Prairie Living	41.6	53960	17 Green Acres	53.9	54217	25 Salt Of The Earth	68.8
53566	32 Rustbelt Traditions	20.5	53961	25 Salt Of The Earth	72.7	54220	17 Green Acres	19.5

ZIP CODE	TOP TAPESTRY CONSUMER TYPE	% 2009 HOUSE-HOLDS	ZIP CODE	TOP TAPESTRY CONSUMER TYPE	% 2009 HOUSE-HOLDS	ZIP CODE	TOP TAPESTRY CONSUMER TYPE	% 2009 HOUSE-HOLDS
54227	17 Green Acres	74.4	54512	31 Rural Resort Dwellers	100.0	54670	37 Prairie Living	100.0
54228	25 Salt Of The Earth	100.0	54513	46 Rooted Rural	88.8	54701	55 College Towns	18.7
54229	17 Green Acres	53.2	54514	50 Heartland Communities	51.9	54703	17 Green Acres	22.2
54230	25 Salt Of The Earth	94.0	54515	46 Rooted Rural	86.1	54720	28 Aspiring Young Families	25.1
54234	15 Silver And Gold	59.0	54517	46 Rooted Rural	100.0	54721	37 Prairie Living	100.0
54235	33 Midlife Junction	30.6	54519	31 Rural Resort Dwellers	100.0	54722	50 Heartland Communities	48.5
54241	32 Rustbelt Traditions	43.6	54520	31 Rural Resort Dwellers	44.4	54723	25 Salt Of The Earth	78.0
54245	25 Salt Of The Earth	98.8	54521	31 Rural Resort Dwellers	67.0	54724	32 Rustbelt Traditions	31.4
54246	31 Rural Resort Dwellers	100.0	54524	31 Rural Resort Dwellers	100.0	54725	42 Southern Satellites	43.5
54247	25 Salt Of The Earth	93.7	54526	46 Rooted Rural	77.5	54726	37 Prairie Living	91.1
54301	14 Prosperous Empty Nesters	17.2	54527	50 Heartland Communities	90.3	54727	25 Salt Of The Earth	48.4
54302	52 Inner City Tenants	16.9	54529	31 Rural Resort Dwellers	98.1	54728	31 Rural Resort Dwellers	38.7
54303	36 Old And Newcomers	23.3	54530	46 Rooted Rural	63.0	54729	17 Green Acres	35.9
54304	29 Rustbelt Retirees	16.0	54531	31 Rural Resort Dwellers	93.5	54730	17 Green Acres	41.1
54311	12 Up And Coming Families	27.4	54534	50 Heartland Communities	67.8	54731	46 Rooted Rural	65.1
54313	12 Up And Coming Families	29.4	54536	50 Heartland Communities	100.0	54732	50 Heartland Communities	44.6
54401	17 Green Acres	20.4	54537	42 Southern Satellites	67.2	54733	37 Prairie Living	74.5
54403	32 Rustbelt Traditions	22.0	54538	31 Rural Resort Dwellers	100.0	54734	25 Salt Of The Earth	85.7
54405	50 Heartland Communities	34.5	54539	31 Rural Resort Dwellers	99.4	54736	50 Heartland Communities	47.0
54406	25 Salt Of The Earth	71.5	54540	31 Rural Resort Dwellers	100.0	54737	37 Prairie Living	92.8
54407	25 Salt Of The Earth	93.0	54541	31 Rural Resort Dwellers	48.2	54738	25 Salt Of The Earth	39.0
54408	25 Salt Of The Earth	71.8	54542	49 Senior Sun Seekers	36.3	54739	17 Green Acres	55.2
54409	25 Salt Of The Earth	29.6	54545	31 Rural Resort Dwellers	100.0	54740	37 Prairie Living	55.4
54410	25 Salt Of The Earth	71.1	54546	42 Southern Satellites	47.7	54741	46 Rooted Rural	55.1
54411	37 Prairie Living	50.0	54547	31 Rural Resort Dwellers	100.0	54742	37 Prairie Living	35.0
54412	25 Salt Of The Earth	72.1	54548	31 Rural Resort Dwellers	75.7	54745	31 Rural Resort Dwellers	46.9
54413	25 Salt Of The Earth	100.0	54550	50 Heartland Communities	100.0	54746	46 Rooted Rural	89.0
54414	25 Salt Of The Earth	79.0	54552	50 Heartland Communities	38.6	54747	37 Prairie Living	52.1
54416	46 Rooted Rural	87.2	54554	31 Rural Resort Dwellers	100.0	54748	25 Salt Of The Earth	49.5
54418	25 Salt Of The Earth	66.3	54555	31 Rural Resort Dwellers	34.7	54749	25 Salt Of The Earth	71.6
54420	37 Prairie Living	100.0	54556	50 Heartland Communities	68.9	54750	37 Prairie Living	75.8
54421	32 Rustbelt Traditions	43.1	54557	31 Rural Resort Dwellers	100.0	54751	55 College Towns	20.4
54422	37 Prairie Living	97.5	54558	31 Rural Resort Dwellers	76.8	54754	46 Rooted Rural	75.9
54423	17 Green Acres	89.3	54559	46 Rooted Rural	100.0	54755	37 Prairie Living	35.8
54424	25 Salt Of The Earth	62.0	54560	31 Rural Resort Dwellers	100.0	54756	46 Rooted Rural	55.1
54425	42 Southern Satellites	71.7	54562	31 Rural Resort Dwellers	100.0	54757	42 Southern Satellites	28.4
54426	37 Prairie Living	35.4	54563	46 Rooted Rural	71.1	54758	37 Prairie Living	38.0
54427	25 Salt Of The Earth	93.3	54564	31 Rural Resort Dwellers	94.5	54759	50 Heartland Communities	69.3
54428	49 Senior Sun Seekers	55.6	54565	50 Heartland Communities	93.1	54761	37 Prairie Living	100.0
54430	25 Salt Of The Earth	100.0	54566	46 Rooted Rural	93.2	54762	25 Salt Of The Earth	65.3
54433	37 Prairie Living	100.0	54568	31 Rural Resort Dwellers	54.5	54763	37 Prairie Living	94.0
54435	25 Salt Of The Earth	63.3	54601	55 College Towns	18.4	54765	37 Prairie Living	100.0
54436	37 Prairie Living	73.2	54603	48 Great Expectations	30.0	54766	37 Prairie Living	99.3
54437	50 Heartland Communities	48.9	54610	37 Prairie Living	44.7	54767	17 Green Acres	48.4
54440	25 Salt Of The Earth	87.7	54611	42 Southern Satellites	71.7	54768	50 Heartland Communities	50.2
54441	17 Green Acres	100.0	54612	37 Prairie Living	42.8	54769	31 Rural Resort Dwellers	76.9
54442	25 Salt Of The Earth	91.9	54613	49 Senior Sun Seekers	82.4	54770	25 Salt Of The Earth	65.5
54443	25 Salt Of The Earth	57.9	54614	25 Salt Of The Earth	45.4	54771	50 Heartland Communities	52.8
54446	37 Prairie Living	63.8	54615	33 Midlife Junction	28.9	54772	37 Prairie Living	54.8
54447	37 Prairie Living	100.0	54616	50 Heartland Communities	52.3	54773	46 Rooted Rural	46.0
54448	25 Salt Of The Earth	45.9	54618	50 Heartland Communities	41.0	54801	50 Heartland Communities	54.6
54449	25 Salt Of The Earth	19.4	54619	37 Prairie Living	58.8	54805	37 Prairie Living	50.3
54451	26 Midland Crowd	22.7	54621	25 Salt Of The Earth	96.0	54806	33 Midlife Junction	31.1
54452	25 Salt Of The Earth	31.6	54622	25 Salt Of The Earth	57.6	54810	31 Rural Resort Dwellers	85.9
54454	25 Salt Of The Earth	100.0	54623	46 Rooted Rural	56.2	54812	48 Great Expectations	27.4
54455	17 Green Acres	33.0	54624	31 Rural Resort Dwellers	84.2	54813	25 Salt Of The Earth	40.3
54456	50 Heartland Communities	47.5	54625	37 Prairie Living	100.0	54814	41 Crossroads	57.1
54457	31 Rural Resort Dwellers	33.2	54626	37 Prairie Living	69.9	54817	31 Rural Resort Dwellers	63.5
54459	46 Rooted Rural	56.7	54627	25 Salt Of The Earth	96.9	54819	50 Heartland Communities	42.3
54460	37 Prairie Living	51.5	54628	37 Prairie Living	99.6	54820	46 Rooted Rural	53.4
54462	49 Senior Sun Seekers	100.0	54629	33 Midlife Junction	42.3	54821	31 Rural Resort Dwellers	99.4
54463	31 Rural Resort Dwellers	91.8	54630	25 Salt Of The Earth	43.5	54822	32 Rustbelt Traditions	55.7
54465	31 Rural Resort Dwellers	71.6	54631	37 Prairie Living	90.1	54824	25 Salt Of The Earth	69.2
54466	25 Salt Of The Earth	49.7	54632	46 Rooted Rural	55.0	54826	50 Heartland Communities	39.8
54467	17 Green Acres	27.9	54634	37 Prairie Living	53.9	54827	31 Rural Resort Dwellers	100.0
54469	29 Rustbelt Retirees	63.9	54635	37 Prairie Living	88.4	54828	46 Rooted Rural	72.4
54470	50 Heartland Communities	54.6	54636	17 Green Acres	65.7	54829	50 Heartland Communities	56.7
54471	17 Green Acres	62.0	54638	37 Prairie Living	97.5	54830	49 Senior Sun Seekers	86.4
54473	25 Salt Of The Earth	39.2	54639	37 Prairie Living	51.9	54832	31 Rural Resort Dwellers	57.0
54474	29 Rustbelt Retirees	36.2	54641	46 Rooted Rural	100.0	54835	46 Rooted Rural	94.0
54475	25 Salt Of The Earth	98.6	54642	37 Prairie Living	91.2	54836	25 Salt Of The Earth	89.2
54476	12 Up And Coming Families	28.4	54644	25 Salt Of The Earth	95.5	54837	46 Rooted Rural	39.0
54479	32 Rustbelt Traditions	39.3	54646	46 Rooted Rural	65.7	54838	31 Rural Resort Dwellers	85.1
54480	25 Salt Of The Earth	98.5	54648	37 Prairie Living	57.3	54839	46 Rooted Rural	62.8
54481	17 Green Acres	21.7	54650	13 In Style	19.0	54840	25 Salt Of The Earth	47.6
54484	25 Salt Of The Earth	42.0	54651	46 Rooted Rural	70.0	54843	31 Rural Resort Dwellers	49.8
54485	31 Rural Resort Dwellers	58.6	54652	46 Rooted Rural	99.2	54844	31 Rural Resort Dwellers	100.0
54486	25 Salt Of The Earth	48.0	54653	26 Midland Crowd	63.8	54845	31 Rural Resort Dwellers	50.8
54487	31 Rural Resort Dwellers	41.2	54655	46 Rooted Rural	61.0	54846	46 Rooted Rural	98.1
54488	37 Prairie Living	100.0	54656	26 Midland Crowd	22.1	54847	31 Rural Resort Dwellers	81.4
54489	25 Salt Of The Earth	72.7	54657	37 Prairie Living	82.3	54848	57 Simple Living	26.5
54490	50 Heartland Communities	48.9	54658	46 Rooted Rural	40.7	54849	17 Green Acres	45.6
54491	46 Rooted Rural	54.6	54659	46 Rooted Rural	63.6	54850	46 Rooted Rural	100.0
54493	46 Rooted Rural	61.0	54660	26 Midland Crowd	21.1	54853	33 Midlife Junction	37.7
54494	32 Rustbelt Traditions	29.2	54661	25 Salt Of The Earth	54.9	54854	46 Rooted Rural	54.4
54495	57 Simple Living	23.8	54664	46 Rooted Rural	83.1	54855	46 Rooted Rural	64.4
54498	37 Prairie Living	56.4	54665	50 Heartland Communities	53.5	54856	37 Prairie Living	37.7
54499	25 Salt Of The Earth	54.6	54666	25 Salt Of The Earth	51.8	54858	50 Heartland Communities	69.4
54501	31 Rural Resort Dwellers	24.9	54667	37 Prairie Living	46.9	54859	31 Rural Resort Dwellers	65.0
54511	31 Rural Resort Dwellers	51.7	54669	32 Rustbelt Traditions	27.4	54862	46 Rooted Rural	100.0

CONSUMER TYPE

ZIP CODE	TOP TAPESTRY CONSUMER TYPE	% 2009 HOUSE-HOLDS	ZIP CODE	TOP TAPESTRY CONSUMER TYPE	% 2009 HOUSE-HOLDS	ZIP CODE	TOP TAPESTRY CONSUMER TYPE	% 2009 HOUSE-HOLDS
54864	25 Salt Of The Earth	68.3	55032	17 Green Acres	99.0	55318	04 Boomburbs	46.1
54865	31 Rural Resort Dwellers	97.5	55033	24 Main Street, USA	28.6	55319	17 Green Acres	47.7
54867	46 Rooted Rural	100.0	55036	31 Rural Resort Dwellers	100.0	55320	17 Green Acres	62.2
54868	33 Midlife Junction	40.6	55037	31 Rural Resort Dwellers	59.3	55321	24 Main Street, USA	42.4
54870	31 Rural Resort Dwellers	96.9	55038	12 Up And Coming Families	73.9	55322	12 Up And Coming Families	69.6
54871	50 Heartland Communities	34.9	55040	17 Green Acres	62.7	55324	31 Rural Resort Dwellers	55.0
54872	31 Rural Resort Dwellers	50.9	55041	33 Midlife Junction	28.5	55325	17 Green Acres	44.2
54873	31 Rural Resort Dwellers	41.1	55042	02 Suburban Splendor	66.4	55327	06 Sophisticated Squires	65.6
54874	25 Salt Of The Earth	63.0	55043	06 Sophisticated Squires	30.7	55328	06 Sophisticated Squires	36.4
54875	46 Rooted Rural	51.3	55044	04 Boomburbs	51.0	55329	25 Salt Of The Earth	93.3
54876	31 Rural Resort Dwellers	99.4	55045	18 Cozy And Comfortable	30.8	55330	06 Sophisticated Squires	36.2
54880	33 Midlife Junction	19.8	55046	17 Green Acres	76.3	55331	02 Suburban Splendor	54.0
54888	31 Rural Resort Dwellers	100.0	55047	07 Exurbanites	67.2	55332	37 Prairie Living	53.3
54889	25 Salt Of The Earth	48.6	55049	26 Midland Crowd	74.4	55333	50 Heartland Communities	77.2
54891	31 Rural Resort Dwellers	38.6	55051	25 Salt Of The Earth	21.3	55334	33 Midlife Junction	44.0
54893	31 Rural Resort Dwellers	76.9	55052	26 Midland Crowd	51.5	55335	50 Heartland Communities	59.0
54895	46 Rooted Rural	81.9	55053	17 Green Acres	85.2	55336	25 Salt Of The Earth	35.4
54896	46 Rooted Rural	60.2	55054	06 Sophisticated Squires	100.0	55337	13 In Style	25.9
54901	32 Rustbelt Traditions	26.0	55055	24 Main Street, USA	73.1	55338	17 Green Acres	54.2
54902	32 Rustbelt Traditions	33.7	55056	12 Up And Coming Families	40.8	55339	17 Green Acres	100.0
54904	28 Aspiring Young Families	26.3	55057	06 Sophisticated Squires	20.5	55340	06 Sophisticated Squires	57.7
54909	25 Salt Of The Earth	59.9	55060	17 Green Acres	20.3	55341	06 Sophisticated Squires	57.8
54911	48 Great Expectations	21.2	55063	31 Rural Resort Dwellers	27.9	55342	50 Heartland Communities	62.8
54913	17 Green Acres	61.7	55065	17 Green Acres	100.0	55343	39 Young And Restless	25.3
54914	32 Rustbelt Traditions	17.5	55066	33 Midlife Junction	26.8	55344	16 Enterprising Professionals	37.2
54915	12 Up And Coming Families	28.7	55067	17 Green Acres	100.0	55345	07 Exurbanites	35.7
54921	25 Salt Of The Earth	52.2	55068	12 Up And Coming Families	29.6	55346	04 Boomburbs	23.8
54922	25 Salt Of The Earth	89.6	55069	32 Rustbelt Traditions	42.6	55347	04 Boomburbs	54.7
54923	25 Salt Of The Earth	54.9	55070	12 Up And Coming Families	96.0	55349	32 Rustbelt Traditions	50.4
54928	37 Prairie Living	100.0	55071	18 Cozy And Comfortable	51.9	55350	24 Main Street, USA	29.1
54929	25 Salt Of The Earth	41.6	55072	31 Rural Resort Dwellers	54.5	55352	06 Sophisticated Squires	37.7
54930	31 Rural Resort Dwellers	97.0	55073	06 Sophisticated Squires	54.8	55353	17 Green Acres	51.8
54932	17 Green Acres	99.2	55074	24 Main Street, USA	72.3	55354	25 Salt Of The Earth	58.8
54935	32 Rustbelt Traditions	30.1	55075	24 Main Street, USA	64.5	55355	25 Salt Of The Earth	24.8
54937	17 Green Acres	38.3	55076	06 Sophisticated Squires	25.4	55356	02 Suburban Splendor	43.4
54940	25 Salt Of The Earth	46.1	55077	39 Young And Restless	36.6	55357	06 Sophisticated Squires	52.9
54941	31 Rural Resort Dwellers	64.7	55079	06 Sophisticated Squires	58.1	55358	17 Green Acres	55.4
54942	12 Up And Coming Families	95.8	55080	17 Green Acres	81.9	55359	06 Sophisticated Squires	34.4
54943	46 Rooted Rural	48.2	55082	02 Suburban Splendor	33.1	55360	17 Green Acres	92.7
54944	17 Green Acres	71.8	55084	24 Main Street, USA	85.0	55362	06 Sophisticated Squires	20.4
54945	33 Midlife Junction	52.7	55087	17 Green Acres	100.0	55363	24 Main Street, USA	53.7
54947	17 Green Acres	83.9	55088	17 Green Acres	58.4	55364	02 Suburban Splendor	26.6
54948	46 Rooted Rural	83.6	55089	17 Green Acres	50.3	55366	25 Salt Of The Earth	100.0
54949	42 Southern Satellites	51.2	55092	06 Sophisticated Squires	46.5	55367	17 Green Acres	100.0
54950	25 Salt Of The Earth	44.2	55101	27 Metro Renters	70.8	55368	17 Green Acres	71.5
54952	32 Rustbelt Traditions	18.3	55102	27 Metro Renters	29.8	55369	06 Sophisticated Squires	38.3
54956	17 Green Acres	19.8	55103	52 Inner City Tenants	35.4	55370	17 Green Acres	100.0
54960	31 Rural Resort Dwellers	89.4	55104	22 Metropolitans	28.5	55371	17 Green Acres	28.9
54961	17 Green Acres	39.1	55105	22 Metropolitans	46.8	55372	12 Up And Coming Families	27.6
54962	25 Salt Of The Earth	94.7	55106	24 Main Street, USA	23.0	55373	41 Crossroads	34.3
54963	25 Salt Of The Earth	54.0	55107	38 Industrious Urban Fringe	21.8	55374	04 Boomburbs	43.5
54964	25 Salt Of The Earth	100.0	55108	39 Young And Restless	29.5	55375	12 Up And Coming Families	99.1
54965	31 Rural Resort Dwellers	75.9	55109	24 Main Street, USA	38.0	55376	12 Up And Coming Families	48.4
54966	42 Southern Satellites	56.5	55110	24 Main Street, USA	17.7	55378	04 Boomburbs	63.1
54967	25 Salt Of The Earth	63.5	55112	07 Exurbanites	24.4	55379	12 Up And Coming Families	40.4
54968	46 Rooted Rural	29.8	55113	13 In Style	30.8	55381	25 Salt Of The Earth	57.8
54970	42 Southern Satellites	44.2	55114	36 Old And Newcomers	71.3	55382	17 Green Acres	90.2
54971	25 Salt Of The Earth	26.0	55115	02 Suburban Splendor	32.2	55384	30 Retirement Communities	70.1
54974	25 Salt Of The Earth	93.4	55116	22 Metropolitans	25.2	55385	32 Rustbelt Traditions	47.8
54977	25 Salt Of The Earth	93.3	55117	36 Old And Newcomers	20.5	55386	04 Boomburbs	61.0
54978	46 Rooted Rural	100.0	55118	24 Main Street, USA	26.2	55387	12 Up And Coming Families	68.5
54979	25 Salt Of The Earth	93.7	55119	28 Aspiring Young Families	15.4	55388	24 Main Street, USA	49.3
54981	25 Salt Of The Earth	32.8	55120	07 Exurbanites	65.4	55389	50 Heartland Communities	42.4
54982	31 Rural Resort Dwellers	38.1	55121	16 Enterprising Professionals	52.3	55390	26 Midland Crowd	82.1
54983	25 Salt Of The Earth	61.6	55122	16 Enterprising Professionals	27.0	55391	02 Suburban Splendor	36.4
54984	49 Senior Sun Seekers	42.8	55123	04 Boomburbs	40.5	55395	24 Main Street, USA	67.2
54986	17 Green Acres	50.4	55124	06 Sophisticated Squires	35.9	55396	37 Prairie Living	36.6
55001	02 Suburban Splendor	63.8	55125	04 Boomburbs	50.6	55397	24 Main Street, USA	73.5
55003	18 Cozy And Comfortable	100.0	55126	13 In Style	34.9	55398	12 Up And Coming Families	51.3
55005	12 Up And Coming Families	47.4	55127	06 Sophisticated Squires	32.4	55401	27 Metro Renters	74.9
55006	33 Midlife Junction	50.6	55128	12 Up And Coming Families	34.4	55402	27 Metro Renters	100.0
55007	25 Salt Of The Earth	51.6	55129	04 Boomburbs	100.0	55403	27 Metro Renters	73.4
55008	17 Green Acres	24.5	55130	60 City Dimensions	22.7	55404	52 Inner City Tenants	26.4
55009	26 Midland Crowd	37.5	55301	12 Up And Coming Families	69.6	55405	27 Metro Renters	51.0
55011	06 Sophisticated Squires	61.2	55302	17 Green Acres	48.2	55406	22 Metropolitans	45.9
55012	17 Green Acres	43.6	55303	06 Sophisticated Squires	37.9	55407	24 Main Street, USA	27.2
55013	17 Green Acres	37.0	55304	06 Sophisticated Squires	58.7	55408	27 Metro Renters	51.5
55014	04 Boomburbs	25.3	55305	36 Old And Newcomers	24.6	55409	22 Metropolitans	25.9
55016	06 Sophisticated Squires	36.4	55306	16 Enterprising Professionals	54.8	55410	22 Metropolitans	44.5
55017	25 Salt Of The Earth	82.6	55307	25 Salt Of The Earth	43.9	55411	51 Metro City Edge	47.6
55018	17 Green Acres	79.4	55308	12 Up And Coming Families	100.0	55412	32 Rustbelt Traditions	33.0
55019	24 Main Street, USA	63.0	55309	12 Up And Coming Families	57.9	55413	36 Old And Newcomers	59.3
55020	06 Sophisticated Squires	100.0	55310	50 Heartland Communities	76.9	55414	63 Dorms To Diplomas	38.8
55021	17 Green Acres	22.4	55311	04 Boomburbs	60.4	55415	65 Social Security Set	41.6
55024	12 Up And Coming Families	67.9	55312	25 Salt Of The Earth	54.1	55416	22 Metropolitans	22.9
55025	06 Sophisticated Squires	44.4	55313	06 Sophisticated Squires	27.3	55417	22 Metropolitans	26.0
55026	17 Green Acres	90.0	55314	25 Salt Of The Earth	61.8	55418	48 Great Expectations	28.0
55027	37 Prairie Living	69.5	55315	06 Sophisticated Squires	99.3	55419	22 Metropolitans	27.5
55030	31 Rural Resort Dwellers	45.3	55316	06 Sophisticated Squires	41.7	55420	18 Cozy And Comfortable	33.3
55031	17 Green Acres	91.7	55317	04 Boomburbs	56.3	55421	36 Old And Newcomers	25.0

ZIP CODE	TOP TAPESTRY CONSUMER TYPE	% 2009 HOUSE-HOLDS	ZIP CODE	TOP TAPESTRY CONSUMER TYPE	% 2009 HOUSE-HOLDS	ZIP CODE	TOP TAPESTRY CONSUMER TYPE	% 2009 HOUSE-HOLDS
55422	18 Cozy And Comfortable	27.6	55785	46 Rooted Rural	79.6	56010	37 Prairie Living	99.5
55423	18 Cozy And Comfortable	34.2	55787	49 Senior Sun Seekers	49.2	56011	17 Green Acres	49.5
55424	01 Top Rung	20.6	55790	31 Rural Resort Dwellers	53.6	56013	50 Heartland Communities	54.4
55425	24 Main Street, USA	18.8	55792	29 Rustbelt Retirees	42.9	56014	37 Prairie Living	100.0
55426	36 Old And Newcomers	21.4	55793	46 Rooted Rural	52.9	56016	37 Prairie Living	61.8
55427	13 In Style	28.8	55795	31 Rural Resort Dwellers	53.6	56017	17 Green Acres	93.9
55428	18 Cozy And Comfortable	22.9	55797	25 Salt Of The Earth	99.6	56019	37 Prairie Living	100.0
55429	18 Cozy And Comfortable	39.6	55798	46 Rooted Rural	86.6	56020	25 Salt Of The Earth	100.0
55430	32 Rustbelt Traditions	37.8	55801	17 Green Acres	100.0	56021	17 Green Acres	100.0
55431	14 Prosperous Empty Nesters	26.3	55802	65 Social Security Set	54.1	56022	37 Prairie Living	100.0
55432	18 Cozy And Comfortable	34.6	55803	17 Green Acres	33.5	56023	37 Prairie Living	100.0
55433	24 Main Street, USA	21.0	55804	18 Cozy And Comfortable	54.9	56024	19 Milk And Cookies	77.9
55434	18 Cozy And Comfortable	23.6	55805	55 College Towns	37.6	56025	37 Prairie Living	100.0
55435	30 Retirement Communities	44.6	55806	48 Great Expectations	40.3	56026	25 Salt Of The Earth	60.5
55436	30 Retirement Communities	30.5	55807	32 Rustbelt Traditions	43.2	56027	50 Heartland Communities	76.1
55437	13 In Style	23.5	55808	41 Crossroads	23.5	56028	25 Salt Of The Earth	77.8
55438	13 In Style	27.6	55810	29 Rustbelt Retirees	25.3	56029	37 Prairie Living	99.1
55439	03 Connoisseurs	50.5	55811	29 Rustbelt Retirees	20.5	56030	17 Green Acres	100.0
55441	13 In Style	41.9	55812	22 Metropolitans	50.0	56031	50 Heartland Communities	18.3
55442	02 Suburban Splendor	38.8	55901	04 Boomburbs	20.6	56032	37 Prairie Living	100.0
55443	04 Boomburbs	29.2	55902	02 Suburban Splendor	24.2	56033	37 Prairie Living	100.0
55444	06 Sophisticated Squires	67.6	55904	48 Great Expectations	14.3	56034	17 Green Acres	98.6
55445	12 Up And Coming Families	37.3	55906	06 Sophisticated Squires	20.0	56035	25 Salt Of The Earth	100.0
55446	04 Boomburbs	78.0	55909	37 Prairie Living	98.7	56036	25 Salt Of The Earth	67.2
55447	02 Suburban Splendor	31.0	55910	37 Prairie Living	69.9	56037	25 Salt Of The Earth	85.2
55448	06 Sophisticated Squires	35.0	55912	29 Rustbelt Retirees	23.2	56039	37 Prairie Living	100.0
55449	12 Up And Coming Families	57.3	55917	25 Salt Of The Earth	36.7	56041	25 Salt Of The Earth	76.3
55454	65 Social Security Set	60.1	55918	32 Rustbelt Traditions	80.8	56042	25 Salt Of The Earth	96.6
55455	63 Dorms To Diplomas	98.1	55919	25 Salt Of The Earth	54.0	56043	37 Prairie Living	100.0
55602	31 Rural Resort Dwellers	100.0	55920	12 Up And Coming Families	35.6	56044	17 Green Acres	52.5
55603	25 Salt Of The Earth	99.3	55921	32 Rustbelt Traditions	36.6	56045	25 Salt Of The Earth	100.0
55604	31 Rural Resort Dwellers	73.0	55922	37 Prairie Living	100.0	56047	37 Prairie Living	100.0
55605	31 Rural Resort Dwellers	100.0	55923	17 Green Acres	49.5	56048	25 Salt Of The Earth	63.4
55606	31 Rural Resort Dwellers	100.0	55924	25 Salt Of The Earth	59.5	56050	25 Salt Of The Earth	55.2
55607	31 Rural Resort Dwellers	80.6	55925	17 Green Acres	98.0	56051	37 Prairie Living	100.0
55612	31 Rural Resort Dwellers	100.0	55926	37 Prairie Living	100.0	56052	25 Salt Of The Earth	67.8
55613	31 Rural Resort Dwellers	100.0	55927	26 Midland Crowd	41.4	56054	37 Prairie Living	62.5
55614	29 Rustbelt Retirees	57.5	55929	37 Prairie Living	73.6	56055	32 Rustbelt Traditions	37.0
55615	31 Rural Resort Dwellers	100.0	55932	19 Milk And Cookies	70.4	56057	25 Salt Of The Earth	41.7
55616	31 Rural Resort Dwellers	34.6	55933	37 Prairie Living	72.7	56058	17 Green Acres	41.2
55702	25 Salt Of The Earth	100.0	55934	19 Milk And Cookies	60.1	56060	37 Prairie Living	100.0
55703	31 Rural Resort Dwellers	41.6	55935	17 Green Acres	94.5	56062	32 Rustbelt Traditions	51.0
55704	46 Rooted Rural	87.6	55936	33 Midlife Junction	64.3	56063	17 Green Acres	76.8
55705	29 Rustbelt Retirees	34.6	55939	50 Heartland Communities	52.3	56065	32 Rustbelt Traditions	52.9
55706	29 Rustbelt Retirees	77.7	55940	32 Rustbelt Traditions	58.8	56068	50 Heartland Communities	75.1
55707	25 Salt Of The Earth	35.8	55941	17 Green Acres	79.4	56069	25 Salt Of The Earth	55.0
55709	50 Heartland Communities	40.9	55943	37 Prairie Living	46.8	56071	17 Green Acres	42.5
55710	17 Green Acres	65.0	55944	19 Milk And Cookies	30.2	56072	50 Heartland Communities	55.4
55711	26 Midland Crowd	77.4	55945	31 Rural Resort Dwellers	51.7	56073	17 Green Acres	25.8
55712	31 Rural Resort Dwellers	100.0	55946	32 Rustbelt Traditions	53.2	56074	17 Green Acres	69.4
55717	31 Rural Resort Dwellers	92.1	55947	17 Green Acres	37.9	56075	37 Prairie Living	100.0
55718	32 Rustbelt Traditions	33.6	55949	33 Midlife Junction	67.4	56078	37 Prairie Living	100.0
55719	50 Heartland Communities	24.7	55951	50 Heartland Communities	78.2	56080	17 Green Acres	100.0
55720	32 Rustbelt Traditions	21.2	55952	26 Midland Crowd	54.8	56081	37 Prairie Living	27.3
55721	25 Salt Of The Earth	64.9	55953	37 Prairie Living	52.1	56082	24 Main Street, USA	19.0
55723	31 Rural Resort Dwellers	41.6	55954	50 Heartland Communities	64.1	56083	37 Prairie Living	100.0
55724	31 Rural Resort Dwellers	83.0	55955	12 Up And Coming Families	72.1	56085	32 Rustbelt Traditions	30.2
55725	15 Silver And Gold	96.0	55956	25 Salt Of The Earth	51.6	56087	50 Heartland Communities	72.6
55726	46 Rooted Rural	97.8	55957	37 Prairie Living	98.5	56088	50 Heartland Communities	65.3
55731	31 Rural Resort Dwellers	39.6	55959	17 Green Acres	86.8	56089	25 Salt Of The Earth	91.9
55732	46 Rooted Rural	51.6	55960	17 Green Acres	52.5	56090	37 Prairie Living	98.9
55733	17 Green Acres	73.0	55961	37 Prairie Living	100.0	56091	37 Prairie Living	100.0
55734	50 Heartland Communities	44.9	55962	37 Prairie Living	96.6	56093	17 Green Acres	21.1
55735	31 Rural Resort Dwellers	90.9	55963	17 Green Acres	73.8	56096	31 Rural Resort Dwellers	35.3
55736	50 Heartland Communities	61.9	55964	26 Midland Crowd	49.6	56097	50 Heartland Communities	51.0
55738	25 Salt Of The Earth	92.9	55965	37 Prairie Living	55.7	56098	50 Heartland Communities	61.8
55741	50 Heartland Communities	53.0	55967	17 Green Acres	100.0	56101	57 Simple Living	29.0
55742	25 Salt Of The Earth	68.6	55968	37 Prairie Living	100.0	56110	25 Salt Of The Earth	72.5
55744	31 Rural Resort Dwellers	20.5	55969	17 Green Acres	95.1	56111	37 Prairie Living	100.0
55746	50 Heartland Communities	22.1	55970	25 Salt Of The Earth	75.1	56113	37 Prairie Living	100.0
55748	50 Heartland Communities	60.9	55971	33 Midlife Junction	39.6	56114	37 Prairie Living	100.0
55749	25 Salt Of The Earth	100.0	55972	33 Midlife Junction	65.5	56115	50 Heartland Communities	55.7
55750	29 Rustbelt Retirees	100.0	55973	37 Prairie Living	100.0	56116	37 Prairie Living	100.0
55751	25 Salt Of The Earth	97.9	55974	37 Prairie Living	100.0	56117	37 Prairie Living	100.0
55752	31 Rural Resort Dwellers	90.2	55975	33 Midlife Junction	34.1	56118	37 Prairie Living	95.3
55756	31 Rural Resort Dwellers	97.0	55976	24 Main Street, USA	28.6	56119	25 Salt Of The Earth	72.2
55757	37 Prairie Living	53.9	55977	37 Prairie Living	90.3	56120	42 Southern Satellites	95.5
55760	31 Rural Resort Dwellers	37.2	55979	26 Midland Crowd	86.1	56121	37 Prairie Living	100.0
55763	31 Rural Resort Dwellers	90.5	55981	33 Midlife Junction	28.4	56122	37 Prairie Living	100.0
55765	46 Rooted Rural	71.7	55982	37 Prairie Living	100.0	56123	37 Prairie Living	100.0
55767	33 Midlife Junction	83.8	55983	25 Salt Of The Earth	75.2	56125	37 Prairie Living	100.0
55768	18 Cozy And Comfortable	28.4	55985	32 Rustbelt Traditions	46.8	56127	37 Prairie Living	100.0
55769	50 Heartland Communities	63.2	55987	32 Rustbelt Traditions	16.1	56128	50 Heartland Communities	58.0
55771	31 Rural Resort Dwellers	50.7	55990	37 Prairie Living	100.0	56129	37 Prairie Living	100.0
55775	29 Rustbelt Retirees	50.8	55991	25 Salt Of The Earth	56.8	56131	50 Heartland Communities	62.0
55779	17 Green Acres	97.8	55992	24 Main Street, USA	41.8	56132	37 Prairie Living	100.0
55780	26 Midland Crowd	100.0	56001	55 College Towns	19.9	56134	37 Prairie Living	100.0
55781	31 Rural Resort Dwellers	50.2	56003	13 In Style	18.9	56136	50 Heartland Communities	64.7
55783	31 Rural Resort Dwellers	68.0	56007	32 Rustbelt Traditions	17.3	56137	37 Prairie Living	100.0
55784	25 Salt Of The Earth	100.0	56009	25 Salt Of The Earth	64.2	56138	37 Prairie Living	100.0

CONSUMER TYPE

ZIP CODE	TOP TAPESTRY CONSUMER TYPE	% 2009 HOUSE-HOLDS
56139	37 Prairie Living	100.0
56141	37 Prairie Living	100.0
56142	50 Heartland Communities	52.7
56143	37 Prairie Living	26.6
56144	37 Prairie Living	100.0
56145	37 Prairie Living	99.4
56146	37 Prairie Living	100.0
56147	37 Prairie Living	100.0
56149	50 Heartland Communities	63.5
56150	50 Heartland Communities	61.9
56151	37 Prairie Living	100.0
56152	50 Heartland Communities	54.6
56153	37 Prairie Living	100.0
56155	37 Prairie Living	100.0
56156	14 Prosperous Empty Nesters	26.3
56157	17 Green Acres	75.3
56158	37 Prairie Living	100.0
56159	50 Heartland Communities	64.7
56160	37 Prairie Living	98.8
56161	37 Prairie Living	100.0
56162	37 Prairie Living	100.0
56164	50 Heartland Communities	35.7
56165	37 Prairie Living	100.0
56166	37 Prairie Living	100.0
56167	37 Prairie Living	100.0
56168	37 Prairie Living	100.0
56169	37 Prairie Living	98.3
56170	37 Prairie Living	99.2
56171	50 Heartland Communities	66.6
56172	50 Heartland Communities	41.6
56173	37 Prairie Living	100.0
56174	37 Prairie Living	100.0
56175	50 Heartland Communities	70.3
56176	50 Heartland Communities	69.2
56178	50 Heartland Communities	55.6
56180	50 Heartland Communities	56.3
56181	50 Heartland Communities	65.3
56183	50 Heartland Communities	53.0
56185	37 Prairie Living	100.0
56186	37 Prairie Living	100.0
56187	32 Rustbelt Traditions	21.3
56201	48 Great Expectations	15.1
56207	37 Prairie Living	100.0
56208	50 Heartland Communities	69.2
56209	33 Midlife Junction	50.7
56210	37 Prairie Living	50.0
56211	37 Prairie Living	100.0
56212	37 Prairie Living	100.0
56214	37 Prairie Living	100.0
56215	50 Heartland Communities	45.6
56216	37 Prairie Living	100.0
56218	37 Prairie Living	100.0
56219	50 Heartland Communities	83.5
56220	50 Heartland Communities	70.4
56221	37 Prairie Living	100.0
56222	50 Heartland Communities	55.3
56223	50 Heartland Communities	59.5
56224	37 Prairie Living	100.0
56225	50 Heartland Communities	83.8
56226	37 Prairie Living	100.0
56227	37 Prairie Living	100.0
56228	25 Salt Of The Earth	86.2
56229	25 Salt Of The Earth	66.8
56230	37 Prairie Living	100.0
56231	37 Prairie Living	100.0
56232	50 Heartland Communities	73.8
56235	37 Prairie Living	100.0
56236	37 Prairie Living	100.0
56237	37 Prairie Living	100.0
56239	37 Prairie Living	100.0
56240	50 Heartland Communities	81.6
56241	29 Rustbelt Retirees	33.3
56243	37 Prairie Living	85.0
56244	37 Prairie Living	100.0
56245	37 Prairie Living	100.0
56248	50 Heartland Communities	76.5
56249	37 Prairie Living	100.0
56251	25 Salt Of The Earth	74.4
56252	46 Rooted Rural	76.3
56253	37 Prairie Living	100.0
56255	37 Prairie Living	100.0
56256	50 Heartland Communities	56.2
56257	37 Prairie Living	100.0
56258	28 Aspiring Young Families	17.4
56260	37 Prairie Living	100.0
56262	37 Prairie Living	100.0
56263	37 Prairie Living	100.0
56264	37 Prairie Living	39.3
56265	33 Midlife Junction	47.7
56266	37 Prairie Living	47.8
56267	37 Prairie Living	25.2
56270	25 Salt Of The Earth	70.2
56271	37 Prairie Living	100.0
56273	25 Salt Of The Earth	47.6
56274	37 Prairie Living	100.0
56276	37 Prairie Living	100.0
56277	29 Rustbelt Retirees	53.8
56278	50 Heartland Communities	82.6
56279	17 Green Acres	76.9
56280	37 Prairie Living	100.0
56281	37 Prairie Living	100.0
56282	37 Prairie Living	88.2
56283	25 Salt Of The Earth	25.8
56284	50 Heartland Communities	61.6
56285	37 Prairie Living	55.9
56287	37 Prairie Living	100.0
56288	33 Midlife Junction	40.6
56289	37 Prairie Living	65.1
56291	37 Prairie Living	100.0
56292	37 Prairie Living	100.0
56293	50 Heartland Communities	62.2
56294	37 Prairie Living	100.0
56295	37 Prairie Living	100.0
56296	50 Heartland Communities	74.8
56297	37 Prairie Living	100.0
56301	63 Dorms To Diplomas	19.9
56303	06 Sophisticated Squires	19.2
56304	28 Aspiring Young Families	17.1
56307	37 Prairie Living	29.3
56308	33 Midlife Junction	35.1
56309	37 Prairie Living	100.0
56310	17 Green Acres	68.9
56311	37 Prairie Living	97.6
56312	37 Prairie Living	54.0
56313	17 Green Acres	100.0
56314	25 Salt Of The Earth	78.5
56315	31 Rural Resort Dwellers	80.7
56316	25 Salt Of The Earth	78.4
56318	25 Salt Of The Earth	72.3
56319	25 Salt Of The Earth	61.5
56320	17 Green Acres	55.2
56323	37 Prairie Living	100.0
56324	31 Rural Resort Dwellers	70.5
56326	37 Prairie Living	90.1
56327	31 Rural Resort Dwellers	57.1
56328	37 Prairie Living	100.0
56329	32 Rustbelt Traditions	34.5
56330	25 Salt Of The Earth	77.6
56331	37 Prairie Living	67.7
56332	25 Salt Of The Earth	66.3
56334	33 Midlife Junction	39.7
56336	25 Salt Of The Earth	73.3
56338	31 Rural Resort Dwellers	59.5
56339	50 Heartland Communities	71.4
56340	25 Salt Of The Earth	45.2
56341	31 Rural Resort Dwellers	100.0
56342	31 Rural Resort Dwellers	78.1
56343	31 Rural Resort Dwellers	100.0
56345	17 Green Acres	22.2
56347	37 Prairie Living	37.3
56349	37 Prairie Living	88.7
56350	46 Rooted Rural	81.3
56352	37 Prairie Living	35.0
56353	17 Green Acres	26.9
56354	31 Rural Resort Dwellers	69.7
56355	25 Salt Of The Earth	91.2
56357	25 Salt Of The Earth	96.6
56358	26 Midland Crowd	44.2
56359	31 Rural Resort Dwellers	65.9
56360	37 Prairie Living	40.5
56361	37 Prairie Living	49.7
56362	29 Rustbelt Retirees	34.3
56363	25 Salt Of The Earth	100.0
56364	37 Prairie Living	46.9
56367	17 Green Acres	50.0
56368	17 Green Acres	52.5
56373	26 Midland Crowd	46.9
56374	28 Aspiring Young Families	35.0
56375	17 Green Acres	100.0
56377	12 Up And Coming Families	72.2
56378	29 Rustbelt Retirees	29.9
56379	28 Aspiring Young Families	33.7
56381	33 Midlife Junction	38.4
56382	37 Prairie Living	84.7
56384	37 Prairie Living	100.0
56385	37 Prairie Living	72.7
56386	31 Rural Resort Dwellers	100.0
56387	39 Young And Restless	46.3
56389	37 Prairie Living	100.0
56401	17 Green Acres	25.3
56425	17 Green Acres	56.6
56431	31 Rural Resort Dwellers	39.9
56433	31 Rural Resort Dwellers	100.0
56434	46 Rooted Rural	100.0
56435	31 Rural Resort Dwellers	80.2
56437	50 Heartland Communities	72.8
56438	50 Heartland Communities	57.5
56440	50 Heartland Communities	77.6
56441	50 Heartland Communities	36.6
56442	15 Silver And Gold	53.2
56443	25 Salt Of The Earth	52.5
56444	31 Rural Resort Dwellers	85.3
56446	50 Heartland Communities	69.7
56447	31 Rural Resort Dwellers	100.0
56448	31 Rural Resort Dwellers	100.0
56449	17 Green Acres	38.9
56450	31 Rural Resort Dwellers	100.0
56452	31 Rural Resort Dwellers	62.7
56453	37 Prairie Living	100.0
56455	50 Heartland Communities	55.9
56456	31 Rural Resort Dwellers	100.0
56458	31 Rural Resort Dwellers	100.0
56461	31 Rural Resort Dwellers	53.7
56464	50 Heartland Communities	39.5
56465	31 Rural Resort Dwellers	78.9
56466	50 Heartland Communities	33.3
56467	31 Rural Resort Dwellers	100.0
56468	31 Rural Resort Dwellers	87.4
56469	31 Rural Resort Dwellers	90.3
56470	31 Rural Resort Dwellers	50.6
56472	31 Rural Resort Dwellers	50.3
56473	31 Rural Resort Dwellers	48.0
56474	50 Heartland Communities	43.8
56475	25 Salt Of The Earth	73.8
56477	37 Prairie Living	47.9
56479	57 Simple Living	20.0
56481	46 Rooted Rural	69.1
56482	37 Prairie Living	26.1
56484	31 Rural Resort Dwellers	64.6
56501	31 Rural Resort Dwellers	39.3
56510	50 Heartland Communities	78.9
56511	31 Rural Resort Dwellers	98.1
56514	32 Rustbelt Traditions	35.4
56515	31 Rural Resort Dwellers	89.9
56516	37 Prairie Living	98.0
56517	37 Prairie Living	97.0
56518	37 Prairie Living	99.3
56519	37 Prairie Living	100.0
56520	32 Rustbelt Traditions	40.1
56521	46 Rooted Rural	60.1
56522	37 Prairie Living	100.0
56523	37 Prairie Living	97.6
56524	37 Prairie Living	78.7
56525	37 Prairie Living	100.0
56527	46 Rooted Rural	64.2
56528	31 Rural Resort Dwellers	99.7
56529	53 Home Town	46.4
56531	50 Heartland Communities	67.7
56533	37 Prairie Living	69.8
56534	37 Prairie Living	59.3
56535	50 Heartland Communities	84.2
56536	37 Prairie Living	94.0
56537	33 Midlife Junction	22.2
56540	50 Heartland Communities	60.0
56542	50 Heartland Communities	38.3
56543	37 Prairie Living	100.0
56544	46 Rooted Rural	35.1
56545	37 Prairie Living	100.0
56546	37 Prairie Living	100.0
56547	26 Midland Crowd	50.9
56548	37 Prairie Living	100.0
56549	33 Midlife Junction	62.6
56550	37 Prairie Living	100.0
56551	31 Rural Resort Dwellers	44.8
56552	25 Salt Of The Earth	89.8
56553	37 Prairie Living	100.0
56554	31 Rural Resort Dwellers	47.2
56556	50 Heartland Communities	84.4
56557	50 Heartland Communities	47.0
56560	55 College Towns	14.2
56562	55 College Towns	100.0
56563	63 Dorms To Diplomas	0.0
56565	37 Prairie Living	100.0
56566	50 Heartland Communities	54.8
56567	50 Heartland Communities	38.5
56568	37 Prairie Living	100.0
56569	46 Rooted Rural	88.0
56570	37 Prairie Living	54.8
56571	31 Rural Resort Dwellers	89.0
56572	31 Rural Resort Dwellers	33.4

ZIP CODE	TOP TAPESTRY CONSUMER TYPE	% 2009 HOUSE-HOLDS	ZIP CODE	TOP TAPESTRY CONSUMER TYPE	% 2009 HOUSE-HOLDS	ZIP CODE	TOP TAPESTRY CONSUMER TYPE	% 2009 HOUSE-HOLDS
56573	50 Heartland Communities	29.7	56737	46 Rooted Rural	98.4	57107	41 Crossroads	48.5
56574	37 Prairie Living	100.0	56738	37 Prairie Living	53.7	57108	13 In Style	100.0
56575	46 Rooted Rural	77.4	56740	37 Prairie Living	100.0	57110	12 Up And Coming Families	56.8
56576	31 Rural Resort Dwellers	100.0	56741	31 Rural Resort Dwellers	100.0	57197	18 Cozy And Comfortable	100.0
56577	31 Rural Resort Dwellers	100.0	56742	50 Heartland Communities	88.2	57201	57 Simple Living	18.1
56578	31 Rural Resort Dwellers	58.9	56744	37 Prairie Living	100.0	57212	50 Heartland Communities	52.8
56579	37 Prairie Living	100.0	56748	37 Prairie Living	98.7	57213	37 Prairie Living	100.0
56580	19 Milk And Cookies	54.2	56750	50 Heartland Communities	35.8	57216	46 Rooted Rural	85.4
56581	37 Prairie Living	100.0	56751	42 Southern Satellites	30.4	57217	37 Prairie Living	100.0
56583	37 Prairie Living	100.0	56754	25 Salt Of The Earth	100.0	57218	37 Prairie Living	100.0
56584	50 Heartland Communities	52.9	56755	37 Prairie Living	100.0	57219	37 Prairie Living	100.0
56585	37 Prairie Living	85.2	56756	26 Midland Crowd	72.8	57220	37 Prairie Living	100.0
56586	31 Rural Resort Dwellers	98.9	56757	50 Heartland Communities	65.5	57221	37 Prairie Living	98.6
56587	31 Rural Resort Dwellers	100.0	56758	37 Prairie Living	81.5	57223	37 Prairie Living	94.9
56588	37 Prairie Living	84.8	56759	37 Prairie Living	87.9	57224	37 Prairie Living	100.0
56589	37 Prairie Living	86.0	56760	37 Prairie Living	91.6	57225	37 Prairie Living	59.9
56590	37 Prairie Living	100.0	56761	25 Salt Of The Earth	63.2	57226	50 Heartland Communities	77.2
56592	37 Prairie Living	84.4	56762	29 Rustbelt Retirees	43.6	57227	37 Prairie Living	100.0
56593	37 Prairie Living	100.0	56763	26 Midland Crowd	66.4	57231	46 Rooted Rural	44.0
56594	37 Prairie Living	100.0	57001	50 Heartland Communities	56.1	57232	37 Prairie Living	100.0
56601	26 Midland Crowd	24.5	57002	25 Salt Of The Earth	77.9	57233	37 Prairie Living	100.0
56621	46 Rooted Rural	46.1	57003	17 Green Acres	74.3	57234	46 Rooted Rural	92.0
56623	33 Midlife Junction	55.8	57004	33 Midlife Junction	51.3	57235	37 Prairie Living	100.0
56626	46 Rooted Rural	99.5	57005	12 Up And Coming Families	85.9	57236	37 Prairie Living	100.0
56627	46 Rooted Rural	99.5	57006	55 College Towns	28.5	57237	37 Prairie Living	100.0
56628	31 Rural Resort Dwellers	100.0	57007	24 Main Street, USA	100.0	57238	37 Prairie Living	100.0
56629	46 Rooted Rural	100.0	57010	37 Prairie Living	96.7	57239	37 Prairie Living	100.0
56630	46 Rooted Rural	70.1	57012	50 Heartland Communities	61.1	57241	37 Prairie Living	98.8
56633	51 Metro City Edge	65.1	57013	32 Rustbelt Traditions	48.7	57242	37 Prairie Living	100.0
56634	50 Heartland Communities	70.4	57014	50 Heartland Communities	75.8	57243	37 Prairie Living	100.0
56636	31 Rural Resort Dwellers	39.9	57015	37 Prairie Living	94.9	57245	37 Prairie Living	100.0
56637	31 Rural Resort Dwellers	100.0	57016	37 Prairie Living	95.1	57246	37 Prairie Living	100.0
56639	31 Rural Resort Dwellers	100.0	57017	37 Prairie Living	100.0	57247	37 Prairie Living	100.0
56641	31 Rural Resort Dwellers	100.0	57018	32 Rustbelt Traditions	55.9	57248	46 Rooted Rural	92.9
56644	50 Heartland Communities	71.7	57020	19 Milk And Cookies	77.8	57249	50 Heartland Communities	75.4
56646	37 Prairie Living	100.0	57021	37 Prairie Living	100.0	57251	37 Prairie Living	100.0
56647	46 Rooted Rural	65.5	57022	33 Midlife Junction	55.0	57252	50 Heartland Communities	46.7
56649	25 Salt Of The Earth	26.4	57024	50 Heartland Communities	59.8	57255	37 Prairie Living	100.0
56650	46 Rooted Rural	48.5	57025	37 Prairie Living	33.0	57256	37 Prairie Living	100.0
56651	46 Rooted Rural	92.3	57026	25 Salt Of The Earth	81.7	57257	37 Prairie Living	70.5
56652	37 Prairie Living	92.5	57027	37 Prairie Living	100.0	57258	37 Prairie Living	100.0
56653	46 Rooted Rural	72.8	57028	33 Midlife Junction	56.8	57259	37 Prairie Living	100.0
56654	46 Rooted Rural	100.0	57029	50 Heartland Communities	69.8	57260	37 Prairie Living	100.0
56655	31 Rural Resort Dwellers	75.4	57030	25 Salt Of The Earth	87.4	57261	37 Prairie Living	100.0
56657	31 Rural Resort Dwellers	100.0	57031	37 Prairie Living	100.0	57262	50 Heartland Communities	47.7
56659	31 Rural Resort Dwellers	86.6	57032	13 In Style	46.3	57263	37 Prairie Living	100.0
56660	46 Rooted Rural	100.0	57033	19 Milk And Cookies	61.3	57264	37 Prairie Living	100.0
56661	46 Rooted Rural	57.8	57034	37 Prairie Living	100.0	57265	37 Prairie Living	100.0
56662	49 Senior Sun Seekers	51.2	57035	25 Salt Of The Earth	87.1	57266	50 Heartland Communities	72.4
56663	26 Midland Crowd	76.3	57036	37 Prairie Living	98.4	57268	37 Prairie Living	100.0
56666	51 Metro City Edge	100.0	57037	50 Heartland Communities	52.3	57269	37 Prairie Living	100.0
56667	46 Rooted Rural	96.1	57038	25 Salt Of The Earth	59.3	57270	50 Heartland Communities	57.0
56668	31 Rural Resort Dwellers	100.0	57039	50 Heartland Communities	42.2	57271	37 Prairie Living	100.0
56669	31 Rural Resort Dwellers	50.0	57040	37 Prairie Living	100.0	57272	37 Prairie Living	100.0
56670	51 Metro City Edge	100.0	57042	33 Midlife Junction	34.8	57273	50 Heartland Communities	59.7
56671	51 Metro City Edge	100.0	57043	50 Heartland Communities	63.6	57274	50 Heartland Communities	61.0
56672	31 Rural Resort Dwellers	54.7	57045	37 Prairie Living	100.0	57276	37 Prairie Living	100.0
56673	26 Midland Crowd	59.5	57046	37 Prairie Living	100.0	57278	37 Prairie Living	100.0
56676	46 Rooted Rural	88.8	57047	37 Prairie Living	100.0	57279	37 Prairie Living	97.9
56678	26 Midland Crowd	100.0	57048	37 Prairie Living	97.0	57301	33 Midlife Junction	19.8
56680	31 Rural Resort Dwellers	86.2	57049	13 In Style	100.0	57311	37 Prairie Living	100.0
56681	31 Rural Resort Dwellers	100.0	57050	37 Prairie Living	100.0	57312	37 Prairie Living	100.0
56682	26 Midland Crowd	100.0	57051	37 Prairie Living	100.0	57313	50 Heartland Communities	59.1
56683	31 Rural Resort Dwellers	100.0	57052	37 Prairie Living	100.0	57314	37 Prairie Living	100.0
56684	37 Prairie Living	100.0	57053	37 Prairie Living	99.3	57315	37 Prairie Living	100.0
56685	46 Rooted Rural	100.0	57054	37 Prairie Living	100.0	57317	37 Prairie Living	100.0
56686	46 Rooted Rural	62.7	57055	17 Green Acres	97.4	57319	50 Heartland Communities	67.4
56688	31 Rural Resort Dwellers	100.0	57057	37 Prairie Living	100.0	57321	37 Prairie Living	100.0
56701	33 Midlife Junction	28.1	57058	50 Heartland Communities	74.9	57322	37 Prairie Living	100.0
56710	37 Prairie Living	100.0	57059	50 Heartland Communities	91.5	57323	37 Prairie Living	100.0
56711	31 Rural Resort Dwellers	100.0	57062	37 Prairie Living	100.0	57324	37 Prairie Living	100.0
56713	37 Prairie Living	93.4	57063	37 Prairie Living	94.9	57325	33 Midlife Junction	62.7
56714	42 Southern Satellites	60.4	57064	12 Up And Coming Families	96.6	57328	50 Heartland Communities	66.0
56715	50 Heartland Communities	96.2	57065	37 Prairie Living	100.0	57329	37 Prairie Living	100.0
56716	48 Great Expectations	22.8	57066	50 Heartland Communities	84.5	57330	37 Prairie Living	100.0
56720	37 Prairie Living	100.0	57067	37 Prairie Living	100.0	57331	37 Prairie Living	100.0
56721	28 Aspiring Young Families	25.6	57068	17 Green Acres	90.3	57332	37 Prairie Living	99.5
56722	37 Prairie Living	100.0	57069	55 College Towns	54.0	57334	37 Prairie Living	100.0
56723	37 Prairie Living	66.2	57070	50 Heartland Communities	81.5	57335	37 Prairie Living	100.0
56724	37 Prairie Living	93.5	57071	26 Midland Crowd	63.8	57337	37 Prairie Living	100.0
56725	37 Prairie Living	75.5	57072	37 Prairie Living	100.0	57339	64 City Commons	50.9
56726	37 Prairie Living	93.7	57073	50 Heartland Communities	66.9	57340	37 Prairie Living	100.0
56727	37 Prairie Living	70.9	57075	31 Rural Resort Dwellers	92.0	57341	37 Prairie Living	100.0
56728	37 Prairie Living	100.0	57076	37 Prairie Living	100.0	57342	37 Prairie Living	100.0
56729	37 Prairie Living	100.0	57077	26 Midland Crowd	79.8	57344	37 Prairie Living	100.0
56732	50 Heartland Communities	54.9	57078	26 Midland Crowd	30.1	57345	50 Heartland Communities	65.4
56733	37 Prairie Living	100.0	57103	28 Aspiring Young Families	27.8	57348	37 Prairie Living	100.0
56734	50 Heartland Communities	93.0	57104	48 Great Expectations	38.0	57349	50 Heartland Communities	69.5
56735	37 Prairie Living	85.4	57105	48 Great Expectations	21.1	57350	50 Heartland Communities	40.8
56736	31 Rural Resort Dwellers	72.3	57106	04 Boomburbs	19.2	57353	37 Prairie Living	100.0

CONSUMER TYPE

ZIP CODE	TOP TAPESTRY CONSUMER TYPE	% 2009 HOUSE-HOLDS	ZIP CODE	TOP TAPESTRY CONSUMER TYPE	% 2009 HOUSE-HOLDS	ZIP CODE	TOP TAPESTRY CONSUMER TYPE	% 2009 HOUSE-HOLDS
57355	37 Prairie Living	100.0	57548	51 Metro City Edge	88.8	57780	37 Prairie Living	100.0
57356	50 Heartland Communities	42.1	57551	50 Heartland Communities	67.5	57782	31 Rural Resort Dwellers	100.0
57359	37 Prairie Living	100.0	57552	37 Prairie Living	100.0	57783	28 Aspiring Young Families	23.2
57362	50 Heartland Communities	78.7	57553	37 Prairie Living	100.0	57785	26 Midland Crowd	27.6
57363	37 Prairie Living	100.0	57555	51 Metro City Edge	76.3	57787	37 Prairie Living	100.0
57364	37 Prairie Living	100.0	57559	37 Prairie Living	100.0	57788	37 Prairie Living	100.0
57365	46 Rooted Rural	98.7	57560	37 Prairie Living	100.0	57790	50 Heartland Communities	61.8
57366	50 Heartland Communities	76.1	57562	37 Prairie Living	100.0	57791	37 Prairie Living	100.0
57368	50 Heartland Communities	69.5	57564	37 Prairie Living	100.0	57792	37 Prairie Living	100.0
57369	50 Heartland Communities	64.3	57566	64 City Commons	74.4	57793	46 Rooted Rural	68.7
57370	37 Prairie Living	98.1	57567	46 Rooted Rural	80.1	57794	51 Metro City Edge	100.0
57371	37 Prairie Living	100.0	57568	37 Prairie Living	100.0	57799	33 Midlife Junction	100.0
57373	50 Heartland Communities	57.7	57569	46 Rooted Rural	73.7	58004	37 Prairie Living	100.0
57374	37 Prairie Living	100.0	57571	37 Prairie Living	100.0	58005	25 Salt Of The Earth	70.1
57375	37 Prairie Living	100.0	57572	51 Metro City Edge	97.2	58006	37 Prairie Living	100.0
57376	50 Heartland Communities	62.7	57574	37 Prairie Living	100.0	58007	37 Prairie Living	100.0
57379	37 Prairie Living	100.0	57576	37 Prairie Living	100.0	58008	37 Prairie Living	100.0
57380	50 Heartland Communities	34.4	57577	51 Metro City Edge	64.5	58009	37 Prairie Living	100.0
57381	37 Prairie Living	100.0	57579	51 Metro City Edge	69.8	58011	37 Prairie Living	100.0
57382	50 Heartland Communities	71.3	57580	37 Prairie Living	57.4	58012	33 Midlife Junction	51.8
57383	37 Prairie Living	100.0	57584	37 Prairie Living	100.0	58013	37 Prairie Living	100.0
57384	37 Prairie Living	100.0	57585	37 Prairie Living	100.0	58015	37 Prairie Living	100.0
57385	50 Heartland Communities	51.8	57601	50 Heartland Communities	47.1	58016	37 Prairie Living	100.0
57386	37 Prairie Living	100.0	57620	37 Prairie Living	100.0	58017	37 Prairie Living	100.0
57401	48 Great Expectations	20.4	57622	64 City Commons	100.0	58018	37 Prairie Living	100.0
57420	37 Prairie Living	100.0	57623	37 Prairie Living	79.6	58021	37 Prairie Living	91.9
57421	37 Prairie Living	100.0	57625	51 Metro City Edge	42.0	58027	50 Heartland Communities	69.6
57422	37 Prairie Living	100.0	57626	37 Prairie Living	100.0	58029	37 Prairie Living	100.0
57424	37 Prairie Living	100.0	57630	46 Rooted Rural	87.5	58030	37 Prairie Living	100.0
57427	37 Prairie Living	100.0	57631	37 Prairie Living	100.0	58031	37 Prairie Living	100.0
57428	37 Prairie Living	100.0	57632	37 Prairie Living	100.0	58032	37 Prairie Living	100.0
57429	37 Prairie Living	100.0	57633	51 Metro City Edge	64.1	58033	37 Prairie Living	100.0
57430	50 Heartland Communities	71.6	57634	37 Prairie Living	100.0	58035	37 Prairie Living	100.0
57432	37 Prairie Living	100.0	57638	50 Heartland Communities	78.0	58036	25 Salt Of The Earth	98.1
57433	37 Prairie Living	100.0	57640	37 Prairie Living	100.0	58038	25 Salt Of The Earth	94.9
57434	37 Prairie Living	100.0	57641	37 Prairie Living	100.0	58040	26 Midland Crowd	76.3
57435	37 Prairie Living	100.0	57642	51 Metro City Edge	82.7	58041	37 Prairie Living	56.1
57436	37 Prairie Living	100.0	57644	37 Prairie Living	100.0	58042	06 Sophisticated Squires	60.5
57437	50 Heartland Communities	74.6	57645	37 Prairie Living	100.0	58043	37 Prairie Living	100.0
57438	50 Heartland Communities	67.5	57646	37 Prairie Living	100.0	58045	50 Heartland Communities	45.2
57440	37 Prairie Living	100.0	57648	37 Prairie Living	100.0	58046	37 Prairie Living	100.0
57441	37 Prairie Living	97.9	57649	37 Prairie Living	100.0	58047	19 Milk And Cookies	42.3
57442	50 Heartland Communities	81.2	57650	37 Prairie Living	100.0	58048	37 Prairie Living	100.0
57445	33 Midlife Junction	70.5	57651	37 Prairie Living	100.0	58049	37 Prairie Living	100.0
57446	37 Prairie Living	100.0	57656	46 Rooted Rural	77.1	58051	32 Rustbelt Traditions	54.3
57448	37 Prairie Living	100.0	57657	56 Rural Bypasses	61.1	58052	37 Prairie Living	100.0
57449	37 Prairie Living	100.0	57658	51 Metro City Edge	100.0	58053	50 Heartland Communities	61.6
57450	37 Prairie Living	100.0	57660	37 Prairie Living	100.0	58054	50 Heartland Communities	75.3
57451	37 Prairie Living	53.2	57701	41 Crossroads	14.7	58056	37 Prairie Living	100.0
57452	37 Prairie Living	100.0	57702	07 Exurbanites	32.2	58057	37 Prairie Living	100.0
57454	37 Prairie Living	100.0	57703	19 Milk And Cookies	55.5	58058	37 Prairie Living	100.0
57455	37 Prairie Living	100.0	57706	40 Military Proximity	76.4	58059	19 Milk And Cookies	61.5
57456	37 Prairie Living	100.0	57714	64 City Commons	45.4	58060	37 Prairie Living	100.0
57457	37 Prairie Living	100.0	57716	51 Metro City Edge	99.4	58061	37 Prairie Living	100.0
57460	37 Prairie Living	97.8	57717	50 Heartland Communities	21.4	58062	37 Prairie Living	100.0
57461	37 Prairie Living	100.0	57718	26 Midland Crowd	99.2	58063	37 Prairie Living	100.0
57465	37 Prairie Living	100.0	57719	41 Crossroads	73.2	58064	37 Prairie Living	100.0
57466	37 Prairie Living	100.0	57720	37 Prairie Living	100.0	58067	37 Prairie Living	100.0
57467	37 Prairie Living	100.0	57722	31 Rural Resort Dwellers	100.0	58068	37 Prairie Living	100.0
57468	37 Prairie Living	100.0	57724	37 Prairie Living	100.0	58069	37 Prairie Living	100.0
57469	50 Heartland Communities	54.0	57725	25 Salt Of The Earth	86.7	58071	37 Prairie Living	100.0
57470	37 Prairie Living	100.0	57730	31 Rural Resort Dwellers	80.7	58072	50 Heartland Communities	23.5
57471	37 Prairie Living	100.0	57732	31 Rural Resort Dwellers	73.2	58075	28 Aspiring Young Families	46.6
57472	37 Prairie Living	100.0	57735	37 Prairie Living	72.3	58076	57 Simple Living	100.0
57473	37 Prairie Living	100.0	57737	37 Prairie Living	100.0	58077	37 Prairie Living	100.0
57474	37 Prairie Living	100.0	57738	31 Rural Resort Dwellers	100.0	58078	12 Up And Coming Families	49.4
57475	37 Prairie Living	100.0	57741	37 Prairie Living	100.0	58079	37 Prairie Living	98.5
57476	37 Prairie Living	100.0	57744	31 Rural Resort Dwellers	94.0	58081	37 Prairie Living	100.0
57477	37 Prairie Living	100.0	57745	31 Rural Resort Dwellers	50.4	58102	28 Aspiring Young Families	13.1
57479	37 Prairie Living	100.0	57747	50 Heartland Communities	58.2	58103	39 Young And Restless	23.0
57481	37 Prairie Living	78.0	57748	37 Prairie Living	100.0	58104	12 Up And Coming Families	37.3
57501	26 Midland Crowd	26.6	57750	37 Prairie Living	100.0	58201	36 Old And Newcomers	31.8
57520	37 Prairie Living	100.0	57751	31 Rural Resort Dwellers	54.8	58203	63 Dorms To Diplomas	19.1
57521	37 Prairie Living	100.0	57752	41 Crossroads	53.0	58204	40 Military Proximity	100.0
57522	26 Midland Crowd	88.1	57754	32 Rustbelt Traditions	37.7	58205	40 Military Proximity	100.0
57523	50 Heartland Communities	75.2	57755	37 Prairie Living	100.0	58210	37 Prairie Living	100.0
57528	37 Prairie Living	100.0	57756	51 Metro City Edge	89.1	58212	37 Prairie Living	100.0
57529	37 Prairie Living	100.0	57758	37 Prairie Living	100.0	58214	33 Midlife Junction	100.0
57531	37 Prairie Living	100.0	57759	31 Rural Resort Dwellers	100.0	58216	37 Prairie Living	100.0
57532	26 Midland Crowd	84.3	57760	50 Heartland Communities	61.6	58218	37 Prairie Living	100.0
57533	50 Heartland Communities	72.3	57761	46 Rooted Rural	60.0	58219	37 Prairie Living	100.0
57534	37 Prairie Living	100.0	57762	37 Prairie Living	100.0	58220	50 Heartland Communities	35.2
57536	37 Prairie Living	73.3	57763	31 Rural Resort Dwellers	69.8	58222	37 Prairie Living	98.6
57537	37 Prairie Living	100.0	57766	31 Rural Resort Dwellers	100.0	58223	37 Prairie Living	100.0
57538	37 Prairie Living	98.0	57767	37 Prairie Living	100.0	58224	37 Prairie Living	100.0
57540	37 Prairie Living	100.0	57769	26 Midland Crowd	86.7	58225	50 Heartland Communities	79.0
57541	37 Prairie Living	100.0	57770	51 Metro City Edge	92.1	58227	37 Prairie Living	100.0
57543	50 Heartland Communities	77.7	57772	51 Metro City Edge	98.4	58228	26 Midland Crowd	55.1
57544	37 Prairie Living	93.0	57775	37 Prairie Living	100.0	58229	37 Prairie Living	100.0
57547	37 Prairie Living	100.0	57779	37 Prairie Living	100.0	58230	37 Prairie Living	100.0

ZIP CODE	TOP TAPESTRY CONSUMER TYPE	% 2009 HOUSE-HOLDS	ZIP CODE	TOP TAPESTRY CONSUMER TYPE	% 2009 HOUSE-HOLDS	ZIP CODE	TOP TAPESTRY CONSUMER TYPE	% 2009 HOUSE-HOLDS
58231	37 Prairie Living	100.0	58422	37 Prairie Living	100.0	58576	46 Rooted Rural	83.0
58233	37 Prairie Living	92.1	58423	37 Prairie Living	100.0	58577	25 Salt Of The Earth	38.0
58235	37 Prairie Living	100.0	58424	37 Prairie Living	100.0	58579	25 Salt Of The Earth	50.7
58237	50 Heartland Communities	40.5	58425	37 Prairie Living	60.6	58580	37 Prairie Living	100.0
58238	37 Prairie Living	100.0	58426	37 Prairie Living	100.0	58581	37 Prairie Living	100.0
58239	37 Prairie Living	100.0	58428	37 Prairie Living	100.0	58601	36 Old And Newcomers	15.6
58240	50 Heartland Communities	77.1	58429	37 Prairie Living	100.0	58620	37 Prairie Living	100.0
58241	17 Green Acres	78.2	58430	37 Prairie Living	100.0	58621	37 Prairie Living	53.8
58243	37 Prairie Living	100.0	58431	37 Prairie Living	100.0	58622	50 Heartland Communities	72.9
58244	37 Prairie Living	100.0	58433	50 Heartland Communities	57.6	58623	37 Prairie Living	61.4
58249	37 Prairie Living	60.6	58436	50 Heartland Communities	73.4	58625	37 Prairie Living	100.0
58250	37 Prairie Living	100.0	58438	37 Prairie Living	100.0	58626	37 Prairie Living	100.0
58251	50 Heartland Communities	68.5	58439	37 Prairie Living	100.0	58627	37 Prairie Living	100.0
58254	50 Heartland Communities	79.1	58440	37 Prairie Living	100.0	58630	25 Salt Of The Earth	78.4
58255	37 Prairie Living	100.0	58441	37 Prairie Living	100.0	58631	50 Heartland Communities	74.0
58256	25 Salt Of The Earth	65.0	58442	37 Prairie Living	100.0	58632	37 Prairie Living	100.0
58257	50 Heartland Communities	57.4	58443	37 Prairie Living	100.0	58634	37 Prairie Living	100.0
58258	17 Green Acres	88.9	58444	37 Prairie Living	100.0	58636	37 Prairie Living	77.5
58259	37 Prairie Living	100.0	58445	37 Prairie Living	100.0	58638	50 Heartland Communities	85.8
58260	37 Prairie Living	100.0	58448	37 Prairie Living	100.0	58639	50 Heartland Communities	64.2
58261	46 Rooted Rural	86.7	58451	37 Prairie Living	100.0	58640	37 Prairie Living	90.7
58262	37 Prairie Living	100.0	58454	37 Prairie Living	100.0	58641	37 Prairie Living	100.0
58265	37 Prairie Living	100.0	58455	37 Prairie Living	100.0	58642	37 Prairie Living	100.0
58266	37 Prairie Living	100.0	58456	37 Prairie Living	100.0	58643	37 Prairie Living	100.0
58267	50 Heartland Communities	66.7	58458	50 Heartland Communities	84.0	58645	37 Prairie Living	100.0
58269	37 Prairie Living	100.0	58460	37 Prairie Living	100.0	58646	37 Prairie Living	100.0
58270	50 Heartland Communities	85.9	58461	37 Prairie Living	100.0	58647	37 Prairie Living	100.0
58271	25 Salt Of The Earth	87.9	58463	37 Prairie Living	100.0	58649	37 Prairie Living	100.0
58272	37 Prairie Living	100.0	58464	37 Prairie Living	100.0	58650	37 Prairie Living	100.0
58273	37 Prairie Living	100.0	58466	37 Prairie Living	100.0	58651	37 Prairie Living	100.0
58274	50 Heartland Communities	74.1	58467	37 Prairie Living	100.0	58652	37 Prairie Living	100.0
58275	25 Salt Of The Earth	57.8	58472	37 Prairie Living	100.0	58653	37 Prairie Living	100.0
58276	37 Prairie Living	100.0	58474	37 Prairie Living	48.8	58654	37 Prairie Living	100.0
58277	37 Prairie Living	100.0	58475	37 Prairie Living	100.0	58655	37 Prairie Living	100.0
58278	17 Green Acres	69.2	58476	37 Prairie Living	100.0	58656	37 Prairie Living	92.8
58281	37 Prairie Living	100.0	58477	37 Prairie Living	100.0	58701	36 Old And Newcomers	20.7
58282	50 Heartland Communities	72.1	58478	37 Prairie Living	100.0	58703	48 Great Expectations	24.1
58301	33 Midlife Junction	39.2	58479	37 Prairie Living	100.0	58704	40 Military Proximity	100.0
58311	37 Prairie Living	100.0	58480	37 Prairie Living	100.0	58705	40 Military Proximity	100.0
58316	26 Midland Crowd	21.4	58481	37 Prairie Living	100.0	58707	55 College Towns	100.0
58317	37 Prairie Living	100.0	58482	50 Heartland Communities	76.2	58710	50 Heartland Communities	66.0
58318	50 Heartland Communities	61.2	58483	37 Prairie Living	100.0	58711	37 Prairie Living	100.0
58321	37 Prairie Living	100.0	58484	37 Prairie Living	100.0	58712	37 Prairie Living	98.2
58323	37 Prairie Living	100.0	58486	37 Prairie Living	100.0	58713	37 Prairie Living	100.0
58324	37 Prairie Living	100.0	58487	37 Prairie Living	100.0	58716	37 Prairie Living	100.0
58325	37 Prairie Living	100.0	58488	37 Prairie Living	100.0	58718	37 Prairie Living	99.2
58327	37 Prairie Living	99.4	58490	37 Prairie Living	100.0	58721	37 Prairie Living	100.0
58329	51 Metro City Edge	53.2	58492	37 Prairie Living	100.0	58722	26 Midland Crowd	80.7
58330	37 Prairie Living	100.0	58494	37 Prairie Living	100.0	58723	37 Prairie Living	98.4
58331	37 Prairie Living	100.0	58495	50 Heartland Communities	79.4	58725	37 Prairie Living	100.0
58332	37 Prairie Living	91.7	58496	37 Prairie Living	100.0	58727	37 Prairie Living	100.0
58338	37 Prairie Living	100.0	58497	37 Prairie Living	100.0	58730	50 Heartland Communities	90.2
58339	37 Prairie Living	100.0	58501	48 Great Expectations	18.9	58731	37 Prairie Living	100.0
58341	50 Heartland Communities	72.6	58503	41 Crossroads	28.7	58733	26 Midland Crowd	68.3
58343	37 Prairie Living	100.0	58504	06 Sophisticated Squires	17.7	58734	37 Prairie Living	100.0
58344	50 Heartland Communities	74.8	58520	37 Prairie Living	100.0	58735	37 Prairie Living	100.0
58345	37 Prairie Living	100.0	58521	37 Prairie Living	74.6	58736	50 Heartland Communities	72.1
58346	37 Prairie Living	100.0	58523	19 Milk And Cookies	35.4	58737	37 Prairie Living	100.0
58348	50 Heartland Communities	63.5	58524	37 Prairie Living	100.0	58740	37 Prairie Living	75.8
58351	37 Prairie Living	88.3	58529	37 Prairie Living	100.0	58741	37 Prairie Living	100.0
58352	37 Prairie Living	100.0	58530	46 Rooted Rural	53.9	58744	37 Prairie Living	100.0
58353	37 Prairie Living	100.0	58531	37 Prairie Living	97.2	58746	37 Prairie Living	50.0
58356	50 Heartland Communities	82.9	58532	37 Prairie Living	100.0	58748	37 Prairie Living	100.0
58357	41 Crossroads	55.5	58533	50 Heartland Communities	74.1	58750	37 Prairie Living	100.0
58361	37 Prairie Living	83.5	58535	37 Prairie Living	100.0	58752	37 Prairie Living	100.0
58362	37 Prairie Living	100.0	58538	51 Metro City Edge	82.2	58755	37 Prairie Living	100.0
58363	37 Prairie Living	100.0	58540	50 Heartland Communities	68.9	58756	37 Prairie Living	100.0
58365	37 Prairie Living	100.0	58541	37 Prairie Living	100.0	58757	51 Metro City Edge	51.1
58366	50 Heartland Communities	74.1	58542	37 Prairie Living	100.0	58758	37 Prairie Living	100.0
58367	50 Heartland Communities	49.1	58544	37 Prairie Living	100.0	58759	37 Prairie Living	100.0
58368	33 Midlife Junction	46.4	58545	19 Milk And Cookies	30.1	58760	37 Prairie Living	100.0
58369	41 Crossroads	100.0	58549	37 Prairie Living	100.0	58761	50 Heartland Communities	67.4
58370	41 Crossroads	58.0	58552	50 Heartland Communities	69.9	58762	37 Prairie Living	100.0
58372	37 Prairie Living	100.0	58554	41 Crossroads	18.0	58763	51 Metro City Edge	71.2
58374	50 Heartland Communities	63.5	58558	17 Green Acres	85.3	58765	50 Heartland Communities	82.6
58377	37 Prairie Living	100.0	58559	37 Prairie Living	97.5	58768	37 Prairie Living	84.0
58380	37 Prairie Living	96.6	58560	37 Prairie Living	68.3	58769	37 Prairie Living	100.0
58381	56 Rural Bypasses	71.7	58561	37 Prairie Living	100.0	58770	50 Heartland Communities	76.6
58382	37 Prairie Living	100.0	58562	37 Prairie Living	100.0	58771	37 Prairie Living	100.0
58384	37 Prairie Living	100.0	58563	50 Heartland Communities	50.7	58772	37 Prairie Living	100.0
58385	37 Prairie Living	100.0	58564	37 Prairie Living	100.0	58773	37 Prairie Living	100.0
58386	37 Prairie Living	100.0	58565	37 Prairie Living	100.0	58775	46 Rooted Rural	80.2
58401	33 Midlife Junction	16.4	58566	37 Prairie Living	100.0	58776	37 Prairie Living	100.0
58405	55 College Towns	100.0	58568	37 Prairie Living	96.7	58778	37 Prairie Living	100.0
58413	50 Heartland Communities	69.7	58569	37 Prairie Living	100.0	58779	37 Prairie Living	85.8
58415	37 Prairie Living	100.0	58570	51 Metro City Edge	62.7	58781	37 Prairie Living	100.0
58416	37 Prairie Living	100.0	58571	46 Rooted Rural	93.4	58782	37 Prairie Living	100.0
58418	37 Prairie Living	100.0	58572	37 Prairie Living	50.0	58783	37 Prairie Living	96.7
58420	37 Prairie Living	100.0	58573	37 Prairie Living	100.0	58784	50 Heartland Communities	75.0
58421	50 Heartland Communities	75.8	58575	50 Heartland Communities	72.3	58785	19 Milk And Cookies	97.2

CONSUMER TYPE

ZIP CODE	TOP TAPESTRY CONSUMER TYPE	% 2009 HOUSE-HOLDS	ZIP CODE	TOP TAPESTRY CONSUMER TYPE	% 2009 HOUSE-HOLDS	ZIP CODE	TOP TAPESTRY CONSUMER TYPE	% 2009 HOUSE-HOLDS
58787	37 Prairie Living	100.0	59212	37 Prairie Living	100.0	59446	37 Prairie Living	100.0
58788	50 Heartland Communities	64.2	59213	37 Prairie Living	100.0	59447	37 Prairie Living	100.0
58789	37 Prairie Living	100.0	59214	37 Prairie Living	100.0	59448	51 Metro City Edge	100.0
58790	50 Heartland Communities	83.0	59215	50 Heartland Communities	66.6	59450	37 Prairie Living	100.0
58792	37 Prairie Living	100.0	59218	50 Heartland Communities	69.5	59451	37 Prairie Living	100.0
58793	50 Heartland Communities	77.6	59219	37 Prairie Living	100.0	59452	37 Prairie Living	100.0
58794	37 Prairie Living	100.0	59221	50 Heartland Communities	57.1	59453	37 Prairie Living	100.0
58795	37 Prairie Living	100.0	59222	37 Prairie Living	100.0	59454	37 Prairie Living	100.0
58801	28 Aspiring Young Families	20.7	59223	31 Rural Resort Dwellers	86.1	59456	37 Prairie Living	100.0
58830	37 Prairie Living	100.0	59225	51 Metro City Edge	73.5	59457	50 Heartland Communities	52.7
58831	37 Prairie Living	100.0	59226	46 Rooted Rural	71.4	59460	37 Prairie Living	100.0
58833	37 Prairie Living	83.7	59230	50 Heartland Communities	30.1	59462	37 Prairie Living	100.0
58835	37 Prairie Living	100.0	59241	37 Prairie Living	100.0	59463	37 Prairie Living	100.0
58838	37 Prairie Living	100.0	59242	37 Prairie Living	100.0	59464	37 Prairie Living	100.0
58843	37 Prairie Living	100.0	59243	37 Prairie Living	100.0	59465	37 Prairie Living	100.0
58844	37 Prairie Living	100.0	59244	37 Prairie Living	100.0	59466	37 Prairie Living	100.0
58845	37 Prairie Living	100.0	59247	37 Prairie Living	100.0	59467	37 Prairie Living	100.0
58847	37 Prairie Living	100.0	59248	31 Rural Resort Dwellers	46.3	59468	37 Prairie Living	84.4
58849	50 Heartland Communities	74.9	59250	37 Prairie Living	100.0	59469	37 Prairie Living	100.0
58852	50 Heartland Communities	80.1	59252	37 Prairie Living	100.0	59471	37 Prairie Living	100.0
58853	37 Prairie Living	100.0	59253	37 Prairie Living	95.0	59472	46 Rooted Rural	80.6
58854	50 Heartland Communities	64.3	59254	37 Prairie Living	50.1	59474	50 Heartland Communities	45.6
58856	37 Prairie Living	100.0	59255	51 Metro City Edge	83.9	59479	37 Prairie Living	100.0
59001	25 Salt Of The Earth	79.3	59256	37 Prairie Living	100.0	59480	46 Rooted Rural	72.4
59002	17 Green Acres	100.0	59257	37 Prairie Living	100.0	59482	37 Prairie Living	100.0
59003	26 Midland Crowd	91.1	59258	37 Prairie Living	95.7	59483	26 Midland Crowd	40.1
59006	26 Midland Crowd	63.1	59259	37 Prairie Living	100.0	59484	37 Prairie Living	100.0
59007	31 Rural Resort Dwellers	100.0	59260	37 Prairie Living	100.0	59486	37 Prairie Living	53.5
59008	31 Rural Resort Dwellers	100.0	59261	37 Prairie Living	100.0	59487	26 Midland Crowd	86.0
59010	37 Prairie Living	100.0	59262	37 Prairie Living	100.0	59489	37 Prairie Living	100.0
59011	37 Prairie Living	32.0	59263	37 Prairie Living	60.1	59501	48 Great Expectations	23.9
59012	26 Midland Crowd	100.0	59270	33 Midlife Junction	40.7	59520	37 Prairie Living	36.6
59014	50 Heartland Communities	54.8	59274	37 Prairie Living	100.0	59521	51 Metro City Edge	72.6
59015	17 Green Acres	81.7	59275	37 Prairie Living	100.0	59522	50 Heartland Communities	67.9
59016	51 Metro City Edge	100.0	59276	37 Prairie Living	100.0	59523	50 Heartland Communities	36.8
59019	25 Salt Of The Earth	39.8	59301	50 Heartland Communities	24.2	59524	46 Rooted Rural	92.0
59022	38 Industrious Urban Fringe	89.3	59311	37 Prairie Living	100.0	59525	37 Prairie Living	100.0
59024	37 Prairie Living	100.0	59312	37 Prairie Living	100.0	59526	51 Metro City Edge	44.9
59025	37 Prairie Living	100.0	59313	50 Heartland Communities	79.3	59527	51 Metro City Edge	100.0
59027	31 Rural Resort Dwellers	100.0	59314	37 Prairie Living	100.0	59528	37 Prairie Living	100.0
59028	31 Rural Resort Dwellers	100.0	59315	37 Prairie Living	100.0	59529	37 Prairie Living	100.0
59029	46 Rooted Rural	87.9	59316	37 Prairie Living	100.0	59530	37 Prairie Living	100.0
59030	22 Metropolitans	55.4	59317	37 Prairie Living	100.0	59531	37 Prairie Living	100.0
59031	46 Rooted Rural	53.8	59318	37 Prairie Living	100.0	59532	37 Prairie Living	100.0
59032	37 Prairie Living	100.0	59322	37 Prairie Living	100.0	59535	37 Prairie Living	100.0
59033	37 Prairie Living	100.0	59324	37 Prairie Living	100.0	59537	37 Prairie Living	100.0
59034	50 Heartland Communities	45.7	59326	37 Prairie Living	100.0	59538	37 Prairie Living	52.0
59037	26 Midland Crowd	60.9	59327	50 Heartland Communities	37.1	59540	37 Prairie Living	100.0
59038	37 Prairie Living	100.0	59330	46 Rooted Rural	31.2	59542	37 Prairie Living	100.0
59039	37 Prairie Living	100.0	59332	37 Prairie Living	100.0	59544	37 Prairie Living	100.0
59041	46 Rooted Rural	44.0	59336	37 Prairie Living	100.0	59545	37 Prairie Living	100.0
59043	51 Metro City Edge	76.0	59337	37 Prairie Living	100.0	59546	37 Prairie Living	100.0
59044	26 Midland Crowd	27.8	59338	37 Prairie Living	100.0	59601	36 Old And Newcomers	19.6
59046	37 Prairie Living	75.5	59339	37 Prairie Living	100.0	59602	26 Midland Crowd	34.2
59047	31 Rural Resort Dwellers	28.9	59341	37 Prairie Living	100.0	59625	63 Dorms To Diplomas	100.0
59050	51 Metro City Edge	30.0	59343	37 Prairie Living	100.0	59632	41 Crossroads	45.7
59052	37 Prairie Living	81.4	59344	37 Prairie Living	100.0	59633	31 Rural Resort Dwellers	85.8
59053	37 Prairie Living	100.0	59345	37 Prairie Living	100.0	59634	07 Exurbanites	33.7
59055	37 Prairie Living	100.0	59347	19 Milk And Cookies	57.2	59635	19 Milk And Cookies	48.1
59057	17 Green Acres	70.2	59349	49 Senior Sun Seekers	79.0	59639	31 Rural Resort Dwellers	100.0
59058	37 Prairie Living	100.0	59351	37 Prairie Living	100.0	59641	37 Prairie Living	100.0
59059	37 Prairie Living	100.0	59353	50 Heartland Communities	60.9	59642	37 Prairie Living	100.0
59061	31 Rural Resort Dwellers	84.8	59354	37 Prairie Living	100.0	59643	37 Prairie Living	68.8
59062	37 Prairie Living	100.0	59401	48 Great Expectations	29.4	59644	50 Heartland Communities	59.7
59063	26 Midland Crowd	100.0	59402	40 Military Proximity	100.0	59645	37 Prairie Living	64.7
59064	37 Prairie Living	100.0	59404	07 Exurbanites	15.9	59647	37 Prairie Living	100.0
59065	31 Rural Resort Dwellers	100.0	59405	33 Midlife Junction	37.4	59648	31 Rural Resort Dwellers	99.7
59067	37 Prairie Living	100.0	59410	37 Prairie Living	100.0	59701	50 Heartland Communities	18.0
59068	33 Midlife Junction	47.9	59411	56 Rural Bypasses	96.8	59711	50 Heartland Communities	41.1
59069	37 Prairie Living	94.0	59412	46 Rooted Rural	57.4	59714	28 Aspiring Young Families	43.6
59070	37 Prairie Living	99.5	59414	26 Midland Crowd	100.0	59715	55 College Towns	38.7
59071	37 Prairie Living	96.4	59416	37 Prairie Living	100.0	59717	63 Dorms To Diplomas	100.0
59072	50 Heartland Communities	54.0	59417	51 Metro City Edge	55.0	59718	22 Metropolitans	27.4
59074	37 Prairie Living	100.0	59418	37 Prairie Living	100.0	59720	31 Rural Resort Dwellers	100.0
59075	26 Midland Crowd	93.2	59419	37 Prairie Living	100.0	59721	37 Prairie Living	100.0
59076	37 Prairie Living	100.0	59420	37 Prairie Living	100.0	59722	50 Heartland Communities	43.8
59077	37 Prairie Living	100.0	59421	31 Rural Resort Dwellers	48.1	59724	37 Prairie Living	100.0
59078	37 Prairie Living	100.0	59422	33 Midlife Junction	38.9	59725	37 Prairie Living	27.4
59079	26 Midland Crowd	82.3	59424	37 Prairie Living	100.0	59727	31 Rural Resort Dwellers	100.0
59085	37 Prairie Living	52.2	59425	33 Midlife Junction	42.8	59729	31 Rural Resort Dwellers	99.9
59086	37 Prairie Living	71.2	59427	33 Midlife Junction	22.6	59730	22 Metropolitans	53.7
59087	37 Prairie Living	100.0	59430	37 Prairie Living	100.0	59731	37 Prairie Living	59.2
59088	46 Rooted Rural	82.5	59433	37 Prairie Living	100.0	59733	31 Rural Resort Dwellers	100.0
59089	37 Prairie Living	96.5	59434	26 Midland Crowd	83.3	59735	37 Prairie Living	100.0
59101	48 Great Expectations	20.3	59436	37 Prairie Living	100.0	59736	31 Rural Resort Dwellers	100.0
59102	33 Midlife Junction	24.1	59440	37 Prairie Living	62.3	59739	37 Prairie Living	100.0
59105	17 Green Acres	19.9	59441	37 Prairie Living	100.0	59741	26 Midland Crowd	55.0
59106	17 Green Acres	46.8	59442	37 Prairie Living	62.5	59745	37 Prairie Living	100.0
59201	50 Heartland Communities	29.8	59443	37 Prairie Living	99.6	59747	37 Prairie Living	100.0
59211	37 Prairie Living	100.0	59444	37 Prairie Living	100.0	59748	17 Green Acres	100.0

ZIP CODE	TOP TAPESTRY CONSUMER TYPE	% 2009 HOUSE-HOLDS	ZIP CODE	TOP TAPESTRY CONSUMER TYPE	% 2009 HOUSE-HOLDS	ZIP CODE	TOP TAPESTRY CONSUMER TYPE	% 2009 HOUSE-HOLDS
59749	31 Rural Resort Dwellers	48.8	60031	04 Boomburbs	43.6	60163	18 Cozy And Comfortable	50.9
59750	17 Green Acres	98.0	60033	24 Main Street, USA	46.9	60164	18 Cozy And Comfortable	30.1
59751	37 Prairie Living	98.1	60034	24 Main Street, USA	71.0	60165	47 Las Casas	100.0
59752	37 Prairie Living	37.5	60035	01 Top Rung	35.6	60169	06 Sophisticated Squires	15.8
59754	46 Rooted Rural	66.6	60037	40 Military Proximity	100.0	60171	36 Old And Newcomers	43.3
59755	31 Rural Resort Dwellers	100.0	60040	20 City Lights	45.7	60172	06 Sophisticated Squires	29.4
59756	31 Rural Resort Dwellers	100.0	60041	17 Green Acres	62.0	60173	39 Young And Restless	41.9
59758	36 Old And Newcomers	76.0	60042	12 Up And Coming Families	58.5	60174	06 Sophisticated Squires	15.5
59759	46 Rooted Rural	44.2	60043	01 Top Rung	95.2	60175	02 Suburban Splendor	47.2
59761	31 Rural Resort Dwellers	100.0	60044	09 Urban Chic	39.0	60176	24 Main Street, USA	71.1
59762	31 Rural Resort Dwellers	100.0	60045	01 Top Rung	66.5	60177	12 Up And Coming Families	46.3
59801	55 College Towns	43.0	60046	12 Up And Coming Families	33.5	60178	24 Main Street, USA	28.8
59802	55 College Towns	32.7	60047	02 Suburban Splendor	53.0	60180	17 Green Acres	54.1
59803	06 Sophisticated Squires	23.7	60048	02 Suburban Splendor	34.0	60181	10 Pleasant-Ville	43.1
59804	26 Midland Crowd	19.9	60050	24 Main Street, USA	20.1	60184	04 Boomburbs	51.6
59808	41 Crossroads	47.5	60051	17 Green Acres	32.8	60185	06 Sophisticated Squires	24.4
59820	17 Green Acres	51.1	60053	05 Wealthy Seaboard Suburbs	47.1	60187	06 Sophisticated Squires	23.8
59821	26 Midland Crowd	98.8	60056	05 Wealthy Seaboard Suburbs	28.8	60188	06 Sophisticated Squires	39.5
59823	31 Rural Resort Dwellers	60.8	60060	04 Boomburbs	30.0	60189	02 Suburban Splendor	38.4
59824	26 Midland Crowd	58.7	60061	02 Suburban Splendor	32.7	60190	06 Sophisticated Squires	59.1
59825	26 Midland Crowd	93.6	60062	03 Connoisseurs	33.3	60191	14 Prosperous Empty Nesters	23.8
59826	31 Rural Resort Dwellers	100.0	60064	60 City Dimensions	22.6	60192	02 Suburban Splendor	46.9
59827	31 Rural Resort Dwellers	100.0	60067	02 Suburban Splendor	23.2	60193	13 In Style	43.3
59828	31 Rural Resort Dwellers	67.1	60068	05 Wealthy Seaboard Suburbs	45.9	60194	13 In Style	23.7
59829	31 Rural Resort Dwellers	65.8	60069	01 Top Rung	43.6	60195	27 Metro Renters	85.1
59831	46 Rooted Rural	71.0	60070	28 Aspiring Young Families	39.5	60201	27 Metro Renters	34.4
59832	37 Prairie Living	84.0	60071	13 In Style	46.7	60202	08 Laptops And Lattes	28.2
59833	17 Green Acres	45.2	60072	06 Sophisticated Squires	93.8	60203	05 Wealthy Seaboard Suburbs	45.6
59834	17 Green Acres	73.3	60073	38 Industrious Urban Fringe	26.1	60208	55 College Towns	55.6
59837	37 Prairie Living	98.0	60074	28 Aspiring Young Families	26.3	60301	27 Metro Renters	100.0
59840	31 Rural Resort Dwellers	40.5	60076	05 Wealthy Seaboard Suburbs	34.1	60302	27 Metro Renters	25.3
59843	31 Rural Resort Dwellers	91.2	60077	30 Retirement Communities	28.8	60304	22 Metropolitans	27.2
59844	31 Rural Resort Dwellers	100.0	60081	06 Sophisticated Squires	46.1	60305	09 Urban Chic	36.2
59845	49 Senior Sun Seekers	92.7	60082	01 Top Rung	100.0	60401	17 Green Acres	33.9
59846	17 Green Acres	93.8	60083	07 Exurbanites	49.8	60402	24 Main Street, USA	60.4
59847	26 Midland Crowd	96.2	60084	06 Sophisticated Squires	31.5	60403	18 Cozy And Comfortable	31.5
59848	49 Senior Sun Seekers	100.0	60085	38 Industrious Urban Fringe	26.0	60404	06 Sophisticated Squires	55.7
59853	31 Rural Resort Dwellers	100.0	60087	18 Cozy And Comfortable	36.8	60406	38 Industrious Urban Fringe	38.3
59854	31 Rural Resort Dwellers	100.0	60088	40 Military Proximity	99.6	60407	32 Rustbelt Traditions	52.1
59858	50 Heartland Communities	64.8	60089	02 Suburban Splendor	31.1	60408	19 Milk And Cookies	43.9
59859	31 Rural Resort Dwellers	74.4	60090	16 Enterprising Professionals	19.9	60409	32 Rustbelt Traditions	30.1
59860	31 Rural Resort Dwellers	42.5	60091	03 Connoisseurs	39.1	60410	06 Sophisticated Squires	48.8
59864	41 Crossroads	22.5	60093	01 Top Rung	65.1	60411	18 Cozy And Comfortable	17.8
59865	26 Midland Crowd	43.5	60096	18 Cozy And Comfortable	49.1	60415	28 Aspiring Young Families	35.1
59866	46 Rooted Rural	100.0	60097	17 Green Acres	32.6	60416	24 Main Street, USA	49.2
59868	31 Rural Resort Dwellers	100.0	60098	24 Main Street, USA	25.4	60417	07 Exurbanites	47.1
59870	31 Rural Resort Dwellers	43.9	60099	38 Industrious Urban Fringe	12.4	60419	34 Family Foundations	47.7
59871	31 Rural Resort Dwellers	100.0	60101	35 International Marketplace	23.7	60420	33 Midlife Junction	27.5
59872	31 Rural Resort Dwellers	62.4	60102	04 Boomburbs	50.5	60421	18 Cozy And Comfortable	54.5
59873	31 Rural Resort Dwellers	70.4	60103	04 Boomburbs	34.0	60422	05 Wealthy Seaboard Suburbs	58.1
59874	31 Rural Resort Dwellers	100.0	60104	34 Family Foundations	44.1	60423	06 Sophisticated Squires	27.3
59875	31 Rural Resort Dwellers	58.6	60106	24 Main Street, USA	23.2	60424	32 Rustbelt Traditions	43.9
59901	26 Midland Crowd	19.2	60107	12 Up And Coming Families	42.7	60425	18 Cozy And Comfortable	39.7
59910	31 Rural Resort Dwellers	100.0	60108	16 Enterprising Professionals	25.0	60426	51 Metro City Edge	39.2
59911	31 Rural Resort Dwellers	100.0	60110	38 Industrious Urban Fringe	43.6	60428	34 Family Foundations	85.3
59912	26 Midland Crowd	35.1	60111	17 Green Acres	93.1	60429	34 Family Foundations	27.6
59914	31 Rural Resort Dwellers	100.0	60112	12 Up And Coming Families	77.3	60430	18 Cozy And Comfortable	28.2
59915	31 Rural Resort Dwellers	100.0	60115	63 Dorms To Diplomas	32.4	60431	12 Up And Coming Families	86.1
59916	31 Rural Resort Dwellers	53.0	60118	13 In Style	30.5	60432	47 Las Casas	27.8
59917	31 Rural Resort Dwellers	35.3	60119	04 Boomburbs	57.3	60433	51 Metro City Edge	34.0
59920	31 Rural Resort Dwellers	57.3	60120	24 Main Street, USA	16.4	60435	24 Main Street, USA	10.7
59922	31 Rural Resort Dwellers	100.0	60123	24 Main Street, USA	17.2	60436	32 Rustbelt Traditions	22.7
59923	46 Rooted Rural	44.9	60124	12 Up And Coming Families	51.2	60437	17 Green Acres	86.7
59925	31 Rural Resort Dwellers	100.0	60126	10 Pleasant-Ville	27.9	60438	18 Cozy And Comfortable	35.0
59928	31 Rural Resort Dwellers	100.0	60129	17 Green Acres	73.2	60439	02 Suburban Splendor	33.3
59929	31 Rural Resort Dwellers	100.0	60130	36 Old And Newcomers	42.3	60440	19 Milk And Cookies	27.3
59930	46 Rooted Rural	100.0	60131	24 Main Street, USA	48.9	60441	12 Up And Coming Families	30.9
59931	31 Rural Resort Dwellers	100.0	60133	06 Sophisticated Squires	23.3	60442	12 Up And Coming Families	42.9
59932	31 Rural Resort Dwellers	100.0	60134	04 Boomburbs	32.4	60443	06 Sophisticated Squires	34.3
59935	49 Senior Sun Seekers	35.5	60135	24 Main Street, USA	41.7	60444	17 Green Acres	47.6
59937	31 Rural Resort Dwellers	27.4	60136	06 Sophisticated Squires	92.1	60445	24 Main Street, USA	31.4
60002	13 In Style	33.2	60137	02 Suburban Splendor	25.0	60446	16 Enterprising Professionals	26.5
60004	05 Wealthy Seaboard Suburbs	36.4	60139	06 Sophisticated Squires	20.6	60447	26 Midland Crowd	49.9
60005	05 Wealthy Seaboard Suburbs	20.8	60140	06 Sophisticated Squires	38.8	60448	06 Sophisticated Squires	36.0
60007	10 Pleasant-Ville	30.7	60141	36 Old And Newcomers	74.2	60449	17 Green Acres	71.4
60008	18 Cozy And Comfortable	21.5	60142	12 Up And Coming Families	31.7	60450	24 Main Street, USA	36.9
60010	02 Suburban Splendor	35.1	60143	07 Exurbanites	37.6	60451	06 Sophisticated Squires	25.0
60012	02 Suburban Splendor	45.6	60145	12 Up And Coming Families	57.5	60452	18 Cozy And Comfortable	33.4
60013	04 Boomburbs	36.8	60146	24 Main Street, USA	57.4	60453	30 Retirement Communities	25.8
60014	06 Sophisticated Squires	21.0	60148	10 Pleasant-Ville	32.6	60455	24 Main Street, USA	29.6
60015	01 Top Rung	32.7	60150	18 Cozy And Comfortable	57.5	60456	32 Rustbelt Traditions	35.4
60016	10 Pleasant-Ville	24.4	60151	06 Sophisticated Squires	44.3	60457	24 Main Street, USA	33.5
60018	10 Pleasant-Ville	41.0	60152	24 Main Street, USA	48.4	60458	28 Aspiring Young Families	49.1
60020	24 Main Street, USA	47.1	60153	34 Family Foundations	38.3	60459	18 Cozy And Comfortable	60.3
60021	06 Sophisticated Squires	34.5	60154	14 Prosperous Empty Nesters	64.6	60460	32 Rustbelt Traditions	65.3
60022	01 Top Rung	88.0	60155	18 Cozy And Comfortable	37.4	60461	14 Prosperous Empty Nesters	43.1
60025	05 Wealthy Seaboard Suburbs	27.3	60156	04 Boomburbs	53.8	60462	13 In Style	19.2
60026	40 Military Proximity	37.7	60157	05 Wealthy Seaboard Suburbs	45.1	60463	05 Wealthy Seaboard Suburbs	38.0
60029	03 Connoisseurs	100.0	60160	35 International Marketplace	33.2	60464	14 Prosperous Empty Nesters	34.0
60030	04 Boomburbs	42.9	60162	24 Main Street, USA	68.3	60465	30 Retirement Communities	32.6

CONSUMER TYPE

ZIP CODE	TOP TAPESTRY CONSUMER TYPE	% 2009 HOUSE-HOLDS	ZIP CODE	TOP TAPESTRY CONSUMER TYPE	% 2009 HOUSE-HOLDS	ZIP CODE	TOP TAPESTRY CONSUMER TYPE	% 2009 HOUSE-HOLDS
60466	18 Cozy And Comfortable	24.4	60619	34 Family Foundations	42.4	61001	31 Rural Resort Dwellers	54.1
60467	05 Wealthy Seaboard Suburbs	59.1	60620	34 Family Foundations	61.0	61006	32 Rustbelt Traditions	76.2
60468	17 Green Acres	45.8	60621	64 City Commons	54.6	61007	25 Salt Of The Earth	76.5
60469	32 Rustbelt Traditions	35.0	60622	23 Trendsetters	48.4	61008	32 Rustbelt Traditions	17.8
60470	25 Salt Of The Earth	85.9	60623	47 Las Casas	48.7	61010	06 Sophisticated Squires	43.2
60471	19 Milk And Cookies	60.6	60624	45 City Strivers	59.8	61011	12 Up And Coming Families	61.0
60472	34 Family Foundations	40.3	60625	35 International Marketplace	49.9	61012	26 Midland Crowd	69.0
60473	18 Cozy And Comfortable	59.4	60626	52 Inner City Tenants	56.1	61014	37 Prairie Living	82.7
60475	32 Rustbelt Traditions	27.2	60628	34 Family Foundations	60.0	61015	17 Green Acres	90.6
60476	29 Rustbelt Retirees	75.5	60629	38 Industrious Urban Fringe	30.4	61016	06 Sophisticated Squires	50.2
60477	06 Sophisticated Squires	26.4	60630	20 City Lights	54.0	61018	25 Salt Of The Earth	74.4
60478	19 Milk And Cookies	43.2	60631	10 Pleasant-Ville	48.2	61019	17 Green Acres	60.5
60479	25 Salt Of The Earth	81.7	60632	47 Las Casas	57.1	61020	17 Green Acres	99.8
60480	17 Green Acres	30.0	60633	29 Rustbelt Retirees	47.3	61021	32 Rustbelt Traditions	27.1
60481	24 Main Street, USA	26.9	60634	24 Main Street, USA	38.8	61024	17 Green Acres	51.0
60482	24 Main Street, USA	62.7	60636	34 Family Foundations	26.7	61025	25 Salt Of The Earth	36.7
60487	12 Up And Coming Families	53.1	60637	45 City Strivers	33.4	61028	50 Heartland Communities	51.0
60490	04 Boomburbs	92.8	60638	24 Main Street, USA	32.6	61030	25 Salt Of The Earth	51.4
60491	06 Sophisticated Squires	48.9	60639	47 Las Casas	54.7	61031	32 Rustbelt Traditions	69.1
60501	38 Industrious Urban Fringe	59.9	60640	23 Trendsetters	33.3	61032	29 Rustbelt Retirees	13.9
60502	04 Boomburbs	68.3	60641	35 International Marketplace	49.0	61036	29 Rustbelt Retirees	29.0
60503	04 Boomburbs	68.6	60642	23 Trendsetters	48.5	61038	25 Salt Of The Earth	49.6
60504	04 Boomburbs	55.5	60643	34 Family Foundations	52.7	61039	25 Salt Of The Earth	93.3
60505	38 Industrious Urban Fringe	36.7	60644	45 City Strivers	66.1	61041	50 Heartland Communities	49.8
60506	38 Industrious Urban Fringe	17.5	60645	35 International Marketplace	27.5	61042	25 Salt Of The Earth	58.8
60510	06 Sophisticated Squires	23.2	60646	05 Wealthy Seaboard Suburbs	39.0	61044	37 Prairie Living	100.0
60511	07 Exurbanites	65.1	60647	35 International Marketplace	37.7	61046	25 Salt Of The Earth	55.6
60512	17 Green Acres	88.1	60649	45 City Strivers	47.0	61047	25 Salt Of The Earth	60.6
60513	10 Pleasant-Ville	32.1	60651	45 City Strivers	51.2	61048	25 Salt Of The Earth	33.7
60514	02 Suburban Splendor	45.5	60652	18 Cozy And Comfortable	43.7	61049	25 Salt Of The Earth	63.8
60515	30 Retirement Communities	21.5	60653	64 City Commons	37.6	61050	37 Prairie Living	100.0
60516	13 In Style	20.5	60654	27 Metro Renters	64.6	61051	25 Salt Of The Earth	97.1
60517	06 Sophisticated Squires	17.6	60655	18 Cozy And Comfortable	50.7	61052	17 Green Acres	100.0
60518	25 Salt Of The Earth	62.1	60656	36 Old And Newcomers	36.6	61053	50 Heartland Communities	44.4
60520	17 Green Acres	94.0	60657	27 Metro Renters	67.6	61054	25 Salt Of The Earth	43.6
60521	01 Top Rung	43.3	60659	35 International Marketplace	45.7	61060	25 Salt Of The Earth	73.4
60523	03 Connoisseurs	34.0	60660	36 Old And Newcomers	34.2	61061	25 Salt Of The Earth	25.5
60525	05 Wealthy Seaboard Suburbs	16.3	60661	27 Metro Renters	84.8	61062	17 Green Acres	49.9
60526	10 Pleasant-Ville	26.6	60706	29 Rustbelt Retirees	37.5	61063	17 Green Acres	42.0
60527	01 Top Rung	17.6	60707	10 Pleasant-Ville	29.1	61064	32 Rustbelt Traditions	61.5
60530	17 Green Acres	59.4	60712	05 Wealthy Seaboard Suburbs	76.8	61065	12 Up And Coming Families	51.9
60531	25 Salt Of The Earth	72.0	60714	10 Pleasant-Ville	32.4	61067	17 Green Acres	67.3
60532	16 Enterprising Professionals	33.2	60803	24 Main Street, USA	35.9	61068	38 Industrious Urban Fringe	17.9
60534	24 Main Street, USA	98.3	60804	47 Las Casas	65.6	61070	37 Prairie Living	69.3
60537	17 Green Acres	60.6	60805	18 Cozy And Comfortable	39.2	61071	32 Rustbelt Traditions	32.1
60538	17 Green Acres	29.3	60827	51 Metro City Edge	38.2	61072	12 Up And Coming Families	34.7
60539	06 Sophisticated Squires	100.0	60901	51 Metro City Edge	18.9	61073	12 Up And Coming Families	23.1
60540	02 Suburban Splendor	37.1	60911	25 Salt Of The Earth	72.5	61074	50 Heartland Communities	40.3
60541	17 Green Acres	99.5	60912	25 Salt Of The Earth	100.0	61075	31 Rural Resort Dwellers	47.3
60542	04 Boomburbs	18.1	60913	17 Green Acres	95.8	61078	25 Salt Of The Earth	50.9
60543	12 Up And Coming Families	44.7	60914	19 Milk And Cookies	25.0	61080	12 Up And Coming Families	25.9
60544	24 Main Street, USA	24.0	60915	32 Rustbelt Traditions	80.3	61081	32 Rustbelt Traditions	18.7
60545	17 Green Acres	66.3	60917	18 Cozy And Comfortable	100.0	61084	25 Salt Of The Earth	50.6
60546	05 Wealthy Seaboard Suburbs	29.1	60918	37 Prairie Living	84.0	61085	50 Heartland Communities	30.4
60548	18 Cozy And Comfortable	27.0	60919	32 Rustbelt Traditions	69.1	61087	29 Rustbelt Retirees	43.4
60549	17 Green Acres	84.6	60921	50 Heartland Communities	89.6	61088	17 Green Acres	92.1
60550	18 Cozy And Comfortable	91.1	60922	25 Salt Of The Earth	63.3	61089	37 Prairie Living	88.6
60551	17 Green Acres	72.0	60924	29 Rustbelt Retirees	55.2	61101	51 Metro City Edge	24.9
60552	17 Green Acres	50.5	60927	17 Green Acres	58.8	61102	51 Metro City Edge	21.2
60553	17 Green Acres	76.7	60928	25 Salt Of The Earth	89.8	61103	32 Rustbelt Traditions	29.7
60554	02 Suburban Splendor	43.4	60929	37 Prairie Living	100.0	61104	60 City Dimensions	49.7
60555	06 Sophisticated Squires	37.5	60930	37 Prairie Living	100.0	61107	29 Rustbelt Retirees	18.1
60556	17 Green Acres	84.3	60931	37 Prairie Living	74.8	61108	32 Rustbelt Traditions	30.6
60558	02 Suburban Splendor	43.0	60934	37 Prairie Living	100.0	61109	53 Home Town	20.6
60559	10 Pleasant-Ville	18.9	60935	25 Salt Of The Earth	92.4	61111	32 Rustbelt Traditions	31.1
60560	12 Up And Coming Families	31.7	60936	29 Rustbelt Retirees	43.5	61112	13 In Style	100.0
60561	07 Exurbanites	34.2	60938	29 Rustbelt Retirees	61.5	61114	13 In Style	35.0
60563	16 Enterprising Professionals	53.3	60940	17 Green Acres	97.2	61115	32 Rustbelt Traditions	39.4
60564	04 Boomburbs	99.4	60941	17 Green Acres	55.9	61201	29 Rustbelt Retirees	17.1
60565	02 Suburban Splendor	67.8	60942	50 Heartland Communities	41.2	61230	25 Salt Of The Earth	100.0
60585	04 Boomburbs	99.4	60946	32 Rustbelt Traditions	73.4	61231	50 Heartland Communities	57.7
60586	04 Boomburbs	56.3	60948	31 Rural Resort Dwellers	52.8	61232	25 Salt Of The Earth	64.4
60601	08 Laptops And Lattes	87.4	60949	42 Southern Satellites	87.7	61234	32 Rustbelt Traditions	72.4
60602	08 Laptops And Lattes	94.3	60950	26 Midland Crowd	39.0	61235	50 Heartland Communities	66.4
60603	22 Metropolitans	52.0	60951	25 Salt Of The Earth	75.1	61238	32 Rustbelt Traditions	47.0
60604	01 Top Rung	89.8	60952	37 Prairie Living	100.0	61240	18 Cozy And Comfortable	29.8
60605	27 Metro Renters	65.7	60953	50 Heartland Communities	57.2	61241	17 Green Acres	26.5
60606	27 Metro Renters	42.0	60954	25 Salt Of The Earth	31.6	61242	25 Salt Of The Earth	83.2
60607	55 College Towns	24.6	60955	42 Southern Satellites	49.7	61243	37 Prairie Living	100.0
60608	58 NeWest Residents	26.9	60957	32 Rustbelt Traditions	65.8	61244	29 Rustbelt Retirees	37.9
60609	58 NeWest Residents	22.6	60959	50 Heartland Communities	70.4	61250	25 Salt Of The Earth	99.3
60610	27 Metro Renters	41.5	60960	50 Heartland Communities	57.2	61251	25 Salt Of The Earth	100.0
60611	08 Laptops And Lattes	51.7	60961	25 Salt Of The Earth	44.5	61252	32 Rustbelt Traditions	38.5
60612	64 City Commons	21.7	60962	37 Prairie Living	100.0	61254	29 Rustbelt Retirees	25.7
60613	27 Metro Renters	67.5	60963	50 Heartland Communities	65.9	61256	29 Rustbelt Retirees	50.9
60614	08 Laptops And Lattes	49.1	60964	32 Rustbelt Traditions	26.3	61257	26 Midland Crowd	59.7
60615	27 Metro Renters	46.7	60966	42 Southern Satellites	46.1	61259	17 Green Acres	68.9
60616	44 Urban Melting Pot	27.0	60968	37 Prairie Living	93.3	61260	25 Salt Of The Earth	54.2
60617	34 Family Foundations	33.4	60970	50 Heartland Communities	35.1	61261	46 Rooted Rural	96.5
60618	35 International Marketplace	63.7	60973	37 Prairie Living	100.0	61262	25 Salt Of The Earth	55.6

ZIP CODE	TOP TAPESTRY CONSUMER TYPE	% 2009 HOUSE-HOLDS	ZIP CODE	TOP TAPESTRY CONSUMER TYPE	% 2009 HOUSE-HOLDS	ZIP CODE	TOP TAPESTRY CONSUMER TYPE	% 2009 HOUSE-HOLDS
61263	32 Rustbelt Traditions	100.0	61447	46 Rooted Rural	70.0	61635	17 Green Acres	100.0
61264	32 Rustbelt Traditions	27.9	61448	25 Salt Of The Earth	34.2	61701	48 Great Expectations	23.8
61265	32 Rustbelt Traditions	21.4	61449	37 Prairie Living	100.0	61704	04 Boomburbs	30.0
61270	25 Salt Of The Earth	50.5	61450	50 Heartland Communities	74.2	61705	07 Exurbanites	28.5
61272	46 Rooted Rural	48.1	61451	25 Salt Of The Earth	93.4	61720	25 Salt Of The Earth	100.0
61273	17 Green Acres	31.0	61452	37 Prairie Living	100.0	61721	37 Prairie Living	100.0
61274	37 Prairie Living	100.0	61453	37 Prairie Living	100.0	61722	17 Green Acres	96.6
61275	25 Salt Of The Earth	91.3	61454	46 Rooted Rural	90.1	61723	32 Rustbelt Traditions	37.4
61277	29 Rustbelt Retirees	41.7	61455	55 College Towns	26.2	61724	25 Salt Of The Earth	97.8
61279	18 Cozy And Comfortable	73.2	61458	50 Heartland Communities	61.3	61725	17 Green Acres	70.7
61281	17 Green Acres	68.6	61459	25 Salt Of The Earth	78.2	61726	32 Rustbelt Traditions	63.6
61282	32 Rustbelt Traditions	40.2	61460	37 Prairie Living	96.5	61727	32 Rustbelt Traditions	25.1
61283	32 Rustbelt Traditions	51.3	61462	53 Home Town	30.9	61728	32 Rustbelt Traditions	70.5
61284	18 Cozy And Comfortable	46.7	61465	29 Rustbelt Retirees	78.2	61729	17 Green Acres	73.1
61285	25 Salt Of The Earth	90.3	61466	25 Salt Of The Earth	97.0	61730	25 Salt Of The Earth	90.2
61301	48 Great Expectations	25.8	61467	25 Salt Of The Earth	67.9	61731	37 Prairie Living	100.0
61310	32 Rustbelt Traditions	42.4	61469	46 Rooted Rural	57.6	61732	19 Milk And Cookies	65.1
61311	25 Salt Of The Earth	89.2	61470	37 Prairie Living	100.0	61733	25 Salt Of The Earth	75.5
61312	25 Salt Of The Earth	63.9	61471	37 Prairie Living	100.0	61734	32 Rustbelt Traditions	28.9
61313	25 Salt Of The Earth	93.8	61472	37 Prairie Living	77.4	61735	17 Green Acres	69.8
61314	32 Rustbelt Traditions	89.9	61473	50 Heartland Communities	36.2	61736	17 Green Acres	86.7
61318	25 Salt Of The Earth	93.7	61474	42 Southern Satellites	81.3	61737	17 Green Acres	100.0
61319	25 Salt Of The Earth	87.5	61475	37 Prairie Living	80.9	61738	18 Cozy And Comfortable	31.1
61320	18 Cozy And Comfortable	79.5	61476	37 Prairie Living	94.5	61739	33 Midlife Junction	46.5
61321	42 Southern Satellites	96.9	61477	37 Prairie Living	55.8	61740	29 Rustbelt Retirees	76.4
61325	25 Salt Of The Earth	68.7	61478	37 Prairie Living	95.3	61741	32 Rustbelt Traditions	41.1
61326	25 Salt Of The Earth	41.2	61479	37 Prairie Living	83.9	61742	17 Green Acres	91.5
61327	25 Salt Of The Earth	76.3	61480	46 Rooted Rural	51.3	61743	17 Green Acres	98.8
61329	32 Rustbelt Traditions	62.1	61482	37 Prairie Living	99.2	61744	25 Salt Of The Earth	66.1
61330	25 Salt Of The Earth	56.8	61483	50 Heartland Communities	36.3	61745	12 Up And Coming Families	42.6
61333	37 Prairie Living	100.0	61484	50 Heartland Communities	90.8	61747	17 Green Acres	95.6
61334	25 Salt Of The Earth	100.0	61485	37 Prairie Living	91.0	61748	12 Up And Coming Families	53.5
61335	25 Salt Of The Earth	69.5	61486	25 Salt Of The Earth	49.1	61749	25 Salt Of The Earth	77.3
61336	25 Salt Of The Earth	60.8	61488	32 Rustbelt Traditions	69.6	61752	17 Green Acres	41.4
61337	25 Salt Of The Earth	60.1	61489	25 Salt Of The Earth	85.5	61753	25 Salt Of The Earth	62.7
61341	17 Green Acres	35.4	61490	50 Heartland Communities	76.6	61754	32 Rustbelt Traditions	63.7
61342	32 Rustbelt Traditions	30.0	61491	50 Heartland Communities	69.8	61755	17 Green Acres	57.8
61344	25 Salt Of The Earth	86.0	61501	50 Heartland Communities	73.9	61756	25 Salt Of The Earth	69.8
61345	25 Salt Of The Earth	99.4	61516	25 Salt Of The Earth	83.7	61759	25 Salt Of The Earth	100.0
61346	25 Salt Of The Earth	89.4	61517	25 Salt Of The Earth	43.9	61760	25 Salt Of The Earth	69.3
61348	50 Heartland Communities	41.5	61519	46 Rooted Rural	100.0	61761	28 Aspiring Young Families	18.3
61349	25 Salt Of The Earth	84.6	61520	50 Heartland Communities	20.0	61764	32 Rustbelt Traditions	19.6
61350	29 Rustbelt Retirees	17.9	61523	32 Rustbelt Traditions	37.9	61769	25 Salt Of The Earth	88.1
61353	25 Salt Of The Earth	100.0	61524	25 Salt Of The Earth	100.0	61770	37 Prairie Living	96.5
61354	29 Rustbelt Retirees	34.0	61525	07 Exurbanites	35.2	61771	37 Prairie Living	77.1
61356	14 Prosperous Empty Nesters	18.8	61526	17 Green Acres	79.5	61772	25 Salt Of The Earth	83.2
61358	42 Southern Satellites	81.8	61528	07 Exurbanites	62.2	61773	37 Prairie Living	100.0
61360	18 Cozy And Comfortable	55.1	61529	32 Rustbelt Traditions	55.6	61774	32 Rustbelt Traditions	85.1
61361	29 Rustbelt Retirees	47.6	61530	29 Rustbelt Retirees	20.2	61775	37 Prairie Living	100.0
61362	29 Rustbelt Retirees	33.6	61531	29 Rustbelt Retirees	50.1	61776	18 Cozy And Comfortable	63.5
61364	50 Heartland Communities	30.1	61532	25 Salt Of The Earth	97.8	61777	25 Salt Of The Earth	77.0
61367	25 Salt Of The Earth	76.9	61533	32 Rustbelt Traditions	59.3	61778	25 Salt Of The Earth	98.5
61368	25 Salt Of The Earth	64.5	61534	17 Green Acres	48.0	61790	55 College Towns	100.0
61369	50 Heartland Communities	82.8	61535	07 Exurbanites	84.1	61801	63 Dorms To Diplomas	35.2
61370	29 Rustbelt Retirees	62.7	61536	25 Salt Of The Earth	63.4	61802	36 Old And Newcomers	19.5
61373	17 Green Acres	54.3	61537	29 Rustbelt Retirees	29.7	61810	37 Prairie Living	100.0
61375	25 Salt Of The Earth	43.3	61540	29 Rustbelt Retirees	84.8	61811	25 Salt Of The Earth	100.0
61376	25 Salt Of The Earth	50.1	61542	57 Simple Living	26.8	61812	37 Prairie Living	100.0
61377	50 Heartland Communities	76.5	61543	25 Salt Of The Earth	91.4	61813	32 Rustbelt Traditions	51.3
61378	25 Salt Of The Earth	87.2	61544	46 Rooted Rural	87.9	61814	25 Salt Of The Earth	67.1
61379	32 Rustbelt Traditions	81.4	61545	25 Salt Of The Earth	76.3	61816	37 Prairie Living	86.0
61401	29 Rustbelt Retirees	19.7	61546	25 Salt Of The Earth	82.9	61817	32 Rustbelt Traditions	60.2
61410	25 Salt Of The Earth	29.5	61547	06 Sophisticated Squires	41.7	61818	32 Rustbelt Traditions	78.7
61411	37 Prairie Living	100.0	61548	06 Sophisticated Squires	26.3	61820	63 Dorms To Diplomas	43.1
61412	46 Rooted Rural	47.0	61550	33 Midlife Junction	40.7	61821	14 Prosperous Empty Nesters	12.8
61413	25 Salt Of The Earth	100.0	61552	07 Exurbanites	100.0	61822	04 Boomburbs	19.2
61414	37 Prairie Living	99.1	61554	32 Rustbelt Traditions	31.2	61830	37 Prairie Living	85.9
61415	37 Prairie Living	38.5	61559	25 Salt Of The Earth	87.1	61831	25 Salt Of The Earth	52.6
61417	37 Prairie Living	72.2	61560	31 Rural Resort Dwellers	87.4	61832	53 Home Town	30.7
61418	46 Rooted Rural	100.0	61561	18 Cozy And Comfortable	35.8	61833	50 Heartland Communities	99.4
61420	50 Heartland Communities	65.3	61563	14 Prosperous Empty Nesters	100.0	61834	25 Salt Of The Earth	28.2
61421	37 Prairie Living	84.6	61565	25 Salt Of The Earth	73.6	61839	25 Salt Of The Earth	94.0
61422	32 Rustbelt Traditions	30.3	61567	25 Salt Of The Earth	100.0	61840	25 Salt Of The Earth	52.9
61423	25 Salt Of The Earth	100.0	61568	17 Green Acres	75.7	61841	46 Rooted Rural	46.2
61425	46 Rooted Rural	71.0	61569	18 Cozy And Comfortable	48.8	61842	25 Salt Of The Earth	48.1
61427	50 Heartland Communities	66.2	61570	32 Rustbelt Traditions	42.4	61843	25 Salt Of The Earth	77.1
61428	31 Rural Resort Dwellers	80.0	61571	18 Cozy And Comfortable	27.0	61844	32 Rustbelt Traditions	54.8
61430	33 Midlife Junction	80.2	61572	25 Salt Of The Earth	100.0	61845	25 Salt Of The Earth	91.4
61431	37 Prairie Living	97.1	61602	57 Simple Living	46.3	61846	50 Heartland Communities	29.4
61432	46 Rooted Rural	97.3	61603	32 Rustbelt Traditions	26.7	61847	25 Salt Of The Earth	88.9
61433	46 Rooted Rural	100.0	61604	32 Rustbelt Traditions	25.3	61849	25 Salt Of The Earth	43.3
61434	50 Heartland Communities	56.4	61605	62 Modest Income Homes	57.3	61850	46 Rooted Rural	93.4
61435	25 Salt Of The Earth	89.2	61606	55 College Towns	54.8	61851	25 Salt Of The Earth	79.8
61436	25 Salt Of The Earth	71.7	61607	29 Rustbelt Retirees	50.3	61852	17 Green Acres	91.9
61437	42 Southern Satellites	67.5	61610	32 Rustbelt Traditions	100.0	61853	19 Milk And Cookies	34.2
61438	37 Prairie Living	99.3	61611	29 Rustbelt Retirees	18.4	61854	32 Rustbelt Traditions	52.5
61440	37 Prairie Living	100.0	61614	22 Metropolitans	29.7	61855	37 Prairie Living	100.0
61441	50 Heartland Communities	65.9	61615	13 In Style	49.3	61856	14 Prosperous Empty Nesters	38.9
61442	42 Southern Satellites	80.2	61616	32 Rustbelt Traditions	52.8	61858	25 Salt Of The Earth	39.7
61443	50 Heartland Communities	35.4	61625	55 College Towns	100.0	61859	19 Milk And Cookies	62.5

CONSUMER TYPE

ZIP CODE	TOP TAPESTRY CONSUMER TYPE	% 2009 HOUSE-HOLDS	ZIP CODE	TOP TAPESTRY CONSUMER TYPE	% 2009 HOUSE-HOLDS	ZIP CODE	TOP TAPESTRY CONSUMER TYPE	% 2009 HOUSE-HOLDS
61862	37 Prairie Living	82.6	62070	46 Rooted Rural	97.1	62320	50 Heartland Communities	60.8
61863	18 Cozy And Comfortable	90.4	62074	50 Heartland Communities	39.9	62321	33 Midlife Junction	50.0
61864	18 Cozy And Comfortable	60.0	62075	50 Heartland Communities	65.2	62323	46 Rooted Rural	97.5
61865	25 Salt Of The Earth	70.2	62079	46 Rooted Rural	64.4	62324	50 Heartland Communities	62.5
61866	48 Great Expectations	23.2	62080	42 Southern Satellites	44.5	62325	37 Prairie Living	76.4
61870	50 Heartland Communities	66.9	62081	46 Rooted Rural	79.2	62326	50 Heartland Communities	62.3
61872	25 Salt Of The Earth	66.7	62082	53 Home Town	50.3	62330	46 Rooted Rural	72.2
61873	12 Up And Coming Families	42.8	62083	46 Rooted Rural	74.6	62334	37 Prairie Living	100.0
61874	16 Enterprising Professionals	36.0	62084	50 Heartland Communities	50.5	62338	25 Salt Of The Earth	65.8
61875	26 Midland Crowd	56.2	62086	46 Rooted Rural	82.9	62339	25 Salt Of The Earth	53.7
61876	46 Rooted Rural	91.9	62087	53 Home Town	61.2	62340	50 Heartland Communities	49.7
61877	33 Midlife Junction	51.1	62088	32 Rustbelt Traditions	45.1	62341	25 Salt Of The Earth	44.6
61878	32 Rustbelt Traditions	84.2	62090	64 City Commons	59.2	62343	37 Prairie Living	63.4
61880	33 Midlife Junction	41.9	62091	25 Salt Of The Earth	67.8	62344	37 Prairie Living	100.0
61882	25 Salt Of The Earth	97.9	62092	50 Heartland Communities	76.3	62345	46 Rooted Rural	99.3
61883	50 Heartland Communities	62.7	62094	50 Heartland Communities	55.5	62346	37 Prairie Living	100.0
61884	17 Green Acres	98.3	62095	32 Rustbelt Traditions	45.9	62347	25 Salt Of The Earth	81.7
61910	25 Salt Of The Earth	48.0	62097	25 Salt Of The Earth	42.5	62348	25 Salt Of The Earth	100.0
61911	42 Southern Satellites	44.7	62201	64 City Commons	43.4	62349	25 Salt Of The Earth	89.0
61912	25 Salt Of The Earth	51.7	62203	34 Family Foundations	66.0	62351	46 Rooted Rural	62.4
61913	46 Rooted Rural	44.8	62204	62 Modest Income Homes	59.2	62352	46 Rooted Rural	69.6
61914	25 Salt Of The Earth	47.2	62205	62 Modest Income Homes	57.3	62353	50 Heartland Communities	53.1
61917	37 Prairie Living	100.0	62206	51 Metro City Edge	46.2	62354	25 Salt Of The Earth	74.0
61919	17 Green Acres	88.4	62207	62 Modest Income Homes	73.3	62355	46 Rooted Rural	90.0
61920	55 College Towns	21.3	62208	29 Rustbelt Retirees	42.7	62356	46 Rooted Rural	97.5
61924	50 Heartland Communities	54.6	62214	25 Salt Of The Earth	61.1	62357	46 Rooted Rural	75.9
61925	25 Salt Of The Earth	67.1	62215	25 Salt Of The Earth	41.1	62358	46 Rooted Rural	40.2
61928	25 Salt Of The Earth	76.5	62217	46 Rooted Rural	99.1	62359	37 Prairie Living	100.0
61929	25 Salt Of The Earth	74.2	62218	17 Green Acres	68.2	62360	32 Rustbelt Traditions	59.5
61930	37 Prairie Living	100.0	62220	48 Great Expectations	26.4	62361	37 Prairie Living	89.6
61931	25 Salt Of The Earth	52.5	62221	28 Aspiring Young Families	31.8	62362	46 Rooted Rural	62.0
61932	37 Prairie Living	100.0	62223	29 Rustbelt Retirees	31.6	62363	50 Heartland Communities	27.4
61933	50 Heartland Communities	89.3	62225	12 Up And Coming Families	58.5	62365	25 Salt Of The Earth	100.0
61937	25 Salt Of The Earth	92.6	62226	48 Great Expectations	21.8	62366	50 Heartland Communities	50.4
61938	32 Rustbelt Traditions	24.8	62230	25 Salt Of The Earth	27.7	62367	37 Prairie Living	100.0
61940	37 Prairie Living	100.0	62231	29 Rustbelt Retirees	19.4	62370	37 Prairie Living	99.6
61942	50 Heartland Communities	61.7	62232	50 Heartland Communities	25.8	62373	37 Prairie Living	83.4
61943	50 Heartland Communities	47.1	62233	50 Heartland Communities	35.0	62374	37 Prairie Living	100.0
61944	50 Heartland Communities	24.2	62234	33 Midlife Junction	21.8	62375	37 Prairie Living	100.0
61951	50 Heartland Communities	39.1	62236	18 Cozy And Comfortable	78.7	62376	25 Salt Of The Earth	76.8
61953	32 Rustbelt Traditions	27.0	62237	25 Salt Of The Earth	38.3	62378	46 Rooted Rural	92.0
61956	32 Rustbelt Traditions	52.7	62238	42 Southern Satellites	82.6	62379	50 Heartland Communities	43.7
61957	25 Salt Of The Earth	67.2	62239	32 Rustbelt Traditions	78.9	62380	37 Prairie Living	100.0
62001	25 Salt Of The Earth	89.9	62240	41 Crossroads	68.8	62401	33 Midlife Junction	31.2
62002	32 Rustbelt Traditions	25.0	62241	25 Salt Of The Earth	81.1	62410	46 Rooted Rural	73.8
62006	37 Prairie Living	94.3	62242	50 Heartland Communities	51.7	62411	25 Salt Of The Earth	35.0
62009	50 Heartland Communities	99.2	62243	18 Cozy And Comfortable	61.3	62413	46 Rooted Rural	87.0
62010	32 Rustbelt Traditions	22.6	62244	25 Salt Of The Earth	58.5	62414	42 Southern Satellites	44.9
62011	46 Rooted Rural	58.2	62245	25 Salt Of The Earth	67.6	62417	50 Heartland Communities	48.8
62012	25 Salt Of The Earth	69.5	62246	33 Midlife Junction	19.9	62418	50 Heartland Communities	38.6
62013	46 Rooted Rural	85.1	62248	17 Green Acres	100.0	62419	42 Southern Satellites	99.4
62014	25 Salt Of The Earth	73.7	62249	17 Green Acres	35.8	62420	50 Heartland Communities	49.5
62015	37 Prairie Living	97.4	62253	46 Rooted Rural	100.0	62421	37 Prairie Living	100.0
62016	50 Heartland Communities	46.1	62254	33 Midlife Junction	68.2	62422	42 Southern Satellites	93.7
62017	50 Heartland Communities	81.5	62255	42 Southern Satellites	60.5	62423	25 Salt Of The Earth	88.3
62018	41 Crossroads	32.9	62257	25 Salt Of The Earth	28.2	62424	25 Salt Of The Earth	99.3
62019	46 Rooted Rural	60.7	62258	18 Cozy And Comfortable	24.7	62425	37 Prairie Living	86.4
62021	17 Green Acres	42.0	62260	17 Green Acres	44.4	62426	42 Southern Satellites	96.1
62022	25 Salt Of The Earth	63.1	62261	25 Salt Of The Earth	83.7	62427	46 Rooted Rural	88.9
62024	29 Rustbelt Retirees	44.9	62262	50 Heartland Communities	47.9	62428	50 Heartland Communities	50.3
62025	22 Metropolitans	34.3	62263	32 Rustbelt Traditions	19.6	62431	42 Southern Satellites	93.3
62027	46 Rooted Rural	59.1	62264	32 Rustbelt Traditions	36.0	62432	46 Rooted Rural	96.1
62028	26 Midland Crowd	60.1	62265	18 Cozy And Comfortable	43.7	62433	50 Heartland Communities	73.7
62030	37 Prairie Living	90.3	62268	25 Salt Of The Earth	100.0	62434	25 Salt Of The Earth	91.5
62031	25 Salt Of The Earth	59.9	62269	13 In Style	23.6	62436	42 Southern Satellites	71.0
62032	46 Rooted Rural	95.6	62271	32 Rustbelt Traditions	49.2	62438	25 Salt Of The Earth	96.1
62033	50 Heartland Communities	50.9	62272	42 Southern Satellites	79.3	62439	29 Rustbelt Retirees	22.8
62034	13 In Style	38.2	62274	50 Heartland Communities	49.2	62440	17 Green Acres	75.7
62035	33 Midlife Junction	34.5	62275	42 Southern Satellites	62.4	62441	25 Salt Of The Earth	38.7
62036	46 Rooted Rural	100.0	62277	42 Southern Satellites	60.7	62442	25 Salt Of The Earth	36.3
62037	26 Midland Crowd	45.2	62278	25 Salt Of The Earth	31.6	62443	42 Southern Satellites	58.9
62040	29 Rustbelt Retirees	30.5	62280	25 Salt Of The Earth	54.1	62445	37 Prairie Living	55.9
62044	50 Heartland Communities	62.8	62281	25 Salt Of The Earth	63.0	62446	46 Rooted Rural	98.1
62045	46 Rooted Rural	65.7	62284	17 Green Acres	43.9	62447	25 Salt Of The Earth	75.0
62047	50 Heartland Communities	95.1	62285	26 Midland Crowd	61.3	62448	50 Heartland Communities	54.4
62048	29 Rustbelt Retirees	59.8	62286	53 Home Town	21.2	62449	50 Heartland Communities	44.2
62049	50 Heartland Communities	35.8	62288	25 Salt Of The Earth	54.9	62450	50 Heartland Communities	36.9
62050	46 Rooted Rural	91.6	62293	33 Midlife Junction	35.6	62451	42 Southern Satellites	39.7
62051	46 Rooted Rural	100.0	62294	28 Aspiring Young Families	28.5	62452	42 Southern Satellites	89.3
62052	50 Heartland Communities	40.3	62295	17 Green Acres	84.7	62454	50 Heartland Communities	42.5
62053	50 Heartland Communities	81.5	62297	46 Rooted Rural	63.6	62458	46 Rooted Rural	55.2
62054	46 Rooted Rural	60.7	62298	17 Green Acres	42.8	62460	46 Rooted Rural	55.7
62056	50 Heartland Communities	39.4	62301	32 Rustbelt Traditions	22.8	62461	37 Prairie Living	87.4
62060	53 Home Town	32.1	62305	26 Midland Crowd	34.3	62462	37 Prairie Living	99.0
62061	32 Rustbelt Traditions	72.7	62311	50 Heartland Communities	91.5	62463	50 Heartland Communities	75.4
62062	13 In Style	37.1	62312	46 Rooted Rural	47.1	62465	25 Salt Of The Earth	97.7
62063	46 Rooted Rural	62.2	62313	37 Prairie Living	100.0	62466	46 Rooted Rural	50.5
62065	50 Heartland Communities	89.6	62314	37 Prairie Living	54.1	62467	25 Salt Of The Earth	94.5
62067	57 Simple Living	60.7	62316	37 Prairie Living	100.0	62468	25 Salt Of The Earth	55.8
62069	50 Heartland Communities	51.6	62319	37 Prairie Living	100.0	62469	26 Midland Crowd	48.8

ZIP CODE	TOP TAPESTRY CONSUMER TYPE	% 2009 HOUSE-HOLDS
62471	50 Heartland Communities	32.2
62473	26 Midland Crowd	86.0
62474	46 Rooted Rural	69.8
62475	37 Prairie Living	50.0
62476	42 Southern Satellites	45.3
62477	46 Rooted Rural	62.8
62478	25 Salt Of The Earth	97.0
62479	25 Salt Of The Earth	74.5
62480	25 Salt Of The Earth	45.9
62481	37 Prairie Living	93.3
62501	25 Salt Of The Earth	60.3
62510	32 Rustbelt Traditions	39.2
62512	25 Salt Of The Earth	100.0
62513	25 Salt Of The Earth	94.8
62514	17 Green Acres	100.0
62515	17 Green Acres	48.8
62517	50 Heartland Communities	100.0
62518	25 Salt Of The Earth	100.0
62520	17 Green Acres	57.6
62521	18 Cozy And Comfortable	21.2
62522	55 College Towns	16.2
62523	65 Social Security Set	98.4
62526	33 Midlife Junction	19.7
62530	32 Rustbelt Traditions	56.5
62531	25 Salt Of The Earth	86.6
62533	25 Salt Of The Earth	82.1
62534	50 Heartland Communities	64.7
62535	07 Exurbanites	100.0
62536	07 Exurbanites	53.6
62538	37 Prairie Living	72.8
62539	32 Rustbelt Traditions	52.1
62543	25 Salt Of The Earth	100.0
62544	25 Salt Of The Earth	54.4
62545	26 Midland Crowd	51.5
62546	29 Rustbelt Retirees	54.2
62547	25 Salt Of The Earth	100.0
62548	29 Rustbelt Retirees	40.5
62549	17 Green Acres	88.9
62550	25 Salt Of The Earth	40.4
62551	32 Rustbelt Traditions	72.2
62553	25 Salt Of The Earth	95.0
62554	25 Salt Of The Earth	58.9
62555	25 Salt Of The Earth	88.7
62556	37 Prairie Living	88.3
62557	50 Heartland Communities	53.8
62558	32 Rustbelt Traditions	55.7
62560	25 Salt Of The Earth	64.3
62561	26 Midland Crowd	36.1
62563	07 Exurbanites	40.6
62565	50 Heartland Communities	31.6
62567	50 Heartland Communities	75.7
62568	50 Heartland Communities	20.0
62571	25 Salt Of The Earth	51.0
62572	26 Midland Crowd	87.5
62573	25 Salt Of The Earth	73.2
62601	37 Prairie Living	100.0
62611	37 Prairie Living	76.5
62612	26 Midland Crowd	52.7
62613	32 Rustbelt Traditions	36.3
62615	32 Rustbelt Traditions	74.2
62617	46 Rooted Rural	100.0
62618	53 Home Town	33.7
62621	37 Prairie Living	73.6
62624	46 Rooted Rural	96.4
62625	17 Green Acres	46.7
62626	33 Midlife Junction	27.2
62627	46 Rooted Rural	90.6
62628	25 Salt Of The Earth	76.6
62629	12 Up And Coming Families	39.0
62630	46 Rooted Rural	64.1
62631	37 Prairie Living	100.0
62633	37 Prairie Living	86.6
62634	37 Prairie Living	63.1
62635	37 Prairie Living	89.2
62638	25 Salt Of The Earth	56.9
62639	25 Salt Of The Earth	50.8
62640	29 Rustbelt Retirees	23.5
62642	32 Rustbelt Traditions	61.7
62643	25 Salt Of The Earth	84.4
62644	50 Heartland Communities	55.2
62649	46 Rooted Rural	77.2
62650	14 Prosperous Empty Nesters	16.2
62655	46 Rooted Rural	98.3
62656	33 Midlife Junction	25.0
62661	26 Midland Crowd	77.7
62664	50 Heartland Communities	31.1
62665	46 Rooted Rural	50.2
62666	25 Salt Of The Earth	93.7
62667	25 Salt Of The Earth	55.8
62668	25 Salt Of The Earth	81.0
62670	32 Rustbelt Traditions	44.0
62671	25 Salt Of The Earth	96.9
62672	46 Rooted Rural	78.6
62673	37 Prairie Living	90.0
62674	50 Heartland Communities	51.7
62675	07 Exurbanites	17.1
62677	17 Green Acres	70.8
62681	50 Heartland Communities	75.5
62682	25 Salt Of The Earth	97.2
62683	37 Prairie Living	100.0
62684	06 Sophisticated Squires	52.6
62685	46 Rooted Rural	72.3
62688	17 Green Acres	58.6
62690	50 Heartland Communities	41.0
62691	50 Heartland Communities	80.4
62692	46 Rooted Rural	38.2
62693	18 Cozy And Comfortable	87.6
62694	50 Heartland Communities	60.5
62701	65 Social Security Set	80.4
62702	32 Rustbelt Traditions	13.8
62703	32 Rustbelt Traditions	21.2
62704	22 Metropolitans	13.3
62707	41 Crossroads	20.8
62711	07 Exurbanites	31.2
62712	07 Exurbanites	53.4
62801	53 Home Town	33.2
62803	37 Prairie Living	100.0
62806	50 Heartland Communities	77.1
62807	46 Rooted Rural	60.2
62808	50 Heartland Communities	57.4
62809	25 Salt Of The Earth	71.2
62810	46 Rooted Rural	86.6
62812	50 Heartland Communities	49.1
62814	46 Rooted Rural	75.5
62815	25 Salt Of The Earth	100.0
62816	46 Rooted Rural	91.6
62817	46 Rooted Rural	100.0
62818	25 Salt Of The Earth	82.6
62819	50 Heartland Communities	100.0
62820	46 Rooted Rural	94.3
62821	50 Heartland Communities	48.6
62822	50 Heartland Communities	74.3
62823	50 Heartland Communities	60.4
62824	46 Rooted Rural	79.6
62827	37 Prairie Living	51.6
62828	37 Prairie Living	53.3
62829	46 Rooted Rural	100.0
62830	50 Heartland Communities	61.2
62831	46 Rooted Rural	75.7
62832	50 Heartland Communities	44.9
62833	25 Salt Of The Earth	87.1
62835	46 Rooted Rural	55.8
62836	46 Rooted Rural	100.0
62837	50 Heartland Communities	75.9
62838	46 Rooted Rural	83.2
62839	50 Heartland Communities	53.1
62842	42 Southern Satellites	100.0
62843	42 Southern Satellites	70.9
62844	50 Heartland Communities	73.3
62846	46 Rooted Rural	100.0
62849	42 Southern Satellites	44.8
62850	46 Rooted Rural	67.9
62851	46 Rooted Rural	64.2
62853	25 Salt Of The Earth	100.0
62854	50 Heartland Communities	57.5
62855	25 Salt Of The Earth	100.0
62858	50 Heartland Communities	38.2
62859	50 Heartland Communities	75.9
62860	46 Rooted Rural	100.0
62862	46 Rooted Rural	97.6
62863	53 Home Town	18.5
62864	46 Rooted Rural	18.8
62865	46 Rooted Rural	79.3
62866	46 Rooted Rural	100.0
62867	50 Heartland Communities	85.4
62868	42 Southern Satellites	68.2
62869	46 Rooted Rural	53.5
62870	50 Heartland Communities	48.4
62871	37 Prairie Living	91.1
62872	26 Midland Crowd	77.9
62875	50 Heartland Communities	76.2
62877	26 Midland Crowd	45.7
62878	42 Southern Satellites	93.2
62880	37 Prairie Living	93.3
62881	25 Salt Of The Earth	19.5
62882	42 Southern Satellites	42.7
62883	46 Rooted Rural	79.1
62884	50 Heartland Communities	55.3
62885	46 Rooted Rural	85.5
62886	42 Southern Satellites	61.5
62887	46 Rooted Rural	56.3
62888	46 Rooted Rural	61.3
62889	25 Salt Of The Earth	71.9
62890	46 Rooted Rural	69.5
62892	25 Salt Of The Earth	100.0
62893	25 Salt Of The Earth	93.8
62894	46 Rooted Rural	86.0
62895	50 Heartland Communities	58.0
62896	50 Heartland Communities	41.5
62897	25 Salt Of The Earth	64.1
62898	26 Midland Crowd	53.3
62899	46 Rooted Rural	100.0
62901	63 Dorms To Diplomas	37.2
62902	55 College Towns	41.5
62903	55 College Towns	69.9
62905	46 Rooted Rural	82.0
62906	50 Heartland Communities	47.2
62907	46 Rooted Rural	100.0
62908	46 Rooted Rural	57.1
62910	42 Southern Satellites	49.9
62912	46 Rooted Rural	93.5
62914	62 Modest Income Homes	46.0
62916	46 Rooted Rural	84.3
62917	46 Rooted Rural	49.8
62918	33 Midlife Junction	38.5
62919	46 Rooted Rural	52.4
62920	46 Rooted Rural	51.6
62922	46 Rooted Rural	66.4
62923	46 Rooted Rural	94.6
62924	32 Rustbelt Traditions	62.4
62926	46 Rooted Rural	47.7
62928	46 Rooted Rural	100.0
62930	50 Heartland Communities	45.6
62931	49 Senior Sun Seekers	79.1
62932	50 Heartland Communities	98.9
62933	33 Midlife Junction	100.0
62934	50 Heartland Communities	79.8
62935	46 Rooted Rural	56.8
62938	46 Rooted Rural	59.0
62939	25 Salt Of The Earth	42.3
62940	50 Heartland Communities	62.6
62941	50 Heartland Communities	72.8
62942	42 Southern Satellites	100.0
62943	46 Rooted Rural	82.0
62946	50 Heartland Communities	47.1
62947	46 Rooted Rural	93.5
62948	50 Heartland Communities	44.8
62950	50 Heartland Communities	93.5
62951	50 Heartland Communities	76.5
62952	50 Heartland Communities	61.3
62954	50 Heartland Communities	97.0
62955	50 Heartland Communities	82.4
62956	50 Heartland Communities	77.8
62957	46 Rooted Rural	100.0
62958	13 In Style	42.0
62959	33 Midlife Junction	17.6
62960	50 Heartland Communities	29.5
62961	46 Rooted Rural	100.0
62962	46 Rooted Rural	100.0
62963	62 Modest Income Homes	100.0
62964	62 Modest Income Homes	45.3
62966	33 Midlife Junction	17.7
62967	46 Rooted Rural	100.0
62970	46 Rooted Rural	90.4
62972	46 Rooted Rural	69.7
62974	46 Rooted Rural	73.9
62975	26 Midland Crowd	51.9
62976	56 Rural Bypasses	90.5
62977	46 Rooted Rural	74.1
62979	50 Heartland Communities	55.2
62982	50 Heartland Communities	100.0
62983	50 Heartland Communities	91.7
62984	50 Heartland Communities	73.0
62985	46 Rooted Rural	100.0
62987	46 Rooted Rural	100.0
62988	56 Rural Bypasses	55.4
62990	46 Rooted Rural	57.6
62992	56 Rural Bypasses	88.8
62994	46 Rooted Rural	95.5
62995	46 Rooted Rural	50.1
62996	46 Rooted Rural	99.7
62997	46 Rooted Rural	100.0
62998	42 Southern Satellites	100.0
62999	50 Heartland Communities	100.0
63005	02 Suburban Splendor	53.3
63010	12 Up And Coming Families	19.5
63011	07 Exurbanites	34.1
63012	19 Milk And Cookies	61.8
63013	17 Green Acres	50.1
63014	25 Salt Of The Earth	72.6

CONSUMER TYPE

ZIP CODE	TOP TAPESTRY CONSUMER TYPE	% 2009 HOUSE-HOLDS	ZIP CODE	TOP TAPESTRY CONSUMER TYPE	% 2009 HOUSE-HOLDS	ZIP CODE	TOP TAPESTRY CONSUMER TYPE	% 2009 HOUSE-HOLDS
63015	26 Midland Crowd	90.5	63147	34 Family Foundations	50.2	63537	50 Heartland Communities	67.1
63016	26 Midland Crowd	67.9	63301	29 Rustbelt Retirees	14.8	63538	37 Prairie Living	100.0
63017	02 Suburban Splendor	25.8	63303	28 Aspiring Young Families	31.6	63539	37 Prairie Living	92.1
63019	18 Cozy And Comfortable	25.2	63304	12 Up And Coming Families	36.5	63540	46 Rooted Rural	91.3
63020	26 Midland Crowd	25.9	63330	31 Rural Resort Dwellers	100.0	63541	37 Prairie Living	100.0
63021	06 Sophisticated Squires	29.2	63332	31 Rural Resort Dwellers	53.1	63543	37 Prairie Living	100.0
63023	26 Midland Crowd	50.6	63333	42 Southern Satellites	66.5	63544	46 Rooted Rural	91.1
63025	04 Boomburbs	61.5	63334	25 Salt Of The Earth	33.2	63545	50 Heartland Communities	67.3
63026	06 Sophisticated Squires	26.2	63336	50 Heartland Communities	50.2	63546	46 Rooted Rural	66.6
63028	26 Midland Crowd	41.0	63339	42 Southern Satellites	91.6	63547	37 Prairie Living	97.6
63030	42 Southern Satellites	66.7	63341	06 Sophisticated Squires	72.6	63548	50 Heartland Communities	76.7
63031	19 Milk And Cookies	21.8	63343	26 Midland Crowd	35.0	63549	50 Heartland Communities	81.7
63033	18 Cozy And Comfortable	28.3	63344	46 Rooted Rural	79.0	63551	46 Rooted Rural	100.0
63034	18 Cozy And Comfortable	31.0	63345	46 Rooted Rural	97.4	63552	50 Heartland Communities	34.8
63036	46 Rooted Rural	94.1	63347	26 Midland Crowd	57.5	63555	50 Heartland Communities	64.0
63037	25 Salt Of The Earth	59.4	63348	17 Green Acres	79.3	63556	53 Home Town	48.2
63038	02 Suburban Splendor	72.6	63349	42 Southern Satellites	63.6	63557	37 Prairie Living	100.0
63039	17 Green Acres	96.3	63350	50 Heartland Communities	58.6	63558	46 Rooted Rural	81.7
63040	04 Boomburbs	99.4	63351	50 Heartland Communities	59.4	63559	46 Rooted Rural	92.7
63041	26 Midland Crowd	71.1	63352	50 Heartland Communities	61.1	63560	37 Prairie Living	96.8
63042	28 Aspiring Young Families	28.1	63353	50 Heartland Communities	70.0	63561	50 Heartland Communities	54.4
63043	18 Cozy And Comfortable	33.7	63357	17 Green Acres	60.4	63563	37 Prairie Living	100.0
63044	24 Main Street, USA	37.5	63359	46 Rooted Rural	50.6	63565	50 Heartland Communities	51.7
63048	50 Heartland Communities	27.9	63361	53 Home Town	41.2	63566	37 Prairie Living	58.7
63049	26 Midland Crowd	40.0	63362	26 Midland Crowd	54.1	63567	46 Rooted Rural	100.0
63050	17 Green Acres	43.7	63363	46 Rooted Rural	63.6	63601	53 Home Town	26.6
63051	26 Midland Crowd	55.1	63366	12 Up And Coming Families	49.0	63620	46 Rooted Rural	100.0
63052	12 Up And Coming Families	41.0	63367	07 Exurbanites	44.4	63621	46 Rooted Rural	98.8
63055	17 Green Acres	81.8	63368	04 Boomburbs	54.8	63622	46 Rooted Rural	52.7
63056	25 Salt Of The Earth	59.2	63369	25 Salt Of The Earth	70.3	63623	46 Rooted Rural	99.7
63060	26 Midland Crowd	51.6	63373	25 Salt Of The Earth	100.0	63624	56 Rural Bypasses	50.6
63061	26 Midland Crowd	86.2	63376	06 Sophisticated Squires	30.7	63625	46 Rooted Rural	100.0
63068	25 Salt Of The Earth	49.1	63377	46 Rooted Rural	39.3	63626	42 Southern Satellites	78.7
63069	26 Midland Crowd	34.1	63379	26 Midland Crowd	46.5	63627	26 Midland Crowd	50.5
63070	41 Crossroads	50.4	63381	17 Green Acres	61.4	63628	42 Southern Satellites	33.2
63071	42 Southern Satellites	100.0	63382	50 Heartland Communities	49.3	63629	42 Southern Satellites	62.2
63072	26 Midland Crowd	95.9	63383	17 Green Acres	33.2	63630	56 Rural Bypasses	42.9
63074	48 Great Expectations	37.0	63384	53 Home Town	38.4	63631	46 Rooted Rural	95.6
63077	42 Southern Satellites	34.9	63385	17 Green Acres	50.1	63633	46 Rooted Rural	96.1
63080	25 Salt Of The Earth	32.9	63386	25 Salt Of The Earth	100.0	63636	46 Rooted Rural	100.0
63084	32 Rustbelt Traditions	32.5	63388	46 Rooted Rural	99.3	63637	46 Rooted Rural	97.3
63087	46 Rooted Rural	73.5	63389	26 Midland Crowd	62.6	63638	42 Southern Satellites	52.3
63088	16 Enterprising Professionals	47.3	63390	26 Midland Crowd	46.1	63640	33 Midlife Junction	35.9
63089	25 Salt Of The Earth	38.5	63401	53 Home Town	30.4	63645	46 Rooted Rural	58.6
63090	17 Green Acres	47.1	63430	42 Southern Satellites	56.8	63648	42 Southern Satellites	53.6
63091	25 Salt Of The Earth	98.2	63431	46 Rooted Rural	72.9	63650	50 Heartland Communities	61.2
63101	52 Inner City Tenants	75.7	63432	37 Prairie Living	100.0	63653	53 Home Town	95.8
63102	27 Metro Renters	92.9	63433	46 Rooted Rural	100.0	63654	46 Rooted Rural	100.0
63103	65 Social Security Set	87.5	63434	37 Prairie Living	100.0	63655	46 Rooted Rural	79.7
63104	36 Old And Newcomers	19.0	63435	53 Home Town	37.5	63656	46 Rooted Rural	84.9
63105	08 Laptops And Lattes	50.5	63436	42 Southern Satellites	59.9	63660	56 Rural Bypasses	68.6
63106	64 City Commons	73.0	63437	50 Heartland Communities	54.2	63662	42 Southern Satellites	59.0
63107	62 Modest Income Homes	66.0	63438	42 Southern Satellites	82.1	63664	42 Southern Satellites	35.5
63108	27 Metro Renters	49.4	63439	37 Prairie Living	71.8	63665	46 Rooted Rural	85.1
63109	32 Rustbelt Traditions	19.7	63440	42 Southern Satellites	43.8	63670	25 Salt Of The Earth	27.7
63110	48 Great Expectations	32.2	63441	46 Rooted Rural	90.1	63673	46 Rooted Rural	34.2
63111	60 City Dimensions	57.7	63443	46 Rooted Rural	82.8	63675	46 Rooted Rural	100.0
63112	62 Modest Income Homes	27.5	63445	50 Heartland Communities	59.0	63701	55 College Towns	18.5
63113	62 Modest Income Homes	70.4	63446	37 Prairie Living	100.0	63703	53 Home Town	33.4
63114	32 Rustbelt Traditions	50.4	63447	50 Heartland Communities	74.4	63730	50 Heartland Communities	59.6
63115	62 Modest Income Homes	65.3	63448	50 Heartland Communities	67.2	63732	25 Salt Of The Earth	92.7
63116	48 Great Expectations	26.2	63450	50 Heartland Communities	88.7	63735	56 Rural Bypasses	72.4
63117	22 Metropolitans	35.4	63451	37 Prairie Living	100.0	63736	26 Midland Crowd	59.5
63118	60 City Dimensions	57.9	63452	50 Heartland Communities	87.6	63739	26 Midland Crowd	95.5
63119	30 Retirement Communities	20.4	63453	37 Prairie Living	100.0	63740	53 Home Town	26.7
63120	62 Modest Income Homes	53.2	63454	25 Salt Of The Earth	69.7	63743	25 Salt Of The Earth	100.0
63121	34 Family Foundations	35.6	63456	50 Heartland Communities	26.3	63744	46 Rooted Rural	100.0
63122	14 Prosperous Empty Nesters	17.6	63457	46 Rooted Rural	99.3	63747	25 Salt Of The Earth	100.0
63123	29 Rustbelt Retirees	33.0	63458	37 Prairie Living	100.0	63748	25 Salt Of The Earth	78.1
63124	03 Connoisseurs	36.0	63459	25 Salt Of The Earth	34.6	63750	46 Rooted Rural	100.0
63125	29 Rustbelt Retirees	39.2	63460	37 Prairie Living	100.0	63751	42 Southern Satellites	60.2
63126	14 Prosperous Empty Nesters	52.3	63461	25 Salt Of The Earth	35.2	63755	17 Green Acres	32.9
63127	30 Retirement Communities	32.9	63462	50 Heartland Communities	53.9	63760	46 Rooted Rural	90.0
63128	14 Prosperous Empty Nesters	42.6	63463	25 Salt Of The Earth	100.0	63763	46 Rooted Rural	80.6
63129	06 Sophisticated Squires	33.7	63464	37 Prairie Living	100.0	63764	42 Southern Satellites	52.0
63130	34 Family Foundations	26.8	63466	37 Prairie Living	96.2	63766	25 Salt Of The Earth	88.4
63131	03 Connoisseurs	47.0	63468	50 Heartland Communities	71.1	63769	25 Salt Of The Earth	99.2
63132	03 Connoisseurs	15.4	63469	50 Heartland Communities	59.0	63770	25 Salt Of The Earth	100.0
63133	62 Modest Income Homes	34.7	63471	25 Salt Of The Earth	100.0	63771	42 Southern Satellites	74.9
63134	51 Metro City Edge	38.8	63472	42 Southern Satellites	75.2	63775	50 Heartland Communities	34.4
63135	51 Metro City Edge	32.6	63473	37 Prairie Living	96.9	63780	25 Salt Of The Earth	40.7
63136	51 Metro City Edge	43.4	63474	46 Rooted Rural	99.1	63781	42 Southern Satellites	99.0
63137	32 Rustbelt Traditions	50.4	63501	33 Midlife Junction	28.5	63782	42 Southern Satellites	100.0
63138	48 Great Expectations	27.9	63530	42 Southern Satellites	78.9	63783	25 Salt Of The Earth	100.0
63139	48 Great Expectations	34.6	63531	37 Prairie Living	100.0	63785	46 Rooted Rural	96.8
63140	64 City Commons	61.9	63532	56 Rural Bypasses	64.7	63787	42 Southern Satellites	54.7
63141	16 Enterprising Professionals	24.5	63533	37 Prairie Living	69.3	63801	42 Southern Satellites	9.9
63143	36 Old And Newcomers	39.5	63534	46 Rooted Rural	90.7	63821	56 Rural Bypasses	70.1
63144	22 Metropolitans	29.7	63535	37 Prairie Living	100.0	63822	53 Home Town	41.7
63146	14 Prosperous Empty Nesters	26.6	63536	37 Prairie Living	97.5	63823	50 Heartland Communities	65.0

ZIP CODE	TOP TAPESTRY CONSUMER TYPE	% 2009 HOUSE-HOLDS	ZIP CODE	TOP TAPESTRY CONSUMER TYPE	% 2009 HOUSE-HOLDS	ZIP CODE	TOP TAPESTRY CONSUMER TYPE	% 2009 HOUSE-HOLDS
63825	50 Heartland Communities	49.3	64064	04 Boomburbs	32.9	64437	37 Prairie Living	68.0
63827	56 Rural Bypasses	99.5	64067	50 Heartland Communities	47.6	64438	37 Prairie Living	100.0
63829	56 Rural Bypasses	70.6	64068	12 Up And Coming Families	22.8	64439	25 Salt Of The Earth	73.0
63830	53 Home Town	34.4	64070	17 Green Acres	100.0	64440	25 Salt Of The Earth	100.0
63833	42 Southern Satellites	89.2	64071	46 Rooted Rural	71.5	64441	37 Prairie Living	100.0
63834	37 Prairie Living	27.8	64074	25 Salt Of The Earth	81.0	64442	37 Prairie Living	88.0
63837	56 Rural Bypasses	87.5	64075	19 Milk And Cookies	43.4	64443	25 Salt Of The Earth	99.8
63841	25 Salt Of The Earth	27.1	64076	26 Midland Crowd	62.8	64444	25 Salt Of The Earth	86.5
63845	53 Home Town	44.8	64077	42 Southern Satellites	61.9	64445	50 Heartland Communities	97.8
63846	42 Southern Satellites	95.3	64078	26 Midland Crowd	48.0	64446	50 Heartland Communities	78.9
63848	53 Home Town	71.3	64079	12 Up And Coming Families	29.0	64448	25 Salt Of The Earth	67.6
63849	56 Rural Bypasses	63.8	64080	12 Up And Coming Families	41.2	64449	42 Southern Satellites	99.0
63851	56 Rural Bypasses	35.5	64081	12 Up And Coming Families	24.1	64451	37 Prairie Living	92.3
63852	56 Rural Bypasses	71.1	64082	06 Sophisticated Squires	69.2	64453	37 Prairie Living	100.0
63855	50 Heartland Communities	45.9	64083	12 Up And Coming Families	47.8	64454	26 Midland Crowd	61.8
63857	53 Home Town	33.7	64084	25 Salt Of The Earth	68.5	64455	37 Prairie Living	100.0
63862	56 Rural Bypasses	88.0	64085	32 Rustbelt Traditions	30.6	64456	50 Heartland Communities	72.2
63863	56 Rural Bypasses	41.0	64086	12 Up And Coming Families	41.3	64457	37 Prairie Living	100.0
63866	56 Rural Bypasses	88.9	64088	17 Green Acres	44.0	64458	37 Prairie Living	100.0
63867	42 Southern Satellites	60.3	64089	12 Up And Coming Families	55.0	64459	25 Salt Of The Earth	100.0
63868	42 Southern Satellites	100.0	64093	28 Aspiring Young Families	23.5	64461	42 Southern Satellites	86.8
63869	50 Heartland Communities	23.4	64096	50 Heartland Communities	75.2	64463	50 Heartland Communities	71.8
63870	42 Southern Satellites	43.1	64097	50 Heartland Communities	63.9	64465	17 Green Acres	27.7
63873	42 Southern Satellites	28.7	64098	17 Green Acres	33.9	64466	37 Prairie Living	100.0
63876	50 Heartland Communities	57.8	64101	27 Metro Renters	100.0	64467	46 Rooted Rural	53.4
63877	42 Southern Satellites	44.6	64105	27 Metro Renters	100.0	64468	55 College Towns	41.3
63879	56 Rural Bypasses	94.2	64106	27 Metro Renters	32.1	64469	50 Heartland Communities	55.4
63901	53 Home Town	24.2	64108	60 City Dimensions	27.7	64470	50 Heartland Communities	71.1
63931	56 Rural Bypasses	95.8	64109	62 Modest Income Homes	42.2	64471	46 Rooted Rural	77.7
63932	46 Rooted Rural	64.4	64110	22 Metropolitans	25.3	64473	37 Prairie Living	100.0
63933	46 Rooted Rural	50.1	64111	39 Young And Restless	22.1	64474	37 Prairie Living	100.0
63934	46 Rooted Rural	69.2	64112	27 Metro Renters	68.8	64475	42 Southern Satellites	98.8
63935	50 Heartland Communities	36.0	64113	03 Connoisseurs	31.6	64476	37 Prairie Living	94.3
63936	42 Southern Satellites	93.1	64114	22 Metropolitans	22.3	64477	50 Heartland Communities	37.4
63937	46 Rooted Rural	43.3	64116	48 Great Expectations	34.5	64479	42 Southern Satellites	99.3
63939	46 Rooted Rural	91.8	64117	32 Rustbelt Traditions	57.5	64480	37 Prairie Living	100.0
63940	56 Rural Bypasses	74.2	64118	28 Aspiring Young Families	17.0	64481	37 Prairie Living	65.0
63941	46 Rooted Rural	100.0	64119	32 Rustbelt Traditions	39.2	64482	50 Heartland Communities	82.2
63942	46 Rooted Rural	100.0	64120	53 Home Town	90.0	64483	46 Rooted Rural	83.2
63943	56 Rural Bypasses	47.5	64123	53 Home Town	72.1	64484	25 Salt Of The Earth	50.6
63944	46 Rooted Rural	66.5	64124	60 City Dimensions	41.4	64485	25 Salt Of The Earth	29.1
63945	26 Midland Crowd	52.8	64125	53 Home Town	100.0	64486	37 Prairie Living	100.0
63950	46 Rooted Rural	100.0	64126	53 Home Town	48.8	64487	37 Prairie Living	95.7
63951	46 Rooted Rural	100.0	64127	62 Modest Income Homes	34.4	64489	37 Prairie Living	54.8
63952	56 Rural Bypasses	84.2	64128	62 Modest Income Homes	66.1	64490	25 Salt Of The Earth	60.7
63953	56 Rural Bypasses	79.1	64129	32 Rustbelt Traditions	43.7	64491	50 Heartland Communities	92.7
63954	56 Rural Bypasses	95.0	64130	62 Modest Income Homes	48.0	64492	25 Salt Of The Earth	81.6
63955	46 Rooted Rural	100.0	64131	36 Old And Newcomers	21.4	64493	25 Salt Of The Earth	57.1
63956	46 Rooted Rural	86.2	64132	51 Metro City Edge	60.5	64494	37 Prairie Living	97.8
63957	50 Heartland Communities	69.3	64133	29 Rustbelt Retirees	35.1	64496	37 Prairie Living	100.0
63960	46 Rooted Rural	54.3	64134	32 Rustbelt Traditions	54.3	64497	26 Midland Crowd	72.3
63961	42 Southern Satellites	53.4	64136	18 Cozy And Comfortable	100.0	64498	37 Prairie Living	100.0
63963	46 Rooted Rural	84.9	64137	36 Old And Newcomers	20.5	64499	37 Prairie Living	98.8
63964	50 Heartland Communities	53.1	64138	18 Cozy And Comfortable	36.4	64501	53 Home Town	25.3
63965	46 Rooted Rural	44.4	64139	18 Cozy And Comfortable	81.1	64503	32 Rustbelt Traditions	46.3
63966	49 Senior Sun Seekers	96.5	64145	15 Silver And Gold	33.5	64504	53 Home Town	35.0
63967	46 Rooted Rural	69.2	64146	33 Midlife Junction	78.5	64505	32 Rustbelt Traditions	28.0
64001	37 Prairie Living	100.0	64147	64 City Commons	74.8	64506	14 Prosperous Empty Nesters	26.1
64011	26 Midland Crowd	37.0	64149	06 Sophisticated Squires	47.1	64507	32 Rustbelt Traditions	26.3
64012	26 Midland Crowd	26.3	64150	52 Inner City Tenants	65.2	64601	50 Heartland Communities	31.8
64014	19 Milk And Cookies	46.8	64151	13 In Style	44.0	64620	37 Prairie Living	65.0
64015	19 Milk And Cookies	53.5	64152	06 Sophisticated Squires	15.3	64622	37 Prairie Living	90.8
64016	32 Rustbelt Traditions	30.9	64153	16 Enterprising Professionals	54.1	64623	37 Prairie Living	74.8
64017	42 Southern Satellites	83.0	64154	16 Enterprising Professionals	52.2	64624	50 Heartland Communities	58.2
64018	17 Green Acres	88.7	64155	12 Up And Coming Families	58.5	64625	46 Rooted Rural	90.7
64019	26 Midland Crowd	46.9	64156	41 Crossroads	54.8	64628	50 Heartland Communities	33.1
64020	50 Heartland Communities	67.2	64157	12 Up And Coming Families	100.0	64630	50 Heartland Communities	73.8
64021	50 Heartland Communities	77.9	64158	12 Up And Coming Families	100.0	64631	50 Heartland Communities	61.4
64022	33 Midlife Junction	68.7	64161	32 Rustbelt Traditions	100.0	64632	50 Heartland Communities	70.2
64024	32 Rustbelt Traditions	25.0	64163	41 Crossroads	87.2	64633	50 Heartland Communities	40.1
64029	12 Up And Coming Families	64.4	64164	41 Crossroads	52.6	64635	46 Rooted Rural	86.8
64030	19 Milk And Cookies	23.0	64165	06 Sophisticated Squires	100.0	64636	50 Heartland Communities	80.2
64034	12 Up And Coming Families	70.7	64166	06 Sophisticated Squires	100.0	64637	46 Rooted Rural	66.2
64035	50 Heartland Communities	69.3	64167	12 Up And Coming Families	100.0	64638	50 Heartland Communities	68.2
64036	42 Southern Satellites	100.0	64401	25 Salt Of The Earth	88.4	64639	37 Prairie Living	100.0
64037	33 Midlife Junction	33.5	64402	50 Heartland Communities	80.5	64640	50 Heartland Communities	58.3
64040	25 Salt Of The Earth	50.7	64421	46 Rooted Rural	100.0	64641	46 Rooted Rural	97.9
64048	17 Green Acres	47.8	64422	37 Prairie Living	100.0	64642	37 Prairie Living	85.1
64050	32 Rustbelt Traditions	29.1	64423	37 Prairie Living	100.0	64643	50 Heartland Communities	85.5
64052	29 Rustbelt Retirees	27.2	64424	50 Heartland Communities	75.1	64644	50 Heartland Communities	66.2
64053	53 Home Town	84.9	64426	37 Prairie Living	96.9	64645	46 Rooted Rural	100.0
64054	32 Rustbelt Traditions	31.2	64427	46 Rooted Rural	67.0	64646	46 Rooted Rural	53.1
64055	29 Rustbelt Retirees	29.0	64428	50 Heartland Communities	70.5	64647	37 Prairie Living	96.6
64056	32 Rustbelt Traditions	36.6	64429	33 Midlife Junction	26.3	64648	50 Heartland Communities	38.5
64057	48 Great Expectations	33.2	64430	25 Salt Of The Earth	83.1	64649	26 Midland Crowd	85.2
64058	19 Milk And Cookies	82.2	64431	50 Heartland Communities	100.0	64650	46 Rooted Rural	92.3
64060	12 Up And Coming Families	56.5	64432	37 Prairie Living	100.0	64651	46 Rooted Rural	99.3
64061	17 Green Acres	50.2	64433	37 Prairie Living	100.0	64652	37 Prairie Living	98.1
64062	17 Green Acres	59.1	64434	37 Prairie Living	99.1	64653	37 Prairie Living	97.7
64063	12 Up And Coming Families	23.8	64436	37 Prairie Living	87.4	64654	37 Prairie Living	100.0

CONSUMER TYPE

ZIP CODE	TOP TAPESTRY CONSUMER TYPE	% 2009 HOUSE-HOLDS	ZIP CODE	TOP TAPESTRY CONSUMER TYPE	% 2009 HOUSE-HOLDS	ZIP CODE	TOP TAPESTRY CONSUMER TYPE	% 2009 HOUSE-HOLDS
64655	37 Prairie Living	100.0	64867	42 Southern Satellites	91.0	65261	50 Heartland Communities	71.9
64656	50 Heartland Communities	100.0	64868	42 Southern Satellites	80.0	65262	26 Midland Crowd	91.2
64657	37 Prairie Living	98.6	64870	48 Great Expectations	38.6	65263	46 Rooted Rural	43.2
64658	50 Heartland Communities	39.8	64873	42 Southern Satellites	60.3	65264	25 Salt Of The Earth	84.1
64659	37 Prairie Living	100.0	64874	42 Southern Satellites	84.1	65265	50 Heartland Communities	39.0
64660	37 Prairie Living	100.0	65001	42 Southern Satellites	58.2	65270	53 Home Town	25.2
64661	46 Rooted Rural	82.7	65010	17 Green Acres	44.8	65274	50 Heartland Communities	69.9
64664	46 Rooted Rural	100.0	65011	46 Rooted Rural	71.3	65275	37 Prairie Living	52.0
64667	46 Rooted Rural	100.0	65013	53 Home Town	45.4	65276	50 Heartland Communities	42.1
64668	50 Heartland Communities	58.5	65014	42 Southern Satellites	68.1	65279	07 Exurbanites	41.3
64670	50 Heartland Communities	68.4	65016	46 Rooted Rural	53.6	65280	46 Rooted Rural	93.6
64671	31 Rural Resort Dwellers	50.3	65017	42 Southern Satellites	59.7	65281	37 Prairie Living	43.3
64672	37 Prairie Living	100.0	65018	50 Heartland Communities	41.0	65282	25 Salt Of The Earth	82.8
64673	50 Heartland Communities	50.1	65020	31 Rural Resort Dwellers	17.2	65283	37 Prairie Living	100.0
64674	50 Heartland Communities	62.0	65023	25 Salt Of The Earth	76.9	65284	26 Midland Crowd	51.1
64676	37 Prairie Living	100.0	65024	50 Heartland Communities	65.9	65285	25 Salt Of The Earth	94.1
64679	50 Heartland Communities	72.3	65025	42 Southern Satellites	75.3	65286	37 Prairie Living	98.7
64681	37 Prairie Living	100.0	65026	42 Southern Satellites	17.6	65287	17 Green Acres	81.2
64682	46 Rooted Rural	55.2	65032	25 Salt Of The Earth	39.4	65301	53 Home Town	21.6
64683	50 Heartland Communities	40.6	65034	42 Southern Satellites	44.1	65305	40 Military Proximity	99.7
64686	46 Rooted Rural	100.0	65035	25 Salt Of The Earth	99.3	65321	37 Prairie Living	97.5
64688	37 Prairie Living	100.0	65037	49 Senior Sun Seekers	51.0	65322	37 Prairie Living	78.6
64689	37 Prairie Living	77.6	65039	17 Green Acres	93.3	65323	46 Rooted Rural	100.0
64701	17 Green Acres	39.4	65040	26 Midland Crowd	77.2	65324	31 Rural Resort Dwellers	39.4
64720	50 Heartland Communities	67.2	65041	50 Heartland Communities	29.7	65325	50 Heartland Communities	65.4
64722	46 Rooted Rural	100.0	65042	26 Midland Crowd	100.0	65326	49 Senior Sun Seekers	100.0
64723	46 Rooted Rural	88.5	65043	26 Midland Crowd	54.0	65329	37 Prairie Living	92.3
64724	50 Heartland Communities	86.9	65046	46 Rooted Rural	85.9	65330	50 Heartland Communities	99.0
64725	32 Rustbelt Traditions	69.0	65047	41 Crossroads	60.9	65332	25 Salt Of The Earth	50.4
64726	37 Prairie Living	94.7	65048	42 Southern Satellites	67.1	65333	42 Southern Satellites	54.3
64728	37 Prairie Living	75.2	65049	15 Silver And Gold	67.1	65334	42 Southern Satellites	57.6
64730	50 Heartland Communities	31.6	65050	42 Southern Satellites	100.0	65335	46 Rooted Rural	57.9
64733	46 Rooted Rural	88.4	65051	25 Salt Of The Earth	41.6	65336	28 Aspiring Young Families	36.7
64734	17 Green Acres	100.0	65052	31 Rural Resort Dwellers	58.3	65337	53 Home Town	58.9
64735	53 Home Town	27.3	65053	17 Green Acres	80.5	65338	50 Heartland Communities	52.3
64738	46 Rooted Rural	97.6	65054	25 Salt Of The Earth	100.0	65339	37 Prairie Living	100.0
64739	25 Salt Of The Earth	80.8	65058	25 Salt Of The Earth	54.6	65340	53 Home Town	30.9
64740	49 Senior Sun Seekers	66.8	65059	26 Midland Crowd	92.0	65344	37 Prairie Living	95.7
64741	46 Rooted Rural	70.0	65061	46 Rooted Rural	93.3	65345	37 Prairie Living	63.2
64742	26 Midland Crowd	72.1	65062	31 Rural Resort Dwellers	100.0	65347	37 Prairie Living	49.9
64744	49 Senior Sun Seekers	20.5	65063	26 Midland Crowd	73.9	65348	46 Rooted Rural	78.6
64745	46 Rooted Rural	100.0	65064	26 Midland Crowd	53.2	65349	50 Heartland Communities	58.4
64746	25 Salt Of The Earth	81.6	65065	31 Rural Resort Dwellers	74.3	65350	32 Rustbelt Traditions	63.9
64747	32 Rustbelt Traditions	42.2	65066	25 Salt Of The Earth	35.8	65351	50 Heartland Communities	58.9
64748	53 Home Town	66.0	65067	42 Southern Satellites	93.3	65354	42 Southern Satellites	94.3
64750	46 Rooted Rural	100.0	65068	25 Salt Of The Earth	74.3	65355	49 Senior Sun Seekers	79.1
64752	46 Rooted Rural	68.9	65069	25 Salt Of The Earth	100.0	65360	50 Heartland Communities	58.3
64755	50 Heartland Communities	32.6	65072	15 Silver And Gold	74.0	65401	33 Midlife Junction	24.4
64756	46 Rooted Rural	100.0	65074	26 Midland Crowd	79.3	65409	55 College Towns	100.0
64759	37 Prairie Living	27.6	65075	37 Prairie Living	100.0	65436	46 Rooted Rural	100.0
64761	42 Southern Satellites	76.7	65076	17 Green Acres	91.2	65438	46 Rooted Rural	52.6
64762	53 Home Town	51.3	65077	42 Southern Satellites	98.8	65439	46 Rooted Rural	100.0
64763	50 Heartland Communities	57.4	65078	50 Heartland Communities	34.3	65440	46 Rooted Rural	100.0
64767	46 Rooted Rural	98.1	65079	15 Silver And Gold	47.1	65441	42 Southern Satellites	82.6
64769	37 Prairie Living	100.0	65080	26 Midland Crowd	100.0	65443	46 Rooted Rural	99.3
64770	37 Prairie Living	94.4	65081	50 Heartland Communities	62.8	65444	46 Rooted Rural	100.0
64771	37 Prairie Living	84.3	65082	46 Rooted Rural	82.0	65446	46 Rooted Rural	78.4
64772	50 Heartland Communities	27.5	65083	42 Southern Satellites	72.6	65449	46 Rooted Rural	90.4
64776	46 Rooted Rural	33.9	65084	50 Heartland Communities	31.6	65452	46 Rooted Rural	96.4
64778	37 Prairie Living	98.7	65085	25 Salt Of The Earth	98.4	65453	50 Heartland Communities	30.9
64779	50 Heartland Communities	88.0	65101	17 Green Acres	26.1	65456	46 Rooted Rural	100.0
64780	37 Prairie Living	100.0	65109	13 In Style	26.3	65457	33 Midlife Junction	72.1
64783	46 Rooted Rural	58.1	65201	55 College Towns	29.6	65459	50 Heartland Communities	40.2
64784	46 Rooted Rural	96.1	65202	28 Aspiring Young Families	43.2	65461	46 Rooted Rural	100.0
64788	46 Rooted Rural	82.1	65203	16 Enterprising Professionals	22.2	65462	46 Rooted Rural	100.0
64790	42 Southern Satellites	100.0	65211	63 Dorms To Diplomas	100.0	65463	42 Southern Satellites	100.0
64801	53 Home Town	24.6	65215	55 College Towns	100.0	65464	46 Rooted Rural	100.0
64804	26 Midland Crowd	19.1	65216	55 College Towns	100.0	65466	46 Rooted Rural	71.4
64831	42 Southern Satellites	62.0	65230	46 Rooted Rural	64.6	65468	46 Rooted Rural	100.0
64832	26 Midland Crowd	85.1	65231	26 Midland Crowd	63.1	65470	46 Rooted Rural	50.3
64833	37 Prairie Living	100.0	65232	46 Rooted Rural	77.9	65473	40 Military Proximity	96.5
64834	17 Green Acres	37.7	65233	33 Midlife Junction	17.1	65479	46 Rooted Rural	92.5
64835	53 Home Town	61.5	65236	50 Heartland Communities	73.5	65483	46 Rooted Rural	67.8
64836	53 Home Town	26.5	65237	42 Southern Satellites	56.0	65484	46 Rooted Rural	100.0
64840	32 Rustbelt Traditions	42.8	65239	25 Salt Of The Earth	99.8	65486	46 Rooted Rural	57.2
64842	42 Southern Satellites	100.0	65240	25 Salt Of The Earth	40.9	65501	46 Rooted Rural	100.0
64843	42 Southern Satellites	86.7	65243	42 Southern Satellites	38.5	65529	46 Rooted Rural	100.0
64844	42 Southern Satellites	87.3	65244	46 Rooted Rural	74.6	65534	46 Rooted Rural	63.0
64847	46 Rooted Rural	78.5	65246	50 Heartland Communities	93.2	65535	42 Southern Satellites	88.4
64848	46 Rooted Rural	48.1	65247	46 Rooted Rural	94.4	65536	42 Southern Satellites	27.7
64850	42 Southern Satellites	26.7	65248	50 Heartland Communities	42.0	65541	46 Rooted Rural	100.0
64854	42 Southern Satellites	59.0	65250	42 Southern Satellites	99.0	65542	46 Rooted Rural	63.1
64855	26 Midland Crowd	50.2	65251	26 Midland Crowd	31.9	65543	46 Rooted Rural	100.0
64856	41 Crossroads	53.3	65254	53 Home Town	48.7	65548	50 Heartland Communities	57.5
64859	37 Prairie Living	49.2	65255	26 Midland Crowd	78.1	65550	46 Rooted Rural	43.2
64861	37 Prairie Living	89.2	65256	26 Midland Crowd	98.1	65552	26 Midland Crowd	60.3
64862	42 Southern Satellites	45.0	65257	50 Heartland Communities	49.4	65555	46 Rooted Rural	100.0
64863	42 Southern Satellites	100.0	65258	42 Southern Satellites	82.4	65556	46 Rooted Rural	41.7
64865	42 Southern Satellites	39.3	65259	42 Southern Satellites	41.3	65557	46 Rooted Rural	91.7
64866	42 Southern Satellites	100.0	65260	25 Salt Of The Earth	94.1	65559	50 Heartland Communities	45.8

ZIP CODE	TOP TAPESTRY CONSUMER TYPE	% 2009 HOUSE-HOLDS
65560	46 Rooted Rural	50.8
65564	46 Rooted Rural	100.0
65565	42 Southern Satellites	35.3
65566	46 Rooted Rural	100.0
65567	42 Southern Satellites	75.9
65570	46 Rooted Rural	100.0
65571	46 Rooted Rural	50.4
65580	46 Rooted Rural	71.4
65582	25 Salt Of The Earth	57.3
65583	26 Midland Crowd	48.6
65584	41 Crossroads	46.2
65586	46 Rooted Rural	100.0
65588	56 Rural Bypasses	64.8
65589	46 Rooted Rural	100.0
65590	42 Southern Satellites	63.7
65591	46 Rooted Rural	94.5
65601	37 Prairie Living	51.0
65603	37 Prairie Living	100.0
65604	46 Rooted Rural	82.6
65605	42 Southern Satellites	46.6
65606	46 Rooted Rural	73.9
65608	46 Rooted Rural	51.5
65609	42 Southern Satellites	85.2
65610	50 Heartland Communities	39.2
65611	49 Senior Sun Seekers	84.3
65612	25 Salt Of The Earth	96.3
65613	33 Midlife Junction	32.1
65614	46 Rooted Rural	95.0
65616	33 Midlife Junction	48.6
65617	26 Midland Crowd	76.3
65618	46 Rooted Rural	100.0
65619	19 Milk And Cookies	47.1
65620	42 Southern Satellites	100.0
65622	46 Rooted Rural	33.7
65623	42 Southern Satellites	98.9
65624	46 Rooted Rural	100.0
65625	46 Rooted Rural	31.3
65626	46 Rooted Rural	56.4
65627	41 Crossroads	96.1
65629	42 Southern Satellites	82.4
65630	26 Midland Crowd	70.3
65631	26 Midland Crowd	66.0
65632	46 Rooted Rural	57.1
65633	50 Heartland Communities	56.8
65634	46 Rooted Rural	95.6
65635	46 Rooted Rural	83.2
65637	46 Rooted Rural	59.5
65638	37 Prairie Living	59.9
65640	46 Rooted Rural	95.0
65641	46 Rooted Rural	47.2
65644	42 Southern Satellites	94.8
65646	46 Rooted Rural	44.8
65647	42 Southern Satellites	93.8
65648	26 Midland Crowd	82.5
65649	50 Heartland Communities	42.9
65650	46 Rooted Rural	99.4
65652	42 Southern Satellites	51.1
65653	49 Senior Sun Seekers	32.1
65654	37 Prairie Living	100.0
65655	46 Rooted Rural	63.7
65656	46 Rooted Rural	60.7
65657	42 Southern Satellites	100.0
65658	49 Senior Sun Seekers	99.4
65660	37 Prairie Living	100.0
65661	50 Heartland Communities	79.1
65662	42 Southern Satellites	67.9
65663	46 Rooted Rural	51.0
65666	46 Rooted Rural	71.6
65667	50 Heartland Communities	40.0
65668	49 Senior Sun Seekers	95.6
65669	26 Midland Crowd	100.0
65672	48 Great Expectations	45.2
65674	50 Heartland Communities	70.1
65675	46 Rooted Rural	89.3
65676	49 Senior Sun Seekers	82.5
65679	46 Rooted Rural	87.5
65680	49 Senior Sun Seekers	63.5
65681	31 Rural Resort Dwellers	77.8
65682	37 Prairie Living	50.3
65685	46 Rooted Rural	84.1
65686	15 Silver And Gold	51.2
65688	42 Southern Satellites	100.0
65689	50 Heartland Communities	58.5
65690	46 Rooted Rural	100.0
65692	46 Rooted Rural	65.8
65702	46 Rooted Rural	100.0
65704	46 Rooted Rural	54.3
65705	42 Southern Satellites	31.4
65706	26 Midland Crowd	20.5
65707	50 Heartland Communities	43.5
65708	25 Salt Of The Earth	23.8
65710	46 Rooted Rural	70.0
65711	37 Prairie Living	22.4
65712	50 Heartland Communities	40.4
65713	46 Rooted Rural	85.6
65714	28 Aspiring Young Families	49.0
65715	37 Prairie Living	82.9
65717	46 Rooted Rural	56.7
65720	42 Southern Satellites	88.9
65721	12 Up And Coming Families	38.0
65722	42 Southern Satellites	74.9
65723	42 Southern Satellites	34.5
65724	49 Senior Sun Seekers	100.0
65725	26 Midland Crowd	56.4
65727	46 Rooted Rural	100.0
65728	26 Midland Crowd	100.0
65729	49 Senior Sun Seekers	67.9
65730	26 Midland Crowd	69.2
65731	46 Rooted Rural	100.0
65732	46 Rooted Rural	96.3
65733	46 Rooted Rural	98.9
65734	42 Southern Satellites	74.1
65735	46 Rooted Rural	100.0
65737	46 Rooted Rural	50.4
65738	26 Midland Crowd	53.1
65739	31 Rural Resort Dwellers	100.0
65740	49 Senior Sun Seekers	99.9
65742	26 Midland Crowd	67.5
65744	46 Rooted Rural	100.0
65745	42 Southern Satellites	100.0
65746	42 Southern Satellites	62.2
65747	31 Rural Resort Dwellers	51.4
65752	37 Prairie Living	99.0
65753	42 Southern Satellites	69.6
65754	26 Midland Crowd	100.0
65755	46 Rooted Rural	100.0
65756	42 Southern Satellites	98.3
65757	26 Midland Crowd	68.6
65759	42 Southern Satellites	70.2
65760	46 Rooted Rural	100.0
65761	49 Senior Sun Seekers	84.0
65762	37 Prairie Living	69.3
65764	37 Prairie Living	92.1
65766	46 Rooted Rural	97.1
65767	46 Rooted Rural	100.0
65768	37 Prairie Living	93.0
65769	42 Southern Satellites	92.9
65770	25 Salt Of The Earth	78.2
65771	26 Midland Crowd	56.7
65772	42 Southern Satellites	98.8
65773	46 Rooted Rural	76.2
65774	46 Rooted Rural	93.3
65775	42 Southern Satellites	20.8
65777	46 Rooted Rural	100.0
65778	46 Rooted Rural	100.0
65779	49 Senior Sun Seekers	60.0
65781	25 Salt Of The Earth	50.5
65783	42 Southern Satellites	88.9
65784	46 Rooted Rural	100.0
65785	46 Rooted Rural	53.6
65786	42 Southern Satellites	46.7
65787	31 Rural Resort Dwellers	56.4
65788	42 Southern Satellites	74.3
65789	46 Rooted Rural	74.0
65790	42 Southern Satellites	100.0
65791	50 Heartland Communities	71.0
65793	50 Heartland Communities	40.8
65802	53 Home Town	31.2
65803	53 Home Town	33.8
65804	33 Midlife Junction	29.6
65806	63 Dorms To Diplomas	29.7
65807	55 College Towns	11.8
65809	07 Exurbanites	46.7
65810	17 Green Acres	24.1
66002	25 Salt Of The Earth	27.2
66006	17 Green Acres	51.6
66007	18 Cozy And Comfortable	54.8
66008	37 Prairie Living	100.0
66010	46 Rooted Rural	100.0
66012	48 Great Expectations	28.0
66013	17 Green Acres	32.7
66014	46 Rooted Rural	93.9
66015	37 Prairie Living	98.5
66016	25 Salt Of The Earth	100.0
66017	37 Prairie Living	100.0
66018	19 Milk And Cookies	77.4
66020	26 Midland Crowd	65.1
66021	19 Milk And Cookies	62.8
66023	37 Prairie Living	72.8
66025	28 Aspiring Young Families	38.1
66026	37 Prairie Living	42.8
66027	40 Military Proximity	98.7
66030	12 Up And Coming Families	28.3
66031	17 Green Acres	100.0
66032	50 Heartland Communities	52.4
66033	37 Prairie Living	83.7
66035	50 Heartland Communities	83.9
66039	46 Rooted Rural	70.9
66040	46 Rooted Rural	57.5
66041	25 Salt Of The Earth	72.7
66042	25 Salt Of The Earth	80.1
66043	19 Milk And Cookies	35.2
66044	63 Dorms To Diplomas	24.5
66045	63 Dorms To Diplomas	100.0
66046	55 College Towns	26.5
66047	22 Metropolitans	47.7
66048	32 Rustbelt Traditions	20.2
66049	13 In Style	38.5
66050	26 Midland Crowd	64.5
66052	25 Salt Of The Earth	59.7
66053	17 Green Acres	43.3
66054	17 Green Acres	57.0
66056	46 Rooted Rural	99.9
66058	37 Prairie Living	100.0
66060	37 Prairie Living	82.1
66061	28 Aspiring Young Families	17.7
66062	04 Boomburbs	26.5
66064	32 Rustbelt Traditions	27.8
66066	46 Rooted Rural	64.4
66067	32 Rustbelt Traditions	31.3
66070	31 Rural Resort Dwellers	51.4
66071	17 Green Acres	39.8
66072	25 Salt Of The Earth	88.9
66073	26 Midland Crowd	64.3
66075	46 Rooted Rural	63.8
66076	46 Rooted Rural	63.9
66078	25 Salt Of The Earth	87.4
66079	25 Salt Of The Earth	100.0
66080	42 Southern Satellites	62.9
66083	17 Green Acres	45.6
66085	04 Boomburbs	43.3
66086	17 Green Acres	65.7
66087	50 Heartland Communities	46.5
66088	37 Prairie Living	47.1
66090	46 Rooted Rural	30.8
66091	46 Rooted Rural	52.2
66092	26 Midland Crowd	35.0
66093	37 Prairie Living	100.0
66094	37 Prairie Living	100.0
66095	46 Rooted Rural	87.5
66097	25 Salt Of The Earth	89.5
66101	62 Modest Income Homes	20.2
66102	53 Home Town	35.1
66103	39 Young And Restless	38.7
66104	51 Metro City Edge	20.2
66105	59 Southwestern Families	76.7
66106	32 Rustbelt Traditions	44.7
66109	32 Rustbelt Traditions	28.9
66111	41 Crossroads	29.9
66112	32 Rustbelt Traditions	22.5
66113	41 Crossroads	100.0
66118	66 Unclassified	100.0
66202	39 Young And Restless	23.2
66203	33 Midlife Junction	20.0
66204	36 Old And Newcomers	20.8
66205	22 Metropolitans	40.7
66206	03 Connoisseurs	49.2
66207	14 Prosperous Empty Nesters	61.2
66208	22 Metropolitans	24.7
66209	02 Suburban Splendor	51.6
66210	16 Enterprising Professionals	38.2
66211	03 Connoisseurs	59.4
66212	14 Prosperous Empty Nesters	18.1
66213	04 Boomburbs	56.2
66214	39 Young And Restless	32.6
66215	39 Young And Restless	19.8
66216	18 Cozy And Comfortable	20.5
66217	02 Suburban Splendor	50.1
66218	04 Boomburbs	72.8
66219	16 Enterprising Professionals	35.3
66220	02 Suburban Splendor	80.2
66221	04 Boomburbs	87.1
66223	04 Boomburbs	100.0
66224	04 Boomburbs	100.0
66226	04 Boomburbs	60.8
66227	07 Exurbanites	59.2
66401	50 Heartland Communities	43.0
66402	19 Milk And Cookies	53.3
66403	37 Prairie Living	100.0
66404	37 Prairie Living	100.0

CONSUMER TYPE

ZIP CODE	TOP TAPESTRY CONSUMER TYPE	% 2009 HOUSE-HOLDS	ZIP CODE	TOP TAPESTRY CONSUMER TYPE	% 2009 HOUSE-HOLDS	ZIP CODE	TOP TAPESTRY CONSUMER TYPE	% 2009 HOUSE-HOLDS
66406	37 Prairie Living	100.0	66710	50 Heartland Communities	70.6	66939	37 Prairie Living	100.0
66407	26 Midland Crowd	95.8	66711	50 Heartland Communities	92.2	66940	37 Prairie Living	100.0
66408	37 Prairie Living	100.0	66712	50 Heartland Communities	97.2	66941	37 Prairie Living	100.0
66409	17 Green Acres	95.1	66713	50 Heartland Communities	35.5	66942	37 Prairie Living	100.0
66411	50 Heartland Communities	84.6	66714	46 Rooted Rural	53.7	66943	50 Heartland Communities	81.3
66412	37 Prairie Living	100.0	66716	46 Rooted Rural	87.3	66944	37 Prairie Living	100.0
66413	50 Heartland Communities	62.6	66717	46 Rooted Rural	100.0	66945	37 Prairie Living	100.0
66414	17 Green Acres	31.5	66720	32 Rustbelt Traditions	27.6	66946	37 Prairie Living	100.0
66415	50 Heartland Communities	87.0	66724	50 Heartland Communities	81.0	66948	37 Prairie Living	100.0
66416	37 Prairie Living	100.0	66725	50 Heartland Communities	50.6	66949	50 Heartland Communities	86.9
66417	37 Prairie Living	84.5	66728	25 Salt Of The Earth	100.0	66951	37 Prairie Living	100.0
66418	25 Salt Of The Earth	100.0	66732	37 Prairie Living	100.0	66952	37 Prairie Living	100.0
66419	37 Prairie Living	84.7	66733	50 Heartland Communities	53.2	66953	37 Prairie Living	92.9
66422	26 Midland Crowd	84.6	66734	37 Prairie Living	90.4	66955	37 Prairie Living	100.0
66423	46 Rooted Rural	92.1	66735	46 Rooted Rural	85.8	66956	50 Heartland Communities	69.3
66424	37 Prairie Living	100.0	66736	50 Heartland Communities	52.7	66958	37 Prairie Living	98.0
66425	37 Prairie Living	100.0	66738	46 Rooted Rural	93.2	66959	37 Prairie Living	100.0
66427	50 Heartland Communities	69.6	66739	42 Southern Satellites	30.0	66960	37 Prairie Living	100.0
66428	37 Prairie Living	100.0	66740	37 Prairie Living	67.5	66961	37 Prairie Living	100.0
66429	25 Salt Of The Earth	77.2	66743	53 Home Town	29.2	66962	37 Prairie Living	100.0
66431	37 Prairie Living	72.8	66746	37 Prairie Living	100.0	66963	37 Prairie Living	98.4
66432	37 Prairie Living	100.0	66748	50 Heartland Communities	77.3	66964	37 Prairie Living	100.0
66434	50 Heartland Communities	37.9	66749	57 Simple Living	16.9	66966	37 Prairie Living	100.0
66436	33 Midlife Junction	26.5	66751	42 Southern Satellites	86.4	66967	50 Heartland Communities	84.2
66438	37 Prairie Living	100.0	66753	37 Prairie Living	91.6	66968	50 Heartland Communities	78.3
66439	50 Heartland Communities	75.9	66754	46 Rooted Rural	100.0	66970	37 Prairie Living	100.0
66440	17 Green Acres	65.8	66755	37 Prairie Living	100.0	67001	25 Salt Of The Earth	85.7
66441	33 Midlife Junction	16.9	66756	46 Rooted Rural	96.6	67002	12 Up And Coming Families	52.7
66442	40 Military Proximity	100.0	66757	42 Southern Satellites	25.6	67003	50 Heartland Communities	93.7
66449	37 Prairie Living	98.2	66758	37 Prairie Living	100.0	67004	50 Heartland Communities	76.0
66451	25 Salt Of The Earth	87.9	66759	46 Rooted Rural	65.8	67005	53 Home Town	29.5
66502	55 College Towns	32.7	66761	37 Prairie Living	100.0	67008	46 Rooted Rural	58.7
66503	16 Enterprising Professionals	29.5	66762	55 College Towns	22.8	67009	50 Heartland Communities	74.9
66506	63 Dorms To Diplomas	100.0	66763	50 Heartland Communities	87.5	67010	17 Green Acres	36.1
66507	25 Salt Of The Earth	59.3	66767	46 Rooted Rural	100.0	67013	32 Rustbelt Traditions	60.0
66508	50 Heartland Communities	65.3	66769	37 Prairie Living	76.9	67016	26 Midland Crowd	100.0
66509	25 Salt Of The Earth	93.7	66770	25 Salt Of The Earth	74.1	67017	17 Green Acres	85.6
66510	25 Salt Of The Earth	97.7	66771	37 Prairie Living	83.5	67018	37 Prairie Living	100.0
66512	17 Green Acres	46.8	66772	37 Prairie Living	100.0	67019	46 Rooted Rural	80.2
66514	26 Midland Crowd	100.0	66773	46 Rooted Rural	68.8	67020	32 Rustbelt Traditions	56.1
66515	37 Prairie Living	100.0	66775	37 Prairie Living	100.0	67021	37 Prairie Living	100.0
66516	37 Prairie Living	100.0	66776	42 Southern Satellites	73.6	67022	50 Heartland Communities	76.8
66517	28 Aspiring Young Families	100.0	66777	49 Senior Sun Seekers	97.2	67023	46 Rooted Rural	94.0
66518	37 Prairie Living	100.0	66778	46 Rooted Rural	100.0	67024	50 Heartland Communities	64.2
66520	37 Prairie Living	100.0	66779	37 Prairie Living	96.1	67025	25 Salt Of The Earth	75.5
66521	50 Heartland Communities	56.8	66780	37 Prairie Living	100.0	67026	17 Green Acres	63.4
66522	37 Prairie Living	100.0	66781	42 Southern Satellites	69.2	67028	37 Prairie Living	100.0
66523	50 Heartland Communities	78.2	66783	50 Heartland Communities	72.3	67029	50 Heartland Communities	78.8
66524	17 Green Acres	50.1	66801	55 College Towns	16.9	67030	17 Green Acres	82.4
66526	26 Midland Crowd	65.1	66830	37 Prairie Living	100.0	67031	25 Salt Of The Earth	52.5
66527	37 Prairie Living	100.0	66833	37 Prairie Living	100.0	67035	37 Prairie Living	100.0
66528	42 Southern Satellites	98.8	66834	37 Prairie Living	100.0	67036	37 Prairie Living	100.0
66531	37 Prairie Living	96.1	66835	25 Salt Of The Earth	97.6	67037	06 Sophisticated Squires	27.8
66532	37 Prairie Living	95.5	66838	37 Prairie Living	100.0	67038	37 Prairie Living	100.0
66533	17 Green Acres	54.7	66839	50 Heartland Communities	52.8	67039	32 Rustbelt Traditions	50.2
66534	50 Heartland Communities	79.3	66840	37 Prairie Living	99.7	67042	32 Rustbelt Traditions	20.6
66535	26 Midland Crowd	100.0	66842	37 Prairie Living	100.0	67045	50 Heartland Communities	81.5
66536	25 Salt Of The Earth	50.3	66843	37 Prairie Living	100.0	67047	49 Senior Sun Seekers	82.8
66537	46 Rooted Rural	83.1	66845	50 Heartland Communities	80.1	67049	37 Prairie Living	100.0
66538	50 Heartland Communities	78.4	66846	50 Heartland Communities	48.8	67050	17 Green Acres	100.0
66539	17 Green Acres	100.0	66849	37 Prairie Living	100.0	67051	37 Prairie Living	87.5
66540	37 Prairie Living	90.5	66850	37 Prairie Living	100.0	67052	26 Midland Crowd	33.5
66541	37 Prairie Living	100.0	66851	50 Heartland Communities	90.5	67053	25 Salt Of The Earth	100.0
66542	07 Exurbanites	62.6	66852	37 Prairie Living	89.6	67054	50 Heartland Communities	91.9
66543	25 Salt Of The Earth	92.8	66853	46 Rooted Rural	82.4	67055	04 Boomburbs	100.0
66544	37 Prairie Living	90.9	66854	46 Rooted Rural	83.8	67056	32 Rustbelt Traditions	42.5
66546	17 Green Acres	85.4	66856	25 Salt Of The Earth	94.3	67057	37 Prairie Living	100.0
66547	17 Green Acres	58.7	66857	37 Prairie Living	100.0	67058	50 Heartland Communities	76.7
66548	50 Heartland Communities	81.2	66858	37 Prairie Living	100.0	67059	37 Prairie Living	100.0
66549	37 Prairie Living	98.1	66859	37 Prairie Living	100.0	67060	25 Salt Of The Earth	31.4
66550	37 Prairie Living	100.0	66860	50 Heartland Communities	67.9	67061	37 Prairie Living	100.0
66552	37 Prairie Living	100.0	66861	31 Rural Resort Dwellers	37.0	67062	26 Midland Crowd	52.1
66554	37 Prairie Living	55.1	66862	37 Prairie Living	100.0	67063	50 Heartland Communities	33.7
66603	60 City Dimensions	54.1	66864	25 Salt Of The Earth	100.0	67065	37 Prairie Living	100.0
66604	33 Midlife Junction	22.0	66865	25 Salt Of The Earth	95.7	67066	37 Prairie Living	100.0
66605	53 Home Town	34.1	66866	37 Prairie Living	62.7	67067	06 Sophisticated Squires	92.8
66606	32 Rustbelt Traditions	30.7	66868	37 Prairie Living	90.6	67068	50 Heartland Communities	33.1
66607	60 City Dimensions	34.7	66869	46 Rooted Rural	56.5	67070	37 Prairie Living	100.0
66608	53 Home Town	51.5	66870	46 Rooted Rural	57.6	67071	37 Prairie Living	100.0
66609	19 Milk And Cookies	31.9	66871	46 Rooted Rural	80.9	67072	26 Midland Crowd	94.7
66610	07 Exurbanites	49.2	66872	50 Heartland Communities	66.7	67073	37 Prairie Living	100.0
66611	22 Metropolitans	23.7	66873	37 Prairie Living	100.0	67074	26 Midland Crowd	67.3
66612	57 Simple Living	25.2	66901	50 Heartland Communities	42.1	67101	17 Green Acres	60.6
66614	13 In Style	19.8	66930	37 Prairie Living	100.0	67102	37 Prairie Living	100.0
66615	12 Up And Coming Families	65.8	66932	37 Prairie Living	100.0	67103	37 Prairie Living	100.0
66616	32 Rustbelt Traditions	49.4	66933	37 Prairie Living	100.0	67104	37 Prairie Living	71.4
66617	17 Green Acres	49.6	66935	50 Heartland Communities	57.3	67105	25 Salt Of The Earth	85.7
66618	17 Green Acres	77.7	66936	37 Prairie Living	100.0	67106	25 Salt Of The Earth	83.6
66619	28 Aspiring Young Families	73.1	66937	37 Prairie Living	100.0	67107	33 Midlife Junction	44.3
66701	53 Home Town	32.1	66938	50 Heartland Communities	74.9	67108	32 Rustbelt Traditions	65.5

ZIP CODE	TOP TAPESTRY CONSUMER TYPE	% 2009 HOUSE-HOLDS	ZIP CODE	TOP TAPESTRY CONSUMER TYPE	% 2009 HOUSE-HOLDS	ZIP CODE	TOP TAPESTRY CONSUMER TYPE	% 2009 HOUSE-HOLDS
67109	37 Prairie Living	100.0	67422	25 Salt Of The Earth	98.4	67567	37 Prairie Living	100.0
67110	19 Milk And Cookies	50.3	67423	37 Prairie Living	100.0	67568	37 Prairie Living	100.0
67111	25 Salt Of The Earth	100.0	67425	37 Prairie Living	96.7	67570	37 Prairie Living	79.8
67112	37 Prairie Living	100.0	67427	37 Prairie Living	100.0	67572	37 Prairie Living	100.0
67114	26 Midland Crowd	25.8	67428	42 Southern Satellites	59.8	67573	37 Prairie Living	100.0
67117	30 Retirement Communities	100.0	67430	50 Heartland Communities	100.0	67574	37 Prairie Living	100.0
67118	25 Salt Of The Earth	100.0	67431	29 Rustbelt Retirees	37.0	67575	37 Prairie Living	100.0
67119	50 Heartland Communities	75.6	67432	50 Heartland Communities	51.5	67576	50 Heartland Communities	63.5
67120	17 Green Acres	74.3	67436	37 Prairie Living	100.0	67578	50 Heartland Communities	85.4
67122	37 Prairie Living	67.0	67437	50 Heartland Communities	93.7	67579	33 Midlife Junction	41.3
67123	32 Rustbelt Traditions	93.9	67438	37 Prairie Living	100.0	67581	37 Prairie Living	100.0
67124	50 Heartland Communities	40.1	67439	33 Midlife Junction	30.2	67583	37 Prairie Living	100.0
67127	50 Heartland Communities	84.1	67441	37 Prairie Living	100.0	67584	37 Prairie Living	100.0
67131	25 Salt Of The Earth	100.0	67442	37 Prairie Living	84.5	67601	22 Metropolitans	21.1
67132	26 Midland Crowd	97.7	67443	25 Salt Of The Earth	70.6	67621	37 Prairie Living	100.0
67133	17 Green Acres	44.2	67444	37 Prairie Living	100.0	67622	37 Prairie Living	100.0
67134	37 Prairie Living	100.0	67445	37 Prairie Living	100.0	67623	37 Prairie Living	100.0
67135	32 Rustbelt Traditions	43.6	67446	50 Heartland Communities	91.9	67625	37 Prairie Living	100.0
67137	37 Prairie Living	92.0	67447	37 Prairie Living	100.0	67626	37 Prairie Living	100.0
67138	37 Prairie Living	100.0	67448	37 Prairie Living	64.3	67627	37 Prairie Living	100.0
67140	37 Prairie Living	100.0	67449	50 Heartland Communities	61.3	67628	37 Prairie Living	100.0
67142	37 Prairie Living	83.8	67450	37 Prairie Living	100.0	67629	37 Prairie Living	100.0
67143	37 Prairie Living	100.0	67451	37 Prairie Living	100.0	67631	37 Prairie Living	100.0
67144	26 Midland Crowd	100.0	67452	37 Prairie Living	100.0	67632	37 Prairie Living	100.0
67146	25 Salt Of The Earth	92.7	67454	50 Heartland Communities	87.3	67634	37 Prairie Living	100.0
67147	17 Green Acres	33.2	67455	50 Heartland Communities	83.4	67635	37 Prairie Living	100.0
67149	17 Green Acres	100.0	67456	33 Midlife Junction	51.0	67637	50 Heartland Communities	43.1
67150	37 Prairie Living	100.0	67457	37 Prairie Living	100.0	67638	37 Prairie Living	100.0
67151	37 Prairie Living	79.5	67458	37 Prairie Living	100.0	67639	37 Prairie Living	97.1
67152	50 Heartland Communities	31.6	67459	37 Prairie Living	100.0	67640	37 Prairie Living	100.0
67154	25 Salt Of The Earth	75.9	67460	33 Midlife Junction	30.9	67642	50 Heartland Communities	85.8
67155	37 Prairie Living	100.0	67464	37 Prairie Living	100.0	67643	37 Prairie Living	100.0
67156	50 Heartland Communities	18.4	67466	50 Heartland Communities	86.0	67644	37 Prairie Living	100.0
67159	37 Prairie Living	100.0	67467	50 Heartland Communities	68.2	67645	37 Prairie Living	100.0
67202	65 Social Security Set	83.6	67468	37 Prairie Living	100.0	67646	37 Prairie Living	100.0
67203	32 Rustbelt Traditions	18.5	67470	17 Green Acres	74.8	67647	37 Prairie Living	100.0
67204	25 Salt Of The Earth	17.5	67473	37 Prairie Living	56.1	67648	37 Prairie Living	100.0
67205	04 Boomburbs	67.7	67474	37 Prairie Living	97.7	67649	37 Prairie Living	100.0
67206	14 Prosperous Empty Nesters	36.2	67475	37 Prairie Living	100.0	67650	37 Prairie Living	100.0
67207	28 Aspiring Young Families	23.8	67476	25 Salt Of The Earth	100.0	67651	37 Prairie Living	100.0
67208	48 Great Expectations	20.9	67478	37 Prairie Living	100.0	67653	37 Prairie Living	100.0
67209	12 Up And Coming Families	38.3	67480	25 Salt Of The Earth	72.1	67654	50 Heartland Communities	88.2
67210	12 Up And Coming Families	20.6	67481	37 Prairie Living	100.0	67656	37 Prairie Living	100.0
67211	53 Home Town	43.9	67482	37 Prairie Living	100.0	67657	37 Prairie Living	100.0
67212	06 Sophisticated Squires	18.0	67483	37 Prairie Living	100.0	67658	37 Prairie Living	100.0
67213	53 Home Town	62.1	67484	37 Prairie Living	100.0	67659	37 Prairie Living	71.4
67214	62 Modest Income Homes	42.9	67485	37 Prairie Living	100.0	67660	37 Prairie Living	100.0
67215	19 Milk And Cookies	49.9	67487	26 Midland Crowd	82.2	67661	50 Heartland Communities	54.2
67216	41 Crossroads	29.4	67490	50 Heartland Communities	80.4	67663	50 Heartland Communities	77.8
67217	32 Rustbelt Traditions	48.2	67491	37 Prairie Living	100.0	67664	37 Prairie Living	100.0
67218	32 Rustbelt Traditions	26.6	67492	37 Prairie Living	100.0	67665	50 Heartland Communities	93.1
67219	19 Milk And Cookies	24.1	67501	53 Home Town	35.4	67669	50 Heartland Communities	79.4
67220	12 Up And Coming Families	41.7	67502	29 Rustbelt Retirees	16.7	67671	29 Rustbelt Retirees	41.1
67221	40 Military Proximity	100.0	67505	42 Southern Satellites	56.2	67672	37 Prairie Living	44.1
67223	06 Sophisticated Squires	78.0	67510	37 Prairie Living	100.0	67673	37 Prairie Living	100.0
67226	04 Boomburbs	34.8	67511	37 Prairie Living	100.0	67675	37 Prairie Living	100.0
67227	17 Green Acres	100.0	67512	37 Prairie Living	100.0	67701	33 Midlife Junction	36.6
67228	04 Boomburbs	100.0	67513	37 Prairie Living	100.0	67730	50 Heartland Communities	77.5
67230	02 Suburban Splendor	41.6	67514	37 Prairie Living	100.0	67731	37 Prairie Living	100.0
67232	26 Midland Crowd	100.0	67516	37 Prairie Living	100.0	67732	37 Prairie Living	100.0
67235	04 Boomburbs	44.9	67518	37 Prairie Living	100.0	67733	37 Prairie Living	100.0
67301	53 Home Town	32.1	67519	37 Prairie Living	100.0	67734	37 Prairie Living	100.0
67330	50 Heartland Communities	77.3	67520	50 Heartland Communities	94.5	67735	50 Heartland Communities	35.8
67332	37 Prairie Living	93.9	67521	37 Prairie Living	100.0	67736	37 Prairie Living	100.0
67333	50 Heartland Communities	74.7	67522	25 Salt Of The Earth	95.6	67737	37 Prairie Living	100.0
67335	50 Heartland Communities	48.7	67523	37 Prairie Living	100.0	67738	37 Prairie Living	100.0
67336	50 Heartland Communities	85.5	67524	46 Rooted Rural	90.6	67739	37 Prairie Living	100.0
67337	50 Heartland Communities	31.5	67525	37 Prairie Living	100.0	67740	37 Prairie Living	100.0
67341	25 Salt Of The Earth	100.0	67526	37 Prairie Living	46.0	67741	37 Prairie Living	100.0
67342	25 Salt Of The Earth	94.6	67529	37 Prairie Living	100.0	67743	37 Prairie Living	100.0
67344	46 Rooted Rural	72.3	67530	33 Midlife Junction	16.0	67744	37 Prairie Living	100.0
67345	37 Prairie Living	91.4	67543	25 Salt Of The Earth	75.2	67745	37 Prairie Living	100.0
67346	46 Rooted Rural	94.7	67544	50 Heartland Communities	75.3	67748	50 Heartland Communities	92.4
67347	46 Rooted Rural	100.0	67545	37 Prairie Living	100.0	67749	50 Heartland Communities	57.7
67349	50 Heartland Communities	84.3	67546	50 Heartland Communities	56.9	67751	37 Prairie Living	100.0
67351	25 Salt Of The Earth	100.0	67547	50 Heartland Communities	88.1	67752	37 Prairie Living	100.0
67352	50 Heartland Communities	83.0	67548	50 Heartland Communities	97.7	67753	37 Prairie Living	100.0
67353	50 Heartland Communities	93.6	67550	50 Heartland Communities	49.9	67756	37 Prairie Living	56.8
67354	42 Southern Satellites	78.0	67552	37 Prairie Living	100.0	67757	37 Prairie Living	100.0
67355	46 Rooted Rural	100.0	67553	37 Prairie Living	100.0	67758	37 Prairie Living	100.0
67356	50 Heartland Communities	76.6	67554	50 Heartland Communities	63.7	67761	37 Prairie Living	100.0
67357	53 Home Town	42.5	67556	37 Prairie Living	100.0	67762	37 Prairie Living	100.0
67360	46 Rooted Rural	88.4	67557	37 Prairie Living	100.0	67764	37 Prairie Living	83.8
67361	50 Heartland Communities	73.2	67559	37 Prairie Living	100.0	67801	38 Industrious Urban Fringe	26.4
67401	53 Home Town	18.6	67560	37 Prairie Living	55.2	67831	37 Prairie Living	100.0
67410	37 Prairie Living	24.6	67561	42 Southern Satellites	56.5	67834	37 Prairie Living	100.0
67416	26 Midland Crowd	70.9	67563	37 Prairie Living	100.0	67835	26 Midland Crowd	75.2
67417	37 Prairie Living	100.0	67564	37 Prairie Living	100.0	67837	37 Prairie Living	100.0
67418	37 Prairie Living	100.0	67565	50 Heartland Communities	71.2	67838	37 Prairie Living	99.8
67420	37 Prairie Living	67.7	67566	37 Prairie Living	100.0	67839	37 Prairie Living	67.9

CONSUMER TYPE

ZIP CODE	TOP TAPESTRY CONSUMER TYPE	% 2009 HOUSE-HOLDS	ZIP CODE	TOP TAPESTRY CONSUMER TYPE	% 2009 HOUSE-HOLDS	ZIP CODE	TOP TAPESTRY CONSUMER TYPE	% 2009 HOUSE-HOLDS
67840	37 Prairie Living	100.0	68110	62 Modest Income Homes	40.4	68371	37 Prairie Living	100.0
67841	37 Prairie Living	100.0	68111	51 Metro City Edge	63.1	68372	17 Green Acres	50.1
67842	37 Prairie Living	100.0	68112	32 Rustbelt Traditions	44.5	68375	37 Prairie Living	79.2
67844	37 Prairie Living	100.0	68113	40 Military Proximity	100.0	68376	50 Heartland Communities	84.9
67846	41 Crossroads	28.5	68114	30 Retirement Communities	18.7	68377	37 Prairie Living	100.0
67849	37 Prairie Living	100.0	68116	04 Boomburbs	46.5	68378	37 Prairie Living	100.0
67850	37 Prairie Living	82.9	68117	32 Rustbelt Traditions	89.4	68379	37 Prairie Living	100.0
67851	19 Milk And Cookies	86.7	68118	04 Boomburbs	42.8	68380	37 Prairie Living	100.0
67853	37 Prairie Living	100.0	68122	12 Up And Coming Families	76.7	68381	50 Heartland Communities	100.0
67854	50 Heartland Communities	67.0	68123	12 Up And Coming Families	24.8	68401	37 Prairie Living	100.0
67855	37 Prairie Living	100.0	68124	14 Prosperous Empty Nesters	29.6	68402	17 Green Acres	100.0
67857	37 Prairie Living	100.0	68127	39 Young And Restless	40.0	68404	17 Green Acres	100.0
67859	41 Crossroads	58.7	68128	12 Up And Coming Families	26.1	68405	33 Midlife Junction	71.3
67860	26 Midland Crowd	75.9	68130	02 Suburban Splendor	29.0	68406	37 Prairie Living	100.0
67861	37 Prairie Living	66.4	68131	39 Young And Restless	28.5	68407	37 Prairie Living	83.7
67862	37 Prairie Living	100.0	68132	36 Old And Newcomers	18.0	68409	25 Salt Of The Earth	77.3
67863	37 Prairie Living	100.0	68133	04 Boomburbs	39.1	68410	25 Salt Of The Earth	35.4
67864	50 Heartland Communities	83.3	68134	18 Cozy And Comfortable	26.9	68413	37 Prairie Living	93.8
67865	37 Prairie Living	100.0	68135	04 Boomburbs	68.0	68414	46 Rooted Rural	98.6
67867	37 Prairie Living	100.0	68136	12 Up And Coming Families	68.0	68415	37 Prairie Living	100.0
67868	37 Prairie Living	100.0	68137	19 Milk And Cookies	49.7	68416	37 Prairie Living	100.0
67869	37 Prairie Living	99.1	68138	12 Up And Coming Families	49.5	68417	37 Prairie Living	100.0
67870	37 Prairie Living	98.5	68142	12 Up And Coming Families	81.8	68418	17 Green Acres	86.4
67871	37 Prairie Living	44.5	68144	14 Prosperous Empty Nesters	16.2	68420	50 Heartland Communities	82.7
67876	37 Prairie Living	100.0	68147	32 Rustbelt Traditions	56.2	68421	50 Heartland Communities	86.1
67877	37 Prairie Living	60.8	68152	14 Prosperous Empty Nesters	23.9	68422	37 Prairie Living	100.0
67878	37 Prairie Living	100.0	68154	39 Young And Restless	30.5	68423	17 Green Acres	100.0
67879	37 Prairie Living	100.0	68157	19 Milk And Cookies	59.9	68424	37 Prairie Living	100.0
67880	26 Midland Crowd	29.5	68164	12 Up And Coming Families	15.0	68428	17 Green Acres	100.0
67882	37 Prairie Living	79.4	68182	14 Prosperous Empty Nesters	0.0	68429	37 Prairie Living	100.0
67901	38 Industrious Urban Fringe	24.6	68198	55 College Towns	0.0	68430	17 Green Acres	87.0
67950	26 Midland Crowd	51.2	68301	37 Prairie Living	84.5	68431	37 Prairie Living	100.0
67951	37 Prairie Living	33.8	68303	37 Prairie Living	97.2	68433	37 Prairie Living	100.0
67952	37 Prairie Living	100.0	68304	37 Prairie Living	100.0	68434	33 Midlife Junction	65.6
67953	37 Prairie Living	100.0	68305	50 Heartland Communities	46.3	68436	37 Prairie Living	100.0
67954	37 Prairie Living	100.0	68307	37 Prairie Living	99.6	68437	46 Rooted Rural	100.0
68001	37 Prairie Living	100.0	68309	50 Heartland Communities	100.0	68439	37 Prairie Living	100.0
68002	25 Salt Of The Earth	67.7	68310	25 Salt Of The Earth	19.6	68440	37 Prairie Living	100.0
68003	32 Rustbelt Traditions	35.5	68313	37 Prairie Living	100.0	68441	37 Prairie Living	100.0
68004	37 Prairie Living	100.0	68314	37 Prairie Living	84.1	68442	46 Rooted Rural	100.0
68005	33 Midlife Junction	23.2	68315	37 Prairie Living	98.5	68443	37 Prairie Living	100.0
68007	17 Green Acres	51.0	68316	37 Prairie Living	100.0	68444	37 Prairie Living	100.0
68008	17 Green Acres	35.1	68317	25 Salt Of The Earth	44.2	68445	37 Prairie Living	100.0
68010	16 Enterprising Professionals	100.0	68318	50 Heartland Communities	91.4	68446	29 Rustbelt Retirees	60.6
68014	37 Prairie Living	100.0	68319	37 Prairie Living	100.0	68447	37 Prairie Living	100.0
68015	46 Rooted Rural	83.5	68320	37 Prairie Living	100.0	68448	37 Prairie Living	100.0
68017	25 Salt Of The Earth	84.0	68321	46 Rooted Rural	100.0	68450	37 Prairie Living	50.5
68018	37 Prairie Living	95.5	68322	37 Prairie Living	100.0	68452	37 Prairie Living	100.0
68019	37 Prairie Living	100.0	68323	37 Prairie Living	100.0	68453	37 Prairie Living	100.0
68020	37 Prairie Living	97.5	68324	37 Prairie Living	100.0	68454	17 Green Acres	90.1
68022	12 Up And Coming Families	36.5	68325	37 Prairie Living	100.0	68455	37 Prairie Living	95.0
68023	06 Sophisticated Squires	42.2	68326	37 Prairie Living	100.0	68456	37 Prairie Living	100.0
68025	32 Rustbelt Traditions	26.7	68327	37 Prairie Living	98.3	68457	46 Rooted Rural	90.0
68028	06 Sophisticated Squires	25.5	68328	37 Prairie Living	100.0	68458	37 Prairie Living	87.7
68029	37 Prairie Living	100.0	68329	37 Prairie Living	100.0	68460	37 Prairie Living	100.0
68030	37 Prairie Living	97.3	68330	37 Prairie Living	100.0	68461	07 Exurbanites	68.4
68031	25 Salt Of The Earth	54.4	68331	37 Prairie Living	100.0	68462	19 Milk And Cookies	74.6
68033	25 Salt Of The Earth	69.4	68332	37 Prairie Living	100.0	68463	25 Salt Of The Earth	67.5
68034	17 Green Acres	90.8	68333	33 Midlife Junction	49.9	68464	37 Prairie Living	95.5
68036	37 Prairie Living	100.0	68335	37 Prairie Living	100.0	68465	25 Salt Of The Earth	90.9
68037	32 Rustbelt Traditions	66.5	68336	17 Green Acres	99.5	68466	50 Heartland Communities	95.9
68038	50 Heartland Communities	75.2	68337	37 Prairie Living	94.7	68467	50 Heartland Communities	18.8
68039	51 Metro City Edge	82.9	68338	37 Prairie Living	100.0	68502	48 Great Expectations	35.9
68040	37 Prairie Living	100.0	68339	17 Green Acres	100.0	68503	48 Great Expectations	28.6
68041	25 Salt Of The Earth	90.8	68340	37 Prairie Living	100.0	68504	39 Young And Restless	27.8
68044	26 Midland Crowd	66.7	68341	25 Salt Of The Earth	75.0	68505	18 Cozy And Comfortable	23.3
68045	50 Heartland Communities	69.3	68342	37 Prairie Living	100.0	68506	13 In Style	16.9
68046	06 Sophisticated Squires	25.2	68343	37 Prairie Living	100.0	68507	32 Rustbelt Traditions	42.9
68047	29 Rustbelt Retirees	37.1	68344	37 Prairie Living	100.0	68508	55 College Towns	27.7
68048	17 Green Acres	32.8	68345	37 Prairie Living	100.0	68510	48 Great Expectations	18.0
68050	37 Prairie Living	100.0	68346	37 Prairie Living	100.0	68512	13 In Style	38.9
68055	37 Prairie Living	100.0	68347	19 Milk And Cookies	80.9	68514	17 Green Acres	92.9
68057	50 Heartland Communities	58.7	68348	37 Prairie Living	100.0	68516	04 Boomburbs	22.6
68059	07 Exurbanites	43.6	68349	37 Prairie Living	94.8	68517	17 Green Acres	89.1
68061	37 Prairie Living	100.0	68350	37 Prairie Living	100.0	68520	07 Exurbanites	85.9
68062	37 Prairie Living	100.0	68351	37 Prairie Living	100.0	68521	28 Aspiring Young Families	23.2
68064	33 Midlife Junction	36.1	68352	50 Heartland Communities	53.3	68522	12 Up And Coming Families	54.2
68065	25 Salt Of The Earth	79.0	68354	37 Prairie Living	100.0	68523	17 Green Acres	100.0
68066	25 Salt Of The Earth	49.9	68355	50 Heartland Communities	85.6	68524	28 Aspiring Young Families	65.1
68067	50 Heartland Communities	84.5	68357	37 Prairie Living	100.0	68526	07 Exurbanites	100.0
68069	07 Exurbanites	47.6	68358	17 Green Acres	87.0	68527	17 Green Acres	77.8
68070	25 Salt Of The Earth	84.7	68359	50 Heartland Communities	72.8	68528	12 Up And Coming Families	73.3
68071	51 Metro City Edge	89.9	68360	17 Green Acres	100.0	68531	17 Green Acres	100.0
68073	19 Milk And Cookies	82.6	68361	37 Prairie Living	61.8	68532	17 Green Acres	100.0
68102	65 Social Security Set	47.5	68362	50 Heartland Communities	100.0	68583	39 Young And Restless	100.0
68104	32 Rustbelt Traditions	44.1	68365	37 Prairie Living	100.0	68588	63 Dorms To Diplomas	100.0
68105	32 Rustbelt Traditions	19.6	68366	25 Salt Of The Earth	90.7	68601	32 Rustbelt Traditions	29.8
68106	32 Rustbelt Traditions	21.9	68367	37 Prairie Living	100.0	68620	37 Prairie Living	74.3
68107	32 Rustbelt Traditions	36.0	68368	25 Salt Of The Earth	87.6	68621	25 Salt Of The Earth	52.3
68108	53 Home Town	41.5	68370	50 Heartland Communities	90.0	68622	37 Prairie Living	100.0

ZIP CODE	TOP TAPESTRY CONSUMER TYPE	% 2009 HOUSE-HOLDS	ZIP CODE	TOP TAPESTRY CONSUMER TYPE	% 2009 HOUSE-HOLDS	ZIP CODE	TOP TAPESTRY CONSUMER TYPE	% 2009 HOUSE-HOLDS
68623	37 Prairie Living	100.0	68771	37 Prairie Living	100.0	68927	37 Prairie Living	100.0
68624	37 Prairie Living	98.3	68773	37 Prairie Living	100.0	68928	37 Prairie Living	97.9
68626	37 Prairie Living	100.0	68774	37 Prairie Living	100.0	68929	37 Prairie Living	93.8
68627	37 Prairie Living	100.0	68776	41 Crossroads	18.6	68930	50 Heartland Communities	70.6
68628	37 Prairie Living	100.0	68777	37 Prairie Living	100.0	68932	37 Prairie Living	100.0
68629	50 Heartland Communities	60.5	68778	37 Prairie Living	100.0	68933	46 Rooted Rural	85.3
68631	37 Prairie Living	100.0	68779	50 Heartland Communities	38.1	68934	37 Prairie Living	100.0
68632	50 Heartland Communities	75.9	68780	37 Prairie Living	100.0	68935	37 Prairie Living	100.0
68633	37 Prairie Living	100.0	68781	37 Prairie Living	51.4	68936	37 Prairie Living	100.0
68635	37 Prairie Living	100.0	68783	37 Prairie Living	93.5	68937	37 Prairie Living	70.7
68636	37 Prairie Living	100.0	68784	50 Heartland Communities	59.8	68938	37 Prairie Living	100.0
68637	37 Prairie Living	100.0	68785	37 Prairie Living	100.0	68939	50 Heartland Communities	53.0
68638	37 Prairie Living	65.6	68786	37 Prairie Living	100.0	68940	37 Prairie Living	100.0
68640	50 Heartland Communities	60.8	68787	33 Midlife Junction	55.3	68941	37 Prairie Living	100.0
68641	37 Prairie Living	100.0	68788	37 Prairie Living	37.3	68942	37 Prairie Living	87.0
68642	37 Prairie Living	100.0	68789	37 Prairie Living	100.0	68943	37 Prairie Living	90.7
68643	37 Prairie Living	100.0	68790	37 Prairie Living	100.0	68944	37 Prairie Living	99.8
68644	37 Prairie Living	98.2	68791	37 Prairie Living	100.0	68945	37 Prairie Living	100.0
68647	25 Salt Of The Earth	73.7	68792	37 Prairie Living	100.0	68946	37 Prairie Living	100.0
68648	37 Prairie Living	100.0	68801	32 Rustbelt Traditions	24.6	68947	37 Prairie Living	100.0
68649	50 Heartland Communities	75.1	68803	33 Midlife Junction	16.7	68948	37 Prairie Living	100.0
68651	37 Prairie Living	100.0	68810	17 Green Acres	74.6	68949	32 Rustbelt Traditions	32.9
68652	37 Prairie Living	100.0	68812	37 Prairie Living	100.0	68950	37 Prairie Living	100.0
68653	37 Prairie Living	74.8	68813	37 Prairie Living	100.0	68952	37 Prairie Living	90.6
68654	37 Prairie Living	100.0	68814	37 Prairie Living	100.0	68954	37 Prairie Living	100.0
68655	37 Prairie Living	100.0	68815	37 Prairie Living	100.0	68955	26 Midland Crowd	77.5
68658	37 Prairie Living	100.0	68816	37 Prairie Living	100.0	68956	37 Prairie Living	100.0
68659	37 Prairie Living	100.0	68817	37 Prairie Living	100.0	68957	37 Prairie Living	100.0
68660	50 Heartland Communities	81.3	68818	17 Green Acres	24.8	68958	37 Prairie Living	96.4
68661	42 Southern Satellites	40.8	68820	37 Prairie Living	100.0	68959	50 Heartland Communities	42.2
68662	37 Prairie Living	100.0	68821	37 Prairie Living	100.0	68960	37 Prairie Living	100.0
68663	37 Prairie Living	100.0	68822	37 Prairie Living	52.0	68961	37 Prairie Living	100.0
68665	37 Prairie Living	100.0	68823	50 Heartland Communities	70.1	68964	37 Prairie Living	100.0
68666	50 Heartland Communities	77.0	68824	37 Prairie Living	100.0	68966	31 Rural Resort Dwellers	84.9
68667	37 Prairie Living	100.0	68825	37 Prairie Living	100.0	68967	37 Prairie Living	100.0
68669	37 Prairie Living	100.0	68826	50 Heartland Communities	63.4	68969	37 Prairie Living	100.0
68701	26 Midland Crowd	20.4	68827	37 Prairie Living	86.8	68970	37 Prairie Living	57.7
68710	37 Prairie Living	100.0	68828	37 Prairie Living	100.0	68971	37 Prairie Living	73.7
68711	37 Prairie Living	100.0	68831	37 Prairie Living	100.0	68972	37 Prairie Living	100.0
68713	37 Prairie Living	100.0	68832	26 Midland Crowd	56.3	68973	37 Prairie Living	100.0
68714	50 Heartland Communities	67.2	68833	37 Prairie Living	100.0	68974	37 Prairie Living	100.0
68715	25 Salt Of The Earth	81.5	68834	37 Prairie Living	100.0	68975	37 Prairie Living	87.3
68716	37 Prairie Living	100.0	68835	37 Prairie Living	100.0	68976	37 Prairie Living	100.0
68717	37 Prairie Living	100.0	68836	42 Southern Satellites	69.4	68977	37 Prairie Living	100.0
68718	50 Heartland Communities	73.3	68837	37 Prairie Living	100.0	68978	50 Heartland Communities	91.5
68719	37 Prairie Living	100.0	68838	37 Prairie Living	100.0	68979	37 Prairie Living	61.8
68720	37 Prairie Living	100.0	68840	42 Southern Satellites	46.5	68980	37 Prairie Living	100.0
68722	37 Prairie Living	100.0	68841	37 Prairie Living	100.0	68981	37 Prairie Living	100.0
68723	37 Prairie Living	100.0	68842	37 Prairie Living	100.0	68982	37 Prairie Living	100.0
68724	37 Prairie Living	62.7	68843	37 Prairie Living	100.0	69001	50 Heartland Communities	41.8
68725	37 Prairie Living	100.0	68844	37 Prairie Living	100.0	69020	46 Rooted Rural	94.1
68726	37 Prairie Living	100.0	68845	13 In Style	27.3	69021	37 Prairie Living	52.8
68727	50 Heartland Communities	76.7	68846	37 Prairie Living	100.0	69022	50 Heartland Communities	56.0
68728	37 Prairie Living	100.0	68847	48 Great Expectations	22.8	69023	37 Prairie Living	100.0
68729	37 Prairie Living	100.0	68849	55 College Towns	100.0	69024	46 Rooted Rural	65.0
68730	37 Prairie Living	100.0	68850	38 Industrious Urban Fringe	36.9	69025	50 Heartland Communities	84.9
68731	41 Crossroads	74.8	68852	37 Prairie Living	100.0	69026	37 Prairie Living	100.0
68732	37 Prairie Living	100.0	68853	50 Heartland Communities	79.5	69027	37 Prairie Living	100.0
68733	37 Prairie Living	83.1	68854	37 Prairie Living	100.0	69028	37 Prairie Living	100.0
68734	37 Prairie Living	100.0	68855	37 Prairie Living	100.0	69029	37 Prairie Living	100.0
68735	37 Prairie Living	100.0	68856	37 Prairie Living	100.0	69030	37 Prairie Living	100.0
68736	37 Prairie Living	100.0	68858	37 Prairie Living	100.0	69032	37 Prairie Living	100.0
68739	50 Heartland Communities	67.1	68859	37 Prairie Living	100.0	69033	37 Prairie Living	54.0
68740	37 Prairie Living	100.0	68860	37 Prairie Living	100.0	69034	46 Rooted Rural	69.1
68741	37 Prairie Living	51.4	68861	17 Green Acres	100.0	69036	37 Prairie Living	100.0
68742	37 Prairie Living	100.0	68862	50 Heartland Communities	51.9	69037	37 Prairie Living	100.0
68743	25 Salt Of The Earth	99.2	68863	37 Prairie Living	100.0	69038	37 Prairie Living	100.0
68745	50 Heartland Communities	67.9	68864	37 Prairie Living	100.0	69039	37 Prairie Living	78.3
68746	37 Prairie Living	100.0	68865	37 Prairie Living	100.0	69040	37 Prairie Living	100.0
68747	37 Prairie Living	100.0	68866	37 Prairie Living	100.0	69041	37 Prairie Living	100.0
68748	42 Southern Satellites	45.4	68869	50 Heartland Communities	72.7	69042	37 Prairie Living	100.0
68749	37 Prairie Living	100.0	68870	17 Green Acres	84.2	69043	37 Prairie Living	100.0
68751	37 Prairie Living	100.0	68871	37 Prairie Living	100.0	69044	50 Heartland Communities	80.1
68752	37 Prairie Living	96.2	68872	37 Prairie Living	100.0	69045	37 Prairie Living	100.0
68753	37 Prairie Living	100.0	68873	33 Midlife Junction	40.7	69046	37 Prairie Living	100.0
68755	37 Prairie Living	100.0	68874	50 Heartland Communities	73.3	69101	17 Green Acres	18.1
68756	37 Prairie Living	51.3	68875	37 Prairie Living	100.0	69120	37 Prairie Living	100.0
68757	37 Prairie Living	100.0	68876	42 Southern Satellites	69.0	69121	37 Prairie Living	100.0
68758	50 Heartland Communities	88.1	68878	37 Prairie Living	100.0	69122	37 Prairie Living	95.6
68759	37 Prairie Living	100.0	68879	37 Prairie Living	100.0	69123	37 Prairie Living	100.0
68760	50 Heartland Communities	79.3	68881	37 Prairie Living	100.0	69125	37 Prairie Living	100.0
68761	37 Prairie Living	100.0	68882	37 Prairie Living	100.0	69127	31 Rural Resort Dwellers	84.6
68763	37 Prairie Living	73.3	68883	37 Prairie Living	99.9	69128	37 Prairie Living	100.0
68764	37 Prairie Living	100.0	68901	32 Rustbelt Traditions	35.7	69129	37 Prairie Living	100.0
68765	37 Prairie Living	100.0	68920	37 Prairie Living	58.1	69130	25 Salt Of The Earth	24.7
68766	37 Prairie Living	100.0	68922	50 Heartland Communities	86.8	69131	37 Prairie Living	100.0
68767	25 Salt Of The Earth	70.2	68923	37 Prairie Living	100.0	69132	37 Prairie Living	100.0
68768	37 Prairie Living	100.0	68924	37 Prairie Living	100.0	69133	37 Prairie Living	100.0
68769	50 Heartland Communities	70.9	68925	37 Prairie Living	100.0	69134	37 Prairie Living	100.0
68770	37 Prairie Living	97.6	68926	50 Heartland Communities	83.5	69138	46 Rooted Rural	29.8

CONSUMER TYPE

ZIP CODE	TOP TAPESTRY CONSUMER TYPE	% 2009 HOUSE-HOLDS	ZIP CODE	TOP TAPESTRY CONSUMER TYPE	% 2009 HOUSE-HOLDS	ZIP CODE	TOP TAPESTRY CONSUMER TYPE	% 2009 HOUSE-HOLDS
69140	37 Prairie Living	50.4	70072	19 Milk And Cookies	18.7	70458	19 Milk And Cookies	24.9
69141	37 Prairie Living	100.0	70075	06 Sophisticated Squires	32.7	70460	19 Milk And Cookies	24.4
69142	37 Prairie Living	100.0	70076	56 Rural Bypasses	100.0	70461	06 Sophisticated Squires	38.2
69143	25 Salt Of The Earth	59.7	70079	18 Cozy And Comfortable	41.8	70462	46 Rooted Rural	66.2
69144	31 Rural Resort Dwellers	100.0	70080	41 Crossroads	96.3	70466	41 Crossroads	42.8
69145	50 Heartland Communities	92.5	70081	66 Unclassified	100.0	70467	56 Rural Bypasses	100.0
69146	31 Rural Resort Dwellers	100.0	70083	56 Rural Bypasses	81.6	70471	13 In Style	23.8
69147	50 Heartland Communities	50.9	70084	25 Salt Of The Earth	31.0	70501	62 Modest Income Homes	29.8
69148	37 Prairie Living	100.0	70085	41 Crossroads	65.3	70503	22 Metropolitans	19.5
69149	37 Prairie Living	100.0	70086	56 Rural Bypasses	100.0	70504	14 Prosperous Empty Nesters	100.0
69150	37 Prairie Living	100.0	70087	28 Aspiring Young Families	49.9	70506	28 Aspiring Young Families	25.6
69151	37 Prairie Living	100.0	70090	42 Southern Satellites	37.1	70507	41 Crossroads	35.0
69152	37 Prairie Living	100.0	70091	56 Rural Bypasses	100.0	70508	13 In Style	27.2
69153	32 Rustbelt Traditions	24.3	70092	19 Milk And Cookies	31.2	70510	26 Midland Crowd	22.6
69154	50 Heartland Communities	77.8	70094	32 Rustbelt Traditions	16.1	70512	56 Rural Bypasses	58.1
69155	37 Prairie Living	95.6	70112	64 City Commons	62.1	70514	56 Rural Bypasses	34.6
69156	37 Prairie Living	100.0	70113	64 City Commons	35.9	70515	56 Rural Bypasses	56.3
69157	37 Prairie Living	100.0	70114	51 Metro City Edge	22.7	70516	26 Midland Crowd	41.2
69161	37 Prairie Living	100.0	70115	22 Metropolitans	23.1	70517	56 Rural Bypasses	47.7
69162	32 Rustbelt Traditions	26.8	70116	08 Laptops And Lattes	22.8	70518	26 Midland Crowd	28.1
69163	37 Prairie Living	91.2	70117	62 Modest Income Homes	25.2	70520	26 Midland Crowd	29.6
69165	37 Prairie Living	91.9	70118	22 Metropolitans	15.7	70525	56 Rural Bypasses	35.4
69166	37 Prairie Living	100.0	70119	22 Metropolitans	19.9	70526	25 Salt Of The Earth	19.2
69167	37 Prairie Living	100.0	70121	36 Old And Newcomers	23.1	70528	42 Southern Satellites	100.0
69168	37 Prairie Living	100.0	70122	34 Family Foundations	28.6	70529	26 Midland Crowd	28.8
69169	37 Prairie Living	94.8	70123	27 Metro Renters	19.2	70531	42 Southern Satellites	100.0
69170	37 Prairie Living	100.0	70124	22 Metropolitans	60.5	70532	56 Rural Bypasses	60.5
69201	50 Heartland Communities	40.2	70125	22 Metropolitans	39.2	70533	42 Southern Satellites	60.5
69210	37 Prairie Living	100.0	70126	34 Family Foundations	30.5	70535	50 Heartland Communities	26.3
69211	37 Prairie Living	100.0	70127	34 Family Foundations	36.4	70537	56 Rural Bypasses	61.5
69212	37 Prairie Living	100.0	70128	19 Milk And Cookies	28.6	70538	56 Rural Bypasses	50.7
69214	37 Prairie Living	100.0	70129	64 City Commons	40.3	70542	56 Rural Bypasses	50.9
69216	37 Prairie Living	100.0	70130	27 Metro Renters	32.8	70543	56 Rural Bypasses	47.5
69217	37 Prairie Living	100.0	70131	18 Cozy And Comfortable	19.4	70544	56 Rural Bypasses	44.7
69218	37 Prairie Living	100.0	70301	26 Midland Crowd	29.4	70546	62 Modest Income Homes	13.9
69221	37 Prairie Living	100.0	70339	42 Southern Satellites	100.0	70548	56 Rural Bypasses	29.0
69301	32 Rustbelt Traditions	27.8	70341	56 Rural Bypasses	52.0	70549	56 Rural Bypasses	48.4
69331	37 Prairie Living	100.0	70342	56 Rural Bypasses	42.0	70552	42 Southern Satellites	100.0
69333	37 Prairie Living	100.0	70343	17 Green Acres	38.7	70554	56 Rural Bypasses	32.7
69334	37 Prairie Living	36.9	70344	46 Rooted Rural	40.6	70555	26 Midland Crowd	97.0
69335	37 Prairie Living	100.0	70345	42 Southern Satellites	39.6	70559	56 Rural Bypasses	100.0
69336	50 Heartland Communities	66.5	70346	51 Metro City Edge	34.7	70560	42 Southern Satellites	18.6
69337	55 College Towns	53.3	70353	56 Rural Bypasses	99.7	70563	17 Green Acres	23.6
69339	50 Heartland Communities	71.0	70354	46 Rooted Rural	60.4	70570	62 Modest Income Homes	33.3
69340	37 Prairie Living	100.0	70355	42 Southern Satellites	100.0	70577	56 Rural Bypasses	62.5
69341	29 Rustbelt Retirees	22.4	70356	56 Rural Bypasses	100.0	70578	42 Southern Satellites	27.7
69343	37 Prairie Living	60.5	70357	56 Rural Bypasses	53.8	70581	42 Southern Satellites	98.0
69345	37 Prairie Living	100.0	70358	46 Rooted Rural	50.3	70582	42 Southern Satellites	27.2
69346	37 Prairie Living	100.0	70359	41 Crossroads	32.9	70583	41 Crossroads	30.9
69347	37 Prairie Living	51.4	70360	06 Sophisticated Squires	13.7	70584	56 Rural Bypasses	32.5
69348	37 Prairie Living	100.0	70363	56 Rural Bypasses	22.1	70586	56 Rural Bypasses	18.2
69350	37 Prairie Living	100.0	70364	28 Aspiring Young Families	17.0	70589	46 Rooted Rural	35.4
69351	37 Prairie Living	100.0	70372	25 Salt Of The Earth	42.0	70591	42 Southern Satellites	28.7
69352	37 Prairie Living	100.0	70374	42 Southern Satellites	61.7	70592	26 Midland Crowd	43.7
69354	37 Prairie Living	100.0	70375	42 Southern Satellites	89.1	70601	62 Modest Income Homes	34.5
69356	37 Prairie Living	53.9	70377	42 Southern Satellites	62.0	70605	07 Exurbanites	21.4
69357	50 Heartland Communities	32.1	70380	42 Southern Satellites	22.0	70607	41 Crossroads	25.5
69358	50 Heartland Communities	54.1	70390	56 Rural Bypasses	43.1	70609	63 Dorms To Diplomas	100.0
69360	50 Heartland Communities	63.1	70392	26 Midland Crowd	51.5	70611	26 Midland Crowd	60.3
69361	48 Great Expectations	18.1	70394	26 Midland Crowd	32.6	70615	34 Family Foundations	24.9
69366	37 Prairie Living	100.0	70395	26 Midland Crowd	71.6	70630	42 Southern Satellites	54.5
69367	37 Prairie Living	100.0	70397	37 Prairie Living	54.9	70631	56 Rural Bypasses	52.7
70001	39 Young And Restless	27.5	70401	55 College Towns	32.3	70632	46 Rooted Rural	80.3
70002	52 Inner City Tenants	19.4	70402	30 Retirement Communities	0.0	70633	50 Heartland Communities	24.4
70003	18 Cozy And Comfortable	34.8	70403	26 Midland Crowd	45.6	70634	42 Southern Satellites	28.5
70005	14 Prosperous Empty Nesters	28.4	70420	26 Midland Crowd	36.3	70637	46 Rooted Rural	65.2
70006	14 Prosperous Empty Nesters	29.9	70422	56 Rural Bypasses	41.0	70639	46 Rooted Rural	100.0
70030	17 Green Acres	46.2	70426	56 Rural Bypasses	74.5	70643	46 Rooted Rural	100.0
70031	25 Salt Of The Earth	88.6	70427	62 Modest Income Homes	37.5	70645	46 Rooted Rural	100.0
70032	29 Rustbelt Retirees	58.1	70431	26 Midland Crowd	55.1	70647	26 Midland Crowd	38.6
70036	46 Rooted Rural	100.0	70433	12 Up And Coming Families	36.3	70648	25 Salt Of The Earth	27.1
70037	26 Midland Crowd	26.4	70435	17 Green Acres	39.3	70650	42 Southern Satellites	100.0
70039	41 Crossroads	57.5	70436	56 Rural Bypasses	97.3	70652	42 Southern Satellites	64.8
70040	26 Midland Crowd	48.5	70437	26 Midland Crowd	61.1	70653	56 Rural Bypasses	35.0
70041	56 Rural Bypasses	53.9	70438	46 Rooted Rural	39.3	70654	56 Rural Bypasses	100.0
70043	50 Heartland Communities	17.0	70441	56 Rural Bypasses	96.3	70655	56 Rural Bypasses	38.2
70047	06 Sophisticated Squires	31.2	70442	46 Rooted Rural	56.2	70656	42 Southern Satellites	47.9
70049	62 Modest Income Homes	42.5	70443	56 Rural Bypasses	42.7	70657	26 Midland Crowd	55.6
70051	56 Rural Bypasses	61.9	70444	56 Rural Bypasses	48.6	70658	46 Rooted Rural	100.0
70052	42 Southern Satellites	65.2	70445	26 Midland Crowd	50.7	70660	42 Southern Satellites	100.0
70053	48 Great Expectations	26.6	70446	26 Midland Crowd	77.2	70661	46 Rooted Rural	52.2
70056	52 Inner City Tenants	20.7	70447	17 Green Acres	79.6	70662	42 Southern Satellites	100.0
70057	26 Midland Crowd	36.7	70448	12 Up And Coming Families	35.6	70663	26 Midland Crowd	20.4
70058	19 Milk And Cookies	26.0	70449	46 Rooted Rural	51.5	70665	41 Crossroads	46.8
70062	64 City Commons	20.0	70450	56 Rural Bypasses	66.2	70668	46 Rooted Rural	21.6
70065	13 In Style	12.4	70452	42 Southern Satellites	31.5	70669	26 Midland Crowd	45.1
70067	42 Southern Satellites	70.4	70453	56 Rural Bypasses	88.6	70706	26 Midland Crowd	70.1
70068	19 Milk And Cookies	38.5	70454	26 Midland Crowd	52.1	70710	41 Crossroads	50.2
70070	06 Sophisticated Squires	30.8	70455	26 Midland Crowd	100.0	70711	26 Midland Crowd	57.4
70071	18 Cozy And Comfortable	36.3	70456	56 Rural Bypasses	90.0	70712	41 Crossroads	100.0

ZIP CODE	TOP TAPESTRY CONSUMER TYPE	% 2009 HOUSE-HOLDS	ZIP CODE	TOP TAPESTRY CONSUMER TYPE	% 2009 HOUSE-HOLDS	ZIP CODE	TOP TAPESTRY CONSUMER TYPE	% 2009 HOUSE-HOLDS
70714	51 Metro City Edge	26.2	71038	56 Rural Bypasses	70.8	71322	62 Modest Income Homes	31.3
70715	56 Rural Bypasses	75.0	71039	56 Rural Bypasses	73.3	71323	46 Rooted Rural	86.5
70719	26 Midland Crowd	46.3	71040	56 Rural Bypasses	46.9	71325	62 Modest Income Homes	53.9
70721	51 Metro City Edge	100.0	71043	56 Rural Bypasses	100.0	71326	56 Rural Bypasses	90.2
70722	56 Rural Bypasses	35.2	71044	56 Rural Bypasses	96.8	71327	56 Rural Bypasses	51.1
70723	56 Rural Bypasses	100.0	71045	56 Rural Bypasses	54.7	71328	26 Midland Crowd	79.7
70725	26 Midland Crowd	100.0	71046	46 Rooted Rural	69.3	71331	42 Southern Satellites	100.0
70726	26 Midland Crowd	61.0	71047	26 Midland Crowd	68.4	71333	56 Rural Bypasses	100.0
70729	41 Crossroads	100.0	71048	56 Rural Bypasses	100.0	71334	62 Modest Income Homes	47.1
70730	26 Midland Crowd	60.0	71049	46 Rooted Rural	59.9	71336	56 Rural Bypasses	64.7
70732	42 Southern Satellites	96.3	71051	46 Rooted Rural	48.7	71340	56 Rural Bypasses	63.0
70733	42 Southern Satellites	100.0	71052	62 Modest Income Homes	26.8	71341	56 Rural Bypasses	58.6
70734	41 Crossroads	59.9	71055	62 Modest Income Homes	20.7	71342	46 Rooted Rural	32.9
70736	56 Rural Bypasses	64.9	71060	26 Midland Crowd	64.4	71343	56 Rural Bypasses	49.9
70737	26 Midland Crowd	81.0	71061	56 Rural Bypasses	95.5	71346	62 Modest Income Homes	47.8
70739	17 Green Acres	28.7	71063	56 Rural Bypasses	100.0	71350	46 Rooted Rural	43.0
70740	56 Rural Bypasses	100.0	71064	56 Rural Bypasses	81.5	71351	56 Rural Bypasses	46.1
70744	42 Southern Satellites	47.3	71065	56 Rural Bypasses	86.4	71353	62 Modest Income Homes	42.7
70748	56 Rural Bypasses	66.7	71067	56 Rural Bypasses	39.3	71354	46 Rooted Rural	84.4
70749	31 Rural Resort Dwellers	55.0	71068	56 Rural Bypasses	49.3	71355	50 Heartland Communities	54.0
70750	56 Rural Bypasses	66.6	71069	56 Rural Bypasses	79.3	71356	50 Heartland Communities	79.1
70752	56 Rural Bypasses	87.9	71070	56 Rural Bypasses	73.9	71357	56 Rural Bypasses	53.0
70753	56 Rural Bypasses	100.0	71071	42 Southern Satellites	60.8	71358	56 Rural Bypasses	61.6
70754	26 Midland Crowd	45.5	71072	46 Rooted Rural	98.4	71360	26 Midland Crowd	30.7
70755	42 Southern Satellites	64.2	71073	46 Rooted Rural	64.4	71362	46 Rooted Rural	56.8
70756	56 Rural Bypasses	86.7	71075	50 Heartland Communities	36.2	71366	62 Modest Income Homes	81.8
70757	56 Rural Bypasses	90.1	71078	26 Midland Crowd	64.8	71367	46 Rooted Rural	55.6
70759	50 Heartland Communities	87.9	71079	56 Rural Bypasses	100.0	71368	56 Rural Bypasses	65.7
70760	62 Modest Income Homes	41.3	71082	56 Rural Bypasses	34.0	71369	56 Rural Bypasses	66.5
70761	56 Rural Bypasses	100.0	71101	62 Modest Income Homes	35.1	71371	46 Rooted Rural	41.9
70762	26 Midland Crowd	78.4	71103	62 Modest Income Homes	71.2	71373	32 Rustbelt Traditions	37.0
70763	26 Midland Crowd	62.1	71104	48 Great Expectations	27.4	71375	62 Modest Income Homes	100.0
70764	50 Heartland Communities	20.7	71105	33 Midlife Junction	27.3	71378	56 Rural Bypasses	54.5
70767	26 Midland Crowd	29.1	71106	62 Modest Income Homes	21.6	71401	56 Rural Bypasses	51.1
70769	12 Up And Coming Families	52.4	71107	26 Midland Crowd	24.4	71403	46 Rooted Rural	81.7
70770	26 Midland Crowd	65.7	71108	51 Metro City Edge	49.5	71404	56 Rural Bypasses	72.6
70772	56 Rural Bypasses	100.0	71109	62 Modest Income Homes	50.7	71405	41 Crossroads	35.8
70773	42 Southern Satellites	54.8	71110	40 Military Proximity	100.0	71406	56 Rural Bypasses	93.7
70774	26 Midland Crowd	63.0	71111	12 Up And Coming Families	11.3	71407	42 Southern Satellites	92.5
70775	26 Midland Crowd	45.7	71112	32 Rustbelt Traditions	18.7	71409	26 Midland Crowd	65.1
70776	26 Midland Crowd	55.6	71115	39 Young And Restless	19.9	71411	56 Rural Bypasses	100.0
70777	26 Midland Crowd	71.7	71118	29 Rustbelt Retirees	21.1	71416	56 Rural Bypasses	90.6
70778	26 Midland Crowd	54.7	71119	18 Cozy And Comfortable	30.2	71417	56 Rural Bypasses	30.2
70780	56 Rural Bypasses	100.0	71129	52 Inner City Tenants	39.3	71418	46 Rooted Rural	58.4
70783	31 Rural Resort Dwellers	51.1	71201	33 Midlife Junction	14.2	71419	46 Rooted Rural	63.3
70785	26 Midland Crowd	60.8	71202	51 Metro City Edge	36.2	71422	56 Rural Bypasses	48.1
70788	56 Rural Bypasses	67.5	71203	26 Midland Crowd	17.8	71423	46 Rooted Rural	45.4
70789	56 Rural Bypasses	93.5	71209	55 College Towns	100.0	71424	46 Rooted Rural	37.8
70791	56 Rural Bypasses	20.9	71219	56 Rural Bypasses	100.0	71425	46 Rooted Rural	100.0
70792	56 Rural Bypasses	100.0	71220	62 Modest Income Homes	20.0	71426	46 Rooted Rural	100.0
70801	27 Metro Renters	100.0	71222	56 Rural Bypasses	60.4	71427	56 Rural Bypasses	100.0
70802	62 Modest Income Homes	61.3	71223	56 Rural Bypasses	96.8	71429	46 Rooted Rural	50.4
70803	63 Dorms To Diplomas	100.0	71225	26 Midland Crowd	100.0	71430	46 Rooted Rural	79.1
70805	51 Metro City Edge	81.6	71226	56 Rural Bypasses	69.8	71432	42 Southern Satellites	86.0
70806	57 Simple Living	17.7	71227	42 Southern Satellites	38.2	71433	56 Rural Bypasses	44.7
70807	62 Modest Income Homes	46.9	71229	56 Rural Bypasses	70.9	71435	56 Rural Bypasses	59.3
70808	22 Metropolitans	27.1	71232	56 Rural Bypasses	47.0	71438	46 Rooted Rural	53.7
70809	27 Metro Renters	15.5	71234	42 Southern Satellites	48.0	71439	46 Rooted Rural	99.9
70810	02 Suburban Splendor	23.1	71235	56 Rural Bypasses	34.3	71441	46 Rooted Rural	66.7
70811	32 Rustbelt Traditions	27.2	71237	56 Rural Bypasses	70.5	71446	46 Rooted Rural	25.2
70812	51 Metro City Edge	61.7	71238	26 Midland Crowd	59.2	71447	56 Rural Bypasses	78.8
70813	64 City Commons	100.0	71241	46 Rooted Rural	35.7	71449	49 Senior Sun Seekers	25.9
70814	19 Milk And Cookies	35.4	71243	46 Rooted Rural	100.0	71450	56 Rural Bypasses	52.7
70815	14 Prosperous Empty Nesters	35.0	71245	57 Simple Living	71.4	71454	56 Rural Bypasses	79.2
70816	39 Young And Restless	30.8	71250	56 Rural Bypasses	82.8	71455	56 Rural Bypasses	79.4
70817	06 Sophisticated Squires	22.2	71251	50 Heartland Communities	34.0	71456	56 Rural Bypasses	100.0
70818	19 Milk And Cookies	27.9	71254	62 Modest Income Homes	54.3	71457	56 Rural Bypasses	16.5
70819	24 Main Street, USA	30.9	71256	56 Rural Bypasses	100.0	71459	40 Military Proximity	99.8
70820	63 Dorms To Diplomas	46.3	71259	46 Rooted Rural	51.3	71461	48 Great Expectations	64.6
71001	56 Rural Bypasses	51.1	71260	56 Rural Bypasses	61.3	71462	46 Rooted Rural	56.8
71002	56 Rural Bypasses	100.0	71261	56 Rural Bypasses	97.4	71463	46 Rooted Rural	34.8
71003	56 Rural Bypasses	100.0	71263	46 Rooted Rural	79.6	71465	42 Southern Satellites	95.1
71004	56 Rural Bypasses	55.0	71264	56 Rural Bypasses	61.3	71466	42 Southern Satellites	100.0
71006	07 Exurbanites	45.0	71266	56 Rural Bypasses	50.8	71467	46 Rooted Rural	56.5
71007	26 Midland Crowd	100.0	71268	56 Rural Bypasses	47.4	71468	46 Rooted Rural	100.0
71008	56 Rural Bypasses	76.9	71269	46 Rooted Rural	37.5	71469	46 Rooted Rural	45.2
71016	56 Rural Bypasses	55.5	71270	55 College Towns	33.1	71472	42 Southern Satellites	98.6
71018	56 Rural Bypasses	72.2	71275	41 Crossroads	66.7	71473	42 Southern Satellites	63.1
71019	56 Rural Bypasses	41.2	71276	56 Rural Bypasses	58.0	71479	56 Rural Bypasses	50.2
71023	46 Rooted Rural	72.3	71277	42 Southern Satellites	77.6	71483	50 Heartland Communities	24.1
71024	46 Rooted Rural	90.0	71280	32 Rustbelt Traditions	44.0	71485	26 Midland Crowd	64.9
71027	42 Southern Satellites	94.1	71282	62 Modest Income Homes	27.1	71486	56 Rural Bypasses	41.3
71028	56 Rural Bypasses	100.0	71286	56 Rural Bypasses	83.0	71601	51 Metro City Edge	34.2
71029	56 Rural Bypasses	100.0	71291	26 Midland Crowd	22.6	71602	26 Midland Crowd	36.4
71030	26 Midland Crowd	86.1	71292	26 Midland Crowd	29.7	71603	25 Salt Of The Earth	15.9
71031	56 Rural Bypasses	66.2	71295	62 Modest Income Homes	24.2	71630	56 Rural Bypasses	100.0
71032	46 Rooted Rural	84.7	71301	62 Modest Income Homes	25.3	71631	56 Rural Bypasses	97.4
71033	26 Midland Crowd	95.9	71302	62 Modest Income Homes	48.0	71635	42 Southern Satellites	44.1
71034	46 Rooted Rural	100.0	71303	07 Exurbanites	22.2	71638	62 Modest Income Homes	41.3
71037	41 Crossroads	32.8	71316	46 Rooted Rural	100.0	71639	62 Modest Income Homes	37.6

CONSUMER TYPE

ZIP CODE	TOP TAPESTRY CONSUMER TYPE	% 2009 HOUSE-HOLDS	ZIP CODE	TOP TAPESTRY CONSUMER TYPE	% 2009 HOUSE-HOLDS	ZIP CODE	TOP TAPESTRY CONSUMER TYPE	% 2009 HOUSE-HOLDS
71640	56 Rural Bypasses	43.3	71923	46 Rooted Rural	26.9	72079	41 Crossroads	47.5
71642	42 Southern Satellites	100.0	71929	46 Rooted Rural	98.7	72080	46 Rooted Rural	100.0
71643	62 Modest Income Homes	51.2	71933	46 Rooted Rural	52.7	72081	42 Southern Satellites	70.5
71644	46 Rooted Rural	38.2	71935	46 Rooted Rural	69.5	72082	56 Rural Bypasses	98.9
71646	42 Southern Satellites	69.3	71937	42 Southern Satellites	85.6	72083	37 Prairie Living	100.0
71647	56 Rural Bypasses	57.1	71940	46 Rooted Rural	61.4	72084	42 Southern Satellites	83.7
71651	46 Rooted Rural	85.7	71941	42 Southern Satellites	64.3	72086	50 Heartland Communities	17.8
71652	42 Southern Satellites	89.6	71942	42 Southern Satellites	100.0	72087	26 Midland Crowd	44.1
71653	56 Rural Bypasses	49.6	71943	42 Southern Satellites	48.3	72088	43 The Elders	65.1
71654	62 Modest Income Homes	32.5	71944	42 Southern Satellites	75.2	72099	40 Military Proximity	100.0
71655	42 Southern Satellites	27.6	71945	46 Rooted Rural	99.5	72101	56 Rural Bypasses	26.2
71656	63 Dorms To Diplomas	100.0	71949	46 Rooted Rural	82.0	72102	42 Southern Satellites	100.0
71658	56 Rural Bypasses	64.6	71950	42 Southern Satellites	57.0	72103	26 Midland Crowd	32.1
71660	42 Southern Satellites	69.0	71952	42 Southern Satellites	100.0	72104	50 Heartland Communities	29.4
71661	56 Rural Bypasses	59.1	71953	50 Heartland Communities	41.0	72105	26 Midland Crowd	100.0
71662	56 Rural Bypasses	47.9	71956	42 Southern Satellites	97.6	72106	42 Southern Satellites	64.0
71663	56 Rural Bypasses	73.6	71957	31 Rural Resort Dwellers	42.8	72110	46 Rooted Rural	44.7
71665	42 Southern Satellites	36.6	71958	46 Rooted Rural	98.5	72111	42 Southern Satellites	57.5
71666	56 Rural Bypasses	98.7	71959	46 Rooted Rural	66.1	72112	42 Southern Satellites	20.5
71667	42 Southern Satellites	56.9	71960	46 Rooted Rural	100.0	72113	12 Up And Coming Families	52.1
71670	42 Southern Satellites	46.4	71961	46 Rooted Rural	100.0	72114	64 City Commons	21.6
71671	50 Heartland Communities	44.9	71962	46 Rooted Rural	99.5	72116	14 Prosperous Empty Nesters	28.2
71674	56 Rural Bypasses	59.6	71964	26 Midland Crowd	80.0	72117	56 Rural Bypasses	38.7
71675	42 Southern Satellites	40.7	71965	46 Rooted Rural	100.0	72118	32 Rustbelt Traditions	34.9
71676	56 Rural Bypasses	89.6	71968	26 Midland Crowd	52.6	72120	19 Milk And Cookies	28.0
71677	42 Southern Satellites	100.0	71969	46 Rooted Rural	100.0	72121	42 Southern Satellites	85.4
71678	56 Rural Bypasses	76.3	71970	46 Rooted Rural	100.0	72122	43 The Elders	44.5
71701	53 Home Town	18.4	71971	37 Prairie Living	100.0	72125	42 Southern Satellites	100.0
71720	56 Rural Bypasses	74.4	71972	42 Southern Satellites	100.0	72126	46 Rooted Rural	53.7
71722	56 Rural Bypasses	53.0	71973	56 Rural Bypasses	100.0	72127	56 Rural Bypasses	72.0
71725	56 Rural Bypasses	97.6	71998	55 College Towns	100.0	72128	42 Southern Satellites	98.7
71726	49 Senior Sun Seekers	49.5	72001	42 Southern Satellites	81.2	72129	42 Southern Satellites	76.7
71730	42 Southern Satellites	17.6	72002	26 Midland Crowd	71.5	72130	42 Southern Satellites	57.4
71740	56 Rural Bypasses	74.4	72003	37 Prairie Living	65.1	72131	46 Rooted Rural	45.0
71742	56 Rural Bypasses	57.5	72004	56 Rural Bypasses	100.0	72132	26 Midland Crowd	65.2
71743	42 Southern Satellites	44.1	72005	56 Rural Bypasses	100.0	72133	56 Rural Bypasses	100.0
71744	42 Southern Satellites	57.4	72006	56 Rural Bypasses	29.9	72134	46 Rooted Rural	100.0
71745	56 Rural Bypasses	62.5	72007	26 Midland Crowd	91.5	72135	26 Midland Crowd	81.2
71747	56 Rural Bypasses	100.0	72010	56 Rural Bypasses	34.5	72136	26 Midland Crowd	100.0
71748	46 Rooted Rural	100.0	72011	26 Midland Crowd	77.5	72137	46 Rooted Rural	52.1
71749	42 Southern Satellites	78.0	72012	26 Midland Crowd	48.1	72140	46 Rooted Rural	100.0
71751	42 Southern Satellites	56.2	72013	46 Rooted Rural	75.3	72141	46 Rooted Rural	89.0
71752	56 Rural Bypasses	50.3	72014	56 Rural Bypasses	100.0	72142	46 Rooted Rural	50.8
71753	56 Rural Bypasses	15.5	72015	18 Cozy And Comfortable	20.2	72143	26 Midland Crowd	19.2
71758	46 Rooted Rural	100.0	72016	42 Southern Satellites	68.1	72149	63 Dorms To Diplomas	100.0
71762	50 Heartland Communities	53.0	72017	56 Rural Bypasses	50.5	72150	42 Southern Satellites	69.9
71763	56 Rural Bypasses	51.2	72019	26 Midland Crowd	54.1	72152	56 Rural Bypasses	100.0
71764	56 Rural Bypasses	52.1	72020	42 Southern Satellites	62.7	72153	46 Rooted Rural	50.5
71765	56 Rural Bypasses	50.6	72021	53 Home Town	33.0	72156	46 Rooted Rural	100.0
71766	42 Southern Satellites	100.0	72022	26 Midland Crowd	42.6	72157	46 Rooted Rural	71.0
71770	56 Rural Bypasses	55.7	72023	12 Up And Coming Families	31.3	72160	50 Heartland Communities	26.5
71801	50 Heartland Communities	20.2	72024	46 Rooted Rural	67.9	72165	46 Rooted Rural	100.0
71822	42 Southern Satellites	48.0	72025	42 Southern Satellites	92.4	72166	37 Prairie Living	100.0
71825	42 Southern Satellites	88.9	72026	42 Southern Satellites	100.0	72167	42 Southern Satellites	61.7
71826	56 Rural Bypasses	65.2	72027	46 Rooted Rural	100.0	72168	56 Rural Bypasses	91.4
71827	56 Rural Bypasses	55.3	72028	46 Rooted Rural	100.0	72170	37 Prairie Living	82.5
71828	42 Southern Satellites	93.5	72029	56 Rural Bypasses	60.8	72173	26 Midland Crowd	94.5
71831	56 Rural Bypasses	100.0	72030	46 Rooted Rural	100.0	72175	56 Rural Bypasses	100.0
71832	42 Southern Satellites	63.3	72031	46 Rooted Rural	82.2	72176	26 Midland Crowd	64.8
71833	42 Southern Satellites	55.2	72032	26 Midland Crowd	26.2	72179	46 Rooted Rural	100.0
71834	56 Rural Bypasses	55.1	72034	28 Aspiring Young Families	24.2	72199	42 Southern Satellites	77.5
71835	46 Rooted Rural	77.3	72035	63 Dorms To Diplomas	100.0	72201	65 Social Security Set	51.2
71836	42 Southern Satellites	53.7	72036	62 Modest Income Homes	49.2	72202	62 Modest Income Homes	31.6
71837	42 Southern Satellites	39.3	72038	42 Southern Satellites	100.0	72204	51 Metro City Edge	35.3
71838	56 Rural Bypasses	77.7	72039	46 Rooted Rural	72.5	72205	22 Metropolitans	18.1
71839	46 Rooted Rural	83.3	72040	46 Rooted Rural	64.2	72206	62 Modest Income Homes	28.9
71841	42 Southern Satellites	95.2	72041	56 Rural Bypasses	54.7	72207	22 Metropolitans	45.2
71842	42 Southern Satellites	90.7	72042	46 Rooted Rural	24.8	72209	51 Metro City Edge	67.0
71845	56 Rural Bypasses	89.6	72044	49 Senior Sun Seekers	97.3	72210	28 Aspiring Young Families	41.5
71846	42 Southern Satellites	56.7	72045	42 Southern Satellites	88.0	72211	16 Enterprising Professionals	30.0
71847	42 Southern Satellites	63.4	72046	56 Rural Bypasses	31.5	72212	13 In Style	22.2
71851	42 Southern Satellites	60.4	72047	42 Southern Satellites	93.9	72223	04 Boomburbs	52.9
71852	42 Southern Satellites	51.8	72048	46 Rooted Rural	100.0	72227	33 Midlife Junction	47.4
71853	56 Rural Bypasses	74.4	72051	46 Rooted Rural	100.0	72301	48 Great Expectations	14.7
71854	46 Rooted Rural	14.1	72052	42 Southern Satellites	100.0	72310	42 Southern Satellites	100.0
71855	46 Rooted Rural	56.7	72055	46 Rooted Rural	85.0	72311	56 Rural Bypasses	100.0
71857	46 Rooted Rural	35.0	72057	42 Southern Satellites	100.0	72313	56 Rural Bypasses	100.0
71858	46 Rooted Rural	42.8	72058	26 Midland Crowd	82.0	72315	41 Crossroads	16.6
71859	56 Rural Bypasses	100.0	72060	56 Rural Bypasses	85.9	72320	56 Rural Bypasses	100.0
71860	56 Rural Bypasses	59.6	72063	46 Rooted Rural	100.0	72324	42 Southern Satellites	92.0
71861	46 Rooted Rural	51.0	72064	46 Rooted Rural	51.8	72326	42 Southern Satellites	78.0
71862	42 Southern Satellites	43.8	72065	26 Midland Crowd	63.8	72327	56 Rural Bypasses	89.2
71864	56 Rural Bypasses	57.1	72066	42 Southern Satellites	100.0	72328	56 Rural Bypasses	100.0
71865	42 Southern Satellites	100.0	72067	49 Senior Sun Seekers	100.0	72329	42 Southern Satellites	100.0
71866	46 Rooted Rural	100.0	72068	42 Southern Satellites	100.0	72330	42 Southern Satellites	97.2
71901	57 Simple Living	23.8	72069	62 Modest Income Homes	67.7	72331	62 Modest Income Homes	41.8
71909	43 The Elders	78.1	72070	46 Rooted Rural	51.4	72333	62 Modest Income Homes	77.2
71913	31 Rural Resort Dwellers	18.9	72072	56 Rural Bypasses	100.0	72335	48 Great Expectations	15.5
71921	46 Rooted Rural	58.6	72073	42 Southern Satellites	58.8	72338	56 Rural Bypasses	100.0
71922	56 Rural Bypasses	100.0	72076	19 Milk And Cookies	14.5	72339	56 Rural Bypasses	100.0

ZIP CODE	TOP TAPESTRY CONSUMER TYPE	% 2009 HOUSE-HOLDS	ZIP CODE	TOP TAPESTRY CONSUMER TYPE	% 2009 HOUSE-HOLDS	ZIP CODE	TOP TAPESTRY CONSUMER TYPE	% 2009 HOUSE-HOLDS
72340	56 Rural Bypasses	100.0	72513	50 Heartland Communities	81.3	72680	46 Rooted Rural	100.0
72341	56 Rural Bypasses	100.0	72515	46 Rooted Rural	100.0	72682	46 Rooted Rural	100.0
72342	64 City Commons	30.6	72517	46 Rooted Rural	100.0	72683	46 Rooted Rural	100.0
72346	42 Southern Satellites	64.8	72519	50 Heartland Communities	59.2	72685	46 Rooted Rural	100.0
72347	46 Rooted Rural	85.9	72520	46 Rooted Rural	100.0	72686	46 Rooted Rural	100.0
72348	56 Rural Bypasses	36.7	72521	42 Southern Satellites	67.2	72687	46 Rooted Rural	55.8
72350	56 Rural Bypasses	95.6	72522	42 Southern Satellites	100.0	72701	22 Metropolitans	22.8
72351	42 Southern Satellites	100.0	72523	42 Southern Satellites	89.4	72703	39 Young And Restless	20.8
72354	56 Rural Bypasses	56.7	72524	46 Rooted Rural	60.8	72704	26 Midland Crowd	37.2
72355	56 Rural Bypasses	61.8	72527	25 Salt Of The Earth	100.0	72712	28 Aspiring Young Families	29.2
72358	53 Home Town	49.3	72528	46 Rooted Rural	100.0	72714	49 Senior Sun Seekers	49.2
72360	56 Rural Bypasses	39.2	72529	49 Senior Sun Seekers	57.7	72715	15 Silver And Gold	65.9
72364	41 Crossroads	33.2	72530	46 Rooted Rural	44.5	72717	46 Rooted Rural	78.0
72365	50 Heartland Communities	39.7	72531	46 Rooted Rural	54.6	72718	17 Green Acres	98.8
72366	56 Rural Bypasses	47.1	72532	46 Rooted Rural	90.4	72719	26 Midland Crowd	100.0
72367	56 Rural Bypasses	100.0	72533	46 Rooted Rural	100.0	72721	46 Rooted Rural	62.8
72368	56 Rural Bypasses	100.0	72534	46 Rooted Rural	61.0	72722	42 Southern Satellites	78.3
72369	56 Rural Bypasses	82.4	72536	46 Rooted Rural	91.0	72727	26 Midland Crowd	78.2
72370	42 Southern Satellites	31.5	72537	49 Senior Sun Seekers	100.0	72729	46 Rooted Rural	100.0
72372	56 Rural Bypasses	51.4	72538	46 Rooted Rural	94.4	72730	26 Midland Crowd	79.7
72373	56 Rural Bypasses	62.7	72539	46 Rooted Rural	100.0	72732	42 Southern Satellites	55.9
72374	56 Rural Bypasses	62.3	72540	46 Rooted Rural	97.2	72734	42 Southern Satellites	73.3
72376	56 Rural Bypasses	56.1	72542	49 Senior Sun Seekers	47.6	72736	42 Southern Satellites	44.3
72379	56 Rural Bypasses	100.0	72543	46 Rooted Rural	33.8	72738	42 Southern Satellites	45.6
72384	56 Rural Bypasses	63.3	72544	49 Senior Sun Seekers	100.0	72739	26 Midland Crowd	60.9
72386	42 Southern Satellites	71.6	72546	46 Rooted Rural	80.0	72740	42 Southern Satellites	38.1
72390	62 Modest Income Homes	37.0	72550	42 Southern Satellites	92.0	72742	37 Prairie Living	63.5
72392	56 Rural Bypasses	100.0	72553	42 Southern Satellites	100.0	72744	42 Southern Satellites	47.0
72394	56 Rural Bypasses	98.1	72554	46 Rooted Rural	79.4	72745	12 Up And Coming Families	58.1
72395	42 Southern Satellites	98.7	72555	56 Rural Bypasses	51.6	72747	37 Prairie Living	81.4
72396	42 Southern Satellites	23.5	72556	50 Heartland Communities	80.0	72749	46 Rooted Rural	100.0
72401	26 Midland Crowd	17.0	72560	46 Rooted Rural	64.4	72751	32 Rustbelt Traditions	36.8
72404	28 Aspiring Young Families	26.8	72561	46 Rooted Rural	94.8	72752	46 Rooted Rural	100.0
72410	56 Rural Bypasses	66.0	72562	42 Southern Satellites	80.4	72753	32 Rustbelt Traditions	30.4
72411	42 Southern Satellites	93.9	72564	46 Rooted Rural	78.6	72756	38 Industrious Urban Fringe	12.8
72412	25 Salt Of The Earth	85.8	72565	46 Rooted Rural	100.0	72758	12 Up And Coming Families	32.0
72413	56 Rural Bypasses	51.2	72566	46 Rooted Rural	83.6	72760	46 Rooted Rural	97.7
72414	46 Rooted Rural	96.6	72567	56 Rural Bypasses	100.0	72761	26 Midland Crowd	42.8
72415	42 Southern Satellites	59.0	72568	42 Southern Satellites	100.0	72762	17 Green Acres	27.7
72416	42 Southern Satellites	83.6	72569	42 Southern Satellites	75.2	72764	28 Aspiring Young Families	22.7
72417	42 Southern Satellites	100.0	72571	42 Southern Satellites	100.0	72768	42 Southern Satellites	85.4
72419	56 Rural Bypasses	86.3	72572	46 Rooted Rural	100.0	72769	42 Southern Satellites	95.3
72421	37 Prairie Living	70.7	72573	50 Heartland Communities	62.0	72773	42 Southern Satellites	77.4
72422	53 Home Town	35.0	72576	46 Rooted Rural	50.1	72774	26 Midland Crowd	75.2
72424	42 Southern Satellites	100.0	72577	37 Prairie Living	100.0	72776	46 Rooted Rural	100.0
72425	42 Southern Satellites	100.0	72578	46 Rooted Rural	100.0	72801	48 Great Expectations	35.8
72426	46 Rooted Rural	87.8	72579	42 Southern Satellites	100.0	72802	25 Salt Of The Earth	20.4
72428	42 Southern Satellites	100.0	72581	31 Rural Resort Dwellers	83.2	72820	46 Rooted Rural	100.0
72429	37 Prairie Living	100.0	72583	46 Rooted Rural	98.8	72821	46 Rooted Rural	82.9
72430	46 Rooted Rural	92.0	72584	46 Rooted Rural	100.0	72823	42 Southern Satellites	65.4
72432	42 Southern Satellites	40.8	72585	46 Rooted Rural	100.0	72824	42 Southern Satellites	81.0
72433	42 Southern Satellites	33.8	72587	46 Rooted Rural	100.0	72826	42 Southern Satellites	100.0
72434	46 Rooted Rural	100.0	72601	46 Rooted Rural	27.0	72827	56 Rural Bypasses	64.3
72435	42 Southern Satellites	100.0	72611	46 Rooted Rural	52.4	72828	56 Rural Bypasses	59.3
72436	42 Southern Satellites	100.0	72616	42 Southern Satellites	59.7	72830	42 Southern Satellites	37.4
72437	42 Southern Satellites	96.5	72617	49 Senior Sun Seekers	100.0	72832	42 Southern Satellites	100.0
72438	56 Rural Bypasses	45.1	72619	49 Senior Sun Seekers	100.0	72833	53 Home Town	40.1
72440	46 Rooted Rural	100.0	72623	46 Rooted Rural	100.0	72834	42 Southern Satellites	41.3
72441	42 Southern Satellites	100.0	72624	46 Rooted Rural	100.0	72835	46 Rooted Rural	100.0
72442	42 Southern Satellites	93.8	72626	50 Heartland Communities	71.7	72837	42 Southern Satellites	54.9
72443	42 Southern Satellites	100.0	72628	46 Rooted Rural	100.0	72838	46 Rooted Rural	71.6
72444	46 Rooted Rural	61.0	72629	46 Rooted Rural	96.5	72839	46 Rooted Rural	100.0
72445	42 Southern Satellites	100.0	72631	49 Senior Sun Seekers	53.3	72840	42 Southern Satellites	100.0
72447	50 Heartland Communities	69.3	72632	31 Rural Resort Dwellers	59.0	72841	46 Rooted Rural	100.0
72449	42 Southern Satellites	100.0	72633	46 Rooted Rural	100.0	72842	42 Southern Satellites	99.4
72450	42 Southern Satellites	37.4	72634	50 Heartland Communities	47.4	72843	46 Rooted Rural	55.2
72453	42 Southern Satellites	100.0	72635	50 Heartland Communities	42.7	72845	42 Southern Satellites	80.0
72454	50 Heartland Communities	57.3	72638	42 Southern Satellites	91.8	72846	42 Southern Satellites	54.6
72455	50 Heartland Communities	27.3	72639	42 Southern Satellites	74.9	72847	46 Rooted Rural	65.7
72456	42 Southern Satellites	96.7	72640	46 Rooted Rural	100.0	72851	46 Rooted Rural	52.1
72457	50 Heartland Communities	93.2	72641	50 Heartland Communities	50.3	72852	46 Rooted Rural	100.0
72458	46 Rooted Rural	75.9	72642	49 Senior Sun Seekers	100.0	72853	42 Southern Satellites	51.8
72459	42 Southern Satellites	91.9	72644	46 Rooted Rural	58.3	72854	46 Rooted Rural	100.0
72460	46 Rooted Rural	100.0	72645	50 Heartland Communities	57.1	72855	50 Heartland Communities	42.8
72461	50 Heartland Communities	60.8	72648	46 Rooted Rural	97.8	72856	42 Southern Satellites	100.0
72464	42 Southern Satellites	100.0	72650	50 Heartland Communities	61.5	72857	56 Rural Bypasses	95.7
72465	46 Rooted Rural	100.0	72651	49 Senior Sun Seekers	76.6	72858	42 Southern Satellites	66.2
72466	46 Rooted Rural	91.0	72653	49 Senior Sun Seekers	64.7	72860	56 Rural Bypasses	60.1
72467	42 Southern Satellites	100.0	72655	46 Rooted Rural	100.0	72863	42 Southern Satellites	83.9
72469	46 Rooted Rural	65.8	72658	46 Rooted Rural	64.2	72865	42 Southern Satellites	72.2
72470	42 Southern Satellites	100.0	72660	42 Southern Satellites	100.0	72901	48 Great Expectations	30.1
72471	56 Rural Bypasses	73.7	72661	49 Senior Sun Seekers	100.0	72903	14 Prosperous Empty Nesters	14.2
72472	53 Home Town	51.9	72662	46 Rooted Rural	100.0	72904	53 Home Town	52.0
72473	50 Heartland Communities	45.0	72663	46 Rooted Rural	100.0	72905	26 Midland Crowd	50.0
72476	50 Heartland Communities	65.1	72666	46 Rooted Rural	100.0	72908	32 Rustbelt Traditions	25.1
72478	42 Southern Satellites	99.1	72668	49 Senior Sun Seekers	100.0	72916	28 Aspiring Young Families	47.5
72479	46 Rooted Rural	56.6	72669	42 Southern Satellites	95.9	72921	26 Midland Crowd	31.0
72482	49 Senior Sun Seekers	60.1	72670	46 Rooted Rural	100.0	72923	26 Midland Crowd	48.4
72501	42 Southern Satellites	37.8	72675	46 Rooted Rural	83.0	72926	42 Southern Satellites	78.2
72512	43 The Elders	39.5	72679	46 Rooted Rural	100.0	72927	50 Heartland Communities	30.3

CONSUMER TYPE

ZIP CODE	TOP TAPESTRY CONSUMER TYPE	% 2009 HOUSE-HOLDS	ZIP CODE	TOP TAPESTRY CONSUMER TYPE	% 2009 HOUSE-HOLDS	ZIP CODE	TOP TAPESTRY CONSUMER TYPE	% 2009 HOUSE-HOLDS
72928	46 Rooted Rural	80.4	73089	17 Green Acres	43.4	73532	50 Heartland Communities	78.8
72930	37 Prairie Living	55.4	73090	46 Rooted Rural	100.0	73533	50 Heartland Communities	20.5
72932	42 Southern Satellites	87.1	73092	46 Rooted Rural	100.0	73537	50 Heartland Communities	84.7
72933	25 Salt Of The Earth	48.9	73093	17 Green Acres	59.4	73538	32 Rustbelt Traditions	45.7
72934	46 Rooted Rural	85.9	73095	46 Rooted Rural	100.0	73539	37 Prairie Living	100.0
72936	26 Midland Crowd	72.1	73096	55 College Towns	26.0	73540	46 Rooted Rural	100.0
72937	42 Southern Satellites	65.9	73098	50 Heartland Communities	73.1	73541	50 Heartland Communities	54.5
72938	42 Southern Satellites	82.4	73099	19 Milk And Cookies	27.9	73542	50 Heartland Communities	44.4
72940	42 Southern Satellites	39.9	73102	65 Social Security Set	95.4	73543	42 Southern Satellites	81.1
72941	25 Salt Of The Earth	53.3	73103	52 Inner City Tenants	30.8	73544	37 Prairie Living	100.0
72943	42 Southern Satellites	93.7	73104	36 Old And Newcomers	37.5	73546	46 Rooted Rural	100.0
72944	42 Southern Satellites	43.3	73105	62 Modest Income Homes	27.1	73547	50 Heartland Communities	65.4
72946	42 Southern Satellites	71.2	73106	60 City Dimensions	44.2	73548	46 Rooted Rural	100.0
72947	46 Rooted Rural	54.0	73107	48 Great Expectations	33.7	73549	26 Midland Crowd	82.7
72948	46 Rooted Rural	72.7	73108	59 Southwestern Families	40.5	73550	50 Heartland Communities	91.9
72949	42 Southern Satellites	38.6	73109	53 Home Town	26.7	73551	37 Prairie Living	100.0
72950	46 Rooted Rural	96.8	73110	48 Great Expectations	17.7	73552	46 Rooted Rural	84.5
72951	46 Rooted Rural	97.6	73111	62 Modest Income Homes	60.8	73553	46 Rooted Rural	100.0
72952	42 Southern Satellites	63.8	73112	48 Great Expectations	15.6	73554	50 Heartland Communities	73.7
72955	42 Southern Satellites	100.0	73114	51 Metro City Edge	36.1	73559	37 Prairie Living	100.0
72956	42 Southern Satellites	21.8	73115	32 Rustbelt Traditions	33.9	73560	46 Rooted Rural	98.1
72958	42 Southern Satellites	51.3	73116	33 Midlife Junction	22.5	73562	42 Southern Satellites	71.0
72959	46 Rooted Rural	60.3	73117	62 Modest Income Homes	66.4	73564	37 Prairie Living	100.0
73002	46 Rooted Rural	99.6	73118	48 Great Expectations	30.6	73565	50 Heartland Communities	78.4
73003	12 Up And Coming Families	43.0	73119	53 Home Town	58.8	73566	50 Heartland Communities	93.2
73004	26 Midland Crowd	71.0	73120	39 Young And Restless	28.4	73568	50 Heartland Communities	100.0
73005	53 Home Town	41.9	73121	14 Prosperous Empty Nesters	42.9	73569	50 Heartland Communities	100.0
73006	46 Rooted Rural	72.8	73122	32 Rustbelt Traditions	25.3	73570	50 Heartland Communities	100.0
73007	26 Midland Crowd	33.2	73127	52 Inner City Tenants	36.2	73571	37 Prairie Living	100.0
73008	14 Prosperous Empty Nesters	18.9	73128	17 Green Acres	34.1	73572	50 Heartland Communities	60.1
73009	46 Rooted Rural	88.1	73129	53 Home Town	48.0	73573	46 Rooted Rural	49.5
73010	26 Midland Crowd	79.6	73130	32 Rustbelt Traditions	29.4	73601	53 Home Town	47.2
73011	50 Heartland Communities	52.7	73131	07 Exurbanites	68.5	73620	46 Rooted Rural	99.4
73012	04 Boomburbs	57.2	73132	19 Milk And Cookies	20.9	73622	46 Rooted Rural	100.0
73013	07 Exurbanites	15.2	73134	36 Old And Newcomers	59.8	73624	48 Great Expectations	87.5
73014	37 Prairie Living	30.0	73135	19 Milk And Cookies	26.5	73625	37 Prairie Living	100.0
73015	50 Heartland Communities	57.2	73139	36 Old And Newcomers	18.9	73626	37 Prairie Living	89.6
73016	26 Midland Crowd	100.0	73141	53 Home Town	33.0	73627	37 Prairie Living	100.0
73017	50 Heartland Communities	53.0	73142	16 Enterprising Professionals	79.6	73628	50 Heartland Communities	75.7
73018	53 Home Town	24.8	73145	40 Military Proximity	100.0	73632	50 Heartland Communities	58.6
73020	17 Green Acres	25.6	73149	53 Home Town	53.4	73638	37 Prairie Living	100.0
73021	37 Prairie Living	100.0	73150	07 Exurbanites	53.1	73639	37 Prairie Living	100.0
73024	37 Prairie Living	100.0	73151	02 Suburban Splendor	96.9	73641	50 Heartland Communities	66.2
73025	17 Green Acres	44.6	73159	19 Milk And Cookies	28.3	73642	37 Prairie Living	100.0
73026	26 Midland Crowd	50.5	73160	19 Milk And Cookies	48.8	73644	53 Home Town	25.2
73027	46 Rooted Rural	47.0	73162	07 Exurbanites	22.1	73645	50 Heartland Communities	65.1
73028	50 Heartland Communities	55.9	73165	17 Green Acres	67.8	73646	37 Prairie Living	100.0
73029	50 Heartland Communities	80.2	73169	26 Midland Crowd	88.0	73647	48 Great Expectations	77.9
73030	50 Heartland Communities	43.6	73170	12 Up And Coming Families	49.4	73650	37 Prairie Living	100.0
73034	16 Enterprising Professionals	17.1	73173	14 Prosperous Empty Nesters	99.6	73651	50 Heartland Communities	77.7
73036	53 Home Town	22.7	73179	26 Midland Crowd	71.0	73654	37 Prairie Living	99.7
73038	50 Heartland Communities	43.9	73401	50 Heartland Communities	20.0	73655	46 Rooted Rural	100.0
73040	50 Heartland Communities	73.4	73430	46 Rooted Rural	100.0	73658	37 Prairie Living	100.0
73041	37 Prairie Living	100.0	73432	46 Rooted Rural	100.0	73659	37 Prairie Living	100.0
73042	46 Rooted Rural	100.0	73433	50 Heartland Communities	42.7	73660	37 Prairie Living	96.1
73043	46 Rooted Rural	100.0	73434	46 Rooted Rural	100.0	73661	37 Prairie Living	100.0
73044	26 Midland Crowd	28.8	73437	46 Rooted Rural	100.0	73662	50 Heartland Communities	95.4
73045	26 Midland Crowd	72.5	73438	50 Heartland Communities	47.9	73663	50 Heartland Communities	65.4
73047	46 Rooted Rural	72.9	73439	49 Senior Sun Seekers	64.8	73664	37 Prairie Living	100.0
73048	37 Prairie Living	57.1	73440	46 Rooted Rural	100.0	73666	37 Prairie Living	100.0
73049	50 Heartland Communities	37.8	73441	46 Rooted Rural	100.0	73667	37 Prairie Living	100.0
73051	46 Rooted Rural	40.3	73442	46 Rooted Rural	100.0	73668	37 Prairie Living	100.0
73052	50 Heartland Communities	37.1	73443	42 Southern Satellites	34.9	73669	50 Heartland Communities	73.5
73053	37 Prairie Living	94.8	73444	56 Rural Bypasses	66.3	73673	37 Prairie Living	75.4
73054	26 Midland Crowd	62.1	73446	46 Rooted Rural	48.8	73701	53 Home Town	58.6
73055	50 Heartland Communities	46.0	73447	42 Southern Satellites	100.0	73703	33 Midlife Junction	37.2
73056	46 Rooted Rural	95.6	73448	50 Heartland Communities	29.5	73705	40 Military Proximity	0.0
73057	50 Heartland Communities	66.2	73449	49 Senior Sun Seekers	60.2	73716	37 Prairie Living	100.0
73058	26 Midland Crowd	65.7	73450	46 Rooted Rural	100.0	73717	50 Heartland Communities	39.7
73059	50 Heartland Communities	61.5	73453	46 Rooted Rural	75.0	73718	37 Prairie Living	100.0
73061	26 Midland Crowd	97.7	73456	50 Heartland Communities	64.0	73719	37 Prairie Living	100.0
73062	50 Heartland Communities	72.1	73458	46 Rooted Rural	95.7	73720	37 Prairie Living	100.0
73063	46 Rooted Rural	100.0	73459	42 Southern Satellites	100.0	73722	37 Prairie Living	85.3
73064	19 Milk And Cookies	41.7	73460	50 Heartland Communities	40.7	73724	46 Rooted Rural	100.0
73065	26 Midland Crowd	67.3	73461	46 Rooted Rural	100.0	73726	37 Prairie Living	100.0
73067	46 Rooted Rural	100.0	73463	46 Rooted Rural	56.3	73727	37 Prairie Living	88.1
73068	26 Midland Crowd	49.4	73481	46 Rooted Rural	100.0	73728	37 Prairie Living	74.5
73069	55 College Towns	23.9	73488	46 Rooted Rural	100.0	73729	37 Prairie Living	100.0
73071	55 College Towns	23.5	73501	53 Home Town	19.7	73730	37 Prairie Living	100.0
73072	63 Dorms To Diplomas	15.6	73503	40 Military Proximity	100.0	73731	37 Prairie Living	100.0
73073	46 Rooted Rural	100.0	73505	28 Aspiring Young Families	14.3	73733	37 Prairie Living	100.0
73074	50 Heartland Communities	61.5	73507	48 Great Expectations	24.9	73734	26 Midland Crowd	100.0
73075	50 Heartland Communities	32.0	73521	53 Home Town	42.4	73735	37 Prairie Living	100.0
73077	53 Home Town	26.4	73523	40 Military Proximity	99.4	73736	37 Prairie Living	100.0
73078	17 Green Acres	92.7	73526	50 Heartland Communities	99.5	73737	50 Heartland Communities	49.9
73079	25 Salt Of The Earth	97.7	73527	26 Midland Crowd	81.9	73738	50 Heartland Communities	77.6
73080	26 Midland Crowd	28.1	73528	46 Rooted Rural	100.0	73739	37 Prairie Living	100.0
73082	46 Rooted Rural	57.9	73529	46 Rooted Rural	68.4	73741	46 Rooted Rural	73.0
73084	34 Family Foundations	29.7	73530	50 Heartland Communities	100.0	73742	46 Rooted Rural	42.0
73086	50 Heartland Communities	36.9	73531	37 Prairie Living	100.0	73744	37 Prairie Living	100.0

ZIP CODE	TOP TAPESTRY CONSUMER TYPE	% 2009 HOUSE-HOLDS	ZIP CODE	TOP TAPESTRY CONSUMER TYPE	% 2009 HOUSE-HOLDS	ZIP CODE	TOP TAPESTRY CONSUMER TYPE	% 2009 HOUSE-HOLDS
73747	37 Prairie Living	100.0	74054	46 Rooted Rural	100.0	74434	26 Midland Crowd	40.2
73749	50 Heartland Communities	95.6	74055	12 Up And Coming Families	43.5	74435	46 Rooted Rural	100.0
73750	29 Rustbelt Retirees	40.5	74056	50 Heartland Communities	60.3	74436	46 Rooted Rural	47.5
73753	37 Prairie Living	79.4	74058	50 Heartland Communities	59.1	74437	50 Heartland Communities	27.6
73754	46 Rooted Rural	89.2	74059	32 Rustbelt Traditions	53.5	74441	46 Rooted Rural	57.4
73755	46 Rooted Rural	100.0	74060	31 Rural Resort Dwellers	35.8	74442	46 Rooted Rural	92.4
73756	37 Prairie Living	100.0	74061	46 Rooted Rural	39.5	74445	50 Heartland Communities	43.2
73757	37 Prairie Living	100.0	74062	46 Rooted Rural	100.0	74447	50 Heartland Communities	27.5
73758	37 Prairie Living	100.0	74063	26 Midland Crowd	41.2	74450	46 Rooted Rural	99.1
73759	50 Heartland Communities	71.4	74066	26 Midland Crowd	20.7	74451	31 Rural Resort Dwellers	55.0
73760	37 Prairie Living	100.0	74070	32 Rustbelt Traditions	35.8	74452	42 Southern Satellites	100.0
73761	37 Prairie Living	100.0	74072	42 Southern Satellites	71.6	74454	42 Southern Satellites	42.7
73762	37 Prairie Living	77.3	74073	26 Midland Crowd	37.7	74455	56 Rural Bypasses	74.8
73763	37 Prairie Living	57.9	74074	26 Midland Crowd	21.5	74457	46 Rooted Rural	43.9
73764	37 Prairie Living	100.0	74075	55 College Towns	23.9	74462	50 Heartland Communities	50.4
73766	37 Prairie Living	100.0	74077	63 Dorms To Diplomas	0.0	74463	56 Rural Bypasses	100.0
73768	37 Prairie Living	100.0	74078	63 Dorms To Diplomas	100.0	74464	48 Great Expectations	25.7
73770	37 Prairie Living	100.0	74079	50 Heartland Communities	59.6	74467	53 Home Town	19.8
73771	37 Prairie Living	100.0	74080	26 Midland Crowd	87.0	74469	50 Heartland Communities	64.0
73772	50 Heartland Communities	38.0	74081	42 Southern Satellites	96.8	74470	46 Rooted Rural	100.0
73773	50 Heartland Communities	70.0	74083	46 Rooted Rural	76.9	74471	42 Southern Satellites	65.2
73801	53 Home Town	30.6	74084	56 Rural Bypasses	83.1	74472	46 Rooted Rural	100.0
73832	37 Prairie Living	100.0	74085	50 Heartland Communities	38.7	74501	46 Rooted Rural	28.7
73834	37 Prairie Living	100.0	74103	65 Social Security Set	58.3	74523	46 Rooted Rural	50.0
73835	37 Prairie Living	97.0	74104	22 Metropolitans	37.8	74525	46 Rooted Rural	54.0
73838	37 Prairie Living	100.0	74105	36 Old And Newcomers	25.6	74528	46 Rooted Rural	100.0
73840	37 Prairie Living	100.0	74106	62 Modest Income Homes	43.0	74531	46 Rooted Rural	100.0
73841	46 Rooted Rural	100.0	74107	32 Rustbelt Traditions	21.2	74533	46 Rooted Rural	100.0
73842	46 Rooted Rural	100.0	74108	26 Midland Crowd	24.2	74534	46 Rooted Rural	100.0
73843	37 Prairie Living	100.0	74110	53 Home Town	59.0	74536	50 Heartland Communities	60.3
73844	37 Prairie Living	100.0	74112	32 Rustbelt Traditions	34.6	74538	46 Rooted Rural	49.0
73848	50 Heartland Communities	70.5	74114	32 Rustbelt Traditions	30.0	74540	46 Rooted Rural	100.0
73851	37 Prairie Living	100.0	74115	53 Home Town	64.5	74543	46 Rooted Rural	100.0
73852	46 Rooted Rural	38.2	74116	52 Inner City Tenants	58.9	74547	50 Heartland Communities	62.2
73853	37 Prairie Living	100.0	74117	25 Salt Of The Earth	66.7	74549	46 Rooted Rural	100.0
73855	37 Prairie Living	100.0	74119	30 Retirement Communities	47.8	74552	46 Rooted Rural	99.3
73857	37 Prairie Living	100.0	74120	22 Metropolitans	27.0	74553	46 Rooted Rural	100.0
73858	50 Heartland Communities	82.5	74126	51 Metro City Edge	58.0	74555	46 Rooted Rural	100.0
73859	50 Heartland Communities	72.5	74127	53 Home Town	38.7	74557	46 Rooted Rural	100.0
73860	37 Prairie Living	54.9	74128	32 Rustbelt Traditions	39.9	74558	46 Rooted Rural	100.0
73931	37 Prairie Living	100.0	74129	28 Aspiring Young Families	32.1	74560	46 Rooted Rural	100.0
73932	37 Prairie Living	68.3	74130	53 Home Town	48.9	74561	49 Senior Sun Seekers	57.2
73933	37 Prairie Living	55.6	74131	41 Crossroads	42.2	74562	46 Rooted Rural	100.0
73937	37 Prairie Living	100.0	74132	19 Milk And Cookies	41.5	74563	50 Heartland Communities	54.2
73938	37 Prairie Living	100.0	74133	39 Young And Restless	25.8	74567	46 Rooted Rural	100.0
73939	55 College Towns	60.9	74134	28 Aspiring Young Families	59.1	74569	46 Rooted Rural	100.0
73942	41 Crossroads	21.4	74135	14 Prosperous Empty Nesters	32.2	74570	46 Rooted Rural	100.0
73944	37 Prairie Living	100.0	74136	39 Young And Restless	48.4	74571	50 Heartland Communities	63.4
73945	37 Prairie Living	67.3	74137	02 Suburban Splendor	56.5	74572	46 Rooted Rural	55.0
73946	37 Prairie Living	100.0	74145	39 Young And Restless	26.7	74574	46 Rooted Rural	100.0
73947	37 Prairie Living	100.0	74146	39 Young And Restless	30.8	74576	46 Rooted Rural	100.0
73949	46 Rooted Rural	61.7	74171	15 Silver And Gold	100.0	74577	46 Rooted Rural	88.6
73950	37 Prairie Living	58.2	74301	50 Heartland Communities	58.3	74578	46 Rooted Rural	43.4
73951	41 Crossroads	77.5	74330	46 Rooted Rural	53.6	74601	53 Home Town	42.6
74002	50 Heartland Communities	51.8	74331	31 Rural Resort Dwellers	48.5	74604	14 Prosperous Empty Nesters	35.4
74003	53 Home Town	37.6	74332	46 Rooted Rural	88.0	74630	46 Rooted Rural	100.0
74006	33 Midlife Junction	29.8	74333	46 Rooted Rural	88.3	74631	53 Home Town	40.5
74008	26 Midland Crowd	26.1	74337	42 Southern Satellites	50.8	74632	37 Prairie Living	100.0
74010	26 Midland Crowd	30.8	74338	42 Southern Satellites	100.0	74633	46 Rooted Rural	74.0
74011	19 Milk And Cookies	44.7	74339	53 Home Town	98.8	74636	37 Prairie Living	100.0
74012	19 Milk And Cookies	35.6	74342	46 Rooted Rural	47.5	74637	50 Heartland Communities	79.0
74014	17 Green Acres	35.1	74343	46 Rooted Rural	46.5	74640	37 Prairie Living	92.9
74015	26 Midland Crowd	84.8	74344	49 Senior Sun Seekers	38.8	74641	46 Rooted Rural	100.0
74016	26 Midland Crowd	45.3	74346	53 Home Town	31.1	74643	37 Prairie Living	100.0
74017	17 Green Acres	18.2	74347	42 Southern Satellites	100.0	74644	46 Rooted Rural	100.0
74019	17 Green Acres	48.9	74352	42 Southern Satellites	61.4	74646	37 Prairie Living	100.0
74020	26 Midland Crowd	35.3	74354	53 Home Town	25.2	74647	46 Rooted Rural	72.4
74021	32 Rustbelt Traditions	20.2	74358	50 Heartland Communities	100.0	74650	37 Prairie Living	100.0
74022	46 Rooted Rural	52.7	74359	42 Southern Satellites	100.0	74651	46 Rooted Rural	100.0
74023	50 Heartland Communities	44.4	74360	56 Rural Bypasses	78.7	74652	50 Heartland Communities	92.8
74026	46 Rooted Rural	100.0	74361	50 Heartland Communities	17.7	74653	50 Heartland Communities	66.1
74027	46 Rooted Rural	77.9	74363	46 Rooted Rural	35.9	74701	33 Midlife Junction	30.0
74028	46 Rooted Rural	51.5	74364	42 Southern Satellites	53.4	74723	46 Rooted Rural	100.0
74029	50 Heartland Communities	73.0	74365	42 Southern Satellites	100.0	74724	46 Rooted Rural	61.8
74030	50 Heartland Communities	58.9	74366	56 Rural Bypasses	58.4	74726	46 Rooted Rural	56.0
74032	41 Crossroads	74.7	74367	31 Rural Resort Dwellers	54.0	74727	50 Heartland Communities	39.2
74033	19 Milk And Cookies	57.3	74368	42 Southern Satellites	100.0	74728	42 Southern Satellites	34.1
74035	50 Heartland Communities	48.6	74369	37 Prairie Living	56.6	74729	50 Heartland Communities	45.8
74036	26 Midland Crowd	60.1	74370	31 Rural Resort Dwellers	36.5	74730	50 Heartland Communities	33.7
74037	12 Up And Coming Families	44.6	74401	62 Modest Income Homes	20.6	74731	46 Rooted Rural	50.1
74038	42 Southern Satellites	100.0	74403	53 Home Town	20.7	74733	56 Rural Bypasses	59.3
74039	42 Southern Satellites	52.2	74421	26 Midland Crowd	59.9	74734	56 Rural Bypasses	79.0
74041	26 Midland Crowd	100.0	74422	56 Rural Bypasses	68.1	74735	46 Rooted Rural	69.2
74042	42 Southern Satellites	100.0	74423	42 Southern Satellites	100.0	74736	46 Rooted Rural	100.0
74044	42 Southern Satellites	58.0	74425	49 Senior Sun Seekers	70.1	74738	46 Rooted Rural	100.0
74045	46 Rooted Rural	95.8	74426	49 Senior Sun Seekers	42.7	74740	56 Rural Bypasses	100.0
74047	26 Midland Crowd	57.4	74427	49 Senior Sun Seekers	73.6	74741	46 Rooted Rural	59.6
74048	50 Heartland Communities	39.0	74428	46 Rooted Rural	73.8	74743	50 Heartland Communities	32.6
74051	26 Midland Crowd	99.7	74429	26 Midland Crowd	26.9	74745	46 Rooted Rural	36.6
74053	26 Midland Crowd	99.9	74432	49 Senior Sun Seekers	47.0	74748	46 Rooted Rural	88.2

ZIP CODE	TOP TAPESTRY CONSUMER TYPE	% 2009 HOUSE-HOLDS	ZIP CODE	TOP TAPESTRY CONSUMER TYPE	% 2009 HOUSE-HOLDS	ZIP CODE	TOP TAPESTRY CONSUMER TYPE	% 2009 HOUSE-HOLDS
74754	42 Southern Satellites	100.0	75035	04 Boomburbs	52.7	75201	27 Metro Renters	87.0
74755	46 Rooted Rural	100.0	75038	39 Young And Restless	64.0	75202	27 Metro Renters	100.0
74756	46 Rooted Rural	100.0	75039	27 Metro Renters	55.0	75203	58 NeWest Residents	41.9
74759	46 Rooted Rural	100.0	75040	19 Milk And Cookies	35.3	75204	27 Metro Renters	63.8
74760	46 Rooted Rural	100.0	75041	38 Industrious Urban Fringe	22.4	75205	01 Top Rung	35.7
74764	42 Southern Satellites	52.3	75042	38 Industrious Urban Fringe	20.1	75206	27 Metro Renters	24.6
74766	56 Rural Bypasses	67.1	75043	19 Milk And Cookies	36.2	75207	66 Unclassified	80.0
74801	53 Home Town	45.3	75044	19 Milk And Cookies	51.5	75208	59 Southwestern Families	26.2
74804	26 Midland Crowd	26.8	75048	12 Up And Coming Families	42.6	75209	09 Urban Chic	19.4
74820	46 Rooted Rural	17.7	75050	39 Young And Restless	21.0	75210	62 Modest Income Homes	49.2
74824	46 Rooted Rural	100.0	75051	38 Industrious Urban Fringe	48.6	75211	58 NeWest Residents	32.0
74825	46 Rooted Rural	32.9	75052	12 Up And Coming Families	35.8	75212	59 Southwestern Families	60.8
74826	46 Rooted Rural	100.0	75054	12 Up And Coming Families	68.5	75214	22 Metropolitans	22.6
74827	46 Rooted Rural	100.0	75056	12 Up And Coming Families	46.3	75215	62 Modest Income Homes	57.4
74829	56 Rural Bypasses	73.3	75057	39 Young And Restless	38.4	75216	62 Modest Income Homes	33.4
74831	46 Rooted Rural	100.0	75058	26 Midland Crowd	53.8	75217	38 Industrious Urban Fringe	44.9
74832	46 Rooted Rural	100.0	75060	38 Industrious Urban Fringe	19.4	75218	14 Prosperous Empty Nesters	24.2
74833	46 Rooted Rural	92.8	75061	38 Industrious Urban Fringe	22.3	75219	27 Metro Renters	36.3
74834	50 Heartland Communities	50.3	75062	39 Young And Restless	21.1	75220	58 NeWest Residents	64.0
74839	56 Rural Bypasses	94.2	75063	16 Enterprising Professionals	66.6	75223	59 Southwestern Families	41.3
74840	46 Rooted Rural	80.4	75065	28 Aspiring Young Families	26.9	75224	38 Industrious Urban Fringe	39.2
74842	37 Prairie Living	100.0	75067	39 Young And Restless	44.4	75225	01 Top Rung	46.5
74843	37 Prairie Living	100.0	75068	12 Up And Coming Families	53.5	75226	27 Metro Renters	31.5
74845	56 Rural Bypasses	85.5	75069	02 Suburban Splendor	11.9	75227	38 Industrious Urban Fringe	31.8
74848	50 Heartland Communities	49.9	75070	04 Boomburbs	85.3	75228	52 Inner City Tenants	28.3
74849	53 Home Town	57.0	75071	12 Up And Coming Families	42.2	75229	03 Connoisseurs	22.2
74850	46 Rooted Rural	100.0	75074	19 Milk And Cookies	17.7	75230	03 Connoisseurs	21.3
74851	26 Midland Crowd	58.0	75075	07 Exurbanites	29.9	75231	39 Young And Restless	33.9
74852	46 Rooted Rural	100.0	75076	31 Rural Resort Dwellers	37.6	75232	34 Family Foundations	47.9
74854	46 Rooted Rural	54.0	75077	12 Up And Coming Families	39.0	75233	59 Southwestern Families	23.9
74855	42 Southern Satellites	42.5	75078	12 Up And Coming Families	90.8	75234	32 Rustbelt Traditions	15.6
74856	56 Rural Bypasses	56.6	75080	52 Inner City Tenants	14.9	75235	58 NeWest Residents	31.1
74857	26 Midland Crowd	85.1	75081	07 Exurbanites	24.5	75236	38 Industrious Urban Fringe	42.6
74859	46 Rooted Rural	37.9	75082	04 Boomburbs	40.6	75237	52 Inner City Tenants	80.7
74860	46 Rooted Rural	97.8	75087	04 Boomburbs	35.4	75238	39 Young And Restless	15.7
74864	50 Heartland Communities	71.5	75088	19 Milk And Cookies	24.7	75240	39 Young And Restless	31.7
74865	50 Heartland Communities	58.7	75089	12 Up And Coming Families	55.7	75241	34 Family Foundations	53.7
74867	46 Rooted Rural	100.0	75090	53 Home Town	25.0	75243	39 Young And Restless	59.1
74868	46 Rooted Rural	37.3	75092	33 Midlife Junction	22.9	75244	13 In Style	21.4
74869	46 Rooted Rural	100.0	75093	04 Boomburbs	34.1	75246	52 Inner City Tenants	41.9
74871	46 Rooted Rural	71.8	75094	04 Boomburbs	78.9	75247	62 Modest Income Homes	100.0
74872	37 Prairie Living	43.4	75098	12 Up And Coming Families	54.0	75248	13 In Style	22.5
74873	46 Rooted Rural	37.2	75102	26 Midland Crowd	79.5	75249	19 Milk And Cookies	100.0
74875	46 Rooted Rural	100.0	75103	46 Rooted Rural	54.8	75251	08 Laptops And Lattes	100.0
74878	46 Rooted Rural	100.0	75104	12 Up And Coming Families	37.1	75252	16 Enterprising Professionals	41.2
74880	46 Rooted Rural	54.7	75105	42 Southern Satellites	100.0	75253	41 Crossroads	68.9
74881	46 Rooted Rural	75.3	75109	26 Midland Crowd	100.0	75254	39 Young And Restless	52.0
74883	50 Heartland Communities	98.9	75110	26 Midland Crowd	16.3	75261	32 Rustbelt Traditions	100.0
74884	50 Heartland Communities	44.0	75114	19 Milk And Cookies	51.5	75287	39 Young And Restless	36.3
74901	53 Home Town	55.6	75115	06 Sophisticated Squires	22.1	75401	53 Home Town	34.7
74902	42 Southern Satellites	75.0	75116	07 Exurbanites	20.3	75402	33 Midlife Junction	30.9
74930	42 Southern Satellites	55.8	75117	46 Rooted Rural	55.6	75407	26 Midland Crowd	77.2
74931	46 Rooted Rural	78.1	75119	26 Midland Crowd	26.1	75409	26 Midland Crowd	94.2
74932	46 Rooted Rural	100.0	75124	46 Rooted Rural	42.5	75410	46 Rooted Rural	63.0
74937	46 Rooted Rural	52.1	75125	41 Crossroads	50.3	75411	17 Green Acres	50.7
74939	46 Rooted Rural	100.0	75126	12 Up And Coming Families	34.5	75412	46 Rooted Rural	100.0
74940	46 Rooted Rural	96.1	75127	46 Rooted Rural	99.4	75414	26 Midland Crowd	69.0
74941	46 Rooted Rural	50.9	75134	19 Milk And Cookies	28.2	75415	46 Rooted Rural	100.0
74944	46 Rooted Rural	100.0	75135	26 Midland Crowd	67.3	75416	46 Rooted Rural	70.7
74948	42 Southern Satellites	66.8	75137	19 Milk And Cookies	33.5	75417	50 Heartland Communities	53.8
74949	46 Rooted Rural	100.0	75140	46 Rooted Rural	46.6	75418	46 Rooted Rural	26.5
74953	50 Heartland Communities	39.1	75141	41 Crossroads	51.0	75420	46 Rooted Rural	100.0
74954	42 Southern Satellites	39.6	75142	26 Midland Crowd	71.6	75421	25 Salt Of The Earth	62.8
74955	53 Home Town	31.5	75143	26 Midland Crowd	26.3	75422	46 Rooted Rural	75.4
74956	25 Salt Of The Earth	60.6	75144	50 Heartland Communities	41.5	75423	26 Midland Crowd	39.7
74957	56 Rural Bypasses	78.8	75146	28 Aspiring Young Families	36.4	75424	26 Midland Crowd	100.0
74959	42 Southern Satellites	60.3	75147	41 Crossroads	52.7	75426	56 Rural Bypasses	36.0
74960	56 Rural Bypasses	33.5	75148	49 Senior Sun Seekers	52.0	75428	55 College Towns	45.7
74962	46 Rooted Rural	78.4	75149	38 Industrious Urban Fringe	22.5	75431	46 Rooted Rural	50.8
74963	56 Rural Bypasses	68.0	75150	19 Milk And Cookies	20.1	75432	46 Rooted Rural	37.0
74964	42 Southern Satellites	100.0	75152	26 Midland Crowd	65.4	75433	46 Rooted Rural	100.0
74965	42 Southern Satellites	53.8	75153	46 Rooted Rural	100.0	75435	46 Rooted Rural	63.3
74966	46 Rooted Rural	64.6	75154	19 Milk And Cookies	25.0	75436	56 Rural Bypasses	58.1
75001	16 Enterprising Professionals	36.0	75155	42 Southern Satellites	100.0	75437	46 Rooted Rural	60.2
75002	04 Boomburbs	62.9	75156	49 Senior Sun Seekers	69.5	75438	46 Rooted Rural	100.0
75006	39 Young And Restless	14.2	75158	26 Midland Crowd	100.0	75439	50 Heartland Communities	85.8
75007	06 Sophisticated Squires	25.6	75159	26 Midland Crowd	38.1	75440	46 Rooted Rural	69.0
75009	06 Sophisticated Squires	49.6	75160	26 Midland Crowd	27.8	75442	26 Midland Crowd	35.0
75010	16 Enterprising Professionals	49.3	75161	26 Midland Crowd	55.1	75446	50 Heartland Communities	37.6
75013	04 Boomburbs	96.3	75163	49 Senior Sun Seekers	60.4	75447	46 Rooted Rural	68.7
75019	04 Boomburbs	54.5	75165	19 Milk And Cookies	11.7	75448	46 Rooted Rural	100.0
75020	53 Home Town	19.2	75166	26 Midland Crowd	100.0	75449	56 Rural Bypasses	75.8
75021	25 Salt Of The Earth	36.7	75167	17 Green Acres	30.9	75450	46 Rooted Rural	100.0
75022	04 Boomburbs	82.1	75169	46 Rooted Rural	34.1	75451	46 Rooted Rural	100.0
75023	02 Suburban Splendor	25.6	75172	41 Crossroads	34.2	75452	26 Midland Crowd	36.2
75024	16 Enterprising Professionals	64.7	75173	26 Midland Crowd	81.9	75453	46 Rooted Rural	84.9
75025	04 Boomburbs	79.2	75180	38 Industrious Urban Fringe	43.1	75454	26 Midland Crowd	96.7
75028	04 Boomburbs	80.0	75181	12 Up And Coming Families	48.9	75455	26 Midland Crowd	28.9
75032	02 Suburban Splendor	47.3	75182	07 Exurbanites	58.2	75457	46 Rooted Rural	44.5
75034	12 Up And Coming Families	27.6	75189	26 Midland Crowd	74.8	75459	26 Midland Crowd	44.2

ZIP CODE	TOP TAPESTRY CONSUMER TYPE	% 2009 HOUSE-HOLDS	ZIP CODE	TOP TAPESTRY CONSUMER TYPE	% 2009 HOUSE-HOLDS	ZIP CODE	TOP TAPESTRY CONSUMER TYPE	% 2009 HOUSE-HOLDS
75460	53 Home Town	25.3	75706	42 Southern Satellites	69.0	75979	46 Rooted Rural	43.6
75462	17 Green Acres	43.2	75707	26 Midland Crowd	36.5	75980	46 Rooted Rural	61.8
75468	46 Rooted Rural	97.5	75708	41 Crossroads	68.9	76001	12 Up And Coming Families	43.4
75469	46 Rooted Rural	100.0	75709	26 Midland Crowd	57.5	76002	04 Boomburbs	60.7
75470	46 Rooted Rural	98.0	75750	46 Rooted Rural	51.5	76006	39 Young And Restless	77.3
75471	42 Southern Satellites	99.2	75751	26 Midland Crowd	22.0	76008	06 Sophisticated Squires	56.2
75472	46 Rooted Rural	100.0	75752	46 Rooted Rural	45.9	76009	41 Crossroads	44.3
75473	46 Rooted Rural	66.4	75754	46 Rooted Rural	82.6	76010	52 Inner City Tenants	34.0
75474	41 Crossroads	36.9	75755	46 Rooted Rural	25.3	76011	39 Young And Restless	52.5
75476	46 Rooted Rural	95.5	75756	46 Rooted Rural	58.9	76012	07 Exurbanites	33.6
75477	50 Heartland Communities	70.5	75757	26 Midland Crowd	61.0	76013	33 Midlife Junction	25.5
75478	46 Rooted Rural	55.6	75758	49 Senior Sun Seekers	30.4	76014	28 Aspiring Young Families	56.9
75479	25 Salt Of The Earth	51.3	75760	46 Rooted Rural	100.0	76015	39 Young And Restless	22.0
75480	31 Rural Resort Dwellers	85.5	75762	17 Green Acres	42.6	76016	06 Sophisticated Squires	28.5
75481	46 Rooted Rural	100.0	75763	49 Senior Sun Seekers	39.0	76017	19 Milk And Cookies	32.1
75482	46 Rooted Rural	15.0	75765	46 Rooted Rural	35.8	76018	12 Up And Coming Families	55.9
75486	46 Rooted Rural	35.0	75766	53 Home Town	25.5	76019	33 Midlife Junction	100.0
75487	56 Rural Bypasses	62.0	75770	46 Rooted Rural	69.6	76020	26 Midland Crowd	36.0
75488	37 Prairie Living	73.8	75771	26 Midland Crowd	35.3	76021	39 Young And Restless	29.1
75490	26 Midland Crowd	53.6	75773	31 Rural Resort Dwellers	37.8	76022	36 Old And Newcomers	36.4
75491	26 Midland Crowd	67.8	75778	46 Rooted Rural	44.7	76023	26 Midland Crowd	99.5
75492	46 Rooted Rural	100.0	75783	31 Rural Resort Dwellers	61.9	76028	19 Milk And Cookies	29.1
75493	26 Midland Crowd	100.0	75784	46 Rooted Rural	100.0	76031	26 Midland Crowd	21.6
75494	50 Heartland Communities	42.5	75785	46 Rooted Rural	53.8	76033	53 Home Town	21.3
75495	26 Midland Crowd	38.5	75789	26 Midland Crowd	35.8	76034	02 Suburban Splendor	84.2
75496	53 Home Town	47.3	75790	46 Rooted Rural	46.3	76035	26 Midland Crowd	98.5
75497	31 Rural Resort Dwellers	86.5	75791	19 Milk And Cookies	42.0	76036	32 Rustbelt Traditions	25.2
75501	26 Midland Crowd	24.2	75792	26 Midland Crowd	76.0	76039	19 Milk And Cookies	31.6
75503	07 Exurbanites	22.3	75798	50 Heartland Communities	0.0	76040	39 Young And Restless	32.5
75550	46 Rooted Rural	100.0	75799	16 Enterprising Professionals	97.0	76041	42 Southern Satellites	80.3
75551	46 Rooted Rural	37.5	75801	48 Great Expectations	19.2	76043	26 Midland Crowd	67.5
75554	46 Rooted Rural	61.0	75803	32 Rustbelt Traditions	18.4	76044	26 Midland Crowd	62.7
75555	46 Rooted Rural	100.0	75831	46 Rooted Rural	50.1	76048	26 Midland Crowd	29.7
75556	46 Rooted Rural	100.0	75833	46 Rooted Rural	68.7	76049	26 Midland Crowd	39.4
75558	26 Midland Crowd	100.0	75835	46 Rooted Rural	28.6	76050	17 Green Acres	42.0
75559	42 Southern Satellites	35.4	75838	46 Rooted Rural	100.0	76051	16 Enterprising Professionals	25.7
75560	46 Rooted Rural	99.8	75839	46 Rooted Rural	77.3	76052	04 Boomburbs	86.2
75561	50 Heartland Communities	33.5	75840	46 Rooted Rural	36.4	76053	29 Rustbelt Retirees	23.4
75563	46 Rooted Rural	57.8	75844	46 Rooted Rural	68.5	76054	07 Exurbanites	20.9
75566	46 Rooted Rural	100.0	75845	46 Rooted Rural	50.4	76055	26 Midland Crowd	50.7
75567	46 Rooted Rural	60.2	75846	41 Crossroads	60.3	76058	41 Crossroads	40.3
75568	50 Heartland Communities	62.0	75847	46 Rooted Rural	61.4	76059	41 Crossroads	43.4
75569	53 Home Town	41.0	75850	46 Rooted Rural	100.0	76060	28 Aspiring Young Families	30.4
75570	42 Southern Satellites	20.3	75851	46 Rooted Rural	63.8	76063	12 Up And Coming Families	26.2
75571	50 Heartland Communities	58.3	75852	46 Rooted Rural	60.4	76064	26 Midland Crowd	60.7
75572	42 Southern Satellites	63.0	75853	46 Rooted Rural	100.0	76065	06 Sophisticated Squires	23.8
75574	46 Rooted Rural	89.7	75855	46 Rooted Rural	82.2	76066	26 Midland Crowd	62.5
75599	50 Heartland Communities	0.0	75856	46 Rooted Rural	100.0	76067	46 Rooted Rural	30.3
75601	33 Midlife Junction	25.9	75859	26 Midland Crowd	72.6	76070	26 Midland Crowd	91.1
75602	62 Modest Income Homes	16.1	75860	46 Rooted Rural	54.6	76071	42 Southern Satellites	50.9
75603	46 Rooted Rural	60.4	75861	46 Rooted Rural	42.6	76073	26 Midland Crowd	100.0
75604	41 Crossroads	13.8	75862	49 Senior Sun Seekers	66.8	76077	26 Midland Crowd	100.0
75605	26 Midland Crowd	20.2	75901	26 Midland Crowd	17.7	76078	26 Midland Crowd	100.0
75630	49 Senior Sun Seekers	76.0	75904	26 Midland Crowd	23.4	76082	26 Midland Crowd	91.9
75631	42 Southern Satellites	51.5	75925	46 Rooted Rural	64.1	76084	42 Southern Satellites	32.5
75633	46 Rooted Rural	26.4	75926	56 Rural Bypasses	57.3	76085	26 Midland Crowd	95.0
75638	46 Rooted Rural	43.7	75928	56 Rural Bypasses	76.9	76086	33 Midlife Junction	44.8
75639	46 Rooted Rural	63.0	75929	46 Rooted Rural	63.2	76087	17 Green Acres	42.4
75640	46 Rooted Rural	41.1	75930	46 Rooted Rural	83.3	76088	26 Midland Crowd	87.4
75643	56 Rural Bypasses	60.5	75931	49 Senior Sun Seekers	66.7	76092	04 Boomburbs	53.7
75644	46 Rooted Rural	49.6	75932	49 Senior Sun Seekers	65.8	76093	42 Southern Satellites	82.9
75645	46 Rooted Rural	53.5	75933	56 Rural Bypasses	77.7	76102	27 Metro Renters	52.6
75647	46 Rooted Rural	33.8	75935	46 Rooted Rural	44.9	76103	59 Southwestern Families	25.7
75650	26 Midland Crowd	91.1	75936	46 Rooted Rural	58.7	76104	62 Modest Income Homes	61.1
75651	42 Southern Satellites	99.1	75937	46 Rooted Rural	100.0	76105	59 Southwestern Families	50.8
75652	53 Home Town	17.8	75938	46 Rooted Rural	84.2	76106	59 Southwestern Families	67.3
75654	46 Rooted Rural	31.6	75939	42 Southern Satellites	51.5	76107	22 Metropolitans	27.5
75656	53 Home Town	43.0	75941	38 Industrious Urban Fringe	27.5	76108	19 Milk And Cookies	15.2
75657	46 Rooted Rural	35.8	75943	46 Rooted Rural	99.5	76109	27 Metro Renters	17.1
75661	56 Rural Bypasses	49.3	75946	56 Rural Bypasses	51.8	76110	59 Southwestern Families	41.2
75662	46 Rooted Rural	17.5	75948	49 Senior Sun Seekers	72.3	76111	53 Home Town	29.9
75667	56 Rural Bypasses	72.4	75949	46 Rooted Rural	40.9	76112	52 Inner City Tenants	25.7
75668	50 Heartland Communities	97.0	75951	46 Rooted Rural	46.0	76114	53 Home Town	35.5
75669	46 Rooted Rural	100.0	75954	42 Southern Satellites	60.7	76115	59 Southwestern Families	50.4
75670	53 Home Town	31.2	75956	46 Rooted Rural	43.2	76116	52 Inner City Tenants	34.1
75672	46 Rooted Rural	45.1	75959	49 Senior Sun Seekers	100.0	76117	32 Rustbelt Traditions	39.6
75681	56 Rural Bypasses	64.2	75960	46 Rooted Rural	46.6	76118	12 Up And Coming Families	33.7
75683	42 Southern Satellites	33.5	75961	55 College Towns	31.6	76119	62 Modest Income Homes	20.3
75684	46 Rooted Rural	51.3	75962	63 Dorms To Diplomas	100.0	76120	39 Young And Restless	64.2
75686	46 Rooted Rural	45.6	75964	41 Crossroads	24.6	76122	48 Great Expectations	100.0
75687	46 Rooted Rural	100.0	75965	55 College Towns	34.5	76123	12 Up And Coming Families	45.7
75689	42 Southern Satellites	100.0	75966	56 Rural Bypasses	52.0	76126	18 Cozy And Comfortable	23.4
75691	42 Southern Satellites	71.8	75968	56 Rural Bypasses	87.7	76127	13 In Style	61.9
75692	26 Midland Crowd	60.7	75969	42 Southern Satellites	74.5	76129	63 Dorms To Diplomas	100.0
75693	17 Green Acres	29.5	75972	50 Heartland Communities	34.1	76131	12 Up And Coming Families	50.5
75701	14 Prosperous Empty Nesters	15.6	75973	56 Rural Bypasses	63.8	76132	39 Young And Restless	52.3
75702	59 Southwestern Families	28.5	75974	56 Rural Bypasses	64.6	76133	28 Aspiring Young Families	15.0
75703	36 Old And Newcomers	19.0	75975	46 Rooted Rural	69.0	76134	19 Milk And Cookies	39.9
75704	42 Southern Satellites	48.7	75976	46 Rooted Rural	100.0	76135	32 Rustbelt Traditions	22.3
75705	46 Rooted Rural	30.7	75977	56 Rural Bypasses	100.0	76137	12 Up And Coming Families	28.1

CONSUMER TYPE

ZIP CODE	TOP TAPESTRY CONSUMER TYPE	% 2009 HOUSE-HOLDS	ZIP CODE	TOP TAPESTRY CONSUMER TYPE	% 2009 HOUSE-HOLDS	ZIP CODE	TOP TAPESTRY CONSUMER TYPE	% 2009 HOUSE-HOLDS
76140	41 Crossroads	16.0	76453	31 Rural Resort Dwellers	100.0	76653	50 Heartland Communities	56.1
76148	19 Milk And Cookies	76.3	76454	50 Heartland Communities	90.7	76655	26 Midland Crowd	46.0
76155	39 Young And Restless	100.0	76455	37 Prairie Living	63.6	76656	46 Rooted Rural	71.5
76164	59 Southwestern Families	83.0	76457	37 Prairie Living	39.8	76657	26 Midland Crowd	31.9
76177	12 Up And Coming Families	81.4	76458	50 Heartland Communities	34.5	76660	46 Rooted Rural	100.0
76179	19 Milk And Cookies	42.7	76459	46 Rooted Rural	100.0	76661	50 Heartland Communities	70.7
76180	28 Aspiring Young Families	22.9	76460	37 Prairie Living	100.0	76664	50 Heartland Communities	68.5
76201	63 Dorms To Diplomas	28.6	76462	46 Rooted Rural	63.7	76665	50 Heartland Communities	52.0
76205	55 College Towns	24.2	76463	31 Rural Resort Dwellers	100.0	76666	46 Rooted Rural	100.0
76207	39 Young And Restless	41.3	76464	46 Rooted Rural	93.4	76667	46 Rooted Rural	41.5
76208	41 Crossroads	45.3	76470	50 Heartland Communities	68.7	76670	56 Rural Bypasses	65.4
76209	28 Aspiring Young Families	25.5	76471	50 Heartland Communities	49.7	76671	49 Senior Sun Seekers	56.3
76210	12 Up And Coming Families	61.5	76472	31 Rural Resort Dwellers	94.3	76673	46 Rooted Rural	100.0
76225	46 Rooted Rural	53.0	76474	37 Prairie Living	100.0	76676	46 Rooted Rural	100.0
76226	07 Exurbanites	39.8	76475	50 Heartland Communities	76.3	76678	46 Rooted Rural	100.0
76227	26 Midland Crowd	54.0	76476	26 Midland Crowd	53.3	76679	46 Rooted Rural	100.0
76228	37 Prairie Living	100.0	76483	50 Heartland Communities	69.6	76680	46 Rooted Rural	100.0
76230	50 Heartland Communities	41.0	76484	46 Rooted Rural	68.9	76681	46 Rooted Rural	99.0
76233	26 Midland Crowd	76.3	76486	46 Rooted Rural	100.0	76682	46 Rooted Rural	63.8
76234	26 Midland Crowd	51.7	76487	26 Midland Crowd	93.0	76687	31 Rural Resort Dwellers	71.9
76238	25 Salt Of The Earth	100.0	76490	46 Rooted Rural	100.0	76689	50 Heartland Communities	28.5
76239	46 Rooted Rural	90.8	76491	37 Prairie Living	100.0	76690	46 Rooted Rural	79.5
76240	53 Home Town	15.8	76501	26 Midland Crowd	23.8	76691	50 Heartland Communities	39.1
76245	49 Senior Sun Seekers	71.9	76502	13 In Style	17.5	76692	46 Rooted Rural	43.6
76247	26 Midland Crowd	84.1	76504	53 Home Town	22.3	76693	50 Heartland Communities	51.3
76248	12 Up And Coming Families	44.3	76511	50 Heartland Communities	43.2	76701	36 Old And Newcomers	48.5
76249	19 Milk And Cookies	36.7	76513	26 Midland Crowd	18.8	76704	62 Modest Income Homes	47.0
76250	25 Salt Of The Earth	100.0	76518	46 Rooted Rural	100.0	76705	53 Home Town	15.1
76251	46 Rooted Rural	100.0	76519	46 Rooted Rural	88.0	76706	63 Dorms To Diplomas	36.3
76252	25 Salt Of The Earth	75.1	76520	53 Home Town	33.1	76707	53 Home Town	36.2
76255	50 Heartland Communities	38.6	76522	28 Aspiring Young Families	20.7	76708	17 Green Acres	24.0
76258	26 Midland Crowd	42.7	76523	26 Midland Crowd	99.8	76710	14 Prosperous Empty Nesters	21.0
76259	26 Midland Crowd	99.8	76524	26 Midland Crowd	90.7	76711	53 Home Town	53.2
76261	46 Rooted Rural	100.0	76525	46 Rooted Rural	51.8	76712	28 Aspiring Young Families	22.9
76262	26 Midland Crowd	31.7	76526	46 Rooted Rural	100.0	76801	53 Home Town	22.4
76263	25 Salt Of The Earth	100.0	76527	26 Midland Crowd	88.5	76802	46 Rooted Rural	60.4
76264	46 Rooted Rural	74.7	76528	50 Heartland Communities	36.0	76820	37 Prairie Living	100.0
76265	31 Rural Resort Dwellers	57.1	76530	50 Heartland Communities	36.3	76821	50 Heartland Communities	60.3
76266	17 Green Acres	40.4	76531	50 Heartland Communities	54.8	76823	46 Rooted Rural	34.3
76270	46 Rooted Rural	52.4	76534	53 Home Town	48.3	76825	50 Heartland Communities	34.9
76271	26 Midland Crowd	80.1	76537	26 Midland Crowd	100.0	76827	31 Rural Resort Dwellers	100.0
76272	26 Midland Crowd	57.0	76538	37 Prairie Living	79.5	76828	37 Prairie Living	100.0
76273	26 Midland Crowd	36.5	76539	26 Midland Crowd	92.1	76831	31 Rural Resort Dwellers	90.9
76301	53 Home Town	29.4	76541	52 Inner City Tenants	55.6	76832	31 Rural Resort Dwellers	100.0
76302	52 Inner City Tenants	38.1	76542	12 Up And Coming Families	33.3	76834	50 Heartland Communities	42.9
76305	46 Rooted Rural	60.8	76543	40 Military Proximity	21.4	76836	37 Prairie Living	100.0
76306	19 Milk And Cookies	25.8	76544	40 Military Proximity	99.7	76837	50 Heartland Communities	79.6
76308	32 Rustbelt Traditions	15.6	76548	12 Up And Coming Families	36.6	76841	31 Rural Resort Dwellers	100.0
76309	53 Home Town	30.3	76549	41 Crossroads	35.8	76842	37 Prairie Living	100.0
76310	19 Milk And Cookies	28.8	76550	53 Home Town	22.7	76844	50 Heartland Communities	58.7
76311	40 Military Proximity	100.0	76554	26 Midland Crowd	74.0	76845	37 Prairie Living	100.0
76351	50 Heartland Communities	42.1	76556	46 Rooted Rural	99.0	76848	31 Rural Resort Dwellers	100.0
76354	53 Home Town	28.0	76557	26 Midland Crowd	41.0	76849	31 Rural Resort Dwellers	47.2
76357	37 Prairie Living	98.5	76559	41 Crossroads	99.2	76852	37 Prairie Living	100.0
76360	50 Heartland Communities	61.2	76561	42 Southern Satellites	93.5	76853	50 Heartland Communities	54.1
76363	37 Prairie Living	100.0	76565	31 Rural Resort Dwellers	100.0	76854	31 Rural Resort Dwellers	100.0
76364	37 Prairie Living	100.0	76566	46 Rooted Rural	100.0	76856	37 Prairie Living	41.3
76365	33 Midlife Junction	21.2	76567	25 Salt Of The Earth	18.1	76857	49 Senior Sun Seekers	65.6
76366	37 Prairie Living	36.3	76569	56 Rural Bypasses	56.3	76858	37 Prairie Living	100.0
76367	32 Rustbelt Traditions	22.5	76570	46 Rooted Rural	42.1	76859	50 Heartland Communities	46.1
76371	50 Heartland Communities	78.1	76571	17 Green Acres	45.4	76861	46 Rooted Rural	61.8
76372	46 Rooted Rural	94.2	76574	38 Industrious Urban Fringe	15.8	76862	37 Prairie Living	100.0
76373	37 Prairie Living	100.0	76577	46 Rooted Rural	60.1	76864	37 Prairie Living	100.0
76374	53 Home Town	28.9	76578	53 Home Town	53.6	76865	37 Prairie Living	100.0
76377	46 Rooted Rural	56.6	76579	26 Midland Crowd	100.0	76866	37 Prairie Living	100.0
76379	37 Prairie Living	100.0	76621	37 Prairie Living	51.4	76869	37 Prairie Living	100.0
76380	50 Heartland Communities	59.1	76622	46 Rooted Rural	97.6	76870	37 Prairie Living	100.0
76384	50 Heartland Communities	37.3	76624	26 Midland Crowd	99.4	76871	37 Prairie Living	100.0
76388	37 Prairie Living	100.0	76626	50 Heartland Communities	63.9	76872	31 Rural Resort Dwellers	70.5
76389	37 Prairie Living	97.5	76627	46 Rooted Rural	50.7	76873	37 Prairie Living	100.0
76401	26 Midland Crowd	17.2	76629	50 Heartland Communities	59.2	76874	31 Rural Resort Dwellers	83.3
76424	53 Home Town	44.6	76630	26 Midland Crowd	100.0	76875	37 Prairie Living	100.0
76426	26 Midland Crowd	40.0	76631	46 Rooted Rural	100.0	76877	50 Heartland Communities	73.2
76427	46 Rooted Rural	100.0	76632	46 Rooted Rural	54.9	76878	53 Home Town	39.9
76429	37 Prairie Living	57.7	76633	17 Green Acres	63.4	76880	37 Prairie Living	100.0
76430	46 Rooted Rural	44.1	76634	31 Rural Resort Dwellers	50.3	76882	37 Prairie Living	100.0
76431	42 Southern Satellites	76.4	76635	53 Home Town	59.2	76883	31 Rural Resort Dwellers	100.0
76432	46 Rooted Rural	99.8	76636	26 Midland Crowd	100.0	76884	37 Prairie Living	100.0
76433	37 Prairie Living	47.6	76637	31 Rural Resort Dwellers	100.0	76885	31 Rural Resort Dwellers	100.0
76435	37 Prairie Living	93.3	76638	17 Green Acres	69.1	76887	37 Prairie Living	88.5
76436	46 Rooted Rural	99.6	76639	46 Rooted Rural	100.0	76888	37 Prairie Living	100.0
76437	50 Heartland Communities	36.3	76640	26 Midland Crowd	97.8	76890	46 Rooted Rural	99.7
76442	50 Heartland Communities	45.6	76641	46 Rooted Rural	59.6	76901	48 Great Expectations	19.1
76443	46 Rooted Rural	58.9	76642	46 Rooted Rural	38.5	76903	59 Southwestern Families	35.1
76444	37 Prairie Living	46.8	76643	19 Milk And Cookies	34.4	76904	14 Prosperous Empty Nesters	15.5
76445	50 Heartland Communities	59.4	76645	53 Home Town	30.6	76905	38 Industrious Urban Fringe	33.7
76446	37 Prairie Living	40.5	76648	46 Rooted Rural	55.9	76908	40 Military Proximity	98.1
76448	50 Heartland Communities	57.0	76649	31 Rural Resort Dwellers	100.0	76909	63 Dorms To Diplomas	100.0
76449	46 Rooted Rural	37.0	76651	26 Midland Crowd	65.8	76930	37 Prairie Living	100.0
76450	50 Heartland Communities	32.7	76652	46 Rooted Rural	76.9	76932	42 Southern Satellites	28.2

ZIP CODE	TOP TAPESTRY CONSUMER TYPE	% 2009 HOUSE-HOLDS	ZIP CODE	TOP TAPESTRY CONSUMER TYPE	% 2009 HOUSE-HOLDS	ZIP CODE	TOP TAPESTRY CONSUMER TYPE	% 2009 HOUSE-HOLDS
76933	50 Heartland Communities	69.6	77079	03 Connoisseurs	30.2	77449	12 Up And Coming Families	57.8
76934	46 Rooted Rural	100.0	77080	58 NeWest Residents	31.5	77450	04 Boomburbs	54.9
76935	31 Rural Resort Dwellers	99.3	77081	58 NeWest Residents	57.8	77455	37 Prairie Living	58.2
76936	59 Southwestern Families	42.1	77082	39 Young And Restless	41.7	77456	42 Southern Satellites	50.8
76937	37 Prairie Living	100.0	77083	19 Milk And Cookies	45.9	77457	31 Rural Resort Dwellers	79.5
76940	37 Prairie Living	100.0	77084	19 Milk And Cookies	37.9	77458	46 Rooted Rural	100.0
76941	46 Rooted Rural	51.5	77085	19 Milk And Cookies	57.2	77459	04 Boomburbs	62.8
76943	59 Southwestern Families	44.0	77086	38 Industrious Urban Fringe	56.6	77461	26 Midland Crowd	51.4
76945	50 Heartland Communities	59.6	77087	59 Southwestern Families	43.9	77465	59 Southwestern Families	30.8
76949	31 Rural Resort Dwellers	100.0	77088	19 Milk And Cookies	22.0	77468	42 Southern Satellites	100.0
76950	37 Prairie Living	31.9	77089	19 Milk And Cookies	34.4	77469	13 In Style	16.9
76951	46 Rooted Rural	77.9	77090	39 Young And Restless	49.1	77471	26 Midland Crowd	24.5
76955	37 Prairie Living	100.0	77091	52 Inner City Tenants	27.8	77474	26 Midland Crowd	35.7
76957	37 Prairie Living	100.0	77092	52 Inner City Tenants	41.7	77477	16 Enterprising Professionals	40.0
77002	27 Metro Renters	79.0	77093	59 Southwestern Families	88.2	77478	03 Connoisseurs	17.0
77003	59 Southwestern Families	50.3	77094	04 Boomburbs	97.6	77479	04 Boomburbs	54.9
77004	62 Modest Income Homes	20.4	77095	04 Boomburbs	52.8	77480	42 Southern Satellites	22.5
77005	01 Top Rung	45.3	77096	14 Prosperous Empty Nesters	20.6	77482	56 Rural Bypasses	35.4
77006	27 Metro Renters	71.2	77098	27 Metro Renters	56.3	77483	37 Prairie Living	100.0
77007	27 Metro Renters	22.1	77099	52 Inner City Tenants	31.6	77484	26 Midland Crowd	66.3
77008	22 Metropolitans	31.6	77301	41 Crossroads	17.9	77485	26 Midland Crowd	39.1
77009	59 Southwestern Families	46.5	77302	41 Crossroads	41.2	77486	33 Midlife Junction	50.4
77010	65 Social Security Set	100.0	77303	26 Midland Crowd	52.4	77488	26 Midland Crowd	20.2
77011	59 Southwestern Families	85.3	77304	13 In Style	24.2	77489	19 Milk And Cookies	77.0
77012	59 Southwestern Families	67.1	77306	41 Crossroads	63.4	77493	19 Milk And Cookies	57.2
77013	58 NeWest Residents	40.5	77316	26 Midland Crowd	90.5	77494	04 Boomburbs	55.0
77014	12 Up And Coming Families	35.7	77318	26 Midland Crowd	59.2	77498	12 Up And Coming Families	36.1
77015	28 Aspiring Young Families	21.2	77320	26 Midland Crowd	25.9	77502	38 Industrious Urban Fringe	34.1
77016	34 Family Foundations	43.9	77327	26 Midland Crowd	29.9	77503	38 Industrious Urban Fringe	55.9
77017	38 Industrious Urban Fringe	39.9	77328	41 Crossroads	34.2	77504	19 Milk And Cookies	18.5
77018	32 Rustbelt Traditions	23.1	77331	49 Senior Sun Seekers	35.9	77505	04 Boomburbs	46.4
77019	08 Laptops And Lattes	33.9	77335	56 Rural Bypasses	53.3	77506	59 Southwestern Families	35.7
77020	59 Southwestern Families	60.9	77336	26 Midland Crowd	50.6	77510	26 Midland Crowd	64.3
77021	62 Modest Income Homes	44.1	77338	19 Milk And Cookies	51.4	77511	26 Midland Crowd	31.9
77022	59 Southwestern Families	79.1	77339	16 Enterprising Professionals	19.8	77514	46 Rooted Rural	48.5
77023	59 Southwestern Families	46.2	77340	63 Dorms To Diplomas	22.4	77515	41 Crossroads	24.5
77024	01 Top Rung	31.7	77345	02 Suburban Splendor	36.0	77517	26 Midland Crowd	62.0
77025	27 Metro Renters	28.8	77346	12 Up And Coming Families	59.7	77518	41 Crossroads	47.7
77026	62 Modest Income Homes	75.5	77351	46 Rooted Rural	32.1	77519	41 Crossroads	100.0
77027	27 Metro Renters	43.8	77354	12 Up And Coming Families	51.0	77520	59 Southwestern Families	26.8
77028	62 Modest Income Homes	65.8	77355	26 Midland Crowd	34.4	77521	19 Milk And Cookies	15.8
77029	59 Southwestern Families	43.6	77356	15 Silver And Gold	42.7	77523	26 Midland Crowd	30.1
77030	27 Metro Renters	38.5	77357	41 Crossroads	80.5	77530	19 Milk And Cookies	40.9
77031	52 Inner City Tenants	29.9	77358	56 Rural Bypasses	26.7	77531	38 Industrious Urban Fringe	30.9
77032	60 City Dimensions	32.8	77359	46 Rooted Rural	81.5	77532	19 Milk And Cookies	23.0
77033	34 Family Foundations	42.0	77360	49 Senior Sun Seekers	100.0	77534	26 Midland Crowd	87.0
77034	38 Industrious Urban Fringe	22.0	77362	26 Midland Crowd	90.2	77535	26 Midland Crowd	46.1
77035	52 Inner City Tenants	36.4	77363	42 Southern Satellites	62.4	77536	06 Sophisticated Squires	37.5
77036	52 Inner City Tenants	54.3	77364	49 Senior Sun Seekers	75.1	77538	26 Midland Crowd	87.1
77037	38 Industrious Urban Fringe	77.0	77365	41 Crossroads	73.4	77539	19 Milk And Cookies	26.3
77038	38 Industrious Urban Fringe	29.2	77371	46 Rooted Rural	30.6	77541	38 Industrious Urban Fringe	29.2
77039	38 Industrious Urban Fringe	64.1	77372	41 Crossroads	61.7	77545	12 Up And Coming Families	66.0
77040	19 Milk And Cookies	26.5	77373	19 Milk And Cookies	63.0	77546	12 Up And Coming Families	27.9
77041	19 Milk And Cookies	38.6	77375	12 Up And Coming Families	43.0	77547	59 Southwestern Families	65.2
77042	39 Young And Restless	64.9	77377	12 Up And Coming Families	63.5	77550	62 Modest Income Homes	12.0
77043	28 Aspiring Young Families	27.6	77378	41 Crossroads	56.0	77551	14 Prosperous Empty Nesters	17.9
77044	26 Midland Crowd	43.3	77379	02 Suburban Splendor	25.2	77554	31 Rural Resort Dwellers	33.9
77045	38 Industrious Urban Fringe	35.1	77380	16 Enterprising Professionals	30.7	77560	56 Rural Bypasses	100.0
77046	08 Laptops And Lattes	100.0	77381	04 Boomburbs	37.7	77562	26 Midland Crowd	36.0
77047	34 Family Foundations	61.6	77382	04 Boomburbs	51.6	77563	07 Exurbanites	25.4
77048	34 Family Foundations	38.0	77384	06 Sophisticated Squires	46.9	77564	42 Southern Satellites	61.4
77049	38 Industrious Urban Fringe	78.7	77385	12 Up And Coming Families	33.6	77565	13 In Style	25.7
77050	34 Family Foundations	41.7	77386	12 Up And Coming Families	73.5	77566	06 Sophisticated Squires	21.4
77051	62 Modest Income Homes	62.4	77388	19 Milk And Cookies	25.2	77568	32 Rustbelt Traditions	20.9
77053	38 Industrious Urban Fringe	34.5	77389	12 Up And Coming Families	39.9	77571	19 Milk And Cookies	38.6
77054	27 Metro Renters	42.2	77396	41 Crossroads	37.3	77573	12 Up And Coming Families	27.7
77055	58 NeWest Residents	39.3	77401	02 Suburban Splendor	33.9	77575	56 Rural Bypasses	32.8
77056	27 Metro Renters	54.1	77406	06 Sophisticated Squires	37.9	77577	26 Midland Crowd	53.9
77057	27 Metro Renters	43.0	77407	04 Boomburbs	97.7	77578	26 Midland Crowd	26.5
77058	39 Young And Restless	57.2	77414	26 Midland Crowd	21.6	77581	12 Up And Coming Families	31.7
77059	02 Suburban Splendor	59.6	77417	26 Midland Crowd	67.2	77583	41 Crossroads	45.0
77060	58 NeWest Residents	41.8	77418	33 Midlife Junction	26.5	77584	12 Up And Coming Families	45.9
77061	52 Inner City Tenants	32.4	77419	46 Rooted Rural	100.0	77585	56 Rural Bypasses	54.0
77062	02 Suburban Splendor	19.7	77420	53 Home Town	58.7	77586	36 Old And Newcomers	19.0
77063	27 Metro Renters	36.8	77422	26 Midland Crowd	30.1	77587	59 Southwestern Families	46.2
77064	12 Up And Coming Families	32.9	77423	38 Industrious Urban Fringe	32.4	77590	32 Rustbelt Traditions	30.3
77065	12 Up And Coming Families	25.9	77426	25 Salt Of The Earth	53.1	77591	34 Family Foundations	28.8
77066	19 Milk And Cookies	32.2	77429	04 Boomburbs	58.1	77597	26 Midland Crowd	52.3
77067	19 Milk And Cookies	21.1	77430	17 Green Acres	62.4	77598	39 Young And Restless	59.8
77068	13 In Style	61.0	77432	42 Southern Satellites	100.0	77611	26 Midland Crowd	34.7
77069	13 In Style	33.9	77433	19 Milk And Cookies	61.1	77612	42 Southern Satellites	72.3
77070	12 Up And Coming Families	24.1	77434	50 Heartland Communities	37.8	77614	42 Southern Satellites	100.0
77071	19 Milk And Cookies	38.4	77435	25 Salt Of The Earth	40.7	77616	42 Southern Satellites	100.0
77072	38 Industrious Urban Fringe	32.1	77437	59 Southwestern Families	20.3	77619	32 Rustbelt Traditions	47.0
77073	28 Aspiring Young Families	64.6	77440	46 Rooted Rural	100.0	77622	26 Midland Crowd	98.0
77074	58 NeWest Residents	27.7	77441	07 Exurbanites	73.5	77624	46 Rooted Rural	100.0
77075	38 Industrious Urban Fringe	39.3	77442	37 Prairie Living	49.4	77625	46 Rooted Rural	30.9
77076	59 Southwestern Families	60.5	77444	42 Southern Satellites	41.6	77627	32 Rustbelt Traditions	30.9
77077	39 Young And Restless	34.1	77445	41 Crossroads	28.7	77630	62 Modest Income Homes	15.0
77078	51 Metro City Edge	44.8	77447	26 Midland Crowd	67.8	77632	17 Green Acres	28.5

CONSUMER TYPE

ZIP CODE	TOP TAPESTRY CONSUMER TYPE	% 2009 HOUSE-HOLDS	ZIP CODE	TOP TAPESTRY CONSUMER TYPE	% 2009 HOUSE-HOLDS	ZIP CODE	TOP TAPESTRY CONSUMER TYPE	% 2009 HOUSE-HOLDS
77640	62 Modest Income Homes	50.2	78040	59 Southwestern Families	91.4	78234	40 Military Proximity	99.9
77642	59 Southwestern Families	14.5	78041	38 Industrious Urban Fringe	34.2	78235	40 Military Proximity	77.2
77650	49 Senior Sun Seekers	84.4	78043	59 Southwestern Families	65.5	78236	40 Military Proximity	85.3
77651	32 Rustbelt Traditions	28.1	78045	12 Up And Coming Families	47.3	78237	59 Southwestern Families	100.0
77656	42 Southern Satellites	27.6	78046	59 Southwestern Families	76.7	78238	36 Old And Newcomers	18.1
77657	26 Midland Crowd	83.9	78052	26 Midland Crowd	45.1	78239	19 Milk And Cookies	31.4
77659	07 Exurbanites	38.5	78055	31 Rural Resort Dwellers	52.5	78240	39 Young And Restless	40.3
77660	42 Southern Satellites	76.9	78056	26 Midland Crowd	100.0	78242	59 Southwestern Families	56.6
77662	26 Midland Crowd	41.7	78057	46 Rooted Rural	100.0	78244	19 Milk And Cookies	55.1
77664	46 Rooted Rural	98.3	78058	31 Rural Resort Dwellers	100.0	78245	19 Milk And Cookies	45.0
77665	42 Southern Satellites	28.1	78059	41 Crossroads	79.6	78247	12 Up And Coming Families	43.2
77701	62 Modest Income Homes	47.9	78061	59 Southwestern Families	73.1	78248	04 Boomburbs	56.3
77702	48 Great Expectations	47.7	78063	31 Rural Resort Dwellers	45.7	78249	12 Up And Coming Families	35.2
77703	62 Modest Income Homes	37.6	78064	26 Midland Crowd	54.8	78250	19 Milk And Cookies	72.1
77705	51 Metro City Edge	24.1	78065	59 Southwestern Families	45.1	78251	12 Up And Coming Families	61.9
77706	07 Exurbanites	26.8	78066	26 Midland Crowd	100.0	78252	41 Crossroads	50.7
77707	19 Milk And Cookies	19.5	78067	59 Southwestern Families	100.0	78253	12 Up And Coming Families	95.3
77708	28 Aspiring Young Families	37.2	78069	38 Industrious Urban Fringe	33.1	78254	12 Up And Coming Families	47.8
77710	52 Inner City Tenants	100.0	78070	07 Exurbanites	60.0	78255	07 Exurbanites	86.0
77713	28 Aspiring Young Families	25.2	78071	46 Rooted Rural	45.1	78256	02 Suburban Splendor	50.7
77801	55 College Towns	40.2	78072	46 Rooted Rural	74.7	78257	03 Connoisseurs	99.5
77802	33 Midlife Junction	19.2	78073	41 Crossroads	68.7	78258	04 Boomburbs	55.8
77803	41 Crossroads	21.0	78074	31 Rural Resort Dwellers	100.0	78259	04 Boomburbs	68.6
77807	41 Crossroads	53.8	78075	46 Rooted Rural	100.0	78260	04 Boomburbs	56.4
77808	26 Midland Crowd	65.6	78076	59 Southwestern Families	64.9	78261	02 Suburban Splendor	100.0
77830	46 Rooted Rural	91.0	78101	26 Midland Crowd	53.8	78263	26 Midland Crowd	46.9
77831	46 Rooted Rural	97.5	78102	46 Rooted Rural	23.4	78264	41 Crossroads	99.6
77833	33 Midlife Junction	26.3	78108	06 Sophisticated Squires	60.4	78266	07 Exurbanites	87.8
77835	37 Prairie Living	47.7	78109	19 Milk And Cookies	51.3	78332	59 Southwestern Families	51.1
77836	46 Rooted Rural	30.0	78111	46 Rooted Rural	100.0	78336	41 Crossroads	35.1
77837	50 Heartland Communities	52.2	78112	41 Crossroads	85.5	78338	59 Southwestern Families	100.0
77840	63 Dorms To Diplomas	77.3	78113	46 Rooted Rural	89.5	78340	46 Rooted Rural	100.0
77845	04 Boomburbs	20.7	78114	26 Midland Crowd	59.1	78343	38 Industrious Urban Fringe	46.8
77850	46 Rooted Rural	100.0	78116	46 Rooted Rural	100.0	78344	59 Southwestern Families	100.0
77853	56 Rural Bypasses	95.2	78117	46 Rooted Rural	100.0	78349	59 Southwestern Families	73.4
77856	46 Rooted Rural	77.0	78118	50 Heartland Communities	42.5	78353	56 Rural Bypasses	100.0
77859	50 Heartland Communities	25.5	78119	53 Home Town	24.0	78355	59 Southwestern Families	77.7
77861	46 Rooted Rural	100.0	78121	26 Midland Crowd	84.1	78357	59 Southwestern Families	84.2
77864	56 Rural Bypasses	46.2	78122	46 Rooted Rural	100.0	78360	59 Southwestern Families	100.0
77865	46 Rooted Rural	99.7	78123	31 Rural Resort Dwellers	60.0	78361	59 Southwestern Families	82.2
77868	59 Southwestern Families	28.3	78124	26 Midland Crowd	66.6	78362	28 Aspiring Young Families	39.4
77871	46 Rooted Rural	55.3	78130	26 Midland Crowd	17.0	78363	59 Southwestern Families	24.4
77872	46 Rooted Rural	98.6	78132	07 Exurbanites	46.0	78368	59 Southwestern Families	47.4
77873	46 Rooted Rural	79.2	78133	31 Rural Resort Dwellers	60.9	78369	59 Southwestern Families	100.0
77879	46 Rooted Rural	36.1	78140	59 Southwestern Families	69.5	78370	59 Southwestern Families	43.1
77880	46 Rooted Rural	88.5	78141	46 Rooted Rural	100.0	78372	26 Midland Crowd	38.0
77901	59 Southwestern Families	27.9	78147	42 Southern Satellites	68.6	78373	31 Rural Resort Dwellers	93.0
77904	26 Midland Crowd	19.6	78148	12 Up And Coming Families	20.2	78374	12 Up And Coming Families	20.7
77905	26 Midland Crowd	38.6	78150	41 Crossroads	100.0	78375	59 Southwestern Families	41.3
77951	59 Southwestern Families	75.4	78151	59 Southwestern Families	65.1	78376	59 Southwestern Families	97.0
77954	56 Rural Bypasses	35.8	78152	17 Green Acres	79.5	78377	50 Heartland Communities	57.3
77957	50 Heartland Communities	39.1	78154	12 Up And Coming Families	42.1	78379	46 Rooted Rural	100.0
77962	46 Rooted Rural	98.0	78155	26 Midland Crowd	42.0	78380	59 Southwestern Families	59.5
77963	46 Rooted Rural	30.5	78159	56 Rural Bypasses	100.0	78382	49 Senior Sun Seekers	25.9
77964	46 Rooted Rural	77.3	78160	46 Rooted Rural	95.0	78383	49 Senior Sun Seekers	48.9
77968	17 Green Acres	53.4	78161	26 Midland Crowd	100.0	78384	59 Southwestern Families	100.0
77971	46 Rooted Rural	40.4	78163	07 Exurbanites	100.0	78385	59 Southwestern Families	100.0
77974	37 Prairie Living	53.1	78164	46 Rooted Rural	74.3	78387	59 Southwestern Families	48.9
77975	46 Rooted Rural	68.9	78201	59 Southwestern Families	43.1	78389	56 Rural Bypasses	84.9
77979	25 Salt Of The Earth	22.5	78202	62 Modest Income Homes	77.0	78390	59 Southwestern Families	37.7
77983	46 Rooted Rural	54.5	78203	59 Southwestern Families	67.4	78391	37 Prairie Living	65.3
77984	50 Heartland Communities	53.3	78204	59 Southwestern Families	84.9	78393	46 Rooted Rural	64.6
77990	46 Rooted Rural	100.0	78205	65 Social Security Set	93.8	78401	60 City Dimensions	26.5
77994	46 Rooted Rural	98.8	78207	59 Southwestern Families	82.8	78402	30 Retirement Communities	99.6
77995	46 Rooted Rural	25.5	78208	60 City Dimensions	42.5	78404	59 Southwestern Families	33.1
78002	26 Midland Crowd	43.3	78209	14 Prosperous Empty Nesters	15.2	78405	59 Southwestern Families	94.3
78003	26 Midland Crowd	36.1	78210	59 Southwestern Families	60.7	78406	59 Southwestern Families	100.0
78004	07 Exurbanites	100.0	78211	59 Southwestern Families	96.7	78407	59 Southwestern Families	48.5
78005	46 Rooted Rural	100.0	78212	59 Southwestern Families	17.8	78408	59 Southwestern Families	44.4
78006	07 Exurbanites	49.5	78213	32 Rustbelt Traditions	26.3	78409	59 Southwestern Families	59.8
78007	46 Rooted Rural	65.7	78214	59 Southwestern Families	82.1	78410	19 Milk And Cookies	36.3
78008	46 Rooted Rural	100.0	78215	52 Inner City Tenants	43.0	78411	32 Rustbelt Traditions	25.2
78009	26 Midland Crowd	86.6	78216	16 Enterprising Professionals	21.6	78412	36 Old And Newcomers	21.9
78010	41 Crossroads	33.8	78217	36 Old And Newcomers	22.4	78413	19 Milk And Cookies	21.6
78011	59 Southwestern Families	56.7	78218	52 Inner City Tenants	16.3	78414	12 Up And Coming Families	28.1
78013	31 Rural Resort Dwellers	47.7	78219	62 Modest Income Homes	19.7	78415	59 Southwestern Families	30.6
78014	59 Southwestern Families	50.2	78220	62 Modest Income Homes	47.1	78416	59 Southwestern Families	74.2
78015	03 Connoisseurs	64.0	78221	59 Southwestern Families	67.2	78417	38 Industrious Urban Fringe	55.8
78016	56 Rural Bypasses	26.5	78222	41 Crossroads	32.9	78418	07 Exurbanites	20.9
78017	59 Southwestern Families	51.6	78223	59 Southwestern Families	23.0	78419	40 Military Proximity	100.0
78019	59 Southwestern Families	99.3	78224	59 Southwestern Families	34.9	78501	38 Industrious Urban Fringe	33.3
78021	46 Rooted Rural	100.0	78225	59 Southwestern Families	100.0	78503	59 Southwestern Families	62.9
78022	46 Rooted Rural	50.8	78226	59 Southwestern Families	62.7	78504	19 Milk And Cookies	19.5
78023	07 Exurbanites	85.1	78227	59 Southwestern Families	34.3	78516	59 Southwestern Families	72.9
78024	31 Rural Resort Dwellers	96.6	78228	59 Southwestern Families	34.8	78520	59 Southwestern Families	61.5
78025	15 Silver And Gold	33.8	78229	39 Young And Restless	60.1	78521	59 Southwestern Families	69.3
78026	59 Southwestern Families	37.6	78230	16 Enterprising Professionals	20.8	78526	59 Southwestern Families	38.0
78027	31 Rural Resort Dwellers	100.0	78231	16 Enterprising Professionals	50.9	78536	56 Rural Bypasses	100.0
78028	46 Rooted Rural	17.9	78232	16 Enterprising Professionals	23.1	78537	59 Southwestern Families	92.7
78039	26 Midland Crowd	96.7	78233	19 Milk And Cookies	41.0	78538	59 Southwestern Families	100.0

ZIP CODE	TOP TAPESTRY CONSUMER TYPE	% 2009 HOUSE-HOLDS	ZIP CODE	TOP TAPESTRY CONSUMER TYPE	% 2009 HOUSE-HOLDS	ZIP CODE	TOP TAPESTRY CONSUMER TYPE	% 2009 HOUSE-HOLDS
78539	59 Southwestern Families	28.2	78672	49 Senior Sun Seekers	97.7	78948	46 Rooted Rural	49.8
78541	59 Southwestern Families	44.9	78675	37 Prairie Living	100.0	78949	46 Rooted Rural	100.0
78542	59 Southwestern Families	81.8	78676	31 Rural Resort Dwellers	63.5	78950	46 Rooted Rural	45.5
78547	59 Southwestern Families	100.0	78677	37 Prairie Living	100.0	78953	46 Rooted Rural	55.9
78548	59 Southwestern Families	100.0	78681	04 Boomburbs	39.4	78954	31 Rural Resort Dwellers	61.2
78549	59 Southwestern Families	100.0	78701	27 Metro Renters	55.4	78956	50 Heartland Communities	44.3
78550	59 Southwestern Families	44.5	78702	59 Southwestern Families	46.3	78957	46 Rooted Rural	41.7
78552	59 Southwestern Families	24.8	78703	27 Metro Renters	31.6	78959	56 Rural Bypasses	92.4
78557	59 Southwestern Families	100.0	78704	52 Inner City Tenants	21.6	78962	46 Rooted Rural	48.4
78559	59 Southwestern Families	51.9	78705	63 Dorms To Diplomas	73.1	78963	46 Rooted Rural	100.0
78560	59 Southwestern Families	96.6	78712	63 Dorms To Diplomas	0.0	79001	37 Prairie Living	100.0
78563	56 Rural Bypasses	94.3	78717	04 Boomburbs	93.1	79005	38 Industrious Urban Fringe	86.8
78566	59 Southwestern Families	57.7	78719	38 Industrious Urban Fringe	99.8	79007	53 Home Town	23.3
78569	59 Southwestern Families	99.8	78721	34 Family Foundations	34.3	79009	59 Southwestern Families	59.8
78570	59 Southwestern Families	88.1	78722	27 Metro Renters	27.1	79011	37 Prairie Living	100.0
78572	59 Southwestern Families	67.2	78723	32 Rustbelt Traditions	24.1	79014	46 Rooted Rural	28.6
78573	59 Southwestern Families	80.1	78724	38 Industrious Urban Fringe	63.7	79015	55 College Towns	36.6
78574	59 Southwestern Families	70.8	78725	19 Milk And Cookies	85.8	79016	55 College Towns	100.0
78575	59 Southwestern Families	59.0	78726	04 Boomburbs	99.2	79018	37 Prairie Living	100.0
78577	59 Southwestern Families	64.0	78727	16 Enterprising Professionals	49.1	79019	37 Prairie Living	63.7
78578	59 Southwestern Families	29.7	78728	16 Enterprising Professionals	50.6	79022	37 Prairie Living	25.0
78580	59 Southwestern Families	88.9	78729	16 Enterprising Professionals	30.9	79027	59 Southwestern Families	51.9
78582	59 Southwestern Families	95.8	78730	02 Suburban Splendor	89.3	79029	59 Southwestern Families	19.2
78583	59 Southwestern Families	85.3	78731	03 Connoisseurs	22.7	79031	59 Southwestern Families	79.6
78584	59 Southwestern Families	100.0	78732	04 Boomburbs	100.0	79034	37 Prairie Living	100.0
78586	59 Southwestern Families	70.7	78733	06 Sophisticated Squires	52.7	79035	37 Prairie Living	45.1
78588	56 Rural Bypasses	100.0	78734	07 Exurbanites	51.3	79036	46 Rooted Rural	48.3
78589	59 Southwestern Families	76.6	78735	16 Enterprising Professionals	38.8	79039	37 Prairie Living	95.9
78590	46 Rooted Rural	95.8	78736	19 Milk And Cookies	75.5	79040	37 Prairie Living	100.0
78591	56 Rural Bypasses	100.0	78737	07 Exurbanites	46.6	79041	50 Heartland Communities	41.2
78593	59 Southwestern Families	81.9	78738	03 Connoisseurs	43.4	79042	37 Prairie Living	100.0
78594	59 Southwestern Families	100.0	78739	04 Boomburbs	92.4	79043	59 Southwestern Families	92.3
78595	59 Southwestern Families	100.0	78741	39 Young And Restless	56.7	79044	37 Prairie Living	100.0
78596	59 Southwestern Families	61.6	78742	41 Crossroads	100.0	79045	59 Southwestern Families	51.6
78597	15 Silver And Gold	100.0	78744	38 Industrious Urban Fringe	61.1	79046	37 Prairie Living	100.0
78598	46 Rooted Rural	100.0	78745	19 Milk And Cookies	27.9	79052	59 Southwestern Families	54.8
78602	26 Midland Crowd	60.6	78746	02 Suburban Splendor	34.2	79056	37 Prairie Living	100.0
78605	26 Midland Crowd	47.5	78747	12 Up And Coming Families	43.3	79057	50 Heartland Communities	100.0
78606	31 Rural Resort Dwellers	60.4	78748	12 Up And Coming Families	35.3	79058	26 Midland Crowd	90.4
78607	49 Senior Sun Seekers	99.3	78749	04 Boomburbs	39.9	79059	37 Prairie Living	100.0
78608	26 Midland Crowd	100.0	78750	02 Suburban Splendor	33.0	79061	37 Prairie Living	100.0
78609	49 Senior Sun Seekers	75.4	78751	27 Metro Renters	44.9	79062	37 Prairie Living	100.0
78610	06 Sophisticated Squires	50.3	78752	52 Inner City Tenants	39.7	79063	37 Prairie Living	100.0
78611	31 Rural Resort Dwellers	35.8	78753	52 Inner City Tenants	41.8	79064	37 Prairie Living	59.9
78612	26 Midland Crowd	66.5	78754	13 In Style	35.2	79065	50 Heartland Communities	33.0
78613	12 Up And Coming Families	53.6	78756	22 Metropolitans	30.1	79068	18 Cozy And Comfortable	50.0
78614	37 Prairie Living	69.1	78757	22 Metropolitans	42.3	79070	37 Prairie Living	36.7
78615	26 Midland Crowd	75.2	78758	39 Young And Restless	38.4	79072	59 Southwestern Families	30.4
78616	26 Midland Crowd	73.1	78759	16 Enterprising Professionals	31.4	79079	50 Heartland Communities	82.8
78617	41 Crossroads	67.5	78801	59 Southwestern Families	40.4	79080	46 Rooted Rural	100.0
78618	31 Rural Resort Dwellers	100.0	78827	59 Southwestern Families	100.0	79081	37 Prairie Living	52.8
78619	06 Sophisticated Squires	45.8	78828	49 Senior Sun Seekers	94.4	79082	37 Prairie Living	96.8
78620	06 Sophisticated Squires	46.4	78829	59 Southwestern Families	100.0	79083	32 Rustbelt Traditions	42.3
78621	26 Midland Crowd	53.6	78830	59 Southwestern Families	95.8	79084	37 Prairie Living	100.0
78623	26 Midland Crowd	87.9	78832	49 Senior Sun Seekers	52.4	79085	42 Southern Satellites	100.0
78624	31 Rural Resort Dwellers	52.0	78833	56 Rural Bypasses	51.4	79086	37 Prairie Living	62.4
78626	12 Up And Coming Families	33.9	78834	59 Southwestern Families	50.5	79087	37 Prairie Living	100.0
78628	07 Exurbanites	33.7	78837	46 Rooted Rural	100.0	79088	59 Southwestern Families	38.0
78629	46 Rooted Rural	21.6	78838	31 Rural Resort Dwellers	92.5	79092	37 Prairie Living	86.3
78631	31 Rural Resort Dwellers	83.4	78839	59 Southwestern Families	99.7	79094	37 Prairie Living	100.0
78632	46 Rooted Rural	100.0	78840	59 Southwestern Families	55.4	79095	37 Prairie Living	39.1
78633	15 Silver And Gold	66.1	78843	40 Military Proximity	100.0	79096	46 Rooted Rural	74.8
78634	12 Up And Coming Families	59.8	78850	46 Rooted Rural	100.0	79097	25 Salt Of The Earth	98.3
78635	31 Rural Resort Dwellers	100.0	78851	50 Heartland Communities	41.8	79098	37 Prairie Living	100.0
78636	31 Rural Resort Dwellers	55.7	78852	59 Southwestern Families	79.4	79101	57 Simple Living	47.4
78638	46 Rooted Rural	51.9	78861	46 Rooted Rural	31.5	79102	59 Southwestern Families	22.8
78639	49 Senior Sun Seekers	72.6	78870	46 Rooted Rural	100.0	79103	32 Rustbelt Traditions	47.5
78640	12 Up And Coming Families	39.5	78872	59 Southwestern Families	100.0	79104	59 Southwestern Families	63.7
78641	12 Up And Coming Families	73.7	78873	31 Rural Resort Dwellers	71.9	79106	32 Rustbelt Traditions	15.3
78642	26 Midland Crowd	65.9	78877	56 Rural Bypasses	73.6	79107	59 Southwestern Families	32.4
78643	33 Midlife Junction	25.3	78879	31 Rural Resort Dwellers	100.0	79108	41 Crossroads	28.1
78644	26 Midland Crowd	26.2	78880	59 Southwestern Families	66.1	79109	33 Midlife Junction	12.0
78645	30 Retirement Communities	25.3	78881	56 Rural Bypasses	77.4	79110	32 Rustbelt Traditions	38.5
78648	50 Heartland Communities	28.7	78883	31 Rural Resort Dwellers	73.8	79111	28 Aspiring Young Families	98.4
78650	46 Rooted Rural	75.1	78884	31 Rural Resort Dwellers	100.0	79118	41 Crossroads	49.0
78652	17 Green Acres	63.0	78885	31 Rural Resort Dwellers	100.0	79119	12 Up And Coming Families	39.1
78653	26 Midland Crowd	44.1	78886	46 Rooted Rural	98.1	79121	02 Suburban Splendor	26.2
78654	46 Rooted Rural	25.1	78931	46 Rooted Rural	100.0	79124	07 Exurbanites	40.9
78655	26 Midland Crowd	76.5	78932	31 Rural Resort Dwellers	80.9	79201	50 Heartland Communities	53.4
78656	41 Crossroads	81.2	78933	46 Rooted Rural	38.4	79220	37 Prairie Living	100.0
78657	15 Silver And Gold	67.4	78934	46 Rooted Rural	42.1	79225	50 Heartland Communities	84.7
78659	26 Midland Crowd	92.2	78935	31 Rural Resort Dwellers	80.7	79226	50 Heartland Communities	61.8
78660	12 Up And Coming Families	63.3	78938	46 Rooted Rural	100.0	79227	50 Heartland Communities	65.0
78662	26 Midland Crowd	81.6	78940	46 Rooted Rural	75.8	79229	37 Prairie Living	100.0
78663	31 Rural Resort Dwellers	100.0	78941	56 Rural Bypasses	55.2	79230	37 Prairie Living	100.0
78664	12 Up And Coming Families	38.7	78942	38 Industrious Urban Fringe	22.9	79234	37 Prairie Living	100.0
78665	12 Up And Coming Families	51.7	78944	46 Rooted Rural	50.8	79235	59 Southwestern Families	50.8
78666	55 College Towns	31.8	78945	37 Prairie Living	32.5	79237	37 Prairie Living	100.0
78669	07 Exurbanites	72.7	78946	46 Rooted Rural	40.5	79239	37 Prairie Living	100.0
78671	31 Rural Resort Dwellers	100.0	78947	26 Midland Crowd	53.8	79240	37 Prairie Living	100.0

CONSUMER TYPE

ZIP CODE	TOP TAPESTRY CONSUMER TYPE	% 2009 HOUSE-HOLDS	ZIP CODE	TOP TAPESTRY CONSUMER TYPE	% 2009 HOUSE-HOLDS	ZIP CODE	TOP TAPESTRY CONSUMER TYPE	% 2009 HOUSE-HOLDS
79241	50 Heartland Communities	43.2	79535	37 Prairie Living	79.2	79903	59 Southwestern Families	55.8
79243	37 Prairie Living	100.0	79536	50 Heartland Communities	39.5	79904	59 Southwestern Families	34.8
79244	37 Prairie Living	100.0	79537	50 Heartland Communities	100.0	79905	59 Southwestern Families	90.4
79245	50 Heartland Communities	99.9	79538	46 Rooted Rural	100.0	79906	40 Military Proximity	90.8
79247	37 Prairie Living	100.0	79539	37 Prairie Living	100.0	79907	59 Southwestern Families	59.6
79248	50 Heartland Communities	62.1	79540	37 Prairie Living	100.0	79908	40 Military Proximity	100.0
79250	50 Heartland Communities	54.4	79541	46 Rooted Rural	46.7	79912	19 Milk And Cookies	17.0
79251	37 Prairie Living	100.0	79543	50 Heartland Communities	50.2	79915	59 Southwestern Families	60.6
79252	50 Heartland Communities	55.6	79544	37 Prairie Living	100.0	79916	59 Southwestern Families	100.0
79255	37 Prairie Living	100.0	79545	50 Heartland Communities	37.6	79918	40 Military Proximity	0.0
79256	37 Prairie Living	100.0	79546	50 Heartland Communities	73.9	79922	02 Suburban Splendor	34.5
79257	37 Prairie Living	100.0	79547	50 Heartland Communities	70.1	79924	38 Industrious Urban Fringe	19.8
79259	50 Heartland Communities	100.0	79548	37 Prairie Living	100.0	79925	29 Rustbelt Retirees	25.0
79261	37 Prairie Living	88.0	79549	59 Southwestern Families	16.7	79927	59 Southwestern Families	97.7
79311	37 Prairie Living	45.8	79553	50 Heartland Communities	78.1	79928	59 Southwestern Families	51.1
79312	37 Prairie Living	99.5	79556	53 Home Town	30.6	79930	59 Southwestern Families	63.6
79313	50 Heartland Communities	100.0	79560	37 Prairie Living	87.0	79932	07 Exurbanites	40.2
79316	37 Prairie Living	34.3	79561	46 Rooted Rural	100.0	79934	19 Milk And Cookies	26.1
79320	37 Prairie Living	100.0	79562	25 Salt Of The Earth	45.7	79935	38 Industrious Urban Fringe	20.3
79322	50 Heartland Communities	50.6	79563	41 Crossroads	94.3	79936	38 Industrious Urban Fringe	38.0
79323	38 Industrious Urban Fringe	25.2	79565	31 Rural Resort Dwellers	100.0	79938	38 Industrious Urban Fringe	72.5
79324	37 Prairie Living	100.0	79566	37 Prairie Living	53.4	79968	55 College Towns	100.0
79325	37 Prairie Living	68.7	79567	37 Prairie Living	30.4	80002	52 Inner City Tenants	34.3
79326	37 Prairie Living	100.0	79601	55 College Towns	28.5	80003	13 In Style	16.1
79329	33 Midlife Junction	44.6	79602	53 Home Town	23.3	80004	13 In Style	22.1
79331	59 Southwestern Families	38.3	79603	53 Home Town	26.8	80005	07 Exurbanites	31.5
79336	59 Southwestern Families	22.6	79605	53 Home Town	15.2	80007	04 Boomburbs	61.3
79339	50 Heartland Communities	40.8	79606	39 Young And Restless	22.8	80010	58 NeWest Residents	42.9
79342	37 Prairie Living	100.0	79607	40 Military Proximity	100.0	80011	18 Cozy And Comfortable	22.4
79343	56 Rural Bypasses	70.5	79697	48 Great Expectations	0.0	80012	28 Aspiring Young Families	31.9
79344	37 Prairie Living	100.0	79698	53 Home Town	100.0	80013	12 Up And Coming Families	38.7
79345	37 Prairie Living	100.0	79699	55 College Towns	100.0	80014	13 In Style	23.2
79346	37 Prairie Living	64.7	79701	59 Southwestern Families	41.1	80015	04 Boomburbs	35.0
79347	50 Heartland Communities	37.0	79703	38 Industrious Urban Fringe	29.6	80016	02 Suburban Splendor	57.9
79351	59 Southwestern Families	75.5	79705	14 Prosperous Empty Nesters	27.0	80017	28 Aspiring Young Families	35.8
79353	37 Prairie Living	100.0	79706	26 Midland Crowd	37.8	80018	07 Exurbanites	72.6
79355	37 Prairie Living	100.0	79707	13 In Style	17.7	80019	06 Sophisticated Squires	100.0
79356	50 Heartland Communities	40.8	79713	37 Prairie Living	100.0	80020	04 Boomburbs	25.6
79357	50 Heartland Communities	60.6	79714	59 Southwestern Families	21.7	80021	12 Up And Coming Families	32.9
79358	37 Prairie Living	94.2	79718	59 Southwestern Families	100.0	80022	38 Industrious Urban Fringe	52.5
79359	59 Southwestern Families	50.5	79719	56 Rural Bypasses	100.0	80023	04 Boomburbs	59.8
79360	37 Prairie Living	25.7	79720	53 Home Town	17.8	80026	04 Boomburbs	27.6
79363	26 Midland Crowd	40.5	79730	46 Rooted Rural	100.0	80027	04 Boomburbs	29.8
79364	50 Heartland Communities	35.4	79731	59 Southwestern Families	48.1	80030	24 Main Street, USA	41.6
79366	31 Rural Resort Dwellers	100.0	79734	46 Rooted Rural	53.4	80031	13 In Style	15.8
79370	50 Heartland Communities	88.3	79735	56 Rural Bypasses	33.4	80033	24 Main Street, USA	29.5
79371	50 Heartland Communities	94.0	79738	37 Prairie Living	100.0	80101	37 Prairie Living	100.0
79373	37 Prairie Living	70.4	79739	37 Prairie Living	100.0	80102	19 Milk And Cookies	47.4
79376	37 Prairie Living	100.0	79741	46 Rooted Rural	100.0	80103	26 Midland Crowd	56.1
79377	37 Prairie Living	100.0	79742	50 Heartland Communities	100.0	80104	13 In Style	24.1
79379	37 Prairie Living	65.3	79743	46 Rooted Rural	100.0	80105	46 Rooted Rural	61.0
79381	38 Industrious Urban Fringe	56.3	79744	42 Southern Satellites	54.6	80106	17 Green Acres	39.9
79382	26 Midland Crowd	64.4	79745	50 Heartland Communities	26.4	80107	06 Sophisticated Squires	84.2
79401	55 College Towns	40.6	79748	37 Prairie Living	100.0	80108	02 Suburban Splendor	63.6
79403	62 Modest Income Homes	24.1	79749	37 Prairie Living	100.0	80109	04 Boomburbs	81.2
79404	59 Southwestern Families	42.1	79752	46 Rooted Rural	32.7	80110	24 Main Street, USA	38.3
79407	26 Midland Crowd	15.0	79754	31 Rural Resort Dwellers	100.0	80111	02 Suburban Splendor	38.4
79409	63 Dorms To Diplomas	100.0	79755	46 Rooted Rural	62.7	80112	02 Suburban Splendor	23.1
79410	55 College Towns	43.2	79756	59 Southwestern Families	26.2	80113	36 Old And Newcomers	24.8
79411	59 Southwestern Families	31.9	79758	25 Salt Of The Earth	52.9	80116	02 Suburban Splendor	51.0
79412	33 Midlife Junction	25.3	79761	59 Southwestern Families	30.9	80117	17 Green Acres	50.3
79413	33 Midlife Junction	29.4	79762	32 Rustbelt Traditions	15.1	80118	02 Suburban Splendor	63.2
79414	48 Great Expectations	30.6	79763	59 Southwestern Families	32.3	80120	13 In Style	16.7
79415	59 Southwestern Families	43.9	79764	41 Crossroads	57.6	80121	07 Exurbanites	28.2
79416	55 College Towns	20.8	79765	07 Exurbanites	44.5	80122	02 Suburban Splendor	23.8
79423	12 Up And Coming Families	25.0	79766	41 Crossroads	45.6	80123	06 Sophisticated Squires	17.8
79424	12 Up And Coming Families	29.2	79772	59 Southwestern Families	62.0	80124	04 Boomburbs	53.6
79501	50 Heartland Communities	59.6	79777	56 Rural Bypasses	100.0	80125	12 Up And Coming Families	63.5
79502	50 Heartland Communities	50.9	79781	42 Southern Satellites	100.0	80126	04 Boomburbs	46.4
79503	50 Heartland Communities	83.5	79782	46 Rooted Rural	38.4	80127	06 Sophisticated Squires	23.8
79504	46 Rooted Rural	60.2	79783	37 Prairie Living	100.0	80128	06 Sophisticated Squires	37.1
79506	50 Heartland Communities	52.8	79789	26 Midland Crowd	100.0	80129	04 Boomburbs	77.0
79508	17 Green Acres	100.0	79821	59 Southwestern Families	93.5	80130	04 Boomburbs	80.3
79510	46 Rooted Rural	71.4	79830	33 Midlife Junction	40.9	80132	02 Suburban Splendor	60.7
79511	46 Rooted Rural	92.0	79832	33 Midlife Junction	75.0	80133	17 Green Acres	45.2
79512	50 Heartland Communities	32.4	79834	46 Rooted Rural	91.2	80134	04 Boomburbs	44.6
79517	37 Prairie Living	100.0	79835	59 Southwestern Families	81.1	80135	07 Exurbanites	28.4
79518	37 Prairie Living	100.0	79836	59 Southwestern Families	76.6	80136	17 Green Acres	100.0
79519	46 Rooted Rural	100.0	79837	46 Rooted Rural	96.1	80137	26 Midland Crowd	72.1
79520	50 Heartland Communities	96.8	79839	59 Southwestern Families	100.0	80138	04 Boomburbs	54.1
79521	50 Heartland Communities	64.9	79842	46 Rooted Rural	100.0	80202	08 Laptops And Lattes	35.1
79525	26 Midland Crowd	92.4	79843	59 Southwestern Families	72.0	80203	27 Metro Renters	94.4
79526	46 Rooted Rural	77.0	79847	46 Rooted Rural	89.7	80204	38 Industrious Urban Fringe	24.7
79527	37 Prairie Living	99.2	79849	59 Southwestern Families	100.0	80205	38 Industrious Urban Fringe	13.3
79528	50 Heartland Communities	76.6	79851	41 Crossroads	99.6	80206	27 Metro Renters	52.8
79529	50 Heartland Communities	100.0	79852	46 Rooted Rural	100.0	80207	34 Family Foundations	28.1
79530	46 Rooted Rural	98.3	79854	46 Rooted Rural	100.0	80208	55 College Towns	66.0
79532	50 Heartland Communities	99.1	79855	59 Southwestern Families	91.3	80209	27 Metro Renters	24.1
79533	46 Rooted Rural	95.7	79901	59 Southwestern Families	38.1	80210	22 Metropolitans	49.5
79534	37 Prairie Living	100.0	79902	59 Southwestern Families	19.3	80211	24 Main Street, USA	23.6

ZIP CODE	TOP TAPESTRY CONSUMER TYPE	% 2009 HOUSE-HOLDS	ZIP CODE	TOP TAPESTRY CONSUMER TYPE	% 2009 HOUSE-HOLDS	ZIP CODE	TOP TAPESTRY CONSUMER TYPE	% 2009 HOUSE-HOLDS
80212	22 Metropolitans	38.4	80530	19 Milk And Cookies	56.2	80827	31 Rural Resort Dwellers	95.6
80214	36 Old And Newcomers	32.3	80534	12 Up And Coming Families	84.7	80828	33 Midlife Junction	78.3
80215	36 Old And Newcomers	38.3	80535	17 Green Acres	56.7	80829	22 Metropolitans	40.6
80216	38 Industrious Urban Fringe	72.2	80536	31 Rural Resort Dwellers	90.8	80830	37 Prairie Living	100.0
80218	27 Metro Renters	83.2	80537	28 Aspiring Young Families	16.5	80831	06 Sophisticated Squires	50.9
80219	38 Industrious Urban Fringe	60.7	80538	12 Up And Coming Families	20.0	80832	26 Midland Crowd	72.1
80220	22 Metropolitans	25.3	80540	07 Exurbanites	50.0	80833	26 Midland Crowd	58.8
80221	24 Main Street, USA	32.8	80542	12 Up And Coming Families	75.9	80834	37 Prairie Living	100.0
80222	36 Old And Newcomers	33.4	80543	38 Industrious Urban Fringe	48.1	80835	37 Prairie Living	98.0
80223	38 Industrious Urban Fringe	34.9	80545	31 Rural Resort Dwellers	100.0	80836	37 Prairie Living	100.0
80224	36 Old And Newcomers	30.8	80547	02 Suburban Splendor	100.0	80840	40 Military Proximity	100.0
80226	18 Cozy And Comfortable	15.8	80549	19 Milk And Cookies	34.9	80861	37 Prairie Living	100.0
80227	13 In Style	24.4	80550	12 Up And Coming Families	61.6	80863	06 Sophisticated Squires	43.5
80228	39 Young And Restless	26.4	80601	12 Up And Coming Families	43.2	80864	26 Midland Crowd	100.0
80229	28 Aspiring Young Families	17.7	80602	04 Boomburbs	40.9	80903	48 Great Expectations	22.7
80230	24 Main Street, USA	39.2	80603	17 Green Acres	64.5	80904	36 Old And Newcomers	20.3
80231	39 Young And Restless	37.3	80610	26 Midland Crowd	69.4	80905	36 Old And Newcomers	47.7
80232	18 Cozy And Comfortable	23.6	80611	37 Prairie Living	100.0	80906	02 Suburban Splendor	21.6
80233	18 Cozy And Comfortable	23.4	80612	26 Midland Crowd	78.6	80907	28 Aspiring Young Families	23.0
80234	39 Young And Restless	26.1	80615	17 Green Acres	72.1	80908	07 Exurbanites	52.3
80235	16 Enterprising Professionals	24.8	80620	26 Midland Crowd	23.7	80909	52 Inner City Tenants	25.2
80236	13 In Style	21.6	80621	38 Industrious Urban Fringe	38.4	80910	28 Aspiring Young Families	20.6
80237	36 Old And Newcomers	19.2	80624	17 Green Acres	71.8	80911	19 Milk And Cookies	43.6
80238	09 Urban Chic	100.0	80631	38 Industrious Urban Fringe	16.6	80913	40 Military Proximity	99.3
80239	12 Up And Coming Families	32.8	80634	12 Up And Coming Families	26.5	80914	40 Military Proximity	100.0
80241	04 Boomburbs	29.9	80639	63 Dorms To Diplomas	100.0	80915	28 Aspiring Young Families	26.1
80246	39 Young And Restless	68.0	80640	17 Green Acres	97.5	80916	19 Milk And Cookies	34.4
80247	39 Young And Restless	48.4	80642	26 Midland Crowd	56.1	80917	36 Old And Newcomers	25.1
80249	12 Up And Coming Families	81.1	80643	17 Green Acres	68.7	80918	28 Aspiring Young Families	19.2
80260	41 Crossroads	37.4	80644	26 Midland Crowd	56.2	80919	16 Enterprising Professionals	24.1
80262	27 Metro Renters	0.0	80645	24 Main Street, USA	34.8	80920	04 Boomburbs	48.1
80301	16 Enterprising Professionals	29.8	80648	26 Midland Crowd	100.0	80921	07 Exurbanites	89.9
80302	63 Dorms To Diplomas	41.5	80649	37 Prairie Living	81.4	80922	12 Up And Coming Families	91.2
80303	09 Urban Chic	22.9	80650	25 Salt Of The Earth	65.6	80923	12 Up And Coming Families	98.2
80304	22 Metropolitans	19.4	80651	26 Midland Crowd	41.0	80924	04 Boomburbs	100.0
80305	09 Urban Chic	34.6	80652	37 Prairie Living	88.1	80925	12 Up And Coming Families	58.6
80309	63 Dorms To Diplomas	0.0	80653	37 Prairie Living	93.7	80926	02 Suburban Splendor	60.2
80401	03 Connoisseurs	15.2	80654	37 Prairie Living	59.4	80927	17 Green Acres	100.0
80403	07 Exurbanites	34.9	80701	50 Heartland Communities	19.8	80928	26 Midland Crowd	88.2
80421	17 Green Acres	46.8	80705	26 Midland Crowd	100.0	80929	12 Up And Coming Families	52.3
80422	22 Metropolitans	100.0	80720	37 Prairie Living	69.4	80930	12 Up And Coming Families	100.0
80423	31 Rural Resort Dwellers	96.4	80721	37 Prairie Living	100.0	80951	41 Crossroads	95.1
80424	16 Enterprising Professionals	64.9	80722	37 Prairie Living	100.0	81001	53 Home Town	12.9
80428	17 Green Acres	77.2	80723	57 Simple Living	23.6	81003	53 Home Town	21.6
80430	37 Prairie Living	100.0	80726	37 Prairie Living	100.0	81004	32 Rustbelt Traditions	29.5
80433	07 Exurbanites	55.6	80727	37 Prairie Living	100.0	81005	29 Rustbelt Retirees	30.3
80435	16 Enterprising Professionals	39.4	80728	37 Prairie Living	100.0	81006	17 Green Acres	26.7
80439	07 Exurbanites	53.1	80729	37 Prairie Living	98.9	81007	12 Up And Coming Families	38.7
80440	12 Up And Coming Families	57.6	80731	37 Prairie Living	100.0	81008	19 Milk And Cookies	33.8
80442	16 Enterprising Professionals	92.4	80733	37 Prairie Living	100.0	81019	31 Rural Resort Dwellers	100.0
80443	16 Enterprising Professionals	90.0	80734	37 Prairie Living	73.2	81020	49 Senior Sun Seekers	95.3
80446	31 Rural Resort Dwellers	50.0	80735	37 Prairie Living	100.0	81021	37 Prairie Living	100.0
80447	31 Rural Resort Dwellers	99.9	80736	37 Prairie Living	100.0	81022	46 Rooted Rural	66.6
80449	31 Rural Resort Dwellers	93.5	80737	50 Heartland Communities	83.5	81023	31 Rural Resort Dwellers	100.0
80451	31 Rural Resort Dwellers	90.9	80740	37 Prairie Living	100.0	81025	46 Rooted Rural	79.6
80452	31 Rural Resort Dwellers	44.3	80741	37 Prairie Living	100.0	81027	37 Prairie Living	100.0
80455	22 Metropolitans	83.9	80742	37 Prairie Living	100.0	81029	37 Prairie Living	100.0
80456	31 Rural Resort Dwellers	100.0	80743	37 Prairie Living	100.0	81036	50 Heartland Communities	80.2
80459	26 Midland Crowd	80.8	80744	37 Prairie Living	99.5	81039	50 Heartland Communities	85.5
80461	33 Midlife Junction	24.2	80745	37 Prairie Living	100.0	81040	31 Rural Resort Dwellers	100.0
80463	31 Rural Resort Dwellers	67.3	80747	37 Prairie Living	100.0	81041	59 Southwestern Families	82.8
80465	06 Sophisticated Squires	44.4	80749	37 Prairie Living	100.0	81043	37 Prairie Living	100.0
80466	22 Metropolitans	51.7	80750	37 Prairie Living	99.0	81044	37 Prairie Living	100.0
80467	26 Midland Crowd	59.1	80751	17 Green Acres	18.0	81045	37 Prairie Living	100.0
80468	17 Green Acres	100.0	80754	37 Prairie Living	100.0	81047	53 Home Town	53.8
80470	07 Exurbanites	72.2	80755	37 Prairie Living	100.0	81049	37 Prairie Living	100.0
80478	31 Rural Resort Dwellers	100.0	80757	37 Prairie Living	100.0	81050	33 Midlife Junction	18.9
80479	37 Prairie Living	100.0	80758	37 Prairie Living	62.8	81052	53 Home Town	16.3
80480	46 Rooted Rural	56.3	80759	37 Prairie Living	51.6	81054	50 Heartland Communities	76.5
80481	22 Metropolitans	62.9	80801	37 Prairie Living	100.0	81055	31 Rural Resort Dwellers	100.0
80482	16 Enterprising Professionals	100.0	80802	37 Prairie Living	100.0	81057	37 Prairie Living	100.0
80487	09 Urban Chic	22.4	80804	37 Prairie Living	100.0	81058	46 Rooted Rural	88.5
80498	16 Enterprising Professionals	87.1	80805	37 Prairie Living	100.0	81059	37 Prairie Living	82.5
80501	12 Up And Coming Families	15.4	80807	46 Rooted Rural	33.9	81062	37 Prairie Living	100.0
80503	13 In Style	41.9	80808	26 Midland Crowd	80.3	81063	50 Heartland Communities	75.4
80504	26 Midland Crowd	35.6	80809	31 Rural Resort Dwellers	65.6	81064	37 Prairie Living	100.0
80510	31 Rural Resort Dwellers	100.0	80810	37 Prairie Living	100.0	81067	53 Home Town	22.2
80512	31 Rural Resort Dwellers	46.1	80812	37 Prairie Living	100.0	81069	31 Rural Resort Dwellers	100.0
80513	12 Up And Coming Families	20.8	80813	31 Rural Resort Dwellers	99.7	81071	37 Prairie Living	100.0
80514	41 Crossroads	55.5	80814	17 Green Acres	68.7	81073	50 Heartland Communities	76.7
80515	31 Rural Resort Dwellers	90.1	80815	50 Heartland Communities	68.3	81076	37 Prairie Living	100.0
80516	07 Exurbanites	52.8	80816	31 Rural Resort Dwellers	46.3	81081	37 Prairie Living	96.9
80517	31 Rural Resort Dwellers	68.2	80817	12 Up And Coming Families	43.1	81082	57 Simple Living	26.9
80520	07 Exurbanites	100.0	80818	37 Prairie Living	86.2	81084	37 Prairie Living	100.0
80521	55 College Towns	35.2	80820	31 Rural Resort Dwellers	100.0	81087	37 Prairie Living	100.0
80523	63 Dorms To Diplomas	100.0	80821	50 Heartland Communities	71.5	81089	50 Heartland Communities	53.9
80524	07 Exurbanites	19.3	80822	37 Prairie Living	100.0	81090	37 Prairie Living	100.0
80525	04 Boomburbs	13.3	80823	37 Prairie Living	100.0	81091	31 Rural Resort Dwellers	89.3
80526	13 In Style	18.0	80824	37 Prairie Living	100.0	81092	37 Prairie Living	100.0
80528	12 Up And Coming Families	78.5	80825	37 Prairie Living	100.0	81101	26 Midland Crowd	18.0

CONSUMER TYPE

ZIP CODE	TOP TAPESTRY CONSUMER TYPE	% 2009 HOUSE-HOLDS	ZIP CODE	TOP TAPESTRY CONSUMER TYPE	% 2009 HOUSE-HOLDS	ZIP CODE	TOP TAPESTRY CONSUMER TYPE	% 2009 HOUSE-HOLDS
81102	55 College Towns	100.0	81527	31 Rural Resort Dwellers	96.5	82435	33 Midlife Junction	19.9
81120	56 Rural Bypasses	77.1	81601	36 Old And Newcomers	24.9	82441	37 Prairie Living	61.9
81121	31 Rural Resort Dwellers	100.0	81610	46 Rooted Rural	100.0	82442	31 Rural Resort Dwellers	99.7
81122	26 Midland Crowd	33.7	81611	08 Laptops And Lattes	54.0	82443	33 Midlife Junction	61.5
81123	46 Rooted Rural	100.0	81615	08 Laptops And Lattes	55.6	82501	41 Crossroads	15.6
81125	38 Industrious Urban Fringe	44.5	81620	16 Enterprising Professionals	76.4	82510	56 Rural Bypasses	73.1
81130	31 Rural Resort Dwellers	100.0	81621	12 Up And Coming Families	36.2	82512	37 Prairie Living	100.0
81132	31 Rural Resort Dwellers	35.8	81623	09 Urban Chic	24.9	82513	31 Rural Resort Dwellers	99.2
81133	46 Rooted Rural	100.0	81624	31 Rural Resort Dwellers	100.0	82514	51 Metro City Edge	95.2
81136	37 Prairie Living	85.6	81625	19 Milk And Cookies	20.0	82516	37 Prairie Living	56.0
81137	41 Crossroads	35.5	81630	31 Rural Resort Dwellers	86.7	82520	33 Midlife Junction	43.3
81140	46 Rooted Rural	49.5	81631	12 Up And Coming Families	77.6	82523	37 Prairie Living	96.1
81143	31 Rural Resort Dwellers	64.3	81632	16 Enterprising Professionals	52.8	82601	32 Rustbelt Traditions	12.0
81144	46 Rooted Rural	25.2	81633	46 Rooted Rural	100.0	82604	19 Milk And Cookies	21.0
81146	37 Prairie Living	57.4	81635	31 Rural Resort Dwellers	79.3	82609	07 Exurbanites	15.7
81147	31 Rural Resort Dwellers	100.0	81637	12 Up And Coming Families	86.7	82620	31 Rural Resort Dwellers	100.0
81149	46 Rooted Rural	65.5	81638	37 Prairie Living	100.0	82633	17 Green Acres	19.3
81151	56 Rural Bypasses	43.0	81639	26 Midland Crowd	45.4	82636	41 Crossroads	63.3
81152	46 Rooted Rural	95.3	81640	37 Prairie Living	76.6	82637	33 Midlife Junction	37.9
81154	31 Rural Resort Dwellers	100.0	81641	25 Salt Of The Earth	37.7	82639	37 Prairie Living	97.9
81155	31 Rural Resort Dwellers	100.0	81642	31 Rural Resort Dwellers	93.0	82642	31 Rural Resort Dwellers	100.0
81201	31 Rural Resort Dwellers	47.9	81643	31 Rural Resort Dwellers	100.0	82643	26 Midland Crowd	100.0
81210	31 Rural Resort Dwellers	57.1	81647	12 Up And Coming Families	69.1	82649	31 Rural Resort Dwellers	73.7
81211	31 Rural Resort Dwellers	73.0	81648	19 Milk And Cookies	55.3	82701	50 Heartland Communities	48.9
81212	33 Midlife Junction	46.7	81650	28 Aspiring Young Families	40.5	82710	37 Prairie Living	100.0
81220	31 Rural Resort Dwellers	100.0	81652	26 Midland Crowd	75.3	82712	37 Prairie Living	100.0
81223	31 Rural Resort Dwellers	100.0	81653	17 Green Acres	100.0	82714	31 Rural Resort Dwellers	100.0
81224	16 Enterprising Professionals	99.8	81654	09 Urban Chic	56.3	82715	31 Rural Resort Dwellers	100.0
81226	33 Midlife Junction	54.3	81657	23 Trendsetters	52.8	82716	26 Midland Crowd	27.0
81228	41 Crossroads	53.5	82001	48 Great Expectations	19.7	82718	06 Sophisticated Squires	30.9
81230	22 Metropolitans	27.3	82005	40 Military Proximity	99.4	82720	37 Prairie Living	98.8
81231	31 Rural Resort Dwellers	54.5	82007	41 Crossroads	49.1	82721	26 Midland Crowd	57.4
81233	31 Rural Resort Dwellers	100.0	82009	07 Exurbanites	36.9	82723	31 Rural Resort Dwellers	100.0
81235	31 Rural Resort Dwellers	100.0	82050	37 Prairie Living	100.0	82725	17 Green Acres	100.0
81236	15 Silver And Gold	100.0	82051	31 Rural Resort Dwellers	100.0	82727	26 Midland Crowd	50.5
81239	31 Rural Resort Dwellers	100.0	82052	31 Rural Resort Dwellers	90.0	82729	25 Salt Of The Earth	63.8
81240	26 Midland Crowd	72.4	82053	37 Prairie Living	74.9	82730	46 Rooted Rural	98.4
81241	31 Rural Resort Dwellers	100.0	82054	17 Green Acres	54.6	82731	26 Midland Crowd	82.3
81243	31 Rural Resort Dwellers	100.0	82055	31 Rural Resort Dwellers	100.0	82732	26 Midland Crowd	100.0
81251	41 Crossroads	100.0	82058	31 Rural Resort Dwellers	100.0	82801	57 Simple Living	20.0
81252	31 Rural Resort Dwellers	100.0	82063	31 Rural Resort Dwellers	100.0	82831	37 Prairie Living	80.0
81253	31 Rural Resort Dwellers	96.9	82070	22 Metropolitans	28.0	82832	31 Rural Resort Dwellers	92.4
81301	55 College Towns	26.0	82072	55 College Towns	48.0	82834	31 Rural Resort Dwellers	44.4
81303	13 In Style	40.5	82081	07 Exurbanites	100.0	82835	37 Prairie Living	100.0
81320	22 Metropolitans	53.6	82082	37 Prairie Living	100.0	82836	31 Rural Resort Dwellers	99.8
81321	26 Midland Crowd	19.9	82083	31 Rural Resort Dwellers	75.6	82838	31 Rural Resort Dwellers	100.0
81323	31 Rural Resort Dwellers	100.0	82084	31 Rural Resort Dwellers	100.0	82839	31 Rural Resort Dwellers	100.0
81324	46 Rooted Rural	100.0	82190	13 In Style	52.9	82842	31 Rural Resort Dwellers	100.0
81325	31 Rural Resort Dwellers	100.0	82201	25 Salt Of The Earth	32.0	82844	31 Rural Resort Dwellers	100.0
81326	26 Midland Crowd	76.2	82210	37 Prairie Living	100.0	82901	26 Midland Crowd	22.6
81327	37 Prairie Living	69.4	82212	31 Rural Resort Dwellers	100.0	82922	31 Rural Resort Dwellers	100.0
81328	31 Rural Resort Dwellers	97.0	82213	31 Rural Resort Dwellers	100.0	82923	31 Rural Resort Dwellers	100.0
81331	37 Prairie Living	100.0	82214	46 Rooted Rural	93.8	82925	31 Rural Resort Dwellers	100.0
81334	59 Southwestern Families	60.6	82215	31 Rural Resort Dwellers	100.0	82930	28 Aspiring Young Families	22.6
81335	37 Prairie Living	100.0	82217	37 Prairie Living	100.0	82933	26 Midland Crowd	99.9
81401	33 Midlife Junction	32.5	82219	31 Rural Resort Dwellers	98.8	82935	17 Green Acres	25.4
81403	31 Rural Resort Dwellers	71.0	82221	37 Prairie Living	100.0	82936	26 Midland Crowd	100.0
81410	46 Rooted Rural	85.1	82222	37 Prairie Living	100.0	82937	26 Midland Crowd	100.0
81411	46 Rooted Rural	100.0	82223	37 Prairie Living	100.0	82938	17 Green Acres	100.0
81413	49 Senior Sun Seekers	55.4	82224	37 Prairie Living	100.0	82941	31 Rural Resort Dwellers	100.0
81415	31 Rural Resort Dwellers	87.3	82225	50 Heartland Communities	77.3	83001	16 Enterprising Professionals	30.7
81416	46 Rooted Rural	19.7	82227	37 Prairie Living	100.0	83011	22 Metropolitans	90.3
81418	31 Rural Resort Dwellers	86.0	82229	25 Salt Of The Earth	55.6	83012	22 Metropolitans	99.3
81419	31 Rural Resort Dwellers	76.2	82240	33 Midlife Junction	26.6	83013	22 Metropolitans	100.0
81422	46 Rooted Rural	100.0	82242	37 Prairie Living	100.0	83014	09 Urban Chic	90.3
81423	31 Rural Resort Dwellers	100.0	82243	37 Prairie Living	100.0	83101	26 Midland Crowd	79.6
81424	46 Rooted Rural	100.0	82244	37 Prairie Living	99.6	83110	25 Salt Of The Earth	63.5
81425	42 Southern Satellites	41.2	82301	32 Rustbelt Traditions	17.4	83111	26 Midland Crowd	100.0
81426	09 Urban Chic	92.0	82310	31 Rural Resort Dwellers	100.0	83112	26 Midland Crowd	85.0
81427	31 Rural Resort Dwellers	100.0	82321	37 Prairie Living	100.0	83113	26 Midland Crowd	90.0
81428	31 Rural Resort Dwellers	66.2	82322	26 Midland Crowd	100.0	83114	25 Salt Of The Earth	100.0
81430	09 Urban Chic	100.0	82323	37 Prairie Living	100.0	83115	31 Rural Resort Dwellers	100.0
81431	46 Rooted Rural	100.0	82325	31 Rural Resort Dwellers	100.0	83118	31 Rural Resort Dwellers	100.0
81432	31 Rural Resort Dwellers	87.8	82327	46 Rooted Rural	93.5	83120	31 Rural Resort Dwellers	93.8
81433	31 Rural Resort Dwellers	100.0	82329	49 Senior Sun Seekers	98.6	83122	26 Midland Crowd	69.1
81434	31 Rural Resort Dwellers	100.0	82331	46 Rooted Rural	50.2	83123	26 Midland Crowd	100.0
81435	08 Laptops And Lattes	64.1	82332	37 Prairie Living	100.0	83126	26 Midland Crowd	98.5
81501	33 Midlife Junction	25.1	82334	31 Rural Resort Dwellers	100.0	83127	31 Rural Resort Dwellers	68.1
81503	18 Cozy And Comfortable	19.1	82336	26 Midland Crowd	99.2	83201	48 Great Expectations	18.8
81504	18 Cozy And Comfortable	24.0	82401	50 Heartland Communities	26.5	83202	41 Crossroads	22.6
81505	33 Midlife Junction	31.4	82410	29 Rustbelt Retirees	61.7	83203	26 Midland Crowd	100.0
81506	30 Retirement Communities	35.3	82411	37 Prairie Living	97.8	83204	48 Great Expectations	27.9
81507	07 Exurbanites	42.4	82414	33 Midlife Junction	29.9	83209	33 Midlife Junction	0.0
81520	28 Aspiring Young Families	50.8	82421	37 Prairie Living	83.2	83210	53 Home Town	36.0
81521	26 Midland Crowd	43.7	82426	50 Heartland Communities	76.9	83211	41 Crossroads	51.3
81522	17 Green Acres	100.0	82428	37 Prairie Living	100.0	83212	37 Prairie Living	100.0
81523	17 Green Acres	100.0	82431	50 Heartland Communities	31.2	83213	46 Rooted Rural	88.3
81524	37 Prairie Living	95.6	82432	37 Prairie Living	96.5	83214	37 Prairie Living	100.0
81525	37 Prairie Living	100.0	82433	37 Prairie Living	95.8	83217	37 Prairie Living	100.0
81526	33 Midlife Junction	55.1	82434	37 Prairie Living	100.0	83220	46 Rooted Rural	94.9

ZIP CODE	TOP TAPESTRY CONSUMER TYPE	% 2009 HOUSE-HOLDS	ZIP CODE	TOP TAPESTRY CONSUMER TYPE	% 2009 HOUSE-HOLDS	ZIP CODE	TOP TAPESTRY CONSUMER TYPE	% 2009 HOUSE-HOLDS
83221	26 Midland Crowd	33.2	83450	37 Prairie Living	100.0	83705	28 Aspiring Young Families	28.6
83226	37 Prairie Living	53.5	83451	42 Southern Satellites	99.5	83706	13 In Style	28.9
83227	31 Rural Resort Dwellers	100.0	83452	26 Midland Crowd	95.4	83709	19 Milk And Cookies	25.4
83228	37 Prairie Living	100.0	83455	12 Up And Coming Families	98.7	83712	36 Old And Newcomers	39.5
83232	37 Prairie Living	100.0	83460	63 Dorms To Diplomas	0.0	83713	04 Boomburbs	34.2
83234	37 Prairie Living	99.0	83462	31 Rural Resort Dwellers	100.0	83714	12 Up And Coming Families	45.3
83235	49 Senior Sun Seekers	92.9	83463	31 Rural Resort Dwellers	100.0	83716	12 Up And Coming Families	65.6
83236	26 Midland Crowd	44.7	83464	37 Prairie Living	100.0	83725	63 Dorms To Diplomas	0.0
83237	25 Salt Of The Earth	82.3	83466	31 Rural Resort Dwellers	100.0	83801	26 Midland Crowd	71.8
83238	37 Prairie Living	88.9	83467	31 Rural Resort Dwellers	51.0	83802	46 Rooted Rural	100.0
83241	37 Prairie Living	100.0	83469	31 Rural Resort Dwellers	100.0	83803	49 Senior Sun Seekers	100.0
83243	37 Prairie Living	100.0	83501	33 Midlife Junction	31.1	83804	46 Rooted Rural	100.0
83244	37 Prairie Living	100.0	83520	31 Rural Resort Dwellers	100.0	83805	46 Rooted Rural	42.9
83245	25 Salt Of The Earth	81.9	83522	33 Midlife Junction	58.7	83809	31 Rural Resort Dwellers	100.0
83246	46 Rooted Rural	100.0	83523	37 Prairie Living	88.9	83810	31 Rural Resort Dwellers	85.1
83250	25 Salt Of The Earth	81.8	83524	46 Rooted Rural	39.8	83811	31 Rural Resort Dwellers	100.0
83251	31 Rural Resort Dwellers	99.0	83525	31 Rural Resort Dwellers	100.0	83812	46 Rooted Rural	100.0
83252	37 Prairie Living	65.2	83526	37 Prairie Living	88.0	83813	31 Rural Resort Dwellers	99.3
83253	49 Senior Sun Seekers	100.0	83530	31 Rural Resort Dwellers	39.9	83814	48 Great Expectations	22.5
83254	25 Salt Of The Earth	36.5	83533	37 Prairie Living	100.0	83815	26 Midland Crowd	45.1
83255	37 Prairie Living	82.5	83535	46 Rooted Rural	77.5	83821	31 Rural Resort Dwellers	100.0
83261	46 Rooted Rural	65.6	83536	50 Heartland Communities	45.5	83822	46 Rooted Rural	100.0
83262	26 Midland Crowd	69.1	83537	37 Prairie Living	93.5	83823	25 Salt Of The Earth	51.6
83263	25 Salt Of The Earth	35.6	83539	31 Rural Resort Dwellers	38.6	83824	46 Rooted Rural	100.0
83271	37 Prairie Living	100.0	83540	26 Midland Crowd	75.2	83827	31 Rural Resort Dwellers	100.0
83272	31 Rural Resort Dwellers	84.9	83541	31 Rural Resort Dwellers	94.5	83830	46 Rooted Rural	100.0
83274	26 Midland Crowd	34.3	83542	49 Senior Sun Seekers	100.0	83832	26 Midland Crowd	92.2
83276	26 Midland Crowd	40.6	83543	37 Prairie Living	100.0	83833	31 Rural Resort Dwellers	99.0
83278	31 Rural Resort Dwellers	93.0	83544	46 Rooted Rural	41.6	83834	46 Rooted Rural	100.0
83283	37 Prairie Living	100.0	83545	37 Prairie Living	86.9	83835	26 Midland Crowd	63.9
83285	31 Rural Resort Dwellers	66.0	83546	46 Rooted Rural	92.6	83836	31 Rural Resort Dwellers	100.0
83286	37 Prairie Living	100.0	83547	49 Senior Sun Seekers	93.5	83837	50 Heartland Communities	57.6
83287	31 Rural Resort Dwellers	100.0	83548	31 Rural Resort Dwellers	56.6	83839	46 Rooted Rural	81.0
83301	48 Great Expectations	12.5	83549	49 Senior Sun Seekers	100.0	83842	31 Rural Resort Dwellers	100.0
83302	37 Prairie Living	100.0	83552	31 Rural Resort Dwellers	61.5	83843	55 College Towns	27.9
83313	24 Main Street, USA	32.1	83553	46 Rooted Rural	47.3	83845	26 Midland Crowd	52.2
83314	37 Prairie Living	100.0	83554	31 Rural Resort Dwellers	100.0	83846	50 Heartland Communities	100.0
83316	37 Prairie Living	53.2	83555	31 Rural Resort Dwellers	100.0	83847	17 Green Acres	35.8
83318	37 Prairie Living	27.0	83601	49 Senior Sun Seekers	100.0	83848	31 Rural Resort Dwellers	100.0
83320	37 Prairie Living	98.4	83602	46 Rooted Rural	87.5	83850	46 Rooted Rural	45.4
83321	37 Prairie Living	100.0	83604	37 Prairie Living	100.0	83851	46 Rooted Rural	64.5
83322	31 Rural Resort Dwellers	100.0	83605	41 Crossroads	21.1	83852	46 Rooted Rural	62.0
83323	37 Prairie Living	100.0	83607	26 Midland Crowd	55.0	83853	37 Prairie Living	100.0
83324	26 Midland Crowd	92.4	83610	37 Prairie Living	100.0	83854	26 Midland Crowd	52.0
83325	37 Prairie Living	100.0	83611	31 Rural Resort Dwellers	100.0	83855	50 Heartland Communities	55.6
83327	31 Rural Resort Dwellers	100.0	83612	46 Rooted Rural	51.0	83856	31 Rural Resort Dwellers	37.1
83328	37 Prairie Living	33.1	83615	31 Rural Resort Dwellers	100.0	83857	46 Rooted Rural	100.0
83330	50 Heartland Communities	49.8	83616	06 Sophisticated Squires	33.5	83858	26 Midland Crowd	83.6
83332	31 Rural Resort Dwellers	48.7	83617	25 Salt Of The Earth	34.7	83860	31 Rural Resort Dwellers	56.2
83333	12 Up And Coming Families	24.0	83619	46 Rooted Rural	35.7	83861	46 Rooted Rural	48.8
83334	41 Crossroads	53.6	83622	31 Rural Resort Dwellers	98.2	83864	31 Rural Resort Dwellers	40.7
83335	37 Prairie Living	100.0	83623	46 Rooted Rural	77.4	83868	50 Heartland Communities	80.2
83336	42 Southern Satellites	35.5	83624	42 Southern Satellites	52.9	83869	26 Midland Crowd	50.5
83338	26 Midland Crowd	27.9	83626	26 Midland Crowd	84.1	83870	46 Rooted Rural	100.0
83340	09 Urban Chic	43.4	83627	37 Prairie Living	87.1	83871	17 Green Acres	93.0
83341	26 Midland Crowd	33.9	83628	53 Home Town	37.5	83872	17 Green Acres	98.9
83342	37 Prairie Living	100.0	83629	46 Rooted Rural	100.0	83873	46 Rooted Rural	27.7
83343	38 Industrious Urban Fringe	50.0	83631	31 Rural Resort Dwellers	90.5	83876	26 Midland Crowd	58.1
83344	37 Prairie Living	100.0	83632	31 Rural Resort Dwellers	100.0	84001	37 Prairie Living	100.0
83346	37 Prairie Living	100.0	83633	37 Prairie Living	100.0	84003	06 Sophisticated Squires	26.4
83347	46 Rooted Rural	49.1	83634	12 Up And Coming Families	55.8	84004	04 Boomburbs	73.8
83348	37 Prairie Living	100.0	83636	26 Midland Crowd	100.0	84005	12 Up And Coming Families	76.2
83349	37 Prairie Living	100.0	83637	31 Rural Resort Dwellers	100.0	84006	18 Cozy And Comfortable	100.0
83350	37 Prairie Living	38.3	83638	31 Rural Resort Dwellers	98.8	84007	46 Rooted Rural	63.5
83352	37 Prairie Living	45.0	83639	37 Prairie Living	53.8	84010	28 Aspiring Young Families	29.0
83355	26 Midland Crowd	55.0	83641	26 Midland Crowd	92.6	84013	26 Midland Crowd	39.1
83401	19 Milk And Cookies	15.6	83642	12 Up And Coming Families	38.1	84014	06 Sophisticated Squires	41.2
83402	48 Great Expectations	15.4	83643	31 Rural Resort Dwellers	100.0	84015	12 Up And Coming Families	46.5
83404	07 Exurbanites	35.6	83644	17 Green Acres	40.5	84017	17 Green Acres	53.9
83406	12 Up And Coming Families	57.1	83645	37 Prairie Living	99.7	84018	06 Sophisticated Squires	100.0
83414	31 Rural Resort Dwellers	100.0	83646	12 Up And Coming Families	71.2	84020	04 Boomburbs	56.8
83420	37 Prairie Living	87.2	83647	26 Midland Crowd	30.9	84021	46 Rooted Rural	66.3
83422	26 Midland Crowd	73.2	83648	40 Military Proximity	93.4	84022	19 Milk And Cookies	89.9
83423	42 Southern Satellites	100.0	83650	37 Prairie Living	100.0	84023	31 Rural Resort Dwellers	100.0
83424	26 Midland Crowd	100.0	83651	48 Great Expectations	23.0	84025	06 Sophisticated Squires	55.7
83425	37 Prairie Living	100.0	83654	31 Rural Resort Dwellers	55.5	84026	56 Rural Bypasses	60.0
83428	31 Rural Resort Dwellers	100.0	83655	46 Rooted Rural	46.8	84028	31 Rural Resort Dwellers	100.0
83429	31 Rural Resort Dwellers	100.0	83657	37 Prairie Living	100.0	84029	26 Midland Crowd	26.9
83431	37 Prairie Living	100.0	83660	46 Rooted Rural	45.5	84031	46 Rooted Rural	100.0
83434	26 Midland Crowd	66.9	83661	25 Salt Of The Earth	36.0	84032	17 Green Acres	39.3
83435	37 Prairie Living	100.0	83669	12 Up And Coming Families	67.2	84033	17 Green Acres	100.0
83436	37 Prairie Living	56.5	83670	37 Prairie Living	100.0	84035	26 Midland Crowd	100.0
83440	26 Midland Crowd	28.3	83672	25 Salt Of The Earth	23.3	84036	17 Green Acres	69.0
83442	26 Midland Crowd	56.7	83676	59 Southwestern Families	38.6	84037	07 Exurbanites	25.8
83443	37 Prairie Living	57.2	83677	49 Senior Sun Seekers	100.0	84038	31 Rural Resort Dwellers	100.0
83444	26 Midland Crowd	97.8	83686	12 Up And Coming Families	52.8	84039	26 Midland Crowd	98.8
83445	46 Rooted Rural	28.9	83687	12 Up And Coming Families	51.6	84040	06 Sophisticated Squires	47.4
83446	31 Rural Resort Dwellers	96.7	83702	22 Metropolitans	32.2	84041	12 Up And Coming Families	34.3
83448	19 Milk And Cookies	59.6	83703	48 Great Expectations	25.8	84042	12 Up And Coming Families	42.4
83449	31 Rural Resort Dwellers	95.9	83704	28 Aspiring Young Families	27.3	84043	12 Up And Coming Families	67.5

CONSUMER TYPE

ZIP CODE	TOP TAPESTRY CONSUMER TYPE	% 2009 HOUSE-HOLDS
84044	19 Milk And Cookies	55.4
84045	04 Boomburbs	64.5
84046	31 Rural Resort Dwellers	100.0
84047	39 Young And Restless	21.8
84049	17 Green Acres	100.0
84050	17 Green Acres	66.5
84051	46 Rooted Rural	100.0
84052	37 Prairie Living	76.6
84053	26 Midland Crowd	100.0
84054	13 In Style	42.6
84056	40 Military Proximity	100.0
84057	28 Aspiring Young Families	33.1
84058	28 Aspiring Young Families	24.0
84060	16 Enterprising Professionals	44.0
84061	17 Green Acres	78.3
84062	12 Up And Coming Families	36.1
84063	56 Rural Bypasses	100.0
84064	37 Prairie Living	99.2
84065	12 Up And Coming Families	54.0
84066	48 Great Expectations	53.8
84067	12 Up And Coming Families	44.2
84069	25 Salt Of The Earth	82.9
84070	28 Aspiring Young Families	43.0
84071	26 Midland Crowd	71.8
84072	46 Rooted Rural	100.0
84073	46 Rooted Rural	74.6
84074	12 Up And Coming Families	58.4
84075	12 Up And Coming Families	70.1
84076	26 Midland Crowd	100.0
84078	26 Midland Crowd	41.8
84080	25 Salt Of The Earth	100.0
84081	12 Up And Coming Families	62.8
84082	17 Green Acres	100.0
84083	58 NeWest Residents	71.1
84084	06 Sophisticated Squires	35.3
84085	56 Rural Bypasses	65.1
84086	37 Prairie Living	100.0
84087	12 Up And Coming Families	49.9
84088	12 Up And Coming Families	55.0
84092	02 Suburban Splendor	53.9
84093	06 Sophisticated Squires	56.7
84094	12 Up And Coming Families	33.4
84095	12 Up And Coming Families	35.7
84096	12 Up And Coming Families	99.9
84097	06 Sophisticated Squires	34.2
84098	09 Urban Chic	40.1
84101	27 Metro Renters	57.8
84102	55 College Towns	41.5
84103	27 Metro Renters	28.5
84104	38 Industrious Urban Fringe	66.8
84105	22 Metropolitans	71.5
84106	24 Main Street, USA	28.6
84107	28 Aspiring Young Families	24.2
84108	22 Metropolitans	25.0
84109	14 Prosperous Empty Nesters	25.5
84111	27 Metro Renters	25.4
84112	01 Top Rung	69.8
84113	63 Dorms To Diplomas	97.8
84115	48 Great Expectations	42.0
84116	38 Industrious Urban Fringe	34.4
84117	36 Old And Newcomers	22.7
84118	19 Milk And Cookies	40.5
84119	38 Industrious Urban Fringe	20.6
84120	19 Milk And Cookies	46.1
84121	07 Exurbanites	24.3
84123	28 Aspiring Young Families	18.7
84124	14 Prosperous Empty Nesters	23.3
84128	12 Up And Coming Families	53.6
84302	32 Rustbelt Traditions	21.5
84305	25 Salt Of The Earth	98.5
84306	25 Salt Of The Earth	91.6
84307	25 Salt Of The Earth	97.7
84308	37 Prairie Living	88.1
84309	25 Salt Of The Earth	74.2
84310	06 Sophisticated Squires	94.2
84311	25 Salt Of The Earth	85.4
84312	25 Salt Of The Earth	73.8
84313	37 Prairie Living	100.0
84314	25 Salt Of The Earth	100.0
84315	17 Green Acres	76.7
84317	06 Sophisticated Squires	66.7
84318	17 Green Acres	78.5
84319	12 Up And Coming Families	41.5
84320	25 Salt Of The Earth	81.0
84321	55 College Towns	23.3
84322	63 Dorms To Diplomas	100.0
84324	17 Green Acres	97.1
84325	17 Green Acres	94.9
84328	17 Green Acres	100.0
84329	37 Prairie Living	100.0
84330	26 Midland Crowd	100.0
84331	26 Midland Crowd	100.0
84332	17 Green Acres	48.5
84333	25 Salt Of The Earth	99.1
84335	17 Green Acres	52.2
84336	26 Midland Crowd	97.4
84337	26 Midland Crowd	28.9
84338	37 Prairie Living	99.4
84339	17 Green Acres	88.8
84340	26 Midland Crowd	52.2
84341	39 Young And Restless	38.8
84401	60 City Dimensions	15.6
84403	07 Exurbanites	26.2
84404	26 Midland Crowd	14.6
84405	14 Prosperous Empty Nesters	14.3
84414	06 Sophisticated Squires	43.4
84501	26 Midland Crowd	19.4
84510	59 Southwestern Families	99.7
84511	26 Midland Crowd	62.6
84520	50 Heartland Communities	100.0
84523	25 Salt Of The Earth	51.3
84525	42 Southern Satellites	87.2
84526	50 Heartland Communities	48.2
84528	26 Midland Crowd	49.4
84531	59 Southwestern Families	100.0
84532	33 Midlife Junction	38.6
84533	41 Crossroads	100.0
84535	25 Salt Of The Earth	36.4
84536	59 Southwestern Families	100.0
84540	26 Midland Crowd	99.1
84542	26 Midland Crowd	100.0
84601	12 Up And Coming Families	24.1
84604	63 Dorms To Diplomas	27.9
84606	63 Dorms To Diplomas	40.8
84621	37 Prairie Living	100.0
84622	42 Southern Satellites	90.1
84624	37 Prairie Living	40.8
84627	55 College Towns	52.9
84628	41 Crossroads	100.0
84629	31 Rural Resort Dwellers	41.0
84630	37 Prairie Living	100.0
84631	37 Prairie Living	48.5
84634	33 Midlife Junction	87.5
84635	25 Salt Of The Earth	83.4
84642	33 Midlife Junction	75.2
84645	26 Midland Crowd	100.0
84647	25 Salt Of The Earth	71.3
84648	32 Rustbelt Traditions	51.8
84651	12 Up And Coming Families	41.0
84653	17 Green Acres	60.0
84654	26 Midland Crowd	47.4
84655	12 Up And Coming Families	60.7
84660	12 Up And Coming Families	39.9
84663	12 Up And Coming Families	33.8
84664	06 Sophisticated Squires	75.6
84701	26 Midland Crowd	34.8
84710	31 Rural Resort Dwellers	100.0
84712	31 Rural Resort Dwellers	100.0
84713	37 Prairie Living	41.8
84714	42 Southern Satellites	82.5
84716	26 Midland Crowd	100.0
84719	31 Rural Resort Dwellers	100.0
84720	12 Up And Coming Families	37.5
84721	28 Aspiring Young Families	40.0
84722	25 Salt Of The Earth	76.9
84726	31 Rural Resort Dwellers	48.5
84728	53 Home Town	100.0
84729	46 Rooted Rural	99.4
84731	37 Prairie Living	83.3
84734	46 Rooted Rural	40.0
84737	26 Midland Crowd	41.1
84738	26 Midland Crowd	41.3
84739	25 Salt Of The Earth	100.0
84741	31 Rural Resort Dwellers	48.6
84743	37 Prairie Living	100.0
84745	26 Midland Crowd	79.3
84747	37 Prairie Living	100.0
84750	37 Prairie Living	100.0
84751	37 Prairie Living	63.5
84753	42 Southern Satellites	88.2
84754	46 Rooted Rural	87.6
84755	46 Rooted Rural	90.0
84756	42 Southern Satellites	91.9
84757	31 Rural Resort Dwellers	100.0
84758	46 Rooted Rural	93.1
84759	31 Rural Resort Dwellers	78.3
84760	31 Rural Resort Dwellers	100.0
84761	46 Rooted Rural	99.1
84765	12 Up And Coming Families	50.7
84766	25 Salt Of The Earth	100.0
84770	28 Aspiring Young Families	24.9
84772	46 Rooted Rural	54.5
84773	31 Rural Resort Dwellers	100.0
84775	31 Rural Resort Dwellers	100.0
84780	49 Senior Sun Seekers	35.4
84781	31 Rural Resort Dwellers	100.0
84782	31 Rural Resort Dwellers	97.4
84783	31 Rural Resort Dwellers	95.0
84790	15 Silver And Gold	24.5
85003	65 Social Security Set	34.1
85004	65 Social Security Set	29.6
85006	58 NeWest Residents	51.3
85007	58 NeWest Residents	36.4
85008	58 NeWest Residents	27.7
85009	59 Southwestern Families	40.6
85012	39 Young And Restless	31.4
85013	36 Old And Newcomers	22.2
85014	36 Old And Newcomers	29.6
85015	52 Inner City Tenants	38.3
85016	52 Inner City Tenants	15.2
85017	38 Industrious Urban Fringe	38.4
85018	52 Inner City Tenants	13.9
85019	58 NeWest Residents	22.9
85020	36 Old And Newcomers	10.1
85021	39 Young And Restless	22.9
85022	39 Young And Restless	15.7
85023	39 Young And Restless	18.9
85024	19 Milk And Cookies	32.9
85027	19 Milk And Cookies	35.5
85028	07 Exurbanites	25.4
85029	28 Aspiring Young Families	17.8
85031	38 Industrious Urban Fringe	76.8
85032	19 Milk And Cookies	27.4
85033	38 Industrious Urban Fringe	67.0
85034	58 NeWest Residents	35.5
85035	38 Industrious Urban Fringe	69.6
85037	12 Up And Coming Families	52.1
85040	59 Southwestern Families	42.6
85041	59 Southwestern Families	35.7
85042	38 Industrious Urban Fringe	32.1
85043	38 Industrious Urban Fringe	53.9
85044	16 Enterprising Professionals	27.2
85045	04 Boomburbs	100.0
85048	04 Boomburbs	60.7
85050	04 Boomburbs	41.1
85051	18 Cozy And Comfortable	29.7
85053	18 Cozy And Comfortable	24.2
85054	16 Enterprising Professionals	99.9
85083	04 Boomburbs	100.0
85085	07 Exurbanites	99.9
85086	06 Sophisticated Squires	89.1
85087	07 Exurbanites	37.2
85201	28 Aspiring Young Families	32.5
85202	39 Young And Restless	30.2
85203	28 Aspiring Young Families	19.1
85204	19 Milk And Cookies	23.1
85205	19 Milk And Cookies	30.7
85206	43 The Elders	41.4
85207	12 Up And Coming Families	29.7
85208	49 Senior Sun Seekers	30.0
85209	12 Up And Coming Families	65.0
85210	52 Inner City Tenants	27.4
85212	12 Up And Coming Families	92.9
85213	06 Sophisticated Squires	31.6
85215	43 The Elders	32.0
85218	15 Silver And Gold	59.1
85219	49 Senior Sun Seekers	45.1
85220	49 Senior Sun Seekers	61.9
85222	31 Rural Resort Dwellers	20.2
85224	19 Milk And Cookies	34.1
85225	12 Up And Coming Families	28.8
85226	12 Up And Coming Families	27.9
85228	56 Rural Bypasses	30.0
85231	49 Senior Sun Seekers	29.4
85232	49 Senior Sun Seekers	60.3
85233	04 Boomburbs	35.5
85234	12 Up And Coming Families	31.4
85236	04 Boomburbs	100.0
85237	29 Rustbelt Retirees	42.5
85238	59 Southwestern Families	98.4
85239	41 Crossroads	92.0
85240	26 Midland Crowd	96.7
85242	06 Sophisticated Squires	46.1
85243	26 Midland Crowd	100.0
85245	56 Rural Bypasses	100.0
85247	62 Modest Income Homes	45.3
85248	43 The Elders	36.0
85249	12 Up And Coming Families	86.1
85250	22 Metropolitans	26.5
85251	36 Old And Newcomers	27.4

ZIP CODE	TOP TAPESTRY CONSUMER TYPE	% 2009 HOUSE-HOLDS
85253	01 Top Rung	60.1
85254	07 Exurbanites	27.9
85255	03 Connoisseurs	49.4
85256	41 Crossroads	92.6
85257	28 Aspiring Young Families	16.0
85258	09 Urban Chic	34.9
85259	02 Suburban Splendor	33.9
85260	16 Enterprising Professionals	29.5
85262	15 Silver And Gold	48.1
85263	15 Silver And Gold	99.7
85264	38 Industrious Urban Fringe	75.1
85266	03 Connoisseurs	80.7
85268	15 Silver And Gold	27.5
85272	59 Southwestern Families	98.7
85273	50 Heartland Communities	97.4
85281	39 Young And Restless	23.7
85282	28 Aspiring Young Families	19.3
85283	39 Young And Restless	19.7
85284	02 Suburban Splendor	52.4
85286	12 Up And Coming Families	49.6
85287	55 College Towns	100.0
85292	41 Crossroads	29.1
85293	41 Crossroads	40.1
85294	26 Midland Crowd	45.8
85295	06 Sophisticated Squires	38.8
85296	04 Boomburbs	81.8
85297	12 Up And Coming Families	69.4
85298	12 Up And Coming Families	98.5
85301	52 Inner City Tenants	24.3
85302	19 Milk And Cookies	31.8
85303	19 Milk And Cookies	27.3
85304	19 Milk And Cookies	34.4
85305	12 Up And Coming Families	61.9
85306	19 Milk And Cookies	46.0
85307	12 Up And Coming Families	51.1
85308	12 Up And Coming Families	22.5
85309	40 Military Proximity	0.0
85310	04 Boomburbs	53.8
85321	49 Senior Sun Seekers	72.0
85322	41 Crossroads	100.0
85323	38 Industrious Urban Fringe	34.6
85324	49 Senior Sun Seekers	100.0
85326	26 Midland Crowd	51.2
85328	41 Crossroads	100.0
85331	04 Boomburbs	28.0
85332	49 Senior Sun Seekers	56.4
85333	59 Southwestern Families	100.0
85335	31 Rural Resort Dwellers	43.7
85337	56 Rural Bypasses	99.7
85338	12 Up And Coming Families	42.0
85339	07 Exurbanites	47.2
85340	52 Inner City Tenants	23.9
85342	46 Rooted Rural	46.8
85343	41 Crossroads	100.0
85344	49 Senior Sun Seekers	36.7
85345	19 Milk And Cookies	29.2
85347	46 Rooted Rural	52.7
85348	49 Senior Sun Seekers	100.0
85350	59 Southwestern Families	71.1
85351	43 The Elders	100.0
85353	38 Industrious Urban Fringe	81.9
85354	41 Crossroads	86.6
85355	06 Sophisticated Squires	99.9
85356	49 Senior Sun Seekers	61.6
85361	46 Rooted Rural	89.2
85362	49 Senior Sun Seekers	96.2
85363	57 Simple Living	56.8
85364	59 Southwestern Families	19.1
85365	49 Senior Sun Seekers	32.3
85367	43 The Elders	57.7
85373	43 The Elders	81.7
85374	43 The Elders	45.3
85375	43 The Elders	100.0
85379	12 Up And Coming Families	70.3
85381	04 Boomburbs	28.1
85382	12 Up And Coming Families	41.0
85383	04 Boomburbs	55.1
85387	43 The Elders	85.8
85388	43 The Elders	55.4
85390	49 Senior Sun Seekers	59.9
85392	12 Up And Coming Families	85.9
85395	15 Silver And Gold	54.2
85396	17 Green Acres	100.0
85501	46 Rooted Rural	26.4
85530	59 Southwestern Families	100.0
85533	46 Rooted Rural	81.3
85534	42 Southern Satellites	47.8
85535	46 Rooted Rural	100.0
85539	46 Rooted Rural	25.8
85540	19 Milk And Cookies	74.6
85541	31 Rural Resort Dwellers	29.7
85542	59 Southwestern Families	83.5
85543	46 Rooted Rural	69.5
85544	31 Rural Resort Dwellers	58.1
85545	49 Senior Sun Seekers	100.0
85546	41 Crossroads	28.4
85550	59 Southwestern Families	100.0
85552	26 Midland Crowd	49.6
85601	49 Senior Sun Seekers	100.0
85602	49 Senior Sun Seekers	70.2
85603	50 Heartland Communities	69.0
85606	49 Senior Sun Seekers	100.0
85607	59 Southwestern Families	57.3
85610	46 Rooted Rural	65.9
85611	15 Silver And Gold	64.7
85613	40 Military Proximity	99.7
85614	43 The Elders	71.6
85615	26 Midland Crowd	57.9
85616	46 Rooted Rural	61.3
85617	49 Senior Sun Seekers	100.0
85618	59 Southwestern Families	51.6
85619	07 Exurbanites	72.9
85621	59 Southwestern Families	64.2
85622	15 Silver And Gold	50.2
85623	46 Rooted Rural	63.8
85624	49 Senior Sun Seekers	89.7
85625	49 Senior Sun Seekers	100.0
85629	26 Midland Crowd	66.7
85630	49 Senior Sun Seekers	100.0
85631	38 Industrious Urban Fringe	26.5
85632	46 Rooted Rural	80.4
85634	51 Metro City Edge	43.9
85635	33 Midlife Junction	26.2
85637	15 Silver And Gold	91.0
85638	49 Senior Sun Seekers	97.5
85640	46 Rooted Rural	73.4
85641	17 Green Acres	73.5
85643	56 Rural Bypasses	27.0
85645	15 Silver And Gold	32.2
85648	19 Milk And Cookies	51.0
85650	07 Exurbanites	37.6
85653	26 Midland Crowd	38.8
85658	31 Rural Resort Dwellers	87.7
85701	48 Great Expectations	18.0
85704	30 Retirement Communities	27.7
85705	52 Inner City Tenants	35.0
85706	58 NeWest Residents	30.1
85707	40 Military Proximity	99.9
85709	29 Rustbelt Retirees	100.0
85710	36 Old And Newcomers	21.5
85711	52 Inner City Tenants	21.2
85712	52 Inner City Tenants	21.3
85713	59 Southwestern Families	32.5
85714	59 Southwestern Families	48.7
85715	13 In Style	34.1
85716	52 Inner City Tenants	31.7
85718	03 Connoisseurs	22.4
85719	55 College Towns	34.3
85721	63 Dorms To Diplomas	100.0
85730	19 Milk And Cookies	42.4
85735	26 Midland Crowd	59.1
85736	41 Crossroads	74.7
85737	04 Boomburbs	42.0
85739	15 Silver And Gold	57.2
85741	19 Milk And Cookies	47.2
85742	12 Up And Coming Families	33.8
85743	12 Up And Coming Families	63.5
85745	07 Exurbanites	22.1
85746	38 Industrious Urban Fringe	24.7
85747	12 Up And Coming Families	53.8
85748	07 Exurbanites	29.7
85749	07 Exurbanites	51.4
85750	13 In Style	21.3
85755	15 Silver And Gold	98.5
85756	49 Senior Sun Seekers	33.0
85757	41 Crossroads	54.3
85901	31 Rural Resort Dwellers	32.2
85920	31 Rural Resort Dwellers	100.0
85922	46 Rooted Rural	100.0
85924	49 Senior Sun Seekers	81.8
85925	26 Midland Crowd	58.0
85928	31 Rural Resort Dwellers	93.0
85929	31 Rural Resort Dwellers	66.0
85935	15 Silver And Gold	51.9
85936	46 Rooted Rural	44.8
85937	26 Midland Crowd	59.1
85938	26 Midland Crowd	50.5
86001	55 College Towns	26.5
86004	17 Green Acres	11.2
86021	26 Midland Crowd	87.9
86022	26 Midland Crowd	93.3
86025	56 Rural Bypasses	25.2
86030	59 Southwestern Families	94.3
86033	41 Crossroads	58.2
86034	59 Southwestern Families	78.1
86035	59 Southwestern Families	84.9
86036	26 Midland Crowd	81.6
86038	31 Rural Resort Dwellers	100.0
86039	59 Southwestern Families	100.0
86040	41 Crossroads	35.9
86042	59 Southwestern Families	100.0
86043	56 Rural Bypasses	94.8
86044	53 Home Town	50.0
86045	41 Crossroads	40.4
86046	31 Rural Resort Dwellers	34.3
86047	59 Southwestern Families	39.2
86053	59 Southwestern Families	98.1
86054	59 Southwestern Families	100.0
86301	14 Prosperous Empty Nesters	28.0
86303	15 Silver And Gold	45.9
86305	15 Silver And Gold	42.5
86314	33 Midlife Junction	43.1
86315	31 Rural Resort Dwellers	99.7
86320	42 Southern Satellites	95.6
86321	41 Crossroads	100.0
86322	49 Senior Sun Seekers	49.3
86323	26 Midland Crowd	45.3
86324	49 Senior Sun Seekers	37.3
86325	31 Rural Resort Dwellers	88.1
86326	33 Midlife Junction	40.1
86327	15 Silver And Gold	39.3
86332	49 Senior Sun Seekers	74.1
86333	49 Senior Sun Seekers	99.8
86334	26 Midland Crowd	81.8
86335	31 Rural Resort Dwellers	94.2
86336	15 Silver And Gold	66.7
86337	49 Senior Sun Seekers	99.7
86343	31 Rural Resort Dwellers	88.0
86351	15 Silver And Gold	100.0
86401	32 Rustbelt Traditions	23.4
86403	31 Rural Resort Dwellers	25.4
86404	49 Senior Sun Seekers	61.8
86406	49 Senior Sun Seekers	31.9
86409	49 Senior Sun Seekers	34.6
86411	31 Rural Resort Dwellers	99.1
86413	49 Senior Sun Seekers	99.4
86426	49 Senior Sun Seekers	80.8
86429	33 Midlife Junction	75.8
86432	41 Crossroads	100.0
86434	51 Metro City Edge	99.8
86435	59 Southwestern Families	100.0
86436	49 Senior Sun Seekers	100.0
86440	31 Rural Resort Dwellers	50.7
86441	49 Senior Sun Seekers	100.0
86442	49 Senior Sun Seekers	70.0
86444	49 Senior Sun Seekers	100.0
86445	49 Senior Sun Seekers	100.0
86502	38 Industrious Urban Fringe	56.7
86503	59 Southwestern Families	79.5
86505	59 Southwestern Families	47.6
86507	59 Southwestern Families	100.0
86510	59 Southwestern Families	87.2
86514	59 Southwestern Families	100.0
86535	59 Southwestern Families	100.0
86538	51 Metro City Edge	48.0
86556	59 Southwestern Families	97.6
87001	38 Industrious Urban Fringe	91.4
87002	26 Midland Crowd	30.3
87004	38 Industrious Urban Fringe	33.0
87005	46 Rooted Rural	57.5
87006	41 Crossroads	80.9
87007	51 Metro City Edge	72.7
87008	07 Exurbanites	100.0
87009	46 Rooted Rural	100.0
87010	13 In Style	90.0
87012	46 Rooted Rural	100.0
87013	59 Southwestern Families	63.6
87014	56 Rural Bypasses	47.7
87015	12 Up And Coming Families	58.1
87016	46 Rooted Rural	100.0
87017	56 Rural Bypasses	76.1
87018	49 Senior Sun Seekers	71.1
87020	46 Rooted Rural	23.4
87021	41 Crossroads	80.7
87023	41 Crossroads	50.6
87024	59 Southwestern Families	71.9
87025	31 Rural Resort Dwellers	87.9
87026	59 Southwestern Families	86.7
87027	49 Senior Sun Seekers	100.0
87028	46 Rooted Rural	100.0

CONSUMER TYPE

ZIP CODE	TOP TAPESTRY CONSUMER TYPE	% 2009 HOUSE-HOLDS	ZIP CODE	TOP TAPESTRY CONSUMER TYPE	% 2009 HOUSE-HOLDS	ZIP CODE	TOP TAPESTRY CONSUMER TYPE	% 2009 HOUSE-HOLDS
87029	46 Rooted Rural	93.4	87557	31 Rural Resort Dwellers	72.5	88119	50 Heartland Communities	68.7
87031	26 Midland Crowd	38.2	87560	56 Rural Bypasses	57.3	88120	37 Prairie Living	100.0
87035	41 Crossroads	60.0	87564	31 Rural Resort Dwellers	85.6	88121	37 Prairie Living	100.0
87036	50 Heartland Communities	77.1	87565	26 Midland Crowd	85.9	88123	37 Prairie Living	100.0
87041	38 Industrious Urban Fringe	65.3	87566	41 Crossroads	71.4	88124	50 Heartland Communities	68.6
87042	26 Midland Crowd	84.0	87567	26 Midland Crowd	100.0	88125	37 Prairie Living	100.0
87043	03 Connoisseurs	46.7	87571	31 Rural Resort Dwellers	37.7	88126	37 Prairie Living	100.0
87044	31 Rural Resort Dwellers	67.4	87573	31 Rural Resort Dwellers	100.0	88130	37 Prairie Living	17.6
87045	56 Rural Bypasses	96.2	87575	31 Rural Resort Dwellers	77.0	88132	37 Prairie Living	100.0
87046	66 Unclassified	100.0	87579	46 Rooted Rural	50.0	88133	37 Prairie Living	100.0
87047	17 Green Acres	47.7	87580	31 Rural Resort Dwellers	100.0	88134	37 Prairie Living	92.1
87048	07 Exurbanites	69.0	87581	26 Midland Crowd	96.9	88135	56 Rural Bypasses	75.6
87052	56 Rural Bypasses	79.1	87701	59 Southwestern Families	21.3	88136	37 Prairie Living	97.9
87053	38 Industrious Urban Fringe	65.2	87711	56 Rural Bypasses	100.0	88201	14 Prosperous Empty Nesters	24.8
87056	13 In Style	58.0	87713	46 Rooted Rural	100.0	88203	50 Heartland Communities	20.6
87059	07 Exurbanites	49.3	87714	31 Rural Resort Dwellers	67.2	88210	50 Heartland Communities	14.7
87060	26 Midland Crowd	100.0	87715	46 Rooted Rural	65.2	88213	37 Prairie Living	100.0
87062	41 Crossroads	95.3	87718	31 Rural Resort Dwellers	100.0	88220	53 Home Town	14.6
87063	46 Rooted Rural	100.0	87722	46 Rooted Rural	100.0	88230	56 Rural Bypasses	34.0
87068	17 Green Acres	56.4	87724	56 Rural Bypasses	100.0	88231	42 Southern Satellites	47.4
87083	29 Rustbelt Retirees	100.0	87728	37 Prairie Living	100.0	88232	59 Southwestern Families	68.0
87102	59 Southwestern Families	32.3	87729	37 Prairie Living	100.0	88240	59 Southwestern Families	31.7
87104	33 Midlife Junction	21.2	87730	37 Prairie Living	100.0	88242	26 Midland Crowd	58.3
87105	38 Industrious Urban Fringe	41.6	87731	31 Rural Resort Dwellers	52.4	88250	26 Midland Crowd	75.4
87106	22 Metropolitans	42.0	87732	46 Rooted Rural	60.5	88252	50 Heartland Communities	37.4
87107	33 Midlife Junction	24.5	87733	37 Prairie Living	100.0	88253	41 Crossroads	75.9
87108	52 Inner City Tenants	22.3	87734	46 Rooted Rural	100.0	88256	56 Rural Bypasses	100.0
87109	36 Old And Newcomers	20.3	87740	50 Heartland Communities	19.2	88260	59 Southwestern Families	33.5
87110	14 Prosperous Empty Nesters	18.1	87742	31 Rural Resort Dwellers	100.0	88264	46 Rooted Rural	100.0
87111	36 Old And Newcomers	20.2	87743	37 Prairie Living	100.0	88265	46 Rooted Rural	100.0
87112	32 Rustbelt Traditions	14.5	87745	31 Rural Resort Dwellers	100.0	88267	46 Rooted Rural	53.6
87113	50 Heartland Communities	36.0	87746	37 Prairie Living	100.0	88301	50 Heartland Communities	86.9
87114	12 Up And Coming Families	41.1	87747	50 Heartland Communities	70.9	88310	26 Midland Crowd	20.0
87116	40 Military Proximity	100.0	87750	46 Rooted Rural	100.0	88312	31 Rural Resort Dwellers	100.0
87120	12 Up And Coming Families	39.1	87752	46 Rooted Rural	100.0	88314	46 Rooted Rural	100.0
87121	38 Industrious Urban Fringe	66.1	87801	41 Crossroads	31.9	88316	46 Rooted Rural	69.1
87122	04 Boomburbs	50.0	87820	49 Senior Sun Seekers	96.7	88317	31 Rural Resort Dwellers	80.4
87123	28 Aspiring Young Families	15.9	87821	31 Rural Resort Dwellers	100.0	88318	37 Prairie Living	100.0
87124	19 Milk And Cookies	41.1	87823	46 Rooted Rural	81.6	88321	46 Rooted Rural	100.0
87131	65 Social Security Set	97.8	87825	46 Rooted Rural	38.3	88324	31 Rural Resort Dwellers	86.7
87144	12 Up And Coming Families	78.6	87827	31 Rural Resort Dwellers	100.0	88330	40 Military Proximity	100.0
87301	59 Southwestern Families	29.8	87828	46 Rooted Rural	100.0	88336	46 Rooted Rural	100.0
87310	56 Rural Bypasses	100.0	87829	31 Rural Resort Dwellers	100.0	88337	46 Rooted Rural	39.5
87312	59 Southwestern Families	62.1	87830	49 Senior Sun Seekers	100.0	88338	46 Rooted Rural	100.0
87313	59 Southwestern Families	53.7	87831	46 Rooted Rural	89.3	88339	31 Rural Resort Dwellers	100.0
87315	46 Rooted Rural	79.5	87901	49 Senior Sun Seekers	80.9	88340	51 Metro City Edge	100.0
87320	59 Southwestern Families	100.0	87930	49 Senior Sun Seekers	100.0	88341	31 Rural Resort Dwellers	86.6
87321	26 Midland Crowd	100.0	87931	49 Senior Sun Seekers	100.0	88343	46 Rooted Rural	100.0
87323	59 Southwestern Families	49.8	87933	49 Senior Sun Seekers	100.0	88344	46 Rooted Rural	100.0
87325	59 Southwestern Families	40.8	87936	59 Southwestern Families	100.0	88345	31 Rural Resort Dwellers	70.5
87327	56 Rural Bypasses	80.9	87937	59 Southwestern Families	100.0	88346	41 Crossroads	60.7
87328	59 Southwestern Families	85.3	87940	59 Southwestern Families	100.0	88347	31 Rural Resort Dwellers	100.0
87401	41 Crossroads	26.5	87941	59 Southwestern Families	100.0	88348	46 Rooted Rural	100.0
87402	07 Exurbanites	24.3	87942	49 Senior Sun Seekers	100.0	88351	46 Rooted Rural	96.1
87410	26 Midland Crowd	62.8	87943	49 Senior Sun Seekers	100.0	88352	46 Rooted Rural	78.8
87412	26 Midland Crowd	56.6	88001	48 Great Expectations	13.0	88353	50 Heartland Communities	100.0
87413	41 Crossroads	50.7	88002	40 Military Proximity	100.0	88354	31 Rural Resort Dwellers	69.7
87415	26 Midland Crowd	100.0	88003	55 College Towns	94.7	88401	50 Heartland Communities	35.2
87416	26 Midland Crowd	100.0	88005	33 Midlife Junction	22.0	88410	37 Prairie Living	100.0
87417	19 Milk And Cookies	61.4	88007	26 Midland Crowd	34.9	88411	49 Senior Sun Seekers	100.0
87418	26 Midland Crowd	100.0	88008	12 Up And Coming Families	43.0	88414	37 Prairie Living	100.0
87419	31 Rural Resort Dwellers	67.6	88011	22 Metropolitans	32.4	88415	50 Heartland Communities	87.6
87420	56 Rural Bypasses	35.2	88012	41 Crossroads	61.2	88416	49 Senior Sun Seekers	100.0
87421	26 Midland Crowd	52.4	88020	46 Rooted Rural	100.0	88417	46 Rooted Rural	100.0
87501	15 Silver And Gold	22.2	88021	59 Southwestern Families	76.7	88418	37 Prairie Living	100.0
87505	22 Metropolitans	16.8	88022	41 Crossroads	91.8	88419	37 Prairie Living	100.0
87506	03 Connoisseurs	20.6	88023	59 Southwestern Families	29.6	88421	49 Senior Sun Seekers	100.0
87507	41 Crossroads	21.4	88025	46 Rooted Rural	100.0	88422	37 Prairie Living	100.0
87508	07 Exurbanites	58.7	88026	56 Rural Bypasses	48.0	88424	37 Prairie Living	100.0
87510	26 Midland Crowd	96.2	88030	56 Rural Bypasses	28.6	88426	49 Senior Sun Seekers	100.0
87513	31 Rural Resort Dwellers	77.4	88039	49 Senior Sun Seekers	100.0	88427	37 Prairie Living	100.0
87514	31 Rural Resort Dwellers	100.0	88041	46 Rooted Rural	95.2	88430	49 Senior Sun Seekers	100.0
87520	31 Rural Resort Dwellers	100.0	88042	49 Senior Sun Seekers	100.0	88431	46 Rooted Rural	100.0
87521	46 Rooted Rural	75.6	88043	50 Heartland Communities	71.2	88434	49 Senior Sun Seekers	97.7
87522	26 Midland Crowd	71.9	88044	59 Southwestern Families	62.8	88435	56 Rural Bypasses	39.4
87524	31 Rural Resort Dwellers	65.9	88045	42 Southern Satellites	38.2	88436	37 Prairie Living	100.0
87527	46 Rooted Rural	100.0	88047	59 Southwestern Families	44.6	88439	49 Senior Sun Seekers	100.0
87528	41 Crossroads	80.9	88048	59 Southwestern Families	100.0	89001	26 Midland Crowd	100.0
87530	26 Midland Crowd	100.0	88049	46 Rooted Rural	99.8	89002	12 Up And Coming Families	42.7
87531	41 Crossroads	59.7	88061	33 Midlife Junction	26.0	89003	33 Midlife Junction	100.0
87532	41 Crossroads	28.7	88063	59 Southwestern Families	100.0	89005	14 Prosperous Empty Nesters	39.4
87535	26 Midland Crowd	78.3	88072	59 Southwestern Families	100.0	89008	49 Senior Sun Seekers	92.0
87537	41 Crossroads	55.3	88081	59 Southwestern Families	59.8	89011	15 Silver And Gold	28.1
87539	26 Midland Crowd	100.0	88101	53 Home Town	15.3	89012	16 Enterprising Professionals	47.1
87540	07 Exurbanites	54.2	88103	40 Military Proximity	100.0	89013	49 Senior Sun Seekers	100.0
87544	06 Sophisticated Squires	22.3	88112	37 Prairie Living	100.0	89014	13 In Style	25.8
87549	46 Rooted Rural	100.0	88113	37 Prairie Living	100.0	89015	12 Up And Coming Families	33.6
87552	41 Crossroads	51.9	88114	37 Prairie Living	100.0	89017	26 Midland Crowd	100.0
87553	56 Rural Bypasses	77.0	88116	37 Prairie Living	95.0	89018	41 Crossroads	80.4
87556	56 Rural Bypasses	37.8	88118	37 Prairie Living	100.0	89019	31 Rural Resort Dwellers	56.3

ZIP CODE	TOP TAPESTRY CONSUMER TYPE	% 2009 HOUSE-HOLDS	ZIP CODE	TOP TAPESTRY CONSUMER TYPE	% 2009 HOUSE-HOLDS	ZIP CODE	TOP TAPESTRY CONSUMER TYPE	% 2009 HOUSE-HOLDS
89020	41 Crossroads	74.4	89427	32 Rustbelt Traditions	100.0	90056	09 Urban Chic	48.1
89021	06 Sophisticated Squires	100.0	89429	46 Rooted Rural	54.1	90057	58 NeWest Residents	72.8
89027	15 Silver And Gold	38.3	89430	31 Rural Resort Dwellers	100.0	90058	58 NeWest Residents	51.1
89029	36 Old And Newcomers	77.2	89431	24 Main Street, USA	21.3	90059	47 Las Casas	49.0
89030	38 Industrious Urban Fringe	51.5	89433	12 Up And Coming Families	43.2	90061	47 Las Casas	67.0
89031	12 Up And Coming Families	88.8	89434	06 Sophisticated Squires	21.8	90062	45 City Strivers	59.9
89032	12 Up And Coming Families	77.3	89436	12 Up And Coming Families	45.3	90063	47 Las Casas	97.0
89040	41 Crossroads	32.1	89440	31 Rural Resort Dwellers	93.7	90064	23 Trendsetters	38.9
89043	31 Rural Resort Dwellers	54.0	89441	06 Sophisticated Squires	47.4	90065	47 Las Casas	31.7
89044	15 Silver And Gold	100.0	89442	41 Crossroads	100.0	90066	23 Trendsetters	43.7
89045	41 Crossroads	100.0	89444	49 Senior Sun Seekers	52.6	90067	08 Laptops And Lattes	100.0
89046	49 Senior Sun Seekers	100.0	89445	26 Midland Crowd	34.1	90068	08 Laptops And Lattes	40.9
89047	46 Rooted Rural	99.2	89447	33 Midlife Junction	24.3	90069	27 Metro Renters	59.7
89048	49 Senior Sun Seekers	64.6	89451	09 Urban Chic	41.6	90071	08 Laptops And Lattes	100.0
89049	26 Midland Crowd	31.6	89460	19 Milk And Cookies	24.6	90077	01 Top Rung	99.8
89052	16 Enterprising Professionals	32.0	89501	65 Social Security Set	75.8	90089	63 Dorms To Diplomas	98.5
89054	31 Rural Resort Dwellers	52.6	89502	52 Inner City Tenants	23.8	90094	09 Urban Chic	100.0
89060	49 Senior Sun Seekers	91.6	89503	18 Cozy And Comfortable	27.7	90095	27 Metro Renters	100.0
89061	49 Senior Sun Seekers	100.0	89506	28 Aspiring Young Families	33.8	90201	47 Las Casas	94.3
89074	16 Enterprising Professionals	20.5	89508	12 Up And Coming Families	43.5	90210	01 Top Rung	57.2
89081	37 Prairie Living	84.5	89509	36 Old And Newcomers	20.0	90211	08 Laptops And Lattes	65.4
89084	37 Prairie Living	100.0	89510	12 Up And Coming Families	56.6	90212	08 Laptops And Lattes	77.3
89086	37 Prairie Living	100.0	89511	07 Exurbanites	29.8	90220	47 Las Casas	37.8
89101	65 Social Security Set	32.9	89512	52 Inner City Tenants	35.7	90221	47 Las Casas	84.1
89102	65 Social Security Set	20.8	89519	03 Connoisseurs	52.2	90222	47 Las Casas	62.9
89103	39 Young And Restless	24.6	89521	12 Up And Coming Families	44.6	90230	22 Metropolitans	28.7
89104	24 Main Street, USA	18.9	89523	12 Up And Coming Families	50.0	90232	09 Urban Chic	32.5
89106	52 Inner City Tenants	21.9	89701	13 In Style	16.4	90240	21 Urban Villages	31.6
89107	18 Cozy And Comfortable	18.8	89703	03 Connoisseurs	28.8	90241	35 International Marketplace	33.7
89108	52 Inner City Tenants	23.1	89704	06 Sophisticated Squires	54.9	90242	21 Urban Villages	53.6
89109	65 Social Security Set	43.9	89705	18 Cozy And Comfortable	72.8	90245	09 Urban Chic	55.8
89110	38 Industrious Urban Fringe	23.6	89706	12 Up And Coming Families	17.2	90247	35 International Marketplace	37.7
89113	16 Enterprising Professionals	87.2	89801	12 Up And Coming Families	33.2	90248	11 Pacific Heights	22.1
89115	52 Inner City Tenants	31.6	89815	12 Up And Coming Families	70.3	90249	21 Urban Villages	20.5
89117	16 Enterprising Professionals	25.0	89820	41 Crossroads	38.9	90250	52 Inner City Tenants	34.0
89118	39 Young And Restless	45.0	89821	26 Midland Crowd	100.0	90254	08 Laptops And Lattes	79.0
89119	52 Inner City Tenants	38.9	89822	26 Midland Crowd	99.9	90255	47 Las Casas	67.0
89120	36 Old And Newcomers	27.0	89823	26 Midland Crowd	60.0	90260	35 International Marketplace	60.7
89121	30 Retirement Communities	12.5	89825	41 Crossroads	85.7	90262	47 Las Casas	68.5
89122	41 Crossroads	16.8	89831	50 Heartland Communities	75.3	90263	09 Urban Chic	100.0
89123	12 Up And Coming Families	33.2	89833	26 Midland Crowd	100.0	90265	09 Urban Chic	51.6
89124	13 In Style	81.2	89834	37 Prairie Living	100.0	90266	08 Laptops And Lattes	33.2
89128	28 Aspiring Young Families	18.6	89835	41 Crossroads	72.7	90270	47 Las Casas	100.0
89129	04 Boomburbs	40.6	90001	47 Las Casas	99.1	90272	01 Top Rung	57.0
89130	12 Up And Coming Families	33.7	90002	47 Las Casas	71.5	90274	03 Connoisseurs	55.9
89131	12 Up And Coming Families	60.9	90003	47 Las Casas	91.6	90275	03 Connoisseurs	57.7
89134	43 The Elders	52.4	90004	58 NeWest Residents	45.7	90277	08 Laptops And Lattes	45.4
89135	13 In Style	100.0	90005	58 NeWest Residents	74.6	90278	09 Urban Chic	59.2
89138	09 Urban Chic	100.0	90006	58 NeWest Residents	73.7	90280	47 Las Casas	69.8
89139	07 Exurbanites	91.8	90007	58 NeWest Residents	33.2	90290	09 Urban Chic	64.7
89141	31 Rural Resort Dwellers	100.0	90008	45 City Strivers	25.1	90291	23 Trendsetters	33.9
89142	12 Up And Coming Families	38.2	90010	44 Urban Melting Pot	43.8	90292	27 Metro Renters	36.1
89143	12 Up And Coming Families	100.0	90011	47 Las Casas	95.9	90293	08 Laptops And Lattes	87.1
89144	04 Boomburbs	50.3	90012	65 Social Security Set	30.8	90301	35 International Marketplace	28.4
89145	18 Cozy And Comfortable	19.1	90013	65 Social Security Set	90.5	90302	52 Inner City Tenants	29.2
89146	36 Old And Newcomers	23.8	90014	65 Social Security Set	99.2	90303	47 Las Casas	34.4
89147	13 In Style	41.6	90015	58 NeWest Residents	67.6	90304	47 Las Casas	72.5
89148	13 In Style	100.0	90016	35 International Marketplace	34.4	90305	34 Family Foundations	31.3
89149	07 Exurbanites	82.0	90017	58 NeWest Residents	93.1	90401	08 Laptops And Lattes	51.5
89154	65 Social Security Set	100.0	90018	35 International Marketplace	47.9	90402	01 Top Rung	53.1
89156	12 Up And Coming Families	32.2	90019	35 International Marketplace	31.1	90403	08 Laptops And Lattes	90.6
89166	07 Exurbanites	100.0	90020	44 Urban Melting Pot	26.0	90404	23 Trendsetters	70.0
89169	52 Inner City Tenants	59.9	90021	65 Social Security Set	50.6	90405	08 Laptops And Lattes	60.2
89178	31 Rural Resort Dwellers	58.6	90022	47 Las Casas	87.8	90501	11 Pacific Heights	28.5
89179	31 Rural Resort Dwellers	100.0	90023	47 Las Casas	88.1	90502	11 Pacific Heights	75.7
89183	12 Up And Coming Families	62.3	90024	08 Laptops And Lattes	44.0	90503	23 Trendsetters	36.8
89191	40 Military Proximity	100.0	90025	27 Metro Renters	49.8	90504	11 Pacific Heights	69.1
89301	33 Midlife Junction	48.5	90026	35 International Marketplace	40.2	90505	09 Urban Chic	27.1
89310	49 Senior Sun Seekers	96.7	90027	23 Trendsetters	40.7	90601	21 Urban Villages	30.0
89311	31 Rural Resort Dwellers	100.0	90028	27 Metro Renters	33.1	90602	58 NeWest Residents	21.6
89316	26 Midland Crowd	100.0	90029	58 NeWest Residents	53.7	90603	10 Pleasant-Ville	45.4
89317	26 Midland Crowd	99.3	90031	47 Las Casas	74.2	90604	21 Urban Villages	43.0
89403	26 Midland Crowd	94.9	90032	47 Las Casas	51.7	90605	21 Urban Villages	53.5
89404	17 Green Acres	100.0	90033	47 Las Casas	62.8	90606	21 Urban Villages	71.5
89405	42 Southern Satellites	98.9	90034	23 Trendsetters	29.4	90620	10 Pleasant-Ville	30.9
89406	17 Green Acres	27.8	90035	23 Trendsetters	58.6	90621	35 International Marketplace	31.5
89408	17 Green Acres	56.9	90036	23 Trendsetters	32.8	90623	11 Pacific Heights	58.5
89409	50 Heartland Communities	100.0	90037	47 Las Casas	52.1	90630	05 Wealthy Seaboard Suburbs	29.0
89410	07 Exurbanites	33.2	90038	58 NeWest Residents	61.3	90631	10 Pleasant-Ville	15.2
89412	42 Southern Satellites	100.0	90039	35 International Marketplace	27.1	90638	10 Pleasant-Ville	45.3
89413	15 Silver And Gold	39.0	90040	47 Las Casas	57.4	90639	30 Retirement Communities	100.0
89414	26 Midland Crowd	100.0	90041	11 Pacific Heights	26.8	90640	21 Urban Villages	25.9
89415	49 Senior Sun Seekers	37.6	90042	35 International Marketplace	24.4	90650	21 Urban Villages	71.1
89418	26 Midland Crowd	100.0	90043	45 City Strivers	32.4	90660	21 Urban Villages	79.2
89419	26 Midland Crowd	38.9	90044	47 Las Casas	34.7	90670	21 Urban Villages	74.3
89420	49 Senior Sun Seekers	100.0	90045	09 Urban Chic	24.2	90680	35 International Marketplace	38.6
89423	07 Exurbanites	58.5	90046	27 Metro Renters	42.2	90701	11 Pacific Heights	38.1
89424	41 Crossroads	100.0	90047	34 Family Foundations	45.6	90703	11 Pacific Heights	91.6
89425	37 Prairie Living	58.3	90048	08 Laptops And Lattes	50.3	90704	35 International Marketplace	59.4
89426	37 Prairie Living	93.7	90049	08 Laptops And Lattes	50.2	90706	35 International Marketplace	41.4

CONSUMER TYPE

ZIP CODE	TOP TAPESTRY CONSUMER TYPE	% 2009 HOUSE-HOLDS	ZIP CODE	TOP TAPESTRY CONSUMER TYPE	% 2009 HOUSE-HOLDS	ZIP CODE	TOP TAPESTRY CONSUMER TYPE	% 2009 HOUSE-HOLDS
90710	35 International Marketplace	48.3	91364	09 Urban Chic	58.8	91941	36 Old And Newcomers	22.3
90712	10 Pleasant-Ville	63.5	91367	23 Trendsetters	26.4	91942	36 Old And Newcomers	31.9
90713	10 Pleasant-Ville	85.3	91371	39 Young And Restless	100.0	91945	21 Urban Villages	29.2
90715	35 International Marketplace	30.6	91377	02 Suburban Splendor	75.2	91950	21 Urban Villages	24.5
90716	47 Las Casas	65.2	91381	04 Boomburbs	75.2	91962	07 Exurbanites	72.5
90717	20 City Lights	26.4	91384	04 Boomburbs	54.4	91963	46 Rooted Rural	83.1
90720	03 Connoisseurs	25.3	91387	06 Sophisticated Squires	23.6	91977	35 International Marketplace	18.0
90723	47 Las Casas	39.8	91390	06 Sophisticated Squires	32.6	91978	13 In Style	41.1
90731	35 International Marketplace	33.6	91401	35 International Marketplace	38.7	91980	46 Rooted Rural	100.0
90732	09 Urban Chic	36.4	91402	58 NeWest Residents	46.8	92003	14 Prosperous Empty Nesters	68.2
90740	43 The Elders	46.3	91403	23 Trendsetters	53.4	92004	31 Rural Resort Dwellers	81.1
90742	08 Laptops And Lattes	100.0	91405	35 International Marketplace	71.9	92007	09 Urban Chic	44.0
90743	09 Urban Chic	100.0	91406	35 International Marketplace	41.8	92008	09 Urban Chic	38.6
90744	47 Las Casas	55.5	91411	23 Trendsetters	44.6	92009	09 Urban Chic	40.9
90745	21 Urban Villages	53.8	91423	23 Trendsetters	44.6	92010	06 Sophisticated Squires	36.0
90746	10 Pleasant-Ville	34.4	91436	01 Top Rung	49.1	92011	09 Urban Chic	38.6
90747	34 Family Foundations	100.0	91501	23 Trendsetters	60.8	92014	03 Connoisseurs	41.9
90755	35 International Marketplace	35.1	91502	35 International Marketplace	59.0	92019	20 City Lights	13.9
90802	27 Metro Renters	30.7	91504	05 Wealthy Seaboard Suburbs	18.9	92020	52 Inner City Tenants	44.7
90803	08 Laptops And Lattes	37.3	91505	23 Trendsetters	31.0	92021	52 Inner City Tenants	27.3
90804	58 NeWest Residents	25.1	91506	09 Urban Chic	36.4	92024	23 Trendsetters	25.4
90805	35 International Marketplace	33.0	91522	23 Trendsetters	100.0	92025	58 NeWest Residents	22.3
90806	35 International Marketplace	32.3	91601	23 Trendsetters	23.5	92026	36 Old And Newcomers	11.9
90807	09 Urban Chic	30.1	91602	23 Trendsetters	68.5	92027	21 Urban Villages	19.4
90808	10 Pleasant-Ville	37.8	91604	09 Urban Chic	32.8	92028	03 Connoisseurs	16.8
90810	21 Urban Villages	58.1	91605	58 NeWest Residents	34.6	92029	03 Connoisseurs	28.8
90813	58 NeWest Residents	78.0	91606	35 International Marketplace	42.5	92036	31 Rural Resort Dwellers	85.9
90814	23 Trendsetters	43.8	91607	23 Trendsetters	73.5	92037	03 Connoisseurs	31.1
90815	05 Wealthy Seaboard Suburbs	53.9	91701	20 City Lights	23.0	92040	52 Inner City Tenants	15.5
90822	38 Industrious Urban Fringe	100.0	91702	21 Urban Villages	40.7	92054	23 Trendsetters	17.6
90840	63 Dorms To Diplomas	100.0	91706	21 Urban Villages	50.2	92055	40 Military Proximity	100.0
91001	09 Urban Chic	23.2	91708	38 Industrious Urban Fringe	91.3	92056	06 Sophisticated Squires	21.2
91006	11 Pacific Heights	37.2	91709	04 Boomburbs	46.0	92057	21 Urban Villages	14.9
91007	11 Pacific Heights	50.9	91710	21 Urban Villages	26.8	92058	40 Military Proximity	28.0
91008	09 Urban Chic	88.8	91711	03 Connoisseurs	22.9	92059	21 Urban Villages	82.9
91010	21 Urban Villages	34.9	91722	21 Urban Villages	63.4	92061	38 Industrious Urban Fringe	78.4
91011	01 Top Rung	47.9	91723	35 International Marketplace	58.4	92064	06 Sophisticated Squires	23.8
91016	35 International Marketplace	45.2	91724	20 City Lights	34.6	92065	06 Sophisticated Squires	27.5
91020	23 Trendsetters	61.2	91730	28 Aspiring Young Families	33.4	92066	31 Rural Resort Dwellers	99.4
91024	09 Urban Chic	69.3	91731	47 Las Casas	46.9	92067	01 Top Rung	100.0
91030	23 Trendsetters	48.7	91732	47 Las Casas	48.3	92069	58 NeWest Residents	17.1
91040	20 City Lights	35.1	91733	47 Las Casas	71.5	92070	46 Rooted Rural	60.7
91042	35 International Marketplace	24.4	91737	06 Sophisticated Squires	39.2	92071	06 Sophisticated Squires	24.0
91101	27 Metro Renters	70.9	91739	12 Up And Coming Families	27.8	92075	09 Urban Chic	37.8
91103	35 International Marketplace	19.3	91740	10 Pleasant-Ville	51.3	92078	14 Prosperous Empty Nesters	31.2
91104	09 Urban Chic	38.0	91741	05 Wealthy Seaboard Suburbs	29.6	92081	06 Sophisticated Squires	19.8
91105	03 Connoisseurs	46.9	91744	21 Urban Villages	74.9	92082	07 Exurbanites	28.7
91106	27 Metro Renters	24.0	91745	11 Pacific Heights	56.5	92083	28 Aspiring Young Families	20.7
91107	23 Trendsetters	29.1	91746	21 Urban Villages	88.5	92084	10 Pleasant-Ville	18.8
91108	01 Top Rung	70.9	91748	11 Pacific Heights	48.4	92086	31 Rural Resort Dwellers	94.1
91123	08 Laptops And Lattes	100.0	91750	02 Suburban Splendor	18.5	92091	01 Top Rung	83.2
91201	44 Urban Melting Pot	41.4	91752	38 Industrious Urban Fringe	23.7	92096	49 Senior Sun Seekers	100.0
91202	44 Urban Melting Pot	33.2	91754	11 Pacific Heights	52.3	92101	65 Social Security Set	33.0
91203	44 Urban Melting Pot	72.3	91755	11 Pacific Heights	47.0	92102	58 NeWest Residents	30.6
91204	35 International Marketplace	57.2	91759	07 Exurbanites	88.4	92103	27 Metro Renters	49.0
91205	44 Urban Melting Pot	65.4	91761	21 Urban Villages	27.6	92104	23 Trendsetters	35.5
91206	44 Urban Melting Pot	46.5	91762	21 Urban Villages	26.1	92105	58 NeWest Residents	47.4
91207	03 Connoisseurs	55.9	91763	21 Urban Villages	48.0	92106	09 Urban Chic	41.7
91208	03 Connoisseurs	37.8	91764	21 Urban Villages	22.2	92107	23 Trendsetters	33.5
91214	11 Pacific Heights	27.1	91765	11 Pacific Heights	52.6	92108	27 Metro Renters	61.8
91301	02 Suburban Splendor	31.0	91766	47 Las Casas	50.8	92109	27 Metro Renters	51.5
91302	01 Top Rung	42.7	91767	21 Urban Villages	46.1	92110	23 Trendsetters	26.1
91303	35 International Marketplace	25.0	91768	47 Las Casas	41.3	92111	35 International Marketplace	18.7
91304	35 International Marketplace	38.6	91770	21 Urban Villages	42.9	92113	47 Las Casas	58.6
91306	35 International Marketplace	31.0	91773	10 Pleasant-Ville	36.5	92114	21 Urban Villages	45.6
91307	05 Wealthy Seaboard Suburbs	43.0	91775	11 Pacific Heights	57.9	92115	23 Trendsetters	23.1
91311	03 Connoisseurs	20.0	91776	11 Pacific Heights	32.6	92116	52 Inner City Tenants	35.1
91316	30 Retirement Communities	35.2	91780	11 Pacific Heights	95.1	92117	20 City Lights	25.9
91320	02 Suburban Splendor	22.0	91784	03 Connoisseurs	45.7	92118	09 Urban Chic	37.1
91321	30 Retirement Communities	14.5	91786	52 Inner City Tenants	28.4	92119	05 Wealthy Seaboard Suburbs	25.9
91324	23 Trendsetters	24.5	91789	11 Pacific Heights	53.0	92120	09 Urban Chic	29.6
91325	23 Trendsetters	34.6	91790	21 Urban Villages	72.2	92121	04 Boomburbs	51.5
91326	03 Connoisseurs	31.0	91791	11 Pacific Heights	28.1	92122	27 Metro Renters	48.7
91330	55 College Towns	100.0	91792	11 Pacific Heights	55.8	92123	16 Enterprising Professionals	24.4
91331	47 Las Casas	49.4	91801	35 International Marketplace	37.8	92124	09 Urban Chic	26.1
91335	35 International Marketplace	36.2	91803	35 International Marketplace	37.4	92126	11 Pacific Heights	55.1
91340	47 Las Casas	55.2	91901	07 Exurbanites	26.9	92127	04 Boomburbs	32.6
91342	21 Urban Villages	58.9	91902	09 Urban Chic	24.8	92128	04 Boomburbs	39.6
91343	58 NeWest Residents	40.1	91905	31 Rural Resort Dwellers	96.5	92129	02 Suburban Splendor	42.4
91344	10 Pleasant-Ville	32.8	91906	46 Rooted Rural	97.0	92130	04 Boomburbs	24.6
91345	21 Urban Villages	48.9	91910	35 International Marketplace	14.2	92131	04 Boomburbs	28.6
91350	04 Boomburbs	28.7	91911	21 Urban Villages	27.9	92134	66 Unclassified	0.0
91351	06 Sophisticated Squires	30.3	91913	11 Pacific Heights	29.1	92135	40 Military Proximity	100.0
91352	47 Las Casas	43.9	91914	12 Up And Coming Families	61.6	92136	40 Military Proximity	100.0
91354	04 Boomburbs	66.7	91915	04 Boomburbs	54.1	92139	21 Urban Villages	27.1
91355	04 Boomburbs	20.7	91916	31 Rural Resort Dwellers	100.0	92140	40 Military Proximity	100.0
91356	36 Old And Newcomers	21.7	91917	31 Rural Resort Dwellers	99.6	92145	40 Military Proximity	100.0
91360	05 Wealthy Seaboard Suburbs	22.7	91932	52 Inner City Tenants	36.7	92152	40 Military Proximity	0.0
91361	09 Urban Chic	38.3	91934	46 Rooted Rural	100.0	92154	21 Urban Villages	38.0
91362	02 Suburban Splendor	23.7	91935	02 Suburban Splendor	43.3	92173	58 NeWest Residents	35.7

ZIP CODE	TOP TAPESTRY CONSUMER TYPE	% 2009 HOUSE-HOLDS	ZIP CODE	TOP TAPESTRY CONSUMER TYPE	% 2009 HOUSE-HOLDS	ZIP CODE	TOP TAPESTRY CONSUMER TYPE	% 2009 HOUSE-HOLDS
92182	63 Dorms To Diplomas	100.0	92382	13 In Style	64.0	92677	02 Suburban Splendor	25.2
92201	58 NeWest Residents	21.0	92384	49 Senior Sun Seekers	100.0	92679	04 Boomburbs	50.9
92203	59 Southwestern Families	37.6	92385	13 In Style	66.8	92683	11 Pacific Heights	43.4
92210	15 Silver And Gold	87.0	92389	49 Senior Sun Seekers	100.0	92688	04 Boomburbs	49.5
92211	15 Silver And Gold	46.5	92392	12 Up And Coming Families	42.3	92691	05 Wealthy Seaboard Suburbs	24.6
92220	38 Industrious Urban Fringe	34.8	92394	24 Main Street, USA	46.8	92692	02 Suburban Splendor	24.6
92223	49 Senior Sun Seekers	34.2	92395	38 Industrious Urban Fringe	25.1	92694	03 Connoisseurs	97.7
92225	38 Industrious Urban Fringe	49.5	92397	31 Rural Resort Dwellers	62.0	92697	63 Dorms To Diplomas	100.0
92227	59 Southwestern Families	29.6	92399	24 Main Street, USA	13.2	92701	58 NeWest Residents	46.0
92230	38 Industrious Urban Fringe	58.4	92401	58 NeWest Residents	98.5	92703	47 Las Casas	53.5
92231	59 Southwestern Families	49.0	92404	52 Inner City Tenants	19.9	92704	21 Urban Villages	29.7
92233	38 Industrious Urban Fringe	43.6	92405	38 Industrious Urban Fringe	36.5	92705	03 Connoisseurs	25.9
92234	12 Up And Coming Families	21.3	92407	38 Industrious Urban Fringe	21.0	92706	47 Las Casas	20.5
92236	47 Las Casas	50.3	92408	38 Industrious Urban Fringe	25.0	92707	21 Urban Villages	33.2
92239	24 Main Street, USA	47.7	92410	58 NeWest Residents	40.8	92708	05 Wealthy Seaboard Suburbs	30.6
92240	38 Industrious Urban Fringe	24.9	92411	59 Southwestern Families	44.3	92780	35 International Marketplace	29.3
92241	49 Senior Sun Seekers	88.0	92501	38 Industrious Urban Fringe	32.5	92782	16 Enterprising Professionals	27.7
92242	49 Senior Sun Seekers	100.0	92503	38 Industrious Urban Fringe	17.4	92801	35 International Marketplace	43.7
92243	38 Industrious Urban Fringe	22.7	92504	24 Main Street, USA	21.4	92802	58 NeWest Residents	27.3
92249	59 Southwestern Families	82.0	92505	21 Urban Villages	28.8	92804	35 International Marketplace	47.2
92250	38 Industrious Urban Fringe	55.1	92506	02 Suburban Splendor	20.1	92805	21 Urban Villages	34.7
92251	12 Up And Coming Families	48.7	92507	16 Enterprising Professionals	19.6	92806	35 International Marketplace	21.6
92252	57 Simple Living	26.3	92508	04 Boomburbs	59.2	92807	03 Connoisseurs	27.5
92253	15 Silver And Gold	48.6	92509	38 Industrious Urban Fringe	30.3	92808	04 Boomburbs	57.6
92254	47 Las Casas	100.0	92518	15 Silver And Gold	100.0	92821	07 Exurbanites	11.8
92256	33 Midlife Junction	88.7	92521	63 Dorms To Diplomas	100.0	92823	05 Wealthy Seaboard Suburbs	61.7
92257	43 The Elders	97.4	92530	12 Up And Coming Families	18.8	92831	39 Young And Restless	24.7
92259	49 Senior Sun Seekers	100.0	92532	12 Up And Coming Families	68.0	92832	23 Trendsetters	30.8
92260	15 Silver And Gold	34.1	92536	31 Rural Resort Dwellers	87.9	92833	21 Urban Villages	26.2
92262	30 Retirement Communities	19.2	92539	49 Senior Sun Seekers	45.5	92835	05 Wealthy Seaboard Suburbs	25.0
92264	15 Silver And Gold	50.7	92543	49 Senior Sun Seekers	24.1	92840	35 International Marketplace	37.1
92267	49 Senior Sun Seekers	100.0	92544	49 Senior Sun Seekers	17.0	92841	21 Urban Villages	34.5
92270	15 Silver And Gold	51.6	92545	49 Senior Sun Seekers	36.8	92843	21 Urban Villages	54.2
92274	47 Las Casas	30.2	92548	49 Senior Sun Seekers	47.2	92844	11 Pacific Heights	39.7
92276	43 The Elders	48.9	92549	31 Rural Resort Dwellers	100.0	92845	05 Wealthy Seaboard Suburbs	64.6
92277	52 Inner City Tenants	25.7	92551	12 Up And Coming Families	58.3	92860	10 Pleasant-Ville	33.9
92278	40 Military Proximity	100.0	92553	38 Industrious Urban Fringe	39.5	92861	03 Connoisseurs	82.1
92280	49 Senior Sun Seekers	71.4	92555	06 Sophisticated Squires	38.2	92862	04 Boomburbs	83.3
92281	59 Southwestern Families	62.7	92557	06 Sophisticated Squires	35.8	92865	05 Wealthy Seaboard Suburbs	17.7
92282	49 Senior Sun Seekers	58.4	92561	31 Rural Resort Dwellers	91.0	92866	09 Urban Chic	25.5
92283	56 Rural Bypasses	34.2	92562	03 Connoisseurs	20.4	92867	10 Pleasant-Ville	20.1
92284	33 Midlife Junction	33.7	92563	12 Up And Coming Families	32.1	92868	35 International Marketplace	31.5
92285	49 Senior Sun Seekers	81.7	92567	26 Midland Crowd	28.2	92869	03 Connoisseurs	23.0
92301	38 Industrious Urban Fringe	70.6	92570	38 Industrious Urban Fringe	53.7	92870	05 Wealthy Seaboard Suburbs	23.5
92304	31 Rural Resort Dwellers	90.9	92571	38 Industrious Urban Fringe	56.8	92879	12 Up And Coming Families	36.9
92305	31 Rural Resort Dwellers	92.0	92582	46 Rooted Rural	70.2	92880	38 Industrious Urban Fringe	67.9
92307	24 Main Street, USA	17.1	92583	49 Senior Sun Seekers	26.6	92881	04 Boomburbs	64.1
92308	38 Industrious Urban Fringe	17.6	92584	17 Green Acres	29.8	92882	04 Boomburbs	25.9
92309	58 NeWest Residents	71.4	92585	33 Midlife Junction	37.6	92883	12 Up And Coming Families	50.1
92310	40 Military Proximity	100.0	92586	43 The Elders	67.6	92886	09 Urban Chic	20.3
92311	24 Main Street, USA	28.6	92587	07 Exurbanites	39.4	92887	02 Suburban Splendor	51.2
92313	10 Pleasant-Ville	25.7	92590	28 Aspiring Young Families	86.2	93001	23 Trendsetters	35.5
92314	31 Rural Resort Dwellers	60.5	92591	12 Up And Coming Families	22.7	93003	09 Urban Chic	11.8
92315	31 Rural Resort Dwellers	55.3	92592	04 Boomburbs	61.7	93004	10 Pleasant-Ville	14.1
92316	38 Industrious Urban Fringe	47.9	92595	26 Midland Crowd	36.1	93010	05 Wealthy Seaboard Suburbs	27.2
92317	07 Exurbanites	100.0	92596	04 Boomburbs	59.3	93012	04 Boomburbs	23.7
92320	49 Senior Sun Seekers	27.4	92602	04 Boomburbs	68.3	93013	09 Urban Chic	27.8
92321	07 Exurbanites	51.9	92603	03 Connoisseurs	75.0	93015	21 Urban Villages	70.4
92322	10 Pleasant-Ville	53.8	92604	03 Connoisseurs	23.4	93021	02 Suburban Splendor	26.4
92324	38 Industrious Urban Fringe	34.1	92606	16 Enterprising Professionals	38.5	93022	09 Urban Chic	53.5
92325	31 Rural Resort Dwellers	27.3	92610	04 Boomburbs	77.6	93023	09 Urban Chic	47.3
92327	50 Heartland Communities	82.7	92612	27 Metro Renters	38.8	93030	21 Urban Villages	41.6
92328	49 Senior Sun Seekers	100.0	92614	02 Suburban Splendor	36.0	93033	21 Urban Villages	57.0
92332	31 Rural Resort Dwellers	78.0	92617	63 Dorms To Diplomas	73.4	93035	21 Urban Villages	23.4
92335	38 Industrious Urban Fringe	31.7	92618	16 Enterprising Professionals	92.1	93036	21 Urban Villages	38.0
92336	12 Up And Coming Families	26.9	92620	02 Suburban Splendor	32.4	93041	35 International Marketplace	45.4
92337	12 Up And Coming Families	43.8	92624	09 Urban Chic	50.3	93042	40 Military Proximity	100.0
92338	49 Senior Sun Seekers	78.6	92625	03 Connoisseurs	38.6	93043	40 Military Proximity	100.0
92339	22 Metropolitans	76.7	92626	23 Trendsetters	22.2	93060	47 Las Casas	29.1
92342	15 Silver And Gold	93.7	92627	23 Trendsetters	33.5	93063	06 Sophisticated Squires	23.7
92344	06 Sophisticated Squires	57.0	92629	09 Urban Chic	46.5	93065	02 Suburban Splendor	18.5
92345	38 Industrious Urban Fringe	23.9	92630	02 Suburban Splendor	22.6	93066	03 Connoisseurs	71.4
92346	38 Industrious Urban Fringe	16.7	92637	43 The Elders	90.5	93067	09 Urban Chic	100.0
92347	46 Rooted Rural	77.0	92646	03 Connoisseurs	22.9	93101	23 Trendsetters	49.0
92350	23 Trendsetters	100.0	92647	05 Wealthy Seaboard Suburbs	25.8	93103	35 International Marketplace	23.2
92352	07 Exurbanites	79.9	92648	23 Trendsetters	24.8	93105	09 Urban Chic	34.6
92354	36 Old And Newcomers	25.5	92649	09 Urban Chic	21.3	93106	66 Unclassified	100.0
92356	46 Rooted Rural	81.7	92651	09 Urban Chic	33.0	93108	03 Connoisseurs	54.3
92358	31 Rural Resort Dwellers	94.5	92653	01 Top Rung	19.8	93109	09 Urban Chic	64.8
92359	24 Main Street, USA	73.6	92655	11 Pacific Heights	82.1	93110	09 Urban Chic	44.5
92363	49 Senior Sun Seekers	29.9	92656	04 Boomburbs	49.2	93111	03 Connoisseurs	39.6
92364	41 Crossroads	66.4	92657	01 Top Rung	53.5	93117	63 Dorms To Diplomas	30.3
92365	49 Senior Sun Seekers	45.1	92660	01 Top Rung	26.6	93202	38 Industrious Urban Fringe	100.0
92368	38 Industrious Urban Fringe	100.0	92661	08 Laptops And Lattes	73.8	93203	47 Las Casas	87.0
92371	26 Midland Crowd	72.8	92662	08 Laptops And Lattes	50.7	93204	38 Industrious Urban Fringe	52.5
92372	31 Rural Resort Dwellers	51.5	92663	08 Laptops And Lattes	41.1	93205	49 Senior Sun Seekers	100.0
92373	03 Connoisseurs	24.9	92672	09 Urban Chic	26.9	93206	38 Industrious Urban Fringe	96.5
92374	10 Pleasant-Ville	16.0	92673	02 Suburban Splendor	49.9	93207	37 Prairie Living	38.9
92376	38 Industrious Urban Fringe	33.4	92675	02 Suburban Splendor	20.9	93210	38 Industrious Urban Fringe	33.9
92377	12 Up And Coming Families	33.7	92676	09 Urban Chic	64.2	93212	38 Industrious Urban Fringe	84.6

CONSUMER TYPE

ZIP CODE	TOP TAPESTRY CONSUMER TYPE	% 2009 HOUSE-HOLDS	ZIP CODE	TOP TAPESTRY CONSUMER TYPE	% 2009 HOUSE-HOLDS	ZIP CODE	TOP TAPESTRY CONSUMER TYPE	% 2009 HOUSE-HOLDS
93215	38 Industrious Urban Fringe	51.0	93465	19 Milk And Cookies	25.7	93704	22 Metropolitans	15.2
93219	59 Southwestern Families	58.1	93501	38 Industrious Urban Fringe	32.6	93705	38 Industrious Urban Fringe	35.7
93221	24 Main Street, USA	44.3	93505	24 Main Street, USA	38.8	93706	38 Industrious Urban Fringe	25.6
93223	38 Industrious Urban Fringe	58.6	93510	06 Sophisticated Squires	75.4	93710	52 Inner City Tenants	28.8
93224	26 Midland Crowd	72.1	93512	31 Rural Resort Dwellers	100.0	93711	03 Connoisseurs	15.7
93225	31 Rural Resort Dwellers	64.2	93513	31 Rural Resort Dwellers	100.0	93720	04 Boomburbs	43.3
93226	31 Rural Resort Dwellers	100.0	93514	07 Exurbanites	34.4	93721	65 Social Security Set	35.7
93230	38 Industrious Urban Fringe	25.0	93516	50 Heartland Communities	49.6	93722	12 Up And Coming Families	38.2
93234	47 Las Casas	60.6	93517	31 Rural Resort Dwellers	100.0	93723	07 Exurbanites	51.9
93235	38 Industrious Urban Fringe	68.1	93518	49 Senior Sun Seekers	56.6	93725	38 Industrious Urban Fringe	34.9
93238	49 Senior Sun Seekers	68.6	93519	49 Senior Sun Seekers	97.8	93726	55 College Towns	24.5
93239	47 Las Casas	94.4	93523	40 Military Proximity	75.3	93727	38 Industrious Urban Fringe	16.1
93240	49 Senior Sun Seekers	100.0	93524	15 Silver And Gold	53.3	93728	38 Industrious Urban Fringe	44.4
93241	47 Las Casas	91.5	93526	31 Rural Resort Dwellers	100.0	93730	02 Suburban Splendor	37.6
93242	38 Industrious Urban Fringe	62.7	93527	46 Rooted Rural	44.3	93741	22 Metropolitans	100.0
93243	26 Midland Crowd	76.2	93528	49 Senior Sun Seekers	100.0	93901	20 City Lights	42.5
93244	07 Exurbanites	75.9	93529	09 Urban Chic	100.0	93905	47 Las Casas	76.7
93245	12 Up And Coming Families	27.0	93531	15 Silver And Gold	80.7	93906	35 International Marketplace	45.3
93247	38 Industrious Urban Fringe	31.6	93532	06 Sophisticated Squires	82.8	93907	07 Exurbanites	31.1
93249	47 Las Casas	100.0	93534	52 Inner City Tenants	16.7	93908	03 Connoisseurs	38.7
93250	47 Las Casas	60.7	93535	38 Industrious Urban Fringe	24.3	93920	09 Urban Chic	85.9
93251	26 Midland Crowd	100.0	93536	10 Pleasant-Ville	16.8	93923	15 Silver And Gold	67.5
93252	46 Rooted Rural	65.2	93541	31 Rural Resort Dwellers	100.0	93924	09 Urban Chic	53.9
93254	37 Prairie Living	100.0	93543	17 Green Acres	43.7	93925	21 Urban Villages	100.0
93255	49 Senior Sun Seekers	100.0	93544	31 Rural Resort Dwellers	69.3	93926	47 Las Casas	58.6
93256	59 Southwestern Families	72.9	93545	57 Simple Living	43.3	93927	47 Las Casas	71.6
93257	38 Industrious Urban Fringe	22.4	93546	09 Urban Chic	66.3	93930	47 Las Casas	57.3
93260	31 Rural Resort Dwellers	93.2	93550	38 Industrious Urban Fringe	34.2	93932	26 Midland Crowd	63.3
93262	31 Rural Resort Dwellers	100.0	93551	06 Sophisticated Squires	26.9	93933	35 International Marketplace	23.0
93263	38 Industrious Urban Fringe	50.3	93552	12 Up And Coming Families	36.9	93940	23 Trendsetters	47.5
93265	31 Rural Resort Dwellers	43.8	93553	17 Green Acres	81.5	93943	40 Military Proximity	100.0
93266	38 Industrious Urban Fringe	90.7	93554	49 Senior Sun Seekers	100.0	93950	09 Urban Chic	63.9
93267	59 Southwestern Families	29.9	93555	07 Exurbanites	13.0	93953	15 Silver And Gold	74.8
93268	53 Home Town	21.1	93560	28 Aspiring Young Families	34.2	93955	35 International Marketplace	32.1
93270	47 Las Casas	42.5	93561	24 Main Street, USA	21.2	93960	47 Las Casas	52.7
93271	15 Silver And Gold	53.9	93562	32 Rustbelt Traditions	98.6	94002	09 Urban Chic	31.5
93272	38 Industrious Urban Fringe	95.8	93563	31 Rural Resort Dwellers	100.0	94005	09 Urban Chic	100.0
93274	38 Industrious Urban Fringe	45.0	93591	38 Industrious Urban Fringe	64.8	94010	23 Trendsetters	24.9
93276	26 Midland Crowd	75.0	93601	31 Rural Resort Dwellers	95.4	94014	11 Pacific Heights	84.3
93277	28 Aspiring Young Families	15.3	93602	31 Rural Resort Dwellers	72.6	94015	11 Pacific Heights	63.5
93280	38 Industrious Urban Fringe	67.7	93604	31 Rural Resort Dwellers	100.0	94019	09 Urban Chic	75.2
93283	49 Senior Sun Seekers	100.0	93608	47 Las Casas	78.5	94020	09 Urban Chic	99.3
93285	49 Senior Sun Seekers	73.4	93609	38 Industrious Urban Fringe	49.3	94021	09 Urban Chic	100.0
93286	59 Southwestern Families	40.3	93610	38 Industrious Urban Fringe	30.4	94022	03 Connoisseurs	42.2
93287	31 Rural Resort Dwellers	100.0	93611	04 Boomburbs	22.4	94024	03 Connoisseurs	50.9
93291	38 Industrious Urban Fringe	23.9	93612	52 Inner City Tenants	24.1	94025	08 Laptops And Lattes	36.5
93292	13 In Style	20.3	93614	31 Rural Resort Dwellers	58.9	94027	01 Top Rung	98.4
93301	57 Simple Living	20.6	93615	47 Las Casas	44.5	94028	01 Top Rung	83.3
93304	38 Industrious Urban Fringe	58.6	93616	59 Southwestern Families	51.6	94030	05 Wealthy Seaboard Suburbs	39.7
93305	58 NeWest Residents	50.4	93618	38 Industrious Urban Fringe	50.1	94035	40 Military Proximity	100.0
93306	38 Industrious Urban Fringe	28.6	93619	04 Boomburbs	35.9	94038	02 Suburban Splendor	47.2
93307	38 Industrious Urban Fringe	56.9	93620	38 Industrious Urban Fringe	74.5	94040	27 Metro Renters	31.7
93308	60 City Dimensions	14.3	93621	31 Rural Resort Dwellers	100.0	94041	23 Trendsetters	46.2
93309	28 Aspiring Young Families	23.6	93622	47 Las Casas	54.4	94043	23 Trendsetters	53.6
93311	12 Up And Coming Families	39.5	93623	22 Metropolitans	97.7	94044	05 Wealthy Seaboard Suburbs	21.7
93312	12 Up And Coming Families	41.2	93625	38 Industrious Urban Fringe	41.2	94060	09 Urban Chic	100.0
93313	12 Up And Coming Families	70.0	93626	49 Senior Sun Seekers	46.5	94061	23 Trendsetters	47.8
93314	02 Suburban Splendor	65.7	93627	47 Las Casas	100.0	94062	01 Top Rung	29.5
93401	55 College Towns	33.2	93630	47 Las Casas	38.2	94063	35 International Marketplace	32.6
93402	09 Urban Chic	24.0	93631	38 Industrious Urban Fringe	39.0	94065	08 Laptops And Lattes	68.5
93405	63 Dorms To Diplomas	35.3	93633	31 Rural Resort Dwellers	54.8	94066	11 Pacific Heights	22.7
93407	63 Dorms To Diplomas	100.0	93635	38 Industrious Urban Fringe	33.8	94070	03 Connoisseurs	43.6
93420	33 Midlife Junction	17.9	93636	06 Sophisticated Squires	67.7	94074	09 Urban Chic	100.0
93422	07 Exurbanites	30.4	93637	38 Industrious Urban Fringe	23.3	94080	11 Pacific Heights	56.0
93426	26 Midland Crowd	56.4	93638	58 NeWest Residents	36.2	94085	16 Enterprising Professionals	48.0
93427	19 Milk And Cookies	45.5	93640	47 Las Casas	83.9	94086	23 Trendsetters	29.7
93428	15 Silver And Gold	96.8	93641	31 Rural Resort Dwellers	100.0	94087	09 Urban Chic	31.5
93429	40 Military Proximity	100.0	93643	31 Rural Resort Dwellers	100.0	94089	11 Pacific Heights	26.3
93430	31 Rural Resort Dwellers	92.8	93644	31 Rural Resort Dwellers	36.2	94102	65 Social Security Set	40.0
93432	31 Rural Resort Dwellers	40.4	93645	31 Rural Resort Dwellers	100.0	94103	23 Trendsetters	43.7
93433	28 Aspiring Young Families	20.1	93646	47 Las Casas	94.4	94104	44 Urban Melting Pot	100.0
93434	21 Urban Villages	61.7	93647	38 Industrious Urban Fringe	46.4	94105	08 Laptops And Lattes	100.0
93436	10 Pleasant-Ville	21.6	93648	47 Las Casas	45.0	94107	08 Laptops And Lattes	49.7
93437	40 Military Proximity	99.5	93650	59 Southwestern Families	31.3	94108	27 Metro Renters	33.6
93441	09 Urban Chic	74.2	93651	17 Green Acres	100.0	94109	27 Metro Renters	45.7
93442	15 Silver And Gold	29.4	93652	21 Urban Villages	100.0	94110	23 Trendsetters	40.3
93444	10 Pleasant-Ville	31.1	93653	31 Rural Resort Dwellers	99.4	94111	08 Laptops And Lattes	73.2
93445	49 Senior Sun Seekers	30.3	93654	38 Industrious Urban Fringe	21.0	94112	11 Pacific Heights	92.1
93446	33 Midlife Junction	17.8	93656	38 Industrious Urban Fringe	73.4	94114	08 Laptops And Lattes	99.9
93449	09 Urban Chic	57.7	93657	47 Las Casas	16.4	94115	08 Laptops And Lattes	52.4
93450	26 Midland Crowd	100.0	93660	47 Las Casas	78.4	94116	11 Pacific Heights	79.0
93451	17 Green Acres	44.7	93662	38 Industrious Urban Fringe	39.7	94117	08 Laptops And Lattes	72.1
93452	31 Rural Resort Dwellers	75.1	93664	31 Rural Resort Dwellers	36.7	94118	08 Laptops And Lattes	49.0
93453	13 In Style	33.3	93667	07 Exurbanites	53.0	94121	11 Pacific Heights	37.5
93454	21 Urban Villages	18.3	93668	38 Industrious Urban Fringe	54.1	94122	11 Pacific Heights	47.9
93455	10 Pleasant-Ville	32.5	93669	31 Rural Resort Dwellers	100.0	94123	08 Laptops And Lattes	95.7
93458	47 Las Casas	26.0	93675	31 Rural Resort Dwellers	90.2	94124	11 Pacific Heights	37.0
93460	09 Urban Chic	54.8	93701	58 NeWest Residents	82.3	94127	03 Connoisseurs	49.2
93461	38 Industrious Urban Fringe	72.1	93702	38 Industrious Urban Fringe	34.4	94129	08 Laptops And Lattes	97.8
93463	09 Urban Chic	25.5	93703	38 Industrious Urban Fringe	46.5	94130	39 Young And Restless	100.0

ZIP CODE	TOP TAPESTRY CONSUMER TYPE	% 2009 HOUSE-HOLDS	ZIP CODE	TOP TAPESTRY CONSUMER TYPE	% 2009 HOUSE-HOLDS	ZIP CODE	TOP TAPESTRY CONSUMER TYPE	% 2009 HOUSE-HOLDS
94131	08 Laptops And Lattes	56.6	94598	03 Connoisseurs	43.1	95050	23 Trendsetters	47.4
94132	11 Pacific Heights	35.8	94599	49 Senior Sun Seekers	49.1	95051	11 Pacific Heights	37.5
94133	08 Laptops And Lattes	39.7	94601	35 International Marketplace	52.5	95053	23 Trendsetters	0.0
94134	11 Pacific Heights	91.0	94602	35 International Marketplace	29.4	95054	27 Metro Renters	38.5
94158	27 Metro Renters	100.0	94603	38 Industrious Urban Fringe	26.3	95060	09 Urban Chic	54.6
94301	08 Laptops And Lattes	40.6	94605	45 City Strivers	38.4	95062	09 Urban Chic	30.0
94303	03 Connoisseurs	20.9	94606	35 International Marketplace	42.5	95064	63 Dorms To Diplomas	95.4
94304	27 Metro Renters	79.0	94607	45 City Strivers	30.7	95065	09 Urban Chic	47.9
94305	63 Dorms To Diplomas	73.3	94608	45 City Strivers	52.4	95066	09 Urban Chic	49.7
94306	09 Urban Chic	48.1	94609	23 Trendsetters	62.4	95070	01 Top Rung	54.4
94401	23 Trendsetters	40.2	94610	27 Metro Renters	56.4	95073	09 Urban Chic	68.6
94402	09 Urban Chic	40.1	94611	03 Connoisseurs	31.1	95076	21 Urban Villages	35.3
94403	09 Urban Chic	35.3	94612	65 Social Security Set	52.9	95110	35 International Marketplace	37.8
94404	09 Urban Chic	46.7	94613	55 College Towns	100.0	95111	21 Urban Villages	34.2
94501	23 Trendsetters	48.5	94618	08 Laptops And Lattes	44.4	95112	35 International Marketplace	31.1
94502	03 Connoisseurs	37.5	94619	09 Urban Chic	27.0	95113	27 Metro Renters	63.1
94503	06 Sophisticated Squires	41.0	94621	45 City Strivers	30.5	95116	47 Las Casas	38.4
94505	07 Exurbanites	70.1	94702	23 Trendsetters	47.8	95117	23 Trendsetters	60.9
94506	01 Top Rung	47.6	94703	23 Trendsetters	80.6	95118	05 Wealthy Seaboard Suburbs	29.0
94507	01 Top Rung	62.6	94704	63 Dorms To Diplomas	56.8	95119	11 Pacific Heights	36.3
94508	09 Urban Chic	65.9	94705	08 Laptops And Lattes	47.3	95120	03 Connoisseurs	41.5
94509	10 Pleasant-Ville	23.3	94706	09 Urban Chic	43.1	95121	11 Pacific Heights	63.6
94510	02 Suburban Splendor	19.9	94707	03 Connoisseurs	64.0	95122	21 Urban Villages	52.6
94512	10 Pleasant-Ville	100.0	94708	03 Connoisseurs	78.2	95123	06 Sophisticated Squires	24.7
94513	04 Boomburbs	55.9	94709	08 Laptops And Lattes	43.3	95124	09 Urban Chic	34.4
94514	46 Rooted Rural	53.5	94710	23 Trendsetters	72.3	95125	09 Urban Chic	37.4
94515	46 Rooted Rural	22.7	94720	63 Dorms To Diplomas	100.0	95126	23 Trendsetters	40.6
94517	03 Connoisseurs	36.6	94801	58 NeWest Residents	17.5	95127	21 Urban Villages	42.8
94518	05 Wealthy Seaboard Suburbs	24.3	94803	05 Wealthy Seaboard Suburbs	29.4	95128	23 Trendsetters	52.5
94519	10 Pleasant-Ville	56.2	94804	45 City Strivers	26.6	95129	11 Pacific Heights	44.4
94520	35 International Marketplace	20.4	94805	05 Wealthy Seaboard Suburbs	30.6	95130	05 Wealthy Seaboard Suburbs	35.3
94521	05 Wealthy Seaboard Suburbs	23.3	94806	21 Urban Villages	23.0	95131	11 Pacific Heights	62.6
94523	09 Urban Chic	26.8	94901	23 Trendsetters	32.7	95132	11 Pacific Heights	88.9
94525	20 City Lights	40.7	94903	09 Urban Chic	34.1	95133	11 Pacific Heights	66.2
94526	03 Connoisseurs	35.7	94904	30 Retirement Communities	35.5	95134	19 Milk And Cookies	43.6
94528	03 Connoisseurs	100.0	94920	01 Top Rung	44.1	95135	15 Silver And Gold	37.8
94530	23 Trendsetters	25.7	94922	15 Silver And Gold	100.0	95136	16 Enterprising Professionals	42.1
94531	04 Boomburbs	88.9	94923	15 Silver And Gold	66.9	95138	04 Boomburbs	59.4
94533	24 Main Street, USA	17.8	94924	09 Urban Chic	100.0	95139	06 Sophisticated Squires	30.2
94534	02 Suburban Splendor	18.3	94925	09 Urban Chic	72.5	95140	03 Connoisseurs	85.7
94535	40 Military Proximity	87.2	94928	28 Aspiring Young Families	22.2	95148	11 Pacific Heights	80.1
94536	11 Pacific Heights	43.5	94929	31 Rural Resort Dwellers	100.0	95202	65 Social Security Set	53.2
94538	11 Pacific Heights	45.7	94930	09 Urban Chic	100.0	95203	24 Main Street, USA	25.4
94539	02 Suburban Splendor	41.7	94931	28 Aspiring Young Families	39.0	95204	24 Main Street, USA	46.2
94541	35 International Marketplace	38.6	94933	09 Urban Chic	100.0	95205	38 Industrious Urban Fringe	66.3
94542	09 Urban Chic	38.2	94937	15 Silver And Gold	63.6	95206	38 Industrious Urban Fringe	36.0
94544	35 International Marketplace	35.7	94938	09 Urban Chic	100.0	95207	24 Main Street, USA	22.3
94545	10 Pleasant-Ville	29.0	94939	09 Urban Chic	42.7	95209	06 Sophisticated Squires	31.9
94546	05 Wealthy Seaboard Suburbs	28.2	94940	37 Prairie Living	100.0	95210	38 Industrious Urban Fringe	22.9
94547	11 Pacific Heights	54.3	94941	09 Urban Chic	57.3	95211	63 Dorms To Diplomas	100.0
94548	21 Urban Villages	100.0	94945	09 Urban Chic	44.2	95212	41 Crossroads	59.6
94549	03 Connoisseurs	42.6	94946	09 Urban Chic	98.8	95215	38 Industrious Urban Fringe	46.4
94550	09 Urban Chic	19.2	94947	09 Urban Chic	32.3	95219	13 In Style	24.3
94551	06 Sophisticated Squires	33.4	94949	09 Urban Chic	53.6	95220	17 Green Acres	25.1
94552	02 Suburban Splendor	74.6	94951	31 Rural Resort Dwellers	38.9	95222	31 Rural Resort Dwellers	62.4
94553	13 In Style	22.4	94952	09 Urban Chic	55.3	95223	31 Rural Resort Dwellers	57.6
94555	11 Pacific Heights	54.9	94954	10 Pleasant-Ville	33.1	95228	31 Rural Resort Dwellers	98.7
94556	03 Connoisseurs	70.5	94956	09 Urban Chic	100.0	95230	25 Salt Of The Earth	39.2
94558	03 Connoisseurs	26.0	94960	09 Urban Chic	71.6	95231	24 Main Street, USA	39.0
94559	35 International Marketplace	36.0	94963	09 Urban Chic	100.0	95232	31 Rural Resort Dwellers	100.0
94560	11 Pacific Heights	50.6	94964	18 Cozy And Comfortable	58.2	95236	10 Pleasant-Ville	41.3
94561	12 Up And Coming Families	34.6	94965	08 Laptops And Lattes	69.5	95237	26 Midland Crowd	50.6
94563	03 Connoisseurs	69.8	94970	09 Urban Chic	100.0	95240	24 Main Street, USA	18.9
94564	20 City Lights	31.7	94971	09 Urban Chic	62.2	95242	13 In Style	24.4
94565	38 Industrious Urban Fringe	18.7	94972	09 Urban Chic	100.0	95245	31 Rural Resort Dwellers	88.2
94566	02 Suburban Splendor	24.3	94973	09 Urban Chic	100.0	95246	31 Rural Resort Dwellers	37.3
94567	31 Rural Resort Dwellers	51.5	95002	21 Urban Villages	100.0	95247	15 Silver And Gold	33.2
94568	16 Enterprising Professionals	26.8	95003	09 Urban Chic	58.6	95249	57 Simple Living	39.5
94569	10 Pleasant-Ville	100.0	95004	10 Pleasant-Ville	42.4	95251	31 Rural Resort Dwellers	100.0
94571	31 Rural Resort Dwellers	40.9	95005	09 Urban Chic	83.5	95252	17 Green Acres	50.2
94572	10 Pleasant-Ville	45.3	95006	09 Urban Chic	100.0	95255	31 Rural Resort Dwellers	41.5
94574	09 Urban Chic	47.8	95008	23 Trendsetters	47.8	95257	31 Rural Resort Dwellers	100.0
94576	09 Urban Chic	100.0	95010	36 Old And Newcomers	43.7	95258	06 Sophisticated Squires	54.4
94577	20 City Lights	25.2	95012	47 Las Casas	62.8	95301	38 Industrious Urban Fringe	26.7
94578	35 International Marketplace	24.0	95013	10 Pleasant-Ville	81.8	95303	21 Urban Villages	63.2
94579	10 Pleasant-Ville	45.3	95014	11 Pacific Heights	41.1	95304	26 Midland Crowd	47.4
94580	10 Pleasant-Ville	48.5	95017	09 Urban Chic	100.0	95306	31 Rural Resort Dwellers	100.0
94582	04 Boomburbs	64.8	95018	09 Urban Chic	87.1	95307	38 Industrious Urban Fringe	34.4
94583	02 Suburban Splendor	48.1	95019	47 Las Casas	42.4	95309	31 Rural Resort Dwellers	100.0
94585	06 Sophisticated Squires	39.6	95020	21 Urban Villages	23.8	95310	49 Senior Sun Seekers	51.7
94586	05 Wealthy Seaboard Suburbs	60.4	95023	21 Urban Villages	37.6	95311	49 Senior Sun Seekers	68.7
94587	11 Pacific Heights	63.5	95030	03 Connoisseurs	35.4	95313	38 Industrious Urban Fringe	78.8
94588	02 Suburban Splendor	36.8	95032	09 Urban Chic	39.9	95315	38 Industrious Urban Fringe	96.2
94589	10 Pleasant-Ville	31.3	95033	09 Urban Chic	41.1	95316	37 Prairie Living	26.2
94590	35 International Marketplace	30.3	95035	11 Pacific Heights	62.6	95317	38 Industrious Urban Fringe	100.0
94591	10 Pleasant-Ville	17.4	95037	35 International Marketplace	21.8	95318	22 Metropolitans	91.8
94592	63 Dorms To Diplomas	100.0	95039	47 Las Casas	42.3	95320	17 Green Acres	21.6
94595	43 The Elders	62.6	95043	37 Prairie Living	99.7	95321	15 Silver And Gold	80.5
94596	27 Metro Renters	38.9	95045	24 Main Street, USA	50.5	95322	24 Main Street, USA	31.7
94597	09 Urban Chic	30.5	95046	03 Connoisseurs	53.1	95323	37 Prairie Living	100.0

CONSUMER TYPE

ZIP CODE	TOP TAPESTRY CONSUMER TYPE	% 2009 HOUSE-HOLDS	ZIP CODE	TOP TAPESTRY CONSUMER TYPE	% 2009 HOUSE-HOLDS	ZIP CODE	TOP TAPESTRY CONSUMER TYPE	% 2009 HOUSE-HOLDS
95324	42 Southern Satellites	35.7	95467	17 Green Acres	94.0	95648	04 Boomburbs	45.4
95326	21 Urban Villages	34.1	95468	31 Rural Resort Dwellers	100.0	95650	07 Exurbanites	28.7
95327	31 Rural Resort Dwellers	34.1	95469	17 Green Acres	58.7	95651	07 Exurbanites	52.2
95329	31 Rural Resort Dwellers	96.1	95470	26 Midland Crowd	51.7	95652	52 Inner City Tenants	59.0
95330	21 Urban Villages	46.5	95472	09 Urban Chic	75.3	95653	38 Industrious Urban Fringe	94.5
95333	38 Industrious Urban Fringe	37.6	95476	09 Urban Chic	19.9	95655	61 High Rise Renters	100.0
95334	47 Las Casas	52.1	95480	15 Silver And Gold	100.0	95658	07 Exurbanites	41.9
95335	31 Rural Resort Dwellers	100.0	95482	24 Main Street, USA	24.9	95659	37 Prairie Living	100.0
95336	10 Pleasant-Ville	26.5	95485	46 Rooted Rural	47.4	95660	24 Main Street, USA	26.9
95337	06 Sophisticated Squires	17.9	95488	31 Rural Resort Dwellers	100.0	95661	16 Enterprising Professionals	37.2
95338	31 Rural Resort Dwellers	79.7	95490	31 Rural Resort Dwellers	23.8	95662	10 Pleasant-Ville	32.2
95340	24 Main Street, USA	18.6	95492	09 Urban Chic	20.1	95663	07 Exurbanites	67.9
95341	47 Las Casas	23.6	95493	31 Rural Resort Dwellers	100.0	95664	07 Exurbanites	99.3
95345	31 Rural Resort Dwellers	100.0	95494	37 Prairie Living	66.7	95665	31 Rural Resort Dwellers	60.3
95346	31 Rural Resort Dwellers	100.0	95497	15 Silver And Gold	100.0	95666	31 Rural Resort Dwellers	70.6
95348	10 Pleasant-Ville	22.0	95501	33 Midlife Junction	20.7	95667	07 Exurbanites	36.7
95350	24 Main Street, USA	27.9	95503	24 Main Street, USA	22.8	95668	46 Rooted Rural	53.8
95351	38 Industrious Urban Fringe	41.6	95511	37 Prairie Living	100.0	95669	31 Rural Resort Dwellers	60.1
95354	24 Main Street, USA	34.2	95514	37 Prairie Living	91.1	95670	24 Main Street, USA	17.7
95355	12 Up And Coming Families	20.8	95519	33 Midlife Junction	22.9	95672	07 Exurbanites	76.9
95356	28 Aspiring Young Families	28.7	95521	55 College Towns	41.9	95673	24 Main Street, USA	53.2
95357	38 Industrious Urban Fringe	17.4	95524	09 Urban Chic	83.8	95674	37 Prairie Living	100.0
95358	38 Industrious Urban Fringe	38.1	95525	07 Exurbanites	41.3	95677	28 Aspiring Young Families	20.5
95360	38 Industrious Urban Fringe	64.6	95526	31 Rural Resort Dwellers	72.7	95678	04 Boomburbs	30.1
95361	24 Main Street, USA	23.9	95527	31 Rural Resort Dwellers	100.0	95679	37 Prairie Living	92.3
95363	12 Up And Coming Families	36.0	95528	31 Rural Resort Dwellers	100.0	95681	17 Green Acres	62.4
95364	31 Rural Resort Dwellers	100.0	95531	31 Rural Resort Dwellers	18.8	95682	13 In Style	37.2
95366	19 Milk And Cookies	33.6	95536	37 Prairie Living	65.5	95683	03 Connoisseurs	81.6
95367	38 Industrious Urban Fringe	30.2	95540	31 Rural Resort Dwellers	18.5	95684	31 Rural Resort Dwellers	56.9
95368	12 Up And Coming Families	48.0	95542	33 Midlife Junction	38.1	95685	31 Rural Resort Dwellers	69.4
95369	38 Industrious Urban Fringe	63.2	95543	31 Rural Resort Dwellers	99.8	95687	06 Sophisticated Squires	21.7
95370	31 Rural Resort Dwellers	22.4	95546	51 Metro City Edge	80.2	95688	07 Exurbanites	29.5
95372	18 Cozy And Comfortable	87.3	95547	31 Rural Resort Dwellers	100.0	95689	15 Silver And Gold	70.1
95374	42 Southern Satellites	88.8	95548	49 Senior Sun Seekers	99.8	95690	37 Prairie Living	49.5
95376	04 Boomburbs	23.3	95549	07 Exurbanites	32.2	95691	06 Sophisticated Squires	30.3
95377	04 Boomburbs	82.7	95550	07 Exurbanites	74.1	95692	38 Industrious Urban Fringe	47.9
95379	31 Rural Resort Dwellers	29.0	95551	24 Main Street, USA	91.5	95693	07 Exurbanites	97.8
95380	38 Industrious Urban Fringe	27.5	95552	49 Senior Sun Seekers	100.0	95694	21 Urban Villages	53.7
95382	16 Enterprising Professionals	29.1	95554	31 Rural Resort Dwellers	92.0	95695	35 International Marketplace	24.8
95383	31 Rural Resort Dwellers	83.2	95555	31 Rural Resort Dwellers	100.0	95698	09 Urban Chic	64.6
95385	38 Industrious Urban Fringe	61.6	95556	46 Rooted Rural	100.0	95701	31 Rural Resort Dwellers	74.0
95386	38 Industrious Urban Fringe	42.8	95558	37 Prairie Living	100.0	95703	31 Rural Resort Dwellers	67.8
95388	38 Industrious Urban Fringe	62.4	95560	31 Rural Resort Dwellers	96.4	95709	31 Rural Resort Dwellers	62.5
95389	22 Metropolitans	91.3	95562	53 Home Town	39.3	95713	07 Exurbanites	44.8
95391	17 Green Acres	98.4	95563	31 Rural Resort Dwellers	100.0	95714	07 Exurbanites	82.8
95401	28 Aspiring Young Families	15.4	95564	48 Great Expectations	100.0	95715	31 Rural Resort Dwellers	100.0
95403	13 In Style	16.0	95565	25 Salt Of The Earth	94.0	95717	31 Rural Resort Dwellers	73.1
95404	03 Connoisseurs	22.9	95567	49 Senior Sun Seekers	59.8	95720	31 Rural Resort Dwellers	60.6
95405	13 In Style	17.5	95568	31 Rural Resort Dwellers	100.0	95721	09 Urban Chic	60.0
95407	21 Urban Villages	48.2	95569	31 Rural Resort Dwellers	62.8	95722	05 Wealthy Seaboard Suburbs	53.6
95409	43 The Elders	24.6	95570	31 Rural Resort Dwellers	64.4	95724	31 Rural Resort Dwellers	100.0
95410	15 Silver And Gold	98.5	95573	31 Rural Resort Dwellers	99.6	95726	10 Pleasant-Ville	41.6
95412	15 Silver And Gold	100.0	95585	37 Prairie Living	96.8	95728	31 Rural Resort Dwellers	100.0
95415	46 Rooted Rural	69.1	95587	37 Prairie Living	88.6	95742	49 Senior Sun Seekers	99.8
95417	46 Rooted Rural	78.0	95589	31 Rural Resort Dwellers	89.7	95746	03 Connoisseurs	38.1
95420	31 Rural Resort Dwellers	100.0	95595	31 Rural Resort Dwellers	56.7	95747	12 Up And Coming Families	39.4
95421	31 Rural Resort Dwellers	91.4	95602	07 Exurbanites	31.6	95757	04 Boomburbs	96.7
95422	49 Senior Sun Seekers	64.5	95603	07 Exurbanites	21.5	95758	04 Boomburbs	44.3
95423	49 Senior Sun Seekers	69.7	95605	38 Industrious Urban Fringe	48.0	95762	04 Boomburbs	61.5
95425	46 Rooted Rural	38.5	95606	09 Urban Chic	74.6	95765	04 Boomburbs	73.6
95427	31 Rural Resort Dwellers	98.5	95607	37 Prairie Living	72.5	95776	12 Up And Coming Families	49.3
95428	33 Midlife Junction	45.2	95608	13 In Style	15.2	95811	27 Metro Renters	67.7
95429	31 Rural Resort Dwellers	100.0	95610	13 In Style	21.1	95814	65 Social Security Set	35.6
95432	15 Silver And Gold	100.0	95612	37 Prairie Living	99.0	95815	60 City Dimensions	19.6
95436	09 Urban Chic	50.5	95614	07 Exurbanites	94.6	95816	27 Metro Renters	50.2
95437	31 Rural Resort Dwellers	47.3	95615	37 Prairie Living	97.4	95817	22 Metropolitans	29.2
95439	13 In Style	66.5	95616	55 College Towns	38.4	95818	09 Urban Chic	21.1
95441	17 Green Acres	62.8	95618	55 College Towns	29.9	95819	22 Metropolitans	36.3
95442	09 Urban Chic	70.1	95619	29 Rustbelt Retirees	67.6	95820	38 Industrious Urban Fringe	44.6
95443	31 Rural Resort Dwellers	100.0	95620	12 Up And Coming Families	36.0	95821	36 Old And Newcomers	35.8
95444	09 Urban Chic	100.0	95621	28 Aspiring Young Families	17.2	95822	24 Main Street, USA	17.6
95445	31 Rural Resort Dwellers	99.9	95623	31 Rural Resort Dwellers	59.9	95823	38 Industrious Urban Fringe	26.7
95446	31 Rural Resort Dwellers	53.8	95624	07 Exurbanites	26.0	95824	38 Industrious Urban Fringe	47.7
95448	09 Urban Chic	33.9	95626	10 Pleasant-Ville	48.3	95825	39 Young And Restless	29.6
95449	38 Industrious Urban Fringe	50.0	95627	38 Industrious Urban Fringe	50.4	95826	28 Aspiring Young Families	29.1
95450	31 Rural Resort Dwellers	100.0	95628	13 In Style	23.7	95827	28 Aspiring Young Families	20.6
95451	31 Rural Resort Dwellers	45.7	95629	31 Rural Resort Dwellers	65.9	95828	38 Industrious Urban Fringe	26.4
95452	07 Exurbanites	54.8	95630	04 Boomburbs	56.9	95829	12 Up And Coming Families	60.4
95453	31 Rural Resort Dwellers	34.4	95631	17 Green Acres	65.2	95830	02 Suburban Splendor	72.1
95454	46 Rooted Rural	75.3	95632	12 Up And Coming Families	30.9	95831	13 In Style	18.0
95456	15 Silver And Gold	72.0	95633	31 Rural Resort Dwellers	44.0	95832	38 Industrious Urban Fringe	97.4
95457	31 Rural Resort Dwellers	34.7	95634	31 Rural Resort Dwellers	98.9	95833	28 Aspiring Young Families	42.9
95458	49 Senior Sun Seekers	96.5	95635	31 Rural Resort Dwellers	100.0	95834	33 Midlife Junction	68.0
95459	31 Rural Resort Dwellers	100.0	95636	31 Rural Resort Dwellers	100.0	95835	12 Up And Coming Families	90.3
95460	15 Silver And Gold	82.9	95637	09 Urban Chic	52.2	95836	46 Rooted Rural	72.2
95461	31 Rural Resort Dwellers	83.9	95638	07 Exurbanites	50.4	95837	09 Urban Chic	89.2
95462	22 Metropolitans	60.3	95640	26 Midland Crowd	42.5	95838	38 Industrious Urban Fringe	19.2
95464	49 Senior Sun Seekers	98.6	95641	49 Senior Sun Seekers	87.9	95841	52 Inner City Tenants	35.6
95465	09 Urban Chic	83.7	95642	31 Rural Resort Dwellers	43.6	95842	28 Aspiring Young Families	27.0
95466	31 Rural Resort Dwellers	69.6	95645	38 Industrious Urban Fringe	74.4	95843	12 Up And Coming Families	52.6

ZIP CODE	TOP TAPESTRY CONSUMER TYPE	% 2009 HOUSE-HOLDS	ZIP CODE	TOP TAPESTRY CONSUMER TYPE	% 2009 HOUSE-HOLDS	ZIP CODE	TOP TAPESTRY CONSUMER TYPE	% 2009 HOUSE-HOLDS
95864	03 Connoisseurs	23.9	96040	31 Rural Resort Dwellers	75.5	96720	10 Pleasant-Ville	16.5
95901	38 Industrious Urban Fringe	19.4	96041	46 Rooted Rural	72.8	96722	09 Urban Chic	100.0
95903	40 Military Proximity	100.0	96044	49 Senior Sun Seekers	60.4	96725	09 Urban Chic	100.0
95910	31 Rural Resort Dwellers	100.0	96046	31 Rural Resort Dwellers	100.0	96726	31 Rural Resort Dwellers	100.0
95912	38 Industrious Urban Fringe	77.6	96047	31 Rural Resort Dwellers	50.0	96727	31 Rural Resort Dwellers	32.3
95914	49 Senior Sun Seekers	100.0	96048	31 Rural Resort Dwellers	100.0	96728	50 Heartland Communities	95.3
95915	49 Senior Sun Seekers	94.1	96050	31 Rural Resort Dwellers	88.4	96729	46 Rooted Rural	66.7
95916	31 Rural Resort Dwellers	72.5	96051	31 Rural Resort Dwellers	100.0	96730	13 In Style	93.8
95917	38 Industrious Urban Fringe	63.0	96052	49 Senior Sun Seekers	63.3	96731	21 Urban Villages	59.4
95918	31 Rural Resort Dwellers	98.3	96054	46 Rooted Rural	84.9	96732	11 Pacific Heights	47.2
95919	49 Senior Sun Seekers	76.5	96055	46 Rooted Rural	56.5	96734	05 Wealthy Seaboard Suburbs	29.8
95920	38 Industrious Urban Fringe	100.0	96056	31 Rural Resort Dwellers	64.6	96738	13 In Style	97.6
95922	31 Rural Resort Dwellers	100.0	96057	31 Rural Resort Dwellers	100.0	96740	13 In Style	29.2
95923	15 Silver And Gold	100.0	96058	46 Rooted Rural	83.4	96741	07 Exurbanites	31.8
95925	49 Senior Sun Seekers	54.9	96059	31 Rural Resort Dwellers	100.0	96742	65 Social Security Set	100.0
95926	63 Dorms To Diplomas	21.2	96062	31 Rural Resort Dwellers	100.0	96743	09 Urban Chic	46.1
95928	63 Dorms To Diplomas	15.2	96063	31 Rural Resort Dwellers	100.0	96744	11 Pacific Heights	54.0
95932	38 Industrious Urban Fringe	56.9	96064	31 Rural Resort Dwellers	76.3	96746	09 Urban Chic	31.3
95934	49 Senior Sun Seekers	100.0	96065	31 Rural Resort Dwellers	100.0	96747	38 Industrious Urban Fringe	100.0
95935	31 Rural Resort Dwellers	62.7	96067	31 Rural Resort Dwellers	77.1	96748	31 Rural Resort Dwellers	43.0
95936	31 Rural Resort Dwellers	100.0	96069	31 Rural Resort Dwellers	100.0	96749	24 Main Street, USA	77.8
95937	46 Rooted Rural	84.2	96071	31 Rural Resort Dwellers	50.5	96750	31 Rural Resort Dwellers	99.8
95938	24 Main Street, USA	28.0	96073	07 Exurbanites	74.1	96752	18 Cozy And Comfortable	36.3
95939	37 Prairie Living	100.0	96075	31 Rural Resort Dwellers	100.0	96753	16 Enterprising Professionals	38.9
95941	49 Senior Sun Seekers	79.6	96076	31 Rural Resort Dwellers	98.9	96754	20 City Lights	64.2
95942	07 Exurbanites	67.8	96080	31 Rural Resort Dwellers	18.8	96755	10 Pleasant-Ville	56.3
95943	37 Prairie Living	78.1	96085	31 Rural Resort Dwellers	100.0	96756	20 City Lights	37.6
95944	31 Rural Resort Dwellers	100.0	96086	31 Rural Resort Dwellers	100.0	96757	46 Rooted Rural	99.7
95945	31 Rural Resort Dwellers	16.9	96087	31 Rural Resort Dwellers	100.0	96760	19 Milk And Cookies	69.2
95946	15 Silver And Gold	59.3	96088	31 Rural Resort Dwellers	100.0	96761	23 Trendsetters	30.0
95947	50 Heartland Communities	49.9	96091	15 Silver And Gold	63.7	96762	20 City Lights	69.0
95948	38 Industrious Urban Fringe	31.0	96093	33 Midlife Junction	79.6	96763	24 Main Street, USA	100.0
95949	07 Exurbanites	29.8	96094	31 Rural Resort Dwellers	55.4	96764	25 Salt Of The Earth	81.5
95951	38 Industrious Urban Fringe	100.0	96096	31 Rural Resort Dwellers	100.0	96766	11 Pacific Heights	36.8
95953	38 Industrious Urban Fringe	79.8	96097	57 Simple Living	44.0	96768	19 Milk And Cookies	38.3
95954	49 Senior Sun Seekers	90.7	96101	31 Rural Resort Dwellers	49.7	96769	10 Pleasant-Ville	78.4
95955	37 Prairie Living	100.0	96103	15 Silver And Gold	88.5	96770	33 Midlife Junction	100.0
95956	31 Rural Resort Dwellers	100.0	96104	37 Prairie Living	67.8	96771	31 Rural Resort Dwellers	88.8
95957	50 Heartland Communities	50.0	96105	31 Rural Resort Dwellers	100.0	96772	31 Rural Resort Dwellers	81.9
95959	31 Rural Resort Dwellers	39.1	96106	15 Silver And Gold	100.0	96773	18 Cozy And Comfortable	100.0
95960	31 Rural Resort Dwellers	100.0	96107	31 Rural Resort Dwellers	74.8	96774	18 Cozy And Comfortable	100.0
95961	38 Industrious Urban Fringe	39.9	96108	31 Rural Resort Dwellers	92.4	96776	34 Family Foundations	52.3
95962	31 Rural Resort Dwellers	100.0	96109	49 Senior Sun Seekers	85.2	96777	46 Rooted Rural	100.0
95963	37 Prairie Living	25.9	96111	31 Rural Resort Dwellers	100.0	96778	46 Rooted Rural	64.9
95965	46 Rooted Rural	21.2	96112	31 Rural Resort Dwellers	100.0	96779	10 Pleasant-Ville	62.7
95966	49 Senior Sun Seekers	18.8	96113	31 Rural Resort Dwellers	78.1	96780	18 Cozy And Comfortable	100.0
95968	46 Rooted Rural	85.9	96114	07 Exurbanites	59.3	96781	29 Rustbelt Retirees	87.4
95969	49 Senior Sun Seekers	21.6	96115	31 Rural Resort Dwellers	100.0	96782	11 Pacific Heights	50.0
95970	37 Prairie Living	100.0	96116	31 Rural Resort Dwellers	100.0	96783	33 Midlife Junction	59.3
95971	13 In Style	27.0	96117	26 Midland Crowd	98.8	96785	31 Rural Resort Dwellers	99.1
95972	49 Senior Sun Seekers	100.0	96118	31 Rural Resort Dwellers	75.6	96786	40 Military Proximity	42.8
95973	07 Exurbanites	16.6	96119	46 Rooted Rural	100.0	96789	12 Up And Coming Families	36.6
95975	31 Rural Resort Dwellers	99.5	96120	17 Green Acres	56.9	96790	09 Urban Chic	100.0
95977	31 Rural Resort Dwellers	76.9	96121	31 Rural Resort Dwellers	100.0	96791	28 Aspiring Young Families	32.5
95979	49 Senior Sun Seekers	91.9	96122	31 Rural Resort Dwellers	43.1	96792	21 Urban Villages	39.4
95981	31 Rural Resort Dwellers	100.0	96123	46 Rooted Rural	100.0	96793	11 Pacific Heights	38.4
95982	17 Green Acres	57.1	96124	31 Rural Resort Dwellers	100.0	96795	10 Pleasant-Ville	44.2
95983	49 Senior Sun Seekers	62.4	96125	31 Rural Resort Dwellers	100.0	96796	11 Pacific Heights	92.4
95984	49 Senior Sun Seekers	100.0	96126	31 Rural Resort Dwellers	100.0	96797	11 Pacific Heights	42.9
95987	38 Industrious Urban Fringe	82.1	96128	26 Midland Crowd	100.0	96813	36 Old And Newcomers	34.2
95988	24 Main Street, USA	38.5	96130	26 Midland Crowd	34.9	96814	44 Urban Melting Pot	27.5
95991	12 Up And Coming Families	17.1	96132	46 Rooted Rural	100.0	96815	36 Old And Newcomers	42.4
95993	10 Pleasant-Ville	18.0	96133	28 Aspiring Young Families	72.3	96816	11 Pacific Heights	70.7
96001	07 Exurbanites	25.7	96134	38 Industrious Urban Fringe	54.7	96817	44 Urban Melting Pot	44.1
96002	17 Green Acres	28.8	96135	31 Rural Resort Dwellers	100.0	96818	40 Military Proximity	34.8
96003	33 Midlife Junction	14.9	96136	26 Midland Crowd	100.0	96819	11 Pacific Heights	70.2
96006	46 Rooted Rural	100.0	96137	15 Silver And Gold	88.6	96821	03 Connoisseurs	70.3
96007	46 Rooted Rural	24.7	96140	09 Urban Chic	100.0	96822	36 Old And Newcomers	33.9
96008	31 Rural Resort Dwellers	100.0	96141	32 Rustbelt Traditions	86.1	96825	09 Urban Chic	37.6
96010	31 Rural Resort Dwellers	100.0	96142	23 Trendsetters	31.5	96826	36 Old And Newcomers	49.0
96013	50 Heartland Communities	61.2	96143	35 International Marketplace	50.3	96853	40 Military Proximity	100.0
96014	31 Rural Resort Dwellers	100.0	96145	09 Urban Chic	50.6	96858	40 Military Proximity	100.0
96015	31 Rural Resort Dwellers	93.3	96146	08 Laptops And Lattes	100.0	96860	40 Military Proximity	100.0
96016	31 Rural Resort Dwellers	91.3	96148	13 In Style	74.0	96861	40 Military Proximity	100.0
96019	24 Main Street, USA	45.0	96150	13 In Style	10.9	96863	40 Military Proximity	100.0
96020	31 Rural Resort Dwellers	86.1	96161	06 Sophisticated Squires	25.3	97001	31 Rural Resort Dwellers	100.0
96021	46 Rooted Rural	32.6	96162	31 Rural Resort Dwellers	86.4	97002	49 Senior Sun Seekers	24.6
96022	31 Rural Resort Dwellers	32.8	96701	11 Pacific Heights	37.3	97004	17 Green Acres	64.4
96023	46 Rooted Rural	100.0	96704	31 Rural Resort Dwellers	29.9	97005	36 Old And Newcomers	41.5
96024	31 Rural Resort Dwellers	99.8	96705	10 Pleasant-Ville	93.1	97006	16 Enterprising Professionals	34.2
96025	57 Simple Living	44.3	96706	12 Up And Coming Families	37.9	97007	04 Boomburbs	22.4
96027	31 Rural Resort Dwellers	73.1	96707	12 Up And Coming Families	33.3	97008	13 In Style	26.2
96028	31 Rural Resort Dwellers	51.9	96708	09 Urban Chic	80.3	97009	07 Exurbanites	51.3
96031	31 Rural Resort Dwellers	100.0	96710	33 Midlife Junction	100.0	97011	31 Rural Resort Dwellers	99.8
96032	31 Rural Resort Dwellers	100.0	96712	09 Urban Chic	67.3	97013	24 Main Street, USA	24.7
96033	31 Rural Resort Dwellers	100.0	96713	31 Rural Resort Dwellers	60.8	97014	26 Midland Crowd	87.2
96034	46 Rooted Rural	87.8	96716	10 Pleasant-Ville	68.2	97015	13 In Style	27.7
96035	46 Rooted Rural	63.1	96717	21 Urban Villages	54.3	97016	25 Salt Of The Earth	38.1
96038	46 Rooted Rural	87.4	96718	46 Rooted Rural	100.0	97017	17 Green Acres	100.0
96039	49 Senior Sun Seekers	55.6	96719	10 Pleasant-Ville	55.0	97018	17 Green Acres	100.0

CONSUMER TYPE

ZIP CODE	TOP TAPESTRY CONSUMER TYPE	% 2009 HOUSE-HOLDS	ZIP CODE	TOP TAPESTRY CONSUMER TYPE	% 2009 HOUSE-HOLDS	ZIP CODE	TOP TAPESTRY CONSUMER TYPE	% 2009 HOUSE-HOLDS
97019	17 Green Acres	65.6	97216	24 Main Street, USA	58.0	97414	49 Senior Sun Seekers	68.2
97021	46 Rooted Rural	91.9	97217	24 Main Street, USA	52.9	97415	49 Senior Sun Seekers	43.8
97022	17 Green Acres	35.2	97218	24 Main Street, USA	72.7	97416	46 Rooted Rural	66.1
97023	17 Green Acres	56.0	97219	13 In Style	26.5	97417	50 Heartland Communities	72.3
97024	24 Main Street, USA	37.1	97220	24 Main Street, USA	50.0	97419	31 Rural Resort Dwellers	58.1
97026	38 Industrious Urban Fringe	55.2	97221	22 Metropolitans	36.9	97420	33 Midlife Junction	21.2
97027	17 Green Acres	37.8	97222	24 Main Street, USA	47.1	97423	33 Midlife Junction	39.3
97028	13 In Style	100.0	97223	13 In Style	36.1	97424	25 Salt Of The Earth	23.1
97029	37 Prairie Living	100.0	97224	04 Boomburbs	17.8	97426	42 Southern Satellites	22.9
97030	24 Main Street, USA	18.8	97225	16 Enterprising Professionals	28.4	97427	25 Salt Of The Earth	100.0
97031	33 Midlife Junction	15.0	97227	52 Inner City Tenants	22.3	97429	31 Rural Resort Dwellers	55.4
97032	41 Crossroads	33.1	97229	02 Suburban Splendor	32.8	97430	37 Prairie Living	54.8
97034	09 Urban Chic	27.8	97230	24 Main Street, USA	29.8	97431	26 Midland Crowd	62.3
97035	13 In Style	39.6	97231	07 Exurbanites	50.1	97434	46 Rooted Rural	75.4
97037	31 Rural Resort Dwellers	37.8	97232	27 Metro Renters	58.3	97435	46 Rooted Rural	80.2
97038	12 Up And Coming Families	28.3	97233	24 Main Street, USA	50.8	97436	31 Rural Resort Dwellers	100.0
97039	37 Prairie Living	75.2	97236	24 Main Street, USA	55.3	97437	31 Rural Resort Dwellers	64.1
97040	31 Rural Resort Dwellers	95.4	97239	27 Metro Renters	38.5	97438	17 Green Acres	86.6
97041	31 Rural Resort Dwellers	40.6	97266	24 Main Street, USA	58.5	97439	49 Senior Sun Seekers	58.5
97042	17 Green Acres	54.2	97267	24 Main Street, USA	32.1	97441	31 Rural Resort Dwellers	100.0
97045	07 Exurbanites	29.7	97301	48 Great Expectations	20.0	97442	46 Rooted Rural	63.5
97048	25 Salt Of The Earth	45.7	97302	36 Old And Newcomers	16.5	97443	31 Rural Resort Dwellers	98.3
97049	13 In Style	64.5	97303	24 Main Street, USA	23.8	97444	15 Silver And Gold	37.8
97050	46 Rooted Rural	100.0	97304	07 Exurbanites	37.3	97446	26 Midland Crowd	71.8
97051	24 Main Street, USA	39.6	97305	52 Inner City Tenants	26.7	97447	31 Rural Resort Dwellers	63.4
97053	17 Green Acres	47.7	97306	13 In Style	40.0	97448	31 Rural Resort Dwellers	22.7
97054	25 Salt Of The Earth	62.6	97317	07 Exurbanites	27.2	97449	49 Senior Sun Seekers	86.3
97055	26 Midland Crowd	34.8	97321	07 Exurbanites	19.1	97450	31 Rural Resort Dwellers	100.0
97056	17 Green Acres	30.5	97322	28 Aspiring Young Families	21.0	97451	17 Green Acres	100.0
97057	31 Rural Resort Dwellers	100.0	97324	31 Rural Resort Dwellers	75.1	97452	26 Midland Crowd	68.0
97058	33 Midlife Junction	23.2	97325	26 Midland Crowd	37.6	97453	49 Senior Sun Seekers	74.5
97060	06 Sophisticated Squires	25.0	97326	31 Rural Resort Dwellers	45.8	97454	31 Rural Resort Dwellers	53.6
97062	02 Suburban Splendor	23.5	97327	25 Salt Of The Earth	61.5	97455	14 Prosperous Empty Nesters	45.8
97063	49 Senior Sun Seekers	99.8	97329	31 Rural Resort Dwellers	100.0	97456	26 Midland Crowd	56.5
97064	26 Midland Crowd	60.3	97330	22 Metropolitans	13.6	97457	46 Rooted Rural	35.3
97065	46 Rooted Rural	99.6	97331	63 Dorms To Diplomas	100.0	97458	50 Heartland Communities	40.3
97067	31 Rural Resort Dwellers	99.1	97333	63 Dorms To Diplomas	19.2	97459	33 Midlife Junction	51.0
97068	02 Suburban Splendor	40.9	97338	31 Rural Resort Dwellers	26.9	97461	25 Salt Of The Earth	68.0
97070	16 Enterprising Professionals	62.1	97341	31 Rural Resort Dwellers	63.4	97462	31 Rural Resort Dwellers	50.3
97071	38 Industrious Urban Fringe	23.6	97342	31 Rural Resort Dwellers	93.7	97463	46 Rooted Rural	56.9
97080	06 Sophisticated Squires	41.1	97343	31 Rural Resort Dwellers	99.1	97465	49 Senior Sun Seekers	100.0
97086	04 Boomburbs	28.5	97344	26 Midland Crowd	77.0	97466	46 Rooted Rural	99.3
97089	07 Exurbanites	100.0	97345	25 Salt Of The Earth	62.5	97467	49 Senior Sun Seekers	65.3
97101	26 Midland Crowd	48.5	97346	46 Rooted Rural	70.3	97469	46 Rooted Rural	34.4
97103	33 Midlife Junction	14.7	97347	26 Midland Crowd	71.5	97470	33 Midlife Junction	20.5
97106	17 Green Acres	72.9	97348	25 Salt Of The Earth	70.9	97471	26 Midland Crowd	17.5
97107	31 Rural Resort Dwellers	98.9	97350	31 Rural Resort Dwellers	100.0	97473	31 Rural Resort Dwellers	100.0
97108	46 Rooted Rural	98.4	97351	28 Aspiring Young Families	35.7	97476	31 Rural Resort Dwellers	96.8
97109	17 Green Acres	100.0	97352	26 Midland Crowd	34.6	97477	48 Great Expectations	22.1
97111	25 Salt Of The Earth	66.4	97355	25 Salt Of The Earth	21.9	97478	17 Green Acres	29.2
97112	31 Rural Resort Dwellers	75.7	97357	26 Midland Crowd	97.1	97479	50 Heartland Communities	39.3
97113	12 Up And Coming Families	37.2	97358	25 Salt Of The Earth	75.9	97480	50 Heartland Communities	85.9
97114	26 Midland Crowd	53.0	97360	25 Salt Of The Earth	57.3	97481	25 Salt Of The Earth	100.0
97115	17 Green Acres	90.6	97361	55 College Towns	40.7	97484	31 Rural Resort Dwellers	100.0
97116	17 Green Acres	47.3	97362	30 Retirement Communities	32.1	97486	31 Rural Resort Dwellers	100.0
97117	07 Exurbanites	73.4	97364	31 Rural Resort Dwellers	100.0	97487	26 Midland Crowd	56.4
97119	17 Green Acres	92.0	97365	31 Rural Resort Dwellers	20.6	97488	31 Rural Resort Dwellers	100.0
97121	24 Main Street, USA	86.2	97366	31 Rural Resort Dwellers	100.0	97489	31 Rural Resort Dwellers	75.4
97122	31 Rural Resort Dwellers	100.0	97367	31 Rural Resort Dwellers	57.3	97490	17 Green Acres	52.3
97123	12 Up And Coming Families	26.9	97368	31 Rural Resort Dwellers	98.4	97492	25 Salt Of The Earth	93.4
97124	16 Enterprising Professionals	19.2	97369	31 Rural Resort Dwellers	100.0	97493	31 Rural Resort Dwellers	62.6
97125	17 Green Acres	100.0	97370	28 Aspiring Young Families	32.0	97495	46 Rooted Rural	100.0
97127	26 Midland Crowd	100.0	97371	37 Prairie Living	41.7	97496	48 Great Expectations	45.3
97128	24 Main Street, USA	38.2	97374	17 Green Acres	31.9	97497	46 Rooted Rural	63.7
97131	31 Rural Resort Dwellers	74.3	97375	17 Green Acres	100.0	97498	31 Rural Resort Dwellers	100.0
97132	17 Green Acres	28.4	97376	31 Rural Resort Dwellers	96.5	97499	42 Southern Satellites	56.0
97133	07 Exurbanites	52.9	97377	37 Prairie Living	67.5	97501	26 Midland Crowd	20.0
97136	49 Senior Sun Seekers	58.4	97378	24 Main Street, USA	48.8	97502	24 Main Street, USA	25.3
97137	26 Midland Crowd	60.1	97380	26 Midland Crowd	97.5	97503	41 Crossroads	47.0
97138	31 Rural Resort Dwellers	47.2	97381	24 Main Street, USA	50.9	97504	30 Retirement Communities	22.9
97140	12 Up And Coming Families	55.0	97383	28 Aspiring Young Families	27.6	97520	22 Metropolitans	40.6
97141	31 Rural Resort Dwellers	32.8	97385	17 Green Acres	81.2	97522	46 Rooted Rural	93.5
97144	17 Green Acres	100.0	97386	50 Heartland Communities	32.4	97523	49 Senior Sun Seekers	43.2
97145	15 Silver And Gold	73.2	97389	26 Midland Crowd	73.0	97524	26 Midland Crowd	56.2
97146	26 Midland Crowd	36.1	97390	15 Silver And Gold	59.7	97525	31 Rural Resort Dwellers	62.0
97148	17 Green Acres	75.8	97391	26 Midland Crowd	29.2	97526	31 Rural Resort Dwellers	24.9
97149	15 Silver And Gold	100.0	97392	07 Exurbanites	46.4	97527	31 Rural Resort Dwellers	52.8
97201	27 Metro Renters	64.8	97394	31 Rural Resort Dwellers	50.6	97530	31 Rural Resort Dwellers	82.9
97202	22 Metropolitans	36.6	97396	32 Rustbelt Traditions	40.4	97531	46 Rooted Rural	39.5
97203	24 Main Street, USA	52.6	97401	63 Dorms To Diplomas	26.8	97532	31 Rural Resort Dwellers	99.4
97204	65 Social Security Set	100.0	97402	26 Midland Crowd	17.0	97534	46 Rooted Rural	100.0
97205	65 Social Security Set	53.6	97403	55 College Towns	28.5	97535	49 Senior Sun Seekers	75.0
97206	24 Main Street, USA	67.2	97404	18 Cozy And Comfortable	29.7	97536	31 Rural Resort Dwellers	82.5
97209	27 Metro Renters	79.8	97405	07 Exurbanites	27.4	97537	31 Rural Resort Dwellers	73.4
97210	27 Metro Renters	51.1	97406	31 Rural Resort Dwellers	100.0	97538	31 Rural Resort Dwellers	85.1
97211	24 Main Street, USA	43.3	97408	13 In Style	29.3	97539	49 Senior Sun Seekers	83.1
97212	05 Wealthy Seaboard Suburbs	21.1	97410	31 Rural Resort Dwellers	82.9	97540	33 Midlife Junction	50.7
97213	24 Main Street, USA	28.6	97411	31 Rural Resort Dwellers	61.7	97541	31 Rural Resort Dwellers	56.1
97214	27 Metro Renters	48.4	97412	37 Prairie Living	100.0	97543	31 Rural Resort Dwellers	100.0
97215	22 Metropolitans	50.4	97413	31 Rural Resort Dwellers	98.6	97544	31 Rural Resort Dwellers	100.0

ZIP CODE	TOP TAPESTRY CONSUMER TYPE	% 2009 HOUSE-HOLDS	ZIP CODE	TOP TAPESTRY CONSUMER TYPE	% 2009 HOUSE-HOLDS	ZIP CODE	TOP TAPESTRY CONSUMER TYPE	% 2009 HOUSE-HOLDS
97601	48 Great Expectations	28.1	97884	31 Rural Resort Dwellers	100.0	98134	27 Metro Renters	92.6
97603	26 Midland Crowd	17.6	97885	46 Rooted Rural	66.4	98136	09 Urban Chic	40.2
97620	37 Prairie Living	100.0	97886	46 Rooted Rural	79.3	98144	44 Urban Melting Pot	19.3
97621	46 Rooted Rural	100.0	97901	37 Prairie Living	100.0	98146	24 Main Street, USA	23.5
97623	49 Senior Sun Seekers	52.9	97903	37 Prairie Living	100.0	98148	36 Old And Newcomers	46.4
97624	49 Senior Sun Seekers	61.2	97904	37 Prairie Living	100.0	98155	10 Pleasant-Ville	21.8
97625	26 Midland Crowd	94.1	97906	37 Prairie Living	100.0	98166	36 Old And Newcomers	18.9
97627	31 Rural Resort Dwellers	82.6	97907	50 Heartland Communities	83.6	98168	24 Main Street, USA	44.3
97630	50 Heartland Communities	32.8	97908	37 Prairie Living	100.0	98177	03 Connoisseurs	26.7
97632	38 Industrious Urban Fringe	56.7	97909	37 Prairie Living	100.0	98178	24 Main Street, USA	25.4
97633	46 Rooted Rural	69.5	97910	37 Prairie Living	100.0	98188	18 Cozy And Comfortable	26.5
97635	46 Rooted Rural	100.0	97911	37 Prairie Living	100.0	98195	63 Dorms To Diplomas	100.0
97636	37 Prairie Living	100.0	97913	37 Prairie Living	38.3	98198	52 Inner City Tenants	18.9
97637	37 Prairie Living	98.5	97914	33 Midlife Junction	27.2	98199	23 Trendsetters	25.9
97638	46 Rooted Rural	100.0	97917	37 Prairie Living	100.0	98201	24 Main Street, USA	29.4
97639	46 Rooted Rural	100.0	97918	46 Rooted Rural	40.1	98203	24 Main Street, USA	33.4
97640	37 Prairie Living	100.0	97920	37 Prairie Living	100.0	98204	28 Aspiring Young Families	31.4
97701	07 Exurbanites	17.7	98001	06 Sophisticated Squires	35.3	98205	12 Up And Coming Families	60.2
97702	26 Midland Crowd	15.3	98002	24 Main Street, USA	28.7	98208	06 Sophisticated Squires	26.1
97707	31 Rural Resort Dwellers	52.5	98003	39 Young And Restless	20.5	98220	37 Prairie Living	75.0
97710	37 Prairie Living	100.0	98004	09 Urban Chic	16.7	98221	17 Green Acres	24.1
97711	37 Prairie Living	100.0	98005	16 Enterprising Professionals	31.6	98223	17 Green Acres	35.3
97712	07 Exurbanites	85.2	98006	02 Suburban Splendor	22.9	98224	31 Rural Resort Dwellers	100.0
97720	50 Heartland Communities	62.5	98007	39 Young And Restless	30.8	98225	55 College Towns	21.2
97721	37 Prairie Living	100.0	98008	05 Wealthy Seaboard Suburbs	41.8	98226	36 Old And Newcomers	31.0
97730	31 Rural Resort Dwellers	100.0	98010	06 Sophisticated Squires	31.9	98229	13 In Style	53.9
97731	46 Rooted Rural	41.1	98011	13 In Style	29.1	98230	31 Rural Resort Dwellers	30.7
97733	46 Rooted Rural	50.6	98012	06 Sophisticated Squires	30.2	98232	31 Rural Resort Dwellers	36.1
97734	26 Midland Crowd	68.3	98014	06 Sophisticated Squires	56.4	98233	24 Main Street, USA	37.2
97735	46 Rooted Rural	100.0	98019	04 Boomburbs	61.3	98236	31 Rural Resort Dwellers	79.8
97737	49 Senior Sun Seekers	100.0	98020	30 Retirement Communities	32.4	98237	46 Rooted Rural	42.9
97738	25 Salt Of The Earth	69.7	98021	06 Sophisticated Squires	43.4	98239	31 Rural Resort Dwellers	48.8
97739	49 Senior Sun Seekers	85.6	98022	24 Main Street, USA	22.1	98240	17 Green Acres	60.2
97741	26 Midland Crowd	39.6	98023	06 Sophisticated Squires	19.3	98241	50 Heartland Communities	68.4
97750	49 Senior Sun Seekers	100.0	98024	17 Green Acres	54.3	98244	17 Green Acres	55.5
97751	37 Prairie Living	100.0	98026	13 In Style	16.3	98245	31 Rural Resort Dwellers	96.9
97752	37 Prairie Living	100.0	98027	02 Suburban Splendor	31.6	98247	17 Green Acres	43.6
97753	31 Rural Resort Dwellers	100.0	98028	13 In Style	21.9	98248	17 Green Acres	31.7
97754	53 Home Town	27.1	98029	04 Boomburbs	63.2	98249	31 Rural Resort Dwellers	100.0
97756	26 Midland Crowd	32.3	98030	06 Sophisticated Squires	20.2	98250	15 Silver And Gold	49.7
97758	17 Green Acres	74.4	98031	06 Sophisticated Squires	32.0	98251	26 Midland Crowd	48.9
97759	31 Rural Resort Dwellers	51.1	98032	16 Enterprising Professionals	21.9	98252	26 Midland Crowd	42.2
97760	31 Rural Resort Dwellers	69.1	98033	09 Urban Chic	24.2	98253	15 Silver And Gold	58.3
97761	51 Metro City Edge	99.6	98034	13 In Style	24.4	98257	15 Silver And Gold	52.5
97801	48 Great Expectations	25.7	98036	06 Sophisticated Squires	24.3	98258	12 Up And Coming Families	33.9
97810	26 Midland Crowd	64.1	98037	36 Old And Newcomers	26.5	98260	31 Rural Resort Dwellers	99.4
97812	37 Prairie Living	100.0	98038	12 Up And Coming Families	34.9	98261	31 Rural Resort Dwellers	58.0
97813	37 Prairie Living	60.6	98039	01 Top Rung	99.5	98262	31 Rural Resort Dwellers	100.0
97814	50 Heartland Communities	32.0	98040	03 Connoisseurs	35.5	98264	17 Green Acres	27.9
97818	26 Midland Crowd	36.5	98042	06 Sophisticated Squires	34.9	98266	41 Crossroads	84.5
97820	26 Midland Crowd	100.0	98043	28 Aspiring Young Families	31.7	98267	31 Rural Resort Dwellers	83.3
97823	37 Prairie Living	100.0	98045	06 Sophisticated Squires	32.3	98270	12 Up And Coming Families	32.8
97824	31 Rural Resort Dwellers	89.5	98047	24 Main Street, USA	63.7	98271	17 Green Acres	22.3
97825	46 Rooted Rural	100.0	98051	26 Midland Crowd	37.9	98272	06 Sophisticated Squires	23.7
97826	46 Rooted Rural	82.0	98052	16 Enterprising Professionals	36.7	98273	24 Main Street, USA	19.3
97827	46 Rooted Rural	46.8	98053	02 Suburban Splendor	80.7	98274	24 Main Street, USA	55.5
97828	31 Rural Resort Dwellers	38.1	98055	36 Old And Newcomers	31.9	98275	16 Enterprising Professionals	21.1
97830	49 Senior Sun Seekers	100.0	98056	13 In Style	15.1	98277	26 Midland Crowd	13.1
97833	37 Prairie Living	83.4	98057	36 Old And Newcomers	46.7	98278	40 Military Proximity	100.0
97834	49 Senior Sun Seekers	57.7	98058	06 Sophisticated Squires	21.4	98279	15 Silver And Gold	70.4
97835	37 Prairie Living	100.0	98059	16 Enterprising Professionals	19.3	98281	31 Rural Resort Dwellers	100.0
97836	37 Prairie Living	48.3	98065	02 Suburban Splendor	55.2	98282	31 Rural Resort Dwellers	62.1
97837	31 Rural Resort Dwellers	79.5	98070	07 Exurbanites	43.1	98283	46 Rooted Rural	51.6
97838	41 Crossroads	23.0	98072	02 Suburban Splendor	44.4	98284	26 Midland Crowd	35.6
97839	37 Prairie Living	100.0	98074	02 Suburban Splendor	44.7	98288	31 Rural Resort Dwellers	100.0
97840	31 Rural Resort Dwellers	100.0	98075	04 Boomburbs	42.3	98290	06 Sophisticated Squires	36.1
97841	37 Prairie Living	100.0	98077	02 Suburban Splendor	67.3	98292	17 Green Acres	35.3
97842	31 Rural Resort Dwellers	100.0	98087	06 Sophisticated Squires	21.2	98294	12 Up And Coming Families	31.0
97843	37 Prairie Living	100.0	98092	07 Exurbanites	33.6	98295	26 Midland Crowd	74.5
97844	41 Crossroads	62.3	98101	27 Metro Renters	88.0	98296	06 Sophisticated Squires	64.7
97845	46 Rooted Rural	44.2	98102	27 Metro Renters	81.9	98303	15 Silver And Gold	100.0
97846	31 Rural Resort Dwellers	56.4	98103	23 Trendsetters	30.7	98304	31 Rural Resort Dwellers	78.3
97848	46 Rooted Rural	80.0	98104	65 Social Security Set	65.9	98305	31 Rural Resort Dwellers	100.0
97850	33 Midlife Junction	15.8	98105	63 Dorms To Diplomas	34.7	98310	36 Old And Newcomers	24.4
97856	37 Prairie Living	100.0	98106	28 Aspiring Young Families	29.3	98311	28 Aspiring Young Families	28.3
97857	46 Rooted Rural	90.4	98107	23 Trendsetters	37.2	98312	48 Great Expectations	20.7
97862	46 Rooted Rural	25.1	98108	11 Pacific Heights	35.0	98315	40 Military Proximity	99.4
97864	37 Prairie Living	100.0	98109	27 Metro Renters	56.2	98320	49 Senior Sun Seekers	97.6
97865	46 Rooted Rural	100.0	98110	02 Suburban Splendor	38.4	98321	26 Midland Crowd	40.2
97867	46 Rooted Rural	89.4	98112	03 Connoisseurs	20.5	98323	12 Up And Coming Families	85.2
97868	46 Rooted Rural	81.9	98115	22 Metropolitans	37.7	98325	31 Rural Resort Dwellers	82.5
97869	46 Rooted Rural	99.7	98116	09 Urban Chic	31.0	98326	49 Senior Sun Seekers	77.0
97870	49 Senior Sun Seekers	68.3	98117	22 Metropolitans	32.9	98327	12 Up And Coming Families	99.8
97873	46 Rooted Rural	99.3	98118	24 Main Street, USA	20.7	98328	17 Green Acres	56.9
97874	49 Senior Sun Seekers	100.0	98119	27 Metro Renters	56.8	98329	26 Midland Crowd	38.8
97875	26 Midland Crowd	40.3	98121	27 Metro Renters	94.8	98330	31 Rural Resort Dwellers	50.3
97876	31 Rural Resort Dwellers	62.0	98122	27 Metro Renters	54.8	98331	46 Rooted Rural	34.2
97877	31 Rural Resort Dwellers	72.7	98125	22 Metropolitans	20.8	98332	07 Exurbanites	53.7
97882	26 Midland Crowd	36.8	98126	22 Metropolitans	18.3	98333	07 Exurbanites	100.0
97883	46 Rooted Rural	54.1	98133	36 Old And Newcomers	26.8	98335	07 Exurbanites	36.9

CONSUMER TYPE

ZIP CODE	TOP TAPESTRY CONSUMER TYPE	% 2009 HOUSE-HOLDS	ZIP CODE	TOP TAPESTRY CONSUMER TYPE	% 2009 HOUSE-HOLDS	ZIP CODE	TOP TAPESTRY CONSUMER TYPE	% 2009 HOUSE-HOLDS
98336	46 Rooted Rural	98.8	98548	49 Senior Sun Seekers	93.5	98822	26 Midland Crowd	93.1
98337	48 Great Expectations	53.9	98550	32 Rustbelt Traditions	34.5	98823	26 Midland Crowd	56.3
98338	17 Green Acres	42.0	98552	46 Rooted Rural	100.0	98826	31 Rural Resort Dwellers	64.3
98339	26 Midland Crowd	67.5	98555	49 Senior Sun Seekers	100.0	98827	31 Rural Resort Dwellers	70.7
98340	15 Silver And Gold	90.3	98557	50 Heartland Communities	38.6	98828	26 Midland Crowd	74.3
98342	12 Up And Coming Families	54.9	98560	31 Rural Resort Dwellers	100.0	98830	37 Prairie Living	100.0
98345	13 In Style	100.0	98562	31 Rural Resort Dwellers	99.7	98831	31 Rural Resort Dwellers	51.7
98346	13 In Style	41.0	98563	17 Green Acres	33.4	98832	37 Prairie Living	99.6
98349	31 Rural Resort Dwellers	58.1	98564	31 Rural Resort Dwellers	66.4	98833	31 Rural Resort Dwellers	100.0
98351	26 Midland Crowd	75.4	98568	46 Rooted Rural	84.4	98834	31 Rural Resort Dwellers	84.1
98354	36 Old And Newcomers	32.5	98569	49 Senior Sun Seekers	41.3	98837	17 Green Acres	21.6
98355	49 Senior Sun Seekers	95.4	98570	46 Rooted Rural	69.7	98840	33 Midlife Junction	35.5
98356	33 Midlife Junction	31.1	98571	49 Senior Sun Seekers	78.0	98841	26 Midland Crowd	29.3
98358	15 Silver And Gold	100.0	98572	46 Rooted Rural	100.0	98843	38 Industrious Urban Fringe	66.4
98359	17 Green Acres	81.7	98575	46 Rooted Rural	100.0	98844	31 Rural Resort Dwellers	34.7
98360	12 Up And Coming Families	55.0	98576	26 Midland Crowd	41.7	98845	37 Prairie Living	95.3
98361	49 Senior Sun Seekers	66.9	98577	25 Salt Of The Earth	35.6	98846	46 Rooted Rural	98.9
98362	33 Midlife Junction	36.3	98579	26 Midland Crowd	87.3	98847	26 Midland Crowd	52.4
98363	31 Rural Resort Dwellers	27.1	98580	26 Midland Crowd	67.6	98848	47 Las Casas	20.8
98365	15 Silver And Gold	96.1	98581	49 Senior Sun Seekers	100.0	98849	46 Rooted Rural	67.4
98366	24 Main Street, USA	23.2	98582	46 Rooted Rural	98.8	98850	41 Crossroads	78.6
98367	17 Green Acres	53.0	98584	31 Rural Resort Dwellers	18.1	98851	46 Rooted Rural	50.5
98368	31 Rural Resort Dwellers	37.2	98585	31 Rural Resort Dwellers	44.8	98852	36 Old And Newcomers	100.0
98370	17 Green Acres	28.9	98586	50 Heartland Communities	49.5	98855	46 Rooted Rural	74.9
98371	24 Main Street, USA	33.1	98587	46 Rooted Rural	100.0	98856	31 Rural Resort Dwellers	61.2
98372	36 Old And Newcomers	18.7	98588	31 Rural Resort Dwellers	56.2	98857	38 Industrious Urban Fringe	67.2
98373	28 Aspiring Young Families	21.5	98589	26 Midland Crowd	67.5	98858	37 Prairie Living	100.0
98374	06 Sophisticated Squires	43.8	98590	50 Heartland Communities	63.5	98859	31 Rural Resort Dwellers	100.0
98375	26 Midland Crowd	38.2	98591	46 Rooted Rural	92.3	98862	31 Rural Resort Dwellers	99.9
98376	31 Rural Resort Dwellers	98.9	98592	31 Rural Resort Dwellers	98.8	98901	17 Green Acres	21.0
98377	49 Senior Sun Seekers	55.2	98593	26 Midland Crowd	78.3	98902	57 Simple Living	15.3
98380	17 Green Acres	73.6	98595	49 Senior Sun Seekers	50.7	98903	17 Green Acres	27.6
98381	41 Crossroads	44.4	98596	26 Midland Crowd	58.1	98908	17 Green Acres	34.4
98382	15 Silver And Gold	33.3	98597	26 Midland Crowd	77.8	98922	31 Rural Resort Dwellers	83.4
98383	39 Young And Restless	25.4	98601	26 Midland Crowd	85.0	98923	26 Midland Crowd	79.7
98387	12 Up And Coming Families	35.1	98602	31 Rural Resort Dwellers	72.3	98926	63 Dorms To Diplomas	20.6
98388	13 In Style	49.9	98603	26 Midland Crowd	74.0	98930	38 Industrious Urban Fringe	58.4
98390	28 Aspiring Young Families	38.4	98604	12 Up And Coming Families	38.5	98932	38 Industrious Urban Fringe	88.9
98391	12 Up And Coming Families	39.3	98605	31 Rural Resort Dwellers	76.8	98933	38 Industrious Urban Fringe	63.8
98392	26 Midland Crowd	53.7	98606	06 Sophisticated Squires	53.5	98935	59 Southwestern Families	49.4
98394	31 Rural Resort Dwellers	76.3	98607	04 Boomburbs	34.2	98936	26 Midland Crowd	73.2
98402	65 Social Security Set	75.2	98610	41 Crossroads	58.3	98937	26 Midland Crowd	48.4
98403	27 Metro Renters	28.4	98611	25 Salt Of The Earth	36.7	98938	38 Industrious Urban Fringe	49.1
98404	38 Industrious Urban Fringe	28.3	98612	31 Rural Resort Dwellers	64.3	98942	17 Green Acres	60.3
98405	24 Main Street, USA	22.9	98613	46 Rooted Rural	86.0	98944	38 Industrious Urban Fringe	56.3
98406	22 Metropolitans	17.8	98616	26 Midland Crowd	100.0	98946	17 Green Acres	66.0
98407	24 Main Street, USA	22.8	98617	46 Rooted Rural	100.0	98947	38 Industrious Urban Fringe	57.5
98408	32 Rustbelt Traditions	53.1	98619	31 Rural Resort Dwellers	100.0	98948	38 Industrious Urban Fringe	58.7
98409	52 Inner City Tenants	25.3	98620	31 Rural Resort Dwellers	37.1	98951	38 Industrious Urban Fringe	35.7
98416	55 College Towns	100.0	98621	31 Rural Resort Dwellers	94.0	98952	38 Industrious Urban Fringe	73.1
98418	48 Great Expectations	43.7	98624	31 Rural Resort Dwellers	100.0	98953	37 Prairie Living	32.3
98421	37 Prairie Living	98.4	98625	17 Green Acres	33.1	99001	33 Midlife Junction	55.0
98422	12 Up And Coming Families	25.1	98626	17 Green Acres	20.2	99003	17 Green Acres	55.4
98424	28 Aspiring Young Families	40.3	98628	50 Heartland Communities	100.0	99004	55 College Towns	38.1
98433	40 Military Proximity	93.9	98629	17 Green Acres	52.7	99005	06 Sophisticated Squires	51.3
98438	40 Military Proximity	100.0	98631	49 Senior Sun Seekers	62.9	99006	33 Midlife Junction	38.1
98439	52 Inner City Tenants	100.0	98632	17 Green Acres	13.7	99008	37 Prairie Living	68.6
98443	17 Green Acres	58.3	98635	31 Rural Resort Dwellers	49.0	99009	26 Midland Crowd	74.2
98444	52 Inner City Tenants	28.8	98638	31 Rural Resort Dwellers	100.0	99011	40 Military Proximity	99.9
98445	18 Cozy And Comfortable	31.5	98640	49 Senior Sun Seekers	100.0	99012	46 Rooted Rural	56.7
98446	17 Green Acres	39.9	98642	17 Green Acres	37.3	99013	51 Metro City Edge	40.0
98447	29 Rustbelt Retirees	100.0	98643	31 Rural Resort Dwellers	100.0	99016	26 Midland Crowd	24.9
98465	36 Old And Newcomers	30.9	98645	26 Midland Crowd	59.9	99017	37 Prairie Living	100.0
98466	36 Old And Newcomers	25.7	98647	46 Rooted Rural	98.1	99018	46 Rooted Rural	79.4
98467	07 Exurbanites	34.6	98648	31 Rural Resort Dwellers	51.2	99019	12 Up And Coming Families	69.7
98498	14 Prosperous Empty Nesters	23.0	98649	25 Salt Of The Earth	83.5	99021	26 Midland Crowd	36.9
98499	52 Inner City Tenants	37.0	98650	31 Rural Resort Dwellers	100.0	99022	24 Main Street, USA	29.5
98501	07 Exurbanites	15.8	98651	31 Rural Resort Dwellers	100.0	99023	07 Exurbanites	94.1
98502	13 In Style	24.4	98660	24 Main Street, USA	26.0	99025	19 Milk And Cookies	42.1
98503	28 Aspiring Young Families	34.7	98661	24 Main Street, USA	22.1	99026	17 Green Acres	42.2
98505	13 In Style	100.0	98662	17 Green Acres	20.8	99027	17 Green Acres	53.5
98506	36 Old And Newcomers	30.4	98663	48 Great Expectations	31.6	99029	37 Prairie Living	57.0
98512	13 In Style	28.1	98664	24 Main Street, USA	30.2	99030	25 Salt Of The Earth	75.2
98513	26 Midland Crowd	22.0	98665	06 Sophisticated Squires	19.5	99031	37 Prairie Living	58.3
98516	06 Sophisticated Squires	36.3	98671	17 Green Acres	49.3	99032	37 Prairie Living	100.0
98520	53 Home Town	11.8	98672	26 Midland Crowd	22.6	99033	50 Heartland Communities	92.5
98524	15 Silver And Gold	41.1	98674	17 Green Acres	44.0	99034	26 Midland Crowd	100.0
98526	46 Rooted Rural	100.0	98675	26 Midland Crowd	69.3	99036	07 Exurbanites	95.6
98528	31 Rural Resort Dwellers	46.1	98682	12 Up And Coming Families	50.4	99037	06 Sophisticated Squires	27.1
98531	33 Midlife Junction	28.1	98683	12 Up And Coming Families	23.1	99040	51 Metro City Edge	71.2
98532	17 Green Acres	18.9	98684	28 Aspiring Young Families	36.0	99101	46 Rooted Rural	64.9
98533	49 Senior Sun Seekers	77.2	98685	06 Sophisticated Squires	39.9	99103	37 Prairie Living	97.3
98535	49 Senior Sun Seekers	60.4	98686	13 In Style	28.0	99105	37 Prairie Living	100.0
98536	49 Senior Sun Seekers	100.0	98801	07 Exurbanites	17.8	99107	31 Rural Resort Dwellers	100.0
98537	25 Salt Of The Earth	59.5	98802	26 Midland Crowd	21.5	99109	31 Rural Resort Dwellers	28.4
98538	46 Rooted Rural	80.9	98812	47 Las Casas	34.8	99110	26 Midland Crowd	61.9
98541	26 Midland Crowd	25.3	98813	42 Southern Satellites	37.9	99111	33 Midlife Junction	56.8
98542	46 Rooted Rural	100.0	98814	31 Rural Resort Dwellers	100.0	99113	37 Prairie Living	97.8
98546	15 Silver And Gold	46.9	98815	26 Midland Crowd	31.3	99114	31 Rural Resort Dwellers	36.3
98547	49 Senior Sun Seekers	58.8	98816	33 Midlife Junction	41.3	99115	49 Senior Sun Seekers	76.8

ZIP CODE	TOP TAPESTRY CONSUMER TYPE	% 2009 HOUSE-HOLDS	ZIP CODE	TOP TAPESTRY CONSUMER TYPE	% 2009 HOUSE-HOLDS	ZIP CODE	TOP TAPESTRY CONSUMER TYPE	% 2009 HOUSE-HOLDS
99116	29 Rustbelt Retirees	27.8	99403	33 Midlife Junction	24.9	99665	51 Metro City Edge	100.0
99117	31 Rural Resort Dwellers	100.0	99501	52 Inner City Tenants	40.6	99667	31 Rural Resort Dwellers	100.0
99118	31 Rural Resort Dwellers	63.8	99502	06 Sophisticated Squires	28.0	99668	56 Rural Bypasses	100.0
99119	31 Rural Resort Dwellers	72.8	99503	52 Inner City Tenants	24.2	99669	17 Green Acres	27.8
99121	31 Rural Resort Dwellers	100.0	99504	28 Aspiring Young Families	23.4	99670	17 Green Acres	100.0
99122	33 Midlife Junction	52.1	99505	40 Military Proximity	100.0	99671	51 Metro City Edge	100.0
99123	31 Rural Resort Dwellers	100.0	99506	40 Military Proximity	100.0	99672	31 Rural Resort Dwellers	73.1
99125	37 Prairie Living	100.0	99507	28 Aspiring Young Families	30.0	99674	31 Rural Resort Dwellers	100.0
99126	46 Rooted Rural	82.0	99508	52 Inner City Tenants	25.9	99676	31 Rural Resort Dwellers	100.0
99128	37 Prairie Living	84.9	99515	06 Sophisticated Squires	37.5	99679	38 Industrious Urban Fringe	100.0
99129	41 Crossroads	65.0	99516	02 Suburban Splendor	56.0	99681	59 Southwestern Families	100.0
99130	37 Prairie Living	97.4	99517	28 Aspiring Young Families	26.2	99682	53 Home Town	100.0
99131	31 Rural Resort Dwellers	100.0	99518	28 Aspiring Young Families	39.2	99684	19 Milk And Cookies	100.0
99133	50 Heartland Communities	70.4	99540	22 Metropolitans	62.1	99685	16 Enterprising Professionals	100.0
99134	37 Prairie Living	100.0	99546	19 Milk And Cookies	100.0	99686	06 Sophisticated Squires	46.7
99135	31 Rural Resort Dwellers	100.0	99547	19 Milk And Cookies	100.0	99688	31 Rural Resort Dwellers	57.2
99136	37 Prairie Living	100.0	99549	19 Milk And Cookies	100.0	99689	26 Midland Crowd	100.0
99137	31 Rural Resort Dwellers	100.0	99551	38 Industrious Urban Fringe	100.0	99691	33 Midlife Junction	100.0
99138	46 Rooted Rural	97.7	99552	38 Industrious Urban Fringe	100.0	99701	28 Aspiring Young Families	23.9
99139	31 Rural Resort Dwellers	56.4	99553	48 Great Expectations	100.0	99702	40 Military Proximity	100.0
99140	50 Heartland Communities	97.1	99554	38 Industrious Urban Fringe	100.0	99703	40 Military Proximity	100.0
99141	31 Rural Resort Dwellers	38.7	99555	38 Industrious Urban Fringe	100.0	99704	31 Rural Resort Dwellers	100.0
99143	37 Prairie Living	99.4	99556	31 Rural Resort Dwellers	74.4	99705	19 Milk And Cookies	50.3
99147	31 Rural Resort Dwellers	100.0	99557	56 Rural Bypasses	98.0	99709	28 Aspiring Young Families	29.3
99148	31 Rural Resort Dwellers	77.6	99558	51 Metro City Edge	100.0	99712	06 Sophisticated Squires	63.7
99150	46 Rooted Rural	86.9	99559	28 Aspiring Young Families	35.7	99714	17 Green Acres	79.8
99153	50 Heartland Communities	72.6	99561	59 Southwestern Families	100.0	99720	51 Metro City Edge	100.0
99156	31 Rural Resort Dwellers	79.2	99563	51 Metro City Edge	100.0	99721	19 Milk And Cookies	100.0
99157	31 Rural Resort Dwellers	100.0	99564	19 Milk And Cookies	100.0	99722	51 Metro City Edge	100.0
99158	37 Prairie Living	100.0	99565	19 Milk And Cookies	100.0	99723	19 Milk And Cookies	66.4
99159	29 Rustbelt Retirees	76.1	99567	06 Sophisticated Squires	67.1	99724	51 Metro City Edge	100.0
99161	33 Midlife Junction	71.4	99568	31 Rural Resort Dwellers	100.0	99726	62 Modest Income Homes	100.0
99163	63 Dorms To Diplomas	43.6	99569	38 Industrious Urban Fringe	100.0	99727	38 Industrious Urban Fringe	100.0
99164	63 Dorms To Diplomas	100.0	99571	48 Great Expectations	50.0	99729	13 In Style	100.0
99166	31 Rural Resort Dwellers	58.4	99572	31 Rural Resort Dwellers	100.0	99730	50 Heartland Communities	100.0
99167	25 Salt Of The Earth	51.9	99573	31 Rural Resort Dwellers	72.8	99733	50 Heartland Communities	100.0
99169	29 Rustbelt Retirees	25.8	99574	13 In Style	53.3	99734	66 Unclassified	100.0
99170	37 Prairie Living	98.4	99575	56 Rural Bypasses	100.0	99736	38 Industrious Urban Fringe	100.0
99171	37 Prairie Living	100.0	99576	13 In Style	58.7	99737	17 Green Acres	61.6
99173	46 Rooted Rural	79.5	99577	06 Sophisticated Squires	39.2	99739	51 Metro City Edge	100.0
99176	37 Prairie Living	100.0	99578	59 Southwestern Families	100.0	99740	50 Heartland Communities	97.6
99179	37 Prairie Living	100.0	99579	19 Milk And Cookies	100.0	99741	51 Metro City Edge	100.0
99180	31 Rural Resort Dwellers	65.3	99580	38 Industrious Urban Fringe	100.0	99742	59 Southwestern Families	100.0
99181	46 Rooted Rural	51.4	99583	48 Great Expectations	100.0	99743	13 In Style	75.0
99185	31 Rural Resort Dwellers	87.6	99585	51 Metro City Edge	100.0	99744	31 Rural Resort Dwellers	85.7
99201	65 Social Security Set	33.6	99586	31 Rural Resort Dwellers	100.0	99745	51 Metro City Edge	100.0
99202	48 Great Expectations	22.1	99587	22 Metropolitans	38.7	99746	51 Metro City Edge	100.0
99203	22 Metropolitans	22.6	99588	31 Rural Resort Dwellers	72.9	99747	19 Milk And Cookies	100.0
99204	36 Old And Newcomers	27.9	99589	59 Southwestern Families	100.0	99748	51 Metro City Edge	100.0
99205	32 Rustbelt Traditions	35.4	99591	19 Milk And Cookies	100.0	99749	38 Industrious Urban Fringe	100.0
99206	33 Midlife Junction	21.7	99602	51 Metro City Edge	100.0	99750	38 Industrious Urban Fringe	100.0
99207	48 Great Expectations	57.0	99603	13 In Style	29.4	99751	38 Industrious Urban Fringe	100.0
99208	07 Exurbanites	17.0	99604	51 Metro City Edge	100.0	99752	45 City Strivers	30.6
99212	48 Great Expectations	33.3	99606	26 Midland Crowd	100.0	99753	51 Metro City Edge	100.0
99216	36 Old And Newcomers	25.0	99607	38 Industrious Urban Fringe	100.0	99755	13 In Style	75.0
99217	36 Old And Newcomers	19.2	99610	31 Rural Resort Dwellers	100.0	99756	31 Rural Resort Dwellers	95.2
99218	07 Exurbanites	32.9	99611	17 Green Acres	28.0	99757	33 Midlife Junction	100.0
99223	13 In Style	19.0	99612	24 Main Street, USA	100.0	99758	62 Modest Income Homes	95.5
99224	07 Exurbanites	20.1	99613	17 Green Acres	89.0	99759	38 Industrious Urban Fringe	100.0
99251	14 Prosperous Empty Nesters	100.0	99614	59 Southwestern Families	100.0	99760	31 Rural Resort Dwellers	100.0
99301	58 NeWest Residents	18.2	99615	13 In Style	29.9	99762	28 Aspiring Young Families	56.2
99320	26 Midland Crowd	31.7	99620	38 Industrious Urban Fringe	100.0	99763	38 Industrious Urban Fringe	100.0
99321	38 Industrious Urban Fringe	100.0	99621	38 Industrious Urban Fringe	100.0	99765	19 Milk And Cookies	55.4
99322	37 Prairie Living	100.0	99622	59 Southwestern Families	100.0	99766	38 Industrious Urban Fringe	100.0
99323	26 Midland Crowd	72.2	99625	26 Midland Crowd	100.0	99767	62 Modest Income Homes	100.0
99324	33 Midlife Junction	37.8	99626	38 Industrious Urban Fringe	100.0	99768	51 Metro City Edge	100.0
99326	38 Industrious Urban Fringe	79.4	99627	33 Midlife Junction	99.3	99769	59 Southwestern Families	100.0
99328	33 Midlife Junction	29.3	99628	38 Industrious Urban Fringe	100.0	99771	19 Milk And Cookies	97.0
99330	26 Midland Crowd	100.0	99630	59 Southwestern Families	100.0	99772	51 Metro City Edge	100.0
99336	28 Aspiring Young Families	16.8	99631	31 Rural Resort Dwellers	100.0	99773	38 Industrious Urban Fringe	100.0
99337	26 Midland Crowd	20.4	99632	38 Industrious Urban Fringe	100.0	99777	62 Modest Income Homes	100.0
99338	06 Sophisticated Squires	49.8	99634	59 Southwestern Families	100.0	99778	51 Metro City Edge	100.0
99341	46 Rooted Rural	74.1	99636	38 Industrious Urban Fringe	100.0	99780	26 Midland Crowd	63.4
99343	38 Industrious Urban Fringe	65.0	99638	19 Milk And Cookies	100.0	99781	51 Metro City Edge	100.0
99344	38 Industrious Urban Fringe	30.0	99639	31 Rural Resort Dwellers	100.0	99782	38 Industrious Urban Fringe	100.0
99347	50 Heartland Communities	66.3	99640	26 Midland Crowd	100.0	99783	51 Metro City Edge	100.0
99348	38 Industrious Urban Fringe	99.6	99645	17 Green Acres	31.8	99784	51 Metro City Edge	100.0
99349	38 Industrious Urban Fringe	100.0	99647	26 Midland Crowd	100.0	99785	51 Metro City Edge	100.0
99350	26 Midland Crowd	31.9	99648	19 Milk And Cookies	100.0	99786	38 Industrious Urban Fringe	100.0
99352	07 Exurbanites	24.2	99649	19 Milk And Cookies	100.0	99788	51 Metro City Edge	100.0
99353	12 Up And Coming Families	45.5	99650	38 Industrious Urban Fringe	100.0	99789	66 Unclassified	100.0
99354	07 Exurbanites	15.9	99654	06 Sophisticated Squires	22.5	99801	13 In Style	32.8
99356	37 Prairie Living	100.0	99655	59 Southwestern Families	100.0	99820	26 Midland Crowd	100.0
99357	47 Las Casas	42.7	99656	56 Rural Bypasses	100.0	99824	13 In Style	100.0
99360	37 Prairie Living	71.5	99658	38 Industrious Urban Fringe	100.0	99825	31 Rural Resort Dwellers	100.0
99361	46 Rooted Rural	62.0	99659	51 Metro City Edge	100.0	99826	31 Rural Resort Dwellers	100.0
99362	14 Prosperous Empty Nesters	15.3	99660	19 Milk And Cookies	100.0	99827	31 Rural Resort Dwellers	96.0
99371	37 Prairie Living	100.0	99661	24 Main Street, USA	100.0	99829	26 Midland Crowd	83.4
99401	31 Rural Resort Dwellers	100.0	99662	51 Metro City Edge	100.0	99833	26 Midland Crowd	61.0
99402	31 Rural Resort Dwellers	100.0	99664	22 Metropolitans	54.1	99835	13 In Style	49.8

CONSUMER TYPE

ZIP CODE	TOP TAPESTRY CONSUMER TYPE	% 2009 HOUSE-HOLDS	ZIP CODE	TOP TAPESTRY CONSUMER TYPE	% 2009 HOUSE-HOLDS	ZIP CODE	TOP TAPESTRY CONSUMER TYPE	% 2009 HOUSE-HOLDS
99840	22 Metropolitans	100.0						
99901	24 Main Street, USA	40.3						
99903	31 Rural Resort Dwellers	100.0						
99919	26 Midland Crowd	100.0						
99921	41 Crossroads	74.2						
99922	25 Salt Of The Earth	100.0						
99923	31 Rural Resort Dwellers	100.0						
99925	41 Crossroads	100.0						
99926	26 Midland Crowd	55.4						
99927	37 Prairie Living	100.0						
99929	31 Rural Resort Dwellers	62.0						
99950	37 Prairie Living	53.3						

Business Data by ZIP Code

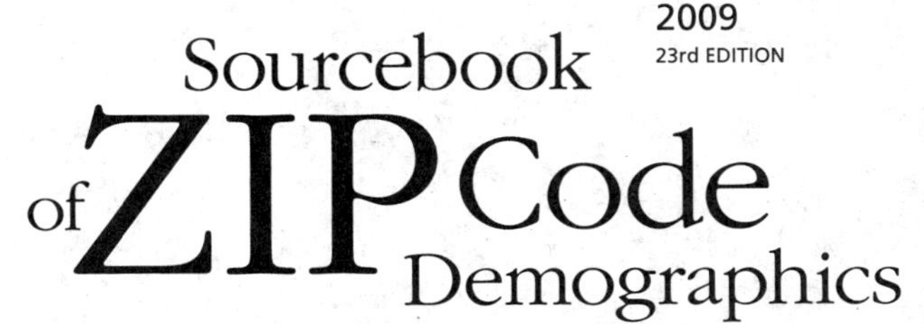

ZIP CODE	2009 Total Firms	2009 Total Employees	TOP INDUSTRY RANKED on 2009 EMPLOYMENT
01001	704	9743	PRIMARY METAL MANUFACTURING
01002	936	8375	EDUCATIONAL SERVICES
01003	29	6649	EDUCATIONAL SERVICES
01004	11	59	OTHER INFORMATION SERVICES
01005	206	1440	EDUCATIONAL SERVICES
01007	383	2457	EDUCATIONAL SERVICES
01008	43	308	ACCOMMODATION
01009	25	185	MISCELLANEOUS MANUFACTURING
01010	134	591	MISCELLANEOUS MANUFACTURING
01011	43	97	EDUCATIONAL SERVICES
01012	31	163	EDUCATIONAL SERVICES
01013	586	6207	EXEC.; LEGIS.; & OTHER SUPPORT
01020	876	9626	EDUCATIONAL SERVICES
01021	2	2	SCENIC & SIGHTSEEING TRANSPORT
01022	81	3181	MISCELLANEOUS MANUFACTURING
01026	46	198	REPAIR AND MAINTENANCE
01027	664	5428	PAPER MANUFACTURING
01028	817	9298	MISCELLANEOUS MANUFACTURING
01029	17	105	ACCOMMODATION
01030	316	2170	EDUCATIONAL SERVICES
01031	45	209	EDUCATIONAL SERVICES
01032	32	127	ACCOMMODATION
01033	219	894	EDUCATIONAL SERVICES
01034	50	301	ACCOMMODATION
01035	455	4461	FOOD SVCS & DRINKING PLACES
01036	188	925	EDUCATIONAL SERVICES
01037	42	315	RELIG.; GRANT; CIVIC; PROF ORG
01038	114	2035	MERCH. WHOLESALERS;NONDUR. GDS
01039	62	235	SPECIAL TRADE CONTRACTORS
01040	1582	27152	RELIG.; GRANT; CIVIC; PROF ORG
01041	7	14	SPECIAL TRADE CONTRACTORS
01050	79	684	EDUCATIONAL SERVICES
01053	49	1780	PROF.; SCIENTIFIC; & TECH SVCS
01054	63	208	TEXTILE MILLS
01056	694	6585	EXEC.; LEGIS.; & OTHER SUPPORT
01057	268	1311	EDUCATIONAL SERVICES
01059	1	1	PROF.; SCIENTIFIC; & TECH SVCS
01060	1447	13537	HOSPITALS
01061	10	12	AMBULATORY HEALTH CARE SVCS
01062	358	2113	AMBULATORY HEALTH CARE SVCS
01063	11	1438	EDUCATIONAL SERVICES
01066	8	64	SPECIAL TRADE CONTRACTORS
01068	59	212	EDUCATIONAL SERVICES
01069	482	6944	HOSPITALS
01070	20	33	ACCOMMODATION
01071	49	449	LEATHER & ALLIED PRODUCT MFG
01072	44	282	EXEC.; LEGIS.; & OTHER SUPPORT
01073	174	1001	FOOD AND BEVERAGE STORES
01074	18	47	FOOD SVCS & DRINKING PLACES
01075	476	4887	EDUCATIONAL SERVICES
01077	372	2920	EDUCATIONAL SERVICES
01079	29	105	SPECIAL TRADE CONTRACTORS
01080	80	434	MOTOR VEHICLE & PARTS DEALERS
01081	46	169	JUSTICE; PUBIC ORDER/SAFETY
01082	348	3197	EDUCATIONAL SERVICES
01083	95	453	EDUCATIONAL SERVICES
01084	6	18	SPECIAL TRADE CONTRACTORS
01085	1401	23576	MERCH. WHOLESALERS;DURABLE GDS
01086	10	79	ADMINISTRATIVE & SUPPORT SVCS
01088	50	558	WOOD PRODUCT MANUFACTURING
01089	1544	17050	FOOD SVCS & DRINKING PLACES
01090	11	22	SPECIAL TRADE CONTRACTORS
01092	36	1636	TEXTILE MILLS
01093	50	325	PLASTICS & RUBBER PRODUCTS MFG
01094	6	24	BLDG MATL & GARDEN EQPMT DLRS
01095	520	3798	EDUCATIONAL SERVICES
01096	130	539	EDUCATIONAL SERVICES
01097	1	2	MERCH. WHOLESALERS;DURABLE GDS
01098	53	157	TRANSIT & GRND PASS. TRANSPORT
01101	14	555	POSTAL SERVICE
01103	1007	10655	PROF.; SCIENTIFIC; & TECH SVCS
01104	845	20842	HOSPITALS
01105	526	7029	JUSTICE; PUBIC ORDER/SAFETY
01106	389	4569	NURSING & RESID. CARE FACILIT.
01107	299	3534	AMBULATORY HEALTH CARE SVCS
01108	510	3516	EDUCATIONAL SERVICES
01109	582	6946	EDUCATIONAL SERVICES
01111	6	8700	INSURANCE CARRIERS & RELATED
01115	84	834	PROF.; SCIENTIFIC; & TECH SVCS
01116	9	8	PROF.; SCIENTIFIC; & TECH SVCS
01118	227	2034	AMBULATORY HEALTH CARE SVCS
01119	205	3127	EDUCATIONAL SERVICES
01128	69	1013	FOOD AND BEVERAGE STORES
01129	268	3123	GENERAL MERCHANDISE STORES
01138	6	18	ADMINISTRATIVE & SUPPORT SVCS
01139	1	0	MERCH. WHOLESALERS;NONDUR. GDS
01144	57	767	INSURANCE CARRIERS & RELATED
01151	283	2569	MERCH. WHOLESALERS;NONDUR. GDS
01152	4	3000	POSTAL SERVICE
01199	46	13080	AMBULATORY HEALTH CARE SVCS
01201	2182	28234	AMBULATORY HEALTH CARE SVCS
01202	12	23	CONSTRUCTION OF BUILDINGS
01220	306	2190	FOOD SVCS & DRINKING PLACES
01222	15	23	CROP PRODUCTION
01223	86	547	EDUCATIONAL SERVICES
01224	9	32	PLASTICS & RUBBER PRODUCTS MFG
01225	94	513	EDUCATIONAL SERVICES
01226	210	3597	PAPER MANUFACTURING
01229	6	5	ADMINISTRATIVE & SUPPORT SVCS
01230	806	5782	EDUCATIONAL SERVICES
01235	76	484	ACCOMMODATION
01236	53	387	EDUCATIONAL SERVICES
01237	218	2162	PROF.; SCIENTIFIC; & TECH SVCS
01238	430	3180	FOOD SVCS & DRINKING PLACES
01240	389	5789	ACCOMMODATION
01242	18	86	MERCH. WHOLESALERS;DURABLE GDS
01243	15	49	MISCELLANEOUS STORE RETAILERS
01244	15	37	EDUCATIONAL SERVICES
01245	37	133	HOSPITALS
01247	664	7030	HOSPITALS
01252	5	4	ACCOMMODATION
01253	46	336	ADMINISTRATIVE & SUPPORT SVCS
01254	62	195	FOOD AND BEVERAGE STORES
01255	39	181	SOCIAL ASSISTANCE
01256	14	26	EDUCATIONAL SERVICES
01257	220	1240	EDUCATIONAL SERVICES
01258	40	529	ACCOMMODATION
01259	17	56	FOOD AND BEVERAGE STORES
01260	8	529	PAPER MANUFACTURING
01262	148	1016	RELIG.; GRANT; CIVIC; PROF ORG
01263	1	90	RELIG.; GRANT; CIVIC; PROF ORG
01264	10	59	JUSTICE; PUBIC ORDER/SAFETY
01266	98	525	ACCOMMODATION
01267	329	4124	EDUCATIONAL SERVICES
01270	20	34	EXEC.; LEGIS.; & OTHER SUPPORT
01301	1092	10199	HOSPITALS
01302	2	3	BROADCASTING
01330	70	267	EDUCATIONAL SERVICES
01331	481	4994	FABRICATED METAL PRODUCT MFG
01337	89	410	MERCH. WHOLESALERS;NONDUR. GDS
01338	17	33	FOOD AND BEVERAGE STORES
01339	66	463	ACCOMMODATION
01340	60	262	TEXTILE MILLS
01341	57	165	EDUCATIONAL SERVICES
01342	60	975	EDUCATIONAL SERVICES
01343	6	10	EXEC.; LEGIS.; & OTHER SUPPORT
01344	35	166	EDUCATIONAL SERVICES
01346	12	22	EXEC.; LEGIS.; & OTHER SUPPORT
01347	3	5	EXEC.; LEGIS.; & OTHER SUPPORT
01349	23	225	PROF.; SCIENTIFIC; & TECH SVCS
01350	5	5	PROF.; SCIENTIFIC; & TECH SVCS
01351	71	261	EDUCATIONAL SERVICES
01354	60	530	TRANSIT & GRND PASS. TRANSPORT
01355	35	146	EDUCATIONAL SERVICES
01360	92	947	EDUCATIONAL SERVICES
01364	325	2157	EDUCATIONAL SERVICES
01366	68	347	EDUCATIONAL SERVICES
01367	25	116	SPECIAL TRADE CONTRACTORS
01368	37	102	EDUCATIONAL SERVICES
01370	257	1213	EDUCATIONAL SERVICES
01373	270	4732	MISCELLANEOUS STORE RETAILERS
01375	105	656	HEAVY & CIVIL ENG. CONSTRUCT'N
01376	203	3337	RELIG.; GRANT; CIVIC; PROF ORG
01378	25	83	EDUCATIONAL SERVICES
01379	39	186	EDUCATIONAL SERVICES
01380	1	1	SUPPORT ACT. FOR TRANSPORT.
01420	1540	15772	EDUCATIONAL SERVICES
01430	181	951	EDUCATIONAL SERVICES
01431	92	323	EDUCATIONAL SERVICES
01432	375	5047	COMPUTER & ELECTRONIC PROD MFG
01434	107	2787	ADMINISTRATIVE & SUPPORT SVCS
01436	68	1102	EXEC.; LEGIS.; & OTHER SUPPORT
01438	20	166	MERCH. WHOLESALERS;NONDUR. GDS
01440	772	9324	HOSPITALS
01441	1	1500	MISCELLANEOUS MANUFACTURING
01450	336	2178	EDUCATIONAL SERVICES
01451	241	1109	PROF.; SCIENTIFIC; & TECH SVCS
01452	132	422	JUSTICE; PUBIC ORDER/SAFETY
01453	1781	19974	HOSPITALS
01460	519	5460	MERCH. WHOLESALERS;DURABLE GDS
01462	375	2287	BLDG MATL & GARDEN EQPMT DLRS
01463	346	1899	EDUCATIONAL SERVICES
01464	202	2283	EXEC.; LEGIS.; & OTHER SUPPORT
01467	11	54	MISCELLANEOUS STORE RETAILERS
01468	113	634	MERCH. WHOLESALERS;DURABLE GDS
01469	201	2414	PROF.; SCIENTIFIC; & TECH SVCS
01471	2	850	PRINT'G & RELATED SUPP'T ACT'S
01472	13	252	PAPER MANUFACTURING
01473	278	2268	REAL ESTATE
01474	53	194	TRANSIT & GRND PASS. TRANSPORT
01475	279	1812	EDUCATIONAL SERVICES
01477	5	109	MISCELLANEOUS MANUFACTURING
01501	986	10710	FOOD SVCS & DRINKING PLACES
01503	127	452	EDUCATIONAL SERVICES
01504	185	970	FOOD AND BEVERAGE STORES
01505	175	1429	EDUCATIONAL SERVICES
01506	90	449	JUSTICE; PUBIC ORDER/SAFETY
01507	419	3246	EDUCATIONAL SERVICES
01508	12	148	JUSTICE; PUBIC ORDER/SAFETY
01509	2	2	CLOTHING & CLOTH'G ACC. STORES
01510	477	5076	PLASTICS & RUBBER PRODUCTS MFG
01515	93	550	EDUCATIONAL SERVICES
01516	216	1198	EDUCATIONAL SERVICES
01518	137	772	EDUCATIONAL SERVICES
01519	208	952	EDUCATIONAL SERVICES
01520	478	3868	EDUCATIONAL SERVICES
01521	43	166	EDUCATIONAL SERVICES
01522	60	292	MERCH. WHOLESALERS;DURABLE GDS
01523	209	1874	EDUCATIONAL SERVICES
01524	242	1675	MERCH. WHOLESALERS;NONDUR. GDS
01525	24	75	GASOLINE STATIONS
01526	11	25	MERCH. WHOLESALERS;DURABLE GDS
01527	534	4846	SPECIAL TRADE CONTRACTORS
01529	57	197	EDUCATIONAL SERVICES
01531	38	127	ACCOMMODATION
01532	767	11785	ADMINISTRATIVE & SUPPORT SVCS
01534	157	1197	NURSING & RESID. CARE FACILIT.
01535	169	1407	PLASTICS & RUBBER PRODUCTS MFG
01536	262	3475	FABRICATED METAL PRODUCT MFG
01537	96	934	GENERAL MERCHANDISE STORES
01538	14	67	MOTOR VEHICLE & PARTS DEALERS
01540	431	3136	PROF.; SCIENTIFIC; & TECH SVCS
01541	126	2480	OTHER INFORMATION SERVICES
01542	69	428	NURSING & RESID. CARE FACILIT.
01543	209	1423	EDUCATIONAL SERVICES
01545	1271	11852	EDUCATIONAL SERVICES
01550	640	7127	MISCELLANEOUS MANUFACTURING
01560	83	328	ELECT'L EQPMT; APP; & COMP MFG
01561	21	282	EDUCATIONAL SERVICES
01562	417	4592	PAPER MANUFACTURING
01564	318	2451	NURSING & RESID. CARE FACILIT.
01566	373	4256	FOOD SVCS & DRINKING PLACES
01568	210	1156	EDUCATIONAL SERVICES
01569	487	3139	EDUCATIONAL SERVICES
01570	620	10843	INSURANCE CARRIERS & RELATED
01571	276	2369	EDUCATIONAL SERVICES
01581	1377	23176	PROF.; SCIENTIFIC; & TECH SVCS
01582	5	2026	UTILITIES
01583	440	5752	JUSTICE; PUBIC ORDER/SAFETY
01585	141	870	RELIG.; GRANT; CIVIC; PROF ORG
01588	356	4444	GENERAL MERCHANDISE STORES
01590	327	2765	EDUCATIONAL SERVICES
01602	529	4119	EDUCATIONAL SERVICES
01603	755	6497	GENERAL MERCHANDISE STORES
01604	1346	12670	FOOD SVCS & DRINKING PLACES
01605	982	19772	AMBULATORY HEALTH CARE SVCS
01606	770	13851	NONMETALLIC MINERAL PROD. MFG
01607	269	3440	SPECIAL TRADE CONTRACTORS
01608	1088	32526	HOSPITALS
01609	1004	7903	EDUCATIONAL SERVICES
01610	715	9791	EDUCATIONAL SERVICES
01611	70	224	EDUCATIONAL SERVICES
01612	117	762	EDUCATIONAL SERVICES
01613	14	49	SOCIAL ASSISTANCE
01614	16	101	EXEC.; LEGIS.; & OTHER SUPPORT
01653	4	6026	INSURANCE CARRIERS & RELATED
01655	64	7410	HOSPITALS
01701	1476	27694	CREDIT INTERMEDIATION & RELATD
01702	1635	24503	MISCELLANEOUS STORE RETAILERS
01703	6	20	REAL ESTATE
01704	3	3	INSURANCE CARRIERS & RELATED
01705	3	5	DATA PROCESS'G
01718	3	6	SPECIAL TRADE CONTRACTORS
01719	216	1617	UNCLASSIFIED ESTABLISHMENTS
01720	1094	10515	EDUCATIONAL SERVICES
01721	603	5008	ADMINISTRATIVE & SUPPORT SVCS
01730	731	23750	COMPUTER & ELECTRONIC PROD MFG
01731	28	795	NAT'L SECURITY & INT'L AFFAIRS
01740	170	2472	ELECTRONICS & APPLIANCE STORES
01741	145	771	EDUCATIONAL SERVICES
01742	1199	13349	MACHINERY MANUFACTURING
01745	25	147	ELECTRONICS & APPLIANCE STORES
01746	628	4600	EDUCATIONAL SERVICES
01747	258	2093	UTILITIES
01748	495	9375	TELECOMMUNICATIONS
01749	825	7589	EDUCATIONAL SERVICES
01752	2053	29947	COMPUTER & ELECTRONIC PROD MFG
01754	483	3045	PROF.; SCIENTIFIC; & TECH SVCS
01756	261	1485	EDUCATIONAL SERVICES
01757	1332	16428	HOSPITALS

BUSINESS DATA

ZIP CODE	2009 Total Firms	2009 Total Employees	TOP INDUSTRY RANKED on 2009 EMPLOYMENT
01760	1937	23764	HOSPITALS
01770	149	703	HEAVY & CIVIL ENG. CONSTRUCT'N
01772	497	5394	EDUCATIONAL SERVICES
01773	228	1571	EDUCATIONAL SERVICES
01775	275	2335	EDUCATIONAL SERVICES
01776	751	6468	EDUCATIONAL SERVICES
01778	461	3798	EDUCATIONAL SERVICES
01784	3	9	RELIG.; GRANT; CIVIC; PROF ORG
01801	3087	42552	ADMINISTRATIVE & SUPPORT SVCS
01803	2164	36473	ADMINISTRATIVE & SUPPORT SVCS
01805	11	316	AMBULATORY HEALTH CARE SVCS
01810	1438	24057	PROF.; SCIENTIFIC; & TECH SVCS
01821	1059	13602	PROF.; SCIENTIFIC; & TECH SVCS
01822	1	10	ADMINISTRATIVE & SUPPORT SVCS
01824	1330	19056	COMPUTER & ELECTRONIC PROD MFG
01826	897	4273	FOOD SVCS & DRINKING PLACES
01827	81	263	EDUCATIONAL SERVICES
01830	945	10792	EDUCATIONAL SERVICES
01831	5	29	TRUCK TRANSPORTATION
01832	541	4520	EDUCATIONAL SERVICES
01833	288	2728	FURNITURE & RELATED PROD. MFG
01834	180	908	EXEC.; LEGIS.; & OTHER SUPPORT
01835	466	5049	AMUSEMENT; GAMBLING;& RECREAT.
01840	817	7706	EDUCATIONAL SERVICES
01841	683	8925	UTILITIES
01842	2	40	WASTE MANAGMT & REMEDIAT'N SVC
01843	759	15230	ADMINISTRATIVE & SUPPORT SVCS
01844	1460	15266	FOOD SVCS & DRINKING PLACES
01845	1174	20333	PROF.; SCIENTIFIC; & TECH SVCS
01850	204	1970	PROF.; SCIENTIFIC; & TECH SVCS
01851	823	9234	SPECIAL TRADE CONTRACTORS
01852	1556	15444	EDUCATIONAL SERVICES
01853	7	10	ADMINISTRATIVE & SUPPORT SVCS
01854	513	7995	EDUCATIONAL SERVICES
01860	181	785	EDUCATIONAL SERVICES
01862	546	10373	RAIL TRANSPORTATION
01863	376	3263	EDUCATIONAL SERVICES
01864	680	5891	MERCH. WHOLESALERS;DURABLE GDS
01865	3	3	UNCLASSIFIED ESTABLISHMENTS
01866	1	5	POSTAL SERVICE
01867	844	5737	EDUCATIONAL SERVICES
01876	1118	13019	PROF.; SCIENTIFIC; & TECH SVCS
01879	509	3861	EDUCATIONAL SERVICES
01880	1498	16370	PROF.; SCIENTIFIC; & TECH SVCS
01885	11	103	AMUSEMENT; GAMBLING;& RECREAT.
01886	880	8586	PROF.; SCIENTIFIC; & TECH SVCS
01887	1128	22992	COMPUTER & ELECTRONIC PROD MFG
01888	12	42	TRUCK TRANSPORTATION
01889	2	3	CREDIT INTERMEDIATION & RELATD
01890	908	7778	HOSPITALS
01901	595	5916	RELIG.; GRANT; CIVIC; PROF ORG
01902	788	4972	EDUCATIONAL SERVICES
01903	1	0	SPECIAL TRADE CONTRACTORS
01904	490	4352	AMBULATORY HEALTH CARE SVCS
01905	596	10204	TRANSPORTATION EQUIPMENT MFG
01906	1215	11964	ADMINISTRATIVE & SUPPORT SVCS
01907	514	3687	FOOD SVCS & DRINKING PLACES
01908	90	397	FOOD SVCS & DRINKING PLACES
01910	1	0	ELECT'L EQPMT; APP; & COMP MFG
01913	705	5568	EDUCATIONAL SERVICES
01915	2116	25627	HOSPITALS
01921	185	654	EDUCATIONAL SERVICES
01922	79	661	EDUCATIONAL SERVICES
01923	1808	22570	FOOD SVCS & DRINKING PLACES
01929	287	1961	FOOD SVCS & DRINKING PLACES
01930	1545	11956	COMPUTER & ELECTRONIC PROD MFG
01931	7	17	CONSTRUCTION OF BUILDINGS
01936	25	19	CONSTRUCTION OF BUILDINGS
01937	1	1	PROF.; SCIENTIFIC; & TECH SVCS
01938	723	5044	PUBLISHING INDUSTRIES
01940	512	3840	PROF.; SCIENTIFIC; & TECH SVCS
01944	304	1603	EDUCATIONAL SERVICES
01945	993	6257	EDUCATIONAL SERVICES
01949	474	4645	PROF.; SCIENTIFIC; & TECH SVCS
01950	1355	11829	HOSPITALS
01951	191	1321	HEAVY & CIVIL ENG. CONSTRUCT'N
01952	538	3253	FOOD SVCS & DRINKING PLACES
01960	2278	24589	FOOD SVCS & DRINKING PLACES
01961	9	48	HEAVY & CIVIL ENG. CONSTRUCT'N
01965	8	81	SECURITIES/COMMODITY CONTRACTS
01966	412	2098	EDUCATIONAL SERVICES
01969	350	2513	FOOD AND BEVERAGE STORES
01970	2077	40191	HOSPITALS
01971	1	0	SPECIAL TRADE CONTRACTORS
01982	235	1674	EDUCATIONAL SERVICES
01983	422	2553	PERFORM'G ARTS; SPEC. SPORTS
01984	134	953	EDUCATIONAL SERVICES
01985	139	995	EDUCATIONAL SERVICES
02018	7	16	SPECIAL TRADE CONTRACTORS
02019	549	5121	FOOD SVCS & DRINKING PLACES

ZIP CODE	2009 Total Firms	2009 Total Employees	TOP INDUSTRY RANKED on 2009 EMPLOYMENT
02020	6	15	AMUSEMENT; GAMBLING;& RECREAT.
02021	1390	30540	ADMINISTRATIVE & SUPPORT SVCS
02025	492	2738	PERFORM'G ARTS; SPEC. SPORTS
02026	1331	14626	FOOD SVCS & DRINKING PLACES
02027	11	27	MERCH. WHOLESALERS;DURABLE GDS
02030	144	799	EDUCATIONAL SERVICES
02032	127	1604	FOOD SVCS & DRINKING PLACES
02035	811	12061	PROF.; SCIENTIFIC; & TECH SVCS
02038	1177	12028	EDUCATIONAL SERVICES
02040	2	2	PROF.; SCIENTIFIC; & TECH SVCS
02041	6	215	RELIG.; GRANT; CIVIC; PROF ORG
02043	1414	12985	CLOTHING & CLOTH'G ACC. STORES
02045	362	1321	FOOD SVCS & DRINKING PLACES
02047	14	21	NAT'L SECURITY & INT'L AFFAIRS
02048	789	11780	MERCH. WHOLESALERS;DURABLE GDS
02050	912	6336	EXEC.; LEGIS.; & OTHER SUPPORT
02051	11	41	SOCIAL ASSISTANCE
02052	472	2859	EDUCATIONAL SERVICES
02053	466	2997	EDUCATIONAL SERVICES
02054	344	2280	FOOD AND BEVERAGE STORES
02056	274	2369	EDUCATIONAL SERVICES
02059	5	4	POSTAL SERVICE
02060	1	260	AMUSEMENT; GAMBLING;& RECREAT.
02061	793	9517	PERSONAL AND LAUNDRY SERVICES
02062	2000	26746	HOSPITALS
02065	1	1	SPECIAL TRADE CONTRACTORS
02066	658	3563	FOOD SVCS & DRINKING PLACES
02067	464	3689	EDUCATIONAL SERVICES
02070	5	10	GENERAL MERCHANDISE STORES
02071	16	166	ADMINISTRATIVE & SUPPORT SVCS
02072	1270	17250	FABRICATED METAL PRODUCT MFG
02081	939	7418	ADMINISTRATIVE & SUPPORT SVCS
02090	659	9276	PUBLISHING INDUSTRIES
02093	585	5154	CLOTHING & CLOTH'G ACC. STORES
02108	2274	37176	CREDIT INTERMEDIATION & RELATD
02109	2232	43683	PROF.; SCIENTIFIC; & TECH SVCS
02110	2622	45710	PROF.; SCIENTIFIC; & TECH SVCS
02111	1496	36904	PROF.; SCIENTIFIC; & TECH SVCS
02112	1	27	SOCIAL ASSISTANCE
02113	344	1453	FOOD SVCS & DRINKING PLACES
02114	1293	40150	HOSPITALS
02115	1006	33079	HOSPITALS
02116	3334	60609	PROF.; SCIENTIFIC; & TECH SVCS
02117	11	28	ADMINISTRATIVE & SUPPORT SVCS
02118	1306	22170	HOSPITALS
02119	936	10229	SOCIAL ASSISTANCE
02120	270	8416	JUSTICE; PUBIC ORDER/SAFETY
02121	479	2735	EDUCATIONAL SERVICES
02122	898	8675	MERCH. WHOLESALERS;DURABLE GDS
02123	4	13	CONSTRUCTION OF BUILDINGS
02124	1049	8526	HOSPITALS
02125	771	16635	PUBLISHING INDUSTRIES
02126	500	2780	EDUCATIONAL SERVICES
02127	1102	13042	MERCH. WHOLESALERS;NONDUR. GDS
02128	1326	14580	SUPPORT ACT. FOR TRANSPORT.
02129	787	13245	HEAVY & CIVIL ENG. CONSTRUCT'N
02130	1183	14525	AMBULATORY HEALTH CARE SVCS
02131	734	6652	SOCIAL ASSISTANCE
02132	849	7847	MOTOR VEHICLE & PARTS DEALERS
02133	36	1210	EXEC.; LEGIS.; & OTHER SUPPORT
02134	954	9223	BROADCASTING
02135	1301	17885	HOSPITALS
02136	780	5956	MERCH. WHOLESALERS;NONDUR. GDS
02137	5	25	MERCH. WHOLESALERS;DURABLE GDS
02138	2274	33170	EDUCATIONAL SERVICES
02139	1814	52329	PROF.; SCIENTIFIC; & TECH SVCS
02140	827	6652	PROF.; SCIENTIFIC; & TECH SVCS
02141	761	9716	PROF.; SCIENTIFIC; & TECH SVCS
02142	626	16399	PROF.; SCIENTIFIC; & TECH SVCS
02143	1147	12434	ADMINISTRATIVE & SUPPORT SVCS
02144	682	4472	PROF.; SCIENTIFIC; & TECH SVCS
02145	595	5184	FOOD AND BEVERAGE STORES
02148	1896	15239	EDUCATIONAL SERVICES
02149	1384	13660	HOSPITALS
02150	1132	17121	FOOD AND BEVERAGE STORES
02151	1159	8694	FOOD SVCS & DRINKING PLACES
02152	523	3530	UTILITIES
02153	1	0	UNCLASSIFIED ESTABLISHMENTS
02155	1998	16213	FOOD AND BEVERAGE STORES
02156	4	1	PROF.; SCIENTIFIC; & TECH SVCS
02163	14	117	OTHER INFORMATION SERVICES
02169	2563	32395	AMBULATORY HEALTH CARE SVCS
02170	424	2627	FOOD SVCS & DRINKING PLACES
02171	553	8607	SECURITIES/COMMODITY CONTRACTS
02176	853	7493	COURIERS AND MESSENGERS
02180	1005	6952	AMBULATORY HEALTH CARE SVCS
02184	2275	26341	FOOD SVCS & DRINKING PLACES
02185	6	18	ADMINISTRATIVE & SUPPORT SVCS
02186	699	5192	EDUCATIONAL SERVICES
02188	538	4552	NURSING & RESID. CARE FACILIT.

ZIP CODE	2009 Total Firms	2009 Total Employees	TOP INDUSTRY RANKED on 2009 EMPLOYMENT
02189	668	6112	SPECIAL TRADE CONTRACTORS
02190	655	7686	HOSPITALS
02191	221	1093	RELIG.; GRANT; CIVIC; PROF ORG
02196	4	44	TRANSIT & GRND PASS. TRANSPORT
02199	289	8530	PROF.; SCIENTIFIC; & TECH SVCS
02201	74	3909	EXEC.; LEGIS.; & OTHER SUPPORT
02203	33	823	ADMIN. HUMAN RESOURCE PROGRAMS
02205	14	2910	POSTAL SERVICE
02210	1263	31562	PROF.; SCIENTIFIC; & TECH SVCS
02215	1008	23978	EDUCATIONAL SERVICES
02216	2	0	PROF.; SCIENTIFIC; & TECH SVCS
02222	53	609	ADMIN. OF ECONOMIC PROGRAMS
02228	2	350	POSTAL SERVICE
02238	12	15	PROF.; SCIENTIFIC; & TECH SVCS
02241	1	1	RELIG.; GRANT; CIVIC; PROF ORG
02269	8	133	SOCIAL ASSISTANCE
02301	2270	30259	EDUCATIONAL SERVICES
02302	574	8125	HOSPITALS
02303	9	12	SPECIAL TRADE CONTRACTORS
02305	4	40	ADMINISTRATIVE & SUPPORT SVCS
02322	340	5412	FABRICATED METAL PRODUCT MFG
02324	679	5746	FOOD SVCS & DRINKING PLACES
02325	2	935	EDUCATIONAL SERVICES
02327	16	99	TRANSIT & GRND PASS. TRANSPORT
02330	382	2548	FOOD MANUFACTURING
02331	12	25	CONSTRUCTION OF BUILDINGS
02332	564	3749	EDUCATIONAL SERVICES
02333	423	2438	FOOD SVCS & DRINKING PLACES
02334	8	11	ADMINISTRATIVE & SUPPORT SVCS
02337	2	3	RELIG.; GRANT; CIVIC; PROF ORG
02338	206	1497	GENERAL MERCHANDISE STORES
02339	1023	7836	EDUCATIONAL SERVICES
02341	311	2102	FOOD SVCS & DRINKING PLACES
02343	418	2905	SPECIAL TRADE CONTRACTORS
02345	45	266	FOOD AND BEVERAGE STORES
02346	881	8067	FOOD SVCS & DRINKING PLACES
02347	418	3282	CLOTHING & CLOTH'G ACC. STORES
02349	2	505	FOOD MANUFACTURING
02350	2	2	POSTAL SERVICE
02351	564	4518	PRINT'G & RELATED SUPP'T ACT'S
02355	5	6	BLDG MATL & GARDEN EQPMT DLRS
02356	366	3238	FOOD AND BEVERAGE STORES
02357	3	606	EDUCATIONAL SERVICES
02358	7	45	ADMINISTRATIVE & SUPPORT SVCS
02359	838	6285	HOSPITALS
02360	2513	22693	FOOD SVCS & DRINKING PLACES
02361	3	12	SPECIAL TRADE CONTRACTORS
02362	15	93	SOCIAL ASSISTANCE
02364	702	5243	EDUCATIONAL SERVICES
02366	13	181	JUSTICE; PUBIC ORDER/SAFETY
02367	112	299	EDUCATIONAL SERVICES
02368	958	8174	FOOD SVCS & DRINKING PLACES
02370	815	7783	PROF.; SCIENTIFIC; & TECH SVCS
02375	634	6216	EDUCATIONAL SERVICES
02379	521	6629	FOOD AND BEVERAGE STORES
02381	4	13	FOOD AND BEVERAGE STORES
02382	468	4232	SPECIAL TRADE CONTRACTORS
02420	737	5639	PROF.; SCIENTIFIC; & TECH SVCS
02421	687	18437	PROF.; SCIENTIFIC; & TECH SVCS
02445	802	7426	EDUCATIONAL SERVICES
02446	1280	9545	CLOTHING & CLOTH'G ACC. STORES
02447	3	12	SPECIAL TRADE CONTRACTORS
02451	1556	27800	PROF.; SCIENTIFIC; & TECH SVCS
02452	558	8349	EDUCATIONAL SERVICES
02453	1324	12431	EDUCATIONAL SERVICES
02454	7	108	ACCOMMODATION
02456	2	1	ADMINISTRATIVE & SUPPORT SVCS
02457	2	2	ACCOMMODATION
02458	722	7188	PROF.; SCIENTIFIC; & TECH SVCS
02459	1245	12072	COMPUTER & ELECTRONIC PROD MFG
02460	382	3328	EDUCATIONAL SERVICES
02461	348	2655	PRIMARY METAL MANUFACTURING
02462	146	3771	HOSPITALS
02464	370	3120	PROF.; SCIENTIFIC; & TECH SVCS
02465	405	3761	JUSTICE; PUBIC ORDER/SAFETY
02466	365	4315	PUBLISHING INDUSTRIES
02467	558	9381	EDUCATIONAL SERVICES
02468	112	487	EDUCATIONAL SERVICES
02471	9	10	SPECIAL TRADE CONTRACTORS
02472	1512	18468	PROF.; SCIENTIFIC; & TECH SVCS
02474	751	3886	EDUCATIONAL SERVICES
02475	1	3	PROF.; SCIENTIFIC; & TECH SVCS
02476	635	4251	EDUCATIONAL SERVICES
02478	630	4652	EXEC.; LEGIS.; & OTHER SUPPORT
02479	3	2	SPECIAL TRADE CONTRACTORS
02481	1175	17886	INSURANCE CARRIERS & RELATED
02482	635	4444	PROF.; SCIENTIFIC; & TECH SVCS
02492	728	5360	EDUCATIONAL SERVICES
02493	369	3408	EDUCATIONAL SERVICES
02494	907	20404	TELECOMMUNICATIONS

ZIP CODE	2009 Total Firms	2009 Total Employ-ees	TOP INDUSTRY RANKED on 2009 EMPLOYMENT
02532	614	4484	AMBULATORY HEALTH CARE SVCS
02534	90	724	MERCH. WHOLESALERS;NONDUR. GDS
02535	150	672	ACCOMMODATION
02536	607	3499	FOOD AND BEVERAGE STORES
02537	168	1287	HOSPITALS
02538	209	1931	FOOD SVCS & DRINKING PLACES
02539	613	3366	FOOD SVCS & DRINKING PLACES
02540	964	8498	FOOD SVCS & DRINKING PLACES
02541	8	6	RELIG.; GRANT; CIVIC; PROF ORG
02542	27	1796	NAT'L SECURITY & INT'L AFFAIRS
02543	85	3600	PROF.; SCIENTIFIC; & TECH SVCS
02552	3	9	ACCOMMODATION
02553	20	92	FOOD SVCS & DRINKING PLACES
02554	1260	8060	FOOD SVCS & DRINKING PLACES
02556	157	1507	ACCOMMODATION
02557	356	2074	FOOD SVCS & DRINKING PLACES
02558	52	423	FOOD SVCS & DRINKING PLACES
02559	196	1318	FABRICATED METAL PRODUCT MFG
02561	81	403	MERCH. WHOLESALERS;NONDUR. GDS
02562	136	792	SPECIAL TRADE CONTRACTORS
02563	690	4688	FOOD SVCS & DRINKING PLACES
02564	28	91	AMUSEMENT; GAMBLING;& RECREAT.
02568	820	3678	HOSPITALS
02571	682	5877	MERCH. WHOLESALERS;DURABLE GDS
02574	25	46	PERSONAL AND LAUNDRY SERVICES
02575	142	492	EDUCATIONAL SERVICES
02576	124	1020	MERCH. WHOLESALERS;DURABLE GDS
02584	14	32	EDUCATIONAL SERVICES
02601	2133	21198	FOOD SVCS & DRINKING PLACES
02630	225	1128	EXEC.; LEGIS.; & OTHER SUPPORT
02631	487	3982	ACCOMMODATION
02632	355	1876	NURSING & RESID. CARE FACILIT.
02633	542	3074	ACCOMMODATION
02634	1	1	REAL ESTATE
02635	123	419	EDUCATIONAL SERVICES
02637	14	47	AMUSEMENT; GAMBLING;& RECREAT.
02638	239	803	FOOD SVCS & DRINKING PLACES
02639	214	1245	ACCOMMODATION
02641	46	254	FOOD SVCS & DRINKING PLACES
02642	234	1342	FOOD SVCS & DRINKING PLACES
02643	36	172	REAL ESTATE
02644	59	768	RELIG.; GRANT; CIVIC; PROF ORG
02645	552	3344	EDUCATIONAL SERVICES
02646	173	1043	FOOD SVCS & DRINKING PLACES
02647	17	146	SPORTG GDS;HOBBY;BOOK; & MUSIC
02648	305	1168	EDUCATIONAL SERVICES
02649	748	5211	FOOD SVCS & DRINKING PLACES
02650	47	379	NURSING & RESID. CARE FACILIT.
02651	57	339	CONSTRUCTION OF BUILDINGS
02652	62	200	ACCOMMODATION
02653	802	5238	FOOD SVCS & DRINKING PLACES
02655	359	1771	RELIG.; GRANT; CIVIC; PROF ORG
02657	677	3820	FOOD SVCS & DRINKING PLACES
02659	63	256	SPECIAL TRADE CONTRACTORS
02660	413	2845	FOOD AND BEVERAGE STORES
02661	19	119	PROF.; SCIENTIFIC; & TECH SVCS
02662	21	81	REAL ESTATE
02663	23	89	ACCOMMODATION
02664	582	5817	EXEC.; LEGIS.; & OTHER SUPPORT
02666	123	474	FOOD SVCS & DRINKING PLACES
02667	292	1539	FOOD SVCS & DRINKING PLACES
02668	167	911	EDUCATIONAL SERVICES
02669	29	147	SPECIAL TRADE CONTRACTORS
02670	122	658	FOOD SVCS & DRINKING PLACES
02671	96	401	ADMINISTRATIVE & SUPPORT SVCS
02672	9	19	MERCH. WHOLESALERS;DURABLE GDS
02673	386	3098	ACCOMMODATION
02675	271	1319	FOOD SVCS & DRINKING PLACES
02702	133	722	FOOD SVCS & DRINKING PLACES
02703	1526	22588	COMPUTER & ELECTRONIC PROD MFG
02712	8	101	FABRICATED METAL PRODUCT MFG
02713	6	4	SUPPORT ACT. FOR TRANSPORT.
02714	33	2	ADMINISTRATIVE & SUPPORT SVCS
02715	135	683	EDUCATIONAL SERVICES
02717	228	1397	EDUCATIONAL SERVICES
02718	112	894	EDUCATIONAL SERVICES
02719	653	6078	FOOD SVCS & DRINKING PLACES
02720	1234	18757	EDUCATIONAL SERVICES
02721	1056	12119	AMBULATORY HEALTH CARE SVCS
02722	44	517	POSTAL SERVICE
02723	454	3833	TEXTILE PRODUCT MILLS
02724	384	3798	FOOD MANUFACTURING
02725	88	1436	UTILITIES
02726	424	3867	FOOD SVCS & DRINKING PLACES
02738	282	2342	UNCLASSIFIED ESTABLISHMENTS
02739	337	1735	EDUCATIONAL SERVICES
02740	1818	23731	HOSPITALS
02741	1	5	TRANSIT & GRND PASS. TRANSPORT
02742	1	0	PERSONAL AND LAUNDRY SERVICES
02743	295	1494	EDUCATIONAL SERVICES
02744	306	2506	LEATHER & ALLIED PRODUCT MFG
02745	739	9062	MERCH. WHOLESALERS;DURABLE GDS
02746	608	5716	TRANSIT & GRND PASS. TRANSPORT
02747	971	12926	EDUCATIONAL SERVICES
02748	318	5662	MERCH. WHOLESALERS;DURABLE GDS
02760	1084	8323	FOOD SVCS & DRINKING PLACES
02761	3	6	BLDG MATL & GARDEN EQPMT DLRS
02762	424	3473	FOOD SVCS & DRINKING PLACES
02763	165	1917	FABRICATED METAL PRODUCT MFG
02764	101	1251	MERCH. WHOLESALERS;DURABLE GDS
02766	477	5407	MERCH. WHOLESALERS;NONDUR. GDS
02767	702	9901	MISCELLANEOUS MANUFACTURING
02768	5	11	TELECOMMUNICATIONS
02769	362	1810	EDUCATIONAL SERVICES
02770	150	708	EDUCATIONAL SERVICES
02771	828	8152	FOOD SVCS & DRINKING PLACES
02777	628	4478	FOOD SVCS & DRINKING PLACES
02779	135	621	EDUCATIONAL SERVICES
02780	1786	25529	EXEC.; LEGIS.; & OTHER SUPPORT
02783	1	700	NONSTORE RETAILERS
02790	666	3251	SPECIAL TRADE CONTRACTORS
02791	13	45	EXEC.; LEGIS.; & OTHER SUPPORT
02801	5	23	FOOD SVCS & DRINKING PLACES
02802	8	30	MOTION PICT. & SOUND RECORDING
02804	85	513	MISCELLANEOUS MANUFACTURING
02806	469	2945	EDUCATIONAL SERVICES
02807	237	1913	ACCOMMODATION
02808	28	322	TEXTILE MILLS
02809	814	7440	EDUCATIONAL SERVICES
02812	32	119	JUSTICE; PUBIC ORDER/SAFETY
02813	326	1296	FOOD SVCS & DRINKING PLACES
02814	211	1288	EDUCATIONAL SERVICES
02815	4	52	EDUCATIONAL SERVICES
02816	930	7346	FOOD SVCS & DRINKING PLACES
02817	217	2629	PROF.; SCIENTIFIC; & TECH SVCS
02818	1008	8881	INSURANCE CARRIERS & RELATED
02822	220	1080	ACCOMMODATION
02823	6	59	MERCH. WHOLESALERS;DURABLE GDS
02824	5	66	FOOD SVCS & DRINKING PLACES
02825	139	482	EDUCATIONAL SERVICES
02826	14	147	PLASTICS & RUBBER PRODUCTS MFG
02827	34	165	EDUCATIONAL SERVICES
02828	332	3140	NURSING & RESID. CARE FACILIT.
02829	16	75	FOOD SVCS & DRINKING PLACES
02830	157	1075	EDUCATIONAL SERVICES
02831	83	592	PROF.; SCIENTIFIC; & TECH SVCS
02832	119	848	MISCELLANEOUS MANUFACTURING
02833	52	85	SOCIAL ASSISTANCE
02835	226	1587	AMUSEMENT; GAMBLING;& RECREAT.
02836	7	212	TEXTILE MILLS
02837	144	564	EDUCATIONAL SERVICES
02838	70	500	NURSING & RESID. CARE FACILIT.
02839	24	138	AMUSEMENT; GAMBLING;& RECREAT.
02840	1768	14043	FOOD SVCS & DRINKING PLACES
02841	27	2250	ADMINISTRATIVE & SUPPORT SVCS
02842	1046	10629	PROF.; SCIENTIFIC; & TECH SVCS
02852	1139	14453	NAT'L SECURITY & INT'L AFFAIRS
02857	285	3444	MERCH. WHOLESALERS;DURABLE GDS
02858	19	94	JUSTICE; PUBIC ORDER/SAFETY
02859	146	1446	NURSING & RESID. CARE FACILIT.
02860	1777	18394	AMBULATORY HEALTH CARE SVCS
02861	658	10116	PROF.; SCIENTIFIC; & TECH SVCS
02862	6	34	SOCIAL ASSISTANCE
02863	413	3723	TEXTILE MILLS
02864	969	7589	FOOD SVCS & DRINKING PLACES
02865	762	20956	INSURANCE CARRIERS & RELATED
02871	625	6510	CONSTRUCTION OF BUILDINGS
02872	9	15	EXEC.; LEGIS.; & OTHER SUPPORT
02873	4	182	ACCOMMODATION
02874	81	265	MUSEUMS; HIST. SITES;& SIMILAR
02875	2	2	POSTAL SERVICE
02876	29	561	MISCELLANEOUS MANUFACTURING
02877	4	40	ADMINISTRATIVE & SUPPORT SVCS
02878	542	2713	EDUCATIONAL SERVICES
02879	1035	8035	AMBULATORY HEALTH CARE SVCS
02880	8	9	ADMINISTRATIVE & SUPPORT SVCS
02881	108	3121	EDUCATIONAL SERVICES
02882	640	5032	FOOD SVCS & DRINKING PLACES
02883	4	0	SPECIAL TRADE CONTRACTORS
02885	563	4442	FOOD SVCS & DRINKING PLACES
02886	2394	39523	INSURANCE CARRIERS & RELATED
02887	5	11	ADMINISTRATIVE & SUPPORT SVCS
02888	1077	10319	SPECIAL TRADE CONTRACTORS
02889	726	3978	EDUCATIONAL SERVICES
02891	1195	10845	FOOD SVCS & DRINKING PLACES
02892	133	2065	ELECT'L EQPMT; APP; & COMP MFG
02893	876	7655	BLDG MATL & GARDEN EQPMT DLRS
02894	16	490	EDUCATIONAL SERVICES
02895	1239	17012	ADMINISTRATIVE & SUPPORT SVCS
02896	405	3455	NURSING & RESID. CARE FACILIT.
02898	105	1267	FOOD AND BEVERAGE STORES
02901	1	0	MERCH. WHOLESALERS;DURABLE GDS
02902	12	24	PUBLISHING INDUSTRIES
02903	2744	47330	HOSPITALS
02904	1401	18906	AMBULATORY HEALTH CARE SVCS
02905	963	13422	HOSPITALS
02906	1107	10645	HOSPITALS
02907	889	12162	MISCELLANEOUS MANUFACTURING
02908	941	16608	EXEC.; LEGIS.; & OTHER SUPPORT
02909	1037	6364	EDUCATIONAL SERVICES
02910	1045	8930	AMBULATORY HEALTH CARE SVCS
02911	380	2404	RELIG.; GRANT; CIVIC; PROF ORG
02912	21	449	OTHER INFORMATION SERVICES
02914	1183	13227	MISCELLANEOUS MANUFACTURING
02915	464	6121	HOSPITALS
02916	332	5387	SPECIAL TRADE CONTRACTORS
02917	726	9726	ADMINISTRATIVE & SUPPORT SVCS
02918	7	1271	EDUCATIONAL SERVICES
02919	1490	12884	INSURANCE CARRIERS & RELATED
02920	1724	23235	ADMIN. HUMAN RESOURCE PROGRAMS
02921	331	4625	FABRICATED METAL PRODUCT MFG
02940	11	31	PROF.; SCIENTIFIC; & TECH SVCS
03031	708	6927	ACCOMMODATION
03032	212	2021	SPECIAL TRADE CONTRACTORS
03033	175	772	EDUCATIONAL SERVICES
03034	180	854	CONSTRUCTION OF BUILDINGS
03036	159	463	EDUCATIONAL SERVICES
03037	126	429	EDUCATIONAL SERVICES
03038	1111	8587	EDUCATIONAL SERVICES
03041	10	36	RELIG.; GRANT; CIVIC; PROF ORG
03042	261	2353	GENERAL MERCHANDISE STORES
03043	53	199	AMUSEMENT; GAMBLING;& RECREAT.
03044	97	531	NURSING & RESID. CARE FACILIT.
03045	481	3483	NURSING & RESID. CARE FACILIT.
03046	72	156	SPECIAL TRADE CONTRACTORS
03047	61	1028	SOCIAL ASSISTANCE
03048	128	480	FOOD SVCS & DRINKING PLACES
03049	296	2255	EDUCATIONAL SERVICES
03051	990	11765	COMPUTER & ELECTRONIC PROD MFG
03052	161	881	EDUCATIONAL SERVICES
03053	1147	12835	FABRICATED METAL PRODUCT MFG
03054	967	13334	PROF.; SCIENTIFIC; & TECH SVCS
03055	766	7601	PRIMARY METAL MANUFACTURING
03057	47	155	EDUCATIONAL SERVICES
03060	2126	26892	HOSPITALS
03061	16	80	ADMINISTRATIVE & SUPPORT SVCS
03062	608	9812	EDUCATIONAL SERVICES
03063	916	12023	FOOD SVCS & DRINKING PLACES
03064	437	4192	PROF.; SCIENTIFIC; & TECH SVCS
03070	163	550	EDUCATIONAL SERVICES
03071	181	985	SPECIAL TRADE CONTRACTORS
03073	6	6	SPECIAL TRADE CONTRACTORS
03076	424	2242	EDUCATIONAL SERVICES
03077	332	2964	GENERAL MERCHANDISE STORES
03079	1793	20646	GENERAL MERCHANDISE STORES
03082	81	147	SPECIAL TRADE CONTRACTORS
03084	60	178	EDUCATIONAL SERVICES
03086	278	2026	PROF.; SCIENTIFIC; & TECH SVCS
03087	451	2848	PROF.; SCIENTIFIC; & TECH SVCS
03101	1491	15534	PROF.; SCIENTIFIC; & TECH SVCS
03102	786	10457	SOCIAL ASSISTANCE
03103	1751	30391	AMBULATORY HEALTH CARE SVCS
03104	986	8051	FOOD SVCS & DRINKING PLACES
03105	12	40	SOCIAL ASSISTANCE
03106	791	9288	EDUCATIONAL SERVICES
03108	14	111	SPECIAL TRADE CONTRACTORS
03109	477	6232	MERCH. WHOLESALERS;DURABLE GDS
03110	1310	11657	PROF.; SCIENTIFIC; & TECH SVCS
03215	56	1031	ACCOMMODATION
03216	105	659	EDUCATIONAL SERVICES
03217	142	1089	WOOD PRODUCT MANUFACTURING
03218	38	92	FOOD AND BEVERAGE STORES
03220	347	2456	EDUCATIONAL SERVICES
03221	131	511	EDUCATIONAL SERVICES
03222	284	2849	MISCELLANEOUS MANUFACTURING
03223	156	721	FOOD SVCS & DRINKING PLACES
03224	75	319	MUSEUMS; HIST. SITES;& SIMILAR
03225	73	282	EDUCATIONAL SERVICES
03226	100	908	SCENIC & SIGHTSEEING TRANSPORT
03227	57	187	FOOD SVCS & DRINKING PLACES
03229	239	1679	MERCH. WHOLESALERS;NONDUR. GDS
03230	41	235	ACCOMMODATION
03231	8	12	CONSTRUCTION OF BUILDINGS
03233	8	28	PROF.; SCIENTIFIC; & TECH SVCS
03234	190	1427	BROADCASTING
03235	326	3420	FABRICATED METAL PRODUCT MFG
03237	74	199	PROF.; SCIENTIFIC; & TECH SVCS
03238	3	182	ADMIN. HUMAN RESOURCE PROGRAMS
03240	31	81	JUSTICE; PUBIC ORDER/SAFETY
03241	41	200	ACCOMMODATION

BUSINESS DATA

ZIP CODE	2009 Total Firms	2009 Total Employees	TOP INDUSTRY RANKED on 2009 EMPLOYMENT	ZIP CODE	2009 Total Firms	2009 Total Employees	TOP INDUSTRY RANKED on 2009 EMPLOYMENT	ZIP CODE	2009 Total Firms	2009 Total Employees	TOP INDUSTRY RANKED on 2009 EMPLOYMENT
03242	223	2490	EDUCATIONAL SERVICES	03592	77	409	FOOD SVCS & DRINKING PLACES	03858	116	572	EDUCATIONAL SERVICES
03243	34	91	EDUCATIONAL SERVICES	03593	15	105	ACCOMMODATION	03859	4	8	NONMETALLIC MINERAL PROD. MFG
03244	333	2189	MERCH. WHOLESALERS;DURABLE GDS	03595	44	178	ACCOMMODATION	03860	562	5890	ACCOMMODATION
03245	94	591	EDUCATIONAL SERVICES	03597	36	298	NURSING & RESID. CARE FACILIT.	03861	163	993	EDUCATIONAL SERVICES
03246	1084	11380	HOSPITALS	03598	167	866	EDUCATIONAL SERVICES	03862	438	2966	MOTOR VEHICLE & PARTS DEALERS
03247	10	15	REAL ESTATE	03601	17	21	EDUCATIONAL SERVICES	03864	195	1122	MACHINERY MANUFACTURING
03249	421	2986	EDUCATIONAL SERVICES	03602	93	406	EDUCATIONAL SERVICES	03865	601	4474	EDUCATIONAL SERVICES
03251	225	3298	ACCOMMODATION	03603	197	1866	ELECT'L EQPMT; APP; & COMP MFG	03866	7	12	MISCELLANEOUS STORE RETAILERS
03252	5	19	TRUCK TRANSPORTATION	03604	3	11	FOOD AND BEVERAGE STORES	03867	966	9944	HOSPITALS
03253	497	3551	FOOD SVCS & DRINKING PLACES	03605	40	159	EDUCATIONAL SERVICES	03868	155	1193	FOOD AND BEVERAGE STORES
03254	211	1918	ACCOMMODATION	03607	4	21	MERCH. WHOLESALERS;DURABLE GDS	03869	100	408	UNCLASSIFIED ESTABLISHMENTS
03255	89	365	FOOD SVCS & DRINKING PLACES	03608	136	1079	FOOD AND BEVERAGE STORES	03870	261	1161	FOOD SVCS & DRINKING PLACES
03256	96	741	EDUCATIONAL SERVICES	03609	35	275	PAPER MANUFACTURING	03871	40	200	AMUSEMENT; GAMBLING;& RECREAT.
03257	355	3542	HOSPITALS	03740	33	123	WOOD PRODUCT MANUFACTURING	03872	176	631	EDUCATIONAL SERVICES
03258	121	633	FOOD SVCS & DRINKING PLACES	03741	124	611	EDUCATIONAL SERVICES	03873	107	392	EDUCATIONAL SERVICES
03259	12	25	CROP PRODUCTION	03743	719	6298	EDUCATIONAL SERVICES	03874	483	6000	UTILITIES
03260	29	263	EDUCATIONAL SERVICES	03745	33	126	EDUCATIONAL SERVICES	03875	20	62	BLDG MATL & GARDEN EQPMT DLRS
03261	199	1068	EDUCATIONAL SERVICES	03746	6	36	WOOD PRODUCT MANUFACTURING	03878	534	5661	GENERAL MERCHANDISE STORES
03262	105	824	RELIG.; GRANT; CIVIC; PROF ORG	03748	162	738	MOTOR VEHICLE & PARTS DEALERS	03882	35	100	EDUCATIONAL SERVICES
03263	166	1737	EDUCATIONAL SERVICES	03749	6	25	MERCH. WHOLESALERS;DURABLE GDS	03883	8	19	EDUCATIONAL SERVICES
03264	423	3277	EDUCATIONAL SERVICES	03750	17	60	PROF.; SCIENTIFIC; & TECH SVCS	03884	77	269	EDUCATIONAL SERVICES
03266	100	573	RELIG.; GRANT; CIVIC; PROF ORG	03751	21	99	NURSING & RESID. CARE FACILIT.	03885	346	3577	LEATHER & ALLIED PRODUCT MFG
03268	36	82	SPECIAL TRADE CONTRACTORS	03752	31	57	EXEC.; LEGIS.; & OTHER SUPPORT	03886	146	853	SPECIAL TRADE CONTRACTORS
03269	77	383	EDUCATIONAL SERVICES	03753	95	471	EDUCATIONAL SERVICES	03887	54	324	WOOD PRODUCT MANUFACTURING
03272	6	9	CONSTRUCTION OF BUILDINGS	03754	7	32	TEXTILE MILLS	03890	39	466	ACCOMMODATION
03273	15	14	MISCELLANEOUS STORE RETAILERS	03755	385	8571	RELIG.; GRANT; CIVIC; PROF ORG	03894	564	3661	EDUCATIONAL SERVICES
03275	406	3797	EDUCATIONAL SERVICES	03756	52	6297	AMBULATORY HEALTH CARE SVCS	03896	32	120	BLDG MATL & GARDEN EQPMT DLRS
03276	473	8712	MERCH. WHOLESALERS;DURABLE GDS	03765	22	115	EDUCATIONAL SERVICES	03897	2	2	TRUCK TRANSPORTATION
03278	154	1004	ELECT'L EQPMT; APP; & COMP MFG	03766	635	8464	MERCH. WHOLESALERS;DURABLE GDS	03901	157	818	EDUCATIONAL SERVICES
03279	34	136	EDUCATIONAL SERVICES	03768	77	533	ACCOMMODATION	03902	71	366	FOOD SVCS & DRINKING PLACES
03280	42	99	EXEC.; LEGIS.; & OTHER SUPPORT	03769	2	7	INSURANCE CARRIERS & RELATED	03903	243	1390	EDUCATIONAL SERVICES
03281	313	1526	EDUCATIONAL SERVICES	03770	27	271	EDUCATIONAL SERVICES	03904	518	4282	SPORTG GDS;HOBBY;BOOK; & MUSIC
03282	43	308	WOOD PRODUCT MANUFACTURING	03771	23	124	EDUCATIONAL SERVICES	03905	41	191	FOOD SVCS & DRINKING PLACES
03284	30	98	BLDG MATL & GARDEN EQPMT DLRS	03773	424	4698	PRIMARY METAL MANUFACTURING	03906	123	2869	TRANSPORTATION EQUIPMENT MFG
03285	62	201	EDUCATIONAL SERVICES	03774	100	1130	NURSING & RESID. CARE FACILIT.	03907	270	2693	FOOD SVCS & DRINKING PLACES
03287	71	398	ACCOMMODATION	03777	65	481	EDUCATIONAL SERVICES	03908	181	1089	EDUCATIONAL SERVICES
03289	11	86	CONSTRUCTION OF BUILDINGS	03779	24	61	EDUCATIONAL SERVICES	03909	675	5851	FOOD SVCS & DRINKING PLACES
03290	95	398	EDUCATIONAL SERVICES	03780	15	137	EDUCATIONAL SERVICES	03910	42	539	AMUSEMENT; GAMBLING;& RECREAT.
03291	5	17	SUPPORT ACT. FOR TRANSPORT.	03781	61	192	RELIG.; GRANT; CIVIC; PROF ORG	03911	20	252	ACCOMMODATION
03293	17	70	ACCOMMODATION	03782	164	661	EDUCATIONAL SERVICES	04001	49	327	RELIG.; GRANT; CIVIC; PROF ORG
03301	2830	50711	AMBULATORY HEALTH CARE SVCS	03784	447	5965	FOOD SVCS & DRINKING PLACES	04002	224	1384	JUSTICE; PUBIC ORDER/SAFETY
03302	13	34	RELIG.; GRANT; CIVIC; PROF ORG	03785	169	847	FOOD AND BEVERAGE STORES	04003	18	186	FOOD SVCS & DRINKING PLACES
03303	333	2926	BLDG MATL & GARDEN EQPMT DLRS	03801	3078	39212	RELIG.; GRANT; CIVIC; PROF ORG	04004	15	28	FOOD SVCS & DRINKING PLACES
03304	398	4396	MOTOR VEHICLE & PARTS DEALERS	03802	23	56	EDUCATIONAL SERVICES	04005	1138	13086	EDUCATIONAL SERVICES
03305	6	1481	ADMIN. OF ECONOMIC PROGRAMS	03803	1	0	NAT'L SECURITY & INT'L AFFAIRS	04006	10	34	FOOD AND BEVERAGE STORES
03307	173	2001	PERFORM'G ARTS; SPEC. SPORTS	03809	187	1026	EDUCATIONAL SERVICES	04008	84	287	EXEC.; LEGIS.; & OTHER SUPPORT
03431	1468	22847	AMBULATORY HEALTH CARE SVCS	03810	59	281	FOOD SVCS & DRINKING PLACES	04009	344	2610	EDUCATIONAL SERVICES
03435	4	11	EDUCATIONAL SERVICES	03811	148	1233	ACCOMMODATION	04010	44	83	ACCOMMODATION
03440	123	532	EDUCATIONAL SERVICES	03812	112	644	ACCOMMODATION	04011	1178	14475	AMBULATORY HEALTH CARE SVCS
03441	9	48	SPECIAL TRADE CONTRACTORS	03813	145	1155	SOCIAL ASSISTANCE	04014	3	38	PROF.; SCIENTIFIC; & TECH SVCS
03442	40	402	PAPER MANUFACTURING	03814	106	974	EDUCATIONAL SERVICES	04015	154	1579	ACCOMMODATION
03443	47	1204	MERCH. WHOLESALERS;NONDUR. GDS	03815	9	23	JUSTICE; PUBIC ORDER/SAFETY	04016	15	227	JUSTICE; PUBIC ORDER/SAFETY
03444	88	495	EDUCATIONAL SERVICES	03816	34	152	RELIG.; GRANT; CIVIC; PROF ORG	04017	28	84	AMUSEMENT; GAMBLING;& RECREAT.
03445	24	48	SPECIAL TRADE CONTRACTORS	03817	35	164	AMBULATORY HEALTH CARE SVCS	04019	2	5	EDUCATIONAL SERVICES
03446	242	2286	MOTOR VEHICLE & PARTS DEALERS	03818	503	2675	EDUCATIONAL SERVICES	04020	90	516	FOOD AND BEVERAGE STORES
03447	92	556	CONSTRUCTION OF BUILDINGS	03819	68	251	EDUCATIONAL SERVICES	04021	164	1338	EDUCATIONAL SERVICES
03448	24	111	CHEMICAL MANUFACTURING	03820	1555	16891	INSURANCE CARRIERS & RELATED	04022	54	228	ACCOMMODATION
03449	67	211	OTHER INFORMATION SERVICES	03821	14	41	SPECIAL TRADE CONTRACTORS	04024	16	118	MERCH. WHOLESALERS;DURABLE GDS
03450	39	192	EDUCATIONAL SERVICES	03822	1	0	INSURANCE CARRIERS & RELATED	04027	135	665	MOTOR VEHICLE & PARTS DEALERS
03451	114	1004	GENERAL MERCHANDISE STORES	03823	56	337	EDUCATIONAL SERVICES	04028	3	47	ACCOMMODATION
03452	271	2674	MACHINERY MANUFACTURING	03824	295	6471	EDUCATIONAL SERVICES	04029	67	229	ACCOMMODATION
03455	106	442	EDUCATIONAL SERVICES	03825	319	1581	EDUCATIONAL SERVICES	04030	84	563	EDUCATIONAL SERVICES
03456	24	103	COMPUTER & ELECTRONIC PROD MFG	03826	79	552	FOOD SVCS & DRINKING PLACES	04032	491	3902	FOOD SVCS & DRINKING PLACES
03457	25	64	JUSTICE; PUBIC ORDER/SAFETY	03827	109	341	EDUCATIONAL SERVICES	04033	4	1000	SPORTG GDS;HOBBY;BOOK; & MUSIC
03458	502	5531	FABRICATED METAL PRODUCT MFG	03830	25	64	FOOD SVCS & DRINKING PLACES	04037	212	2208	ADMINISTRATIVE & SUPPORT SVCS
03461	204	2160	EDUCATIONAL SERVICES	03832	12	31	ACCOMMODATION	04038	546	4606	NURSING & RESID. CARE FACILIT.
03462	51	440	ADMINISTRATIVE & SUPPORT SVCS	03833	1166	11100	EDUCATIONAL SERVICES	04039	361	2075	EDUCATIONAL SERVICES
03464	28	128	WOOD PRODUCT MANUFACTURING	03835	241	1290	EDUCATIONAL SERVICES	04040	93	529	ACCOMMODATION
03465	75	244	EDUCATIONAL SERVICES	03836	64	330	OTHER INFORMATION SERVICES	04041	33	570	EDUCATIONAL SERVICES
03466	35	284	PRINT'G & RELATED SUPP'T ACT'S	03837	41	226	ACCOMMODATION	04042	136	714	JUSTICE; PUBIC ORDER/SAFETY
03467	71	551	NURSING & RESID. CARE FACILIT.	03838	58	1016	AMUSEMENT; GAMBLING;& RECREAT.	04043	656	5036	FOOD SVCS & DRINKING PLACES
03468	2	2	POSTAL SERVICE	03839	123	441	SPECIAL TRADE CONTRACTORS	04046	490	2890	ACCOMMODATION
03469	38	148	WOOD PRODUCT MANUFACTURING	03840	281	1896	SPORTG GDS;HOBBY;BOOK; & MUSIC	04047	58	306	ACCOMMODATION
03470	171	1363	MERCH. WHOLESALERS;DURABLE GDS	03841	300	2742	MOTOR VEHICLE & PARTS DEALERS	04048	101	499	EDUCATIONAL SERVICES
03561	582	5516	HOSPITALS	03842	890	6658	FOOD SVCS & DRINKING PLACES	04049	92	215	EDUCATIONAL SERVICES
03570	427	4494	PAPER MANUFACTURING	03843	10	32	PUBLISHING INDUSTRIES	04050	19	50	OTHER INFORMATION SERVICES
03574	127	594	EDUCATIONAL SERVICES	03844	178	932	EDUCATIONAL SERVICES	04051	74	214	EDUCATIONAL SERVICES
03575	20	1300	ACCOMMODATION	03845	67	379	FOOD SVCS & DRINKING PLACES	04054	17	130	FOOD SVCS & DRINKING PLACES
03576	238	1991	ACCOMMODATION	03846	80	836	ACCOMMODATION	04055	245	1766	ACCOMMODATION
03579	49	208	SPORTG GDS;HOBBY;BOOK; & MUSIC	03847	3	7	ACCOMMODATION	04056	15	29	MUSEUMS; HIST. SITES;& SIMILAR
03580	129	1951	MUSEUMS; HIST. SITES;& SIMILAR	03848	284	2068	MERCH. WHOLESALERS;DURABLE GDS	04057	7	74	EDUCATIONAL SERVICES
03581	290	2346	GENERAL MERCHANDISE STORES	03849	72	781	ACCOMMODATION	04061	32	97	CONSTRUCTION OF BUILDINGS
03582	92	444	EDUCATIONAL SERVICES	03850	22	116	AMUSEMENT; GAMBLING;& RECREAT.	04062	831	7338	MOTOR VEHICLE & PARTS DEALERS
03583	55	558	AMUSEMENT; GAMBLING;& RECREAT.	03851	108	596	PLASTICS & RUBBER PRODUCTS MFG	04063	16	99	ACCOMMODATION
03584	288	2165	HOSPITALS	03852	11	14	POSTAL SERVICE	04064	386	2472	ACCOMMODATION
03585	101	846	FABRICATED METAL PRODUCT MFG	03853	20	237	ACCOMMODATION	04066	24	62	CONSTRUCTION OF BUILDINGS
03586	40	137	ACCOMMODATION	03854	40	583	ACCOMMODATION	04068	34	237	MERCH. WHOLESALERS;DURABLE GDS
03588	48	171	MERCH. WHOLESALERS;DURABLE GDS	03855	91	409	FOOD SVCS & DRINKING PLACES	04069	31	112	EDUCATIONAL SERVICES
03589	1	30	AMUSEMENT; GAMBLING;& RECREAT.	03856	65	755	TRANSPORTATION EQUIPMENT MFG	04070	16	34	SPECIAL TRADE CONTRACTORS
03590	41	105	EDUCATIONAL SERVICES	03857	237	1484	EDUCATIONAL SERVICES	04071	229	1418	ACCOMMODATION

ZIP CODE	2009 Total Firms	2009 Total Employ-ees	TOP INDUSTRY RANKED on 2009 EMPLOYMENT
04072	778	8221	AMBULATORY HEALTH CARE SVCS
04073	747	8842	AMBULATORY HEALTH CARE SVCS
04074	1232	16163	FOOD AND BEVERAGE STORES
04076	72	185	EDUCATIONAL SERVICES
04077	21	122	ACCOMMODATION
04078	20	104	FOOD AND BEVERAGE STORES
04079	121	349	EDUCATIONAL SERVICES
04082	3	3	POSTAL SERVICE
04083	163	996	EDUCATIONAL SERVICES
04084	255	3246	ELECT'L EQPMT; APP; & COMP MFG
04085	30	154	ACCOMMODATION
04086	428	3882	EDUCATIONAL SERVICES
04087	122	976	EDUCATIONAL SERVICES
04088	51	343	ACCOMMODATION
04090	566	4589	FOOD SVCS & DRINKING PLACES
04091	19	46	SPECIAL TRADE CONTRACTORS
04092	901	14763	PROF.; SCIENTIFIC; & TECH SVCS
04093	263	1409	EDUCATIONAL SERVICES
04094	8	403	MISCELLANEOUS STORE RETAILERS
04095	16	74	JUSTICE; PUBIC ORDER/SAFETY
04096	542	3740	CLOTHING & CLOTH'G ACC. STORES
04097	135	399	SPECIAL TRADE CONTRACTORS
04098	8	16	CONSTRUCTION OF BUILDINGS
04101	3124	35032	PROF.; SCIENTIFIC; & TECH SVCS
04102	930	25663	RELIG.; GRANT; CIVIC; PROF ORG
04103	1456	16221	EDUCATIONAL SERVICES
04104	46	143	PROF.; SCIENTIFIC; & TECH SVCS
04105	623	4627	EDUCATIONAL SERVICES
04106	1643	24223	INSURANCE CARRIERS & RELATED
04107	232	1492	EDUCATIONAL SERVICES
04108	42	173	FOOD SVCS & DRINKING PLACES
04109	7	14	PERSONAL AND LAUNDRY SERVICES
04110	25	243	ADMINISTRATIVE & SUPPORT SVCS
04112	14	22	FOOD AND BEVERAGE STORES
04116	10	28	ADMINISTRATIVE & SUPPORT SVCS
04122	1	8	CREDIT INTERMEDIATION & RELATD
04210	1211	18236	MERCH. WHOLESALERS;NONDUR. GDS
04212	4	2	INSURANCE CARRIERS & RELATED
04216	32	221	WOOD PRODUCT MANUFACTURING
04217	293	1954	FOOD SVCS & DRINKING PLACES
04219	42	190	ACCOMMODATION
04220	66	310	ADMINISTRATIVE & SUPPORT SVCS
04221	27	352	ACCOMMODATION
04222	70	151	EDUCATIONAL SERVICES
04223	2	32	RAIL TRANSPORTATION
04224	81	645	WOOD PRODUCT MANUFACTURING
04225	2	11	FOOD SVCS & DRINKING PLACES
04226	1	1	POSTAL SERVICE
04227	1	12	JUSTICE; PUBIC ORDER/SAFETY
04228	1	1	SUPPORT ACT. FOR TRANSPORT.
04230	2	2	SECURITIES/COMMODITY CONTRACTS
04231	11	76	ACCOMMODATION
04234	6	10	AMBULATORY HEALTH CARE SVCS
04236	106	443	EDUCATIONAL SERVICES
04237	11	12	ACCOMMODATION
04238	31	230	EDUCATIONAL SERVICES
04239	119	2210	PAPER MANUFACTURING
04240	1769	26979	AMBULATORY HEALTH CARE SVCS
04241	5	13	ADMINISTRATIVE & SUPPORT SVCS
04243	3	0	REAL ESTATE
04250	123	1326	PRINT'G & RELATED SUPP'T ACT'S
04252	137	1067	WOOD PRODUCT MANUFACTURING
04253	56	262	EDUCATIONAL SERVICES
04254	121	776	WOOD PRODUCT MANUFACTURING
04255	29	131	WOOD PRODUCT MANUFACTURING
04256	110	759	EDUCATIONAL SERVICES
04257	137	1045	EDUCATIONAL SERVICES
04258	49	254	SPECIAL TRADE CONTRACTORS
04259	97	738	EDUCATIONAL SERVICES
04260	260	1656	EDUCATIONAL SERVICES
04261	29	556	ADMINISTRATIVE & SUPPORT SVCS
04262	5	5	WAREHOUSING AND STORAGE
04263	53	374	ACCOMMODATION
04265	41	327	TEXTILE MILLS
04266	11	33	FOOD SVCS & DRINKING PLACES
04267	5	1	AMUSEMENT; GAMBLING;& RECREAT.
04268	259	2334	HOSPITALS
04270	214	2620	MOTOR VEHICLE & PARTS DEALERS
04271	23	61	JUSTICE; PUBIC ORDER/SAFETY
04274	169	1950	ACCOMMODATION
04275	12	25	FURN. & HOME FURNISHGS STORES
04276	268	3120	PAPER MANUFACTURING
04280	144	796	EDUCATIONAL SERVICES
04281	204	2391	EDUCATIONAL SERVICES
04282	206	1454	EDUCATIONAL SERVICES
04284	29	243	ACCOMMODATION
04285	32	147	ACCOMMODATION
04286	7	9	MISCELLANEOUS STORE RETAILERS
04287	41	200	MISCELLANEOUS MANUFACTURING
04288	3	20	WOOD PRODUCT MANUFACTURING

ZIP CODE	2009 Total Firms	2009 Total Employ-ees	TOP INDUSTRY RANKED on 2009 EMPLOYMENT
04289	57	341	NURSING & RESID. CARE FACILIT.
04290	30	58	FOOD AND BEVERAGE STORES
04291	5	7	CONSTRUCTION OF BUILDINGS
04292	22	121	EDUCATIONAL SERVICES
04294	135	1035	MERCH. WHOLESALERS;NONDUR. GDS
04330	1755	25758	HOSPITALS
04332	6	22	SPECIAL TRADE CONTRACTORS
04333	112	5804	ADMIN. OF ECONOMIC PROGRAMS
04338	1	0	SPECIAL TRADE CONTRACTORS
04341	9	97	REAL ESTATE
04342	29	109	MISCELLANEOUS STORE RETAILERS
04343	9	37	SOCIAL ASSISTANCE
04344	117	844	NURSING & RESID. CARE FACILIT.
04345	440	3622	EDUCATIONAL SERVICES
04346	43	241	FOOD AND BEVERAGE STORES
04347	194	1171	FOOD SVCS & DRINKING PLACES
04348	79	516	BLDG MATL & GARDEN EQPMT DLRS
04349	27	272	ACCOMMODATION
04350	66	275	EDUCATIONAL SERVICES
04351	142	770	BLDG MATL & GARDEN EQPMT DLRS
04352	49	172	ACCOMMODATION
04353	42	194	EDUCATIONAL SERVICES
04354	37	93	EDUCATIONAL SERVICES
04355	73	460	EDUCATIONAL SERVICES
04357	117	893	EDUCATIONAL SERVICES
04358	132	651	EDUCATIONAL SERVICES
04359	7	40	EDUCATIONAL SERVICES
04360	15	47	JUSTICE; PUBIC ORDER/SAFETY
04363	57	236	EDUCATIONAL SERVICES
04364	264	2167	MERCH. WHOLESALERS;NONDUR. GDS
04401	2920	42762	HOSPITALS
04402	20	36	SPECIAL TRADE CONTRACTORS
04406	21	52	SOCIAL ASSISTANCE
04408	11	38	TELECOMMUNICATIONS
04410	21	71	BLDG MATL & GARDEN EQPMT DLRS
04411	29	70	EDUCATIONAL SERVICES
04412	606	8965	HOSPITALS
04413	5	9	ACCOMMODATION
04414	33	182	EXEC.; LEGIS.; & OTHER SUPPORT
04415	5	13	MERCH. WHOLESALERS;NONDUR. GDS
04416	228	2362	PAPER MANUFACTURING
04417	9	10	EXEC.; LEGIS.; & OTHER SUPPORT
04418	29	102	EDUCATIONAL SERVICES
04419	71	382	EDUCATIONAL SERVICES
04420	1	189	EDUCATIONAL SERVICES
04421	55	303	FOOD SVCS & DRINKING PLACES
04422	34	399	EXEC.; LEGIS.; & OTHER SUPPORT
04424	45	369	SECURITIES/COMMODITY CONTRACTS
04426	272	2341	HOSPITALS
04427	71	452	EDUCATIONAL SERVICES
04428	72	462	RELIG.; GRANT; CIVIC; PROF ORG
04429	146	829	EDUCATIONAL SERVICES
04430	70	769	PAPER MANUFACTURING
04431	6	20	ACCOMMODATION
04434	31	148	EDUCATIONAL SERVICES
04435	21	74	MERCH. WHOLESALERS;NONDUR. GDS
04438	24	65	CONSTRUCTION OF BUILDINGS
04441	148	889	HOSPITALS
04442	24	88	FOOD SVCS & DRINKING PLACES
04443	86	1226	SPORTG GDS;HOBBY;BOOK; & MUSIC
04444	302	2384	EDUCATIONAL SERVICES
04448	50	267	NURSING & RESID. CARE FACILIT.
04449	26	88	CONSTRUCTION OF BUILDINGS
04450	31	185	WOOD PRODUCT MANUFACTURING
04451	8	64	FORESTRY AND LOGGING
04453	14	27	EDUCATIONAL SERVICES
04455	26	164	RELIG.; GRANT; CIVIC; PROF ORG
04456	46	162	EDUCATIONAL SERVICES
04457	255	2715	EDUCATIONAL SERVICES
04459	29	154	EDUCATIONAL SERVICES
04460	55	430	MERCH. WHOLESALERS;NONDUR. GDS
04461	51	349	EDUCATIONAL SERVICES
04462	220	1652	HOSPITALS
04463	81	1771	FABRICATED METAL PRODUCT MFG
04464	26	106	FURNITURE & RELATED PROD. MFG
04468	285	3149	PROF.; SCIENTIFIC; & TECH SVCS
04469	13	2700	EDUCATIONAL SERVICES
04471	8	70	FORESTRY AND LOGGING
04472	60	500	CONSTRUCTION OF BUILDINGS
04473	198	10731	EDUCATIONAL SERVICES
04474	107	501	EDUCATIONAL SERVICES
04475	8	15	SPORTG GDS;HOBBY;BOOK; & MUSIC
04476	30	269	NURSING & RESID. CARE FACILIT.
04478	35	157	ACCOMMODATION
04479	33	220	CONSTRUCTION OF BUILDINGS
04481	16	121	ADMINISTRATIVE & SUPPORT SVCS
04485	10	46	EXEC.; LEGIS.; & OTHER SUPPORT
04487	11	33	FOOD AND BEVERAGE STORES
04488	20	76	NURSING & RESID. CARE FACILIT.
04489	8	349	HEAVY & CIVIL ENG. CONSTRUCT'N

ZIP CODE	2009 Total Firms	2009 Total Employ-ees	TOP INDUSTRY RANKED on 2009 EMPLOYMENT
04490	10	233	UNCLASSIFIED ESTABLISHMENTS
04491	11	37	FOOD AND BEVERAGE STORES
04492	5	58	FORESTRY AND LOGGING
04493	58	217	EDUCATIONAL SERVICES
04495	10	55	EDUCATIONAL SERVICES
04496	115	394	EDUCATIONAL SERVICES
04497	10	51	PAPER MANUFACTURING
04530	599	4957	EDUCATIONAL SERVICES
04535	19	46	EXEC.; LEGIS.; & OTHER SUPPORT
04537	144	554	CONSTRUCTION OF BUILDINGS
04538	294	2849	ACCOMMODATION
04539	80	172	MUSEUMS; HIST. SITES;& SIMILAR
04541	2	2	POSTAL SERVICE
04543	338	3209	HOSPITALS
04544	23	293	TRANSPORTATION EQUIPMENT MFG
04547	31	133	FABRICATED METAL PRODUCT MFG
04548	50	359	FOOD SVCS & DRINKING PLACES
04551	29	62	RELIG.; GRANT; CIVIC; PROF ORG
04553	150	761	ELECT'L EQPMT; APP; & COMP MFG
04554	63	283	FOOD SVCS & DRINKING PLACES
04555	70	403	ADMINISTRATIVE & SUPPORT SVCS
04556	84	354	EDUCATIONAL SERVICES
04558	17	86	EDUCATIONAL SERVICES
04562	75	277	FOOD SVCS & DRINKING PLACES
04563	28	63	CONSTRUCTION OF BUILDINGS
04564	29	210	FABRICATED METAL PRODUCT MFG
04565	7	156	ACCOMMODATION
04568	42	78	EDUCATIONAL SERVICES
04571	6	34	FOOD AND BEVERAGE STORES
04572	227	1737	EDUCATIONAL SERVICES
04573	27	86	OTHER INFORMATION SERVICES
04574	53	185	EDUCATIONAL SERVICES
04575	7	123	ADMIN. OF HOUSING PROGRAMS
04576	42	179	ACCOMMODATION
04578	272	1519	EDUCATIONAL SERVICES
04579	101	514	FOOD SVCS & DRINKING PLACES
04605	969	8478	HOSPITALS
04606	28	121	MERCH. WHOLESALERS;NONDUR. GDS
04607	55	180	AMBULATORY HEALTH CARE SVCS
04609	546	6374	PROF.; SCIENTIFIC; & TECH SVCS
04611	20	75	FOOD MANUFACTURING
04612	27	93	ADMINISTRATIVE & SUPPORT SVCS
04613	7	11	FOOD AND BEVERAGE STORES
04614	216	1552	HOSPITALS
04616	43	296	TRANSPORTATION EQUIPMENT MFG
04617	36	137	ACCOMMODATION
04619	282	2356	HOSPITALS
04622	65	404	MERCH. WHOLESALERS;NONDUR. GDS
04623	59	430	FOOD AND BEVERAGE STORES
04624	8	14	FOOD AND BEVERAGE STORES
04625	11	15	AMUSEMENT; GAMBLING;& RECREAT.
04626	20	244	NAT'L SECURITY & INT'L AFFAIRS
04627	86	700	RELIG.; GRANT; CIVIC; PROF ORG
04628	20	60	EDUCATIONAL SERVICES
04629	1	0	PROF.; SCIENTIFIC; & TECH SVCS
04630	52	937	BROADCASTING
04631	103	422	EDUCATIONAL SERVICES
04634	59	139	EDUCATIONAL SERVICES
04635	11	11	FOOD AND BEVERAGE STORES
04637	14	33	ACCOMMODATION
04640	114	648	CONSTRUCTION OF BUILDINGS
04642	8	49	ACCOMMODATION
04643	44	519	MISCELLANEOUS MANUFACTURING
04644	11	102	SPECIAL TRADE CONTRACTORS
04645	10	12	FOOD AND BEVERAGE STORES
04646	8	58	FOOD SVCS & DRINKING PLACES
04648	29	111	PROF.; SCIENTIFIC; & TECH SVCS
04649	64	316	EDUCATIONAL SERVICES
04650	10	24	SPECIAL TRADE CONTRACTORS
04652	81	621	EDUCATIONAL SERVICES
04653	23	219	TRANSPORTATION EQUIPMENT MFG
04654	276	2457	HOSPITALS
04655	26	150	JUSTICE; PUBIC ORDER/SAFETY
04657	4	15	CONSTRUCTION OF BUILDINGS
04658	73	865	FOOD AND BEVERAGE STORES
04660	95	287	AMUSEMENT; GAMBLING;& RECREAT.
04662	87	640	ACCOMMODATION
04664	54	308	EDUCATIONAL SERVICES
04666	37	118	EDUCATIONAL SERVICES
04667	34	211	EDUCATIONAL SERVICES
04668	50	383	APPAREL MANUFACTURING
04669	17	207	FABRICATED METAL PRODUCT MFG
04671	11	32	EDUCATIONAL SERVICES
04672	3	47	PROF.; SCIENTIFIC; & TECH SVCS
04673	11	44	FOOD AND BEVERAGE STORES
04674	10	15	MUSEUMS; HIST. SITES;& SIMILAR
04675	13	155	MISCELLANEOUS STORE RETAILERS
04676	34	119	EDUCATIONAL SERVICES
04677	18	48	SPORTG GDS;HOBBY;BOOK; & MUSIC
04679	215	1525	MOTOR VEHICLE & PARTS DEALERS

BUSINESS DATA

ZIP CODE	2009 Total Firms	2009 Total Employ-ees	TOP INDUSTRY RANKED on 2009 EMPLOYMENT
04680	36	120	TRANSPORTATION EQUIPMENT MFG
04681	96	401	FOOD AND BEVERAGE STORES
04683	6	36	PROF.; SCIENTIFIC; & TECH SVCS
04684	48	236	CONSTRUCTION OF BUILDINGS
04685	44	67	EDUCATIONAL SERVICES
04686	6	9	EDUCATIONAL SERVICES
04691	15	65	FOOD MANUFACTURING
04693	43	602	NAT'L SECURITY & INT'L AFFAIRS
04694	82	927	PAPER MANUFACTURING
04730	530	4562	RELIG.; GRANT; CIVIC; PROF ORG
04732	85	667	WOOD PRODUCT MANUFACTURING
04733	6	16	EDUCATIONAL SERVICES
04734	18	53	TRUCK TRANSPORTATION
04735	26	89	FABRICATED METAL PRODUCT MFG
04736	476	4870	HOSPITALS
04738	1	1	RELIG.; GRANT; CIVIC; PROF ORG
04739	55	557	SOCIAL ASSISTANCE
04740	37	1162	FOOD MANUFACTURING
04742	118	724	EDUCATIONAL SERVICES
04743	279	2757	HOSPITALS
04744	7	65	SUPPORT ACTIVITIES: AGR./FOR.
04745	44	399	EDUCATIONAL SERVICES
04746	9	24	HOSPITALS
04747	68	346	EDUCATIONAL SERVICES
04750	74	1059	NAT'L SECURITY & INT'L AFFAIRS
04751	2	309	NAT'L SECURITY & INT'L AFFAIRS
04756	181	2257	PAPER MANUFACTURING
04757	59	258	CONSTRUCTION OF BUILDINGS
04758	79	586	NURSING & RESID. CARE FACILIT.
04760	25	84	CROP PRODUCTION
04761	20	277	WOOD PRODUCT MANUFACTURING
04762	12	54	EDUCATIONAL SERVICES
04763	30	213	WOOD PRODUCT MANUFACTURING
04764	4	7	ACCOMMODATION
04765	75	384	NURSING & RESID. CARE FACILIT.
04766	9	16	EXEC.; LEGIS.; & OTHER SUPPORT
04768	14	80	WOOD PRODUCT MANUFACTURING
04769	687	10401	AMBULATORY HEALTH CARE SVCS
04772	33	179	MERCH. WHOLESALERS;NONDUR. GDS
04773	6	45	TRUCK TRANSPORTATION
04774	28	106	JUSTICE; PUBIC ORDER/SAFETY
04775	1	2	POSTAL SERVICE
04776	33	129	JUSTICE; PUBIC ORDER/SAFETY
04777	13	164	EDUCATIONAL SERVICES
04779	15	57	FOOD SVCS & DRINKING PLACES
04780	16	37	ACCOMMODATION
04781	10	42	EDUCATIONAL SERVICES
04783	11	27	EDUCATIONAL SERVICES
04785	96	787	NURSING & RESID. CARE FACILIT.
04786	51	298	EDUCATIONAL SERVICES
04787	10	47	REAL ESTATE
04841	755	6410	FOOD SVCS & DRINKING PLACES
04843	453	3711	NURSING & RESID. CARE FACILIT.
04846	6	32	EDUCATIONAL SERVICES
04847	60	251	ACCOMMODATION
04848	49	185	EDUCATIONAL SERVICES
04849	193	729	FOOD SVCS & DRINKING PLACES
04850	7	14	BROADCASTING
04851	6	15	EXEC.; LEGIS.; & OTHER SUPPORT
04852	11	70	ACCOMMODATION
04853	32	101	EDUCATIONAL SERVICES
04854	60	187	SPECIAL TRADE CONTRACTORS
04855	12	80	CONSTRUCTION OF BUILDINGS
04856	362	2935	EDUCATIONAL SERVICES
04858	46	225	AMBULATORY HEALTH CARE SVCS
04859	18	191	AMUSEMENT; GAMBLING;& RECREAT.
04860	69	236	MERCH. WHOLESALERS;NONDUR. GDS
04861	172	1530	JUSTICE; PUBIC ORDER/SAFETY
04862	159	508	EDUCATIONAL SERVICES
04863	73	351	FOOD SVCS & DRINKING PLACES
04864	176	951	FABRICATED METAL PRODUCT MFG
04865	15	73	CONSTRUCTION OF BUILDINGS
04901	1327	20330	HOSPITALS
04903	3	42	BLDG MATL & GARDEN EQPMT DLRS
04910	44	188	EDUCATIONAL SERVICES
04911	41	187	HEAVY & CIVIL ENG. CONSTRUCT'N
04912	29	168	FORESTRY AND LOGGING
04915	618	5478	HOSPITALS
04917	83	757	WOOD PRODUCT MANUFACTURING
04918	20	164	FOOD SVCS & DRINKING PLACES
04920	81	550	MOTOR VEHICLE & PARTS DEALERS
04921	47	216	ACCOMMODATION
04922	22	450	FURNITURE & RELATED PROD. MFG
04923	13	29	LEATHER & ALLIED PRODUCT MFG
04924	38	167	EDUCATIONAL SERVICES
04925	8	59	MOTOR VEHICLE & PARTS DEALERS
04926	16	82	BLDG MATL & GARDEN EQPMT DLRS
04927	67	701	MERCH. WHOLESALERS;DURABLE GDS
04928	63	223	FABRICATED METAL PRODUCT MFG
04929	31	203	MERCH. WHOLESALERS;DURABLE GDS

ZIP CODE	2009 Total Firms	2009 Total Employ-ees	TOP INDUSTRY RANKED on 2009 EMPLOYMENT
04930	150	990	EDUCATIONAL SERVICES
04932	29	115	RELIG.; GRANT; CIVIC; PROF ORG
04933	3	22	MERCH. WHOLESALERS;DURABLE GDS
04935	2	3	POSTAL SERVICE
04936	29	219	RELIG.; GRANT; CIVIC; PROF ORG
04937	247	1883	EDUCATIONAL SERVICES
04938	499	4813	HOSPITALS
04939	11	30	EDUCATIONAL SERVICES
04940	5	11	MERCH. WHOLESALERS;DURABLE GDS
04941	41	250	ACCOMMODATION
04942	34	193	MISCELLANEOUS MANUFACTURING
04943	53	534	LEATHER & ALLIED PRODUCT MFG
04944	9	380	EDUCATIONAL SERVICES
04945	94	620	FORESTRY AND LOGGING
04947	166	1424	ACCOMMODATION
04949	36	149	EDUCATIONAL SERVICES
04950	189	1224	EDUCATIONAL SERVICES
04951	27	59	EDUCATIONAL SERVICES
04952	49	180	MERCH. WHOLESALERS;NONDUR. GDS
04953	218	1577	EDUCATIONAL SERVICES
04954	10	16	PLASTICS & RUBBER PRODUCTS MFG
04955	42	117	EDUCATIONAL SERVICES
04956	23	99	WOOD PRODUCT MANUFACTURING
04957	130	836	CLOTHING & CLOTH'G ACC. STORES
04958	58	394	EDUCATIONAL SERVICES
04961	29	47	ACCOMMODATION
04962	9	62	MISCELLANEOUS MANUFACTURING
04963	247	1745	EDUCATIONAL SERVICES
04964	21	116	FOOD SVCS & DRINKING PLACES
04965	66	556	GENERAL MERCHANDISE STORES
04966	60	174	EDUCATIONAL SERVICES
04967	160	4356	CONSTRUCTION OF BUILDINGS
04969	28	154	NURSING & RESID. CARE FACILIT.
04970	181	678	FOOD SVCS & DRINKING PLACES
04971	44	136	EDUCATIONAL SERVICES
04972	1	1	SPECIAL TRADE CONTRACTORS
04973	40	250	MERCH. WHOLESALERS;DURABLE GDS
04974	137	857	EDUCATIONAL SERVICES
04975	4	20	REAL ESTATE
04976	557	8155	PAPER MANUFACTURING
04978	31	388	AMBULATORY HEALTH CARE SVCS
04979	48	121	EDUCATIONAL SERVICES
04981	61	174	FOOD SVCS & DRINKING PLACES
04982	37	222	WOOD PRODUCT MANUFACTURING
04983	60	280	EDUCATIONAL SERVICES
04984	4	8	FURNITURE & RELATED PROD. MFG
04985	31	532	MOTOR VEHICLE & PARTS DEALERS
04986	54	494	EDUCATIONAL SERVICES
04987	28	88	FOOD AND BEVERAGE STORES
04988	110	575	EDUCATIONAL SERVICES
04989	101	517	WOOD PRODUCT MANUFACTURING
04992	11	30	FOOD AND BEVERAGE STORES
05001	491	4072	POSTAL SERVICE
05009	14	714	HOSPITALS
05030	38	228	EXEC.; LEGIS.; & OTHER SUPPORT
05031	27	133	ACCOMMODATION
05032	111	846	PLASTICS & RUBBER PRODUCTS MFG
05033	170	1228	FABRICATED METAL PRODUCT MFG
05034	27	81	FURN. & HOME FURNISHGS STORES
05035	27	146	MERCH. WHOLESALERS;DURABLE GDS
05036	17	138	SPECIAL TRADE CONTRACTORS
05037	28	433	AMUSEMENT; GAMBLING;& RECREAT.
05038	84	401	EDUCATIONAL SERVICES
05039	15	29	EXEC.; LEGIS.; & OTHER SUPPORT
05040	21	126	EDUCATIONAL SERVICES
05041	7	41	MOTOR VEHICLE & PARTS DEALERS
05042	14	66	UTILITIES
05043	30	294	FURNITURE & RELATED PROD. MFG
05045	83	683	ACCOMMODATION
05046	52	159	JUSTICE; PUBIC ORDER/SAFETY
05047	81	195	SOCIAL ASSISTANCE
05048	79	372	EDUCATIONAL SERVICES
05049	4	15	FOOD SVCS & DRINKING PLACES
05050	2	3	BLDG MATL & GARDEN EQPMT DLRS
05051	33	142	EDUCATIONAL SERVICES
05052	11	78	MACHINERY MANUFACTURING
05053	13	38	PUBLISHING INDUSTRIES
05054	5	48	BLDG MATL & GARDEN EQPMT DLRS
05055	164	877	MERCH. WHOLESALERS;NONDUR. GDS
05056	31	428	ACCOMMODATION
05058	12	111	ACCOMMODATION
05059	81	939	ACCOMMODATION
05060	250	2213	HOSPITALS
05061	20	340	EDUCATIONAL SERVICES
05062	23	72	EDUCATIONAL SERVICES
05065	56	230	EDUCATIONAL SERVICES
05067	13	67	EDUCATIONAL SERVICES
05068	121	714	EDUCATIONAL SERVICES
05069	12	60	REPAIR AND MAINTENANCE
05070	16	56	EDUCATIONAL SERVICES

ZIP CODE	2009 Total Firms	2009 Total Employ-ees	TOP INDUSTRY RANKED on 2009 EMPLOYMENT
05071	14	83	FOOD SVCS & DRINKING PLACES
05072	16	35	CROP PRODUCTION
05073	10	49	AMBULATORY HEALTH CARE SVCS
05074	27	268	EDUCATIONAL SERVICES
05075	32	91	EXEC.; LEGIS.; & OTHER SUPPORT
05076	7	14	PRINT'G & RELATED SUPP'T ACT'S
05077	32	258	MERCH. WHOLESALERS;DURABLE GDS
05079	19	73	EDUCATIONAL SERVICES
05081	53	512	EDUCATIONAL SERVICES
05083	17	49	EDUCATIONAL SERVICES
05084	9	17	MISCELLANEOUS MANUFACTURING
05085	7	6	POSTAL SERVICE
05086	17	48	FOOD AND BEVERAGE STORES
05088	36	234	TRANSIT & GRND PASS. TRANSPORT
05089	221	1833	HOSPITALS
05091	371	2164	FOOD SVCS & DRINKING PLACES
05101	278	2292	MISCELLANEOUS MANUFACTURING
05141	3	5	GASOLINE STATIONS
05142	45	190	BROADCASTING
05143	273	1252	PRINT'G & RELATED SUPP'T ACT'S
05146	40	179	ACCOMMODATION
05148	60	305	EDUCATIONAL SERVICES
05149	302	3655	ACCOMMODATION
05150	64	1005	BLDG MATL & GARDEN EQPMT DLRS
05151	61	202	JUSTICE; PUBIC ORDER/SAFETY
05152	11	121	AMUSEMENT; GAMBLING;& RECREAT.
05153	39	120	EDUCATIONAL SERVICES
05154	44	212	EDUCATIONAL SERVICES
05155	32	1324	ACCOMMODATION
05156	460	3660	HOSPITALS
05158	87	1086	REPAIR AND MAINTENANCE
05159	11	94	ELECT'L EQPMT; APP; & COMP MFG
05161	25	132	GENERAL MERCHANDISE STORES
05201	903	10442	HOSPITALS
05250	152	983	MISCELLANEOUS MANUFACTURING
05251	98	479	EDUCATIONAL SERVICES
05252	21	45	PLASTICS & RUBBER PRODUCTS MFG
05253	31	179	MISCELLANEOUS MANUFACTURING
05254	155	1105	ACCOMMODATION
05255	475	3049	FOOD SVCS & DRINKING PLACES
05257	89	743	MERCH. WHOLESALERS;DURABLE GDS
05260	5	51	JUSTICE; PUBIC ORDER/SAFETY
05261	64	304	EDUCATIONAL SERVICES
05262	105	538	PLASTICS & RUBBER PRODUCTS MFG
05301	1261	12068	EDUCATIONAL SERVICES
05302	7	23	RELIG.; GRANT; CIVIC; PROF ORG
05304	1	49	CHEMICAL MANUFACTURING
05340	42	196	REAL ESTATE
05341	34	89	EDUCATIONAL SERVICES
05342	36	170	EDUCATIONAL SERVICES
05343	37	108	EDUCATIONAL SERVICES
05344	27	198	EDUCATIONAL SERVICES
05345	90	432	EDUCATIONAL SERVICES
05346	166	1185	EDUCATIONAL SERVICES
05350	23	76	EDUCATIONAL SERVICES
05351	4	9	CONSTRUCTION OF BUILDINGS
05352	17	97	JUSTICE; PUBIC ORDER/SAFETY
05353	71	717	AMBULATORY HEALTH CARE SVCS
05354	52	851	UTILITIES
05355	20	46	EDUCATIONAL SERVICES
05356	136	1991	ACCOMMODATION
05357	7	15	AMUSEMENT; GAMBLING;& RECREAT.
05358	9	31	EDUCATIONAL SERVICES
05359	20	59	ACCOMMODATION
05360	14	22	EXEC.; LEGIS.; & OTHER SUPPORT
05361	25	93	EDUCATIONAL SERVICES
05362	10	29	JUSTICE; PUBIC ORDER/SAFETY
05363	209	2485	ACCOMMODATION
05401	2190	32354	AMBULATORY HEALTH CARE SVCS
05402	11	28	ADMINISTRATIVE & SUPPORT SVCS
05403	1405	19418	FOOD SVCS & DRINKING PLACES
05404	279	2992	SOCIAL ASSISTANCE
05405	21	357	OTHER INFORMATION SERVICES
05406	13	65	RELIG.; GRANT; CIVIC; PROF ORG
05407	3	2	CONSTRUCTION OF BUILDINGS
05408	175	1472	NURSING & RESID. CARE FACILIT.
05439	2	585	EDUCATIONAL SERVICES
05440	79	305	EDUCATIONAL SERVICES
05441	17	64	EDUCATIONAL SERVICES
05442	7	18	EDUCATIONAL SERVICES
05443	334	1480	EDUCATIONAL SERVICES
05444	80	261	ACCOMMODATION
05445	155	520	EDUCATIONAL SERVICES
05446	844	8367	AMBULATORY HEALTH CARE SVCS
05447	11	28	FOOD SVCS & DRINKING PLACES
05448	18	41	SPECIAL TRADE CONTRACTORS
05450	189	1394	FOOD SVCS & DRINKING PLACES
05451	17	18	RELIG.; GRANT; CIVIC; PROF ORG
05452	911	7153	EDUCATIONAL SERVICES
05453	3	8	ADMINISTRATIVE & SUPPORT SVCS

ZIP CODE	2009 Total Firms	2009 Total Employ-ees	TOP INDUSTRY RANKED on 2009 EMPLOYMENT	ZIP CODE	2009 Total Firms	2009 Total Employ-ees	TOP INDUSTRY RANKED on 2009 EMPLOYMENT	ZIP CODE	2009 Total Firms	2009 Total Employ-ees	TOP INDUSTRY RANKED on 2009 EMPLOYMENT
05454	122	881	EDUCATIONAL SERVICES	05738	43	165	ELECTRONICS & APPLIANCE STORES	06006	1	0	POSTAL SERVICE
05455	30	131	EDUCATIONAL SERVICES	05739	64	310	FURNITURE & RELATED PROD. MFG	06010	2151	19445	FABRICATED METAL PRODUCT MFG
05456	52	265	EDUCATIONAL SERVICES	05740	19	36	MERCH. WHOLESALERS;NONDUR. GDS	06011	8	24	PROF.; SCIENTIFIC; & TECH SVCS
05457	43	144	EXEC.; LEGIS.; & OTHER SUPPORT	05741	3	13	HEAVY & CIVIL ENG. CONSTRUCT'N	06013	249	1197	EDUCATIONAL SERVICES
05458	79	258	EDUCATIONAL SERVICES	05742	14	31	JUSTICE; PUBIC ORDER/SAFETY	06016	132	993	MERCH. WHOLESALERS;NONDUR. GDS
05459	56	334	EDUCATIONAL SERVICES	05743	164	1076	EDUCATIONAL SERVICES	06018	233	3052	MISCELLANEOUS MANUFACTURING
05460	16	289	ACCOMMODATION	05744	13	64	TRUCK TRANSPORTATION	06019	740	4058	FOOD SVCS & DRINKING PLACES
05461	186	1023	EDUCATIONAL SERVICES	05745	9	128	FURNITURE & RELATED PROD. MFG	06020	1	5	MACHINERY MANUFACTURING
05462	54	117	EDUCATIONAL SERVICES	05746	5	8	MERCH. WHOLESALERS;NONDUR. GDS	06021	33	84	SOCIAL ASSISTANCE
05463	24	40	EDUCATIONAL SERVICES	05747	14	66	WOOD PRODUCT MANUFACTURING	06023	75	1243	MOTOR VEHICLE & PARTS DEALERS
05464	107	1522	ACCOMMODATION	05748	20	137	EDUCATIONAL SERVICES	06024	19	129	SPECIAL TRADE CONTRACTORS
05465	162	799	EDUCATIONAL SERVICES	05750	14	57	NURSING & RESID. CARE FACILIT.	06025	5	6	TRANSPORTATION EQUIPMENT MFG
05466	6	8	MOTOR VEHICLE & PARTS DEALERS	05751	211	5951	ACCOMMODATION	06026	361	4834	NAT'L SECURITY & INT'L AFFAIRS
05468	388	3484	EDUCATIONAL SERVICES	05753	760	8060	EDUCATIONAL SERVICES	06027	50	149	EDUCATIONAL SERVICES
05469	29	76	EDUCATIONAL SERVICES	05757	39	105	JUSTICE; PUBIC ORDER/SAFETY	06028	2	4	POSTAL SERVICE
05470	20	68	SPECIAL TRADE CONTRACTORS	05758	26	101	EDUCATIONAL SERVICES	06029	476	2694	EDUCATIONAL SERVICES
05471	36	123	ACCOMMODATION	05759	98	1152	NONSTORE RETAILERS	06030	47	222	AMBULATORY HEALTH CARE SVCS
05472	100	399	SPECIAL TRADE CONTRACTORS	05760	50	171	EDUCATIONAL SERVICES	06031	59	403	EDUCATIONAL SERVICES
05473	45	136	CONSTRUCTION OF BUILDINGS	05761	46	110	FOOD SVCS & DRINKING PLACES	06032	1788	33937	EDUCATIONAL SERVICES
05474	50	405	ACCOMMODATION	05762	28	115	FABRICATED METAL PRODUCT MFG	06033	1958	18084	SOCIAL ASSISTANCE
05476	84	635	EDUCATIONAL SERVICES	05763	109	556	EDUCATIONAL SERVICES	06034	7	7	SPECIAL TRADE CONTRACTORS
05477	217	1287	ACCOMMODATION	05764	142	944	EDUCATIONAL SERVICES	06035	394	2341	SOCIAL ASSISTANCE
05478	823	7686	HOSPITALS	05765	52	222	EDUCATIONAL SERVICES	06037	1151	10714	ADMINISTRATIVE & SUPPORT SVCS
05479	2	0	RELIG.; GRANT; CIVIC; PROF ORG	05766	17	50	EDUCATIONAL SERVICES	06039	126	1344	ACCOMMODATION
05481	9	12	SPECIAL TRADE CONTRACTORS	05767	73	386	EDUCATIONAL SERVICES	06040	1629	12945	RELIG.; GRANT; CIVIC; PROF ORG
05482	414	3711	NURSING & RESID. CARE FACILIT.	05768	11	32	ADMINISTRATIVE & SUPPORT SVCS	06042	1201	17951	AMBULATORY HEALTH CARE SVCS
05483	34	84	MERCH. WHOLESALERS;NONDUR. GDS	05769	39	282	ACCOMMODATION	06043	218	1364	EDUCATIONAL SERVICES
05485	8	185	PAPER MANUFACTURING	05770	67	225	TELECOMMUNICATIONS	06045	8	26	WASTE MANAGMT & REMEDIAT'N SVC
05486	90	507	ACCOMMODATION	05772	23	144	FOOD SVCS & DRINKING PLACES	06050	15	188	POSTAL SERVICE
05487	47	152	EDUCATIONAL SERVICES	05773	91	463	EDUCATIONAL SERVICES	06051	1188	13416	FABRICATED METAL PRODUCT MFG
05488	280	2376	EDUCATIONAL SERVICES	05774	22	102	ACCOMMODATION	06052	348	7228	HOSPITALS
05489	66	238	RELIG.; GRANT; CIVIC; PROF ORG	05775	27	231	MERCH. WHOLESALERS;DURABLE GDS	06053	588	7576	EDUCATIONAL SERVICES
05490	10	66	EDUCATIONAL SERVICES	05776	10	38	ELECT'L EQPMT; APP; & COMP MFG	06057	232	2430	PROF.; SCIENTIFIC; & TECH SVCS
05491	285	3434	MOTOR VEHICLE & PARTS DEALERS	05777	106	474	EDUCATIONAL SERVICES	06058	106	346	EDUCATIONAL SERVICES
05492	17	35	EDUCATIONAL SERVICES	05778	22	58	EDUCATIONAL SERVICES	06059	10	7	SPECIAL TRADE CONTRACTORS
05494	43	195	SPECIAL TRADE CONTRACTORS	05819	695	7295	EDUCATIONAL SERVICES	06060	53	165	ACCOMMODATION
05495	1033	12032	BLDG MATL & GARDEN EQPMT DLRS	05820	19	66	EDUCATIONAL SERVICES	06061	11	77	SOCIAL ASSISTANCE
05601	11	12	SPECIAL TRADE CONTRACTORS	05821	53	191	RELIG.; GRANT; CIVIC; PROF ORG	06062	1044	12369	SPECIAL TRADE CONTRACTORS
05602	1131	13757	HOSPITALS	05822	99	623	NURSING & RESID. CARE FACILIT.	06063	125	695	EDUCATIONAL SERVICES
05603	1	100	ADMIN. OF ECONOMIC PROGRAMS	05823	3	1	FABRICATED METAL PRODUCT MFG	06064	3	0	FURNITURE & RELATED PROD. MFG
05604	5	292	INSURANCE CARRIERS & RELATED	05824	46	222	EDUCATIONAL SERVICES	06065	18	42	MERCH. WHOLESALERS;DURABLE GDS
05609	21	394	EXEC.; LEGIS.; & OTHER SUPPORT	05825	16	112	TRUCK TRANSPORTATION	06066	1331	13188	HOSPITALS
05620	19	742	ADMIN. OF ECONOMIC PROGRAMS	05826	29	107	JUSTICE; PUBIC ORDER/SAFETY	06067	1221	14456	PROF.; SCIENTIFIC; & TECH SVCS
05633	21	586	EXEC.; LEGIS.; & OTHER SUPPORT	05827	15	258	ACCOMMODATION	06068	144	796	NURSING & RESID. CARE FACILIT.
05640	3	3	FOOD AND BEVERAGE STORES	05828	82	327	EDUCATIONAL SERVICES	06069	211	1797	AMBULATORY HEALTH CARE SVCS
05641	947	8359	EDUCATIONAL SERVICES	05829	161	1185	SPECIAL TRADE CONTRACTORS	06070	831	6584	EDUCATIONAL SERVICES
05647	37	549	ANIMAL PRODUCTION	05830	50	433	MACHINERY MANUFACTURING	06071	369	3114	HOSPITALS
05648	19	41	FURN. & HOME FURNISHGS STORES	05832	36	337	ACCOMMODATION	06072	7	10	REPAIR AND MAINTENANCE
05649	25	102	EXEC.; LEGIS.; & OTHER SUPPORT	05833	7	31	FOOD AND BEVERAGE STORES	06073	154	648	EDUCATIONAL SERVICES
05650	24	58	FOOD MANUFACTURING	05836	20	40	FOOD MANUFACTURING	06074	1388	13930	PROF.; SCIENTIFIC; & TECH SVCS
05651	80	503	CONSTRUCTION OF BUILDINGS	05837	5	12	EDUCATIONAL SERVICES	06075	34	20	PROF.; SCIENTIFIC; & TECH SVCS
05652	21	124	EDUCATIONAL SERVICES	05838	4	11	MOTOR VEHICLE & PARTS DEALERS	06076	415	3965	HOSPITALS
05653	9	38	EXEC.; LEGIS.; & OTHER SUPPORT	05839	23	129	NURSING & RESID. CARE FACILIT.	06077	3	50	JUSTICE; PUBIC ORDER/SAFETY
05654	21	193	MISCELLANEOUS STORE RETAILERS	05840	1	17	HEAVY & CIVIL ENG. CONSTRUCT'N	06078	413	4116	JUSTICE; PUBIC ORDER/SAFETY
05655	110	612	EDUCATIONAL SERVICES	05841	31	277	ACCOMMODATION	06079	1	1	POSTAL SERVICE
05656	124	962	EDUCATIONAL SERVICES	05842	9	10	MISCELLANEOUS STORE RETAILERS	06081	58	164	EDUCATIONAL SERVICES
05657	10	34	MUSEUMS; HIST. SITES;& SIMILAR	05843	151	759	EDUCATIONAL SERVICES	06082	1757	23706	INSURANCE CARRIERS & RELATED
05658	42	108	JUSTICE; PUBIC ORDER/SAFETY	05845	40	217	MERCH. WHOLESALERS;DURABLE GDS	06083	11	20	REAL ESTATE
05660	81	377	EDUCATIONAL SERVICES	05846	70	293	FURNITURE & RELATED PROD. MFG	06084	559	3706	EDUCATIONAL SERVICES
05661	428	3523	HOSPITALS	05847	19	65	EDUCATIONAL SERVICES	06085	241	1446	JUSTICE; PUBIC ORDER/SAFETY
05662	3	7	FOOD AND BEVERAGE STORES	05848	14	43	ACCOMMODATION	06088	572	6017	FOOD SVCS & DRINKING PLACES
05663	214	1988	EDUCATIONAL SERVICES	05849	49	188	FURNITURE & RELATED PROD. MFG	06089	132	4739	INSURANCE CARRIERS & RELATED
05664	7	59	SPORTG GDS;HOBBY;BOOK; & MUSIC	05850	7	162	EDUCATIONAL SERVICES	06090	32	41	RELIG.; GRANT; CIVIC; PROF ORG
05665	3	12	WOOD PRODUCT MANUFACTURING	05851	304	3332	EDUCATIONAL SERVICES	06091	11	1	POSTAL SERVICE
05666	6	17	EXEC.; LEGIS.; & OTHER SUPPORT	05853	16	38	FOOD AND BEVERAGE STORES	06092	119	976	MOTOR VEHICLE & PARTS DEALERS
05667	78	473	EDUCATIONAL SERVICES	05855	489	4876	HOSPITALS	06093	78	580	MERCH. WHOLESALERS;NONDUR. GDS
05669	24	190	ACCOMMODATION	05857	28	151	MISCELLANEOUS STORE RETAILERS	06094	3	3	ADMINISTRATIVE & SUPPORT SVCS
05670	22	176	MOTOR VEHICLE & PARTS DEALERS	05858	6	14	SPECIAL TRADE CONTRACTORS	06095	1327	21511	MACHINERY MANUFACTURING
05671	26	1785	ADMIN. HUMAN RESOURCE PROGRAMS	05859	59	625	ACCOMMODATION	06096	718	12489	EXEC.; LEGIS.; & OTHER SUPPORT
05672	534	5998	ACCOMMODATION	05860	95	560	EDUCATIONAL SERVICES	06098	539	4065	EDUCATIONAL SERVICES
05673	416	1778	FOOD SVCS & DRINKING PLACES	05861	3	6	SPECIAL TRADE CONTRACTORS	06101	4	9	POSTAL SERVICE
05674	157	1421	ACCOMMODATION	05862	23	96	RELIG.; GRANT; CIVIC; PROF ORG	06102	50	3	AMBULATORY HEALTH CARE SVCS
05675	27	85	SPECIAL TRADE CONTRACTORS	05863	6	48	POSTAL SERVICE	06103	1434	27417	PROF.; SCIENTIFIC; & TECH SVCS
05676	348	3446	PROF.; SCIENTIFIC; & TECH SVCS	05866	18	59	EDUCATIONAL SERVICES	06105	1009	19243	HOSPITALS
05677	84	525	COMPUTER & ELECTRONIC PROD MFG	05867	24	115	EDUCATIONAL SERVICES	06106	2131	26653	EXEC.; LEGIS.; & OTHER SUPPORT
05678	18	184	NONMETALLIC MINERAL PROD. MFG	05868	23	90	JUSTICE; PUBIC ORDER/SAFETY	06107	1133	9713	EDUCATIONAL SERVICES
05679	90	592	EDUCATIONAL SERVICES	05871	52	128	EDUCATIONAL SERVICES	06108	1564	26831	MERCH. WHOLESALERS;DURABLE GDS
05680	45	165	EDUCATIONAL SERVICES	05872	18	54	EDUCATIONAL SERVICES	06109	1137	10174	MERCH. WHOLESALERS;DURABLE GDS
05681	22	52	UNCLASSIFIED ESTABLISHMENTS	05873	30	64	EDUCATIONAL SERVICES	06110	853	8730	FABRICATED METAL PRODUCT MFG
05682	17	58	EDUCATIONAL SERVICES	05874	23	56	CHEMICAL MANUFACTURING	06111	1607	25168	HEAVY & CIVIL ENG. CONSTRUCT'N
05701	1635	16483	AMBULATORY HEALTH CARE SVCS	05875	10	41	SPORTG GDS;HOBBY;BOOK; & MUSIC	06112	443	8318	SOCIAL ASSISTANCE
05702	8	5	MISCELLANEOUS STORE RETAILERS	05901	1	28	ACCOMMODATION	06114	1014	10940	FABRICATED METAL PRODUCT MFG
05730	15	23	GENERAL MERCHANDISE STORES	05902	6	519	FURNITURE & RELATED PROD. MFG	06115	22	6375	HOSPITALS
05731	13	45	ACCOMMODATION	05903	41	134	EDUCATIONAL SERVICES	06117	440	8315	EDUCATIONAL SERVICES
05732	56	259	AMBULATORY HEALTH CARE SVCS	05904	8	143	PAPER MANUFACTURING	06118	506	5249	EDUCATIONAL SERVICES
05733	274	1534	EDUCATIONAL SERVICES	05905	27	85	JUSTICE; PUBIC ORDER/SAFETY	06119	554	2930	EDUCATIONAL SERVICES
05734	52	136	EDUCATIONAL SERVICES	05906	29	134	SPECIAL TRADE CONTRACTORS	06120	566	8318	PERFORM'G ARTS; SPEC. SPORTS
05735	147	1216	EDUCATIONAL SERVICES	05907	16	45	EXEC.; LEGIS.; & OTHER SUPPORT	06123	2	7	REPAIR AND MAINTENANCE
05736	33	151	MERCH. WHOLESALERS;DURABLE GDS	06001	1183	9451	PROF.; SCIENTIFIC; & TECH SVCS	06127	2	0	RELIG.; GRANT; CIVIC; PROF ORG
05737	19	145	ACCOMMODATION	06002	1375	15687	NURSING & RESID. CARE FACILIT.	06128	2	2	CONSTRUCTION OF BUILDINGS

BUSINESS DATA

ZIP CODE	2009 Total Firms	2009 Total Employ-ees	TOP INDUSTRY RANKED on 2009 EMPLOYMENT	ZIP CODE	2009 Total Firms	2009 Total Employ-ees	TOP INDUSTRY RANKED on 2009 EMPLOYMENT	ZIP CODE	2009 Total Firms	2009 Total Employ-ees	TOP INDUSTRY RANKED on 2009 EMPLOYMENT
06129	4	3	INSURANCE CARRIERS & RELATED	06388	3	12	SUPPORT ACT. FOR TRANSPORT.	06615	1113	11856	PROF.; SCIENTIFIC; & TECH SVCS
06131	2	1	WASTE MANAGMT & REMEDIAT'N SVC	06389	10	85	JUSTICE; PUBIC ORDER/SAFETY	06701	3	2	PERSONAL AND LAUNDRY SERVICES
06132	2	5	PROF.; SCIENTIFIC; & TECH SVCS	06390	92	482	AMUSEMENT; GAMBLING;& RECREAT.	06702	753	8238	JUSTICE; PUBIC ORDER/SAFETY
06133	6	11	ADMINISTRATIVE & SUPPORT SVCS	06401	653	4917	EDUCATIONAL SERVICES	06704	679	5077	EDUCATIONAL SERVICES
06134	6	57	SOCIAL ASSISTANCE	06403	205	1172	SPECIAL TRADE CONTRACTORS	06705	911	9424	NURSING & RESID. CARE FACILIT.
06137	5	7	SPECIAL TRADE CONTRACTORS	06404	4	5	MISCELLANEOUS STORE RETAILERS	06706	547	6779	HOSPITALS
06141	3	5	MERCH. WHOLESALERS;DURABLE GDS	06405	1922	15936	FOOD SVCS & DRINKING PLACES	06708	1120	13233	AMBULATORY HEALTH CARE SVCS
06142	2	2	SPECIAL TRADE CONTRACTORS	06409	101	937	PROF.; SCIENTIFIC; & TECH SVCS	06710	154	1061	EDUCATIONAL SERVICES
06143	1	1	BLDG MATL & GARDEN EQPMT DLRS	06410	1313	15784	MERCH. WHOLESALERS;NONDUR. GDS	06712	384	1935	EDUCATIONAL SERVICES
06146	2	7	ADMINISTRATIVE & SUPPORT SVCS	06412	243	2603	ELECT'L EQPMT; APP; & COMP MFG	06716	640	3385	FABRICATED METAL PRODUCT MFG
06147	4	5	SPECIAL TRADE CONTRACTORS	06413	720	4919	CHEMICAL MANUFACTURING	06720	1	0	UNCLASSIFIED ESTABLISHMENTS
06156	6	10002	INSURANCE CARRIERS & RELATED	06414	5	17	ADMINISTRATIVE & SUPPORT SVCS	06721	3	12	PROF.; SCIENTIFIC; & TECH SVCS
06183	7	4022	INSURANCE CARRIERS & RELATED	06415	652	4408	EDUCATIONAL SERVICES	06722	1	0	REPAIR AND MAINTENANCE
06226	697	8572	EDUCATIONAL SERVICES	06416	734	7100	FOOD SVCS & DRINKING PLACES	06750	120	622	PROF.; SCIENTIFIC; & TECH SVCS
06230	3	8	MERCH. WHOLESALERS;DURABLE GDS	06417	257	1456	MISCELLANEOUS STORE RETAILERS	06751	209	810	HOSPITALS
06231	49	137	AMBULATORY HEALTH CARE SVCS	06418	531	5698	HOSPITALS	06752	60	291	EXEC.; LEGIS.; & OTHER SUPPORT
06232	79	508	ACCOMMODATION	06419	261	587	EDUCATIONAL SERVICES	06753	31	39	EXEC.; LEGIS.; & OTHER SUPPORT
06233	4	4	POSTAL SERVICE	06420	152	663	EDUCATIONAL SERVICES	06754	87	303	FURNITURE & RELATED PROD. MFG
06234	252	1685	FOOD SVCS & DRINKING PLACES	06422	338	2104	EDUCATIONAL SERVICES	06755	38	130	WOOD PRODUCT MANUFACTURING
06235	84	365	EDUCATIONAL SERVICES	06423	202	789	PERFORM'G ARTS; SPEC. SPORTS	06756	139	640	MERCH. WHOLESALERS;NONDUR. GDS
06237	190	1440	EDUCATIONAL SERVICES	06424	439	2018	EDUCATIONAL SERVICES	06757	238	1662	EDUCATIONAL SERVICES
06238	303	1307	EDUCATIONAL SERVICES	06426	545	3367	PROF.; SCIENTIFIC; & TECH SVCS	06758	4	48	ACCOMMODATION
06239	481	4056	EDUCATIONAL SERVICES	06437	1281	7724	AMBULATORY HEALTH CARE SVCS	06759	477	3352	EDUCATIONAL SERVICES
06241	201	3995	MERCH. WHOLESALERS;NONDUR. GDS	06438	164	616	RELIG.; GRANT; CIVIC; PROF ORG	06762	389	4658	CHEMICAL MANUFACTURING
06242	59	372	TRANSPORTATION EQUIPMENT MFG	06439	8	32	CONSTRUCTION OF BUILDINGS	06763	92	354	FOOD SVCS & DRINKING PLACES
06243	12	39	MERCH. WHOLESALERS;DURABLE GDS	06440	9	22	MISCELLANEOUS STORE RETAILERS	06770	915	7428	EDUCATIONAL SERVICES
06244	5	16	FURNITURE & RELATED PROD. MFG	06441	183	752	EDUCATIONAL SERVICES	06776	1371	10362	PAPER MANUFACTURING
06245	1	2	FOOD AND BEVERAGE STORES	06442	56	355	ELECT'L EQPMT; APP; & COMP MFG	06777	115	515	FOOD SVCS & DRINKING PLACES
06246	3	2	FOOD AND BEVERAGE STORES	06443	970	5796	EDUCATIONAL SERVICES	06778	28	46	EDUCATIONAL SERVICES
06247	74	263	EDUCATIONAL SERVICES	06444	11	42	FURN. & HOME FURNISHGS STORES	06779	202	1109	EDUCATIONAL SERVICES
06248	261	1582	EDUCATIONAL SERVICES	06447	291	1786	INSURANCE CARRIERS & RELATED	06781	12	56	AMUSEMENT; GAMBLING;& RECREAT.
06249	195	1527	SPECIAL TRADE CONTRACTORS	06450	1322	15074	EDUCATIONAL SERVICES	06782	157	650	EDUCATIONAL SERVICES
06250	170	1778	HOSPITALS	06451	795	9971	AMBULATORY HEALTH CARE SVCS	06783	100	249	JUSTICE; PUBIC ORDER/SAFETY
06251	2	9	MERCH. WHOLESALERS;NONDUR. GDS	06455	233	2051	COMPUTER & ELECTRONIC PROD MFG	06784	142	435	EDUCATIONAL SERVICES
06254	134	967	BLDG MATL & GARDEN EQPMT DLRS	06456	10	15	RELIG.; GRANT; CIVIC; PROF ORG	06785	14	100	EDUCATIONAL SERVICES
06255	110	929	EDUCATIONAL SERVICES	06457	2267	29456	HOSPITALS	06786	286	2974	FABRICATED METAL PRODUCT MFG
06256	119	1889	GENERAL MERCHANDISE STORES	06459	6	80	OTHER INFORMATION SERVICES	06787	418	3437	FABRICATED METAL PRODUCT MFG
06258	45	540	EDUCATIONAL SERVICES	06460	2682	24159	FOOD SVCS & DRINKING PLACES	06790	1647	16343	AMBULATORY HEALTH CARE SVCS
06259	116	1159	FABRICATED METAL PRODUCT MFG	06461	454	7007	FOOD SVCS & DRINKING PLACES	06791	181	733	SPECIAL TRADE CONTRACTORS
06260	626	6706	HOSPITALS	06467	54	567	NONMETALLIC MINERAL PROD. MFG	06793	69	470	EDUCATIONAL SERVICES
06262	13	130	MISCELLANEOUS STORE RETAILERS	06468	947	6562	EDUCATIONAL SERVICES	06794	127	680	EDUCATIONAL SERVICES
06263	9	266	COMPUTER & ELECTRONIC PROD MFG	06469	114	815	EDUCATIONAL SERVICES	06795	734	7790	FABRICATED METAL PRODUCT MFG
06264	39	204	EDUCATIONAL SERVICES	06470	895	7288	PUBLISHING INDUSTRIES	06796	46	451	ACCOMMODATION
06266	31	302	FABRICATED METAL PRODUCT MFG	06471	381	2650	NURSING & RESID. CARE FACILIT.	06798	707	2748	FOOD SVCS & DRINKING PLACES
06267	14	199	SOCIAL ASSISTANCE	06472	216	2399	COMPUTER & ELECTRONIC PROD MFG	06801	1025	8047	AMBULATORY HEALTH CARE SVCS
06268	324	3053	FOOD SVCS & DRINKING PLACES	06473	1592	20892	MISCELLANEOUS MANUFACTURING	06804	1043	7201	EDUCATIONAL SERVICES
06269	24	549	PERSONAL AND LAUNDRY SERVICES	06475	1131	7100	FOOD SVCS & DRINKING PLACES	06807	349	1542	FOOD SVCS & DRINKING PLACES
06277	125	683	FOOD SVCS & DRINKING PLACES	06477	875	8860	FOOD SVCS & DRINKING PLACES	06810	3098	39383	HOSPITALS
06278	127	798	ACCOMMODATION	06478	517	2965	EDUCATIONAL SERVICES	06811	1205	8491	FOOD AND BEVERAGE STORES
06279	178	1043	FOOD SVCS & DRINKING PLACES	06479	348	3747	NURSING & RESID. CARE FACILIT.	06812	361	1810	EDUCATIONAL SERVICES
06280	112	840	NURSING & RESID. CARE FACILIT.	06480	462	3321	EDUCATIONAL SERVICES	06813	10	34	SPECIAL TRADE CONTRACTORS
06281	231	1836	EDUCATIONAL SERVICES	06481	35	206	PLASTICS & RUBBER PRODUCTS MFG	06816	2	352	PRINT'G & RELATED SUPP'T ACT'S
06282	16	144	ACCOMMODATION	06482	291	1768	NURSING & RESID. CARE FACILIT.	06817	2	0	CHEMICAL MANUFACTURING
06320	1578	15890	HOSPITALS	06483	616	4614	SPECIAL TRADE CONTRACTORS	06820	1085	9334	FOOD SVCS & DRINKING PLACES
06330	84	616	PAPER MANUFACTURING	06484	1831	21751	PROF.; SCIENTIFIC; & TECH SVCS	06824	1737	11262	EDUCATIONAL SERVICES
06331	136	524	EDUCATIONAL SERVICES	06487	1	3	RELIG.; GRANT; CIVIC; PROF ORG	06825	1013	11121	EDUCATIONAL SERVICES
06332	20	181	EDUCATIONAL SERVICES	06488	1023	8926	EDUCATIONAL SERVICES	06828	6	1405	COMPUTER & ELECTRONIC PROD MFG
06333	351	2177	JUSTICE; PUBIC ORDER/SAFETY	06489	1412	13083	EDUCATIONAL SERVICES	06829	29	42	RELIG.; GRANT; CIVIC; PROF ORG
06334	119	1040	MERCH. WHOLESALERS;NONDUR. GDS	06491	5	304	WOOD PRODUCT MANUFACTURING	06830	2645	24775	SECURITIES/COMMODITY CONTRACTS
06335	181	1297	EDUCATIONAL SERVICES	06492	2304	26006	AMBULATORY HEALTH CARE SVCS	06831	668	8737	BLDG MATL & GARDEN EQPMT DLRS
06336	7	203	CHEMICAL MANUFACTURING	06498	446	3747	FABRICATED METAL PRODUCT MFG	06836	9	37	ADMINISTRATIVE & SUPPORT SVCS
06338	4	47	JUSTICE; PUBIC ORDER/SAFETY	06504	7	12	AMBULATORY HEALTH CARE SVCS	06838	9	25	CONSTRUCTION OF BUILDINGS
06339	244	12552	ACCOMMODATION	06505	1	3	PROF.; SCIENTIFIC; & TECH SVCS	06840	1170	6675	EDUCATIONAL SERVICES
06340	1188	14347	CHEMICAL MANUFACTURING	06506	1	0	NAT'L SECURITY & INT'L AFFAIRS	06850	888	11500	AMBULATORY HEALTH CARE SVCS
06349	16	242	NAT'L SECURITY & INT'L AFFAIRS	06510	1270	16436	AMBULATORY HEALTH CARE SVCS	06851	1866	18035	AMBULATORY HEALTH CARE SVCS
06350	1	0	RELIG.; GRANT; CIVIC; PROF ORG	06511	2423	35634	EDUCATIONAL SERVICES	06852	7	175	PETROLEUM & COAL PRODUCTS MFG
06351	464	3322	EDUCATIONAL SERVICES	06512	961	7210	FOOD AND BEVERAGE STORES	06853	179	758	EDUCATIONAL SERVICES
06353	38	116	REPAIR AND MAINTENANCE	06513	791	7486	AMBULATORY HEALTH CARE SVCS	06854	1406	17466	MISCELLANEOUS MANUFACTURING
06354	92	708	MISCELLANEOUS STORE RETAILERS	06514	997	9133	EDUCATIONAL SERVICES	06855	480	5080	MERCH. WHOLESALERS;DURABLE GDS
06355	915	7849	FOOD SVCS & DRINKING PLACES	06515	481	6734	EDUCATIONAL SERVICES	06856	5	10	CONSTRUCTION OF BUILDINGS
06357	445	3872	JUSTICE; PUBIC ORDER/SAFETY	06516	1692	20046	AMBULATORY HEALTH CARE SVCS	06857	3	710	MERCH. WHOLESALERS;DURABLE GDS
06359	195	1582	FOOD SVCS & DRINKING PLACES	06517	487	4856	RELIG.; GRANT; CIVIC; PROF ORG	06858	1	10	FURN. & HOME FURNISHGS STORES
06360	1702	17085	AMBULATORY HEALTH CARE SVCS	06518	921	6798	AMBULATORY HEALTH CARE SVCS	06870	361	2057	ACCOMMODATION
06365	183	771	EDUCATIONAL SERVICES	06519	592	12924	HOSPITALS	06875	16	26	EXEC.; LEGIS.; & OTHER SUPPORT
06370	144	1447	EDUCATIONAL SERVICES	06520	2	0	PUBLISHING INDUSTRIES	06876	4	10	RELIG.; GRANT; CIVIC; PROF ORG
06371	570	2854	EDUCATIONAL SERVICES	06524	240	1303	EDUCATIONAL SERVICES	06877	1369	11490	CHEMICAL MANUFACTURING
06372	13	29	PROF.; SCIENTIFIC; & TECH SVCS	06525	492	4648	NURSING & RESID. CARE FACILIT.	06878	224	1618	EDUCATIONAL SERVICES
06373	14	53	EXEC.; LEGIS.; & OTHER SUPPORT	06530	1	1	REAL ESTATE	06880	2603	17912	PROF.; SCIENTIFIC; & TECH SVCS
06374	390	3293	MERCH. WHOLESALERS;DURABLE GDS	06534	2	1	CONSTRUCTION OF BUILDINGS	06881	4	2	AMUSEMENT; GAMBLING;& RECREAT.
06375	76	575	RELIG.; GRANT; CIVIC; PROF ORG	06601	4	4	ADMINISTRATIVE & SUPPORT SVCS	06883	327	1892	EDUCATIONAL SERVICES
06376	5	3	REAL ESTATE	06602	3	6	CREDIT INTERMEDIATION & RELATD	06890	310	2399	PROF.; SCIENTIFIC; & TECH SVCS
06377	77	445	EDUCATIONAL SERVICES	06604	1435	19670	JUSTICE; PUBIC ORDER/SAFETY	06896	358	1916	EDUCATIONAL SERVICES
06378	446	1733	FOOD SVCS & DRINKING PLACES	06605	683	7025	EDUCATIONAL SERVICES	06897	1241	10362	PROF.; SCIENTIFIC; & TECH SVCS
06379	328	3332	MACHINERY MANUFACTURING	06606	1216	9601	HOSPITALS	06901	1540	22692	PROF.; SCIENTIFIC; & TECH SVCS
06380	68	589	TRANSIT & GRND PASS. TRANSPORT	06607	339	3068	TRANSPORTATION EQUIPMENT MFG	06902	3032	32516	PROF.; SCIENTIFIC; & TECH SVCS
06382	369	3987	FOOD SVCS & DRINKING PLACES	06608	420	2580	EXEC.; LEGIS.; & OTHER SUPPORT	06903	415	1859	EDUCATIONAL SERVICES
06383	2	290	PAPER MANUFACTURING	06610	609	8213	HOSPITALS	06904	10	90	AMUSEMENT; GAMBLING;& RECREAT.
06384	77	278	EDUCATIONAL SERVICES	06611	1564	17065	AMBULATORY HEALTH CARE SVCS	06905	1428	14233	PROF.; SCIENTIFIC; & TECH SVCS
06385	826	11585	GENERAL MERCHANDISE STORES	06612	213	1201	CREDIT INTERMEDIATION & RELATD	06906	494	3574	OTHER INFORMATION SERVICES
06387	15	477	FABRICATED METAL PRODUCT MFG	06614	919	8152	AMBULATORY HEALTH CARE SVCS	06907	459	2922	COMPUTER & ELECTRONIC PROD MFG

ZIP CODE	2009 Total Firms	2009 Total Employees	TOP INDUSTRY RANKED on 2009 EMPLOYMENT	ZIP CODE	2009 Total Firms	2009 Total Employees	TOP INDUSTRY RANKED on 2009 EMPLOYMENT	ZIP CODE	2009 Total Firms	2009 Total Employees	TOP INDUSTRY RANKED on 2009 EMPLOYMENT
06910	2	6	POSTAL SERVICE	07095	1500	18234	EXEC.; LEGIS.; & OTHER SUPPORT	07522	377	2250	EDUCATIONAL SERVICES
06911	1	4	INSURANCE CARRIERS & RELATED	07096	3	5	PERFORM'G ARTS; SPEC. SPORTS	07524	453	2801	EDUCATIONAL SERVICES
06921	2	6	REAL ESTATE	07097	5	379	RELIG.; GRANT; CIVIC; PROF ORG	07538	3	2	PROF.; SCIENTIFIC; & TECH SVCS
06922	2	3	CREDIT INTERMEDIATION & RELATD	07099	6	41	RELIG.; GRANT; CIVIC; PROF ORG	07543	2	9	UNCLASSIFIED ESTABLISHMENTS
06926	4	1814	MERCH. WHOLESALERS;DURABLE GDS	07101	7	50	FURNITURE & RELATED PROD. MFG	07601	3971	45015	HOSPITALS
06927	4	300	CREDIT INTERMEDIATION & RELATD	07102	2554	54826	INSURANCE CARRIERS & RELATED	07602	7	39	TRANSIT & GRND PASS. TRANSPORT
07001	502	9094	MOTOR VEHICLE & PARTS DEALERS	07103	939	21467	HOSPITALS	07603	265	1138	EDUCATIONAL SERVICES
07002	2037	19636	EDUCATIONAL SERVICES	07104	1120	9656	EDUCATIONAL SERVICES	07604	681	4344	FOOD SVCS & DRINKING PLACES
07003	1885	14348	EDUCATIONAL SERVICES	07105	2274	23311	INSURANCE CARRIERS & RELATED	07605	343	2534	COMPUTER & ELECTRONIC PROD MFG
07004	2203	27075	PROF.; SCIENTIFIC; & TECH SVCS	07106	443	2178	EDUCATIONAL SERVICES	07606	398	5315	MERCH. WHOLESALERS;NONDUR. GDS
07005	879	6076	PROF.; SCIENTIFIC; & TECH SVCS	07107	715	5109	EDUCATIONAL SERVICES	07607	345	3652	PROF.; SCIENTIFIC; & TECH SVCS
07006	1450	12873	PROF.; SCIENTIFIC; & TECH SVCS	07108	445	2759	EDUCATIONAL SERVICES	07608	243	6154	MOTOR VEHICLE & PARTS DEALERS
07007	11	52	SPECIAL TRADE CONTRACTORS	07109	1160	11607	HOSPITALS	07620	80	378	AMUSEMENT; GAMBLING;& RECREAT.
07008	608	6532	MERCH. WHOLESALERS;NONDUR. GDS	07110	1096	10108	MERCH. WHOLESALERS;NONDUR. GDS	07621	933	4770	EDUCATIONAL SERVICES
07009	522	6040	HOSPITALS	07111	1504	11596	EDUCATIONAL SERVICES	07624	665	3387	PERSONAL AND LAUNDRY SERVICES
07010	717	2585	FOOD SVCS & DRINKING PLACES	07112	505	6306	HOSPITALS	07626	288	1667	EDUCATIONAL SERVICES
07011	1529	9690	FOOD AND BEVERAGE STORES	07114	1117	27840	AIR TRANSPORTATION	07627	107	648	EDUCATIONAL SERVICES
07012	539	6197	FURN. & HOME FURNISHGS STORES	07188	1	0	SPECIAL TRADE CONTRACTORS	07628	543	2246	EDUCATIONAL SERVICES
07013	1259	8365	EDUCATIONAL SERVICES	07201	1918	22976	MERCH. WHOLESALERS;NONDUR. GDS	07630	292	2500	AMBULATORY HEALTH CARE SVCS
07014	329	6543	COMPUTER & ELECTRONIC PROD MFG	07202	948	15560	EXEC.; LEGIS.; & OTHER SUPPORT	07631	2024	14974	HOSPITALS
07015	6	11	PROF.; SCIENTIFIC; & TECH SVCS	07203	677	5354	MERCH. WHOLESALERS;DURABLE GDS	07632	897	9716	MERCH. WHOLESALERS;NONDUR. GDS
07016	1253	14169	ELECT'L EQPMT; APP; & COMP MFG	07204	427	2489	EDUCATIONAL SERVICES	07640	140	883	UTILITIES
07017	713	8657	EXEC.; LEGIS.; & OTHER SUPPORT	07205	853	6804	MERCH. WHOLESALERS;DURABLE GDS	07641	118	679	EDUCATIONAL SERVICES
07018	981	10037	AMBULATORY HEALTH CARE SVCS	07206	663	6069	TRUCK TRANSPORTATION	07642	381	2563	EDUCATIONAL SERVICES
07019	4	35	ADMINISTRATIVE & SUPPORT SVCS	07207	5	71	ADMINISTRATIVE & SUPPORT SVCS	07643	477	3497	MERCH. WHOLESALERS;DURABLE GDS
07020	599	4391	FOOD SVCS & DRINKING PLACES	07208	775	6184	EDUCATIONAL SERVICES	07644	812	4967	EDUCATIONAL SERVICES
07021	46	226	EDUCATIONAL SERVICES	07302	1711	21470	JUSTICE; PUBIC ORDER/SAFETY	07645	568	16654	FOOD AND BEVERAGE STORES
07022	577	3287	MERCH. WHOLESALERS;DURABLE GDS	07303	3	6	CLOTHING & CLOTH'G ACC. STORES	07646	321	2112	EDUCATIONAL SERVICES
07023	287	1513	HOSPITALS	07304	1051	7660	EDUCATIONAL SERVICES	07647	417	6168	NURSING & RESID. CARE FACILIT.
07024	2208	10805	REAL ESTATE	07305	1343	14557	EDUCATIONAL SERVICES	07648	299	2284	NURSING & RESID. CARE FACILIT.
07026	1041	6820	SPECIAL TRADE CONTRACTORS	07306	2307	22441	EDUCATIONAL SERVICES	07649	502	3433	PROF.; SCIENTIFIC; & TECH SVCS
07027	300	2625	FOOD AND BEVERAGE STORES	07307	923	4267	EDUCATIONAL SERVICES	07650	943	3420	SPECIAL TRADE CONTRACTORS
07028	161	1143	EDUCATIONAL SERVICES	07310	548	7774	SECURITIES/COMMODITY CONTRACTS	07652	2548	37424	CLOTHING & CLOTH'G ACC. STORES
07029	558	4049	FOOD MANUFACTURING	07311	41	3280	SECURITIES/COMMODITY CONTRACTS	07653	19	82	CONSTRUCTION OF BUILDINGS
07030	2272	15421	EDUCATIONAL SERVICES	07399	7	3525	SECURITIES/COMMODITY CONTRACTS	07656	473	6442	RENTAL AND LEASING SERVICES
07031	472	3922	RELIG.; GRANT; CIVIC; PROF ORG	07401	315	3599	EDUCATIONAL SERVICES	07657	801	5002	PLASTICS & RUBBER PRODUCTS MFG
07032	1518	17054	TRUCK TRANSPORTATION	07403	285	1496	SOCIAL ASSISTANCE	07660	409	4771	RELIG.; GRANT; CIVIC; PROF ORG
07033	701	14922	CHEMICAL MANUFACTURING	07405	881	4828	EDUCATIONAL SERVICES	07661	417	2553	EDUCATIONAL SERVICES
07034	212	745	AMBULATORY HEALTH CARE SVCS	07407	791	8161	MERCH. WHOLESALERS;NONDUR. GDS	07662	522	4571	PROF.; SCIENTIFIC; & TECH SVCS
07035	393	4096	NURSING & RESID. CARE FACILIT.	07410	1618	13269	EDUCATIONAL SERVICES	07663	828	11233	MERCH. WHOLESALERS;DURABLE GDS
07036	1994	19474	MERCH. WHOLESALERS;DURABLE GDS	07416	379	2624	FOOD SVCS & DRINKING PLACES	07666	1676	12661	EDUCATIONAL SERVICES
07039	1735	22791	AMBULATORY HEALTH CARE SVCS	07417	522	9375	MISCELLANEOUS MANUFACTURING	07670	635	3697	EDUCATIONAL SERVICES
07040	938	5987	TRANSIT & GRND PASS. TRANSPORT	07418	39	118	SPECIAL TRADE CONTRACTORS	07675	1336	9364	HOSPITALS
07041	779	5450	PROF.; SCIENTIFIC; & TECH SVCS	07419	334	1946	PLASTICS & RUBBER PRODUCTS MFG	07676	247	1139	FOOD SVCS & DRINKING PLACES
07042	1770	11680	PROF.; SCIENTIFIC; & TECH SVCS	07420	151	1656	NURSING & RESID. CARE FACILIT.	07677	323	6624	PROF.; SCIENTIFIC; & TECH SVCS
07043	494	3906	SPECIAL TRADE CONTRACTORS	07421	267	903	FOOD AND BEVERAGE STORES	07701	2361	18513	HOSPITALS
07044	748	4693	PERSONAL AND LAUNDRY SERVICES	07422	82	212	RELIG.; GRANT; CIVIC; PROF ORG	07702	701	6412	AMBULATORY HEALTH CARE SVCS
07045	594	3384	MERCH. WHOLESALERS;DURABLE GDS	07423	234	1063	EDUCATIONAL SERVICES	07703	36	374	HOSPITALS
07046	269	2618	EDUCATIONAL SERVICES	07424	1414	11091	PROF.; SCIENTIFIC; & TECH SVCS	07704	246	956	EDUCATIONAL SERVICES
07047	1628	16407	MERCH. WHOLESALERS;DURABLE GDS	07428	27	272	AMUSEMENT; GAMBLING;& RECREAT.	07710	15	74	EDUCATIONAL SERVICES
07050	1126	8752	EDUCATIONAL SERVICES	07430	1112	12822	MERCH. WHOLESALERS;DURABLE GDS	07711	107	460	FOOD SVCS & DRINKING PLACES
07051	6	28	CREDIT INTERMEDIATION & RELATD	07432	606	3932	PROF.; SCIENTIFIC; & TECH SVCS	07712	1810	12497	EDUCATIONAL SERVICES
07052	1886	15841	AMBULATORY HEALTH CARE SVCS	07435	259	766	ACCOMMODATION	07716	467	2199	NURSING & RESID. CARE FACILIT.
07054	2570	57475	PROF.; SCIENTIFIC; & TECH SVCS	07436	663	7056	UNCLASSIFIED ESTABLISHMENTS	07717	153	553	PROF.; SCIENTIFIC; & TECH SVCS
07055	2390	15292	HOSPITALS	07438	338	2669	EDUCATIONAL SERVICES	07718	156	781	SPECIAL TRADE CONTRACTORS
07057	342	2844	MERCH. WHOLESALERS;NONDUR. GDS	07439	74	381	EDUCATIONAL SERVICES	07719	1293	8696	FOOD SVCS & DRINKING PLACES
07058	346	5748	MERCH. WHOLESALERS;DURABLE GDS	07440	210	814	PLASTICS & RUBBER PRODUCTS MFG	07720	206	764	FOOD SVCS & DRINKING PLACES
07059	762	9770	INSURANCE CARRIERS & RELATED	07442	650	2439	EDUCATIONAL SERVICES	07721	85	961	EDUCATIONAL SERVICES
07060	1810	14084	HOSPITALS	07444	491	4630	NURSING & RESID. CARE FACILIT.	07722	484	2977	EDUCATIONAL SERVICES
07061	5	14	SPECIAL TRADE CONTRACTORS	07446	1189	9834	MERCH. WHOLESALERS;DURABLE GDS	07723	151	805	AMUSEMENT; GAMBLING;& RECREAT.
07062	459	7746	INSURANCE CARRIERS & RELATED	07450	1748	10806	HOSPITALS	07724	1565	18417	PROF.; SCIENTIFIC; & TECH SVCS
07063	189	1865	PROF.; SCIENTIFIC; & TECH SVCS	07451	12	42	TRANSIT & GRND PASS. TRANSPORT	07726	1865	17070	ADMINISTRATIVE & SUPPORT SVCS
07064	79	646	NONMETALLIC MINERAL PROD. MFG	07452	546	4257	EDUCATIONAL SERVICES	07727	721	7824	UTILITIES
07065	1197	10054	HOSPITALS	07456	455	2842	ACCOMMODATION	07728	3269	35929	HOSPITALS
07066	808	6681	EDUCATIONAL SERVICES	07457	294	3327	REPAIR AND MAINTENANCE	07730	738	6419	EDUCATIONAL SERVICES
07067	343	1979	EDUCATIONAL SERVICES	07458	524	5515	PUBLISHING INDUSTRIES	07731	1402	9758	ADMINISTRATIVE & SUPPORT SVCS
07068	557	13849	PROF.; SCIENTIFIC; & TECH SVCS	07460	78	277	EXEC.; LEGIS.; & OTHER SUPPORT	07732	192	1711	FOOD SVCS & DRINKING PLACES
07069	477	5797	GENERAL MERCHANDISE STORES	07461	714	3279	EDUCATIONAL SERVICES	07733	640	10868	MOTOR VEHICLE & PARTS DEALERS
07070	1152	6118	PROF.; SCIENTIFIC; & TECH SVCS	07462	414	6017	ACCOMMODATION	07734	329	2069	TRANSIT & GRND PASS. TRANSPORT
07071	1156	11156	PROF.; SCIENTIFIC; & TECH SVCS	07463	480	3045	EDUCATIONAL SERVICES	07735	787	5164	FOOD SVCS & DRINKING PLACES
07072	853	12800	MERCH. WHOLESALERS;DURABLE GDS	07465	171	1145	RELIG.; GRANT; CIVIC; PROF ORG	07737	88	888	TRANSIT & GRND PASS. TRANSPORT
07073	727	9849	PERFORM'G ARTS; SPEC. SPORTS	07470	2919	39189	EDUCATIONAL SERVICES	07738	218	1982	EDUCATIONAL SERVICES
07074	368	6015	MERCH. WHOLESALERS;DURABLE GDS	07474	31	49	MACHINERY MANUFACTURING	07739	320	2251	AMBULATORY HEALTH CARE SVCS
07075	241	3302	EDUCATIONAL SERVICES	07480	563	2913	EDUCATIONAL SERVICES	07740	1251	10855	HOSPITALS
07076	891	7041	EDUCATIONAL SERVICES	07481	839	5059	NURSING & RESID. CARE FACILIT.	07746	596	4078	EDUCATIONAL SERVICES
07077	41	289	EDUCATIONAL SERVICES	07495	67	1402	ADMINISTRATIVE & SUPPORT SVCS	07747	1330	8139	EDUCATIONAL SERVICES
07078	617	9652	PROF.; SCIENTIFIC; & TECH SVCS	07501	1158	8518	EDUCATIONAL SERVICES	07748	973	9190	EDUCATIONAL SERVICES
07079	730	4739	EDUCATIONAL SERVICES	07502	340	2006	EDUCATIONAL SERVICES	07750	128	517	FOOD SVCS & DRINKING PLACES
07080	1605	19881	MERCH. WHOLESALERS;DURABLE GDS	07503	830	9685	AMBULATORY HEALTH CARE SVCS	07751	591	4266	EDUCATIONAL SERVICES
07081	1116	10375	PROF.; SCIENTIFIC; & TECH SVCS	07504	243	1571	BLDG MATL & GARDEN EQPMT DLRS	07752	13	35	CONSTRUCTION OF BUILDINGS
07082	123	735	MISCELLANEOUS MANUFACTURING	07505	786	9515	JUSTICE; PUBIC ORDER/SAFETY	07753	1530	26643	HOSPITALS
07083	2743	29597	RELIG.; GRANT; CIVIC; PROF ORG	07506	915	6540	EDUCATIONAL SERVICES	07754	8	44	SPORTG GDS;HOBBY;BOOK; & MUSIC
07086	328	10455	SECURITIES/COMMODITY CONTRACTS	07507	11	23	ADMINISTRATIVE & SUPPORT SVCS	07755	398	2855	FOOD SVCS & DRINKING PLACES
07087	2281	10780	EDUCATIONAL SERVICES	07508	742	4503	EDUCATIONAL SERVICES	07756	153	887	NURSING & RESID. CARE FACILIT.
07088	140	1527	BLDG MATL & GARDEN EQPMT DLRS	07509	7	7	SPECIAL TRADE CONTRACTORS	07757	185	4017	PERFORM'G ARTS; SPEC. SPORTS
07090	1568	10285	EDUCATIONAL SERVICES	07510	3	1200	POSTAL SERVICE	07758	113	732	EDUCATIONAL SERVICES
07091	14	49	ADMINISTRATIVE & SUPPORT SVCS	07511	6	28	ELECTRONICS & APPLIANCE STORES	07760	356	2912	EDUCATIONAL SERVICES
07092	492	5389	PROF.; SCIENTIFIC; & TECH SVCS	07512	949	14528	EXEC.; LEGIS.; & OTHER SUPPORT	07762	563	3429	REAL ESTATE
07093	1669	7569	EDUCATIONAL SERVICES	07513	305	2342	MERCH. WHOLESALERS;DURABLE GDS	07763	21	86	CONSTRUCTION OF BUILDINGS
07094	1276	29027	CLOTHING & CLOTH'G ACC. STORES	07514	462	4327	AMBULATORY HEALTH CARE SVCS	07764	450	3995	PROF.; SCIENTIFIC; & TECH SVCS

BUSINESS DATA

ZIP CODE	2009 Total Firms	2009 Total Employees	TOP INDUSTRY RANKED on 2009 EMPLOYMENT
07765	8	24	SOCIAL ASSISTANCE
07799	3	195	RELIG.; GRANT; CIVIC; PROF ORG
07801	1208	14808	FABRICATED METAL PRODUCT MFG
07802	4	8	HEALTH & PERSONAL CARE STORES
07803	142	873	MERCH. WHOLESALERS;DURABLE GDS
07806	23	200	ADMINISTRATIVE & SUPPORT SVCS
07820	47	251	AMUSEMENT; GAMBLING;& RECREAT.
07821	303	1923	NURSING & RESID. CARE FACILIT.
07822	114	588	PROF.; SCIENTIFIC; & TECH SVCS
07823	416	2977	MERCH. WHOLESALERS;NONDUR. GDS
07825	503	2351	EDUCATIONAL SERVICES
07826	363	3099	INSURANCE CARRIERS & RELATED
07827	161	887	FOOD AND BEVERAGE STORES
07828	511	3558	MERCH. WHOLESALERS;NONDUR. GDS
07829	8	50	FABRICATED METAL PRODUCT MFG
07830	376	1568	EDUCATIONAL SERVICES
07831	4	5	FOOD AND BEVERAGE STORES
07832	172	810	GASOLINE STATIONS
07833	15	293	TRUCK TRANSPORTATION
07834	1142	14835	HOSPITALS
07836	580	6033	ADMINISTRATIVE & SUPPORT SVCS
07837	4	3	SPECIAL TRADE CONTRACTORS
07838	145	831	EDUCATIONAL SERVICES
07839	5	12	SOCIAL ASSISTANCE
07840	1423	13033	AMBULATORY HEALTH CARE SVCS
07842	10	88	REPAIR AND MAINTENANCE
07843	323	1538	EDUCATIONAL SERVICES
07844	64	445	ADMINISTRATIVE & SUPPORT SVCS
07845	15	32	FOOD SVCS & DRINKING PLACES
07846	14	62	EDUCATIONAL SERVICES
07847	171	1088	BLDG MATL & GARDEN EQPMT DLRS
07848	256	1810	SPECIAL TRADE CONTRACTORS
07849	355	1807	FOOD SVCS & DRINKING PLACES
07850	212	1181	PRINT'G & RELATED SUPP'T ACT'S
07851	24	119	JUSTICE; PUBIC ORDER/SAFETY
07852	286	2443	FOOD SVCS & DRINKING PLACES
07853	416	1712	EDUCATIONAL SERVICES
07855	7	14	HEAVY & CIVIL ENG. CONSTRUCT'N
07856	244	1878	PROF.; SCIENTIFIC; & TECH SVCS
07857	220	1048	FOOD AND BEVERAGE STORES
07860	1516	12986	EXEC.; LEGIS.; & OTHER SUPPORT
07863	133	833	EXEC.; LEGIS.; & OTHER SUPPORT
07865	98	945	NAT'L SECURITY & INT'L AFFAIRS
07866	1305	12701	GENERAL MERCHANDISE STORES
07869	1036	9428	EDUCATIONAL SERVICES
07870	10	48	RELIG.; GRANT; CIVIC; PROF ORG
07871	1072	6911	EDUCATIONAL SERVICES
07874	292	2659	EDUCATIONAL SERVICES
07875	30	118	EDUCATIONAL SERVICES
07876	564	3721	EDUCATIONAL SERVICES
07877	8	87	TRANSIT & GRND PASS. TRANSPORT
07878	21	108	MUSEUMS; HIST. SITES;& SIMILAR
07879	17	51	PROF.; SCIENTIFIC; & TECH SVCS
07880	6	15	ADMINISTRATIVE & SUPPORT SVCS
07881	3	62	FOOD MANUFACTURING
07882	705	5295	EDUCATIONAL SERVICES
07885	382	4733	ADMINISTRATIVE & SUPPORT SVCS
07890	1	900	INSURANCE CARRIERS & RELATED
07901	1478	13355	HOSPITALS
07902	11	108	RELIG.; GRANT; CIVIC; PROF ORG
07920	768	11166	TELECOMMUNICATIONS
07921	461	5789	PROF.; SCIENTIFIC; & TECH SVCS
07922	620	6095	AMBULATORY HEALTH CARE SVCS
07924	622	3064	FOOD AND BEVERAGE STORES
07926	23	382	EDUCATIONAL SERVICES
07927	276	5490	PROF.; SCIENTIFIC; & TECH SVCS
07928	796	5752	EDUCATIONAL SERVICES
07930	790	4494	FOOD AND BEVERAGE STORES
07931	163	1098	RELIG.; GRANT; CIVIC; PROF ORG
07932	808	19946	MISCELLANEOUS MANUFACTURING
07933	122	1039	FOOD SVCS & DRINKING PLACES
07934	98	988	EDUCATIONAL SERVICES
07935	33	87	MERCH. WHOLESALERS;NONDUR. GDS
07936	987	16909	CHEMICAL MANUFACTURING
07938	43	655	RELIG.; GRANT; CIVIC; PROF ORG
07939	12	32	AMUSEMENT; GAMBLING;& RECREAT.
07940	790	10578	AMBULATORY HEALTH CARE SVCS
07945	437	2507	EDUCATIONAL SERVICES
07946	262	706	PROF.; SCIENTIFIC; & TECH SVCS
07950	653	12339	CHEMICAL MANUFACTURING
07960	3368	44449	PROF.; SCIENTIFIC; & TECH SVCS
07961	21	103	JUSTICE; PUBIC ORDER/SAFETY
07962	12	67	SOCIAL ASSISTANCE
07963	10	67	RELIG.; GRANT; CIVIC; PROF ORG
07970	51	552	ACCOMMODATION
07974	532	14333	CHEMICAL MANUFACTURING
07976	41	234	JUSTICE; PUBIC ORDER/SAFETY
07977	96	913	HOSPITALS
07978	44	320	REAL ESTATE
07979	23	53	JUSTICE; PUBIC ORDER/SAFETY
07980	189	1269	FOOD AND BEVERAGE STORES
07981	628	12935	TELECOMMUNICATIONS
07999	2	950	RELIG.; GRANT; CIVIC; PROF ORG
08001	45	594	EDUCATIONAL SERVICES
08002	1614	25838	HOSPITALS
08003	1437	14033	PROF.; SCIENTIFIC; & TECH SVCS
08004	342	2240	RELIG.; GRANT; CIVIC; PROF ORG
08005	721	2685	UTILITIES
08006	99	543	MERCH. WHOLESALERS;NONDUR. GDS
08007	203	1712	PAPER MANUFACTURING
08008	894	6297	FOOD SVCS & DRINKING PLACES
08009	834	7201	RELIG.; GRANT; CIVIC; PROF ORG
08010	265	1639	EDUCATIONAL SERVICES
08011	4	21	MISCELLANEOUS MANUFACTURING
08012	1666	16690	MOTOR VEHICLE & PARTS DEALERS
08014	65	957	COMPUTER & ELECTRONIC PROD MFG
08015	308	2702	HOSPITALS
08016	1467	19339	GENERAL MERCHANDISE STORES
08018	31	338	EDUCATIONAL SERVICES
08019	49	165	EDUCATIONAL SERVICES
08020	85	595	NURSING & RESID. CARE FACILIT.
08021	1125	8023	FOOD SVCS & DRINKING PLACES
08022	262	2544	MERCH. WHOLESALERS;DURABLE GDS
08023	20	1567	MERCH. WHOLESALERS;NONDUR. GDS
08025	4	3	POSTAL SERVICE
08026	186	1447	AMBULATORY HEALTH CARE SVCS
08027	116	1758	RELIG.; GRANT; CIVIC; PROF ORG
08028	709	6676	EDUCATIONAL SERVICES
08029	102	581	PROF.; SCIENTIFIC; & TECH SVCS
08030	511	4539	EDUCATIONAL SERVICES
08031	432	5761	POSTAL SERVICE
08032	8	106	PLASTICS & RUBBER PRODUCTS MFG
08033	1058	5462	PROF.; SCIENTIFIC; & TECH SVCS
08034	1534	12830	PROF.; SCIENTIFIC; & TECH SVCS
08035	415	2230	EDUCATIONAL SERVICES
08036	359	2515	SPECIAL TRADE CONTRACTORS
08037	1200	13432	HOSPITALS
08038	16	146	EXEC.; LEGIS.; & OTHER SUPPORT
08039	20	127	EDUCATIONAL SERVICES
08041	36	161	EDUCATIONAL SERVICES
08042	5	7	POSTAL SERVICE
08043	1509	25851	HOSPITALS
08045	90	1301	BLDG MATL & GARDEN EQPMT DLRS
08046	656	6755	HOSPITALS
08048	418	6058	HEALTH & PERSONAL CARE STORES
08049	122	891	EDUCATIONAL SERVICES
08050	996	8954	HOSPITALS
08051	242	1829	FOOD SVCS & DRINKING PLACES
08052	627	5563	FOOD SVCS & DRINKING PLACES
08053	2213	98581	AMBULATORY HEALTH CARE SVCS
08054	2187	32317	PROF.; SCIENTIFIC; & TECH SVCS
08055	1348	11578	EDUCATIONAL SERVICES
08056	89	858	SPECIAL TRADE CONTRACTORS
08057	1589	19753	COMPUTER & ELECTRONIC PROD MFG
08059	182	1269	FOOD SVCS & DRINKING PLACES
08060	1236	20565	HOSPITALS
08061	34	273	AMBULATORY HEALTH CARE SVCS
08062	435	3080	EDUCATIONAL SERVICES
08063	57	344	EDUCATIONAL SERVICES
08064	14	2076	ADMIN. HUMAN RESOURCE PROGRAMS
08065	214	1748	EDUCATIONAL SERVICES
08066	377	5646	MERCH. WHOLESALERS;NONDUR. GDS
08067	71	977	NONMETALLIC MINERAL PROD. MFG
08068	245	5101	ADMINISTRATIVE & SUPPORT SVCS
08069	409	3379	EDUCATIONAL SERVICES
08070	470	3301	FOOD SVCS & DRINKING PLACES
08071	470	3485	SPORTG GDS;HOBBY;BOOK; & MUSIC
08072	21	159	EDUCATIONAL SERVICES
08073	26	464	MACHINERY MANUFACTURING
08074	23	142	MERCH. WHOLESALERS;NONDUR. GDS
08075	959	7365	EDUCATIONAL SERVICES
08077	952	9141	MERCH. WHOLESALERS;DURABLE GDS
08078	339	4536	AMBULATORY HEALTH CARE SVCS
08079	474	5006	PROF.; SCIENTIFIC; & TECH SVCS
08080	1232	13585	EDUCATIONAL SERVICES
08081	720	5033	EDUCATIONAL SERVICES
08083	279	1597	EDUCATIONAL SERVICES
08084	276	4211	EDUCATIONAL SERVICES
08085	721	10869	PROF.; SCIENTIFIC; & TECH SVCS
08086	232	7819	PUBLISHING INDUSTRIES
08087	742	5484	TRANSPORTATION EQUIPMENT MFG
08088	799	4857	EDUCATIONAL SERVICES
08089	127	528	SPECIAL TRADE CONTRACTORS
08090	182	730	AMBULATORY HEALTH CARE SVCS
08091	610	6908	MERCH. WHOLESALERS;DURABLE GDS
08092	189	1480	SPECIAL TRADE CONTRACTORS
08093	326	3457	EDUCATIONAL SERVICES
08094	1219	7624	EDUCATIONAL SERVICES
08095	61	255	WAREHOUSING AND STORAGE
08096	1942	18511	FOOD SVCS & DRINKING PLACES
08097	179	1458	AMBULATORY HEALTH CARE SVCS
08098	410	3753	CONSTRUCTION OF BUILDINGS
08099	7	22	ADMINISTRATIVE & SUPPORT SVCS
08101	3	1	RELIG.; GRANT; CIVIC; PROF ORG
08102	431	7309	EDUCATIONAL SERVICES
08103	814	22486	HOSPITALS
08104	510	4565	EDUCATIONAL SERVICES
08105	461	3523	EDUCATIONAL SERVICES
08106	353	1953	FOOD SVCS & DRINKING PLACES
08107	346	1863	EDUCATIONAL SERVICES
08108	777	5971	EDUCATIONAL SERVICES
08109	1112	9988	TRANSIT & GRND PASS. TRANSPORT
08110	876	14950	MERCH. WHOLESALERS;NONDUR. GDS
08201	503	3349	EDUCATIONAL SERVICES
08202	285	2340	FOOD SVCS & DRINKING PLACES
08203	368	2268	EDUCATIONAL SERVICES
08204	1130	9404	FOOD SVCS & DRINKING PLACES
08205	715	5810	ACCOMMODATION
08210	1083	12356	HOSPITALS
08212	24	164	MISCELLANEOUS STORE RETAILERS
08213	24	583	TRANSIT & GRND PASS. TRANSPORT
08214	55	522	EDUCATIONAL SERVICES
08215	494	2980	RELIG.; GRANT; CIVIC; PROF ORG
08217	28	257	EDUCATIONAL SERVICES
08218	8	10	MERCH. WHOLESALERS;NONDUR. GDS
08219	26	110	AIR TRANSPORTATION
08220	5	61	FOOD SVCS & DRINKING PLACES
08221	493	3780	NURSING & RESID. CARE FACILIT.
08223	292	1417	FOOD SVCS & DRINKING PLACES
08224	20	183	JUSTICE; PUBIC ORDER/SAFETY
08225	713	5492	EXEC.; LEGIS.; & OTHER SUPPORT
08226	1209	7020	FOOD SVCS & DRINKING PLACES
08230	296	1725	ACCOMMODATION
08231	11	45	MUSEUMS; HIST. SITES;& SIMILAR
08232	1011	10077	EDUCATIONAL SERVICES
08234	1492	19313	PROF.; SCIENTIFIC; & TECH SVCS
08240	76	2851	HOSPITALS
08241	42	135	EDUCATIONAL SERVICES
08242	289	2373	FOOD SVCS & DRINKING PLACES
08243	275	1730	FOOD SVCS & DRINKING PLACES
08244	718	6426	AMBULATORY HEALTH CARE SVCS
08245	8	49	RELIG.; GRANT; CIVIC; PROF ORG
08246	22	96	JUSTICE; PUBIC ORDER/SAFETY
08247	251	1553	FOOD SVCS & DRINKING PLACES
08248	16	223	FOOD SVCS & DRINKING PLACES
08250	45	213	EXEC.; LEGIS.; & OTHER SUPPORT
08251	186	779	FOOD SVCS & DRINKING PLACES
08252	15	23	RELIG.; GRANT; CIVIC; PROF ORG
08260	1441	10950	FOOD SVCS & DRINKING PLACES
08270	265	3006	EXEC.; LEGIS.; & OTHER SUPPORT
08302	1573	15616	EXEC.; LEGIS.; & OTHER SUPPORT
08310	114	1261	NONMETALLIC MINERAL PROD. MFG
08311	73	728	REPAIR AND MAINTENANCE
08312	196	2053	HEAVY & CIVIL ENG. CONSTRUCT'N
08313	11	224	CROP PRODUCTION
08314	10	691	JUSTICE; PUBIC ORDER/SAFETY
08315	14	56	MERCH. WHOLESALERS;DURABLE GDS
08316	14	93	FOOD AND BEVERAGE STORES
08317	48	193	EDUCATIONAL SERVICES
08318	449	3511	SOCIAL ASSISTANCE
08319	33	152	EDUCATIONAL SERVICES
08320	21	111	RELIG.; GRANT; CIVIC; PROF ORG
08321	11	16	ACCOMMODATION
08322	282	1491	EDUCATIONAL SERVICES
08323	45	329	MERCH. WHOLESALERS;NONDUR. GDS
08324	9	10	RELIG.; GRANT; CIVIC; PROF ORG
08326	58	378	TEXTILE MILLS
08327	25	623	JUSTICE; PUBIC ORDER/SAFETY
08328	58	387	FOOD SVCS & DRINKING PLACES
08329	13	95	MINING (EXCEPT OIL AND GAS)
08330	988	10888	EDUCATIONAL SERVICES
08332	1019	10874	EDUCATIONAL SERVICES
08340	33	47	FABRICATED METAL PRODUCT MFG
08341	51	283	EDUCATIONAL SERVICES
08342	13	27	RELIG.; GRANT; CIVIC; PROF ORG
08343	100	576	EDUCATIONAL SERVICES
08344	183	1003	EDUCATIONAL SERVICES
08345	26	215	EDUCATIONAL SERVICES
08346	12	26	MUSEUMS; HIST. SITES;& SIMILAR
08347	19	242	FOOD MANUFACTURING
08348	14	189	EDUCATIONAL SERVICES
08349	78	656	EDUCATIONAL SERVICES
08350	24	199	EDUCATIONAL SERVICES
08352	32	370	FOOD MANUFACTURING
08353	25	166	CROP PRODUCTION
08360	2264	25901	AMBULATORY HEALTH CARE SVCS
08361	383	5373	EXEC.; LEGIS.; & OTHER SUPPORT
08362	11	35	SOCIAL ASSISTANCE
08401	2253	85500	ACCOMMODATION
08402	350	2259	FOOD SVCS & DRINKING PLACES

ZIP CODE	2009 Total Firms	2009 Total Employ-ees	TOP INDUSTRY RANKED on 2009 EMPLOYMENT	ZIP CODE	2009 Total Firms	2009 Total Employ-ees	TOP INDUSTRY RANKED on 2009 EMPLOYMENT	ZIP CODE	2009 Total Firms	2009 Total Employ-ees	TOP INDUSTRY RANKED on 2009 EMPLOYMENT
08403	71	256	FOOD SVCS & DRINKING PLACES	08759	559	5516	NURSING & RESID. CARE FACILIT.	10019	8155	150864	PROF.; SCIENTIFIC; & TECH SVCS
08404	8	47	PERSONAL AND LAUNDRY SERVICES	08801	260	2567	EDUCATIONAL SERVICES	10020	1126	40405	PUBLISHING INDUSTRIES
08406	432	2216	FOOD AND BEVERAGE STORES	08802	181	624	EDUCATIONAL SERVICES	10021	3007	19647	AMBULATORY HEALTH CARE SVCS
08501	275	1799	EDUCATIONAL SERVICES	08803	3	27	JUSTICE; PUBIC ORDER/SAFETY	10022	11612	152254	PROF.; SCIENTIFIC; & TECH SVCS
08502	299	1721	HOSPITALS	08804	147	781	PROF.; SCIENTIFIC; & TECH SVCS	10023	3212	34069	PERFORM'G ARTS; SPEC. SPORTS
08504	4	5	SPECIAL TRADE CONTRACTORS	08805	761	3700	FOOD SVCS & DRINKING PLACES	10024	2935	19757	MUSEUMS; HIST. SITES;& SIMILAR
08505	762	6842	FOOD SVCS & DRINKING PLACES	08807	1674	44136	CHEMICAL MANUFACTURING	10025	2776	18456	FURNITURE & RELATED PROD. MFG
08510	166	1674	TRANSIT & GRND PASS. TRANSPORT	08808	17	131	MERCH. WHOLESALERS;NONDUR. GDS	10026	698	2888	EDUCATIONAL SERVICES
08511	53	232	FOOD SVCS & DRINKING PLACES	08809	665	8600	HEAVY & CIVIL ENG. CONSTRUCT'N	10027	1947	17054	EDUCATIONAL SERVICES
08512	666	9165	PROF.; SCIENTIFIC; & TECH SVCS	08810	397	7023	MERCH. WHOLESALERS;NONDUR. GDS	10028	2634	16244	MUSEUMS; HIST. SITES;& SIMILAR
08514	156	1061	BLDG MATL & GARDEN EQPMT DLRS	08812	797	5153	EDUCATIONAL SERVICES	10029	2295	31985	HOSPITALS
08515	100	831	AMUSEMENT; GAMBLING;& RECREAT.	08816	2140	21569	EDUCATIONAL SERVICES	10030	579	3352	EDUCATIONAL SERVICES
08518	135	1515	MERCH. WHOLESALERS;DURABLE GDS	08817	1743	23036	PROF.; SCIENTIFIC; & TECH SVCS	10031	1164	6175	EDUCATIONAL SERVICES
08520	995	11940	SECURITIES/COMMODITY CONTRACTS	08818	12	21	PROF.; SCIENTIFIC; & TECH SVCS	10032	1378	25129	HOSPITALS
08525	300	1354	PROF.; SCIENTIFIC; & TECH SVCS	08820	1128	13714	HOSPITALS	10033	1438	6821	EDUCATIONAL SERVICES
08526	3	20	SPECIAL TRADE CONTRACTORS	08821	17	155	PROF.; SCIENTIFIC; & TECH SVCS	10034	927	4643	EDUCATIONAL SERVICES
08527	1353	11500	AMUSEMENT; GAMBLING;& RECREAT.	08822	2196	17734	HOSPITALS	10035	1202	14629	EXEC.; LEGIS.; & OTHER SUPPORT
08528	76	732	MINING (EXCEPT OIL AND GAS)	08823	267	987	FOOD AND BEVERAGE STORES	10036	10174	137830	PROF.; SCIENTIFIC; & TECH SVCS
08530	567	2806	EDUCATIONAL SERVICES	08824	217	1400	EDUCATIONAL SERVICES	10037	399	2263	REAL ESTATE
08533	255	1098	EDUCATIONAL SERVICES	08825	347	2186	JUSTICE; PUBIC ORDER/SAFETY	10038	3585	55584	JUSTICE; PUBIC ORDER/SAFETY
08534	707	7719	MERCH. WHOLESALERS;NONDUR. GDS	08826	195	1623	EXEC.; LEGIS.; & OTHER SUPPORT	10039	383	2034	SOCIAL ASSISTANCE
08535	216	1185	ADMINISTRATIVE & SUPPORT SVCS	08827	270	1550	FOOD SVCS & DRINKING PLACES	10040	787	5115	EDUCATIONAL SERVICES
08536	443	4742	EDUCATIONAL SERVICES	08828	38	124	ADMINISTRATIVE & SUPPORT SVCS	10041	51	2167	SECURITIES/COMMODITY CONTRACTS
08540	3118	71701	PROF.; SCIENTIFIC; & TECH SVCS	08829	152	820	EDUCATIONAL SERVICES	10043	2	0	CREDIT INTERMEDIATION & RELATD
08541	1	0	EDUCATIONAL SERVICES	08830	1033	12681	PROF.; SCIENTIFIC; & TECH SVCS	10044	174	5320	EXEC.; LEGIS.; & OTHER SUPPORT
08542	678	5985	FOOD SVCS & DRINKING PLACES	08831	1234	12636	PROF.; SCIENTIFIC; & TECH SVCS	10045	4	3015	CREDIT INTERMEDIATION & RELATD
08543	15	27	PROF.; SCIENTIFIC; & TECH SVCS	08832	56	1052	TRUCK TRANSPORTATION	10055	35	2406	INSURANCE CARRIERS & RELATED
08544	16	4700	EDUCATIONAL SERVICES	08833	582	3844	PROF.; SCIENTIFIC; & TECH SVCS	10065	3318	57586	HOSPITALS
08550	546	5869	PROF.; SCIENTIFIC; & TECH SVCS	08835	370	2633	MERCH. WHOLESALERS;DURABLE GDS	10069	66	574	CONSTRUCTION OF BUILDINGS
08551	238	1637	PROF.; SCIENTIFIC; & TECH SVCS	08836	177	1014	EDUCATIONAL SERVICES	10075	1644	11740	HOSPITALS
08553	57	301	FOOD SVCS & DRINKING PLACES	08837	1524	28804	PROF.; SCIENTIFIC; & TECH SVCS	10080	2	15000	SECURITIES/COMMODITY CONTRACTS
08554	71	326	FOOD AND BEVERAGE STORES	08840	1135	5964	EDUCATIONAL SERVICES	10081	3	200	CONSTRUCTION OF BUILDINGS
08555	25	77	EDUCATIONAL SERVICES	08844	1509	11661	EDUCATIONAL SERVICES	10101	2	2	MERCH. WHOLESALERS;DURABLE GDS
08556	21	44	FOOD SVCS & DRINKING PLACES	08846	804	6598	BLDG MATL & GARDEN EQPMT DLRS	10103	157	3657	PROF.; SCIENTIFIC; & TECH SVCS
08557	28	502	EDUCATIONAL SERVICES	08848	345	1431	EDUCATIONAL SERVICES	10104	84	10773	SECURITIES/COMMODITY CONTRACTS
08558	334	13333	NURSING & RESID. CARE FACILIT.	08850	335	2317	BLDG MATL & GARDEN EQPMT DLRS	10105	86	9081	PROF.; SCIENTIFIC; & TECH SVCS
08559	183	536	SPECIAL TRADE CONTRACTORS	08852	519	11538	PUBLISHING INDUSTRIES	10106	128	2396	FOOD SVCS & DRINKING PLACES
08560	86	2099	CHEMICAL MANUFACTURING	08853	174	511	EDUCATIONAL SERVICES	10107	379	1617	PROF.; SCIENTIFIC; & TECH SVCS
08561	76	504	PROF.; SCIENTIFIC; & TECH SVCS	08854	1639	28715	PROF.; SCIENTIFIC; & TECH SVCS	10108	1	3	PERFORM'G ARTS; SPEC. SPORTS
08562	215	1496	EDUCATIONAL SERVICES	08855	7	43	NONSTORE RETAILERS	10110	241	1994	PROF.; SCIENTIFIC; & TECH SVCS
08601	2	23	RELIG.; GRANT; CIVIC; PROF ORG	08857	1077	10445	HOSPITALS	10111	324	3951	SECURITIES/COMMODITY CONTRACTS
08604	1	0	UNCLASSIFIED ESTABLISHMENTS	08858	61	605	PUBLISHING INDUSTRIES	10112	218	7992	MOTION PICT. & SOUND RECORDING
08605	1	0	RELIG.; GRANT; CIVIC; PROF ORG	08859	363	3081	EDUCATIONAL SERVICES	10113	5	8	ADMINISTRATIVE & SUPPORT SVCS
08606	2	2	CONSTRUCTION OF BUILDINGS	08861	1561	15357	EDUCATIONAL SERVICES	10115	109	1356	RELIG.; GRANT; CIVIC; PROF ORG
08607	2	12	EDUCATIONAL SERVICES	08862	5	3	MISCELLANEOUS STORE RETAILERS	10116	5	19	CONSTRUCTION OF BUILDINGS
08608	828	20147	EXEC.; LEGIS.; & OTHER SUPPORT	08863	300	1949	CHEMICAL MANUFACTURING	10118	1072	7203	PROF.; SCIENTIFIC; & TECH SVCS
08609	428	5070	EXEC.; LEGIS.; & OTHER SUPPORT	08865	1351	14737	RELIG.; GRANT; CIVIC; PROF ORG	10119	556	7522	PROF.; SCIENTIFIC; & TECH SVCS
08610	841	4747	EDUCATIONAL SERVICES	08867	244	1309	ADMINISTRATIVE & SUPPORT SVCS	10120	133	4784	CLOTHING & CLOTH'G ACC. STORES
08611	811	24061	EXEC.; LEGIS.; & OTHER SUPPORT	08868	6	66	EDUCATIONAL SERVICES	10121	208	3317	PUBLISHING INDUSTRIES
08618	876	21540	PROF.; SCIENTIFIC; & TECH SVCS	08869	452	7498	CHEMICAL MANUFACTURING	10122	216	1595	PROF.; SCIENTIFIC; & TECH SVCS
08619	1508	16295	PROF.; SCIENTIFIC; & TECH SVCS	08870	7	19	PROF.; SCIENTIFIC; & TECH SVCS	10123	354	3770	ACCOMMODATION
08620	279	2337	EXEC.; LEGIS.; & OTHER SUPPORT	08871	1	10	WASTE MANAGMT & REMEDIAT'N SVC	10128	2712	28831	HOSPITALS
08625	7	1301	RELIG.; GRANT; CIVIC; PROF ORG	08872	541	5524	JUSTICE; PUBIC ORDER/SAFETY	10129	1	1	PUBLISHING INDUSTRIES
08628	542	12883	INSURANCE CARRIERS & RELATED	08873	1851	26691	PROF.; SCIENTIFIC; & TECH SVCS	10138	1	1000	INSURANCE CARRIERS & RELATED
08629	147	3032	HOSPITALS	08875	10	17	SPECIAL TRADE CONTRACTORS	10150	13	35	FABRICATED METAL PRODUCT MFG
08638	1018	15109	JUSTICE; PUBIC ORDER/SAFETY	08876	2090	21105	MISCELLANEOUS MANUFACTURING	10151	97	954	SECURITIES/COMMODITY CONTRACTS
08640	71	621	JUSTICE; PUBIC ORDER/SAFETY	08879	725	4915	FOOD SVCS & DRINKING PLACES	10152	168	770	SECURITIES/COMMODITY CONTRACTS
08641	60	4110	NAT'L SECURITY & INT'L AFFAIRS	08880	111	502	EDUCATIONAL SERVICES	10153	124	4063	PROF.; SCIENTIFIC; & TECH SVCS
08648	1677	20816	PROF.; SCIENTIFIC; & TECH SVCS	08882	709	4585	MOTOR VEHICLE & PARTS DEALERS	10154	63	3634	PROF.; SCIENTIFIC; & TECH SVCS
08650	18	66	MERCH. WHOLESALERS;DURABLE GDS	08884	280	1847	PAPER MANUFACTURING	10155	210	1582	PROF.; SCIENTIFIC; & TECH SVCS
08666	2	3	EXEC.; LEGIS.; & OTHER SUPPORT	08885	8	33	SOCIAL ASSISTANCE	10156	4	17	ADMINISTRATIVE & SUPPORT SVCS
08690	653	9216	HOSPITALS	08886	157	551	MOTOR VEHICLE & PARTS DEALERS	10158	74	4243	SECURITIES/COMMODITY CONTRACTS
08691	685	10041	MERCH. WHOLESALERS;DURABLE GDS	08887	35	208	EDUCATIONAL SERVICES	10159	6	15	PERFORM'G ARTS; SPEC. SPORTS
08701	2689	32335	EDUCATIONAL SERVICES	08888	55	226	PROF.; SCIENTIFIC; & TECH SVCS	10162	31	53	REAL ESTATE
08720	36	467	NURSING & RESID. CARE FACILIT.	08889	482	8324	CHEMICAL MANUFACTURING	10163	3	7	NONSTORE RETAILERS
08721	636	4858	EDUCATIONAL SERVICES	08890	9	88	BROADCASTING	10165	694	4438	PROF.; SCIENTIFIC; & TECH SVCS
08722	227	1100	EDUCATIONAL SERVICES	08899	5	46	RELIG.; GRANT; CIVIC; PROF ORG	10166	202	6981	SECURITIES/COMMODITY CONTRACTS
08723	1333	9347	FOOD SVCS & DRINKING PLACES	08901	2425	31025	HOSPITALS	10167	233	4392	CREDIT INTERMEDIATION & RELATD
08724	1185	9981	HOSPITALS	08902	1400	18389	BLDG MATL & GARDEN EQPMT DLRS	10168	396	2801	ADMINISTRATIVE & SUPPORT SVCS
08730	248	1119	FOOD SVCS & DRINKING PLACES	08903	4	3	ELECTRONICS & APPLIANCE STORES	10169	549	3880	SECURITIES/COMMODITY CONTRACTS
08731	756	3982	FOOD SVCS & DRINKING PLACES	08904	519	2615	EDUCATIONAL SERVICES	10170	502	4383	ADMINISTRATIVE & SUPPORT SVCS
08732	76	307	EDUCATIONAL SERVICES	08906	4	9	PROF.; SCIENTIFIC; & TECH SVCS	10171	34	4988	CREDIT INTERMEDIATION & RELATD
08733	189	4446	MUSEUMS; HIST. SITES;& SIMILAR	08933	1	2000	MISCELLANEOUS MANUFACTURING	10172	64	620	CREDIT INTERMEDIATION & RELATD
08734	244	1827	EDUCATIONAL SERVICES	10001	14192	123759	PROF.; SCIENTIFIC; & TECH SVCS	10173	17	812	PROF.; SCIENTIFIC; & TECH SVCS
08735	197	1028	FOOD SVCS & DRINKING PLACES	10002	4067	21006	SOCIAL ASSISTANCE	10174	252	3236	PROF.; SCIENTIFIC; & TECH SVCS
08736	997	7236	AMUSEMENT; GAMBLING;& RECREAT.	10003	6345	77457	AMBULATORY HEALTH CARE SVCS	10175	211	1664	ADMINISTRATIVE & SUPPORT SVCS
08738	49	154	REAL ESTATE	10004	2489	53057	PROF.; SCIENTIFIC; & TECH SVCS	10176	149	1082	PROF.; SCIENTIFIC; & TECH SVCS
08739	27	56	CONSTRUCTION OF BUILDINGS	10005	2687	38097	PROF.; SCIENTIFIC; & TECH SVCS	10177	93	1424	PROF.; SCIENTIFIC; & TECH SVCS
08740	48	126	FOOD SVCS & DRINKING PLACES	10006	1496	18366	PROF.; SCIENTIFIC; & TECH SVCS	10178	72	6011	PROF.; SCIENTIFIC; & TECH SVCS
08741	65	339	FOOD SVCS & DRINKING PLACES	10007	2334	37570	EXEC.; LEGIS.; & OTHER SUPPORT	10179	6	6177	SECURITIES/COMMODITY CONTRACTS
08742	1568	8714	AMUSEMENT; GAMBLING;& RECREAT.	10008	5	6	PROF.; SCIENTIFIC; & TECH SVCS	10185	3	2	MOTION PICT. & SOUND RECORDING
08750	331	2187	REAL ESTATE	10009	1713	6624	FOOD SVCS & DRINKING PLACES	10199	7	1600	POSTAL SERVICE
08751	296	2438	AMUSEMENT; GAMBLING;& RECREAT.	10010	5510	59964	PROF.; SCIENTIFIC; & TECH SVCS	10260	1	0	CREDIT INTERMEDIATION & RELATD
08752	160	1117	FOOD SVCS & DRINKING PLACES	10011	6611	71519	PROF.; SCIENTIFIC; & TECH SVCS	10268	1	100	RELIG.; GRANT; CIVIC; PROF ORG
08753	3376	26446	FOOD SVCS & DRINKING PLACES	10012	4548	29158	PROF.; SCIENTIFIC; & TECH SVCS	10270	20	5593	INSURANCE CARRIERS & RELATED
08754	33	86	ADMINISTRATIVE & SUPPORT SVCS	10013	7535	51536	PROF.; SCIENTIFIC; & TECH SVCS	10271	145	6052	PROF.; SCIENTIFIC; & TECH SVCS
08755	1309	14099	HOSPITALS	10014	3331	34221	PROF.; SCIENTIFIC; & TECH SVCS	10274	2	12	PUBLISHING INDUSTRIES
08756	2	1	RELIG.; GRANT; CIVIC; PROF ORG	10016	10335	96830	PROF.; SCIENTIFIC; & TECH SVCS	10278	89	1894	ADMIN. OF ECONOMIC PROGRAMS
08757	317	2287	SOCIAL ASSISTANCE	10017	8831	136690	PROF.; SCIENTIFIC; & TECH SVCS	10279	151	1237	PROF.; SCIENTIFIC; & TECH SVCS
08758	208	1193	RELIG.; GRANT; CIVIC; PROF ORG	10018	12437	110903	PROF.; SCIENTIFIC; & TECH SVCS	10280	282	874	RELIG.; GRANT; CIVIC; PROF ORG

BUSINESS DATA

ZIP CODE	2009 Total Firms	2009 Total Employees	TOP INDUSTRY RANKED on 2009 EMPLOYMENT
10281	176	11774	PROF.; SCIENTIFIC; & TECH SVCS
10282	159	1781	SECURITIES/COMMODITY CONTRACTS
10285	14	6776	CREDIT INTERMEDIATION & RELATD
10286	4	2031	MANAGMT OF COMPANIES & ENTERP.
10301	1190	9786	EDUCATIONAL SERVICES
10302	689	5038	RELIG.; GRANT; CIVIC; PROF ORG
10303	609	5830	BLDG MATL & GARDEN EQPMT DLRS
10304	985	9890	RELIG.; GRANT; CIVIC; PROF ORG
10305	1191	10664	AMBULATORY HEALTH CARE SVCS
10306	1407	9495	EDUCATIONAL SERVICES
10307	378	1608	EDUCATIONAL SERVICES
10308	540	2687	EDUCATIONAL SERVICES
10309	1045	7111	MERCH. WHOLESALERS;DURABLE GDS
10310	847	4918	SOCIAL ASSISTANCE
10311	30	47	TELECOMMUNICATIONS
10312	1091	5979	EDUCATIONAL SERVICES
10313	3	1	WASTE MANAGMT & REMEDIAT'N SVC
10314	2426	25548	EDUCATIONAL SERVICES
10451	1360	53568	HOSPITALS
10452	1312	8294	EDUCATIONAL SERVICES
10453	1257	10415	EDUCATIONAL SERVICES
10454	1064	9313	SPECIAL TRADE CONTRACTORS
10455	1407	11320	EDUCATIONAL SERVICES
10456	1259	7476	EDUCATIONAL SERVICES
10457	1509	17234	HOSPITALS
10458	1857	16267	EDUCATIONAL SERVICES
10459	1103	5369	EDUCATIONAL SERVICES
10460	973	7346	EDUCATIONAL SERVICES
10461	2185	25419	HOSPITALS
10462	1933	10495	AMBULATORY HEALTH CARE SVCS
10463	1442	10695	NURSING & RESID. CARE FACILIT.
10464	215	1091	FOOD SVCS & DRINKING PLACES
10465	738	5563	EDUCATIONAL SERVICES
10466	1374	9012	AMBULATORY HEALTH CARE SVCS
10467	2157	12216	HOSPITALS
10468	1183	14552	EDUCATIONAL SERVICES
10469	1331	9116	NURSING & RESID. CARE FACILIT.
10470	489	2299	EDUCATIONAL SERVICES
10471	511	8284	NURSING & RESID. CARE FACILIT.
10472	999	4479	EDUCATIONAL SERVICES
10473	637	8707	EDUCATIONAL SERVICES
10474	1086	14115	MERCH. WHOLESALERS;NONDUR. GDS
10475	617	9801	NURSING & RESID. CARE FACILIT.
10501	23	43	PROF.; SCIENTIFIC; & TECH SVCS
10502	343	2248	EDUCATIONAL SERVICES
10503	6	6	REAL ESTATE
10504	536	6273	COMPUTER & ELECTRONIC PROD MFG
10505	70	498	FOOD SVCS & DRINKING PLACES
10506	281	1495	EDUCATIONAL SERVICES
10507	559	7613	INSURANCE CARRIERS & RELATED
10509	1185	10327	EDUCATIONAL SERVICES
10510	469	3936	EDUCATIONAL SERVICES
10511	127	1796	ADMIN. OF ECONOMIC PROGRAMS
10512	938	7352	HOSPITALS
10514	386	3046	EDUCATIONAL SERVICES
10516	361	1813	ACCOMMODATION
10517	17	73	EDUCATIONAL SERVICES
10518	85	641	EDUCATIONAL SERVICES
10519	58	367	JUSTICE; PUBIC ORDER/SAFETY
10520	506	2892	EDUCATIONAL SERVICES
10521	2	0	SECURITIES/COMMODITY CONTRACTS
10522	457	3876	EDUCATIONAL SERVICES
10523	1085	13119	ADMINISTRATIVE & SUPPORT SVCS
10524	169	981	RELIG.; GRANT; CIVIC; PROF ORG
10526	61	549	MOTOR VEHICLE & PARTS DEALERS
10527	19	200	ACCOMMODATION
10528	632	4784	PROF.; SCIENTIFIC; & TECH SVCS
10530	571	3707	EDUCATIONAL SERVICES
10532	531	11854	ADMINISTRATIVE & SUPPORT SVCS
10533	334	2483	RELIG.; GRANT; CIVIC; PROF ORG
10535	107	908	AMUSEMENT; GAMBLING;& RECREAT.
10536	444	2383	HOSPITALS
10537	22	14	PROF.; SCIENTIFIC; & TECH SVCS
10538	851	4605	FOOD SVCS & DRINKING PLACES
10540	37	670	EDUCATIONAL SERVICES
10541	841	4420	EDUCATIONAL SERVICES
10542	12	60	FOOD AND BEVERAGE STORES
10543	1250	8315	EDUCATIONAL SERVICES
10545	8	62	NONSTORE RETAILERS
10546	98	815	SPECIAL TRADE CONTRACTORS
10547	271	2403	GENERAL MERCHANDISE STORES
10548	131	3005	HOSPITALS
10549	1218	10587	AMBULATORY HEALTH CARE SVCS
10550	1858	14051	SPECIAL TRADE CONTRACTORS
10552	369	4139	NURSING & RESID. CARE FACILIT.
10553	296	2257	MERCH. WHOLESALERS;DURABLE GDS
10558	1	10	CREDIT INTERMEDIATION & RELATD
10560	185	1032	EDUCATIONAL SERVICES
10562	1008	7433	EDUCATIONAL SERVICES
10566	1006	7559	AMBULATORY HEALTH CARE SVCS
10567	521	5264	NURSING & RESID. CARE FACILIT.
10570	638	4685	PUBLISHING INDUSTRIES
10573	1842	14742	EDUCATIONAL SERVICES
10576	219	833	MISCELLANEOUS STORE RETAILERS
10577	413	12701	MERCH. WHOLESALERS;NONDUR. GDS
10578	30	208	NURSING & RESID. CARE FACILIT.
10579	262	1221	EDUCATIONAL SERVICES
10580	793	9712	RELIG.; GRANT; CIVIC; PROF ORG
10583	1581	10561	EDUCATIONAL SERVICES
10587	14	12	FOOD SVCS & DRINKING PLACES
10588	116	673	EDUCATIONAL SERVICES
10589	314	3751	BEVERAGE & TOBACCO PRODUCT MFG
10590	223	974	EDUCATIONAL SERVICES
10591	1372	15278	AMBULATORY HEALTH CARE SVCS
10594	329	2267	EDUCATIONAL SERVICES
10595	499	14680	EXEC.; LEGIS.; & OTHER SUPPORT
10596	33	77	MERCH. WHOLESALERS;DURABLE GDS
10597	15	42	AMUSEMENT; GAMBLING;& RECREAT.
10598	1053	10187	EDUCATIONAL SERVICES
10601	2551	30076	EXEC.; LEGIS.; & OTHER SUPPORT
10602	6	36	BLDG MATL & GARDEN EQPMT DLRS
10603	748	6612	MERCH. WHOLESALERS;DURABLE GDS
10604	903	17663	ELECTRONICS & APPLIANCE STORES
10605	800	21022	GENERAL MERCHANDISE STORES
10606	760	6336	PROF.; SCIENTIFIC; & TECH SVCS
10607	425	3182	AMUSEMENT; GAMBLING;& RECREAT.
10610	6	26	RELIG.; GRANT; CIVIC; PROF ORG
10701	2071	20304	HOSPITALS
10702	3	0	CONSTRUCTION OF BUILDINGS
10703	401	6966	FABRICATED METAL PRODUCT MFG
10704	1182	7539	FOOD SVCS & DRINKING PLACES
10705	903	4501	TRANSIT & GRND PASS. TRANSPORT
10706	339	2921	EDUCATIONAL SERVICES
10707	396	2339	SPECIAL TRADE CONTRACTORS
10708	635	4657	HOSPITALS
10709	430	2835	EDUCATIONAL SERVICES
10710	986	10176	BLDG MATL & GARDEN EQPMT DLRS
10801	2247	16562	NURSING & RESID. CARE FACILIT.
10802	3	2	PROF.; SCIENTIFIC; & TECH SVCS
10803	570	4579	SPECIAL TRADE CONTRACTORS
10804	359	2306	EDUCATIONAL SERVICES
10805	311	3594	NURSING & RESID. CARE FACILIT.
10901	1007	10784	EDUCATIONAL SERVICES
10910	3	28	REAL ESTATE
10911	13	293	ACCOMMODATION
10912	6	19	ADMINISTRATIVE & SUPPORT SVCS
10913	245	2206	MERCH. WHOLESALERS;DURABLE GDS
10914	31	64	SOCIAL ASSISTANCE
10915	41	170	SPECIAL TRADE CONTRACTORS
10916	116	1011	RELIG.; GRANT; CIVIC; PROF ORG
10917	385	6070	EDUCATIONAL SERVICES
10918	432	3465	EDUCATIONAL SERVICES
10919	51	299	JUSTICE; PUBIC ORDER/SAFETY
10920	386	3405	RELIG.; GRANT; CIVIC; PROF ORG
10921	297	1784	EDUCATIONAL SERVICES
10922	37	157	EDUCATIONAL SERVICES
10923	261	1609	FOOD AND BEVERAGE STORES
10924	899	11586	EDUCATIONAL SERVICES
10925	170	499	EDUCATIONAL SERVICES
10926	146	1003	PROF.; SCIENTIFIC; & TECH SVCS
10927	378	2847	NURSING & RESID. CARE FACILIT.
10928	219	1072	EDUCATIONAL SERVICES
10930	159	430	AMBULATORY HEALTH CARE SVCS
10931	67	949	BLDG MATL & GARDEN EQPMT DLRS
10932	10	118	JUSTICE; PUBIC ORDER/SAFETY
10933	12	13	AMUSEMENT; GAMBLING;& RECREAT.
10940	1882	20939	HOSPITALS
10941	602	7480	FOOD SVCS & DRINKING PLACES
10949	9	16	SPECIAL TRADE CONTRACTORS
10950	1157	7128	GENERAL MERCHANDISE STORES
10952	1163	5418	EDUCATIONAL SERVICES
10953	24	243	MERCH. WHOLESALERS;NONDUR. GDS
10954	1237	11251	EDUCATIONAL SERVICES
10956	1369	9765	JUSTICE; PUBIC ORDER/SAFETY
10958	116	915	MOTOR VEHICLE & PARTS DEALERS
10959	7	17	MERCH. WHOLESALERS;DURABLE GDS
10960	954	8088	HOSPITALS
10962	380	7143	HOSPITALS
10963	101	879	JUSTICE; PUBIC ORDER/SAFETY
10964	45	1753	EDUCATIONAL SERVICES
10965	643	10015	MERCH. WHOLESALERS;NONDUR. GDS
10968	134	497	FOOD SVCS & DRINKING PLACES
10969	125	577	MERCH. WHOLESALERS;NONDUR. GDS
10970	470	6920	ADMIN. HUMAN RESOURCE PROGRAMS
10973	112	1325	EDUCATIONAL SERVICES
10974	128	680	NONSTORE RETAILERS
10975	21	66	JUSTICE; PUBIC ORDER/SAFETY
10976	56	627	EDUCATIONAL SERVICES
10977	1693	11392	EDUCATIONAL SERVICES
10979	7	1	SPECIAL TRADE CONTRACTORS
10980	455	3013	NONMETALLIC MINERAL PROD. MFG
10981	44	132	RENTAL AND LEASING SERVICES
10982	50	411	HOSPITALS
10983	196	1461	MERCH. WHOLESALERS;DURABLE GDS
10984	56	714	EDUCATIONAL SERVICES
10985	12	29	HEAVY & CIVIL ENG. CONSTRUCT'N
10986	45	122	CONSTRUCTION OF BUILDINGS
10987	159	1828	ADMINISTRATIVE & SUPPORT SVCS
10988	34	133	REAL ESTATE
10989	318	2617	PROF.; SCIENTIFIC; & TECH SVCS
10990	1089	6411	EDUCATIONAL SERVICES
10992	287	1624	RELIG.; GRANT; CIVIC; PROF ORG
10993	155	1953	HOSPITALS
10994	725	10038	EDUCATIONAL SERVICES
10996	101	1414	HOSPITALS
10998	49	122	FOOD SVCS & DRINKING PLACES
11001	1015	6085	PROF.; SCIENTIFIC; & TECH SVCS
11002	3	25	ADMINISTRATIVE & SUPPORT SVCS
11003	1127	8392	PERFORM'G ARTS; SPEC. SPORTS
11004	295	2016	EDUCATIONAL SERVICES
11005	48	439	MERCH. WHOLESALERS;DURABLE GDS
11010	906	5600	EDUCATIONAL SERVICES
11020	147	1176	EDUCATIONAL SERVICES
11021	2636	14108	PROF.; SCIENTIFIC; & TECH SVCS
11022	2	0	UNCLASSIFIED ESTABLISHMENTS
11023	418	2824	EDUCATIONAL SERVICES
11024	207	1127	EDUCATIONAL SERVICES
11030	1161	12694	AMBULATORY HEALTH CARE SVCS
11040	1811	25851	HOSPITALS
11041	2	30	INSURANCE CARRIERS & RELATED
11042	778	13649	AMBULATORY HEALTH CARE SVCS
11050	1658	17645	EDUCATIONAL SERVICES
11096	474	4317	TRANSIT & GRND PASS. TRANSPORT
11101	4561	71672	TRANSIT & GRND PASS. TRANSPORT
11102	998	5904	HOSPITALS
11103	1598	6610	EDUCATIONAL SERVICES
11104	798	5006	SOCIAL ASSISTANCE
11105	1258	7595	EDUCATIONAL SERVICES
11106	1489	9206	EDUCATIONAL SERVICES
11109	35	115	EDUCATIONAL SERVICES
11201	3851	57611	EDUCATIONAL SERVICES
11202	8	24	SOCIAL ASSISTANCE
11203	1850	15140	EXEC.; LEGIS.; & OTHER SUPPORT
11204	2398	10296	EDUCATIONAL SERVICES
11205	1642	12726	EDUCATIONAL SERVICES
11206	1829	15494	AMBULATORY HEALTH CARE SVCS
11207	1906	13849	EDUCATIONAL SERVICES
11208	1476	13187	EDUCATIONAL SERVICES
11209	2228	13739	HOSPITALS
11210	1561	7708	EDUCATIONAL SERVICES
11211	3971	19268	EDUCATIONAL SERVICES
11212	1488	9458	EDUCATIONAL SERVICES
11213	1346	9902	HOSPITALS
11214	1969	12415	EDUCATIONAL SERVICES
11215	2474	20171	HOSPITALS
11216	1529	6949	EDUCATIONAL SERVICES
11217	1751	14845	EXEC.; LEGIS.; & OTHER SUPPORT
11218	2178	9548	EDUCATIONAL SERVICES
11219	3606	15751	EDUCATIONAL SERVICES
11220	2613	17577	HOSPITALS
11221	1210	7287	EDUCATIONAL SERVICES
11222	2055	17282	FABRICATED METAL PRODUCT MFG
11223	2493	10824	EDUCATIONAL SERVICES
11224	861	7870	NURSING & RESID. CARE FACILIT.
11225	1203	5237	EDUCATIONAL SERVICES
11226	2110	9639	EDUCATIONAL SERVICES
11228	850	5321	HOSPITALS
11229	2091	12693	EDUCATIONAL SERVICES
11230	2633	12979	EDUCATIONAL SERVICES
11231	1448	10791	TRANSIT & GRND PASS. TRANSPORT
11232	1902	14965	MERCH. WHOLESALERS;DURABLE GDS
11233	939	5642	EDUCATIONAL SERVICES
11234	2406	15364	AMBULATORY HEALTH CARE SVCS
11235	2396	18332	EDUCATIONAL SERVICES
11236	1783	11668	EDUCATIONAL SERVICES
11237	1344	10600	HOSPITALS
11238	1387	9679	EDUCATIONAL SERVICES
11239	142	2502	FOOD SVCS & DRINKING PLACES
11241	88	633	ADMINISTRATIVE & SUPPORT SVCS
11242	199	662	PROF.; SCIENTIFIC; & TECH SVCS
11243	11	33	AMBULATORY HEALTH CARE SVCS
11245	2	7	SOCIAL ASSISTANCE
11247	1	0	ADMINISTRATIVE & SUPPORT SVCS
11248	3	101	FOOD SVCS & DRINKING PLACES
11251	3	4	MISCELLANEOUS STORE RETAILERS
11252	9	7	CLOTHING & CLOTH'G ACC. STORES
11256	5	552	RELIG.; GRANT; CIVIC; PROF ORG
11351	9	4859	PROF.; SCIENTIFIC; & TECH SVCS
11352	2	9	RELIG.; GRANT; CIVIC; PROF ORG
11354	3405	18541	NURSING & RESID. CARE FACILIT.

ZIP CODE	2009 Total Firms	2009 Total Employees	TOP INDUSTRY RANKED on 2009 EMPLOYMENT	ZIP CODE	2009 Total Firms	2009 Total Employees	TOP INDUSTRY RANKED on 2009 EMPLOYMENT	ZIP CODE	2009 Total Firms	2009 Total Employees	TOP INDUSTRY RANKED on 2009 EMPLOYMENT
11355	1710	11192	HOSPITALS	11580	1560	12370	HOSPITALS	11801	2893	23844	PROF.; SCIENTIFIC; & TECH SVCS
11356	913	7476	SPECIAL TRADE CONTRACTORS	11581	890	6694	GENERAL MERCHANDISE STORES	11802	7	28	CHEMICAL MANUFACTURING
11357	1097	7184	MISCELLANEOUS STORE RETAILERS	11582	5	46	PERSONAL AND LAUNDRY SERVICES	11803	1824	19874	EDUCATIONAL SERVICES
11358	1371	5055	EDUCATIONAL SERVICES	11590	2344	25910	FOOD SVCS & DRINKING PLACES	11804	145	1701	TRUCK TRANSPORTATION
11359	18	96	CLOTHING & CLOTH'G ACC. STORES	11596	454	2788	FOOD SVCS & DRINKING PLACES	11855	1	0	UNCLASSIFIED ESTABLISHMENTS
11360	345	3369	HOSPITALS	11598	433	3573	NURSING & RESID. CARE FACILIT.	11901	1663	20031	JUSTICE; PUBIC ORDER/SAFETY
11361	1288	7869	EDUCATIONAL SERVICES	11599	4	801	POSTAL SERVICE	11930	198	1223	FOOD SVCS & DRINKING PLACES
11362	536	14893	ADMIN. ENVIRO. QUALITY PROGRMS	11691	858	10646	EDUCATIONAL SERVICES	11931	77	365	FOOD SVCS & DRINKING PLACES
11363	187	1155	MERCH. WHOLESALERS;DURABLE GDS	11692	187	2005	NURSING & RESID. CARE FACILIT.	11932	424	2789	REAL ESTATE
11364	577	4621	EDUCATIONAL SERVICES	11693	225	1637	FOOD MANUFACTURING	11933	239	2499	AMUSEMENT; GAMBLING;& RECREAT.
11365	640	5729	EDUCATIONAL SERVICES	11694	479	3217	EDUCATIONAL SERVICES	11934	428	2384	EDUCATIONAL SERVICES
11366	568	2637	EDUCATIONAL SERVICES	11695	4	16	MUSEUMS; HIST. SITES;& SIMILAR	11935	224	1107	EDUCATIONAL SERVICES
11367	759	4720	EDUCATIONAL SERVICES	11697	61	639	REAL ESTATE	11937	1127	7089	FOOD SVCS & DRINKING PLACES
11368	2292	11867	ADMIN. OF ECONOMIC PROGRAMS	11701	1289	13178	HOSPITALS	11939	29	43	CROP PRODUCTION
11369	431	5345	ACCOMMODATION	11702	772	4610	FOOD SVCS & DRINKING PLACES	11940	217	753	NURSING & RESID. CARE FACILIT.
11370	385	4187	AIR TRANSPORTATION	11703	403	2675	EDUCATIONAL SERVICES	11941	138	707	EDUCATIONAL SERVICES
11371	123	2608	RENTAL AND LEASING SERVICES	11704	1732	12071	SPECIAL TRADE CONTRACTORS	11942	160	700	FOOD SVCS & DRINKING PLACES
11372	2667	9499	EDUCATIONAL SERVICES	11705	268	2410	FOOD MANUFACTURING	11944	315	2194	FOOD SVCS & DRINKING PLACES
11373	1964	19267	HOSPITALS	11706	2508	26639	MERCH. WHOLESALERS;NONDUR. GDS	11946	669	3751	FOOD SVCS & DRINKING PLACES
11374	1227	7848	AMBULATORY HEALTH CARE SVCS	11709	163	1208	FOOD SVCS & DRINKING PLACES	11947	79	425	JUSTICE; PUBIC ORDER/SAFETY
11375	2461	15958	HOSPITALS	11710	1448	7353	EDUCATIONAL SERVICES	11948	27	210	BLDG MATL & GARDEN EQPMT DLRS
11377	2188	20487	ADMIN. ENVIRO. QUALITY PROGRMS	11713	389	4030	EDUCATIONAL SERVICES	11949	284	1077	EDUCATIONAL SERVICES
11378	1443	15570	MERCH. WHOLESALERS;NONDUR. GDS	11714	841	16211	BROADCASTING	11950	285	727	FOOD SVCS & DRINKING PLACES
11379	716	3950	EDUCATIONAL SERVICES	11715	169	746	FOOD SVCS & DRINKING PLACES	11951	211	1150	EDUCATIONAL SERVICES
11385	2921	18258	EDUCATIONAL SERVICES	11716	1831	26681	SPECIAL TRADE CONTRACTORS	11952	312	1815	EDUCATIONAL SERVICES
11411	332	1179	EDUCATIONAL SERVICES	11717	1131	12198	EDUCATIONAL SERVICES	11953	382	3377	EDUCATIONAL SERVICES
11412	701	2551	EDUCATIONAL SERVICES	11718	122	522	SPECIAL TRADE CONTRACTORS	11954	433	2817	ACCOMMODATION
11413	830	5553	SUPPORT ACT. FOR TRANSPORT.	11719	149	1297	NURSING & RESID. CARE FACILIT.	11955	109	900	EDUCATIONAL SERVICES
11414	556	3613	FOOD SVCS & DRINKING PLACES	11720	756	6864	EDUCATIONAL SERVICES	11956	16	28	AMUSEMENT; GAMBLING;& RECREAT.
11415	580	2836	PROF.; SCIENTIFIC; & TECH SVCS	11721	178	804	FOOD SVCS & DRINKING PLACES	11957	39	121	EDUCATIONAL SERVICES
11416	662	4797	EDUCATIONAL SERVICES	11722	793	8393	EDUCATIONAL SERVICES	11958	73	368	JUSTICE; PUBIC ORDER/SAFETY
11417	728	4210	EDUCATIONAL SERVICES	11724	161	909	EDUCATIONAL SERVICES	11959	185	1003	SPECIAL TRADE CONTRACTORS
11418	1208	9200	RELIG.; GRANT; CIVIC; PROF ORG	11725	1568	15296	GENERAL MERCHANDISE STORES	11960	24	80	EDUCATIONAL SERVICES
11419	1220	4401	REAL ESTATE	11726	777	6370	EDUCATIONAL SERVICES	11961	183	1277	EDUCATIONAL SERVICES
11420	737	4658	PERFORM'G ARTS; SPEC. SPORTS	11727	650	3524	UTILITIES	11962	45	136	AMUSEMENT; GAMBLING;& RECREAT.
11421	654	2646	REAL ESTATE	11729	1998	12983	FABRICATED METAL PRODUCT MFG	11963	509	2285	EDUCATIONAL SERVICES
11422	560	2685	PROF.; SCIENTIFIC; & TECH SVCS	11730	563	3283	PROF.; SCIENTIFIC; & TECH SVCS	11964	189	758	JUSTICE; PUBIC ORDER/SAFETY
11423	617	3802	HOSPITALS	11731	1052	6149	EDUCATIONAL SERVICES	11965	44	207	RELIG.; GRANT; CIVIC; PROF ORG
11424	19	141	EXEC.; LEGIS.; & OTHER SUPPORT	11732	166	1127	REAL ESTATE	11967	683	5946	MERCH. WHOLESALERS;NONDUR. GDS
11425	2	500	ADMIN. HUMAN RESOURCE PROGRAMS	11733	854	7204	AMBULATORY HEALTH CARE SVCS	11968	1405	10837	HOSPITALS
11426	373	2052	EXEC.; LEGIS.; & OTHER SUPPORT	11735	3207	33246	PROF.; SCIENTIFIC; & TECH SVCS	11969	19	57	TRANSIT & GRND PASS. TRANSPORT
11427	304	3846	EXEC.; LEGIS.; & OTHER SUPPORT	11738	468	3268	EXEC.; LEGIS.; & OTHER SUPPORT	11970	13	44	ACCOMMODATION
11428	586	3080	REAL ESTATE	11739	70	361	REPAIR AND MAINTENANCE	11971	362	1992	EXEC.; LEGIS.; & OTHER SUPPORT
11429	441	2012	HEAVY & CIVIL ENG. CONSTRUCT'N	11740	325	2953	COMPUTER & ELECTRONIC PROD MFG	11972	85	360	MERCH. WHOLESALERS;DURABLE GDS
11430	497	15952	SUPPORT ACT. FOR TRANSPORT.	11741	1177	8592	FURN. & HOME FURNISHGS STORES	11973	12	5787	PROF.; SCIENTIFIC; & TECH SVCS
11431	2	1	RELIG.; GRANT; CIVIC; PROF ORG	11742	407	5807	MERCH. WHOLESALERS;NONDUR. GDS	11975	131	923	JUSTICE; PUBIC ORDER/SAFETY
11432	2236	18591	RELIG.; GRANT; CIVIC; PROF ORG	11743	2650	19910	HOSPITALS	11976	196	714	FOOD SVCS & DRINKING PLACES
11433	748	7041	EXEC.; LEGIS.; & OTHER SUPPORT	11746	2375	24812	SPORTG GDS;HOBBY;BOOK; & MUSIC	11977	126	638	NURSING & RESID. CARE FACILIT.
11434	1768	15191	TRANSIT & GRND PASS. TRANSPORT	11747	2356	43863	PROF.; SCIENTIFIC; & TECH SVCS	11978	525	5352	FOOD SVCS & DRINKING PLACES
11435	1385	10315	BLDG MATL & GARDEN EQPMT DLRS	11749	699	10031	PROF.; SCIENTIFIC; & TECH SVCS	11980	306	8441	JUSTICE; PUBIC ORDER/SAFETY
11436	235	1729	ACCOMMODATION	11751	587	4766	EDUCATIONAL SERVICES	12007	8	53	NONMETALLIC MINERAL PROD. MFG
11439	3	1633	EDUCATIONAL SERVICES	11752	253	1298	EDUCATIONAL SERVICES	12008	19	80	JUSTICE; PUBIC ORDER/SAFETY
11451	9	803	OTHER INFORMATION SERVICES	11753	1144	15530	PROF.; SCIENTIFIC; & TECH SVCS	12009	293	2521	FOOD AND BEVERAGE STORES
11501	2100	27618	EXEC.; LEGIS.; & OTHER SUPPORT	11754	496	6083	HOSPITALS	12010	1049	13737	HOSPITALS
11507	303	1965	EDUCATIONAL SERVICES	11755	494	4415	CLOTHING & CLOTH'G ACC. STORES	12015	120	502	EDUCATIONAL SERVICES
11509	103	1105	FOOD SVCS & DRINKING PLACES	11756	1201	7112	EDUCATIONAL SERVICES	12016	1	2	FOOD AND BEVERAGE STORES
11510	1199	5691	EDUCATIONAL SERVICES	11757	1630	10539	EDUCATIONAL SERVICES	12017	20	28	PUBLISHING INDUSTRIES
11514	544	5853	FOOD SVCS & DRINKING PLACES	11758	2010	12023	EDUCATIONAL SERVICES	12018	169	1035	EDUCATIONAL SERVICES
11516	705	2680	EDUCATIONAL SERVICES	11762	524	6729	MERCH. WHOLESALERS;DURABLE GDS	12019	336	1727	AMBULATORY HEALTH CARE SVCS
11518	358	2024	RELIG.; GRANT; CIVIC; PROF ORG	11763	1085	9063	NURSING & RESID. CARE FACILIT.	12020	1080	12996	EXEC.; LEGIS.; & OTHER SUPPORT
11520	1942	19860	MERCH. WHOLESALERS;DURABLE GDS	11764	437	3989	CONSTRUCTION OF BUILDINGS	12022	58	274	EDUCATIONAL SERVICES
11530	2968	31616	PROF.; SCIENTIFIC; & TECH SVCS	11765	21	53	SOCIAL ASSISTANCE	12023	64	559	EDUCATIONAL SERVICES
11531	1	1	PERSONAL AND LAUNDRY SERVICES	11766	422	2123	RELIG.; GRANT; CIVIC; PROF ORG	12024	4	3	POSTAL SERVICE
11542	1356	11814	WHOLESALE ELEC. MRKTS & AGENTS	11767	435	2521	AMBULATORY HEALTH CARE SVCS	12025	175	599	FOOD SVCS & DRINKING PLACES
11545	514	6985	CREDIT INTERMEDIATION & RELATD	11768	952	5180	EDUCATIONAL SERVICES	12027	153	1180	EDUCATIONAL SERVICES
11547	44	135	SPECIAL TRADE CONTRACTORS	11769	359	4395	EDUCATIONAL SERVICES	12028	11	35	JUSTICE; PUBIC ORDER/SAFETY
11548	274	7550	EDUCATIONAL SERVICES	11770	96	644	FOOD SVCS & DRINKING PLACES	12029	98	757	SOCIAL ASSISTANCE
11549	10	2758	EDUCATIONAL SERVICES	11771	622	3701	EDUCATIONAL SERVICES	12031	7	14	EXEC.; LEGIS.; & OTHER SUPPORT
11550	2227	14027	EDUCATIONAL SERVICES	11772	1905	15974	EDUCATIONAL SERVICES	12032	47	124	EDUCATIONAL SERVICES
11552	1007	6278	EDUCATIONAL SERVICES	11776	890	6661	SOCIAL ASSISTANCE	12033	329	2609	EDUCATIONAL SERVICES
11553	1024	9641	NURSING & RESID. CARE FACILIT.	11777	731	13351	OTHER INFORMATION SERVICES	12035	25	147	JUSTICE; PUBIC ORDER/SAFETY
11554	1229	14043	HOSPITALS	11778	430	2895	EDUCATIONAL SERVICES	12036	12	26	SPORTG GDS;HOBBY;BOOK; & MUSIC
11556	230	7348	OTHER INFORMATION SERVICES	11779	2305	23806	PROF.; SCIENTIFIC; & TECH SVCS	12037	362	1616	PLASTICS & RUBBER PRODUCTS MFG
11557	561	3521	EDUCATIONAL SERVICES	11780	685	4861	MOTOR VEHICLE & PARTS DEALERS	12040	7	188	EDUCATIONAL SERVICES
11558	488	2476	FOOD SVCS & DRINKING PLACES	11782	875	4569	MOTOR VEHICLE & PARTS DEALERS	12041	19	82	EDUCATIONAL SERVICES
11559	467	3851	EDUCATIONAL SERVICES	11783	630	3903	EDUCATIONAL SERVICES	12042	16	74	FOOD SVCS & DRINKING PLACES
11560	405	2350	EDUCATIONAL SERVICES	11784	632	4987	EDUCATIONAL SERVICES	12043	406	4738	EDUCATIONAL SERVICES
11561	1115	7330	EDUCATIONAL SERVICES	11786	137	1639	EDUCATIONAL SERVICES	12045	15	102	JUSTICE; PUBIC ORDER/SAFETY
11563	1360	7900	PROF.; SCIENTIFIC; & TECH SVCS	11787	1896	17277	HOSPITALS	12046	23	170	JUSTICE; PUBIC ORDER/SAFETY
11565	275	1169	EDUCATIONAL SERVICES	11788	2153	39796	MERCH. WHOLESALERS;DURABLE GDS	12047	575	6694	AMBULATORY HEALTH CARE SVCS
11566	1271	7512	EDUCATIONAL SERVICES	11789	108	230	PROF.; SCIENTIFIC; & TECH SVCS	12050	5	11	SPECIAL TRADE CONTRACTORS
11568	127	3124	EDUCATIONAL SERVICES	11790	566	4439	AMBULATORY HEALTH CARE SVCS	12051	176	2408	JUSTICE; PUBIC ORDER/SAFETY
11569	62	262	FOOD AND BEVERAGE STORES	11791	1484	14837	PROF.; SCIENTIFIC; & TECH SVCS	12052	41	147	EDUCATIONAL SERVICES
11570	1578	24839	AMBULATORY HEALTH CARE SVCS	11792	274	1918	SOCIAL ASSISTANCE	12053	76	605	EDUCATIONAL SERVICES
11571	4	6	MISCELLANEOUS STORE RETAILERS	11793	1025	6532	FOOD SVCS & DRINKING PLACES	12054	537	4555	EDUCATIONAL SERVICES
11572	1486	12295	HOSPITALS	11794	71	32484	EDUCATIONAL SERVICES	12055	2	4	RELIG.; GRANT; CIVIC; PROF ORG
11575	322	2344	EDUCATIONAL SERVICES	11795	675	12680	HOSPITALS	12056	97	528	SPECIAL TRADE CONTRACTORS
11576	619	3875	MOTOR VEHICLE & PARTS DEALERS	11796	109	905	EDUCATIONAL SERVICES	12057	36	159	FOOD SVCS & DRINKING PLACES
11577	645	4108	EDUCATIONAL SERVICES	11797	759	15538	INSURANCE CARRIERS & RELATED	12058	21	42	FOOD SVCS & DRINKING PLACES
11579	270	907	JUSTICE; PUBIC ORDER/SAFETY	11798	355	2964	EDUCATIONAL SERVICES	12059	33	126	PROF.; SCIENTIFIC; & TECH SVCS

BUSINESS DATA

ZIP CODE	2009 Total Firms	2009 Total Employees	TOP INDUSTRY RANKED on 2009 EMPLOYMENT	ZIP CODE	2009 Total Firms	2009 Total Employees	TOP INDUSTRY RANKED on 2009 EMPLOYMENT	ZIP CODE	2009 Total Firms	2009 Total Employees	TOP INDUSTRY RANKED on 2009 EMPLOYMENT
12060	57	106	PROF.; SCIENTIFIC; & TECH SVCS	12184	254	1740	NURSING & RESID. CARE FACILIT.	12432	17	145	EDUCATIONAL SERVICES
12061	411	4294	EDUCATIONAL SERVICES	12185	41	146	JUSTICE; PUBIC ORDER/SAFETY	12433	18	43	UNCLASSIFIED ESTABLISHMENTS
12062	33	73	BLDG MATL & GARDEN EQPMT DLRS	12186	186	2083	EDUCATIONAL SERVICES	12434	53	202	EDUCATIONAL SERVICES
12063	12	11	PRINT'G & RELATED SUPP'T ACT'S	12187	17	41	FABRICATED METAL PRODUCT MFG	12435	17	64	ACCOMMODATION
12064	11	26	POSTAL SERVICE	12188	241	4620	MISCELLANEOUS MANUFACTURING	12436	27	73	EXEC.; LEGIS.; & OTHER SUPPORT
12065	1870	18670	PROF.; SCIENTIFIC; & TECH SVCS	12189	414	6424	NAT'L SECURITY & INT'L AFFAIRS	12438	9	20	WOOD PRODUCT MANUFACTURING
12066	49	149	JUSTICE; PUBIC ORDER/SAFETY	12190	47	154	EDUCATIONAL SERVICES	12439	34	280	ACCOMMODATION
12067	51	733	NONMETALLIC MINERAL PROD. MFG	12192	111	889	MERCH. WHOLESALERS;NONDUR. GDS	12440	91	364	ACCOMMODATION
12068	170	2436	PRIMARY METAL MANUFACTURING	12193	55	298	FABRICATED METAL PRODUCT MFG	12441	4	445	ACCOMMODATION
12069	6	18	EXEC.; LEGIS.; & OTHER SUPPORT	12194	10	34	EXEC.; LEGIS.; & OTHER SUPPORT	12442	111	1686	ADMINISTRATIVE & SUPPORT SVCS
12070	21	83	AMUSEMENT; GAMBLING;& RECREAT.	12195	22	340	PERFORM'G ARTS; SPEC. SPORTS	12443	105	574	TRANSIT & GRND PASS. TRANSPORT
12071	7	16	CROP PRODUCTION	12196	100	585	FOOD AND BEVERAGE STORES	12444	16	37	EXEC.; LEGIS.; & OTHER SUPPORT
12072	118	1145	JUSTICE; PUBIC ORDER/SAFETY	12197	68	250	EDUCATIONAL SERVICES	12446	148	799	AMUSEMENT; GAMBLING;& RECREAT.
12073	6	8	RELIG.; GRANT; CIVIC; PROF ORG	12198	189	1624	EDUCATIONAL SERVICES	12448	4	11	NURSING & RESID. CARE FACILIT.
12074	105	768	EDUCATIONAL SERVICES	12201	8	1229	EXEC.; LEGIS.; & OTHER SUPPORT	12449	127	2217	NURSING & RESID. CARE FACILIT.
12075	136	995	NURSING & RESID. CARE FACILIT.	12202	356	3627	RELIG.; GRANT; CIVIC; PROF ORG	12450	6	6	MERCH. WHOLESALERS;DURABLE GDS
12076	36	302	UTILITIES	12203	1296	23393	PROF.; SCIENTIFIC; & TECH SVCS	12451	40	385	BLDG MATL & GARDEN EQPMT DLRS
12077	239	10412	CONSTRUCTION OF BUILDINGS	12204	467	9509	HOSPITALS	12452	10	18	HEAVY & CIVIL ENG. CONSTRUCT'N
12078	819	7714	HOSPITALS	12205	2968	37309	FOOD SVCS & DRINKING PLACES	12453	12	65	FOOD SVCS & DRINKING PLACES
12082	20	110	MUSEUMS; HIST. SITES;& SIMILAR	12206	1031	11227	AMBULATORY HEALTH CARE SVCS	12454	11	19	SPECIAL TRADE CONTRACTORS
12083	170	1106	EDUCATIONAL SERVICES	12207	1118	18460	EXEC.; LEGIS.; & OTHER SUPPORT	12455	214	1275	JUSTICE; PUBIC ORDER/SAFETY
12084	223	2486	AMUSEMENT; GAMBLING;& RECREAT.	12208	638	40100	AMBULATORY HEALTH CARE SVCS	12456	15	127	NONMETALLIC MINERAL PROD. MFG
12085	38	1221	EDUCATIONAL SERVICES	12209	205	2087	EXEC.; LEGIS.; & OTHER SUPPORT	12457	45	343	ACCOMMODATION
12086	32	231	JUSTICE; PUBIC ORDER/SAFETY	12210	735	6498	RELIG.; GRANT; CIVIC; PROF ORG	12458	49	1268	JUSTICE; PUBIC ORDER/SAFETY
12087	23	101	TRUCK TRANSPORTATION	12211	454	9592	INSURANCE CARRIERS & RELATED	12459	7	5	EDUCATIONAL SERVICES
12089	12	64	BLDG MATL & GARDEN EQPMT DLRS	12212	9	6	ADMINISTRATIVE & SUPPORT SVCS	12460	19	483	MERCH. WHOLESALERS;NONDUR. GDS
12090	205	1625	PROF.; SCIENTIFIC; & TECH SVCS	12220	8	41	FOOD SVCS & DRINKING PLACES	12461	32	59	EDUCATIONAL SERVICES
12092	27	670	PLASTICS & RUBBER PRODUCTS MFG	12222	22	7216	EDUCATIONAL SERVICES	12463	34	116	FABRICATED METAL PRODUCT MFG
12093	34	139	EDUCATIONAL SERVICES	12223	91	9910	EXEC.; LEGIS.; & OTHER SUPPORT	12464	96	434	RELIG.; GRANT; CIVIC; PROF ORG
12094	30	44	EDUCATIONAL SERVICES	12224	7	20	PUBLISHING INDUSTRIES	12465	16	53	JUSTICE; PUBIC ORDER/SAFETY
12095	721	8058	EXEC.; LEGIS.; & OTHER SUPPORT	12226	22	1579	JUSTICE; PUBIC ORDER/SAFETY	12466	114	1181	EDUCATIONAL SERVICES
12106	139	579	PROF.; SCIENTIFIC; & TECH SVCS	12227	2	53	OTHER INFORMATION SERVICES	12468	47	132	FOOD AND BEVERAGE STORES
12107	11	64	JUSTICE; PUBIC ORDER/SAFETY	12228	2	0	ADMIN. OF ECONOMIC PROGRAMS	12469	14	35	BLDG MATL & GARDEN EQPMT DLRS
12108	65	192	EXEC.; LEGIS.; & OTHER SUPPORT	12230	9	1119	OTHER INFORMATION SERVICES	12470	10	28	SPECIAL TRADE CONTRACTORS
12110	1638	25165	PROF.; SCIENTIFIC; & TECH SVCS	12231	4	558	EXEC.; LEGIS.; & OTHER SUPPORT	12471	13	67	JUSTICE; PUBIC ORDER/SAFETY
12115	12	20	BLDG MATL & GARDEN EQPMT DLRS	12232	7	134	ADMIN. OF ECONOMIC PROGRAMS	12472	100	383	ADMINISTRATIVE & SUPPORT SVCS
12116	23	38	EXEC.; LEGIS.; & OTHER SUPPORT	12233	8	3996	EXEC.; LEGIS.; & OTHER SUPPORT	12473	22	131	ACCOMMODATION
12117	139	703	EDUCATIONAL SERVICES	12234	4	343	EXEC.; LEGIS.; & OTHER SUPPORT	12474	75	404	EDUCATIONAL SERVICES
12118	383	3542	MERCH. WHOLESALERS;NONDUR. GDS	12235	5	739	ADMIN. OF ECONOMIC PROGRAMS	12475	12	70	PERFORM'G ARTS; SPEC. SPORTS
12120	12	105	EXEC.; LEGIS.; & OTHER SUPPORT	12236	5	220	EXEC.; LEGIS.; & OTHER SUPPORT	12477	736	3689	PROF.; SCIENTIFIC; & TECH SVCS
12121	31	172	JUSTICE; PUBIC ORDER/SAFETY	12237	1	300	AMBULATORY HEALTH CARE SVCS	12480	33	457	ACCOMMODATION
12122	206	491	FOOD AND BEVERAGE STORES	12238	1	3	EXEC.; LEGIS.; & OTHER SUPPORT	12481	80	506	EXEC.; LEGIS.; & OTHER SUPPORT
12123	182	854	EDUCATIONAL SERVICES	12239	3	506	EXEC.; LEGIS.; & OTHER SUPPORT	12482	20	247	JUSTICE; PUBIC ORDER/SAFETY
12124	22	268	PERFORM'G ARTS; SPEC. SPORTS	12240	11	1650	ADMIN. HUMAN RESOURCE PROGRAMS	12483	8	8	ACCOMMODATION
12125	123	828	EDUCATIONAL SERVICES	12242	8	215	JUSTICE; PUBIC ORDER/SAFETY	12484	158	1506	EDUCATIONAL SERVICES
12128	6	7	ADMINISTRATIVE & SUPPORT SVCS	12243	1	50	ADMIN. HUMAN RESOURCE PROGRAMS	12485	110	632	EDUCATIONAL SERVICES
12130	38	61	EXEC.; LEGIS.; & OTHER SUPPORT	12245	1	0	EXEC.; LEGIS.; & OTHER SUPPORT	12486	30	136	TRANSIT & GRND PASS. TRANSPORT
12131	14	73	MUSEUMS; HIST. SITES;& SIMILAR	12246	2	45	ADMIN. HUMAN RESOURCE PROGRAMS	12487	57	753	MERCH. WHOLESALERS;NONDUR. GDS
12132	20	49	SUPPORT ACTIVITIES: AGR./FOR.	12247	5	1638	EXEC.; LEGIS.; & OTHER SUPPORT	12489	27	99	HEAVY & CIVIL ENG. CONSTRUCT'N
12133	9	113	PAPER MANUFACTURING	12248	7	24	EXEC.; LEGIS.; & OTHER SUPPORT	12490	7	16	PROF.; SCIENTIFIC; & TECH SVCS
12134	170	888	EDUCATIONAL SERVICES	12257	1	0	ADMIN. OF ECONOMIC PROGRAMS	12491	87	397	FABRICATED METAL PRODUCT MFG
12136	54	219	ANIMAL PRODUCTION	12260	18	602	PROF.; SCIENTIFIC; & TECH SVCS	12492	11	11	WOOD PRODUCT MANUFACTURING
12137	46	299	FOOD SVCS & DRINKING PLACES	12288	1	1000	POSTAL SERVICE	12493	17	180	SOCIAL ASSISTANCE
12138	52	308	TEXTILE MILLS	12301	1	1	MACHINERY MANUFACTURING	12494	28	86	FOOD SVCS & DRINKING PLACES
12139	26	74	EXEC.; LEGIS.; & OTHER SUPPORT	12302	839	11266	NAT'L SECURITY & INT'L AFFAIRS	12495	14	24	PROF.; SCIENTIFIC; & TECH SVCS
12140	36	297	JUSTICE; PUBIC ORDER/SAFETY	12303	819	7984	EDUCATIONAL SERVICES	12496	171	1406	SPORTG GDS;HOBBY;BOOK; & MUSIC
12141	7	35	JUSTICE; PUBIC ORDER/SAFETY	12304	740	10664	EXEC.; LEGIS.; & OTHER SUPPORT	12498	344	1687	MACHINERY MANUFACTURING
12143	227	1717	SPECIAL TRADE CONTRACTORS	12305	770	12412	RELIG.; GRANT; CIVIC; PROF ORG	12501	162	1300	EDUCATIONAL SERVICES
12144	734	7544	PROF.; SCIENTIFIC; & TECH SVCS	12306	810	9411	FOOD AND BEVERAGE STORES	12502	47	268	PAPER MANUFACTURING
12147	25	171	OTHER INFORMATION SERVICES	12307	222	2734	COMPUTER & ELECTRONIC PROD MFG	12503	30	60	CROP PRODUCTION
12148	91	646	FOOD SVCS & DRINKING PLACES	12308	413	6610	HOSPITALS	12504	10	673	EDUCATIONAL SERVICES
12149	59	694	CONSTRUCTION OF BUILDINGS	12309	703	11111	PROF.; SCIENTIFIC; & TECH SVCS	12506	4	4	POSTAL SERVICE
12150	32	145	SPECIAL TRADE CONTRACTORS	12325	1	0	UNCLASSIFIED ESTABLISHMENTS	12507	7	15	RELIG.; GRANT; CIVIC; PROF ORG
12151	54	362	PUBLISHING INDUSTRIES	12345	5	4810	MERCH. WHOLESALERS;DURABLE GDS	12508	574	5546	JUSTICE; PUBIC ORDER/SAFETY
12153	30	64	EXEC.; LEGIS.; & OTHER SUPPORT	12401	2562	27467	AMBULATORY HEALTH CARE SVCS	12510	15	85	SPECIAL TRADE CONTRACTORS
12154	90	463	EDUCATIONAL SERVICES	12402	8	25	NURSING & RESID. CARE FACILIT.	12511	1	0	HOSPITALS
12155	36	317	EDUCATIONAL SERVICES	12404	103	444	AMUSEMENT; GAMBLING;& RECREAT.	12512	9	44	JUSTICE; PUBIC ORDER/SAFETY
12156	30	497	FOOD AND BEVERAGE STORES	12405	16	93	ACCOMMODATION	12513	50	442	ADMIN. HUMAN RESOURCE PROGRAMS
12157	233	2234	EDUCATIONAL SERVICES	12406	75	148	RELIG.; GRANT; CIVIC; PROF ORG	12514	77	163	EDUCATIONAL SERVICES
12158	147	1236	CHEMICAL MANUFACTURING	12407	20	113	TRUCK TRANSPORTATION	12515	42	165	WAREHOUSING AND STORAGE
12159	214	2011	SOCIAL ASSISTANCE	12409	30	75	HEAVY & CIVIL ENG. CONSTRUCT'N	12516	98	655	ACCOMMODATION
12160	15	29	GASOLINE STATIONS	12410	22	48	ACCOMMODATION	12517	22	72	PROF.; SCIENTIFIC; & TECH SVCS
12161	15	208	NONMETALLIC MINERAL PROD. MFG	12411	13	50	FABRICATED METAL PRODUCT MFG	12518	244	1612	HOSPITALS
12164	66	419	ACCOMMODATION	12412	37	620	EDUCATIONAL SERVICES	12520	83	431	EDUCATIONAL SERVICES
12165	27	130	EXEC.; LEGIS.; & OTHER SUPPORT	12413	173	1185	EDUCATIONAL SERVICES	12521	61	966	EDUCATIONAL SERVICES
12166	20	140	BLDG MATL & GARDEN EQPMT DLRS	12414	563	4276	EDUCATIONAL SERVICES	12522	171	1344	EDUCATIONAL SERVICES
12167	126	1217	EDUCATIONAL SERVICES	12416	4	5	PROF.; SCIENTIFIC; & TECH SVCS	12523	44	224	ACCOMMODATION
12168	72	239	SPECIAL TRADE CONTRACTORS	12417	12	19	AMUSEMENT; GAMBLING;& RECREAT.	12524	827	9144	AMBULATORY HEALTH CARE SVCS
12169	13	16	ADMINISTRATIVE & SUPPORT SVCS	12418	10	9	HEAVY & CIVIL ENG. CONSTRUCT'N	12525	124	530	ACCOMMODATION
12170	89	413	ADMINISTRATIVE & SUPPORT SVCS	12419	11	186	EDUCATIONAL SERVICES	12526	193	1131	PROF.; SCIENTIFIC; & TECH SVCS
12172	11	128	JUSTICE; PUBIC ORDER/SAFETY	12420	8	57	JUSTICE; PUBIC ORDER/SAFETY	12527	9	87	JUSTICE; PUBIC ORDER/SAFETY
12173	42	88	MERCH. WHOLESALERS;DURABLE GDS	12421	4	1	FOOD AND BEVERAGE STORES	12528	505	3850	EDUCATIONAL SERVICES
12174	13	48	JUSTICE; PUBIC ORDER/SAFETY	12422	12	167	TEXTILE MILLS	12529	132	466	PUBLISHING INDUSTRIES
12175	29	182	JUSTICE; PUBIC ORDER/SAFETY	12423	60	349	AMUSEMENT; GAMBLING;& RECREAT.	12530	6	13	REAL ESTATE
12176	3	53	FABRICATED METAL PRODUCT MFG	12424	7	75	ACCOMMODATION	12531	81	682	ACCOMMODATION
12177	13	56	JUSTICE; PUBIC ORDER/SAFETY	12427	14	30	MERCH. WHOLESALERS;DURABLE GDS	12533	846	13973	COMPUTER & ELECTRONIC PROD MFG
12180	1983	29838	EDUCATIONAL SERVICES	12428	336	3780	EDUCATIONAL SERVICES	12534	1065	9944	HOSPITALS
12181	2	2	CROP PRODUCTION	12429	24	84	RELIG.; GRANT; CIVIC; PROF ORG	12537	11	31	FOOD AND BEVERAGE STORES
12182	350	3017	FOOD AND BEVERAGE STORES	12430	59	231	ACCOMMODATION	12538	511	4218	EDUCATIONAL SERVICES
12183	137	1621	MERCH. WHOLESALERS;DURABLE GDS	12431	41	165	JUSTICE; PUBIC ORDER/SAFETY	12540	287	2651	EDUCATIONAL SERVICES

ZIP CODE	2009 Total Firms	2009 Total Employees	TOP INDUSTRY RANKED on 2009 EMPLOYMENT
12541	26	63	AMBULATORY HEALTH CARE SVCS
12542	187	1028	EDUCATIONAL SERVICES
12543	78	1018	TRUCK TRANSPORTATION
12544	14	127	SOCIAL ASSISTANCE
12545	311	2478	EDUCATIONAL SERVICES
12546	243	901	FOOD AND BEVERAGE STORES
12547	99	715	BEVERAGE & TOBACCO PRODUCT MFG
12548	65	376	SOCIAL ASSISTANCE
12549	484	3365	FOOD SVCS & DRINKING PLACES
12550	2617	26339	EDUCATIONAL SERVICES
12551	4	19	SOCIAL ASSISTANCE
12553	934	8862	AMBULATORY HEALTH CARE SVCS
12555	3	850	POSTAL SERVICE
12561	781	9684	EDUCATIONAL SERVICES
12563	305	2154	SOCIAL ASSISTANCE
12564	361	2720	EDUCATIONAL SERVICES
12565	51	554	PLASTICS & RUBBER PRODUCTS MFG
12566	344	2168	EDUCATIONAL SERVICES
12567	221	1015	EDUCATIONAL SERVICES
12568	24	265	PERFORM'G ARTS; SPEC. SPORTS
12569	329	2035	HOSPITALS
12570	151	491	EDUCATIONAL SERVICES
12571	615	2797	EDUCATIONAL SERVICES
12572	719	5305	NURSING & RESID. CARE FACILIT.
12574	12	28	CONSTRUCTION OF BUILDINGS
12575	64	706	ADMINISTRATIVE & SUPPORT SVCS
12577	53	323	JUSTICE; PUBIC ORDER/SAFETY
12578	85	705	JUSTICE; PUBIC ORDER/SAFETY
12580	116	1085	EDUCATIONAL SERVICES
12581	104	425	EXEC.; LEGIS.; & OTHER SUPPORT
12582	101	1294	JUSTICE; PUBIC ORDER/SAFETY
12583	97	220	FOOD SVCS & DRINKING PLACES
12584	64	1005	FOOD AND BEVERAGE STORES
12585	25	216	ACCOMMODATION
12586	369	3096	FOOD AND BEVERAGE STORES
12588	9	11	MOTOR VEHICLE & PARTS DEALERS
12589	285	2551	JUSTICE; PUBIC ORDER/SAFETY
12590	1256	8494	EDUCATIONAL SERVICES
12592	33	2126	SOCIAL ASSISTANCE
12594	118	990	EDUCATIONAL SERVICES
12601	2365	29231	EDUCATIONAL SERVICES
12602	7	40	SOCIAL ASSISTANCE
12603	1467	14618	EDUCATIONAL SERVICES
12604	4	18	EDUCATIONAL SERVICES
12701	785	8949	SOCIAL ASSISTANCE
12719	60	475	ACCOMMODATION
12720	19	262	PERFORM'G ARTS; SPEC. SPORTS
12721	145	483	MERCH. WHOLESALERS;DURABLE GDS
12722	6	209	ACCOMMODATION
12723	76	1132	ACCOMMODATION
12724	8	34	ELECTRONICS & APPLIANCE STORES
12725	16	170	ACCOMMODATION
12726	49	255	SPECIAL TRADE CONTRACTORS
12727	4	7	SPECIAL TRADE CONTRACTORS
12729	41	209	EDUCATIONAL SERVICES
12732	39	282	EDUCATIONAL SERVICES
12733	46	378	EDUCATIONAL SERVICES
12734	67	683	ACCOMMODATION
12736	9	52	TRUCK TRANSPORTATION
12737	47	561	ACCOMMODATION
12738	8	12	PROF.; SCIENTIFIC; & TECH SVCS
12740	72	545	PROF.; SCIENTIFIC; & TECH SVCS
12741	19	51	HOSPITALS
12742	13	59	SUPPORT ACT. FOR TRANSPORT.
12743	10	17	RELIG.; GRANT; CIVIC; PROF ORG
12745	9	53	EXEC.; LEGIS.; & OTHER SUPPORT
12746	29	235	EXEC.; LEGIS.; & OTHER SUPPORT
12747	38	318	AMBULATORY HEALTH CARE SVCS
12748	117	801	EDUCATIONAL SERVICES
12749	31	147	CHEMICAL MANUFACTURING
12750	9	26	ADMIN. OF ECONOMIC PROGRAMS
12751	35	216	BEVERAGE & TOBACCO PRODUCT MFG
12752	17	41	MERCH. WHOLESALERS;NONDUR. GDS
12754	464	3960	NURSING & RESID. CARE FACILIT.
12758	163	954	ACCOMMODATION
12759	43	880	RELIG.; GRANT; CIVIC; PROF ORG
12760	18	96	MISCELLANEOUS MANUFACTURING
12762	31	336	HEAVY & CIVIL ENG. CONSTRUCT'N
12763	29	367	REAL ESTATE
12764	116	644	ACCOMMODATION
12765	21	176	ACCOMMODATION
12766	18	16	PROF.; SCIENTIFIC; & TECH SVCS
12767	2	3	POSTAL SERVICE
12768	38	459	ACCOMMODATION
12769	3	5	SUPPORT ACTIVITIES: AGR./FOR.
12770	10	35	SCENIC & SIGHTSEEING TRANSPORT
12771	609	4402	HOSPITALS
12775	105	967	INSURANCE CARRIERS & RELATED
12776	130	826	ACCOMMODATION
12777	26	127	PERFORM'G ARTS; SPEC. SPORTS

ZIP CODE	2009 Total Firms	2009 Total Employees	TOP INDUSTRY RANKED on 2009 EMPLOYMENT
12778	11	8	CONSTRUCTION OF BUILDINGS
12779	140	1842	PROF.; SCIENTIFIC; & TECH SVCS
12780	55	332	RELIG.; GRANT; CIVIC; PROF ORG
12781	9	317	SUPPORT ACTIVITIES: AGR./FOR.
12783	52	263	RELIG.; GRANT; CIVIC; PROF ORG
12784	6	10	MERCH. WHOLESALERS;NONDUR. GDS
12785	20	60	NURSING & RESID. CARE FACILIT.
12786	71	315	JUSTICE; PUBIC ORDER/SAFETY
12787	17	65	CONSTRUCTION OF BUILDINGS
12788	66	655	JUSTICE; PUBIC ORDER/SAFETY
12789	89	319	ACCOMMODATION
12790	153	1319	ACCOMMODATION
12791	28	113	TRANSIT & GRND PASS. TRANSPORT
12792	11	10	FOOD AND BEVERAGE STORES
12801	929	13204	HOSPITALS
12803	299	2487	EDUCATIONAL SERVICES
12804	1198	15237	FOOD SVCS & DRINKING PLACES
12808	11	8	POSTAL SERVICE
12809	81	756	NURSING & RESID. CARE FACILIT.
12810	20	94	CONSTRUCTION OF BUILDINGS
12811	10	7	POSTAL SERVICE
12812	28	175	MUSEUMS; HIST. SITES;& SIMILAR
12814	154	1474	ACCOMMODATION
12815	52	764	ACCOMMODATION
12816	204	1103	EDUCATIONAL SERVICES
12817	160	698	FOOD SVCS & DRINKING PLACES
12819	6	16	REAL ESTATE
12820	13	105	JUSTICE; PUBIC ORDER/SAFETY
12821	12	732	JUSTICE; PUBIC ORDER/SAFETY
12822	153	901	EDUCATIONAL SERVICES
12823	5	27	FABRICATED METAL PRODUCT MFG
12824	40	319	ACCOMMODATION
12827	101	394	SPECIAL TRADE CONTRACTORS
12828	287	4040	EXEC.; LEGIS.; & OTHER SUPPORT
12831	287	2049	MERCH. WHOLESALERS;DURABLE GDS
12832	200	2517	EDUCATIONAL SERVICES
12833	87	329	EDUCATIONAL SERVICES
12834	291	1609	NONMETALLIC MINERAL PROD. MFG
12835	69	246	EXEC.; LEGIS.; & OTHER SUPPORT
12836	38	82	EXEC.; LEGIS.; & OTHER SUPPORT
12837	36	73	NURSING & RESID. CARE FACILIT.
12838	24	195	EDUCATIONAL SERVICES
12839	371	3195	EDUCATIONAL SERVICES
12841	5	11	MUSEUMS; HIST. SITES;& SIMILAR
12842	116	582	EXEC.; LEGIS.; & OTHER SUPPORT
12843	14	23	MOTOR VEHICLE & PARTS DEALERS
12844	13	148	ACCOMMODATION
12845	613	7313	FOOD SVCS & DRINKING PLACES
12846	130	585	EDUCATIONAL SERVICES
12847	87	524	ACCOMMODATION
12848	4	63	MISCELLANEOUS MANUFACTURING
12849	17	119	NONMETALLIC MINERAL PROD. MFG
12850	40	166	ACCOMMODATION
12851	27	44	EXEC.; LEGIS.; & OTHER SUPPORT
12852	46	156	EDUCATIONAL SERVICES
12853	125	1381	ACCOMMODATION
12854	9	22	SOCIAL ASSISTANCE
12855	13	37	ACCOMMODATION
12856	14	236	ACCOMMODATION
12857	21	125	EDUCATIONAL SERVICES
12858	2	152	FOOD SVCS & DRINKING PLACES
12859	28	201	FOOD SVCS & DRINKING PLACES
12860	28	414	EDUCATIONAL SERVICES
12861	15	167	JUSTICE; PUBIC ORDER/SAFETY
12862	6	33	BLDG MATL & GARDEN EQPMT DLRS
12863	14	128	JUSTICE; PUBIC ORDER/SAFETY
12864	8	40	ACCOMMODATION
12865	106	935	EDUCATIONAL SERVICES
12866	2071	48156	MERCH. WHOLESALERS;DURABLE GDS
12870	141	620	RELIG.; GRANT; CIVIC; PROF ORG
12871	140	976	EDUCATIONAL SERVICES
12872	6	9	REPAIR AND MAINTENANCE
12873	10	22	FOOD AND BEVERAGE STORES
12874	11	155	OTHER INFORMATION SERVICES
12878	27	142	ACCOMMODATION
12883	261	2564	WHOLESALE ELEC. MRKTS & AGENTS
12884	8	9	EXEC.; LEGIS.; & OTHER SUPPORT
12885	244	2270	ACCOMMODATION
12886	15	42	BLDG MATL & GARDEN EQPMT DLRS
12887	135	975	EDUCATIONAL SERVICES
12901	1968	26839	AMBULATORY HEALTH CARE SVCS
12903	119	1194	ADMINISTRATIVE & SUPPORT SVCS
12910	45	376	JUSTICE; PUBIC ORDER/SAFETY
12911	2	2	MERCH. WHOLESALERS;DURABLE GDS
12912	124	448	EDUCATIONAL SERVICES
12913	26	59	EDUCATIONAL SERVICES
12914	14	83	JUSTICE; PUBIC ORDER/SAFETY
12915	7	21	SPECIAL TRADE CONTRACTORS
12916	55	455	EDUCATIONAL SERVICES
12917	32	127	FOOD SVCS & DRINKING PLACES

ZIP CODE	2009 Total Firms	2009 Total Employees	TOP INDUSTRY RANKED on 2009 EMPLOYMENT
12918	34	121	JUSTICE; PUBIC ORDER/SAFETY
12919	234	2558	PROF.; SCIENTIFIC; & TECH SVCS
12920	87	654	EDUCATIONAL SERVICES
12921	112	768	EDUCATIONAL SERVICES
12922	7	11	GASOLINE STATIONS
12923	22	40	SPECIAL TRADE CONTRACTORS
12924	11	292	EDUCATIONAL SERVICES
12926	49	223	JUSTICE; PUBIC ORDER/SAFETY
12927	22	153	JUSTICE; PUBIC ORDER/SAFETY
12928	85	285	EXEC.; LEGIS.; & OTHER SUPPORT
12929	45	1476	JUSTICE; PUBIC ORDER/SAFETY
12930	15	23	FOOD SVCS & DRINKING PLACES
12932	160	1817	SOCIAL ASSISTANCE
12933	14	122	EDUCATIONAL SERVICES
12934	28	47	FOOD AND BEVERAGE STORES
12935	40	309	EDUCATIONAL SERVICES
12936	36	51	FOOD SVCS & DRINKING PLACES
12937	49	331	EDUCATIONAL SERVICES
12939	13	19	FOOD AND BEVERAGE STORES
12941	45	282	BLDG MATL & GARDEN EQPMT DLRS
12942	48	150	ACCOMMODATION
12943	39	262	EDUCATIONAL SERVICES
12944	180	974	MERCH. WHOLESALERS;DURABLE GDS
12945	19	99	ACCOMMODATION
12946	532	4707	ACCOMMODATION
12950	30	134	JUSTICE; PUBIC ORDER/SAFETY
12952	15	23	GASOLINE STATIONS
12953	737	9261	JUSTICE; PUBIC ORDER/SAFETY
12955	6	56	ACCOMMODATION
12956	34	436	EDUCATIONAL SERVICES
12957	41	196	CROP PRODUCTION
12958	62	306	MERCH. WHOLESALERS;DURABLE GDS
12959	40	54	FOOD AND BEVERAGE STORES
12960	7	15	CONSTRUCTION OF BUILDINGS
12961	5	16	FOOD AND BEVERAGE STORES
12962	101	522	MERCH. WHOLESALERS;DURABLE GDS
12964	1	0	UNCLASSIFIED ESTABLISHMENTS
12965	35	203	MISCELLANEOUS MANUFACTURING
12966	55	196	JUSTICE; PUBIC ORDER/SAFETY
12967	24	200	MERCH. WHOLESALERS;NONDUR. GDS
12969	8	35	JUSTICE; PUBIC ORDER/SAFETY
12970	30	158	EDUCATIONAL SERVICES
12972	170	1693	EDUCATIONAL SERVICES
12973	5	33	EXEC.; LEGIS.; & OTHER SUPPORT
12974	101	710	EXEC.; LEGIS.; & OTHER SUPPORT
12975	8	19	WATER TRANSPORTATION
12976	2	3	POSTAL SERVICE
12977	26	756	JUSTICE; PUBIC ORDER/SAFETY
12978	10	28	FOOD AND BEVERAGE STORES
12979	113	1854	CHEMICAL MANUFACTURING
12980	30	182	EDUCATIONAL SERVICES
12981	59	376	EDUCATIONAL SERVICES
12983	542	4460	AMBULATORY HEALTH CARE SVCS
12985	17	75	EXEC.; LEGIS.; & OTHER SUPPORT
12986	260	3230	EXEC.; LEGIS.; & OTHER SUPPORT
12987	11	13	CONSTRUCTION OF BUILDINGS
12989	23	52	EXEC.; LEGIS.; & OTHER SUPPORT
12992	120	980	EDUCATIONAL SERVICES
12993	109	588	EDUCATIONAL SERVICES
12996	90	842	TEXTILE MILLS
12997	114	1147	ACCOMMODATION
13020	4	3	POSTAL SERVICE
13021	1704	19880	EDUCATIONAL SERVICES
13022	1	4	ADMINISTRATIVE & SUPPORT SVCS
13024	4	842	JUSTICE; PUBIC ORDER/SAFETY
13026	52	750	EDUCATIONAL SERVICES
13027	1016	8375	WHOLESALE ELEC. MRKTS & AGENTS
13028	32	156	WOOD PRODUCT MANUFACTURING
13029	248	1286	FOOD SVCS & DRINKING PLACES
13030	111	536	SPORTG GDS;HOBBY;BOOK; & MUSIC
13031	550	5462	EDUCATIONAL SERVICES
13032	356	3634	EDUCATIONAL SERVICES
13033	109	929	EDUCATIONAL SERVICES
13034	28	100	EDUCATIONAL SERVICES
13035	375	2964	EDUCATIONAL SERVICES
13036	316	2512	EDUCATIONAL SERVICES
13037	289	2901	EDUCATIONAL SERVICES
13039	728	7131	MOTOR VEHICLE & PARTS DEALERS
13040	80	411	EDUCATIONAL SERVICES
13041	302	2169	SPORTG GDS;HOBBY;BOOK; & MUSIC
13042	47	166	EDUCATIONAL SERVICES
13043	4	14	CONSTRUCTION OF BUILDINGS
13044	69	241	FOOD AND BEVERAGE STORES
13045	1256	22078	EDUCATIONAL SERVICES
13051	2	2	POSTAL SERVICE
13052	45	273	EDUCATIONAL SERVICES
13053	164	1716	EDUCATIONAL SERVICES
13054	32	145	EDUCATIONAL SERVICES
13056	2	0	RELIG.; GRANT; CIVIC; PROF ORG
13057	1653	29345	TRANSPORTATION EQUIPMENT MFG

BUSINESS DATA

ZIP CODE	2009 Total Firms	2009 Total Employees	TOP INDUSTRY RANKED on 2009 EMPLOYMENT	ZIP CODE	2009 Total Firms	2009 Total Employees	TOP INDUSTRY RANKED on 2009 EMPLOYMENT	ZIP CODE	2009 Total Firms	2009 Total Employees	TOP INDUSTRY RANKED on 2009 EMPLOYMENT
13060	152	1488	MISCELLANEOUS MANUFACTURING	13210	1237	27415	AMBULATORY HEALTH CARE SVCS	13428	73	776	PUBLISHING INDUSTRIES
13061	25	127	JUSTICE; PUBIC ORDER/SAFETY	13211	435	5984	EDUCATIONAL SERVICES	13431	80	827	EDUCATIONAL SERVICES
13062	6	7	MISCELLANEOUS STORE RETAILERS	13212	1158	12768	INSURANCE CARRIERS & RELATED	13433	48	145	EDUCATIONAL SERVICES
13063	53	400	ACCOMMODATION	13214	662	7120	FOOD SVCS & DRINKING PLACES	13435	13	45	JUSTICE; PUBIC ORDER/SAFETY
13064	43	125	MUSEUMS; HIST. SITES;& SIMILAR	13215	384	4948	HOSPITALS	13436	31	88	EXEC.; LEGIS.; & OTHER SUPPORT
13065	6	4	SPECIAL TRADE CONTRACTORS	13217	14	257	POSTAL SERVICE	13437	17	67	JUSTICE; PUBIC ORDER/SAFETY
13066	724	5909	FOOD SVCS & DRINKING PLACES	13218	1	35	POSTAL SERVICE	13438	77	461	EDUCATIONAL SERVICES
13068	100	894	RELIG.; GRANT; CIVIC; PROF ORG	13219	600	6302	FOOD AND BEVERAGE STORES	13439	131	689	EDUCATIONAL SERVICES
13069	820	8681	AMBULATORY HEALTH CARE SVCS	13220	22	713	POSTAL SERVICE	13440	1342	15981	JUSTICE; PUBIC ORDER/SAFETY
13071	31	136	MERCH. WHOLESALERS;DURABLE GDS	13221	3	7	CREDIT INTERMEDIATION & RELATD	13441	95	2494	TRANSIT & GRND PASS. TRANSPORT
13072	23	179	JUSTICE; PUBIC ORDER/SAFETY	13224	330	3558	RELIG.; GRANT; CIVIC; PROF ORG	13442	1	4	ADMINISTRATIVE & SUPPORT SVCS
13073	172	929	EDUCATIONAL SERVICES	13235	1	2	DATA PROCESS'G	13450	5	5	POSTAL SERVICE
13074	90	997	EDUCATIONAL SERVICES	13244	48	4916	EDUCATIONAL SERVICES	13452	121	1159	EDUCATIONAL SERVICES
13076	39	128	JUSTICE; PUBIC ORDER/SAFETY	13261	41	397	JUSTICE; PUBIC ORDER/SAFETY	13454	21	105	MUSEUMS; HIST. SITES;& SIMILAR
13077	213	1325	EDUCATIONAL SERVICES	13290	200	2969	CLOTHING & CLOTH'G ACC. STORES	13455	14	239	WOOD PRODUCT MANUFACTURING
13078	259	2485	NURSING & RESID. CARE FACILIT.	13301	8	38	ADMIN. OF ECONOMIC PROGRAMS	13456	80	892	EDUCATIONAL SERVICES
13080	104	715	EDUCATIONAL SERVICES	13302	31	142	EDUCATIONAL SERVICES	13457	8	37	JUSTICE; PUBIC ORDER/SAFETY
13081	38	110	BEVERAGE & TOBACCO PRODUCT MFG	13303	13	46	ACCOMMODATION	13459	80	893	GENERAL MERCHANDISE STORES
13082	108	579	FABRICATED METAL PRODUCT MFG	13304	117	808	MERCH. WHOLESALERS;DURABLE GDS	13460	186	1523	EDUCATIONAL SERVICES
13083	54	189	TRUCK TRANSPORTATION	13305	19	309	EDUCATIONAL SERVICES	13461	91	462	FOOD AND BEVERAGE STORES
13084	180	1197	EDUCATIONAL SERVICES	13308	51	396	MERCH. WHOLESALERS;DURABLE GDS	13464	23	68	WOOD PRODUCT MANUFACTURING
13087	8	61	ADMINISTRATIVE & SUPPORT SVCS	13309	240	2161	EDUCATIONAL SERVICES	13468	14	35	UNCLASSIFIED ESTABLISHMENTS
13088	1242	20835	AMBULATORY HEALTH CARE SVCS	13310	38	167	MISCELLANEOUS STORE RETAILERS	13469	20	141	JUSTICE; PUBIC ORDER/SAFETY
13089	2	0	MISCELLANEOUS STORE RETAILERS	13312	9	27	SPECIAL TRADE CONTRACTORS	13470	9	10	HEAVY & CIVIL ENG. CONSTRUCT'N
13090	883	9385	FOOD SVCS & DRINKING PLACES	13313	24	143	EXEC.; LEGIS.; & OTHER SUPPORT	13471	35	311	EXEC.; LEGIS.; & OTHER SUPPORT
13092	51	319	ANIMAL PRODUCTION	13314	25	144	EDUCATIONAL SERVICES	13472	19	70	AMUSEMENT; GAMBLING;& RECREAT.
13093	3	202	UTILITIES	13315	20	90	REPAIR AND MAINTENANCE	13473	39	512	EDUCATIONAL SERVICES
13101	53	545	EDUCATIONAL SERVICES	13316	185	1882	PRIMARY METAL MANUFACTURING	13475	10	88	EDUCATIONAL SERVICES
13102	10	40	EDUCATIONAL SERVICES	13317	139	1630	FOOD MANUFACTURING	13476	147	1055	PERFORM'G ARTS; SPEC. SPORTS
13103	6	6	FOOD AND BEVERAGE STORES	13318	16	37	FOOD MANUFACTURING	13477	23	64	BLDG MATL & GARDEN EQPMT DLRS
13104	566	4121	FURN. & HOME FURNISHGS STORES	13319	47	286	TRANSPORTATION EQUIPMENT MFG	13478	81	10311	ADMINISTRATIVE & SUPPORT SVCS
13107	4	52	FOOD AND BEVERAGE STORES	13320	69	435	EDUCATIONAL SERVICES	13479	19	111	FOOD SVCS & DRINKING PLACES
13108	244	1999	EDUCATIONAL SERVICES	13321	21	126	AMBULATORY HEALTH CARE SVCS	13480	111	796	EDUCATIONAL SERVICES
13110	55	93	FOOD SVCS & DRINKING PLACES	13322	27	285	PRIMARY METAL MANUFACTURING	13482	5	7	FOOD AND BEVERAGE STORES
13111	23	41	CONSTRUCTION OF BUILDINGS	13323	343	3676	NURSING & RESID. CARE FACILIT.	13483	6	18	REAL ESTATE
13112	35	225	FOOD MANUFACTURING	13324	43	103	FORESTRY AND LOGGING	13484	5	4	SPECIAL TRADE CONTRACTORS
13113	7	61	JUSTICE; PUBIC ORDER/SAFETY	13325	31	99	EDUCATIONAL SERVICES	13485	12	22	SUPPORT ACTIVITIES: AGR./FOR.
13114	199	2099	EDUCATIONAL SERVICES	13326	525	11534	HOSPITALS	13486	25	112	ACCOMMODATION
13115	19	300	EDUCATIONAL SERVICES	13327	75	266	PAPER MANUFACTURING	13488	8	14	TRUCK TRANSPORTATION
13116	70	435	EDUCATIONAL SERVICES	13328	33	145	JUSTICE; PUBIC ORDER/SAFETY	13489	17	71	EDUCATIONAL SERVICES
13117	11	58	EXEC.; LEGIS.; & OTHER SUPPORT	13329	121	947	EDUCATIONAL SERVICES	13490	67	985	EDUCATIONAL SERVICES
13118	166	1398	JUSTICE; PUBIC ORDER/SAFETY	13331	32	88	ACCOMMODATION	13491	81	509	EDUCATIONAL SERVICES
13119	2	5	PROF.; SCIENTIFIC; & TECH SVCS	13332	89	291	ACCOMMODATION	13492	292	2109	TRANSPORTATION EQUIPMENT MFG
13120	82	822	EDUCATIONAL SERVICES	13333	9	19	FOOD SVCS & DRINKING PLACES	13493	44	341	MERCH. WHOLESALERS;DURABLE GDS
13121	12	44	EXEC.; LEGIS.; & OTHER SUPPORT	13334	19	68	EXEC.; LEGIS.; & OTHER SUPPORT	13494	13	93	ACCOMMODATION
13122	47	138	SPECIAL TRADE CONTRACTORS	13335	47	1260	INSURANCE CARRIERS & RELATED	13495	185	2022	MOTOR VEHICLE & PARTS DEALERS
13123	10	63	EDUCATIONAL SERVICES	13337	30	121	EXEC.; LEGIS.; & OTHER SUPPORT	13501	1189	20767	EDUCATIONAL SERVICES
13124	2	2	CONSTRUCTION OF BUILDINGS	13338	53	321	FOOD AND BEVERAGE STORES	13502	1339	27952	MERCH. WHOLESALERS;DURABLE GDS
13126	1195	13576	EDUCATIONAL SERVICES	13339	159	819	EDUCATIONAL SERVICES	13503	7	13	ADMINISTRATIVE & SUPPORT SVCS
13131	96	1179	EDUCATIONAL SERVICES	13340	199	1817	EDUCATIONAL SERVICES	13504	7	509	POSTAL SERVICE
13132	52	168	RELIG.; GRANT; CIVIC; PROF ORG	13341	5	8	RELIG.; GRANT; CIVIC; PROF ORG	13601	2011	27431	EDUCATIONAL SERVICES
13134	10	11	HEAVY & CIVIL ENG. CONSTRUCT'N	13342	9	64	EXEC.; LEGIS.; & OTHER SUPPORT	13602	50	705	NAT'L SECURITY & INT'L AFFAIRS
13135	308	1739	EDUCATIONAL SERVICES	13343	40	251	EDUCATIONAL SERVICES	13603	29	133	CONSTRUCTION OF BUILDINGS
13136	12	25	HEAVY & CIVIL ENG. CONSTRUCT'N	13345	15	56	ACCOMMODATION	13605	133	1591	EDUCATIONAL SERVICES
13137	5	8	SPECIAL TRADE CONTRACTORS	13346	203	2723	EDUCATIONAL SERVICES	13606	63	895	EDUCATIONAL SERVICES
13138	17	110	JUSTICE; PUBIC ORDER/SAFETY	13348	40	207	JUSTICE; PUBIC ORDER/SAFETY	13607	220	2114	ACCOMMODATION
13139	11	70	EDUCATIONAL SERVICES	13350	515	5346	EDUCATIONAL SERVICES	13608	26	128	EDUCATIONAL SERVICES
13140	115	859	EDUCATIONAL SERVICES	13352	2	2	POSTAL SERVICE	13611	21	279	EDUCATIONAL SERVICES
13141	28	134	MERCH. WHOLESALERS;DURABLE GDS	13353	10	34	EXEC.; LEGIS.; & OTHER SUPPORT	13612	53	281	EDUCATIONAL SERVICES
13142	333	2380	MACHINERY MANUFACTURING	13354	67	859	EDUCATIONAL SERVICES	13613	53	454	EDUCATIONAL SERVICES
13143	59	455	EDUCATIONAL SERVICES	13355	16	33	NURSING & RESID. CARE FACILIT.	13614	12	65	JUSTICE; PUBIC ORDER/SAFETY
13144	21	46	FOOD AND BEVERAGE STORES	13357	238	2797	FABRICATED METAL PRODUCT MFG	13615	30	201	PAPER MANUFACTURING
13145	80	425	EDUCATIONAL SERVICES	13360	83	314	FOOD SVCS & DRINKING PLACES	13616	21	344	FOOD SVCS & DRINKING PLACES
13146	64	254	CROP PRODUCTION	13361	10	24	MINING (EXCEPT OIL AND GAS)	13617	443	8717	EDUCATIONAL SERVICES
13147	30	102	CROP PRODUCTION	13362	11	100	JUSTICE; PUBIC ORDER/SAFETY	13618	121	886	JUSTICE; PUBIC ORDER/SAFETY
13148	355	4206	MACHINERY MANUFACTURING	13363	38	219	EXEC.; LEGIS.; & OTHER SUPPORT	13619	284	2455	EDUCATIONAL SERVICES
13152	500	3236	FOOD SVCS & DRINKING PLACES	13364	10	43	FOOD SVCS & DRINKING PLACES	13620	40	175	SPECIAL TRADE CONTRACTORS
13153	15	1963	MISCELLANEOUS MANUFACTURING	13365	277	2417	HOSPITALS	13621	9	52	CONSTRUCTION OF BUILDINGS
13154	3	5	RELIG.; GRANT; CIVIC; PROF ORG	13367	506	4844	EDUCATIONAL SERVICES	13622	72	340	EDUCATIONAL SERVICES
13155	31	215	EDUCATIONAL SERVICES	13368	68	397	SPORTG GDS;HOBBY;BOOK; & MUSIC	13623	5	30	MUSEUMS; HIST. SITES;& SIMILAR
13156	38	255	MUSEUMS; HIST. SITES;& SIMILAR	13401	6	523	FURNITURE & RELATED PROD. MFG	13624	237	1647	EDUCATIONAL SERVICES
13157	43	529	FOOD SVCS & DRINKING PLACES	13402	75	279	EDUCATIONAL SERVICES	13625	36	193	EDUCATIONAL SERVICES
13158	37	598	ACCOMMODATION	13403	219	4399	JUSTICE; PUBIC ORDER/SAFETY	13626	45	240	EDUCATIONAL SERVICES
13159	201	1772	EDUCATIONAL SERVICES	13404	7	36	EXEC.; LEGIS.; & OTHER SUPPORT	13627	3	15	INSURANCE CARRIERS & RELATED
13160	76	617	EDUCATIONAL SERVICES	13406	28	108	FOOD SVCS & DRINKING PLACES	13628	8	13	CREDIT INTERMEDIATION & RELATD
13162	18	93	FOOD SVCS & DRINKING PLACES	13407	141	1129	EDUCATIONAL SERVICES	13630	47	270	EDUCATIONAL SERVICES
13163	62	814	JUSTICE; PUBIC ORDER/SAFETY	13408	108	1289	EDUCATIONAL SERVICES	13631	3	17	TRUCK TRANSPORTATION
13164	75	926	MERCH. WHOLESALERS;NONDUR. GDS	13409	53	616	MACHINERY MANUFACTURING	13632	22	43	ELECTRONICS & APPLIANCE STORES
13165	498	5609	EXEC.; LEGIS.; & OTHER SUPPORT	13410	23	124	AMBULATORY HEALTH CARE SVCS	13633	2	8	MACHINERY MANUFACTURING
13166	171	949	FOOD SVCS & DRINKING PLACES	13411	131	1093	INSURANCE CARRIERS & RELATED	13634	73	538	EDUCATIONAL SERVICES
13167	74	337	MOTOR VEHICLE & PARTS DEALERS	13413	933	14563	INSURANCE CARRIERS & RELATED	13635	29	58	REPAIR AND MAINTENANCE
13201	9	32	REAL ESTATE	13415	1	1	CONSTRUCTION OF BUILDINGS	13636	16	42	EXEC.; LEGIS.; & OTHER SUPPORT
13202	1905	46869	ADMIN. HUMAN RESOURCE PROGRAMS	13416	85	411	EDUCATIONAL SERVICES	13637	117	987	GENERAL MERCHANDISE STORES
13203	740	13180	AMBULATORY HEALTH CARE SVCS	13417	127	1411	EDUCATIONAL SERVICES	13638	14	89	FOOD SVCS & DRINKING PLACES
13204	1226	16213	RELIG.; GRANT; CIVIC; PROF ORG	13418	4	2	BLDG MATL & GARDEN EQPMT DLRS	13639	3	0	POSTAL SERVICE
13205	485	5682	AMBULATORY HEALTH CARE SVCS	13420	210	1764	AMUSEMENT; GAMBLING;& RECREAT.	13640	30	275	AMUSEMENT; GAMBLING;& RECREAT.
13206	1171	11135	SPECIAL TRADE CONTRACTORS	13421	592	12255	MISCELLANEOUS MANUFACTURING	13641	10	82	FOOD SVCS & DRINKING PLACES
13207	247	2042	EDUCATIONAL SERVICES	13424	119	5266	JUSTICE; PUBIC ORDER/SAFETY	13642	317	3882	EDUCATIONAL SERVICES
13208	841	7226	EDUCATIONAL SERVICES	13425	53	409	MERCH. WHOLESALERS;DURABLE GDS	13643	12	55	JUSTICE; PUBIC ORDER/SAFETY
13209	670	7111	MERCH. WHOLESALERS;DURABLE GDS	13426	8	40	JUSTICE; PUBIC ORDER/SAFETY	13645	5	38	NONMETALLIC MINERAL PROD. MFG

ZIP CODE	2009 Total Firms	2009 Total Employ-ees	TOP INDUSTRY RANKED on 2009 EMPLOYMENT
13646	106	299	EDUCATIONAL SERVICES
13647	9	57	JUSTICE; PUBIC ORDER/SAFETY
13648	61	533	EDUCATIONAL SERVICES
13649	3	5	FOOD AND BEVERAGE STORES
13650	47	198	FOOD SVCS & DRINKING PLACES
13651	14	47	AMUSEMENT; GAMBLING;& RECREAT.
13652	33	108	EXEC.; LEGIS.; & OTHER SUPPORT
13654	66	602	FOOD AND BEVERAGE STORES
13655	182	2505	EXEC.; LEGIS.; & OTHER SUPPORT
13656	56	490	FOOD MANUFACTURING
13658	43	263	EDUCATIONAL SERVICES
13659	15	25	EXEC.; LEGIS.; & OTHER SUPPORT
13660	38	272	EDUCATIONAL SERVICES
13661	28	134	EDUCATIONAL SERVICES
13662	694	8678	PRIMARY METAL MANUFACTURING
13664	39	250	EDUCATIONAL SERVICES
13665	17	83	JUSTICE; PUBIC ORDER/SAFETY
13666	6	17	HEAVY & CIVIL ENG. CONSTRUCT'N
13667	62	300	PAPER MANUFACTURING
13668	81	1019	EDUCATIONAL SERVICES
13669	542	7520	HOSPITALS
13670	11	23	GASOLINE STATIONS
13671	1	0	JUSTICE; PUBIC ORDER/SAFETY
13672	24	191	EDUCATIONAL SERVICES
13673	57	583	EDUCATIONAL SERVICES
13674	11	34	MERCH. WHOLESALERS;NONDUR. GDS
13675	7	9	MISCELLANEOUS MANUFACTURING
13676	548	6828	EDUCATIONAL SERVICES
13677	2	1	UTILITIES
13678	5	22	MERCH. WHOLESALERS;DURABLE GDS
13679	35	208	ACCOMMODATION
13680	10	71	SOCIAL ASSISTANCE
13681	12	34	INSURANCE CARRIERS & RELATED
13682	12	96	JUSTICE; PUBIC ORDER/SAFETY
13683	20	57	EXEC.; LEGIS.; & OTHER SUPPORT
13684	31	71	JUSTICE; PUBIC ORDER/SAFETY
13685	86	601	EDUCATIONAL SERVICES
13687	12	46	MERCH. WHOLESALERS;DURABLE GDS
13690	42	332	HOSPITALS
13691	59	322	JUSTICE; PUBIC ORDER/SAFETY
13692	16	54	CONSTRUCTION OF BUILDINGS
13693	18	66	JUSTICE; PUBIC ORDER/SAFETY
13694	58	235	BLDG MATL & GARDEN EQPMT DLRS
13695	7	28	EDUCATIONAL SERVICES
13696	4	3	BLDG MATL & GARDEN EQPMT DLRS
13697	35	165	JUSTICE; PUBIC ORDER/SAFETY
13730	124	849	EDUCATIONAL SERVICES
13731	95	205	EDUCATIONAL SERVICES
13732	188	1401	EDUCATIONAL SERVICES
13733	191	703	EDUCATIONAL SERVICES
13734	24	42	EDUCATIONAL SERVICES
13736	42	74	MERCH. WHOLESALERS;DURABLE GDS
13738	4	12	MERCH. WHOLESALERS;DURABLE GDS
13739	13	49	SPECIAL TRADE CONTRACTORS
13740	34	73	PROF.; SCIENTIFIC; & TECH SVCS
13743	119	665	EDUCATIONAL SERVICES
13744	27	62	WOOD PRODUCT MANUFACTURING
13745	37	139	WASTE MANAGMT & REMEDIAT'N SVC
13746	41	282	SOCIAL ASSISTANCE
13747	8	116	CONSTRUCTION OF BUILDINGS
13748	120	4171	MERCH. WHOLESALERS;NONDUR. GDS
13749	1	1	POSTAL SERVICE
13750	39	189	EDUCATIONAL SERVICES
13751	17	27	EXEC.; LEGIS.; & OTHER SUPPORT
13752	17	22	AMUSEMENT; GAMBLING;& RECREAT.
13753	333	2825	EDUCATIONAL SERVICES
13754	217	1332	SOCIAL ASSISTANCE
13755	85	444	EDUCATIONAL SERVICES
13756	23	67	MINING (EXCEPT OIL AND GAS)
13757	16	63	JUSTICE; PUBIC ORDER/SAFETY
13758	2	23	JUSTICE; PUBIC ORDER/SAFETY
13760	1493	14303	EDUCATIONAL SERVICES
13761	1	2	PUBLISHING INDUSTRIES
13762	1	7	ADMINISTRATIVE & SUPPORT SVCS
13763	1	0	RELIG.; GRANT; CIVIC; PROF ORG
13774	8	16	SOCIAL ASSISTANCE
13775	56	214	EDUCATIONAL SERVICES
13776	36	237	EDUCATIONAL SERVICES
13777	16	57	ADMINISTRATIVE & SUPPORT SVCS
13778	261	2493	UNCLASSIFIED ESTABLISHMENTS
13780	36	80	EDUCATIONAL SERVICES
13782	41	255	EXEC.; LEGIS.; & OTHER SUPPORT
13783	221	1465	ACCOMMODATION
13784	12	64	JUSTICE; PUBIC ORDER/SAFETY
13786	8	29	SPECIAL TRADE CONTRACTORS
13787	86	975	EDUCATIONAL SERVICES
13788	44	899	CHEMICAL MANUFACTURING
13790	973	15478	HOSPITALS
13794	6	14	NONMETALLIC MINERAL PROD. MFG
13795	119	2199	PRINT'G & RELATED SUPP'T ACT'S
13796	27	195	EDUCATIONAL SERVICES
13797	50	109	MUSEUMS; HIST. SITES;& SIMILAR
13801	25	101	JUSTICE; PUBIC ORDER/SAFETY
13802	53	227	EDUCATIONAL SERVICES
13803	119	970	EDUCATIONAL SERVICES
13804	29	230	ADMIN. HUMAN RESOURCE PROGRAMS
13806	8	47	JUSTICE; PUBIC ORDER/SAFETY
13807	57	310	EDUCATIONAL SERVICES
13808	74	586	EDUCATIONAL SERVICES
13809	35	130	MERCH. WHOLESALERS;DURABLE GDS
13810	20	37	BLDG MATL & GARDEN EQPMT DLRS
13811	117	576	EDUCATIONAL SERVICES
13812	58	923	AMUSEMENT; GAMBLING;& RECREAT.
13813	22	113	BLDG MATL & GARDEN EQPMT DLRS
13814	15	51	EDUCATIONAL SERVICES
13815	870	11317	PROF.; SCIENTIFIC; & TECH SVCS
13820	1146	13382	EDUCATIONAL SERVICES
13825	83	520	EDUCATIONAL SERVICES
13826	5	2	REPAIR AND MAINTENANCE
13827	625	9338	COMPUTER & ELECTRONIC PROD MFG
13830	155	937	HOSPITALS
13832	13	26	ACCOMMODATION
13833	72	303	BLDG MATL & GARDEN EQPMT DLRS
13834	7	91	BLDG MATL & GARDEN EQPMT DLRS
13835	24	113	JUSTICE; PUBIC ORDER/SAFETY
13838	274	6870	AMBULATORY HEALTH CARE SVCS
13839	24	469	EDUCATIONAL SERVICES
13840	4	21	PERSONAL AND LAUNDRY SERVICES
13841	20	92	RELIG.; GRANT; CIVIC; PROF ORG
13842	17	322	EDUCATIONAL SERVICES
13843	45	175	EDUCATIONAL SERVICES
13844	14	128	JUSTICE; PUBIC ORDER/SAFETY
13845	20	171	EDUCATIONAL SERVICES
13846	10	35	EDUCATIONAL SERVICES
13847	10	96	JUSTICE; PUBIC ORDER/SAFETY
13848	2	3	PAPER MANUFACTURING
13849	141	582	WOOD PRODUCT MANUFACTURING
13850	1101	17154	EDUCATIONAL SERVICES
13851	3	5	REAL ESTATE
13856	325	2201	EDUCATIONAL SERVICES
13859	6	33	JUSTICE; PUBIC ORDER/SAFETY
13860	6	15	GASOLINE STATIONS
13861	29	173	MERCH. WHOLESALERS;NONDUR. GDS
13862	147	1143	EDUCATIONAL SERVICES
13863	9	31	JUSTICE; PUBIC ORDER/SAFETY
13864	13	34	SPECIAL TRADE CONTRACTORS
13865	178	924	EDUCATIONAL SERVICES
13901	1336	16036	PROF.; SCIENTIFIC; & TECH SVCS
13902	30	2402	UTILITIES
13903	510	9478	HOSPITALS
13904	380	6599	FOOD MANUFACTURING
13905	1047	14751	EDUCATIONAL SERVICES
14001	238	3964	MERCH. WHOLESALERS;DURABLE GDS
14004	288	4251	JUSTICE; PUBIC ORDER/SAFETY
14005	37	368	EDUCATIONAL SERVICES
14006	239	2925	EDUCATIONAL SERVICES
14008	22	68	RELIG.; GRANT; CIVIC; PROF ORG
14009	219	2987	PROF.; SCIENTIFIC; & TECH SVCS
14010	2	71	EDUCATIONAL SERVICES
14011	165	2574	JUSTICE; PUBIC ORDER/SAFETY
14012	59	641	EDUCATIONAL SERVICES
14013	34	156	JUSTICE; PUBIC ORDER/SAFETY
14020	1130	14623	HOSPITALS
14021	3	20	REAL ESTATE
14024	34	101	CROP PRODUCTION
14025	82	352	FOOD SVCS & DRINKING PLACES
14026	78	644	SPECIAL TRADE CONTRACTORS
14027	13	81	JUSTICE; PUBIC ORDER/SAFETY
14028	26	289	WAREHOUSING AND STORAGE
14029	4	12	EXEC.; LEGIS.; & OTHER SUPPORT
14030	87	603	FOOD SVCS & DRINKING PLACES
14031	417	5017	MISCELLANEOUS MANUFACTURING
14032	183	911	SPECIAL TRADE CONTRACTORS
14033	61	218	EDUCATIONAL SERVICES
14034	49	964	JUSTICE; PUBIC ORDER/SAFETY
14035	5	8	FOOD SVCS & DRINKING PLACES
14036	112	3583	AMUSEMENT; GAMBLING;& RECREAT.
14037	19	113	AMBULATORY HEALTH CARE SVCS
14038	11	55	MERCH. WHOLESALERS;DURABLE GDS
14039	3	8	MINING (EXCEPT OIL AND GAS)
14040	52	402	PERFORM'G ARTS; SPEC. SPORTS
14041	5	3	POSTAL SERVICE
14042	68	461	ACCOMMODATION
14043	969	13121	CREDIT INTERMEDIATION & RELATD
14047	159	852	FOOD SVCS & DRINKING PLACES
14048	586	8581	MERCH. WHOLESALERS;NONDUR. GDS
14051	403	2715	EDUCATIONAL SERVICES
14052	689	8555	MERCH. WHOLESALERS;DURABLE GDS
14054	27	88	MERCH. WHOLESALERS;DURABLE GDS
14055	24	76	EXEC.; LEGIS.; & OTHER SUPPORT
14056	35	211	EDUCATIONAL SERVICES
14057	197	2304	EDUCATIONAL SERVICES
14058	57	785	MERCH. WHOLESALERS;NONDUR. GDS
14059	308	4385	TRANSPORTATION EQUIPMENT MFG
14060	7	32	TRUCK TRANSPORTATION
14061	9	19	EXEC.; LEGIS.; & OTHER SUPPORT
14062	62	409	EDUCATIONAL SERVICES
14063	506	5035	EDUCATIONAL SERVICES
14065	23	57	ACCOMMODATION
14066	32	643	EDUCATIONAL SERVICES
14067	132	782	NURSING & RESID. CARE FACILIT.
14068	221	6218	PROF.; SCIENTIFIC; & TECH SVCS
14069	26	596	ACCOMMODATION
14070	204	3819	HOSPITALS
14072	449	5482	AMUSEMENT; GAMBLING;& RECREAT.
14075	1259	14155	EDUCATIONAL SERVICES
14080	141	876	EDUCATIONAL SERVICES
14081	140	3673	AMBULATORY HEALTH CARE SVCS
14082	19	92	CONSTRUCTION OF BUILDINGS
14083	9	19	FABRICATED METAL PRODUCT MFG
14085	71	481	EDUCATIONAL SERVICES
14086	708	11613	PROF.; SCIENTIFIC; & TECH SVCS
14091	10	43	JUSTICE; PUBIC ORDER/SAFETY
14092	377	3370	NURSING & RESID. CARE FACILIT.
14094	1628	23923	TRANSPORTATION EQUIPMENT MFG
14095	2	3	PROF.; SCIENTIFIC; & TECH SVCS
14098	66	805	EDUCATIONAL SERVICES
14101	40	367	NURSING & RESID. CARE FACILIT.
14102	28	81	EXEC.; LEGIS.; & OTHER SUPPORT
14103	339	3518	EDUCATIONAL SERVICES
14105	120	1441	EDUCATIONAL SERVICES
14107	9	463	WASTE MANAGMT & REMEDIAT'N SVC
14108	136	1360	HOSPITALS
14109	5	684	EDUCATIONAL SERVICES
14110	14	57	FOOD AND BEVERAGE STORES
14111	120	961	EDUCATIONAL SERVICES
14112	2	2	POSTAL SERVICE
14113	16	145	BLDG MATL & GARDEN EQPMT DLRS
14120	1208	11234	EDUCATIONAL SERVICES
14125	74	1110	NONMETALLIC MINERAL PROD. MFG
14126	31	103	FOOD SVCS & DRINKING PLACES
14127	1188	16124	EDUCATIONAL SERVICES
14129	14	118	EXEC.; LEGIS.; & OTHER SUPPORT
14130	21	104	EXEC.; LEGIS.; & OTHER SUPPORT
14131	95	1323	RELIG.; GRANT; CIVIC; PROF ORG
14132	161	2762	EDUCATIONAL SERVICES
14133	5	41	EXEC.; LEGIS.; & OTHER SUPPORT
14134	15	344	SOCIAL ASSISTANCE
14135	24	114	JUSTICE; PUBIC ORDER/SAFETY
14136	166	1070	MERCH. WHOLESALERS;NONDUR. GDS
14138	51	537	EDUCATIONAL SERVICES
14139	36	210	EDUCATIONAL SERVICES
14140	7	88	JUSTICE; PUBIC ORDER/SAFETY
14141	363	4179	GENERAL MERCHANDISE STORES
14143	33	166	FOOD SVCS & DRINKING PLACES
14144	4	38	EDUCATIONAL SERVICES
14145	32	157	MERCH. WHOLESALERS;NONDUR. GDS
14150	1526	21198	AMBULATORY HEALTH CARE SVCS
14151	6	11	SOCIAL ASSISTANCE
14167	27	192	ACCOMMODATION
14168	3	8	FOOD AND BEVERAGE STORES
14169	16	117	JUSTICE; PUBIC ORDER/SAFETY
14170	56	448	AMBULATORY HEALTH CARE SVCS
14171	45	725	PROF.; SCIENTIFIC; & TECH SVCS
14172	96	639	MERCH. WHOLESALERS;NONDUR. GDS
14173	39	252	FOOD SVCS & DRINKING PLACES
14174	125	972	EDUCATIONAL SERVICES
14201	364	4455	EDUCATIONAL SERVICES
14202	1628	33654	PROF.; SCIENTIFIC; & TECH SVCS
14203	889	19065	HOSPITALS
14204	319	3754	EDUCATIONAL SERVICES
14205	2	41	CONSTRUCTION OF BUILDINGS
14206	744	9227	MERCH. WHOLESALERS;DURABLE GDS
14207	838	15150	TRANSPORTATION EQUIPMENT MFG
14208	200	2788	EDUCATIONAL SERVICES
14209	483	12078	EDUCATIONAL SERVICES
14210	495	6116	EDUCATIONAL SERVICES
14211	508	4333	TRANSIT & GRND PASS. TRANSPORT
14212	379	2754	FOOD AND BEVERAGE STORES
14213	426	7200	FOOD MANUFACTURING
14214	622	9195	HOSPITALS
14215	823	14949	HOSPITALS
14216	691	4793	FOOD SVCS & DRINKING PLACES
14217	842	8274	HOSPITALS
14218	526	5564	RELIG.; GRANT; CIVIC; PROF ORG
14219	556	9524	TRANSPORTATION EQUIPMENT MFG
14220	451	6692	HOSPITALS
14221	3297	50462	AMBULATORY HEALTH CARE SVCS
14222	486	7873	HOSPITALS
14223	455	5212	EDUCATIONAL SERVICES

ZIP CODE	2009 Total Firms	2009 Total Employ-ees	TOP INDUSTRY RANKED on 2009 EMPLOYMENT
14224	1462	18233	AMBULATORY HEALTH CARE SVCS
14225	1689	24592	PROF.; SCIENTIFIC; & TECH SVCS
14226	1535	17044	FOOD SVCS & DRINKING PLACES
14227	666	12484	NURSING & RESID. CARE FACILIT.
14228	857	16344	PROF.; SCIENTIFIC; & TECH SVCS
14231	13	48	ADMINISTRATIVE & SUPPORT SVCS
14240	3	1001	POSTAL SERVICE
14241	1	60	POSTAL SERVICE
14260	22	1242	EDUCATIONAL SERVICES
14261	3	53	RELIG.; GRANT; CIVIC; PROF ORG
14263	12	6158	AMBULATORY HEALTH CARE SVCS
14301	605	6610	AMBULATORY HEALTH CARE SVCS
14302	3	464	CHEMICAL MANUFACTURING
14303	311	8396	AMUSEMENT; GAMBLING;& RECREAT.
14304	1150	13891	FOOD SVCS & DRINKING PLACES
14305	429	4410	RELIG.; GRANT; CIVIC; PROF ORG
14410	2	1	MISCELLANEOUS MANUFACTURING
14411	448	4818	SOCIAL ASSISTANCE
14413	14	49	MERCH. WHOLESALERS;NONDUR. GDS
14414	267	3067	MERCH. WHOLESALERS;NONDUR. GDS
14415	8	12	CROP PRODUCTION
14416	122	1413	EDUCATIONAL SERVICES
14418	44	102	BEVERAGE & TOBACCO PRODUCT MFG
14420	585	8729	EDUCATIONAL SERVICES
14422	51	289	MACHINERY MANUFACTURING
14423	161	1789	COMPUTER & ELECTRONIC PROD MFG
14424	1318	18025	NURSING & RESID. CARE FACILIT.
14425	234	3417	PERFORM'G ARTS; SPEC. SPORTS
14427	72	748	ACCOMMODATION
14428	188	1426	EDUCATIONAL SERVICES
14429	9	8	EXEC.; LEGIS.; & OTHER SUPPORT
14430	11	16	EXEC.; LEGIS.; & OTHER SUPPORT
14432	211	3076	EDUCATIONAL SERVICES
14433	123	1333	CONSTRUCTION OF BUILDINGS
14435	52	460	ADMIN. ENVIRO. QUALITY PROGRMS
14437	383	3216	HOSPITALS
14441	10	98	SPECIAL TRADE CONTRACTORS
14443	9	323	SPORTG GDS;HOBBY;BOOK; & MUSIC
14445	404	4282	EDUCATIONAL SERVICES
14449	6	21	MERCH. WHOLESALERS;DURABLE GDS
14450	1305	14311	EDUCATIONAL SERVICES
14452	6	54	AMUSEMENT; GAMBLING;& RECREAT.
14453	21	351	RENTAL AND LEASING SERVICES
14454	435	5196	EDUCATIONAL SERVICES
14456	902	11288	HOSPITALS
14461	30	157	CONSTRUCTION OF BUILDINGS
14462	25	48	EXEC.; LEGIS.; & OTHER SUPPORT
14463	20	102	MERCH. WHOLESALERS;NONDUR. GDS
14464	132	675	FOOD AND BEVERAGE STORES
14466	57	227	JUSTICE; PUBIC ORDER/SAFETY
14467	263	3739	EDUCATIONAL SERVICES
14468	389	2239	EDUCATIONAL SERVICES
14469	225	1603	PROF.; SCIENTIFIC; & TECH SVCS
14470	132	1193	EDUCATIONAL SERVICES
14471	154	1234	EDUCATIONAL SERVICES
14472	291	2129	EDUCATIONAL SERVICES
14475	15	51	ELECTRONICS & APPLIANCE STORES
14476	33	323	EDUCATIONAL SERVICES
14477	17	143	TRUCK TRANSPORTATION
14478	23	387	EDUCATIONAL SERVICES
14479	4	6	SPECIAL TRADE CONTRACTORS
14480	96	582	FOOD SVCS & DRINKING PLACES
14481	55	510	MERCH. WHOLESALERS;NONDUR. GDS
14482	299	2861	EDUCATIONAL SERVICES
14485	139	1066	EDUCATIONAL SERVICES
14486	10	21	MERCH. WHOLESALERS;DURABLE GDS
14487	140	1098	EDUCATIONAL SERVICES
14488	4	0	POSTAL SERVICE
14489	290	3302	EXEC.; LEGIS.; & OTHER SUPPORT
14502	354	3652	ADMINISTRATIVE & SUPPORT SVCS
14504	45	412	EXEC.; LEGIS.; & OTHER SUPPORT
14505	142	884	EDUCATIONAL SERVICES
14506	101	550	FOOD SVCS & DRINKING PLACES
14507	55	211	FOOD MANUFACTURING
14508	6	43	JUSTICE; PUBIC ORDER/SAFETY
14510	196	2465	ADMIN. HUMAN RESOURCE PROGRAMS
14511	18	95	MUSEUMS; HIST. SITES;& SIMILAR
14512	191	986	BEVERAGE & TOBACCO PRODUCT MFG
14513	558	11244	AMBULATORY HEALTH CARE SVCS
14514	125	943	RELIG.; GRANT; CIVIC; PROF ORG
14515	6	6	POSTAL SERVICE
14516	50	363	MISCELLANEOUS MANUFACTURING
14517	101	714	EDUCATIONAL SERVICES
14518	5	253	MISCELLANEOUS MANUFACTURING
14519	379	2409	MISCELLANEOUS MANUFACTURING
14520	8	197	EDUCATIONAL SERVICES
14521	99	744	EDUCATIONAL SERVICES
14522	329	2734	PLASTICS & RUBBER PRODUCTS MFG
14525	78	1063	EDUCATIONAL SERVICES
14526	560	4818	EDUCATIONAL SERVICES

ZIP CODE	2009 Total Firms	2009 Total Employ-ees	TOP INDUSTRY RANKED on 2009 EMPLOYMENT
14527	611	6352	AMBULATORY HEALTH CARE SVCS
14529	5	11	FOOD SVCS & DRINKING PLACES
14530	189	1690	EDUCATIONAL SERVICES
14532	194	2862	UNCLASSIFIED ESTABLISHMENTS
14533	36	329	CHEMICAL MANUFACTURING
14534	1185	12025	PROF.; SCIENTIFIC; & TECH SVCS
14536	23	93	ACCOMMODATION
14537	5	31	TRUCK TRANSPORTATION
14538	10	45	JUSTICE; PUBIC ORDER/SAFETY
14539	12	230	EDUCATIONAL SERVICES
14541	60	1436	JUSTICE; PUBIC ORDER/SAFETY
14542	9	13	EXEC.; LEGIS.; & OTHER SUPPORT
14543	123	1283	EDUCATIONAL SERVICES
14544	70	505	EDUCATIONAL SERVICES
14545	7	5	FOOD SVCS & DRINKING PLACES
14546	163	1960	MERCH. WHOLESALERS;DURABLE GDS
14547	10	23	SPECIAL TRADE CONTRACTORS
14548	88	991	EDUCATIONAL SERVICES
14549	7	36	ACCOMMODATION
14550	46	434	FOOD AND BEVERAGE STORES
14551	214	2665	EDUCATIONAL SERVICES
14555	55	193	FOOD SVCS & DRINKING PLACES
14556	6	404	JUSTICE; PUBIC ORDER/SAFETY
14557	5	53	JUSTICE; PUBIC ORDER/SAFETY
14558	3	6	AMUSEMENT; GAMBLING;& RECREAT.
14559	550	5215	EDUCATIONAL SERVICES
14560	45	102	CONSTRUCTION OF BUILDINGS
14561	75	402	CROP PRODUCTION
14563	10	46	BLDG MATL & GARDEN EQPMT DLRS
14564	864	10644	FOOD SVCS & DRINKING PLACES
14568	109	812	EDUCATIONAL SERVICES
14569	321	3493	HOSPITALS
14571	28	129	FOOD AND BEVERAGE STORES
14572	156	1791	EDUCATIONAL SERVICES
14580	1422	17573	AMBULATORY HEALTH CARE SVCS
14585	18	83	MERCH. WHOLESALERS;DURABLE GDS
14586	146	7084	ADMINISTRATIVE & SUPPORT SVCS
14588	11	457	RELIG.; GRANT; CIVIC; PROF ORG
14589	220	2724	EDUCATIONAL SERVICES
14590	188	2008	MISCELLANEOUS MANUFACTURING
14591	47	436	PRIMARY METAL MANUFACTURING
14592	22	166	FORESTRY AND LOGGING
14602	8	57	PROF.; SCIENTIFIC; & TECH SVCS
14603	8	51	POSTAL SERVICE
14604	681	11827	PROF.; SCIENTIFIC; & TECH SVCS
14605	433	5862	EDUCATIONAL SERVICES
14606	987	16167	TRANSPORTATION EQUIPMENT MFG
14607	1274	15341	FURN. & HOME FURNISHGS STORES
14608	460	5596	EDUCATIONAL SERVICES
14609	964	8304	EDUCATIONAL SERVICES
14610	503	9207	TELECOMMUNICATIONS
14611	707	15565	HOSPITALS
14612	668	6466	EDUCATIONAL SERVICES
14613	256	3051	EDUCATIONAL SERVICES
14614	903	13249	PROF.; SCIENTIFIC; & TECH SVCS
14615	470	6089	FOOD SVCS & DRINKING PLACES
14616	475	4010	FOOD AND BEVERAGE STORES
14617	506	4168	EDUCATIONAL SERVICES
14618	1379	15784	AMBULATORY HEALTH CARE SVCS
14619	165	6020	CONSTRUCTION OF BUILDINGS
14620	768	16834	HOSPITALS
14621	1032	19244	HOSPITALS
14622	366	3899	AMUSEMENT; GAMBLING;& RECREAT.
14623	1980	38645	PROF.; SCIENTIFIC; & TECH SVCS
14624	1520	24996	FOOD AND BEVERAGE STORES
14625	624	8439	PROF.; SCIENTIFIC; & TECH SVCS
14626	1136	11491	GENERAL MERCHANDISE STORES
14627	13	283	EDUCATIONAL SERVICES
14642	132	2772	AMBULATORY HEALTH CARE SVCS
14643	1	0	CREDIT INTERMEDIATION & RELATD
14644	1	2	CREDIT INTERMEDIATION & RELATD
14646	2	0	TELECOMMUNICATIONS
14647	7	3655	INSURANCE CARRIERS & RELATED
14649	1	0	SPECIAL TRADE CONTRACTORS
14650	7	1832	MACHINERY MANUFACTURING
14652	5	32	ELECTRONICS & APPLIANCE STORES
14653	3	1015	PIPELINE TRANSPORTATION
14692	28	2425	POSTAL SERVICE
14694	1	650	PRINT'G & RELATED SUPP'T ACT'S
14701	1746	24738	AMBULATORY HEALTH CARE SVCS
14702	6	14	SPECIAL TRADE CONTRACTORS
14706	166	1349	EDUCATIONAL SERVICES
14707	8	11	HEAVY & CIVIL ENG. CONSTRUCT'N
14708	1	0	JUSTICE; PUBIC ORDER/SAFETY
14709	58	289	JUSTICE; PUBIC ORDER/SAFETY
14710	96	506	EDUCATIONAL SERVICES
14711	54	280	EDUCATIONAL SERVICES
14712	125	1118	FOOD SVCS & DRINKING PLACES
14714	5	18	SOCIAL ASSISTANCE
14715	80	312	FABRICATED METAL PRODUCT MFG

ZIP CODE	2009 Total Firms	2009 Total Employ-ees	TOP INDUSTRY RANKED on 2009 EMPLOYMENT
14716	95	650	EDUCATIONAL SERVICES
14717	18	35	ADMINISTRATIVE & SUPPORT SVCS
14718	84	428	SOCIAL ASSISTANCE
14719	69	757	MERCH. WHOLESALERS;DURABLE GDS
14720	19	91	TRANSIT & GRND PASS. TRANSPORT
14721	5	9	FOOD SVCS & DRINKING PLACES
14722	87	789	ACCOMMODATION
14723	40	157	SPECIAL TRADE CONTRACTORS
14724	90	1365	AMUSEMENT; GAMBLING;& RECREAT.
14726	17	103	FOOD AND BEVERAGE STORES
14727	182	1722	EDUCATIONAL SERVICES
14728	37	131	ACCOMMODATION
14729	22	77	ACCOMMODATION
14730	10	19	RELIG.; GRANT; CIVIC; PROF ORG
14731	183	2320	ACCOMMODATION
14732	29	123	JUSTICE; PUBIC ORDER/SAFETY
14733	238	4737	FABRICATED METAL PRODUCT MFG
14735	81	463	EDUCATIONAL SERVICES
14736	51	98	ACCOMMODATION
14737	117	537	EDUCATIONAL SERVICES
14738	110	734	EDUCATIONAL SERVICES
14739	58	503	MERCH. WHOLESALERS;NONDUR. GDS
14740	34	721	NURSING & RESID. CARE FACILIT.
14741	43	295	TRANSIT & GRND PASS. TRANSPORT
14742	7	184	NURSING & RESID. CARE FACILIT.
14743	36	245	EDUCATIONAL SERVICES
14744	33	564	EDUCATIONAL SERVICES
14745	5	3	POSTAL SERVICE
14747	47	164	EDUCATIONAL SERVICES
14748	14	69	FOOD SVCS & DRINKING PLACES
14750	322	5268	MERCH. WHOLESALERS;DURABLE GDS
14751	5	8	HEAVY & CIVIL ENG. CONSTRUCT'N
14752	19	19	RELIG.; GRANT; CIVIC; PROF ORG
14753	44	143	SOCIAL ASSISTANCE
14754	15	30	EXEC.; LEGIS.; & OTHER SUPPORT
14755	114	1971	JUSTICE; PUBIC ORDER/SAFETY
14756	5	27	CONSTRUCTION OF BUILDINGS
14757	344	3902	JUSTICE; PUBIC ORDER/SAFETY
14758	1	2	POSTAL SERVICE
14760	996	16772	PROF.; SCIENTIFIC; & TECH SVCS
14766	7	10	HEAVY & CIVIL ENG. CONSTRUCT'N
14767	45	341	EDUCATIONAL SERVICES
14769	28	129	JUSTICE; PUBIC ORDER/SAFETY
14770	90	782	EDUCATIONAL SERVICES
14772	107	942	EDUCATIONAL SERVICES
14774	11	65	EDUCATIONAL SERVICES
14775	91	436	EDUCATIONAL SERVICES
14777	33	96	EDUCATIONAL SERVICES
14778	6	840	EDUCATIONAL SERVICES
14779	339	6868	AMUSEMENT; GAMBLING;& RECREAT.
14781	102	386	EDUCATIONAL SERVICES
14782	46	395	EDUCATIONAL SERVICES
14783	21	84	MISCELLANEOUS STORE RETAILERS
14784	26	58	SPECIAL TRADE CONTRACTORS
14785	16	67	ACCOMMODATION
14786	4	13	PROF.; SCIENTIFIC; & TECH SVCS
14787	344	2044	MACHINERY MANUFACTURING
14788	8	15	SPORTG GDS;HOBBY;BOOK; & MUSIC
14801	150	903	EDUCATIONAL SERVICES
14802	91	1388	EDUCATIONAL SERVICES
14803	51	307	NONMETALLIC MINERAL PROD. MFG
14804	36	242	EDUCATIONAL SERVICES
14805	17	23	ACCOMMODATION
14806	69	344	EDUCATIONAL SERVICES
14807	75	579	FOOD MANUFACTURING
14808	16	55	MERCH. WHOLESALERS;DURABLE GDS
14809	80	476	EDUCATIONAL SERVICES
14810	594	6137	MERCH. WHOLESALERS;DURABLE GDS
14812	40	311	JUSTICE; PUBIC ORDER/SAFETY
14813	151	1774	EXEC.; LEGIS.; & OTHER SUPPORT
14814	118	1111	MISCELLANEOUS MANUFACTURING
14815	11	97	EDUCATIONAL SERVICES
14816	20	37	FOOD AND BEVERAGE STORES
14817	49	238	SOCIAL ASSISTANCE
14818	57	166	EXEC.; LEGIS.; & OTHER SUPPORT
14819	9	5	EXEC.; LEGIS.; & OTHER SUPPORT
14820	7	26	EDUCATIONAL SERVICES
14821	61	757	MERCH. WHOLESALERS;NONDUR. GDS
14822	36	141	EDUCATIONAL SERVICES
14823	106	485	EDUCATIONAL SERVICES
14824	16	124	FORESTRY AND LOGGING
14825	27	408	MERCH. WHOLESALERS;DURABLE GDS
14826	62	281	HEAVY & CIVIL ENG. CONSTRUCT'N
14827	7	16	BLDG MATL & GARDEN EQPMT DLRS
14830	820	9411	PROF.; SCIENTIFIC; & TECH SVCS
14831	1	500	MERCH. WHOLESALERS;DURABLE GDS
14836	15	204	EDUCATIONAL SERVICES
14837	170	1093	EDUCATIONAL SERVICES
14838	23	74	AMUSEMENT; GAMBLING;& RECREAT.
14839	19	34	HEAVY & CIVIL ENG. CONSTRUCT'N

ZIP CODE	2009 Total Firms	2009 Total Employ-ees	TOP INDUSTRY RANKED on 2009 EMPLOYMENT
14840	143	1007	FABRICATED METAL PRODUCT MFG
14841	46	187	BEVERAGE & TOBACCO PRODUCT MFG
14842	21	80	ACCOMMODATION
14843	595	8175	MISCELLANEOUS MANUFACTURING
14845	903	12115	MERCH. WHOLESALERS;DURABLE GDS
14846	10	77	ACCOMMODATION
14847	81	208	FOOD SVCS & DRINKING PLACES
14850	2594	30579	EDUCATIONAL SERVICES
14851	11	86	RELIG.; GRANT; CIVIC; PROF ORG
14852	4	5	ADMINISTRATIVE & SUPPORT SVCS
14853	72	2370	EDUCATIONAL SERVICES
14854	11	33	GASOLINE STATIONS
14855	20	159	EDUCATIONAL SERVICES
14856	9	57	FOOD SVCS & DRINKING PLACES
14857	6	156	EDUCATIONAL SERVICES
14858	24	79	EXEC.; LEGIS.; & OTHER SUPPORT
14859	7	31	JUSTICE; PUBIC ORDER/SAFETY
14860	44	235	BEVERAGE & TOBACCO PRODUCT MFG
14861	24	75	SPECIAL TRADE CONTRACTORS
14863	4	3	POSTAL SERVICE
14864	26	50	MISCELLANEOUS MANUFACTURING
14865	124	1392	HOSPITALS
14867	106	513	EDUCATIONAL SERVICES
14869	49	409	EDUCATIONAL SERVICES
14870	280	4612	GENERAL MERCHANDISE STORES
14871	88	571	NONMETALLIC MINERAL PROD. MFG
14872	16	51	BLDG MATL & GARDEN EQPMT DLRS
14873	87	463	BLDG MATL & GARDEN EQPMT DLRS
14874	23	27	EXEC.; LEGIS.; & OTHER SUPPORT
14876	9	63	AMUSEMENT; GAMBLING;& RECREAT.
14877	10	16	PROF.; SCIENTIFIC; & TECH SVCS
14878	24	60	BEVERAGE & TOBACCO PRODUCT MFG
14879	34	177	EDUCATIONAL SERVICES
14880	38	226	EDUCATIONAL SERVICES
14881	19	154	EDUCATIONAL SERVICES
14882	136	1120	FOOD AND BEVERAGE STORES
14883	113	522	EDUCATIONAL SERVICES
14884	6	544	ACCOMMODATION
14885	19	136	EDUCATIONAL SERVICES
14886	261	1304	EDUCATIONAL SERVICES
14887	7	60	ACCOMMODATION
14889	40	249	EDUCATIONAL SERVICES
14891	290	3070	EDUCATIONAL SERVICES
14892	276	2135	NURSING & RESID. CARE FACILIT.
14893	16	27	MACHINERY MANUFACTURING
14894	22	66	MERCH. WHOLESALERS;NONDUR. GDS
14895	417	5879	MACHINERY MANUFACTURING
14897	29	118	EDUCATIONAL SERVICES
14898	42	171	JUSTICE; PUBIC ORDER/SAFETY
14901	926	14318	EDUCATIONAL SERVICES
14902	3	7	EXEC.; LEGIS.; & OTHER SUPPORT
14903	439	5056	FOOD SVCS & DRINKING PLACES
14904	366	3577	PAPER MANUFACTURING
14905	211	3118	HOSPITALS
15001	892	7365	SECURITIES/COMMODITY CONTRACTS
15003	475	3730	PRIMARY METAL MANUFACTURING
15004	14	76	WOOD PRODUCT MANUFACTURING
15005	205	1286	FOOD SVCS & DRINKING PLACES
15006	11	21	RELIG.; GRANT; CIVIC; PROF ORG
15007	55	236	MOTOR VEHICLE & PARTS DEALERS
15009	662	14155	HOSPITALS
15010	1013	9793	SPECIAL TRADE CONTRACTORS
15012	712	6501	FOOD SVCS & DRINKING PLACES
15014	89	3381	PRIMARY METAL MANUFACTURING
15015	38	236	AMUSEMENT; GAMBLING;& RECREAT.
15017	927	10795	HOSPITALS
15018	16	133	MACHINERY MANUFACTURING
15019	26	53	FOOD AND BEVERAGE STORES
15020	10	104	MERCH. WHOLESALERS;NONDUR. GDS
15021	306	2869	PUBLISHING INDUSTRIES
15022	484	4093	FURN. & HOME FURNISHGS STORES
15024	292	4195	MACHINERY MANUFACTURING
15025	526	9300	HOSPITALS
15026	124	1048	SUPPORT ACT. FOR TRANSPORT.
15027	63	294	FABRICATED METAL PRODUCT MFG
15028	2	2	POSTAL SERVICE
15030	64	734	BLDG MATL & GARDEN EQPMT DLRS
15031	34	347	CONSTRUCTION OF BUILDINGS
15032	10	7	POSTAL SERVICE
15033	198	1207	FABRICATED METAL PRODUCT MFG
15034	79	450	TRANSIT & GRND PASS. TRANSPORT
15035	73	388	SPECIAL TRADE CONTRACTORS
15037	400	2811	EDUCATIONAL SERVICES
15038	13	91	AMBULATORY HEALTH CARE SVCS
15042	146	1118	PROF.; SCIENTIFIC; & TECH SVCS
15043	36	245	SUPPORT ACT. FOR TRANSPORT.
15044	824	7755	FOOD SVCS & DRINKING PLACES
15045	132	825	MERCH. WHOLESALERS;DURABLE GDS
15046	65	428	FABRICATED METAL PRODUCT MFG
15047	12	26	FURNITURE & RELATED PROD. MFG
15049	17	434	RELIG.; GRANT; CIVIC; PROF ORG
15050	54	341	EDUCATIONAL SERVICES
15051	26	1290	MISCELLANEOUS MANUFACTURING
15052	76	459	FOOD SVCS & DRINKING PLACES
15053	5	10	CONSTRUCTION OF BUILDINGS
15054	10	169	CHEMICAL MANUFACTURING
15055	62	1310	TELECOMMUNICATIONS
15056	128	2133	PRIMARY METAL MANUFACTURING
15057	257	1806	EDUCATIONAL SERVICES
15059	146	1326	PRIMARY METAL MANUFACTURING
15060	30	230	AMUSEMENT; GAMBLING;& RECREAT.
15061	580	7540	EDUCATIONAL SERVICES
15062	290	2174	EDUCATIONAL SERVICES
15063	419	4414	HOSPITALS
15064	44	304	MERCH. WHOLESALERS;DURABLE GDS
15065	437	5817	HOSPITALS
15066	390	2420	FOOD SVCS & DRINKING PLACES
15067	63	438	NONMETALLIC MINERAL PROD. MFG
15068	1389	13986	PRIMARY METAL MANUFACTURING
15069	2	53	ADMINISTRATIVE & SUPPORT SVCS
15071	348	3364	EDUCATIONAL SERVICES
15072	4	2	POSTAL SERVICE
15074	356	3587	SOCIAL ASSISTANCE
15075	7	21	SPECIAL TRADE CONTRACTORS
15076	60	459	EDUCATIONAL SERVICES
15077	9	78	MINING (EXCEPT OIL AND GAS)
15078	18	109	FABRICATED METAL PRODUCT MFG
15081	13	51	PROF.; SCIENTIFIC; & TECH SVCS
15082	7	8	UNCLASSIFIED ESTABLISHMENTS
15083	39	61	SPECIAL TRADE CONTRACTORS
15084	553	5323	PUBLISHING INDUSTRIES
15085	214	1488	HEAVY & CIVIL ENG. CONSTRUCT'N
15086	203	8332	TELECOMMUNICATIONS
15087	13	23	FABRICATED METAL PRODUCT MFG
15088	53	578	MERCH. WHOLESALERS;NONDUR. GDS
15089	201	1332	PROF.; SCIENTIFIC; & TECH SVCS
15090	1165	9351	MOTOR VEHICLE & PARTS DEALERS
15091	8	116	AMUSEMENT; GAMBLING;& RECREAT.
15095	2	43	SPECIAL TRADE CONTRACTORS
15096	1	280	RELIG.; GRANT; CIVIC; PROF ORG
15101	740	6527	MERCH. WHOLESALERS;DURABLE GDS
15102	1044	8476	FOOD SVCS & DRINKING PLACES
15104	234	3511	SPECIAL TRADE CONTRACTORS
15106	981	7705	PROF.; SCIENTIFIC; & TECH SVCS
15108	1540	26555	PROF.; SCIENTIFIC; & TECH SVCS
15110	162	1284	FABRICATED METAL PRODUCT MFG
15112	132	909	MERCH. WHOLESALERS;DURABLE GDS
15116	405	3069	EDUCATIONAL SERVICES
15120	670	7347	FOOD SVCS & DRINKING PLACES
15122	627	11882	GENERAL MERCHANDISE STORES
15123	145	1242	CLOTHING & CLOTH'G ACC. STORES
15126	222	1128	EDUCATIONAL SERVICES
15127	17	93	MISCELLANEOUS MANUFACTURING
15129	180	1071	EDUCATIONAL SERVICES
15131	343	2479	FOOD SVCS & DRINKING PLACES
15132	822	8225	RELIG.; GRANT; CIVIC; PROF ORG
15133	93	575	EDUCATIONAL SERVICES
15134	1	0	HEAVY & CIVIL ENG. CONSTRUCT'N
15135	79	635	MERCH. WHOLESALERS;DURABLE GDS
15136	869	8234	SPECIAL TRADE CONTRACTORS
15137	446	4934	MERCH. WHOLESALERS;NONDUR. GDS
15139	357	4068	MERCH. WHOLESALERS;DURABLE GDS
15140	86	399	EXEC.; LEGIS.; & OTHER SUPPORT
15142	45	377	AMUSEMENT; GAMBLING;& RECREAT.
15143	839	12001	HOSPITALS
15144	167	1207	CHEMICAL MANUFACTURING
15145	262	1728	MERCH. WHOLESALERS;DURABLE GDS
15146	1897	27287	HOSPITALS
15147	408	4219	FOOD MANUFACTURING
15148	124	2102	TRANSPORTATION EQUIPMENT MFG
15201	691	6867	PRIMARY METAL MANUFACTURING
15202	619	4566	HOSPITALS
15203	914	11924	FOOD SVCS & DRINKING PLACES
15204	152	822	SPECIAL TRADE CONTRACTORS
15205	1376	24381	MERCH. WHOLESALERS;NONDUR. GDS
15206	996	11745	EDUCATIONAL SERVICES
15207	210	1804	EXEC.; LEGIS.; & OTHER SUPPORT
15208	287	3176	EDUCATIONAL SERVICES
15209	358	2756	SPECIAL TRADE CONTRACTORS
15210	561	2614	EDUCATIONAL SERVICES
15211	196	1345	FOOD SVCS & DRINKING PLACES
15212	1174	18216	HOSPITALS
15213	1285	27869	EDUCATIONAL SERVICES
15214	158	1444	EDUCATIONAL SERVICES
15215	580	5840	HOSPITALS
15216	714	5196	FOOD SVCS & DRINKING PLACES
15217	784	6859	NURSING & RESID. CARE FACILIT.
15218	436	3627	AMBULATORY HEALTH CARE SVCS
15219	2290	38208	PROF.; SCIENTIFIC; & TECH SVCS
15220	1248	17151	BROADCASTING
15221	941	7591	EDUCATIONAL SERVICES
15222	2493	72375	PROF.; SCIENTIFIC; & TECH SVCS
15223	338	4865	JUSTICE; PUBIC ORDER/SAFETY
15224	473	6356	HOSPITALS
15225	140	2412	MERCH. WHOLESALERS;DURABLE GDS
15226	347	3161	FOOD SVCS & DRINKING PLACES
15227	594	4039	EDUCATIONAL SERVICES
15228	613	4504	FOOD SVCS & DRINKING PLACES
15229	365	3360	EDUCATIONAL SERVICES
15230	5	1	ADMINISTRATIVE & SUPPORT SVCS
15231	112	1633	FOOD SVCS & DRINKING PLACES
15232	492	6960	HOSPITALS
15233	361	8720	JUSTICE; PUBIC ORDER/SAFETY
15234	638	4120	FOOD SVCS & DRINKING PLACES
15235	1242	11854	FOOD SVCS & DRINKING PLACES
15236	1130	10531	FOOD SVCS & DRINKING PLACES
15237	2240	21713	FOOD SVCS & DRINKING PLACES
15238	1044	18276	PROF.; SCIENTIFIC; & TECH SVCS
15239	611	5074	EDUCATIONAL SERVICES
15240	8	4005	EXEC.; LEGIS.; & OTHER SUPPORT
15241	848	7280	FOOD SVCS & DRINKING PLACES
15242	8	19	MISCELLANEOUS STORE RETAILERS
15243	225	4921	NURSING & RESID. CARE FACILIT.
15244	3	9	SPECIAL TRADE CONTRACTORS
15258	4	7014	CREDIT INTERMEDIATION & RELATD
15259	1	0	MISCELLANEOUS MANUFACTURING
15260	25	9721	EDUCATIONAL SERVICES
15261	10	419	AMBULATORY HEALTH CARE SVCS
15272	6	1316	PROF.; SCIENTIFIC; & TECH SVCS
15275	207	7536	PROF.; SCIENTIFIC; & TECH SVCS
15276	80	2024	ADMINISTRATIVE & SUPPORT SVCS
15282	2	1139	EDUCATIONAL SERVICES
15290	2	6	POSTAL SERVICE
15301	2470	26561	FOOD SVCS & DRINKING PLACES
15310	12	10	RELIG.; GRANT; CIVIC; PROF ORG
15311	23	60	MERCH. WHOLESALERS;DURABLE GDS
15312	106	475	EDUCATIONAL SERVICES
15313	25	102	AMUSEMENT; GAMBLING;& RECREAT.
15314	177	1313	EDUCATIONAL SERVICES
15315	19	92	EDUCATIONAL SERVICES
15316	7	53	FABRICATED METAL PRODUCT MFG
15317	1970	20500	PROF.; SCIENTIFIC; & TECH SVCS
15320	222	1053	EDUCATIONAL SERVICES
15321	113	457	SPECIAL TRADE CONTRACTORS
15322	37	107	NURSING & RESID. CARE FACILIT.
15323	130	902	EDUCATIONAL SERVICES
15324	18	33	MACHINERY MANUFACTURING
15325	6	22	JUSTICE; PUBIC ORDER/SAFETY
15327	22	85	MERCH. WHOLESALERS;DURABLE GDS
15329	36	258	SOCIAL ASSISTANCE
15330	207	2437	BLDG MATL & GARDEN EQPMT DLRS
15331	32	112	JUSTICE; PUBIC ORDER/SAFETY
15332	214	1523	SPECIAL TRADE CONTRACTORS
15333	80	494	EDUCATIONAL SERVICES
15334	4	9	EXEC.; LEGIS.; & OTHER SUPPORT
15336	4	4	MISCELLANEOUS STORE RETAILERS
15337	26	98	EDUCATIONAL SERVICES
15338	40	286	EDUCATIONAL SERVICES
15339	7	34	FOOD SVCS & DRINKING PLACES
15340	103	290	FOOD SVCS & DRINKING PLACES
15341	17	75	SPECIAL TRADE CONTRACTORS
15342	146	2107	MERCH. WHOLESALERS;NONDUR. GDS
15344	64	543	APPAREL MANUFACTURING
15345	39	61	EXEC.; LEGIS.; & OTHER SUPPORT
15346	8	32	EXEC.; LEGIS.; & OTHER SUPPORT
15347	52	970	PERFORM'G ARTS; SPEC. SPORTS
15348	14	40	FOOD AND BEVERAGE STORES
15349	69	678	MOTOR VEHICLE & PARTS DEALERS
15350	7	63	EDUCATIONAL SERVICES
15351	6	37	JUSTICE; PUBIC ORDER/SAFETY
15352	26	95	SUPPORT ACTIVITIES FOR MINING
15353	5	23	JUSTICE; PUBIC ORDER/SAFETY
15357	68	511	RELIG.; GRANT; CIVIC; PROF ORG
15358	32	152	JUSTICE; PUBIC ORDER/SAFETY
15359	21	81	JUSTICE; PUBIC ORDER/SAFETY
15360	62	164	NONMETALLIC MINERAL PROD. MFG
15361	2	1	REPAIR AND MAINTENANCE
15362	18	29	SPECIAL TRADE CONTRACTORS
15363	19	27	CREDIT INTERMEDIATION & RELATD
15364	13	60	FABRICATED METAL PRODUCT MFG
15365	4	7	EXEC.; LEGIS.; & OTHER SUPPORT
15366	2	2	POSTAL SERVICE
15367	126	538	TRANSIT & GRND PASS. TRANSPORT
15368	10	29	SOCIAL ASSISTANCE
15370	725	9435	JUSTICE; PUBIC ORDER/SAFETY
15376	36	121	MERCH. WHOLESALERS;DURABLE GDS
15377	20	531	MINING (EXCEPT OIL AND GAS)
15378	9	26	PRINT'G & RELATED SUPP'T ACT'S
15379	8	4	POSTAL SERVICE
15380	31	93	SPECIAL TRADE CONTRACTORS

ZIP CODE	2009 Total Firms	2009 Total Employ-ees	TOP INDUSTRY RANKED on 2009 EMPLOYMENT	ZIP CODE	2009 Total Firms	2009 Total Employ-ees	TOP INDUSTRY RANKED on 2009 EMPLOYMENT	ZIP CODE	2009 Total Firms	2009 Total Employ-ees	TOP INDUSTRY RANKED on 2009 EMPLOYMENT
15401	1749	20047	FOOD SVCS & DRINKING PLACES	15544	5	5	POSTAL SERVICE	15693	17	104	MINING (EXCEPT OIL AND GAS)
15410	4	33	ADMINISTRATIVE & SUPPORT SVCS	15545	71	270	EDUCATIONAL SERVICES	15695	5	34	RELIG.; GRANT; CIVIC; PROF ORG
15411	25	84	WOOD PRODUCT MANUFACTURING	15546	8	7	PERSONAL AND LAUNDRY SERVICES	15696	33	210	PROF.; SCIENTIFIC; & TECH SVCS
15412	17	61	CHEMICAL MANUFACTURING	15547	27	243	HEALTH & PERSONAL CARE STORES	15697	181	1720	COMPUTER & ELECTRONIC PROD MFG
15413	8	65	FABRICATED METAL PRODUCT MFG	15548	3	2	BLDG MATL & GARDEN EQPMT DLRS	15698	33	241	MERCH. WHOLESALERS;NONDUR. GDS
15415	5	94	MINING (EXCEPT OIL AND GAS)	15549	3	4	FOOD SVCS & DRINKING PLACES	15701	1523	17681	FOOD SVCS & DRINKING PLACES
15416	3	23	RELIG.; GRANT; CIVIC; PROF ORG	15550	48	191	EXEC.; LEGIS.; & OTHER SUPPORT	15705	12	2394	EDUCATIONAL SERVICES
15417	300	1875	MOTOR VEHICLE & PARTS DEALERS	15551	10	29	EDUCATIONAL SERVICES	15710	3	3	GASOLINE STATIONS
15419	115	9319	EDUCATIONAL SERVICES	15552	189	1361	EDUCATIONAL SERVICES	15711	11	63	JUSTICE; PUBIC ORDER/SAFETY
15420	6	14	SOCIAL ASSISTANCE	15553	5	18	RELIG.; GRANT; CIVIC; PROF ORG	15712	3	3	POSTAL SERVICE
15421	20	65	ACCOMMODATION	15554	70	362	EDUCATIONAL SERVICES	15713	5	6	MERCH. WHOLESALERS;DURABLE GDS
15422	1	2	POSTAL SERVICE	15557	136	1026	JUSTICE; PUBIC ORDER/SAFETY	15714	222	1357	EDUCATIONAL SERVICES
15423	49	609	EDUCATIONAL SERVICES	15558	81	483	TRUCK TRANSPORTATION	15715	33	169	MERCH. WHOLESALERS;DURABLE GDS
15424	83	451	EDUCATIONAL SERVICES	15559	59	204	MUSEUMS; HIST. SITES;& SIMILAR	15716	21	160	SUPPORT ACTIVITIES FOR MINING
15425	755	5424	EDUCATIONAL SERVICES	15560	19	110	EDUCATIONAL SERVICES	15717	418	3642	MERCH. WHOLESALERS;DURABLE GDS
15427	20	48	RELIG.; GRANT; CIVIC; PROF ORG	15561	8	17	EDUCATIONAL SERVICES	15720	14	41	JUSTICE; PUBIC ORDER/SAFETY
15428	39	316	AMUSEMENT; GAMBLING;& RECREAT.	15562	15	148	HEAVY & CIVIL ENG. CONSTRUCT'N	15721	10	17	WOOD PRODUCT MANUFACTURING
15429	3	7	AMUSEMENT; GAMBLING;& RECREAT.	15563	118	898	MERCH. WHOLESALERS;DURABLE GDS	15722	104	556	EDUCATIONAL SERVICES
15430	3	3	POSTAL SERVICE	15564	3	3	RELIG.; GRANT; CIVIC; PROF ORG	15723	1	1	POSTAL SERVICE
15431	120	700	AMBULATORY HEALTH CARE SVCS	15565	4	31	PRIMARY METAL MANUFACTURING	15724	61	229	JUSTICE; PUBIC ORDER/SAFETY
15432	19	63	REPAIR AND MAINTENANCE	15601	3148	36706	FOOD SVCS & DRINKING PLACES	15725	31	107	SUPPORT ACTIVITIES FOR MINING
15433	10	75	EDUCATIONAL SERVICES	15610	116	324	FOOD SVCS & DRINKING PLACES	15727	3	2	POSTAL SERVICE
15434	7	51	NURSING & RESID. CARE FACILIT.	15611	30	354	MOTOR VEHICLE & PARTS DEALERS	15728	117	851	MINING (EXCEPT OIL AND GAS)
15435	11	18	REPAIR AND MAINTENANCE	15612	11	155	EDUCATIONAL SERVICES	15729	34	415	EDUCATIONAL SERVICES
15436	76	383	FOOD AND BEVERAGE STORES	15613	377	2164	MACHINERY MANUFACTURING	15730	8	27	MUSEUMS; HIST. SITES;& SIMILAR
15437	92	2542	ACCOMMODATION	15615	4	2	POSTAL SERVICE	15731	4	4	GASOLINE STATIONS
15438	54	177	JUSTICE; PUBIC ORDER/SAFETY	15616	5	17	BLDG MATL & GARDEN EQPMT DLRS	15732	30	63	EDUCATIONAL SERVICES
15440	3	1	POSTAL SERVICE	15617	13	24	FOOD SVCS & DRINKING PLACES	15733	2	19	NURSING & RESID. CARE FACILIT.
15442	68	982	SOCIAL ASSISTANCE	15618	72	639	PRIMARY METAL MANUFACTURING	15734	14	222	MERCH. WHOLESALERS;DURABLE GDS
15443	1	2	POSTAL SERVICE	15619	9	26	REPAIR AND MAINTENANCE	15736	55	296	EDUCATIONAL SERVICES
15444	13	54	JUSTICE; PUBIC ORDER/SAFETY	15620	23	127	JUSTICE; PUBIC ORDER/SAFETY	15737	11	20	RELIG.; GRANT; CIVIC; PROF ORG
15445	108	850	SPECIAL TRADE CONTRACTORS	15621	8	69	JUSTICE; PUBIC ORDER/SAFETY	15738	4	5	FOOD AND BEVERAGE STORES
15446	25	77	TELECOMMUNICATIONS	15622	58	1450	ACCOMMODATION	15739	4	1	RELIG.; GRANT; CIVIC; PROF ORG
15447	5	11	NURSING & RESID. CARE FACILIT.	15623	13	62	EDUCATIONAL SERVICES	15741	6	6	CLOTHING & CLOTH'G ACC. STORES
15448	1	2	POSTAL SERVICE	15624	21	157	FOOD SVCS & DRINKING PLACES	15742	18	81	FABRICATED METAL PRODUCT MFG
15449	3	4	POSTAL SERVICE	15625	7	33	EXEC.; LEGIS.; & OTHER SUPPORT	15744	8	78	MINING (EXCEPT OIL AND GAS)
15450	10	75	JUSTICE; PUBIC ORDER/SAFETY	15626	249	2600	GENERAL MERCHANDISE STORES	15745	7	10	EXEC.; LEGIS.; & OTHER SUPPORT
15451	13	76	MINING (EXCEPT OIL AND GAS)	15627	185	1053	EDUCATIONAL SERVICES	15746	16	393	NURSING & RESID. CARE FACILIT.
15454	4	3	POSTAL SERVICE	15628	92	462	AMUSEMENT; GAMBLING;& RECREAT.	15747	38	234	EDUCATIONAL SERVICES
15455	7	69	FOOD SVCS & DRINKING PLACES	15629	14	32	RELIG.; GRANT; CIVIC; PROF ORG	15748	213	1549	UTILITIES
15456	91	1451	AMBULATORY HEALTH CARE SVCS	15631	23	190	FOOD MANUFACTURING	15750	4	11	MERCH. WHOLESALERS;DURABLE GDS
15458	68	338	EDUCATIONAL SERVICES	15632	340	4031	FABRICATED METAL PRODUCT MFG	15752	3	5	RELIG.; GRANT; CIVIC; PROF ORG
15459	75	474	NURSING & RESID. CARE FACILIT.	15633	8	70	MACHINERY MANUFACTURING	15753	9	32	WASTE MANAGMT & REMEDIAT'N SVC
15460	1	1	POSTAL SERVICE	15634	13	45	FOOD SVCS & DRINKING PLACES	15754	7	47	COMPUTER & ELECTRONIC PROD MFG
15461	146	977	MACHINERY MANUFACTURING	15635	7	11	REPAIR AND MAINTENANCE	15756	3	2	FOOD SVCS & DRINKING PLACES
15462	18	85	EDUCATIONAL SERVICES	15636	116	720	EXEC.; LEGIS.; & OTHER SUPPORT	15757	64	258	EDUCATIONAL SERVICES
15463	6	10	CONSTRUCTION OF BUILDINGS	15637	80	506	EDUCATIONAL SERVICES	15758	6	18	BLDG MATL & GARDEN EQPMT DLRS
15464	32	498	MUSEUMS; HIST. SITES;& SIMILAR	15638	3	5	RELIG.; GRANT; CIVIC; PROF ORG	15759	65	533	EDUCATIONAL SERVICES
15465	18	230	TRANSPORTATION EQUIPMENT MFG	15639	62	469	PROF.; SCIENTIFIC; & TECH SVCS	15760	2	12	SPECIAL TRADE CONTRACTORS
15466	10	17	CREDIT INTERMEDIATION & RELATD	15640	2	3	POSTAL SERVICE	15761	2	26	SPECIAL TRADE CONTRACTORS
15467	2	6	CONSTRUCTION OF BUILDINGS	15641	9	36	JUSTICE; PUBIC ORDER/SAFETY	15762	24	139	TRANSPORTATION EQUIPMENT MFG
15468	58	268	JUSTICE; PUBIC ORDER/SAFETY	15642	1448	11758	FOOD SVCS & DRINKING PLACES	15764	8	26	TRUCK TRANSPORTATION
15469	59	266	JUSTICE; PUBIC ORDER/SAFETY	15644	671	5719	MERCH. WHOLESALERS;DURABLE GDS	15765	64	431	BLDG MATL & GARDEN EQPMT DLRS
15470	30	361	PRINT'G & RELATED SUPP'T ACT'S	15646	44	127	RELIG.; GRANT; CIVIC; PROF ORG	15767	669	5626	FOOD SVCS & DRINKING PLACES
15472	8	24	MERCH. WHOLESALERS;DURABLE GDS	15647	12	33	FABRICATED METAL PRODUCT MFG	15770	8	44	PROF.; SCIENTIFIC; & TECH SVCS
15473	145	906	EDUCATIONAL SERVICES	15650	1293	15896	MACHINERY MANUFACTURING	15771	21	154	MERCH. WHOLESALERS;NONDUR. GDS
15474	61	218	EDUCATIONAL SERVICES	15655	27	441	AMUSEMENT; GAMBLING;& RECREAT.	15772	34	173	NURSING & RESID. CARE FACILIT.
15475	53	108	EDUCATIONAL SERVICES	15656	344	4900	PRIMARY METAL MANUFACTURING	15773	16	143	SPECIAL TRADE CONTRACTORS
15476	3	2	POSTAL SERVICE	15658	471	2929	AMUSEMENT; GAMBLING;& RECREAT.	15774	101	808	SPECIAL TRADE CONTRACTORS
15477	25	177	PAPER MANUFACTURING	15660	4	102	PRIMARY METAL MANUFACTURING	15775	3	6	POSTAL SERVICE
15478	147	1009	UTILITIES	15661	37	559	PRIMARY METAL MANUFACTURING	15777	7	9	FOOD AND BEVERAGE STORES
15479	57	1343	SPORTG GDS;HOBBY;BOOK; & MUSIC	15662	3	7	WASTE MANAGMT & REMEDIAT'N SVC	15778	2	12	BLDG MATL & GARDEN EQPMT DLRS
15480	54	339	PROF.; SCIENTIFIC; & TECH SVCS	15663	23	183	RELIG.; GRANT; CIVIC; PROF ORG	15779	12	735	HOSPITALS
15482	19	86	FOOD SVCS & DRINKING PLACES	15664	13	110	FURN. & HOME FURNISHGS STORES	15780	4	31	JUSTICE; PUBIC ORDER/SAFETY
15483	10	71	MERCH. WHOLESALERS;DURABLE GDS	15665	53	246	JUSTICE; PUBIC ORDER/SAFETY	15781	2	2	POSTAL SERVICE
15484	4	5	POSTAL SERVICE	15666	761	7889	COMPUTER & ELECTRONIC PROD MFG	15783	3	3	POSTAL SERVICE
15486	45	145	SPECIAL TRADE CONTRACTORS	15668	643	6515	MISCELLANEOUS MANUFACTURING	15784	6	5	REPAIR AND MAINTENANCE
15488	11	51	TRUCK TRANSPORTATION	15670	148	837	PROF.; SCIENTIFIC; & TECH SVCS	15801	1074	15044	HOSPITALS
15489	4	44	MERCH. WHOLESALERS;NONDUR. GDS	15671	9	53	FABRICATED METAL PRODUCT MFG	15821	13	40	FOOD AND BEVERAGE STORES
15490	33	67	MERCH. WHOLESALERS;DURABLE GDS	15672	176	2452	FOOD AND BEVERAGE STORES	15822	2	0	AMUSEMENT; GAMBLING;& RECREAT.
15492	3	0	MERCH. WHOLESALERS;DURABLE GDS	15673	45	236	FOOD AND BEVERAGE STORES	15823	31	259	MACHINERY MANUFACTURING
15501	1176	14284	HOSPITALS	15674	46	272	MERCH. WHOLESALERS;DURABLE GDS	15824	196	1600	FABRICATED METAL PRODUCT MFG
15502	9	346	ACCOMMODATION	15675	29	272	ADMINISTRATIVE & SUPPORT SVCS	15825	581	6561	EDUCATIONAL SERVICES
15510	3	1185	JUSTICE; PUBIC ORDER/SAFETY	15676	33	171	JUSTICE; PUBIC ORDER/SAFETY	15827	7	37	SECURITIES/COMMODITY CONTRACTS
15520	4	4	POSTAL SERVICE	15677	21	105	EDUCATIONAL SERVICES	15828	19	35	ACCOMMODATION
15521	65	391	PLASTICS & RUBBER PRODUCTS MFG	15678	27	124	JUSTICE; PUBIC ORDER/SAFETY	15829	32	115	JUSTICE; PUBIC ORDER/SAFETY
15522	811	7578	MERCH. WHOLESALERS;DURABLE GDS	15679	92	569	EDUCATIONAL SERVICES	15831	4	15	REPAIR AND MAINTENANCE
15530	182	1309	EDUCATIONAL SERVICES	15680	14	57	EDUCATIONAL SERVICES	15832	14	17	EXEC.; LEGIS.; & OTHER SUPPORT
15531	122	809	EDUCATIONAL SERVICES	15681	141	1230	FABRICATED METAL PRODUCT MFG	15834	249	2043	PRIMARY METAL MANUFACTURING
15532	2	3	RELIG.; GRANT; CIVIC; PROF ORG	15682	7	116	REAL ESTATE	15840	79	750	CHEMICAL MANUFACTURING
15533	88	1354	FOOD SVCS & DRINKING PLACES	15683	300	3293	HEAVY & CIVIL ENG. CONSTRUCT'N	15841	8	24	HOSPITALS
15534	13	17	POSTAL SERVICE	15684	25	38	RELIG.; GRANT; CIVIC; PROF ORG	15845	122	1182	PAPER MANUFACTURING
15535	41	107	WOOD PRODUCT MANUFACTURING	15685	11	36	JUSTICE; PUBIC ORDER/SAFETY	15846	117	741	FABRICATED METAL PRODUCT MFG
15536	11	41	WOOD PRODUCT MANUFACTURING	15686	28	410	EDUCATIONAL SERVICES	15847	5	6	EXEC.; LEGIS.; & OTHER SUPPORT
15537	401	3351	HOSPITALS	15687	62	336	JUSTICE; PUBIC ORDER/SAFETY	15848	29	74	AMBULATORY HEALTH CARE SVCS
15538	11	15	SPECIAL TRADE CONTRACTORS	15688	13	101	SPECIAL TRADE CONTRACTORS	15849	46	442	MINING (EXCEPT OIL AND GAS)
15539	20	158	EDUCATIONAL SERVICES	15689	10	58	RELIG.; GRANT; CIVIC; PROF ORG	15851	203	1233	MACHINERY MANUFACTURING
15540	6	179	MINING (EXCEPT OIL AND GAS)	15690	290	1814	JUSTICE; PUBIC ORDER/SAFETY	15853	363	4196	EXEC.; LEGIS.; & OTHER SUPPORT
15541	115	602	NONSTORE RETAILERS	15691	5	23	FABRICATED METAL PRODUCT MFG	15856	19	39	FURN. & HOME FURNISHGS STORES
15542	22	52	SPECIAL TRADE CONTRACTORS	15692	16	28	FOOD AND BEVERAGE STORES	15857	729	9445	CHEMICAL MANUFACTURING

ZIP CODE	2009 Total Firms	2009 Total Employ-ees	TOP INDUSTRY RANKED on 2009 EMPLOYMENT
15860	36	122	FOOD SVCS & DRINKING PLACES
15861	6	23	ADMIN. OF ECONOMIC PROGRAMS
15863	6	18	CONSTRUCTION OF BUILDINGS
15864	39	326	NONMETALLIC MINERAL PROD. MFG
15865	49	278	PRIMARY METAL MANUFACTURING
15866	5	7	FOOD MANUFACTURING
15868	55	150	EDUCATIONAL SERVICES
15870	36	224	FABRICATED METAL PRODUCT MFG
15901	569	6671	AMBULATORY HEALTH CARE SVCS
15902	330	2603	MERCH. WHOLESALERS;DURABLE GDS
15904	1026	14834	FOOD SVCS & DRINKING PLACES
15905	647	12516	HOSPITALS
15906	287	2996	EDUCATIONAL SERVICES
15907	3	0	INSURANCE CARRIERS & RELATED
15909	161	733	JUSTICE; PUBIC ORDER/SAFETY
15920	27	303	EDUCATIONAL SERVICES
15921	23	94	MOTOR VEHICLE & PARTS DEALERS
15922	9	20	EXEC.; LEGIS.; & OTHER SUPPORT
15923	57	318	EDUCATIONAL SERVICES
15924	18	140	EDUCATIONAL SERVICES
15925	5	7	NONSTORE RETAILERS
15926	91	434	NONSTORE RETAILERS
15927	16	75	UTILITIES
15928	63	725	EDUCATIONAL SERVICES
15929	5	8	GENERAL MERCHANDISE STORES
15930	5	9	RELIG.; GRANT; CIVIC; PROF ORG
15931	641	7777	PROF.; SCIENTIFIC; & TECH SVCS
15934	16	112	MACHINERY MANUFACTURING
15935	84	407	MERCH. WHOLESALERS;DURABLE GDS
15936	50	215	RELIG.; GRANT; CIVIC; PROF ORG
15937	14	123	JUSTICE; PUBIC ORDER/SAFETY
15938	58	250	EDUCATIONAL SERVICES
15940	57	1038	EDUCATIONAL SERVICES
15942	33	206	MERCH. WHOLESALERS;DURABLE GDS
15943	91	398	FOOD AND BEVERAGE STORES
15944	98	857	UTILITIES
15945	9	32	FOOD SVCS & DRINKING PLACES
15946	183	1301	JUSTICE; PUBIC ORDER/SAFETY
15948	10	33	JUSTICE; PUBIC ORDER/SAFETY
15949	21	66	RELIG.; GRANT; CIVIC; PROF ORG
15951	31	151	JUSTICE; PUBIC ORDER/SAFETY
15952	43	213	REPAIR AND MAINTENANCE
15953	1	1	SOCIAL ASSISTANCE
15954	52	390	TRUCK TRANSPORTATION
15955	55	552	EDUCATIONAL SERVICES
15956	61	361	APPAREL MANUFACTURING
15957	14	124	HEAVY & CIVIL ENG. CONSTRUCT'N
15958	51	486	WOOD PRODUCT MANUFACTURING
15959	12	24	MOTOR VEHICLE & PARTS DEALERS
15960	12	63	MINING (EXCEPT OIL AND GAS)
15961	16	47	RELIG.; GRANT; CIVIC; PROF ORG
15962	15	66	FOOD SVCS & DRINKING PLACES
15963	345	3305	HOSPITALS
16001	2287	24129	HOSPITALS
16002	567	4880	MERCH. WHOLESALERS;DURABLE GDS
16003	6	11	ADMINISTRATIVE & SUPPORT SVCS
16018	1	300	ADMINISTRATIVE & SUPPORT SVCS
16020	35	139	EXEC.; LEGIS.; & OTHER SUPPORT
16022	12	44	EDUCATIONAL SERVICES
16023	136	2810	FABRICATED METAL PRODUCT MFG
16024	14	442	MACHINERY MANUFACTURING
16025	172	672	NURSING & RESID. CARE FACILIT.
16027	18	58	ADMINISTRATIVE & SUPPORT SVCS
16028	85	369	JUSTICE; PUBIC ORDER/SAFETY
16029	28	358	MERCH. WHOLESALERS;DURABLE GDS
16030	18	102	GASOLINE STATIONS
16033	258	1669	MISCELLANEOUS STORE RETAILERS
16034	61	294	HEAVY & CIVIL ENG. CONSTRUCT'N
16035	3	3	MERCH. WHOLESALERS;NONDUR. GDS
16036	28	160	EDUCATIONAL SERVICES
16037	217	2484	MERCH. WHOLESALERS;NONDUR. GDS
16038	137	874	FOOD SVCS & DRINKING PLACES
16039	4	207	EDUCATIONAL SERVICES
16040	18	20	GASOLINE STATIONS
16041	41	721	EDUCATIONAL SERVICES
16045	71	1963	PRIMARY METAL MANUFACTURING
16046	560	5288	FOOD SVCS & DRINKING PLACES
16048	5	103	JUSTICE; PUBIC ORDER/SAFETY
16049	88	492	MISCELLANEOUS STORE RETAILERS
16050	55	497	CHEMICAL MANUFACTURING
16051	137	1055	WASTE MANAGMT & REMEDIAT'N SVC
16052	99	441	EDUCATIONAL SERVICES
16053	100	432	SPECIAL TRADE CONTRACTORS
16054	13	18	UTILITIES
16055	298	2103	SPECIAL TRADE CONTRACTORS
16056	285	3244	MISCELLANEOUS MANUFACTURING
16057	423	3461	EDUCATIONAL SERVICES
16058	3	7	EDUCATIONAL SERVICES
16059	318	2571	MOTOR VEHICLE & PARTS DEALERS
16061	95	556	ADMINISTRATIVE & SUPPORT SVCS
16063	407	4478	PROF.; SCIENTIFIC; & TECH SVCS
16066	1344	17765	MERCH. WHOLESALERS;DURABLE GDS
16101	1766	17277	FOOD SVCS & DRINKING PLACES
16102	174	1356	TRANSPORTATION EQUIPMENT MFG
16103	3	20	FABRICATED METAL PRODUCT MFG
16105	550	6698	HOSPITALS
16107	5	7	SOCIAL ASSISTANCE
16108	4	302	PROF.; SCIENTIFIC; & TECH SVCS
16110	12	50	FABRICATED METAL PRODUCT MFG
16111	30	100	FOOD AND BEVERAGE STORES
16112	50	555	EDUCATIONAL SERVICES
16113	15	101	ACCOMMODATION
16114	17	48	EXEC.; LEGIS.; & OTHER SUPPORT
16115	114	1040	WOOD PRODUCT MANUFACTURING
16116	62	226	JUSTICE; PUBIC ORDER/SAFETY
16117	628	5792	FABRICATED METAL PRODUCT MFG
16120	44	249	BLDG MATL & GARDEN EQPMT DLRS
16121	202	3088	HOSPITALS
16123	58	1064	PLASTICS & RUBBER PRODUCTS MFG
16124	63	273	COMPUTER & ELECTRONIC PROD MFG
16125	634	7814	PRIMARY METAL MANUFACTURING
16127	758	9373	EDUCATIONAL SERVICES
16130	91	510	EDUCATIONAL SERVICES
16131	21	83	MERCH. WHOLESALERS;DURABLE GDS
16132	31	169	MERCH. WHOLESALERS;DURABLE GDS
16133	42	210	SUPPORT ACTIVITIES FOR MINING
16134	132	755	EDUCATIONAL SERVICES
16136	32	489	PRIMARY METAL MANUFACTURING
16137	471	5376	JUSTICE; PUBIC ORDER/SAFETY
16140	12	30	BLDG MATL & GARDEN EQPMT DLRS
16141	33	162	JUSTICE; PUBIC ORDER/SAFETY
16142	182	1388	FOOD MANUFACTURING
16143	79	396	MISCELLANEOUS MANUFACTURING
16145	135	655	CONSTRUCTION OF BUILDINGS
16146	562	7819	HOSPITALS
16148	863	10966	FOOD SVCS & DRINKING PLACES
16150	235	1516	FOOD MANUFACTURING
16151	12	27	AMBULATORY HEALTH CARE SVCS
16153	91	382	EDUCATIONAL SERVICES
16154	93	434	PRIMARY METAL MANUFACTURING
16155	7	53	AMUSEMENT; GAMBLING;& RECREAT.
16156	109	423	WASTE MANAGMT & REMEDIAT'N SVC
16157	105	1118	NONMETALLIC MINERAL PROD. MFG
16159	153	2093	TRUCK TRANSPORTATION
16160	18	68	FOOD SVCS & DRINKING PLACES
16161	51	1215	PRIMARY METAL MANUFACTURING
16172	3	478	EDUCATIONAL SERVICES
16201	848	8844	HOSPITALS
16210	20	65	MERCH. WHOLESALERS;DURABLE GDS
16211	2	4	MERCH. WHOLESALERS;DURABLE GDS
16212	8	18	FOOD SVCS & DRINKING PLACES
16213	7	24	CONSTRUCTION OF BUILDINGS
16214	601	7455	EDUCATIONAL SERVICES
16217	21	133	ACCOMMODATION
16218	40	226	TRANSIT & GRND PASS. TRANSPORT
16220	5	15	FOOD SVCS & DRINKING PLACES
16221	2	1	POSTAL SERVICE
16222	45	214	WOOD PRODUCT MANUFACTURING
16223	11	45	TRUCK TRANSPORTATION
16224	29	236	WOOD PRODUCT MANUFACTURING
16225	5	5	EXEC.; LEGIS.; & OTHER SUPPORT
16226	287	2191	EDUCATIONAL SERVICES
16228	5	27	JUSTICE; PUBIC ORDER/SAFETY
16229	201	2415	MACHINERY MANUFACTURING
16230	18	80	EDUCATIONAL SERVICES
16232	154	1198	EDUCATIONAL SERVICES
16233	36	341	MERCH. WHOLESALERS;DURABLE GDS
16234	7	10	UTILITIES
16235	36	89	FOOD SVCS & DRINKING PLACES
16236	11	56	JUSTICE; PUBIC ORDER/SAFETY
16238	8	13	EDUCATIONAL SERVICES
16239	77	529	NURSING & RESID. CARE FACILIT.
16240	28	115	TRUCK TRANSPORTATION
16242	199	1008	EDUCATIONAL SERVICES
16244	15	83	FOOD AND BEVERAGE STORES
16245	4	3	POSTAL SERVICE
16246	11	56	FURN. & HOME FURNISHGS STORES
16248	93	435	EDUCATIONAL SERVICES
16249	77	322	EDUCATIONAL SERVICES
16250	5	38	BLDG MATL & GARDEN EQPMT DLRS
16253	2	4	MOTOR VEHICLE & PARTS DEALERS
16254	166	1780	WOOD PRODUCT MANUFACTURING
16255	63	609	NURSING & RESID. CARE FACILIT.
16256	24	76	BEVERAGE & TOBACCO PRODUCT MFG
16258	42	827	BLDG MATL & GARDEN EQPMT DLRS
16259	33	43	GASOLINE STATIONS
16260	6	31	FOOD SVCS & DRINKING PLACES
16261	1	0	POSTAL SERVICE
16262	103	1249	FOOD MANUFACTURING
16263	10	36	UTILITIES
16301	548	6507	RAIL TRANSPORTATION
16311	24	139	SUPPORT ACTIVITIES FOR MINING
16312	3	2	AMUSEMENT; GAMBLING;& RECREAT.
16313	49	382	JUSTICE; PUBIC ORDER/SAFETY
16314	237	1225	PLASTICS & RUBBER PRODUCTS MFG
16316	270	1645	MACHINERY MANUFACTURING
16317	39	195	REPAIR AND MAINTENANCE
16319	117	1372	GENERAL MERCHANDISE STORES
16321	7	22	FOOD SVCS & DRINKING PLACES
16322	7	91	MERCH. WHOLESALERS;DURABLE GDS
16323	798	10553	PROF.; SCIENTIFIC; & TECH SVCS
16326	28	130	JUSTICE; PUBIC ORDER/SAFETY
16327	84	349	EDUCATIONAL SERVICES
16328	6	12	FOOD SVCS & DRINKING PLACES
16329	8	1048	FABRICATED METAL PRODUCT MFG
16331	5	33	FOOD MANUFACTURING
16332	3	4	SPECIAL TRADE CONTRACTORS
16333	11	35	RELIG.; GRANT; CIVIC; PROF ORG
16334	15	270	MISCELLANEOUS MANUFACTURING
16335	1595	17494	MACHINERY MANUFACTURING
16340	45	213	FABRICATED METAL PRODUCT MFG
16341	62	303	PRIMARY METAL MANUFACTURING
16342	46	1263	ADMIN. HUMAN RESOURCE PROGRAMS
16343	43	412	TRUCK TRANSPORTATION
16344	19	41	SPECIAL TRADE CONTRACTORS
16345	89	444	EDUCATIONAL SERVICES
16346	185	2920	HOSPITALS
16347	84	461	JUSTICE; PUBIC ORDER/SAFETY
16350	82	341	JUSTICE; PUBIC ORDER/SAFETY
16351	67	210	EDUCATIONAL SERVICES
16352	4	9	MERCH. WHOLESALERS;DURABLE GDS
16353	153	585	EDUCATIONAL SERVICES
16354	500	3851	MERCH. WHOLESALERS;DURABLE GDS
16360	59	465	MERCH. WHOLESALERS;DURABLE GDS
16361	8	54	REPAIR AND MAINTENANCE
16362	24	46	EDUCATIONAL SERVICES
16364	34	78	BLDG MATL & GARDEN EQPMT DLRS
16365	975	12044	HOSPITALS
16366	1	700	CLOTHING & CLOTH'G ACC. STORES
16370	9	37	SPECIAL TRADE CONTRACTORS
16371	149	1140	NURSING & RESID. CARE FACILIT.
16372	25	141	JUSTICE; PUBIC ORDER/SAFETY
16373	142	1148	SOCIAL ASSISTANCE
16374	37	201	WASTE MANAGMT & REMEDIAT'N SVC
16375	5	6	RELIG.; GRANT; CIVIC; PROF ORG
16388	1	0	MISCELLANEOUS MANUFACTURING
16401	145	707	FOOD SVCS & DRINKING PLACES
16402	16	90	JUSTICE; PUBIC ORDER/SAFETY
16403	179	1643	JUSTICE; PUBIC ORDER/SAFETY
16404	87	221	BLDG MATL & GARDEN EQPMT DLRS
16405	20	75	JUSTICE; PUBIC ORDER/SAFETY
16406	123	826	NURSING & RESID. CARE FACILIT.
16407	458	4965	PLASTICS & RUBBER PRODUCTS MFG
16410	36	202	FABRICATED METAL PRODUCT MFG
16411	28	71	JUSTICE; PUBIC ORDER/SAFETY
16412	382	3083	FOOD SVCS & DRINKING PLACES
16413	4	3	POSTAL SERVICE
16415	321	4405	PRIMARY METAL MANUFACTURING
16416	10	68	JUSTICE; PUBIC ORDER/SAFETY
16417	329	2624	NURSING & RESID. CARE FACILIT.
16420	12	30	ACCOMMODATION
16421	70	844	PLASTICS & RUBBER PRODUCTS MFG
16422	13	27	EXEC.; LEGIS.; & OTHER SUPPORT
16423	90	812	CONSTRUCTION OF BUILDINGS
16424	194	1120	EDUCATIONAL SERVICES
16426	122	762	ELECTRONICS & APPLIANCE STORES
16427	7	39	EDUCATIONAL SERVICES
16428	474	4006	FOOD MANUFACTURING
16430	6	171	ACCOMMODATION
16433	197	2293	MERCH. WHOLESALERS;DURABLE GDS
16434	72	747	WOOD PRODUCT MANUFACTURING
16435	62	148	FABRICATED METAL PRODUCT MFG
16436	17	43	RELIG.; GRANT; CIVIC; PROF ORG
16438	262	1747	MISCELLANEOUS MANUFACTURING
16440	23	75	AMUSEMENT; GAMBLING;& RECREAT.
16441	352	1898	MERCH. WHOLESALERS;NONDUR. GDS
16442	76	265	JUSTICE; PUBIC ORDER/SAFETY
16443	41	123	FOOD SVCS & DRINKING PLACES
16444	5	1063	EDUCATIONAL SERVICES
16475	1	570	JUSTICE; PUBIC ORDER/SAFETY
16501	938	16253	EXEC.; LEGIS.; & OTHER SUPPORT
16502	542	6918	FABRICATED METAL PRODUCT MFG
16503	436	7392	PRIMARY METAL MANUFACTURING
16504	308	3782	RELIG.; GRANT; CIVIC; PROF ORG
16505	1070	11410	FOOD SVCS & DRINKING PLACES
16506	922	12074	ADMINISTRATIVE & SUPPORT SVCS
16507	433	8750	SOCIAL ASSISTANCE
16508	693	7449	PROF.; SCIENTIFIC; & TECH SVCS
16509	994	17708	ACCOMMODATION
16510	662	6502	FOOD SVCS & DRINKING PLACES

BUSINESS DATA

ZIP CODE	2009 Total Firms	2009 Total Employees	TOP INDUSTRY RANKED on 2009 EMPLOYMENT
16511	261	3397	JUSTICE; PUBIC ORDER/SAFETY
16512	12	187	RELIG.; GRANT; CIVIC; PROF ORG
16514	7	59	ADMINISTRATIVE & SUPPORT SVCS
16515	2	300	POSTAL SERVICE
16522	1	50	CREDIT INTERMEDIATION & RELATD
16530	7	2506	INSURANCE CARRIERS & RELATED
16531	5	18	SPECIAL TRADE CONTRACTORS
16534	2	350	PUBLISHING INDUSTRIES
16541	13	728	EDUCATIONAL SERVICES
16544	42	5661	HOSPITALS
16546	5	415	EDUCATIONAL SERVICES
16550	20	6874	HOSPITALS
16553	1	600	CREDIT INTERMEDIATION & RELATD
16563	3	622	EDUCATIONAL SERVICES
16565	173	2114	CLOTHING & CLOTH'G ACC. STORES
16601	1040	15057	RAIL TRANSPORTATION
16602	1681	21036	FOOD SVCS & DRINKING PLACES
16603	16	52	ADMINISTRATIVE & SUPPORT SVCS
16611	86	776	PAPER MANUFACTURING
16613	33	194	JUSTICE; PUBIC ORDER/SAFETY
16616	1	38	WOOD PRODUCT MANUFACTURING
16617	120	1031	EDUCATIONAL SERVICES
16619	9	17	UNCLASSIFIED ESTABLISHMENTS
16620	9	16	NURSING & RESID. CARE FACILIT.
16621	18	54	AMBULATORY HEALTH CARE SVCS
16622	4	5	MACHINERY MANUFACTURING
16623	15	98	ADMINISTRATIVE & SUPPORT SVCS
16624	4	12	SPECIAL TRADE CONTRACTORS
16625	131	1851	PRINT'G & RELATED SUPP'T ACT'S
16627	64	235	GENERAL MERCHANDISE STORES
16629	3	21	EDUCATIONAL SERVICES
16630	178	2007	JUSTICE; PUBIC ORDER/SAFETY
16631	15	98	MOTOR VEHICLE & PARTS DEALERS
16633	5	38	EDUCATIONAL SERVICES
16634	7	15	MERCH. WHOLESALERS;DURABLE GDS
16635	534	6201	NAT'L SECURITY & INT'L AFFAIRS
16636	22	49	FOOD SVCS & DRINKING PLACES
16637	74	487	MERCH. WHOLESALERS;DURABLE GDS
16638	1	150	ACCOMMODATION
16639	28	180	PRIMARY METAL MANUFACTURING
16640	16	255	EDUCATIONAL SERVICES
16641	62	335	EDUCATIONAL SERVICES
16644	14	35	RELIG.; GRANT; CIVIC; PROF ORG
16645	8	156	FURNITURE & RELATED PROD. MFG
16646	75	578	SOCIAL ASSISTANCE
16647	17	105	AMUSEMENT; GAMBLING;& RECREAT.
16648	618	9429	NURSING & RESID. CARE FACILIT.
16650	53	262	WASTE MANAGMT & REMEDIAT'N SVC
16651	112	1151	JUSTICE; PUBIC ORDER/SAFETY
16652	707	6805	JUSTICE; PUBIC ORDER/SAFETY
16654	2	650	JUSTICE; PUBIC ORDER/SAFETY
16655	20	147	CONSTRUCTION OF BUILDINGS
16656	45	104	TRUCK TRANSPORTATION
16657	35	144	ACCOMMODATION
16659	24	102	EDUCATIONAL SERVICES
16660	11	55	JUSTICE; PUBIC ORDER/SAFETY
16661	21	98	NONSTORE RETAILERS
16662	233	1926	LEATHER & ALLIED PRODUCT MFG
16663	3	1	POSTAL SERVICE
16664	39	211	PETROLEUM & COAL PRODUCTS MFG
16665	32	120	SPECIAL TRADE CONTRACTORS
16666	86	303	EDUCATIONAL SERVICES
16667	33	90	FOOD SVCS & DRINKING PLACES
16668	120	734	EDUCATIONAL SERVICES
16669	77	265	RELIG.; GRANT; CIVIC; PROF ORG
16670	1	1	PROF.; SCIENTIFIC; & TECH SVCS
16671	21	26	CONSTRUCTION OF BUILDINGS
16672	5	60	PETROLEUM & COAL PRODUCTS MFG
16673	214	3278	PAPER MANUFACTURING
16674	11	46	EDUCATIONAL SERVICES
16675	1	1	MERCH. WHOLESALERS;DURABLE GDS
16677	5	7	SPECIAL TRADE CONTRACTORS
16678	112	701	LEATHER & ALLIED PRODUCT MFG
16679	10	18	MERCH. WHOLESALERS;NONDUR. GDS
16680	13	27	PROF.; SCIENTIFIC; & TECH SVCS
16681	3	5	MACHINERY MANUFACTURING
16683	16	144	ANIMAL PRODUCTION
16684	33	1467	AMUSEMENT; GAMBLING;& RECREAT.
16685	2	2	RELIG.; GRANT; CIVIC; PROF ORG
16686	394	3748	EDUCATIONAL SERVICES
16689	17	206	FOOD SVCS & DRINKING PLACES
16691	4	2	POSTAL SERVICE
16692	19	182	EDUCATIONAL SERVICES
16693	108	1052	RELIG.; GRANT; CIVIC; PROF ORG
16694	8	4	POSTAL SERVICE
16695	46	158	MERCH. WHOLESALERS;NONDUR. GDS
16701	842	10507	FABRICATED METAL PRODUCT MFG
16720	53	170	EDUCATIONAL SERVICES
16724	7	77	UTILITIES
16725	9	35	FOOD SVCS & DRINKING PLACES

ZIP CODE	2009 Total Firms	2009 Total Employees	TOP INDUSTRY RANKED on 2009 EMPLOYMENT
16726	10	85	EXEC.; LEGIS.; & OTHER SUPPORT
16727	6	35	EXEC.; LEGIS.; & OTHER SUPPORT
16728	2	2	FOOD AND BEVERAGE STORES
16729	18	278	EDUCATIONAL SERVICES
16730	2	10	FOOD SVCS & DRINKING PLACES
16731	85	606	FURNITURE & RELATED PROD. MFG
16732	4	12	SPECIAL TRADE CONTRACTORS
16733	4	3	EXEC.; LEGIS.; & OTHER SUPPORT
16734	5	10	EXEC.; LEGIS.; & OTHER SUPPORT
16735	297	2149	HOSPITALS
16738	58	583	MERCH. WHOLESALERS;DURABLE GDS
16740	55	253	JUSTICE; PUBIC ORDER/SAFETY
16743	171	1554	NONMETALLIC MINERAL PROD. MFG
16744	7	10	SPECIAL TRADE CONTRACTORS
16745	9	19	REPAIR AND MAINTENANCE
16746	40	342	MERCH. WHOLESALERS;NONDUR. GDS
16748	105	678	EDUCATIONAL SERVICES
16749	210	1825	EDUCATIONAL SERVICES
16750	6	47	HEAVY & CIVIL ENG. CONSTRUCT'N
16801	1974	22525	FOOD SVCS & DRINKING PLACES
16802	47	1837	UNCLASSIFIED ESTABLISHMENTS
16803	690	13689	ACCOMMODATION
16804	9	54	MISCELLANEOUS MANUFACTURING
16805	1	4	PROF.; SCIENTIFIC; & TECH SVCS
16820	23	64	BLDG MATL & GARDEN EQPMT DLRS
16821	9	29	FOOD SVCS & DRINKING PLACES
16822	55	418	WOOD PRODUCT MANUFACTURING
16823	865	8980	JUSTICE; PUBIC ORDER/SAFETY
16825	15	436	TRUCK TRANSPORTATION
16826	12	84	EDUCATIONAL SERVICES
16827	130	844	FOOD SVCS & DRINKING PLACES
16828	184	1706	HOSPITALS
16829	14	103	MERCH. WHOLESALERS;DURABLE GDS
16830	824	9895	HOSPITALS
16832	12	64	MUSEUMS; HIST. SITES;& SIMILAR
16833	183	1503	JUSTICE; PUBIC ORDER/SAFETY
16834	9	47	FABRICATED METAL PRODUCT MFG
16835	9	16	EXEC.; LEGIS.; & OTHER SUPPORT
16836	31	115	EDUCATIONAL SERVICES
16837	2	1	ADMINISTRATIVE & SUPPORT SVCS
16838	46	192	REAL ESTATE
16839	7	14	FOOD SVCS & DRINKING PLACES
16840	10	12	RELIG.; GRANT; CIVIC; PROF ORG
16841	84	470	MERCH. WHOLESALERS;NONDUR. GDS
16843	25	354	EXEC.; LEGIS.; & OTHER SUPPORT
16844	50	124	SPECIAL TRADE CONTRACTORS
16845	26	152	MINING (EXCEPT OIL AND GAS)
16847	26	233	FOOD AND BEVERAGE STORES
16848	11	92	GASOLINE STATIONS
16849	5	34	FOOD AND BEVERAGE STORES
16850	5	8	EXEC.; LEGIS.; & OTHER SUPPORT
16851	36	98	FOOD SVCS & DRINKING PLACES
16852	3	60	ACCOMMODATION
16853	73	806	GASOLINE STATIONS
16854	64	210	RELIG.; GRANT; CIVIC; PROF ORG
16855	7	8	SPECIAL TRADE CONTRACTORS
16856	3	35	FABRICATED METAL PRODUCT MFG
16858	70	355	EDUCATIONAL SERVICES
16859	8	24	MERCH. WHOLESALERS;DURABLE GDS
16860	5	7	CONSTRUCTION OF BUILDINGS
16861	3	6	EXEC.; LEGIS.; & OTHER SUPPORT
16863	12	48	MACHINERY MANUFACTURING
16864	2	2	PERSONAL AND LAUNDRY SERVICES
16865	23	92	SPECIAL TRADE CONTRACTORS
16866	442	5377	JUSTICE; PUBIC ORDER/SAFETY
16868	21	320	SPECIAL TRADE CONTRACTORS
16870	161	636	EDUCATIONAL SERVICES
16871	2	3	EXEC.; LEGIS.; & OTHER SUPPORT
16872	25	75	EDUCATIONAL SERVICES
16873	4	11	HEAVY & CIVIL ENG. CONSTRUCT'N
16874	56	295	FOOD SVCS & DRINKING PLACES
16875	138	733	EDUCATIONAL SERVICES
16876	6	37	FORESTRY AND LOGGING
16877	27	96	PROF.; SCIENTIFIC; & TECH SVCS
16878	25	88	EDUCATIONAL SERVICES
16879	11	82	JUSTICE; PUBIC ORDER/SAFETY
16881	63	1907	MERCH. WHOLESALERS;DURABLE GDS
16882	13	37	ACCOMMODATION
16901	706	5967	HOSPITALS
16910	6	10	FOOD AND BEVERAGE STORES
16911	5	27	WASTE MANAGMT & REMEDIAT'N SVC
16912	89	1965	TRANSPORTATION EQUIPMENT MFG
16914	35	111	TRANSIT & GRND PASS. TRANSPORT
16915	381	3655	HOSPITALS
16917	74	221	FOOD SVCS & DRINKING PLACES
16920	81	888	PLASTICS & RUBBER PRODUCTS MFG
16921	38	75	ACCOMMODATION
16922	138	617	PRIMARY METAL MANUFACTURING
16923	47	164	UTILITIES
16925	78	263	PRIMARY METAL MANUFACTURING

ZIP CODE	2009 Total Firms	2009 Total Employees	TOP INDUSTRY RANKED on 2009 EMPLOYMENT
16926	23	43	NURSING & RESID. CARE FACILIT.
16927	28	156	SOCIAL ASSISTANCE
16928	49	188	JUSTICE; PUBIC ORDER/SAFETY
16929	76	216	FOOD AND BEVERAGE STORES
16930	61	353	WOOD PRODUCT MANUFACTURING
16932	19	48	RELIG.; GRANT; CIVIC; PROF ORG
16933	372	3432	EDUCATIONAL SERVICES
16935	59	244	FOOD AND BEVERAGE STORES
16936	52	233	FOOD AND BEVERAGE STORES
16937	5	36	JUSTICE; PUBIC ORDER/SAFETY
16938	43	149	ACCOMMODATION
16939	5	30	RELIG.; GRANT; CIVIC; PROF ORG
16940	13	32	SPECIAL TRADE CONTRACTORS
16941	4	2	RELIG.; GRANT; CIVIC; PROF ORG
16942	21	51	FOOD AND BEVERAGE STORES
16943	12	37	AMBULATORY HEALTH CARE SVCS
16945	7	10	MISCELLANEOUS MANUFACTURING
16946	83	532	EDUCATIONAL SERVICES
16947	273	2523	EDUCATIONAL SERVICES
16948	76	409	EDUCATIONAL SERVICES
16950	113	863	PLASTICS & RUBBER PRODUCTS MFG
17001	10	19	SPECIAL TRADE CONTRACTORS
17002	20	252	BLDG MATL & GARDEN EQPMT DLRS
17003	339	3439	NAT'L SECURITY & INT'L AFFAIRS
17004	174	2636	MACHINERY MANUFACTURING
17005	30	46	FOOD SVCS & DRINKING PLACES
17006	39	144	EDUCATIONAL SERVICES
17007	120	1075	EDUCATIONAL SERVICES
17009	139	2031	PRIMARY METAL MANUFACTURING
17010	35	243	NURSING & RESID. CARE FACILIT.
17011	1818	33257	PROF.; SCIENTIFIC; & TECH SVCS
17013	1619	19041	GENERAL MERCHANDISE STORES
17014	5	9	REPAIR AND MAINTENANCE
17015	712	10865	TRUCK TRANSPORTATION
17016	39	688	NURSING & RESID. CARE FACILIT.
17017	54	247	FISHING; HUNTING AND TRAPPING
17018	123	359	EDUCATIONAL SERVICES
17019	590	4452	SPECIAL TRADE CONTRACTORS
17020	259	1782	EDUCATIONAL SERVICES
17021	40	116	POSTAL SERVICE
17022	826	9932	NURSING & RESID. CARE FACILIT.
17023	187	1456	GENERAL MERCHANDISE STORES
17024	54	393	EDUCATIONAL SERVICES
17025	375	2805	EDUCATIONAL SERVICES
17026	107	2508	FOOD MANUFACTURING
17027	10	852	EDUCATIONAL SERVICES
17028	143	1460	ACCOMMODATION
17029	6	100	NURSING & RESID. CARE FACILIT.
17030	55	689	FABRICATED METAL PRODUCT MFG
17032	240	1646	EDUCATIONAL SERVICES
17033	848	34741	HOSPITALS
17034	84	388	FOOD SVCS & DRINKING PLACES
17035	20	50	EDUCATIONAL SERVICES
17036	514	3994	FOOD SVCS & DRINKING PLACES
17037	35	102	JUSTICE; PUBIC ORDER/SAFETY
17038	226	2445	MERCH. WHOLESALERS;DURABLE GDS
17039	6	30	FOOD SVCS & DRINKING PLACES
17040	71	179	CREDIT INTERMEDIATION & RELATD
17041	4	7	SUPPORT ACTIVITIES: AGR./FOR.
17042	1715	18762	HOSPITALS
17043	670	5270	FOOD SVCS & DRINKING PLACES
17044	873	9887	HOSPITALS
17045	98	486	WOOD PRODUCT MANUFACTURING
17046	751	5923	EDUCATIONAL SERVICES
17047	98	531	EDUCATIONAL SERVICES
17048	139	1058	EDUCATIONAL SERVICES
17049	96	720	CONSTRUCTION OF BUILDINGS
17050	1173	17380	FOOD SVCS & DRINKING PLACES
17051	114	643	EDUCATIONAL SERVICES
17052	27	157	MINING (EXCEPT OIL AND GAS)
17053	137	627	PETROLEUM & COAL PRODUCTS MFG
17054	4	26	ADMINISTRATIVE & SUPPORT SVCS
17055	1270	16445	SOCIAL ASSISTANCE
17056	8	37	BROADCASTING
17057	716	11117	EDUCATIONAL SERVICES
17058	44	385	RELIG.; GRANT; CIVIC; PROF ORG
17059	394	4356	FOOD MANUFACTURING
17060	32	169	MERCH. WHOLESALERS;DURABLE GDS
17061	319	2812	MERCH. WHOLESALERS;DURABLE GDS
17062	108	604	EDUCATIONAL SERVICES
17063	82	450	FURNITURE & RELATED PROD. MFG
17064	45	244	PERFORM'G ARTS; SPEC. SPORTS
17065	131	1202	COMPUTER & ELECTRONIC PROD MFG
17066	188	1915	MERCH. WHOLESALERS;DURABLE GDS
17067	485	5472	NURSING & RESID. CARE FACILIT.
17068	209	1322	JUSTICE; PUBIC ORDER/SAFETY
17069	9	18	MERCH. WHOLESALERS;DURABLE GDS
17070	590	4509	FOOD SVCS & DRINKING PLACES
17072	38	466	BLDG MATL & GARDEN EQPMT DLRS
17073	113	562	FURNITURE & RELATED PROD. MFG

ZIP CODE	2009 Total Firms	2009 Total Employ-ees	TOP INDUSTRY RANKED on 2009 EMPLOYMENT	ZIP CODE	2009 Total Firms	2009 Total Employ-ees	TOP INDUSTRY RANKED on 2009 EMPLOYMENT	ZIP CODE	2009 Total Firms	2009 Total Employ-ees	TOP INDUSTRY RANKED on 2009 EMPLOYMENT
17074	287	1216	FOOD AND BEVERAGE STORES	17270	4	2	AMUSEMENT; GAMBLING;& RECREAT.	17537	12	24	MISCELLANEOUS STORE RETAILERS
17075	7	5	FOOD AND BEVERAGE STORES	17271	21	225	EDUCATIONAL SERVICES	17538	188	2590	EDUCATIONAL SERVICES
17076	12	87	MOTOR VEHICLE & PARTS DEALERS	17272	6	26	AMUSEMENT; GAMBLING;& RECREAT.	17540	424	5353	PLASTICS & RUBBER PRODUCTS MFG
17077	13	384	TRUCK TRANSPORTATION	17301	121	674	FOOD SVCS & DRINKING PLACES	17543	1299	17180	CHEMICAL MANUFACTURING
17078	567	4219	PROF.; SCIENTIFIC; & TECH SVCS	17302	51	79	RELIG.; GRANT; CIVIC; PROF ORG	17545	937	12616	MERCH. WHOLESALERS;DURABLE GDS
17080	13	42	FOOD SVCS & DRINKING PLACES	17303	23	115	EDUCATIONAL SERVICES	17547	161	2346	INSURANCE CARRIERS & RELATED
17081	15	103	JUSTICE; PUBIC ORDER/SAFETY	17304	75	589	FOOD MANUFACTURING	17549	2	0	BLDG MATL & GARDEN EQPMT DLRS
17082	109	444	PERFORM'G ARTS; SPEC. SPORTS	17306	20	246	JUSTICE; PUBIC ORDER/SAFETY	17550	28	173	JUSTICE; PUBIC ORDER/SAFETY
17083	13	115	FOOD SVCS & DRINKING PLACES	17307	214	1642	FOOD MANUFACTURING	17551	183	2385	EDUCATIONAL SERVICES
17084	125	1340	COMPUTER & ELECTRONIC PROD MFG	17309	67	253	EDUCATIONAL SERVICES	17552	535	6052	FOOD SVCS & DRINKING PLACES
17085	3	5	PRINT'G & RELATED SUPP'T ACT'S	17310	8	74	EDUCATIONAL SERVICES	17554	187	2693	PUBLISHING INDUSTRIES
17086	71	293	RELIG.; GRANT; CIVIC; PROF ORG	17311	19	113	JUSTICE; PUBIC ORDER/SAFETY	17555	141	1290	SPECIAL TRADE CONTRACTORS
17087	94	677	WOOD PRODUCT MANUFACTURING	17312	4	45	FOOD AND BEVERAGE STORES	17557	707	10858	FOOD MANUFACTURING
17088	69	827	FURNITURE & RELATED PROD. MFG	17313	266	2688	CONSTRUCTION OF BUILDINGS	17560	99	1074	RELIG.; GRANT; CIVIC; PROF ORG
17090	148	775	JUSTICE; PUBIC ORDER/SAFETY	17314	138	1161	UTILITIES	17562	179	1323	BLDG MATL & GARDEN EQPMT DLRS
17093	25	459	EDUCATIONAL SERVICES	17315	486	3731	FOOD AND BEVERAGE STORES	17563	92	329	JUSTICE; PUBIC ORDER/SAFETY
17094	73	785	FURNITURE & RELATED PROD. MFG	17316	198	1109	FOOD AND BEVERAGE STORES	17564	3	14	MERCH. WHOLESALERS;DURABLE GDS
17097	17	59	MERCH. WHOLESALERS;NONDUR. GDS	17317	18	183	EDUCATIONAL SERVICES	17565	64	310	EDUCATIONAL SERVICES
17098	72	423	JUSTICE; PUBIC ORDER/SAFETY	17318	67	1443	PRINT'G & RELATED SUPP'T ACT'S	17566	464	3785	FOOD AND BEVERAGE STORES
17099	41	319	JUSTICE; PUBIC ORDER/SAFETY	17319	266	1624	ELECT'L EQPMT; APP; & COMP MFG	17567	41	616	MERCH. WHOLESALERS;DURABLE GDS
17101	1174	29504	EXEC.; LEGIS.; & OTHER SUPPORT	17320	194	2365	ACCOMMODATION	17568	8	141	SPECIAL TRADE CONTRACTORS
17102	388	3007	RELIG.; GRANT; CIVIC; PROF ORG	17321	53	354	EDUCATIONAL SERVICES	17569	174	546	MERCH. WHOLESALERS;DURABLE GDS
17103	431	4730	HOSPITALS	17322	89	400	PLASTICS & RUBBER PRODUCTS MFG	17570	6	369	FOOD MANUFACTURING
17104	592	14417	PROF.; SCIENTIFIC; & TECH SVCS	17323	10	31	UTILITIES	17572	163	1700	FOOD SVCS & DRINKING PLACES
17105	10	141	POSTAL SERVICE	17324	79	831	FOOD AND BEVERAGE STORES	17575	4	3	POSTAL SERVICE
17106	8	24	WASTE MANAGMT & REMEDIAT'N SVC	17325	1628	15598	EDUCATIONAL SERVICES	17576	28	528	FOOD SVCS & DRINKING PLACES
17107	3	1205	TRUCK TRANSPORTATION	17327	237	2170	CHEMICAL MANUFACTURING	17578	197	1108	SPECIAL TRADE CONTRACTORS
17108	7	43	EXEC.; LEGIS.; & OTHER SUPPORT	17329	45	147	EDUCATIONAL SERVICES	17579	231	1263	ACCOMMODATION
17109	975	15354	HOSPITALS	17331	2076	26089	FOOD SVCS & DRINKING PLACES	17580	10	92	NONMETALLIC MINERAL PROD. MFG
17110	1277	31565	HOSPITALS	17337	1	1	POSTAL SERVICE	17581	64	766	SPECIAL TRADE CONTRACTORS
17111	1295	19583	FOOD SVCS & DRINKING PLACES	17339	226	1556	EDUCATIONAL SERVICES	17582	44	266	EDUCATIONAL SERVICES
17112	1423	15842	RELIG.; GRANT; CIVIC; PROF ORG	17340	348	2681	FURNITURE & RELATED PROD. MFG	17583	1	0	JUSTICE; PUBIC ORDER/SAFETY
17113	287	2969	PRIMARY METAL MANUFACTURING	17342	28	284	FOOD AND BEVERAGE STORES	17584	335	5561	NURSING & RESID. CARE FACILIT.
17120	82	4552	ADMIN. OF ECONOMIC PROGRAMS	17343	6	12	MERCH. WHOLESALERS;NONDUR. GDS	17585	6	42	AMUSEMENT; GAMBLING;& RECREAT.
17121	3	5023	ADMIN. OF ECONOMIC PROGRAMS	17344	88	513	RELIG.; GRANT; CIVIC; PROF ORG	17601	3023	48449	FABRICATED METAL PRODUCT MFG
17124	3	408	ADMIN. OF ECONOMIC PROGRAMS	17345	208	2126	EDUCATIONAL SERVICES	17602	2053	38219	HOSPITALS
17125	2	10	EXEC.; LEGIS.; & OTHER SUPPORT	17347	95	885	FABRICATED METAL PRODUCT MFG	17603	2632	27859	FOOD SVCS & DRINKING PLACES
17126	3	131	EXEC.; LEGIS.; & OTHER SUPPORT	17349	199	1530	MISCELLANEOUS MANUFACTURING	17604	12	754	POSTAL SERVICE
17128	2	1504	EXEC.; LEGIS.; & OTHER SUPPORT	17350	461	5851	FOOD MANUFACTURING	17605	8	12	PROF.; SCIENTIFIC; & TECH SVCS
17177	2	2004	INSURANCE CARRIERS & RELATED	17352	38	116	PROF.; SCIENTIFIC; & TECH SVCS	17606	5	7	SPECIAL TRADE CONTRACTORS
17201	1474	19828	NURSING & RESID. CARE FACILIT.	17353	67	600	FOOD MANUFACTURING	17607	1	2	CONSTRUCTION OF BUILDINGS
17202	1044	9776	FOOD SVCS & DRINKING PLACES	17354	1	0	JUSTICE; PUBIC ORDER/SAFETY	17608	5	6	UTILITIES
17210	2	4	PUBLISHING INDUSTRIES	17355	9	18	ADMIN. OF ECONOMIC PROGRAMS	17701	2166	30717	HOSPITALS
17211	9	28	GENERAL MERCHANDISE STORES	17356	591	5239	FURNITURE & RELATED PROD. MFG	17702	343	2127	SPECIAL TRADE CONTRACTORS
17212	13	13	MERCH. WHOLESALERS;DURABLE GDS	17358	6	46	HEAVY & CIVIL ENG. CONSTRUCT'N	17703	2	31	AMBULATORY HEALTH CARE SVCS
17213	9	11	POSTAL SERVICE	17360	95	466	MERCH. WHOLESALERS;DURABLE GDS	17720	9	7	CONSTRUCTION OF BUILDINGS
17214	64	1147	PUBLISHING INDUSTRIES	17361	348	3056	DATA PROCESS'G	17721	58	942	TRANSIT & GRND PASS. TRANSPORT
17215	5	5	ACCOMMODATION	17362	280	2333	PAPER MANUFACTURING	17723	4	3	GASOLINE STATIONS
17217	36	112	PROF.; SCIENTIFIC; & TECH SVCS	17363	205	1052	FOOD AND BEVERAGE STORES	17724	224	1686	PLASTICS & RUBBER PRODUCTS MFG
17219	10	14	BROADCASTING	17364	96	855	TRUCK TRANSPORTATION	17726	6	10	RELIG.; GRANT; CIVIC; PROF ORG
17220	18	38	AMBULATORY HEALTH CARE SVCS	17365	86	580	PRIMARY METAL MANUFACTURING	17727	4	6	ACCOMMODATION
17221	25	191	CROP PRODUCTION	17366	82	278	SPECIAL TRADE CONTRACTORS	17728	115	529	JUSTICE; PUBIC ORDER/SAFETY
17222	203	1146	AMBULATORY HEALTH CARE SVCS	17368	211	1336	PRIMARY METAL MANUFACTURING	17729	10	16	MUSEUMS; HIST. SITES;& SIMILAR
17223	21	246	EXEC.; LEGIS.; & OTHER SUPPORT	17370	108	812	SPECIAL TRADE CONTRACTORS	17730	19	142	WASTE MANAGMT & REMEDIAT'N SVC
17224	70	314	WOOD PRODUCT MANUFACTURING	17371	20	89	JUSTICE; PUBIC ORDER/SAFETY	17731	35	117	AMUSEMENT; GAMBLING;& RECREAT.
17225	623	7086	NONMETALLIC MINERAL PROD. MFG	17372	119	521	EDUCATIONAL SERVICES	17735	5	5	RELIG.; GRANT; CIVIC; PROF ORG
17228	29	90	MACHINERY MANUFACTURING	17375	1	500	FOOD MANUFACTURING	17737	191	853	EDUCATIONAL SERVICES
17229	29	253	CONSTRUCTION OF BUILDINGS	17401	993	12714	PAPER MANUFACTURING	17738	2	11	SUPPORT ACTIVITIES: AGR./FOR.
17231	14	49	MERCH. WHOLESALERS;NONDUR. GDS	17402	1661	25974	FOOD SVCS & DRINKING PLACES	17739	7	3	MOTOR VEHICLE & PARTS DEALERS
17232	4	22	EDUCATIONAL SERVICES	17403	1519	26902	EDUCATIONAL SERVICES	17740	384	3083	EDUCATIONAL SERVICES
17233	308	4766	PROF.; SCIENTIFIC; & TECH SVCS	17404	1173	17386	FOOD SVCS & DRINKING PLACES	17742	8	77	EDUCATIONAL SERVICES
17235	32	104	SPECIAL TRADE CONTRACTORS	17405	9	97	UNCLASSIFIED ESTABLISHMENTS	17744	75	383	FOOD SVCS & DRINKING PLACES
17236	263	2874	ACCOMMODATION	17406	728	14940	MERCH. WHOLESALERS;DURABLE GDS	17745	684	4856	EXEC.; LEGIS.; & OTHER SUPPORT
17237	32	322	EDUCATIONAL SERVICES	17407	61	422	FURNITURE & RELATED PROD. MFG	17747	66	333	EDUCATIONAL SERVICES
17238	50	344	JUSTICE; PUBIC ORDER/SAFETY	17408	602	8185	MISCELLANEOUS MANUFACTURING	17748	28	3771	PAPER MANUFACTURING
17239	7	6	REPAIR AND MAINTENANCE	17501	190	1553	MERCH. WHOLESALERS;DURABLE GDS	17749	10	20	NURSING & RESID. CARE FACILIT.
17240	92	359	EXEC.; LEGIS.; & OTHER SUPPORT	17502	63	367	SPECIAL TRADE CONTRACTORS	17750	3	24	NONMETALLIC MINERAL PROD. MFG
17241	348	2073	EDUCATIONAL SERVICES	17503	5	8	FOOD SVCS & DRINKING PLACES	17751	275	3265	GENERAL MERCHANDISE STORES
17243	70	564	NURSING & RESID. CARE FACILIT.	17504	4	9	ADMINISTRATIVE & SUPPORT SVCS	17752	135	2227	FURNITURE & RELATED PROD. MFG
17244	59	192	SPECIAL TRADE CONTRACTORS	17505	129	1131	FOOD SVCS & DRINKING PLACES	17754	535	5804	NURSING & RESID. CARE FACILIT.
17246	8	22	JUSTICE; PUBIC ORDER/SAFETY	17506	43	630	MERCH. WHOLESALERS;DURABLE GDS	17756	526	7825	MACHINERY MANUFACTURING
17247	6	205	NURSING & RESID. CARE FACILIT.	17507	31	752	SPECIAL TRADE CONTRACTORS	17758	44	123	FOOD SVCS & DRINKING PLACES
17249	12	128	MERCH. WHOLESALERS;NONDUR. GDS	17508	56	530	SPECIAL TRADE CONTRACTORS	17760	16	167	FOOD SVCS & DRINKING PLACES
17250	6	9	FOOD SVCS & DRINKING PLACES	17509	126	737	NURSING & RESID. CARE FACILIT.	17762	18	125	JUSTICE; PUBIC ORDER/SAFETY
17251	7	12	BLDG MATL & GARDEN EQPMT DLRS	17512	501	5299	MERCH. WHOLESALERS;DURABLE GDS	17763	17	51	AMUSEMENT; GAMBLING;& RECREAT.
17252	101	645	TRUCK TRANSPORTATION	17516	103	1041	ANIMAL PRODUCTION	17764	121	770	HOSPITALS
17253	5	8	INSURANCE CARRIERS & RELATED	17517	464	7030	PROF.; SCIENTIFIC; & TECH SVCS	17765	22	41	FOOD SVCS & DRINKING PLACES
17254	20	302	EDUCATIONAL SERVICES	17518	19	59	PROF.; SCIENTIFIC; & TECH SVCS	17768	12	30	WOOD PRODUCT MANUFACTURING
17255	44	197	WOOD PRODUCT MANUFACTURING	17519	161	2809	WOOD PRODUCT MANUFACTURING	17769	4	20	ACCOMMODATION
17256	6	1283	MACHINERY MANUFACTURING	17520	198	2972	TRUCK TRANSPORTATION	17771	65	420	ADMINISTRATIVE & SUPPORT SVCS
17257	747	9728	MERCH. WHOLESALERS;DURABLE GDS	17521	6	26	PRINT'G & RELATED SUPP'T ACT'S	17772	77	590	EDUCATIONAL SERVICES
17260	30	115	RELIG.; GRANT; CIVIC; PROF ORG	17522	1471	17455	HOSPITALS	17773	2	3	SUPPORT ACTIVITIES: AGR./FOR.
17261	7	1215	SOCIAL ASSISTANCE	17527	262	1890	FOOD SVCS & DRINKING PLACES	17774	20	50	SPECIAL TRADE CONTRACTORS
17262	27	129	FOOD SVCS & DRINKING PLACES	17528	13	72	APPAREL MANUFACTURING	17776	12	23	MUSEUMS; HIST. SITES;& SIMILAR
17263	22	57	REAL ESTATE	17529	132	781	FOOD MANUFACTURING	17777	177	1078	NURSING & RESID. CARE FACILIT.
17264	54	228	EDUCATIONAL SERVICES	17532	80	266	TRANSIT & GRND PASS. TRANSPORT	17778	1	2	FOOD SVCS & DRINKING PLACES
17265	13	20	SPECIAL TRADE CONTRACTORS	17533	6	5	SPECIAL TRADE CONTRACTORS	17779	29	177	PROF.; SCIENTIFIC; & TECH SVCS
17266	22	87	SPECIAL TRADE CONTRACTORS	17534	110	825	FOOD MANUFACTURING	17801	732	7015	ADMIN. HUMAN RESOURCE PROGRAMS
17267	92	381	EDUCATIONAL SERVICES	17535	89	488	EDUCATIONAL SERVICES	17810	49	768	RELIG.; GRANT; CIVIC; PROF ORG
17268	922	7811	PROF.; SCIENTIFIC; & TECH SVCS	17536	56	233	TRUCK TRANSPORTATION	17812	85	408	MERCH. WHOLESALERS;DURABLE GDS

BUSINESS DATA

ZIP CODE	2009 Total Firms	2009 Total Employ-ees	TOP INDUSTRY RANKED on 2009 EMPLOYMENT
17813	65	822	MISCELLANEOUS STORE RETAILERS
17814	185	971	PRIMARY METAL MANUFACTURING
17815	1266	13882	PROF.; SCIENTIFIC; & TECH SVCS
17820	144	751	WOOD PRODUCT MANUFACTURING
17821	665	6565	HOSPITALS
17822	39	8322	HOSPITALS
17823	46	202	SUPPORT ACT. FOR TRANSPORT.
17824	141	2306	AMUSEMENT; GAMBLING;& RECREAT.
17827	29	119	FURNITURE & RELATED PROD. MFG
17829	14	41	SPECIAL TRADE CONTRACTORS
17830	104	464	EDUCATIONAL SERVICES
17831	31	283	FOOD SVCS & DRINKING PLACES
17832	10	45	MINING (EXCEPT OIL AND GAS)
17833	24	2559	FURN. & HOME FURNISHGS STORES
17834	105	304	NURSING & RESID. CARE FACILIT.
17835	18	40	FOOD AND BEVERAGE STORES
17836	3	16	SPECIAL TRADE CONTRACTORS
17837	976	12591	AMBULATORY HEALTH CARE SVCS
17839	1	13	GASOLINE STATIONS
17840	5	8	MERCH. WHOLESALERS;DURABLE GDS
17841	82	367	UNCLASSIFIED ESTABLISHMENTS
17842	290	2378	BLDG MATL & GARDEN EQPMT DLRS
17844	419	2652	BLDG MATL & GARDEN EQPMT DLRS
17845	57	338	JUSTICE; PUBIC ORDER/SAFETY
17846	135	741	EDUCATIONAL SERVICES
17847	408	6655	MERCH. WHOLESALERS;NONDUR. GDS
17850	34	287	MERCH. WHOLESALERS;DURABLE GDS
17851	282	1916	PAPER MANUFACTURING
17853	105	483	WOOD PRODUCT MANUFACTURING
17855	37	334	EDUCATIONAL SERVICES
17856	86	1891	MISCELLANEOUS MANUFACTURING
17857	277	3457	FOOD MANUFACTURING
17858	13	17	MERCH. WHOLESALERS;NONDUR. GDS
17859	101	511	NURSING & RESID. CARE FACILIT.
17860	66	1121	BLDG MATL & GARDEN EQPMT DLRS
17861	6	48	HEAVY & CIVIL ENG. CONSTRUCT'N
17862	15	135	APPAREL MANUFACTURING
17864	46	146	SPECIAL TRADE CONTRACTORS
17865	7	7	REPAIR AND MAINTENANCE
17866	213	3552	JUSTICE; PUBIC ORDER/SAFETY
17867	3	5	TRUCK TRANSPORTATION
17868	29	724	CHEMICAL MANUFACTURING
17870	673	7539	EXEC.; LEGIS.; & OTHER SUPPORT
17872	404	2132	HEALTH & PERSONAL CARE STORES
17876	104	1093	FOOD SVCS & DRINKING PLACES
17877	3	1	PERSONAL AND LAUNDRY SERVICES
17878	43	168	NURSING & RESID. CARE FACILIT.
17880	1	2	POSTAL SERVICE
17881	47	127	EDUCATIONAL SERVICES
17882	4	5	RELIG.; GRANT; CIVIC; PROF ORG
17883	11	25	SPORTG GDS;HOBBY;BOOK; & MUSIC
17884	16	58	MERCH. WHOLESALERS;NONDUR. GDS
17885	7	12	ACCOMMODATION
17886	15	159	CREDIT INTERMEDIATION & RELATD
17887	13	73	ADMINISTRATIVE & SUPPORT SVCS
17888	9	11	POSTAL SERVICE
17889	93	567	MINING (EXCEPT OIL AND GAS)
17901	1091	14650	JUSTICE; PUBIC ORDER/SAFETY
17920	7	6	MOTOR VEHICLE & PARTS DEALERS
17921	221	2676	PROF.; SCIENTIFIC; & TECH SVCS
17922	69	484	MERCH. WHOLESALERS;NONDUR. GDS
17923	10	35	TRUCK TRANSPORTATION
17925	7	7	RELIG.; GRANT; CIVIC; PROF ORG
17929	64	1684	PRIMARY METAL MANUFACTURING
17930	10	18	MERCH. WHOLESALERS;DURABLE GDS
17931	304	3078	JUSTICE; PUBIC ORDER/SAFETY
17932	1	558	JUSTICE; PUBIC ORDER/SAFETY
17933	22	184	MERCH. WHOLESALERS;DURABLE GDS
17934	8	44	MERCH. WHOLESALERS;DURABLE GDS
17935	40	171	RELIG.; GRANT; CIVIC; PROF ORG
17936	9	231	MISCELLANEOUS STORE RETAILERS
17938	92	741	FABRICATED METAL PRODUCT MFG
17941	31	496	MERCH. WHOLESALERS;NONDUR. GDS
17942	8	15	SPECIAL TRADE CONTRACTORS
17943	12	22	FOOD SVCS & DRINKING PLACES
17944	13	53	FOOD SVCS & DRINKING PLACES
17945	6	9	MISCELLANEOUS STORE RETAILERS
17946	5	17	EXEC.; LEGIS.; & OTHER SUPPORT
17948	158	803	EDUCATIONAL SERVICES
17949	10	37	MERCH. WHOLESALERS;NONDUR. GDS
17951	16	933	EDUCATIONAL SERVICES
17952	6	8	EXEC.; LEGIS.; & OTHER SUPPORT
17953	16	99	RELIG.; GRANT; CIVIC; PROF ORG
17954	171	1305	JUSTICE; PUBIC ORDER/SAFETY
17957	8	258	JUSTICE; PUBIC ORDER/SAFETY
17959	38	78	UTILITIES
17960	116	572	MERCH. WHOLESALERS;DURABLE GDS
17961	292	2637	NURSING & RESID. CARE FACILIT.
17963	272	2260	WOOD PRODUCT MANUFACTURING
17964	22	106	NURSING & RESID. CARE FACILIT.
17965	49	157	MERCH. WHOLESALERS;NONDUR. GDS
17966	2	4	NONSTORE RETAILERS
17967	67	497	BLDG MATL & GARDEN EQPMT DLRS
17968	14	161	MERCH. WHOLESALERS;NONDUR. GDS
17970	142	1757	GENERAL MERCHANDISE STORES
17972	443	4216	EDUCATIONAL SERVICES
17974	3	82	RELIG.; GRANT; CIVIC; PROF ORG
17976	230	1443	NURSING & RESID. CARE FACILIT.
17978	17	110	TRUCK TRANSPORTATION
17979	8	94	TRANSPORTATION EQUIPMENT MFG
17980	136	603	EDUCATIONAL SERVICES
17981	105	1499	WAREHOUSING AND STORAGE
17982	10	38	PROF.; SCIENTIFIC; & TECH SVCS
17983	92	399	RELIG.; GRANT; CIVIC; PROF ORG
17985	27	49	CONSTRUCTION OF BUILDINGS
18002	74	833	POSTAL SERVICE
18010	2	4	PROF.; SCIENTIFIC; & TECH SVCS
18011	87	529	PRIMARY METAL MANUFACTURING
18012	2	2	RELIG.; GRANT; CIVIC; PROF ORG
18013	579	3865	APPAREL MANUFACTURING
18014	432	3401	SPECIAL TRADE CONTRACTORS
18015	877	14519	HOSPITALS
18016	7	249	POSTAL SERVICE
18017	1355	24508	HOSPITALS
18018	1556	12582	EDUCATIONAL SERVICES
18020	687	8664	EDUCATIONAL SERVICES
18030	24	109	FOOD SVCS & DRINKING PLACES
18031	158	3605	TELECOMMUNICATIONS
18032	232	1240	EDUCATIONAL SERVICES
18034	244	5025	MISCELLANEOUS MANUFACTURING
18035	24	87	RELIG.; GRANT; CIVIC; PROF ORG
18036	387	2500	ELECT'L EQPMT; APP; & COMP MFG
18037	211	1011	SPECIAL TRADE CONTRACTORS
18038	61	213	MACHINERY MANUFACTURING
18039	12	27	PAPER MANUFACTURING
18040	373	6441	FABRICATED METAL PRODUCT MFG
18041	162	3890	FURNITURE & RELATED PROD. MFG
18042	1756	14089	HOSPITALS
18043	5	13	ADMINISTRATIVE & SUPPORT SVCS
18044	12	65	EDUCATIONAL SERVICES
18045	946	11100	FOOD SVCS & DRINKING PLACES
18046	12	94	FOOD SVCS & DRINKING PLACES
18049	779	5709	MOTOR VEHICLE & PARTS DEALERS
18051	113	1246	FOOD SVCS & DRINKING PLACES
18052	1163	12661	FOOD SVCS & DRINKING PLACES
18053	43	102	WOOD PRODUCT MANUFACTURING
18054	120	733	FABRICATED METAL PRODUCT MFG
18055	385	2045	EDUCATIONAL SERVICES
18056	29	175	EDUCATIONAL SERVICES
18058	123	588	RELIG.; GRANT; CIVIC; PROF ORG
18059	33	139	AMBULATORY HEALTH CARE SVCS
18060	8	119	NURSING & RESID. CARE FACILIT.
18062	417	5196	PROF.; SCIENTIFIC; & TECH SVCS
18063	38	177	TRUCK TRANSPORTATION
18064	786	8007	EXEC.; LEGIS.; & OTHER SUPPORT
18065	23	161	FOOD SVCS & DRINKING PLACES
18066	185	1079	EDUCATIONAL SERVICES
18067	541	3625	EDUCATIONAL SERVICES
18068	6	15	RELIG.; GRANT; CIVIC; PROF ORG
18069	208	1672	EDUCATIONAL SERVICES
18070	32	196	MERCH. WHOLESALERS;DURABLE GDS
18071	350	2787	HOSPITALS
18072	229	1709	WASTE MANAGMT & REMEDIAT'N SVC
18073	311	2334	MERCH. WHOLESALERS;DURABLE GDS
18074	104	407	MACHINERY MANUFACTURING
18076	92	646	FOOD AND BEVERAGE STORES
18077	68	159	JUSTICE; PUBIC ORDER/SAFETY
18078	216	1861	EDUCATIONAL SERVICES
18079	11	17	RELIG.; GRANT; CIVIC; PROF ORG
18080	284	1400	EDUCATIONAL SERVICES
18081	37	78	REAL ESTATE
18083	62	514	MERCH. WHOLESALERS;DURABLE GDS
18084	22	84	PROF.; SCIENTIFIC; & TECH SVCS
18085	30	468	FURNITURE & RELATED PROD. MFG
18086	5	24	FOOD MANUFACTURING
18087	134	1626	FOOD SVCS & DRINKING PLACES
18088	265	1575	FOOD SVCS & DRINKING PLACES
18091	321	1934	FOOD SVCS & DRINKING PLACES
18092	84	354	MERCH. WHOLESALERS;NONDUR. GDS
18098	2	0	PUBLISHING INDUSTRIES
18101	662	8609	UTILITIES
18102	1419	11651	AMBULATORY HEALTH CARE SVCS
18103	1657	28376	HOSPITALS
18104	1880	21324	EDUCATIONAL SERVICES
18105	14	76	SOCIAL ASSISTANCE
18106	680	11227	MERCH. WHOLESALERS;DURABLE GDS
18109	1117	17267	COMPUTER & ELECTRONIC PROD MFG
18195	60	5209	MISCELLANEOUS MANUFACTURING
18201	1276	10001	HOSPITALS
18202	741	15368	AMBULATORY HEALTH CARE SVCS
18210	107	470	EDUCATIONAL SERVICES
18211	37	136	MINING (EXCEPT OIL AND GAS)
18212	5	3	POSTAL SERVICE
18214	47	238	FURNITURE & RELATED PROD. MFG
18216	28	186	UNCLASSIFIED ESTABLISHMENTS
18218	58	575	HOSPITALS
18219	92	346	JUSTICE; PUBIC ORDER/SAFETY
18220	15	373	FURNITURE & RELATED PROD. MFG
18221	6	38	PERFORM'G ARTS; SPEC. SPORTS
18222	241	1658	EDUCATIONAL SERVICES
18223	3	63	NONSTORE RETAILERS
18224	161	899	FOOD MANUFACTURING
18225	12	34	FOOD AND BEVERAGE STORES
18229	400	2325	FOOD SVCS & DRINKING PLACES
18230	1	0	POSTAL SERVICE
18231	7	25	JUSTICE; PUBIC ORDER/SAFETY
18232	133	870	JUSTICE; PUBIC ORDER/SAFETY
18234	7	26	NONSTORE RETAILERS
18235	791	6863	HOSPITALS
18237	117	923	BEVERAGE & TOBACCO PRODUCT MFG
18239	5	17	SUPPORT ACTIVITIES: AGR./FOR.
18240	111	2703	MOTOR VEHICLE & PARTS DEALERS
18241	33	33	AMBULATORY HEALTH CARE SVCS
18242	3	2	GASOLINE STATIONS
18244	18	198	MOTOR VEHICLE & PARTS DEALERS
18245	8	6	REPAIR AND MAINTENANCE
18246	11	27	NURSING & RESID. CARE FACILIT.
18247	7	17	CONSTRUCTION OF BUILDINGS
18248	17	51	REAL ESTATE
18249	114	756	AMUSEMENT; GAMBLING;& RECREAT.
18250	65	197	RELIG.; GRANT; CIVIC; PROF ORG
18251	34	116	BLDG MATL & GARDEN EQPMT DLRS
18252	531	4002	EDUCATIONAL SERVICES
18254	16	36	FOOD SVCS & DRINKING PLACES
18255	125	1044	ACCOMMODATION
18256	9	21	MERCH. WHOLESALERS;NONDUR. GDS
18301	906	9490	AMBULATORY HEALTH CARE SVCS
18302	240	1589	ACCOMMODATION
18320	17	196	ACCOMMODATION
18321	98	1027	FOOD SVCS & DRINKING PLACES
18322	384	2867	FOOD AND BEVERAGE STORES
18323	10	58	FOOD SVCS & DRINKING PLACES
18324	120	3537	ACCOMMODATION
18325	91	352	ACCOMMODATION
18326	161	1005	MISCELLANEOUS MANUFACTURING
18327	56	444	COMPUTER & ELECTRONIC PROD MFG
18328	163	1241	EDUCATIONAL SERVICES
18330	131	497	NURSING & RESID. CARE FACILIT.
18331	82	295	FOOD MANUFACTURING
18332	48	158	ACCOMMODATION
18333	74	382	FOOD SVCS & DRINKING PLACES
18334	44	160	PERFORM'G ARTS; SPEC. SPORTS
18335	109	417	FOOD SVCS & DRINKING PLACES
18336	163	1468	FOOD AND BEVERAGE STORES
18337	608	4013	EXEC.; LEGIS.; & OTHER SUPPORT
18340	4	22	JUSTICE; PUBIC ORDER/SAFETY
18341	13	53	ADMINISTRATIVE & SUPPORT SVCS
18342	75	329	TRANSPORTATION EQUIPMENT MFG
18343	136	595	FABRICATED METAL PRODUCT MFG
18344	370	3238	GENERAL MERCHANDISE STORES
18346	105	594	TRUCK TRANSPORTATION
18347	153	391	PROF.; SCIENTIFIC; & TECH SVCS
18349	11	427	ACCOMMODATION
18350	99	743	AMUSEMENT; GAMBLING;& RECREAT.
18351	49	204	PLASTICS & RUBBER PRODUCTS MFG
18352	46	172	FOOD SVCS & DRINKING PLACES
18353	247	714	PROF.; SCIENTIFIC; & TECH SVCS
18354	82	277	EDUCATIONAL SERVICES
18355	55	906	ACCOMMODATION
18356	35	1549	ACCOMMODATION
18357	5	324	AMUSEMENT; GAMBLING;& RECREAT.
18360	1755	12788	FOOD SVCS & DRINKING PLACES
18370	56	2064	MISCELLANEOUS MANUFACTURING
18371	4	135	AMUSEMENT; GAMBLING;& RECREAT.
18372	404	4014	TRUCK TRANSPORTATION
18403	276	3194	EDUCATIONAL SERVICES
18405	68	522	ACCOMMODATION
18407	571	4908	HOSPITALS
18410	41	256	JUSTICE; PUBIC ORDER/SAFETY
18411	980	12440	PROF.; SCIENTIFIC; & TECH SVCS
18413	75	343	CONSTRUCTION OF BUILDINGS
18414	163	595	SPECIAL TRADE CONTRACTORS
18415	25	118	EDUCATIONAL SERVICES
18416	27	91	EDUCATIONAL SERVICES
18417	29	288	ACCOMMODATION
18419	121	1064	EDUCATIONAL SERVICES
18420	25	69	TRANSIT & GRND PASS. TRANSPORT
18421	174	1285	EDUCATIONAL SERVICES
18424	157	752	NURSING & RESID. CARE FACILIT.
18425	31	63	FOOD AND BEVERAGE STORES

ZIP CODE	2009 Total Firms	2009 Total Employ-ees	TOP INDUSTRY RANKED on 2009 EMPLOYMENT	ZIP CODE	2009 Total Firms	2009 Total Employ-ees	TOP INDUSTRY RANKED on 2009 EMPLOYMENT	ZIP CODE	2009 Total Firms	2009 Total Employ-ees	TOP INDUSTRY RANKED on 2009 EMPLOYMENT
18426	137	574	FOOD AND BEVERAGE STORES	18655	193	674	EDUCATIONAL SERVICES	18950	31	193	SPORTG GDS;HOBBY;BOOK; & MUSIC
18427	175	998	FOOD AND BEVERAGE STORES	18656	87	188	SPECIAL TRADE CONTRACTORS	18951	1622	14472	EDUCATIONAL SERVICES
18428	531	5364	ACCOMMODATION	18657	728	5157	FOOD SVCS & DRINKING PLACES	18953	27	50	SPECIAL TRADE CONTRACTORS
18430	1	0	RELIG.; GRANT; CIVIC; PROF ORG	18660	80	180	MOTOR VEHICLE & PARTS DEALERS	18954	384	2506	FOOD AND BEVERAGE STORES
18431	880	9196	HOSPITALS	18661	209	1692	EXEC.; LEGIS.; & OTHER SUPPORT	18955	54	433	CONSTRUCTION OF BUILDINGS
18433	209	1095	EDUCATIONAL SERVICES	18701	667	8117	TELECOMMUNICATIONS	18956	14	227	TRANSIT & GRND PASS. TRANSPORT
18434	140	1099	MERCH. WHOLESALERS;DURABLE GDS	18702	2218	29968	FOOD SVCS & DRINKING PLACES	18957	14	24	SPECIAL TRADE CONTRACTORS
18435	31	284	RELIG.; GRANT; CIVIC; PROF ORG	18703	9	126	RENTAL AND LEASING SERVICES	18958	8	28	MERCH. WHOLESALERS;DURABLE GDS
18436	386	1768	EDUCATIONAL SERVICES	18704	1732	14708	AMBULATORY HEALTH CARE SVCS	18960	393	5860	HOSPITALS
18437	17	229	ACCOMMODATION	18705	526	3735	EDUCATIONAL SERVICES	18962	40	184	MERCH. WHOLESALERS;DURABLE GDS
18438	50	612	ACCOMMODATION	18706	605	9458	MERCH. WHOLESALERS;DURABLE GDS	18963	53	133	EDUCATIONAL SERVICES
18439	31	496	ACCOMMODATION	18707	517	5177	MISCELLANEOUS STORE RETAILERS	18964	602	8207	FOOD MANUFACTURING
18440	23	172	EDUCATIONAL SERVICES	18708	305	2036	RELIG.; GRANT; CIVIC; PROF ORG	18966	1599	12795	PROF.; SCIENTIFIC; & TECH SVCS
18441	16	39	MOTOR VEHICLE & PARTS DEALERS	18709	216	1257	FOOD SVCS & DRINKING PLACES	18968	11	68	PROF.; SCIENTIFIC; & TECH SVCS
18443	6	6	POSTAL SERVICE	18711	92	10184	EXEC.; LEGIS.; & OTHER SUPPORT	18969	450	5615	MISCELLANEOUS MANUFACTURING
18444	377	2482	NURSING & RESID. CARE FACILIT.	18764	8	13920	HOSPITALS	18970	38	508	FABRICATED METAL PRODUCT MFG
18445	99	690	SOCIAL ASSISTANCE	18765	3	51	NURSING & RESID. CARE FACILIT.	18971	19	110	TRUCK TRANSPORTATION
18446	130	410	MINING (EXCEPT OIL AND GAS)	18766	3	510	EDUCATIONAL SERVICES	18972	99	207	TRANSIT & GRND PASS. TRANSPORT
18447	421	3655	PROF.; SCIENTIFIC; & TECH SVCS	18801	512	3048	JUSTICE; PUBIC ORDER/SAFETY	18974	1837	21303	PROF.; SCIENTIFIC; & TECH SVCS
18448	1	1700	COMPUTER & ELECTRONIC PROD MFG	18810	172	1183	FABRICATED METAL PRODUCT MFG	18976	736	8671	FOOD SVCS & DRINKING PLACES
18449	2	1	PROF.; SCIENTIFIC; & TECH SVCS	18812	31	70	SPECIAL TRADE CONTRACTORS	18977	163	708	PROF.; SCIENTIFIC; & TECH SVCS
18451	40	129	BLDG MATL & GARDEN EQPMT DLRS	18813	9	44	ACCOMMODATION	18979	7	8	FOOD AND BEVERAGE STORES
18452	183	1274	HOSPITALS	18814	10	117	WASTE MANAGMT & REMEDIAT'N SVC	18980	47	65	CONSTRUCTION OF BUILDINGS
18453	34	38	ADMIN. ENVIRO. QUALITY PROGRMS	18815	9	68	ACCOMMODATION	18981	5	30	MERCH. WHOLESALERS;DURABLE GDS
18454	8	74	ACCOMMODATION	18816	16	247	EDUCATIONAL SERVICES	19001	740	10541	HOSPITALS
18455	11	163	ACCOMMODATION	18817	30	162	EDUCATIONAL SERVICES	19002	1228	9187	EDUCATIONAL SERVICES
18456	13	23	CONSTRUCTION OF BUILDINGS	18818	41	171	EDUCATIONAL SERVICES	19003	1116	8551	HOSPITALS
18457	32	71	ACCOMMODATION	18820	6	39	JUSTICE; PUBIC ORDER/SAFETY	19004	1316	16173	CREDIT INTERMEDIATION & RELATD
18458	79	310	EDUCATIONAL SERVICES	18821	72	225	FABRICATED METAL PRODUCT MFG	19006	1306	12470	HOSPITALS
18459	19	254	MISCELLANEOUS MANUFACTURING	18822	133	650	FOOD SVCS & DRINKING PLACES	19007	1261	18476	MERCH. WHOLESALERS;NONDUR. GDS
18460	16	107	ACCOMMODATION	18823	23	106	FOOD SVCS & DRINKING PLACES	19008	895	9055	AMBULATORY HEALTH CARE SVCS
18461	20	368	ACCOMMODATION	18824	44	73	MINING (EXCEPT OIL AND GAS)	19009	41	419	EDUCATIONAL SERVICES
18462	9	15	CROP PRODUCTION	18825	25	18	REPAIR AND MAINTENANCE	19010	1110	12316	HOSPITALS
18463	30	125	AMBULATORY HEALTH CARE SVCS	18826	75	701	EDUCATIONAL SERVICES	19012	231	3204	HOSPITALS
18464	45	184	SPECIAL TRADE CONTRACTORS	18827	8	31	COMPUTER & ELECTRONIC PROD MFG	19013	1061	15187	HOSPITALS
18465	39	195	ACCOMMODATION	18828	19	41	GASOLINE STATIONS	19014	799	8996	MERCH. WHOLESALERS;DURABLE GDS
18466	233	11766	RELIG.; GRANT; CIVIC; PROF ORG	18829	26	50	FOOD AND BEVERAGE STORES	19015	376	2916	FOOD AND BEVERAGE STORES
18469	13	1030	ACCOMMODATION	18830	31	85	FOOD SVCS & DRINKING PLACES	19016	1	0	SPECIAL TRADE CONTRACTORS
18470	89	209	ACCOMMODATION	18831	25	137	SPECIAL TRADE CONTRACTORS	19017	95	181	JUSTICE; PUBIC ORDER/SAFETY
18471	45	275	SOCIAL ASSISTANCE	18832	66	222	TRUCK TRANSPORTATION	19018	585	4764	FOOD AND BEVERAGE STORES
18472	138	1722	JUSTICE; PUBIC ORDER/SAFETY	18833	56	138	MERCH. WHOLESALERS;NONDUR. GDS	19020	2431	30617	MERCH. WHOLESALERS;DURABLE GDS
18473	21	121	APPAREL MANUFACTURING	18834	166	886	FOOD SVCS & DRINKING PLACES	19021	263	2797	PROF.; SCIENTIFIC; & TECH SVCS
18501	6	14	SPECIAL TRADE CONTRACTORS	18837	122	319	EDUCATIONAL SERVICES	19022	188	2583	GENERAL MERCHANDISE STORES
18503	1038	14333	BROADCASTING	18840	467	11930	AMBULATORY HEALTH CARE SVCS	19023	585	4605	HOSPITALS
18504	630	4099	EDUCATIONAL SERVICES	18842	13	28	ACCOMMODATION	19025	210	2361	SECURITIES/COMMODITY CONTRACTS
18505	703	7966	RELIG.; GRANT; CIVIC; PROF ORG	18843	29	91	REPAIR AND MAINTENANCE	19026	758	6617	HOSPITALS
18507	385	5709	ACCOMMODATION	18844	44	98	MERCH. WHOLESALERS;DURABLE GDS	19027	709	4842	SOCIAL ASSISTANCE
18508	714	10003	HOSPITALS	18845	9	20	FOOD SVCS & DRINKING PLACES	19028	64	369	SPECIAL TRADE CONTRACTORS
18509	637	6681	EDUCATIONAL SERVICES	18846	12	17	FORESTRY AND LOGGING	19029	275	2733	ACCOMMODATION
18510	409	9927	HOSPITALS	18847	178	873	EDUCATIONAL SERVICES	19030	632	13017	FOOD AND BEVERAGE STORES
18512	713	9718	EDUCATIONAL SERVICES	18848	535	6987	MERCH. WHOLESALERS;NONDUR. GDS	19031	293	2376	FOOD AND BEVERAGE STORES
18515	4	601	PROF.; SCIENTIFIC; & TECH SVCS	18850	60	298	EDUCATIONAL SERVICES	19032	325	2955	EDUCATIONAL SERVICES
18517	214	3237	TRUCK TRANSPORTATION	18851	19	17	FOOD AND BEVERAGE STORES	19033	355	2856	FOOD AND BEVERAGE STORES
18518	329	2846	APPAREL MANUFACTURING	18853	177	2002	FOOD MANUFACTURING	19034	685	11611	PROF.; SCIENTIFIC; & TECH SVCS
18519	335	4112	GENERAL MERCHANDISE STORES	18854	121	573	AMBULATORY HEALTH CARE SVCS	19035	112	1010	AMUSEMENT; GAMBLING;& RECREAT.
18601	3	7	FABRICATED METAL PRODUCT MFG	18901	2053	22548	EXEC.; LEGIS.; & OTHER SUPPORT	19036	318	2160	ADMINISTRATIVE & SUPPORT SVCS
18602	22	78	INSURANCE CARRIERS & RELATED	18902	573	5940	MOTOR VEHICLE & PARTS DEALERS	19037	6	108	FABRICATED METAL PRODUCT MFG
18603	718	6306	HOSPITALS	18910	35	54	ADMINISTRATIVE & SUPPORT SVCS	19038	1198	9546	EDUCATIONAL SERVICES
18610	192	1077	REAL ESTATE	18911	10	23	REPAIR AND MAINTENANCE	19039	19	77	REAL ESTATE
18611	4	6	FOOD SVCS & DRINKING PLACES	18912	192	1153	NURSING & RESID. CARE FACILIT.	19040	865	6274	INSURANCE CARRIERS & RELATED
18612	676	8105	PRINT'G & RELATED SUPP'T ACT'S	18913	21	43	FOOD AND BEVERAGE STORES	19041	352	2665	EDUCATIONAL SERVICES
18614	176	581	MACHINERY MANUFACTURING	18914	622	5184	PRINT'G & RELATED SUPP'T ACT'S	19043	169	5840	RENTAL AND LEASING SERVICES
18615	65	138	AMUSEMENT; GAMBLING;& RECREAT.	18915	219	3202	MOTOR VEHICLE & PARTS DEALERS	19044	1038	33823	TELECOMMUNICATIONS
18616	48	268	NURSING & RESID. CARE FACILIT.	18916	10	426	MERCH. WHOLESALERS;DURABLE GDS	19046	1298	13027	HOSPITALS
18617	26	41	GASOLINE STATIONS	18917	146	593	FOOD SVCS & DRINKING PLACES	19047	1908	25381	MOTOR VEHICLE & PARTS DEALERS
18618	125	419	FOOD SVCS & DRINKING PLACES	18918	4	17	AMUSEMENT; GAMBLING;& RECREAT.	19050	818	4604	EDUCATIONAL SERVICES
18619	10	95	ACCOMMODATION	18920	39	98	MERCH. WHOLESALERS;DURABLE GDS	19052	8	311	JUSTICE; PUBIC ORDER/SAFETY
18621	155	664	SPECIAL TRADE CONTRACTORS	18921	17	28	BLDG MATL & GARDEN EQPMT DLRS	19053	1759	16504	PROF.; SCIENTIFIC; & TECH SVCS
18622	18	12	AMBULATORY HEALTH CARE SVCS	18922	10	22	REPAIR AND MAINTENANCE	19054	303	1873	EDUCATIONAL SERVICES
18623	79	306	BLDG MATL & GARDEN EQPMT DLRS	18923	45	202	CLOTHING & CLOTH'G ACC. STORES	19055	176	1377	EDUCATIONAL SERVICES
18624	35	647	ACCOMMODATION	18924	32	463	MOTOR VEHICLE & PARTS DEALERS	19056	418	3637	ADMINISTRATIVE & SUPPORT SVCS
18625	45	388	PROF.; SCIENTIFIC; & TECH SVCS	18925	123	633	EDUCATIONAL SERVICES	19057	777	5919	PUBLISHING INDUSTRIES
18626	54	396	NURSING & RESID. CARE FACILIT.	18927	84	155	EDUCATIONAL SERVICES	19058	7	74	ADMINISTRATIVE & SUPPORT SVCS
18627	27	288	EDUCATIONAL SERVICES	18928	21	167	ADMINISTRATIVE & SUPPORT SVCS	19061	814	7006	PLASTICS & RUBBER PRODUCTS MFG
18628	8	130	EDUCATIONAL SERVICES	18929	293	1775	EDUCATIONAL SERVICES	19063	2324	24940	SOCIAL ASSISTANCE
18629	63	3568	MERCH. WHOLESALERS;NONDUR. GDS	18930	80	381	EDUCATIONAL SERVICES	19064	1121	11624	EDUCATIONAL SERVICES
18630	88	634	TRUCK TRANSPORTATION	18931	144	1739	FOOD SVCS & DRINKING PLACES	19065	1	1	RAIL TRANSPORTATION
18631	37	274	MISCELLANEOUS MANUFACTURING	18932	42	266	FOOD SVCS & DRINKING PLACES	19066	99	947	EDUCATIONAL SERVICES
18632	18	82	EDUCATIONAL SERVICES	18933	10	43	FOOD SVCS & DRINKING PLACES	19067	1895	15075	PROF.; SCIENTIFIC; & TECH SVCS
18634	438	3161	EDUCATIONAL SERVICES	18934	19	74	PROF.; SCIENTIFIC; & TECH SVCS	19070	213	1573	EDUCATIONAL SERVICES
18635	103	508	TRUCK TRANSPORTATION	18935	10	16	PROF.; SCIENTIFIC; & TECH SVCS	19072	492	2426	PROF.; SCIENTIFIC; & TECH SVCS
18636	45	71	AMBULATORY HEALTH CARE SVCS	18936	375	6119	MISCELLANEOUS STORE RETAILERS	19073	1008	10606	PROF.; SCIENTIFIC; & TECH SVCS
18640	940	10598	TRUCK TRANSPORTATION	18938	709	3606	FOOD SVCS & DRINKING PLACES	19074	127	580	EDUCATIONAL SERVICES
18641	241	1551	FOOD SVCS & DRINKING PLACES	18940	1485	15026	EDUCATIONAL SERVICES	19075	213	2258	CONSTRUCTION OF BUILDINGS
18642	127	1038	BLDG MATL & GARDEN EQPMT DLRS	18942	199	1005	MERCH. WHOLESALERS;DURABLE GDS	19076	212	1489	EDUCATIONAL SERVICES
18643	503	4231	MOTOR VEHICLE & PARTS DEALERS	18943	9	66	HEAVY & CIVIL ENG. CONSTRUCT'N	19078	312	2487	HOSPITALS
18644	397	2062	FABRICATED METAL PRODUCT MFG	18944	693	4825	EDUCATIONAL SERVICES	19079	325	3111	EDUCATIONAL SERVICES
18651	304	1429	EDUCATIONAL SERVICES	18946	19	111	CROP PRODUCTION	19081	278	2073	EDUCATIONAL SERVICES
18653	2	50	EDUCATIONAL SERVICES	18947	279	1897	SPECIAL TRADE CONTRACTORS	19082	1363	8461	FOOD AND BEVERAGE STORES
18654	3	2	POSTAL SERVICE	18949	116	1149	MISCELLANEOUS MANUFACTURING	19083	1189	6399	AMBULATORY HEALTH CARE SVCS

BUSINESS DATA

ZIP CODE	2009 Total Firms	2009 Total Employees	TOP INDUSTRY RANKED on 2009 EMPLOYMENT
19085	167	9225	SECURITIES/COMMODITY CONTRACTS
19086	182	1161	EDUCATIONAL SERVICES
19087	2367	27359	PROF.; SCIENTIFIC; & TECH SVCS
19088	1	900	PUBLISHING INDUSTRIES
19090	1290	19922	NAT'L SECURITY & INT'L AFFAIRS
19094	128	823	FOOD SVCS & DRINKING PLACES
19095	211	2579	EDUCATIONAL SERVICES
19096	445	4227	EDUCATIONAL SERVICES
19101	7	29	CONSTRUCTION OF BUILDINGS
19102	2060	37014	PROF.; SCIENTIFIC; & TECH SVCS
19103	3776	94957	PROF.; SCIENTIFIC; & TECH SVCS
19104	1604	54406	HOSPITALS
19105	8	14	NONSTORE RETAILERS
19106	2241	41686	INSURANCE CARRIERS & RELATED
19107	2495	52463	EXEC.; LEGIS.; & OTHER SUPPORT
19108	54	446	DATA PROCESS'G
19109	73	1214	PROF.; SCIENTIFIC; & TECH SVCS
19110	101	1402	JUSTICE; PUBIC ORDER/SAFETY
19111	1096	12053	HOSPITALS
19112	72	4051	CLOTHING & CLOTH'G ACC. STORES
19113	79	5106	AMBULATORY HEALTH CARE SVCS
19114	720	17030	AMBULATORY HEALTH CARE SVCS
19115	964	10960	AMBULATORY HEALTH CARE SVCS
19116	798	9598	FOOD MANUFACTURING
19118	622	5733	HOSPITALS
19119	533	4450	NURSING & RESID. CARE FACILIT.
19120	1218	6712	EDUCATIONAL SERVICES
19121	698	4191	EDUCATIONAL SERVICES
19122	522	6537	SOCIAL ASSISTANCE
19123	981	12740	ADMINISTRATIVE & SUPPORT SVCS
19124	1702	20002	TRANSPORTATION EQUIPMENT MFG
19125	698	6034	HOSPITALS
19126	261	1859	NURSING & RESID. CARE FACILIT.
19127	366	3072	FOOD SVCS & DRINKING PLACES
19128	832	7764	HOSPITALS
19129	241	5339	HOSPITALS
19130	883	22914	PUBLISHING INDUSTRIES
19131	948	11745	EDUCATIONAL SERVICES
19132	882	7559	MOTOR VEHICLE & PARTS DEALERS
19133	707	4214	SOCIAL ASSISTANCE
19134	1543	17790	HOSPITALS
19135	899	5898	FOOD AND BEVERAGE STORES
19136	972	9051	MERCH. WHOLESALERS;DURABLE GDS
19137	359	3990	TRANSIT & GRND PASS. TRANSPORT
19138	532	2206	EDUCATIONAL SERVICES
19139	995	5765	EDUCATIONAL SERVICES
19140	1368	20451	AMBULATORY HEALTH CARE SVCS
19141	703	7494	EDUCATIONAL SERVICES
19142	568	2801	EDUCATIONAL SERVICES
19143	960	6701	HOSPITALS
19144	1250	11791	EDUCATIONAL SERVICES
19145	1061	12170	EXEC.; LEGIS.; & OTHER SUPPORT
19146	964	6481	EDUCATIONAL SERVICES
19147	1671	9471	FOOD SVCS & DRINKING PLACES
19148	1513	21311	RELIG.; GRANT; CIVIC; PROF ORG
19149	931	6162	FOOD AND BEVERAGE STORES
19150	437	2702	FOOD AND BEVERAGE STORES
19151	574	3255	EDUCATIONAL SERVICES
19152	684	7260	HOSPITALS
19153	568	30992	SUPPORT ACT. FOR TRANSPORT.
19154	805	19459	MERCH. WHOLESALERS;NONDUR. GDS
19160	1	0	RELIG.; GRANT; CIVIC; PROF ORG
19176	1	0	FOOD SVCS & DRINKING PLACES
19181	1	300	INSURANCE CARRIERS & RELATED
19192	6	8800	INSURANCE CARRIERS & RELATED
19255	1	0	EXEC.; LEGIS.; & OTHER SUPPORT
19301	849	7012	HOSPITALS
19310	92	1422	EDUCATIONAL SERVICES
19311	276	3115	CROP PRODUCTION
19312	683	10476	PROF.; SCIENTIFIC; & TECH SVCS
19316	14	40	SPECIAL TRADE CONTRACTORS
19317	601	4941	MERCH. WHOLESALERS;NONDUR. GDS
19318	11	104	NURSING & RESID. CARE FACILIT.
19319	14	335	EDUCATIONAL SERVICES
19320	1097	11574	HOSPITALS
19330	136	413	TRANSIT & GRND PASS. TRANSPORT
19331	87	2401	MISCELLANEOUS MANUFACTURING
19333	255	3665	REAL ESTATE
19335	1340	11519	EDUCATIONAL SERVICES
19339	2	1004	INSURANCE CARRIERS & RELATED
19341	1765	27976	PROF.; SCIENTIFIC; & TECH SVCS
19342	591	7213	EDUCATIONAL SERVICES
19343	255	2077	TRANSIT & GRND PASS. TRANSPORT
19344	323	2974	NURSING & RESID. CARE FACILIT.
19345	7	934	EDUCATIONAL SERVICES
19346	6	41	PLASTICS & RUBBER PRODUCTS MFG
19347	28	70	FOOD SVCS & DRINKING PLACES
19348	1078	12633	NURSING & RESID. CARE FACILIT.
19350	188	1229	CROP PRODUCTION
19351	9	25	BLDG MATL & GARDEN EQPMT DLRS
19352	78	236	WHOLESALE ELEC. MRKTS & AGENTS
19353	12	26	PROF.; SCIENTIFIC; & TECH SVCS
19354	5	6	POSTAL SERVICE
19355	1768	40787	PROF.; SCIENTIFIC; & TECH SVCS
19357	20	65	ACCOMMODATION
19358	6	46	PAPER MANUFACTURING
19360	25	117	SUPPORT ACT. FOR TRANSPORT.
19362	119	1533	FOOD MANUFACTURING
19363	528	3856	EDUCATIONAL SERVICES
19365	276	1857	GENERAL MERCHANDISE STORES
19366	2	3	POSTAL SERVICE
19367	11	38	MERCH. WHOLESALERS;NONDUR. GDS
19369	32	300	FOOD SVCS & DRINKING PLACES
19371	2	2	POSTAL SERVICE
19372	153	1557	GENERAL MERCHANDISE STORES
19373	41	628	JUSTICE; PUBIC ORDER/SAFETY
19374	81	2047	CROP PRODUCTION
19375	36	94	REAL ESTATE
19376	23	102	FABRICATED METAL PRODUCT MFG
19380	2036	27089	PROF.; SCIENTIFIC; & TECH SVCS
19381	9	99	PROF.; SCIENTIFIC; & TECH SVCS
19382	1957	18883	FOOD SVCS & DRINKING PLACES
19383	5	71	OTHER INFORMATION SERVICES
19390	380	4043	EDUCATIONAL SERVICES
19395	42	327	EDUCATIONAL SERVICES
19399	11	1113	POSTAL SERVICE
19401	2059	23830	HOSPITALS
19403	1549	16399	EDUCATIONAL SERVICES
19404	12	410	JUSTICE; PUBIC ORDER/SAFETY
19405	284	1706	WASTE MANAGMT & REMEDIAT'N SVC
19406	2533	51780	COMPUTER & ELECTRONIC PROD MFG
19407	9	303	EDUCATIONAL SERVICES
19408	5	7	REPAIR AND MAINTENANCE
19409	14	37	CONSTRUCTION OF BUILDINGS
19421	11	22	PROF.; SCIENTIFIC; & TECH SVCS
19422	1102	14188	PROF.; SCIENTIFIC; & TECH SVCS
19423	16	44	REPAIR AND MAINTENANCE
19424	2	7	CREDIT INTERMEDIATION & RELATD
19425	413	2689	SPECIAL TRADE CONTRACTORS
19426	1061	14567	CHEMICAL MANUFACTURING
19428	1739	31264	PROF.; SCIENTIFIC; & TECH SVCS
19430	11	29	CONSTRUCTION OF BUILDINGS
19432	18	602	EDUCATIONAL SERVICES
19435	31	476	NURSING & RESID. CARE FACILIT.
19436	28	931	NURSING & RESID. CARE FACILIT.
19437	25	45	PROF.; SCIENTIFIC; & TECH SVCS
19438	627	11274	INSURANCE CARRIERS & RELATED
19440	586	11362	FOOD MANUFACTURING
19442	57	786	PROF.; SCIENTIFIC; & TECH SVCS
19443	44	631	MISCELLANEOUS MANUFACTURING
19444	328	3108	PROF.; SCIENTIFIC; & TECH SVCS
19446	1771	19520	NURSING & RESID. CARE FACILIT.
19450	28	160	FOOD SVCS & DRINKING PLACES
19451	9	256	FOOD SVCS & DRINKING PLACES
19453	28	189	PROF.; SCIENTIFIC; & TECH SVCS
19454	1050	12022	FOOD SVCS & DRINKING PLACES
19456	140	3262	SECURITIES/COMMODITY CONTRACTS
19457	27	334	SPORTG GDS;HOBBY;BOOK; & MUSIC
19460	1519	11805	HOSPITALS
19462	1073	14642	PROF.; SCIENTIFIC; & TECH SVCS
19464	2033	18650	EDUCATIONAL SERVICES
19465	566	4264	EDUCATIONAL SERVICES
19468	920	12830	HEAVY & CIVIL ENG. CONSTRUCT'N
19470	17	52	FOOD SVCS & DRINKING PLACES
19472	22	40	BLDG MATL & GARDEN EQPMT DLRS
19473	323	2780	EDUCATIONAL SERVICES
19474	288	2929	SPECIAL TRADE CONTRACTORS
19475	314	2022	NAT'L SECURITY & INT'L AFFAIRS
19477	136	3711	PROF.; SCIENTIFIC; & TECH SVCS
19478	10	192	ACCOMMODATION
19480	118	529	SPECIAL TRADE CONTRACTORS
19481	13	114	JUSTICE; PUBIC ORDER/SAFETY
19482	5	29	HEAVY & CIVIL ENG. CONSTRUCT'N
19484	2	0	PAPER MANUFACTURING
19486	21	948	CHEMICAL MANUFACTURING
19490	102	1279	NURSING & RESID. CARE FACILIT.
19492	42	370	EDUCATIONAL SERVICES
19501	77	940	APPAREL MANUFACTURING
19503	77	666	MERCH. WHOLESALERS;DURABLE GDS
19504	128	436	EDUCATIONAL SERVICES
19505	144	1136	GENERAL MERCHANDISE STORES
19506	210	1099	EDUCATIONAL SERVICES
19507	150	899	NONMETALLIC MINERAL PROD. MFG
19508	487	3304	EDUCATIONAL SERVICES
19510	165	1769	PROF.; SCIENTIFIC; & TECH SVCS
19511	16	42	BLDG MATL & GARDEN EQPMT DLRS
19512	708	5766	EDUCATIONAL SERVICES
19516	13	48	PROF.; SCIENTIFIC; & TECH SVCS
19518	413	3186	PROF.; SCIENTIFIC; & TECH SVCS
19519	4	5	REPAIR AND MAINTENANCE
19520	256	2535	GENERAL MERCHANDISE STORES
19522	508	3497	EDUCATIONAL SERVICES
19523	8	127	EDUCATIONAL SERVICES
19525	414	3076	FOOD SVCS & DRINKING PLACES
19526	457	5933	PROF.; SCIENTIFIC; & TECH SVCS
19529	94	363	EDUCATIONAL SERVICES
19530	552	6500	EDUCATIONAL SERVICES
19533	362	5192	FURNITURE & RELATED PROD. MFG
19534	70	478	CROP PRODUCTION
19535	7	28	CONSTRUCTION OF BUILDINGS
19536	18	31	RELIG.; GRANT; CIVIC; PROF ORG
19538	25	41	RELIG.; GRANT; CIVIC; PROF ORG
19539	104	490	FOOD AND BEVERAGE STORES
19540	319	1978	MERCH. WHOLESALERS;DURABLE GDS
19541	50	142	SPECIAL TRADE CONTRACTORS
19542	9	7	SPECIAL TRADE CONTRACTORS
19543	336	3689	TRANSPORTATION EQUIPMENT MFG
19544	16	93	MERCH. WHOLESALERS;DURABLE GDS
19545	30	127	FOOD SVCS & DRINKING PLACES
19547	217	1462	EDUCATIONAL SERVICES
19548	12	80	FABRICATED METAL PRODUCT MFG
19549	12	136	RAIL TRANSPORTATION
19550	22	190	SOCIAL ASSISTANCE
19551	191	2792	FOOD AND BEVERAGE STORES
19554	39	296	MERCH. WHOLESALERS;NONDUR. GDS
19555	150	1458	PRIMARY METAL MANUFACTURING
19559	22	190	PRIMARY METAL MANUFACTURING
19560	310	3685	GENERAL MERCHANDISE STORES
19562	98	1648	NURSING & RESID. CARE FACILIT.
19564	13	78	FOOD SVCS & DRINKING PLACES
19565	185	3040	RELIG.; GRANT; CIVIC; PROF ORG
19567	165	1446	LEATHER & ALLIED PRODUCT MFG
19601	1544	18486	PROF.; SCIENTIFIC; & TECH SVCS
19602	539	5709	EDUCATIONAL SERVICES
19603	4	4	MOTION PICT. & SOUND RECORDING
19604	392	6074	HOSPITALS
19605	1229	17989	MISCELLANEOUS MANUFACTURING
19606	906	9540	GENERAL MERCHANDISE STORES
19607	834	11570	RENTAL AND LEASING SERVICES
19608	648	7025	MISCELLANEOUS MANUFACTURING
19609	333	3115	EDUCATIONAL SERVICES
19610	1363	23516	AMBULATORY HEALTH CARE SVCS
19611	609	17338	AMBULATORY HEALTH CARE SVCS
19612	15	420	POSTAL SERVICE
19701	915	7405	FOOD SVCS & DRINKING PLACES
19702	1318	19987	ADMIN. HUMAN RESOURCE PROGRAMS
19703	485	4015	PRIMARY METAL MANUFACTURING
19706	125	1328	PETROLEUM & COAL PRODUCTS MFG
19707	605	4790	REAL ESTATE
19708	4	13	PROF.; SCIENTIFIC; & TECH SVCS
19709	1018	7393	FOOD SVCS & DRINKING PLACES
19710	13	67	ACCOMMODATION
19711	1818	16060	FOOD SVCS & DRINKING PLACES
19712	1	550	HEALTH & PERSONAL CARE STORES
19713	1172	15982	AMBULATORY HEALTH CARE SVCS
19714	17	63	CONSTRUCTION OF BUILDINGS
19715	6	8	PUBLISHING INDUSTRIES
19716	32	497	PERFORM'G ARTS; SPEC. SPORTS
19717	2	20	AMBULATORY HEALTH CARE SVCS
19718	30	7884	HOSPITALS
19720	2267	35857	ADMIN. HUMAN RESOURCE PROGRAMS
19730	44	331	EDUCATIONAL SERVICES
19731	14	41	JUSTICE; PUBIC ORDER/SAFETY
19732	6	39	SECURITIES/COMMODITY CONTRACTS
19733	15	75	MOTOR VEHICLE & PARTS DEALERS
19734	188	1632	CONSTRUCTION OF BUILDINGS
19735	4	501	MUSEUMS; HIST. SITES;& SIMILAR
19736	24	114	PAPER MANUFACTURING
19801	3311	35931	PROF.; SCIENTIFIC; & TECH SVCS
19802	820	6918	EDUCATIONAL SERVICES
19803	1488	19751	PROF.; SCIENTIFIC; & TECH SVCS
19804	1017	15991	PERFORM'G ARTS; SPEC. SPORTS
19805	1277	16633	HOSPITALS
19806	584	5757	INSURANCE CARRIERS & RELATED
19807	392	4200	EDUCATIONAL SERVICES
19808	1524	15627	FOOD SVCS & DRINKING PLACES
19809	650	7873	SECURITIES/COMMODITY CONTRACTS
19810	998	6078	EDUCATIONAL SERVICES
19850	3	20	WASTE MANAGMT & REMEDIAT'N SVC
19880	3	3	CHEMICAL MANUFACTURING
19884	4	15	CREDIT INTERMEDIATION & RELATD
19890	1	3	SECURITIES/COMMODITY CONTRACTS
19897	1	0	CHEMICAL MANUFACTURING
19898	15	1368	CHEMICAL MANUFACTURING
19899	9	12	REAL ESTATE
19901	1828	30336	EXEC.; LEGIS.; & OTHER SUPPORT
19902	39	7596	EXEC.; LEGIS.; & OTHER SUPPORT
19903	9	69	ADMIN. OF ECONOMIC PROGRAMS
19904	1197	13462	EDUCATIONAL SERVICES
19930	247	1843	FOOD SVCS & DRINKING PLACES

ZIP CODE	2009 Total Firms	2009 Total Employees	TOP INDUSTRY RANKED on 2009 EMPLOYMENT
19931	12	27	SPECIAL TRADE CONTRACTORS
19933	257	2214	EDUCATIONAL SERVICES
19934	377	3906	EDUCATIONAL SERVICES
19936	25	153	NONSTORE RETAILERS
19938	124	1598	MISCELLANEOUS MANUFACTURING
19939	198	905	BLDG MATL & GARDEN EQPMT DLRS
19940	248	1627	FURN. & HOME FURNISHGS STORES
19941	44	107	RELIG.; GRANT; CIVIC; PROF ORG
19943	221	1222	EDUCATIONAL SERVICES
19944	121	1052	FOOD SVCS & DRINKING PLACES
19945	182	766	SPECIAL TRADE CONTRACTORS
19946	73	584	MERCH. WHOLESALERS;DURABLE GDS
19947	968	10767	EXEC.; LEGIS.; & OTHER SUPPORT
19950	208	1519	CONSTRUCTION OF BUILDINGS
19951	76	1068	FOOD MANUFACTURING
19952	290	2753	AMUSEMENT; GAMBLING;& RECREAT.
19953	92	353	SPECIAL TRADE CONTRACTORS
19954	32	121	JUSTICE; PUBIC ORDER/SAFETY
19955	15	170	FABRICATED METAL PRODUCT MFG
19956	547	2803	EDUCATIONAL SERVICES
19958	1118	8415	AMBULATORY HEALTH CARE SVCS
19960	101	478	SPECIAL TRADE CONTRACTORS
19961	8	74	JUSTICE; PUBIC ORDER/SAFETY
19962	84	228	EDUCATIONAL SERVICES
19963	917	11222	HOSPITALS
19964	25	87	BLDG MATL & GARDEN EQPMT DLRS
19966	744	8435	WHOLESALE ELEC. MRKTS & AGENTS
19967	98	649	FOOD AND BEVERAGE STORES
19968	345	1594	ADMINISTRATIVE & SUPPORT SVCS
19969	7	28	MERCH. WHOLESALERS;DURABLE GDS
19970	332	1682	FOOD SVCS & DRINKING PLACES
19971	1339	11816	FOOD SVCS & DRINKING PLACES
19973	923	14334	ANIMAL PRODUCTION
19975	416	5569	FOOD MANUFACTURING
19977	637	5423	JUSTICE; PUBIC ORDER/SAFETY
19979	13	38	TRANSIT & GRND PASS. TRANSPORT
19980	23	371	EDUCATIONAL SERVICES
20001	2546	51542	PROF.; SCIENTIFIC; & TECH SVCS
20002	2435	26127	EDUCATIONAL SERVICES
20003	1440	13062	PROF.; SCIENTIFIC; & TECH SVCS
20004	1437	39046	PROF.; SCIENTIFIC; & TECH SVCS
20005	3611	49860	PROF.; SCIENTIFIC; & TECH SVCS
20006	2595	39084	PROF.; SCIENTIFIC; & TECH SVCS
20007	2470	26332	PROF.; SCIENTIFIC; & TECH SVCS
20008	1140	13139	NAT'L SECURITY & INT'L AFFAIRS
20009	2371	20244	RELIG.; GRANT; CIVIC; PROF ORG
20010	787	17818	HOSPITALS
20011	1409	8432	EDUCATIONAL SERVICES
20012	519	2869	PROF.; SCIENTIFIC; & TECH SVCS
20013	11	21	TELECOMMUNICATIONS
20015	691	5751	FOOD SVCS & DRINKING PLACES
20016	1424	21955	EDUCATIONAL SERVICES
20017	612	7850	HOSPITALS
20018	697	6913	SPECIAL TRADE CONTRACTORS
20019	841	9956	MERCH. WHOLESALERS;NONDUR. GDS
20020	913	6627	EDUCATIONAL SERVICES
20024	725	19550	JUSTICE; PUBIC ORDER/SAFETY
20027	6	19	BLDG MATL & GARDEN EQPMT DLRS
20030	2	1	PROF.; SCIENTIFIC; & TECH SVCS
20032	566	9546	ADMIN. HUMAN RESOURCE PROGRAMS
20033	1	0	PROF.; SCIENTIFIC; & TECH SVCS
20035	4	21	RELIG.; GRANT; CIVIC; PROF ORG
20036	4627	56886	PROF.; SCIENTIFIC; & TECH SVCS
20037	1252	32315	PROF.; SCIENTIFIC; & TECH SVCS
20039	2	1	REAL ESTATE
20040	6	14	RELIG.; GRANT; CIVIC; PROF ORG
20041	2	6	AIR TRANSPORTATION
20043	1	0	PROF.; SCIENTIFIC; & TECH SVCS
20044	7	530	JUSTICE; PUBIC ORDER/SAFETY
20045	218	1045	PUBLISHING INDUSTRIES
20047	1	15	ADMINISTRATIVE & SUPPORT SVCS
20049	4	1646	RELIG.; GRANT; CIVIC; PROF ORG
20050	26	70	PERSONAL AND LAUNDRY SERVICES
20052	24	10560	EDUCATIONAL SERVICES
20053	3	0	PROF.; SCIENTIFIC; & TECH SVCS
20056	2	3	ADMINISTRATIVE & SUPPORT SVCS
20057	16	637	MANAGMT OF COMPANIES & ENTERP.
20059	20	4882	EDUCATIONAL SERVICES
20060	16	2438	HOSPITALS
20062	5	1108	ADMINISTRATIVE & SUPPORT SVCS
20064	18	759	OTHER INFORMATION SERVICES
20065	3	800	INSURANCE CARRIERS & RELATED
20066	4	3509	POSTAL SERVICE
20068	6	2009	UTILITIES
20071	4	2865	PUBLISHING INDUSTRIES
20074	1	5	HEAVY & CIVIL ENG. CONSTRUCT'N
20076	6	2001	INSURANCE CARRIERS & RELATED
20080	4	108	MANAGMT OF COMPANIES & ENTERP.
20090	6	14	RELIG.; GRANT; CIVIC; PROF ORG
20105	202	939	EDUCATIONAL SERVICES
20106	99	257	CONSTRUCTION OF BUILDINGS
20107	26	9	FOOD AND BEVERAGE STORES
20108	25	109	ADMINISTRATIVE & SUPPORT SVCS
20109	1738	23290	SPECIAL TRADE CONTRACTORS
20110	2433	30957	COMPUTER & ELECTRONIC PROD MFG
20111	783	6337	SPECIAL TRADE CONTRACTORS
20112	462	3029	EDUCATIONAL SERVICES
20113	4	10	REAL ESTATE
20115	258	1554	PROF.; SCIENTIFIC; & TECH SVCS
20116	6	7	ADMINISTRATIVE & SUPPORT SVCS
20117	335	1738	EDUCATIONAL SERVICES
20118	10	28	PERFORM'G ARTS; SPEC. SPORTS
20119	108	621	SPECIAL TRADE CONTRACTORS
20120	472	7742	ADMINISTRATIVE & SUPPORT SVCS
20121	656	4885	FOOD SVCS & DRINKING PLACES
20122	21	98	PERFORM'G ARTS; SPEC. SPORTS
20124	265	3836	UNCLASSIFIED ESTABLISHMENTS
20128	6	11	FOOD AND BEVERAGE STORES
20129	28	45	PROF.; SCIENTIFIC; & TECH SVCS
20130	7	35	FOOD SVCS & DRINKING PLACES
20131	7	23	AMUSEMENT; GAMBLING;& RECREAT.
20132	585	4506	EDUCATIONAL SERVICES
20134	11	40	TRANSIT & GRND PASS. TRANSPORT
20135	88	216	JUSTICE; PUBIC ORDER/SAFETY
20136	279	3565	SUPPORT ACT. FOR TRANSPORT.
20137	41	97	PROF.; SCIENTIFIC; & TECH SVCS
20138	25	181	CHEMICAL MANUFACTURING
20139	5	36	MISCELLANEOUS STORE RETAILERS
20140	5	8	PROF.; SCIENTIFIC; & TECH SVCS
20141	110	468	EDUCATIONAL SERVICES
20142	5	16	SPECIAL TRADE CONTRACTORS
20143	40	207	ADMINISTRATIVE & SUPPORT SVCS
20144	32	86	SPECIAL TRADE CONTRACTORS
20146	6	25	ADMINISTRATIVE & SUPPORT SVCS
20147	1246	15526	TELECOMMUNICATIONS
20148	268	2397	EDUCATIONAL SERVICES
20151	1955	36038	PROF.; SCIENTIFIC; & TECH SVCS
20152	404	3625	ADMINISTRATIVE & SUPPORT SVCS
20153	25	284	ADMINISTRATIVE & SUPPORT SVCS
20155	687	6111	SPECIAL TRADE CONTRACTORS
20156	7	25	CONSTRUCTION OF BUILDINGS
20158	100	420	EDUCATIONAL SERVICES
20159	2	2	PROF.; SCIENTIFIC; & TECH SVCS
20160	9	19	PROF.; SCIENTIFIC; & TECH SVCS
20163	1	0	POSTAL SERVICE
20164	1194	9911	EDUCATIONAL SERVICES
20165	650	5481	FOOD SVCS & DRINKING PLACES
20166	1942	38831	SPECIAL TRADE CONTRACTORS
20167	14	198	SPECIAL TRADE CONTRACTORS
20168	5	45	ADMINISTRATIVE & SUPPORT SVCS
20169	485	2861	REAL ESTATE
20170	1780	17562	PROF.; SCIENTIFIC; & TECH SVCS
20171	1006	19326	PROF.; SCIENTIFIC; & TECH SVCS
20172	15	141	BLDG MATL & GARDEN EQPMT DLRS
20175	1195	11423	EXEC.; LEGIS.; & OTHER SUPPORT
20176	1467	17443	HOSPITALS
20177	18	53	SPECIAL TRADE CONTRACTORS
20178	3	5	SPECIAL TRADE CONTRACTORS
20180	154	518	AMUSEMENT; GAMBLING;& RECREAT.
20181	218	1404	SPECIAL TRADE CONTRACTORS
20182	2	7	SPECIAL TRADE CONTRACTORS
20184	52	317	CROP PRODUCTION
20185	2	1	ADMINISTRATIVE & SUPPORT SVCS
20186	1145	10273	FOOD SVCS & DRINKING PLACES
20187	378	3377	SPECIAL TRADE CONTRACTORS
20188	11	15	ADMINISTRATIVE & SUPPORT SVCS
20190	1521	28707	PROF.; SCIENTIFIC; & TECH SVCS
20191	1092	14076	PROF.; SCIENTIFIC; & TECH SVCS
20192	5	3037	ADMIN. ENVIRO. QUALITY PROGRMS
20194	166	1110	EDUCATIONAL SERVICES
20195	9	15	SPECIAL TRADE CONTRACTORS
20197	52	201	EDUCATIONAL SERVICES
20198	110	829	EDUCATIONAL SERVICES
20201	12	2716	ADMIN. HUMAN RESOURCE PROGRAMS
20202	4	39	MUSEUMS; HIST. SITES;& SIMILAR
20204	1	11	OTHER INFORMATION SERVICES
20210	19	1454	SOCIAL ASSISTANCE
20212	1	0	ADMIN. OF ECONOMIC PROGRAMS
20216	1	0	EXEC.; LEGIS.; & OTHER SUPPORT
20217	41	504	OTHER INFORMATION SERVICES
20219	1	406	EXEC.; LEGIS.; & OTHER SUPPORT
20220	9	41	CREDIT INTERMEDIATION & RELATD
20221	1	0	EXEC.; LEGIS.; & OTHER SUPPORT
20222	1	0	ADMINISTRATIVE & SUPPORT SVCS
20223	1	0	JUSTICE; PUBIC ORDER/SAFETY
20224	7	621	SPECIAL TRADE CONTRACTORS
20226	2	0	EXEC.; LEGIS.; & OTHER SUPPORT
20227	1	7	SPECIAL TRADE CONTRACTORS
20228	3	1818	PRINT'G & RELATED SUPP'T ACT'S
20229	1	5	EXEC.; LEGIS.; & OTHER SUPPORT
20230	24	9781	PROF.; SCIENTIFIC; & TECH SVCS
20237	2	12	PROF.; SCIENTIFIC; & TECH SVCS
20238	2	412	MUSEUMS; HIST. SITES;& SIMILAR
20239	2	0	SECURITIES/COMMODITY CONTRACTS
20240	20	261	EXEC.; LEGIS.; & OTHER SUPPORT
20241	3	3	RELIG.; GRANT; CIVIC; PROF ORG
20242	6	587	EXEC.; LEGIS.; & OTHER SUPPORT
20245	1	630	ADMIN. ENVIRO. QUALITY PROGRMS
20250	29	2927	ADMIN. OF ECONOMIC PROGRAMS
20260	7	3005	POSTAL SERVICE
20268	1	50	ADMIN. OF ECONOMIC PROGRAMS
20306	11	1164	AMBULATORY HEALTH CARE SVCS
20307	27	453	AMBULATORY HEALTH CARE SVCS
20317	4	709	NURSING & RESID. CARE FACILIT.
20318	1	0	NAT'L SECURITY & INT'L AFFAIRS
20319	11	74	FOOD SVCS & DRINKING PLACES
20340	2	3	PERSONAL AND LAUNDRY SERVICES
20372	1	3	FOOD SVCS & DRINKING PLACES
20373	10	139	NAT'L SECURITY & INT'L AFFAIRS
20374	22	124	NAT'L SECURITY & INT'L AFFAIRS
20375	6	1085	NAT'L SECURITY & INT'L AFFAIRS
20380	1	0	NAT'L SECURITY & INT'L AFFAIRS
20390	2	1357	NAT'L SECURITY & INT'L AFFAIRS
20392	4	9	ADMINISTRATIVE & SUPPORT SVCS
20393	1	400	NAT'L SECURITY & INT'L AFFAIRS
20401	3	11	CREDIT INTERMEDIATION & RELATD
20402	1	0	MERCH. WHOLESALERS;DURABLE GDS
20403	1	4	SPORTG GDS;HOBBY;BOOK; & MUSIC
20405	8	144	EXEC.; LEGIS.; & OTHER SUPPORT
20407	7	36	JUSTICE; PUBIC ORDER/SAFETY
20408	5	456	EXEC.; LEGIS.; & OTHER SUPPORT
20410	9	110	EXEC.; LEGIS.; & OTHER SUPPORT
20415	4	32	OTHER INFORMATION SERVICES
20418	15	278	RELIG.; GRANT; CIVIC; PROF ORG
20419	2	152	ADMIN. OF ECONOMIC PROGRAMS
20420	8	1629	PERSONAL AND LAUNDRY SERVICES
20422	15	1755	AMBULATORY HEALTH CARE SVCS
20424	1	0	ADMIN. OF ECONOMIC PROGRAMS
20425	2	3	EXEC.; LEGIS.; & OTHER SUPPORT
20426	3	14	FOOD SVCS & DRINKING PLACES
20427	1	70	ADMIN. OF ECONOMIC PROGRAMS
20429	3	26	SOCIAL ASSISTANCE
20431	5	4002	EXEC.; LEGIS.; & OTHER SUPPORT
20433	14	8109	SECURITIES/COMMODITY CONTRACTS
20436	1	2	CREDIT INTERMEDIATION & RELATD
20437	1	0	PROF.; SCIENTIFIC; & TECH SVCS
20439	33	331	EXEC.; LEGIS.; & OTHER SUPPORT
20441	1	100	PROF.; SCIENTIFIC; & TECH SVCS
20442	9	84	JUSTICE; PUBIC ORDER/SAFETY
20444	1	8	ADMIN. ENVIRO. QUALITY PROGRMS
20447	1	900	ADMIN. HUMAN RESOURCE PROGRAMS
20451	4	251	NAT'L SECURITY & INT'L AFFAIRS
20460	2	0	ADMIN. ENVIRO. QUALITY PROGRMS
20463	1	0	EXEC.; LEGIS.; & OTHER SUPPORT
20472	2	1900	JUSTICE; PUBIC ORDER/SAFETY
20500	17	0	BROADCASTING
20503	6	0	PUBLISHING INDUSTRIES
20505	1	0	NAT'L SECURITY & INT'L AFFAIRS
20506	4	53	OTHER INFORMATION SERVICES
20507	1	0	ADMIN. HUMAN RESOURCE PROGRAMS
20508	6	160	EXEC.; LEGIS.; & OTHER SUPPORT
20510	108	162	EXEC.; LEGIS.; & OTHER SUPPORT
20515	457	365	EXEC.; LEGIS.; & OTHER SUPPORT
20520	17	85	PROF.; SCIENTIFIC; & TECH SVCS
20521	1	1	SPORTG GDS;HOBBY;BOOK; & MUSIC
20522	1	1	CONSTRUCTION OF BUILDINGS
20523	6	12	SPORTG GDS;HOBBY;BOOK; & MUSIC
20526	5	550	NAT'L SECURITY & INT'L AFFAIRS
20527	1	200	EXEC.; LEGIS.; & OTHER SUPPORT
20528	2	17	SPECIAL TRADE CONTRACTORS
20530	21	153	FUNDS; TRUSTS; & OTHER FINANCE
20531	1	0	EXEC.; LEGIS.; & OTHER SUPPORT
20534	6	49	ELECT'L EQPMT; APP; & COMP MFG
20535	5	8050	JUSTICE; PUBIC ORDER/SAFETY
20536	2	0	PROF.; SCIENTIFIC; & TECH SVCS
20537	1	0	PROF.; SCIENTIFIC; & TECH SVCS
20540	21	5435	OTHER INFORMATION SERVICES
20542	3	148	OTHER INFORMATION SERVICES
20543	7	355	EXEC.; LEGIS.; & OTHER SUPPORT
20546	1	6	CREDIT INTERMEDIATION & RELATD
20547	7	402	NAT'L SECURITY & INT'L AFFAIRS
20548	7	5688	PUBLISHING INDUSTRIES
20549	3	1	FOOD AND BEVERAGE STORES
20551	4	3373	MONETARY AUTH. - CENTRAL BANK
20552	7	223	EXEC.; LEGIS.; & OTHER SUPPORT
20553	4	3135	OTHER INFORMATION SERVICES
20554	3	4	OTHER INFORMATION SERVICES
20560	21	6220	MUSEUMS; HIST. SITES;& SIMILAR
20565	3	1140	EXEC.; LEGIS.; & OTHER SUPPORT
20566	5	835	PERFORM'G ARTS; SPEC. SPORTS

ZIP CODE	2009 Total Firms	2009 Total Employees	TOP INDUSTRY RANKED on 2009 EMPLOYMENT	ZIP CODE	2009 Total Firms	2009 Total Employees	TOP INDUSTRY RANKED on 2009 EMPLOYMENT	ZIP CODE	2009 Total Firms	2009 Total Employees	TOP INDUSTRY RANKED on 2009 EMPLOYMENT
20571	2	412	CREDIT INTERMEDIATION & RELATD	20712	172	743	EDUCATIONAL SERVICES	20857	1	0	ADMIN. HUMAN RESOURCE PROGRAMS
20572	1	50	ADMIN. OF ECONOMIC PROGRAMS	20714	124	520	FOOD SVCS & DRINKING PLACES	20859	12	23	REAL ESTATE
20573	2	126	ADMIN. OF ECONOMIC PROGRAMS	20715	852	6319	EDUCATIONAL SERVICES	20860	97	1580	NURSING & RESID. CARE FACILIT.
20576	2	55	EXEC.; LEGIS.; & OTHER SUPPORT	20716	825	7864	FOOD SVCS & DRINKING PLACES	20861	105	381	ADMINISTRATIVE & SUPPORT SVCS
20577	4	550	RELIG.; GRANT; CIVIC; PROF ORG	20717	7	65	REPAIR AND MAINTENANCE	20862	12	182	ADMINISTRATIVE & SUPPORT SVCS
20579	3	18	NAT'L SECURITY & INT'L AFFAIRS	20718	11	52	SPECIAL TRADE CONTRACTORS	20866	392	3238	EDUCATIONAL SERVICES
20580	3	6	ADMIN. OF ECONOMIC PROGRAMS	20720	406	1981	SPECIAL TRADE CONTRACTORS	20868	35	231	MACHINERY MANUFACTURING
20585	12	158	CONSTRUCTION OF BUILDINGS	20721	428	2488	EDUCATIONAL SERVICES	20871	281	3572	CONSTRUCTION OF BUILDINGS
20590	18	5643	HEAVY & CIVIL ENG. CONSTRUCT'N	20722	252	1935	SPECIAL TRADE CONTRACTORS	20872	458	2476	EDUCATIONAL SERVICES
20591	3	6	PERSONAL AND LAUNDRY SERVICES	20723	556	14420	EDUCATIONAL SERVICES	20874	1172	10292	EDUCATIONAL SERVICES
20593	13	76	FOOD SVCS & DRINKING PLACES	20724	312	8259	MERCH. WHOLESALERS;DURABLE GDS	20875	19	29	SPECIAL TRADE CONTRACTORS
20594	1	360	ADMIN. OF ECONOMIC PROGRAMS	20725	7	22	PERFORM'G ARTS; SPEC. SPORTS	20876	465	8552	COMPUTER & ELECTRONIC PROD MFG
20597	1	0	CONSTRUCTION OF BUILDINGS	20731	4	13	TRUCK TRANSPORTATION	20877	2310	20325	RELIG.; GRANT; CIVIC; PROF ORG
20601	1135	9121	FOOD SVCS & DRINKING PLACES	20732	181	1243	FOOD SVCS & DRINKING PLACES	20878	1493	23378	CONSTRUCTION OF BUILDINGS
20602	755	7784	AMBULATORY HEALTH CARE SVCS	20733	53	120	FOOD SVCS & DRINKING PLACES	20879	1464	20329	COMPUTER & ELECTRONIC PROD MFG
20603	607	7984	GENERAL MERCHANDISE STORES	20735	1304	12151	SPECIAL TRADE CONTRACTORS	20880	19	47	PROF.; SCIENTIFIC; & TECH SVCS
20604	13	24	ADMINISTRATIVE & SUPPORT SVCS	20736	309	2142	EDUCATIONAL SERVICES	20882	349	1895	ADMINISTRATIVE & SUPPORT SVCS
20606	4	4	POSTAL SERVICE	20737	447	3703	EDUCATIONAL SERVICES	20884	4	5	SPECIAL TRADE CONTRACTORS
20607	210	1222	SPORTG GDS;HOBBY;BOOK; & MUSIC	20738	9	21	REAL ESTATE	20885	8	23	ADMINISTRATIVE & SUPPORT SVCS
20608	18	246	UTILITIES	20740	1049	26013	EDUCATIONAL SERVICES	20886	425	3083	EDUCATIONAL SERVICES
20609	30	90	SPECIAL TRADE CONTRACTORS	20741	6	41	REAL ESTATE	20889	31	7756	AMBULATORY HEALTH CARE SVCS
20610	12	116	RELIG.; GRANT; CIVIC; PROF ORG	20742	29	921	OTHER INFORMATION SERVICES	20891	3	3	TRANSIT & GRND PASS. TRANSPORT
20611	34	442	JUSTICE; PUBIC ORDER/SAFETY	20743	1353	11653	SPECIAL TRADE CONTRACTORS	20892	61	5133	PROF.; SCIENTIFIC; & TECH SVCS
20612	10	37	FOOD SVCS & DRINKING PLACES	20744	1058	6104	EDUCATIONAL SERVICES	20894	2	684	OTHER INFORMATION SERVICES
20613	290	1858	MERCH. WHOLESALERS;DURABLE GDS	20745	832	7049	EDUCATIONAL SERVICES	20895	1186	10409	FOOD SVCS & DRINKING PLACES
20615	10	75	FOOD SVCS & DRINKING PLACES	20746	714	6731	PROF.; SCIENTIFIC; & TECH SVCS	20896	32	53	SOCIAL ASSISTANCE
20616	121	848	FOOD AND BEVERAGE STORES	20747	1096	9685	EDUCATIONAL SERVICES	20898	15	1267	POSTAL SERVICE
20617	22	249	EDUCATIONAL SERVICES	20748	1346	9067	MOTOR VEHICLE & PARTS DEALERS	20899	5	2129	ADMIN. OF ECONOMIC PROGRAMS
20618	24	270	ADMINISTRATIVE & SUPPORT SVCS	20749	10	14	PROF.; SCIENTIFIC; & TECH SVCS	20901	768	6047	EDUCATIONAL SERVICES
20619	411	5998	PROF.; SCIENTIFIC; & TECH SVCS	20750	7	12	ADMINISTRATIVE & SUPPORT SVCS	20902	1428	10450	EDUCATIONAL SERVICES
20620	56	467	SPECIAL TRADE CONTRACTORS	20751	147	846	FOOD SVCS & DRINKING PLACES	20903	374	3439	REAL ESTATE
20621	20	121	EDUCATIONAL SERVICES	20752	2	1	PROF.; SCIENTIFIC; & TECH SVCS	20904	1311	14403	MOTOR VEHICLE & PARTS DEALERS
20622	218	2040	NURSING & RESID. CARE FACILIT.	20753	3	0	SPECIAL TRADE CONTRACTORS	20905	346	1887	EDUCATIONAL SERVICES
20623	43	424	EDUCATIONAL SERVICES	20754	366	2052	REAL ESTATE	20906	1041	7583	EDUCATIONAL SERVICES
20624	36	74	MERCH. WHOLESALERS;DURABLE GDS	20755	82	939	EDUCATIONAL SERVICES	20907	7	9	SPORTG GDS;HOBBY;BOOK; & MUSIC
20625	15	106	FOOD SVCS & DRINKING PLACES	20757	8	12	ADMINISTRATIVE & SUPPORT SVCS	20908	2	16	TRANSIT & GRND PASS. TRANSPORT
20626	9	29	AMUSEMENT; GAMBLING;& RECREAT.	20758	20	46	SPECIAL TRADE CONTRACTORS	20910	2981	30854	PROF.; SCIENTIFIC; & TECH SVCS
20627	5	8	ADMINISTRATIVE & SUPPORT SVCS	20759	125	1428	EDUCATIONAL SERVICES	20911	1	0	PUBLISHING INDUSTRIES
20628	11	39	MERCH. WHOLESALERS;DURABLE GDS	20762	92	2968	HOSPITALS	20912	741	6509	HOSPITALS
20629	20	41	AMUSEMENT; GAMBLING;& RECREAT.	20763	164	2287	MERCH. WHOLESALERS;DURABLE GDS	20913	4	5	REPAIR AND MAINTENANCE
20630	8	23	AMUSEMENT; GAMBLING;& RECREAT.	20764	85	352	EDUCATIONAL SERVICES	20914	18	44	PROF.; SCIENTIFIC; & TECH SVCS
20632	15	77	SPECIAL TRADE CONTRACTORS	20765	43	317	FOOD SVCS & DRINKING PLACES	20915	12	39	PROF.; SCIENTIFIC; & TECH SVCS
20634	93	714	EDUCATIONAL SERVICES	20768	4	11	ADMINISTRATIVE & SUPPORT SVCS	20916	12	42	SOCIAL ASSISTANCE
20635	5	97	EDUCATIONAL SERVICES	20769	134	837	COMPUTER & ELECTRONIC PROD MFG	20918	5	10	ADMINISTRATIVE & SUPPORT SVCS
20636	256	2567	COMPUTER & ELECTRONIC PROD MFG	20770	1114	26007	SPACE RESEARCH AND TECHNOLOGY	21001	850	11517	HEALTH & PERSONAL CARE STORES
20637	153	1085	SOCIAL ASSISTANCE	20771	9	20624	COMPUTER & ELECTRONIC PROD MFG	21005	51	594	NONSTORE RETAILERS
20639	306	1946	EDUCATIONAL SERVICES	20772	1355	12158	SPECIAL TRADE CONTRACTORS	21009	442	4514	PROF.; SCIENTIFIC; & TECH SVCS
20640	205	1511	EDUCATIONAL SERVICES	20773	8	96	MERCH. WHOLESALERS;NONDUR. GDS	21010	13	133	CREDIT INTERMEDIATION & RELATD
20643	2	1	FOOD AND BEVERAGE STORES	20774	1349	20582	EDUCATIONAL SERVICES	21012	479	3451	SOCIAL ASSISTANCE
20645	11	119	AMUSEMENT; GAMBLING;& RECREAT.	20775	13	30	PROF.; SCIENTIFIC; & TECH SVCS	21013	110	370	SPECIAL TRADE CONTRACTORS
20646	820	10073	EDUCATIONAL SERVICES	20776	76	419	ADMINISTRATIVE & SUPPORT SVCS	21014	1962	22017	EXEC.; LEGIS.; & OTHER SUPPORT
20650	547	6425	HOSPITALS	20777	136	612	RELIG.; GRANT; CIVIC; PROF ORG	21015	700	6431	FOOD SVCS & DRINKING PLACES
20653	656	7896	PROF.; SCIENTIFIC; & TECH SVCS	20778	90	369	ADMINISTRATIVE & SUPPORT SVCS	21017	155	3588	MERCH. WHOLESALERS;DURABLE GDS
20656	15	215	EDUCATIONAL SERVICES	20779	63	316	SPECIAL TRADE CONTRACTORS	21018	4	16	SPECIAL TRADE CONTRACTORS
20657	282	1597	EDUCATIONAL SERVICES	20781	810	9100	SPECIAL TRADE CONTRACTORS	21020	3	2	MERCH. WHOLESALERS;DURABLE GDS
20658	24	476	MISCELLANEOUS STORE RETAILERS	20782	739	6103	EDUCATIONAL SERVICES	21022	22	458	EDUCATIONAL SERVICES
20659	448	2151	SPECIAL TRADE CONTRACTORS	20783	788	6345	NAT'L SECURITY & INT'L AFFAIRS	21023	17	58	SPORTG GDS;HOBBY;BOOK; & MUSIC
20660	4	127	EDUCATIONAL SERVICES	20784	484	3872	EDUCATIONAL SERVICES	21027	7	17	RELIG.; GRANT; CIVIC; PROF ORG
20661	4	5	SUPPORT ACTIVITIES: AGR./FOR.	20785	1201	24119	FOOD AND BEVERAGE STORES	21028	144	898	HEAVY & CIVIL ENG. CONSTRUCT'N
20662	39	196	EDUCATIONAL SERVICES	20787	1	1	EDUCATIONAL SERVICES	21029	342	2730	MOTOR VEHICLE & PARTS DEALERS
20664	83	692	EDUCATIONAL SERVICES	20790	5	4024	POSTAL SERVICE	21030	1419	23795	CHEMICAL MANUFACTURING
20667	13	93	EDUCATIONAL SERVICES	20791	6	18	REAL ESTATE	21031	336	9959	PROF.; SCIENTIFIC; & TECH SVCS
20670	38	551	HOSPITALS	20792	3	8	TRANSIT & GRND PASS. TRANSPORT	21032	223	2426	ADMIN. OF ECONOMIC PROGRAMS
20674	16	147	EDUCATIONAL SERVICES	20794	801	14992	MERCH. WHOLESALERS;NONDUR. GDS	21034	133	390	EDUCATIONAL SERVICES
20675	30	411	EDUCATIONAL SERVICES	20812	31	136	FOOD SVCS & DRINKING PLACES	21035	227	1785	MERCH. WHOLESALERS;NONDUR. GDS
20676	53	159	EDUCATIONAL SERVICES	20814	3619	42683	PROF.; SCIENTIFIC; & TECH SVCS	21036	66	337	EXEC.; LEGIS.; & OTHER SUPPORT
20677	50	206	TRANSIT & GRND PASS. TRANSPORT	20815	1165	14615	INSURANCE CARRIERS & RELATED	21037	759	5881	FOOD SVCS & DRINKING PLACES
20678	934	12108	EXEC.; LEGIS.; & OTHER SUPPORT	20816	564	4010	FOOD AND BEVERAGE STORES	21040	619	5113	FOOD SVCS & DRINKING PLACES
20680	39	168	EDUCATIONAL SERVICES	20817	1518	18982	ACCOMMODATION	21041	17	43	PROF.; SCIENTIFIC; & TECH SVCS
20682	2	44	ACCOMMODATION	20818	103	419	PROF.; SCIENTIFIC; & TECH SVCS	21042	1193	9422	EDUCATIONAL SERVICES
20684	33	1099	NAT'L SECURITY & INT'L AFFAIRS	20824	7	17	PROF.; SCIENTIFIC; & TECH SVCS	21043	1186	11607	EDUCATIONAL SERVICES
20685	113	454	EDUCATIONAL SERVICES	20825	5	6	PROF.; SCIENTIFIC; & TECH SVCS	21044	1791	17274	PROF.; SCIENTIFIC; & TECH SVCS
20686	19	532	EDUCATIONAL SERVICES	20827	14	184	UTILITIES	21045	1780	20827	PROF.; SCIENTIFIC; & TECH SVCS
20687	6	23	MOTOR VEHICLE & PARTS DEALERS	20830	11	83	ADMINISTRATIVE & SUPPORT SVCS	21046	1266	23316	PROF.; SCIENTIFIC; & TECH SVCS
20688	229	2930	FOOD SVCS & DRINKING PLACES	20832	742	6856	HOSPITALS	21047	440	3285	CONSTRUCTION OF BUILDINGS
20689	52	285	EDUCATIONAL SERVICES	20833	156	558	ADMINISTRATIVE & SUPPORT SVCS	21048	364	2043	SPECIAL TRADE CONTRACTORS
20690	23	153	EDUCATIONAL SERVICES	20837	193	1291	REPAIR AND MAINTENANCE	21050	577	4424	SPECIAL TRADE CONTRACTORS
20692	30	52	CONSTRUCTION OF BUILDINGS	20838	20	55	SPECIAL TRADE CONTRACTORS	21051	15	21	PROF.; SCIENTIFIC; & TECH SVCS
20693	13	28	EDUCATIONAL SERVICES	20839	22	157	AMUSEMENT; GAMBLING;& RECREAT.	21052	6	2	RELIG.; GRANT; CIVIC; PROF ORG
20695	311	2591	SPECIAL TRADE CONTRACTORS	20841	142	944	JUSTICE; PUBIC ORDER/SAFETY	21053	52	742	RELIG.; GRANT; CIVIC; PROF ORG
20701	190	5478	PROF.; SCIENTIFIC; & TECH SVCS	20842	97	582	PROF.; SCIENTIFIC; & TECH SVCS	21054	466	4619	FOOD SVCS & DRINKING PLACES
20703	4	5	REAL ESTATE	20847	5	4	PROF.; SCIENTIFIC; & TECH SVCS	21056	13	46	AMUSEMENT; GAMBLING;& RECREAT.
20704	11	20	HEAVY & CIVIL ENG. CONSTRUCT'N	20848	11	14	FURN. & HOME FURNISHGS STORES	21057	113	763	SPECIAL TRADE CONTRACTORS
20705	1674	23720	SPECIAL TRADE CONTRACTORS	20849	13	44	RELIG.; GRANT; CIVIC; PROF ORG	21060	626	9212	JUSTICE; PUBIC ORDER/SAFETY
20706	1529	22463	PROF.; SCIENTIFIC; & TECH SVCS	20850	4112	52586	PROF.; SCIENTIFIC; & TECH SVCS	21061	2405	24444	FOOD SVCS & DRINKING PLACES
20707	2014	20190	AMBULATORY HEALTH CARE SVCS	20851	249	1502	EDUCATIONAL SERVICES	21062	4	42	ADMIN. OF ECONOMIC PROGRAMS
20708	351	2449	PROF.; SCIENTIFIC; & TECH SVCS	20852	3143	53583	ADMIN. HUMAN RESOURCE PROGRAMS	21071	34	411	FOOD MANUFACTURING
20709	7	10	ADMINISTRATIVE & SUPPORT SVCS	20853	443	2402	EDUCATIONAL SERVICES	21074	483	4610	EDUCATIONAL SERVICES
20710	320	2692	CONSTRUCTION OF BUILDINGS	20854	1145	9122	EDUCATIONAL SERVICES	21075	975	12624	PROF.; SCIENTIFIC; & TECH SVCS
20711	173	1130	SPECIAL TRADE CONTRACTORS	20855	660	8114	PROF.; SCIENTIFIC; & TECH SVCS	21076	900	17913	ADMINISTRATIVE & SUPPORT SVCS

ZIP CODE	2009 Total Firms	2009 Total Employ-ees	TOP INDUSTRY RANKED on 2009 EMPLOYMENT	ZIP CODE	2009 Total Firms	2009 Total Employ-ees	TOP INDUSTRY RANKED on 2009 EMPLOYMENT	ZIP CODE	2009 Total Firms	2009 Total Employ-ees	TOP INDUSTRY RANKED on 2009 EMPLOYMENT
21077	42	935	MACHINERY MANUFACTURING	21270	1	3	ADMINISTRATIVE & SUPPORT SVCS	21663	282	2027	FOOD SVCS & DRINKING PLACES
21078	671	6191	HOSPITALS	21278	1	0	PUBLISHING INDUSTRIES	21664	21	153	EDUCATIONAL SERVICES
21082	31	123	EDUCATIONAL SERVICES	21281	1	0	ADMINISTRATIVE & SUPPORT SVCS	21665	10	21	AMUSEMENT; GAMBLING;& RECREAT.
21084	287	1404	CONSTRUCTION OF BUILDINGS	21282	21	34	FOOD SVCS & DRINKING PLACES	21666	599	4071	EDUCATIONAL SERVICES
21085	461	3141	EDUCATIONAL SERVICES	21284	9	25	PRINT'G & RELATED SUPP'T ACT'S	21667	13	46	ADMINISTRATIVE & SUPPORT SVCS
21087	178	730	SPECIAL TRADE CONTRACTORS	21285	6	18	ADMIN. OF ECONOMIC PROGRAMS	21668	55	360	EDUCATIONAL SERVICES
21088	1	18	BLDG MATL & GARDEN EQPMT DLRS	21286	1283	18507	PROF.; SCIENTIFIC; & TECH SVCS	21669	13	104	JUSTICE; PUBIC ORDER/SAFETY
21090	694	16053	MERCH. WHOLESALERS;DURABLE GDS	21287	105	10108	HOSPITALS	21670	3	1	POSTAL SERVICE
21092	2	11	CONSTRUCTION OF BUILDINGS	21290	1	29	EDUCATIONAL SERVICES	21671	58	380	ACCOMMODATION
21093	2038	25325	PROF.; SCIENTIFIC; & TECH SVCS	21401	4433	50829	FOOD SVCS & DRINKING PLACES	21672	8	8	FOOD AND BEVERAGE STORES
21094	16	46	SECURITIES/COMMODITY CONTRACTS	21402	40	778	RELIG.; GRANT; CIVIC; PROF ORG	21673	116	508	JUSTICE; PUBIC ORDER/SAFETY
21102	266	1644	NURSING & RESID. CARE FACILIT.	21403	988	6258	FOOD SVCS & DRINKING PLACES	21675	6	75	JUSTICE; PUBIC ORDER/SAFETY
21104	141	1378	CONSTRUCTION OF BUILDINGS	21404	13	8	MOTOR VEHICLE & PARTS DEALERS	21676	14	17	FURNITURE & RELATED PROD. MFG
21105	7	11	CREDIT INTERMEDIATION & RELATD	21405	13	13	FOOD SVCS & DRINKING PLACES	21677	8	27	MERCH. WHOLESALERS;NONDUR. GDS
21106	10	7	ADMINISTRATIVE & SUPPORT SVCS	21409	422	3872	COMPUTER & ELECTRONIC PROD MFG	21678	65	600	SOCIAL ASSISTANCE
21108	788	8308	HEAVY & CIVIL ENG. CONSTRUCT'N	21411	1	400	EXEC.; LEGIS.; & OTHER SUPPORT	21679	36	127	SPECIAL TRADE CONTRACTORS
21111	172	1140	EDUCATIONAL SERVICES	21501	3	0	SPECIAL TRADE CONTRACTORS	21701	2591	27826	HOSPITALS
21113	595	5975	ADMINISTRATIVE & SUPPORT SVCS	21502	2036	27989	HOSPITALS	21702	1235	20070	NAT'L SECURITY & INT'L AFFAIRS
21114	804	7222	FOOD SVCS & DRINKING PLACES	21503	1	1	POSTAL SERVICE	21703	964	15490	ADMINISTRATIVE & SUPPORT SVCS
21117	2131	31558	INSURANCE CARRIERS & RELATED	21504	1	2	POSTAL SERVICE	21704	943	14081	FOOD SVCS & DRINKING PLACES
21120	200	970	EDUCATIONAL SERVICES	21505	3	3	SPORTG GDS;HOBBY;BOOK; & MUSIC	21705	23	82	TELECOMMUNICATIONS
21122	1527	9999	FOOD SVCS & DRINKING PLACES	21520	105	812	EDUCATIONAL SERVICES	21709	1	5	CREDIT INTERMEDIATION & RELATD
21123	11	41	CONSTRUCTION OF BUILDINGS	21521	27	180	MERCH. WHOLESALERS;DURABLE GDS	21710	84	661	COMPUTER & ELECTRONIC PROD MFG
21128	186	1067	PROF.; SCIENTIFIC; & TECH SVCS	21522	9	7	EDUCATIONAL SERVICES	21711	23	71	GASOLINE STATIONS
21130	3	92	EXEC.; LEGIS.; & OTHER SUPPORT	21523	10	71	CREDIT INTERMEDIATION & RELATD	21713	261	1831	NURSING & RESID. CARE FACILIT.
21131	264	1625	AMUSEMENT; GAMBLING;& RECREAT.	21524	16	92	FOOD AND BEVERAGE STORES	21714	12	21	AMUSEMENT; GAMBLING;& RECREAT.
21132	65	388	EDUCATIONAL SERVICES	21528	5	96	MERCH. WHOLESALERS;DURABLE GDS	21715	4	11	RELIG.; GRANT; CIVIC; PROF ORG
21133	755	5949	HOSPITALS	21529	19	79	SPECIAL TRADE CONTRACTORS	21716	153	1033	EDUCATIONAL SERVICES
21136	1084	6790	EDUCATIONAL SERVICES	21530	55	457	AMUSEMENT; GAMBLING;& RECREAT.	21717	32	197	ADMINISTRATIVE & SUPPORT SVCS
21139	3	25	SOCIAL ASSISTANCE	21531	86	297	EDUCATIONAL SERVICES	21718	10	12	SPECIAL TRADE CONTRACTORS
21140	56	241	FOOD SVCS & DRINKING PLACES	21532	416	4971	EDUCATIONAL SERVICES	21719	34	149	FOOD SVCS & DRINKING PLACES
21144	419	4021	WHOLESALE ELEC. MRKTS & AGENTS	21536	168	1386	NURSING & RESID. CARE FACILIT.	21720	9	177	CONSTRUCTION OF BUILDINGS
21146	1052	7117	EDUCATIONAL SERVICES	21538	15	32	EDUCATIONAL SERVICES	21721	5	7	RELIG.; GRANT; CIVIC; PROF ORG
21150	5	10	PROF.; SCIENTIFIC; & TECH SVCS	21539	70	574	EDUCATIONAL SERVICES	21722	141	916	SPECIAL TRADE CONTRACTORS
21152	227	6761	PROF.; SCIENTIFIC; & TECH SVCS	21540	9	1251	PAPER MANUFACTURING	21723	35	94	OTHER INFORMATION SERVICES
21153	52	907	EDUCATIONAL SERVICES	21541	155	2523	ACCOMMODATION	21727	180	2762	EDUCATIONAL SERVICES
21154	153	1031	AMUSEMENT; GAMBLING;& RECREAT.	21542	16	37	RELIG.; GRANT; CIVIC; PROF ORG	21733	24	41	SPECIAL TRADE CONTRACTORS
21155	88	469	SPECIAL TRADE CONTRACTORS	21543	5	12	REPAIR AND MAINTENANCE	21734	21	124	RELIG.; GRANT; CIVIC; PROF ORG
21156	12	24	RELIG.; GRANT; CIVIC; PROF ORG	21545	21	208	EDUCATIONAL SERVICES	21737	60	713	TRANSIT & GRND PASS. TRANSPORT
21157	2088	25486	AMBULATORY HEALTH CARE SVCS	21550	888	7979	FOOD SVCS & DRINKING PLACES	21738	126	764	EDUCATIONAL SERVICES
21158	319	2725	RELIG.; GRANT; CIVIC; PROF ORG	21555	28	85	EDUCATIONAL SERVICES	21740	3108	42172	FOOD SVCS & DRINKING PLACES
21160	112	582	SOCIAL ASSISTANCE	21556	3	5	RELIG.; GRANT; CIVIC; PROF ORG	21741	3	4	PROF.; SCIENTIFIC; & TECH SVCS
21161	143	575	SPECIAL TRADE CONTRACTORS	21557	32	73	RELIG.; GRANT; CIVIC; PROF ORG	21742	856	16369	CREDIT INTERMEDIATION & RELATD
21162	285	3809	SPECIAL TRADE CONTRACTORS	21560	2	1	NONSTORE RETAILERS	21746	6	2812	JUSTICE; PUBIC ORDER/SAFETY
21163	130	339	EDUCATIONAL SERVICES	21561	68	292	SOCIAL ASSISTANCE	21750	169	1688	MERCH. WHOLESALERS;DURABLE GDS
21201	2497	45378	PROF.; SCIENTIFIC; & TECH SVCS	21562	91	795	NURSING & RESID. CARE FACILIT.	21754	219	2260	SPECIAL TRADE CONTRACTORS
21202	2856	51364	PROF.; SCIENTIFIC; & TECH SVCS	21601	1831	19256	AMBULATORY HEALTH CARE SVCS	21755	148	580	SPECIAL TRADE CONTRACTORS
21203	31	79	BLDG MATL & GARDEN EQPMT DLRS	21607	17	255	FABRICATED METAL PRODUCT MFG	21756	78	160	SPECIAL TRADE CONTRACTORS
21204	2208	31230	HOSPITALS	21609	3	5	SUPPORT ACT. FOR TRANSPORT.	21757	76	303	CROP PRODUCTION
21205	527	10757	EDUCATIONAL SERVICES	21610	11	13	MERCH. WHOLESALERS;DURABLE GDS	21758	88	381	FOOD AND BEVERAGE STORES
21206	834	5588	EDUCATIONAL SERVICES	21612	21	49	RELIG.; GRANT; CIVIC; PROF ORG	21759	1	1	POSTAL SERVICE
21207	986	8089	EDUCATIONAL SERVICES	21613	1033	10894	FOOD SVCS & DRINKING PLACES	21762	29	104	EDUCATIONAL SERVICES
21208	1735	14149	AMBULATORY HEALTH CARE SVCS	21617	465	3792	EDUCATIONAL SERVICES	21765	18	163	JUSTICE; PUBIC ORDER/SAFETY
21209	730	7982	PROF.; SCIENTIFIC; & TECH SVCS	21619	310	1485	FOOD AND BEVERAGE STORES	21766	16	49	SPECIAL TRADE CONTRACTORS
21210	398	3972	EDUCATIONAL SERVICES	21620	812	7463	EDUCATIONAL SERVICES	21767	38	564	BLDG MATL & GARDEN EQPMT DLRS
21211	896	12736	INSURANCE CARRIERS & RELATED	21622	26	71	EDUCATIONAL SERVICES	21769	335	1653	EDUCATIONAL SERVICES
21212	806	6931	RELIG.; GRANT; CIVIC; PROF ORG	21623	61	205	EDUCATIONAL SERVICES	21770	149	684	EDUCATIONAL SERVICES
21213	593	4686	EDUCATIONAL SERVICES	21624	7	8	FURNITURE & RELATED PROD. MFG	21771	989	6163	SPECIAL TRADE CONTRACTORS
21214	538	3448	EDUCATIONAL SERVICES	21625	66	769	FOOD MANUFACTURING	21773	174	956	SPECIAL TRADE CONTRACTORS
21215	1862	26202	HOSPITALS	21626	5	2	POSTAL SERVICE	21774	246	1250	EDUCATIONAL SERVICES
21216	516	2970	EDUCATIONAL SERVICES	21627	4	2	POSTAL SERVICE	21775	3	52	JUSTICE; PUBIC ORDER/SAFETY
21217	888	6530	EDUCATIONAL SERVICES	21628	12	60	PROF.; SCIENTIFIC; & TECH SVCS	21776	162	1278	OTHER INFORMATION SERVICES
21218	1596	14944	HOSPITALS	21629	492	3918	SPECIAL TRADE CONTRACTORS	21777	32	598	FABRICATED METAL PRODUCT MFG
21219	268	5034	PRIMARY METAL MANUFACTURING	21631	59	204	HOSPITALS	21778	21	96	SPECIAL TRADE CONTRACTORS
21220	961	8378	TRANSPORTATION EQUIPMENT MFG	21632	255	2604	PLASTICS & RUBBER PRODUCTS MFG	21779	24	61	PROF.; SCIENTIFIC; & TECH SVCS
21221	1149	9544	EDUCATIONAL SERVICES	21634	20	216	FOOD AND BEVERAGE STORES	21780	27	90	SPECIAL TRADE CONTRACTORS
21222	1390	15021	EDUCATIONAL SERVICES	21635	82	349	JUSTICE; PUBIC ORDER/SAFETY	21781	8	72	EDUCATIONAL SERVICES
21223	904	9038	HOSPITALS	21636	31	266	SPECIAL TRADE CONTRACTORS	21782	104	419	FOOD SVCS & DRINKING PLACES
21224	2231	32900	MERCH. WHOLESALERS;DURABLE GDS	21638	195	1466	FOOD SVCS & DRINKING PLACES	21783	218	1380	EDUCATIONAL SERVICES
21225	768	6731	HOSPITALS	21639	129	572	EDUCATIONAL SERVICES	21784	1262	13106	SPECIAL TRADE CONTRACTORS
21226	520	8892	MERCH. WHOLESALERS;NONDUR. GDS	21640	18	49	ADMINISTRATIVE & SUPPORT SVCS	21787	270	2057	MERCH. WHOLESALERS;DURABLE GDS
21227	1411	20745	AMBULATORY HEALTH CARE SVCS	21641	10	15	CREDIT INTERMEDIATION & RELATD	21788	423	3666	CONSTRUCTION OF BUILDINGS
21228	1727	23621	NURSING & RESID. CARE FACILIT.	21643	160	2224	FOOD AND BEVERAGE STORES	21790	4	7	PROF.; SCIENTIFIC; & TECH SVCS
21229	846	9202	HOSPITALS	21644	5	11	ELECT'L EQPMT; APP; & COMP MFG	21791	150	935	EDUCATIONAL SERVICES
21230	1607	27471	ADMIN. OF ECONOMIC PROGRAMS	21645	35	424	BLDG MATL & GARDEN EQPMT DLRS	21793	270	2037	CHEMICAL MANUFACTURING
21231	766	8570	PROF.; SCIENTIFIC; & TECH SVCS	21647	17	39	ACCOMMODATION	21794	71	416	JUSTICE; PUBIC ORDER/SAFETY
21233	3	1006	POSTAL SERVICE	21648	9	54	NURSING & RESID. CARE FACILIT.	21795	311	6084	NURSING & RESID. CARE FACILIT.
21234	1575	15089	NURSING & RESID. CARE FACILIT.	21649	28	74	MACHINERY MANUFACTURING	21797	279	2095	ADMINISTRATIVE & SUPPORT SVCS
21235	3	18	HEAVY & CIVIL ENG. CONSTRUCT'N	21650	10	64	ANIMAL PRODUCTION	21798	84	802	ADMINISTRATIVE & SUPPORT SVCS
21236	1523	19407	FOOD SVCS & DRINKING PLACES	21651	92	541	JUSTICE; PUBIC ORDER/SAFETY	21801	2026	29138	HOSPITALS
21237	1170	16176	HOSPITALS	21652	6	12	CONSTRUCTION OF BUILDINGS	21802	14	128	ADMINISTRATIVE & SUPPORT SVCS
21239	337	4524	HEALTH & PERSONAL CARE STORES	21653	5	6	SPECIAL TRADE CONTRACTORS	21803	6	7	WHOLESALE ELEC. MRKTS & AGENTS
21240	127	11720	MERCH. WHOLESALERS;DURABLE GDS	21654	87	528	AMUSEMENT; GAMBLING;& RECREAT.	21804	1278	16261	EDUCATIONAL SERVICES
21241	3	6	CREDIT INTERMEDIATION & RELATD	21655	157	781	MERCH. WHOLESALERS;NONDUR. GDS	21810	8	12	PROF.; SCIENTIFIC; & TECH SVCS
21244	1107	19487	ADMIN. HUMAN RESOURCE PROGRAMS	21657	37	158	MERCH. WHOLESALERS;DURABLE GDS	21811	917	7436	HOSPITALS
21250	5	87	OTHER INFORMATION SERVICES	21658	273	1900	CLOTHING & CLOTH'G ACC. STORES	21813	137	1005	RELIG.; GRANT; CIVIC; PROF ORG
21251	5	45	OTHER INFORMATION SERVICES	21659	28	74	SPECIAL TRADE CONTRACTORS	21814	10	21	SPECIAL TRADE CONTRACTORS
21252	13	151	OTHER INFORMATION SERVICES	21660	123	2184	EDUCATIONAL SERVICES	21817	223	2298	NURSING & RESID. CARE FACILIT.
21264	1	2	AMBULATORY HEALTH CARE SVCS	21661	145	740	FOOD AND BEVERAGE STORES	21821	20	43	EDUCATIONAL SERVICES
21268	1	11	AMBULATORY HEALTH CARE SVCS	21662	27	43	ACCOMMODATION	21822	63	328	PETROLEUM & COAL PRODUCTS MFG

BUSINESS DATA

ZIP CODE	2009 Total Firms	2009 Total Employ-ees	TOP INDUSTRY RANKED on 2009 EMPLOYMENT	ZIP CODE	2009 Total Firms	2009 Total Employ-ees	TOP INDUSTRY RANKED on 2009 EMPLOYMENT	ZIP CODE	2009 Total Firms	2009 Total Employ-ees	TOP INDUSTRY RANKED on 2009 EMPLOYMENT
21824	20	46	ADMINISTRATIVE & SUPPORT SVCS	22180	1231	8643	FOOD SVCS & DRINKING PLACES	22526	1	5	SPECIAL TRADE CONTRACTORS
21826	163	1171	FOOD SVCS & DRINKING PLACES	22181	164	870	EDUCATIONAL SERVICES	22528	1	2	POSTAL SERVICE
21829	11	14	MERCH. WHOLESALERS;NONDUR. GDS	22182	1975	30279	PROF.; SCIENTIFIC; & TECH SVCS	22529	3	2	POSTAL SERVICE
21830	88	513	SPECIAL TRADE CONTRACTORS	22183	12	24	PROF.; SCIENTIFIC; & TECH SVCS	22530	3	4	POSTAL SERVICE
21835	15	217	WOOD PRODUCT MANUFACTURING	22191	1420	12745	EDUCATIONAL SERVICES	22534	34	57	SPECIAL TRADE CONTRACTORS
21836	5	3	POSTAL SERVICE	22192	1915	22885	EXEC.; LEGIS.; & OTHER SUPPORT	22535	30	91	JUSTICE; PUBIC ORDER/SAFETY
21837	69	455	EDUCATIONAL SERVICES	22193	1001	6538	EDUCATIONAL SERVICES	22538	6	50	ACCOMMODATION
21838	42	338	RELIG.; GRANT; CIVIC; PROF ORG	22194	17	58	TRANSIT & GRND PASS. TRANSPORT	22539	110	451	MERCH. WHOLESALERS;NONDUR. GDS
21840	7	10	ACCOMMODATION	22195	15	65	ADMINISTRATIVE & SUPPORT SVCS	22542	45	154	SPECIAL TRADE CONTRACTORS
21841	41	352	EDUCATIONAL SERVICES	22199	4	7	ADMINISTRATIVE & SUPPORT SVCS	22544	2	2	POSTAL SERVICE
21842	1799	20585	FOOD SVCS & DRINKING PLACES	22201	1714	22305	PROF.; SCIENTIFIC; & TECH SVCS	22545	1	2	POSTAL SERVICE
21843	9	30	TRANSIT & GRND PASS. TRANSPORT	22202	1381	21788	PROF.; SCIENTIFIC; & TECH SVCS	22546	273	2723	FOOD SVCS & DRINKING PLACES
21849	82	299	SPECIAL TRADE CONTRACTORS	22203	890	17632	PROF.; SCIENTIFIC; & TECH SVCS	22548	4	35	FISHING; HUNTING AND TRAPPING
21850	90	321	SPECIAL TRADE CONTRACTORS	22204	867	7198	EDUCATIONAL SERVICES	22551	325	1865	EDUCATIONAL SERVICES
21851	387	4071	PROF.; SCIENTIFIC; & TECH SVCS	22205	357	4928	RELIG.; GRANT; CIVIC; PROF ORG	22552	6	44	WOOD PRODUCT MANUFACTURING
21852	3	12	FORESTRY AND LOGGING	22206	476	5395	FOOD SVCS & DRINKING PLACES	22553	328	3359	EDUCATIONAL SERVICES
21853	298	3284	EDUCATIONAL SERVICES	22207	812	7446	EDUCATIONAL SERVICES	22554	1251	12036	EXEC.; LEGIS.; & OTHER SUPPORT
21856	35	189	EDUCATIONAL SERVICES	22209	948	18936	PROF.; SCIENTIFIC; & TECH SVCS	22555	16	43	PROF.; SCIENTIFIC; & TECH SVCS
21861	44	186	WOOD PRODUCT MANUFACTURING	22210	11	43	SECURITIES/COMMODITY CONTRACTS	22556	412	4607	EDUCATIONAL SERVICES
21862	7	24	CONSTRUCTION OF BUILDINGS	22211	34	617	RELIG.; GRANT; CIVIC; PROF ORG	22558	2	71	MUSEUMS; HIST. SITES;& SIMILAR
21863	242	2374	EXEC.; LEGIS.; & OTHER SUPPORT	22213	44	466	EDUCATIONAL SERVICES	22560	471	4160	FOOD SVCS & DRINKING PLACES
21864	13	22	SOCIAL ASSISTANCE	22214	9	210	BLDG MATL & GARDEN EQPMT DLRS	22565	18	84	MOTOR VEHICLE & PARTS DEALERS
21865	8	10	SPECIAL TRADE CONTRACTORS	22217	1	0	OTHER INFORMATION SERVICES	22567	71	226	EDUCATIONAL SERVICES
21866	9	47	JUSTICE; PUBIC ORDER/SAFETY	22230	3	1221	ADMIN. HUMAN RESOURCE PROGRAMS	22570	6	42	HEAVY & CIVIL ENG. CONSTRUCT'N
21867	5	38	MUSEUMS; HIST. SITES;& SIMILAR	22301	502	3160	FOOD SVCS & DRINKING PLACES	22572	342	2475	NURSING & RESID. CARE FACILIT.
21869	41	77	EDUCATIONAL SERVICES	22302	521	6320	EDUCATIONAL SERVICES	22576	37	404	ACCOMMODATION
21871	65	662	ADMIN. HUMAN RESOURCE PROGRAMS	22303	278	2851	PROF.; SCIENTIFIC; & TECH SVCS	22577	3	5	POSTAL SERVICE
21872	32	154	SPECIAL TRADE CONTRACTORS	22304	1413	16702	PROF.; SCIENTIFIC; & TECH SVCS	22578	148	700	RELIG.; GRANT; CIVIC; PROF ORG
21874	52	365	INSURANCE CARRIERS & RELATED	22305	322	3575	FOOD SVCS & DRINKING PLACES	22579	11	26	SPECIAL TRADE CONTRACTORS
21875	160	983	EDUCATIONAL SERVICES	22306	732	8987	SOCIAL ASSISTANCE	22580	100	446	PROF.; SCIENTIFIC; & TECH SVCS
21901	521	5544	EDUCATIONAL SERVICES	22307	182	1995	EDUCATIONAL SERVICES	22581	2	14	WOOD PRODUCT MANUFACTURING
21902	8	73	ADMIN. HUMAN RESOURCE PROGRAMS	22308	194	1460	EDUCATIONAL SERVICES	22601	2115	27271	EDUCATIONAL SERVICES
21903	184	1590	EDUCATIONAL SERVICES	22309	687	4334	EDUCATIONAL SERVICES	22602	741	9587	FOOD SVCS & DRINKING PLACES
21904	148	811	JUSTICE; PUBIC ORDER/SAFETY	22310	841	7791	PROF.; SCIENTIFIC; & TECH SVCS	22603	615	10450	FOOD SVCS & DRINKING PLACES
21911	391	2444	EDUCATIONAL SERVICES	22311	285	7223	PROF.; SCIENTIFIC; & TECH SVCS	22604	33	73	SOCIAL ASSISTANCE
21912	25	116	SOCIAL ASSISTANCE	22312	992	11774	SPECIAL TRADE CONTRACTORS	22610	60	146	SPECIAL TRADE CONTRACTORS
21913	45	320	JUSTICE; PUBIC ORDER/SAFETY	22313	12	15	TRUCK TRANSPORTATION	22611	396	3616	PRINT'G & RELATED SUPP'T ACT'S
21914	20	147	FOOD SVCS & DRINKING PLACES	22314	4007	44848	PROF.; SCIENTIFIC; & TECH SVCS	22620	97	448	EDUCATIONAL SERVICES
21915	148	1137	EDUCATIONAL SERVICES	22315	410	4989	FOOD SVCS & DRINKING PLACES	22623	9	5	RELIG.; GRANT; CIVIC; PROF ORG
21916	7	74	EDUCATIONAL SERVICES	22320	5	16	RELIG.; GRANT; CIVIC; PROF ORG	22624	76	744	SPECIAL TRADE CONTRACTORS
21917	54	297	EDUCATIONAL SERVICES	22331	7	176	INSURANCE CARRIERS & RELATED	22625	58	369	EDUCATIONAL SERVICES
21918	91	304	EDUCATIONAL SERVICES	22332	6	28	RELIG.; GRANT; CIVIC; PROF ORG	22626	5	6	FOOD AND BEVERAGE STORES
21919	53	222	ACCOMMODATION	22401	2138	22809	FOOD SVCS & DRINKING PLACES	22627	36	98	FOOD SVCS & DRINKING PLACES
21920	7	91	HEAVY & CIVIL ENG. CONSTRUCT'N	22402	4	10	RELIG.; GRANT; CIVIC; PROF ORG	22630	1501	12899	EDUCATIONAL SERVICES
21921	1530	16735	MISCELLANEOUS MANUFACTURING	22403	7	131	ADMINISTRATIVE & SUPPORT SVCS	22637	47	232	AMBULATORY HEALTH CARE SVCS
21922	7	24	ADMINISTRATIVE & SUPPORT SVCS	22404	22	59	ADMINISTRATIVE & SUPPORT SVCS	22639	16	257	BEVERAGE & TOBACCO PRODUCT MFG
21930	19	341	FOOD SVCS & DRINKING PLACES	22405	813	7033	EDUCATIONAL SERVICES	22640	15	82	EDUCATIONAL SERVICES
22003	1789	12450	PROF.; SCIENTIFIC; & TECH SVCS	22406	603	6205	MERCH. WHOLESALERS;NONDUR. GDS	22641	13	25	SPECIAL TRADE CONTRACTORS
22009	8	18	SOCIAL ASSISTANCE	22407	1477	14358	FOOD SVCS & DRINKING PLACES	22642	73	168	BEVERAGE & TOBACCO PRODUCT MFG
22015	776	6477	FOOD SVCS & DRINKING PLACES	22408	1178	13215	MOTOR VEHICLE & PARTS DEALERS	22643	15	31	CROP PRODUCTION
22025	236	1626	FOOD SVCS & DRINKING PLACES	22412	2	3503	INSURANCE CARRIERS & RELATED	22644	64	114	CONSTRUCTION OF BUILDINGS
22026	482	3281	EDUCATIONAL SERVICES	22427	198	1284	JUSTICE; PUBIC ORDER/SAFETY	22645	107	841	MISCELLANEOUS MANUFACTURING
22027	72	652	PROF.; SCIENTIFIC; & TECH SVCS	22430	1	2	POSTAL SERVICE	22646	18	135	RELIG.; GRANT; CIVIC; PROF ORG
22030	3424	53863	EDUCATIONAL SERVICES	22432	62	330	AMBULATORY HEALTH CARE SVCS	22649	1	2	RELIG.; GRANT; CIVIC; PROF ORG
22031	1872	25417	PROF.; SCIENTIFIC; & TECH SVCS	22433	2	6	MERCH. WHOLESALERS;DURABLE GDS	22650	18	62	EDUCATIONAL SERVICES
22032	423	4487	EDUCATIONAL SERVICES	22435	126	672	TRANSPORTATION EQUIPMENT MFG	22652	49	68	SPECIAL TRADE CONTRACTORS
22033	1082	22212	PROF.; SCIENTIFIC; & TECH SVCS	22436	7	2	POSTAL SERVICE	22654	13	28	ACCOMMODATION
22035	86	4880	EXEC.; LEGIS.; & OTHER SUPPORT	22437	15	36	MERCH. WHOLESALERS;DURABLE GDS	22655	417	2351	EDUCATIONAL SERVICES
22037	2	3500	PETROLEUM & COAL PRODUCTS MFG	22438	12	54	GASOLINE STATIONS	22656	48	724	SPECIAL TRADE CONTRACTORS
22038	17	38	SPECIAL TRADE CONTRACTORS	22442	4	9	MERCH. WHOLESALERS;DURABLE GDS	22657	376	4306	TRANSPORTATION EQUIPMENT MFG
22039	364	2037	EDUCATIONAL SERVICES	22443	274	1518	FOOD SVCS & DRINKING PLACES	22660	55	228	GASOLINE STATIONS
22040	5	37	JUSTICE; PUBIC ORDER/SAFETY	22446	6	17	ADMIN. OF ECONOMIC PROGRAMS	22663	62	307	JUSTICE; PUBIC ORDER/SAFETY
22041	994	8868	PROF.; SCIENTIFIC; & TECH SVCS	22448	51	765	PROF.; SCIENTIFIC; & TECH SVCS	22664	591	4574	EDUCATIONAL SERVICES
22042	1138	30480	HOSPITALS	22451	3	3	ADMINISTRATIVE & SUPPORT SVCS	22701	1440	13721	EDUCATIONAL SERVICES
22043	683	6713	PROF.; SCIENTIFIC; & TECH SVCS	22454	24	70	SPECIAL TRADE CONTRACTORS	22709	12	78	NURSING & RESID. CARE FACILIT.
22044	600	5101	MOTOR VEHICLE & PARTS DEALERS	22460	44	156	NURSING & RESID. CARE FACILIT.	22711	4	2	FURNITURE & RELATED PROD. MFG
22046	1245	10657	FURN. & HOME FURNISHGS STORES	22463	6	14	SPECIAL TRADE CONTRACTORS	22712	214	1765	EDUCATIONAL SERVICES
22060	115	5521	EXEC.; LEGIS.; & OTHER SUPPORT	22469	53	215	EDUCATIONAL SERVICES	22713	29	258	PROF.; SCIENTIFIC; & TECH SVCS
22066	555	2515	FOOD SVCS & DRINKING PLACES	22471	14	9	CONSTRUCTION OF BUILDINGS	22714	46	207	JUSTICE; PUBIC ORDER/SAFETY
22079	1122	11329	SPECIAL TRADE CONTRACTORS	22472	6	367	JUSTICE; PUBIC ORDER/SAFETY	22715	22	34	FABRICATED METAL PRODUCT MFG
22101	1573	11816	PROF.; SCIENTIFIC; & TECH SVCS	22473	202	863	EDUCATIONAL SERVICES	22716	22	49	ADMINISTRATIVE & SUPPORT SVCS
22102	2096	56925	PROF.; SCIENTIFIC; & TECH SVCS	22476	6	8	SOCIAL ASSISTANCE	22718	27	657	BLDG MATL & GARDEN EQPMT DLRS
22103	4	13	HEALTH & PERSONAL CARE STORES	22480	82	773	ACCOMMODATION	22719	7	15	WOOD PRODUCT MANUFACTURING
22106	4	18	PROF.; SCIENTIFIC; & TECH SVCS	22481	1	2	POSTAL SERVICE	22720	17	65	SPECIAL TRADE CONTRACTORS
22107	2	0	OTHER INFORMATION SERVICES	22482	394	3517	GENERAL MERCHANDISE STORES	22721	3	1	PROF.; SCIENTIFIC; & TECH SVCS
22108	1	0	PUBLISHING INDUSTRIES	22485	628	4976	PROF.; SCIENTIFIC; & TECH SVCS	22722	7	7	SPECIAL TRADE CONTRACTORS
22116	24	265	ADMINISTRATIVE & SUPPORT SVCS	22488	41	451	WOOD PRODUCT MANUFACTURING	22723	7	27	GENERAL MERCHANDISE STORES
22121	11	875	MUSEUMS; HIST. SITES;& SIMILAR	22501	27	172	MANAGMT OF COMPANIES & ENTERP.	22724	41	83	PROF.; SCIENTIFIC; & TECH SVCS
22122	30	878	PRINT'G & RELATED SUPP'T ACT'S	22503	140	557	EDUCATIONAL SERVICES	22725	8	47	BEVERAGE & TOBACCO PRODUCT MFG
22124	350	2489	EDUCATIONAL SERVICES	22504	6	17	SPECIAL TRADE CONTRACTORS	22726	29	233	NURSING & RESID. CARE FACILIT.
22125	125	378	FOOD SVCS & DRINKING PLACES	22507	31	100	NONMETALLIC MINERAL PROD. MFG	22727	302	1633	EDUCATIONAL SERVICES
22134	199	1336	EDUCATIONAL SERVICES	22508	243	1078	FOOD SVCS & DRINKING PLACES	22728	87	594	MACHINERY MANUFACTURING
22135	2	1003	EDUCATIONAL SERVICES	22509	3	0	POSTAL SERVICE	22729	11	335	JUSTICE; PUBIC ORDER/SAFETY
22150	1436	17215	PROF.; SCIENTIFIC; & TECH SVCS	22511	53	361	MERCH. WHOLESALERS;NONDUR. GDS	22730	5	1	GENERAL MERCHANDISE STORES
22151	626	10053	PUBLISHING INDUSTRIES	22513	2	5	REAL ESTATE	22731	5	50	ADMIN. OF ECONOMIC PROGRAMS
22152	471	5791	EDUCATIONAL SERVICES	22514	67	738	EDUCATIONAL SERVICES	22732	10	29	EDUCATIONAL SERVICES
22153	564	6978	MERCH. WHOLESALERS;DURABLE GDS	22517	4	18	TRANSIT & GRND PASS. TRANSPORT	22733	42	237	CROP PRODUCTION
22159	8	1260	PUBLISHING INDUSTRIES	22520	245	1342	EXEC.; LEGIS.; & OTHER SUPPORT	22734	105	567	EDUCATIONAL SERVICES
22161	1	0	MISCELLANEOUS MANUFACTURING	22523	1	1	POSTAL SERVICE	22735	31	67	SPECIAL TRADE CONTRACTORS
22172	206	963	EDUCATIONAL SERVICES	22524	9	40	MERCH. WHOLESALERS;NONDUR. GDS	22736	10	88	SOCIAL ASSISTANCE

ZIP CODE	2009 Total Firms	2009 Total Employ-ees	TOP INDUSTRY RANKED on 2009 EMPLOYMENT	ZIP CODE	2009 Total Firms	2009 Total Employ-ees	TOP INDUSTRY RANKED on 2009 EMPLOYMENT	ZIP CODE	2009 Total Firms	2009 Total Employ-ees	TOP INDUSTRY RANKED on 2009 EMPLOYMENT
22737	52	160	JUSTICE; PUBIC ORDER/SAFETY	23002	400	2442	SPECIAL TRADE CONTRACTORS	23149	208	1265	EDUCATIONAL SERVICES
22738	39	107	FOOD SVCS & DRINKING PLACES	23003	6	22	SPECIAL TRADE CONTRACTORS	23150	419	7536	COMPUTER & ELECTRONIC PROD MFG
22740	84	139	MISCELLANEOUS STORE RETAILERS	23004	32	305	NONMETALLIC MINERAL PROD. MFG	23153	13	24	GENERAL MERCHANDISE STORES
22741	15	112	CROP PRODUCTION	23005	1640	19978	SPECIAL TRADE CONTRACTORS	23154	4	2	RELIG.; GRANT; CIVIC; PROF ORG
22742	33	69	PROF.; SCIENTIFIC; & TECH SVCS	23009	156	898	NONMETALLIC MINERAL PROD. MFG	23155	1	35	FOOD AND BEVERAGE STORES
22743	8	105	ACCOMMODATION	23011	34	61	MERCH. WHOLESALERS;DURABLE GDS	23156	46	235	REAL ESTATE
22746	4	4	POSTAL SERVICE	23014	1	351	JUSTICE; PUBIC ORDER/SAFETY	23160	5	623	JUSTICE; PUBIC ORDER/SAFETY
22747	158	747	EDUCATIONAL SERVICES	23015	88	321	SPECIAL TRADE CONTRACTORS	23161	5	54	RELIG.; GRANT; CIVIC; PROF ORG
22748	8	36	FOOD AND BEVERAGE STORES	23018	8	43	MERCH. WHOLESALERS;NONDUR. GDS	23162	4	8	CONSTRUCTION OF BUILDINGS
22749	11	19	CROP PRODUCTION	23021	3	1	POSTAL SERVICE	23163	6	7	RELIG.; GRANT; CIVIC; PROF ORG
22801	2111	29193	FOOD SVCS & DRINKING PLACES	23022	25	65	CONSTRUCTION OF BUILDINGS	23168	199	1906	AMBULATORY HEALTH CARE SVCS
22802	726	10401	PRINT'G & RELATED SUPP'T ACT'S	23023	4	38	EDUCATIONAL SERVICES	23169	50	218	SPECIAL TRADE CONTRACTORS
22803	7	17	MERCH. WHOLESALERS;DURABLE GDS	23024	113	372	JUSTICE; PUBIC ORDER/SAFETY	23170	1	5	CROP PRODUCTION
22807	8	1725	EDUCATIONAL SERVICES	23025	5	37	AMUSEMENT; GAMBLING;& RECREAT.	23173	18	495	EDUCATIONAL SERVICES
22810	49	271	BLDG MATL & GARDEN EQPMT DLRS	23027	31	125	RELIG.; GRANT; CIVIC; PROF ORG	23175	136	598	MISCELLANEOUS STORE RETAILERS
22811	13	99	JUSTICE; PUBIC ORDER/SAFETY	23030	197	1338	EDUCATIONAL SERVICES	23176	8	13	SPECIAL TRADE CONTRACTORS
22812	216	5061	EDUCATIONAL SERVICES	23031	3	77	EDUCATIONAL SERVICES	23177	21	72	AMBULATORY HEALTH CARE SVCS
22815	238	1822	EDUCATIONAL SERVICES	23032	9	30	SPECIAL TRADE CONTRACTORS	23178	5	6	ADMINISTRATIVE & SUPPORT SVCS
22820	8	10	CONSTRUCTION OF BUILDINGS	23035	34	190	TEXTILE MILLS	23180	7	24	JUSTICE; PUBIC ORDER/SAFETY
22821	197	2227	MERCH. WHOLESALERS;NONDUR. GDS	23038	32	74	PIPELINE TRANSPORTATION	23181	247	2486	PAPER MANUFACTURING
22824	305	4156	TELECOMMUNICATIONS	23039	35	131	EDUCATIONAL SERVICES	23183	28	106	MERCH. WHOLESALERS;DURABLE GDS
22827	310	3455	CHEMICAL MANUFACTURING	23040	140	856	EDUCATIONAL SERVICES	23184	6	7	MISCELLANEOUS STORE RETAILERS
22830	28	83	EDUCATIONAL SERVICES	23043	158	646	AMUSEMENT; GAMBLING;& RECREAT.	23185	2051	27880	FOOD SVCS & DRINKING PLACES
22831	24	530	MERCH. WHOLESALERS;NONDUR. GDS	23045	5	42	MERCH. WHOLESALERS;DURABLE GDS	23186	4	4851	EDUCATIONAL SERVICES
22832	25	81	AMUSEMENT; GAMBLING;& RECREAT.	23047	91	6809	AMUSEMENT; GAMBLING;& RECREAT.	23187	17	51	ADMINISTRATIVE & SUPPORT SVCS
22833	3	3	POSTAL SERVICE	23050	15	33	CONSTRUCTION OF BUILDINGS	23188	1516	15401	FOOD SVCS & DRINKING PLACES
22834	32	111	EDUCATIONAL SERVICES	23055	83	919	FURN. & HOME FURNISHGS STORES	23190	6	16	FOOD AND BEVERAGE STORES
22835	624	4803	APPAREL MANUFACTURING	23056	16	32	ADMIN. OF ECONOMIC PROGRAMS	23192	189	827	EDUCATIONAL SERVICES
22840	104	4175	AMUSEMENT; GAMBLING;& RECREAT.	23058	21	59	HEAVY & CIVIL ENG. CONSTRUCT'N	23218	10	45	EXEC.; LEGIS.; & OTHER SUPPORT
22841	108	1775	SPECIAL TRADE CONTRACTORS	23059	904	13743	BLDG MATL & GARDEN EQPMT DLRS	23219	2263	53406	PROF.; SCIENTIFIC; & TECH SVCS
22842	257	1963	FURNITURE & RELATED PROD. MFG	23060	1249	20087	INSURANCE CARRIERS & RELATED	23220	1471	20537	MUSEUMS; HIST. SITES;& SIMILAR
22843	38	163	EDUCATIONAL SERVICES	23061	788	7271	EDUCATIONAL SERVICES	23221	540	3876	FOOD SVCS & DRINKING PLACES
22844	244	1860	PRIMARY METAL MANUFACTURING	23062	88	888	EDUCATIONAL SERVICES	23222	593	3877	EDUCATIONAL SERVICES
22845	8	16	CONSTRUCTION OF BUILDINGS	23063	247	1976	EDUCATIONAL SERVICES	23223	1036	10035	EDUCATIONAL SERVICES
22846	50	489	EDUCATIONAL SERVICES	23064	5	43	ACCOMMODATION	23224	1384	13107	TRUCK TRANSPORTATION
22847	41	417	EDUCATIONAL SERVICES	23065	32	67	RELIG.; GRANT; CIVIC; PROF ORG	23225	1388	18015	HOSPITALS
22848	2	5	INSURANCE CARRIERS & RELATED	23066	6	79	MUSEUMS; HIST. SITES;& SIMILAR	23226	1098	12189	AMBULATORY HEALTH CARE SVCS
22849	165	1155	EDUCATIONAL SERVICES	23067	4	1	BLDG MATL & GARDEN EQPMT DLRS	23227	699	8512	NURSING & RESID. CARE FACILIT.
22850	19	16	REPAIR AND MAINTENANCE	23068	5	21	FOOD SVCS & DRINKING PLACES	23228	1459	15975	SPECIAL TRADE CONTRACTORS
22851	185	959	WOOD PRODUCT MANUFACTURING	23069	187	3826	EXEC.; LEGIS.; & OTHER SUPPORT	23229	1190	11267	HOSPITALS
22853	127	2147	MERCH. WHOLESALERS;NONDUR. GDS	23070	5	9	SPECIAL TRADE CONTRACTORS	23230	2124	34126	INSURANCE CARRIERS & RELATED
22901	1983	39567	EDUCATIONAL SERVICES	23071	57	243	JUSTICE; PUBIC ORDER/SAFETY	23231	1008	12849	CHEMICAL MANUFACTURING
22902	2200	19028	EXEC.; LEGIS.; & OTHER SUPPORT	23072	436	2142	AMBULATORY HEALTH CARE SVCS	23232	4	2217	POSTAL SERVICE
22903	1949	29295	AMBULATORY HEALTH CARE SVCS	23075	201	1234	EDUCATIONAL SERVICES	23233	1112	13515	FOOD SVCS & DRINKING PLACES
22904	25	1315	OTHER INFORMATION SERVICES	23076	28	112	NAT'L SECURITY & INT'L AFFAIRS	23234	831	14653	BEVERAGE & TOBACCO PRODUCT MFG
22905	10	21	SPECIAL TRADE CONTRACTORS	23079	8	9	PERFORM'G ARTS; SPEC. SPORTS	23235	2105	26742	JUSTICE; PUBIC ORDER/SAFETY
22906	29	53	PROF.; SCIENTIFIC; & TECH SVCS	23081	1	15	EXEC.; LEGIS.; & OTHER SUPPORT	23236	1057	9608	PROF.; SCIENTIFIC; & TECH SVCS
22908	389	6442	AMBULATORY HEALTH CARE SVCS	23083	49	436	FOOD MANUFACTURING	23237	660	7936	MERCH. WHOLESALERS;DURABLE GDS
22909	2	1305	INSURANCE CARRIERS & RELATED	23084	33	49	RELIG.; GRANT; CIVIC; PROF ORG	23238	649	10074	MOTOR VEHICLE & PARTS DEALERS
22910	1	0	MERCH. WHOLESALERS;DURABLE GDS	23085	44	249	EXEC.; LEGIS.; & OTHER SUPPORT	23242	16	29	SPECIAL TRADE CONTRACTORS
22911	884	10363	COMPUTER & ELECTRONIC PROD MFG	23086	162	1308	EXEC.; LEGIS.; & OTHER SUPPORT	23249	9	2098	AMBULATORY HEALTH CARE SVCS
22920	111	516	EDUCATIONAL SERVICES	23089	93	338	HEAVY & CIVIL ENG. CONSTRUCT'N	23250	53	1186	ADMIN. OF ECONOMIC PROGRAMS
22922	84	509	UTILITIES	23090	10	31	CLOTHING & CLOTH'G ACC. STORES	23255	12	78	INSURANCE CARRIERS & RELATED
22923	123	324	SPECIAL TRADE CONTRACTORS	23091	5	133	UNCLASSIFIED ESTABLISHMENTS	23260	7	13	MUSEUMS; HIST. SITES;& SIMILAR
22924	3	4	POSTAL SERVICE	23092	23	317	EDUCATIONAL SERVICES	23261	6	24	SOCIAL ASSISTANCE
22931	16	201	MERCH. WHOLESALERS;NONDUR. GDS	23093	429	3783	EXEC.; LEGIS.; & OTHER SUPPORT	23269	3	0	CREDIT INTERMEDIATION & RELATD
22932	274	1663	EDUCATIONAL SERVICES	23101	1	4	PROF.; SCIENTIFIC; & TECH SVCS	23273	5	36	EXEC.; LEGIS.; & OTHER SUPPORT
22935	18	104	RELIG.; GRANT; CIVIC; PROF ORG	23102	41	179	SOCIAL ASSISTANCE	23279	1	400	INSURANCE CARRIERS & RELATED
22936	131	633	TRANSPORTATION EQUIPMENT MFG	23103	198	1783	NONMETALLIC MINERAL PROD. MFG	23284	57	1990	EDUCATIONAL SERVICES
22937	27	58	EDUCATIONAL SERVICES	23105	3	10	GASOLINE STATIONS	23288	1	30	FOOD SVCS & DRINKING PLACES
22938	40	136	ADMINISTRATIVE & SUPPORT SVCS	23106	43	175	AMBULATORY HEALTH CARE SVCS	23294	1073	14474	FOOD SVCS & DRINKING PLACES
22939	273	7996	HOSPITALS	23107	1	0	POSTAL SERVICE	23297	4	2308	EXEC.; LEGIS.; & OTHER SUPPORT
22940	48	130	CONSTRUCTION OF BUILDINGS	23108	1	1	ADMINISTRATIVE & SUPPORT SVCS	23298	144	15212	HOSPITALS
22942	233	3322	GENERAL MERCHANDISE STORES	23109	232	1158	EDUCATIONAL SERVICES	23301	140	867	JUSTICE; PUBIC ORDER/SAFETY
22943	24	53	ADMINISTRATIVE & SUPPORT SVCS	23110	34	169	EDUCATIONAL SERVICES	23303	20	99	JUSTICE; PUBIC ORDER/SAFETY
22945	11	35	RELIG.; GRANT; CIVIC; PROF ORG	23111	1207	11379	FOOD SVCS & DRINKING PLACES	23304	2	15	INSURANCE CARRIERS & RELATED
22946	8	13	PROF.; SCIENTIFIC; & TECH SVCS	23112	1445	15246	FOOD SVCS & DRINKING PLACES	23306	94	530	NURSING & RESID. CARE FACILIT.
22947	150	645	AMUSEMENT; GAMBLING;& RECREAT.	23113	1045	9186	FOOD SVCS & DRINKING PLACES	23307	22	18	PERSONAL AND LAUNDRY SERVICES
22948	8	19	ACCOMMODATION	23114	324	2792	HOSPITALS	23308	33	39	PERSONAL AND LAUNDRY SERVICES
22949	163	1305	UTILITIES	23115	10	63	FOOD AND BEVERAGE STORES	23310	292	2492	FOOD SVCS & DRINKING PLACES
22952	43	225	SPECIAL TRADE CONTRACTORS	23116	713	9314	FOOD AND BEVERAGE STORES	23313	2	1	POSTAL SERVICE
22957	6	29	MUSEUMS; HIST. SITES;& SIMILAR	23117	258	1025	EDUCATIONAL SERVICES	23314	169	727	EDUCATIONAL SERVICES
22958	87	1542	ACCOMMODATION	23119	6	12	SPECIAL TRADE CONTRACTORS	23315	31	102	EDUCATIONAL SERVICES
22959	58	293	WOOD PRODUCT MANUFACTURING	23120	119	491	EDUCATIONAL SERVICES	23316	35	341	MERCH. WHOLESALERS;NONDUR. GDS
22960	577	4646	EDUCATIONAL SERVICES	23123	37	356	AMBULATORY HEALTH CARE SVCS	23320	3185	48294	PROF.; SCIENTIFIC; & TECH SVCS
22963	420	2280	EDUCATIONAL SERVICES	23124	109	992	HOSPITALS	23321	1035	10080	FOOD SVCS & DRINKING PLACES
22964	22	96	CROP PRODUCTION	23125	5	11	ACCOMMODATION	23322	1442	13240	JUSTICE; PUBIC ORDER/SAFETY
22965	7	38	PERSONAL AND LAUNDRY SERVICES	23126	16	35	AMBULATORY HEALTH CARE SVCS	23323	887	10115	MERCH. WHOLESALERS;DURABLE GDS
22967	65	223	AMUSEMENT; GAMBLING;& RECREAT.	23127	7	34	PROF.; SCIENTIFIC; & TECH SVCS	23324	620	7113	MERCH. WHOLESALERS;DURABLE GDS
22968	381	1922	SPECIAL TRADE CONTRACTORS	23128	15	18	SPECIAL TRADE CONTRACTORS	23325	292	2136	EDUCATIONAL SERVICES
22969	26	38	FURNITURE & RELATED PROD. MFG	23129	57	466	MERCH. WHOLESALERS;DURABLE GDS	23326	1	0	NAT'L SECURITY & INT'L AFFAIRS
22971	22	67	CONSTRUCTION OF BUILDINGS	23130	5	5	CONSTRUCTION OF BUILDINGS	23327	6	5	ADMINISTRATIVE & SUPPORT SVCS
22972	17	52	ADMINISTRATIVE & SUPPORT SVCS	23131	14	44	FOOD AND BEVERAGE STORES	23328	17	74	SPECIAL TRADE CONTRACTORS
22973	229	1323	EDUCATIONAL SERVICES	23138	17	74	BLDG MATL & GARDEN EQPMT DLRS	23336	265	1493	ACCOMMODATION
22974	145	794	SPECIAL TRADE CONTRACTORS	23139	799	4333	EDUCATIONAL SERVICES	23337	23	1389	SPACE RESEARCH AND TECHNOLOGY
22976	7	64	MERCH. WHOLESALERS;NONDUR. GDS	23140	178	999	SPECIAL TRADE CONTRACTORS	23341	9	8	MINING (EXCEPT OIL AND GAS)
22980	1211	12005	PAPER MANUFACTURING	23141	169	749	FOOD AND BEVERAGE STORES	23347	52	362	JUSTICE; PUBIC ORDER/SAFETY
22987	3	4	FOOD AND BEVERAGE STORES	23146	177	1477	SPECIAL TRADE CONTRACTORS	23350	210	2078	MERCH. WHOLESALERS;NONDUR. GDS
22989	2	200	EDUCATIONAL SERVICES	23147	5	23	MUSEUMS; HIST. SITES;& SIMILAR	23354	17	85	AMBULATORY HEALTH CARE SVCS
23001	4	5	MERCH. WHOLESALERS;NONDUR. GDS	23148	32	136	EDUCATIONAL SERVICES	23356	20	121	REAL ESTATE

BUSINESS DATA

ZIP CODE	2009 Total Firms	2009 Total Employ-ees	TOP INDUSTRY RANKED on 2009 EMPLOYMENT	ZIP CODE	2009 Total Firms	2009 Total Employ-ees	TOP INDUSTRY RANKED on 2009 EMPLOYMENT	ZIP CODE	2009 Total Firms	2009 Total Employ-ees	TOP INDUSTRY RANKED on 2009 EMPLOYMENT
23357	10	14	PROF.; SCIENTIFIC; & TECH SVCS	23605	478	4856	PROF.; SCIENTIFIC; & TECH SVCS	23899	19	49	WOOD PRODUCT MANUFACTURING
23358	4	21	FOOD AND BEVERAGE STORES	23606	1724	19379	PROF.; SCIENTIFIC; & TECH SVCS	23901	873	7974	HOSPITALS
23359	15	31	ADMINISTRATIVE & SUPPORT SVCS	23607	796	27012	TRANSPORTATION EQUIPMENT MFG	23909	3	760	EDUCATIONAL SERVICES
23389	3	4	POSTAL SERVICE	23608	977	7988	EDUCATIONAL SERVICES	23915	13	170	JUSTICE; PUBIC ORDER/SAFETY
23395	9	80	ACCOMMODATION	23609	8	13	SCENIC & SIGHTSEEING TRANSPORT	23917	107	1407	JUSTICE; PUBIC ORDER/SAFETY
23397	32	471	EXEC.; LEGIS.; & OTHER SUPPORT	23612	6	50	CONSTRUCTION OF BUILDINGS	23919	118	554	SUPPORT ACT. FOR TRANSPORT.
23398	4	15	ACCOMMODATION	23630	5	1015	CLOTHING & CLOTH'G ACC. STORES	23920	73	257	TEXTILE MILLS
23401	18	78	MOTOR VEHICLE & PARTS DEALERS	23651	18	81	FOOD SVCS & DRINKING PLACES	23921	107	709	EDUCATIONAL SERVICES
23404	3	32	BLDG MATL & GARDEN EQPMT DLRS	23661	602	8716	SPECIAL TRADE CONTRACTORS	23922	73	1712	JUSTICE; PUBIC ORDER/SAFETY
23405	29	155	EDUCATIONAL SERVICES	23662	310	2372	RELIG.; GRANT; CIVIC; PROF ORG	23923	113	597	EDUCATIONAL SERVICES
23407	16	575	FOOD MANUFACTURING	23663	300	2488	EDUCATIONAL SERVICES	23924	235	1397	NONMETALLIC MINERAL PROD. MFG
23408	3	1	RELIG.; GRANT; CIVIC; PROF ORG	23664	121	286	AMUSEMENT; GAMBLING;& RECREAT.	23927	269	1721	PROF.; SCIENTIFIC; & TECH SVCS
23409	4	28	BLDG MATL & GARDEN EQPMT DLRS	23665	65	729	NAT'L SECURITY & INT'L AFFAIRS	23930	187	1276	EDUCATIONAL SERVICES
23410	89	628	EDUCATIONAL SERVICES	23666	1801	21372	FOOD SVCS & DRINKING PLACES	23934	10	12	CROP PRODUCTION
23412	1	1	RELIG.; GRANT; CIVIC; PROF ORG	23667	11	1291	HOSPITALS	23936	239	1540	JUSTICE; PUBIC ORDER/SAFETY
23413	75	1397	HOSPITALS	23668	4	167	FOOD SVCS & DRINKING PLACES	23937	61	276	WOOD PRODUCT MANUFACTURING
23414	13	89	NURSING & RESID. CARE FACILIT.	23669	1121	12559	ADMINISTRATIVE & SUPPORT SVCS	23938	9	16	FOOD SVCS & DRINKING PLACES
23415	71	310	JUSTICE; PUBIC ORDER/SAFETY	23670	10	223	POSTAL SERVICE	23939	7	13	REPAIR AND MAINTENANCE
23416	41	402	EDUCATIONAL SERVICES	23681	1	3000	SPACE RESEARCH AND TECHNOLOGY	23941	1	0	RELIG.; GRANT; CIVIC; PROF ORG
23417	216	841	NURSING & RESID. CARE FACILIT.	23690	132	977	EXEC.; LEGIS.; & OTHER SUPPORT	23942	20	58	MUSEUMS; HIST. SITES;& SIMILAR
23418	133	1203	AMBULATORY HEALTH CARE SVCS	23691	3	41	PROF.; SCIENTIFIC; & TECH SVCS	23943	15	63	JUSTICE; PUBIC ORDER/SAFETY
23420	75	225	SPECIAL TRADE CONTRACTORS	23692	769	6514	EDUCATIONAL SERVICES	23944	180	1283	MERCH. WHOLESALERS;DURABLE GDS
23421	150	1488	FOOD MANUFACTURING	23693	587	5527	GENERAL MERCHANDISE STORES	23947	169	1492	MERCH. WHOLESALERS;DURABLE GDS
23422	11	13	RELIG.; GRANT; CIVIC; PROF ORG	23694	4	2	PROF.; SCIENTIFIC; & TECH SVCS	23950	143	1199	FABRICATED METAL PRODUCT MFG
23423	10	30	REAL ESTATE	23696	65	331	BEVERAGE & TOBACCO PRODUCT MFG	23952	29	129	JUSTICE; PUBIC ORDER/SAFETY
23424	1	2	POSTAL SERVICE	23701	724	6726	EDUCATIONAL SERVICES	23954	28	77	SPECIAL TRADE CONTRACTORS
23426	6	26	FOOD MANUFACTURING	23702	280	2568	PERSONAL AND LAUNDRY SERVICES	23955	23	132	JUSTICE; PUBIC ORDER/SAFETY
23427	10	46	MERCH. WHOLESALERS;NONDUR. GDS	23703	503	6080	EDUCATIONAL SERVICES	23958	47	79	GASOLINE STATIONS
23429	2	0	CROP PRODUCTION	23704	931	13516	HOSPITALS	23959	22	58	EDUCATIONAL SERVICES
23430	614	7074	MERCH. WHOLESALERS;NONDUR. GDS	23705	6	27	TRANSPORTATION EQUIPMENT MFG	23960	45	93	EXEC.; LEGIS.; & OTHER SUPPORT
23431	2	6	HEAVY & CIVIL ENG. CONSTRUCT'N	23707	515	11595	HOSPITALS	23962	12	36	WASTE MANAGMT & REMEDIAT'N SVC
23432	44	145	JUSTICE; PUBIC ORDER/SAFETY	23708	11	50	FOOD AND BEVERAGE STORES	23963	11	39	RELIG.; GRANT; CIVIC; PROF ORG
23433	25	161	BLDG MATL & GARDEN EQPMT DLRS	23709	39	4811	NAT'L SECURITY & INT'L AFFAIRS	23964	22	145	WOOD PRODUCT MANUFACTURING
23434	1602	19953	EXEC.; LEGIS.; & OTHER SUPPORT	23801	56	1030	NAT'L SECURITY & INT'L AFFAIRS	23966	39	111	SOCIAL ASSISTANCE
23435	463	4460	GENERAL MERCHANDISE STORES	23803	1311	11322	AMBULATORY HEALTH CARE SVCS	23967	16	77	EDUCATIONAL SERVICES
23436	20	21	FOOD SVCS & DRINKING PLACES	23804	2	6	ADMINISTRATIVE & SUPPORT SVCS	23968	22	219	EDUCATIONAL SERVICES
23437	68	259	EDUCATIONAL SERVICES	23805	571	7641	HOSPITALS	23970	568	6145	HOSPITALS
23438	42	132	MERCH. WHOLESALERS;DURABLE GDS	23806	5	1003	EDUCATIONAL SERVICES	23974	135	1042	JUSTICE; PUBIC ORDER/SAFETY
23439	4	26	TRANSIT & GRND PASS. TRANSPORT	23821	42	312	EDUCATIONAL SERVICES	23976	18	268	WOOD PRODUCT MANUFACTURING
23440	24	89	EDUCATIONAL SERVICES	23824	347	2425	NAT'L SECURITY & INT'L AFFAIRS	24001	2	2	DATA PROCESS'G
23441	30	152	HEAVY & CIVIL ENG. CONSTRUCT'N	23827	48	529	TEXTILE PRODUCT MILLS	24004	1	1	SOCIAL ASSISTANCE
23442	51	1706	FOOD MANUFACTURING	23828	16	16	FOOD MANUFACTURING	24007	1	0	PROF.; SCIENTIFIC; & TECH SVCS
23443	3	5	ACCOMMODATION	23829	37	506	JUSTICE; PUBIC ORDER/SAFETY	24011	650	8079	PROF.; SCIENTIFIC; & TECH SVCS
23450	10	23	ADMINISTRATIVE & SUPPORT SVCS	23830	27	219	SPECIAL TRADE CONTRACTORS	24012	1590	23120	FOOD SVCS & DRINKING PLACES
23451	2166	18819	FOOD SVCS & DRINKING PLACES	23831	964	8843	FOOD SVCS & DRINKING PLACES	24013	290	3055	SPECIAL TRADE CONTRACTORS
23452	3202	42105	MOTOR VEHICLE & PARTS DEALERS	23832	680	16660	EXEC.; LEGIS.; & OTHER SUPPORT	24014	671	12655	AMBULATORY HEALTH CARE SVCS
23453	579	8585	EDUCATIONAL SERVICES	23833	27	186	JUSTICE; PUBIC ORDER/SAFETY	24015	477	3874	EDUCATIONAL SERVICES
23454	2010	24591	AMBULATORY HEALTH CARE SVCS	23834	1169	13872	GENERAL MERCHANDISE STORES	24016	912	12856	JUSTICE; PUBIC ORDER/SAFETY
23455	1508	16090	PROF.; SCIENTIFIC; & TECH SVCS	23836	388	6233	MERCH. WHOLESALERS;DURABLE GDS	24017	650	6862	SPECIAL TRADE CONTRACTORS
23456	1068	11829	EDUCATIONAL SERVICES	23837	177	1650	JUSTICE; PUBIC ORDER/SAFETY	24018	1859	17244	FOOD SVCS & DRINKING PLACES
23457	112	582	CROP PRODUCTION	23838	200	799	EDUCATIONAL SERVICES	24019	908	13941	MISCELLANEOUS MANUFACTURING
23458	4	22	ADMINISTRATIVE & SUPPORT SVCS	23839	24	342	EDUCATIONAL SERVICES	24020	2	0	POSTAL SERVICE
23459	8	30	RELIG.; GRANT; CIVIC; PROF ORG	23840	27	67	NURSING & RESID. CARE FACILIT.	24022	6	11	PROF.; SCIENTIFIC; & TECH SVCS
23460	29	321	NAT'L SECURITY & INT'L AFFAIRS	23841	136	1077	EDUCATIONAL SERVICES	24025	2	8	MERCH. WHOLESALERS;DURABLE GDS
23461	8	29	ACCOMMODATION	23842	102	1839	MERCH. WHOLESALERS;DURABLE GDS	24028	3	3	CONSTRUCTION OF BUILDINGS
23462	2993	36556	PROF.; SCIENTIFIC; & TECH SVCS	23843	8	40	MERCH. WHOLESALERS;DURABLE GDS	24031	2	20	TRUCK TRANSPORTATION
23463	5	2514	PROF.; SCIENTIFIC; & TECH SVCS	23844	11	11	MISCELLANEOUS STORE RETAILERS	24032	1	7	SPECIAL TRADE CONTRACTORS
23464	1633	14663	EDUCATIONAL SERVICES	23845	19	64	FORESTRY AND LOGGING	24034	2	28	MUSEUMS; HIST. SITES;& SIMILAR
23466	15	33	CONSTRUCTION OF BUILDINGS	23846	10	7	FURN. & HOME FURNISHGS STORES	24035	2	3	SPECIAL TRADE CONTRACTORS
23467	15	61	PERFORM'G ARTS; SPEC. SPORTS	23847	613	5934	FOOD SVCS & DRINKING PLACES	24038	1	4	PROF.; SCIENTIFIC; & TECH SVCS
23471	23	48	SCENIC & SIGHTSEEING TRANSPORT	23850	12	37	CONSTRUCTION OF BUILDINGS	24042	1	900	RAIL TRANSPORTATION
23480	17	56	EXEC.; LEGIS.; & OTHER SUPPORT	23851	701	7483	MERCH. WHOLESALERS;NONDUR. GDS	24053	66	286	AMBULATORY HEALTH CARE SVCS
23483	2	28	NONSTORE RETAILERS	23856	19	103	MINING (EXCEPT OIL AND GAS)	24054	120	783	FURNITURE & RELATED PROD. MFG
23486	5	21	MERCH. WHOLESALERS;NONDUR. GDS	23857	33	307	FORESTRY AND LOGGING	24055	374	2466	FURNITURE & RELATED PROD. MFG
23487	195	1116	EDUCATIONAL SERVICES	23860	816	9777	CHEMICAL MANUFACTURING	24058	4	3	RELIG.; GRANT; CIVIC; PROF ORG
23488	2	0	POSTAL SERVICE	23866	46	162	CHEMICAL MANUFACTURING	24059	27	44	EDUCATIONAL SERVICES
23501	14	57	CLOTHING & CLOTH'G ACC. STORES	23867	67	983	WHOLESALE ELEC. MRKTS & AGENTS	24060	1317	16003	FOOD SVCS & DRINKING PLACES
23502	2120	35959	AMBULATORY HEALTH CARE SVCS	23868	277	3587	EDUCATIONAL SERVICES	24061	25	903	PROF.; SCIENTIFIC; & TECH SVCS
23503	353	2046	EDUCATIONAL SERVICES	23870	1	900	JUSTICE; PUBIC ORDER/SAFETY	24062	8	26	MISCELLANEOUS MANUFACTURING
23504	565	6741	EDUCATIONAL SERVICES	23872	72	515	BEVERAGE & TOBACCO PRODUCT MFG	24063	4	7	SPECIAL TRADE CONTRACTORS
23505	774	9682	HOSPITALS	23873	1	1	POSTAL SERVICE	24064	93	756	MINING (EXCEPT OIL AND GAS)
23506	1	0	PUBLISHING INDUSTRIES	23874	22	124	EDUCATIONAL SERVICES	24065	148	545	WOOD PRODUCT MANUFACTURING
23507	260	11139	HOSPITALS	23875	320	3257	EDUCATIONAL SERVICES	24066	161	904	EDUCATIONAL SERVICES
23508	365	3139	EDUCATIONAL SERVICES	23876	8	19	RELIG.; GRANT; CIVIC; PROF ORG	24067	47	202	SPECIAL TRADE CONTRACTORS
23509	280	2308	EDUCATIONAL SERVICES	23878	33	111	EDUCATIONAL SERVICES	24068	11	12	AMBULATORY HEALTH CARE SVCS
23510	1775	30666	PUBLISHING INDUSTRIES	23879	20	303	WOOD PRODUCT MANUFACTURING	24069	32	36	BLDG MATL & GARDEN EQPMT DLRS
23511	110	2323	CREDIT INTERMEDIATION & RELATD	23881	27	78	CROP PRODUCTION	24070	27	697	HOSPITALS
23513	749	9349	RELIG.; GRANT; CIVIC; PROF ORG	23882	99	667	AMBULATORY HEALTH CARE SVCS	24072	25	99	EDUCATIONAL SERVICES
23514	6	33	SOCIAL ASSISTANCE	23883	121	1447	UTILITIES	24073	1486	15014	FOOD SVCS & DRINKING PLACES
23517	658	5731	FOOD SVCS & DRINKING PLACES	23884	27	553	EXEC.; LEGIS.; & OTHER SUPPORT	24076	30	228	MISCELLANEOUS STORE RETAILERS
23518	876	7199	FOOD SVCS & DRINKING PLACES	23885	46	107	AMBULATORY HEALTH CARE SVCS	24077	61	650	EDUCATIONAL SERVICES
23521	68	1546	NAT'L SECURITY & INT'L AFFAIRS	23887	14	35	GASOLINE STATIONS	24078	321	2528	ADMINISTRATIVE & SUPPORT SVCS
23523	193	7180	TRANSPORTATION EQUIPMENT MFG	23888	94	543	FOOD SVCS & DRINKING PLACES	24079	34	158	EDUCATIONAL SERVICES
23529	11	3362	EDUCATIONAL SERVICES	23889	8	37	GASOLINE STATIONS	24082	10	61	EDUCATIONAL SERVICES
23541	5	12	ADMINISTRATIVE & SUPPORT SVCS	23890	171	1711	MERCH. WHOLESALERS;NONDUR. GDS	24083	202	2263	REPAIR AND MAINTENANCE
23551	1	4	FOOD SVCS & DRINKING PLACES	23891	3	300	JUSTICE; PUBIC ORDER/SAFETY	24084	365	6783	MOTOR VEHICLE & PARTS DEALERS
23601	1149	11664	HOSPITALS	23893	5	3	FOOD AND BEVERAGE STORES	24085	42	341	MACHINERY MANUFACTURING
23602	1355	16357	FOOD SVCS & DRINKING PLACES	23894	5	19	FORESTRY AND LOGGING	24086	7	6	POSTAL SERVICE
23603	111	3381	MERCH. WHOLESALERS;DURABLE GDS	23897	16	12	ACCOMMODATION	24087	79	675	EDUCATIONAL SERVICES
23604	44	1137	NAT'L SECURITY & INT'L AFFAIRS	23898	35	154	NURSING & RESID. CARE FACILIT.	24088	101	975	EDUCATIONAL SERVICES

ZIP CODE	2009 Total Firms	2009 Total Employ-ees	TOP INDUSTRY RANKED on 2009 EMPLOYMENT
24089	86	198	CLOTHING & CLOTH'G ACC. STORES
24090	169	1880	EXEC.; LEGIS.; & OTHER SUPPORT
24091	392	2638	TELECOMMUNICATIONS
24092	71	275	EDUCATIONAL SERVICES
24093	18	232	UTILITIES
24095	59	267	EDUCATIONAL SERVICES
24101	198	960	FOOD AND BEVERAGE STORES
24102	42	128	EDUCATIONAL SERVICES
24104	93	382	REAL ESTATE
24105	8	6	FOOD MANUFACTURING
24111	8	7	REPAIR AND MAINTENANCE
24112	1874	20017	FURNITURE & RELATED PROD. MFG
24114	3	2	HOSPITALS
24115	2	5	ACCOMMODATION
24120	87	588	CHEMICAL MANUFACTURING
24121	471	2400	EDUCATIONAL SERVICES
24122	55	289	MERCH. WHOLESALERS;DURABLE GDS
24124	112	1048	PAPER MANUFACTURING
24126	7	13	MISCELLANEOUS STORE RETAILERS
24127	132	545	EDUCATIONAL SERVICES
24128	32	83	SPECIAL TRADE CONTRACTORS
24129	3	52	MACHINERY MANUFACTURING
24130	3	1	POSTAL SERVICE
24131	13	45	FOOD SVCS & DRINKING PLACES
24132	2	2	POSTAL SERVICE
24133	47	209	JUSTICE; PUBIC ORDER/SAFETY
24134	265	2177	AMBULATORY HEALTH CARE SVCS
24136	102	547	ACCOMMODATION
24137	62	271	AMUSEMENT; GAMBLING;& RECREAT.
24138	23	51	FOOD AND BEVERAGE STORES
24139	9	10	POSTAL SERVICE
24141	773	6954	MACHINERY MANUFACTURING
24142	4	1388	EDUCATIONAL SERVICES
24143	2	7	PROF.; SCIENTIFIC; & TECH SVCS
24146	3	2	POSTAL SERVICE
24147	56	479	NURSING & RESID. CARE FACILIT.
24148	249	2922	ADMINISTRATIVE & SUPPORT SVCS
24149	68	526	EDUCATIONAL SERVICES
24150	16	247	NONMETALLIC MINERAL PROD. MFG
24151	953	10219	WOOD PRODUCT MANUFACTURING
24153	1872	28952	HOSPITALS
24161	13	10	PROF.; SCIENTIFIC; & TECH SVCS
24162	67	284	EDUCATIONAL SERVICES
24165	45	146	AMBULATORY HEALTH CARE SVCS
24167	2	5	POSTAL SERVICE
24168	29	1533	FURNITURE & RELATED PROD. MFG
24171	413	3907	HOSPITALS
24174	30	190	MERCH. WHOLESALERS;DURABLE GDS
24175	252	1788	FOOD SVCS & DRINKING PLACES
24176	47	123	SUPPORT ACT. FOR TRANSPORT.
24177	6	237	TRANSPORTATION EQUIPMENT MFG
24178	2	2	SPECIAL TRADE CONTRACTORS
24179	641	5203	MISCELLANEOUS MANUFACTURING
24184	145	509	EDUCATIONAL SERVICES
24185	29	255	MERCH. WHOLESALERS;DURABLE GDS
24201	833	9803	FOOD SVCS & DRINKING PLACES
24202	474	6630	FOOD SVCS & DRINKING PLACES
24203	2	8	SPECIAL TRADE CONTRACTORS
24209	3	6	CONSTRUCTION OF BUILDINGS
24210	1162	11017	HOSPITALS
24211	269	1131	CONSTRUCTION OF BUILDINGS
24212	5	44	PROF.; SCIENTIFIC; & TECH SVCS
24215	2	18	MERCH. WHOLESALERS;DURABLE GDS
24216	84	696	MINING (EXCEPT OIL AND GAS)
24217	6	31	TRUCK TRANSPORTATION
24218	10	75	EDUCATIONAL SERVICES
24219	370	4760	EDUCATIONAL SERVICES
24220	11	114	EDUCATIONAL SERVICES
24221	5	12	POSTAL SERVICE
24224	110	719	EDUCATIONAL SERVICES
24225	27	310	UTILITIES
24226	40	162	EDUCATIONAL SERVICES
24228	233	1943	HOSPITALS
24230	238	1343	EDUCATIONAL SERVICES
24236	133	825	MACHINERY MANUFACTURING
24237	22	131	JUSTICE; PUBIC ORDER/SAFETY
24239	9	9	GASOLINE STATIONS
24243	28	148	EDUCATIONAL SERVICES
24244	146	1676	NURSING & RESID. CARE FACILIT.
24245	29	107	EDUCATIONAL SERVICES
24246	6	15	RELIG.; GRANT; CIVIC; PROF ORG
24248	58	451	EDUCATIONAL SERVICES
24250	15	76	EDUCATIONAL SERVICES
24251	274	1841	NAT'L SECURITY & INT'L AFFAIRS
24256	99	412	REPAIR AND MAINTENANCE
24258	17	43	EDUCATIONAL SERVICES
24260	121	1024	EDUCATIONAL SERVICES
24263	190	1487	EDUCATIONAL SERVICES
24265	15	262	MINING (EXCEPT OIL AND GAS)
24266	464	3598	FOOD SVCS & DRINKING PLACES
24269	7	27	BLDG MATL & GARDEN EQPMT DLRS
24270	11	10	AMBULATORY HEALTH CARE SVCS
24271	46	239	EDUCATIONAL SERVICES
24272	20	271	EDUCATIONAL SERVICES
24273	450	6630	MERCH. WHOLESALERS;DURABLE GDS
24277	226	2071	HOSPITALS
24279	146	596	EDUCATIONAL SERVICES
24280	46	421	SPECIAL TRADE CONTRACTORS
24281	53	468	MISCELLANEOUS MANUFACTURING
24282	25	653	NONSTORE RETAILERS
24283	122	748	FOOD AND BEVERAGE STORES
24290	120	932	FOOD AND BEVERAGE STORES
24292	20	95	JUSTICE; PUBIC ORDER/SAFETY
24293	399	3856	EDUCATIONAL SERVICES
24301	494	5107	FURNITURE & RELATED PROD. MFG
24311	68	2954	TRANSPORTATION EQUIPMENT MFG
24312	37	98	JUSTICE; PUBIC ORDER/SAFETY
24313	9	26	MERCH. WHOLESALERS;DURABLE GDS
24314	37	749	MERCH. WHOLESALERS;NONDUR. GDS
24315	103	1220	ELECT'L EQPMT; APP; & COMP MFG
24316	3	6	MUSEUMS; HIST. SITES;& SIMILAR
24317	103	471	EDUCATIONAL SERVICES
24318	6	8	POSTAL SERVICE
24319	194	2230	MISCELLANEOUS STORE RETAILERS
24322	4	0	SPECIAL TRADE CONTRACTORS
24323	13	17	PROF.; SCIENTIFIC; & TECH SVCS
24324	38	260	TRUCK TRANSPORTATION
24325	13	45	JUSTICE; PUBIC ORDER/SAFETY
24326	20	75	AMBULATORY HEALTH CARE SVCS
24327	8	355	EDUCATIONAL SERVICES
24328	66	247	ACCOMMODATION
24330	65	261	EDUCATIONAL SERVICES
24333	715	9019	FURNITURE & RELATED PROD. MFG
24340	134	787	EDUCATIONAL SERVICES
24343	427	5152	APPAREL MANUFACTURING
24347	19	272	ACCOMMODATION
24348	192	1696	EDUCATIONAL SERVICES
24350	20	38	MERCH. WHOLESALERS;DURABLE GDS
24351	6	33	JUSTICE; PUBIC ORDER/SAFETY
24352	23	195	NURSING & RESID. CARE FACILIT.
24354	652	9511	HOSPITALS
24360	158	1028	GASOLINE STATIONS
24361	80	448	EDUCATIONAL SERVICES
24363	36	216	EDUCATIONAL SERVICES
24366	33	266	EDUCATIONAL SERVICES
24368	136	1087	PLASTICS & RUBBER PRODUCTS MFG
24370	151	950	EDUCATIONAL SERVICES
24374	12	58	EDUCATIONAL SERVICES
24375	28	197	EDUCATIONAL SERVICES
24377	6	11	CREDIT INTERMEDIATION & RELATD
24378	30	62	AMBULATORY HEALTH CARE SVCS
24380	70	206	EDUCATIONAL SERVICES
24381	90	585	RENTAL AND LEASING SERVICES
24382	945	12245	MISCELLANEOUS MANUFACTURING
24401	1557	16344	FOOD SVCS & DRINKING PLACES
24402	6	12	PUBLISHING INDUSTRIES
24411	4	0	POSTAL SERVICE
24412	4	12	HOSPITALS
24413	21	40	COMPUTER & ELECTRONIC PROD MFG
24415	2	2	MISCELLANEOUS STORE RETAILERS
24416	315	2968	EDUCATIONAL SERVICES
24421	75	251	EDUCATIONAL SERVICES
24422	209	1336	NURSING & RESID. CARE FACILIT.
24426	634	7406	PAPER MANUFACTURING
24430	34	614	JUSTICE; PUBIC ORDER/SAFETY
24431	38	122	MISCELLANEOUS STORE RETAILERS
24432	12	42	JUSTICE; PUBIC ORDER/SAFETY
24433	2	2	SPECIAL TRADE CONTRACTORS
24435	65	424	MISCELLANEOUS MANUFACTURING
24437	26	177	EDUCATIONAL SERVICES
24438	2	1	UTILITIES
24439	34	482	ACCOMMODATION
24440	41	282	JUSTICE; PUBIC ORDER/SAFETY
24441	109	965	PLASTICS & RUBBER PRODUCTS MFG
24442	4	22	SOCIAL ASSISTANCE
24445	149	2096	AMUSEMENT; GAMBLING;& RECREAT.
24448	14	335	PLASTICS & RUBBER PRODUCTS MFG
24450	909	8056	EDUCATIONAL SERVICES
24457	29	622	APPAREL MANUFACTURING
24458	28	75	RELIG.; GRANT; CIVIC; PROF ORG
24459	27	38	AMBULATORY HEALTH CARE SVCS
24460	52	415	ACCOMMODATION
24463	8	29	SPECIAL TRADE CONTRACTORS
24464	7	15	ACCOMMODATION
24465	145	582	EDUCATIONAL SERVICES
24467	46	341	MERCH. WHOLESALERS;DURABLE GDS
24468	2	0	GENERAL MERCHANDISE STORES
24469	14	17	REPAIR AND MAINTENANCE
24471	27	74	ADMINISTRATIVE & SUPPORT SVCS
24472	64	544	GASOLINE STATIONS
24473	16	62	ACCOMMODATION
24474	9	31	REPAIR AND MAINTENANCE
24476	10	21	MOTOR VEHICLE & PARTS DEALERS
24477	235	4714	PROF.; SCIENTIFIC; & TECH SVCS
24479	29	142	EDUCATIONAL SERVICES
24482	270	5042	EXEC.; LEGIS.; & OTHER SUPPORT
24483	13	72	EXEC.; LEGIS.; & OTHER SUPPORT
24484	84	253	EXEC.; LEGIS.; & OTHER SUPPORT
24485	6	6	FABRICATED METAL PRODUCT MFG
24486	116	1837	TRUCK TRANSPORTATION
24487	16	40	TELECOMMUNICATIONS
24501	1376	21415	HOSPITALS
24502	1687	21939	FOOD SVCS & DRINKING PLACES
24503	410	5275	HOSPITALS
24504	646	12416	PROF.; SCIENTIFIC; & TECH SVCS
24505	6	14	CONSTRUCTION OF BUILDINGS
24506	15	350	POSTAL SERVICE
24513	1	1500	CLOTHING & CLOTH'G ACC. STORES
24514	1	100	RELIG.; GRANT; CIVIC; PROF ORG
24517	326	4334	TEXTILE MILLS
24520	44	605	MOTOR VEHICLE & PARTS DEALERS
24521	356	3334	MACHINERY MANUFACTURING
24522	372	3229	FURNITURE & RELATED PROD. MFG
24523	824	6874	FOOD SVCS & DRINKING PLACES
24526	41	634	PAPER MANUFACTURING
24527	84	2115	SPORTG GDS;HOBBY;BOOK; & MUSIC
24528	174	1379	TEXTILE MILLS
24529	32	170	CROP PRODUCTION
24530	17	44	FOOD AND BEVERAGE STORES
24531	344	3859	EXEC.; LEGIS.; & OTHER SUPPORT
24533	2	2	POSTAL SERVICE
24534	26	132	TEXTILE MILLS
24535	4	2	POSTAL SERVICE
24536	4	16	FORESTRY AND LOGGING
24538	96	669	TRUCK TRANSPORTATION
24539	3	167	MERCH. WHOLESALERS;NONDUR. GDS
24540	1347	13365	FOOD SVCS & DRINKING PLACES
24541	1305	21746	HOSPITALS
24543	5	11	PERSONAL AND LAUNDRY SERVICES
24549	69	290	EDUCATIONAL SERVICES
24550	98	369	BLDG MATL & GARDEN EQPMT DLRS
24551	640	6626	PROF.; SCIENTIFIC; & TECH SVCS
24553	36	470	FABRICATED METAL PRODUCT MFG
24554	74	557	MISCELLANEOUS MANUFACTURING
24555	58	134	RELIG.; GRANT; CIVIC; PROF ORG
24556	70	276	FOOD AND BEVERAGE STORES
24557	277	2000	EDUCATIONAL SERVICES
24558	275	1438	JUSTICE; PUBIC ORDER/SAFETY
24562	3	2	MERCH. WHOLESALERS;DURABLE GDS
24563	132	581	SPECIAL TRADE CONTRACTORS
24565	17	89	WOOD PRODUCT MANUFACTURING
24566	13	12	POSTAL SERVICE
24569	19	47	WOOD PRODUCT MANUFACTURING
24570	1	0	POSTAL SERVICE
24571	36	53	RELIG.; GRANT; CIVIC; PROF ORG
24572	446	4770	EDUCATIONAL SERVICES
24574	71	398	EDUCATIONAL SERVICES
24576	7	172	EDUCATIONAL SERVICES
24577	87	379	EDUCATIONAL SERVICES
24578	48	519	ACCOMMODATION
24579	38	421	ELECT'L EQPMT; APP; & COMP MFG
24580	11	30	RELIG.; GRANT; CIVIC; PROF ORG
24586	106	694	BLDG MATL & GARDEN EQPMT DLRS
24588	339	3076	EXEC.; LEGIS.; & OTHER SUPPORT
24589	49	369	EDUCATIONAL SERVICES
24590	234	954	TEXTILE PRODUCT MILLS
24592	901	9378	GENERAL MERCHANDISE STORES
24593	32	138	SPECIAL TRADE CONTRACTORS
24594	33	183	WOOD PRODUCT MANUFACTURING
24595	4	364	EDUCATIONAL SERVICES
24597	22	63	EDUCATIONAL SERVICES
24598	50	118	TRUCK TRANSPORTATION
24599	9	29	WOOD PRODUCT MANUFACTURING
24601	2	2	POSTAL SERVICE
24602	3	3	POSTAL SERVICE
24603	37	401	MINING (EXCEPT OIL AND GAS)
24604	4	14	BROADCASTING
24605	424	4962	EDUCATIONAL SERVICES
24606	6	12	AMBULATORY HEALTH CARE SVCS
24607	10	139	ACCOMMODATION
24608	6	2	CROP PRODUCTION
24609	234	2561	EDUCATIONAL SERVICES
24612	16	50	EXEC.; LEGIS.; & OTHER SUPPORT
24613	20	104	SPECIAL TRADE CONTRACTORS
24614	443	3311	EDUCATIONAL SERVICES
24619	2	22	NONSTORE RETAILERS
24620	61	254	EDUCATIONAL SERVICES
24622	5	16	MINING (EXCEPT OIL AND GAS)
24624	14	61	ADMIN. ENVIRO. QUALITY PROGRMS
24627	2	392	PETROLEUM & COAL PRODUCTS MFG

BUSINESS DATA

ZIP CODE	2009 Total Firms	2009 Total Employees	TOP INDUSTRY RANKED on 2009 EMPLOYMENT	ZIP CODE	2009 Total Firms	2009 Total Employees	TOP INDUSTRY RANKED on 2009 EMPLOYMENT	ZIP CODE	2009 Total Firms	2009 Total Employees	TOP INDUSTRY RANKED on 2009 EMPLOYMENT
24628	22	122	MINING (EXCEPT OIL AND GAS)	24898	4	4	REPAIR AND MAINTENANCE	25106	24	71	TRUCK TRANSPORTATION
24630	166	1307	COMPUTER & ELECTRONIC PROD MFG	24901	700	5998	FOOD SVCS & DRINKING PLACES	25107	9	64	MINING (EXCEPT OIL AND GAS)
24631	122	1173	WHOLESALE ELEC. MRKTS & AGENTS	24902	23	190	COMPUTER & ELECTRONIC PROD MFG	25108	5	25	EDUCATIONAL SERVICES
24634	8	101	EDUCATIONAL SERVICES	24910	85	293	FOOD SVCS & DRINKING PLACES	25109	7	44	EDUCATIONAL SERVICES
24635	31	92	EXEC.; LEGIS.; & OTHER SUPPORT	24915	15	28	ACCOMMODATION	25110	6	19	ADMINISTRATIVE & SUPPORT SVCS
24637	91	1088	GENERAL MERCHANDISE STORES	24916	10	51	GASOLINE STATIONS	25111	6	31	ELECT'L EQPMT; APP; & COMP MFG
24639	47	409	MINING (EXCEPT OIL AND GAS)	24918	14	42	JUSTICE; PUBIC ORDER/SAFETY	25112	26	1494	MERCH. WHOLESALERS;NONDUR. GDS
24640	1	6	MERCH. WHOLESALERS;DURABLE GDS	24920	15	276	MERCH. WHOLESALERS;DURABLE GDS	25113	19	145	NURSING & RESID. CARE FACILIT.
24641	426	3327	AMBULATORY HEALTH CARE SVCS	24924	15	159	HOSPITALS	25114	11	53	JUSTICE; PUBIC ORDER/SAFETY
24646	4	35	NURSING & RESID. CARE FACILIT.	24925	30	183	BLDG MATL & GARDEN EQPMT DLRS	25118	10	51	RELIG.; GRANT; CIVIC; PROF ORG
24649	32	277	MINING (EXCEPT OIL AND GAS)	24927	8	79	JUSTICE; PUBIC ORDER/SAFETY	25119	7	13	UTILITIES
24651	397	2950	EDUCATIONAL SERVICES	24931	20	158	EDUCATIONAL SERVICES	25121	9	47	SPECIAL TRADE CONTRACTORS
24656	118	1721	PETROLEUM & COAL PRODUCTS MFG	24934	12	83	EDUCATIONAL SERVICES	25123	19	61	EDUCATIONAL SERVICES
24657	13	86	MINING (EXCEPT OIL AND GAS)	24935	12	29	BLDG MATL & GARDEN EQPMT DLRS	25124	7	15	ADMINISTRATIVE & SUPPORT SVCS
24658	2	2	POSTAL SERVICE	24938	45	126	EDUCATIONAL SERVICES	25125	11	63	JUSTICE; PUBIC ORDER/SAFETY
24701	1098	11057	RAIL TRANSPORTATION	24941	27	82	FOOD AND BEVERAGE STORES	25126	8	51	ADMIN. ENVIRO. QUALITY PROGRMS
24712	63	928	EDUCATIONAL SERVICES	24943	1	3	SUPPORT ACT. FOR TRANSPORT.	25130	191	1692	EDUCATIONAL SERVICES
24714	1	5	WOOD PRODUCT MANUFACTURING	24944	18	223	PROF.; SCIENTIFIC; & TECH SVCS	25132	3	42	MINING (EXCEPT OIL AND GAS)
24715	27	57	JUSTICE; PUBIC ORDER/SAFETY	24945	10	15	MERCH. WHOLESALERS;DURABLE GDS	25133	7	15	GASOLINE STATIONS
24716	4	7	FOOD AND BEVERAGE STORES	24946	40	285	JUSTICE; PUBIC ORDER/SAFETY	25134	5	3	POSTAL SERVICE
24719	2	2	POSTAL SERVICE	24951	32	307	NURSING & RESID. CARE FACILIT.	25136	112	834	HOSPITALS
24724	3	0	FOOD AND BEVERAGE STORES	24954	217	1281	ACCOMMODATION	25139	11	29	ADMIN. OF ECONOMIC PROGRAMS
24726	10	63	WHOLESALE ELEC. MRKTS & AGENTS	24957	11	93	AMBULATORY HEALTH CARE SVCS	25140	18	391	PETROLEUM & COAL PRODUCTS MFG
24729	1	0	POSTAL SERVICE	24962	7	7	GASOLINE STATIONS	25141	5	23	WOOD PRODUCT MANUFACTURING
24731	6	11	FOOD AND BEVERAGE STORES	24963	93	336	EDUCATIONAL SERVICES	25142	2	0	POSTAL SERVICE
24732	5	10	RELIG.; GRANT; CIVIC; PROF ORG	24966	23	220	CROP PRODUCTION	25143	405	4247	MERCH. WHOLESALERS;DURABLE GDS
24733	7	13	FOOD AND BEVERAGE STORES	24970	189	2242	HOSPITALS	25148	5	9	PERSONAL AND LAUNDRY SERVICES
24736	21	113	EDUCATIONAL SERVICES	24974	1	0	POSTAL SERVICE	25149	2	4	BLDG MATL & GARDEN EQPMT DLRS
24737	12	47	EDUCATIONAL SERVICES	24976	19	60	ANIMAL PRODUCTION	25152	7	19	SOCIAL ASSISTANCE
24738	2	3	FOOD AND BEVERAGE STORES	24977	6	47	FOOD AND BEVERAGE STORES	25154	5	5	REPAIR AND MAINTENANCE
24739	11	3	ADMINISTRATIVE & SUPPORT SVCS	24981	15	85	BLDG MATL & GARDEN EQPMT DLRS	25156	12	45	AMUSEMENT; GAMBLING;& RECREAT.
24740	1479	13216	HOSPITALS	24983	112	766	COMPUTER & ELECTRONIC PROD MFG	25159	144	2487	MERCH. WHOLESALERS;DURABLE GDS
24747	16	46	MERCH. WHOLESALERS;DURABLE GDS	24985	3	4	FOOD AND BEVERAGE STORES	25160	2	8	FABRICATED METAL PRODUCT MFG
24751	2	5	AMBULATORY HEALTH CARE SVCS	24986	208	2218	PROF.; SCIENTIFIC; & TECH SVCS	25161	8	49	JUSTICE; PUBIC ORDER/SAFETY
24801	279	2766	EXEC.; LEGIS.; & OTHER SUPPORT	24991	12	73	WASTE MANAGMT & REMEDIAT'N SVC	25162	16	201	MINING (EXCEPT OIL AND GAS)
24808	15	31	EDUCATIONAL SERVICES	24993	3	5	BEVERAGE & TOBACCO PRODUCT MFG	25164	10	22	MERCH. WHOLESALERS;DURABLE GDS
24811	4	32	EDUCATIONAL SERVICES	25002	17	224	MACHINERY MANUFACTURING	25165	12	112	JUSTICE; PUBIC ORDER/SAFETY
24813	6	5	UTILITIES	25003	71	1063	WHOLESALE ELEC. MRKTS & AGENTS	25168	26	180	CROP PRODUCTION
24815	5	32	JUSTICE; PUBIC ORDER/SAFETY	25005	12	121	CONSTRUCTION OF BUILDINGS	25169	3	5	SPECIAL TRADE CONTRACTORS
24816	3	35	EDUCATIONAL SERVICES	25007	7	1	RELIG.; GRANT; CIVIC; PROF ORG	25173	9	43	RELIG.; GRANT; CIVIC; PROF ORG
24817	32	106	AMBULATORY HEALTH CARE SVCS	25008	2	1	MERCH. WHOLESALERS;NONDUR. GDS	25174	6	19	FOOD AND BEVERAGE STORES
24818	26	261	CONSTRUCTION OF BUILDINGS	25009	8	147	SPECIAL TRADE CONTRACTORS	25177	757	7403	MERCH. WHOLESALERS;DURABLE GDS
24822	3	93	EDUCATIONAL SERVICES	25011	8	34	JUSTICE; PUBIC ORDER/SAFETY	25180	1	0	RELIG.; GRANT; CIVIC; PROF ORG
24823	6	12	JUSTICE; PUBIC ORDER/SAFETY	25015	141	2009	CHEMICAL MANUFACTURING	25181	16	615	MINING (EXCEPT OIL AND GAS)
24826	3	118	MINING (EXCEPT OIL AND GAS)	25019	13	756	MINING (EXCEPT OIL AND GAS)	25183	4	52	JUSTICE; PUBIC ORDER/SAFETY
24827	16	45	EDUCATIONAL SERVICES	25021	5	16	FOOD AND BEVERAGE STORES	25185	3	391	JUSTICE; PUBIC ORDER/SAFETY
24828	10	23	PRIMARY METAL MANUFACTURING	25022	2	2	POSTAL SERVICE	25186	54	459	EDUCATIONAL SERVICES
24829	4	14	SOCIAL ASSISTANCE	25024	5	30	TRUCK TRANSPORTATION	25187	59	72	MERCH. WHOLESALERS;DURABLE GDS
24830	2	2	POSTAL SERVICE	25025	1	0	RELIG.; GRANT; CIVIC; PROF ORG	25193	16	601	MINING (EXCEPT OIL AND GAS)
24831	2	1	POSTAL SERVICE	25026	12	25	BLDG MATL & GARDEN EQPMT DLRS	25201	4	32	EDUCATIONAL SERVICES
24834	1	3	RELIG.; GRANT; CIVIC; PROF ORG	25028	8	137	MINING (EXCEPT OIL AND GAS)	25202	19	98	EDUCATIONAL SERVICES
24836	35	346	AMBULATORY HEALTH CARE SVCS	25030	6	17	EDUCATIONAL SERVICES	25203	5	32	MISCELLANEOUS STORE RETAILERS
24839	20	78	EDUCATIONAL SERVICES	25031	8	46	PROF.; SCIENTIFIC; & TECH SVCS	25204	4	308	MINING (EXCEPT OIL AND GAS)
24842	3	5	SPECIAL TRADE CONTRACTORS	25033	42	1330	MERCH. WHOLESALERS;DURABLE GDS	25205	9	54	ADMIN. OF ECONOMIC PROGRAMS
24843	1	1	POSTAL SERVICE	25035	49	349	ADMIN. OF ECONOMIC PROGRAMS	25206	18	93	EDUCATIONAL SERVICES
24844	63	412	EDUCATIONAL SERVICES	25036	5	5	MISCELLANEOUS STORE RETAILERS	25208	32	1934	MINING (EXCEPT OIL AND GAS)
24845	10	31	BLDG MATL & GARDEN EQPMT DLRS	25039	25	627	MINING (EXCEPT OIL AND GAS)	25209	74	772	MINING (EXCEPT OIL AND GAS)
24846	2	1	RELIG.; GRANT; CIVIC; PROF ORG	25040	11	22	FOOD AND BEVERAGE STORES	25211	2	5	CONSTRUCTION OF BUILDINGS
24847	3	23	SOCIAL ASSISTANCE	25043	122	814	EDUCATIONAL SERVICES	25213	180	1627	EDUCATIONAL SERVICES
24848	1	2	POSTAL SERVICE	25044	5	31	EDUCATIONAL SERVICES	25214	7	76	REPAIR AND MAINTENANCE
24849	13	64	ADMINISTRATIVE & SUPPORT SVCS	25045	146	786	EDUCATIONAL SERVICES	25234	36	290	HEAVY & CIVIL ENG. CONSTRUCT'N
24850	15	18	FOOD AND BEVERAGE STORES	25047	6	17	MINING (EXCEPT OIL AND GAS)	25235	7	3	BLDG MATL & GARDEN EQPMT DLRS
24851	19	63	WOOD PRODUCT MANUFACTURING	25048	6	12	AMBULATORY HEALTH CARE SVCS	25239	22	120	EDUCATIONAL SERVICES
24853	29	379	GENERAL MERCHANDISE STORES	25049	14	188	EDUCATIONAL SERVICES	25241	22	74	EDUCATIONAL SERVICES
24854	7	107	RELIG.; GRANT; CIVIC; PROF ORG	25051	1	2	POSTAL SERVICE	25243	17	50	JUSTICE; PUBIC ORDER/SAFETY
24855	2	7	GASOLINE STATIONS	25053	165	1662	FOOD SVCS & DRINKING PLACES	25244	4	4	CONSTRUCTION OF BUILDINGS
24857	7	18	SPECIAL TRADE CONTRACTORS	25054	5	158	MINING (EXCEPT OIL AND GAS)	25245	9	17	CONSTRUCTION OF BUILDINGS
24859	1	15	UTILITIES	25057	4	5	ADMINISTRATIVE & SUPPORT SVCS	25247	12	27	EDUCATIONAL SERVICES
24860	17	47	FABRICATED METAL PRODUCT MFG	25059	19	190	BLDG MATL & GARDEN EQPMT DLRS	25248	38	256	SPECIAL TRADE CONTRACTORS
24861	12	14	FOOD AND BEVERAGE STORES	25060	4	9	MISCELLANEOUS STORE RETAILERS	25251	7	57	EDUCATIONAL SERVICES
24862	1	1	MOTOR VEHICLE & PARTS DEALERS	25061	3	2	POSTAL SERVICE	25252	5	32	EDUCATIONAL SERVICES
24866	1	3	FOOD AND BEVERAGE STORES	25062	2	3	GENERAL MERCHANDISE STORES	25253	11	43	EXEC.; LEGIS.; & OTHER SUPPORT
24867	10	185	NURSING & RESID. CARE FACILIT.	25063	13	52	EDUCATIONAL SERVICES	25259	5	3	POSTAL SERVICE
24868	70	250	MINING (EXCEPT OIL AND GAS)	25064	384	3734	NURSING & RESID. CARE FACILIT.	25260	69	689	GENERAL MERCHANDISE STORES
24869	1	2	POSTAL SERVICE	25067	22	126	EXEC.; LEGIS.; & OTHER SUPPORT	25261	5	37	HEAVY & CIVIL ENG. CONSTRUCT'N
24870	160	728	FOOD SVCS & DRINKING PLACES	25070	70	699	TRANSPORTATION EQUIPMENT MFG	25262	29	243	MERCH. WHOLESALERS;DURABLE GDS
24871	3	4	MINING (EXCEPT OIL AND GAS)	25071	231	1667	FOOD SVCS & DRINKING PLACES	25264	4	8	GASOLINE STATIONS
24872	7	23	EXEC.; LEGIS.; & OTHER SUPPORT	25075	17	442	MINING (EXCEPT OIL AND GAS)	25265	48	563	UTILITIES
24873	4	7	SPECIAL TRADE CONTRACTORS	25076	7	97	MINING (EXCEPT OIL AND GAS)	25266	16	112	JUSTICE; PUBIC ORDER/SAFETY
24874	199	1624	HEAVY & CIVIL ENG. CONSTRUCT'N	25079	2	2	POSTAL SERVICE	25267	14	68	TEXTILE PRODUCT MILLS
24878	2	1	POSTAL SERVICE	25081	9	148	EDUCATIONAL SERVICES	25268	4	16	EXEC.; LEGIS.; & OTHER SUPPORT
24879	7	13	FOOD AND BEVERAGE STORES	25082	23	99	FOOD MANUFACTURING	25270	13	113	BLDG MATL & GARDEN EQPMT DLRS
24880	10	27	SPECIAL TRADE CONTRACTORS	25083	11	83	PERFORM'G ARTS; SPEC. SPORTS	25271	525	4828	GENERAL MERCHANDISE STORES
24881	13	84	CONSTRUCTION OF BUILDINGS	25085	41	239	FOOD AND BEVERAGE STORES	25275	28	110	EDUCATIONAL SERVICES
24882	2	4	POSTAL SERVICE	25086	24	289	NURSING & RESID. CARE FACILIT.	25276	338	2559	HOSPITALS
24884	3	6	GASOLINE STATIONS	25088	4	2	SUPPORT ACTIVITIES FOR MINING	25285	5	40	UTILITIES
24888	4	17	MINING (EXCEPT OIL AND GAS)	25090	7	15	ACCOMMODATION	25286	24	164	CREDIT INTERMEDIATION & RELATD
24892	76	357	EDUCATIONAL SERVICES	25093	6	3	POSTAL SERVICE	25287	15	575	WATER TRANSPORTATION
24894	3	2	POSTAL SERVICE	25102	10	58	SUPPORT ACT. FOR TRANSPORT.	25301	1590	28008	HOSPITALS
24895	6	30	ADMIN. HUMAN RESOURCE PROGRAMS	25103	10	42	BLDG MATL & GARDEN EQPMT DLRS	25302	699	6274	PROF.; SCIENTIFIC; & TECH SVCS

ZIP CODE	2009 Total Firms	2009 Total Employ-ees	TOP INDUSTRY RANKED on 2009 EMPLOYMENT
25303	438	5501	MERCH. WHOLESALERS;NONDUR. GDS
25304	522	10233	HOSPITALS
25305	134	5766	EXEC.; LEGIS.; & OTHER SUPPORT
25306	129	1515	MINING (EXCEPT OIL AND GAS)
25309	550	7866	FOOD SVCS & DRINKING PLACES
25311	483	7076	MERCH. WHOLESALERS;DURABLE GDS
25312	442	4997	MOTOR VEHICLE & PARTS DEALERS
25313	490	6064	FOOD SVCS & DRINKING PLACES
25314	321	3114	PIPELINE TRANSPORTATION
25315	134	1027	NURSING & RESID. CARE FACILIT.
25317	1	1000	ADMIN. OF ECONOMIC PROGRAMS
25320	115	907	TRANSPORTATION EQUIPMENT MFG
25321	1	2	RELIG.; GRANT; CIVIC; PROF ORG
25322	1	0	ADMINISTRATIVE & SUPPORT SVCS
25323	1	1	REAL ESTATE
25325	1	2	ADMINISTRATIVE & SUPPORT SVCS
25326	3	2	SUPPORT ACTIVITIES FOR MINING
25329	4	6	RELIG.; GRANT; CIVIC; PROF ORG
25330	1	0	EXEC.; LEGIS.; & OTHER SUPPORT
25333	2	8	HEAVY & CIVIL ENG. CONSTRUCT'N
25337	1	1	RELIG.; GRANT; CIVIC; PROF ORG
25339	4	13	SUPPORT ACTIVITIES FOR MINING
25356	7	26	SPECIAL TRADE CONTRACTORS
25357	1	9	ADMINISTRATIVE & SUPPORT SVCS
25358	3	4	MERCH. WHOLESALERS;DURABLE GDS
25360	4	7	MERCH. WHOLESALERS;DURABLE GDS
25361	2	4	CREDIT INTERMEDIATION & RELATD
25362	6	9	REAL ESTATE
25364	7	21	TRUCK TRANSPORTATION
25365	4	3	ADMINISTRATIVE & SUPPORT SVCS
25387	27	211	FOOD SVCS & DRINKING PLACES
25389	123	1404	CLOTHING & CLOTH'G ACC. STORES
25396	1	1200	TELECOMMUNICATIONS
25401	1060	13705	HOSPITALS
25402	11	18	RELIG.; GRANT; CIVIC; PROF ORG
25403	151	2612	PROF.; SCIENTIFIC; & TECH SVCS
25404	531	4630	PLASTICS & RUBBER PRODUCTS MFG
25405	213	2602	PRINT'G & RELATED SUPP'T ACT'S
25410	1	0	RELIG.; GRANT; CIVIC; PROF ORG
25411	434	3274	EDUCATIONAL SERVICES
25413	117	563	EDUCATIONAL SERVICES
25414	584	5330	PERFORM'G ARTS; SPEC. SPORTS
25419	127	687	MERCH. WHOLESALERS;NONDUR. GDS
25420	30	93	EDUCATIONAL SERVICES
25421	4	10	SPECIAL TRADE CONTRACTORS
25422	15	20	FOOD AND BEVERAGE STORES
25423	8	105	PAPER MANUFACTURING
25425	210	1343	MUSEUMS; HIST. SITES;& SIMILAR
25427	224	1549	EDUCATIONAL SERVICES
25428	277	2040	FOOD SVCS & DRINKING PLACES
25430	189	2690	NONSTORE RETAILERS
25431	15	55	JUSTICE; PUBIC ORDER/SAFETY
25432	4	135	MINING (EXCEPT OIL AND GAS)
25434	40	208	JUSTICE; PUBIC ORDER/SAFETY
25437	3	2	POSTAL SERVICE
25438	202	2650	PROF.; SCIENTIFIC; & TECH SVCS
25440	3	0	CONSTRUCTION OF BUILDINGS
25441	9	45	FOOD SVCS & DRINKING PLACES
25442	28	306	EDUCATIONAL SERVICES
25443	251	1775	FOOD SVCS & DRINKING PLACES
25444	18	101	JUSTICE; PUBIC ORDER/SAFETY
25446	22	115	PERFORM'G ARTS; SPEC. SPORTS
25501	7	11	BLDG MATL & GARDEN EQPMT DLRS
25502	17	518	MERCH. WHOLESALERS;NONDUR. GDS
25503	7	106	EDUCATIONAL SERVICES
25504	716	8393	FOOD SVCS & DRINKING PLACES
25505	8	30	SPECIAL TRADE CONTRACTORS
25506	58	271	EDUCATIONAL SERVICES
25507	89	843	PLASTICS & RUBBER PRODUCTS MFG
25508	238	1850	MOTOR VEHICLE & PARTS DEALERS
25510	73	521	SUPPORT ACTIVITIES FOR MINING
25511	13	132	TRUCK TRANSPORTATION
25512	18	348	MINING (EXCEPT OIL AND GAS)
25514	65	456	EDUCATIONAL SERVICES
25515	27	137	TRUCK TRANSPORTATION
25517	8	47	EDUCATIONAL SERVICES
25520	6	15	WOOD PRODUCT MANUFACTURING
25521	21	169	EDUCATIONAL SERVICES
25523	144	1372	EDUCATIONAL SERVICES
25524	50	274	EDUCATIONAL SERVICES
25526	778	6886	HOSPITALS
25529	17	76	TRANSIT & GRND PASS. TRANSPORT
25530	182	1677	CHEMICAL MANUFACTURING
25534	1	2	POSTAL SERVICE
25535	90	482	HEAVY & CIVIL ENG. CONSTRUCT'N
25537	44	367	WHOLESALE ELEC. MRKTS & AGENTS
25540	4	6	MERCH. WHOLESALERS;DURABLE GDS
25541	235	1579	FOOD AND BEVERAGE STORES
25545	78	775	EDUCATIONAL SERVICES
25547	24	127	MINING (EXCEPT OIL AND GAS)

ZIP CODE	2009 Total Firms	2009 Total Employ-ees	TOP INDUSTRY RANKED on 2009 EMPLOYMENT
25550	384	3148	MERCH. WHOLESALERS;DURABLE GDS
25555	27	392	MERCH. WHOLESALERS;DURABLE GDS
25557	12	60	EDUCATIONAL SERVICES
25559	30	174	FABRICATED METAL PRODUCT MFG
25560	237	1907	PROF.; SCIENTIFIC; & TECH SVCS
25562	2	2	INSURANCE CARRIERS & RELATED
25564	11	8	HEAVY & CIVIL ENG. CONSTRUCT'N
25565	7	37	JUSTICE; PUBIC ORDER/SAFETY
25567	7	9	SPECIAL TRADE CONTRACTORS
25569	26	116	GENERAL MERCHANDISE STORES
25570	186	1988	EXEC.; LEGIS.; & OTHER SUPPORT
25571	48	210	EDUCATIONAL SERVICES
25573	17	76	MERCH. WHOLESALERS;NONDUR. GDS
25601	516	5650	HOSPITALS
25606	12	87	EDUCATIONAL SERVICES
25607	12	49	JUSTICE; PUBIC ORDER/SAFETY
25608	8	7	FOOD AND BEVERAGE STORES
25611	6	26	RELIG.; GRANT; CIVIC; PROF ORG
25612	2	21	EDUCATIONAL SERVICES
25614	10	54	FOOD AND BEVERAGE STORES
25617	12	32	MERCH. WHOLESALERS;DURABLE GDS
25621	135	924	MERCH. WHOLESALERS;DURABLE GDS
25624	8	50	JUSTICE; PUBIC ORDER/SAFETY
25625	47	1157	WOOD PRODUCT MANUFACTURING
25628	14	61	FOOD AND BEVERAGE STORES
25630	8	43	TRUCK TRANSPORTATION
25632	20	194	MERCH. WHOLESALERS;DURABLE GDS
25634	11	186	EDUCATIONAL SERVICES
25635	104	697	MINING (EXCEPT OIL AND GAS)
25637	29	312	FOOD AND BEVERAGE STORES
25638	18	92	EDUCATIONAL SERVICES
25639	9	29	EDUCATIONAL SERVICES
25644	4	13	GASOLINE STATIONS
25646	41	180	MOTOR VEHICLE & PARTS DEALERS
25647	15	43	SPECIAL TRADE CONTRACTORS
25649	31	131	NURSING & RESID. CARE FACILIT.
25650	5	6	POSTAL SERVICE
25651	12	132	MINING (EXCEPT OIL AND GAS)
25652	17	87	MERCH. WHOLESALERS;DURABLE GDS
25653	31	226	MERCH. WHOLESALERS;DURABLE GDS
25654	7	353	MINING (EXCEPT OIL AND GAS)
25661	319	2846	EDUCATIONAL SERVICES
25665	4	10	GASOLINE STATIONS
25666	2	0	POSTAL SERVICE
25667	13	62	AMBULATORY HEALTH CARE SVCS
25669	15	81	EDUCATIONAL SERVICES
25670	83	515	EDUCATIONAL SERVICES
25671	20	333	PETROLEUM & COAL PRODUCTS MFG
25672	3	4	POSTAL SERVICE
25674	66	342	MOTOR VEHICLE & PARTS DEALERS
25676	33	394	MINING (EXCEPT OIL AND GAS)
25678	56	287	EDUCATIONAL SERVICES
25685	17	956	MINING (EXCEPT OIL AND GAS)
25686	2	5	REAL ESTATE
25688	9	35	NONMETALLIC MINERAL PROD. MFG
25690	7	20	ELECT'L EQPMT; APP; & COMP MFG
25691	1	1	POSTAL SERVICE
25692	6	22	MINING (EXCEPT OIL AND GAS)
25696	21	144	BLDG MATL & GARDEN EQPMT DLRS
25701	1567	22580	AMBULATORY HEALTH CARE SVCS
25702	271	5702	HOSPITALS
25703	239	4946	RELIG.; GRANT; CIVIC; PROF ORG
25704	408	5614	HOSPITALS
25705	477	7683	MERCH. WHOLESALERS;DURABLE GDS
25708	2	10	SOCIAL ASSISTANCE
25711	1	2	DATA PROCESS'G
25712	1	0	UNCLASSIFIED ESTABLISHMENTS
25716	1	20	PROF.; SCIENTIFIC; & TECH SVCS
25718	2	1	WHOLESALE ELEC. MRKTS & AGENTS
25722	2	40	JUSTICE; PUBIC ORDER/SAFETY
25727	1	5	PROF.; SCIENTIFIC; & TECH SVCS
25728	1	2	MERCH. WHOLESALERS;DURABLE GDS
25729	1	8	FOOD SVCS & DRINKING PLACES
25755	11	2242	EDUCATIONAL SERVICES
25801	1876	20897	HOSPITALS
25802	6	2	INSURANCE CARRIERS & RELATED
25810	3	3	POSTAL SERVICE
25811	3	6	GASOLINE STATIONS
25812	63	486	NURSING & RESID. CARE FACILIT.
25813	256	2498	FOOD SVCS & DRINKING PLACES
25817	15	18	MACHINERY MANUFACTURING
25818	30	130	HEAVY & CIVIL ENG. CONSTRUCT'N
25820	7	23	ACCOMMODATION
25823	30	155	EDUCATIONAL SERVICES
25825	22	28	MERCH. WHOLESALERS;NONDUR. GDS
25826	2	2	POSTAL SERVICE
25827	104	537	MERCH. WHOLESALERS;DURABLE GDS
25831	19	88	MUSEUMS; HIST. SITES;& SIMILAR
25832	95	750	ACCOMMODATION
25836	11	16	SPECIAL TRADE CONTRACTORS

ZIP CODE	2009 Total Firms	2009 Total Employ-ees	TOP INDUSTRY RANKED on 2009 EMPLOYMENT
25837	5	9	BROADCASTING
25839	15	98	EDUCATIONAL SERVICES
25840	252	1867	FOOD SVCS & DRINKING PLACES
25841	12	69	WOOD PRODUCT MANUFACTURING
25843	28	1538	OTHER INFORMATION SERVICES
25844	37	288	EDUCATIONAL SERVICES
25845	13	40	EDUCATIONAL SERVICES
25846	16	325	ADMIN. ENVIRO. QUALITY PROGRMS
25848	5	8	UTILITIES
25849	6	92	MERCH. WHOLESALERS;DURABLE GDS
25851	8	32	MOTOR VEHICLE & PARTS DEALERS
25853	3	2	POSTAL SERVICE
25854	39	631	ACCOMMODATION
25855	12	286	AMBULATORY HEALTH CARE SVCS
25857	4	12	MERCH. WHOLESALERS;DURABLE GDS
25860	2	32	WASTE MANAGMT & REMEDIAT'N SVC
25862	17	606	SCENIC & SIGHTSEEING TRANSPORT
25864	5	13	FABRICATED METAL PRODUCT MFG
25865	14	117	MERCH. WHOLESALERS;DURABLE GDS
25866	7	23	AMBULATORY HEALTH CARE SVCS
25868	14	88	EDUCATIONAL SERVICES
25870	6	39	RELIG.; GRANT; CIVIC; PROF ORG
25871	32	361	MOTION PICT. & SOUND RECORDING
25873	26	327	GENERAL MERCHANDISE STORES
25875	4	7	ADMINISTRATIVE & SUPPORT SVCS
25876	8	129	ACCOMMODATION
25878	19	75	SOCIAL ASSISTANCE
25879	6	507	SCENIC & SIGHTSEEING TRANSPORT
25880	211	1785	GENERAL MERCHANDISE STORES
25882	101	657	RAIL TRANSPORTATION
25901	450	3867	FOOD SVCS & DRINKING PLACES
25902	2	2	POSTAL SERVICE
25904	7	10	EXEC.; LEGIS.; & OTHER SUPPORT
25906	6	17	FABRICATED METAL PRODUCT MFG
25907	1	2	TRANSIT & GRND PASS. TRANSPORT
25908	3	2	POSTAL SERVICE
25909	29	186	RELIG.; GRANT; CIVIC; PROF ORG
25911	6	21	SPECIAL TRADE CONTRACTORS
25913	7	27	UTILITIES
25915	12	51	WHOLESALE ELEC. MRKTS & AGENTS
25916	1	0	POSTAL SERVICE
25917	35	374	MINING (EXCEPT OIL AND GAS)
25918	83	326	EDUCATIONAL SERVICES
25919	6	3	POSTAL SERVICE
25920	7	131	PROF.; SCIENTIFIC; & TECH SVCS
25921	92	928	ADMINISTRATIVE & SUPPORT SVCS
25922	8	48	EDUCATIONAL SERVICES
25927	14	63	MERCH. WHOLESALERS;DURABLE GDS
25928	5	4	MERCH. WHOLESALERS;DURABLE GDS
25932	14	32	AMBULATORY HEALTH CARE SVCS
25936	4	2	SCENIC & SIGHTSEEING TRANSPORT
25938	14	18	SPECIAL TRADE CONTRACTORS
25942	2	3	POSTAL SERVICE
25951	242	1823	RAIL TRANSPORTATION
25958	10	76	EDUCATIONAL SERVICES
25962	149	976	RELIG.; GRANT; CIVIC; PROF ORG
25965	1	0	SPECIAL TRADE CONTRACTORS
25966	3	18	WASTE MANAGMT & REMEDIAT'N SVC
25969	11	35	EDUCATIONAL SERVICES
25971	19	71	EDUCATIONAL SERVICES
25972	1	2	POSTAL SERVICE
25976	36	127	EDUCATIONAL SERVICES
25977	2	1	ACCOMMODATION
25978	16	70	WOOD PRODUCT MANUFACTURING
25979	17	410	MUSEUMS; HIST. SITES;& SIMILAR
25981	18	100	WHOLESALE ELEC. MRKTS & AGENTS
25984	68	655	MINING (EXCEPT OIL AND GAS)
25985	7	26	JUSTICE; PUBIC ORDER/SAFETY
25986	4	28	CONSTRUCTION OF BUILDINGS
25989	6	8	MERCH. WHOLESALERS;DURABLE GDS
26003	2090	33179	HOSPITALS
26030	21	211	PRIMARY METAL MANUFACTURING
26031	46	467	FOOD SVCS & DRINKING PLACES
26032	20	127	WHOLESALE ELEC. MRKTS & AGENTS
26033	76	406	EDUCATIONAL SERVICES
26034	154	5324	PERFORM'G ARTS; SPEC. SPORTS
26035	39	147	FABRICATED METAL PRODUCT MFG
26036	6	415	MINING (EXCEPT OIL AND GAS)
26037	172	1418	PRIMARY METAL MANUFACTURING
26038	76	1310	HOSPITALS
26039	12	890	NONSTORE RETAILERS
26040	43	236	EDUCATIONAL SERVICES
26041	518	4564	FOOD SVCS & DRINKING PLACES
26047	130	1752	EDUCATIONAL SERVICES
26050	58	2747	MERCH. WHOLESALERS;DURABLE GDS
26055	32	192	CHEMICAL MANUFACTURING
26056	11	128	FOOD AND BEVERAGE STORES
26058	3	62	TRUCK TRANSPORTATION
26059	164	2632	MERCH. WHOLESALERS;DURABLE GDS
26060	35	557	MISCELLANEOUS MANUFACTURING

BUSINESS DATA

ZIP CODE	2009 Total Firms	2009 Total Employ-ees	TOP INDUSTRY RANKED on 2009 EMPLOYMENT	ZIP CODE	2009 Total Firms	2009 Total Employ-ees	TOP INDUSTRY RANKED on 2009 EMPLOYMENT	ZIP CODE	2009 Total Firms	2009 Total Employ-ees	TOP INDUSTRY RANKED on 2009 EMPLOYMENT
26062	805	10257	PRIMARY METAL MANUFACTURING	26296	1	1	JUSTICE; PUBIC ORDER/SAFETY	26561	1	0	POSTAL SERVICE
26070	265	2058	EDUCATIONAL SERVICES	26298	2	3	FOOD AND BEVERAGE STORES	26562	9	47	PROF.; SCIENTIFIC; & TECH SVCS
26074	20	173	BLDG MATL & GARDEN EQPMT DLRS	26301	1473	17124	HOSPITALS	26563	4	12	EDUCATIONAL SERVICES
26075	5	56	JUSTICE; PUBIC ORDER/SAFETY	26302	10	42	MERCH. WHOLESALERS;DURABLE GDS	26566	2	6	PROF.; SCIENTIFIC; & TECH SVCS
26101	1902	21956	HOSPITALS	26306	2	3004	JUSTICE; PUBIC ORDER/SAFETY	26568	9	35	FOOD SVCS & DRINKING PLACES
26102	4	15	EXEC.; LEGIS.; & OTHER SUPPORT	26320	17	40	SUPPORT ACTIVITIES FOR MINING	26570	67	1169	PETROLEUM & COAL PRODUCTS MFG
26103	1	2	NONSTORE RETAILERS	26321	6	19	EDUCATIONAL SERVICES	26571	57	362	EDUCATIONAL SERVICES
26104	462	4636	EDUCATIONAL SERVICES	26323	40	432	ELECT'L EQPMT; APP; & COMP MFG	26572	1	2	POSTAL SERVICE
26105	517	5539	GENERAL MERCHANDISE STORES	26325	4	5	CONSTRUCTION OF BUILDINGS	26574	12	119	UTILITIES
26106	2	3	CONSTRUCTION OF BUILDINGS	26330	822	7926	SUPPORT ACT. FOR TRANSPORT.	26575	52	201	EDUCATIONAL SERVICES
26120	1	850	CLOTHING & CLOTH'G ACC. STORES	26335	40	154	EDUCATIONAL SERVICES	26576	4	9	WAREHOUSING AND STORAGE
26133	15	34	ADMIN. ENVIRO. QUALITY PROGRMS	26337	29	67	MUSEUMS; HIST. SITES;& SIMILAR	26578	3	10	MISCELLANEOUS STORE RETAILERS
26134	42	872	MERCH. WHOLESALERS;NONDUR. GDS	26338	3	12	UTILITIES	26581	10	38	JUSTICE; PUBIC ORDER/SAFETY
26136	11	32	SPECIAL TRADE CONTRACTORS	26339	2	5	FOOD SVCS & DRINKING PLACES	26582	133	1833	MINING (EXCEPT OIL AND GAS)
26137	10	12	UTILITIES	26342	4	3	GASOLINE STATIONS	26585	3	8	POSTAL SERVICE
26141	2	32	WOOD PRODUCT MANUFACTURING	26346	55	266	EDUCATIONAL SERVICES	26586	6	3	UTILITIES
26142	27	181	SPECIAL TRADE CONTRACTORS	26347	29	150	EDUCATIONAL SERVICES	26587	4	7	UTILITIES
26143	120	664	EDUCATIONAL SERVICES	26348	5	17	FORESTRY AND LOGGING	26588	37	142	EDUCATIONAL SERVICES
26146	27	205	PRIMARY METAL MANUFACTURING	26349	2	2	POSTAL SERVICE	26590	17	97	MINING (EXCEPT OIL AND GAS)
26147	122	860	HOSPITALS	26351	190	1558	EDUCATIONAL SERVICES	26591	27	156	FABRICATED METAL PRODUCT MFG
26148	3	5	WOOD PRODUCT MANUFACTURING	26354	326	3174	PLASTICS & RUBBER PRODUCTS MFG	26601	251	1855	EDUCATIONAL SERVICES
26149	82	398	EDUCATIONAL SERVICES	26361	5	26	FOOD MANUFACTURING	26610	20	128	PROF.; SCIENTIFIC; & TECH SVCS
26150	139	2444	MOTOR VEHICLE & PARTS DEALERS	26362	163	880	EDUCATIONAL SERVICES	26611	3	6	MERCH. WHOLESALERS;DURABLE GDS
26151	11	97	EDUCATIONAL SERVICES	26366	7	290	UTILITIES	26615	1	0	RELIG.; GRANT; CIVIC; PROF ORG
26155	443	5006	MERCH. WHOLESALERS;NONDUR. GDS	26369	12	55	WASTE MANAGMT & REMEDIAT'N SVC	26617	1	1	POSTAL SERVICE
26159	72	457	FABRICATED METAL PRODUCT MFG	26372	15	47	SUPPORT ACTIVITIES: AGR./FOR.	26619	2	11	PROF.; SCIENTIFIC; & TECH SVCS
26160	7	9	SPECIAL TRADE CONTRACTORS	26374	10	42	CONSTRUCTION OF BUILDINGS	26621	33	130	ADMINISTRATIVE & SUPPORT SVCS
26161	5	35	MERCH. WHOLESALERS;DURABLE GDS	26376	2	1	FOOD AND BEVERAGE STORES	26623	21	77	EDUCATIONAL SERVICES
26162	1	0	TRUCK TRANSPORTATION	26377	10	40	BLDG MATL & GARDEN EQPMT DLRS	26624	155	1148	FOOD AND BEVERAGE STORES
26164	238	3739	PRIMARY METAL MANUFACTURING	26378	98	1113	SUPPORT ACTIVITIES FOR MINING	26627	8	144	MERCH. WHOLESALERS;DURABLE GDS
26167	15	129	EDUCATIONAL SERVICES	26384	9	22	WOOD PRODUCT MANUFACTURING	26629	8	84	MOTOR VEHICLE & PARTS DEALERS
26169	11	18	UTILITIES	26385	64	391	EDUCATIONAL SERVICES	26631	1	1	POSTAL SERVICE
26170	199	1113	FOOD SVCS & DRINKING PLACES	26386	37	195	EDUCATIONAL SERVICES	26636	4	8	RELIG.; GRANT; CIVIC; PROF ORG
26175	104	949	SOCIAL ASSISTANCE	26404	13	125	CONSTRUCTION OF BUILDINGS	26651	560	4403	GENERAL MERCHANDISE STORES
26178	16	120	MERCH. WHOLESALERS;DURABLE GDS	26405	12	107	CONSTRUCTION OF BUILDINGS	26656	9	48	MISCELLANEOUS STORE RETAILERS
26180	32	209	SOCIAL ASSISTANCE	26408	57	452	ADMINISTRATIVE & SUPPORT SVCS	26660	11	49	BLDG MATL & GARDEN EQPMT DLRS
26181	80	2973	CHEMICAL MANUFACTURING	26410	27	154	AMBULATORY HEALTH CARE SVCS	26662	12	55	REPAIR AND MAINTENANCE
26184	26	220	MERCH. WHOLESALERS;DURABLE GDS	26411	5	7	POSTAL SERVICE	26667	8	248	MINING (EXCEPT OIL AND GAS)
26187	175	1151	EDUCATIONAL SERVICES	26412	3	5	POSTAL SERVICE	26671	2	4	POSTAL SERVICE
26201	826	7705	AMBULATORY HEALTH CARE SVCS	26415	90	683	JUSTICE; PUBIC ORDER/SAFETY	26676	12	21	FORESTRY AND LOGGING
26202	13	328	COMPUTER & ELECTRONIC PROD MFG	26416	276	2352	EDUCATIONAL SERVICES	26678	21	73	MACHINERY MANUFACTURING
26203	6	85	MINING (EXCEPT OIL AND GAS)	26419	42	346	UTILITIES	26679	38	195	FOOD AND BEVERAGE STORES
26205	100	874	WOOD PRODUCT MANUFACTURING	26421	5	5	POSTAL SERVICE	26680	3	3	MERCH. WHOLESALERS;DURABLE GDS
26206	65	702	MINING (EXCEPT OIL AND GAS)	26422	9	16	UTILITIES	26681	34	155	EDUCATIONAL SERVICES
26208	11	124	AMBULATORY HEALTH CARE SVCS	26424	4	6	FOOD AND BEVERAGE STORES	26690	5	7	UTILITIES
26209	38	2883	ACCOMMODATION	26425	30	110	EDUCATIONAL SERVICES	26691	5	11	MACHINERY MANUFACTURING
26210	5	7	ADMIN. ENVIRO. QUALITY PROGRMS	26426	128	1204	EDUCATIONAL SERVICES	26704	100	429	JUSTICE; PUBIC ORDER/SAFETY
26215	1	0	RELIG.; GRANT; CIVIC; PROF ORG	26430	12	94	NONSTORE RETAILERS	26705	23	105	EDUCATIONAL SERVICES
26217	11	41	EDUCATIONAL SERVICES	26431	187	1246	EDUCATIONAL SERVICES	26707	10	10	CREDIT INTERMEDIATION & RELATD
26218	29	114	EDUCATIONAL SERVICES	26434	2	2	POSTAL SERVICE	26710	38	439	SOCIAL ASSISTANCE
26222	13	62	MERCH. WHOLESALERS;DURABLE GDS	26435	3	5	FOOD AND BEVERAGE STORES	26711	96	492	EDUCATIONAL SERVICES
26224	8	11	AMBULATORY HEALTH CARE SVCS	26436	7	40	WOOD PRODUCT MANUFACTURING	26714	7	6	SPECIAL TRADE CONTRACTORS
26228	3	11	UTILITIES	26437	13	18	PIPELINE TRANSPORTATION	26716	18	72	WOOD PRODUCT MANUFACTURING
26229	5	18	MERCH. WHOLESALERS;DURABLE GDS	26438	3	41	JUSTICE; PUBIC ORDER/SAFETY	26717	15	111	JUSTICE; PUBIC ORDER/SAFETY
26230	5	18	EDUCATIONAL SERVICES	26440	10	43	JUSTICE; PUBIC ORDER/SAFETY	26719	71	473	JUSTICE; PUBIC ORDER/SAFETY
26234	35	137	AMBULATORY HEALTH CARE SVCS	26443	4	23	EDUCATIONAL SERVICES	26720	4	18	PROF.; SCIENTIFIC; & TECH SVCS
26236	4	21	ACCOMMODATION	26444	48	150	EDUCATIONAL SERVICES	26722	9	63	BLDG MATL & GARDEN EQPMT DLRS
26237	7	9	ADMINISTRATIVE & SUPPORT SVCS	26447	20	281	AMUSEMENT; GAMBLING;& RECREAT.	26726	535	6600	UNCLASSIFIED ESTABLISHMENTS
26238	17	97	MINING (EXCEPT OIL AND GAS)	26448	10	40	JUSTICE; PUBIC ORDER/SAFETY	26731	3	19	SUPPORT ACT. FOR TRANSPORT.
26241	896	9824	HOSPITALS	26451	25	129	EDUCATIONAL SERVICES	26739	35	229	MERCH. WHOLESALERS;DURABLE GDS
26250	125	947	JUSTICE; PUBIC ORDER/SAFETY	26452	358	3387	HOSPITALS	26743	16	123	JUSTICE; PUBIC ORDER/SAFETY
26253	72	1515	WOOD PRODUCT MANUFACTURING	26456	113	657	EDUCATIONAL SERVICES	26750	33	109	JUSTICE; PUBIC ORDER/SAFETY
26254	11	23	ACCOMMODATION	26461	2	1	MOTOR VEHICLE & PARTS DEALERS	26753	115	938	REPAIR AND MAINTENANCE
26257	8	45	EDUCATIONAL SERVICES	26463	2	5	UTILITIES	26755	16	14	FOOD SVCS & DRINKING PLACES
26259	18	174	MERCH. WHOLESALERS;DURABLE GDS	26501	915	11284	AMBULATORY HEALTH CARE SVCS	26757	353	3348	EDUCATIONAL SERVICES
26260	102	1472	ACCOMMODATION	26502	3	2	FOOD AND BEVERAGE STORES	26761	12	28	TRUCK TRANSPORTATION
26261	95	684	EDUCATIONAL SERVICES	26504	5	23	RELIG.; GRANT; CIVIC; PROF ORG	26763	27	101	JUSTICE; PUBIC ORDER/SAFETY
26263	4	6	TRANSPORTATION EQUIPMENT MFG	26505	1675	19547	FOOD SVCS & DRINKING PLACES	26764	114	750	HOSPITALS
26264	19	47	MERCH. WHOLESALERS;DURABLE GDS	26506	107	3355	AMBULATORY HEALTH CARE SVCS	26767	21	93	SUPPORT ACT. FOR TRANSPORT.
26266	5	64	EDUCATIONAL SERVICES	26507	10	79	MERCH. WHOLESALERS;DURABLE GDS	26801	71	498	EDUCATIONAL SERVICES
26267	5	14	SPECIAL TRADE CONTRACTORS	26508	724	8062	ACCOMMODATION	26802	33	81	EDUCATIONAL SERVICES
26268	3	0	CONSTRUCTION OF BUILDINGS	26519	33	178	ADMIN. OF ECONOMIC PROGRAMS	26804	3	36	EDUCATIONAL SERVICES
26269	5	104	EDUCATIONAL SERVICES	26520	18	135	EDUCATIONAL SERVICES	26807	170	1171	AMBULATORY HEALTH CARE SVCS
26270	32	98	EDUCATIONAL SERVICES	26521	33	252	EDUCATIONAL SERVICES	26808	6	610	ACCOMMODATION
26271	6	66	BLDG MATL & GARDEN EQPMT DLRS	26524	1	0	POSTAL SERVICE	26810	34	97	TELECOMMUNICATIONS
26273	13	42	OTHER INFORMATION SERVICES	26525	134	873	WOOD PRODUCT MANUFACTURING	26812	69	109	MUSEUMS; HIST. SITES;& SIMILAR
26275	15	25	SOCIAL ASSISTANCE	26527	2	22	JUSTICE; PUBIC ORDER/SAFETY	26814	10	164	MERCH. WHOLESALERS;DURABLE GDS
26276	4	2	POSTAL SERVICE	26531	9	38	REPAIR AND MAINTENANCE	26815	14	221	NAT'L SECURITY & INT'L AFFAIRS
26278	4	8	MERCH. WHOLESALERS;DURABLE GDS	26534	20	189	SPECIAL TRADE CONTRACTORS	26817	10	18	GENERAL MERCHANDISE STORES
26280	51	423	WOOD PRODUCT MANUFACTURING	26537	308	2729	EDUCATIONAL SERVICES	26818	8	35	TRUCK TRANSPORTATION
26282	3	13	MINING (EXCEPT OIL AND GAS)	26541	46	370	MINING (EXCEPT OIL AND GAS)	26823	7	125	CROP PRODUCTION
26283	9	31	CONSTRUCTION OF BUILDINGS	26542	59	291	JUSTICE; PUBIC ORDER/SAFETY	26833	27	89	EDUCATIONAL SERVICES
26285	7	25	MERCH. WHOLESALERS;DURABLE GDS	26543	9	31	RELIG.; GRANT; CIVIC; PROF ORG	26836	315	4606	FOOD MANUFACTURING
26287	154	1222	EXEC.; LEGIS.; & OTHER SUPPORT	26544	6	55	CONSTRUCTION OF BUILDINGS	26838	1	0	CONSTRUCTION OF BUILDINGS
26288	132	973	HOSPITALS	26546	4	30	RELIG.; GRANT; CIVIC; PROF ORG	26845	6	21	EDUCATIONAL SERVICES
26289	1	2	SPECIAL TRADE CONTRACTORS	26547	80	497	MERCH. WHOLESALERS;DURABLE GDS	26847	312	2829	HOSPITALS
26291	24	214	WOOD PRODUCT MANUFACTURING	26554	1746	16642	FOOD SVCS & DRINKING PLACES	26851	71	309	SPECIAL TRADE CONTRACTORS
26292	54	477	SOCIAL ASSISTANCE	26555	6	46	PROF.; SCIENTIFIC; & TECH SVCS	26852	6	5	BEVERAGE & TOBACCO PRODUCT MFG
26293	14	66	FOOD SVCS & DRINKING PLACES	26559	17	86	EDUCATIONAL SERVICES	26855	12	102	SPECIAL TRADE CONTRACTORS
26294	10	60	JUSTICE; PUBIC ORDER/SAFETY	26560	3	1	PERSONAL AND LAUNDRY SERVICES	26865	11	53	ACCOMMODATION

ZIP CODE	2009 Total Firms	2009 Total Employees	TOP INDUSTRY RANKED on 2009 EMPLOYMENT	ZIP CODE	2009 Total Firms	2009 Total Employees	TOP INDUSTRY RANKED on 2009 EMPLOYMENT	ZIP CODE	2009 Total Firms	2009 Total Employees	TOP INDUSTRY RANKED on 2009 EMPLOYMENT
26866	26	43	PROF.; SCIENTIFIC; & TECH SVCS	27259	13	87	EDUCATIONAL SERVICES	27503	78	301	EDUCATIONAL SERVICES
26884	15	71	ACCOMMODATION	27260	2619	22329	FURNITURE & RELATED PROD. MFG	27504	515	3828	SPECIAL TRADE CONTRACTORS
26886	1	1	RELIG.; GRANT; CIVIC; PROF ORG	27261	16	52	REAL ESTATE	27505	111	341	EDUCATIONAL SERVICES
27006	427	2727	NURSING & RESID. CARE FACILIT.	27262	1878	20577	HOSPITALS	27506	32	984	EDUCATIONAL SERVICES
27007	47	136	ACCOMMODATION	27263	1535	16728	FURNITURE & RELATED PROD. MFG	27507	21	30	HEAVY & CIVIL ENG. CONSTRUCT'N
27009	55	148	REPAIR AND MAINTENANCE	27264	1	1	ADMINISTRATIVE & SUPPORT SVCS	27508	85	861	EDUCATIONAL SERVICES
27010	10	17	CONSTRUCTION OF BUILDINGS	27265	1561	13785	FOOD SVCS & DRINKING PLACES	27509	138	8834	UNCLASSIFIED ESTABLISHMENTS
27011	134	1155	EDUCATIONAL SERVICES	27278	1153	8149	PROF.; SCIENTIFIC; & TECH SVCS	27510	519	3881	FOOD SVCS & DRINKING PLACES
27012	829	6829	FOOD SVCS & DRINKING PLACES	27281	39	153	ACCOMMODATION	27511	2197	19183	EDUCATIONAL SERVICES
27013	131	3787	MISCELLANEOUS MANUFACTURING	27282	523	4818	FURN. & HOME FURNISHGS STORES	27512	35	109	ADMINISTRATIVE & SUPPORT SVCS
27014	51	445	APPAREL MANUFACTURING	27283	56	192	MERCH. WHOLESALERS;NONDUR. GDS	27513	1413	22741	TELECOMMUNICATIONS
27016	125	1462	EXEC.; LEGIS.; & OTHER SUPPORT	27284	1825	18952	INSURANCE CARRIERS & RELATED	27514	1666	24214	HOSPITALS
27017	350	3659	EDUCATIONAL SERVICES	27285	12	9	CONSTRUCTION OF BUILDINGS	27515	17	51	HEALTH & PERSONAL CARE STORES
27018	219	1488	EDUCATIONAL SERVICES	27288	1047	9536	TRUCK TRANSPORTATION	27516	781	6465	EDUCATIONAL SERVICES
27019	72	228	EDUCATIONAL SERVICES	27291	37	72	SPECIAL TRADE CONTRACTORS	27517	757	6858	PROF.; SCIENTIFIC; & TECH SVCS
27020	129	732	BLDG MATL & GARDEN EQPMT DLRS	27292	1780	16862	JUSTICE; PUBIC ORDER/SAFETY	27518	1067	22403	HOSPITALS
27021	493	4078	FOOD SVCS & DRINKING PLACES	27293	5	9	MERCH. WHOLESALERS;DURABLE GDS	27519	416	3262	EDUCATIONAL SERVICES
27022	28	204	EDUCATIONAL SERVICES	27295	955	8569	CONSTRUCTION OF BUILDINGS	27520	1080	7534	FOOD SVCS & DRINKING PLACES
27023	248	1469	EDUCATIONAL SERVICES	27298	302	2203	FURNITURE & RELATED PROD. MFG	27521	155	754	EDUCATIONAL SERVICES
27024	56	327	BLDG MATL & GARDEN EQPMT DLRS	27299	64	647	BLDG MATL & GARDEN EQPMT DLRS	27522	373	4168	MACHINERY MANUFACTURING
27025	440	3757	TEXTILE MILLS	27301	188	3326	FURN. & HOME FURNISHGS STORES	27523	299	2559	FOOD SVCS & DRINKING PLACES
27027	132	1342	TEXTILE MILLS	27302	783	9212	FOOD SVCS & DRINKING PLACES	27524	270	1197	EDUCATIONAL SERVICES
27028	977	9790	EDUCATIONAL SERVICES	27305	36	36	NURSING & RESID. CARE FACILIT.	27525	220	1572	CHEMICAL MANUFACTURING
27030	1704	19742	APPAREL MANUFACTURING	27306	205	2093	MERCH. WHOLESALERS;DURABLE GDS	27526	1219	9253	FOOD SVCS & DRINKING PLACES
27031	1	0	SPECIAL TRADE CONTRACTORS	27310	166	892	FOOD SVCS & DRINKING PLACES	27527	193	2876	MERCH. WHOLESALERS;DURABLE GDS
27040	170	936	EDUCATIONAL SERVICES	27311	61	190	RELIG.; GRANT; CIVIC; PROF ORG	27528	4	21	PROF.; SCIENTIFIC; & TECH SVCS
27041	322	2000	EDUCATIONAL SERVICES	27312	691	4336	NURSING & RESID. CARE FACILIT.	27529	1719	17583	FOOD SVCS & DRINKING PLACES
27042	14	615	MERCH. WHOLESALERS;DURABLE GDS	27313	144	813	NURSING & RESID. CARE FACILIT.	27530	1567	18969	HOSPITALS
27043	100	367	EDUCATIONAL SERVICES	27314	24	243	CLOTHING & CLOTH'G ACC. STORES	27531	33	61	PROF.; SCIENTIFIC; & TECH SVCS
27045	240	2695	MACHINERY MANUFACTURING	27315	50	314	CONSTRUCTION OF BUILDINGS	27532	4	9	SPECIAL TRADE CONTRACTORS
27046	41	136	EDUCATIONAL SERVICES	27316	264	2404	EDUCATIONAL SERVICES	27533	4	7	PERSONAL AND LAUNDRY SERVICES
27047	26	162	TRUCK TRANSPORTATION	27317	576	6312	FURNITURE & RELATED PROD. MFG	27534	1259	17621	FOOD SVCS & DRINKING PLACES
27048	184	1175	NONMETALLIC MINERAL PROD. MFG	27320	1221	12834	EDUCATIONAL SERVICES	27536	1071	9745	FOOD SVCS & DRINKING PLACES
27049	1	2	POSTAL SERVICE	27323	2	2	ADMINISTRATIVE & SUPPORT SVCS	27537	462	4995	EDUCATIONAL SERVICES
27050	62	330	EDUCATIONAL SERVICES	27325	181	898	WOOD PRODUCT MANUFACTURING	27539	352	5111	FABRICATED METAL PRODUCT MFG
27051	214	1599	EDUCATIONAL SERVICES	27326	51	177	EDUCATIONAL SERVICES	27540	538	3909	EDUCATIONAL SERVICES
27052	298	1850	BEVERAGE & TOBACCO PRODUCT MFG	27330	1565	16972	AMBULATORY HEALTH CARE SVCS	27541	76	209	EDUCATIONAL SERVICES
27053	63	331	BLDG MATL & GARDEN EQPMT DLRS	27331	10	50	NONSTORE RETAILERS	27542	234	1626	FOOD SVCS & DRINKING PLACES
27054	48	324	EDUCATIONAL SERVICES	27332	745	10565	MERCH. WHOLESALERS;NONDUR. GDS	27543	3	5	POSTAL SERVICE
27055	586	6851	TEXTILE MILLS	27340	14	116	JUSTICE; PUBIC ORDER/SAFETY	27544	78	466	EDUCATIONAL SERVICES
27101	1943	25761	PROF.; SCIENTIFIC; & TECH SVCS	27341	202	971	FURNITURE & RELATED PROD. MFG	27545	682	5358	FOOD SVCS & DRINKING PLACES
27102	10	18	SPECIAL TRADE CONTRACTORS	27342	3	63	EDUCATIONAL SERVICES	27546	608	5696	JUSTICE; PUBIC ORDER/SAFETY
27103	2779	38423	HOSPITALS	27343	33	109	EDUCATIONAL SERVICES	27549	786	5540	EDUCATIONAL SERVICES
27104	801	7054	FOOD SVCS & DRINKING PLACES	27344	719	7938	MERCH. WHOLESALERS;NONDUR. GDS	27551	30	91	BLDG MATL & GARDEN EQPMT DLRS
27105	1367	27643	PROF.; SCIENTIFIC; & TECH SVCS	27349	76	277	EDUCATIONAL SERVICES	27552	6	24	AMBULATORY HEALTH CARE SVCS
27106	1345	17127	RELIG.; GRANT; CIVIC; PROF ORG	27350	173	810	FURNITURE & RELATED PROD. MFG	27553	35	671	JUSTICE; PUBIC ORDER/SAFETY
27107	1101	9203	FOOD MANUFACTURING	27351	27	44	RELIG.; GRANT; CIVIC; PROF ORG	27555	23	148	EDUCATIONAL SERVICES
27108	1	5	TRANSIT & GRND PASS. TRANSPORT	27355	72	371	FURNITURE & RELATED PROD. MFG	27556	16	208	EDUCATIONAL SERVICES
27109	8	1823	EDUCATIONAL SERVICES	27356	94	1084	MERCH. WHOLESALERS;NONDUR. GDS	27557	130	1190	APPAREL MANUFACTURING
27110	7	528	EDUCATIONAL SERVICES	27357	215	1870	CONSTRUCTION OF BUILDINGS	27559	67	1342	WOOD PRODUCT MANUFACTURING
27113	6	13	FABRICATED METAL PRODUCT MFG	27358	325	1133	HEAVY & CIVIL ENG. CONSTRUCT'N	27560	1413	27024	PROF.; SCIENTIFIC; & TECH SVCS
27114	12	28	TRUCK TRANSPORTATION	27359	8	1651	MOTOR VEHICLE & PARTS DEALERS	27562	52	749	PAPER MANUFACTURING
27115	3	7	ADMIN. OF ECONOMIC PROGRAMS	27360	1919	19274	TRUCK TRANSPORTATION	27563	129	719	APPAREL MANUFACTURING
27116	8	24	ADMINISTRATIVE & SUPPORT SVCS	27361	10	30	CONSTRUCTION OF BUILDINGS	27565	880	10409	CHEMICAL MANUFACTURING
27117	4	4	ADMINISTRATIVE & SUPPORT SVCS	27370	344	2080	EDUCATIONAL SERVICES	27568	43	351	EDUCATIONAL SERVICES
27120	3	4	FOOD SVCS & DRINKING PLACES	27371	408	4217	JUSTICE; PUBIC ORDER/SAFETY	27569	154	970	EDUCATIONAL SERVICES
27127	860	7770	EDUCATIONAL SERVICES	27373	2	4	SPECIAL TRADE CONTRACTORS	27570	3	3	SPORTG GDS;HOBBY;BOOK; & MUSIC
27130	3	11	PROF.; SCIENTIFIC; & TECH SVCS	27374	56	800	SPECIAL TRADE CONTRACTORS	27571	134	709	FOOD SVCS & DRINKING PLACES
27150	1	2	MISCELLANEOUS MANUFACTURING	27375	66	2294	EXEC.; LEGIS.; & OTHER SUPPORT	27572	130	331	SPECIAL TRADE CONTRACTORS
27157	61	17768	AMBULATORY HEALTH CARE SVCS	27376	364	2062	FOOD AND BEVERAGE STORES	27573	841	8574	GENERAL MERCHANDISE STORES
27201	14	42	GASOLINE STATIONS	27377	134	2414	ELECT'L EQPMT; APP; & COMP MFG	27574	261	1253	EDUCATIONAL SERVICES
27202	6	56	MERCH. WHOLESALERS;DURABLE GDS	27379	322	2136	EDUCATIONAL SERVICES	27576	413	3383	FOOD SVCS & DRINKING PLACES
27203	1667	17463	MERCH. WHOLESALERS;DURABLE GDS	27401	2061	41727	HOSPITALS	27577	1251	15119	COMPUTER & ELECTRONIC PROD MFG
27204	10	38	REPAIR AND MAINTENANCE	27402	12	37	SPECIAL TRADE CONTRACTORS	27581	32	48	SPECIAL TRADE CONTRACTORS
27205	813	12460	FURNITURE & RELATED PROD. MFG	27403	966	8894	HOSPITALS	27582	18	155	EDUCATIONAL SERVICES
27207	91	551	EDUCATIONAL SERVICES	27404	15	15	PRINT'G & RELATED SUPP'T ACT'S	27583	111	1672	MANAGMT OF COMPANIES & ENTERP.
27208	51	124	EDUCATIONAL SERVICES	27405	1889	19753	AMBULATORY HEALTH CARE SVCS	27584	6	23	FOOD SVCS & DRINKING PLACES
27209	176	2523	PRIMARY METAL MANUFACTURING	27406	1973	22552	SPECIAL TRADE CONTRACTORS	27586	3	47	EDUCATIONAL SERVICES
27212	39	337	JUSTICE; PUBIC ORDER/SAFETY	27407	2802	28923	FOOD SVCS & DRINKING PLACES	27587	1520	9735	EDUCATIONAL SERVICES
27213	11	49	TRUCK TRANSPORTATION	27408	1616	17331	FOOD SVCS & DRINKING PLACES	27588	12	18	SPECIAL TRADE CONTRACTORS
27214	211	2087	PRINT'G & RELATED SUPP'T ACT'S	27409	1561	34910	MERCH. WHOLESALERS;DURABLE GDS	27589	317	2229	EDUCATIONAL SERVICES
27215	2201	31962	AMBULATORY HEALTH CARE SVCS	27410	1591	20739	FOOD AND BEVERAGE STORES	27591	516	3952	MERCH. WHOLESALERS;DURABLE GDS
27216	11	29	REAL ESTATE	27411	22	440	NONSTORE RETAILERS	27592	185	621	EDUCATIONAL SERVICES
27217	982	8292	APPAREL MANUFACTURING	27412	11	1987	AMBULATORY HEALTH CARE SVCS	27593	14	136	EDUCATIONAL SERVICES
27229	119	803	APPAREL MANUFACTURING	27413	1	1	PROF.; SCIENTIFIC; & TECH SVCS	27594	4	6	MISCELLANEOUS STORE RETAILERS
27230	2	201	TEXTILE MILLS	27415	11	11	REPAIR AND MAINTENANCE	27596	407	3923	MERCH. WHOLESALERS;DURABLE GDS
27231	40	53	RELIG.; GRANT; CIVIC; PROF ORG	27416	9	12	ADMINISTRATIVE & SUPPORT SVCS	27597	606	5279	MERCH. WHOLESALERS;NONDUR. GDS
27233	90	544	CONSTRUCTION OF BUILDINGS	27417	12	17	MERCH. WHOLESALERS;DURABLE GDS	27599	61	2340	AMBULATORY HEALTH CARE SVCS
27235	149	2427	MERCH. WHOLESALERS;NONDUR. GDS	27419	16	88	ADMINISTRATIVE & SUPPORT SVCS	27601	1614	23515	EXEC.; LEGIS.; & OTHER SUPPORT
27239	304	1727	EDUCATIONAL SERVICES	27420	5	753	PROF.; SCIENTIFIC; & TECH SVCS	27602	5	14	EXEC.; LEGIS.; & OTHER SUPPORT
27242	40	245	EXEC.; LEGIS.; & OTHER SUPPORT	27425	5	33	RELIG.; GRANT; CIVIC; PROF ORG	27603	2503	28745	EXEC.; LEGIS.; & OTHER SUPPORT
27243	92	349	EDUCATIONAL SERVICES	27427	6	23	SECURITIES/COMMODITY CONTRACTS	27604	2211	27656	EXEC.; LEGIS.; & OTHER SUPPORT
27244	206	3334	EDUCATIONAL SERVICES	27429	13	12	SPECIAL TRADE CONTRACTORS	27605	628	7072	REAL ESTATE
27247	4	3	SPECIAL TRADE CONTRACTORS	27435	1	0	ADMINISTRATIVE & SUPPORT SVCS	27606	1369	14933	PROF.; SCIENTIFIC; & TECH SVCS
27248	112	568	EDUCATIONAL SERVICES	27438	10	25	RELIG.; GRANT; CIVIC; PROF ORG	27607	1481	25802	HOSPITALS
27249	248	1414	EDUCATIONAL SERVICES	27455	507	4695	AMBULATORY HEALTH CARE SVCS	27608	451	3209	RELIG.; GRANT; CIVIC; PROF ORG
27252	55	238	EDUCATIONAL SERVICES	27495	3	5	CREDIT INTERMEDIATION & RELATD	27609	3210	32479	CREDIT INTERMEDIATION & RELATD
27253	827	7991	EDUCATIONAL SERVICES	27498	2	1	CREDIT INTERMEDIATION & RELATD	27610	1609	25928	EXEC.; LEGIS.; & OTHER SUPPORT
27256	6	16	SUPPORT ACT. FOR TRANSPORT.	27501	422	2528	EDUCATIONAL SERVICES	27611	12	27	TRUCK TRANSPORTATION
27258	161	2362	EDUCATIONAL SERVICES	27502	995	6911	FOOD SVCS & DRINKING PLACES	27612	1988	21067	PROF.; SCIENTIFIC; & TECH SVCS

BUSINESS DATA

ZIP CODE	2009 Total Firms	2009 Total Employ-ees	TOP INDUSTRY RANKED on 2009 EMPLOYMENT
27613	869	6583	EDUCATIONAL SERVICES
27614	695	11340	AMBULATORY HEALTH CARE SVCS
27615	2798	19734	PROF.; SCIENTIFIC; & TECH SVCS
27616	1544	15034	FOOD SVCS & DRINKING PLACES
27617	790	12089	SPECIAL TRADE CONTRACTORS
27619	23	97	ADMINISTRATIVE & SUPPORT SVCS
27620	7	31	SPECIAL TRADE CONTRACTORS
27622	12	29	RELIG.; GRANT; CIVIC; PROF ORG
27623	17	228	RENTAL AND LEASING SERVICES
27624	22	69	ADMINISTRATIVE & SUPPORT SVCS
27627	10	19	FOOD AND BEVERAGE STORES
27628	6	49	FOOD SVCS & DRINKING PLACES
27629	12	38	SPECIAL TRADE CONTRACTORS
27636	7	13	ADMINISTRATIVE & SUPPORT SVCS
27656	1	900	INSURANCE CARRIERS & RELATED
27658	9	20	SPORTG GDS;HOBBY;BOOK; & MUSIC
27661	4	20	SPECIAL TRADE CONTRACTORS
27675	7	23	ADMINISTRATIVE & SUPPORT SVCS
27676	4	22	RELIG.; GRANT; CIVIC; PROF ORG
27695	24	222	RELIG.; GRANT; CIVIC; PROF ORG
27697	5	830	ADMIN. OF ECONOMIC PROGRAMS
27699	12	892	ADMIN. HUMAN RESOURCE PROGRAMS
27701	1558	18452	MERCH. WHOLESALERS;NONDUR. GDS
27702	6	8	RELIG.; GRANT; CIVIC; PROF ORG
27703	1357	19154	PROF.; SCIENTIFIC; & TECH SVCS
27704	1123	13266	AMBULATORY HEALTH CARE SVCS
27705	1632	28904	EDUCATIONAL SERVICES
27707	1594	16374	EDUCATIONAL SERVICES
27708	21	253	OTHER INFORMATION SERVICES
27709	199	26992	TELECOMMUNICATIONS
27710	161	10676	HOSPITALS
27711	6	597	PROF.; SCIENTIFIC; & TECH SVCS
27712	284	3041	EDUCATIONAL SERVICES
27713	1704	19454	PROF.; SCIENTIFIC; & TECH SVCS
27715	11	88	ADMINISTRATIVE & SUPPORT SVCS
27717	8	16	MISCELLANEOUS STORE RETAILERS
27722	7	28	ADMINISTRATIVE & SUPPORT SVCS
27801	542	5656	EDUCATIONAL SERVICES
27802	10	64	MERCH. WHOLESALERS;DURABLE GDS
27803	537	3611	EDUCATIONAL SERVICES
27804	1990	27967	AMBULATORY HEALTH CARE SVCS
27805	92	412	FOOD AND BEVERAGE STORES
27806	100	1742	MINING (EXCEPT OIL AND GAS)
27807	147	883	EDUCATIONAL SERVICES
27808	90	314	EDUCATIONAL SERVICES
27809	157	2366	WHOLESALE ELEC. MRKTS & AGENTS
27810	237	1195	HOSPITALS
27811	8	30	SOCIAL ASSISTANCE
27812	93	540	EDUCATIONAL SERVICES
27813	22	121	SPECIAL TRADE CONTRACTORS
27814	38	95	RELIG.; GRANT; CIVIC; PROF ORG
27815	1	0	PROF.; SCIENTIFIC; & TECH SVCS
27816	55	132	MISCELLANEOUS MANUFACTURING
27817	175	1060	EDUCATIONAL SERVICES
27818	17	44	CROP PRODUCTION
27819	17	44	JUSTICE; PUBIC ORDER/SAFETY
27820	72	566	AMBULATORY HEALTH CARE SVCS
27821	14	24	GASOLINE STATIONS
27822	199	1827	PRINT'G & RELATED SUPP'T ACT'S
27823	207	1681	BLDG MATL & GARDEN EQPMT DLRS
27824	53	350	CREDIT INTERMEDIATION & RELATD
27825	14	157	SOCIAL ASSISTANCE
27826	36	399	MERCH. WHOLESALERS;NONDUR. GDS
27827	16	25	SPECIAL TRADE CONTRACTORS
27828	360	3368	WHOLESALE ELEC. MRKTS & AGENTS
27829	44	133	SOCIAL ASSISTANCE
27830	136	614	EDUCATIONAL SERVICES
27831	56	414	AMBULATORY HEALTH CARE SVCS
27832	65	542	EDUCATIONAL SERVICES
27833	1	0	BLDG MATL & GARDEN EQPMT DLRS
27834	2253	53606	HOSPITALS
27835	12	33	ACCOMMODATION
27836	4	6	INSURANCE CARRIERS & RELATED
27837	95	281	EDUCATIONAL SERVICES
27839	147	2151	EXEC.; LEGIS.; & OTHER SUPPORT
27840	21	322	MISCELLANEOUS MANUFACTURING
27841	6	6	SPECIAL TRADE CONTRACTORS
27842	34	158	CONSTRUCTION OF BUILDINGS
27843	21	104	CROP PRODUCTION
27844	52	238	EDUCATIONAL SERVICES
27845	138	1357	JUSTICE; PUBIC ORDER/SAFETY
27846	61	317	EDUCATIONAL SERVICES
27847	15	143	AMBULATORY HEALTH CARE SVCS
27849	46	239	WOOD PRODUCT MANUFACTURING
27850	247	1100	EDUCATIONAL SERVICES
27851	101	486	EDUCATIONAL SERVICES
27852	60	122	SPECIAL TRADE CONTRACTORS
27853	6	12	PERFORM'G ARTS; SPEC. SPORTS
27855	204	1575	EDUCATIONAL SERVICES
27856	450	4329	EXEC.; LEGIS.; & OTHER SUPPORT

ZIP CODE	2009 Total Firms	2009 Total Employ-ees	TOP INDUSTRY RANKED on 2009 EMPLOYMENT
27857	33	71	EDUCATIONAL SERVICES
27858	1895	17590	FOOD SVCS & DRINKING PLACES
27860	105	549	CROP PRODUCTION
27861	4	1	EXEC.; LEGIS.; & OTHER SUPPORT
27862	11	85	EDUCATIONAL SERVICES
27863	166	1002	EDUCATIONAL SERVICES
27864	115	1060	EDUCATIONAL SERVICES
27865	75	446	EDUCATIONAL SERVICES
27866	15	280	HEAVY & CIVIL ENG. CONSTRUCT'N
27867	3	24	NURSING & RESID. CARE FACILIT.
27868	14	94	EDUCATIONAL SERVICES
27869	85	711	NURSING & RESID. CARE FACILIT.
27870	1105	10454	FOOD SVCS & DRINKING PLACES
27871	147	1476	UNCLASSIFIED ESTABLISHMENTS
27872	15	35	FOOD AND BEVERAGE STORES
27873	8	19	GASOLINE STATIONS
27874	182	1150	EDUCATIONAL SERVICES
27875	9	19	SPORTG GDS;HOBBY;BOOK; & MUSIC
27876	56	284	PAPER MANUFACTURING
27877	14	437	CHEMICAL MANUFACTURING
27878	71	343	FOOD SVCS & DRINKING PLACES
27879	16	74	SPECIAL TRADE CONTRACTORS
27880	65	733	BLDG MATL & GARDEN EQPMT DLRS
27881	3	3	GENERAL MERCHANDISE STORES
27882	204	2096	MERCH. WHOLESALERS;NONDUR. GDS
27883	92	448	EDUCATIONAL SERVICES
27884	32	142	EDUCATIONAL SERVICES
27885	91	803	JUSTICE; PUBIC ORDER/SAFETY
27886	803	11008	MERCH. WHOLESALERS;NONDUR. GDS
27887	8	535	EXEC.; LEGIS.; & OTHER SUPPORT
27888	46	99	ADMIN. ENVIRO. QUALITY PROGRMS
27889	1321	14309	TEXTILE MILLS
27890	146	1779	EDUCATIONAL SERVICES
27891	117	2376	MERCH. WHOLESALERS;DURABLE GDS
27892	691	5569	EDUCATIONAL SERVICES
27893	1906	31862	MERCH. WHOLESALERS;DURABLE GDS
27894	7	25	MUSEUMS; HIST. SITES;& SIMILAR
27895	3	6	PROF.; SCIENTIFIC; & TECH SVCS
27896	611	5256	FOOD SVCS & DRINKING PLACES
27897	46	155	TRANSPORTATION EQUIPMENT MFG
27906	2	16	HOSPITALS
27909	1723	19172	EXEC.; LEGIS.; & OTHER SUPPORT
27910	596	6400	AMBULATORY HEALTH CARE SVCS
27915	98	648	FOOD SVCS & DRINKING PLACES
27916	13	11	SPECIAL TRADE CONTRACTORS
27917	39	531	EDUCATIONAL SERVICES
27919	27	50	MERCH. WHOLESALERS;NONDUR. GDS
27920	138	770	ACCOMMODATION
27921	134	943	EDUCATIONAL SERVICES
27922	30	768	PRIMARY METAL MANUFACTURING
27923	59	253	JUSTICE; PUBIC ORDER/SAFETY
27924	68	292	CONSTRUCTION OF BUILDINGS
27925	191	1215	CROP PRODUCTION
27926	23	81	PROF.; SCIENTIFIC; & TECH SVCS
27927	232	1551	REAL ESTATE
27928	78	391	MERCH. WHOLESALERS;NONDUR. GDS
27929	80	422	EXEC.; LEGIS.; & OTHER SUPPORT
27932	593	5699	HOSPITALS
27935	25	68	FOOD SVCS & DRINKING PLACES
27936	68	167	FOOD SVCS & DRINKING PLACES
27937	52	230	EDUCATIONAL SERVICES
27938	92	892	EDUCATIONAL SERVICES
27939	116	522	FOOD AND BEVERAGE STORES
27941	67	281	SPECIAL TRADE CONTRACTORS
27942	19	88	CONSTRUCTION OF BUILDINGS
27943	98	556	ADMIN. OF ECONOMIC PROGRAMS
27944	375	2009	EXEC.; LEGIS.; & OTHER SUPPORT
27946	18	85	MERCH. WHOLESALERS;NONDUR. GDS
27947	49	176	FOOD SVCS & DRINKING PLACES
27948	780	4380	FOOD SVCS & DRINKING PLACES
27949	806	5446	FOOD SVCS & DRINKING PLACES
27950	35	182	MOTOR VEHICLE & PARTS DEALERS
27953	33	298	TRANSPORTATION EQUIPMENT MFG
27954	485	3077	MUSEUMS; HIST. SITES;& SIMILAR
27956	19	139	EXEC.; LEGIS.; & OTHER SUPPORT
27957	32	182	MERCH. WHOLESALERS;NONDUR. GDS
27958	222	1687	EDUCATIONAL SERVICES
27959	517	4486	FOOD SVCS & DRINKING PLACES
27960	127	654	FOOD SVCS & DRINKING PLACES
27962	392	4003	PAPER MANUFACTURING
27964	67	261	BLDG MATL & GARDEN EQPMT DLRS
27965	29	111	EDUCATIONAL SERVICES
27966	131	400	SPECIAL TRADE CONTRACTORS
27967	8	41	EDUCATIONAL SERVICES
27968	48	210	FOOD SVCS & DRINKING PLACES
27969	3	9	WASTE MANAGMT & REMEDIAT'N SVC
27970	78	376	WOOD PRODUCT MANUFACTURING
27972	18	56	REAL ESTATE
27973	30	140	EDUCATIONAL SERVICES
27974	29	57	REPAIR AND MAINTENANCE

ZIP CODE	2009 Total Firms	2009 Total Employ-ees	TOP INDUSTRY RANKED on 2009 EMPLOYMENT
27976	56	146	JUSTICE; PUBIC ORDER/SAFETY
27978	14	70	SUPPORT ACTIVITIES: AGR./FOR.
27979	53	242	EDUCATIONAL SERVICES
27980	45	182	EDUCATIONAL SERVICES
27981	101	608	TRANSPORTATION EQUIPMENT MFG
27982	19	92	AMUSEMENT; GAMBLING;& RECREAT.
27983	394	2823	EDUCATIONAL SERVICES
27985	17	219	EDUCATIONAL SERVICES
27986	95	1138	ADMINISTRATIVE & SUPPORT SVCS
28001	1356	12515	FOOD SVCS & DRINKING PLACES
28002	9	32	ADMINISTRATIVE & SUPPORT SVCS
28006	21	70	SPECIAL TRADE CONTRACTORS
28007	43	267	MERCH. WHOLESALERS;NONDUR. GDS
28009	42	253	EDUCATIONAL SERVICES
28010	3	124	RELIG.; GRANT; CIVIC; PROF ORG
28012	701	6472	EDUCATIONAL SERVICES
28016	344	2567	FABRICATED METAL PRODUCT MFG
28017	52	813	EDUCATIONAL SERVICES
28018	107	761	EDUCATIONAL SERVICES
28019	19	29	RELIG.; GRANT; CIVIC; PROF ORG
28020	38	112	EDUCATIONAL SERVICES
28021	381	2804	FURNITURE & RELATED PROD. MFG
28023	386	2628	EDUCATIONAL SERVICES
28024	11	96	EDUCATIONAL SERVICES
28025	2009	23854	PERSONAL AND LAUNDRY SERVICES
28026	8	11	FABRICATED METAL PRODUCT MFG
28027	1839	25839	FOOD SVCS & DRINKING PLACES
28031	1358	8584	FOOD SVCS & DRINKING PLACES
28032	81	668	EDUCATIONAL SERVICES
28033	36	356	UTILITIES
28034	467	2871	EDUCATIONAL SERVICES
28035	1	30	OTHER INFORMATION SERVICES
28036	471	4142	MERCH. WHOLESALERS;DURABLE GDS
28037	845	5377	FOOD SVCS & DRINKING PLACES
28038	7	17	RELIG.; GRANT; CIVIC; PROF ORG
28039	24	413	BLDG MATL & GARDEN EQPMT DLRS
28040	123	498	SPECIAL TRADE CONTRACTORS
28041	31	198	EDUCATIONAL SERVICES
28042	31	202	EDUCATIONAL SERVICES
28043	1011	9390	PLASTICS & RUBBER PRODUCTS MFG
28052	1454	20939	JUSTICE; PUBIC ORDER/SAFETY
28053	12	56	ADMIN. OF ECONOMIC PROGRAMS
28054	1789	20830	HOSPITALS
28055	3	29	ADMINISTRATIVE & SUPPORT SVCS
28056	835	7154	FOOD SVCS & DRINKING PLACES
28070	22	43	ADMINISTRATIVE & SUPPORT SVCS
28071	51	468	HEAVY & CIVIL ENG. CONSTRUCT'N
28072	25	86	SPECIAL TRADE CONTRACTORS
28073	78	1961	MERCH. WHOLESALERS;DURABLE GDS
28074	2	2	MISCELLANEOUS MANUFACTURING
28075	462	3051	BLDG MATL & GARDEN EQPMT DLRS
28076	13	329	APPAREL MANUFACTURING
28077	7	48	JUSTICE; PUBIC ORDER/SAFETY
28078	1563	18874	UTILITIES
28079	1032	7490	SPECIAL TRADE CONTRACTORS
28080	95	1141	FABRICATED METAL PRODUCT MFG
28081	500	3466	NURSING & RESID. CARE FACILIT.
28082	6	15	SUPPORT ACT. FOR TRANSPORT.
28083	870	7342	FOOD SVCS & DRINKING PLACES
28086	752	7915	TRANSFORTATION EQUIPMENT MFG
28088	82	564	EDUCATIONAL SERVICES
28089	20	91	EDUCATIONAL SERVICES
28090	155	847	EDUCATIONAL SERVICES
28091	55	684	APPAREL MANUFACTURING
28092	1293	14511	EXEC.; LEGIS.; & OTHER SUPPORT
28093	10	37	SOCIAL ASSISTANCE
28097	208	1184	FOOD SVCS & DRINKING PLACES
28098	145	1204	MOTOR VEHICLE & PARTS DEALERS
28101	35	159	TEXTILE MILLS
28102	4	12	RELIG.; GRANT; CIVIC; PROF ORG
28103	280	2818	MERCH. WHOLESALERS;NONDUR. GDS
28104	714	5631	SPECIAL TRADE CONTRACTORS
28105	1886	20275	GENERAL MERCHANDISE STORES
28106	38	122	MERCH. WHOLESALERS;DURABLE GDS
28107	250	1645	HEAVY & CIVIL ENG. CONSTRUCT'N
28108	35	89	MERCH. WHOLESALERS;DURABLE GDS
28109	6	81	EDUCATIONAL SERVICES
28110	1805	25356	SPECIAL TRADE CONTRACTORS
28111	15	36	SPECIAL TRADE CONTRACTORS
28112	785	10013	FOOD MANUFACTURING
28114	101	836	APPAREL MANUFACTURING
28115	1138	10468	EDUCATIONAL SERVICES
28117	1661	17641	BLDG MATL & GARDEN EQPMT DLRS
28119	63	170	EDUCATIONAL SERVICES
28120	574	6755	RELIG.; GRANT; CIVIC; PROF ORG
28123	6	14	MACHINERY MANUFACTURING
28124	164	1354	TEXTILE MILLS
28125	52	474	EDUCATIONAL SERVICES
28126	8	33	WASTE MANAGMT & REMEDIAT'N SVC
28127	163	1369	MISCELLANEOUS MANUFACTURING

ZIP CODE	2009 Total Firms	2009 Total Employ-ees	TOP INDUSTRY RANKED on 2009 EMPLOYMENT	ZIP CODE	2009 Total Firms	2009 Total Employ-ees	TOP INDUSTRY RANKED on 2009 EMPLOYMENT	ZIP CODE	2009 Total Firms	2009 Total Employ-ees	TOP INDUSTRY RANKED on 2009 EMPLOYMENT
28128	233	1962	PLASTICS & RUBBER PRODUCTS MFG	28302	18	16	SPECIAL TRADE CONTRACTORS	28408	14	26	SPECIAL TRADE CONTRACTORS
28129	190	1201	EDUCATIONAL SERVICES	28303	2048	17690	FOOD SVCS & DRINKING PLACES	28409	496	1748	EDUCATIONAL SERVICES
28130	20	71	TRUCK TRANSPORTATION	28304	1361	16817	AMBULATORY HEALTH CARE SVCS	28411	735	4486	FOOD SVCS & DRINKING PLACES
28133	79	552	HEAVY & CIVIL ENG. CONSTRUCT'N	28305	463	3434	AMBULATORY HEALTH CARE SVCS	28412	1075	9193	FOOD SVCS & DRINKING PLACES
28134	871	10602	GENERAL MERCHANDISE STORES	28306	1195	11929	EDUCATIONAL SERVICES	28420	86	417	EDUCATIONAL SERVICES
28135	100	750	FABRICATED METAL PRODUCT MFG	28307	160	2486	EDUCATIONAL SERVICES	28421	42	130	CONSTRUCTION OF BUILDINGS
28136	20	89	JUSTICE; PUBIC ORDER/SAFETY	28308	40	243	PROF.; SCIENTIFIC; & TECH SVCS	28422	264	2206	EXEC.; LEGIS.; & OTHER SUPPORT
28137	81	7457	MERCH. WHOLESALERS;DURABLE GDS	28309	8	25	CONSTRUCTION OF BUILDINGS	28423	54	199	AMBULATORY HEALTH CARE SVCS
28138	222	1673	SPECIAL TRADE CONTRACTORS	28310	32	1263	SUPPORT ACT. FOR TRANSPORT.	28424	14	322	JUSTICE; PUBIC ORDER/SAFETY
28139	719	6216	PROF.; SCIENTIFIC; & TECH SVCS	28311	713	9300	PLASTICS & RUBBER PRODUCTS MFG	28425	438	5048	EXEC.; LEGIS.; & OTHER SUPPORT
28144	1308	16350	HOSPITALS	28312	498	4248	EDUCATIONAL SERVICES	28428	451	6280	TRUCK TRANSPORTATION
28145	3	6	SUPPORT ACT. FOR TRANSPORT.	28314	875	8647	FOOD SVCS & DRINKING PLACES	28429	254	2580	JUSTICE; PUBIC ORDER/SAFETY
28146	515	6295	EDUCATIONAL SERVICES	28315	614	6571	FOOD SVCS & DRINKING PLACES	28430	41	235	EDUCATIONAL SERVICES
28147	713	10759	FOOD AND BEVERAGE STORES	28318	74	354	EDUCATIONAL SERVICES	28431	227	1499	AMBULATORY HEALTH CARE SVCS
28150	1307	14728	MERCH. WHOLESALERS;DURABLE GDS	28319	2	1	POSTAL SERVICE	28432	27	46	SOCIAL ASSISTANCE
28151	7	18	ADMINISTRATIVE & SUPPORT SVCS	28320	266	1168	EDUCATIONAL SERVICES	28433	147	643	CROP PRODUCTION
28152	830	8945	EDUCATIONAL SERVICES	28323	56	245	EDUCATIONAL SERVICES	28434	42	120	ADMINISTRATIVE & SUPPORT SVCS
28159	96	757	EDUCATIONAL SERVICES	28325	17	35	SPECIAL TRADE CONTRACTORS	28435	38	199	ADMINISTRATIVE & SUPPORT SVCS
28160	262	6498	FABRICATED METAL PRODUCT MFG	28326	194	947	EDUCATIONAL SERVICES	28436	57	304	HEAVY & CIVIL ENG. CONSTRUCT'N
28163	76	726	MERCH. WHOLESALERS;DURABLE GDS	28327	469	3357	JUSTICE; PUBIC ORDER/SAFETY	28438	31	137	RELIG.; GRANT; CIVIC; PROF ORG
28164	360	2327	FABRICATED METAL PRODUCT MFG	28328	1258	13199	FOOD MANUFACTURING	28439	104	544	CONSTRUCTION OF BUILDINGS
28166	266	2287	TRANSPORTATION EQUIPMENT MFG	28329	7	36	JUSTICE; PUBIC ORDER/SAFETY	28441	113	783	APPAREL MANUFACTURING
28167	41	120	RELIG.; GRANT; CIVIC; PROF ORG	28330	7	213	PAPER MANUFACTURING	28442	32	180	EDUCATIONAL SERVICES
28168	162	1677	BLDG MATL & GARDEN EQPMT DLRS	28331	1	2	POSTAL SERVICE	28443	517	2420	EDUCATIONAL SERVICES
28169	9	43	JUSTICE; PUBIC ORDER/SAFETY	28332	35	337	EDUCATIONAL SERVICES	28444	85	6258	RELIG.; GRANT; CIVIC; PROF ORG
28170	622	5792	HOSPITALS	28333	124	2104	BLDG MATL & GARDEN EQPMT DLRS	28445	413	2318	REAL ESTATE
28173	732	3100	RELIG.; GRANT; CIVIC; PROF ORG	28334	1209	12280	ELECT'L EQPMT; APP; & COMP MFG	28447	33	151	CROP PRODUCTION
28174	145	1487	EDUCATIONAL SERVICES	28335	1	1	INSURANCE CARRIERS & RELATED	28448	26	46	BLDG MATL & GARDEN EQPMT DLRS
28201	2	4	TELECOMMUNICATIONS	28337	622	4620	EDUCATIONAL SERVICES	28449	88	479	FOOD SVCS & DRINKING PLACES
28202	2005	46169	PROF.; SCIENTIFIC; & TECH SVCS	28338	155	1136	TEXTILE MILLS	28450	56	808	NURSING & RESID. CARE FACILIT.
28203	1839	15048	PROF.; SCIENTIFIC; & TECH SVCS	28339	245	2021	GENERAL MERCHANDISE STORES	28451	691	6558	TEXTILE MILLS
28204	1176	10920	AMBULATORY HEALTH CARE SVCS	28340	280	1771	EDUCATIONAL SERVICES	28452	22	77	SPECIAL TRADE CONTRACTORS
28205	2261	13300	EDUCATIONAL SERVICES	28341	133	1549	FOOD MANUFACTURING	28453	90	583	TRUCK TRANSPORTATION
28206	1131	16161	MERCH. WHOLESALERS;DURABLE GDS	28342	19	178	MERCH. WHOLESALERS;NONDUR. GDS	28454	42	206	EXEC.; LEGIS.; & OTHER SUPPORT
28207	573	7350	AMBULATORY HEALTH CARE SVCS	28343	28	85	EDUCATIONAL SERVICES	28455	38	49	EDUCATIONAL SERVICES
28208	2088	29005	MERCH. WHOLESALERS;DURABLE GDS	28344	57	402	FOOD MANUFACTURING	28456	108	1934	PAPER MANUFACTURING
28209	1203	10998	PROF.; SCIENTIFIC; & TECH SVCS	28345	337	3490	EDUCATIONAL SERVICES	28457	189	1868	EDUCATIONAL SERVICES
28210	1520	14711	PROF.; SCIENTIFIC; & TECH SVCS	28347	25	456	JUSTICE; PUBIC ORDER/SAFETY	28458	210	2660	FOOD MANUFACTURING
28211	1622	21806	FOOD SVCS & DRINKING PLACES	28348	621	6753	MERCH. WHOLESALERS;DURABLE GDS	28459	96	555	REPAIR AND MAINTENANCE
28212	1244	10546	MOTOR VEHICLE & PARTS DEALERS	28349	266	4256	TEXTILE MILLS	28460	284	1334	FOOD SVCS & DRINKING PLACES
28213	1067	10570	INSURANCE CARRIERS & RELATED	28350	9	34	HOSPITALS	28461	865	7233	ADMINISTRATIVE & SUPPORT SVCS
28214	684	6918	EDUCATIONAL SERVICES	28351	104	1305	TEXTILE MILLS	28462	476	2590	AMBULATORY HEALTH CARE SVCS
28215	843	5188	EDUCATIONAL SERVICES	28352	977	10276	HOSPITALS	28463	302	1475	EDUCATIONAL SERVICES
28216	1391	16359	FOOD SVCS & DRINKING PLACES	28353	2	3	CROP PRODUCTION	28464	43	826	FOOD MANUFACTURING
28217	2552	34721	PROF.; SCIENTIFIC; & TECH SVCS	28355	9	58	MINING (EXCEPT OIL AND GAS)	28465	295	1154	EXEC.; LEGIS.; & OTHER SUPPORT
28218	9	29	REAL ESTATE	28356	87	293	UNCLASSIFIED ESTABLISHMENTS	28466	552	2785	FOOD SVCS & DRINKING PLACES
28219	6	25	MOTOR VEHICLE & PARTS DEALERS	28357	51	1680	FOOD MANUFACTURING	28467	303	1926	FOOD SVCS & DRINKING PLACES
28220	11	102	PROF.; SCIENTIFIC; & TECH SVCS	28358	1723	19671	HOSPITALS	28468	175	1633	AMUSEMENT; GAMBLING;& RECREAT.
28221	7	31	SPECIAL TRADE CONTRACTORS	28359	4	4	ADMINISTRATIVE & SUPPORT SVCS	28469	404	2887	REAL ESTATE
28222	10	18	RELIG.; GRANT; CIVIC; PROF ORG	28360	292	7284	EDUCATIONAL SERVICES	28470	644	5478	FOOD SVCS & DRINKING PLACES
28223	13	427	WHOLESALE ELEC. MRKTS & AGENTS	28362	1	30	MACHINERY MANUFACTURING	28472	1181	10342	AMBULATORY HEALTH CARE SVCS
28224	10	33	SPECIAL TRADE CONTRACTORS	28363	25	111	MERCH. WHOLESALERS;DURABLE GDS	28478	92	329	EDUCATIONAL SERVICES
28226	1484	12952	PROF.; SCIENTIFIC; & TECH SVCS	28364	299	3882	FOOD MANUFACTURING	28479	67	389	NURSING & RESID. CARE FACILIT.
28227	1492	10692	MOTOR VEHICLE & PARTS DEALERS	28365	515	7088	FOOD AND BEVERAGE STORES	28480	225	2181	FOOD SVCS & DRINKING PLACES
28228	4	5701	MANAGMT OF COMPANIES & ENTERP.	28366	168	1604	NONMETALLIC MINERAL PROD. MFG	28501	958	10051	AMBULATORY HEALTH CARE SVCS
28229	12	34	ADMINISTRATIVE & SUPPORT SVCS	28367	13	10	GASOLINE STATIONS	28502	4	22	EXEC.; LEGIS.; & OTHER SUPPORT
28230	1	0	AMBULATORY HEALTH CARE SVCS	28368	34	28	RELIG.; GRANT; CIVIC; PROF ORG	28503	5	6	PROF.; SCIENTIFIC; & TECH SVCS
28231	3	6	RELIG.; GRANT; CIVIC; PROF ORG	28369	37	150	EDUCATIONAL SERVICES	28504	886	16392	EXEC.; LEGIS.; & OTHER SUPPORT
28232	3	2	FABRICATED METAL PRODUCT MFG	28370	6	13	MISCELLANEOUS STORE RETAILERS	28508	27	156	EDUCATIONAL SERVICES
28233	3	3	HEALTH & PERSONAL CARE STORES	28371	107	488	SPECIAL TRADE CONTRACTORS	28509	34	186	BLDG MATL & GARDEN EQPMT DLRS
28234	6	21	NONSTORE RETAILERS	28372	390	5056	AMBULATORY HEALTH CARE SVCS	28510	41	1416	ACCOMMODATION
28235	4	234	ADMINISTRATIVE & SUPPORT SVCS	28373	70	227	WASTE MANAGMT & REMEDIAT'N SVC	28511	18	205	FOOD MANUFACTURING
28236	1	1	AMBULATORY HEALTH CARE SVCS	28374	694	13964	HOSPITALS	28512	286	2406	FOOD SVCS & DRINKING PLACES
28237	2	1	SPECIAL TRADE CONTRACTORS	28375	6	6	SCENIC & SIGHTSEEING TRANSPORT	28513	302	3362	ADMINISTRATIVE & SUPPORT SVCS
28241	21	43	ADMINISTRATIVE & SUPPORT SVCS	28376	811	7933	MERCH. WHOLESALERS;NONDUR. GDS	28515	160	1182	EDUCATIONAL SERVICES
28242	1	0	UTILITIES	28377	319	2556	EDUCATIONAL SERVICES	28516	645	5233	WOOD PRODUCT MANUFACTURING
28243	1	6	PAPER MANUFACTURING	28378	1	1	POSTAL SERVICE	28518	244	1367	EDUCATIONAL SERVICES
28244	60	1359	ADMINISTRATIVE & SUPPORT SVCS	28379	1072	9850	APPAREL MANUFACTURING	28519	41	144	MOTOR VEHICLE & PARTS DEALERS
28246	24	270	PROF.; SCIENTIFIC; & TECH SVCS	28382	205	1278	MERCH. WHOLESALERS;DURABLE GDS	28520	12	112	WATER TRANSPORTATION
28247	29	80	CONSTRUCTION OF BUILDINGS	28383	163	1020	EDUCATIONAL SERVICES	28521	52	229	EDUCATIONAL SERVICES
28256	8	14	SPECIAL TRADE CONTRACTORS	28384	300	2949	ANIMAL PRODUCTION	28522	5	12	PLASTICS & RUBBER PRODUCTS MFG
28262	1341	21821	FOOD SVCS & DRINKING PLACES	28385	78	477	EDUCATIONAL SERVICES	28523	55	297	EDUCATIONAL SERVICES
28266	9	21	ADMINISTRATIVE & SUPPORT SVCS	28386	79	300	SPECIAL TRADE CONTRACTORS	28524	16	62	MERCH. WHOLESALERS;NONDUR. GDS
28269	1665	26666	TRUCK TRANSPORTATION	28387	1090	8813	FOOD SVCS & DRINKING PLACES	28525	57	376	MERCH. WHOLESALERS;NONDUR. GDS
28270	890	6270	EDUCATIONAL SERVICES	28388	11	34	PROF.; SCIENTIFIC; & TECH SVCS	28526	64	157	CROP PRODUCTION
28271	20	63	SPECIAL TRADE CONTRACTORS	28390	576	3962	FOOD SVCS & DRINKING PLACES	28527	19	39	RELIG.; GRANT; CIVIC; PROF ORG
28273	1932	62352	INSURANCE CARRIERS & RELATED	28391	135	645	FOOD AND BEVERAGE STORES	28528	6	6	SUPPORT ACT. FOR TRANSPORT.
28274	1	0	EDUCATIONAL SERVICES	28392	44	6485	MERCH. WHOLESALERS;NONDUR. GDS	28529	57	642	NURSING & RESID. CARE FACILIT.
28277	2130	20745	FOOD SVCS & DRINKING PLACES	28393	46	440	FOOD MANUFACTURING	28530	165	2746	CHEMICAL MANUFACTURING
28278	260	2070	MACHINERY MANUFACTURING	28394	177	732	EDUCATIONAL SERVICES	28531	51	282	MUSEUMS; HIST. SITES;& SIMILAR
28280	39	525	PROF.; SCIENTIFIC; & TECH SVCS	28395	70	277	EDUCATIONAL SERVICES	28532	665	4706	FOOD SVCS & DRINKING PLACES
28281	78	575	PROF.; SCIENTIFIC; & TECH SVCS	28396	53	2743	TEXTILE MILLS	28533	44	479	HOSPITALS
28282	34	594	PROF.; SCIENTIFIC; & TECH SVCS	28398	282	2826	ANIMAL PRODUCTION	28537	4	10	MERCH. WHOLESALERS;NONDUR. GDS
28284	23	145	PROF.; SCIENTIFIC; & TECH SVCS	28399	43	139	CROP PRODUCTION	28538	46	219	FURN. & HOME FURNISHGS STORES
28285	14	684	REAL ESTATE	28401	2393	29442	HOSPITALS	28539	178	925	SOCIAL ASSISTANCE
28287	17	54	PROF.; SCIENTIFIC; & TECH SVCS	28402	14	129	PROF.; SCIENTIFIC; & TECH SVCS	28540	1679	14236	EDUCATIONAL SERVICES
28288	2	40	SECURITIES/COMMODITY CONTRACTS	28403	3542	33765	FOOD SVCS & DRINKING PLACES	28541	8	10	PROF.; SCIENTIFIC; & TECH SVCS
28297	3	5	REAL ESTATE	28404	7	29	SPECIAL TRADE CONTRACTORS	28542	14	50	FOOD SVCS & DRINKING PLACES
28299	9	8	PROF.; SCIENTIFIC; & TECH SVCS	28405	1960	26429	SPORTG GDS;HOBBY;BOOK; & MUSIC	28543	9	36	ADMIN. HUMAN RESOURCE PROGRAMS
28301	1765	21751	JUSTICE; PUBIC ORDER/SAFETY	28406	25	68	SPECIAL TRADE CONTRACTORS	28544	77	584	FOOD SVCS & DRINKING PLACES

BUSINESS DATA

ZIP CODE	2009 Total Firms	2009 Total Employ-ees	TOP INDUSTRY RANKED on 2009 EMPLOYMENT	ZIP CODE	2009 Total Firms	2009 Total Employ-ees	TOP INDUSTRY RANKED on 2009 EMPLOYMENT	ZIP CODE	2009 Total Firms	2009 Total Employ-ees	TOP INDUSTRY RANKED on 2009 EMPLOYMENT
28545	4	7	CREDIT INTERMEDIATION & RELATD	28662	13	130	BLDG MATL & GARDEN EQPMT DLRS	28759	238	2100	MERCH. WHOLESALERS;NONDUR. GDS
28546	1424	19209	FOOD SVCS & DRINKING PLACES	28663	25	129	EDUCATIONAL SERVICES	28760	7	11	SPECIAL TRADE CONTRACTORS
28547	32	2078	HOSPITALS	28664	5	37	ANIMAL PRODUCTION	28761	113	958	NURSING & RESID. CARE FACILIT.
28551	320	2030	EDUCATIONAL SERVICES	28665	42	55	RELIG.; GRANT; CIVIC; PROF ORG	28762	143	1889	MERCH. WHOLESALERS;DURABLE GDS
28552	8	11	FOOD MANUFACTURING	28666	12	178	EDUCATIONAL SERVICES	28763	35	94	SUPPORT ACTIVITIES: AGR./FOR.
28553	18	29	PROF.; SCIENTIFIC; & TECH SVCS	28667	9	25	FOOD AND BEVERAGE STORES	28765	3	8	SPORTG GDS;HOBBY;BOOK; & MUSIC
28554	15	517	EXEC.; LEGIS.; & OTHER SUPPORT	28668	22	382	RELIG.; GRANT; CIVIC; PROF ORG	28766	28	94	HEAVY & CIVIL ENG. CONSTRUCT'N
28555	134	504	EDUCATIONAL SERVICES	28669	68	544	WOOD PRODUCT MANUFACTURING	28768	244	1243	GENERAL MERCHANDISE STORES
28556	25	55	TRANSPORTATION EQUIPMENT MFG	28670	72	419	EDUCATIONAL SERVICES	28770	13	159	FOOD SVCS & DRINKING PLACES
28557	1450	11628	FOOD SVCS & DRINKING PLACES	28671	60	701	MISCELLANEOUS MANUFACTURING	28771	309	2663	FURNITURE & RELATED PROD. MFG
28560	1364	11883	HOSPITALS	28672	5	12	FURNITURE & RELATED PROD. MFG	28772	80	700	FABRICATED METAL PRODUCT MFG
28561	14	35	BLDG MATL & GARDEN EQPMT DLRS	28673	99	548	EDUCATIONAL SERVICES	28773	120	466	NURSING & RESID. CARE FACILIT.
28562	1503	15764	AMBULATORY HEALTH CARE SVCS	28675	431	2900	MISCELLANEOUS MANUFACTURING	28774	76	752	HEAVY & CIVIL ENG. CONSTRUCT'N
28563	4	5	EXEC.; LEGIS.; & OTHER SUPPORT	28676	97	456	SPECIAL TRADE CONTRACTORS	28775	27	46	PROF.; SCIENTIFIC; & TECH SVCS
28564	6	14	CONSTRUCTION OF BUILDINGS	28677	1584	19649	HOSPITALS	28776	15	356	MACHINERY MANUFACTURING
28570	503	3673	EDUCATIONAL SERVICES	28678	79	575	MERCH. WHOLESALERS;DURABLE GDS	28777	516	5245	EDUCATIONAL SERVICES
28571	164	641	MERCH. WHOLESALERS;NONDUR. GDS	28679	65	245	EDUCATIONAL SERVICES	28778	297	3163	TEXTILE MILLS
28572	192	791	FOOD AND BEVERAGE STORES	28680	3	8	SPECIAL TRADE CONTRACTORS	28779	758	8973	HOSPITALS
28573	83	936	AMBULATORY HEALTH CARE SVCS	28681	695	7522	FURNITURE & RELATED PROD. MFG	28781	32	100	EDUCATIONAL SERVICES
28574	306	1582	EDUCATIONAL SERVICES	28682	43	121	MOTOR VEHICLE & PARTS DEALERS	28782	346	1544	NURSING & RESID. CARE FACILIT.
28575	35	242	REAL ESTATE	28683	23	38	FOOD AND BEVERAGE STORES	28783	28	132	CONSTRUCTION OF BUILDINGS
28577	17	243	NURSING & RESID. CARE FACILIT.	28684	39	60	NURSING & RESID. CARE FACILIT.	28784	9	93	ACCOMMODATION
28578	79	394	EDUCATIONAL SERVICES	28685	39	134	EDUCATIONAL SERVICES	28785	163	1005	MERCH. WHOLESALERS;DURABLE GDS
28579	21	109	EDUCATIONAL SERVICES	28687	8	16	SOCIAL ASSISTANCE	28786	1260	10704	SOCIAL ASSISTANCE
28580	369	2765	EDUCATIONAL SERVICES	28688	6	42	MERCH. WHOLESALERS;NONDUR. GDS	28787	528	4468	MERCH. WHOLESALERS;DURABLE GDS
28581	6	7	HEAVY & CIVIL ENG. CONSTRUCT'N	28689	63	644	MERCH. WHOLESALERS;DURABLE GDS	28788	5	48	SOCIAL ASSISTANCE
28582	17	39	PROF.; SCIENTIFIC; & TECH SVCS	28690	287	5018	TEXTILE MILLS	28789	141	913	FOOD SVCS & DRINKING PLACES
28583	7	26	TELECOMMUNICATIONS	28691	1	1	MUSEUMS; HIST. SITES;& SIMILAR	28790	55	708	ACCOMMODATION
28584	529	2915	FOOD SVCS & DRINKING PLACES	28692	131	417	SPECIAL TRADE CONTRACTORS	28791	548	5509	HOSPITALS
28585	163	732	EDUCATIONAL SERVICES	28693	51	301	EDUCATIONAL SERVICES	28792	1830	16900	FOOD SVCS & DRINKING PLACES
28586	211	2064	EXEC.; LEGIS.; & OTHER SUPPORT	28694	527	3555	TELECOMMUNICATIONS	28793	14	100	AMBULATORY HEALTH CARE SVCS
28587	11	41	CROP PRODUCTION	28697	749	9581	EDUCATIONAL SERVICES	28801	2751	41482	HOSPITALS
28589	3	9	HEAVY & CIVIL ENG. CONSTRUCT'N	28698	43	171	EDUCATIONAL SERVICES	28802	23	38	SPECIAL TRADE CONTRACTORS
28590	510	5178	EDUCATIONAL SERVICES	28699	1	1	POSTAL SERVICE	28803	1601	25917	AMBULATORY HEALTH CARE SVCS
28594	171	1037	REAL ESTATE	28701	51	193	PROF.; SCIENTIFIC; & TECH SVCS	28804	787	8151	ACCOMMODATION
28601	2107	27760	FURNITURE & RELATED PROD. MFG	28702	10	14	ACCOMMODATION	28805	843	9788	FOOD SVCS & DRINKING PLACES
28602	2065	29647	FOOD SVCS & DRINKING PLACES	28704	937	10899	MACHINERY MANUFACTURING	28806	1730	20483	FOOD SVCS & DRINKING PLACES
28603	20	42	ADMINISTRATIVE & SUPPORT SVCS	28705	185	975	EDUCATIONAL SERVICES	28810	1	1	POSTAL SERVICE
28604	668	5534	ACCOMMODATION	28707	7	98	ACCOMMODATION	28813	15	215	TRANSIT & GRND PASS. TRANSPORT
28605	383	3460	ACCOMMODATION	28708	16	20	HEAVY & CIVIL ENG. CONSTRUCT'N	28814	17	29	PROF.; SCIENTIFIC; & TECH SVCS
28606	34	202	SOCIAL ASSISTANCE	28709	62	237	ELECT'L EQPMT; APP; & COMP MFG	28815	11	76	PRINT'G & RELATED SUPP'T ACT'S
28607	1789	17338	FOOD SVCS & DRINKING PLACES	28710	11	78	SOCIAL ASSISTANCE	28816	14	24	INSURANCE CARRIERS & RELATED
28608	2	3	OTHER INFORMATION SERVICES	28711	543	5146	NURSING & RESID. CARE FACILIT.	28901	277	2189	RELIG.; GRANT; CIVIC; PROF ORG
28609	112	2227	MERCH. WHOLESALERS;DURABLE GDS	28712	1061	8506	ACCOMMODATION	28902	40	132	EDUCATIONAL SERVICES
28610	208	6766	RENTAL AND LEASING SERVICES	28713	468	3708	FOOD SVCS & DRINKING PLACES	28903	1	1	POSTAL SERVICE
28611	17	129	EDUCATIONAL SERVICES	28714	576	4412	EDUCATIONAL SERVICES	28904	431	2117	EDUCATIONAL SERVICES
28612	194	2219	HOSPITALS	28715	592	4509	EDUCATIONAL SERVICES	28905	59	782	TEXTILE MILLS
28613	715	12574	FURNITURE & RELATED PROD. MFG	28716	407	4693	PAPER MANUFACTURING	28906	945	6999	HOSPITALS
28615	53	150	RELIG.; GRANT; CIVIC; PROF ORG	28717	347	2700	REAL ESTATE	28909	20	51	FABRICATED METAL PRODUCT MFG
28616	17	195	RELIG.; GRANT; CIVIC; PROF ORG	28718	46	91	JUSTICE; PUBIC ORDER/SAFETY	29001	69	321	RELIG.; GRANT; CIVIC; PROF ORG
28617	56	290	MISCELLANEOUS STORE RETAILERS	28719	343	8730	AMUSEMENT; GAMBLING;& RECREAT.	29002	9	35	HEALTH & PERSONAL CARE STORES
28618	70	422	SOCIAL ASSISTANCE	28720	47	267	MISCELLANEOUS STORE RETAILERS	29003	285	2284	HOSPITALS
28619	30	743	MUSEUMS; HIST. SITES;& SIMILAR	28721	291	3406	HOSPITALS	29006	353	3787	FOOD MANUFACTURING
28621	565	7030	HOSPITALS	28722	324	2920	RELIG.; GRANT; CIVIC; PROF ORG	29009	78	753	TEXTILE MILLS
28622	62	336	EDUCATIONAL SERVICES	28723	144	607	EDUCATIONAL SERVICES	29010	474	3682	JUSTICE; PUBIC ORDER/SAFETY
28623	33	185	MISCELLANEOUS STORE RETAILERS	28724	9	21	RELIG.; GRANT; CIVIC; PROF ORG	29014	24	83	POSTAL SERVICE
28624	50	155	EDUCATIONAL SERVICES	28725	55	256	FOOD SVCS & DRINKING PLACES	29015	21	101	EDUCATIONAL SERVICES
28625	1145	17016	MERCH. WHOLESALERS;DURABLE GDS	28726	102	1813	ELECT'L EQPMT; APP; & COMP MFG	29016	399	15683	PROF.; SCIENTIFIC; & TECH SVCS
28626	65	138	BLDG MATL & GARDEN EQPMT DLRS	28727	7	33	EXEC.; LEGIS.; & OTHER SUPPORT	29018	96	488	TRUCK TRANSPORTATION
28627	38	264	ACCOMMODATION	28728	33	616	PLASTICS & RUBBER PRODUCTS MFG	29020	1174	10345	HOSPITALS
28628	22	110	AMBULATORY HEALTH CARE SVCS	28729	85	521	AMUSEMENT; GAMBLING;& RECREAT.	29021	8	8	SPECIAL TRADE CONTRACTORS
28629	7	25	FOOD SVCS & DRINKING PLACES	28730	270	1232	COMPUTER & ELECTRONIC PROD MFG	29030	76	351	BLDG MATL & GARDEN EQPMT DLRS
28630	488	4528	APPAREL MANUFACTURING	28731	272	2532	NURSING & RESID. CARE FACILIT.	29031	25	717	TEXTILE MILLS
28631	20	63	BLDG MATL & GARDEN EQPMT DLRS	28732	608	7787	PLASTICS & RUBBER PRODUCTS MFG	29032	52	496	WOOD PRODUCT MANUFACTURING
28633	1	400	FURNITURE & RELATED PROD. MFG	28733	12	124	JUSTICE; PUBIC ORDER/SAFETY	29033	512	5693	PRIMARY METAL MANUFACTURING
28634	139	758	EDUCATIONAL SERVICES	28734	1375	10044	FOOD SVCS & DRINKING PLACES	29036	525	4108	PROF.; SCIENTIFIC; & TECH SVCS
28635	58	322	EDUCATIONAL SERVICES	28735	5	4	POSTAL SERVICE	29037	16	12	HEAVY & CIVIL ENG. CONSTRUCT'N
28636	91	1328	FURNITURE & RELATED PROD. MFG	28736	55	139	SCENIC & SIGHTSEEING TRANSPORT	29038	51	393	EDUCATIONAL SERVICES
28637	135	2248	APPAREL MANUFACTURING	28737	7	3	LEATHER & ALLIED PRODUCT MFG	29039	41	265	EDUCATIONAL SERVICES
28638	332	4787	EDUCATIONAL SERVICES	28738	3	13	ADMINISTRATIVE & SUPPORT SVCS	29040	129	477	EDUCATIONAL SERVICES
28640	301	3273	TEXTILE MILLS	28739	480	4070	ACCOMMODATION	29041	8	7	EXEC.; LEGIS.; & OTHER SUPPORT
28641	12	67	JUSTICE; PUBIC ORDER/SAFETY	28740	19	82	EDUCATIONAL SERVICES	29042	159	1653	WOOD PRODUCT MANUFACTURING
28642	208	1611	PROF.; SCIENTIFIC; & TECH SVCS	28741	434	2843	FOOD SVCS & DRINKING PLACES	29044	153	1487	PAPER MANUFACTURING
28643	84	437	COMPUTER & ELECTRONIC PROD MFG	28742	78	311	ACCOMMODATION	29045	335	3024	EDUCATIONAL SERVICES
28644	58	283	RELIG.; GRANT; CIVIC; PROF ORG	28743	91	393	ACCOMMODATION	29046	3	35	EDUCATIONAL SERVICES
28645	1463	19912	FURN. & HOME FURNISHGS STORES	28744	12	55	SPECIAL TRADE CONTRACTORS	29047	105	1003	FOOD AND BEVERAGE STORES
28646	81	1384	AMBULATORY HEALTH CARE SVCS	28745	26	221	ACCOMMODATION	29048	149	418	FOOD AND BEVERAGE STORES
28647	13	73	ACCOMMODATION	28746	164	1433	AMUSEMENT; GAMBLING;& RECREAT.	29051	28	187	CROP PRODUCTION
28649	14	17	FABRICATED METAL PRODUCT MFG	28747	97	397	ACCOMMODATION	29052	28	114	EDUCATIONAL SERVICES
28650	310	3322	FURNITURE & RELATED PROD. MFG	28748	230	798	SPECIAL TRADE CONTRACTORS	29053	277	1949	HEAVY & CIVIL ENG. CONSTRUCT'N
28651	124	731	EDUCATIONAL SERVICES	28749	15	119	FOOD SVCS & DRINKING PLACES	29054	204	1633	EDUCATIONAL SERVICES
28652	3	9	MERCH. WHOLESALERS;NONDUR. GDS	28750	12	124	TEXTILE MILLS	29055	155	869	HEAVY & CIVIL ENG. CONSTRUCT'N
28653	2	7	REAL ESTATE	28751	260	1485	AMUSEMENT; GAMBLING;& RECREAT.	29056	84	471	EDUCATIONAL SERVICES
28654	87	373	EDUCATIONAL SERVICES	28752	1046	13834	CHEMICAL MANUFACTURING	29058	133	545	MUSEUMS; HIST. SITES;& SIMILAR
28655	1855	26019	HOSPITALS	28753	278	2159	AMBULATORY HEALTH CARE SVCS	29059	257	1827	EDUCATIONAL SERVICES
28657	410	3157	EXEC.; LEGIS.; & OTHER SUPPORT	28754	229	1681	EDUCATIONAL SERVICES	29061	200	2871	SPECIAL TRADE CONTRACTORS
28658	960	14516	FURNITURE & RELATED PROD. MFG	28755	13	187	WHOLESALE ELEC. MRKTS & AGENTS	29062	4	2	GENERAL MERCHANDISE STORES
28659	1023	10616	HOSPITALS	28756	93	828	TEXTILE MILLS	29063	1021	7783	EDUCATIONAL SERVICES
28660	30	359	EDUCATIONAL SERVICES	28757	20	410	SPORTG GDS;HOBBY;BOOK; & MUSIC	29065	17	173	ADMINISTRATIVE & SUPPORT SVCS
28661	5	59	PAPER MANUFACTURING	28758	14	347	FOOD AND BEVERAGE STORES	29067	270	1429	EDUCATIONAL SERVICES

ZIP CODE	2009 Total Firms	2009 Total Employees	TOP INDUSTRY RANKED on 2009 EMPLOYMENT
29069	124	589	EDUCATIONAL SERVICES
29070	314	1758	APPAREL MANUFACTURING
29071	25	180	TRUCK TRANSPORTATION
29072	2037	22375	JUSTICE; PUBIC ORDER/SAFETY
29073	806	5958	EDUCATIONAL SERVICES
29074	6	35	ACCOMMODATION
29075	53	253	HEAVY & CIVIL ENG. CONSTRUCT'N
29078	459	5909	PROF.; SCIENTIFIC; & TECH SVCS
29080	78	357	RELIG.; GRANT; CIVIC; PROF ORG
29081	67	155	CREDIT INTERMEDIATION & RELATD
29082	24	39	FOOD AND BEVERAGE STORES
29101	89	1834	APPAREL MANUFACTURING
29102	931	6200	HOSPITALS
29104	59	161	FURNITURE & RELATED PROD. MFG
29105	41	416	MERCH. WHOLESALERS;NONDUR. GDS
29107	68	482	EDUCATIONAL SERVICES
29108	961	11892	MERCH. WHOLESALERS;NONDUR. GDS
29111	27	107	EDUCATIONAL SERVICES
29112	132	566	EDUCATIONAL SERVICES
29113	45	173	MERCH. WHOLESALERS;NONDUR. GDS
29114	68	498	FURNITURE & RELATED PROD. MFG
29115	1517	18813	EDUCATIONAL SERVICES
29116	5	25	SOCIAL ASSISTANCE
29117	2	55	EDUCATIONAL SERVICES
29118	430	8099	HOSPITALS
29122	9	54	AMBULATORY HEALTH CARE SVCS
29123	116	1002	EDUCATIONAL SERVICES
29125	95	338	EDUCATIONAL SERVICES
29126	39	179	EDUCATIONAL SERVICES
29127	200	1546	WOOD PRODUCT MANUFACTURING
29128	73	523	JUSTICE; PUBIC ORDER/SAFETY
29129	90	917	CROP PRODUCTION
29130	154	1115	NURSING & RESID. CARE FACILIT.
29132	2	8	SPECIAL TRADE CONTRACTORS
29133	34	210	WOOD PRODUCT MANUFACTURING
29135	354	2486	EDUCATIONAL SERVICES
29137	50	275	MERCH. WHOLESALERS;DURABLE GDS
29138	380	2021	EDUCATIONAL SERVICES
29142	277	1887	FOOD SVCS & DRINKING PLACES
29143	5	79	CROP PRODUCTION
29145	16	84	CROP PRODUCTION
29146	42	112	TRUCK TRANSPORTATION
29147	2	25	EXEC.; LEGIS.; & OTHER SUPPORT
29148	271	1569	MISCELLANEOUS MANUFACTURING
29150	2491	27487	HOSPITALS
29151	14	21	EXEC.; LEGIS.; & OTHER SUPPORT
29152	64	503	EDUCATIONAL SERVICES
29153	494	5906	MISCELLANEOUS MANUFACTURING
29154	625	6577	RELIG.; GRANT; CIVIC; PROF ORG
29160	175	1451	FABRICATED METAL PRODUCT MFG
29161	284	1177	TRANSPORTATION EQUIPMENT MFG
29162	132	780	JUSTICE; PUBIC ORDER/SAFETY
29163	39	128	EDUCATIONAL SERVICES
29164	139	722	EDUCATIONAL SERVICES
29166	24	350	FOOD MANUFACTURING
29168	53	196	MACHINERY MANUFACTURING
29169	1552	21425	HOSPITALS
29170	665	7418	EDUCATIONAL SERVICES
29171	12	39	SPECIAL TRADE CONTRACTORS
29172	278	4111	MERCH. WHOLESALERS;DURABLE GDS
29175	12	29	RELIG.; GRANT; CIVIC; PROF ORG
29177	11	160	CLOTHING & CLOTH'G ACC. STORES
29178	90	953	MERCH. WHOLESALERS;NONDUR. GDS
29180	519	4584	EXEC.; LEGIS.; & OTHER SUPPORT
29201	3547	57938	FOOD SVCS & DRINKING PLACES
29202	19	163	EDUCATIONAL SERVICES
29203	1444	29328	FOOD SVCS & DRINKING PLACES
29204	1133	11207	EDUCATIONAL SERVICES
29205	1113	8892	FOOD SVCS & DRINKING PLACES
29206	918	6202	FOOD SVCS & DRINKING PLACES
29207	65	1334	SPECIAL TRADE CONTRACTORS
29208	58	1178	EDUCATIONAL SERVICES
29209	1064	12521	HOSPITALS
29210	2057	35016	JUSTICE; PUBIC ORDER/SAFETY
29211	3	8	HEAVY & CIVIL ENG. CONSTRUCT'N
29212	1170	14543	FOOD SVCS & DRINKING PLACES
29216	2	409	ADMIN. OF ECONOMIC PROGRAMS
29217	1	0	UNCLASSIFIED ESTABLISHMENTS
29219	3	3	INSURANCE CARRIERS & RELATED
29220	5	2864	AMBULATORY HEALTH CARE SVCS
29221	8	22	ADMINISTRATIVE & SUPPORT SVCS
29223	1823	18092	FOOD SVCS & DRINKING PLACES
29224	12	27	SPECIAL TRADE CONTRACTORS
29226	1	20	SECURITIES/COMMODITY CONTRACTS
29228	1	1	AMUSEMENT; GAMBLING;& RECREAT.
29229	762	7656	FOOD SVCS & DRINKING PLACES
29230	4	33	ADMINISTRATIVE & SUPPORT SVCS
29240	2	9	SPECIAL TRADE CONTRACTORS
29250	9	49	ADMINISTRATIVE & SUPPORT SVCS
29260	8	22	SPECIAL TRADE CONTRACTORS

ZIP CODE	2009 Total Firms	2009 Total Employees	TOP INDUSTRY RANKED on 2009 EMPLOYMENT
29290	4	15	ADMINISTRATIVE & SUPPORT SVCS
29301	1436	13910	FOOD SVCS & DRINKING PLACES
29302	1053	10073	EDUCATIONAL SERVICES
29303	1594	31011	HOSPITALS
29304	14	55	PROF.; SCIENTIFIC; & TECH SVCS
29305	4	30	SOCIAL ASSISTANCE
29306	998	11524	EXEC.; LEGIS.; & OTHER SUPPORT
29307	764	11562	NURSING & RESID. CARE FACILIT.
29316	647	3991	FOOD SVCS & DRINKING PLACES
29318	1	1	PROF.; SCIENTIFIC; & TECH SVCS
29319	6	700	FOOD SVCS & DRINKING PLACES
29320	4	2	POSTAL SERVICE
29321	48	335	NONMETALLIC MINERAL PROD. MFG
29322	158	1244	EDUCATIONAL SERVICES
29323	375	1909	EDUCATIONAL SERVICES
29324	4	3	FOOD SVCS & DRINKING PLACES
29325	519	8376	SOCIAL ASSISTANCE
29329	4	8	RELIG.; GRANT; CIVIC; PROF ORG
29330	202	1468	EDUCATIONAL SERVICES
29331	1	1	RELIG.; GRANT; CIVIC; PROF ORG
29332	49	299	FABRICATED METAL PRODUCT MFG
29333	9	32	SPECIAL TRADE CONTRACTORS
29334	539	11885	MERCH. WHOLESALERS;DURABLE GDS
29335	81	843	TEXTILE MILLS
29336	3	8	RELIG.; GRANT; CIVIC; PROF ORG
29338	2	22	SPECIAL TRADE CONTRACTORS
29340	602	7518	MERCH. WHOLESALERS;NONDUR. GDS
29341	798	10207	FOOD SVCS & DRINKING PLACES
29342	2	4	RELIG.; GRANT; CIVIC; PROF ORG
29346	5	8	JUSTICE; PUBIC ORDER/SAFETY
29348	5	105	REAL ESTATE
29349	657	5638	NURSING & RESID. CARE FACILIT.
29351	37	149	EDUCATIONAL SERVICES
29353	105	1184	GENERAL MERCHANDISE STORES
29355	20	171	MISCELLANEOUS MANUFACTURING
29356	349	2999	TEXTILE PRODUCT MILLS
29360	907	8382	EDUCATIONAL SERVICES
29364	17	133	TELECOMMUNICATIONS
29365	261	3239	APPAREL MANUFACTURING
29368	10	41	JUSTICE; PUBIC ORDER/SAFETY
29369	187	940	EDUCATIONAL SERVICES
29370	21	54	RELIG.; GRANT; CIVIC; PROF ORG
29372	107	556	EDUCATIONAL SERVICES
29373	6	19	EXEC.; LEGIS.; & OTHER SUPPORT
29374	67	287	JUSTICE; PUBIC ORDER/SAFETY
29375	11	35	ADMINISTRATIVE & SUPPORT SVCS
29376	291	2895	MERCH. WHOLESALERS;DURABLE GDS
29377	2	3	POSTAL SERVICE
29378	3	3	POSTAL SERVICE
29379	796	6949	FABRICATED METAL PRODUCT MFG
29384	76	208	EDUCATIONAL SERVICES
29385	165	2193	TEXTILE PRODUCT MILLS
29386	2	35	PAPER MANUFACTURING
29388	370	2110	EDUCATIONAL SERVICES
29395	3	183	MISCELLANEOUS STORE RETAILERS
29401	2187	23185	FOOD SVCS & DRINKING PLACES
29402	13	71	SPECIAL TRADE CONTRACTORS
29403	1084	17986	HOSPITALS
29404	42	280	ACCOMMODATION
29405	1796	26760	PROF.; SCIENTIFIC; & TECH SVCS
29406	1932	30080	FOOD SVCS & DRINKING PLACES
29407	2715	25046	MERCH. WHOLESALERS;NONDUR. GDS
29409	6	637	EDUCATIONAL SERVICES
29410	317	3355	MERCH. WHOLESALERS;NONDUR. GDS
29412	1187	9106	ADMIN. ENVIRO. QUALITY PROGRMS
29413	9	14	ADMINISTRATIVE & SUPPORT SVCS
29414	757	10281	HOSPITALS
29415	4	32	ADMINISTRATIVE & SUPPORT SVCS
29416	13	42	ADMINISTRATIVE & SUPPORT SVCS
29417	14	32	HEAVY & CIVIL ENG. CONSTRUCT'N
29418	1646	21219	TRANSPORTATION EQUIPMENT MFG
29419	13	49	PROF.; SCIENTIFIC; & TECH SVCS
29420	271	2727	EDUCATIONAL SERVICES
29422	10	67	SPECIAL TRADE CONTRACTORS
29423	16	98	ADMINISTRATIVE & SUPPORT SVCS
29424	8	176	EDUCATIONAL SERVICES
29425	87	9798	AMBULATORY HEALTH CARE SVCS
29426	19	47	MERCH. WHOLESALERS;DURABLE GDS
29429	85	377	ADMINISTRATIVE & SUPPORT SVCS
29430	2	0	CREDIT INTERMEDIATION & RELATD
29431	119	546	AMUSEMENT; GAMBLING;& RECREAT.
29432	71	261	EDUCATIONAL SERVICES
29433	7	91	UTILITIES
29434	22	53	EXEC.; LEGIS.; & OTHER SUPPORT
29435	98	343	EDUCATIONAL SERVICES
29436	109	348	EDUCATIONAL SERVICES
29437	50	1581	EXEC.; LEGIS.; & OTHER SUPPORT
29438	167	695	REAL ESTATE
29439	90	512	FOOD SVCS & DRINKING PLACES
29440	1416	13041	EDUCATIONAL SERVICES

ZIP CODE	2009 Total Firms	2009 Total Employees	TOP INDUSTRY RANKED on 2009 EMPLOYMENT
29442	5	4	ADMINISTRATIVE & SUPPORT SVCS
29445	922	9578	EDUCATIONAL SERVICES
29446	52	154	CONSTRUCTION OF BUILDINGS
29447	3	1	RELIG.; GRANT; CIVIC; PROF ORG
29448	83	836	MERCH. WHOLESALERS;DURABLE GDS
29449	235	1353	EDUCATIONAL SERVICES
29450	87	1842	HEAVY & CIVIL ENG. CONSTRUCT'N
29451	208	2278	ACCOMMODATION
29452	15	75	TRUCK TRANSPORTATION
29453	42	258	RELIG.; GRANT; CIVIC; PROF ORG
29455	800	7350	AMUSEMENT; GAMBLING;& RECREAT.
29456	485	4607	EXEC.; LEGIS.; & OTHER SUPPORT
29457	7	11	CONSTRUCTION OF BUILDINGS
29458	106	453	EDUCATIONAL SERVICES
29461	1316	16019	EDUCATIONAL SERVICES
29464	2939	25175	FOOD SVCS & DRINKING PLACES
29465	35	125	REAL ESTATE
29466	540	3662	EDUCATIONAL SERVICES
29468	44	369	ADMIN. OF ECONOMIC PROGRAMS
29469	14	25	RELIG.; GRANT; CIVIC; PROF ORG
29470	133	969	SPECIAL TRADE CONTRACTORS
29471	35	102	SPECIAL TRADE CONTRACTORS
29472	196	1654	JUSTICE; PUBIC ORDER/SAFETY
29474	35	67	RELIG.; GRANT; CIVIC; PROF ORG
29475	63	159	SOCIAL ASSISTANCE
29476	1	50	CHEMICAL MANUFACTURING
29477	354	2953	EXEC.; LEGIS.; & OTHER SUPPORT
29479	225	1509	MERCH. WHOLESALERS;NONDUR. GDS
29481	45	234	TEXTILE PRODUCT MILLS
29482	82	609	FOOD SVCS & DRINKING PLACES
29483	2185	20418	FOOD SVCS & DRINKING PLACES
29484	17	41	SPECIAL TRADE CONTRACTORS
29485	1040	8196	HOSPITALS
29487	59	221	ACCOMMODATION
29488	1216	10413	EDUCATIONAL SERVICES
29492	603	6119	PROF.; SCIENTIFIC; & TECH SVCS
29493	7	109	WOOD PRODUCT MANUFACTURING
29501	2601	31913	FOOD SVCS & DRINKING PLACES
29502	8	12	ADMINISTRATIVE & SUPPORT SVCS
29503	7	47	SOCIAL ASSISTANCE
29504	10	34	ADMINISTRATIVE & SUPPORT SVCS
29505	723	7939	HOSPITALS
29506	659	10677	AMBULATORY HEALTH CARE SVCS
29510	353	2329	EDUCATIONAL SERVICES
29511	203	1090	EDUCATIONAL SERVICES
29512	642	6914	JUSTICE; PUBIC ORDER/SAFETY
29516	19	250	RELIG.; GRANT; CIVIC; PROF ORG
29518	42	155	EDUCATIONAL SERVICES
29519	1	2	POSTAL SERVICE
29520	571	6373	FABRICATED METAL PRODUCT MFG
29525	50	354	MERCH. WHOLESALERS;DURABLE GDS
29526	2155	26095	TELECOMMUNICATIONS
29527	443	2526	NURSING & RESID. CARE FACILIT.
29528	13	28	SPECIAL TRADE CONTRACTORS
29530	90	220	EDUCATIONAL SERVICES
29532	727	6634	EDUCATIONAL SERVICES
29536	707	8776	FOOD MANUFACTURING
29540	74	1386	PRIMARY METAL MANUFACTURING
29541	124	1444	JUSTICE; PUBIC ORDER/SAFETY
29543	9	126	NURSING & RESID. CARE FACILIT.
29544	90	323	EDUCATIONAL SERVICES
29545	38	291	EDUCATIONAL SERVICES
29546	39	114	FOOD SVCS & DRINKING PLACES
29547	46	443	GASOLINE STATIONS
29550	1046	18920	FABRICATED METAL PRODUCT MFG
29551	4	7	ADMINISTRATIVE & SUPPORT SVCS
29554	303	2759	PLASTICS & RUBBER PRODUCTS MFG
29555	205	1334	CHEMICAL MANUFACTURING
29556	718	5996	TELECOMMUNICATIONS
29560	637	5523	MISCELLANEOUS STORE RETAILERS
29563	81	333	EDUCATIONAL SERVICES
29564	35	146	TEXTILE PRODUCT MILLS
29565	157	1075	PAPER MANUFACTURING
29566	878	4451	EDUCATIONAL SERVICES
29567	15	48	SOCIAL ASSISTANCE
29568	392	1432	AMUSEMENT; GAMBLING;& RECREAT.
29569	669	4131	HOSPITALS
29570	92	532	EDUCATIONAL SERVICES
29571	599	5098	APPAREL MANUFACTURING
29572	1025	16419	ACCOMMODATION
29573	2	6	SUPPORT ACTIVITIES: AGR./FOR.
29574	453	4901	RELIG.; GRANT; CIVIC; PROF ORG
29575	977	9772	INSURANCE CARRIERS & RELATED
29576	1299	9950	FOOD SVCS & DRINKING PLACES
29577	3594	38083	FOOD SVCS & DRINKING PLACES
29578	23	92	SOCIAL ASSISTANCE
29579	1081	8635	FOOD SVCS & DRINKING PLACES
29580	20	200	FOOD MANUFACTURING
29581	93	295	EDUCATIONAL SERVICES
29582	1455	11087	FOOD SVCS & DRINKING PLACES

BUSINESS DATA

ZIP CODE	2009 Total Firms	2009 Total Employ-ees	TOP INDUSTRY RANKED on 2009 EMPLOYMENT	ZIP CODE	2009 Total Firms	2009 Total Employ-ees	TOP INDUSTRY RANKED on 2009 EMPLOYMENT	ZIP CODE	2009 Total Firms	2009 Total Employ-ees	TOP INDUSTRY RANKED on 2009 EMPLOYMENT
29583	131	722	EDUCATIONAL SERVICES	29685	37	330	AMUSEMENT; GAMBLING;& RECREAT.	29904	17	960	UNCLASSIFIED ESTABLISHMENTS
29584	49	160	EDUCATIONAL SERVICES	29686	14	111	EDUCATIONAL SERVICES	29905	9	41	AMUSEMENT; GAMBLING;& RECREAT.
29585	917	5854	FOOD SVCS & DRINKING PLACES	29687	1018	6865	EDUCATIONAL SERVICES	29906	786	6441	FOOD SVCS & DRINKING PLACES
29587	14	23	SPECIAL TRADE CONTRACTORS	29688	4	13	OTHER INFORMATION SERVICES	29907	407	2826	EDUCATIONAL SERVICES
29588	1290	7868	EDUCATIONAL SERVICES	29689	63	185	FABRICATED METAL PRODUCT MFG	29909	221	2107	FOOD SVCS & DRINKING PLACES
29589	1	5	MERCH. WHOLESALERS;DURABLE GDS	29690	609	5607	EDUCATIONAL SERVICES	29910	1784	12003	FOOD SVCS & DRINKING PLACES
29590	70	520	UNCLASSIFIED ESTABLISHMENTS	29691	360	2683	EDUCATIONAL SERVICES	29911	37	124	RELIG.; GRANT; CIVIC; PROF ORG
29591	149	720	MERCH. WHOLESALERS;NONDUR. GDS	29692	136	1425	EDUCATIONAL SERVICES	29912	10	29	GASOLINE STATIONS
29592	11	15	TEXTILE MILLS	29693	349	2845	MERCH. WHOLESALERS;DURABLE GDS	29914	2	7	EXEC.; LEGIS.; & OTHER SUPPORT
29593	51	2192	TEXTILE MILLS	29695	1	5	BLDG MATL & GARDEN EQPMT DLRS	29915	35	446	ACCOMMODATION
29594	5	51	MERCH. WHOLESALERS;NONDUR. GDS	29696	125	1720	PROF.; SCIENTIFIC; & TECH SVCS	29916	15	222	PLASTICS & RUBBER PRODUCTS MFG
29596	39	495	TEXTILE MILLS	29697	262	3471	TEXTILE PRODUCT MILLS	29918	179	1100	EDUCATIONAL SERVICES
29597	4	11	ADMINISTRATIVE & SUPPORT SVCS	29702	242	1935	TEXTILE MILLS	29920	227	1407	ACCOMMODATION
29598	6	11	REAL ESTATE	29703	1	2	POSTAL SERVICE	29921	9	93	BLDG MATL & GARDEN EQPMT DLRS
29601	2225	30579	EXEC.; LEGIS.; & OTHER SUPPORT	29704	51	1458	PAPER MANUFACTURING	29922	25	53	RELIG.; GRANT; CIVIC; PROF ORG
29602	13	797	POSTAL SERVICE	29706	819	7311	APPAREL MANUFACTURING	29923	7	11	EXEC.; LEGIS.; & OTHER SUPPORT
29603	1	4	MISCELLANEOUS STORE RETAILERS	29707	303	2522	MERCH. WHOLESALERS;NONDUR. GDS	29924	347	2804	PAPER MANUFACTURING
29604	5	8	POSTAL SERVICE	29708	844	9947	AMUSEMENT; GAMBLING;& RECREAT.	29925	51	139	SPECIAL TRADE CONTRACTORS
29605	1527	37538	HOSPITALS	29709	314	1825	EXEC.; LEGIS.; & OTHER SUPPORT	29926	1730	13153	AMBULATORY HEALTH CARE SVCS
29606	16	920	COMPUTER & ELECTRONIC PROD MFG	29710	758	5196	EDUCATIONAL SERVICES	29927	442	3823	SPECIAL TRADE CONTRACTORS
29607	3707	54101	FOOD SVCS & DRINKING PLACES	29712	73	144	FOOD SVCS & DRINKING PLACES	29928	2108	19554	FOOD SVCS & DRINKING PLACES
29608	11	17	ADMINISTRATIVE & SUPPORT SVCS	29714	66	1135	APPAREL MANUFACTURING	29929	25	62	CROP PRODUCTION
29609	1367	11893	FOOD SVCS & DRINKING PLACES	29715	682	8958	FABRICATED METAL PRODUCT MFG	29931	6	20	EDUCATIONAL SERVICES
29610	1	45	POSTAL SERVICE	29716	12	15	REAL ESTATE	29932	19	171	EDUCATIONAL SERVICES
29611	1032	8589	FOOD SVCS & DRINKING PLACES	29717	26	122	EDUCATIONAL SERVICES	29933	2	9	MERCH. WHOLESALERS;DURABLE GDS
29612	1	50	TRUCK TRANSPORTATION	29718	152	728	TELECOMMUNICATIONS	29934	19	46	SOCIAL ASSISTANCE
29613	6	51	OTHER INFORMATION SERVICES	29720	1843	18546	APPAREL MANUFACTURING	29935	207	1403	FOOD SVCS & DRINKING PLACES
29614	7	126	EDUCATIONAL SERVICES	29721	10	32	INSURANCE CARRIERS & RELATED	29936	654	5316	CONSTRUCTION OF BUILDINGS
29615	2140	31667	PROF.; SCIENTIFIC; & TECH SVCS	29724	6	27	JUSTICE; PUBIC ORDER/SAFETY	29938	61	122	ADMINISTRATIVE & SUPPORT SVCS
29616	19	74	POSTAL SERVICE	29726	29	79	MINING (EXCEPT OIL AND GAS)	29939	7	6	MISCELLANEOUS STORE RETAILERS
29617	487	3264	EDUCATIONAL SERVICES	29727	27	67	CONSTRUCTION OF BUILDINGS	29940	65	481	EDUCATIONAL SERVICES
29620	602	5262	APPAREL MANUFACTURING	29728	381	3869	GENERAL MERCHANDISE STORES	29941	19	196	REAL ESTATE
29621	1911	32605	HOSPITALS	29729	127	1689	NONMETALLIC MINERAL PROD. MFG	29943	13	16	MERCH. WHOLESALERS;DURABLE GDS
29622	15	20	ADMINISTRATIVE & SUPPORT SVCS	29730	2341	22729	EDUCATIONAL SERVICES	29944	165	1127	EDUCATIONAL SERVICES
29623	5	14	ADMINISTRATIVE & SUPPORT SVCS	29731	13	17	EXEC.; LEGIS.; & OTHER SUPPORT	29945	150	757	ACCOMMODATION
29624	810	6861	JUSTICE; PUBIC ORDER/SAFETY	29732	1929	17929	AMBULATORY HEALTH CARE SVCS	30002	135	974	EDUCATIONAL SERVICES
29625	772	8124	PLASTICS & RUBBER PRODUCTS MFG	29733	9	921	EDUCATIONAL SERVICES	30003	3	9	CREDIT INTERMEDIATION & RELATD
29626	276	6534	WHOLESALE ELEC. MRKTS & AGENTS	29734	2	22	RELIG.; GRANT; CIVIC; PROF ORG	30004	2485	29361	TELECOMMUNICATIONS
29627	401	3114	SPECIAL TRADE CONTRACTORS	29741	56	189	EDUCATIONAL SERVICES	30005	1756	27271	PROF.; SCIENTIFIC; & TECH SVCS
29628	75	682	TEXTILE PRODUCT MILLS	29742	51	110	GASOLINE STATIONS	30006	10	103	ADMINISTRATIVE & SUPPORT SVCS
29630	234	2106	EDUCATIONAL SERVICES	29743	17	51	JUSTICE; PUBIC ORDER/SAFETY	30007	13	27	CREDIT INTERMEDIATION & RELATD
29631	498	4235	FOOD SVCS & DRINKING PLACES	29744	6	110	NONMETALLIC MINERAL PROD. MFG	30008	740	5391	EXEC.; LEGIS.; & OTHER SUPPORT
29632	2	0	PERFORM'G ARTS; SPEC. SPORTS	29745	767	8099	JUSTICE; PUBIC ORDER/SAFETY	30009	1508	16990	PROF.; SCIENTIFIC; & TECH SVCS
29633	5	33	ADMIN. OF ECONOMIC PROGRAMS	29801	1362	18585	EXEC.; LEGIS.; & OTHER SUPPORT	30010	17	47	REPAIR AND MAINTENANCE
29634	13	307	OTHER INFORMATION SERVICES	29802	13	196	EXEC.; LEGIS.; & OTHER SUPPORT	30011	279	2748	MERCH. WHOLESALERS;NONDUR. GDS
29635	33	75	GASOLINE STATIONS	29803	1088	10405	FOOD SVCS & DRINKING PLACES	30012	1334	16213	ELECT'L EQPMT; APP; & COMP MFG
29636	6	12	RELIG.; GRANT; CIVIC; PROF ORG	29804	6	9	SPECIAL TRADE CONTRACTORS	30013	1388	16078	FOOD SVCS & DRINKING PLACES
29638	69	358	WOOD PRODUCT MANUFACTURING	29805	126	2413	TEXTILE PRODUCT MILLS	30014	1762	20276	EDUCATIONAL SERVICES
29639	55	504	EDUCATIONAL SERVICES	29808	1	14000	UTILITIES	30015	9	27	SPECIAL TRADE CONTRACTORS
29640	1222	12377	NURSING & RESID. CARE FACILIT.	29809	89	594	FOOD SVCS & DRINKING PLACES	30016	714	3535	EDUCATIONAL SERVICES
29641	8	11	SPECIAL TRADE CONTRACTORS	29810	225	1312	FORESTRY AND LOGGING	30017	434	2320	FOOD SVCS & DRINKING PLACES
29642	552	4672	NURSING & RESID. CARE FACILIT.	29812	503	4627	EXEC.; LEGIS.; & OTHER SUPPORT	30018	14	66	ADMINISTRATIVE & SUPPORT SVCS
29643	75	511	BLDG MATL & GARDEN EQPMT DLRS	29813	2	2	REPAIR AND MAINTENANCE	30019	871	7312	FOOD AND BEVERAGE STORES
29644	471	7021	COMPUTER & ELECTRONIC PROD MFG	29816	27	60	JUSTICE; PUBIC ORDER/SAFETY	30021	412	2738	EDUCATIONAL SERVICES
29645	178	1429	FOOD AND BEVERAGE STORES	29817	129	1339	MACHINERY MANUFACTURING	30022	2333	32269	PERSONAL AND LAUNDRY SERVICES
29646	1061	15883	HOSPITALS	29819	24	113	HEAVY & CIVIL ENG. CONSTRUCT'N	30023	16	30	PROF.; SCIENTIFIC; & TECH SVCS
29647	1	350	NONSTORE RETAILERS	29821	44	173	EXEC.; LEGIS.; & OTHER SUPPORT	30024	2811	30419	MERCH. WHOLESALERS;DURABLE GDS
29648	6	18	RELIG.; GRANT; CIVIC; PROF ORG	29822	33	385	FOOD AND BEVERAGE STORES	30025	288	2373	PLASTICS & RUBBER PRODUCTS MFG
29649	1255	18808	RENTAL AND LEASING SERVICES	29824	302	3064	EDUCATIONAL SERVICES	30028	452	2848	EDUCATIONAL SERVICES
29650	1414	14290	MERCH. WHOLESALERS;NONDUR. GDS	29826	16	24	REPAIR AND MAINTENANCE	30030	1567	25283	EXEC.; LEGIS.; & OTHER SUPPORT
29651	1241	20208	MOTOR VEHICLE & PARTS DEALERS	29827	126	1741	JUSTICE; PUBIC ORDER/SAFETY	30031	13	27	SOCIAL ASSISTANCE
29652	3	4	DATA PROCESS'G	29828	23	139	EDUCATIONAL SERVICES	30032	1556	17641	JUSTICE; PUBIC ORDER/SAFETY
29653	119	881	TRANSPORTATION EQUIPMENT MFG	29829	155	1667	EDUCATIONAL SERVICES	30033	1158	15511	HEALTH & PERSONAL CARE STORES
29654	239	2361	TRANSPORTATION EQUIPMENT MFG	29831	75	1488	PAPER MANUFACTURING	30034	1194	11131	EDUCATIONAL SERVICES
29655	175	935	EDUCATIONAL SERVICES	29832	177	1917	APPAREL MANUFACTURING	30035	1015	8695	MERCH. WHOLESALERS;DURABLE GDS
29656	2	3	SPECIAL TRADE CONTRACTORS	29834	27	238	FOOD SVCS & DRINKING PLACES	30036	10	24	SPECIAL TRADE CONTRACTORS
29657	299	3227	COMPUTER & ELECTRONIC PROD MFG	29835	292	1761	NURSING & RESID. CARE FACILIT.	30037	11	29	PROF.; SCIENTIFIC; & TECH SVCS
29658	10	109	MOTOR VEHICLE & PARTS DEALERS	29836	11	8	POSTAL SERVICE	30038	1108	7089	FOOD SVCS & DRINKING PLACES
29659	11	12	GASOLINE STATIONS	29838	15	72	CONSTRUCTION OF BUILDINGS	30039	806	5719	EDUCATIONAL SERVICES
29661	127	1099	NONMETALLIC MINERAL PROD. MFG	29839	7	38	JUSTICE; PUBIC ORDER/SAFETY	30040	2477	17821	FOOD MANUFACTURING
29662	581	3548	FOOD SVCS & DRINKING PLACES	29840	15	12	FURN. & HOME FURNISHGS STORES	30041	1594	12645	FOOD SVCS & DRINKING PLACES
29664	41	216	ACCOMMODATION	29841	1027	7992	FOOD SVCS & DRINKING PLACES	30042	13	36	ADMINISTRATIVE & SUPPORT SVCS
29665	1	2	POSTAL SERVICE	29842	220	1755	CHEMICAL MANUFACTURING	30043	2364	24475	PROF.; SCIENTIFIC; & TECH SVCS
29666	149	963	EDUCATIONAL SERVICES	29843	25	105	WOOD PRODUCT MANUFACTURING	30044	1655	10418	EDUCATIONAL SERVICES
29667	11	42	PROF.; SCIENTIFIC; & TECH SVCS	29844	1	1	POSTAL SERVICE	30045	3029	45037	EXEC.; LEGIS.; & OTHER SUPPORT
29669	256	2041	JUSTICE; PUBIC ORDER/SAFETY	29845	45	67	SPECIAL TRADE CONTRACTORS	30046	13	36	SOCIAL ASSISTANCE
29670	305	2393	EDUCATIONAL SERVICES	29846	1	0	POSTAL SERVICE	30047	2185	12148	EDUCATIONAL SERVICES
29671	546	5438	EXEC.; LEGIS.; & OTHER SUPPORT	29847	74	626	JUSTICE; PUBIC ORDER/SAFETY	30048	23	44	ADMINISTRATIVE & SUPPORT SVCS
29672	301	3781	HOSPITALS	29848	26	13	POSTAL SERVICE	30049	11	22	ADMINISTRATIVE & SUPPORT SVCS
29673	811	8526	EDUCATIONAL SERVICES	29849	11	10	CROP PRODUCTION	30052	1613	10142	EDUCATIONAL SERVICES
29675	2	31	WOOD PRODUCT MANUFACTURING	29850	3	2	POSTAL SERVICE	30054	221	1176	SPECIAL TRADE CONTRACTORS
29676	122	605	EDUCATIONAL SERVICES	29851	134	636	EDUCATIONAL SERVICES	30055	68	512	MERCH. WHOLESALERS;NONDUR. GDS
29677	11	1350	PLASTICS & RUBBER PRODUCTS MFG	29853	187	2143	MACHINERY MANUFACTURING	30056	53	153	HEAVY & CIVIL ENG. CONSTRUCT'N
29678	1070	9396	ELECT'L EQPMT; APP; & COMP MFG	29856	29	56	SPECIAL TRADE CONTRACTORS	30058	1366	9620	EDUCATIONAL SERVICES
29679	2	2	ADMINISTRATIVE & SUPPORT SVCS	29860	215	1728	TRUCK TRANSPORTATION	30060	2786	43913	AMBULATORY HEALTH CARE SVCS
29680	539	4739	FOOD SVCS & DRINKING PLACES	29861	5	14	ADMINISTRATIVE & SUPPORT SVCS	30061	17	57	SPECIAL TRADE CONTRACTORS
29681	1212	13429	COMPUTER & ELECTRONIC PROD MFG	29899	1	300	JUSTICE; PUBIC ORDER/SAFETY	30062	2833	32299	PROF.; SCIENTIFIC; & TECH SVCS
29682	73	397	EDUCATIONAL SERVICES	29901	11	43	SOCIAL ASSISTANCE	30063	2	8204	TRANSPORTATION EQUIPMENT MFG
29683	7	348	APPAREL MANUFACTURING	29902	997	9598	HOSPITALS	30064	1456	10274	FOOD SVCS & DRINKING PLACES
29684	88	817	CHEMICAL MANUFACTURING	29903	8	21	ADMINISTRATIVE & SUPPORT SVCS	30065	14	39	ADMINISTRATIVE & SUPPORT SVCS

ZIP CODE	2009 Total Firms	2009 Total Employ-ees	TOP INDUSTRY RANKED on 2009 EMPLOYMENT	ZIP CODE	2009 Total Firms	2009 Total Employ-ees	TOP INDUSTRY RANKED on 2009 EMPLOYMENT	ZIP CODE	2009 Total Firms	2009 Total Employ-ees	TOP INDUSTRY RANKED on 2009 EMPLOYMENT
30066	2438	20004	EDUCATIONAL SERVICES	30169	3	10	PERFORM'G ARTS; SPEC. SPORTS	30309	2522	46262	PROF.; SCIENTIFIC; & TECH SVCS
30067	2506	26635	FURN. & HOME FURNISHGS STORES	30170	69	266	EDUCATIONAL SERVICES	30310	1057	8341	EDUCATIONAL SERVICES
30068	1213	9348	EDUCATIONAL SERVICES	30171	49	247	TRANSPORTATION EQUIPMENT MFG	30311	786	4967	AMBULATORY HEALTH CARE SVCS
30069	20	1487	NAT'L SECURITY & INT'L AFFAIRS	30172	5	11	HEALTH & PERSONAL CARE STORES	30312	901	8794	HOSPITALS
30070	28	271	APPAREL MANUFACTURING	30173	83	267	EDUCATIONAL SERVICES	30313	293	4677	BEVERAGE & TOBACCO PRODUCT MFG
30071	3013	38033	MERCH. WHOLESALERS;DURABLE GDS	30175	114	359	NONMETALLIC MINERAL PROD. MFG	30314	396	4707	EDUCATIONAL SERVICES
30072	19	31	JUSTICE; PUBIC ORDER/SAFETY	30176	269	2848	FABRICATED METAL PRODUCT MFG	30315	999	15275	PERFORM'G ARTS; SPEC. SPORTS
30074	9	14	PUBLISHING INDUSTRIES	30177	30	483	NONMETALLIC MINERAL PROD. MFG	30316	1042	9907	JUSTICE; PUBIC ORDER/SAFETY
30075	2539	18650	REAL ESTATE	30178	69	274	EDUCATIONAL SERVICES	30317	365	1836	EDUCATIONAL SERVICES
30076	2603	25877	PROF.; SCIENTIFIC; & TECH SVCS	30179	249	1678	EDUCATIONAL SERVICES	30318	2692	32151	CHEMICAL MANUFACTURING
30077	19	44	PROF.; SCIENTIFIC; & TECH SVCS	30180	971	8779	FOOD SVCS & DRINKING PLACES	30319	1069	23822	COMPUTER & ELECTRONIC PROD MFG
30078	1611	14190	FOOD SVCS & DRINKING PLACES	30182	51	344	PERFORM'G ARTS; SPEC. SPORTS	30320	231	4934	RENTAL AND LEASING SERVICES
30079	155	8422	EXEC.; LEGIS.; & OTHER SUPPORT	30183	105	611	EDUCATIONAL SERVICES	30321	8	23	HEAVY & CIVIL ENG. CONSTRUCT'N
30080	2395	22171	FOOD SVCS & DRINKING PLACES	30184	126	598	ACCOMMODATION	30322	79	26382	EDUCATIONAL SERVICES
30081	18	44	ADMINISTRATIVE & SUPPORT SVCS	30185	83	498	ADMINISTRATIVE & SUPPORT SVCS	30324	1418	15321	TRANSIT & GRND PASS. TRANSPORT
30082	674	8616	PROF.; SCIENTIFIC; & TECH SVCS	30187	163	897	MERCH. WHOLESALERS;DURABLE GDS	30325	5	6	MERCH. WHOLESALERS;DURABLE GDS
30083	1635	12762	EDUCATIONAL SERVICES	30188	2097	12717	FOOD SVCS & DRINKING PLACES	30326	1773	25686	PROF.; SCIENTIFIC; & TECH SVCS
30084	2613	28715	AMBULATORY HEALTH CARE SVCS	30189	1233	8777	EDUCATIONAL SERVICES	30327	774	10860	INSURANCE CARRIERS & RELATED
30085	11	41	CONSTRUCTION OF BUILDINGS	30204	428	3818	EDUCATIONAL SERVICES	30328	3215	44665	PROF.; SCIENTIFIC; & TECH SVCS
30086	11	16	PROF.; SCIENTIFIC; & TECH SVCS	30205	81	299	SPECIAL TRADE CONTRACTORS	30329	1461	29530	ADMIN. HUMAN RESOURCE PROGRAMS
30087	1042	7080	FOOD SVCS & DRINKING PLACES	30206	46	105	MERCH. WHOLESALERS;NONDUR. GDS	30330	17	138	ELECTRONICS & APPLIANCE STORES
30088	441	1602	FOOD SVCS & DRINKING PLACES	30212	2	2	ADMINISTRATIVE & SUPPORT SVCS	30331	1286	12966	EDUCATIONAL SERVICES
30090	66	2639	JUSTICE; PUBIC ORDER/SAFETY	30213	724	8533	EDUCATIONAL SERVICES	30332	18	4809	EDUCATIONAL SERVICES
30091	10	8	CONSTRUCTION OF BUILDINGS	30214	2099	16640	AMBULATORY HEALTH CARE SVCS	30333	1	1	ADMINISTRATIVE & SUPPORT SVCS
30092	2266	29869	PROF.; SCIENTIFIC; & TECH SVCS	30215	584	3134	EDUCATIONAL SERVICES	30334	231	10775	EXEC.; LEGIS.; & OTHER SUPPORT
30093	2176	20648	MERCH. WHOLESALERS;DURABLE GDS	30216	34	78	JUSTICE; PUBIC ORDER/SAFETY	30336	964	22178	MERCH. WHOLESALERS;DURABLE GDS
30094	715	4876	EDUCATIONAL SERVICES	30217	225	1794	EDUCATIONAL SERVICES	30337	669	9853	ACCOMMODATION
30095	11	20	ADMINISTRATIVE & SUPPORT SVCS	30218	49	187	TRANSPORTATION EQUIPMENT MFG	30338	1892	21408	REPAIR AND MAINTENANCE
30096	3693	42318	PROF.; SCIENTIFIC; & TECH SVCS	30220	92	394	EDUCATIONAL SERVICES	30339	3292	54252	PROF.; SCIENTIFIC; & TECH SVCS
30097	2019	22289	PROF.; SCIENTIFIC; & TECH SVCS	30222	158	2116	UNCLASSIFIED ESTABLISHMENTS	30340	2177	17718	SPECIAL TRADE CONTRACTORS
30098	1	2000	INSURANCE CARRIERS & RELATED	30223	1342	12081	FOOD SVCS & DRINKING PLACES	30341	2392	19726	PROF.; SCIENTIFIC; & TECH SVCS
30099	1	1600	SECURITIES/COMMODITY CONTRACTS	30224	769	10423	HOSPITALS	30342	2111	28157	AMBULATORY HEALTH CARE SVCS
30101	1470	9868	FOOD SVCS & DRINKING PLACES	30228	642	4454	EDUCATIONAL SERVICES	30343	1	1	ADMINISTRATIVE & SUPPORT SVCS
30102	768	4186	ADMINISTRATIVE & SUPPORT SVCS	30229	16	36	FOOD AND BEVERAGE STORES	30344	1335	14430	HOSPITALS
30103	400	3238	ACCOMMODATION	30230	182	1369	TEXTILE MILLS	30345	954	8585	PROF.; SCIENTIFIC; & TECH SVCS
30104	46	98	FABRICATED METAL PRODUCT MFG	30233	655	6948	EXEC.; LEGIS.; & OTHER SUPPORT	30346	861	19095	ACCOMMODATION
30105	52	721	FURN. & HOME FURNISHGS STORES	30234	41	288	MERCH. WHOLESALERS;DURABLE GDS	30347	2	5	PROF.; SCIENTIFIC; & TECH SVCS
30106	828	9903	HOSPITALS	30236	1860	14631	JUSTICE; PUBIC ORDER/SAFETY	30349	2027	18657	MERCH. WHOLESALERS;DURABLE GDS
30107	366	3164	MERCH. WHOLESALERS;DURABLE GDS	30237	6	30	ADMINISTRATIVE & SUPPORT SVCS	30350	1191	11225	PROF.; SCIENTIFIC; & TECH SVCS
30108	234	2013	APPAREL MANUFACTURING	30238	400	2288	EDUCATIONAL SERVICES	30354	768	17340	PROF.; SCIENTIFIC; & TECH SVCS
30109	1	1	FURN. & HOME FURNISHGS STORES	30240	1317	19269	AMBULATORY HEALTH CARE SVCS	30355	18	63	POSTAL SERVICE
30110	486	3738	FOOD SVCS & DRINKING PLACES	30241	798	8454	FOOD SVCS & DRINKING PLACES	30356	16	36	SECURITIES/COMMODITY CONTRACTS
30111	5	15	ADMINISTRATIVE & SUPPORT SVCS	30248	572	4192	EDUCATIONAL SERVICES	30357	7	12	BEVERAGE & TOBACCO PRODUCT MFG
30112	6	18	INSURANCE CARRIERS & RELATED	30250	16	257	GENERAL MERCHANDISE STORES	30358	9	19	CONSTRUCTION OF BUILDINGS
30113	182	1134	EDUCATIONAL SERVICES	30251	73	404	HEAVY & CIVIL ENG. CONSTRUCT'N	30359	16	27	PROF.; SCIENTIFIC; & TECH SVCS
30114	1675	14579	FOOD SVCS & DRINKING PLACES	30252	592	2979	EDUCATIONAL SERVICES	30360	667	10613	UNCLASSIFIED ESTABLISHMENTS
30115	996	7936	EDUCATIONAL SERVICES	30253	1963	21381	FOOD SVCS & DRINKING PLACES	30361	244	3239	PROF.; SCIENTIFIC; & TECH SVCS
30116	457	4430	EDUCATIONAL SERVICES	30256	27	83	MERCH. WHOLESALERS;NONDUR. GDS	30362	5	6	INSURANCE CARRIERS & RELATED
30117	1874	18997	HOSPITALS	30257	70	399	ADMINISTRATIVE & SUPPORT SVCS	30363	203	4567	PROF.; SCIENTIFIC; & TECH SVCS
30118	1	147	FOOD SVCS & DRINKING PLACES	30258	43	393	TEXTILE MILLS	30364	5	8	PROF.; SCIENTIFIC; & TECH SVCS
30119	2	4022	MERCH. WHOLESALERS;DURABLE GDS	30259	48	205	EDUCATIONAL SERVICES	30366	7	8	PROF.; SCIENTIFIC; & TECH SVCS
30120	1956	17002	FURN. & HOME FURNISHGS STORES	30260	1216	16171	FOOD SVCS & DRINKING PLACES	30369	4	2005	POSTAL SERVICE
30121	756	9862	FOOD SVCS & DRINKING PLACES	30261	1	0	RELIG.; GRANT; CIVIC; PROF ORG	30374	1	0	UNCLASSIFIED ESTABLISHMENTS
30122	785	13895	CONSTRUCTION OF BUILDINGS	30263	1937	15350	EDUCATIONAL SERVICES	30375	2	6	UNCLASSIFIED ESTABLISHMENTS
30123	4	16	JUSTICE; PUBIC ORDER/SAFETY	30264	7	31	ADMINISTRATIVE & SUPPORT SVCS	30377	3	2	MISCELLANEOUS STORE RETAILERS
30124	75	422	EDUCATIONAL SERVICES	30265	867	13610	FOOD SVCS & DRINKING PLACES	30378	1	60	POSTAL SERVICE
30125	730	6361	MERCH. WHOLESALERS;DURABLE GDS	30266	13	83	FOOD AND BEVERAGE STORES	30384	2	12	BLDG MATL & GARDEN EQPMT DLRS
30126	1024	8120	EDUCATIONAL SERVICES	30268	280	3194	MERCH. WHOLESALERS;DURABLE GDS	30401	599	5554	EDUCATIONAL SERVICES
30127	1085	7304	EDUCATIONAL SERVICES	30269	1513	17785	FOOD SVCS & DRINKING PLACES	30410	36	353	EDUCATIONAL SERVICES
30129	2	4	MERCH. WHOLESALERS;DURABLE GDS	30271	7	17	CONSTRUCTION OF BUILDINGS	30411	88	778	JUSTICE; PUBIC ORDER/SAFETY
30132	983	6072	EDUCATIONAL SERVICES	30272	16	76	FOOD AND BEVERAGE STORES	30412	7	14	REPAIR AND MAINTENANCE
30133	7	18	PROF.; SCIENTIFIC; & TECH SVCS	30273	197	770	EDUCATIONAL SERVICES	30413	43	88	ADMINISTRATIVE & SUPPORT SVCS
30134	1481	11595	EXEC.; LEGIS.; & OTHER SUPPORT	30274	1150	10223	HOSPITALS	30414	9	79	EDUCATIONAL SERVICES
30135	1449	12588	FOOD SVCS & DRINKING PLACES	30275	3	7	RELIG.; GRANT; CIVIC; PROF ORG	30415	211	1301	EDUCATIONAL SERVICES
30137	42	562	CHEMICAL MANUFACTURING	30276	217	1324	APPAREL MANUFACTURING	30417	368	4298	FOOD MANUFACTURING
30138	2	2	POSTAL SERVICE	30277	313	1852	EDUCATIONAL SERVICES	30420	44	82	JUSTICE; PUBIC ORDER/SAFETY
30139	117	556	EDUCATIONAL SERVICES	30281	2174	16533	FOOD SVCS & DRINKING PLACES	30421	47	249	CROP PRODUCTION
30140	1	37	PLASTICS & RUBBER PRODUCTS MFG	30284	17	70	SOCIAL ASSISTANCE	30423	5	6	GASOLINE STATIONS
30141	845	6446	FOOD SVCS & DRINKING PLACES	30285	13	720	PRINT'G & RELATED SUPP'T ACT'S	30424	8	232	TEXTILE MILLS
30142	27	128	HEAVY & CIVIL ENG. CONSTRUCT'N	30286	870	7127	EDUCATIONAL SERVICES	30425	17	59	FOOD AND BEVERAGE STORES
30143	1103	8551	FABRICATED METAL PRODUCT MFG	30287	1	1	PROF.; SCIENTIFIC; & TECH SVCS	30426	14	24	GASOLINE STATIONS
30144	2820	35553	FOOD SVCS & DRINKING PLACES	30288	255	5335	TRUCK TRANSPORTATION	30427	307	4696	MERCH. WHOLESALERS;NONDUR. GDS
30145	117	533	EDUCATIONAL SERVICES	30289	24	63	BLDG MATL & GARDEN EQPMT DLRS	30428	90	535	HOSPITALS
30146	5	6	MACHINERY MANUFACTURING	30290	449	3241	EDUCATIONAL SERVICES	30429	17	212	WOOD PRODUCT MANUFACTURING
30147	67	507	EDUCATIONAL SERVICES	30291	564	7238	MOTOR VEHICLE & PARTS DEALERS	30434	277	2394	EDUCATIONAL SERVICES
30148	98	510	NONMETALLIC MINERAL PROD. MFG	30292	67	242	HEAVY & CIVIL ENG. CONSTRUCT'N	30436	380	3286	EDUCATIONAL SERVICES
30149	5	553	OTHER INFORMATION SERVICES	30293	77	529	EDUCATIONAL SERVICES	30439	434	2846	EDUCATIONAL SERVICES
30150	10	81	EDUCATIONAL SERVICES	30294	662	6304	TRUCK TRANSPORTATION	30441	67	226	FOOD SVCS & DRINKING PLACES
30151	24	62	TELECOMMUNICATIONS	30295	237	1630	EDUCATIONAL SERVICES	30442	240	2144	WOOD PRODUCT MANUFACTURING
30152	930	8000	EDUCATIONAL SERVICES	30296	362	1208	EDUCATIONAL SERVICES	30445	109	814	EDUCATIONAL SERVICES
30153	440	3790	FOOD MANUFACTURING	30297	1274	15391	MERCH. WHOLESALERS;NONDUR. GDS	30446	51	154	ELECTRONICS & APPLIANCE STORES
30154	9	9	REPAIR AND MAINTENANCE	30298	4	5	BLDG MATL & GARDEN EQPMT DLRS	30447	1	0	POSTAL SERVICE
30156	18	43	TRUCK TRANSPORTATION	30301	13	60	TRANSIT & GRND PASS. TRANSPORT	30448	4	6	WASTE MANAGMT & REMEDIAT'N SVC
30157	573	3731	EDUCATIONAL SERVICES	30302	10	47	ADMINISTRATIVE & SUPPORT SVCS	30449	8	7	JUSTICE; PUBIC ORDER/SAFETY
30160	3	8	CONSTRUCTION OF BUILDINGS	30303	4946	80462	PROF.; SCIENTIFIC; & TECH SVCS	30450	82	585	APPAREL MANUFACTURING
30161	1581	19451	EDUCATIONAL SERVICES	30304	4	81	CREDIT INTERMEDIATION & RELATD	30451	5	104	NURSING & RESID. CARE FACILIT.
30162	5	23	SOCIAL ASSISTANCE	30305	2884	30989	PROF.; SCIENTIFIC; & TECH SVCS	30452	52	251	SPECIAL TRADE CONTRACTORS
30164	1	1	REPAIR AND MAINTENANCE	30306	743	6029	FOOD SVCS & DRINKING PLACES	30453	216	2075	JUSTICE; PUBIC ORDER/SAFETY
30165	1470	19051	HOSPITALS	30307	707	5569	FOOD SVCS & DRINKING PLACES	30454	7	5	POSTAL SERVICE
30168	765	9314	MERCH. WHOLESALERS;DURABLE GDS	30308	1413	33257	PROF.; SCIENTIFIC; & TECH SVCS	30455	21	60	RELIG.; GRANT; CIVIC; PROF ORG

BUSINESS DATA

ZIP CODE	2009 Total Firms	2009 Total Employ-ees	TOP INDUSTRY RANKED on 2009 EMPLOYMENT	ZIP CODE	2009 Total Firms	2009 Total Employ-ees	TOP INDUSTRY RANKED on 2009 EMPLOYMENT	ZIP CODE	2009 Total Firms	2009 Total Employ-ees	TOP INDUSTRY RANKED on 2009 EMPLOYMENT
30456	48	267	EDUCATIONAL SERVICES	30607	345	4004	FOOD SVCS & DRINKING PLACES	30813	497	5678	JUSTICE; PUBIC ORDER/SAFETY
30457	227	1481	TEXTILE MILLS	30608	5	37	CONSTRUCTION OF BUILDINGS	30814	188	959	EDUCATIONAL SERVICES
30458	1976	17523	FOOD SVCS & DRINKING PLACES	30609	5	125	REAL ESTATE	30815	585	3189	EDUCATIONAL SERVICES
30459	12	45	SPECIAL TRADE CONTRACTORS	30619	17	94	ADMINISTRATIVE & SUPPORT SVCS	30816	44	179	NURSING & RESID. CARE FACILIT.
30460	12	150	OTHER INFORMATION SERVICES	30620	129	1403	FOOD MANUFACTURING	30817	396	1590	EDUCATIONAL SERVICES
30461	335	1504	EDUCATIONAL SERVICES	30621	99	536	NURSING & RESID. CARE FACILIT.	30818	18	107	PROF.; SCIENTIFIC; & TECH SVCS
30464	17	1879	MERCH. WHOLESALERS;NONDUR. GDS	30622	554	5805	MISCELLANEOUS STORE RETAILERS	30819	1	10	MERCH. WHOLESALERS;DURABLE GDS
30467	606	3939	FABRICATED METAL PRODUCT MFG	30623	7	8	GASOLINE STATIONS	30820	17	70	MERCH. WHOLESALERS;DURABLE GDS
30470	13	16	REPAIR AND MAINTENANCE	30624	62	131	RELIG.; GRANT; CIVIC; PROF ORG	30821	22	34	PERSONAL AND LAUNDRY SERVICES
30471	149	740	EDUCATIONAL SERVICES	30625	52	97	SPECIAL TRADE CONTRACTORS	30822	5	3	FISHING; HUNTING AND TRAPPING
30473	61	285	WHOLESALE ELEC. MRKTS & AGENTS	30627	31	63	MISCELLANEOUS STORE RETAILERS	30823	42	118	SPECIAL TRADE CONTRACTORS
30474	930	9873	MACHINERY MANUFACTURING	30628	98	685	SPECIAL TRADE CONTRACTORS	30824	712	8418	SPECIAL TRADE CONTRACTORS
30475	2	1	REAL ESTATE	30629	99	631	NURSING & RESID. CARE FACILIT.	30828	158	1177	EDUCATIONAL SERVICES
30477	87	1098	MERCH. WHOLESALERS;DURABLE GDS	30630	105	632	PROF.; SCIENTIFIC; & TECH SVCS	30830	503	5548	PROF.; SCIENTIFIC; & TECH SVCS
30501	3019	44622	HOSPITALS	30631	91	300	EDUCATIONAL SERVICES	30833	195	2315	MERCH. WHOLESALERS;DURABLE GDS
30502	3	19	PROF.; SCIENTIFIC; & TECH SVCS	30633	238	1963	EXEC.; LEGIS.; & OTHER SUPPORT	30901	1747	30783	AMBULATORY HEALTH CARE SVCS
30503	10	225	ADMINISTRATIVE & SUPPORT SVCS	30634	43	100	CROP PRODUCTION	30903	6	3	CONSTRUCTION OF BUILDINGS
30504	685	8910	MERCH. WHOLESALERS;DURABLE GDS	30635	815	7289	MERCH. WHOLESALERS;DURABLE GDS	30904	1068	12076	HOSPITALS
30506	719	3650	EDUCATIONAL SERVICES	30638	2	5	TRUCK TRANSPORTATION	30905	121	1838	COMPUTER & ELECTRONIC PROD MFG
30507	506	6573	FOOD MANUFACTURING	30639	19	218	EDUCATIONAL SERVICES	30906	1797	21589	EDUCATIONAL SERVICES
30510	130	2421	APPAREL MANUFACTURING	30641	35	189	SPECIAL TRADE CONTRACTORS	30907	2466	19793	FOOD SVCS & DRINKING PLACES
30511	139	915	NURSING & RESID. CARE FACILIT.	30642	571	5279	REAL ESTATE	30909	2082	22491	FOOD SVCS & DRINKING PLACES
30512	1103	6553	CREDIT INTERMEDIATION & RELATD	30643	690	5978	MERCH. WHOLESALERS;NONDUR. GDS	30912	76	13727	AMBULATORY HEALTH CARE SVCS
30513	969	5761	EDUCATIONAL SERVICES	30645	5	25	AMBULATORY HEALTH CARE SVCS	30914	2	2	REAL ESTATE
30514	12	27	RELIG.; GRANT; CIVIC; PROF ORG	30646	129	676	FOOD AND BEVERAGE STORES	30916	3	6	MERCH. WHOLESALERS;DURABLE GDS
30515	14	31	ADMINISTRATIVE & SUPPORT SVCS	30647	24	104	EDUCATIONAL SERVICES	30917	11	17	REPAIR AND MAINTENANCE
30516	37	173	EDUCATIONAL SERVICES	30648	117	777	EDUCATIONAL SERVICES	30919	8	15	SPECIAL TRADE CONTRACTORS
30517	369	5124	UNCLASSIFIED ESTABLISHMENTS	30650	669	5979	FOOD SVCS & DRINKING PLACES	31001	58	754	JUSTICE; PUBIC ORDER/SAFETY
30518	2275	20041	AMUSEMENT; GAMBLING;& RECREAT.	30655	954	9642	RELIG.; GRANT; CIVIC; PROF ORG	31002	56	396	MERCH. WHOLESALERS;DURABLE GDS
30519	1074	11278	FOOD SVCS & DRINKING PLACES	30656	199	1195	APPAREL MANUFACTURING	31003	8	24	CREDIT INTERMEDIATION & RELATD
30520	96	266	WOOD PRODUCT MANUFACTURING	30660	39	150	CROP PRODUCTION	31004	21	86	SPECIAL TRADE CONTRACTORS
30521	194	2162	EDUCATIONAL SERVICES	30662	323	2580	NURSING & RESID. CARE FACILIT.	31005	154	1187	ADMINISTRATIVE & SUPPORT SVCS
30522	30	54	RELIG.; GRANT; CIVIC; PROF ORG	30663	82	291	WHOLESALE ELEC. MRKTS & AGENTS	31006	212	1476	EXEC.; LEGIS.; & OTHER SUPPORT
30523	676	4284	FABRICATED METAL PRODUCT MFG	30664	3	9	MERCH. WHOLESALERS;NONDUR. GDS	31007	26	215	SOCIAL ASSISTANCE
30525	528	3463	ACCOMMODATION	30665	9	46	EDUCATIONAL SERVICES	31008	476	3162	MERCH. WHOLESALERS;DURABLE GDS
30527	139	414	FOOD SVCS & DRINKING PLACES	30666	163	1105	PROF.; SCIENTIFIC; & TECH SVCS	31009	38	121	JUSTICE; PUBIC ORDER/SAFETY
30528	992	6165	EDUCATIONAL SERVICES	30667	16	52	RELIG.; GRANT; CIVIC; PROF ORG	31010	1	0	RELIG.; GRANT; CIVIC; PROF ORG
30529	660	5794	FOOD SVCS & DRINKING PLACES	30668	61	235	FURN. & HOME FURNISHGS STORES	31011	16	63	MACHINERY MANUFACTURING
30530	81	660	WOOD PRODUCT MANUFACTURING	30669	107	637	EDUCATIONAL SERVICES	31012	34	275	JUSTICE; PUBIC ORDER/SAFETY
30531	639	5714	MISCELLANEOUS MANUFACTURING	30671	5	11	CROP PRODUCTION	31013	3	140	NONMETALLIC MINERAL PROD. MFG
30533	1038	6492	FOOD SVCS & DRINKING PLACES	30673	542	3445	MERCH. WHOLESALERS;DURABLE GDS	31014	368	3752	EDUCATIONAL SERVICES
30534	1116	7809	FOOD SVCS & DRINKING PLACES	30677	764	4725	EDUCATIONAL SERVICES	31015	957	9177	HOSPITALS
30535	216	2234	HOSPITALS	30678	30	124	REAL ESTATE	31016	36	49	CONSTRUCTION OF BUILDINGS
30536	319	1035	MISCELLANEOUS MANUFACTURING	30680	1275	11887	EDUCATIONAL SERVICES	31017	21	52	JUSTICE; PUBIC ORDER/SAFETY
30537	103	798	ACCOMMODATION	30683	124	708	FABRICATED METAL PRODUCT MFG	31018	32	596	JUSTICE; PUBIC ORDER/SAFETY
30538	131	1164	FURNITURE & RELATED PROD. MFG	30701	1560	19135	TEXTILE PRODUCT MILLS	31019	57	136	MERCH. WHOLESALERS;NONDUR. GDS
30539	9	31	NONMETALLIC MINERAL PROD. MFG	30703	5	17	ADMINISTRATIVE & SUPPORT SVCS	31020	48	696	NONMETALLIC MINERAL PROD. MFG
30540	1409	8813	FOOD MANUFACTURING	30705	820	10693	TEXTILE PRODUCT MILLS	31021	1505	17084	HOSPITALS
30541	19	32	RELIG.; GRANT; CIVIC; PROF ORG	30707	326	3099	FURN. & HOME FURNISHGS STORES	31022	42	459	WOOD PRODUCT MANUFACTURING
30542	810	7332	FOOD MANUFACTURING	30708	2	9	MINING (EXCEPT OIL AND GAS)	31023	533	5562	EDUCATIONAL SERVICES
30543	51	191	HEAVY & CIVIL ENG. CONSTRUCT'N	30710	78	297	EDUCATIONAL SERVICES	31024	777	7088	WOOD PRODUCT MANUFACTURING
30544	2	0	MERCH. WHOLESALERS;DURABLE GDS	30711	37	105	OTHER INFORMATION SERVICES	31025	20	38	AMBULATORY HEALTH CARE SVCS
30545	242	1158	ACCOMMODATION	30719	1	0	SUPPORT ACT. FOR TRANSPORT.	31027	257	3119	SPECIAL TRADE CONTRACTORS
30546	513	2786	REAL ESTATE	30720	1752	22250	TEXTILE MILLS	31028	214	1550	GENERAL MERCHANDISE STORES
30547	147	894	EDUCATIONAL SERVICES	30721	1822	26934	TEXTILE PRODUCT MILLS	31029	615	4927	EDUCATIONAL SERVICES
30548	336	2215	EDUCATIONAL SERVICES	30722	9	46	SOCIAL ASSISTANCE	31030	498	6191	EDUCATIONAL SERVICES
30549	648	5211	EDUCATIONAL SERVICES	30724	16	472	TEXTILE PRODUCT MILLS	31031	147	1813	NONMETALLIC MINERAL PROD. MFG
30552	55	128	FOOD AND BEVERAGE STORES	30725	85	721	TEXTILE MILLS	31032	405	2606	EDUCATIONAL SERVICES
30553	352	4356	UNCLASSIFIED ESTABLISHMENTS	30726	1	2	POSTAL SERVICE	31033	38	42	RELIG.; GRANT; CIVIC; PROF ORG
30554	149	502	SPECIAL TRADE CONTRACTORS	30728	660	8009	MERCH. WHOLESALERS;DURABLE GDS	31034	6	832	JUSTICE; PUBIC ORDER/SAFETY
30555	93	314	FOOD SVCS & DRINKING PLACES	30730	33	220	EDUCATIONAL SERVICES	31035	24	107	TRANSIT & GRND PASS. TRANSPORT
30557	45	106	RELIG.; GRANT; CIVIC; PROF ORG	30731	57	1050	APPAREL MANUFACTURING	31036	446	3238	JUSTICE; PUBIC ORDER/SAFETY
30558	102	467	EDUCATIONAL SERVICES	30732	6	41	ADMINISTRATIVE & SUPPORT SVCS	31037	55	558	JUSTICE; PUBIC ORDER/SAFETY
30559	93	193	EDUCATIONAL SERVICES	30733	29	249	PLASTICS & RUBBER PRODUCTS MFG	31038	13	44	EXEC.; LEGIS.; & OTHER SUPPORT
30560	125	318	EDUCATIONAL SERVICES	30734	58	230	SPORTG GDS;HOBBY;BOOK; & MUSIC	31039	6	4	RELIG.; GRANT; CIVIC; PROF ORG
30562	36	221	ACCOMMODATION	30735	86	376	EDUCATIONAL SERVICES	31040	3	29	SOCIAL ASSISTANCE
30563	113	597	EDUCATIONAL SERVICES	30736	1053	8519	EDUCATIONAL SERVICES	31041	17	108	NURSING & RESID. CARE FACILIT.
30564	97	1767	FOOD MANUFACTURING	30738	82	358	REPAIR AND MAINTENANCE	31042	93	1148	EDUCATIONAL SERVICES
30565	62	241	SPECIAL TRADE CONTRACTORS	30739	141	1315	EDUCATIONAL SERVICES	31044	133	910	NURSING & RESID. CARE FACILIT.
30566	307	3737	EDUCATIONAL SERVICES	30740	125	524	EDUCATIONAL SERVICES	31045	2	2	POSTAL SERVICE
30567	114	3795	FOOD MANUFACTURING	30741	612	4345	EDUCATIONAL SERVICES	31046	90	759	UTILITIES
30568	51	749	TEXTILE MILLS	30742	531	7452	HOSPITALS	31047	80	1537	MERCH. WHOLESALERS;DURABLE GDS
30571	99	449	EDUCATIONAL SERVICES	30746	23	1226	FURN. & HOME FURNISHGS STORES	31049	35	89	CONSTRUCTION OF BUILDINGS
30572	39	164	EDUCATIONAL SERVICES	30747	462	3094	EDUCATIONAL SERVICES	31050	12	49	JUSTICE; PUBIC ORDER/SAFETY
30573	26	225	RELIG.; GRANT; CIVIC; PROF ORG	30750	50	525	EDUCATIONAL SERVICES	31051	8	21	SUPPORT ACTIVITIES: AGR./FOR.
30575	35	283	CONSTRUCTION OF BUILDINGS	30751	5	63	BLDG MATL & GARDEN EQPMT DLRS	31052	146	780	EDUCATIONAL SERVICES
30576	71	570	EDUCATIONAL SERVICES	30752	356	3376	TEXTILE PRODUCT MILLS	31054	74	1000	BLDG MATL & GARDEN EQPMT DLRS
30577	914	10734	TEXTILE MILLS	30753	127	1379	JUSTICE; PUBIC ORDER/SAFETY	31055	294	3454	MACHINERY MANUFACTURING
30580	3	16	SPECIAL TRADE CONTRACTORS	30755	169	1433	EDUCATIONAL SERVICES	31057	47	174	NURSING & RESID. CARE FACILIT.
30581	10	22	REPAIR AND MAINTENANCE	30756	14	84	FOOD SVCS & DRINKING PLACES	31058	13	78	MERCH. WHOLESALERS;DURABLE GDS
30582	178	1388	ACCOMMODATION	30757	39	276	HOSPITALS	31059	5	7	CONSTRUCTION OF BUILDINGS
30597	1	350	EDUCATIONAL SERVICES	30802	189	1466	JUSTICE; PUBIC ORDER/SAFETY	31060	41	158	BLDG MATL & GARDEN EQPMT DLRS
30598	3	258	EDUCATIONAL SERVICES	30803	16	55	JUSTICE; PUBIC ORDER/SAFETY	31061	1547	16810	EDUCATIONAL SERVICES
30599	1	430	MERCH. WHOLESALERS;NONDUR. GDS	30805	50	205	EDUCATIONAL SERVICES	31062	6	336	NURSING & RESID. CARE FACILIT.
30601	1144	17962	FOOD MANUFACTURING	30806	2	2	FOOD AND BEVERAGE STORES	31063	249	1574	FOOD MANUFACTURING
30602	273	19268	EDUCATIONAL SERVICES	30807	7	101	MERCH. WHOLESALERS;DURABLE GDS	31064	285	2274	EDUCATIONAL SERVICES
30603	4	14	RELIG.; GRANT; CIVIC; PROF ORG	30808	60	513	MERCH. WHOLESALERS;NONDUR. GDS	31065	27	62	NONSTORE RETAILERS
30604	17	41	ADMINISTRATIVE & SUPPORT SVCS	30809	1098	11674	EDUCATIONAL SERVICES	31066	9	113	MERCH. WHOLESALERS;NONDUR. GDS
30605	1014	7788	FOOD SVCS & DRINKING PLACES	30810	70	358	SOCIAL ASSISTANCE	31067	7	83	NURSING & RESID. CARE FACILIT.
30606	1746	20683	HOSPITALS	30812	7	1230	HOSPITALS	31068	113	1802	PAPER MANUFACTURING

ZIP CODE	2009 Total Firms	2009 Total Employ-ees	TOP INDUSTRY RANKED on 2009 EMPLOYMENT
31069	760	10434	SPECIAL TRADE CONTRACTORS
31070	38	384	EDUCATIONAL SERVICES
31071	28	142	NURSING & RESID. CARE FACILIT.
31072	23	72	INSURANCE CARRIERS & RELATED
31075	69	476	EDUCATIONAL SERVICES
31076	105	992	UTILITIES
31077	34	94	MERCH. WHOLESALERS;DURABLE GDS
31078	201	1008	EDUCATIONAL SERVICES
31079	106	630	EDUCATIONAL SERVICES
31081	4	9	HEAVY & CIVIL ENG. CONSTRUCT'N
31082	558	7207	NONMETALLIC MINERAL PROD. MFG
31083	5	32	SPECIAL TRADE CONTRACTORS
31084	1	0	POSTAL SERVICE
31085	24	216	MERCH. WHOLESALERS;NONDUR. GDS
31086	4	17	ADMINISTRATIVE & SUPPORT SVCS
31087	219	1187	EDUCATIONAL SERVICES
31088	1332	13473	EDUCATIONAL SERVICES
31089	98	1001	ADMIN. OF ECONOMIC PROGRAMS
31090	29	191	NURSING & RESID. CARE FACILIT.
31091	127	1326	JUSTICE; PUBIC ORDER/SAFETY
31092	299	2113	FOOD MANUFACTURING
31093	1153	12252	FOOD SVCS & DRINKING PLACES
31094	16	26	FOOD AND BEVERAGE STORES
31095	7	8	ELECTRONICS & APPLIANCE STORES
31096	224	2979	JUSTICE; PUBIC ORDER/SAFETY
31097	27	57	ADMINISTRATIVE & SUPPORT SVCS
31098	108	21554	NAT'L SECURITY & INT'L AFFAIRS
31099	4	18	SOCIAL ASSISTANCE
31106	8	24	RELIG.; GRANT; CIVIC; PROF ORG
31107	7	8	PROF.; SCIENTIFIC; & TECH SVCS
31119	6	11	WHOLESALE ELEC. MRKTS & AGENTS
31126	3	3	PROF.; SCIENTIFIC; & TECH SVCS
31131	9	25	REAL ESTATE
31139	11	26	SECURITIES/COMMODITY CONTRACTS
31141	8	21	PUBLISHING INDUSTRIES
31145	14	28	ADMINISTRATIVE & SUPPORT SVCS
31146	6	34	PROF.; SCIENTIFIC; & TECH SVCS
31150	3	7	ADMINISTRATIVE & SUPPORT SVCS
31156	4	5	SPECIAL TRADE CONTRACTORS
31201	1551	21797	HOSPITALS
31202	4	5	HEAVY & CIVIL ENG. CONSTRUCT'N
31203	2	3	REPAIR AND MAINTENANCE
31204	1330	9400	EDUCATIONAL SERVICES
31205	3	3	ADMINISTRATIVE & SUPPORT SVCS
31206	1416	15531	FOOD SVCS & DRINKING PLACES
31207	9	1461	EDUCATIONAL SERVICES
31208	10	233	JUSTICE; PUBIC ORDER/SAFETY
31209	7	15	SPECIAL TRADE CONTRACTORS
31210	1586	18033	FOOD SVCS & DRINKING PLACES
31211	514	4335	EDUCATIONAL SERVICES
31212	1	0	MERCH. WHOLESALERS;DURABLE GDS
31213	6	683	POSTAL SERVICE
31216	491	7533	MERCH. WHOLESALERS;DURABLE GDS
31217	472	6511	HOSPITALS
31220	262	2155	EDUCATIONAL SERVICES
31221	8	19	MERCH. WHOLESALERS;DURABLE GDS
31295	4	2540	INSURANCE CARRIERS & RELATED
31297	1	4	MERCH. WHOLESALERS;DURABLE GDS
31301	41	145	REAL ESTATE
31302	173	716	SPECIAL TRADE CONTRACTORS
31303	22	110	ADMINISTRATIVE & SUPPORT SVCS
31304	14	41	TRANSPORTATION EQUIPMENT MFG
31305	315	2387	REAL ESTATE
31307	12	37	SOCIAL ASSISTANCE
31308	136	300	SPECIAL TRADE CONTRACTORS
31309	21	62	BLDG MATL & GARDEN EQPMT DLRS
31310	6	16	CONSTRUCTION OF BUILDINGS
31312	199	1144	EDUCATIONAL SERVICES
31313	1220	10284	EDUCATIONAL SERVICES
31314	63	20527	NAT'L SECURITY & INT'L AFFAIRS
31315	17	333	EDUCATIONAL SERVICES
31316	155	869	EDUCATIONAL SERVICES
31318	6	157	PAPER MANUFACTURING
31319	9	50	SPECIAL TRADE CONTRACTORS
31320	246	1501	EDUCATIONAL SERVICES
31321	230	1425	EDUCATIONAL SERVICES
31322	757	7031	FOOD SVCS & DRINKING PLACES
31323	43	1002	CHEMICAL MANUFACTURING
31324	770	4739	FOOD SVCS & DRINKING PLACES
31326	690	7842	MERCH. WHOLESALERS;DURABLE GDS
31327	12	59	ADMIN. ENVIRO. QUALITY PROGRMS
31328	283	1256	FOOD SVCS & DRINKING PLACES
31329	361	2857	EXEC.; LEGIS.; & OTHER SUPPORT
31331	161	432	FOOD SVCS & DRINKING PLACES
31333	18	175	PLASTICS & RUBBER PRODUCTS MFG
31401	2210	21905	EDUCATIONAL SERVICES
31402	12	45	SUPPORT ACT. FOR TRANSPORT.
31403	7	15	ADMINISTRATIVE & SUPPORT SVCS
31404	1020	17898	AMBULATORY HEALTH CARE SVCS
31405	1892	23948	AMBULATORY HEALTH CARE SVCS
31406	2416	21828	AMBULATORY HEALTH CARE SVCS
31407	259	5042	FOOD MANUFACTURING
31408	1125	20418	TRANSPORTATION EQUIPMENT MFG
31409	25	175	NAT'L SECURITY & INT'L AFFAIRS
31410	646	4053	FOOD SVCS & DRINKING PLACES
31411	163	1680	AMUSEMENT; GAMBLING;& RECREAT.
31412	13	46	SOCIAL ASSISTANCE
31414	3	3	AMUSEMENT; GAMBLING;& RECREAT.
31415	490	9274	PAPER MANUFACTURING
31416	19	40	ADMINISTRATIVE & SUPPORT SVCS
31418	4	5	SUPPORT ACT. FOR TRANSPORT.
31419	1076	15075	HOSPITALS
31420	8	45	SOCIAL ASSISTANCE
31421	16	963	ACCOMMODATION
31501	1036	9594	HOSPITALS
31502	9	36	RELIG.; GRANT; CIVIC; PROF ORG
31503	517	6923	JUSTICE; PUBIC ORDER/SAFETY
31510	540	3961	FOOD MANUFACTURING
31512	38	224	EDUCATIONAL SERVICES
31513	685	6401	PROF.; SCIENTIFIC; & TECH SVCS
31515	1	0	SOCIAL ASSISTANCE
31516	450	3233	EDUCATIONAL SERVICES
31518	21	54	SUPPORT ACTIVITIES: AGR./FOR.
31519	75	325	EDUCATIONAL SERVICES
31520	1748	17689	HOSPITALS
31521	6	11	ADMINISTRATIVE & SUPPORT SVCS
31522	1008	12002	ACCOMMODATION
31523	384	2798	FOOD SVCS & DRINKING PLACES
31524	10	1918	JUSTICE; PUBIC ORDER/SAFETY
31525	858	12697	JUSTICE; PUBIC ORDER/SAFETY
31527	82	2249	ACCOMMODATION
31532	15	35	BLDG MATL & GARDEN EQPMT DLRS
31533	1006	9868	MERCH. WHOLESALERS;NONDUR. GDS
31534	1	2	DATA PROCESS'G
31535	225	3760	FABRICATED METAL PRODUCT MFG
31537	327	2564	EDUCATIONAL SERVICES
31539	467	4410	APPAREL MANUFACTURING
31542	73	533	SPECIAL TRADE CONTRACTORS
31543	66	151	JUSTICE; PUBIC ORDER/SAFETY
31544	21	23	RELIG.; GRANT; CIVIC; PROF ORG
31545	646	6618	PAPER MANUFACTURING
31546	173	1163	EDUCATIONAL SERVICES
31547	41	9816	NAT'L SECURITY & INT'L AFFAIRS
31548	731	5918	FOOD SVCS & DRINKING PLACES
31549	47	214	ADMINISTRATIVE & SUPPORT SVCS
31550	25	141	EDUCATIONAL SERVICES
31551	20	63	TRUCK TRANSPORTATION
31552	19	213	BROADCASTING
31553	244	1446	EDUCATIONAL SERVICES
31554	129	1129	FURN. & HOME FURNISHGS STORES
31555	48	200	EDUCATIONAL SERVICES
31556	5	13	WOOD PRODUCT MANUFACTURING
31557	109	582	SPECIAL TRADE CONTRACTORS
31558	736	4846	EDUCATIONAL SERVICES
31560	58	320	FURNITURE & RELATED PROD. MFG
31561	14	1348	ACCOMMODATION
31562	32	113	EDUCATIONAL SERVICES
31563	29	158	MERCH. WHOLESALERS;DURABLE GDS
31564	6	12	FOOD AND BEVERAGE STORES
31565	46	152	AMUSEMENT; GAMBLING;& RECREAT.
31566	81	402	EDUCATIONAL SERVICES
31567	11	79	EDUCATIONAL SERVICES
31568	16	51	SPECIAL TRADE CONTRACTORS
31569	197	1731	EXEC.; LEGIS.; & OTHER SUPPORT
31598	5	15	SOCIAL ASSISTANCE
31599	1	357	JUSTICE; PUBIC ORDER/SAFETY
31601	1960	24180	FOOD SVCS & DRINKING PLACES
31602	1416	15196	HOSPITALS
31603	6	31	SOCIAL ASSISTANCE
31604	6	9	ADMINISTRATIVE & SUPPORT SVCS
31605	291	1858	AMBULATORY HEALTH CARE SVCS
31606	97	349	WAREHOUSING AND STORAGE
31620	448	3931	FOOD SVCS & DRINKING PLACES
31622	42	346	WOOD PRODUCT MANUFACTURING
31623	3	6	RELIG.; GRANT; CIVIC; PROF ORG
31624	7	88	GASOLINE STATIONS
31625	7	22	CROP PRODUCTION
31626	63	146	FOOD MANUFACTURING
31627	11	179	MERCH. WHOLESALERS;NONDUR. GDS
31629	18	50	MERCH. WHOLESALERS;DURABLE GDS
31630	7	32	CONSTRUCTION OF BUILDINGS
31631	21	71	MUSEUMS; HIST. SITES;& SIMILAR
31632	186	1191	EDUCATIONAL SERVICES
31634	213	2411	FABRICATED METAL PRODUCT MFG
31635	182	1399	EDUCATIONAL SERVICES
31636	344	3304	PAPER MANUFACTURING
31637	75	198	ADMIN. OF ECONOMIC PROGRAMS
31638	32	141	EDUCATIONAL SERVICES
31639	379	3716	TEXTILE MILLS
31641	22	49	MERCH. WHOLESALERS;DURABLE GDS
31642	167	868	EDUCATIONAL SERVICES
31643	339	2608	NURSING & RESID. CARE FACILIT.
31645	54	176	FOOD SVCS & DRINKING PLACES
31647	57	465	EDUCATIONAL SERVICES
31648	36	189	EDUCATIONAL SERVICES
31649	10	18	FABRICATED METAL PRODUCT MFG
31650	75	1019	WOOD PRODUCT MANUFACTURING
31698	6	1613	EDUCATIONAL SERVICES
31699	36	401	HOSPITALS
31701	1758	22077	HOSPITALS
31702	4	48	ADMINISTRATIVE & SUPPORT SVCS
31703	2	22	ADMINISTRATIVE & SUPPORT SVCS
31704	19	147	MISCELLANEOUS STORE RETAILERS
31705	890	13188	MOTOR VEHICLE & PARTS DEALERS
31706	1	1	MISCELLANEOUS STORE RETAILERS
31707	1588	16748	FOOD SVCS & DRINKING PLACES
31708	15	22	PROF.; SCIENTIFIC; & TECH SVCS
31709	825	8071	EDUCATIONAL SERVICES
31711	20	60	EXEC.; LEGIS.; & OTHER SUPPORT
31712	22	221	BLDG MATL & GARDEN EQPMT DLRS
31714	279	3055	ADMINISTRATIVE & SUPPORT SVCS
31716	47	260	EDUCATIONAL SERVICES
31719	262	3613	MERCH. WHOLESALERS;DURABLE GDS
31720	16	59	JUSTICE; PUBIC ORDER/SAFETY
31721	269	2653	MERCH. WHOLESALERS;NONDUR. GDS
31722	15	22	MACHINERY MANUFACTURING
31727	4	10	SUPPORT ACT. FOR TRANSPORT.
31730	435	6144	FOOD MANUFACTURING
31733	28	126	EDUCATIONAL SERVICES
31735	23	181	MERCH. WHOLESALERS;DURABLE GDS
31738	53	1419	MERCH. WHOLESALERS;DURABLE GDS
31739	1	0	JUSTICE; PUBIC ORDER/SAFETY
31743	17	47	ANIMAL PRODUCTION
31744	81	485	SECURITIES/COMMODITY CONTRACTS
31747	12	57	NONSTORE RETAILERS
31749	32	182	MACHINERY MANUFACTURING
31750	698	8743	MERCH. WHOLESALERS;DURABLE GDS
31753	17	86	EDUCATIONAL SERVICES
31756	10	62	EDUCATIONAL SERVICES
31757	333	2454	EDUCATIONAL SERVICES
31760	6	27	BLDG MATL & GARDEN EQPMT DLRS
31763	578	4841	EDUCATIONAL SERVICES
31764	53	149	TELECOMMUNICATIONS
31765	58	121	SUPPORT ACTIVITIES: AGR./FOR.
31768	989	10737	CLOTHING & CLOTH'G ACC. STORES
31769	2	3	POSTAL SERVICE
31771	75	1493	MERCH. WHOLESALERS;NONDUR. GDS
31772	15	39	PERSONAL AND LAUNDRY SERVICES
31773	63	951	CHEMICAL MANUFACTURING
31774	236	2411	EDUCATIONAL SERVICES
31775	74	750	MERCH. WHOLESALERS;NONDUR. GDS
31776	9	310	SUPPORT ACT. FOR TRANSPORT.
31778	48	113	SPECIAL TRADE CONTRACTORS
31779	239	2025	JUSTICE; PUBIC ORDER/SAFETY
31780	67	436	NURSING & RESID. CARE FACILIT.
31781	31	82	FOOD SVCS & DRINKING PLACES
31782	3	1	GASOLINE STATIONS
31783	16	126	AMUSEMENT; GAMBLING;& RECREAT.
31784	17	60	MERCH. WHOLESALERS;NONDUR. GDS
31787	31	160	FOOD AND BEVERAGE STORES
31788	291	5460	FOOD MANUFACTURING
31789	28	79	PLASTICS & RUBBER PRODUCTS MFG
31790	49	202	MERCH. WHOLESALERS;DURABLE GDS
31791	444	3008	EDUCATIONAL SERVICES
31792	1471	19318	HOSPITALS
31793	312	5736	APPAREL MANUFACTURING
31794	1495	15718	MERCH. WHOLESALERS;DURABLE GDS
31795	40	306	CROP PRODUCTION
31796	41	101	MERCH. WHOLESALERS;NONDUR. GDS
31798	14	27	CONSTRUCTION OF BUILDINGS
31799	8	18	SOCIAL ASSISTANCE
31801	22	51	JUSTICE; PUBIC ORDER/SAFETY
31803	170	1546	MERCH. WHOLESALERS;NONDUR. GDS
31804	108	313	EDUCATIONAL SERVICES
31805	88	440	EDUCATIONAL SERVICES
31806	130	1201	BLDG MATL & GARDEN EQPMT DLRS
31807	37	248	EDUCATIONAL SERVICES
31808	143	919	HEAVY & CIVIL ENG. CONSTRUCT'N
31810	22	26	RELIG.; GRANT; CIVIC; PROF ORG
31811	181	1114	EDUCATIONAL SERVICES
31812	11	64	NONMETALLIC MINERAL PROD. MFG
31814	2	2	PAPER MANUFACTURING
31815	88	392	EDUCATIONAL SERVICES
31816	264	1757	EDUCATIONAL SERVICES
31820	126	2247	TRANSPORTATION EQUIPMENT MFG
31821	7	53	REPAIR AND MAINTENANCE
31822	196	2208	ACCOMMODATION
31823	17	1319	FOOD MANUFACTURING
31824	55	422	BLDG MATL & GARDEN EQPMT DLRS
31825	70	262	NURSING & RESID. CARE FACILIT.

BUSINESS DATA

ZIP CODE	2009 Total Firms	2009 Total Employees	TOP INDUSTRY RANKED on 2009 EMPLOYMENT
31826	31	103	FABRICATED METAL PRODUCT MFG
31827	88	743	ADMIN. HUMAN RESOURCE PROGRAMS
31829	12	34	RELIG.; GRANT; CIVIC; PROF ORG
31830	99	611	NURSING & RESID. CARE FACILIT.
31831	101	317	NURSING & RESID. CARE FACILIT.
31832	6	30	FOOD AND BEVERAGE STORES
31833	307	5313	ADMINISTRATIVE & SUPPORT SVCS
31836	25	36	EXEC.; LEGIS.; & OTHER SUPPORT
31901	1509	29107	EXEC.; LEGIS.; & OTHER SUPPORT
31902	5	5	MOTOR VEHICLE & PARTS DEALERS
31903	578	3687	EDUCATIONAL SERVICES
31904	1987	22119	AMBULATORY HEALTH CARE SVCS
31905	189	36144	NAT'L SECURITY & INT'L AFFAIRS
31906	761	6164	EDUCATIONAL SERVICES
31907	1270	14656	EDUCATIONAL SERVICES
31908	14	39	ADMINISTRATIVE & SUPPORT SVCS
31909	1240	12981	FOOD SVCS & DRINKING PLACES
31914	2	1	AIR TRANSPORTATION
31917	7	57	CONSTRUCTION OF BUILDINGS
31995	1	30	ACCOMMODATION
31999	5	5711	UNCLASSIFIED ESTABLISHMENTS
32003	553	6043	FOOD SVCS & DRINKING PLACES
32004	15	50	SPECIAL TRADE CONTRACTORS
32006	10	21	MERCH. WHOLESALERS;DURABLE GDS
32007	15	192	SPECIAL TRADE CONTRACTORS
32008	200	1023	BLDG MATL & GARDEN EQPMT DLRS
32009	28	97	EDUCATIONAL SERVICES
32011	358	2112	FOOD SVCS & DRINKING PLACES
32013	5	8	FURNITURE & RELATED PROD. MFG
32024	278	1271	EDUCATIONAL SERVICES
32025	822	10416	HOSPITALS
32026	3	0	JUSTICE; PUBIC ORDER/SAFETY
32030	3	4	BLDG MATL & GARDEN EQPMT DLRS
32033	89	808	MERCH. WHOLESALERS;NONDUR. GDS
32034	1534	11717	AMUSEMENT; GAMBLING;& RECREAT.
32035	19	183	REAL ESTATE
32038	132	611	EDUCATIONAL SERVICES
32040	121	607	EDUCATIONAL SERVICES
32041	11	43	BLDG MATL & GARDEN EQPMT DLRS
32042	3	2	POSTAL SERVICE
32043	678	8832	JUSTICE; PUBIC ORDER/SAFETY
32044	37	143	EDUCATIONAL SERVICES
32046	233	1338	HEAVY & CIVIL ENG. CONSTRUCT'N
32050	8	13	PROF.; SCIENTIFIC; & TECH SVCS
32052	242	2142	JUSTICE; PUBIC ORDER/SAFETY
32053	72	453	PERFORM'G ARTS; SPEC. SPORTS
32054	261	4970	JUSTICE; PUBIC ORDER/SAFETY
32055	1157	11157	HOSPITALS
32056	17	60	SPECIAL TRADE CONTRACTORS
32058	77	527	JUSTICE; PUBIC ORDER/SAFETY
32059	63	268	ANIMAL PRODUCTION
32060	384	4650	FOOD MANUFACTURING
32061	3	4	REAL ESTATE
32062	31	179	BLDG MATL & GARDEN EQPMT DLRS
32063	533	8008	HOSPITALS
32064	539	4935	EXEC.; LEGIS.; & OTHER SUPPORT
32065	683	4098	EDUCATIONAL SERVICES
32066	217	1955	JUSTICE; PUBIC ORDER/SAFETY
32067	19	43	SOCIAL ASSISTANCE
32068	800	7251	FURN. & HOME FURNISHGS STORES
32071	54	148	MERCH. WHOLESALERS;DURABLE GDS
32072	11	53	SUPPORT ACTIVITIES: AGR./FOR.
32073	1962	20439	FOOD SVCS & DRINKING PLACES
32079	30	270	NURSING & RESID. CARE FACILIT.
32080	934	5025	FOOD SVCS & DRINKING PLACES
32081	79	649	EDUCATIONAL SERVICES
32082	1061	11630	AMUSEMENT; GAMBLING;& RECREAT.
32083	25	1237	JUSTICE; PUBIC ORDER/SAFETY
32084	2244	20138	EXEC.; LEGIS.; & OTHER SUPPORT
32085	30	73	ADMINISTRATIVE & SUPPORT SVCS
32086	1232	10367	AMBULATORY HEALTH CARE SVCS
32087	68	875	JUSTICE; PUBIC ORDER/SAFETY
32091	777	6965	JUSTICE; PUBIC ORDER/SAFETY
32092	579	6026	REAL ESTATE
32094	55	186	WOOD PRODUCT MANUFACTURING
32095	299	2305	SPECIAL TRADE CONTRACTORS
32096	98	1486	CHEMICAL MANUFACTURING
32097	490	5176	EXEC.; LEGIS.; & OTHER SUPPORT
32099	3	2	CREDIT INTERMEDIATION & RELATD
32102	114	354	FOOD SVCS & DRINKING PLACES
32105	10	200	MERCH. WHOLESALERS;NONDUR. GDS
32110	792	5228	SPECIAL TRADE CONTRACTORS
32111	2	203	MACHINERY MANUFACTURING
32112	207	1637	BLDG MATL & GARDEN EQPMT DLRS
32113	223	820	EDUCATIONAL SERVICES
32114	2915	38963	HOSPITALS
32115	12	56	SOCIAL ASSISTANCE
32117	1740	15328	AMBULATORY HEALTH CARE SVCS
32118	1241	10666	ACCOMMODATION
32119	1192	7185	ADMINISTRATIVE & SUPPORT SVCS
32120	14	24	PROF.; SCIENTIFIC; & TECH SVCS
32121	4	12	ADMINISTRATIVE & SUPPORT SVCS
32122	3	3	HEAVY & CIVIL ENG. CONSTRUCT'N
32123	1	2	REAL ESTATE
32124	243	4380	JUSTICE; PUBIC ORDER/SAFETY
32125	9	27	SPECIAL TRADE CONTRACTORS
32126	5	6	ADMINISTRATIVE & SUPPORT SVCS
32127	1373	8639	FOOD SVCS & DRINKING PLACES
32128	393	2060	EDUCATIONAL SERVICES
32129	620	5073	EDUCATIONAL SERVICES
32130	162	1278	MISCELLANEOUS MANUFACTURING
32131	180	1098	JUSTICE; PUBIC ORDER/SAFETY
32132	456	2674	SPECIAL TRADE CONTRACTORS
32133	2	2	MERCH. WHOLESALERS;DURABLE GDS
32134	192	694	EDUCATIONAL SERVICES
32135	26	49	SPECIAL TRADE CONTRACTORS
32136	402	2077	MOTOR VEHICLE & PARTS DEALERS
32137	1527	8837	FOOD SVCS & DRINKING PLACES
32138	7	22	AMBULATORY HEALTH CARE SVCS
32139	25	61	JUSTICE; PUBIC ORDER/SAFETY
32140	32	85	EDUCATIONAL SERVICES
32141	396	2008	TRANSPORTATION EQUIPMENT MFG
32142	10	1300	SPORTG GDS;HOBBY;BOOK; & MUSIC
32145	158	697	SOCIAL ASSISTANCE
32147	28	180	MERCH. WHOLESALERS;DURABLE GDS
32148	195	954	EDUCATIONAL SERVICES
32149	1	50	MINING (EXCEPT OIL AND GAS)
32157	3	7	GASOLINE STATIONS
32158	12	17	REPAIR AND MAINTENANCE
32159	1012	10111	FOOD SVCS & DRINKING PLACES
32160	1	2	POSTAL SERVICE
32162	459	5882	NURSING & RESID. CARE FACILIT.
32163	1	0	SPECIAL TRADE CONTRACTORS
32164	566	6369	PROF.; SCIENTIFIC; & TECH SVCS
32168	1628	8693	EXEC.; LEGIS.; & OTHER SUPPORT
32169	516	3006	FOOD SVCS & DRINKING PLACES
32170	24	68	MERCH. WHOLESALERS;DURABLE GDS
32173	11	24	NONMETALLIC MINERAL PROD. MFG
32174	2380	21823	HOSPITALS
32175	17	39	CONSTRUCTION OF BUILDINGS
32176	605	3751	FOOD SVCS & DRINKING PLACES
32177	1416	14551	PAPER MANUFACTURING
32178	23	46	SPECIAL TRADE CONTRACTORS
32179	190	629	SPECIAL TRADE CONTRACTORS
32180	164	1767	MERCH. WHOLESALERS;NONDUR. GDS
32181	72	149	HEAVY & CIVIL ENG. CONSTRUCT'N
32182	29	80	ACCOMMODATION
32183	3	5	PROF.; SCIENTIFIC; & TECH SVCS
32185	3	6	CONSTRUCTION OF BUILDINGS
32187	75	361	EDUCATIONAL SERVICES
32189	74	157	SPECIAL TRADE CONTRACTORS
32190	32	315	MERCH. WHOLESALERS;NONDUR. GDS
32192	12	88	MERCH. WHOLESALERS;DURABLE GDS
32193	64	149	OTHER INFORMATION SERVICES
32195	141	664	SUPPORT ACTIVITIES: AGR./FOR.
32201	3	1	SPECIAL TRADE CONTRACTORS
32202	1468	42839	EXEC.; LEGIS.; & OTHER SUPPORT
32203	12	2017	POSTAL SERVICE
32204	1024	20540	HOSPITALS
32205	1363	9545	FOOD SVCS & DRINKING PLACES
32206	952	12021	MERCH. WHOLESALERS;DURABLE GDS
32207	2859	37636	HOSPITALS
32208	960	6442	EDUCATIONAL SERVICES
32209	888	15612	AMBULATORY HEALTH CARE SVCS
32210	2291	16835	REPAIR AND MAINTENANCE
32211	1373	10417	ADMINISTRATIVE & SUPPORT SVCS
32212	81	977	NAT'L SECURITY & INT'L AFFAIRS
32214	8	2612	HOSPITALS
32216	2635	36623	AMBULATORY HEALTH CARE SVCS
32217	1082	7346	ADMINISTRATIVE & SUPPORT SVCS
32218	1679	21107	FOOD SVCS & DRINKING PLACES
32219	396	5229	MERCH. WHOLESALERS;DURABLE GDS
32220	346	5901	TRUCK TRANSPORTATION
32221	501	3996	EDUCATIONAL SERVICES
32222	163	867	FOOD SVCS & DRINKING PLACES
32223	953	6120	FOOD SVCS & DRINKING PLACES
32224	856	19432	HOSPITALS
32225	1807	17834	FOOD SVCS & DRINKING PLACES
32226	453	7044	MERCH. WHOLESALERS;DURABLE GDS
32227	4	18	REAL ESTATE
32228	32	356	UNCLASSIFIED ESTABLISHMENTS
32229	3	74	POSTAL SERVICE
32232	1	1	PROF.; SCIENTIFIC; & TECH SVCS
32233	710	8953	POSTAL SERVICE
32234	155	1982	MISCELLANEOUS MANUFACTURING
32235	14	190	SPECIAL TRADE CONTRACTORS
32236	15	34	WASTE MANAGMT & REMEDIAT'N SVC
32237	2	4	BLDG MATL & GARDEN EQPMT DLRS
32238	8	12	SPECIAL TRADE CONTRACTORS
32239	10	44	ADMINISTRATIVE & SUPPORT SVCS
32240	19	82	SPECIAL TRADE CONTRACTORS
32241	39	119	HEAVY & CIVIL ENG. CONSTRUCT'N
32244	800	8503	MOTOR VEHICLE & PARTS DEALERS
32245	19	37	ELECTRONICS & APPLIANCE STORES
32246	1449	18518	SECURITIES/COMMODITY CONTRACTS
32247	8	12	RELIG.; GRANT; CIVIC; PROF ORG
32250	1774	13523	FOOD SVCS & DRINKING PLACES
32254	1395	24587	FOOD AND BEVERAGE STORES
32255	7	14	RELIG.; GRANT; CIVIC; PROF ORG
32256	3008	50937	PROF.; SCIENTIFIC; & TECH SVCS
32257	1710	13175	FOOD SVCS & DRINKING PLACES
32258	480	10785	CREDIT INTERMEDIATION & RELATD
32259	790	5874	FURN. & HOME FURNISHGS STORES
32260	18	29	INSURANCE CARRIERS & RELATED
32266	290	2120	EDUCATIONAL SERVICES
32277	452	3557	AMBULATORY HEALTH CARE SVCS
32301	2907	28307	PROF.; SCIENTIFIC; & TECH SVCS
32302	13	26	UNCLASSIFIED ESTABLISHMENTS
32303	2456	21366	PROF.; SCIENTIFIC; & TECH SVCS
32304	1141	14903	FOOD SVCS & DRINKING PLACES
32305	547	2912	SPECIAL TRADE CONTRACTORS
32306	30	5734	EDUCATIONAL SERVICES
32307	12	3723	EDUCATIONAL SERVICES
32308	2021	26257	HOSPITALS
32309	885	5604	FOOD SVCS & DRINKING PLACES
32310	482	4864	SUPPORT ACT. FOR TRANSPORT.
32311	324	2915	GENERAL MERCHANDISE STORES
32312	854	6314	EDUCATIONAL SERVICES
32314	12	21	PROF.; SCIENTIFIC; & TECH SVCS
32315	9	23	SPECIAL TRADE CONTRACTORS
32316	4	8	ADMINISTRATIVE & SUPPORT SVCS
32317	246	1633	PROF.; SCIENTIFIC; & TECH SVCS
32318	15	64	ADMINISTRATIVE & SUPPORT SVCS
32320	381	1798	FOOD SVCS & DRINKING PLACES
32321	208	1755	EDUCATIONAL SERVICES
32322	241	786	REAL ESTATE
32323	7	7	UTILITIES
32324	179	5826	HOSPITALS
32326	4	7	JUSTICE; PUBIC ORDER/SAFETY
32327	741	5188	JUSTICE; PUBIC ORDER/SAFETY
32328	296	1376	JUSTICE; PUBIC ORDER/SAFETY
32329	3	3	CLOTHING & CLOTH'G ACC. STORES
32330	13	26	GASOLINE STATIONS
32331	109	603	SOCIAL ASSISTANCE
32332	46	153	EDUCATIONAL SERVICES
32333	328	2563	MERCH. WHOLESALERS;DURABLE GDS
32334	70	1225	ACCOMMODATION
32336	55	221	ACCOMMODATION
32337	5	21	FOOD AND BEVERAGE STORES
32340	514	4467	FOOD MANUFACTURING
32341	2	5	EXEC.; LEGIS.; & OTHER SUPPORT
32343	104	2015	PROF.; SCIENTIFIC; & TECH SVCS
32344	528	2805	JUSTICE; PUBIC ORDER/SAFETY
32346	104	388	FOOD SVCS & DRINKING PLACES
32347	455	3098	EDUCATIONAL SERVICES
32348	336	4581	MISCELLANEOUS MANUFACTURING
32350	17	36	EDUCATIONAL SERVICES
32351	783	10304	JUSTICE; PUBIC ORDER/SAFETY
32352	80	445	MINING (EXCEPT OIL AND GAS)
32353	3	31	JUSTICE; PUBIC ORDER/SAFETY
32355	42	156	PETROLEUM & COAL PRODUCTS MFG
32356	4	2	SUPPORT ACTIVITIES: AGR./FOR.
32357	2	3	FOOD AND BEVERAGE STORES
32358	74	213	PROF.; SCIENTIFIC; & TECH SVCS
32359	74	311	ACCOMMODATION
32360	11	52	UTILITIES
32361	2	19	FOOD AND BEVERAGE STORES
32362	8	19	PROF.; SCIENTIFIC; & TECH SVCS
32399	191	26133	EXEC.; LEGIS.; & OTHER SUPPORT
32401	2065	23906	AMBULATORY HEALTH CARE SVCS
32402	15	20	SPECIAL TRADE CONTRACTORS
32403	146	1981	AMBULATORY HEALTH CARE SVCS
32404	966	8209	TRANSPORTATION EQUIPMENT MFG
32405	2075	23620	AMBULATORY HEALTH CARE SVCS
32406	5	11	SPECIAL TRADE CONTRACTORS
32407	884	8280	FOOD SVCS & DRINKING PLACES
32408	822	6924	FOOD SVCS & DRINKING PLACES
32409	176	1167	EDUCATIONAL SERVICES
32410	13	57	FOOD SVCS & DRINKING PLACES
32411	1	3	PROF.; SCIENTIFIC; & TECH SVCS
32412	3	4	SPECIAL TRADE CONTRACTORS
32413	811	5624	FOOD SVCS & DRINKING PLACES
32417	15	14	CONSTRUCTION OF BUILDINGS
32420	50	181	SPECIAL TRADE CONTRACTORS
32421	90	778	TRUCK TRANSPORTATION
32422	1	2	POSTAL SERVICE
32423	23	48	CROP PRODUCTION
32424	424	2763	JUSTICE; PUBIC ORDER/SAFETY
32425	439	3592	EXEC.; LEGIS.; & OTHER SUPPORT
32426	25	112	JUSTICE; PUBIC ORDER/SAFETY

ZIP CODE	2009 Total Firms	2009 Total Employ-ees	TOP INDUSTRY RANKED on 2009 EMPLOYMENT
32427	21	61	JUSTICE; PUBIC ORDER/SAFETY
32428	551	6499	APPAREL MANUFACTURING
32430	27	107	EDUCATIONAL SERVICES
32431	111	434	EDUCATIONAL SERVICES
32432	2	2	POSTAL SERVICE
32433	477	3417	JUSTICE; PUBIC ORDER/SAFETY
32434	1	4	FOOD AND BEVERAGE STORES
32435	307	4473	HEAVY & CIVIL ENG. CONSTRUCT'N
32437	18	136	PERFORM'G ARTS; SPEC. SPORTS
32438	42	102	NURSING & RESID. CARE FACILIT.
32439	307	1966	SPECIAL TRADE CONTRACTORS
32440	214	1587	EDUCATIONAL SERVICES
32442	72	211	EDUCATIONAL SERVICES
32443	43	92	FOOD AND BEVERAGE STORES
32444	584	5625	CREDIT INTERMEDIATION & RELATD
32445	46	240	EXEC.; LEGIS.; & OTHER SUPPORT
32446	726	6840	EDUCATIONAL SERVICES
32447	4	3	RENTAL AND LEASING SERVICES
32448	379	3587	GENERAL MERCHANDISE STORES
32449	8	21	MERCH. WHOLESALERS;NONDUR. GDS
32452	4	5	POSTAL SERVICE
32455	90	413	EDUCATIONAL SERVICES
32456	726	3519	EXEC.; LEGIS.; & OTHER SUPPORT
32457	1	1	SPECIAL TRADE CONTRACTORS
32459	1070	5957	FOOD SVCS & DRINKING PLACES
32460	107	1031	JUSTICE; PUBIC ORDER/SAFETY
32461	9	56	FOOD AND BEVERAGE STORES
32462	74	282	EDUCATIONAL SERVICES
32463	7	14	FOOD AND BEVERAGE STORES
32464	64	155	SOCIAL ASSISTANCE
32465	226	1563	JUSTICE; PUBIC ORDER/SAFETY
32466	110	446	EDUCATIONAL SERVICES
32501	982	19300	HOSPITALS
32502	1271	14747	PROF.; SCIENTIFIC; & TECH SVCS
32503	1466	14518	HOSPITALS
32504	1565	32541	HOSPITALS
32505	1590	14872	MOTOR VEHICLE & PARTS DEALERS
32506	873	6311	GENERAL MERCHANDISE STORES
32507	1004	6090	FOOD SVCS & DRINKING PLACES
32508	151	17699	NAT'L SECURITY & INT'L AFFAIRS
32509	18	250	JUSTICE; PUBIC ORDER/SAFETY
32511	16	4142	NAT'L SECURITY & INT'L AFFAIRS
32512	8	117	AMBULATORY HEALTH CARE SVCS
32513	5	11	SPECIAL TRADE CONTRACTORS
32514	1201	22274	EDUCATIONAL SERVICES
32516	8	8	SPECIAL TRADE CONTRACTORS
32520	1	400	UTILITIES
32522	1	2	SUPPORT ACTIVITIES: AGR./FOR.
32523	1	0	PROF.; SCIENTIFIC; & TECH SVCS
32524	13	22	EDUCATIONAL SERVICES
32526	703	4962	FOOD SVCS & DRINKING PLACES
32530	6	9	RELIG.; GRANT; CIVIC; PROF ORG
32531	148	556	EDUCATIONAL SERVICES
32533	562	8331	TEXTILE PRODUCT MILLS
32534	789	6353	GENERAL MERCHANDISE STORES
32535	133	1218	JUSTICE; PUBIC ORDER/SAFETY
32536	1011	7683	FOOD SVCS & DRINKING PLACES
32537	2	2	SPECIAL TRADE CONTRACTORS
32538	20	230	JUSTICE; PUBIC ORDER/SAFETY
32539	417	5947	JUSTICE; PUBIC ORDER/SAFETY
32540	26	141	FOOD SVCS & DRINKING PLACES
32541	1894	16045	FOOD SVCS & DRINKING PLACES
32542	110	3252	HOSPITALS
32544	46	279	FOOD AND BEVERAGE STORES
32547	1550	13338	HOSPITALS
32548	1908	19562	EXEC.; LEGIS.; & OTHER SUPPORT
32549	20	42	SPECIAL TRADE CONTRACTORS
32550	829	10147	AMUSEMENT; GAMBLING;& RECREAT.
32560	6	19	PERFORM'G ARTS; SPEC. SPORTS
32561	655	5200	FOOD SVCS & DRINKING PLACES
32562	14	54	AMBULATORY HEALTH CARE SVCS
32563	914	5344	FOOD SVCS & DRINKING PLACES
32564	53	179	MERCH. WHOLESALERS;DURABLE GDS
32565	214	1414	EDUCATIONAL SERVICES
32566	921	4435	FOOD SVCS & DRINKING PLACES
32567	111	292	EDUCATIONAL SERVICES
32568	84	417	PAPER MANUFACTURING
32569	525	3498	GENERAL MERCHANDISE STORES
32570	1089	8723	FOOD SVCS & DRINKING PLACES
32571	937	6504	FOOD SVCS & DRINKING PLACES
32572	9	25	ADMINISTRATIVE & SUPPORT SVCS
32577	130	348	CONSTRUCTION OF BUILDINGS
32578	1047	8619	EDUCATIONAL SERVICES
32579	343	2406	JUSTICE; PUBIC ORDER/SAFETY
32580	161	1413	ELECTRONICS & APPLIANCE STORES
32583	591	5080	JUSTICE; PUBIC ORDER/SAFETY
32588	14	24	ADMINISTRATIVE & SUPPORT SVCS
32591	7	19	MOTION PICT. & SOUND RECORDING
32601	1927	18609	JUSTICE; PUBIC ORDER/SAFETY
32602	16	44	PROF.; SCIENTIFIC; & TECH SVCS
32603	124	1274	FOOD SVCS & DRINKING PLACES
32604	10	27	RELIG.; GRANT; CIVIC; PROF ORG
32605	868	10732	AMBULATORY HEALTH CARE SVCS
32606	1066	10564	AMBULATORY HEALTH CARE SVCS
32607	850	7789	AMBULATORY HEALTH CARE SVCS
32608	1189	19823	FOOD SVCS & DRINKING PLACES
32609	1208	13368	EXEC.; LEGIS.; & OTHER SUPPORT
32610	77	44425	EDUCATIONAL SERVICES
32611	41	2469	PERFORM'G ARTS; SPEC. SPORTS
32614	12	29	CONSTRUCTION OF BUILDINGS
32615	587	6021	GENERAL MERCHANDISE STORES
32616	13	40	ADMINISTRATIVE & SUPPORT SVCS
32617	127	357	EDUCATIONAL SERVICES
32618	150	598	FABRICATED METAL PRODUCT MFG
32619	110	556	EDUCATIONAL SERVICES
32621	198	1823	JUSTICE; PUBIC ORDER/SAFETY
32622	39	169	SPECIAL TRADE CONTRACTORS
32625	124	446	FOOD SVCS & DRINKING PLACES
32626	505	3306	GENERAL MERCHANDISE STORES
32627	8	22	ADMINISTRATIVE & SUPPORT SVCS
32628	205	2143	JUSTICE; PUBIC ORDER/SAFETY
32631	9	40	ADMINISTRATIVE & SUPPORT SVCS
32633	2	2	POSTAL SERVICE
32634	9	12	MISCELLANEOUS STORE RETAILERS
32635	14	55	ADMINISTRATIVE & SUPPORT SVCS
32639	10	15	MERCH. WHOLESALERS;DURABLE GDS
32640	253	2078	MERCH. WHOLESALERS;DURABLE GDS
32641	263	4546	EDUCATIONAL SERVICES
32643	435	2199	FOOD SVCS & DRINKING PLACES
32644	2	1	RELIG.; GRANT; CIVIC; PROF ORG
32648	18	53	BLDG MATL & GARDEN EQPMT DLRS
32653	469	6964	MERCH. WHOLESALERS;DURABLE GDS
32654	1	2	PERSONAL AND LAUNDRY SERVICES
32655	9	12	SPECIAL TRADE CONTRACTORS
32656	343	2471	EDUCATIONAL SERVICES
32658	18	57	MOTOR VEHICLE & PARTS DEALERS
32662	8	2	SUPPORT ACT. FOR TRANSPORT.
32663	12	19	SPECIAL TRADE CONTRACTORS
32664	63	79	CROP PRODUCTION
32666	180	715	ACCOMMODATION
32667	146	723	MUSEUMS; HIST. SITES;& SIMILAR
32668	118	345	RELIG.; GRANT; CIVIC; PROF ORG
32669	466	3192	PROF.; SCIENTIFIC; & TECH SVCS
32680	164	534	EDUCATIONAL SERVICES
32681	27	182	MERCH. WHOLESALERS;NONDUR. GDS
32683	12	44	SOCIAL ASSISTANCE
32686	162	1272	MERCH. WHOLESALERS;NONDUR. GDS
32692	22	79	FOOD SVCS & DRINKING PLACES
32693	362	2485	JUSTICE; PUBIC ORDER/SAFETY
32694	89	284	FOOD SVCS & DRINKING PLACES
32696	444	2796	TRANSPORTATION EQUIPMENT MFG
32697	11	145	TRUCK TRANSPORTATION
32701	1932	15057	AMBULATORY HEALTH CARE SVCS
32702	77	406	NURSING & RESID. CARE FACILIT.
32703	2290	19674	MERCH. WHOLESALERS;DURABLE GDS
32704	37	135	SPECIAL TRADE CONTRACTORS
32706	16	50	PERSONAL AND LAUNDRY SERVICES
32707	1788	11750	PROF.; SCIENTIFIC; & TECH SVCS
32708	1275	8344	SPECIAL TRADE CONTRACTORS
32709	67	450	MERCH. WHOLESALERS;NONDUR. GDS
32710	4	15	SPECIAL TRADE CONTRACTORS
32712	976	5928	EDUCATIONAL SERVICES
32713	699	3455	SPECIAL TRADE CONTRACTORS
32714	2505	22120	FOOD AND BEVERAGE STORES
32715	12	25	ADMINISTRATIVE & SUPPORT SVCS
32716	24	45	MERCH. WHOLESALERS;DURABLE GDS
32718	12	60	MERCH. WHOLESALERS;DURABLE GDS
32719	15	49	CONSTRUCTION OF BUILDINGS
32720	2030	16652	EXEC.; LEGIS.; & OTHER SUPPORT
32721	17	34	ADMINISTRATIVE & SUPPORT SVCS
32722	1	1	EDUCATIONAL SERVICES
32724	1055	10255	EDUCATIONAL SERVICES
32725	1118	6699	EDUCATIONAL SERVICES
32726	1226	7676	FOOD SVCS & DRINKING PLACES
32727	17	20	CONSTRUCTION OF BUILDINGS
32728	10	52	SPECIAL TRADE CONTRACTORS
32730	369	2178	FOOD SVCS & DRINKING PLACES
32732	179	698	SPECIAL TRADE CONTRACTORS
32733	27	84	SPECIAL TRADE CONTRACTORS
32735	55	134	MERCH. WHOLESALERS;NONDUR. GDS
32736	288	1616	MERCH. WHOLESALERS;NONDUR. GDS
32738	564	2592	SPECIAL TRADE CONTRACTORS
32739	12	34	ADMINISTRATIVE & SUPPORT SVCS
32744	151	422	EDUCATIONAL SERVICES
32746	1997	28210	PROF.; SCIENTIFIC; & TECH SVCS
32747	15	34	ADMINISTRATIVE & SUPPORT SVCS
32750	3083	22581	SPECIAL TRADE CONTRACTORS
32751	1991	24548	INSURANCE CARRIERS & RELATED
32752	21	32	CONSTRUCTION OF BUILDINGS
32753	6	13	ADMINISTRATIVE & SUPPORT SVCS
32754	238	1088	EDUCATIONAL SERVICES
32756	19	25	CONSTRUCTION OF BUILDINGS
32757	1412	10351	EDUCATIONAL SERVICES
32759	108	284	FABRICATED METAL PRODUCT MFG
32762	33	120	SPECIAL TRADE CONTRACTORS
32763	1411	9573	FOOD SVCS & DRINKING PLACES
32764	153	377	SPECIAL TRADE CONTRACTORS
32765	1967	14860	EDUCATIONAL SERVICES
32766	187	527	EDUCATIONAL SERVICES
32767	47	216	EDUCATIONAL SERVICES
32768	19	130	MERCH. WHOLESALERS;NONDUR. GDS
32771	2573	27858	SPECIAL TRADE CONTRACTORS
32772	7	10	CONSTRUCTION OF BUILDINGS
32773	1132	12353	JUSTICE; PUBIC ORDER/SAFETY
32774	12	27	SPECIAL TRADE CONTRACTORS
32775	13	20	FOOD SVCS & DRINKING PLACES
32776	302	1391	SPECIAL TRADE CONTRACTORS
32777	9	9	MISCELLANEOUS STORE RETAILERS
32778	1189	11879	EXEC.; LEGIS.; & OTHER SUPPORT
32779	1204	6808	PROF.; SCIENTIFIC; & TECH SVCS
32780	1389	13513	JUSTICE; PUBIC ORDER/SAFETY
32781	8	10	SPECIAL TRADE CONTRACTORS
32783	4	8	ADMINISTRATIVE & SUPPORT SVCS
32784	431	1925	EDUCATIONAL SERVICES
32789	3666	24854	PROF.; SCIENTIFIC; & TECH SVCS
32790	36	95	PROF.; SCIENTIFIC; & TECH SVCS
32791	34	73	PROF.; SCIENTIFIC; & TECH SVCS
32792	2775	22964	EDUCATIONAL SERVICES
32793	16	70	MISCELLANEOUS MANUFACTURING
32794	15	32	DATA PROCESS'G
32795	29	80	SPECIAL TRADE CONTRACTORS
32796	681	9280	HOSPITALS
32798	101	901	MERCH. WHOLESALERS;NONDUR. GDS
32799	2	2	CREDIT INTERMEDIATION & RELATD
32801	3487	44940	PROF.; SCIENTIFIC; & TECH SVCS
32802	22	336	SOCIAL ASSISTANCE
32803	2725	42583	HOSPITALS
32804	2044	19090	AMBULATORY HEALTH CARE SVCS
32805	1595	17634	MERCH. WHOLESALERS;DURABLE GDS
32806	1752	38477	HOSPITALS
32807	1774	10861	SPECIAL TRADE CONTRACTORS
32808	1861	18803	SPECIAL TRADE CONTRACTORS
32809	2614	35281	EDUCATIONAL SERVICES
32810	1458	19931	ADMINISTRATIVE & SUPPORT SVCS
32811	1312	15145	ADMINISTRATIVE & SUPPORT SVCS
32812	1731	5235	RENTAL AND LEASING SERVICES
32814	260	1600	PROF.; SCIENTIFIC; & TECH SVCS
32815	11	59	HEAVY & CIVIL ENG. CONSTRUCT'N
32816	31	4627	EDUCATIONAL SERVICES
32817	1035	9385	FOOD SVCS & DRINKING PLACES
32818	788	5919	FOOD SVCS & DRINKING PLACES
32819	3429	53965	ACCOMMODATION
32820	175	1506	SUPPORT ACT. FOR TRANSPORT.
32821	775	19761	ACCOMMODATION
32822	1427	14627	FOOD SVCS & DRINKING PLACES
32824	1056	17723	MERCH. WHOLESALERS;DURABLE GDS
32825	608	4613	EDUCATIONAL SERVICES
32826	533	11182	PROF.; SCIENTIFIC; & TECH SVCS
32827	258	7887	RENTAL AND LEASING SERVICES
32828	784	7235	FOOD SVCS & DRINKING PLACES
32829	167	1286	EDUCATIONAL SERVICES
32830	481	43775	ACCOMMODATION
32831	7	1773	JUSTICE; PUBIC ORDER/SAFETY
32832	164	2277	RELIG.; GRANT; CIVIC; PROF ORG
32833	113	332	MERCH. WHOLESALERS;DURABLE GDS
32835	1005	8121	EDUCATIONAL SERVICES
32836	398	6160	ACCOMMODATION
32837	1515	19861	ACCOMMODATION
32839	1129	12839	FOOD SVCS & DRINKING PLACES
32853	12	14	PROF.; SCIENTIFIC; & TECH SVCS
32854	15	18	PUBLISHING INDUSTRIES
32855	6	11	PROF.; SCIENTIFIC; & TECH SVCS
32856	20	45	PERFORM'G ARTS; SPEC. SPORTS
32857	7	27	SPECIAL TRADE CONTRACTORS
32858	5	9	BLDG MATL & GARDEN EQPMT DLRS
32859	12	14	ADMINISTRATIVE & SUPPORT SVCS
32860	10	122	ADMINISTRATIVE & SUPPORT SVCS
32861	11	36	ADMINISTRATIVE & SUPPORT SVCS
32862	5	2029	POSTAL SERVICE
32867	7	10	MOTOR VEHICLE & PARTS DEALERS
32868	18	55	SOCIAL ASSISTANCE
32869	13	36	TRANSIT & GRND PASS. TRANSPORT
32872	4	6	REAL ESTATE
32877	17	20	SPECIAL TRADE CONTRACTORS
32878	21	50	HEAVY & CIVIL ENG. CONSTRUCT'N
32887	4	2210	PUBLISHING INDUSTRIES
32891	1	1100	PROF.; SCIENTIFIC; & TECH SVCS
32893	3	40	EXEC.; LEGIS.; & OTHER SUPPORT
32899	11	2533	EXEC.; LEGIS.; & OTHER SUPPORT
32901	2093	30412	HOSPITALS

BUSINESS DATA

ZIP CODE	2009 Total Firms	2009 Total Employ-ees	TOP INDUSTRY RANKED on 2009 EMPLOYMENT	ZIP CODE	2009 Total Firms	2009 Total Employ-ees	TOP INDUSTRY RANKED on 2009 EMPLOYMENT	ZIP CODE	2009 Total Firms	2009 Total Employ-ees	TOP INDUSTRY RANKED on 2009 EMPLOYMENT
32902	11	47	CONSTRUCTION OF BUILDINGS	33043	330	1400	ACCOMMODATION	33174	922	5886	PROF.; SCIENTIFIC; & TECH SVCS
32903	447	2344	FOOD SVCS & DRINKING PLACES	33045	9	14	CONSTRUCTION OF BUILDINGS	33175	1412	8675	EDUCATIONAL SERVICES
32904	1513	18703	TRANSPORTATION EQUIPMENT MFG	33050	876	6838	FOOD SVCS & DRINKING PLACES	33176	2538	33901	AMBULATORY HEALTH CARE SVCS
32905	947	11866	COMPUTER & ELECTRONIC PROD MFG	33051	49	167	REAL ESTATE	33177	722	5974	EDUCATIONAL SERVICES
32906	8	16	TRANSIT & GRND PASS. TRANSPORT	33052	10	27	SPECIAL TRADE CONTRACTORS	33178	2525	42326	ADMINISTRATIVE & SUPPORT SVCS
32907	597	5400	FOOD SVCS & DRINKING PLACES	33054	1584	13718	EDUCATIONAL SERVICES	33179	1268	17124	CONSTRUCTION OF BUILDINGS
32908	80	669	EDUCATIONAL SERVICES	33055	450	2683	EDUCATIONAL SERVICES	33180	2219	19658	REAL ESTATE
32909	458	2613	EDUCATIONAL SERVICES	33056	688	5967	EDUCATIONAL SERVICES	33181	1277	13440	MOTION PICT. & SOUND RECORDING
32910	8	16	MERCH. WHOLESALERS;DURABLE GDS	33060	1765	12368	JUSTICE; PUBIC ORDER/SAFETY	33182	138	1129	SUPPORT ACT. FOR TRANSPORT.
32911	5	5	PROF.; SCIENTIFIC; & TECH SVCS	33061	13	26	ADMINISTRATIVE & SUPPORT SVCS	33183	812	6580	EDUCATIONAL SERVICES
32912	10	18	REAL ESTATE	33062	1331	8719	MOTOR VEHICLE & PARTS DEALERS	33184	491	2774	FOOD AND BEVERAGE STORES
32919	5	530	COMPUTER & ELECTRONIC PROD MFG	33063	1846	18640	PROF.; SCIENTIFIC; & TECH SVCS	33185	386	2529	EDUCATIONAL SERVICES
32920	614	6033	PROF.; SCIENTIFIC; & TECH SVCS	33064	2691	25298	MERCH. WHOLESALERS;DURABLE GDS	33186	4426	24664	FOOD SVCS & DRINKING PLACES
32922	1405	9821	EDUCATIONAL SERVICES	33065	2456	20470	PROF.; SCIENTIFIC; & TECH SVCS	33187	329	1994	MERCH. WHOLESALERS;NONDUR. GDS
32923	13	41	RELIG.; GRANT; CIVIC; PROF ORG	33066	192	859	EDUCATIONAL SERVICES	33189	557	4874	GENERAL MERCHANDISE STORES
32924	4	9	SPECIAL TRADE CONTRACTORS	33067	935	6732	GENERAL MERCHANDISE STORES	33190	63	844	AMBULATORY HEALTH CARE SVCS
32925	52	2996	NAT'L SECURITY & INT'L AFFAIRS	33068	815	5257	EDUCATIONAL SERVICES	33193	361	1494	EDUCATIONAL SERVICES
32926	851	6729	SPECIAL TRADE CONTRACTORS	33069	2986	35852	SPECIAL TRADE CONTRACTORS	33194	66	708	ACCOMMODATION
32927	631	4563	FOOD AND BEVERAGE STORES	33070	408	2638	HOSPITALS	33196	662	6518	COMPUTER & ELECTRONIC PROD MFG
32931	939	8052	FOOD SVCS & DRINKING PLACES	33071	1245	11143	FOOD SVCS & DRINKING PLACES	33197	13	28	SPECIAL TRADE CONTRACTORS
32932	10	18	ADMINISTRATIVE & SUPPORT SVCS	33073	1409	14797	MOTOR VEHICLE & PARTS DEALERS	33199	10	1511	EDUCATIONAL SERVICES
32934	573	5253	MERCH. WHOLESALERS;DURABLE GDS	33074	9	15	SECURITIES/COMMODITY CONTRACTS	33222	7	38	GENERAL MERCHANDISE STORES
32935	1964	17353	BROADCASTING	33075	14	36	ADMINISTRATIVE & SUPPORT SVCS	33231	2	3	RELIG.; GRANT; CIVIC; PROF ORG
32936	20	30	SPECIAL TRADE CONTRACTORS	33076	822	6244	EDUCATIONAL SERVICES	33233	9	20	PROF.; SCIENTIFIC; & TECH SVCS
32937	1045	6602	FOOD SVCS & DRINKING PLACES	33077	23	59	NONMETALLIC MINERAL PROD. MFG	33234	4	4	MOTION PICT. & SOUND RECORDING
32940	1195	16054	EXEC.; LEGIS.; & OTHER SUPPORT	33081	8	9	MERCH. WHOLESALERS;DURABLE GDS	33238	1	1	ADMINISTRATIVE & SUPPORT SVCS
32941	16	27	SPECIAL TRADE CONTRACTORS	33082	21	503	POSTAL SERVICE	33239	5	14	PROF.; SCIENTIFIC; & TECH SVCS
32948	135	1024	MERCH. WHOLESALERS;NONDUR. GDS	33083	4	9	PERSONAL AND LAUNDRY SERVICES	33242	2	3	SPECIAL TRADE CONTRACTORS
32949	101	214	MERCH. WHOLESALERS;NONDUR. GDS	33084	5	5	SUPPORT ACTIVITIES: AGR./FOR.	33243	9	44	HEAVY & CIVIL ENG. CONSTRUCT'N
32950	146	939	PROF.; SCIENTIFIC; & TECH SVCS	33090	13	46	SPECIAL TRADE CONTRACTORS	33245	4	18	POSTAL SERVICE
32951	307	1195	FOOD AND BEVERAGE STORES	33092	9	31	SPECIAL TRADE CONTRACTORS	33247	2	8	ADMINISTRATIVE & SUPPORT SVCS
32952	860	8001	FOOD SVCS & DRINKING PLACES	33093	10	40	AMBULATORY HEALTH CARE SVCS	33255	9	18	ADMINISTRATIVE & SUPPORT SVCS
32953	1019	8215	FOOD SVCS & DRINKING PLACES	33097	11	33	PROF.; SCIENTIFIC; & TECH SVCS	33256	30	93	ADMINISTRATIVE & SUPPORT SVCS
32954	19	39	SPECIAL TRADE CONTRACTORS	33101	19	16	PERFORM'G ARTS; SPEC. SPORTS	33257	5	8	ADMINISTRATIVE & SUPPORT SVCS
32955	1283	13769	HOSPITALS	33107	1	40	PROF.; SCIENTIFIC; & TECH SVCS	33261	7	16	ADMINISTRATIVE & SUPPORT SVCS
32956	6	5	CONSTRUCTION OF BUILDINGS	33109	80	609	AMUSEMENT; GAMBLING;& RECREAT.	33265	19	37	MERCH. WHOLESALERS;DURABLE GDS
32957	9	20	RELIG.; GRANT; CIVIC; PROF ORG	33110	7	630	NONSTORE RETAILERS	33266	13	16	SPECIAL TRADE CONTRACTORS
32958	1012	6357	FOOD SVCS & DRINKING PLACES	33111	1	6	CONSTRUCTION OF BUILDINGS	33269	7	11	PROF.; SCIENTIFIC; & TECH SVCS
32959	6	8	SPECIAL TRADE CONTRACTORS	33112	14	330	PROF.; SCIENTIFIC; & TECH SVCS	33280	6	25	PROF.; SCIENTIFIC; & TECH SVCS
32960	2672	25145	AMBULATORY HEALTH CARE SVCS	33114	22	66	SUPPORT ACT. FOR TRANSPORT.	33283	17	46	PERSONAL AND LAUNDRY SERVICES
32961	17	73	CONSTRUCTION OF BUILDINGS	33116	19	100	PROF.; SCIENTIFIC; & TECH SVCS	33296	7	25	MERCH. WHOLESALERS;NONDUR. GDS
32962	766	4294	SPECIAL TRADE CONTRACTORS	33119	1	0	POSTAL SERVICE	33299	15	963	PROF.; SCIENTIFIC; & TECH SVCS
32963	842	6081	REAL ESTATE	33122	2356	19820	MERCH. WHOLESALERS;DURABLE GDS	33301	2576	40393	EXEC.; LEGIS.; & OTHER SUPPORT
32964	12	42	PROF.; SCIENTIFIC; & TECH SVCS	33125	1858	13267	HOSPITALS	33302	15	33	RELIG.; GRANT; CIVIC; PROF ORG
32965	9	26	TRUCK TRANSPORTATION	33126	3235	45753	MERCH. WHOLESALERS;DURABLE GDS	33303	10	61	SPECIAL TRADE CONTRACTORS
32966	696	6637	FOOD SVCS & DRINKING PLACES	33127	1399	10153	EDUCATIONAL SERVICES	33304	1592	11930	PROF.; SCIENTIFIC; & TECH SVCS
32967	637	5632	MERCH. WHOLESALERS;NONDUR. GDS	33128	409	7612	EXEC.; LEGIS.; & OTHER SUPPORT	33305	689	4642	FOOD SVCS & DRINKING PLACES
32968	355	2077	FOOD MANUFACTURING	33129	494	2523	REAL ESTATE	33306	953	5476	REAL ESTATE
32969	5	4	SPECIAL TRADE CONTRACTORS	33130	1398	13885	PROF.; SCIENTIFIC; & TECH SVCS	33307	17	46	SPECIAL TRADE CONTRACTORS
32970	24	642	MERCH. WHOLESALERS;NONDUR. GDS	33131	3534	36356	PROF.; SCIENTIFIC; & TECH SVCS	33308	2229	18148	HOSPITALS
32971	5	5	RELIG.; GRANT; CIVIC; PROF ORG	33132	1507	16406	ADMINISTRATIVE & SUPPORT SVCS	33309	3793	52533	ADMINISTRATIVE & SUPPORT SVCS
32976	203	889	REAL ESTATE	33133	2032	18187	HOSPITALS	33310	20	129	SPECIAL TRADE CONTRACTORS
32978	3	9	ADMINISTRATIVE & SUPPORT SVCS	33134	4125	35330	PROF.; SCIENTIFIC; & TECH SVCS	33311	2900	17910	EDUCATIONAL SERVICES
33001	29	169	ADMIN. ENVIRO. QUALITY PROGRMS	33135	1639	8274	EDUCATIONAL SERVICES	33312	2417	23403	ADMINISTRATIVE & SUPPORT SVCS
33002	1	0	POSTAL SERVICE	33136	543	23706	HOSPITALS	33313	1494	13013	EDUCATIONAL SERVICES
33004	1198	10494	ACCOMMODATION	33137	1419	19876	CONSTRUCTION OF BUILDINGS	33314	1841	16981	HOSPITALS
33008	8	13	WASTE MANAGMT & REMEDIAT'N SVC	33138	1462	8206	EDUCATIONAL SERVICES	33315	1167	14583	SUPPORT ACT. FOR TRANSPORT.
33009	2116	14309	FOOD SVCS & DRINKING PLACES	33139	3676	31353	FOOD SVCS & DRINKING PLACES	33316	2069	28162	HOSPITALS
33010	2081	14544	BROADCASTING	33140	1145	14547	ACCOMMODATION	33317	1658	16037	MOTOR VEHICLE & PARTS DEALERS
33011	4	9	ADMINISTRATIVE & SUPPORT SVCS	33141	1136	6671	PROF.; SCIENTIFIC; & TECH SVCS	33318	11	68	TRANSIT & GRND PASS. TRANSPORT
33012	2824	17202	AMBULATORY HEALTH CARE SVCS	33142	3338	30250	MERCH. WHOLESALERS;DURABLE GDS	33319	1346	9748	EXEC.; LEGIS.; & OTHER SUPPORT
33013	1066	9010	HOSPITALS	33143	1991	17596	HOSPITALS	33320	9	38	NONSTORE RETAILERS
33014	2195	24970	MISCELLANEOUS MANUFACTURING	33144	1885	9778	MOTOR VEHICLE & PARTS DEALERS	33321	1236	14711	MISCELLANEOUS MANUFACTURING
33015	1164	8110	EDUCATIONAL SERVICES	33145	1276	6859	PROF.; SCIENTIFIC; & TECH SVCS	33322	1015	8134	COMPUTER & ELECTRONIC PROD MFG
33016	2835	20423	MERCH. WHOLESALERS;DURABLE GDS	33146	1180	14057	EXEC.; LEGIS.; & OTHER SUPPORT	33323	1219	15212	CLOTHING & CLOTH'G ACC. STORES
33017	14	62	FOOD SVCS & DRINKING PLACES	33147	1406	12910	EDUCATIONAL SERVICES	33324	2094	21823	FOOD SVCS & DRINKING PLACES
33018	978	6565	EDUCATIONAL SERVICES	33149	666	5539	FOOD SVCS & DRINKING PLACES	33325	772	8289	MERCH. WHOLESALERS;NONDUR. GDS
33019	596	3771	ACCOMMODATION	33150	766	6888	HOSPITALS	33326	1355	36594	SPECIAL TRADE CONTRACTORS
33020	2791	21357	ADMINISTRATIVE & SUPPORT SVCS	33151	1	3	POSTAL SERVICE	33327	369	1372	EDUCATIONAL SERVICES
33021	2709	35343	HOSPITALS	33152	25	2165	POSTAL SERVICE	33328	1066	8072	EDUCATIONAL SERVICES
33022	14	474	BLDG MATL & GARDEN EQPMT DLRS	33153	8	18	EDUCATIONAL SERVICES	33329	16	47	HEAVY & CIVIL ENG. CONSTRUCT'N
33023	2307	14006	BROADCASTING	33154	854	7089	REAL ESTATE	33330	624	4376	FOOD AND BEVERAGE STORES
33024	2399	18869	FOOD SVCS & DRINKING PLACES	33155	3299	20806	HOSPITALS	33331	743	13475	AMBULATORY HEALTH CARE SVCS
33025	1021	15226	EDUCATIONAL SERVICES	33156	2236	21799	PROF.; SCIENTIFIC; & TECH SVCS	33332	283	3376	JUSTICE; PUBIC ORDER/SAFETY
33026	1105	9818	FOOD SVCS & DRINKING PLACES	33157	2543	20537	PROF.; SCIENTIFIC; & TECH SVCS	33334	2443	18463	ADMINISTRATIVE & SUPPORT SVCS
33027	1094	14733	INSURANCE CARRIERS & RELATED	33158	123	536	RELIG.; GRANT; CIVIC; PROF ORG	33335	16	54	SUPPORT ACT. FOR TRANSPORT.
33028	475	5718	HOSPITALS	33159	68	1372	NONSTORE RETAILERS	33337	1	4700	ADMINISTRATIVE & SUPPORT SVCS
33029	832	7682	EDUCATIONAL SERVICES	33160	1517	21728	REAL ESTATE	33338	9	11	REPAIR AND MAINTENANCE
33030	1224	11100	EXEC.; LEGIS.; & OTHER SUPPORT	33161	1492	11547	EDUCATIONAL SERVICES	33339	6	4	PROF.; SCIENTIFIC; & TECH SVCS
33031	236	2516	MERCH. WHOLESALERS;NONDUR. GDS	33162	1914	12111	EDUCATIONAL SERVICES	33345	14	98	POSTAL SERVICE
33032	499	3044	EDUCATIONAL SERVICES	33163	4	19	HEAVY & CIVIL ENG. CONSTRUCT'N	33346	4	8	MERCH. WHOLESALERS;NONDUR. GDS
33033	547	4335	EDUCATIONAL SERVICES	33164	5	18	MISCELLANEOUS STORE RETAILERS	33348	4	8	SUPPORT ACT. FOR TRANSPORT.
33034	436	6720	GENERAL MERCHANDISE STORES	33165	1883	10029	EDUCATIONAL SERVICES	33349	3	3	ADMINISTRATIVE & SUPPORT SVCS
33035	66	596	SOCIAL ASSISTANCE	33166	7038	58928	MERCH. WHOLESALERS;DURABLE GDS	33351	2150	17166	AMBULATORY HEALTH CARE SVCS
33036	475	4158	FOOD SVCS & DRINKING PLACES	33167	442	5430	MERCH. WHOLESALERS;NONDUR. GDS	33355	16	46	SPECIAL TRADE CONTRACTORS
33037	930	6770	AMUSEMENT; GAMBLING;& RECREAT.	33168	673	4088	EDUCATIONAL SERVICES	33359	2	2	ADMINISTRATIVE & SUPPORT SVCS
33039	22	338	NAT'L SECURITY & INT'L AFFAIRS	33169	2054	22252	HOSPITALS	33388	129	1039	CLOTHING & CLOTH'G ACC. STORES
33040	2737	23131	FOOD SVCS & DRINKING PLACES	33170	328	3437	MERCH. WHOLESALERS;NONDUR. GDS	33394	96	1434	SECURITIES/COMMODITY CONTRACTS
33041	16	60	ADMIN. OF ECONOMIC PROGRAMS	33172	3603	45237	JUSTICE; PUBIC ORDER/SAFETY	33401	3359	31378	PROF.; SCIENTIFIC; & TECH SVCS
33042	269	985	ACCOMMODATION	33173	1366	15245	JUSTICE; PUBIC ORDER/SAFETY	33402	14	31	ADMINISTRATIVE & SUPPORT SVCS

ZIP CODE	2009 Total Firms	2009 Total Employ-ees	TOP INDUSTRY RANKED on 2009 EMPLOYMENT	ZIP CODE	2009 Total Firms	2009 Total Employ-ees	TOP INDUSTRY RANKED on 2009 EMPLOYMENT	ZIP CODE	2009 Total Firms	2009 Total Employ-ees	TOP INDUSTRY RANKED on 2009 EMPLOYMENT
33403	1120	8105	MOTOR VEHICLE & PARTS DEALERS	33523	550	4105	REAL ESTATE	33679	15	93	MERCH. WHOLESALERS;DURABLE GDS
33404	1820	19435	MERCH. WHOLESALERS;DURABLE GDS	33524	13	299	SPECIAL TRADE CONTRACTORS	33680	2	9	WOOD PRODUCT MANUFACTURING
33405	1308	8517	PUBLISHING INDUSTRIES	33525	711	6334	JUSTICE; PUBIC ORDER/SAFETY	33681	10	22	ADMINISTRATIVE & SUPPORT SVCS
33406	1403	15341	JUSTICE; PUBIC ORDER/SAFETY	33526	10	17	SUPPORT ACT. FOR TRANSPORT.	33682	19	36	ADMINISTRATIVE & SUPPORT SVCS
33407	1991	29566	HOSPITALS	33527	279	2753	MERCH. WHOLESALERS;NONDUR. GDS	33684	17	39	SPECIAL TRADE CONTRACTORS
33408	1617	14719	PROF.; SCIENTIFIC; & TECH SVCS	33530	3	16	RELIG.; GRANT; CIVIC; PROF ORG	33685	17	88	ADMINISTRATIVE & SUPPORT SVCS
33409	2547	23561	ADMINISTRATIVE & SUPPORT SVCS	33534	242	2032	EDUCATIONAL SERVICES	33686	1	2	CONSTRUCTION OF BUILDINGS
33410	2411	27046	HOSPITALS	33537	21	92	EDUCATIONAL SERVICES	33687	14	54	SPECIAL TRADE CONTRACTORS
33411	2418	25402	MERCH. WHOLESALERS;DURABLE GDS	33538	127	500	BLDG MATL & GARDEN EQPMT DLRS	33688	37	108	ADMINISTRATIVE & SUPPORT SVCS
33412	559	2859	AMUSEMENT; GAMBLING;& RECREAT.	33539	19	51	SPECIAL TRADE CONTRACTORS	33689	4	5	SUPPORT ACT. FOR TRANSPORT.
33413	403	4065	SPECIAL TRADE CONTRACTORS	33540	141	680	AMBULATORY HEALTH CARE SVCS	33690	1	0	REPAIR AND MAINTENANCE
33414	2055	14613	FOOD SVCS & DRINKING PLACES	33541	452	4160	HOSPITALS	33694	15	70	PERFORM'G ARTS; SPEC. SPORTS
33415	1254	7146	MOTOR VEHICLE & PARTS DEALERS	33542	765	5808	RELIG.; GRANT; CIVIC; PROF ORG	33701	1815	23474	HOSPITALS
33416	28	1245	RELIG.; GRANT; CIVIC; PROF ORG	33543	316	2756	ACCOMMODATION	33702	1078	12556	BROADCASTING
33417	624	4156	NURSING & RESID. CARE FACILIT.	33544	557	4636	FOOD SVCS & DRINKING PLACES	33703	461	3471	AMBULATORY HEALTH CARE SVCS
33418	934	7668	AMUSEMENT; GAMBLING;& RECREAT.	33545	99	903	EDUCATIONAL SERVICES	33704	622	3947	FOOD SVCS & DRINKING PLACES
33419	7	19	REPAIR AND MAINTENANCE	33547	291	2170	EDUCATIONAL SERVICES	33705	631	7428	HOSPITALS
33420	25	90	SPECIAL TRADE CONTRACTORS	33548	339	1698	FOOD SVCS & DRINKING PLACES	33706	873	8160	ACCOMMODATION
33421	24	72	ADMINISTRATIVE & SUPPORT SVCS	33549	759	5047	SPECIAL TRADE CONTRACTORS	33707	968	7996	NURSING & RESID. CARE FACILIT.
33422	13	30	REPAIR AND MAINTENANCE	33550	7	22	PROF.; SCIENTIFIC; & TECH SVCS	33708	691	4842	FOOD SVCS & DRINKING PLACES
33424	11	31	REAL ESTATE	33556	749	5550	SPECIAL TRADE CONTRACTORS	33709	736	6210	FOOD SVCS & DRINKING PLACES
33425	15	127	ADMINISTRATIVE & SUPPORT SVCS	33558	290	2376	EDUCATIONAL SERVICES	33710	1443	13326	FOOD SVCS & DRINKING PLACES
33426	1988	19226	FOOD SVCS & DRINKING PLACES	33559	293	1891	PROF.; SCIENTIFIC; & TECH SVCS	33711	584	7915	EDUCATIONAL SERVICES
33427	11	36	COMPUTER & ELECTRONIC PROD MFG	33563	1437	16666	FOOD AND BEVERAGE STORES	33712	556	4962	EDUCATIONAL SERVICES
33428	1130	8595	SOCIAL ASSISTANCE	33564	4	45	MERCH. WHOLESALERS;NONDUR. GDS	33713	1318	12771	EXEC.; LEGIS.; & OTHER SUPPORT
33429	22	80	SPECIAL TRADE CONTRACTORS	33565	247	2506	MERCH. WHOLESALERS;NONDUR. GDS	33714	779	10969	SPECIAL TRADE CONTRACTORS
33430	635	12170	JUSTICE; PUBIC ORDER/SAFETY	33566	412	7637	FOOD MANUFACTURING	33715	205	1038	REAL ESTATE
33431	3534	39851	EDUCATIONAL SERVICES	33567	169	1378	EDUCATIONAL SERVICES	33716	569	33603	BROADCASTING
33432	3026	20591	PROF.; SCIENTIFIC; & TECH SVCS	33568	28	75	COURIERS AND MESSENGERS	33729	1	3000	BROADCASTING
33433	1363	12131	NURSING & RESID. CARE FACILIT.	33569	299	2603	FOOD AND BEVERAGE STORES	33730	2	250	POSTAL SERVICE
33434	1034	10038	CLOTHING & CLOTH'G ACC. STORES	33570	482	3453	JUSTICE; PUBIC ORDER/SAFETY	33731	17	100	INSURANCE CARRIERS & RELATED
33435	1309	9643	HOSPITALS	33571	5	14	ADMINISTRATIVE & SUPPORT SVCS	33732	11	29	NONSTORE RETAILERS
33436	870	6570	AMUSEMENT; GAMBLING;& RECREAT.	33572	351	2782	MERCH. WHOLESALERS;NONDUR. GDS	33733	18	51	ADMINISTRATIVE & SUPPORT SVCS
33437	552	3095	AMBULATORY HEALTH CARE SVCS	33573	332	4935	NURSING & RESID. CARE FACILIT.	33734	12	37	ELECTRONICS & APPLIANCE STORES
33438	23	225	EDUCATIONAL SERVICES	33574	13	667	EDUCATIONAL SERVICES	33736	6	20	ADMINISTRATIVE & SUPPORT SVCS
33439	1	250	FOOD MANUFACTURING	33575	4	21	CONSTRUCTION OF BUILDINGS	33737	1	1	ELECTRONICS & APPLIANCE STORES
33440	618	5711	CROP PRODUCTION	33576	169	1101	FOOD SVCS & DRINKING PLACES	33738	8	19	SPECIAL TRADE CONTRACTORS
33441	1841	11628	FOOD SVCS & DRINKING PLACES	33578	736	7784	FOOD SVCS & DRINKING PLACES	33740	1	1	PROF.; SCIENTIFIC; & TECH SVCS
33442	1727	27907	PROF.; SCIENTIFIC; & TECH SVCS	33579	153	1080	MERCH. WHOLESALERS;NONDUR. GDS	33741	2	18	AMUSEMENT; GAMBLING;& RECREAT.
33443	11	52	SPECIAL TRADE CONTRACTORS	33583	14	142	SPECIAL TRADE CONTRACTORS	33742	10	12	ADMINISTRATIVE & SUPPORT SVCS
33444	1218	8395	SPECIAL TRADE CONTRACTORS	33584	595	8177	FURN. & HOME FURNISHGS STORES	33743	30	80	ADMINISTRATIVE & SUPPORT SVCS
33445	1208	11944	PROF.; SCIENTIFIC; & TECH SVCS	33585	61	583	UTILITIES	33744	6	2100	AMBULATORY HEALTH CARE SVCS
33446	576	5647	ADMINISTRATIVE & SUPPORT SVCS	33586	12	573	MISCELLANEOUS STORE RETAILERS	33747	5	7	NONSTORE RETAILERS
33447	2	4	PROF.; SCIENTIFIC; & TECH SVCS	33587	1	1	POSTAL SERVICE	33755	1151	7892	RELIG.; GRANT; CIVIC; PROF ORG
33448	1	6	ELECTRONICS & APPLIANCE STORES	33592	266	2212	SPECIAL TRADE CONTRACTORS	33756	1791	20253	CREDIT INTERMEDIATION & RELATD
33449	281	2231	ADMINISTRATIVE & SUPPORT SVCS	33593	13	64	CROP PRODUCTION	33757	14	107	SPECIAL TRADE CONTRACTORS
33454	19	41	PROF.; SCIENTIFIC; & TECH SVCS	33594	374	2685	FOOD SVCS & DRINKING PLACES	33758	22	128	ADMINISTRATIVE & SUPPORT SVCS
33455	726	4737	FOOD AND BEVERAGE STORES	33595	11	20	ADMINISTRATIVE & SUPPORT SVCS	33759	780	9993	FOOD SVCS & DRINKING PLACES
33458	2832	22275	PROF.; SCIENTIFIC; & TECH SVCS	33596	477	3877	EDUCATIONAL SERVICES	33760	844	15120	MERCH. WHOLESALERS;DURABLE GDS
33459	4	15	CROP PRODUCTION	33597	159	856	PROF.; SCIENTIFIC; & TECH SVCS	33761	1328	11128	FOOD SVCS & DRINKING PLACES
33460	1285	5956	EDUCATIONAL SERVICES	33598	227	1971	CROP PRODUCTION	33762	1257	19748	SPECIAL TRADE CONTRACTORS
33461	1382	11798	EDUCATIONAL SERVICES	33601	25	205	ADMINISTRATIVE & SUPPORT SVCS	33763	482	4425	MOTOR VEHICLE & PARTS DEALERS
33462	1198	11364	HOSPITALS	33602	2510	39556	PROF.; SCIENTIFIC; & TECH SVCS	33764	1021	17956	MISCELLANEOUS MANUFACTURING
33463	1387	9093	EDUCATIONAL SERVICES	33603	730	6130	EDUCATIONAL SERVICES	33765	1419	14879	EXEC.; LEGIS.; & OTHER SUPPORT
33464	5	1000	PUBLISHING INDUSTRIES	33604	1311	6679	EDUCATIONAL SERVICES	33766	15	33	ADMINISTRATIVE & SUPPORT SVCS
33465	11	114	SOCIAL ASSISTANCE	33605	1285	21186	JUSTICE; PUBIC ORDER/SAFETY	33767	513	4927	ACCOMMODATION
33466	11	21	BROADCASTING	33606	1564	22391	HOSPITALS	33770	1033	11812	AMBULATORY HEALTH CARE SVCS
33467	1328	9954	PROF.; SCIENTIFIC; & TECH SVCS	33607	3020	58468	HOSPITALS	33771	1221	12411	FOOD SVCS & DRINKING PLACES
33468	34	66	ADMINISTRATIVE & SUPPORT SVCS	33609	2174	23249	PROF.; SCIENTIFIC; & TECH SVCS	33772	866	8218	NURSING & RESID. CARE FACILIT.
33469	851	3855	FOOD SVCS & DRINKING PLACES	33610	1688	29684	ACCOMMODATION	33773	975	17608	PROF.; SCIENTIFIC; & TECH SVCS
33470	869	5283	HOSPITALS	33611	1027	10773	BROADCASTING	33774	558	5596	AMBULATORY HEALTH CARE SVCS
33471	213	1538	ADMINISTRATIVE & SUPPORT SVCS	33612	2261	45910	HOSPITALS	33775	36	73	PROF.; SCIENTIFIC; & TECH SVCS
33472	348	2935	MERCH. WHOLESALERS;NONDUR. GDS	33613	1030	11268	AMBULATORY HEALTH CARE SVCS	33776	225	1668	EDUCATIONAL SERVICES
33473	44	369	ADMINISTRATIVE & SUPPORT SVCS	33614	2043	22088	ADMINISTRATIVE & SUPPORT SVCS	33777	571	9396	PROF.; SCIENTIFIC; & TECH SVCS
33474	16	30	SPECIAL TRADE CONTRACTORS	33615	954	7168	EDUCATIONAL SERVICES	33778	418	5776	JUSTICE; PUBIC ORDER/SAFETY
33475	14	49	SPECIAL TRADE CONTRACTORS	33616	143	2160	ADMIN. HUMAN RESOURCE PROGRAMS	33779	21	118	ADMINISTRATIVE & SUPPORT SVCS
33476	157	1395	NURSING & RESID. CARE FACILIT.	33617	1241	11316	FOOD SVCS & DRINKING PLACES	33780	19	82	EXEC.; LEGIS.; & OTHER SUPPORT
33477	826	5685	FOOD SVCS & DRINKING PLACES	33618	1910	15648	FOOD SVCS & DRINKING PLACES	33781	1571	21024	NURSING & RESID. CARE FACILIT.
33478	501	4776	TRANSPORTATION EQUIPMENT MFG	33619	2661	40396	MERCH. WHOLESALERS;DURABLE GDS	33782	473	5781	MACHINERY MANUFACTURING
33480	1279	13187	AMUSEMENT; GAMBLING;& RECREAT.	33620	25	14270	EDUCATIONAL SERVICES	33784	4	4	SPECIAL TRADE CONTRACTORS
33481	15	75	PROF.; SCIENTIFIC; & TECH SVCS	33621	49	1106	HOSPITALS	33785	253	1619	FOOD SVCS & DRINKING PLACES
33482	12	47	ADMINISTRATIVE & SUPPORT SVCS	33622	12	133	FOOD SVCS & DRINKING PLACES	33786	16	41	ACCOMMODATION
33483	1736	11692	MOTOR VEHICLE & PARTS DEALERS	33623	14	46	SUPPORT ACT. FOR TRANSPORT.	33801	2133	23357	PROF.; SCIENTIFIC; & TECH SVCS
33484	883	7712	HOSPITALS	33624	837	7122	ADMINISTRATIVE & SUPPORT SVCS	33802	11	32	HEAVY & CIVIL ENG. CONSTRUCT'N
33486	775	8522	HOSPITALS	33625	733	6838	FOOD SVCS & DRINKING PLACES	33803	1350	12925	FOOD SVCS & DRINKING PLACES
33487	1991	28437	PROF.; SCIENTIFIC; & TECH SVCS	33626	795	8465	PROF.; SCIENTIFIC; & TECH SVCS	33804	27	73	ADMINISTRATIVE & SUPPORT SVCS
33488	8	19	ADMINISTRATIVE & SUPPORT SVCS	33629	1114	6759	EDUCATIONAL SERVICES	33805	639	16390	AMBULATORY HEALTH CARE SVCS
33493	87	2655	WHOLESALE ELEC. MRKTS & AGENTS	33630	5	139	POSTAL SERVICE	33806	10	36	ADMINISTRATIVE & SUPPORT SVCS
33496	510	5013	AMUSEMENT; GAMBLING;& RECREAT.	33634	1872	29469	PROF.; SCIENTIFIC; & TECH SVCS	33807	29	74	ADMINISTRATIVE & SUPPORT SVCS
33497	19	33	WASTE MANAGMT & REMEDIAT'N SVC	33635	247	1809	EDUCATIONAL SERVICES	33809	986	11068	FOOD SVCS & DRINKING PLACES
33498	574	2912	EDUCATIONAL SERVICES	33637	469	6690	PROF.; SCIENTIFIC; & TECH SVCS	33810	509	3200	EDUCATIONAL SERVICES
33499	1	100	NONSTORE RETAILERS	33646	20	63	PROF.; SCIENTIFIC; & TECH SVCS	33811	671	9491	INSURANCE CARRIERS & RELATED
33503	4	801	MERCH. WHOLESALERS;NONDUR. GDS	33647	888	10856	EDUCATIONAL SERVICES	33812	153	1008	JUSTICE; PUBIC ORDER/SAFETY
33508	13	24	ADMINISTRATIVE & SUPPORT SVCS	33655	6	0	MISCELLANEOUS STORE RETAILERS	33813	1280	9459	FOOD SVCS & DRINKING PLACES
33509	33	66	ADMINISTRATIVE & SUPPORT SVCS	33660	1	0	COURIERS AND MESSENGERS	33815	588	9021	FOOD MANUFACTURING
33510	495	3824	EDUCATIONAL SERVICES	33672	3	81	SPECIAL TRADE CONTRACTORS	33820	13	92	EDUCATIONAL SERVICES
33511	2599	23856	FOOD SVCS & DRINKING PLACES	33673	3	3	ADMINISTRATIVE & SUPPORT SVCS	33823	895	9975	TRUCK TRANSPORTATION
33513	500	4969	JUSTICE; PUBIC ORDER/SAFETY	33674	4	5	RENTAL AND LEASING SERVICES	33825	741	6402	EDUCATIONAL SERVICES
33514	40	259	FOOD MANUFACTURING	33675	6	6	PROF.; SCIENTIFIC; & TECH SVCS	33826	2	2	ADMINISTRATIVE & SUPPORT SVCS
33521	28	1257	JUSTICE; PUBIC ORDER/SAFETY	33677	6	119	SOCIAL ASSISTANCE	33827	46	223	EDUCATIONAL SERVICES

BUSINESS DATA

ZIP CODE	2009 Total Firms	2009 Total Employ-ees	TOP INDUSTRY RANKED on 2009 EMPLOYMENT	ZIP CODE	2009 Total Firms	2009 Total Employ-ees	TOP INDUSTRY RANKED on 2009 EMPLOYMENT	ZIP CODE	2009 Total Firms	2009 Total Employ-ees	TOP INDUSTRY RANKED on 2009 EMPLOYMENT
33830	1183	22436	JUSTICE; PUBIC ORDER/SAFETY	33952	1355	8514	AMBULATORY HEALTH CARE SVCS	34241	268	1534	AMUSEMENT; GAMBLING;& RECREAT.
33831	9	23	HOSPITALS	33953	396	2293	SPECIAL TRADE CONTRACTORS	34242	412	2254	REAL ESTATE
33834	138	1444	FOOD AND BEVERAGE STORES	33954	388	2475	SPECIAL TRADE CONTRACTORS	34243	1543	19731	TRANSPORTATION EQUIPMENT MFG
33835	10	11	CHEMICAL MANUFACTURING	33955	186	1296	JUSTICE; PUBIC ORDER/SAFETY	34250	14	117	SUPPORT ACT. FOR TRANSPORT.
33836	3	6	SPECIAL TRADE CONTRACTORS	33956	176	806	FOOD AND BEVERAGE STORES	34251	198	616	CROP PRODUCTION
33837	341	3916	AMBULATORY HEALTH CARE SVCS	33957	630	3938	FOOD SVCS & DRINKING PLACES	34264	9	21	BLDG MATL & GARDEN EQPMT DLRS
33838	199	2552	FOOD MANUFACTURING	33960	25	231	BLDG MATL & GARDEN EQPMT DLRS	34265	2	2	SPECIAL TRADE CONTRACTORS
33839	80	651	EDUCATIONAL SERVICES	33965	6	973	EDUCATIONAL SERVICES	34266	947	8714	HOSPITALS
33840	6	120	MERCH. WHOLESALERS;NONDUR. GDS	33966	1005	16971	EXEC.; LEGIS.; & OTHER SUPPORT	34267	5	38	SPECIAL TRADE CONTRACTORS
33841	216	1592	MERCH. WHOLESALERS;NONDUR. GDS	33967	522	3151	SPECIAL TRADE CONTRACTORS	34268	13	1440	SUPPORT ACTIVITIES: AGR./FOR.
33843	230	2262	MERCH. WHOLESALERS;NONDUR. GDS	33970	16	37	ELECTRONICS & APPLIANCE STORES	34269	90	1420	MERCH. WHOLESALERS;DURABLE GDS
33844	864	6891	EDUCATIONAL SERVICES	33971	553	5018	SPECIAL TRADE CONTRACTORS	34270	7	328	MERCH. WHOLESALERS;DURABLE GDS
33845	4	26	SPECIAL TRADE CONTRACTORS	33972	121	251	CONSTRUCTION OF BUILDINGS	34272	5	93	AMUSEMENT; GAMBLING;& RECREAT.
33846	16	55	CONSTRUCTION OF BUILDINGS	33973	65	151	SPECIAL TRADE CONTRACTORS	34274	11	17	PROF.; SCIENTIFIC; & TECH SVCS
33847	6	11	FOOD AND BEVERAGE STORES	33974	64	384	EDUCATIONAL SERVICES	34275	567	5934	PLASTICS & RUBBER PRODUCTS MFG
33848	14	79	HEAVY & CIVIL ENG. CONSTRUCT'N	33975	4	16	CROP PRODUCTION	34276	40	73	MISCELLANEOUS STORE RETAILERS
33849	16	84	MINING (EXCEPT OIL AND GAS)	33976	62	81	SPECIAL TRADE CONTRACTORS	34277	28	49	ADMINISTRATIVE & SUPPORT SVCS
33850	196	1568	EDUCATIONAL SERVICES	33980	568	5474	NURSING & RESID. CARE FACILIT.	34278	3	2	REPAIR AND MAINTENANCE
33851	62	575	SUPPORT ACTIVITIES: AGR./FOR.	33981	159	727	FOOD AND BEVERAGE STORES	34280	10	23	REPAIR AND MAINTENANCE
33852	795	4848	EDUCATIONAL SERVICES	33982	335	3373	EDUCATIONAL SERVICES	34282	11	19	SPECIAL TRADE CONTRACTORS
33853	666	5801	WHOLESALE ELEC. MRKTS & AGENTS	33983	221	1595	GENERAL MERCHANDISE STORES	34284	25	103	PERFORM'G ARTS; SPEC. SPORTS
33854	1	0	CONSTRUCTION OF BUILDINGS	33990	1539	12309	EXEC.; LEGIS.; & OTHER SUPPORT	34285	1572	12654	AMBULATORY HEALTH CARE SVCS
33855	26	69	UTILITIES	33991	550	4672	EDUCATIONAL SERVICES	34286	165	447	SPECIAL TRADE CONTRACTORS
33856	7	12	FOOD SVCS & DRINKING PLACES	33993	282	978	EDUCATIONAL SERVICES	34287	596	3635	FOOD SVCS & DRINKING PLACES
33857	58	356	CROP PRODUCTION	33994	9	9	ANIMAL PRODUCTION	34288	90	625	EDUCATIONAL SERVICES
33858	10	12	GASOLINE STATIONS	34101	37	108	TRANSIT & GRND PASS. TRANSPORT	34289	92	787	MERCH. WHOLESALERS;DURABLE GDS
33859	321	4214	EXEC.; LEGIS.; & OTHER SUPPORT	34102	2475	21088	AMBULATORY HEALTH CARE SVCS	34290	14	31	SPECIAL TRADE CONTRACTORS
33860	499	6633	MERCH. WHOLESALERS;NONDUR. GDS	34103	1413	11894	REAL ESTATE	34291	54	581	EDUCATIONAL SERVICES
33862	8	13	SPECIAL TRADE CONTRACTORS	34104	2154	15738	SPECIAL TRADE CONTRACTORS	34292	458	4708	ADMINISTRATIVE & SUPPORT SVCS
33863	2	7	MISCELLANEOUS STORE RETAILERS	34105	444	5306	AMUSEMENT; GAMBLING;& RECREAT.	34293	959	6039	GENERAL MERCHANDISE STORES
33865	19	99	MERCH. WHOLESALERS;DURABLE GDS	34106	17	58	WASTE MANAGMT & REMEDIAT'N SVC	34295	10	16	ADMINISTRATIVE & SUPPORT SVCS
33867	5	184	ACCOMMODATION	34107	6	12	ADMINISTRATIVE & SUPPORT SVCS	34420	991	5434	SPECIAL TRADE CONTRACTORS
33868	188	1684	JUSTICE; PUBIC ORDER/SAFETY	34108	1090	9567	ACCOMMODATION	34421	26	39	ADMINISTRATIVE & SUPPORT SVCS
33870	1641	14404	FOOD SVCS & DRINKING PLACES	34109	2415	17350	SPECIAL TRADE CONTRACTORS	34423	14	13	PROF.; SCIENTIFIC; & TECH SVCS
33871	5	12	SOCIAL ASSISTANCE	34110	1255	12137	NURSING & RESID. CARE FACILIT.	34428	453	4300	HOSPITALS
33872	243	2806	HOSPITALS	34112	1324	8082	JUSTICE; PUBIC ORDER/SAFETY	34429	889	5554	FOOD SVCS & DRINKING PLACES
33873	574	5054	EDUCATIONAL SERVICES	34113	509	4332	FOOD AND BEVERAGE STORES	34430	9	45	MERCH. WHOLESALERS;DURABLE GDS
33875	236	1593	EXEC.; LEGIS.; & OTHER SUPPORT	34114	506	4475	UNCLASSIFIED ESTABLISHMENTS	34431	179	748	EDUCATIONAL SERVICES
33876	211	1249	FOOD SVCS & DRINKING PLACES	34116	1060	4266	EDUCATIONAL SERVICES	34432	501	2665	GENERAL MERCHANDISE STORES
33877	20	304	FOOD MANUFACTURING	34117	466	2185	SPECIAL TRADE CONTRACTORS	34433	148	464	EDUCATIONAL SERVICES
33880	1621	15144	FOOD SVCS & DRINKING PLACES	34119	841	5331	EDUCATIONAL SERVICES	34434	128	518	EDUCATIONAL SERVICES
33881	1147	14638	HOSPITALS	34120	677	5580	MERCH. WHOLESALERS;NONDUR. GDS	34436	215	647	ACCOMMODATION
33882	7	36	PROF.; SCIENTIFIC; & TECH SVCS	34133	27	52	SPECIAL TRADE CONTRACTORS	34442	442	2400	PROF.; SCIENTIFIC; & TECH SVCS
33883	15	43	HEAVY & CIVIL ENG. CONSTRUCT'N	34134	1253	8852	FOOD SVCS & DRINKING PLACES	34445	12	24	AMUSEMENT; GAMBLING;& RECREAT.
33884	652	4547	NURSING & RESID. CARE FACILIT.	34135	1970	12735	HEAVY & CIVIL ENG. CONSTRUCT'N	34446	442	1539	FOOD SVCS & DRINKING PLACES
33885	4	14	SPECIAL TRADE CONTRACTORS	34136	4	38	COURIERS AND MESSENGERS	34447	17	47	HEALTH & PERSONAL CARE STORES
33888	1	1000	INSURANCE CARRIERS & RELATED	34137	7	36	JUSTICE; PUBIC ORDER/SAFETY	34448	434	3332	MOTOR VEHICLE & PARTS DEALERS
33890	129	817	MERCH. WHOLESALERS;NONDUR. GDS	34138	17	29	MUSEUMS; HIST. SITES;& SIMILAR	34449	125	447	HEAVY & CIVIL ENG. CONSTRUCT'N
33896	135	1916	FOOD SVCS & DRINKING PLACES	34139	87	440	EDUCATIONAL SERVICES	34450	725	4969	FOOD SVCS & DRINKING PLACES
33897	206	1778	ACCOMMODATION	34140	23	130	FOOD SVCS & DRINKING PLACES	34451	17	28	ADMINISTRATIVE & SUPPORT SVCS
33898	251	2960	SUPPORT ACTIVITIES: AGR./FOR.	34141	19	179	MUSEUMS; HIST. SITES;& SIMILAR	34452	308	4584	AMBULATORY HEALTH CARE SVCS
33901	2886	34309	HOSPITALS	34142	668	8395	MERCH. WHOLESALERS;NONDUR. GDS	34453	485	3035	GENERAL MERCHANDISE STORES
33902	14	37	TRANSIT & GRND PASS. TRANSPORT	34143	2	4	ADMINISTRATIVE & SUPPORT SVCS	34460	8	12	ELECTRONICS & APPLIANCE STORES
33903	1244	6998	FOOD SVCS & DRINKING PLACES	34145	1272	7813	REAL ESTATE	34461	519	5649	EDUCATIONAL SERVICES
33904	1986	11361	REAL ESTATE	34146	28	126	SPECIAL TRADE CONTRACTORS	34464	6	7	SPECIAL TRADE CONTRACTORS
33905	1273	13407	SPECIAL TRADE CONTRACTORS	34201	135	1619	FOOD SVCS & DRINKING PLACES	34465	396	1880	AMBULATORY HEALTH CARE SVCS
33906	31	94	CONSTRUCTION OF BUILDINGS	34202	618	5296	ADMINISTRATIVE & SUPPORT SVCS	34470	1786	13306	FOOD SVCS & DRINKING PLACES
33907	2538	21072	FOOD SVCS & DRINKING PLACES	34203	1133	10546	SPECIAL TRADE CONTRACTORS	34471	2178	27613	HOSPITALS
33908	1942	15058	NURSING & RESID. CARE FACILIT.	34204	16	41	ADMINISTRATIVE & SUPPORT SVCS	34472	528	3703	COMPUTER & ELECTRONIC PROD MFG
33909	912	4642	SPECIAL TRADE CONTRACTORS	34205	1687	13038	AMBULATORY HEALTH CARE SVCS	34473	280	1472	FOOD SVCS & DRINKING PLACES
33910	21	34	CONSTRUCTION OF BUILDINGS	34206	13	26	PROF.; SCIENTIFIC; & TECH SVCS	34474	1058	18940	PROF.; SCIENTIFIC; & TECH SVCS
33911	6	13	MERCH. WHOLESALERS;DURABLE GDS	34207	1141	9140	FOOD SVCS & DRINKING PLACES	34475	1069	15741	JUSTICE; PUBIC ORDER/SAFETY
33912	1480	16148	FOOD SVCS & DRINKING PLACES	34208	1049	16833	HOSPITALS	34476	410	1551	AMBULATORY HEALTH CARE SVCS
33913	835	10289	ADMINISTRATIVE & SUPPORT SVCS	34209	905	9989	HOSPITALS	34477	20	150	SPECIAL TRADE CONTRACTORS
33914	859	4399	REAL ESTATE	34210	571	6526	FOOD SVCS & DRINKING PLACES	34478	48	396	POSTAL SERVICE
33915	31	67	SPECIAL TRADE CONTRACTORS	34211	195	1850	CROP PRODUCTION	34479	408	1888	SPECIAL TRADE CONTRACTORS
33916	1209	12014	SPECIAL TRADE CONTRACTORS	34212	157	1080	EDUCATIONAL SERVICES	34480	711	3310	SPECIAL TRADE CONTRACTORS
33917	793	4902	UTILITIES	34215	59	395	FOOD SVCS & DRINKING PLACES	34481	440	3357	GENERAL MERCHANDISE STORES
33918	12	80	FOOD MANUFACTURING	34216	85	615	FOOD SVCS & DRINKING PLACES	34482	648	4745	FOOD SVCS & DRINKING PLACES
33919	1573	9312	AMBULATORY HEALTH CARE SVCS	34217	331	1927	FOOD SVCS & DRINKING PLACES	34483	11	27	BLDG MATL & GARDEN EQPMT DLRS
33920	183	849	EDUCATIONAL SERVICES	34218	3	7	TRANSIT & GRND PASS. TRANSPORT	34484	123	487	SPECIAL TRADE CONTRACTORS
33921	188	1224	ACCOMMODATION	34219	258	1564	BLDG MATL & GARDEN EQPMT DLRS	34487	4	10	TRANSIT & GRND PASS. TRANSPORT
33922	193	737	ACCOMMODATION	34220	7	36	ADMINISTRATIVE & SUPPORT SVCS	34488	306	1732	AMUSEMENT; GAMBLING;& RECREAT.
33924	100	837	FOOD SVCS & DRINKING PLACES	34221	1108	11380	MERCH. WHOLESALERS;NONDUR. GDS	34489	14	25	PROF.; SCIENTIFIC; & TECH SVCS
33927	1	2	RELIG.; GRANT; CIVIC; PROF ORG	34222	404	3292	CLOTHING & CLOTH'G ACC. STORES	34491	650	3738	GENERAL MERCHANDISE STORES
33928	1004	7794	FOOD SVCS & DRINKING PLACES	34223	918	5192	REAL ESTATE	34492	5	11	ADMINISTRATIVE & SUPPORT SVCS
33930	23	345	CROP PRODUCTION	34224	600	3048	FOOD SVCS & DRINKING PLACES	34498	21	137	EDUCATIONAL SERVICES
33931	796	4858	FOOD SVCS & DRINKING PLACES	34228	368	3548	REAL ESTATE	34601	1468	12420	EXEC.; LEGIS.; & OTHER SUPPORT
33932	7	17	ADMINISTRATIVE & SUPPORT SVCS	34229	263	1895	GENERAL MERCHANDISE STORES	34602	191	2654	GENERAL MERCHANDISE STORES
33935	750	6446	SUPPORT ACTIVITIES: AGR./FOR.	34230	55	110	PROF.; SCIENTIFIC; & TECH SVCS	34603	10	19	AMUSEMENT; GAMBLING;& RECREAT.
33936	735	3992	FOOD AND BEVERAGE STORES	34231	1948	12313	FOOD SVCS & DRINKING PLACES	34604	285	3439	OTHER INFORMATION SERVICES
33938	21	79	HEAVY & CIVIL ENG. CONSTRUCT'N	34232	1402	12522	PROF.; SCIENTIFIC; & TECH SVCS	34605	11	38	MERCH. WHOLESALERS;DURABLE GDS
33944	12	54	MERCH. WHOLESALERS;DURABLE GDS	34233	1266	13840	HOSPITALS	34606	1071	7406	FOOD SVCS & DRINKING PLACES
33945	11	44	ACCOMMODATION	34234	973	8226	SPECIAL TRADE CONTRACTORS	34607	271	945	REAL ESTATE
33946	87	822	FOOD SVCS & DRINKING PLACES	34235	261	1825	NURSING & RESID. CARE FACILIT.	34608	461	1930	NURSING & RESID. CARE FACILIT.
33947	106	643	EDUCATIONAL SERVICES	34236	2530	21331	EXEC.; LEGIS.; & OTHER SUPPORT	34609	879	5406	EDUCATIONAL SERVICES
33948	828	10114	EXEC.; LEGIS.; & OTHER SUPPORT	34237	1011	12892	JUSTICE; PUBIC ORDER/SAFETY	34610	235	1004	HEAVY & CIVIL ENG. CONSTRUCT'N
33949	19	52	SPECIAL TRADE CONTRACTORS	34238	626	6899	NURSING & RESID. CARE FACILIT.	34611	16	57	SOCIAL ASSISTANCE
33950	1331	10745	HOSPITALS	34239	1237	17139	AMBULATORY HEALTH CARE SVCS	34613	803	7219	GENERAL MERCHANDISE STORES
33951	27	67	SOCIAL ASSISTANCE	34240	1220	14025	SPECIAL TRADE CONTRACTORS	34614	128	614	NONMETALLIC MINERAL PROD. MFG

ZIP CODE	2009 Total Firms	2009 Total Employ-ees	TOP INDUSTRY RANKED on 2009 EMPLOYMENT	ZIP CODE	2009 Total Firms	2009 Total Employ-ees	TOP INDUSTRY RANKED on 2009 EMPLOYMENT	ZIP CODE	2009 Total Firms	2009 Total Employ-ees	TOP INDUSTRY RANKED on 2009 EMPLOYMENT
34636	3	4	FOOD AND BEVERAGE STORES	34974	816	5106	FOOD SVCS & DRINKING PLACES	35123	8	37	RELIG.; GRANT; CIVIC; PROF ORG
34637	40	1551	JUSTICE; PUBIC ORDER/SAFETY	34979	12	52	TRUCK TRANSPORTATION	35124	1583	16524	MERCH. WHOLESALERS;DURABLE GDS
34638	260	3441	EDUCATIONAL SERVICES	34981	249	4611	MERCH. WHOLESALERS;NONDUR. GDS	35125	549	4948	FOOD SVCS & DRINKING PLACES
34639	612	4394	FOOD SVCS & DRINKING PLACES	34982	1189	10020	EXEC.; LEGIS.; & OTHER SUPPORT	35126	443	2572	EDUCATIONAL SERVICES
34652	1677	12775	HOSPITALS	34983	917	3234	EDUCATIONAL SERVICES	35127	145	1255	RELIG.; GRANT; CIVIC; PROF ORG
34653	807	6840	NURSING & RESID. CARE FACILIT.	34984	644	2867	EXEC.; LEGIS.; & OTHER SUPPORT	35128	258	1919	INSURANCE CARRIERS & RELATED
34654	606	5754	EXEC.; LEGIS.; & OTHER SUPPORT	34985	13	23	SPECIAL TRADE CONTRACTORS	35130	53	176	JUSTICE; PUBIC ORDER/SAFETY
34655	821	7083	EDUCATIONAL SERVICES	34986	901	7359	FOOD SVCS & DRINKING PLACES	35131	71	563	NONMETALLIC MINERAL PROD. MFG
34656	22	48	TRANSIT & GRND PASS. TRANSPORT	34987	141	491	ADMINISTRATIVE & SUPPORT SVCS	35133	56	229	EDUCATIONAL SERVICES
34660	7	60	FOOD SVCS & DRINKING PLACES	34988	11	24	ADMINISTRATIVE & SUPPORT SVCS	35135	34	169	CONSTRUCTION OF BUILDINGS
34661	5	9	MOTOR VEHICLE & PARTS DEALERS	34990	1099	8056	SPECIAL TRADE CONTRACTORS	35136	84	694	APPAREL MANUFACTURING
34667	1370	11353	AMBULATORY HEALTH CARE SVCS	34991	18	51	SPECIAL TRADE CONTRACTORS	35137	10	370	MERCH. WHOLESALERS;DURABLE GDS
34668	1482	11560	FOOD SVCS & DRINKING PLACES	34992	13	35	ADMINISTRATIVE & SUPPORT SVCS	35139	3	3	POSTAL SERVICE
34669	404	1992	EDUCATIONAL SERVICES	34994	3195	25559	AMBULATORY HEALTH CARE SVCS	35142	3	43	MACHINERY MANUFACTURING
34673	20	41	MERCH. WHOLESALERS;DURABLE GDS	34995	20	66	SOCIAL ASSISTANCE	35143	51	240	WOOD PRODUCT MANUFACTURING
34674	18	52	SPECIAL TRADE CONTRACTORS	34996	640	6785	EXEC.; LEGIS.; & OTHER SUPPORT	35144	5	0	GASOLINE STATIONS
34677	1110	11393	SPECIAL TRADE CONTRACTORS	34997	1743	12677	MOTOR VEHICLE & PARTS DEALERS	35146	225	1899	JUSTICE; PUBIC ORDER/SAFETY
34679	7	11	ADMINISTRATIVE & SUPPORT SVCS	35004	281	2698	MERCH. WHOLESALERS;DURABLE GDS	35147	84	284	MOTOR VEHICLE & PARTS DEALERS
34680	20	79	SPECIAL TRADE CONTRACTORS	35005	157	1183	EDUCATIONAL SERVICES	35148	191	1487	EDUCATIONAL SERVICES
34681	18	25	PROF.; SCIENTIFIC; & TECH SVCS	35006	51	846	MINING (EXCEPT OIL AND GAS)	35149	9	332	TRUCK TRANSPORTATION
34682	30	108	NONSTORE RETAILERS	35007	1049	9350	HOSPITALS	35150	829	9641	HOSPITALS
34683	840	5458	EDUCATIONAL SERVICES	35010	906	14245	MISCELLANEOUS MANUFACTURING	35151	110	1971	CHEMICAL MANUFACTURING
34684	1045	11310	NURSING & RESID. CARE FACILIT.	35011	2	5	RELIG.; GRANT; CIVIC; PROF ORG	35160	934	9610	EDUCATIONAL SERVICES
34685	340	2977	REAL ESTATE	35013	4	9	FOOD SVCS & DRINKING PLACES	35161	1	2	ADMINISTRATIVE & SUPPORT SVCS
34688	148	967	EDUCATIONAL SERVICES	35014	54	329	EDUCATIONAL SERVICES	35171	68	549	PAPER MANUFACTURING
34689	1503	10687	FOOD SVCS & DRINKING PLACES	35015	5	23	POSTAL SERVICE	35172	52	237	MERCH. WHOLESALERS;DURABLE GDS
34690	324	2024	ADMINISTRATIVE & SUPPORT SVCS	35016	592	4448	FOOD SVCS & DRINKING PLACES	35173	866	7641	SPECIAL TRADE CONTRACTORS
34691	465	3062	ADMINISTRATIVE & SUPPORT SVCS	35019	41	564	BLDG MATL & GARDEN EQPMT DLRS	35175	93	323	AMUSEMENT; GAMBLING;& RECREAT.
34692	10	14	ADMINISTRATIVE & SUPPORT SVCS	35020	1180	9129	JUSTICE; PUBIC ORDER/SAFETY	35176	20	93	FABRICATED METAL PRODUCT MFG
34695	576	4673	HOSPITALS	35021	3	6	ADMINISTRATIVE & SUPPORT SVCS	35178	61	418	PLASTICS & RUBBER PRODUCTS MFG
34697	19	31	ADMINISTRATIVE & SUPPORT SVCS	35022	746	10886	HOSPITALS	35179	168	1143	TRUCK TRANSPORTATION
34698	1299	13011	HOSPITALS	35023	671	5156	EXEC.; LEGIS.; & OTHER SUPPORT	35180	346	2116	RELIG.; GRANT; CIVIC; PROF ORG
34705	80	665	NONMETALLIC MINERAL PROD. MFG	35031	182	1713	FOOD MANUFACTURING	35181	1	2	POSTAL SERVICE
34711	2016	13956	EDUCATIONAL SERVICES	35032	2	2	AMBULATORY HEALTH CARE SVCS	35182	1	2	POSTAL SERVICE
34712	22	48	ADMINISTRATIVE & SUPPORT SVCS	35033	49	543	MACHINERY MANUFACTURING	35183	7	14	RELIG.; GRANT; CIVIC; PROF ORG
34713	4	12	ADMINISTRATIVE & SUPPORT SVCS	35034	102	1375	SPECIAL TRADE CONTRACTORS	35184	83	334	EDUCATIONAL SERVICES
34714	397	3102	HEALTH & PERSONAL CARE STORES	35035	34	312	WOOD PRODUCT MANUFACTURING	35185	14	92	WOOD PRODUCT MANUFACTURING
34715	402	2482	JUSTICE; PUBIC ORDER/SAFETY	35036	13	35	JUSTICE; PUBIC ORDER/SAFETY	35186	71	426	PROF.; SCIENTIFIC; & TECH SVCS
34729	4	3	POSTAL SERVICE	35040	426	4506	GENERAL MERCHANDISE STORES	35187	7	25	RELIG.; GRANT; CIVIC; PROF ORG
34731	367	1817	SPECIAL TRADE CONTRACTORS	35041	1	0	RELIG.; GRANT; CIVIC; PROF ORG	35188	119	630	EDUCATIONAL SERVICES
34734	47	336	ADMINISTRATIVE & SUPPORT SVCS	35042	216	1358	HOSPITALS	35201	9	77	PROF.; SCIENTIFIC; & TECH SVCS
34736	505	3910	BLDG MATL & GARDEN EQPMT DLRS	35043	266	1146	FOOD SVCS & DRINKING PLACES	35202	8	26	SOCIAL ASSISTANCE
34737	120	1560	AMUSEMENT; GAMBLING;& RECREAT.	35044	244	2421	EDUCATIONAL SERVICES	35203	2100	38138	UTILITIES
34739	39	174	ADMINISTRATIVE & SUPPORT SVCS	35045	708	4942	FOOD SVCS & DRINKING PLACES	35204	470	6408	SUPPORT ACT. FOR TRANSPORT.
34740	1	1	PROF.; SCIENTIFIC; & TECH SVCS	35046	89	1429	MISCELLANEOUS MANUFACTURING	35205	1134	17019	HOSPITALS
34741	2582	21158	AMBULATORY HEALTH CARE SVCS	35048	12	145	EDUCATIONAL SERVICES	35206	507	3133	EDUCATIONAL SERVICES
34742	15	33	ADMINISTRATIVE & SUPPORT SVCS	35049	110	605	EDUCATIONAL SERVICES	35207	300	6371	MERCH. WHOLESALERS;DURABLE GDS
34743	502	1927	EDUCATIONAL SERVICES	35051	341	4757	RELIG.; GRANT; CIVIC; PROF ORG	35208	392	2293	EDUCATIONAL SERVICES
34744	2075	14178	EDUCATIONAL SERVICES	35052	4	316	NURSING & RESID. CARE FACILIT.	35209	3075	38062	HOSPITALS
34745	19	33	SPECIAL TRADE CONTRACTORS	35053	43	95	SPECIAL TRADE CONTRACTORS	35210	1094	17489	CREDIT INTERMEDIATION & RELATD
34746	1642	14445	ACCOMMODATION	35054	95	426	CONSTRUCTION OF BUILDINGS	35211	695	10131	MERCH. WHOLESALERS;DURABLE GDS
34747	1080	14309	ACCOMMODATION	35055	1477	16856	MERCH. WHOLESALERS;DURABLE GDS	35212	362	5701	TRANSPORTATION EQUIPMENT MFG
34748	2046	19607	HOSPITALS	35056	1	2	EXEC.; LEGIS.; & OTHER SUPPORT	35213	411	6378	HOSPITALS
34749	15	25	ADMINISTRATIVE & SUPPORT SVCS	35057	281	2192	WHOLESALE ELEC. MRKTS & AGENTS	35214	509	5002	TRUCK TRANSPORTATION
34753	93	276	HEAVY & CIVIL ENG. CONSTRUCT'N	35058	330	4790	HOSPITALS	35215	1035	11461	FURNITURE & RELATED PROD. MFG
34755	20	47	FOOD AND BEVERAGE STORES	35060	10	125	SPECIAL TRADE CONTRACTORS	35216	1878	14707	MOTOR VEHICLE & PARTS DEALERS
34756	133	358	EDUCATIONAL SERVICES	35061	53	538	UNCLASSIFIED ESTABLISHMENTS	35217	645	17031	MERCH. WHOLESALERS;DURABLE GDS
34758	243	3320	WHOLESALE ELEC. MRKTS & AGENTS	35062	160	879	FOOD SVCS & DRINKING PLACES	35218	276	2327	MOTOR VEHICLE & PARTS DEALERS
34759	265	1813	FOOD AND BEVERAGE STORES	35063	28	138	EDUCATIONAL SERVICES	35219	4	39	TRUCK TRANSPORTATION
34760	31	167	PROF.; SCIENTIFIC; & TECH SVCS	35064	383	6766	PRIMARY METAL MANUFACTURING	35220	7	10	AMBULATORY HEALTH CARE SVCS
34761	1271	17482	ACCOMMODATION	35068	226	1735	FOOD SVCS & DRINKING PLACES	35221	113	1467	EDUCATIONAL SERVICES
34762	54	1353	WASTE MANAGMT & REMEDIAT'N SVC	35070	20	95	CONSTRUCTION OF BUILDINGS	35222	691	10075	MERCH. WHOLESALERS;DURABLE GDS
34769	1058	9108	FOOD SVCS & DRINKING PLACES	35071	621	4818	FOOD SVCS & DRINKING PLACES	35223	837	8066	INSURANCE CARRIERS & RELATED
34770	18	83	SPECIAL TRADE CONTRACTORS	35072	84	702	FURNITURE & RELATED PROD. MFG	35224	119	874	RELIG.; GRANT; CIVIC; PROF ORG
34771	383	1536	EDUCATIONAL SERVICES	35073	90	539	EDUCATIONAL SERVICES	35226	575	4686	CONSTRUCTION OF BUILDINGS
34772	369	1536	SPECIAL TRADE CONTRACTORS	35074	10	97	FOOD AND BEVERAGE STORES	35228	242	1725	MISCELLANEOUS STORE RETAILERS
34773	70	556	ANIMAL PRODUCTION	35077	355	3110	EDUCATIONAL SERVICES	35229	10	1088	EDUCATIONAL SERVICES
34777	9	43	CONSTRUCTION OF BUILDINGS	35078	92	529	SPECIAL TRADE CONTRACTORS	35231	3	1	ADMINISTRATIVE & SUPPORT SVCS
34778	6	18	REPAIR AND MAINTENANCE	35079	106	426	EDUCATIONAL SERVICES	35233	1051	28258	AMBULATORY HEALTH CARE SVCS
34785	545	5976	SPECIAL TRADE CONTRACTORS	35080	283	1822	MACHINERY MANUFACTURING	35234	325	8329	HOSPITALS
34786	577	2442	EDUCATIONAL SERVICES	35082	1	2	POSTAL SERVICE	35235	785	10530	AMBULATORY HEALTH CARE SVCS
34787	1860	14045	EDUCATIONAL SERVICES	35083	70	73	MERCH. WHOLESALERS;NONDUR. GDS	35236	13	36	BLDG MATL & GARDEN EQPMT DLRS
34788	585	5063	FOOD SVCS & DRINKING PLACES	35085	163	904	EDUCATIONAL SERVICES	35238	10	175	MINING (EXCEPT OIL AND GAS)
34789	3	6	REPAIR AND MAINTENANCE	35087	45	238	ADMIN. OF ECONOMIC PROGRAMS	35242	1921	23377	NONSTORE RETAILERS
34797	35	57	FOOD MANUFACTURING	35089	36	158	CONSTRUCTION OF BUILDINGS	35243	1297	14860	PROF.; SCIENTIFIC; & TECH SVCS
34945	313	5312	JUSTICE; PUBIC ORDER/SAFETY	35091	25	187	EDUCATIONAL SERVICES	35244	1907	21807	FOOD SVCS & DRINKING PLACES
34946	359	4328	TRANSPORTATION EQUIPMENT MFG	35094	506	4368	MERCH. WHOLESALERS;DURABLE GDS	35249	120	12478	HOSPITALS
34947	543	11101	EXEC.; LEGIS.; & OTHER SUPPORT	35096	197	7202	TRANSPORTATION EQUIPMENT MFG	35253	8	60	MINING (EXCEPT OIL AND GAS)
34948	5	13	SOCIAL ASSISTANCE	35097	53	383	EDUCATIONAL SERVICES	35254	3	353	EDUCATIONAL SERVICES
34949	217	792	FOOD SVCS & DRINKING PLACES	35098	9	74	SPECIAL TRADE CONTRACTORS	35255	4	4	PROF.; SCIENTIFIC; & TECH SVCS
34950	1220	10335	HOSPITALS	35111	264	2799	MERCH. WHOLESALERS;NONDUR. GDS	35259	3	5	PERFORM'G ARTS; SPEC. SPORTS
34951	274	1902	SPECIAL TRADE CONTRACTORS	35112	16	40	EXEC.; LEGIS.; & OTHER SUPPORT	35260	9	115	ADMINISTRATIVE & SUPPORT SVCS
34952	1980	15818	AMBULATORY HEALTH CARE SVCS	35114	45	384	EDUCATIONAL SERVICES	35261	6	40	ADMINISTRATIVE & SUPPORT SVCS
34953	973	3781	GENERAL MERCHANDISE STORES	35115	320	2749	EDUCATIONAL SERVICES	35266	12	36	ADMINISTRATIVE & SUPPORT SVCS
34954	6	11	BLDG MATL & GARDEN EQPMT DLRS	35116	73	421	EDUCATIONAL SERVICES	35283	2	370	EXEC.; LEGIS.; & OTHER SUPPORT
34956	215	2229	JUSTICE; PUBIC ORDER/SAFETY	35117	106	506	BLDG MATL & GARDEN EQPMT DLRS	35285	5	13	CREDIT INTERMEDIATION & RELATD
34957	1185	7605	FOOD SVCS & DRINKING PLACES	35118	73	294	NONSTORE RETAILERS	35288	1	0	CREDIT INTERMEDIATION & RELATD
34958	3	4	ADMINISTRATIVE & SUPPORT SVCS	35119	1	2	POSTAL SERVICE	35290	3	330	CREDIT INTERMEDIATION & RELATD
34972	969	7775	JUSTICE; PUBIC ORDER/SAFETY	35120	175	875	EDUCATIONAL SERVICES	35294	18	5150	HOSPITALS
34973	12	46	ANIMAL PRODUCTION	35121	693	4891	EDUCATIONAL SERVICES	35401	1937	33033	HOSPITALS

BUSINESS DATA

ZIP CODE	2009 Total Firms	2009 Total Employees	TOP INDUSTRY RANKED on 2009 EMPLOYMENT	ZIP CODE	2009 Total Firms	2009 Total Employees	TOP INDUSTRY RANKED on 2009 EMPLOYMENT	ZIP CODE	2009 Total Firms	2009 Total Employees	TOP INDUSTRY RANKED on 2009 EMPLOYMENT
35402	8	18	CONSTRUCTION OF BUILDINGS	35603	717	7590	FOOD SVCS & DRINKING PLACES	35816	1138	10462	FOOD SVCS & DRINKING PLACES
35403	2	2	ADMINISTRATIVE & SUPPORT SVCS	35610	31	124	EDUCATIONAL SERVICES	35824	179	4248	CHEMICAL MANUFACTURING
35404	713	8283	AMBULATORY HEALTH CARE SVCS	35611	1221	11446	FOOD SVCS & DRINKING PLACES	35893	4	475	CREDIT INTERMEDIATION & RELATD
35405	1036	14707	BLDG MATL & GARDEN EQPMT DLRS	35612	3	7	ADMINISTRATIVE & SUPPORT SVCS	35896	8	670	EDUCATIONAL SERVICES
35406	359	5346	AMBULATORY HEALTH CARE SVCS	35613	275	2135	COMPUTER & ELECTRONIC PROD MFG	35898	36	407	ADMINISTRATIVE & SUPPORT SVCS
35407	9	10	SPECIAL TRADE CONTRACTORS	35614	93	510	MISCELLANEOUS MANUFACTURING	35899	9	104	PERFORM'G ARTS; SPEC. SPORTS
35440	3	9	SPECIAL TRADE CONTRACTORS	35615	5	18	SUPPORT ACTIVITIES: AGR./FOR.	35901	1261	13250	EXEC.; LEGIS.; & OTHER SUPPORT
35441	20	103	EDUCATIONAL SERVICES	35616	119	1356	RELIG.; GRANT; CIVIC; PROF ORG	35902	5	573	EXEC.; LEGIS.; & OTHER SUPPORT
35442	168	1278	NONMETALLIC MINERAL PROD. MFG	35617	1	2	POSTAL SERVICE	35903	570	11279	FOOD MANUFACTURING
35443	30	113	EDUCATIONAL SERVICES	35618	78	2602	PAPER MANUFACTURING	35904	372	4432	EDUCATIONAL SERVICES
35444	111	2337	MINING (EXCEPT OIL AND GAS)	35619	78	471	EDUCATIONAL SERVICES	35905	169	1344	SPECIAL TRADE CONTRACTORS
35446	23	113	EDUCATIONAL SERVICES	35620	137	930	MERCH. WHOLESALERS;NONDUR. GDS	35906	516	4911	FOOD SVCS & DRINKING PLACES
35447	144	1124	HOSPITALS	35621	70	268	EDUCATIONAL SERVICES	35907	164	755	FOOD SVCS & DRINKING PLACES
35448	2	0	FISHING; HUNTING AND TRAPPING	35622	109	1075	NURSING & RESID. CARE FACILIT.	35950	896	10225	MERCH. WHOLESALERS;NONDUR. GDS
35449	1	2	POSTAL SERVICE	35630	2047	23393	FOOD SVCS & DRINKING PLACES	35951	207	1941	NURSING & RESID. CARE FACILIT.
35452	56	196	EDUCATIONAL SERVICES	35631	4	25	CONSTRUCTION OF BUILDINGS	35952	197	793	FOOD SVCS & DRINKING PLACES
35453	278	2623	MISCELLANEOUS MANUFACTURING	35632	5	607	EDUCATIONAL SERVICES	35953	212	1179	EDUCATIONAL SERVICES
35456	65	456	EDUCATIONAL SERVICES	35633	327	2440	FURNITURE & RELATED PROD. MFG	35954	395	3468	GENERAL MERCHANDISE STORES
35457	4	3	MERCH. WHOLESALERS;DURABLE GDS	35634	241	1850	EDUCATIONAL SERVICES	35956	141	886	TRUCK TRANSPORTATION
35458	5	16	GASOLINE STATIONS	35640	681	5853	MACHINERY MANUFACTURING	35957	594	8458	FOOD MANUFACTURING
35459	20	141	WASTE MANAGMT & REMEDIAT'N SVC	35643	71	302	CONSTRUCTION OF BUILDINGS	35958	70	233	PROF.; SCIENTIFIC; & TECH SVCS
35460	14	184	WOOD PRODUCT MANUFACTURING	35645	271	1556	EDUCATIONAL SERVICES	35959	117	435	EDUCATIONAL SERVICES
35461	30	43	RELIG.; GRANT; CIVIC; PROF ORG	35646	111	900	SPECIAL TRADE CONTRACTORS	35960	583	3692	GENERAL MERCHANDISE STORES
35462	245	2140	AMUSEMENT; GAMBLING;& RECREAT.	35647	14	218	EDUCATIONAL SERVICES	35961	135	1807	FOOD MANUFACTURING
35463	22	72	EDUCATIONAL SERVICES	35648	68	377	EDUCATIONAL SERVICES	35962	129	1232	EDUCATIONAL SERVICES
35464	16	52	SOCIAL ASSISTANCE	35649	14	106	MERCH. WHOLESALERS;NONDUR. GDS	35963	16	25	GASOLINE STATIONS
35466	126	670	EDUCATIONAL SERVICES	35650	470	3076	FOOD SVCS & DRINKING PLACES	35964	21	228	EDUCATIONAL SERVICES
35468	1	0	POSTAL SERVICE	35651	14	116	EDUCATIONAL SERVICES	35966	67	314	RELIG.; GRANT; CIVIC; PROF ORG
35469	11	34	HEAVY & CIVIL ENG. CONSTRUCT'N	35652	283	1143	FOOD SVCS & DRINKING PLACES	35967	794	10123	APPAREL MANUFACTURING
35470	243	2200	EDUCATIONAL SERVICES	35653	519	4259	HOSPITALS	35968	217	3685	APPAREL MANUFACTURING
35471	1	65	WOOD PRODUCT MANUFACTURING	35654	188	1376	MACHINERY MANUFACTURING	35971	141	1118	NURSING & RESID. CARE FACILIT.
35473	315	1680	SPECIAL TRADE CONTRACTORS	35660	442	4290	HOSPITALS	35972	11	66	ACCOMMODATION
35474	146	965	MERCH. WHOLESALERS;DURABLE GDS	35661	863	12040	MERCH. WHOLESALERS;DURABLE GDS	35973	35	122	EDUCATIONAL SERVICES
35475	166	1106	EDUCATIONAL SERVICES	35662	6	7	RENTAL AND LEASING SERVICES	35974	83	518	EDUCATIONAL SERVICES
35476	737	13437	GENERAL MERCHANDISE STORES	35670	117	814	EDUCATIONAL SERVICES	35975	13	16	FOOD AND BEVERAGE STORES
35477	12	50	EDUCATIONAL SERVICES	35671	91	3751	TRANSPORTATION EQUIPMENT MFG	35976	897	10566	FOOD MANUFACTURING
35478	6	86	SPECIAL TRADE CONTRACTORS	35672	104	542	EDUCATIONAL SERVICES	35978	168	886	MERCH. WHOLESALERS;NONDUR. GDS
35480	23	31	RELIG.; GRANT; CIVIC; PROF ORG	35673	187	1969	PRIMARY METAL MANUFACTURING	35979	38	208	EDUCATIONAL SERVICES
35481	121	568	NURSING & RESID. CARE FACILIT.	35674	573	5230	EDUCATIONAL SERVICES	35980	48	155	EDUCATIONAL SERVICES
35482	3	2	MERCH. WHOLESALERS;DURABLE GDS	35677	34	170	EDUCATIONAL SERVICES	35981	77	603	EDUCATIONAL SERVICES
35486	4	13	CREDIT INTERMEDIATION & RELATD	35739	154	877	JUSTICE; PUBIC ORDER/SAFETY	35983	104	1494	MOTOR VEHICLE & PARTS DEALERS
35487	34	950	EDUCATIONAL SERVICES	35740	88	2674	TEXTILE PRODUCT MILLS	35984	66	489	REAL ESTATE
35490	78	2618	TRANSPORTATION EQUIPMENT MFG	35741	92	693	FABRICATED METAL PRODUCT MFG	35986	360	3367	EDUCATIONAL SERVICES
35491	2	4	FISHING; HUNTING AND TRAPPING	35742	3	8	CONSTRUCTION OF BUILDINGS	35987	78	740	FABRICATED METAL PRODUCT MFG
35501	1089	10653	FOOD SVCS & DRINKING PLACES	35744	38	179	ADMIN. OF ECONOMIC PROGRAMS	35988	58	357	EDUCATIONAL SERVICES
35502	5	15	SOCIAL ASSISTANCE	35745	3	3	PROF.; SCIENTIFIC; & TECH SVCS	35989	60	736	TEXTILE PRODUCT MILLS
35503	253	1508	EDUCATIONAL SERVICES	35746	6	4	CROP PRODUCTION	35990	28	108	EDUCATIONAL SERVICES
35504	236	1504	NURSING & RESID. CARE FACILIT.	35747	144	683	EDUCATIONAL SERVICES	36003	51	331	MISCELLANEOUS MANUFACTURING
35540	89	767	WOOD PRODUCT MANUFACTURING	35748	145	658	EDUCATIONAL SERVICES	36005	38	191	MERCH. WHOLESALERS;NONDUR. GDS
35541	86	384	EDUCATIONAL SERVICES	35749	241	1463	EDUCATIONAL SERVICES	36006	28	126	EDUCATIONAL SERVICES
35542	10	22	EXEC.; LEGIS.; & OTHER SUPPORT	35750	309	1517	EDUCATIONAL SERVICES	36008	2	6	FOOD MANUFACTURING
35543	39	241	EDUCATIONAL SERVICES	35751	6	13	CONSTRUCTION OF BUILDINGS	36009	60	405	TRUCK TRANSPORTATION
35544	17	41	CONSTRUCTION OF BUILDINGS	35752	53	283	EDUCATIONAL SERVICES	36010	154	2221	GENERAL MERCHANDISE STORES
35545	16	206	MERCH. WHOLESALERS;DURABLE GDS	35754	149	627	FABRICATED METAL PRODUCT MFG	36013	15	65	EDUCATIONAL SERVICES
35546	75	735	MINING (EXCEPT OIL AND GAS)	35755	17	103	ACCOMMODATION	36015	5	480	PAPER MANUFACTURING
35548	36	304	CLOTHING & CLOTH'G ACC. STORES	35756	160	2617	MERCH. WHOLESALERS;DURABLE GDS	36016	148	1019	JUSTICE; PUBIC ORDER/SAFETY
35549	114	625	EDUCATIONAL SERVICES	35757	181	877	NURSING & RESID. CARE FACILIT.	36017	54	318	JUSTICE; PUBIC ORDER/SAFETY
35550	99	765	NURSING & RESID. CARE FACILIT.	35758	1502	14047	FOOD SVCS & DRINKING PLACES	36020	17	194	NONMETALLIC MINERAL PROD. MFG
35551	1	30	ANIMAL PRODUCTION	35759	159	1088	FOOD AND BEVERAGE STORES	36022	112	648	EDUCATIONAL SERVICES
35552	21	87	JUSTICE; PUBIC ORDER/SAFETY	35760	131	620	EDUCATIONAL SERVICES	36024	169	1038	FURNITURE & RELATED PROD. MFG
35553	181	1788	EDUCATIONAL SERVICES	35761	163	614	EDUCATIONAL SERVICES	36025	86	874	JUSTICE; PUBIC ORDER/SAFETY
35554	15	70	MINING (EXCEPT OIL AND GAS)	35762	3	3	POSTAL SERVICE	36026	24	75	CONSTRUCTION OF BUILDINGS
35555	471	3475	AMBULATORY HEALTH CARE SVCS	35763	274	1671	FOOD SVCS & DRINKING PLACES	36027	771	7508	FABRICATED METAL PRODUCT MFG
35559	5	3	EXEC.; LEGIS.; & OTHER SUPPORT	35764	16	106	MERCH. WHOLESALERS;NONDUR. GDS	36028	30	80	BLDG MATL & GARDEN EQPMT DLRS
35560	4	9	GASOLINE STATIONS	35765	80	354	EDUCATIONAL SERVICES	36029	30	22	ADMINISTRATIVE & SUPPORT SVCS
35563	124	1526	CONSTRUCTION OF BUILDINGS	35766	3	23	EDUCATIONAL SERVICES	36030	10	6	FOOD AND BEVERAGE STORES
35564	46	1219	MERCH. WHOLESALERS;NONDUR. GDS	35767	2	2	POSTAL SERVICE	36031	6	3	POSTAL SERVICE
35565	466	5637	FURNITURE & RELATED PROD. MFG	35768	738	9306	ADMINISTRATIVE & SUPPORT SVCS	36032	69	767	MISCELLANEOUS MANUFACTURING
35570	447	4206	WOOD PRODUCT MANUFACTURING	35769	259	2127	FOOD SVCS & DRINKING PLACES	36033	126	826	HOSPITALS
35571	20	49	EXEC.; LEGIS.; & OTHER SUPPORT	35771	76	256	EDUCATIONAL SERVICES	36034	15	20	CONSTRUCTION OF BUILDINGS
35572	18	57	TRUCK TRANSPORTATION	35772	147	1422	TEXTILE PRODUCT MILLS	36035	50	209	EDUCATIONAL SERVICES
35573	2	3	EXEC.; LEGIS.; & OTHER SUPPORT	35773	196	871	EDUCATIONAL SERVICES	36036	30	127	EDUCATIONAL SERVICES
35574	24	71	TRUCK TRANSPORTATION	35774	5	98	HOSPITALS	36037	671	5228	FOOD SVCS & DRINKING PLACES
35575	24	615	WOOD PRODUCT MANUFACTURING	35775	14	30	RELIG.; GRANT; CIVIC; PROF ORG	36038	8	37	JUSTICE; PUBIC ORDER/SAFETY
35576	77	486	WOOD PRODUCT MANUFACTURING	35776	56	223	EDUCATIONAL SERVICES	36039	6	2	POSTAL SERVICE
35577	6	11	SUPPORT ACT. FOR TRANSPORT.	35801	2948	36467	HOSPITALS	36040	222	1072	EDUCATIONAL SERVICES
35578	53	276	EDUCATIONAL SERVICES	35802	993	9104	PROF.; SCIENTIFIC; & TECH SVCS	36041	42	323	TRUCK TRANSPORTATION
35579	48	311	EDUCATIONAL SERVICES	35803	576	6439	MERCH. WHOLESALERS;DURABLE GDS	36042	17	25	RELIG.; GRANT; CIVIC; PROF ORG
35580	69	591	MINING (EXCEPT OIL AND GAS)	35804	21	147	FISHING; HUNTING AND TRAPPING	36043	87	1109	SPECIAL TRADE CONTRACTORS
35581	78	873	REAL ESTATE	35805	1242	20964	COMPUTER & ELECTRONIC PROD MFG	36046	37	62	REPAIR AND MAINTENANCE
35582	177	2669	NURSING & RESID. CARE FACILIT.	35806	1135	19931	PROF.; SCIENTIFIC; & TECH SVCS	36047	26	170	MERCH. WHOLESALERS;DURABLE GDS
35584	19	118	EDUCATIONAL SERVICES	35807	4	36	EDUCATIONAL SERVICES	36048	44	237	EDUCATIONAL SERVICES
35585	25	72	HEAVY & CIVIL ENG. CONSTRUCT'N	35808	29	191	PROF.; SCIENTIFIC; & TECH SVCS	36049	234	2241	FOOD MANUFACTURING
35586	134	1099	MERCH. WHOLESALERS;DURABLE GDS	35809	2	22	SPECIAL TRADE CONTRACTORS	36051	30	119	EDUCATIONAL SERVICES
35587	11	44	EDUCATIONAL SERVICES	35810	788	7778	EDUCATIONAL SERVICES	36052	16	29	MERCH. WHOLESALERS;NONDUR. GDS
35592	266	2642	TRUCK TRANSPORTATION	35811	828	10988	WHOLESALE ELEC. MRKTS & AGENTS	36053	41	74	EDUCATIONAL SERVICES
35593	21	94	EDUCATIONAL SERVICES	35812	1	0	COMPUTER & ELECTRONIC PROD MFG	36054	460	2707	FOOD AND BEVERAGE STORES
35594	333	3077	MERCH. WHOLESALERS;DURABLE GDS	35813	4	310	POSTAL SERVICE	36057	10	462	PRIMARY METAL MANUFACTURING
35601	2347	32181	HOSPITALS	35814	7	29	SPECIAL TRADE CONTRACTORS	36061	1	0	FOOD AND BEVERAGE STORES
35602	5	65	ADMINISTRATIVE & SUPPORT SVCS	35815	15	23	CONSTRUCTION OF BUILDINGS	36062	1	100	BLDG MATL & GARDEN EQPMT DLRS

ZIP CODE	2009 Total Firms	2009 Total Employ-ees	TOP INDUSTRY RANKED on 2009 EMPLOYMENT
36064	137	751	CONSTRUCTION OF BUILDINGS
36065	16	67	GENERAL MERCHANDISE STORES
36066	550	8689	GENERAL MERCHANDISE STORES
36067	890	7037	MERCH. WHOLESALERS;NONDUR. GDS
36068	4	5	SPECIAL TRADE CONTRACTORS
36069	87	490	JUSTICE; PUBIC ORDER/SAFETY
36071	12	14	HEAVY & CIVIL ENG. CONSTRUCT'N
36072	1	0	ADMINISTRATIVE & SUPPORT SVCS
36075	65	1608	PERFORM'G ARTS; SPEC. SPORTS
36078	398	3838	TRANSPORTATION EQUIPMENT MFG
36079	158	3121	PRIMARY METAL MANUFACTURING
36080	34	62	CONSTRUCTION OF BUILDINGS
36081	778	7574	EDUCATIONAL SERVICES
36082	6	23	OTHER INFORMATION SERVICES
36083	394	4066	HOSPITALS
36087	1	4	POSTAL SERVICE
36088	68	1225	EDUCATIONAL SERVICES
36089	336	3218	FOOD MANUFACTURING
36091	53	187	EDUCATIONAL SERVICES
36092	682	7310	EDUCATIONAL SERVICES
36093	172	624	SPECIAL TRADE CONTRACTORS
36101	5	39	ADMINISTRATIVE & SUPPORT SVCS
36102	1	6	TELECOMMUNICATIONS
36104	1915	25917	EXEC.; LEGIS.; & OTHER SUPPORT
36105	440	8602	WHOLESALE ELEC. MRKTS & AGENTS
36106	1009	9237	AMBULATORY HEALTH CARE SVCS
36107	518	3933	FOOD SVCS & DRINKING PLACES
36108	795	12842	NAT'L SECURITY & INT'L AFFAIRS
36109	812	11865	ELECT'L EQPMT; APP; & COMP MFG
36110	393	7789	EXEC.; LEGIS.; & OTHER SUPPORT
36111	284	2121	EDUCATIONAL SERVICES
36112	45	1314	NAT'L SECURITY & INT'L AFFAIRS
36113	3	15	CONSTRUCTION OF BUILDINGS
36114	22	144	NAT'L SECURITY & INT'L AFFAIRS
36115	3	1	PROF.; SCIENTIFIC; & TECH SVCS
36116	1258	16182	RELIG.; GRANT; CIVIC; PROF ORG
36117	2656	25525	FOOD SVCS & DRINKING PLACES
36119	4	500	POSTAL SERVICE
36120	2	7	ADMINISTRATIVE & SUPPORT SVCS
36121	7	119	POSTAL SERVICE
36123	7	76	INSURANCE CARRIERS & RELATED
36124	15	30	EDUCATIONAL SERVICES
36125	4	7	ADMINISTRATIVE & SUPPORT SVCS
36130	104	5307	EXEC.; LEGIS.; & OTHER SUPPORT
36131	12	684	EXEC.; LEGIS.; & OTHER SUPPORT
36132	1	43	EXEC.; LEGIS.; & OTHER SUPPORT
36201	1220	11643	FOOD SVCS & DRINKING PLACES
36202	10	13	AMUSEMENT; GAMBLING;& RECREAT.
36203	946	10865	FOOD SVCS & DRINKING PLACES
36204	1	1	RENTAL AND LEASING SERVICES
36205	40	545	EDUCATIONAL SERVICES
36206	344	3228	GENERAL MERCHANDISE STORES
36207	580	7972	PROF.; SCIENTIFIC; & TECH SVCS
36250	151	995	EDUCATIONAL SERVICES
36251	198	3911	WOOD PRODUCT MANUFACTURING
36253	8	83	CREDIT INTERMEDIATION & RELATD
36254	3	6	TRUCK TRANSPORTATION
36255	10	48	EDUCATIONAL SERVICES
36256	33	181	EDUCATIONAL SERVICES
36257	2	3	POSTAL SERVICE
36258	18	109	HEAVY & CIVIL ENG. CONSTRUCT'N
36260	77	1053	FURNITURE & RELATED PROD. MFG
36261	4	3	SPECIAL TRADE CONTRACTORS
36262	19	88	EDUCATIONAL SERVICES
36263	12	52	PROF.; SCIENTIFIC; & TECH SVCS
36264	272	2121	CONSTRUCTION OF BUILDINGS
36265	480	5432	EDUCATIONAL SERVICES
36266	180	1350	NURSING & RESID. CARE FACILIT.
36267	4	29	HEAVY & CIVIL ENG. CONSTRUCT'N
36268	95	789	FABRICATED METAL PRODUCT MFG
36269	11	15	POSTAL SERVICE
36271	90	572	MERCH. WHOLESALERS;DURABLE GDS
36272	283	2924	MISCELLANEOUS MANUFACTURING
36273	75	429	EDUCATIONAL SERVICES
36274	438	2681	MERCH. WHOLESALERS;NONDUR. GDS
36275	2	70	EDUCATIONAL SERVICES
36276	64	1476	FABRICATED METAL PRODUCT MFG
36277	62	379	EDUCATIONAL SERVICES
36278	207	1159	EDUCATIONAL SERVICES
36279	30	238	RELIG.; GRANT; CIVIC; PROF ORG
36280	70	243	EDUCATIONAL SERVICES
36301	1794	18955	HOSPITALS
36302	14	117	POSTAL SERVICE
36303	2335	29077	EXEC.; LEGIS.; & OTHER SUPPORT
36304	4	38	SPECIAL TRADE CONTRACTORS
36305	517	4174	MERCH. WHOLESALERS;DURABLE GDS
36310	278	2629	TEXTILE PRODUCT MILLS
36311	46	529	HEAVY & CIVIL ENG. CONSTRUCT'N
36312	155	1643	TRUCK TRANSPORTATION
36313	4	12	MERCH. WHOLESALERS;DURABLE GDS
36314	7	8	BROADCASTING
36316	38	80	UTILITIES
36317	4	5	FOOD AND BEVERAGE STORES
36318	10	23	JUSTICE; PUBIC ORDER/SAFETY
36319	65	1057	UTILITIES
36320	79	604	WHOLESALE ELEC. MRKTS & AGENTS
36321	40	529	OIL AND GAS EXTRACTION
36322	358	1925	FOOD SVCS & DRINKING PLACES
36323	273	2137	INSURANCE CARRIERS & RELATED
36330	1328	11564	EDUCATIONAL SERVICES
36331	8	13	ADMINISTRATIVE & SUPPORT SVCS
36340	357	3827	MERCH. WHOLESALERS;DURABLE GDS
36343	36	82	JUSTICE; PUBIC ORDER/SAFETY
36344	174	941	NURSING & RESID. CARE FACILIT.
36345	226	1700	CONSTRUCTION OF BUILDINGS
36346	18	1128	FOOD MANUFACTURING
36349	7	25	PROF.; SCIENTIFIC; & TECH SVCS
36350	138	1988	PLASTICS & RUBBER PRODUCTS MFG
36351	88	527	EXEC.; LEGIS.; & OTHER SUPPORT
36352	131	644	EDUCATIONAL SERVICES
36353	29	42	EXEC.; LEGIS.; & OTHER SUPPORT
36360	823	6069	FOOD SVCS & DRINKING PLACES
36361	2	14	MERCH. WHOLESALERS;DURABLE GDS
36362	76	5183	SUPPORT ACT. FOR TRANSPORT.
36370	7	14	RELIG.; GRANT; CIVIC; PROF ORG
36371	21	142	MERCH. WHOLESALERS;DURABLE GDS
36373	10	45	MERCH. WHOLESALERS;DURABLE GDS
36374	11	59	EDUCATIONAL SERVICES
36375	174	691	EDUCATIONAL SERVICES
36376	49	382	EDUCATIONAL SERVICES
36401	357	3359	TRUCK TRANSPORTATION
36420	719	5564	FOOD SVCS & DRINKING PLACES
36421	194	4265	TEXTILE PRODUCT MILLS
36425	42	238	WOOD PRODUCT MANUFACTURING
36426	662	6068	PAPER MANUFACTURING
36427	1	2	INSURANCE CARRIERS & RELATED
36429	2	33	FORESTRY AND LOGGING
36432	61	652	BLDG MATL & GARDEN EQPMT DLRS
36435	7	15	GASOLINE STATIONS
36436	6	13	MERCH. WHOLESALERS;DURABLE GDS
36439	45	383	EDUCATIONAL SERVICES
36441	149	930	REPAIR AND MAINTENANCE
36442	181	937	SPECIAL TRADE CONTRACTORS
36444	20	25	ADMIN. OF ECONOMIC PROGRAMS
36445	116	798	FURNITURE & RELATED PROD. MFG
36446	15	397	WOOD PRODUCT MANUFACTURING
36449	1	1	RELIG.; GRANT; CIVIC; PROF ORG
36451	257	1844	EDUCATIONAL SERVICES
36453	41	197	EDUCATIONAL SERVICES
36454	4	4	FOOD AND BEVERAGE STORES
36455	13	52	EDUCATIONAL SERVICES
36456	34	152	EDUCATIONAL SERVICES
36457	2	0	POSTAL SERVICE
36458	9	104	BLDG MATL & GARDEN EQPMT DLRS
36460	661	5602	HOSPITALS
36461	2	2	MERCH. WHOLESALERS;DURABLE GDS
36462	1	18	CLOTHING & CLOTH'G ACC. STORES
36467	365	3114	AMBULATORY HEALTH CARE SVCS
36470	8	971	PAPER MANUFACTURING
36471	29	416	WOOD PRODUCT MANUFACTURING
36473	3	2	SUPPORT ACTIVITIES: AGR./FOR.
36474	35	198	EDUCATIONAL SERVICES
36475	40	161	TRUCK TRANSPORTATION
36476	5	20	MACHINERY MANUFACTURING
36477	132	620	EDUCATIONAL SERVICES
36480	52	124	EDUCATIONAL SERVICES
36481	18	40	RELIG.; GRANT; CIVIC; PROF ORG
36482	20	28	RELIG.; GRANT; CIVIC; PROF ORG
36483	12	17	POSTAL SERVICE
36502	720	6360	TRUCK TRANSPORTATION
36503	1	17	JUSTICE; PUBIC ORDER/SAFETY
36504	3	21	EXEC.; LEGIS.; & OTHER SUPPORT
36505	39	926	CHEMICAL MANUFACTURING
36507	727	8794	FURNITURE & RELATED PROD. MFG
36509	143	1589	TRANSPORTATION EQUIPMENT MFG
36511	33	547	FOOD MANUFACTURING
36512	13	240	CHEMICAL MANUFACTURING
36513	14	18	FOOD SVCS & DRINKING PLACES
36518	213	1283	EDUCATIONAL SERVICES
36521	58	250	CONSTRUCTION OF BUILDINGS
36522	218	1665	EDUCATIONAL SERVICES
36523	62	563	MERCH. WHOLESALERS;NONDUR. GDS
36524	44	144	EDUCATIONAL SERVICES
36525	66	604	SPECIAL TRADE CONTRACTORS
36526	1378	11316	AMBULATORY HEALTH CARE SVCS
36527	538	4416	FOOD SVCS & DRINKING PLACES
36528	83	611	MUSEUMS; HIST. SITES;& SIMILAR
36529	6	7	POSTAL SERVICE
36530	265	1309	EDUCATIONAL SERVICES
36532	1318	8929	HOSPITALS
36533	17	28	SPECIAL TRADE CONTRACTORS
36535	1527	12815	FOOD SVCS & DRINKING PLACES
36536	14	176	UNCLASSIFIED ESTABLISHMENTS
36538	5	9	RELIG.; GRANT; CIVIC; PROF ORG
36539	20	74	EDUCATIONAL SERVICES
36540	8	13	FOOD AND BEVERAGE STORES
36541	199	1136	EDUCATIONAL SERVICES
36542	971	7713	REAL ESTATE
36543	12	80	EDUCATIONAL SERVICES
36544	154	1509	EDUCATIONAL SERVICES
36545	409	4156	PAPER MANUFACTURING
36547	26	46	ADMINISTRATIVE & SUPPORT SVCS
36548	33	144	EDUCATIONAL SERVICES
36549	126	470	RELIG.; GRANT; CIVIC; PROF ORG
36550	10	12	FOOD SVCS & DRINKING PLACES
36551	271	2899	BLDG MATL & GARDEN EQPMT DLRS
36553	78	2334	CHEMICAL MANUFACTURING
36555	48	135	FOOD SVCS & DRINKING PLACES
36556	5	4	POSTAL SERVICE
36558	101	390	EDUCATIONAL SERVICES
36559	29	34	ADMINISTRATIVE & SUPPORT SVCS
36560	84	1029	HOSPITALS
36561	725	5742	FOOD SVCS & DRINKING PLACES
36562	24	95	EDUCATIONAL SERVICES
36564	18	697	RELIG.; GRANT; CIVIC; PROF ORG
36567	541	3662	FOOD SVCS & DRINKING PLACES
36568	11	25	UTILITIES
36569	13	17	ADMINISTRATIVE & SUPPORT SVCS
36571	731	6390	FOOD SVCS & DRINKING PLACES
36572	109	965	EDUCATIONAL SERVICES
36574	40	218	TRUCK TRANSPORTATION
36575	470	3226	EDUCATIONAL SERVICES
36576	84	520	HEAVY & CIVIL ENG. CONSTRUCT'N
36577	7	17	ADMINISTRATIVE & SUPPORT SVCS
36578	49	204	EDUCATIONAL SERVICES
36579	35	89	EDUCATIONAL SERVICES
36580	208	1305	UTILITIES
36581	3	27	FORESTRY AND LOGGING
36582	972	10737	MERCH. WHOLESALERS;DURABLE GDS
36583	13	20	SPECIAL TRADE CONTRACTORS
36584	7	25	TRUCK TRANSPORTATION
36585	12	32	FOOD SVCS & DRINKING PLACES
36587	142	662	EDUCATIONAL SERVICES
36590	2	9	BLDG MATL & GARDEN EQPMT DLRS
36601	18	80	SUPPORT ACT. FOR TRANSPORT.
36602	1043	12453	PROF.; SCIENTIFIC; & TECH SVCS
36603	377	6594	TRANSPORTATION EQUIPMENT MFG
36604	481	7770	AMBULATORY HEALTH CARE SVCS
36605	494	3860	EDUCATIONAL SERVICES
36606	1687	20327	MOTOR VEHICLE & PARTS DEALERS
36607	603	11083	HOSPITALS
36608	1962	21841	HOSPITALS
36609	1185	13442	AMBULATORY HEALTH CARE SVCS
36610	402	5934	PAPER MANUFACTURING
36611	178	2201	CHEMICAL MANUFACTURING
36612	168	1632	FOOD AND BEVERAGE STORES
36613	216	1481	EDUCATIONAL SERVICES
36615	103	3427	COMPUTER & ELECTRONIC PROD MFG
36616	8	18	NONSTORE RETAILERS
36617	314	7236	HOSPITALS
36618	442	5855	EDUCATIONAL SERVICES
36619	627	7110	FOOD SVCS & DRINKING PLACES
36621	2	300	SECURITIES/COMMODITY CONTRACTS
36622	5	717	CREDIT INTERMEDIATION & RELATD
36628	1	0	ADMIN. ENVIRO. QUALITY PROGRMS
36633	6	26	EXEC.; LEGIS.; & OTHER SUPPORT
36640	1	3	PROF.; SCIENTIFIC; & TECH SVCS
36652	1	4	BROADCASTING
36660	6	5	CONSTRUCTION OF BUILDINGS
36663	2	9	CONSTRUCTION OF BUILDINGS
36670	2	1	AMBULATORY HEALTH CARE SVCS
36671	2	6	CONSTRUCTION OF BUILDINGS
36675	2	200	RELIG.; GRANT; CIVIC; PROF ORG
36685	12	33	ADMINISTRATIVE & SUPPORT SVCS
36688	15	419	AMBULATORY HEALTH CARE SVCS
36689	12	28	BLDG MATL & GARDEN EQPMT DLRS
36691	16	71	SOCIAL ASSISTANCE
36693	958	12392	MERCH. WHOLESALERS;DURABLE GDS
36695	1087	9080	PROF.; SCIENTIFIC; & TECH SVCS
36701	1028	9536	HOSPITALS
36702	3	14	FOOD MANUFACTURING
36703	451	6529	PAPER MANUFACTURING
36720	10	41	EDUCATIONAL SERVICES
36722	17	136	TELECOMMUNICATIONS
36723	3	7	EXEC.; LEGIS.; & OTHER SUPPORT
36726	289	2235	EXEC.; LEGIS.; & OTHER SUPPORT
36727	1	1	POSTAL SERVICE
36728	12	39	CONSTRUCTION OF BUILDINGS
36732	563	6387	PAPER MANUFACTURING
36736	31	105	EDUCATIONAL SERVICES

BUSINESS DATA

ZIP CODE	2009 Total Firms	2009 Total Employ-ees	TOP INDUSTRY RANKED on 2009 EMPLOYMENT
36738	25	84	CROP PRODUCTION
36740	19	47	JUSTICE; PUBIC ORDER/SAFETY
36741	1	2	POSTAL SERVICE
36742	41	104	TRUCK TRANSPORTATION
36744	268	3790	HOSPITALS
36745	3	3	RELIG.; GRANT; CIVIC; PROF ORG
36748	188	1785	WOOD PRODUCT MANUFACTURING
36749	11	40	JUSTICE; PUBIC ORDER/SAFETY
36750	95	1020	WOOD PRODUCT MANUFACTURING
36751	11	43	EDUCATIONAL SERVICES
36752	68	206	WAREHOUSING AND STORAGE
36753	4	39	WOOD PRODUCT MANUFACTURING
36754	6	6	FOOD AND BEVERAGE STORES
36756	233	1909	EDUCATIONAL SERVICES
36758	20	269	BLDG MATL & GARDEN EQPMT DLRS
36759	27	52	CROP PRODUCTION
36761	21	158	SOCIAL ASSISTANCE
36763	6	14	FOOD AND BEVERAGE STORES
36764	8	57	MERCH. WHOLESALERS;DURABLE GDS
36765	21	117	EDUCATIONAL SERVICES
36766	3	6	FOOD AND BEVERAGE STORES
36767	36	170	EDUCATIONAL SERVICES
36768	31	101	BLDG MATL & GARDEN EQPMT DLRS
36769	76	1193	PAPER MANUFACTURING
36773	11	18	RELIG.; GRANT; CIVIC; PROF ORG
36775	19	63	EDUCATIONAL SERVICES
36776	21	41	SOCIAL ASSISTANCE
36782	50	233	EDUCATIONAL SERVICES
36783	43	121	HEAVY & CIVIL ENG. CONSTRUCT'N
36784	354	2658	GENERAL MERCHANDISE STORES
36785	33	132	PETROLEUM & COAL PRODUCTS MFG
36786	97	930	FOOD MANUFACTURING
36790	6	22	FORESTRY AND LOGGING
36792	20	114	EDUCATIONAL SERVICES
36793	6	13	CONSTRUCTION OF BUILDINGS
36801	1328	15940	HOSPITALS
36803	11	57	FOOD SVCS & DRINKING PLACES
36804	355	3786	MERCH. WHOLESALERS;DURABLE GDS
36830	1361	14642	FOOD SVCS & DRINKING PLACES
36831	11	59	ADMIN. OF ECONOMIC PROGRAMS
36832	411	5820	FOOD SVCS & DRINKING PLACES
36849	38	799	PROF.; SCIENTIFIC; & TECH SVCS
36850	52	210	EDUCATIONAL SERVICES
36851	8	843	MERCH. WHOLESALERS;DURABLE GDS
36852	40	254	GASOLINE STATIONS
36853	353	2466	NURSING & RESID. CARE FACILIT.
36854	448	4068	EDUCATIONAL SERVICES
36855	22	54	EDUCATIONAL SERVICES
36856	50	217	HEAVY & CIVIL ENG. CONSTRUCT'N
36858	14	40	JUSTICE; PUBIC ORDER/SAFETY
36860	56	182	FISHING; HUNTING AND TRAPPING
36861	50	147	SPECIAL TRADE CONTRACTORS
36862	236	2184	TRUCK TRANSPORTATION
36863	425	2793	MERCH. WHOLESALERS;DURABLE GDS
36865	9	62	EDUCATIONAL SERVICES
36866	81	328	EDUCATIONAL SERVICES
36867	976	10940	HOSPITALS
36868	4	3	ADMINISTRATIVE & SUPPORT SVCS
36869	318	4170	MERCH. WHOLESALERS;DURABLE GDS
36870	276	1363	FOOD AND BEVERAGE STORES
36871	33	221	MACHINERY MANUFACTURING
36874	86	475	EDUCATIONAL SERVICES
36875	68	463	EDUCATIONAL SERVICES
36877	183	1250	EDUCATIONAL SERVICES
36879	22	68	FOOD SVCS & DRINKING PLACES
36901	4	27	SOCIAL ASSISTANCE
36904	264	1734	SPECIAL TRADE CONTRACTORS
36907	35	186	MERCH. WHOLESALERS;DURABLE GDS
36908	123	524	EDUCATIONAL SERVICES
36910	3	3	MERCH. WHOLESALERS;DURABLE GDS
36912	43	69	RELIG.; GRANT; CIVIC; PROF ORG
36913	7	53	OIL AND GAS EXTRACTION
36915	10	8	RELIG.; GRANT; CIVIC; PROF ORG
36916	47	2428	PAPER MANUFACTURING
36919	65	236	BLDG MATL & GARDEN EQPMT DLRS
36921	27	157	MERCH. WHOLESALERS;DURABLE GDS
36922	10	7	RELIG.; GRANT; CIVIC; PROF ORG
36925	106	1042	MACHINERY MANUFACTURING
37010	62	286	SOCIAL ASSISTANCE
37011	13	28	PROF.; SCIENTIFIC; & TECH SVCS
37012	67	441	TELECOMMUNICATIONS
37013	1202	11673	FOOD SVCS & DRINKING PLACES
37014	68	187	SPECIAL TRADE CONTRACTORS
37015	509	6516	ELECT'L EQPMT; APP; & COMP MFG
37016	20	55	EDUCATIONAL SERVICES
37018	30	47	FOOD SVCS & DRINKING PLACES
37019	27	246	CONSTRUCTION OF BUILDINGS
37020	88	435	EDUCATIONAL SERVICES
37022	84	256	EDUCATIONAL SERVICES
37023	12	53	MERCH. WHOLESALERS;DURABLE GDS

ZIP CODE	2009 Total Firms	2009 Total Employ-ees	TOP INDUSTRY RANKED on 2009 EMPLOYMENT
37024	33	73	ADMINISTRATIVE & SUPPORT SVCS
37025	86	338	SPECIAL TRADE CONTRACTORS
37026	28	165	TRUCK TRANSPORTATION
37027	3233	40147	MOTOR VEHICLE & PARTS DEALERS
37028	12	22	CONSTRUCTION OF BUILDINGS
37029	96	674	ACCOMMODATION
37030	371	2893	EDUCATIONAL SERVICES
37031	31	89	RELIG.; GRANT; CIVIC; PROF ORG
37032	62	218	EDUCATIONAL SERVICES
37033	343	2592	EDUCATIONAL SERVICES
37034	144	836	EDUCATIONAL SERVICES
37035	28	93	EDUCATIONAL SERVICES
37036	126	947	JUSTICE; PUBIC ORDER/SAFETY
37037	79	359	EDUCATIONAL SERVICES
37040	2050	29403	FOOD SVCS & DRINKING PLACES
37041	5	6	BLDG MATL & GARDEN EQPMT DLRS
37042	943	6838	EDUCATIONAL SERVICES
37043	962	9340	HOSPITALS
37044	2	702	EDUCATIONAL SERVICES
37046	84	210	EDUCATIONAL SERVICES
37047	54	425	EDUCATIONAL SERVICES
37048	55	176	CONSTRUCTION OF BUILDINGS
37049	73	361	EDUCATIONAL SERVICES
37050	45	807	UTILITIES
37051	27	51	SPECIAL TRADE CONTRACTORS
37052	43	319	EDUCATIONAL SERVICES
37055	1216	13023	FOOD SVCS & DRINKING PLACES
37056	2	3	RELIG.; GRANT; CIVIC; PROF ORG
37057	15	15	POSTAL SERVICE
37058	278	1720	EDUCATIONAL SERVICES
37059	28	72	ACCOMMODATION
37060	68	408	EDUCATIONAL SERVICES
37061	274	1643	SOCIAL ASSISTANCE
37062	253	1776	ELECT'L EQPMT; APP; & COMP MFG
37063	2	0	ADMINISTRATIVE & SUPPORT SVCS
37064	2186	18368	EDUCATIONAL SERVICES
37065	14	68	CONSTRUCTION OF BUILDINGS
37066	1548	17926	EDUCATIONAL SERVICES
37067	1830	31142	TELECOMMUNICATIONS
37068	17	94	PERSONAL AND LAUNDRY SERVICES
37069	309	1875	EDUCATIONAL SERVICES
37070	12	20	SPECIAL TRADE CONTRACTORS
37071	5	41	RELIG.; GRANT; CIVIC; PROF ORG
37072	1268	12156	GENERAL MERCHANDISE STORES
37073	247	1297	ELECT'L EQPMT; APP; & COMP MFG
37074	240	1764	EDUCATIONAL SERVICES
37075	1801	15619	FOOD SVCS & DRINKING PLACES
37076	949	11014	FOOD SVCS & DRINKING PLACES
37077	23	71	SPECIAL TRADE CONTRACTORS
37078	42	254	FOOD SVCS & DRINKING PLACES
37079	36	114	SPECIAL TRADE CONTRACTORS
37080	188	947	SPECIAL TRADE CONTRACTORS
37082	156	1112	EDUCATIONAL SERVICES
37083	557	3717	EDUCATIONAL SERVICES
37085	54	320	EDUCATIONAL SERVICES
37086	677	15521	MERCH. WHOLESALERS;DURABLE GDS
37087	1666	18993	FOOD SVCS & DRINKING PLACES
37088	4	12	SPORTG GDS;HOBBY;BOOK; & MUSIC
37090	403	8161	COMPUTER & ELECTRONIC PROD MFG
37091	735	9014	EDUCATIONAL SERVICES
37095	72	339	EDUCATIONAL SERVICES
37096	214	1605	TRANSPORTATION EQUIPMENT MFG
37097	81	524	MERCH. WHOLESALERS;DURABLE GDS
37098	123	727	EDUCATIONAL SERVICES
37101	138	692	EDUCATIONAL SERVICES
37110	1594	11333	BLDG MATL & GARDEN EQPMT DLRS
37111	2	2	CONSTRUCTION OF BUILDINGS
37115	1373	15317	MOTOR VEHICLE & PARTS DEALERS
37116	11	27	SOCIAL ASSISTANCE
37118	24	27	ELECTRONICS & APPLIANCE STORES
37119	1	1	POSTAL SERVICE
37121	13	26	CONSTRUCTION OF BUILDINGS
37122	1027	8478	FOOD SVCS & DRINKING PLACES
37127	300	5137	MERCH. WHOLESALERS;NONDUR. GDS
37128	543	4384	EDUCATIONAL SERVICES
37129	2354	26746	FOOD SVCS & DRINKING PLACES
37130	1600	17259	HOSPITALS
37131	3	2600	INSURANCE CARRIERS & RELATED
37132	10	2576	EDUCATIONAL SERVICES
37133	15	129	MISCELLANEOUS MANUFACTURING
37134	111	811	CHEMICAL MANUFACTURING
37135	152	758	SPECIAL TRADE CONTRACTORS
37136	13	13	FOOD AND BEVERAGE STORES
37137	24	192	RELIG.; GRANT; CIVIC; PROF ORG
37138	509	3845	CHEMICAL MANUFACTURING
37140	7	14	ACCOMMODATION
37141	17	62	JUSTICE; PUBIC ORDER/SAFETY
37142	20	162	NURSING & RESID. CARE FACILIT.
37143	85	326	EDUCATIONAL SERVICES
37144	42	121	EDUCATIONAL SERVICES

ZIP CODE	2009 Total Firms	2009 Total Employ-ees	TOP INDUSTRY RANKED on 2009 EMPLOYMENT
37145	27	71	WOOD PRODUCT MANUFACTURING
37146	182	1369	EDUCATIONAL SERVICES
37148	486	6938	FABRICATED METAL PRODUCT MFG
37149	31	165	SOCIAL ASSISTANCE
37150	169	1117	FOOD AND BEVERAGE STORES
37151	9	30	SPECIAL TRADE CONTRACTORS
37152	10	53	MERCH. WHOLESALERS;DURABLE GDS
37153	54	239	EDUCATIONAL SERVICES
37160	1189	13445	FOOD MANUFACTURING
37161	1	450	MISCELLANEOUS MANUFACTURING
37162	5	13	HEAVY & CIVIL ENG. CONSTRUCT'N
37166	510	6198	TRANSPORTATION EQUIPMENT MFG
37167	1341	24495	TRANSPORTATION EQUIPMENT MFG
37171	12	24	SPECIAL TRADE CONTRACTORS
37172	1014	16186	MERCH. WHOLESALERS;DURABLE GDS
37174	535	9317	TRANSPORTATION EQUIPMENT MFG
37175	16	53	WOOD PRODUCT MANUFACTURING
37178	41	134	EDUCATIONAL SERVICES
37179	125	740	EDUCATIONAL SERVICES
37180	32	317	EDUCATIONAL SERVICES
37181	35	73	FOOD AND BEVERAGE STORES
37183	65	373	EDUCATIONAL SERVICES
37184	96	400	EDUCATIONAL SERVICES
37185	433	3154	EDUCATIONAL SERVICES
37186	241	1081	EDUCATIONAL SERVICES
37187	156	1401	TRANSPORTATION EQUIPMENT MFG
37188	433	3841	FOOD SVCS & DRINKING PLACES
37189	104	1072	SPECIAL TRADE CONTRACTORS
37190	334	1933	HOSPITALS
37191	64	332	EDUCATIONAL SERVICES
37201	587	11571	JUSTICE; PUBIC ORDER/SAFETY
37202	12	194	POSTAL SERVICE
37203	3715	56639	HOSPITALS
37204	1324	18628	PROF.; SCIENTIFIC; & TECH SVCS
37205	1113	14791	HOSPITALS
37206	733	8161	RELIG.; GRANT; CIVIC; PROF ORG
37207	1378	11616	EDUCATIONAL SERVICES
37208	699	7931	HOSPITALS
37209	1464	18363	EDUCATIONAL SERVICES
37210	1865	28935	MERCH. WHOLESALERS;DURABLE GDS
37211	3191	30242	SPECIAL TRADE CONTRACTORS
37212	1166	15579	HOSPITALS
37213	114	2127	MERCH. WHOLESALERS;DURABLE GDS
37214	1958	37381	ACCOMMODATION
37215	1384	12064	FOOD SVCS & DRINKING PLACES
37216	498	3545	EDUCATIONAL SERVICES
37217	1485	19223	PROF.; SCIENTIFIC; & TECH SVCS
37218	444	4221	NURSING & RESID. CARE FACILIT.
37219	554	10597	PROF.; SCIENTIFIC; & TECH SVCS
37220	298	2182	EDUCATIONAL SERVICES
37221	944	5727	FOOD SVCS & DRINKING PLACES
37222	17	68	ADMINISTRATIVE & SUPPORT SVCS
37224	4	4	MERCH. WHOLESALERS;DURABLE GDS
37228	395	9012	PROF.; SCIENTIFIC; & TECH SVCS
37229	24	35	ADMINISTRATIVE & SUPPORT SVCS
37230	4	13	ADMINISTRATIVE & SUPPORT SVCS
37232	157	54415	AMBULATORY HEALTH CARE SVCS
37234	9	3309	SPORTG GDS;HOBBY;BOOK; & MUSIC
37235	2	20	REAL ESTATE
37236	10	3149	HOSPITALS
37237	2	25	CREDIT INTERMEDIATION & RELATD
37238	32	1407	PROF.; SCIENTIFIC; & TECH SVCS
37240	16	479	OTHER INFORMATION SERVICES
37241	1	4	SPECIAL TRADE CONTRACTORS
37242	14	1599	EXEC.; LEGIS.; & OTHER SUPPORT
37243	363	11663	ADMIN. HUMAN RESOURCE PROGRAMS
37245	30	1216	ADMIN. OF ECONOMIC PROGRAMS
37246	2	12	CREDIT INTERMEDIATION & RELATD
37247	13	649	JUSTICE; PUBIC ORDER/SAFETY
37250	2	1203	INSURANCE CARRIERS & RELATED
37301	99	393	EDUCATIONAL SERVICES
37302	47	156	EDUCATIONAL SERVICES
37303	1199	13297	FOOD SVCS & DRINKING PLACES
37305	39	78	RELIG.; GRANT; CIVIC; PROF ORG
37306	50	152	JUSTICE; PUBIC ORDER/SAFETY
37307	198	1192	MOTOR VEHICLE & PARTS DEALERS
37308	23	79	EDUCATIONAL SERVICES
37309	54	1363	PAPER MANUFACTURING
37310	129	1715	CHEMICAL MANUFACTURING
37311	1548	26805	RELIG.; GRANT; CIVIC; PROF ORG
37312	1055	14735	FOOD SVCS & DRINKING PLACES
37313	75	555	SOCIAL ASSISTANCE
37314	5	8	TRUCK TRANSPORTATION
37315	35	3970	FOOD MANUFACTURING
37316	2	24	BLDG MATL & GARDEN EQPMT DLRS
37317	128	599	HOSPITALS
37318	58	335	EDUCATIONAL SERVICES
37320	12	27	RELIG.; GRANT; CIVIC; PROF ORG
37321	711	9442	FURN. & HOME FURNISHGS STORES
37322	201	2049	TEXTILE MILLS

ZIP CODE	2009 Total Firms	2009 Total Employ-ees	TOP INDUSTRY RANKED on 2009 EMPLOYMENT	ZIP CODE	2009 Total Firms	2009 Total Employ-ees	TOP INDUSTRY RANKED on 2009 EMPLOYMENT	ZIP CODE	2009 Total Firms	2009 Total Employ-ees	TOP INDUSTRY RANKED on 2009 EMPLOYMENT
37323	480	3657	MERCH. WHOLESALERS;NONDUR. GDS	37605	5	11	CONSTRUCTION OF BUILDINGS	37801	1075	16414	TRANSPORTATION EQUIPMENT MFG
37324	193	3803	TRANSPORTATION EQUIPMENT MFG	37614	13	2599	EDUCATIONAL SERVICES	37802	16	40	BLDG MATL & GARDEN EQPMT DLRS
37325	25	64	RELIG.; GRANT; CIVIC; PROF ORG	37615	580	7389	SOCIAL ASSISTANCE	37803	370	2545	EDUCATIONAL SERVICES
37326	62	592	NURSING & RESID. CARE FACILIT.	37616	77	1658	MISCELLANEOUS STORE RETAILERS	37804	1009	16594	CREDIT INTERMEDIATION & RELATD
37327	509	3499	MACHINERY MANUFACTURING	37617	526	4685	EDUCATIONAL SERVICES	37806	72	926	PROF.; SCIENTIFIC; & TECH SVCS
37328	23	139	WOOD PRODUCT MANUFACTURING	37618	258	1336	EDUCATIONAL SERVICES	37807	354	2392	EDUCATIONAL SERVICES
37329	90	540	EDUCATIONAL SERVICES	37620	1551	19696	HOSPITALS	37809	31	2363	MERCH. WHOLESALERS;DURABLE GDS
37330	98	548	FABRICATED METAL PRODUCT MFG	37621	9	417	POSTAL SERVICE	37810	16	88	EDUCATIONAL SERVICES
37331	259	3561	MISCELLANEOUS MANUFACTURING	37625	3	9	PERFORM'G ARTS; SPEC. SPORTS	37811	40	299	TRUCK TRANSPORTATION
37332	45	171	EXEC.; LEGIS.; & OTHER SUPPORT	37640	82	195	WOOD PRODUCT MANUFACTURING	37813	759	12634	PROF.; SCIENTIFIC; & TECH SVCS
37333	7	58	BLDG MATL & GARDEN EQPMT DLRS	37641	130	663	EDUCATIONAL SERVICES	37814	1330	15658	HOSPITALS
37334	917	8630	ELECTRONICS & APPLIANCE STORES	37642	252	2465	MACHINERY MANUFACTURING	37815	10	133	PROF.; SCIENTIFIC; & TECH SVCS
37335	30	152	EDUCATIONAL SERVICES	37643	1130	10643	EXEC.; LEGIS.; & OTHER SUPPORT	37818	97	832	EDUCATIONAL SERVICES
37336	53	167	JUSTICE; PUBIC ORDER/SAFETY	37644	2	2	SPECIAL TRADE CONTRACTORS	37819	8	29	BLDG MATL & GARDEN EQPMT DLRS
37337	13	25	BLDG MATL & GARDEN EQPMT DLRS	37645	87	392	AMBULATORY HEALTH CARE SVCS	37820	111	1038	SPECIAL TRADE CONTRACTORS
37338	36	145	EDUCATIONAL SERVICES	37650	393	4711	CHEMICAL MANUFACTURING	37821	847	9720	MERCH. WHOLESALERS;DURABLE GDS
37339	57	223	MISCELLANEOUS MANUFACTURING	37656	78	370	JUSTICE; PUBIC ORDER/SAFETY	37822	6	17	PROF.; SCIENTIFIC; & TECH SVCS
37340	14	120	TRANSPORTATION EQUIPMENT MFG	37657	10	14	WOOD PRODUCT MANUFACTURING	37825	237	4930	FURNITURE & RELATED PROD. MFG
37341	193	1093	EDUCATIONAL SERVICES	37658	103	507	EDUCATIONAL SERVICES	37826	70	652	APPAREL MANUFACTURING
37342	56	196	EDUCATIONAL SERVICES	37659	577	3565	EDUCATIONAL SERVICES	37828	54	845	SPECIAL TRADE CONTRACTORS
37343	1216	10008	FOOD SVCS & DRINKING PLACES	37660	2041	39208	PAPER MANUFACTURING	37829	30	118	EDUCATIONAL SERVICES
37345	65	370	WOOD PRODUCT MANUFACTURING	37662	7	21	SPECIAL TRADE CONTRACTORS	37830	1496	32369	PROF.; SCIENTIFIC; & TECH SVCS
37347	407	3367	FOOD SVCS & DRINKING PLACES	37663	477	5346	CONSTRUCTION OF BUILDINGS	37831	13	22	REPAIR AND MAINTENANCE
37348	13	43	BEVERAGE & TOBACCO PRODUCT MFG	37664	680	6593	FOOD SVCS & DRINKING PLACES	37840	263	1202	EDUCATIONAL SERVICES
37349	1	4	PROF.; SCIENTIFIC; & TECH SVCS	37665	93	373	FOOD SVCS & DRINKING PLACES	37841	524	3165	EDUCATIONAL SERVICES
37350	51	400	PROF.; SCIENTIFIC; & TECH SVCS	37669	1	500	PRINT'G & RELATED SUPP'T ACT'S	37843	44	152	CONSTRUCTION OF BUILDINGS
37351	3	307	MERCH. WHOLESALERS;NONDUR. GDS	37680	10	28	EDUCATIONAL SERVICES	37845	17	331	EXEC.; LEGIS.; & OTHER SUPPORT
37352	137	1225	BEVERAGE & TOBACCO PRODUCT MFG	37681	92	646	SOCIAL ASSISTANCE	37846	38	127	EDUCATIONAL SERVICES
37353	74	586	EXEC.; LEGIS.; & OTHER SUPPORT	37682	11	206	EDUCATIONAL SERVICES	37847	62	655	MISCELLANEOUS MANUFACTURING
37354	537	3751	FOOD SVCS & DRINKING PLACES	37683	460	4370	JUSTICE; PUBIC ORDER/SAFETY	37848	4	14	PROF.; SCIENTIFIC; & TECH SVCS
37355	849	10033	TRANSPORTATION EQUIPMENT MFG	37684	18	3259	OTHER INFORMATION SERVICES	37849	657	4410	EDUCATIONAL SERVICES
37356	187	1021	FOOD SVCS & DRINKING PLACES	37686	180	3209	UNCLASSIFIED ESTABLISHMENTS	37852	53	202	EDUCATIONAL SERVICES
37357	164	1115	FABRICATED METAL PRODUCT MFG	37687	97	485	EDUCATIONAL SERVICES	37853	89	1311	TEXTILE PRODUCT MILLS
37359	6	7	POSTAL SERVICE	37688	25	63	JUSTICE; PUBIC ORDER/SAFETY	37854	370	3686	MISCELLANEOUS MANUFACTURING
37360	32	154	BEVERAGE & TOBACCO PRODUCT MFG	37690	50	367	MACHINERY MANUFACTURING	37857	683	7320	TRANSPORTATION EQUIPMENT MFG
37361	41	423	FOOD SVCS & DRINKING PLACES	37691	19	32	TRUCK TRANSPORTATION	37860	82	2095	TRANSPORTATION EQUIPMENT MFG
37362	32	116	EDUCATIONAL SERVICES	37692	100	1098	PLASTICS & RUBBER PRODUCTS MFG	37861	227	1372	EDUCATIONAL SERVICES
37363	648	6364	TRANSPORTATION EQUIPMENT MFG	37694	40	151	MINING (EXCEPT OIL AND GAS)	37862	1520	14088	FOOD SVCS & DRINKING PLACES
37364	3	7	BLDG MATL & GARDEN EQPMT DLRS	37701	681	18094	EDUCATIONAL SERVICES	37863	894	9951	FOOD SVCS & DRINKING PLACES
37365	46	174	EDUCATIONAL SERVICES	37705	100	880	WOOD PRODUCT MANUFACTURING	37864	6	11	WASTE MANAGMT & REMEDIAT'N SVC
37366	27	223	MISCELLANEOUS MANUFACTURING	37707	2	6	MOTOR VEHICLE & PARTS DEALERS	37865	447	3259	CHEMICAL MANUFACTURING
37367	458	8558	FOOD AND BEVERAGE STORES	37708	166	1659	WOOD PRODUCT MANUFACTURING	37866	23	72	EDUCATIONAL SERVICES
37369	12	56	JUSTICE; PUBIC ORDER/SAFETY	37709	76	287	FOOD SVCS & DRINKING PLACES	37868	4	39	PROF.; SCIENTIFIC; & TECH SVCS
37370	64	255	EDUCATIONAL SERVICES	37710	25	118	MINING (EXCEPT OIL AND GAS)	37869	164	1233	EDUCATIONAL SERVICES
37371	4	34	SPECIAL TRADE CONTRACTORS	37711	110	1289	WOOD PRODUCT MANUFACTURING	37870	60	194	FABRICATED METAL PRODUCT MFG
37373	81	386	EDUCATIONAL SERVICES	37713	14	30	PROF.; SCIENTIFIC; & TECH SVCS	37871	167	913	EDUCATIONAL SERVICES
37374	14	70	MERCH. WHOLESALERS;DURABLE GDS	37714	94	1180	FABRICATED METAL PRODUCT MFG	37872	61	501	TELECOMMUNICATIONS
37375	88	629	FOOD SVCS & DRINKING PLACES	37715	26	351	NONSTORE RETAILERS	37873	93	2106	TRANSPORTATION EQUIPMENT MFG
37376	10	62	MINING (EXCEPT OIL AND GAS)	37716	915	11557	EDUCATIONAL SERVICES	37874	533	4528	NONMETALLIC MINERAL PROD. MFG
37377	304	1990	NURSING & RESID. CARE FACILIT.	37717	2	8	MOTOR VEHICLE & PARTS DEALERS	37876	712	4598	EDUCATIONAL SERVICES
37378	10	49	MERCH. WHOLESALERS;DURABLE GDS	37719	4	53	EDUCATIONAL SERVICES	37877	131	831	SPECIAL TRADE CONTRACTORS
37379	477	4292	UTILITIES	37721	171	1169	JUSTICE; PUBIC ORDER/SAFETY	37878	9	8	RELIG.; GRANT; CIVIC; PROF ORG
37380	238	1995	PRIMARY METAL MANUFACTURING	37722	99	531	EDUCATIONAL SERVICES	37879	260	2852	HOSPITALS
37381	219	1289	WOOD PRODUCT MANUFACTURING	37723	28	266	MINING (EXCEPT OIL AND GAS)	37880	51	204	FOOD SVCS & DRINKING PLACES
37382	2	12	WAREHOUSING AND STORAGE	37724	68	260	EDUCATIONAL SERVICES	37881	30	224	NONSTORE RETAILERS
37383	7	718	EDUCATIONAL SERVICES	37725	447	3947	FOOD SVCS & DRINKING PLACES	37882	189	855	ACCOMMODATION
37384	1	69	CONSTRUCTION OF BUILDINGS	37726	52	97	EDUCATIONAL SERVICES	37885	165	3791	REPAIR AND MAINTENANCE
37385	208	1069	EDUCATIONAL SERVICES	37727	22	69	EDUCATIONAL SERVICES	37886	81	812	ACCOMMODATION
37387	163	604	EDUCATIONAL SERVICES	37729	14	79	EDUCATIONAL SERVICES	37887	283	2023	JUSTICE; PUBIC ORDER/SAFETY
37388	1150	12150	FOOD SVCS & DRINKING PLACES	37730	1	3	RELIG.; GRANT; CIVIC; PROF ORG	37888	40	227	EDUCATIONAL SERVICES
37389	5	3533	EXEC.; LEGIS.; & OTHER SUPPORT	37731	6	40	EDUCATIONAL SERVICES	37890	174	2060	TRUCK TRANSPORTATION
37391	32	47	UTILITIES	37732	6	5	GASOLINE STATIONS	37891	44	254	FURNITURE & RELATED PROD. MFG
37394	12	44	BLDG MATL & GARDEN EQPMT DLRS	37733	7	43	MUSEUMS; HIST. SITES;& SIMILAR	37892	67	206	TRUCK TRANSPORTATION
37396	2	5	MERCH. WHOLESALERS;DURABLE GDS	37737	123	445	EDUCATIONAL SERVICES	37901	12	45	ADMINISTRATIVE & SUPPORT SVCS
37397	161	858	EDUCATIONAL SERVICES	37738	1024	8979	ACCOMMODATION	37902	914	13879	CREDIT INTERMEDIATION & RELATD
37398	662	6845	GENERAL MERCHANDISE STORES	37742	107	543	EDUCATIONAL SERVICES	37909	541	9672	AMBULATORY HEALTH CARE SVCS
37401	14	17	PROF.; SCIENTIFIC; & TECH SVCS	37743	763	8573	NURSING & RESID. CARE FACILIT.	37912	884	9174	FOOD SVCS & DRINKING PLACES
37402	1120	25142	INSURANCE CARRIERS & RELATED	37744	7	24	ADMINISTRATIVE & SUPPORT SVCS	37914	723	9381	TRANSPORTATION EQUIPMENT MFG
37403	536	15114	AMBULATORY HEALTH CARE SVCS	37745	1105	12648	EXEC.; LEGIS.; & OTHER SUPPORT	37915	244	3995	JUSTICE; PUBIC ORDER/SAFETY
37404	782	14388	HOSPITALS	37748	640	5480	FOOD SVCS & DRINKING PLACES	37916	395	13819	AMBULATORY HEALTH CARE SVCS
37405	880	9434	MACHINERY MANUFACTURING	37752	139	1149	EDUCATIONAL SERVICES	37917	1629	19293	HOSPITALS
37406	657	13146	PROF.; SCIENTIFIC; & TECH SVCS	37753	27	168	SCENIC & SIGHTSEEING TRANSPORT	37918	1447	11874	FOOD SVCS & DRINKING PLACES
37407	471	5967	SPECIAL TRADE CONTRACTORS	37754	68	245	EDUCATIONAL SERVICES	37919	2780	29028	FOOD SVCS & DRINKING PLACES
37408	448	4926	MERCH. WHOLESALERS;DURABLE GDS	37755	95	341	UTILITIES	37920	1360	17367	HOSPITALS
37409	164	1533	HEALTH & PERSONAL CARE STORES	37756	182	1741	EDUCATIONAL SERVICES	37921	1171	19149	ADMINISTRATIVE & SUPPORT SVCS
37410	137	1556	MERCH. WHOLESALERS;DURABLE GDS	37757	290	2651	GENERAL MERCHANDISE STORES	37922	1729	21519	PROF.; SCIENTIFIC; & TECH SVCS
37411	803	6228	FOOD SVCS & DRINKING PLACES	37760	461	5196	EDUCATIONAL SERVICES	37923	1674	15379	HOSPITALS
37412	854	9856	MISCELLANEOUS MANUFACTURING	37762	147	1476	HOSPITALS	37924	546	7144	FOOD SVCS & DRINKING PLACES
37414	14	52	HEAVY & CIVIL ENG. CONSTRUCT'N	37763	500	3607	EDUCATIONAL SERVICES	37927	5	5	ADMINISTRATIVE & SUPPORT SVCS
37415	817	6429	FOOD SVCS & DRINKING PLACES	37764	201	1867	FOOD SVCS & DRINKING PLACES	37928	13	19	ADMINISTRATIVE & SUPPORT SVCS
37416	621	6212	PROF.; SCIENTIFIC; & TECH SVCS	37765	7	11	FOOD SVCS & DRINKING PLACES	37929	86	764	PROF.; SCIENTIFIC; & TECH SVCS
37419	271	3829	TRUCK TRANSPORTATION	37766	651	4605	EDUCATIONAL SERVICES	37930	22	88	MERCH. WHOLESALERS;DURABLE GDS
37421	3044	35016	FOOD SVCS & DRINKING PLACES	37769	162	1443	FOOD SVCS & DRINKING PLACES	37931	491	5019	EDUCATIONAL SERVICES
37422	9	24	FOOD SVCS & DRINKING PLACES	37770	45	135	MISCELLANEOUS STORE RETAILERS	37932	784	14643	MERCH. WHOLESALERS;DURABLE GDS
37424	12	19	EDUCATIONAL SERVICES	37771	681	6555	FOOD SVCS & DRINKING PLACES	37933	22	60	CONSTRUCTION OF BUILDINGS
37450	68	738	PROF.; SCIENTIFIC; & TECH SVCS	37772	322	2408	FOOD SVCS & DRINKING PLACES	37934	1214	11860	FOOD SVCS & DRINKING PLACES
37501	2	0	MERCH. WHOLESALERS;DURABLE GDS	37774	555	6584	MOTOR VEHICLE & PARTS DEALERS	37938	329	2386	PERSONAL AND LAUNDRY SERVICES
37601	1621	21951	FOOD SVCS & DRINKING PLACES	37777	343	5260	HOSPITALS	37939	11	23	MERCH. WHOLESALERS;DURABLE GDS
37602	14	32	PROF.; SCIENTIFIC; & TECH SVCS	37778	2	5	WAREHOUSING AND STORAGE	37940	13	22	ADMINISTRATIVE & SUPPORT SVCS
37604	1646	29410	HOSPITALS	37779	49	369	NONMETALLIC MINERAL PROD. MFG	37950	21	651	POSTAL SERVICE

BUSINESS DATA

ZIP CODE	2009 Total Firms	2009 Total Employees	TOP INDUSTRY RANKED on 2009 EMPLOYMENT	ZIP CODE	2009 Total Firms	2009 Total Employees	TOP INDUSTRY RANKED on 2009 EMPLOYMENT	ZIP CODE	2009 Total Firms	2009 Total Employees	TOP INDUSTRY RANKED on 2009 EMPLOYMENT
37996	45	1461	EDUCATIONAL SERVICES	38134	2479	28689	EXEC.; LEGIS.; & OTHER SUPPORT	38342	34	84	EXEC.; LEGIS.; & OTHER SUPPORT
37997	1	8	CREDIT INTERMEDIATION & RELATD	38135	330	2112	EDUCATIONAL SERVICES	38343	563	5889	MERCH. WHOLESALERS;NONDUR. GDS
37998	4	434	EDUCATIONAL SERVICES	38136	3	811	POSTAL SERVICE	38344	418	5052	HEAVY & CIVIL ENG. CONSTRUCT'N
38001	253	1765	EDUCATIONAL SERVICES	38137	178	9401	SECURITIES/COMMODITY CONTRACTS	38345	13	76	EDUCATIONAL SERVICES
38002	715	7373	HOSPITALS	38138	1581	17173	AMBULATORY HEALTH CARE SVCS	38347	9	57	TRUCK TRANSPORTATION
38004	194	1007	FOOD SVCS & DRINKING PLACES	38139	216	1213	EDUCATIONAL SERVICES	38348	20	58	NAT'L SECURITY & INT'L AFFAIRS
38006	145	1851	FOOD MANUFACTURING	38141	466	9814	PROF.; SCIENTIFIC; & TECH SVCS	38351	756	8850	TRANSPORTATION EQUIPMENT MFG
38007	1	0	POSTAL SERVICE	38145	1	800	UTILITIES	38352	8	41	BLDG MATL & GARDEN EQPMT DLRS
38008	451	3930	HOSPITALS	38150	1	23	EDUCATIONAL SERVICES	38355	105	580	EDUCATIONAL SERVICES
38010	3	3	CHEMICAL MANUFACTURING	38152	26	497	OTHER INFORMATION SERVICES	38356	35	206	ADMIN. ENVIRO. QUALITY PROGRMS
38011	151	1107	EDUCATIONAL SERVICES	38157	119	739	CREDIT INTERMEDIATION & RELATD	38357	46	149	EDUCATIONAL SERVICES
38012	607	6058	PLASTICS & RUBBER PRODUCTS MFG	38161	5	154	JUSTICE; PUBIC ORDER/SAFETY	38358	445	6021	FABRICATED METAL PRODUCT MFG
38014	10	33	MERCH. WHOLESALERS;DURABLE GDS	38167	3	2	CONSTRUCTION OF BUILDINGS	38359	21	85	CLOTHING & CLOTH'G ACC. STORES
38015	35	405	SPECIAL TRADE CONTRACTORS	38168	6	36	CREDIT INTERMEDIATION & RELATD	38361	9	7	POSTAL SERVICE
38016	867	9329	FOOD SVCS & DRINKING PLACES	38173	3	11	SPECIAL TRADE CONTRACTORS	38362	17	72	HEAVY & CIVIL ENG. CONSTRUCT'N
38017	1745	18960	SPECIAL TRADE CONTRACTORS	38174	10	102	HOSPITALS	38363	303	2375	AMBULATORY HEALTH CARE SVCS
38018	1298	10784	FOOD SVCS & DRINKING PLACES	38175	11	33	ADMINISTRATIVE & SUPPORT SVCS	38365	20	174	MUSEUMS; HIST. SITES;& SIMILAR
38019	743	6226	EDUCATIONAL SERVICES	38177	13	21	COURIERS AND MESSENGERS	38366	48	273	EDUCATIONAL SERVICES
38021	6	9	CREDIT INTERMEDIATION & RELATD	38181	2	1	MISCELLANEOUS STORE RETAILERS	38367	44	218	EDUCATIONAL SERVICES
38023	57	274	EDUCATIONAL SERVICES	38182	1	1	INSURANCE CARRIERS & RELATED	38368	35	172	TRUCK TRANSPORTATION
38024	1282	13847	PRINT'G & RELATED SUPP'T ACT'S	38183	25	90	BLDG MATL & GARDEN EQPMT DLRS	38369	89	544	MERCH. WHOLESALERS;NONDUR. GDS
38027	15	220	HEALTH & PERSONAL CARE STORES	38184	13	42	SPECIAL TRADE CONTRACTORS	38370	20	32	FOOD SVCS & DRINKING PLACES
38028	169	619	EDUCATIONAL SERVICES	38186	4	49	CONSTRUCTION OF BUILDINGS	38371	19	31	CREDIT INTERMEDIATION & RELATD
38029	12	26	ADMINISTRATIVE & SUPPORT SVCS	38187	6	11	REAL ESTATE	38372	728	6799	EDUCATIONAL SERVICES
38030	10	56	EDUCATIONAL SERVICES	38190	9	16	ADMINISTRATIVE & SUPPORT SVCS	38374	71	289	EDUCATIONAL SERVICES
38034	57	236	MISCELLANEOUS MANUFACTURING	38193	2	700	COMPUTER & ELECTRONIC PROD MFG	38375	454	4222	ELECT'L EQPMT; APP; & COMP MFG
38036	31	512	MISCELLANEOUS MANUFACTURING	38197	1	3000	MERCH. WHOLESALERS;NONDUR. GDS	38376	28	90	EXEC.; LEGIS.; & OTHER SUPPORT
38037	26	92	CREDIT INTERMEDIATION & RELATD	38201	347	3398	EDUCATIONAL SERVICES	38378	1	2	POSTAL SERVICE
38039	55	362	PLASTICS & RUBBER PRODUCTS MFG	38220	52	460	EDUCATIONAL SERVICES	38379	24	139	UNCLASSIFIED ESTABLISHMENTS
38040	162	957	EDUCATIONAL SERVICES	38221	67	249	EDUCATIONAL SERVICES	38380	6	10	MACHINERY MANUFACTURING
38041	48	260	BLDG MATL & GARDEN EQPMT DLRS	38222	77	405	ACCOMMODATION	38381	39	1136	CHEMICAL MANUFACTURING
38042	18	38	SPECIAL TRADE CONTRACTORS	38223	3	8	MERCH. WHOLESALERS;NONDUR. GDS	38382	395	3125	EDUCATIONAL SERVICES
38044	17	81	TRUCK TRANSPORTATION	38224	31	135	JUSTICE; PUBIC ORDER/SAFETY	38387	2	5	POSTAL SERVICE
38045	1	2	MISCELLANEOUS STORE RETAILERS	38225	270	2061	EDUCATIONAL SERVICES	38388	35	251	FOOD SVCS & DRINKING PLACES
38046	9	12	ADMINISTRATIVE & SUPPORT SVCS	38226	4	20	CROP PRODUCTION	38389	6	11	FOOD AND BEVERAGE STORES
38048	3	8	RELIG.; GRANT; CIVIC; PROF ORG	38229	77	560	MINING (EXCEPT OIL AND GAS)	38390	11	14	FOOD AND BEVERAGE STORES
38049	96	605	ADMINISTRATIVE & SUPPORT SVCS	38230	118	829	MACHINERY MANUFACTURING	38391	28	327	MERCH. WHOLESALERS;NONDUR. GDS
38050	47	199	EDUCATIONAL SERVICES	38231	44	943	CROP PRODUCTION	38392	14	46	SUPPORT ACTIVITIES: AGR./FOR.
38052	112	1405	MACHINERY MANUFACTURING	38232	55	209	EDUCATIONAL SERVICES	38393	1	1	POSTAL SERVICE
38053	815	6975	EDUCATIONAL SERVICES	38233	72	623	MERCH. WHOLESALERS;DURABLE GDS	38401	2141	22852	EDUCATIONAL SERVICES
38054	11	325	PROF.; SCIENTIFIC; & TECH SVCS	38235	16	105	APPAREL MANUFACTURING	38402	10	21	SPECIAL TRADE CONTRACTORS
38055	1	0	PROF.; SCIENTIFIC; & TECH SVCS	38236	3	2	POSTAL SERVICE	38425	79	885	JUSTICE; PUBIC ORDER/SAFETY
38057	84	766	PRIMARY METAL MANUFACTURING	38237	506	5782	TRANSPORTATION EQUIPMENT MFG	38449	130	982	WOOD PRODUCT MANUFACTURING
38058	224	1259	EDUCATIONAL SERVICES	38238	1	950	EDUCATIONAL SERVICES	38450	108	901	WOOD PRODUCT MANUFACTURING
38059	164	2341	FOOD MANUFACTURING	38240	55	229	APPAREL MANUFACTURING	38451	54	217	EDUCATIONAL SERVICES
38060	233	1189	FOOD SVCS & DRINKING PLACES	38241	14	57	MERCH. WHOLESALERS;NONDUR. GDS	38452	11	31	FORESTRY AND LOGGING
38061	13	64	WOOD PRODUCT MANUFACTURING	38242	966	9865	AMBULATORY HEALTH CARE SVCS	38453	4	1	RELIG.; GRANT; CIVIC; PROF ORG
38063	477	5531	FABRICATED METAL PRODUCT MFG	38251	65	453	AMUSEMENT; GAMBLING;& RECREAT.	38454	11	13	SPECIAL TRADE CONTRACTORS
38066	90	833	FOOD AND BEVERAGE STORES	38253	20	29	MERCH. WHOLESALERS;DURABLE GDS	38455	23	82	EDUCATIONAL SERVICES
38067	16	64	RELIG.; GRANT; CIVIC; PROF ORG	38254	9	16	ACCOMMODATION	38456	79	323	EDUCATIONAL SERVICES
38068	458	2902	EDUCATIONAL SERVICES	38255	70	323	JUSTICE; PUBIC ORDER/SAFETY	38457	16	40	JUSTICE; PUBIC ORDER/SAFETY
38069	50	230	GASOLINE STATIONS	38256	49	211	ACCOMMODATION	38459	9	112	FOOD SVCS & DRINKING PLACES
38070	5	5	FOOD AND BEVERAGE STORES	38257	124	637	APPAREL MANUFACTURING	38460	13	20	RELIG.; GRANT; CIVIC; PROF ORG
38071	2	2	POSTAL SERVICE	38258	43	244	EDUCATIONAL SERVICES	38461	24	107	EDUCATIONAL SERVICES
38075	102	740	JUSTICE; PUBIC ORDER/SAFETY	38259	23	64	EDUCATIONAL SERVICES	38462	366	2550	EDUCATIONAL SERVICES
38076	11	43	EDUCATIONAL SERVICES	38260	104	632	RELIG.; GRANT; CIVIC; PROF ORG	38463	41	298	FABRICATED METAL PRODUCT MFG
38077	8	11	MERCH. WHOLESALERS;NONDUR. GDS	38261	923	12043	PLASTICS & RUBBER PRODUCTS MFG	38464	971	11063	TRANSPORTATION EQUIPMENT MFG
38079	156	1456	JUSTICE; PUBIC ORDER/SAFETY	38271	5	19	CREDIT INTERMEDIATION & RELATD	38468	117	584	APPAREL MANUFACTURING
38080	67	422	SOCIAL ASSISTANCE	38281	2	1	MOTION PICT. & SOUND RECORDING	38469	139	756	EDUCATIONAL SERVICES
38083	4	4	CONSTRUCTION OF BUILDINGS	38301	1951	34084	HOSPITALS	38471	14	27	JUSTICE; PUBIC ORDER/SAFETY
38088	31	151	ADMINISTRATIVE & SUPPORT SVCS	38302	7	85	TRUCK TRANSPORTATION	38472	48	236	EDUCATIONAL SERVICES
38101	17	44	PUBLISHING INDUSTRIES	38303	3	100	AMBULATORY HEALTH CARE SVCS	38473	32	120	EDUCATIONAL SERVICES
38103	2512	43901	JUSTICE; PUBIC ORDER/SAFETY	38305	2386	31772	FOOD SVCS & DRINKING PLACES	38474	223	1982	MERCH. WHOLESALERS;DURABLE GDS
38104	1769	26649	HOSPITALS	38308	7	57	CONSTRUCTION OF BUILDINGS	38475	3	8	BLDG MATL & GARDEN EQPMT DLRS
38105	464	10890	HOSPITALS	38310	220	2275	MISCELLANEOUS MANUFACTURING	38476	15	40	EDUCATIONAL SERVICES
38106	907	8824	TRUCK TRANSPORTATION	38311	7	31	WASTE MANAGMT & REMEDIAT'N SVC	38477	26	109	AMBULATORY HEALTH CARE SVCS
38107	564	4141	EDUCATIONAL SERVICES	38313	22	124	EDUCATIONAL SERVICES	38478	761	7941	MERCH. WHOLESALERS;NONDUR. GDS
38108	472	5981	CHEMICAL MANUFACTURING	38314	1	4	COURIERS AND MESSENGERS	38481	44	158	MISCELLANEOUS MANUFACTURING
38109	1086	13250	TRUCK TRANSPORTATION	38315	54	310	ADMIN. OF ECONOMIC PROGRAMS	38482	31	102	EDUCATIONAL SERVICES
38110	1	13	PROF.; SCIENTIFIC; & TECH SVCS	38316	93	419	EDUCATIONAL SERVICES	38483	84	367	EDUCATIONAL SERVICES
38111	1426	11309	FOOD SVCS & DRINKING PLACES	38317	62	700	NURSING & RESID. CARE FACILIT.	38485	340	2822	EDUCATIONAL SERVICES
38112	834	15986	EDUCATIONAL SERVICES	38318	5	5	POSTAL SERVICE	38486	9	14	BLDG MATL & GARDEN EQPMT DLRS
38113	6	359	GENERAL MERCHANDISE STORES	38320	468	3999	GENERAL MERCHANDISE STORES	38487	17	28	FOOD AND BEVERAGE STORES
38114	841	8131	ELECT'L EQPMT; APP; & COMP MFG	38321	38	93	SPECIAL TRADE CONTRACTORS	38488	44	129	EDUCATIONAL SERVICES
38115	1771	16060	FOOD SVCS & DRINKING PLACES	38324	4	5	CREDIT INTERMEDIATION & RELATD	38501	2092	22185	AMBULATORY HEALTH CARE SVCS
38116	1860	22555	TRUCK TRANSPORTATION	38326	160	1180	PAPER MANUFACTURING	38502	13	24	RELIG.; GRANT; CIVIC; PROF ORG
38117	1692	17442	FOOD SVCS & DRINKING PLACES	38327	42	177	CONSTRUCTION OF BUILDINGS	38503	14	100	REPAIR AND MAINTENANCE
38118	2720	48878	MERCH. WHOLESALERS;NONDUR. GDS	38328	14	24	FOOD SVCS & DRINKING PLACES	38504	39	133	EDUCATIONAL SERVICES
38119	1615	20290	HOSPITALS	38329	147	737	EDUCATIONAL SERVICES	38505	4	1420	EDUCATIONAL SERVICES
38120	931	31085	HOSPITALS	38330	125	1055	EDUCATIONAL SERVICES	38506	702	8662	EXEC.; LEGIS.; & OTHER SUPPORT
38122	965	8350	FOOD SVCS & DRINKING PLACES	38331	2	2	POSTAL SERVICE	38541	37	166	EDUCATIONAL SERVICES
38124	6	16	ADMINISTRATIVE & SUPPORT SVCS	38332	19	64	APPAREL MANUFACTURING	38543	11	17	AMUSEMENT; GAMBLING;& RECREAT.
38125	1012	12639	MERCH. WHOLESALERS;DURABLE GDS	38333	4	23	ACCOMMODATION	38544	171	714	EDUCATIONAL SERVICES
38126	357	4954	SOCIAL ASSISTANCE	38334	29	50	FORESTRY AND LOGGING	38545	20	66	EXEC.; LEGIS.; & OTHER SUPPORT
38127	829	6418	EDUCATIONAL SERVICES	38336	1	0	POSTAL SERVICE	38547	16	457	PRIMARY METAL MANUFACTURING
38128	1113	12570	HOSPITALS	38337	20	50	EDUCATIONAL SERVICES	38548	14	14	POSTAL SERVICE
38130	3	4	SPECIAL TRADE CONTRACTORS	38338	20	71	REPAIR AND MAINTENANCE	38549	204	1251	TRANSPORTATION EQUIPMENT MFG
38131	81	1058	ADMINISTRATIVE & SUPPORT SVCS	38339	13	34	MERCH. WHOLESALERS;DURABLE GDS	38550	3	9	PLASTICS & RUBBER PRODUCTS MFG
38132	147	3276	MERCH. WHOLESALERS;DURABLE GDS	38340	453	3738	EDUCATIONAL SERVICES	38551	253	1674	EDUCATIONAL SERVICES
38133	1420	22560	FOOD SVCS & DRINKING PLACES	38341	44	266	GASOLINE STATIONS	38552	15	15	REPAIR AND MAINTENANCE

ZIP CODE	2009 Total Firms	2009 Total Employees	TOP INDUSTRY RANKED on 2009 EMPLOYMENT
38553	122	433	CONSTRUCTION OF BUILDINGS
38554	16	60	EDUCATIONAL SERVICES
38555	1304	13691	FOOD SVCS & DRINKING PLACES
38556	614	4169	AMBULATORY HEALTH CARE SVCS
38557	9	36	NONMETALLIC MINERAL PROD. MFG
38558	62	913	AMUSEMENT; GAMBLING;& RECREAT.
38559	41	170	WOOD PRODUCT MANUFACTURING
38560	16	96	MISCELLANEOUS MANUFACTURING
38562	292	1939	FABRICATED METAL PRODUCT MFG
38563	121	1839	TRANSPORTATION EQUIPMENT MFG
38564	15	30	FOOD SVCS & DRINKING PLACES
38565	32	96	EDUCATIONAL SERVICES
38567	10	22	MERCH. WHOLESALERS;DURABLE GDS
38568	34	121	EDUCATIONAL SERVICES
38569	7	38	ADMIN. ENVIRO. QUALITY PROGRMS
38570	546	4992	PRIMARY METAL MANUFACTURING
38571	413	1971	FOOD SVCS & DRINKING PLACES
38572	197	1101	EDUCATIONAL SERVICES
38573	32	82	RELIG.; GRANT; CIVIC; PROF ORG
38574	217	2585	FOOD MANUFACTURING
38575	35	237	MERCH. WHOLESALERS;DURABLE GDS
38577	25	93	CROP PRODUCTION
38578	26	245	SPECIAL TRADE CONTRACTORS
38579	15	80	ACCOMMODATION
38580	45	162	EDUCATIONAL SERVICES
38581	107	444	TRUCK TRANSPORTATION
38582	37	160	FOOD SVCS & DRINKING PLACES
38583	831	6664	MERCH. WHOLESALERS;DURABLE GDS
38585	147	1070	GENERAL MERCHANDISE STORES
38587	24	65	EDUCATIONAL SERVICES
38588	21	37	WOOD PRODUCT MANUFACTURING
38589	2	4	HEAVY & CIVIL ENG. CONSTRUCT'N
38601	18	71	RELIG.; GRANT; CIVIC; PROF ORG
38602	3	29	ADMIN. ENVIRO. QUALITY PROGRMS
38603	129	842	EDUCATIONAL SERVICES
38606	854	8990	MERCH. WHOLESALERS;DURABLE GDS
38610	60	2080	FURNITURE & RELATED PROD. MFG
38611	359	1980	EDUCATIONAL SERVICES
38614	892	8782	EDUCATIONAL SERVICES
38617	14	30	RELIG.; GRANT; CIVIC; PROF ORG
38618	176	748	EDUCATIONAL SERVICES
38619	101	434	EDUCATIONAL SERVICES
38620	22	60	RELIG.; GRANT; CIVIC; PROF ORG
38621	46	159	JUSTICE; PUBIC ORDER/SAFETY
38622	11	16	EXEC.; LEGIS.; & OTHER SUPPORT
38623	2	1	POSTAL SERVICE
38625	13	115	MERCH. WHOLESALERS;DURABLE GDS
38626	11	33	CROP PRODUCTION
38627	11	37	CONSTRUCTION OF BUILDINGS
38628	4	2	FOOD AND BEVERAGE STORES
38629	25	251	EDUCATIONAL SERVICES
38630	3	12	SUPPORT ACTIVITIES: AGR./FOR.
38631	32	263	MERCH. WHOLESALERS;DURABLE GDS
38632	676	5995	EDUCATIONAL SERVICES
38633	28	334	TRUCK TRANSPORTATION
38635	551	4268	EDUCATIONAL SERVICES
38637	536	4947	FOOD SVCS & DRINKING PLACES
38638	18	96	EDUCATIONAL SERVICES
38639	23	150	FOOD MANUFACTURING
38641	31	208	EDUCATIONAL SERVICES
38642	22	90	CROP PRODUCTION
38643	36	274	EDUCATIONAL SERVICES
38644	23	993	ACCOMMODATION
38645	30	315	SUPPORT ACTIVITIES: AGR./FOR.
38646	181	1077	HOSPITALS
38647	9	13	POSTAL SERVICE
38649	8	62	MERCH. WHOLESALERS;DURABLE GDS
38650	57	298	EDUCATIONAL SERVICES
38651	94	624	EXEC.; LEGIS.; & OTHER SUPPORT
38652	702	9703	FURNITURE & RELATED PROD. MFG
38654	1248	12493	FOOD SVCS & DRINKING PLACES
38655	1609	16633	ELECT'L EQPMT; APP; & COMP MFG
38658	22	123	EDUCATIONAL SERVICES
38659	54	303	EDUCATIONAL SERVICES
38661	21	87	GASOLINE STATIONS
38663	481	4946	FURN. & HOME FURNISHGS STORES
38664	121	9851	AMUSEMENT; GAMBLING;& RECREAT.
38665	24	115	EDUCATIONAL SERVICES
38666	191	1419	APPAREL MANUFACTURING
38668	538	6469	EDUCATIONAL SERVICES
38669	2	7	SUPPORT ACTIVITIES: AGR./FOR.
38670	15	47	PERFORM'G ARTS; SPEC. SPORTS
38671	1456	16063	FOOD SVCS & DRINKING PLACES
38672	239	2370	SUPPORT ACT. FOR TRANSPORT.
38673	6	92	UNCLASSIFIED ESTABLISHMENTS
38674	13	61	MERCH. WHOLESALERS;NONDUR. GDS
38676	347	2382	EDUCATIONAL SERVICES
38677	25	319	PUBLISHING INDUSTRIES
38679	10	47	JUSTICE; PUBIC ORDER/SAFETY
38680	93	822	MISCELLANEOUS MANUFACTURING

ZIP CODE	2009 Total Firms	2009 Total Employees	TOP INDUSTRY RANKED on 2009 EMPLOYMENT
38683	112	659	ELECT'L EQPMT; APP; & COMP MFG
38685	16	39	JUSTICE; PUBIC ORDER/SAFETY
38686	1	70	RELIG.; GRANT; CIVIC; PROF ORG
38701	1235	11292	HOSPITALS
38702	3	5	SOCIAL ASSISTANCE
38703	574	6713	HOSPITALS
38704	2	7	WASTE MANAGMT & REMEDIAT'N SVC
38720	7	22	CONSTRUCTION OF BUILDINGS
38721	29	153	EDUCATIONAL SERVICES
38722	16	112	EDUCATIONAL SERVICES
38723	10	245	EDUCATIONAL SERVICES
38725	29	177	EDUCATIONAL SERVICES
38726	6	7	FOOD AND BEVERAGE STORES
38730	54	433	SPORTG GDS;HOBBY;BOOK; & MUSIC
38731	3	31	SUPPORT ACTIVITIES: AGR./FOR.
38732	860	7963	MERCH. WHOLESALERS;NONDUR. GDS
38733	28	994	EDUCATIONAL SERVICES
38736	8	11	RELIG.; GRANT; CIVIC; PROF ORG
38737	95	1635	JUSTICE; PUBIC ORDER/SAFETY
38738	3	1580	JUSTICE; PUBIC ORDER/SAFETY
38739	4	46	RELIG.; GRANT; CIVIC; PROF ORG
38740	12	161	NURSING & RESID. CARE FACILIT.
38744	24	90	TRUCK TRANSPORTATION
38745	2	3	POSTAL SERVICE
38746	13	16	SUPPORT ACTIVITIES: AGR./FOR.
38748	121	1045	EDUCATIONAL SERVICES
38751	503	4617	GENERAL MERCHANDISE STORES
38753	64	322	NURSING & RESID. CARE FACILIT.
38754	46	914	FOOD MANUFACTURING
38756	271	1610	FURNITURE & RELATED PROD. MFG
38759	28	171	EDUCATIONAL SERVICES
38760	12	18	EXEC.; LEGIS.; & OTHER SUPPORT
38761	45	680	EDUCATIONAL SERVICES
38762	108	537	AMBULATORY HEALTH CARE SVCS
38764	9	23	EXEC.; LEGIS.; & OTHER SUPPORT
38765	1	8	RELIG.; GRANT; CIVIC; PROF ORG
38767	2	3	POSTAL SERVICE
38768	1	0	POSTAL SERVICE
38769	95	1099	FABRICATED METAL PRODUCT MFG
38771	104	1168	HOSPITALS
38772	5	363	CROP PRODUCTION
38773	63	326	EDUCATIONAL SERVICES
38774	77	368	EDUCATIONAL SERVICES
38776	19	567	ADMIN. OF ECONOMIC PROGRAMS
38778	55	271	TRUCK TRANSPORTATION
38780	1	2	POSTAL SERVICE
38781	7	14	NURSING & RESID. CARE FACILIT.
38801	1725	20494	AMBULATORY HEALTH CARE SVCS
38802	6	15	MERCH. WHOLESALERS;DURABLE GDS
38803	7	35	SPECIAL TRADE CONTRACTORS
38804	1300	18155	ELECT'L EQPMT; APP; & COMP MFG
38820	2	3	POSTAL SERVICE
38821	545	5735	AMBULATORY HEALTH CARE SVCS
38824	227	1599	SPORTG GDS;HOBBY;BOOK; & MUSIC
38825	1	2	POSTAL SERVICE
38826	75	1936	FURNITURE & RELATED PROD. MFG
38827	129	1272	MOTOR VEHICLE & PARTS DEALERS
38828	35	146	EDUCATIONAL SERVICES
38829	625	6951	MISCELLANEOUS STORE RETAILERS
38833	62	888	TRUCK TRANSPORTATION
38834	1280	14054	MISCELLANEOUS MANUFACTURING
38835	4	4	SPECIAL TRADE CONTRACTORS
38838	21	73	EXEC.; LEGIS.; & OTHER SUPPORT
38839	17	44	MOTOR VEHICLE & PARTS DEALERS
38841	64	3986	FURNITURE & RELATED PROD. MFG
38843	589	5414	EDUCATIONAL SERVICES
38844	6	36	WASTE MANAGMT & REMEDIAT'N SVC
38846	27	279	EDUCATIONAL SERVICES
38847	73	857	APPAREL MANUFACTURING
38848	6	37	JUSTICE; PUBIC ORDER/SAFETY
38849	77	1279	FURNITURE & RELATED PROD. MFG
38850	70	872	FURNITURE & RELATED PROD. MFG
38851	399	4332	FURNITURE & RELATED PROD. MFG
38852	387	3154	FABRICATED METAL PRODUCT MFG
38855	148	509	EDUCATIONAL SERVICES
38856	29	440	APPAREL MANUFACTURING
38857	43	597	EDUCATIONAL SERVICES
38858	138	1563	FURNITURE & RELATED PROD. MFG
38859	10	53	EDUCATIONAL SERVICES
38860	204	2656	FURNITURE & RELATED PROD. MFG
38862	46	235	EDUCATIONAL SERVICES
38863	673	7511	FURNITURE & RELATED PROD. MFG
38864	14	39	FURN. & HOME FURNISHGS STORES
38865	63	269	TRUCK TRANSPORTATION
38866	269	3244	FURNITURE & RELATED PROD. MFG
38868	121	2310	FABRICATED METAL PRODUCT MFG
38869	35	463	PLASTICS & RUBBER PRODUCTS MFG
38870	69	309	EDUCATIONAL SERVICES
38871	15	101	WASTE MANAGMT & REMEDIAT'N SVC
38873	77	601	MERCH. WHOLESALERS;DURABLE GDS

ZIP CODE	2009 Total Firms	2009 Total Employees	TOP INDUSTRY RANKED on 2009 EMPLOYMENT
38874	4	11	AMBULATORY HEALTH CARE SVCS
38876	36	272	MISCELLANEOUS STORE RETAILERS
38877	5	35	HEAVY & CIVIL ENG. CONSTRUCT'N
38878	75	466	MERCH. WHOLESALERS;NONDUR. GDS
38879	118	2101	MACHINERY MANUFACTURING
38880	3	69	EDUCATIONAL SERVICES
38901	981	11535	MISCELLANEOUS MANUFACTURING
38902	2	2	INSURANCE CARRIERS & RELATED
38913	6	10	FOOD SVCS & DRINKING PLACES
38914	11	37	RELIG.; GRANT; CIVIC; PROF ORG
38915	179	1221	WOOD PRODUCT MANUFACTURING
38916	222	1528	HOSPITALS
38917	90	232	EXEC.; LEGIS.; & OTHER SUPPORT
38920	10	19	CONSTRUCTION OF BUILDINGS
38921	199	1334	EDUCATIONAL SERVICES
38922	96	392	EDUCATIONAL SERVICES
38923	11	19	SPECIAL TRADE CONTRACTORS
38924	8	27	CONSTRUCTION OF BUILDINGS
38925	27	105	MERCH. WHOLESALERS;DURABLE GDS
38926	3	23	SUPPORT ACTIVITIES: AGR./FOR.
38927	14	99	NAT'L SECURITY & INT'L AFFAIRS
38928	9	66	SOCIAL ASSISTANCE
38929	13	72	SUPPORT ACTIVITIES: AGR./FOR.
38930	1239	14906	HOSPITALS
38940	23	54	HEAVY & CIVIL ENG. CONSTRUCT'N
38941	96	2150	FOOD MANUFACTURING
38943	7	5	PROF.; SCIENTIFIC; & TECH SVCS
38944	15	81	SUPPORT ACTIVITIES: AGR./FOR.
38945	1	28	SUPPORT ACTIVITIES: AGR./FOR.
38946	8	37	SUPPORT ACTIVITIES: AGR./FOR.
38947	22	156	EDUCATIONAL SERVICES
38948	38	120	FOOD SVCS & DRINKING PLACES
38949	1	3	CONSTRUCTION OF BUILDINGS
38950	5	3	FURNITURE & RELATED PROD. MFG
38951	36	185	ADMIN. HUMAN RESOURCE PROGRAMS
38952	14	218	ANIMAL PRODUCTION
38953	5	17	MERCH. WHOLESALERS;DURABLE GDS
38954	13	95	MERCH. WHOLESALERS;DURABLE GDS
38955	3	2	UTILITIES
38957	47	321	EDUCATIONAL SERVICES
38958	1	0	AIR TRANSPORTATION
38959	2	2	POSTAL SERVICE
38961	8	83	GASOLINE STATIONS
38962	1	2	POSTAL SERVICE
38963	46	534	ADMINISTRATIVE & SUPPORT SVCS
38964	5	15	SUPPORT ACTIVITIES: AGR./FOR.
38965	283	2617	TRANSPORTATION EQUIPMENT MFG
38966	30	176	EDUCATIONAL SERVICES
38967	334	2289	EDUCATIONAL SERVICES
39038	275	1527	AMBULATORY HEALTH CARE SVCS
39039	50	170	PLASTICS & RUBBER PRODUCTS MFG
39040	57	318	EDUCATIONAL SERVICES
39041	91	549	SPECIAL TRADE CONTRACTORS
39042	969	8603	FOOD SVCS & DRINKING PLACES
39043	10	21	MOTION PICT. & SOUND RECORDING
39044	23	48	SPECIAL TRADE CONTRACTORS
39045	12	138	EDUCATIONAL SERVICES
39046	723	12436	TRANSPORTATION EQUIPMENT MFG
39047	670	3260	SPECIAL TRADE CONTRACTORS
39051	487	5577	FOOD MANUFACTURING
39054	18	175	CROP PRODUCTION
39056	809	9357	COMPUTER & ELECTRONIC PROD MFG
39057	15	118	EDUCATIONAL SERVICES
39058	4	15	BROADCASTING
39059	302	2518	MERCH. WHOLESALERS;DURABLE GDS
39060	5	25	MERCH. WHOLESALERS;DURABLE GDS
39061	1	0	RELIG.; GRANT; CIVIC; PROF ORG
39062	14	38	GASOLINE STATIONS
39063	132	1350	TRANSPORTATION EQUIPMENT MFG
39066	92	604	MERCH. WHOLESALERS;NONDUR. GDS
39067	21	85	EDUCATIONAL SERVICES
39069	167	1128	EDUCATIONAL SERVICES
39071	182	1051	PROF.; SCIENTIFIC; & TECH SVCS
39072	1	0	SPECIAL TRADE CONTRACTORS
39073	423	2477	EDUCATIONAL SERVICES
39074	519	8573	FOOD MANUFACTURING
39077	8	99	EDUCATIONAL SERVICES
39078	33	88	MERCH. WHOLESALERS;DURABLE GDS
39079	42	651	EDUCATIONAL SERVICES
39080	25	68	MERCH. WHOLESALERS;NONDUR. GDS
39082	9	17	RELIG.; GRANT; CIVIC; PROF ORG
39083	369	5191	FOOD MANUFACTURING
39086	44	132	MERCH. WHOLESALERS;DURABLE GDS
39087	3	4	POSTAL SERVICE
39088	28	89	SUPPORT ACTIVITIES: AGR./FOR.
39090	577	5032	HOSPITALS
39092	56	421	EDUCATIONAL SERVICES
39094	42	152	CLOTHING & CLOTH'G ACC. STORES
39095	247	2417	HOSPITALS
39096	30	1120	EDUCATIONAL SERVICES

BUSINESS DATA

ZIP CODE	2009 Total Firms	2009 Total Employ-ees	TOP INDUSTRY RANKED on 2009 EMPLOYMENT
39097	39	186	CROP PRODUCTION
39098	3	4	SUPPORT ACTIVITIES: AGR./FOR.
39107	4	5	GASOLINE STATIONS
39108	30	110	EDUCATIONAL SERVICES
39109	7	57	EDUCATIONAL SERVICES
39110	1114	10301	FOOD SVCS & DRINKING PLACES
39111	422	5313	SOCIAL ASSISTANCE
39113	30	123	JUSTICE; PUBIC ORDER/SAFETY
39114	342	2125	EDUCATIONAL SERVICES
39115	6	19	SUPPORT ACTIVITIES: AGR./FOR.
39116	49	187	EDUCATIONAL SERVICES
39117	222	2067	MERCH. WHOLESALERS;NONDUR. GDS
39119	93	530	HEAVY & CIVIL ENG. CONSTRUCT'N
39120	1564	14481	EDUCATIONAL SERVICES
39121	2	7	ADMINISTRATIVE & SUPPORT SVCS
39122	3	5	BLDG MATL & GARDEN EQPMT DLRS
39130	14	41	SPECIAL TRADE CONTRACTORS
39140	70	334	FOOD AND BEVERAGE STORES
39144	19	21	PROF.; SCIENTIFIC; & TECH SVCS
39145	146	1841	INSURANCE CARRIERS & RELATED
39146	57	264	GASOLINE STATIONS
39148	2	151	EDUCATIONAL SERVICES
39149	17	106	EDUCATIONAL SERVICES
39150	267	2953	MERCH. WHOLESALERS;NONDUR. GDS
39151	23	212	EDUCATIONAL SERVICES
39152	6	13	FORESTRY AND LOGGING
39153	134	1070	MERCH. WHOLESALERS;DURABLE GDS
39154	254	4528	EDUCATIONAL SERVICES
39156	16	430	PAPER MANUFACTURING
39157	1986	21163	INSURANCE CARRIERS & RELATED
39158	18	36	WASTE MANAGMT & REMEDIAT'N SVC
39159	192	1311	EDUCATIONAL SERVICES
39160	23	96	EDUCATIONAL SERVICES
39161	5	55	POSTAL SERVICE
39162	4	10	RELIG.; GRANT; CIVIC; PROF ORG
39163	1	0	RELIG.; GRANT; CIVIC; PROF ORG
39165	4	9	WASTE MANAGMT & REMEDIAT'N SVC
39166	5	14	RELIG.; GRANT; CIVIC; PROF ORG
39167	16	80	MERCH. WHOLESALERS;NONDUR. GDS
39168	140	1136	FABRICATED METAL PRODUCT MFG
39169	72	308	SUPPORT ACTIVITIES: AGR./FOR.
39170	195	775	EDUCATIONAL SERVICES
39171	1	2	POSTAL SERVICE
39173	4	3	MERCH. WHOLESALERS;DURABLE GDS
39174	13	309	EDUCATIONAL SERVICES
39175	103	676	EDUCATIONAL SERVICES
39176	74	446	NURSING & RESID. CARE FACILIT.
39177	5	12	WAREHOUSING AND STORAGE
39179	13	45	EDUCATIONAL SERVICES
39180	1275	21272	EXEC.; LEGIS.; & OTHER SUPPORT
39181	4	20	SOCIAL ASSISTANCE
39182	3	26	SOCIAL ASSISTANCE
39183	575	6408	MERCH. WHOLESALERS;NONDUR. GDS
39189	62	555	ADMINISTRATIVE & SUPPORT SVCS
39190	5	19	MUSEUMS; HIST. SITES;& SIMILAR
39191	94	802	EDUCATIONAL SERVICES
39192	30	79	RELIG.; GRANT; CIVIC; PROF ORG
39193	5	3313	HOSPITALS
39194	672	5130	EDUCATIONAL SERVICES
39201	1345	22895	EXEC.; LEGIS.; & OTHER SUPPORT
39202	815	23576	HOSPITALS
39203	271	1707	EDUCATIONAL SERVICES
39204	932	10464	HOSPITALS
39205	9	154	EXEC.; LEGIS.; & OTHER SUPPORT
39206	1118	8531	EDUCATIONAL SERVICES
39207	3	7	SPECIAL TRADE CONTRACTORS
39208	1221	14261	JUSTICE; PUBIC ORDER/SAFETY
39209	1150	12629	EDUCATIONAL SERVICES
39210	55	1054	EDUCATIONAL SERVICES
39211	1194	12840	FOOD SVCS & DRINKING PLACES
39212	634	3932	EDUCATIONAL SERVICES
39213	742	10137	UTILITIES
39215	5	3	RELIG.; GRANT; CIVIC; PROF ORG
39216	873	34275	HOSPITALS
39217	11	83	EDUCATIONAL SERVICES
39218	447	7450	TRUCK TRANSPORTATION
39225	1	5	CLOTHING & CLOTH'G ACC. STORES
39232	1241	19779	AMBULATORY HEALTH CARE SVCS
39236	19	22	REAL ESTATE
39269	27	375	JUSTICE; PUBIC ORDER/SAFETY
39272	449	4663	FOOD SVCS & DRINKING PLACES
39282	6	24	SOCIAL ASSISTANCE
39283	1	0	ADMINISTRATIVE & SUPPORT SVCS
39284	5	10	CREDIT INTERMEDIATION & RELATD
39286	5	19	UNCLASSIFIED ESTABLISHMENTS
39288	8	13	BLDG MATL & GARDEN EQPMT DLRS
39289	2	1	PROF.; SCIENTIFIC; & TECH SVCS
39296	11	24	CONSTRUCTION OF BUILDINGS
39298	3	3	PROF.; SCIENTIFIC; & TECH SVCS
39301	1932	26465	HOSPITALS
39302	4	23	RELIG.; GRANT; CIVIC; PROF ORG
39303	5	5	SUPPORT ACTIVITIES: AGR./FOR.
39304	2	3	INSURANCE CARRIERS & RELATED
39305	531	3785	EDUCATIONAL SERVICES
39307	539	9477	NAT'L SECURITY & INT'L AFFAIRS
39309	46	383	EXEC.; LEGIS.; & OTHER SUPPORT
39320	28	48	EXEC.; LEGIS.; & OTHER SUPPORT
39322	40	183	EDUCATIONAL SERVICES
39323	15	16	POSTAL SERVICE
39324	5	20	RELIG.; GRANT; CIVIC; PROF ORG
39325	105	570	EDUCATIONAL SERVICES
39326	12	23	SPORTG GDS;HOBBY;BOOK; & MUSIC
39327	124	1370	EDUCATIONAL SERVICES
39328	194	1379	EDUCATIONAL SERVICES
39330	59	627	EDUCATIONAL SERVICES
39332	43	93	MISCELLANEOUS STORE RETAILERS
39335	24	68	FOOD AND BEVERAGE STORES
39336	11	96	GASOLINE STATIONS
39337	17	24	RELIG.; GRANT; CIVIC; PROF ORG
39338	36	79	FOOD AND BEVERAGE STORES
39339	569	6037	MERCH. WHOLESALERS;DURABLE GDS
39341	307	2365	EDUCATIONAL SERVICES
39342	46	325	NURSING & RESID. CARE FACILIT.
39345	303	4296	MERCH. WHOLESALERS;DURABLE GDS
39346	73	391	MERCH. WHOLESALERS;NONDUR. GDS
39347	21	31	GASOLINE STATIONS
39348	6	11	EXEC.; LEGIS.; & OTHER SUPPORT
39350	918	11606	EXEC.; LEGIS.; & OTHER SUPPORT
39352	7	13	TRUCK TRANSPORTATION
39354	26	78	NAT'L SECURITY & INT'L AFFAIRS
39355	294	2726	EDUCATIONAL SERVICES
39356	24	31	CONSTRUCTION OF BUILDINGS
39358	31	371	EDUCATIONAL SERVICES
39359	40	944	FOOD MANUFACTURING
39360	69	257	SPECIAL TRADE CONTRACTORS
39361	50	369	WOOD PRODUCT MANUFACTURING
39362	51	229	FORESTRY AND LOGGING
39363	21	67	FOOD AND BEVERAGE STORES
39364	49	200	BLDG MATL & GARDEN EQPMT DLRS
39365	153	1340	FOOD MANUFACTURING
39366	13	49	MERCH. WHOLESALERS;DURABLE GDS
39367	576	5354	EDUCATIONAL SERVICES
39401	2028	26773	HOSPITALS
39402	1872	20614	FOOD SVCS & DRINKING PLACES
39403	4	13	BLDG MATL & GARDEN EQPMT DLRS
39404	15	58	CONSTRUCTION OF BUILDINGS
39406	8	3192	EDUCATIONAL SERVICES
39407	9	55	NAT'L SECURITY & INT'L AFFAIRS
39421	83	489	EDUCATIONAL SERVICES
39422	283	3698	FOOD MANUFACTURING
39423	48	640	WOOD PRODUCT MANUFACTURING
39425	41	328	EDUCATIONAL SERVICES
39426	191	931	EDUCATIONAL SERVICES
39427	20	70	EDUCATIONAL SERVICES
39428	374	4929	FOOD MANUFACTURING
39429	822	8437	GENERAL MERCHANDISE STORES
39436	1	1	POSTAL SERVICE
39437	355	4890	EDUCATIONAL SERVICES
39439	129	822	EDUCATIONAL SERVICES
39440	1429	21737	FOOD MANUFACTURING
39441	9	54	BROADCASTING
39442	7	21	FORESTRY AND LOGGING
39443	416	3764	EDUCATIONAL SERVICES
39451	191	1265	EDUCATIONAL SERVICES
39452	710	4555	HOSPITALS
39455	179	1450	MERCH. WHOLESALERS;DURABLE GDS
39456	29	79	EDUCATIONAL SERVICES
39457	7	23	SUPPORT ACTIVITIES FOR MINING
39459	67	1345	FOOD MANUFACTURING
39460	3	2	RELIG.; GRANT; CIVIC; PROF ORG
39461	10	21	FORESTRY AND LOGGING
39462	94	1005	FORESTRY AND LOGGING
39463	7	20	RAIL TRANSPORTATION
39464	25	28	WASTE MANAGMT & REMEDIAT'N SVC
39465	513	3606	EDUCATIONAL SERVICES
39466	1189	7967	EDUCATIONAL SERVICES
39470	422	2988	EXEC.; LEGIS.; & OTHER SUPPORT
39474	244	1693	AMBULATORY HEALTH CARE SVCS
39475	325	2734	EXEC.; LEGIS.; & OTHER SUPPORT
39476	185	1260	EDUCATIONAL SERVICES
39477	37	396	SUPPORT ACTIVITIES FOR MINING
39478	39	523	BLDG MATL & GARDEN EQPMT DLRS
39479	96	557	EDUCATIONAL SERVICES
39480	48	179	EXEC.; LEGIS.; & OTHER SUPPORT
39481	25	154	EDUCATIONAL SERVICES
39482	161	976	EDUCATIONAL SERVICES
39483	111	580	EDUCATIONAL SERVICES
39501	1562	18010	HOSPITALS
39502	5	122	RELIG.; GRANT; CIVIC; PROF ORG
39503	1793	21758	FOOD SVCS & DRINKING PLACES
39505	14	32	SPECIAL TRADE CONTRACTORS
39506	7	59	ADMINISTRATIVE & SUPPORT SVCS
39507	886	11254	HOSPITALS
39520	638	5296	AMUSEMENT; GAMBLING;& RECREAT.
39521	3	5	REPAIR AND MAINTENANCE
39522	2	6	OTHER INFORMATION SERVICES
39525	193	1538	PROF.; SCIENTIFIC; & TECH SVCS
39529	45	2240	NAT'L SECURITY & INT'L AFFAIRS
39530	742	16710	ACCOMMODATION
39531	802	15205	RELIG.; GRANT; CIVIC; PROF ORG
39532	756	4544	EDUCATIONAL SERVICES
39533	7	43	SOCIAL ASSISTANCE
39534	63	839	FOOD AND BEVERAGE STORES
39535	6	1	CONSTRUCTION OF BUILDINGS
39540	462	3769	FOOD SVCS & DRINKING PLACES
39552	13	218	TRANSPORTATION EQUIPMENT MFG
39553	564	4318	EDUCATIONAL SERVICES
39555	77	454	EDUCATIONAL SERVICES
39556	174	1195	EDUCATIONAL SERVICES
39558	2	8	MERCH. WHOLESALERS;NONDUR. GDS
39560	514	4301	NURSING & RESID. CARE FACILIT.
39561	25	151	MERCH. WHOLESALERS;DURABLE GDS
39562	257	1621	CONSTRUCTION OF BUILDINGS
39563	541	4788	EDUCATIONAL SERVICES
39564	1278	9454	FOOD SVCS & DRINKING PLACES
39565	295	1545	EDUCATIONAL SERVICES
39566	15	35	PROF.; SCIENTIFIC; & TECH SVCS
39567	898	17223	TRANSPORTATION EQUIPMENT MFG
39568	5	20	EXEC.; LEGIS.; & OTHER SUPPORT
39569	2	25	PROF.; SCIENTIFIC; & TECH SVCS
39571	339	2884	CHEMICAL MANUFACTURING
39572	34	58	EXEC.; LEGIS.; & OTHER SUPPORT
39573	95	618	EDUCATIONAL SERVICES
39574	226	1076	SPECIAL TRADE CONTRACTORS
39576	247	1621	GENERAL MERCHANDISE STORES
39577	471	5867	EXEC.; LEGIS.; & OTHER SUPPORT
39581	362	8795	SOCIAL ASSISTANCE
39595	1	0	UNCLASSIFIED ESTABLISHMENTS
39601	1092	11272	AMBULATORY HEALTH CARE SVCS
39602	3	5	ADMINISTRATIVE & SUPPORT SVCS
39603	1	0	ADMINISTRATIVE & SUPPORT SVCS
39629	74	348	EDUCATIONAL SERVICES
39630	73	518	SUPPORT ACT. FOR TRANSPORT.
39631	107	806	HOSPITALS
39632	3	57	RELIG.; GRANT; CIVIC; PROF ORG
39633	32	74	MERCH. WHOLESALERS;DURABLE GDS
39635	7	201	WOOD PRODUCT MANUFACTURING
39638	109	493	EXEC.; LEGIS.; & OTHER SUPPORT
39641	47	218	CONSTRUCTION OF BUILDINGS
39643	23	66	SOCIAL ASSISTANCE
39645	163	1148	EDUCATIONAL SERVICES
39647	16	60	BLDG MATL & GARDEN EQPMT DLRS
39648	1143	12421	PRIMARY METAL MANUFACTURING
39649	1	2	ADMINISTRATIVE & SUPPORT SVCS
39652	213	1949	FOOD MANUFACTURING
39653	187	1093	EDUCATIONAL SERVICES
39654	244	2103	PAPER MANUFACTURING
39656	12	15	RELIG.; GRANT; CIVIC; PROF ORG
39657	69	251	FORESTRY AND LOGGING
39661	31	121	TRUCK TRANSPORTATION
39662	10	89	SUPPORT ACTIVITIES FOR MINING
39663	49	506	BLDG MATL & GARDEN EQPMT DLRS
39664	27	60	RELIG.; GRANT; CIVIC; PROF ORG
39665	7	16	RELIG.; GRANT; CIVIC; PROF ORG
39666	238	3035	FOOD MANUFACTURING
39667	377	2386	EDUCATIONAL SERVICES
39668	8	27	PIPELINE TRANSPORTATION
39669	200	1336	JUSTICE; PUBIC ORDER/SAFETY
39701	1016	13272	EDUCATIONAL SERVICES
39702	693	6367	NURSING & RESID. CARE FACILIT.
39703	4	30	EXEC.; LEGIS.; & OTHER SUPPORT
39704	3	12	ADMINISTRATIVE & SUPPORT SVCS
39705	720	9864	HOSPITALS
39710	45	760	SUPPORT ACT. FOR TRANSPORT.
39730	459	3341	CONSTRUCTION OF BUILDINGS
39735	273	1998	NURSING & RESID. CARE FACILIT.
39736	32	422	NONMETALLIC MINERAL PROD. MFG
39737	5	12	LEATHER & ALLIED PRODUCT MFG
39739	67	700	FOOD MANUFACTURING
39740	90	477	EDUCATIONAL SERVICES
39741	13	47	EDUCATIONAL SERVICES
39743	51	867	PAPER MANUFACTURING
39744	230	1783	EDUCATIONAL SERVICES
39745	19	416	ACCOMMODATION
39746	60	420	REPAIR AND MAINTENANCE
39747	49	285	EDUCATIONAL SERVICES
39750	56	270	EDUCATIONAL SERVICES
39751	18	42	RELIG.; GRANT; CIVIC; PROF ORG
39752	63	308	MERCH. WHOLESALERS;DURABLE GDS
39753	27	1191	EDUCATIONAL SERVICES

ZIP CODE	2009 Total Firms	2009 Total Employees	TOP INDUSTRY RANKED on 2009 EMPLOYMENT	ZIP CODE	2009 Total Firms	2009 Total Employees	TOP INDUSTRY RANKED on 2009 EMPLOYMENT	ZIP CODE	2009 Total Firms	2009 Total Employees	TOP INDUSTRY RANKED on 2009 EMPLOYMENT
39755	12	56	EDUCATIONAL SERVICES	40066	10	34	SPECIAL TRADE CONTRACTORS	40280	8	715	EDUCATIONAL SERVICES
39756	22	92	CHEMICAL MANUFACTURING	40067	135	1769	FOOD MANUFACTURING	40291	695	4508	FOOD SVCS & DRINKING PLACES
39759	1391	15259	FOOD SVCS & DRINKING PLACES	40068	41	319	MERCH. WHOLESALERS;NONDUR. GDS	40292	20	3108	EDUCATIONAL SERVICES
39760	1	1	PROF.; SCIENTIFIC; & TECH SVCS	40069	288	2250	TRANSPORTATION EQUIPMENT MFG	40299	2290	32042	MERCH. WHOLESALERS;DURABLE GDS
39762	158	10956	EDUCATIONAL SERVICES	40070	19	73	MERCH. WHOLESALERS;NONDUR. GDS	40310	18	144	EDUCATIONAL SERVICES
39766	40	103	EDUCATIONAL SERVICES	40071	299	1447	EDUCATIONAL SERVICES	40311	164	1031	HOSPITALS
39767	9	43	TRUCK TRANSPORTATION	40075	8	12	TRUCK TRANSPORTATION	40312	127	696	WOOD PRODUCT MANUFACTURING
39769	39	94	EXEC.; LEGIS.; & OTHER SUPPORT	40076	32	190	EDUCATIONAL SERVICES	40313	27	79	EDUCATIONAL SERVICES
39771	9	79	EXEC.; LEGIS.; & OTHER SUPPORT	40077	11	38	FOOD SVCS & DRINKING PLACES	40316	5	62	EDUCATIONAL SERVICES
39772	35	141	EDUCATIONAL SERVICES	40078	26	145	EDUCATIONAL SERVICES	40317	3	24	JUSTICE; PUBIC ORDER/SAFETY
39773	672	6576	EDUCATIONAL SERVICES	40104	28	165	MINING (EXCEPT OIL AND GAS)	40319	4	5	PROF.; SCIENTIFIC; & TECH SVCS
39776	26	75	MERCH. WHOLESALERS;DURABLE GDS	40107	24	156	EDUCATIONAL SERVICES	40322	163	819	EDUCATIONAL SERVICES
39813	89	584	FOOD AND BEVERAGE STORES	40108	473	3066	CHEMICAL MANUFACTURING	40324	1243	20249	TRANSPORTATION EQUIPMENT MFG
39815	51	441	CHEMICAL MANUFACTURING	40109	85	1018	REPAIR AND MAINTENANCE	40328	15	23	MERCH. WHOLESALERS;DURABLE GDS
39817	510	5170	PAPER MANUFACTURING	40110	9	479	BEVERAGE & TOBACCO PRODUCT MFG	40330	612	6917	TRANSPORTATION EQUIPMENT MFG
39818	5	22	REAL ESTATE	40111	51	218	EDUCATIONAL SERVICES	40334	3	71	NURSING & RESID. CARE FACILIT.
39819	465	5143	HOSPITALS	40115	14	39	EDUCATIONAL SERVICES	40336	321	2389	APPAREL MANUFACTURING
39823	464	2636	EDUCATIONAL SERVICES	40117	50	200	EDUCATIONAL SERVICES	40337	75	338	WOOD PRODUCT MANUFACTURING
39824	7	21	CROP PRODUCTION	40118	150	1140	EDUCATIONAL SERVICES	40339	3	5	FOOD AND BEVERAGE STORES
39825	23	79	CROP PRODUCTION	40119	34	177	ACCOMMODATION	40340	13	31	SUPPORT ACT. FOR TRANSPORT.
39826	15	39	NURSING & RESID. CARE FACILIT.	40121	124	1155	PROF.; SCIENTIFIC; & TECH SVCS	40342	550	5098	EDUCATIONAL SERVICES
39827	81	387	BLDG MATL & GARDEN EQPMT DLRS	40129	4	12	CREDIT INTERMEDIATION & RELATD	40346	15	193	MISCELLANEOUS MANUFACTURING
39828	634	6487	BLDG MATL & GARDEN EQPMT DLRS	40140	11	20	FABRICATED METAL PRODUCT MFG	40347	130	921	SUPPORT ACTIVITIES: AGR./FOR.
39829	5	6	MERCH. WHOLESALERS;NONDUR. GDS	40142	30	35	SPECIAL TRADE CONTRACTORS	40348	23	517	MINING (EXCEPT OIL AND GAS)
39832	15	917	PAPER MANUFACTURING	40143	286	2452	AMBULATORY HEALTH CARE SVCS	40350	2	1	PERSONAL AND LAUNDRY SERVICES
39834	53	237	SOCIAL ASSISTANCE	40144	39	357	EDUCATIONAL SERVICES	40351	871	8270	HOSPITALS
39836	8	18	CROP PRODUCTION	40145	8	9	CROP PRODUCTION	40353	840	9673	PLASTICS & RUBBER PRODUCTS MFG
39837	250	1512	HOSPITALS	40146	132	574	RELIG.; GRANT; CIVIC; PROF ORG	40355	6	27	JUSTICE; PUBIC ORDER/SAFETY
39840	247	1839	EDUCATIONAL SERVICES	40150	75	475	GASOLINE STATIONS	40356	1487	15176	SPECIAL TRADE CONTRACTORS
39841	22	159	FORESTRY AND LOGGING	40152	46	197	JUSTICE; PUBIC ORDER/SAFETY	40357	11	27	GASOLINE STATIONS
39842	311	2436	EDUCATIONAL SERVICES	40153	6	20	RELIG.; GRANT; CIVIC; PROF ORG	40358	10	118	CONSTRUCTION OF BUILDINGS
39845	345	2687	EDUCATIONAL SERVICES	40155	45	662	SPECIAL TRADE CONTRACTORS	40359	210	1775	EDUCATIONAL SERVICES
39846	74	693	APPAREL MANUFACTURING	40157	32	99	EDUCATIONAL SERVICES	40360	210	1774	EDUCATIONAL SERVICES
39851	93	782	CONSTRUCTION OF BUILDINGS	40159	1	0	REAL ESTATE	40361	664	7031	CROP PRODUCTION
39852	1	2	POSTAL SERVICE	40160	767	7189	FOOD SVCS & DRINKING PLACES	40362	1	8	PROF.; SCIENTIFIC; & TECH SVCS
39854	83	525	EDUCATIONAL SERVICES	40161	7	12	BLDG MATL & GARDEN EQPMT DLRS	40363	3	100	RELIG.; GRANT; CIVIC; PROF ORG
39859	30	78	MERCH. WHOLESALERS;NONDUR. GDS	40162	59	204	EDUCATIONAL SERVICES	40370	32	37	SPECIAL TRADE CONTRACTORS
39861	25	88	PAPER MANUFACTURING	40165	1055	12244	EDUCATIONAL SERVICES	40371	63	203	EDUCATIONAL SERVICES
39862	46	135	CROP PRODUCTION	40170	14	22	FURN. & HOME FURNISHGS STORES	40372	42	132	FOOD AND BEVERAGE STORES
39866	35	129	EXEC.; LEGIS.; & OTHER SUPPORT	40171	2	2	EDUCATIONAL SERVICES	40374	29	214	CONSTRUCTION OF BUILDINGS
39867	5	31	FORESTRY AND LOGGING	40175	214	1011	EDUCATIONAL SERVICES	40376	24	161	MUSEUMS; HIST. SITES;& SIMILAR
39870	77	552	PROF.; SCIENTIFIC; & TECH SVCS	40176	16	19	SPECIAL TRADE CONTRACTORS	40379	59	243	EDUCATIONAL SERVICES
39877	17	43	CROP PRODUCTION	40177	56	210	EDUCATIONAL SERVICES	40380	246	1793	EDUCATIONAL SERVICES
39885	20	71	BLDG MATL & GARDEN EQPMT DLRS	40178	13	24	GASOLINE STATIONS	40383	856	9000	PROF.; SCIENTIFIC; & TECH SVCS
39886	66	281	MERCH. WHOLESALERS;DURABLE GDS	40201	12	151	EXEC.; LEGIS.; & OTHER SUPPORT	40385	44	201	EDUCATIONAL SERVICES
39897	74	440	SOCIAL ASSISTANCE	40202	3123	83119	HOSPITALS	40387	22	35	FOOD AND BEVERAGE STORES
39901	2	9	PROF.; SCIENTIFIC; & TECH SVCS	40203	1059	17492	MERCH. WHOLESALERS;DURABLE GDS	40390	125	1451	EDUCATIONAL SERVICES
40003	35	154	SPECIAL TRADE CONTRACTORS	40204	858	9721	FOOD SVCS & DRINKING PLACES	40391	1198	15283	UTILITIES
40004	1042	12183	TRANSPORTATION EQUIPMENT MFG	40205	937	9951	NURSING & RESID. CARE FACILIT.	40392	3	4	ADMINISTRATIVE & SUPPORT SVCS
40006	113	640	EDUCATIONAL SERVICES	40206	990	11359	FOOD MANUFACTURING	40402	97	1129	MISCELLANEOUS MANUFACTURING
40007	5	52	SPECIAL TRADE CONTRACTORS	40207	2257	27118	HOSPITALS	40403	761	8371	MOTOR VEHICLE & PARTS DEALERS
40008	88	357	EDUCATIONAL SERVICES	40208	488	5960	MERCH. WHOLESALERS;DURABLE GDS	40405	2	2	POSTAL SERVICE
40009	12	28	SPECIAL TRADE CONTRACTORS	40209	327	12821	EDUCATIONAL SERVICES	40409	61	366	NURSING & RESID. CARE FACILIT.
40010	68	1084	EDUCATIONAL SERVICES	40210	375	8999	BEVERAGE & TOBACCO PRODUCT MFG	40410	11	266	SPECIAL TRADE CONTRACTORS
40011	50	324	JUSTICE; PUBIC ORDER/SAFETY	40211	756	7981	MERCH. WHOLESALERS;DURABLE GDS	40419	64	227	EDUCATIONAL SERVICES
40012	18	44	CREDIT INTERMEDIATION & RELATD	40212	339	3216	EDUCATIONAL SERVICES	40422	1183	15369	HOSPITALS
40013	83	382	EDUCATIONAL SERVICES	40213	1096	34578	TRUCK TRANSPORTATION	40423	4	5	EDUCATIONAL SERVICES
40014	554	3180	EDUCATIONAL SERVICES	40214	1145	11894	MERCH. WHOLESALERS;NONDUR. GDS	40434	18	72	PERFORM'G ARTS; SPEC. SPORTS
40018	5	6	TRUCK TRANSPORTATION	40215	370	5148	HOSPITALS	40437	89	337	EDUCATIONAL SERVICES
40019	136	1245	MERCH. WHOLESALERS;DURABLE GDS	40216	1181	13345	FOOD SVCS & DRINKING PLACES	40440	61	218	EDUCATIONAL SERVICES
40020	6	10	FOOD AND BEVERAGE STORES	40217	482	5820	HOSPITALS	40442	8	11	REPAIR AND MAINTENANCE
40022	19	116	AMUSEMENT; GAMBLING;& RECREAT.	40218	1536	20947	BROADCASTING	40444	333	1723	EDUCATIONAL SERVICES
40023	64	258	SPECIAL TRADE CONTRACTORS	40219	1267	25623	MISCELLANEOUS STORE RETAILERS	40445	14	21	RELIG.; GRANT; CIVIC; PROF ORG
40025	1	2	POSTAL SERVICE	40220	917	10140	FOOD SVCS & DRINKING PLACES	40447	231	1821	EDUCATIONAL SERVICES
40026	86	692	EDUCATIONAL SERVICES	40221	3	9	SUPPORT ACT. FOR TRANSPORT.	40448	5	54	EDUCATIONAL SERVICES
40027	7	73	FOOD SVCS & DRINKING PLACES	40222	1555	17398	FOOD SVCS & DRINKING PLACES	40452	2	0	CONSTRUCTION OF BUILDINGS
40031	712	7785	JUSTICE; PUBIC ORDER/SAFETY	40223	1468	25541	INSURANCE CARRIERS & RELATED	40456	367	3068	EDUCATIONAL SERVICES
40033	478	6545	REAL ESTATE	40224	2	0	BLDG MATL & GARDEN EQPMT DLRS	40460	4	8	MERCH. WHOLESALERS;DURABLE GDS
40036	6	34	MINING (EXCEPT OIL AND GAS)	40225	6	1502	ELECT'L EQPMT; APP; & COMP MFG	40461	40	137	EDUCATIONAL SERVICES
40037	44	587	BEVERAGE & TOBACCO PRODUCT MFG	40228	415	4059	EDUCATIONAL SERVICES	40464	8	12	UTILITIES
40040	18	39	JUSTICE; PUBIC ORDER/SAFETY	40229	577	7017	MERCH. WHOLESALERS;DURABLE GDS	40468	49	168	EDUCATIONAL SERVICES
40041	3	257	RELIG.; GRANT; CIVIC; PROF ORG	40231	3	157	POSTAL SERVICE	40472	44	150	WOOD PRODUCT MANUFACTURING
40045	47	413	FABRICATED METAL PRODUCT MFG	40232	9	12	REAL ESTATE	40473	14	323	PERFORM'G ARTS; SPEC. SPORTS
40046	21	46	RELIG.; GRANT; CIVIC; PROF ORG	40233	6	5	CONSTRUCTION OF BUILDINGS	40475	1818	21813	EDUCATIONAL SERVICES
40047	416	2947	EDUCATIONAL SERVICES	40241	779	15675	TRANSPORTATION EQUIPMENT MFG	40476	4	3	MERCH. WHOLESALERS;DURABLE GDS
40048	6	138	RELIG.; GRANT; CIVIC; PROF ORG	40242	170	1371	SOCIAL ASSISTANCE	40481	28	109	EDUCATIONAL SERVICES
40049	2	3	POSTAL SERVICE	40243	872	6465	FOOD SVCS & DRINKING PLACES	40484	403	3429	EDUCATIONAL SERVICES
40050	98	684	EDUCATIONAL SERVICES	40245	511	4595	MERCH. WHOLESALERS;NONDUR. GDS	40486	29	177	EDUCATIONAL SERVICES
40051	98	983	GASOLINE STATIONS	40250	8	20	SPECIAL TRADE CONTRACTORS	40488	2	2	SPORTG GDS;HOBBY;BOOK; & MUSIC
40052	11	41	PUBLISHING INDUSTRIES	40252	12	76	ADMINISTRATIVE & SUPPORT SVCS	40489	45	253	EDUCATIONAL SERVICES
40055	35	169	GASOLINE STATIONS	40253	12	62	AIR TRANSPORTATION	40492	2	2	RELIG.; GRANT; CIVIC; PROF ORG
40056	75	523	RELIG.; GRANT; CIVIC; PROF ORG	40256	4	60	ACCOMMODATION	40495	1	1	RELIG.; GRANT; CIVIC; PROF ORG
40057	52	293	MERCH. WHOLESALERS;NONDUR. GDS	40257	7	10	ADMINISTRATIVE & SUPPORT SVCS	40502	1011	8385	HOSPITALS
40058	9	20	MERCH. WHOLESALERS;NONDUR. GDS	40258	641	9414	FOOD SVCS & DRINKING PLACES	40503	2126	22128	FOOD SVCS & DRINKING PLACES
40059	448	2066	FOOD SVCS & DRINKING PLACES	40259	10	31	SPECIAL TRADE CONTRACTORS	40504	1060	15490	HOSPITALS
40060	16	35	SPECIAL TRADE CONTRACTORS	40261	1	1	PROF.; SCIENTIFIC; & TECH SVCS	40505	1406	14766	SPECIAL TRADE CONTRACTORS
40061	4	259	EDUCATIONAL SERVICES	40268	4	6	CONSTRUCTION OF BUILDINGS	40506	8	10882	EDUCATIONAL SERVICES
40062	2	2	POSTAL SERVICE	40269	13	17	PROF.; SCIENTIFIC; & TECH SVCS	40507	1156	14562	PROF.; SCIENTIFIC; & TECH SVCS
40063	2	191	INSURANCE CARRIERS & RELATED	40270	1	4	PROF.; SCIENTIFIC; & TECH SVCS	40508	882	10947	HOSPITALS
40065	986	11887	TRANSPORTATION EQUIPMENT MFG	40272	660	5823	EDUCATIONAL SERVICES	40509	1765	23146	FOOD SVCS & DRINKING PLACES

BUSINESS DATA

ZIP CODE	2009 Total Firms	2009 Total Employ-ees	TOP INDUSTRY RANKED on 2009 EMPLOYMENT	ZIP CODE	2009 Total Firms	2009 Total Employ-ees	TOP INDUSTRY RANKED on 2009 EMPLOYMENT	ZIP CODE	2009 Total Firms	2009 Total Employ-ees	TOP INDUSTRY RANKED on 2009 EMPLOYMENT
40510	177	6290	UNCLASSIFIED ESTABLISHMENTS	40940	7	97	RELIG.; GRANT; CIVIC; PROF ORG	41128	3	6	FURN. & HOME FURNISHGS STORES
40511	1232	29796	MACHINERY MANUFACTURING	40941	8	22	PROF.; SCIENTIFIC; & TECH SVCS	41129	291	3319	OIL AND GAS EXTRACTION
40513	402	3756	FOOD SVCS & DRINKING PLACES	40943	11	86	EDUCATIONAL SERVICES	41132	2	3	SPECIAL TRADE CONTRACTORS
40514	127	560	HEALTH & PERSONAL CARE STORES	40944	1	1	POSTAL SERVICE	41139	190	1299	NURSING & RESID. CARE FACILIT.
40515	425	2513	FOOD SVCS & DRINKING PLACES	40946	1	0	RELIG.; GRANT; CIVIC; PROF ORG	41141	37	196	EDUCATIONAL SERVICES
40516	79	565	PROF.; SCIENTIFIC; & TECH SVCS	40949	19	58	MOTOR VEHICLE & PARTS DEALERS	41142	2	3	POSTAL SERVICE
40517	878	6108	EDUCATIONAL SERVICES	40953	5	5	FOOD AND BEVERAGE STORES	41143	514	5055	FOOD MANUFACTURING
40522	13	35	SPECIAL TRADE CONTRACTORS	40955	1	2	POSTAL SERVICE	41144	304	2416	EDUCATIONAL SERVICES
40523	8	21	REPAIR AND MAINTENANCE	40958	3	4	SPECIAL TRADE CONTRACTORS	41146	4	14	NONMETALLIC MINERAL PROD. MFG
40524	11	33	ELECTRONICS & APPLIANCE STORES	40962	542	3453	EDUCATIONAL SERVICES	41149	9	42	EDUCATIONAL SERVICES
40533	6	8	SPECIAL TRADE CONTRACTORS	40964	2	4	POSTAL SERVICE	41159	7	37	OIL AND GAS EXTRACTION
40536	104	15182	HOSPITALS	40965	638	6900	GENERAL MERCHANDISE STORES	41160	1	2	POSTAL SERVICE
40544	6	6	SUPPORT ACTIVITIES: AGR./FOR.	40972	24	248	EDUCATIONAL SERVICES	41164	250	1844	EDUCATIONAL SERVICES
40546	2	60	RELIG.; GRANT; CIVIC; PROF ORG	40977	253	2357	EDUCATIONAL SERVICES	41166	10	36	MERCH. WHOLESALERS;DURABLE GDS
40555	20	42	REPAIR AND MAINTENANCE	40979	5	3	POSTAL SERVICE	41168	37	536	SOCIAL ASSISTANCE
40579	2	1	MERCH. WHOLESALERS;DURABLE GDS	40982	2	2	POSTAL SERVICE	41169	227	1719	TRANSPORTATION EQUIPMENT MFG
40583	2	2	MERCH. WHOLESALERS;DURABLE GDS	40983	5	6	SPECIAL TRADE CONTRACTORS	41171	146	738	EDUCATIONAL SERVICES
40588	11	32	SOCIAL ASSISTANCE	40988	13	160	MINING (EXCEPT OIL AND GAS)	41173	3	4	POSTAL SERVICE
40591	7	17	ADMINISTRATIVE & SUPPORT SVCS	40995	1	2	POSTAL SERVICE	41174	19	75	ADMINISTRATIVE & SUPPORT SVCS
40601	2162	50388	NAT'L SECURITY & INT'L AFFAIRS	40997	2	2	POSTAL SERVICE	41175	164	932	NONMETALLIC MINERAL PROD. MFG
40602	1	1	PROF.; SCIENTIFIC; & TECH SVCS	41001	406	3387	EDUCATIONAL SERVICES	41179	237	1936	EDUCATIONAL SERVICES
40603	1	2	ADMINISTRATIVE & SUPPORT SVCS	41002	76	311	EDUCATIONAL SERVICES	41180	9	36	JUSTICE; PUBIC ORDER/SAFETY
40604	6	133	EXEC.; LEGIS.; & OTHER SUPPORT	41003	28	82	JUSTICE; PUBIC ORDER/SAFETY	41181	4	22	MERCH. WHOLESALERS;NONDUR. GDS
40621	6	2925	ADMIN. HUMAN RESOURCE PROGRAMS	41004	124	602	EDUCATIONAL SERVICES	41183	28	260	SPECIAL TRADE CONTRACTORS
40622	1	2000	EXEC.; LEGIS.; & OTHER SUPPORT	41005	456	4836	JUSTICE; PUBIC ORDER/SAFETY	41189	43	201	EDUCATIONAL SERVICES
40701	1175	12638	FOOD SVCS & DRINKING PLACES	41006	98	1093	NONMETALLIC MINERAL PROD. MFG	41201	4	0	HEALTH & PERSONAL CARE STORES
40702	4	5	CONSTRUCTION OF BUILDINGS	41007	45	294	RELIG.; GRANT; CIVIC; PROF ORG	41203	17	30	REPAIR AND MAINTENANCE
40724	1	0	JUSTICE; PUBIC ORDER/SAFETY	41008	394	4846	CHEMICAL MANUFACTURING	41204	8	22	JUSTICE; PUBIC ORDER/SAFETY
40729	103	890	EDUCATIONAL SERVICES	41010	39	143	FOOD SVCS & DRINKING PLACES	41214	18	1021	MINING (EXCEPT OIL AND GAS)
40734	55	775	RELIG.; GRANT; CIVIC; PROF ORG	41011	1445	16444	CONSTRUCTION OF BUILDINGS	41216	13	51	MERCH. WHOLESALERS;DURABLE GDS
40737	12	14	MERCH. WHOLESALERS;NONDUR. GDS	41012	3	8	PROF.; SCIENTIFIC; & TECH SVCS	41219	34	140	JUSTICE; PUBIC ORDER/SAFETY
40740	40	216	WASTE MANAGMT & REMEDIAT'N SVC	41014	150	6984	AMBULATORY HEALTH CARE SVCS	41222	65	444	SOCIAL ASSISTANCE
40741	1257	13678	GENERAL MERCHANDISE STORES	41015	462	4346	EDUCATIONAL SERVICES	41224	214	1867	EDUCATIONAL SERVICES
40743	7	43	ADMINISTRATIVE & SUPPORT SVCS	41016	129	744	PAPER MANUFACTURING	41226	1	0	RELIG.; GRANT; CIVIC; PROF ORG
40744	372	3587	DATA PROCESS'G	41017	1354	23091	HOSPITALS	41230	405	2999	EDUCATIONAL SERVICES
40755	5	9	RELIG.; GRANT; CIVIC; PROF ORG	41018	897	12409	PROF.; SCIENTIFIC; & TECH SVCS	41231	26	115	MINING (EXCEPT OIL AND GAS)
40759	16	85	EDUCATIONAL SERVICES	41022	5	13	WASTE MANAGMT & REMEDIAT'N SVC	41232	29	128	RELIG.; GRANT; CIVIC; PROF ORG
40763	3	24	MINING (EXCEPT OIL AND GAS)	41030	109	689	FOOD SVCS & DRINKING PLACES	41234	5	4	POSTAL SERVICE
40769	464	4919	EDUCATIONAL SERVICES	41031	507	5190	PAPER MANUFACTURING	41238	20	74	TRUCK TRANSPORTATION
40771	14	59	JUSTICE; PUBIC ORDER/SAFETY	41033	23	49	BLDG MATL & GARDEN EQPMT DLRS	41240	519	5719	SOCIAL ASSISTANCE
40801	5	412	MINING (EXCEPT OIL AND GAS)	41034	11	28	REAL ESTATE	41250	14	771	MINING (EXCEPT OIL AND GAS)
40803	2	6	AMBULATORY HEALTH CARE SVCS	41035	303	2685	FOOD SVCS & DRINKING PLACES	41254	7	9	SPECIAL TRADE CONTRACTORS
40806	99	619	EDUCATIONAL SERVICES	41037	2	0	POSTAL SERVICE	41255	13	48	TRUCK TRANSPORTATION
40807	14	66	ACCOMMODATION	41039	28	119	EDUCATIONAL SERVICES	41256	79	490	TELECOMMUNICATIONS
40808	5	8	PROF.; SCIENTIFIC; & TECH SVCS	41040	233	1285	EDUCATIONAL SERVICES	41257	3	4	MERCH. WHOLESALERS;NONDUR. GDS
40810	30	192	EDUCATIONAL SERVICES	41041	369	2976	HOSPITALS	41260	7	8	SPECIAL TRADE CONTRACTORS
40813	4	4	POSTAL SERVICE	41042	2415	39896	FOOD SVCS & DRINKING PLACES	41262	14	61	FOOD AND BEVERAGE STORES
40815	15	127	EDUCATIONAL SERVICES	41043	33	211	NONMETALLIC MINERAL PROD. MFG	41263	6	29	HEAVY & CIVIL ENG. CONSTRUCT'N
40816	3	52	MINING (EXCEPT OIL AND GAS)	41044	19	76	TRUCK TRANSPORTATION	41264	8	28	TRUCK TRANSPORTATION
40818	3	1	RELIG.; GRANT; CIVIC; PROF ORG	41045	51	1192	PRIMARY METAL MANUFACTURING	41265	22	699	HEAVY & CIVIL ENG. CONSTRUCT'N
40819	7	13	GASOLINE STATIONS	41046	29	131	UNCLASSIFIED ESTABLISHMENTS	41267	53	353	EDUCATIONAL SERVICES
40820	3	5	MINING (EXCEPT OIL AND GAS)	41048	448	17087	SUPPORT ACT. FOR TRANSPORT.	41268	9	49	JUSTICE; PUBIC ORDER/SAFETY
40823	156	1565	MINING (EXCEPT OIL AND GAS)	41049	20	107	SPECIAL TRADE CONTRACTORS	41271	4	33	EDUCATIONAL SERVICES
40824	8	35	HEAVY & CIVIL ENG. CONSTRUCT'N	41051	368	4077	EDUCATIONAL SERVICES	41274	22	196	EDUCATIONAL SERVICES
40826	8	48	EDUCATIONAL SERVICES	41052	6	17	NURSING & RESID. CARE FACILIT.	41301	215	1208	EDUCATIONAL SERVICES
40827	8	12	FOOD AND BEVERAGE STORES	41053	5	3	RELIG.; GRANT; CIVIC; PROF ORG	41311	238	2074	SOCIAL ASSISTANCE
40828	121	1310	MINING (EXCEPT OIL AND GAS)	41054	2	2	POSTAL SERVICE	41313	7	24	EDUCATIONAL SERVICES
40829	12	567	MERCH. WHOLESALERS;DURABLE GDS	41055	35	93	FOOD AND BEVERAGE STORES	41314	155	905	EDUCATIONAL SERVICES
40830	3	31	MINING (EXCEPT OIL AND GAS)	41056	730	9595	ELECT'L EQPMT; APP; & COMP MFG	41317	3	4	ACCOMMODATION
40831	433	4949	AMBULATORY HEALTH CARE SVCS	41059	55	290	MERCH. WHOLESALERS;DURABLE GDS	41332	32	165	MERCH. WHOLESALERS;DURABLE GDS
40840	8	264	MINING (EXCEPT OIL AND GAS)	41061	1	2	RELIG.; GRANT; CIVIC; PROF ORG	41333	1	1	REPAIR AND MAINTENANCE
40843	6	602	MINING (EXCEPT OIL AND GAS)	41062	1	2	POSTAL SERVICE	41338	4	22	JUSTICE; PUBIC ORDER/SAFETY
40844	10	69	EDUCATIONAL SERVICES	41063	39	163	EDUCATIONAL SERVICES	41339	386	2952	EDUCATIONAL SERVICES
40845	2	1	FOOD AND BEVERAGE STORES	41064	67	212	NURSING & RESID. CARE FACILIT.	41348	12	95	EDUCATIONAL SERVICES
40847	4	4	FOOD AND BEVERAGE STORES	41065	1	2	POSTAL SERVICE	41352	4	8	MERCH. WHOLESALERS;NONDUR. GDS
40849	4	12	SPECIAL TRADE CONTRACTORS	41071	817	8825	FOOD SVCS & DRINKING PLACES	41360	11	111	SOCIAL ASSISTANCE
40854	24	285	CONSTRUCTION OF BUILDINGS	41072	1	1	SCENIC & SIGHTSEEING TRANSPORT	41365	8	30	EDUCATIONAL SERVICES
40855	17	36	ADMINISTRATIVE & SUPPORT SVCS	41073	186	1637	FOOD SVCS & DRINKING PLACES	41366	2	3	CONSTRUCTION OF BUILDINGS
40856	3	3	POSTAL SERVICE	41074	111	1013	EDUCATIONAL SERVICES	41367	3	4	RELIG.; GRANT; CIVIC; PROF ORG
40858	3	4	FOOD AND BEVERAGE STORES	41075	404	4696	HOSPITALS	41385	5	42	RELIG.; GRANT; CIVIC; PROF ORG
40862	10	75	MINING (EXCEPT OIL AND GAS)	41076	505	7000	FOOD SVCS & DRINKING PLACES	41386	4	17	JUSTICE; PUBIC ORDER/SAFETY
40863	9	290	MINING (EXCEPT OIL AND GAS)	41080	32	286	RELIG.; GRANT; CIVIC; PROF ORG	41390	2	1	FOOD AND BEVERAGE STORES
40865	5	20	MERCH. WHOLESALERS;DURABLE GDS	41081	1	8	MERCH. WHOLESALERS;NONDUR. GDS	41397	8	46	SUPPORT ACT. FOR TRANSPORT.
40868	21	18	BLDG MATL & GARDEN EQPMT DLRS	41083	10	24	NURSING & RESID. CARE FACILIT.	41408	5	36	EDUCATIONAL SERVICES
40870	10	86	FABRICATED METAL PRODUCT MFG	41085	14	206	EDUCATIONAL SERVICES	41413	3	62	PUBLISHING INDUSTRIES
40873	25	95	EDUCATIONAL SERVICES	41086	29	200	FOOD SVCS & DRINKING PLACES	41421	2	0	POSTAL SERVICE
40874	5	7	FOOD AND BEVERAGE STORES	41091	232	2082	EDUCATIONAL SERVICES	41425	24	79	EDUCATIONAL SERVICES
40902	5	83	MINING (EXCEPT OIL AND GAS)	41092	56	405	EDUCATIONAL SERVICES	41426	2	3	POSTAL SERVICE
40903	3	4	SPECIAL TRADE CONTRACTORS	41093	26	142	WOOD PRODUCT MANUFACTURING	41451	2	1	PERSONAL AND LAUNDRY SERVICES
40906	441	3988	EDUCATIONAL SERVICES	41094	375	4105	FOOD SVCS & DRINKING PLACES	41464	12	92	MINING (EXCEPT OIL AND GAS)
40913	17	233	ACCOMMODATION	41095	162	1735	PRIMARY METAL MANUFACTURING	41465	397	2699	EDUCATIONAL SERVICES
40914	10	43	SUPPORT ACTIVITIES: AGR./FOR.	41096	16	29	HEAVY & CIVIL ENG. CONSTRUCT'N	41472	386	2997	JUSTICE; PUBIC ORDER/SAFETY
40915	16	60	HEAVY & CIVIL ENG. CONSTRUCT'N	41097	265	1916	EDUCATIONAL SERVICES	41477	4	13	FOOD AND BEVERAGE STORES
40921	6	12	TRUCK TRANSPORTATION	41098	5	11	RAIL TRANSPORTATION	41501	1350	17904	HEALTH & PERSONAL CARE STORES
40923	7	14	SOCIAL ASSISTANCE	41099	5	2157	EDUCATIONAL SERVICES	41502	3	27	MINING (EXCEPT OIL AND GAS)
40927	3	6	FOOD AND BEVERAGE STORES	41101	1341	24794	AMBULATORY HEALTH CARE SVCS	41503	146	1607	HOSPITALS
40930	7	65	EDUCATIONAL SERVICES	41102	658	6571	EDUCATIONAL SERVICES	41512	12	68	SOCIAL ASSISTANCE
40932	4	10	GENERAL MERCHANDISE STORES	41105	9	113	AMBULATORY HEALTH CARE SVCS	41513	10	52	ADMIN. OF ECONOMIC PROGRAMS
40935	29	121	EDUCATIONAL SERVICES	41121	18	103	EDUCATIONAL SERVICES	41514	97	783	MINING (EXCEPT OIL AND GAS)
40939	6	119	EDUCATIONAL SERVICES	41124	23	116	EDUCATIONAL SERVICES	41517	5	43	EDUCATIONAL SERVICES

ZIP CODE	2009 Total Firms	2009 Total Employ-ees	TOP INDUSTRY RANKED on 2009 EMPLOYMENT	ZIP CODE	2009 Total Firms	2009 Total Employ-ees	TOP INDUSTRY RANKED on 2009 EMPLOYMENT	ZIP CODE	2009 Total Firms	2009 Total Employ-ees	TOP INDUSTRY RANKED on 2009 EMPLOYMENT
41519	11	57	SPECIAL TRADE CONTRACTORS	41749	260	2004	HOSPITALS	42071	1196	13641	FOOD SVCS & DRINKING PLACES
41520	14	114	EDUCATIONAL SERVICES	41751	24	213	SUPPORT ACT. FOR TRANSPORT.	42076	24	30	ACCOMMODATION
41522	125	732	EDUCATIONAL SERVICES	41754	5	14	MINING (EXCEPT OIL AND GAS)	42078	80	409	HOSPITALS
41524	39	480	MINING (EXCEPT OIL AND GAS)	41759	17	372	MINING (EXCEPT OIL AND GAS)	42079	28	69	JUSTICE; PUBIC ORDER/SAFETY
41527	8	26	PRINT'G & RELATED SUPP'T ACT'S	41760	7	28	AMBULATORY HEALTH CARE SVCS	42081	97	563	EDUCATIONAL SERVICES
41528	31	104	MINING (EXCEPT OIL AND GAS)	41762	5	11	MERCH. WHOLESALERS;DURABLE GDS	42082	30	147	EDUCATIONAL SERVICES
41531	6	9	FOOD AND BEVERAGE STORES	41763	9	65	MINING (EXCEPT OIL AND GAS)	42083	5	4	FOOD AND BEVERAGE STORES
41534	1	2	POSTAL SERVICE	41764	14	54	MINING (EXCEPT OIL AND GAS)	42084	1	1	POSTAL SERVICE
41535	4	1	CLOTHING & CLOTH'G ACC. STORES	41766	4	10	CONSTRUCTION OF BUILDINGS	42085	15	34	RELIG.; GRANT; CIVIC; PROF ORG
41537	117	653	EDUCATIONAL SERVICES	41772	4	4	MISCELLANEOUS STORE RETAILERS	42086	85	1303	UTILITIES
41538	2	1	PERSONAL AND LAUNDRY SERVICES	41773	48	304	MINING (EXCEPT OIL AND GAS)	42087	121	1210	PAPER MANUFACTURING
41539	32	1088	MINING (EXCEPT OIL AND GAS)	41774	33	254	PETROLEUM & COAL PRODUCTS MFG	42088	52	231	EDUCATIONAL SERVICES
41540	4	53	EDUCATIONAL SERVICES	41775	4	12	AMBULATORY HEALTH CARE SVCS	42101	2122	31742	EDUCATIONAL SERVICES
41542	1	2	POSTAL SERVICE	41776	48	190	MINING (EXCEPT OIL AND GAS)	42102	16	41	SOCIAL ASSISTANCE
41543	10	19	MERCH. WHOLESALERS;NONDUR. GDS	41777	12	42	EDUCATIONAL SERVICES	42103	542	4699	APPAREL MANUFACTURING
41544	23	100	FOOD AND BEVERAGE STORES	41778	3	8	SOCIAL ASSISTANCE	42104	1088	14955	FOOD SVCS & DRINKING PLACES
41547	3	6	POSTAL SERVICE	41804	10	33	GASOLINE STATIONS	42120	26	81	CROP PRODUCTION
41548	20	60	FOOD AND BEVERAGE STORES	41810	4	18	PRINT'G & RELATED SUPP'T ACT'S	42122	60	319	AMUSEMENT; GAMBLING;& RECREAT.
41549	4	219	MINING (EXCEPT OIL AND GAS)	41812	5	31	MINING (EXCEPT OIL AND GAS)	42123	16	25	HEAVY & CIVIL ENG. CONSTRUCT'N
41553	66	499	NURSING & RESID. CARE FACILIT.	41815	11	61	CONSTRUCTION OF BUILDINGS	42124	1	1	FOOD AND BEVERAGE STORES
41554	7	26	JUSTICE; PUBIC ORDER/SAFETY	41817	12	85	MINING (EXCEPT OIL AND GAS)	42127	282	1702	FOOD SVCS & DRINKING PLACES
41555	8	24	JUSTICE; PUBIC ORDER/SAFETY	41819	4	48	NONMETALLIC MINERAL PROD. MFG	42128	1	1	SPORTG GDS;HOBBY;BOOK; & MUSIC
41557	21	62	HEAVY & CIVIL ENG. CONSTRUCT'N	41821	2	2	POSTAL SERVICE	42129	247	2046	MERCH. WHOLESALERS;DURABLE GDS
41558	11	120	MINING (EXCEPT OIL AND GAS)	41822	262	1680	EDUCATIONAL SERVICES	42130	3	5	GENERAL MERCHANDISE STORES
41559	16	80	FOOD AND BEVERAGE STORES	41824	30	234	GASOLINE STATIONS	42131	4	7	TRANSIT & GRND PASS. TRANSPORT
41560	19	179	EDUCATIONAL SERVICES	41825	4	4	POSTAL SERVICE	42133	40	180	RELIG.; GRANT; CIVIC; PROF ORG
41561	1	1	POSTAL SERVICE	41826	17	155	MISCELLANEOUS STORE RETAILERS	42134	635	8768	PROF.; SCIENTIFIC; & TECH SVCS
41562	24	145	SUPPORT ACT. FOR TRANSPORT.	41828	20	191	MINING (EXCEPT OIL AND GAS)	42140	49	278	EDUCATIONAL SERVICES
41563	2	4	GASOLINE STATIONS	41831	35	416	MINING (EXCEPT OIL AND GAS)	42141	1500	16549	AMBULATORY HEALTH CARE SVCS
41564	22	333	NONSTORE RETAILERS	41832	4	52	EDUCATIONAL SERVICES	42151	2	5	FOOD SVCS & DRINKING PLACES
41566	5	52	WASTE MANAGMT & REMEDIAT'N SVC	41833	2	3	FOOD AND BEVERAGE STORES	42152	14	40	BLDG MATL & GARDEN EQPMT DLRS
41567	10	55	AMBULATORY HEALTH CARE SVCS	41834	16	101	EDUCATIONAL SERVICES	42153	2	2	POSTAL SERVICE
41568	8	39	EDUCATIONAL SERVICES	41835	6	21	EDUCATIONAL SERVICES	42154	16	35	NONSTORE RETAILERS
41571	11	29	EXEC.; LEGIS.; & OTHER SUPPORT	41836	17	60	SPECIAL TRADE CONTRACTORS	42156	23	250	AMUSEMENT; GAMBLING;& RECREAT.
41572	93	449	MINING (EXCEPT OIL AND GAS)	41837	23	261	REAL ESTATE	42157	20	31	SPECIAL TRADE CONTRACTORS
41601	111	838	EDUCATIONAL SERVICES	41838	8	6	SUPPORT ACT. FOR TRANSPORT.	42159	9	181	BEVERAGE & TOBACCO PRODUCT MFG
41602	14	92	JUSTICE; PUBIC ORDER/SAFETY	41839	20	592	MINING (EXCEPT OIL AND GAS)	42160	55	347	SPECIAL TRADE CONTRACTORS
41603	29	127	MINING (EXCEPT OIL AND GAS)	41840	64	252	FOOD AND BEVERAGE STORES	42163	2	0	UTILITIES
41604	5	23	MINING (EXCEPT OIL AND GAS)	41843	16	95	MINING (EXCEPT OIL AND GAS)	42164	500	3786	EDUCATIONAL SERVICES
41605	67	532	MERCH. WHOLESALERS;NONDUR. GDS	41844	22	296	EDUCATIONAL SERVICES	42166	49	281	WOOD PRODUCT MANUFACTURING
41606	16	122	EDUCATIONAL SERVICES	41845	1	0	POSTAL SERVICE	42167	296	2951	EDUCATIONAL SERVICES
41607	5	7	FOOD MANUFACTURING	41847	22	273	MINING (EXCEPT OIL AND GAS)	42170	38	605	TRUCK TRANSPORTATION
41612	16	41	FOOD AND BEVERAGE STORES	41848	4	31	MINING (EXCEPT OIL AND GAS)	42171	116	622	EDUCATIONAL SERVICES
41615	7	66	PROF.; SCIENTIFIC; & TECH SVCS	41849	3	5	MERCH. WHOLESALERS;NONDUR. GDS	42202	59	418	APPAREL MANUFACTURING
41616	8	34	JUSTICE; PUBIC ORDER/SAFETY	41855	4	34	MINING (EXCEPT OIL AND GAS)	42204	7	20	MERCH. WHOLESALERS;NONDUR. GDS
41619	4	18	MOTOR VEHICLE & PARTS DEALERS	41858	417	4819	MINING (EXCEPT OIL AND GAS)	42206	139	847	EDUCATIONAL SERVICES
41621	5	8	CREDIT INTERMEDIATION & RELATD	41859	4	17	AMBULATORY HEALTH CARE SVCS	42207	25	67	CONSTRUCTION OF BUILDINGS
41622	14	287	EDUCATIONAL SERVICES	41861	2	110	MINING (EXCEPT OIL AND GAS)	42210	156	937	EDUCATIONAL SERVICES
41630	29	77	JUSTICE; PUBIC ORDER/SAFETY	41862	16	118	EDUCATIONAL SERVICES	42211	421	3657	SPECIAL TRADE CONTRACTORS
41631	29	289	EDUCATIONAL SERVICES	42001	1624	19315	FOOD SVCS & DRINKING PLACES	42214	25	28	CREDIT INTERMEDIATION & RELATD
41632	2	22	EDUCATIONAL SERVICES	42002	17	25	SPECIAL TRADE CONTRACTORS	42215	15	30	RELIG.; GRANT; CIVIC; PROF ORG
41635	112	791	SPECIAL TRADE CONTRACTORS	42003	1532	20745	HOSPITALS	42216	1	1	PERSONAL AND LAUNDRY SERVICES
41636	14	114	JUSTICE; PUBIC ORDER/SAFETY	42020	28	155	TRANSPORTATION EQUIPMENT MFG	42217	80	304	EDUCATIONAL SERVICES
41640	14	66	SUPPORT ACTIVITIES FOR MINING	42021	36	162	WOOD PRODUCT MANUFACTURING	42220	215	1681	APPAREL MANUFACTURING
41642	60	588	MERCH. WHOLESALERS;DURABLE GDS	42022	8	18	BLDG MATL & GARDEN EQPMT DLRS	42221	5	3	POSTAL SERVICE
41643	15	110	NURSING & RESID. CARE FACILIT.	42023	105	502	SOCIAL ASSISTANCE	42223	106	25889	EXEC.; LEGIS.; & OTHER SUPPORT
41645	23	138	CONSTRUCTION OF BUILDINGS	42024	48	148	PROF.; SCIENTIFIC; & TECH SVCS	42232	18	25	FOOD AND BEVERAGE STORES
41647	69	661	HOSPITALS	42025	686	5320	EDUCATIONAL SERVICES	42234	110	604	MERCH. WHOLESALERS;NONDUR. GDS
41649	135	1035	HOSPITALS	42027	31	128	SPECIAL TRADE CONTRACTORS	42236	20	132	EDUCATIONAL SERVICES
41650	7	7	UTILITIES	42028	21	78	EDUCATIONAL SERVICES	42240	1783	25586	HOSPITALS
41651	12	60	MINING (EXCEPT OIL AND GAS)	42029	277	4609	PETROLEUM & COAL PRODUCTS MFG	42241	4	2	SPECIAL TRADE CONTRACTORS
41653	720	6955	HOSPITALS	42031	141	1087	EDUCATIONAL SERVICES	42252	1	0	POSTAL SERVICE
41655	9	14	SPECIAL TRADE CONTRACTORS	42032	10	106	WATER TRANSPORTATION	42254	8	17	MERCH. WHOLESALERS;DURABLE GDS
41659	56	582	PROF.; SCIENTIFIC; & TECH SVCS	42033	1	2	POSTAL SERVICE	42256	98	468	EDUCATIONAL SERVICES
41660	6	82	MINING (EXCEPT OIL AND GAS)	42035	33	83	JUSTICE; PUBIC ORDER/SAFETY	42259	30	459	ACCOMMODATION
41663	1	2	POSTAL SERVICE	42036	16	26	SPECIAL TRADE CONTRACTORS	42261	304	2389	EDUCATIONAL SERVICES
41666	22	32	GASOLINE STATIONS	42037	2	2	FOOD AND BEVERAGE STORES	42262	187	1027	FOOD SVCS & DRINKING PLACES
41667	10	11	FOOD AND BEVERAGE STORES	42038	217	1376	JUSTICE; PUBIC ORDER/SAFETY	42265	20	76	EDUCATIONAL SERVICES
41669	27	190	JUSTICE; PUBIC ORDER/SAFETY	42039	38	210	TELECOMMUNICATIONS	42266	61	265	NURSING & RESID. CARE FACILIT.
41701	1003	10457	EDUCATIONAL SERVICES	42040	32	62	JUSTICE; PUBIC ORDER/SAFETY	42273	10	14	SPORTG GDS;HOBBY;BOOK; & MUSIC
41702	3	11	SUPPORT ACT. FOR TRANSPORT.	42041	213	1807	MERCH. WHOLESALERS;NONDUR. GDS	42274	26	58	MINING (EXCEPT OIL AND GAS)
41712	7	56	EDUCATIONAL SERVICES	42044	63	574	MUSEUMS; HIST. SITES;& SIMILAR	42275	10	21	WOOD PRODUCT MANUFACTURING
41713	3	17	SPECIAL TRADE CONTRACTORS	42045	96	1425	FOOD SVCS & DRINKING PLACES	42276	624	6494	MERCH. WHOLESALERS;DURABLE GDS
41714	10	25	FOOD AND BEVERAGE STORES	42047	7	5	CROP PRODUCTION	42280	1	1	SPECIAL TRADE CONTRACTORS
41719	18	70	MOTOR VEHICLE & PARTS DEALERS	42048	79	444	ACCOMMODATION	42285	7	73	EDUCATIONAL SERVICES
41721	32	506	SOCIAL ASSISTANCE	42049	57	116	FOOD SVCS & DRINKING PLACES	42286	25	62	AMUSEMENT; GAMBLING;& RECREAT.
41722	25	308	MINING (EXCEPT OIL AND GAS)	42050	146	1056	AMBULATORY HEALTH CARE SVCS	42301	1555	22239	FOOD SVCS & DRINKING PLACES
41723	5	54	EDUCATIONAL SERVICES	42051	53	1642	FOOD MANUFACTURING	42302	6	16	JUSTICE; PUBIC ORDER/SAFETY
41725	10	18	SPECIAL TRADE CONTRACTORS	42053	124	1801	CHEMICAL MANUFACTURING	42303	1589	22335	HOSPITALS
41727	25	755	WOOD PRODUCT MANUFACTURING	42054	13	18	MERCH. WHOLESALERS;NONDUR. GDS	42304	1	1	ADMINISTRATIVE & SUPPORT SVCS
41729	13	102	EDUCATIONAL SERVICES	42055	66	566	NURSING & RESID. CARE FACILIT.	42320	279	3745	ANIMAL PRODUCTION
41731	29	421	MINING (EXCEPT OIL AND GAS)	42056	115	684	NURSING & RESID. CARE FACILIT.	42321	3	6	TRANSPORTATION EQUIPMENT MFG
41735	2	2	POSTAL SERVICE	42058	53	268	SUPPORT ACT. FOR TRANSPORT.	42322	10	51	MERCH. WHOLESALERS;DURABLE GDS
41736	1	2	POSTAL SERVICE	42060	7	30	JUSTICE; PUBIC ORDER/SAFETY	42323	25	265	EDUCATIONAL SERVICES
41739	2	2	POSTAL SERVICE	42061	10	67	EDUCATIONAL SERVICES	42324	9	8	GASOLINE STATIONS
41740	17	184	UTILITIES	42063	5	33	JUSTICE; PUBIC ORDER/SAFETY	42325	32	210	MERCH. WHOLESALERS;NONDUR. GDS
41743	7	9	FORESTRY AND LOGGING	42064	274	2424	HOSPITALS	42326	3	3	MOTOR VEHICLE & PARTS DEALERS
41745	4	11	FOOD SVCS & DRINKING PLACES	42066	897	8878	EDUCATIONAL SERVICES	42327	149	1033	EDUCATIONAL SERVICES
41746	16	165	SOCIAL ASSISTANCE	42069	26	99	SOCIAL ASSISTANCE	42328	24	287	UTILITIES
41747	1	1	POSTAL SERVICE	42070	8	16	FOOD AND BEVERAGE STORES	42330	372	3171	GENERAL MERCHANDISE STORES

BUSINESS DATA

ZIP CODE	2009 Total Firms	2009 Total Employ-ees	TOP INDUSTRY RANKED on 2009 EMPLOYMENT	ZIP CODE	2009 Total Firms	2009 Total Employ-ees	TOP INDUSTRY RANKED on 2009 EMPLOYMENT	ZIP CODE	2009 Total Firms	2009 Total Employ-ees	TOP INDUSTRY RANKED on 2009 EMPLOYMENT
42332	4	7	SUPPORT ACT. FOR TRANSPORT.	42649	12	40	WOOD PRODUCT MANUFACTURING	43066	40	190	EDUCATIONAL SERVICES
42333	18	93	EDUCATIONAL SERVICES	42653	299	1628	FOOD SVCS & DRINKING PLACES	43067	41	251	MERCH. WHOLESALERS;NONDUR. GDS
42334	4	4	POSTAL SERVICE	42701	2307	31065	MERCH. WHOLESALERS;DURABLE GDS	43068	1597	18511	CLOTHING & CLOTH'G ACC. STORES
42337	40	609	ADMIN. ENVIRO. QUALITY PROGRMS	42702	15	42	SOCIAL ASSISTANCE	43070	14	167	MACHINERY MANUFACTURING
42338	9	29	FURNITURE & RELATED PROD. MFG	42712	32	68	MERCH. WHOLESALERS;DURABLE GDS	43071	80	334	SPECIAL TRADE CONTRACTORS
42339	15	26	MUSEUMS; HIST. SITES;& SIMILAR	42713	40	208	MERCH. WHOLESALERS;DURABLE GDS	43072	141	1670	TRANSPORTATION EQUIPMENT MFG
42343	49	634	FURNITURE & RELATED PROD. MFG	42715	6	17	BLDG MATL & GARDEN EQPMT DLRS	43073	9	413	ADMINISTRATIVE & SUPPORT SVCS
42344	22	237	COMPUTER & ELECTRONIC PROD MFG	42716	30	75	RELIG.; GRANT; CIVIC; PROF ORG	43074	460	3660	TRANSPORTATION EQUIPMENT MFG
42345	384	3820	EDUCATIONAL SERVICES	42717	260	1906	EDUCATIONAL SERVICES	43076	168	860	EDUCATIONAL SERVICES
42347	243	2052	EDUCATIONAL SERVICES	42718	973	11198	BLDG MATL & GARDEN EQPMT DLRS	43077	4	13	CONSTRUCTION OF BUILDINGS
42348	144	2478	PRIMARY METAL MANUFACTURING	42719	3	1	SOCIAL ASSISTANCE	43078	881	9615	COMPUTER & ELECTRONIC PROD MFG
42349	13	66	EDUCATIONAL SERVICES	42721	85	361	EDUCATIONAL SERVICES	43080	135	916	EDUCATIONAL SERVICES
42350	21	79	FOOD SVCS & DRINKING PLACES	42722	15	31	CREDIT INTERMEDIATION & RELATD	43081	2033	26050	HOSPITALS
42351	92	1741	PRIMARY METAL MANUFACTURING	42724	77	787	EDUCATIONAL SERVICES	43082	789	11525	PROF.; SCIENTIFIC; & TECH SVCS
42352	69	383	EDUCATIONAL SERVICES	42726	106	512	EDUCATIONAL SERVICES	43083	3	5	RELIG.; GRANT; CIVIC; PROF ORG
42354	10	45	PRIMARY METAL MANUFACTURING	42728	576	4617	EDUCATIONAL SERVICES	43084	12	36	EXEC.; LEGIS.; & OTHER SUPPORT
42355	27	139	SPECIAL TRADE CONTRACTORS	42729	18	77	EDUCATIONAL SERVICES	43085	1598	20462	INSURANCE CARRIERS & RELATED
42356	2	76	RELIG.; GRANT; CIVIC; PROF ORG	42731	3	5	ADMINISTRATIVE & SUPPORT SVCS	43086	25	76	PERFORM'G ARTS; SPEC. SPORTS
42361	3	10	CROP PRODUCTION	42732	25	75	RELIG.; GRANT; CIVIC; PROF ORG	43093	4	10	INSURANCE CARRIERS & RELATED
42364	1	2	POSTAL SERVICE	42733	11	22	WOOD PRODUCT MANUFACTURING	43101	11	19	CREDIT INTERMEDIATION & RELATD
42366	72	767	FABRICATED METAL PRODUCT MFG	42740	58	379	FOOD SVCS & DRINKING PLACES	43102	72	797	EDUCATIONAL SERVICES
42367	63	599	AMBULATORY HEALTH CARE SVCS	42741	4	1	ADMINISTRATIVE & SUPPORT SVCS	43103	236	1537	EDUCATIONAL SERVICES
42368	7	8	GENERAL MERCHANDISE STORES	42742	1	0	POSTAL SERVICE	43105	229	1147	PAPER MANUFACTURING
42369	8	34	JUSTICE; PUBIC ORDER/SAFETY	42743	300	1958	EDUCATIONAL SERVICES	43106	23	223	EDUCATIONAL SERVICES
42370	5	29	JUSTICE; PUBIC ORDER/SAFETY	42746	28	104	EDUCATIONAL SERVICES	43107	80	710	MISCELLANEOUS MANUFACTURING
42371	8	20	SPECIAL TRADE CONTRACTORS	42748	321	2334	PERSONAL AND LAUNDRY SERVICES	43109	22	269	SPECIAL TRADE CONTRACTORS
42372	51	193	FOOD AND BEVERAGE STORES	42749	190	2468	MISCELLANEOUS MANUFACTURING	43110	697	7080	FOOD SVCS & DRINKING PLACES
42374	12	154	WOOD PRODUCT MANUFACTURING	42753	4	5	SPORTG GDS;HOBBY;BOOK; & MUSIC	43111	5	15	EDUCATIONAL SERVICES
42375	5	38	JUSTICE; PUBIC ORDER/SAFETY	42754	567	6231	MERCH. WHOLESALERS;NONDUR. GDS	43112	190	1321	EDUCATIONAL SERVICES
42376	82	378	JUSTICE; PUBIC ORDER/SAFETY	42755	1	1	SOCIAL ASSISTANCE	43113	1049	11721	FOOD SVCS & DRINKING PLACES
42378	58	279	EDUCATIONAL SERVICES	42757	52	103	UTILITIES	43115	27	126	NURSING & RESID. CARE FACILIT.
42402	3	1	RELIG.; GRANT; CIVIC; PROF ORG	42758	4	3	RELIG.; GRANT; CIVIC; PROF ORG	43116	21	122	EDUCATIONAL SERVICES
42404	59	492	SPECIAL TRADE CONTRACTORS	42759	8	38	APPAREL MANUFACTURING	43117	5	15	MERCH. WHOLESALERS;NONDUR. GDS
42406	42	252	EDUCATIONAL SERVICES	42762	7	69	WOOD PRODUCT MANUFACTURING	43119	278	1659	EDUCATIONAL SERVICES
42408	147	1310	PLASTICS & RUBBER PRODUCTS MFG	42764	9	13	RELIG.; GRANT; CIVIC; PROF ORG	43123	1684	22083	MERCH. WHOLESALERS;DURABLE GDS
42409	81	598	EDUCATIONAL SERVICES	42765	247	1712	FURN. & HOME FURNISHGS STORES	43125	483	12217	UNCLASSIFIED ESTABLISHMENTS
42410	42	197	EDUCATIONAL SERVICES	42776	53	311	EDUCATIONAL SERVICES	43126	37	55	EDUCATIONAL SERVICES
42411	28	380	JUSTICE; PUBIC ORDER/SAFETY	42782	14	54	EDUCATIONAL SERVICES	43127	5	50	WOOD PRODUCT MANUFACTURING
42413	57	808	MERCH. WHOLESALERS;NONDUR. GDS	42784	55	198	SPECIAL TRADE CONTRACTORS	43128	187	1784	FOOD SVCS & DRINKING PLACES
42419	2	4	CONSTRUCTION OF BUILDINGS	42788	6	9	RELIG.; GRANT; CIVIC; PROF ORG	43130	2234	28600	NONMETALLIC MINERAL PROD. MFG
42420	1473	19395	PRIMARY METAL MANUFACTURING	43001	55	237	JUSTICE; PUBIC ORDER/SAFETY	43135	108	508	WOOD PRODUCT MANUFACTURING
42431	1262	18328	HOSPITALS	43002	8	162	TRANSPORTATION EQUIPMENT MFG	43136	32	221	RELIG.; GRANT; CIVIC; PROF ORG
42436	12	14	INSURANCE CARRIERS & RELATED	43003	60	423	ACCOMMODATION	43137	174	1640	PERFORM'G ARTS; SPEC. SPORTS
42437	299	2952	MERCH. WHOLESALERS;DURABLE GDS	43004	246	3570	PUBLISHING INDUSTRIES	43138	735	6261	FOOD SVCS & DRINKING PLACES
42440	24	73	FABRICATED METAL PRODUCT MFG	43005	14	219	EDUCATIONAL SERVICES	43140	661	7813	JUSTICE; PUBIC ORDER/SAFETY
42441	34	538	MINING (EXCEPT OIL AND GAS)	43006	6	45	ACCOMMODATION	43142	7	4	EXEC.; LEGIS.; & OTHER SUPPORT
42442	73	422	EDUCATIONAL SERVICES	43007	3	6	POSTAL SERVICE	43143	141	1524	FABRICATED METAL PRODUCT MFG
42444	11	24	FOOD AND BEVERAGE STORES	43008	55	497	FOOD SVCS & DRINKING PLACES	43144	11	16	PERSONAL AND LAUNDRY SERVICES
42445	427	3823	FOOD MANUFACTURING	43009	29	80	AMUSEMENT; GAMBLING;& RECREAT.	43145	44	145	UTILITIES
42450	141	665	FOOD SVCS & DRINKING PLACES	43010	11	58	JUSTICE; PUBIC ORDER/SAFETY	43146	165	1390	JUSTICE; PUBIC ORDER/SAFETY
42451	9	19	MACHINERY MANUFACTURING	43011	142	939	EDUCATIONAL SERVICES	43147	789	6892	FOOD SVCS & DRINKING PLACES
42452	38	2325	FOOD MANUFACTURING	43013	39	137	JUSTICE; PUBIC ORDER/SAFETY	43148	38	121	EDUCATIONAL SERVICES
42453	18	55	JUSTICE; PUBIC ORDER/SAFETY	43014	117	508	EDUCATIONAL SERVICES	43149	71	193	CONSTRUCTION OF BUILDINGS
42455	93	639	NURSING & RESID. CARE FACILIT.	43015	1563	17082	EDUCATIONAL SERVICES	43150	48	199	EDUCATIONAL SERVICES
42456	25	119	EDUCATIONAL SERVICES	43016	1054	16749	PROF.; SCIENTIFIC; & TECH SVCS	43151	11	49	TRUCK TRANSPORTATION
42457	3	4	POSTAL SERVICE	43017	2094	38759	HEALTH & PERSONAL CARE STORES	43152	19	97	ACCOMMODATION
42458	14	118	EDUCATIONAL SERVICES	43018	15	58	SPECIAL TRADE CONTRACTORS	43153	16	67	CROP PRODUCTION
42459	139	1000	MINING (EXCEPT OIL AND GAS)	43019	200	1915	HEAVY & CIVIL ENG. CONSTRUCT'N	43154	34	48	HEAVY & CIVIL ENG. CONSTRUCT'N
42460	2	2	POSTAL SERVICE	43021	174	1245	BLDG MATL & GARDEN EQPMT DLRS	43155	63	346	EDUCATIONAL SERVICES
42461	29	244	EDUCATIONAL SERVICES	43022	66	962	EDUCATIONAL SERVICES	43156	9	39	FOOD AND BEVERAGE STORES
42462	23	68	FOOD SVCS & DRINKING PLACES	43023	442	3495	EDUCATIONAL SERVICES	43157	11	61	JUSTICE; PUBIC ORDER/SAFETY
42463	4	8	EXEC.; LEGIS.; & OTHER SUPPORT	43025	258	8202	NONSTORE RETAILERS	43158	9	18	SPECIAL TRADE CONTRACTORS
42464	35	120	WOOD PRODUCT MANUFACTURING	43026	1615	19213	FOOD SVCS & DRINKING PLACES	43160	857	8921	PLASTICS & RUBBER PRODUCTS MFG
42501	1236	13510	FOOD SVCS & DRINKING PLACES	43027	8	39	PIPELINE TRANSPORTATION	43162	208	2379	PROF.; SCIENTIFIC; & TECH SVCS
42502	7	26	SOCIAL ASSISTANCE	43028	106	495	EDUCATIONAL SERVICES	43163	1	4	RELIG.; GRANT; CIVIC; PROF ORG
42503	673	8937	AMBULATORY HEALTH CARE SVCS	43029	8	86	RELIG.; GRANT; CIVIC; PROF ORG	43164	47	374	EDUCATIONAL SERVICES
42516	3	19	NONMETALLIC MINERAL PROD. MFG	43030	7	431	ADMIN. OF ECONOMIC PROGRAMS	43201	1018	11887	PROF.; SCIENTIFIC; & TECH SVCS
42518	64	385	SPECIAL TRADE CONTRACTORS	43031	329	3172	FOOD MANUFACTURING	43202	534	6015	MISCELLANEOUS STORE RETAILERS
42519	95	886	WOOD PRODUCT MANUFACTURING	43032	8	9	FOOD AND BEVERAGE STORES	43203	271	1841	PROF.; SCIENTIFIC; & TECH SVCS
42528	21	695	WOOD PRODUCT MANUFACTURING	43033	24	204	JUSTICE; PUBIC ORDER/SAFETY	43204	1033	13818	JUSTICE; PUBIC ORDER/SAFETY
42533	16	148	MERCH. WHOLESALERS;DURABLE GDS	43035	650	8562	PROF.; SCIENTIFIC; & TECH SVCS	43205	582	22177	HOSPITALS
42539	391	2469	EDUCATIONAL SERVICES	43036	5	3	POSTAL SERVICE	43206	612	10754	INSURANCE CARRIERS & RELATED
42541	10	98	MERCH. WHOLESALERS;DURABLE GDS	43037	15	85	JUSTICE; PUBIC ORDER/SAFETY	43207	1435	29786	CREDIT INTERMEDIATION & RELATD
42544	95	403	FOOD SVCS & DRINKING PLACES	43040	1023	21187	TRANSPORTATION EQUIPMENT MFG	43209	741	6363	EDUCATIONAL SERVICES
42553	118	642	EDUCATIONAL SERVICES	43041	1	2000	CHEMICAL MANUFACTURING	43210	186	40296	EDUCATIONAL SERVICES
42558	3	17	JUSTICE; PUBIC ORDER/SAFETY	43044	94	592	EDUCATIONAL SERVICES	43211	512	4532	EDUCATIONAL SERVICES
42564	4	4	MOTION PICT. & SOUND RECORDING	43045	42	204	EDUCATIONAL SERVICES	43212	1276	12337	FOOD SVCS & DRINKING PLACES
42565	13	49	EDUCATIONAL SERVICES	43046	108	686	GASOLINE STATIONS	43213	1529	24800	MERCH. WHOLESALERS;DURABLE GDS
42566	10	29	BLDG MATL & GARDEN EQPMT DLRS	43047	1	1	FOOD AND BEVERAGE STORES	43214	1301	25655	AMBULATORY HEALTH CARE SVCS
42567	79	551	MERCH. WHOLESALERS;DURABLE GDS	43048	3	3	POSTAL SERVICE	43215	4257	110893	PROF.; SCIENTIFIC; & TECH SVCS
42602	355	5421	MERCH. WHOLESALERS;NONDUR. GDS	43050	1341	14693	MACHINERY MANUFACTURING	43216	15	2216	POSTAL SERVICE
42603	5	7	BLDG MATL & GARDEN EQPMT DLRS	43054	513	7032	INSURANCE CARRIERS & RELATED	43217	74	2087	COURIERS AND MESSENGERS
42629	260	2674	CLOTHING & CLOTH'G ACC. STORES	43055	2294	25583	INSURANCE CARRIERS & RELATED	43218	4	7	PROF.; SCIENTIFIC; & TECH SVCS
42631	4	7	FOOD AND BEVERAGE STORES	43056	706	9271	FOOD SVCS & DRINKING PLACES	43219	1728	36240	FOOD SVCS & DRINKING PLACES
42633	580	6669	EDUCATIONAL SERVICES	43058	9	18	SPECIAL TRADE CONTRACTORS	43220	1231	11215	FOOD SVCS & DRINKING PLACES
42634	25	75	JUSTICE; PUBIC ORDER/SAFETY	43060	59	317	EDUCATIONAL SERVICES	43221	902	8278	EDUCATIONAL SERVICES
42635	103	667	EDUCATIONAL SERVICES	43061	81	383	MERCH. WHOLESALERS;NONDUR. GDS	43222	299	15492	HOSPITALS
42638	6	10	MOTOR VEHICLE & PARTS DEALERS	43062	738	4918	BLDG MATL & GARDEN EQPMT DLRS	43223	773	11056	NURSING & RESID. CARE FACILIT.
42642	618	4415	HOSPITALS	43064	539	5939	SPECIAL TRADE CONTRACTORS	43224	819	9407	GENERAL MERCHANDISE STORES
42647	89	1109	EDUCATIONAL SERVICES	43065	957	7826	FOOD SVCS & DRINKING PLACES	43226	3	2	SUPPORT ACTIVITIES: AGR./FOR.

ZIP CODE	2009 Total Firms	2009 Total Employ-ees	TOP INDUSTRY RANKED on 2009 EMPLOYMENT	ZIP CODE	2009 Total Firms	2009 Total Employ-ees	TOP INDUSTRY RANKED on 2009 EMPLOYMENT	ZIP CODE	2009 Total Firms	2009 Total Employ-ees	TOP INDUSTRY RANKED on 2009 EMPLOYMENT
43227	398	3122	EDUCATIONAL SERVICES	43463	16	51	RELIG.; GRANT; CIVIC; PROF ORG	43718	74	608	EDUCATIONAL SERVICES
43228	1836	36782	PROF.; SCIENTIFIC; & TECH SVCS	43464	19	69	WASTE MANAGMT & REMEDIAT'N SVC	43719	68	282	JUSTICE; PUBIC ORDER/SAFETY
43229	1919	40923	JUSTICE; PUBIC ORDER/SAFETY	43465	116	2403	BLDG MATL & GARDEN EQPMT DLRS	43720	18	46	ACCOMMODATION
43230	1703	23629	CLOTHING & CLOTH'G ACC. STORES	43466	46	229	REPAIR AND MAINTENANCE	43721	5	12	REPAIR AND MAINTENANCE
43231	853	9776	NURSING & RESID. CARE FACILIT.	43467	5	27	PETROLEUM & COAL PRODUCTS MFG	43722	13	48	FOOD SVCS & DRINKING PLACES
43232	1122	14606	GENERAL MERCHANDISE STORES	43468	12	472	RELIG.; GRANT; CIVIC; PROF ORG	43723	167	2786	PLASTICS & RUBBER PRODUCTS MFG
43234	2	3	SUPPORT ACTIVITIES FOR MINING	43469	89	825	MERCH. WHOLESALERS;DURABLE GDS	43724	301	2544	PRIMARY METAL MANUFACTURING
43235	1558	21368	BLDG MATL & GARDEN EQPMT DLRS	43501	14	40	RELIG.; GRANT; CIVIC; PROF ORG	43725	1068	12273	FOOD SVCS & DRINKING PLACES
43236	10	51	POSTAL SERVICE	43502	356	9860	FURNITURE & RELATED PROD. MFG	43727	18	35	FOOD MANUFACTURING
43240	591	11621	FOOD SVCS & DRINKING PLACES	43504	19	162	JUSTICE; PUBIC ORDER/SAFETY	43728	25	74	JUSTICE; PUBIC ORDER/SAFETY
43266	3	502	EXEC.; LEGIS.; & OTHER SUPPORT	43505	11	63	CONSTRUCTION OF BUILDINGS	43730	48	279	EDUCATIONAL SERVICES
43301	7	24	CONSTRUCTION OF BUILDINGS	43506	721	10229	PLASTICS & RUBBER PRODUCTS MFG	43731	122	902	PRIMARY METAL MANUFACTURING
43302	2022	26765	MERCH. WHOLESALERS;DURABLE GDS	43511	17	105	JUSTICE; PUBIC ORDER/SAFETY	43732	33	197	MUSEUMS; HIST. SITES;& SIMILAR
43310	82	343	TRUCK TRANSPORTATION	43512	1177	16642	PRIMARY METAL MANUFACTURING	43733	5	357	MISCELLANEOUS MANUFACTURING
43311	882	11146	MERCH. WHOLESALERS;DURABLE GDS	43515	230	2123	PRIMARY METAL MANUFACTURING	43734	32	266	EDUCATIONAL SERVICES
43314	65	401	EDUCATIONAL SERVICES	43516	96	773	TRANSPORTATION EQUIPMENT MFG	43735	6	72	AMUSEMENT; GAMBLING;& RECREAT.
43315	120	1317	TRANSPORTATION EQUIPMENT MFG	43517	140	1919	FABRICATED METAL PRODUCT MFG	43736	4	15	JUSTICE; PUBIC ORDER/SAFETY
43316	168	2236	PLASTICS & RUBBER PRODUCTS MFG	43518	78	754	MISCELLANEOUS MANUFACTURING	43738	11	2	CONSTRUCTION OF BUILDINGS
43317	30	138	NURSING & RESID. CARE FACILIT.	43519	6	33	ADMINISTRATIVE & SUPPORT SVCS	43739	36	235	MERCH. WHOLESALERS;DURABLE GDS
43318	74	422	EDUCATIONAL SERVICES	43520	7	6	MERCH. WHOLESALERS;DURABLE GDS	43740	13	30	TRUCK TRANSPORTATION
43319	45	2370	TRUCK TRANSPORTATION	43521	87	713	TRANSPORTATION EQUIPMENT MFG	43746	26	88	EDUCATIONAL SERVICES
43320	35	178	HEAVY & CIVIL ENG. CONSTRUCT'N	43522	121	631	FOOD SVCS & DRINKING PLACES	43747	15	23	BROADCASTING
43321	10	130	SOCIAL ASSISTANCE	43523	5	14	MERCH. WHOLESALERS;NONDUR. GDS	43748	41	198	EXEC.; LEGIS.; & OTHER SUPPORT
43322	16	89	EDUCATIONAL SERVICES	43524	41	228	EDUCATIONAL SERVICES	43749	36	214	ACCOMMODATION
43323	19	150	ANIMAL PRODUCTION	43525	23	77	EDUCATIONAL SERVICES	43750	1	5	RELIG.; GRANT; CIVIC; PROF ORG
43324	72	357	EDUCATIONAL SERVICES	43526	190	1877	FABRICATED METAL PRODUCT MFG	43752	6	9	UTILITIES
43325	13	194	EDUCATIONAL SERVICES	43527	69	368	NURSING & RESID. CARE FACILIT.	43754	21	85	MERCH. WHOLESALERS;DURABLE GDS
43326	515	6489	EXEC.; LEGIS.; & OTHER SUPPORT	43528	896	12185	FOOD SVCS & DRINKING PLACES	43755	46	231	EDUCATIONAL SERVICES
43330	5	33	FOOD SVCS & DRINKING PLACES	43529	8	59	EDUCATIONAL SERVICES	43756	260	2055	EDUCATIONAL SERVICES
43331	137	790	NURSING & RESID. CARE FACILIT.	43530	2	4	POSTAL SERVICE	43757	4	10	GASOLINE STATIONS
43332	57	326	FABRICATED METAL PRODUCT MFG	43531	7	11	ADMINISTRATIVE & SUPPORT SVCS	43758	76	593	WOOD PRODUCT MANUFACTURING
43333	25	201	EDUCATIONAL SERVICES	43532	94	924	EDUCATIONAL SERVICES	43759	23	126	MERCH. WHOLESALERS;DURABLE GDS
43334	127	650	FOOD SVCS & DRINKING PLACES	43533	52	380	TRANSPORTATION EQUIPMENT MFG	43760	19	116	MERCH. WHOLESALERS;NONDUR. GDS
43335	1	300	FOOD MANUFACTURING	43534	50	295	EDUCATIONAL SERVICES	43761	3	3	FOOD AND BEVERAGE STORES
43336	5	21	RELIG.; GRANT; CIVIC; PROF ORG	43535	21	147	MACHINERY MANUFACTURING	43762	135	1361	NURSING & RESID. CARE FACILIT.
43337	25	201	EDUCATIONAL SERVICES	43536	10	37	CROP PRODUCTION	43764	351	3606	EDUCATIONAL SERVICES
43338	414	3083	FOOD SVCS & DRINKING PLACES	43537	1428	23005	PROF.; SCIENTIFIC; & TECH SVCS	43766	22	77	JUSTICE; PUBIC ORDER/SAFETY
43340	48	404	MERCH. WHOLESALERS;NONDUR. GDS	43540	41	675	EDUCATIONAL SERVICES	43767	39	134	MISCELLANEOUS MANUFACTURING
43341	18	70	REPAIR AND MAINTENANCE	43541	4	6	MERCH. WHOLESALERS;NONDUR. GDS	43768	19	66	JUSTICE; PUBIC ORDER/SAFETY
43342	84	439	ADMINISTRATIVE & SUPPORT SVCS	43542	96	651	SPECIAL TRADE CONTRACTORS	43771	55	153	EDUCATIONAL SERVICES
43343	25	136	PRIMARY METAL MANUFACTURING	43543	244	2896	TRANSPORTATION EQUIPMENT MFG	43772	31	99	JUSTICE; PUBIC ORDER/SAFETY
43344	142	709	EDUCATIONAL SERVICES	43545	654	8241	PROF.; SCIENTIFIC; & TECH SVCS	43773	60	178	JUSTICE; PUBIC ORDER/SAFETY
43345	19	81	EDUCATIONAL SERVICES	43547	12	48	SPECIAL TRADE CONTRACTORS	43777	90	455	EDUCATIONAL SERVICES
43346	5	29	JUSTICE; PUBIC ORDER/SAFETY	43548	22	59	RELIG.; GRANT; CIVIC; PROF ORG	43778	17	70	SOCIAL ASSISTANCE
43347	29	95	MACHINERY MANUFACTURING	43549	28	187	MERCH. WHOLESALERS;NONDUR. GDS	43779	25	155	EDUCATIONAL SERVICES
43348	109	1631	TRANSPORTATION EQUIPMENT MFG	43550	4	34	MERCH. WHOLESALERS;NONDUR. GDS	43780	46	241	EDUCATIONAL SERVICES
43349	12	72	EDUCATIONAL SERVICES	43551	1485	22056	FOOD SVCS & DRINKING PLACES	43782	29	103	PAPER MANUFACTURING
43350	9	139	EDUCATIONAL SERVICES	43552	6	25	PROF.; SCIENTIFIC; & TECH SVCS	43783	107	566	SOCIAL ASSISTANCE
43351	472	7722	MERCH. WHOLESALERS;DURABLE GDS	43553	30	255	EDUCATIONAL SERVICES	43786	3	6	FOOD SVCS & DRINKING PLACES
43356	44	330	FOOD SVCS & DRINKING PLACES	43554	89	963	FABRICATED METAL PRODUCT MFG	43787	54	172	EDUCATIONAL SERVICES
43357	153	1315	EDUCATIONAL SERVICES	43555	20	571	FABRICATED METAL PRODUCT MFG	43788	16	17	POSTAL SERVICE
43358	61	195	MERCH. WHOLESALERS;NONDUR. GDS	43556	68	290	EDUCATIONAL SERVICES	43789	2	3	REPAIR AND MAINTENANCE
43359	15	35	SPECIAL TRADE CONTRACTORS	43557	94	953	RELIG.; GRANT; CIVIC; PROF ORG	43791	6	11	PERSONAL AND LAUNDRY SERVICES
43360	20	434	ACCOMMODATION	43558	412	5172	AIR TRANSPORTATION	43793	264	1691	EXEC.; LEGIS.; & OTHER SUPPORT
43402	1243	18389	FOOD SVCS & DRINKING PLACES	43560	1305	14386	HOSPITALS	43802	21	89	EDUCATIONAL SERVICES
43403	22	3365	EDUCATIONAL SERVICES	43565	16	97	EDUCATIONAL SERVICES	43803	5	27	MERCH. WHOLESALERS;DURABLE GDS
43406	36	419	MERCH. WHOLESALERS;DURABLE GDS	43566	231	2383	NONMETALLIC MINERAL PROD. MFG	43804	79	866	ELECT'L EQPMT; APP; & COMP MFG
43407	9	53	EDUCATIONAL SERVICES	43567	568	6765	TRANSPORTATION EQUIPMENT MFG	43805	2	0	POSTAL SERVICE
43408	10	60	MINING (EXCEPT OIL AND GAS)	43569	54	372	FOOD MANUFACTURING	43811	28	497	UTILITIES
43410	302	3639	EDUCATIONAL SERVICES	43570	97	1109	TRANSPORTATION EQUIPMENT MFG	43812	859	10176	EXEC.; LEGIS.; & OTHER SUPPORT
43412	89	370	EDUCATIONAL SERVICES	43571	179	1865	EDUCATIONAL SERVICES	43821	146	811	EDUCATIONAL SERVICES
43413	35	171	MISCELLANEOUS STORE RETAILERS	43601	3	305	POSTAL SERVICE	43822	87	885	SPORTG GDS;HOBBY;BOOK; & MUSIC
43414	6	506	CHEMICAL MANUFACTURING	43604	1641	29524	JUSTICE; PUBIC ORDER/SAFETY	43824	37	149	TRUCK TRANSPORTATION
43416	94	1576	PRIMARY METAL MANUFACTURING	43605	580	4999	EDUCATIONAL SERVICES	43828	1	0	SOCIAL ASSISTANCE
43420	1303	17067	PLASTICS & RUBBER PRODUCTS MFG	43606	1029	22163	HOSPITALS	43830	85	506	FOOD SVCS & DRINKING PLACES
43430	145	1559	FOOD SVCS & DRINKING PLACES	43607	651	6915	SPECIAL TRADE CONTRACTORS	43832	255	2597	PLASTICS & RUBBER PRODUCTS MFG
43431	118	1138	PERSONAL AND LAUNDRY SERVICES	43608	384	11200	HOSPITALS	43836	6	26	EDUCATIONAL SERVICES
43432	16	85	EDUCATIONAL SERVICES	43609	477	4232	EDUCATIONAL SERVICES	43837	22	297	FURNITURE & RELATED PROD. MFG
43433	6	462	NONMETALLIC MINERAL PROD. MFG	43610	87	1093	TRANSIT & GRND PASS. TRANSPORT	43840	24	78	JUSTICE; PUBIC ORDER/SAFETY
43434	3	2	POSTAL SERVICE	43611	422	5137	NONMETALLIC MINERAL PROD. MFG	43842	4	28	CONSTRUCTION OF BUILDINGS
43435	25	201	SOCIAL ASSISTANCE	43612	1285	20557	TRANSPORTATION EQUIPMENT MFG	43843	16	81	FOOD SVCS & DRINKING PLACES
43437	9	15	WASTE MANAGMT & REMEDIAT'N SVC	43613	825	6342	EDUCATIONAL SERVICES	43844	99	617	EDUCATIONAL SERVICES
43438	44	181	ACCOMMODATION	43614	947	18893	HOSPITALS	43845	122	1044	NURSING & RESID. CARE FACILIT.
43439	2	3	POSTAL SERVICE	43615	1527	13740	FOOD SVCS & DRINKING PLACES	43901	51	251	NURSING & RESID. CARE FACILIT.
43440	247	1630	ACCOMMODATION	43616	691	12123	HOSPITALS	43902	3	553	PETROLEUM & COAL PRODUCTS MFG
43441	2	2	POSTAL SERVICE	43617	533	5960	FOOD SVCS & DRINKING PLACES	43903	45	106	RELIG.; GRANT; CIVIC; PROF ORG
43442	23	78	EDUCATIONAL SERVICES	43618	65	594	ACCOMMODATION	43905	6	20	HEAVY & CIVIL ENG. CONSTRUCT'N
43443	58	207	CROP PRODUCTION	43619	370	6211	PROF.; SCIENTIFIC; & TECH SVCS	43906	310	2909	HOSPITALS
43445	16	57	SPECIAL TRADE CONTRACTORS	43620	139	2243	NURSING & RESID. CARE FACILIT.	43907	278	2391	MERCH. WHOLESALERS;DURABLE GDS
43446	13	12	FOOD SVCS & DRINKING PLACES	43623	1305	15019	FOOD SVCS & DRINKING PLACES	43908	47	1344	MERCH. WHOLESALERS;DURABLE GDS
43447	125	1396	TRUCK TRANSPORTATION	43635	8	16	REAL ESTATE	43909	2	6	NONMETALLIC MINERAL PROD. MFG
43449	253	2588	EXEC.; LEGIS.; & OTHER SUPPORT	43659	2	1209	NONMETALLIC MINERAL PROD. MFG	43910	50	368	EDUCATIONAL SERVICES
43450	96	1172	TRANSPORTATION EQUIPMENT MFG	43660	4	594	PUBLISHING INDUSTRIES	43912	213	1754	FOOD SVCS & DRINKING PLACES
43451	38	344	TRUCK TRANSPORTATION	43697	7	12	INSURANCE CARRIERS & RELATED	43913	53	619	UTILITIES
43452	853	6922	FOOD SVCS & DRINKING PLACES	43701	2439	38192	HOSPITALS	43915	35	109	RELIG.; GRANT; CIVIC; PROF ORG
43456	130	807	FOOD SVCS & DRINKING PLACES	43702	7	17	CONSTRUCTION OF BUILDINGS	43916	13	42	SPECIAL TRADE CONTRACTORS
43457	26	147	EDUCATIONAL SERVICES	43711	5	7	SPECIAL TRADE CONTRACTORS	43917	73	365	RELIG.; GRANT; CIVIC; PROF ORG
43458	5	49	EDUCATIONAL SERVICES	43713	255	2002	HOSPITALS	43920	873	10235	REAL ESTATE
43460	240	2782	FOOD SVCS & DRINKING PLACES	43716	42	559	MINING (EXCEPT OIL AND GAS)	43925	12	87	AMUSEMENT; GAMBLING;& RECREAT.
43462	15	86	TRUCK TRANSPORTATION	43717	16	53	FOOD SVCS & DRINKING PLACES	43926	10	34	REAL ESTATE

BUSINESS DATA

ZIP CODE	2009 Total Firms	2009 Total Employ-ees	TOP INDUSTRY RANKED on 2009 EMPLOYMENT	ZIP CODE	2009 Total Firms	2009 Total Employ-ees	TOP INDUSTRY RANKED on 2009 EMPLOYMENT	ZIP CODE	2009 Total Firms	2009 Total Employ-ees	TOP INDUSTRY RANKED on 2009 EMPLOYMENT
43927	2	3	POSTAL SERVICE	44081	255	2801	MERCH. WHOLESALERS;NONDUR. GDS	44242	2	35	HEALTH & PERSONAL CARE STORES
43928	1	6	NURSING & RESID. CARE FACILIT.	44082	28	97	EDUCATIONAL SERVICES	44243	16	3833	PERFORM'G ARTS; SPEC. SPORTS
43930	11	436	EDUCATIONAL SERVICES	44084	82	529	HOSPITALS	44250	14	119	EDUCATIONAL SERVICES
43931	16	1920	PRIMARY METAL MANUFACTURING	44085	57	204	AMBULATORY HEALTH CARE SVCS	44251	26	4768	INSURANCE CARRIERS & RELATED
43932	10	44	EDUCATIONAL SERVICES	44086	60	768	BLDG MATL & GARDEN EQPMT DLRS	44253	95	344	PROF.; SCIENTIFIC; & TECH SVCS
43933	13	525	MINING (EXCEPT OIL AND GAS)	44087	1133	19599	TRANSPORTATION EQUIPMENT MFG	44254	180	1610	EDUCATIONAL SERVICES
43934	10	23	FABRICATED METAL PRODUCT MFG	44088	3	6	WASTE MANAGMT & REMEDIAT'N SVC	44255	243	2116	RELIG.; GRANT; CIVIC; PROF ORG
43935	339	4081	HOSPITALS	44089	519	3244	FOOD SVCS & DRINKING PLACES	44256	2455	26464	FOOD SVCS & DRINKING PLACES
43937	1	0	JUSTICE; PUBIC ORDER/SAFETY	44090	328	3501	PLASTICS & RUBBER PRODUCTS MFG	44258	16	74	ELECTRONICS & APPLIANCE STORES
43938	125	855	EDUCATIONAL SERVICES	44092	815	10470	MERCH. WHOLESALERS;NONDUR. GDS	44260	311	3032	PLASTICS & RUBBER PRODUCTS MFG
43939	15	92	JUSTICE; PUBIC ORDER/SAFETY	44093	25	73	JUSTICE; PUBIC ORDER/SAFETY	44262	121	1066	SPECIAL TRADE CONTRACTORS
43940	5	17	EXEC.; LEGIS.; & OTHER SUPPORT	44094	2227	22252	HOSPITALS	44264	161	1819	FOOD SVCS & DRINKING PLACES
43941	1	0	POSTAL SERVICE	44095	986	8895	FOOD SVCS & DRINKING PLACES	44265	21	479	TRANSPORTATION EQUIPMENT MFG
43942	68	391	EXEC.; LEGIS.; & OTHER SUPPORT	44096	12	17	ADMINISTRATIVE & SUPPORT SVCS	44266	1076	12610	HOSPITALS
43943	42	383	EDUCATIONAL SERVICES	44099	39	188	RELIG.; GRANT; CIVIC; PROF ORG	44270	214	1916	FOOD AND BEVERAGE STORES
43944	60	216	EDUCATIONAL SERVICES	44101	12	63	POSTAL SERVICE	44272	183	1883	EDUCATIONAL SERVICES
43945	65	410	EDUCATIONAL SERVICES	44102	1222	12863	SOCIAL ASSISTANCE	44273	220	2320	MERCH. WHOLESALERS;DURABLE GDS
43946	58	228	MERCH. WHOLESALERS;DURABLE GDS	44103	1077	12698	SOCIAL ASSISTANCE	44274	33	515	PLASTICS & RUBBER PRODUCTS MFG
43947	116	1256	MACHINERY MANUFACTURING	44104	593	6221	EDUCATIONAL SERVICES	44275	69	298	REPAIR AND MAINTENANCE
43948	30	106	EXEC.; LEGIS.; & OTHER SUPPORT	44105	1059	18126	PROF.; SCIENTIFIC; & TECH SVCS	44276	52	261	EDUCATIONAL SERVICES
43950	826	11098	FOOD SVCS & DRINKING PLACES	44106	853	34323	AMBULATORY HEALTH CARE SVCS	44278	670	6820	MACHINERY MANUFACTURING
43951	10	24	RELIG.; GRANT; CIVIC; PROF ORG	44107	1508	13994	EDUCATIONAL SERVICES	44280	204	4948	MISCELLANEOUS MANUFACTURING
43952	1032	18933	HOSPITALS	44108	438	3659	EDUCATIONAL SERVICES	44281	926	10695	FOOD SVCS & DRINKING PLACES
43953	426	3071	AMBULATORY HEALTH CARE SVCS	44109	1244	15139	SOCIAL ASSISTANCE	44282	13	26	SPECIAL TRADE CONTRACTORS
43961	22	724	UTILITIES	44110	662	6404	MACHINERY MANUFACTURING	44285	4	14	RELIG.; GRANT; CIVIC; PROF ORG
43962	6	276	NONMETALLIC MINERAL PROD. MFG	44111	1189	15629	AMBULATORY HEALTH CARE SVCS	44286	417	17447	PRIMARY METAL MANUFACTURING
43963	49	258	RELIG.; GRANT; CIVIC; PROF ORG	44112	601	7788	MERCH. WHOLESALERS;DURABLE GDS	44287	128	989	PLASTICS & RUBBER PRODUCTS MFG
43964	233	1883	CHEMICAL MANUFACTURING	44113	2343	50721	PROF.; SCIENTIFIC; & TECH SVCS	44288	91	595	EDUCATIONAL SERVICES
43967	3	13	REPAIR AND MAINTENANCE	44114	2280	75827	PROF.; SCIENTIFIC; & TECH SVCS	44301	459	3572	EDUCATIONAL SERVICES
43968	171	952	RELIG.; GRANT; CIVIC; PROF ORG	44115	1300	50095	CREDIT INTERMEDIATION & RELATD	44302	214	1706	AMBULATORY HEALTH CARE SVCS
43970	1	2	POSTAL SERVICE	44116	1126	9212	FOOD SVCS & DRINKING PLACES	44303	332	3315	NURSING & RESID. CARE FACILIT.
43971	38	553	PRIMARY METAL MANUFACTURING	44117	389	12841	MACHINERY MANUFACTURING	44304	343	6192	HOSPITALS
43972	8	20	MERCH. WHOLESALERS;DURABLE GDS	44118	1217	10752	EDUCATIONAL SERVICES	44305	563	7988	FOOD AND BEVERAGE STORES
43973	52	340	PRINT'G & RELATED SUPP'T ACT'S	44119	456	4524	NURSING & RESID. CARE FACILIT.	44306	706	10120	EXEC.; LEGIS.; & OTHER SUPPORT
43974	8	71	MERCH. WHOLESALERS;DURABLE GDS	44120	957	6482	EDUCATIONAL SERVICES	44307	237	6212	HOSPITALS
43976	52	800	EDUCATIONAL SERVICES	44121	870	6092	AMBULATORY HEALTH CARE SVCS	44308	821	17681	JUSTICE; PUBIC ORDER/SAFETY
43977	56	167	PROF.; SCIENTIFIC; & TECH SVCS	44122	2866	38141	AMBULATORY HEALTH CARE SVCS	44309	18	1189	POSTAL SERVICE
43981	11	55	JUSTICE; PUBIC ORDER/SAFETY	44123	376	2707	EDUCATIONAL SERVICES	44310	1037	14903	HOSPITALS
43983	11	21	FOOD SVCS & DRINKING PLACES	44124	1608	22326	HOSPITALS	44311	518	8523	PROF.; SCIENTIFIC; & TECH SVCS
43985	9	24	EXEC.; LEGIS.; & OTHER SUPPORT	44125	1247	22248	MERCH. WHOLESALERS;DURABLE GDS	44312	1087	10645	FOOD SVCS & DRINKING PLACES
43986	43	265	EDUCATIONAL SERVICES	44126	540	3744	REAL ESTATE	44313	940	9863	SPORTG GDS;HOBBY;BOOK; & MUSIC
43988	69	274	EDUCATIONAL SERVICES	44127	273	3506	FABRICATED METAL PRODUCT MFG	44314	443	3296	EDUCATIONAL SERVICES
44001	672	6281	FOOD SVCS & DRINKING PLACES	44128	1429	17241	PROF.; SCIENTIFIC; & TECH SVCS	44315	2	918	COMPUTER & ELECTRONIC PROD MFG
44003	189	2061	AMBULATORY HEALTH CARE SVCS	44129	1062	14029	HOSPITALS	44316	4	6003	PLASTICS & RUBBER PRODUCTS MFG
44004	1392	15255	FOOD SVCS & DRINKING PLACES	44130	2112	36319	PROF.; SCIENTIFIC; & TECH SVCS	44317	4	1125	PLASTICS & RUBBER PRODUCTS MFG
44005	9	42	RELIG.; GRANT; CIVIC; PROF ORG	44131	1789	24214	PROF.; SCIENTIFIC; & TECH SVCS	44319	1042	9596	FOOD SVCS & DRINKING PLACES
44010	105	1432	PLASTICS & RUBBER PRODUCTS MFG	44132	470	4298	AMBULATORY HEALTH CARE SVCS	44320	609	5024	AMBULATORY HEALTH CARE SVCS
44011	659	8640	MERCH. WHOLESALERS;DURABLE GDS	44133	1052	8158	FOOD SVCS & DRINKING PLACES	44321	409	4503	PROF.; SCIENTIFIC; & TECH SVCS
44012	545	10817	TRANSPORTATION EQUIPMENT MFG	44134	906	8238	FOOD SVCS & DRINKING PLACES	44322	26	464	GENERAL MERCHANDISE STORES
44017	717	10731	EDUCATIONAL SERVICES	44135	889	21418	SPACE RESEARCH AND TECHNOLOGY	44325	14	2340	EDUCATIONAL SERVICES
44021	219	1990	PLASTICS & RUBBER PRODUCTS MFG	44136	1128	12685	FOOD SVCS & DRINKING PLACES	44326	5	523	OTHER INFORMATION SERVICES
44022	767	4556	EDUCATIONAL SERVICES	44137	656	6361	EDUCATIONAL SERVICES	44328	5	10	CREDIT INTERMEDIATION & RELATD
44023	857	6306	PLASTICS & RUBBER PRODUCTS MFG	44138	375	3657	PUBLISHING INDUSTRIES	44333	1671	28398	PROF.; SCIENTIFIC; & TECH SVCS
44024	1014	9730	HOSPITALS	44139	1492	26371	FOOD MANUFACTURING	44334	13	18	MISCELLANEOUS STORE RETAILERS
44026	560	4259	EDUCATIONAL SERVICES	44140	322	2343	EDUCATIONAL SERVICES	44372	3	16	SOCIAL ASSISTANCE
44028	279	1935	AMUSEMENT; GAMBLING;& RECREAT.	44141	684	10495	HOSPITALS	44401	63	274	EDUCATIONAL SERVICES
44030	483	4460	EDUCATIONAL SERVICES	44142	607	10328	TRANSPORTATION EQUIPMENT MFG	44402	72	546	EDUCATIONAL SERVICES
44032	26	107	SUPPORT ACTIVITIES FOR MINING	44143	1042	24073	INSURANCE CARRIERS & RELATED	44403	190	1399	TRUCK TRANSPORTATION
44033	9	92	MERCH. WHOLESALERS;DURABLE GDS	44144	507	18062	PRINT'G & RELATED SUPP'T ACT'S	44404	18	84	BLDG MATL & GARDEN EQPMT DLRS
44035	2518	38173	EXEC.; LEGIS.; & OTHER SUPPORT	44145	1905	25541	PROF.; SCIENTIFIC; & TECH SVCS	44405	149	1032	EDUCATIONAL SERVICES
44036	9	27	ADMINISTRATIVE & SUPPORT SVCS	44146	1594	27094	TRANSPORTATION EQUIPMENT MFG	44406	842	7064	PROF.; SCIENTIFIC; & TECH SVCS
44039	633	5540	EDUCATIONAL SERVICES	44147	640	7232	PROF.; SCIENTIFIC; & TECH SVCS	44408	483	5089	FOOD SVCS & DRINKING PLACES
44040	95	1234	EDUCATIONAL SERVICES	44149	494	8736	FABRICATED METAL PRODUCT MFG	44410	590	3771	EDUCATIONAL SERVICES
44041	561	4467	HOSPITALS	44181	2	300	POSTAL SERVICE	44411	56	343	JUSTICE; PUBIC ORDER/SAFETY
44044	335	2528	MERCH. WHOLESALERS;DURABLE GDS	44195	100	13146	AMBULATORY HEALTH CARE SVCS	44412	48	314	MERCH. WHOLESALERS;DURABLE GDS
44045	31	689	FOOD SVCS & DRINKING PLACES	44199	42	705	JUSTICE; PUBIC ORDER/SAFETY	44413	246	2121	MERCH. WHOLESALERS;DURABLE GDS
44046	46	233	NURSING & RESID. CARE FACILIT.	44201	87	405	EDUCATIONAL SERVICES	44416	3	8	ADMINISTRATIVE & SUPPORT SVCS
44047	389	4456	EXEC.; LEGIS.; & OTHER SUPPORT	44202	764	8597	MERCH. WHOLESALERS;DURABLE GDS	44417	20	85	JUSTICE; PUBIC ORDER/SAFETY
44048	93	697	NURSING & RESID. CARE FACILIT.	44203	1317	18743	PROF.; SCIENTIFIC; & TECH SVCS	44418	27	145	NURSING & RESID. CARE FACILIT.
44049	8	23	JUSTICE; PUBIC ORDER/SAFETY	44210	21	183	MUSEUMS; HIST. SITES;& SIMILAR	44420	574	4749	MERCH. WHOLESALERS;DURABLE GDS
44050	139	1486	SPECIAL TRADE CONTRACTORS	44211	2	1	HEAVY & CIVIL ENG. CONSTRUCT'N	44422	6	28	WAREHOUSING AND STORAGE
44052	683	6681	EDUCATIONAL SERVICES	44212	1030	9468	FOOD SVCS & DRINKING PLACES	44423	54	376	EDUCATIONAL SERVICES
44053	536	10102	AMBULATORY HEALTH CARE SVCS	44214	123	830	CLOTHING & CLOTH'G ACC. STORES	44424	18	85	EXEC.; LEGIS.; & OTHER SUPPORT
44054	265	3042	EDUCATIONAL SERVICES	44215	32	130	FOOD SVCS & DRINKING PLACES	44425	529	3960	MERCH. WHOLESALERS;DURABLE GDS
44055	421	5936	PRIMARY METAL MANUFACTURING	44216	158	653	MERCH. WHOLESALERS;DURABLE GDS	44427	33	229	SOCIAL ASSISTANCE
44056	512	8292	FOOD SVCS & DRINKING PLACES	44217	105	484	EDUCATIONAL SERVICES	44428	118	835	MISCELLANEOUS MANUFACTURING
44057	577	4838	NURSING & RESID. CARE FACILIT.	44221	935	12035	EDUCATIONAL SERVICES	44429	91	421	EDUCATIONAL SERVICES
44060	2900	36950	FOOD SVCS & DRINKING PLACES	44222	2	3	CONSTRUCTION OF BUILDINGS	44430	57	480	EDUCATIONAL SERVICES
44061	16	54	AMBULATORY HEALTH CARE SVCS	44223	628	7397	MERCH. WHOLESALERS;DURABLE GDS	44431	138	992	EDUCATIONAL SERVICES
44062	491	8549	FURNITURE & RELATED PROD. MFG	44224	1212	14500	FOOD SVCS & DRINKING PLACES	44432	457	4076	SOCIAL ASSISTANCE
44064	63	245	SPECIAL TRADE CONTRACTORS	44230	267	1396	EDUCATIONAL SERVICES	44436	117	1171	SPECIAL TRADE CONTRACTORS
44065	290	2708	ADMINISTRATIVE & SUPPORT SVCS	44231	255	1668	FOOD SVCS & DRINKING PLACES	44437	76	567	EDUCATIONAL SERVICES
44067	613	5312	HOSPITALS	44232	39	97	JUSTICE; PUBIC ORDER/SAFETY	44438	86	947	NURSING & RESID. CARE FACILIT.
44068	47	891	PLASTICS & RUBBER PRODUCTS MFG	44233	228	1539	SPECIAL TRADE CONTRACTORS	44439	15	168	PLASTICS & RUBBER PRODUCTS MFG
44070	1318	14031	FOOD SVCS & DRINKING PLACES	44234	71	869	RELIG.; GRANT; CIVIC; PROF ORG	44440	121	1690	EXEC.; LEGIS.; & OTHER SUPPORT
44072	205	916	ADMINISTRATIVE & SUPPORT SVCS	44235	21	52	ADMINISTRATIVE & SUPPORT SVCS	44441	36	184	JUSTICE; PUBIC ORDER/SAFETY
44074	411	5155	SECURITIES/COMMODITY CONTRACTS	44236	1373	13825	SPORTG GDS;HOBBY;BOOK; & MUSIC	44442	115	750	EDUCATIONAL SERVICES
44076	162	1550	FURNITURE & RELATED PROD. MFG	44237	1	400	PROF.; SCIENTIFIC; & TECH SVCS	44443	89	540	FOOD SVCS & DRINKING PLACES
44077	1879	19844	EDUCATIONAL SERVICES	44240	1246	20583	EDUCATIONAL SERVICES	44444	301	2329	FOOD SVCS & DRINKING PLACES
44080	42	165	FOOD SVCS & DRINKING PLACES	44241	505	8100	PLASTICS & RUBBER PRODUCTS MFG	44445	77	475	SPECIAL TRADE CONTRACTORS

ZIP CODE	2009 Total Firms	2009 Total Employ-ees	TOP INDUSTRY RANKED on 2009 EMPLOYMENT	ZIP CODE	2009 Total Firms	2009 Total Employ-ees	TOP INDUSTRY RANKED on 2009 EMPLOYMENT	ZIP CODE	2009 Total Firms	2009 Total Employ-ees	TOP INDUSTRY RANKED on 2009 EMPLOYMENT
44446	994	13104	FOOD SVCS & DRINKING PLACES	44666	58	370	ACCOMMODATION	44865	91	490	MERCH. WHOLESALERS;DURABLE GDS
44449	34	76	CONSTRUCTION OF BUILDINGS	44667	497	6593	FOOD MANUFACTURING	44866	40	71	PROF.; SCIENTIFIC; & TECH SVCS
44450	47	287	EDUCATIONAL SERVICES	44669	37	156	TRUCK TRANSPORTATION	44867	40	163	ADMINISTRATIVE & SUPPORT SVCS
44451	212	2758	PROF.; SCIENTIFIC; & TECH SVCS	44670	14	45	JUSTICE; PUBIC ORDER/SAFETY	44870	2077	44351	AMUSEMENT; GAMBLING;& RECREAT.
44452	254	2641	NURSING & RESID. CARE FACILIT.	44671	6	19	PERFORM'G ARTS; SPEC. SPORTS	44871	11	22	SOCIAL ASSISTANCE
44453	7	18	FOOD SVCS & DRINKING PLACES	44672	159	2110	NURSING & RESID. CARE FACILIT.	44874	17	26	RELIG.; GRANT; CIVIC; PROF ORG
44454	31	130	MERCH. WHOLESALERS;DURABLE GDS	44675	42	350	ACCOMMODATION	44875	437	5584	PRIMARY METAL MANUFACTURING
44455	51	298	PROF.; SCIENTIFIC; & TECH SVCS	44676	133	813	NONMETALLIC MINERAL PROD. MFG	44878	65	431	FABRICATED METAL PRODUCT MFG
44460	1008	13131	AMBULATORY HEALTH CARE SVCS	44677	118	1136	EDUCATIONAL SERVICES	44880	39	306	EDUCATIONAL SERVICES
44470	59	309	JUSTICE; PUBIC ORDER/SAFETY	44678	3	11	SPECIAL TRADE CONTRACTORS	44881	4	3	POSTAL SERVICE
44471	285	2671	PRIMARY METAL MANUFACTURING	44680	164	1192	PLASTICS & RUBBER PRODUCTS MFG	44882	87	648	EDUCATIONAL SERVICES
44473	166	1680	PLASTICS & RUBBER PRODUCTS MFG	44681	308	2950	FOOD SVCS & DRINKING PLACES	44883	1093	12478	EDUCATIONAL SERVICES
44481	575	16119	TRANSPORTATION EQUIPMENT MFG	44682	19	126	EDUCATIONAL SERVICES	44887	25	71	EDUCATIONAL SERVICES
44482	4	5	MERCH. WHOLESALERS;DURABLE GDS	44683	290	2661	MERCH. WHOLESALERS;DURABLE GDS	44888	1	1600	PRINT'G & RELATED SUPP'T ACT'S
44483	1146	16291	HOSPITALS	44685	664	7523	EDUCATIONAL SERVICES	44889	120	464	ACCOMMODATION
44484	920	11031	AMBULATORY HEALTH CARE SVCS	44687	43	646	NURSING & RESID. CARE FACILIT.	44890	328	5255	MACHINERY MANUFACTURING
44485	327	2837	PRIMARY METAL MANUFACTURING	44688	90	640	FOOD AND BEVERAGE STORES	44901	12	357	POSTAL SERVICE
44486	1	5000	ELECT'L EQPMT; APP; & COMP MFG	44689	31	271	PLASTICS & RUBBER PRODUCTS MFG	44902	704	7196	JUSTICE; PUBIC ORDER/SAFETY
44490	21	153	FABRICATED METAL PRODUCT MFG	44690	36	987	MERCH. WHOLESALERS;NONDUR. GDS	44903	753	16226	HOSPITALS
44491	47	130	EXEC.; LEGIS.; & OTHER SUPPORT	44691	2042	25913	EDUCATIONAL SERVICES	44904	383	3152	MERCH. WHOLESALERS;DURABLE GDS
44492	5	24	EDUCATIONAL SERVICES	44693	7	49	ACCOMMODATION	44905	487	4232	JUSTICE; PUBIC ORDER/SAFETY
44493	6	31	JUSTICE; PUBIC ORDER/SAFETY	44695	31	498	WOOD PRODUCT MANUFACTURING	44906	1068	16261	TRANSPORTATION EQUIPMENT MFG
44501	10	840	POSTAL SERVICE	44697	24	119	MUSEUMS; HIST. SITES;& SIMILAR	44907	569	5980	COMPUTER & ELECTRONIC PROD MFG
44502	516	5959	FABRICATED METAL PRODUCT MFG	44699	17	32	WOOD PRODUCT MANUFACTURING	45001	34	110	FOOD SVCS & DRINKING PLACES
44503	517	7254	PROF.; SCIENTIFIC; & TECH SVCS	44701	3	16	REAL ESTATE	45002	394	2986	SPECIAL TRADE CONTRACTORS
44504	189	22280	AMBULATORY HEALTH CARE SVCS	44702	698	10794	JUSTICE; PUBIC ORDER/SAFETY	45003	32	283	ACCOMMODATION
44505	804	10442	AMBULATORY HEALTH CARE SVCS	44703	187	1467	SPECIAL TRADE CONTRACTORS	45004	2	5	SPECIAL TRADE CONTRACTORS
44506	123	942	SOCIAL ASSISTANCE	44704	110	1900	FABRICATED METAL PRODUCT MFG	45005	962	12959	HOSPITALS
44507	234	1877	EDUCATIONAL SERVICES	44705	529	9569	FOOD MANUFACTURING	45011	1955	24151	EDUCATIONAL SERVICES
44509	458	5364	EDUCATIONAL SERVICES	44706	522	16008	FABRICATED METAL PRODUCT MFG	45012	1	2	INSURANCE CARRIERS & RELATED
44510	78	1536	PRIMARY METAL MANUFACTURING	44707	500	10948	SUPPORT ACT. FOR TRANSPORT.	45013	1168	10163	FOOD SVCS & DRINKING PLACES
44511	341	2067	FOOD AND BEVERAGE STORES	44708	958	11639	HOSPITALS	45014	1808	34212	INSURANCE CARRIERS & RELATED
44512	2297	27122	FOOD SVCS & DRINKING PLACES	44709	550	6834	AMBULATORY HEALTH CARE SVCS	45015	385	4370	MERCH. WHOLESALERS;DURABLE GDS
44513	7	25	PROF.; SCIENTIFIC; & TECH SVCS	44710	179	10915	AMBULATORY HEALTH CARE SVCS	45018	10	16	SPECIAL TRADE CONTRACTORS
44514	836	8173	FOOD SVCS & DRINKING PLACES	44711	9	15	UTILITIES	45030	678	7025	FOOD SVCS & DRINKING PLACES
44515	1161	14816	FOOD SVCS & DRINKING PLACES	44714	205	1569	NURSING & RESID. CARE FACILIT.	45032	13	53	JUSTICE; PUBIC ORDER/SAFETY
44555	23	2753	EDUCATIONAL SERVICES	44718	1364	15503	FOOD SVCS & DRINKING PLACES	45033	7	82	JUSTICE; PUBIC ORDER/SAFETY
44601	1297	15933	FOOD AND BEVERAGE STORES	44720	1958	31229	MERCH. WHOLESALERS;DURABLE GDS	45034	26	99	EDUCATIONAL SERVICES
44606	161	1599	FABRICATED METAL PRODUCT MFG	44721	261	1738	EDUCATIONAL SERVICES	45036	1306	17595	JUSTICE; PUBIC ORDER/SAFETY
44607	4	8	FOOD AND BEVERAGE STORES	44730	154	1177	EDUCATIONAL SERVICES	45039	378	2962	COMPUTER & ELECTRONIC PROD MFG
44608	76	530	MERCH. WHOLESALERS;DURABLE GDS	44735	10	24	NONSTORE RETAILERS	45040	1472	32864	MERCH. WHOLESALERS;DURABLE GDS
44609	98	694	EDUCATIONAL SERVICES	44750	2	252	MISCELLANEOUS MANUFACTURING	45041	63	587	SPECIAL TRADE CONTRACTORS
44610	154	1485	PLASTICS & RUBBER PRODUCTS MFG	44767	18	3017	NONSTORE RETAILERS	45042	773	7065	EDUCATIONAL SERVICES
44611	33	269	SPECIAL TRADE CONTRACTORS	44802	17	272	CONSTRUCTION OF BUILDINGS	45044	1493	13885	FOOD SVCS & DRINKING PLACES
44612	151	1563	MISCELLANEOUS MANUFACTURING	44804	29	219	EDUCATIONAL SERVICES	45050	360	5458	SPECIAL TRADE CONTRACTORS
44613	67	1276	FOOD MANUFACTURING	44805	1233	16548	EDUCATIONAL SERVICES	45051	2	172	NURSING & RESID. CARE FACILIT.
44614	351	3359	WHOLESALE ELEC. MRKTS & AGENTS	44807	80	463	EDUCATIONAL SERVICES	45052	100	982	CHEMICAL MANUFACTURING
44615	463	3616	EXEC.; LEGIS.; & OTHER SUPPORT	44809	36	182	EDUCATIONAL SERVICES	45053	59	217	SPECIAL TRADE CONTRACTORS
44617	17	362	BLDG MATL & GARDEN EQPMT DLRS	44811	435	5878	PLASTICS & RUBBER PRODUCTS MFG	45054	41	439	SOCIAL ASSISTANCE
44618	194	1702	BLDG MATL & GARDEN EQPMT DLRS	44813	207	1354	SPECIAL TRADE CONTRACTORS	45055	6	24	FABRICATED METAL PRODUCT MFG
44619	22	82	BLDG MATL & GARDEN EQPMT DLRS	44814	75	380	EDUCATIONAL SERVICES	45056	648	5866	FOOD SVCS & DRINKING PLACES
44620	34	106	EDUCATIONAL SERVICES	44815	33	348	MINING (EXCEPT OIL AND GAS)	45061	12	17	CREDIT INTERMEDIATION & RELATD
44621	117	1187	HOSPITALS	44816	26	408	MERCH. WHOLESALERS;DURABLE GDS	45062	21	115	EDUCATIONAL SERVICES
44622	778	11605	AMBULATORY HEALTH CARE SVCS	44817	28	366	EDUCATIONAL SERVICES	45063	16	124	SPECIAL TRADE CONTRACTORS
44624	92	641	SPECIAL TRADE CONTRACTORS	44818	55	287	FOOD SVCS & DRINKING PLACES	45064	32	147	NURSING & RESID. CARE FACILIT.
44625	28	144	ACCOMMODATION	44820	759	8037	FABRICATED METAL PRODUCT MFG	45065	70	332	SOCIAL ASSISTANCE
44626	64	548	CONSTRUCTION OF BUILDINGS	44822	73	358	EDUCATIONAL SERVICES	45066	691	8066	FOOD SVCS & DRINKING PLACES
44627	94	594	PLASTICS & RUBBER PRODUCTS MFG	44824	103	632	EDUCATIONAL SERVICES	45067	215	2441	BEVERAGE & TOBACCO PRODUCT MFG
44628	21	130	MINING (EXCEPT OIL AND GAS)	44825	8	32	EDUCATIONAL SERVICES	45068	305	1616	FOOD SVCS & DRINKING PLACES
44629	71	799	FABRICATED METAL PRODUCT MFG	44826	27	285	EDUCATIONAL SERVICES	45069	2142	27223	FOOD SVCS & DRINKING PLACES
44630	19	100	FOOD AND BEVERAGE STORES	44827	212	1843	NONMETALLIC MINERAL PROD. MFG	45070	12	32	EDUCATIONAL SERVICES
44631	1	0	RELIG.; GRANT; CIVIC; PROF ORG	44828	9	143	RELIG.; GRANT; CIVIC; PROF ORG	45071	14	23	REPAIR AND MAINTENANCE
44632	502	4986	FOOD SVCS & DRINKING PLACES	44830	591	6841	REPAIR AND MAINTENANCE	45101	65	350	FOOD SVCS & DRINKING PLACES
44633	88	1213	PLASTICS & RUBBER PRODUCTS MFG	44833	556	5226	MACHINERY MANUFACTURING	45102	537	6383	INSURANCE CARRIERS & RELATED
44634	47	180	MERCH. WHOLESALERS;DURABLE GDS	44836	56	885	NURSING & RESID. CARE FACILIT.	45103	865	14399	REPAIR AND MAINTENANCE
44636	54	1097	FOOD MANUFACTURING	44837	75	635	EDUCATIONAL SERVICES	45105	1	0	POSTAL SERVICE
44637	75	830	FURNITURE & RELATED PROD. MFG	44838	17	161	MERCH. WHOLESALERS;NONDUR. GDS	45106	279	1932	NONSTORE RETAILERS
44638	28	132	EDUCATIONAL SERVICES	44839	390	5326	RELIG.; GRANT; CIVIC; PROF ORG	45107	235	2603	TRANSPORTATION EQUIPMENT MFG
44639	6	7	RELIG.; GRANT; CIVIC; PROF ORG	44840	69	343	EDUCATIONAL SERVICES	45110	3	15	GASOLINE STATIONS
44640	2	2	POSTAL SERVICE	44841	11	237	RELIG.; GRANT; CIVIC; PROF ORG	45111	17	209	CONSTRUCTION OF BUILDINGS
44641	527	4917	EDUCATIONAL SERVICES	44842	258	2168	EDUCATIONAL SERVICES	45112	4	6	RELIG.; GRANT; CIVIC; PROF ORG
44643	112	771	EDUCATIONAL SERVICES	44843	76	458	EDUCATIONAL SERVICES	45113	61	395	EDUCATIONAL SERVICES
44644	127	1709	FABRICATED METAL PRODUCT MFG	44844	19	73	SPECIAL TRADE CONTRACTORS	45114	5	4	MERCH. WHOLESALERS;DURABLE GDS
44645	54	268	MERCH. WHOLESALERS;DURABLE GDS	44845	2	0	HEALTH & PERSONAL CARE STORES	45115	2	2	POSTAL SERVICE
44646	1388	18624	HOSPITALS	44846	185	3269	EDUCATIONAL SERVICES	45118	91	590	EDUCATIONAL SERVICES
44647	457	5197	FABRICATED METAL PRODUCT MFG	44847	110	1535	ADMINISTRATIVE & SUPPORT SVCS	45119	4	7	GASOLINE STATIONS
44648	6	10	PROF.; SCIENTIFIC; & TECH SVCS	44848	6	12	RELIG.; GRANT; CIVIC; PROF ORG	45120	77	656	EDUCATIONAL SERVICES
44650	4	11	FOOD AND BEVERAGE STORES	44849	49	111	FOOD SVCS & DRINKING PLACES	45121	352	3163	AMBULATORY HEALTH CARE SVCS
44651	19	99	MACHINERY MANUFACTURING	44850	12	39	EDUCATIONAL SERVICES	45122	229	1384	EDUCATIONAL SERVICES
44652	8	87	CHEMICAL MANUFACTURING	44851	149	1275	EDUCATIONAL SERVICES	45123	249	2151	ADMINISTRATIVE & SUPPORT SVCS
44653	33	665	MERCH. WHOLESALERS;DURABLE GDS	44853	37	566	FOOD MANUFACTURING	45130	55	266	EDUCATIONAL SERVICES
44654	783	7642	NURSING & RESID. CARE FACILIT.	44854	57	641	PRINT'G & RELATED SUPP'T ACT'S	45131	15	84	JUSTICE; PUBIC ORDER/SAFETY
44656	76	417	EDUCATIONAL SERVICES	44855	33	177	MERCH. WHOLESALERS;NONDUR. GDS	45132	6	6	FOOD AND BEVERAGE STORES
44657	371	4634	PRIMARY METAL MANUFACTURING	44856	6	48	EDUCATIONAL SERVICES	45133	817	7784	AMBULATORY HEALTH CARE SVCS
44659	34	419	CONSTRUCTION OF BUILDINGS	44857	961	12034	HOSPITALS	45135	84	1167	MISCELLANEOUS MANUFACTURING
44660	17	836	BLDG MATL & GARDEN EQPMT DLRS	44859	41	167	NONMETALLIC MINERAL PROD. MFG	45138	7	92	EDUCATIONAL SERVICES
44661	16	90	JUSTICE; PUBIC ORDER/SAFETY	44860	6	27	ACCOMMODATION	45140	1204	13486	ADMINISTRATIVE & SUPPORT SVCS
44662	225	2636	FOOD MANUFACTURING	44861	16	340	CHEMICAL MANUFACTURING	45142	94	457	EDUCATIONAL SERVICES
44663	1117	11832	FOOD SVCS & DRINKING PLACES	44862	27	98	FOOD SVCS & DRINKING PLACES	45144	123	1569	UTILITIES
44665	12	59	JUSTICE; PUBIC ORDER/SAFETY	44864	68	1259	NONMETALLIC MINERAL PROD. MFG	45145	3	4	POSTAL SERVICE

BUSINESS DATA

ZIP CODE	2009 Total Firms	2009 Total Employees	TOP INDUSTRY RANKED on 2009 EMPLOYMENT
45146	18	36	EXEC.; LEGIS.; & OTHER SUPPORT
45147	16	175	PROF.; SCIENTIFIC; & TECH SVCS
45148	17	50	ADMINISTRATIVE & SUPPORT SVCS
45150	1361	15925	FOOD SVCS & DRINKING PLACES
45152	189	1021	EDUCATIONAL SERVICES
45153	31	182	SPECIAL TRADE CONTRACTORS
45154	238	2493	EDUCATIONAL SERVICES
45155	14	110	EDUCATIONAL SERVICES
45156	2	2	POSTAL SERVICE
45157	215	1119	EDUCATIONAL SERVICES
45158	17	97	JUSTICE; PUBIC ORDER/SAFETY
45159	55	647	PLASTICS & RUBBER PRODUCTS MFG
45160	40	186	EXEC.; LEGIS.; & OTHER SUPPORT
45162	61	508	FOOD MANUFACTURING
45164	8	20	NURSING & RESID. CARE FACILIT.
45166	2	2	PERFORM'G ARTS; SPEC. SPORTS
45167	106	992	NURSING & RESID. CARE FACILIT.
45168	46	195	EDUCATIONAL SERVICES
45169	118	1214	TRANSPORTATION EQUIPMENT MFG
45171	137	689	EDUCATIONAL SERVICES
45172	9	46	JUSTICE; PUBIC ORDER/SAFETY
45174	62	216	INSURANCE CARRIERS & RELATED
45176	215	1273	MISCELLANEOUS MANUFACTURING
45177	1018	25321	AIR TRANSPORTATION
45201	3	8	ADMINISTRATIVE & SUPPORT SVCS
45202	3462	97932	PROF.; SCIENTIFIC; & TECH SVCS
45203	353	6617	PROF.; SCIENTIFIC; & TECH SVCS
45204	200	4406	EXEC.; LEGIS.; & OTHER SUPPORT
45205	275	2013	EDUCATIONAL SERVICES
45206	656	6710	PROF.; SCIENTIFIC; & TECH SVCS
45207	129	2303	EDUCATIONAL SERVICES
45208	688	5759	FOOD SVCS & DRINKING PLACES
45209	599	9558	FOOD SVCS & DRINKING PLACES
45211	999	8891	FOOD SVCS & DRINKING PLACES
45212	725	10097	AMBULATORY HEALTH CARE SVCS
45213	342	4733	BLDG MATL & GARDEN EQPMT DLRS
45214	492	6703	FABRICATED METAL PRODUCT MFG
45215	1366	26176	TRANSPORTATION EQUIPMENT MFG
45216	405	5770	SOCIAL ASSISTANCE
45217	236	3505	FOOD MANUFACTURING
45218	64	530	EDUCATIONAL SERVICES
45219	664	12173	HOSPITALS
45220	340	7893	HOSPITALS
45221	24	10106	EDUCATIONAL SERVICES
45222	2	11	POSTAL SERVICE
45223	508	5058	MERCH. WHOLESALERS;DURABLE GDS
45224	417	3712	NURSING & RESID. CARE FACILIT.
45225	286	3518	FABRICATED METAL PRODUCT MFG
45226	384	5572	ADMIN. HUMAN RESOURCE PROGRAMS
45227	818	12015	MERCH. WHOLESALERS;DURABLE GDS
45228	32	213	AMUSEMENT; GAMBLING;& RECREAT.
45229	448	13827	RELIG.; GRANT; CIVIC; PROF ORG
45230	665	4696	AMBULATORY HEALTH CARE SVCS
45231	995	8459	EDUCATIONAL SERVICES
45232	190	4744	MERCH. WHOLESALERS;NONDUR. GDS
45233	323	3448	EDUCATIONAL SERVICES
45234	1	0	POSTAL SERVICE
45235	1	0	POSTAL SERVICE
45236	1413	19143	FOOD SVCS & DRINKING PLACES
45237	802	10693	EDUCATIONAL SERVICES
45238	1010	10022	FOOD SVCS & DRINKING PLACES
45239	650	7271	HOSPITALS
45240	816	12533	FOOD SVCS & DRINKING PLACES
45241	1808	31703	MERCH. WHOLESALERS;DURABLE GDS
45242	2571	42585	AMBULATORY HEALTH CARE SVCS
45243	438	3652	EDUCATIONAL SERVICES
45244	729	6661	MERCH. WHOLESALERS;DURABLE GDS
45245	939	13678	FOOD SVCS & DRINKING PLACES
45246	1777	38243	HEALTH & PERSONAL CARE STORES
45247	684	5015	FOOD SVCS & DRINKING PLACES
45248	464	4324	EDUCATIONAL SERVICES
45249	867	12669	FOOD SVCS & DRINKING PLACES
45250	1	24	SPECIAL TRADE CONTRACTORS
45251	651	8230	FOOD SVCS & DRINKING PLACES
45252	72	1317	OTHER INFORMATION SERVICES
45253	9	15	SPECIAL TRADE CONTRACTORS
45254	9	23	ADMINISTRATIVE & SUPPORT SVCS
45255	849	8448	FOOD SVCS & DRINKING PLACES
45258	4	20	TRANSIT & GRND PASS. TRANSPORT
45262	3	6	MERCH. WHOLESALERS;DURABLE GDS
45263	10	4075	CREDIT INTERMEDIATION & RELATD
45267	23	5411	HOSPITALS
45275	24	267	RENTAL AND LEASING SERVICES
45301	6	9	ACCOMMODATION
45302	104	3800	MACHINERY MANUFACTURING
45303	64	474	EDUCATIONAL SERVICES
45304	172	1110	EDUCATIONAL SERVICES
45305	284	1702	EDUCATIONAL SERVICES
45306	78	559	PLASTICS & RUBBER PRODUCTS MFG
45307	13	43	EXEC.; LEGIS.; & OTHER SUPPORT
45308	90	764	TRUCK TRANSPORTATION
45309	342	3915	PLASTICS & RUBBER PRODUCTS MFG
45310	12	142	TRUCK TRANSPORTATION
45311	125	757	EDUCATIONAL SERVICES
45312	30	252	EDUCATIONAL SERVICES
45314	86	1215	EDUCATIONAL SERVICES
45315	187	3285	EDUCATIONAL SERVICES
45316	3	28	SOCIAL ASSISTANCE
45317	16	88	BLDG MATL & GARDEN EQPMT DLRS
45318	210	1747	HEALTH & PERSONAL CARE STORES
45319	23	266	TRANSPORTATION EQUIPMENT MFG
45320	623	6468	TRANSPORTATION EQUIPMENT MFG
45321	28	78	PLASTICS & RUBBER PRODUCTS MFG
45322	573	4829	FOOD SVCS & DRINKING PLACES
45323	134	1064	FOOD SVCS & DRINKING PLACES
45324	1108	13045	FOOD SVCS & DRINKING PLACES
45325	73	274	JUSTICE; PUBIC ORDER/SAFETY
45326	32	672	MERCH. WHOLESALERS;DURABLE GDS
45327	278	1746	EDUCATIONAL SERVICES
45328	21	302	MISCELLANEOUS MANUFACTURING
45330	23	66	WOOD PRODUCT MANUFACTURING
45331	1139	12255	ELECT'L EQPMT; APP; & COMP MFG
45332	21	65	JUSTICE; PUBIC ORDER/SAFETY
45333	29	192	EDUCATIONAL SERVICES
45334	86	2471	TRANSPORTATION EQUIPMENT MFG
45335	148	1195	EDUCATIONAL SERVICES
45336	6	69	FOOD SVCS & DRINKING PLACES
45337	34	153	HEAVY & CIVIL ENG. CONSTRUCT'N
45338	156	2627	HEALTH & PERSONAL CARE STORES
45339	31	118	FOOD SVCS & DRINKING PLACES
45340	11	26	CONSTRUCTION OF BUILDINGS
45341	68	342	JUSTICE; PUBIC ORDER/SAFETY
45342	1113	19987	PROF.; SCIENTIFIC; & TECH SVCS
45343	5	10	SPECIAL TRADE CONTRACTORS
45344	444	3744	FOOD SVCS & DRINKING PLACES
45345	137	1032	SOCIAL ASSISTANCE
45346	64	609	EDUCATIONAL SERVICES
45347	116	1197	EDUCATIONAL SERVICES
45348	21	129	MERCH. WHOLESALERS;NONDUR. GDS
45349	32	97	JUSTICE; PUBIC ORDER/SAFETY
45350	14	101	JUSTICE; PUBIC ORDER/SAFETY
45351	15	162	FOOD MANUFACTURING
45352	12	28	RELIG.; GRANT; CIVIC; PROF ORG
45353	3	32	EDUCATIONAL SERVICES
45354	23	108	EDUCATIONAL SERVICES
45356	951	11480	EDUCATIONAL SERVICES
45358	14	257	EDUCATIONAL SERVICES
45359	56	253	EDUCATIONAL SERVICES
45360	10	94	JUSTICE; PUBIC ORDER/SAFETY
45361	7	6	RELIG.; GRANT; CIVIC; PROF ORG
45362	23	211	MERCH. WHOLESALERS;NONDUR. GDS
45363	41	1111	BLDG MATL & GARDEN EQPMT DLRS
45365	1189	24826	MERCH. WHOLESALERS;DURABLE GDS
45368	116	1148	TRANSPORTATION EQUIPMENT MFG
45369	44	458	ADMINISTRATIVE & SUPPORT SVCS
45370	79	404	SPECIAL TRADE CONTRACTORS
45371	691	11779	HOSPITALS
45372	10	39	RELIG.; GRANT; CIVIC; PROF ORG
45373	1390	21896	HOSPITALS
45374	2	1300	MISCELLANEOUS MANUFACTURING
45377	658	10592	TRANSPORTATION EQUIPMENT MFG
45378	12	57	JUSTICE; PUBIC ORDER/SAFETY
45380	217	2238	MISCELLANEOUS MANUFACTURING
45381	142	957	EDUCATIONAL SERVICES
45382	35	110	SUPPORT ACTIVITIES: AGR./FOR.
45383	165	1253	EDUCATIONAL SERVICES
45384	14	581	EDUCATIONAL SERVICES
45385	1192	14677	HOSPITALS
45387	256	3066	NURSING & RESID. CARE FACILIT.
45388	13	49	TRUCK TRANSPORTATION
45389	17	41	FOOD SVCS & DRINKING PLACES
45390	101	564	EDUCATIONAL SERVICES
45401	9	1507	POSTAL SERVICE
45402	1873	33013	PROF.; SCIENTIFIC; & TECH SVCS
45403	503	4644	FABRICATED METAL PRODUCT MFG
45404	761	16313	HOSPITALS
45405	516	5775	HOSPITALS
45406	520	6157	HOSPITALS
45408	328	6152	PRINT'G & RELATED SUPP'T ACT'S
45409	469	11878	HOSPITALS
45410	329	2884	ADMINISTRATIVE & SUPPORT SVCS
45413	2	20	SECURITIES/COMMODITY CONTRACTS
45414	1516	20332	FOOD SVCS & DRINKING PLACES
45415	496	5853	FOOD AND BEVERAGE STORES
45416	154	1473	NURSING & RESID. CARE FACILIT.
45417	190	1825	MACHINERY MANUFACTURING
45418	155	2038	JUSTICE; PUBIC ORDER/SAFETY
45419	430	3162	EDUCATIONAL SERVICES
45420	722	11546	CREDIT INTERMEDIATION & RELATD
45422	43	3148	EXEC.; LEGIS.; & OTHER SUPPORT
45423	49	858	SECURITIES/COMMODITY CONTRACTS
45424	1348	15399	FOOD SVCS & DRINKING PLACES
45426	419	5018	EXEC.; LEGIS.; & OTHER SUPPORT
45427	251	1687	FOOD MANUFACTURING
45428	9	1610	HOSPITALS
45429	1097	17567	AMBULATORY HEALTH CARE SVCS
45430	205	4991	TELECOMMUNICATIONS
45431	937	11245	PROF.; SCIENTIFIC; & TECH SVCS
45432	652	6391	PROF.; SCIENTIFIC; & TECH SVCS
45433	98	1788	JUSTICE; PUBIC ORDER/SAFETY
45434	359	4756	FABRICATED METAL PRODUCT MFG
45435	20	2900	EDUCATIONAL SERVICES
45437	3	9	POSTAL SERVICE
45439	772	13698	MERCH. WHOLESALERS;DURABLE GDS
45440	570	8016	NONSTORE RETAILERS
45441	7	28	ADMINISTRATIVE & SUPPORT SVCS
45449	581	7555	MACHINERY MANUFACTURING
45458	898	7655	PROF.; SCIENTIFIC; & TECH SVCS
45459	2316	25533	FOOD SVCS & DRINKING PLACES
45469	14	3037	EDUCATIONAL SERVICES
45475	11	43	ADMINISTRATIVE & SUPPORT SVCS
45479	4	3561	TELECOMMUNICATIONS
45490	1	0	POSTAL SERVICE
45501	17	281	POSTAL SERVICE
45502	651	11048	TRANSPORTATION EQUIPMENT MFG
45503	846	10126	FOOD SVCS & DRINKING PLACES
45504	891	23156	HOSPITALS
45505	651	10532	INSURANCE CARRIERS & RELATED
45506	322	3856	FABRICATED METAL PRODUCT MFG
45601	2008	31240	AMBULATORY HEALTH CARE SVCS
45612	119	588	EDUCATIONAL SERVICES
45613	74	407	EDUCATIONAL SERVICES
45614	75	770	NURSING & RESID. CARE FACILIT.
45616	14	52	BLDG MATL & GARDEN EQPMT DLRS
45617	7	16	GASOLINE STATIONS
45618	5	11	MERCH. WHOLESALERS;NONDUR. GDS
45619	178	973	EDUCATIONAL SERVICES
45620	34	735	ADMINISTRATIVE & SUPPORT SVCS
45621	16	29	GASOLINE STATIONS
45622	11	21	HEAVY & CIVIL ENG. CONSTRUCT'N
45623	41	153	EDUCATIONAL SERVICES
45624	4	9	MERCH. WHOLESALERS;NONDUR. GDS
45628	105	738	EDUCATIONAL SERVICES
45629	59	1524	JUSTICE; PUBIC ORDER/SAFETY
45630	9	25	CONSTRUCTION OF BUILDINGS
45631	706	9358	HOSPITALS
45633	6	43	JUSTICE; PUBIC ORDER/SAFETY
45634	34	373	NONMETALLIC MINERAL PROD. MFG
45636	1	4	FOOD SVCS & DRINKING PLACES
45638	722	6175	EDUCATIONAL SERVICES
45640	732	8371	FOOD MANUFACTURING
45642	2	0	SPECIAL TRADE CONTRACTORS
45643	1	2	POSTAL SERVICE
45644	78	310	EDUCATIONAL SERVICES
45645	29	116	SPECIAL TRADE CONTRACTORS
45646	21	240	EDUCATIONAL SERVICES
45647	37	100	TRUCK TRANSPORTATION
45648	228	1840	EDUCATIONAL SERVICES
45650	3	3	FOOD SVCS & DRINKING PLACES
45651	225	2040	EDUCATIONAL SERVICES
45652	47	754	WOOD PRODUCT MANUFACTURING
45653	102	671	EDUCATIONAL SERVICES
45654	22	68	TRUCK TRANSPORTATION
45656	138	770	EDUCATIONAL SERVICES
45657	31	63	WOOD PRODUCT MANUFACTURING
45658	20	156	UTILITIES
45659	21	178	HOSPITALS
45660	199	1782	WOOD PRODUCT MANUFACTURING
45661	251	4034	CHEMICAL MANUFACTURING
45662	1430	17953	HOSPITALS
45663	144	1103	EDUCATIONAL SERVICES
45669	221	1429	EDUCATIONAL SERVICES
45671	5	50	JUSTICE; PUBIC ORDER/SAFETY
45672	25	69	SOCIAL ASSISTANCE
45673	15	22	BLDG MATL & GARDEN EQPMT DLRS
45674	48	872	EDUCATIONAL SERVICES
45677	1	1	POSTAL SERVICE
45678	9	31	FOOD SVCS & DRINKING PLACES
45679	76	877	HOSPITALS
45680	307	4231	GENERAL MERCHANDISE STORES
45681	14	58	EDUCATIONAL SERVICES
45682	59	244	EDUCATIONAL SERVICES
45684	22	70	FOOD AND BEVERAGE STORES
45685	10	43	MERCH. WHOLESALERS;DURABLE GDS
45686	38	186	EDUCATIONAL SERVICES
45688	5	4	FOOD AND BEVERAGE STORES
45690	478	7427	WOOD PRODUCT MANUFACTURING
45692	272	2797	MERCH. WHOLESALERS;NONDUR. GDS
45693	390	3210	GENERAL MERCHANDISE STORES
45694	385	2478	FOOD SVCS & DRINKING PLACES

ZIP CODE	2009 Total Firms	2009 Total Employ-ees	TOP INDUSTRY RANKED on 2009 EMPLOYMENT	ZIP CODE	2009 Total Firms	2009 Total Employ-ees	TOP INDUSTRY RANKED on 2009 EMPLOYMENT	ZIP CODE	2009 Total Firms	2009 Total Employ-ees	TOP INDUSTRY RANKED on 2009 EMPLOYMENT
45695	13	47	EDUCATIONAL SERVICES	45848	36	358	HOSPITALS	46071	112	720	EDUCATIONAL SERVICES
45696	12	81	EDUCATIONAL SERVICES	45849	31	135	EDUCATIONAL SERVICES	46072	458	3967	HOSPITALS
45697	100	758	RELIG.; GRANT; CIVIC; PROF ORG	45850	67	525	EDUCATIONAL SERVICES	46074	622	5932	EDUCATIONAL SERVICES
45698	8	58	EDUCATIONAL SERVICES	45851	19	498	PLASTICS & RUBBER PRODUCTS MFG	46075	129	1311	MERCH. WHOLESALERS;DURABLE GDS
45701	1196	12902	FOOD SVCS & DRINKING PLACES	45853	88	6584	MACHINERY MANUFACTURING	46076	39	253	FABRICATED METAL PRODUCT MFG
45710	135	547	EDUCATIONAL SERVICES	45854	17	29	MERCH. WHOLESALERS;DURABLE GDS	46077	817	6488	SPECIAL TRADE CONTRACTORS
45711	32	126	EDUCATIONAL SERVICES	45855	6	54	MERCH. WHOLESALERS;NONDUR. GDS	46082	20	94	MERCH. WHOLESALERS;DURABLE GDS
45712	13	128	MERCH. WHOLESALERS;DURABLE GDS	45856	165	1835	UNCLASSIFIED ESTABLISHMENTS	46102	8	50	JUSTICE; PUBIC ORDER/SAFETY
45713	13	98	HEAVY & CIVIL ENG. CONSTRUCT'N	45858	75	2969	FOOD MANUFACTURING	46103	9	109	EDUCATIONAL SERVICES
45714	344	2359	MERCH. WHOLESALERS;NONDUR. GDS	45859	10	27	CROP PRODUCTION	46104	14	86	FABRICATED METAL PRODUCT MFG
45715	133	1148	PRIMARY METAL MANUFACTURING	45860	50	625	EDUCATIONAL SERVICES	46105	64	367	EDUCATIONAL SERVICES
45716	5	9	CONSTRUCTION OF BUILDINGS	45861	10	33	FOOD SVCS & DRINKING PLACES	46106	158	936	SPECIAL TRADE CONTRACTORS
45719	21	134	EDUCATIONAL SERVICES	45862	32	152	GASOLINE STATIONS	46107	336	7452	HOSPITALS
45720	12	35	BLDG MATL & GARDEN EQPMT DLRS	45863	51	237	MERCH. WHOLESALERS;DURABLE GDS	46110	12	120	CONSTRUCTION OF BUILDINGS
45723	71	454	CONSTRUCTION OF BUILDINGS	45864	19	294	EDUCATIONAL SERVICES	46111	17	96	EDUCATIONAL SERVICES
45724	15	48	SUPPORT ACTIVITIES FOR MINING	45865	186	3288	MACHINERY MANUFACTURING	46112	872	9155	MERCH. WHOLESALERS;DURABLE GDS
45727	10	162	NONSTORE RETAILERS	45866	6	6	RELIG.; GRANT; CIVIC; PROF ORG	46113	195	1732	FOOD SVCS & DRINKING PLACES
45729	14	106	SUPPORT ACTIVITIES FOR MINING	45867	34	334	EDUCATIONAL SERVICES	46115	41	117	JUSTICE; PUBIC ORDER/SAFETY
45732	110	473	ACCOMMODATION	45868	13	31	FURN. & HOME FURNISHGS STORES	46117	17	405	EDUCATIONAL SERVICES
45734	13	41	EDUCATIONAL SERVICES	45869	136	4419	COMPUTER & ELECTRONIC PROD MFG	46118	113	926	EDUCATIONAL SERVICES
45735	22	58	AMBULATORY HEALTH CARE SVCS	45870	5	52	FABRICATED METAL PRODUCT MFG	46120	260	1636	FOOD SVCS & DRINKING PLACES
45739	3	1	PERSONAL AND LAUNDRY SERVICES	45871	70	427	WOOD PRODUCT MANUFACTURING	46121	82	407	MACHINERY MANUFACTURING
45740	12	31	JUSTICE; PUBIC ORDER/SAFETY	45872	130	2010	FOOD AND BEVERAGE STORES	46122	510	4235	EXEC.; LEGIS.; & OTHER SUPPORT
45741	9	9	MERCH. WHOLESALERS;DURABLE GDS	45873	98	1315	MISCELLANEOUS MANUFACTURING	46123	911	10197	FOOD SVCS & DRINKING PLACES
45742	61	407	MISCELLANEOUS MANUFACTURING	45874	38	194	EXEC.; LEGIS.; & OTHER SUPPORT	46124	354	4894	WOOD PRODUCT MANUFACTURING
45743	10	48	SPECIAL TRADE CONTRACTORS	45875	463	4273	MERCH. WHOLESALERS;DURABLE GDS	46125	17	291	EDUCATIONAL SERVICES
45744	62	260	OIL AND GAS EXTRACTION	45876	92	944	FABRICATED METAL PRODUCT MFG	46126	104	565	EDUCATIONAL SERVICES
45745	20	63	EDUCATIONAL SERVICES	45877	79	731	RELIG.; GRANT; CIVIC; PROF ORG	46127	4	25	MERCH. WHOLESALERS;NONDUR. GDS
45746	12	24	SPORTG GDS;HOBBY;BOOK; & MUSIC	45879	279	3328	MERCH. WHOLESALERS;DURABLE GDS	46128	37	175	JUSTICE; PUBIC ORDER/SAFETY
45750	1400	20580	HOSPITALS	45880	70	719	RELIG.; GRANT; CIVIC; PROF ORG	46129	3	16	MERCH. WHOLESALERS;NONDUR. GDS
45760	128	894	SOCIAL ASSISTANCE	45881	18	264	EDUCATIONAL SERVICES	46130	45	142	FABRICATED METAL PRODUCT MFG
45761	24	115	ADMIN. HUMAN RESOURCE PROGRAMS	45882	81	712	NURSING & RESID. CARE FACILIT.	46131	1162	12753	HOSPITALS
45764	249	2467	EDUCATIONAL SERVICES	45883	105	1156	FOOD MANUFACTURING	46133	23	114	EDUCATIONAL SERVICES
45766	20	29	MERCH. WHOLESALERS;DURABLE GDS	45884	4	3	POSTAL SERVICE	46135	704	9748	JUSTICE; PUBIC ORDER/SAFETY
45767	64	252	EDUCATIONAL SERVICES	45885	491	5811	HOSPITALS	46140	1283	16530	FOOD SVCS & DRINKING PLACES
45768	53	185	FOOD AND BEVERAGE STORES	45886	10	35	WAREHOUSING AND STORAGE	46142	1434	12504	FOOD SVCS & DRINKING PLACES
45769	260	1974	FOOD SVCS & DRINKING PLACES	45887	106	930	EDUCATIONAL SERVICES	46143	1072	12601	FOOD SVCS & DRINKING PLACES
45770	11	180	MERCH. WHOLESALERS;DURABLE GDS	45888	17	62	SPECIAL TRADE CONTRACTORS	46144	4	15	MERCH. WHOLESALERS;DURABLE GDS
45771	63	309	EDUCATIONAL SERVICES	45889	24	196	EDUCATIONAL SERVICES	46146	9	23	FURN. & HOME FURNISHGS STORES
45772	32	250	EDUCATIONAL SERVICES	45890	28	122	EDUCATIONAL SERVICES	46147	72	183	FOOD AND BEVERAGE STORES
45773	21	193	SUPPORT ACTIVITIES FOR MINING	45891	687	10353	MERCH. WHOLESALERS;DURABLE GDS	46148	182	1368	EDUCATIONAL SERVICES
45775	27	96	JUSTICE; PUBIC ORDER/SAFETY	45893	8	15	EXEC.; LEGIS.; & OTHER SUPPORT	46149	61	415	EDUCATIONAL SERVICES
45776	15	22	MOTOR VEHICLE & PARTS DEALERS	45894	13	65	FABRICATED METAL PRODUCT MFG	46150	18	89	UTILITIES
45778	26	413	EDUCATIONAL SERVICES	45895	739	6422	FOOD SVCS & DRINKING PLACES	46151	975	8898	AMBULATORY HEALTH CARE SVCS
45779	21	89	EDUCATIONAL SERVICES	45896	56	331	EDUCATIONAL SERVICES	46154	11	191	TELECOMMUNICATIONS
45780	119	975	NURSING & RESID. CARE FACILIT.	45897	4	6	ACCOMMODATION	46155	7	46	EDUCATIONAL SERVICES
45782	15	82	FOOD AND BEVERAGE STORES	45898	26	132	FOOD SVCS & DRINKING PLACES	46156	51	223	FOOD MANUFACTURING
45783	22	107	FOOD AND BEVERAGE STORES	45899	6	14	FOOD SVCS & DRINKING PLACES	46157	99	513	EDUCATIONAL SERVICES
45784	60	405	EDUCATIONAL SERVICES	46001	303	2254	EDUCATIONAL SERVICES	46158	703	7264	FOOD SVCS & DRINKING PLACES
45786	64	623	UTILITIES	46011	292	4447	HOSPITALS	46160	146	693	ACCOMMODATION
45787	3	1	SPORTG GDS;HOBBY;BOOK; & MUSIC	46012	542	5887	EDUCATIONAL SERVICES	46161	84	949	MISCELLANEOUS MANUFACTURING
45788	19	73	CONSTRUCTION OF BUILDINGS	46013	577	8336	FOOD SVCS & DRINKING PLACES	46162	9	48	JUSTICE; PUBIC ORDER/SAFETY
45789	2	3	OIL AND GAS EXTRACTION	46015	8	23	SOCIAL ASSISTANCE	46163	233	1385	EDUCATIONAL SERVICES
45801	1121	20426	HOSPITALS	46016	1025	12485	PROF.; SCIENTIFIC; & TECH SVCS	46164	85	294	UTILITIES
45802	9	55	UNCLASSIFIED ESTABLISHMENTS	46017	145	986	ADMINISTRATIVE & SUPPORT SVCS	46165	45	183	EDUCATIONAL SERVICES
45804	714	13683	SPECIAL TRADE CONTRACTORS	46018	4	7	REAL ESTATE	46166	31	142	MACHINERY MANUFACTURING
45805	875	10648	FOOD SVCS & DRINKING PLACES	46030	101	719	EDUCATIONAL SERVICES	46167	129	937	FABRICATED METAL PRODUCT MFG
45806	307	3405	EDUCATIONAL SERVICES	46031	50	246	MERCH. WHOLESALERS;NONDUR. GDS	46168	1025	16787	UTILITIES
45807	386	3135	FABRICATED METAL PRODUCT MFG	46032	2946	38820	INSURANCE CARRIERS & RELATED	46170	2	1	POSTAL SERVICE
45808	23	195	GASOLINE STATIONS	46033	494	4120	FOOD SVCS & DRINKING PLACES	46171	36	167	WOOD PRODUCT MANUFACTURING
45809	8	40	EDUCATIONAL SERVICES	46034	200	869	FOOD SVCS & DRINKING PLACES	46172	83	477	EDUCATIONAL SERVICES
45810	157	1936	EDUCATIONAL SERVICES	46035	34	89	JUSTICE; PUBIC ORDER/SAFETY	46173	499	4674	RELIG.; GRANT; CIVIC; PROF ORG
45812	43	102	JUSTICE; PUBIC ORDER/SAFETY	46036	338	4117	TRANSPORTATION EQUIPMENT MFG	46175	15	42	FABRICATED METAL PRODUCT MFG
45813	105	1041	NONMETALLIC MINERAL PROD. MFG	46037	768	10598	CREDIT INTERMEDIATION & RELATD	46176	1072	16925	NONMETALLIC MINERAL PROD. MFG
45814	54	347	NURSING & RESID. CARE FACILIT.	46038	1132	11275	FOOD SVCS & DRINKING PLACES	46180	30	70	REPAIR AND MAINTENANCE
45815	2	1	PRINT'G & RELATED SUPP'T ACT'S	46039	12	16	BLDG MATL & GARDEN EQPMT DLRS	46181	155	720	EDUCATIONAL SERVICES
45816	14	20	RELIG.; GRANT; CIVIC; PROF ORG	46040	252	1276	EDUCATIONAL SERVICES	46182	44	411	NURSING & RESID. CARE FACILIT.
45817	241	4299	PLASTICS & RUBBER PRODUCTS MFG	46041	772	12828	MERCH. WHOLESALERS;NONDUR. GDS	46183	9	77	EDUCATIONAL SERVICES
45819	14	29	TELECOMMUNICATIONS	46044	61	386	EDUCATIONAL SERVICES	46184	343	2085	EDUCATIONAL SERVICES
45820	17	56	CHEMICAL MANUFACTURING	46045	2	2	REPAIR AND MAINTENANCE	46186	40	60	MACHINERY MANUFACTURING
45821	29	118	FOOD SVCS & DRINKING PLACES	46047	6	20	FOOD MANUFACTURING	46201	936	12729	MERCH. WHOLESALERS;DURABLE GDS
45822	829	7994	FOOD SVCS & DRINKING PLACES	46048	19	55	JUSTICE; PUBIC ORDER/SAFETY	46202	1643	133813	EDUCATIONAL SERVICES
45826	14	113	FOOD SVCS & DRINKING PLACES	46049	13	31	BLDG MATL & GARDEN EQPMT DLRS	46203	1290	14061	MERCH. WHOLESALERS;DURABLE GDS
45827	61	435	MACHINERY MANUFACTURING	46050	41	112	MACHINERY MANUFACTURING	46204	2840	63475	PROF.; SCIENTIFIC; & TECH SVCS
45828	236	2792	HOSPITALS	46051	72	585	MERCH. WHOLESALERS;DURABLE GDS	46205	1060	11895	ADMINISTRATIVE & SUPPORT SVCS
45830	160	1183	EDUCATIONAL SERVICES	46052	868	9166	HOSPITALS	46206	21	47	TRUCK TRANSPORTATION
45831	93	925	FABRICATED METAL PRODUCT MFG	46055	167	724	ADMINISTRATIVE & SUPPORT SVCS	46207	1	0	MERCH. WHOLESALERS;DURABLE GDS
45832	59	526	EDUCATIONAL SERVICES	46056	49	287	SPECIAL TRADE CONTRACTORS	46208	747	9152	EDUCATIONAL SERVICES
45833	390	4526	FOOD MANUFACTURING	46057	43	221	EDUCATIONAL SERVICES	46214	530	9180	AMBULATORY HEALTH CARE SVCS
45835	12	168	EDUCATIONAL SERVICES	46058	62	320	NURSING & RESID. CARE FACILIT.	46216	220	3184	PROF.; SCIENTIFIC; & TECH SVCS
45836	38	179	PLASTICS & RUBBER PRODUCTS MFG	46060	1477	16523	FOOD SVCS & DRINKING PLACES	46217	737	9253	SPECIAL TRADE CONTRACTORS
45837	7	9	MERCH. WHOLESALERS;DURABLE GDS	46061	13	87	CONSTRUCTION OF BUILDINGS	46218	1000	9075	SPECIAL TRADE CONTRACTORS
45838	1	12	WAREHOUSING AND STORAGE	46062	454	3339	AMBULATORY HEALTH CARE SVCS	46219	1613	32371	REPAIR AND MAINTENANCE
45839	10	41	SOCIAL ASSISTANCE	46063	11	583	FOOD MANUFACTURING	46220	2169	15461	FOOD SVCS & DRINKING PLACES
45840	2399	39350	EDUCATIONAL SERVICES	46064	426	4532	JUSTICE; PUBIC ORDER/SAFETY	46221	545	7794	EDUCATIONAL SERVICES
45841	12	44	RELIG.; GRANT; CIVIC; PROF ORG	46065	103	654	NURSING & RESID. CARE FACILIT.	46222	1089	17662	TRANSPORTATION EQUIPMENT MFG
45843	65	514	TRANSPORTATION EQUIPMENT MFG	46067	5	14	MERCH. WHOLESALERS;NONDUR. GDS	46223	1	9	EDUCATIONAL SERVICES
45844	124	405	EDUCATIONAL SERVICES	46068	71	444	EDUCATIONAL SERVICES	46224	737	7290	FOOD SVCS & DRINKING PLACES
45845	122	978	MACHINERY MANUFACTURING	46069	176	1391	FABRICATED METAL PRODUCT MFG	46225	677	13434	CHEMICAL MANUFACTURING
45846	156	2011	FOOD MANUFACTURING	46070	43	311	FABRICATED METAL PRODUCT MFG	46226	1292	13868	EDUCATIONAL SERVICES

BUSINESS DATA

ZIP CODE	2009 Total Firms	2009 Total Employ-ees	TOP INDUSTRY RANKED on 2009 EMPLOYMENT
46227	1879	18563	FOOD SVCS & DRINKING PLACES
46228	198	1033	EDUCATIONAL SERVICES
46229	796	8424	FOOD SVCS & DRINKING PLACES
46230	4	11	REAL ESTATE
46231	186	4567	SPECIAL TRADE CONTRACTORS
46234	386	3461	HEAVY & CIVIL ENG. CONSTRUCT'N
46235	259	4511	CLOTHING & CLOTH'G ACC. STORES
46236	635	5055	EDUCATIONAL SERVICES
46237	766	8777	FOOD SVCS & DRINKING PLACES
46239	530	5231	SPECIAL TRADE CONTRACTORS
46240	2199	31500	PROF.; SCIENTIFIC; & TECH SVCS
46241	1564	31208	TRANSPORTATION EQUIPMENT MFG
46242	7	24	TRANSIT & GRND PASS. TRANSPORT
46244	2	1	MINING (EXCEPT OIL AND GAS)
46247	7	12	SPECIAL TRADE CONTRACTORS
46249	9	2795	NAT'L SECURITY & INT'L AFFAIRS
46250	1897	25332	FOOD SVCS & DRINKING PLACES
46251	3	60	CONSTRUCTION OF BUILDINGS
46253	7	14	SPORTG GDS;HOBBY;BOOK; & MUSIC
46254	1082	12820	FOOD SVCS & DRINKING PLACES
46255	2	35	CREDIT INTERMEDIATION & RELATD
46256	892	16415	CHEMICAL MANUFACTURING
46259	162	1348	EDUCATIONAL SERVICES
46260	992	32359	HOSPITALS
46268	2019	37912	MERCH. WHOLESALERS;NONDUR. GDS
46278	651	13364	HOSPITALS
46280	281	3953	CONSTRUCTION OF BUILDINGS
46282	46	5990	INSURANCE CARRIERS & RELATED
46285	10	6094	MERCH. WHOLESALERS;NONDUR. GDS
46290	179	6296	COMPUTER & ELECTRONIC PROD MFG
46298	1	0	POSTAL SERVICE
46301	17	59	JUSTICE; PUBIC ORDER/SAFETY
46302	8	164	EDUCATIONAL SERVICES
46303	293	1687	EDUCATIONAL SERVICES
46304	912	14547	PRIMARY METAL MANUFACTURING
46307	1640	17866	JUSTICE; PUBIC ORDER/SAFETY
46308	10	47	PRINT'G & RELATED SUPP'T ACT'S
46310	477	2358	FOOD SVCS & DRINKING PLACES
46311	511	4559	FOOD SVCS & DRINKING PLACES
46312	745	10071	AMUSEMENT; GAMBLING;& RECREAT.
46319	590	5437	ADMINISTRATIVE & SUPPORT SVCS
46320	639	15931	HOSPITALS
46321	841	12688	HOSPITALS
46322	1008	9758	FOOD SVCS & DRINKING PLACES
46323	452	5771	EDUCATIONAL SERVICES
46324	484	3831	EDUCATIONAL SERVICES
46325	3	11	RELIG.; GRANT; CIVIC; PROF ORG
46327	249	3514	PRIMARY METAL MANUFACTURING
46340	24	68	SPECIAL TRADE CONTRACTORS
46341	219	1626	EDUCATIONAL SERVICES
46342	823	8096	HOSPITALS
46345	40	606	CHEMICAL MANUFACTURING
46346	22	89	EDUCATIONAL SERVICES
46347	109	744	MERCH. WHOLESALERS;DURABLE GDS
46348	37	162	EDUCATIONAL SERVICES
46349	73	255	SPECIAL TRADE CONTRACTORS
46350	1501	19391	HOSPITALS
46352	6	39	ADMINISTRATIVE & SUPPORT SVCS
46355	4	14	SPECIAL TRADE CONTRACTORS
46356	443	3874	TRANSPORTATION EQUIPMENT MFG
46360	1849	25004	AMUSEMENT; GAMBLING;& RECREAT.
46361	7	24	OTHER INFORMATION SERVICES
46365	10	13	CROP PRODUCTION
46366	179	989	EDUCATIONAL SERVICES
46368	1042	11887	FOOD SVCS & DRINKING PLACES
46371	81	707	FOOD SVCS & DRINKING PLACES
46372	37	207	EDUCATIONAL SERVICES
46373	374	3463	EDUCATIONAL SERVICES
46374	22	239	NURSING & RESID. CARE FACILIT.
46375	896	10285	FOOD SVCS & DRINKING PLACES
46376	20	67	ADMINISTRATIVE & SUPPORT SVCS
46377	30	83	ADMINISTRATIVE & SUPPORT SVCS
46379	3	8	FOOD SVCS & DRINKING PLACES
46380	1	30	FABRICATED METAL PRODUCT MFG
46381	8	39	JUSTICE; PUBIC ORDER/SAFETY
46382	40	380	EDUCATIONAL SERVICES
46383	1984	27311	HOSPITALS
46384	24	58	CONSTRUCTION OF BUILDINGS
46385	808	5957	EDUCATIONAL SERVICES
46390	93	608	FOOD SVCS & DRINKING PLACES
46391	132	3008	JUSTICE; PUBIC ORDER/SAFETY
46392	148	1199	EDUCATIONAL SERVICES
46393	23	70	JUSTICE; PUBIC ORDER/SAFETY
46394	293	4594	MERCH. WHOLESALERS;NONDUR. GDS
46401	3	9	POSTAL SERVICE
46402	438	5730	EXEC.; LEGIS.; & OTHER SUPPORT
46403	307	2178	FOOD SVCS & DRINKING PLACES
46404	332	2295	EDUCATIONAL SERVICES
46405	274	1864	GASOLINE STATIONS
46406	299	3228	EDUCATIONAL SERVICES

ZIP CODE	2009 Total Firms	2009 Total Employ-ees	TOP INDUSTRY RANKED on 2009 EMPLOYMENT
46407	323	1955	EDUCATIONAL SERVICES
46408	565	5543	EDUCATIONAL SERVICES
46409	218	1526	EDUCATIONAL SERVICES
46410	2295	31500	HOSPITALS
46411	9	27	ADMINISTRATIVE & SUPPORT SVCS
46501	124	771	EDUCATIONAL SERVICES
46502	13	28	BLDG MATL & GARDEN EQPMT DLRS
46504	89	706	FABRICATED METAL PRODUCT MFG
46506	321	4209	MERCH. WHOLESALERS;DURABLE GDS
46507	284	5367	TRANSPORTATION EQUIPMENT MFG
46508	11	51	FABRICATED METAL PRODUCT MFG
46510	47	216	SPECIAL TRADE CONTRACTORS
46511	151	1510	EDUCATIONAL SERVICES
46513	6	9	RELIG.; GRANT; CIVIC; PROF ORG
46514	1689	31340	MOTOR VEHICLE & PARTS DEALERS
46515	13	37	SOCIAL ASSISTANCE
46516	1513	23922	TRANSPORTATION EQUIPMENT MFG
46517	763	14315	MERCH. WHOLESALERS;DURABLE GDS
46524	46	117	SPECIAL TRADE CONTRACTORS
46526	1184	24259	HOSPITALS
46527	8	16	ADMINISTRATIVE & SUPPORT SVCS
46528	566	9310	TRANSPORTATION EQUIPMENT MFG
46530	687	7146	ADMIN. OF ECONOMIC PROGRAMS
46531	22	73	GASOLINE STATIONS
46532	59	486	EDUCATIONAL SERVICES
46534	468	3666	EDUCATIONAL SERVICES
46536	127	1047	EDUCATIONAL SERVICES
46537	35	183	FOOD SVCS & DRINKING PLACES
46538	140	835	PLASTICS & RUBBER PRODUCTS MFG
46539	86	855	FOOD MANUFACTURING
46540	394	9444	MERCH. WHOLESALERS;DURABLE GDS
46542	145	3909	MACHINERY MANUFACTURING
46543	61	578	TRANSPORTATION EQUIPMENT MFG
46544	884	13459	CHEMICAL MANUFACTURING
46545	1523	22823	FOOD SVCS & DRINKING PLACES
46546	5	24	MERCH. WHOLESALERS;DURABLE GDS
46550	439	7101	MERCH. WHOLESALERS;DURABLE GDS
46552	191	2773	FABRICATED METAL PRODUCT MFG
46553	173	3784	TRANSPORTATION EQUIPMENT MFG
46554	121	935	PRIMARY METAL MANUFACTURING
46555	194	1102	FOOD SVCS & DRINKING PLACES
46556	47	5850	EDUCATIONAL SERVICES
46561	293	1702	RELIG.; GRANT; CIVIC; PROF ORG
46562	183	1420	MERCH. WHOLESALERS;DURABLE GDS
46563	1134	13817	FABRICATED METAL PRODUCT MFG
46565	292	2681	TRANSPORTATION EQUIPMENT MFG
46567	431	3831	TRANSPORTATION EQUIPMENT MFG
46570	18	123	MERCH. WHOLESALERS;NONDUR. GDS
46571	149	3271	TRANSPORTATION EQUIPMENT MFG
46572	5	3	POSTAL SERVICE
46573	160	2472	MERCH. WHOLESALERS;DURABLE GDS
46574	237	2387	BLDG MATL & GARDEN EQPMT DLRS
46580	1231	18221	PRINT'G & RELATED SUPP'T ACT'S
46581	16	470	PRIMARY METAL MANUFACTURING
46582	371	7102	MISCELLANEOUS MANUFACTURING
46590	115	1102	EDUCATIONAL SERVICES
46595	15	60	MERCH. WHOLESALERS;DURABLE GDS
46601	1145	25002	HOSPITALS
46604	1	5	MERCH. WHOLESALERS;DURABLE GDS
46613	304	3418	ADMINISTRATIVE & SUPPORT SVCS
46614	751	9220	FOOD SVCS & DRINKING PLACES
46615	382	4026	EDUCATIONAL SERVICES
46616	107	699	EDUCATIONAL SERVICES
46617	437	6820	RELIG.; GRANT; CIVIC; PROF ORG
46619	527	6267	MERCH. WHOLESALERS;DURABLE GDS
46624	7	10	TRANSIT & GRND PASS. TRANSPORT
46626	3	1110	PUBLISHING INDUSTRIES
46628	857	17666	TRANSPORTATION EQUIPMENT MFG
46634	4	4	PERFORM'G ARTS; SPEC. SPORTS
46635	255	2990	AMBULATORY HEALTH CARE SVCS
46637	492	5442	FOOD SVCS & DRINKING PLACES
46660	7	15	FURN. & HOME FURNISHGS STORES
46680	4	2	FABRICATED METAL PRODUCT MFG
46701	221	3760	TRANSPORTATION EQUIPMENT MFG
46702	45	146	EDUCATIONAL SERVICES
46703	956	8901	FOOD SVCS & DRINKING PLACES
46704	21	130	UTILITIES
46705	67	968	TRANSPORTATION EQUIPMENT MFG
46706	732	10229	TRANSPORTATION EQUIPMENT MFG
46710	139	2107	TRANSPORTATION EQUIPMENT MFG
46711	290	3221	NURSING & RESID. CARE FACILIT.
46713	6	7	SPECIAL TRADE CONTRACTORS
46714	652	8720	MERCH. WHOLESALERS;DURABLE GDS
46721	140	4622	FABRICATED METAL PRODUCT MFG
46723	197	1598	PROF.; SCIENTIFIC; & TECH SVCS
46725	876	9959	FABRICATED METAL PRODUCT MFG
46730	33	165	FOOD AND BEVERAGE STORES
46731	20	101	TELECOMMUNICATIONS
46732	64	309	ELECT'L EQPMT; APP; & COMP MFG
46733	752	9353	TRANSPORTATION EQUIPMENT MFG

ZIP CODE	2009 Total Firms	2009 Total Employ-ees	TOP INDUSTRY RANKED on 2009 EMPLOYMENT
46737	309	3536	FABRICATED METAL PRODUCT MFG
46738	217	3064	EDUCATIONAL SERVICES
46740	79	975	FOOD MANUFACTURING
46741	102	1333	SPECIAL TRADE CONTRACTORS
46742	95	769	MACHINERY MANUFACTURING
46743	66	567	SPECIAL TRADE CONTRACTORS
46745	35	328	PROF.; SCIENTIFIC; & TECH SVCS
46746	129	1529	MERCH. WHOLESALERS;DURABLE GDS
46747	41	327	FABRICATED METAL PRODUCT MFG
46748	118	648	MERCH. WHOLESALERS;DURABLE GDS
46750	875	11386	COMPUTER & ELECTRONIC PROD MFG
46755	571	9549	TRANSPORTATION EQUIPMENT MFG
46759	8	24	ANIMAL PRODUCTION
46760	25	88	FABRICATED METAL PRODUCT MFG
46761	387	4259	EDUCATIONAL SERVICES
46763	50	515	MACHINERY MANUFACTURING
46764	38	247	COMPUTER & ELECTRONIC PROD MFG
46765	138	731	EDUCATIONAL SERVICES
46766	14	43	JUSTICE; PUBIC ORDER/SAFETY
46767	212	3765	TRANSPORTATION EQUIPMENT MFG
46769	1	9	SPECIAL TRADE CONTRACTORS
46770	95	1085	SPECIAL TRADE CONTRACTORS
46771	6	5	MOTOR VEHICLE & PARTS DEALERS
46772	52	786	EDUCATIONAL SERVICES
46773	82	714	TRANSPORTATION EQUIPMENT MFG
46774	477	6215	FOOD SVCS & DRINKING PLACES
46776	58	551	FOOD MANUFACTURING
46777	169	1859	MERCH. WHOLESALERS;DURABLE GDS
46778	7	6	POSTAL SERVICE
46779	37	106	EDUCATIONAL SERVICES
46780	1	1	REPAIR AND MAINTENANCE
46781	22	151	EDUCATIONAL SERVICES
46782	4	30	JUSTICE; PUBIC ORDER/SAFETY
46783	168	4113	TRANSPORTATION EQUIPMENT MFG
46784	65	349	EDUCATIONAL SERVICES
46785	37	752	FABRICATED METAL PRODUCT MFG
46786	18	255	SPECIAL TRADE CONTRACTORS
46787	113	1090	MISCELLANEOUS STORE RETAILERS
46788	55	231	MACHINERY MANUFACTURING
46789	17	53	GASOLINE STATIONS
46791	21	279	TRUCK TRANSPORTATION
46792	150	1753	PERSONAL AND LAUNDRY SERVICES
46793	123	1398	FABRICATED METAL PRODUCT MFG
46794	23	216	MACHINERY MANUFACTURING
46795	115	548	ELECT'L EQPMT; APP; & COMP MFG
46796	13	70	EDUCATIONAL SERVICES
46797	118	4424	MOTOR VEHICLE & PARTS DEALERS
46798	29	135	WASTE MANAGMT & REMEDIAT'N SVC
46799	21	54	FOOD AND BEVERAGE STORES
46802	1348	28651	PROF.; SCIENTIFIC; & TECH SVCS
46803	617	14554	MERCH. WHOLESALERS;DURABLE GDS
46804	1413	22699	AMBULATORY HEALTH CARE SVCS
46805	1243	25299	SOCIAL ASSISTANCE
46806	446	4323	RELIG.; GRANT; CIVIC; PROF ORG
46807	316	2275	EDUCATIONAL SERVICES
46808	984	18674	MERCH. WHOLESALERS;DURABLE GDS
46809	577	12161	MACHINERY MANUFACTURING
46814	215	2214	EDUCATIONAL SERVICES
46815	660	5542	FOOD SVCS & DRINKING PLACES
46816	286	2279	EDUCATIONAL SERVICES
46818	684	12740	MISCELLANEOUS MANUFACTURING
46819	102	1202	EDUCATIONAL SERVICES
46825	1471	19685	FOOD SVCS & DRINKING PLACES
46835	522	6296	FOOD SVCS & DRINKING PLACES
46845	378	7054	HOSPITALS
46850	1	0	RELIG.; GRANT; CIVIC; PROF ORG
46851	2	10	NONMETALLIC MINERAL PROD. MFG
46856	1	20	SOCIAL ASSISTANCE
46857	2	30	MISCELLANEOUS MANUFACTURING
46858	1	4	MISCELLANEOUS STORE RETAILERS
46859	1	2	SPECIAL TRADE CONTRACTORS
46862	1	0	PROF.; SCIENTIFIC; & TECH SVCS
46863	1	0	REAL ESTATE
46864	1	1	PERFORM'G ARTS; SPEC. SPORTS
46865	1	0	ADMINISTRATIVE & SUPPORT SVCS
46866	1	1	ADMINISTRATIVE & SUPPORT SVCS
46868	3	7	ADMINISTRATIVE & SUPPORT SVCS
46869	1	0	PROF.; SCIENTIFIC; & TECH SVCS
46885	12	40	ADMINISTRATIVE & SUPPORT SVCS
46895	3	14	PERFORM'G ARTS; SPEC. SPORTS
46896	3	10	ADMINISTRATIVE & SUPPORT SVCS
46898	14	41	SPECIAL TRADE CONTRACTORS
46899	6	4	SPECIAL TRADE CONTRACTORS
46901	1457	18895	TRANSPORTATION EQUIPMENT MFG
46902	1271	26619	COMPUTER & ELECTRONIC PROD MFG
46903	2	2	SPECIAL TRADE CONTRACTORS
46904	8	154	MOTOR VEHICLE & PARTS DEALERS
46910	90	940	EDUCATIONAL SERVICES
46911	28	117	RELIG.; GRANT; CIVIC; PROF ORG
46912	1	2	MERCH. WHOLESALERS;DURABLE GDS

ZIP CODE	2009 Total Firms	2009 Total Employ-ees	TOP INDUSTRY RANKED on 2009 EMPLOYMENT	ZIP CODE	2009 Total Firms	2009 Total Employ-ees	TOP INDUSTRY RANKED on 2009 EMPLOYMENT	ZIP CODE	2009 Total Firms	2009 Total Employ-ees	TOP INDUSTRY RANKED on 2009 EMPLOYMENT
46913	21	47	CHEMICAL MANUFACTURING	47043	216	1107	EXEC.; LEGIS.; & OTHER SUPPORT	47302	727	9098	FABRICATED METAL PRODUCT MFG
46914	71	957	JUSTICE; PUBIC ORDER/SAFETY	47060	168	1041	RELIG.; GRANT; CIVIC; PROF ORG	47303	989	15114	HOSPITALS
46915	39	221	JUSTICE; PUBIC ORDER/SAFETY	47102	147	1397	FOOD MANUFACTURING	47304	874	11653	FOOD SVCS & DRINKING PLACES
46916	9	15	JUSTICE; PUBIC ORDER/SAFETY	47104	1	1	ACCOMMODATION	47305	471	6353	JUSTICE; PUBIC ORDER/SAFETY
46917	65	235	EDUCATIONAL SERVICES	47106	110	1154	WOOD PRODUCT MANUFACTURING	47306	33	859	EDUCATIONAL SERVICES
46919	72	522	EDUCATIONAL SERVICES	47107	2	7	RELIG.; GRANT; CIVIC; PROF ORG	47307	3	1	SPECIAL TRADE CONTRACTORS
46920	19	50	JUSTICE; PUBIC ORDER/SAFETY	47108	72	600	CHEMICAL MANUFACTURING	47308	12	14	CONSTRUCTION OF BUILDINGS
46922	3	11	FOOD AND BEVERAGE STORES	47110	12	49	EDUCATIONAL SERVICES	47320	98	939	FOOD SVCS & DRINKING PLACES
46923	289	3972	FOOD AND BEVERAGE STORES	47111	302	2661	EDUCATIONAL SERVICES	47322	2	2	CONSTRUCTION OF BUILDINGS
46926	39	236	EDUCATIONAL SERVICES	47112	707	7402	FOOD SVCS & DRINKING PLACES	47324	10	26	WAREHOUSING AND STORAGE
46928	144	893	EDUCATIONAL SERVICES	47114	5	5	POSTAL SERVICE	47325	7	28	ADMINISTRATIVE & SUPPORT SVCS
46929	147	945	MERCH. WHOLESALERS;DURABLE GDS	47115	32	186	GENERAL MERCHANDISE STORES	47326	31	283	FOOD SVCS & DRINKING PLACES
46930	6	8	SPECIAL TRADE CONTRACTORS	47116	17	66	EDUCATIONAL SERVICES	47327	192	1575	FOOD SVCS & DRINKING PLACES
46931	21	306	EDUCATIONAL SERVICES	47117	60	2497	AMUSEMENT; GAMBLING;& RECREAT.	47330	156	914	EDUCATIONAL SERVICES
46932	70	296	EDUCATIONAL SERVICES	47118	97	458	EXEC.; LEGIS.; & OTHER SUPPORT	47331	815	7943	TRANSPORTATION EQUIPMENT MFG
46933	208	2364	FOOD SVCS & DRINKING PLACES	47119	273	2221	FOOD SVCS & DRINKING PLACES	47334	113	1345	FOOD SVCS & DRINKING PLACES
46936	123	810	NURSING & RESID. CARE FACILIT.	47120	18	70	FABRICATED METAL PRODUCT MFG	47335	15	29	EDUCATIONAL SERVICES
46937	4	16	PERSONAL AND LAUNDRY SERVICES	47122	189	1151	EDUCATIONAL SERVICES	47336	103	911	MERCH. WHOLESALERS;DURABLE GDS
46938	57	232	EDUCATIONAL SERVICES	47123	1	0	POSTAL SERVICE	47337	10	33	TRUCK TRANSPORTATION
46939	52	345	FABRICATED METAL PRODUCT MFG	47124	79	321	EDUCATIONAL SERVICES	47338	69	619	MACHINERY MANUFACTURING
46940	48	301	NURSING & RESID. CARE FACILIT.	47125	37	92	FOOD SVCS & DRINKING PLACES	47339	10	13	FABRICATED METAL PRODUCT MFG
46941	26	63	SPECIAL TRADE CONTRACTORS	47126	86	508	JUSTICE; PUBIC ORDER/SAFETY	47340	74	299	AMUSEMENT; GAMBLING;& RECREAT.
46943	11	68	EDUCATIONAL SERVICES	47129	871	13647	FOOD SVCS & DRINKING PLACES	47341	34	213	EDUCATIONAL SERVICES
46945	11	48	REPAIR AND MAINTENANCE	47130	1475	21294	HOSPITALS	47342	74	726	EDUCATIONAL SERVICES
46946	2	3	RELIG.; GRANT; CIVIC; PROF ORG	47131	6	9	INSURANCE CARRIERS & RELATED	47344	6	22	JUSTICE; PUBIC ORDER/SAFETY
46947	1020	16441	MERCH. WHOLESALERS;NONDUR. GDS	47135	23	205	RELIG.; GRANT; CIVIC; PROF ORG	47345	34	78	PROF.; SCIENTIFIC; & TECH SVCS
46950	9	12	POSTAL SERVICE	47136	57	297	EDUCATIONAL SERVICES	47346	153	1214	MERCH. WHOLESALERS;DURABLE GDS
46951	26	97	CONSTRUCTION OF BUILDINGS	47137	57	427	NONMETALLIC MINERAL PROD. MFG	47348	311	3246	PAPER MANUFACTURING
46952	875	11996	AMBULATORY HEALTH CARE SVCS	47138	62	208	EDUCATIONAL SERVICES	47351	9	44	EDUCATIONAL SERVICES
46953	741	12242	EDUCATIONAL SERVICES	47139	2	1	RELIG.; GRANT; CIVIC; PROF ORG	47352	22	46	AMUSEMENT; GAMBLING;& RECREAT.
46957	16	112	MERCH. WHOLESALERS;DURABLE GDS	47140	91	523	EDUCATIONAL SERVICES	47353	225	1452	MISCELLANEOUS MANUFACTURING
46958	15	52	COMPUTER & ELECTRONIC PROD MFG	47141	14	26	POSTAL SERVICE	47354	20	42	FOOD SVCS & DRINKING PLACES
46959	2	9	MERCH. WHOLESALERS;NONDUR. GDS	47142	21	230	WOOD PRODUCT MANUFACTURING	47355	91	876	MERCH. WHOLESALERS;DURABLE GDS
46960	33	114	EDUCATIONAL SERVICES	47143	57	414	TRUCK TRANSPORTATION	47356	141	882	EDUCATIONAL SERVICES
46961	5	28	JUSTICE; PUBIC ORDER/SAFETY	47145	42	166	EDUCATIONAL SERVICES	47357	15	46	JUSTICE; PUBIC ORDER/SAFETY
46962	338	3831	RELIG.; GRANT; CIVIC; PROF ORG	47146	7	30	RELIG.; GRANT; CIVIC; PROF ORG	47358	31	365	EDUCATIONAL SERVICES
46965	3	75	FABRICATED METAL PRODUCT MFG	47147	17	122	PROF.; SCIENTIFIC; & TECH SVCS	47359	101	748	FABRICATED METAL PRODUCT MFG
46967	4	8	MERCH. WHOLESALERS;DURABLE GDS	47150	1868	26710	EDUCATIONAL SERVICES	47360	21	67	CREDIT INTERMEDIATION & RELATD
46968	3	2	EXEC.; LEGIS.; & OTHER SUPPORT	47151	8	11	REAL ESTATE	47361	30	81	TRUCK TRANSPORTATION
46970	749	8604	MERCH. WHOLESALERS;DURABLE GDS	47160	11	38	EDUCATIONAL SERVICES	47362	972	13224	AMBULATORY HEALTH CARE SVCS
46971	8	141	CONSTRUCTION OF BUILDINGS	47161	69	384	FURN. & HOME FURNISHGS STORES	47366	14	90	GASOLINE STATIONS
46974	30	77	REPAIR AND MAINTENANCE	47162	31	258	EDUCATIONAL SERVICES	47367	4	30	WAREHOUSING AND STORAGE
46975	707	6197	MERCH. WHOLESALERS;DURABLE GDS	47163	18	54	NONMETALLIC MINERAL PROD. MFG	47368	57	511	EDUCATIONAL SERVICES
46977	3	1	MISCELLANEOUS STORE RETAILERS	47164	79	437	EDUCATIONAL SERVICES	47369	41	131	EDUCATIONAL SERVICES
46978	44	325	EDUCATIONAL SERVICES	47165	160	771	EDUCATIONAL SERVICES	47370	6	8	EDUCATIONAL SERVICES
46979	96	751	EDUCATIONAL SERVICES	47166	40	478	EDUCATIONAL SERVICES	47371	545	5929	TRANSPORTATION EQUIPMENT MFG
46980	1	0	POSTAL SERVICE	47167	669	5581	MISCELLANEOUS MANUFACTURING	47373	49	245	JUSTICE; PUBIC ORDER/SAFETY
46982	67	558	FURNITURE & RELATED PROD. MFG	47170	655	5723	FOOD SVCS & DRINKING PLACES	47374	2098	30983	HOSPITALS
46984	11	20	SPECIAL TRADE CONTRACTORS	47172	409	5590	TRUCK TRANSPORTATION	47375	12	21	SOCIAL ASSISTANCE
46985	43	127	BLDG MATL & GARDEN EQPMT DLRS	47174	4	12	NONSTORE RETAILERS	47380	33	200	FABRICATED METAL PRODUCT MFG
46986	68	465	TRUCK TRANSPORTATION	47175	16	36	WOOD PRODUCT MANUFACTURING	47381	5	4	MISCELLANEOUS STORE RETAILERS
46987	49	217	EDUCATIONAL SERVICES	47177	25	157	ACCOMMODATION	47382	10	122	MERCH. WHOLESALERS;DURABLE GDS
46988	22	58	MERCH. WHOLESALERS;NONDUR. GDS	47190	4	2	EXEC.; LEGIS.; & OTHER SUPPORT	47383	65	642	EDUCATIONAL SERVICES
46989	81	1095	EDUCATIONAL SERVICES	47201	1829	29625	AMBULATORY HEALTH CARE SVCS	47384	40	138	PRIMARY METAL MANUFACTURING
46990	23	134	MACHINERY MANUFACTURING	47202	11	43	SOCIAL ASSISTANCE	47385	44	986	MISCELLANEOUS MANUFACTURING
46991	41	410	FOOD AND BEVERAGE STORES	47203	467	4304	EDUCATIONAL SERVICES	47386	11	53	BLDG MATL & GARDEN EQPMT DLRS
46992	711	9290	TRANSPORTATION EQUIPMENT MFG	47220	252	1775	EDUCATIONAL SERVICES	47387	32	218	EDUCATIONAL SERVICES
46994	58	698	EDUCATIONAL SERVICES	47223	35	265	AMBULATORY HEALTH CARE SVCS	47388	21	119	MERCH. WHOLESALERS;NONDUR. GDS
46995	7	11	ADMINISTRATIVE & SUPPORT SVCS	47224	13	57	JUSTICE; PUBIC ORDER/SAFETY	47390	201	2565	TRANSPORTATION EQUIPMENT MFG
46996	342	3949	TRANSPORTATION EQUIPMENT MFG	47225	3	6	RELIG.; GRANT; CIVIC; PROF ORG	47392	5	7	FOOD AND BEVERAGE STORES
46998	3	3	POSTAL SERVICE	47226	6	48	EDUCATIONAL SERVICES	47393	20	43	JUSTICE; PUBIC ORDER/SAFETY
47001	427	3913	MERCH. WHOLESALERS;DURABLE GDS	47227	21	121	EDUCATIONAL SERVICES	47394	367	3675	MACHINERY MANUFACTURING
47003	35	65	BLDG MATL & GARDEN EQPMT DLRS	47228	4	4	POSTAL SERVICE	47396	196	2158	EDUCATIONAL SERVICES
47006	549	11109	MISCELLANEOUS MANUFACTURING	47229	91	821	TRANSPORTATION EQUIPMENT MFG	47401	1174	13342	FOOD SVCS & DRINKING PLACES
47010	7	38	CREDIT INTERMEDIATION & RELATD	47230	28	115	EDUCATIONAL SERVICES	47402	18	122	AMBULATORY HEALTH CARE SVCS
47011	19	34	ADMINISTRATIVE & SUPPORT SVCS	47231	24	129	JUSTICE; PUBIC ORDER/SAFETY	47403	877	12623	HOSPITALS
47012	379	3327	MERCH. WHOLESALERS;DURABLE GDS	47232	40	151	RELIG.; GRANT; CIVIC; PROF ORG	47404	1542	18997	FOOD SVCS & DRINKING PLACES
47016	18	84	EDUCATIONAL SERVICES	47234	23	68	MINING (EXCEPT OIL AND GAS)	47405	61	10137	EDUCATIONAL SERVICES
47017	28	48	JUSTICE; PUBIC ORDER/SAFETY	47235	27	79	JUSTICE; PUBIC ORDER/SAFETY	47406	29	340	RELIG.; GRANT; CIVIC; PROF ORG
47018	140	1031	NURSING & RESID. CARE FACILIT.	47236	2	8	TRUCK TRANSPORTATION	47407	8	55	MERCH. WHOLESALERS;DURABLE GDS
47019	9	11	CREDIT INTERMEDIATION & RELATD	47240	957	12755	TRANSPORTATION EQUIPMENT MFG	47408	511	5089	FOOD SVCS & DRINKING PLACES
47020	26	1148	AMUSEMENT; GAMBLING;& RECREAT.	47243	138	1098	EDUCATIONAL SERVICES	47420	7	15	ADMIN. ENVIRO. QUALITY PROGRMS
47021	10	57	INSURANCE CARRIERS & RELATED	47244	15	42	JUSTICE; PUBIC ORDER/SAFETY	47421	1044	10998	HOSPITALS
47022	55	232	EDUCATIONAL SERVICES	47245	3	48	EDUCATIONAL SERVICES	47424	313	2151	EDUCATIONAL SERVICES
47023	36	74	NONMETALLIC MINERAL PROD. MFG	47246	118	754	EDUCATIONAL SERVICES	47426	9	27	ADMINISTRATIVE & SUPPORT SVCS
47024	59	209	EDUCATIONAL SERVICES	47247	8	51	ELECTRONICS & APPLIANCE STORES	47427	14	39	JUSTICE; PUBIC ORDER/SAFETY
47025	854	12384	AMUSEMENT; GAMBLING;& RECREAT.	47249	3	4	FOOD SVCS & DRINKING PLACES	47429	205	1710	MISCELLANEOUS MANUFACTURING
47030	66	123	MISCELLANEOUS STORE RETAILERS	47250	1114	13694	TRANSPORTATION EQUIPMENT MFG	47430	1	1	POSTAL SERVICE
47031	142	814	EDUCATIONAL SERVICES	47260	53	246	CONSTRUCTION OF BUILDINGS	47431	22	42	NONMETALLIC MINERAL PROD. MFG
47032	65	353	CONSTRUCTION OF BUILDINGS	47263	6	17	TRUCK TRANSPORTATION	47432	230	1762	ACCOMMODATION
47033	2	2	POSTAL SERVICE	47264	23	97	ACCOMMODATION	47433	96	416	NURSING & RESID. CARE FACILIT.
47034	31	212	WOOD PRODUCT MANUFACTURING	47265	721	7581	WAREHOUSING AND STORAGE	47434	5	7	RELIG.; GRANT; CIVIC; PROF ORG
47035	3	15	MISCELLANEOUS STORE RETAILERS	47270	14	24	SPECIAL TRADE CONTRACTORS	47435	4	154	CLOTHING & CLOTH'G ACC. STORES
47036	41	324	RELIG.; GRANT; CIVIC; PROF ORG	47272	41	110	ACCOMMODATION	47436	25	95	EDUCATIONAL SERVICES
47037	148	848	RELIG.; GRANT; CIVIC; PROF ORG	47273	34	141	EDUCATIONAL SERVICES	47437	5	15	FABRICATED METAL PRODUCT MFG
47038	27	172	MERCH. WHOLESALERS;DURABLE GDS	47274	1241	18605	MERCH. WHOLESALERS;DURABLE GDS	47438	109	760	EDUCATIONAL SERVICES
47039	2	2	MISCELLANEOUS STORE RETAILERS	47280	26	385	EDUCATIONAL SERVICES	47439	1	0	POSTAL SERVICE
47040	192	890	EDUCATIONAL SERVICES	47281	27	105	ADMIN. ENVIRO. QUALITY PROGRMS	47441	373	3096	EDUCATIONAL SERVICES
47041	187	1389	PRINT'G & RELATED SUPP'T ACT'S	47282	37	81	EXEC.; LEGIS.; & OTHER SUPPORT	47443	38	239	EDUCATIONAL SERVICES
47042	234	1621	JUSTICE; PUBIC ORDER/SAFETY	47283	91	431	BLDG MATL & GARDEN EQPMT DLRS	47445	2	11	EXEC.; LEGIS.; & OTHER SUPPORT

BUSINESS DATA

ZIP CODE	2009 Total Firms	2009 Total Employ-ees	TOP INDUSTRY RANKED on 2009 EMPLOYMENT	ZIP CODE	2009 Total Firms	2009 Total Employ-ees	TOP INDUSTRY RANKED on 2009 EMPLOYMENT	ZIP CODE	2009 Total Firms	2009 Total Employ-ees	TOP INDUSTRY RANKED on 2009 EMPLOYMENT
47446	327	2564	FABRICATED METAL PRODUCT MFG	47629	14	39	ADMINISTRATIVE & SUPPORT SVCS	47876	8	503	RELIG.; GRANT; CIVIC; PROF ORG
47448	503	3093	ACCOMMODATION	47630	909	9906	MERCH. WHOLESALERS;DURABLE GDS	47878	11	61	JUSTICE; PUBIC ORDER/SAFETY
47449	11	103	FOOD MANUFACTURING	47631	93	806	ACCOMMODATION	47879	61	232	TRUCK TRANSPORTATION
47451	45	378	NONMETALLIC MINERAL PROD. MFG	47633	113	1244	EDUCATIONAL SERVICES	47880	1	2	POSTAL SERVICE
47452	158	1957	WAREHOUSING AND STORAGE	47634	36	119	EDUCATIONAL SERVICES	47881	7	16	EXEC.; LEGIS.; & OTHER SUPPORT
47453	17	69	JUSTICE; PUBIC ORDER/SAFETY	47635	243	2013	UTILITIES	47882	324	3367	TRANSPORTATION EQUIPMENT MFG
47454	369	3228	HEAVY & CIVIL ENG. CONSTRUCT'N	47637	22	64	EDUCATIONAL SERVICES	47884	7	74	NONMETALLIC MINERAL PROD. MFG
47455	9	48	EDUCATIONAL SERVICES	47638	71	273	EDUCATIONAL SERVICES	47885	201	1270	EDUCATIONAL SERVICES
47456	13	17	RELIG.; GRANT; CIVIC; PROF ORG	47639	142	1076	FOOD SVCS & DRINKING PLACES	47901	630	5497	PROF.; SCIENTIFIC; & TECH SVCS
47457	5	15	CONSTRUCTION OF BUILDINGS	47640	18	33	PIPELINE TRANSPORTATION	47902	6	13	PROF.; SCIENTIFIC; & TECH SVCS
47458	10	18	ADMINISTRATIVE & SUPPORT SVCS	47647	1	1	PERSONAL AND LAUNDRY SERVICES	47903	20	43	SPECIAL TRADE CONTRACTORS
47459	71	122	FOOD SVCS & DRINKING PLACES	47648	156	747	EDUCATIONAL SERVICES	47904	787	12802	AMBULATORY HEALTH CARE SVCS
47460	417	3854	MISCELLANEOUS MANUFACTURING	47649	33	393	MINING (EXCEPT OIL AND GAS)	47905	1597	25082	MERCH. WHOLESALERS;DURABLE GDS
47462	57	425	PLASTICS & RUBBER PRODUCTS MFG	47654	7	45	EDUCATIONAL SERVICES	47906	994	14280	FOOD SVCS & DRINKING PLACES
47463	15	16	BLDG MATL & GARDEN EQPMT DLRS	47660	159	1499	MINING (EXCEPT OIL AND GAS)	47907	43	16346	EDUCATIONAL SERVICES
47464	9	69	EDUCATIONAL SERVICES	47665	77	736	UTILITIES	47909	584	8159	MERCH. WHOLESALERS;DURABLE GDS
47465	44	394	EDUCATIONAL SERVICES	47666	27	80	ADMINISTRATIVE & SUPPORT SVCS	47916	2	2	POSTAL SERVICE
47467	1	0	POSTAL SERVICE	47670	635	11960	TRANSPORTATION EQUIPMENT MFG	47917	13	20	UTILITIES
47468	29	116	EDUCATIONAL SERVICES	47683	5	8	RELIG.; GRANT; CIVIC; PROF ORG	47918	219	2545	PRIMARY METAL MANUFACTURING
47469	56	208	FOOD AND BEVERAGE STORES	47702	1	0	MISCELLANEOUS STORE RETAILERS	47920	53	242	EDUCATIONAL SERVICES
47470	30	56	TRUCK TRANSPORTATION	47704	1	1	RELIG.; GRANT; CIVIC; PROF ORG	47921	37	237	FOOD SVCS & DRINKING PLACES
47471	82	359	FOOD SVCS & DRINKING PLACES	47706	2	2	SPORTG GDS;HOBBY;BOOK; & MUSIC	47922	69	440	MERCH. WHOLESALERS;NONDUR. GDS
47501	666	7814	FOOD MANUFACTURING	47708	690	14190	CREDIT INTERMEDIATION & RELATD	47923	118	672	MERCH. WHOLESALERS;DURABLE GDS
47512	135	885	MINING (EXCEPT OIL AND GAS)	47710	890	16799	PERSONAL AND LAUNDRY SERVICES	47924	8	12	RELIG.; GRANT; CIVIC; PROF ORG
47513	53	331	ACCOMMODATION	47711	1247	17862	MERCH. WHOLESALERS;DURABLE GDS	47925	10	56	EDUCATIONAL SERVICES
47514	9	376	JUSTICE; PUBIC ORDER/SAFETY	47712	749	11287	EDUCATIONAL SERVICES	47926	28	150	MERCH. WHOLESALERS;NONDUR. GDS
47515	22	18	CONSTRUCTION OF BUILDINGS	47713	412	5774	AMBULATORY HEALTH CARE SVCS	47928	73	733	EDUCATIONAL SERVICES
47516	23	112	EDUCATIONAL SERVICES	47714	925	14426	HOSPITALS	47929	21	106	EDUCATIONAL SERVICES
47519	22	321	MINING (EXCEPT OIL AND GAS)	47715	1918	27205	FOOD SVCS & DRINKING PLACES	47930	27	178	WOOD PRODUCT MANUFACTURING
47520	109	580	FURNITURE & RELATED PROD. MFG	47716	13	15	ADMINISTRATIVE & SUPPORT SVCS	47932	215	1532	EDUCATIONAL SERVICES
47521	30	130	EDUCATIONAL SERVICES	47719	4	510	ADMINISTRATIVE & SUPPORT SVCS	47933	1039	14471	PRINT'G & RELATED SUPP'T ACT'S
47522	26	9702	NAT'L SECURITY & INT'L AFFAIRS	47720	382	4391	SPECIAL TRADE CONTRACTORS	47940	36	212	NAT'L SECURITY & INT'L AFFAIRS
47523	128	1288	PLASTICS & RUBBER PRODUCTS MFG	47721	3	4501	FOOD MANUFACTURING	47941	30	253	MERCH. WHOLESALERS;DURABLE GDS
47524	8	29	MISCELLANEOUS STORE RETAILERS	47722	1	506	EDUCATIONAL SERVICES	47942	27	102	TRUCK TRANSPORTATION
47525	11	22	ACCOMMODATION	47724	6	14	SPECIAL TRADE CONTRACTORS	47943	21	267	ANIMAL PRODUCTION
47527	54	609	FOOD MANUFACTURING	47725	431	7398	PLASTICS & RUBBER PRODUCTS MFG	47944	175	1203	FOOD SVCS & DRINKING PLACES
47528	21	314	EDUCATIONAL SERVICES	47727	2	5011	ELECT'L EQPMT; APP; & COMP MFG	47946	95	815	MERCH. WHOLESALERS;NONDUR. GDS
47529	41	446	EDUCATIONAL SERVICES	47728	7	18	SPECIAL TRADE CONTRACTORS	47948	66	427	PLASTICS & RUBBER PRODUCTS MFG
47531	16	146	MINING (EXCEPT OIL AND GAS)	47733	1	3	MISCELLANEOUS STORE RETAILERS	47949	35	121	PERFORM'G ARTS; SPEC. SPORTS
47532	177	4977	FURNITURE & RELATED PROD. MFG	47736	2	5	CONSTRUCTION OF BUILDINGS	47950	15	37	SPECIAL TRADE CONTRACTORS
47535	16	112	RELIG.; GRANT; CIVIC; PROF ORG	47744	2	420	MANAGMT OF COMPANIES & ENTERP.	47951	171	1323	PRIMARY METAL MANUFACTURING
47536	6	21	WOOD PRODUCT MANUFACTURING	47747	9	7030	HOSPITALS	47952	63	216	MISCELLANEOUS MANUFACTURING
47537	11	30	SUPPORT ACTIVITIES: AGR./FOR.	47750	4	3214	HOSPITALS	47954	64	258	SOCIAL ASSISTANCE
47541	52	306	ANIMAL PRODUCTION	47801	2	5	ADMINISTRATIVE & SUPPORT SVCS	47955	55	324	UTILITIES
47542	384	8049	FURNITURE & RELATED PROD. MFG	47802	1336	17049	FOOD SVCS & DRINKING PLACES	47957	49	184	EXEC.; LEGIS.; & OTHER SUPPORT
47545	11	260	PROF.; SCIENTIFIC; & TECH SVCS	47803	526	6693	NAT'L SECURITY & INT'L AFFAIRS	47958	6	22	MACHINERY MANUFACTURING
47546	1069	17628	FURNITURE & RELATED PROD. MFG	47804	416	11311	HOSPITALS	47959	110	656	FURN. & HOME FURNISHGS STORES
47547	8	26	ADMINISTRATIVE & SUPPORT SVCS	47805	230	2397	TRANSPORTATION EQUIPMENT MFG	47960	762	7658	AMUSEMENT; GAMBLING;& RECREAT.
47549	5	1165	MERCH. WHOLESALERS;DURABLE GDS	47807	959	14150	AMBULATORY HEALTH CARE SVCS	47962	3	51	MERCH. WHOLESALERS;DURABLE GDS
47550	20	109	EDUCATIONAL SERVICES	47808	6	16	ELECTRONICS & APPLIANCE STORES	47963	93	471	EDUCATIONAL SERVICES
47551	19	409	EDUCATIONAL SERVICES	47809	9	1831	EDUCATIONAL SERVICES	47964	17	1	POSTAL SERVICE
47552	8	163	EDUCATIONAL SERVICES	47811	1	2600	SPORTG GDS;HOBBY;BOOK; & MUSIC	47965	18	107	EDUCATIONAL SERVICES
47553	297	1720	FOOD SVCS & DRINKING PLACES	47830	4	36	JUSTICE; PUBIC ORDER/SAFETY	47966	40	1135	PROF.; SCIENTIFIC; & TECH SVCS
47556	4	38	FOOD SVCS & DRINKING PLACES	47831	2	2	POSTAL SERVICE	47967	30	288	FOOD AND BEVERAGE STORES
47557	30	172	CROP PRODUCTION	47832	39	885	PLASTICS & RUBBER PRODUCTS MFG	47968	24	95	EDUCATIONAL SERVICES
47558	178	1401	EDUCATIONAL SERVICES	47833	25	28	POSTAL SERVICE	47969	6	16	WAREHOUSING AND STORAGE
47561	40	436	FOOD AND BEVERAGE STORES	47834	642	5956	EDUCATIONAL SERVICES	47970	52	414	MISCELLANEOUS MANUFACTURING
47562	192	1008	CONSTRUCTION OF BUILDINGS	47836	9	12	FOOD AND BEVERAGE STORES	47971	46	216	PLASTICS & RUBBER PRODUCTS MFG
47564	31	324	TRUCK TRANSPORTATION	47837	16	80	WOOD PRODUCT MANUFACTURING	47974	22	130	TRUCK TRANSPORTATION
47567	253	2581	UTILITIES	47838	58	291	EDUCATIONAL SERVICES	47975	24	94	EDUCATIONAL SERVICES
47568	39	158	MERCH. WHOLESALERS;NONDUR. GDS	47840	31	119	GASOLINE STATIONS	47977	128	1332	FABRICATED METAL PRODUCT MFG
47574	2	25	ACCOMMODATION	47841	89	430	EDUCATIONAL SERVICES	47978	576	5152	FOOD SVCS & DRINKING PLACES
47575	37	385	FURNITURE & RELATED PROD. MFG	47842	292	3306	MERCH. WHOLESALERS;NONDUR. GDS	47980	56	386	MERCH. WHOLESALERS;NONDUR. GDS
47576	16	76	FORESTRY AND LOGGING	47845	2	0	POSTAL SERVICE	47981	28	97	MERCH. WHOLESALERS;NONDUR. GDS
47577	45	1277	EDUCATIONAL SERVICES	47846	13	27	FABRICATED METAL PRODUCT MFG	47982	4	14	MERCH. WHOLESALERS;NONDUR. GDS
47578	22	41	RELIG.; GRANT; CIVIC; PROF ORG	47847	32	102	CROP PRODUCTION	47983	9	11	RELIG.; GRANT; CIVIC; PROF ORG
47579	86	1974	AMUSEMENT; GAMBLING;& RECREAT.	47848	46	172	MACHINERY MANUFACTURING	47986	3	15	MERCH. WHOLESALERS;NONDUR. GDS
47580	6	12	TRUCK TRANSPORTATION	47849	9	50	UTILITIES	47987	118	2262	TRANSPORTATION EQUIPMENT MFG
47581	124	1248	EDUCATIONAL SERVICES	47850	51	422	EDUCATIONAL SERVICES	47988	1	0	FOOD AND BEVERAGE STORES
47584	6	7	SPECIAL TRADE CONTRACTORS	47851	4	81	PLASTICS & RUBBER PRODUCTS MFG	47989	54	181	EDUCATIONAL SERVICES
47585	8	22	ADMINISTRATIVE & SUPPORT SVCS	47852	4	2	POSTAL SERVICE	47990	39	130	FOOD SVCS & DRINKING PLACES
47586	468	4699	PRIMARY METAL MANUFACTURING	47853	11	22	MACHINERY MANUFACTURING	47991	37	338	MERCH. WHOLESALERS;DURABLE GDS
47588	26	271	TRANSPORTATION EQUIPMENT MFG	47854	19	457	SPECIAL TRADE CONTRACTORS	47992	44	111	FOOD SVCS & DRINKING PLACES
47590	7	18	WASTE MANAGMT & REMEDIAT'N SVC	47855	15	88	EDUCATIONAL SERVICES	47993	134	1194	FABRICATED METAL PRODUCT MFG
47591	1190	16149	HOSPITALS	47857	7	115	NURSING & RESID. CARE FACILIT.	47994	19	62	MERCH. WHOLESALERS;DURABLE GDS
47596	6	20	CROP PRODUCTION	47858	10	47	MINING (EXCEPT OIL AND GAS)	47995	88	842	COMPUTER & ELECTRONIC PROD MFG
47597	23	66	JUSTICE; PUBIC ORDER/SAFETY	47859	27	277	ACCOMMODATION	47996	17	24	SPECIAL TRADE CONTRACTORS
47598	74	384	MINING (EXCEPT OIL AND GAS)	47860	8	25	JUSTICE; PUBIC ORDER/SAFETY	47997	7	10	TELECOMMUNICATIONS
47601	515	4764	JUSTICE; PUBIC ORDER/SAFETY	47861	15	54	RELIG.; GRANT; CIVIC; PROF ORG	48001	324	2257	EDUCATIONAL SERVICES
47610	142	1242	COMPUTER & ELECTRONIC PROD MFG	47862	44	483	WOOD PRODUCT MANUFACTURING	48002	63	122	PROF.; SCIENTIFIC; & TECH SVCS
47611	41	186	EXEC.; LEGIS.; & OTHER SUPPORT	47863	5	8	SPECIAL TRADE CONTRACTORS	48003	204	1591	EDUCATIONAL SERVICES
47612	33	142	SPECIAL TRADE CONTRACTORS	47865	2	5	UTILITIES	48004	4	14	ADMINISTRATIVE & SUPPORT SVCS
47613	60	306	FOOD SVCS & DRINKING PLACES	47866	14	360	MINING (EXCEPT OIL AND GAS)	48005	187	1397	EDUCATIONAL SERVICES
47614	2	2	POSTAL SERVICE	47868	52	96	JUSTICE; PUBIC ORDER/SAFETY	48006	52	222	FABRICATED METAL PRODUCT MFG
47615	26	207	TRANSPORTATION EQUIPMENT MFG	47869	3	6	GASOLINE STATIONS	48009	1978	14309	PROF.; SCIENTIFIC; & TECH SVCS
47616	21	39	RELIG.; GRANT; CIVIC; PROF ORG	47870	6	19	JUSTICE; PUBIC ORDER/SAFETY	48012	21	47	CONSTRUCTION OF BUILDINGS
47617	5	19	RELIG.; GRANT; CIVIC; PROF ORG	47871	15	110	EDUCATIONAL SERVICES	48014	131	731	EDUCATIONAL SERVICES
47618	3	22	MERCH. WHOLESALERS;NONDUR. GDS	47872	305	2837	JUSTICE; PUBIC ORDER/SAFETY	48015	338	5453	MOTOR VEHICLE & PARTS DEALERS
47619	48	233	EDUCATIONAL SERVICES	47874	58	993	PLASTICS & RUBBER PRODUCTS MFG	48017	533	3665	MERCH. WHOLESALERS;DURABLE GDS
47620	500	6546	PLASTICS & RUBBER PRODUCTS MFG	47875	8	14	MISCELLANEOUS STORE RETAILERS	48021	975	6226	FOOD SVCS & DRINKING PLACES

ZIP CODE	2009 Total Firms	2009 Total Employ-ees	TOP INDUSTRY RANKED on 2009 EMPLOYMENT
48022	59	161	EDUCATIONAL SERVICES
48023	176	1587	EDUCATIONAL SERVICES
48025	1047	8507	PROF.; SCIENTIFIC; & TECH SVCS
48026	755	9420	MACHINERY MANUFACTURING
48027	49	143	AMUSEMENT; GAMBLING;& RECREAT.
48028	41	190	RELIG.; GRANT; CIVIC; PROF ORG
48030	589	3845	EDUCATIONAL SERVICES
48032	48	127	SPECIAL TRADE CONTRACTORS
48033	1315	20936	PROF.; SCIENTIFIC; & TECH SVCS
48034	1507	19554	PROF.; SCIENTIFIC; & TECH SVCS
48035	1141	10798	FOOD SVCS & DRINKING PLACES
48036	965	10380	AMBULATORY HEALTH CARE SVCS
48037	13	32	SPECIAL TRADE CONTRACTORS
48038	1357	14667	HOSPITALS
48039	383	2744	FABRICATED METAL PRODUCT MFG
48040	367	4375	PLASTICS & RUBBER PRODUCTS MFG
48041	117	567	EDUCATIONAL SERVICES
48042	533	4866	MACHINERY MANUFACTURING
48043	1145	18720	HOSPITALS
48044	708	5461	EDUCATIONAL SERVICES
48045	682	5446	AMUSEMENT; GAMBLING;& RECREAT.
48046	6	255	POSTAL SERVICE
48047	886	7207	AMBULATORY HEALTH CARE SVCS
48048	179	1295	JUSTICE; PUBIC ORDER/SAFETY
48049	82	308	SPECIAL TRADE CONTRACTORS
48050	60	364	BLDG MATL & GARDEN EQPMT DLRS
48051	702	8700	FABRICATED METAL PRODUCT MFG
48054	202	2639	HOSPITALS
48059	590	5652	FOOD SVCS & DRINKING PLACES
48060	1857	23577	HOSPITALS
48061	1	0	POSTAL SERVICE
48062	370	5506	ADMINISTRATIVE & SUPPORT SVCS
48063	64	278	SPECIAL TRADE CONTRACTORS
48064	108	579	CONSTRUCTION OF BUILDINGS
48065	460	5925	MACHINERY MANUFACTURING
48066	1784	21411	FOOD SVCS & DRINKING PLACES
48067	1553	11247	FOOD SVCS & DRINKING PLACES
48068	15	27	PROF.; SCIENTIFIC; & TECH SVCS
48069	77	326	PROF.; SCIENTIFIC; & TECH SVCS
48070	170	802	AMBULATORY HEALTH CARE SVCS
48071	1708	24590	PROF.; SCIENTIFIC; & TECH SVCS
48072	608	3662	EDUCATIONAL SERVICES
48073	1167	26482	HOSPITALS
48074	307	2142	EDUCATIONAL SERVICES
48075	3026	29004	PROF.; SCIENTIFIC; & TECH SVCS
48076	2070	19570	PROF.; SCIENTIFIC; & TECH SVCS
48079	418	4074	PLASTICS & RUBBER PRODUCTS MFG
48080	976	8749	FOOD SVCS & DRINKING PLACES
48081	636	5093	RELIG.; GRANT; CIVIC; PROF ORG
48082	331	3357	UNCLASSIFIED ESTABLISHMENTS
48083	2524	38927	PROF.; SCIENTIFIC; & TECH SVCS
48084	2285	35781	PROF.; SCIENTIFIC; & TECH SVCS
48085	747	4921	EDUCATIONAL SERVICES
48088	481	5681	EDUCATIONAL SERVICES
48089	1397	20685	TRUCK TRANSPORTATION
48090	8	380	POSTAL SERVICE
48091	1104	16917	TRANSPORTATION EQUIPMENT MFG
48092	969	14264	NAT'L SECURITY & INT'L AFFAIRS
48093	866	31341	TRANSPORTATION EQUIPMENT MFG
48094	324	1919	CONSTRUCTION OF BUILDINGS
48095	272	1900	FOOD SVCS & DRINKING PLACES
48096	119	714	SPECIAL TRADE CONTRACTORS
48097	175	1079	NURSING & RESID. CARE FACILIT.
48098	810	17729	PROF.; SCIENTIFIC; & TECH SVCS
48099	19	38	ADMINISTRATIVE & SUPPORT SVCS
48101	699	7882	FOOD SVCS & DRINKING PLACES
48103	2479	24343	FOOD SVCS & DRINKING PLACES
48104	2735	24868	FOOD SVCS & DRINKING PLACES
48105	1085	16584	EDUCATIONAL SERVICES
48106	30	127	PERSONAL AND LAUNDRY SERVICES
48107	17	142	RELIG.; GRANT; CIVIC; PROF ORG
48108	1816	29206	PROF.; SCIENTIFIC; & TECH SVCS
48109	229	42367	EDUCATIONAL SERVICES
48110	3	12	DATA PROCESS'G
48111	1046	18855	TRANSPORTATION EQUIPMENT MFG
48112	7	23	MUSEUMS; HIST. SITES;& SIMILAR
48113	7	12	DATA PROCESS'G
48114	706	5076	AMBULATORY HEALTH CARE SVCS
48116	1553	16196	FOOD SVCS & DRINKING PLACES
48117	248	2095	EDUCATIONAL SERVICES
48118	636	10044	AMBULATORY HEALTH CARE SVCS
48120	243	9837	PRIMARY METAL MANUFACTURING
48121	5	9	SPECIAL TRADE CONTRACTORS
48122	261	2786	SPECIAL TRADE CONTRACTORS
48123	2	2	SPECIAL TRADE CONTRACTORS
48124	1160	28151	AMBULATORY HEALTH CARE SVCS
48125	408	3479	EDUCATIONAL SERVICES
48126	1877	34210	INSURANCE CARRIERS & RELATED
48127	877	6222	FOOD SVCS & DRINKING PLACES
48128	214	3157	EDUCATIONAL SERVICES
48130	582	6308	ELECTRONICS & APPLIANCE STORES
48131	252	3054	FOOD SVCS & DRINKING PLACES
48133	174	1314	FOOD SVCS & DRINKING PLACES
48134	475	7144	TRANSPORTATION EQUIPMENT MFG
48135	824	8678	HOSPITALS
48136	2	12	SPECIAL TRADE CONTRACTORS
48137	115	494	CROP PRODUCTION
48138	237	1499	AMUSEMENT; GAMBLING;& RECREAT.
48139	71	888	TRANSPORTATION EQUIPMENT MFG
48140	83	648	EDUCATIONAL SERVICES
48141	498	4200	EDUCATIONAL SERVICES
48143	17	124	EDUCATIONAL SERVICES
48144	372	1958	FOOD SVCS & DRINKING PLACES
48145	65	228	AMUSEMENT; GAMBLING;& RECREAT.
48146	695	5678	FOOD SVCS & DRINKING PLACES
48150	2356	42039	PROF.; SCIENTIFIC; & TECH SVCS
48151	9	23	ADMINISTRATIVE & SUPPORT SVCS
48152	1686	23002	CREDIT INTERMEDIATION & RELATD
48153	7	11	CONSTRUCTION OF BUILDINGS
48154	1077	12241	HOSPITALS
48157	32	132	FOOD SVCS & DRINKING PLACES
48158	265	1779	MISCELLANEOUS MANUFACTURING
48159	62	227	MERCH. WHOLESALERS;DURABLE GDS
48160	411	4224	TRANSPORTATION EQUIPMENT MFG
48161	1069	11138	EDUCATIONAL SERVICES
48162	941	13500	TRANSPORTATION EQUIPMENT MFG
48164	226	1516	EDUCATIONAL SERVICES
48165	271	3166	MERCH. WHOLESALERS;DURABLE GDS
48166	157	2453	PROF.; SCIENTIFIC; & TECH SVCS
48167	940	7968	FOOD AND BEVERAGE STORES
48168	367	5351	TRANSPORTATION EQUIPMENT MFG
48169	444	2283	EDUCATIONAL SERVICES
48170	2290	35490	TRANSPORTATION EQUIPMENT MFG
48173	224	1297	FOOD SVCS & DRINKING PLACES
48174	1236	20436	TRANSPORTATION EQUIPMENT MFG
48175	7	25	ADMINISTRATIVE & SUPPORT SVCS
48176	862	10550	PLASTICS & RUBBER PRODUCTS MFG
48177	7	37	SPECIAL TRADE CONTRACTORS
48178	833	4991	EDUCATIONAL SERVICES
48179	56	299	RELIG.; GRANT; CIVIC; PROF ORG
48180	1768	27495	FOOD SVCS & DRINKING PLACES
48182	495	3685	EDUCATIONAL SERVICES
48183	1186	26215	HOSPITALS
48184	771	14801	WHOLESALE ELEC. MRKTS & AGENTS
48185	1507	17153	FOOD SVCS & DRINKING PLACES
48186	623	5430	EDUCATIONAL SERVICES
48187	1391	15072	TRANSPORTATION EQUIPMENT MFG
48188	635	6706	MERCH. WHOLESALERS;NONDUR. GDS
48189	450	3062	EXEC.; LEGIS.; & OTHER SUPPORT
48190	8	39	JUSTICE; PUBIC ORDER/SAFETY
48191	62	212	ADMINISTRATIVE & SUPPORT SVCS
48192	853	9419	HOSPITALS
48193	463	5405	NURSING & RESID. CARE FACILIT.
48195	854	10790	FOOD SVCS & DRINKING PLACES
48197	1823	23246	HOSPITALS
48198	983	13324	TRANSPORTATION EQUIPMENT MFG
48201	890	54598	SOCIAL ASSISTANCE
48202	897	38165	EDUCATIONAL SERVICES
48203	971	9601	PROF.; SCIENTIFIC; & TECH SVCS
48204	689	4642	JUSTICE; PUBIC ORDER/SAFETY
48205	839	4088	EDUCATIONAL SERVICES
48206	336	1511	EDUCATIONAL SERVICES
48207	1068	20980	BEVERAGE & TOBACCO PRODUCT MFG
48208	351	3360	EDUCATIONAL SERVICES
48209	736	6960	EDUCATIONAL SERVICES
48210	608	5342	MERCH. WHOLESALERS;DURABLE GDS
48211	332	11170	TRANSPORTATION EQUIPMENT MFG
48212	964	9374	TRANSPORTATION EQUIPMENT MFG
48213	663	4745	EDUCATIONAL SERVICES
48214	547	8107	HOSPITALS
48215	357	5078	TRANSPORTATION EQUIPMENT MFG
48216	433	4593	RELIG.; GRANT; CIVIC; PROF ORG
48217	200	2249	PROF.; SCIENTIFIC; & TECH SVCS
48218	178	1591	NONMETALLIC MINERAL PROD. MFG
48219	1188	6320	EDUCATIONAL SERVICES
48220	1182	10876	EDUCATIONAL SERVICES
48221	941	5547	EDUCATIONAL SERVICES
48222	2	23	MOTOR VEHICLE & PARTS DEALERS
48223	580	3253	EDUCATIONAL SERVICES
48224	908	4472	EDUCATIONAL SERVICES
48225	473	3773	CLOTHING & CLOTH'G ACC. STORES
48226	2218	63087	PROF.; SCIENTIFIC; & TECH SVCS
48227	1214	5989	EDUCATIONAL SERVICES
48228	1182	7593	EDUCATIONAL SERVICES
48229	181	844	EDUCATIONAL SERVICES
48230	580	5033	HOSPITALS
48231	3	3	NONSTORE RETAILERS
48232	6	32	MERCH. WHOLESALERS;NONDUR. GDS
48233	2	33	POSTAL SERVICE
48234	884	9980	TRANSPORTATION EQUIPMENT MFG
48235	1121	8318	HOSPITALS
48236	1108	15956	HOSPITALS
48237	1470	11757	ADMINISTRATIVE & SUPPORT SVCS
48238	834	5729	EDUCATIONAL SERVICES
48239	1084	13631	PROF.; SCIENTIFIC; & TECH SVCS
48240	506	3022	EDUCATIONAL SERVICES
48242	110	3629	FOOD SVCS & DRINKING PLACES
48243	133	10901	TRANSPORTATION EQUIPMENT MFG
48244	2	152	SOCIAL ASSISTANCE
48265	5	120	CREDIT INTERMEDIATION & RELATD
48268	1	0	ADMINISTRATIVE & SUPPORT SVCS
48288	2	0	UNCLASSIFIED ESTABLISHMENTS
48301	496	3947	FOOD SVCS & DRINKING PLACES
48302	927	9735	PROF.; SCIENTIFIC; & TECH SVCS
48303	9	14	POSTAL SERVICE
48304	877	11914	PROF.; SCIENTIFIC; & TECH SVCS
48306	461	3134	EDUCATIONAL SERVICES
48307	1917	21800	AMBULATORY HEALTH CARE SVCS
48308	20	206	POSTAL SERVICE
48309	1146	20261	MACHINERY MANUFACTURING
48310	1072	8445	TRANSPORTATION EQUIPMENT MFG
48311	10	21	SOCIAL ASSISTANCE
48312	917	22337	TRANSPORTATION EQUIPMENT MFG
48313	902	12999	FOOD SVCS & DRINKING PLACES
48314	772	10689	TRANSPORTATION EQUIPMENT MFG
48315	1137	14169	FOOD SVCS & DRINKING PLACES
48316	711	5398	EDUCATIONAL SERVICES
48317	1159	8441	SPECIAL TRADE CONTRACTORS
48318	13	47	ADMINISTRATIVE & SUPPORT SVCS
48320	347	2326	FOOD SVCS & DRINKING PLACES
48321	3	5	TELECOMMUNICATIONS
48322	1371	9818	AMBULATORY HEALTH CARE SVCS
48323	503	3894	EDUCATIONAL SERVICES
48324	274	1740	AMUSEMENT; GAMBLING;& RECREAT.
48325	12	33	MOTION PICT. & SOUND RECORDING
48326	1593	58561	TRANSPORTATION EQUIPMENT MFG
48327	784	5708	FOOD SVCS & DRINKING PLACES
48328	1110	11450	EXEC.; LEGIS.; & OTHER SUPPORT
48329	867	6995	MERCH. WHOLESALERS;DURABLE GDS
48330	22	16	WASTE MANAGMT & REMEDIAT'N SVC
48331	800	17384	PROF.; SCIENTIFIC; & TECH SVCS
48332	10	9	MERCH. WHOLESALERS;DURABLE GDS
48333	6	223	POSTAL SERVICE
48334	2044	20752	PROF.; SCIENTIFIC; & TECH SVCS
48335	953	13474	PROF.; SCIENTIFIC; & TECH SVCS
48336	1389	15276	AMBULATORY HEALTH CARE SVCS
48340	568	5944	TRANSPORTATION EQUIPMENT MFG
48341	764	21545	HOSPITALS
48342	773	10348	WHOLESALE ELEC. MRKTS & AGENTS
48343	4	555	POSTAL SERVICE
48346	1032	8096	FOOD SVCS & DRINKING PLACES
48347	14	84	PROF.; SCIENTIFIC; & TECH SVCS
48348	507	3788	EDUCATIONAL SERVICES
48350	208	1100	MACHINERY MANUFACTURING
48353	253	1952	EDUCATIONAL SERVICES
48356	206	1178	FOOD SVCS & DRINKING PLACES
48357	367	2179	EDUCATIONAL SERVICES
48359	361	10022	TRANSPORTATION EQUIPMENT MFG
48360	289	2352	EDUCATIONAL SERVICES
48361	6	3	PROF.; SCIENTIFIC; & TECH SVCS
48362	469	3438	FOOD SVCS & DRINKING PLACES
48363	102	577	EDUCATIONAL SERVICES
48366	4	5	POSTAL SERVICE
48367	130	618	FOOD SVCS & DRINKING PLACES
48370	38	157	AMUSEMENT; GAMBLING;& RECREAT.
48371	755	5908	FOOD SVCS & DRINKING PLACES
48374	278	4434	EDUCATIONAL SERVICES
48375	1453	17120	FOOD SVCS & DRINKING PLACES
48376	15	91	POSTAL SERVICE
48377	807	14822	GENERAL MERCHANDISE STORES
48380	132	5145	PROF.; SCIENTIFIC; & TECH SVCS
48381	697	4840	FOOD SVCS & DRINKING PLACES
48382	595	5817	HOSPITALS
48383	198	1639	FOOD AND BEVERAGE STORES
48386	436	3130	BLDG MATL & GARDEN EQPMT DLRS
48387	14	32	ADMINISTRATIVE & SUPPORT SVCS
48390	1263	14227	MISCELLANEOUS MANUFACTURING
48393	1007	16419	TRANSPORTATION EQUIPMENT MFG
48401	27	62	AMBULATORY HEALTH CARE SVCS
48410	6	13	BLDG MATL & GARDEN EQPMT DLRS
48411	7	16	FABRICATED METAL PRODUCT MFG
48412	93	670	EDUCATIONAL SERVICES
48413	504	5229	FOOD SVCS & DRINKING PLACES
48414	46	164	EDUCATIONAL SERVICES
48415	390	3549	FOOD SVCS & DRINKING PLACES
48416	167	938	EDUCATIONAL SERVICES
48417	50	143	TELECOMMUNICATIONS
48418	98	539	EDUCATIONAL SERVICES
48419	58	228	EDUCATIONAL SERVICES
48420	671	4751	FOOD SVCS & DRINKING PLACES

BUSINESS DATA

ZIP CODE	2009 Total Firms	2009 Total Employ-ees	TOP INDUSTRY RANKED on 2009 EMPLOYMENT	ZIP CODE	2009 Total Firms	2009 Total Employ-ees	TOP INDUSTRY RANKED on 2009 EMPLOYMENT	ZIP CODE	2009 Total Firms	2009 Total Employ-ees	TOP INDUSTRY RANKED on 2009 EMPLOYMENT
48421	110	324	ACCOMMODATION	48628	45	188	MACHINERY MANUFACTURING	48806	48	295	EDUCATIONAL SERVICES
48422	215	1621	EDUCATIONAL SERVICES	48629	472	2953	FOOD SVCS & DRINKING PLACES	48807	18	34	MERCH. WHOLESALERS;DURABLE GDS
48423	770	6253	FOOD SVCS & DRINKING PLACES	48630	5	22	CREDIT INTERMEDIATION & RELATD	48808	113	667	AMUSEMENT; GAMBLING;& RECREAT.
48426	21	47	MERCH. WHOLESALERS;DURABLE GDS	48631	160	1242	NURSING & RESID. CARE FACILIT.	48809	322	2415	FABRICATED METAL PRODUCT MFG
48427	113	1112	FABRICATED METAL PRODUCT MFG	48632	74	256	SOCIAL ASSISTANCE	48811	166	2362	HOSPITALS
48428	141	535	EDUCATIONAL SERVICES	48633	14	55	PIPELINE TRANSPORTATION	48812	10	91	MISCELLANEOUS MANUFACTURING
48429	261	1985	NONMETALLIC MINERAL PROD. MFG	48634	136	704	FOOD SVCS & DRINKING PLACES	48813	760	7845	EXEC.; LEGIS.; & OTHER SUPPORT
48430	1369	10516	FOOD SVCS & DRINKING PLACES	48635	40	104	ACCOMMODATION	48815	59	163	EDUCATIONAL SERVICES
48432	12	26	SPORTG GDS;HOBBY;BOOK; & MUSIC	48636	23	80	GASOLINE STATIONS	48816	7	12	WAREHOUSING AND STORAGE
48433	722	5440	EDUCATIONAL SERVICES	48637	91	800	MERCH. WHOLESALERS;NONDUR. GDS	48817	222	2643	EDUCATIONAL SERVICES
48434	5	5	FOOD AND BEVERAGE STORES	48638	369	3666	PROF.; SCIENTIFIC; & TECH SVCS	48818	90	277	FOOD SVCS & DRINKING PLACES
48435	40	100	SOCIAL ASSISTANCE	48640	1574	14890	EDUCATIONAL SERVICES	48819	64	287	EDUCATIONAL SERVICES
48436	55	203	EDUCATIONAL SERVICES	48641	8	55	PROF.; SCIENTIFIC; & TECH SVCS	48820	450	2470	FOOD SVCS & DRINKING PLACES
48437	41	532	EDUCATIONAL SERVICES	48642	834	10802	SPECIAL TRADE CONTRACTORS	48821	175	1288	NURSING & RESID. CARE FACILIT.
48438	202	1179	EDUCATIONAL SERVICES	48647	267	1336	FOOD SVCS & DRINKING PLACES	48822	45	132	SPECIAL TRADE CONTRACTORS
48439	1348	20570	HOSPITALS	48649	52	182	MERCH. WHOLESALERS;NONDUR. GDS	48823	1755	22502	FOOD SVCS & DRINKING PLACES
48440	50	115	JUSTICE; PUBIC ORDER/SAFETY	48650	333	2274	EDUCATIONAL SERVICES	48824	79	2807	AMBULATORY HEALTH CARE SVCS
48441	165	1095	HOSPITALS	48651	195	960	EXEC.; LEGIS.; & OTHER SUPPORT	48825	8	153	FOOD MANUFACTURING
48442	664	4619	EDUCATIONAL SERVICES	48652	27	80	RELIG.; GRANT; CIVIC; PROF ORG	48826	8	16	PERSONAL AND LAUNDRY SERVICES
48444	429	4741	FOOD MANUFACTURING	48653	403	2977	EDUCATIONAL SERVICES	48827	366	3214	EDUCATIONAL SERVICES
48445	43	290	EDUCATIONAL SERVICES	48654	149	1217	EDUCATIONAL SERVICES	48829	165	1020	FOOD SVCS & DRINKING PLACES
48446	1347	14579	FABRICATED METAL PRODUCT MFG	48655	189	1171	MISCELLANEOUS MANUFACTURING	48830	2	1	PROF.; SCIENTIFIC; & TECH SVCS
48449	67	298	EXEC.; LEGIS.; & OTHER SUPPORT	48656	114	339	FOOD SVCS & DRINKING PLACES	48831	93	721	EDUCATIONAL SERVICES
48450	207	1356	FABRICATED METAL PRODUCT MFG	48657	229	1386	EDUCATIONAL SERVICES	48832	26	48	FURN. & HOME FURNISHGS STORES
48451	289	1798	EDUCATIONAL SERVICES	48658	294	2800	JUSTICE; PUBIC ORDER/SAFETY	48833	5	14	NURSING & RESID. CARE FACILIT.
48453	291	1881	HOSPITALS	48659	63	485	NURSING & RESID. CARE FACILIT.	48834	29	71	EDUCATIONAL SERVICES
48454	20	48	SPECIAL TRADE CONTRACTORS	48661	739	5560	FOOD SVCS & DRINKING PLACES	48835	72	450	EDUCATIONAL SERVICES
48455	291	1420	PLASTICS & RUBBER PRODUCTS MFG	48662	27	78	EXEC.; LEGIS.; & OTHER SUPPORT	48836	429	3230	TRANSPORTATION EQUIPMENT MFG
48456	30	83	BLDG MATL & GARDEN EQPMT DLRS	48667	3	26	MERCH. WHOLESALERS;NONDUR. GDS	48837	563	4360	FOOD AND BEVERAGE STORES
48457	266	1250	EDUCATIONAL SERVICES	48670	18	2189	HOSPITALS	48838	727	8007	MACHINERY MANUFACTURING
48458	504	3360	EDUCATIONAL SERVICES	48674	10	2939	CHEMICAL MANUFACTURING	48840	330	1825	EDUCATIONAL SERVICES
48460	79	510	EDUCATIONAL SERVICES	48686	1	1281	MISCELLANEOUS MANUFACTURING	48841	19	60	RELIG.; GRANT; CIVIC; PROF ORG
48461	197	1428	EDUCATIONAL SERVICES	48701	33	127	WAREHOUSING AND STORAGE	48842	574	6077	EDUCATIONAL SERVICES
48462	366	2075	ADMINISTRATIVE & SUPPORT SVCS	48703	155	985	FOOD SVCS & DRINKING PLACES	48843	1626	19884	EDUCATIONAL SERVICES
48463	116	528	EDUCATIONAL SERVICES	48705	14	25	SPECIAL TRADE CONTRACTORS	48844	10	18	ADMINISTRATIVE & SUPPORT SVCS
48464	33	141	EDUCATIONAL SERVICES	48706	1631	18768	FOOD SVCS & DRINKING PLACES	48845	15	72	CONSTRUCTION OF BUILDINGS
48465	15	59	CONSTRUCTION OF BUILDINGS	48708	1212	14107	HOSPITALS	48846	636	10182	JUSTICE; PUBIC ORDER/SAFETY
48466	40	249	EDUCATIONAL SERVICES	48710	8	1154	EDUCATIONAL SERVICES	48847	292	2266	EDUCATIONAL SERVICES
48467	137	523	FOOD SVCS & DRINKING PLACES	48720	42	203	FABRICATED METAL PRODUCT MFG	48848	162	1236	EDUCATIONAL SERVICES
48468	44	187	SPECIAL TRADE CONTRACTORS	48721	14	33	SPECIAL TRADE CONTRACTORS	48849	207	1249	FOOD AND BEVERAGE STORES
48469	84	403	ACCOMMODATION	48722	192	2212	FOOD SVCS & DRINKING PLACES	48850	164	1506	EDUCATIONAL SERVICES
48470	17	74	RELIG.; GRANT; CIVIC; PROF ORG	48723	622	7298	EXEC.; LEGIS.; & OTHER SUPPORT	48851	29	62	EXEC.; LEGIS.; & OTHER SUPPORT
48471	422	4039	HOSPITALS	48724	32	148	RELIG.; GRANT; CIVIC; PROF ORG	48852	12	40	MERCH. WHOLESALERS;DURABLE GDS
48472	40	159	PLASTICS & RUBBER PRODUCTS MFG	48725	122	635	FOOD SVCS & DRINKING PLACES	48853	21	70	JUSTICE; PUBIC ORDER/SAFETY
48473	458	3443	EDUCATIONAL SERVICES	48726	229	2418	BLDG MATL & GARDEN EQPMT DLRS	48854	715	8239	PLASTICS & RUBBER PRODUCTS MFG
48475	92	930	PLASTICS & RUBBER PRODUCTS MFG	48727	28	520	MACHINERY MANUFACTURING	48855	394	2764	TRANSPORTATION EQUIPMENT MFG
48476	27	144	BLDG MATL & GARDEN EQPMT DLRS	48728	10	28	FOOD SVCS & DRINKING PLACES	48856	37	225	EDUCATIONAL SERVICES
48480	5	49	JUSTICE; PUBIC ORDER/SAFETY	48729	11	18	POSTAL SERVICE	48857	83	404	EDUCATIONAL SERVICES
48501	11	32	HEAVY & CIVIL ENG. CONSTRUCT'N	48730	303	2075	FOOD SVCS & DRINKING PLACES	48858	1776	25250	ACCOMMODATION
48502	571	10015	CREDIT INTERMEDIATION & RELATD	48731	57	974	TRANSPORTATION EQUIPMENT MFG	48859	9	256	PUBLISHING INDUSTRIES
48503	987	16424	HOSPITALS	48732	278	3280	FOOD SVCS & DRINKING PLACES	48860	25	146	FOOD AND BEVERAGE STORES
48504	839	7239	FOOD SVCS & DRINKING PLACES	48733	46	211	EDUCATIONAL SERVICES	48861	41	121	SPECIAL TRADE CONTRACTORS
48505	632	3883	EDUCATIONAL SERVICES	48734	411	7267	FOOD SVCS & DRINKING PLACES	48862	3	1	PROF.; SCIENTIFIC; & TECH SVCS
48506	793	12552	TRANSPORTATION EQUIPMENT MFG	48735	30	83	WHOLESALE ELEC. MRKTS & AGENTS	48863	3	13	CHEMICAL MANUFACTURING
48507	1884	24344	FOOD SVCS & DRINKING PLACES	48736	1	1	POSTAL SERVICE	48864	1290	15708	FOOD SVCS & DRINKING PLACES
48509	489	4836	FOOD SVCS & DRINKING PLACES	48737	59	179	FOOD AND BEVERAGE STORES	48865	35	79	EDUCATIONAL SERVICES
48519	217	2182	HEALTH & PERSONAL CARE STORES	48738	37	88	RELIG.; GRANT; CIVIC; PROF ORG	48866	105	729	NURSING & RESID. CARE FACILIT.
48529	476	3530	SPECIAL TRADE CONTRACTORS	48739	217	1066	EDUCATIONAL SERVICES	48867	1090	10922	SOCIAL ASSISTANCE
48532	910	11754	AMBULATORY HEALTH CARE SVCS	48740	178	689	EXEC.; LEGIS.; & OTHER SUPPORT	48870	6	0	CONSTRUCTION OF BUILDINGS
48550	3	3100	TRANSPORTATION EQUIPMENT MFG	48741	62	292	EDUCATIONAL SERVICES	48871	36	205	SOCIAL ASSISTANCE
48554	2	0	MERCH. WHOLESALERS;DURABLE GDS	48742	103	959	EDUCATIONAL SERVICES	48872	241	1166	EDUCATIONAL SERVICES
48556	1	3999	TRANSPORTATION EQUIPMENT MFG	48743	13	27	FOOD SVCS & DRINKING PLACES	48873	30	195	WOOD PRODUCT MANUFACTURING
48557	1	3	AMBULATORY HEALTH CARE SVCS	48744	95	720	EDUCATIONAL SERVICES	48874	6	10	FOOD SVCS & DRINKING PLACES
48601	1223	28739	TRANSPORTATION EQUIPMENT MFG	48745	31	59	RELIG.; GRANT; CIVIC; PROF ORG	48875	320	2743	TRANSPORTATION EQUIPMENT MFG
48602	991	16587	AMBULATORY HEALTH CARE SVCS	48746	240	1359	EDUCATIONAL SERVICES	48876	103	816	EDUCATIONAL SERVICES
48603	1155	13458	FOOD SVCS & DRINKING PLACES	48747	38	103	MERCH. WHOLESALERS;NONDUR. GDS	48877	46	115	SPECIAL TRADE CONTRACTORS
48604	833	13916	FOOD SVCS & DRINKING PLACES	48748	49	264	NONMETALLIC MINERAL PROD. MFG	48878	65	500	PROF.; SCIENTIFIC; & TECH SVCS
48605	1	3	PERFORM'G ARTS; SPEC. SPORTS	48749	39	380	SOCIAL ASSISTANCE	48879	685	7267	SPECIAL TRADE CONTRACTORS
48606	1	0	RELIG.; GRANT; CIVIC; PROF ORG	48750	473	4142	PLASTICS & RUBBER PRODUCTS MFG	48880	254	2324	JUSTICE; PUBIC ORDER/SAFETY
48607	294	4754	ADMINISTRATIVE & SUPPORT SVCS	48754	25	128	EDUCATIONAL SERVICES	48881	113	840	FOOD MANUFACTURING
48608	5	2	AIR TRANSPORTATION	48755	163	2273	PRIMARY METAL MANUFACTURING	48882	13	75	EDUCATIONAL SERVICES
48609	459	3765	FOOD AND BEVERAGE STORES	48756	108	400	RELIG.; GRANT; CIVIC; PROF ORG	48883	154	994	EDUCATIONAL SERVICES
48610	57	222	MERCH. WHOLESALERS;DURABLE GDS	48757	134	1125	EDUCATIONAL SERVICES	48884	103	565	HOSPITALS
48611	224	1257	EDUCATIONAL SERVICES	48758	11	118	FOOD SVCS & DRINKING PLACES	48885	18	360	EDUCATIONAL SERVICES
48612	235	1420	MACHINERY MANUFACTURING	48759	140	1166	FOOD MANUFACTURING	48886	63	109	BLDG MATL & GARDEN EQPMT DLRS
48613	8	13	RELIG.; GRANT; CIVIC; PROF ORG	48760	11	20	POSTAL SERVICE	48888	257	2042	EXEC.; LEGIS.; & OTHER SUPPORT
48614	33	87	JUSTICE; PUBIC ORDER/SAFETY	48761	24	82	WOOD PRODUCT MANUFACTURING	48889	19	46	FOOD AND BEVERAGE STORES
48615	87	620	EDUCATIONAL SERVICES	48762	50	126	AMUSEMENT; GAMBLING;& RECREAT.	48890	62	444	PRIMARY METAL MANUFACTURING
48616	321	1877	EDUCATIONAL SERVICES	48763	304	3602	PROF.; SCIENTIFIC; & TECH SVCS	48891	64	323	EDUCATIONAL SERVICES
48617	474	4811	HOSPITALS	48764	1	1	CONSTRUCTION OF BUILDINGS	48892	135	827	EDUCATIONAL SERVICES
48618	158	1279	MISCELLANEOUS MANUFACTURING	48765	19	61	NONMETALLIC MINERAL PROD. MFG	48893	128	843	MISCELLANEOUS MANUFACTURING
48619	18	61	RELIG.; GRANT; CIVIC; PROF ORG	48766	39	216	EDUCATIONAL SERVICES	48894	56	374	EDUCATIONAL SERVICES
48620	11	28	MERCH. WHOLESALERS;NONDUR. GDS	48767	55	161	EDUCATIONAL SERVICES	48895	450	3194	TRANSPORTATION EQUIPMENT MFG
48621	68	614	TRANSPORTATION EQUIPMENT MFG	48768	263	2742	EDUCATIONAL SERVICES	48896	14	652	MACHINERY MANUFACTURING
48622	183	1385	CHEMICAL MANUFACTURING	48769	2	4	SPECIAL TRADE CONTRACTORS	48897	43	215	EDUCATIONAL SERVICES
48623	418	2718	EDUCATIONAL SERVICES	48770	83	340	EDUCATIONAL SERVICES	48901	7	58	CONSTRUCTION OF BUILDINGS
48624	586	4222	FOOD SVCS & DRINKING PLACES	48787	1	501	INSURANCE CARRIERS & RELATED	48906	1197	12639	RELIG.; GRANT; CIVIC; PROF ORG
48625	420	2426	EDUCATIONAL SERVICES	48801	599	8719	EDUCATIONAL SERVICES	48908	6	4	ADMINISTRATIVE & SUPPORT SVCS
48626	211	2048	COMPUTER & ELECTRONIC PROD MFG	48804	10	31	ADMINISTRATIVE & SUPPORT SVCS	48909	14	127	ADMINISTRATIVE & SUPPORT SVCS
48627	7	35	REAL ESTATE	48805	5	7	ADMINISTRATIVE & SUPPORT SVCS	48910	1093	15967	HOSPITALS

ZIP CODE	2009 Total Firms	2009 Total Employ-ees	TOP INDUSTRY RANKED on 2009 EMPLOYMENT	ZIP CODE	2009 Total Firms	2009 Total Employ-ees	TOP INDUSTRY RANKED on 2009 EMPLOYMENT	ZIP CODE	2009 Total Firms	2009 Total Employ-ees	TOP INDUSTRY RANKED on 2009 EMPLOYMENT
48911	1132	14133	FOOD SVCS & DRINKING PLACES	49089	24	32	SPECIAL TRADE CONTRACTORS	49287	52	173	JUSTICE; PUBIC ORDER/SAFETY
48912	1144	26452	RELIG.; GRANT; CIVIC; PROF ORG	49090	788	8115	FOOD SVCS & DRINKING PLACES	49288	49	181	EDUCATIONAL SERVICES
48913	26	4557	ADMIN. HUMAN RESOURCE PROGRAMS	49091	828	10538	EDUCATIONAL SERVICES	49289	10	69	CHEMICAL MANUFACTURING
48915	179	8054	HOSPITALS	49092	77	761	GENERAL MERCHANDISE STORES	49301	529	3954	ADMINISTRATIVE & SUPPORT SVCS
48917	1691	37987	INSURANCE CARRIERS & RELATED	49093	782	8268	TRANSPORTATION EQUIPMENT MFG	49302	158	1204	MERCH. WHOLESALERS;DURABLE GDS
48918	10	144	EXEC.; LEGIS.; & OTHER SUPPORT	49094	136	626	EDUCATIONAL SERVICES	49303	23	135	MERCH. WHOLESALERS;NONDUR. GDS
48919	1	310	PUBLISHING INDUSTRIES	49095	37	133	ACCOMMODATION	49304	253	1541	AMBULATORY HEALTH CARE SVCS
48922	6	1005	EXEC.; LEGIS.; & OTHER SUPPORT	49096	71	406	EDUCATIONAL SERVICES	49305	62	213	FOOD SVCS & DRINKING PLACES
48924	3	810	POSTAL SERVICE	49097	284	2437	PLASTICS & RUBBER PRODUCTS MFG	49306	281	2618	EDUCATIONAL SERVICES
48933	1072	29592	EDUCATIONAL SERVICES	49098	200	1864	MOTOR VEHICLE & PARTS DEALERS	49307	832	8498	FOOD SVCS & DRINKING PLACES
48951	2	1325	INSURANCE CARRIERS & RELATED	49099	186	2182	MISCELLANEOUS STORE RETAILERS	49309	31	73	OTHER INFORMATION SERVICES
49001	1042	21892	CHEMICAL MANUFACTURING	49101	112	452	MACHINERY MANUFACTURING	49310	81	342	EDUCATIONAL SERVICES
49002	1167	18879	MISCELLANEOUS MANUFACTURING	49102	44	829	AMBULATORY HEALTH CARE SVCS	49311	4	11	GASOLINE STATIONS
49003	14	111	ADMINISTRATIVE & SUPPORT SVCS	49103	351	2855	EDUCATIONAL SERVICES	49312	6	12	FOOD MANUFACTURING
49004	348	3635	MERCH. WHOLESALERS;DURABLE GDS	49104	14	1172	EDUCATIONAL SERVICES	49314	10	63	MERCH. WHOLESALERS;DURABLE GDS
49005	2	1	ADMINISTRATIVE & SUPPORT SVCS	49106	217	3272	UTILITIES	49315	701	10118	MERCH. WHOLESALERS;NONDUR. GDS
49006	490	5433	EDUCATIONAL SERVICES	49107	297	2106	RELIG.; GRANT; CIVIC; PROF ORG	49316	647	9617	UNCLASSIFIED ESTABLISHMENTS
49007	1279	23360	HOSPITALS	49111	118	665	EDUCATIONAL SERVICES	49317	3	68	FOOD SVCS & DRINKING PLACES
49008	668	16522	EDUCATIONAL SERVICES	49112	260	1812	EDUCATIONAL SERVICES	49318	30	204	CROP PRODUCTION
49009	1326	15811	FOOD SVCS & DRINKING PLACES	49113	52	222	FABRICATED METAL PRODUCT MFG	49319	361	3002	EDUCATIONAL SERVICES
49010	661	8749	CHEMICAL MANUFACTURING	49115	12	54	EXEC.; LEGIS.; & OTHER SUPPORT	49320	9	20	FOOD SVCS & DRINKING PLACES
49011	73	296	EDUCATIONAL SERVICES	49116	36	278	REPAIR AND MAINTENANCE	49321	651	7884	FOOD SVCS & DRINKING PLACES
49012	153	1070	AMUSEMENT; GAMBLING;& RECREAT.	49117	391	2286	FOOD SVCS & DRINKING PLACES	49322	18	30	EDUCATIONAL SERVICES
49013	183	1260	EDUCATIONAL SERVICES	49119	16	222	MERCH. WHOLESALERS;DURABLE GDS	49323	194	921	EDUCATIONAL SERVICES
49014	704	9873	MERCH. WHOLESALERS;NONDUR. GDS	49120	1209	11489	EDUCATIONAL SERVICES	49325	41	181	WOOD PRODUCT MANUFACTURING
49015	1103	10421	FOOD SVCS & DRINKING PLACES	49125	107	674	GASOLINE STATIONS	49326	49	173	ACCOMMODATION
49016	21	46	ADMINISTRATIVE & SUPPORT SVCS	49126	40	327	MERCH. WHOLESALERS;DURABLE GDS	49327	198	1772	MERCH. WHOLESALERS;NONDUR. GDS
49017	735	10061	HOSPITALS	49127	382	3497	FOOD SVCS & DRINKING PLACES	49328	108	575	MACHINERY MANUFACTURING
49019	8	47	AMBULATORY HEALTH CARE SVCS	49128	174	1715	EXEC.; LEGIS.; & OTHER SUPPORT	49329	218	1581	RELIG.; GRANT; CIVIC; PROF ORG
49020	4	16	FOOD SVCS & DRINKING PLACES	49129	56	252	FOOD SVCS & DRINKING PLACES	49330	116	991	SPECIAL TRADE CONTRACTORS
49021	123	526	EDUCATIONAL SERVICES	49130	57	543	RELIG.; GRANT; CIVIC; PROF ORG	49331	519	3995	EDUCATIONAL SERVICES
49022	1455	25273	RELIG.; GRANT; CIVIC; PROF ORG	49201	1501	31395	PROF.; SCIENTIFIC; & TECH SVCS	49332	98	421	MOTOR VEHICLE & PARTS DEALERS
49023	8	21	RELIG.; GRANT; CIVIC; PROF ORG	49202	1284	15968	FOOD SVCS & DRINKING PLACES	49333	259	1864	EDUCATIONAL SERVICES
49024	1092	11073	AMBULATORY HEALTH CARE SVCS	49203	1157	11725	FABRICATED METAL PRODUCT MFG	49335	24	136	SPECIAL TRADE CONTRACTORS
49026	78	755	CROP PRODUCTION	49204	11	27	PERFORM'G ARTS; SPEC. SPORTS	49336	72	423	EDUCATIONAL SERVICES
49027	5	2	POSTAL SERVICE	49220	99	578	EDUCATIONAL SERVICES	49337	365	2605	TRANSPORTATION EQUIPMENT MFG
49028	152	1416	TRANSPORTATION EQUIPMENT MFG	49221	1515	20808	EDUCATIONAL SERVICES	49338	51	271	RELIG.; GRANT; CIVIC; PROF ORG
49029	32	70	JUSTICE; PUBIC ORDER/SAFETY	49224	419	4586	EDUCATIONAL SERVICES	49339	37	167	PERFORM'G ARTS; SPEC. SPORTS
49030	63	303	EDUCATIONAL SERVICES	49227	38	76	MISCELLANEOUS STORE RETAILERS	49340	106	6864	SECURITIES/COMMODITY CONTRACTS
49031	274	2426	JUSTICE; PUBIC ORDER/SAFETY	49228	252	2170	MISCELLANEOUS MANUFACTURING	49341	1023	7237	EDUCATIONAL SERVICES
49032	177	1783	EDUCATIONAL SERVICES	49229	70	257	EDUCATIONAL SERVICES	49342	30	62	GENERAL MERCHANDISE STORES
49033	18	29	SPECIAL TRADE CONTRACTORS	49230	380	2128	FOOD SVCS & DRINKING PLACES	49343	111	395	EDUCATIONAL SERVICES
49034	73	447	EDUCATIONAL SERVICES	49232	55	264	EDUCATIONAL SERVICES	49344	74	324	FOOD AND BEVERAGE STORES
49035	4	8	FOOD AND BEVERAGE STORES	49233	62	285	EDUCATIONAL SERVICES	49345	418	4552	EDUCATIONAL SERVICES
49036	1089	11855	MERCH. WHOLESALERS;DURABLE GDS	49234	109	874	EDUCATIONAL SERVICES	49346	113	763	FOOD AND BEVERAGE STORES
49037	785	18357	TRANSPORTATION EQUIPMENT MFG	49235	44	77	CROP PRODUCTION	49347	24	46	ADMINISTRATIVE & SUPPORT SVCS
49038	358	5688	RELIG.; GRANT; CIVIC; PROF ORG	49236	189	2063	NONMETALLIC MINERAL PROD. MFG	49348	410	4709	EDUCATIONAL SERVICES
49040	102	787	MACHINERY MANUFACTURING	49237	114	672	EDUCATIONAL SERVICES	49349	253	2151	EDUCATIONAL SERVICES
49041	32	113	FOOD SVCS & DRINKING PLACES	49238	56	220	CROP PRODUCTION	49351	4	4000	LEATHER & ALLIED PRODUCT MFG
49042	143	1720	EDUCATIONAL SERVICES	49239	5	2	REPAIR AND MAINTENANCE	49355	7	18510	PROF.; SCIENTIFIC; & TECH SVCS
49043	50	507	EDUCATIONAL SERVICES	49240	235	1110	MACHINERY MANUFACTURING	49401	344	3053	FOOD SVCS & DRINKING PLACES
49045	170	1083	EDUCATIONAL SERVICES	49241	60	252	EDUCATIONAL SERVICES	49402	39	74	ACCOMMODATION
49046	253	1403	EDUCATIONAL SERVICES	49242	697	7294	EDUCATIONAL SERVICES	49403	58	467	CROP PRODUCTION
49047	574	6083	ADMINISTRATIVE & SUPPORT SVCS	49245	140	1241	FABRICATED METAL PRODUCT MFG	49404	359	12437	TRUCK TRANSPORTATION
49048	978	17293	HOSPITALS	49246	73	567	EDUCATIONAL SERVICES	49405	41	280	EDUCATIONAL SERVICES
49050	42	136	EDUCATIONAL SERVICES	49247	200	1625	FABRICATED METAL PRODUCT MFG	49406	121	758	FOOD SVCS & DRINKING PLACES
49051	42	191	JUSTICE; PUBIC ORDER/SAFETY	49248	25	48	WAREHOUSING AND STORAGE	49408	237	1415	EDUCATIONAL SERVICES
49052	22	103	CROP PRODUCTION	49249	66	189	FOOD SVCS & DRINKING PLACES	49409	48	374	FOOD AND BEVERAGE STORES
49053	193	2631	TRANSPORTATION EQUIPMENT MFG	49250	270	2771	FABRICATED METAL PRODUCT MFG	49410	40	115	WOOD PRODUCT MANUFACTURING
49055	177	1098	SPORTG GDS;HOBBY;BOOK; & MUSIC	49251	166	1054	FABRICATED METAL PRODUCT MFG	49411	37	260	PRINT'G & RELATED SUPP'T ACT'S
49056	50	687	MERCH. WHOLESALERS;NONDUR. GDS	49252	140	2288	ELECT'L EQPMT; APP; & COMP MFG	49412	561	6323	MERCH. WHOLESALERS;NONDUR. GDS
49057	199	1458	EDUCATIONAL SERVICES	49253	83	284	MOTOR VEHICLE & PARTS DEALERS	49415	208	1718	PRIMARY METAL MANUFACTURING
49058	752	7661	HOSPITALS	49254	149	1329	EDUCATIONAL SERVICES	49416	9	17	FOOD SVCS & DRINKING PLACES
49060	58	610	EDUCATIONAL SERVICES	49255	23	52	CROP PRODUCTION	49417	1462	17551	EDUCATIONAL SERVICES
49061	43	299	ACCOMMODATION	49256	124	933	RELIG.; GRANT; CIVIC; PROF ORG	49418	1408	17128	FOOD SVCS & DRINKING PLACES
49062	2	4	FOOD AND BEVERAGE STORES	49257	3	2	FABRICATED METAL PRODUCT MFG	49419	212	1362	SPECIAL TRADE CONTRACTORS
49063	2	1	RELIG.; GRANT; CIVIC; PROF ORG	49258	8	42	FABRICATED METAL PRODUCT MFG	49420	331	3222	MERCH. WHOLESALERS;NONDUR. GDS
49064	92	1320	EDUCATIONAL SERVICES	49259	67	168	EXEC.; LEGIS.; & OTHER SUPPORT	49421	122	576	EDUCATIONAL SERVICES
49065	158	1557	FOOD MANUFACTURING	49261	54	553	EDUCATIONAL SERVICES	49422	11	138	REAL ESTATE
49066	19	44	FOOD AND BEVERAGE STORES	49262	58	285	EDUCATIONAL SERVICES	49423	2021	32662	MERCH. WHOLESALERS;DURABLE GDS
49067	136	551	EDUCATIONAL SERVICES	49263	5	13	EXEC.; LEGIS.; & OTHER SUPPORT	49424	1632	21237	EDUCATIONAL SERVICES
49068	736	7469	TRANSPORTATION EQUIPMENT MFG	49264	35	301	SOCIAL ASSISTANCE	49425	70	492	EDUCATIONAL SERVICES
49070	78	441	EDUCATIONAL SERVICES	49265	182	1350	EDUCATIONAL SERVICES	49426	867	7686	EDUCATIONAL SERVICES
49071	263	2255	PLASTICS & RUBBER PRODUCTS MFG	49266	65	164	FABRICATED METAL PRODUCT MFG	49427	17	167	FOOD SVCS & DRINKING PLACES
49072	109	1524	TRANSPORTATION EQUIPMENT MFG	49267	170	2111	AMUSEMENT; GAMBLING;& RECREAT.	49428	848	7911	EDUCATIONAL SERVICES
49073	106	599	FOOD SVCS & DRINKING PLACES	49268	20	86	JUSTICE; PUBIC ORDER/SAFETY	49429	4	21	PAPER MANUFACTURING
49074	4	103	RELIG.; GRANT; CIVIC; PROF ORG	49269	119	1588	TRANSPORTATION EQUIPMENT MFG	49430	2	72	NURSING & RESID. CARE FACILIT.
49075	15	49	MERCH. WHOLESALERS;NONDUR. GDS	49270	130	880	EDUCATIONAL SERVICES	49431	917	9798	FOOD SVCS & DRINKING PLACES
49076	90	693	EDUCATIONAL SERVICES	49271	53	148	EDUCATIONAL SERVICES	49434	9	117	FOOD SVCS & DRINKING PLACES
49077	59	109	FOOD SVCS & DRINKING PLACES	49272	50	157	JUSTICE; PUBIC ORDER/SAFETY	49435	136	873	BLDG MATL & GARDEN EQPMT DLRS
49078	280	4293	EDUCATIONAL SERVICES	49274	88	587	EDUCATIONAL SERVICES	49436	81	475	ACCOMMODATION
49079	591	6930	HOSPITALS	49276	15	88	PROF.; SCIENTIFIC; & TECH SVCS	49437	225	1296	EDUCATIONAL SERVICES
49080	549	6146	FOOD MANUFACTURING	49277	48	180	MISCELLANEOUS MANUFACTURING	49440	278	3392	EXEC.; LEGIS.; & OTHER SUPPORT
49081	16	36	SPECIAL TRADE CONTRACTORS	49279	26	123	EDUCATIONAL SERVICES	49441	1238	15167	EDUCATIONAL SERVICES
49082	165	1281	EDUCATIONAL SERVICES	49281	9	71	FABRICATED METAL PRODUCT MFG	49442	1145	14542	EDUCATIONAL SERVICES
49083	301	2055	SPECIAL TRADE CONTRACTORS	49282	11	99	ACCOMMODATION	49443	5	4	SPECIAL TRADE CONTRACTORS
49084	6	101	MISCELLANEOUS MANUFACTURING	49283	120	1439	EDUCATIONAL SERVICES	49444	1270	16348	HOSPITALS
49085	1299	21678	HOSPITALS	49284	81	460	EDUCATIONAL SERVICES	49445	603	5742	MERCH. WHOLESALERS;NONDUR. GDS
49087	231	1501	FOOD SVCS & DRINKING PLACES	49285	207	1144	EDUCATIONAL SERVICES	49446	72	585	FOOD MANUFACTURING
49088	79	315	EDUCATIONAL SERVICES	49286	527	4695	FOOD SVCS & DRINKING PLACES	49448	134	1826	MOTOR VEHICLE & PARTS DEALERS

BUSINESS DATA

ZIP CODE	2009 Total Firms	2009 Total Employees	TOP INDUSTRY RANKED on 2009 EMPLOYMENT	ZIP CODE	2009 Total Firms	2009 Total Employees	TOP INDUSTRY RANKED on 2009 EMPLOYMENT	ZIP CODE	2009 Total Firms	2009 Total Employees	TOP INDUSTRY RANKED on 2009 EMPLOYMENT
49449	153	713	FOOD SVCS & DRINKING PLACES	49664	89	490	EDUCATIONAL SERVICES	49795	69	519	FABRICATED METAL PRODUCT MFG
49450	55	279	FOOD AND BEVERAGE STORES	49665	131	565	EDUCATIONAL SERVICES	49796	31	96	REPAIR AND MAINTENANCE
49451	146	1158	PRIMARY METAL MANUFACTURING	49666	7	4	FOOD AND BEVERAGE STORES	49797	22	83	FOOD AND BEVERAGE STORES
49452	46	1184	ANIMAL PRODUCTION	49667	27	79	CONSTRUCTION OF BUILDINGS	49799	73	238	ADMINISTRATIVE & SUPPORT SVCS
49453	276	1613	FOOD SVCS & DRINKING PLACES	49668	151	850	EDUCATIONAL SERVICES	49801	843	9892	HOSPITALS
49454	178	951	EDUCATIONAL SERVICES	49670	121	488	ACCOMMODATION	49802	275	3389	MERCH. WHOLESALERS;DURABLE GDS
49455	222	1683	MERCH. WHOLESALERS;NONDUR. GDS	49673	8	4	MERCH. WHOLESALERS;NONDUR. GDS	49805	10	17	GASOLINE STATIONS
49456	560	6588	FURNITURE & RELATED PROD. MFG	49674	10	55	FOOD SVCS & DRINKING PLACES	49806	29	69	ACCOMMODATION
49457	158	810	ACCOMMODATION	49675	81	472	EDUCATIONAL SERVICES	49807	79	330	WASTE MANAGMT & REMEDIAT'N SVC
49458	12	60	FOOD SVCS & DRINKING PLACES	49676	97	271	FOOD AND BEVERAGE STORES	49808	24	311	ACCOMMODATION
49459	56	699	MERCH. WHOLESALERS;NONDUR. GDS	49677	307	3179	FOOD MANUFACTURING	49812	46	259	WOOD PRODUCT MANUFACTURING
49460	219	1491	JUSTICE; PUBIC ORDER/SAFETY	49679	32	99	MUSEUMS; HIST. SITES;& SIMILAR	49814	38	147	AMUSEMENT; GAMBLING;& RECREAT.
49461	357	3046	EDUCATIONAL SERVICES	49680	58	215	SUPPORT ACTIVITIES FOR MINING	49815	20	120	RAIL TRANSPORTATION
49464	861	15053	FURNITURE & RELATED PROD. MFG	49682	323	2011	AMUSEMENT; GAMBLING;& RECREAT.	49816	46	127	EXEC.; LEGIS.; & OTHER SUPPORT
49468	7	17	PROF.; SCIENTIFIC; & TECH SVCS	49683	50	426	AMUSEMENT; GAMBLING;& RECREAT.	49817	20	87	EDUCATIONAL SERVICES
49501	26	102	UNCLASSIFIED ESTABLISHMENTS	49684	2968	32515	HOSPITALS	49818	20	78	CROP PRODUCTION
49502	3	2	REPAIR AND MAINTENANCE	49685	22	43	PUBLISHING INDUSTRIES	49819	6	14	EDUCATIONAL SERVICES
49503	3093	82579	HOSPITALS	49686	2183	21156	EDUCATIONAL SERVICES	49820	76	173	ACCOMMODATION
49504	1329	15455	MERCH. WHOLESALERS;DURABLE GDS	49688	57	352	BROADCASTING	49821	25	53	WOOD PRODUCT MANUFACTURING
49505	846	12177	MACHINERY MANUFACTURING	49689	90	268	FOOD AND BEVERAGE STORES	49822	8	14	HEALTH & PERSONAL CARE STORES
49506	937	24857	HOSPITALS	49690	292	3090	AMUSEMENT; GAMBLING;& RECREAT.	49825	12	77	EDUCATIONAL SERVICES
49507	936	8981	MERCH. WHOLESALERS;DURABLE GDS	49696	10	36	SPECIAL TRADE CONTRACTORS	49826	7	10	FOOD AND BEVERAGE STORES
49508	1204	12514	FOOD AND BEVERAGE STORES	49701	263	2211	FOOD SVCS & DRINKING PLACES	49827	44	176	EDUCATIONAL SERVICES
49509	956	13555	FOOD AND BEVERAGE STORES	49705	14	201	PRIMARY METAL MANUFACTURING	49829	1147	12876	PAPER MANUFACTURING
49510	3	0	ADMINISTRATIVE & SUPPORT SVCS	49706	179	713	SPECIAL TRADE CONTRACTORS	49831	27	150	EDUCATIONAL SERVICES
49512	1846	44614	MERCH. WHOLESALERS;DURABLE GDS	49707	1257	12307	HOSPITALS	49833	7	13	FOOD AND BEVERAGE STORES
49514	7	9	SPECIAL TRADE CONTRACTORS	49709	173	854	REAL ESTATE	49834	5	9	MISCELLANEOUS STORE RETAILERS
49515	9	8	ADMINISTRATIVE & SUPPORT SVCS	49710	23	32	ACCOMMODATION	49835	30	62	MUSEUMS; HIST. SITES;& SIMILAR
49516	9	15	SUPPORT ACTIVITIES: AGR./FOR.	49711	1	1	RELIG.; GRANT; CIVIC; PROF ORG	49836	34	63	CONSTRUCTION OF BUILDINGS
49518	10	12	REAL ESTATE	49712	385	2889	PLASTICS & RUBBER PRODUCTS MFG	49837	311	2797	REPAIR AND MAINTENANCE
49519	739	10340	HOSPITALS	49713	106	516	AMUSEMENT; GAMBLING;& RECREAT.	49838	20	33	ACCOMMODATION
49523	2	2	REAL ESTATE	49715	96	1516	ACCOMMODATION	49839	55	168	EDUCATIONAL SERVICES
49525	1384	14773	EDUCATIONAL SERVICES	49716	40	81	AMUSEMENT; GAMBLING;& RECREAT.	49840	33	216	MINING (EXCEPT OIL AND GAS)
49528	2	2	ADMINISTRATIVE & SUPPORT SVCS	49717	6	6	POSTAL SERVICE	49841	232	1469	EDUCATIONAL SERVICES
49530	2	376	PUBLISHING INDUSTRIES	49718	31	76	RELIG.; GRANT; CIVIC; PROF ORG	49845	16	2478	FOOD SVCS & DRINKING PLACES
49534	814	11292	MERCH. WHOLESALERS;NONDUR. GDS	49719	121	770	EDUCATIONAL SERVICES	49847	29	211	WOOD PRODUCT MANUFACTURING
49544	655	16286	PROF.; SCIENTIFIC; & TECH SVCS	49720	657	5575	FOOD SVCS & DRINKING PLACES	49848	8	44	MERCH. WHOLESALERS;DURABLE GDS
49546	2176	24130	AMBULATORY HEALTH CARE SVCS	49721	771	5360	GENERAL MERCHANDISE STORES	49849	425	5553	MINING (EXCEPT OIL AND GAS)
49548	1572	28547	TRANSPORTATION EQUIPMENT MFG	49722	18	49	CONSTRUCTION OF BUILDINGS	49852	3	9	GASOLINE STATIONS
49550	4	0	MISCELLANEOUS STORE RETAILERS	49723	7	43	FOOD SVCS & DRINKING PLACES	49853	41	111	ACCOMMODATION
49560	7	560	RELIG.; GRANT; CIVIC; PROF ORG	49724	28	107	UTILITIES	49854	354	2806	AMUSEMENT; GAMBLING;& RECREAT.
49588	1	0	AMBULATORY HEALTH CARE SVCS	49725	60	267	EDUCATIONAL SERVICES	49855	1750	20863	HOSPITALS
49601	1138	16440	EDUCATIONAL SERVICES	49726	115	621	ACCOMMODATION	49858	521	5511	EDUCATIONAL SERVICES
49610	36	1809	ACCOMMODATION	49727	260	2370	PRIMARY METAL MANUFACTURING	49861	34	95	JUSTICE; PUBIC ORDER/SAFETY
49611	22	32	OTHER INFORMATION SERVICES	49728	21	59	FOOD SVCS & DRINKING PLACES	49862	317	2611	JUSTICE; PUBIC ORDER/SAFETY
49612	58	177	BLDG MATL & GARDEN EQPMT DLRS	49729	60	339	FOOD SVCS & DRINKING PLACES	49863	6	17	MACHINERY MANUFACTURING
49613	40	157	AMUSEMENT; GAMBLING;& RECREAT.	49730	89	265	MERCH. WHOLESALERS;NONDUR. GDS	49864	4	2	POSTAL SERVICE
49614	124	635	EDUCATIONAL SERVICES	49733	47	144	JUSTICE; PUBIC ORDER/SAFETY	49866	312	2829	EDUCATIONAL SERVICES
49615	351	2655	ACCOMMODATION	49734	8	17	PROF.; SCIENTIFIC; & TECH SVCS	49868	333	3093	HOSPITALS
49616	127	1198	MISCELLANEOUS MANUFACTURING	49735	1249	11947	FOOD SVCS & DRINKING PLACES	49870	176	1415	EDUCATIONAL SERVICES
49617	220	1000	EXEC.; LEGIS.; & OTHER SUPPORT	49736	22	53	EXEC.; LEGIS.; & OTHER SUPPORT	49871	12	735	MINING (EXCEPT OIL AND GAS)
49618	14	87	EXEC.; LEGIS.; & OTHER SUPPORT	49738	571	5195	HOSPITALS	49872	8	22	EXEC.; LEGIS.; & OTHER SUPPORT
49619	35	231	EDUCATIONAL SERVICES	49740	534	4585	FOOD SVCS & DRINKING PLACES	49873	4	8	FOOD SVCS & DRINKING PLACES
49620	98	312	EDUCATIONAL SERVICES	49743	15	34	FOOD MANUFACTURING	49874	52	511	NURSING & RESID. CARE FACILIT.
49621	105	287	SPECIAL TRADE CONTRACTORS	49744	25	109	EDUCATIONAL SERVICES	49876	40	858	MERCH. WHOLESALERS;DURABLE GDS
49622	126	883	MERCH. WHOLESALERS;DURABLE GDS	49745	36	85	AMUSEMENT; GAMBLING;& RECREAT.	49877	1	0	EXEC.; LEGIS.; & OTHER SUPPORT
49623	18	44	FOOD SVCS & DRINKING PLACES	49746	140	1069	EDUCATIONAL SERVICES	49878	96	488	WOOD PRODUCT MANUFACTURING
49625	45	148	MERCH. WHOLESALERS;NONDUR. GDS	49747	70	156	FOOD SVCS & DRINKING PLACES	49879	50	182	EDUCATIONAL SERVICES
49626	7	7	POSTAL SERVICE	49748	12	15	ACCOMMODATION	49880	27	114	EDUCATIONAL SERVICES
49627	19	114	EXEC.; LEGIS.; & OTHER SUPPORT	49749	258	1244	FOOD SVCS & DRINKING PLACES	49881	19	285	WOOD PRODUCT MANUFACTURING
49628	22	82	FOOD SVCS & DRINKING PLACES	49751	54	141	SUPPORT ACTIVITIES FOR MINING	49883	19	57	WOOD PRODUCT MANUFACTURING
49629	241	1395	FOOD SVCS & DRINKING PLACES	49752	28	74	FOOD SVCS & DRINKING PLACES	49884	21	105	JUSTICE; PUBIC ORDER/SAFETY
49630	120	474	CROP PRODUCTION	49753	50	165	EDUCATIONAL SERVICES	49885	51	114	ADMINISTRATIVE & SUPPORT SVCS
49631	206	1579	FOOD MANUFACTURING	49755	49	214	ADMINISTRATIVE & SUPPORT SVCS	49886	27	230	FORESTRY AND LOGGING
49632	41	161	FOOD AND BEVERAGE STORES	49756	179	1346	REPAIR AND MAINTENANCE	49887	121	642	NURSING & RESID. CARE FACILIT.
49633	95	320	EDUCATIONAL SERVICES	49757	188	2288	ACCOMMODATION	49891	42	94	FOOD MANUFACTURING
49634	6	389	MERCH. WHOLESALERS;NONDUR. GDS	49759	52	152	BLDG MATL & GARDEN EQPMT DLRS	49892	40	152	MISCELLANEOUS STORE RETAILERS
49635	200	1697	HOSPITALS	49760	30	51	FOOD SVCS & DRINKING PLACES	49893	37	97	FOOD AND BEVERAGE STORES
49636	148	1029	ADMINISTRATIVE & SUPPORT SVCS	49761	3	11	AMUSEMENT; GAMBLING;& RECREAT.	49894	17	196	RAIL TRANSPORTATION
49637	101	1486	FOOD MANUFACTURING	49762	49	154	FOOD SVCS & DRINKING PLACES	49895	40	136	GENERAL MERCHANDISE STORES
49638	17	34	ADMIN. ENVIRO. QUALITY PROGRMS	49764	12	73	AMUSEMENT; GAMBLING;& RECREAT.	49896	24	271	EDUCATIONAL SERVICES
49639	39	171	EXEC.; LEGIS.; & OTHER SUPPORT	49765	170	1186	EDUCATIONAL SERVICES	49901	9	13	EXEC.; LEGIS.; & OTHER SUPPORT
49640	106	697	MANAGMT OF COMPANIES & ENTERP.	49766	65	245	FOOD SVCS & DRINKING PLACES	49902	10	21	FOOD SVCS & DRINKING PLACES
49642	16	78	TRANSIT & GRND PASS. TRANSPORT	49768	60	208	ACCOMMODATION	49903	11	156	WOOD PRODUCT MANUFACTURING
49643	209	1529	ACCOMMODATION	49769	83	526	EDUCATIONAL SERVICES	49905	39	171	SPECIAL TRADE CONTRACTORS
49644	59	183	SUPPORT ACTIVITIES: AGR./FOR.	49770	1384	13549	HOSPITALS	49908	141	2206	ACCOMMODATION
49645	87	319	EDUCATIONAL SERVICES	49774	75	399	EDUCATIONAL SERVICES	49910	27	147	EDUCATIONAL SERVICES
49646	500	5028	SPECIAL TRADE CONTRACTORS	49775	16	20	REAL ESTATE	49911	176	1225	BLDG MATL & GARDEN EQPMT DLRS
49648	64	651	FOOD MANUFACTURING	49776	71	311	MERCH. WHOLESALERS;NONDUR. GDS	49912	67	216	FOOD AND BEVERAGE STORES
49649	241	1316	NURSING & RESID. CARE FACILIT.	49777	46	283	MINING (EXCEPT OIL AND GAS)	49913	381	2328	EDUCATIONAL SERVICES
49650	102	261	AMUSEMENT; GAMBLING;& RECREAT.	49779	290	1724	MINING (EXCEPT OIL AND GAS)	49915	42	247	PERSONAL AND LAUNDRY SERVICES
49651	346	1638	FABRICATED METAL PRODUCT MFG	49780	63	460	EDUCATIONAL SERVICES	49916	94	566	RELIG.; GRANT; CIVIC; PROF ORG
49653	95	295	FOOD SVCS & DRINKING PLACES	49781	329	2671	FOOD SVCS & DRINKING PLACES	49917	4	5	EDUCATIONAL SERVICES
49654	104	944	FOOD SVCS & DRINKING PLACES	49782	121	387	FOOD SVCS & DRINKING PLACES	49918	31	222	ACCOMMODATION
49655	72	563	EDUCATIONAL SERVICES	49783	1001	10616	ACCOMMODATION	49919	16	57	NURSING & RESID. CARE FACILIT.
49656	40	98	EDUCATIONAL SERVICES	49788	73	1843	EXEC.; LEGIS.; & OTHER SUPPORT	49920	238	1764	EDUCATIONAL SERVICES
49657	129	937	EDUCATIONAL SERVICES	49790	1	1	FOOD SVCS & DRINKING PLACES	49921	2	5	BLDG MATL & GARDEN EQPMT DLRS
49659	246	1229	EDUCATIONAL SERVICES	49791	10	20	GASOLINE STATIONS	49922	28	282	MISCELLANEOUS MANUFACTURING
49660	698	6597	AMUSEMENT; GAMBLING;& RECREAT.	49792	6	12	WOOD PRODUCT MANUFACTURING	49925	35	276	EDUCATIONAL SERVICES
49663	146	679	EDUCATIONAL SERVICES	49793	18	37	ACCOMMODATION	49927	13	40	EDUCATIONAL SERVICES

ZIP CODE	2009 Total Firms	2009 Total Employ-ees	TOP INDUSTRY RANKED on 2009 EMPLOYMENT
49929	9	55	ACCOMMODATION
49930	329	3278	HOSPITALS
49931	527	7151	EDUCATIONAL SERVICES
49934	22	237	NURSING & RESID. CARE FACILIT.
49935	336	2543	HOSPITALS
49938	477	4260	REPAIR AND MAINTENANCE
49945	88	375	EDUCATIONAL SERVICES
49946	238	1971	EDUCATIONAL SERVICES
49947	39	378	JUSTICE; PUBIC ORDER/SAFETY
49948	28	79	EXEC.; LEGIS.; & OTHER SUPPORT
49950	53	261	ACCOMMODATION
49952	3	4	FOOD AND BEVERAGE STORES
49953	245	1412	PAPER MANUFACTURING
49955	16	155	EDUCATIONAL SERVICES
49958	32	71	EXEC.; LEGIS.; & OTHER SUPPORT
49959	10	23	EXEC.; LEGIS.; & OTHER SUPPORT
49960	8	15	FOOD SVCS & DRINKING PLACES
49961	7	7	FOOD SVCS & DRINKING PLACES
49962	11	9	EDUCATIONAL SERVICES
49963	31	201	WOOD PRODUCT MANUFACTURING
49964	6	14	FORESTRY AND LOGGING
49965	23	120	ACCOMMODATION
49967	27	93	EXEC.; LEGIS.; & OTHER SUPPORT
49968	98	1033	ACCOMMODATION
49969	76	1414	ACCOMMODATION
49970	8	31	JUSTICE; PUBIC ORDER/SAFETY
49971	34	177	MERCH. WHOLESALERS;DURABLE GDS
50001	6	8	SUPPORT ACTIVITIES: AGR./FOR.
50002	84	756	EDUCATIONAL SERVICES
50003	287	2760	EXEC.; LEGIS.; & OTHER SUPPORT
50005	29	111	FABRICATED METAL PRODUCT MFG
50006	64	441	EDUCATIONAL SERVICES
50007	17	102	EDUCATIONAL SERVICES
50008	22	110	MISCELLANEOUS MANUFACTURING
50009	424	7630	PERFORM'G ARTS; SPEC. SPORTS
50010	1491	22662	FOOD SVCS & DRINKING PLACES
50011	36	7615	EDUCATIONAL SERVICES
50012	1	75	BROADCASTING
50014	476	4440	FOOD SVCS & DRINKING PLACES
50020	80	419	EDUCATIONAL SERVICES
50021	646	10559	FOOD AND BEVERAGE STORES
50022	521	5091	NURSING & RESID. CARE FACILIT.
50023	664	7883	EDUCATIONAL SERVICES
50025	234	1737	PROF.; SCIENTIFIC; & TECH SVCS
50026	14	47	MERCH. WHOLESALERS;NONDUR. GDS
50027	15	53	JUSTICE; PUBIC ORDER/SAFETY
50028	50	281	EDUCATIONAL SERVICES
50029	34	69	WAREHOUSING AND STORAGE
50031	4	5	SUPPORT ACTIVITIES: AGR./FOR.
50032	7	10	HEAVY & CIVIL ENG. CONSTRUCT'N
50033	11	48	FOOD AND BEVERAGE STORES
50034	24	225	EDUCATIONAL SERVICES
50035	95	709	EDUCATIONAL SERVICES
50036	639	7063	EDUCATIONAL SERVICES
50038	10	67	SPECIAL TRADE CONTRACTORS
50039	16	34	GASOLINE STATIONS
50040	19	63	EDUCATIONAL SERVICES
50041	7	45	SPECIAL TRADE CONTRACTORS
50042	19	33	SUPPORT ACTIVITIES: AGR./FOR.
50043	1	5	WAREHOUSING AND STORAGE
50044	23	272	EDUCATIONAL SERVICES
50046	37	89	EDUCATIONAL SERVICES
50047	154	1313	DATA PROCESS'G
50048	47	139	CONSTRUCTION OF BUILDINGS
50049	297	4418	FOOD AND BEVERAGE STORES
50050	37	95	EDUCATIONAL SERVICES
50051	14	17	CROP PRODUCTION
50052	5	8	WAREHOUSING AND STORAGE
50054	87	544	EDUCATIONAL SERVICES
50055	18	79	EDUCATIONAL SERVICES
50056	60	217	EDUCATIONAL SERVICES
50057	7	26	MERCH. WHOLESALERS;NONDUR. GDS
50058	116	932	EDUCATIONAL SERVICES
50059	1	1	REPAIR AND MAINTENANCE
50060	149	1551	AMBULATORY HEALTH CARE SVCS
50061	51	124	HEAVY & CIVIL ENG. CONSTRUCT'N
50062	8	45	EDUCATIONAL SERVICES
50063	66	638	EDUCATIONAL SERVICES
50064	4	15	WAREHOUSING AND STORAGE
50065	13	28	CROP PRODUCTION
50066	8	5	WAREHOUSING AND STORAGE
50067	9	23	FOOD SVCS & DRINKING PLACES
50068	4	4	CONSTRUCTION OF BUILDINGS
50069	42	167	EDUCATIONAL SERVICES
50070	26	186	FABRICATED METAL PRODUCT MFG
50071	55	195	EDUCATIONAL SERVICES
50072	75	502	EDUCATIONAL SERVICES
50073	19	107	SPECIAL TRADE CONTRACTORS
50074	16	23	AMUSEMENT; GAMBLING;& RECREAT.
50075	46	194	JUSTICE; PUBIC ORDER/SAFETY
50076	76	418	EDUCATIONAL SERVICES
50078	7	11	JUSTICE; PUBIC ORDER/SAFETY
50101	4	12	MERCH. WHOLESALERS;NONDUR. GDS
50102	7	9	CHEMICAL MANUFACTURING
50103	11	72	EDUCATIONAL SERVICES
50104	6	17	MERCH. WHOLESALERS;NONDUR. GDS
50105	44	277	EDUCATIONAL SERVICES
50106	35	268	EDUCATIONAL SERVICES
50107	40	329	EDUCATIONAL SERVICES
50108	12	41	ANIMAL PRODUCTION
50109	53	631	TRUCK TRANSPORTATION
50110	4	72	AMBULATORY HEALTH CARE SVCS
50111	328	3811	SPECIAL TRADE CONTRACTORS
50112	529	7707	EDUCATIONAL SERVICES
50115	202	1432	FOOD AND BEVERAGE STORES
50116	4	11	ADMINISTRATIVE & SUPPORT SVCS
50117	5	27	FOOD SVCS & DRINKING PLACES
50118	15	109	EDUCATIONAL SERVICES
50119	9	41	MINING (EXCEPT OIL AND GAS)
50120	14	17	CROP PRODUCTION
50122	72	360	EDUCATIONAL SERVICES
50123	36	170	MERCH. WHOLESALERS;NONDUR. GDS
50124	122	900	EDUCATIONAL SERVICES
50125	685	6251	EDUCATIONAL SERVICES
50126	425	3839	EDUCATIONAL SERVICES
50127	2	2	MERCH. WHOLESALERS;DURABLE GDS
50128	10	16	GASOLINE STATIONS
50129	406	2421	HOSPITALS
50130	79	510	EDUCATIONAL SERVICES
50131	642	11249	EDUCATIONAL SERVICES
50132	14	37	FOOD SVCS & DRINKING PLACES
50133	15	59	JUSTICE; PUBIC ORDER/SAFETY
50134	27	122	PROF.; SCIENTIFIC; & TECH SVCS
50135	59	291	TRANSPORTATION EQUIPMENT MFG
50136	28	87	FABRICATED METAL PRODUCT MFG
50137	10	10	FOOD MANUFACTURING
50138	467	4974	HOSPITALS
50139	26	173	SPECIAL TRADE CONTRACTORS
50140	62	995	EDUCATIONAL SERVICES
50141	42	118	EDUCATIONAL SERVICES
50142	30	246	HEAVY & CIVIL ENG. CONSTRUCT'N
50143	16	54	CREDIT INTERMEDIATION & RELATD
50144	110	940	EDUCATIONAL SERVICES
50145	4	76	EDUCATIONAL SERVICES
50146	13	15	CONSTRUCTION OF BUILDINGS
50147	28	101	EDUCATIONAL SERVICES
50148	18	18	RELIG.; GRANT; CIVIC; PROF ORG
50149	18	49	SOCIAL ASSISTANCE
50150	19	59	FOOD AND BEVERAGE STORES
50151	24	83	SPECIAL TRADE CONTRACTORS
50152	2	4	POSTAL SERVICE
50153	47	265	MACHINERY MANUFACTURING
50154	17	64	EDUCATIONAL SERVICES
50155	6	13	MERCH. WHOLESALERS;NONDUR. GDS
50156	107	732	NURSING & RESID. CARE FACILIT.
50157	30	191	MERCH. WHOLESALERS;NONDUR. GDS
50158	1250	20447	HOSPITALS
50160	18	265	EDUCATIONAL SERVICES
50161	47	200	EDUCATIONAL SERVICES
50162	26	85	HEAVY & CIVIL ENG. CONSTRUCT'N
50163	30	194	EDUCATIONAL SERVICES
50164	33	119	EDUCATIONAL SERVICES
50165	3	3	BLDG MATL & GARDEN EQPMT DLRS
50166	32	156	EDUCATIONAL SERVICES
50167	39	64	WAREHOUSING AND STORAGE
50168	20	81	EDUCATIONAL SERVICES
50169	51	533	JUSTICE; PUBIC ORDER/SAFETY
50170	92	455	EDUCATIONAL SERVICES
50171	202	1790	TRANSPORTATION EQUIPMENT MFG
50173	13	59	FOOD SVCS & DRINKING PLACES
50174	30	128	EDUCATIONAL SERVICES
50201	327	3494	EXEC.; LEGIS.; & OTHER SUPPORT
50206	29	213	NURSING & RESID. CARE FACILIT.
50207	89	721	EDUCATIONAL SERVICES
50208	806	9652	MISCELLANEOUS MANUFACTURING
50210	32	117	FABRICATED METAL PRODUCT MFG
50211	211	1463	EDUCATIONAL SERVICES
50212	149	622	EDUCATIONAL SERVICES
50213	336	3351	AMUSEMENT; GAMBLING;& RECREAT.
50214	12	48	FOOD MANUFACTURING
50216	181	1743	FOOD MANUFACTURING
50217	39	118	MACHINERY MANUFACTURING
50218	3	6	RELIG.; GRANT; CIVIC; PROF ORG
50219	611	9527	MUSEUMS; HIST. SITES;& SIMILAR
50220	340	4304	FOOD MANUFACTURING
50222	7	9	MERCH. WHOLESALERS;NONDUR. GDS
50223	13	23	EXEC.; LEGIS.; & OTHER SUPPORT
50225	77	615	EDUCATIONAL SERVICES
50226	96	687	SOCIAL ASSISTANCE
50227	2	1	POSTAL SERVICE
50228	54	515	EDUCATIONAL SERVICES
50229	23	47	SPECIAL TRADE CONTRACTORS
50230	57	306	EDUCATIONAL SERVICES
50231	14	29	BLDG MATL & GARDEN EQPMT DLRS
50232	20	126	SUPPORT ACT. FOR TRANSPORT.
50233	34	200	MERCH. WHOLESALERS;DURABLE GDS
50234	7	110	AMUSEMENT; GAMBLING;& RECREAT.
50235	16	70	EDUCATIONAL SERVICES
50236	34	309	PROF.; SCIENTIFIC; & TECH SVCS
50237	58	261	SPECIAL TRADE CONTRACTORS
50238	26	85	EDUCATIONAL SERVICES
50239	10	22	CROP PRODUCTION
50240	69	268	INSURANCE CARRIERS & RELATED
50241	13	27	SPECIAL TRADE CONTRACTORS
50242	14	43	JUSTICE; PUBIC ORDER/SAFETY
50243	4	18	SPECIAL TRADE CONTRACTORS
50244	53	457	PROF.; SCIENTIFIC; & TECH SVCS
50246	36	101	JUSTICE; PUBIC ORDER/SAFETY
50247	63	480	EDUCATIONAL SERVICES
50248	196	2463	FABRICATED METAL PRODUCT MFG
50249	78	464	REPAIR AND MAINTENANCE
50250	131	874	FOOD SVCS & DRINKING PLACES
50251	109	761	FOOD MANUFACTURING
50252	1	1	SPECIAL TRADE CONTRACTORS
50254	5	7	CROP PRODUCTION
50255	4	109	EDUCATIONAL SERVICES
50256	11	48	WASTE MANAGMT & REMEDIAT'N SVC
50257	42	253	EDUCATIONAL SERVICES
50258	50	232	TRUCK TRANSPORTATION
50259	3	11	BLDG MATL & GARDEN EQPMT DLRS
50261	38	254	EDUCATIONAL SERVICES
50262	6	9	RELIG.; GRANT; CIVIC; PROF ORG
50263	284	3258	PRINT'G & RELATED SUPP'T ACT'S
50264	6	7	POSTAL SERVICE
50265	1220	14176	INSURANCE CARRIERS & RELATED
50266	1816	37651	INSURANCE CARRIERS & RELATED
50268	24	44	FOOD AND BEVERAGE STORES
50269	8	8	RELIG.; GRANT; CIVIC; PROF ORG
50271	41	347	MERCH. WHOLESALERS;NONDUR. GDS
50272	3	4	POSTAL SERVICE
50273	367	2818	FOOD SVCS & DRINKING PLACES
50274	17	27	FOOD SVCS & DRINKING PLACES
50275	11	6	MERCH. WHOLESALERS;NONDUR. GDS
50276	62	1571	SOCIAL ASSISTANCE
50277	28	73	CHEMICAL MANUFACTURING
50278	60	176	NURSING & RESID. CARE FACILIT.
50301	5	17	SOCIAL ASSISTANCE
50302	2	1	RELIG.; GRANT; CIVIC; PROF ORG
50304	1	0	RELIG.; GRANT; CIVIC; PROF ORG
50305	7	28	RELIG.; GRANT; CIVIC; PROF ORG
50307	1	0	SPECIAL TRADE CONTRACTORS
50309	2111	50248	INSURANCE CARRIERS & RELATED
50310	1049	7755	FOOD SVCS & DRINKING PLACES
50311	603	7077	EDUCATIONAL SERVICES
50312	743	7247	EDUCATIONAL SERVICES
50313	1149	17798	MOTOR VEHICLE & PARTS DEALERS
50314	464	14263	HOSPITALS
50315	855	11011	ADMINISTRATIVE & SUPPORT SVCS
50316	504	6792	HOSPITALS
50317	937	11401	FOOD MANUFACTURING
50318	1	0	POSTAL SERVICE
50319	172	10997	ADMIN. HUMAN RESOURCE PROGRAMS
50320	392	3339	FOOD SVCS & DRINKING PLACES
50321	385	13373	TRUCK TRANSPORTATION
50322	1720	20926	AMBULATORY HEALTH CARE SVCS
50323	160	2733	CREDIT INTERMEDIATION & RELATD
50325	1045	14057	FOOD SVCS & DRINKING PLACES
50327	272	3211	FOOD SVCS & DRINKING PLACES
50328	1	2000	INSURANCE CARRIERS & RELATED
50333	3	12	PROF.; SCIENTIFIC; & TECH SVCS
50391	1	901	INSURANCE CARRIERS & RELATED
50392	7	12027	INSURANCE CARRIERS & RELATED
50395	2	420	POSTAL SERVICE
50398	5	2000	INSURANCE CARRIERS & RELATED
50401	1597	23706	HOSPITALS
50402	6	32	SOCIAL ASSISTANCE
50420	18	55	BLDG MATL & GARDEN EQPMT DLRS
50421	158	1866	FABRICATED METAL PRODUCT MFG
50423	134	1069	FOOD MANUFACTURING
50424	94	581	EDUCATIONAL SERVICES
50426	8	33	FOOD SVCS & DRINKING PLACES
50427	5	10	MERCH. WHOLESALERS;DURABLE GDS
50428	625	5098	EDUCATIONAL SERVICES
50430	23	91	EDUCATIONAL SERVICES
50431	17	31	MACHINERY MANUFACTURING
50432	21	77	EDUCATIONAL SERVICES
50433	14	21	WAREHOUSING AND STORAGE
50434	25	111	MINING (EXCEPT OIL AND GAS)
50435	35	152	MERCH. WHOLESALERS;DURABLE GDS
50436	322	8821	MERCH. WHOLESALERS;DURABLE GDS

BUSINESS DATA

ZIP CODE	2009 Total Firms	2009 Total Employ-ees	TOP INDUSTRY RANKED on 2009 EMPLOYMENT	ZIP CODE	2009 Total Firms	2009 Total Employ-ees	TOP INDUSTRY RANKED on 2009 EMPLOYMENT	ZIP CODE	2009 Total Firms	2009 Total Employ-ees	TOP INDUSTRY RANKED on 2009 EMPLOYMENT
50438	223	1966	TRANSPORTATION EQUIPMENT MFG	50569	29	66	SPECIAL TRADE CONTRACTORS	50677	539	7896	INSURANCE CARRIERS & RELATED
50439	6	67	ANIMAL PRODUCTION	50570	12	36	WAREHOUSING AND STORAGE	50680	51	246	EDUCATIONAL SERVICES
50440	31	85	JUSTICE; PUBIC ORDER/SAFETY	50571	35	64	WAREHOUSING AND STORAGE	50681	10	20	EXEC.; LEGIS.; & OTHER SUPPORT
50441	288	2770	MERCH. WHOLESALERS;DURABLE GDS	50573	12	28	JUSTICE; PUBIC ORDER/SAFETY	50682	86	699	PLASTICS & RUBBER PRODUCTS MFG
50444	21	75	JUSTICE; PUBIC ORDER/SAFETY	50574	185	1292	EDUCATIONAL SERVICES	50701	1091	16461	ADMINISTRATIVE & SUPPORT SVCS
50446	23	59	WAREHOUSING AND STORAGE	50575	44	245	NURSING & RESID. CARE FACILIT.	50702	917	16705	HOSPITALS
50447	60	268	NURSING & RESID. CARE FACILIT.	50576	18	261	FOOD MANUFACTURING	50703	916	19334	HOSPITALS
50448	32	91	JUSTICE; PUBIC ORDER/SAFETY	50577	23	83	FOOD MANUFACTURING	50704	20	67	ADMINISTRATIVE & SUPPORT SVCS
50449	26	82	MERCH. WHOLESALERS;NONDUR. GDS	50578	39	95	EDUCATIONAL SERVICES	50706	5	2	SPECIAL TRADE CONTRACTORS
50450	191	2377	MOTOR VEHICLE & PARTS DEALERS	50579	160	1007	EDUCATIONAL SERVICES	50707	192	1370	FOOD SVCS & DRINKING PLACES
50451	22	61	PROF.; SCIENTIFIC; & TECH SVCS	50581	45	178	NURSING & RESID. CARE FACILIT.	50801	533	5478	MACHINERY MANUFACTURING
50452	42	439	EDUCATIONAL SERVICES	50582	9	38	SPECIAL TRADE CONTRACTORS	50830	47	473	EDUCATIONAL SERVICES
50453	27	67	FURNITURE & RELATED PROD. MFG	50583	226	1346	EXEC.; LEGIS.; & OTHER SUPPORT	50831	8	13	FOOD SVCS & DRINKING PLACES
50454	4	8	WAREHOUSING AND STORAGE	50585	58	452	EDUCATIONAL SERVICES	50833	156	732	EDUCATIONAL SERVICES
50455	17	59	REPAIR AND MAINTENANCE	50586	18	28	CREDIT INTERMEDIATION & RELATD	50835	4	12	MERCH. WHOLESALERS;NONDUR. GDS
50456	53	380	EDUCATIONAL SERVICES	50588	622	8999	FOOD MANUFACTURING	50836	10	48	JUSTICE; PUBIC ORDER/SAFETY
50457	18	26	MERCH. WHOLESALERS;NONDUR. GDS	50590	53	339	TRANSPORTATION EQUIPMENT MFG	50837	19	62	EDUCATIONAL SERVICES
50458	90	367	NURSING & RESID. CARE FACILIT.	50591	14	30	FOOD SVCS & DRINKING PLACES	50839	3	6	MERCH. WHOLESALERS;DURABLE GDS
50459	178	1755	AMUSEMENT; GAMBLING;& RECREAT.	50592	4	8	FOOD SVCS & DRINKING PLACES	50840	28	224	FOOD AND BEVERAGE STORES
50460	9	18	FURN. & HOME FURNISHGS STORES	50593	5	10	SPECIAL TRADE CONTRACTORS	50841	220	1285	EDUCATIONAL SERVICES
50461	277	2325	TEXTILE MILLS	50594	19	30	FOOD MANUFACTURING	50842	3	5	POSTAL SERVICE
50464	27	77	JUSTICE; PUBIC ORDER/SAFETY	50595	484	7192	ELECT'L EQPMT; APP; & COMP MFG	50843	29	113	MERCH. WHOLESALERS;NONDUR. GDS
50465	28	83	MERCH. WHOLESALERS;NONDUR. GDS	50597	128	739	WAREHOUSING AND STORAGE	50845	21	106	EDUCATIONAL SERVICES
50466	86	517	TRANSPORTATION EQUIPMENT MFG	50598	50	149	FOOD MANUFACTURING	50846	35	246	RELIG.; GRANT; CIVIC; PROF ORG
50467	8	14	FOOD SVCS & DRINKING PLACES	50599	20	53	MERCH. WHOLESALERS;DURABLE GDS	50847	5	8	MERCH. WHOLESALERS;DURABLE GDS
50468	81	582	EDUCATIONAL SERVICES	50601	105	703	EDUCATIONAL SERVICES	50848	4	4	ANIMAL PRODUCTION
50469	81	381	EDUCATIONAL SERVICES	50602	121	750	RELIG.; GRANT; CIVIC; PROF ORG	50849	177	1709	NONMETALLIC MINERAL PROD. MFG
50470	19	64	MISCELLANEOUS STORE RETAILERS	50603	22	32	SPECIAL TRADE CONTRACTORS	50851	120	1287	MERCH. WHOLESALERS;NONDUR. GDS
50471	40	101	ANIMAL PRODUCTION	50604	68	536	EDUCATIONAL SERVICES	50853	56	271	EDUCATIONAL SERVICES
50472	123	966	EDUCATIONAL SERVICES	50605	8	12	POSTAL SERVICE	50854	187	1237	EDUCATIONAL SERVICES
50473	10	13	RELIG.; GRANT; CIVIC; PROF ORG	50606	30	358	EDUCATIONAL SERVICES	50857	10	18	WAREHOUSING AND STORAGE
50475	78	752	MACHINERY MANUFACTURING	50607	35	47	WAREHOUSING AND STORAGE	50858	21	97	EDUCATIONAL SERVICES
50476	46	251	AMBULATORY HEALTH CARE SVCS	50608	5	17	WAREHOUSING AND STORAGE	50859	15	36	EDUCATIONAL SERVICES
50477	15	40	ANIMAL PRODUCTION	50609	18	108	RELIG.; GRANT; CIVIC; PROF ORG	50860	6	13	MOTOR VEHICLE & PARTS DEALERS
50478	52	302	MERCH. WHOLESALERS;DURABLE GDS	50611	17	55	JUSTICE; PUBIC ORDER/SAFETY	50861	7	10	MERCH. WHOLESALERS;DURABLE GDS
50479	32	165	MACHINERY MANUFACTURING	50612	6	18	WAREHOUSING AND STORAGE	50862	3	3	GENERAL MERCHANDISE STORES
50480	62	237	NURSING & RESID. CARE FACILIT.	50613	1406	19729	FOOD SVCS & DRINKING PLACES	50863	9	7	POSTAL SERVICE
50481	3	7	MERCH. WHOLESALERS;NONDUR. GDS	50614	6	165	PERFORM'G ARTS; SPEC. SPORTS	50864	97	494	EDUCATIONAL SERVICES
50482	48	214	RELIG.; GRANT; CIVIC; PROF ORG	50616	465	5616	CHEMICAL MANUFACTURING	51001	94	1129	TRUCK TRANSPORTATION
50483	39	185	AMUSEMENT; GAMBLING;& RECREAT.	50619	100	454	EDUCATIONAL SERVICES	51002	97	455	EDUCATIONAL SERVICES
50484	32	75	EDUCATIONAL SERVICES	50620	2	7	MERCH. WHOLESALERS;DURABLE GDS	51003	87	382	SPECIAL TRADE CONTRACTORS
50501	1661	18378	FOOD SVCS & DRINKING PLACES	50621	63	710	EDUCATIONAL SERVICES	51004	47	252	EDUCATIONAL SERVICES
50510	57	404	EDUCATIONAL SERVICES	50622	105	786	SPECIAL TRADE CONTRACTORS	51005	85	478	EDUCATIONAL SERVICES
50511	528	4945	AMBULATORY HEALTH CARE SVCS	50623	2	5	WAREHOUSING AND STORAGE	51006	52	295	NURSING & RESID. CARE FACILIT.
50514	85	961	FABRICATED METAL PRODUCT MFG	50624	49	376	EDUCATIONAL SERVICES	51007	15	55	EDUCATIONAL SERVICES
50515	24	30	FOOD SVCS & DRINKING PLACES	50625	57	185	EDUCATIONAL SERVICES	51008	12	34	CREDIT INTERMEDIATION & RELATD
50516	25	57	SPECIAL TRADE CONTRACTORS	50626	53	277	EDUCATIONAL SERVICES	51009	17	40	CHEMICAL MANUFACTURING
50517	80	531	FABRICATED METAL PRODUCT MFG	50627	220	1829	EDUCATIONAL SERVICES	51010	30	51	REPAIR AND MAINTENANCE
50518	9	43	EDUCATIONAL SERVICES	50628	46	272	EDUCATIONAL SERVICES	51012	409	4040	FOOD MANUFACTURING
50519	27	136	EDUCATIONAL SERVICES	50629	84	436	EDUCATIONAL SERVICES	51014	25	83	EDUCATIONAL SERVICES
50520	8	24	PROF.; SCIENTIFIC; & TECH SVCS	50630	73	754	FOOD MANUFACTURING	51015	1	1	SPECIAL TRADE CONTRACTORS
50521	8	222	EDUCATIONAL SERVICES	50631	16	52	JUSTICE; PUBIC ORDER/SAFETY	51016	49	258	NURSING & RESID. CARE FACILIT.
50522	43	253	SOCIAL ASSISTANCE	50632	36	151	EDUCATIONAL SERVICES	51018	19	57	JUSTICE; PUBIC ORDER/SAFETY
50523	26	142	EDUCATIONAL SERVICES	50633	17	26	RELIG.; GRANT; CIVIC; PROF ORG	51019	32	122	MERCH. WHOLESALERS;DURABLE GDS
50524	29	51	MERCH. WHOLESALERS;NONDUR. GDS	50634	25	123	EDUCATIONAL SERVICES	51020	30	180	JUSTICE; PUBIC ORDER/SAFETY
50525	242	2368	DATA PROCESS'G	50635	61	299	NURSING & RESID. CARE FACILIT.	51022	34	171	ANIMAL PRODUCTION
50527	6	9	POSTAL SERVICE	50636	106	575	EDUCATIONAL SERVICES	51023	157	1405	MISCELLANEOUS MANUFACTURING
50528	16	45	WAREHOUSING AND STORAGE	50638	209	1648	MERCH. WHOLESALERS;DURABLE GDS	51024	49	412	EDUCATIONAL SERVICES
50529	45	447	MACHINERY MANUFACTURING	50641	46	153	MUSEUMS; HIST. SITES;& SIMILAR	51025	113	1007	FURNITURE & RELATED PROD. MFG
50530	74	394	ACCOMMODATION	50642	23	148	GASOLINE STATIONS	51026	51	106	MERCH. WHOLESALERS;NONDUR. GDS
50531	10	42	UNCLASSIFIED ESTABLISHMENTS	50643	117	986	EDUCATIONAL SERVICES	51027	55	321	MERCH. WHOLESALERS;NONDUR. GDS
50532	34	183	MERCH. WHOLESALERS;NONDUR. GDS	50644	476	4437	HOSPITALS	51028	104	492	EDUCATIONAL SERVICES
50533	166	1274	NURSING & RESID. CARE FACILIT.	50645	41	121	TRUCK TRANSPORTATION	51029	18	26	MERCH. WHOLESALERS;NONDUR. GDS
50535	42	121	EDUCATIONAL SERVICES	50647	75	514	FABRICATED METAL PRODUCT MFG	51030	60	307	SPECIAL TRADE CONTRACTORS
50536	281	2878	AMUSEMENT; GAMBLING;& RECREAT.	50648	193	1450	EDUCATIONAL SERVICES	51031	566	5706	FOOD SVCS & DRINKING PLACES
50538	34	333	FOOD MANUFACTURING	50649	7	29	BLDG MATL & GARDEN EQPMT DLRS	51033	18	21	ANIMAL PRODUCTION
50539	39	118	EDUCATIONAL SERVICES	50650	31	82	TRUCK TRANSPORTATION	51034	118	723	EDUCATIONAL SERVICES
50540	37	163	NURSING & RESID. CARE FACILIT.	50651	176	4090	RELIG.; GRANT; CIVIC; PROF ORG	51035	124	628	EDUCATIONAL SERVICES
50541	39	184	MINING (EXCEPT OIL AND GAS)	50652	9	20	AIR TRANSPORTATION	51036	30	120	ANIMAL PRODUCTION
50542	63	362	WAREHOUSING AND STORAGE	50653	22	34	WAREHOUSING AND STORAGE	51037	15	37	SPECIAL TRADE CONTRACTORS
50543	89	390	NURSING & RESID. CARE FACILIT.	50654	20	41	RELIG.; GRANT; CIVIC; PROF ORG	51038	42	148	CONSTRUCTION OF BUILDINGS
50544	26	91	MERCH. WHOLESALERS;DURABLE GDS	50655	36	140	EDUCATIONAL SERVICES	51039	79	442	EDUCATIONAL SERVICES
50545	5	15	RELIG.; GRANT; CIVIC; PROF ORG	50657	1	0	ADMIN. ENVIRO. QUALITY PROGRMS	51040	243	1638	HOSPITALS
50546	14	110	TELECOMMUNICATIONS	50658	96	399	EDUCATIONAL SERVICES	51041	331	4104	FOOD MANUFACTURING
50548	355	3093	EDUCATIONAL SERVICES	50659	340	3334	FABRICATED METAL PRODUCT MFG	51044	15	39	HEAVY & CIVIL ENG. CONSTRUCT'N
50551	12	15	ANIMAL PRODUCTION	50660	32	180	EDUCATIONAL SERVICES	51045	9	30	MERCH. WHOLESALERS;NONDUR. GDS
50552	13	18	FOOD MANUFACTURING	50662	353	2986	EDUCATIONAL SERVICES	51046	96	540	EDUCATIONAL SERVICES
50554	97	1171	MACHINERY MANUFACTURING	50664	12	36	MERCH. WHOLESALERS;NONDUR. GDS	51047	41	98	NURSING & RESID. CARE FACILIT.
50556	20	44	CREDIT INTERMEDIATION & RELATD	50665	107	480	EDUCATIONAL SERVICES	51048	19	63	EDUCATIONAL SERVICES
50557	40	92	JUSTICE; PUBIC ORDER/SAFETY	50666	36	135	EDUCATIONAL SERVICES	51049	28	133	MACHINERY MANUFACTURING
50558	23	65	SPECIAL TRADE CONTRACTORS	50667	21	69	MINING (EXCEPT OIL AND GAS)	51050	148	896	EDUCATIONAL SERVICES
50559	26	54	WAREHOUSING AND STORAGE	50668	63	209	EDUCATIONAL SERVICES	51051	6	20	WAREHOUSING AND STORAGE
50560	35	93	EDUCATIONAL SERVICES	50669	112	1103	CONSTRUCTION OF BUILDINGS	51052	30	162	CONSTRUCTION OF BUILDINGS
50561	23	147	FOOD MANUFACTURING	50670	84	695	MACHINERY MANUFACTURING	51053	83	478	EDUCATIONAL SERVICES
50562	31	137	EDUCATIONAL SERVICES	50671	16	36	CROP PRODUCTION	51054	161	3835	TELECOMMUNICATIONS
50563	107	576	EDUCATIONAL SERVICES	50672	26	64	PETROLEUM & COAL PRODUCTS MFG	51055	65	1220	FOOD SVCS & DRINKING PLACES
50565	14	28	MERCH. WHOLESALERS;NONDUR. GDS	50673	3	6	SPORTG GDS;HOBBY;BOOK; & MUSIC	51056	17	39	GASOLINE STATIONS
50566	21	88	WAREHOUSING AND STORAGE	50674	151	1171	TRANSPORTATION EQUIPMENT MFG	51058	64	261	NURSING & RESID. CARE FACILIT.
50567	13	22	MERCH. WHOLESALERS;NONDUR. GDS	50675	121	1068	FABRICATED METAL PRODUCT MFG	51060	26	124	BLDG MATL & GARDEN EQPMT DLRS
50568	55	406	EDUCATIONAL SERVICES	50676	96	470	EDUCATIONAL SERVICES	51061	17	75	EDUCATIONAL SERVICES

ZIP CODE	2009 Total Firms	2009 Total Employ-ees	TOP INDUSTRY RANKED on 2009 EMPLOYMENT	ZIP CODE	2009 Total Firms	2009 Total Employ-ees	TOP INDUSTRY RANKED on 2009 EMPLOYMENT	ZIP CODE	2009 Total Firms	2009 Total Employ-ees	TOP INDUSTRY RANKED on 2009 EMPLOYMENT
51062	8	22	ANIMAL PRODUCTION	51520	10	109	FOOD MANUFACTURING	52046	81	742	EDUCATIONAL SERVICES
51063	27	346	NURSING & RESID. CARE FACILIT.	51521	126	877	EDUCATIONAL SERVICES	52047	20	37	EXEC.; LEGIS.; & OTHER SUPPORT
51101	861	14227	HOSPITALS	51523	13	38	WAREHOUSING AND STORAGE	52048	11	44	JUSTICE; PUBIC ORDER/SAFETY
51102	15	47	SOCIAL ASSISTANCE	51525	42	171	EDUCATIONAL SERVICES	52049	89	553	PLASTICS & RUBBER PRODUCTS MFG
51103	422	4587	FOOD SVCS & DRINKING PLACES	51526	65	342	TRUCK TRANSPORTATION	52050	8	21	FOOD SVCS & DRINKING PLACES
51104	474	6456	HOSPITALS	51527	37	100	TRUCK TRANSPORTATION	52052	175	1498	NURSING & RESID. CARE FACILIT.
51105	400	5559	AMBULATORY HEALTH CARE SVCS	51528	37	146	EDUCATIONAL SERVICES	52053	35	113	MERCH. WHOLESALERS;DURABLE GDS
51106	949	15162	FOOD MANUFACTURING	51529	89	713	EDUCATIONAL SERVICES	52054	40	170	WOOD PRODUCT MANUFACTURING
51108	171	1858	GENERAL MERCHANDISE STORES	51530	45	139	NURSING & RESID. CARE FACILIT.	52056	11	62	EDUCATIONAL SERVICES
51109	78	497	CONSTRUCTION OF BUILDINGS	51531	79	439	EDUCATIONAL SERVICES	52057	439	4517	ELECT'L EQPMT; APP; & COMP MFG
51111	96	3932	FOOD MANUFACTURING	51532	26	71	EDUCATIONAL SERVICES	52060	429	3899	MERCH. WHOLESALERS;NONDUR. GDS
51201	346	4494	SOCIAL ASSISTANCE	51533	42	152	TELECOMMUNICATIONS	52064	44	191	EDUCATIONAL SERVICES
51230	21	54	CROP PRODUCTION	51534	284	3008	SOCIAL ASSISTANCE	52065	39	219	MUSEUMS; HIST. SITES;& SIMILAR
51231	23	85	PLASTICS & RUBBER PRODUCTS MFG	51535	133	622	EDUCATIONAL SERVICES	52066	2	4	REPAIR AND MAINTENANCE
51232	40	112	FOOD SVCS & DRINKING PLACES	51536	15	68	WAREHOUSING AND STORAGE	52068	130	2312	EDUCATIONAL SERVICES
51234	44	569	MACHINERY MANUFACTURING	51537	481	4168	NONSTORE RETAILERS	52069	124	700	EDUCATIONAL SERVICES
51235	53	173	MERCH. WHOLESALERS;DURABLE GDS	51540	9	68	EDUCATIONAL SERVICES	52070	38	138	JUSTICE; PUBIC ORDER/SAFETY
51237	91	716	MACHINERY MANUFACTURING	51541	15	30	CROP PRODUCTION	52071	16	58	FOOD SVCS & DRINKING PLACES
51238	88	643	PLASTICS & RUBBER PRODUCTS MFG	51542	20	94	ACCOMMODATION	52072	18	139	JUSTICE; PUBIC ORDER/SAFETY
51239	130	1041	EDUCATIONAL SERVICES	51543	35	118	JUSTICE; PUBIC ORDER/SAFETY	52073	32	88	SPECIAL TRADE CONTRACTORS
51240	94	550	EDUCATIONAL SERVICES	51544	43	135	EDUCATIONAL SERVICES	52074	13	18	FOOD SVCS & DRINKING PLACES
51241	78	462	FOOD MANUFACTURING	51545	14	23	ACCOMMODATION	52075	14	36	FOOD SVCS & DRINKING PLACES
51242	29	156	MERCH. WHOLESALERS;NONDUR. GDS	51546	155	955	PRINT'G & RELATED SUPP'T ACT'S	52076	124	747	NURSING & RESID. CARE FACILIT.
51243	32	141	EDUCATIONAL SERVICES	51548	10	86	BROADCASTING	52077	22	35	REPAIR AND MAINTENANCE
51244	7	11	SPECIAL TRADE CONTRACTORS	51549	18	92	MERCH. WHOLESALERS;DURABLE GDS	52078	23	106	BLDG MATL & GARDEN EQPMT DLRS
51245	107	567	HOSPITALS	51550	4	5	FOOD SVCS & DRINKING PLACES	52079	21	48	SPECIAL TRADE CONTRACTORS
51246	232	1723	EDUCATIONAL SERVICES	51551	63	359	EDUCATIONAL SERVICES	52101	740	8030	EDUCATIONAL SERVICES
51247	235	2864	FABRICATED METAL PRODUCT MFG	51552	17	46	FOOD SVCS & DRINKING PLACES	52132	75	780	EDUCATIONAL SERVICES
51248	112	706	NURSING & RESID. CARE FACILIT.	51553	33	127	EXEC.; LEGIS.; & OTHER SUPPORT	52133	13	37	SUPPORT ACTIVITIES: AGR./FOR.
51249	206	1755	EDUCATIONAL SERVICES	51554	5	30	FOOD SVCS & DRINKING PLACES	52134	19	54	GASOLINE STATIONS
51250	379	6419	MERCH. WHOLESALERS;DURABLE GDS	51555	198	1809	FOOD SVCS & DRINKING PLACES	52135	57	258	MERCH. WHOLESALERS;NONDUR. GDS
51301	802	9308	HOSPITALS	51556	18	32	BLDG MATL & GARDEN EQPMT DLRS	52136	319	3414	MERCH. WHOLESALERS;DURABLE GDS
51331	132	1242	FOOD SVCS & DRINKING PLACES	51557	30	182	EDUCATIONAL SERVICES	52140	22	91	ACCOMMODATION
51333	13	32	CROP PRODUCTION	51558	33	80	SOCIAL ASSISTANCE	52141	44	349	EDUCATIONAL SERVICES
51334	377	3393	EDUCATIONAL SERVICES	51559	46	344	EDUCATIONAL SERVICES	52142	83	705	EDUCATIONAL SERVICES
51338	56	353	EDUCATIONAL SERVICES	51560	102	1118	FOOD MANUFACTURING	52144	69	243	TRUCK TRANSPORTATION
51340	11	42	CREDIT INTERMEDIATION & RELATD	51561	33	164	PERFORM'G ARTS; SPEC. SPORTS	52146	55	171	ACCOMMODATION
51341	9	61	EDUCATIONAL SERVICES	51562	22	246	TRUCK TRANSPORTATION	52147	33	94	FOOD AND BEVERAGE STORES
51342	69	559	RELIG.; GRANT; CIVIC; PROF ORG	51563	17	21	EXEC.; LEGIS.; & OTHER SUPPORT	52149	2	0	TELECOMMUNICATIONS
51343	6	8	CROP PRODUCTION	51564	21	71	CONSTRUCTION OF BUILDINGS	52151	119	1058	MISCELLANEOUS MANUFACTURING
51345	12	132	MERCH. WHOLESALERS;NONDUR. GDS	51565	14	44	BLDG MATL & GARDEN EQPMT DLRS	52154	46	175	CONSTRUCTION OF BUILDINGS
51346	136	885	NURSING & RESID. CARE FACILIT.	51566	415	4437	FABRICATED METAL PRODUCT MFG	52155	55	193	SPECIAL TRADE CONTRACTORS
51347	73	473	PRIMARY METAL MANUFACTURING	51570	41	377	TRANSIT & GRND PASS. TRANSPORT	52156	30	76	CREDIT INTERMEDIATION & RELATD
51350	20	62	MERCH. WHOLESALERS;DURABLE GDS	51571	13	16	CONSTRUCTION OF BUILDINGS	52157	67	439	EDUCATIONAL SERVICES
51351	236	1543	FOOD SVCS & DRINKING PLACES	51572	21	53	EXEC.; LEGIS.; & OTHER SUPPORT	52158	29	206	PETROLEUM & COAL PRODUCTS MFG
51354	49	261	CROP PRODUCTION	51573	72	265	EDUCATIONAL SERVICES	52159	154	1216	EDUCATIONAL SERVICES
51355	96	1034	FOOD SVCS & DRINKING PLACES	51575	46	365	EDUCATIONAL SERVICES	52160	55	183	JUSTICE; PUBIC ORDER/SAFETY
51357	51	290	EDUCATIONAL SERVICES	51576	38	614	MERCH. WHOLESALERS;DURABLE GDS	52161	91	603	ADMINISTRATIVE & SUPPORT SVCS
51358	84	379	EDUCATIONAL SERVICES	51577	105	368	FOOD SVCS & DRINKING PLACES	52162	179	2260	FOOD MANUFACTURING
51360	569	5139	TRANSPORTATION EQUIPMENT MFG	51578	13	14	SPECIAL TRADE CONTRACTORS	52163	23	105	FOOD MANUFACTURING
51363	10	57	WAREHOUSING AND STORAGE	51579	118	834	TRANSPORTATION EQUIPMENT MFG	52164	9	14	WAREHOUSING AND STORAGE
51364	35	272	ADMINISTRATIVE & SUPPORT SVCS	51601	348	3524	FABRICATED METAL PRODUCT MFG	52165	46	108	MERCH. WHOLESALERS;NONDUR. GDS
51365	22	221	SOCIAL ASSISTANCE	51630	7	10	POSTAL SERVICE	52166	11	49	FOOD SVCS & DRINKING PLACES
51366	25	40	SUPPORT ACTIVITIES: AGR./FOR.	51631	15	88	TRANSPORTATION EQUIPMENT MFG	52168	26	105	AMUSEMENT; GAMBLING;& RECREAT.
51401	829	10005	FABRICATED METAL PRODUCT MFG	51632	335	3395	FABRICATED METAL PRODUCT MFG	52169	15	29	FABRICATED METAL PRODUCT MFG
51430	48	295	WAREHOUSING AND STORAGE	51636	23	61	TELECOMMUNICATIONS	52170	29	57	EDUCATIONAL SERVICES
51431	20	51	JUSTICE; PUBIC ORDER/SAFETY	51637	7	106	EDUCATIONAL SERVICES	52171	44	399	MERCH. WHOLESALERS;NONDUR. GDS
51432	6	57	AMUSEMENT; GAMBLING;& RECREAT.	51638	51	240	EDUCATIONAL SERVICES	52172	383	2751	EDUCATIONAL SERVICES
51433	29	87	FOOD SVCS & DRINKING PLACES	51639	27	172	EDUCATIONAL SERVICES	52175	193	1921	TRANSPORTATION EQUIPMENT MFG
51436	61	280	FOOD AND BEVERAGE STORES	51640	82	616	EDUCATIONAL SERVICES	52201	38	340	FOOD SVCS & DRINKING PLACES
51439	35	107	EDUCATIONAL SERVICES	51645	9	6	WAREHOUSING AND STORAGE	52202	40	244	EDUCATIONAL SERVICES
51440	20	72	WAREHOUSING AND STORAGE	51646	44	218	TRUCK TRANSPORTATION	52203	133	964	FOOD SVCS & DRINKING PLACES
51441	9	14	MERCH. WHOLESALERS;DURABLE GDS	51647	8	8	WAREHOUSING AND STORAGE	52204	2	2604	ELECT'L EQPMT; APP; & COMP MFG
51442	518	6645	FOOD MANUFACTURING	51648	22	184	GASOLINE STATIONS	52205	334	3392	JUSTICE; PUBIC ORDER/SAFETY
51443	69	353	EDUCATIONAL SERVICES	51649	12	42	CREDIT INTERMEDIATION & RELATD	52206	63	238	CLOTHING & CLOTH'G ACC. STORES
51444	22	67	CONSTRUCTION OF BUILDINGS	51650	13	25	MERCH. WHOLESALERS;DURABLE GDS	52207	24	31	FOOD SVCS & DRINKING PLACES
51445	223	2306	REPAIR AND MAINTENANCE	51651	3	3	POSTAL SERVICE	52208	167	1065	MISCELLANEOUS MANUFACTURING
51446	45	169	EDUCATIONAL SERVICES	51652	99	612	EDUCATIONAL SERVICES	52209	76	339	MERCH. WHOLESALERS;NONDUR. GDS
51447	15	7	HEAVY & CIVIL ENG. CONSTRUCT'N	51653	50	373	EDUCATIONAL SERVICES	52210	16	57	PRIMARY METAL MANUFACTURING
51448	35	55	FOOD SVCS & DRINKING PLACES	51654	7	8	CROP PRODUCTION	52211	158	894	EDUCATIONAL SERVICES
51449	113	1457	RELIG.; GRANT; CIVIC; PROF ORG	51656	2	1	POSTAL SERVICE	52212	20	21	POSTAL SERVICE
51450	103	770	EDUCATIONAL SERVICES	52001	1654	31491	MERCH. WHOLESALERS;DURABLE GDS	52213	121	541	MOTOR VEHICLE & PARTS DEALERS
51451	9	11	WAREHOUSING AND STORAGE	52002	734	11725	FOOD SVCS & DRINKING PLACES	52214	98	595	EDUCATIONAL SERVICES
51452	18	42	FOOD AND BEVERAGE STORES	52003	626	9773	ADMINISTRATIVE & SUPPORT SVCS	52215	20	59	JUSTICE; PUBIC ORDER/SAFETY
51453	39	123	EDUCATIONAL SERVICES	52004	21	47	SPECIAL TRADE CONTRACTORS	52216	77	385	EDUCATIONAL SERVICES
51454	84	306	EDUCATIONAL SERVICES	52030	22	102	EDUCATIONAL SERVICES	52217	28	31	FURNITURE & RELATED PROD. MFG
51455	139	1049	EDUCATIONAL SERVICES	52031	193	1303	MISCELLANEOUS MANUFACTURING	52218	39	204	EDUCATIONAL SERVICES
51458	118	487	EDUCATIONAL SERVICES	52032	35	197	REAL ESTATE	52219	12	39	MERCH. WHOLESALERS;NONDUR. GDS
51459	4	77	FOOD MANUFACTURING	52033	182	1415	BLDG MATL & GARDEN EQPMT DLRS	52220	17	50	ADMINISTRATIVE & SUPPORT SVCS
51460	3	4	POSTAL SERVICE	52035	19	116	EDUCATIONAL SERVICES	52221	9	24	SPECIAL TRADE CONTRACTORS
51461	41	293	EDUCATIONAL SERVICES	52036	2	12	GASOLINE STATIONS	52222	38	61	SPECIAL TRADE CONTRACTORS
51462	43	275	MACHINERY MANUFACTURING	52037	29	133	EDUCATIONAL SERVICES	52223	57	617	MACHINERY MANUFACTURING
51463	44	122	MERCH. WHOLESALERS;NONDUR. GDS	52038	15	40	ACCOMMODATION	52224	119	611	EDUCATIONAL SERVICES
51465	20	47	GASOLINE STATIONS	52039	22	97	TRUCK TRANSPORTATION	52225	15	49	EXEC.; LEGIS.; & OTHER SUPPORT
51466	95	431	NURSING & RESID. CARE FACILIT.	52040	310	3602	WOOD PRODUCT MANUFACTURING	52227	67	267	SPECIAL TRADE CONTRACTORS
51467	47	154	EDUCATIONAL SERVICES	52041	53	347	MACHINERY MANUFACTURING	52228	98	465	SPECIAL TRADE CONTRACTORS
51501	1040	19145	AMUSEMENT; GAMBLING;& RECREAT.	52042	75	703	MERCH. WHOLESALERS;DURABLE GDS	52229	33	47	EXEC.; LEGIS.; & OTHER SUPPORT
51502	12	33	MERCH. WHOLESALERS;DURABLE GDS	52043	222	1482	EDUCATIONAL SERVICES	52231	8	33	WAREHOUSING AND STORAGE
51503	1126	16953	REAL ESTATE	52044	4	9	PROF.; SCIENTIFIC; & TECH SVCS	52232	8	12	CREDIT INTERMEDIATION & RELATD
51510	101	1026	TRUCK TRANSPORTATION	52045	71	612	EDUCATIONAL SERVICES	52233	380	5853	ADMINISTRATIVE & SUPPORT SVCS

BUSINESS DATA

ZIP CODE	2009 Total Firms	2009 Total Employees	TOP INDUSTRY RANKED on 2009 EMPLOYMENT	ZIP CODE	2009 Total Firms	2009 Total Employees	TOP INDUSTRY RANKED on 2009 EMPLOYMENT	ZIP CODE	2009 Total Firms	2009 Total Employees	TOP INDUSTRY RANKED on 2009 EMPLOYMENT
52235	38	601	MANAGMT OF COMPANIES & ENTERP.	52535	36	109	PIPELINE TRANSPORTATION	52732	1175	16093	PLASTICS & RUBBER PRODUCTS MFG
52236	25	88	BLDG MATL & GARDEN EQPMT DLRS	52536	20	129	EDUCATIONAL SERVICES	52733	4	13	PRIMARY METAL MANUFACTURING
52237	48	220	MERCH. WHOLESALERS;NONDUR. GDS	52537	387	2377	HOSPITALS	52737	7	13	MERCH. WHOLESALERS;DURABLE GDS
52240	1595	17817	FOOD SVCS & DRINKING PLACES	52540	38	90	CREDIT INTERMEDIATION & RELATD	52738	131	2124	FOOD MANUFACTURING
52241	889	13129	FOOD SVCS & DRINKING PLACES	52542	30	124	EDUCATIONAL SERVICES	52739	15	27	FOOD AND BEVERAGE STORES
52242	132	20722	AMBULATORY HEALTH CARE SVCS	52543	4	4	RELIG.; GRANT; CIVIC; PROF ORG	52742	362	3689	MISCELLANEOUS MANUFACTURING
52243	3	2400	PROF.; SCIENTIFIC; & TECH SVCS	52544	459	4704	PLASTICS & RUBBER PRODUCTS MFG	52745	32	48	FOOD AND BEVERAGE STORES
52244	32	63	ADMINISTRATIVE & SUPPORT SVCS	52548	3	4	MERCH. WHOLESALERS;NONDUR. GDS	52746	28	75	EDUCATIONAL SERVICES
52245	454	8144	AMBULATORY HEALTH CARE SVCS	52549	14	45	MINING (EXCEPT OIL AND GAS)	52747	110	848	EDUCATIONAL SERVICES
52246	439	7475	HOSPITALS	52550	9	27	FOOD SVCS & DRINKING PLACES	52748	349	3420	PRINT'G & RELATED SUPP'T ACT'S
52247	315	1754	EDUCATIONAL SERVICES	52551	24	109	EDUCATIONAL SERVICES	52749	9	20	MERCH. WHOLESALERS;NONDUR. GDS
52248	83	486	NURSING & RESID. CARE FACILIT.	52552	20	28	GASOLINE STATIONS	52750	24	173	EDUCATIONAL SERVICES
52249	56	253	NURSING & RESID. CARE FACILIT.	52553	67	1146	FOOD MANUFACTURING	52751	44	177	JUSTICE; PUBIC ORDER/SAFETY
52251	18	48	JUSTICE; PUBIC ORDER/SAFETY	52554	50	616	EDUCATIONAL SERVICES	52752	14	40	FOOD SVCS & DRINKING PLACES
52253	117	496	MERCH. WHOLESALERS;DURABLE GDS	52555	6	11	GASOLINE STATIONS	52753	164	879	FOOD SVCS & DRINKING PLACES
52254	48	161	EDUCATIONAL SERVICES	52556	887	7780	PRIMARY METAL MANUFACTURING	52754	22	324	EDUCATIONAL SERVICES
52255	55	274	ADMINISTRATIVE & SUPPORT SVCS	52557	4	116	EDUCATIONAL SERVICES	52755	56	431	EDUCATIONAL SERVICES
52257	10	8	ADMINISTRATIVE & SUPPORT SVCS	52560	9	18	RELIG.; GRANT; CIVIC; PROF ORG	52756	62	240	EDUCATIONAL SERVICES
52301	193	1260	PRINT'G & RELATED SUPP'T ACT'S	52561	36	193	MERCH. WHOLESALERS;NONDUR. GDS	52757	23	56	REPAIR AND MAINTENANCE
52302	1035	10565	EDUCATIONAL SERVICES	52562	2	4	BLDG MATL & GARDEN EQPMT DLRS	52758	23	34	MOTOR VEHICLE & PARTS DEALERS
52305	26	37	TELECOMMUNICATIONS	52563	37	80	MERCH. WHOLESALERS;NONDUR. GDS	52759	3	5	RELIG.; GRANT; CIVIC; PROF ORG
52306	64	245	NURSING & RESID. CARE FACILIT.	52565	207	1591	MERCH. WHOLESALERS;DURABLE GDS	52760	6	205	MACHINERY MANUFACTURING
52307	23	103	EDUCATIONAL SERVICES	52566	3	4	GENERAL MERCHANDISE STORES	52761	1155	18710	FURNITURE & RELATED PROD. MFG
52308	20	93	EDUCATIONAL SERVICES	52567	21	62	EDUCATIONAL SERVICES	52765	21	87	ACCOMMODATION
52309	16	23	SUPPORT ACTIVITIES: AGR./FOR.	52568	4	3	POSTAL SERVICE	52766	26	65	BLDG MATL & GARDEN EQPMT DLRS
52310	331	3156	PLASTICS & RUBBER PRODUCTS MFG	52569	12	26	FOOD SVCS & DRINKING PLACES	52767	14	75	NURSING & RESID. CARE FACILIT.
52312	6	1	POSTAL SERVICE	52570	22	128	MERCH. WHOLESALERS;DURABLE GDS	52768	40	276	MOTOR VEHICLE & PARTS DEALERS
52313	13	29	MERCH. WHOLESALERS;NONDUR. GDS	52571	71	432	EDUCATIONAL SERVICES	52769	24	80	JUSTICE; PUBIC ORDER/SAFETY
52314	220	1592	EDUCATIONAL SERVICES	52572	46	216	EDUCATIONAL SERVICES	52772	298	2071	EDUCATIONAL SERVICES
52315	48	126	EDUCATIONAL SERVICES	52573	12	19	TRUCK TRANSPORTATION	52773	109	1043	FOOD SVCS & DRINKING PLACES
52316	72	450	EDUCATIONAL SERVICES	52574	17	87	JUSTICE; PUBIC ORDER/SAFETY	52774	8	33	GASOLINE STATIONS
52317	419	4416	PLASTICS & RUBBER PRODUCTS MFG	52576	20	68	WASTE MANAGMT & REMEDIAT'N SVC	52776	217	2402	FOOD MANUFACTURING
52318	40	365	MISCELLANEOUS MANUFACTURING	52577	788	7083	EDUCATIONAL SERVICES	52777	64	314	EDUCATIONAL SERVICES
52319	3	33	ADMIN. OF ECONOMIC PROGRAMS	52580	18	278	EDUCATIONAL SERVICES	52778	152	1690	MERCH. WHOLESALERS;DURABLE GDS
52320	58	259	EDUCATIONAL SERVICES	52581	10	34	MINING (EXCEPT OIL AND GAS)	52801	439	9285	PROF.; SCIENTIFIC; & TECH SVCS
52321	27	73	EDUCATIONAL SERVICES	52583	9	43	BLDG MATL & GARDEN EQPMT DLRS	52802	495	8056	MERCH. WHOLESALERS;NONDUR. GDS
52322	86	360	EDUCATIONAL SERVICES	52584	18	38	PUBLISHING INDUSTRIES	52803	798	15262	HOSPITALS
52323	38	66	EDUCATIONAL SERVICES	52585	39	171	TRUCK TRANSPORTATION	52804	572	6524	EDUCATIONAL SERVICES
52324	73	828	UTILITIES	52586	9	18	CROP PRODUCTION	52805	2	0	TRANSIT & GRND PASS. TRANSPORT
52325	8	15	RELIG.; GRANT; CIVIC; PROF ORG	52588	6	6	CONSTRUCTION OF BUILDINGS	52806	1208	20001	FOOD SVCS & DRINKING PLACES
52326	23	60	FOOD SVCS & DRINKING PLACES	52590	34	241	EDUCATIONAL SERVICES	52807	1105	15640	FOOD SVCS & DRINKING PLACES
52327	94	514	EDUCATIONAL SERVICES	52591	200	1554	EDUCATIONAL SERVICES	52808	5	22	SPECIAL TRADE CONTRACTORS
52328	43	283	EDUCATIONAL SERVICES	52593	4	3	POSTAL SERVICE	52809	9	27	ADMINISTRATIVE & SUPPORT SVCS
52329	26	77	MERCH. WHOLESALERS;DURABLE GDS	52594	5	9	WOOD PRODUCT MANUFACTURING	53001	56	278	MERCH. WHOLESALERS;NONDUR. GDS
52330	21	71	FOOD SVCS & DRINKING PLACES	52595	5	42	EDUCATIONAL SERVICES	53002	97	1321	FABRICATED METAL PRODUCT MFG
52332	82	254	BROADCASTING	52601	1225	14623	FOOD SVCS & DRINKING PLACES	53003	26	153	SPECIAL TRADE CONTRACTORS
52333	172	954	NURSING & RESID. CARE FACILIT.	52619	17	19	GASOLINE STATIONS	53004	115	1275	FOOD MANUFACTURING
52334	19	115	CONSTRUCTION OF BUILDINGS	52620	52	253	MACHINERY MANUFACTURING	53005	2310	27036	PROF.; SCIENTIFIC; & TECH SVCS
52335	37	65	UNCLASSIFIED ESTABLISHMENTS	52621	23	115	EDUCATIONAL SERVICES	53006	54	1171	MERCH. WHOLESALERS;DURABLE GDS
52336	87	366	EDUCATIONAL SERVICES	52623	99	470	EDUCATIONAL SERVICES	53007	328	4070	MACHINERY MANUFACTURING
52337	34	245	EDUCATIONAL SERVICES	52624	21	84	EDUCATIONAL SERVICES	53008	21	354	GENERAL MERCHANDISE STORES
52338	106	477	RELIG.; GRANT; CIVIC; PROF ORG	52625	99	614	EDUCATIONAL SERVICES	53010	248	1891	EDUCATIONAL SERVICES
52339	153	1161	EXEC.; LEGIS.; & OTHER SUPPORT	52626	55	194	EDUCATIONAL SERVICES	53011	51	190	GASOLINE STATIONS
52340	54	301	EDUCATIONAL SERVICES	52627	532	6465	MERCH. WHOLESALERS;NONDUR. GDS	53012	854	6742	EDUCATIONAL SERVICES
52341	23	54	SPECIAL TRADE CONTRACTORS	52630	16	25	ANIMAL PRODUCTION	53013	105	762	PRIMARY METAL MANUFACTURING
52342	180	1252	EDUCATIONAL SERVICES	52631	25	277	CROP PRODUCTION	53014	368	4056	FOOD MANUFACTURING
52344	9	33	FOOD SVCS & DRINKING PLACES	52632	650	9261	MERCH. WHOLESALERS;DURABLE GDS	53015	84	1104	EDUCATIONAL SERVICES
52345	61	360	EDUCATIONAL SERVICES	52635	23	60	MOTOR VEHICLE & PARTS DEALERS	53016	16	225	FOOD MANUFACTURING
52346	80	327	EDUCATIONAL SERVICES	52637	126	1473	NONMETALLIC MINERAL PROD. MFG	53017	79	261	EDUCATIONAL SERVICES
52347	110	1040	MACHINERY MANUFACTURING	52638	21	1035	FABRICATED METAL PRODUCT MFG	53018	496	4806	FOOD SVCS & DRINKING PLACES
52348	3	2	FOOD AND BEVERAGE STORES	52639	52	832	FOOD AND BEVERAGE STORES	53019	70	900	TRUCK TRANSPORTATION
52349	376	3017	AMBULATORY HEALTH CARE SVCS	52640	62	330	NURSING & RESID. CARE FACILIT.	53020	150	1452	ACCOMMODATION
52350	2	1	RELIG.; GRANT; CIVIC; PROF ORG	52641	625	9877	MERCH. WHOLESALERS;DURABLE GDS	53021	145	1327	EDUCATIONAL SERVICES
52351	35	365	TRUCK TRANSPORTATION	52644	15	62	WAREHOUSING AND STORAGE	53022	836	12604	PLASTICS & RUBBER PRODUCTS MFG
52352	36	204	EDUCATIONAL SERVICES	52645	99	599	EDUCATIONAL SERVICES	53023	31	188	TRANSPORTATION EQUIPMENT MFG
52353	497	4604	RELIG.; GRANT; CIVIC; PROF ORG	52646	11	57	MERCH. WHOLESALERS;NONDUR. GDS	53024	671	7492	MERCH. WHOLESALERS;DURABLE GDS
52354	16	28	MERCH. WHOLESALERS;NONDUR. GDS	52647	16	150	CONSTRUCTION OF BUILDINGS	53026	11	45	MUSEUMS; HIST. SITES;& SIMILAR
52355	7	7	EXEC.; LEGIS.; & OTHER SUPPORT	52648	6	157	CREDIT INTERMEDIATION & RELATD	53027	727	11170	EDUCATIONAL SERVICES
52356	150	630	NURSING & RESID. CARE FACILIT.	52649	34	78	EDUCATIONAL SERVICES	53029	920	8180	EDUCATIONAL SERVICES
52358	199	1116	SPECIAL TRADE CONTRACTORS	52650	24	86	MERCH. WHOLESALERS;NONDUR. GDS	53031	9	34	CLOTHING & CLOTH'G ACC. STORES
52359	16	41	TRUCK TRANSPORTATION	52651	36	110	EDUCATIONAL SERVICES	53032	181	3325	MERCH. WHOLESALERS;DURABLE GDS
52361	287	3697	MACHINERY MANUFACTURING	52652	8	14	RELIG.; GRANT; CIVIC; PROF ORG	53033	152	915	FOOD SVCS & DRINKING PLACES
52362	64	387	EDUCATIONAL SERVICES	52653	185	1315	PLASTICS & RUBBER PRODUCTS MFG	53034	65	633	FABRICATED METAL PRODUCT MFG
52401	775	15377	PROF.; SCIENTIFIC; & TECH SVCS	52654	88	350	EDUCATIONAL SERVICES	53035	82	539	FABRICATED METAL PRODUCT MFG
52402	2041	27725	FOOD SVCS & DRINKING PLACES	52655	332	7025	HOSPITALS	53036	121	1022	FABRICATED METAL PRODUCT MFG
52403	559	7062	HOSPITALS	52656	103	784	TRUCK TRANSPORTATION	53037	317	3474	PERSONAL AND LAUNDRY SERVICES
52404	1707	47967	TRUCK TRANSPORTATION	52657	8	35	MERCH. WHOLESALERS;NONDUR. GDS	53038	206	2747	PLASTICS & RUBBER PRODUCTS MFG
52405	449	4625	EDUCATIONAL SERVICES	52658	36	277	TRUCK TRANSPORTATION	53039	214	3608	EXEC.; LEGIS.; & OTHER SUPPORT
52406	17	57	PROF.; SCIENTIFIC; & TECH SVCS	52659	63	416	TRUCK TRANSPORTATION	53040	250	2715	FABRICATED METAL PRODUCT MFG
52408	2	2	OTHER INFORMATION SERVICES	52660	15	55	MERCH. WHOLESALERS;NONDUR. GDS	53042	252	2667	MACHINERY MANUFACTURING
52409	4	10	TRUCK TRANSPORTATION	52701	13	23	TRUCK TRANSPORTATION	53044	86	10222	FABRICATED METAL PRODUCT MFG
52410	19	86	CONSTRUCTION OF BUILDINGS	52720	17	160	FOOD MANUFACTURING	53045	1257	17721	FOOD SVCS & DRINKING PLACES
52411	129	1984	INSURANCE CARRIERS & RELATED	52721	30	82	EDUCATIONAL SERVICES	53046	101	938	ADMINISTRATIVE & SUPPORT SVCS
52498	3	7010	COMPUTER & ELECTRONIC PROD MFG	52722	1359	22018	MERCH. WHOLESALERS;DURABLE GDS	53047	11	37	CREDIT INTERMEDIATION & RELATD
52499	10	13012	PROF.; SCIENTIFIC; & TECH SVCS	52726	124	872	TRUCK TRANSPORTATION	53048	125	2960	PRINT'G & RELATED SUPP'T ACT'S
52501	1278	19156	FOOD MANUFACTURING	52727	4	3	NONSTORE RETAILERS	53049	79	536	FOOD SVCS & DRINKING PLACES
52530	29	75	SOCIAL ASSISTANCE	52728	49	620	BLDG MATL & GARDEN EQPMT DLRS	53050	290	3965	FABRICATED METAL PRODUCT MFG
52531	288	2380	FABRICATED METAL PRODUCT MFG	52729	46	116	EDUCATIONAL SERVICES	53051	1815	32638	GENERAL MERCHANDISE STORES
52533	50	84	RELIG.; GRANT; CIVIC; PROF ORG	52730	134	1639	PLASTICS & RUBBER PRODUCTS MFG	53052	6	18	MOTOR VEHICLE & PARTS DEALERS
52534	11	18	SPECIAL TRADE CONTRACTORS	52731	25	85	JUSTICE; PUBIC ORDER/SAFETY	53056	37	304	CHEMICAL MANUFACTURING

ZIP CODE	2009 Total Firms	2009 Total Employ-ees	TOP INDUSTRY RANKED on 2009 EMPLOYMENT	ZIP CODE	2009 Total Firms	2009 Total Employ-ees	TOP INDUSTRY RANKED on 2009 EMPLOYMENT	ZIP CODE	2009 Total Firms	2009 Total Employ-ees	TOP INDUSTRY RANKED on 2009 EMPLOYMENT
53057	64	476	EDUCATIONAL SERVICES	53184	208	2221	MISCELLANEOUS MANUFACTURING	53542	2	12	FOOD SVCS & DRINKING PLACES
53058	106	1511	ADMINISTRATIVE & SUPPORT SVCS	53185	497	3854	EDUCATIONAL SERVICES	53543	76	472	EDUCATIONAL SERVICES
53059	44	143	EDUCATIONAL SERVICES	53186	2183	31872	MERCH. WHOLESALERS;DURABLE GDS	53544	26	128	EDUCATIONAL SERVICES
53060	28	223	SPECIAL TRADE CONTRACTORS	53187	17	113	MERCH. WHOLESALERS;NONDUR. GDS	53545	1466	19439	FOOD SVCS & DRINKING PLACES
53061	177	1925	EDUCATIONAL SERVICES	53188	1490	29466	INSURANCE CARRIERS & RELATED	53546	937	23196	TRANSPORTATION EQUIPMENT MFG
53063	60	640	TRUCK TRANSPORTATION	53189	741	5978	SPECIAL TRADE CONTRACTORS	53547	15	65	CREDIT INTERMEDIATION & RELATD
53064	27	289	MACHINERY MANUFACTURING	53190	573	7443	EDUCATIONAL SERVICES	53548	732	10023	AMBULATORY HEALTH CARE SVCS
53065	59	371	EDUCATIONAL SERVICES	53191	149	1058	EDUCATIONAL SERVICES	53549	433	5697	BLDG MATL & GARDEN EQPMT DLRS
53066	1316	17682	REPAIR AND MAINTENANCE	53192	37	1151	EDUCATIONAL SERVICES	53550	40	341	MERCH. WHOLESALERS;NONDUR. GDS
53069	57	264	FOOD SVCS & DRINKING PLACES	53194	2	4	POSTAL SERVICE	53551	312	3214	FOOD SVCS & DRINKING PLACES
53070	153	1196	PLASTICS & RUBBER PRODUCTS MFG	53195	17	84	MERCH. WHOLESALERS;DURABLE GDS	53553	17	33	EXEC.; LEGIS.; & OTHER SUPPORT
53072	1221	13753	EDUCATIONAL SERVICES	53201	30	71	SOCIAL ASSISTANCE	53554	45	365	EDUCATIONAL SERVICES
53073	598	8144	FOOD MANUFACTURING	53202	3139	59467	INSURANCE CARRIERS & RELATED	53555	305	2281	MACHINERY MANUFACTURING
53074	599	6352	FOOD SVCS & DRINKING PLACES	53203	692	18682	CREDIT INTERMEDIATION & RELATD	53556	53	173	GASOLINE STATIONS
53075	134	1756	PRINT'G & RELATED SUPP'T ACT'S	53204	1277	15342	MACHINERY MANUFACTURING	53557	23	79	TRUCK TRANSPORTATION
53076	188	2229	SPORTG GDS;HOBBY;BOOK; & MUSIC	53205	359	3624	EDUCATIONAL SERVICES	53558	374	2705	EDUCATIONAL SERVICES
53078	48	251	FOOD AND BEVERAGE STORES	53206	627	2769	EDUCATIONAL SERVICES	53559	152	1175	EDUCATIONAL SERVICES
53079	38	503	FOOD AND BEVERAGE STORES	53207	1391	22660	SUPPORT ACT. FOR TRANSPORT.	53560	164	1952	REAL ESTATE
53080	265	3224	PRIMARY METAL MANUFACTURING	53208	1080	11588	MERCH. WHOLESALERS;NONDUR. GDS	53561	42	345	ACCOMMODATION
53081	1936	30231	AMBULATORY HEALTH CARE SVCS	53209	1638	21060	SPECIAL TRADE CONTRACTORS	53562	1396	18281	FOOD SVCS & DRINKING PLACES
53082	8	11	INSURANCE CARRIERS & RELATED	53210	845	44106	FOOD AND BEVERAGE STORES	53563	356	2507	EDUCATIONAL SERVICES
53083	539	9533	HOSPITALS	53211	963	14330	EDUCATIONAL SERVICES	53565	212	2044	MERCH. WHOLESALERS;NONDUR. GDS
53085	403	4447	BLDG MATL & GARDEN EQPMT DLRS	53212	1318	28712	AMBULATORY HEALTH CARE SVCS	53566	907	11889	NONSTORE RETAILERS
53086	314	2278	EDUCATIONAL SERVICES	53213	925	9013	AMBULATORY HEALTH CARE SVCS	53569	37	185	FOOD SVCS & DRINKING PLACES
53088	29	245	SPECIAL TRADE CONTRACTORS	53214	1648	26659	MACHINERY MANUFACTURING	53570	95	470	EDUCATIONAL SERVICES
53089	537	9249	PRINT'G & RELATED SUPP'T ACT'S	53215	1421	22096	HOSPITALS	53571	9	43	SPECIAL TRADE CONTRACTORS
53090	498	4124	PROF.; SCIENTIFIC; & TECH SVCS	53216	920	7871	EDUCATIONAL SERVICES	53572	417	2404	FOOD SVCS & DRINKING PLACES
53091	59	284	FOOD AND BEVERAGE STORES	53217	1476	14800	EDUCATIONAL SERVICES	53573	122	771	MACHINERY MANUFACTURING
53092	1539	17608	MERCH. WHOLESALERS;DURABLE GDS	53218	861	8404	NAT'L SECURITY & INT'L AFFAIRS	53574	176	1469	NURSING & RESID. CARE FACILIT.
53093	37	333	SPECIAL TRADE CONTRACTORS	53219	849	7126	PROF.; SCIENTIFIC; & TECH SVCS	53575	466	3767	EDUCATIONAL SERVICES
53094	856	9262	EDUCATIONAL SERVICES	53220	807	9062	FOOD SVCS & DRINKING PLACES	53576	66	465	EDUCATIONAL SERVICES
53095	1467	20593	AMBULATORY HEALTH CARE SVCS	53221	904	11549	FOOD SVCS & DRINKING PLACES	53577	60	693	CONSTRUCTION OF BUILDINGS
53097	209	2581	EDUCATIONAL SERVICES	53222	805	11791	GENERAL MERCHANDISE STORES	53578	239	2747	MERCH. WHOLESALERS;DURABLE GDS
53098	272	4196	AMBULATORY HEALTH CARE SVCS	53223	1073	22635	MISCELLANEOUS MANUFACTURING	53579	56	319	FOOD AND BEVERAGE STORES
53099	6	21	FOOD SVCS & DRINKING PLACES	53224	629	12793	PROF.; SCIENTIFIC; & TECH SVCS	53580	10	62	CONSTRUCTION OF BUILDINGS
53101	7	23	NONMETALLIC MINERAL PROD. MFG	53225	619	10188	NURSING & RESID. CARE FACILIT.	53581	600	6126	ELECT'L EQPMT; APP; & COMP MFG
53102	1	0	POSTAL SERVICE	53226	1948	34985	HOSPITALS	53582	41	162	FOOD SVCS & DRINKING PLACES
53103	226	1573	FOOD SVCS & DRINKING PLACES	53227	1120	17697	HOSPITALS	53583	285	3271	MISCELLANEOUS MANUFACTURING
53104	175	1667	COMPUTER & ELECTRONIC PROD MFG	53228	412	5929	MOTOR VEHICLE & PARTS DEALERS	53584	2	1	HEAVY & CIVIL ENG. CONSTRUCT'N
53105	1097	11789	EDUCATIONAL SERVICES	53233	710	25558	EDUCATIONAL SERVICES	53585	84	386	WOOD PRODUCT MANUFACTURING
53108	170	1853	MERCH. WHOLESALERS;DURABLE GDS	53234	3	3	REAL ESTATE	53586	91	562	MOTOR VEHICLE & PARTS DEALERS
53109	4	104	ACCOMMODATION	53235	297	3933	RELIG.; GRANT; CIVIC; PROF ORG	53587	58	263	EDUCATIONAL SERVICES
53110	619	9440	FABRICATED METAL PRODUCT MFG	53237	5	29	TRUCK TRANSPORTATION	53588	241	2733	NONMETALLIC MINERAL PROD. MFG
53114	99	1398	FOOD MANUFACTURING	53259	1	2	CREDIT INTERMEDIATION & RELATD	53589	782	8899	MERCH. WHOLESALERS;DURABLE GDS
53115	751	7725	UTILITIES	53263	1	30	FURN. & HOME FURNISHGS STORES	53590	1104	11819	FOOD SVCS & DRINKING PLACES
53118	206	1319	EDUCATIONAL SERVICES	53288	2	205	SECURITIES/COMMODITY CONTRACTS	53593	835	7383	EDUCATIONAL SERVICES
53119	160	1271	FOOD SVCS & DRINKING PLACES	53290	4	5303	MANAGMT OF COMPANIES & ENTERP.	53594	169	2402	TRANSPORTATION EQUIPMENT MFG
53120	332	3445	EDUCATIONAL SERVICES	53295	23	2633	HOSPITALS	53595	1	4000	CLOTHING & CLOTH'G ACC. STORES
53121	845	9204	EDUCATIONAL SERVICES	53401	4	20	SOCIAL ASSISTANCE	53597	647	7013	EDUCATIONAL SERVICES
53122	416	3448	BLDG MATL & GARDEN EQPMT DLRS	53402	806	4824	EDUCATIONAL SERVICES	53598	84	2838	HEALTH & PERSONAL CARE STORES
53125	89	414	RELIG.; GRANT; CIVIC; PROF ORG	53403	1302	17752	CHEMICAL MANUFACTURING	53599	7	12	HEALTH & PERSONAL CARE STORES
53126	305	2578	MERCH. WHOLESALERS;DURABLE GDS	53404	559	7354	SOCIAL ASSISTANCE	53701	28	68	PERSONAL AND LAUNDRY SERVICES
53127	55	235	EDUCATIONAL SERVICES	53405	643	8447	EDUCATIONAL SERVICES	53702	263	19623	SOCIAL ASSISTANCE
53128	195	925	FOOD SVCS & DRINKING PLACES	53406	1055	13377	FOOD SVCS & DRINKING PLACES	53703	2593	39946	EXEC.; LEGIS.; & OTHER SUPPORT
53129	519	7700	ADMINISTRATIVE & SUPPORT SVCS	53408	12	29	ADMINISTRATIVE & SUPPORT SVCS	53704	2333	37410	FOOD MANUFACTURING
53130	448	4060	FOOD SVCS & DRINKING PLACES	53501	11	67	SPECIAL TRADE CONTRACTORS	53705	1080	15982	NURSING & RESID. CARE FACILIT.
53132	1061	13203	MACHINERY MANUFACTURING	53502	70	289	EDUCATIONAL SERVICES	53706	212	28858	EDUCATIONAL SERVICES
53137	50	197	FURNITURE & RELATED PROD. MFG	53503	61	254	SPECIAL TRADE CONTRACTORS	53707	17	148	INSURANCE CARRIERS & RELATED
53138	9	43	FABRICATED METAL PRODUCT MFG	53504	70	255	EDUCATIONAL SERVICES	53708	54	162	EXEC.; LEGIS.; & OTHER SUPPORT
53139	75	351	EDUCATIONAL SERVICES	53505	13	27	AMUSEMENT; GAMBLING;& RECREAT.	53711	1612	21747	PROF.; SCIENTIFIC; & TECH SVCS
53140	1109	10439	JUSTICE; PUBIC ORDER/SAFETY	53506	29	38	FOOD SVCS & DRINKING PLACES	53713	1482	30831	INSURANCE CARRIERS & RELATED
53141	10	38	AMUSEMENT; GAMBLING;& RECREAT.	53507	71	461	MISCELLANEOUS MANUFACTURING	53714	619	7580	POSTAL SERVICE
53142	1045	11501	FOOD SVCS & DRINKING PLACES	53508	188	1210	EDUCATIONAL SERVICES	53715	577	11201	HOSPITALS
53143	648	10173	HOSPITALS	53510	75	610	FOOD MANUFACTURING	53716	1228	12011	AMBULATORY HEALTH CARE SVCS
53144	851	14169	EDUCATIONAL SERVICES	53511	1541	18300	EDUCATIONAL SERVICES	53717	717	16855	AMBULATORY HEALTH CARE SVCS
53146	247	1714	EDUCATIONAL SERVICES	53512	8	45	SOCIAL ASSISTANCE	53718	863	16596	REPAIR AND MAINTENANCE
53147	1077	11272	ACCOMMODATION	53515	101	653	CLOTHING & CLOTH'G ACC. STORES	53719	1953	20902	PROF.; SCIENTIFIC; & TECH SVCS
53148	21	148	MOTOR VEHICLE & PARTS DEALERS	53516	80	383	EDUCATIONAL SERVICES	53725	5	7	SPECIAL TRADE CONTRACTORS
53149	624	5525	EDUCATIONAL SERVICES	53517	68	387	FOOD AND BEVERAGE STORES	53726	125	1819	EDUCATIONAL SERVICES
53150	732	6688	MERCH. WHOLESALERS;DURABLE GDS	53518	60	137	TELECOMMUNICATIONS	53744	32	82	ADMINISTRATIVE & SUPPORT SVCS
53151	1415	23921	PROF.; SCIENTIFIC; & TECH SVCS	53520	237	1940	TRANSPORTATION EQUIPMENT MFG	53783	11	2493	INSURANCE CARRIERS & RELATED
53152	13	81	CONSTRUCTION OF BUILDINGS	53521	99	325	EDUCATIONAL SERVICES	53784	4	660	PROF.; SCIENTIFIC; & TECH SVCS
53153	111	871	ELECT'L EQPMT; APP; & COMP MFG	53522	45	316	PRIMARY METAL MANUFACTURING	53788	1	340	UTILITIES
53154	1027	21161	TRANSPORTATION EQUIPMENT MFG	53523	236	1290	EDUCATIONAL SERVICES	53792	125	23509	AMBULATORY HEALTH CARE SVCS
53156	115	1074	CHEMICAL MANUFACTURING	53525	143	1296	EDUCATIONAL SERVICES	53801	23	59	CROP PRODUCTION
53157	25	65	JUSTICE; PUBIC ORDER/SAFETY	53526	41	151	FOOD MANUFACTURING	53802	13	32	FOOD MANUFACTURING
53158	425	8666	MERCH. WHOLESALERS;DURABLE GDS	53527	309	3039	MERCH. WHOLESALERS;NONDUR. GDS	53803	43	177	EDUCATIONAL SERVICES
53159	7	33	MISCELLANEOUS MANUFACTURING	53528	219	1640	PLASTICS & RUBBER PRODUCTS MFG	53804	72	298	MERCH. WHOLESALERS;NONDUR. GDS
53167	38	357	JUSTICE; PUBIC ORDER/SAFETY	53529	90	352	PLASTICS & RUBBER PRODUCTS MFG	53805	250	2407	EXEC.; LEGIS.; & OTHER SUPPORT
53168	240	2060	BLDG MATL & GARDEN EQPMT DLRS	53530	259	1574	EDUCATIONAL SERVICES	53806	83	447	UTILITIES
53170	79	697	FOOD MANUFACTURING	53531	148	1598	FABRICATED METAL PRODUCT MFG	53807	167	1663	MERCH. WHOLESALERS;NONDUR. GDS
53171	21	176	JUSTICE; PUBIC ORDER/SAFETY	53532	513	6017	PROF.; SCIENTIFIC; & TECH SVCS	53808	56	780	NONSTORE RETAILERS
53172	431	4553	MISCELLANEOUS STORE RETAILERS	53533	421	3482	HOSPITALS	53809	186	1620	EDUCATIONAL SERVICES
53176	4	4	SPECIAL TRADE CONTRACTORS	53534	358	3129	EDUCATIONAL SERVICES	53810	14	58	JUSTICE; PUBIC ORDER/SAFETY
53177	434	8537	JUSTICE; PUBIC ORDER/SAFETY	53535	5	8	SPECIAL TRADE CONTRACTORS	53811	96	606	EDUCATIONAL SERVICES
53178	111	420	RELIG.; GRANT; CIVIC; PROF ORG	53536	290	2655	MERCH. WHOLESALERS;NONDUR. GDS	53812	43	254	HEAVY & CIVIL ENG. CONSTRUCT'N
53179	90	536	MERCH. WHOLESALERS;DURABLE GDS	53537	49	316	TRUCK TRANSPORTATION	53813	374	3185	NURSING & RESID. CARE FACILIT.
53181	209	1196	JUSTICE; PUBIC ORDER/SAFETY	53538	751	11583	AMBULATORY HEALTH CARE SVCS	53816	21	55	CROP PRODUCTION
53182	360	3764	EXEC.; LEGIS.; & OTHER SUPPORT	53540	6	19	BLDG MATL & GARDEN EQPMT DLRS	53817	13	108	EDUCATIONAL SERVICES
53183	143	868	EDUCATIONAL SERVICES	53541	27	88	EDUCATIONAL SERVICES	53818	596	6547	EDUCATIONAL SERVICES

BUSINESS DATA

ZIP CODE	2009 Total Firms	2009 Total Employ-ees	TOP INDUSTRY RANKED on 2009 EMPLOYMENT
53820	101	383	EDUCATIONAL SERVICES
53821	526	6785	MERCH. WHOLESALERS;DURABLE GDS
53824	1	150	RELIG.; GRANT; CIVIC; PROF ORG
53825	13	34	MERCH. WHOLESALERS;NONDUR. GDS
53826	39	238	EDUCATIONAL SERVICES
53827	9	38	JUSTICE; PUBIC ORDER/SAFETY
53901	762	11582	HOSPITALS
53910	164	1662	PAPER MANUFACTURING
53911	71	362	PROF.; SCIENTIFIC; & TECH SVCS
53913	1082	18640	ACCOMMODATION
53916	1005	11521	SOCIAL ASSISTANCE
53919	72	365	EDUCATIONAL SERVICES
53920	19	58	EDUCATIONAL SERVICES
53922	37	46	SOCIAL ASSISTANCE
53923	58	782	FOOD MANUFACTURING
53924	42	260	EDUCATIONAL SERVICES
53925	358	3223	FOOD SVCS & DRINKING PLACES
53926	36	132	CONSTRUCTION OF BUILDINGS
53927	4	2	FOOD SVCS & DRINKING PLACES
53928	9	6	POSTAL SERVICE
53929	107	880	EDUCATIONAL SERVICES
53930	47	299	PLASTICS & RUBBER PRODUCTS MFG
53931	17	402	MERCH. WHOLESALERS;NONDUR. GDS
53932	74	1159	SPECIAL TRADE CONTRACTORS
53933	116	1195	JUSTICE; PUBIC ORDER/SAFETY
53934	187	1273	EDUCATIONAL SERVICES
53935	23	283	FOOD AND BEVERAGE STORES
53936	25	91	EDUCATIONAL SERVICES
53937	40	114	TRUCK TRANSPORTATION
53939	19	52	CONSTRUCTION OF BUILDINGS
53940	84	1026	FOOD SVCS & DRINKING PLACES
53941	105	322	BLDG MATL & GARDEN EQPMT DLRS
53942	12	17	MERCH. WHOLESALERS;NONDUR. GDS
53943	42	171	SPECIAL TRADE CONTRACTORS
53944	67	292	WOOD PRODUCT MANUFACTURING
53946	167	1247	MERCH. WHOLESALERS;DURABLE GDS
53947	12	18	FOOD SVCS & DRINKING PLACES
53948	401	4151	EXEC.; LEGIS.; & OTHER SUPPORT
53949	300	1875	EDUCATIONAL SERVICES
53950	161	1341	TRANSPORTATION EQUIPMENT MFG
53951	57	280	EXEC.; LEGIS.; & OTHER SUPPORT
53952	125	835	PRIMARY METAL MANUFACTURING
53953	10	29	FOOD SVCS & DRINKING PLACES
53954	170	1138	SPECIAL TRADE CONTRACTORS
53955	215	1264	EDUCATIONAL SERVICES
53956	139	1022	NURSING & RESID. CARE FACILIT.
53957	3	3	SUPPORT ACTIVITIES: AGR./FOR.
53959	571	7521	MERCH. WHOLESALERS;DURABLE GDS
53960	98	468	EDUCATIONAL SERVICES
53961	34	68	EDUCATIONAL SERVICES
53962	17	310	RELIG.; GRANT; CIVIC; PROF ORG
53963	396	5157	OTHER INFORMATION SERVICES
53964	154	2649	FOOD MANUFACTURING
53965	765	11770	FOOD SVCS & DRINKING PLACES
53968	91	252	FOOD SVCS & DRINKING PLACES
53969	19	438	EXEC.; LEGIS.; & OTHER SUPPORT
54001	401	3286	HEAVY & CIVIL ENG. CONSTRUCT'N
54002	325	3329	BLDG MATL & GARDEN EQPMT DLRS
54003	23	201	PRINT'G & RELATED SUPP'T ACT'S
54004	67	314	EDUCATIONAL SERVICES
54005	167	1049	EDUCATIONAL SERVICES
54006	31	97	JUSTICE; PUBIC ORDER/SAFETY
54007	48	88	ANIMAL PRODUCTION
54009	82	1020	ACCOMMODATION
54010	7	31	FOOD SVCS & DRINKING PLACES
54011	294	2661	EXEC.; LEGIS.; & OTHER SUPPORT
54013	111	765	EDUCATIONAL SERVICES
54014	89	669	FABRICATED METAL PRODUCT MFG
54015	87	1014	EDUCATIONAL SERVICES
54016	1308	11386	FOOD SVCS & DRINKING PLACES
54017	652	6390	FOOD SVCS & DRINKING PLACES
54020	274	3686	TRANSPORTATION EQUIPMENT MFG
54021	203	1471	EDUCATIONAL SERVICES
54022	707	6448	EDUCATIONAL SERVICES
54023	137	884	FURNITURE & RELATED PROD. MFG
54024	318	3356	HOSPITALS
54025	264	2167	EDUCATIONAL SERVICES
54026	61	123	ADMINISTRATIVE & SUPPORT SVCS
54027	33	187	FOOD MANUFACTURING
54028	108	1201	FABRICATED METAL PRODUCT MFG
54082	36	191	SPECIAL TRADE CONTRACTORS
54101	97	424	FOOD SVCS & DRINKING PLACES
54102	33	87	FOOD SVCS & DRINKING PLACES
54103	19	39	GENERAL MERCHANDISE STORES
54104	49	165	FOOD SVCS & DRINKING PLACES
54106	138	562	SPECIAL TRADE CONTRACTORS
54107	162	1323	EDUCATIONAL SERVICES
54110	204	3288	MACHINERY MANUFACTURING
54111	68	215	FOOD SVCS & DRINKING PLACES
54112	91	608	EDUCATIONAL SERVICES
54113	61	1561	PAPER MANUFACTURING
54114	368	2018	FOOD SVCS & DRINKING PLACES
54115	1525	19571	SPECIAL TRADE CONTRACTORS
54119	15	253	EDUCATIONAL SERVICES
54120	8	13	CONSTRUCTION OF BUILDINGS
54121	191	1033	EXEC.; LEGIS.; & OTHER SUPPORT
54123	9	31	TRUCK TRANSPORTATION
54124	142	1402	EDUCATIONAL SERVICES
54125	39	298	WOOD PRODUCT MANUFACTURING
54126	131	532	MERCH. WHOLESALERS;NONDUR. GDS
54127	4	5	FOOD SVCS & DRINKING PLACES
54128	61	443	FOOD SVCS & DRINKING PLACES
54129	108	633	EDUCATIONAL SERVICES
54130	879	10354	PAPER MANUFACTURING
54131	3	1	ADMINISTRATIVE & SUPPORT SVCS
54135	152	2874	EXEC.; LEGIS.; & OTHER SUPPORT
54136	222	3352	MERCH. WHOLESALERS;NONDUR. GDS
54137	28	112	EDUCATIONAL SERVICES
54138	120	512	ACCOMMODATION
54139	105	855	MERCH. WHOLESALERS;NONDUR. GDS
54140	324	5085	FOOD AND BEVERAGE STORES
54141	69	251	FOOD SVCS & DRINKING PLACES
54143	810	11717	TRANSPORTATION EQUIPMENT MFG
54149	81	306	FOOD SVCS & DRINKING PLACES
54150	12	361	WOOD PRODUCT MANUFACTURING
54151	182	1907	PAPER MANUFACTURING
54152	15	68	MERCH. WHOLESALERS;NONDUR. GDS
54153	397	4025	REPAIR AND MAINTENANCE
54154	250	2224	EDUCATIONAL SERVICES
54155	226	1867	EXEC.; LEGIS.; & OTHER SUPPORT
54156	63	531	NONMETALLIC MINERAL PROD. MFG
54157	225	2484	NURSING & RESID. CARE FACILIT.
54159	36	94	WOOD PRODUCT MANUFACTURING
54160	11	63	MACHINERY MANUFACTURING
54161	85	518	MACHINERY MANUFACTURING
54162	328	3491	REPAIR AND MAINTENANCE
54165	270	2621	SOCIAL ASSISTANCE
54166	906	8782	FOOD SVCS & DRINKING PLACES
54169	96	439	FOOD SVCS & DRINKING PLACES
54170	78	436	EDUCATIONAL SERVICES
54171	69	232	EDUCATIONAL SERVICES
54173	138	522	FOOD SVCS & DRINKING PLACES
54174	118	1026	EDUCATIONAL SERVICES
54175	53	234	FOOD SVCS & DRINKING PLACES
54177	111	858	EDUCATIONAL SERVICES
54180	113	725	EDUCATIONAL SERVICES
54182	3	58	MERCH. WHOLESALERS;NONDUR. GDS
54201	265	2369	WOOD PRODUCT MANUFACTURING
54202	116	520	FOOD SVCS & DRINKING PLACES
54204	71	410	EDUCATIONAL SERVICES
54205	89	328	FOOD SVCS & DRINKING PLACES
54207	12	55	JUSTICE; PUBIC ORDER/SAFETY
54208	233	2030	CROP PRODUCTION
54209	174	1065	ACCOMMODATION
54210	84	350	ACCOMMODATION
54211	99	469	ACCOMMODATION
54212	191	1300	FOOD SVCS & DRINKING PLACES
54213	42	119	CONSTRUCTION OF BUILDINGS
54214	18	80	CONSTRUCTION OF BUILDINGS
54215	13	70	FOOD SVCS & DRINKING PLACES
54216	285	2636	UTILITIES
54217	266	2199	EDUCATIONAL SERVICES
54220	1803	26980	FOOD MANUFACTURING
54221	9	11	PROF.; SCIENTIFIC; & TECH SVCS
54226	8	26	TRANSIT & GRND PASS. TRANSPORT
54227	43	185	PERFORM'G ARTS; SPEC. SPORTS
54228	108	944	EDUCATIONAL SERVICES
54229	134	680	MISCELLANEOUS MANUFACTURING
54230	133	871	EDUCATIONAL SERVICES
54232	46	672	MACHINERY MANUFACTURING
54234	269	1560	FOOD SVCS & DRINKING PLACES
54235	1161	13276	UNCLASSIFIED ESTABLISHMENTS
54240	8	4	CREDIT INTERMEDIATION & RELATD
54241	498	6590	MISCELLANEOUS MANUFACTURING
54245	109	1314	EDUCATIONAL SERVICES
54246	96	412	ACCOMMODATION
54247	55	186	GASOLINE STATIONS
54301	1388	27209	HOSPITALS
54302	1177	14551	MERCH. WHOLESALERS;NONDUR. GDS
54303	1487	25064	AMUSEMENT; GAMBLING;& RECREAT.
54304	2001	36874	FOOD SVCS & DRINKING PLACES
54305	9	115	AMBULATORY HEALTH CARE SVCS
54306	1	3	CONSTRUCTION OF BUILDINGS
54307	24	133	AMBULATORY HEALTH CARE SVCS
54308	5	4	CONSTRUCTION OF BUILDINGS
54311	1062	14937	HOSPITALS
54313	1117	12670	TRUCK TRANSPORTATION
54324	4	4	REAL ESTATE
54344	3	2000	INSURANCE CARRIERS & RELATED
54401	1498	29832	AMBULATORY HEALTH CARE SVCS
54402	9	16	ELECTRONICS & APPLIANCE STORES
54403	1085	13051	JUSTICE; PUBIC ORDER/SAFETY
54405	167	1655	FOOD MANUFACTURING
54406	156	1231	TRUCK TRANSPORTATION
54407	46	209	PRINT'G & RELATED SUPP'T ACT'S
54408	31	78	WOOD PRODUCT MANUFACTURING
54409	737	7244	FOOD SVCS & DRINKING PLACES
54410	42	934	TRUCK TRANSPORTATION
54411	138	654	EDUCATIONAL SERVICES
54412	63	561	EDUCATIONAL SERVICES
54413	12	103	MERCH. WHOLESALERS;NONDUR. GDS
54414	88	432	SPECIAL TRADE CONTRACTORS
54415	7	48	GASOLINE STATIONS
54416	77	1010	PERFORM'G ARTS; SPEC. SPORTS
54417	9	515	PAPER MANUFACTURING
54418	23	78	CROP PRODUCTION
54420	33	125	MERCH. WHOLESALERS;NONDUR. GDS
54421	110	1258	EDUCATIONAL SERVICES
54422	28	371	FOOD MANUFACTURING
54423	70	184	BLDG MATL & GARDEN EQPMT DLRS
54424	46	194	AMUSEMENT; GAMBLING;& RECREAT.
54425	78	968	WOOD PRODUCT MANUFACTURING
54426	102	745	EDUCATIONAL SERVICES
54427	24	49	FOOD SVCS & DRINKING PLACES
54428	80	601	EDUCATIONAL SERVICES
54429	8	21	EDUCATIONAL SERVICES
54430	5	43	ACCOMMODATION
54432	1	0	SPORTG GDS;HOBBY;BOOK; & MUSIC
54433	67	501	EDUCATIONAL SERVICES
54434	4	6	FOOD AND BEVERAGE STORES
54435	59	148	JUSTICE; PUBIC ORDER/SAFETY
54436	48	321	FOOD AND BEVERAGE STORES
54437	94	877	FOOD MANUFACTURING
54439	2	1	RELIG.; GRANT; CIVIC; PROF ORG
54440	83	378	SPECIAL TRADE CONTRACTORS
54441	14	63	REPAIR AND MAINTENANCE
54442	21	43	CONSTRUCTION OF BUILDINGS
54443	64	427	EDUCATIONAL SERVICES
54446	97	690	EDUCATIONAL SERVICES
54447	17	34	EXEC.; LEGIS.; & OTHER SUPPORT
54448	153	2194	FOOD MANUFACTURING
54449	1197	22549	AMBULATORY HEALTH CARE SVCS
54450	23	223	WOOD PRODUCT MANUFACTURING
54451	604	6623	FABRICATED METAL PRODUCT MFG
54452	709	8693	BLDG MATL & GARDEN EQPMT DLRS
54454	31	239	FOOD AND BEVERAGE STORES
54455	514	6292	BLDG MATL & GARDEN EQPMT DLRS
54456	351	3098	EXEC.; LEGIS.; & OTHER SUPPORT
54457	308	2403	AMUSEMENT; GAMBLING;& RECREAT.
54458	10	37	ACCOMMODATION
54459	43	118	WOOD PRODUCT MANUFACTURING
54460	80	648	NURSING & RESID. CARE FACILIT.
54462	12	142	ACCOMMODATION
54463	35	48	ACCOMMODATION
54464	7	20	SPECIAL TRADE CONTRACTORS
54465	35	116	JUSTICE; PUBIC ORDER/SAFETY
54466	98	728	EDUCATIONAL SERVICES
54467	529	7884	FOOD MANUFACTURING
54469	59	1214	PAPER MANUFACTURING
54470	84	528	NURSING & RESID. CARE FACILIT.
54471	44	182	EDUCATIONAL SERVICES
54473	103	516	EDUCATIONAL SERVICES
54474	225	6085	NONMETALLIC MINERAL PROD. MFG
54475	59	347	JUSTICE; PUBIC ORDER/SAFETY
54476	801	10687	MERCH. WHOLESALERS;DURABLE GDS
54479	128	1288	FOOD MANUFACTURING
54480	43	172	EDUCATIONAL SERVICES
54481	1740	31235	INSURANCE CARRIERS & RELATED
54484	147	1810	FABRICATED METAL PRODUCT MFG
54485	17	31	ACCOMMODATION
54486	76	272	WOOD PRODUCT MANUFACTURING
54487	513	4762	MOTOR VEHICLE & PARTS DEALERS
54488	35	104	CROP PRODUCTION
54489	45	447	MERCH. WHOLESALERS;NONDUR. GDS
54490	25	186	RELIG.; GRANT; CIVIC; PROF ORG
54491	62	436	WOOD PRODUCT MANUFACTURING
54492	1	300	SPORTG GDS;HOBBY;BOOK; & MUSIC
54493	18	56	FOOD MANUFACTURING
54494	1309	12155	EDUCATIONAL SERVICES
54495	415	7551	PAPER MANUFACTURING
54498	67	302	MERCH. WHOLESALERS;DURABLE GDS
54499	167	1691	FOOD AND BEVERAGE STORES
54501	1335	11957	FOOD SVCS & DRINKING PLACES
54511	60	153	SPECIAL TRADE CONTRACTORS
54512	141	522	ACCOMMODATION
54513	11	20	FORESTRY AND LOGGING
54514	56	279	WOOD PRODUCT MANUFACTURING
54515	21	60	EDUCATIONAL SERVICES
54517	17	78	NAT'L SECURITY & INT'L AFFAIRS
54519	82	178	SPECIAL TRADE CONTRACTORS

ZIP CODE	2009 Total Firms	2009 Total Employees	TOP INDUSTRY RANKED on 2009 EMPLOYMENT	ZIP CODE	2009 Total Firms	2009 Total Employees	TOP INDUSTRY RANKED on 2009 EMPLOYMENT	ZIP CODE	2009 Total Firms	2009 Total Employees	TOP INDUSTRY RANKED on 2009 EMPLOYMENT
54520	345	1895	AMUSEMENT; GAMBLING;& RECREAT.	54664	87	282	EDUCATIONAL SERVICES	54843	946	7314	ACCOMMODATION
54521	761	4518	FOOD SVCS & DRINKING PLACES	54665	561	4544	NURSING & RESID. CARE FACILIT.	54844	30	57	BLDG MATL & GARDEN EQPMT DLRS
54524	29	121	MOTOR VEHICLE & PARTS DEALERS	54666	91	541	ACCOMMODATION	54845	10	47	CONSTRUCTION OF BUILDINGS
54525	6	14	ADMINISTRATIVE & SUPPORT SVCS	54667	232	1572	EDUCATIONAL SERVICES	54846	6	30	EXEC.; LEGIS.; & OTHER SUPPORT
54526	31	142	PRINT'G & RELATED SUPP'T ACT'S	54669	308	3687	EDUCATIONAL SERVICES	54847	205	773	ACCOMMODATION
54527	45	274	EDUCATIONAL SERVICES	54670	60	273	TRUCK TRANSPORTATION	54848	419	4876	BLDG MATL & GARDEN EQPMT DLRS
54529	30	96	FOOD SVCS & DRINKING PLACES	54701	2154	27182	AMBULATORY HEALTH CARE SVCS	54849	75	206	FOOD SVCS & DRINKING PLACES
54530	30	738	BLDG MATL & GARDEN EQPMT DLRS	54702	21	76	ADMINISTRATIVE & SUPPORT SVCS	54850	72	297	FOOD SVCS & DRINKING PLACES
54531	81	227	COMPUTER & ELECTRONIC PROD MFG	54703	1434	27332	AMBULATORY HEALTH CARE SVCS	54853	187	1327	WOOD PRODUCT MANUFACTURING
54532	1	0	SPORTG GDS;HOBBY;BOOK; & MUSIC	54720	287	3124	PROF.; SCIENTIFIC; & TECH SVCS	54854	44	309	EDUCATIONAL SERVICES
54534	249	1816	RELIG.; GRANT; CIVIC; PROF ORG	54721	40	121	EDUCATIONAL SERVICES	54855	28	118	CONSTRUCTION OF BUILDINGS
54536	8	69	CONSTRUCTION OF BUILDINGS	54722	121	981	EDUCATIONAL SERVICES	54856	64	180	ELECTRONICS & APPLIANCE STORES
54537	18	57	JUSTICE; PUBIC ORDER/SAFETY	54723	51	124	FOOD SVCS & DRINKING PLACES	54857	12	48	FOOD SVCS & DRINKING PLACES
54538	114	734	COMPUTER & ELECTRONIC PROD MFG	54724	320	2384	MOTOR VEHICLE & PARTS DEALERS	54858	93	340	JUSTICE; PUBIC ORDER/SAFETY
54539	74	169	SPECIAL TRADE CONTRACTORS	54725	82	395	EDUCATIONAL SERVICES	54859	128	1082	FOOD MANUFACTURING
54540	123	511	FOOD SVCS & DRINKING PLACES	54726	50	135	AMBULATORY HEALTH CARE SVCS	54861	48	1180	ADMINISTRATIVE & SUPPORT SVCS
54541	73	911	WOOD PRODUCT MANUFACTURING	54727	159	1318	EDUCATIONAL SERVICES	54862	12	27	FORESTRY AND LOGGING
54542	31	87	WOOD PRODUCT MANUFACTURING	54728	290	1931	ACCOMMODATION	54864	49	334	MERCH. WHOLESALERS;NONDUR. GDS
54543	5	12	EXEC.; LEGIS.; & OTHER SUPPORT	54729	1336	18921	EDUCATIONAL SERVICES	54865	39	217	EDUCATIONAL SERVICES
54545	146	655	ACCOMMODATION	54730	129	861	EDUCATIONAL SERVICES	54867	30	108	WOOD PRODUCT MANUFACTURING
54546	55	539	WOOD PRODUCT MANUFACTURING	54731	25	70	FOOD SVCS & DRINKING PLACES	54868	934	10503	AMBULATORY HEALTH CARE SVCS
54547	176	678	WOOD PRODUCT MANUFACTURING	54732	121	811	EDUCATIONAL SERVICES	54870	67	161	ACCOMMODATION
54548	618	4837	AMBULATORY HEALTH CARE SVCS	54733	62	259	TELECOMMUNICATIONS	54871	179	1645	EXEC.; LEGIS.; & OTHER SUPPORT
54550	12	18	FOOD SVCS & DRINKING PLACES	54734	19	75	MERCH. WHOLESALERS;DURABLE GDS	54872	312	1811	EDUCATIONAL SERVICES
54552	311	3396	PAPER MANUFACTURING	54735	18	219	FOOD SVCS & DRINKING PLACES	54873	178	624	EDUCATIONAL SERVICES
54554	74	530	NURSING & RESID. CARE FACILIT.	54736	300	2016	EDUCATIONAL SERVICES	54874	72	284	NURSING & RESID. CARE FACILIT.
54555	402	3518	PAPER MANUFACTURING	54737	19	120	EXEC.; LEGIS.; & OTHER SUPPORT	54875	34	70	WOOD PRODUCT MANUFACTURING
54556	91	839	MERCH. WHOLESALERS;DURABLE GDS	54738	107	309	DATA PROCESS'G	54876	82	217	BLDG MATL & GARDEN EQPMT DLRS
54557	88	226	FOOD SVCS & DRINKING PLACES	54739	107	483	EDUCATIONAL SERVICES	54880	1660	18618	FOOD SVCS & DRINKING PLACES
54558	163	775	FOOD SVCS & DRINKING PLACES	54740	82	595	EDUCATIONAL SERVICES	54888	78	332	FOOD SVCS & DRINKING PLACES
54559	25	33	FOOD SVCS & DRINKING PLACES	54741	34	182	JUSTICE; PUBIC ORDER/SAFETY	54889	120	2253	AMUSEMENT; GAMBLING;& RECREAT.
54560	47	204	ACCOMMODATION	54742	141	743	EDUCATIONAL SERVICES	54890	5	10	FOOD AND BEVERAGE STORES
54561	8	11	ACCOMMODATION	54743	9	111	EDUCATIONAL SERVICES	54891	214	1162	EDUCATIONAL SERVICES
54562	167	860	ACCOMMODATION	54745	93	485	FOOD SVCS & DRINKING PLACES	54893	211	1553	EXEC.; LEGIS.; & OTHER SUPPORT
54563	17	196	EDUCATIONAL SERVICES	54746	15	37	ANIMAL PRODUCTION	54895	53	244	EDUCATIONAL SERVICES
54564	20	61	JUSTICE; PUBIC ORDER/SAFETY	54747	134	764	RELIG.; GRANT; CIVIC; PROF ORG	54896	116	445	EDUCATIONAL SERVICES
54565	8	136	ACCOMMODATION	54748	28	235	FOOD MANUFACTURING	54901	1343	18636	EDUCATIONAL SERVICES
54566	76	653	AMUSEMENT; GAMBLING;& RECREAT.	54749	41	167	SPECIAL TRADE CONTRACTORS	54902	1045	15276	MERCH. WHOLESALERS;DURABLE GDS
54568	367	2832	HOSPITALS	54750	42	168	NONMETALLIC MINERAL PROD. MFG	54903	16	30	RELIG.; GRANT; CIVIC; PROF ORG
54601	2177	43963	AMBULATORY HEALTH CARE SVCS	54751	1039	13064	EDUCATIONAL SERVICES	54904	769	11285	HOSPITALS
54602	21	109	ADMINISTRATIVE & SUPPORT SVCS	54754	58	265	FOOD SVCS & DRINKING PLACES	54906	1	500	NONSTORE RETAILERS
54603	762	10994	FOOD SVCS & DRINKING PLACES	54755	314	1994	TRUCK TRANSPORTATION	54909	80	451	EDUCATIONAL SERVICES
54610	151	1027	UTILITIES	54756	53	172	FOOD SVCS & DRINKING PLACES	54911	1642	30396	INSURANCE CARRIERS & RELATED
54611	45	201	FOOD MANUFACTURING	54757	123	442	EDUCATIONAL SERVICES	54912	29	85	ADMINISTRATIVE & SUPPORT SVCS
54612	189	4584	FURNITURE & RELATED PROD. MFG	54758	191	1865	FOOD SVCS & DRINKING PLACES	54913	1101	13534	FOOD SVCS & DRINKING PLACES
54613	53	132	AMUSEMENT; GAMBLING;& RECREAT.	54759	67	479	FOOD SVCS & DRINKING PLACES	54914	1861	28309	MERCH. WHOLESALERS;DURABLE GDS
54614	75	759	FORESTRY AND LOGGING	54760	32	199	NURSING & RESID. CARE FACILIT.	54915	993	13477	FOOD SVCS & DRINKING PLACES
54615	566	5644	EXEC.; LEGIS.; & OTHER SUPPORT	54761	53	227	NURSING & RESID. CARE FACILIT.	54919	3	1903	INSURANCE CARRIERS & RELATED
54616	93	690	EDUCATIONAL SERVICES	54762	58	333	EDUCATIONAL SERVICES	54921	53	403	SUPPORT ACT. FOR TRANSPORT.
54618	87	512	NAT'L SECURITY & INT'L AFFAIRS	54763	60	347	MERCH. WHOLESALERS;DURABLE GDS	54922	38	130	JUSTICE; PUBIC ORDER/SAFETY
54619	119	550	EDUCATIONAL SERVICES	54764	3	8	FOOD SVCS & DRINKING PLACES	54923	415	4629	AMBULATORY HEALTH CARE SVCS
54620	4	2	MERCH. WHOLESALERS;DURABLE GDS	54765	14	41	MOTOR VEHICLE & PARTS DEALERS	54926	6	8	MERCH. WHOLESALERS;NONDUR. GDS
54621	39	140	MERCH. WHOLESALERS;NONDUR. GDS	54766	51	166	MERCH. WHOLESALERS;NONDUR. GDS	54927	8	40	FOOD SVCS & DRINKING PLACES
54622	119	429	FOOD MANUFACTURING	54767	129	1018	EDUCATIONAL SERVICES	54928	10	18	FOOD SVCS & DRINKING PLACES
54623	89	372	FOOD SVCS & DRINKING PLACES	54768	190	1537	EXEC.; LEGIS.; & OTHER SUPPORT	54929	384	3791	FABRICATED METAL PRODUCT MFG
54624	70	402	EDUCATIONAL SERVICES	54769	27	99	ACCOMMODATION	54930	98	504	CROP PRODUCTION
54625	10	42	JUSTICE; PUBIC ORDER/SAFETY	54770	90	425	EDUCATIONAL SERVICES	54931	37	372	FURN. & HOME FURNISHGS STORES
54626	29	58	EXEC.; LEGIS.; & OTHER SUPPORT	54771	207	1154	FOOD SVCS & DRINKING PLACES	54932	33	115	TRUCK TRANSPORTATION
54627	75	330	TRANSPORTATION EQUIPMENT MFG	54772	31	101	SPECIAL TRADE CONTRACTORS	54933	27	105	FURNITURE & RELATED PROD. MFG
54628	50	83	GASOLINE STATIONS	54773	173	1994	EXEC.; LEGIS.; & OTHER SUPPORT	54934	8	31	SPECIAL TRADE CONTRACTORS
54629	103	819	EDUCATIONAL SERVICES	54801	513	3040	FOOD SVCS & DRINKING PLACES	54935	1770	26375	MOTOR VEHICLE & PARTS DEALERS
54630	157	1452	MACHINERY MANUFACTURING	54805	59	521	FOOD MANUFACTURING	54936	12	514	SPECIAL TRADE CONTRACTORS
54631	76	379	CROP PRODUCTION	54806	723	7040	EDUCATIONAL SERVICES	54937	712	12207	AMBULATORY HEALTH CARE SVCS
54632	52	182	UTILITIES	54810	156	1044	EDUCATIONAL SERVICES	54940	155	628	ACCOMMODATION
54634	173	1280	HOSPITALS	54812	293	6210	WAREHOUSING AND STORAGE	54941	253	2161	ACCOMMODATION
54635	82	337	MERCH. WHOLESALERS;NONDUR. GDS	54813	31	111	FABRICATED METAL PRODUCT MFG	54942	297	3382	MISCELLANEOUS STORE RETAILERS
54636	277	2656	EDUCATIONAL SERVICES	54814	242	1617	FOOD SVCS & DRINKING PLACES	54943	71	226	CROP PRODUCTION
54637	10	42	AMUSEMENT; GAMBLING;& RECREAT.	54816	7	11	FOOD SVCS & DRINKING PLACES	54944	268	1609	EDUCATIONAL SERVICES
54638	49	746	SOCIAL ASSISTANCE	54817	109	837	ACCOMMODATION	54945	161	1601	PUBLISHING INDUSTRIES
54639	114	645	FOOD MANUFACTURING	54818	1	0	EXEC.; LEGIS.; & OTHER SUPPORT	54946	7	833	HOSPITALS
54641	4	46	WOOD PRODUCT MANUFACTURING	54819	126	656	EDUCATIONAL SERVICES	54947	70	242	FOOD SVCS & DRINKING PLACES
54642	57	290	EDUCATIONAL SERVICES	54820	58	215	EXEC.; LEGIS.; & OTHER SUPPORT	54948	11	34	TRUCK TRANSPORTATION
54643	9	57	UNCLASSIFIED ESTABLISHMENTS	54821	191	667	ACCOMMODATION	54949	154	913	EDUCATIONAL SERVICES
54644	35	78	FOOD MANUFACTURING	54822	193	949	EDUCATIONAL SERVICES	54950	133	1466	WOOD PRODUCT MANUFACTURING
54645	7	37	FOOD AND BEVERAGE STORES	54824	77	304	RELIG.; GRANT; CIVIC; PROF ORG	54952	836	15125	AMBULATORY HEALTH CARE SVCS
54646	150	961	MERCH. WHOLESALERS;DURABLE GDS	54826	25	85	FOOD MANUFACTURING	54956	1651	32004	PAPER MANUFACTURING
54648	50	179	MERCH. WHOLESALERS;NONDUR. GDS	54827	26	86	ACCOMMODATION	54957	6	40	EXEC.; LEGIS.; & OTHER SUPPORT
54649	12	82	JUSTICE; PUBIC ORDER/SAFETY	54828	20	49	ACCOMMODATION	54960	87	260	FOOD SVCS & DRINKING PLACES
54650	854	12161	FOOD SVCS & DRINKING PLACES	54829	286	2210	FOOD MANUFACTURING	54961	551	6726	FOOD MANUFACTURING
54651	52	424	EDUCATIONAL SERVICES	54830	150	816	AMUSEMENT; GAMBLING;& RECREAT.	54962	41	75	HEAVY & CIVIL ENG. CONSTRUCT'N
54652	54	172	FOOD SVCS & DRINKING PLACES	54832	48	232	EDUCATIONAL SERVICES	54963	220	3431	PROF.; SCIENTIFIC; & TECH SVCS
54653	13	33	WOOD PRODUCT MANUFACTURING	54834	3	2	ACCOMMODATION	54964	36	96	SOCIAL ASSISTANCE
54654	18	127	EDUCATIONAL SERVICES	54835	41	90	SPECIAL TRADE CONTRACTORS	54965	35	30	EDUCATIONAL SERVICES
54655	84	495	EDUCATIONAL SERVICES	54836	18	31	SPECIAL TRADE CONTRACTORS	54966	131	1044	CROP PRODUCTION
54656	768	8802	FABRICATED METAL PRODUCT MFG	54837	205	1212	EDUCATIONAL SERVICES	54967	34	171	EXEC.; LEGIS.; & OTHER SUPPORT
54657	7	8	FOOD SVCS & DRINKING PLACES	54838	66	187	JUSTICE; PUBIC ORDER/SAFETY	54968	182	928	CONSTRUCTION OF BUILDINGS
54658	93	306	FOOD SVCS & DRINKING PLACES	54839	25	37	EXEC.; LEGIS.; & OTHER SUPPORT	54969	17	77	EDUCATIONAL SERVICES
54659	45	241	NONMETALLIC MINERAL PROD. MFG	54840	213	1979	MERCH. WHOLESALERS;DURABLE GDS	54970	95	842	JUSTICE; PUBIC ORDER/SAFETY
54660	737	9388	HOSPITALS	54841	21	172	ACCOMMODATION	54971	487	8577	MISCELLANEOUS MANUFACTURING
54661	97	607	FOOD SVCS & DRINKING PLACES	54842	11	80	HEAVY & CIVIL ENG. CONSTRUCT'N	54974	46	623	EDUCATIONAL SERVICES

BUSINESS DATA

ZIP CODE	2009 Total Firms	2009 Total Employ-ees	TOP INDUSTRY RANKED on 2009 EMPLOYMENT	ZIP CODE	2009 Total Firms	2009 Total Employ-ees	TOP INDUSTRY RANKED on 2009 EMPLOYMENT	ZIP CODE	2009 Total Firms	2009 Total Employ-ees	TOP INDUSTRY RANKED on 2009 EMPLOYMENT
54976	4	3	RELIG.; GRANT; CIVIC; PROF ORG	55109	1438	18281	FOOD SVCS & DRINKING PLACES	55364	428	2197	EDUCATIONAL SERVICES
54977	37	171	TRUCK TRANSPORTATION	55110	1612	22130	EDUCATIONAL SERVICES	55366	11	23	GASOLINE STATIONS
54978	14	93	TRANSPORTATION EQUIPMENT MFG	55111	148	4320	MISCELLANEOUS STORE RETAILERS	55367	32	120	MERCH. WHOLESALERS;NONDUR. GDS
54979	46	193	FOOD SVCS & DRINKING PLACES	55112	1258	25730	SOCIAL ASSISTANCE	55368	128	1311	EDUCATIONAL SERVICES
54980	7	18	FOOD SVCS & DRINKING PLACES	55113	2274	38064	FOOD SVCS & DRINKING PLACES	55369	1764	24822	FOOD SVCS & DRINKING PLACES
54981	850	9115	PRIMARY METAL MANUFACTURING	55114	890	13346	AMBULATORY HEALTH CARE SVCS	55370	27	280	FURNITURE & RELATED PROD. MFG
54982	441	3614	MOTOR VEHICLE & PARTS DEALERS	55115	179	1472	EDUCATIONAL SERVICES	55371	504	6849	HOSPITALS
54983	200	1712	PLASTICS & RUBBER PRODUCTS MFG	55116	695	9423	WHOLESALE ELEC. MRKTS & AGENTS	55372	801	23399	AMUSEMENT; GAMBLING;& RECREAT.
54984	153	1083	ACCOMMODATION	55117	1122	13905	EDUCATIONAL SERVICES	55373	181	2182	MERCH. WHOLESALERS;DURABLE GDS
54985	17	2224	OTHER INFORMATION SERVICES	55118	1030	11538	FOOD SVCS & DRINKING PLACES	55374	639	8074	MERCH. WHOLESALERS;DURABLE GDS
54986	177	1587	EDUCATIONAL SERVICES	55119	519	5807	EDUCATIONAL SERVICES	55375	113	628	EDUCATIONAL SERVICES
55001	129	559	AMUSEMENT; GAMBLING;& RECREAT.	55120	380	9434	AIR TRANSPORTATION	55376	344	4336	WAREHOUSING AND STORAGE
55003	96	5501	PROF.; SCIENTIFIC; & TECH SVCS	55121	1116	27845	AIR TRANSPORTATION	55377	3	7	GASOLINE STATIONS
55005	95	519	FABRICATED METAL PRODUCT MFG	55122	999	12907	INSURANCE CARRIERS & RELATED	55378	747	8323	EDUCATIONAL SERVICES
55006	109	837	EDUCATIONAL SERVICES	55123	406	11971	PROF.; SCIENTIFIC; & TECH SVCS	55379	1271	22077	EXEC.; LEGIS.; & OTHER SUPPORT
55007	36	56	AMUSEMENT; GAMBLING;& RECREAT.	55124	1224	15063	FOOD SVCS & DRINKING PLACES	55380	3	6	RELIG.; GRANT; CIVIC; PROF ORG
55008	647	7794	HOSPITALS	55125	1387	20921	INSURANCE CARRIERS & RELATED	55381	54	246	EDUCATIONAL SERVICES
55009	362	3882	MERCH. WHOLESALERS;DURABLE GDS	55126	845	12647	PROF.; SCIENTIFIC; & TECH SVCS	55382	111	286	FOOD SVCS & DRINKING PLACES
55010	9	73	SPECIAL TRADE CONTRACTORS	55127	437	6485	ADMINISTRATIVE & SUPPORT SVCS	55384	96	1367	NURSING & RESID. CARE FACILIT.
55011	278	1679	SPECIAL TRADE CONTRACTORS	55128	845	8237	PROF.; SCIENTIFIC; & TECH SVCS	55385	38	217	MERCH. WHOLESALERS;NONDUR. GDS
55012	114	3193	EXEC.; LEGIS.; & OTHER SUPPORT	55129	226	1902	EDUCATIONAL SERVICES	55386	167	1725	RELIG.; GRANT; CIVIC; PROF ORG
55013	182	1696	NURSING & RESID. CARE FACILIT.	55130	372	3958	AMBULATORY HEALTH CARE SVCS	55387	474	5945	HOSPITALS
55014	568	5571	SPECIAL TRADE CONTRACTORS	55144	14	12361	MISCELLANEOUS MANUFACTURING	55388	185	1081	EDUCATIONAL SERVICES
55016	567	5898	EDUCATIONAL SERVICES	55146	3	2302	EXEC.; LEGIS.; & OTHER SUPPORT	55389	100	394	RELIG.; GRANT; CIVIC; PROF ORG
55017	17	70	MERCH. WHOLESALERS;NONDUR. GDS	55150	21	128	CLOTHING & CLOTH'G ACC. STORES	55390	80	335	RELIG.; GRANT; CIVIC; PROF ORG
55018	34	174	MERCH. WHOLESALERS;NONDUR. GDS	55155	179	13959	ADMIN. OF ECONOMIC PROGRAMS	55391	1166	14579	FOOD MANUFACTURING
55019	79	590	RELIG.; GRANT; CIVIC; PROF ORG	55164	2	30	POSTAL SERVICE	55392	9	60	CREDIT INTERMEDIATION & RELATD
55020	86	423	PERFORM'G ARTS; SPEC. SPORTS	55165	4	2	BLDG MATL & GARDEN EQPMT DLRS	55395	135	1934	SUPPORT ACT. FOR TRANSPORT.
55021	1093	13061	EDUCATIONAL SERVICES	55175	1	1	PROF.; SCIENTIFIC; & TECH SVCS	55396	121	668	MERCH. WHOLESALERS;DURABLE GDS
55024	594	4636	EDUCATIONAL SERVICES	55191	1	6	TRANSIT & GRND PASS. TRANSPORT	55397	49	1424	RELIG.; GRANT; CIVIC; PROF ORG
55025	1031	8743	FOOD SVCS & DRINKING PLACES	55301	347	3167	CLOTHING & CLOTH'G ACC. STORES	55398	307	1683	EDUCATIONAL SERVICES
55026	14	120	AMUSEMENT; GAMBLING;& RECREAT.	55302	357	2719	TELECOMMUNICATIONS	55401	1453	17772	PROF.; SCIENTIFIC; & TECH SVCS
55027	118	651	CHEMICAL MANUFACTURING	55303	1772	21336	EDUCATIONAL SERVICES	55402	2401	53768	PROF.; SCIENTIFIC; & TECH SVCS
55029	9	33	FOOD SVCS & DRINKING PLACES	55304	1030	9272	EDUCATIONAL SERVICES	55403	991	21739	GENERAL MERCHANDISE STORES
55030	25	58	FOOD SVCS & DRINKING PLACES	55305	1412	30735	AMBULATORY HEALTH CARE SVCS	55404	1110	22348	HOSPITALS
55031	68	438	FOOD SVCS & DRINKING PLACES	55306	706	9836	COMPUTER & ELECTRONIC PROD MFG	55405	737	6454	EDUCATIONAL SERVICES
55032	92	414	BLDG MATL & GARDEN EQPMT DLRS	55307	129	1071	FOOD MANUFACTURING	55406	1174	11106	EDUCATIONAL SERVICES
55033	1134	12787	MISCELLANEOUS STORE RETAILERS	55308	276	2747	UTILITIES	55407	998	17145	AMBULATORY HEALTH CARE SVCS
55036	3	4	FOOD AND BEVERAGE STORES	55309	441	4512	BLDG MATL & GARDEN EQPMT DLRS	55408	1475	9179	FOOD SVCS & DRINKING PLACES
55037	221	2251	FOOD SVCS & DRINKING PLACES	55310	89	673	EDUCATIONAL SERVICES	55409	303	3071	NURSING & RESID. CARE FACILIT.
55038	422	3751	PRINT'G & RELATED SUPP'T ACT'S	55311	560	6718	MISCELLANEOUS MANUFACTURING	55410	509	3127	FOOD SVCS & DRINKING PLACES
55040	342	2139	FOOD SVCS & DRINKING PLACES	55312	39	190	EDUCATIONAL SERVICES	55411	855	11935	MERCH. WHOLESALERS;DURABLE GDS
55041	320	3543	PRIMARY METAL MANUFACTURING	55313	855	9706	JUSTICE; PUBIC ORDER/SAFETY	55412	317	2360	EDUCATIONAL SERVICES
55042	345	2408	PROF.; SCIENTIFIC; & TECH SVCS	55314	51	593	FOOD MANUFACTURING	55413	1074	27137	HOSPITALS
55043	128	569	HEAVY & CIVIL ENG. CONSTRUCT'N	55315	105	342	EDUCATIONAL SERVICES	55414	1219	16075	FOOD SVCS & DRINKING PLACES
55044	1330	13755	EDUCATIONAL SERVICES	55316	429	4897	EDUCATIONAL SERVICES	55415	690	18707	JUSTICE; PUBIC ORDER/SAFETY
55045	216	1640	PLASTICS & RUBBER PRODUCTS MFG	55317	750	14655	MISCELLANEOUS MANUFACTURING	55416	2150	26567	PROF.; SCIENTIFIC; & TECH SVCS
55046	101	1016	EXEC.; LEGIS.; & OTHER SUPPORT	55318	896	15455	COMPUTER & ELECTRONIC PROD MFG	55417	414	5367	HOSPITALS
55047	90	323	ACCOMMODATION	55319	114	668	MERCH. WHOLESALERS;DURABLE GDS	55418	981	10024	PROF.; SCIENTIFIC; & TECH SVCS
55049	108	1273	REAL ESTATE	55320	155	1204	FOOD AND BEVERAGE STORES	55419	659	5892	PROF.; SCIENTIFIC; & TECH SVCS
55051	458	3806	EDUCATIONAL SERVICES	55321	224	2599	PROF.; SCIENTIFIC; & TECH SVCS	55420	1337	19624	RENTAL AND LEASING SERVICES
55052	62	560	ACCOMMODATION	55322	86	406	SPECIAL TRADE CONTRACTORS	55421	769	12168	PROF.; SCIENTIFIC; & TECH SVCS
55053	35	537	MERCH. WHOLESALERS;NONDUR. GDS	55323	1	0	SPECIAL TRADE CONTRACTORS	55422	1050	26067	SOCIAL ASSISTANCE
55054	36	211	SPECIAL TRADE CONTRACTORS	55324	33	157	NURSING & RESID. CARE FACILIT.	55423	1032	14100	ELECTRONICS & APPLIANCE STORES
55055	155	2058	BLDG MATL & GARDEN EQPMT DLRS	55325	157	996	MERCH. WHOLESALERS;DURABLE GDS	55424	356	3324	EXEC.; LEGIS.; & OTHER SUPPORT
55056	452	4321	EDUCATIONAL SERVICES	55327	90	338	EDUCATIONAL SERVICES	55425	1243	27093	FUNDS; TRUSTS; & OTHER FINANCE
55057	808	10487	EDUCATIONAL SERVICES	55328	332	3379	EDUCATIONAL SERVICES	55426	1349	31258	HOSPITALS
55060	1211	20005	NONMETALLIC MINERAL PROD. MFG	55329	89	807	EDUCATIONAL SERVICES	55427	1126	14393	FOOD MANUFACTURING
55063	384	3017	EDUCATIONAL SERVICES	55330	1334	13084	FOOD SVCS & DRINKING PLACES	55428	1199	21843	NURSING & RESID. CARE FACILIT.
55065	38	234	EDUCATIONAL SERVICES	55331	796	5649	FOOD SVCS & DRINKING PLACES	55429	658	6678	EDUCATIONAL SERVICES
55066	880	10635	FOOD SVCS & DRINKING PLACES	55332	101	577	NURSING & RESID. CARE FACILIT.	55430	753	11820	COMPUTER & ELECTRONIC PROD MFG
55067	2	0	MISCELLANEOUS STORE RETAILERS	55333	36	176	NURSING & RESID. CARE FACILIT.	55431	1162	22208	MOTOR VEHICLE & PARTS DEALERS
55068	557	6524	PETROLEUM & COAL PRODUCTS MFG	55334	176	2185	MERCH. WHOLESALERS;NONDUR. GDS	55432	1398	23652	MERCH. WHOLESALERS;DURABLE GDS
55069	178	2008	JUSTICE; PUBIC ORDER/SAFETY	55335	67	313	EDUCATIONAL SERVICES	55433	1011	20069	MACHINERY MANUFACTURING
55070	170	1446	EDUCATIONAL SERVICES	55336	326	4097	FOOD MANUFACTURING	55434	771	6849	FOOD SVCS & DRINKING PLACES
55071	117	1230	PETROLEUM & COAL PRODUCTS MFG	55337	2327	26417	AMBULATORY HEALTH CARE SVCS	55435	2076	35843	HOSPITALS
55072	137	1486	JUSTICE; PUBIC ORDER/SAFETY	55338	28	122	MERCH. WHOLESALERS;NONDUR. GDS	55436	355	2826	FOOD MANUFACTURING
55073	100	409	ADMINISTRATIVE & SUPPORT SVCS	55339	28	157	HEAVY & CIVIL ENG. CONSTRUCT'N	55437	696	12182	PROF.; SCIENTIFIC; & TECH SVCS
55074	52	468	HEAVY & CIVIL ENG. CONSTRUCT'N	55340	344	5245	TRANSPORTATION EQUIPMENT MFG	55438	342	5966	PROF.; SCIENTIFIC; & TECH SVCS
55075	601	8168	EDUCATIONAL SERVICES	55341	77	493	EDUCATIONAL SERVICES	55439	1117	16861	PERSONAL AND LAUNDRY SERVICES
55076	473	6116	EDUCATIONAL SERVICES	55342	106	1042	MACHINERY MANUFACTURING	55440	11	71	SPECIAL TRADE CONTRACTORS
55077	290	5838	MISCELLANEOUS MANUFACTURING	55343	1594	29676	MERCH. WHOLESALERS;DURABLE GDS	55441	1260	22001	PROF.; SCIENTIFIC; & TECH SVCS
55079	148	823	RELIG.; GRANT; CIVIC; PROF ORG	55344	2027	46413	PROF.; SCIENTIFIC; & TECH SVCS	55442	341	10573	INSURANCE CARRIERS & RELATED
55080	52	217	PRIMARY METAL MANUFACTURING	55345	769	9369	MERCH. WHOLESALERS;DURABLE GDS	55443	652	8249	AMBULATORY HEALTH CARE SVCS
55082	1567	16533	FOOD SVCS & DRINKING PLACES	55346	357	3292	MERCH. WHOLESALERS;DURABLE GDS	55444	224	886	EDUCATIONAL SERVICES
55084	72	714	ACCOMMODATION	55347	406	3978	EDUCATIONAL SERVICES	55445	465	8671	MACHINERY MANUFACTURING
55085	17	105	CREDIT INTERMEDIATION & RELATD	55349	142	1274	SPECIAL TRADE CONTRACTORS	55446	270	5494	SOCIAL ASSISTANCE
55087	5	11	NURSING & RESID. CARE FACILIT.	55350	964	14650	COMPUTER & ELECTRONIC PROD MFG	55447	1218	19364	MISCELLANEOUS MANUFACTURING
55088	40	180	SPECIAL TRADE CONTRACTORS	55352	267	2266	SPECIAL TRADE CONTRACTORS	55448	620	8845	FOOD SVCS & DRINKING PLACES
55089	46	2652	AMUSEMENT; GAMBLING;& RECREAT.	55353	137	921	ACCOMMODATION	55449	1038	12282	FOOD SVCS & DRINKING PLACES
55090	34	168	FOOD SVCS & DRINKING PLACES	55354	84	846	CONSTRUCTION OF BUILDINGS	55450	106	3632	SUPPORT ACT. FOR TRANSPORT.
55092	262	4011	HOSPITALS	55355	486	4969	NURSING & RESID. CARE FACILIT.	55454	345	15489	AMBULATORY HEALTH CARE SVCS
55101	1464	37487	HOSPITALS	55356	299	2396	SPECIAL TRADE CONTRACTORS	55455	226	35387	EDUCATIONAL SERVICES
55102	1312	29794	EDUCATIONAL SERVICES	55357	131	1108	SPECIAL TRADE CONTRACTORS	55458	7	40	MERCH. WHOLESALERS;NONDUR. GDS
55103	614	7025	SOCIAL ASSISTANCE	55358	236	2378	HEAVY & CIVIL ENG. CONSTRUCT'N	55474	5	7100	SECURITIES/COMMODITY CONTRACTS
55104	2089	24005	AMBULATORY HEALTH CARE SVCS	55359	305	2371	SPECIAL TRADE CONTRACTORS	55479	4	98	SECURITIES/COMMODITY CONTRACTS
55105	812	8014	FOOD SVCS & DRINKING PLACES	55360	55	211	EDUCATIONAL SERVICES	55480	1	3	SECURITIES/COMMODITY CONTRACTS
55106	918	9601	EDUCATIONAL SERVICES	55361	4	120	AMUSEMENT; GAMBLING;& RECREAT.	55487	89	1521	EXEC.; LEGIS.; & OTHER SUPPORT
55107	592	11766	SOCIAL ASSISTANCE	55362	649	7853	EDUCATIONAL SERVICES	55488	4	2853	PUBLISHING INDUSTRIES
55108	574	17929	EDUCATIONAL SERVICES	55363	96	498	WOOD PRODUCT MANUFACTURING	55601	33	131	ACCOMMODATION

ZIP CODE	2009 Total Firms	2009 Total Employ-ees	TOP INDUSTRY RANKED on 2009 EMPLOYMENT	ZIP CODE	2009 Total Firms	2009 Total Employ-ees	TOP INDUSTRY RANKED on 2009 EMPLOYMENT	ZIP CODE	2009 Total Firms	2009 Total Employ-ees	TOP INDUSTRY RANKED on 2009 EMPLOYMENT
55602	9	14	PROF.; SCIENTIFIC; & TECH SVCS	55807	478	5665	SPECIAL TRADE CONTRACTORS	56017	33	261	EDUCATIONAL SERVICES
55603	26	117	EDUCATIONAL SERVICES	55808	107	800	EDUCATIONAL SERVICES	56019	41	144	EDUCATIONAL SERVICES
55604	344	2261	ACCOMMODATION	55810	253	1949	ACCOMMODATION	56020	13	46	FOOD AND BEVERAGE STORES
55605	43	562	ACCOMMODATION	55811	1245	19860	EDUCATIONAL SERVICES	56021	46	225	NONMETALLIC MINERAL PROD. MFG
55606	13	22	CONSTRUCTION OF BUILDINGS	55812	266	4722	EDUCATIONAL SERVICES	56022	7	18	CHEMICAL MANUFACTURING
55607	11	14	ACCOMMODATION	55815	4	41	ADMINISTRATIVE & SUPPORT SVCS	56023	29	96	EDUCATIONAL SERVICES
55609	19	49	AMUSEMENT; GAMBLING;& RECREAT.	55816	16	94	MISCELLANEOUS STORE RETAILERS	56024	63	359	BLDG MATL & GARDEN EQPMT DLRS
55612	62	640	ACCOMMODATION	55901	1843	28665	COMPUTER & ELECTRONIC PROD MFG	56025	41	94	SPECIAL TRADE CONTRACTORS
55613	16	135	PROF.; SCIENTIFIC; & TECH SVCS	55902	951	18947	HOSPITALS	56026	56	375	MACHINERY MANUFACTURING
55614	112	1049	MINING (EXCEPT OIL AND GAS)	55903	57	203	WASTE MANAGMT & REMEDIAT'N SVC	56027	40	283	TRUCK TRANSPORTATION
55615	34	303	FOOD SVCS & DRINKING PLACES	55904	1206	18442	EXEC.; LEGIS.; & OTHER SUPPORT	56028	68	389	FOOD SVCS & DRINKING PLACES
55616	329	3718	FOOD SVCS & DRINKING PLACES	55905	153	512	AMBULATORY HEALTH CARE SVCS	56029	96	129	TRUCK TRANSPORTATION
55701	1	4	FOOD AND BEVERAGE STORES	55906	594	5223	EDUCATIONAL SERVICES	56030	4	22	GASOLINE STATIONS
55702	12	26	FOOD SVCS & DRINKING PLACES	55909	61	701	NURSING & RESID. CARE FACILIT.	56031	729	9422	AMBULATORY HEALTH CARE SVCS
55703	16	76	REPAIR AND MAINTENANCE	55910	51	265	FOOD MANUFACTURING	56032	19	66	BLDG MATL & GARDEN EQPMT DLRS
55704	34	147	JUSTICE; PUBIC ORDER/SAFETY	55912	1029	16499	MERCH. WHOLESALERS;NONDUR. GDS	56033	24	48	RELIG.; GRANT; CIVIC; PROF ORG
55705	120	668	HOSPITALS	55917	146	979	EDUCATIONAL SERVICES	56034	21	27	PIPELINE TRANSPORTATION
55706	76	563	MINING (EXCEPT OIL AND GAS)	55918	35	248	PROF.; SCIENTIFIC; & TECH SVCS	56035	24	232	AMBULATORY HEALTH CARE SVCS
55707	88	458	EDUCATIONAL SERVICES	55919	24	40	GASOLINE STATIONS	56036	53	337	MERCH. WHOLESALERS;DURABLE GDS
55708	54	513	ACCOMMODATION	55920	188	1369	EDUCATIONAL SERVICES	56037	48	171	EDUCATIONAL SERVICES
55709	92	342	FOOD SVCS & DRINKING PLACES	55921	278	2284	EXEC.; LEGIS.; & OTHER SUPPORT	56039	28	171	EDUCATIONAL SERVICES
55710	32	89	FOOD SVCS & DRINKING PLACES	55922	42	76	ANIMAL PRODUCTION	56041	49	170	PETROLEUM & COAL PRODUCTS MFG
55711	21	71	NURSING & RESID. CARE FACILIT.	55923	172	1442	NURSING & RESID. CARE FACILIT.	56042	42	105	MERCH. WHOLESALERS;NONDUR. GDS
55712	11	74	PROF.; SCIENTIFIC; & TECH SVCS	55924	37	270	ANIMAL PRODUCTION	56043	24	120	FABRICATED METAL PRODUCT MFG
55713	35	459	SOCIAL ASSISTANCE	55925	36	172	GASOLINE STATIONS	56044	65	192	EDUCATIONAL SERVICES
55716	13	45	MOTOR VEHICLE & PARTS DEALERS	55926	28	121	MERCH. WHOLESALERS;DURABLE GDS	56045	28	73	MERCH. WHOLESALERS;DURABLE GDS
55717	12	79	SPECIAL TRADE CONTRACTORS	55927	177	1501	EDUCATIONAL SERVICES	56046	12	51	BLDG MATL & GARDEN EQPMT DLRS
55718	187	2249	ACCOMMODATION	55929	28	134	HEAVY & CIVIL ENG. CONSTRUCT'N	56047	6	22	SPECIAL TRADE CONTRACTORS
55719	183	1578	RELIG.; GRANT; CIVIC; PROF ORG	55931	27	78	TRUCK TRANSPORTATION	56048	136	712	EDUCATIONAL SERVICES
55720	672	9963	AMUSEMENT; GAMBLING;& RECREAT.	55932	70	476	EDUCATIONAL SERVICES	56050	50	317	PLASTICS & RUBBER PRODUCTS MFG
55721	91	716	UTILITIES	55933	14	51	MERCH. WHOLESALERS;NONDUR. GDS	56051	29	98	MERCH. WHOLESALERS;DURABLE GDS
55722	62	339	EDUCATIONAL SERVICES	55934	104	659	EDUCATIONAL SERVICES	56052	15	41	CONSTRUCTION OF BUILDINGS
55723	174	1266	MERCH. WHOLESALERS;NONDUR. GDS	55935	30	282	FABRICATED METAL PRODUCT MFG	56054	41	158	FOOD MANUFACTURING
55724	47	155	FOOD SVCS & DRINKING PLACES	55936	92	569	NURSING & RESID. CARE FACILIT.	56055	153	1279	MERCH. WHOLESALERS;DURABLE GDS
55725	26	82	ELECT'L EQPMT; APP; & COMP MFG	55939	137	697	NURSING & RESID. CARE FACILIT.	56056	15	85	CHEMICAL MANUFACTURING
55726	43	242	EDUCATIONAL SERVICES	55940	102	925	EDUCATIONAL SERVICES	56057	161	1669	MERCH. WHOLESALERS;NONDUR. GDS
55731	417	2774	AMUSEMENT; GAMBLING;& RECREAT.	55941	61	165	EDUCATIONAL SERVICES	56058	248	2816	PRIMARY METAL MANUFACTURING
55732	31	97	JUSTICE; PUBIC ORDER/SAFETY	55942	1	0	FURN. & HOME FURNISHGS STORES	56060	22	67	JUSTICE; PUBIC ORDER/SAFETY
55733	104	639	EDUCATIONAL SERVICES	55943	146	791	TELECOMMUNICATIONS	56062	170	1632	FOOD MANUFACTURING
55734	244	2232	EDUCATIONAL SERVICES	55944	255	2124	EDUCATIONAL SERVICES	56063	95	447	SPECIAL TRADE CONTRACTORS
55735	60	443	EDUCATIONAL SERVICES	55945	44	204	MISCELLANEOUS MANUFACTURING	56065	126	763	EDUCATIONAL SERVICES
55736	80	426	EDUCATIONAL SERVICES	55946	105	739	MERCH. WHOLESALERS;DURABLE GDS	56068	53	262	EDUCATIONAL SERVICES
55738	16	590	MINING (EXCEPT OIL AND GAS)	55947	310	2097	SOCIAL ASSISTANCE	56069	137	1686	FOOD MANUFACTURING
55741	105	509	TRANSIT & GRND PASS. TRANSPORT	55949	161	627	FOOD SVCS & DRINKING PLACES	56071	436	4775	SPECIAL TRADE CONTRACTORS
55742	6	8	FOOD AND BEVERAGE STORES	55950	7	31	EDUCATIONAL SERVICES	56072	86	538	RELIG.; GRANT; CIVIC; PROF ORG
55744	1200	11628	PAPER MANUFACTURING	55951	67	413	EDUCATIONAL SERVICES	56073	1023	12517	FOOD MANUFACTURING
55746	931	10802	MINING (EXCEPT OIL AND GAS)	55952	113	1598	PROF.; SCIENTIFIC; & TECH SVCS	56074	74	482	EDUCATIONAL SERVICES
55748	50	139	MOTOR VEHICLE & PARTS DEALERS	55953	23	169	EDUCATIONAL SERVICES	56075	5	20	EDUCATIONAL SERVICES
55749	2	3	ACCOMMODATION	55954	89	424	EDUCATIONAL SERVICES	56078	20	34	FOOD AND BEVERAGE STORES
55750	45	278	JUSTICE; PUBIC ORDER/SAFETY	55955	115	581	JUSTICE; PUBIC ORDER/SAFETY	56080	30	398	EDUCATIONAL SERVICES
55751	28	128	EDUCATIONAL SERVICES	55956	62	317	EDUCATIONAL SERVICES	56081	304	2755	FOOD MANUFACTURING
55752	4	5	POSTAL SERVICE	55957	28	57	SPECIAL TRADE CONTRACTORS	56082	421	5033	EDUCATIONAL SERVICES
55753	42	1138	PRIMARY METAL MANUFACTURING	55959	58	365	TRANSIT & GRND PASS. TRANSPORT	56083	43	190	MERCH. WHOLESALERS;DURABLE GDS
55756	13	39	ACCOMMODATION	55960	83	316	FOOD SVCS & DRINKING PLACES	56084	3	0	TRUCK TRANSPORTATION
55757	18	60	MERCH. WHOLESALERS;NONDUR. GDS	55961	21	120	NURSING & RESID. CARE FACILIT.	56085	289	3183	MISCELLANEOUS MANUFACTURING
55758	7	7	POSTAL SERVICE	55962	41	130	EDUCATIONAL SERVICES	56087	179	2048	NURSING & RESID. CARE FACILIT.
55760	188	1255	EDUCATIONAL SERVICES	55963	195	1757	EDUCATIONAL SERVICES	56088	92	991	MERCH. WHOLESALERS;NONDUR. GDS
55763	7	24	CONSTRUCTION OF BUILDINGS	55964	199	1795	FOOD MANUFACTURING	56089	12	15	SPECIAL TRADE CONTRACTORS
55764	17	91	EXEC.; LEGIS.; & OTHER SUPPORT	55965	171	1364	EXEC.; LEGIS.; & OTHER SUPPORT	56090	30	78	FOOD AND BEVERAGE STORES
55765	29	75	FURN. & HOME FURNISHGS STORES	55967	43	165	CONSTRUCTION OF BUILDINGS	56091	22	91	CROP PRODUCTION
55766	3	6	EXEC.; LEGIS.; & OTHER SUPPORT	55968	3	2	ACCOMMODATION	56093	529	7732	PRINT'G & RELATED SUPP'T ACT'S
55767	224	2347	HOSPITALS	55969	35	142	SPECIAL TRADE CONTRACTORS	56096	137	988	EDUCATIONAL SERVICES
55768	81	4378	PRIMARY METAL MANUFACTURING	55970	33	143	EDUCATIONAL SERVICES	56097	193	1549	EDUCATIONAL SERVICES
55769	87	405	EDUCATIONAL SERVICES	55971	166	1201	EDUCATIONAL SERVICES	56098	126	816	NURSING & RESID. CARE FACILIT.
55771	121	539	ACCOMMODATION	55972	212	1289	EDUCATIONAL SERVICES	56101	355	3453	BLDG MATL & GARDEN EQPMT DLRS
55772	4	9	EXEC.; LEGIS.; & OTHER SUPPORT	55973	17	37	WAREHOUSING AND STORAGE	56110	109	686	EDUCATIONAL SERVICES
55775	27	77	AMUSEMENT; GAMBLING;& RECREAT.	55974	151	1094	MISCELLANEOUS MANUFACTURING	56111	17	33	CREDIT INTERMEDIATION & RELATD
55779	92	527	EDUCATIONAL SERVICES	55975	188	1158	EDUCATIONAL SERVICES	56113	8	14	FOOD SVCS & DRINKING PLACES
55780	10	77	RELIG.; GRANT; CIVIC; PROF ORG	55976	224	1927	NURSING & RESID. CARE FACILIT.	56114	14	34	GENERAL MERCHANDISE STORES
55781	15	59	FOOD SVCS & DRINKING PLACES	55977	2	4	CROP PRODUCTION	56115	65	247	NURSING & RESID. CARE FACILIT.
55782	13	89	MUSEUMS; HIST. SITES;& SIMILAR	55979	19	88	MISCELLANEOUS MANUFACTURING	56116	18	72	EDUCATIONAL SERVICES
55783	53	144	FOOD SVCS & DRINKING PLACES	55981	273	2885	HOSPITALS	56117	13	25	ANIMAL PRODUCTION
55784	1	0	CONSTRUCTION OF BUILDINGS	55982	13	14	FOOD SVCS & DRINKING PLACES	56118	26	271	FOOD SVCS & DRINKING PLACES
55785	9	20	CONSTRUCTION OF BUILDINGS	55983	81	693	GASOLINE STATIONS	56119	16	65	EDUCATIONAL SERVICES
55786	7	77	EXEC.; LEGIS.; & OTHER SUPPORT	55985	64	351	HEAVY & CIVIL ENG. CONSTRUCT'N	56120	34	295	FOOD MANUFACTURING
55787	7	10	POSTAL SERVICE	55987	1463	24471	MERCH. WHOLESALERS;DURABLE GDS	56121	19	32	REPAIR AND MAINTENANCE
55790	134	1147	AMUSEMENT; GAMBLING;& RECREAT.	55988	3	18	FABRICATED METAL PRODUCT MFG	56122	38	169	MERCH. WHOLESALERS;NONDUR. GDS
55791	3	35	JUSTICE; PUBIC ORDER/SAFETY	55990	53	188	EDUCATIONAL SERVICES	56123	39	132	MUSEUMS; HIST. SITES;& SIMILAR
55792	815	9871	NURSING & RESID. CARE FACILIT.	55991	65	182	TRANSIT & GRND PASS. TRANSPORT	56125	5	12	WAREHOUSING AND STORAGE
55793	11	30	AMUSEMENT; GAMBLING;& RECREAT.	55992	249	1841	MERCH. WHOLESALERS;NONDUR. GDS	56127	23	139	NONMETALLIC MINERAL PROD. MFG
55795	51	409	EXEC.; LEGIS.; & OTHER SUPPORT	56001	2374	36742	HOSPITALS	56128	123	1542	PLASTICS & RUBBER PRODUCTS MFG
55796	6	24	CONSTRUCTION OF BUILDINGS	56002	25	92	BROADCASTING	56129	40	225	EDUCATIONAL SERVICES
55797	29	275	EDUCATIONAL SERVICES	56003	433	5961	PRINT'G & RELATED SUPP'T ACT'S	56131	79	540	NURSING & RESID. CARE FACILIT.
55798	15	34	BLDG MATL & GARDEN EQPMT DLRS	56007	960	14835	HOSPITALS	56132	20	53	FOOD SVCS & DRINKING PLACES
55801	1	0	PROF.; SCIENTIFIC; & TECH SVCS	56009	54	223	EDUCATIONAL SERVICES	56134	15	21	CREDIT INTERMEDIATION & RELATD
55802	1378	19975	PROF.; SCIENTIFIC; & TECH SVCS	56010	56	240	MERCH. WHOLESALERS;NONDUR. GDS	56136	81	571	HOSPITALS
55803	512	2402	TRANSIT & GRND PASS. TRANSPORT	56011	232	1777	EDUCATIONAL SERVICES	56137	46	214	MERCH. WHOLESALERS;NONDUR. GDS
55804	356	2299	EDUCATIONAL SERVICES	56013	401	3372	EDUCATIONAL SERVICES	56138	38	254	NURSING & RESID. CARE FACILIT.
55805	335	28871	HOSPITALS	56014	44	131	ANIMAL PRODUCTION	56139	19	75	SPECIAL TRADE CONTRACTORS
55806	415	3773	RELIG.; GRANT; CIVIC; PROF ORG	56016	49	183	WASTE MANAGMT & REMEDIAT'N SVC	56140	4	20	FOOD SVCS & DRINKING PLACES

BUSINESS DATA

ZIP CODE	2009 Total Firms	2009 Total Employ-ees	TOP INDUSTRY RANKED on 2009 EMPLOYMENT	ZIP CODE	2009 Total Firms	2009 Total Employ-ees	TOP INDUSTRY RANKED on 2009 EMPLOYMENT	ZIP CODE	2009 Total Firms	2009 Total Employ-ees	TOP INDUSTRY RANKED on 2009 EMPLOYMENT
56141	10	19	MERCH. WHOLESALERS;NONDUR. GDS	56270	48	1283	AMUSEMENT; GAMBLING;& RECREAT.	56379	529	7702	ADMINISTRATIVE & SUPPORT SVCS
56142	90	338	EXEC.; LEGIS.; & OTHER SUPPORT	56271	60	354	MERCH. WHOLESALERS;NONDUR. GDS	56381	108	658	NURSING & RESID. CARE FACILIT.
56143	276	2653	EDUCATIONAL SERVICES	56273	224	1509	NURSING & RESID. CARE FACILIT.	56382	53	303	EDUCATIONAL SERVICES
56144	40	136	NURSING & RESID. CARE FACILIT.	56274	13	22	CROP PRODUCTION	56384	53	448	EDUCATIONAL SERVICES
56145	23	121	EDUCATIONAL SERVICES	56276	18	123	HEAVY & CIVIL ENG. CONSTRUCT'N	56385	37	277	MACHINERY MANUFACTURING
56146	2	2	SPECIAL TRADE CONTRACTORS	56277	239	1564	NURSING & RESID. CARE FACILIT.	56386	25	64	ACCOMMODATION
56147	5	5	POSTAL SERVICE	56278	213	1495	EDUCATIONAL SERVICES	56387	590	9037	FOOD SVCS & DRINKING PLACES
56149	100	413	EDUCATIONAL SERVICES	56279	47	110	CROP PRODUCTION	56389	4	8	RELIG.; GRANT; CIVIC; PROF ORG
56150	133	901	EDUCATIONAL SERVICES	56280	15	92	MACHINERY MANUFACTURING	56401	1655	17747	FOOD SVCS & DRINKING PLACES
56151	44	123	MERCH. WHOLESALERS;DURABLE GDS	56281	42	560	HEAVY & CIVIL ENG. CONSTRUCT'N	56425	446	6752	GENERAL MERCHANDISE STORES
56152	61	1276	EXEC.; LEGIS.; & OTHER SUPPORT	56282	53	284	EDUCATIONAL SERVICES	56431	486	3682	HOSPITALS
56153	18	70	PERSONAL AND LAUNDRY SERVICES	56283	409	3731	EDUCATIONAL SERVICES	56433	77	355	EXEC.; LEGIS.; & OTHER SUPPORT
56155	32	89	SPECIAL TRADE CONTRACTORS	56284	91	1691	FOOD MANUFACTURING	56434	9	18	FOOD SVCS & DRINKING PLACES
56156	345	3562	EDUCATIONAL SERVICES	56285	55	260	FABRICATED METAL PRODUCT MFG	56435	115	513	BLDG MATL & GARDEN EQPMT DLRS
56157	14	75	EDUCATIONAL SERVICES	56287	3	3	FOOD SVCS & DRINKING PLACES	56436	8	18	ACCOMMODATION
56158	12	55	UNCLASSIFIED ESTABLISHMENTS	56288	227	1307	FOOD SVCS & DRINKING PLACES	56437	39	121	FOOD MANUFACTURING
56159	115	1054	EDUCATIONAL SERVICES	56289	32	66	FOOD SVCS & DRINKING PLACES	56438	79	482	FOOD MANUFACTURING
56160	12	34	CREDIT INTERMEDIATION & RELATD	56291	11	36	FOOD SVCS & DRINKING PLACES	56440	74	347	NURSING & RESID. CARE FACILIT.
56161	22	72	EDUCATIONAL SERVICES	56292	37	109	FOOD SVCS & DRINKING PLACES	56441	178	2438	HOSPITALS
56162	14	46	FOOD SVCS & DRINKING PLACES	56293	74	616	WOOD PRODUCT MANUFACTURING	56442	301	1332	REAL ESTATE
56164	346	3144	EDUCATIONAL SERVICES	56294	9	43	FOOD SVCS & DRINKING PLACES	56443	55	181	UTILITIES
56165	8	32	SUPPORT ACT. FOR TRANSPORT.	56295	19	45	INSURANCE CARRIERS & RELATED	56444	136	1466	AMUSEMENT; GAMBLING;& RECREAT.
56166	4	20	NURSING & RESID. CARE FACILIT.	56296	171	1058	EDUCATIONAL SERVICES	56446	81	293	EDUCATIONAL SERVICES
56167	19	427	MERCH. WHOLESALERS;NONDUR. GDS	56297	37	260	FURNITURE & RELATED PROD. MFG	56447	91	313	FOOD SVCS & DRINKING PLACES
56168	21	44	RELIG.; GRANT; CIVIC; PROF ORG	56301	1756	25874	FOOD SVCS & DRINKING PLACES	56448	26	89	AMUSEMENT; GAMBLING;& RECREAT.
56169	34	141	EDUCATIONAL SERVICES	56302	30	147	SPECIAL TRADE CONTRACTORS	56449	25	86	HEAVY & CIVIL ENG. CONSTRUCT'N
56170	38	120	EDUCATIONAL SERVICES	56303	951	23643	HOSPITALS	56450	58	331	FOOD SVCS & DRINKING PLACES
56171	83	341	EDUCATIONAL SERVICES	56304	502	9387	NURSING & RESID. CARE FACILIT.	56452	183	863	AMBULATORY HEALTH CARE SVCS
56172	241	1667	EDUCATIONAL SERVICES	56307	233	1700	EDUCATIONAL SERVICES	56453	19	30	CONSTRUCTION OF BUILDINGS
56173	9	11	CREDIT INTERMEDIATION & RELATD	56308	1475	16886	EDUCATIONAL SERVICES	56455	53	303	PLASTICS & RUBBER PRODUCTS MFG
56174	25	71	CREDIT INTERMEDIATION & RELATD	56309	80	433	SPECIAL TRADE CONTRACTORS	56456	13	147	FABRICATED METAL PRODUCT MFG
56175	151	1010	AMBULATORY HEALTH CARE SVCS	56310	145	1054	FABRICATED METAL PRODUCT MFG	56458	13	50	ACCOMMODATION
56176	63	394	EDUCATIONAL SERVICES	56311	55	479	EDUCATIONAL SERVICES	56461	84	285	SPECIAL TRADE CONTRACTORS
56177	2	2	FOOD AND BEVERAGE STORES	56312	97	663	PROF.; SCIENTIFIC; & TECH SVCS	56464	176	1094	NURSING & RESID. CARE FACILIT.
56178	110	875	HOSPITALS	56313	8	25	FOOD SVCS & DRINKING PLACES	56465	104	855	FABRICATED METAL PRODUCT MFG
56180	55	242	EDUCATIONAL SERVICES	56314	28	62	TRUCK TRANSPORTATION	56466	110	823	FOOD MANUFACTURING
56181	49	211	MERCH. WHOLESALERS;NONDUR. GDS	56315	111	486	EDUCATIONAL SERVICES	56467	126	417	ACCOMMODATION
56183	64	396	EDUCATIONAL SERVICES	56316	70	461	FOOD MANUFACTURING	56468	307	3088	AMUSEMENT; GAMBLING;& RECREAT.
56185	35	77	WAREHOUSING AND STORAGE	56317	6	58	MERCH. WHOLESALERS;NONDUR. GDS	56469	31	115	MACHINERY MANUFACTURING
56186	14	54	RELIG.; GRANT; CIVIC; PROF ORG	56318	31	156	ACCOMMODATION	56470	731	5479	FOOD MANUFACTURING
56187	736	9698	FOOD MANUFACTURING	56319	51	229	ADMINISTRATIVE & SUPPORT SVCS	56472	469	4780	ACCOMMODATION
56201	1271	22810	FOOD AND BEVERAGE STORES	56320	233	4184	NONMETALLIC MINERAL PROD. MFG	56473	98	698	EDUCATIONAL SERVICES
56207	15	30	WAREHOUSING AND STORAGE	56321	15	827	EDUCATIONAL SERVICES	56474	249	1407	NURSING & RESID. CARE FACILIT.
56208	120	1253	JUSTICE; PUBIC ORDER/SAFETY	56323	27	122	EDUCATIONAL SERVICES	56475	59	389	TELECOMMUNICATIONS
56209	96	657	EDUCATIONAL SERVICES	56324	59	272	ADMINISTRATIVE & SUPPORT SVCS	56477	105	630	EDUCATIONAL SERVICES
56211	21	42	WAREHOUSING AND STORAGE	56325	18	122	CONSTRUCTION OF BUILDINGS	56478	1	1	NURSING & RESID. CARE FACILIT.
56212	37	125	BLDG MATL & GARDEN EQPMT DLRS	56326	88	423	NURSING & RESID. CARE FACILIT.	56479	214	2934	HOSPITALS
56214	36	163	NURSING & RESID. CARE FACILIT.	56327	21	41	RELIG.; GRANT; CIVIC; PROF ORG	56481	66	285	EDUCATIONAL SERVICES
56215	279	2683	MERCH. WHOLESALERS;DURABLE GDS	56328	4	17	RELIG.; GRANT; CIVIC; PROF ORG	56482	405	4813	EDUCATIONAL SERVICES
56216	27	201	CROP PRODUCTION	56329	239	2301	EXEC.; LEGIS.; & OTHER SUPPORT	56484	473	3345	FOOD SVCS & DRINKING PLACES
56218	21	66	ANIMAL PRODUCTION	56330	31	300	WOOD PRODUCT MANUFACTURING	56501	1049	11246	HOSPITALS
56219	56	331	NURSING & RESID. CARE FACILIT.	56331	87	404	SPECIAL TRADE CONTRACTORS	56502	11	43	PETROLEUM & COAL PRODUCTS MFG
56220	157	1539	HOSPITALS	56332	82	191	SPECIAL TRADE CONTRACTORS	56510	190	1241	EDUCATIONAL SERVICES
56221	55	285	EDUCATIONAL SERVICES	56333	11	29	FOOD SVCS & DRINKING PLACES	56511	67	530	FABRICATED METAL PRODUCT MFG
56222	118	719	NURSING & RESID. CARE FACILIT.	56334	339	3673	HOSPITALS	56514	155	888	EDUCATIONAL SERVICES
56223	76	515	EDUCATIONAL SERVICES	56335	18	47	MERCH. WHOLESALERS;DURABLE GDS	56515	193	860	NURSING & RESID. CARE FACILIT.
56224	21	46	UTILITIES	56336	81	297	MISCELLANEOUS MANUFACTURING	56516	14	31	GASOLINE STATIONS
56225	40	206	EDUCATIONAL SERVICES	56338	23	52	SPECIAL TRADE CONTRACTORS	56517	20	41	CROP PRODUCTION
56226	14	59	WHOLESALE ELEC. MRKTS & AGENTS	56339	94	418	TELECOMMUNICATIONS	56518	15	32	EDUCATIONAL SERVICES
56227	9	8	REPAIR AND MAINTENANCE	56340	57	761	TRANSPORTATION EQUIPMENT MFG	56519	16	46	EDUCATIONAL SERVICES
56228	36	319	FABRICATED METAL PRODUCT MFG	56341	5	9	FOOD AND BEVERAGE STORES	56520	212	1579	EDUCATIONAL SERVICES
56229	72	1018	FURNITURE & RELATED PROD. MFG	56342	154	851	EDUCATIONAL SERVICES	56521	39	146	ACCOMMODATION
56230	40	108	UTILITIES	56343	61	332	ACCOMMODATION	56522	16	82	EDUCATIONAL SERVICES
56231	18	92	MERCH. WHOLESALERS;DURABLE GDS	56345	661	9888	TRANSPORTATION EQUIPMENT MFG	56523	28	148	EDUCATIONAL SERVICES
56232	149	1618	EDUCATIONAL SERVICES	56347	309	3074	PRINT'G & RELATED SUPP'T ACT'S	56524	17	54	SPORTG GDS;HOBBY;BOOK; & MUSIC
56235	26	80	BLDG MATL & GARDEN EQPMT DLRS	56349	42	143	TRANSIT & GRND PASS. TRANSPORT	56525	16	40	INSURANCE CARRIERS & RELATED
56236	16	23	CROP PRODUCTION	56350	12	39	FOOD SVCS & DRINKING PLACES	56527	25	95	SPECIAL TRADE CONTRACTORS
56237	31	129	GASOLINE STATIONS	56352	296	3343	FOOD AND BEVERAGE STORES	56528	113	196	ACCOMMODATION
56239	19	54	CHEMICAL MANUFACTURING	56353	292	2521	EDUCATIONAL SERVICES	56529	103	922	GENERAL MERCHANDISE STORES
56240	53	326	NURSING & RESID. CARE FACILIT.	56354	54	236	BLDG MATL & GARDEN EQPMT DLRS	56531	184	800	AMBULATORY HEALTH CARE SVCS
56241	243	2318	AMUSEMENT; GAMBLING;& RECREAT.	56355	29	101	SPECIAL TRADE CONTRACTORS	56533	13	27	FOOD AND BEVERAGE STORES
56243	56	506	EDUCATIONAL SERVICES	56356	20	89	NURSING & RESID. CARE FACILIT.	56534	33	122	SPECIAL TRADE CONTRACTORS
56244	74	481	MERCH. WHOLESALERS;DURABLE GDS	56357	13	38	FURNITURE & RELATED PROD. MFG	56535	86	785	EDUCATIONAL SERVICES
56245	19	95	WAREHOUSING AND STORAGE	56358	69	482	EDUCATIONAL SERVICES	56536	24	77	MERCH. WHOLESALERS;NONDUR. GDS
56248	65	184	EDUCATIONAL SERVICES	56359	155	3433	AMUSEMENT; GAMBLING;& RECREAT.	56537	1008	12738	EDUCATIONAL SERVICES
56249	14	38	WAREHOUSING AND STORAGE	56360	175	914	EDUCATIONAL SERVICES	56538	8	19	SOCIAL ASSISTANCE
56251	37	199	ADMINISTRATIVE & SUPPORT SVCS	56361	144	837	EDUCATIONAL SERVICES	56540	154	781	EDUCATIONAL SERVICES
56252	66	420	EDUCATIONAL SERVICES	56362	332	2623	HOSPITALS	56541	11	19	INSURANCE CARRIERS & RELATED
56253	31	148	CONSTRUCTION OF BUILDINGS	56363	10	54	FURNITURE & RELATED PROD. MFG	56542	224	1334	NURSING & RESID. CARE FACILIT.
56255	23	88	JUSTICE; PUBIC ORDER/SAFETY	56364	153	1053	EDUCATIONAL SERVICES	56543	7	12	FOOD MANUFACTURING
56256	188	1228	NURSING & RESID. CARE FACILIT.	56367	173	1354	WOOD PRODUCT MANUFACTURING	56544	139	1042	EDUCATIONAL SERVICES
56257	37	72	MERCH. WHOLESALERS;NONDUR. GDS	56368	163	642	SPECIAL TRADE CONTRACTORS	56545	25	175	EDUCATIONAL SERVICES
56258	852	11558	MERCH. WHOLESALERS;NONDUR. GDS	56369	27	215	HEAVY & CIVIL ENG. CONSTRUCT'N	56546	15	31	MERCH. WHOLESALERS;DURABLE GDS
56260	34	181	WAREHOUSING AND STORAGE	56371	7	15	SPORTG GDS;HOBBY;BOOK; & MUSIC	56547	83	546	EDUCATIONAL SERVICES
56262	41	82	RELIG.; GRANT; CIVIC; PROF ORG	56373	74	494	EDUCATIONAL SERVICES	56548	53	411	NURSING & RESID. CARE FACILIT.
56263	20	83	EDUCATIONAL SERVICES	56374	284	2399	EDUCATIONAL SERVICES	56549	152	1168	MOTION PICT. & SOUND RECORDING
56264	84	747	EDUCATIONAL SERVICES	56375	28	169	TRANSIT & GRND PASS. TRANSPORT	56550	24	94	EDUCATIONAL SERVICES
56265	441	5022	AMBULATORY HEALTH CARE SVCS	56376	24	157	WASTE MANAGMT & REMEDIAT'N SVC	56551	122	546	NURSING & RESID. CARE FACILIT.
56266	78	564	CONSTRUCTION OF BUILDINGS	56377	340	4306	PAPER MANUFACTURING	56552	16	28	GASOLINE STATIONS
56267	420	4776	EDUCATIONAL SERVICES	56378	476	4194	EDUCATIONAL SERVICES	56553	11	31	CONSTRUCTION OF BUILDINGS

ZIP CODE	2009 Total Firms	2009 Total Employ-ees	TOP INDUSTRY RANKED on 2009 EMPLOYMENT	ZIP CODE	2009 Total Firms	2009 Total Employ-ees	TOP INDUSTRY RANKED on 2009 EMPLOYMENT	ZIP CODE	2009 Total Firms	2009 Total Employ-ees	TOP INDUSTRY RANKED on 2009 EMPLOYMENT
56554	99	618	EDUCATIONAL SERVICES	56714	55	273	EDUCATIONAL SERVICES	57061	11	16	WAREHOUSING AND STORAGE
56556	80	274	NURSING & RESID. CARE FACILIT.	56715	21	132	TRUCK TRANSPORTATION	57062	62	496	JUSTICE; PUBIC ORDER/SAFETY
56557	181	1312	EDUCATIONAL SERVICES	56716	449	5878	FOOD MANUFACTURING	57063	35	176	ACCOMMODATION
56560	1343	15209	EDUCATIONAL SERVICES	56720	9	7	FOOD MANUFACTURING	57064	234	1535	SPECIAL TRADE CONTRACTORS
56561	13	43	TRUCK TRANSPORTATION	56721	378	4024	EDUCATIONAL SERVICES	57065	9	9	POSTAL SERVICE
56562	10	738	EDUCATIONAL SERVICES	56722	7	11	AIR TRANSPORTATION	57066	124	737	NURSING & RESID. CARE FACILIT.
56563	6	50	OTHER INFORMATION SERVICES	56723	29	160	EDUCATIONAL SERVICES	57067	8	13	WAREHOUSING AND STORAGE
56565	3	2	AIR TRANSPORTATION	56724	6	13	AIR TRANSPORTATION	57068	42	139	EDUCATIONAL SERVICES
56566	13	154	AMUSEMENT; GAMBLING;& RECREAT.	56725	26	146	EDUCATIONAL SERVICES	57069	422	5371	MUSEUMS; HIST. SITES;& SIMILAR
56567	186	1034	EDUCATIONAL SERVICES	56726	102	499	EDUCATIONAL SERVICES	57070	72	617	NURSING & RESID. CARE FACILIT.
56568	15	26	CROP PRODUCTION	56727	42	218	FABRICATED METAL PRODUCT MFG	57071	102	541	CROP PRODUCTION
56569	32	221	AMBULATORY HEALTH CARE SVCS	56728	139	944	HOSPITALS	57072	15	18	TRUCK TRANSPORTATION
56570	43	96	ACCOMMODATION	56729	11	21	MERCH. WHOLESALERS;DURABLE GDS	57073	35	204	EDUCATIONAL SERVICES
56571	162	784	ACCOMMODATION	56731	4	14	UTILITIES	57075	34	198	PETROLEUM & COAL PRODUCTS MFG
56572	253	1971	FOOD MANUFACTURING	56732	104	721	EDUCATIONAL SERVICES	57076	15	93	CROP PRODUCTION
56573	523	4815	ADMINISTRATIVE & SUPPORT SVCS	56733	26	100	EDUCATIONAL SERVICES	57077	45	282	MERCH. WHOLESALERS;NONDUR. GDS
56574	12	24	RELIG.; GRANT; CIVIC; PROF ORG	56734	36	101	MERCH. WHOLESALERS;NONDUR. GDS	57078	1049	14417	ADMIN. HUMAN RESOURCE PROGRAMS
56575	37	78	EDUCATIONAL SERVICES	56735	39	111	EDUCATIONAL SERVICES	57079	1	9	PROF.; SCIENTIFIC; & TECH SVCS
56576	41	67	BLDG MATL & GARDEN EQPMT DLRS	56736	57	194	MERCH. WHOLESALERS;NONDUR. GDS	57101	34	67	SPECIAL TRADE CONTRACTORS
56577	1	1	PERSONAL AND LAUNDRY SERVICES	56737	47	297	SPECIAL TRADE CONTRACTORS	57103	940	12422	FOOD MANUFACTURING
56578	21	36	ACCOMMODATION	56738	76	290	EDUCATIONAL SERVICES	57104	2358	42117	CREDIT INTERMEDIATION & RELATD
56579	54	270	EDUCATIONAL SERVICES	56740	6	1	EXEC.; LEGIS.; & OTHER SUPPORT	57105	1524	32140	HOSPITALS
56580	33	86	HEAVY & CIVIL ENG. CONSTRUCT'N	56741	5	17	ACCOMMODATION	57106	1175	15322	FOOD SVCS & DRINKING PLACES
56581	20	82	JUSTICE; PUBIC ORDER/SAFETY	56742	42	171	EDUCATIONAL SERVICES	57107	357	7001	MOTOR VEHICLE & PARTS DEALERS
56583	13	17	SUPPORT ACTIVITIES: AGR./FOR.	56744	32	196	SPECIAL TRADE CONTRACTORS	57108	744	7705	AMBULATORY HEALTH CARE SVCS
56584	65	407	NURSING & RESID. CARE FACILIT.	56748	31	109	EDUCATIONAL SERVICES	57109	32	87	SPECIAL TRADE CONTRACTORS
56585	42	297	EDUCATIONAL SERVICES	56750	165	1010	EDUCATIONAL SERVICES	57110	328	3192	FOOD AND BEVERAGE STORES
56586	89	414	EDUCATIONAL SERVICES	56751	317	4807	MERCH. WHOLESALERS;DURABLE GDS	57118	7	23	TRUCK TRANSPORTATION
56587	116	270	SPECIAL TRADE CONTRACTORS	56754	33	151	WAREHOUSING AND STORAGE	57193	2	450	INSURANCE CARRIERS & RELATED
56588	19	32	GASOLINE STATIONS	56755	14	33	RELIG.; GRANT; CIVIC; PROF ORG	57197	9	442	EDUCATIONAL SERVICES
56589	44	279	EDUCATIONAL SERVICES	56756	6	15	AMBULATORY HEALTH CARE SVCS	57198	4	1105	ADMIN. ENVIRO. QUALITY PROGRMS
56590	34	90	SPECIAL TRADE CONTRACTORS	56757	63	398	EDUCATIONAL SERVICES	57201	1394	16749	FOOD SVCS & DRINKING PLACES
56591	11	386	EXEC.; LEGIS.; & OTHER SUPPORT	56758	13	18	FOOD SVCS & DRINKING PLACES	57212	93	648	SPECIAL TRADE CONTRACTORS
56592	34	129	MERCH. WHOLESALERS;DURABLE GDS	56759	8	14	GASOLINE STATIONS	57213	19	30	EDUCATIONAL SERVICES
56593	9	25	FOOD AND BEVERAGE STORES	56760	17	52	EDUCATIONAL SERVICES	57214	7	21	CONSTRUCTION OF BUILDINGS
56594	18	54	MERCH. WHOLESALERS;DURABLE GDS	56761	24	36	PROF.; SCIENTIFIC; & TECH SVCS	57216	44	585	FOOD AND BEVERAGE STORES
56601	1715	21182	EDUCATIONAL SERVICES	56762	157	1258	EDUCATIONAL SERVICES	57217	7	17	TRUCK TRANSPORTATION
56619	9	11	SPECIAL TRADE CONTRACTORS	56763	188	4569	BLDG MATL & GARDEN EQPMT DLRS	57218	12	14	INSURANCE CARRIERS & RELATED
56621	257	1883	FABRICATED METAL PRODUCT MFG	57001	54	487	EDUCATIONAL SERVICES	57219	30	235	NURSING & RESID. CARE FACILIT.
56623	233	1619	ACCOMMODATION	57002	32	124	CHEMICAL MANUFACTURING	57220	31	127	FOOD MANUFACTURING
56626	24	234	EDUCATIONAL SERVICES	57003	47	220	EDUCATIONAL SERVICES	57221	31	173	NURSING & RESID. CARE FACILIT.
56627	25	109	MERCH. WHOLESALERS;DURABLE GDS	57004	204	1366	EDUCATIONAL SERVICES	57223	39	173	EDUCATIONAL SERVICES
56628	97	1086	SOCIAL ASSISTANCE	57005	325	3231	MERCH. WHOLESALERS;DURABLE GDS	57224	16	78	RELIG.; GRANT; CIVIC; PROF ORG
56629	6	44	EDUCATIONAL SERVICES	57006	1150	17201	EDUCATIONAL SERVICES	57225	131	669	EDUCATIONAL SERVICES
56630	175	1312	EDUCATIONAL SERVICES	57007	8	323	NONSTORE RETAILERS	57226	138	1135	EDUCATIONAL SERVICES
56631	3	6	FOOD AND BEVERAGE STORES	57010	9	51	MACHINERY MANUFACTURING	57227	18	54	FOOD SVCS & DRINKING PLACES
56633	197	1928	AMUSEMENT; GAMBLING;& RECREAT.	57012	45	271	RELIG.; GRANT; CIVIC; PROF ORG	57231	130	867	MERCH. WHOLESALERS;DURABLE GDS
56634	90	618	NURSING & RESID. CARE FACILIT.	57013	205	2140	MACHINERY MANUFACTURING	57232	16	35	FOOD SVCS & DRINKING PLACES
56636	244	1770	HOSPITALS	57014	61	257	NURSING & RESID. CARE FACILIT.	57233	6	7	BLDG MATL & GARDEN EQPMT DLRS
56637	11	46	EDUCATIONAL SERVICES	57015	25	145	PETROLEUM & COAL PRODUCTS MFG	57234	70	301	RELIG.; GRANT; CIVIC; PROF ORG
56639	25	32	MOTOR VEHICLE & PARTS DEALERS	57016	32	172	EDUCATIONAL SERVICES	57235	20	83	EDUCATIONAL SERVICES
56641	24	35	ACCOMMODATION	57017	34	465	ELECT'L EQPMT; APP; & COMP MFG	57236	7	13	WAREHOUSING AND STORAGE
56644	41	204	MERCH. WHOLESALERS;NONDUR. GDS	57018	52	406	EDUCATIONAL SERVICES	57237	46	182	MERCH. WHOLESALERS;DURABLE GDS
56646	19	87	MERCH. WHOLESALERS;NONDUR. GDS	57020	39	108	FOOD SVCS & DRINKING PLACES	57238	17	52	ANIMAL PRODUCTION
56647	28	45	ACCOMMODATION	57021	15	22	WASTE MANAGMT & REMEDIAT'N SVC	57239	11	28	ACCOMMODATION
56649	520	5116	PAPER MANUFACTURING	57022	185	1276	EDUCATIONAL SERVICES	57241	62	430	EDUCATIONAL SERVICES
56650	52	204	EDUCATIONAL SERVICES	57024	13	42	PROF.; SCIENTIFIC; & TECH SVCS	57242	12	41	PRIMARY METAL MANUFACTURING
56651	26	24	TRANSIT & GRND PASS. TRANSPORT	57025	113	1500	EDUCATIONAL SERVICES	57243	10	70	EDUCATIONAL SERVICES
56652	19	40	FOOD SVCS & DRINKING PLACES	57026	84	517	MERCH. WHOLESALERS;DURABLE GDS	57245	7	19	EDUCATIONAL SERVICES
56653	57	341	AMBULATORY HEALTH CARE SVCS	57027	3	4	CONSTRUCTION OF BUILDINGS	57246	3	29	WAREHOUSING AND STORAGE
56654	2	4	POSTAL SERVICE	57028	171	1670	AMUSEMENT; GAMBLING;& RECREAT.	57247	7	42	MUSEUMS; HIST. SITES;& SIMILAR
56655	170	470	FOOD AND BEVERAGE STORES	57029	116	1309	NURSING & RESID. CARE FACILIT.	57248	40	466	FOOD MANUFACTURING
56657	32	135	EXEC.; LEGIS.; & OTHER SUPPORT	57030	94	573	EDUCATIONAL SERVICES	57249	63	355	EDUCATIONAL SERVICES
56659	7	7	ACCOMMODATION	57031	23	554	GASOLINE STATIONS	57251	4	52	NONMETALLIC MINERAL PROD. MFG
56660	12	23	TRANSPORTATION EQUIPMENT MFG	57032	130	968	FURNITURE & RELATED PROD. MFG	57252	315	2956	MERCH. WHOLESALERS;DURABLE GDS
56661	60	271	EDUCATIONAL SERVICES	57033	164	904	FOOD SVCS & DRINKING PLACES	57255	26	160	DATA PROCESS'G
56662	52	105	FOOD SVCS & DRINKING PLACES	57034	28	223	NURSING & RESID. CARE FACILIT.	57256	2	1	RELIG.; GRANT; CIVIC; PROF ORG
56663	6	17	ACCOMMODATION	57035	50	175	EDUCATIONAL SERVICES	57257	8	30	SPECIAL TRADE CONTRACTORS
56666	13	133	EDUCATIONAL SERVICES	57036	43	170	EDUCATIONAL SERVICES	57258	10	60	SUPPORT ACTIVITIES: AGR./FOR.
56667	17	21	ADMINISTRATIVE & SUPPORT SVCS	57037	51	326	EDUCATIONAL SERVICES	57259	17	75	EDUCATIONAL SERVICES
56668	16	102	MISCELLANEOUS MANUFACTURING	57038	45	208	JUSTICE; PUBIC ORDER/SAFETY	57260	51	367	NURSING & RESID. CARE FACILIT.
56669	32	70	ACCOMMODATION	57039	119	868	EDUCATIONAL SERVICES	57261	20	135	EDUCATIONAL SERVICES
56670	22	106	EXEC.; LEGIS.; & OTHER SUPPORT	57040	13	92	CONSTRUCTION OF BUILDINGS	57262	321	2327	EDUCATIONAL SERVICES
56671	108	1579	AMUSEMENT; GAMBLING;& RECREAT.	57041	7	186	TRANSPORTATION EQUIPMENT MFG	57263	12	64	EDUCATIONAL SERVICES
56672	135	756	EDUCATIONAL SERVICES	57042	405	3764	EDUCATIONAL SERVICES	57264	13	40	CREDIT INTERMEDIATION & RELATD
56673	21	62	FOOD SVCS & DRINKING PLACES	57043	76	594	NURSING & RESID. CARE FACILIT.	57265	5	6	CONSTRUCTION OF BUILDINGS
56676	44	174	TELECOMMUNICATIONS	57045	65	412	NURSING & RESID. CARE FACILIT.	57266	24	157	EDUCATIONAL SERVICES
56678	49	292	WOOD PRODUCT MANUFACTURING	57046	12	24	FOOD MANUFACTURING	57268	38	165	TELECOMMUNICATIONS
56679	8	9	PROF.; SCIENTIFIC; & TECH SVCS	57047	7	7	MERCH. WHOLESALERS;NONDUR. GDS	57269	6	18	SPECIAL TRADE CONTRACTORS
56680	9	15	ACCOMMODATION	57048	26	98	EDUCATIONAL SERVICES	57270	23	76	PROF.; SCIENTIFIC; & TECH SVCS
56681	27	65	ACCOMMODATION	57049	275	5173	FOOD MANUFACTURING	57271	7	11	WAREHOUSING AND STORAGE
56683	25	76	MERCH. WHOLESALERS;DURABLE GDS	57050	7	9	POSTAL SERVICE	57272	6	15	WAREHOUSING AND STORAGE
56684	13	40	MERCH. WHOLESALERS;DURABLE GDS	57051	17	50	RELIG.; GRANT; CIVIC; PROF ORG	57273	42	233	RELIG.; GRANT; CIVIC; PROF ORG
56685	9	39	ACCOMMODATION	57052	24	59	BLDG MATL & GARDEN EQPMT DLRS	57274	214	1745	NURSING & RESID. CARE FACILIT.
56686	51	148	JUSTICE; PUBIC ORDER/SAFETY	57053	137	701	EDUCATIONAL SERVICES	57276	69	305	NURSING & RESID. CARE FACILIT.
56688	3	3	ACCOMMODATION	57054	16	93	EDUCATIONAL SERVICES	57278	29	203	EDUCATIONAL SERVICES
56701	572	8938	ELECTRONICS & APPLIANCE STORES	57055	34	131	EDUCATIONAL SERVICES	57279	41	278	EDUCATIONAL SERVICES
56710	23	50	WAREHOUSING AND STORAGE	57057	5	44	EDUCATIONAL SERVICES	57301	1030	12237	FOOD SVCS & DRINKING PLACES
56711	14	39	ACCOMMODATION	57058	143	1243	PROF.; SCIENTIFIC; & TECH SVCS	57311	70	460	EDUCATIONAL SERVICES
56713	62	436	EDUCATIONAL SERVICES	57059	69	482	EDUCATIONAL SERVICES	57312	26	751	MERCH. WHOLESALERS;NONDUR. GDS

BUSINESS DATA

ZIP CODE	2009 Total Firms	2009 Total Employ-ees	TOP INDUSTRY RANKED on 2009 EMPLOYMENT
57313	104	499	HOSPITALS
57314	21	192	CROP PRODUCTION
57315	57	190	EDUCATIONAL SERVICES
57317	33	174	EDUCATIONAL SERVICES
57319	57	224	NURSING & RESID. CARE FACILIT.
57321	20	35	CONSTRUCTION OF BUILDINGS
57322	8	45	CROP PRODUCTION
57323	15	23	FOOD SVCS & DRINKING PLACES
57324	8	14	MERCH. WHOLESALERS;NONDUR. GDS
57325	276	1873	EDUCATIONAL SERVICES
57328	93	581	RELIG.; GRANT; CIVIC; PROF ORG
57329	3	5	MERCH. WHOLESALERS;NONDUR. GDS
57330	27	99	RELIG.; GRANT; CIVIC; PROF ORG
57331	15	51	CONSTRUCTION OF BUILDINGS
57332	43	147	EDUCATIONAL SERVICES
57334	35	105	BLDG MATL & GARDEN EQPMT DLRS
57335	15	49	AMBULATORY HEALTH CARE SVCS
57337	7	25	MERCH. WHOLESALERS;NONDUR. GDS
57339	70	663	EXEC.; LEGIS.; & OTHER SUPPORT
57340	6	15	SUPPORT ACTIVITIES: AGR./FOR.
57341	16	25	AMUSEMENT; GAMBLING;& RECREAT.
57342	21	39	CREDIT INTERMEDIATION & RELATD
57344	8	19	SPECIAL TRADE CONTRACTORS
57345	102	554	EDUCATIONAL SERVICES
57346	4	319	EDUCATIONAL SERVICES
57348	25	74	HEAVY & CIVIL ENG. CONSTRUCT'N
57349	114	806	ADMINISTRATIVE & SUPPORT SVCS
57350	745	7297	FOOD SVCS & DRINKING PLACES
57353	28	293	EDUCATIONAL SERVICES
57354	5	25	WAREHOUSING AND STORAGE
57355	89	881	CROP PRODUCTION
57356	98	968	AMUSEMENT; GAMBLING;& RECREAT.
57358	4	11	FOOD SVCS & DRINKING PLACES
57359	41	84	OTHER INFORMATION SERVICES
57361	14	319	EDUCATIONAL SERVICES
57362	190	1205	EDUCATIONAL SERVICES
57363	33	119	EDUCATIONAL SERVICES
57364	8	11	RELIG.; GRANT; CIVIC; PROF ORG
57365	30	593	ACCOMMODATION
57366	118	1168	NURSING & RESID. CARE FACILIT.
57367	20	85	ADMIN. ENVIRO. QUALITY PROGRMS
57368	101	498	NURSING & RESID. CARE FACILIT.
57369	175	1225	HOSPITALS
57370	27	42	CROP PRODUCTION
57371	9	31	JUSTICE; PUBIC ORDER/SAFETY
57373	11	31	MERCH. WHOLESALERS;NONDUR. GDS
57374	17	51	NONMETALLIC MINERAL PROD. MFG
57375	47	138	EDUCATIONAL SERVICES
57376	42	241	RELIG.; GRANT; CIVIC; PROF ORG
57379	2	0	ANIMAL PRODUCTION
57380	162	1522	EDUCATIONAL SERVICES
57381	35	170	JUSTICE; PUBIC ORDER/SAFETY
57382	116	620	EDUCATIONAL SERVICES
57383	43	204	NURSING & RESID. CARE FACILIT.
57384	27	173	EDUCATIONAL SERVICES
57385	101	547	MERCH. WHOLESALERS;NONDUR. GDS
57386	8	48	WAREHOUSING AND STORAGE
57401	1615	19130	HOSPITALS
57402	8	65	FOOD SVCS & DRINKING PLACES
57420	3	3	AMUSEMENT; GAMBLING;& RECREAT.
57421	7	29	ANIMAL PRODUCTION
57422	11	40	FABRICATED METAL PRODUCT MFG
57424	8	15	FOOD SVCS & DRINKING PLACES
57426	3	5	ANIMAL PRODUCTION
57427	16	87	TELECOMMUNICATIONS
57428	55	432	HOSPITALS
57429	3	3	RELIG.; GRANT; CIVIC; PROF ORG
57430	172	1161	MERCH. WHOLESALERS;DURABLE GDS
57432	26	90	CREDIT INTERMEDIATION & RELATD
57433	23	82	JUSTICE; PUBIC ORDER/SAFETY
57434	22	77	EDUCATIONAL SERVICES
57435	11	41	RELIG.; GRANT; CIVIC; PROF ORG
57436	24	200	CROP PRODUCTION
57437	81	581	EDUCATIONAL SERVICES
57438	120	613	EDUCATIONAL SERVICES
57439	4	27	MERCH. WHOLESALERS;DURABLE GDS
57440	12	96	CROP PRODUCTION
57441	24	93	EDUCATIONAL SERVICES
57442	144	901	HOSPITALS
57445	128	658	EDUCATIONAL SERVICES
57446	27	99	FOOD MANUFACTURING
57448	22	83	RELIG.; GRANT; CIVIC; PROF ORG
57449	6	3	FOOD SVCS & DRINKING PLACES
57450	52	333	EXEC.; LEGIS.; & OTHER SUPPORT
57451	116	768	CROP PRODUCTION
57452	8	39	EDUCATIONAL SERVICES
57454	22	88	EDUCATIONAL SERVICES
57455	12	25	FOOD MANUFACTURING
57456	65	251	RELIG.; GRANT; CIVIC; PROF ORG
57457	6	23	JUSTICE; PUBIC ORDER/SAFETY
57460	6	11	CROP PRODUCTION
57461	23	120	EDUCATIONAL SERVICES
57465	12	29	CROP PRODUCTION
57466	11	29	JUSTICE; PUBIC ORDER/SAFETY
57467	20	59	JUSTICE; PUBIC ORDER/SAFETY
57468	13	34	FOOD SVCS & DRINKING PLACES
57469	209	1638	EXEC.; LEGIS.; & OTHER SUPPORT
57470	4	1	RELIG.; GRANT; CIVIC; PROF ORG
57471	42	194	ANIMAL PRODUCTION
57472	89	389	NURSING & RESID. CARE FACILIT.
57473	6	10	MERCH. WHOLESALERS;DURABLE GDS
57474	16	39	FISHING; HUNTING AND TRAPPING
57475	13	36	JUSTICE; PUBIC ORDER/SAFETY
57476	28	124	EDUCATIONAL SERVICES
57477	11	22	CREDIT INTERMEDIATION & RELATD
57479	20	173	EDUCATIONAL SERVICES
57481	12	276	REPAIR AND MAINTENANCE
57501	1155	14290	EXEC.; LEGIS.; & OTHER SUPPORT
57520	9	61	AMUSEMENT; GAMBLING;& RECREAT.
57521	5	2	POSTAL SERVICE
57522	26	79	GASOLINE STATIONS
57523	105	495	EDUCATIONAL SERVICES
57528	31	152	EDUCATIONAL SERVICES
57529	16	43	AMUSEMENT; GAMBLING;& RECREAT.
57531	14	31	AMUSEMENT; GAMBLING;& RECREAT.
57532	189	1756	EDUCATIONAL SERVICES
57533	139	943	NURSING & RESID. CARE FACILIT.
57534	5	16	MERCH. WHOLESALERS;NONDUR. GDS
57536	34	190	EDUCATIONAL SERVICES
57537	12	21	CROP PRODUCTION
57538	6	10	POSTAL SERVICE
57540	3	17	CONSTRUCTION OF BUILDINGS
57541	3	8	SUPPORT ACTIVITIES: AGR./FOR.
57543	112	522	EDUCATIONAL SERVICES
57544	52	293	EXEC.; LEGIS.; & OTHER SUPPORT
57547	7	4	EDUCATIONAL SERVICES
57548	72	617	EXEC.; LEGIS.; & OTHER SUPPORT
57551	106	579	EDUCATIONAL SERVICES
57552	27	66	EDUCATIONAL SERVICES
57553	9	12	PROF.; SCIENTIFIC; & TECH SVCS
57555	127	1337	EDUCATIONAL SERVICES
57559	83	426	EDUCATIONAL SERVICES
57560	7	23	EDUCATIONAL SERVICES
57562	3	5	MISCELLANEOUS STORE RETAILERS
57563	3	9	EDUCATIONAL SERVICES
57564	98	463	EDUCATIONAL SERVICES
57566	9	67	EDUCATIONAL SERVICES
57567	112	761	NURSING & RESID. CARE FACILIT.
57568	63	225	EDUCATIONAL SERVICES
57569	24	136	AMUSEMENT; GAMBLING;& RECREAT.
57570	106	2052	SOCIAL ASSISTANCE
57571	3	3	ANIMAL PRODUCTION
57572	15	349	EDUCATIONAL SERVICES
57574	3	1	ANIMAL PRODUCTION
57576	17	61	GASOLINE STATIONS
57577	18	261	EDUCATIONAL SERVICES
57579	70	503	EDUCATIONAL SERVICES
57580	330	2334	EDUCATIONAL SERVICES
57584	11	20	ANIMAL PRODUCTION
57585	11	20	EDUCATIONAL SERVICES
57601	306	2423	FOOD AND BEVERAGE STORES
57620	83	407	EDUCATIONAL SERVICES
57621	7	33	EDUCATIONAL SERVICES
57622	6	18	EDUCATIONAL SERVICES
57623	56	322	EDUCATIONAL SERVICES
57625	269	2906	EXEC.; LEGIS.; & OTHER SUPPORT
57626	74	345	EDUCATIONAL SERVICES
57630	1	0	POSTAL SERVICE
57631	24	33	FOOD AND BEVERAGE STORES
57632	68	270	MERCH. WHOLESALERS;NONDUR. GDS
57633	45	206	EDUCATIONAL SERVICES
57634	2	0	ANIMAL PRODUCTION
57636	2	1	SUPPORT ACT. FOR TRANSPORT.
57638	139	854	MERCH. WHOLESALERS;NONDUR. GDS
57639	6	20	EDUCATIONAL SERVICES
57640	3	4	MERCH. WHOLESALERS;NONDUR. GDS
57641	42	195	EDUCATIONAL SERVICES
57642	110	587	EDUCATIONAL SERVICES
57644	12	26	JUSTICE; PUBIC ORDER/SAFETY
57645	7	15	POSTAL SERVICE
57646	19	45	EXEC.; LEGIS.; & OTHER SUPPORT
57648	32	144	FOOD MANUFACTURING
57649	11	16	ANIMAL PRODUCTION
57651	8	8	FOOD AND BEVERAGE STORES
57652	10	60	EDUCATIONAL SERVICES
57656	66	343	EDUCATIONAL SERVICES
57657	4	5	ANIMAL PRODUCTION
57658	5	65	EDUCATIONAL SERVICES
57660	3	5	MERCH. WHOLESALERS;NONDUR. GDS
57661	3	9	AMBULATORY HEALTH CARE SVCS
57701	2517	35705	AMBULATORY HEALTH CARE SVCS
57702	1462	14561	CONSTRUCTION OF BUILDINGS
57703	421	5164	ADMINISTRATIVE & SUPPORT SVCS
57706	32	5202	NAT'L SECURITY & INT'L AFFAIRS
57709	50	205	PERFORM'G ARTS; SPEC. SPORTS
57714	12	142	EDUCATIONAL SERVICES
57716	8	115	EDUCATIONAL SERVICES
57717	330	2478	EDUCATIONAL SERVICES
57718	197	1051	ADMINISTRATIVE & SUPPORT SVCS
57719	129	843	EDUCATIONAL SERVICES
57720	75	299	EDUCATIONAL SERVICES
57722	14	45	EXEC.; LEGIS.; & OTHER SUPPORT
57724	17	84	RELIG.; GRANT; CIVIC; PROF ORG
57725	5	14	RELIG.; GRANT; CIVIC; PROF ORG
57730	360	3014	ACCOMMODATION
57732	211	3466	AMUSEMENT; GAMBLING;& RECREAT.
57735	65	227	EDUCATIONAL SERVICES
57737	6	8	EDUCATIONAL SERVICES
57738	3	6	EDUCATIONAL SERVICES
57741	8	15	EXEC.; LEGIS.; & OTHER SUPPORT
57744	52	585	MISCELLANEOUS STORE RETAILERS
57745	171	1242	ACCOMMODATION
57747	324	2087	HOSPITALS
57748	11	49	EDUCATIONAL SERVICES
57750	16	331	MUSEUMS; HIST. SITES;& SIMILAR
57751	109	1099	FOOD SVCS & DRINKING PLACES
57752	49	811	EDUCATIONAL SERVICES
57754	143	945	ACCOMMODATION
57755	1	3	ANIMAL PRODUCTION
57756	14	149	EDUCATIONAL SERVICES
57758	5	5	EDUCATIONAL SERVICES
57759	10	142	SUPPORT ACTIVITIES: AGR./FOR.
57760	53	307	EDUCATIONAL SERVICES
57761	31	218	EDUCATIONAL SERVICES
57762	10	17	RELIG.; GRANT; CIVIC; PROF ORG
57763	13	55	EDUCATIONAL SERVICES
57764	16	230	EDUCATIONAL SERVICES
57766	8	20	EXEC.; LEGIS.; & OTHER SUPPORT
57767	2	1	SPECIAL TRADE CONTRACTORS
57769	99	461	EDUCATIONAL SERVICES
57770	212	2496	EXEC.; LEGIS.; & OTHER SUPPORT
57772	23	209	EDUCATIONAL SERVICES
57773	8	17	FOOD SVCS & DRINKING PLACES
57775	3	3	SUPPORT ACT. FOR TRANSPORT.
57776	1	0	POSTAL SERVICE
57779	14	68	ANIMAL PRODUCTION
57780	9	16	PROF.; SCIENTIFIC; & TECH SVCS
57782	2	0	TRUCK TRANSPORTATION
57783	660	6451	CREDIT INTERMEDIATION & RELATD
57785	396	3069	FOOD SVCS & DRINKING PLACES
57787	14	54	FOOD MANUFACTURING
57788	9	30	ANIMAL PRODUCTION
57790	94	614	TELECOMMUNICATIONS
57791	11	45	PROF.; SCIENTIFIC; & TECH SVCS
57792	2	1	FOOD AND BEVERAGE STORES
57793	56	333	WOOD PRODUCT MANUFACTURING
57794	5	10	AMUSEMENT; GAMBLING;& RECREAT.
57799	2	324	EDUCATIONAL SERVICES
58001	11	103	WOOD PRODUCT MANUFACTURING
58002	2	2	TELECOMMUNICATIONS
58004	7	19	TRANSPORTATION EQUIPMENT MFG
58005	14	32	SPECIAL TRADE CONTRACTORS
58006	41	354	SOCIAL ASSISTANCE
58007	7	16	WAREHOUSING AND STORAGE
58008	9	15	MERCH. WHOLESALERS;NONDUR. GDS
58011	40	113	EDUCATIONAL SERVICES
58012	125	882	EDUCATIONAL SERVICES
58013	11	32	AIR TRANSPORTATION
58015	19	73	CONSTRUCTION OF BUILDINGS
58016	17	93	TRUCK TRANSPORTATION
58017	18	23	CROP PRODUCTION
58018	14	94	EDUCATIONAL SERVICES
58021	12	47	MISCELLANEOUS STORE RETAILERS
58027	91	748	MERCH. WHOLESALERS;NONDUR. GDS
58029	7	16	CROP PRODUCTION
58030	31	308	SUPPORT ACTIVITIES: AGR./FOR.
58031	16	19	CREDIT INTERMEDIATION & RELATD
58032	70	354	FABRICATED METAL PRODUCT MFG
58033	27	66	ACCOMMODATION
58035	28	84	CROP PRODUCTION
58036	11	125	REPAIR AND MAINTENANCE
58038	19	155	FOOD MANUFACTURING
58040	60	994	MACHINERY MANUFACTURING
58041	81	1010	ACCOMMODATION
58042	46	192	BLDG MATL & GARDEN EQPMT DLRS
58043	13	20	CROP PRODUCTION
58045	137	1240	FOOD MANUFACTURING
58046	36	277	SPECIAL TRADE CONTRACTORS
58047	70	415	FOOD AND BEVERAGE STORES
58048	39	189	EDUCATIONAL SERVICES

ZIP CODE	2009 Total Firms	2009 Total Employ-ees	TOP INDUSTRY RANKED on 2009 EMPLOYMENT
58049	19	35	JUSTICE; PUBIC ORDER/SAFETY
58051	55	520	EDUCATIONAL SERVICES
58052	21	37	RELIG.; GRANT; CIVIC; PROF ORG
58053	65	230	MERCH. WHOLESALERS;DURABLE GDS
58054	175	1404	NURSING & RESID. CARE FACILIT.
58056	12	23	WAREHOUSING AND STORAGE
58057	1	1	RELIG.; GRANT; CIVIC; PROF ORG
58058	8	30	UTILITIES
58059	29	183	WAREHOUSING AND STORAGE
58060	69	395	EDUCATIONAL SERVICES
58061	26	71	CROP PRODUCTION
58062	10	9	DATA PROCESS'G
58063	11	51	JUSTICE; PUBIC ORDER/SAFETY
58064	35	172	EDUCATIONAL SERVICES
58065	3	4	WAREHOUSING AND STORAGE
58067	23	52	CONSTRUCTION OF BUILDINGS
58068	20	60	WAREHOUSING AND STORAGE
58069	1	1	SPECIAL TRADE CONTRACTORS
58071	22	117	EDUCATIONAL SERVICES
58072	511	5231	EDUCATIONAL SERVICES
58075	489	5559	FOOD MANUFACTURING
58076	3	357	EDUCATIONAL SERVICES
58077	23	47	PROF.; SCIENTIFIC; & TECH SVCS
58078	878	9058	MACHINERY MANUFACTURING
58079	25	77	CONSTRUCTION OF BUILDINGS
58081	37	159	EDUCATIONAL SERVICES
58102	1839	41963	AMBULATORY HEALTH CARE SVCS
58103	2917	41725	FOOD SVCS & DRINKING PLACES
58104	702	8890	PROF.; SCIENTIFIC; & TECH SVCS
58105	13	139	ADMIN. OF ECONOMIC PROGRAMS
58106	48	227	DATA PROCESS'G
58107	31	136	ADMINISTRATIVE & SUPPORT SVCS
58108	8	51	SPECIAL TRADE CONTRACTORS
58109	2	1	REPAIR AND MAINTENANCE
58121	5	2013	INSURANCE CARRIERS & RELATED
58122	8	7496	EDUCATIONAL SERVICES
58124	3	28	CREDIT INTERMEDIATION & RELATD
58126	1	0	EDUCATIONAL SERVICES
58201	1567	28636	AMBULATORY HEALTH CARE SVCS
58202	40	3851	EDUCATIONAL SERVICES
58203	791	11302	SPECIAL TRADE CONTRACTORS
58204	14	191	EDUCATIONAL SERVICES
58205	20	82	RELIG.; GRANT; CIVIC; PROF ORG
58206	8	17	ADMINISTRATIVE & SUPPORT SVCS
58208	6	13	ADMINISTRATIVE & SUPPORT SVCS
58210	20	58	EDUCATIONAL SERVICES
58212	39	151	NURSING & RESID. CARE FACILIT.
58214	10	47	ACCOMMODATION
58216	10	45	PUBLISHING INDUSTRIES
58218	23	147	EDUCATIONAL SERVICES
58219	1	1	REPAIR AND MAINTENANCE
58220	251	1662	CONSTRUCTION OF BUILDINGS
58222	34	105	CROP PRODUCTION
58223	9	31	BLDG MATL & GARDEN EQPMT DLRS
58224	4	9	WAREHOUSING AND STORAGE
58225	85	621	FOOD MANUFACTURING
58227	49	196	EDUCATIONAL SERVICES
58228	39	256	FOOD SVCS & DRINKING PLACES
58229	9	24	JUSTICE; PUBIC ORDER/SAFETY
58230	85	439	EDUCATIONAL SERVICES
58231	31	216	MERCH. WHOLESALERS;DURABLE GDS
58233	15	47	MERCH. WHOLESALERS;NONDUR. GDS
58235	25	94	CROP PRODUCTION
58236	4	5	WAREHOUSING AND STORAGE
58237	369	3427	MISCELLANEOUS MANUFACTURING
58238	9	15	CROP PRODUCTION
58239	7	8	FOOD AND BEVERAGE STORES
58240	52	299	NURSING & RESID. CARE FACILIT.
58241	8	13	CROP PRODUCTION
58243	49	228	CROP PRODUCTION
58244	10	102	EDUCATIONAL SERVICES
58249	239	1430	NURSING & RESID. CARE FACILIT.
58250	21	27	MERCH. WHOLESALERS;NONDUR. GDS
58251	107	641	EDUCATIONAL SERVICES
58254	46	260	EDUCATIONAL SERVICES
58255	1	2	EXEC.; LEGIS.; & OTHER SUPPORT
58256	26	116	EDUCATIONAL SERVICES
58257	146	1106	EDUCATIONAL SERVICES
58258	3	14	SPECIAL TRADE CONTRACTORS
58259	32	166	MERCH. WHOLESALERS;DURABLE GDS
58260	13	187	CONSTRUCTION OF BUILDINGS
58261	58	452	TRUCK TRANSPORTATION
58262	13	65	NURSING & RESID. CARE FACILIT.
58265	39	213	EDUCATIONAL SERVICES
58266	12	13	CROP PRODUCTION
58267	72	660	HOSPITALS
58269	18	93	NURSING & RESID. CARE FACILIT.
58270	160	934	NURSING & RESID. CARE FACILIT.
58271	66	1078	TRANSPORTATION EQUIPMENT MFG
58272	23	66	EDUCATIONAL SERVICES
58273	14	25	FOOD SVCS & DRINKING PLACES
58274	44	161	WAREHOUSING AND STORAGE
58275	15	41	WAREHOUSING AND STORAGE
58276	43	193	CROP PRODUCTION
58277	14	25	MERCH. WHOLESALERS;NONDUR. GDS
58278	58	315	BROADCASTING
58281	6	11	FOOD SVCS & DRINKING PLACES
58282	100	547	NURSING & RESID. CARE FACILIT.
58301	675	6321	EDUCATIONAL SERVICES
58310	1	1	WAREHOUSING AND STORAGE
58311	5	8	CHEMICAL MANUFACTURING
58313	11	7	MERCH. WHOLESALERS;NONDUR. GDS
58316	144	5024	EXEC.; LEGIS.; & OTHER SUPPORT
58317	17	59	WAREHOUSING AND STORAGE
58318	289	1900	EDUCATIONAL SERVICES
58321	12	13	FOOD SVCS & DRINKING PLACES
58323	4	11	MERCH. WHOLESALERS;NONDUR. GDS
58324	136	582	NURSING & RESID. CARE FACILIT.
58325	9	14	RAIL TRANSPORTATION
58327	14	35	WAREHOUSING AND STORAGE
58329	86	822	EDUCATIONAL SERVICES
58330	23	75	EDUCATIONAL SERVICES
58331	9	30	JUSTICE; PUBIC ORDER/SAFETY
58332	20	36	MERCH. WHOLESALERS;NONDUR. GDS
58335	111	1525	EXEC.; LEGIS.; & OTHER SUPPORT
58338	17	20	MERCH. WHOLESALERS;NONDUR. GDS
58339	6	15	MERCH. WHOLESALERS;NONDUR. GDS
58341	181	1339	AMBULATORY HEALTH CARE SVCS
58343	2	4	BEVERAGE & TOBACCO PRODUCT MFG
58344	88	380	RELIG.; GRANT; CIVIC; PROF ORG
58345	11	30	SOCIAL ASSISTANCE
58346	41	227	EDUCATIONAL SERVICES
58348	49	254	MACHINERY MANUFACTURING
58351	50	168	EDUCATIONAL SERVICES
58352	28	108	EDUCATIONAL SERVICES
58353	2	4	POSTAL SERVICE
58355	8	15	WAREHOUSING AND STORAGE
58356	145	820	NURSING & RESID. CARE FACILIT.
58357	7	28	EDUCATIONAL SERVICES
58361	16	34	FOOD SVCS & DRINKING PLACES
58362	9	7	SPECIAL TRADE CONTRACTORS
58363	2	2	WAREHOUSING AND STORAGE
58365	25	140	JUSTICE; PUBIC ORDER/SAFETY
58366	61	340	EDUCATIONAL SERVICES
58367	169	1030	HOSPITALS
58368	268	1897	HOSPITALS
58369	29	110	EDUCATIONAL SERVICES
58370	15	544	AMUSEMENT; GAMBLING;& RECREAT.
58372	12	29	SUPPORT ACTIVITIES: AGR./FOR.
58374	23	83	JUSTICE; PUBIC ORDER/SAFETY
58377	18	43	EDUCATIONAL SERVICES
58379	6	57	SOCIAL ASSISTANCE
58380	32	106	MERCH. WHOLESALERS;NONDUR. GDS
58381	19	127	EDUCATIONAL SERVICES
58382	9	9	WAREHOUSING AND STORAGE
58384	27	45	FOOD SVCS & DRINKING PLACES
58385	10	67	EDUCATIONAL SERVICES
58386	13	42	PROF.; SCIENTIFIC; & TECH SVCS
58401	913	10809	SOCIAL ASSISTANCE
58402	8	29	SOCIAL ASSISTANCE
58405	2	155	EDUCATIONAL SERVICES
58413	106	688	RELIG.; GRANT; CIVIC; PROF ORG
58415	1	2	GASOLINE STATIONS
58416	58	187	ACCOMMODATION
58418	42	71	CROP PRODUCTION
58420	11	31	EDUCATIONAL SERVICES
58421	223	1768	FOOD MANUFACTURING
58422	14	41	JUSTICE; PUBIC ORDER/SAFETY
58423	15	23	CROP PRODUCTION
58424	38	97	SPECIAL TRADE CONTRACTORS
58425	190	843	HOSPITALS
58426	10	20	MERCH. WHOLESALERS;NONDUR. GDS
58428	17	122	MERCH. WHOLESALERS;NONDUR. GDS
58429	17	23	ACCOMMODATION
58430	4	17	JUSTICE; PUBIC ORDER/SAFETY
58431	8	7	FOOD SVCS & DRINKING PLACES
58433	83	584	CROP PRODUCTION
58436	142	851	EDUCATIONAL SERVICES
58438	50	263	EDUCATIONAL SERVICES
58439	19	48	EDUCATIONAL SERVICES
58440	10	31	FOOD SVCS & DRINKING PLACES
58441	22	115	CONSTRUCTION OF BUILDINGS
58442	32	154	EDUCATIONAL SERVICES
58443	22	44	CROP PRODUCTION
58444	26	74	EDUCATIONAL SERVICES
58445	16	27	CROP PRODUCTION
58448	29	77	MERCH. WHOLESALERS;DURABLE GDS
58451	25	50	CROP PRODUCTION
58452	2	0	PERSONAL AND LAUNDRY SERVICES
58454	22	41	REPAIR AND MAINTENANCE
58455	14	91	JUSTICE; PUBIC ORDER/SAFETY
58456	39	124	RELIG.; GRANT; CIVIC; PROF ORG
58458	129	697	EDUCATIONAL SERVICES
58460	11	68	ELECT'L EQPMT; APP; & COMP MFG
58461	29	99	EDUCATIONAL SERVICES
58463	80	336	CONSTRUCTION OF BUILDINGS
58464	27	51	CROP PRODUCTION
58466	21	88	EDUCATIONAL SERVICES
58467	82	251	CROP PRODUCTION
58472	21	67	EDUCATIONAL SERVICES
58474	196	1273	MACHINERY MANUFACTURING
58475	12	19	MERCH. WHOLESALERS;NONDUR. GDS
58476	22	81	ADMIN. ENVIRO. QUALITY PROGRMS
58477	6	8	CROP PRODUCTION
58478	15	19	EDUCATIONAL SERVICES
58479	9	68	EDUCATIONAL SERVICES
58480	17	33	MERCH. WHOLESALERS;NONDUR. GDS
58481	14	91	FOOD MANUFACTURING
58482	93	509	TELECOMMUNICATIONS
58483	24	67	FOOD SVCS & DRINKING PLACES
58484	8	25	RELIG.; GRANT; CIVIC; PROF ORG
58486	32	41	CROP PRODUCTION
58487	27	137	SUPPORT ACTIVITIES: AGR./FOR.
58488	17	25	JUSTICE; PUBIC ORDER/SAFETY
58490	15	28	MERCH. WHOLESALERS;NONDUR. GDS
58492	29	118	EDUCATIONAL SERVICES
58494	27	109	EDUCATIONAL SERVICES
58495	111	805	RELIG.; GRANT; CIVIC; PROF ORG
58496	30	48	CROP PRODUCTION
58497	14	41	CROP PRODUCTION
58501	2046	29594	AMBULATORY HEALTH CARE SVCS
58502	30	45	PUBLISHING INDUSTRIES
58503	865	11622	FOOD SVCS & DRINKING PLACES
58504	1359	16896	SPECIAL TRADE CONTRACTORS
58505	114	3430	ADMIN. OF ECONOMIC PROGRAMS
58506	8	77	TEXTILE PRODUCT MILLS
58507	5	11	CONSTRUCTION OF BUILDINGS
58520	13	20	EDUCATIONAL SERVICES
58521	18	47	BLDG MATL & GARDEN EQPMT DLRS
58523	234	3036	OIL AND GAS EXTRACTION
58524	10	10	ACCOMMODATION
58528	7	42	EDUCATIONAL SERVICES
58529	63	227	EDUCATIONAL SERVICES
58530	98	733	UTILITIES
58531	8	28	ADMIN. ENVIRO. QUALITY PROGRMS
58532	13	14	TRUCK TRANSPORTATION
58533	84	450	AMBULATORY HEALTH CARE SVCS
58535	37	163	EDUCATIONAL SERVICES
58538	136	2470	EXEC.; LEGIS.; & OTHER SUPPORT
58540	149	1031	EDUCATIONAL SERVICES
58541	13	30	PROF.; SCIENTIFIC; & TECH SVCS
58542	16	28	FOOD SVCS & DRINKING PLACES
58544	35	149	EDUCATIONAL SERVICES
58545	208	1304	EDUCATIONAL SERVICES
58549	8	17	MERCH. WHOLESALERS;DURABLE GDS
58552	147	899	EDUCATIONAL SERVICES
58554	938	8441	EDUCATIONAL SERVICES
58558	21	79	MERCH. WHOLESALERS;DURABLE GDS
58559	23	22	FOOD SVCS & DRINKING PLACES
58560	7	25	ADMIN. ENVIRO. QUALITY PROGRMS
58561	85	419	RELIG.; GRANT; CIVIC; PROF ORG
58562	23	49	FABRICATED METAL PRODUCT MFG
58563	90	561	EDUCATIONAL SERVICES
58564	6	70	RELIG.; GRANT; CIVIC; PROF ORG
58565	26	151	ACCOMMODATION
58566	12	16	EDUCATIONAL SERVICES
58568	23	75	EDUCATIONAL SERVICES
58569	7	14	SOCIAL ASSISTANCE
58570	18	56	EDUCATIONAL SERVICES
58571	53	468	UTILITIES
58572	22	54	GASOLINE STATIONS
58573	37	284	RELIG.; GRANT; CIVIC; PROF ORG
58575	71	236	HOSPITALS
58576	56	1288	UTILITIES
58577	135	776	EDUCATIONAL SERVICES
58579	39	316	EDUCATIONAL SERVICES
58580	27	38	WASTE MANAGMT & REMEDIAT'N SVC
58581	19	50	EDUCATIONAL SERVICES
58601	1238	12588	FOOD SVCS & DRINKING PLACES
58602	9	24	SOCIAL ASSISTANCE
58620	27	27	RELIG.; GRANT; CIVIC; PROF ORG
58621	171	642	MERCH. WHOLESALERS;DURABLE GDS
58622	119	789	SPECIAL TRADE CONTRACTORS
58623	215	1350	FOOD SVCS & DRINKING PLACES
58625	13	19	SPECIAL TRADE CONTRACTORS
58626	14	27	JUSTICE; PUBIC ORDER/SAFETY
58627	5	20	EDUCATIONAL SERVICES
58630	11	28	INSURANCE CARRIERS & RELATED
58631	74	404	NURSING & RESID. CARE FACILIT.
58632	21	56	EDUCATIONAL SERVICES

BUSINESS DATA

ZIP CODE	2009 Total Firms	2009 Total Employ-ees	TOP INDUSTRY RANKED on 2009 EMPLOYMENT	ZIP CODE	2009 Total Firms	2009 Total Employ-ees	TOP INDUSTRY RANKED on 2009 EMPLOYMENT	ZIP CODE	2009 Total Firms	2009 Total Employ-ees	TOP INDUSTRY RANKED on 2009 EMPLOYMENT
58634	19	93	CONSTRUCTION OF BUILDINGS	58843	26	39	REPAIR AND MAINTENANCE	59211	5	10	POSTAL SERVICE
58636	46	144	EDUCATIONAL SERVICES	58844	14	30	WAREHOUSING AND STORAGE	59212	14	76	EDUCATIONAL SERVICES
58638	72	253	EDUCATIONAL SERVICES	58845	33	122	EDUCATIONAL SERVICES	59213	18	159	EDUCATIONAL SERVICES
58639	170	1384	HOSPITALS	58847	23	38	OIL AND GAS EXTRACTION	59214	5	5	ANIMAL PRODUCTION
58640	90	438	FOOD SVCS & DRINKING PLACES	58849	64	455	EDUCATIONAL SERVICES	59215	124	776	EDUCATIONAL SERVICES
58641	4	7	RELIG.; GRANT; CIVIC; PROF ORG	58852	138	994	EDUCATIONAL SERVICES	59217	4	8	POSTAL SERVICE
58642	24	68	EXEC.; LEGIS.; & OTHER SUPPORT	58853	27	423	AMBULATORY HEALTH CARE SVCS	59218	63	373	HOSPITALS
58643	19	84	SPECIAL TRADE CONTRACTORS	58854	228	1403	FOOD SVCS & DRINKING PLACES	59219	10	11	TRUCK TRANSPORTATION
58645	98	544	MISCELLANEOUS STORE RETAILERS	58856	9	18	WAREHOUSING AND STORAGE	59221	49	199	SPECIAL TRADE CONTRACTORS
58646	86	500	AMBULATORY HEALTH CARE SVCS	59001	119	320	EDUCATIONAL SERVICES	59222	14	26	SPECIAL TRADE CONTRACTORS
58647	61	392	EDUCATIONAL SERVICES	59002	6	36	PERFORM'G ARTS; SPEC. SPORTS	59223	24	84	ADMIN. ENVIRO. QUALITY PROGRMS
58649	20	59	SPECIAL TRADE CONTRACTORS	59003	41	221	EDUCATIONAL SERVICES	59225	24	153	EDUCATIONAL SERVICES
58650	35	100	FOOD AND BEVERAGE STORES	59006	22	41	ADMIN. OF ECONOMIC PROGRAMS	59226	24	40	FOOD SVCS & DRINKING PLACES
58651	30	87	JUSTICE; PUBIC ORDER/SAFETY	59007	4	5	FOOD SVCS & DRINKING PLACES	59230	363	2254	HOSPITALS
58652	61	300	PROF.; SCIENTIFIC; & TECH SVCS	59008	22	55	EDUCATIONAL SERVICES	59231	6	12	TRANSPORTATION EQUIPMENT MFG
58653	37	231	EDUCATIONAL SERVICES	59010	5	11	ANIMAL PRODUCTION	59240	2	1	POSTAL SERVICE
58654	7	101	SOCIAL ASSISTANCE	59011	269	1584	MINING (EXCEPT OIL AND GAS)	59241	23	50	EDUCATIONAL SERVICES
58655	28	111	EDUCATIONAL SERVICES	59012	10	16	EXEC.; LEGIS.; & OTHER SUPPORT	59242	8	61	EDUCATIONAL SERVICES
58656	21	87	SECURITIES/COMMODITY CONTRACTS	59013	5	10	SPECIAL TRADE CONTRACTORS	59243	21	80	SPECIAL TRADE CONTRACTORS
58701	1901	21933	HOSPITALS	59014	79	302	EDUCATIONAL SERVICES	59244	4	2	SUPPORT ACTIVITIES: AGR./FOR.
58702	23	53	CONSTRUCTION OF BUILDINGS	59015	23	106	EDUCATIONAL SERVICES	59247	19	81	EDUCATIONAL SERVICES
58703	526	6300	INSURANCE CARRIERS & RELATED	59016	15	222	EDUCATIONAL SERVICES	59248	24	56	EDUCATIONAL SERVICES
58704	11	254	EDUCATIONAL SERVICES	59018	34	388	ANIMAL PRODUCTION	59250	19	103	EDUCATIONAL SERVICES
58705	50	1039	ADMINISTRATIVE & SUPPORT SVCS	59019	232	1483	MINING (EXCEPT OIL AND GAS)	59252	6	7	GASOLINE STATIONS
58707	3	832	EDUCATIONAL SERVICES	59020	33	191	FOOD SVCS & DRINKING PLACES	59253	8	35	EDUCATIONAL SERVICES
58710	32	61	EDUCATIONAL SERVICES	59022	96	1721	EXEC.; LEGIS.; & OTHER SUPPORT	59254	200	1265	NURSING & RESID. CARE FACILIT.
58711	21	33	CONSTRUCTION OF BUILDINGS	59024	15	49	EDUCATIONAL SERVICES	59255	145	1594	EXEC.; LEGIS.; & OTHER SUPPORT
58712	4	5	HEAVY & CIVIL ENG. CONSTRUCT'N	59025	21	312	MINING (EXCEPT OIL AND GAS)	59256	8	15	NAT'L SECURITY & INT'L AFFAIRS
58713	1	0	POSTAL SERVICE	59026	7	20	MERCH. WHOLESALERS;NONDUR. GDS	59257	5	5	POSTAL SERVICE
58716	7	15	SPECIAL TRADE CONTRACTORS	59027	49	332	MERCH. WHOLESALERS;DURABLE GDS	59258	7	11	ANIMAL PRODUCTION
58718	57	282	CONSTRUCTION OF BUILDINGS	59028	27	91	ACCOMMODATION	59259	25	91	EDUCATIONAL SERVICES
58721	81	301	JUSTICE; PUBIC ORDER/SAFETY	59029	16	135	EDUCATIONAL SERVICES	59260	9	12	CROP PRODUCTION
58722	45	195	EDUCATIONAL SERVICES	59030	104	932	ACCOMMODATION	59261	28	136	EDUCATIONAL SERVICES
58723	17	18	MERCH. WHOLESALERS;NONDUR. GDS	59031	8	35	MUSEUMS; HIST. SITES;& SIMILAR	59262	19	70	EDUCATIONAL SERVICES
58725	19	36	AMBULATORY HEALTH CARE SVCS	59032	19	87	EDUCATIONAL SERVICES	59263	134	681	TELECOMMUNICATIONS
58727	19	39	RELIG.; GRANT; CIVIC; PROF ORG	59033	6	2	EDUCATIONAL SERVICES	59270	503	4273	SPECIAL TRADE CONTRACTORS
58730	151	769	NURSING & RESID. CARE FACILIT.	59034	307	1788	EDUCATIONAL SERVICES	59273	3	1	FURN. & HOME FURNISHGS STORES
58731	12	13	HEAVY & CIVIL ENG. CONSTRUCT'N	59035	34	143	ACCOMMODATION	59274	10	16	CROP PRODUCTION
58733	14	42	EDUCATIONAL SERVICES	59036	115	584	HOSPITALS	59275	21	88	EDUCATIONAL SERVICES
58734	17	40	AMUSEMENT; GAMBLING;& RECREAT.	59037	76	255	UTILITIES	59276	4	5	CROP PRODUCTION
58735	3	8	POSTAL SERVICE	59038	55	135	EDUCATIONAL SERVICES	59301	657	5512	NURSING & RESID. CARE FACILIT.
58736	27	110	EDUCATIONAL SERVICES	59039	4	14	ACCOMMODATION	59311	16	17	GASOLINE STATIONS
58737	17	13	WAREHOUSING AND STORAGE	59041	86	298	EDUCATIONAL SERVICES	59312	5	3	AIR TRANSPORTATION
58740	38	145	EDUCATIONAL SERVICES	59043	119	1146	EXEC.; LEGIS.; & OTHER SUPPORT	59313	237	1601	SPECIAL TRADE CONTRACTORS
58741	30	91	EDUCATIONAL SERVICES	59044	398	4054	PIPELINE TRANSPORTATION	59314	3	6	ANIMAL PRODUCTION
58744	12	19	RAIL TRANSPORTATION	59046	23	61	EDUCATIONAL SERVICES	59315	9	12	MERCH. WHOLESALERS;NONDUR. GDS
58746	118	765	HOSPITALS	59047	875	4760	FOOD SVCS & DRINKING PLACES	59316	3	2	PROF.; SCIENTIFIC; & TECH SVCS
58748	8	11	WAREHOUSING AND STORAGE	59050	31	283	EDUCATIONAL SERVICES	59317	127	456	EDUCATIONAL SERVICES
58750	27	62	MERCH. WHOLESALERS;NONDUR. GDS	59052	17	87	ACCOMMODATION	59318	5	4	CONSTRUCTION OF BUILDINGS
58752	32	101	EDUCATIONAL SERVICES	59053	22	159	ANIMAL PRODUCTION	59322	2	4	EDUCATIONAL SERVICES
58755	6	12	OIL AND GAS EXTRACTION	59054	24	41	EDUCATIONAL SERVICES	59323	98	1476	MINING (EXCEPT OIL AND GAS)
58756	14	47	EDUCATIONAL SERVICES	59055	14	10	ANIMAL PRODUCTION	59324	66	318	EDUCATIONAL SERVICES
58757	32	334	EDUCATIONAL SERVICES	59057	21	50	PROF.; SCIENTIFIC; & TECH SVCS	59326	10	21	JUSTICE; PUBIC ORDER/SAFETY
58758	12	15	REPAIR AND MAINTENANCE	59058	3	6	SPORTG GDS;HOBBY;BOOK; & MUSIC	59327	183	1199	EXEC.; LEGIS.; & OTHER SUPPORT
58759	36	98	EDUCATIONAL SERVICES	59059	13	14	ANIMAL PRODUCTION	59330	471	4453	NURSING & RESID. CARE FACILIT.
58760	14	71	SPECIAL TRADE CONTRACTORS	59061	20	48	JUSTICE; PUBIC ORDER/SAFETY	59332	3	3	SPORTG GDS;HOBBY;BOOK; & MUSIC
58761	101	525	EDUCATIONAL SERVICES	59062	1	4	SPORTG GDS;HOBBY;BOOK; & MUSIC	59333	1	0	SUPPORT ACTIVITIES: AGR./FOR.
58762	32	95	EDUCATIONAL SERVICES	59063	50	268	EDUCATIONAL SERVICES	59336	12	40	JUSTICE; PUBIC ORDER/SAFETY
58763	249	2945	EDUCATIONAL SERVICES	59064	8	19	UNCLASSIFIED ESTABLISHMENTS	59337	87	284	EDUCATIONAL SERVICES
58765	27	98	ADMINISTRATIVE & SUPPORT SVCS	59065	20	185	ACCOMMODATION	59338	4	21	EDUCATIONAL SERVICES
58768	7	8	WAREHOUSING AND STORAGE	59066	17	165	EDUCATIONAL SERVICES	59339	11	15	PROF.; SCIENTIFIC; & TECH SVCS
58769	10	16	FOOD SVCS & DRINKING PLACES	59067	11	68	EDUCATIONAL SERVICES	59343	1	1	FOOD MANUFACTURING
58770	66	379	RELIG.; GRANT; CIVIC; PROF ORG	59068	386	2159	FOOD SVCS & DRINKING PLACES	59344	15	47	EDUCATIONAL SERVICES
58771	30	102	EDUCATIONAL SERVICES	59069	15	63	EDUCATIONAL SERVICES	59345	2	4	ANIMAL PRODUCTION
58772	33	98	PROF.; SCIENTIFIC; & TECH SVCS	59070	34	105	CONSTRUCTION OF BUILDINGS	59347	11	36	EDUCATIONAL SERVICES
58773	55	146	EDUCATIONAL SERVICES	59071	7	27	ANIMAL PRODUCTION	59349	89	294	EDUCATIONAL SERVICES
58775	21	161	EDUCATIONAL SERVICES	59072	251	1085	HOSPITALS	59351	6	6	POSTAL SERVICE
58776	13	28	MERCH. WHOLESALERS;NONDUR. GDS	59074	32	135	ANIMAL PRODUCTION	59353	72	246	EDUCATIONAL SERVICES
58778	5	12	FOOD SVCS & DRINKING PLACES	59075	10	46	EDUCATIONAL SERVICES	59401	1063	9257	ADMINISTRATIVE & SUPPORT SVCS
58779	23	45	EDUCATIONAL SERVICES	59077	4	6	ANIMAL PRODUCTION	59402	38	3571	NAT'L SECURITY & INT'L AFFAIRS
58781	31	82	EDUCATIONAL SERVICES	59078	4	6	EDUCATIONAL SERVICES	59403	27	82	NURSING & RESID. CARE FACILIT.
58782	33	112	EDUCATIONAL SERVICES	59079	69	345	EDUCATIONAL SERVICES	59404	860	7826	FOOD SVCS & DRINKING PLACES
58783	24	39	MERCH. WHOLESALERS;NONDUR. GDS	59081	8	46	ACCOMMODATION	59405	1490	19116	AMBULATORY HEALTH CARE SVCS
58784	192	1519	AMBULATORY HEALTH CARE SVCS	59082	6	4	SPECIAL TRADE CONTRACTORS	59406	13	27	SPECIAL TRADE CONTRACTORS
58785	29	171	EDUCATIONAL SERVICES	59084	1	5	ANIMAL PRODUCTION	59410	82	224	ACCOMMODATION
58787	12	18	WAREHOUSING AND STORAGE	59085	13	34	ANIMAL PRODUCTION	59411	17	28	EDUCATIONAL SERVICES
58788	80	392	SOCIAL ASSISTANCE	59086	42	128	EDUCATIONAL SERVICES	59412	62	198	EDUCATIONAL SERVICES
58789	23	56	ADMIN. ENVIRO. QUALITY PROGRMS	59087	38	95	EDUCATIONAL SERVICES	59414	104	949	RELIG.; GRANT; CIVIC; PROF ORG
58790	74	556	RELIG.; GRANT; CIVIC; PROF ORG	59088	56	242	EDUCATIONAL SERVICES	59416	21	43	EDUCATIONAL SERVICES
58792	5	36	WAREHOUSING AND STORAGE	59089	9	52	EDUCATIONAL SERVICES	59417	275	6714	EXEC.; LEGIS.; & OTHER SUPPORT
58793	58	321	RELIG.; GRANT; CIVIC; PROF ORG	59101	3606	47614	AMBULATORY HEALTH CARE SVCS	59418	1	1	POSTAL SERVICE
58794	9	63	POSTAL SERVICE	59102	2752	25802	FOOD SVCS & DRINKING PLACES	59419	6	15	EDUCATIONAL SERVICES
58795	21	32	FOOD SVCS & DRINKING PLACES	59103	29	26	SPECIAL TRADE CONTRACTORS	59420	22	116	SUPPORT ACTIVITIES: AGR./FOR.
58801	1260	11368	SUPPORT ACTIVITIES FOR MINING	59104	54	72	SPECIAL TRADE CONTRACTORS	59421	64	387	EDUCATIONAL SERVICES
58802	15	21	CONSTRUCTION OF BUILDINGS	59105	929	5212	FOOD SVCS & DRINKING PLACES	59422	239	1041	CROP PRODUCTION
58830	14	25	JUSTICE; PUBIC ORDER/SAFETY	59106	317	2296	EDUCATIONAL SERVICES	59424	5	8	MOTOR VEHICLE & PARTS DEALERS
58831	35	116	EDUCATIONAL SERVICES	59107	21	63	REPAIR AND MAINTENANCE	59425	281	1630	AMBULATORY HEALTH CARE SVCS
58833	11	11	POSTAL SERVICE	59108	26	112	ADMINISTRATIVE & SUPPORT SVCS	59427	349	1894	ANIMAL PRODUCTION
58835	20	32	OIL AND GAS EXTRACTION	59117	1	100	CREDIT INTERMEDIATION & RELATD	59430	26	132	EDUCATIONAL SERVICES
58838	8	30	CONSTRUCTION OF BUILDINGS	59201	246	1769	HOSPITALS	59432	16	23	ANIMAL PRODUCTION

ZIP CODE	2009 Total Firms	2009 Total Employ-ees	TOP INDUSTRY RANKED on 2009 EMPLOYMENT	ZIP CODE	2009 Total Firms	2009 Total Employ-ees	TOP INDUSTRY RANKED on 2009 EMPLOYMENT	ZIP CODE	2009 Total Firms	2009 Total Employ-ees	TOP INDUSTRY RANKED on 2009 EMPLOYMENT
59433	29	81	EDUCATIONAL SERVICES	59703	7	15	SPECIAL TRADE CONTRACTORS	59865	157	1001	EXEC.; LEGIS.; & OTHER SUPPORT
59434	45	145	ACCOMMODATION	59710	31	63	MINING (EXCEPT OIL AND GAS)	59866	51	279	WOOD PRODUCT MANUFACTURING
59435	8	55	MERCH. WHOLESALERS;DURABLE GDS	59711	406	2847	ACCOMMODATION	59867	4	4	FOOD SVCS & DRINKING PLACES
59436	136	739	EDUCATIONAL SERVICES	59713	16	31	FOOD SVCS & DRINKING PLACES	59868	176	762	WOOD PRODUCT MANUFACTURING
59440	6	17	WASTE MANAGMT & REMEDIAT'N SVC	59714	868	5196	SPECIAL TRADE CONTRACTORS	59870	409	2088	EDUCATIONAL SERVICES
59441	2	1	SCENIC & SIGHTSEEING TRANSPORT	59715	2526	19955	FOOD SVCS & DRINKING PLACES	59871	12	45	EXEC.; LEGIS.; & OTHER SUPPORT
59442	185	828	NURSING & RESID. CARE FACILIT.	59716	403	3067	ACCOMMODATION	59872	158	838	EDUCATIONAL SERVICES
59443	27	51	EDUCATIONAL SERVICES	59717	32	592	EDUCATIONAL SERVICES	59873	266	1444	EDUCATIONAL SERVICES
59444	13	30	CROP PRODUCTION	59718	1575	12253	PROF.; SCIENTIFIC; & TECH SVCS	59874	60	195	WOOD PRODUCT MANUFACTURING
59446	31	120	EDUCATIONAL SERVICES	59719	30	104	SPECIAL TRADE CONTRACTORS	59875	193	968	WOOD PRODUCT MANUFACTURING
59447	20	51	EDUCATIONAL SERVICES	59720	37	113	MINING (EXCEPT OIL AND GAS)	59901	3813	31731	AMBULATORY HEALTH CARE SVCS
59448	14	177	EDUCATIONAL SERVICES	59721	12	28	EDUCATIONAL SERVICES	59903	68	105	SPECIAL TRADE CONTRACTORS
59450	15	54	EDUCATIONAL SERVICES	59722	234	2559	JUSTICE; PUBIC ORDER/SAFETY	59904	33	90	SPECIAL TRADE CONTRACTORS
59451	5	11	MINING (EXCEPT OIL AND GAS)	59724	6	23	FOOD SVCS & DRINKING PLACES	59910	10	35	ACCOMMODATION
59452	25	118	ANIMAL PRODUCTION	59725	519	3021	EDUCATIONAL SERVICES	59911	632	2775	FOOD SVCS & DRINKING PLACES
59453	12	39	EDUCATIONAL SERVICES	59727	11	17	RELIG.; GRANT; CIVIC; PROF ORG	59912	707	5860	CONSTRUCTION OF BUILDINGS
59454	22	44	SECURITIES/COMMODITY CONTRACTS	59728	12	20	EDUCATIONAL SERVICES	59913	30	66	FOOD SVCS & DRINKING PLACES
59456	11	30	CROP PRODUCTION	59729	358	944	ACCOMMODATION	59914	15	42	BEVERAGE & TOBACCO PRODUCT MFG
59457	560	4155	NURSING & RESID. CARE FACILIT.	59730	152	1060	ACCOMMODATION	59915	21	41	RELIG.; GRANT; CIVIC; PROF ORG
59460	19	36	SPECIAL TRADE CONTRACTORS	59731	7	6	EDUCATIONAL SERVICES	59916	6	29	ACCOMMODATION
59461	2	2	CROP PRODUCTION	59732	4	4	EDUCATIONAL SERVICES	59917	420	1456	AMUSEMENT; GAMBLING;& RECREAT.
59462	7	33	REPAIR AND MAINTENANCE	59733	10	34	ACCOMMODATION	59918	31	216	WOOD PRODUCT MANUFACTURING
59463	10	16	ACCOMMODATION	59735	27	81	EDUCATIONAL SERVICES	59919	57	259	EXEC.; LEGIS.; & OTHER SUPPORT
59464	21	113	EDUCATIONAL SERVICES	59736	26	54	PERSONAL AND LAUNDRY SERVICES	59920	32	87	EDUCATIONAL SERVICES
59465	19	106	ACCOMMODATION	59739	38	150	EDUCATIONAL SERVICES	59921	1	0	POSTAL SERVICE
59466	18	91	OIL AND GAS EXTRACTION	59740	21	29	FOOD SVCS & DRINKING PLACES	59922	159	929	ACCOMMODATION
59467	16	223	ANIMAL PRODUCTION	59741	176	1062	EDUCATIONAL SERVICES	59923	655	3795	SUPPORT ACTIVITIES: AGR./FOR.
59468	23	76	EDUCATIONAL SERVICES	59743	18	45	FOOD SVCS & DRINKING PLACES	59925	51	186	EDUCATIONAL SERVICES
59469	11	17	MERCH. WHOLESALERS;NONDUR. GDS	59745	19	122	TRUCK TRANSPORTATION	59926	11	36	FOOD SVCS & DRINKING PLACES
59471	17	67	EDUCATIONAL SERVICES	59746	10	26	ACCOMMODATION	59927	17	86	FORESTRY AND LOGGING
59472	15	283	EDUCATIONAL SERVICES	59747	17	16	MERCH. WHOLESALERS;NONDUR. GDS	59928	4	9	GENERAL MERCHANDISE STORES
59474	288	1781	HOSPITALS	59748	7	119	EDUCATIONAL SERVICES	59929	7	23	ACCOMMODATION
59477	18	102	EDUCATIONAL SERVICES	59749	119	528	EDUCATIONAL SERVICES	59930	35	66	FURN. & HOME FURNISHGS STORES
59479	73	317	SUPPORT ACTIVITIES: AGR./FOR.	59750	11	243	MISCELLANEOUS MANUFACTURING	59931	15	26	POSTAL SERVICE
59480	10	39	JUSTICE; PUBIC ORDER/SAFETY	59751	5	6	SPORTG GDS;HOBBY;BOOK; & MUSIC	59932	69	246	EDUCATIONAL SERVICES
59482	58	210	EDUCATIONAL SERVICES	59752	186	1405	UNCLASSIFIED ESTABLISHMENTS	59933	3	2	SPECIAL TRADE CONTRACTORS
59483	24	64	ANIMAL PRODUCTION	59754	88	321	EDUCATIONAL SERVICES	59934	25	42	EDUCATIONAL SERVICES
59484	35	201	ADMINISTRATIVE & SUPPORT SVCS	59755	64	472	RELIG.; GRANT; CIVIC; PROF ORG	59935	164	607	EXEC.; LEGIS.; & OTHER SUPPORT
59485	21	104	ANIMAL PRODUCTION	59756	14	558	HOSPITALS	59936	52	921	MUSEUMS; HIST. SITES;& SIMILAR
59486	72	651	EDUCATIONAL SERVICES	59758	318	2027	ACCOMMODATION	59937	1118	7204	ACCOMMODATION
59487	24	135	EDUCATIONAL SERVICES	59759	176	812	MINING (EXCEPT OIL AND GAS)	60001	2	6	NONSTORE RETAILERS
59489	30	84	EDUCATIONAL SERVICES	59760	7	46	EDUCATIONAL SERVICES	60002	975	6524	FOOD SVCS & DRINKING PLACES
59501	770	7423	CREDIT INTERMEDIATION & RELATD	59761	40	101	ANIMAL PRODUCTION	60004	1957	23130	TELECOMMUNICATIONS
59520	100	352	EDUCATIONAL SERVICES	59762	26	69	SPORTG GDS;HOBBY;BOOK; & MUSIC	60005	1969	30829	HOSPITALS
59521	71	2134	EXEC.; LEGIS.; & OTHER SUPPORT	59771	38	42	REAL ESTATE	60006	11	38	SPECIAL TRADE CONTRACTORS
59522	145	766	EDUCATIONAL SERVICES	59772	25	47	SPECIAL TRADE CONTRACTORS	60007	3598	56915	MERCH. WHOLESALERS;DURABLE GDS
59523	200	849	EDUCATIONAL SERVICES	59773	1	1	EDUCATIONAL SERVICES	60008	1181	18667	COMPUTER & ELECTRONIC PROD MFG
59524	20	62	EDUCATIONAL SERVICES	59801	2109	17493	FOOD SVCS & DRINKING PLACES	60009	5	31	FABRICATED METAL PRODUCT MFG
59525	21	3113	UNCLASSIFIED ESTABLISHMENTS	59802	1424	14964	EXEC.; LEGIS.; & OTHER SUPPORT	60010	2365	24944	HOSPITALS
59526	95	1038	EXEC.; LEGIS.; & OTHER SUPPORT	59803	355	1294	EDUCATIONAL SERVICES	60011	28	91	AMBULATORY HEALTH CARE SVCS
59527	30	263	EDUCATIONAL SERVICES	59804	327	4796	HOSPITALS	60012	346	5124	MERCH. WHOLESALERS;DURABLE GDS
59528	20	54	CROP PRODUCTION	59806	60	145	ADMINISTRATIVE & SUPPORT SVCS	60013	792	7284	EDUCATIONAL SERVICES
59529	9	20	CROP PRODUCTION	59807	21	24	INSURANCE CARRIERS & RELATED	60014	2263	24816	EDUCATIONAL SERVICES
59530	12	52	JUSTICE; PUBIC ORDER/SAFETY	59808	1167	16691	FOOD SVCS & DRINKING PLACES	60015	1779	46381	MISCELLANEOUS MANUFACTURING
59531	29	38	CROP PRODUCTION	59812	41	1953	EDUCATIONAL SERVICES	60016	1736	18217	EDUCATIONAL SERVICES
59532	7	9	MERCH. WHOLESALERS;NONDUR. GDS	59820	52	156	EDUCATIONAL SERVICES	60017	6	11	SPECIAL TRADE CONTRACTORS
59535	9	4	ANIMAL PRODUCTION	59821	93	466	EDUCATIONAL SERVICES	60018	2261	47883	PROF.; SCIENTIFIC; & TECH SVCS
59537	9	26	CROP PRODUCTION	59823	62	1284	WOOD PRODUCT MANUFACTURING	60020	414	3107	FOOD SVCS & DRINKING PLACES
59538	240	1365	EDUCATIONAL SERVICES	59824	64	230	EDUCATIONAL SERVICES	60021	208	1274	FOOD SVCS & DRINKING PLACES
59540	35	135	EDUCATIONAL SERVICES	59825	83	225	EDUCATIONAL SERVICES	60022	342	3085	MUSEUMS; HIST. SITES;& SIMILAR
59542	24	84	EDUCATIONAL SERVICES	59826	71	155	EDUCATIONAL SERVICES	60025	1809	16993	RELIG.; GRANT; CIVIC; PROF ORG
59544	13	74	EDUCATIONAL SERVICES	59827	11	38	ACCOMMODATION	60026	685	11796	MERCH. WHOLESALERS;DURABLE GDS
59545	11	7	CROP PRODUCTION	59828	166	574	EDUCATIONAL SERVICES	60029	17	238	RELIG.; GRANT; CIVIC; PROF ORG
59546	12	28	PROF.; SCIENTIFIC; & TECH SVCS	59829	124	791	EDUCATIONAL SERVICES	60030	1171	11065	EDUCATIONAL SERVICES
59547	8	19	EDUCATIONAL SERVICES	59830	8	27	ADMIN. OF ECONOMIC PROGRAMS	60031	1639	22829	AMUSEMENT; GAMBLING;& RECREAT.
59601	2526	33247	ADMIN. HUMAN RESOURCE PROGRAMS	59831	13	54	JUSTICE; PUBIC ORDER/SAFETY	60033	501	3668	EDUCATIONAL SERVICES
59602	600	4755	NAT'L SECURITY & INT'L AFFAIRS	59832	54	229	CONSTRUCTION OF BUILDINGS	60034	101	917	MACHINERY MANUFACTURING
59604	29	52	RELIG.; GRANT; CIVIC; PROF ORG	59833	177	810	EDUCATIONAL SERVICES	60035	1950	16063	PAPER MANUFACTURING
59620	7	419	ADMIN. ENVIRO. QUALITY PROGRMS	59834	81	336	EDUCATIONAL SERVICES	60037	8	53	NAT'L SECURITY & INT'L AFFAIRS
59623	8	440	EXEC.; LEGIS.; & OTHER SUPPORT	59835	1	1	CONSTRUCTION OF BUILDINGS	60039	19	63	FOOD AND BEVERAGE STORES
59624	22	29	RELIG.; GRANT; CIVIC; PROF ORG	59837	16	38	MERCH. WHOLESALERS;NONDUR. GDS	60040	234	1668	FOOD SVCS & DRINKING PLACES
59625	2	232	EDUCATIONAL SERVICES	59840	1064	6635	FOOD SVCS & DRINKING PLACES	60041	243	1513	EDUCATIONAL SERVICES
59626	13	32	ADMIN. OF HOUSING PROGRAMS	59841	7	25	EDUCATIONAL SERVICES	60042	223	1481	MERCH. WHOLESALERS;DURABLE GDS
59631	10	17	FOOD SVCS & DRINKING PLACES	59842	7	157	GASOLINE STATIONS	60043	92	477	EXEC.; LEGIS.; & OTHER SUPPORT
59632	112	888	EXEC.; LEGIS.; & OTHER SUPPORT	59843	17	19	ANIMAL PRODUCTION	60044	718	7357	ADMINISTRATIVE & SUPPORT SVCS
59633	7	7	ANIMAL PRODUCTION	59844	32	117	FABRICATED METAL PRODUCT MFG	60045	1295	23889	INSURANCE CARRIERS & RELATED
59634	108	788	NONMETALLIC MINERAL PROD. MFG	59845	97	409	EDUCATIONAL SERVICES	60046	806	5520	NURSING & RESID. CARE FACILIT.
59635	161	964	EDUCATIONAL SERVICES	59846	29	84	SUPPORT ACTIVITIES: AGR./FOR.	60047	1663	16184	FOOD SVCS & DRINKING PLACES
59636	9	936	AMBULATORY HEALTH CARE SVCS	59847	206	987	EDUCATIONAL SERVICES	60048	1949	23060	HOSPITALS
59638	6	209	MINING (EXCEPT OIL AND GAS)	59848	3	1	AMBULATORY HEALTH CARE SVCS	60049	10	1153	INSURANCE CARRIERS & RELATED
59639	128	624	MISCELLANEOUS STORE RETAILERS	59851	13	41	CREDIT INTERMEDIATION & RELATD	60050	1222	18684	HOSPITALS
59640	7	47	ACCOMMODATION	59853	54	207	EDUCATIONAL SERVICES	60051	782	6334	GENERAL MERCHANDISE STORES
59642	2	4	TRUCK TRANSPORTATION	59854	36	84	AMUSEMENT; GAMBLING;& RECREAT.	60053	993	14493	PROF.; SCIENTIFIC; & TECH SVCS
59643	5	27	SPECIAL TRADE CONTRACTORS	59855	90	2011	EXEC.; LEGIS.; & OTHER SUPPORT	60056	1623	19374	MERCH. WHOLESALERS;DURABLE GDS
59644	194	1082	EDUCATIONAL SERVICES	59856	5	13	EDUCATIONAL SERVICES	60060	1524	21311	MISCELLANEOUS MANUFACTURING
59645	137	574	ANIMAL PRODUCTION	59858	117	826	ANIMAL PRODUCTION	60061	1110	18196	PROF.; SCIENTIFIC; & TECH SVCS
59647	4	18	MERCH. WHOLESALERS;DURABLE GDS	59859	204	1001	HOSPITALS	60062	3930	67112	INSURANCE CARRIERS & RELATED
59648	49	280	CROP PRODUCTION	59860	821	4278	EXEC.; LEGIS.; & OTHER SUPPORT	60064	359	28699	CHEMICAL MANUFACTURING
59701	1733	15725	SOCIAL ASSISTANCE	59863	7	13	FOOD SVCS & DRINKING PLACES	60065	25	58	REPAIR AND MAINTENANCE
59702	10	13	CONSTRUCTION OF BUILDINGS	59864	381	2471	HOSPITALS	60067	1738	15354	EDUCATIONAL SERVICES

BUSINESS DATA

ZIP CODE	2009 Total Firms	2009 Total Employ-ees	TOP INDUSTRY RANKED on 2009 EMPLOYMENT	ZIP CODE	2009 Total Firms	2009 Total Employ-ees	TOP INDUSTRY RANKED on 2009 EMPLOYMENT	ZIP CODE	2009 Total Firms	2009 Total Employ-ees	TOP INDUSTRY RANKED on 2009 EMPLOYMENT
60068	1779	19724	HOSPITALS	60176	530	8937	FOOD SVCS & DRINKING PLACES	60465	533	5544	EDUCATIONAL SERVICES
60069	654	23811	FUNDS; TRUSTS; & OTHER FINANCE	60177	710	7762	FOOD SVCS & DRINKING PLACES	60466	576	8651	EDUCATIONAL SERVICES
60070	424	3520	CREDIT INTERMEDIATION & RELATD	60178	904	10606	EDUCATIONAL SERVICES	60467	740	5728	AMBULATORY HEALTH CARE SVCS
60071	249	2240	COMPUTER & ELECTRONIC PROD MFG	60179	7	12600	GENERAL MERCHANDISE STORES	60468	238	1857	MOTOR VEHICLE & PARTS DEALERS
60072	79	998	FABRICATED METAL PRODUCT MFG	60180	104	1573	SPECIAL TRADE CONTRACTORS	60469	146	1136	SPECIAL TRADE CONTRACTORS
60073	985	8222	FOOD SVCS & DRINKING PLACES	60181	1953	23092	EDUCATIONAL SERVICES	60470	25	122	NONMETALLIC MINERAL PROD. MFG
60074	963	7637	EDUCATIONAL SERVICES	60183	20	189	EDUCATIONAL SERVICES	60471	241	1739	EXEC.; LEGIS.; & OTHER SUPPORT
60075	8	48	RENTAL AND LEASING SERVICES	60184	83	423	JUSTICE; PUBIC ORDER/SAFETY	60472	126	1150	RELIG.; GRANT; CIVIC; PROF ORG
60076	1567	14232	TRANSPORTATION EQUIPMENT MFG	60185	1618	19433	MERCH. WHOLESALERS;NONDUR. GDS	60473	1004	11264	EDUCATIONAL SERVICES
60077	1885	28477	PROF.; SCIENTIFIC; & TECH SVCS	60186	6	20	SPECIAL TRADE CONTRACTORS	60474	23	138	FOOD AND BEVERAGE STORES
60078	10	20	MERCH. WHOLESALERS;DURABLE GDS	60187	1786	18809	JUSTICE; PUBIC ORDER/SAFETY	60475	276	1630	EDUCATIONAL SERVICES
60079	11	64	AMUSEMENT; GAMBLING;& RECREAT.	60188	1539	25823	MERCH. WHOLESALERS;DURABLE GDS	60476	101	1171	PETROLEUM & COAL PRODUCTS MFG
60081	341	3516	ELECT'L EQPMT; APP; & COMP MFG	60189	798	6621	FOOD SVCS & DRINKING PLACES	60477	1261	16360	PUBLISHING INDUSTRIES
60082	7	55	RELIG.; GRANT; CIVIC; PROF ORG	60190	353	10444	HOSPITALS	60478	373	2232	EDUCATIONAL SERVICES
60083	164	1323	EDUCATIONAL SERVICES	60191	1025	17687	MERCH. WHOLESALERS;DURABLE GDS	60479	22	27	CONSTRUCTION OF BUILDINGS
60084	782	9309	UNCLASSIFIED ESTABLISHMENTS	60192	338	6553	MERCH. WHOLESALERS;DURABLE GDS	60480	168	1072	MACHINERY MANUFACTURING
60085	2076	29343	HOSPITALS	60193	1266	11819	MERCH. WHOLESALERS;DURABLE GDS	60481	422	2769	EDUCATIONAL SERVICES
60087	535	4742	EDUCATIONAL SERVICES	60194	552	6683	EDUCATIONAL SERVICES	60482	315	1820	FOOD SVCS & DRINKING PLACES
60088	66	1024	NONSTORE RETAILERS	60195	357	2450	FOOD SVCS & DRINKING PLACES	60487	463	6532	AMBULATORY HEALTH CARE SVCS
60089	1566	19527	PROF.; SCIENTIFIC; & TECH SVCS	60196	26	3440	INSURANCE CARRIERS & RELATED	60490	317	4087	FOOD SVCS & DRINKING PLACES
60090	1603	26293	PROF.; SCIENTIFIC; & TECH SVCS	60199	2	0	CREDIT INTERMEDIATION & RELATD	60491	648	4121	EDUCATIONAL SERVICES
60091	1140	7694	EDUCATIONAL SERVICES	60201	2457	33106	EDUCATIONAL SERVICES	60499	4	8	MERCH. WHOLESALERS;NONDUR. GDS
60093	1547	10917	EDUCATIONAL SERVICES	60202	1102	10354	HOSPITALS	60501	418	4552	EDUCATIONAL SERVICES
60095	2	3	WASTE MANAGMT & REMEDIAT'N SVC	60203	85	388	CHEMICAL MANUFACTURING	60502	645	8169	PROF.; SCIENTIFIC; & TECH SVCS
60096	161	898	FOOD SVCS & DRINKING PLACES	60204	11	22	PROF.; SCIENTIFIC; & TECH SVCS	60503	131	829	TRUCK TRANSPORTATION
60097	186	696	FOOD SVCS & DRINKING PLACES	60208	28	1085	EDUCATIONAL SERVICES	60504	1112	18644	FOOD SVCS & DRINKING PLACES
60098	1366	19362	HOSPITALS	60301	561	4485	FOOD SVCS & DRINKING PLACES	60505	1295	15212	EXEC.; LEGIS.; & OTHER SUPPORT
60099	697	7291	EDUCATIONAL SERVICES	60302	1353	14526	HOSPITALS	60506	1612	27686	AMBULATORY HEALTH CARE SVCS
60101	2130	25208	MERCH. WHOLESALERS;DURABLE GDS	60303	13	35	ADMINISTRATIVE & SUPPORT SVCS	60507	7	34	RELIG.; GRANT; CIVIC; PROF ORG
60102	1095	9680	FOOD SVCS & DRINKING PLACES	60304	481	4097	HOSPITALS	60510	1291	17883	EXEC.; LEGIS.; & OTHER SUPPORT
60103	984	6468	EDUCATIONAL SERVICES	60305	375	4401	EDUCATIONAL SERVICES	60511	86	619	FUNDS; TRUSTS; & OTHER FINANCE
60104	469	6218	TRANSPORTATION EQUIPMENT MFG	60401	208	1210	FOOD SVCS & DRINKING PLACES	60512	39	314	MERCH. WHOLESALERS;NONDUR. GDS
60106	1740	19917	MERCH. WHOLESALERS;DURABLE GDS	60402	1265	10866	AMBULATORY HEALTH CARE SVCS	60513	576	5528	MUSEUMS; HIST. SITES;& SIMILAR
60107	740	7640	FOOD SVCS & DRINKING PLACES	60403	551	4391	TRANSIT & GRND PASS. TRANSPORT	60514	300	2087	EDUCATIONAL SERVICES
60108	1350	15881	GENERAL MERCHANDISE STORES	60404	528	4480	SPECIAL TRADE CONTRACTORS	60515	2480	40509	ADMINISTRATIVE & SUPPORT SVCS
60109	36	543	EDUCATIONAL SERVICES	60406	729	9097	HOSPITALS	60516	721	4934	EDUCATIONAL SERVICES
60110	611	6410	EDUCATIONAL SERVICES	60407	42	185	SOCIAL ASSISTANCE	60517	901	14572	PROF.; SCIENTIFIC; & TECH SVCS
60111	17	22	POSTAL SERVICE	60408	143	835	EDUCATIONAL SERVICES	60518	107	451	EDUCATIONAL SERVICES
60112	100	692	SPECIAL TRADE CONTRACTORS	60409	1151	8727	EDUCATIONAL SERVICES	60519	9	269	WASTE MANAGMT & REMEDIAT'N SVC
60113	29	155	EDUCATIONAL SERVICES	60410	379	4450	MERCH. WHOLESALERS;NONDUR. GDS	60520	101	505	EDUCATIONAL SERVICES
60115	1256	18217	FOOD SVCS & DRINKING PLACES	60411	1961	27205	MERCH. WHOLESALERS;DURABLE GDS	60521	1263	9380	AMBULATORY HEALTH CARE SVCS
60118	1051	8692	GENERAL MERCHANDISE STORES	60412	2	3	PERSONAL AND LAUNDRY SERVICES	60522	16	21	REAL ESTATE
60119	470	2984	SPECIAL TRADE CONTRACTORS	60415	526	6847	TRUCK TRANSPORTATION	60523	1944	33252	FOOD SVCS & DRINKING PLACES
60120	1277	16835	HOSPITALS	60416	262	2079	CONSTRUCTION OF BUILDINGS	60525	1807	25795	TRANSPORTATION EQUIPMENT MFG
60121	12	195	SOCIAL ASSISTANCE	60417	499	3286	EDUCATIONAL SERVICES	60526	260	3130	EDUCATIONAL SERVICES
60123	2045	28296	EDUCATIONAL SERVICES	60419	496	3648	EDUCATIONAL SERVICES	60527	1596	19920	PROF.; SCIENTIFIC; & TECH SVCS
60124	497	4524	PROF.; SCIENTIFIC; & TECH SVCS	60420	223	2786	PRINT'G & RELATED SUPP'T ACT'S	60530	20	134	MACHINERY MANUFACTURING
60126	2334	31901	AMBULATORY HEALTH CARE SVCS	60421	126	994	CHEMICAL MANUFACTURING	60531	58	337	EDUCATIONAL SERVICES
60129	12	14	TRUCK TRANSPORTATION	60422	323	2741	EDUCATIONAL SERVICES	60532	1534	20433	TELECOMMUNICATIONS
60130	661	6582	FOOD SVCS & DRINKING PLACES	60423	1215	10761	FOOD SVCS & DRINKING PLACES	60534	346	2732	EDUCATIONAL SERVICES
60131	1106	19339	MERCH. WHOLESALERS;DURABLE GDS	60424	69	496	EDUCATIONAL SERVICES	60536	7	22	EDUCATIONAL SERVICES
60133	626	7183	ADMINISTRATIVE & SUPPORT SVCS	60425	216	2344	COMPUTER & ELECTRONIC PROD MFG	60537	16	45	TRUCK TRANSPORTATION
60134	1607	15279	FOOD SVCS & DRINKING PLACES	60426	911	12912	ADMINISTRATIVE & SUPPORT SVCS	60538	484	9986	MERCH. WHOLESALERS;DURABLE GDS
60135	227	1244	EDUCATIONAL SERVICES	60428	381	3246	JUSTICE; PUBIC ORDER/SAFETY	60539	9	1309	RELIG.; GRANT; CIVIC; PROF ORG
60136	178	1174	SPECIAL TRADE CONTRACTORS	60429	492	4614	HOSPITALS	60540	2442	31433	HOSPITALS
60137	1629	18477	EDUCATIONAL SERVICES	60430	1034	10972	AMBULATORY HEALTH CARE SVCS	60541	110	692	EDUCATIONAL SERVICES
60138	17	60	ADMINISTRATIVE & SUPPORT SVCS	60431	564	7633	GENERAL MERCHANDISE STORES	60542	459	4987	MACHINERY MANUFACTURING
60139	821	10964	MERCH. WHOLESALERS;DURABLE GDS	60432	944	12644	JUSTICE; PUBIC ORDER/SAFETY	60543	1015	8010	FOOD SVCS & DRINKING PLACES
60140	400	3467	WOOD PRODUCT MANUFACTURING	60433	421	6616	MERCH. WHOLESALERS;DURABLE GDS	60544	772	9190	EDUCATIONAL SERVICES
60141	19	93	HOSPITALS	60434	11	263	ADMINISTRATIVE & SUPPORT SVCS	60545	322	3212	EDUCATIONAL SERVICES
60142	609	6010	REAL ESTATE	60435	1842	23565	HOSPITALS	60546	631	5019	CLOTHING & CLOTH'G ACC. STORES
60143	1008	24579	MISCELLANEOUS MANUFACTURING	60436	621	12340	MERCH. WHOLESALERS;DURABLE GDS	60548	469	3596	EDUCATIONAL SERVICES
60144	20	176	ADMINISTRATIVE & SUPPORT SVCS	60437	15	12	MERCH. WHOLESALERS;NONDUR. GDS	60549	24	412	EDUCATIONAL SERVICES
60145	62	421	UNCLASSIFIED ESTABLISHMENTS	60438	1087	11215	FOOD SVCS & DRINKING PLACES	60550	65	463	NURSING & RESID. CARE FACILIT.
60146	80	658	BLDG MATL & GARDEN EQPMT DLRS	60439	884	13275	MISCELLANEOUS MANUFACTURING	60551	119	1062	JUSTICE; PUBIC ORDER/SAFETY
60147	17	333	COMPUTER & ELECTRONIC PROD MFG	60440	1471	22985	PROF.; SCIENTIFIC; & TECH SVCS	60552	120	811	EDUCATIONAL SERVICES
60148	2601	30565	FOOD SVCS & DRINKING PLACES	60441	971	7594	JUSTICE; PUBIC ORDER/SAFETY	60553	24	70	MERCH. WHOLESALERS;NONDUR. GDS
60150	66	573	EDUCATIONAL SERVICES	60442	233	1238	EDUCATIONAL SERVICES	60554	387	2607	EDUCATIONAL SERVICES
60151	160	1717	MERCH. WHOLESALERS;NONDUR. GDS	60443	759	9486	GENERAL MERCHANDISE STORES	60555	726	16023	MERCH. WHOLESALERS;NONDUR. GDS
60152	459	4082	MERCH. WHOLESALERS;DURABLE GDS	60444	63	523	EDUCATIONAL SERVICES	60556	78	448	MERCH. WHOLESALERS;NONDUR. GDS
60153	640	21037	HOSPITALS	60445	890	9996	FOOD SVCS & DRINKING PLACES	60557	7	115	NONMETALLIC MINERAL PROD. MFG
60154	764	9090	COMPUTER & ELECTRONIC PROD MFG	60446	865	13105	EDUCATIONAL SERVICES	60558	349	2694	EDUCATIONAL SERVICES
60155	482	10627	MERCH. WHOLESALERS;DURABLE GDS	60447	366	3330	EDUCATIONAL SERVICES	60559	1285	14658	TRUCK TRANSPORTATION
60156	532	3723	FOOD SVCS & DRINKING PLACES	60448	1118	7984	FOOD SVCS & DRINKING PLACES	60560	783	6375	EDUCATIONAL SERVICES
60157	74	615	AMUSEMENT; GAMBLING;& RECREAT.	60449	341	2489	MACHINERY MANUFACTURING	60561	668	6737	FOOD SVCS & DRINKING PLACES
60159	4	5	MERCH. WHOLESALERS;DURABLE GDS	60450	1004	9797	FOOD SVCS & DRINKING PLACES	60563	2745	35650	PROF.; SCIENTIFIC; & TECH SVCS
60160	1123	24766	HOSPITALS	60451	1063	7319	EDUCATIONAL SERVICES	60564	1121	9818	EDUCATIONAL SERVICES
60161	3	7	PERSONAL AND LAUNDRY SERVICES	60452	681	7218	HOSPITALS	60565	643	3718	EDUCATIONAL SERVICES
60162	442	7711	REPAIR AND MAINTENANCE	60453	1775	20722	HOSPITALS	60566	10	28	CONSTRUCTION OF BUILDINGS
60163	156	2166	EDUCATIONAL SERVICES	60454	8	17	PROF.; SCIENTIFIC; & TECH SVCS	60567	23	66	REPAIR AND MAINTENANCE
60164	449	9281	MERCH. WHOLESALERS;NONDUR. GDS	60455	895	11499	PROF.; SCIENTIFIC; & TECH SVCS	60585	678	5341	FOOD SVCS & DRINKING PLACES
60165	153	973	AMUSEMENT; GAMBLING;& RECREAT.	60456	57	491	JUSTICE; PUBIC ORDER/SAFETY	60586	540	3941	EDUCATIONAL SERVICES
60168	8	54	PROF.; SCIENTIFIC; & TECH SVCS	60457	439	3091	FOOD SVCS & DRINKING PLACES	60598	8	10	PROF.; SCIENTIFIC; & TECH SVCS
60169	1009	16464	HOSPITALS	60458	257	1324	EDUCATIONAL SERVICES	60599	1	3	MERCH. WHOLESALERS;DURABLE GDS
60170	7	0	FOOD AND BEVERAGE STORES	60459	559	5221	EDUCATIONAL SERVICES	60601	3389	86266	PROF.; SCIENTIFIC; & TECH SVCS
60171	331	5135	EDUCATIONAL SERVICES	60460	39	140	EDUCATIONAL SERVICES	60602	2858	45520	PROF.; SCIENTIFIC; & TECH SVCS
60172	1111	8041	MERCH. WHOLESALERS;DURABLE GDS	60461	300	2561	AMBULATORY HEALTH CARE SVCS	60603	2291	55423	PROF.; SCIENTIFIC; & TECH SVCS
60173	2571	44395	PROF.; SCIENTIFIC; & TECH SVCS	60462	1756	20352	FOOD SVCS & DRINKING PLACES	60604	1730	41065	PROF.; SCIENTIFIC; & TECH SVCS
60174	2200	27745	FOOD SVCS & DRINKING PLACES	60463	785	9662	HOSPITALS	60605	1449	19649	EDUCATIONAL SERVICES
60175	612	4303	EDUCATIONAL SERVICES	60464	248	2578	EDUCATIONAL SERVICES	60606	3985	100888	PROF.; SCIENTIFIC; & TECH SVCS

ZIP CODE	2009 Total Firms	2009 Total Employ-ees	TOP INDUSTRY RANKED on 2009 EMPLOYMENT	ZIP CODE	2009 Total Firms	2009 Total Employ-ees	TOP INDUSTRY RANKED on 2009 EMPLOYMENT	ZIP CODE	2009 Total Firms	2009 Total Employ-ees	TOP INDUSTRY RANKED on 2009 EMPLOYMENT
60607	2451	44273	EDUCATIONAL SERVICES	60931	16	189	EDUCATIONAL SERVICES	61074	173	2359	NAT'L SECURITY & INT'L AFFAIRS
60608	2116	37813	AMBULATORY HEALTH CARE SVCS	60932	7	24	CONSTRUCTION OF BUILDINGS	61075	42	148	EDUCATIONAL SERVICES
60609	1770	30051	FOOD MANUFACTURING	60933	14	40	JUSTICE; PUBIC ORDER/SAFETY	61077	20	210	PROF.; SCIENTIFIC; & TECH SVCS
60610	1737	18777	PROF.; SCIENTIFIC; & TECH SVCS	60934	4	6	POSTAL SERVICE	61078	79	373	EDUCATIONAL SERVICES
60611	4399	81147	FOOD SVCS & DRINKING PLACES	60935	19	92	FOOD SVCS & DRINKING PLACES	61079	10	97	JUSTICE; PUBIC ORDER/SAFETY
60612	1726	67931	HOSPITALS	60936	232	2611	MISCELLANEOUS MANUFACTURING	61080	462	4387	NONMETALLIC MINERAL PROD. MFG
60613	1601	11642	FOOD SVCS & DRINKING PLACES	60938	132	1114	FOOD SVCS & DRINKING PLACES	61081	925	13917	MERCH. WHOLESALERS;DURABLE GDS
60614	2943	29377	FOOD SVCS & DRINKING PLACES	60939	3	24	WAREHOUSING AND STORAGE	61084	79	433	EDUCATIONAL SERVICES
60615	981	6059	EDUCATIONAL SERVICES	60940	87	810	PLASTICS & RUBBER PRODUCTS MFG	61085	207	1607	TRANSPORTATION EQUIPMENT MFG
60616	1864	29128	HOSPITALS	60941	83	740	EDUCATIONAL SERVICES	61087	112	468	FOOD AND BEVERAGE STORES
60617	1652	15616	EDUCATIONAL SERVICES	60942	278	1938	EDUCATIONAL SERVICES	61088	135	1079	EDUCATIONAL SERVICES
60618	2841	21543	EDUCATIONAL SERVICES	60944	26	162	EDUCATIONAL SERVICES	61089	22	165	COMPUTER & ELECTRONIC PROD MFG
60619	1787	9691	EDUCATIONAL SERVICES	60945	18	69	RAIL TRANSPORTATION	61091	4	8	NONMETALLIC MINERAL PROD. MFG
60620	1450	10284	EDUCATIONAL SERVICES	60946	20	141	EDUCATIONAL SERVICES	61101	887	10679	EXEC.; LEGIS.; & OTHER SUPPORT
60621	647	5057	EDUCATIONAL SERVICES	60948	41	290	FOOD MANUFACTURING	61102	472	5404	MERCH. WHOLESALERS;DURABLE GDS
60622	1798	16840	HOSPITALS	60949	22	67	WAREHOUSING AND STORAGE	61103	744	14187	AMBULATORY HEALTH CARE SVCS
60623	1736	13993	EDUCATIONAL SERVICES	60950	369	4753	PROF.; SCIENTIFIC; & TECH SVCS	61104	1078	20986	SOCIAL ASSISTANCE
60624	924	9363	EDUCATIONAL SERVICES	60951	24	25	MOTOR VEHICLE & PARTS DEALERS	61105	1	1	MUSEUMS; HIST. SITES;& SIMILAR
60625	1709	14434	EDUCATIONAL SERVICES	60952	32	108	MERCH. WHOLESALERS;DURABLE GDS	61106	2	6	MERCH. WHOLESALERS;DURABLE GDS
60626	1039	8636	EDUCATIONAL SERVICES	60953	97	503	EDUCATIONAL SERVICES	61107	1119	11736	AMBULATORY HEALTH CARE SVCS
60628	1508	14053	EDUCATIONAL SERVICES	60954	242	3282	MERCH. WHOLESALERS;NONDUR. GDS	61108	1633	27133	AMBULATORY HEALTH CARE SVCS
60629	1443	12332	EDUCATIONAL SERVICES	60955	85	570	SOCIAL ASSISTANCE	61109	1056	16643	MERCH. WHOLESALERS;DURABLE GDS
60630	1554	12989	MERCH. WHOLESALERS;DURABLE GDS	60956	5	10	FOOD MANUFACTURING	61110	10	37	GENERAL MERCHANDISE STORES
60631	1354	17613	PROF.; SCIENTIFIC; & TECH SVCS	60957	288	2106	NURSING & RESID. CARE FACILIT.	61111	1232	17309	PROF.; SCIENTIFIC; & TECH SVCS
60632	1719	20068	EDUCATIONAL SERVICES	60959	42	215	NURSING & RESID. CARE FACILIT.	61112	225	2922	CLOTHING & CLOTH'G ACC. STORES
60633	290	6447	WHOLESALE ELEC. MRKTS & AGENTS	60960	33	63	FOOD AND BEVERAGE STORES	61114	475	6018	EDUCATIONAL SERVICES
60634	1810	13634	EDUCATIONAL SERVICES	60961	16	82	EDUCATIONAL SERVICES	61115	653	6317	EDUCATIONAL SERVICES
60636	874	6830	EDUCATIONAL SERVICES	60962	41	181	MERCH. WHOLESALERS;NONDUR. GDS	61125	16	832	POSTAL SERVICE
60637	974	25444	EDUCATIONAL SERVICES	60963	67	395	FOOD MANUFACTURING	61126	8	12	MISCELLANEOUS MANUFACTURING
60638	1612	26088	FABRICATED METAL PRODUCT MFG	60964	174	1123	EDUCATIONAL SERVICES	61130	3	4	PROF.; SCIENTIFIC; & TECH SVCS
60639	2303	20569	FOOD SVCS & DRINKING PLACES	60966	52	207	NURSING & RESID. CARE FACILIT.	61131	1	10	REAL ESTATE
60640	2148	21793	EDUCATIONAL SERVICES	60967	9	66	POSTAL SERVICE	61132	9	81	ADMINISTRATIVE & SUPPORT SVCS
60641	1954	14764	EDUCATIONAL SERVICES	60968	10	63	EDUCATIONAL SERVICES	61201	1588	21987	PROF.; SCIENTIFIC; & TECH SVCS
60642	1674	20087	PROF.; SCIENTIFIC; & TECH SVCS	60969	9	123	MERCH. WHOLESALERS;DURABLE GDS	61204	6	18	ADMINISTRATIVE & SUPPORT SVCS
60643	1428	10226	EDUCATIONAL SERVICES	60970	426	3839	HOSPITALS	61230	30	141	JUSTICE; PUBIC ORDER/SAFETY
60644	943	9027	EDUCATIONAL SERVICES	60973	25	90	RELIG.; GRANT; CIVIC; PROF ORG	61231	330	2111	NURSING & RESID. CARE FACILIT.
60645	843	5159	EDUCATIONAL SERVICES	60974	12	46	EDUCATIONAL SERVICES	61232	41	380	ACCOMMODATION
60646	1197	11598	PROF.; SCIENTIFIC; & TECH SVCS	61001	49	170	JUSTICE; PUBIC ORDER/SAFETY	61233	24	44	FOOD AND BEVERAGE STORES
60647	2597	19955	FOOD SVCS & DRINKING PLACES	61006	83	785	FOOD MANUFACTURING	61234	75	348	EDUCATIONAL SERVICES
60649	1038	7681	HOSPITALS	61007	24	71	CROP PRODUCTION	61235	75	345	EDUCATIONAL SERVICES
60651	1210	9565	EDUCATIONAL SERVICES	61008	982	16408	TRANSPORTATION EQUIPMENT MFG	61236	4	2	POSTAL SERVICE
60652	763	7800	MERCH. WHOLESALERS;NONDUR. GDS	61010	211	2380	MERCH. WHOLESALERS;DURABLE GDS	61237	15	69	FOOD MANUFACTURING
60653	736	5774	EDUCATIONAL SERVICES	61011	65	318	EDUCATIONAL SERVICES	61238	187	1444	EXEC.; LEGIS.; & OTHER SUPPORT
60654	3205	43535	PROF.; SCIENTIFIC; & TECH SVCS	61012	39	205	FABRICATED METAL PRODUCT MFG	61239	29	117	EXEC.; LEGIS.; & OTHER SUPPORT
60655	446	3046	EDUCATIONAL SERVICES	61013	25	140	MOTOR VEHICLE & PARTS DEALERS	61240	164	1358	NURSING & RESID. CARE FACILIT.
60656	593	5910	ADMINISTRATIVE & SUPPORT SVCS	61014	42	280	MACHINERY MANUFACTURING	61241	194	928	FOOD SVCS & DRINKING PLACES
60657	2550	24494	HOSPITALS	61015	29	119	ADMINISTRATIVE & SUPPORT SVCS	61242	50	687	CHEMICAL MANUFACTURING
60659	1659	9568	EDUCATIONAL SERVICES	61016	141	1329	AMUSEMENT; GAMBLING;& RECREAT.	61243	14	78	AMUSEMENT; GAMBLING;& RECREAT.
60660	1017	7869	FOOD SVCS & DRINKING PLACES	61018	31	470	MERCH. WHOLESALERS;NONDUR. GDS	61244	723	10380	MACHINERY MANUFACTURING
60661	1111	26472	PROF.; SCIENTIFIC; & TECH SVCS	61019	72	322	RELIG.; GRANT; CIVIC; PROF ORG	61250	105	490	EDUCATIONAL SERVICES
60666	293	11165	SUPPORT ACT. FOR TRANSPORT.	61020	62	289	PROF.; SCIENTIFIC; & TECH SVCS	61251	6	8	POSTAL SERVICE
60668	1	4	SUPPORT ACT. FOR TRANSPORT.	61021	963	12418	HOSPITALS	61252	186	1492	FABRICATED METAL PRODUCT MFG
60670	7	277	CREDIT INTERMEDIATION & RELATD	61024	99	615	EDUCATIONAL SERVICES	61254	671	5166	FOOD SVCS & DRINKING PLACES
60674	1	20	BROADCASTING	61025	141	1459	MERCH. WHOLESALERS;DURABLE GDS	61256	32	142	EDUCATIONAL SERVICES
60675	1	0	SECURITIES/COMMODITY CONTRACTS	61027	6	19	BLDG MATL & GARDEN EQPMT DLRS	61257	49	2772	FOOD MANUFACTURING
60680	16	40	PROF.; SCIENTIFIC; & TECH SVCS	61028	120	463	NURSING & RESID. CARE FACILIT.	61258	9	22	MERCH. WHOLESALERS;DURABLE GDS
60681	1	2	PERSONAL AND LAUNDRY SERVICES	61030	99	450	EDUCATIONAL SERVICES	61259	15	69	BLDG MATL & GARDEN EQPMT DLRS
60685	2	0	SECURITIES/COMMODITY CONTRACTS	61031	61	303	NURSING & RESID. CARE FACILIT.	61260	30	163	EDUCATIONAL SERVICES
60690	22	54	SPECIAL TRADE CONTRACTORS	61032	1520	19622	MISCELLANEOUS MANUFACTURING	61261	28	124	NURSING & RESID. CARE FACILIT.
60693	1	100	MERCH. WHOLESALERS;DURABLE GDS	61036	588	5720	ACCOMMODATION	61262	20	60	FOOD MANUFACTURING
60697	1	0	CREDIT INTERMEDIATION & RELATD	61037	6	20	EDUCATIONAL SERVICES	61263	17	81	EDUCATIONAL SERVICES
60699	9	14321	POSTAL SERVICE	61038	45	170	PROF.; SCIENTIFIC; & TECH SVCS	61264	483	6666	ADMINISTRATIVE & SUPPORT SVCS
60701	2	1000	POSTAL SERVICE	61039	32	91	CREDIT INTERMEDIATION & RELATD	61265	2373	34677	AMBULATORY HEALTH CARE SVCS
60706	827	13965	ADMINISTRATIVE & SUPPORT SVCS	61041	57	424	FABRICATED METAL PRODUCT MFG	61266	7	5	SPECIAL TRADE CONTRACTORS
60707	953	9314	MOTOR VEHICLE & PARTS DEALERS	61042	18	72	ELECT'L EQPMT; APP; & COMP MFG	61270	314	2964	COMPUTER & ELECTRONIC PROD MFG
60712	926	24564	PROF.; SCIENTIFIC; & TECH SVCS	61043	6	35	CREDIT INTERMEDIATION & RELATD	61272	31	157	EDUCATIONAL SERVICES
60714	1729	27329	NURSING & RESID. CARE FACILIT.	61044	8	21	CROP PRODUCTION	61273	124	730	EDUCATIONAL SERVICES
60803	947	14995	MERCH. WHOLESALERS;DURABLE GDS	61046	150	952	FOOD SVCS & DRINKING PLACES	61274	15	141	MERCH. WHOLESALERS;NONDUR. GDS
60804	1373	16580	EDUCATIONAL SERVICES	61047	36	137	JUSTICE; PUBIC ORDER/SAFETY	61275	96	565	EDUCATIONAL SERVICES
60805	749	7661	HOSPITALS	61048	206	1696	EDUCATIONAL SERVICES	61276	10	11	PROF.; SCIENTIFIC; & TECH SVCS
60827	530	4275	EDUCATIONAL SERVICES	61049	8	159	MACHINERY MANUFACTURING	61277	120	1150	MISCELLANEOUS MANUFACTURING
60901	1601	21532	HOSPITALS	61050	25	41	CROP PRODUCTION	61278	27	129	CREDIT INTERMEDIATION & RELATD
60910	45	180	PROF.; SCIENTIFIC; & TECH SVCS	61051	81	436	FABRICATED METAL PRODUCT MFG	61279	43	151	JUSTICE; PUBIC ORDER/SAFETY
60911	49	384	JUSTICE; PUBIC ORDER/SAFETY	61052	38	111	EDUCATIONAL SERVICES	61281	61	319	EDUCATIONAL SERVICES
60912	20	52	BLDG MATL & GARDEN EQPMT DLRS	61053	129	734	EDUCATIONAL SERVICES	61282	218	3055	HOSPITALS
60913	47	174	EDUCATIONAL SERVICES	61054	142	2476	PRINT'G & RELATED SUPP'T ACT'S	61283	45	197	EDUCATIONAL SERVICES
60914	896	11241	FOOD SVCS & DRINKING PLACES	61057	2	112	SOCIAL ASSISTANCE	61284	42	374	EDUCATIONAL SERVICES
60915	559	6815	FOOD SVCS & DRINKING PLACES	61059	3	4	FOOD SVCS & DRINKING PLACES	61285	47	448	MERCH. WHOLESALERS;NONDUR. GDS
60917	12	43	RELIG.; GRANT; CIVIC; PROF ORG	61060	51	240	EDUCATIONAL SERVICES	61299	5	182	CONSTRUCTION OF BUILDINGS
60918	36	138	PIPELINE TRANSPORTATION	61061	438	2809	MACHINERY MANUFACTURING	61301	494	4966	EDUCATIONAL SERVICES
60919	14	40	WOOD PRODUCT MANUFACTURING	61062	76	444	EDUCATIONAL SERVICES	61310	146	1112	FOOD MANUFACTURING
60920	6	15	CREDIT INTERMEDIATION & RELATD	61063	156	1024	EDUCATIONAL SERVICES	61311	3	3	AIR TRANSPORTATION
60921	56	392	PRIMARY METAL MANUFACTURING	61064	160	2342	SPECIAL TRADE CONTRACTORS	61312	8	10	SPECIAL TRADE CONTRACTORS
60922	62	307	EDUCATIONAL SERVICES	61065	166	964	EDUCATIONAL SERVICES	61313	15	252	NONMETALLIC MINERAL PROD. MFG
60924	109	616	MERCH. WHOLESALERS;NONDUR. GDS	61067	23	49	HEAVY & CIVIL ENG. CONSTRUCT'N	61314	23	127	UNCLASSIFIED ESTABLISHMENTS
60926	4	2	RELIG.; GRANT; CIVIC; PROF ORG	61068	634	6866	FOOD AND BEVERAGE STORES	61315	10	24	EDUCATIONAL SERVICES
60927	88	480	EDUCATIONAL SERVICES	61070	29	53	SPECIAL TRADE CONTRACTORS	61316	7	39	TRUCK TRANSPORTATION
60928	42	204	SPECIAL TRADE CONTRACTORS	61071	493	4155	FOOD SVCS & DRINKING PLACES	61317	15	86	EDUCATIONAL SERVICES
60929	42	184	JUSTICE; PUBIC ORDER/SAFETY	61072	246	2762	EDUCATIONAL SERVICES	61318	24	55	ADMIN. OF ECONOMIC PROGRAMS
60930	27	264	NURSING & RESID. CARE FACILIT.	61073	527	4019	MERCH. WHOLESALERS;NONDUR. GDS	61319	30	176	MINING (EXCEPT OIL AND GAS)

BUSINESS DATA

ZIP CODE	2009 Total Firms	2009 Total Employ-ees	TOP INDUSTRY RANKED on 2009 EMPLOYMENT
61320	10	31	JUSTICE; PUBIC ORDER/SAFETY
61321	8	12	POSTAL SERVICE
61322	34	166	EDUCATIONAL SERVICES
61323	4	42	MISCELLANEOUS MANUFACTURING
61324	1	2	POSTAL SERVICE
61325	28	166	EDUCATIONAL SERVICES
61326	75	634	MISCELLANEOUS STORE RETAILERS
61327	68	458	CHEMICAL MANUFACTURING
61328	2	4	WAREHOUSING AND STORAGE
61329	40	258	PLASTICS & RUBBER PRODUCTS MFG
61330	49	192	EDUCATIONAL SERVICES
61331	3	4	WAREHOUSING AND STORAGE
61332	10	21	FABRICATED METAL PRODUCT MFG
61333	12	20	WAREHOUSING AND STORAGE
61334	29	213	FOOD SVCS & DRINKING PLACES
61335	25	194	SPECIAL TRADE CONTRACTORS
61336	15	44	RELIG.; GRANT; CIVIC; PROF ORG
61337	16	74	EDUCATIONAL SERVICES
61338	23	187	EDUCATIONAL SERVICES
61340	17	277	FABRICATED METAL PRODUCT MFG
61341	279	2102	EDUCATIONAL SERVICES
61342	399	4454	FOOD MANUFACTURING
61344	9	23	TRUCK TRANSPORTATION
61345	27	255	MACHINERY MANUFACTURING
61346	1	1	RELIG.; GRANT; CIVIC; PROF ORG
61348	168	2150	EDUCATIONAL SERVICES
61349	37	177	EDUCATIONAL SERVICES
61350	1191	14800	EDUCATIONAL SERVICES
61353	43	167	EDUCATIONAL SERVICES
61354	703	9240	FOOD SVCS & DRINKING PLACES
61356	669	7403	BLDG MATL & GARDEN EQPMT DLRS
61358	12	31	NONMETALLIC MINERAL PROD. MFG
61359	9	15	CROP PRODUCTION
61360	142	872	EDUCATIONAL SERVICES
61361	70	218	MUSEUMS; HIST. SITES;& SIMILAR
61362	196	2637	HOSPITALS
61363	10	35	JUSTICE; PUBIC ORDER/SAFETY
61364	627	6098	MACHINERY MANUFACTURING
61367	49	318	ACCOMMODATION
61368	50	169	EDUCATIONAL SERVICES
61369	67	1020	FOOD MANUFACTURING
61370	32	133	EDUCATIONAL SERVICES
61371	11	45	FOOD SVCS & DRINKING PLACES
61372	11	76	NONMETALLIC MINERAL PROD. MFG
61373	111	1031	FOOD SVCS & DRINKING PLACES
61374	8	33	EDUCATIONAL SERVICES
61375	28	173	EDUCATIONAL SERVICES
61376	85	491	NURSING & RESID. CARE FACILIT.
61377	62	716	FOOD MANUFACTURING
61378	14	42	SECURITIES/COMMODITY CONTRACTS
61379	46	166	JUSTICE; PUBIC ORDER/SAFETY
61401	1584	19015	AMBULATORY HEALTH CARE SVCS
61402	1	6	ADMINISTRATIVE & SUPPORT SVCS
61410	117	501	EDUCATIONAL SERVICES
61411	23	45	MERCH. WHOLESALERS;NONDUR. GDS
61412	55	218	EDUCATIONAL SERVICES
61413	41	223	EDUCATIONAL SERVICES
61414	45	112	JUSTICE; PUBIC ORDER/SAFETY
61415	59	331	EDUCATIONAL SERVICES
61416	3	4	POSTAL SERVICE
61417	9	18	WAREHOUSING AND STORAGE
61418	31	280	EDUCATIONAL SERVICES
61419	22	66	FOOD SVCS & DRINKING PLACES
61420	52	115	MERCH. WHOLESALERS;NONDUR. GDS
61421	61	210	EDUCATIONAL SERVICES
61422	166	1339	FABRICATED METAL PRODUCT MFG
61423	14	31	FABRICATED METAL PRODUCT MFG
61424	7	17	CONSTRUCTION OF BUILDINGS
61425	17	48	FOOD AND BEVERAGE STORES
61426	1	2	POSTAL SERVICE
61427	67	405	EDUCATIONAL SERVICES
61428	37	153	AMUSEMENT; GAMBLING;& RECREAT.
61430	15	42	JUSTICE; PUBIC ORDER/SAFETY
61431	14	25	JUSTICE; PUBIC ORDER/SAFETY
61432	39	157	TELECOMMUNICATIONS
61433	4	12	WAREHOUSING AND STORAGE
61434	175	1542	MOTOR VEHICLE & PARTS DEALERS
61435	4	5	RELIG.; GRANT; CIVIC; PROF ORG
61436	25	79	ACCOMMODATION
61437	29	220	AMBULATORY HEALTH CARE SVCS
61438	33	164	BLDG MATL & GARDEN EQPMT DLRS
61439	5	5	POSTAL SERVICE
61440	34	93	EDUCATIONAL SERVICES
61441	23	74	CREDIT INTERMEDIATION & RELATD
61442	37	92	JUSTICE; PUBIC ORDER/SAFETY
61443	580	6951	EDUCATIONAL SERVICES
61447	27	63	JUSTICE; PUBIC ORDER/SAFETY
61448	127	846	NURSING & RESID. CARE FACILIT.
61449	19	50	ADMINISTRATIVE & SUPPORT SVCS
61450	77	365	EDUCATIONAL SERVICES
61451	10	16	AMUSEMENT; GAMBLING;& RECREAT.
61452	10	13	MERCH. WHOLESALERS;NONDUR. GDS
61453	19	32	TRUCK TRANSPORTATION
61454	21	59	AMBULATORY HEALTH CARE SVCS
61455	904	10116	FOOD SVCS & DRINKING PLACES
61458	33	75	JUSTICE; PUBIC ORDER/SAFETY
61459	8	22	JUSTICE; PUBIC ORDER/SAFETY
61460	5	114	AMUSEMENT; GAMBLING;& RECREAT.
61462	531	5249	FOOD MANUFACTURING
61465	68	170	FOOD SVCS & DRINKING PLACES
61466	8	17	SUPPORT ACTIVITIES: AGR./FOR.
61467	42	175	EDUCATIONAL SERVICES
61468	1	0	SPECIAL TRADE CONTRACTORS
61469	99	303	JUSTICE; PUBIC ORDER/SAFETY
61470	16	108	NURSING & RESID. CARE FACILIT.
61471	13	35	CREDIT INTERMEDIATION & RELATD
61472	17	22	CROP PRODUCTION
61473	73	393	EDUCATIONAL SERVICES
61474	12	65	FOOD SVCS & DRINKING PLACES
61475	13	53	EDUCATIONAL SERVICES
61476	10	36	CONSTRUCTION OF BUILDINGS
61477	15	33	WOOD PRODUCT MANUFACTURING
61478	5	106	MERCH. WHOLESALERS;NONDUR. GDS
61479	6	141	MERCH. WHOLESALERS;NONDUR. GDS
61480	76	364	NURSING & RESID. CARE FACILIT.
61482	28	128	EDUCATIONAL SERVICES
61483	99	638	AMBULATORY HEALTH CARE SVCS
61484	35	123	PRIMARY METAL MANUFACTURING
61485	33	94	TRUCK TRANSPORTATION
61486	88	387	EDUCATIONAL SERVICES
61488	34	155	JUSTICE; PUBIC ORDER/SAFETY
61489	44	232	EDUCATIONAL SERVICES
61490	61	329	MERCH. WHOLESALERS;NONDUR. GDS
61491	109	659	EDUCATIONAL SERVICES
61501	79	380	EDUCATIONAL SERVICES
61516	24	86	EDUCATIONAL SERVICES
61517	89	757	MACHINERY MANUFACTURING
61519	4	5	SPECIAL TRADE CONTRACTORS
61520	615	5363	EDUCATIONAL SERVICES
61523	343	2192	FOOD SVCS & DRINKING PLACES
61524	5	24	JUSTICE; PUBIC ORDER/SAFETY
61525	135	834	EDUCATIONAL SERVICES
61526	19	208	FABRICATED METAL PRODUCT MFG
61528	65	450	SPECIAL TRADE CONTRACTORS
61529	93	582	EDUCATIONAL SERVICES
61530	250	2718	EDUCATIONAL SERVICES
61531	124	989	AMBULATORY HEALTH CARE SVCS
61532	10	43	CONSTRUCTION OF BUILDINGS
61533	72	546	EDUCATIONAL SERVICES
61534	30	143	EDUCATIONAL SERVICES
61535	34	96	FOOD SVCS & DRINKING PLACES
61536	79	357	ADMINISTRATIVE & SUPPORT SVCS
61537	150	1088	EDUCATIONAL SERVICES
61539	7	20	MERCH. WHOLESALERS;NONDUR. GDS
61540	169	997	FABRICATED METAL PRODUCT MFG
61541	8	40	TRUCK TRANSPORTATION
61542	176	1047	EDUCATIONAL SERVICES
61543	5	6	REPAIR AND MAINTENANCE
61544	25	202	EDUCATIONAL SERVICES
61545	20	121	ACCOMMODATION
61546	108	497	EDUCATIONAL SERVICES
61547	62	363	CHEMICAL MANUFACTURING
61548	332	2960	EDUCATIONAL SERVICES
61550	737	15403	PROF.; SCIENTIFIC; & TECH SVCS
61552	39	423	MERCH. WHOLESALERS;DURABLE GDS
61553	11	107	JUSTICE; PUBIC ORDER/SAFETY
61554	1387	15873	FOOD SVCS & DRINKING PLACES
61555	6	58	SPECIAL TRADE CONTRACTORS
61558	1	500	INSURANCE CARRIERS & RELATED
61559	95	664	FOOD MANUFACTURING
61560	20	38	FOOD SVCS & DRINKING PLACES
61561	118	1126	SPECIAL TRADE CONTRACTORS
61562	7	22	FOOD SVCS & DRINKING PLACES
61563	12	44	JUSTICE; PUBIC ORDER/SAFETY
61564	23	152	EDUCATIONAL SERVICES
61565	26	100	EDUCATIONAL SERVICES
61567	12	88	EXEC.; LEGIS.; & OTHER SUPPORT
61568	182	1035	SOCIAL ASSISTANCE
61569	28	167	SPECIAL TRADE CONTRACTORS
61570	66	330	EDUCATIONAL SERVICES
61571	616	5165	EDUCATIONAL SERVICES
61572	36	97	EXEC.; LEGIS.; & OTHER SUPPORT
61601	8	603	POSTAL SERVICE
61602	879	11698	PROF.; SCIENTIFIC; & TECH SVCS
61603	629	19233	AMBULATORY HEALTH CARE SVCS
61604	919	11457	JUSTICE; PUBIC ORDER/SAFETY
61605	357	3954	EDUCATIONAL SERVICES
61606	252	2875	EDUCATIONAL SERVICES
61607	450	5770	CREDIT INTERMEDIATION & RELATD
61610	157	805	EDUCATIONAL SERVICES
61611	1057	14261	AMUSEMENT; GAMBLING;& RECREAT.
61612	18	55	SOCIAL ASSISTANCE
61613	100	1770	GENERAL MERCHANDISE STORES
61614	1373	14412	AMBULATORY HEALTH CARE SVCS
61615	1243	21947	FOOD SVCS & DRINKING PLACES
61616	335	2571	EDUCATIONAL SERVICES
61625	6	82	OTHER INFORMATION SERVICES
61629	2	2507	MACHINERY MANUFACTURING
61630	1	0	UNCLASSIFIED ESTABLISHMENTS
61633	1	68	INSURANCE CARRIERS & RELATED
61634	1	210	SECURITIES/COMMODITY CONTRACTS
61635	1	1491	EDUCATIONAL SERVICES
61636	16	2070	HOSPITALS
61637	7	10663	HOSPITALS
61641	1	1300	PRIMARY METAL MANUFACTURING
61643	3	514	PUBLISHING INDUSTRIES
61650	2	0	CONSTRUCTION OF BUILDINGS
61651	2	7	TRANSIT & GRND PASS. TRANSPORT
61652	3	22	SPECIAL TRADE CONTRACTORS
61653	2	2	PRINT'G & RELATED SUPP'T ACT'S
61654	1	2	PROF.; SCIENTIFIC; & TECH SVCS
61701	1897	30171	RELIG.; GRANT; CIVIC; PROF ORG
61702	42	133	PROF.; SCIENTIFIC; & TECH SVCS
61704	1226	15093	FOOD SVCS & DRINKING PLACES
61705	238	3435	FOOD MANUFACTURING
61710	7	32018	INSURANCE CARRIERS & RELATED
61720	8	20	BLDG MATL & GARDEN EQPMT DLRS
61721	23	84	JUSTICE; PUBIC ORDER/SAFETY
61722	15	43	JUSTICE; PUBIC ORDER/SAFETY
61723	79	452	TRUCK TRANSPORTATION
61724	16	21	MERCH. WHOLESALERS;NONDUR. GDS
61725	54	158	EXEC.; LEGIS.; & OTHER SUPPORT
61726	104	683	NURSING & RESID. CARE FACILIT.
61727	416	4317	UTILITIES
61728	50	248	EDUCATIONAL SERVICES
61729	35	224	SPECIAL TRADE CONTRACTORS
61730	17	35	EXEC.; LEGIS.; & OTHER SUPPORT
61731	9	97	RELIG.; GRANT; CIVIC; PROF ORG
61732	44	135	SPECIAL TRADE CONTRACTORS
61733	34	322	PROF.; SCIENTIFIC; & TECH SVCS
61734	83	717	EDUCATIONAL SERVICES
61735	14	55	EXEC.; LEGIS.; & OTHER SUPPORT
61736	48	341	EDUCATIONAL SERVICES
61737	22	60	MERCH. WHOLESALERS;DURABLE GDS
61738	193	1721	CONSTRUCTION OF BUILDINGS
61739	251	1737	FABRICATED METAL PRODUCT MFG
61740	59	421	EDUCATIONAL SERVICES
61741	85	586	EDUCATIONAL SERVICES
61742	63	671	MERCH. WHOLESALERS;DURABLE GDS
61743	16	115	MERCH. WHOLESALERS;NONDUR. GDS
61744	91	731	MERCH. WHOLESALERS;DURABLE GDS
61745	109	496	EDUCATIONAL SERVICES
61747	58	499	AMBULATORY HEALTH CARE SVCS
61748	73	316	JUSTICE; PUBIC ORDER/SAFETY
61749	19	72	JUSTICE; PUBIC ORDER/SAFETY
61750	5	14	EXEC.; LEGIS.; & OTHER SUPPORT
61751	1	2	FOOD SVCS & DRINKING PLACES
61752	134	868	FOOD SVCS & DRINKING PLACES
61753	107	552	FOOD SVCS & DRINKING PLACES
61754	50	254	FOOD SVCS & DRINKING PLACES
61755	122	634	EDUCATIONAL SERVICES
61756	60	344	EDUCATIONAL SERVICES
61758	3	14	FOOD SVCS & DRINKING PLACES
61759	60	287	FOOD SVCS & DRINKING PLACES
61760	102	825	FABRICATED METAL PRODUCT MFG
61761	1223	23806	EDUCATIONAL SERVICES
61764	640	8406	JUSTICE; PUBIC ORDER/SAFETY
61769	23	82	EDUCATIONAL SERVICES
61770	42	131	FOOD SVCS & DRINKING PLACES
61771	18	81	AMUSEMENT; GAMBLING;& RECREAT.
61772	14	29	CROP PRODUCTION
61773	31	82	JUSTICE; PUBIC ORDER/SAFETY
61774	31	195	EDUCATIONAL SERVICES
61775	13	33	CROP PRODUCTION
61776	36	187	MISCELLANEOUS MANUFACTURING
61777	33	98	SPECIAL TRADE CONTRACTORS
61778	11	34	EXEC.; LEGIS.; & OTHER SUPPORT
61790	12	279	EDUCATIONAL SERVICES
61801	754	15595	HOSPITALS
61802	681	9890	MERCH. WHOLESALERS;NONDUR. GDS
61803	7	14	ADMINISTRATIVE & SUPPORT SVCS
61810	15	81	CHEMICAL MANUFACTURING
61811	15	21	ADMINISTRATIVE & SUPPORT SVCS
61812	9	56	EDUCATIONAL SERVICES
61813	79	665	MACHINERY MANUFACTURING
61814	36	224	EDUCATIONAL SERVICES
61815	12	99	SPECIAL TRADE CONTRACTORS
61816	16	87	EDUCATIONAL SERVICES
61817	80	380	EDUCATIONAL SERVICES
61818	45	375	REPAIR AND MAINTENANCE

ZIP CODE	2009 Total Firms	2009 Total Employees	TOP INDUSTRY RANKED on 2009 EMPLOYMENT	ZIP CODE	2009 Total Firms	2009 Total Employees	TOP INDUSTRY RANKED on 2009 EMPLOYMENT	ZIP CODE	2009 Total Firms	2009 Total Employees	TOP INDUSTRY RANKED on 2009 EMPLOYMENT
61820	1987	35398	EDUCATIONAL SERVICES	62016	165	1094	HOSPITALS	62233	274	3039	ADMIN. HUMAN RESOURCE PROGRAMS
61821	840	11732	EDUCATIONAL SERVICES	62017	31	328	CONSTRUCTION OF BUILDINGS	62234	1103	9684	FOOD SVCS & DRINKING PLACES
61822	704	13268	SPORTG GDS;HOBBY;BOOK; & MUSIC	62018	64	339	EDUCATIONAL SERVICES	62236	498	4924	INSURANCE CARRIERS & RELATED
61824	5	7	PERFORM'G ARTS; SPEC. SPORTS	62019	13	18	FOOD AND BEVERAGE STORES	62237	68	322	NURSING & RESID. CARE FACILIT.
61825	1	0	ELECTRONICS & APPLIANCE STORES	62021	18	109	MERCH. WHOLESALERS;DURABLE GDS	62238	18	191	TRUCK TRANSPORTATION
61826	20	71	ADMINISTRATIVE & SUPPORT SVCS	62022	21	61	MERCH. WHOLESALERS;DURABLE GDS	62239	130	1062	EDUCATIONAL SERVICES
61830	21	30	OTHER INFORMATION SERVICES	62023	1	0	POSTAL SERVICE	62240	43	162	BLDG MATL & GARDEN EQPMT DLRS
61831	7	12	AMUSEMENT; GAMBLING;& RECREAT.	62024	311	8540	PRIMARY METAL MANUFACTURING	62241	25	35	EXEC.; LEGIS.; & OTHER SUPPORT
61832	1545	17463	EDUCATIONAL SERVICES	62025	1292	15374	PROF.; SCIENTIFIC; & TECH SVCS	62242	55	240	EDUCATIONAL SERVICES
61833	93	784	CONSTRUCTION OF BUILDINGS	62026	8	5365	EDUCATIONAL SERVICES	62243	192	1629	ELECT'L EQPMT; APP; & COMP MFG
61834	336	7567	WHOLESALE ELEC. MRKTS & AGENTS	62027	16	20	FOOD SVCS & DRINKING PLACES	62244	23	101	REAL ESTATE
61839	19	114	EDUCATIONAL SERVICES	62028	20	279	EDUCATIONAL SERVICES	62245	61	408	MERCH. WHOLESALERS;DURABLE GDS
61840	19	106	WAREHOUSING AND STORAGE	62030	1	1	POSTAL SERVICE	62246	406	3679	EXEC.; LEGIS.; & OTHER SUPPORT
61841	52	175	BLDG MATL & GARDEN EQPMT DLRS	62031	18	65	MINING (EXCEPT OIL AND GAS)	62247	1	0	POSTAL SERVICE
61842	141	626	EDUCATIONAL SERVICES	62032	32	126	JUSTICE; PUBIC ORDER/SAFETY	62248	18	117	TRUCK TRANSPORTATION
61843	78	508	MISCELLANEOUS MANUFACTURING	62033	157	892	MERCH. WHOLESALERS;DURABLE GDS	62249	597	6968	ELECT'L EQPMT; APP; & COMP MFG
61844	38	112	EDUCATIONAL SERVICES	62034	382	3662	AMBULATORY HEALTH CARE SVCS	62250	25	142	FABRICATED METAL PRODUCT MFG
61845	10	13	ADMINISTRATIVE & SUPPORT SVCS	62035	466	4600	EDUCATIONAL SERVICES	62252	4	30	JUSTICE; PUBIC ORDER/SAFETY
61846	123	899	EDUCATIONAL SERVICES	62036	11	11	MERCH. WHOLESALERS;DURABLE GDS	62253	31	77	FOOD SVCS & DRINKING PLACES
61847	45	275	NURSING & RESID. CARE FACILIT.	62037	122	866	AMUSEMENT; GAMBLING;& RECREAT.	62254	189	1551	EDUCATIONAL SERVICES
61848	11	81	MERCH. WHOLESALERS;NONDUR. GDS	62040	1461	16237	RELIG.; GRANT; CIVIC; PROF ORG	62255	20	63	SPECIAL TRADE CONTRACTORS
61849	66	330	EDUCATIONAL SERVICES	62044	74	396	EDUCATIONAL SERVICES	62256	11	37	FOOD SVCS & DRINKING PLACES
61850	10	4	POSTAL SERVICE	62045	8	70	JUSTICE; PUBIC ORDER/SAFETY	62257	98	616	EDUCATIONAL SERVICES
61851	14	113	PROF.; SCIENTIFIC; & TECH SVCS	62046	48	290	MERCH. WHOLESALERS;DURABLE GDS	62258	247	2013	EDUCATIONAL SERVICES
61852	6	28	JUSTICE; PUBIC ORDER/SAFETY	62047	121	549	EDUCATIONAL SERVICES	62259	2	1082	JUSTICE; PUBIC ORDER/SAFETY
61853	307	2245	EDUCATIONAL SERVICES	62048	70	803	MACHINERY MANUFACTURING	62260	199	1411	MERCH. WHOLESALERS;DURABLE GDS
61854	51	325	FURNITURE & RELATED PROD. MFG	62049	361	3057	JUSTICE; PUBIC ORDER/SAFETY	62261	5	12	ADMIN. ENVIRO. QUALITY PROGRMS
61855	3	3	WAREHOUSING AND STORAGE	62050	9	16	CROP PRODUCTION	62262	39	265	EDUCATIONAL SERVICES
61856	355	2435	FOOD SVCS & DRINKING PLACES	62051	27	67	EXEC.; LEGIS.; & OTHER SUPPORT	62263	339	3436	TRUCK TRANSPORTATION
61857	4	7	SPORTG GDS;HOBBY;BOOK; & MUSIC	62052	529	4376	FOOD SVCS & DRINKING PLACES	62264	107	751	EDUCATIONAL SERVICES
61858	80	522	GASOLINE STATIONS	62053	20	100	EXEC.; LEGIS.; & OTHER SUPPORT	62265	107	730	NURSING & RESID. CARE FACILIT.
61859	40	212	FOOD SVCS & DRINKING PLACES	62054	10	14	MINING (EXCEPT OIL AND GAS)	62266	3	7	UTILITIES
61862	13	38	FOOD SVCS & DRINKING PLACES	62056	573	5865	FOOD SVCS & DRINKING PLACES	62268	26	63	EDUCATIONAL SERVICES
61863	14	130	JUSTICE; PUBIC ORDER/SAFETY	62058	33	108	ACCOMMODATION	62269	1013	10021	FOOD SVCS & DRINKING PLACES
61864	48	291	EDUCATIONAL SERVICES	62059	34	469	PERFORM'G ARTS; SPEC. SPORTS	62271	78	552	FOOD SVCS & DRINKING PLACES
61865	37	90	EDUCATIONAL SERVICES	62060	177	1357	EDUCATIONAL SERVICES	62272	63	224	SPECIAL TRADE CONTRACTORS
61866	511	6711	BLDG MATL & GARDEN EQPMT DLRS	62061	47	141	EDUCATIONAL SERVICES	62273	11	23	WAREHOUSING AND STORAGE
61870	37	357	MINING (EXCEPT OIL AND GAS)	62062	253	2552	HOSPITALS	62274	286	2794	JUSTICE; PUBIC ORDER/SAFETY
61871	22	115	EDUCATIONAL SERVICES	62063	32	111	JUSTICE; PUBIC ORDER/SAFETY	62275	76	305	FOOD SVCS & DRINKING PLACES
61872	21	71	EXEC.; LEGIS.; & OTHER SUPPORT	62065	3	8	RELIG.; GRANT; CIVIC; PROF ORG	62277	39	136	EDUCATIONAL SERVICES
61873	129	757	EDUCATIONAL SERVICES	62067	40	237	SPECIAL TRADE CONTRACTORS	62278	305	2910	HOSPITALS
61874	202	2101	NURSING & RESID. CARE FACILIT.	62069	97	629	MERCH. WHOLESALERS;NONDUR. GDS	62279	11	5	RELIG.; GRANT; CIVIC; PROF ORG
61875	25	46	MISCELLANEOUS MANUFACTURING	62070	4	6	FOOD SVCS & DRINKING PLACES	62280	8	59	MINING (EXCEPT OIL AND GAS)
61876	34	359	EDUCATIONAL SERVICES	62071	14	245	FOOD MANUFACTURING	62281	65	296	EDUCATIONAL SERVICES
61877	47	157	MERCH. WHOLESALERS;NONDUR. GDS	62074	27	56	EDUCATIONAL SERVICES	62282	28	225	TRUCK TRANSPORTATION
61878	46	298	WOOD PRODUCT MANUFACTURING	62075	143	759	EDUCATIONAL SERVICES	62284	17	28	SPECIAL TRADE CONTRACTORS
61880	88	652	EDUCATIONAL SERVICES	62076	2	7	TRUCK TRANSPORTATION	62285	90	416	EDUCATIONAL SERVICES
61882	21	123	EDUCATIONAL SERVICES	62077	9	50	JUSTICE; PUBIC ORDER/SAFETY	62286	355	2887	PRIMARY METAL MANUFACTURING
61883	128	816	EDUCATIONAL SERVICES	62078	4	3	EXEC.; LEGIS.; & OTHER SUPPORT	62288	120	1128	FOOD MANUFACTURING
61884	20	53	PROF.; SCIENTIFIC; & TECH SVCS	62079	12	100	EDUCATIONAL SERVICES	62289	13	31	EDUCATIONAL SERVICES
61910	215	2200	MERCH. WHOLESALERS;NONDUR. GDS	62080	62	401	EDUCATIONAL SERVICES	62292	21	94	JUSTICE; PUBIC ORDER/SAFETY
61911	291	2453	FURNITURE & RELATED PROD. MFG	62081	8	31	FOOD SVCS & DRINKING PLACES	62293	142	1482	EDUCATIONAL SERVICES
61912	48	222	RELIG.; GRANT; CIVIC; PROF ORG	62082	85	490	MERCH. WHOLESALERS;NONDUR. GDS	62294	363	2520	FOOD SVCS & DRINKING PLACES
61913	67	201	EDUCATIONAL SERVICES	62083	10	33	SOCIAL ASSISTANCE	62295	35	304	EDUCATIONAL SERVICES
61914	60	310	EDUCATIONAL SERVICES	62084	74	1377	MERCH. WHOLESALERS;NONDUR. GDS	62297	7	9	RELIG.; GRANT; CIVIC; PROF ORG
61917	15	18	POSTAL SERVICE	62085	4	14	EXEC.; LEGIS.; & OTHER SUPPORT	62298	612	4232	FOOD SVCS & DRINKING PLACES
61919	24	48	MERCH. WHOLESALERS;NONDUR. GDS	62086	27	62	EDUCATIONAL SERVICES	62301	1768	26967	AMBULATORY HEALTH CARE SVCS
61920	898	16617	PUBLISHING INDUSTRIES	62087	58	507	PROF.; SCIENTIFIC; & TECH SVCS	62305	674	9157	MERCH. WHOLESALERS;NONDUR. GDS
61924	74	444	NURSING & RESID. CARE FACILIT.	62088	219	2338	EDUCATIONAL SERVICES	62306	3	2	REAL ESTATE
61925	21	96	FOOD SVCS & DRINKING PLACES	62089	25	50	FOOD SVCS & DRINKING PLACES	62311	51	189	EDUCATIONAL SERVICES
61928	20	39	MERCH. WHOLESALERS;DURABLE GDS	62090	39	118	JUSTICE; PUBIC ORDER/SAFETY	62312	81	538	EDUCATIONAL SERVICES
61929	28	380	UNCLASSIFIED ESTABLISHMENTS	62091	5	18	MERCH. WHOLESALERS;NONDUR. GDS	62313	6	7	WAREHOUSING AND STORAGE
61930	15	11	FOOD SVCS & DRINKING PLACES	62092	110	726	EDUCATIONAL SERVICES	62314	13	23	WASTE MANAGMT & REMEDIAT'N SVC
61931	29	81	EDUCATIONAL SERVICES	62093	8	19	HEAVY & CIVIL ENG. CONSTRUCT'N	62316	29	166	EDUCATIONAL SERVICES
61932	17	97	EDUCATIONAL SERVICES	62094	39	164	TRUCK TRANSPORTATION	62319	5	12	SUPPORT ACTIVITIES: AGR./FOR.
61933	55	976	SUPPORT ACTIVITIES: AGR./FOR.	62095	437	4306	FOOD SVCS & DRINKING PLACES	62320	101	640	EDUCATIONAL SERVICES
61936	9	11	SPECIAL TRADE CONTRACTORS	62097	55	175	EDUCATIONAL SERVICES	62321	258	3081	ELECT'L EQPMT; APP; & COMP MFG
61937	75	332	EDUCATIONAL SERVICES	62098	3	2	EXEC.; LEGIS.; & OTHER SUPPORT	62323	13	10	ADMINISTRATIVE & SUPPORT SVCS
61938	1129	17340	AMBULATORY HEALTH CARE SVCS	62201	426	5202	EDUCATIONAL SERVICES	62324	38	112	CONSTRUCTION OF BUILDINGS
61940	8	26	JUSTICE; PUBIC ORDER/SAFETY	62203	181	1640	SOCIAL ASSISTANCE	62325	10	27	MERCH. WHOLESALERS;NONDUR. GDS
61941	3	9	EXEC.; LEGIS.; & OTHER SUPPORT	62204	131	925	EDUCATIONAL SERVICES	62326	100	646	MERCH. WHOLESALERS;DURABLE GDS
61942	40	247	SOCIAL ASSISTANCE	62205	275	3213	EDUCATIONAL SERVICES	62329	6	17	CREDIT INTERMEDIATION & RELATD
61943	78	296	EDUCATIONAL SERVICES	62206	438	6057	PROF.; SCIENTIFIC; & TECH SVCS	62330	60	263	EDUCATIONAL SERVICES
61944	575	5665	BLDG MATL & GARDEN EQPMT DLRS	62207	204	2321	RAIL TRANSPORTATION	62334	6	25	MERCH. WHOLESALERS;NONDUR. GDS
61949	6	14	WAREHOUSING AND STORAGE	62208	953	11065	FOOD SVCS & DRINKING PLACES	62336	6	40	MERCH. WHOLESALERS;NONDUR. GDS
61951	333	2804	MACHINERY MANUFACTURING	62214	39	108	CONSTRUCTION OF BUILDINGS	62338	19	46	HEAVY & CIVIL ENG. CONSTRUCT'N
61953	388	2747	FOOD SVCS & DRINKING PLACES	62215	64	441	SPECIAL TRADE CONTRACTORS	62339	47	308	SPECIAL TRADE CONTRACTORS
61955	7	40	JUSTICE; PUBIC ORDER/SAFETY	62216	63	528	NURSING & RESID. CARE FACILIT.	62340	64	320	EDUCATIONAL SERVICES
61956	79	500	EDUCATIONAL SERVICES	62217	29	170	MERCH. WHOLESALERS;DURABLE GDS	62341	135	901	MISCELLANEOUS MANUFACTURING
61957	56	314	EDUCATIONAL SERVICES	62218	37	106	EDUCATIONAL SERVICES	62343	20	80	EDUCATIONAL SERVICES
62001	53	381	FOOD AND BEVERAGE STORES	62219	27	108	EDUCATIONAL SERVICES	62344	4	4	CONSTRUCTION OF BUILDINGS
62002	1397	19179	HOSPITALS	62220	1017	12992	HOSPITALS	62345	14	106	EDUCATIONAL SERVICES
62006	17	87	JUSTICE; PUBIC ORDER/SAFETY	62221	504	4869	EDUCATIONAL SERVICES	62346	7	7	SPECIAL TRADE CONTRACTORS
62009	62	340	FOOD SVCS & DRINKING PLACES	62222	7	15	SPECIAL TRADE CONTRACTORS	62347	53	403	EDUCATIONAL SERVICES
62010	306	2328	FOOD SVCS & DRINKING PLACES	62223	502	5904	FOOD SVCS & DRINKING PLACES	62348	9	31	SPECIAL TRADE CONTRACTORS
62011	8	43	MISCELLANEOUS STORE RETAILERS	62225	76	4305	NAT'L SECURITY & INT'L AFFAIRS	62349	17	40	EDUCATIONAL SERVICES
62012	166	782	PROF.; SCIENTIFIC; & TECH SVCS	62226	1065	11046	HOSPITALS	62351	68	385	RELIG.; GRANT; CIVIC; PROF ORG
62013	28	106	EDUCATIONAL SERVICES	62230	293	3404	CONSTRUCTION OF BUILDINGS	62352	14	25	FOOD SVCS & DRINKING PLACES
62014	109	618	EDUCATIONAL SERVICES	62231	317	2660	FOOD SVCS & DRINKING PLACES	62353	192	3138	MERCH. WHOLESALERS;NONDUR. GDS
62015	18	31	FABRICATED METAL PRODUCT MFG	62232	178	1767	FOOD SVCS & DRINKING PLACES	62354	105	529	ACCOMMODATION

BUSINESS DATA

ZIP CODE	2009 Total Firms	2009 Total Employ-ees	TOP INDUSTRY RANKED on 2009 EMPLOYMENT	ZIP CODE	2009 Total Firms	2009 Total Employ-ees	TOP INDUSTRY RANKED on 2009 EMPLOYMENT	ZIP CODE	2009 Total Firms	2009 Total Employ-ees	TOP INDUSTRY RANKED on 2009 EMPLOYMENT
62355	20	53	ACCOMMODATION	62520	27	69	CONSTRUCTION OF BUILDINGS	62681	244	1841	CONSTRUCTION OF BUILDINGS
62356	17	26	EXEC.; LEGIS.; & OTHER SUPPORT	62521	1079	14697	MERCH. WHOLESALERS;NONDUR. GDS	62682	18	87	JUSTICE; PUBIC ORDER/SAFETY
62357	9	19	ANIMAL PRODUCTION	62522	413	4238	FOOD SVCS & DRINKING PLACES	62683	4	2	POSTAL SERVICE
62358	20	73	JUSTICE; PUBIC ORDER/SAFETY	62523	495	5879	JUSTICE; PUBIC ORDER/SAFETY	62684	97	746	NURSING & RESID. CARE FACILIT.
62359	9	44	SUPPORT ACTIVITIES: AGR./FOR.	62524	8	11	ADMINISTRATIVE & SUPPORT SVCS	62685	53	248	MERCH. WHOLESALERS;NONDUR. GDS
62360	50	335	EDUCATIONAL SERVICES	62525	5	65	AMUSEMENT; GAMBLING;& RECREAT.	62688	23	85	JUSTICE; PUBIC ORDER/SAFETY
62361	19	55	FOOD AND BEVERAGE STORES	62526	1348	30326	UNCLASSIFIED ESTABLISHMENTS	62689	9	20	SOCIAL ASSISTANCE
62362	16	53	EDUCATIONAL SERVICES	62530	63	344	EDUCATIONAL SERVICES	62690	176	1579	EDUCATIONAL SERVICES
62363	370	3144	NURSING & RESID. CARE FACILIT.	62531	49	328	EDUCATIONAL SERVICES	62691	157	1190	BLDG MATL & GARDEN EQPMT DLRS
62365	16	31	FOOD AND BEVERAGE STORES	62532	8	66	PETROLEUM & COAL PRODUCTS MFG	62692	85	362	EDUCATIONAL SERVICES
62366	55	219	EDUCATIONAL SERVICES	62533	65	434	MINING (EXCEPT OIL AND GAS)	62693	58	853	MINING (EXCEPT OIL AND GAS)
62367	44	153	EDUCATIONAL SERVICES	62534	39	465	FOOD SVCS & DRINKING PLACES	62694	130	1069	HEAVY & CIVIL ENG. CONSTRUCT'N
62370	20	72	FOOD SVCS & DRINKING PLACES	62535	202	2513	FOOD SVCS & DRINKING PLACES	62695	10	50	NONMETALLIC MINERAL PROD. MFG
62373	2	9	BLDG MATL & GARDEN EQPMT DLRS	62536	21	83	ADMINISTRATIVE & SUPPORT SVCS	62701	711	17886	INSURANCE CARRIERS & RELATED
62374	11	21	MERCH. WHOLESALERS;DURABLE GDS	62537	17	82	MERCH. WHOLESALERS;DURABLE GDS	62702	1509	38882	NAT'L SECURITY & INT'L AFFAIRS
62375	12	96	BLDG MATL & GARDEN EQPMT DLRS	62538	12	31	MERCH. WHOLESALERS;NONDUR. GDS	62703	1705	23132	EDUCATIONAL SERVICES
62376	33	158	WAREHOUSING AND STORAGE	62539	42	275	BLDG MATL & GARDEN EQPMT DLRS	62704	2190	22001	FOOD SVCS & DRINKING PLACES
62378	22	55	ADMINISTRATIVE & SUPPORT SVCS	62540	53	343	UTILITIES	62705	27	19	SPECIAL TRADE CONTRACTORS
62379	81	287	EDUCATIONAL SERVICES	62541	5	17	MERCH. WHOLESALERS;NONDUR. GDS	62706	44	2152	EXEC.; LEGIS.; & OTHER SUPPORT
62380	4	8	MERCH. WHOLESALERS;NONDUR. GDS	62543	14	25	WAREHOUSING AND STORAGE	62707	355	7572	RELIG.; GRANT; CIVIC; PROF ORG
62401	1368	18331	FOOD SVCS & DRINKING PLACES	62544	67	466	EDUCATIONAL SERVICES	62708	10	9	ADMINISTRATIVE & SUPPORT SVCS
62410	23	146	JUSTICE; PUBIC ORDER/SAFETY	62545	31	89	FABRICATED METAL PRODUCT MFG	62711	507	5378	PROF.; SCIENTIFIC; & TECH SVCS
62411	202	1177	NURSING & RESID. CARE FACILIT.	62546	70	231	EDUCATIONAL SERVICES	62712	177	1580	PROF.; SCIENTIFIC; & TECH SVCS
62413	10	28	WAREHOUSING AND STORAGE	62547	30	127	MERCH. WHOLESALERS;NONDUR. GDS	62713	3	1215	INSURANCE CARRIERS & RELATED
62414	56	240	EDUCATIONAL SERVICES	62548	59	389	EDUCATIONAL SERVICES	62756	16	510	EXEC.; LEGIS.; & OTHER SUPPORT
62417	96	672	NURSING & RESID. CARE FACILIT.	62549	181	1724	MERCH. WHOLESALERS;DURABLE GDS	62761	3	204	ADMIN. HUMAN RESOURCE PROGRAMS
62418	55	394	TRUCK TRANSPORTATION	62550	106	573	NURSING & RESID. CARE FACILIT.	62762	2	196	ADMIN. HUMAN RESOURCE PROGRAMS
62419	4	4	POSTAL SERVICE	62551	22	307	EDUCATIONAL SERVICES	62764	12	1436	EXEC.; LEGIS.; & OTHER SUPPORT
62420	233	1765	EDUCATIONAL SERVICES	62553	11	36	MERCH. WHOLESALERS;NONDUR. GDS	62767	1	0	ADMIN. OF ECONOMIC PROGRAMS
62421	17	35	ADMINISTRATIVE & SUPPORT SVCS	62554	35	303	EDUCATIONAL SERVICES	62769	7	3878	HOSPITALS
62422	38	219	EDUCATIONAL SERVICES	62555	14	24	WAREHOUSING AND STORAGE	62777	2	22	EDUCATIONAL SERVICES
62423	8	2	MOTOR VEHICLE & PARTS DEALERS	62556	9	23	TRUCK TRANSPORTATION	62781	16	2429	HOSPITALS
62424	67	534	EDUCATIONAL SERVICES	62557	313	2680	CONSTRUCTION OF BUILDINGS	62791	14	56	HEAVY & CIVIL ENG. CONSTRUCT'N
62425	13	29	BROADCASTING	62558	97	479	EDUCATIONAL SERVICES	62794	3	76	ADMIN. OF ECONOMIC PROGRAMS
62426	29	93	JUSTICE; PUBIC ORDER/SAFETY	62560	89	538	EDUCATIONAL SERVICES	62801	920	10903	EDUCATIONAL SERVICES
62427	40	171	PRIMARY METAL MANUFACTURING	62561	118	865	EDUCATIONAL SERVICES	62803	36	308	SOCIAL ASSISTANCE
62428	116	877	MACHINERY MANUFACTURING	62563	161	1030	PROF.; SCIENTIFIC; & TECH SVCS	62805	5	9	MISCELLANEOUS MANUFACTURING
62431	24	136	EDUCATIONAL SERVICES	62565	438	6204	PROF.; SCIENTIFIC; & TECH SVCS	62806	174	1779	MACHINERY MANUFACTURING
62432	18	27	CROP PRODUCTION	62567	46	253	EDUCATIONAL SERVICES	62807	17	59	FABRICATED METAL PRODUCT MFG
62433	37	263	EDUCATIONAL SERVICES	62568	704	6454	HOSPITALS	62808	38	146	EDUCATIONAL SERVICES
62434	9	31	MERCH. WHOLESALERS;NONDUR. GDS	62570	10	18	FOOD SVCS & DRINKING PLACES	62809	2	10	SPECIAL TRADE CONTRACTORS
62435	1	0	MOTOR VEHICLE & PARTS DEALERS	62571	45	117	EDUCATIONAL SERVICES	62810	32	67	EDUCATIONAL SERVICES
62436	7	21	SPECIAL TRADE CONTRACTORS	62572	10	10	ADMINISTRATIVE & SUPPORT SVCS	62811	8	18	WAREHOUSING AND STORAGE
62438	6	7	PROF.; SCIENTIFIC; & TECH SVCS	62573	50	511	EDUCATIONAL SERVICES	62812	576	4115	TRANSPORTATION EQUIPMENT MFG
62439	351	3186	MISCELLANEOUS MANUFACTURING	62601	13	33	EDUCATIONAL SERVICES	62814	44	221	EDUCATIONAL SERVICES
62440	20	53	RELIG.; GRANT; CIVIC; PROF ORG	62610	8	58	MERCH. WHOLESALERS;DURABLE GDS	62815	9	6	POSTAL SERVICE
62441	260	2665	COMPUTER & ELECTRONIC PROD MFG	62611	41	135	MERCH. WHOLESALERS;NONDUR. GDS	62816	22	72	SPECIAL TRADE CONTRACTORS
62442	90	771	EDUCATIONAL SERVICES	62612	79	472	EDUCATIONAL SERVICES	62817	16	22	CROP PRODUCTION
62443	28	78	ANIMAL PRODUCTION	62613	92	468	EDUCATIONAL SERVICES	62818	26	70	MERCH. WHOLESALERS;NONDUR. GDS
62444	3	18	MINING (EXCEPT OIL AND GAS)	62615	171	1162	COMPUTER & ELECTRONIC PROD MFG	62819	8	20	BLDG MATL & GARDEN EQPMT DLRS
62445	31	164	JUSTICE; PUBIC ORDER/SAFETY	62617	21	89	HEAVY & CIVIL ENG. CONSTRUCT'N	62820	8	18	MERCH. WHOLESALERS;NONDUR. GDS
62446	28	115	CROP PRODUCTION	62618	284	4101	FOOD MANUFACTURING	62821	416	3266	EDUCATIONAL SERVICES
62447	101	584	EDUCATIONAL SERVICES	62621	36	207	EDUCATIONAL SERVICES	62822	94	594	EDUCATIONAL SERVICES
62448	299	1894	EDUCATIONAL SERVICES	62622	3	15	MERCH. WHOLESALERS;NONDUR. GDS	62823	74	269	EDUCATIONAL SERVICES
62449	118	625	EDUCATIONAL SERVICES	62624	14	97	PETROLEUM & COAL PRODUCTS MFG	62824	70	389	EDUCATIONAL SERVICES
62450	630	6293	MERCH. WHOLESALERS;DURABLE GDS	62625	24	94	EDUCATIONAL SERVICES	62825	3	9	EXEC.; LEGIS.; & OTHER SUPPORT
62451	92	345	EDUCATIONAL SERVICES	62626	449	4646	EDUCATIONAL SERVICES	62827	57	300	EDUCATIONAL SERVICES
62452	7	13	SPECIAL TRADE CONTRACTORS	62627	41	97	EDUCATIONAL SERVICES	62828	44	223	DATA PROCESS'G
62454	481	6445	PETROLEUM & COAL PRODUCTS MFG	62628	22	76	CREDIT INTERMEDIATION & RELATD	62829	8	17	CROP PRODUCTION
62458	96	634	CROP PRODUCTION	62629	302	1976	EDUCATIONAL SERVICES	62830	47	173	FOOD SVCS & DRINKING PLACES
62459	17	189	EDUCATIONAL SERVICES	62630	15	21	CREDIT INTERMEDIATION & RELATD	62831	18	72	ACCOMMODATION
62460	35	136	MERCH. WHOLESALERS;NONDUR. GDS	62631	13	138	EDUCATIONAL SERVICES	62832	365	3324	PERFORM'G ARTS; SPEC. SPORTS
62461	29	132	MACHINERY MANUFACTURING	62633	25	164	BLDG MATL & GARDEN EQPMT DLRS	62833	8	6	MERCH. WHOLESALERS;NONDUR. GDS
62462	34	132	BLDG MATL & GARDEN EQPMT DLRS	62634	40	89	WAREHOUSING AND STORAGE	62834	1	0	EXEC.; LEGIS.; & OTHER SUPPORT
62463	45	189	MERCH. WHOLESALERS;DURABLE GDS	62635	24	66	EDUCATIONAL SERVICES	62835	42	278	TELECOMMUNICATIONS
62464	2	18	PIPELINE TRANSPORTATION	62638	36	235	FOOD SVCS & DRINKING PLACES	62836	17	47	MANAGMT OF COMPANIES & ENTERP.
62465	33	163	EDUCATIONAL SERVICES	62639	3	18	MERCH. WHOLESALERS;NONDUR. GDS	62837	480	4345	TRANSPORTATION EQUIPMENT MFG
62466	80	487	EDUCATIONAL SERVICES	62640	115	1484	PERSONAL AND LAUNDRY SERVICES	62838	67	408	FOOD AND BEVERAGE STORES
62467	103	2222	FURNITURE & RELATED PROD. MFG	62642	34	205	EDUCATIONAL SERVICES	62839	351	3457	TRANSPORTATION EQUIPMENT MFG
62468	104	698	EDUCATIONAL SERVICES	62643	15	61	EDUCATIONAL SERVICES	62841	6	15	EXEC.; LEGIS.; & OTHER SUPPORT
62469	8	11	TRUCK TRANSPORTATION	62644	221	1877	HOSPITALS	62842	28	68	SPECIAL TRADE CONTRACTORS
62471	485	5842	RELIG.; GRANT; CIVIC; PROF ORG	62649	18	79	SOCIAL ASSISTANCE	62843	2	7	WAREHOUSING AND STORAGE
62473	26	118	AMBULATORY HEALTH CARE SVCS	62650	1191	14852	EDUCATIONAL SERVICES	62844	104	889	RELIG.; GRANT; CIVIC; PROF ORG
62474	29	55	SPECIAL TRADE CONTRACTORS	62655	23	75	BLDG MATL & GARDEN EQPMT DLRS	62846	27	755	EDUCATIONAL SERVICES
62475	5	35	MERCH. WHOLESALERS;NONDUR. GDS	62656	796	8188	EDUCATIONAL SERVICES	62848	34	103	JUSTICE; PUBIC ORDER/SAFETY
62476	70	207	FOOD AND BEVERAGE STORES	62660	3	5	RELIG.; GRANT; CIVIC; PROF ORG	62849	42	158	EDUCATIONAL SERVICES
62477	30	113	MERCH. WHOLESALERS;DURABLE GDS	62661	35	96	EXEC.; LEGIS.; & OTHER SUPPORT	62850	21	45	EDUCATIONAL SERVICES
62478	6	6	UNCLASSIFIED ESTABLISHMENTS	62663	9	24	SUPPORT ACTIVITIES: AGR./FOR.	62851	9	18	CONSTRUCTION OF BUILDINGS
62479	17	48	MERCH. WHOLESALERS;DURABLE GDS	62664	103	883	EDUCATIONAL SERVICES	62852	8	3	POSTAL SERVICE
62480	23	65	JUSTICE; PUBIC ORDER/SAFETY	62665	55	573	CHEMICAL MANUFACTURING	62853	17	68	JUSTICE; PUBIC ORDER/SAFETY
62481	6	10	GASOLINE STATIONS	62666	16	53	EDUCATIONAL SERVICES	62854	50	212	EDUCATIONAL SERVICES
62501	60	334	EDUCATIONAL SERVICES	62667	19	51	CREDIT INTERMEDIATION & RELATD	62855	3	7	EDUCATIONAL SERVICES
62510	84	1818	MERCH. WHOLESALERS;DURABLE GDS	62668	45	136	EDUCATIONAL SERVICES	62856	10	29	MERCH. WHOLESALERS;DURABLE GDS
62512	11	25	EXEC.; LEGIS.; & OTHER SUPPORT	62670	101	576	EDUCATIONAL SERVICES	62857	1	2	POSTAL SERVICE
62513	61	239	EDUCATIONAL SERVICES	62671	16	55	TRUCK TRANSPORTATION	62858	212	868	EDUCATIONAL SERVICES
62514	8	28	EXEC.; LEGIS.; & OTHER SUPPORT	62672	11	18	RELIG.; GRANT; CIVIC; PROF ORG	62859	265	1469	EDUCATIONAL SERVICES
62515	39	302	EDUCATIONAL SERVICES	62673	28	77	CROP PRODUCTION	62860	14	12	CONSTRUCTION OF BUILDINGS
62517	7	7	PROF.; SCIENTIFIC; & TECH SVCS	62674	43	292	EDUCATIONAL SERVICES	62861	1	1	POSTAL SERVICE
62518	8	30	WAREHOUSING AND STORAGE	62675	261	1633	EDUCATIONAL SERVICES	62862	9	45	TRUCK TRANSPORTATION
62519	5	61	CREDIT INTERMEDIATION & RELATD	62677	84	389	EDUCATIONAL SERVICES	62863	466	3709	EDUCATIONAL SERVICES

ZIP CODE	2009 Total Firms	2009 Total Employ-ees	TOP INDUSTRY RANKED on 2009 EMPLOYMENT	ZIP CODE	2009 Total Firms	2009 Total Employ-ees	TOP INDUSTRY RANKED on 2009 EMPLOYMENT	ZIP CODE	2009 Total Firms	2009 Total Employ-ees	TOP INDUSTRY RANKED on 2009 EMPLOYMENT
62864	1450	24745	MOTOR VEHICLE & PARTS DEALERS	62965	3	3	MISCELLANEOUS STORE RETAILERS	63090	1102	12400	SPECIAL TRADE CONTRACTORS
62865	39	193	EDUCATIONAL SERVICES	62966	645	6100	EDUCATIONAL SERVICES	63091	46	259	TRUCK TRANSPORTATION
62866	4	7	FOOD SVCS & DRINKING PLACES	62967	9	11	UTILITIES	63099	8	3201	EDUCATIONAL SERVICES
62867	14	23	MERCH. WHOLESALERS;NONDUR. GDS	62969	35	119	EXEC.; LEGIS.; & OTHER SUPPORT	63101	948	25873	ADMINISTRATIVE & SUPPORT SVCS
62868	58	402	EDUCATIONAL SERVICES	62970	19	110	PRIMARY METAL MANUFACTURING	63102	737	23211	PROF.; SCIENTIFIC; & TECH SVCS
62869	99	577	EDUCATIONAL SERVICES	62971	2	3	POSTAL SERVICE	63103	1132	46229	EDUCATIONAL SERVICES
62870	63	350	NURSING & RESID. CARE FACILIT.	62972	23	424	ACCOMMODATION	63104	898	15996	EDUCATIONAL SERVICES
62871	25	347	MERCH. WHOLESALERS;NONDUR. GDS	62973	2	1	FOOD AND BEVERAGE STORES	63105	2227	52489	JUSTICE; PUBIC ORDER/SAFETY
62872	19	74	EDUCATIONAL SERVICES	62974	29	70	EDUCATIONAL SERVICES	63106	393	7259	HOSPITALS
62874	6	9	FOOD SVCS & DRINKING PLACES	62975	14	35	MISCELLANEOUS STORE RETAILERS	63107	302	1962	EDUCATIONAL SERVICES
62875	37	196	CONSTRUCTION OF BUILDINGS	62976	16	72	RELIG.; GRANT; CIVIC; PROF ORG	63108	1311	13212	FOOD SVCS & DRINKING PLACES
62876	7	16	RELIG.; GRANT; CIVIC; PROF ORG	62977	21	134	MACHINERY MANUFACTURING	63109	804	4832	FOOD SVCS & DRINKING PLACES
62877	15	51	WAREHOUSING AND STORAGE	62979	66	356	MINING (EXCEPT OIL AND GAS)	63110	1090	39164	HOSPITALS
62878	5	1	REAL ESTATE	62982	66	502	HOSPITALS	63111	522	4232	RELIG.; GRANT; CIVIC; PROF ORG
62879	2	3	RELIG.; GRANT; CIVIC; PROF ORG	62983	31	114	JUSTICE; PUBIC ORDER/SAFETY	63112	473	3464	EDUCATIONAL SERVICES
62880	35	201	FOOD AND BEVERAGE STORES	62984	89	384	TRUCK TRANSPORTATION	63113	470	3088	RELIG.; GRANT; CIVIC; PROF ORG
62881	591	6094	TRUCK TRANSPORTATION	62985	31	66	EDUCATIONAL SERVICES	63114	1367	13410	SPECIAL TRADE CONTRACTORS
62882	72	434	EDUCATIONAL SERVICES	62987	26	41	SPECIAL TRADE CONTRACTORS	63115	532	4608	SOCIAL ASSISTANCE
62883	6	20	MINING (EXCEPT OIL AND GAS)	62988	54	315	EDUCATIONAL SERVICES	63116	900	7327	FOOD SVCS & DRINKING PLACES
62884	89	427	EDUCATIONAL SERVICES	62990	11	20	JUSTICE; PUBIC ORDER/SAFETY	63117	935	13586	HOSPITALS
62885	13	23	SUPPORT ACTIVITIES: AGR./FOR.	62992	55	854	EDUCATIONAL SERVICES	63118	936	15090	BEVERAGE & TOBACCO PRODUCT MFG
62886	5	9	WOOD PRODUCT MANUFACTURING	62994	18	59	MERCH. WHOLESALERS;DURABLE GDS	63119	1650	16531	EDUCATIONAL SERVICES
62887	13	17	CROP PRODUCTION	62995	205	2081	JUSTICE; PUBIC ORDER/SAFETY	63120	262	4153	MACHINERY MANUFACTURING
62888	44	206	MACHINERY MANUFACTURING	62996	6	3	POSTAL SERVICE	63121	597	6434	HEALTH & PERSONAL CARE STORES
62889	16	63	EDUCATIONAL SERVICES	62997	12	23	EXEC.; LEGIS.; & OTHER SUPPORT	63122	1992	20817	EDUCATIONAL SERVICES
62890	64	205	EDUCATIONAL SERVICES	62998	15	332	CHEMICAL MANUFACTURING	63123	1337	13677	FOOD SVCS & DRINKING PLACES
62891	11	14	EXEC.; LEGIS.; & OTHER SUPPORT	62999	49	321	EDUCATIONAL SERVICES	63124	524	7160	EDUCATIONAL SERVICES
62892	15	91	PIPELINE TRANSPORTATION	63001	1	0	JUSTICE; PUBIC ORDER/SAFETY	63125	1001	12457	HOSPITALS
62893	23	71	SPECIAL TRADE CONTRACTORS	63005	1378	16758	PROF.; SCIENTIFIC; & TECH SVCS	63126	776	7327	FOOD SVCS & DRINKING PLACES
62894	20	116	EDUCATIONAL SERVICES	63006	34	117	ADMINISTRATIVE & SUPPORT SVCS	63127	612	8401	PROF.; SCIENTIFIC; & TECH SVCS
62895	90	423	EDUCATIONAL SERVICES	63010	1176	11248	FOOD SVCS & DRINKING PLACES	63128	1017	18986	HOSPITALS
62896	454	3714	AMBULATORY HEALTH CARE SVCS	63011	2069	19439	EDUCATIONAL SERVICES	63129	1379	11892	FOOD SVCS & DRINKING PLACES
62897	35	332	ACCOMMODATION	63012	175	1158	MERCH. WHOLESALERS;NONDUR. GDS	63130	826	9589	EDUCATIONAL SERVICES
62898	43	261	EDUCATIONAL SERVICES	63013	44	182	EDUCATIONAL SERVICES	63131	1425	27883	SECURITIES/COMMODITY CONTRACTS
62899	80	479	ELECT'L EQPMT; APP; & COMP MFG	63014	19	36	CONSTRUCTION OF BUILDINGS	63132	1403	23598	PROF.; SCIENTIFIC; & TECH SVCS
62901	1275	24572	EDUCATIONAL SERVICES	63015	24	80	ADMINISTRATIVE & SUPPORT SVCS	63133	346	4265	MERCH. WHOLESALERS;DURABLE GDS
62902	145	995	MERCH. WHOLESALERS;NONDUR. GDS	63016	195	918	NURSING & RESID. CARE FACILIT.	63134	502	7497	ACCOMMODATION
62903	67	651	EDUCATIONAL SERVICES	63017	2118	35647	PROF.; SCIENTIFIC; & TECH SVCS	63135	502	3988	EDUCATIONAL SERVICES
62905	24	157	MERCH. WHOLESALERS;NONDUR. GDS	63019	293	1788	FOOD SVCS & DRINKING PLACES	63136	1173	13048	HOSPITALS
62906	392	3509	HOSPITALS	63020	567	3954	EDUCATIONAL SERVICES	63137	280	3705	EXEC.; LEGIS.; & OTHER SUPPORT
62907	62	185	FOOD AND BEVERAGE STORES	63021	971	8372	EDUCATIONAL SERVICES	63138	377	3321	EDUCATIONAL SERVICES
62908	15	27	EXEC.; LEGIS.; & OTHER SUPPORT	63022	24	46	SPECIAL TRADE CONTRACTORS	63139	837	10998	FOOD SVCS & DRINKING PLACES
62909	3	17	MERCH. WHOLESALERS;NONDUR. GDS	63023	81	285	EDUCATIONAL SERVICES	63140	26	156	JUSTICE; PUBIC ORDER/SAFETY
62910	59	215	EDUCATIONAL SERVICES	63024	2	1	ADMINISTRATIVE & SUPPORT SVCS	63141	2911	49261	SOCIAL ASSISTANCE
62912	30	108	EDUCATIONAL SERVICES	63025	564	5279	MACHINERY MANUFACTURING	63143	626	7719	FOOD SVCS & DRINKING PLACES
62914	185	1610	RELIG.; GRANT; CIVIC; PROF ORG	63026	1755	41293	TRANSPORTATION EQUIPMENT MFG	63144	920	11496	PROF.; SCIENTIFIC; & TECH SVCS
62915	22	64	JUSTICE; PUBIC ORDER/SAFETY	63028	1030	11107	AMBULATORY HEALTH CARE SVCS	63145	44	2296	PERFORM'G ARTS; SPEC. SPORTS
62916	27	246	EDUCATIONAL SERVICES	63030	1	1	SPECIAL TRADE CONTRACTORS	63146	1620	27925	MERCH. WHOLESALERS;DURABLE GDS
62917	57	315	NURSING & RESID. CARE FACILIT.	63031	1189	10447	EDUCATIONAL SERVICES	63147	498	9555	TRUCK TRANSPORTATION
62918	310	2382	BROADCASTING	63032	11	15	SPECIAL TRADE CONTRACTORS	63151	25	143	DATA PROCESS'G
62919	41	302	NONMETALLIC MINERAL PROD. MFG	63033	1008	9896	FOOD SVCS & DRINKING PLACES	63155	4	5555	POSTAL SERVICE
62920	94	659	EDUCATIONAL SERVICES	63034	289	2046	GENERAL MERCHANDISE STORES	63156	3	1	ADMINISTRATIVE & SUPPORT SVCS
62921	9	15	ADMINISTRATIVE & SUPPORT SVCS	63036	13	82	JUSTICE; PUBIC ORDER/SAFETY	63157	3	72	ADMINISTRATIVE & SUPPORT SVCS
62922	57	264	REPAIR AND MAINTENANCE	63037	123	913	MERCH. WHOLESALERS;DURABLE GDS	63158	2	0	AMBULATORY HEALTH CARE SVCS
62923	16	68	MERCH. WHOLESALERS;DURABLE GDS	63038	152	1147	EDUCATIONAL SERVICES	63160	2	200	HOSPITALS
62924	67	338	WASTE MANAGMT & REMEDIAT'N SVC	63039	31	236	JUSTICE; PUBIC ORDER/SAFETY	63163	2	0	SOCIAL ASSISTANCE
62926	53	284	EDUCATIONAL SERVICES	63040	252	1839	FOOD AND BEVERAGE STORES	63164	5	3903	UNCLASSIFIED ESTABLISHMENTS
62927	6	35	JUSTICE; PUBIC ORDER/SAFETY	63041	6	9	AMBULATORY HEALTH CARE SVCS	63166	12	25	MERCH. WHOLESALERS;NONDUR. GDS
62928	20	44	FOOD SVCS & DRINKING PLACES	63042	1033	19173	COMPUTER & ELECTRONIC PROD MFG	63167	4	5025	PROF.; SCIENTIFIC; & TECH SVCS
62930	211	1762	EDUCATIONAL SERVICES	63043	1178	22988	MERCH. WHOLESALERS;DURABLE GDS	63169	1	1	PROF.; SCIENTIFIC; & TECH SVCS
62931	75	279	EDUCATIONAL SERVICES	63044	1234	27714	HOSPITALS	63177	3	11	MISCELLANEOUS STORE RETAILERS
62932	35	217	MINING (EXCEPT OIL AND GAS)	63045	397	11375	PROF.; SCIENTIFIC; & TECH SVCS	63178	4	6	MERCH. WHOLESALERS;DURABLE GDS
62933	56	381	HEALTH & PERSONAL CARE STORES	63047	1	1	POSTAL SERVICE	63188	14	14	ADMINISTRATIVE & SUPPORT SVCS
62934	42	143	TELECOMMUNICATIONS	63048	143	1969	PRIMARY METAL MANUFACTURING	63199	2	80	POSTAL SERVICE
62935	68	1110	PETROLEUM & COAL PRODUCTS MFG	63049	518	3494	FOOD SVCS & DRINKING PLACES	63301	2180	27062	AMUSEMENT; GAMBLING;& RECREAT.
62938	135	935	SOCIAL ASSISTANCE	63050	517	4944	EXEC.; LEGIS.; & OTHER SUPPORT	63302	26	51	PROF.; SCIENTIFIC; & TECH SVCS
62939	92	626	EDUCATIONAL SERVICES	63051	304	1866	EDUCATIONAL SERVICES	63303	1152	11198	FOOD SVCS & DRINKING PLACES
62940	5	9	ANIMAL PRODUCTION	63052	572	3363	EDUCATIONAL SERVICES	63304	1249	12324	TELECOMMUNICATIONS
62941	18	271	MERCH. WHOLESALERS;DURABLE GDS	63053	16	100	FOOD SVCS & DRINKING PLACES	63330	5	16	ADMIN. ENVIRO. QUALITY PROGRMS
62942	20	59	EDUCATIONAL SERVICES	63055	64	332	SPECIAL TRADE CONTRACTORS	63332	63	294	AMUSEMENT; GAMBLING;& RECREAT.
62943	14	30	UTILITIES	63056	31	46	RELIG.; GRANT; CIVIC; PROF ORG	63333	23	66	EDUCATIONAL SERVICES
62946	670	5823	EDUCATIONAL SERVICES	63057	3	39	NURSING & RESID. CARE FACILIT.	63334	334	2878	JUSTICE; PUBIC ORDER/SAFETY
62947	12	72	TRANSIT & GRND PASS. TRANSPORT	63060	38	196	EDUCATIONAL SERVICES	63336	80	587	EDUCATIONAL SERVICES
62948	485	3637	FOOD SVCS & DRINKING PLACES	63061	1	6	RELIG.; GRANT; CIVIC; PROF ORG	63338	6	10	FOOD AND BEVERAGE STORES
62949	17	38	FOOD SVCS & DRINKING PLACES	63065	8	182	NURSING & RESID. CARE FACILIT.	63339	23	73	MERCH. WHOLESALERS;DURABLE GDS
62950	11	22	FOOD SVCS & DRINKING PLACES	63066	2	3	MOTION PICT. & SOUND RECORDING	63341	87	429	SPECIAL TRADE CONTRACTORS
62951	174	809	EDUCATIONAL SERVICES	63068	207	1809	TRANSPORTATION EQUIPMENT MFG	63342	4	10	CREDIT INTERMEDIATION & RELATD
62952	130	606	EDUCATIONAL SERVICES	63069	575	5606	MERCH. WHOLESALERS;DURABLE GDS	63343	160	815	EDUCATIONAL SERVICES
62953	15	334	UTILITIES	63070	167	2038	NONMETALLIC MINERAL PROD. MFG	63344	48	201	SPECIAL TRADE CONTRACTORS
62954	24	236	EDUCATIONAL SERVICES	63071	27	88	EDUCATIONAL SERVICES	63345	14	55	JUSTICE; PUBIC ORDER/SAFETY
62955	3	11	GASOLINE STATIONS	63072	51	110	EDUCATIONAL SERVICES	63346	4	18	FOOD AND BEVERAGE STORES
62956	34	437	EXEC.; LEGIS.; & OTHER SUPPORT	63073	16	240	AMUSEMENT; GAMBLING;& RECREAT.	63347	35	85	CONSTRUCTION OF BUILDINGS
62957	29	89	EDUCATIONAL SERVICES	63074	518	5853	GENERAL MERCHANDISE STORES	63348	156	668	GASOLINE STATIONS
62958	64	328	FOOD SVCS & DRINKING PLACES	63077	395	2806	EDUCATIONAL SERVICES	63349	65	326	ANIMAL PRODUCTION
62959	1489	16243	FOOD SVCS & DRINKING PLACES	63079	15	216	ADMINISTRATIVE & SUPPORT SVCS	63350	24	144	MINING (EXCEPT OIL AND GAS)
62960	491	5789	FOOD SVCS & DRINKING PLACES	63080	653	6557	GENERAL MERCHANDISE STORES	63351	98	642	CONSTRUCTION OF BUILDINGS
62961	3	10	RELIG.; GRANT; CIVIC; PROF ORG	63084	775	8100	JUSTICE; PUBIC ORDER/SAFETY	63352	39	251	EDUCATIONAL SERVICES
62962	9	24	EXEC.; LEGIS.; & OTHER SUPPORT	63087	12	18	ADMINISTRATIVE & SUPPORT SVCS	63353	252	2266	EDUCATIONAL SERVICES
62963	32	257	COMPUTER & ELECTRONIC PROD MFG	63088	394	3541	FOOD SVCS & DRINKING PLACES	63357	149	970	NURSING & RESID. CARE FACILIT.
62964	73	511	EDUCATIONAL SERVICES	63089	147	672	HEAVY & CIVIL ENG. CONSTRUCT'N	63359	36	65	RELIG.; GRANT; CIVIC; PROF ORG

BUSINESS DATA

ZIP CODE	2009 Total Firms	2009 Total Employ-ees	TOP INDUSTRY RANKED on 2009 EMPLOYMENT
63361	270	1509	EDUCATIONAL SERVICES
63362	156	1102	FOOD AND BEVERAGE STORES
63363	75	579	FABRICATED METAL PRODUCT MFG
63365	47	116	RELIG.; GRANT; CIVIC; PROF ORG
63366	1615	15942	EDUCATIONAL SERVICES
63367	567	4044	HOSPITALS
63368	878	13468	CREDIT INTERMEDIATION & RELATD
63369	57	361	SPECIAL TRADE CONTRACTORS
63370	6	6	RELIG.; GRANT; CIVIC; PROF ORG
63373	38	79	TRANSIT & GRND PASS. TRANSPORT
63376	2422	25559	FOOD SVCS & DRINKING PLACES
63377	81	430	NURSING & RESID. CARE FACILIT.
63378	1	1	SUPPORT ACT. FOR TRANSPORT.
63379	944	8089	MERCH. WHOLESALERS;DURABLE GDS
63381	19	25	SPECIAL TRADE CONTRACTORS
63382	170	1817	JUSTICE; PUBIC ORDER/SAFETY
63383	700	4928	EDUCATIONAL SERVICES
63384	75	409	EDUCATIONAL SERVICES
63385	1148	10683	TRANSPORTATION EQUIPMENT MFG
63386	25	93	JUSTICE; PUBIC ORDER/SAFETY
63387	7	13	PROF.; SCIENTIFIC; & TECH SVCS
63388	24	91	EDUCATIONAL SERVICES
63389	169	790	EDUCATIONAL SERVICES
63390	241	1940	FURNITURE & RELATED PROD. MFG
63401	1039	12104	EDUCATIONAL SERVICES
63430	22	73	EDUCATIONAL SERVICES
63431	4	38	MERCH. WHOLESALERS;NONDUR. GDS
63432	10	13	FOOD SVCS & DRINKING PLACES
63433	1	5	EXEC.; LEGIS.; & OTHER SUPPORT
63434	32	205	EDUCATIONAL SERVICES
63435	160	1025	COMPUTER & ELECTRONIC PROD MFG
63436	50	451	EDUCATIONAL SERVICES
63437	70	370	RELIG.; GRANT; CIVIC; PROF ORG
63438	9	7	FOOD AND BEVERAGE STORES
63439	5	10	UNCLASSIFIED ESTABLISHMENTS
63440	49	197	UNCLASSIFIED ESTABLISHMENTS
63441	26	79	EDUCATIONAL SERVICES
63442	2	34	WOOD PRODUCT MANUFACTURING
63443	10	22	MERCH. WHOLESALERS;DURABLE GDS
63445	221	1191	RELIG.; GRANT; CIVIC; PROF ORG
63446	26	46	AMUSEMENT; GAMBLING;& RECREAT.
63447	52	508	MANAGMT OF COMPANIES & ENTERP.
63448	57	457	AMUSEMENT; GAMBLING;& RECREAT.
63450	2	2	POSTAL SERVICE
63451	17	27	SPECIAL TRADE CONTRACTORS
63452	47	502	EDUCATIONAL SERVICES
63453	7	32	EDUCATIONAL SERVICES
63454	15	43	PROF.; SCIENTIFIC; & TECH SVCS
63456	204	2539	PRIMARY METAL MANUFACTURING
63457	49	160	EXEC.; LEGIS.; & OTHER SUPPORT
63458	12	174	FOOD SVCS & DRINKING PLACES
63459	132	608	EXEC.; LEGIS.; & OTHER SUPPORT
63460	16	98	WOOD PRODUCT MANUFACTURING
63461	272	2527	RELIG.; GRANT; CIVIC; PROF ORG
63462	92	382	PLASTICS & RUBBER PRODUCTS MFG
63463	20	89	EDUCATIONAL SERVICES
63464	4	4	TRUCK TRANSPORTATION
63465	13	55	EDUCATIONAL SERVICES
63466	4	2	MISCELLANEOUS STORE RETAILERS
63467	1	0	POSTAL SERVICE
63468	150	1087	FABRICATED METAL PRODUCT MFG
63469	72	382	EDUCATIONAL SERVICES
63471	60	258	GASOLINE STATIONS
63472	27	71	GASOLINE STATIONS
63473	7	18	UTILITIES
63474	29	92	EDUCATIONAL SERVICES
63501	992	10459	EDUCATIONAL SERVICES
63530	29	154	EDUCATIONAL SERVICES
63531	16	22	MERCH. WHOLESALERS;NONDUR. GDS
63532	49	264	EDUCATIONAL SERVICES
63533	19	78	EDUCATIONAL SERVICES
63534	25	75	EDUCATIONAL SERVICES
63535	4	9	WHOLESALE ELEC. MRKTS & AGENTS
63536	19	49	FOOD AND BEVERAGE STORES
63537	147	845	EDUCATIONAL SERVICES
63538	9	27	CONSTRUCTION OF BUILDINGS
63539	13	25	FISHING; HUNTING AND TRAPPING
63540	2	0	POSTAL SERVICE
63541	9	23	SOCIAL ASSISTANCE
63543	10	38	EDUCATIONAL SERVICES
63544	20	31	REPAIR AND MAINTENANCE
63545	45	238	EDUCATIONAL SERVICES
63546	29	69	FOOD AND BEVERAGE STORES
63547	21	89	TELECOMMUNICATIONS
63548	90	401	GASOLINE STATIONS
63549	87	454	RELIG.; GRANT; CIVIC; PROF ORG
63551	10	15	PROF.; SCIENTIFIC; & TECH SVCS
63552	463	4176	FOOD MANUFACTURING
63555	255	1497	EDUCATIONAL SERVICES
63556	191	2138	FOOD MANUFACTURING

ZIP CODE	2009 Total Firms	2009 Total Employ-ees	TOP INDUSTRY RANKED on 2009 EMPLOYMENT
63557	7	7	MERCH. WHOLESALERS;DURABLE GDS
63558	23	138	EDUCATIONAL SERVICES
63559	30	160	EDUCATIONAL SERVICES
63560	4	4	POSTAL SERVICE
63561	38	358	EDUCATIONAL SERVICES
63563	25	83	FOOD AND BEVERAGE STORES
63565	240	1239	CROP PRODUCTION
63566	8	18	ADMINISTRATIVE & SUPPORT SVCS
63567	5	15	BLDG MATL & GARDEN EQPMT DLRS
63601	645	7873	EDUCATIONAL SERVICES
63620	47	294	NONMETALLIC MINERAL PROD. MFG
63621	41	188	RELIG.; GRANT; CIVIC; PROF ORG
63622	26	64	EDUCATIONAL SERVICES
63623	28	166	NURSING & RESID. CARE FACILIT.
63624	86	417	EDUCATIONAL SERVICES
63625	14	55	EDUCATIONAL SERVICES
63626	10	22	SOCIAL ASSISTANCE
63627	106	547	EDUCATIONAL SERVICES
63628	390	2924	EXEC.; LEGIS.; & OTHER SUPPORT
63629	45	561	MINING (EXCEPT OIL AND GAS)
63630	68	433	EDUCATIONAL SERVICES
63631	39	189	EDUCATIONAL SERVICES
63633	34	205	EXEC.; LEGIS.; & OTHER SUPPORT
63636	13	13	GASOLINE STATIONS
63637	23	80	JUSTICE; PUBIC ORDER/SAFETY
63638	141	1454	EDUCATIONAL SERVICES
63640	1184	13065	HOSPITALS
63645	439	3562	HOSPITALS
63648	27	50	JUSTICE; PUBIC ORDER/SAFETY
63650	224	1272	EDUCATIONAL SERVICES
63651	3	1	POSTAL SERVICE
63653	28	231	EDUCATIONAL SERVICES
63654	45	371	EDUCATIONAL SERVICES
63655	37	152	EDUCATIONAL SERVICES
63656	6	120	PROF.; SCIENTIFIC; & TECH SVCS
63660	62	754	JUSTICE; PUBIC ORDER/SAFETY
63662	54	295	EDUCATIONAL SERVICES
63663	52	294	FOOD SVCS & DRINKING PLACES
63664	427	3425	SOCIAL ASSISTANCE
63665	5	5	RELIG.; GRANT; CIVIC; PROF ORG
63666	3	19	MERCH. WHOLESALERS;NONDUR. GDS
63670	540	6378	CHEMICAL MANUFACTURING
63673	53	127	NURSING & RESID. CARE FACILIT.
63674	2	5	CONSTRUCTION OF BUILDINGS
63675	3	1	RELIG.; GRANT; CIVIC; PROF ORG
63701	1465	16980	HOSPITALS
63702	20	56	ADMINISTRATIVE & SUPPORT SVCS
63703	1140	16024	AMBULATORY HEALTH CARE SVCS
63730	131	961	TRUCK TRANSPORTATION
63732	38	271	WOOD PRODUCT MANUFACTURING
63735	32	110	EDUCATIONAL SERVICES
63736	102	945	EDUCATIONAL SERVICES
63737	2	5	HEAVY & CIVIL ENG. CONSTRUCT'N
63738	1	2	POSTAL SERVICE
63739	6	20	MUSEUMS; HIST. SITES;& SIMILAR
63740	138	1263	EDUCATIONAL SERVICES
63742	6	14	BEVERAGE & TOBACCO PRODUCT MFG
63743	4	6	FABRICATED METAL PRODUCT MFG
63744	26	156	EDUCATIONAL SERVICES
63745	7	16	GASOLINE STATIONS
63746	3	20	RELIG.; GRANT; CIVIC; PROF ORG
63747	3	13	REAL ESTATE
63748	25	74	FOOD SVCS & DRINKING PLACES
63750	2	3	ADMINISTRATIVE & SUPPORT SVCS
63751	16	30	ACCOMMODATION
63752	7	22	MISCELLANEOUS MANUFACTURING
63755	901	9591	PAPER MANUFACTURING
63758	15	69	BLDG MATL & GARDEN EQPMT DLRS
63760	6	34	EDUCATIONAL SERVICES
63763	1	1	POSTAL SERVICE
63764	236	1484	NURSING & RESID. CARE FACILIT.
63766	24	49	EDUCATIONAL SERVICES
63767	14	50	RELIG.; GRANT; CIVIC; PROF ORG
63769	37	248	EDUCATIONAL SERVICES
63770	10	64	TRUCK TRANSPORTATION
63771	84	744	EDUCATIONAL SERVICES
63774	4	7	MERCH. WHOLESALERS;DURABLE GDS
63775	656	8211	TRANSPORTATION EQUIPMENT MFG
63776	4	557	FOOD MANUFACTURING
63779	12	33	FOOD SVCS & DRINKING PLACES
63780	221	2032	WOOD PRODUCT MANUFACTURING
63781	22	111	APPAREL MANUFACTURING
63782	1	1	POSTAL SERVICE
63783	4	32	NURSING & RESID. CARE FACILIT.
63784	10	15	FOOD AND BEVERAGE STORES
63785	12	26	CONSTRUCTION OF BUILDINGS
63787	11	148	EDUCATIONAL SERVICES
63801	1315	13944	AMBULATORY HEALTH CARE SVCS
63820	4	9	SUPPORT ACTIVITIES: AGR./FOR.
63821	26	117	JUSTICE; PUBIC ORDER/SAFETY

ZIP CODE	2009 Total Firms	2009 Total Employ-ees	TOP INDUSTRY RANKED on 2009 EMPLOYMENT
63822	123	640	WOOD PRODUCT MANUFACTURING
63823	37	238	NURSING & RESID. CARE FACILIT.
63824	3	4	POSTAL SERVICE
63825	156	1254	EDUCATIONAL SERVICES
63826	3	81	AMBULATORY HEALTH CARE SVCS
63827	12	47	RELIG.; GRANT; CIVIC; PROF ORG
63828	3	7	EXEC.; LEGIS.; & OTHER SUPPORT
63829	46	241	FOOD AND BEVERAGE STORES
63830	328	2873	AMUSEMENT; GAMBLING;& RECREAT.
63833	3	6	MERCH. WHOLESALERS;NONDUR. GDS
63834	275	2099	TRANSIT & GRND PASS. TRANSPORT
63837	26	260	EDUCATIONAL SERVICES
63839	17	201	EDUCATIONAL SERVICES
63840	10	87	EDUCATIONAL SERVICES
63841	643	6149	MERCH. WHOLESALERS;DURABLE GDS
63845	184	1416	EDUCATIONAL SERVICES
63846	29	194	EDUCATIONAL SERVICES
63847	1	1	POSTAL SERVICE
63848	57	305	EDUCATIONAL SERVICES
63849	3	9	MOTOR VEHICLE & PARTS DEALERS
63850	1	1	POSTAL SERVICE
63851	197	2740	HOSPITALS
63852	35	261	EDUCATIONAL SERVICES
63853	10	52	MISCELLANEOUS STORE RETAILERS
63855	39	252	TRUCK TRANSPORTATION
63857	677	5755	ELECT'L EQPMT; APP; & COMP MFG
63860	6	42	AMBULATORY HEALTH CARE SVCS
63862	46	275	RELIG.; GRANT; CIVIC; PROF ORG
63863	335	2271	TRANSPORTATION EQUIPMENT MFG
63866	28	478	UTILITIES
63867	38	347	GASOLINE STATIONS
63868	22	43	RELIG.; GRANT; CIVIC; PROF ORG
63869	196	2610	PRIMARY METAL MANUFACTURING
63870	40	126	MACHINERY MANUFACTURING
63873	199	2040	SOCIAL ASSISTANCE
63874	17	128	EDUCATIONAL SERVICES
63875	1	0	POSTAL SERVICE
63876	81	529	NURSING & RESID. CARE FACILIT.
63877	134	867	EDUCATIONAL SERVICES
63878	1	2	POSTAL SERVICE
63879	29	129	EDUCATIONAL SERVICES
63880	3	9	SUPPORT ACTIVITIES: AGR./FOR.
63881	2	3	CROP PRODUCTION
63882	17	43	JUSTICE; PUBIC ORDER/SAFETY
63901	1565	20647	HOSPITALS
63902	9	14	SPECIAL TRADE CONTRACTORS
63931	3	4	SUPPORT ACTIVITIES: AGR./FOR.
63932	38	301	EDUCATIONAL SERVICES
63933	117	925	AMBULATORY HEALTH CARE SVCS
63934	5	5	FABRICATED METAL PRODUCT MFG
63935	436	2701	AMBULATORY HEALTH CARE SVCS
63936	31	1007	MISCELLANEOUS STORE RETAILERS
63937	66	508	EDUCATIONAL SERVICES
63939	47	141	FURNITURE & RELATED PROD. MFG
63940	29	118	EDUCATIONAL SERVICES
63941	11	24	NURSING & RESID. CARE FACILIT.
63942	9	42	EDUCATIONAL SERVICES
63943	26	114	JUSTICE; PUBIC ORDER/SAFETY
63944	85	510	EDUCATIONAL SERVICES
63945	18	69	EDUCATIONAL SERVICES
63950	3	9	TRUCK TRANSPORTATION
63951	3	24	JUSTICE; PUBIC ORDER/SAFETY
63952	8	11	MERCH. WHOLESALERS;NONDUR. GDS
63953	45	261	EDUCATIONAL SERVICES
63954	56	306	EDUCATIONAL SERVICES
63955	12	12	MERCH. WHOLESALERS;DURABLE GDS
63956	41	100	ACCOMMODATION
63957	272	2231	EDUCATIONAL SERVICES
63960	126	684	EDUCATIONAL SERVICES
63961	50	162	EDUCATIONAL SERVICES
63962	1	1	RELIG.; GRANT; CIVIC; PROF ORG
63964	17	51	RELIG.; GRANT; CIVIC; PROF ORG
63965	205	1033	WOOD PRODUCT MANUFACTURING
63966	73	249	ADMIN. ENVIRO. QUALITY PROGRMS
63967	39	143	MINING (EXCEPT OIL AND GAS)
64001	45	194	EDUCATIONAL SERVICES
64011	88	543	MERCH. WHOLESALERS;DURABLE GDS
64012	891	7145	FOOD SVCS & DRINKING PLACES
64013	23	113	EXEC.; LEGIS.; & OTHER SUPPORT
64014	683	8886	FOOD SVCS & DRINKING PLACES
64015	1172	8405	EDUCATIONAL SERVICES
64016	144	577	PERSONAL AND LAUNDRY SERVICES
64017	7	5	REPAIR AND MAINTENANCE
64018	26	105	EDUCATIONAL SERVICES
64019	75	418	EDUCATIONAL SERVICES
64020	184	1814	NURSING & RESID. CARE FACILIT.
64021	33	48	RELIG.; GRANT; CIVIC; PROF ORG
64022	10	13	CROP PRODUCTION
64024	505	5010	FOOD MANUFACTURING
64028	12	21	CREDIT INTERMEDIATION & RELATD

ZIP CODE	2009 Total Firms	2009 Total Employ-ees	TOP INDUSTRY RANKED on 2009 EMPLOYMENT	ZIP CODE	2009 Total Firms	2009 Total Employ-ees	TOP INDUSTRY RANKED on 2009 EMPLOYMENT	ZIP CODE	2009 Total Firms	2009 Total Employ-ees	TOP INDUSTRY RANKED on 2009 EMPLOYMENT
64029	376	3352	TRANSPORTATION EQUIPMENT MFG	64149	14	18	SPECIAL TRADE CONTRACTORS	64494	19	76	EDUCATIONAL SERVICES
64030	944	15263	TRANSPORTATION EQUIPMENT MFG	64150	301	4800	AMUSEMENT; GAMBLING;& RECREAT.	64496	11	28	CROP PRODUCTION
64034	155	932	MERCH. WHOLESALERS;DURABLE GDS	64151	539	4513	FOOD SVCS & DRINKING PLACES	64497	6	13	POSTAL SERVICE
64035	26	102	EDUCATIONAL SERVICES	64152	687	4625	EDUCATIONAL SERVICES	64498	13	40	HEAVY & CIVIL ENG. CONSTRUCT'N
64036	27	85	EXEC.; LEGIS.; & OTHER SUPPORT	64153	657	13642	ADMINISTRATIVE & SUPPORT SVCS	64499	3	4	SPECIAL TRADE CONTRACTORS
64037	414	2678	EXEC.; LEGIS.; & OTHER SUPPORT	64154	265	3569	FOOD SVCS & DRINKING PLACES	64501	745	8785	JUSTICE; PUBIC ORDER/SAFETY
64040	268	1030	EDUCATIONAL SERVICES	64155	404	5086	GENERAL MERCHANDISE STORES	64502	8	35	SPECIAL TRADE CONTRACTORS
64048	108	369	EDUCATIONAL SERVICES	64156	37	387	EDUCATIONAL SERVICES	64503	400	6424	MERCH. WHOLESALERS;DURABLE GDS
64050	881	7470	RELIG.; GRANT; CIVIC; PROF ORG	64157	146	1750	FOOD SVCS & DRINKING PLACES	64504	330	6361	FOOD MANUFACTURING
64051	10	22	INSURANCE CARRIERS & RELATED	64158	67	1398	GENERAL MERCHANDISE STORES	64505	279	2354	AMUSEMENT; GAMBLING;& RECREAT.
64052	362	2556	WASTE MANAGMT & REMEDIAT'N SVC	64161	173	9487	AMUSEMENT; GAMBLING;& RECREAT.	64506	1168	18751	HOSPITALS
64053	101	584	EDUCATIONAL SERVICES	64163	43	1599	PROF.; SCIENTIFIC; & TECH SVCS	64507	446	10318	AMBULATORY HEALTH CARE SVCS
64054	106	636	FOOD SVCS & DRINKING PLACES	64164	13	98	EDUCATIONAL SERVICES	64508	6	16	SPECIAL TRADE CONTRACTORS
64055	1475	15809	FOOD SVCS & DRINKING PLACES	64165	6	44	RELIG.; GRANT; CIVIC; PROF ORG	64601	697	6646	FOOD SVCS & DRINKING PLACES
64056	284	4116	INSURANCE CARRIERS & RELATED	64167	4	18	FURNITURE & RELATED PROD. MFG	64620	8	53	JUSTICE; PUBIC ORDER/SAFETY
64057	585	7296	FOOD SVCS & DRINKING PLACES	64168	3	4	CONSTRUCTION OF BUILDINGS	64622	13	16	FOOD SVCS & DRINKING PLACES
64058	122	1279	EDUCATIONAL SERVICES	64171	14	11	MOTION PICT. & SOUND RECORDING	64623	23	74	EDUCATIONAL SERVICES
64060	410	2891	EDUCATIONAL SERVICES	64180	1	0	TELECOMMUNICATIONS	64624	57	236	NURSING & RESID. CARE FACILIT.
64061	77	957	PRIMARY METAL MANUFACTURING	64188	16	31	PERFORM'G ARTS; SPEC. SPORTS	64625	13	49	TELECOMMUNICATIONS
64062	124	901	EDUCATIONAL SERVICES	64190	8	29	FOOD SVCS & DRINKING PLACES	64628	319	2580	GENERAL MERCHANDISE STORES
64063	1101	9329	FOOD SVCS & DRINKING PLACES	64192	13	18	CLOTHING & CLOTH'G ACC. STORES	64630	16	34	EXEC.; LEGIS.; & OTHER SUPPORT
64064	473	4780	MERCH. WHOLESALERS;DURABLE GDS	64195	2	4	AIR TRANSPORTATION	64631	29	123	EDUCATIONAL SERVICES
64065	9	768	EDUCATIONAL SERVICES	64197	2	1100	NAT'L SECURITY & INT'L AFFAIRS	64632	20	71	EDUCATIONAL SERVICES
64066	9	19	MERCH. WHOLESALERS;NONDUR. GDS	64198	1	6	OTHER INFORMATION SERVICES	64633	303	2041	EDUCATIONAL SERVICES
64067	331	2178	EDUCATIONAL SERVICES	64199	1	1	PERFORM'G ARTS; SPEC. SPORTS	64635	16	54	EDUCATIONAL SERVICES
64068	1389	23261	TRANSPORTATION EQUIPMENT MFG	64401	26	68	MINING (EXCEPT OIL AND GAS)	64636	10	22	EDUCATIONAL SERVICES
64069	16	41	SPECIAL TRADE CONTRACTORS	64402	184	1515	MACHINERY MANUFACTURING	64637	17	54	JUSTICE; PUBIC ORDER/SAFETY
64070	93	410	EDUCATIONAL SERVICES	64420	8	19	FOOD SVCS & DRINKING PLACES	64638	14	28	MINING (EXCEPT OIL AND GAS)
64071	32	77	JUSTICE; PUBIC ORDER/SAFETY	64421	18	35	EDUCATIONAL SERVICES	64639	3	31	MERCH. WHOLESALERS;NONDUR. GDS
64072	16	22	EDUCATIONAL SERVICES	64422	7	23	SPECIAL TRADE CONTRACTORS	64640	195	1200	FABRICATED METAL PRODUCT MFG
64073	1	15	MERCH. WHOLESALERS;DURABLE GDS	64423	25	86	EDUCATIONAL SERVICES	64641	29	123	EDUCATIONAL SERVICES
64074	14	24	CREDIT INTERMEDIATION & RELATD	64424	363	2580	FOOD SVCS & DRINKING PLACES	64642	27	103	EDUCATIONAL SERVICES
64075	342	2377	FOOD SVCS & DRINKING PLACES	64426	10	21	MANAGMT OF COMPANIES & ENTERP.	64643	31	173	PERSONAL AND LAUNDRY SERVICES
64076	363	1866	EDUCATIONAL SERVICES	64427	9	30	GASOLINE STATIONS	64644	125	611	EDUCATIONAL SERVICES
64077	60	374	PLASTICS & RUBBER PRODUCTS MFG	64428	41	260	EDUCATIONAL SERVICES	64645	7	10	ADMIN. OF ECONOMIC PROGRAMS
64078	193	1884	FABRICATED METAL PRODUCT MFG	64429	475	6217	HEAVY & CIVIL ENG. CONSTRUCT'N	64646	6	29	EDUCATIONAL SERVICES
64079	494	3068	FOOD SVCS & DRINKING PLACES	64430	17	49	CHEMICAL MANUFACTURING	64647	11	63	EDUCATIONAL SERVICES
64080	362	1929	EDUCATIONAL SERVICES	64431	15	30	HEAVY & CIVIL ENG. CONSTRUCT'N	64648	95	382	EDUCATIONAL SERVICES
64081	606	11006	NURSING & RESID. CARE FACILIT.	64432	3	2	POSTAL SERVICE	64649	10	90	EDUCATIONAL SERVICES
64082	225	2219	FOOD SVCS & DRINKING PLACES	64433	7	89	EDUCATIONAL SERVICES	64650	43	174	PROF.; SCIENTIFIC; & TECH SVCS
64083	373	3085	GENERAL MERCHANDISE STORES	64434	14	90	EDUCATIONAL SERVICES	64651	23	39	EXEC.; LEGIS.; & OTHER SUPPORT
64084	22	40	MINING (EXCEPT OIL AND GAS)	64436	14	46	EDUCATIONAL SERVICES	64652	13	79	EDUCATIONAL SERVICES
64085	337	3274	CHEMICAL MANUFACTURING	64437	47	222	EDUCATIONAL SERVICES	64653	40	123	EXEC.; LEGIS.; & OTHER SUPPORT
64086	773	8623	FOOD SVCS & DRINKING PLACES	64438	6	2	POSTAL SERVICE	64654	5	3	MERCH. WHOLESALERS;NONDUR. GDS
64088	29	37	CONSTRUCTION OF BUILDINGS	64439	60	349	EDUCATIONAL SERVICES	64655	5	59	MERCH. WHOLESALERS;NONDUR. GDS
64089	344	2175	HOSPITALS	64440	15	95	EDUCATIONAL SERVICES	64656	9	75	EDUCATIONAL SERVICES
64090	12	35	EDUCATIONAL SERVICES	64441	4	8	EXEC.; LEGIS.; & OTHER SUPPORT	64657	3	5	POSTAL SERVICE
64092	7	53	ACCOMMODATION	64442	58	388	EDUCATIONAL SERVICES	64658	144	2189	PUBLISHING INDUSTRIES
64093	1199	14875	EDUCATIONAL SERVICES	64443	30	73	EDUCATIONAL SERVICES	64659	42	148	EDUCATIONAL SERVICES
64096	52	427	CROP PRODUCTION	64444	42	116	EDUCATIONAL SERVICES	64660	20	72	EDUCATIONAL SERVICES
64097	60	327	EDUCATIONAL SERVICES	64445	10	20	MERCH. WHOLESALERS;NONDUR. GDS	64661	38	186	EDUCATIONAL SERVICES
64098	178	1191	ACCOMMODATION	64446	73	269	EDUCATIONAL SERVICES	64664	10	9	CONSTRUCTION OF BUILDINGS
64101	208	1117	CHEMICAL MANUFACTURING	64448	32	325	EDUCATIONAL SERVICES	64667	20	62	EDUCATIONAL SERVICES
64102	143	2139	ADMINISTRATIVE & SUPPORT SVCS	64449	7	11	RELIG.; GRANT; CIVIC; PROF ORG	64668	53	263	EDUCATIONAL SERVICES
64105	797	25548	PROF.; SCIENTIFIC; & TECH SVCS	64451	31	285	SPECIAL TRADE CONTRACTORS	64670	36	185	EDUCATIONAL SERVICES
64106	1111	35541	EXEC.; LEGIS.; & OTHER SUPPORT	64453	9	22	FOOD SVCS & DRINKING PLACES	64671	34	144	EDUCATIONAL SERVICES
64108	1495	46591	MERCH. WHOLESALERS;NONDUR. GDS	64454	73	380	NURSING & RESID. CARE FACILIT.	64672	5	13	POSTAL SERVICE
64109	306	3220	EDUCATIONAL SERVICES	64455	18	108	EDUCATIONAL SERVICES	64673	162	871	CROP PRODUCTION
64110	470	4853	EDUCATIONAL SERVICES	64456	104	598	EDUCATIONAL SERVICES	64674	24	86	EDUCATIONAL SERVICES
64111	1734	28361	AMBULATORY HEALTH CARE SVCS	64457	10	59	EDUCATIONAL SERVICES	64676	6	10	CREDIT INTERMEDIATION & RELATD
64112	832	15256	PROF.; SCIENTIFIC; & TECH SVCS	64458	4	17	CROP PRODUCTION	64679	21	85	SPECIAL TRADE CONTRACTORS
64113	357	1928	FOOD AND BEVERAGE STORES	64459	12	45	EDUCATIONAL SERVICES	64680	2	0	RAIL TRANSPORTATION
64114	1296	18569	RELIG.; GRANT; CIVIC; PROF ORG	64461	40	256	FABRICATED METAL PRODUCT MFG	64681	16	27	JUSTICE; PUBIC ORDER/SAFETY
64116	1463	23041	ACCOMMODATION	64463	77	364	EDUCATIONAL SERVICES	64682	17	127	EDUCATIONAL SERVICES
64117	307	9141	MERCH. WHOLESALERS;DURABLE GDS	64465	118	382	EDUCATIONAL SERVICES	64683	427	3892	FOOD MANUFACTURING
64118	1089	10309	EDUCATIONAL SERVICES	64466	27	276	ANIMAL PRODUCTION	64686	3	4	POSTAL SERVICE
64119	730	6540	GENERAL MERCHANDISE STORES	64467	1	1	POSTAL SERVICE	64688	11	7	POSTAL SERVICE
64120	506	16030	MERCH. WHOLESALERS;NONDUR. GDS	64468	693	9334	EDUCATIONAL SERVICES	64689	22	170	EDUCATIONAL SERVICES
64121	1	0	NONSTORE RETAILERS	64469	120	602	EDUCATIONAL SERVICES	64701	837	7262	EDUCATIONAL SERVICES
64123	140	1362	FOOD AND BEVERAGE STORES	64470	155	645	FOOD SVCS & DRINKING PLACES	64720	102	567	EDUCATIONAL SERVICES
64124	246	1891	EDUCATIONAL SERVICES	64471	18	28	MERCH. WHOLESALERS;DURABLE GDS	64722	16	148	EDUCATIONAL SERVICES
64125	80	881	PAPER MANUFACTURING	64473	103	427	EDUCATIONAL SERVICES	64723	34	78	CONSTRUCTION OF BUILDINGS
64126	202	2335	FABRICATED METAL PRODUCT MFG	64474	20	100	EDUCATIONAL SERVICES	64724	107	618	EDUCATIONAL SERVICES
64127	552	5744	EDUCATIONAL SERVICES	64475	8	40	EDUCATIONAL SERVICES	64725	68	328	EDUCATIONAL SERVICES
64128	258	3492	HOSPITALS	64476	16	86	EDUCATIONAL SERVICES	64726	16	18	MERCH. WHOLESALERS;DURABLE GDS
64129	331	7603	PERFORM'G ARTS; SPEC. SPORTS	64477	166	1221	EDUCATIONAL SERVICES	64728	10	83	EDUCATIONAL SERVICES
64130	417	6123	EDUCATIONAL SERVICES	64479	27	99	EDUCATIONAL SERVICES	64730	434	3452	EDUCATIONAL SERVICES
64131	813	14673	PROF.; SCIENTIFIC; & TECH SVCS	64480	7	10	MERCH. WHOLESALERS;NONDUR. GDS	64733	37	121	EDUCATIONAL SERVICES
64132	340	7220	HOSPITALS	64481	36	128	CROP PRODUCTION	64734	49	364	EDUCATIONAL SERVICES
64133	1182	13985	PROF.; SCIENTIFIC; & TECH SVCS	64482	201	1211	EDUCATIONAL SERVICES	64735	823	6494	FOOD MANUFACTURING
64134	464	3373	EDUCATIONAL SERVICES	64483	12	137	EDUCATIONAL SERVICES	64738	29	65	FOOD AND BEVERAGE STORES
64136	68	633	FOOD SVCS & DRINKING PLACES	64484	37	135	EDUCATIONAL SERVICES	64739	28	504	EDUCATIONAL SERVICES
64137	185	3752	PROF.; SCIENTIFIC; & TECH SVCS	64485	290	1864	EDUCATIONAL SERVICES	64740	52	146	EDUCATIONAL SERVICES
64138	499	4916	EDUCATIONAL SERVICES	64486	21	37	SPECIAL TRADE CONTRACTORS	64741	17	90	MERCH. WHOLESALERS;NONDUR. GDS
64139	34	265	EDUCATIONAL SERVICES	64487	27	53	FOOD SVCS & DRINKING PLACES	64742	76	359	EDUCATIONAL SERVICES
64141	10	30	PROF.; SCIENTIFIC; & TECH SVCS	64489	94	739	EDUCATIONAL SERVICES	64743	16	84	EDUCATIONAL SERVICES
64145	299	5353	FOOD SVCS & DRINKING PLACES	64490	53	204	EDUCATIONAL SERVICES	64744	348	2376	EDUCATIONAL SERVICES
64146	27	54	ADMINISTRATIVE & SUPPORT SVCS	64491	154	676	EDUCATIONAL SERVICES	64745	7	24	JUSTICE; PUBIC ORDER/SAFETY
64147	33	510	MERCH. WHOLESALERS;DURABLE GDS	64492	26	79	FOOD MANUFACTURING	64746	48	225	EDUCATIONAL SERVICES
64148	7	26	SPECIAL TRADE CONTRACTORS	64493	11	19	ACCOMMODATION	64747	109	400	MERCH. WHOLESALERS;NONDUR. GDS

BUSINESS DATA

ZIP CODE	2009 Total Firms	2009 Total Employees	TOP INDUSTRY RANKED on 2009 EMPLOYMENT	ZIP CODE	2009 Total Firms	2009 Total Employees	TOP INDUSTRY RANKED on 2009 EMPLOYMENT	ZIP CODE	2009 Total Firms	2009 Total Employees	TOP INDUSTRY RANKED on 2009 EMPLOYMENT
64748	62	393	EDUCATIONAL SERVICES	65050	23	590	REAL ESTATE	65305	33	6728	NAT'L SECURITY & INT'L AFFAIRS
64750	3	7	WAREHOUSING AND STORAGE	65051	217	1592	EDUCATIONAL SERVICES	65320	26	81	PERFORM'G ARTS; SPEC. SPORTS
64752	30	118	EDUCATIONAL SERVICES	65052	115	1050	AMUSEMENT; GAMBLING;& RECREAT.	65321	21	52	JUSTICE; PUBIC ORDER/SAFETY
64755	86	570	EDUCATIONAL SERVICES	65053	34	99	SPECIAL TRADE CONTRACTORS	65322	36	114	EDUCATIONAL SERVICES
64756	12	19	ANIMAL PRODUCTION	65054	31	112	MERCH. WHOLESALERS;NONDUR. GDS	65323	45	248	EDUCATIONAL SERVICES
64759	412	3900	FURNITURE & RELATED PROD. MFG	65055	2	3	RELIG.; GRANT; CIVIC; PROF ORG	65324	75	366	EDUCATIONAL SERVICES
64761	42	175	EDUCATIONAL SERVICES	65058	36	309	MERCH. WHOLESALERS;NONDUR. GDS	65325	171	741	EDUCATIONAL SERVICES
64762	54	218	INSURANCE CARRIERS & RELATED	65059	33	436	EDUCATIONAL SERVICES	65326	39	190	JUSTICE; PUBIC ORDER/SAFETY
64763	54	221	NURSING & RESID. CARE FACILIT.	65061	30	53	RELIG.; GRANT; CIVIC; PROF ORG	65327	16	48	SPECIAL TRADE CONTRACTORS
64765	3	18	WAREHOUSING AND STORAGE	65062	1	0	RELIG.; GRANT; CIVIC; PROF ORG	65329	13	13	RELIG.; GRANT; CIVIC; PROF ORG
64767	9	8	PRINT'G & RELATED SUPP'T ACT'S	65063	86	563	EDUCATIONAL SERVICES	65330	13	49	MINING (EXCEPT OIL AND GAS)
64769	17	66	MACHINERY MANUFACTURING	65064	11	34	SPECIAL TRADE CONTRACTORS	65332	36	101	EDUCATIONAL SERVICES
64770	38	122	EDUCATIONAL SERVICES	65065	1026	11444	FOOD SVCS & DRINKING PLACES	65333	16	63	EDUCATIONAL SERVICES
64771	6	13	CONSTRUCTION OF BUILDINGS	65066	339	3127	PRINT'G & RELATED SUPP'T ACT'S	65334	21	191	EDUCATIONAL SERVICES
64772	693	5639	PLASTICS & RUBBER PRODUCTS MFG	65067	10	8	CROP PRODUCTION	65335	12	11	WAREHOUSING AND STORAGE
64776	172	1317	SOCIAL ASSISTANCE	65068	19	76	EDUCATIONAL SERVICES	65336	190	1013	FOOD SVCS & DRINKING PLACES
64778	15	43	MERCH. WHOLESALERS;DURABLE GDS	65069	28	123	WAREHOUSING AND STORAGE	65337	43	332	MERCH. WHOLESALERS;DURABLE GDS
64779	113	502	EDUCATIONAL SERVICES	65072	54	150	RELIG.; GRANT; CIVIC; PROF ORG	65338	152	807	SPECIAL TRADE CONTRACTORS
64780	20	94	FOOD MANUFACTURING	65074	83	349	EDUCATIONAL SERVICES	65339	23	130	SPECIAL TRADE CONTRACTORS
64781	6	28	EDUCATIONAL SERVICES	65075	39	252	NURSING & RESID. CARE FACILIT.	65340	697	8115	MERCH. WHOLESALERS;NONDUR. GDS
64783	26	65	EDUCATIONAL SERVICES	65076	13	34	RELIG.; GRANT; CIVIC; PROF ORG	65344	19	45	EDUCATIONAL SERVICES
64784	45	168	CROP PRODUCTION	65077	19	25	ACCOMMODATION	65345	5	6	BLDG MATL & GARDEN EQPMT DLRS
64788	58	156	JUSTICE; PUBIC ORDER/SAFETY	65078	112	655	EDUCATIONAL SERVICES	65347	18	29	FOOD SVCS & DRINKING PLACES
64790	19	88	EDUCATIONAL SERVICES	65079	361	1537	REAL ESTATE	65348	35	193	EDUCATIONAL SERVICES
64801	2235	29316	EDUCATIONAL SERVICES	65080	20	38	SPECIAL TRADE CONTRACTORS	65349	105	782	MACHINERY MANUFACTURING
64802	9	17	ADMINISTRATIVE & SUPPORT SVCS	65081	130	1262	JUSTICE; PUBIC ORDER/SAFETY	65350	26	189	EDUCATIONAL SERVICES
64803	21	32	ELECTRONICS & APPLIANCE STORES	65082	61	301	NURSING & RESID. CARE FACILIT.	65351	107	548	EDUCATIONAL SERVICES
64804	1817	29755	HOSPITALS	65083	5	8	MERCH. WHOLESALERS;DURABLE GDS	65354	20	36	FOOD SVCS & DRINKING PLACES
64830	31	85	JUSTICE; PUBIC ORDER/SAFETY	65084	344	2122	GENERAL MERCHANDISE STORES	65355	563	2734	FOOD SVCS & DRINKING PLACES
64831	265	1542	EDUCATIONAL SERVICES	65085	53	414	EDUCATIONAL SERVICES	65360	195	1104	HOSPITALS
64832	24	90	UTILITIES	65101	1661	32169	EXEC.; LEGIS.; & OTHER SUPPORT	65401	1484	16131	HOSPITALS
64833	15	89	ANIMAL PRODUCTION	65102	12	84	ADMIN. OF ECONOMIC PROGRAMS	65402	10	24	SOCIAL ASSISTANCE
64834	153	771	EDUCATIONAL SERVICES	65105	1	76	EXEC.; LEGIS.; & OTHER SUPPORT	65409	5	1280	EDUCATIONAL SERVICES
64835	41	218	EDUCATIONAL SERVICES	65108	1	3	SPECIAL TRADE CONTRACTORS	65436	1	0	RELIG.; GRANT; CIVIC; PROF ORG
64836	898	11797	FOOD MANUFACTURING	65109	1813	25868	ADMIN. OF ECONOMIC PROGRAMS	65438	88	526	FURN. & HOME FURNISHGS STORES
64840	100	727	EDUCATIONAL SERVICES	65110	10	46	SPECIAL TRADE CONTRACTORS	65439	6	94	MINING (EXCEPT OIL AND GAS)
64841	18	492	TRUCK TRANSPORTATION	65201	2005	29856	HOSPITALS	65440	12	290	MINING (EXCEPT OIL AND GAS)
64842	22	44	WOOD PRODUCT MANUFACTURING	65202	1182	14833	FOOD SVCS & DRINKING PLACES	65441	137	1083	APPAREL MANUFACTURING
64843	86	493	SUPPORT ACTIVITIES: AGR./FOR.	65203	1764	23531	INSURANCE CARRIERS & RELATED	65443	5	2	GENERAL MERCHANDISE STORES
64844	134	564	EDUCATIONAL SERVICES	65205	41	293	PROF.; SCIENTIFIC; & TECH SVCS	65444	17	27	CROP PRODUCTION
64847	22	44	PROF.; SCIENTIFIC; & TECH SVCS	65211	218	28462	EDUCATIONAL SERVICES	65446	15	19	WOOD PRODUCT MANUFACTURING
64848	14	139	FOOD MANUFACTURING	65212	60	8186	AMBULATORY HEALTH CARE SVCS	65449	13	45	ACCOMMODATION
64849	3	5	POSTAL SERVICE	65215	1	25	EDUCATIONAL SERVICES	65452	109	657	EDUCATIONAL SERVICES
64850	1009	14203	HOSPITALS	65216	1	276	EDUCATIONAL SERVICES	65453	356	2912	MERCH. WHOLESALERS;DURABLE GDS
64854	146	2205	FOOD MANUFACTURING	65217	1	900	INSURANCE CARRIERS & RELATED	65456	12	16	FABRICATED METAL PRODUCT MFG
64855	47	173	RELIG.; GRANT; CIVIC; PROF ORG	65218	2	1005	INSURANCE CARRIERS & RELATED	65457	8	20	WASTE MANAGMT & REMEDIAT'N SVC
64856	230	1064	JUSTICE; PUBIC ORDER/SAFETY	65230	13	21	NURSING & RESID. CARE FACILIT.	65459	179	789	EDUCATIONAL SERVICES
64857	11	10	EXEC.; LEGIS.; & OTHER SUPPORT	65231	108	438	REPAIR AND MAINTENANCE	65461	6	6	FOOD AND BEVERAGE STORES
64858	7	12	EDUCATIONAL SERVICES	65232	7	9	PROF.; SCIENTIFIC; & TECH SVCS	65462	27	95	EDUCATIONAL SERVICES
64859	12	23	FOOD MANUFACTURING	65233	591	6723	AMUSEMENT; GAMBLING;& RECREAT.	65463	17	24	CONSTRUCTION OF BUILDINGS
64861	33	126	EDUCATIONAL SERVICES	65236	88	461	EDUCATIONAL SERVICES	65464	4	21	FURNITURE & RELATED PROD. MFG
64862	125	1033	EDUCATIONAL SERVICES	65237	37	138	EDUCATIONAL SERVICES	65466	137	567	EDUCATIONAL SERVICES
64863	82	1565	MERCH. WHOLESALERS;NONDUR. GDS	65239	30	93	EDUCATIONAL SERVICES	65468	4	3	REPAIR AND MAINTENANCE
64864	4	4	POSTAL SERVICE	65240	215	1802	ELECT'L EQPMT; APP; & COMP MFG	65470	22	61	EDUCATIONAL SERVICES
64865	193	1734	AMUSEMENT; GAMBLING;& RECREAT.	65243	15	21	POSTAL SERVICE	65473	135	2890	NONSTORE RETAILERS
64866	29	43	BLDG MATL & GARDEN EQPMT DLRS	65244	20	532	UTILITIES	65479	6	10	AMUSEMENT; GAMBLING;& RECREAT.
64867	22	123	EDUCATIONAL SERVICES	65246	6	4	MERCH. WHOLESALERS;NONDUR. GDS	65483	344	2309	HOSPITALS
64868	10	30	ELECTRONICS & APPLIANCE STORES	65247	17	40	HEAVY & CIVIL ENG. CONSTRUCT'N	65484	2	3	SUPPORT ACTIVITIES: AGR./FOR.
64869	3	3	WAREHOUSING AND STORAGE	65248	218	1294	NURSING & RESID. CARE FACILIT.	65486	118	604	EDUCATIONAL SERVICES
64870	442	4000	MISCELLANEOUS MANUFACTURING	65250	9	14	MERCH. WHOLESALERS;DURABLE GDS	65501	9	39	JUSTICE; PUBIC ORDER/SAFETY
64873	11	20	ADMINISTRATIVE & SUPPORT SVCS	65251	765	7635	EDUCATIONAL SERVICES	65529	1	3	SPECIAL TRADE CONTRACTORS
64874	55	276	EDUCATIONAL SERVICES	65254	96	519	PRIMARY METAL MANUFACTURING	65532	1	1	POSTAL SERVICE
65001	15	49	JUSTICE; PUBIC ORDER/SAFETY	65255	84	565	EDUCATIONAL SERVICES	65534	16	197	EDUCATIONAL SERVICES
65010	152	1090	EDUCATIONAL SERVICES	65256	45	347	EDUCATIONAL SERVICES	65535	41	143	SPORTG GDS;HOBBY;BOOK; & MUSIC
65011	42	122	BROADCASTING	65257	45	205	EDUCATIONAL SERVICES	65536	1513	14011	MERCH. WHOLESALERS;DURABLE GDS
65013	117	758	EDUCATIONAL SERVICES	65258	6	32	EDUCATIONAL SERVICES	65541	3	4	SPECIAL TRADE CONTRACTORS
65014	72	255	SPECIAL TRADE CONTRACTORS	65259	114	560	EDUCATIONAL SERVICES	65542	170	1119	EDUCATIONAL SERVICES
65016	21	66	SPECIAL TRADE CONTRACTORS	65260	13	13	PERSONAL AND LAUNDRY SERVICES	65543	4	5	CROP PRODUCTION
65017	27	64	SPECIAL TRADE CONTRACTORS	65261	73	390	EDUCATIONAL SERVICES	65546	1	2	POSTAL SERVICE
65018	334	2764	ANIMAL PRODUCTION	65262	65	1039	GASOLINE STATIONS	65548	250	2072	MACHINERY MANUFACTURING
65020	985	6930	EDUCATIONAL SERVICES	65263	42	167	EDUCATIONAL SERVICES	65550	62	222	JUSTICE; PUBIC ORDER/SAFETY
65023	32	70	BLDG MATL & GARDEN EQPMT DLRS	65264	41	152	CREDIT INTERMEDIATION & RELATD	65552	26	323	EDUCATIONAL SERVICES
65024	38	216	APPAREL MANUFACTURING	65265	737	6978	HOSPITALS	65555	24	82	EDUCATIONAL SERVICES
65025	14	36	EDUCATIONAL SERVICES	65270	796	9392	EDUCATIONAL SERVICES	65556	191	1229	EDUCATIONAL SERVICES
65026	527	4402	ELECT'L EQPMT; APP; & COMP MFG	65274	55	432	EDUCATIONAL SERVICES	65557	19	33	PROF.; SCIENTIFIC; & TECH SVCS
65032	40	427	EDUCATIONAL SERVICES	65275	171	800	EDUCATIONAL SERVICES	65559	349	2029	RELIG.; GRANT; CIVIC; PROF ORG
65034	16	32	MERCH. WHOLESALERS;NONDUR. GDS	65276	70	392	EDUCATIONAL SERVICES	65560	584	4635	EDUCATIONAL SERVICES
65035	59	626	WOOD PRODUCT MANUFACTURING	65278	3	38	EDUCATIONAL SERVICES	65564	2	6	MERCH. WHOLESALERS;DURABLE GDS
65036	2	4	ADMIN. ENVIRO. QUALITY PROGRMS	65279	63	305	BEVERAGE & TOBACCO PRODUCT MFG	65565	318	2259	MOTOR VEHICLE & PARTS DEALERS
65037	318	1502	REAL ESTATE	65280	3	3	FABRICATED METAL PRODUCT MFG	65566	70	1064	MINING (EXCEPT OIL AND GAS)
65038	30	267	NURSING & RESID. CARE FACILIT.	65281	191	1013	EDUCATIONAL SERVICES	65567	47	448	EDUCATIONAL SERVICES
65039	45	144	AMUSEMENT; GAMBLING;& RECREAT.	65282	4	26	ACCOMMODATION	65570	12	41	EDUCATIONAL SERVICES
65040	16	19	SPECIAL TRADE CONTRACTORS	65283	16	40	UTILITIES	65571	111	493	EDUCATIONAL SERVICES
65041	351	2397	EDUCATIONAL SERVICES	65284	54	367	EDUCATIONAL SERVICES	65580	16	81	RENTAL AND LEASING SERVICES
65042	4	11	MERCH. WHOLESALERS;DURABLE GDS	65285	12	24	MOTOR VEHICLE & PARTS DEALERS	65582	138	925	MERCH. WHOLESALERS;NONDUR. GDS
65043	204	1888	ELECT'L EQPMT; APP; & COMP MFG	65286	6	11	MERCH. WHOLESALERS;NONDUR. GDS	65583	364	2375	EDUCATIONAL SERVICES
65046	39	138	SPECIAL TRADE CONTRACTORS	65287	6	2	POSTAL SERVICE	65584	515	3718	FOOD SVCS & DRINKING PLACES
65047	74	537	MERCH. WHOLESALERS;DURABLE GDS	65299	2	0	POSTAL SERVICE	65586	1	2	POSTAL SERVICE
65048	3	5	MERCH. WHOLESALERS;DURABLE GDS	65301	1577	20109	FOOD MANUFACTURING	65588	87	570	APPAREL MANUFACTURING
65049	643	4556	REAL ESTATE	65302	8	25	SOCIAL ASSISTANCE	65589	2	1	POSTAL SERVICE

ZIP CODE	2009 Total Firms	2009 Total Employ-ees	TOP INDUSTRY RANKED on 2009 EMPLOYMENT	ZIP CODE	2009 Total Firms	2009 Total Employ-ees	TOP INDUSTRY RANKED on 2009 EMPLOYMENT	ZIP CODE	2009 Total Firms	2009 Total Employ-ees	TOP INDUSTRY RANKED on 2009 EMPLOYMENT
65590	20	56	EDUCATIONAL SERVICES	65721	1000	7163	FOOD SVCS & DRINKING PLACES	66024	42	509	MERCH. WHOLESALERS;NONDUR. GDS
65591	22	60	MERCH. WHOLESALERS;DURABLE GDS	65722	28	138	TRUCK TRANSPORTATION	66025	162	959	EDUCATIONAL SERVICES
65601	13	21	APPAREL MANUFACTURING	65723	98	476	EDUCATIONAL SERVICES	66026	19	49	EDUCATIONAL SERVICES
65603	10	13	CHEMICAL MANUFACTURING	65724	51	144	ACCOMMODATION	66027	69	3953	NAT'L SECURITY & INT'L AFFAIRS
65604	157	758	EDUCATIONAL SERVICES	65725	83	427	EDUCATIONAL SERVICES	66030	410	3581	EDUCATIONAL SERVICES
65605	469	3343	FOOD SVCS & DRINKING PLACES	65726	6	443	EDUCATIONAL SERVICES	66031	57	3182	FOOD MANUFACTURING
65606	142	846	EDUCATIONAL SERVICES	65727	13	12	FABRICATED METAL PRODUCT MFG	66032	288	1889	HOSPITALS
65608	405	2635	MACHINERY MANUFACTURING	65728	1	1	POSTAL SERVICE	66033	26	131	REPAIR AND MAINTENANCE
65609	19	79	EDUCATIONAL SERVICES	65729	13	57	JUSTICE; PUBIC ORDER/SAFETY	66035	50	382	EDUCATIONAL SERVICES
65610	121	572	EDUCATIONAL SERVICES	65730	6	13	MOTION PICT. & SOUND RECORDING	66036	11	33	RENTAL AND LEASING SERVICES
65611	71	302	EDUCATIONAL SERVICES	65731	5	18	SPECIAL TRADE CONTRACTORS	66039	15	40	EXEC.; LEGIS.; & OTHER SUPPORT
65612	27	232	TRUCK TRANSPORTATION	65732	28	182	RELIG.; GRANT; CIVIC; PROF ORG	66040	157	955	UTILITIES
65613	944	13093	NURSING & RESID. CARE FACILIT.	65733	17	45	JUSTICE; PUBIC ORDER/SAFETY	66041	22	59	EDUCATIONAL SERVICES
65614	19	78	HEAVY & CIVIL ENG. CONSTRUCT'N	65734	85	621	EDUCATIONAL SERVICES	66042	15	24	RELIG.; GRANT; CIVIC; PROF ORG
65615	23	317	PUBLISHING INDUSTRIES	65735	6	21	ADMINISTRATIVE & SUPPORT SVCS	66043	214	2648	JUSTICE; PUBIC ORDER/SAFETY
65616	2612	29639	ACCOMMODATION	65737	561	2779	EDUCATIONAL SERVICES	66044	1557	20769	AMBULATORY HEALTH CARE SVCS
65617	41	219	RELIG.; GRANT; CIVIC; PROF ORG	65738	529	4729	EDUCATIONAL SERVICES	66045	47	3723	EDUCATIONAL SERVICES
65618	2	2	MERCH. WHOLESALERS;DURABLE GDS	65739	60	1135	FOOD SVCS & DRINKING PLACES	66046	776	12527	PROF.; SCIENTIFIC; & TECH SVCS
65619	168	1088	SPECIAL TRADE CONTRACTORS	65740	79	144	ACCOMMODATION	66047	482	6490	SOCIAL ASSISTANCE
65620	5	11	REPAIR AND MAINTENANCE	65741	2	4	MISCELLANEOUS STORE RETAILERS	66048	1211	13494	EDUCATIONAL SERVICES
65622	411	2652	MERCH. WHOLESALERS;NONDUR. GDS	65742	372	1835	EDUCATIONAL SERVICES	66049	783	8216	FOOD SVCS & DRINKING PLACES
65623	12	56	ANIMAL PRODUCTION	65744	2	20	EDUCATIONAL SERVICES	66050	62	215	EDUCATIONAL SERVICES
65624	71	189	FOOD SVCS & DRINKING PLACES	65745	55	174	JUSTICE; PUBIC ORDER/SAFETY	66051	16	42	SPECIAL TRADE CONTRACTORS
65625	494	5378	FOOD MANUFACTURING	65746	185	1040	EDUCATIONAL SERVICES	66052	41	271	CROP PRODUCTION
65626	44	125	RELIG.; GRANT; CIVIC; PROF ORG	65747	252	954	JUSTICE; PUBIC ORDER/SAFETY	66053	295	1902	EDUCATIONAL SERVICES
65627	13	32	PROF.; SCIENTIFIC; & TECH SVCS	65752	5	6	PROF.; SCIENTIFIC; & TECH SVCS	66054	62	378	EDUCATIONAL SERVICES
65629	7	122	EDUCATIONAL SERVICES	65753	99	547	EDUCATIONAL SERVICES	66056	138	577	EDUCATIONAL SERVICES
65630	10	85	REAL ESTATE	65754	30	143	EDUCATIONAL SERVICES	66058	10	17	MOTOR VEHICLE & PARTS DEALERS
65631	73	596	EDUCATIONAL SERVICES	65755	11	33	MERCH. WHOLESALERS;NONDUR. GDS	66060	48	177	EDUCATIONAL SERVICES
65632	55	367	EDUCATIONAL SERVICES	65756	13	53	CONSTRUCTION OF BUILDINGS	66061	1899	34874	HOSPITALS
65633	157	846	EDUCATIONAL SERVICES	65757	206	2112	TRUCK TRANSPORTATION	66062	2120	26456	FOOD SVCS & DRINKING PLACES
65634	16	30	WOOD PRODUCT MANUFACTURING	65759	25	103	EDUCATIONAL SERVICES	66063	22	76	PUBLISHING INDUSTRIES
65635	16	114	EDUCATIONAL SERVICES	65760	19	41	RENTAL AND LEASING SERVICES	66064	207	1825	HOSPITALS
65636	5	10	SPECIAL TRADE CONTRACTORS	65761	61	307	EDUCATIONAL SERVICES	66066	162	834	EDUCATIONAL SERVICES
65637	33	239	EDUCATIONAL SERVICES	65762	10	43	EDUCATIONAL SERVICES	66067	711	8666	MERCH. WHOLESALERS;DURABLE GDS
65638	9	16	HEAVY & CIVIL ENG. CONSTRUCT'N	65764	19	25	FOOD AND BEVERAGE STORES	66070	49	147	EDUCATIONAL SERVICES
65640	10	8	CONSTRUCTION OF BUILDINGS	65765	2	2	FOOD AND BEVERAGE STORES	66071	506	4234	EDUCATIONAL SERVICES
65641	87	177	FOOD SVCS & DRINKING PLACES	65766	2	3	MERCH. WHOLESALERS;DURABLE GDS	66072	33	131	EDUCATIONAL SERVICES
65644	31	63	SPECIAL TRADE CONTRACTORS	65767	66	545	EDUCATIONAL SERVICES	66073	92	409	EDUCATIONAL SERVICES
65645	3	13	JUSTICE; PUBIC ORDER/SAFETY	65768	9	8	SPECIAL TRADE CONTRACTORS	66075	175	710	JUSTICE; PUBIC ORDER/SAFETY
65646	41	111	EDUCATIONAL SERVICES	65769	61	368	FOOD MANUFACTURING	66076	34	190	EDUCATIONAL SERVICES
65647	50	302	EDUCATIONAL SERVICES	65770	46	228	EDUCATIONAL SERVICES	66078	18	44	FOOD SVCS & DRINKING PLACES
65648	147	752	EDUCATIONAL SERVICES	65771	50	190	ADMINISTRATIVE & SUPPORT SVCS	66079	18	154	MOTOR VEHICLE & PARTS DEALERS
65649	44	276	ADMINISTRATIVE & SUPPORT SVCS	65772	44	278	EDUCATIONAL SERVICES	66080	29	328	EDUCATIONAL SERVICES
65650	10	21	MOTOR VEHICLE & PARTS DEALERS	65773	12	19	ACCOMMODATION	66083	237	2020	MISCELLANEOUS MANUFACTURING
65652	79	443	JUSTICE; PUBIC ORDER/SAFETY	65774	29	168	EDUCATIONAL SERVICES	66085	324	2770	EDUCATIONAL SERVICES
65653	323	2106	EDUCATIONAL SERVICES	65775	1468	14502	AMBULATORY HEALTH CARE SVCS	66086	245	1742	EDUCATIONAL SERVICES
65654	11	64	EDUCATIONAL SERVICES	65777	10	27	RELIG.; GRANT; CIVIC; PROF ORG	66087	111	484	EXEC.; LEGIS.; & OTHER SUPPORT
65655	186	1068	EDUCATIONAL SERVICES	65778	19	168	EDUCATIONAL SERVICES	66088	121	534	EDUCATIONAL SERVICES
65656	144	692	EDUCATIONAL SERVICES	65779	80	332	EDUCATIONAL SERVICES	66090	115	854	MERCH. WHOLESALERS;DURABLE GDS
65657	2	0	RELIG.; GRANT; CIVIC; PROF ORG	65781	213	1141	EDUCATIONAL SERVICES	66091	12	42	UTILITIES
65658	35	162	MOTOR VEHICLE & PARTS DEALERS	65783	6	8	SPECIAL TRADE CONTRACTORS	66092	93	631	EDUCATIONAL SERVICES
65660	2	6	PROF.; SCIENTIFIC; & TECH SVCS	65784	2	1	FOOD AND BEVERAGE STORES	66093	21	77	EDUCATIONAL SERVICES
65661	152	823	PROF.; SCIENTIFIC; & TECH SVCS	65785	322	1250	EDUCATIONAL SERVICES	66094	32	273	AMUSEMENT; GAMBLING;& RECREAT.
65662	29	88	RELIG.; GRANT; CIVIC; PROF ORG	65786	62	264	EDUCATIONAL SERVICES	66095	34	94	EDUCATIONAL SERVICES
65663	46	268	EDUCATIONAL SERVICES	65787	23	119	RELIG.; GRANT; CIVIC; PROF ORG	66097	37	165	HOSPITALS
65664	22	46	EDUCATIONAL SERVICES	65788	19	45	RELIG.; GRANT; CIVIC; PROF ORG	66101	770	10441	EXEC.; LEGIS.; & OTHER SUPPORT
65666	4	5	REPAIR AND MAINTENANCE	65789	51	477	MERCH. WHOLESALERS;DURABLE GDS	66102	793	8679	EDUCATIONAL SERVICES
65667	131	528	EDUCATIONAL SERVICES	65790	11	30	JUSTICE; PUBIC ORDER/SAFETY	66103	593	5171	SPECIAL TRADE CONTRACTORS
65668	142	707	EDUCATIONAL SERVICES	65791	233	1301	EDUCATIONAL SERVICES	66104	320	2195	EDUCATIONAL SERVICES
65669	76	388	EDUCATIONAL SERVICES	65793	238	2069	EDUCATIONAL SERVICES	66105	395	6012	MERCH. WHOLESALERS;DURABLE GDS
65672	399	2537	EDUCATIONAL SERVICES	65801	35	858	POSTAL SERVICE	66106	842	10908	MERCH. WHOLESALERS;NONDUR. GDS
65673	6	29	PUBLISHING INDUSTRIES	65802	2266	37567	EDUCATIONAL SERVICES	66109	349	2221	EDUCATIONAL SERVICES
65674	96	573	EDUCATIONAL SERVICES	65803	1941	31870	SPORTG GDS;HOBBY;BOOK; & MUSIC	66110	3	4	CONSTRUCTION OF BUILDINGS
65675	16	88	EDUCATIONAL SERVICES	65804	3136	52391	HOSPITALS	66111	531	9764	FURN. & HOME FURNISHGS STORES
65676	14	33	ACCOMMODATION	65806	873	12290	FOOD MANUFACTURING	66112	504	5867	HOSPITALS
65679	94	316	EDUCATIONAL SERVICES	65807	2322	36912	HOSPITALS	66113	1	1	PERFORM'G ARTS; SPEC. SPORTS
65680	19	38	CONSTRUCTION OF BUILDINGS	65808	39	84	SPECIAL TRADE CONTRACTORS	66115	200	8261	TRANSPORTATION EQUIPMENT MFG
65681	100	360	MACHINERY MANUFACTURING	65809	246	4760	SECURITIES/COMMODITY CONTRACTS	66118	60	989	TRUCK TRANSPORTATION
65682	89	727	MERCH. WHOLESALERS;DURABLE GDS	65810	471	2933	FOOD SVCS & DRINKING PLACES	66160	62	6033	AMBULATORY HEALTH CARE SVCS
65685	13	68	EDUCATIONAL SERVICES	65814	21	99	INSURANCE CARRIERS & RELATED	66201	20	127	INSURANCE CARRIERS & RELATED
65686	264	1321	ACCOMMODATION	65897	22	6140	OTHER INFORMATION SERVICES	66202	1231	23891	PROF.; SCIENTIFIC; & TECH SVCS
65688	4	4	CONSTRUCTION OF BUILDINGS	65898	2	3050	SPORTG GDS;HOBBY;BOOK; & MUSIC	66203	893	8270	CREDIT INTERMEDIATION & RELATD
65689	202	2515	TRUCK TRANSPORTATION	65899	1	0	INSURANCE CARRIERS & RELATED	66204	920	11575	HOSPITALS
65690	3	12	RELIG.; GRANT; CIVIC; PROF ORG	66002	565	6788	EDUCATIONAL SERVICES	66205	589	6758	GENERAL MERCHANDISE STORES
65692	27	204	WOOD PRODUCT MANUFACTURING	66006	261	1671	EDUCATIONAL SERVICES	66206	358	3254	EDUCATIONAL SERVICES
65702	12	18	MERCH. WHOLESALERS;DURABLE GDS	66007	194	1273	EDUCATIONAL SERVICES	66207	499	3331	EDUCATIONAL SERVICES
65704	141	1612	UNCLASSIFIED ESTABLISHMENTS	66008	10	123	EDUCATIONAL SERVICES	66208	664	5807	REAL ESTATE
65705	114	827	EDUCATIONAL SERVICES	66010	27	55	EDUCATIONAL SERVICES	66209	599	7150	FOOD SVCS & DRINKING PLACES
65706	644	4486	EDUCATIONAL SERVICES	66012	463	3570	GENERAL MERCHANDISE STORES	66210	1689	26100	PROF.; SCIENTIFIC; & TECH SVCS
65707	87	414	EDUCATIONAL SERVICES	66013	77	619	ADMINISTRATIVE & SUPPORT SVCS	66211	1154	23663	PROF.; SCIENTIFIC; & TECH SVCS
65708	585	10230	PRIMARY METAL MANUFACTURING	66014	11	26	MERCH. WHOLESALERS;DURABLE GDS	66212	1542	15723	FOOD SVCS & DRINKING PLACES
65710	27	313	EDUCATIONAL SERVICES	66015	29	127	EDUCATIONAL SERVICES	66213	960	11867	INSURANCE CARRIERS & RELATED
65711	463	2909	GENERAL MERCHANDISE STORES	66016	7	14	EDUCATIONAL SERVICES	66214	1125	19128	PROF.; SCIENTIFIC; & TECH SVCS
65712	415	4274	SOCIAL ASSISTANCE	66017	11	65	EDUCATIONAL SERVICES	66215	1746	25924	MERCH. WHOLESALERS;DURABLE GDS
65713	26	185	EDUCATIONAL SERVICES	66018	185	2115	PAPER MANUFACTURING	66216	631	5300	ADMINISTRATIVE & SUPPORT SVCS
65714	1141	8850	ADMINISTRATIVE & SUPPORT SVCS	66019	3	7	POSTAL SERVICE	66217	230	6800	MACHINERY MANUFACTURING
65715	1	5	MERCH. WHOLESALERS;NONDUR. GDS	66020	31	184	EDUCATIONAL SERVICES	66218	184	1733	SPECIAL TRADE CONTRACTORS
65717	65	508	EDUCATIONAL SERVICES	66021	55	256	ACCOMMODATION	66219	518	21031	UNCLASSIFIED ESTABLISHMENTS
65720	9	14	FOOD MANUFACTURING	66023	47	209	EDUCATIONAL SERVICES	66220	85	528	AMUSEMENT; GAMBLING;& RECREAT.

BUSINESS DATA

ZIP CODE	2009 Total Firms	2009 Total Employees	TOP INDUSTRY RANKED on 2009 EMPLOYMENT
66221	282	2543	FOOD SVCS & DRINKING PLACES
66222	6	5	SPECIAL TRADE CONTRACTORS
66223	706	6772	FOOD SVCS & DRINKING PLACES
66224	221	1725	EDUCATIONAL SERVICES
66225	30	80	ADMINISTRATIVE & SUPPORT SVCS
66226	238	3553	SPECIAL TRADE CONTRACTORS
66227	192	3035	MERCH. WHOLESALERS;DURABLE GDS
66250	4	1202	NONSTORE RETAILERS
66251	8	2007	TELECOMMUNICATIONS
66282	15	35	REAL ESTATE
66283	14	57	ADMINISTRATIVE & SUPPORT SVCS
66285	40	111	UNCLASSIFIED ESTABLISHMENTS
66286	7	31	SPECIAL TRADE CONTRACTORS
66401	104	614	FOOD AND BEVERAGE STORES
66402	55	471	JUSTICE; PUBIC ORDER/SAFETY
66403	42	159	UTILITIES
66404	12	160	EDUCATIONAL SERVICES
66406	33	211	SOCIAL ASSISTANCE
66407	21	367	REPAIR AND MAINTENANCE
66408	28	349	FOOD MANUFACTURING
66409	41	151	EDUCATIONAL SERVICES
66411	45	411	NONMETALLIC MINERAL PROD. MFG
66412	12	31	INSURANCE CARRIERS & RELATED
66413	59	290	EDUCATIONAL SERVICES
66414	53	306	EDUCATIONAL SERVICES
66415	42	200	NURSING & RESID. CARE FACILIT.
66416	13	12	RELIG.; GRANT; CIVIC; PROF ORG
66417	19	91	PROF.; SCIENTIFIC; & TECH SVCS
66418	10	34	EDUCATIONAL SERVICES
66419	11	16	RELIG.; GRANT; CIVIC; PROF ORG
66420	2	0	POSTAL SERVICE
66422	16	37	EDUCATIONAL SERVICES
66423	50	210	EDUCATIONAL SERVICES
66424	40	124	EDUCATIONAL SERVICES
66425	40	116	JUSTICE; PUBIC ORDER/SAFETY
66427	71	350	NURSING & RESID. CARE FACILIT.
66428	12	17	MERCH. WHOLESALERS;NONDUR. GDS
66429	24	155	SPECIAL TRADE CONTRACTORS
66431	18	41	BLDG MATL & GARDEN EQPMT DLRS
66432	10	18	PIPELINE TRANSPORTATION
66434	366	2653	EDUCATIONAL SERVICES
66436	380	2422	EDUCATIONAL SERVICES
66438	20	156	PROF.; SCIENTIFIC; & TECH SVCS
66439	198	1040	EXEC.; LEGIS.; & OTHER SUPPORT
66440	53	181	EDUCATIONAL SERVICES
66441	1023	10123	EDUCATIONAL SERVICES
66442	109	16040	NAT'L SECURITY & INT'L AFFAIRS
66449	28	102	NURSING & RESID. CARE FACILIT.
66451	125	975	EDUCATIONAL SERVICES
66501	4	7	RELIG.; GRANT; CIVIC; PROF ORG
66502	1792	25527	PROF.; SCIENTIFIC; & TECH SVCS
66503	319	4076	INSURANCE CARRIERS & RELATED
66505	10	22	NAT'L SECURITY & INT'L AFFAIRS
66506	28	921	PROF.; SCIENTIFIC; & TECH SVCS
66507	32	221	FOOD SVCS & DRINKING PLACES
66508	301	3135	FABRICATED METAL PRODUCT MFG
66509	77	1513	AMUSEMENT; GAMBLING;& RECREAT.
66510	30	179	EDUCATIONAL SERVICES
66512	129	809	EDUCATIONAL SERVICES
66514	41	681	EXEC.; LEGIS.; & OTHER SUPPORT
66515	21	37	JUSTICE; PUBIC ORDER/SAFETY
66516	10	17	GASOLINE STATIONS
66517	31	114	EDUCATIONAL SERVICES
66518	8	12	MISCELLANEOUS STORE RETAILERS
66520	26	62	EDUCATIONAL SERVICES
66521	99	663	HOSPITALS
66522	1	1	POSTAL SERVICE
66523	208	1252	CONSTRUCTION OF BUILDINGS
66524	81	424	EDUCATIONAL SERVICES
66526	35	99	EDUCATIONAL SERVICES
66527	16	524	AMUSEMENT; GAMBLING;& RECREAT.
66528	21	48	EDUCATIONAL SERVICES
66531	50	239	EDUCATIONAL SERVICES
66532	24	68	FOOD AND BEVERAGE STORES
66533	80	446	EDUCATIONAL SERVICES
66534	193	2469	FABRICATED METAL PRODUCT MFG
66535	44	219	EDUCATIONAL SERVICES
66536	162	1308	EDUCATIONAL SERVICES
66537	38	141	EDUCATIONAL SERVICES
66538	268	2234	MISCELLANEOUS MANUFACTURING
66539	90	372	EDUCATIONAL SERVICES
66540	13	20	EXEC.; LEGIS.; & OTHER SUPPORT
66541	24	101	CONSTRUCTION OF BUILDINGS
66542	79	1015	EDUCATIONAL SERVICES
66543	19	94	FOOD SVCS & DRINKING PLACES
66544	20	35	EDUCATIONAL SERVICES
66546	29	182	SPECIAL TRADE CONTRACTORS
66547	363	2951	MACHINERY MANUFACTURING
66548	54	426	TRANSPORTATION EQUIPMENT MFG
66549	72	435	EXEC.; LEGIS.; & OTHER SUPPORT

ZIP CODE	2009 Total Firms	2009 Total Employees	TOP INDUSTRY RANKED on 2009 EMPLOYMENT
66550	22	65	EDUCATIONAL SERVICES
66552	19	51	FABRICATED METAL PRODUCT MFG
66554	25	84	EDUCATIONAL SERVICES
66601	16	56	SPECIAL TRADE CONTRACTORS
66603	647	9997	JUSTICE; PUBIC ORDER/SAFETY
66604	1155	17178	FOOD SVCS & DRINKING PLACES
66605	351	2259	EDUCATIONAL SERVICES
66606	500	8594	HOSPITALS
66607	324	6212	CLOTHING & CLOTH'G ACC. STORES
66608	428	4168	BLDG MATL & GARDEN EQPMT DLRS
66609	310	6711	PRINT'G & RELATED SUPP'T ACT'S
66610	126	447	EDUCATIONAL SERVICES
66611	490	6806	NURSING & RESID. CARE FACILIT.
66612	500	15658	EXEC.; LEGIS.; & OTHER SUPPORT
66614	1027	9199	NURSING & RESID. CARE FACILIT.
66615	173	2427	BROADCASTING
66616	112	760	EDUCATIONAL SERVICES
66617	180	1339	EDUCATIONAL SERVICES
66618	297	6464	PLASTICS & RUBBER PRODUCTS MFG
66619	151	2758	NAT'L SECURITY & INT'L AFFAIRS
66620	5	144	EXEC.; LEGIS.; & OTHER SUPPORT
66621	8	122	RELIG.; GRANT; CIVIC; PROF ORG
66622	9	319	EXEC.; LEGIS.; & OTHER SUPPORT
66624	1	250	POSTAL SERVICE
66629	3	3910	INSURANCE CARRIERS & RELATED
66636	1	600	SECURITIES/COMMODITY CONTRACTS
66667	6	12	ADMINISTRATIVE & SUPPORT SVCS
66675	4	5	ADMINISTRATIVE & SUPPORT SVCS
66683	30	171	JUSTICE; PUBIC ORDER/SAFETY
66701	605	6926	INSURANCE CARRIERS & RELATED
66710	28	55	FISHING; HUNTING AND TRAPPING
66711	32	58	UTILITIES
66712	93	354	EDUCATIONAL SERVICES
66713	246	1874	PAPER MANUFACTURING
66714	5	8	OIL AND GAS EXTRACTION
66716	30	67	FOOD SVCS & DRINKING PLACES
66717	19	131	EDUCATIONAL SERVICES
66720	592	6920	MERCH. WHOLESALERS;DURABLE GDS
66724	44	206	EDUCATIONAL SERVICES
66725	375	2497	PRINT'G & RELATED SUPP'T ACT'S
66728	12	16	SPECIAL TRADE CONTRACTORS
66732	9	11	FOOD SVCS & DRINKING PLACES
66733	127	657	EXEC.; LEGIS.; & OTHER SUPPORT
66734	14	14	MUSEUMS; HIST. SITES;& SIMILAR
66735	9	13	ADMINISTRATIVE & SUPPORT SVCS
66736	283	1604	EDUCATIONAL SERVICES
66738	25	19	AMUSEMENT; GAMBLING;& RECREAT.
66739	163	1515	MERCH. WHOLESALERS;DURABLE GDS
66740	23	173	COMPUTER & ELECTRONIC PROD MFG
66741	5	1	REPAIR AND MAINTENANCE
66742	23	99	HEAVY & CIVIL ENG. CONSTRUCT'N
66743	301	2124	RELIG.; GRANT; CIVIC; PROF ORG
66746	26	40	JUSTICE; PUBIC ORDER/SAFETY
66748	105	898	MERCH. WHOLESALERS;DURABLE GDS
66749	443	4106	PLASTICS & RUBBER PRODUCTS MFG
66751	34	173	BLDG MATL & GARDEN EQPMT DLRS
66753	47	95	EDUCATIONAL SERVICES
66754	9	7	FOOD AND BEVERAGE STORES
66755	45	301	EDUCATIONAL SERVICES
66756	37	110	FOOD SVCS & DRINKING PLACES
66757	178	3117	REPAIR AND MAINTENANCE
66758	7	17	JUSTICE; PUBIC ORDER/SAFETY
66759	1	0	POSTAL SERVICE
66760	2	18	ADMINISTRATIVE & SUPPORT SVCS
66761	14	45	MERCH. WHOLESALERS;NONDUR. GDS
66762	1176	13987	FOOD SVCS & DRINKING PLACES
66763	149	1195	FOOD MANUFACTURING
66767	38	147	NURSING & RESID. CARE FACILIT.
66769	17	27	JUSTICE; PUBIC ORDER/SAFETY
66770	43	672	EDUCATIONAL SERVICES
66771	55	531	NURSING & RESID. CARE FACILIT.
66772	16	21	SPECIAL TRADE CONTRACTORS
66773	24	179	MERCH. WHOLESALERS;DURABLE GDS
66775	15	28	TRUCK TRANSPORTATION
66776	41	204	FOOD SVCS & DRINKING PLACES
66777	28	83	UNCLASSIFIED ESTABLISHMENTS
66778	5	144	MERCH. WHOLESALERS;DURABLE GDS
66779	36	139	EDUCATIONAL SERVICES
66780	22	34	CONSTRUCTION OF BUILDINGS
66781	45	130	EDUCATIONAL SERVICES
66782	9	20	MUSEUMS; HIST. SITES;& SIMILAR
66783	131	712	EDUCATIONAL SERVICES
66801	1313	17027	FOOD MANUFACTURING
66830	8	36	EDUCATIONAL SERVICES
66833	23	84	EDUCATIONAL SERVICES
66834	35	132	EDUCATIONAL SERVICES
66835	38	120	EDUCATIONAL SERVICES
66838	11	14	FOOD MANUFACTURING
66839	291	2063	HOSPITALS
66840	29	91	JUSTICE; PUBIC ORDER/SAFETY

ZIP CODE	2009 Total Firms	2009 Total Employees	TOP INDUSTRY RANKED on 2009 EMPLOYMENT
66842	25	89	FOOD SVCS & DRINKING PLACES
66843	12	68	MINING (EXCEPT OIL AND GAS)
66845	105	409	EDUCATIONAL SERVICES
66846	269	1636	EDUCATIONAL SERVICES
66849	24	64	ANIMAL PRODUCTION
66850	6	10	ACCOMMODATION
66851	27	136	FOOD SVCS & DRINKING PLACES
66852	34	203	FURNITURE & RELATED PROD. MFG
66853	23	93	EDUCATIONAL SERVICES
66854	43	307	RELIG.; GRANT; CIVIC; PROF ORG
66855	3	5	CONSTRUCTION OF BUILDINGS
66856	78	380	FOOD SVCS & DRINKING PLACES
66857	33	155	EDUCATIONAL SERVICES
66858	19	42	OIL AND GAS EXTRACTION
66859	16	117	EDUCATIONAL SERVICES
66860	76	315	SPECIAL TRADE CONTRACTORS
66861	198	1294	RELIG.; GRANT; CIVIC; PROF ORG
66862	5	5	JUSTICE; PUBIC ORDER/SAFETY
66863	2	2	POSTAL SERVICE
66864	13	60	EDUCATIONAL SERVICES
66865	42	218	EDUCATIONAL SERVICES
66866	63	407	NURSING & RESID. CARE FACILIT.
66868	20	70	EDUCATIONAL SERVICES
66869	48	211	FOOD SVCS & DRINKING PLACES
66870	5	17	MERCH. WHOLESALERS;NONDUR. GDS
66871	66	292	BLDG MATL & GARDEN EQPMT DLRS
66872	43	122	EDUCATIONAL SERVICES
66873	14	41	JUSTICE; PUBIC ORDER/SAFETY
66901	391	3592	EDUCATIONAL SERVICES
66930	7	6	GASOLINE STATIONS
66932	10	36	JUSTICE; PUBIC ORDER/SAFETY
66933	17	47	JUSTICE; PUBIC ORDER/SAFETY
66935	214	1573	NURSING & RESID. CARE FACILIT.
66936	17	89	JUSTICE; PUBIC ORDER/SAFETY
66937	43	173	RELIG.; GRANT; CIVIC; PROF ORG
66938	60	308	NURSING & RESID. CARE FACILIT.
66939	34	178	MERCH. WHOLESALERS;DURABLE GDS
66940	14	37	EDUCATIONAL SERVICES
66941	8	16	CREDIT INTERMEDIATION & RELATD
66942	9	17	EXEC.; LEGIS.; & OTHER SUPPORT
66943	39	141	FOOD MANUFACTURING
66944	13	19	FOOD MANUFACTURING
66945	56	417	AMBULATORY HEALTH CARE SVCS
66946	3	11	SUPPORT ACTIVITIES: AGR./FOR.
66948	23	102	NURSING & RESID. CARE FACILIT.
66949	41	108	EDUCATIONAL SERVICES
66951	50	208	NURSING & RESID. CARE FACILIT.
66952	22	83	GASOLINE STATIONS
66953	41	279	MERCH. WHOLESALERS;DURABLE GDS
66955	10	83	SUPPORT ACTIVITIES: AGR./FOR.
66956	92	624	EXEC.; LEGIS.; & OTHER SUPPORT
66958	13	32	CONSTRUCTION OF BUILDINGS
66959	12	19	JUSTICE; PUBIC ORDER/SAFETY
66960	8	11	FOOD SVCS & DRINKING PLACES
66961	5	11	MERCH. WHOLESALERS;NONDUR. GDS
66962	20	52	MERCH. WHOLESALERS;NONDUR. GDS
66963	13	37	WAREHOUSING AND STORAGE
66964	14	23	TRUCK TRANSPORTATION
66966	36	161	EDUCATIONAL SERVICES
66967	184	1242	EDUCATIONAL SERVICES
66968	142	731	EDUCATIONAL SERVICES
66970	9	16	AMUSEMENT; GAMBLING;& RECREAT.
67001	48	322	EDUCATIONAL SERVICES
67002	419	3692	EDUCATIONAL SERVICES
67003	229	1335	EDUCATIONAL SERVICES
67004	60	226	EDUCATIONAL SERVICES
67005	636	7551	SUPPORT ACT. FOR TRANSPORT.
67008	15	49	JUSTICE; PUBIC ORDER/SAFETY
67009	55	354	EDUCATIONAL SERVICES
67010	439	3041	EDUCATIONAL SERVICES
67012	4	12	FOOD SVCS & DRINKING PLACES
67013	114	498	EDUCATIONAL SERVICES
67016	14	98	EDUCATIONAL SERVICES
67017	66	357	EDUCATIONAL SERVICES
67018	6	7	WAREHOUSING AND STORAGE
67019	39	275	EDUCATIONAL SERVICES
67020	79	382	EDUCATIONAL SERVICES
67021	7	15	REPAIR AND MAINTENANCE
67022	103	451	HOSPITALS
67023	14	21	ANIMAL PRODUCTION
67024	45	199	EDUCATIONAL SERVICES
67025	132	968	EDUCATIONAL SERVICES
67026	189	827	EDUCATIONAL SERVICES
67028	14	21	WAREHOUSING AND STORAGE
67029	109	470	EDUCATIONAL SERVICES
67030	80	1034	UNCLASSIFIED ESTABLISHMENTS
67031	111	440	EDUCATIONAL SERVICES
67035	65	280	NURSING & RESID. CARE FACILIT.
67036	10	32	WAREHOUSING AND STORAGE
67037	685	5960	EDUCATIONAL SERVICES

ZIP CODE	2009 Total Firms	2009 Total Employ-ees	TOP INDUSTRY RANKED on 2009 EMPLOYMENT	ZIP CODE	2009 Total Firms	2009 Total Employ-ees	TOP INDUSTRY RANKED on 2009 EMPLOYMENT	ZIP CODE	2009 Total Firms	2009 Total Employ-ees	TOP INDUSTRY RANKED on 2009 EMPLOYMENT
67038	24	102	NURSING & RESID. CARE FACILIT.	67220	285	6954	CHEMICAL MANUFACTURING	67481	44	187	EDUCATIONAL SERVICES
67039	66	326	EDUCATIONAL SERVICES	67221	18	94	EDUCATIONAL SERVICES	67482	10	12	WAREHOUSING AND STORAGE
67041	6	58	EDUCATIONAL SERVICES	67223	8	39	SPECIAL TRADE CONTRACTORS	67483	14	51	CREDIT INTERMEDIATION & RELATD
67042	861	10610	EDUCATIONAL SERVICES	67226	781	16550	EDUCATIONAL SERVICES	67484	40	125	EDUCATIONAL SERVICES
67045	237	1265	HOSPITALS	67227	7	159	ADMINISTRATIVE & SUPPORT SVCS	67485	37	197	MACHINERY MANUFACTURING
67047	22	99	FISHING; HUNTING AND TRAPPING	67228	23	160	EDUCATIONAL SERVICES	67487	47	209	EDUCATIONAL SERVICES
67049	9	15	EXEC.; LEGIS.; & OTHER SUPPORT	67230	124	336	EDUCATIONAL SERVICES	67490	87	396	EDUCATIONAL SERVICES
67050	51	388	SOCIAL ASSISTANCE	67232	4	8	PROF.; SCIENTIFIC; & TECH SVCS	67491	13	86	EDUCATIONAL SERVICES
67051	15	31	JUSTICE; PUBIC ORDER/SAFETY	67235	159	1014	SOCIAL ASSISTANCE	67492	18	41	MINING (EXCEPT OIL AND GAS)
67052	212	2908	EDUCATIONAL SERVICES	67260	17	2632	EDUCATIONAL SERVICES	67501	1529	18883	JUSTICE; PUBIC ORDER/SAFETY
67053	43	535	RELIG.; GRANT; CIVIC; PROF ORG	67275	4	25	ADMINISTRATIVE & SUPPORT SVCS	67502	581	7738	AMBULATORY HEALTH CARE SVCS
67054	103	628	HOSPITALS	67276	2	1200	POSTAL SERVICE	67504	11	24	SPECIAL TRADE CONTRACTORS
67056	140	1027	WOOD PRODUCT MANUFACTURING	67277	18	63	PROF.; SCIENTIFIC; & TECH SVCS	67505	141	2029	MERCH. WHOLESALERS;NONDUR. GDS
67057	29	77	FOOD SVCS & DRINKING PLACES	67278	16	28	SUPPORT ACTIVITIES: AGR./FOR.	67510	12	16	SOCIAL ASSISTANCE
67058	134	892	HOSPITALS	67301	740	8273	HOSPITALS	67511	13	24	CREDIT INTERMEDIATION & RELATD
67059	54	282	EDUCATIONAL SERVICES	67330	78	322	EDUCATIONAL SERVICES	67512	12	29	PIPELINE TRANSPORTATION
67060	342	2216	EDUCATIONAL SERVICES	67332	23	122	FOOD MANUFACTURING	67513	8	7	WAREHOUSING AND STORAGE
67061	12	12	CREDIT INTERMEDIATION & RELATD	67333	140	1314	PLASTICS & RUBBER PRODUCTS MFG	67514	39	91	FOOD SVCS & DRINKING PLACES
67062	171	3226	WAREHOUSING AND STORAGE	67334	4	4	POSTAL SERVICE	67515	3	7	JUSTICE; PUBIC ORDER/SAFETY
67063	188	1562	EDUCATIONAL SERVICES	67335	129	1107	PLASTICS & RUBBER PRODUCTS MFG	67516	37	92	EDUCATIONAL SERVICES
67065	11	18	WAREHOUSING AND STORAGE	67336	79	445	EDUCATIONAL SERVICES	67518	8	10	WAREHOUSING AND STORAGE
67066	17	215	FOOD MANUFACTURING	67337	616	8094	NURSING & RESID. CARE FACILIT.	67519	15	20	WAREHOUSING AND STORAGE
67067	89	554	SPECIAL TRADE CONTRACTORS	67340	16	38	FOOD SVCS & DRINKING PLACES	67520	22	48	EDUCATIONAL SERVICES
67068	279	2224	HOSPITALS	67341	4	9	BLDG MATL & GARDEN EQPMT DLRS	67521	8	34	MERCH. WHOLESALERS;DURABLE GDS
67070	129	452	HOSPITALS	67342	54	202	GASOLINE STATIONS	67522	72	717	EDUCATIONAL SERVICES
67071	9	2	ANIMAL PRODUCTION	67344	31	47	NURSING & RESID. CARE FACILIT.	67523	31	82	EDUCATIONAL SERVICES
67072	8	48	JUSTICE; PUBIC ORDER/SAFETY	67345	6	5	FOOD AND BEVERAGE STORES	67524	34	300	REPAIR AND MAINTENANCE
67073	8	11	FABRICATED METAL PRODUCT MFG	67346	17	51	TRANSPORTATION EQUIPMENT MFG	67525	87	300	SPECIAL TRADE CONTRACTORS
67074	39	320	EDUCATIONAL SERVICES	67347	15	21	RELIG.; GRANT; CIVIC; PROF ORG	67526	203	846	EDUCATIONAL SERVICES
67101	205	1694	EDUCATIONAL SERVICES	67349	85	339	RELIG.; GRANT; CIVIC; PROF ORG	67529	12	27	JUSTICE; PUBIC ORDER/SAFETY
67102	2	0	RELIG.; GRANT; CIVIC; PROF ORG	67351	11	23	FURN. & HOME FURNISHGS STORES	67530	1138	11816	EDUCATIONAL SERVICES
67103	17	32	MERCH. WHOLESALERS;DURABLE GDS	67352	31	207	EDUCATIONAL SERVICES	67543	81	553	EDUCATIONAL SERVICES
67104	213	1519	MERCH. WHOLESALERS;DURABLE GDS	67353	36	125	EDUCATIONAL SERVICES	67544	212	1190	COMPUTER & ELECTRONIC PROD MFG
67105	4	7	CROP PRODUCTION	67354	23	67	EDUCATIONAL SERVICES	67545	16	84	FOOD MANUFACTURING
67106	18	31	TRUCK TRANSPORTATION	67355	7	10	HEAVY & CIVIL ENG. CONSTRUCT'N	67546	88	575	NURSING & RESID. CARE FACILIT.
67107	153	1831	MACHINERY MANUFACTURING	67356	145	806	JUSTICE; PUBIC ORDER/SAFETY	67547	138	662	EXEC.; LEGIS.; & OTHER SUPPORT
67108	50	264	RELIG.; GRANT; CIVIC; PROF ORG	67357	581	8349	HOSPITALS	67548	135	750	FURNITURE & RELATED PROD. MFG
67109	34	153	EDUCATIONAL SERVICES	67360	7	11	FOOD AND BEVERAGE STORES	67550	301	2988	HOSPITALS
67110	190	1626	EDUCATIONAL SERVICES	67361	138	771	EDUCATIONAL SERVICES	67552	46	317	FABRICATED METAL PRODUCT MFG
67111	8	8	RELIG.; GRANT; CIVIC; PROF ORG	67363	2	4	POSTAL SERVICE	67553	6	9	EXEC.; LEGIS.; & OTHER SUPPORT
67112	17	30	FUNDS; TRUSTS; & OTHER FINANCE	67364	13	84	EDUCATIONAL SERVICES	67554	241	1828	EDUCATIONAL SERVICES
67114	1017	10336	SPECIAL TRADE CONTRACTORS	67401	2447	33084	FOOD MANUFACTURING	67556	23	35	JUSTICE; PUBIC ORDER/SAFETY
67117	42	866	EDUCATIONAL SERVICES	67402	11	25	ADMINISTRATIVE & SUPPORT SVCS	67557	54	137	EDUCATIONAL SERVICES
67118	41	284	PRIMARY METAL MANUFACTURING	67410	566	4019	GENERAL MERCHANDISE STORES	67559	1	3	WAREHOUSING AND STORAGE
67119	93	319	EDUCATIONAL SERVICES	67416	41	124	JUSTICE; PUBIC ORDER/SAFETY	67560	204	959	SPECIAL TRADE CONTRACTORS
67120	24	95	BEVERAGE & TOBACCO PRODUCT MFG	67417	7	4	FOOD SVCS & DRINKING PLACES	67561	50	225	EDUCATIONAL SERVICES
67122	4	7	POSTAL SERVICE	67418	17	32	JUSTICE; PUBIC ORDER/SAFETY	67563	20	63	EDUCATIONAL SERVICES
67123	31	111	EDUCATIONAL SERVICES	67420	310	2922	HOSPITALS	67564	10	6	POSTAL SERVICE
67124	583	4500	HOSPITALS	67422	60	243	EDUCATIONAL SERVICES	67565	35	172	EDUCATIONAL SERVICES
67127	38	219	NURSING & RESID. CARE FACILIT.	67423	15	32	MERCH. WHOLESALERS;NONDUR. GDS	67566	17	52	EDUCATIONAL SERVICES
67131	9	8	MOTOR VEHICLE & PARTS DEALERS	67425	24	63	EDUCATIONAL SERVICES	67567	20	62	ANIMAL PRODUCTION
67132	15	100	EDUCATIONAL SERVICES	67427	32	91	PETROLEUM & COAL PRODUCTS MFG	67568	12	8	POSTAL SERVICE
67133	147	809	EDUCATIONAL SERVICES	67428	74	303	EDUCATIONAL SERVICES	67570	48	248	EDUCATIONAL SERVICES
67134	28	50	SPECIAL TRADE CONTRACTORS	67430	43	124	EDUCATIONAL SERVICES	67572	51	359	HOSPITALS
67135	80	466	EDUCATIONAL SERVICES	67431	82	415	EDUCATIONAL SERVICES	67573	12	4	MERCH. WHOLESALERS;DURABLE GDS
67137	29	126	EDUCATIONAL SERVICES	67432	370	3014	MACHINERY MANUFACTURING	67574	19	93	EDUCATIONAL SERVICES
67138	35	72	ANIMAL PRODUCTION	67436	33	63	WAREHOUSING AND STORAGE	67575	28	200	MERCH. WHOLESALERS;DURABLE GDS
67140	38	165	EDUCATIONAL SERVICES	67437	72	375	EDUCATIONAL SERVICES	67576	166	592	NURSING & RESID. CARE FACILIT.
67142	14	61	SPECIAL TRADE CONTRACTORS	67438	14	51	MACHINERY MANUFACTURING	67578	91	531	EDUCATIONAL SERVICES
67143	8	19	NONMETALLIC MINERAL PROD. MFG	67439	214	2375	NURSING & RESID. CARE FACILIT.	67579	136	817	MACHINERY MANUFACTURING
67144	62	384	EDUCATIONAL SERVICES	67441	34	214	NURSING & RESID. CARE FACILIT.	67581	30	59	EDUCATIONAL SERVICES
67146	59	237	EDUCATIONAL SERVICES	67442	7	20	WAREHOUSING AND STORAGE	67583	43	147	EDUCATIONAL SERVICES
67147	275	2854	MACHINERY MANUFACTURING	67443	74	319	EDUCATIONAL SERVICES	67584	33	94	JUSTICE; PUBIC ORDER/SAFETY
67149	37	171	FABRICATED METAL PRODUCT MFG	67444	20	47	FABRICATED METAL PRODUCT MFG	67585	24	189	FOOD SVCS & DRINKING PLACES
67150	9	0	CROP PRODUCTION	67445	36	145	EDUCATIONAL SERVICES	67601	1546	16157	EDUCATIONAL SERVICES
67151	17	54	EDUCATIONAL SERVICES	67446	52	169	TELECOMMUNICATIONS	67621	29	127	EDUCATIONAL SERVICES
67152	490	4432	PROF.; SCIENTIFIC; & TECH SVCS	67447	8	10	MERCH. WHOLESALERS;NONDUR. GDS	67622	32	160	EDUCATIONAL SERVICES
67154	52	303	NURSING & RESID. CARE FACILIT.	67448	37	292	EDUCATIONAL SERVICES	67623	16	38	SOCIAL ASSISTANCE
67155	14	15	POSTAL SERVICE	67449	177	1824	NURSING & RESID. CARE FACILIT.	67625	21	26	RELIG.; GRANT; CIVIC; PROF ORG
67156	708	8323	EDUCATIONAL SERVICES	67450	33	130	EDUCATIONAL SERVICES	67626	6	37	BROADCASTING
67159	23	77	SPECIAL TRADE CONTRACTORS	67451	40	138	EDUCATIONAL SERVICES	67627	2	6	RELIG.; GRANT; CIVIC; PROF ORG
67201	32	1169	TRANSPORTATION EQUIPMENT MFG	67452	15	29	FOOD SVCS & DRINKING PLACES	67628	4	6	WAREHOUSING AND STORAGE
67202	1481	22433	CREDIT INTERMEDIATION & RELATD	67454	23	165	MINING (EXCEPT OIL AND GAS)	67629	8	11	MACHINERY MANUFACTURING
67203	1365	14838	JUSTICE; PUBIC ORDER/SAFETY	67455	162	856	JUSTICE; PUBIC ORDER/SAFETY	67631	14	13	MERCH. WHOLESALERS;DURABLE GDS
67204	477	2564	EDUCATIONAL SERVICES	67456	202	1339	EDUCATIONAL SERVICES	67632	17	25	EDUCATIONAL SERVICES
67205	580	5928	FOOD SVCS & DRINKING PLACES	67457	58	207	NURSING & RESID. CARE FACILIT.	67634	17	25	MISCELLANEOUS MANUFACTURING
67206	1016	16005	PROF.; SCIENTIFIC; & TECH SVCS	67458	24	83	FOOD SVCS & DRINKING PLACES	67635	6	5	WAREHOUSING AND STORAGE
67207	1018	12675	GENERAL MERCHANDISE STORES	67459	13	75	MACHINERY MANUFACTURING	67637	141	711	RELIG.; GRANT; CIVIC; PROF ORG
67208	883	7247	AMBULATORY HEALTH CARE SVCS	67460	844	9839	EDUCATIONAL SERVICES	67638	17	30	MERCH. WHOLESALERS;DURABLE GDS
67209	942	18004	COMPUTER & ELECTRONIC PROD MFG	67464	44	235	RELIG.; GRANT; CIVIC; PROF ORG	67639	8	50	EDUCATIONAL SERVICES
67210	187	23278	TRANSPORTATION EQUIPMENT MFG	67466	46	145	EDUCATIONAL SERVICES	67640	28	101	PROF.; SCIENTIFIC; & TECH SVCS
67211	1102	11989	PROF.; SCIENTIFIC; & TECH SVCS	67467	173	1150	RELIG.; GRANT; CIVIC; PROF ORG	67642	214	993	EXEC.; LEGIS.; & OTHER SUPPORT
67212	1027	7747	FOOD SVCS & DRINKING PLACES	67468	13	33	FABRICATED METAL PRODUCT MFG	67643	24	33	RELIG.; GRANT; CIVIC; PROF ORG
67213	997	13659	FABRICATED METAL PRODUCT MFG	67470	14	46	ADMINISTRATIVE & SUPPORT SVCS	67644	25	87	ACCOMMODATION
67214	1253	22518	HOSPITALS	67473	133	913	MACHINERY MANUFACTURING	67645	38	394	TELECOMMUNICATIONS
67215	145	6059	MOTOR VEHICLE & PARTS DEALERS	67474	9	13	REAL ESTATE	67646	62	241	EDUCATIONAL SERVICES
67216	616	6483	FOOD SVCS & DRINKING PLACES	67475	7	17	ANIMAL PRODUCTION	67647	22	167	CROP PRODUCTION
67217	614	9822	EDUCATIONAL SERVICES	67476	5	14	SPECIAL TRADE CONTRACTORS	67648	57	284	MACHINERY MANUFACTURING
67218	640	12128	HOSPITALS	67478	7	11	FOOD SVCS & DRINKING PLACES	67649	19	56	EDUCATIONAL SERVICES
67219	512	12320	MACHINERY MANUFACTURING	67480	45	702	MERCH. WHOLESALERS;DURABLE GDS	67650	27	68	SPECIAL TRADE CONTRACTORS

BUSINESS DATA

ZIP CODE	2009 Total Firms	2009 Total Employ-ees	TOP INDUSTRY RANKED on 2009 EMPLOYMENT
67651	46	214	EDUCATIONAL SERVICES
67653	15	37	SUPPORT ACTIVITIES: AGR./FOR.
67654	299	2425	JUSTICE; PUBIC ORDER/SAFETY
67656	6	21	WAREHOUSING AND STORAGE
67657	36	170	EDUCATIONAL SERVICES
67658	6	14	BLDG MATL & GARDEN EQPMT DLRS
67659	8	14	CROP PRODUCTION
67660	2	5	REPAIR AND MAINTENANCE
67661	292	2036	MERCH. WHOLESALERS;DURABLE GDS
67663	193	1232	UNCLASSIFIED ESTABLISHMENTS
67664	17	29	TRUCK TRANSPORTATION
67665	308	2014	FOOD SVCS & DRINKING PLACES
67667	5	11	REPAIR AND MAINTENANCE
67669	184	862	EXEC.; LEGIS.; & OTHER SUPPORT
67671	90	704	RELIG.; GRANT; CIVIC; PROF ORG
67672	242	1450	HOSPITALS
67673	8	5	GASOLINE STATIONS
67674	1	0	SPORTG GDS;HOBBY;BOOK; & MUSIC
67675	6	7	EXEC.; LEGIS.; & OTHER SUPPORT
67701	517	3592	FOOD SVCS & DRINKING PLACES
67730	172	797	EDUCATIONAL SERVICES
67731	46	233	EDUCATIONAL SERVICES
67732	31	168	TELECOMMUNICATIONS
67733	7	30	MERCH. WHOLESALERS;DURABLE GDS
67734	6	6	MERCH. WHOLESALERS;NONDUR. GDS
67735	355	2798	EDUCATIONAL SERVICES
67736	42	91	HEAVY & CIVIL ENG. CONSTRUCT'N
67737	48	260	EDUCATIONAL SERVICES
67738	40	135	EDUCATIONAL SERVICES
67739	13	31	CREDIT INTERMEDIATION & RELATD
67740	179	1015	EDUCATIONAL SERVICES
67741	24	52	WAREHOUSING AND STORAGE
67743	12	19	UTILITIES
67744	6	9	SPECIAL TRADE CONTRACTORS
67745	24	59	EDUCATIONAL SERVICES
67747	7	13	MERCH. WHOLESALERS;NONDUR. GDS
67748	210	1489	EDUCATIONAL SERVICES
67749	201	1052	HOSPITALS
67751	24	37	RELIG.; GRANT; CIVIC; PROF ORG
67752	140	894	EXEC.; LEGIS.; & OTHER SUPPORT
67753	26	102	ANIMAL PRODUCTION
67756	171	810	EDUCATIONAL SERVICES
67757	40	115	EDUCATIONAL SERVICES
67758	142	515	EDUCATIONAL SERVICES
67761	12	17	ANIMAL PRODUCTION
67762	22	52	EDUCATIONAL SERVICES
67764	38	121	EDUCATIONAL SERVICES
67801	1240	18532	FOOD MANUFACTURING
67831	133	560	EDUCATIONAL SERVICES
67834	63	398	EDUCATIONAL SERVICES
67835	191	1326	ANIMAL PRODUCTION
67836	14	54	ANIMAL PRODUCTION
67837	58	191	EDUCATIONAL SERVICES
67838	49	236	EDUCATIONAL SERVICES
67839	179	946	EDUCATIONAL SERVICES
67840	13	11	PIPELINE TRANSPORTATION
67841	20	67	EDUCATIONAL SERVICES
67842	27	115	ANIMAL PRODUCTION
67843	5	149	EXEC.; LEGIS.; & OTHER SUPPORT
67844	47	211	EDUCATIONAL SERVICES
67846	1612	15666	EDUCATIONAL SERVICES
67849	32	88	ANIMAL PRODUCTION
67850	24	108	MERCH. WHOLESALERS;NONDUR. GDS
67851	76	3983	FOOD MANUFACTURING
67853	53	263	EDUCATIONAL SERVICES
67854	94	434	HOSPITALS
67855	173	845	ANIMAL PRODUCTION
67857	16	23	OIL AND GAS EXTRACTION
67859	28	222	EDUCATIONAL SERVICES
67860	186	1185	HOSPITALS
67861	173	943	EDUCATIONAL SERVICES
67862	19	41	CROP PRODUCTION
67863	24	66	FOOD MANUFACTURING
67864	173	979	EDUCATIONAL SERVICES
67865	51	353	EDUCATIONAL SERVICES
67867	95	554	EDUCATIONAL SERVICES
67868	12	61	ANIMAL PRODUCTION
67869	68	481	CROP PRODUCTION
67870	116	1063	ANIMAL PRODUCTION
67871	357	2066	ANIMAL PRODUCTION
67876	46	261	EDUCATIONAL SERVICES
67877	158	947	EDUCATIONAL SERVICES
67878	213	1433	EDUCATIONAL SERVICES
67879	143	631	NURSING & RESID. CARE FACILIT.
67880	501	3770	EDUCATIONAL SERVICES
67882	14	270	MERCH. WHOLESALERS;NONDUR. GDS
67901	1169	11674	FOOD MANUFACTURING
67905	3	6	REAL ESTATE
67950	235	1351	HOSPITALS
67951	330	1842	EDUCATIONAL SERVICES
67952	39	185	EDUCATIONAL SERVICES
67953	12	47	UTILITIES
67954	37	188	EDUCATIONAL SERVICES
68001	3	2	MERCH. WHOLESALERS;NONDUR. GDS
68002	89	442	EDUCATIONAL SERVICES
68003	185	1491	ACCOMMODATION
68004	55	209	EDUCATIONAL SERVICES
68005	788	10919	SECURITIES/COMMODITY CONTRACTS
68007	144	655	WASTE MANAGMT & REMEDIAT'N SVC
68008	590	6566	MERCH. WHOLESALERS;DURABLE GDS
68010	30	1549	SOCIAL ASSISTANCE
68014	7	12	FOOD SVCS & DRINKING PLACES
68015	23	198	EDUCATIONAL SERVICES
68016	10	22	HEAVY & CIVIL ENG. CONSTRUCT'N
68017	46	398	FURN. & HOME FURNISHGS STORES
68018	11	25	CREDIT INTERMEDIATION & RELATD
68019	19	66	JUSTICE; PUBIC ORDER/SAFETY
68020	37	108	EXEC.; LEGIS.; & OTHER SUPPORT
68022	400	4489	PUBLISHING INDUSTRIES
68023	92	754	PLASTICS & RUBBER PRODUCTS MFG
68025	1211	16325	MERCH. WHOLESALERS;NONDUR. GDS
68026	6	13	ADMINISTRATIVE & SUPPORT SVCS
68028	398	3008	AMUSEMENT; GAMBLING;& RECREAT.
68029	21	75	MACHINERY MANUFACTURING
68030	29	115	EDUCATIONAL SERVICES
68031	91	484	EDUCATIONAL SERVICES
68033	16	115	EDUCATIONAL SERVICES
68034	26	33	ADMINISTRATIVE & SUPPORT SVCS
68036	13	41	SUPPORT ACTIVITIES: AGR./FOR.
68037	92	915	NONMETALLIC MINERAL PROD. MFG
68038	64	446	RELIG.; GRANT; CIVIC; PROF ORG
68039	52	1131	EXEC.; LEGIS.; & OTHER SUPPORT
68040	14	25	CREDIT INTERMEDIATION & RELATD
68041	42	584	BLDG MATL & GARDEN EQPMT DLRS
68042	5	7	FOOD SVCS & DRINKING PLACES
68044	22	135	BLDG MATL & GARDEN EQPMT DLRS
68045	108	636	EDUCATIONAL SERVICES
68046	789	9529	PROF.; SCIENTIFIC; & TECH SVCS
68047	111	1222	MACHINERY MANUFACTURING
68048	421	2493	NURSING & RESID. CARE FACILIT.
68050	26	74	EDUCATIONAL SERVICES
68055	14	34	EDUCATIONAL SERVICES
68056	1	49	SOCIAL ASSISTANCE
68057	73	485	EDUCATIONAL SERVICES
68058	6	9	GASOLINE STATIONS
68059	116	525	EDUCATIONAL SERVICES
68061	159	683	EDUCATIONAL SERVICES
68062	13	156	MACHINERY MANUFACTURING
68063	25	53	GASOLINE STATIONS
68064	133	3149	PRIMARY METAL MANUFACTURING
68065	43	162	EDUCATIONAL SERVICES
68066	314	3021	AMUSEMENT; GAMBLING;& RECREAT.
68067	60	274	EXEC.; LEGIS.; & OTHER SUPPORT
68068	6	17	MERCH. WHOLESALERS;NONDUR. GDS
68069	106	633	MERCH. WHOLESALERS;NONDUR. GDS
68070	28	138	UNCLASSIFIED ESTABLISHMENTS
68071	70	1202	EXEC.; LEGIS.; & OTHER SUPPORT
68072	4	26	JUSTICE; PUBIC ORDER/SAFETY
68073	51	259	EDUCATIONAL SERVICES
68101	2	2	PROF.; SCIENTIFIC; & TECH SVCS
68102	1060	24991	PROF.; SCIENTIFIC; & TECH SVCS
68103	11	44	MERCH. WHOLESALERS;DURABLE GDS
68104	634	5081	SOCIAL ASSISTANCE
68105	487	13716	AMBULATORY HEALTH CARE SVCS
68106	669	8092	FOOD AND BEVERAGE STORES
68107	894	10474	FOOD MANUFACTURING
68108	407	4992	POSTAL SERVICE
68109	2	3	POSTAL SERVICE
68110	396	7851	FURNITURE & RELATED PROD. MFG
68111	381	4075	EDUCATIONAL SERVICES
68112	297	4354	SOCIAL ASSISTANCE
68113	68	1443	HOSPITALS
68114	1687	38925	DATA PROCESS'G
68116	409	4638	FOOD SVCS & DRINKING PLACES
68117	504	8296	MERCH. WHOLESALERS;DURABLE GDS
68118	242	3311	FOOD SVCS & DRINKING PLACES
68122	268	9925	MERCH. WHOLESALERS;NONDUR. GDS
68123	448	6479	FOOD SVCS & DRINKING PLACES
68124	681	12911	HOSPITALS
68127	1465	26485	MERCH. WHOLESALERS;DURABLE GDS
68128	520	9452	PROF.; SCIENTIFIC; & TECH SVCS
68130	740	9183	FOOD SVCS & DRINKING PLACES
68131	617	13209	INSURANCE CARRIERS & RELATED
68132	396	3959	BROADCASTING
68133	93	1171	GENERAL MERCHANDISE STORES
68134	1196	11857	ADMINISTRATIVE & SUPPORT SVCS
68135	262	2752	EDUCATIONAL SERVICES
68136	171	999	SPECIAL TRADE CONTRACTORS
68137	1656	28136	MERCH. WHOLESALERS;DURABLE GDS
68138	486	11099	MERCH. WHOLESALERS;DURABLE GDS
68139	18	25	ADMINISTRATIVE & SUPPORT SVCS
68142	32	108	AMUSEMENT; GAMBLING;& RECREAT.
68144	1862	20118	FOOD SVCS & DRINKING PLACES
68145	16	89	ADMINISTRATIVE & SUPPORT SVCS
68147	134	987	EDUCATIONAL SERVICES
68152	179	2062	MERCH. WHOLESALERS;DURABLE GDS
68154	1325	27385	CREDIT INTERMEDIATION & RELATD
68155	1	1	SPECIAL TRADE CONTRACTORS
68157	39	453	EDUCATIONAL SERVICES
68164	714	12472	PROF.; SCIENTIFIC; & TECH SVCS
68172	1	0	PROF.; SCIENTIFIC; & TECH SVCS
68175	5	5236	INSURANCE CARRIERS & RELATED
68178	26	2979	EDUCATIONAL SERVICES
68179	6	5390	RAIL TRANSPORTATION
68182	12	3367	EDUCATIONAL SERVICES
68183	119	2022	EXEC.; LEGIS.; & OTHER SUPPORT
68197	4	1526	CREDIT INTERMEDIATION & RELATD
68198	58	14169	AMBULATORY HEALTH CARE SVCS
68301	56	382	NURSING & RESID. CARE FACILIT.
68303	6	7	POSTAL SERVICE
68304	10	19	MERCH. WHOLESALERS;NONDUR. GDS
68305	273	2185	MACHINERY MANUFACTURING
68307	21	43	CONSTRUCTION OF BUILDINGS
68309	4	5	FOOD SVCS & DRINKING PLACES
68310	855	9340	EXEC.; LEGIS.; & OTHER SUPPORT
68313	25	49	RELIG.; GRANT; CIVIC; PROF ORG
68314	7	17	FOOD SVCS & DRINKING PLACES
68315	13	29	HEAVY & CIVIL ENG. CONSTRUCT'N
68316	17	63	EDUCATIONAL SERVICES
68317	59	183	EDUCATIONAL SERVICES
68318	24	120	EDUCATIONAL SERVICES
68319	25	88	ADMINISTRATIVE & SUPPORT SVCS
68320	4	5	CROP PRODUCTION
68321	19	960	CHEMICAL MANUFACTURING
68322	38	325	EDUCATIONAL SERVICES
68323	14	25	POSTAL SERVICE
68324	5	15	WAREHOUSING AND STORAGE
68325	20	61	MERCH. WHOLESALERS;NONDUR. GDS
68326	15	39	WAREHOUSING AND STORAGE
68327	29	62	WAREHOUSING AND STORAGE
68328	12	27	MACHINERY MANUFACTURING
68329	18	151	EDUCATIONAL SERVICES
68330	8	22	FOOD SVCS & DRINKING PLACES
68331	32	73	FABRICATED METAL PRODUCT MFG
68332	2	3	POSTAL SERVICE
68333	298	5045	FOOD MANUFACTURING
68335	41	161	EDUCATIONAL SERVICES
68336	16	31	GASOLINE STATIONS
68337	18	70	MERCH. WHOLESALERS;NONDUR. GDS
68338	16	82	EDUCATIONAL SERVICES
68339	41	170	FOOD SVCS & DRINKING PLACES
68340	54	613	MACHINERY MANUFACTURING
68341	26	514	MACHINERY MANUFACTURING
68342	38	280	SPECIAL TRADE CONTRACTORS
68343	35	239	MERCH. WHOLESALERS;NONDUR. GDS
68344	11	17	FURNITURE & RELATED PROD. MFG
68345	12	32	MINING (EXCEPT OIL AND GAS)
68346	10	15	UNCLASSIFIED ESTABLISHMENTS
68347	63	285	POSTAL SERVICE
68348	10	27	MERCH. WHOLESALERS;NONDUR. GDS
68349	47	160	EDUCATIONAL SERVICES
68350	5	225	BLDG MATL & GARDEN EQPMT DLRS
68351	47	350	EDUCATIONAL SERVICES
68352	314	2514	HOSPITALS
68354	45	261	SOCIAL ASSISTANCE
68355	351	2345	EDUCATIONAL SERVICES
68357	18	42	FABRICATED METAL PRODUCT MFG
68358	55	733	EDUCATIONAL SERVICES
68359	75	559	AMBULATORY HEALTH CARE SVCS
68360	12	31	SPECIAL TRADE CONTRACTORS
68361	196	1517	EDUCATIONAL SERVICES
68362	2	11	FOOD SVCS & DRINKING PLACES
68364	7	13	MERCH. WHOLESALERS;NONDUR. GDS
68365	18	46	FOOD SVCS & DRINKING PLACES
68366	45	245	WAREHOUSING AND STORAGE
68367	17	34	GASOLINE STATIONS
68368	29	201	UTILITIES
68370	170	999	HOSPITALS
68371	102	791	AMBULATORY HEALTH CARE SVCS
68372	74	263	SPECIAL TRADE CONTRACTORS
68375	12	13	FOOD SVCS & DRINKING PLACES
68376	78	492	EDUCATIONAL SERVICES
68377	17	77	FOOD SVCS & DRINKING PLACES
68378	27	113	EDUCATIONAL SERVICES
68380	3	44	EDUCATIONAL SERVICES
68381	6	10	REPAIR AND MAINTENANCE
68382	2	4	MISCELLANEOUS MANUFACTURING
68401	25	130	FOOD SVCS & DRINKING PLACES
68402	32	173	EDUCATIONAL SERVICES
68403	7	7	WAREHOUSING AND STORAGE

ZIP CODE	2009 Total Firms	2009 Total Employ-ees	TOP INDUSTRY RANKED on 2009 EMPLOYMENT	ZIP CODE	2009 Total Firms	2009 Total Employ-ees	TOP INDUSTRY RANKED on 2009 EMPLOYMENT	ZIP CODE	2009 Total Firms	2009 Total Employ-ees	TOP INDUSTRY RANKED on 2009 EMPLOYMENT
68404	26	90	SPECIAL TRADE CONTRACTORS	68628	53	160	EDUCATIONAL SERVICES	68771	75	360	EDUCATIONAL SERVICES
68405	114	1119	EDUCATIONAL SERVICES	68629	48	420	MERCH. WHOLESALERS;NONDUR. GDS	68773	16	62	CROP PRODUCTION
68406	22	155	FOOD SVCS & DRINKING PLACES	68631	16	58	CONSTRUCTION OF BUILDINGS	68774	6	2	MERCH. WHOLESALERS;NONDUR. GDS
68407	24	132	MISCELLANEOUS STORE RETAILERS	68632	190	1935	NURSING & RESID. CARE FACILIT.	68776	511	5807	INSURANCE CARRIERS & RELATED
68409	42	275	EDUCATIONAL SERVICES	68633	61	337	NURSING & RESID. CARE FACILIT.	68777	63	265	EDUCATIONAL SERVICES
68410	490	4510	MERCH. WHOLESALERS;DURABLE GDS	68634	15	61	FOOD MANUFACTURING	68778	73	116	EDUCATIONAL SERVICES
68413	17	63	NONSTORE RETAILERS	68635	19	26	EDUCATIONAL SERVICES	68779	137	787	NURSING & RESID. CARE FACILIT.
68414	8	18	POSTAL SERVICE	68636	86	410	EDUCATIONAL SERVICES	68780	73	356	NURSING & RESID. CARE FACILIT.
68415	34	131	EDUCATIONAL SERVICES	68637	22	94	MERCH. WHOLESALERS;NONDUR. GDS	68781	69	509	HOSPITALS
68416	8	47	ANIMAL PRODUCTION	68638	102	479	NURSING & RESID. CARE FACILIT.	68783	75	372	NURSING & RESID. CARE FACILIT.
68417	11	16	CONSTRUCTION OF BUILDINGS	68640	73	500	EDUCATIONAL SERVICES	68784	74	1373	MERCH. WHOLESALERS;NONDUR. GDS
68418	39	130	EDUCATIONAL SERVICES	68641	47	233	EDUCATIONAL SERVICES	68785	9	159	SPECIAL TRADE CONTRACTORS
68419	9	13	CREDIT INTERMEDIATION & RELATD	68642	86	463	MERCH. WHOLESALERS;NONDUR. GDS	68786	62	217	NURSING & RESID. CARE FACILIT.
68420	94	458	FOOD MANUFACTURING	68643	56	263	EDUCATIONAL SERVICES	68787	334	3362	TRANSPORTATION EQUIPMENT MFG
68421	20	53	FOOD AND BEVERAGE STORES	68644	37	659	MERCH. WHOLESALERS;DURABLE GDS	68788	299	2450	AMBULATORY HEALTH CARE SVCS
68422	25	70	SPECIAL TRADE CONTRACTORS	68647	18	81	MERCH. WHOLESALERS;NONDUR. GDS	68789	6	17	CREDIT INTERMEDIATION & RELATD
68423	25	173	JUSTICE; PUBIC ORDER/SAFETY	68648	13	18	FOOD SVCS & DRINKING PLACES	68790	27	107	EDUCATIONAL SERVICES
68424	35	287	WAREHOUSING AND STORAGE	68649	97	494	NURSING & RESID. CARE FACILIT.	68791	150	755	EDUCATIONAL SERVICES
68428	36	216	EDUCATIONAL SERVICES	68651	98	433	RELIG.; GRANT; CIVIC; PROF ORG	68792	20	99	EDUCATIONAL SERVICES
68429	8	10	WHOLESALE ELEC. MRKTS & AGENTS	68652	47	166	EDUCATIONAL SERVICES	68801	1165	16915	FOOD MANUFACTURING
68430	57	253	SPECIAL TRADE CONTRACTORS	68653	34	180	NONMETALLIC MINERAL PROD. MFG	68802	15	29	ADMINISTRATIVE & SUPPORT SVCS
68431	15	29	FOOD SVCS & DRINKING PLACES	68654	29	158	EDUCATIONAL SERVICES	68803	1199	16573	HOSPITALS
68433	8	25	ANIMAL PRODUCTION	68655	4	6	WAREHOUSING AND STORAGE	68810	42	524	PLASTICS & RUBBER PRODUCTS MFG
68434	387	4067	EDUCATIONAL SERVICES	68658	24	84	EDUCATIONAL SERVICES	68812	13	82	EDUCATIONAL SERVICES
68436	46	247	NONSTORE RETAILERS	68659	3	8	TRUCK TRANSPORTATION	68813	24	37	RELIG.; GRANT; CIVIC; PROF ORG
68437	11	12	MUSEUMS; HIST. SITES;& SIMILAR	68660	66	804	FOOD AND BEVERAGE STORES	68814	64	170	EDUCATIONAL SERVICES
68438	4	6	INSURANCE CARRIERS & RELATED	68661	213	3750	FOOD MANUFACTURING	68815	45	182	EDUCATIONAL SERVICES
68439	16	18	EDUCATIONAL SERVICES	68662	41	306	CHEMICAL MANUFACTURING	68816	10	22	CREDIT INTERMEDIATION & RELATD
68440	4	9	FOOD SVCS & DRINKING PLACES	68663	38	145	MERCH. WHOLESALERS;DURABLE GDS	68817	18	33	MERCH. WHOLESALERS;NONDUR. GDS
68441	7	17	SPECIAL TRADE CONTRACTORS	68664	25	447	MACHINERY MANUFACTURING	68818	397	3311	TELECOMMUNICATIONS
68442	24	97	EDUCATIONAL SERVICES	68665	46	296	WAREHOUSING AND STORAGE	68820	11	20	MERCH. WHOLESALERS;NONDUR. GDS
68443	39	150	EDUCATIONAL SERVICES	68666	89	417	NURSING & RESID. CARE FACILIT.	68821	18	24	ANIMAL PRODUCTION
68444	9	21	FOOD SVCS & DRINKING PLACES	68667	3	4	FOOD SVCS & DRINKING PLACES	68822	365	2867	MISCELLANEOUS MANUFACTURING
68445	11	29	CREDIT INTERMEDIATION & RELATD	68669	22	46	MACHINERY MANUFACTURING	68823	182	952	NURSING & RESID. CARE FACILIT.
68446	161	1541	MERCH. WHOLESALERS;NONDUR. GDS	68701	1398	19057	HOSPITALS	68824	49	293	EDUCATIONAL SERVICES
68447	25	84	EDUCATIONAL SERVICES	68702	7	8	ADMINISTRATIVE & SUPPORT SVCS	68825	56	339	EDUCATIONAL SERVICES
68448	12	25	SPECIAL TRADE CONTRACTORS	68710	37	187	EDUCATIONAL SERVICES	68826	219	1651	EDUCATIONAL SERVICES
68450	172	1265	MERCH. WHOLESALERS;NONDUR. GDS	68711	4	1	MERCH. WHOLESALERS;DURABLE GDS	68827	27	110	FOOD AND BEVERAGE STORES
68452	3	25	JUSTICE; PUBIC ORDER/SAFETY	68713	158	1108	EDUCATIONAL SERVICES	68828	7	6	SOCIAL ASSISTANCE
68453	8	13	MERCH. WHOLESALERS;NONDUR. GDS	68714	144	626	HOSPITALS	68831	32	70	RELIG.; GRANT; CIVIC; PROF ORG
68454	20	55	INSURANCE CARRIERS & RELATED	68715	56	644	EDUCATIONAL SERVICES	68832	83	658	EDUCATIONAL SERVICES
68455	32	62	CROP PRODUCTION	68716	67	316	NURSING & RESID. CARE FACILIT.	68833	18	56	EDUCATIONAL SERVICES
68456	50	504	EDUCATIONAL SERVICES	68717	10	21	CREDIT INTERMEDIATION & RELATD	68834	10	9	POSTAL SERVICE
68457	11	19	MERCH. WHOLESALERS;DURABLE GDS	68718	126	654	WAREHOUSING AND STORAGE	68835	18	64	EDUCATIONAL SERVICES
68458	10	18	CONSTRUCTION OF BUILDINGS	68719	13	20	CREDIT INTERMEDIATION & RELATD	68836	70	420	FOOD SVCS & DRINKING PLACES
68460	35	304	MACHINERY MANUFACTURING	68720	20	61	MERCH. WHOLESALERS;NONDUR. GDS	68837	5	9	CROP PRODUCTION
68461	22	139	ADMINISTRATIVE & SUPPORT SVCS	68722	55	349	NURSING & RESID. CARE FACILIT.	68838	13	54	FOOD AND BEVERAGE STORES
68462	138	2119	FOOD AND BEVERAGE STORES	68723	22	87	JUSTICE; PUBIC ORDER/SAFETY	68840	121	1655	FOOD MANUFACTURING
68463	88	610	EDUCATIONAL SERVICES	68724	31	128	EXEC.; LEGIS.; & OTHER SUPPORT	68841	39	160	EDUCATIONAL SERVICES
68464	22	47	NURSING & RESID. CARE FACILIT.	68725	40	100	EDUCATIONAL SERVICES	68842	58	174	RELIG.; GRANT; CIVIC; PROF ORG
68465	104	659	EDUCATIONAL SERVICES	68726	60	254	FOOD MANUFACTURING	68843	54	185	EDUCATIONAL SERVICES
68466	70	394	RELIG.; GRANT; CIVIC; PROF ORG	68727	46	253	EDUCATIONAL SERVICES	68844	10	18	MERCH. WHOLESALERS;NONDUR. GDS
68467	568	7264	TRUCK TRANSPORTATION	68728	13	56	RELIG.; GRANT; CIVIC; PROF ORG	68845	454	5967	EDUCATIONAL SERVICES
68501	30	768	POSTAL SERVICE	68729	116	695	EDUCATIONAL SERVICES	68846	14	25	CREDIT INTERMEDIATION & RELATD
68502	876	18258	HOSPITALS	68730	89	332	EDUCATIONAL SERVICES	68847	1323	23920	SPORTG GDS;HOBBY;BOOK; & MUSIC
68503	354	5330	BROADCASTING	68731	101	656	JUSTICE; PUBIC ORDER/SAFETY	68848	20	78	ADMINISTRATIVE & SUPPORT SVCS
68504	889	10672	FOOD SVCS & DRINKING PLACES	68732	15	19	WHOLESALE ELEC. MRKTS & AGENTS	68849	7	156	NONSTORE RETAILERS
68505	585	6149	GENERAL MERCHANDISE STORES	68733	37	266	EDUCATIONAL SERVICES	68850	526	8176	FOOD MANUFACTURING
68506	1045	20575	HOSPITALS	68734	5	9	MERCH. WHOLESALERS;NONDUR. GDS	68852	21	139	EDUCATIONAL SERVICES
68507	488	6774	MACHINERY MANUFACTURING	68735	71	251	EDUCATIONAL SERVICES	68853	111	795	RELIG.; GRANT; CIVIC; PROF ORG
68508	1852	36627	ADMIN. HUMAN RESOURCE PROGRAMS	68736	20	65	MERCH. WHOLESALERS;NONDUR. GDS	68854	31	105	ACCOMMODATION
68509	2	3	EXEC.; LEGIS.; & OTHER SUPPORT	68738	3	10	GASOLINE STATIONS	68855	15	18	CREDIT INTERMEDIATION & RELATD
68510	1133	21400	INSURANCE CARRIERS & RELATED	68739	233	1386	EXEC.; LEGIS.; & OTHER SUPPORT	68856	32	136	EDUCATIONAL SERVICES
68512	374	8005	MERCH. WHOLESALERS;NONDUR. GDS	68740	29	99	CREDIT INTERMEDIATION & RELATD	68858	15	63	ANIMAL PRODUCTION
68514	15	116	MOTOR VEHICLE & PARTS DEALERS	68741	17	45	HEAVY & CIVIL ENG. CONSTRUCT'N	68859	31	135	JUSTICE; PUBIC ORDER/SAFETY
68516	1302	14567	FOOD SVCS & DRINKING PLACES	68742	12	15	EDUCATIONAL SERVICES	68860	19	88	JUSTICE; PUBIC ORDER/SAFETY
68517	29	642	CHEMICAL MANUFACTURING	68743	37	249	TELECOMMUNICATIONS	68861	3	20	FOOD MANUFACTURING
68520	52	912	EDUCATIONAL SERVICES	68745	95	601	EDUCATIONAL SERVICES	68862	247	1635	EXEC.; LEGIS.; & OTHER SUPPORT
68521	775	11250	FOOD SVCS & DRINKING PLACES	68746	29	116	HOSPITALS	68863	46	210	EDUCATIONAL SERVICES
68522	233	4054	EXEC.; LEGIS.; & OTHER SUPPORT	68747	3	25	NONMETALLIC MINERAL PROD. MFG	68864	35	131	EDUCATIONAL SERVICES
68523	40	186	BLDG MATL & GARDEN EQPMT DLRS	68748	105	2626	FOOD MANUFACTURING	68865	38	227	MERCH. WHOLESALERS;NONDUR. GDS
68524	110	7075	SUPPORT ACT. FOR TRANSPORT.	68749	4	15	TRUCK TRANSPORTATION	68866	32	115	EDUCATIONAL SERVICES
68526	137	2298	GENERAL MERCHANDISE STORES	68751	5	10	GASOLINE STATIONS	68869	117	985	FOOD AND BEVERAGE STORES
68527	30	81	SPECIAL TRADE CONTRACTORS	68752	21	54	EXEC.; LEGIS.; & OTHER SUPPORT	68870	16	50	EDUCATIONAL SERVICES
68528	274	3887	MOTOR VEHICLE & PARTS DEALERS	68753	2	1	RELIG.; GRANT; CIVIC; PROF ORG	68871	9	5	ADMIN. OF ECONOMIC PROGRAMS
68529	4	7	INSURANCE CARRIERS & RELATED	68755	12	22	FOOD SVCS & DRINKING PLACES	68872	20	67	EDUCATIONAL SERVICES
68531	2	6	SUPPORT ACTIVITIES: AGR./FOR.	68756	180	1246	EDUCATIONAL SERVICES	68873	161	1020	HOSPITALS
68532	12	29	PROF.; SCIENTIFIC; & TECH SVCS	68757	30	71	EDUCATIONAL SERVICES	68874	59	226	NURSING & RESID. CARE FACILIT.
68542	23	58	ADMINISTRATIVE & SUPPORT SVCS	68758	64	357	EDUCATIONAL SERVICES	68875	40	144	EDUCATIONAL SERVICES
68583	27	1437	EDUCATIONAL SERVICES	68759	17	20	GASOLINE STATIONS	68876	78	352	EDUCATIONAL SERVICES
68588	47	2298	EDUCATIONAL SERVICES	68760	92	546	EDUCATIONAL SERVICES	68878	22	120	EDUCATIONAL SERVICES
68601	1406	19689	FABRICATED METAL PRODUCT MFG	68761	19	67	JUSTICE; PUBIC ORDER/SAFETY	68879	33	112	EDUCATIONAL SERVICES
68602	13	14	BLDG MATL & GARDEN EQPMT DLRS	68763	375	2330	FOOD SVCS & DRINKING PLACES	68881	4	4	ANIMAL PRODUCTION
68620	204	1654	HOSPITALS	68764	50	192	EDUCATIONAL SERVICES	68882	24	92	EDUCATIONAL SERVICES
68621	13	25	CONSTRUCTION OF BUILDINGS	68765	90	543	HOSPITALS	68883	95	654	ADMINISTRATIVE & SUPPORT SVCS
68622	55	338	MERCH. WHOLESALERS;NONDUR. GDS	68766	18	39	PROF.; SCIENTIFIC; & TECH SVCS	68901	1342	15895	EDUCATIONAL SERVICES
68623	7	18	WAREHOUSING AND STORAGE	68767	161	734	EDUCATIONAL SERVICES	68902	6	22	ADMINISTRATIVE & SUPPORT SVCS
68624	29	128	EDUCATIONAL SERVICES	68768	32	101	WAREHOUSING AND STORAGE	68920	122	634	NURSING & RESID. CARE FACILIT.
68626	28	183	MERCH. WHOLESALERS;NONDUR. GDS	68769	115	797	EDUCATIONAL SERVICES	68922	105	728	SUPPORT ACTIVITIES: AGR./FOR.
68627	40	132	EDUCATIONAL SERVICES	68770	83	377	NURSING & RESID. CARE FACILIT.	68923	9	6	SPECIAL TRADE CONTRACTORS

BUSINESS DATA

ZIP CODE	2009 Total Firms	2009 Total Employ-ees	TOP INDUSTRY RANKED on 2009 EMPLOYMENT	ZIP CODE	2009 Total Firms	2009 Total Employ-ees	TOP INDUSTRY RANKED on 2009 EMPLOYMENT	ZIP CODE	2009 Total Firms	2009 Total Employ-ees	TOP INDUSTRY RANKED on 2009 EMPLOYMENT
68924	51	743	BROADCASTING	69132	9	40	MERCH. WHOLESALERS;NONDUR. GDS	70039	151	1714	GENERAL MERCHANDISE STORES
68925	13	68	HEAVY & CIVIL ENG. CONSTRUCT'N	69133	21	63	EDUCATIONAL SERVICES	70040	23	219	SCENIC & SIGHTSEEING TRANSPORT
68926	54	211	NURSING & RESID. CARE FACILIT.	69134	23	113	BLDG MATL & GARDEN EQPMT DLRS	70041	61	246	RELIG.; GRANT; CIVIC; PROF ORG
68927	60	320	NURSING & RESID. CARE FACILIT.	69138	245	1834	EDUCATIONAL SERVICES	70043	585	6777	PETROLEUM & COAL PRODUCTS MFG
68928	19	49	EDUCATIONAL SERVICES	69140	155	1014	NURSING & RESID. CARE FACILIT.	70044	3	6	SPECIAL TRADE CONTRACTORS
68929	4	14	FOOD AND BEVERAGE STORES	69141	15	184	FABRICATED METAL PRODUCT MFG	70047	263	3039	EDUCATIONAL SERVICES
68930	84	505	EDUCATIONAL SERVICES	69142	14	88	SUPPORT ACTIVITIES: AGR./FOR.	70049	59	326	EDUCATIONAL SERVICES
68932	29	120	NURSING & RESID. CARE FACILIT.	69143	59	451	EDUCATIONAL SERVICES	70050	3	199	FOOD MANUFACTURING
68933	75	771	EXEC.; LEGIS.; & OTHER SUPPORT	69144	18	50	TELECOMMUNICATIONS	70051	58	1084	PETROLEUM & COAL PRODUCTS MFG
68934	12	28	CONSTRUCTION OF BUILDINGS	69145	237	1588	COMPUTER & ELECTRONIC PROD MFG	70052	107	1788	CHEMICAL MANUFACTURING
68935	46	195	NURSING & RESID. CARE FACILIT.	69146	18	47	SOCIAL ASSISTANCE	70053	1081	11929	JUSTICE; PUBIC ORDER/SAFETY
68936	10	89	WAREHOUSING AND STORAGE	69147	31	98	SPORTG GDS;HOBBY;BOOK; & MUSIC	70054	9	85	EXEC.; LEGIS.; & OTHER SUPPORT
68937	96	402	NURSING & RESID. CARE FACILIT.	69148	11	20	FOOD SVCS & DRINKING PLACES	70055	9	13	SPECIAL TRADE CONTRACTORS
68938	30	194	EDUCATIONAL SERVICES	69149	28	97	EDUCATIONAL SERVICES	70056	1013	9385	HOSPITALS
68939	120	577	EDUCATIONAL SERVICES	69150	41	94	SPECIAL TRADE CONTRACTORS	70057	120	3600	MERCH. WHOLESALERS;NONDUR. GDS
68940	16	118	CHEMICAL MANUFACTURING	69151	24	98	EDUCATIONAL SERVICES	70058	1392	20825	EXEC.; LEGIS.; & OTHER SUPPORT
68941	18	47	BLDG MATL & GARDEN EQPMT DLRS	69152	90	470	AMUSEMENT; GAMBLING;& RECREAT.	70059	10	24	MOTOR VEHICLE & PARTS DEALERS
68942	19	51	WAREHOUSING AND STORAGE	69153	436	3171	EDUCATIONAL SERVICES	70062	1839	15070	SPECIAL TRADE CONTRACTORS
68943	15	38	TRUCK TRANSPORTATION	69154	77	518	HOSPITALS	70063	12	39	ADMINISTRATIVE & SUPPORT SVCS
68944	33	210	NURSING & RESID. CARE FACILIT.	69155	58	344	MERCH. WHOLESALERS;DURABLE GDS	70064	15	23	ADMINISTRATIVE & SUPPORT SVCS
68945	7	43	ANIMAL PRODUCTION	69156	25	121	EDUCATIONAL SERVICES	70065	1184	10727	FOOD SVCS & DRINKING PLACES
68946	5	11	EXEC.; LEGIS.; & OTHER SUPPORT	69157	7	18	CREDIT INTERMEDIATION & RELATD	70067	82	773	PRIMARY METAL MANUFACTURING
68947	25	168	EDUCATIONAL SERVICES	69160	2	1007	SPORTG GDS;HOBBY;BOOK; & MUSIC	70068	1020	10204	AMBULATORY HEALTH CARE SVCS
68948	28	86	SECURITIES/COMMODITY CONTRACTS	69161	3	3	FOOD SVCS & DRINKING PLACES	70069	6	10	REPAIR AND MAINTENANCE
68949	440	4714	MISCELLANEOUS MANUFACTURING	69162	462	4062	MERCH. WHOLESALERS;DURABLE GDS	70070	327	2735	EDUCATIONAL SERVICES
68950	14	34	CROP PRODUCTION	69163	54	187	EDUCATIONAL SERVICES	70071	148	1047	EDUCATIONAL SERVICES
68952	5	25	NURSING & RESID. CARE FACILIT.	69165	79	943	UTILITIES	70072	1339	13536	HOSPITALS
68954	5	30	PROF.; SCIENTIFIC; & TECH SVCS	69166	71	264	EDUCATIONAL SERVICES	70073	9	17	SPECIAL TRADE CONTRACTORS
68955	52	352	HEAVY & CIVIL ENG. CONSTRUCT'N	69167	32	87	EDUCATIONAL SERVICES	70075	53	725	PETROLEUM & COAL PRODUCTS MFG
68956	34	319	NURSING & RESID. CARE FACILIT.	69168	19	45	WAREHOUSING AND STORAGE	70076	9	319	MERCH. WHOLESALERS;NONDUR. GDS
68957	29	113	EDUCATIONAL SERVICES	69169	45	180	EDUCATIONAL SERVICES	70078	8	8	FOOD SVCS & DRINKING PLACES
68958	40	135	EDUCATIONAL SERVICES	69170	22	31	ADMIN. OF ECONOMIC PROGRAMS	70079	107	2464	PETROLEUM & COAL PRODUCTS MFG
68959	238	1935	AMBULATORY HEALTH CARE SVCS	69171	2	7	ANIMAL PRODUCTION	70080	59	351	EDUCATIONAL SERVICES
68960	6	7	WAREHOUSING AND STORAGE	69201	327	1928	AMUSEMENT; GAMBLING;& RECREAT.	70082	4	19	SUPPORT ACTIVITIES FOR MINING
68961	53	297	EDUCATIONAL SERVICES	69210	204	1413	EDUCATIONAL SERVICES	70083	52	403	WAREHOUSING AND STORAGE
68964	4	6	POSTAL SERVICE	69211	19	54	EDUCATIONAL SERVICES	70084	207	3401	EDUCATIONAL SERVICES
68966	35	99	EXEC.; LEGIS.; & OTHER SUPPORT	69212	8	54	CROP PRODUCTION	70085	69	332	EDUCATIONAL SERVICES
68967	80	318	EDUCATIONAL SERVICES	69214	18	40	BLDG MATL & GARDEN EQPMT DLRS	70086	53	564	CHEMICAL MANUFACTURING
68969	1	1	FOOD AND BEVERAGE STORES	69216	12	37	EDUCATIONAL SERVICES	70087	332	5841	MERCH. WHOLESALERS;DURABLE GDS
68970	124	586	MOTOR VEHICLE & PARTS DEALERS	69217	40	104	ACCOMMODATION	70090	138	951	MUSEUMS; HIST. SITES;& SIMILAR
68971	30	100	FOOD SVCS & DRINKING PLACES	69218	23	60	EXEC.; LEGIS.; & OTHER SUPPORT	70091	75	531	MERCH. WHOLESALERS;NONDUR. GDS
68972	8	9	POSTAL SERVICE	69219	2	3	SUPPORT ACTIVITIES: AGR./FOR.	70092	47	152	SPECIAL TRADE CONTRACTORS
68973	28	94	EDUCATIONAL SERVICES	69220	3	7	MOTOR VEHICLE & PARTS DEALERS	70094	567	13528	SPECIAL TRADE CONTRACTORS
68974	14	36	GASOLINE STATIONS	69221	12	17	SUPPORT ACTIVITIES: AGR./FOR.	70096	2	22	PROF.; SCIENTIFIC; & TECH SVCS
68975	2	3	WAREHOUSING AND STORAGE	69301	467	4270	RELIG.; GRANT; CIVIC; PROF ORG	70112	1309	43757	HOSPITALS
68976	8	15	FOOD SVCS & DRINKING PLACES	69331	4	5	CROP PRODUCTION	70113	510	10820	POSTAL SERVICE
68977	13	30	PUBLISHING INDUSTRIES	69333	31	72	ANIMAL PRODUCTION	70114	698	5968	EDUCATIONAL SERVICES
68978	174	1105	HOSPITALS	69334	85	359	EDUCATIONAL SERVICES	70115	1313	13494	HOSPITALS
68979	127	824	EDUCATIONAL SERVICES	69335	2	0	AMBULATORY HEALTH CARE SVCS	70116	727	5004	FOOD SVCS & DRINKING PLACES
68980	20	89	MERCH. WHOLESALERS;NONDUR. GDS	69336	161	1138	EDUCATIONAL SERVICES	70117	602	4246	NAT'L SECURITY & INT'L AFFAIRS
68981	14	22	RELIG.; GRANT; CIVIC; PROF ORG	69337	416	2889	EDUCATIONAL SERVICES	70118	904	16787	EDUCATIONAL SERVICES
68982	33	151	EDUCATIONAL SERVICES	69339	99	650	EDUCATIONAL SERVICES	70119	1583	20001	JUSTICE; PUBIC ORDER/SAFETY
69001	616	5487	FOOD SVCS & DRINKING PLACES	69340	4	13	ADMIN. ENVIRO. QUALITY PROGRMS	70121	747	26386	HOSPITALS
69020	32	89	EDUCATIONAL SERVICES	69341	461	4376	EXEC.; LEGIS.; & OTHER SUPPORT	70122	402	5194	UNCLASSIFIED ESTABLISHMENTS
69021	147	690	EDUCATIONAL SERVICES	69343	168	1040	EDUCATIONAL SERVICES	70123	2028	30415	MERCH. WHOLESALERS;DURABLE GDS
69022	139	953	HOSPITALS	69345	23	163	EDUCATIONAL SERVICES	70124	362	2513	ADMIN. OF ECONOMIC PROGRAMS
69023	9	22	MERCH. WHOLESALERS;NONDUR. GDS	69346	43	116	EDUCATIONAL SERVICES	70125	396	6496	TRANSIT & GRND PASS. TRANSPORT
69024	34	219	EDUCATIONAL SERVICES	69347	62	228	NURSING & RESID. CARE FACILIT.	70126	406	5962	EDUCATIONAL SERVICES
69025	96	508	EDUCATIONAL SERVICES	69348	88	397	EDUCATIONAL SERVICES	70127	426	2445	BLDG MATL & GARDEN EQPMT DLRS
69026	10	51	MERCH. WHOLESALERS;NONDUR. GDS	69350	77	232	ANIMAL PRODUCTION	70128	119	1295	MOTOR VEHICLE & PARTS DEALERS
69027	9	15	MUSEUMS; HIST. SITES;& SIMILAR	69351	7	8	REPAIR AND MAINTENANCE	70129	266	6950	SPACE RESEARCH AND TECHNOLOGY
69028	48	144	EDUCATIONAL SERVICES	69352	26	332	MISCELLANEOUS MANUFACTURING	70130	2855	49095	ACCOMMODATION
69029	19	56	ANIMAL PRODUCTION	69353	3	16	FOOD AND BEVERAGE STORES	70131	327	1932	NURSING & RESID. CARE FACILIT.
69030	19	26	EDUCATIONAL SERVICES	69354	2	3	EDUCATIONAL SERVICES	70139	75	2471	MERCH. WHOLESALERS;NONDUR. GDS
69032	42	175	EDUCATIONAL SERVICES	69355	8	12	PROF.; SCIENTIFIC; & TECH SVCS	70141	3	38	ADMIN. OF ECONOMIC PROGRAMS
69033	213	1505	EDUCATIONAL SERVICES	69356	49	295	EDUCATIONAL SERVICES	70142	5	10	CREDIT INTERMEDIATION & RELATD
69034	44	180	EDUCATIONAL SERVICES	69357	120	619	EDUCATIONAL SERVICES	70143	6	1248	SUPPORT ACT. FOR TRANSPORT.
69036	1	3	WAREHOUSING AND STORAGE	69358	88	888	RAIL TRANSPORTATION	70146	11	64	NAT'L SECURITY & INT'L AFFAIRS
69037	6	64	POSTAL SERVICE	69360	96	527	EDUCATIONAL SERVICES	70148	4	3175	EDUCATIONAL SERVICES
69038	32	280	MERCH. WHOLESALERS;NONDUR. GDS	69361	1200	12987	HOSPITALS	70149	1	15	NAT'L SECURITY & INT'L AFFAIRS
69039	4	2	MERCH. WHOLESALERS;NONDUR. GDS	69363	5	4	PRINT'G & RELATED SUPP'T ACT'S	70150	6	13	SPECIAL TRADE CONTRACTORS
69040	39	240	RELIG.; GRANT; CIVIC; PROF ORG	69365	10	40	FOOD AND BEVERAGE STORES	70151	3	12	CONSTRUCTION OF BUILDINGS
69041	5	8	ADMIN. ENVIRO. QUALITY PROGRMS	69366	21	37	ANIMAL PRODUCTION	70152	1	5	PERFORM'G ARTS; SPEC. SPORTS
69042	8	17	EXEC.; LEGIS.; & OTHER SUPPORT	69367	7	5	EDUCATIONAL SERVICES	70163	189	2783	PROF.; SCIENTIFIC; & TECH SVCS
69043	37	132	CONSTRUCTION OF BUILDINGS	70001	1729	18165	ADMINISTRATIVE & SUPPORT SVCS	70165	2	506	EXEC.; LEGIS.; & OTHER SUPPORT
69044	59	338	NURSING & RESID. CARE FACILIT.	70002	2502	32307	AMBULATORY HEALTH CARE SVCS	70170	127	1826	PROF.; SCIENTIFIC; & TECH SVCS
69045	74	336	EDUCATIONAL SERVICES	70003	938	9204	EDUCATIONAL SERVICES	70174	5	10	MERCH. WHOLESALERS;DURABLE GDS
69046	9	9	SPECIAL TRADE CONTRACTORS	70004	21	64	SPECIAL TRADE CONTRACTORS	70175	7	55	PERSONAL AND LAUNDRY SERVICES
69101	1486	14401	HOSPITALS	70005	1051	8872	PROF.; SCIENTIFIC; & TECH SVCS	70177	3	13	ADMINISTRATIVE & SUPPORT SVCS
69103	6	10	SPECIAL TRADE CONTRACTORS	70006	1017	9741	AMBULATORY HEALTH CARE SVCS	70178	2	0	ADMINISTRATIVE & SUPPORT SVCS
69120	67	241	EDUCATIONAL SERVICES	70009	6	20	ADMINISTRATIVE & SUPPORT SVCS	70179	11	35	ADMINISTRATIVE & SUPPORT SVCS
69121	41	87	ANIMAL PRODUCTION	70010	6	14	MERCH. WHOLESALERS;DURABLE GDS	70181	4	18	ADMINISTRATIVE & SUPPORT SVCS
69122	39	263	GASOLINE STATIONS	70011	8	13	CONSTRUCTION OF BUILDINGS	70182	2	0	ELECTRONICS & APPLIANCE STORES
69123	40	144	EDUCATIONAL SERVICES	70030	62	568	SUPPORT ACT. FOR TRANSPORT.	70183	10	32	ADMINISTRATIVE & SUPPORT SVCS
69125	21	41	ANIMAL PRODUCTION	70031	16	232	WAREHOUSING AND STORAGE	70184	1	1	SOCIAL ASSISTANCE
69127	37	160	ACCOMMODATION	70032	103	702	RELIG.; GRANT; CIVIC; PROF ORG	70185	6	20	PROF.; SCIENTIFIC; & TECH SVCS
69128	8	7	EXEC.; LEGIS.; & OTHER SUPPORT	70033	13	348	ADMINISTRATIVE & SUPPORT SVCS	70186	1	0	SPECIAL TRADE CONTRACTORS
69129	88	374	EDUCATIONAL SERVICES	70036	20	79	SPECIAL TRADE CONTRACTORS	70187	6	19	SPECIAL TRADE CONTRACTORS
69130	307	3163	TRANSPORTATION EQUIPMENT MFG	70037	686	9259	SPECIAL TRADE CONTRACTORS	70301	1456	12495	EDUCATIONAL SERVICES
69131	27	142	EDUCATIONAL SERVICES	70038	20	252	REPAIR AND MAINTENANCE	70302	4	18	PROF.; SCIENTIFIC; & TECH SVCS

ZIP CODE	2009 Total Firms	2009 Total Employees	TOP INDUSTRY RANKED on 2009 EMPLOYMENT
70310	3	778	EDUCATIONAL SERVICES
70339	130	892	EDUCATIONAL SERVICES
70340	61	2820	SUPPORT ACT. FOR TRANSPORT.
70341	45	407	EDUCATIONAL SERVICES
70342	145	1789	HEAVY & CIVIL ENG. CONSTRUCT'N
70343	91	702	EDUCATIONAL SERVICES
70344	123	695	EDUCATIONAL SERVICES
70345	382	4003	SCENIC & SIGHTSEEING TRANSPORT
70346	390	3605	EDUCATIONAL SERVICES
70352	5	13	FOOD SVCS & DRINKING PLACES
70353	59	484	MERCH. WHOLESALERS;NONDUR. GDS
70354	206	2695	SCENIC & SIGHTSEEING TRANSPORT
70355	6	49	CROP PRODUCTION
70356	73	941	TRANSPORTATION EQUIPMENT MFG
70357	252	3113	SPECIAL TRADE CONTRACTORS
70358	94	690	FOOD SVCS & DRINKING PLACES
70359	129	879	FOOD SVCS & DRINKING PLACES
70360	2234	27172	AMBULATORY HEALTH CARE SVCS
70361	9	25	FOOD SVCS & DRINKING PLACES
70363	1038	18734	SPECIAL TRADE CONTRACTORS
70364	988	8217	FOOD SVCS & DRINKING PLACES
70371	1	2	POSTAL SERVICE
70372	59	334	EDUCATIONAL SERVICES
70373	119	1246	TRANSPORTATION EQUIPMENT MFG
70374	265	3691	TRANSPORTATION EQUIPMENT MFG
70375	50	213	FOOD SVCS & DRINKING PLACES
70377	74	306	EDUCATIONAL SERVICES
70380	1369	14855	SPECIAL TRADE CONTRACTORS
70381	2	1	INSURANCE CARRIERS & RELATED
70390	173	1971	EDUCATIONAL SERVICES
70391	45	323	FOOD MANUFACTURING
70392	271	2071	GENERAL MERCHANDISE STORES
70393	16	173	FOOD AND BEVERAGE STORES
70394	338	2796	EDUCATIONAL SERVICES
70395	136	1534	SPECIAL TRADE CONTRACTORS
70397	23	119	FOOD AND BEVERAGE STORES
70401	1060	11413	EXEC.; LEGIS.; & OTHER SUPPORT
70402	7	96	OTHER INFORMATION SERVICES
70403	1105	15279	HOSPITALS
70404	6	63	WHOLESALE ELEC. MRKTS & AGENTS
70420	272	1338	FOOD SVCS & DRINKING PLACES
70421	8	75	FOOD SVCS & DRINKING PLACES
70422	549	4186	EXEC.; LEGIS.; & OTHER SUPPORT
70426	84	722	JUSTICE; PUBIC ORDER/SAFETY
70427	749	7190	PAPER MANUFACTURING
70429	1	2	EXEC.; LEGIS.; & OTHER SUPPORT
70431	121	396	EDUCATIONAL SERVICES
70433	2659	26811	JUSTICE; PUBIC ORDER/SAFETY
70434	28	78	SPECIAL TRADE CONTRACTORS
70435	411	1839	MERCH. WHOLESALERS;DURABLE GDS
70436	9	48	REAL ESTATE
70437	273	784	EDUCATIONAL SERVICES
70438	663	6499	UNCLASSIFIED ESTABLISHMENTS
70441	152	1329	EDUCATIONAL SERVICES
70442	15	41	FISHING; HUNTING AND TRAPPING
70443	192	1354	ADMIN. HUMAN RESOURCE PROGRAMS
70444	228	1723	EDUCATIONAL SERVICES
70445	282	1520	HOSPITALS
70446	85	555	EDUCATIONAL SERVICES
70447	321	1821	TRANSPORTATION EQUIPMENT MFG
70448	1089	6057	EDUCATIONAL SERVICES
70449	57	294	FOOD SVCS & DRINKING PLACES
70450	33	149	EDUCATIONAL SERVICES
70451	21	423	WOOD PRODUCT MANUFACTURING
70452	341	1623	EDUCATIONAL SERVICES
70453	24	157	MERCH. WHOLESALERS;NONDUR. GDS
70454	613	3912	EDUCATIONAL SERVICES
70455	50	1248	GENERAL MERCHANDISE STORES
70456	61	566	TRANSPORTATION EQUIPMENT MFG
70458	2164	12850	FOOD SVCS & DRINKING PLACES
70459	21	34	SPECIAL TRADE CONTRACTORS
70460	724	7592	EXEC.; LEGIS.; & OTHER SUPPORT
70461	846	8277	MOTOR VEHICLE & PARTS DEALERS
70462	125	609	EDUCATIONAL SERVICES
70463	19	56	JUSTICE; PUBIC ORDER/SAFETY
70464	6	3	POSTAL SERVICE
70465	15	68	SOCIAL ASSISTANCE
70466	116	522	WASTE MANAGMT & REMEDIAT'N SVC
70469	15	160	ADMINISTRATIVE & SUPPORT SVCS
70470	33	86	PROF.; SCIENTIFIC; & TECH SVCS
70471	1559	12235	INSURANCE CARRIERS & RELATED
70501	1858	19157	JUSTICE; PUBIC ORDER/SAFETY
70502	4	7	PROF.; SCIENTIFIC; & TECH SVCS
70503	2233	22070	AMBULATORY HEALTH CARE SVCS
70504	9	1887	EDUCATIONAL SERVICES
70505	7	7	ADMINISTRATIVE & SUPPORT SVCS
70506	1813	26836	EXEC.; LEGIS.; & OTHER SUPPORT
70507	549	6227	SPECIAL TRADE CONTRACTORS
70508	2348	30425	SPECIAL TRADE CONTRACTORS
70509	12	64	SOCIAL ASSISTANCE
70510	982	8891	JUSTICE; PUBIC ORDER/SAFETY
70511	1	3	SOCIAL ASSISTANCE
70512	120	943	EDUCATIONAL SERVICES
70513	9	777	FOOD MANUFACTURING
70514	74	481	FABRICATED METAL PRODUCT MFG
70515	86	503	JUSTICE; PUBIC ORDER/SAFETY
70516	15	82	EDUCATIONAL SERVICES
70517	781	6042	EDUCATIONAL SERVICES
70518	914	15585	SPECIAL TRADE CONTRACTORS
70519	2	400	MERCH. WHOLESALERS;NONDUR. GDS
70520	392	2865	SPECIAL TRADE CONTRACTORS
70521	24	164	EDUCATIONAL SERVICES
70522	45	892	CHEMICAL MANUFACTURING
70523	35	1559	AMUSEMENT; GAMBLING;& RECREAT.
70524	10	4	POSTAL SERVICE
70525	274	1983	EDUCATIONAL SERVICES
70526	818	7962	HOSPITALS
70527	3	15	AMBULATORY HEALTH CARE SVCS
70528	85	984	REPAIR AND MAINTENANCE
70529	217	1511	EDUCATIONAL SERVICES
70531	19	130	GASOLINE STATIONS
70532	71	453	EXEC.; LEGIS.; & OTHER SUPPORT
70533	117	734	EDUCATIONAL SERVICES
70534	13	69	EDUCATIONAL SERVICES
70535	744	5756	EDUCATIONAL SERVICES
70537	14	98	SPECIAL TRADE CONTRACTORS
70538	513	4345	EDUCATIONAL SERVICES
70540	3	6	CONSTRUCTION OF BUILDINGS
70541	63	448	EDUCATIONAL SERVICES
70542	117	494	NURSING & RESID. CARE FACILIT.
70543	74	709	EDUCATIONAL SERVICES
70544	252	2361	FOOD MANUFACTURING
70546	653	6626	HOSPITALS
70548	333	2286	AMBULATORY HEALTH CARE SVCS
70549	123	877	MERCH. WHOLESALERS;NONDUR. GDS
70550	27	64	ELECT'L EQPMT; APP; & COMP MFG
70551	21	125	EDUCATIONAL SERVICES
70552	57	502	TRANSPORTATION EQUIPMENT MFG
70554	202	1543	HOSPITALS
70555	152	1417	SPECIAL TRADE CONTRACTORS
70556	21	119	MERCH. WHOLESALERS;NONDUR. GDS
70558	7	26	FOOD AND BEVERAGE STORES
70559	24	145	EDUCATIONAL SERVICES
70560	2013	24800	SPECIAL TRADE CONTRACTORS
70562	6	33	SOCIAL ASSISTANCE
70563	378	4636	EDUCATIONAL SERVICES
70569	8	24	FOOD AND BEVERAGE STORES
70570	1351	13857	GENERAL MERCHANDISE STORES
70571	2	5	JUSTICE; PUBIC ORDER/SAFETY
70575	4	6	GASOLINE STATIONS
70576	35	436	EDUCATIONAL SERVICES
70577	115	719	EDUCATIONAL SERVICES
70578	438	3416	EDUCATIONAL SERVICES
70580	1	2	POSTAL SERVICE
70581	23	91	EDUCATIONAL SERVICES
70582	476	4383	JUSTICE; PUBIC ORDER/SAFETY
70583	492	5737	SPECIAL TRADE CONTRACTORS
70584	140	742	EDUCATIONAL SERVICES
70585	30	49	UTILITIES
70586	653	5178	EDUCATIONAL SERVICES
70589	82	507	EDUCATIONAL SERVICES
70591	150	1042	NURSING & RESID. CARE FACILIT.
70592	306	2749	SPECIAL TRADE CONTRACTORS
70596	7	7	PROF.; SCIENTIFIC; & TECH SVCS
70598	7	17	UNCLASSIFIED ESTABLISHMENTS
70601	2471	34652	HOSPITALS
70602	8	217	MUSEUMS; HIST. SITES;& SIMILAR
70605	952	8230	FOOD SVCS & DRINKING PLACES
70606	13	28	MISCELLANEOUS STORE RETAILERS
70607	574	5843	FOOD SVCS & DRINKING PLACES
70609	6	1585	EDUCATIONAL SERVICES
70611	407	2269	EDUCATIONAL SERVICES
70612	7	21	ADMINISTRATIVE & SUPPORT SVCS
70615	445	12025	JUSTICE; PUBIC ORDER/SAFETY
70616	3	6	MERCH. WHOLESALERS;DURABLE GDS
70629	58	631	PROF.; SCIENTIFIC; & TECH SVCS
70630	22	219	BLDG MATL & GARDEN EQPMT DLRS
70631	123	1307	UNCLASSIFIED ESTABLISHMENTS
70632	18	129	RENTAL AND LEASING SERVICES
70633	272	2351	JUSTICE; PUBIC ORDER/SAFETY
70634	853	9168	ADMINISTRATIVE & SUPPORT SVCS
70637	24	69	MERCH. WHOLESALERS;DURABLE GDS
70638	37	84	EDUCATIONAL SERVICES
70639	14	84	EDUCATIONAL SERVICES
70640	11	62	EDUCATIONAL SERVICES
70643	15	151	SPECIAL TRADE CONTRACTORS
70644	4	62	EDUCATIONAL SERVICES
70645	55	285	EDUCATIONAL SERVICES
70646	14	21	FOOD SVCS & DRINKING PLACES
70647	162	1021	EDUCATIONAL SERVICES
70648	271	1873	ADMINISTRATIVE & SUPPORT SVCS
70650	20	402	SUPPORT ACTIVITIES FOR MINING
70651	4	4	RELIG.; GRANT; CIVIC; PROF ORG
70652	35	311	EDUCATIONAL SERVICES
70653	65	404	EDUCATIONAL SERVICES
70654	5	15	RENTAL AND LEASING SERVICES
70655	128	820	JUSTICE; PUBIC ORDER/SAFETY
70656	65	238	EDUCATIONAL SERVICES
70657	64	148	RELIG.; GRANT; CIVIC; PROF ORG
70658	29	86	EDUCATIONAL SERVICES
70659	47	383	EDUCATIONAL SERVICES
70660	17	89	EDUCATIONAL SERVICES
70661	38	235	EDUCATIONAL SERVICES
70662	11	23	FOOD AND BEVERAGE STORES
70663	994	9560	FOOD SVCS & DRINKING PLACES
70664	4	22	MOTOR VEHICLE & PARTS DEALERS
70665	304	9198	PETROLEUM & COAL PRODUCTS MFG
70668	150	3309	PERFORM'G ARTS; SPEC. SPORTS
70669	336	9551	CHEMICAL MANUFACTURING
70706	271	1467	EDUCATIONAL SERVICES
70707	6	41	SPECIAL TRADE CONTRACTORS
70710	83	1050	SPECIAL TRADE CONTRACTORS
70711	142	800	EDUCATIONAL SERVICES
70712	4	9	MUSEUMS; HIST. SITES;& SIMILAR
70714	507	4228	EDUCATIONAL SERVICES
70715	28	424	PLASTICS & RUBBER PRODUCTS MFG
70718	1	11	ADMIN. OF ECONOMIC PROGRAMS
70719	89	1103	TRANSPORTATION EQUIPMENT MFG
70721	17	569	MERCH. WHOLESALERS;NONDUR. GDS
70722	278	1887	EDUCATIONAL SERVICES
70723	127	3767	EXEC.; LEGIS.; & OTHER SUPPORT
70725	32	369	SUPPORT ACT. FOR TRANSPORT.
70726	1485	10065	FOOD SVCS & DRINKING PLACES
70727	7	9	ADMINISTRATIVE & SUPPORT SVCS
70728	2	22	FOOD AND BEVERAGE STORES
70729	29	162	BLDG MATL & GARDEN EQPMT DLRS
70730	59	171	RELIG.; GRANT; CIVIC; PROF ORG
70732	15	51	EXEC.; LEGIS.; & OTHER SUPPORT
70733	45	181	EDUCATIONAL SERVICES
70734	188	5490	MERCH. WHOLESALERS;NONDUR. GDS
70736	7	5	ADMINISTRATIVE & SUPPORT SVCS
70737	1611	14219	FOOD SVCS & DRINKING PLACES
70738	2	2	SUPPORT ACT. FOR TRANSPORT.
70739	243	2133	SPECIAL TRADE CONTRACTORS
70740	51	226	FOOD SVCS & DRINKING PLACES
70743	2	13	BLDG MATL & GARDEN EQPMT DLRS
70744	71	675	ADMINISTRATIVE & SUPPORT SVCS
70747	22	21	FOOD AND BEVERAGE STORES
70748	156	2508	HOSPITALS
70749	19	49	CONSTRUCTION OF BUILDINGS
70750	54	589	PETROLEUM & COAL PRODUCTS MFG
70752	26	206	HEAVY & CIVIL ENG. CONSTRUCT'N
70753	29	88	WAREHOUSING AND STORAGE
70754	260	1907	EDUCATIONAL SERVICES
70755	85	419	FOOD AND BEVERAGE STORES
70756	13	71	SPECIAL TRADE CONTRACTORS
70757	71	503	EDUCATIONAL SERVICES
70759	37	237	JUSTICE; PUBIC ORDER/SAFETY
70760	418	3960	UTILITIES
70761	23	63	BLDG MATL & GARDEN EQPMT DLRS
70762	18	32	REAL ESTATE
70763	53	359	FABRICATED METAL PRODUCT MFG
70764	617	5192	MERCH. WHOLESALERS;NONDUR. GDS
70765	1	3	REPAIR AND MAINTENANCE
70767	732	8833	SPECIAL TRADE CONTRACTORS
70769	872	8391	FABRICATED METAL PRODUCT MFG
70770	37	232	EDUCATIONAL SERVICES
70772	21	88	JUSTICE; PUBIC ORDER/SAFETY
70773	18	81	EDUCATIONAL SERVICES
70774	177	1170	EDUCATIONAL SERVICES
70775	352	4618	JUSTICE; PUBIC ORDER/SAFETY
70776	112	3796	CHEMICAL MANUFACTURING
70777	58	521	MERCH. WHOLESALERS;DURABLE GDS
70778	63	472	FOOD SVCS & DRINKING PLACES
70780	18	141	RENTAL AND LEASING SERVICES
70782	15	42	EDUCATIONAL SERVICES
70783	21	76	UTILITIES
70784	2	4	POSTAL SERVICE
70785	430	4065	FABRICATED METAL PRODUCT MFG
70786	4	10	SPECIAL TRADE CONTRACTORS
70788	94	717	FOOD MANUFACTURING
70789	21	20	EXEC.; LEGIS.; & OTHER SUPPORT
70791	743	9420	PAPER MANUFACTURING
70801	501	5610	PROF.; SCIENTIFIC; & TECH SVCS
70802	1680	36953	EXEC.; LEGIS.; & OTHER SUPPORT
70803	72	1562	PROF.; SCIENTIFIC; & TECH SVCS
70804	4	52	JUSTICE; PUBIC ORDER/SAFETY
70805	1091	14252	MERCH. WHOLESALERS;NONDUR. GDS
70806	2560	28074	EXEC.; LEGIS.; & OTHER SUPPORT
70807	468	6271	JUSTICE; PUBIC ORDER/SAFETY

BUSINESS DATA

ZIP CODE	2009 Total Firms	2009 Total Employ-ees	TOP INDUSTRY RANKED on 2009 EMPLOYMENT	ZIP CODE	2009 Total Firms	2009 Total Employ-ees	TOP INDUSTRY RANKED on 2009 EMPLOYMENT	ZIP CODE	2009 Total Firms	2009 Total Employ-ees	TOP INDUSTRY RANKED on 2009 EMPLOYMENT
70808	1646	27124	AMBULATORY HEALTH CARE SVCS	71108	585	4581	EDUCATIONAL SERVICES	71322	276	2466	WOOD PRODUCT MANUFACTURING
70809	2603	41742	PROF.; SCIENTIFIC; & TECH SVCS	71109	763	8134	BLDG MATL & GARDEN EQPMT DLRS	71323	16	102	NURSING & RESID. CARE FACILIT.
70810	1283	16638	ADMINISTRATIVE & SUPPORT SVCS	71110	49	1877	RELIG.; GRANT; CIVIC; PROF ORG	71324	5	20	EXEC.; LEGIS.; & OTHER SUPPORT
70811	271	1560	EDUCATIONAL SERVICES	71111	2054	28778	AMUSEMENT; GAMBLING;& RECREAT.	71325	35	388	SOCIAL ASSISTANCE
70812	84	631	EDUCATIONAL SERVICES	71112	782	7346	FOOD SVCS & DRINKING PLACES	71326	23	120	SOCIAL ASSISTANCE
70813	17	377	JUSTICE; PUBIC ORDER/SAFETY	71113	2	0	SPECIAL TRADE CONTRACTORS	71327	97	1057	JUSTICE; PUBIC ORDER/SAFETY
70814	622	5392	MERCH. WHOLESALERS;DURABLE GDS	71115	369	7630	HOSPITALS	71328	90	405	EDUCATIONAL SERVICES
70815	1462	16166	EDUCATIONAL SERVICES	71118	799	8019	HOSPITALS	71329	3	4	TRUCK TRANSPORTATION
70816	2475	25267	PROF.; SCIENTIFIC; & TECH SVCS	71119	197	1884	MERCH. WHOLESALERS;DURABLE GDS	71330	4	5	POSTAL SERVICE
70817	985	8217	SPECIAL TRADE CONTRACTORS	71129	557	11184	MACHINERY MANUFACTURING	71331	19	82	EDUCATIONAL SERVICES
70818	346	2143	FOOD AND BEVERAGE STORES	71130	1	1	RELIG.; GRANT; CIVIC; PROF ORG	71333	8	41	CONSTRUCTION OF BUILDINGS
70819	157	1142	MOTOR VEHICLE & PARTS DEALERS	71133	8	13	ADMINISTRATIVE & SUPPORT SVCS	71334	327	2369	EDUCATIONAL SERVICES
70820	192	2305	CHEMICAL MANUFACTURING	71134	3	11	RELIG.; GRANT; CIVIC; PROF ORG	71336	32	216	EDUCATIONAL SERVICES
70821	14	42	TRANSIT & GRND PASS. TRANSPORT	71135	13	64	ADMINISTRATIVE & SUPPORT SVCS	71339	10	21	MERCH. WHOLESALERS;NONDUR. GDS
70825	10	89	TELECOMMUNICATIONS	71136	7	37	OIL AND GAS EXTRACTION	71340	54	408	JUSTICE; PUBIC ORDER/SAFETY
70827	104	122	PROF.; SCIENTIFIC; & TECH SVCS	71137	2	1	BLDG MATL & GARDEN EQPMT DLRS	71341	54	467	FOOD MANUFACTURING
70836	169	3036	CLOTHING & CLOTH'G ACC. STORES	71138	5	9	SPECIAL TRADE CONTRACTORS	71342	419	2625	HOSPITALS
70837	4	19	SPECIAL TRADE CONTRACTORS	71148	2	8	SPECIAL TRADE CONTRACTORS	71343	261	1748	SOCIAL ASSISTANCE
70874	4	12	ADMINISTRATIVE & SUPPORT SVCS	71149	3	13	ADMINISTRATIVE & SUPPORT SVCS	71345	6	85	EDUCATIONAL SERVICES
70879	18	41	REAL ESTATE	71162	1	8	ADMINISTRATIVE & SUPPORT SVCS	71346	93	469	FOOD SVCS & DRINKING PLACES
70884	5	11	RELIG.; GRANT; CIVIC; PROF ORG	71166	2	6	HEALTH & PERSONAL CARE STORES	71348	2	3	POSTAL SERVICE
70892	3	2	TRANSIT & GRND PASS. TRANSPORT	71171	4	5	PROF.; SCIENTIFIC; & TECH SVCS	71350	152	1374	GENERAL MERCHANDISE STORES
70893	1	2	RELIG.; GRANT; CIVIC; PROF ORG	71172	2	18	ADMINISTRATIVE & SUPPORT SVCS	71351	477	5805	AMUSEMENT; GAMBLING;& RECREAT.
70894	2	0	SECURITIES/COMMODITY CONTRACTS	71201	2549	25887	PROF.; SCIENTIFIC; & TECH SVCS	71353	55	319	AMBULATORY HEALTH CARE SVCS
70895	9	19	SPECIAL TRADE CONTRACTORS	71202	637	8096	HOSPITALS	71354	36	223	CROP PRODUCTION
70896	1	4	ADMINISTRATIVE & SUPPORT SVCS	71203	1194	15166	FOOD SVCS & DRINKING PLACES	71355	57	207	EDUCATIONAL SERVICES
70898	7	17	FOOD MANUFACTURING	71207	2	1	PROF.; SCIENTIFIC; & TECH SVCS	71356	13	37	EDUCATIONAL SERVICES
71001	263	2790	FOOD MANUFACTURING	71209	5	1255	EDUCATIONAL SERVICES	71357	83	442	EDUCATIONAL SERVICES
71002	4	3	EXEC.; LEGIS.; & OTHER SUPPORT	71210	5	9	RELIG.; GRANT; CIVIC; PROF ORG	71358	19	292	FOOD MANUFACTURING
71003	35	185	SPECIAL TRADE CONTRACTORS	71211	10	87	HEAVY & CIVIL ENG. CONSTRUCT'N	71360	1130	16659	EXEC.; LEGIS.; & OTHER SUPPORT
71004	29	206	EDUCATIONAL SERVICES	71218	6	11	BLDG MATL & GARDEN EQPMT DLRS	71361	3	10	ADMINISTRATIVE & SUPPORT SVCS
71006	244	2222	JUSTICE; PUBIC ORDER/SAFETY	71219	20	131	EDUCATIONAL SERVICES	71362	43	366	EDUCATIONAL SERVICES
71007	17	104	SPECIAL TRADE CONTRACTORS	71220	822	7318	PAPER MANUFACTURING	71363	6	7	ADMIN. ENVIRO. QUALITY PROGRMS
71008	21	112	EDUCATIONAL SERVICES	71221	1	2	EXEC.; LEGIS.; & OTHER SUPPORT	71366	127	755	EDUCATIONAL SERVICES
71009	36	68	GENERAL MERCHANDISE STORES	71222	92	579	AMBULATORY HEALTH CARE SVCS	71367	17	18	JUSTICE; PUBIC ORDER/SAFETY
71016	40	185	EDUCATIONAL SERVICES	71223	32	63	CROP PRODUCTION	71368	49	192	AMBULATORY HEALTH CARE SVCS
71018	60	317	RELIG.; GRANT; CIVIC; PROF ORG	71225	138	707	EDUCATIONAL SERVICES	71369	97	561	EXEC.; LEGIS.; & OTHER SUPPORT
71019	323	2365	EDUCATIONAL SERVICES	71226	60	149	SOCIAL ASSISTANCE	71371	34	158	OIL AND GAS EXTRACTION
71021	45	255	MACHINERY MANUFACTURING	71227	88	591	RELIG.; GRANT; CIVIC; PROF ORG	71373	360	3196	JUSTICE; PUBIC ORDER/SAFETY
71023	57	245	EDUCATIONAL SERVICES	71229	33	106	JUSTICE; PUBIC ORDER/SAFETY	71375	41	291	JUSTICE; PUBIC ORDER/SAFETY
71024	22	142	EDUCATIONAL SERVICES	71230	29	102	SUPPORT ACTIVITIES: AGR./FOR.	71377	4	9	TRANSPORTATION EQUIPMENT MFG
71027	44	270	HEAVY & CIVIL ENG. CONSTRUCT'N	71232	247	2158	PRIMARY METAL MANUFACTURING	71378	67	1236	MERCH. WHOLESALERS;NONDUR. GDS
71028	48	200	EDUCATIONAL SERVICES	71233	16	74	GASOLINE STATIONS	71401	3	4	FOOD AND BEVERAGE STORES
71029	28	57	MERCH. WHOLESALERS;NONDUR. GDS	71234	89	313	NONMETALLIC MINERAL PROD. MFG	71403	49	279	EDUCATIONAL SERVICES
71030	24	41	ADMINISTRATIVE & SUPPORT SVCS	71235	78	419	UTILITIES	71404	14	95	EDUCATIONAL SERVICES
71031	19	93	SPECIAL TRADE CONTRACTORS	71237	37	321	JUSTICE; PUBIC ORDER/SAFETY	71405	170	1365	EDUCATIONAL SERVICES
71032	54	171	RELIG.; GRANT; CIVIC; PROF ORG	71238	33	58	RELIG.; GRANT; CIVIC; PROF ORG	71406	7	24	EDUCATIONAL SERVICES
71033	121	786	GASOLINE STATIONS	71240	2	3	POSTAL SERVICE	71407	16	118	SUPPORT ACTIVITIES: AGR./FOR.
71034	16	36	RELIG.; GRANT; CIVIC; PROF ORG	71241	418	4541	FOOD MANUFACTURING	71409	149	1061	EDUCATIONAL SERVICES
71037	350	2283	EDUCATIONAL SERVICES	71242	10	114	EDUCATIONAL SERVICES	71410	11	41	EDUCATIONAL SERVICES
71038	138	992	EDUCATIONAL SERVICES	71243	18	104	SUPPORT ACTIVITIES: AGR./FOR.	71411	77	600	WOOD PRODUCT MANUFACTURING
71039	26	39	RELIG.; GRANT; CIVIC; PROF ORG	71245	95	1390	EDUCATIONAL SERVICES	71414	7	25	FOOD SVCS & DRINKING PLACES
71040	360	3249	JUSTICE; PUBIC ORDER/SAFETY	71247	49	294	AMBULATORY HEALTH CARE SVCS	71415	15	42	JUSTICE; PUBIC ORDER/SAFETY
71043	17	48	RELIG.; GRANT; CIVIC; PROF ORG	71249	2	7	RELIG.; GRANT; CIVIC; PROF ORG	71416	26	77	EDUCATIONAL SERVICES
71044	22	42	FOOD AND BEVERAGE STORES	71250	17	44	CROP PRODUCTION	71417	142	1165	MERCH. WHOLESALERS;DURABLE GDS
71045	7	4	RELIG.; GRANT; CIVIC; PROF ORG	71251	329	2537	EDUCATIONAL SERVICES	71418	298	2088	EDUCATIONAL SERVICES
71046	18	37	SUPPORT ACTIVITIES FOR MINING	71253	12	62	EDUCATIONAL SERVICES	71419	30	159	EDUCATIONAL SERVICES
71047	197	1030	FABRICATED METAL PRODUCT MFG	71254	288	2378	EXEC.; LEGIS.; & OTHER SUPPORT	71422	41	858	WOOD PRODUCT MANUFACTURING
71048	25	131	JUSTICE; PUBIC ORDER/SAFETY	71256	19	14	RELIG.; GRANT; CIVIC; PROF ORG	71423	70	547	EDUCATIONAL SERVICES
71049	114	591	EDUCATIONAL SERVICES	71259	81	391	AMBULATORY HEALTH CARE SVCS	71424	14	80	EDUCATIONAL SERVICES
71050	4	1	RELIG.; GRANT; CIVIC; PROF ORG	71260	74	205	CREDIT INTERMEDIATION & RELATD	71425	4	19	FOOD SVCS & DRINKING PLACES
71051	39	196	EDUCATIONAL SERVICES	71261	72	544	NURSING & RESID. CARE FACILIT.	71426	4	24	CONSTRUCTION OF BUILDINGS
71052	473	4466	PAPER MANUFACTURING	71263	332	2622	EDUCATIONAL SERVICES	71427	1	1	RELIG.; GRANT; CIVIC; PROF ORG
71055	925	8169	EDUCATIONAL SERVICES	71264	25	70	CROP PRODUCTION	71428	1	3	MERCH. WHOLESALERS;DURABLE GDS
71058	2	7	RELIG.; GRANT; CIVIC; PROF ORG	71266	26	148	FOOD AND BEVERAGE STORES	71429	81	1681	PAPER MANUFACTURING
71060	59	177	EDUCATIONAL SERVICES	71268	38	160	EDUCATIONAL SERVICES	71430	106	657	BLDG MATL & GARDEN EQPMT DLRS
71061	85	510	SPECIAL TRADE CONTRACTORS	71269	445	2958	EDUCATIONAL SERVICES	71432	18	71	EDUCATIONAL SERVICES
71063	25	98	EDUCATIONAL SERVICES	71270	1358	14485	EDUCATIONAL SERVICES	71433	98	421	EDUCATIONAL SERVICES
71064	124	576	EDUCATIONAL SERVICES	71272	1	35	OTHER INFORMATION SERVICES	71435	61	303	JUSTICE; PUBIC ORDER/SAFETY
71065	43	115	EDUCATIONAL SERVICES	71273	4	7	INSURANCE CARRIERS & RELATED	71438	25	70	FOOD AND BEVERAGE STORES
71066	5	6	FOOD AND BEVERAGE STORES	71275	46	880	NONMETALLIC MINERAL PROD. MFG	71439	23	185	EDUCATIONAL SERVICES
71067	45	394	PETROLEUM & COAL PRODUCTS MFG	71276	9	39	CROP PRODUCTION	71440	5	26	BLDG MATL & GARDEN EQPMT DLRS
71068	126	562	AMBULATORY HEALTH CARE SVCS	71277	31	96	EDUCATIONAL SERVICES	71441	10	30	EDUCATIONAL SERVICES
71069	17	68	SUPPORT ACTIVITIES FOR MINING	71279	18	133	EDUCATIONAL SERVICES	71446	1016	8445	FOOD SVCS & DRINKING PLACES
71070	46	176	FORESTRY AND LOGGING	71280	115	1637	ADMINISTRATIVE & SUPPORT SVCS	71447	15	578	WOOD PRODUCT MANUFACTURING
71071	75	736	PLASTICS & RUBBER PRODUCTS MFG	71281	8	53	REAL ESTATE	71448	3	16	MERCH. WHOLESALERS;DURABLE GDS
71072	24	99	EDUCATIONAL SERVICES	71282	409	3549	EDUCATIONAL SERVICES	71449	505	3784	SOCIAL ASSISTANCE
71073	85	964	SPECIAL TRADE CONTRACTORS	71286	17	47	SPECIAL TRADE CONTRACTORS	71450	18	105	EDUCATIONAL SERVICES
71075	306	2690	PAPER MANUFACTURING	71291	1556	12954	HOSPITALS	71452	3	11	AMUSEMENT; GAMBLING;& RECREAT.
71078	108	515	EDUCATIONAL SERVICES	71292	760	11119	MERCH. WHOLESALERS;NONDUR. GDS	71454	46	216	EDUCATIONAL SERVICES
71079	6	41	EDUCATIONAL SERVICES	71294	5	3	SPECIAL TRADE CONTRACTORS	71455	7	20	MERCH. WHOLESALERS;DURABLE GDS
71080	7	30	SUPPORT ACTIVITIES: AGR./FOR.	71295	520	4474	EDUCATIONAL SERVICES	71456	28	91	RELIG.; GRANT; CIVIC; PROF ORG
71082	225	1542	EDUCATIONAL SERVICES	71301	1928	25532	HOSPITALS	71457	1338	12261	EDUCATIONAL SERVICES
71101	1768	26516	HOSPITALS	71302	429	5081	EDUCATIONAL SERVICES	71459	162	3379	EXEC.; LEGIS.; & OTHER SUPPORT
71102	3	1565	POSTAL SERVICE	71303	1097	11049	FOOD SVCS & DRINKING PLACES	71460	3	3	POSTAL SERVICE
71103	566	16492	HOSPITALS	71306	2	16	SPECIAL TRADE CONTRACTORS	71461	29	270	EXEC.; LEGIS.; & OTHER SUPPORT
71104	652	4479	EDUCATIONAL SERVICES	71307	3	12	BLDG MATL & GARDEN EQPMT DLRS	71462	18	96	EDUCATIONAL SERVICES
71105	1559	18064	HOSPITALS	71309	1	0	PROF.; SCIENTIFIC; & TECH SVCS	71463	314	2395	WOOD PRODUCT MANUFACTURING
71106	1409	14009	AMBULATORY HEALTH CARE SVCS	71315	6	12	CONSTRUCTION OF BUILDINGS	71465	127	728	HOSPITALS
71107	1190	12808	ADMINISTRATIVE & SUPPORT SVCS	71320	3	4	UTILITIES	71466	2	1	SPORTG GDS;HOBBY;BOOK; & MUSIC

ZIP CODE	2009 Total Firms	2009 Total Employ-ees	TOP INDUSTRY RANKED on 2009 EMPLOYMENT
71467	74	643	WOOD PRODUCT MANUFACTURING
71468	15	79	EDUCATIONAL SERVICES
71469	46	307	EDUCATIONAL SERVICES
71471	1	0	RELIG.; GRANT; CIVIC; PROF ORG
71472	6	10	FOOD AND BEVERAGE STORES
71473	11	8	EXEC.; LEGIS.; & OTHER SUPPORT
71474	15	104	EDUCATIONAL SERVICES
71475	3	4	MOTOR VEHICLE & PARTS DEALERS
71477	8	114	MOTOR VEHICLE & PARTS DEALERS
71479	45	183	SUPPORT ACTIVITIES FOR MINING
71480	16	80	EDUCATIONAL SERVICES
71483	438	3843	JUSTICE; PUBIC ORDER/SAFETY
71485	68	468	EXEC.; LEGIS.; & OTHER SUPPORT
71486	131	1203	MERCH. WHOLESALERS;DURABLE GDS
71497	4	45	EDUCATIONAL SERVICES
71601	1159	12734	PAPER MANUFACTURING
71602	469	7298	FOOD MANUFACTURING
71603	944	10651	HOSPITALS
71611	10	15	ADMINISTRATIVE & SUPPORT SVCS
71612	1	0	BLDG MATL & GARDEN EQPMT DLRS
71613	5	15	ADMINISTRATIVE & SUPPORT SVCS
71630	33	556	MERCH. WHOLESALERS;NONDUR. GDS
71631	12	34	JUSTICE; PUBIC ORDER/SAFETY
71635	617	5225	RELIG.; GRANT; CIVIC; PROF ORG
71638	121	1023	EDUCATIONAL SERVICES
71639	325	2438	EDUCATIONAL SERVICES
71640	135	822	APPAREL MANUFACTURING
71642	12	52	FORESTRY AND LOGGING
71643	40	531	JUSTICE; PUBIC ORDER/SAFETY
71644	34	741	JUSTICE; PUBIC ORDER/SAFETY
71646	215	1270	EDUCATIONAL SERVICES
71647	73	448	EDUCATIONAL SERVICES
71651	4	11	ACCOMMODATION
71652	34	141	TRUCK TRANSPORTATION
71653	293	1845	EDUCATIONAL SERVICES
71654	254	2034	EDUCATIONAL SERVICES
71655	670	5879	EDUCATIONAL SERVICES
71657	2	2	SPECIAL TRADE CONTRACTORS
71658	9	21	SOCIAL ASSISTANCE
71659	4	12	CROP PRODUCTION
71660	6	27	RELIG.; GRANT; CIVIC; PROF ORG
71661	10	42	CREDIT INTERMEDIATION & RELATD
71662	4	11	MERCH. WHOLESALERS;NONDUR. GDS
71663	46	292	PROF.; SCIENTIFIC; & TECH SVCS
71665	184	998	EDUCATIONAL SERVICES
71666	2	12	PROF.; SCIENTIFIC; & TECH SVCS
71667	264	2195	APPAREL MANUFACTURING
71670	39	136	CROP PRODUCTION
71671	386	3346	EDUCATIONAL SERVICES
71674	21	68	CROP PRODUCTION
71675	29	88	FABRICATED METAL PRODUCT MFG
71676	36	108	EDUCATIONAL SERVICES
71677	8	50	SUPPORT ACTIVITIES: AGR./FOR.
71678	2	6	FOOD SVCS & DRINKING PLACES
71701	897	9060	COMPUTER & ELECTRONIC PROD MFG
71711	5	14	FOOD MANUFACTURING
71720	75	418	MERCH. WHOLESALERS;DURABLE GDS
71721	4	128	WOOD PRODUCT MANUFACTURING
71722	4	16	MUSEUMS; HIST. SITES;& SIMILAR
71724	17	146	MERCH. WHOLESALERS;DURABLE GDS
71725	19	120	WOOD PRODUCT MANUFACTURING
71726	45	65	FOOD AND BEVERAGE STORES
71728	2	0	POSTAL SERVICE
71730	1762	19676	FOOD MANUFACTURING
71731	5	8	SPECIAL TRADE CONTRACTORS
71740	37	854	CHEMICAL MANUFACTURING
71742	351	2737	BLDG MATL & GARDEN EQPMT DLRS
71743	107	713	RELIG.; GRANT; CIVIC; PROF ORG
71744	169	1138	CHEMICAL MANUFACTURING
71745	17	54	TRUCK TRANSPORTATION
71747	35	354	WOOD PRODUCT MANUFACTURING
71748	1	0	RELIG.; GRANT; CIVIC; PROF ORG
71749	96	535	EDUCATIONAL SERVICES
71750	3	8	FOOD SVCS & DRINKING PLACES
71751	20	38	ACCOMMODATION
71752	20	109	EDUCATIONAL SERVICES
71753	869	8774	MERCH. WHOLESALERS;DURABLE GDS
71754	1	1	SPECIAL TRADE CONTRACTORS
71758	24	172	WOOD PRODUCT MANUFACTURING
71759	22	113	MERCH. WHOLESALERS;NONDUR. GDS
71762	115	911	EDUCATIONAL SERVICES
71763	38	320	EDUCATIONAL SERVICES
71764	94	345	EDUCATIONAL SERVICES
71765	78	443	EDUCATIONAL SERVICES
71766	13	19	UTILITIES
71768	4	1	OIL AND GAS EXTRACTION
71770	42	309	WOOD PRODUCT MANUFACTURING
71772	3	12	FORESTRY AND LOGGING
71801	741	10605	FOOD MANUFACTURING
71802	3	17	MUSEUMS; HIST. SITES;& SIMILAR
71820	2	1	GASOLINE STATIONS
71822	351	3446	PAPER MANUFACTURING
71823	1	0	OTHER INFORMATION SERVICES
71825	22	220	EDUCATIONAL SERVICES
71826	62	316	EDUCATIONAL SERVICES
71827	7	11	POSTAL SERVICE
71831	8	14	FISHING; HUNTING AND TRAPPING
71832	412	5130	MERCH. WHOLESALERS;NONDUR. GDS
71833	93	666	WOOD PRODUCT MANUFACTURING
71834	29	105	EDUCATIONAL SERVICES
71835	20	101	EDUCATIONAL SERVICES
71836	105	558	TRUCK TRANSPORTATION
71837	108	661	EDUCATIONAL SERVICES
71838	30	43	EDUCATIONAL SERVICES
71839	25	62	FOOD SVCS & DRINKING PLACES
71840	3	5	RELIG.; GRANT; CIVIC; PROF ORG
71841	22	296	SPECIAL TRADE CONTRACTORS
71842	47	276	EDUCATIONAL SERVICES
71845	147	786	EDUCATIONAL SERVICES
71846	77	273	EDUCATIONAL SERVICES
71847	1	0	POSTAL SERVICE
71851	67	372	EDUCATIONAL SERVICES
71852	416	7244	FOOD MANUFACTURING
71853	9	9	CROP PRODUCTION
71854	1303	13708	MERCH. WHOLESALERS;DURABLE GDS
71855	6	5	POSTAL SERVICE
71857	239	2306	PETROLEUM & COAL PRODUCTS MFG
71858	26	172	EDUCATIONAL SERVICES
71859	13	92	EDUCATIONAL SERVICES
71860	108	792	FURNITURE & RELATED PROD. MFG
71861	48	240	EDUCATIONAL SERVICES
71862	27	297	MUSEUMS; HIST. SITES;& SIMILAR
71864	5	0	POSTAL SERVICE
71865	6	23	MERCH. WHOLESALERS;DURABLE GDS
71866	28	68	EDUCATIONAL SERVICES
71901	1652	22393	MERCH. WHOLESALERS;DURABLE GDS
71902	7	10	INSURANCE CARRIERS & RELATED
71903	15	29	RELIG.; GRANT; CIVIC; PROF ORG
71909	481	2822	AMBULATORY HEALTH CARE SVCS
71910	2	2	SOCIAL ASSISTANCE
71913	2243	19278	FOOD SVCS & DRINKING PLACES
71914	10	28	ADMINISTRATIVE & SUPPORT SVCS
71920	1	2	ACCOMMODATION
71921	84	674	TRUCK TRANSPORTATION
71922	7	70	WOOD PRODUCT MANUFACTURING
71923	635	7080	EDUCATIONAL SERVICES
71929	110	522	EDUCATIONAL SERVICES
71933	22	39	MERCH. WHOLESALERS;DURABLE GDS
71935	13	19	RENTAL AND LEASING SERVICES
71937	42	288	EDUCATIONAL SERVICES
71940	50	185	EDUCATIONAL SERVICES
71941	38	144	EDUCATIONAL SERVICES
71942	3	15	WASTE MANAGMT & REMEDIAT'N SVC
71943	237	1698	WOOD PRODUCT MANUFACTURING
71944	15	56	FOOD MANUFACTURING
71945	44	352	WOOD PRODUCT MANUFACTURING
71949	55	441	EDUCATIONAL SERVICES
71950	35	265	EDUCATIONAL SERVICES
71952	3	4	FOOD AND BEVERAGE STORES
71953	722	5855	APPAREL MANUFACTURING
71956	33	486	WOOD PRODUCT MANUFACTURING
71957	235	1690	ACCOMMODATION
71958	151	972	EDUCATIONAL SERVICES
71959	14	38	JUSTICE; PUBIC ORDER/SAFETY
71960	45	276	EDUCATIONAL SERVICES
71961	18	82	EDUCATIONAL SERVICES
71962	8	12	POSTAL SERVICE
71964	96	981	EDUCATIONAL SERVICES
71965	13	45	ADMINISTRATIVE & SUPPORT SVCS
71968	111	664	SPECIAL TRADE CONTRACTORS
71969	3	3	CROP PRODUCTION
71970	9	14	FOOD AND BEVERAGE STORES
71971	20	55	EDUCATIONAL SERVICES
71972	6	37	EDUCATIONAL SERVICES
71973	37	853	FOOD MANUFACTURING
71998	4	385	EDUCATIONAL SERVICES
71999	2	22	OTHER INFORMATION SERVICES
72001	8	7	CROP PRODUCTION
72002	243	1877	SOCIAL ASSISTANCE
72003	13	32	AIR TRANSPORTATION
72004	58	226	EDUCATIONAL SERVICES
72005	8	25	RELIG.; GRANT; CIVIC; PROF ORG
72006	142	1102	AMBULATORY HEALTH CARE SVCS
72007	54	147	RELIG.; GRANT; CIVIC; PROF ORG
72010	222	1528	EDUCATIONAL SERVICES
72011	75	1081	MERCH. WHOLESALERS;DURABLE GDS
72012	384	2658	EDUCATIONAL SERVICES
72013	33	239	EDUCATIONAL SERVICES
72014	4	15	SUPPORT ACTIVITIES: AGR./FOR.
72015	1122	9820	JUSTICE; PUBIC ORDER/SAFETY
72016	60	180	EDUCATIONAL SERVICES
72017	10	21	FOOD AND BEVERAGE STORES
72018	14	59	SPECIAL TRADE CONTRACTORS
72019	481	3968	MOTOR VEHICLE & PARTS DEALERS
72020	65	208	EDUCATIONAL SERVICES
72021	270	1938	APPAREL MANUFACTURING
72022	696	5336	FOOD SVCS & DRINKING PLACES
72023	1002	7208	EDUCATIONAL SERVICES
72024	125	700	EDUCATIONAL SERVICES
72025	17	45	EDUCATIONAL SERVICES
72026	7	13	EDUCATIONAL SERVICES
72027	27	176	EDUCATIONAL SERVICES
72028	15	61	EDUCATIONAL SERVICES
72029	121	625	EDUCATIONAL SERVICES
72030	15	26	JUSTICE; PUBIC ORDER/SAFETY
72031	434	3385	EDUCATIONAL SERVICES
72032	1801	19984	FOOD SVCS & DRINKING PLACES
72033	10	18	SPECIAL TRADE CONTRACTORS
72034	991	9235	AMBULATORY HEALTH CARE SVCS
72035	10	1600	EDUCATIONAL SERVICES
72036	29	69	JUSTICE; PUBIC ORDER/SAFETY
72037	4	37	MACHINERY MANUFACTURING
72038	2	2	MISCELLANEOUS STORE RETAILERS
72039	60	403	SPECIAL TRADE CONTRACTORS
72040	116	597	EDUCATIONAL SERVICES
72041	50	113	EDUCATIONAL SERVICES
72042	250	2451	LEATHER & ALLIED PRODUCT MFG
72043	6	12	HEAVY & CIVIL ENG. CONSTRUCT'N
72044	18	39	PUBLISHING INDUSTRIES
72045	28	207	SPECIAL TRADE CONTRACTORS
72046	156	973	SOCIAL ASSISTANCE
72047	12	45	EDUCATIONAL SERVICES
72048	1	0	POSTAL SERVICE
72051	25	104	EDUCATIONAL SERVICES
72052	3	11	PIPELINE TRANSPORTATION
72053	4	15	RELIG.; GRANT; CIVIC; PROF ORG
72055	31	179	EDUCATIONAL SERVICES
72057	10	6	RELIG.; GRANT; CIVIC; PROF ORG
72058	352	1961	EDUCATIONAL SERVICES
72059	3	0	AIR TRANSPORTATION
72060	8	15	POSTAL SERVICE
72061	13	125	EDUCATIONAL SERVICES
72063	16	82	EDUCATIONAL SERVICES
72064	121	840	EDUCATIONAL SERVICES
72065	78	246	FOOD SVCS & DRINKING PLACES
72066	2	5	GASOLINE STATIONS
72067	171	780	EDUCATIONAL SERVICES
72068	12	48	JUSTICE; PUBIC ORDER/SAFETY
72069	39	101	SOCIAL ASSISTANCE
72070	21	33	MINING (EXCEPT OIL AND GAS)
72072	11	9	RELIG.; GRANT; CIVIC; PROF ORG
72073	22	93	EDUCATIONAL SERVICES
72074	4	10	MERCH. WHOLESALERS;NONDUR. GDS
72075	4	12	MUSEUMS; HIST. SITES;& SIMILAR
72076	1058	10078	SOCIAL ASSISTANCE
72078	9	33	CREDIT INTERMEDIATION & RELATD
72079	12	693	OTHER INFORMATION SERVICES
72080	7	10	POSTAL SERVICE
72081	131	815	NURSING & RESID. CARE FACILIT.
72082	51	270	EDUCATIONAL SERVICES
72083	14	50	SPORTG GDS;HOBBY;BOOK; & MUSIC
72084	20	101	WOOD PRODUCT MANUFACTURING
72085	2	1	RELIG.; GRANT; CIVIC; PROF ORG
72086	346	3595	FABRICATED METAL PRODUCT MFG
72087	38	138	FOOD AND BEVERAGE STORES
72088	95	666	RELIG.; GRANT; CIVIC; PROF ORG
72089	7	13	CONSTRUCTION OF BUILDINGS
72099	44	341	CLOTHING & CLOTH'G ACC. STORES
72101	123	884	EDUCATIONAL SERVICES
72102	31	106	MERCH. WHOLESALERS;DURABLE GDS
72103	276	2461	MERCH. WHOLESALERS;DURABLE GDS
72104	729	7365	EDUCATIONAL SERVICES
72105	18	2	REAL ESTATE
72106	142	689	EDUCATIONAL SERVICES
72107	13	259	CONSTRUCTION OF BUILDINGS
72108	4	20	ANIMAL PRODUCTION
72110	690	5476	EDUCATIONAL SERVICES
72111	14	69	EDUCATIONAL SERVICES
72112	501	4470	PRIMARY METAL MANUFACTURING
72113	802	9778	MERCH. WHOLESALERS;DURABLE GDS
72114	977	14940	HOSPITALS
72115	10	11	ELECTRONICS & APPLIANCE STORES
72116	1097	8901	FOOD SVCS & DRINKING PLACES
72117	950	14364	TRUCK TRANSPORTATION
72118	737	5947	EDUCATIONAL SERVICES
72120	963	6327	ADMINISTRATIVE & SUPPORT SVCS
72121	63	512	EDUCATIONAL SERVICES
72122	31	102	EDUCATIONAL SERVICES
72123	13	46	MERCH. WHOLESALERS;NONDUR. GDS
72124	7	6	SPECIAL TRADE CONTRACTORS

BUSINESS DATA

ZIP CODE	2009 Total Firms	2009 Total Employ-ees	TOP INDUSTRY RANKED on 2009 EMPLOYMENT	ZIP CODE	2009 Total Firms	2009 Total Employ-ees	TOP INDUSTRY RANKED on 2009 EMPLOYMENT	ZIP CODE	2009 Total Firms	2009 Total Employ-ees	TOP INDUSTRY RANKED on 2009 EMPLOYMENT
72125	23	100	NONSTORE RETAILERS	72338	2	12	MERCH. WHOLESALERS;NONDUR. GDS	72462	12	42	JUSTICE; PUBIC ORDER/SAFETY
72126	188	987	EXEC.; LEGIS.; & OTHER SUPPORT	72339	4	13	JUSTICE; PUBIC ORDER/SAFETY	72464	3	1	RELIG.; GRANT; CIVIC; PROF ORG
72127	52	489	MERCH. WHOLESALERS;DURABLE GDS	72340	1	0	RELIG.; GRANT; CIVIC; PROF ORG	72465	1	2	POSTAL SERVICE
72128	14	94	EDUCATIONAL SERVICES	72341	4	13	JUSTICE; PUBIC ORDER/SAFETY	72466	17	22	GASOLINE STATIONS
72129	27	137	MACHINERY MANUFACTURING	72342	318	2722	EDUCATIONAL SERVICES	72467	10	2290	EDUCATIONAL SERVICES
72130	23	23	RELIG.; GRANT; CIVIC; PROF ORG	72346	19	116	FOOD SVCS & DRINKING PLACES	72469	18	171	EDUCATIONAL SERVICES
72131	109	578	EDUCATIONAL SERVICES	72347	30	99	CROP PRODUCTION	72470	13	43	WAREHOUSING AND STORAGE
72132	79	560	UTILITIES	72348	96	470	EDUCATIONAL SERVICES	72471	32	104	EDUCATIONAL SERVICES
72133	2	1	RELIG.; GRANT; CIVIC; PROF ORG	72350	26	54	JUSTICE; PUBIC ORDER/SAFETY	72472	292	2529	EDUCATIONAL SERVICES
72134	9	22	MERCH. WHOLESALERS;NONDUR. GDS	72351	23	134	EDUCATIONAL SERVICES	72473	71	515	EDUCATIONAL SERVICES
72135	105	179	ADMINISTRATIVE & SUPPORT SVCS	72352	1	0	POSTAL SERVICE	72474	1	3	RELIG.; GRANT; CIVIC; PROF ORG
72136	11	34	TRUCK TRANSPORTATION	72353	2	2	POSTAL SERVICE	72475	25	146	FOOD MANUFACTURING
72137	67	639	EDUCATIONAL SERVICES	72354	95	354	EDUCATIONAL SERVICES	72476	357	3716	AMBULATORY HEALTH CARE SVCS
72139	8	11	FURNITURE & RELATED PROD. MFG	72355	42	337	EDUCATIONAL SERVICES	72478	2	115	RELIG.; GRANT; CIVIC; PROF ORG
72140	18	26	WAREHOUSING AND STORAGE	72358	38	260	JUSTICE; PUBIC ORDER/SAFETY	72479	77	387	EDUCATIONAL SERVICES
72141	20	33	SPECIAL TRADE CONTRACTORS	72359	15	145	EDUCATIONAL SERVICES	72482	21	85	EDUCATIONAL SERVICES
72142	81	175	SPECIAL TRADE CONTRACTORS	72360	267	1553	EDUCATIONAL SERVICES	72501	1220	17027	FOOD MANUFACTURING
72143	1551	16601	AMBULATORY HEALTH CARE SVCS	72364	358	2879	EDUCATIONAL SERVICES	72503	5	19	MOTION PICT. & SOUND RECORDING
72145	5	18	PROF.; SCIENTIFIC; & TECH SVCS	72365	148	1420	EDUCATIONAL SERVICES	72512	93	467	NURSING & RESID. CARE FACILIT.
72149	8	1172	EDUCATIONAL SERVICES	72366	95	585	EDUCATIONAL SERVICES	72513	226	1437	GENERAL MERCHANDISE STORES
72150	406	3084	FABRICATED METAL PRODUCT MFG	72367	5	12	WAREHOUSING AND STORAGE	72517	10	77	EDUCATIONAL SERVICES
72152	17	63	SPECIAL TRADE CONTRACTORS	72368	22	38	RELIG.; GRANT; CIVIC; PROF ORG	72519	129	725	EDUCATIONAL SERVICES
72153	110	468	EDUCATIONAL SERVICES	72369	3	5	FOOD AND BEVERAGE STORES	72520	5	2	CONSTRUCTION OF BUILDINGS
72156	11	18	SPECIAL TRADE CONTRACTORS	72370	341	5054	MISCELLANEOUS STORE RETAILERS	72521	132	910	EDUCATIONAL SERVICES
72157	21	46	SPECIAL TRADE CONTRACTORS	72372	50	185	EDUCATIONAL SERVICES	72522	6	65	EDUCATIONAL SERVICES
72160	566	5970	MACHINERY MANUFACTURING	72373	62	221	EXEC.; LEGIS.; & OTHER SUPPORT	72523	30	222	EDUCATIONAL SERVICES
72164	2	2	POSTAL SERVICE	72374	18	139	SOCIAL ASSISTANCE	72524	12	77	MERCH. WHOLESALERS;NONDUR. GDS
72165	2	2	FORESTRY AND LOGGING	72376	39	158	SPECIAL TRADE CONTRACTORS	72525	2	4	SPECIAL TRADE CONTRACTORS
72166	8	13	ADMIN. ENVIRO. QUALITY PROGRMS	72377	3	3	POSTAL SERVICE	72526	6	70	EDUCATIONAL SERVICES
72167	11	11	POSTAL SERVICE	72379	3	1	RELIG.; GRANT; CIVIC; PROF ORG	72527	7	13	CROP PRODUCTION
72168	8	218	JUSTICE; PUBIC ORDER/SAFETY	72383	2	1	RELIG.; GRANT; CIVIC; PROF ORG	72528	6	2	REPAIR AND MAINTENANCE
72169	3	4	CROP PRODUCTION	72384	30	270	EDUCATIONAL SERVICES	72529	93	555	EXEC.; LEGIS.; & OTHER SUPPORT
72170	4	6	FOOD SVCS & DRINKING PLACES	72386	39	143	EDUCATIONAL SERVICES	72530	37	225	ACCOMMODATION
72173	172	895	EDUCATIONAL SERVICES	72387	4	24	EDUCATIONAL SERVICES	72531	12	17	ACCOMMODATION
72175	13	26	SPECIAL TRADE CONTRACTORS	72389	3	4	AMBULATORY HEALTH CARE SVCS	72532	30	119	SPECIAL TRADE CONTRACTORS
72176	75	423	EDUCATIONAL SERVICES	72390	353	2753	EDUCATIONAL SERVICES	72533	12	33	FOOD SVCS & DRINKING PLACES
72178	3	18	ELECTRONICS & APPLIANCE STORES	72391	3	5	CROP PRODUCTION	72534	12	147	EDUCATIONAL SERVICES
72179	6	26	EDUCATIONAL SERVICES	72392	28	221	MERCH. WHOLESALERS;NONDUR. GDS	72536	21	85	BLDG MATL & GARDEN EQPMT DLRS
72180	3	10	RELIG.; GRANT; CIVIC; PROF ORG	72394	14	35	SUPPORT ACTIVITIES: AGR./FOR.	72537	34	69	AMUSEMENT; GAMBLING;& RECREAT.
72181	11	81	JUSTICE; PUBIC ORDER/SAFETY	72395	46	327	EDUCATIONAL SERVICES	72538	8	22	GASOLINE STATIONS
72182	5	26	JUSTICE; PUBIC ORDER/SAFETY	72396	572	4235	MERCH. WHOLESALERS;NONDUR. GDS	72539	9	16	REAL ESTATE
72183	11	110	EXEC.; LEGIS.; & OTHER SUPPORT	72401	2845	34154	AMBULATORY HEALTH CARE SVCS	72540	6	70	MERCH. WHOLESALERS;DURABLE GDS
72190	14	24	CONSTRUCTION OF BUILDINGS	72402	5	19	FURN. & HOME FURNISHGS STORES	72542	382	1516	EDUCATIONAL SERVICES
72199	10	2658	ACCOMMODATION	72403	20	72	REPAIR AND MAINTENANCE	72543	699	5332	MISCELLANEOUS MANUFACTURING
72201	1956	38362	PROF.; SCIENTIFIC; & TECH SVCS	72404	585	6729	EDUCATIONAL SERVICES	72544	28	47	ACCOMMODATION
72202	980	15373	TELECOMMUNICATIONS	72410	6	28	JUSTICE; PUBIC ORDER/SAFETY	72546	4	15	REPAIR AND MAINTENANCE
72203	22	42	CONSTRUCTION OF BUILDINGS	72411	39	417	EDUCATIONAL SERVICES	72550	11	19	PERSONAL AND LAUNDRY SERVICES
72204	1444	16385	EDUCATIONAL SERVICES	72412	5	12	GASOLINE STATIONS	72553	6	10	FOOD SVCS & DRINKING PLACES
72205	1900	101448	AMBULATORY HEALTH CARE SVCS	72413	12	32	UTILITIES	72554	101	487	EDUCATIONAL SERVICES
72206	1177	13552	MERCH. WHOLESALERS;DURABLE GDS	72414	9	12	MACHINERY MANUFACTURING	72555	4	12	JUSTICE; PUBIC ORDER/SAFETY
72207	600	3792	SOCIAL ASSISTANCE	72415	45	301	NONMETALLIC MINERAL PROD. MFG	72556	218	1610	EDUCATIONAL SERVICES
72209	1562	22967	ADMIN. OF ECONOMIC PROGRAMS	72416	101	403	ELECT'L EQPMT; APP; & COMP MFG	72560	604	3945	FOOD SVCS & DRINKING PLACES
72210	440	3197	TRUCK TRANSPORTATION	72417	80	572	EDUCATIONAL SERVICES	72561	23	199	EDUCATIONAL SERVICES
72211	1521	18363	FOOD SVCS & DRINKING PLACES	72419	53	330	COMPUTER & ELECTRONIC PROD MFG	72562	58	201	EDUCATIONAL SERVICES
72212	644	7784	DATA PROCESS'G	72421	14	70	SUPPORT ACTIVITIES: AGR./FOR.	72564	14	61	EDUCATIONAL SERVICES
72214	10	20	ADMINISTRATIVE & SUPPORT SVCS	72422	202	1887	FURNITURE & RELATED PROD. MFG	72565	15	32	PROF.; SCIENTIFIC; & TECH SVCS
72215	8	6	SPECIAL TRADE CONTRACTORS	72425	11	25	FOOD AND BEVERAGE STORES	72566	15	42	EXEC.; LEGIS.; & OTHER SUPPORT
72216	5	3	CONSTRUCTION OF BUILDINGS	72426	21	129	SUPPORT ACTIVITIES: AGR./FOR.	72567	14	36	JUSTICE; PUBIC ORDER/SAFETY
72217	10	615	ADMINISTRATIVE & SUPPORT SVCS	72427	1	2	POSTAL SERVICE	72568	41	222	EDUCATIONAL SERVICES
72219	4	3	AMUSEMENT; GAMBLING;& RECREAT.	72428	9	8	FOOD AND BEVERAGE STORES	72569	2	6	POSTAL SERVICE
72221	13	22	CONSTRUCTION OF BUILDINGS	72429	25	68	MERCH. WHOLESALERS;DURABLE GDS	72571	5	3	MERCH. WHOLESALERS;DURABLE GDS
72222	7	10	ADMINISTRATIVE & SUPPORT SVCS	72430	3	5	MERCH. WHOLESALERS;NONDUR. GDS	72572	6	7	FOOD AND BEVERAGE STORES
72223	744	5813	CREDIT INTERMEDIATION & RELATD	72431	12	20	AIR TRANSPORTATION	72573	5	10	NURSING & RESID. CARE FACILIT.
72225	15	14	PROF.; SCIENTIFIC; & TECH SVCS	72432	202	1288	EDUCATIONAL SERVICES	72575	2	5	REAL ESTATE
72227	455	3213	FOOD SVCS & DRINKING PLACES	72433	94	736	EDUCATIONAL SERVICES	72576	215	1281	UTILITIES
72231	6	162	RELIG.; GRANT; CIVIC; PROF ORG	72434	73	329	EDUCATIONAL SERVICES	72577	5	4	POSTAL SERVICE
72260	2	21	TRUCK TRANSPORTATION	72435	9	47	WHOLESALE ELEC. MRKTS & AGENTS	72578	1	0	POSTAL SERVICE
72301	1131	15294	TRUCK TRANSPORTATION	72436	11	22	GASOLINE STATIONS	72579	21	109	EDUCATIONAL SERVICES
72303	8	19	MUSEUMS; HIST. SITES;& SIMILAR	72437	77	440	EDUCATIONAL SERVICES	72581	20	88	SPECIAL TRADE CONTRACTORS
72310	8	119	EDUCATIONAL SERVICES	72438	76	386	CROP PRODUCTION	72583	39	195	EDUCATIONAL SERVICES
72311	6	21	ADMINISTRATIVE & SUPPORT SVCS	72439	4	11	FOOD MANUFACTURING	72584	9	64	EDUCATIONAL SERVICES
72312	5	11	FOOD SVCS & DRINKING PLACES	72440	16	176	EDUCATIONAL SERVICES	72585	1	1	POSTAL SERVICE
72313	5	11	CROP PRODUCTION	72441	4	16	UTILITIES	72587	1	1	POSTAL SERVICE
72315	998	12376	MERCH. WHOLESALERS;DURABLE GDS	72442	151	795	EDUCATIONAL SERVICES	72601	1599	14864	EDUCATIONAL SERVICES
72316	6	29	SPECIAL TRADE CONTRACTORS	72443	49	778	TRANSPORTATION EQUIPMENT MFG	72602	15	59	RELIG.; GRANT; CIVIC; PROF ORG
72320	6	406	JUSTICE; PUBIC ORDER/SAFETY	72444	29	234	EDUCATIONAL SERVICES	72611	60	396	EDUCATIONAL SERVICES
72321	8	101	EDUCATIONAL SERVICES	72445	2	9	AIR TRANSPORTATION	72613	2	2	TRANSIT & GRND PASS. TRANSPORT
72322	13	52	FOOD SVCS & DRINKING PLACES	72447	71	646	EDUCATIONAL SERVICES	72615	6	52	FOOD MANUFACTURING
72324	54	212	EDUCATIONAL SERVICES	72449	3	7	FOOD SVCS & DRINKING PLACES	72616	469	5682	FOOD MANUFACTURING
72325	5	29	CROP PRODUCTION	72450	1252	17190	TRANSPORTATION EQUIPMENT MFG	72617	7	19	FOOD AND BEVERAGE STORES
72326	44	261	PLASTICS & RUBBER PRODUCTS MFG	72451	1	0	PROF.; SCIENTIFIC; & TECH SVCS	72619	165	611	AMUSEMENT; GAMBLING;& RECREAT.
72327	50	211	SUPPORT ACTIVITIES: AGR./FOR.	72453	3	5	POSTAL SERVICE	72623	11	16	SPECIAL TRADE CONTRACTORS
72328	1	1	POSTAL SERVICE	72454	216	1843	FURNITURE & RELATED PROD. MFG	72624	17	13	GASOLINE STATIONS
72329	2	4	WAREHOUSING AND STORAGE	72455	469	3406	FOOD SVCS & DRINKING PLACES	72626	64	299	EDUCATIONAL SERVICES
72330	12	31	JUSTICE; PUBIC ORDER/SAFETY	72456	15	42	WOOD PRODUCT MANUFACTURING	72628	30	207	EDUCATIONAL SERVICES
72331	83	674	EDUCATIONAL SERVICES	72457	17	92	EDUCATIONAL SERVICES	72629	17	33	CONSTRUCTION OF BUILDINGS
72332	5	28	EDUCATIONAL SERVICES	72458	10	26	MUSEUMS; HIST. SITES;& SIMILAR	72630	27	21	AMUSEMENT; GAMBLING;& RECREAT.
72333	63	198	EDUCATIONAL SERVICES	72459	24	88	CONSTRUCTION OF BUILDINGS	72631	173	584	FOOD SVCS & DRINKING PLACES
72335	746	6898	EDUCATIONAL SERVICES	72460	13	60	EDUCATIONAL SERVICES	72632	670	3667	FOOD SVCS & DRINKING PLACES
72336	6	6	EXEC.; LEGIS.; & OTHER SUPPORT	72461	109	781	APPAREL MANUFACTURING	72633	34	128	EDUCATIONAL SERVICES

ZIP CODE	2009 Total Firms	2009 Total Employ-ees	TOP INDUSTRY RANKED on 2009 EMPLOYMENT
72634	299	4546	MISCELLANEOUS STORE RETAILERS
72635	154	756	APPAREL MANUFACTURING
72636	5	1	ACCOMMODATION
72638	196	2546	FOOD MANUFACTURING
72639	5	29	ACCOMMODATION
72640	6	8	ACCOMMODATION
72641	180	1127	EXEC.; LEGIS.; & OTHER SUPPORT
72642	77	334	ACCOMMODATION
72644	147	510	EDUCATIONAL SERVICES
72645	57	173	EDUCATIONAL SERVICES
72648	13	41	ADMINISTRATIVE & SUPPORT SVCS
72650	218	1332	EDUCATIONAL SERVICES
72651	72	522	REPAIR AND MAINTENANCE
72653	1617	14010	MERCH. WHOLESALERS;NONDUR. GDS
72654	13	33	AMUSEMENT; GAMBLING;& RECREAT.
72655	15	78	EDUCATIONAL SERVICES
72658	66	349	EDUCATIONAL SERVICES
72660	13	24	ACCOMMODATION
72661	24	33	ACCOMMODATION
72662	101	313	EDUCATIONAL SERVICES
72663	5	10	PROF.; SCIENTIFIC; & TECH SVCS
72666	15	39	FOOD AND BEVERAGE STORES
72668	17	26	ACCOMMODATION
72669	4	45	MERCH. WHOLESALERS;DURABLE GDS
72670	18	32	ACCOMMODATION
72672	43	77	JUSTICE; PUBIC ORDER/SAFETY
72675	54	146	WOOD PRODUCT MANUFACTURING
72677	20	76	JUSTICE; PUBIC ORDER/SAFETY
72679	3	27	SUPPORT ACTIVITIES: AGR./FOR.
72680	30	134	EDUCATIONAL SERVICES
72682	27	453	EDUCATIONAL SERVICES
72683	5	11	UTILITIES
72685	50	181	EDUCATIONAL SERVICES
72686	6	4	POSTAL SERVICE
72687	345	1877	EDUCATIONAL SERVICES
72701	1809	25579	EDUCATIONAL SERVICES
72702	25	34	PROF.; SCIENTIFIC; & TECH SVCS
72703	1974	23197	HOSPITALS
72704	456	5031	MOTOR VEHICLE & PARTS DEALERS
72711	6	38	HEAVY & CIVIL ENG. CONSTRUCT'N
72712	2333	26595	GENERAL MERCHANDISE STORES
72714	266	1577	RELIG.; GRANT; CIVIC; PROF ORG
72715	154	883	AMUSEMENT; GAMBLING;& RECREAT.
72716	2	10000	GENERAL MERCHANDISE STORES
72717	14	13	CROP PRODUCTION
72718	50	101	JUSTICE; PUBIC ORDER/SAFETY
72719	110	624	EDUCATIONAL SERVICES
72721	7	38	WOOD PRODUCT MANUFACTURING
72722	81	2817	ANIMAL PRODUCTION
72727	81	407	EDUCATIONAL SERVICES
72728	30	828	TRUCK TRANSPORTATION
72729	6	3	SUPPORT ACT. FOR TRANSPORT.
72730	219	1509	EDUCATIONAL SERVICES
72732	114	276	EDUCATIONAL SERVICES
72733	7	11	SPECIAL TRADE CONTRACTORS
72734	260	2751	FOOD MANUFACTURING
72735	5	16	HEAVY & CIVIL ENG. CONSTRUCT'N
72736	188	1192	EDUCATIONAL SERVICES
72737	15	157	EDUCATIONAL SERVICES
72738	47	194	MERCH. WHOLESALERS;NONDUR. GDS
72739	29	243	SPECIAL TRADE CONTRACTORS
72740	378	2700	FOOD MANUFACTURING
72741	4	81	AMBULATORY HEALTH CARE SVCS
72742	34	151	EDUCATIONAL SERVICES
72744	189	1065	MISCELLANEOUS STORE RETAILERS
72745	393	4398	TRUCK TRANSPORTATION
72747	13	17	ADMINISTRATIVE & SUPPORT SVCS
72749	12	36	RELIG.; GRANT; CIVIC; PROF ORG
72751	161	723	EDUCATIONAL SERVICES
72752	7	13	PROF.; SCIENTIFIC; & TECH SVCS
72753	238	1272	EDUCATIONAL SERVICES
72756	1786	21645	FOOD MANUFACTURING
72757	14	14	PROF.; SCIENTIFIC; & TECH SVCS
72758	858	10023	EDUCATIONAL SERVICES
72760	19	192	EDUCATIONAL SERVICES
72761	862	8973	MERCH. WHOLESALERS;DURABLE GDS
72762	1251	17923	AMBULATORY HEALTH CARE SVCS
72764	1971	26299	FOOD MANUFACTURING
72765	9	13	SOCIAL ASSISTANCE
72766	11	32	FURN. & HOME FURNISHGS STORES
72768	42	87	MINING (EXCEPT OIL AND GAS)
72769	13	114	CROP PRODUCTION
72770	30	519	TRUCK TRANSPORTATION
72773	12	54	MISCELLANEOUS STORE RETAILERS
72774	120	450	EDUCATIONAL SERVICES
72776	6	21	TEXTILE PRODUCT MILLS
72801	1210	11381	EDUCATIONAL SERVICES
72802	773	10602	FOOD MANUFACTURING
72811	8	19	SOCIAL ASSISTANCE
72812	6	31	CONSTRUCTION OF BUILDINGS
72820	1	1	SPECIAL TRADE CONTRACTORS
72821	51	234	BEVERAGE & TOBACCO PRODUCT MFG
72823	188	1769	EDUCATIONAL SERVICES
72824	39	109	EDUCATIONAL SERVICES
72826	5	4	EXEC.; LEGIS.; & OTHER SUPPORT
72827	4	1	TRUCK TRANSPORTATION
72828	9	40	EDUCATIONAL SERVICES
72829	17	100	MISCELLANEOUS STORE RETAILERS
72830	753	8937	FOOD MANUFACTURING
72832	25	79	EDUCATIONAL SERVICES
72833	228	1700	EDUCATIONAL SERVICES
72834	282	3027	FOOD MANUFACTURING
72835	10	23	FOOD AND BEVERAGE STORES
72837	158	800	EDUCATIONAL SERVICES
72838	6	7	AMUSEMENT; GAMBLING;& RECREAT.
72839	4	0	HEAVY & CIVIL ENG. CONSTRUCT'N
72840	30	106	EDUCATIONAL SERVICES
72841	3	24	PERSONAL AND LAUNDRY SERVICES
72842	38	161	EDUCATIONAL SERVICES
72843	39	332	EDUCATIONAL SERVICES
72845	44	510	TRANSPORTATION EQUIPMENT MFG
72846	73	357	EDUCATIONAL SERVICES
72847	46	145	EDUCATIONAL SERVICES
72851	9	83	MERCH. WHOLESALERS;DURABLE GDS
72852	8	51	EDUCATIONAL SERVICES
72853	70	546	EDUCATIONAL SERVICES
72854	17	23	WOOD PRODUCT MANUFACTURING
72855	348	2805	MACHINERY MANUFACTURING
72856	16	17	MISCELLANEOUS STORE RETAILERS
72857	74	281	CONSTRUCTION OF BUILDINGS
72858	68	364	EDUCATIONAL SERVICES
72860	15	55	MISCELLANEOUS STORE RETAILERS
72863	49	425	FOOD MANUFACTURING
72865	33	409	MACHINERY MANUFACTURING
72901	2070	27760	AMBULATORY HEALTH CARE SVCS
72902	14	86	AMBULATORY HEALTH CARE SVCS
72903	1474	22317	FOOD SVCS & DRINKING PLACES
72904	478	12034	MERCH. WHOLESALERS;NONDUR. GDS
72905	18	1128	NAT'L SECURITY & INT'L AFFAIRS
72906	7	109	WOOD PRODUCT MANUFACTURING
72908	478	13516	ELECT'L EQPMT; APP; & COMP MFG
72913	11	17	SPECIAL TRADE CONTRACTORS
72914	3	7	SPECIAL TRADE CONTRACTORS
72916	253	4136	MERCH. WHOLESALERS;DURABLE GDS
72917	17	33	REPAIR AND MAINTENANCE
72918	3	9	CONSTRUCTION OF BUILDINGS
72919	7	730	NURSING & RESID. CARE FACILIT.
72921	340	3002	FOOD SVCS & DRINKING PLACES
72923	167	1681	SPECIAL TRADE CONTRACTORS
72926	17	37	GASOLINE STATIONS
72927	279	2612	FOOD MANUFACTURING
72928	21	229	EDUCATIONAL SERVICES
72930	10	42	SOCIAL ASSISTANCE
72932	37	367	EDUCATIONAL SERVICES
72933	162	983	NURSING & RESID. CARE FACILIT.
72934	11	38	SOCIAL ASSISTANCE
72935	6	16	EXEC.; LEGIS.; & OTHER SUPPORT
72936	373	2494	EDUCATIONAL SERVICES
72937	56	255	EDUCATIONAL SERVICES
72938	35	208	EDUCATIONAL SERVICES
72940	46	106	SOCIAL ASSISTANCE
72941	78	429	EDUCATIONAL SERVICES
72943	46	271	EDUCATIONAL SERVICES
72944	100	592	WOOD PRODUCT MANUFACTURING
72945	12	39	CHEMICAL MANUFACTURING
72946	74	331	EDUCATIONAL SERVICES
72947	109	632	EDUCATIONAL SERVICES
72948	11	31	MERCH. WHOLESALERS;NONDUR. GDS
72949	390	3648	MERCH. WHOLESALERS;NONDUR. GDS
72950	8	14	MUSEUMS; HIST. SITES;& SIMILAR
72951	50	175	AMBULATORY HEALTH CARE SVCS
72952	32	86	SPECIAL TRADE CONTRACTORS
72955	5	4	POSTAL SERVICE
72956	1236	13363	FOOD MANUFACTURING
72957	10	46	PRIMARY METAL MANUFACTURING
72958	328	2746	FOOD MANUFACTURING
72959	45	138	JUSTICE; PUBIC ORDER/SAFETY
73001	4	24	JUSTICE; PUBIC ORDER/SAFETY
73002	30	204	EDUCATIONAL SERVICES
73003	734	4029	FOOD SVCS & DRINKING PLACES
73004	27	181	EDUCATIONAL SERVICES
73005	431	3527	EDUCATIONAL SERVICES
73006	132	718	EDUCATIONAL SERVICES
73007	82	355	RELIG.; GRANT; CIVIC; PROF ORG
73008	798	6104	EDUCATIONAL SERVICES
73009	68	501	EDUCATIONAL SERVICES
73010	335	2118	EDUCATIONAL SERVICES
73011	14	26	CONSTRUCTION OF BUILDINGS
73012	230	1096	EDUCATIONAL SERVICES
73013	1677	14524	FOOD SVCS & DRINKING PLACES
73014	55	319	FOOD SVCS & DRINKING PLACES
73015	183	1128	REAL ESTATE
73016	44	325	EDUCATIONAL SERVICES
73017	56	278	EDUCATIONAL SERVICES
73018	1189	11746	FOOD SVCS & DRINKING PLACES
73019	41	1438	EDUCATIONAL SERVICES
73020	427	2509	EDUCATIONAL SERVICES
73021	17	50	MUSEUMS; HIST. SITES;& SIMILAR
73022	20	406	EDUCATIONAL SERVICES
73023	7	11	SPECIAL TRADE CONTRACTORS
73024	24	252	NURSING & RESID. CARE FACILIT.
73025	159	756	EDUCATIONAL SERVICES
73026	204	1594	EDUCATIONAL SERVICES
73027	30	107	EDUCATIONAL SERVICES
73028	158	713	EDUCATIONAL SERVICES
73029	74	322	EDUCATIONAL SERVICES
73030	223	1494	MACHINERY MANUFACTURING
73031	39	84	EDUCATIONAL SERVICES
73032	10	22	JUSTICE; PUBIC ORDER/SAFETY
73033	38	98	BLDG MATL & GARDEN EQPMT DLRS
73034	1811	16145	EDUCATIONAL SERVICES
73036	816	8625	EDUCATIONAL SERVICES
73038	74	314	EDUCATIONAL SERVICES
73040	100	345	EDUCATIONAL SERVICES
73041	12	31	JUSTICE; PUBIC ORDER/SAFETY
73042	26	113	EDUCATIONAL SERVICES
73043	6	13	WAREHOUSING AND STORAGE
73044	882	5407	EDUCATIONAL SERVICES
73045	273	1807	EDUCATIONAL SERVICES
73047	189	1072	SPECIAL TRADE CONTRACTORS
73048	97	463	EDUCATIONAL SERVICES
73049	136	842	EDUCATIONAL SERVICES
73050	25	973	EXEC.; LEGIS.; & OTHER SUPPORT
73051	132	1528	EXEC.; LEGIS.; & OTHER SUPPORT
73052	320	2707	SPECIAL TRADE CONTRACTORS
73053	37	187	EDUCATIONAL SERVICES
73054	91	306	EDUCATIONAL SERVICES
73055	331	2423	EDUCATIONAL SERVICES
73056	19	65	MERCH. WHOLESALERS;NONDUR. GDS
73057	76	526	EDUCATIONAL SERVICES
73058	12	6	SUPPORT ACTIVITIES: AGR./FOR.
73059	93	421	EDUCATIONAL SERVICES
73061	50	302	EDUCATIONAL SERVICES
73062	54	205	EDUCATIONAL SERVICES
73063	19	52	EDUCATIONAL SERVICES
73064	584	3949	EDUCATIONAL SERVICES
73065	399	2816	AMUSEMENT; GAMBLING;& RECREAT.
73066	48	234	EDUCATIONAL SERVICES
73067	36	278	SPECIAL TRADE CONTRACTORS
73068	331	1777	EDUCATIONAL SERVICES
73069	2222	28793	SUPPORT ACTIVITIES FOR MINING
73070	45	117	CONSTRUCTION OF BUILDINGS
73071	824	18212	HOSPITALS
73072	1157	11023	FOOD SVCS & DRINKING PLACES
73073	14	138	EDUCATIONAL SERVICES
73074	26	114	EDUCATIONAL SERVICES
73075	491	4711	EXEC.; LEGIS.; & OTHER SUPPORT
73077	320	3360	TRANSPORTATION EQUIPMENT MFG
73078	253	6063	DATA PROCESS'G
73079	14	101	SPECIAL TRADE CONTRACTORS
73080	473	2564	FOOD SVCS & DRINKING PLACES
73082	101	546	EDUCATIONAL SERVICES
73083	77	164	ADMINISTRATIVE & SUPPORT SVCS
73084	143	1006	HOSPITALS
73085	21	54	SPECIAL TRADE CONTRACTORS
73086	474	3355	NURSING & RESID. CARE FACILIT.
73089	289	1763	ANIMAL PRODUCTION
73090	35	220	EDUCATIONAL SERVICES
73092	45	188	EDUCATIONAL SERVICES
73093	88	760	EDUCATIONAL SERVICES
73095	48	307	EDUCATIONAL SERVICES
73096	611	5242	FOOD SVCS & DRINKING PLACES
73097	41	80	MERCH. WHOLESALERS;DURABLE GDS
73098	113	812	UNCLASSIFIED ESTABLISHMENTS
73099	1399	12386	MERCH. WHOLESALERS;DURABLE GDS
73101	28	35	RELIG.; GRANT; CIVIC; PROF ORG
73102	1609	34548	HOSPITALS
73103	443	5628	AMBULATORY HEALTH CARE SVCS
73104	530	22049	AMBULATORY HEALTH CARE SVCS
73105	787	18094	EXEC.; LEGIS.; & OTHER SUPPORT
73106	838	8680	INSURANCE CARRIERS & RELATED
73107	1271	15723	INSURANCE CARRIERS & RELATED
73108	951	15604	COURIERS AND MESSENGERS
73109	1149	9614	HOSPITALS
73110	1218	17011	EDUCATIONAL SERVICES
73111	479	7593	ADMIN. OF ECONOMIC PROGRAMS
73112	2460	31522	HOSPITALS
73113	16	73	SPECIAL TRADE CONTRACTORS
73114	834	12973	PROF.; SCIENTIFIC; & TECH SVCS
73115	620	6022	MISCELLANEOUS STORE RETAILERS

BUSINESS DATA

ZIP CODE	2009 Total Firms	2009 Total Employees	TOP INDUSTRY RANKED on 2009 EMPLOYMENT	ZIP CODE	2009 Total Firms	2009 Total Employees	TOP INDUSTRY RANKED on 2009 EMPLOYMENT	ZIP CODE	2009 Total Firms	2009 Total Employees	TOP INDUSTRY RANKED on 2009 EMPLOYMENT
73116	1902	15941	PROF.; SCIENTIFIC; & TECH SVCS	73502	23	97	EXEC.; LEGIS.; & OTHER SUPPORT	73717	421	2918	EDUCATIONAL SERVICES
73117	322	7339	ADMIN. HUMAN RESOURCE PROGRAMS	73503	92	2745	HOSPITALS	73718	35	175	MERCH. WHOLESALERS;NONDUR. GDS
73118	1524	21621	OIL AND GAS EXTRACTION	73505	1253	17953	EDUCATIONAL SERVICES	73719	10	15	WAREHOUSING AND STORAGE
73119	858	6945	HOSPITALS	73506	13	41	FABRICATED METAL PRODUCT MFG	73720	8	21	GASOLINE STATIONS
73120	1469	17174	HOSPITALS	73507	470	3091	EDUCATIONAL SERVICES	73722	28	133	EDUCATIONAL SERVICES
73121	152	2181	MERCH. WHOLESALERS;DURABLE GDS	73520	6	13	UNCLASSIFIED ESTABLISHMENTS	73724	107	447	EDUCATIONAL SERVICES
73122	423	2644	EDUCATIONAL SERVICES	73521	895	9596	FOOD MANUFACTURING	73726	36	153	SECURITIES/COMMODITY CONTRACTS
73123	25	89	ADMINISTRATIVE & SUPPORT SVCS	73522	6	91	EDUCATIONAL SERVICES	73727	8	31	MERCH. WHOLESALERS;DURABLE GDS
73125	4	53	PROF.; SCIENTIFIC; & TECH SVCS	73523	13	4725	NAT'L SECURITY & INT'L AFFAIRS	73728	142	840	EXEC.; LEGIS.; & OTHER SUPPORT
73126	2	2	PERFORM'G ARTS; SPEC. SPORTS	73526	56	192	EDUCATIONAL SERVICES	73729	34	56	SPECIAL TRADE CONTRACTORS
73127	1312	17075	MERCH. WHOLESALERS;DURABLE GDS	73527	90	558	EDUCATIONAL SERVICES	73730	35	222	EDUCATIONAL SERVICES
73128	507	7720	TRUCK TRANSPORTATION	73528	32	156	EDUCATIONAL SERVICES	73731	18	23	WAREHOUSING AND STORAGE
73129	1076	12121	MERCH. WHOLESALERS;DURABLE GDS	73529	150	893	EDUCATIONAL SERVICES	73733	13	46	EXEC.; LEGIS.; & OTHER SUPPORT
73130	498	3378	FOOD SVCS & DRINKING PLACES	73530	22	116	EDUCATIONAL SERVICES	73734	44	237	EDUCATIONAL SERVICES
73131	159	3137	PLASTICS & RUBBER PRODUCTS MFG	73531	7	11	SUPPORT ACT. FOR TRANSPORT.	73735	21	114	EDUCATIONAL SERVICES
73132	1128	10962	INSURANCE CARRIERS & RELATED	73532	27	369	NONMETALLIC MINERAL PROD. MFG	73736	6	14	POSTAL SERVICE
73134	591	11064	FOOD SVCS & DRINKING PLACES	73533	1278	11776	SPECIAL TRADE CONTRACTORS	73737	259	1520	SPECIAL TRADE CONTRACTORS
73135	323	6523	MERCH. WHOLESALERS;DURABLE GDS	73534	17	52	AMUSEMENT; GAMBLING;& RECREAT.	73738	54	323	EDUCATIONAL SERVICES
73136	2	0	PROF.; SCIENTIFIC; & TECH SVCS	73537	27	78	EDUCATIONAL SERVICES	73739	21	58	JUSTICE; PUBIC ORDER/SAFETY
73137	7	12	CONSTRUCTION OF BUILDINGS	73538	163	763	EDUCATIONAL SERVICES	73741	65	367	ADMINISTRATIVE & SUPPORT SVCS
73139	890	7709	FOOD SVCS & DRINKING PLACES	73539	6	19	RELIG.; GRANT; CIVIC; PROF ORG	73742	234	1602	SPECIAL TRADE CONTRACTORS
73140	23	40	SPECIAL TRADE CONTRACTORS	73540	9	8	RELIG.; GRANT; CIVIC; PROF ORG	73743	6	16	EDUCATIONAL SERVICES
73141	229	2053	GENERAL MERCHANDISE STORES	73541	57	357	NONMETALLIC MINERAL PROD. MFG	73744	8	26	JUSTICE; PUBIC ORDER/SAFETY
73142	251	2375	SOCIAL ASSISTANCE	73542	278	1270	EDUCATIONAL SERVICES	73746	11	15	CREDIT INTERMEDIATION & RELATD
73143	13	38	MOTOR VEHICLE & PARTS DEALERS	73543	17	169	EDUCATIONAL SERVICES	73747	10	17	MERCH. WHOLESALERS;NONDUR. GDS
73144	11	8	ADMINISTRATIVE & SUPPORT SVCS	73544	14	28	CREDIT INTERMEDIATION & RELATD	73749	44	120	EDUCATIONAL SERVICES
73145	46	22802	TRANSPORTATION EQUIPMENT MFG	73546	55	178	EDUCATIONAL SERVICES	73750	487	4331	TELECOMMUNICATIONS
73146	8	28	SOCIAL ASSISTANCE	73547	48	444	JUSTICE; PUBIC ORDER/SAFETY	73753	22	233	MERCH. WHOLESALERS;NONDUR. GDS
73147	15	16	MERCH. WHOLESALERS;DURABLE GDS	73548	12	139	TRUCK TRANSPORTATION	73754	41	273	EDUCATIONAL SERVICES
73148	4	56	SPECIAL TRADE CONTRACTORS	73549	8	5	SPECIAL TRADE CONTRACTORS	73755	35	90	TRUCK TRANSPORTATION
73149	525	7983	MOTOR VEHICLE & PARTS DEALERS	73550	141	982	EDUCATIONAL SERVICES	73756	28	47	EDUCATIONAL SERVICES
73150	124	719	NAT'L SECURITY & INT'L AFFAIRS	73551	2	10	WAREHOUSING AND STORAGE	73757	5	26	JUSTICE; PUBIC ORDER/SAFETY
73151	11	15	GENERAL MERCHANDISE STORES	73552	23	317	SOCIAL ASSISTANCE	73758	19	58	JUSTICE; PUBIC ORDER/SAFETY
73152	3	7	ADMIN. OF ECONOMIC PROGRAMS	73554	178	1001	EDUCATIONAL SERVICES	73759	123	773	EDUCATIONAL SERVICES
73153	26	98	CLOTHING & CLOTH'G ACC. STORES	73555	10	152	JUSTICE; PUBIC ORDER/SAFETY	73760	29	130	WASTE MANAGMT & REMEDIAT'N SVC
73154	19	41	SPECIAL TRADE CONTRACTORS	73556	6	14	EXEC.; LEGIS.; & OTHER SUPPORT	73761	24	76	JUSTICE; PUBIC ORDER/SAFETY
73155	9	8	ADMINISTRATIVE & SUPPORT SVCS	73557	22	75	FOOD SVCS & DRINKING PLACES	73762	107	1023	MACHINERY MANUFACTURING
73156	29	51	MERCH. WHOLESALERS;NONDUR. GDS	73559	16	58	EDUCATIONAL SERVICES	73763	164	902	EDUCATIONAL SERVICES
73157	26	138	PRINT'G & RELATED SUPP'T ACT'S	73560	16	109	RELIG.; GRANT; CIVIC; PROF ORG	73764	8	97	EDUCATIONAL SERVICES
73159	789	10091	SUPPORT ACT. FOR TRANSPORT.	73562	21	140	EDUCATIONAL SERVICES	73766	67	341	EDUCATIONAL SERVICES
73160	1726	15431	ADMINISTRATIVE & SUPPORT SVCS	73564	23	50	MERCH. WHOLESALERS;DURABLE GDS	73768	58	554	SPECIAL TRADE CONTRACTORS
73162	525	3323	FOOD SVCS & DRINKING PLACES	73565	48	302	EDUCATIONAL SERVICES	73770	10	1943	PROF.; SCIENTIFIC; & TECH SVCS
73165	108	801	SPECIAL TRADE CONTRACTORS	73566	83	326	NURSING & RESID. CARE FACILIT.	73771	34	183	EXEC.; LEGIS.; & OTHER SUPPORT
73169	71	5736	ADMIN. OF ECONOMIC PROGRAMS	73567	24	176	EDUCATIONAL SERVICES	73772	295	1834	ADMINISTRATIVE & SUPPORT SVCS
73170	592	3815	EDUCATIONAL SERVICES	73568	58	239	EDUCATIONAL SERVICES	73773	49	362	EDUCATIONAL SERVICES
73172	34	91	ADMINISTRATIVE & SUPPORT SVCS	73569	29	87	MERCH. WHOLESALERS;DURABLE GDS	73801	1002	9911	SPECIAL TRADE CONTRACTORS
73173	76	989	SPECIAL TRADE CONTRACTORS	73570	39	251	EDUCATIONAL SERVICES	73802	6	25	HEAVY & CIVIL ENG. CONSTRUCT'N
73178	1	0	CONSTRUCTION OF BUILDINGS	73571	3	1	POSTAL SERVICE	73832	116	383	EXEC.; LEGIS.; & OTHER SUPPORT
73179	280	9190	MISCELLANEOUS STORE RETAILERS	73572	154	835	AMBULATORY HEALTH CARE SVCS	73834	124	753	EDUCATIONAL SERVICES
73189	39	66	REAL ESTATE	73573	133	676	EDUCATIONAL SERVICES	73835	16	49	JUSTICE; PUBIC ORDER/SAFETY
73190	4	5	MERCH. WHOLESALERS;DURABLE GDS	73601	591	6181	FOOD MANUFACTURING	73838	17	12	RELIG.; GRANT; CIVIC; PROF ORG
73194	1	1500	EXEC.; LEGIS.; & OTHER SUPPORT	73620	45	236	JUSTICE; PUBIC ORDER/SAFETY	73840	29	85	EDUCATIONAL SERVICES
73195	4	1	RENTAL AND LEASING SERVICES	73622	10	63	MERCH. WHOLESALERS;DURABLE GDS	73841	31	563	JUSTICE; PUBIC ORDER/SAFETY
73198	1	0	ADMINISTRATIVE & SUPPORT SVCS	73624	60	726	SPECIAL TRADE CONTRACTORS	73842	56	199	EDUCATIONAL SERVICES
73401	1775	20368	PLASTICS & RUBBER PRODUCTS MFG	73625	16	117	EDUCATIONAL SERVICES	73843	41	137	EDUCATIONAL SERVICES
73402	10	27	RELIG.; GRANT; CIVIC; PROF ORG	73626	38	222	EDUCATIONAL SERVICES	73844	24	122	MACHINERY MANUFACTURING
73403	4	4	ELECTRONICS & APPLIANCE STORES	73627	20	45	JUSTICE; PUBIC ORDER/SAFETY	73848	162	640	EDUCATIONAL SERVICES
73425	7	159	SPECIAL TRADE CONTRACTORS	73628	149	685	EDUCATIONAL SERVICES	73851	11	29	SPECIAL TRADE CONTRACTORS
73430	21	263	EDUCATIONAL SERVICES	73632	209	1201	EDUCATIONAL SERVICES	73852	103	730	EDUCATIONAL SERVICES
73432	23	594	MOTOR VEHICLE & PARTS DEALERS	73638	11	56	EXEC.; LEGIS.; & OTHER SUPPORT	73853	19	124	EDUCATIONAL SERVICES
73433	72	471	EDUCATIONAL SERVICES	73639	40	101	EDUCATIONAL SERVICES	73855	4	3	SUPPORT ACTIVITIES: AGR./FOR.
73434	8	10	SPECIAL TRADE CONTRACTORS	73641	19	39	EXEC.; LEGIS.; & OTHER SUPPORT	73857	25	56	EDUCATIONAL SERVICES
73435	15	160	EDUCATIONAL SERVICES	73642	14	31	ANIMAL PRODUCTION	73858	132	717	SPECIAL TRADE CONTRACTORS
73436	10	21	JUSTICE; PUBIC ORDER/SAFETY	73644	850	7318	SPECIAL TRADE CONTRACTORS	73859	113	583	EDUCATIONAL SERVICES
73437	4	4	POSTAL SERVICE	73645	84	352	EDUCATIONAL SERVICES	73860	118	675	EDUCATIONAL SERVICES
73438	152	1020	SPECIAL TRADE CONTRACTORS	73646	9	8	POSTAL SERVICE	73901	9	17	UTILITIES
73439	275	1289	EDUCATIONAL SERVICES	73647	27	129	RENTAL AND LEASING SERVICES	73931	26	98	SPECIAL TRADE CONTRACTORS
73440	7	11	TRUCK TRANSPORTATION	73648	11	56	MERCH. WHOLESALERS;NONDUR. GDS	73932	223	1028	SPECIAL TRADE CONTRACTORS
73441	2	1	POSTAL SERVICE	73650	35	220	EDUCATIONAL SERVICES	73933	179	713	EDUCATIONAL SERVICES
73442	12	29	OIL AND GAS EXTRACTION	73651	227	1802	HOSPITALS	73937	20	56	EDUCATIONAL SERVICES
73443	151	655	EDUCATIONAL SERVICES	73654	70	224	EDUCATIONAL SERVICES	73938	39	139	EDUCATIONAL SERVICES
73444	9	12	FOOD AND BEVERAGE STORES	73655	40	179	ACCOMMODATION	73939	54	240	EDUCATIONAL SERVICES
73446	369	4947	MERCH. WHOLESALERS;DURABLE GDS	73658	20	54	JUSTICE; PUBIC ORDER/SAFETY	73942	950	7871	MERCH. WHOLESALERS;NONDUR. GDS
73447	19	57	EDUCATIONAL SERVICES	73659	11	20	JUSTICE; PUBIC ORDER/SAFETY	73944	29	82	EDUCATIONAL SERVICES
73448	239	1481	EDUCATIONAL SERVICES	73660	34	145	EDUCATIONAL SERVICES	73945	119	772	EDUCATIONAL SERVICES
73449	41	274	WASTE MANAGMT & REMEDIAT'N SVC	73661	21	61	WAREHOUSING AND STORAGE	73946	13	8	ACCOMMODATION
73450	20	120	EDUCATIONAL SERVICES	73662	213	1567	JUSTICE; PUBIC ORDER/SAFETY	73947	36	112	ANIMAL PRODUCTION
73453	9	12	MERCH. WHOLESALERS;DURABLE GDS	73663	127	594	SPECIAL TRADE CONTRACTORS	73949	102	708	CROP PRODUCTION
73455	12	56	FOOD MANUFACTURING	73664	55	248	EDUCATIONAL SERVICES	73950	61	365	EDUCATIONAL SERVICES
73456	93	346	EDUCATIONAL SERVICES	73666	21	212	SPECIAL TRADE CONTRACTORS	73951	26	99	EDUCATIONAL SERVICES
73458	14	438	FABRICATED METAL PRODUCT MFG	73667	74	218	JUSTICE; PUBIC ORDER/SAFETY	74001	21	45	EDUCATIONAL SERVICES
73459	29	1358	AMUSEMENT; GAMBLING;& RECREAT.	73668	5	10	FOOD SVCS & DRINKING PLACES	74002	90	637	MERCH. WHOLESALERS;NONDUR. GDS
73460	270	2254	AMBULATORY HEALTH CARE SVCS	73669	88	673	MACHINERY MANUFACTURING	74003	759	7005	PROF.; SCIENTIFIC; & TECH SVCS
73461	22	79	EDUCATIONAL SERVICES	73673	18	40	UNCLASSIFIED ESTABLISHMENTS	74004	2	913	PROF.; SCIENTIFIC; & TECH SVCS
73463	112	767	EDUCATIONAL SERVICES	73701	1363	14130	HOSPITALS	74005	2	1	SPECIAL TRADE CONTRACTORS
73481	77	501	SPECIAL TRADE CONTRACTORS	73702	11	42	EXEC.; LEGIS.; & OTHER SUPPORT	74006	1008	9630	SOCIAL ASSISTANCE
73487	7	13	OIL AND GAS EXTRACTION	73703	1058	9438	FOOD SVCS & DRINKING PLACES	74008	708	4991	EDUCATIONAL SERVICES
73488	3	7	OIL AND GAS EXTRACTION	73705	12	141	PROF.; SCIENTIFIC; & TECH SVCS	74010	372	2156	EDUCATIONAL SERVICES
73491	112	737	EDUCATIONAL SERVICES	73706	1	0	UNCLASSIFIED ESTABLISHMENTS	74011	392	3189	PROF.; SCIENTIFIC; & TECH SVCS
73501	1505	14329	EXEC.; LEGIS.; & OTHER SUPPORT	73716	26	106	EDUCATIONAL SERVICES	74012	2212	23526	EDUCATIONAL SERVICES

ZIP CODE	2009 Total Firms	2009 Total Employees	TOP INDUSTRY RANKED on 2009 EMPLOYMENT	ZIP CODE	2009 Total Firms	2009 Total Employees	TOP INDUSTRY RANKED on 2009 EMPLOYMENT	ZIP CODE	2009 Total Firms	2009 Total Employees	TOP INDUSTRY RANKED on 2009 EMPLOYMENT
74013	23	39	ADMINISTRATIVE & SUPPORT SVCS	74136	1748	32650	AMBULATORY HEALTH CARE SVCS	74464	1257	12632	EDUCATIONAL SERVICES
74014	417	2679	MACHINERY MANUFACTURING	74137	794	7056	FOOD SVCS & DRINKING PLACES	74465	24	107	EXEC.; LEGIS.; & OTHER SUPPORT
74015	440	6098	MERCH. WHOLESALERS;DURABLE GDS	74145	1940	19827	ADMINISTRATIVE & SUPPORT SVCS	74467	572	3800	MERCH. WHOLESALERS;DURABLE GDS
74016	152	854	EDUCATIONAL SERVICES	74146	1573	20606	ADMINISTRATIVE & SUPPORT SVCS	74468	6	47	EDUCATIONAL SERVICES
74017	1212	28981	RENTAL AND LEASING SERVICES	74147	19	75	SPECIAL TRADE CONTRACTORS	74469	103	794	EDUCATIONAL SERVICES
74018	17	40	ADMINISTRATIVE & SUPPORT SVCS	74148	2	2	ADMINISTRATIVE & SUPPORT SVCS	74470	50	293	EDUCATIONAL SERVICES
74019	273	2505	MERCH. WHOLESALERS;DURABLE GDS	74149	4	22	SPECIAL TRADE CONTRACTORS	74471	24	119	EDUCATIONAL SERVICES
74020	267	1510	FOOD SVCS & DRINKING PLACES	74150	11	16	ADMINISTRATIVE & SUPPORT SVCS	74472	21	84	EDUCATIONAL SERVICES
74021	389	1771	EDUCATIONAL SERVICES	74152	25	97	EDUCATIONAL SERVICES	74477	2	1	SPECIAL TRADE CONTRACTORS
74022	38	173	EDUCATIONAL SERVICES	74153	16	42	TRUCK TRANSPORTATION	74501	1437	14378	FOOD SVCS & DRINKING PLACES
74023	521	3849	FOOD SVCS & DRINKING PLACES	74155	14	971	PERSONAL AND LAUNDRY SERVICES	74502	11	72	ADMINISTRATIVE & SUPPORT SVCS
74026	53	314	EDUCATIONAL SERVICES	74157	11	15	SPECIAL TRADE CONTRACTORS	74521	11	46	EDUCATIONAL SERVICES
74027	15	60	SPECIAL TRADE CONTRACTORS	74158	9	10	TRUCK TRANSPORTATION	74522	12	127	SPECIAL TRADE CONTRACTORS
74028	44	235	EDUCATIONAL SERVICES	74159	21	102	ELECTRONICS & APPLIANCE STORES	74523	364	2290	EDUCATIONAL SERVICES
74029	226	1718	MERCH. WHOLESALERS;NONDUR. GDS	74169	14	64	ADMINISTRATIVE & SUPPORT SVCS	74525	442	3233	MERCH. WHOLESALERS;DURABLE GDS
74030	221	1566	EDUCATIONAL SERVICES	74170	30	50	ADMINISTRATIVE & SUPPORT SVCS	74528	2	3	POSTAL SERVICE
74031	14	120	EDUCATIONAL SERVICES	74171	8	1067	EDUCATIONAL SERVICES	74529	2	1	GASOLINE STATIONS
74032	33	197	EDUCATIONAL SERVICES	74172	33	4156	PIPELINE TRANSPORTATION	74530	3	3	RELIG.; GRANT; CIVIC; PROF ORG
74033	206	1364	EDUCATIONAL SERVICES	74301	533	4790	NURSING & RESID. CARE FACILIT.	74531	30	114	EDUCATIONAL SERVICES
74034	7	15	GASOLINE STATIONS	74330	77	547	EDUCATIONAL SERVICES	74533	21	170	EDUCATIONAL SERVICES
74035	144	990	JUSTICE; PUBIC ORDER/SAFETY	74331	236	1363	ACCOMMODATION	74534	3	22	MISCELLANEOUS STORE RETAILERS
74036	176	927	EDUCATIONAL SERVICES	74332	45	367	GASOLINE STATIONS	74535	12	24	MERCH. WHOLESALERS;NONDUR. GDS
74037	507	4037	AMUSEMENT; GAMBLING;& RECREAT.	74333	32	164	EDUCATIONAL SERVICES	74536	116	502	EDUCATIONAL SERVICES
74038	35	129	PERFORM'G ARTS; SPEC. SPORTS	74335	3	3	MERCH. WHOLESALERS;DURABLE GDS	74538	191	1496	EDUCATIONAL SERVICES
74039	64	242	SPECIAL TRADE CONTRACTORS	74337	189	1668	UTILITIES	74540	3	2	SPECIAL TRADE CONTRACTORS
74041	68	510	EDUCATIONAL SERVICES	74338	127	775	EDUCATIONAL SERVICES	74543	6	7	RELIG.; GRANT; CIVIC; PROF ORG
74042	14	25	EXEC.; LEGIS.; & OTHER SUPPORT	74339	94	453	EDUCATIONAL SERVICES	74545	5	6	ADMINISTRATIVE & SUPPORT SVCS
74043	8	29	MERCH. WHOLESALERS;NONDUR. GDS	74340	51	139	PERFORM'G ARTS; SPEC. SPORTS	74546	23	279	EDUCATIONAL SERVICES
74044	216	1468	EDUCATIONAL SERVICES	74342	21	83	JUSTICE; PUBIC ORDER/SAFETY	74547	110	803	EDUCATIONAL SERVICES
74045	7	26	JUSTICE; PUBIC ORDER/SAFETY	74343	112	524	EDUCATIONAL SERVICES	74549	4	2	FOOD SVCS & DRINKING PLACES
74046	2	16	EDUCATIONAL SERVICES	74344	902	5222	FOOD SVCS & DRINKING PLACES	74552	30	142	PIPELINE TRANSPORTATION
74047	122	878	EDUCATIONAL SERVICES	74345	13	15	SPECIAL TRADE CONTRACTORS	74553	44	170	EDUCATIONAL SERVICES
74048	250	1914	EDUCATIONAL SERVICES	74346	296	2277	EXEC.; LEGIS.; & OTHER SUPPORT	74554	81	598	SPECIAL TRADE CONTRACTORS
74050	1	2	POSTAL SERVICE	74347	106	620	EDUCATIONAL SERVICES	74555	14	141	EDUCATIONAL SERVICES
74051	67	603	TRUCK TRANSPORTATION	74349	97	333	EDUCATIONAL SERVICES	74556	6	11	PROF.; SCIENTIFIC; & TECH SVCS
74052	48	348	EDUCATIONAL SERVICES	74350	105	492	FOOD SVCS & DRINKING PLACES	74557	7	64	EDUCATIONAL SERVICES
74053	121	686	EDUCATIONAL SERVICES	74352	189	1235	SPECIAL TRADE CONTRACTORS	74558	16	64	EDUCATIONAL SERVICES
74054	8	32	OIL AND GAS EXTRACTION	74354	836	9317	AMUSEMENT; GAMBLING;& RECREAT.	74559	6	156	EDUCATIONAL SERVICES
74055	1101	10630	FOOD SVCS & DRINKING PLACES	74355	1	1	ADMINISTRATIVE & SUPPORT SVCS	74560	14	120	EDUCATIONAL SERVICES
74056	434	2233	EXEC.; LEGIS.; & OTHER SUPPORT	74358	13	92	REPAIR AND MAINTENANCE	74561	83	355	AMBULATORY HEALTH CARE SVCS
74058	217	1327	EDUCATIONAL SERVICES	74359	17	169	EDUCATIONAL SERVICES	74562	32	174	EDUCATIONAL SERVICES
74059	172	1238	EDUCATIONAL SERVICES	74360	34	256	EDUCATIONAL SERVICES	74563	47	333	SPECIAL TRADE CONTRACTORS
74060	19	229	EDUCATIONAL SERVICES	74361	779	9519	MOTOR VEHICLE & PARTS DEALERS	74565	26	309	EDUCATIONAL SERVICES
74061	38	255	EDUCATIONAL SERVICES	74362	10	36	WASTE MANAGMT & REMEDIAT'N SVC	74567	4	7	MISCELLANEOUS STORE RETAILERS
74062	19	202	EDUCATIONAL SERVICES	74363	53	603	EDUCATIONAL SERVICES	74569	34	569	JUSTICE; PUBIC ORDER/SAFETY
74063	940	11117	PRIMARY METAL MANUFACTURING	74364	30	142	ANIMAL PRODUCTION	74570	25	223	EDUCATIONAL SERVICES
74066	1087	11139	SOCIAL ASSISTANCE	74365	149	824	EDUCATIONAL SERVICES	74571	177	1924	HOSPITALS
74067	14	60	ADMINISTRATIVE & SUPPORT SVCS	74366	32	209	ANIMAL PRODUCTION	74572	20	145	EDUCATIONAL SERVICES
74068	3	4	JUSTICE; PUBIC ORDER/SAFETY	74367	9	29	JUSTICE; PUBIC ORDER/SAFETY	74574	15	91	EXEC.; LEGIS.; & OTHER SUPPORT
74070	404	2127	EDUCATIONAL SERVICES	74368	6	39	EDUCATIONAL SERVICES	74576	1	2	POSTAL SERVICE
74071	5	13	FOOD AND BEVERAGE STORES	74369	69	396	EDUCATIONAL SERVICES	74577	8	123	EDUCATIONAL SERVICES
74072	49	660	EDUCATIONAL SERVICES	74370	103	701	AMUSEMENT; GAMBLING;& RECREAT.	74578	319	3262	EDUCATIONAL SERVICES
74073	124	618	EDUCATIONAL SERVICES	74401	1320	15497	HOSPITALS	74601	1230	14972	PETROLEUM & COAL PRODUCTS MFG
74074	1422	12425	EXEC.; LEGIS.; & OTHER SUPPORT	74402	12	12	PROF.; SCIENTIFIC; & TECH SVCS	74602	11	44	SOCIAL ASSISTANCE
74075	630	8296	FOOD SVCS & DRINKING PLACES	74403	1035	11019	BLDG MATL & GARDEN EQPMT DLRS	74604	259	1419	NURSING & RESID. CARE FACILIT.
74076	23	158	ADMINISTRATIVE & SUPPORT SVCS	74421	141	893	EDUCATIONAL SERVICES	74630	39	220	FABRICATED METAL PRODUCT MFG
74077	2	26	EDUCATIONAL SERVICES	74422	13	62	EDUCATIONAL SERVICES	74631	337	2560	EDUCATIONAL SERVICES
74078	194	10962	EDUCATIONAL SERVICES	74423	25	100	JUSTICE; PUBIC ORDER/SAFETY	74632	27	207	FOOD SVCS & DRINKING PLACES
74079	249	2367	MERCH. WHOLESALERS;DURABLE GDS	74425	28	344	SOCIAL ASSISTANCE	74633	17	55	OIL AND GAS EXTRACTION
74080	61	421	COMPUTER & ELECTRONIC PROD MFG	74426	336	2218	FOOD SVCS & DRINKING PLACES	74636	9	46	EDUCATIONAL SERVICES
74081	16	88	FABRICATED METAL PRODUCT MFG	74427	62	182	FOOD SVCS & DRINKING PLACES	74637	82	491	EDUCATIONAL SERVICES
74082	3	3	RELIG.; GRANT; CIVIC; PROF ORG	74428	20	99	EDUCATIONAL SERVICES	74640	15	54	JUSTICE; PUBIC ORDER/SAFETY
74083	22	114	HEAVY & CIVIL ENG. CONSTRUCT'N	74429	404	2345	EDUCATIONAL SERVICES	74641	25	176	UNCLASSIFIED ESTABLISHMENTS
74084	32	132	EDUCATIONAL SERVICES	74430	31	247	EDUCATIONAL SERVICES	74643	33	161	EDUCATIONAL SERVICES
74085	71	398	FABRICATED METAL PRODUCT MFG	74431	20	168	EDUCATIONAL SERVICES	74644	10	12	ANIMAL PRODUCTION
74101	19	122	PERSONAL AND LAUNDRY SERVICES	74432	513	2887	AMBULATORY HEALTH CARE SVCS	74646	2	4	WAREHOUSING AND STORAGE
74103	973	16727	PROF.; SCIENTIFIC; & TECH SVCS	74434	230	1717	ADMINISTRATIVE & SUPPORT SVCS	74647	163	1401	AMUSEMENT; GAMBLING;& RECREAT.
74104	878	20553	HOSPITALS	74435	122	704	ACCOMMODATION	74650	19	75	EDUCATIONAL SERVICES
74105	1523	8648	FOOD SVCS & DRINKING PLACES	74436	135	708	EDUCATIONAL SERVICES	74651	17	383	EDUCATIONAL SERVICES
74106	390	3673	EDUCATIONAL SERVICES	74437	412	2907	NONMETALLIC MINERAL PROD. MFG	74652	46	232	EDUCATIONAL SERVICES
74107	844	14126	MACHINERY MANUFACTURING	74438	9	43	JUSTICE; PUBIC ORDER/SAFETY	74653	157	1195	EDUCATIONAL SERVICES
74108	144	1787	NONMETALLIC MINERAL PROD. MFG	74441	89	1220	BLDG MATL & GARDEN EQPMT DLRS	74701	1341	14215	EDUCATIONAL SERVICES
74110	428	5049	MERCH. WHOLESALERS;DURABLE GDS	74442	23	118	EDUCATIONAL SERVICES	74702	5	16	GASOLINE STATIONS
74112	970	12612	PUBLISHING INDUSTRIES	74444	4	11	FOOD AND BEVERAGE STORES	74720	16	248	EDUCATIONAL SERVICES
74114	671	6210	EDUCATIONAL SERVICES	74445	83	485	EDUCATIONAL SERVICES	74721	3	3	SOCIAL ASSISTANCE
74115	959	11766	RENTAL AND LEASING SERVICES	74446	22	96	RELIG.; GRANT; CIVIC; PROF ORG	74722	22	163	EDUCATIONAL SERVICES
74116	617	16277	TRANSPORTATION EQUIPMENT MFG	74447	814	6959	EDUCATIONAL SERVICES	74723	34	207	EDUCATIONAL SERVICES
74117	58	6274	TELECOMMUNICATIONS	74450	17	90	EDUCATIONAL SERVICES	74724	5	5	FOOD AND BEVERAGE STORES
74119	734	13956	INSURANCE CARRIERS & RELATED	74451	94	1169	MERCH. WHOLESALERS;NONDUR. GDS	74726	46	227	EDUCATIONAL SERVICES
74120	647	8846	JUSTICE; PUBIC ORDER/SAFETY	74452	18	108	EDUCATIONAL SERVICES	74727	57	381	EDUCATIONAL SERVICES
74126	181	844	EDUCATIONAL SERVICES	74454	67	406	EDUCATIONAL SERVICES	74728	495	5098	FOOD MANUFACTURING
74127	428	5805	HOSPITALS	74455	55	229	EDUCATIONAL SERVICES	74729	77	260	EDUCATIONAL SERVICES
74128	401	4847	ADMINISTRATIVE & SUPPORT SVCS	74456	8	166	EDUCATIONAL SERVICES	74730	107	761	EDUCATIONAL SERVICES
74129	619	5070	MOTOR VEHICLE & PARTS DEALERS	74457	4	6	POSTAL SERVICE	74731	34	69	FOOD SVCS & DRINKING PLACES
74130	29	253	EDUCATIONAL SERVICES	74458	2	3	EXEC.; LEGIS.; & OTHER SUPPORT	74733	83	410	EDUCATIONAL SERVICES
74131	200	3268	FABRICATED METAL PRODUCT MFG	74459	2	3	EXEC.; LEGIS.; & OTHER SUPPORT	74734	22	131	EDUCATIONAL SERVICES
74132	224	2865	SUPPORT ACT. FOR TRANSPORT.	74460	16	112	EDUCATIONAL SERVICES	74735	39	376	SPECIAL TRADE CONTRACTORS
74133	2171	27572	FOOD SVCS & DRINKING PLACES	74461	1	23	EDUCATIONAL SERVICES	74736	16	43	JUSTICE; PUBIC ORDER/SAFETY
74134	220	5475	CREDIT INTERMEDIATION & RELATD	74462	359	2709	AMBULATORY HEALTH CARE SVCS	74737	6	9	FOOD AND BEVERAGE STORES
74135	1796	20913	RENTAL AND LEASING SERVICES	74463	9	172	JUSTICE; PUBIC ORDER/SAFETY	74738	18	415	AMUSEMENT; GAMBLING;& RECREAT.

BUSINESS DATA

ZIP CODE	2009 Total Firms	2009 Total Employ-ees	TOP INDUSTRY RANKED on 2009 EMPLOYMENT	ZIP CODE	2009 Total Firms	2009 Total Employ-ees	TOP INDUSTRY RANKED on 2009 EMPLOYMENT	ZIP CODE	2009 Total Firms	2009 Total Employ-ees	TOP INDUSTRY RANKED on 2009 EMPLOYMENT
74740	39	223	EDUCATIONAL SERVICES	74956	31	181	EDUCATIONAL SERVICES	75103	733	4290	FOOD SVCS & DRINKING PLACES
74741	27	110	MERCH. WHOLESALERS;DURABLE GDS	74957	41	334	EDUCATIONAL SERVICES	75104	1455	10226	FOOD SVCS & DRINKING PLACES
74743	492	4199	SOCIAL ASSISTANCE	74959	171	1158	AMBULATORY HEALTH CARE SVCS	75105	4	22	MERCH. WHOLESALERS;DURABLE GDS
74745	543	4434	EDUCATIONAL SERVICES	74960	418	4105	FOOD MANUFACTURING	75106	36	56	TRANSIT & GRND PASS. TRANSPORT
74747	8	5	SOCIAL ASSISTANCE	74962	142	832	EDUCATIONAL SERVICES	75109	157	2312	NONMETALLIC MINERAL PROD. MFG
74748	7	9	MERCH. WHOLESALERS;NONDUR. GDS	74963	11	30	EDUCATIONAL SERVICES	75110	1334	12040	EDUCATIONAL SERVICES
74750	17	32	JUSTICE; PUBIC ORDER/SAFETY	74964	59	375	EDUCATIONAL SERVICES	75114	155	733	EDUCATIONAL SERVICES
74752	3	3	POSTAL SERVICE	74965	104	1098	ELECT'L EQPMT; APP; & COMP MFG	75115	1787	11701	FOOD SVCS & DRINKING PLACES
74753	3	6	SOCIAL ASSISTANCE	74966	73	520	EDUCATIONAL SERVICES	75116	1147	6480	EDUCATIONAL SERVICES
74754	9	10	RELIG.; GRANT; CIVIC; PROF ORG	75001	3266	38984	PROF.; SCIENTIFIC; & TECH SVCS	75117	148	667	EDUCATIONAL SERVICES
74755	6	14	JUSTICE; PUBIC ORDER/SAFETY	75002	1181	8047	EDUCATIONAL SERVICES	75118	3	1	POSTAL SERVICE
74756	21	171	HEAVY & CIVIL ENG. CONSTRUCT'N	75006	3560	44754	MERCH. WHOLESALERS;DURABLE GDS	75119	906	10754	FABRICATED METAL PRODUCT MFG
74759	28	174	EDUCATIONAL SERVICES	75007	1151	13984	FOOD SVCS & DRINKING PLACES	75120	2	2	RELIG.; GRANT; CIVIC; PROF ORG
74760	1	1	POSTAL SERVICE	75009	297	1719	EDUCATIONAL SERVICES	75121	13	50	MERCH. WHOLESALERS;DURABLE GDS
74761	3	24	EDUCATIONAL SERVICES	75010	422	4775	AMBULATORY HEALTH CARE SVCS	75123	29	74	CONSTRUCTION OF BUILDINGS
74764	196	2243	PAPER MANUFACTURING	75011	48	210	REAL ESTATE	75124	99	536	EDUCATIONAL SERVICES
74766	65	677	WOOD PRODUCT MANUFACTURING	75013	1143	13242	FOOD SVCS & DRINKING PLACES	75125	173	1708	EDUCATIONAL SERVICES
74801	955	7591	EDUCATIONAL SERVICES	75014	8	29	MERCH. WHOLESALERS;DURABLE GDS	75126	806	5039	EDUCATIONAL SERVICES
74802	11	24	ADMINISTRATIVE & SUPPORT SVCS	75015	12	43	PETROLEUM & COAL PRODUCTS MFG	75127	27	262	EDUCATIONAL SERVICES
74804	876	13825	AMUSEMENT; GAMBLING;& RECREAT.	75016	10	25	INSURANCE CARRIERS & RELATED	75132	21	69	MERCH. WHOLESALERS;DURABLE GDS
74818	9	28	SOCIAL ASSISTANCE	75017	7	24	SPECIAL TRADE CONTRACTORS	75134	359	3243	EDUCATIONAL SERVICES
74820	1417	14113	HOSPITALS	75019	1089	16516	PROF.; SCIENTIFIC; & TECH SVCS	75135	191	1000	EDUCATIONAL SERVICES
74821	17	32	TRUCK TRANSPORTATION	75020	1000	12210	SOCIAL ASSISTANCE	75137	577	6250	FURNITURE & RELATED PROD. MFG
74824	28	172	EDUCATIONAL SERVICES	75021	229	1152	SPECIAL TRADE CONTRACTORS	75138	20	26	SPECIAL TRADE CONTRACTORS
74825	73	498	EDUCATIONAL SERVICES	75022	461	3782	FOOD SVCS & DRINKING PLACES	75140	224	1628	NURSING & RESID. CARE FACILIT.
74826	25	160	EDUCATIONAL SERVICES	75023	1455	8066	FOOD SVCS & DRINKING PLACES	75141	210	2553	MACHINERY MANUFACTURING
74827	9	44	HEAVY & CIVIL ENG. CONSTRUCT'N	75024	1260	48204	MISCELLANEOUS MANUFACTURING	75142	602	4397	EDUCATIONAL SERVICES
74829	40	293	JUSTICE; PUBIC ORDER/SAFETY	75025	539	3589	EDUCATIONAL SERVICES	75143	426	2118	EDUCATIONAL SERVICES
74830	15	132	EDUCATIONAL SERVICES	75026	25	87	PROF.; SCIENTIFIC; & TECH SVCS	75144	93	503	EDUCATIONAL SERVICES
74831	22	74	RELIG.; GRANT; CIVIC; PROF ORG	75027	22	77	SPECIAL TRADE CONTRACTORS	75146	680	5704	EDUCATIONAL SERVICES
74832	36	185	EDUCATIONAL SERVICES	75028	1050	10820	EDUCATIONAL SERVICES	75147	267	1738	MACHINERY MANUFACTURING
74833	13	40	JUSTICE; PUBIC ORDER/SAFETY	75029	27	81	CONSTRUCTION OF BUILDINGS	75148	235	1488	EDUCATIONAL SERVICES
74834	371	3322	INSURANCE CARRIERS & RELATED	75030	31	96	SPECIAL TRADE CONTRACTORS	75149	1790	17514	EDUCATIONAL SERVICES
74836	14	33	JUSTICE; PUBIC ORDER/SAFETY	75032	779	5774	EDUCATIONAL SERVICES	75150	2549	23362	FOOD SVCS & DRINKING PLACES
74837	24	134	EDUCATIONAL SERVICES	75034	2970	26858	FOOD SVCS & DRINKING PLACES	75151	7	18	ADMINISTRATIVE & SUPPORT SVCS
74839	26	81	EDUCATIONAL SERVICES	75035	528	3702	EDUCATIONAL SERVICES	75152	86	569	EDUCATIONAL SERVICES
74840	32	211	EDUCATIONAL SERVICES	75038	1255	28938	PROF.; SCIENTIFIC; & TECH SVCS	75153	15	50	CREDIT INTERMEDIATION & RELATD
74842	31	165	EDUCATIONAL SERVICES	75039	1229	28863	HEALTH & PERSONAL CARE STORES	75154	770	4304	EDUCATIONAL SERVICES
74843	5	17	EDUCATIONAL SERVICES	75040	1751	18215	EXEC.; LEGIS.; & OTHER SUPPORT	75155	51	486	EDUCATIONAL SERVICES
74844	10	40	MERCH. WHOLESALERS;NONDUR. GDS	75041	1665	16097	MERCH. WHOLESALERS;DURABLE GDS	75156	552	2892	FOOD SVCS & DRINKING PLACES
74845	22	108	FOOD SVCS & DRINKING PLACES	75042	1610	22762	REPAIR AND MAINTENANCE	75157	12	27	BLDG MATL & GARDEN EQPMT DLRS
74848	335	2053	EDUCATIONAL SERVICES	75043	1322	8793	EDUCATIONAL SERVICES	75158	68	816	ADMINISTRATIVE & SUPPORT SVCS
74849	101	1006	AMBULATORY HEALTH CARE SVCS	75044	630	4552	HOSPITALS	75159	579	4154	MERCH. WHOLESALERS;DURABLE GDS
74850	13	14	AMBULATORY HEALTH CARE SVCS	75045	13	16	REPAIR AND MAINTENANCE	75160	1320	12182	MERCH. WHOLESALERS;DURABLE GDS
74851	232	1569	EDUCATIONAL SERVICES	75046	13	14	PROF.; SCIENTIFIC; & TECH SVCS	75161	123	614	GASOLINE STATIONS
74852	32	101	EDUCATIONAL SERVICES	75047	9	21	PROF.; SCIENTIFIC; & TECH SVCS	75163	50	217	EDUCATIONAL SERVICES
74854	45	177	EDUCATIONAL SERVICES	75048	327	1848	EDUCATIONAL SERVICES	75164	7	14	EXEC.; LEGIS.; & OTHER SUPPORT
74855	114	561	MERCH. WHOLESALERS;DURABLE GDS	75049	13	30	CONSTRUCTION OF BUILDINGS	75165	1424	13971	EDUCATIONAL SERVICES
74856	28	286	MINING (EXCEPT OIL AND GAS)	75050	3469	32210	MERCH. WHOLESALERS;DURABLE GDS	75166	81	259	FOOD SVCS & DRINKING PLACES
74857	120	293	MERCH. WHOLESALERS;DURABLE GDS	75051	1543	14871	TRANSPORTATION EQUIPMENT MFG	75167	126	1196	PROF.; SCIENTIFIC; & TECH SVCS
74859	269	2171	AMUSEMENT; GAMBLING;& RECREAT.	75052	1418	13789	FOOD SVCS & DRINKING PLACES	75168	12	18	BLDG MATL & GARDEN EQPMT DLRS
74860	29	180	EDUCATIONAL SERVICES	75053	21	69	MISCELLANEOUS MANUFACTURING	75169	428	2523	EDUCATIONAL SERVICES
74864	182	963	CREDIT INTERMEDIATION & RELATD	75054	55	166	EDUCATIONAL SERVICES	75172	66	805	TRUCK TRANSPORTATION
74865	38	417	EDUCATIONAL SERVICES	75056	859	7465	PROF.; SCIENTIFIC; & TECH SVCS	75173	109	659	EDUCATIONAL SERVICES
74866	11	36	SPECIAL TRADE CONTRACTORS	75057	1179	15614	MERCH. WHOLESALERS;DURABLE GDS	75180	707	4818	SPECIAL TRADE CONTRACTORS
74867	25	137	EDUCATIONAL SERVICES	75058	84	578	NURSING & RESID. CARE FACILIT.	75181	387	1896	EDUCATIONAL SERVICES
74868	609	4998	EDUCATIONAL SERVICES	75060	1130	8079	EDUCATIONAL SERVICES	75182	251	2452	MERCH. WHOLESALERS;DURABLE GDS
74869	14	15	RELIG.; GRANT; CIVIC; PROF ORG	75061	1926	20183	SPECIAL TRADE CONTRACTORS	75185	18	29	REAL ESTATE
74871	59	374	EDUCATIONAL SERVICES	75062	2165	30464	PROF.; SCIENTIFIC; & TECH SVCS	75187	14	32	PERFORM'G ARTS; SPEC. SPORTS
74872	96	535	EDUCATIONAL SERVICES	75063	1589	31262	PROF.; SCIENTIFIC; & TECH SVCS	75189	557	2523	EDUCATIONAL SERVICES
74873	301	1723	EDUCATIONAL SERVICES	75065	392	2291	FOOD SVCS & DRINKING PLACES	75201	3720	64374	PROF.; SCIENTIFIC; & TECH SVCS
74875	31	64	JUSTICE; PUBIC ORDER/SAFETY	75067	1972	20418	FOOD SVCS & DRINKING PLACES	75202	1225	17584	PROF.; SCIENTIFIC; & TECH SVCS
74878	42	169	EDUCATIONAL SERVICES	75068	471	2566	EDUCATIONAL SERVICES	75203	700	9849	HOSPITALS
74880	65	488	EDUCATIONAL SERVICES	75069	1940	20225	PROF.; SCIENTIFIC; & TECH SVCS	75204	2365	18130	PROF.; SCIENTIFIC; & TECH SVCS
74881	97	607	EDUCATIONAL SERVICES	75070	1444	15462	INSURANCE CARRIERS & RELATED	75205	1666	10411	FOOD SVCS & DRINKING PLACES
74883	96	1057	HEAVY & CIVIL ENG. CONSTRUCT'N	75071	801	9241	TRANSPORTATION EQUIPMENT MFG	75206	3153	22678	FOOD SVCS & DRINKING PLACES
74884	276	2325	EXEC.; LEGIS.; & OTHER SUPPORT	75074	2977	33904	EDUCATIONAL SERVICES	75207	3270	28480	ACCOMMODATION
74901	56	413	EDUCATIONAL SERVICES	75075	2030	34536	EDUCATIONAL SERVICES	75208	1775	10628	EDUCATIONAL SERVICES
74902	152	1898	AMUSEMENT; GAMBLING;& RECREAT.	75076	287	1887	EDUCATIONAL SERVICES	75209	998	8163	MOTOR VEHICLE & PARTS DEALERS
74930	33	156	EDUCATIONAL SERVICES	75077	765	5483	FOOD SVCS & DRINKING PLACES	75210	255	2220	FOOD AND BEVERAGE STORES
74931	5	48	EDUCATIONAL SERVICES	75078	325	1807	EDUCATIONAL SERVICES	75211	1524	14309	COMPUTER & ELECTRONIC PROD MFG
74932	39	320	EDUCATIONAL SERVICES	75080	3369	34240	EDUCATIONAL SERVICES	75212	912	13054	MERCH. WHOLESALERS;DURABLE GDS
74935	7	41	EDUCATIONAL SERVICES	75081	3615	30885	MERCH. WHOLESALERS;DURABLE GDS	75214	1189	6244	RELIG.; GRANT; CIVIC; PROF ORG
74936	15	73	EDUCATIONAL SERVICES	75082	554	16716	SPECIAL TRADE CONTRACTORS	75215	929	9823	EDUCATIONAL SERVICES
74937	158	1075	EDUCATIONAL SERVICES	75083	47	178	TRANSIT & GRND PASS. TRANSPORT	75216	1399	6095	EDUCATIONAL SERVICES
74939	18	262	JUSTICE; PUBIC ORDER/SAFETY	75085	17	30	ELECTRONICS & APPLIANCE STORES	75217	1793	9953	EDUCATIONAL SERVICES
74940	42	305	EDUCATIONAL SERVICES	75086	57	330	REPAIR AND MAINTENANCE	75218	1126	7196	HOSPITALS
74941	82	300	EDUCATIONAL SERVICES	75087	1670	11421	FOOD SVCS & DRINKING PLACES	75219	2636	22194	PROF.; SCIENTIFIC; & TECH SVCS
74942	6	94	EDUCATIONAL SERVICES	75088	1056	8950	EDUCATIONAL SERVICES	75220	3032	27646	FOOD SVCS & DRINKING PLACES
74943	3	2	POSTAL SERVICE	75089	270	1406	EDUCATIONAL SERVICES	75221	18	16	CLOTHING & CLOTH'G ACC. STORES
74944	43	190	EDUCATIONAL SERVICES	75090	1651	19099	LEATHER & ALLIED PRODUCT MFG	75222	35	65	REPAIR AND MAINTENANCE
74945	10	117	MERCH. WHOLESALERS;DURABLE GDS	75091	9	19	ADMINISTRATIVE & SUPPORT SVCS	75223	537	3084	MERCH. WHOLESALERS;DURABLE GDS
74946	20	161	MERCH. WHOLESALERS;NONDUR. GDS	75092	617	6243	HOSPITALS	75224	1018	5521	EDUCATIONAL SERVICES
74947	3	31	EDUCATIONAL SERVICES	75093	2679	30494	FOOD SVCS & DRINKING PLACES	75225	2455	18801	FOOD SVCS & DRINKING PLACES
74948	192	1658	TRUCK TRANSPORTATION	75094	242	1571	EDUCATIONAL SERVICES	75226	941	6233	FOOD SVCS & DRINKING PLACES
74949	7	30	SUPPORT ACTIVITIES: AGR./FOR.	75097	8	20	ADMINISTRATIVE & SUPPORT SVCS	75227	1258	9976	TRUCK TRANSPORTATION
74951	64	275	UTILITIES	75098	779	7885	TRANSPORTATION EQUIPMENT MFG	75228	2020	11991	EDUCATIONAL SERVICES
74953	702	6304	EDUCATIONAL SERVICES	75099	1	0	RELIG.; GRANT; CIVIC; PROF ORG	75229	3089	27709	SUPPORT ACT. FOR TRANSPORT.
74954	168	1881	FABRICATED METAL PRODUCT MFG	75101	15	28	MERCH. WHOLESALERS;NONDUR. GDS	75230	2071	28382	HOSPITALS
74955	605	4980	EDUCATIONAL SERVICES	75102	11	44	TRUCK TRANSPORTATION	75231	2675	30728	PROF.; SCIENTIFIC; & TECH SVCS

ZIP CODE	2009 Total Firms	2009 Total Employees	TOP INDUSTRY RANKED on 2009 EMPLOYMENT	ZIP CODE	2009 Total Firms	2009 Total Employees	TOP INDUSTRY RANKED on 2009 EMPLOYMENT	ZIP CODE	2009 Total Firms	2009 Total Employees	TOP INDUSTRY RANKED on 2009 EMPLOYMENT
75232	610	3541	EDUCATIONAL SERVICES	75438	18	109	EDUCATIONAL SERVICES	75630	93	304	EDUCATIONAL SERVICES
75233	355	2741	EDUCATIONAL SERVICES	75439	20	78	EDUCATIONAL SERVICES	75631	70	753	SPECIAL TRADE CONTRACTORS
75234	2632	37485	PROF.; SCIENTIFIC; & TECH SVCS	75440	319	1581	EDUCATIONAL SERVICES	75633	777	7069	SPECIAL TRADE CONTRACTORS
75235	1510	43124	HOSPITALS	75441	4	11	CREDIT INTERMEDIATION & RELATD	75636	7	15	CHEMICAL MANUFACTURING
75236	349	10251	MERCH. WHOLESALERS;DURABLE GDS	75442	272	1834	EDUCATIONAL SERVICES	75637	4	28	JUSTICE; PUBIC ORDER/SAFETY
75237	907	11760	GENERAL MERCHANDISE STORES	75443	6	3	POSTAL SERVICE	75638	206	1339	EDUCATIONAL SERVICES
75238	2065	15748	MERCH. WHOLESALERS;DURABLE GDS	75444	25	50	RELIG.; GRANT; CIVIC; PROF ORG	75639	64	304	SPECIAL TRADE CONTRACTORS
75240	4118	35144	PROF.; SCIENTIFIC; & TECH SVCS	75446	124	650	EDUCATIONAL SERVICES	75640	72	386	EDUCATIONAL SERVICES
75241	547	5137	TRUCK TRANSPORTATION	75447	13	230	EDUCATIONAL SERVICES	75641	2	0	POSTAL SERVICE
75242	68	698	JUSTICE; PUBIC ORDER/SAFETY	75448	16	32	RELIG.; GRANT; CIVIC; PROF ORG	75642	27	303	EDUCATIONAL SERVICES
75243	3597	31169	TELECOMMUNICATIONS	75449	45	167	EDUCATIONAL SERVICES	75643	30	265	ACCOMMODATION
75244	2558	28024	ADMINISTRATIVE & SUPPORT SVCS	75450	1	3	POSTAL SERVICE	75644	588	4142	EDUCATIONAL SERVICES
75246	326	18262	AMBULATORY HEALTH CARE SVCS	75451	18	72	OIL AND GAS EXTRACTION	75645	133	374	SPECIAL TRADE CONTRACTORS
75247	2298	38415	PROF.; SCIENTIFIC; & TECH SVCS	75452	122	783	EDUCATIONAL SERVICES	75647	422	3105	EDUCATIONAL SERVICES
75248	2441	11696	PROF.; SCIENTIFIC; & TECH SVCS	75453	74	221	EDUCATIONAL SERVICES	75650	166	914	MINING (EXCEPT OIL AND GAS)
75249	92	396	EDUCATIONAL SERVICES	75454	173	1153	PROF.; SCIENTIFIC; & TECH SVCS	75651	67	349	EDUCATIONAL SERVICES
75250	1	1	PROF.; SCIENTIFIC; & TECH SVCS	75455	1217	13184	FOOD MANUFACTURING	75652	579	5997	EDUCATIONAL SERVICES
75251	888	12903	PROF.; SCIENTIFIC; & TECH SVCS	75456	6	9	SPECIAL TRADE CONTRACTORS	75653	4	4	SPECIAL TRADE CONTRACTORS
75252	1771	9742	REAL ESTATE	75457	301	3273	MERCH. WHOLESALERS;DURABLE GDS	75654	363	3129	EDUCATIONAL SERVICES
75253	343	1545	EDUCATIONAL SERVICES	75458	8	40	EDUCATIONAL SERVICES	75656	165	1272	FOOD MANUFACTURING
75254	2365	24324	FOOD SVCS & DRINKING PLACES	75459	100	867	AMBULATORY HEALTH CARE SVCS	75657	403	1856	FOOD SVCS & DRINKING PLACES
75260	3	1502	RELIG.; GRANT; CIVIC; PROF ORG	75460	1584	17891	HOSPITALS	75658	2	3	MUSEUMS; HIST. SITES;& SIMILAR
75261	250	18764	TRUCK TRANSPORTATION	75461	9	15	CONSTRUCTION OF BUILDINGS	75659	7	181	SPECIAL TRADE CONTRACTORS
75265	4	0	FABRICATED METAL PRODUCT MFG	75462	346	2057	GENERAL MERCHANDISE STORES	75660	4	30	ADMINISTRATIVE & SUPPORT SVCS
75266	2	250	DATA PROCESS'G	75468	13	82	EDUCATIONAL SERVICES	75661	74	246	RAIL TRANSPORTATION
75270	97	3112	PROF.; SCIENTIFIC; & TECH SVCS	75469	13	44	EDUCATIONAL SERVICES	75662	1130	13523	SPECIAL TRADE CONTRACTORS
75275	11	2854	EDUCATIONAL SERVICES	75470	5	6	SPECIAL TRADE CONTRACTORS	75663	12	22	SPECIAL TRADE CONTRACTORS
75277	1	0	PROF.; SCIENTIFIC; & TECH SVCS	75471	22	48	RELIG.; GRANT; CIVIC; PROF ORG	75666	4	51	EDUCATIONAL SERVICES
75283	4	4	LESSRS OF NONFIN. INTANG.	75472	85	266	PRIMARY METAL MANUFACTURING	75667	31	191	EDUCATIONAL SERVICES
75286	1	200	SPECIAL TRADE CONTRACTORS	75473	79	424	CONSTRUCTION OF BUILDINGS	75668	94	1945	PRIMARY METAL MANUFACTURING
75287	1143	6458	FOOD SVCS & DRINKING PLACES	75474	383	1843	EDUCATIONAL SERVICES	75669	5	3	SPECIAL TRADE CONTRACTORS
75303	1	0	SPECIAL TRADE CONTRACTORS	75475	4	7	POSTAL SERVICE	75670	1220	12083	EDUCATIONAL SERVICES
75313	2	3	ADMINISTRATIVE & SUPPORT SVCS	75476	19	59	ADMINISTRATIVE & SUPPORT SVCS	75671	11	12	CONSTRUCTION OF BUILDINGS
75315	2	0	SPECIAL TRADE CONTRACTORS	75477	19	122	EDUCATIONAL SERVICES	75672	499	4895	FURNITURE & RELATED PROD. MFG
75336	7	26	SPECIAL TRADE CONTRACTORS	75478	7	51	EDUCATIONAL SERVICES	75680	15	62	UTILITIES
75339	8	22	SPECIAL TRADE CONTRACTORS	75479	52	329	NURSING & RESID. CARE FACILIT.	75681	82	414	EDUCATIONAL SERVICES
75342	3	8	UNCLASSIFIED ESTABLISHMENTS	75480	36	134	REAL ESTATE	75682	38	592	EDUCATIONAL SERVICES
75354	11	12	SPECIAL TRADE CONTRACTORS	75481	13	71	EDUCATIONAL SERVICES	75683	131	680	EDUCATIONAL SERVICES
75355	13	30	ADMINISTRATIVE & SUPPORT SVCS	75482	1149	10974	MERCH. WHOLESALERS;NONDUR. GDS	75684	146	853	EDUCATIONAL SERVICES
75356	6	0	CONSTRUCTION OF BUILDINGS	75483	6	79	CREDIT INTERMEDIATION & RELATD	75685	5	8	MERCH. WHOLESALERS;NONDUR. GDS
75357	8	15	ADMINISTRATIVE & SUPPORT SVCS	75485	6	31	JUSTICE; PUBIC ORDER/SAFETY	75686	446	3178	FOOD MANUFACTURING
75359	8	56	SOCIAL ASSISTANCE	75486	45	469	TRANSPORTATION EQUIPMENT MFG	75687	17	119	EDUCATIONAL SERVICES
75360	13	21	INSURANCE CARRIERS & RELATED	75487	58	131	MERCH. WHOLESALERS;DURABLE GDS	75688	7	369	MERCH. WHOLESALERS;DURABLE GDS
75367	19	54	EDUCATIONAL SERVICES	75488	16	60	MERCH. WHOLESALERS;NONDUR. GDS	75689	18	52	MERCH. WHOLESALERS;DURABLE GDS
75370	34	117	SPECIAL TRADE CONTRACTORS	75489	39	369	EDUCATIONAL SERVICES	75691	126	1154	EDUCATIONAL SERVICES
75371	1	10	PUBLISHING INDUSTRIES	75490	61	426	EDUCATIONAL SERVICES	75692	142	1377	HEAVY & CIVIL ENG. CONSTRUCT'N
75372	16	34	SPECIAL TRADE CONTRACTORS	75491	131	571	EDUCATIONAL SERVICES	75693	207	1777	SPECIAL TRADE CONTRACTORS
75373	1	1	SPECIAL TRADE CONTRACTORS	75492	8	33	FOOD SVCS & DRINKING PLACES	75694	6	16	AMBULATORY HEALTH CARE SVCS
75374	20	79	PERSONAL AND LAUNDRY SERVICES	75493	32	164	EDUCATIONAL SERVICES	75701	2278	50502	AMBULATORY HEALTH CARE SVCS
75376	10	32	COURIERS AND MESSENGERS	75494	432	3016	MERCH. WHOLESALERS;DURABLE GDS	75702	1980	24826	AMBULATORY HEALTH CARE SVCS
75378	4	0	FABRICATED METAL PRODUCT MFG	75495	256	1716	EDUCATIONAL SERVICES	75703	1856	16878	FOOD SVCS & DRINKING PLACES
75379	28	69	ADMINISTRATIVE & SUPPORT SVCS	75496	89	497	PAPER MANUFACTURING	75704	315	2367	MERCH. WHOLESALERS;DURABLE GDS
75380	25	82	TRANSPORTATION EQUIPMENT MFG	75497	103	364	EDUCATIONAL SERVICES	75705	48	624	SPECIAL TRADE CONTRACTORS
75381	18	47	SPECIAL TRADE CONTRACTORS	75501	1572	16440	EDUCATIONAL SERVICES	75706	233	4198	FABRICATED METAL PRODUCT MFG
75382	24	74	ADMINISTRATIVE & SUPPORT SVCS	75503	1426	19060	HOSPITALS	75707	467	9106	MACHINERY MANUFACTURING
75387	1	0	WHOLESALE ELEC. MRKTS & AGENTS	75504	30	303	BLDG MATL & GARDEN EQPMT DLRS	75708	368	5453	HOSPITALS
75390	33	20407	AMBULATORY HEALTH CARE SVCS	75505	6	7	RELIG.; GRANT; CIVIC; PROF ORG	75709	168	2020	PLASTICS & RUBBER PRODUCTS MFG
75397	1	0	PROF.; SCIENTIFIC; & TECH SVCS	75507	3	1	OTHER INFORMATION SERVICES	75710	8	20	PROF.; SCIENTIFIC; & TECH SVCS
75398	2	1500	POSTAL SERVICE	75550	16	141	WOOD PRODUCT MANUFACTURING	75711	23	70	SPECIAL TRADE CONTRACTORS
75401	812	7130	HOSPITALS	75551	544	4673	RELIG.; GRANT; CIVIC; PROF ORG	75712	2	4	NONMETALLIC MINERAL PROD. MFG
75402	796	12994	TELECOMMUNICATIONS	75554	44	265	EDUCATIONAL SERVICES	75713	21	77	ADMINISTRATIVE & SUPPORT SVCS
75403	8	17	ADMINISTRATIVE & SUPPORT SVCS	75555	19	48	CONSTRUCTION OF BUILDINGS	75750	98	859	HEAVY & CIVIL ENG. CONSTRUCT'N
75404	4	105	SPECIAL TRADE CONTRACTORS	75556	28	139	EDUCATIONAL SERVICES	75751	1108	8858	EDUCATIONAL SERVICES
75407	302	1273	EDUCATIONAL SERVICES	75558	28	252	WOOD PRODUCT MANUFACTURING	75752	163	612	ADMINISTRATIVE & SUPPORT SVCS
75409	226	1376	EDUCATIONAL SERVICES	75559	150	908	EDUCATIONAL SERVICES	75754	158	836	BLDG MATL & GARDEN EQPMT DLRS
75410	130	834	EDUCATIONAL SERVICES	75560	21	151	UTILITIES	75755	217	2660	SPORTG GDS;HOBBY;BOOK; & MUSIC
75411	20	24	TRUCK TRANSPORTATION	75561	131	630	EDUCATIONAL SERVICES	75756	118	445	EDUCATIONAL SERVICES
75412	7	11	RELIG.; GRANT; CIVIC; PROF ORG	75562	3	4	FOOD SVCS & DRINKING PLACES	75757	291	1254	EDUCATIONAL SERVICES
75413	6	8	RELIG.; GRANT; CIVIC; PROF ORG	75563	194	1147	EDUCATIONAL SERVICES	75758	219	867	EDUCATIONAL SERVICES
75414	76	436	EDUCATIONAL SERVICES	75564	2	12	SUPPORT ACTIVITIES FOR MINING	75759	8	28	FOOD AND BEVERAGE STORES
75415	4	2	POSTAL SERVICE	75565	4	72	EDUCATIONAL SERVICES	75760	61	332	EDUCATIONAL SERVICES
75416	112	252	FABRICATED METAL PRODUCT MFG	75566	16	15	EXEC.; LEGIS.; & OTHER SUPPORT	75762	312	1914	ACCOMMODATION
75417	78	363	EDUCATIONAL SERVICES	75567	68	391	EDUCATIONAL SERVICES	75763	198	990	EDUCATIONAL SERVICES
75418	563	5032	JUSTICE; PUBIC ORDER/SAFETY	75568	79	407	TRANSPORTATION EQUIPMENT MFG	75764	2	3	FOOD AND BEVERAGE STORES
75420	22	38	MERCH. WHOLESALERS;DURABLE GDS	75569	114	1051	FABRICATED METAL PRODUCT MFG	75765	283	1656	EDUCATIONAL SERVICES
75421	20	63	UTILITIES	75570	374	4075	EXEC.; LEGIS.; & OTHER SUPPORT	75766	956	10796	EDUCATIONAL SERVICES
75422	60	420	EDUCATIONAL SERVICES	75571	69	379	EDUCATIONAL SERVICES	75770	51	273	EDUCATIONAL SERVICES
75423	54	166	EDUCATIONAL SERVICES	75572	100	1683	PAPER MANUFACTURING	75771	607	4859	SOCIAL ASSISTANCE
75424	70	287	EDUCATIONAL SERVICES	75573	33	426	EDUCATIONAL SERVICES	75772	19	27	ANIMAL PRODUCTION
75425	3	4	POSTAL SERVICE	75574	24	217	EDUCATIONAL SERVICES	75773	566	3021	GENERAL MERCHANDISE STORES
75426	272	2118	FABRICATED METAL PRODUCT MFG	75599	2	23	OTHER INFORMATION SERVICES	75778	85	336	EDUCATIONAL SERVICES
75428	394	4066	JUSTICE; PUBIC ORDER/SAFETY	75601	1500	14568	HOSPITALS	75779	14	126	EDUCATIONAL SERVICES
75429	5	6	CONSTRUCTION OF BUILDINGS	75602	672	11940	CHEMICAL MANUFACTURING	75780	33	356	EDUCATIONAL SERVICES
75431	52	420	EDUCATIONAL SERVICES	75603	301	5124	AMBULATORY HEALTH CARE SVCS	75782	22	88	JUSTICE; PUBIC ORDER/SAFETY
75432	168	761	EDUCATIONAL SERVICES	75604	1614	13909	SPECIAL TRADE CONTRACTORS	75783	396	2821	EDUCATIONAL SERVICES
75433	96	426	EDUCATIONAL SERVICES	75605	1215	13183	FOOD SVCS & DRINKING PLACES	75784	11	79	BLDG MATL & GARDEN EQPMT DLRS
75434	2	1	MERCH. WHOLESALERS;NONDUR. GDS	75606	17	8	TRANSIT & GRND PASS. TRANSPORT	75785	309	3876	HOSPITALS
75435	39	104	EDUCATIONAL SERVICES	75607	9	16	UNCLASSIFIED ESTABLISHMENTS	75788	1	2	POSTAL SERVICE
75436	39	159	EDUCATIONAL SERVICES	75608	18	22	PROF.; SCIENTIFIC; & TECH SVCS	75789	203	1649	BLDG MATL & GARDEN EQPMT DLRS
75437	8	20	MISCELLANEOUS STORE RETAILERS	75615	7	11	ADMINISTRATIVE & SUPPORT SVCS	75790	158	1679	ACCOMMODATION

BUSINESS DATA

ZIP CODE	2009 Total Firms	2009 Total Employees	TOP INDUSTRY RANKED on 2009 EMPLOYMENT
75791	443	2940	EDUCATIONAL SERVICES
75792	92	526	EDUCATIONAL SERVICES
75798	2	1	ADMINISTRATIVE & SUPPORT SVCS
75799	1	792	EDUCATIONAL SERVICES
75801	1149	10291	HOSPITALS
75802	6	8	TRANSIT & GRND PASS. TRANSPORT
75803	226	2499	GENERAL MERCHANDISE STORES
75831	251	2068	CONSTRUCTION OF BUILDINGS
75832	12	267	EDUCATIONAL SERVICES
75833	218	1191	EDUCATIONAL SERVICES
75834	2	2	POSTAL SERVICE
75835	628	4465	EDUCATIONAL SERVICES
75838	15	36	PROF.; SCIENTIFIC; & TECH SVCS
75839	105	710	EDUCATIONAL SERVICES
75840	480	3080	FOOD SVCS & DRINKING PLACES
75844	166	1021	FABRICATED METAL PRODUCT MFG
75845	134	699	EDUCATIONAL SERVICES
75846	120	1906	PRIMARY METAL MANUFACTURING
75847	33	275	EDUCATIONAL SERVICES
75848	6	12	SPECIAL TRADE CONTRACTORS
75849	9	204	EDUCATIONAL SERVICES
75850	23	68	PETROLEUM & COAL PRODUCTS MFG
75851	50	777	JUSTICE; PUBIC ORDER/SAFETY
75852	18	784	JUSTICE; PUBIC ORDER/SAFETY
75853	48	120	BLDG MATL & GARDEN EQPMT DLRS
75855	54	462	SPECIAL TRADE CONTRACTORS
75856	14	19	REPAIR AND MAINTENANCE
75858	5	9	HOSPITALS
75859	63	362	MERCH. WHOLESALERS;DURABLE GDS
75860	205	1934	JUSTICE; PUBIC ORDER/SAFETY
75861	42	3177	JUSTICE; PUBIC ORDER/SAFETY
75862	347	1917	EDUCATIONAL SERVICES
75865	3	33	ACCOMMODATION
75901	1711	14979	FOOD SVCS & DRINKING PLACES
75902	7	477	MACHINERY MANUFACTURING
75903	2	0	SPECIAL TRADE CONTRACTORS
75904	1125	15900	FOOD MANUFACTURING
75915	7	17	SPECIAL TRADE CONTRACTORS
75925	121	758	EDUCATIONAL SERVICES
75926	31	163	EDUCATIONAL SERVICES
75928	19	143	WOOD PRODUCT MANUFACTURING
75929	49	219	EDUCATIONAL SERVICES
75930	15	26	SPECIAL TRADE CONTRACTORS
75931	53	694	ACCOMMODATION
75932	56	252	EDUCATIONAL SERVICES
75933	14	20	FOOD AND BEVERAGE STORES
75934	6	1406	MERCH. WHOLESALERS;DURABLE GDS
75935	685	6428	FOOD MANUFACTURING
75936	26	474	EDUCATIONAL SERVICES
75937	26	112	EDUCATIONAL SERVICES
75938	67	350	EDUCATIONAL SERVICES
75939	131	1248	PAPER MANUFACTURING
75941	200	3115	MERCH. WHOLESALERS;DURABLE GDS
75942	2	3	FABRICATED METAL PRODUCT MFG
75943	27	112	EDUCATIONAL SERVICES
75944	30	118	EDUCATIONAL SERVICES
75946	108	590	EDUCATIONAL SERVICES
75948	276	1506	EDUCATIONAL SERVICES
75949	149	843	EDUCATIONAL SERVICES
75951	929	6394	EDUCATIONAL SERVICES
75954	87	551	EDUCATIONAL SERVICES
75956	248	1163	UTILITIES
75958	5	5	MERCH. WHOLESALERS;DURABLE GDS
75959	40	54	ACCOMMODATION
75960	7	10	MERCH. WHOLESALERS;DURABLE GDS
75961	907	11656	FOOD MANUFACTURING
75962	12	1435	EDUCATIONAL SERVICES
75963	11	35	NONMETALLIC MINERAL PROD. MFG
75964	590	5373	WOOD PRODUCT MANUFACTURING
75965	640	6139	FOOD SVCS & DRINKING PLACES
75966	199	1196	EDUCATIONAL SERVICES
75968	66	850	MERCH. WHOLESALERS;DURABLE GDS
75969	57	1713	EDUCATIONAL SERVICES
75972	267	1911	EDUCATIONAL SERVICES
75973	51	278	EDUCATIONAL SERVICES
75974	73	412	EDUCATIONAL SERVICES
75975	139	802	EDUCATIONAL SERVICES
75976	49	186	EDUCATIONAL SERVICES
75977	8	14	PETROLEUM & COAL PRODUCTS MFG
75978	7	385	EDUCATIONAL SERVICES
75979	390	2534	EDUCATIONAL SERVICES
75980	61	263	EDUCATIONAL SERVICES
76001	655	4937	MERCH. WHOLESALERS;DURABLE GDS
76002	199	1348	EDUCATIONAL SERVICES
76003	38	74	PROF.; SCIENTIFIC; & TECH SVCS
76004	25	35	SPECIAL TRADE CONTRACTORS
76005	4	15	TRUCK TRANSPORTATION
76006	805	7583	PROF.; SCIENTIFIC; & TECH SVCS
76007	4	7	SPECIAL TRADE CONTRACTORS
76008	425	2205	EDUCATIONAL SERVICES
76009	484	3839	MERCH. WHOLESALERS;DURABLE GDS
76010	1700	14810	TRANSPORTATION EQUIPMENT MFG
76011	2400	36440	FOOD SVCS & DRINKING PLACES
76012	1100	9783	HOSPITALS
76013	1806	12969	EDUCATIONAL SERVICES
76014	386	4206	EDUCATIONAL SERVICES
76015	1388	13601	FOOD SVCS & DRINKING PLACES
76016	704	4835	EDUCATIONAL SERVICES
76017	1052	12098	FOOD SVCS & DRINKING PLACES
76018	516	6089	FOOD SVCS & DRINKING PLACES
76019	8	8981	TELECOMMUNICATIONS
76020	707	5145	EDUCATIONAL SERVICES
76021	1173	12672	FOOD SVCS & DRINKING PLACES
76022	586	6423	HOSPITALS
76023	182	917	SPECIAL TRADE CONTRACTORS
76028	1805	14507	FOOD SVCS & DRINKING PLACES
76031	442	4768	EXEC.; LEGIS.; & OTHER SUPPORT
76033	1312	13293	SPECIAL TRADE CONTRACTORS
76034	885	7209	EDUCATIONAL SERVICES
76035	86	1057	SPECIAL TRADE CONTRACTORS
76036	510	3397	EDUCATIONAL SERVICES
76039	517	4594	EDUCATIONAL SERVICES
76040	921	11145	FOOD SVCS & DRINKING PLACES
76041	6	20	ADMINISTRATIVE & SUPPORT SVCS
76043	361	3659	UTILITIES
76044	119	1587	MACHINERY MANUFACTURING
76048	1030	7812	NURSING & RESID. CARE FACILIT.
76049	823	4284	SPECIAL TRADE CONTRACTORS
76050	155	1334	EDUCATIONAL SERVICES
76051	2235	28939	FOOD SVCS & DRINKING PLACES
76052	252	2729	PROF.; SCIENTIFIC; & TECH SVCS
76053	1413	9900	CLOTHING & CLOTH'G ACC. STORES
76054	653	5904	FOOD SVCS & DRINKING PLACES
76055	87	506	WASTE MANAGMT & REMEDIAT'N SVC
76058	308	1443	FOOD SVCS & DRINKING PLACES
76059	96	935	EDUCATIONAL SERVICES
76060	505	3170	SPECIAL TRADE CONTRACTORS
76061	10	82	EDUCATIONAL SERVICES
76063	1863	21011	EDUCATIONAL SERVICES
76064	67	546	EDUCATIONAL SERVICES
76065	792	8048	PRIMARY METAL MANUFACTURING
76066	79	586	EDUCATIONAL SERVICES
76067	879	8292	EDUCATIONAL SERVICES
76068	3	4	SPECIAL TRADE CONTRACTORS
76070	11	66	EDUCATIONAL SERVICES
76071	70	749	RELIG.; GRANT; CIVIC; PROF ORG
76073	75	725	EDUCATIONAL SERVICES
76077	16	155	SPECIAL TRADE CONTRACTORS
76078	143	1876	EDUCATIONAL SERVICES
76082	406	2252	EDUCATIONAL SERVICES
76084	108	1129	PROF.; SCIENTIFIC; & TECH SVCS
76085	121	509	SPECIAL TRADE CONTRACTORS
76086	1368	11716	FOOD SVCS & DRINKING PLACES
76087	678	4866	FOOD SVCS & DRINKING PLACES
76088	249	1294	SPECIAL TRADE CONTRACTORS
76092	1505	19170	ADMINISTRATIVE & SUPPORT SVCS
76093	72	376	EDUCATIONAL SERVICES
76094	11	20	SPECIAL TRADE CONTRACTORS
76095	23	47	SPECIAL TRADE CONTRACTORS
76096	22	266	HEALTH & PERSONAL CARE STORES
76097	17	39	ADMINISTRATIVE & SUPPORT SVCS
76098	10	21	SPECIAL TRADE CONTRACTORS
76099	29	89	SPECIAL TRADE CONTRACTORS
76101	19	221	ADMINISTRATIVE & SUPPORT SVCS
76102	2274	46968	PROF.; SCIENTIFIC; & TECH SVCS
76103	476	4483	RELIG.; GRANT; CIVIC; PROF ORG
76104	1346	34252	HOSPITALS
76105	560	4207	EDUCATIONAL SERVICES
76106	932	15434	MERCH. WHOLESALERS;DURABLE GDS
76107	2361	26765	AMBULATORY HEALTH CARE SVCS
76108	729	18104	COMPUTER & ELECTRONIC PROD MFG
76109	886	11778	PROF.; SCIENTIFIC; & TECH SVCS
76110	988	8648	EDUCATIONAL SERVICES
76111	1088	11159	SPECIAL TRADE CONTRACTORS
76112	1166	7137	EDUCATIONAL SERVICES
76113	5	4	SPORTG GDS;HOBBY;BOOK; & MUSIC
76114	683	5515	GENERAL MERCHANDISE STORES
76115	598	5958	EDUCATIONAL SERVICES
76116	2174	16853	FOOD SVCS & DRINKING PLACES
76117	1481	13716	SPECIAL TRADE CONTRACTORS
76118	680	9707	MERCH. WHOLESALERS;DURABLE GDS
76119	1096	13091	EDUCATIONAL SERVICES
76120	329	3962	INSURANCE CARRIERS & RELATED
76121	25	106	FOOD SVCS & DRINKING PLACES
76122	1	4	PROF.; SCIENTIFIC; & TECH SVCS
76123	173	1272	EDUCATIONAL SERVICES
76124	18	35	HEAVY & CIVIL ENG. CONSTRUCT'N
76126	548	4004	SPECIAL TRADE CONTRACTORS
76127	35	685	RELIG.; GRANT; CIVIC; PROF ORG
76129	11	1667	EDUCATIONAL SERVICES
76131	314	9146	RAIL TRANSPORTATION
76132	1068	21137	AMBULATORY HEALTH CARE SVCS
76133	1142	8645	EDUCATIONAL SERVICES
76134	384	48022	MISCELLANEOUS MANUFACTURING
76135	685	6227	FOOD SVCS & DRINKING PLACES
76136	16	337	REAL ESTATE
76137	854	16970	FOOD SVCS & DRINKING PLACES
76140	873	13860	WHOLESALE ELEC. MRKTS & AGENTS
76147	13	38	REAL ESTATE
76148	689	5012	FOOD SVCS & DRINKING PLACES
76155	178	15159	AIR TRANSPORTATION
76161	15	87	PROF.; SCIENTIFIC; & TECH SVCS
76162	7	15	ADMINISTRATIVE & SUPPORT SVCS
76163	14	21	SPECIAL TRADE CONTRACTORS
76164	716	5685	FOOD SVCS & DRINKING PLACES
76177	237	7780	SECURITIES/COMMODITY CONTRACTS
76179	846	9085	EDUCATIONAL SERVICES
76180	1942	21050	FOOD SVCS & DRINKING PLACES
76181	3	13	SPECIAL TRADE CONTRACTORS
76182	22	32	ADMINISTRATIVE & SUPPORT SVCS
76185	17	32	REAL ESTATE
76196	27	995	EXEC.; LEGIS.; & OTHER SUPPORT
76201	1640	16891	HOSPITALS
76202	33	68	ADMINISTRATIVE & SUPPORT SVCS
76203	7	180	FOOD SVCS & DRINKING PLACES
76204	7	54	SOCIAL ASSISTANCE
76205	991	14608	JUSTICE; PUBIC ORDER/SAFETY
76206	6	19	PROF.; SCIENTIFIC; & TECH SVCS
76207	289	6292	MOTOR VEHICLE & PARTS DEALERS
76208	329	4460	PROF.; SCIENTIFIC; & TECH SVCS
76209	408	8934	EDUCATIONAL SERVICES
76210	519	10154	EDUCATIONAL SERVICES
76225	106	577	SPECIAL TRADE CONTRACTORS
76226	327	2008	EDUCATIONAL SERVICES
76227	443	2917	ADMINISTRATIVE & SUPPORT SVCS
76228	27	93	EDUCATIONAL SERVICES
76230	525	3279	SPECIAL TRADE CONTRACTORS
76233	72	470	EDUCATIONAL SERVICES
76234	892	7366	GENERAL MERCHANDISE STORES
76238	13	139	EDUCATIONAL SERVICES
76239	25	69	EDUCATIONAL SERVICES
76240	1307	12914	EDUCATIONAL SERVICES
76241	10	43	PROF.; SCIENTIFIC; & TECH SVCS
76244	22	74	MERCH. WHOLESALERS;NONDUR. GDS
76245	48	274	REPAIR AND MAINTENANCE
76246	3	4	SPECIAL TRADE CONTRACTORS
76247	240	3313	EDUCATIONAL SERVICES
76248	1431	12140	EDUCATIONAL SERVICES
76249	155	868	EDUCATIONAL SERVICES
76250	23	231	EDUCATIONAL SERVICES
76251	48	199	JUSTICE; PUBIC ORDER/SAFETY
76252	205	1403	DATA PROCESS'G
76253	4	67	SPECIAL TRADE CONTRACTORS
76255	258	1438	EDUCATIONAL SERVICES
76258	276	2354	EDUCATIONAL SERVICES
76259	93	1050	SPECIAL TRADE CONTRACTORS
76261	11	18	EDUCATIONAL SERVICES
76262	638	10033	REAL ESTATE
76263	12	16	SUPPORT ACTIVITIES: AGR./FOR.
76264	23	99	EDUCATIONAL SERVICES
76265	62	413	EDUCATIONAL SERVICES
76266	370	3753	GENERAL MERCHANDISE STORES
76267	8	84	EDUCATIONAL SERVICES
76268	12	54	EDUCATIONAL SERVICES
76270	27	63	SPECIAL TRADE CONTRACTORS
76271	54	291	EDUCATIONAL SERVICES
76272	123	1044	TRUCK TRANSPORTATION
76273	291	1811	EDUCATIONAL SERVICES
76301	1445	14896	HOSPITALS
76302	458	5440	PROF.; SCIENTIFIC; & TECH SVCS
76305	170	2107	PRIMARY METAL MANUFACTURING
76306	501	5515	FOOD SVCS & DRINKING PLACES
76307	10	5	RELIG.; GRANT; CIVIC; PROF ORG
76308	1188	13366	FOOD SVCS & DRINKING PLACES
76309	433	3338	EDUCATIONAL SERVICES
76310	477	5183	NONMETALLIC MINERAL PROD. MFG
76311	74	721	MOTOR VEHICLE & PARTS DEALERS
76351	121	896	EDUCATIONAL SERVICES
76352	6	20	UTILITIES
76354	319	2128	EDUCATIONAL SERVICES
76357	15	69	EDUCATIONAL SERVICES
76360	153	1158	MERCH. WHOLESALERS;DURABLE GDS
76363	9	29	EDUCATIONAL SERVICES
76364	7	41	EDUCATIONAL SERVICES
76365	214	1281	MOTOR VEHICLE & PARTS DEALERS
76366	69	353	EDUCATIONAL SERVICES
76367	282	3144	EXEC.; LEGIS.; & OTHER SUPPORT
76369	14	42	EDUCATIONAL SERVICES
76370	17	78	MERCH. WHOLESALERS;DURABLE GDS
76371	99	472	EDUCATIONAL SERVICES

ZIP CODE	2009 Total Firms	2009 Total Employ-ees	TOP INDUSTRY RANKED on 2009 EMPLOYMENT	ZIP CODE	2009 Total Firms	2009 Total Employ-ees	TOP INDUSTRY RANKED on 2009 EMPLOYMENT	ZIP CODE	2009 Total Firms	2009 Total Employ-ees	TOP INDUSTRY RANKED on 2009 EMPLOYMENT
76372	36	149	EDUCATIONAL SERVICES	76543	879	9685	FOOD SVCS & DRINKING PLACES	76707	289	3378	NAT'L SECURITY & INT'L AFFAIRS
76373	6	5	CHEMICAL MANUFACTURING	76544	214	5374	HOSPITALS	76708	505	7439	SOCIAL ASSISTANCE
76374	220	2270	MERCH. WHOLESALERS;NONDUR. GDS	76547	12	29	SPECIAL TRADE CONTRACTORS	76710	1946	20655	FOOD SVCS & DRINKING PLACES
76377	14	150	EDUCATIONAL SERVICES	76548	605	5371	AMBULATORY HEALTH CARE SVCS	76711	314	4852	HOSPITALS
76379	22	30	FOOD AND BEVERAGE STORES	76549	295	4198	EDUCATIONAL SERVICES	76712	1151	27993	PROF.; SCIENTIFIC; & TECH SVCS
76380	245	1520	AMBULATORY HEALTH CARE SVCS	76550	576	4482	EDUCATIONAL SERVICES	76714	11	13	MOTOR VEHICLE & PARTS DEALERS
76384	607	6284	HOSPITALS	76554	49	276	EDUCATIONAL SERVICES	76715	1	3	HEAVY & CIVIL ENG. CONSTRUCT'N
76388	8	24	SUPPORT ACTIVITIES: AGR./FOR.	76556	40	275	EDUCATIONAL SERVICES	76798	5	2400	EDUCATIONAL SERVICES
76389	66	472	EDUCATIONAL SERVICES	76557	107	529	EDUCATIONAL SERVICES	76801	1136	13656	EDUCATIONAL SERVICES
76401	1338	10874	FOOD SVCS & DRINKING PLACES	76558	2	0	POSTAL SERVICE	76802	257	1716	EDUCATIONAL SERVICES
76402	3	1099	EDUCATIONAL SERVICES	76559	61	469	EDUCATIONAL SERVICES	76803	1	0	REAL ESTATE
76424	540	3585	EXEC.; LEGIS.; & OTHER SUPPORT	76561	14	153	EDUCATIONAL SERVICES	76804	5	10	CONSTRUCTION OF BUILDINGS
76426	578	6726	SPECIAL TRADE CONTRACTORS	76564	3	24	FABRICATED METAL PRODUCT MFG	76820	1	1	POSTAL SERVICE
76427	29	166	EDUCATIONAL SERVICES	76565	11	1	POSTAL SERVICE	76821	273	1777	FABRICATED METAL PRODUCT MFG
76429	7	26	UTILITIES	76566	10	23	MERCH. WHOLESALERS;DURABLE GDS	76823	68	373	EDUCATIONAL SERVICES
76430	197	1152	SPECIAL TRADE CONTRACTORS	76567	396	3593	MERCH. WHOLESALERS;DURABLE GDS	76824	18	24	ACCOMMODATION
76431	111	1415	SUPPORT ACTIVITIES FOR MINING	76569	56	441	EDUCATIONAL SERVICES	76825	401	2794	UNCLASSIFIED ESTABLISHMENTS
76432	26	194	EDUCATIONAL SERVICES	76570	94	364	EDUCATIONAL SERVICES	76827	4	39	EDUCATIONAL SERVICES
76433	40	115	JUSTICE; PUBIC ORDER/SAFETY	76571	307	1289	FOOD SVCS & DRINKING PLACES	76828	16	13	ANIMAL PRODUCTION
76435	21	87	MERCH. WHOLESALERS;NONDUR. GDS	76573	4	17	TRUCK TRANSPORTATION	76831	5	11	RELIG.; GRANT; CIVIC; PROF ORG
76436	10	7	POSTAL SERVICE	76574	731	6723	SPECIAL TRADE CONTRACTORS	76832	37	131	EDUCATIONAL SERVICES
76437	231	1257	SPECIAL TRADE CONTRACTORS	76577	81	289	EDUCATIONAL SERVICES	76834	321	1838	EDUCATIONAL SERVICES
76439	2	1	POSTAL SERVICE	76578	28	186	EDUCATIONAL SERVICES	76836	12	2	SUPPORT ACTIVITIES: AGR./FOR.
76442	387	2394	EDUCATIONAL SERVICES	76579	90	925	PRIMARY METAL MANUFACTURING	76837	91	829	JUSTICE; PUBIC ORDER/SAFETY
76443	103	392	EDUCATIONAL SERVICES	76598	1	330	EXEC.; LEGIS.; & OTHER SUPPORT	76841	4	47	JUSTICE; PUBIC ORDER/SAFETY
76444	219	1286	EDUCATIONAL SERVICES	76599	3	35	RELIG.; GRANT; CIVIC; PROF ORG	76842	6	11	MERCH. WHOLESALERS;NONDUR. GDS
76445	24	38	FOOD SVCS & DRINKING PLACES	76621	25	162	EDUCATIONAL SERVICES	76844	201	1080	RELIG.; GRANT; CIVIC; PROF ORG
76446	291	1674	EDUCATIONAL SERVICES	76622	12	95	EDUCATIONAL SERVICES	76845	7	17	INSURANCE CARRIERS & RELATED
76448	416	2871	PRIMARY METAL MANUFACTURING	76623	17	241	MERCH. WHOLESALERS;NONDUR. GDS	76848	2	3	MERCH. WHOLESALERS;NONDUR. GDS
76449	162	941	ACCOMMODATION	76624	43	282	EDUCATIONAL SERVICES	76849	275	1533	FOOD SVCS & DRINKING PLACES
76450	842	5078	FOOD SVCS & DRINKING PLACES	76626	33	339	EDUCATIONAL SERVICES	76852	15	37	EDUCATIONAL SERVICES
76452	2	31	ANIMAL PRODUCTION	76627	34	152	EDUCATIONAL SERVICES	76853	71	324	EDUCATIONAL SERVICES
76453	42	215	EDUCATIONAL SERVICES	76628	4	5	UTILITIES	76854	10	13	ANIMAL PRODUCTION
76454	83	575	MERCH. WHOLESALERS;NONDUR. GDS	76629	79	517	EDUCATIONAL SERVICES	76855	2	20	FOOD SVCS & DRINKING PLACES
76455	32	162	EDUCATIONAL SERVICES	76630	36	280	MERCH. WHOLESALERS;DURABLE GDS	76856	261	1039	EDUCATIONAL SERVICES
76457	177	703	EDUCATIONAL SERVICES	76631	10	66	EDUCATIONAL SERVICES	76857	26	178	EDUCATIONAL SERVICES
76458	338	2765	SPECIAL TRADE CONTRACTORS	76632	31	201	EDUCATIONAL SERVICES	76858	14	26	MERCH. WHOLESALERS;NONDUR. GDS
76459	4	14	MERCH. WHOLESALERS;DURABLE GDS	76633	121	559	EDUCATIONAL SERVICES	76859	136	520	EDUCATIONAL SERVICES
76460	18	45	TRUCK TRANSPORTATION	76634	326	2166	NURSING & RESID. CARE FACILIT.	76861	39	242	EDUCATIONAL SERVICES
76461	6	96	EDUCATIONAL SERVICES	76635	39	420	PRIMARY METAL MANUFACTURING	76862	9	19	UTILITIES
76462	90	324	AMUSEMENT; GAMBLING;& RECREAT.	76636	29	207	EDUCATIONAL SERVICES	76864	44	84	EDUCATIONAL SERVICES
76463	17	106	FOOD SVCS & DRINKING PLACES	76637	29	101	EDUCATIONAL SERVICES	76865	6	2	MACHINERY MANUFACTURING
76464	19	61	EDUCATIONAL SERVICES	76638	64	389	EDUCATIONAL SERVICES	76866	32	132	EDUCATIONAL SERVICES
76465	7	18	EDUCATIONAL SERVICES	76639	33	248	EDUCATIONAL SERVICES	76869	7	9	ANIMAL PRODUCTION
76466	15	71	GENERAL MERCHANDISE STORES	76640	150	1086	EDUCATIONAL SERVICES	76870	14	50	EDUCATIONAL SERVICES
76467	10	15	ANIMAL PRODUCTION	76641	33	200	EDUCATIONAL SERVICES	76871	48	150	EDUCATIONAL SERVICES
76468	34	63	FOOD AND BEVERAGE STORES	76642	296	2315	EDUCATIONAL SERVICES	76872	36	79	EDUCATIONAL SERVICES
76469	7	14	FOOD AND BEVERAGE STORES	76643	299	2307	INSURANCE CARRIERS & RELATED	76873	4	1	POSTAL SERVICE
76470	139	1700	SPECIAL TRADE CONTRACTORS	76644	1	1	RELIG.; GRANT; CIVIC; PROF ORG	76874	2	3	GASOLINE STATIONS
76471	47	220	EDUCATIONAL SERVICES	76645	679	5523	EDUCATIONAL SERVICES	76875	15	54	EDUCATIONAL SERVICES
76472	57	377	EDUCATIONAL SERVICES	76648	95	438	EDUCATIONAL SERVICES	76877	335	1753	EDUCATIONAL SERVICES
76474	9	39	EDUCATIONAL SERVICES	76649	25	169	ACCOMMODATION	76878	103	358	EDUCATIONAL SERVICES
76475	57	256	EDUCATIONAL SERVICES	76650	4	2	MISCELLANEOUS MANUFACTURING	76880	18	73	JUSTICE; PUBIC ORDER/SAFETY
76476	78	566	SUPPORT ACTIVITIES FOR MINING	76651	93	806	EDUCATIONAL SERVICES	76882	6	10	REAL ESTATE
76481	25	31	NONSTORE RETAILERS	76652	26	165	EDUCATIONAL SERVICES	76883	2	6	ANIMAL PRODUCTION
76483	82	384	EDUCATIONAL SERVICES	76653	38	242	NONMETALLIC MINERAL PROD. MFG	76884	25	96	EDUCATIONAL SERVICES
76484	61	346	JUSTICE; PUBIC ORDER/SAFETY	76654	13	15	UTILITIES	76885	1	2	AMUSEMENT; GAMBLING;& RECREAT.
76485	5	15	JUSTICE; PUBIC ORDER/SAFETY	76655	194	1274	EDUCATIONAL SERVICES	76886	8	73	EDUCATIONAL SERVICES
76486	31	225	EDUCATIONAL SERVICES	76656	52	270	EDUCATIONAL SERVICES	76887	25	145	MERCH. WHOLESALERS;DURABLE GDS
76487	39	185	EDUCATIONAL SERVICES	76657	248	2787	MERCH. WHOLESALERS;DURABLE GDS	76888	4	5	ACCOMMODATION
76490	2	3	RELIG.; GRANT; CIVIC; PROF ORG	76660	25	62	EDUCATIONAL SERVICES	76890	18	114	SPECIAL TRADE CONTRACTORS
76491	18	54	EDUCATIONAL SERVICES	76661	319	2337	JUSTICE; PUBIC ORDER/SAFETY	76901	825	7298	FOOD SVCS & DRINKING PLACES
76501	660	8979	MERCH. WHOLESALERS;DURABLE GDS	76664	107	1241	EXEC.; LEGIS.; & OTHER SUPPORT	76902	5	11	RELIG.; GRANT; CIVIC; PROF ORG
76502	865	9716	FOOD SVCS & DRINKING PLACES	76665	184	1049	EDUCATIONAL SERVICES	76903	1780	20670	FOOD AND BEVERAGE STORES
76503	8	33	SPECIAL TRADE CONTRACTORS	76666	3	2	POSTAL SERVICE	76904	1067	11279	FOOD SVCS & DRINKING PLACES
76504	1277	21304	AMBULATORY HEALTH CARE SVCS	76667	503	5059	EDUCATIONAL SERVICES	76905	159	2577	MISCELLANEOUS MANUFACTURING
76505	10	15	SPECIAL TRADE CONTRACTORS	76670	31	127	EDUCATIONAL SERVICES	76906	10	10	CONSTRUCTION OF BUILDINGS
76508	24	21483	AMBULATORY HEALTH CARE SVCS	76671	39	138	JUSTICE; PUBIC ORDER/SAFETY	76908	23	459	NAT'L SECURITY & INT'L AFFAIRS
76511	65	696	JUSTICE; PUBIC ORDER/SAFETY	76673	14	57	EDUCATIONAL SERVICES	76909	11	185	FOOD AND BEVERAGE STORES
76513	997	10322	EDUCATIONAL SERVICES	76676	6	41	EDUCATIONAL SERVICES	76930	7	26	JUSTICE; PUBIC ORDER/SAFETY
76518	18	146	EDUCATIONAL SERVICES	76678	9	18	GASOLINE STATIONS	76932	177	1597	SPECIAL TRADE CONTRACTORS
76519	9	15	RELIG.; GRANT; CIVIC; PROF ORG	76679	17	37	ADMIN. ENVIRO. QUALITY PROGRMS	76933	59	500	ADMINISTRATIVE & SUPPORT SVCS
76520	344	2677	EDUCATIONAL SERVICES	76680	11	43	UNCLASSIFIED ESTABLISHMENTS	76934	14	722	EDUCATIONAL SERVICES
76522	828	6996	EDUCATIONAL SERVICES	76681	15	46	MINING (EXCEPT OIL AND GAS)	76935	35	250	EDUCATIONAL SERVICES
76523	4	2	FOOD AND BEVERAGE STORES	76682	66	550	EDUCATIONAL SERVICES	76936	137	818	SPECIAL TRADE CONTRACTORS
76524	53	477	EDUCATIONAL SERVICES	76684	4	18	FABRICATED METAL PRODUCT MFG	76937	19	24	SUPPORT ACTIVITIES: AGR./FOR.
76525	54	178	EDUCATIONAL SERVICES	76685	3	2	UTILITIES	76939	2	5	SUPPORT ACTIVITIES FOR MINING
76526	5	1	POSTAL SERVICE	76686	7	24	MINING (EXCEPT OIL AND GAS)	76940	5	15	MACHINERY MANUFACTURING
76527	118	1002	EDUCATIONAL SERVICES	76687	30	92	SPECIAL TRADE CONTRACTORS	76941	76	437	EDUCATIONAL SERVICES
76528	602	4797	GENERAL MERCHANDISE STORES	76689	107	643	EDUCATIONAL SERVICES	76943	247	1463	SPECIAL TRADE CONTRACTORS
76530	63	509	EDUCATIONAL SERVICES	76690	34	309	BLDG MATL & GARDEN EQPMT DLRS	76945	89	374	EDUCATIONAL SERVICES
76531	320	1813	EDUCATIONAL SERVICES	76691	273	1569	EDUCATIONAL SERVICES	76949	4	18	OIL AND GAS EXTRACTION
76533	8	24	SPECIAL TRADE CONTRACTORS	76692	382	2417	EDUCATIONAL SERVICES	76950	300	2305	SPECIAL TRADE CONTRACTORS
76534	59	375	EDUCATIONAL SERVICES	76693	47	359	FABRICATED METAL PRODUCT MFG	76951	75	302	EDUCATIONAL SERVICES
76537	103	820	EDUCATIONAL SERVICES	76701	832	9991	JUSTICE; PUBIC ORDER/SAFETY	76953	1	1	POSTAL SERVICE
76538	29	84	EDUCATIONAL SERVICES	76702	24	849	POSTAL SERVICE	76955	10	34	MERCH. WHOLESALERS;NONDUR. GDS
76539	75	435	MINING (EXCEPT OIL AND GAS)	76703	5	12	CONSTRUCTION OF BUILDINGS	76957	12	187	EDUCATIONAL SERVICES
76540	13	1234	EDUCATIONAL SERVICES	76704	270	3605	HEAVY & CIVIL ENG. CONSTRUCT'N	76958	13	115	EDUCATIONAL SERVICES
76541	1254	9506	PUBLISHING INDUSTRIES	76705	761	11377	TRANSPORTATION EQUIPMENT MFG	77001	21	47	TRANSIT & GRND PASS. TRANSPORT
76542	723	6742	EDUCATIONAL SERVICES	76706	967	9023	FOOD SVCS & DRINKING PLACES	77002	4985	123438	PROF.; SCIENTIFIC; & TECH SVCS

BUSINESS DATA

ZIP CODE	2009 Total Firms	2009 Total Employees	TOP INDUSTRY RANKED on 2009 EMPLOYMENT
77003	688	9479	FOOD MANUFACTURING
77004	1527	13656	EDUCATIONAL SERVICES
77005	1360	12589	EDUCATIONAL SERVICES
77006	1680	11585	FOOD SVCS & DRINKING PLACES
77007	1920	19769	PROF.; SCIENTIFIC; & TECH SVCS
77008	2346	21456	PROF.; SCIENTIFIC; & TECH SVCS
77009	1287	9789	EDUCATIONAL SERVICES
77010	447	12883	PROF.; SCIENTIFIC; & TECH SVCS
77011	832	7717	MERCH. WHOLESALERS;DURABLE GDS
77012	467	6706	RELIG.; GRANT; CIVIC; PROF ORG
77013	463	6373	TRUCK TRANSPORTATION
77014	915	5501	PROF.; SCIENTIFIC; & TECH SVCS
77015	1787	21856	MACHINERY MANUFACTURING
77016	662	3005	EDUCATIONAL SERVICES
77017	1235	11222	EDUCATIONAL SERVICES
77018	1612	14541	SPECIAL TRADE CONTRACTORS
77019	1158	15558	INSURANCE CARRIERS & RELATED
77020	993	13105	MERCH. WHOLESALERS;DURABLE GDS
77021	1117	7829	EDUCATIONAL SERVICES
77022	1377	11628	SPECIAL TRADE CONTRACTORS
77023	995	12432	EDUCATIONAL SERVICES
77024	3451	33379	PROF.; SCIENTIFIC; & TECH SVCS
77025	941	9903	GENERAL MERCHANDISE STORES
77026	717	6570	MERCH. WHOLESALERS;DURABLE GDS
77027	3203	35653	PROF.; SCIENTIFIC; & TECH SVCS
77028	704	7423	MERCH. WHOLESALERS;DURABLE GDS
77029	1313	23737	MERCH. WHOLESALERS;DURABLE GDS
77030	1129	82978	HOSPITALS
77031	507	5713	MERCH. WHOLESALERS;NONDUR. GDS
77032	1505	34995	SPECIAL TRADE CONTRACTORS
77033	591	3254	MERCH. WHOLESALERS;DURABLE GDS
77034	1333	13239	FOOD SVCS & DRINKING PLACES
77035	915	6083	FOOD AND BEVERAGE STORES
77036	4535	25382	PROF.; SCIENTIFIC; & TECH SVCS
77037	1270	9835	MOTOR VEHICLE & PARTS DEALERS
77038	511	4322	MERCH. WHOLESALERS;DURABLE GDS
77039	869	10933	FABRICATED METAL PRODUCT MFG
77040	2396	40679	MERCH. WHOLESALERS;DURABLE GDS
77041	2706	56654	SPECIAL TRADE CONTRACTORS
77042	2883	38937	PROF.; SCIENTIFIC; & TECH SVCS
77043	1672	20549	MERCH. WHOLESALERS;DURABLE GDS
77044	431	3906	PRIMARY METAL MANUFACTURING
77045	783	5767	EDUCATIONAL SERVICES
77046	599	18476	PROF.; SCIENTIFIC; & TECH SVCS
77047	464	4350	SPECIAL TRADE CONTRACTORS
77048	300	3017	MERCH. WHOLESALERS;DURABLE GDS
77049	539	8184	EDUCATIONAL SERVICES
77050	93	730	EDUCATIONAL SERVICES
77051	544	4763	FABRICATED METAL PRODUCT MFG
77052	2	2	PROF.; SCIENTIFIC; & TECH SVCS
77053	325	3220	EDUCATIONAL SERVICES
77054	1528	31396	PERFORM'G ARTS; SPEC. SPORTS
77055	2856	25937	MERCH. WHOLESALERS;DURABLE GDS
77056	3972	70482	PROF.; SCIENTIFIC; & TECH SVCS
77057	4365	30797	PROF.; SCIENTIFIC; & TECH SVCS
77058	1742	28598	PROF.; SCIENTIFIC; & TECH SVCS
77059	179	943	JUSTICE; PUBIC ORDER/SAFETY
77060	2757	23932	PROF.; SCIENTIFIC; & TECH SVCS
77061	846	10158	MERCH. WHOLESALERS;DURABLE GDS
77062	479	3755	FOOD AND BEVERAGE STORES
77063	2462	17672	PROF.; SCIENTIFIC; & TECH SVCS
77064	1083	17846	MERCH. WHOLESALERS;DURABLE GDS
77065	1221	12664	FOOD SVCS & DRINKING PLACES
77066	665	6263	SPECIAL TRADE CONTRACTORS
77067	658	21798	MACHINERY MANUFACTURING
77068	849	6226	ADMINISTRATIVE & SUPPORT SVCS
77069	1191	8017	FOOD SVCS & DRINKING PLACES
77070	2566	22707	FOOD SVCS & DRINKING PLACES
77071	561	3088	REPAIR AND MAINTENANCE
77072	1504	23176	PROF.; SCIENTIFIC; & TECH SVCS
77073	842	14733	SPECIAL TRADE CONTRACTORS
77074	2318	26552	HOSPITALS
77075	820	9683	MERCH. WHOLESALERS;DURABLE GDS
77076	987	7595	EDUCATIONAL SERVICES
77077	2302	26594	PERSONAL AND LAUNDRY SERVICES
77078	200	3313	TRUCK TRANSPORTATION
77079	2313	33336	SUPPORT ACTIVITIES FOR MINING
77080	1348	9091	EDUCATIONAL SERVICES
77081	2277	16709	PROF.; SCIENTIFIC; & TECH SVCS
77082	1321	14708	PROF.; SCIENTIFIC; & TECH SVCS
77083	1193	6945	EDUCATIONAL SERVICES
77084	2803	21696	PROF.; SCIENTIFIC; & TECH SVCS
77085	178	1058	EDUCATIONAL SERVICES
77086	750	11449	SPECIAL TRADE CONTRACTORS
77087	1686	15498	PROF.; SCIENTIFIC; & TECH SVCS
77088	817	4747	EDUCATIONAL SERVICES
77089	808	8924	EDUCATIONAL SERVICES
77090	1631	18403	HOSPITALS
77091	985	8405	FOOD MANUFACTURING
77092	3207	28846	MERCH. WHOLESALERS;DURABLE GDS
77093	1329	8626	EDUCATIONAL SERVICES
77094	294	4237	PROF.; SCIENTIFIC; & TECH SVCS
77095	1276	13346	EDUCATIONAL SERVICES
77096	1005	9722	EDUCATIONAL SERVICES
77098	2463	23321	PROF.; SCIENTIFIC; & TECH SVCS
77099	1440	10480	PROF.; SCIENTIFIC; & TECH SVCS
77201	2	80	POSTAL SERVICE
77204	23	1419	NONSTORE RETAILERS
77205	9	13	REAL ESTATE
77206	6	8	FOOD AND BEVERAGE STORES
77207	12	11	TRUCK TRANSPORTATION
77208	3	2	ADMINISTRATIVE & SUPPORT SVCS
77210	2	1	PERFORM'G ARTS; SPEC. SPORTS
77213	5	9	SPECIAL TRADE CONTRACTORS
77215	9	26	REPAIR AND MAINTENANCE
77218	15	85	REAL ESTATE
77219	16	27	PROF.; SCIENTIFIC; & TECH SVCS
77220	3	9	WHOLESALE ELEC. MRKTS & AGENTS
77221	6	2	PROF.; SCIENTIFIC; & TECH SVCS
77222	10	18	ADMINISTRATIVE & SUPPORT SVCS
77223	3	3	PROF.; SCIENTIFIC; & TECH SVCS
77224	7	30	CONSTRUCTION OF BUILDINGS
77225	3	2	OTHER INFORMATION SERVICES
77226	1	0	RELIG.; GRANT; CIVIC; PROF ORG
77227	19	58	MERCH. WHOLESALERS;DURABLE GDS
77228	1	0	RELIG.; GRANT; CIVIC; PROF ORG
77229	7	8	ADMINISTRATIVE & SUPPORT SVCS
77230	7	8	ACCOMMODATION
77231	9	14	SOCIAL ASSISTANCE
77233	8	4	PROF.; SCIENTIFIC; & TECH SVCS
77234	5	11	ADMINISTRATIVE & SUPPORT SVCS
77235	11	24	SUPPORT ACTIVITIES: AGR./FOR.
77236	4	8	AMUSEMENT; GAMBLING;& RECREAT.
77237	2	5	TRUCK TRANSPORTATION
77238	3	12	OIL AND GAS EXTRACTION
77240	5	7	REPAIR AND MAINTENANCE
77241	5	6	MERCH. WHOLESALERS;DURABLE GDS
77242	29	102	REAL ESTATE
77243	11	65	SPECIAL TRADE CONTRACTORS
77244	14	82	ADMINISTRATIVE & SUPPORT SVCS
77245	9	56	TRUCK TRANSPORTATION
77249	1	4	SPECIAL TRADE CONTRACTORS
77251	15	34	SPECIAL TRADE CONTRACTORS
77252	11	57	AMBULATORY HEALTH CARE SVCS
77253	7	32	REAL ESTATE
77254	9	20	PROF.; SCIENTIFIC; & TECH SVCS
77255	6	7	FURN. & HOME FURNISHGS STORES
77256	6	52	AMBULATORY HEALTH CARE SVCS
77257	25	85	TRANSIT & GRND PASS. TRANSPORT
77258	13	23	PERFORM'G ARTS; SPEC. SPORTS
77259	12	16	PERFORM'G ARTS; SPEC. SPORTS
77261	2	2	FOOD SVCS & DRINKING PLACES
77262	1	0	PROF.; SCIENTIFIC; & TECH SVCS
77263	19	109	OTHER INFORMATION SERVICES
77265	6	6	PERSONAL AND LAUNDRY SERVICES
77266	11	25	PERSONAL AND LAUNDRY SERVICES
77267	17	224	PRINT'G & RELATED SUPP'T ACT'S
77268	25	68	ADMINISTRATIVE & SUPPORT SVCS
77269	31	54	TRUCK TRANSPORTATION
77270	19	59	NONSTORE RETAILERS
77271	17	140	REPAIR AND MAINTENANCE
77272	15	124	NURSING & RESID. CARE FACILIT.
77273	8	32	MERCH. WHOLESALERS;DURABLE GDS
77274	6	11	BLDG MATL & GARDEN EQPMT DLRS
77275	10	32	MERCH. WHOLESALERS;DURABLE GDS
77277	24	29	PROF.; SCIENTIFIC; & TECH SVCS
77279	7	13	SPECIAL TRADE CONTRACTORS
77280	16	27	INSURANCE CARRIERS & RELATED
77282	13	51	ADMINISTRATIVE & SUPPORT SVCS
77284	28	71	ADMINISTRATIVE & SUPPORT SVCS
77287	5	26	SPECIAL TRADE CONTRACTORS
77288	1	25	ADMINISTRATIVE & SUPPORT SVCS
77289	14	80	CONSTRUCTION OF BUILDINGS
77290	7	7	REAL ESTATE
77291	3	4	PROF.; SCIENTIFIC; & TECH SVCS
77292	29	37	PROF.; SCIENTIFIC; & TECH SVCS
77293	11	164	ADMINISTRATIVE & SUPPORT SVCS
77301	1979	17884	EXEC.; LEGIS.; & OTHER SUPPORT
77302	280	1197	EDUCATIONAL SERVICES
77303	440	4962	MERCH. WHOLESALERS;DURABLE GDS
77304	1089	14434	HOSPITALS
77305	43	98	SPECIAL TRADE CONTRACTORS
77306	214	2319	EDUCATIONAL SERVICES
77315	1	3	CREDIT INTERMEDIATION & RELATD
77316	226	1012	EDUCATIONAL SERVICES
77318	281	1789	SPECIAL TRADE CONTRACTORS
77320	562	9401	EXEC.; LEGIS.; & OTHER SUPPORT
77325	32	162	DATA PROCESS'G
77326	3	2	POSTAL SERVICE
77327	708	5919	EDUCATIONAL SERVICES
77328	168	904	MERCH. WHOLESALERS;DURABLE GDS
77331	248	1069	EDUCATIONAL SERVICES
77332	5	78	EDUCATIONAL SERVICES
77333	7	5	FOOD AND BEVERAGE STORES
77334	5	10	HEALTH & PERSONAL CARE STORES
77335	78	254	EDUCATIONAL SERVICES
77336	264	1796	SPECIAL TRADE CONTRACTORS
77338	2072	20361	FOOD SVCS & DRINKING PLACES
77339	1613	12565	FOOD SVCS & DRINKING PLACES
77340	1174	12138	EDUCATIONAL SERVICES
77342	12	16	SPECIAL TRADE CONTRACTORS
77345	287	2054	FOOD AND BEVERAGE STORES
77346	1021	7007	FOOD SVCS & DRINKING PLACES
77347	26	49	SPECIAL TRADE CONTRACTORS
77350	12	119	EDUCATIONAL SERVICES
77351	1194	9326	EXEC.; LEGIS.; & OTHER SUPPORT
77353	9	48	SPECIAL TRADE CONTRACTORS
77354	900	5605	SPECIAL TRADE CONTRACTORS
77355	461	3994	EDUCATIONAL SERVICES
77356	876	4787	FOOD SVCS & DRINKING PLACES
77357	409	4339	EDUCATIONAL SERVICES
77358	113	1403	EDUCATIONAL SERVICES
77359	40	59	CONSTRUCTION OF BUILDINGS
77360	178	826	EDUCATIONAL SERVICES
77362	203	651	FABRICATED METAL PRODUCT MFG
77363	87	3886	AMUSEMENT; GAMBLING;& RECREAT.
77364	36	90	RELIG.; GRANT; CIVIC; PROF ORG
77365	679	4310	GENERAL MERCHANDISE STORES
77367	22	109	FOOD AND BEVERAGE STORES
77368	7	31	JUSTICE; PUBIC ORDER/SAFETY
77369	14	76	JUSTICE; PUBIC ORDER/SAFETY
77371	159	888	EDUCATIONAL SERVICES
77372	209	1380	EDUCATIONAL SERVICES
77373	1131	7851	EDUCATIONAL SERVICES
77374	4	52	SPECIAL TRADE CONTRACTORS
77375	1592	15841	AMBULATORY HEALTH CARE SVCS
77376	3	7	EDUCATIONAL SERVICES
77377	611	4171	EDUCATIONAL SERVICES
77378	358	3477	EDUCATIONAL SERVICES
77379	2049	14457	FOOD SVCS & DRINKING PLACES
77380	2419	31192	FOOD SVCS & DRINKING PLACES
77381	592	10170	PROF.; SCIENTIFIC; & TECH SVCS
77382	408	3553	EDUCATIONAL SERVICES
77383	27	98	CONSTRUCTION OF BUILDINGS
77384	367	4343	FOOD SVCS & DRINKING PLACES
77385	649	7395	FOOD SVCS & DRINKING PLACES
77386	907	4571	REPAIR AND MAINTENANCE
77387	37	93	MISCELLANEOUS STORE RETAILERS
77388	1057	7702	EDUCATIONAL SERVICES
77389	371	1623	EDUCATIONAL SERVICES
77391	19	68	PERFORM'G ARTS; SPEC. SPORTS
77393	22	54	ADMINISTRATIVE & SUPPORT SVCS
77396	732	6275	JUSTICE; PUBIC ORDER/SAFETY
77399	3	156	PROF.; SCIENTIFIC; & TECH SVCS
77401	1176	9173	PROF.; SCIENTIFIC; & TECH SVCS
77402	21	96	MERCH. WHOLESALERS;DURABLE GDS
77404	8	41	MERCH. WHOLESALERS;DURABLE GDS
77406	574	4170	BLDG MATL & GARDEN EQPMT DLRS
77407	160	1354	AMUSEMENT; GAMBLING;& RECREAT.
77410	26	70	ADMINISTRATIVE & SUPPORT SVCS
77411	14	16	ADMINISTRATIVE & SUPPORT SVCS
77412	10	146	EDUCATIONAL SERVICES
77413	42	58	SUPPORT ACT. FOR TRANSPORT.
77414	1034	7399	HOSPITALS
77415	6	5	POSTAL SERVICE
77417	31	519	MERCH. WHOLESALERS;DURABLE GDS
77418	424	2703	EDUCATIONAL SERVICES
77419	51	208	EDUCATIONAL SERVICES
77420	82	626	FOOD AND BEVERAGE STORES
77422	366	1882	EXEC.; LEGIS.; & OTHER SUPPORT
77423	303	3512	MACHINERY MANUFACTURING
77426	50	187	FOOD AND BEVERAGE STORES
77428	1	3	RELIG.; GRANT; CIVIC; PROF ORG
77429	1615	13162	EDUCATIONAL SERVICES
77430	42	184	CROP PRODUCTION
77431	1	0	POSTAL SERVICE
77432	5	6	CROP PRODUCTION
77433	559	4135	EDUCATIONAL SERVICES
77434	201	909	HOSPITALS
77435	149	994	FURNITURE & RELATED PROD. MFG
77436	8	2	POSTAL SERVICE
77437	786	7050	SPECIAL TRADE CONTRACTORS
77440	10	102	EDUCATIONAL SERVICES
77441	138	781	ELECT'L EQPMT; APP; & COMP MFG
77442	45	274	MERCH. WHOLESALERS;DURABLE GDS
77443	17	56	BLDG MATL & GARDEN EQPMT DLRS
77444	14	73	TRUCK TRANSPORTATION
77445	437	3806	MOTOR VEHICLE & PARTS DEALERS
77446	49	827	EDUCATIONAL SERVICES
77447	154	830	UTILITIES

ZIP CODE	2009 Total Firms	2009 Total Employ-ees	TOP INDUSTRY RANKED on 2009 EMPLOYMENT
77448	19	127	SPECIAL TRADE CONTRACTORS
77449	905	9595	EDUCATIONAL SERVICES
77450	1881	11682	FOOD SVCS & DRINKING PLACES
77451	15	55	EDUCATIONAL SERVICES
77452	4	10	MACHINERY MANUFACTURING
77453	4	121	MISCELLANEOUS MANUFACTURING
77454	6	27	AIR TRANSPORTATION
77455	51	645	EDUCATIONAL SERVICES
77456	43	229	HEAVY & CIVIL ENG. CONSTRUCT'N
77457	50	162	FOOD SVCS & DRINKING PLACES
77458	7	32	ADMINISTRATIVE & SUPPORT SVCS
77459	950	7632	EDUCATIONAL SERVICES
77460	7	15	ELECTRONICS & APPLIANCE STORES
77461	224	1328	EDUCATIONAL SERVICES
77463	20	2565	PETROLEUM & COAL PRODUCTS MFG
77464	15	110	EDUCATIONAL SERVICES
77465	236	1379	EDUCATIONAL SERVICES
77466	16	65	FOOD SVCS & DRINKING PLACES
77467	5	75	ADMIN. OF ECONOMIC PROGRAMS
77468	3	3	POSTAL SERVICE
77469	913	12901	EDUCATIONAL SERVICES
77470	5	32	JUSTICE; PUBIC ORDER/SAFETY
77471	1341	12808	EDUCATIONAL SERVICES
77473	18	232	MERCH. WHOLESALERS;DURABLE GDS
77474	489	5455	TRANSPORTATION EQUIPMENT MFG
77475	16	99	UTILITIES
77476	63	162	MERCH. WHOLESALERS;DURABLE GDS
77477	1968	25300	MERCH. WHOLESALERS;DURABLE GDS
77478	1683	35051	CONSTRUCTION OF BUILDINGS
77479	1253	14845	EDUCATIONAL SERVICES
77480	166	1000	EDUCATIONAL SERVICES
77481	14	112	MERCH. WHOLESALERS;NONDUR. GDS
77482	45	300	EDUCATIONAL SERVICES
77483	11	32	CONSTRUCTION OF BUILDINGS
77484	365	2488	EDUCATIONAL SERVICES
77485	76	274	SPECIAL TRADE CONTRACTORS
77486	245	1349	FOOD SVCS & DRINKING PLACES
77487	44	100	SPECIAL TRADE CONTRACTORS
77488	609	4616	EDUCATIONAL SERVICES
77489	599	3408	EDUCATIONAL SERVICES
77491	33	78	TRANSIT & GRND PASS. TRANSPORT
77492	10	11	CONSTRUCTION OF BUILDINGS
77493	671	4275	EDUCATIONAL SERVICES
77494	1129	12514	EDUCATIONAL SERVICES
77496	22	69	ADMINISTRATIVE & SUPPORT SVCS
77497	17	64	ADMINISTRATIVE & SUPPORT SVCS
77498	535	4588	EDUCATIONAL SERVICES
77501	9	357	POSTAL SERVICE
77502	1099	15035	EDUCATIONAL SERVICES
77503	575	7289	SPECIAL TRADE CONTRACTORS
77504	800	9095	HOSPITALS
77505	816	9684	EDUCATIONAL SERVICES
77506	813	11406	CHEMICAL MANUFACTURING
77507	128	6286	CHEMICAL MANUFACTURING
77508	10	22	SPECIAL TRADE CONTRACTORS
77510	354	2298	EDUCATIONAL SERVICES
77511	1392	13326	CHEMICAL MANUFACTURING
77512	9	19	TRANSIT & GRND PASS. TRANSPORT
77514	238	1623	JUSTICE; PUBIC ORDER/SAFETY
77515	1035	11186	EXEC.; LEGIS.; & OTHER SUPPORT
77516	2	11	AMUSEMENT; GAMBLING;& RECREAT.
77517	81	419	EDUCATIONAL SERVICES
77518	183	744	FOOD SVCS & DRINKING PLACES
77519	28	113	WOOD PRODUCT MANUFACTURING
77520	1315	11857	EDUCATIONAL SERVICES
77521	1212	16458	HOSPITALS
77522	15	32	SPECIAL TRADE CONTRACTORS
77523	360	6955	MERCH. WHOLESALERS;DURABLE GDS
77530	724	11146	CHEMICAL MANUFACTURING
77531	605	5692	SPECIAL TRADE CONTRACTORS
77532	528	5627	SPECIAL TRADE CONTRACTORS
77533	28	146	JUSTICE; PUBIC ORDER/SAFETY
77534	66	469	EDUCATIONAL SERVICES
77535	481	4338	JUSTICE; PUBIC ORDER/SAFETY
77536	916	10549	SPECIAL TRADE CONTRACTORS
77538	18	93	EDUCATIONAL SERVICES
77539	800	6937	NONMETALLIC MINERAL PROD. MFG
77541	715	14816	MERCH. WHOLESALERS;NONDUR. GDS
77542	3	1	PERSONAL AND LAUNDRY SERVICES
77545	133	1144	EDUCATIONAL SERVICES
77546	1571	11911	FOOD SVCS & DRINKING PLACES
77547	159	2092	FABRICATED METAL PRODUCT MFG
77549	20	44	REAL ESTATE
77550	1530	16883	INSURANCE CARRIERS & RELATED
77551	793	7589	FOOD SVCS & DRINKING PLACES
77552	12	29	SUPPORT ACT. FOR TRANSPORT.
77553	8	319	EDUCATIONAL SERVICES
77554	483	4204	REPAIR AND MAINTENANCE
77555	76	11832	AMBULATORY HEALTH CARE SVCS
77560	27	125	RELIG.; GRANT; CIVIC; PROF ORG
77561	35	466	EDUCATIONAL SERVICES
77562	226	1778	EDUCATIONAL SERVICES
77563	240	1036	EDUCATIONAL SERVICES
77564	33	111	AMBULATORY HEALTH CARE SVCS
77565	463	5031	FOOD SVCS & DRINKING PLACES
77566	954	9657	AMBULATORY HEALTH CARE SVCS
77568	536	7127	CHEMICAL MANUFACTURING
77571	1234	20715	CHEMICAL MANUFACTURING
77572	15	31	ADMINISTRATIVE & SUPPORT SVCS
77573	1576	12528	EDUCATIONAL SERVICES
77574	14	33	REAL ESTATE
77575	664	4413	FOOD SVCS & DRINKING PLACES
77577	39	109	RENTAL AND LEASING SERVICES
77578	304	1860	EDUCATIONAL SERVICES
77580	111	2163	EDUCATIONAL SERVICES
77581	1583	13362	EDUCATIONAL SERVICES
77582	31	262	MERCH. WHOLESALERS;DURABLE GDS
77583	276	3975	SPECIAL TRADE CONTRACTORS
77584	990	7580	FOOD SVCS & DRINKING PLACES
77585	36	263	SPECIAL TRADE CONTRACTORS
77586	587	4579	FOOD SVCS & DRINKING PLACES
77587	676	4671	FOOD AND BEVERAGE STORES
77588	16	47	WOOD PRODUCT MANUFACTURING
77590	1001	11775	MERCH. WHOLESALERS;NONDUR. GDS
77591	335	5078	HOSPITALS
77592	8	37	BLDG MATL & GARDEN EQPMT DLRS
77597	44	206	FOOD SVCS & DRINKING PLACES
77598	1309	15774	FOOD SVCS & DRINKING PLACES
77611	356	2496	EDUCATIONAL SERVICES
77612	217	2046	EDUCATIONAL SERVICES
77613	39	249	EDUCATIONAL SERVICES
77614	59	480	EDUCATIONAL SERVICES
77615	39	1403	PAPER MANUFACTURING
77616	15	74	EDUCATIONAL SERVICES
77617	21	33	ACCOMMODATION
77619	363	3112	EDUCATIONAL SERVICES
77622	33	294	MERCH. WHOLESALERS;DURABLE GDS
77623	24	42	SPECIAL TRADE CONTRACTORS
77624	14	105	BLDG MATL & GARDEN EQPMT DLRS
77625	295	1837	SPECIAL TRADE CONTRACTORS
77626	40	130	FOOD SVCS & DRINKING PLACES
77627	1112	7916	PROF.; SCIENTIFIC; & TECH SVCS
77629	30	51	MERCH. WHOLESALERS;DURABLE GDS
77630	1275	14072	TRANSPORTATION EQUIPMENT MFG
77631	2	1	ADMINISTRATIVE & SUPPORT SVCS
77632	403	3273	EDUCATIONAL SERVICES
77639	11	245	PROF.; SCIENTIFIC; & TECH SVCS
77640	676	13140	MERCH. WHOLESALERS;DURABLE GDS
77642	1099	11599	EDUCATIONAL SERVICES
77643	1	1	SPECIAL TRADE CONTRACTORS
77650	186	652	FOOD SVCS & DRINKING PLACES
77651	345	4415	CHEMICAL MANUFACTURING
77655	45	1038	HEAVY & CIVIL ENG. CONSTRUCT'N
77656	622	5024	EDUCATIONAL SERVICES
77657	571	2539	EDUCATIONAL SERVICES
77659	164	976	EDUCATIONAL SERVICES
77660	33	106	EDUCATIONAL SERVICES
77661	15	40	HEAVY & CIVIL ENG. CONSTRUCT'N
77662	838	5863	EDUCATIONAL SERVICES
77663	30	141	ADMINISTRATIVE & SUPPORT SVCS
77664	46	234	EDUCATIONAL SERVICES
77665	280	2141	EDUCATIONAL SERVICES
77670	2	3	UTILITIES
77701	1557	24253	HOSPITALS
77702	580	7303	HOSPITALS
77703	463	4795	ADMINISTRATIVE & SUPPORT SVCS
77704	13	62	ADMINISTRATIVE & SUPPORT SVCS
77705	1122	17332	PROF.; SCIENTIFIC; & TECH SVCS
77706	1431	12316	FOOD SVCS & DRINKING PLACES
77707	932	11567	MERCH. WHOLESALERS;DURABLE GDS
77708	360	3363	ADMIN. OF ECONOMIC PROGRAMS
77709	1	1	REAL ESTATE
77710	3	1200	EDUCATIONAL SERVICES
77713	278	2711	PLASTICS & RUBBER PRODUCTS MFG
77720	13	41	CONSTRUCTION OF BUILDINGS
77726	15	45	BLDG MATL & GARDEN EQPMT DLRS
77801	386	3172	MERCH. WHOLESALERS;DURABLE GDS
77802	1128	16355	HOSPITALS
77803	956	10707	FOOD MANUFACTURING
77805	31	80	SOCIAL ASSISTANCE
77806	4	7	FOOD SVCS & DRINKING PLACES
77807	159	2778	HEAVY & CIVIL ENG. CONSTRUCT'N
77808	390	2939	SPECIAL TRADE CONTRACTORS
77830	110	619	UTILITIES
77831	38	97	JUSTICE; PUBIC ORDER/SAFETY
77833	1358	15547	EDUCATIONAL SERVICES
77834	8	115	MOTION PICT. & SOUND RECORDING
77835	78	296	EDUCATIONAL SERVICES
77836	397	2321	FOOD SVCS & DRINKING PLACES
77837	65	245	EDUCATIONAL SERVICES
77840	1307	15809	FOOD SVCS & DRINKING PLACES
77841	5	18	CONSTRUCTION OF BUILDINGS
77842	15	52	ADMINISTRATIVE & SUPPORT SVCS
77843	26	12252	PUBLISHING INDUSTRIES
77845	953	11153	PROF.; SCIENTIFIC; & TECH SVCS
77850	2	2	POSTAL SERVICE
77852	15	49	OIL AND GAS EXTRACTION
77853	40	208	SPECIAL TRADE CONTRACTORS
77855	8	25	MERCH. WHOLESALERS;NONDUR. GDS
77856	182	1098	EDUCATIONAL SERVICES
77857	10	69	EDUCATIONAL SERVICES
77859	291	1635	FOOD SVCS & DRINKING PLACES
77861	45	292	EDUCATIONAL SERVICES
77862	13	18	SPECIAL TRADE CONTRACTORS
77863	10	22	ACCOMMODATION
77864	376	3511	MERCH. WHOLESALERS;NONDUR. GDS
77865	54	162	SPECIAL TRADE CONTRACTORS
77866	6	7	RELIG.; GRANT; CIVIC; PROF ORG
77867	3	60	EDUCATIONAL SERVICES
77868	603	7564	HOSPITALS
77870	4	7	UTILITIES
77871	104	393	EDUCATIONAL SERVICES
77872	37	237	EDUCATIONAL SERVICES
77873	30	145	EDUCATIONAL SERVICES
77875	1	1	PROF.; SCIENTIFIC; & TECH SVCS
77876	17	47	UTILITIES
77878	38	244	EDUCATIONAL SERVICES
77879	139	771	EDUCATIONAL SERVICES
77880	33	71	MUSEUMS; HIST. SITES;& SIMILAR
77881	7	35	FOOD SVCS & DRINKING PLACES
77882	5	21	SUPPORT ACTIVITIES: AGR./FOR.
77901	2173	24513	EDUCATIONAL SERVICES
77902	9	9	EDUCATIONAL SERVICES
77903	15	19	ADMINISTRATIVE & SUPPORT SVCS
77904	1084	12631	HOSPITALS
77905	413	4148	SPECIAL TRADE CONTRACTORS
77950	4	5	POSTAL SERVICE
77951	30	167	EDUCATIONAL SERVICES
77954	425	4003	EXEC.; LEGIS.; & OTHER SUPPORT
77957	381	2581	SPECIAL TRADE CONTRACTORS
77960	6	15	SUPPORT ACT. FOR TRANSPORT.
77962	140	920	SPECIAL TRADE CONTRACTORS
77963	230	1141	EDUCATIONAL SERVICES
77964	380	2508	EDUCATIONAL SERVICES
77967	2	2	POSTAL SERVICE
77968	44	199	EDUCATIONAL SERVICES
77969	1	0	POSTAL SERVICE
77970	22	63	ANIMAL PRODUCTION
77971	29	3730	MERCH. WHOLESALERS;NONDUR. GDS
77973	3	4	WAREHOUSING AND STORAGE
77974	10	77	EDUCATIONAL SERVICES
77975	96	589	EDUCATIONAL SERVICES
77976	13	221	UTILITIES
77977	11	84	EDUCATIONAL SERVICES
77978	68	3470	PLASTICS & RUBBER PRODUCTS MFG
77979	653	5557	SPECIAL TRADE CONTRACTORS
77982	106	384	FOOD SVCS & DRINKING PLACES
77983	88	255	EDUCATIONAL SERVICES
77984	185	4220	MERCH. WHOLESALERS;DURABLE GDS
77986	1	1	POSTAL SERVICE
77987	7	31	EDUCATIONAL SERVICES
77988	14	59	SPECIAL TRADE CONTRACTORS
77989	3	18	PIPELINE TRANSPORTATION
77990	30	197	EDUCATIONAL SERVICES
77991	17	164	EDUCATIONAL SERVICES
77993	6	11	EXEC.; LEGIS.; & OTHER SUPPORT
77994	21	33	EDUCATIONAL SERVICES
77995	364	4752	MERCH. WHOLESALERS;NONDUR. GDS
78001	23	9	ANIMAL PRODUCTION
78002	84	361	EDUCATIONAL SERVICES
78003	522	2776	ACCOMMODATION
78004	11	31	ADMINISTRATIVE & SUPPORT SVCS
78005	15	96	MERCH. WHOLESALERS;NONDUR. GDS
78006	1484	10693	INSURANCE CARRIERS & RELATED
78007	2	5	FOOD AND BEVERAGE STORES
78008	14	47	ACCOMMODATION
78009	277	2536	EDUCATIONAL SERVICES
78010	116	648	EDUCATIONAL SERVICES
78011	43	272	EDUCATIONAL SERVICES
78012	8	308	UTILITIES
78013	256	1206	ACCOMMODATION
78014	212	1149	JUSTICE; PUBIC ORDER/SAFETY
78015	109	811	EDUCATIONAL SERVICES
78016	302	1919	EDUCATIONAL SERVICES
78017	114	1087	JUSTICE; PUBIC ORDER/SAFETY
78019	43	412	SPECIAL TRADE CONTRACTORS
78021	24	19	TRUCK TRANSPORTATION
78022	252	1229	SPECIAL TRADE CONTRACTORS
78023	552	3821	SPECIAL TRADE CONTRACTORS
78024	105	1100	ACCOMMODATION

BUSINESS DATA

ZIP CODE	2009 Total Firms	2009 Total Employ-ees	TOP INDUSTRY RANKED on 2009 EMPLOYMENT
78025	266	1576	ACCOMMODATION
78026	213	1817	EDUCATIONAL SERVICES
78027	22	37	MUSEUMS; HIST. SITES;& SIMILAR
78028	2493	19319	HOSPITALS
78029	31	45	SPECIAL TRADE CONTRACTORS
78039	48	200	EDUCATIONAL SERVICES
78040	1764	15383	EDUCATIONAL SERVICES
78041	2900	30382	FOOD SVCS & DRINKING PLACES
78042	3	3	HEALTH & PERSONAL CARE STORES
78043	932	8587	EDUCATIONAL SERVICES
78044	16	150	SPECIAL TRADE CONTRACTORS
78045	1842	21503	SUPPORT ACT. FOR TRANSPORT.
78046	400	5019	EDUCATIONAL SERVICES
78050	6	30	EDUCATIONAL SERVICES
78052	205	1426	EDUCATIONAL SERVICES
78054	6	44	SOCIAL ASSISTANCE
78055	68	349	EDUCATIONAL SERVICES
78056	19	91	MINING (EXCEPT OIL AND GAS)
78057	11	32	GASOLINE STATIONS
78058	62	218	RELIG.; GRANT; CIVIC; PROF ORG
78059	58	650	EDUCATIONAL SERVICES
78060	2	12	FOOD SVCS & DRINKING PLACES
78061	360	2667	EDUCATIONAL SERVICES
78062	2	5	MACHINERY MANUFACTURING
78063	254	820	AMBULATORY HEALTH CARE SVCS
78064	548	3988	MACHINERY MANUFACTURING
78065	160	1206	EDUCATIONAL SERVICES
78066	13	24	SPECIAL TRADE CONTRACTORS
78067	23	222	PROF.; SCIENTIFIC; & TECH SVCS
78069	71	380	MERCH. WHOLESALERS;DURABLE GDS
78070	386	2253	EDUCATIONAL SERVICES
78071	170	1228	PETROLEUM & COAL PRODUCTS MFG
78072	73	260	EDUCATIONAL SERVICES
78073	137	765	HEAVY & CIVIL ENG. CONSTRUCT'N
78074	11	33	JUSTICE; PUBIC ORDER/SAFETY
78075	5	26	GASOLINE STATIONS
78076	468	3521	EDUCATIONAL SERVICES
78101	177	621	FOOD SVCS & DRINKING PLACES
78102	804	7449	EXEC.; LEGIS.; & OTHER SUPPORT
78104	2	4	SPECIAL TRADE CONTRACTORS
78107	8	10	GASOLINE STATIONS
78108	267	1960	EDUCATIONAL SERVICES
78109	506	5384	CONSTRUCTION OF BUILDINGS
78112	105	638	SPECIAL TRADE CONTRACTORS
78113	40	236	EDUCATIONAL SERVICES
78114	515	3231	EDUCATIONAL SERVICES
78115	9	90	EDUCATIONAL SERVICES
78116	9	14	ANIMAL PRODUCTION
78117	10	22	UNCLASSIFIED ESTABLISHMENTS
78118	190	1339	EDUCATIONAL SERVICES
78119	222	1826	JUSTICE; PUBIC ORDER/SAFETY
78121	190	956	FOOD SVCS & DRINKING PLACES
78122	14	10	NONSTORE RETAILERS
78123	69	693	NONMETALLIC MINERAL PROD. MFG
78124	133	1087	EDUCATIONAL SERVICES
78125	1	1	RELIG.; GRANT; CIVIC; PROF ORG
78130	2552	27300	FOOD SVCS & DRINKING PLACES
78131	22	37	SOCIAL ASSISTANCE
78132	488	6358	MERCH. WHOLESALERS;DURABLE GDS
78133	610	1812	ACCOMMODATION
78135	2	567	PRINT'G & RELATED SUPP'T ACT'S
78140	85	787	EDUCATIONAL SERVICES
78141	17	58	EDUCATIONAL SERVICES
78142	4	2	SECURITIES/COMMODITY CONTRACTS
78144	4	11	MUSEUMS; HIST. SITES;& SIMILAR
78145	7	49	EDUCATIONAL SERVICES
78146	32	208	EDUCATIONAL SERVICES
78147	58	364	FOOD MANUFACTURING
78148	709	5590	ADMINISTRATIVE & SUPPORT SVCS
78150	75	1535	EDUCATIONAL SERVICES
78151	42	290	EDUCATIONAL SERVICES
78152	67	217	SPECIAL TRADE CONTRACTORS
78154	1075	13078	FOOD SVCS & DRINKING PLACES
78155	1772	27272	MOTOR VEHICLE & PARTS DEALERS
78156	9	26	SOCIAL ASSISTANCE
78159	23	45	NURSING & RESID. CARE FACILIT.
78160	89	433	EDUCATIONAL SERVICES
78161	16	21	SPECIAL TRADE CONTRACTORS
78162	8	32	PROF.; SCIENTIFIC; & TECH SVCS
78163	461	1821	SPECIAL TRADE CONTRACTORS
78164	156	723	MERCH. WHOLESALERS;DURABLE GDS
78201	2102	17496	AMBULATORY HEALTH CARE SVCS
78202	323	2532	EDUCATIONAL SERVICES
78203	185	1657	FOOD MANUFACTURING
78204	567	7720	FOOD AND BEVERAGE STORES
78205	2111	36440	FOOD SVCS & DRINKING PLACES
78206	27	236	JUSTICE; PUBIC ORDER/SAFETY
78207	1594	37252	EDUCATIONAL SERVICES
78208	163	1952	EDUCATIONAL SERVICES
78209	3032	23501	FOOD SVCS & DRINKING PLACES

ZIP CODE	2009 Total Firms	2009 Total Employ-ees	TOP INDUSTRY RANKED on 2009 EMPLOYMENT
78210	883	7569	EDUCATIONAL SERVICES
78211	766	6404	EDUCATIONAL SERVICES
78212	2106	21023	EDUCATIONAL SERVICES
78213	1557	10638	EDUCATIONAL SERVICES
78214	645	5223	EDUCATIONAL SERVICES
78215	431	6962	AMBULATORY HEALTH CARE SVCS
78216	4989	53907	PROF.; SCIENTIFIC; & TECH SVCS
78217	2894	25890	AMBULATORY HEALTH CARE SVCS
78218	1400	16042	FOOD AND BEVERAGE STORES
78219	1024	23056	MACHINERY MANUFACTURING
78220	472	4574	EDUCATIONAL SERVICES
78221	966	8418	NONMETALLIC MINERAL PROD. MFG
78222	549	6875	MERCH. WHOLESALERS;DURABLE GDS
78223	1070	10232	NURSING & RESID. CARE FACILIT.
78224	570	8311	FOOD SVCS & DRINKING PLACES
78225	246	1590	FOOD SVCS & DRINKING PLACES
78226	195	3354	PROF.; SCIENTIFIC; & TECH SVCS
78227	1099	10482	FOOD SVCS & DRINKING PLACES
78228	1529	12161	EDUCATIONAL SERVICES
78229	2246	51188	HOSPITALS
78230	2249	21792	FOOD SVCS & DRINKING PLACES
78231	287	2252	HEAVY & CIVIL ENG. CONSTRUCT'N
78232	2108	19910	FOOD SVCS & DRINKING PLACES
78233	1275	12361	MOTOR VEHICLE & PARTS DEALERS
78234	104	3642	AMBULATORY HEALTH CARE SVCS
78235	50	452	PROF.; SCIENTIFIC; & TECH SVCS
78236	140	6588	HOSPITALS
78237	841	6170	EDUCATIONAL SERVICES
78238	2103	28222	MISCELLANEOUS MANUFACTURING
78239	377	3563	NURSING & RESID. CARE FACILIT.
78240	1083	10328	SOCIAL ASSISTANCE
78242	237	1651	EDUCATIONAL SERVICES
78243	1	1	OTHER INFORMATION SERVICES
78244	340	2953	EDUCATIONAL SERVICES
78245	473	11195	CREDIT INTERMEDIATION & RELATD
78246	20	47	AMUSEMENT; GAMBLING;& RECREAT.
78247	1204	13222	EDUCATIONAL SERVICES
78248	355	3274	REAL ESTATE
78249	1104	33211	ADMINISTRATIVE & SUPPORT SVCS
78250	906	7109	FOOD SVCS & DRINKING PLACES
78251	872	15846	AMUSEMENT; GAMBLING;& RECREAT.
78252	118	1981	EDUCATIONAL SERVICES
78253	264	1346	EDUCATIONAL SERVICES
78254	408	3080	EDUCATIONAL SERVICES
78255	219	1247	AMUSEMENT; GAMBLING;& RECREAT.
78256	229	3766	CLOTHING & CLOTH'G ACC. STORES
78257	356	3549	FOOD SVCS & DRINKING PLACES
78258	1346	11310	AMBULATORY HEALTH CARE SVCS
78259	321	5817	MISCELLANEOUS MANUFACTURING
78260	250	1726	SPECIAL TRADE CONTRACTORS
78261	53	237	CONSTRUCTION OF BUILDINGS
78263	255	2406	EDUCATIONAL SERVICES
78264	240	3354	MERCH. WHOLESALERS;DURABLE GDS
78265	26	70	ELECTRONICS & APPLIANCE STORES
78266	327	6607	GENERAL MERCHANDISE STORES
78268	30	80	SUPPORT ACTIVITIES FOR MINING
78269	27	61	MACHINERY MANUFACTURING
78270	27	48	ADMINISTRATIVE & SUPPORT SVCS
78278	32	92	PROF.; SCIENTIFIC; & TECH SVCS
78279	25	97	FABRICATED METAL PRODUCT MFG
78280	5	6	REPAIR AND MAINTENANCE
78283	3	14	HEAVY & CIVIL ENG. CONSTRUCT'N
78284	4	1700	POSTAL SERVICE
78288	9	306	INSURANCE CARRIERS & RELATED
78291	2	0	SPECIAL TRADE CONTRACTORS
78292	4	2	ANIMAL PRODUCTION
78293	3	15	SPECIAL TRADE CONTRACTORS
78294	1	0	ADMINISTRATIVE & SUPPORT SVCS
78295	1	4	PERFORM'G ARTS; SPEC. SPORTS
78296	1	1	PROF.; SCIENTIFIC; & TECH SVCS
78297	4	2	SUPPORT ACT. FOR TRANSPORT.
78299	1	0	PROF.; SCIENTIFIC; & TECH SVCS
78330	30	231	EDUCATIONAL SERVICES
78332	1208	14486	SPECIAL TRADE CONTRACTORS
78333	5	45	SPECIAL TRADE CONTRACTORS
78335	3	5	PROF.; SCIENTIFIC; & TECH SVCS
78336	528	5169	SPECIAL TRADE CONTRACTORS
78338	2	0	POSTAL SERVICE
78339	22	263	EDUCATIONAL SERVICES
78340	7	19	FOOD MANUFACTURING
78341	56	601	EDUCATIONAL SERVICES
78342	12	259	EDUCATIONAL SERVICES
78343	90	431	EXEC.; LEGIS.; & OTHER SUPPORT
78344	26	286	EDUCATIONAL SERVICES
78347	5	10	CROP PRODUCTION
78349	24	48	EXEC.; LEGIS.; & OTHER SUPPORT
78350	4	8	MERCH. WHOLESALERS;DURABLE GDS
78351	20	166	EDUCATIONAL SERVICES
78352	7	29	MERCH. WHOLESALERS;DURABLE GDS
78353	32	58	EDUCATIONAL SERVICES

ZIP CODE	2009 Total Firms	2009 Total Employ-ees	TOP INDUSTRY RANKED on 2009 EMPLOYMENT
78355	299	1969	EDUCATIONAL SERVICES
78357	165	1586	EDUCATIONAL SERVICES
78358	85	432	FOOD SVCS & DRINKING PLACES
78359	49	643	CHEMICAL MANUFACTURING
78361	245	1423	EXEC.; LEGIS.; & OTHER SUPPORT
78362	292	3769	FABRICATED METAL PRODUCT MFG
78363	1074	8385	EDUCATIONAL SERVICES
78364	5	26	NAT'L SECURITY & INT'L AFFAIRS
78368	262	1812	EDUCATIONAL SERVICES
78369	48	173	PETROLEUM & COAL PRODUCTS MFG
78370	75	445	FOOD SVCS & DRINKING PLACES
78371	5	17	FOOD SVCS & DRINKING PLACES
78372	124	636	EDUCATIONAL SERVICES
78373	486	2757	REAL ESTATE
78374	489	3250	EDUCATIONAL SERVICES
78375	118	605	SPECIAL TRADE CONTRACTORS
78376	7	77	FOOD AND BEVERAGE STORES
78377	249	1631	SPECIAL TRADE CONTRACTORS
78379	90	319	FOOD SVCS & DRINKING PLACES
78380	621	4641	EDUCATIONAL SERVICES
78381	18	22	SPECIAL TRADE CONTRACTORS
78382	1191	5569	FOOD SVCS & DRINKING PLACES
78383	57	298	ANIMAL PRODUCTION
78384	153	1380	EXEC.; LEGIS.; & OTHER SUPPORT
78385	20	153	EDUCATIONAL SERVICES
78387	346	2644	EXEC.; LEGIS.; & OTHER SUPPORT
78389	33	350	EDUCATIONAL SERVICES
78390	132	691	HOSPITALS
78391	9	35	WAREHOUSING AND STORAGE
78393	73	522	EDUCATIONAL SERVICES
78401	1125	19264	EXEC.; LEGIS.; & OTHER SUPPORT
78402	87	1212	AMUSEMENT; GAMBLING;& RECREAT.
78403	12	17	UNCLASSIFIED ESTABLISHMENTS
78404	663	7386	HOSPITALS
78405	731	11186	EDUCATIONAL SERVICES
78406	88	1415	RENTAL AND LEASING SERVICES
78407	92	2383	PETROLEUM & COAL PRODUCTS MFG
78408	798	9537	MERCH. WHOLESALERS;DURABLE GDS
78409	337	9926	SPECIAL TRADE CONTRACTORS
78410	771	6358	EDUCATIONAL SERVICES
78411	1987	23700	HOSPITALS
78412	1065	8715	FOOD SVCS & DRINKING PLACES
78413	996	6601	FOOD SVCS & DRINKING PLACES
78414	534	4773	AMBULATORY HEALTH CARE SVCS
78415	1332	10292	MOTOR VEHICLE & PARTS DEALERS
78416	312	5891	EDUCATIONAL SERVICES
78417	210	2230	FOOD SVCS & DRINKING PLACES
78418	837	5351	EDUCATIONAL SERVICES
78419	33	556	SUPPORT ACT. FOR TRANSPORT.
78426	2	2	SUPPORT ACTIVITIES: AGR./FOR.
78427	12	40	SOCIAL ASSISTANCE
78460	3	1	HEAVY & CIVIL ENG. CONSTRUCT'N
78463	3	16	ADMINISTRATIVE & SUPPORT SVCS
78465	1	3	ADMINISTRATIVE & SUPPORT SVCS
78466	14	20	ADMINISTRATIVE & SUPPORT SVCS
78467	11	12	AMUSEMENT; GAMBLING;& RECREAT.
78468	16	51	PERSONAL AND LAUNDRY SERVICES
78469	10	29	CREDIT INTERMEDIATION & RELATD
78470	62	501	PROF.; SCIENTIFIC; & TECH SVCS
78471	87	1079	PROF.; SCIENTIFIC; & TECH SVCS
78472	2	0	RELIG.; GRANT; CIVIC; PROF ORG
78473	69	257	PROF.; SCIENTIFIC; & TECH SVCS
78475	82	322	PROF.; SCIENTIFIC; & TECH SVCS
78476	100	407	PROF.; SCIENTIFIC; & TECH SVCS
78477	69	2128	INSURANCE CARRIERS & RELATED
78478	63	831	PROF.; SCIENTIFIC; & TECH SVCS
78480	6	45	COMPUTER & ELECTRONIC PROD MFG
78501	3743	34212	EDUCATIONAL SERVICES
78502	36	153	CONSTRUCTION OF BUILDINGS
78503	1248	21025	HOSPITALS
78504	1889	17040	FOOD SVCS & DRINKING PLACES
78505	2	4	CONSTRUCTION OF BUILDINGS
78516	545	5117	EDUCATIONAL SERVICES
78520	2080	22043	EDUCATIONAL SERVICES
78521	2513	30947	EDUCATIONAL SERVICES
78522	3	1	EXEC.; LEGIS.; & OTHER SUPPORT
78523	4	3	REPAIR AND MAINTENANCE
78526	674	8261	EDUCATIONAL SERVICES
78535	22	119	SOCIAL ASSISTANCE
78536	4	6	MISCELLANEOUS STORE RETAILERS
78537	558	5334	EDUCATIONAL SERVICES
78538	128	1632	EDUCATIONAL SERVICES
78539	1790	21434	EDUCATIONAL SERVICES
78540	14	17	PERFORM'G ARTS; SPEC. SPORTS
78541	637	7426	MERCH. WHOLESALERS;NONDUR. GDS
78542	644	7098	JUSTICE; PUBIC ORDER/SAFETY
78543	180	1550	EDUCATIONAL SERVICES
78545	28	103	ADMINISTRATIVE & SUPPORT SVCS
78547	6	14	EDUCATIONAL SERVICES
78548	20	176	EDUCATIONAL SERVICES

ZIP CODE	2009 Total Firms	2009 Total Employees	TOP INDUSTRY RANKED on 2009 EMPLOYMENT	ZIP CODE	2009 Total Firms	2009 Total Employees	TOP INDUSTRY RANKED on 2009 EMPLOYMENT	ZIP CODE	2009 Total Firms	2009 Total Employees	TOP INDUSTRY RANKED on 2009 EMPLOYMENT
78549	15	85	EDUCATIONAL SERVICES	78652	168	1198	SPECIAL TRADE CONTRACTORS	78766	24	37	SPECIAL TRADE CONTRACTORS
78550	2632	28340	AMBULATORY HEALTH CARE SVCS	78653	355	3156	EDUCATIONAL SERVICES	78767	41	252	CREDIT INTERMEDIATION & RELATD
78551	9	10	REAL ESTATE	78654	1134	7865	EDUCATIONAL SERVICES	78768	61	208	EXEC.; LEGIS.; & OTHER SUPPORT
78552	752	9149	EDUCATIONAL SERVICES	78655	57	259	FOOD SVCS & DRINKING PLACES	78778	5	108	ADMINISTRATIVE & SUPPORT SVCS
78553	6	2	FOOD AND BEVERAGE STORES	78656	36	178	UTILITIES	78779	1	180	ADMIN. OF ECONOMIC PROGRAMS
78557	603	3996	MERCH. WHOLESALERS;DURABLE GDS	78657	218	1679	ACCOMMODATION	78780	2	50	REAL ESTATE
78558	15	52	AMBULATORY HEALTH CARE SVCS	78659	42	78	REPAIR AND MAINTENANCE	78801	934	8895	MERCH. WHOLESALERS;NONDUR. GDS
78559	265	2314	EDUCATIONAL SERVICES	78660	1269	9874	SPECIAL TRADE CONTRACTORS	78802	8	6	SPECIAL TRADE CONTRACTORS
78560	96	4801	EDUCATIONAL SERVICES	78661	14	252	EDUCATIONAL SERVICES	78827	15	43	EDUCATIONAL SERVICES
78561	13	138	EDUCATIONAL SERVICES	78662	34	198	EDUCATIONAL SERVICES	78828	31	114	EDUCATIONAL SERVICES
78562	20	309	EDUCATIONAL SERVICES	78663	34	93	SPECIAL TRADE CONTRACTORS	78829	34	178	EDUCATIONAL SERVICES
78563	18	105	MERCH. WHOLESALERS;NONDUR. GDS	78664	1783	18785	FOOD SVCS & DRINKING PLACES	78830	22	151	SPECIAL TRADE CONTRACTORS
78564	4	26	PETROLEUM & COAL PRODUCTS MFG	78665	440	4929	EDUCATIONAL SERVICES	78832	124	618	UTILITIES
78565	5	25	BLDG MATL & GARDEN EQPMT DLRS	78666	2816	26312	FOOD SVCS & DRINKING PLACES	78833	101	289	EDUCATIONAL SERVICES
78566	279	2554	EDUCATIONAL SERVICES	78667	22	77	SOCIAL ASSISTANCE	78834	282	2723	SOCIAL ASSISTANCE
78567	31	3478	TRANSPORTATION EQUIPMENT MFG	78669	319	1113	AMUSEMENT; GAMBLING;& RECREAT.	78836	10	112	SUPPORT ACTIVITIES FOR MINING
78568	1	2	POSTAL SERVICE	78670	6	6	REPAIR AND MAINTENANCE	78837	38	195	ADMIN. OF ECONOMIC PROGRAMS
78569	58	365	CROP PRODUCTION	78671	49	348	MUSEUMS; HIST. SITES;& SIMILAR	78838	46	388	FOOD AND BEVERAGE STORES
78570	627	5512	EDUCATIONAL SERVICES	78672	31	101	JUSTICE; PUBIC ORDER/SAFETY	78839	225	2238	MERCH. WHOLESALERS;NONDUR. GDS
78572	2450	19359	EDUCATIONAL SERVICES	78673	4	68	CHEMICAL MANUFACTURING	78840	1539	13792	EDUCATIONAL SERVICES
78573	450	3258	EDUCATIONAL SERVICES	78674	9	15	GASOLINE STATIONS	78841	1	11	EXEC.; LEGIS.; & OTHER SUPPORT
78574	491	3829	EDUCATIONAL SERVICES	78675	9	53	JUSTICE; PUBIC ORDER/SAFETY	78842	1	0	MISCELLANEOUS MANUFACTURING
78575	81	1444	RELIG.; GRANT; CIVIC; PROF ORG	78676	695	3184	EDUCATIONAL SERVICES	78843	30	1711	NAT'L SECURITY & INT'L AFFAIRS
78576	83	407	EDUCATIONAL SERVICES	78677	1	1	POSTAL SERVICE	78850	53	253	EDUCATIONAL SERVICES
78577	2265	21776	PROF.; SCIENTIFIC; & TECH SVCS	78680	29	64	PROF.; SCIENTIFIC; & TECH SVCS	78851	6	5	ANIMAL PRODUCTION
78578	406	3110	EDUCATIONAL SERVICES	78681	1277	14085	HOSPITALS	78852	1464	12452	EDUCATIONAL SERVICES
78579	78	1545	PAPER MANUFACTURING	78682	1	21000	COMPUTER & ELECTRONIC PROD MFG	78853	1	0	RELIG.; GRANT; CIVIC; PROF ORG
78580	333	3365	JUSTICE; PUBIC ORDER/SAFETY	78683	8	6	TRANSIT & GRND PASS. TRANSPORT	78860	7	19	ANIMAL PRODUCTION
78582	783	6267	EDUCATIONAL SERVICES	78691	20	47	ADMINISTRATIVE & SUPPORT SVCS	78861	462	3347	EXEC.; LEGIS.; & OTHER SUPPORT
78583	111	1116	EDUCATIONAL SERVICES	78701	4413	65281	EXEC.; LEGIS.; & OTHER SUPPORT	78870	29	179	EDUCATIONAL SERVICES
78584	332	2101	EDUCATIONAL SERVICES	78702	1389	13800	SOCIAL ASSISTANCE	78871	23	17	MINING (EXCEPT OIL AND GAS)
78585	2	8	JUSTICE; PUBIC ORDER/SAFETY	78703	1162	15873	NAT'L SECURITY & INT'L AFFAIRS	78872	38	291	EDUCATIONAL SERVICES
78586	871	8299	EDUCATIONAL SERVICES	78704	2906	31810	FOOD SVCS & DRINKING PLACES	78873	182	615	EDUCATIONAL SERVICES
78588	39	286	EDUCATIONAL SERVICES	78705	1134	17526	HOSPITALS	78877	47	194	EXEC.; LEGIS.; & OTHER SUPPORT
78589	663	4775	EDUCATIONAL SERVICES	78708	29	101	CONSTRUCTION OF BUILDINGS	78879	14	23	ACCOMMODATION
78590	11	117	EDUCATIONAL SERVICES	78709	46	146	ADMINISTRATIVE & SUPPORT SVCS	78880	147	508	TELECOMMUNICATIONS
78591	7	18	ANIMAL PRODUCTION	78710	1	800	POSTAL SERVICE	78881	83	326	EDUCATIONAL SERVICES
78592	12	174	EDUCATIONAL SERVICES	78711	22	631	EXEC.; LEGIS.; & OTHER SUPPORT	78883	18	27	ACCOMMODATION
78593	41	493	CROP PRODUCTION	78712	55	23376	EDUCATIONAL SERVICES	78884	117	386	RELIG.; GRANT; CIVIC; PROF ORG
78594	16	71	AMBULATORY HEALTH CARE SVCS	78713	11	101	OTHER INFORMATION SERVICES	78885	22	26	ANIMAL PRODUCTION
78595	68	720	AMBULATORY HEALTH CARE SVCS	78714	27	125	SPECIAL TRADE CONTRACTORS	78886	10	17	FOOD MANUFACTURING
78596	1441	17201	EDUCATIONAL SERVICES	78715	32	57	PROF.; SCIENTIFIC; & TECH SVCS	78931	2	4	CLOTHING & CLOTH'G ACC. STORES
78597	498	4825	FOOD SVCS & DRINKING PLACES	78716	44	226	RELIG.; GRANT; CIVIC; PROF ORG	78932	38	108	EDUCATIONAL SERVICES
78598	39	126	EXEC.; LEGIS.; & OTHER SUPPORT	78717	392	3481	FOOD SVCS & DRINKING PLACES	78933	30	90	FURNITURE & RELATED PROD. MFG
78599	2	2	SPECIAL TRADE CONTRACTORS	78718	8	38	TRANSIT & GRND PASS. TRANSPORT	78934	452	3279	FOOD SVCS & DRINKING PLACES
78602	1144	8419	EDUCATIONAL SERVICES	78719	135	6980	SUPPORT ACT. FOR TRANSPORT.	78935	20	328	MACHINERY MANUFACTURING
78604	7	5	FOOD AND BEVERAGE STORES	78720	62	187	PROF.; SCIENTIFIC; & TECH SVCS	78938	10	23	FOOD AND BEVERAGE STORES
78605	128	789	SPECIAL TRADE CONTRACTORS	78721	253	6091	COMPUTER & ELECTRONIC PROD MFG	78940	80	305	FOOD SVCS & DRINKING PLACES
78606	251	1313	UTILITIES	78722	287	2993	FOOD SVCS & DRINKING PLACES	78941	153	991	MERCH. WHOLESALERS;NONDUR. GDS
78607	3	3	CONSTRUCTION OF BUILDINGS	78723	960	8121	EDUCATIONAL SERVICES	78942	506	4281	SPECIAL TRADE CONTRACTORS
78608	16	29	HEAVY & CIVIL ENG. CONSTRUCT'N	78724	303	7018	COMPUTER & ELECTRONIC PROD MFG	78943	3	11	SPECIAL TRADE CONTRACTORS
78609	101	290	RELIG.; GRANT; CIVIC; PROF ORG	78725	53	2100	MERCH. WHOLESALERS;DURABLE GDS	78944	62	289	MERCH. WHOLESALERS;NONDUR. GDS
78610	648	6991	EDUCATIONAL SERVICES	78726	329	4688	MISCELLANEOUS MANUFACTURING	78945	634	4131	GENERAL MERCHANDISE STORES
78611	645	4245	ACCOMMODATION	78727	726	11188	MERCH. WHOLESALERS;DURABLE GDS	78946	17	21	POSTAL SERVICE
78612	180	1023	EDUCATIONAL SERVICES	78728	918	13641	MISCELLANEOUS MANUFACTURING	78947	107	517	EDUCATIONAL SERVICES
78613	1766	14604	EDUCATIONAL SERVICES	78729	777	8965	INSURANCE CARRIERS & RELATED	78948	12	53	FOOD SVCS & DRINKING PLACES
78614	24	11	CHEMICAL MANUFACTURING	78730	396	4054	PROF.; SCIENTIFIC; & TECH SVCS	78949	8	27	MISCELLANEOUS MANUFACTURING
78615	37	158	EDUCATIONAL SERVICES	78731	1640	13719	PROF.; SCIENTIFIC; & TECH SVCS	78950	70	289	SPECIAL TRADE CONTRACTORS
78616	58	144	WASTE MANAGMT & REMEDIAT'N SVC	78732	216	1083	EDUCATIONAL SERVICES	78951	4	2	GENERAL MERCHANDISE STORES
78617	236	1471	EDUCATIONAL SERVICES	78733	203	920	PROF.; SCIENTIFIC; & TECH SVCS	78952	21	19	TRANSPORTATION EQUIPMENT MFG
78618	20	51	JUSTICE; PUBIC ORDER/SAFETY	78734	1041	6355	AMUSEMENT; GAMBLING;& RECREAT.	78953	22	71	EDUCATIONAL SERVICES
78619	75	532	FOOD SVCS & DRINKING PLACES	78735	774	13313	COMPUTER & ELECTRONIC PROD MFG	78954	66	259	FOOD SVCS & DRINKING PLACES
78620	561	3332	EDUCATIONAL SERVICES	78736	340	1649	SPECIAL TRADE CONTRACTORS	78956	280	2456	TRANSPORTATION EQUIPMENT MFG
78621	485	3278	CONSTRUCTION OF BUILDINGS	78737	443	1979	PROF.; SCIENTIFIC; & TECH SVCS	78957	315	2335	HOSPITALS
78622	14	27	GASOLINE STATIONS	78738	652	4413	FOOD SVCS & DRINKING PLACES	78959	64	1010	FOOD AND BEVERAGE STORES
78623	16	54	FOOD SVCS & DRINKING PLACES	78739	159	730	EDUCATIONAL SERVICES	78960	8	105	OIL AND GAS EXTRACTION
78624	1441	9236	FOOD SVCS & DRINKING PLACES	78741	830	13570	COMPUTER & ELECTRONIC PROD MFG	78961	16	0	CROP PRODUCTION
78626	1177	13117	EXEC.; LEGIS.; & OTHER SUPPORT	78742	51	613	SPECIAL TRADE CONTRACTORS	78962	218	1593	MACHINERY MANUFACTURING
78627	26	91	ADMINISTRATIVE & SUPPORT SVCS	78744	894	17156	PROF.; SCIENTIFIC; & TECH SVCS	78963	21	26	SPECIAL TRADE CONTRACTORS
78628	898	5179	EDUCATIONAL SERVICES	78745	1937	18221	FOOD SVCS & DRINKING PLACES	79001	17	57	EDUCATIONAL SERVICES
78629	556	5271	MERCH. WHOLESALERS;NONDUR. GDS	78746	3047	32889	PROF.; SCIENTIFIC; & TECH SVCS	79002	3	4	ACCOMMODATION
78630	23	41	ADMINISTRATIVE & SUPPORT SVCS	78747	180	1128	SPECIAL TRADE CONTRACTORS	79003	15	14	FOOD SVCS & DRINKING PLACES
78631	101	275	EDUCATIONAL SERVICES	78748	947	6366	FOOD SVCS & DRINKING PLACES	79005	72	676	FOOD MANUFACTURING
78632	37	156	MERCH. WHOLESALERS;NONDUR. GDS	78749	544	5043	EDUCATIONAL SERVICES	79007	789	8011	PETROLEUM & COAL PRODUCTS MFG
78633	263	1300	CONSTRUCTION OF BUILDINGS	78750	1437	8764	FOOD SVCS & DRINKING PLACES	79008	4	770	PETROLEUM & COAL PRODUCTS MFG
78634	392	3628	CONSTRUCTION OF BUILDINGS	78751	741	18570	ADMIN. HUMAN RESOURCE PROGRAMS	79009	48	267	EDUCATIONAL SERVICES
78635	8	34	SOCIAL ASSISTANCE	78752	1224	15582	EDUCATIONAL SERVICES	79010	39	1089	ANIMAL PRODUCTION
78636	212	1629	UTILITIES	78753	1663	26413	ADMIN. ENVIRO. QUALITY PROGRMS	79011	9	75	EDUCATIONAL SERVICES
78638	56	114	HEAVY & CIVIL ENG. CONSTRUCT'N	78754	768	16330	AMBULATORY HEALTH CARE SVCS	79012	20	500	EDUCATIONAL SERVICES
78639	289	1392	NURSING & RESID. CARE FACILIT.	78755	40	74	REAL ESTATE	79013	57	5359	FOOD MANUFACTURING
78640	457	4193	EDUCATIONAL SERVICES	78756	878	9766	ADMIN. HUMAN RESOURCE PROGRAMS	79014	327	2167	SPECIAL TRADE CONTRACTORS
78641	821	5341	EDUCATIONAL SERVICES	78757	1608	12252	FOOD SVCS & DRINKING PLACES	79015	656	3849	EDUCATIONAL SERVICES
78642	360	1925	EDUCATIONAL SERVICES	78758	2350	27839	ADMINISTRATIVE & SUPPORT SVCS	79016	9	1540	EDUCATIONAL SERVICES
78643	416	2328	HOSPITALS	78759	3134	39285	PROF.; SCIENTIFIC; & TECH SVCS	79018	26	113	EDUCATIONAL SERVICES
78644	716	5370	EDUCATIONAL SERVICES	78760	11	101	PUBLISHING INDUSTRIES	79019	99	482	EDUCATIONAL SERVICES
78645	384	1678	EDUCATIONAL SERVICES	78761	9	14	PERSONAL AND LAUNDRY SERVICES	79021	19	130	EDUCATIONAL SERVICES
78646	20	29	CONSTRUCTION OF BUILDINGS	78762	1	20	ADMINISTRATIVE & SUPPORT SVCS	79022	692	4888	RAIL TRANSPORTATION
78648	389	2307	SOCIAL ASSISTANCE	78763	30	60	PROF.; SCIENTIFIC; & TECH SVCS	79024	35	146	EDUCATIONAL SERVICES
78650	22	63	EDUCATIONAL SERVICES	78764	15	15	RELIG.; GRANT; CIVIC; PROF ORG	79025	30	115	FOOD MANUFACTURING
78651	1	7	TRANSIT & GRND PASS. TRANSPORT	78765	24	33	PROF.; SCIENTIFIC; & TECH SVCS	79027	273	1446	ANIMAL PRODUCTION

BUSINESS DATA

ZIP CODE	2009 Total Firms	2009 Total Employees	TOP INDUSTRY RANKED on 2009 EMPLOYMENT	ZIP CODE	2009 Total Firms	2009 Total Employees	TOP INDUSTRY RANKED on 2009 EMPLOYMENT	ZIP CODE	2009 Total Firms	2009 Total Employees	TOP INDUSTRY RANKED on 2009 EMPLOYMENT
79029	694	5738	EDUCATIONAL SERVICES	79241	100	513	EDUCATIONAL SERVICES	79504	147	649	MOTOR VEHICLE & PARTS DEALERS
79031	49	513	EDUCATIONAL SERVICES	79243	13	24	JUSTICE; PUBIC ORDER/SAFETY	79505	29	86	JUSTICE; PUBIC ORDER/SAFETY
79032	14	75	ANIMAL PRODUCTION	79244	70	243	EDUCATIONAL SERVICES	79506	28	96	EDUCATIONAL SERVICES
79033	8	49	SPECIAL TRADE CONTRACTORS	79245	158	743	EDUCATIONAL SERVICES	79508	81	410	SPECIAL TRADE CONTRACTORS
79034	54	262	EDUCATIONAL SERVICES	79247	7	4	EXEC.; LEGIS.; & OTHER SUPPORT	79510	257	1320	EDUCATIONAL SERVICES
79035	208	3137	FOOD MANUFACTURING	79248	113	457	EDUCATIONAL SERVICES	79511	57	506	EDUCATIONAL SERVICES
79036	113	1012	EDUCATIONAL SERVICES	79250	47	293	EDUCATIONAL SERVICES	79512	275	1906	EXEC.; LEGIS.; & OTHER SUPPORT
79039	56	293	EDUCATIONAL SERVICES	79251	3	8	MERCH. WHOLESALERS;NONDUR. GDS	79516	2	2	POSTAL SERVICE
79040	93	754	EDUCATIONAL SERVICES	79252	208	1067	NONMETALLIC MINERAL PROD. MFG	79517	9	15	SPECIAL TRADE CONTRACTORS
79041	82	426	EDUCATIONAL SERVICES	79255	33	90	CREDIT INTERMEDIATION & RELATD	79518	7	6	SUPPORT ACTIVITIES: AGR./FOR.
79042	48	306	EDUCATIONAL SERVICES	79256	34	85	CLOTHING & CLOTH'G ACC. STORES	79519	1	0	REAL ESTATE
79043	60	399	EDUCATIONAL SERVICES	79257	77	217	EDUCATIONAL SERVICES	79520	132	993	SPECIAL TRADE CONTRACTORS
79044	35	128	EDUCATIONAL SERVICES	79258	3	18	CROP PRODUCTION	79521	231	1150	JUSTICE; PUBIC ORDER/SAFETY
79045	871	7421	EDUCATIONAL SERVICES	79259	4	3	AIR TRANSPORTATION	79525	87	486	EDUCATIONAL SERVICES
79046	42	97	EDUCATIONAL SERVICES	79261	38	120	EDUCATIONAL SERVICES	79526	20	116	EDUCATIONAL SERVICES
79051	6	4	WAREHOUSING AND STORAGE	79311	129	577	EDUCATIONAL SERVICES	79527	28	184	EDUCATIONAL SERVICES
79052	49	282	EDUCATIONAL SERVICES	79312	37	266	EDUCATIONAL SERVICES	79528	53	255	NURSING & RESID. CARE FACILIT.
79053	25	167	EDUCATIONAL SERVICES	79313	31	201	EDUCATIONAL SERVICES	79529	116	699	SUPPORT ACTIVITIES FOR MINING
79054	20	121	EDUCATIONAL SERVICES	79314	5	9	TRUCK TRANSPORTATION	79530	28	112	EDUCATIONAL SERVICES
79056	12	30	EXEC.; LEGIS.; & OTHER SUPPORT	79316	441	3398	EDUCATIONAL SERVICES	79532	25	122	EDUCATIONAL SERVICES
79057	82	335	EDUCATIONAL SERVICES	79320	6	2	SUPPORT ACTIVITIES: AGR./FOR.	79533	22	328	MINING (EXCEPT OIL AND GAS)
79058	11	146	PETROLEUM & COAL PRODUCTS MFG	79322	126	714	HOSPITALS	79534	2	8	MERCH. WHOLESALERS;NONDUR. GDS
79059	56	322	AMBULATORY HEALTH CARE SVCS	79323	285	2522	SPECIAL TRADE CONTRACTORS	79535	6	177	MERCH. WHOLESALERS;DURABLE GDS
79061	16	44	EDUCATIONAL SERVICES	79324	2	4	SUPPORT ACTIVITIES: AGR./FOR.	79536	159	1161	EDUCATIONAL SERVICES
79062	8	61	EDUCATIONAL SERVICES	79325	118	873	EDUCATIONAL SERVICES	79537	21	53	SPECIAL TRADE CONTRACTORS
79063	29	152	EDUCATIONAL SERVICES	79326	7	5	CHEMICAL MANUFACTURING	79538	6	59	EDUCATIONAL SERVICES
79064	124	1122	EDUCATIONAL SERVICES	79329	101	567	EDUCATIONAL SERVICES	79539	5	26	EDUCATIONAL SERVICES
79065	1118	9016	SPECIAL TRADE CONTRACTORS	79330	3	9	EXEC.; LEGIS.; & OTHER SUPPORT	79540	4	5	GASOLINE STATIONS
79066	8	6	OIL AND GAS EXTRACTION	79331	522	3957	JUSTICE; PUBIC ORDER/SAFETY	79541	13	14	EXEC.; LEGIS.; & OTHER SUPPORT
79068	141	833	EDUCATIONAL SERVICES	79336	647	6545	EDUCATIONAL SERVICES	79543	57	409	EDUCATIONAL SERVICES
79070	578	4631	SPECIAL TRADE CONTRACTORS	79339	301	2770	TEXTILE MILLS	79544	20	109	EDUCATIONAL SERVICES
79072	1168	12446	FOOD AND BEVERAGE STORES	79342	20	228	EDUCATIONAL SERVICES	79545	78	465	EDUCATIONAL SERVICES
79073	10	12	FOOD MANUFACTURING	79343	53	465	EDUCATIONAL SERVICES	79546	95	653	EDUCATIONAL SERVICES
79077	4	27	EDUCATIONAL SERVICES	79344	10	43	EDUCATIONAL SERVICES	79547	38	160	EDUCATIONAL SERVICES
79078	10	56	UTILITIES	79345	18	146	EDUCATIONAL SERVICES	79549	759	6704	SPECIAL TRADE CONTRACTORS
79079	197	1073	EDUCATIONAL SERVICES	79346	120	496	MERCH. WHOLESALERS;DURABLE GDS	79550	3	4	FOOD AND BEVERAGE STORES
79080	30	143	PIPELINE TRANSPORTATION	79347	363	2651	EDUCATIONAL SERVICES	79553	197	1324	EDUCATIONAL SERVICES
79081	226	1800	EDUCATIONAL SERVICES	79350	22	174	EDUCATIONAL SERVICES	79556	660	5224	EDUCATIONAL SERVICES
79082	25	219	EDUCATIONAL SERVICES	79351	71	378	EDUCATIONAL SERVICES	79560	6	8	RELIG.; GRANT; CIVIC; PROF ORG
79083	87	490	EDUCATIONAL SERVICES	79353	4	15	EDUCATIONAL SERVICES	79561	20	120	EDUCATIONAL SERVICES
79084	177	760	EDUCATIONAL SERVICES	79355	120	479	EDUCATIONAL SERVICES	79562	104	458	EDUCATIONAL SERVICES
79085	7	104	ANIMAL PRODUCTION	79356	254	1320	SOCIAL ASSISTANCE	79563	53	871	GASOLINE STATIONS
79086	108	1572	PETROLEUM & COAL PRODUCTS MFG	79357	94	454	EDUCATIONAL SERVICES	79565	15	140	EDUCATIONAL SERVICES
79087	63	270	EDUCATIONAL SERVICES	79358	31	232	EDUCATIONAL SERVICES	79566	17	19	PETROLEUM & COAL PRODUCTS MFG
79088	269	2035	EDUCATIONAL SERVICES	79359	108	734	EDUCATIONAL SERVICES	79567	154	1106	PROF.; SCIENTIFIC; & TECH SVCS
79091	19	18	ADMIN. ENVIRO. QUALITY PROGRMS	79360	487	3476	EDUCATIONAL SERVICES	79601	1440	18804	HOSPITALS
79092	95	412	EDUCATIONAL SERVICES	79363	98	718	EDUCATIONAL SERVICES	79602	1225	10586	SPECIAL TRADE CONTRACTORS
79093	5	16	WAREHOUSING AND STORAGE	79364	274	1769	EDUCATIONAL SERVICES	79603	683	5380	EDUCATIONAL SERVICES
79094	2	4	ANIMAL PRODUCTION	79366	22	55	EXEC.; LEGIS.; & OTHER SUPPORT	79604	19	44	HEAVY & CIVIL ENG. CONSTRUCT'N
79095	166	1091	EDUCATIONAL SERVICES	79367	21	221	EDUCATIONAL SERVICES	79605	1275	10662	FOOD SVCS & DRINKING PLACES
79096	150	863	EDUCATIONAL SERVICES	79369	4	24	SUPPORT ACTIVITIES: AGR./FOR.	79606	712	9212	FOOD SVCS & DRINKING PLACES
79097	56	211	HEAVY & CIVIL ENG. CONSTRUCT'N	79370	114	579	EDUCATIONAL SERVICES	79607	50	306	COMPUTER & ELECTRONIC PROD MFG
79098	21	122	WAREHOUSING AND STORAGE	79371	51	363	EDUCATIONAL SERVICES	79608	24	71	CONSTRUCTION OF BUILDINGS
79101	1565	16378	JUSTICE; PUBIC ORDER/SAFETY	79372	83	877	SPECIAL TRADE CONTRACTORS	79697	3	11	OTHER INFORMATION SERVICES
79102	596	5741	SPORTG GDS;HOBBY;BOOK; & MUSIC	79373	129	946	EDUCATIONAL SERVICES	79698	1	20	OTHER INFORMATION SERVICES
79103	289	3908	GENERAL MERCHANDISE STORES	79376	9	25	OIL AND GAS EXTRACTION	79699	3	880	EDUCATIONAL SERVICES
79104	240	1868	RELIG.; GRANT; CIVIC; PROF ORG	79377	21	108	SPECIAL TRADE CONTRACTORS	79701	3157	23993	SPECIAL TRADE CONTRACTORS
79105	23	106	PROF.; SCIENTIFIC; & TECH SVCS	79378	9	143	EDUCATIONAL SERVICES	79702	23	151	SOCIAL ASSISTANCE
79106	1595	23439	HOSPITALS	79379	32	417	EDUCATIONAL SERVICES	79703	649	8062	HOSPITALS
79107	842	8535	JUSTICE; PUBIC ORDER/SAFETY	79380	6	103	EDUCATIONAL SERVICES	79704	6	17	CHEMICAL MANUFACTURING
79108	321	7572	FOOD MANUFACTURING	79381	26	218	EDUCATIONAL SERVICES	79705	1492	12855	EDUCATIONAL SERVICES
79109	2666	17086	FOOD SVCS & DRINKING PLACES	79382	172	1582	EDUCATIONAL SERVICES	79706	821	10985	SPECIAL TRADE CONTRACTORS
79110	683	5047	ADMINISTRATIVE & SUPPORT SVCS	79383	19	89	EDUCATIONAL SERVICES	79707	629	6245	FOOD SVCS & DRINKING PLACES
79111	52	1960	MOTOR VEHICLE & PARTS DEALERS	79401	1338	15278	JUSTICE; PUBIC ORDER/SAFETY	79708	14	42	UNCLASSIFIED ESTABLISHMENTS
79114	35	47	SPECIAL TRADE CONTRACTORS	79402	1	430	POSTAL SERVICE	79710	9	3	SUPPORT ACTIVITIES FOR MINING
79116	15	30	ADMINISTRATIVE & SUPPORT SVCS	79403	481	8202	EDUCATIONAL SERVICES	79711	14	483	POSTAL SERVICE
79117	2	6	SPECIAL TRADE CONTRACTORS	79404	798	12407	MERCH. WHOLESALERS;DURABLE GDS	79713	21	148	SUPPORT ACTIVITIES: AGR./FOR.
79118	642	7926	MERCH. WHOLESALERS;NONDUR. GDS	79407	693	7423	TELECOMMUNICATIONS	79714	555	5633	SPECIAL TRADE CONTRACTORS
79119	380	4375	SPORTG GDS;HOBBY;BOOK; & MUSIC	79408	19	35	RELIG.; GRANT; CIVIC; PROF ORG	79718	38	203	EDUCATIONAL SERVICES
79120	18	6719	EXEC.; LEGIS.; & OTHER SUPPORT	79409	29	8722	EDUCATIONAL SERVICES	79719	7	31	UTILITIES
79121	283	2671	GENERAL MERCHANDISE STORES	79410	858	17430	AMBULATORY HEALTH CARE SVCS	79720	1163	10753	HOSPITALS
79124	362	4048	NURSING & RESID. CARE FACILIT.	79411	286	2336	EDUCATIONAL SERVICES	79721	4	11	SPECIAL TRADE CONTRACTORS
79159	9	20	PERFORM'G ARTS; SPEC. SPORTS	79412	505	4391	TELECOMMUNICATIONS	79730	19	140	UTILITIES
79201	335	2765	HOSPITALS	79413	767	6467	AMBULATORY HEALTH CARE SVCS	79731	193	1676	SPECIAL TRADE CONTRACTORS
79220	6	36	EDUCATIONAL SERVICES	79414	748	7784	FOOD SVCS & DRINKING PLACES	79733	25	218	EDUCATIONAL SERVICES
79221	2	61	MERCH. WHOLESALERS;NONDUR. GDS	79415	542	8977	HOSPITALS	79734	141	1529	RELIG.; GRANT; CIVIC; PROF ORG
79223	5	2	SPECIAL TRADE CONTRACTORS	79416	561	6579	FOOD SVCS & DRINKING PLACES	79735	564	5389	SUPPORT ACTIVITIES FOR MINING
79225	34	149	HOSPITALS	79423	1461	15342	AMBULATORY HEALTH CARE SVCS	79738	24	188	EDUCATIONAL SERVICES
79226	194	892	EDUCATIONAL SERVICES	79424	1696	14397	FOOD SVCS & DRINKING PLACES	79739	65	374	EDUCATIONAL SERVICES
79227	109	470	EDUCATIONAL SERVICES	79430	60	793	AMBULATORY HEALTH CARE SVCS	79740	1	3	ANIMAL PRODUCTION
79229	34	112	FOOD SVCS & DRINKING PLACES	79452	5	64	POSTAL SERVICE	79741	37	249	SPECIAL TRADE CONTRACTORS
79230	6	14	SUPPORT ACTIVITIES: AGR./FOR.	79453	19	64	SOCIAL ASSISTANCE	79742	29	111	EDUCATIONAL SERVICES
79231	4	27	SUPPORT ACTIVITIES: AGR./FOR.	79457	4	71	EXEC.; LEGIS.; & OTHER SUPPORT	79743	21	142	EDUCATIONAL SERVICES
79233	12	40	TRUCK TRANSPORTATION	79464	27	145	CONSTRUCTION OF BUILDINGS	79744	101	915	SPECIAL TRADE CONTRACTORS
79234	7	4	SUPPORT ACTIVITIES: AGR./FOR.	79490	7	42	POSTAL SERVICE	79745	266	1598	SPECIAL TRADE CONTRACTORS
79235	201	1703	EDUCATIONAL SERVICES	79493	32	60	SPECIAL TRADE CONTRACTORS	79748	8	42	RELIG.; GRANT; CIVIC; PROF ORG
79236	23	106	ANIMAL PRODUCTION	79499	9	12	SECURITIES/COMMODITY CONTRACTS	79749	20	95	EDUCATIONAL SERVICES
79237	17	87	EDUCATIONAL SERVICES	79501	168	1147	HOSPITALS	79752	122	960	EDUCATIONAL SERVICES
79239	7	55	SUPPORT ACTIVITIES: AGR./FOR.	79502	110	526	CONSTRUCTION OF BUILDINGS	79754	16	27	EXEC.; LEGIS.; & OTHER SUPPORT
79240	2	7	SUPPORT ACTIVITIES: AGR./FOR.	79503	7	16	EDUCATIONAL SERVICES	79755	24	180	OIL AND GAS EXTRACTION

ZIP CODE	2009 Total Firms	2009 Total Employ-ees	TOP INDUSTRY RANKED on 2009 EMPLOYMENT
79756	407	3195	SPECIAL TRADE CONTRACTORS
79758	48	112	BROADCASTING
79759	2	1	POSTAL SERVICE
79760	9	46	EXEC.; LEGIS.; & OTHER SUPPORT
79761	1780	18277	HOSPITALS
79762	1436	13856	FOOD SVCS & DRINKING PLACES
79763	745	8510	EDUCATIONAL SERVICES
79764	902	8900	MERCH. WHOLESALERS;DURABLE GDS
79765	487	5656	SPECIAL TRADE CONTRACTORS
79766	185	4175	SPECIAL TRADE CONTRACTORS
79768	24	58	OIL AND GAS EXTRACTION
79769	3	6	MERCH. WHOLESALERS;NONDUR. GDS
79770	10	85	OIL AND GAS EXTRACTION
79772	459	4352	CROP PRODUCTION
79776	5	41	TRUCK TRANSPORTATION
79777	19	316	NURSING & RESID. CARE FACILIT.
79778	68	227	EDUCATIONAL SERVICES
79780	4	10	SOCIAL ASSISTANCE
79781	44	71	TRUCK TRANSPORTATION
79782	168	1273	EDUCATIONAL SERVICES
79783	3	18	FOOD MANUFACTURING
79785	11	21	JUSTICE; PUBIC ORDER/SAFETY
79786	4	14	MUSEUMS; HIST. SITES;& SIMILAR
79788	21	245	SPECIAL TRADE CONTRACTORS
79789	37	154	JUSTICE; PUBIC ORDER/SAFETY
79821	226	2437	PRIMARY METAL MANUFACTURING
79830	513	3106	EDUCATIONAL SERVICES
79831	6	13	ANIMAL PRODUCTION
79834	21	323	MUSEUMS; HIST. SITES;& SIMILAR
79835	363	2554	EDUCATIONAL SERVICES
79836	112	644	EDUCATIONAL SERVICES
79837	53	254	EDUCATIONAL SERVICES
79838	160	1392	FOOD SVCS & DRINKING PLACES
79839	40	262	EDUCATIONAL SERVICES
79842	57	232	ACCOMMODATION
79843	205	1285	MERCH. WHOLESALERS;NONDUR. GDS
79845	171	928	EDUCATIONAL SERVICES
79846	1	0	ANIMAL PRODUCTION
79847	30	58	ANIMAL PRODUCTION
79848	122	318	EDUCATIONAL SERVICES
79849	103	989	EDUCATIONAL SERVICES
79851	66	288	JUSTICE; PUBIC ORDER/SAFETY
79852	83	886	ACCOMMODATION
79853	28	321	EDUCATIONAL SERVICES
79854	5	22	EDUCATIONAL SERVICES
79855	175	852	GASOLINE STATIONS
79901	1671	26829	EXEC.; LEGIS.; & OTHER SUPPORT
79902	1560	24508	HOSPITALS
79903	964	6389	PROF.; SCIENTIFIC; & TECH SVCS
79904	608	4281	EDUCATIONAL SERVICES
79905	1061	17427	AMBULATORY HEALTH CARE SVCS
79906	197	4863	TRANSPORTATION EQUIPMENT MFG
79907	1158	15850	EDUCATIONAL SERVICES
79908	10	693	JUSTICE; PUBIC ORDER/SAFETY
79910	2	0	POSTAL SERVICE
79911	4	5	SUPPORT ACT. FOR TRANSPORT.
79912	2309	26377	FOOD SVCS & DRINKING PLACES
79913	28	53	CONSTRUCTION OF BUILDINGS
79914	5	51	PROF.; SCIENTIFIC; & TECH SVCS
79915	1262	14303	MERCH. WHOLESALERS;DURABLE GDS
79916	60	344	FOOD SVCS & DRINKING PLACES
79918	9	40	FOOD SVCS & DRINKING PLACES
79920	11	2170	HOSPITALS
79922	335	3159	MOTOR VEHICLE & PARTS DEALERS
79923	7	19	CONSTRUCTION OF BUILDINGS
79924	1011	11621	EDUCATIONAL SERVICES
79925	2529	33980	FOOD SVCS & DRINKING PLACES
79926	4	3	ADMINISTRATIVE & SUPPORT SVCS
79927	661	7104	MERCH. WHOLESALERS;DURABLE GDS
79928	430	5550	TRUCK TRANSPORTATION
79929	2	9	ADMINISTRATIVE & SUPPORT SVCS
79930	489	4595	EDUCATIONAL SERVICES
79931	2	7	ADMINISTRATIVE & SUPPORT SVCS
79932	540	4657	FOOD SVCS & DRINKING PLACES
79934	95	1234	EDUCATIONAL SERVICES
79935	794	9332	ELECTRONICS & APPLIANCE STORES
79936	2576	27554	FOOD SVCS & DRINKING PLACES
79937	7	25	SPORTG GDS;HOBBY;BOOK; & MUSIC
79938	426	3353	EDUCATIONAL SERVICES
79942	2	3	UNCLASSIFIED ESTABLISHMENTS
79943	1	0	PERSONAL AND LAUNDRY SERVICES
79946	1	0	PROF.; SCIENTIFIC; & TECH SVCS
79948	2	50	SOCIAL ASSISTANCE
79968	10	2786	EDUCATIONAL SERVICES
79996	9	12	SPECIAL TRADE CONTRACTORS
79997	7	9	MISCELLANEOUS MANUFACTURING
80001	30	153	ADMINISTRATIVE & SUPPORT SVCS
80002	1472	12789	FOOD SVCS & DRINKING PLACES
80003	941	8488	FOOD SVCS & DRINKING PLACES
80004	672	4771	EDUCATIONAL SERVICES
80005	415	2894	EDUCATIONAL SERVICES
80006	22	73	ADMINISTRATIVE & SUPPORT SVCS
80007	188	2028	MACHINERY MANUFACTURING
80010	931	5461	EDUCATIONAL SERVICES
80011	1804	31004	MERCH. WHOLESALERS;DURABLE GDS
80012	1411	19382	FOOD SVCS & DRINKING PLACES
80013	696	5403	EDUCATIONAL SERVICES
80014	1980	19539	FOOD SVCS & DRINKING PLACES
80015	1076	7216	EDUCATIONAL SERVICES
80016	724	6321	FOOD SVCS & DRINKING PLACES
80017	348	2664	FOOD SVCS & DRINKING PLACES
80018	64	265	EDUCATIONAL SERVICES
80019	21	394	FURNITURE & RELATED PROD. MFG
80020	1653	16448	FOOD SVCS & DRINKING PLACES
80021	1248	24438	PROF.; SCIENTIFIC; & TECH SVCS
80022	1463	23287	TRUCK TRANSPORTATION
80023	297	2206	FOOD SVCS & DRINKING PLACES
80024	3	31	SPECIAL TRADE CONTRACTORS
80025	11	48	MUSEUMS; HIST. SITES;& SIMILAR
80026	1098	11027	PROF.; SCIENTIFIC; & TECH SVCS
80027	1309	19575	PROF.; SCIENTIFIC; & TECH SVCS
80030	534	3513	EDUCATIONAL SERVICES
80031	965	9303	FOOD SVCS & DRINKING PLACES
80033	1821	19793	HOSPITALS
80034	23	51	WASTE MANAGMT & REMEDIAT'N SVC
80035	23	78	ADMINISTRATIVE & SUPPORT SVCS
80036	8	14	REAL ESTATE
80037	9	17	SPECIAL TRADE CONTRACTORS
80038	23	112	PUBLISHING INDUSTRIES
80040	5	69	SPECIAL TRADE CONTRACTORS
80041	6	5	MERCH. WHOLESALERS;DURABLE GDS
80042	9	16	PERSONAL AND LAUNDRY SERVICES
80044	16	32	FABRICATED METAL PRODUCT MFG
80045	79	6700	HOSPITALS
80046	39	106	REAL ESTATE
80047	21	153	SOCIAL ASSISTANCE
80101	20	79	JUSTICE; PUBIC ORDER/SAFETY
80102	176	500	SPECIAL TRADE CONTRACTORS
80103	146	637	EDUCATIONAL SERVICES
80104	1119	12234	EXEC.; LEGIS.; & OTHER SUPPORT
80105	70	179	EDUCATIONAL SERVICES
80106	100	423	ACCOMMODATION
80107	430	1706	EDUCATIONAL SERVICES
80108	522	3851	FOOD SVCS & DRINKING PLACES
80109	455	5147	JUSTICE; PUBIC ORDER/SAFETY
80110	2122	23179	SPECIAL TRADE CONTRACTORS
80111	3263	52223	INSURANCE CARRIERS & RELATED
80112	3986	74730	PROF.; SCIENTIFIC; & TECH SVCS
80113	1009	8780	HOSPITALS
80116	217	1100	HEAVY & CIVIL ENG. CONSTRUCT'N
80117	126	760	EDUCATIONAL SERVICES
80118	147	696	NURSING & RESID. CARE FACILIT.
80120	1768	18243	EXEC.; LEGIS.; & OTHER SUPPORT
80121	479	4163	MOTOR VEHICLE & PARTS DEALERS
80122	1105	10016	FOOD SVCS & DRINKING PLACES
80123	1447	14439	FOOD SVCS & DRINKING PLACES
80124	994	15940	FOOD SVCS & DRINKING PLACES
80125	446	14833	COMPUTER & ELECTRONIC PROD MFG
80126	769	6453	EDUCATIONAL SERVICES
80127	1363	10101	FOOD SVCS & DRINKING PLACES
80128	660	3428	EDUCATIONAL SERVICES
80129	714	8470	REAL ESTATE
80130	231	1874	EDUCATIONAL SERVICES
80131	23	113	FABRICATED METAL PRODUCT MFG
80132	718	4701	EDUCATIONAL SERVICES
80133	120	605	FOOD SVCS & DRINKING PLACES
80134	1530	10618	FOOD SVCS & DRINKING PLACES
80135	200	1341	SPECIAL TRADE CONTRACTORS
80136	183	591	FOOD SVCS & DRINKING PLACES
80137	77	930	EDUCATIONAL SERVICES
80138	680	4714	FOOD SVCS & DRINKING PLACES
80150	9	19	MOTOR VEHICLE & PARTS DEALERS
80151	8	58	EDUCATIONAL SERVICES
80155	30	57	PROF.; SCIENTIFIC; & TECH SVCS
80160	21	40	SPECIAL TRADE CONTRACTORS
80161	34	122	ADMINISTRATIVE & SUPPORT SVCS
80162	31	72	SPECIAL TRADE CONTRACTORS
80163	45	122	SPECIAL TRADE CONTRACTORS
80165	1	20	MUSEUMS; HIST. SITES;& SIMILAR
80201	29	54	UNCLASSIFIED ESTABLISHMENTS
80202	4935	69726	PROF.; SCIENTIFIC; & TECH SVCS
80203	2030	28495	PROF.; SCIENTIFIC; & TECH SVCS
80204	1753	45898	EDUCATIONAL SERVICES
80205	1223	11399	PROF.; SCIENTIFIC; & TECH SVCS
80206	2113	17036	AMBULATORY HEALTH CARE SVCS
80207	555	8700	PRINT'G & RELATED SUPP'T ACT'S
80208	10	39	EDUCATIONAL SERVICES
80209	1299	8728	FOOD SVCS & DRINKING PLACES
80210	1556	12948	EDUCATIONAL SERVICES
80211	1362	11271	EDUCATIONAL SERVICES
80212	603	4624	FOOD AND BEVERAGE STORES
80214	1143	10632	ADMINISTRATIVE & SUPPORT SVCS
80215	1182	11910	ADMIN. OF ECONOMIC PROGRAMS
80216	2148	39280	MERCH. WHOLESALERS;DURABLE GDS
80217	10	41	ADMINISTRATIVE & SUPPORT SVCS
80218	942	9547	HOSPITALS
80219	1045	5880	EDUCATIONAL SERVICES
80220	963	16353	EDUCATIONAL SERVICES
80221	1094	12821	EDUCATIONAL SERVICES
80222	2000	24138	ADMIN. OF ECONOMIC PROGRAMS
80223	1589	24222	PRINT'G & RELATED SUPP'T ACT'S
80224	666	5450	CONSTRUCTION OF BUILDINGS
80225	14	46	SOCIAL ASSISTANCE
80226	1305	12748	SOCIAL ASSISTANCE
80227	933	6680	EDUCATIONAL SERVICES
80228	1221	13060	PROF.; SCIENTIFIC; & TECH SVCS
80229	1333	18739	EXEC.; LEGIS.; & OTHER SUPPORT
80230	221	4522	AMBULATORY HEALTH CARE SVCS
80231	1248	10926	REAL ESTATE
80232	522	3303	FOOD SVCS & DRINKING PLACES
80233	938	9135	FOOD SVCS & DRINKING PLACES
80234	1048	11415	FOOD SVCS & DRINKING PLACES
80235	314	4906	PROF.; SCIENTIFIC; & TECH SVCS
80236	194	2991	EDUCATIONAL SERVICES
80237	1171	18124	PROF.; SCIENTIFIC; & TECH SVCS
80238	316	5047	FOOD SVCS & DRINKING PLACES
80239	1135	18727	MERCH. WHOLESALERS;DURABLE GDS
80241	387	5040	EDUCATIONAL SERVICES
80246	923	14129	ADMIN. HUMAN RESOURCE PROGRAMS
80247	236	1931	AMBULATORY HEALTH CARE SVCS
80248	4	4	PROF.; SCIENTIFIC; & TECH SVCS
80249	294	15943	SUPPORT ACT. FOR TRANSPORT.
80250	31	76	SOCIAL ASSISTANCE
80260	572	4874	EDUCATIONAL SERVICES
80262	27	145	AMBULATORY HEALTH CARE SVCS
80264	69	712	PROF.; SCIENTIFIC; & TECH SVCS
80265	62	1715	PROF.; SCIENTIFIC; & TECH SVCS
80266	7	3101	POSTAL SERVICE
80273	3	0	INSURANCE CARRIERS & RELATED
80274	4	2010	CREDIT INTERMEDIATION & RELATD
80279	1	0	UNCLASSIFIED ESTABLISHMENTS
80280	3	602	EXEC.; LEGIS.; & OTHER SUPPORT
80290	53	957	PROF.; SCIENTIFIC; & TECH SVCS
80293	97	951	ADMINISTRATIVE & SUPPORT SVCS
80294	26	492	JUSTICE; PUBIC ORDER/SAFETY
80295	7	173	PROF.; SCIENTIFIC; & TECH SVCS
80299	1	0	UNCLASSIFIED ESTABLISHMENTS
80301	2748	39929	COMPUTER & ELECTRONIC PROD MFG
80302	2670	20953	FOOD SVCS & DRINKING PLACES
80303	1267	10409	PROF.; SCIENTIFIC; & TECH SVCS
80304	984	9381	SOCIAL ASSISTANCE
80305	525	7014	EXEC.; LEGIS.; & OTHER SUPPORT
80306	47	107	ACCOMMODATION
80307	9	28	PROF.; SCIENTIFIC; & TECH SVCS
80308	40	145	ADMINISTRATIVE & SUPPORT SVCS
80309	52	8186	EDUCATIONAL SERVICES
80310	1	4	RELIG.; GRANT; CIVIC; PROF ORG
80321	1	0	UNCLASSIFIED ESTABLISHMENTS
80401	2451	32747	PROF.; SCIENTIFIC; & TECH SVCS
80402	14	28	PROF.; SCIENTIFIC; & TECH SVCS
80403	589	10539	EXEC.; LEGIS.; & OTHER SUPPORT
80419	44	1341	EXEC.; LEGIS.; & OTHER SUPPORT
80420	42	70	REAL ESTATE
80421	261	1019	ACCOMMODATION
80422	154	3657	AMUSEMENT; GAMBLING;& RECREAT.
80423	11	20	MOTOR VEHICLE & PARTS DEALERS
80424	972	9074	ACCOMMODATION
80425	10	17	SUPPORT ACTIVITIES: AGR./FOR.
80426	2	1	POSTAL SERVICE
80427	63	460	AMUSEMENT; GAMBLING;& RECREAT.
80428	24	186	ACCOMMODATION
80430	9	15	ANIMAL PRODUCTION
80432	9	34	ACCOMMODATION
80433	391	1558	FOOD AND BEVERAGE STORES
80434	3	1	TRUCK TRANSPORTATION
80435	540	7369	ACCOMMODATION
80436	31	187	EXEC.; LEGIS.; & OTHER SUPPORT
80437	57	83	PROF.; SCIENTIFIC; & TECH SVCS
80438	30	836	MINING (EXCEPT OIL AND GAS)
80439	1462	6881	EDUCATIONAL SERVICES
80440	275	1537	ACCOMMODATION
80442	256	1185	AMUSEMENT; GAMBLING;& RECREAT.
80443	612	5514	ACCOMMODATION
80444	114	1013	ACCOMMODATION
80446	421	2604	ACCOMMODATION
80447	214	955	AMUSEMENT; GAMBLING;& RECREAT.
80448	6	43	ACCOMMODATION
80449	31	108	CONSTRUCTION OF BUILDINGS
80451	68	317	JUSTICE; PUBIC ORDER/SAFETY
80452	249	1437	FOOD SVCS & DRINKING PLACES

ZIP CODE	2009 Total Firms	2009 Total Employees	TOP INDUSTRY RANKED on 2009 EMPLOYMENT
80453	15	17	ADMINISTRATIVE & SUPPORT SVCS
80454	45	233	ACCOMMODATION
80455	14	73	JUSTICE; PUBIC ORDER/SAFETY
80456	22	37	REAL ESTATE
80457	40	81	FOOD SVCS & DRINKING PLACES
80459	169	827	EDUCATIONAL SERVICES
80461	375	1932	EDUCATIONAL SERVICES
80463	17	31	AMUSEMENT; GAMBLING;& RECREAT.
80465	353	1652	FOOD SVCS & DRINKING PLACES
80466	174	961	ACCOMMODATION
80467	82	731	MINING (EXCEPT OIL AND GAS)
80468	16	73	ACCOMMODATION
80469	10	17	RELIG.; GRANT; CIVIC; PROF ORG
80470	166	498	SPECIAL TRADE CONTRACTORS
80471	2	2	POSTAL SERVICE
80473	4	8	ACCOMMODATION
80474	22	57	SPECIAL TRADE CONTRACTORS
80475	9	14	ACCOMMODATION
80476	17	79	RAIL TRANSPORTATION
80477	30	61	SPECIAL TRADE CONTRACTORS
80478	60	381	ACCOMMODATION
80479	5	3	RENTAL AND LEASING SERVICES
80480	130	526	FOOD SVCS & DRINKING PLACES
80481	17	69	ACCOMMODATION
80482	264	3686	ACCOMMODATION
80483	38	149	EDUCATIONAL SERVICES
80487	1754	15431	ACCOMMODATION
80488	24	45	SPECIAL TRADE CONTRACTORS
80497	16	100	ADMINISTRATIVE & SUPPORT SVCS
80498	466	4001	BLDG MATL & GARDEN EQPMT DLRS
80501	2926	28009	FOOD SVCS & DRINKING PLACES
80502	39	75	ADMINISTRATIVE & SUPPORT SVCS
80503	682	8039	PROF.; SCIENTIFIC; & TECH SVCS
80504	703	7587	SPECIAL TRADE CONTRACTORS
80510	34	150	ACCOMMODATION
80511	5	650	SOCIAL ASSISTANCE
80512	79	346	ADMIN. ENVIRO. QUALITY PROGRMS
80513	477	3247	WOOD PRODUCT MANUFACTURING
80514	88	682	FABRICATED METAL PRODUCT MFG
80515	14	48	AMUSEMENT; GAMBLING;& RECREAT.
80516	472	2810	SPECIAL TRADE CONTRACTORS
80517	1008	6523	FOOD SVCS & DRINKING PLACES
80520	34	184	EXEC.; LEGIS.; & OTHER SUPPORT
80521	855	8931	EDUCATIONAL SERVICES
80522	34	2610	EXEC.; LEGIS.; & OTHER SUPPORT
80523	32	8598	EDUCATIONAL SERVICES
80524	2985	28416	HOSPITALS
80525	2774	32367	PROF.; SCIENTIFIC; & TECH SVCS
80526	1013	7584	PROF.; SCIENTIFIC; & TECH SVCS
80527	39	133	SPECIAL TRADE CONTRACTORS
80528	374	7506	ELECTRONICS & APPLIANCE STORES
80530	101	824	MERCH. WHOLESALERS;NONDUR. GDS
80532	5	12	ACCOMMODATION
80533	12	30	FOOD AND BEVERAGE STORES
80534	334	2012	FOOD SVCS & DRINKING PLACES
80535	120	642	EDUCATIONAL SERVICES
80536	52	171	RELIG.; GRANT; CIVIC; PROF ORG
80537	2047	14871	SPECIAL TRADE CONTRACTORS
80538	1523	18839	FOOD SVCS & DRINKING PLACES
80539	23	37	ADMINISTRATIVE & SUPPORT SVCS
80540	233	761	FOOD SVCS & DRINKING PLACES
80541	3	7	CONSTRUCTION OF BUILDINGS
80542	111	449	CHEMICAL MANUFACTURING
80543	91	759	CONSTRUCTION OF BUILDINGS
80544	71	183	PROF.; SCIENTIFIC; & TECH SVCS
80545	63	192	ACCOMMODATION
80546	24	59	GASOLINE STATIONS
80547	23	201	FURNITURE & RELATED PROD. MFG
80549	226	1171	BLDG MATL & GARDEN EQPMT DLRS
80550	866	7280	MACHINERY MANUFACTURING
80601	1101	11241	EXEC.; LEGIS.; & OTHER SUPPORT
80602	231	1157	EDUCATIONAL SERVICES
80603	219	1883	SPECIAL TRADE CONTRACTORS
80610	117	391	EDUCATIONAL SERVICES
80611	38	88	EDUCATIONAL SERVICES
80612	21	88	UTILITIES
80614	32	128	SPECIAL TRADE CONTRACTORS
80615	232	1319	EDUCATIONAL SERVICES
80620	316	3094	SOCIAL ASSISTANCE
80621	375	4440	EDUCATIONAL SERVICES
80622	20	47	EDUCATIONAL SERVICES
80623	29	245	EDUCATIONAL SERVICES
80624	19	171	ANIMAL PRODUCTION
80631	2185	28323	AMBULATORY HEALTH CARE SVCS
80632	8	13	SPECIAL TRADE CONTRACTORS
80633	16	51	SPECIAL TRADE CONTRACTORS
80634	1758	15983	FOOD SVCS & DRINKING PLACES
80638	1	1300	INSURANCE CARRIERS & RELATED
80639	14	5130	OTHER INFORMATION SERVICES
80640	345	7118	TRUCK TRANSPORTATION

ZIP CODE	2009 Total Firms	2009 Total Employees	TOP INDUSTRY RANKED on 2009 EMPLOYMENT
80642	114	646	MERCH. WHOLESALERS;NONDUR. GDS
80643	122	483	EDUCATIONAL SERVICES
80644	79	676	EDUCATIONAL SERVICES
80645	160	1166	AMUSEMENT; GAMBLING;& RECREAT.
80646	17	169	TRUCK TRANSPORTATION
80648	40	139	PROF.; SCIENTIFIC; & TECH SVCS
80649	9	71	PROF.; SCIENTIFIC; & TECH SVCS
80650	36	157	EDUCATIONAL SERVICES
80651	150	1167	MERCH. WHOLESALERS;NONDUR. GDS
80652	35	251	ADMINISTRATIVE & SUPPORT SVCS
80653	26	167	JUSTICE; PUBIC ORDER/SAFETY
80654	148	862	ANIMAL PRODUCTION
80701	773	8216	FOOD MANUFACTURING
80705	9	21	SPECIAL TRADE CONTRACTORS
80720	161	774	EDUCATIONAL SERVICES
80721	16	55	WAREHOUSING AND STORAGE
80722	15	61	FOOD SVCS & DRINKING PLACES
80723	297	2246	NURSING & RESID. CARE FACILIT.
80726	25	91	GASOLINE STATIONS
80727	19	25	CROP PRODUCTION
80728	50	195	EDUCATIONAL SERVICES
80729	28	125	EDUCATIONAL SERVICES
80731	118	743	MERCH. WHOLESALERS;NONDUR. GDS
80732	2	6	FOOD SVCS & DRINKING PLACES
80733	12	183	INSURANCE CARRIERS & RELATED
80734	257	1361	CROP PRODUCTION
80735	33	162	ANIMAL PRODUCTION
80736	15	177	ANIMAL PRODUCTION
80737	144	936	FOOD MANUFACTURING
80740	7	7	CROP PRODUCTION
80741	27	245	EDUCATIONAL SERVICES
80742	18	63	EDUCATIONAL SERVICES
80743	35	327	EDUCATIONAL SERVICES
80744	25	110	EDUCATIONAL SERVICES
80745	3	2	PROF.; SCIENTIFIC; & TECH SVCS
80746	2	10	WAREHOUSING AND STORAGE
80747	24	124	EDUCATIONAL SERVICES
80749	13	32	EDUCATIONAL SERVICES
80750	7	33	HEAVY & CIVIL ENG. CONSTRUCT'N
80751	899	7556	JUSTICE; PUBIC ORDER/SAFETY
80754	14	20	MISCELLANEOUS STORE RETAILERS
80755	4	23	JUSTICE; PUBIC ORDER/SAFETY
80757	18	47	EDUCATIONAL SERVICES
80758	265	1952	SPECIAL TRADE CONTRACTORS
80759	289	2071	CROP PRODUCTION
80801	19	82	EDUCATIONAL SERVICES
80802	7	11	EXEC.; LEGIS.; & OTHER SUPPORT
80804	31	50	ADMIN. OF ECONOMIC PROGRAMS
80805	11	69	CROP PRODUCTION
80807	346	2152	ADMINISTRATIVE & SUPPORT SVCS
80808	168	804	EDUCATIONAL SERVICES
80809	67	334	AMUSEMENT; GAMBLING;& RECREAT.
80810	120	627	SPECIAL TRADE CONTRACTORS
80812	11	12	POSTAL SERVICE
80813	151	2788	AMUSEMENT; GAMBLING;& RECREAT.
80814	114	541	EDUCATIONAL SERVICES
80815	86	314	EDUCATIONAL SERVICES
80816	116	344	ACCOMMODATION
80817	434	3955	FOOD SVCS & DRINKING PLACES
80818	22	33	EXEC.; LEGIS.; & OTHER SUPPORT
80819	37	272	SOCIAL ASSISTANCE
80820	19	170	EXEC.; LEGIS.; & OTHER SUPPORT
80821	80	418	HOSPITALS
80822	23	87	EDUCATIONAL SERVICES
80823	15	45	EDUCATIONAL SERVICES
80824	21	65	RELIG.; GRANT; CIVIC; PROF ORG
80825	43	131	EDUCATIONAL SERVICES
80827	57	215	RELIG.; GRANT; CIVIC; PROF ORG
80828	216	1799	JUSTICE; PUBIC ORDER/SAFETY
80829	333	1859	FOOD SVCS & DRINKING PLACES
80830	10	23	COMPUTER & ELECTRONIC PROD MFG
80831	406	2038	EDUCATIONAL SERVICES
80832	20	21	ANIMAL PRODUCTION
80833	24	165	EDUCATIONAL SERVICES
80834	27	72	EDUCATIONAL SERVICES
80835	60	353	EDUCATIONAL SERVICES
80836	72	383	MERCH. WHOLESALERS;NONDUR. GDS
80840	90	1308	HOSPITALS
80860	27	938	MINING (EXCEPT OIL AND GAS)
80861	11	32	EDUCATIONAL SERVICES
80862	3	5	ANIMAL PRODUCTION
80863	626	3733	EDUCATIONAL SERVICES
80864	24	63	EDUCATIONAL SERVICES
80866	15	45	FOOD SVCS & DRINKING PLACES
80901	37	40	SPECIAL TRADE CONTRACTORS
80902	13	245	EDUCATIONAL SERVICES
80903	2689	29935	EDUCATIONAL SERVICES
80904	1003	8195	SOCIAL ASSISTANCE
80905	850	9702	MOTOR VEHICLE & PARTS DEALERS
80906	1236	20103	ADMINISTRATIVE & SUPPORT SVCS

ZIP CODE	2009 Total Firms	2009 Total Employees	TOP INDUSTRY RANKED on 2009 EMPLOYMENT
80907	2047	31414	HOSPITALS
80908	404	2088	MERCH. WHOLESALERS;DURABLE GDS
80909	2352	25753	HOSPITALS
80910	760	13931	EDUCATIONAL SERVICES
80911	474	3411	EDUCATIONAL SERVICES
80912	4	4803	NAT'L SECURITY & INT'L AFFAIRS
80913	88	829	SPECIAL TRADE CONTRACTORS
80914	36	9648	NAT'L SECURITY & INT'L AFFAIRS
80915	983	9513	SPECIAL TRADE CONTRACTORS
80916	649	8708	EDUCATIONAL SERVICES
80917	697	4391	EDUCATIONAL SERVICES
80918	2211	15501	FOOD SVCS & DRINKING PLACES
80919	841	37912	INSURANCE CARRIERS & RELATED
80920	1457	21495	FOOD SVCS & DRINKING PLACES
80921	343	5408	RELIG.; GRANT; CIVIC; PROF ORG
80922	330	4928	FOOD SVCS & DRINKING PLACES
80923	288	2145	EDUCATIONAL SERVICES
80924	30	111	FOOD SVCS & DRINKING PLACES
80925	46	126	CONSTRUCTION OF BUILDINGS
80926	47	112	SPECIAL TRADE CONTRACTORS
80927	9	5	WASTE MANAGMT & REMEDIAT'N SVC
80928	22	123	EDUCATIONAL SERVICES
80929	23	129	ADMINISTRATIVE & SUPPORT SVCS
80930	19	33	TELECOMMUNICATIONS
80931	11	64	INSURANCE CARRIERS & RELATED
80932	23	20	ADMINISTRATIVE & SUPPORT SVCS
80933	12	12	CONSTRUCTION OF BUILDINGS
80934	8	17	RELIG.; GRANT; CIVIC; PROF ORG
80935	17	56	SPECIAL TRADE CONTRACTORS
80936	35	54	SPECIAL TRADE CONTRACTORS
80937	10	7	PUBLISHING INDUSTRIES
80938	4	6	ADMINISTRATIVE & SUPPORT SVCS
80939	30	527	BLDG MATL & GARDEN EQPMT DLRS
80949	23	131	CONSTRUCTION OF BUILDINGS
80951	22	297	WASTE MANAGMT & REMEDIAT'N SVC
80960	14	47	ADMINISTRATIVE & SUPPORT SVCS
80962	41	158	SPECIAL TRADE CONTRACTORS
80970	11	23	SPECIAL TRADE CONTRACTORS
81001	632	10586	EDUCATIONAL SERVICES
81002	9	22	SPECIAL TRADE CONTRACTORS
81003	1401	19994	HOSPITALS
81004	760	10013	ADMINISTRATIVE & SUPPORT SVCS
81005	672	5468	FOOD SVCS & DRINKING PLACES
81006	397	2816	EDUCATIONAL SERVICES
81007	633	4133	SPECIAL TRADE CONTRACTORS
81008	790	8360	FOOD SVCS & DRINKING PLACES
81019	115	365	FOOD SVCS & DRINKING PLACES
81020	33	98	TRUCK TRANSPORTATION
81021	1	2	ANIMAL PRODUCTION
81022	41	297	EDUCATIONAL SERVICES
81023	54	130	EDUCATIONAL SERVICES
81024	8	13	CONSTRUCTION OF BUILDINGS
81025	15	68	SOCIAL ASSISTANCE
81027	5	35	EDUCATIONAL SERVICES
81029	18	56	EDUCATIONAL SERVICES
81030	17	58	EDUCATIONAL SERVICES
81033	9	614	JUSTICE; PUBIC ORDER/SAFETY
81036	96	548	EXEC.; LEGIS.; & OTHER SUPPORT
81038	4	810	HOSPITALS
81039	95	441	EDUCATIONAL SERVICES
81040	16	49	EDUCATIONAL SERVICES
81041	26	384	FOOD AND BEVERAGE STORES
81043	4	4	SUPPORT ACTIVITIES: AGR./FOR.
81044	9	73	JUSTICE; PUBIC ORDER/SAFETY
81045	9	13	EXEC.; LEGIS.; & OTHER SUPPORT
81046	1	2	POSTAL SERVICE
81047	81	450	EDUCATIONAL SERVICES
81049	9	39	EDUCATIONAL SERVICES
81050	515	4980	HOSPITALS
81052	580	4133	EDUCATIONAL SERVICES
81054	170	1162	JUSTICE; PUBIC ORDER/SAFETY
81055	136	484	EDUCATIONAL SERVICES
81057	14	185	EDUCATIONAL SERVICES
81058	28	211	EDUCATIONAL SERVICES
81059	1	200	JUSTICE; PUBIC ORDER/SAFETY
81062	11	325	JUSTICE; PUBIC ORDER/SAFETY
81063	92	516	EDUCATIONAL SERVICES
81064	11	43	EDUCATIONAL SERVICES
81067	215	1312	EDUCATIONAL SERVICES
81069	85	361	CONSTRUCTION OF BUILDINGS
81071	48	86	EDUCATIONAL SERVICES
81073	149	1121	NURSING & RESID. CARE FACILIT.
81076	13	15	EXEC.; LEGIS.; & OTHER SUPPORT
81077	20	201	EDUCATIONAL SERVICES
81081	2	2	ANIMAL PRODUCTION
81082	720	5232	EDUCATIONAL SERVICES
81084	11	15	AIR TRANSPORTATION
81087	7	86	EDUCATIONAL SERVICES
81089	277	2295	NURSING & RESID. CARE FACILIT.
81090	59	365	EDUCATIONAL SERVICES

ZIP CODE	2009 Total Firms	2009 Total Employ-ees	TOP INDUSTRY RANKED on 2009 EMPLOYMENT	ZIP CODE	2009 Total Firms	2009 Total Employ-ees	TOP INDUSTRY RANKED on 2009 EMPLOYMENT	ZIP CODE	2009 Total Firms	2009 Total Employ-ees	TOP INDUSTRY RANKED on 2009 EMPLOYMENT
81091	36	308	CONSTRUCTION OF BUILDINGS	81418	56	353	REAL ESTATE	82073	16	60	AMUSEMENT; GAMBLING;& RECREAT.
81092	35	176	EDUCATIONAL SERVICES	81419	257	1068	EDUCATIONAL SERVICES	82081	2	8	CROP PRODUCTION
81101	939	7731	EDUCATIONAL SERVICES	81420	1	0	POSTAL SERVICE	82082	109	537	EDUCATIONAL SERVICES
81120	86	338	MINING (EXCEPT OIL AND GAS)	81422	60	272	EDUCATIONAL SERVICES	82083	41	188	EDUCATIONAL SERVICES
81121	38	68	MUSEUMS; HIST. SITES;& SIMILAR	81423	152	530	SPECIAL TRADE CONTRACTORS	82084	6	3	ANIMAL PRODUCTION
81122	561	4692	ACCOMMODATION	81424	89	394	UTILITIES	82190	54	1307	ACCOMMODATION
81123	43	266	EDUCATIONAL SERVICES	81425	150	1041	MERCH. WHOLESALERS;NONDUR. GDS	82201	358	2295	UTILITIES
81124	6	6	SPECIAL TRADE CONTRACTORS	81426	1	1	EXEC.; LEGIS.; & OTHER SUPPORT	82210	23	125	EDUCATIONAL SERVICES
81125	143	1313	MERCH. WHOLESALERS;NONDUR. GDS	81427	193	783	ACCOMMODATION	82212	18	109	MUSEUMS; HIST. SITES;& SIMILAR
81126	2	0	POSTAL SERVICE	81428	260	1343	MINING (EXCEPT OIL AND GAS)	82213	30	170	ACCOMMODATION
81127	8	9	SPORTG GDS;HOBBY;BOOK; & MUSIC	81429	16	57	ADMIN. ENVIRO. QUALITY PROGRMS	82214	73	374	EDUCATIONAL SERVICES
81128	11	10	RELIG.; GRANT; CIVIC; PROF ORG	81430	26	55	JUSTICE; PUBIC ORDER/SAFETY	82215	3	1	POSTAL SERVICE
81129	14	151	EDUCATIONAL SERVICES	81431	13	24	WASTE MANAGMT & REMEDIAT'N SVC	82217	7	12	FOOD SVCS & DRINKING PLACES
81130	113	502	ACCOMMODATION	81432	231	798	FOOD SVCS & DRINKING PLACES	82218	1	0	POSTAL SERVICE
81131	96	178	RELIG.; GRANT; CIVIC; PROF ORG	81433	139	484	FOOD SVCS & DRINKING PLACES	82221	19	65	EDUCATIONAL SERVICES
81132	159	737	EDUCATIONAL SERVICES	81434	22	665	MERCH. WHOLESALERS;DURABLE GDS	82222	8	25	OIL AND GAS EXTRACTION
81133	51	164	FOOD SVCS & DRINKING PLACES	81435	740	5348	ACCOMMODATION	82223	45	178	EDUCATIONAL SERVICES
81136	15	57	FOOD MANUFACTURING	81501	2384	26147	HOSPITALS	82225	151	650	EXEC.; LEGIS.; & OTHER SUPPORT
81137	383	2529	BROADCASTING	81502	52	146	SPECIAL TRADE CONTRACTORS	82227	3	13	GASOLINE STATIONS
81138	3	7	ANIMAL PRODUCTION	81503	351	2338	ADMINISTRATIVE & SUPPORT SVCS	82229	2	3	EDUCATIONAL SERVICES
81140	94	469	EDUCATIONAL SERVICES	81504	523	5732	SPECIAL TRADE CONTRACTORS	82240	512	3844	EDUCATIONAL SERVICES
81141	34	96	EDUCATIONAL SERVICES	81505	1208	14960	SPECIAL TRADE CONTRACTORS	82243	3	3	CROP PRODUCTION
81143	26	138	EDUCATIONAL SERVICES	81506	543	7002	AMBULATORY HEALTH CARE SVCS	82244	8	39	EDUCATIONAL SERVICES
81144	438	3145	MERCH. WHOLESALERS;NONDUR. GDS	81507	307	1396	FOOD AND BEVERAGE STORES	82301	555	5205	JUSTICE; PUBIC ORDER/SAFETY
81146	33	229	EDUCATIONAL SERVICES	81520	292	1749	FOOD SVCS & DRINKING PLACES	82310	11	3	PRIMARY METAL MANUFACTURING
81147	1667	5277	FOOD SVCS & DRINKING PLACES	81521	386	3096	EDUCATIONAL SERVICES	82321	73	282	CONSTRUCTION OF BUILDINGS
81148	6	10	FOOD MANUFACTURING	81522	29	187	ACCOMMODATION	82322	15	86	OIL AND GAS EXTRACTION
81149	67	490	EDUCATIONAL SERVICES	81523	16	21	ANIMAL PRODUCTION	82323	13	28	EXEC.; LEGIS.; & OTHER SUPPORT
81151	19	62	SPECIAL TRADE CONTRACTORS	81524	54	158	MINING (EXCEPT OIL AND GAS)	82324	30	62	ACCOMMODATION
81152	86	507	EDUCATIONAL SERVICES	81525	19	27	ANIMAL PRODUCTION	82325	81	363	ANIMAL PRODUCTION
81154	140	527	AMUSEMENT; GAMBLING;& RECREAT.	81526	228	1253	CROP PRODUCTION	82327	59	334	MINING (EXCEPT OIL AND GAS)
81155	12	24	PRINT'G & RELATED SUPP'T ACT'S	81527	48	182	BLDG MATL & GARDEN EQPMT DLRS	82329	34	71	EDUCATIONAL SERVICES
81157	4	2	SPECIAL TRADE CONTRACTORS	81601	1663	13373	ADMINISTRATIVE & SUPPORT SVCS	82331	250	1088	AMUSEMENT; GAMBLING;& RECREAT.
81201	801	4131	FOOD SVCS & DRINKING PLACES	81602	28	36	SPECIAL TRADE CONTRACTORS	82332	11	17	RELIG.; GRANT; CIVIC; PROF ORG
81210	19	296	AMUSEMENT; GAMBLING;& RECREAT.	81610	23	46	FOOD AND BEVERAGE STORES	82334	23	464	CONSTRUCTION OF BUILDINGS
81211	509	3396	JUSTICE; PUBIC ORDER/SAFETY	81611	1804	14299	FOOD SVCS & DRINKING PLACES	82335	2	9	FOOD SVCS & DRINKING PLACES
81212	1102	11694	JUSTICE; PUBIC ORDER/SAFETY	81612	83	327	DATA PROCESS'G	82336	59	609	SPECIAL TRADE CONTRACTORS
81215	10	38	SPECIAL TRADE CONTRACTORS	81615	310	5808	REAL ESTATE	82401	492	3713	EDUCATIONAL SERVICES
81220	17	31	SOCIAL ASSISTANCE	81620	864	8763	ACCOMMODATION	82410	139	1214	AMBULATORY HEALTH CARE SVCS
81221	4	7	POSTAL SERVICE	81621	666	4154	EDUCATIONAL SERVICES	82411	31	139	EDUCATIONAL SERVICES
81222	6	10	ACCOMMODATION	81623	1092	5395	SPECIAL TRADE CONTRACTORS	82412	16	60	TELECOMMUNICATIONS
81223	55	309	JUSTICE; PUBIC ORDER/SAFETY	81624	62	331	EDUCATIONAL SERVICES	82414	1292	8349	ACCOMMODATION
81224	494	4217	ACCOMMODATION	81625	679	4937	EDUCATIONAL SERVICES	82420	32	191	CONSTRUCTION OF BUILDINGS
81225	2	3	ELECTRONICS & APPLIANCE STORES	81626	9	12	PROF.; SCIENTIFIC; & TECH SVCS	82421	16	73	EDUCATIONAL SERVICES
81226	232	1211	EDUCATIONAL SERVICES	81630	43	229	SPECIAL TRADE CONTRACTORS	82422	7	4	UTILITIES
81227	3	350	ACCOMMODATION	81631	633	4897	EXEC.; LEGIS.; & OTHER SUPPORT	82423	14	60	MINING (EXCEPT OIL AND GAS)
81228	2	2	PROF.; SCIENTIFIC; & TECH SVCS	81632	672	5851	ACCOMMODATION	82426	181	1123	SPECIAL TRADE CONTRACTORS
81230	678	4041	FOOD SVCS & DRINKING PLACES	81635	212	1737	SPECIAL TRADE CONTRACTORS	82428	18	54	ANIMAL PRODUCTION
81231	4	315	EDUCATIONAL SERVICES	81636	1	1	PROF.; SCIENTIFIC; & TECH SVCS	82430	6	41	PIPELINE TRANSPORTATION
81232	2	6	ACCOMMODATION	81637	336	1906	SPECIAL TRADE CONTRACTORS	82431	230	2146	EDUCATIONAL SERVICES
81233	26	95	JUSTICE; PUBIC ORDER/SAFETY	81638	8	15	ANIMAL PRODUCTION	82432	16	92	EDUCATIONAL SERVICES
81235	126	374	ACCOMMODATION	81639	121	710	EDUCATIONAL SERVICES	82433	77	167	EDUCATIONAL SERVICES
81236	45	201	ACCOMMODATION	81640	24	32	MINING (EXCEPT OIL AND GAS)	82434	5	3	MUSEUMS; HIST. SITES;& SIMILAR
81237	2	4	ACCOMMODATION	81641	289	2051	SPECIAL TRADE CONTRACTORS	82435	557	3861	EDUCATIONAL SERVICES
81239	5	11	FOOD AND BEVERAGE STORES	81642	3	4	ACCOMMODATION	82440	16	35	BLDG MATL & GARDEN EQPMT DLRS
81240	168	760	MISCELLANEOUS MANUFACTURING	81643	38	609	ACCOMMODATION	82441	24	82	FOOD SVCS & DRINKING PLACES
81241	9	14	ADMIN. ENVIRO. QUALITY PROGRMS	81645	130	737	FOOD SVCS & DRINKING PLACES	82442	97	437	EDUCATIONAL SERVICES
81242	41	182	BLDG MATL & GARDEN EQPMT DLRS	81646	7	7	PROF.; SCIENTIFIC; & TECH SVCS	82443	349	2260	EDUCATIONAL SERVICES
81243	5	67	ACCOMMODATION	81647	235	1640	ADMINISTRATIVE & SUPPORT SVCS	82450	7	8	SPECIAL TRADE CONTRACTORS
81244	6	10	EXEC.; LEGIS.; & OTHER SUPPORT	81648	163	1659	EDUCATIONAL SERVICES	82501	1013	7948	EDUCATIONAL SERVICES
81248	5	19	POSTAL SERVICE	81649	13	123	AMUSEMENT; GAMBLING;& RECREAT.	82510	27	138	UTILITIES
81251	12	25	ACCOMMODATION	81650	778	5768	SPECIAL TRADE CONTRACTORS	82512	17	15	ANIMAL PRODUCTION
81252	264	975	EDUCATIONAL SERVICES	81652	246	835	SPECIAL TRADE CONTRACTORS	82513	311	1248	ACCOMMODATION
81253	16	33	ACCOMMODATION	81653	14	107	ANIMAL PRODUCTION	82514	56	733	ADMIN. HUMAN RESOURCE PROGRAMS
81301	3086	20556	ACCOMMODATION	81654	92	352	SPECIAL TRADE CONTRACTORS	82515	12	35	FOOD SVCS & DRINKING PLACES
81302	115	276	SPECIAL TRADE CONTRACTORS	81655	33	647	SPECIAL TRADE CONTRACTORS	82516	11	25	AMUSEMENT; GAMBLING;& RECREAT.
81303	760	6182	SPECIAL TRADE CONTRACTORS	81656	33	96	HEAVY & CIVIL ENG. CONSTRUCT'N	82520	819	7090	EDUCATIONAL SERVICES
81320	8	29	SOCIAL ASSISTANCE	81657	797	9151	FOOD SVCS & DRINKING PLACES	82523	32	331	EDUCATIONAL SERVICES
81321	1171	8076	EDUCATIONAL SERVICES	81658	47	52	SPECIAL TRADE CONTRACTORS	82524	7	138	EDUCATIONAL SERVICES
81323	293	988	SUPPORT ACTIVITIES: AGR./FOR.	82001	2150	27303	AMBULATORY HEALTH CARE SVCS	82601	2285	23277	EDUCATIONAL SERVICES
81324	108	573	EDUCATIONAL SERVICES	82002	35	947	EXEC.; LEGIS.; & OTHER SUPPORT	82602	23	66	TRUCK TRANSPORTATION
81325	5	5	TRANSIT & GRND PASS. TRANSPORT	82003	38	112	SPECIAL TRADE CONTRACTORS	82604	929	9941	SPECIAL TRADE CONTRACTORS
81326	122	322	MINING (EXCEPT OIL AND GAS)	82005	34	310	HOSPITALS	82605	14	346	CONSTRUCTION OF BUILDINGS
81327	24	31	GASOLINE STATIONS	82006	1	300	ADMIN. ENVIRO. QUALITY PROGRMS	82609	578	6005	GENERAL MERCHANDISE STORES
81328	239	1211	MERCH. WHOLESALERS;NONDUR. GDS	82007	521	7230	EDUCATIONAL SERVICES	82615	2	0	SUPPORT ACTIVITIES: AGR./FOR.
81329	11	1	POSTAL SERVICE	82009	877	13748	NAT'L SECURITY & INT'L AFFAIRS	82620	21	101	ACCOMMODATION
81330	10	842	EXEC.; LEGIS.; & OTHER SUPPORT	82050	22	75	CROP PRODUCTION	82633	484	3368	HOSPITALS
81331	27	78	TELECOMMUNICATIONS	82051	2	4	EXEC.; LEGIS.; & OTHER SUPPORT	82635	17	216	SPECIAL TRADE CONTRACTORS
81332	55	110	SUPPORT ACTIVITIES: AGR./FOR.	82052	3	5	GASOLINE STATIONS	82636	113	1291	FOOD SVCS & DRINKING PLACES
81334	33	2219	BROADCASTING	82053	41	191	GASOLINE STATIONS	82637	160	1051	UTILITIES
81335	16	35	BLDG MATL & GARDEN EQPMT DLRS	82054	23	34	SPECIAL TRADE CONTRACTORS	82638	1	2	FOOD SVCS & DRINKING PLACES
81401	1579	12540	FOOD SVCS & DRINKING PLACES	82055	26	89	ACCOMMODATION	82639	68	271	EDUCATIONAL SERVICES
81402	17	80	EDUCATIONAL SERVICES	82058	1	4	ACCOMMODATION	82640	4	32	SPECIAL TRADE CONTRACTORS
81403	297	1152	SPECIAL TRADE CONTRACTORS	82059	6	64	CONSTRUCTION OF BUILDINGS	82642	17	114	OIL AND GAS EXTRACTION
81410	46	222	FOOD AND BEVERAGE STORES	82060	4	3	ACCOMMODATION	82643	27	222	EDUCATIONAL SERVICES
81411	4	9	FOOD MANUFACTURING	82061	3	1	EDUCATIONAL SERVICES	82644	145	1502	COMPUTER & ELECTRONIC PROD MFG
81413	275	1359	REPAIR AND MAINTENANCE	82063	5	47	ACCOMMODATION	82646	1	0	MERCH. WHOLESALERS;DURABLE GDS
81414	9	20	MISCELLANEOUS STORE RETAILERS	82070	995	8454	FOOD SVCS & DRINKING PLACES	82648	4	20	OIL AND GAS EXTRACTION
81415	85	224	ANIMAL PRODUCTION	82071	20	3173	EDUCATIONAL SERVICES	82649	67	467	EDUCATIONAL SERVICES
81416	726	5791	FOOD SVCS & DRINKING PLACES	82072	464	4896	EDUCATIONAL SERVICES	82701	289	1772	EDUCATIONAL SERVICES

ZIP CODE	2009 Total Firms	2009 Total Employ-ees	TOP INDUSTRY RANKED on 2009 EMPLOYMENT	ZIP CODE	2009 Total Firms	2009 Total Employ-ees	TOP INDUSTRY RANKED on 2009 EMPLOYMENT	ZIP CODE	2009 Total Firms	2009 Total Employ-ees	TOP INDUSTRY RANKED on 2009 EMPLOYMENT
82710	5	13	FOOD AND BEVERAGE STORES	83223	6	3	SPECIAL TRADE CONTRACTORS	83428	41	112	EDUCATIONAL SERVICES
82711	2	2	ANIMAL PRODUCTION	83226	271	1152	EDUCATIONAL SERVICES	83429	127	510	ACCOMMODATION
82712	9	33	FOOD SVCS & DRINKING PLACES	83227	35	131	MINING (EXCEPT OIL AND GAS)	83431	24	738	FOOD MANUFACTURING
82714	8	30	EXEC.; LEGIS.; & OTHER SUPPORT	83228	9	34	FOOD MANUFACTURING	83433	11	37	FOOD SVCS & DRINKING PLACES
82715	1	2	ACCOMMODATION	83232	15	207	EDUCATIONAL SERVICES	83434	25	215	MERCH. WHOLESALERS;NONDUR. GDS
82716	1128	12435	MINING (EXCEPT OIL AND GAS)	83233	3	5	ANIMAL PRODUCTION	83435	16	28	CROP PRODUCTION
82717	27	70	SPECIAL TRADE CONTRACTORS	83234	37	175	GASOLINE STATIONS	83436	24	218	MERCH. WHOLESALERS;NONDUR. GDS
82718	824	10559	MINING (EXCEPT OIL AND GAS)	83235	5	8	CROP PRODUCTION	83438	5	1	TRUCK TRANSPORTATION
82720	65	472	WOOD PRODUCT MANUFACTURING	83236	43	357	FOOD MANUFACTURING	83440	1082	11258	EDUCATIONAL SERVICES
82721	107	504	EDUCATIONAL SERVICES	83237	23	204	FABRICATED METAL PRODUCT MFG	83441	2	470	PRINT'G & RELATED SUPP'T ACT'S
82723	16	41	JUSTICE; PUBIC ORDER/SAFETY	83238	2	2	TRUCK TRANSPORTATION	83442	503	4048	EDUCATIONAL SERVICES
82725	7	24	EDUCATIONAL SERVICES	83239	8	27	EDUCATIONAL SERVICES	83443	54	633	MERCH. WHOLESALERS;NONDUR. GDS
82727	31	156	EDUCATIONAL SERVICES	83241	72	372	EDUCATIONAL SERVICES	83444	45	158	JUSTICE; PUBIC ORDER/SAFETY
82729	163	1035	HOSPITALS	83243	6	5	TRUCK TRANSPORTATION	83445	373	2837	JUSTICE; PUBIC ORDER/SAFETY
82730	64	281	SPECIAL TRADE CONTRACTORS	83244	23	39	ANIMAL PRODUCTION	83446	9	32	SUPPORT ACTIVITIES: AGR./FOR.
82731	2	13	EDUCATIONAL SERVICES	83245	47	312	ACCOMMODATION	83448	51	429	MERCH. WHOLESALERS;NONDUR. GDS
82732	72	5635	MINING (EXCEPT OIL AND GAS)	83246	66	262	ACCOMMODATION	83449	34	196	RELIG.; GRANT; CIVIC; PROF ORG
82801	1486	12934	HOSPITALS	83250	44	212	GASOLINE STATIONS	83450	89	430	EDUCATIONAL SERVICES
82831	12	40	UTILITIES	83251	75	323	EDUCATIONAL SERVICES	83451	21	70	TRUCK TRANSPORTATION
82832	18	36	FOOD SVCS & DRINKING PLACES	83252	187	940	HOSPITALS	83452	58	151	SPECIAL TRADE CONTRACTORS
82833	26	116	EDUCATIONAL SERVICES	83253	24	21	ANIMAL PRODUCTION	83454	9	88	MERCH. WHOLESALERS;NONDUR. GDS
82834	475	3208	FOOD SVCS & DRINKING PLACES	83254	190	1312	HOSPITALS	83455	146	859	HEAVY & CIVIL ENG. CONSTRUCT'N
82835	15	86	EDUCATIONAL SERVICES	83255	23	61	NURSING & RESID. CARE FACILIT.	83460	1	41	BROADCASTING
82836	39	136	EDUCATIONAL SERVICES	83256	3	3	REPAIR AND MAINTENANCE	83462	14	29	SCENIC & SIGHTSEEING TRANSPORT
82837	4	5	ANIMAL PRODUCTION	83261	25	86	EDUCATIONAL SERVICES	83463	5	4	AMUSEMENT; GAMBLING;& RECREAT.
82838	7	23	AMUSEMENT; GAMBLING;& RECREAT.	83262	21	403	WAREHOUSING AND STORAGE	83464	17	64	EDUCATIONAL SERVICES
82839	45	289	EDUCATIONAL SERVICES	83263	300	2097	EDUCATIONAL SERVICES	83465	3	0	ANIMAL PRODUCTION
82842	27	110	FOOD SVCS & DRINKING PLACES	83271	26	282	DATA PROCESS'G	83466	21	153	SUPPORT ACTIVITIES: AGR./FOR.
82844	1	70	ACCOMMODATION	83272	11	16	ADMINISTRATIVE & SUPPORT SVCS	83467	529	2882	SUPPORT ACTIVITIES: AGR./FOR.
82901	1407	16197	SPECIAL TRADE CONTRACTORS	83274	247	1815	FOOD MANUFACTURING	83468	4	9	EDUCATIONAL SERVICES
82902	11	35	REPAIR AND MAINTENANCE	83276	241	2325	CHEMICAL MANUFACTURING	83469	3	3	ACCOMMODATION
82922	19	45	FOOD SVCS & DRINKING PLACES	83277	3	11	EXEC.; LEGIS.; & OTHER SUPPORT	83501	1820	20449	FABRICATED METAL PRODUCT MFG
82923	66	488	SPECIAL TRADE CONTRACTORS	83278	71	533	ACCOMMODATION	83520	12	211	ADMIN. ENVIRO. QUALITY PROGRMS
82925	19	62	ACCOMMODATION	83281	4	7	TRUCK TRANSPORTATION	83522	114	754	NONMETALLIC MINERAL PROD. MFG
82929	4	290	ACCOMMODATION	83283	3	21	EDUCATIONAL SERVICES	83523	38	250	EDUCATIONAL SERVICES
82930	805	7500	SOCIAL ASSISTANCE	83285	6	12	ADMIN. ENVIRO. QUALITY PROGRMS	83524	26	133	PROF.; SCIENTIFIC; & TECH SVCS
82931	4	10	ADMINISTRATIVE & SUPPORT SVCS	83286	17	25	SPECIAL TRADE CONTRACTORS	83525	32	205	WOOD PRODUCT MANUFACTURING
82932	43	145	SPECIAL TRADE CONTRACTORS	83287	12	47	AMUSEMENT; GAMBLING;& RECREAT.	83526	12	73	FURNITURE & RELATED PROD. MFG
82933	47	214	GASOLINE STATIONS	83301	3001	30781	HOSPITALS	83530	381	2164	WOOD PRODUCT MANUFACTURING
82934	12	61	UTILITIES	83302	13	19	JUSTICE; PUBIC ORDER/SAFETY	83531	5	13	MISCELLANEOUS STORE RETAILERS
82935	515	6788	MERCH. WHOLESALERS;NONDUR. GDS	83303	27	293	MUSEUMS; HIST. SITES;& SIMILAR	83533	4	8	FOOD MANUFACTURING
82936	3	1	OIL AND GAS EXTRACTION	83311	30	177	TELECOMMUNICATIONS	83535	25	76	EDUCATIONAL SERVICES
82937	161	1313	CONSTRUCTION OF BUILDINGS	83312	18	114	CROP PRODUCTION	83536	195	1111	WOOD PRODUCT MANUFACTURING
82938	6	19	CONSTRUCTION OF BUILDINGS	83313	290	1523	SPECIAL TRADE CONTRACTORS	83537	57	266	EDUCATIONAL SERVICES
82939	116	1197	TELECOMMUNICATIONS	83314	29	151	EDUCATIONAL SERVICES	83539	113	543	EDUCATIONAL SERVICES
82941	502	3329	HEAVY & CIVIL ENG. CONSTRUCT'N	83316	352	2212	FOOD AND BEVERAGE STORES	83540	65	573	EDUCATIONAL SERVICES
82942	7	853	MINING (EXCEPT OIL AND GAS)	83318	1024	8948	MERCH. WHOLESALERS;NONDUR. GDS	83541	27	64	CROP PRODUCTION
82943	15	269	REPAIR AND MAINTENANCE	83320	40	192	EDUCATIONAL SERVICES	83542	4	8	AMUSEMENT; GAMBLING;& RECREAT.
82944	11	12	ANIMAL PRODUCTION	83321	27	186	EDUCATIONAL SERVICES	83543	54	284	JUSTICE; PUBIC ORDER/SAFETY
82945	10	17	EXEC.; LEGIS.; & OTHER SUPPORT	83323	48	337	ANIMAL PRODUCTION	83544	351	2522	SUPPORT ACTIVITIES: AGR./FOR.
83001	1924	14243	FOOD SVCS & DRINKING PLACES	83324	22	97	EDUCATIONAL SERVICES	83545	14	23	MISCELLANEOUS MANUFACTURING
83002	34	71	POSTAL SERVICE	83325	39	300	MERCH. WHOLESALERS;NONDUR. GDS	83546	44	225	FORESTRY AND LOGGING
83011	13	213	EDUCATIONAL SERVICES	83327	71	303	MERCH. WHOLESALERS;DURABLE GDS	83547	6	36	MOTOR VEHICLE & PARTS DEALERS
83012	33	638	MUSEUMS; HIST. SITES;& SIMILAR	83328	188	967	EDUCATIONAL SERVICES	83548	3	7	MERCH. WHOLESALERS;NONDUR. GDS
83013	46	2918	ACCOMMODATION	83330	298	2342	NURSING & RESID. CARE FACILIT.	83549	104	375	FOOD SVCS & DRINKING PLACES
83014	160	1056	EDUCATIONAL SERVICES	83332	116	509	EDUCATIONAL SERVICES	83552	22	40	FOOD AND BEVERAGE STORES
83025	69	1520	ACCOMMODATION	83333	762	4067	PROF.; SCIENTIFIC; & TECH SVCS	83553	41	222	WOOD PRODUCT MANUFACTURING
83101	200	2250	MINING (EXCEPT OIL AND GAS)	83334	42	266	EDUCATIONAL SERVICES	83554	38	152	AMBULATORY HEALTH CARE SVCS
83110	291	2210	HOSPITALS	83335	59	358	EDUCATIONAL SERVICES	83555	19	46	JUSTICE; PUBIC ORDER/SAFETY
83111	5	5	ADMIN. ENVIRO. QUALITY PROGRMS	83336	161	897	MOTOR VEHICLE & PARTS DEALERS	83601	7	5	EXEC.; LEGIS.; & OTHER SUPPORT
83112	19	52	AMUSEMENT; GAMBLING;& RECREAT.	83337	1	1	FABRICATED METAL PRODUCT MFG	83602	3	11	ADMIN. OF ECONOMIC PROGRAMS
83113	206	1112	SPECIAL TRADE CONTRACTORS	83338	807	7590	MERCH. WHOLESALERS;NONDUR. GDS	83604	40	140	EDUCATIONAL SERVICES
83114	49	226	GASOLINE STATIONS	83340	944	6159	FOOD SVCS & DRINKING PLACES	83605	1303	16145	JUSTICE; PUBIC ORDER/SAFETY
83115	33	70	JUSTICE; PUBIC ORDER/SAFETY	83341	164	1127	EDUCATIONAL SERVICES	83606	19	102	ADMINISTRATIVE & SUPPORT SVCS
83116	45	270	AMBULATORY HEALTH CARE SVCS	83342	54	2314	UTILITIES	83607	470	3160	EDUCATIONAL SERVICES
83118	62	211	CONSTRUCTION OF BUILDINGS	83343	7	41	WHOLESALE ELEC. MRKTS & AGENTS	83610	75	358	TELECOMMUNICATIONS
83120	39	77	FABRICATED METAL PRODUCT MFG	83344	40	288	CROP PRODUCTION	83611	196	1326	EXEC.; LEGIS.; & OTHER SUPPORT
83121	1	2	POSTAL SERVICE	83346	60	733	MINING (EXCEPT OIL AND GAS)	83612	125	597	SUPPORT ACTIVITIES: AGR./FOR.
83122	6	9	MISCELLANEOUS MANUFACTURING	83347	156	2260	FOOD MANUFACTURING	83615	113	736	ACCOMMODATION
83123	76	486	SPECIAL TRADE CONTRACTORS	83348	7	35	CROP PRODUCTION	83616	1150	6596	FOOD SVCS & DRINKING PLACES
83124	5	42	PIPELINE TRANSPORTATION	83349	25	165	FOOD MANUFACTURING	83617	531	3221	EDUCATIONAL SERVICES
83126	8	31	ADMINISTRATIVE & SUPPORT SVCS	83350	590	4245	MERCH. WHOLESALERS;NONDUR. GDS	83619	313	2731	WOOD PRODUCT MANUFACTURING
83127	191	790	REAL ESTATE	83352	141	1261	EDUCATIONAL SERVICES	83622	108	522	SUPPORT ACTIVITIES: AGR./FOR.
83128	133	562	CONSTRUCTION OF BUILDINGS	83353	82	1248	ACCOMMODATION	83623	87	1204	ADMINISTRATIVE & SUPPORT SVCS
83201	1711	19834	MERCH. WHOLESALERS;DURABLE GDS	83355	216	1385	ANIMAL PRODUCTION	83624	65	401	MERCH. WHOLESALERS;NONDUR. GDS
83202	575	5454	GENERAL MERCHANDISE STORES	83401	1562	14410	PROF.; SCIENTIFIC; & TECH SVCS	83626	27	213	EDUCATIONAL SERVICES
83203	41	1413	EXEC.; LEGIS.; & OTHER SUPPORT	83402	1590	17677	CHEMICAL MANUFACTURING	83627	20	88	SOCIAL ASSISTANCE
83204	580	6080	PROF.; SCIENTIFIC; & TECH SVCS	83403	16	40	PERSONAL AND LAUNDRY SERVICES	83628	156	1139	EDUCATIONAL SERVICES
83205	5	16	ADMINISTRATIVE & SUPPORT SVCS	83404	1000	13267	AMBULATORY HEALTH CARE SVCS	83629	62	370	MOTOR VEHICLE & PARTS DEALERS
83206	9	15	PROF.; SCIENTIFIC; & TECH SVCS	83405	13	46	MUSEUMS; HIST. SITES;& SIMILAR	83630	2	8	MINING (EXCEPT OIL AND GAS)
83209	17	1770	EDUCATIONAL SERVICES	83406	339	4235	GENERAL MERCHANDISE STORES	83631	71	287	SUPPORT ACTIVITIES: AGR./FOR.
83210	130	1447	EDUCATIONAL SERVICES	83414	21	332	ACCOMMODATION	83632	8	22	EXEC.; LEGIS.; & OTHER SUPPORT
83211	270	2583	FOOD MANUFACTURING	83415	2	30	AMBULATORY HEALTH CARE SVCS	83633	6	32	CROP PRODUCTION
83212	11	29	CROP PRODUCTION	83420	183	791	EDUCATIONAL SERVICES	83634	352	3594	JUSTICE; PUBIC ORDER/SAFETY
83213	165	714	HOSPITALS	83421	3	8	SPORTG GDS;HOBBY;BOOK; & MUSIC	83635	3	10	HEAVY & CIVIL ENG. CONSTRUCT'N
83214	14	132	EDUCATIONAL SERVICES	83422	311	1584	PROF.; SCIENTIFIC; & TECH SVCS	83636	5	4	MERCH. WHOLESALERS;DURABLE GDS
83215	1	2	FOOD SVCS & DRINKING PLACES	83423	77	697	FOOD MANUFACTURING	83637	23	42	ACCOMMODATION
83217	28	147	EDUCATIONAL SERVICES	83424	4	8	RENTAL AND LEASING SERVICES	83638	645	3785	SUPPORT ACTIVITIES: AGR./FOR.
83220	1	2	CONSTRUCTION OF BUILDINGS	83425	27	361	MERCH. WHOLESALERS;NONDUR. GDS	83639	105	581	EDUCATIONAL SERVICES
83221	896	9877	HOSPITALS	83427	29	108	EDUCATIONAL SERVICES	83641	84	404	EDUCATIONAL SERVICES

ZIP CODE	2009 Total Firms	2009 Total Employees	TOP INDUSTRY RANKED on 2009 EMPLOYMENT	ZIP CODE	2009 Total Firms	2009 Total Employees	TOP INDUSTRY RANKED on 2009 EMPLOYMENT	ZIP CODE	2009 Total Firms	2009 Total Employees	TOP INDUSTRY RANKED on 2009 EMPLOYMENT
83642	2273	26163	AMBULATORY HEALTH CARE SVCS	83849	75	412	EDUCATIONAL SERVICES	84072	13	52	EDUCATIONAL SERVICES
83643	3	1	ACCOMMODATION	83850	85	379	RELIG.; GRANT; CIVIC; PROF ORG	84073	11	64	SPECIAL TRADE CONTRACTORS
83644	216	932	EDUCATIONAL SERVICES	83851	75	750	AMBULATORY HEALTH CARE SVCS	84074	951	8802	EDUCATIONAL SERVICES
83645	24	114	TELECOMMUNICATIONS	83852	183	1269	FOOD SVCS & DRINKING PLACES	84075	252	2424	EDUCATIONAL SERVICES
83646	548	3391	EDUCATIONAL SERVICES	83853	7	22	EXEC.; LEGIS.; & OTHER SUPPORT	84076	3	53	RELIG.; GRANT; CIVIC; PROF ORG
83647	700	4544	EDUCATIONAL SERVICES	83854	1274	11168	MERCH. WHOLESALERS;DURABLE GDS	84078	1203	11016	SPECIAL TRADE CONTRACTORS
83648	48	10637	NAT'L SECURITY & INT'L AFFAIRS	83855	74	352	EDUCATIONAL SERVICES	84079	1	8	ADMINISTRATIVE & SUPPORT SVCS
83650	24	251	JUSTICE; PUBIC ORDER/SAFETY	83856	288	1615	WOOD PRODUCT MANUFACTURING	84080	8	20	EDUCATIONAL SERVICES
83651	1369	11262	FOOD SVCS & DRINKING PLACES	83857	18	403	WOOD PRODUCT MANUFACTURING	84081	286	5011	EDUCATIONAL SERVICES
83652	6	8	CLOTHING & CLOTH'G ACC. STORES	83858	351	2620	EDUCATIONAL SERVICES	84082	15	33	SPECIAL TRADE CONTRACTORS
83653	23	60	SOCIAL ASSISTANCE	83860	158	738	GENERAL MERCHANDISE STORES	84083	97	908	EXEC.; LEGIS.; & OTHER SUPPORT
83654	86	533	SUPPORT ACTIVITIES: AGR./FOR.	83861	331	2548	WOOD PRODUCT MANUFACTURING	84084	634	6686	FOOD SVCS & DRINKING PLACES
83655	127	552	EDUCATIONAL SERVICES	83864	1358	9647	ACCOMMODATION	84085	4	9	ANIMAL PRODUCTION
83656	15	67	EDUCATIONAL SERVICES	83865	3	7	ADMINISTRATIVE & SUPPORT SVCS	84086	14	27	SUPPORT ACTIVITIES: AGR./FOR.
83657	8	12	JUSTICE; PUBIC ORDER/SAFETY	83866	8	28	MERCH. WHOLESALERS;DURABLE GDS	84087	358	3167	SPECIAL TRADE CONTRACTORS
83660	173	1181	MERCH. WHOLESALERS;NONDUR. GDS	83867	10	308	NURSING & RESID. CARE FACILIT.	84088	1212	14922	SPECIAL TRADE CONTRACTORS
83661	395	2637	FOOD AND BEVERAGE STORES	83868	38	390	GENERAL MERCHANDISE STORES	84089	6	14	HEAVY & CIVIL ENG. CONSTRUCT'N
83666	4	9	GASOLINE STATIONS	83869	99	373	EDUCATIONAL SERVICES	84090	17	48	FOOD AND BEVERAGE STORES
83669	188	696	REAL ESTATE	83870	13	16	FOOD AND BEVERAGE STORES	84091	24	98	SPECIAL TRADE CONTRACTORS
83670	14	57	FORESTRY AND LOGGING	83871	68	310	EDUCATIONAL SERVICES	84092	402	4676	PERSONAL AND LAUNDRY SERVICES
83671	3	3	ACCOMMODATION	83872	12	22	CONSTRUCTION OF BUILDINGS	84093	477	3090	EDUCATIONAL SERVICES
83672	348	2344	FOOD AND BEVERAGE STORES	83873	150	885	MINING (EXCEPT OIL AND GAS)	84094	620	6557	AMBULATORY HEALTH CARE SVCS
83676	95	1053	FOOD MANUFACTURING	83874	1	0	ADMIN. OF ECONOMIC PROGRAMS	84095	1173	15724	PROF.; SCIENTIFIC; & TECH SVCS
83677	9	9	ACCOMMODATION	83876	46	2922	AMUSEMENT; GAMBLING;& RECREAT.	84096	305	1643	EDUCATIONAL SERVICES
83680	23	107	SPECIAL TRADE CONTRACTORS	83877	31	88	SPECIAL TRADE CONTRACTORS	84097	996	13232	PROF.; SCIENTIFIC; & TECH SVCS
83686	743	7825	AMBULATORY HEALTH CARE SVCS	84001	44	248	EDUCATIONAL SERVICES	84098	778	7657	ACCOMMODATION
83687	1130	18550	FOOD MANUFACTURING	84002	3	1	SPECIAL TRADE CONTRACTORS	84101	1717	29887	ACCOMMODATION
83701	43	99	PROF.; SCIENTIFIC; & TECH SVCS	84003	1413	15329	EDUCATIONAL SERVICES	84102	902	11680	FOOD SVCS & DRINKING PLACES
83702	3040	35329	PROF.; SCIENTIFIC; & TECH SVCS	84004	201	1383	MERCH. WHOLESALERS;NONDUR. GDS	84103	501	5459	ADMIN. HUMAN RESOURCE PROGRAMS
83703	506	7025	ADMIN. OF ECONOMIC PROGRAMS	84005	90	764	EXEC.; LEGIS.; & OTHER SUPPORT	84104	1813	40637	MISCELLANEOUS MANUFACTURING
83704	2088	23381	FOOD SVCS & DRINKING PLACES	84006	15	231	MINING (EXCEPT OIL AND GAS)	84105	568	3270	EDUCATIONAL SERVICES
83705	1515	19463	NAT'L SECURITY & INT'L AFFAIRS	84007	9	41	FOOD AND BEVERAGE STORES	84106	1478	12238	FOOD SVCS & DRINKING PLACES
83706	1487	20656	HOSPITALS	84008	2	130	MINING (EXCEPT OIL AND GAS)	84107	3044	38848	HOSPITALS
83707	46	116	FABRICATED METAL PRODUCT MFG	84010	1735	16571	FOOD AND BEVERAGE STORES	84108	516	9846	AMBULATORY HEALTH CARE SVCS
83708	3	169	POSTAL SERVICE	84011	14	105	SPECIAL TRADE CONTRACTORS	84109	703	6502	PROF.; SCIENTIFIC; & TECH SVCS
83709	1688	18074	FOOD SVCS & DRINKING PLACES	84013	13	33	EDUCATIONAL SERVICES	84110	23	115	SPECIAL TRADE CONTRACTORS
83711	22	75	SPECIAL TRADE CONTRACTORS	84014	458	5395	FOOD SVCS & DRINKING PLACES	84111	2014	29621	PROF.; SCIENTIFIC; & TECH SVCS
83712	298	8750	HOSPITALS	84015	1258	17449	MISCELLANEOUS MANUFACTURING	84112	79	11271	EDUCATIONAL SERVICES
83713	870	9973	SOCIAL ASSISTANCE	84016	16	833	EDUCATIONAL SERVICES	84113	65	4084	AMBULATORY HEALTH CARE SVCS
83714	1398	11564	SPECIAL TRADE CONTRACTORS	84017	156	1208	EXEC.; LEGIS.; & OTHER SUPPORT	84114	50	1532	EXEC.; LEGIS.; & OTHER SUPPORT
83715	4	8	RENTAL AND LEASING SERVICES	84020	1543	24540	NAT'L SECURITY & INT'L AFFAIRS	84115	2900	38064	MISCELLANEOUS MANUFACTURING
83716	367	17522	COMPUTER & ELECTRONIC PROD MFG	84021	169	1297	EXEC.; LEGIS.; & OTHER SUPPORT	84116	870	24388	EXEC.; LEGIS.; & OTHER SUPPORT
83717	9	41	CONSTRUCTION OF BUILDINGS	84022	26	301	COMPUTER & ELECTRONIC PROD MFG	84117	1255	7767	PROF.; SCIENTIFIC; & TECH SVCS
83719	39	160	SPECIAL TRADE CONTRACTORS	84023	39	336	SOCIAL ASSISTANCE	84118	1101	12572	EDUCATIONAL SERVICES
83720	27	555	EXEC.; LEGIS.; & OTHER SUPPORT	84024	3	3	ADMINISTRATIVE & SUPPORT SVCS	84119	2216	47888	ADMINISTRATIVE & SUPPORT SVCS
83722	1	2	EXEC.; LEGIS.; & OTHER SUPPORT	84025	397	4667	EXEC.; LEGIS.; & OTHER SUPPORT	84120	884	29793	TRUCK TRANSPORTATION
83724	26	268	EXEC.; LEGIS.; & OTHER SUPPORT	84026	64	369	EXEC.; LEGIS.; & OTHER SUPPORT	84121	1730	20056	FOOD SVCS & DRINKING PLACES
83725	23	5020	EDUCATIONAL SERVICES	84027	20	55	RENTAL AND LEASING SERVICES	84122	27	1304	SUPPORT ACT. FOR TRANSPORT.
83728	1	30	TRUCK TRANSPORTATION	84028	99	590	ACCOMMODATION	84123	1284	19243	EDUCATIONAL SERVICES
83729	1	12	FABRICATED METAL PRODUCT MFG	84029	184	1672	WASTE MANAGMT & REMEDIAT'N SVC	84124	720	6699	HOSPITALS
83735	5	335	ADMIN. OF ECONOMIC PROGRAMS	84031	8	35	FOOD SVCS & DRINKING PLACES	84125	7	13	REAL ESTATE
83801	142	1601	AMUSEMENT; GAMBLING;& RECREAT.	84032	737	4558	EDUCATIONAL SERVICES	84126	5	8	ELECTRONICS & APPLIANCE STORES
83802	8	59	EXEC.; LEGIS.; & OTHER SUPPORT	84033	15	84	PROF.; SCIENTIFIC; & TECH SVCS	84127	7	15	MISCELLANEOUS MANUFACTURING
83803	47	268	NAT'L SECURITY & INT'L AFFAIRS	84034	9	18	EXEC.; LEGIS.; & OTHER SUPPORT	84128	216	2016	EDUCATIONAL SERVICES
83804	27	143	AMUSEMENT; GAMBLING;& RECREAT.	84035	21	138	TRUCK TRANSPORTATION	84132	153	7992	HOSPITALS
83805	455	3202	EDUCATIONAL SERVICES	84036	220	1123	EDUCATIONAL SERVICES	84133	16	586	MANAGMT OF COMPANIES & ENTERP.
83806	14	35	EDUCATIONAL SERVICES	84037	732	5363	EDUCATIONAL SERVICES	84134	1	45	ADMIN. OF ECONOMIC PROGRAMS
83808	6	4	POSTAL SERVICE	84038	18	125	EDUCATIONAL SERVICES	84138	37	345	ADMIN. ENVIRO. QUALITY PROGRMS
83809	6	17	CONSTRUCTION OF BUILDINGS	84039	16	84	EDUCATIONAL SERVICES	84139	12	1799	PROF.; SCIENTIFIC; & TECH SVCS
83810	41	133	FORESTRY AND LOGGING	84040	246	1532	EDUCATIONAL SERVICES	84141	1	7	AMBULATORY HEALTH CARE SVCS
83811	71	219	HEAVY & CIVIL ENG. CONSTRUCT'N	84041	1743	21922	FOOD SVCS & DRINKING PLACES	84143	37	2274	HOSPITALS
83812	6	17	WOOD PRODUCT MANUFACTURING	84042	547	7740	PROF.; SCIENTIFIC; & TECH SVCS	84144	10	443	GENERAL MERCHANDISE STORES
83813	26	50	SPECIAL TRADE CONTRACTORS	84043	908	10211	EDUCATIONAL SERVICES	84145	2	0	MERCH. WHOLESALERS;NONDUR. GDS
83814	2142	21997	AMBULATORY HEALTH CARE SVCS	84044	334	5783	COMPUTER & ELECTRONIC PROD MFG	84147	1	6	PERFORM'G ARTS; SPEC. SPORTS
83815	1090	11753	GENERAL MERCHANDISE STORES	84045	140	938	FOOD AND BEVERAGE STORES	84148	23	1535	HOSPITALS
83816	39	88	PROF.; SCIENTIFIC; & TECH SVCS	84046	50	242	JUSTICE; PUBIC ORDER/SAFETY	84150	30	1266	RELIG.; GRANT; CIVIC; PROF ORG
83821	20	69	ADMIN. ENVIRO. QUALITY PROGRMS	84047	2045	19944	CREDIT INTERMEDIATION & RELATD	84151	2	0	PROF.; SCIENTIFIC; & TECH SVCS
83822	82	422	WOOD PRODUCT MANUFACTURING	84049	143	1206	ACCOMMODATION	84152	16	341	PROF.; SCIENTIFIC; & TECH SVCS
83823	51	242	FORESTRY AND LOGGING	84050	265	1721	EDUCATIONAL SERVICES	84157	16	40	SPECIAL TRADE CONTRACTORS
83824	7	58	EDUCATIONAL SERVICES	84051	6	20	ACCOMMODATION	84158	13	34	MERCH. WHOLESALERS;DURABLE GDS
83825	16	160	HEALTH & PERSONAL CARE STORES	84052	32	470	MERCH. WHOLESALERS;NONDUR. GDS	84165	12	61	CONSTRUCTION OF BUILDINGS
83826	17	61	PROF.; SCIENTIFIC; & TECH SVCS	84053	23	184	CONSTRUCTION OF BUILDINGS	84170	15	13	ADMINISTRATIVE & SUPPORT SVCS
83827	18	44	ADMINISTRATIVE & SUPPORT SVCS	84054	659	13667	ADMINISTRATIVE & SUPPORT SVCS	84171	27	64	CONSTRUCTION OF BUILDINGS
83830	24	93	NONMETALLIC MINERAL PROD. MFG	84055	47	197	EDUCATIONAL SERVICES	84180	15	465	INSURANCE CARRIERS & RELATED
83832	41	220	EDUCATIONAL SERVICES	84056	73	548	GASOLINE STATIONS	84184	2	600	CREDIT INTERMEDIATION & RELATD
83833	57	429	EDUCATIONAL SERVICES	84057	1460	14555	AMBULATORY HEALTH CARE SVCS	84190	78	5363	EXEC.; LEGIS.; & OTHER SUPPORT
83834	8	49	ACCOMMODATION	84058	1093	12476	PROF.; SCIENTIFIC; & TECH SVCS	84199	4	8	POSTAL SERVICE
83835	947	6198	SPECIAL TRADE CONTRACTORS	84059	19	52	ADMINISTRATIVE & SUPPORT SVCS	84201	1	0	NAT'L SECURITY & INT'L AFFAIRS
83836	59	229	ACCOMMODATION	84060	1307	13253	ACCOMMODATION	84301	18	114	MERCH. WHOLESALERS;NONDUR. GDS
83837	240	2232	ACCOMMODATION	84061	21	157	MINING (EXCEPT OIL AND GAS)	84302	788	9150	TRANSPORTATION EQUIPMENT MFG
83839	38	179	SPECIAL TRADE CONTRACTORS	84062	801	5240	EDUCATIONAL SERVICES	84304	2	8	FOOD MANUFACTURING
83840	27	116	WOOD PRODUCT MANUFACTURING	84063	16	32	FOOD SVCS & DRINKING PLACES	84305	5	8	EXEC.; LEGIS.; & OTHER SUPPORT
83841	14	203	WOOD PRODUCT MANUFACTURING	84064	50	203	EDUCATIONAL SERVICES	84306	6	40	MERCH. WHOLESALERS;NONDUR. GDS
83842	3	5	FOOD AND BEVERAGE STORES	84065	914	7237	EDUCATIONAL SERVICES	84307	44	2065	COMPUTER & ELECTRONIC PROD MFG
83843	1009	9306	FOOD SVCS & DRINKING PLACES	84066	540	5489	SPECIAL TRADE CONTRACTORS	84308	1	2	MACHINERY MANUFACTURING
83844	13	320	PUBLISHING INDUSTRIES	84067	597	4937	FOOD SVCS & DRINKING PLACES	84309	5	35	SPECIAL TRADE CONTRACTORS
83845	36	310	WOOD PRODUCT MANUFACTURING	84068	31	114	TRANSIT & GRND PASS. TRANSPORT	84310	144	1246	ACCOMMODATION
83846	32	588	MINING (EXCEPT OIL AND GAS)	84069	6	2	ELECTRONICS & APPLIANCE STORES	84311	15	69	EDUCATIONAL SERVICES
83847	39	358	FORESTRY AND LOGGING	84070	2102	27606	PROF.; SCIENTIFIC; & TECH SVCS	84312	52	498	EDUCATIONAL SERVICES
83848	16	80	ACCOMMODATION	84071	10	643	PROF.; SCIENTIFIC; & TECH SVCS	84314	15	77	WAREHOUSING AND STORAGE

BUSINESS DATA

ZIP CODE	2009 Total Firms	2009 Total Employ-ees	TOP INDUSTRY RANKED on 2009 EMPLOYMENT	ZIP CODE	2009 Total Firms	2009 Total Employ-ees	TOP INDUSTRY RANKED on 2009 EMPLOYMENT	ZIP CODE	2009 Total Firms	2009 Total Employ-ees	TOP INDUSTRY RANKED on 2009 EMPLOYMENT
84315	84	532	CONSTRUCTION OF BUILDINGS	84643	15	69	NURSING & RESID. CARE FACILIT.	85002	9	19	ADMINISTRATIVE & SUPPORT SVCS
84316	6	5	EDUCATIONAL SERVICES	84644	8	21	GASOLINE STATIONS	85003	1195	23848	JUSTICE; PUBIC ORDER/SAFETY
84317	90	806	ACCOMMODATION	84645	33	249	FURNITURE & RELATED PROD. MFG	85004	2069	39466	PROF.; SCIENTIFIC; & TECH SVCS
84318	79	633	SPORTG GDS;HOBBY;BOOK; & MUSIC	84646	51	1943	FOOD MANUFACTURING	85005	13	52	SOCIAL ASSISTANCE
84319	145	2606	FOOD MANUFACTURING	84647	196	1269	EDUCATIONAL SERVICES	85006	983	15446	HOSPITALS
84320	50	653	PLASTICS & RUBBER PRODUCTS MFG	84648	317	2623	FOOD SVCS & DRINKING PLACES	85007	1162	33027	EXEC.; LEGIS.; & OTHER SUPPORT
84321	1429	23208	MISCELLANEOUS MANUFACTURING	84649	11	13	CONSTRUCTION OF BUILDINGS	85008	1511	25161	PROF.; SCIENTIFIC; & TECH SVCS
84322	53	974	EDUCATIONAL SERVICES	84651	575	6314	MERCH. WHOLESALERS;NONDUR. GDS	85009	2338	44908	MERCH. WHOLESALERS;DURABLE GDS
84323	12	46	SOCIAL ASSISTANCE	84652	19	165	MINING (EXCEPT OIL AND GAS)	85010	3	4	SUPPORT ACTIVITIES: AGR./FOR.
84324	14	22	EXEC.; LEGIS.; & OTHER SUPPORT	84653	165	1294	CHEMICAL MANUFACTURING	85011	26	98	ADMINISTRATIVE & SUPPORT SVCS
84325	21	139	PROF.; SCIENTIFIC; & TECH SVCS	84654	137	1651	MINING (EXCEPT OIL AND GAS)	85012	1687	30762	RELIG.; GRANT; CIVIC; PROF ORG
84326	25	191	EDUCATIONAL SERVICES	84655	121	1005	MERCH. WHOLESALERS;NONDUR. GDS	85013	944	22310	HOSPITALS
84327	17	48	SPECIAL TRADE CONTRACTORS	84656	10	29	GASOLINE STATIONS	85014	1654	15882	PROF.; SCIENTIFIC; & TECH SVCS
84328	26	81	AMBULATORY HEALTH CARE SVCS	84657	15	117	NONMETALLIC MINERAL PROD. MFG	85015	1292	11383	HOSPITALS
84329	1	9	EDUCATIONAL SERVICES	84660	915	8970	EDUCATIONAL SERVICES	85016	3446	39944	PROF.; SCIENTIFIC; & TECH SVCS
84330	7	444	PRIMARY METAL MANUFACTURING	84662	33	99	EDUCATIONAL SERVICES	85017	1445	14090	MERCH. WHOLESALERS;DURABLE GDS
84331	3	1	RELIG.; GRANT; CIVIC; PROF ORG	84663	812	11965	MERCH. WHOLESALERS;NONDUR. GDS	85018	1994	17134	FOOD SVCS & DRINKING PLACES
84332	144	1194	FOOD AND BEVERAGE STORES	84664	168	1241	CONSTRUCTION OF BUILDINGS	85019	600	10452	SPECIAL TRADE CONTRACTORS
84333	59	1061	FOOD MANUFACTURING	84665	11	92	ACCOMMODATION	85020	1723	23775	HOSPITALS
84334	9	31	GASOLINE STATIONS	84667	9	29	ADMINISTRATIVE & SUPPORT SVCS	85021	1504	23675	INSURANCE CARRIERS & RELATED
84335	221	2114	FOOD AND BEVERAGE STORES	84701	578	5165	FOOD SVCS & DRINKING PLACES	85022	1191	8723	FOOD SVCS & DRINKING PLACES
84336	19	99	GASOLINE STATIONS	84710	5	15	CONSTRUCTION OF BUILDINGS	85023	730	9914	MOTOR VEHICLE & PARTS DEALERS
84337	349	4651	FURNITURE & RELATED PROD. MFG	84711	11	27	SPECIAL TRADE CONTRACTORS	85024	513	6830	SPECIAL TRADE CONTRACTORS
84338	6	40	FOOD SVCS & DRINKING PLACES	84712	13	39	ACCOMMODATION	85026	4	25	POSTAL SERVICE
84339	71	567	EDUCATIONAL SERVICES	84713	242	1657	HOSPITALS	85027	2371	32832	SPECIAL TRADE CONTRACTORS
84340	73	374	GASOLINE STATIONS	84714	25	212	UTILITIES	85028	1157	8435	REAL ESTATE
84341	766	11189	HOSPITALS	84715	42	238	EDUCATIONAL SERVICES	85029	1487	18709	INSURANCE CARRIERS & RELATED
84401	2295	27765	SPECIAL TRADE CONTRACTORS	84716	31	146	EDUCATIONAL SERVICES	85030	2	65	TRANSIT & GRND PASS. TRANSPORT
84402	10	27	SPECIAL TRADE CONTRACTORS	84718	17	115	RELIG.; GRANT; CIVIC; PROF ORG	85031	586	9595	EXEC.; LEGIS.; & OTHER SUPPORT
84403	1061	14248	HOSPITALS	84719	50	563	ACCOMMODATION	85032	2747	20330	FOOD SVCS & DRINKING PLACES
84404	1348	19294	EDUCATIONAL SERVICES	84720	908	7824	FOOD SVCS & DRINKING PLACES	85033	780	6674	EDUCATIONAL SERVICES
84405	1095	16009	PROF.; SCIENTIFIC; & TECH SVCS	84721	731	6640	PROF.; SCIENTIFIC; & TECH SVCS	85034	1785	53994	SUPPORT ACT. FOR TRANSPORT.
84407	1	2	EXEC.; LEGIS.; & OTHER SUPPORT	84722	9	4	CONSTRUCTION OF BUILDINGS	85035	357	4037	FOOD SVCS & DRINKING PLACES
84408	15	126	EDUCATIONAL SERVICES	84723	32	147	UNCLASSIFIED ESTABLISHMENTS	85036	7	79	SOCIAL ASSISTANCE
84409	10	17	SPECIAL TRADE CONTRACTORS	84724	27	53	SPECIAL TRADE CONTRACTORS	85037	557	5680	HOSPITALS
84412	9	26	ADMINISTRATIVE & SUPPORT SVCS	84725	51	352	RELIG.; GRANT; CIVIC; PROF ORG	85038	1	2	INSURANCE CARRIERS & RELATED
84414	339	2297	EDUCATIONAL SERVICES	84726	74	380	TELECOMMUNICATIONS	85040	2229	44674	MERCH. WHOLESALERS;DURABLE GDS
84415	3	4	CONSTRUCTION OF BUILDINGS	84728	15	37	MINING (EXCEPT OIL AND GAS)	85041	617	4966	EDUCATIONAL SERVICES
84501	748	7141	FOOD SVCS & DRINKING PLACES	84729	16	23	FOOD AND BEVERAGE STORES	85042	619	7327	EDUCATIONAL SERVICES
84510	2	53	EDUCATIONAL SERVICES	84730	7	11	SPECIAL TRADE CONTRACTORS	85043	1003	27741	TRUCK TRANSPORTATION
84511	214	1521	EDUCATIONAL SERVICES	84731	1	0	RELIG.; GRANT; CIVIC; PROF ORG	85044	1404	15457	PROF.; SCIENTIFIC; & TECH SVCS
84512	28	127	ACCOMMODATION	84734	34	161	TELECOMMUNICATIONS	85045	69	154	AMUSEMENT; GAMBLING;& RECREAT.
84513	162	826	JUSTICE; PUBIC ORDER/SAFETY	84735	25	54	UTILITIES	85046	42	171	PROF.; SCIENTIFIC; & TECH SVCS
84516	3	5	SPECIAL TRADE CONTRACTORS	84736	4	2	SOCIAL ASSISTANCE	85048	935	6919	EDUCATIONAL SERVICES
84518	18	108	SUPPORT ACT. FOR TRANSPORT.	84737	518	4928	MERCH. WHOLESALERS;DURABLE GDS	85050	640	6930	FOOD SVCS & DRINKING PLACES
84520	35	164	MINING (EXCEPT OIL AND GAS)	84738	108	692	ACCOMMODATION	85051	1232	9638	FOOD SVCS & DRINKING PLACES
84521	11	26	NURSING & RESID. CARE FACILIT.	84739	12	23	GASOLINE STATIONS	85053	793	9323	INSURANCE CARRIERS & RELATED
84522	22	171	MINING (EXCEPT OIL AND GAS)	84740	23	52	EDUCATIONAL SERVICES	85054	381	6787	FOOD SVCS & DRINKING PLACES
84523	44	212	RELIG.; GRANT; CIVIC; PROF ORG	84741	370	3069	REPAIR AND MAINTENANCE	85060	21	39	PROF.; SCIENTIFIC; & TECH SVCS
84525	95	839	FOOD SVCS & DRINKING PLACES	84742	10	12	CONSTRUCTION OF BUILDINGS	85061	5	5	ADMINISTRATIVE & SUPPORT SVCS
84526	116	809	MINING (EXCEPT OIL AND GAS)	84743	2	1	EXEC.; LEGIS.; & OTHER SUPPORT	85063	9	9	SPECIAL TRADE CONTRACTORS
84528	102	1966	MINING (EXCEPT OIL AND GAS)	84744	13	115	EDUCATIONAL SERVICES	85064	41	180	REAL ESTATE
84530	14	44	PIPELINE TRANSPORTATION	84745	59	496	RELIG.; GRANT; CIVIC; PROF ORG	85066	10	29	ADMINISTRATIVE & SUPPORT SVCS
84531	15	110	ACCOMMODATION	84746	26	46	FOOD SVCS & DRINKING PLACES	85067	34	89	PROF.; SCIENTIFIC; & TECH SVCS
84532	804	4970	FOOD SVCS & DRINKING PLACES	84747	73	674	EDUCATIONAL SERVICES	85068	31	114	PROF.; SCIENTIFIC; & TECH SVCS
84533	21	476	AMUSEMENT; GAMBLING;& RECREAT.	84749	6	6	BLDG MATL & GARDEN EQPMT DLRS	85069	44	104	RELIG.; GRANT; CIVIC; PROF ORG
84534	36	312	AMBULATORY HEALTH CARE SVCS	84750	24	90	EDUCATIONAL SERVICES	85070	9	17	ADMINISTRATIVE & SUPPORT SVCS
84535	202	1519	HOSPITALS	84751	77	955	ANIMAL PRODUCTION	85071	25	69	CONSTRUCTION OF BUILDINGS
84536	19	506	ACCOMMODATION	84752	24	131	EDUCATIONAL SERVICES	85072	1	400	PETROLEUM & COAL PRODUCTS MFG
84537	34	468	COMPUTER & ELECTRONIC PROD MFG	84753	1	12	FOOD MANUFACTURING	85074	2	6	CONSTRUCTION OF BUILDINGS
84539	10	91	EDUCATIONAL SERVICES	84754	69	289	EDUCATIONAL SERVICES	85075	3	2	SUPPORT ACT. FOR TRANSPORT.
84540	5	17	GASOLINE STATIONS	84755	19	226	ACCOMMODATION	85076	20	87	MISCELLANEOUS STORE RETAILERS
84542	44	461	MINING (EXCEPT OIL AND GAS)	84756	9	7	CROP PRODUCTION	85077	1	2	MERCH. WHOLESALERS;DURABLE GDS
84601	1263	15344	SPECIAL TRADE CONTRACTORS	84757	32	61	GASOLINE STATIONS	85078	23	40	MERCH. WHOLESALERS;DURABLE GDS
84602	12	3547	ADMINISTRATIVE & SUPPORT SVCS	84758	33	126	EDUCATIONAL SERVICES	85079	7	4	MISCELLANEOUS MANUFACTURING
84603	11	43	BROADCASTING	84759	199	1068	EDUCATIONAL SERVICES	85080	47	94	MERCH. WHOLESALERS;NONDUR. GDS
84604	1511	20812	HOSPITALS	84760	6	55	EDUCATIONAL SERVICES	85082	20	93	ADMINISTRATIVE & SUPPORT SVCS
84605	9	45	PROF.; SCIENTIFIC; & TECH SVCS	84761	147	704	EXEC.; LEGIS.; & OTHER SUPPORT	85083	98	491	EDUCATIONAL SERVICES
84606	650	10624	ELECTRONICS & APPLIANCE STORES	84762	41	149	REAL ESTATE	85085	523	3818	FOOD SVCS & DRINKING PLACES
84620	29	268	TRUCK TRANSPORTATION	84763	12	52	NURSING & RESID. CARE FACILIT.	85086	828	6623	ADMIN. ENVIRO. QUALITY PROGRMS
84621	1	0	RELIG.; GRANT; CIVIC; PROF ORG	84764	26	1638	ACCOMMODATION	85087	119	512	SPECIAL TRADE CONTRACTORS
84622	40	213	TRUCK TRANSPORTATION	84765	115	487	AMUSEMENT; GAMBLING;& RECREAT.	85201	1646	16109	FOOD SVCS & DRINKING PLACES
84623	6	22	ANIMAL PRODUCTION	84766	1	6	MUSEUMS; HIST. SITES;& SIMILAR	85202	1440	23459	HOSPITALS
84624	302	2569	UTILITIES	84767	96	1220	FOOD SVCS & DRINKING PLACES	85203	1093	8640	ADMINISTRATIVE & SUPPORT SVCS
84626	19	111	MERCH. WHOLESALERS;NONDUR. GDS	84770	2476	23024	HOSPITALS	85204	1657	16339	FOOD SVCS & DRINKING PLACES
84627	222	1229	GENERAL MERCHANDISE STORES	84771	22	63	MERCH. WHOLESALERS;DURABLE GDS	85205	1128	8677	FOOD SVCS & DRINKING PLACES
84628	34	73	EDUCATIONAL SERVICES	84772	4	37	GASOLINE STATIONS	85206	1476	20967	HOSPITALS
84629	65	272	DATA PROCESS'G	84773	10	48	SUPPORT ACTIVITIES: AGR./FOR.	85207	747	4920	EDUCATIONAL SERVICES
84630	9	30	SPORTG GDS;HOBBY;BOOK; & MUSIC	84774	19	47	ANIMAL PRODUCTION	85208	264	1407	EDUCATIONAL SERVICES
84631	228	1849	CROP PRODUCTION	84775	55	246	ACCOMMODATION	85209	654	7631	FOOD SVCS & DRINKING PLACES
84632	22	100	EDUCATIONAL SERVICES	84776	34	244	ACCOMMODATION	85210	2309	26148	MERCH. WHOLESALERS;DURABLE GDS
84633	16	82	EDUCATIONAL SERVICES	84779	20	107	ANIMAL PRODUCTION	85211	31	110	CONSTRUCTION OF BUILDINGS
84634	127	1755	JUSTICE; PUBIC ORDER/SAFETY	84780	429	3538	FOOD SVCS & DRINKING PLACES	85212	345	6228	PROF.; SCIENTIFIC; & TECH SVCS
84635	15	48	MERCH. WHOLESALERS;NONDUR. GDS	84781	9	10	MERCH. WHOLESALERS;NONDUR. GDS	85213	703	5341	EDUCATIONAL SERVICES
84636	11	27	CROP PRODUCTION	84782	27	136	CONSTRUCTION OF BUILDINGS	85214	27	40	SPECIAL TRADE CONTRACTORS
84637	12	47	JUSTICE; PUBIC ORDER/SAFETY	84783	7	6	HEAVY & CIVIL ENG. CONSTRUCT'N	85215	778	14245	TRANSPORTATION EQUIPMENT MFG
84638	2	90	NONMETALLIC MINERAL PROD. MFG	84784	64	600	SPECIAL TRADE CONTRACTORS	85216	24	45	REPAIR AND MAINTENANCE
84639	14	104	PRINT'G & RELATED SUPP'T ACT'S	84790	1379	24304	CLOTHING & CLOTH'G ACC. STORES	85217	18	18	SPECIAL TRADE CONTRACTORS
84640	5	10	ANIMAL PRODUCTION	84791	7	9	PROF.; SCIENTIFIC; & TECH SVCS	85218	270	2936	AMUSEMENT; GAMBLING;& RECREAT.
84642	192	944	NAT'L SECURITY & INT'L AFFAIRS	85001	13	40	PROF.; SCIENTIFIC; & TECH SVCS	85219	480	2585	EXEC.; LEGIS.; & OTHER SUPPORT

ZIP CODE	2009 Total Firms	2009 Total Employ-ees	TOP INDUSTRY RANKED on 2009 EMPLOYMENT	ZIP CODE	2009 Total Firms	2009 Total Employ-ees	TOP INDUSTRY RANKED on 2009 EMPLOYMENT	ZIP CODE	2009 Total Firms	2009 Total Employ-ees	TOP INDUSTRY RANKED on 2009 EMPLOYMENT
85220	965	7017	MOTOR VEHICLE & PARTS DEALERS	85324	100	451	FOOD SVCS & DRINKING PLACES	85603	467	4517	ADMIN. OF HOUSING PROGRAMS
85221	12	273	EDUCATIONAL SERVICES	85325	28	83	CROP PRODUCTION	85605	28	164	FOOD AND BEVERAGE STORES
85222	1483	14056	FOOD SVCS & DRINKING PLACES	85326	631	4689	JUSTICE; PUBIC ORDER/SAFETY	85606	34	351	UTILITIES
85223	110	550	EDUCATIONAL SERVICES	85327	30	108	BLDG MATL & GARDEN EQPMT DLRS	85607	528	4867	JUSTICE; PUBIC ORDER/SAFETY
85224	1596	14830	HOSPITALS	85328	4	24	CROP PRODUCTION	85608	2	16	SOCIAL ASSISTANCE
85225	2006	22183	JUSTICE; PUBIC ORDER/SAFETY	85329	13	355	CROP PRODUCTION	85609	11	63	MINING (EXCEPT OIL AND GAS)
85226	1707	37055	COMPUTER & ELECTRONIC PROD MFG	85331	935	5204	FOOD SVCS & DRINKING PLACES	85610	62	373	SOCIAL ASSISTANCE
85227	2	12	ADMINISTRATIVE & SUPPORT SVCS	85332	49	179	CROP PRODUCTION	85611	17	85	EDUCATIONAL SERVICES
85228	391	3967	EXEC.; LEGIS.; & OTHER SUPPORT	85333	24	102	MISCELLANEOUS STORE RETAILERS	85613	70	2326	RELIG.; GRANT; CIVIC; PROF ORG
85230	24	106	SPECIAL TRADE CONTRACTORS	85334	63	372	EDUCATIONAL SERVICES	85614	336	5081	MINING (EXCEPT OIL AND GAS)
85231	243	2306	EDUCATIONAL SERVICES	85335	325	3627	EDUCATIONAL SERVICES	85615	178	642	SPECIAL TRADE CONTRACTORS
85232	282	7695	EXEC.; LEGIS.; & OTHER SUPPORT	85336	12	364	SUPPORT ACTIVITIES: AGR./FOR.	85616	137	597	EDUCATIONAL SERVICES
85233	1450	23275	SPECIAL TRADE CONTRACTORS	85337	94	970	EDUCATIONAL SERVICES	85617	21	221	FOOD SVCS & DRINKING PLACES
85234	1400	10403	EDUCATIONAL SERVICES	85338	661	8147	PROF.; SCIENTIFIC; & TECH SVCS	85618	54	288	ADMIN. HUMAN RESOURCE PROGRAMS
85235	26	1900	PRIMARY METAL MANUFACTURING	85339	333	2223	EDUCATIONAL SERVICES	85619	23	111	ACCOMMODATION
85236	84	114	FOOD AND BEVERAGE STORES	85340	471	2851	EDUCATIONAL SERVICES	85620	12	100	EDUCATIONAL SERVICES
85237	81	730	RELIG.; GRANT; CIVIC; PROF ORG	85341	8	96	FOOD AND BEVERAGE STORES	85621	1232	12388	FOOD AND BEVERAGE STORES
85238	121	1413	REAL ESTATE	85342	33	50	EDUCATIONAL SERVICES	85622	97	956	REAL ESTATE
85239	309	2872	AMUSEMENT; GAMBLING;& RECREAT.	85343	6	91	EDUCATIONAL SERVICES	85623	126	997	EDUCATIONAL SERVICES
85240	193	786	EDUCATIONAL SERVICES	85344	548	5714	EXEC.; LEGIS.; & OTHER SUPPORT	85624	70	373	EDUCATIONAL SERVICES
85241	20	186	JUSTICE; PUBIC ORDER/SAFETY	85345	1239	15173	SPECIAL TRADE CONTRACTORS	85625	103	262	EDUCATIONAL SERVICES
85242	729	4673	EXEC.; LEGIS.; & OTHER SUPPORT	85346	346	1277	RELIG.; GRANT; CIVIC; PROF ORG	85626	13	81	EDUCATIONAL SERVICES
85243	202	1552	GENERAL MERCHANDISE STORES	85347	25	277	CROP PRODUCTION	85627	6	28	EDUCATIONAL SERVICES
85244	31	92	ADMINISTRATIVE & SUPPORT SVCS	85348	122	298	EDUCATIONAL SERVICES	85628	3	8	ADMINISTRATIVE & SUPPORT SVCS
85245	10	74	ANIMAL PRODUCTION	85349	242	3069	FOOD AND BEVERAGE STORES	85629	139	2197	MISCELLANEOUS STORE RETAILERS
85246	31	76	ADMINISTRATIVE & SUPPORT SVCS	85350	282	3796	FOOD SVCS & DRINKING PLACES	85630	48	194	EDUCATIONAL SERVICES
85247	152	1488	EXEC.; LEGIS.; & OTHER SUPPORT	85351	764	12351	HOSPITALS	85631	76	741	EDUCATIONAL SERVICES
85248	679	9032	CONSTRUCTION OF BUILDINGS	85352	19	101	CROP PRODUCTION	85632	44	193	EDUCATIONAL SERVICES
85249	431	2447	EDUCATIONAL SERVICES	85353	487	17638	SPECIAL TRADE CONTRACTORS	85633	20	141	MUSEUMS; HIST. SITES;& SIMILAR
85250	778	8046	PROF.; SCIENTIFIC; & TECH SVCS	85354	83	411	GASOLINE STATIONS	85634	168	4515	EXEC.; LEGIS.; & OTHER SUPPORT
85251	3609	40266	HOSPITALS	85355	88	441	MERCH. WHOLESALERS;NONDUR. GDS	85635	1543	15138	FOOD SVCS & DRINKING PLACES
85252	50	234	PERFORM'G ARTS; SPEC. SPORTS	85356	112	994	AMUSEMENT; GAMBLING;& RECREAT.	85636	32	75	CONSTRUCTION OF BUILDINGS
85253	934	10655	ACCOMMODATION	85357	25	79	EDUCATIONAL SERVICES	85637	96	343	FOOD AND BEVERAGE STORES
85254	2275	25026	FOOD SVCS & DRINKING PLACES	85358	18	15	MOTOR VEHICLE & PARTS DEALERS	85638	160	573	FOOD SVCS & DRINKING PLACES
85255	1509	20607	FOOD SVCS & DRINKING PLACES	85359	2	1	ELECTRONICS & APPLIANCE STORES	85639	5	176	EDUCATIONAL SERVICES
85256	112	2693	EDUCATIONAL SERVICES	85360	25	172	FOOD SVCS & DRINKING PLACES	85640	51	180	REAL ESTATE
85257	804	15800	PROF.; SCIENTIFIC; & TECH SVCS	85361	56	395	MERCH. WHOLESALERS;DURABLE GDS	85641	218	1144	EDUCATIONAL SERVICES
85258	1956	22435	INSURANCE CARRIERS & RELATED	85362	39	84	FOOD SVCS & DRINKING PLACES	85643	391	3368	EDUCATIONAL SERVICES
85259	490	7455	AMBULATORY HEALTH CARE SVCS	85363	186	1937	NURSING & RESID. CARE FACILIT.	85644	1	25	ADMIN. ENVIRO. QUALITY PROGRMS
85260	4497	44950	PROF.; SCIENTIFIC; & TECH SVCS	85364	2233	26157	EDUCATIONAL SERVICES	85645	20	55	ACCOMMODATION
85261	40	75	PUBLISHING INDUSTRIES	85365	1417	22763	FOOD SVCS & DRINKING PLACES	85646	54	275	AMUSEMENT; GAMBLING;& RECREAT.
85262	325	5232	AMUSEMENT; GAMBLING;& RECREAT.	85366	31	240	FURNITURE & RELATED PROD. MFG	85648	271	2234	FOOD AND BEVERAGE STORES
85263	36	345	HEAVY & CIVIL ENG. CONSTRUCT'N	85367	331	2599	CROP PRODUCTION	85650	291	1891	SPECIAL TRADE CONTRACTORS
85264	67	1499	AMUSEMENT; GAMBLING;& RECREAT.	85369	17	7786	NAT'L SECURITY & INT'L AFFAIRS	85652	18	24	SPECIAL TRADE CONTRACTORS
85266	338	2837	AMUSEMENT; GAMBLING;& RECREAT.	85371	10	60	CROP PRODUCTION	85653	234	2738	EXEC.; LEGIS.; & OTHER SUPPORT
85267	62	213	MERCH. WHOLESALERS;DURABLE GDS	85372	16	25	ADMINISTRATIVE & SUPPORT SVCS	85654	18	252	NONMETALLIC MINERAL PROD. MFG
85268	984	5388	FOOD SVCS & DRINKING PLACES	85373	185	1428	NURSING & RESID. CARE FACILIT.	85658	99	920	AMUSEMENT; GAMBLING;& RECREAT.
85269	30	48	ADMINISTRATIVE & SUPPORT SVCS	85374	1149	11510	FOOD SVCS & DRINKING PLACES	85670	1	0	NAT'L SECURITY & INT'L AFFAIRS
85271	25	56	CONSTRUCTION OF BUILDINGS	85375	430	5029	HOSPITALS	85701	1255	20973	EXEC.; LEGIS.; & OTHER SUPPORT
85272	56	906	PROF.; SCIENTIFIC; & TECH SVCS	85376	2	0	UNCLASSIFIED ESTABLISHMENTS	85702	21	42	RELIG.; GRANT; CIVIC; PROF ORG
85273	84	574	EDUCATIONAL SERVICES	85377	340	2269	ACCOMMODATION	85703	12	37	NURSING & RESID. CARE FACILIT.
85274	22	63	ADMINISTRATIVE & SUPPORT SVCS	85378	5	26	ELECTRONICS & APPLIANCE STORES	85704	1481	15626	FOOD SVCS & DRINKING PLACES
85275	22	58	SPECIAL TRADE CONTRACTORS	85379	231	1723	EDUCATIONAL SERVICES	85705	3340	37181	SPECIAL TRADE CONTRACTORS
85277	35	61	CONSTRUCTION OF BUILDINGS	85380	21	34	PROF.; SCIENTIFIC; & TECH SVCS	85706	865	13274	EDUCATIONAL SERVICES
85278	12	13	PUBLISHING INDUSTRIES	85381	750	6805	AMBULATORY HEALTH CARE SVCS	85707	63	648	GENERAL MERCHANDISE STORES
85280	27	55	CONSTRUCTION OF BUILDINGS	85382	934	13568	FOOD SVCS & DRINKING PLACES	85708	6	87	EDUCATIONAL SERVICES
85281	3478	56840	PROF.; SCIENTIFIC; & TECH SVCS	85383	439	2230	SPECIAL TRADE CONTRACTORS	85709	39	1033	EDUCATIONAL SERVICES
85282	3093	37857	PROF.; SCIENTIFIC; & TECH SVCS	85385	21	72	ADMINISTRATIVE & SUPPORT SVCS	85710	1811	18437	FOOD SVCS & DRINKING PLACES
85283	1632	20452	ADMINISTRATIVE & SUPPORT SVCS	85387	78	202	ADMINISTRATIVE & SUPPORT SVCS	85711	2228	30584	AMBULATORY HEALTH CARE SVCS
85284	1242	22781	MERCH. WHOLESALERS;DURABLE GDS	85388	96	766	EDUCATIONAL SERVICES	85712	2253	28435	AMBULATORY HEALTH CARE SVCS
85285	41	163	ADMINISTRATIVE & SUPPORT SVCS	85390	549	3711	AMBULATORY HEALTH CARE SVCS	85713	1615	25923	NONSTORE RETAILERS
85286	574	6904	GENERAL MERCHANDISE STORES	85392	499	4997	EDUCATIONAL SERVICES	85714	1015	21852	PUBLISHING INDUSTRIES
85287	51	13171	EDUCATIONAL SERVICES	85395	486	6447	FOOD SVCS & DRINKING PLACES	85715	757	7311	FOOD SVCS & DRINKING PLACES
85290	1	30	ADMINISTRATIVE & SUPPORT SVCS	85396	100	483	EDUCATIONAL SERVICES	85716	1494	13816	FOOD SVCS & DRINKING PLACES
85291	5	17	SPECIAL TRADE CONTRACTORS	85501	586	4365	JUSTICE; PUBIC ORDER/SAFETY	85717	23	101	ADMINISTRATIVE & SUPPORT SVCS
85292	31	127	EDUCATIONAL SERVICES	85502	4	3	SPECIAL TRADE CONTRACTORS	85718	1101	11904	REAL ESTATE
85293	74	1405	MERCH. WHOLESALERS;NONDUR. GDS	85530	4	24	WASTE MANAGMT & REMEDIAT'N SVC	85719	2001	21175	FOOD SVCS & DRINKING PLACES
85294	92	737	FOOD SVCS & DRINKING PLACES	85531	8	29	HEAVY & CIVIL ENG. CONSTRUCT'N	85721	38	16055	EDUCATIONAL SERVICES
85295	704	4299	FOOD SVCS & DRINKING PLACES	85532	31	1276	MINING (EXCEPT OIL AND GAS)	85722	1	10	PUBLISHING INDUSTRIES
85296	742	6921	FOOD SVCS & DRINKING PLACES	85533	112	406	EXEC.; LEGIS.; & OTHER SUPPORT	85723	19	1205	HOSPITALS
85297	374	4933	TRUCK TRANSPORTATION	85534	94	597	EDUCATIONAL SERVICES	85724	73	5005	AMBULATORY HEALTH CARE SVCS
85298	179	873	FOOD SVCS & DRINKING PLACES	85535	1	4	ADMINISTRATIVE & SUPPORT SVCS	85725	2	20	MERCH. WHOLESALERS;DURABLE GDS
85299	66	198	SPECIAL TRADE CONTRACTORS	85536	13	173	EDUCATIONAL SERVICES	85726	13	12	PROF.; SCIENTIFIC; & TECH SVCS
85301	2273	25095	SPECIAL TRADE CONTRACTORS	85539	105	973	MINING (EXCEPT OIL AND GAS)	85728	31	57	REAL ESTATE
85302	658	8252	WOOD PRODUCT MANUFACTURING	85540	69	3001	MINING (EXCEPT OIL AND GAS)	85730	493	4023	ADMINISTRATIVE & SUPPORT SVCS
85303	390	6553	MERCH. WHOLESALERS;DURABLE GDS	85541	1062	7154	FOOD SVCS & DRINKING PLACES	85731	31	124	SPECIAL TRADE CONTRACTORS
85304	406	3404	EDUCATIONAL SERVICES	85542	19	388	EXEC.; LEGIS.; & OTHER SUPPORT	85732	54	121	SPECIAL TRADE CONTRACTORS
85305	236	2717	FOOD SVCS & DRINKING PLACES	85543	79	459	EDUCATIONAL SERVICES	85733	24	50	PROF.; SCIENTIFIC; & TECH SVCS
85306	811	9998	HOSPITALS	85544	128	436	JUSTICE; PUBIC ORDER/SAFETY	85734	14	21	ADMINISTRATIVE & SUPPORT SVCS
85307	192	2745	MERCH. WHOLESALERS;DURABLE GDS	85545	36	131	AMUSEMENT; GAMBLING;& RECREAT.	85735	144	1234	AMUSEMENT; GAMBLING;& RECREAT.
85308	2302	20456	FOOD SVCS & DRINKING PLACES	85546	659	7066	REPAIR AND MAINTENANCE	85736	23	138	EDUCATIONAL SERVICES
85309	42	289	AMBULATORY HEALTH CARE SVCS	85547	24	56	SOCIAL ASSISTANCE	85737	372	4602	COMPUTER & ELECTRONIC PROD MFG
85310	343	3193	SPECIAL TRADE CONTRACTORS	85548	6	3	REAL ESTATE	85738	10	45	HEAVY & CIVIL ENG. CONSTRUCT'N
85311	19	37	SPECIAL TRADE CONTRACTORS	85550	122	1623	EXEC.; LEGIS.; & OTHER SUPPORT	85739	337	3088	ACCOMMODATION
85312	33	138	AMBULATORY HEALTH CARE SVCS	85551	11	46	EDUCATIONAL SERVICES	85740	29	104	AMBULATORY HEALTH CARE SVCS
85318	61	235	CONSTRUCTION OF BUILDINGS	85552	163	2120	EDUCATIONAL SERVICES	85741	1200	15075	FOOD SVCS & DRINKING PLACES
85320	29	542	MERCH. WHOLESALERS;NONDUR. GDS	85553	65	198	FOOD SVCS & DRINKING PLACES	85742	287	2944	EDUCATIONAL SERVICES
85321	181	1027	EDUCATIONAL SERVICES	85554	34	163	SUPPORT ACTIVITIES: AGR./FOR.	85743	498	6764	HEAVY & CIVIL ENG. CONSTRUCT'N
85322	14	60	UTILITIES	85601	3	4	OTHER INFORMATION SERVICES	85744	2	1502	COMPUTER & ELECTRONIC PROD MFG
85323	625	38446	PERFORM'G ARTS; SPEC. SPORTS	85602	409	3147	FOOD SVCS & DRINKING PLACES	85745	942	14257	HOSPITALS

BUSINESS DATA

ZIP CODE	2009 Total Firms	2009 Total Employees	TOP INDUSTRY RANKED on 2009 EMPLOYMENT
85746	429	6371	TELECOMMUNICATIONS
85747	289	3146	FOOD SVCS & DRINKING PLACES
85748	266	2251	FOOD SVCS & DRINKING PLACES
85749	440	2524	EDUCATIONAL SERVICES
85750	379	4616	ACCOMMODATION
85751	33	91	CHEMICAL MANUFACTURING
85752	44	107	ADMINISTRATIVE & SUPPORT SVCS
85754	15	27	ADMINISTRATIVE & SUPPORT SVCS
85755	225	2308	AMUSEMENT; GAMBLING;& RECREAT.
85756	447	13826	COMPUTER & ELECTRONIC PROD MFG
85757	89	633	EDUCATIONAL SERVICES
85775	1	8	HEALTH & PERSONAL CARE STORES
85901	1011	9368	HOSPITALS
85902	28	61	CONSTRUCTION OF BUILDINGS
85911	25	308	EDUCATIONAL SERVICES
85912	6	10	JUSTICE; PUBIC ORDER/SAFETY
85920	57	199	EXEC.; LEGIS.; & OTHER SUPPORT
85922	4	2	EDUCATIONAL SERVICES
85923	15	24	SPECIAL TRADE CONTRACTORS
85924	30	125	EDUCATIONAL SERVICES
85925	150	718	EDUCATIONAL SERVICES
85926	7	43	EDUCATIONAL SERVICES
85927	48	260	ACCOMMODATION
85928	118	507	EDUCATIONAL SERVICES
85929	472	3338	EDUCATIONAL SERVICES
85930	16	92	EDUCATIONAL SERVICES
85931	18	39	EDUCATIONAL SERVICES
85932	8	32	WOOD PRODUCT MANUFACTURING
85933	148	695	ACCOMMODATION
85934	16	17	CONSTRUCTION OF BUILDINGS
85935	375	2239	ACCOMMODATION
85936	227	1644	EXEC.; LEGIS.; & OTHER SUPPORT
85937	315	2644	PAPER MANUFACTURING
85938	189	1468	UTILITIES
85939	137	843	FOOD SVCS & DRINKING PLACES
85940	32	99	EDUCATIONAL SERVICES
85941	152	3280	EXEC.; LEGIS.; & OTHER SUPPORT
85942	3	6	OTHER INFORMATION SERVICES
86001	2212	25961	AMBULATORY HEALTH CARE SVCS
86002	32	76	SPECIAL TRADE CONTRACTORS
86003	52	100	SPECIAL TRADE CONTRACTORS
86004	1714	15583	FOOD SVCS & DRINKING PLACES
86011	16	278	OTHER INFORMATION SERVICES
86015	23	645	PAPER MANUFACTURING
86016	5	48	GENERAL MERCHANDISE STORES
86017	46	239	AMUSEMENT; GAMBLING;& RECREAT.
86018	28	86	EDUCATIONAL SERVICES
86020	26	493	ACCOMMODATION
86021	96	657	EDUCATIONAL SERVICES
86022	88	571	EDUCATIONAL SERVICES
86023	97	3411	ACCOMMODATION
86024	34	158	EXEC.; LEGIS.; & OTHER SUPPORT
86025	331	3943	EXEC.; LEGIS.; & OTHER SUPPORT
86028	2	80	MUSEUMS; HIST. SITES;& SIMILAR
86029	5	49	EDUCATIONAL SERVICES
86030	12	64	EDUCATIONAL SERVICES
86031	4	26	MERCH. WHOLESALERS;DURABLE GDS
86032	33	571	UTILITIES
86033	125	2769	EDUCATIONAL SERVICES
86034	58	1458	EXEC.; LEGIS.; & OTHER SUPPORT
86035	26	245	EDUCATIONAL SERVICES
86036	14	158	SCENIC & SIGHTSEEING TRANSPORT
86038	21	178	ACCOMMODATION
86039	43	714	EXEC.; LEGIS.; & OTHER SUPPORT
86040	470	6067	ADMINISTRATIVE & SUPPORT SVCS
86042	18	373	HOSPITALS
86043	24	195	EXEC.; LEGIS.; & OTHER SUPPORT
86044	8	114	EDUCATIONAL SERVICES
86045	191	2448	EDUCATIONAL SERVICES
86046	342	2287	FOOD SVCS & DRINKING PLACES
86047	411	4320	JUSTICE; PUBIC ORDER/SAFETY
86052	7	211	ACCOMMODATION
86053	12	187	ADMIN. ENVIRO. QUALITY PROGRMS
86054	16	163	EDUCATIONAL SERVICES
86301	1875	20511	EDUCATIONAL SERVICES
86302	31	63	SPECIAL TRADE CONTRACTORS
86303	792	5242	EXEC.; LEGIS.; & OTHER SUPPORT
86304	44	75	ADMINISTRATIVE & SUPPORT SVCS
86305	813	6743	AMBULATORY HEALTH CARE SVCS
86312	44	142	SPECIAL TRADE CONTRACTORS
86313	10	608	HOSPITALS
86314	1224	11237	EDUCATIONAL SERVICES
86315	70	956	PERFORM'G ARTS; SPEC. SPORTS
86320	52	300	MINING (EXCEPT OIL AND GAS)
86321	49	855	MINING (EXCEPT OIL AND GAS)
86322	561	4177	JUSTICE; PUBIC ORDER/SAFETY
86323	587	3434	EDUCATIONAL SERVICES
86324	119	1139	EDUCATIONAL SERVICES
86325	145	510	SPECIAL TRADE CONTRACTORS
86326	1242	9294	AMBULATORY HEALTH CARE SVCS

ZIP CODE	2009 Total Firms	2009 Total Employees	TOP INDUSTRY RANKED on 2009 EMPLOYMENT
86327	217	1210	SPECIAL TRADE CONTRACTORS
86329	41	245	EDUCATIONAL SERVICES
86330	2	0	FOOD MANUFACTURING
86331	124	362	FOOD SVCS & DRINKING PLACES
86332	28	150	SUPPORT ACTIVITIES: AGR./FOR.
86333	162	1027	EDUCATIONAL SERVICES
86334	59	107	SPECIAL TRADE CONTRACTORS
86335	106	482	EDUCATIONAL SERVICES
86336	1442	10134	ACCOMMODATION
86337	95	412	EDUCATIONAL SERVICES
86338	15	91	CONSTRUCTION OF BUILDINGS
86339	25	36	PROF.; SCIENTIFIC; & TECH SVCS
86340	20	25	ADMINISTRATIVE & SUPPORT SVCS
86341	17	53	PUBLISHING INDUSTRIES
86342	13	46	FOOD SVCS & DRINKING PLACES
86343	11	31	FOOD SVCS & DRINKING PLACES
86351	320	2052	ACCOMMODATION
86401	1246	11663	JUSTICE; PUBIC ORDER/SAFETY
86402	29	58	ADMIN. OF ECONOMIC PROGRAMS
86403	2349	16463	FOOD SVCS & DRINKING PLACES
86404	415	2414	GENERAL MERCHANDISE STORES
86405	64	135	CONSTRUCTION OF BUILDINGS
86406	508	2385	EDUCATIONAL SERVICES
86409	1041	8342	HOSPITALS
86411	2	7	MERCH. WHOLESALERS;NONDUR. GDS
86412	2	6	MOTION PICT. & SOUND RECORDING
86413	195	922	TRUCK TRANSPORTATION
86426	540	3330	AMUSEMENT; GAMBLING;& RECREAT.
86427	14	34	REAL ESTATE
86429	238	1707	FOOD SVCS & DRINKING PLACES
86430	6	42	WASTE MANAGMT & REMEDIAT'N SVC
86431	12	55	FOOD SVCS & DRINKING PLACES
86432	49	205	EDUCATIONAL SERVICES
86433	28	52	MISCELLANEOUS STORE RETAILERS
86434	60	652	EXEC.; LEGIS.; & OTHER SUPPORT
86435	18	66	EDUCATIONAL SERVICES
86436	43	156	ADMIN. OF ECONOMIC PROGRAMS
86437	7	22	MUSEUMS; HIST. SITES;& SIMILAR
86438	13	36	REAL ESTATE
86439	9	23	SPECIAL TRADE CONTRACTORS
86440	310	1424	EDUCATIONAL SERVICES
86441	56	194	EDUCATIONAL SERVICES
86442	1302	8554	GENERAL MERCHANDISE STORES
86443	4	153	ACCOMMODATION
86444	43	121	MERCH. WHOLESALERS;DURABLE GDS
86445	9	46	ADMIN. ENVIRO. QUALITY PROGRMS
86446	10	18	SPECIAL TRADE CONTRACTORS
86502	20	143	EDUCATIONAL SERVICES
86503	226	2616	EDUCATIONAL SERVICES
86504	104	1843	UTILITIES
86505	91	2295	EDUCATIONAL SERVICES
86506	10	57	EDUCATIONAL SERVICES
86507	10	61	EDUCATIONAL SERVICES
86508	14	165	GASOLINE STATIONS
86510	27	475	EDUCATIONAL SERVICES
86511	28	458	EDUCATIONAL SERVICES
86512	85	1541	EDUCATIONAL SERVICES
86514	34	492	EDUCATIONAL SERVICES
86515	367	3338	JUSTICE; PUBIC ORDER/SAFETY
86520	1	0	EXEC.; LEGIS.; & OTHER SUPPORT
86535	9	7	RELIG.; GRANT; CIVIC; PROF ORG
86538	20	1387	EDUCATIONAL SERVICES
86540	2	40	EDUCATIONAL SERVICES
86544	7	64	EDUCATIONAL SERVICES
86545	6	125	EDUCATIONAL SERVICES
86547	2	34	EDUCATIONAL SERVICES
86556	12	364	EDUCATIONAL SERVICES
87001	32	702	AMUSEMENT; GAMBLING;& RECREAT.
87002	647	6422	EDUCATIONAL SERVICES
87004	452	5798	AMUSEMENT; GAMBLING;& RECREAT.
87005	8	43	EDUCATIONAL SERVICES
87006	6	13	EXEC.; LEGIS.; & OTHER SUPPORT
87007	22	499	AMUSEMENT; GAMBLING;& RECREAT.
87008	149	480	FOOD SVCS & DRINKING PLACES
87010	70	140	MISCELLANEOUS STORE RETAILERS
87011	3	4	MERCH. WHOLESALERS;NONDUR. GDS
87012	5	41	EXEC.; LEGIS.; & OTHER SUPPORT
87013	149	1075	EDUCATIONAL SERVICES
87014	11	81	EDUCATIONAL SERVICES
87015	248	1065	EDUCATIONAL SERVICES
87016	97	918	ADMINISTRATIVE & SUPPORT SVCS
87017	14	267	EDUCATIONAL SERVICES
87018	6	41	EDUCATIONAL SERVICES
87020	499	4451	EDUCATIONAL SERVICES
87021	108	1253	JUSTICE; PUBIC ORDER/SAFETY
87022	30	369	JUSTICE; PUBIC ORDER/SAFETY
87023	5	37	EDUCATIONAL SERVICES
87024	46	445	EDUCATIONAL SERVICES
87025	53	223	ACCOMMODATION
87026	72	1158	EXEC.; LEGIS.; & OTHER SUPPORT

ZIP CODE	2009 Total Firms	2009 Total Employees	TOP INDUSTRY RANKED on 2009 EMPLOYMENT
87027	4	16	OIL AND GAS EXTRACTION
87028	3	3	RELIG.; GRANT; CIVIC; PROF ORG
87029	18	64	MERCH. WHOLESALERS;NONDUR. GDS
87031	846	7564	JUSTICE; PUBIC ORDER/SAFETY
87032	13	95	SOCIAL ASSISTANCE
87034	27	286	EDUCATIONAL SERVICES
87035	260	1787	FOOD SVCS & DRINKING PLACES
87036	84	365	EDUCATIONAL SERVICES
87037	7	47	EXEC.; LEGIS.; & OTHER SUPPORT
87038	4	89	EDUCATIONAL SERVICES
87040	3	15	CONSTRUCTION OF BUILDINGS
87041	11	70	EDUCATIONAL SERVICES
87042	77	386	ADMINISTRATIVE & SUPPORT SVCS
87043	113	404	SPECIAL TRADE CONTRACTORS
87044	7	5	UTILITIES
87045	15	341	PAPER MANUFACTURING
87046	3	2	GASOLINE STATIONS
87047	87	365	EDUCATIONAL SERVICES
87048	337	1123	PROF.; SCIENTIFIC; & TECH SVCS
87049	19	218	HOSPITALS
87051	7	27	EDUCATIONAL SERVICES
87052	11	274	RELIG.; GRANT; CIVIC; PROF ORG
87053	46	140	EXEC.; LEGIS.; & OTHER SUPPORT
87056	17	27	HEAVY & CIVIL ENG. CONSTRUCT'N
87059	287	1222	NONMETALLIC MINERAL PROD. MFG
87060	3	89	EDUCATIONAL SERVICES
87061	11	23	ACCOMMODATION
87062	14	86	EDUCATIONAL SERVICES
87063	6	33	CROP PRODUCTION
87064	1	0	FOOD AND BEVERAGE STORES
87068	172	826	SPECIAL TRADE CONTRACTORS
87070	7	69	GASOLINE STATIONS
87072	8	120	OTHER INFORMATION SERVICES
87083	9	96	AMUSEMENT; GAMBLING;& RECREAT.
87101	6	59	POSTAL SERVICE
87102	2622	42571	EXEC.; LEGIS.; & OTHER SUPPORT
87103	16	57	MERCH. WHOLESALERS;NONDUR. GDS
87104	657	5246	FOOD SVCS & DRINKING PLACES
87105	1240	11364	EDUCATIONAL SERVICES
87106	1431	38040	HOSPITALS
87107	2785	34670	SPECIAL TRADE CONTRACTORS
87108	1669	20488	HOSPITALS
87109	2964	39718	PROF.; SCIENTIFIC; & TECH SVCS
87110	3583	32760	PROF.; SCIENTIFIC; & TECH SVCS
87111	1699	12643	FOOD SVCS & DRINKING PLACES
87112	2025	13044	FOOD SVCS & DRINKING PLACES
87113	1007	20749	SPECIAL TRADE CONTRACTORS
87114	1525	13627	FOOD SVCS & DRINKING PLACES
87115	1	0	UNCLASSIFIED ESTABLISHMENTS
87116	8	116	EDUCATIONAL SERVICES
87117	67	1543	PROF.; SCIENTIFIC; & TECH SVCS
87119	8	7	CONSTRUCTION OF BUILDINGS
87120	1163	8133	FOOD SVCS & DRINKING PLACES
87121	997	11626	FOOD SVCS & DRINKING PLACES
87122	417	3080	REAL ESTATE
87123	1107	10237	PROF.; SCIENTIFIC; & TECH SVCS
87124	1417	15716	COMPUTER & ELECTRONIC PROD MFG
87125	23	97	SOCIAL ASSISTANCE
87131	119	19796	EDUCATIONAL SERVICES
87144	292	4164	NONSTORE RETAILERS
87153	3	3	NONSTORE RETAILERS
87154	23	56	CONSTRUCTION OF BUILDINGS
87158	1	0	UTILITIES
87165	1	1	MISCELLANEOUS STORE RETAILERS
87174	47	174	FURNITURE & RELATED PROD. MFG
87176	21	29	PROF.; SCIENTIFIC; & TECH SVCS
87181	21	39	REAL ESTATE
87184	12	123	SPECIAL TRADE CONTRACTORS
87185	3	4	ADMIN. ENVIRO. QUALITY PROGRMS
87187	3	6	BLDG MATL & GARDEN EQPMT DLRS
87190	19	72	ADMINISTRATIVE & SUPPORT SVCS
87191	26	87	INSURANCE CARRIERS & RELATED
87192	28	50	PROF.; SCIENTIFIC; & TECH SVCS
87193	37	73	CONSTRUCTION OF BUILDINGS
87194	8	9	SECURITIES/COMMODITY CONTRACTS
87195	9	27	MERCH. WHOLESALERS;NONDUR. GDS
87196	17	16	PROF.; SCIENTIFIC; & TECH SVCS
87197	16	25	SPECIAL TRADE CONTRACTORS
87198	20	35	SOCIAL ASSISTANCE
87199	55	132	SPECIAL TRADE CONTRACTORS
87301	1426	17320	HOSPITALS
87305	8	17	RELIG.; GRANT; CIVIC; PROF ORG
87310	1	90	ADMINISTRATIVE & SUPPORT SVCS
87311	13	140	EDUCATIONAL SERVICES
87312	6	47	MISCELLANEOUS STORE RETAILERS
87313	164	1274	EDUCATIONAL SERVICES
87315	11	19	HEAVY & CIVIL ENG. CONSTRUCT'N
87316	24	594	EDUCATIONAL SERVICES
87317	17	154	FOOD AND BEVERAGE STORES
87319	8	38	RELIG.; GRANT; CIVIC; PROF ORG

ZIP CODE	2009 Total Firms	2009 Total Employees	TOP INDUSTRY RANKED on 2009 EMPLOYMENT
87321	53	485	EXEC.; LEGIS.; & OTHER SUPPORT
87322	4	111	EDUCATIONAL SERVICES
87323	72	661	EDUCATIONAL SERVICES
87325	44	398	EDUCATIONAL SERVICES
87326	30	176	EDUCATIONAL SERVICES
87327	113	2460	EXEC.; LEGIS.; & OTHER SUPPORT
87328	25	223	EDUCATIONAL SERVICES
87347	9	300	PETROLEUM & COAL PRODUCTS MFG
87357	32	487	EDUCATIONAL SERVICES
87364	1	2	RELIG.; GRANT; CIVIC; PROF ORG
87365	2	3	MISCELLANEOUS STORE RETAILERS
87375	6	23	EXEC.; LEGIS.; & OTHER SUPPORT
87401	2588	26884	SPECIAL TRADE CONTRACTORS
87402	673	7961	EDUCATIONAL SERVICES
87410	616	4968	MACHINERY MANUFACTURING
87412	14	50	JUSTICE; PUBIC ORDER/SAFETY
87413	425	5535	SPECIAL TRADE CONTRACTORS
87415	82	370	SPECIAL TRADE CONTRACTORS
87416	38	783	UTILITIES
87417	160	1206	EDUCATIONAL SERVICES
87418	19	937	MINING (EXCEPT OIL AND GAS)
87419	26	217	SUPPORT ACTIVITIES FOR MINING
87420	226	2605	JUSTICE; PUBIC ORDER/SAFETY
87421	32	1584	UTILITIES
87455	22	231	EDUCATIONAL SERVICES
87461	10	18	EDUCATIONAL SERVICES
87499	43	63	ADMINISTRATIVE & SUPPORT SVCS
87501	2566	23222	EXEC.; LEGIS.; & OTHER SUPPORT
87502	87	311	RELIG.; GRANT; CIVIC; PROF ORG
87503	13	211	EXEC.; LEGIS.; & OTHER SUPPORT
87504	69	88	CONSTRUCTION OF BUILDINGS
87505	3121	31258	EXEC.; LEGIS.; & OTHER SUPPORT
87506	404	4088	AMUSEMENT; GAMBLING;& RECREAT.
87507	2028	16828	FOOD SVCS & DRINKING PLACES
87508	631	3495	EDUCATIONAL SERVICES
87510	43	157	ACCOMMODATION
87511	28	245	EDUCATIONAL SERVICES
87512	3	11	ACCOMMODATION
87513	21	38	ADMINISTRATIVE & SUPPORT SVCS
87514	54	177	EDUCATIONAL SERVICES
87515	8	20	SUPPORT ACTIVITIES: AGR./FOR.
87516	3	6	CONSTRUCTION OF BUILDINGS
87517	3	4	MISCELLANEOUS MANUFACTURING
87518	2	2	PROF.; SCIENTIFIC; & TECH SVCS
87519	6	33	JUSTICE; PUBIC ORDER/SAFETY
87520	151	657	RAIL TRANSPORTATION
87521	16	29	JUSTICE; PUBIC ORDER/SAFETY
87522	45	283	FOOD SVCS & DRINKING PLACES
87523	7	24	EDUCATIONAL SERVICES
87524	14	23	ACCOMMODATION
87525	42	941	ACCOMMODATION
87527	20	79	JUSTICE; PUBIC ORDER/SAFETY
87528	103	2121	EXEC.; LEGIS.; & OTHER SUPPORT
87529	92	433	FOOD SVCS & DRINKING PLACES
87530	24	283	AMBULATORY HEALTH CARE SVCS
87531	16	76	MOTOR VEHICLE & PARTS DEALERS
87532	791	7667	EDUCATIONAL SERVICES
87533	12	112	EXEC.; LEGIS.; & OTHER SUPPORT
87535	23	323	SPORTG GDS;HOBBY;BOOK; & MUSIC
87537	17	170	CONSTRUCTION OF BUILDINGS
87540	44	145	EDUCATIONAL SERVICES
87543	1	5	ADMINISTRATIVE & SUPPORT SVCS
87544	650	7275	PROF.; SCIENTIFIC; & TECH SVCS
87545	3	7266	EDUCATIONAL SERVICES
87548	4	2	HEAVY & CIVIL ENG. CONSTRUCT'N
87549	29	444	EDUCATIONAL SERVICES
87551	16	65	REPAIR AND MAINTENANCE
87552	121	516	EDUCATIONAL SERVICES
87553	44	309	EDUCATIONAL SERVICES
87554	1	1	POSTAL SERVICE
87556	116	400	EDUCATIONAL SERVICES
87557	97	474	EDUCATIONAL SERVICES
87558	132	842	ACCOMMODATION
87560	21	143	EDUCATIONAL SERVICES
87562	11	15	NONSTORE RETAILERS
87564	7	33	EDUCATIONAL SERVICES
87565	7	9	FURNITURE & RELATED PROD. MFG
87566	44	1168	AMUSEMENT; GAMBLING;& RECREAT.
87567	18	57	EDUCATIONAL SERVICES
87569	2	2	PROF.; SCIENTIFIC; & TECH SVCS
87571	1348	12990	CREDIT INTERMEDIATION & RELATD
87573	6	64	ACCOMMODATION
87574	15	17	CONSTRUCTION OF BUILDINGS
87575	63	432	EDUCATIONAL SERVICES
87577	11	31	HEAVY & CIVIL ENG. CONSTRUCT'N
87578	19	47	JUSTICE; PUBIC ORDER/SAFETY
87579	7	37	ACCOMMODATION
87580	1	2	REAL ESTATE
87581	3	6	MERCH. WHOLESALERS;DURABLE GDS
87582	49	97	EDUCATIONAL SERVICES
87583	7	56	POSTAL SERVICE
87592	20	76	AMUSEMENT; GAMBLING;& RECREAT.
87594	19	56	SPECIAL TRADE CONTRACTORS
87701	824	7607	EDUCATIONAL SERVICES
87710	229	1263	ACCOMMODATION
87711	21	50	EDUCATIONAL SERVICES
87712	7	40	AMBULATORY HEALTH CARE SVCS
87713	5	4	CREDIT INTERMEDIATION & RELATD
87714	77	1282	SOCIAL ASSISTANCE
87715	17	26	FOOD SVCS & DRINKING PLACES
87718	69	199	ACCOMMODATION
87722	9	9	CONSTRUCTION OF BUILDINGS
87723	5	4	CONSTRUCTION OF BUILDINGS
87724	1	3	AMBULATORY HEALTH CARE SVCS
87728	16	50	EDUCATIONAL SERVICES
87729	2	2	PERFORM'G ARTS; SPEC. SPORTS
87730	2	2	ANIMAL PRODUCTION
87731	9	111	RELIG.; GRANT; CIVIC; PROF ORG
87732	92	799	EDUCATIONAL SERVICES
87733	39	91	EXEC.; LEGIS.; & OTHER SUPPORT
87734	6	5	ANIMAL PRODUCTION
87735	2	0	ANIMAL PRODUCTION
87736	1	0	POSTAL SERVICE
87740	428	3442	EXEC.; LEGIS.; & OTHER SUPPORT
87742	9	67	AMUSEMENT; GAMBLING;& RECREAT.
87743	42	104	EDUCATIONAL SERVICES
87745	10	45	JUSTICE; PUBIC ORDER/SAFETY
87746	4	4	ANIMAL PRODUCTION
87747	81	446	NURSING & RESID. CARE FACILIT.
87749	5	7	SUPPORT ACTIVITIES: AGR./FOR.
87750	1	86	NURSING & RESID. CARE FACILIT.
87752	31	72	EDUCATIONAL SERVICES
87753	8	19	MUSEUMS; HIST. SITES;& SIMILAR
87801	443	4892	EDUCATIONAL SERVICES
87820	3	35	SPORTG GDS;HOBBY;BOOK; & MUSIC
87821	35	55	EDUCATIONAL SERVICES
87823	16	80	GASOLINE STATIONS
87824	13	50	EXEC.; LEGIS.; & OTHER SUPPORT
87825	87	395	EDUCATIONAL SERVICES
87827	28	34	ANIMAL PRODUCTION
87828	9	19	EDUCATIONAL SERVICES
87829	51	238	EDUCATIONAL SERVICES
87830	92	361	EDUCATIONAL SERVICES
87831	5	15	ADMIN. ENVIRO. QUALITY PROGRMS
87832	23	63	ADMIN. ENVIRO. QUALITY PROGRMS
87901	443	2809	NURSING & RESID. CARE FACILIT.
87930	16	260	FOOD MANUFACTURING
87931	23	119	CONSTRUCTION OF BUILDINGS
87933	1	2	POSTAL SERVICE
87935	97	446	ACCOMMODATION
87936	7	38	EDUCATIONAL SERVICES
87937	108	984	FOOD AND BEVERAGE STORES
87939	2	0	JUSTICE; PUBIC ORDER/SAFETY
87940	12	84	CROP PRODUCTION
87941	9	102	FOOD AND BEVERAGE STORES
87942	26	98	PERSONAL AND LAUNDRY SERVICES
87943	10	32	SUPPORT ACTIVITIES: AGR./FOR.
88001	1549	15238	FOOD SVCS & DRINKING PLACES
88002	19	201	EDUCATIONAL SERVICES
88003	26	4159	EDUCATIONAL SERVICES
88004	31	642	JUSTICE; PUBIC ORDER/SAFETY
88005	1182	10650	AMBULATORY HEALTH CARE SVCS
88006	11	22	ADMINISTRATIVE & SUPPORT SVCS
88007	421	6519	EXEC.; LEGIS.; & OTHER SUPPORT
88008	107	2397	HOSPITALS
88009	4	1	CREDIT INTERMEDIATION & RELATD
88011	838	12147	AMBULATORY HEALTH CARE SVCS
88012	237	2098	SPACE RESEARCH AND TECHNOLOGY
88013	3	2	CONSTRUCTION OF BUILDINGS
88020	35	250	MERCH. WHOLESALERS;NONDUR. GDS
88021	129	1758	EDUCATIONAL SERVICES
88022	42	179	CONSTRUCTION OF BUILDINGS
88023	86	409	EDUCATIONAL SERVICES
88024	4	79	MERCH. WHOLESALERS;NONDUR. GDS
88025	9	15	ANIMAL PRODUCTION
88026	32	109	EXEC.; LEGIS.; & OTHER SUPPORT
88027	2	15	FOOD AND BEVERAGE STORES
88028	30	139	EDUCATIONAL SERVICES
88029	53	560	AMBULATORY HEALTH CARE SVCS
88030	671	6865	FOOD MANUFACTURING
88031	1	0	SOCIAL ASSISTANCE
88032	12	50	SPECIAL TRADE CONTRACTORS
88033	6	27	NONSTORE RETAILERS
88034	3	8	ANIMAL PRODUCTION
88036	7	432	HOSPITALS
88038	14	36	ANIMAL PRODUCTION
88039	35	75	FOOD SVCS & DRINKING PLACES
88040	6	12	HEAVY & CIVIL ENG. CONSTRUCT'N
88041	13	52	EDUCATIONAL SERVICES
88042	25	96	MISCELLANEOUS STORE RETAILERS
88043	25	456	CHEMICAL MANUFACTURING
88044	36	274	FOOD AND BEVERAGE STORES
88045	220	1244	FOOD SVCS & DRINKING PLACES
88046	90	670	FOOD SVCS & DRINKING PLACES
88047	72	755	MERCH. WHOLESALERS;NONDUR. GDS
88048	34	506	ANIMAL PRODUCTION
88049	36	67	JUSTICE; PUBIC ORDER/SAFETY
88051	3	9	ANIMAL PRODUCTION
88052	9	25	FOOD SVCS & DRINKING PLACES
88053	9	32	FOOD SVCS & DRINKING PLACES
88054	9	263	MERCH. WHOLESALERS;NONDUR. GDS
88055	2	1	ANIMAL PRODUCTION
88056	17	58	MISCELLANEOUS STORE RETAILERS
88058	14	103	EDUCATIONAL SERVICES
88061	861	10120	RELIG.; GRANT; CIVIC; PROF ORG
88062	3	3	MISCELLANEOUS STORE RETAILERS
88063	96	1395	PERFORM'G ARTS; SPEC. SPORTS
88065	17	322	MINING (EXCEPT OIL AND GAS)
88072	22	162	CROP PRODUCTION
88081	82	442	EDUCATIONAL SERVICES
88101	1720	15353	EDUCATIONAL SERVICES
88102	9	22	RELIG.; GRANT; CIVIC; PROF ORG
88103	33	620	HOSPITALS
88112	11	12	CROP PRODUCTION
88113	6	227	ANIMAL PRODUCTION
88114	5	19	SPECIAL TRADE CONTRACTORS
88115	16	135	EDUCATIONAL SERVICES
88116	36	79	EDUCATIONAL SERVICES
88118	18	154	EDUCATIONAL SERVICES
88119	141	595	EDUCATIONAL SERVICES
88120	13	66	EDUCATIONAL SERVICES
88121	13	111	EDUCATIONAL SERVICES
88122	1	1	FOOD AND BEVERAGE STORES
88124	42	239	EDUCATIONAL SERVICES
88125	11	43	JUSTICE; PUBIC ORDER/SAFETY
88126	1	0	CROP PRODUCTION
88130	594	5263	EDUCATIONAL SERVICES
88132	4	3	POSTAL SERVICE
88133	1	0	POSTAL SERVICE
88134	1	3	MERCH. WHOLESALERS;DURABLE GDS
88135	65	409	ANIMAL PRODUCTION
88136	5	6	MERCH. WHOLESALERS;NONDUR. GDS
88201	1369	12120	FOOD SVCS & DRINKING PLACES
88202	31	119	AMUSEMENT; GAMBLING;& RECREAT.
88203	811	7653	EDUCATIONAL SERVICES
88210	619	8115	OIL AND GAS EXTRACTION
88211	4	1	ANIMAL PRODUCTION
88213	5	0	ANIMAL PRODUCTION
88220	1339	13933	PROF.; SCIENTIFIC; & TECH SVCS
88221	3	2	SPECIAL TRADE CONTRACTORS
88230	104	756	EDUCATIONAL SERVICES
88231	152	1694	HEAVY & CIVIL ENG. CONSTRUCT'N
88232	43	404	EDUCATIONAL SERVICES
88240	1684	19440	SPECIAL TRADE CONTRACTORS
88241	8	12	SPECIAL TRADE CONTRACTORS
88242	77	323	SPECIAL TRADE CONTRACTORS
88250	21	19	EDUCATIONAL SERVICES
88252	98	595	EDUCATIONAL SERVICES
88253	31	153	EDUCATIONAL SERVICES
88254	14	14	MACHINERY MANUFACTURING
88255	36	425	SPECIAL TRADE CONTRACTORS
88256	52	282	EDUCATIONAL SERVICES
88260	476	4160	SPECIAL TRADE CONTRACTORS
88262	4	0	ANIMAL PRODUCTION
88263	2	3	UTILITIES
88264	12	37	JUSTICE; PUBIC ORDER/SAFETY
88265	10	66	UTILITIES
88267	91	303	EDUCATIONAL SERVICES
88268	11	433	ACCOMMODATION
88301	103	501	EDUCATIONAL SERVICES
88310	1427	11053	FOOD SVCS & DRINKING PLACES
88311	16	50	SPECIAL TRADE CONTRACTORS
88312	129	765	ACCOMMODATION
88314	3	8	ADMINISTRATIVE & SUPPORT SVCS
88316	113	384	EDUCATIONAL SERVICES
88317	128	769	ACCOMMODATION
88318	40	137	EDUCATIONAL SERVICES
88321	15	35	ANIMAL PRODUCTION
88323	6	52	ACCOMMODATION
88324	4	13	MISCELLANEOUS STORE RETAILERS
88325	21	47	FABRICATED METAL PRODUCT MFG
88330	49	928	NAT'L SECURITY & INT'L AFFAIRS
88336	46	208	EDUCATIONAL SERVICES
88337	41	195	EDUCATIONAL SERVICES
88338	16	48	MUSEUMS; HIST. SITES;& SIMILAR
88339	62	79	SUPPORT ACTIVITIES: AGR./FOR.
88340	115	3210	AMUSEMENT; GAMBLING;& RECREAT.
88341	8	21	ACCOMMODATION
88342	4	12	PROF.; SCIENTIFIC; & TECH SVCS
88343	4	8	ANIMAL PRODUCTION

BUSINESS DATA

ZIP CODE	2009 Total Firms	2009 Total Employees	TOP INDUSTRY RANKED on 2009 EMPLOYMENT	ZIP CODE	2009 Total Firms	2009 Total Employees	TOP INDUSTRY RANKED on 2009 EMPLOYMENT	ZIP CODE	2009 Total Firms	2009 Total Employees	TOP INDUSTRY RANKED on 2009 EMPLOYMENT
88344	7	17	ANIMAL PRODUCTION	89103	3734	43270	AMUSEMENT; GAMBLING;& RECREAT.	89413	20	26	SUPPORT ACTIVITIES: AGR./FOR.
88345	953	5518	FOOD SVCS & DRINKING PLACES	89104	3016	21584	FOOD SVCS & DRINKING PLACES	89414	9	1804	MINING (EXCEPT OIL AND GAS)
88346	136	1733	PERFORM'G ARTS; SPEC. SPORTS	89105	21	66	PERSONAL AND LAUNDRY SERVICES	89415	176	1679	PROF.; SCIENTIFIC; & TECH SVCS
88347	7	123	ACCOMMODATION	89106	1480	25774	PUBLISHING INDUSTRIES	89418	12	250	MINING (EXCEPT OIL AND GAS)
88348	9	24	FOOD AND BEVERAGE STORES	89107	1445	12169	UTILITIES	89419	159	1604	JUSTICE; PUBIC ORDER/SAFETY
88349	7	96	PROF.; SCIENTIFIC; & TECH SVCS	89108	1414	10387	SPECIAL TRADE CONTRACTORS	89420	2	7	SPECIAL TRADE CONTRACTORS
88350	28	89	JUSTICE; PUBIC ORDER/SAFETY	89109	3966	153915	ACCOMMODATION	89421	17	122	EDUCATIONAL SERVICES
88351	6	43	FOOD SVCS & DRINKING PLACES	89110	1084	7237	EDUCATIONAL SERVICES	89422	12	15	ADMIN. OF ECONOMIC PROGRAMS
88352	136	855	EDUCATIONAL SERVICES	89111	91	3658	PERFORM'G ARTS; SPEC. SPORTS	89423	777	8332	REAL ESTATE
88353	52	183	EDUCATIONAL SERVICES	89112	18	52	PUBLISHING INDUSTRIES	89424	16	150	EDUCATIONAL SERVICES
88354	5	8	FOOD SVCS & DRINKING PLACES	89113	719	8548	MERCH. WHOLESALERS;DURABLE GDS	89425	13	30	MACHINERY MANUFACTURING
88355	12	11	CONSTRUCTION OF BUILDINGS	89114	18	39	PROF.; SCIENTIFIC; & TECH SVCS	89426	9	27	SUPPORT ACTIVITIES: AGR./FOR.
88401	400	2783	FOOD SVCS & DRINKING PLACES	89115	1515	16866	SPECIAL TRADE CONTRACTORS	89427	31	238	SOCIAL ASSISTANCE
88410	8	28	MISCELLANEOUS STORE RETAILERS	89116	19	46	ADMINISTRATIVE & SUPPORT SVCS	89428	6	23	JUSTICE; PUBIC ORDER/SAFETY
88411	2	1	CROP PRODUCTION	89117	2772	22463	REAL ESTATE	89429	179	1143	PROF.; SCIENTIFIC; & TECH SVCS
88414	7	8	FOOD AND BEVERAGE STORES	89118	3364	57996	TRANSIT & GRND PASS. TRANSPORT	89430	25	111	EDUCATIONAL SERVICES
88415	218	1277	EDUCATIONAL SERVICES	89119	4395	70082	ACCOMMODATION	89431	2582	36930	SPECIAL TRADE CONTRACTORS
88416	21	52	JUSTICE; PUBIC ORDER/SAFETY	89120	2284	19324	ADMINISTRATIVE & SUPPORT SVCS	89432	41	104	SPECIAL TRADE CONTRACTORS
88417	5	7	ANIMAL PRODUCTION	89121	2762	18861	FOOD SVCS & DRINKING PLACES	89433	151	978	EDUCATIONAL SERVICES
88418	28	155	EDUCATIONAL SERVICES	89122	540	11247	AMUSEMENT; GAMBLING;& RECREAT.	89434	554	10344	AMUSEMENT; GAMBLING;& RECREAT.
88419	25	17	ANIMAL PRODUCTION	89123	1930	12784	FOOD SVCS & DRINKING PLACES	89435	26	58	ADMINISTRATIVE & SUPPORT SVCS
88422	4	2	ANIMAL PRODUCTION	89124	57	692	AMUSEMENT; GAMBLING;& RECREAT.	89436	435	3121	FOOD SVCS & DRINKING PLACES
88424	6	3	SUPPORT ACTIVITIES: AGR./FOR.	89125	10	34	PROF.; SCIENTIFIC; & TECH SVCS	89438	6	943	MINING (EXCEPT OIL AND GAS)
88426	86	396	EDUCATIONAL SERVICES	89126	25	71	MOTOR VEHICLE & PARTS DEALERS	89439	88	2823	NONSTORE RETAILERS
88427	3	27	JUSTICE; PUBIC ORDER/SAFETY	89127	2	2	PERSONAL AND LAUNDRY SERVICES	89440	174	689	FOOD SVCS & DRINKING PLACES
88430	17	21	HEAVY & CIVIL ENG. CONSTRUCT'N	89128	2234	20479	AMBULATORY HEALTH CARE SVCS	89441	167	1257	EDUCATIONAL SERVICES
88431	3	26	ANIMAL PRODUCTION	89129	932	6642	FOOD SVCS & DRINKING PLACES	89442	22	95	EDUCATIONAL SERVICES
88433	1	0	ANIMAL PRODUCTION	89130	1363	11054	FOOD SVCS & DRINKING PLACES	89444	65	224	CONSTRUCTION OF BUILDINGS
88434	29	174	REPAIR AND MAINTENANCE	89131	646	4266	EDUCATIONAL SERVICES	89445	567	4701	ACCOMMODATION
88435	245	1934	ADMINISTRATIVE & SUPPORT SVCS	89132	7	17	ADMINISTRATIVE & SUPPORT SVCS	89446	6	8	UNCLASSIFIED ESTABLISHMENTS
88436	3	39	JUSTICE; PUBIC ORDER/SAFETY	89133	36	79	ADMINISTRATIVE & SUPPORT SVCS	89447	351	2816	CROP PRODUCTION
88439	9	27	JUSTICE; PUBIC ORDER/SAFETY	89134	599	3699	REAL ESTATE	89448	204	1603	SCENIC & SIGHTSEEING TRANSPORT
89001	63	270	GASOLINE STATIONS	89135	561	6844	FOOD SVCS & DRINKING PLACES	89449	444	14011	AMUSEMENT; GAMBLING;& RECREAT.
89002	289	2105	EDUCATIONAL SERVICES	89136	25	88	ELECTRONICS & APPLIANCE STORES	89450	38	115	SPORTG GDS;HOBBY;BOOK; & MUSIC
89003	51	337	ACCOMMODATION	89137	14	35	CONSTRUCTION OF BUILDINGS	89451	672	5142	ACCOMMODATION
89004	20	298	MUSEUMS; HIST. SITES;& SIMILAR	89138	103	179	EDUCATIONAL SERVICES	89452	15	21	PROF.; SCIENTIFIC; & TECH SVCS
89005	794	5393	EXEC.; LEGIS.; & OTHER SUPPORT	89139	666	7371	MERCH. WHOLESALERS;NONDUR. GDS	89460	248	1237	EDUCATIONAL SERVICES
89006	9	11	REPAIR AND MAINTENANCE	89140	6	11	PROF.; SCIENTIFIC; & TECH SVCS	89501	1083	17309	AMUSEMENT; GAMBLING;& RECREAT.
89007	23	115	EDUCATIONAL SERVICES	89141	265	1291	EDUCATIONAL SERVICES	89502	4733	63767	FOOD SVCS & DRINKING PLACES
89008	93	588	EXEC.; LEGIS.; & OTHER SUPPORT	89142	218	1781	EDUCATIONAL SERVICES	89503	992	12146	AMBULATORY HEALTH CARE SVCS
89009	31	99	ADMINISTRATIVE & SUPPORT SVCS	89143	85	295	EDUCATIONAL SERVICES	89504	15	25	CONSTRUCTION OF BUILDINGS
89010	10	68	MINING (EXCEPT OIL AND GAS)	89144	402	8664	HOSPITALS	89505	15	47	ADMINISTRATIVE & SUPPORT SVCS
89011	800	10950	SPECIAL TRADE CONTRACTORS	89145	839	8753	ACCOMMODATION	89506	584	7922	EDUCATIONAL SERVICES
89012	486	2980	FOOD SVCS & DRINKING PLACES	89146	3029	21820	PROF.; SCIENTIFIC; & TECH SVCS	89507	23	43	RELIG.; GRANT; CIVIC; PROF ORG
89013	37	111	EXEC.; LEGIS.; & OTHER SUPPORT	89147	1381	9978	FOOD SVCS & DRINKING PLACES	89508	81	487	EDUCATIONAL SERVICES
89014	1947	22259	FOOD SVCS & DRINKING PLACES	89148	666	6892	PROF.; SCIENTIFIC; & TECH SVCS	89509	1577	10016	AMBULATORY HEALTH CARE SVCS
89015	1242	18828	EXEC.; LEGIS.; & OTHER SUPPORT	89149	637	6524	FOOD SVCS & DRINKING PLACES	89510	80	255	EXEC.; LEGIS.; & OTHER SUPPORT
89016	7	19	CONSTRUCTION OF BUILDINGS	89150	2	5	CREDIT INTERMEDIATION & RELATD	89511	1654	18471	PROF.; SCIENTIFIC; & TECH SVCS
89017	9	38	GASOLINE STATIONS	89152	3	25	SOCIAL ASSISTANCE	89512	775	11816	EXEC.; LEGIS.; & OTHER SUPPORT
89018	30	806	JUSTICE; PUBIC ORDER/SAFETY	89154	24	6093	PERFORM'G ARTS; SPEC. SPORTS	89513	31	77	REPAIR AND MAINTENANCE
89019	170	12074	ACCOMMODATION	89155	45	317	EXEC.; LEGIS.; & OTHER SUPPORT	89515	27	53	ADMINISTRATIVE & SUPPORT SVCS
89020	30	212	PERSONAL AND LAUNDRY SERVICES	89156	281	1540	EDUCATIONAL SERVICES	89519	262	2229	PROF.; SCIENTIFIC; & TECH SVCS
89021	95	338	EDUCATIONAL SERVICES	89157	6	37	ADMINISTRATIVE & SUPPORT SVCS	89520	3	3	AMBULATORY HEALTH CARE SVCS
89022	5	9	FOOD SVCS & DRINKING PLACES	89160	5	8	ADMINISTRATIVE & SUPPORT SVCS	89521	790	11233	MISCELLANEOUS MANUFACTURING
89023	1	0	PROF.; SCIENTIFIC; & TECH SVCS	89161	12	217	NONMETALLIC MINERAL PROD. MFG	89523	528	12323	CONSTRUCTION OF BUILDINGS
89024	14	51	AMUSEMENT; GAMBLING;& RECREAT.	89162	12	40	DATA PROCESS'G	89533	30	65	ADMINISTRATIVE & SUPPORT SVCS
89025	61	848	UTILITIES	89163	1	3000	CREDIT INTERMEDIATION & RELATD	89557	33	1112	PERFORM'G ARTS; SPEC. SPORTS
89027	626	7303	AMUSEMENT; GAMBLING;& RECREAT.	89165	5	142	NONMETALLIC MINERAL PROD. MFG	89570	21	32	ADMINISTRATIVE & SUPPORT SVCS
89028	6	35	TRANSIT & GRND PASS. TRANSPORT	89166	24	124	CONSTRUCTION OF BUILDINGS	89595	11	158	FOOD SVCS & DRINKING PLACES
89029	366	16947	ACCOMMODATION	89169	1710	18064	ACCOMMODATION	89701	1658	23085	EXEC.; LEGIS.; & OTHER SUPPORT
89030	1697	39404	ADMIN. OF ECONOMIC PROGRAMS	89170	11	25	MISCELLANEOUS STORE RETAILERS	89702	38	78	ADMINISTRATIVE & SUPPORT SVCS
89031	518	2978	EDUCATIONAL SERVICES	89173	7	12	PROF.; SCIENTIFIC; & TECH SVCS	89703	874	4283	HOSPITALS
89032	970	16379	TRANSIT & GRND PASS. TRANSPORT	89177	1	6100	AMUSEMENT; GAMBLING;& RECREAT.	89704	113	409	AMUSEMENT; GAMBLING;& RECREAT.
89033	25	70	TRUCK TRANSPORTATION	89178	148	471	EDUCATIONAL SERVICES	89705	203	2814	GENERAL MERCHANDISE STORES
89034	1	0	CONSTRUCTION OF BUILDINGS	89179	10	4	CONSTRUCTION OF BUILDINGS	89706	1617	12137	ADMIN. HUMAN RESOURCE PROGRAMS
89036	14	38	RELIG.; GRANT; CIVIC; PROF ORG	89180	29	41	MISCELLANEOUS STORE RETAILERS	89711	4	37	JUSTICE; PUBIC ORDER/SAFETY
89039	10	68	HEAVY & CIVIL ENG. CONSTRUCT'N	89183	496	6005	AMUSEMENT; GAMBLING;& RECREAT.	89713	5	1282	SOCIAL ASSISTANCE
89040	158	966	EDUCATIONAL SERVICES	89191	87	9632	NAT'L SECURITY & INT'L AFFAIRS	89714	1	0	PERFORM'G ARTS; SPEC. SPORTS
89041	16	29	TELECOMMUNICATIONS	89193	37	176	PROF.; SCIENTIFIC; & TECH SVCS	89721	14	41	ADMINISTRATIVE & SUPPORT SVCS
89042	46	253	EDUCATIONAL SERVICES	89199	1	0	POSTAL SERVICE	89801	1603	13723	ACCOMMODATION
89043	75	273	JUSTICE; PUBIC ORDER/SAFETY	89301	312	3081	JUSTICE; PUBIC ORDER/SAFETY	89802	7	68	HEALTH & PERSONAL CARE STORES
89044	104	497	PROF.; SCIENTIFIC; & TECH SVCS	89310	52	120	EXEC.; LEGIS.; & OTHER SUPPORT	89803	18	60	SOCIAL ASSISTANCE
89045	30	150	EDUCATIONAL SERVICES	89311	7	80	MUSEUMS; HIST. SITES;& SIMILAR	89815	196	840	EDUCATIONAL SERVICES
89046	47	377	AMUSEMENT; GAMBLING;& RECREAT.	89314	8	19	AMBULATORY HEALTH CARE SVCS	89820	167	1446	EDUCATIONAL SERVICES
89047	16	61	MINING (EXCEPT OIL AND GAS)	89315	2	4	PROF.; SCIENTIFIC; & TECH SVCS	89821	20	665	MINING (EXCEPT OIL AND GAS)
89048	602	4867	AMUSEMENT; GAMBLING;& RECREAT.	89316	73	553	MUSEUMS; HIST. SITES;& SIMILAR	89822	91	612	CONSTRUCTION OF BUILDINGS
89049	227	1235	JUSTICE; PUBIC ORDER/SAFETY	89317	8	49	EDUCATIONAL SERVICES	89823	9	10	ANIMAL PRODUCTION
89052	1666	16143	AMBULATORY HEALTH CARE SVCS	89318	15	51	EDUCATIONAL SERVICES	89824	2	7	ANIMAL PRODUCTION
89053	17	42	SPECIAL TRADE CONTRACTORS	89319	3	501	MINING (EXCEPT OIL AND GAS)	89825	63	899	AMUSEMENT; GAMBLING;& RECREAT.
89054	6	34	PROF.; SCIENTIFIC; & TECH SVCS	89402	124	779	ACCOMMODATION	89826	8	11	ACCOMMODATION
89060	148	1015	JUSTICE; PUBIC ORDER/SAFETY	89403	240	2848	HOSPITALS	89828	26	97	EDUCATIONAL SERVICES
89061	40	297	EDUCATIONAL SERVICES	89404	8	112	MINING (EXCEPT OIL AND GAS)	89830	10	13	FOOD SVCS & DRINKING PLACES
89074	1495	20282	PROF.; SCIENTIFIC; & TECH SVCS	89405	5	165	NONMETALLIC MINERAL PROD. MFG	89831	7	11	ACCOMMODATION
89077	7	35	ADMINISTRATIVE & SUPPORT SVCS	89406	1073	8322	EDUCATIONAL SERVICES	89832	51	462	EXEC.; LEGIS.; & OTHER SUPPORT
89081	385	10787	MERCH. WHOLESALERS;DURABLE GDS	89407	8	25	CONSTRUCTION OF BUILDINGS	89833	16	32	ANIMAL PRODUCTION
89084	196	1578	EDUCATIONAL SERVICES	89408	481	4184	MERCH. WHOLESALERS;DURABLE GDS	89834	10	122	ANIMAL PRODUCTION
89085	20	18	CONSTRUCTION OF BUILDINGS	89409	18	118	MINING (EXCEPT OIL AND GAS)	89835	154	766	FOOD SVCS & DRINKING PLACES
89086	24	33	REAL ESTATE	89410	745	4223	FOOD SVCS & DRINKING PLACES	89883	100	2998	ACCOMMODATION
89101	2900	44459	ACCOMMODATION	89411	57	393	MISCELLANEOUS STORE RETAILERS	90001	1405	10160	MERCH. WHOLESALERS;DURABLE GDS
89102	4769	41055	HOSPITALS	89412	20	137	EDUCATIONAL SERVICES	90002	437	2809	EDUCATIONAL SERVICES

ZIP CODE	2009 Total Firms	2009 Total Employ-ees	TOP INDUSTRY RANKED on 2009 EMPLOYMENT	ZIP CODE	2009 Total Firms	2009 Total Employ-ees	TOP INDUSTRY RANKED on 2009 EMPLOYMENT	ZIP CODE	2009 Total Firms	2009 Total Employ-ees	TOP INDUSTRY RANKED on 2009 EMPLOYMENT
90003	1480	7527	EDUCATIONAL SERVICES	90222	436	4446	EDUCATIONAL SERVICES	90640	2305	25322	EDUCATIONAL SERVICES
90004	1735	8008	EDUCATIONAL SERVICES	90223	2	2	ADMINISTRATIVE & SUPPORT SVCS	90650	2133	20123	EDUCATIONAL SERVICES
90005	1407	6945	REAL ESTATE	90224	1	0	ADMINISTRATIVE & SUPPORT SVCS	90651	8	24	ADMINISTRATIVE & SUPPORT SVCS
90006	2374	9782	EDUCATIONAL SERVICES	90230	1873	23832	GENERAL MERCHANDISE STORES	90652	3	3	REAL ESTATE
90007	1519	13780	RELIG.; GRANT; CIVIC; PROF ORG	90231	31	359	CLOTHING & CLOTH'G ACC. STORES	90660	1488	44055	CLOTHING & CLOTH'G ACC. STORES
90008	1190	5228	EDUCATIONAL SERVICES	90232	1838	25780	MOTION PICT. & SOUND RECORDING	90661	4	4	TRUCK TRANSPORTATION
90009	35	150	POSTAL SERVICE	90239	12	10	PROF.; SCIENTIFIC; & TECH SVCS	90662	1	1	TRANSIT & GRND PASS. TRANSPORT
90010	4687	28224	PROF.; SCIENTIFIC; & TECH SVCS	90240	834	4572	REAL ESTATE	90670	3453	54958	MERCH. WHOLESALERS;DURABLE GDS
90011	1555	10599	EDUCATIONAL SERVICES	90241	1951	20934	FOOD SVCS & DRINKING PLACES	90680	1151	6971	FOOD SVCS & DRINKING PLACES
90012	2398	52103	JUSTICE; PUBIC ORDER/SAFETY	90242	800	15359	AMBULATORY HEALTH CARE SVCS	90701	961	5117	FOOD SVCS & DRINKING PLACES
90013	2301	20809	PROF.; SCIENTIFIC; & TECH SVCS	90245	2190	32191	PROF.; SCIENTIFIC; & TECH SVCS	90702	8	20	SPECIAL TRADE CONTRACTORS
90014	4463	13815	MERCH. WHOLESALERS;DURABLE GDS	90247	1526	12913	AMUSEMENT; GAMBLING;& RECREAT.	90703	2241	32360	MOTOR VEHICLE & PARTS DEALERS
90015	5366	29303	FOOD SVCS & DRINKING PLACES	90248	2295	33987	MOTOR VEHICLE & PARTS DEALERS	90704	390	3212	FOOD SVCS & DRINKING PLACES
90016	1356	11218	FOOD AND BEVERAGE STORES	90249	1514	13806	MERCH. WHOLESALERS;DURABLE GDS	90706	2102	14674	HOSPITALS
90017	2683	39231	PROF.; SCIENTIFIC; & TECH SVCS	90250	2421	22229	ADMINISTRATIVE & SUPPORT SVCS	90707	9	21	SPECIAL TRADE CONTRACTORS
90018	1096	5946	NURSING & RESID. CARE FACILIT.	90251	5	7	ADMINISTRATIVE & SUPPORT SVCS	90710	723	7408	AMBULATORY HEALTH CARE SVCS
90019	1919	7935	EDUCATIONAL SERVICES	90254	1248	6276	FOOD SVCS & DRINKING PLACES	90711	8	11	RELIG.; GRANT; CIVIC; PROF ORG
90020	1357	6619	RELIG.; GRANT; CIVIC; PROF ORG	90255	2242	13560	EDUCATIONAL SERVICES	90712	972	12952	FOOD SVCS & DRINKING PLACES
90021	2738	28795	APPAREL MANUFACTURING	90260	1018	6431	EDUCATIONAL SERVICES	90713	477	3993	EDUCATIONAL SERVICES
90022	1918	15570	EDUCATIONAL SERVICES	90261	5	808	ADMIN. OF ECONOMIC PROGRAMS	90714	16	197	POSTAL SERVICE
90023	1612	18394	MERCH. WHOLESALERS;NONDUR. GDS	90262	1272	10000	EDUCATIONAL SERVICES	90715	225	1232	EDUCATIONAL SERVICES
90024	2023	52571	EDUCATIONAL SERVICES	90263	6	1036	EDUCATIONAL SERVICES	90716	376	9995	AMUSEMENT; GAMBLING;& RECREAT.
90025	4166	30523	PROF.; SCIENTIFIC; & TECH SVCS	90264	20	63	RELIG.; GRANT; CIVIC; PROF ORG	90717	959	4329	FOOD SVCS & DRINKING PLACES
90026	1457	10656	RELIG.; GRANT; CIVIC; PROF ORG	90265	1383	7233	FOOD SVCS & DRINKING PLACES	90720	1621	15228	HOSPITALS
90027	2025	24344	HOSPITALS	90266	1908	14562	FOOD SVCS & DRINKING PLACES	90721	6	12	ADMINISTRATIVE & SUPPORT SVCS
90028	2983	23499	FOOD SVCS & DRINKING PLACES	90267	26	67	PROF.; SCIENTIFIC; & TECH SVCS	90723	1987	18035	FABRICATED METAL PRODUCT MFG
90029	1289	5180	FOOD SVCS & DRINKING PLACES	90270	473	3066	EDUCATIONAL SERVICES	90731	1869	14358	EDUCATIONAL SERVICES
90030	1	0	NONSTORE RETAILERS	90272	983	5426	EDUCATIONAL SERVICES	90732	453	4287	HOSPITALS
90031	933	8530	EDUCATIONAL SERVICES	90274	1159	7302	EDUCATIONAL SERVICES	90733	12	22	ADMINISTRATIVE & SUPPORT SVCS
90032	653	8287	EDUCATIONAL SERVICES	90275	734	5141	EDUCATIONAL SERVICES	90734	9	9	PROF.; SCIENTIFIC; & TECH SVCS
90033	1079	27644	HOSPITALS	90277	2024	11293	FOOD SVCS & DRINKING PLACES	90740	921	9022	COMPUTER & ELECTRONIC PROD MFG
90034	1710	14504	HOSPITALS	90278	1241	8910	MACHINERY MANUFACTURING	90742	85	365	FOOD SVCS & DRINKING PLACES
90035	1494	8383	FOOD SVCS & DRINKING PLACES	90280	2025	20036	EDUCATIONAL SERVICES	90743	7	1	PROF.; SCIENTIFIC; & TECH SVCS
90036	3064	27047	BROADCASTING	90290	242	775	SOCIAL ASSISTANCE	90744	1443	11456	MERCH. WHOLESALERS;DURABLE GDS
90037	1134	5534	EDUCATIONAL SERVICES	90291	1489	7418	FOOD SVCS & DRINKING PLACES	90745	1415	30670	MERCH. WHOLESALERS;DURABLE GDS
90038	1539	15027	MOTION PICT. & SOUND RECORDING	90292	1613	13211	PROF.; SCIENTIFIC; & TECH SVCS	90746	1215	13233	MERCH. WHOLESALERS;DURABLE GDS
90039	1156	11503	MUSEUMS; HIST. SITES;& SIMILAR	90293	385	2088	EXEC.; LEGIS.; & OTHER SUPPORT	90747	10	785	EDUCATIONAL SERVICES
90040	1753	41544	MERCH. WHOLESALERS;DURABLE GDS	90294	17	19	CONSTRUCTION OF BUILDINGS	90748	3	21	SUPPORT ACT. FOR TRANSPORT.
90041	1108	7111	EDUCATIONAL SERVICES	90295	38	146	PROF.; SCIENTIFIC; & TECH SVCS	90749	10	28	RELIG.; GRANT; CIVIC; PROF ORG
90042	1057	5065	EDUCATIONAL SERVICES	90296	4	11	SPECIAL TRADE CONTRACTORS	90755	1173	13010	MERCH. WHOLESALERS;DURABLE GDS
90043	1143	4938	EDUCATIONAL SERVICES	90301	2091	16206	HOSPITALS	90801	11	6	REPAIR AND MAINTENANCE
90044	1058	6240	EDUCATIONAL SERVICES	90302	750	4972	PROF.; SCIENTIFIC; & TECH SVCS	90802	2248	31860	JUSTICE; PUBIC ORDER/SAFETY
90045	3315	46433	SUPPORT ACT. FOR TRANSPORT.	90303	566	4805	ACCOMMODATION	90803	1346	9772	FOOD SVCS & DRINKING PLACES
90046	2595	12578	FOOD SVCS & DRINKING PLACES	90304	650	4185	EDUCATIONAL SERVICES	90804	1176	8452	EDUCATIONAL SERVICES
90047	1060	5749	EDUCATIONAL SERVICES	90305	330	1512	PERFORM'G ARTS; SPEC. SPORTS	90805	1494	13225	EDUCATIONAL SERVICES
90048	2914	25691	AMBULATORY HEALTH CARE SVCS	90306	1	0	PROF.; SCIENTIFIC; & TECH SVCS	90806	1403	30571	HOSPITALS
90049	1518	13805	PROF.; SCIENTIFIC; & TECH SVCS	90307	1	1	WASTE MANAGMT & REMEDIAT'N SVC	90807	1543	11246	FOOD SVCS & DRINKING PLACES
90050	4	8	MOTION PICT. & SOUND RECORDING	90308	3	9	REPAIR AND MAINTENANCE	90808	941	8664	EDUCATIONAL SERVICES
90051	6	9	WASTE MANAGMT & REMEDIAT'N SVC	90309	3	6	RELIG.; GRANT; CIVIC; PROF ORG	90809	18	50	PROF.; SCIENTIFIC; & TECH SVCS
90052	6	115	POSTAL SERVICE	90310	1	3	PERFORM'G ARTS; SPEC. SPORTS	90810	735	16186	EDUCATIONAL SERVICES
90053	2	3	REAL ESTATE	90312	1	0	EXEC.; LEGIS.; & OTHER SUPPORT	90813	1518	13017	EDUCATIONAL SERVICES
90055	1	4	MERCH. WHOLESALERS;DURABLE GDS	90401	2593	27695	FOOD SVCS & DRINKING PLACES	90814	324	1546	EDUCATIONAL SERVICES
90056	242	2795	REAL ESTATE	90402	280	912	FOOD SVCS & DRINKING PLACES	90815	965	11934	EDUCATIONAL SERVICES
90057	1781	8540	AMBULATORY HEALTH CARE SVCS	90403	1333	8346	FOOD SVCS & DRINKING PLACES	90822	11	600	HOSPITALS
90058	2118	50538	FOOD MANUFACTURING	90404	2149	29042	PROF.; SCIENTIFIC; & TECH SVCS	90831	142	1447	PROF.; SCIENTIFIC; & TECH SVCS
90059	434	9098	HOSPITALS	90405	2109	14077	PROF.; SCIENTIFIC; & TECH SVCS	90832	5	54	SOCIAL ASSISTANCE
90060	1	0	HEALTH & PERSONAL CARE STORES	90406	29	51	REPAIR AND MAINTENANCE	90840	18	1176	EDUCATIONAL SERVICES
90061	711	7707	EDUCATIONAL SERVICES	90408	10	13	MERCH. WHOLESALERS;DURABLE GDS	90844	2	180	PUBLISHING INDUSTRIES
90062	445	2239	EDUCATIONAL SERVICES	90409	15	20	TRANSIT & GRND PASS. TRANSPORT	90846	2	3000	TRANSPORTATION EQUIPMENT MFG
90063	842	11743	JUSTICE; PUBIC ORDER/SAFETY	90410	1	10	MOTION PICT. & SOUND RECORDING	90853	17	94	PROF.; SCIENTIFIC; & TECH SVCS
90064	2513	27301	PROF.; SCIENTIFIC; & TECH SVCS	90501	2550	29732	WHOLESALE ELEC. MRKTS & AGENTS	90895	2	1100	MISCELLANEOUS STORE RETAILERS
90065	1064	9555	EDUCATIONAL SERVICES	90502	954	18209	AMBULATORY HEALTH CARE SVCS	91001	804	4322	SOCIAL ASSISTANCE
90066	1906	24520	JUSTICE; PUBIC ORDER/SAFETY	90503	2473	33382	HOSPITALS	91003	6	50	SOCIAL ASSISTANCE
90067	2149	39903	PROF.; SCIENTIFIC; & TECH SVCS	90504	886	9786	COMPUTER & ELECTRONIC PROD MFG	91006	1834	12363	PROF.; SCIENTIFIC; & TECH SVCS
90068	773	9261	SPECIAL TRADE CONTRACTORS	90505	3052	32287	FOOD SVCS & DRINKING PLACES	91007	1240	15265	PROF.; SCIENTIFIC; & TECH SVCS
90069	2266	18180	FOOD SVCS & DRINKING PLACES	90506	5	38	OTHER INFORMATION SERVICES	91008	26	67	FURN. & HOME FURNISHGS STORES
90071	1417	39886	PROF.; SCIENTIFIC; & TECH SVCS	90507	7	30	ADMINISTRATIVE & SUPPORT SVCS	91009	8	9	PUBLISHING INDUSTRIES
90072	3	6	POSTAL SERVICE	90508	2	2	CONSTRUCTION OF BUILDINGS	91010	691	10947	PROF.; SCIENTIFIC; & TECH SVCS
90073	46	4044	HOSPITALS	90510	21	317	RELIG.; GRANT; CIVIC; PROF ORG	91011	733	5182	EDUCATIONAL SERVICES
90075	3	0	WHOLESALE ELEC. MRKTS & AGENTS	90601	945	13163	MERCH. WHOLESALERS;DURABLE GDS	91012	21	38	PROF.; SCIENTIFIC; & TECH SVCS
90076	2	22	AMBULATORY HEALTH CARE SVCS	90602	947	11197	NURSING & RESID. CARE FACILIT.	91016	1767	18181	PROF.; SCIENTIFIC; & TECH SVCS
90077	168	2155	EDUCATIONAL SERVICES	90603	605	4549	FOOD SVCS & DRINKING PLACES	91017	11	23	INSURANCE CARRIERS & RELATED
90078	22	89	MOTION PICT. & SOUND RECORDING	90604	413	2597	EDUCATIONAL SERVICES	91020	531	2719	FOOD SVCS & DRINKING PLACES
90079	584	1720	MERCH. WHOLESALERS;NONDUR. GDS	90605	919	7910	EDUCATIONAL SERVICES	91021	6	24	ADMINISTRATIVE & SUPPORT SVCS
90083	9	6	PUBLISHING INDUSTRIES	90606	736	5774	EDUCATIONAL SERVICES	91023	4	19	HEAVY & CIVIL ENG. CONSTRUCT'N
90086	6	2	CREDIT INTERMEDIATION & RELATD	90607	17	33	ADMINISTRATIVE & SUPPORT SVCS	91024	435	2229	FOOD SVCS & DRINKING PLACES
90089	39	1450	HOSPITALS	90608	15	84	PERSONAL AND LAUNDRY SERVICES	91025	8	23	MISCELLANEOUS MANUFACTURING
90091	1	0	PROF.; SCIENTIFIC; & TECH SVCS	90609	11	32	WASTE MANAGMT & REMEDIAT'N SVC	91030	962	7838	RELIG.; GRANT; CIVIC; PROF ORG
90093	5	6	MERCH. WHOLESALERS;DURABLE GDS	90612	1	4	AMBULATORY HEALTH CARE SVCS	91031	15	23	ADMINISTRATIVE & SUPPORT SVCS
90094	23	851	PERFORM'G ARTS; SPEC. SPORTS	90620	1336	18502	FOOD SVCS & DRINKING PLACES	91040	586	2481	EDUCATIONAL SERVICES
90095	232	33724	EDUCATIONAL SERVICES	90621	1563	11413	MOTOR VEHICLE & PARTS DEALERS	91041	18	43	SPECIAL TRADE CONTRACTORS
90201	1826	17156	EDUCATIONAL SERVICES	90622	13	134	POSTAL SERVICE	91042	639	2832	EDUCATIONAL SERVICES
90202	2	37	SPECIAL TRADE CONTRACTORS	90623	440	5002	HOSPITALS	91043	7	8	SPECIAL TRADE CONTRACTORS
90209	31	159	ADMINISTRATIVE & SUPPORT SVCS	90630	1806	23294	INSURANCE CARRIERS & RELATED	91046	22	49	REAL ESTATE
90210	3741	25098	REAL ESTATE	90631	2209	14952	FOOD SVCS & DRINKING PLACES	91066	13	163	MERCH. WHOLESALERS;NONDUR. GDS
90211	2161	12014	AMBULATORY HEALTH CARE SVCS	90632	13	13	ADMINISTRATIVE & SUPPORT SVCS	91077	7	7	MERCH. WHOLESALERS;DURABLE GDS
90212	2259	15379	PROF.; SCIENTIFIC; & TECH SVCS	90633	14	26	HEAVY & CIVIL ENG. CONSTRUCT'N	91101	2992	32612	CREDIT INTERMEDIATION & RELATD
90213	33	104	TRANSIT & GRND PASS. TRANSPORT	90637	15	40	MISCELLANEOUS STORE RETAILERS	91102	9	812	PRINT'G & RELATED SUPP'T ACT'S
90220	1322	24403	MERCH. WHOLESALERS;DURABLE GDS	90638	1308	15781	FOOD SVCS & DRINKING PLACES	91103	879	12115	REAL ESTATE
90221	1504	17583	PRIMARY METAL MANUFACTURING	90639	2	50	EDUCATIONAL SERVICES	91104	1176	5165	EDUCATIONAL SERVICES

BUSINESS DATA

ZIP CODE	2009 Total Firms	2009 Total Employees	TOP INDUSTRY RANKED on 2009 EMPLOYMENT	ZIP CODE	2009 Total Firms	2009 Total Employees	TOP INDUSTRY RANKED on 2009 EMPLOYMENT	ZIP CODE	2009 Total Firms	2009 Total Employees	TOP INDUSTRY RANKED on 2009 EMPLOYMENT
91105	1366	22882	HOSPITALS	91383	6	1	NONSTORE RETAILERS	91763	1571	14676	FOOD SVCS & DRINKING PLACES
91106	1086	6454	PROF.; SCIENTIFIC; & TECH SVCS	91384	410	2442	FOOD SVCS & DRINKING PLACES	91764	1460	17541	FOOD SVCS & DRINKING PLACES
91107	1869	16127	PROF.; SCIENTIFIC; & TECH SVCS	91385	13	114	MERCH. WHOLESALERS;DURABLE GDS	91765	1385	10362	PROF.; SCIENTIFIC; & TECH SVCS
91108	514	2685	EDUCATIONAL SERVICES	91386	30	59	SPECIAL TRADE CONTRACTORS	91766	1617	16780	MERCH. WHOLESALERS;DURABLE GDS
91109	22	7628	PROF.; SCIENTIFIC; & TECH SVCS	91387	500	2874	SPECIAL TRADE CONTRACTORS	91767	1401	15961	HOSPITALS
91114	6	59	EDUCATIONAL SERVICES	91390	357	1601	EDUCATIONAL SERVICES	91768	948	18654	EDUCATIONAL SERVICES
91115	6	37	SOCIAL ASSISTANCE	91392	18	107	ADMINISTRATIVE & SUPPORT SVCS	91769	13	182	POSTAL SERVICE
91116	7	12	MERCH. WHOLESALERS;DURABLE GDS	91393	8	9	MERCH. WHOLESALERS;DURABLE GDS	91770	1552	11442	FOOD SVCS & DRINKING PLACES
91117	10	25	PROF.; SCIENTIFIC; & TECH SVCS	91394	28	78	SPECIAL TRADE CONTRACTORS	91773	1636	19547	SPECIAL TRADE CONTRACTORS
91118	3	8	PROF.; SCIENTIFIC; & TECH SVCS	91395	14	90	ADMINISTRATIVE & SUPPORT SVCS	91775	246	2038	BLDG MATL & GARDEN EQPMT DLRS
91121	1	375	MERCH. WHOLESALERS;NONDUR. GDS	91396	11	9	REAL ESTATE	91776	2045	12060	EDUCATIONAL SERVICES
91124	6	2212	PROF.; SCIENTIFIC; & TECH SVCS	91401	1895	11972	SPECIAL TRADE CONTRACTORS	91778	10	33	MERCH. WHOLESALERS;DURABLE GDS
91125	12	4052	EDUCATIONAL SERVICES	91402	1420	9070	FOOD SVCS & DRINKING PLACES	91780	975	5504	EDUCATIONAL SERVICES
91182	2	64	AMBULATORY HEALTH CARE SVCS	91403	2183	16144	PROF.; SCIENTIFIC; & TECH SVCS	91784	442	2946	GENERAL MERCHANDISE STORES
91188	5	1503	AMBULATORY HEALTH CARE SVCS	91404	5	2	CONSTRUCTION OF BUILDINGS	91785	42	234	POSTAL SERVICE
91201	1105	12765	MERCH. WHOLESALERS;DURABLE GDS	91405	1891	13217	AMBULATORY HEALTH CARE SVCS	91786	3526	29735	AMBULATORY HEALTH CARE SVCS
91202	777	3493	EDUCATIONAL SERVICES	91406	3286	29436	MERCH. WHOLESALERS;DURABLE GDS	91788	19	81	POSTAL SERVICE
91203	1779	42053	FOOD MANUFACTURING	91407	9	8	SPECIAL TRADE CONTRACTORS	91789	2095	22007	MERCH. WHOLESALERS;NONDUR. GDS
91204	1684	14233	MOTOR VEHICLE & PARTS DEALERS	91408	10	83	ADMINISTRATIVE & SUPPORT SVCS	91790	1434	21983	HOSPITALS
91205	1536	7092	EDUCATIONAL SERVICES	91409	21	29	INSURANCE CARRIERS & RELATED	91791	744	7450	FOOD SVCS & DRINKING PLACES
91206	848	9187	HOSPITALS	91411	1504	10620	PROF.; SCIENTIFIC; & TECH SVCS	91792	356	1562	FOOD SVCS & DRINKING PLACES
91207	201	569	PROF.; SCIENTIFIC; & TECH SVCS	91412	8	2	SPECIAL TRADE CONTRACTORS	91793	16	189	POSTAL SERVICE
91208	562	4699	EDUCATIONAL SERVICES	91413	38	110	SPECIAL TRADE CONTRACTORS	91801	1819	12515	EDUCATIONAL SERVICES
91209	24	68	WASTE MANAGMT & REMEDIAT'N SVC	91416	28	96	ADMINISTRATIVE & SUPPORT SVCS	91802	12	261	POSTAL SERVICE
91210	327	3981	CLOTHING & CLOTH'G ACC. STORES	91423	1820	12733	AMBULATORY HEALTH CARE SVCS	91803	1043	10893	HEAVY & CIVIL ENG. CONSTRUCT'N
91214	1124	5318	EDUCATIONAL SERVICES	91426	22	28	EDUCATIONAL SERVICES	91901	626	5729	AMUSEMENT; GAMBLING;& RECREAT.
91221	15	28	SPECIAL TRADE CONTRACTORS	91436	2480	17660	PROF.; SCIENTIFIC; & TECH SVCS	91902	448	2512	FOOD SVCS & DRINKING PLACES
91222	11	7	PROF.; SCIENTIFIC; & TECH SVCS	91496	1	0	GENERAL MERCHANDISE STORES	91903	30	55	SPECIAL TRADE CONTRACTORS
91224	16	33	INSURANCE CARRIERS & RELATED	91501	230	1332	PROF.; SCIENTIFIC; & TECH SVCS	91905	57	234	NAT'L SECURITY & INT'L AFFAIRS
91225	10	30	PROF.; SCIENTIFIC; & TECH SVCS	91502	2147	20276	FOOD SVCS & DRINKING PLACES	91906	85	794	AMUSEMENT; GAMBLING;& RECREAT.
91226	12	45	TRANSIT & GRND PASS. TRANSPORT	91503	13	27	MISCELLANEOUS STORE RETAILERS	91908	28	164	PROF.; SCIENTIFIC; & TECH SVCS
91301	1914	14458	FOOD SVCS & DRINKING PLACES	91504	907	16903	PROF.; SCIENTIFIC; & TECH SVCS	91909	10	11	REAL ESTATE
91302	1546	16116	PROF.; SCIENTIFIC; & TECH SVCS	91505	2336	31114	AMBULATORY HEALTH CARE SVCS	91910	2651	26118	SPECIAL TRADE CONTRACTORS
91303	2164	15202	MOTOR VEHICLE & PARTS DEALERS	91506	1173	7690	EDUCATIONAL SERVICES	91911	2354	16961	EDUCATIONAL SERVICES
91304	1457	17052	MOTOR VEHICLE & PARTS DEALERS	91507	10	31	REAL ESTATE	91912	26	55	ADMINISTRATIVE & SUPPORT SVCS
91305	4	5	PERFORM'G ARTS; SPEC. SPORTS	91508	11	20	SPECIAL TRADE CONTRACTORS	91913	257	1682	EDUCATIONAL SERVICES
91306	796	3408	FOOD SVCS & DRINKING PLACES	91510	26	130	MOTION PICT. & SOUND RECORDING	91914	464	3893	REAL ESTATE
91307	770	7458	AMBULATORY HEALTH CARE SVCS	91521	17	6509	AMUSEMENT; GAMBLING;& RECREAT.	91915	299	2730	FOOD SVCS & DRINKING PLACES
91308	36	82	PROF.; SCIENTIFIC; & TECH SVCS	91522	9	1307	MOTION PICT. & SOUND RECORDING	91916	61	257	EDUCATIONAL SERVICES
91309	21	49	ADMINISTRATIVE & SUPPORT SVCS	91523	9	1560	BROADCASTING	91917	27	88	RELIG.; GRANT; CIVIC; PROF ORG
91310	4	9	REPAIR AND MAINTENANCE	91601	2198	10698	EDUCATIONAL SERVICES	91921	16	185	MISCELLANEOUS STORE RETAILERS
91311	3363	41883	MERCH. WHOLESALERS;DURABLE GDS	91602	850	4735	FOOD SVCS & DRINKING PLACES	91931	15	50	HEAVY & CIVIL ENG. CONSTRUCT'N
91313	28	125	PROF.; SCIENTIFIC; & TECH SVCS	91603	9	18	MOTION PICT. & SOUND RECORDING	91932	466	3285	EDUCATIONAL SERVICES
91316	1473	7823	REAL ESTATE	91604	2050	12213	FOOD SVCS & DRINKING PLACES	91933	7	6	SPECIAL TRADE CONTRACTORS
91319	22	47	ADMINISTRATIVE & SUPPORT SVCS	91605	2771	19349	MERCH. WHOLESALERS;DURABLE GDS	91934	34	83	ACCOMMODATION
91320	1553	19272	PROF.; SCIENTIFIC; & TECH SVCS	91606	1297	9236	INSURANCE CARRIERS & RELATED	91935	222	843	EDUCATIONAL SERVICES
91321	1577	8412	EDUCATIONAL SERVICES	91607	939	5259	AMBULATORY HEALTH CARE SVCS	91941	2333	12631	MOTOR VEHICLE & PARTS DEALERS
91322	63	99	MISCELLANEOUS STORE RETAILERS	91608	195	3881	FOOD SVCS & DRINKING PLACES	91942	1110	14942	HOSPITALS
91324	2675	18244	FOOD SVCS & DRINKING PLACES	91609	2	3000	EDUCATIONAL SERVICES	91943	16	24	SPECIAL TRADE CONTRACTORS
91325	982	11072	MISCELLANEOUS MANUFACTURING	91610	5	13	RELIG.; GRANT; CIVIC; PROF ORG	91944	42	148	ADMINISTRATIVE & SUPPORT SVCS
91326	544	4378	HEALTH & PERSONAL CARE STORES	91614	13	46	PUBLISHING INDUSTRIES	91945	810	6763	WASTE MANAGMT & REMEDIAT'N SVC
91327	29	67	ADMINISTRATIVE & SUPPORT SVCS	91615	7	437	RENTAL AND LEASING SERVICES	91946	11	41	ADMINISTRATIVE & SUPPORT SVCS
91328	15	26	SECURITIES/COMMODITY CONTRACTS	91616	2	21	SPECIAL TRADE CONTRACTORS	91948	9	48	JUSTICE; PUBIC ORDER/SAFETY
91329	9	3539	COMPUTER & ELECTRONIC PROD MFG	91617	11	19	PROF.; SCIENTIFIC; & TECH SVCS	91950	2384	20984	MOTOR VEHICLE & PARTS DEALERS
91330	26	4395	EDUCATIONAL SERVICES	91618	1	0	PERFORM'G ARTS; SPEC. SPORTS	91951	3	5	CONSTRUCTION OF BUILDINGS
91331	1799	15377	EDUCATIONAL SERVICES	91701	848	5028	EDUCATIONAL SERVICES	91962	63	271	EDUCATIONAL SERVICES
91333	2	0	SPECIAL TRADE CONTRACTORS	91702	1439	16774	EDUCATIONAL SERVICES	91963	17	103	SOCIAL ASSISTANCE
91334	2	3	EDUCATIONAL SERVICES	91706	2229	35020	MERCH. WHOLESALERS;NONDUR. GDS	91976	12	15	SPECIAL TRADE CONTRACTORS
91335	2273	11545	EDUCATIONAL SERVICES	91708	121	2067	TRUCK TRANSPORTATION	91977	1121	7271	EDUCATIONAL SERVICES
91337	16	21	PROF.; SCIENTIFIC; & TECH SVCS	91709	1300	7708	EDUCATIONAL SERVICES	91978	276	2418	EDUCATIONAL SERVICES
91340	1497	15001	MERCH. WHOLESALERS;NONDUR. GDS	91710	3314	39392	MERCH. WHOLESALERS;DURABLE GDS	91979	20	58	TRUCK TRANSPORTATION
91341	6	135	SPECIAL TRADE CONTRACTORS	91711	1294	15046	EDUCATIONAL SERVICES	91980	69	336	RELIG.; GRANT; CIVIC; PROF ORG
91342	1633	33050	MERCH. WHOLESALERS;DURABLE GDS	91715	10	926	POSTAL SERVICE	92003	214	1705	MERCH. WHOLESALERS;NONDUR. GDS
91343	1119	10812	EDUCATIONAL SERVICES	91722	832	7724	FOOD SVCS & DRINKING PLACES	92004	203	1260	ACCOMMODATION
91344	1660	11090	EDUCATIONAL SERVICES	91723	1575	11461	HOSPITALS	92007	381	1690	FOOD SVCS & DRINKING PLACES
91345	601	7083	HOSPITALS	91724	752	7116	RELIG.; GRANT; CIVIC; PROF ORG	92008	3046	34982	MERCH. WHOLESALERS;DURABLE GDS
91346	12	24	SPECIAL TRADE CONTRACTORS	91729	55	278	POSTAL SERVICE	92009	798	7119	FOOD SVCS & DRINKING PLACES
91350	1429	8364	EDUCATIONAL SERVICES	91730	4068	39932	PROF.; SCIENTIFIC; & TECH SVCS	92010	409	6410	PROF.; SCIENTIFIC; & TECH SVCS
91351	1294	7263	EDUCATIONAL SERVICES	91731	1759	16275	EDUCATIONAL SERVICES	92011	946	13822	FOOD SVCS & DRINKING PLACES
91352	2390	25002	WASTE MANAGMT & REMEDIAT'N SVC	91732	1038	6614	EDUCATIONAL SERVICES	92013	30	49	PROF.; SCIENTIFIC; & TECH SVCS
91353	14	26	HEAVY & CIVIL ENG. CONSTRUCT'N	91733	2662	18612	MERCH. WHOLESALERS;DURABLE GDS	92014	1115	6857	FOOD SVCS & DRINKING PLACES
91354	249	1547	EDUCATIONAL SERVICES	91734	3	112	POSTAL SERVICE	92018	69	148	PROF.; SCIENTIFIC; & TECH SVCS
91355	3240	47346	AMUSEMENT; GAMBLING;& RECREAT.	91735	1	0	CREDIT INTERMEDIATION & RELATD	92019	822	9903	AMUSEMENT; GAMBLING;& RECREAT.
91356	2388	13660	AMBULATORY HEALTH CARE SVCS	91737	372	2203	EDUCATIONAL SERVICES	92020	3199	31859	EDUCATIONAL SERVICES
91357	28	159	ADMINISTRATIVE & SUPPORT SVCS	91739	792	9369	FOOD SVCS & DRINKING PLACES	92021	1863	12115	FOOD SVCS & DRINKING PLACES
91358	13	33	CLOTHING & CLOTH'G ACC. STORES	91740	1311	9204	FOOD SVCS & DRINKING PLACES	92022	31	70	SPECIAL TRADE CONTRACTORS
91359	59	141	ADMINISTRATIVE & SUPPORT SVCS	91741	779	7594	EDUCATIONAL SERVICES	92023	66	187	ADMINISTRATIVE & SUPPORT SVCS
91360	2130	15446	FOOD SVCS & DRINKING PLACES	91743	16	90	TRANSIT & GRND PASS. TRANSPORT	92024	3195	20538	FOOD SVCS & DRINKING PLACES
91361	1706	15934	PROF.; SCIENTIFIC; & TECH SVCS	91744	1500	14714	EDUCATIONAL SERVICES	92025	3216	30608	SOCIAL ASSISTANCE
91362	2532	31761	INSURANCE CARRIERS & RELATED	91745	1558	13790	MERCH. WHOLESALERS;DURABLE GDS	92026	758	6338	ACCOMMODATION
91363	1	650	INSURANCE CARRIERS & RELATED	91746	1482	24100	MERCH. WHOLESALERS;NONDUR. GDS	92027	792	6941	EDUCATIONAL SERVICES
91364	2728	16035	PROF.; SCIENTIFIC; & TECH SVCS	91747	4	275	POSTAL SERVICE	92028	1608	10580	MERCH. WHOLESALERS;NONDUR. GDS
91365	27	74	ADMINISTRATIVE & SUPPORT SVCS	91748	2508	25495	FOOD SVCS & DRINKING PLACES	92029	1579	16600	SPECIAL TRADE CONTRACTORS
91367	2689	40428	INSURANCE CARRIERS & RELATED	91750	1103	10650	EDUCATIONAL SERVICES	92030	30	53	ADMINISTRATIVE & SUPPORT SVCS
91371	6	1062	EDUCATIONAL SERVICES	91752	681	11717	MERCH. WHOLESALERS;DURABLE GDS	92033	47	96	CONSTRUCTION OF BUILDINGS
91372	26	67	CONSTRUCTION OF BUILDINGS	91754	1632	16486	JUSTICE; PUBIC ORDER/SAFETY	92036	268	1248	ACCOMMODATION
91376	38	198	INSURANCE CARRIERS & RELATED	91755	488	3288	CREDIT INTERMEDIATION & RELATD	92037	3232	35829	PROF.; SCIENTIFIC; & TECH SVCS
91377	210	1196	EDUCATIONAL SERVICES	91759	16	54	RELIG.; GRANT; CIVIC; PROF ORG	92038	57	92	ELECTRONICS & APPLIANCE STORES
91380	68	220	MERCH. WHOLESALERS;DURABLE GDS	91761	3296	60007	SUPPORT ACT. FOR TRANSPORT.	92039	12	11	SPECIAL TRADE CONTRACTORS
91381	437	5030	FOOD SVCS & DRINKING PLACES	91762	1927	11649	EDUCATIONAL SERVICES	92040	1085	10494	AMUSEMENT; GAMBLING;& RECREAT.

ZIP CODE	2009 Total Firms	2009 Total Employ-ees	TOP INDUSTRY RANKED on 2009 EMPLOYMENT
92046	39	90	MERCH. WHOLESALERS;DURABLE GDS
92049	10	8	ADMINISTRATIVE & SUPPORT SVCS
92051	19	34	SPECIAL TRADE CONTRACTORS
92052	36	285	ADMINISTRATIVE & SUPPORT SVCS
92054	2050	13804	FOOD SVCS & DRINKING PLACES
92055	71	2266	HOSPITALS
92056	1273	18186	HOSPITALS
92057	470	4658	EDUCATIONAL SERVICES
92058	718	6153	EDUCATIONAL SERVICES
92059	43	2105	AMUSEMENT; GAMBLING;& RECREAT.
92060	18	89	EDUCATIONAL SERVICES
92061	98	1225	AMUSEMENT; GAMBLING;& RECREAT.
92064	2365	28808	MERCH. WHOLESALERS;DURABLE GDS
92065	1258	7019	EDUCATIONAL SERVICES
92066	14	17	SUPPORT ACTIVITIES: AGR./FOR.
92067	63	178	PROF.; SCIENTIFIC; & TECH SVCS
92068	7	27	AMBULATORY HEALTH CARE SVCS
92069	1491	14926	ADMINISTRATIVE & SUPPORT SVCS
92070	53	669	ACCOMMODATION
92071	1737	15664	SPECIAL TRADE CONTRACTORS
92072	39	79	ADMINISTRATIVE & SUPPORT SVCS
92074	28	50	SPECIAL TRADE CONTRACTORS
92075	1457	7565	FOOD SVCS & DRINKING PLACES
92078	1878	16692	FOOD SVCS & DRINKING PLACES
92079	31	136	SPECIAL TRADE CONTRACTORS
92081	1681	22679	PROF.; SCIENTIFIC; & TECH SVCS
92082	618	5693	AMUSEMENT; GAMBLING;& RECREAT.
92083	1410	10778	EDUCATIONAL SERVICES
92084	1525	9921	MERCH. WHOLESALERS;NONDUR. GDS
92085	57	164	SPECIAL TRADE CONTRACTORS
92086	64	496	AMUSEMENT; GAMBLING;& RECREAT.
92088	37	84	SPECIAL TRADE CONTRACTORS
92091	519	3759	REAL ESTATE
92093	61	19647	EDUCATIONAL SERVICES
92096	5	484	EDUCATIONAL SERVICES
92101	5863	87548	PROF.; SCIENTIFIC; & TECH SVCS
92102	995	11962	JUSTICE; PUBIC ORDER/SAFETY
92103	2414	26246	HOSPITALS
92104	1195	6135	FOOD SVCS & DRINKING PLACES
92105	1089	7730	EDUCATIONAL SERVICES
92106	875	8703	CHEMICAL MANUFACTURING
92107	910	3615	FOOD SVCS & DRINKING PLACES
92108	3233	45441	PROF.; SCIENTIFIC; & TECH SVCS
92109	2238	21792	AMUSEMENT; GAMBLING;& RECREAT.
92110	2413	29921	FOOD SVCS & DRINKING PLACES
92111	3419	40420	ADMINISTRATIVE & SUPPORT SVCS
92112	16	66	ADMINISTRATIVE & SUPPORT SVCS
92113	960	18786	SPECIAL TRADE CONTRACTORS
92114	555	3541	EDUCATIONAL SERVICES
92115	1522	9363	EDUCATIONAL SERVICES
92116	808	3108	FOOD SVCS & DRINKING PLACES
92117	1541	10433	EDUCATIONAL SERVICES
92118	807	8025	ACCOMMODATION
92119	343	1785	EDUCATIONAL SERVICES
92120	1427	16765	AMBULATORY HEALTH CARE SVCS
92121	3886	87293	PROF.; SCIENTIFIC; & TECH SVCS
92122	1297	14125	REAL ESTATE
92123	2591	78879	HOSPITALS
92124	355	2637	EDUCATIONAL SERVICES
92126	2555	22860	FOOD SVCS & DRINKING PLACES
92127	985	15620	PROF.; SCIENTIFIC; & TECH SVCS
92128	1687	19660	FOOD SVCS & DRINKING PLACES
92129	780	4269	EDUCATIONAL SERVICES
92130	1459	14752	PROF.; SCIENTIFIC; & TECH SVCS
92131	937	11695	PROF.; SCIENTIFIC; & TECH SVCS
92132	9	723	NAT'L SECURITY & INT'L AFFAIRS
92134	30	5670	NAT'L SECURITY & INT'L AFFAIRS
92135	33	36217	NAT'L SECURITY & INT'L AFFAIRS
92136	38	43219	NAT'L SECURITY & INT'L AFFAIRS
92137	6	19	TRUCK TRANSPORTATION
92138	56	239	SPECIAL TRADE CONTRACTORS
92139	173	1593	EDUCATIONAL SERVICES
92140	13	2867	NAT'L SECURITY & INT'L AFFAIRS
92142	17	35	ADMINISTRATIVE & SUPPORT SVCS
92143	2	1	REPAIR AND MAINTENANCE
92145	29	1189	NAT'L SECURITY & INT'L AFFAIRS
92147	8	2547	EXEC.; LEGIS.; & OTHER SUPPORT
92149	2	4	TRANSIT & GRND PASS. TRANSPORT
92150	26	104	CREDIT INTERMEDIATION & RELATD
92152	8	77	EXEC.; LEGIS.; & OTHER SUPPORT
92153	4	8	CONSTRUCTION OF BUILDINGS
92154	2140	23177	MISCELLANEOUS MANUFACTURING
92155	10	108	NAT'L SECURITY & INT'L AFFAIRS
92158	5	410	PROF.; SCIENTIFIC; & TECH SVCS
92159	32	84	ADMINISTRATIVE & SUPPORT SVCS
92160	12	73	HOSPITALS
92161	23	1889	AMBULATORY HEALTH CARE SVCS
92162	4	9	RELIG.; GRANT; CIVIC; PROF ORG
92163	20	34	PROF.; SCIENTIFIC; & TECH SVCS
92164	15	18	SPECIAL TRADE CONTRACTORS
92165	4	5	PROF.; SCIENTIFIC; & TECH SVCS
92166	23	45	ADMINISTRATIVE & SUPPORT SVCS
92167	26	83	PUBLISHING INDUSTRIES
92168	14	201	RENTAL AND LEASING SERVICES
92169	29	48	TRUCK TRANSPORTATION
92170	3	2	SPECIAL TRADE CONTRACTORS
92171	18	107	ADMINISTRATIVE & SUPPORT SVCS
92172	26	206	ADMINISTRATIVE & SUPPORT SVCS
92173	785	6727	CLOTHING & CLOTH'G ACC. STORES
92174	6	4	SPECIAL TRADE CONTRACTORS
92175	24	93	BLDG MATL & GARDEN EQPMT DLRS
92176	12	21	PROF.; SCIENTIFIC; & TECH SVCS
92177	26	60	SPECIAL TRADE CONTRACTORS
92178	13	20	ADMINISTRATIVE & SUPPORT SVCS
92179	3	1206	EXEC.; LEGIS.; & OTHER SUPPORT
92182	30	3184	AMUSEMENT; GAMBLING;& RECREAT.
92186	1	110	INSURANCE CARRIERS & RELATED
92190	13	24	HEAVY & CIVIL ENG. CONSTRUCT'N
92191	6	25	PROF.; SCIENTIFIC; & TECH SVCS
92192	34	301	EDUCATIONAL SERVICES
92193	18	95	ADMINISTRATIVE & SUPPORT SVCS
92195	6	8	PROF.; SCIENTIFIC; & TECH SVCS
92196	17	33	RENTAL AND LEASING SERVICES
92198	35	58	NONMETALLIC MINERAL PROD. MFG
92199	3	12	FOOD SVCS & DRINKING PLACES
92201	1843	17111	JUSTICE; PUBIC ORDER/SAFETY
92202	16	354	EXEC.; LEGIS.; & OTHER SUPPORT
92203	488	6490	AMUSEMENT; GAMBLING;& RECREAT.
92210	279	3877	ACCOMMODATION
92211	1374	12451	ADMINISTRATIVE & SUPPORT SVCS
92220	793	8251	ACCOMMODATION
92222	2	0	CROP PRODUCTION
92223	769	5342	EDUCATIONAL SERVICES
92225	622	5120	JUSTICE; PUBIC ORDER/SAFETY
92226	5	9	TRUCK TRANSPORTATION
92227	727	7246	FOOD MANUFACTURING
92230	187	3492	AMUSEMENT; GAMBLING;& RECREAT.
92231	1051	7231	EDUCATIONAL SERVICES
92232	1	0	SPECIAL TRADE CONTRACTORS
92233	101	2444	JUSTICE; PUBIC ORDER/SAFETY
92234	1541	12148	MOTOR VEHICLE & PARTS DEALERS
92235	24	48	SPECIAL TRADE CONTRACTORS
92236	613	9792	MERCH. WHOLESALERS;NONDUR. GDS
92239	25	143	GASOLINE STATIONS
92240	572	3104	EDUCATIONAL SERVICES
92241	117	503	MOTOR VEHICLE & PARTS DEALERS
92242	40	197	ACCOMMODATION
92243	2029	25868	EXEC.; LEGIS.; & OTHER SUPPORT
92244	9	5	CONSTRUCTION OF BUILDINGS
92247	33	69	SPECIAL TRADE CONTRACTORS
92248	8	9	REPAIR AND MAINTENANCE
92249	53	505	EDUCATIONAL SERVICES
92250	201	2428	SUPPORT ACTIVITIES: AGR./FOR.
92251	346	3799	JUSTICE; PUBIC ORDER/SAFETY
92252	213	1852	HOSPITALS
92253	1126	14851	EDUCATIONAL SERVICES
92254	91	803	CROP PRODUCTION
92255	45	116	SPECIAL TRADE CONTRACTORS
92256	107	299	SPECIAL TRADE CONTRACTORS
92257	48	190	ANIMAL PRODUCTION
92258	95	742	MERCH. WHOLESALERS;DURABLE GDS
92259	17	46	TRUCK TRANSPORTATION
92260	2723	22869	FOOD SVCS & DRINKING PLACES
92261	59	118	SPECIAL TRADE CONTRACTORS
92262	2256	17914	FOOD SVCS & DRINKING PLACES
92263	103	207	FABRICATED METAL PRODUCT MFG
92264	961	7496	ACCOMMODATION
92266	20	34	FOOD AND BEVERAGE STORES
92267	23	154	ACCOMMODATION
92268	24	40	FOOD SVCS & DRINKING PLACES
92270	1037	14763	AMBULATORY HEALTH CARE SVCS
92273	17	161	EDUCATIONAL SERVICES
92274	253	5093	MERCH. WHOLESALERS;NONDUR. GDS
92275	27	244	GASOLINE STATIONS
92276	328	3740	ADMINISTRATIVE & SUPPORT SVCS
92277	455	2497	EDUCATIONAL SERVICES
92278	26	657	HOSPITALS
92280	2	18	EXEC.; LEGIS.; & OTHER SUPPORT
92281	54	451	EDUCATIONAL SERVICES
92282	19	98	EDUCATIONAL SERVICES
92283	98	2067	AMUSEMENT; GAMBLING;& RECREAT.
92284	952	5730	FOOD SVCS & DRINKING PLACES
92285	42	112	RELIG.; GRANT; CIVIC; PROF ORG
92286	28	52	SPECIAL TRADE CONTRACTORS
92301	402	4507	EDUCATIONAL SERVICES
92304	6	24	GASOLINE STATIONS
92305	38	183	ACCOMMODATION
92307	1087	7571	HOSPITALS
92308	773	6082	EDUCATIONAL SERVICES
92309	54	636	FOOD SVCS & DRINKING PLACES
92310	68	739	COMPUTER & ELECTRONIC PROD MFG
92311	1105	9300	FOOD SVCS & DRINKING PLACES
92312	5	10	SPECIAL TRADE CONTRACTORS
92313	360	2912	EDUCATIONAL SERVICES
92314	355	986	PROF.; SCIENTIFIC; & TECH SVCS
92315	761	6796	ACCOMMODATION
92316	767	8777	TRUCK TRANSPORTATION
92317	146	859	FOOD SVCS & DRINKING PLACES
92318	8	9	DATA PROCESS'G
92320	227	41794	RELIG.; GRANT; CIVIC; PROF ORG
92321	44	238	RELIG.; GRANT; CIVIC; PROF ORG
92322	29	89	MERCH. WHOLESALERS;DURABLE GDS
92324	1652	19500	EDUCATIONAL SERVICES
92325	383	1357	EDUCATIONAL SERVICES
92326	7	35	RELIG.; GRANT; CIVIC; PROF ORG
92327	27	107	MERCH. WHOLESALERS;DURABLE GDS
92328	23	1021	MUSEUMS; HIST. SITES;& SIMILAR
92329	16	23	ADMINISTRATIVE & SUPPORT SVCS
92331	2	5	PROF.; SCIENTIFIC; & TECH SVCS
92332	1	1	MOTOR VEHICLE & PARTS DEALERS
92333	31	152	RELIG.; GRANT; CIVIC; PROF ORG
92334	22	35	PERFORM'G ARTS; SPEC. SPORTS
92335	2732	29034	HOSPITALS
92336	974	8202	GENERAL MERCHANDISE STORES
92337	918	16863	MERCH. WHOLESALERS;DURABLE GDS
92338	4	73	FOOD AND BEVERAGE STORES
92339	28	172	ACCOMMODATION
92340	42	112	CONSTRUCTION OF BUILDINGS
92341	20	68	ACCOMMODATION
92342	122	602	FOOD SVCS & DRINKING PLACES
92344	238	1218	CONSTRUCTION OF BUILDINGS
92345	2202	14236	EDUCATIONAL SERVICES
92346	903	9335	REAL ESTATE
92347	23	149	EDUCATIONAL SERVICES
92350	5	366	AMBULATORY HEALTH CARE SVCS
92352	497	2971	EDUCATIONAL SERVICES
92354	579	19648	HOSPITALS
92356	164	1143	MINING (EXCEPT OIL AND GAS)
92357	7	1437	HOSPITALS
92358	32	288	ACCOMMODATION
92359	205	1065	NURSING & RESID. CARE FACILIT.
92363	349	2182	FOOD SVCS & DRINKING PLACES
92364	5	24	AMBULATORY HEALTH CARE SVCS
92365	61	256	EDUCATIONAL SERVICES
92366	2	140	MINING (EXCEPT OIL AND GAS)
92368	38	408	MERCH. WHOLESALERS;DURABLE GDS
92369	9	113	ADMIN. ENVIRO. QUALITY PROGRMS
92371	295	2998	EDUCATIONAL SERVICES
92372	72	238	EDUCATIONAL SERVICES
92373	1910	18507	PROF.; SCIENTIFIC; & TECH SVCS
92374	1270	13202	EDUCATIONAL SERVICES
92375	22	23	ADMINISTRATIVE & SUPPORT SVCS
92376	1690	11985	EDUCATIONAL SERVICES
92377	292	3755	EDUCATIONAL SERVICES
92378	59	315	BLDG MATL & GARDEN EQPMT DLRS
92382	204	1461	ACCOMMODATION
92384	20	78	EDUCATIONAL SERVICES
92385	29	115	SUPPORT ACTIVITIES: AGR./FOR.
92386	26	59	CONSTRUCTION OF BUILDINGS
92389	13	33	PROF.; SCIENTIFIC; & TECH SVCS
92391	86	328	EDUCATIONAL SERVICES
92392	1333	11024	FOOD SVCS & DRINKING PLACES
92393	31	67	SPECIAL TRADE CONTRACTORS
92394	331	2745	COMPUTER & ELECTRONIC PROD MFG
92395	1952	16490	HOSPITALS
92397	151	1850	ACCOMMODATION
92398	63	532	EDUCATIONAL SERVICES
92399	1349	6714	EDUCATIONAL SERVICES
92401	582	5951	ADMIN. OF ECONOMIC PROGRAMS
92402	12	15	RELIG.; GRANT; CIVIC; PROF ORG
92404	1131	10639	AMUSEMENT; GAMBLING;& RECREAT.
92405	577	4417	EDUCATIONAL SERVICES
92406	14	48	CONSTRUCTION OF BUILDINGS
92407	836	10727	EDUCATIONAL SERVICES
92408	2010	22954	FOOD SVCS & DRINKING PLACES
92410	1299	10516	EDUCATIONAL SERVICES
92411	440	7050	HOSPITALS
92412	11	50	ADMINISTRATIVE & SUPPORT SVCS
92413	13	16	RELIG.; GRANT; CIVIC; PROF ORG
92415	123	7100	JUSTICE; PUBIC ORDER/SAFETY
92418	30	866	EXEC.; LEGIS.; & OTHER SUPPORT
92423	11	23	AMUSEMENT; GAMBLING;& RECREAT.
92427	19	59	SPECIAL TRADE CONTRACTORS
92501	1602	18788	PROF.; SCIENTIFIC; & TECH SVCS
92502	18	73	EXEC.; LEGIS.; & OTHER SUPPORT
92503	2649	21473	FOOD SVCS & DRINKING PLACES
92504	1334	19122	MOTOR VEHICLE & PARTS DEALERS
92505	847	9229	AMBULATORY HEALTH CARE SVCS
92506	1930	14052	EDUCATIONAL SERVICES
92507	2396	30984	MERCH. WHOLESALERS;DURABLE GDS

BUSINESS DATA

ZIP CODE	2009 Total Firms	2009 Total Employ-ees	TOP INDUSTRY RANKED on 2009 EMPLOYMENT	ZIP CODE	2009 Total Firms	2009 Total Employ-ees	TOP INDUSTRY RANKED on 2009 EMPLOYMENT	ZIP CODE	2009 Total Firms	2009 Total Employ-ees	TOP INDUSTRY RANKED on 2009 EMPLOYMENT
92508	688	4426	FOOD SVCS & DRINKING PLACES	92659	35	85	RENTAL AND LEASING SERVICES	92881	760	8665	FOOD SVCS & DRINKING PLACES
92509	1367	15328	EDUCATIONAL SERVICES	92660	4980	49370	PROF.; SCIENTIFIC; & TECH SVCS	92882	1673	17580	EXEC.; LEGIS.; & OTHER SUPPORT
92513	20	41	SPECIAL TRADE CONTRACTORS	92661	182	849	FOOD SVCS & DRINKING PLACES	92883	401	4812	MERCH. WHOLESALERS;DURABLE GDS
92514	11	12	SPECIAL TRADE CONTRACTORS	92662	176	591	FOOD SVCS & DRINKING PLACES	92885	26	179	POSTAL SERVICE
92515	10	37	SPECIAL TRADE CONTRACTORS	92663	1985	19940	HOSPITALS	92886	1539	8385	FOOD SVCS & DRINKING PLACES
92516	38	78	MERCH. WHOLESALERS;DURABLE GDS	92672	1960	8894	FOOD SVCS & DRINKING PLACES	92887	770	7727	FOOD SVCS & DRINKING PLACES
92517	26	333	OTHER INFORMATION SERVICES	92673	1264	9260	PROF.; SCIENTIFIC; & TECH SVCS	92899	1	0	POSTAL SERVICE
92518	86	1018	NURSING & RESID. CARE FACILIT.	92674	44	202	POSTAL SERVICE	93001	2058	16196	FOOD SVCS & DRINKING PLACES
92519	4	22	MERCH. WHOLESALERS;NONDUR. GDS	92675	2303	13643	AMBULATORY HEALTH CARE SVCS	93002	45	89	PERSONAL AND LAUNDRY SERVICES
92521	6	4544	EDUCATIONAL SERVICES	92676	87	260	PROF.; SCIENTIFIC; & TECH SVCS	93003	4259	40615	PROF.; SCIENTIFIC; & TECH SVCS
92522	22	39329	EXEC.; LEGIS.; & OTHER SUPPORT	92677	2364	14187	FOOD SVCS & DRINKING PLACES	93004	607	3194	SPECIAL TRADE CONTRACTORS
92530	1442	9289	EDUCATIONAL SERVICES	92678	19	60	POSTAL SERVICE	93005	12	14	SPECIAL TRADE CONTRACTORS
92531	17	39	ADMINISTRATIVE & SUPPORT SVCS	92679	620	2152	EDUCATIONAL SERVICES	93006	42	149	RENTAL AND LEASING SERVICES
92532	264	2154	GENERAL MERCHANDISE STORES	92683	3835	22170	FOOD SVCS & DRINKING PLACES	93007	11	44	INSURANCE CARRIERS & RELATED
92536	69	281	ACCOMMODATION	92684	16	40	SPECIAL TRADE CONTRACTORS	93009	77	10288	JUSTICE; PUBIC ORDER/SAFETY
92539	146	660	AMUSEMENT; GAMBLING;& RECREAT.	92685	6	143	POSTAL SERVICE	93010	2173	17102	FOOD SVCS & DRINKING PLACES
92543	1355	10768	HOSPITALS	92688	1291	15170	PROF.; SCIENTIFIC; & TECH SVCS	93011	62	407	INSURANCE CARRIERS & RELATED
92544	742	4459	EDUCATIONAL SERVICES	92690	47	375	POSTAL SERVICE	93012	1146	21796	MERCH. WHOLESALERS;DURABLE GDS
92545	650	8316	GENERAL MERCHANDISE STORES	92691	2568	23554	AMBULATORY HEALTH CARE SVCS	93013	807	7541	MISCELLANEOUS MANUFACTURING
92546	21	14	SPECIAL TRADE CONTRACTORS	92692	1233	8035	REAL ESTATE	93014	15	39	PROF.; SCIENTIFIC; & TECH SVCS
92548	86	316	PROF.; SCIENTIFIC; & TECH SVCS	92693	22	29	SPECIAL TRADE CONTRACTORS	93015	435	2995	MERCH. WHOLESALERS;NONDUR. GDS
92549	309	1210	EDUCATIONAL SERVICES	92694	318	2225	FOOD SVCS & DRINKING PLACES	93016	8	12	SUPPORT ACTIVITIES: AGR./FOR.
92551	195	2724	HEALTH & PERSONAL CARE STORES	92697	71	19715	EDUCATIONAL SERVICES	93020	19	98	REAL ESTATE
92552	21	29	ADMINISTRATIVE & SUPPORT SVCS	92698	1	5	ADMINISTRATIVE & SUPPORT SVCS	93021	1260	12160	MERCH. WHOLESALERS;DURABLE GDS
92553	2012	13246	FOOD SVCS & DRINKING PLACES	92701	2163	24137	JUSTICE; PUBIC ORDER/SAFETY	93022	197	501	FOOD SVCS & DRINKING PLACES
92554	10	22	MERCH. WHOLESALERS;DURABLE GDS	92702	10	16	POSTAL SERVICE	93023	995	6435	ACCOMMODATION
92555	293	5304	HOSPITALS	92703	1270	9501	EXEC.; LEGIS.; & OTHER SUPPORT	93024	19	20	MISCELLANEOUS STORE RETAILERS
92556	17	33	SPECIAL TRADE CONTRACTORS	92704	2678	32241	EDUCATIONAL SERVICES	93030	2281	29655	MERCH. WHOLESALERS;NONDUR. GDS
92557	551	4058	EDUCATIONAL SERVICES	92705	4845	55898	PROF.; SCIENTIFIC; & TECH SVCS	93031	26	48	PROF.; SCIENTIFIC; & TECH SVCS
92561	63	310	ACCOMMODATION	92706	926	7593	CREDIT INTERMEDIATION & RELATD	93032	5	14	SPECIAL TRADE CONTRACTORS
92562	2346	16853	FOOD SVCS & DRINKING PLACES	92707	1491	21775	PROF.; SCIENTIFIC; & TECH SVCS	93033	1106	13300	EDUCATIONAL SERVICES
92563	893	6183	EDUCATIONAL SERVICES	92708	2696	25367	PROF.; SCIENTIFIC; & TECH SVCS	93034	4	2	CONSTRUCTION OF BUILDINGS
92564	26	37	SPORTG GDS;HOBBY;BOOK; & MUSIC	92711	18	44	SOCIAL ASSISTANCE	93035	480	2331	FOOD SVCS & DRINKING PLACES
92567	154	1086	MERCH. WHOLESALERS;NONDUR. GDS	92728	17	262	POSTAL SERVICE	93036	1445	16868	FOOD SVCS & DRINKING PLACES
92570	895	7246	BLDG MATL & GARDEN EQPMT DLRS	92735	3	15	PROF.; SCIENTIFIC; & TECH SVCS	93040	27	184	EDUCATIONAL SERVICES
92571	557	5469	FOOD SVCS & DRINKING PLACES	92780	3900	34893	ADMINISTRATIVE & SUPPORT SVCS	93041	430	2910	FOOD SVCS & DRINKING PLACES
92572	7	10	SPECIAL TRADE CONTRACTORS	92781	44	246	POSTAL SERVICE	93042	25	5041	NAT'L SECURITY & INT'L AFFAIRS
92581	12	28	CONSTRUCTION OF BUILDINGS	92782	399	5851	MOTOR VEHICLE & PARTS DEALERS	93043	10	9904	NAT'L SECURITY & INT'L AFFAIRS
92582	191	1123	FOOD SVCS & DRINKING PLACES	92799	24	58	FOOD SVCS & DRINKING PLACES	93044	9	160	RELIG.; GRANT; CIVIC; PROF ORG
92583	694	4814	EDUCATIONAL SERVICES	92801	2803	23861	PROF.; SCIENTIFIC; & TECH SVCS	93060	944	8619	EDUCATIONAL SERVICES
92584	450	2830	EDUCATIONAL SERVICES	92802	1133	16720	ACCOMMODATION	93061	1	3	EDUCATIONAL SERVICES
92585	208	2350	UTILITIES	92803	11	177	POSTAL SERVICE	93062	43	224	RELIG.; GRANT; CIVIC; PROF ORG
92586	503	2457	NURSING & RESID. CARE FACILIT.	92804	1997	10188	EDUCATIONAL SERVICES	93063	1716	12799	FOOD SVCS & DRINKING PLACES
92587	362	1520	SPECIAL TRADE CONTRACTORS	92805	2482	26384	EXEC.; LEGIS.; & OTHER SUPPORT	93064	6	62	ACCOMMODATION
92589	60	188	SPECIAL TRADE CONTRACTORS	92806	3247	44946	MERCH. WHOLESALERS;DURABLE GDS	93065	3214	27967	FOOD SVCS & DRINKING PLACES
92590	2622	17899	MERCH. WHOLESALERS;DURABLE GDS	92807	2293	25480	PROF.; SCIENTIFIC; & TECH SVCS	93066	176	1884	MERCH. WHOLESALERS;NONDUR. GDS
92591	1290	16560	FOOD SVCS & DRINKING PLACES	92808	570	4498	FOOD SVCS & DRINKING PLACES	93067	86	508	PUBLISHING INDUSTRIES
92592	1053	12023	AMUSEMENT; GAMBLING;& RECREAT.	92809	9	50	POSTAL SERVICE	93094	18	48	ADMINISTRATIVE & SUPPORT SVCS
92593	33	121	ADMINISTRATIVE & SUPPORT SVCS	92811	6	17	DATA PROCESS'G	93101	3693	28859	PROF.; SCIENTIFIC; & TECH SVCS
92595	518	3383	HOSPITALS	92812	13	17	SPECIAL TRADE CONTRACTORS	93102	29	168	RELIG.; GRANT; CIVIC; PROF ORG
92596	238	1072	EDUCATIONAL SERVICES	92814	11	22	SPECIAL TRADE CONTRACTORS	93103	957	10889	PERSONAL AND LAUNDRY SERVICES
92599	5	4550	NONSTORE RETAILERS	92815	12	34	INSURANCE CARRIERS & RELATED	93105	1527	15902	RELIG.; GRANT; CIVIC; PROF ORG
92602	367	6833	FOOD SVCS & DRINKING PLACES	92816	4	4	INSURANCE CARRIERS & RELATED	93106	17	6301	EDUCATIONAL SERVICES
92603	196	1307	EDUCATIONAL SERVICES	92817	30	75	MERCH. WHOLESALERS;DURABLE GDS	93107	3	68	FOOD SVCS & DRINKING PLACES
92604	1220	7883	FOOD SVCS & DRINKING PLACES	92821	3087	42807	PROF.; SCIENTIFIC; & TECH SVCS	93108	704	5747	ACCOMMODATION
92605	19	33	PRINT'G & RELATED SUPP'T ACT'S	92822	18	130	POSTAL SERVICE	93109	315	3609	EDUCATIONAL SERVICES
92606	1083	21136	TELECOMMUNICATIONS	92823	61	3332	REAL ESTATE	93110	498	6281	JUSTICE; PUBIC ORDER/SAFETY
92607	36	299	POSTAL SERVICE	92825	5	23	HEALTH & PERSONAL CARE STORES	93111	733	6278	MERCH. WHOLESALERS;NONDUR. GDS
92609	28	53	REPAIR AND MAINTENANCE	92831	2172	21229	EDUCATIONAL SERVICES	93116	24	81	PROF.; SCIENTIFIC; & TECH SVCS
92610	453	9714	ELECTRONICS & APPLIANCE STORES	92832	1375	10046	FOOD SVCS & DRINKING PLACES	93117	1693	19453	PROF.; SCIENTIFIC; & TECH SVCS
92612	2616	31486	PROF.; SCIENTIFIC; & TECH SVCS	92833	1319	8403	MERCH. WHOLESALERS;DURABLE GDS	93118	12	32	ADMINISTRATIVE & SUPPORT SVCS
92614	2948	47991	PROF.; SCIENTIFIC; & TECH SVCS	92834	22	303	POSTAL SERVICE	93120	19	34	BLDG MATL & GARDEN EQPMT DLRS
92615	31	50	SPECIAL TRADE CONTRACTORS	92835	913	11752	HOSPITALS	93121	20	70	TRUCK TRANSPORTATION
92616	9	5	MERCH. WHOLESALERS;DURABLE GDS	92836	8	8	ADMINISTRATIVE & SUPPORT SVCS	93130	47	63	PROF.; SCIENTIFIC; & TECH SVCS
92617	86	3415	PROF.; SCIENTIFIC; & TECH SVCS	92837	7	14	CHEMICAL MANUFACTURING	93140	32	120	SPECIAL TRADE CONTRACTORS
92618	3638	72703	PROF.; SCIENTIFIC; & TECH SVCS	92838	21	36	SPECIAL TRADE CONTRACTORS	93150	28	36	PROF.; SCIENTIFIC; & TECH SVCS
92619	31	68	REAL ESTATE	92840	1423	10139	EDUCATIONAL SERVICES	93160	40	211	TRANSIT & GRND PASS. TRANSPORT
92620	555	3993	BLDG MATL & GARDEN EQPMT DLRS	92841	1353	16061	MERCH. WHOLESALERS;DURABLE GDS	93190	23	34	MERCH. WHOLESALERS;NONDUR. GDS
92623	21	704	POSTAL SERVICE	92842	35	111	SPECIAL TRADE CONTRACTORS	93201	21	92	EDUCATIONAL SERVICES
92624	400	1794	ADMINISTRATIVE & SUPPORT SVCS	92843	2190	13811	EDUCATIONAL SERVICES	93202	66	384	EDUCATIONAL SERVICES
92625	647	3939	PERSONAL AND LAUNDRY SERVICES	92844	955	4134	EDUCATIONAL SERVICES	93203	258	11686	PROF.; SCIENTIFIC; & TECH SVCS
92626	4194	63190	PROF.; SCIENTIFIC; & TECH SVCS	92845	377	2119	EDUCATIONAL SERVICES	93204	154	836	EDUCATIONAL SERVICES
92627	3539	20722	FOOD SVCS & DRINKING PLACES	92846	6	37	POSTAL SERVICE	93205	25	71	CREDIT INTERMEDIATION & RELATD
92628	25	60	ADMINISTRATIVE & SUPPORT SVCS	92856	19	170	SPECIAL TRADE CONTRACTORS	93206	135	1624	MERCH. WHOLESALERS;NONDUR. GDS
92629	1299	9974	ACCOMMODATION	92857	12	30	TRUCK TRANSPORTATION	93207	18	359	JUSTICE; PUBIC ORDER/SAFETY
92630	3045	27031	PROF.; SCIENTIFIC; & TECH SVCS	92859	22	79	CONSTRUCTION OF BUILDINGS	93208	5	11	ACCOMMODATION
92637	249	3943	REAL ESTATE	92860	1027	12078	JUSTICE; PUBIC ORDER/SAFETY	93210	372	7707	JUSTICE; PUBIC ORDER/SAFETY
92646	1188	6617	EDUCATIONAL SERVICES	92861	173	824	EDUCATIONAL SERVICES	93212	272	6325	JUSTICE; PUBIC ORDER/SAFETY
92647	2882	24762	FOOD SVCS & DRINKING PLACES	92863	36	475	POSTAL SERVICE	93215	861	10055	MERCH. WHOLESALERS;NONDUR. GDS
92648	2216	16881	FOOD SVCS & DRINKING PLACES	92865	1755	21405	ADMINISTRATIVE & SUPPORT SVCS	93216	2	11	SPECIAL TRADE CONTRACTORS
92649	1924	19014	HEALTH & PERSONAL CARE STORES	92866	908	6350	EDUCATIONAL SERVICES	93218	30	150	EDUCATIONAL SERVICES
92650	3	26	RELIG.; GRANT; CIVIC; PROF ORG	92867	3054	24742	ADMINISTRATIVE & SUPPORT SVCS	93219	97	1150	ADMINISTRATIVE & SUPPORT SVCS
92651	2100	12807	FOOD SVCS & DRINKING PLACES	92868	2435	40642	HOSPITALS	93220	9	864	BEVERAGE & TOBACCO PRODUCT MFG
92652	53	115	MERCH. WHOLESALERS;DURABLE GDS	92869	949	5155	EDUCATIONAL SERVICES	93221	483	4345	MERCH. WHOLESALERS;NONDUR. GDS
92653	3272	25512	HOSPITALS	92870	2014	14486	FOOD SVCS & DRINKING PLACES	93222	9	58	PROF.; SCIENTIFIC; & TECH SVCS
92654	29	346	POSTAL SERVICE	92871	22	140	POSTAL SERVICE	93223	168	1254	EDUCATIONAL SERVICES
92655	170	700	EDUCATIONAL SERVICES	92877	21	69	HEAVY & CIVIL ENG. CONSTRUCT'N	93224	31	491	OIL AND GAS EXTRACTION
92656	1458	14096	PROF.; SCIENTIFIC; & TECH SVCS	92878	47	174	POSTAL SERVICE	93225	262	984	REAL ESTATE
92657	177	1459	FOOD SVCS & DRINKING PLACES	92879	1885	22391	FOOD SVCS & DRINKING PLACES	93226	22	171	RELIG.; GRANT; CIVIC; PROF ORG
92658	38	667	POSTAL SERVICE	92880	1273	18293	PROF.; SCIENTIFIC; & TECH SVCS	93227	29	581	MERCH. WHOLESALERS;DURABLE GDS

ZIP CODE	2009 Total Firms	2009 Total Employees	TOP INDUSTRY RANKED on 2009 EMPLOYMENT
93230	1994	22930	EDUCATIONAL SERVICES
93232	13	25	CONSTRUCTION OF BUILDINGS
93234	161	1451	MERCH. WHOLESALERS;NONDUR. GDS
93235	64	504	MERCH. WHOLESALERS;NONDUR. GDS
93237	1	1	RELIG.; GRANT; CIVIC; PROF ORG
93238	136	630	FOOD SVCS & DRINKING PLACES
93239	56	849	FOOD MANUFACTURING
93240	338	1422	EDUCATIONAL SERVICES
93241	262	2328	FOOD MANUFACTURING
93242	62	335	EDUCATIONAL SERVICES
93243	151	1650	GASOLINE STATIONS
93244	29	159	EDUCATIONAL SERVICES
93245	605	7643	AMUSEMENT; GAMBLING;& RECREAT.
93246	24	8865	NAT'L SECURITY & INT'L AFFAIRS
93247	377	3874	MERCH. WHOLESALERS;NONDUR. GDS
93249	65	1431	MERCH. WHOLESALERS;NONDUR. GDS
93250	172	2734	MERCH. WHOLESALERS;NONDUR. GDS
93251	29	869	OIL AND GAS EXTRACTION
93252	40	398	EDUCATIONAL SERVICES
93254	41	288	CROP PRODUCTION
93255	6	6	GASOLINE STATIONS
93256	113	907	FOOD AND BEVERAGE STORES
93257	1905	20509	EDUCATIONAL SERVICES
93258	14	41	TRUCK TRANSPORTATION
93260	10	8	ANIMAL PRODUCTION
93261	23	167	EDUCATIONAL SERVICES
93262	14	276	ACCOMMODATION
93263	462	4893	FOOD AND BEVERAGE STORES
93265	174	706	SUPPORT ACTIVITIES: AGR./FOR.
93266	36	470	WOOD PRODUCT MANUFACTURING
93267	98	851	MERCH. WHOLESALERS;NONDUR. GDS
93268	447	4676	CONSTRUCTION OF BUILDINGS
93270	103	1115	MERCH. WHOLESALERS;NONDUR. GDS
93271	149	1115	UNCLASSIFIED ESTABLISHMENTS
93272	103	962	ANIMAL PRODUCTION
93274	1946	17750	FOOD SVCS & DRINKING PLACES
93275	15	17	PROF.; SCIENTIFIC; & TECH SVCS
93276	5	791	SPECIAL TRADE CONTRACTORS
93277	1951	19093	FOOD SVCS & DRINKING PLACES
93278	26	54	ADMINISTRATIVE & SUPPORT SVCS
93279	29	57	NURSING & RESID. CARE FACILIT.
93280	419	3475	EDUCATIONAL SERVICES
93282	1	0	POSTAL SERVICE
93283	32	181	EDUCATIONAL SERVICES
93285	75	261	AMUSEMENT; GAMBLING;& RECREAT.
93286	204	1890	MERCH. WHOLESALERS;NONDUR. GDS
93287	4	15	JUSTICE; PUBIC ORDER/SAFETY
93290	15	87	ADMINISTRATIVE & SUPPORT SVCS
93291	2217	26912	HOSPITALS
93292	1275	12019	MOTOR VEHICLE & PARTS DEALERS
93301	2930	28657	HOSPITALS
93302	29	40	ADMINISTRATIVE & SUPPORT SVCS
93303	8	7	ADMINISTRATIVE & SUPPORT SVCS
93304	1422	10855	EDUCATIONAL SERVICES
93305	1022	7718	HOSPITALS
93306	1203	8695	EDUCATIONAL SERVICES
93307	1539	19485	WHOLESALE ELEC. MRKTS & AGENTS
93308	2538	36609	SPECIAL TRADE CONTRACTORS
93309	2742	24234	AMBULATORY HEALTH CARE SVCS
93311	640	10883	INSURANCE CARRIERS & RELATED
93312	1106	7712	EDUCATIONAL SERVICES
93313	1150	15110	MOTOR VEHICLE & PARTS DEALERS
93314	467	5111	SPECIAL TRADE CONTRACTORS
93380	16	38	PROF.; SCIENTIFIC; & TECH SVCS
93383	2	3	MERCH. WHOLESALERS;DURABLE GDS
93384	22	33	ADMINISTRATIVE & SUPPORT SVCS
93385	3	7	ADMINISTRATIVE & SUPPORT SVCS
93386	24	25	ADMINISTRATIVE & SUPPORT SVCS
93387	3	4	ADMINISTRATIVE & SUPPORT SVCS
93388	7	5	ADMINISTRATIVE & SUPPORT SVCS
93389	46	61	ADMINISTRATIVE & SUPPORT SVCS
93390	31	247	SPECIAL TRADE CONTRACTORS
93401	3503	30342	PROF.; SCIENTIFIC; & TECH SVCS
93402	583	2120	ADMINISTRATIVE & SUPPORT SVCS
93403	41	168	EXEC.; LEGIS.; & OTHER SUPPORT
93405	708	10310	FOOD SVCS & DRINKING PLACES
93406	72	101	MERCH. WHOLESALERS;DURABLE GDS
93407	19	1809	EDUCATIONAL SERVICES
93408	35	1224	EXEC.; LEGIS.; & OTHER SUPPORT
93409	2	200	HOSPITALS
93410	1	40	PUBLISHING INDUSTRIES
93412	25	57	SPECIAL TRADE CONTRACTORS
93420	1490	8666	FOOD SVCS & DRINKING PLACES
93421	41	46	ADMINISTRATIVE & SUPPORT SVCS
93422	1597	9321	HOSPITALS
93423	59	98	SPECIAL TRADE CONTRACTORS
93424	108	1988	UTILITIES
93426	49	370	ACCOMMODATION
93427	384	2517	FOOD SVCS & DRINKING PLACES
93428	519	1997	FOOD SVCS & DRINKING PLACES

ZIP CODE	2009 Total Firms	2009 Total Employees	TOP INDUSTRY RANKED on 2009 EMPLOYMENT
93429	9	48	FOOD SVCS & DRINKING PLACES
93430	173	521	FOOD SVCS & DRINKING PLACES
93432	40	122	FOOD SVCS & DRINKING PLACES
93433	667	3526	FOOD SVCS & DRINKING PLACES
93434	120	1160	SUPPORT ACTIVITIES: AGR./FOR.
93435	8	9	BEVERAGE & TOBACCO PRODUCT MFG
93436	1323	12492	EXEC.; LEGIS.; & OTHER SUPPORT
93437	56	402	EDUCATIONAL SERVICES
93438	18	31	SPECIAL TRADE CONTRACTORS
93440	75	278	ANIMAL PRODUCTION
93441	139	903	EDUCATIONAL SERVICES
93442	804	4102	FOOD SVCS & DRINKING PLACES
93443	35	51	SPECIAL TRADE CONTRACTORS
93444	501	2282	FOOD SVCS & DRINKING PLACES
93445	153	656	EDUCATIONAL SERVICES
93446	2536	16776	EDUCATIONAL SERVICES
93447	73	123	SPECIAL TRADE CONTRACTORS
93448	49	139	SPECIAL TRADE CONTRACTORS
93449	647	4504	FOOD SVCS & DRINKING PLACES
93450	27	246	TRUCK TRANSPORTATION
93451	131	3512	NAT'L SECURITY & INT'L AFFAIRS
93452	48	640	EXEC.; LEGIS.; & OTHER SUPPORT
93453	145	352	MERCH. WHOLESALERS;NONDUR. GDS
93454	1917	16704	FOOD SVCS & DRINKING PLACES
93455	1398	13280	EDUCATIONAL SERVICES
93456	43	291	FOOD AND BEVERAGE STORES
93457	28	54	CONSTRUCTION OF BUILDINGS
93458	833	9602	ADMINISTRATIVE & SUPPORT SVCS
93460	359	4365	SPORTG GDS;HOBBY;BOOK; & MUSIC
93461	41	586	ADMINISTRATIVE & SUPPORT SVCS
93463	715	4691	PROF.; SCIENTIFIC; & TECH SVCS
93464	17	36	TRANSIT & GRND PASS. TRANSPORT
93465	483	2825	AMBULATORY HEALTH CARE SVCS
93475	3	3	SPECIAL TRADE CONTRACTORS
93483	13	30	TRANSIT & GRND PASS. TRANSPORT
93501	246	2287	FOOD SVCS & DRINKING PLACES
93502	1	0	RELIG.; GRANT; CIVIC; PROF ORG
93504	3	3	PROF.; SCIENTIFIC; & TECH SVCS
93505	215	923	REAL ESTATE
93510	286	1236	FOOD SVCS & DRINKING PLACES
93512	19	62	EDUCATIONAL SERVICES
93513	62	299	EDUCATIONAL SERVICES
93514	846	5948	FOOD SVCS & DRINKING PLACES
93515	12	17	EXEC.; LEGIS.; & OTHER SUPPORT
93516	75	1339	MINING (EXCEPT OIL AND GAS)
93517	113	805	EXEC.; LEGIS.; & OTHER SUPPORT
93518	30	70	EDUCATIONAL SERVICES
93519	1	1	GASOLINE STATIONS
93522	1	38	POSTAL SERVICE
93523	46	1848	SPACE RESEARCH AND TECHNOLOGY
93524	32	16276	NAT'L SECURITY & INT'L AFFAIRS
93526	71	1085	EXEC.; LEGIS.; & OTHER SUPPORT
93527	68	198	MERCH. WHOLESALERS;DURABLE GDS
93528	8	11	UTILITIES
93529	75	607	ACCOMMODATION
93530	3	26	HEAVY & CIVIL ENG. CONSTRUCT'N
93531	19	43	INSURANCE CARRIERS & RELATED
93532	59	2368	JUSTICE; PUBIC ORDER/SAFETY
93534	2396	27220	EDUCATIONAL SERVICES
93535	976	9099	EDUCATIONAL SERVICES
93536	1052	11232	JUSTICE; PUBIC ORDER/SAFETY
93539	42	262	RELIG.; GRANT; CIVIC; PROF ORG
93541	66	339	FOOD SVCS & DRINKING PLACES
93542	1	8	MERCH. WHOLESALERS;DURABLE GDS
93543	223	1338	EDUCATIONAL SERVICES
93544	21	130	AMUSEMENT; GAMBLING;& RECREAT.
93545	132	804	EDUCATIONAL SERVICES
93546	804	8419	ACCOMMODATION
93549	20	576	FOOD AND BEVERAGE STORES
93550	1944	11175	EDUCATIONAL SERVICES
93551	1205	11924	FOOD SVCS & DRINKING PLACES
93552	335	2435	EDUCATIONAL SERVICES
93553	51	169	EDUCATIONAL SERVICES
93554	12	39	TELECOMMUNICATIONS
93555	1035	19740	NAT'L SECURITY & INT'L AFFAIRS
93556	12	58	PROF.; SCIENTIFIC; & TECH SVCS
93560	322	1334	EDUCATIONAL SERVICES
93561	919	5563	FOOD SVCS & DRINKING PLACES
93562	50	962	CHEMICAL MANUFACTURING
93563	20	134	RELIG.; GRANT; CIVIC; PROF ORG
93581	24	43	PROF.; SCIENTIFIC; & TECH SVCS
93584	7	8	SPECIAL TRADE CONTRACTORS
93586	8	23	ADMINISTRATIVE & SUPPORT SVCS
93590	23	43	SPECIAL TRADE CONTRACTORS
93591	116	862	TRANSPORTATION EQUIPMENT MFG
93599	1	6	COMPUTER & ELECTRONIC PROD MFG
93601	78	257	NURSING & RESID. CARE FACILIT.
93602	140	630	NURSING & RESID. CARE FACILIT.
93603	14	42	ACCOMMODATION
93604	64	783	ACCOMMODATION

ZIP CODE	2009 Total Firms	2009 Total Employees	TOP INDUSTRY RANKED on 2009 EMPLOYMENT
93605	13	70	SUPPORT ACTIVITIES: AGR./FOR.
93606	15	90	PAPER MANUFACTURING
93607	4	1	ANIMAL PRODUCTION
93608	18	254	ANIMAL PRODUCTION
93609	134	1226	FOOD MANUFACTURING
93610	429	4468	JUSTICE; PUBIC ORDER/SAFETY
93611	854	7942	EDUCATIONAL SERVICES
93612	2053	14686	FOOD SVCS & DRINKING PLACES
93613	59	121	ADMINISTRATIVE & SUPPORT SVCS
93614	379	2386	AMUSEMENT; GAMBLING;& RECREAT.
93615	70	1838	MERCH. WHOLESALERS;NONDUR. GDS
93616	43	598	MISCELLANEOUS STORE RETAILERS
93618	667	10324	MERCH. WHOLESALERS;NONDUR. GDS
93619	414	2626	EDUCATIONAL SERVICES
93620	219	1261	EDUCATIONAL SERVICES
93621	23	358	SOCIAL ASSISTANCE
93622	261	2939	MERCH. WHOLESALERS;NONDUR. GDS
93623	21	391	ACCOMMODATION
93624	45	1386	ADMINISTRATIVE & SUPPORT SVCS
93625	211	3119	ADMINISTRATIVE & SUPPORT SVCS
93626	66	493	EXEC.; LEGIS.; & OTHER SUPPORT
93627	9	527	FOOD MANUFACTURING
93628	3	151	RELIG.; GRANT; CIVIC; PROF ORG
93630	450	3418	EDUCATIONAL SERVICES
93631	440	5095	MERCH. WHOLESALERS;NONDUR. GDS
93633	7	561	MUSEUMS; HIST. SITES;& SIMILAR
93634	16	611	ACCOMMODATION
93635	984	8036	EDUCATIONAL SERVICES
93636	355	3795	HOSPITALS
93637	1194	15701	EDUCATIONAL SERVICES
93638	738	6007	EDUCATIONAL SERVICES
93639	11	43	CONSTRUCTION OF BUILDINGS
93640	174	3259	MERCH. WHOLESALERS;DURABLE GDS
93641	17	139	ACCOMMODATION
93642	1	15	PERSONAL AND LAUNDRY SERVICES
93643	142	459	MUSEUMS; HIST. SITES;& SIMILAR
93644	864	4263	FOOD SVCS & DRINKING PLACES
93645	22	356	DATA PROCESS'G
93646	158	1638	MERCH. WHOLESALERS;NONDUR. GDS
93647	160	1287	MERCH. WHOLESALERS;NONDUR. GDS
93648	170	1961	MERCH. WHOLESALERS;NONDUR. GDS
93649	3	22	UTILITIES
93650	192	2481	ADMINISTRATIVE & SUPPORT SVCS
93651	80	499	SUPPORT ACTIVITIES: AGR./FOR.
93652	13	460	ADMINISTRATIVE & SUPPORT SVCS
93653	38	237	NONMETALLIC MINERAL PROD. MFG
93654	713	10144	MERCH. WHOLESALERS;NONDUR. GDS
93656	123	745	EDUCATIONAL SERVICES
93657	742	7069	EDUCATIONAL SERVICES
93660	72	692	CROP PRODUCTION
93661	1	0	SPECIAL TRADE CONTRACTORS
93662	745	8240	FOOD MANUFACTURING
93664	114	380	ACCOMMODATION
93665	10	134	MERCH. WHOLESALERS;NONDUR. GDS
93666	11	146	MERCH. WHOLESALERS;NONDUR. GDS
93667	55	332	EDUCATIONAL SERVICES
93668	35	399	EDUCATIONAL SERVICES
93669	6	139	ACCOMMODATION
93670	6	21	EDUCATIONAL SERVICES
93673	20	211	MERCH. WHOLESALERS;NONDUR. GDS
93675	60	248	ACCOMMODATION
93701	501	2923	FOOD AND BEVERAGE STORES
93702	894	6656	EDUCATIONAL SERVICES
93703	1067	8541	HOSPITALS
93704	1205	9642	EDUCATIONAL SERVICES
93705	600	3232	EDUCATIONAL SERVICES
93706	1182	18861	ANIMAL PRODUCTION
93707	4	2	SPECIAL TRADE CONTRACTORS
93708	1	1	ADMINISTRATIVE & SUPPORT SVCS
93709	1	0	MERCH. WHOLESALERS;NONDUR. GDS
93710	2046	19856	FOOD SVCS & DRINKING PLACES
93711	2410	19565	PROF.; SCIENTIFIC; & TECH SVCS
93712	1	7	SPECIAL TRADE CONTRACTORS
93714	2	0	ELECTRONICS & APPLIANCE STORES
93717	1	0	ADMINISTRATIVE & SUPPORT SVCS
93718	1	1	PROF.; SCIENTIFIC; & TECH SVCS
93720	1956	27721	HOSPITALS
93721	1529	39902	AMBULATORY HEALTH CARE SVCS
93722	2120	15413	SPECIAL TRADE CONTRACTORS
93723	145	834	EDUCATIONAL SERVICES
93724	3	48	JUSTICE; PUBIC ORDER/SAFETY
93725	882	14937	MERCH. WHOLESALERS;DURABLE GDS
93726	1491	11925	FOOD SVCS & DRINKING PLACES
93727	2203	24110	PROF.; SCIENTIFIC; & TECH SVCS
93728	727	4334	FOOD SVCS & DRINKING PLACES
93729	60	114	ADMINISTRATIVE & SUPPORT SVCS
93730	158	1158	AMUSEMENT; GAMBLING;& RECREAT.
93740	13	2666	EDUCATIONAL SERVICES
93741	2	0	EDUCATIONAL SERVICES
93744	16	14	PRINT'G & RELATED SUPP'T ACT'S

BUSINESS DATA

ZIP CODE	2009 Total Firms	2009 Total Employ-ees	TOP INDUSTRY RANKED on 2009 EMPLOYMENT	ZIP CODE	2009 Total Firms	2009 Total Employ-ees	TOP INDUSTRY RANKED on 2009 EMPLOYMENT	ZIP CODE	2009 Total Firms	2009 Total Employ-ees	TOP INDUSTRY RANKED on 2009 EMPLOYMENT
93745	5	6	ADMINISTRATIVE & SUPPORT SVCS	94089	917	25125	MERCH. WHOLESALERS;DURABLE GDS	94531	632	5882	FOOD SVCS & DRINKING PLACES
93747	16	83	CONSTRUCTION OF BUILDINGS	94101	4	0	SPECIAL TRADE CONTRACTORS	94533	2666	27333	FOOD SVCS & DRINKING PLACES
93750	2	8	POSTAL SERVICE	94102	3014	44475	ACCOMMODATION	94534	1112	11879	FOOD SVCS & DRINKING PLACES
93755	26	350	RELIG.; GRANT; CIVIC; PROF ORG	94103	4747	57253	EXEC.; LEGIS.; & OTHER SUPPORT	94535	102	1448	EXEC.; LEGIS.; & OTHER SUPPORT
93761	1	15	RELIG.; GRANT; CIVIC; PROF ORG	94104	2878	30258	PROF.; SCIENTIFIC; & TECH SVCS	94536	1474	7469	EDUCATIONAL SERVICES
93772	1	0	PROF.; SCIENTIFIC; & TECH SVCS	94105	2930	84914	PROF.; SCIENTIFIC; & TECH SVCS	94537	23	27	SUPPORT ACTIVITIES: AGR./FOR.
93775	3	4	INSURANCE CARRIERS & RELATED	94106	1	2	PROF.; SCIENTIFIC; & TECH SVCS	94538	3806	61280	COMPUTER & ELECTRONIC PROD MFG
93776	5	4	SPECIAL TRADE CONTRACTORS	94107	2877	28293	PROF.; SCIENTIFIC; & TECH SVCS	94539	1438	29168	COMPUTER & ELECTRONIC PROD MFG
93777	1	0	PERFORM'G ARTS; SPEC. SPORTS	94108	2602	25548	PROF.; SCIENTIFIC; & TECH SVCS	94540	17	60	PROF.; SCIENTIFIC; & TECH SVCS
93778	1	1	ADMINISTRATIVE & SUPPORT SVCS	94109	2855	27621	FURN. & HOME FURNISHGS STORES	94541	2176	11708	PROF.; SCIENTIFIC; & TECH SVCS
93780	1	500	PROF.; SCIENTIFIC; & TECH SVCS	94110	3154	22756	HOSPITALS	94542	131	2092	EDUCATIONAL SERVICES
93786	1	0	PUBLISHING INDUSTRIES	94111	3546	51731	PROF.; SCIENTIFIC; & TECH SVCS	94543	5	9	SPECIAL TRADE CONTRACTORS
93790	4	3	BLDG MATL & GARDEN EQPMT DLRS	94112	1429	6298	EDUCATIONAL SERVICES	94544	1890	22851	MERCH. WHOLESALERS;DURABLE GDS
93791	5	4	MERCH. WHOLESALERS;DURABLE GDS	94114	1316	6289	FOOD SVCS & DRINKING PLACES	94545	2567	41317	MERCH. WHOLESALERS;DURABLE GDS
93792	1	2	CLOTHING & CLOTH'G ACC. STORES	94115	1898	19140	HOSPITALS	94546	1256	8235	HOSPITALS
93793	4	31	ADMINISTRATIVE & SUPPORT SVCS	94116	874	5927	HOSPITALS	94547	352	3650	COMPUTER & ELECTRONIC PROD MFG
93794	5	23	TRANSIT & GRND PASS. TRANSPORT	94117	1105	8625	RELIG.; GRANT; CIVIC; PROF ORG	94548	20	111	EDUCATIONAL SERVICES
93901	2651	34851	MERCH. WHOLESALERS;NONDUR. GDS	94118	1987	15577	HOSPITALS	94549	1599	8498	FOOD SVCS & DRINKING PLACES
93902	30	99	SPECIAL TRADE CONTRACTORS	94119	14	30	RENTAL AND LEASING SERVICES	94550	1883	29923	PROF.; SCIENTIFIC; & TECH SVCS
93905	789	7026	EDUCATIONAL SERVICES	94120	2	21	ADMINISTRATIVE & SUPPORT SVCS	94551	1756	23425	PROF.; SCIENTIFIC; & TECH SVCS
93906	1076	13436	ADMINISTRATIVE & SUPPORT SVCS	94121	989	6954	HOSPITALS	94552	220	1037	EDUCATIONAL SERVICES
93907	763	7929	GENERAL MERCHANDISE STORES	94122	1766	5914	FOOD SVCS & DRINKING PLACES	94553	2065	26043	EXEC.; LEGIS.; & OTHER SUPPORT
93908	482	4558	MERCH. WHOLESALERS;NONDUR. GDS	94123	1490	7891	FOOD SVCS & DRINKING PLACES	94555	337	3450	COMPUTER & ELECTRONIC PROD MFG
93912	35	57	SPECIAL TRADE CONTRACTORS	94124	2097	21999	SPECIAL TRADE CONTRACTORS	94556	501	5027	EDUCATIONAL SERVICES
93915	2	1	SPECIAL TRADE CONTRACTORS	94125	2	5	RELIG.; GRANT; CIVIC; PROF ORG	94557	4	4	UTILITIES
93920	91	1145	ACCOMMODATION	94126	10	9	ADMINISTRATIVE & SUPPORT SVCS	94558	3002	27945	EDUCATIONAL SERVICES
93921	72	208	FOOD SVCS & DRINKING PLACES	94127	686	6239	ADMINISTRATIVE & SUPPORT SVCS	94559	2012	15948	FOOD SVCS & DRINKING PLACES
93922	65	112	ADMINISTRATIVE & SUPPORT SVCS	94128	151	7798	UNCLASSIFIED ESTABLISHMENTS	94560	1509	17868	FOOD SVCS & DRINKING PLACES
93923	1640	10069	FOOD SVCS & DRINKING PLACES	94129	256	4471	SUPPORT ACT. FOR TRANSPORT.	94561	664	3742	EDUCATIONAL SERVICES
93924	380	1477	ACCOMMODATION	94130	44	409	EDUCATIONAL SERVICES	94562	37	864	BEVERAGE & TOBACCO PRODUCT MFG
93925	34	343	CROP PRODUCTION	94131	532	1767	EDUCATIONAL SERVICES	94563	767	3560	EDUCATIONAL SERVICES
93926	188	3804	ADMINISTRATIVE & SUPPORT SVCS	94132	621	13121	EDUCATIONAL SERVICES	94564	746	4790	FOOD SVCS & DRINKING PLACES
93927	287	4288	SUPPORT ACTIVITIES: AGR./FOR.	94133	2074	17302	FOOD SVCS & DRINKING PLACES	94565	1599	15789	EDUCATIONAL SERVICES
93928	3	7	RELIG.; GRANT; CIVIC; PROF ORG	94134	587	3162	EDUCATIONAL SERVICES	94566	2091	24240	REAL ESTATE
93930	464	5122	FOOD MANUFACTURING	94137	1	0	CREDIT INTERMEDIATION & RELATD	94567	31	86	CROP PRODUCTION
93932	13	50	EDUCATIONAL SERVICES	94140	6	9	SPECIAL TRADE CONTRACTORS	94568	1776	17657	FOOD SVCS & DRINKING PLACES
93933	634	4665	FOOD SVCS & DRINKING PLACES	94141	11	22	PUBLISHING INDUSTRIES	94569	6	12	FOOD SVCS & DRINKING PLACES
93940	3306	30373	FOOD SVCS & DRINKING PLACES	94142	16	9	MERCH. WHOLESALERS;DURABLE GDS	94570	9	13	PROF.; SCIENTIFIC; & TECH SVCS
93942	65	157	SPECIAL TRADE CONTRACTORS	94143	168	36206	EDUCATIONAL SERVICES	94571	339	1962	FOOD SVCS & DRINKING PLACES
93943	11	1526	NAT'L SECURITY & INT'L AFFAIRS	94146	17	27	SPECIAL TRADE CONTRACTORS	94572	169	1376	PETROLEUM & COAL PRODUCTS MFG
93944	9	18	OTHER INFORMATION SERVICES	94147	25	98	ADMINISTRATIVE & SUPPORT SVCS	94573	57	1181	BEVERAGE & TOBACCO PRODUCT MFG
93950	869	5040	EDUCATIONAL SERVICES	94150	1	1	PERSONAL AND LAUNDRY SERVICES	94574	1016	9710	BEVERAGE & TOBACCO PRODUCT MFG
93953	144	4544	ACCOMMODATION	94158	103	1284	PROF.; SCIENTIFIC; & TECH SVCS	94576	12	17	BEVERAGE & TOBACCO PRODUCT MFG
93954	17	251	CROP PRODUCTION	94159	17	43	REAL ESTATE	94577	2749	33122	MERCH. WHOLESALERS;DURABLE GDS
93955	1077	9347	EXEC.; LEGIS.; & OTHER SUPPORT	94163	1	1000	MANAGMT OF COMPANIES & ENTERP.	94578	1046	12423	HOSPITALS
93960	329	5462	MERCH. WHOLESALERS;NONDUR. GDS	94164	16	76	TRANSIT & GRND PASS. TRANSPORT	94579	272	2041	EDUCATIONAL SERVICES
93962	15	89	EDUCATIONAL SERVICES	94172	1	0	MISCELLANEOUS STORE RETAILERS	94580	434	5711	EDUCATIONAL SERVICES
94002	988	8911	EDUCATIONAL SERVICES	94188	21	28	SPECIAL TRADE CONTRACTORS	94581	49	91	OTHER INFORMATION SERVICES
94005	410	8813	MERCH. WHOLESALERS;DURABLE GDS	94236	1	6	ADMINISTRATIVE & SUPPORT SVCS	94582	215	1311	EDUCATIONAL SERVICES
94010	3079	31041	HOSPITALS	94249	2	8	EXEC.; LEGIS.; & OTHER SUPPORT	94583	2642	38599	PETROLEUM & COAL PRODUCTS MFG
94011	55	112	SPECIAL TRADE CONTRACTORS	94301	1695	15524	AMBULATORY HEALTH CARE SVCS	94585	582	3218	FOOD SVCS & DRINKING PLACES
94014	1004	10512	MOTOR VEHICLE & PARTS DEALERS	94302	25	35	CONSTRUCTION OF BUILDINGS	94586	76	1007	BLDG MATL & GARDEN EQPMT DLRS
94015	1226	16163	HOSPITALS	94303	1258	13655	PROF.; SCIENTIFIC; & TECH SVCS	94587	1500	19663	MERCH. WHOLESALERS;DURABLE GDS
94017	12	27	ADMINISTRATIVE & SUPPORT SVCS	94304	517	29685	AMBULATORY HEALTH CARE SVCS	94588	2051	48971	PROF.; SCIENTIFIC; & TECH SVCS
94018	38	122	EDUCATIONAL SERVICES	94305	102	3441	OTHER INFORMATION SERVICES	94589	529	8688	HOSPITALS
94019	907	6344	MERCH. WHOLESALERS;NONDUR. GDS	94306	1242	9606	PROF.; SCIENTIFIC; & TECH SVCS	94590	2296	10999	EDUCATIONAL SERVICES
94020	72	360	SOCIAL ASSISTANCE	94309	4	0	EDUCATIONAL SERVICES	94591	1050	7856	FOOD SVCS & DRINKING PLACES
94021	12	51	ACCOMMODATION	94401	1899	9221	FOOD SVCS & DRINKING PLACES	94592	93	2228	EDUCATIONAL SERVICES
94022	1382	7171	PROF.; SCIENTIFIC; & TECH SVCS	94402	1436	11714	PROF.; SCIENTIFIC; & TECH SVCS	94595	539	3297	NURSING & RESID. CARE FACILIT.
94023	31	52	PROF.; SCIENTIFIC; & TECH SVCS	94403	1902	22585	SECURITIES/COMMODITY CONTRACTS	94596	3509	27837	PROF.; SCIENTIFIC; & TECH SVCS
94024	433	2599	EDUCATIONAL SERVICES	94404	1246	25036	DATA PROCESS'G	94597	893	9194	INSURANCE CARRIERS & RELATED
94025	2393	33802	PROF.; SCIENTIFIC; & TECH SVCS	94497	1	450	POSTAL SERVICE	94598	1137	14605	HOSPITALS
94026	49	124	REPAIR AND MAINTENANCE	94501	2447	15693	PROF.; SCIENTIFIC; & TECH SVCS	94599	198	2367	HOSPITALS
94027	140	1375	EDUCATIONAL SERVICES	94502	353	4971	PROF.; SCIENTIFIC; & TECH SVCS	94601	1567	10017	EDUCATIONAL SERVICES
94028	204	1436	NURSING & RESID. CARE FACILIT.	94503	502	4320	FOOD MANUFACTURING	94602	805	4465	HOSPITALS
94030	796	5248	ACCOMMODATION	94505	265	1187	REAL ESTATE	94603	554	8041	WASTE MANAGMT & REMEDIAT'N SVC
94035	29	131	EDUCATIONAL SERVICES	94506	508	2700	FOOD SVCS & DRINKING PLACES	94604	18	164	INSURANCE CARRIERS & RELATED
94037	64	213	EDUCATIONAL SERVICES	94507	560	2861	PROF.; SCIENTIFIC; & TECH SVCS	94605	781	4370	EDUCATIONAL SERVICES
94038	115	448	HOSPITALS	94508	127	2726	EDUCATIONAL SERVICES	94606	1009	5923	MERCH. WHOLESALERS;NONDUR. GDS
94039	8	15	NONSTORE RETAILERS	94509	2114	15889	EDUCATIONAL SERVICES	94607	2299	31520	PROF.; SCIENTIFIC; & TECH SVCS
94040	1348	12705	HOSPITALS	94510	1691	13798	PROF.; SCIENTIFIC; & TECH SVCS	94608	1867	24475	CHEMICAL MANUFACTURING
94041	675	6700	PROF.; SCIENTIFIC; & TECH SVCS	94511	106	358	AMUSEMENT; GAMBLING;& RECREAT.	94609	1217	11975	AMBULATORY HEALTH CARE SVCS
94042	11	34	SPECIAL TRADE CONTRACTORS	94512	2	20	SPECIAL TRADE CONTRACTORS	94610	1021	5667	PROF.; SCIENTIFIC; & TECH SVCS
94043	1730	24147	PROF.; SCIENTIFIC; & TECH SVCS	94513	1824	11584	EDUCATIONAL SERVICES	94611	1415	12476	HOSPITALS
94044	1063	4720	FOOD SVCS & DRINKING PLACES	94514	71	754	ADMIN. ENVIRO. QUALITY PROGRMS	94612	3436	37937	PROF.; SCIENTIFIC; & TECH SVCS
94060	95	728	CROP PRODUCTION	94515	506	3597	ACCOMMODATION	94613	11	122	EDUCATIONAL SERVICES
94061	730	4049	FOOD SVCS & DRINKING PLACES	94516	12	34	EDUCATIONAL SERVICES	94614	13	27	PROF.; SCIENTIFIC; & TECH SVCS
94062	786	4249	EDUCATIONAL SERVICES	94517	380	1401	FOOD AND BEVERAGE STORES	94615	2	0	POSTAL SERVICE
94063	3001	29219	PROF.; SCIENTIFIC; & TECH SVCS	94518	733	4968	EDUCATIONAL SERVICES	94617	1	0	ADMINISTRATIVE & SUPPORT SVCS
94064	34	53	ADMINISTRATIVE & SUPPORT SVCS	94519	519	2924	EDUCATIONAL SERVICES	94618	550	4667	EDUCATIONAL SERVICES
94065	443	22881	PUBLISHING INDUSTRIES	94520	3418	38815	PROF.; SCIENTIFIC; & TECH SVCS	94619	489	2683	EDUCATIONAL SERVICES
94066	1379	11760	FOOD SVCS & DRINKING PLACES	94521	829	5263	EDUCATIONAL SERVICES	94620	16	22	CONSTRUCTION OF BUILDINGS
94070	2309	15554	TRANSIT & GRND PASS. TRANSPORT	94522	20	26	ADMINISTRATIVE & SUPPORT SVCS	94621	1592	19747	ADMINISTRATIVE & SUPPORT SVCS
94074	12	42	ELECTRONICS & APPLIANCE STORES	94523	1650	14155	FOOD SVCS & DRINKING PLACES	94623	12	34	RELIG.; GRANT; CIVIC; PROF ORG
94080	3263	40926	CHEMICAL MANUFACTURING	94524	23	35	SPECIAL TRADE CONTRACTORS	94661	8	18	MERCH. WHOLESALERS;NONDUR. GDS
94083	25	43	SPECIAL TRADE CONTRACTORS	94525	119	1111	FOOD MANUFACTURING	94662	6	9	SPECIAL TRADE CONTRACTORS
94085	1222	27465	MERCH. WHOLESALERS;DURABLE GDS	94526	1755	9338	REAL ESTATE	94666	1	7	PERSONAL AND LAUNDRY SERVICES
94086	1278	16406	COMPUTER & ELECTRONIC PROD MFG	94527	9	23	ADMINISTRATIVE & SUPPORT SVCS	94701	25	48	SPECIAL TRADE CONTRACTORS
94087	1710	10857	FOOD SVCS & DRINKING PLACES	94528	18	108	AMUSEMENT; GAMBLING;& RECREAT.	94702	656	3919	EXEC.; LEGIS.; & OTHER SUPPORT
94088	20	46	REAL ESTATE	94530	891	5806	FOOD SVCS & DRINKING PLACES	94703	508	2722	RELIG.; GRANT; CIVIC; PROF ORG

ZIP CODE	2009 Total Firms	2009 Total Employ-ees	TOP INDUSTRY RANKED on 2009 EMPLOYMENT	ZIP CODE	2009 Total Firms	2009 Total Employ-ees	TOP INDUSTRY RANKED on 2009 EMPLOYMENT	ZIP CODE	2009 Total Firms	2009 Total Employ-ees	TOP INDUSTRY RANKED on 2009 EMPLOYMENT
94704	1665	17239	MISCELLANEOUS STORE RETAILERS	95020	2019	24837	MISCELLANEOUS STORE RETAILERS	95173	4	15	SPECIAL TRADE CONTRACTORS
94705	735	7356	HOSPITALS	95021	14	41	SOCIAL ASSISTANCE	95190	3	1000	PUBLISHING INDUSTRIES
94706	768	3128	EDUCATIONAL SERVICES	95023	1553	12417	EDUCATIONAL SERVICES	95191	1	1	RELIG.; GRANT; CIVIC; PROF ORG
94707	636	2362	FOOD SVCS & DRINKING PLACES	95024	17	56	CROP PRODUCTION	95192	3	2025	EDUCATIONAL SERVICES
94708	167	444	SOCIAL ASSISTANCE	95030	988	6174	FOOD SVCS & DRINKING PLACES	95193	6	2	ADMINISTRATIVE & SUPPORT SVCS
94709	444	3234	EDUCATIONAL SERVICES	95031	48	93	ELECTRONICS & APPLIANCE STORES	95196	2	80	UTILITIES
94710	1530	22266	FOOD AND BEVERAGE STORES	95032	1194	12011	HOSPITALS	95201	16	21	PERFORM'G ARTS; SPEC. SPORTS
94712	7	15	FOOD SVCS & DRINKING PLACES	95033	245	672	EDUCATIONAL SERVICES	95202	952	23822	EXEC.; LEGIS.; & OTHER SUPPORT
94720	129	29606	EDUCATIONAL SERVICES	95035	2638	42021	MACHINERY MANUFACTURING	95203	595	7911	HOSPITALS
94801	710	8718	TRANSIT & GRND PASS. TRANSPORT	95036	12	24	RELIG.; GRANT; CIVIC; PROF ORG	95204	910	9850	HOSPITALS
94802	3	5	TRUCK TRANSPORTATION	95037	1721	18041	EDUCATIONAL SERVICES	95205	1570	13498	SPECIAL TRADE CONTRACTORS
94803	638	2827	EDUCATIONAL SERVICES	95038	33	66	SPECIAL TRADE CONTRACTORS	95206	983	16485	EDUCATIONAL SERVICES
94804	1375	13180	EXEC.; LEGIS.; & OTHER SUPPORT	95039	96	2049	CROP PRODUCTION	95207	2295	17519	FOOD SVCS & DRINKING PLACES
94805	368	1845	ADMIN. HUMAN RESOURCE PROGRAMS	95041	17	30	PROF.; SCIENTIFIC; & TECH SVCS	95208	18	157	POSTAL SERVICE
94806	1136	11439	HOSPITALS	95042	5	2	CONSTRUCTION OF BUILDINGS	95209	456	4589	NURSING & RESID. CARE FACILIT.
94807	5	31	PROF.; SCIENTIFIC; & TECH SVCS	95043	40	189	BEVERAGE & TOBACCO PRODUCT MFG	95210	601	6462	AMBULATORY HEALTH CARE SVCS
94808	3	6	ADMINISTRATIVE & SUPPORT SVCS	95044	7	33	SPORTG GDS;HOBBY;BOOK; & MUSIC	95211	14	1053	AMBULATORY HEALTH CARE SVCS
94820	16	27	REAL ESTATE	95045	183	3753	MERCH. WHOLESALERS;NONDUR. GDS	95212	267	4144	GENERAL MERCHANDISE STORES
94901	4315	23255	PROF.; SCIENTIFIC; & TECH SVCS	95046	258	1407	AMUSEMENT; GAMBLING;& RECREAT.	95213	8	11	SPECIAL TRADE CONTRACTORS
94903	2044	14677	JUSTICE; PUBIC ORDER/SAFETY	95050	2745	28490	PROF.; SCIENTIFIC; & TECH SVCS	95215	670	13575	WAREHOUSING AND STORAGE
94904	626	6935	HOSPITALS	95051	1721	22230	COMPUTER & ELECTRONIC PROD MFG	95219	652	7055	FOOD SVCS & DRINKING PLACES
94912	44	225	MOTION PICT. & SOUND RECORDING	95052	17	18	REAL ESTATE	95220	173	1695	BEVERAGE & TOBACCO PRODUCT MFG
94913	21	42	SUPPORT ACTIVITIES: AGR./FOR.	95053	8	1220	EDUCATIONAL SERVICES	95221	31	200	EDUCATIONAL SERVICES
94914	19	23	ADMINISTRATIVE & SUPPORT SVCS	95054	2917	59618	COMPUTER & ELECTRONIC PROD MFG	95222	369	2185	FOOD SVCS & DRINKING PLACES
94915	36	226	PROF.; SCIENTIFIC; & TECH SVCS	95055	15	18	DATA PROCESS'G	95223	339	1729	ACCOMMODATION
94920	606	3311	PROF.; SCIENTIFIC; & TECH SVCS	95056	5	0	SPECIAL TRADE CONTRACTORS	95224	40	126	EDUCATIONAL SERVICES
94922	30	57	FOOD SVCS & DRINKING PLACES	95060	3081	31603	EXEC.; LEGIS.; & OTHER SUPPORT	95225	26	77	JUSTICE; PUBIC ORDER/SAFETY
94923	131	1099	FOOD SVCS & DRINKING PLACES	95061	57	110	CONSTRUCTION OF BUILDINGS	95227	44	235	FOOD SVCS & DRINKING PLACES
94924	103	331	FOOD SVCS & DRINKING PLACES	95062	2109	10869	AMBULATORY HEALTH CARE SVCS	95228	168	664	ACCOMMODATION
94925	806	6945	FOOD SVCS & DRINKING PLACES	95063	57	69	PROF.; SCIENTIFIC; & TECH SVCS	95229	21	86	CONSTRUCTION OF BUILDINGS
94926	1	500	INSURANCE CARRIERS & RELATED	95064	28	4822	EDUCATIONAL SERVICES	95230	25	180	BLDG MATL & GARDEN EQPMT DLRS
94927	29	84	SPECIAL TRADE CONTRACTORS	95065	388	4521	HOSPITALS	95231	138	3917	JUSTICE; PUBIC ORDER/SAFETY
94928	1447	13252	EDUCATIONAL SERVICES	95066	904	7700	COMPUTER & ELECTRONIC PROD MFG	95232	11	10	CROP PRODUCTION
94929	17	27	ACCOMMODATION	95067	27	63	PROF.; SCIENTIFIC; & TECH SVCS	95233	21	59	SUPPORT ACTIVITIES: AGR./FOR.
94930	427	1748	FOOD SVCS & DRINKING PLACES	95070	961	5753	EDUCATIONAL SERVICES	95234	10	105	MERCH. WHOLESALERS;NONDUR. GDS
94931	629	3527	REPAIR AND MAINTENANCE	95071	8	11	CONSTRUCTION OF BUILDINGS	95236	119	1880	ANIMAL PRODUCTION
94933	31	101	RELIG.; GRANT; CIVIC; PROF ORG	95073	749	3700	FOOD SVCS & DRINKING PLACES	95237	144	980	MERCH. WHOLESALERS;NONDUR. GDS
94937	65	252	PROF.; SCIENTIFIC; & TECH SVCS	95075	30	108	FOOD SVCS & DRINKING PLACES	95240	2210	23516	FOOD MANUFACTURING
94938	32	70	PUBLISHING INDUSTRIES	95076	2765	26254	MERCH. WHOLESALERS;NONDUR. GDS	95241	35	155	ADMINISTRATIVE & SUPPORT SVCS
94939	616	3780	FOOD SVCS & DRINKING PLACES	95077	17	93	ADMINISTRATIVE & SUPPORT SVCS	95242	699	8964	HOSPITALS
94940	23	129	FOOD AND BEVERAGE STORES	95101	15	2002	POSTAL SERVICE	95245	61	144	CONSTRUCTION OF BUILDINGS
94941	1939	8971	FOOD SVCS & DRINKING PLACES	95103	10	127	MISCELLANEOUS MANUFACTURING	95246	39	135	FOOD AND BEVERAGE STORES
94942	67	134	SPECIAL TRADE CONTRACTORS	95106	1	10	ADMINISTRATIVE & SUPPORT SVCS	95247	305	1221	BEVERAGE & TOBACCO PRODUCT MFG
94945	1349	10108	PROF.; SCIENTIFIC; & TECH SVCS	95108	3	26	BROADCASTING	95248	16	56	EDUCATIONAL SERVICES
94946	44	132	HEAVY & CIVIL ENG. CONSTRUCT'N	95109	11	40	MERCH. WHOLESALERS;NONDUR. GDS	95249	355	2888	HOSPITALS
94947	632	3920	ADMINISTRATIVE & SUPPORT SVCS	95110	1812	25569	TELECOMMUNICATIONS	95250	5	13	CROP PRODUCTION
94948	73	194	ADMINISTRATIVE & SUPPORT SVCS	95111	954	5656	EDUCATIONAL SERVICES	95251	26	122	ADMINISTRATIVE & SUPPORT SVCS
94949	1169	7710	PROF.; SCIENTIFIC; & TECH SVCS	95112	4562	43913	SPECIAL TRADE CONTRACTORS	95252	345	1576	EDUCATIONAL SERVICES
94950	19	151	FOOD SVCS & DRINKING PLACES	95113	1548	27618	EXEC.; LEGIS.; & OTHER SUPPORT	95253	14	45	SPECIAL TRADE CONTRACTORS
94951	146	516	SPECIAL TRADE CONTRACTORS	95116	1095	6247	HOSPITALS	95254	21	49	FOOD SVCS & DRINKING PLACES
94952	2420	14921	FOOD SVCS & DRINKING PLACES	95117	648	2918	MOTOR VEHICLE & PARTS DEALERS	95255	101	172	JUSTICE; PUBIC ORDER/SAFETY
94953	38	71	AMBULATORY HEALTH CARE SVCS	95118	898	6776	FOOD SVCS & DRINKING PLACES	95257	19	20	ACCOMMODATION
94954	1269	16918	PROF.; SCIENTIFIC; & TECH SVCS	95119	511	11308	HOSPITALS	95258	69	352	MERCH. WHOLESALERS;DURABLE GDS
94955	27	57	UNCLASSIFIED ESTABLISHMENTS	95120	705	4481	PROF.; SCIENTIFIC; & TECH SVCS	95267	22	56	SOCIAL ASSISTANCE
94956	218	796	EXEC.; LEGIS.; & OTHER SUPPORT	95121	510	4075	EDUCATIONAL SERVICES	95269	32	75	SPECIAL TRADE CONTRACTORS
94957	101	508	RELIG.; GRANT; CIVIC; PROF ORG	95122	1294	9079	EDUCATIONAL SERVICES	95301	807	7414	EDUCATIONAL SERVICES
94960	841	3615	EDUCATIONAL SERVICES	95123	1632	10296	FOOD SVCS & DRINKING PLACES	95303	32	816	BLDG MATL & GARDEN EQPMT DLRS
94963	31	190	EDUCATIONAL SERVICES	95124	1319	9356	AMBULATORY HEALTH CARE SVCS	95304	691	7286	FOOD SVCS & DRINKING PLACES
94964	9	1210	JUSTICE; PUBIC ORDER/SAFETY	95125	2376	12297	PROF.; SCIENTIFIC; & TECH SVCS	95305	24	70	MERCH. WHOLESALERS;DURABLE GDS
94965	1540	6553	PROF.; SCIENTIFIC; & TECH SVCS	95126	1692	12231	PROF.; SCIENTIFIC; & TECH SVCS	95306	32	74	REAL ESTATE
94966	51	169	RELIG.; GRANT; CIVIC; PROF ORG	95127	935	5499	EDUCATIONAL SERVICES	95307	1048	8299	EDUCATIONAL SERVICES
94970	69	357	FOOD SVCS & DRINKING PLACES	95128	2120	22463	HOSPITALS	95309	8	357	ADMIN. OF ECONOMIC PROGRAMS
94971	44	195	EDUCATIONAL SERVICES	95129	1674	12068	FOOD SVCS & DRINKING PLACES	95310	95	565	ACCOMMODATION
94972	20	58	FOOD SVCS & DRINKING PLACES	95130	216	1722	FOOD SVCS & DRINKING PLACES	95311	76	199	ACCOMMODATION
94973	61	109	RELIG.; GRANT; CIVIC; PROF ORG	95131	1953	42322	MERCH. WHOLESALERS;DURABLE GDS	95312	7	37	EDUCATIONAL SERVICES
94975	31	44	SPECIAL TRADE CONTRACTORS	95132	536	3107	EDUCATIONAL SERVICES	95313	62	476	MERCH. WHOLESALERS;NONDUR. GDS
94976	24	40	CONSTRUCTION OF BUILDINGS	95133	626	11338	SPECIAL TRADE CONTRACTORS	95314	2	2	ACCOMMODATION
94977	16	13	PROF.; SCIENTIFIC; & TECH SVCS	95134	541	39074	COMPUTER & ELECTRONIC PROD MFG	95315	127	747	EDUCATIONAL SERVICES
94978	29	47	CONSTRUCTION OF BUILDINGS	95135	238	1689	EDUCATIONAL SERVICES	95316	163	874	EDUCATIONAL SERVICES
94979	46	56	SPECIAL TRADE CONTRACTORS	95136	579	5529	MOTOR VEHICLE & PARTS DEALERS	95317	14	148	JUSTICE; PUBIC ORDER/SAFETY
94998	2	3200	INSURANCE CARRIERS & RELATED	95138	286	8268	COMPUTER & ELECTRONIC PROD MFG	95318	26	199	ACCOMMODATION
94999	1	6	POSTAL SERVICE	95139	93	551	EDUCATIONAL SERVICES	95319	45	354	EDUCATIONAL SERVICES
95001	61	107	NURSING & RESID. CARE FACILIT.	95140	13	67	PROF.; SCIENTIFIC; & TECH SVCS	95320	374	3228	EDUCATIONAL SERVICES
95002	73	2433	ADMINISTRATIVE & SUPPORT SVCS	95141	8	1637	ELECTRONICS & APPLIANCE STORES	95321	215	1169	FOOD SVCS & DRINKING PLACES
95003	1239	7048	FOOD SVCS & DRINKING PLACES	95148	497	3612	EDUCATIONAL SERVICES	95322	251	2684	FOOD SVCS & DRINKING PLACES
95004	96	640	MERCH. WHOLESALERS;NONDUR. GDS	95150	40	81	ADMINISTRATIVE & SUPPORT SVCS	95323	27	479	EDUCATIONAL SERVICES
95005	272	698	POSTAL SERVICE	95151	7	9	PROF.; SCIENTIFIC; & TECH SVCS	95324	230	2407	FOOD SVCS & DRINKING PLACES
95006	338	1700	BROADCASTING	95152	12	23	CONSTRUCTION OF BUILDINGS	95325	4	2	ANIMAL PRODUCTION
95007	17	24	FOOD SVCS & DRINKING PLACES	95153	24	88	ADMINISTRATIVE & SUPPORT SVCS	95326	302	2482	MERCH. WHOLESALERS;NONDUR. GDS
95008	3780	27331	ADMINISTRATIVE & SUPPORT SVCS	95154	24	73	ADMINISTRATIVE & SUPPORT SVCS	95327	265	2621	JUSTICE; PUBIC ORDER/SAFETY
95009	26	62	CONSTRUCTION OF BUILDINGS	95155	8	18	HEAVY & CIVIL ENG. CONSTRUCT'N	95328	37	218	EDUCATIONAL SERVICES
95010	889	7128	FOOD SVCS & DRINKING PLACES	95156	6	10	SPECIAL TRADE CONTRACTORS	95329	82	438	ACCOMMODATION
95011	27	133	CONSTRUCTION OF BUILDINGS	95157	20	26	ELECTRONICS & APPLIANCE STORES	95330	355	5809	MERCH. WHOLESALERS;DURABLE GDS
95012	276	2564	EDUCATIONAL SERVICES	95158	21	41	INSURANCE CARRIERS & RELATED	95333	62	1341	CROP PRODUCTION
95013	14	28	SPORTG GDS;HOBBY;BOOK; & MUSIC	95159	23	69	ADMINISTRATIVE & SUPPORT SVCS	95334	247	6142	PROF.; SCIENTIFIC; & TECH SVCS
95014	2147	25448	COMPUTER & ELECTRONIC PROD MFG	95160	26	88	PERFORM'G ARTS; SPEC. SPORTS	95335	22	142	SOCIAL ASSISTANCE
95015	29	54	EDUCATIONAL SERVICES	95161	12	10	ADMINISTRATIVE & SUPPORT SVCS	95336	1171	9618	EDUCATIONAL SERVICES
95017	38	453	WOOD PRODUCT MANUFACTURING	95164	6	10	SPECIAL TRADE CONTRACTORS	95337	591	6338	EDUCATIONAL SERVICES
95018	416	2023	JUSTICE; PUBIC ORDER/SAFETY	95170	9	11	NONSTORE RETAILERS	95338	704	3413	SUPPORT ACTIVITIES: AGR./FOR.
95019	232	1231	AMBULATORY HEALTH CARE SVCS	95172	2	1	ADMINISTRATIVE & SUPPORT SVCS	95340	1607	12664	AMBULATORY HEALTH CARE SVCS

BUSINESS DATA

ZIP CODE	2009 Total Firms	2009 Total Employ-ees	TOP INDUSTRY RANKED on 2009 EMPLOYMENT	ZIP CODE	2009 Total Firms	2009 Total Employ-ees	TOP INDUSTRY RANKED on 2009 EMPLOYMENT	ZIP CODE	2009 Total Firms	2009 Total Employ-ees	TOP INDUSTRY RANKED on 2009 EMPLOYMENT
95341	653	10421	EDUCATIONAL SERVICES	95457	203	1092	EDUCATIONAL SERVICES	95610	1807	13060	FOOD SVCS & DRINKING PLACES
95343	1	619	EDUCATIONAL SERVICES	95458	76	227	EDUCATIONAL SERVICES	95611	44	51	SPECIAL TRADE CONTRACTORS
95344	27	65	MERCH. WHOLESALERS;DURABLE GDS	95459	18	67	FOOD AND BEVERAGE STORES	95612	78	375	SUPPORT ACTIVITIES: AGR./FOR.
95345	28	96	ACCOMMODATION	95460	344	1384	ACCOMMODATION	95613	38	217	SCENIC & SIGHTSEEING TRANSPORT
95346	43	206	SUPPORT ACTIVITIES: AGR./FOR.	95461	285	1983	UTILITIES	95614	94	376	EDUCATIONAL SERVICES
95347	4	176	UTILITIES	95462	60	224	RELIG.; GRANT; CIVIC; PROF ORG	95615	48	1037	MERCH. WHOLESALERS;NONDUR. GDS
95348	657	12787	AMBULATORY HEALTH CARE SVCS	95463	6	18	WOOD PRODUCT MANUFACTURING	95616	1513	31324	EDUCATIONAL SERVICES
95350	2438	23033	HOSPITALS	95464	87	723	AMUSEMENT; GAMBLING;& RECREAT.	95617	52	66	ADMINISTRATIVE & SUPPORT SVCS
95351	1338	12720	EDUCATIONAL SERVICES	95465	143	864	ACCOMMODATION	95618	430	4564	PROF.; SCIENTIFIC; & TECH SVCS
95352	37	98	SPECIAL TRADE CONTRACTORS	95466	69	467	BEVERAGE & TOBACCO PRODUCT MFG	95619	319	1550	SPECIAL TRADE CONTRACTORS
95353	30	7090	UNCLASSIFIED ESTABLISHMENTS	95467	95	449	FOOD SVCS & DRINKING PLACES	95620	700	6374	FOOD SVCS & DRINKING PLACES
95354	2011	35969	BEVERAGE & TOBACCO PRODUCT MFG	95468	99	960	EXEC.; LEGIS.; & OTHER SUPPORT	95621	626	4962	GENERAL MERCHANDISE STORES
95355	1324	14627	HOSPITALS	95469	52	513	CROP PRODUCTION	95623	162	526	EDUCATIONAL SERVICES
95356	1392	15673	MOTOR VEHICLE & PARTS DEALERS	95470	191	1027	AMUSEMENT; GAMBLING;& RECREAT.	95624	2014	14281	EDUCATIONAL SERVICES
95357	380	6598	FOOD MANUFACTURING	95471	1	5	FOOD SVCS & DRINKING PLACES	95625	7	69	ADMIN. OF ECONOMIC PROGRAMS
95358	698	11249	MERCH. WHOLESALERS;NONDUR. GDS	95472	1732	7930	EDUCATIONAL SERVICES	95626	120	643	PERSONAL AND LAUNDRY SERVICES
95360	264	2096	FOOD MANUFACTURING	95473	71	121	PROF.; SCIENTIFIC; & TECH SVCS	95627	74	579	EDUCATIONAL SERVICES
95361	1241	9536	FOOD MANUFACTURING	95476	2080	13158	ACCOMMODATION	95628	2087	8796	FOOD SVCS & DRINKING PLACES
95363	544	4495	FOOD MANUFACTURING	95480	3	3	EDUCATIONAL SERVICES	95629	21	19	POSTAL SERVICE
95364	32	761	ACCOMMODATION	95481	8	21	FOOD SVCS & DRINKING PLACES	95630	2960	24024	FOOD SVCS & DRINKING PLACES
95365	67	570	EDUCATIONAL SERVICES	95482	2080	16264	EDUCATIONAL SERVICES	95631	220	1184	EDUCATIONAL SERVICES
95366	450	4891	FOOD SVCS & DRINKING PLACES	95485	135	548	EDUCATIONAL SERVICES	95632	616	4707	EDUCATIONAL SERVICES
95367	454	3453	FOOD SVCS & DRINKING PLACES	95486	1	2	POSTAL SERVICE	95633	73	198	EDUCATIONAL SERVICES
95368	279	2257	EDUCATIONAL SERVICES	95487	8	109	RELIG.; GRANT; CIVIC; PROF ORG	95634	172	730	EDUCATIONAL SERVICES
95369	30	121	EDUCATIONAL SERVICES	95488	14	22	ACCOMMODATION	95635	38	135	BLDG MATL & GARDEN EQPMT DLRS
95370	1792	13330	HOSPITALS	95490	642	3703	EDUCATIONAL SERVICES	95636	16	45	ACCOMMODATION
95372	42	201	EDUCATIONAL SERVICES	95492	952	6497	FOOD SVCS & DRINKING PLACES	95637	5	36	SUPPORT ACTIVITIES: AGR./FOR.
95373	5	12	MOTOR VEHICLE & PARTS DEALERS	95493	5	38	SPECIAL TRADE CONTRACTORS	95638	53	178	EDUCATIONAL SERVICES
95374	38	283	ANIMAL PRODUCTION	95494	7	14	BEVERAGE & TOBACCO PRODUCT MFG	95639	8	11	CROP PRODUCTION
95375	7	65	UTILITIES	95497	25	212	ACCOMMODATION	95640	199	2893	JUSTICE; PUBIC ORDER/SAFETY
95376	1470	12358	EDUCATIONAL SERVICES	95501	2062	20979	HOSPITALS	95641	147	771	CROP PRODUCTION
95377	359	5576	FOOD AND BEVERAGE STORES	95502	68	138	SOCIAL ASSISTANCE	95642	736	6899	AMUSEMENT; GAMBLING;& RECREAT.
95378	32	64	ADMINISTRATIVE & SUPPORT SVCS	95503	597	5164	MOTOR VEHICLE & PARTS DEALERS	95645	43	142	AIR TRANSPORTATION
95379	108	1008	AMUSEMENT; GAMBLING;& RECREAT.	95511	5	13	SUPPORT ACTIVITIES: AGR./FOR.	95646	25	89	FOOD SVCS & DRINKING PLACES
95380	1872	20816	FOOD MANUFACTURING	95514	3	22	EDUCATIONAL SERVICES	95648	942	9111	AMUSEMENT; GAMBLING;& RECREAT.
95381	40	143	ADMINISTRATIVE & SUPPORT SVCS	95518	35	60	PROF.; SCIENTIFIC; & TECH SVCS	95650	658	4454	SPECIAL TRADE CONTRACTORS
95382	733	7953	EDUCATIONAL SERVICES	95519	484	2729	FOOD SVCS & DRINKING PLACES	95651	40	381	SCENIC & SIGHTSEEING TRANSPORT
95383	247	890	FOOD SVCS & DRINKING PLACES	95521	1115	9305	EDUCATIONAL SERVICES	95652	146	2660	MERCH. WHOLESALERS;DURABLE GDS
95385	17	99	WOOD PRODUCT MANUFACTURING	95524	51	169	EDUCATIONAL SERVICES	95653	19	173	HEAVY & CIVIL ENG. CONSTRUCT'N
95386	203	1240	EDUCATIONAL SERVICES	95525	72	739	AMUSEMENT; GAMBLING;& RECREAT.	95654	10	250	MERCH. WHOLESALERS;DURABLE GDS
95387	61	600	FOOD SVCS & DRINKING PLACES	95526	24	196	EDUCATIONAL SERVICES	95655	102	3228	EXEC.; LEGIS.; & OTHER SUPPORT
95388	134	1050	EDUCATIONAL SERVICES	95527	11	40	EDUCATIONAL SERVICES	95656	21	42	BEVERAGE & TOBACCO PRODUCT MFG
95389	51	690	ACCOMMODATION	95528	21	159	ADMINISTRATIVE & SUPPORT SVCS	95658	273	1211	SPECIAL TRADE CONTRACTORS
95391	34	118	ADMINISTRATIVE & SUPPORT SVCS	95531	895	6398	EDUCATIONAL SERVICES	95659	38	182	EDUCATIONAL SERVICES
95401	2406	19121	FOOD SVCS & DRINKING PLACES	95532	5	0	ADMINISTRATIVE & SUPPORT SVCS	95660	1144	8773	SPECIAL TRADE CONTRACTORS
95402	127	505	POSTAL SERVICE	95534	4	3	AMBULATORY HEALTH CARE SVCS	95661	2699	28016	FOOD SVCS & DRINKING PLACES
95403	2540	27307	EXEC.; LEGIS.; & OTHER SUPPORT	95536	170	623	FOOD SVCS & DRINKING PLACES	95662	1163	4871	EDUCATIONAL SERVICES
95404	2429	18841	MISCELLANEOUS STORE RETAILERS	95537	14	68	CHEMICAL MANUFACTURING	95663	88	355	SPECIAL TRADE CONTRACTORS
95405	916	10897	HOSPITALS	95538	1	2	PROF.; SCIENTIFIC; & TECH SVCS	95664	30	48	JUSTICE; PUBIC ORDER/SAFETY
95406	41	211	SPECIAL TRADE CONTRACTORS	95540	582	4382	EDUCATIONAL SERVICES	95665	252	1158	TELECOMMUNICATIONS
95407	1562	18749	SPECIAL TRADE CONTRACTORS	95542	212	1033	ACCOMMODATION	95666	233	519	FOOD SVCS & DRINKING PLACES
95409	752	3577	NURSING & RESID. CARE FACILIT.	95543	22	161	SUPPORT ACTIVITIES: AGR./FOR.	95667	2078	15247	HOSPITALS
95410	53	199	ACCOMMODATION	95545	4	9	EDUCATIONAL SERVICES	95668	57	924	MERCH. WHOLESALERS;NONDUR. GDS
95412	14	38	EDUCATIONAL SERVICES	95546	113	869	AMBULATORY HEALTH CARE SVCS	95669	131	638	FOOD SVCS & DRINKING PLACES
95415	93	497	EDUCATIONAL SERVICES	95547	30	84	EDUCATIONAL SERVICES	95670	2044	29448	INSURANCE CARRIERS & RELATED
95416	18	45	SPECIAL TRADE CONTRACTORS	95548	68	531	RELIG.; GRANT; CIVIC; PROF ORG	95671	2	200	JUSTICE; PUBIC ORDER/SAFETY
95417	5	258	MERCH. WHOLESALERS;DURABLE GDS	95549	20	50	SUPPORT ACTIVITIES: AGR./FOR.	95672	92	414	EDUCATIONAL SERVICES
95418	13	599	UNCLASSIFIED ESTABLISHMENTS	95550	9	358	MERCH. WHOLESALERS;DURABLE GDS	95673	403	2643	MERCH. WHOLESALERS;DURABLE GDS
95419	9	15	SUPPORT ACT. FOR TRANSPORT.	95551	33	139	RELIG.; GRANT; CIVIC; PROF ORG	95674	23	163	MERCH. WHOLESALERS;NONDUR. GDS
95420	22	35	CONSTRUCTION OF BUILDINGS	95552	14	26	ACCOMMODATION	95675	9	18	UTILITIES
95421	52	283	ACCOMMODATION	95553	28	158	EDUCATIONAL SERVICES	95676	24	185	MERCH. WHOLESALERS;DURABLE GDS
95422	505	3096	HOSPITALS	95554	20	24	ACCOMMODATION	95677	1175	10288	EDUCATIONAL SERVICES
95423	123	1056	CROP PRODUCTION	95555	34	89	FORESTRY AND LOGGING	95678	2152	22763	FOOD SVCS & DRINKING PLACES
95424	4	11	SPECIAL TRADE CONTRACTORS	95556	28	106	SUPPORT ACTIVITIES: AGR./FOR.	95679	2	2	SCENIC & SIGHTSEEING TRANSPORT
95425	405	2626	WOOD PRODUCT MANUFACTURING	95558	31	136	FOOD MANUFACTURING	95680	4	3	PROF.; SCIENTIFIC; & TECH SVCS
95426	78	217	SPORTG GDS;HOBBY;BOOK; & MUSIC	95559	10	23	BLDG MATL & GARDEN EQPMT DLRS	95681	24	77	MERCH. WHOLESALERS;DURABLE GDS
95427	17	49	FABRICATED METAL PRODUCT MFG	95560	108	699	BLDG MATL & GARDEN EQPMT DLRS	95682	1247	6708	FOOD SVCS & DRINKING PLACES
95428	102	475	EDUCATIONAL SERVICES	95562	71	291	EDUCATIONAL SERVICES	95683	205	963	EDUCATIONAL SERVICES
95430	33	94	ACCOMMODATION	95563	13	52	SUPPORT ACTIVITIES: AGR./FOR.	95684	80	277	EDUCATIONAL SERVICES
95431	4	2112	HOSPITALS	95564	17	305	MERCH. WHOLESALERS;NONDUR. GDS	95685	297	1569	ACCOMMODATION
95432	33	131	ACCOMMODATION	95565	28	646	FORESTRY AND LOGGING	95686	26	204	MISCELLANEOUS STORE RETAILERS
95433	10	18	FOOD AND BEVERAGE STORES	95567	73	728	AMUSEMENT; GAMBLING;& RECREAT.	95687	1282	12820	FOOD SVCS & DRINKING PLACES
95435	3	168	MERCH. WHOLESALERS;NONDUR. GDS	95568	11	29	SUPPORT ACTIVITIES: AGR./FOR.	95688	1762	16340	EXEC.; LEGIS.; & OTHER SUPPORT
95436	241	1285	EDUCATIONAL SERVICES	95569	9	19	ACCOMMODATION	95689	53	87	MOTION PICT. & SOUND RECORDING
95437	1005	6669	FOOD SVCS & DRINKING PLACES	95570	108	572	AMUSEMENT; GAMBLING;& RECREAT.	95690	190	993	MERCH. WHOLESALERS;NONDUR. GDS
95439	50	268	FOOD MANUFACTURING	95571	13	104	ADMIN. ENVIRO. QUALITY PROGRMS	95691	1533	18917	MERCH. WHOLESALERS;NONDUR. GDS
95441	140	1168	BEVERAGE & TOBACCO PRODUCT MFG	95573	111	468	FOOD SVCS & DRINKING PLACES	95692	110	958	FOOD AND BEVERAGE STORES
95442	184	763	FOOD SVCS & DRINKING PLACES	95585	24	146	EDUCATIONAL SERVICES	95693	176	377	EDUCATIONAL SERVICES
95443	10	17	SUPPORT ACT. FOR TRANSPORT.	95587	11	24	MISCELLANEOUS STORE RETAILERS	95694	268	2503	FOOD AND BEVERAGE STORES
95444	52	341	BEVERAGE & TOBACCO PRODUCT MFG	95589	53	154	ACCOMMODATION	95695	1547	15626	AMBULATORY HEALTH CARE SVCS
95445	226	776	ACCOMMODATION	95595	8	14	EDUCATIONAL SERVICES	95696	56	122	SPECIAL TRADE CONTRACTORS
95446	249	1583	BEVERAGE & TOBACCO PRODUCT MFG	95601	24	90	FOOD SVCS & DRINKING PLACES	95697	12	122	SUPPORT ACTIVITIES: AGR./FOR.
95448	1357	9034	BEVERAGE & TOBACCO PRODUCT MFG	95602	672	7767	MISCELLANEOUS MANUFACTURING	95698	13	145	HEAVY & CIVIL ENG. CONSTRUCT'N
95449	89	1847	BEVERAGE & TOBACCO PRODUCT MFG	95603	2323	26455	ADMIN. HUMAN RESOURCE PROGRAMS	95699	5	17	ACCOMMODATION
95450	24	123	ACCOMMODATION	95604	84	157	SPECIAL TRADE CONTRACTORS	95701	32	79	EDUCATIONAL SERVICES
95451	416	1930	SUPPORT ACTIVITIES: AGR./FOR.	95605	339	7945	FOOD AND BEVERAGE STORES	95703	52	141	SPECIAL TRADE CONTRACTORS
95452	94	727	BEVERAGE & TOBACCO PRODUCT MFG	95606	7	2509	AMUSEMENT; GAMBLING;& RECREAT.	95709	134	904	WOOD PRODUCT MANUFACTURING
95453	1050	6506	EXEC.; LEGIS.; & OTHER SUPPORT	95607	6	10	FOOD SVCS & DRINKING PLACES	95712	13	24	SPECIAL TRADE CONTRACTORS
95454	111	630	EDUCATIONAL SERVICES	95608	2104	16210	HOSPITALS	95713	274	1425	FOOD SVCS & DRINKING PLACES
95456	41	396	ACCOMMODATION	95609	47	73	ELECTRONICS & APPLIANCE STORES	95714	15	32	FOOD SVCS & DRINKING PLACES

ZIP CODE	2009 Total Firms	2009 Total Employees	TOP INDUSTRY RANKED on 2009 EMPLOYMENT
95715	13	70	ACCOMMODATION
95717	9	55	JUSTICE; PUBIC ORDER/SAFETY
95720	14	27	PERSONAL AND LAUNDRY SERVICES
95721	2	46	ACCOMMODATION
95722	207	578	EDUCATIONAL SERVICES
95724	11	771	ACCOMMODATION
95726	218	1052	FOOD SVCS & DRINKING PLACES
95728	69	1689	ACCOMMODATION
95735	11	752	ACCOMMODATION
95736	20	184	AMBULATORY HEALTH CARE SVCS
95741	31	56	ACCOMMODATION
95742	1379	19812	SPECIAL TRADE CONTRACTORS
95746	576	3418	EDUCATIONAL SERVICES
95747	618	10367	PROF.; SCIENTIFIC; & TECH SVCS
95757	259	2589	MOTOR VEHICLE & PARTS DEALERS
95758	1393	11161	FOOD SVCS & DRINKING PLACES
95759	63	267	OTHER INFORMATION SERVICES
95762	1266	9708	ELECTRONICS & APPLIANCE STORES
95763	52	99	PROF.; SCIENTIFIC; & TECH SVCS
95765	741	9639	MERCH. WHOLESALERS;DURABLE GDS
95776	692	12309	FOOD MANUFACTURING
95798	3	3	PROF.; SCIENTIFIC; & TECH SVCS
95811	1200	16646	JUSTICE; PUBIC ORDER/SAFETY
95812	45	67	PERFORM'G ARTS; SPEC. SPORTS
95813	5	104	POSTAL SERVICE
95814	3528	58054	ADMIN. HUMAN RESOURCE PROGRAMS
95815	2011	26157	FOOD SVCS & DRINKING PLACES
95816	1491	17230	AMBULATORY HEALTH CARE SVCS
95817	453	34064	AMBULATORY HEALTH CARE SVCS
95818	868	6198	FOOD SVCS & DRINKING PLACES
95819	847	14439	HOSPITALS
95820	1019	12327	RELIG.; GRANT; CIVIC; PROF ORG
95821	1938	11729	FOOD SVCS & DRINKING PLACES
95822	1144	9784	EDUCATIONAL SERVICES
95823	2151	16269	EDUCATIONAL SERVICES
95824	650	5730	FOOD MANUFACTURING
95825	3073	29604	HOSPITALS
95826	1612	20538	PROF.; SCIENTIFIC; & TECH SVCS
95827	1347	23873	ADMIN. ENVIRO. QUALITY PROGRMS
95828	1516	16718	SPECIAL TRADE CONTRACTORS
95829	447	3371	EDUCATIONAL SERVICES
95830	17	389	FOOD MANUFACTURING
95831	717	4214	EDUCATIONAL SERVICES
95832	113	1144	EDUCATIONAL SERVICES
95833	874	11297	PROF.; SCIENTIFIC; & TECH SVCS
95834	1266	19804	PROF.; SCIENTIFIC; & TECH SVCS
95835	332	1838	EDUCATIONAL SERVICES
95836	2	27	AIR TRANSPORTATION
95837	66	1594	SUPPORT ACT. FOR TRANSPORT.
95838	784	7870	MERCH. WHOLESALERS;DURABLE GDS
95841	1326	9560	SPECIAL TRADE CONTRACTORS
95842	542	3450	FOOD SVCS & DRINKING PLACES
95843	490	3355	EDUCATIONAL SERVICES
95851	5	19	MERCH. WHOLESALERS;DURABLE GDS
95852	5	18	PROF.; SCIENTIFIC; & TECH SVCS
95853	5	7	FOOD AND BEVERAGE STORES
95860	26	467	AMUSEMENT; GAMBLING;& RECREAT.
95864	664	4848	PROF.; SCIENTIFIC; & TECH SVCS
95865	13	28	ADMIN. ENVIRO. QUALITY PROGRMS
95866	9	70	ADMINISTRATIVE & SUPPORT SVCS
95901	1224	12087	HOSPITALS
95903	61	618	EDUCATIONAL SERVICES
95910	10	24	MINING (EXCEPT OIL AND GAS)
95912	124	1144	TRUCK TRANSPORTATION
95913	15	85	CROP PRODUCTION
95914	23	39	CONSTRUCTION OF BUILDINGS
95915	3	12	SUPPORT ACTIVITIES: AGR./FOR.
95916	37	134	EDUCATIONAL SERVICES
95917	92	691	EDUCATIONAL SERVICES
95918	57	158	EDUCATIONAL SERVICES
95919	63	155	CREDIT INTERMEDIATION & RELATD
95920	13	69	ADMINISTRATIVE & SUPPORT SVCS
95922	27	157	SUPPORT ACTIVITIES: AGR./FOR.
95923	13	32	ACCOMMODATION
95924	32	60	CONSTRUCTION OF BUILDINGS
95925	14	146	EDUCATIONAL SERVICES
95926	2132	18689	HOSPITALS
95927	133	229	PROF.; SCIENTIFIC; & TECH SVCS
95928	2422	21154	FOOD SVCS & DRINKING PLACES
95929	11	2427	EDUCATIONAL SERVICES
95930	11	13	MERCH. WHOLESALERS;DURABLE GDS
95932	447	3536	AMUSEMENT; GAMBLING;& RECREAT.
95934	15	56	FORESTRY AND LOGGING
95935	15	106	EDUCATIONAL SERVICES
95936	74	281	EXEC.; LEGIS.; & OTHER SUPPORT
95937	126	233	FOOD SVCS & DRINKING PLACES
95938	183	1082	MERCH. WHOLESALERS;NONDUR. GDS
95939	25	115	EDUCATIONAL SERVICES
95941	6	43	MUSEUMS; HIST. SITES;& SIMILAR
95942	50	101	EDUCATIONAL SERVICES

ZIP CODE	2009 Total Firms	2009 Total Employees	TOP INDUSTRY RANKED on 2009 EMPLOYMENT
95943	48	475	RELIG.; GRANT; CIVIC; PROF ORG
95944	3	4	POSTAL SERVICE
95945	2467	14673	HOSPITALS
95946	411	1317	EDUCATIONAL SERVICES
95947	110	406	AMBULATORY HEALTH CARE SVCS
95948	429	3701	MERCH. WHOLESALERS;NONDUR. GDS
95949	835	3533	EDUCATIONAL SERVICES
95950	15	63	EXEC.; LEGIS.; & OTHER SUPPORT
95951	53	391	EDUCATIONAL SERVICES
95953	186	1607	EDUCATIONAL SERVICES
95954	263	864	EDUCATIONAL SERVICES
95955	54	329	FOOD MANUFACTURING
95956	12	20	EDUCATIONAL SERVICES
95957	37	189	SUPPORT ACTIVITIES: AGR./FOR.
95958	6	21	SUPPORT ACTIVITIES: AGR./FOR.
95959	1326	6803	EDUCATIONAL SERVICES
95960	43	57	GASOLINE STATIONS
95961	236	3211	EDUCATIONAL SERVICES
95962	59	309	ACCOMMODATION
95963	560	3263	EDUCATIONAL SERVICES
95965	1041	10413	FOOD MANUFACTURING
95966	915	6228	AMUSEMENT; GAMBLING;& RECREAT.
95967	38	53	SPECIAL TRADE CONTRACTORS
95968	33	129	EDUCATIONAL SERVICES
95969	1369	7943	HOSPITALS
95970	25	155	SPECIAL TRADE CONTRACTORS
95971	492	3877	EXEC.; LEGIS.; & OTHER SUPPORT
95972	4	7	RELIG.; GRANT; CIVIC; PROF ORG
95973	1374	10050	PROF.; SCIENTIFIC; & TECH SVCS
95974	3	3	EXEC.; LEGIS.; & OTHER SUPPORT
95975	82	200	PROF.; SCIENTIFIC; & TECH SVCS
95977	38	105	SUPPORT ACTIVITIES: AGR./FOR.
95978	8	7	POSTAL SERVICE
95979	22	105	SUPPORT ACTIVITIES: AGR./FOR.
95980	4	7	ADMIN. OF ECONOMIC PROGRAMS
95981	15	56	MERCH. WHOLESALERS;DURABLE GDS
95982	71	473	EDUCATIONAL SERVICES
95983	18	41	ANIMAL PRODUCTION
95984	6	6	FOOD AND BEVERAGE STORES
95986	13	16	ACCOMMODATION
95987	199	1952	FOOD SVCS & DRINKING PLACES
95988	470	4534	EXEC.; LEGIS.; & OTHER SUPPORT
95991	1926	19657	AMBULATORY HEALTH CARE SVCS
95992	36	88	ADMINISTRATIVE & SUPPORT SVCS
95993	940	10269	PROF.; SCIENTIFIC; & TECH SVCS
96001	2455	22095	HOSPITALS
96002	2286	16446	PROF.; SCIENTIFIC; & TECH SVCS
96003	1668	17611	EDUCATIONAL SERVICES
96006	23	115	EXEC.; LEGIS.; & OTHER SUPPORT
96007	982	6031	EDUCATIONAL SERVICES
96008	58	239	EDUCATIONAL SERVICES
96009	48	346	EDUCATIONAL SERVICES
96010	9	75	SUPPORT ACTIVITIES: AGR./FOR.
96011	5	11	EDUCATIONAL SERVICES
96013	233	1885	EDUCATIONAL SERVICES
96014	10	390	AMUSEMENT; GAMBLING;& RECREAT.
96015	22	137	NURSING & RESID. CARE FACILIT.
96016	14	88	TRUCK TRANSPORTATION
96017	11	103	EDUCATIONAL SERVICES
96019	304	1887	EDUCATIONAL SERVICES
96020	258	1422	WOOD PRODUCT MANUFACTURING
96021	504	4841	WOOD PRODUCT MANUFACTURING
96022	418	2859	FOOD AND BEVERAGE STORES
96023	54	262	WOOD PRODUCT MANUFACTURING
96024	19	49	EDUCATIONAL SERVICES
96025	120	810	RAIL TRANSPORTATION
96027	140	446	ACCOMMODATION
96028	106	709	HOSPITALS
96029	4	10	EDUCATIONAL SERVICES
96031	5	11	EDUCATIONAL SERVICES
96032	151	544	EDUCATIONAL SERVICES
96033	14	126	ACCOMMODATION
96034	10	23	EDUCATIONAL SERVICES
96035	68	580	HEAVY & CIVIL ENG. CONSTRUCT'N
96037	7	16	MERCH. WHOLESALERS;NONDUR. GDS
96038	20	89	NURSING & RESID. CARE FACILIT.
96039	85	388	SUPPORT ACTIVITIES: AGR./FOR.
96040	16	53	SUPPORT ACTIVITIES: AGR./FOR.
96041	105	531	EDUCATIONAL SERVICES
96044	35	206	ANIMAL PRODUCTION
96046	10	18	PERSONAL AND LAUNDRY SERVICES
96047	23	73	EDUCATIONAL SERVICES
96048	16	53	MERCH. WHOLESALERS;DURABLE GDS
96049	56	95	WASTE MANAGMT & REMEDIAT'N SVC
96050	28	59	JUSTICE; PUBIC ORDER/SAFETY
96051	68	318	EDUCATIONAL SERVICES
96052	69	148	ACCOMMODATION
96054	8	17	ANIMAL PRODUCTION
96055	123	540	FOOD AND BEVERAGE STORES
96056	61	188	EDUCATIONAL SERVICES

ZIP CODE	2009 Total Firms	2009 Total Employees	TOP INDUSTRY RANKED on 2009 EMPLOYMENT
96057	89	430	EXEC.; LEGIS.; & OTHER SUPPORT
96058	32	204	ADMIN. OF ECONOMIC PROGRAMS
96059	23	68	PERSONAL AND LAUNDRY SERVICES
96061	6	12	ACCOMMODATION
96062	31	96	EDUCATIONAL SERVICES
96063	10	34	SUPPORT ACTIVITIES: AGR./FOR.
96064	110	332	EDUCATIONAL SERVICES
96065	12	28	EDUCATIONAL SERVICES
96067	599	13072	ADMINISTRATIVE & SUPPORT SVCS
96068	7	4	POSTAL SERVICE
96069	24	72	EDUCATIONAL SERVICES
96070	2	60	SCENIC & SIGHTSEEING TRANSPORT
96071	12	37	ACCOMMODATION
96073	219	916	EDUCATIONAL SERVICES
96074	11	88	JUSTICE; PUBIC ORDER/SAFETY
96075	10	49	JUSTICE; PUBIC ORDER/SAFETY
96076	2	2	SPECIAL TRADE CONTRACTORS
96078	6	7	POSTAL SERVICE
96079	6	6	AMUSEMENT; GAMBLING;& RECREAT.
96080	1481	13345	MERCH. WHOLESALERS;DURABLE GDS
96084	8	55	AMBULATORY HEALTH CARE SVCS
96085	3	4	EXEC.; LEGIS.; & OTHER SUPPORT
96086	9	23	EDUCATIONAL SERVICES
96087	40	132	EDUCATIONAL SERVICES
96088	135	428	EDUCATIONAL SERVICES
96089	6	9	NURSING & RESID. CARE FACILIT.
96090	13	9	POSTAL SERVICE
96091	29	223	ACCOMMODATION
96092	23	163	ANIMAL PRODUCTION
96093	380	2809	EXEC.; LEGIS.; & OTHER SUPPORT
96094	253	1686	EDUCATIONAL SERVICES
96095	4	175	EXEC.; LEGIS.; & OTHER SUPPORT
96096	22	56	SUPPORT ACTIVITIES: AGR./FOR.
96097	777	5999	JUSTICE; PUBIC ORDER/SAFETY
96099	55	120	PROF.; SCIENTIFIC; & TECH SVCS
96101	429	2803	EXEC.; LEGIS.; & OTHER SUPPORT
96103	175	782	FOOD SVCS & DRINKING PLACES
96104	77	260	HOSPITALS
96105	22	57	FOOD SVCS & DRINKING PLACES
96106	24	178	ACCOMMODATION
96107	34	68	FOOD AND BEVERAGE STORES
96108	2	4	POSTAL SERVICE
96109	32	129	EDUCATIONAL SERVICES
96110	7	20	ANIMAL PRODUCTION
96112	9	10	AMBULATORY HEALTH CARE SVCS
96113	35	697	NAT'L SECURITY & INT'L AFFAIRS
96114	69	296	EDUCATIONAL SERVICES
96115	5	6	POSTAL SERVICE
96116	11	57	JUSTICE; PUBIC ORDER/SAFETY
96117	12	70	EDUCATIONAL SERVICES
96118	74	620	HOSPITALS
96119	6	5	POSTAL SERVICE
96120	77	329	EDUCATIONAL SERVICES
96121	7	22	UTILITIES
96122	266	1350	AMBULATORY HEALTH CARE SVCS
96123	11	56	JUSTICE; PUBIC ORDER/SAFETY
96124	14	27	ACCOMMODATION
96125	36	115	ACCOMMODATION
96126	30	155	SUPPORT ACTIVITIES: AGR./FOR.
96127	5	14	CONSTRUCTION OF BUILDINGS
96128	19	74	SUPPORT ACTIVITIES: AGR./FOR.
96129	37	131	PROF.; SCIENTIFIC; & TECH SVCS
96130	876	6935	EDUCATIONAL SERVICES
96132	1	0	JUSTICE; PUBIC ORDER/SAFETY
96133	6	16	SUPPORT ACTIVITIES: AGR./FOR.
96134	136	886	MERCH. WHOLESALERS;NONDUR. GDS
96135	2	3	ANIMAL PRODUCTION
96136	2	26	UTILITIES
96137	233	651	EDUCATIONAL SERVICES
96140	89	445	FOOD SVCS & DRINKING PLACES
96141	63	524	ACCOMMODATION
96142	67	255	MUSEUMS; HIST. SITES;& SIMILAR
96143	312	1237	FOOD SVCS & DRINKING PLACES
96145	736	4061	FOOD SVCS & DRINKING PLACES
96146	141	2453	ACCOMMODATION
96148	104	447	FOOD SVCS & DRINKING PLACES
96150	1827	17248	ACCOMMODATION
96151	41	143	MOTION PICT. & SOUND RECORDING
96152	2	5	INSURANCE CARRIERS & RELATED
96154	2	4	PROF.; SCIENTIFIC; & TECH SVCS
96155	9	8	ADMINISTRATIVE & SUPPORT SVCS
96156	15	19	CONSTRUCTION OF BUILDINGS
96158	41	56	ADMINISTRATIVE & SUPPORT SVCS
96160	74	170	ACCOMMODATION
96161	1560	9882	ACCOMMODATION
96162	47	76	CONSTRUCTION OF BUILDINGS
96701	1798	18934	FOOD SVCS & DRINKING PLACES
96703	27	122	CONSTRUCTION OF BUILDINGS
96704	153	854	CROP PRODUCTION
96705	54	670	MERCH. WHOLESALERS;NONDUR. GDS

BUSINESS DATA

ZIP CODE	2009 Total Firms	2009 Total Employees	TOP INDUSTRY RANKED on 2009 EMPLOYMENT	ZIP CODE	2009 Total Firms	2009 Total Employees	TOP INDUSTRY RANKED on 2009 EMPLOYMENT	ZIP CODE	2009 Total Firms	2009 Total Employees	TOP INDUSTRY RANKED on 2009 EMPLOYMENT
96706	463	4512	EDUCATIONAL SERVICES	96808	10	8	ADMINISTRATIVE & SUPPORT SVCS	97065	48	294	FOOD SVCS & DRINKING PLACES
96707	816	15337	MERCH. WHOLESALERS;DURABLE GDS	96809	10	38	MERCH. WHOLESALERS;DURABLE GDS	97067	126	640	ACCOMMODATION
96708	307	751	EDUCATIONAL SERVICES	96810	7	2	FOOD AND BEVERAGE STORES	97068	775	4700	EDUCATIONAL SERVICES
96709	22	51	PERFORM'G ARTS; SPEC. SPORTS	96812	12	15	INSURANCE CARRIERS & RELATED	97070	1031	19348	MERCH. WHOLESALERS;DURABLE GDS
96710	9	49	CROP PRODUCTION	96813	5246	66295	PROF.; SCIENTIFIC; & TECH SVCS	97071	933	11430	FOOD AND BEVERAGE STORES
96712	341	2028	FOOD SVCS & DRINKING PLACES	96814	3533	36737	FOOD SVCS & DRINKING PLACES	97075	68	146	SPECIAL TRADE CONTRACTORS
96713	108	1074	ACCOMMODATION	96815	2488	36852	ACCOMMODATION	97077	3	15	GENERAL MERCHANDISE STORES
96714	206	865	FOOD SVCS & DRINKING PLACES	96816	1763	14697	FOOD SVCS & DRINKING PLACES	97080	563	5198	EDUCATIONAL SERVICES
96715	7	4	AMUSEMENT; GAMBLING;& RECREAT.	96817	3024	36643	AMBULATORY HEALTH CARE SVCS	97086	718	7179	GENERAL MERCHANDISE STORES
96716	127	496	FOOD SVCS & DRINKING PLACES	96818	466	4916	EDUCATIONAL SERVICES	97089	291	1429	SPECIAL TRADE CONTRACTORS
96717	93	545	ADMINISTRATIVE & SUPPORT SVCS	96819	3135	57050	MERCH. WHOLESALERS;DURABLE GDS	97101	104	584	EDUCATIONAL SERVICES
96718	6	147	ACCOMMODATION	96820	57	168	MERCH. WHOLESALERS;DURABLE GDS	97102	9	15	ACCOMMODATION
96719	75	495	CONSTRUCTION OF BUILDINGS	96821	321	2087	NURSING & RESID. CARE FACILIT.	97103	1054	6961	FOOD SVCS & DRINKING PLACES
96720	2923	27515	FOOD SVCS & DRINKING PLACES	96822	695	7379	EDUCATIONAL SERVICES	97106	147	717	EDUCATIONAL SERVICES
96721	31	50	PROF.; SCIENTIFIC; & TECH SVCS	96823	53	93	PROF.; SCIENTIFIC; & TECH SVCS	97107	21	104	MERCH. WHOLESALERS;NONDUR. GDS
96722	146	1936	ACCOMMODATION	96824	36	72	PERSONAL AND LAUNDRY SERVICES	97108	17	56	EDUCATIONAL SERVICES
96725	121	447	EDUCATIONAL SERVICES	96825	786	4825	FOOD SVCS & DRINKING PLACES	97109	10	41	EDUCATIONAL SERVICES
96726	45	107	CROP PRODUCTION	96826	1401	10944	HOSPITALS	97110	252	1581	FOOD SVCS & DRINKING PLACES
96727	197	879	EDUCATIONAL SERVICES	96827	9	30	PUBLISHING INDUSTRIES	97111	120	509	FOOD AND BEVERAGE STORES
96728	24	39	TELECOMMUNICATIONS	96828	21	23	PERSONAL AND LAUNDRY SERVICES	97112	98	279	EDUCATIONAL SERVICES
96729	30	308	EDUCATIONAL SERVICES	96830	56	124	TRANSIT & GRND PASS. TRANSPORT	97113	300	3500	FOOD MANUFACTURING
96730	18	54	EDUCATIONAL SERVICES	96836	8	6	RELIG.; GRANT; CIVIC; PROF ORG	97114	134	1539	MERCH. WHOLESALERS;NONDUR. GDS
96731	82	1632	ACCOMMODATION	96837	10	19	MERCH. WHOLESALERS;DURABLE GDS	97115	118	505	BEVERAGE & TOBACCO PRODUCT MFG
96732	1523	17768	GENERAL MERCHANDISE STORES	96839	43	48	PROF.; SCIENTIFIC; & TECH SVCS	97116	707	6328	NURSING & RESID. CARE FACILIT.
96733	52	135	PERFORM'G ARTS; SPEC. SPORTS	96843	1	0	COMPUTER & ELECTRONIC PROD MFG	97117	18	63	EDUCATIONAL SERVICES
96734	1630	11643	EDUCATIONAL SERVICES	96848	3	60	UNCLASSIFIED ESTABLISHMENTS	97118	32	209	WOOD PRODUCT MANUFACTURING
96737	47	145	FOOD SVCS & DRINKING PLACES	96850	100	966	JUSTICE; PUBIC ORDER/SAFETY	97119	122	867	WOOD PRODUCT MANUFACTURING
96738	285	3405	ACCOMMODATION	96853	42	379	ACCOMMODATION	97121	46	413	FOOD MANUFACTURING
96739	50	79	SPECIAL TRADE CONTRACTORS	96854	11	228	NAT'L SECURITY & INT'L AFFAIRS	97122	18	113	SUPPORT ACTIVITIES: AGR./FOR.
96740	2615	18183	ACCOMMODATION	96857	33	23881	CREDIT INTERMEDIATION & RELATD	97123	1662	15656	HOSPITALS
96741	179	848	MUSEUMS; HIST. SITES;& SIMILAR	96858	18	74	CREDIT INTERMEDIATION & RELATD	97124	1538	29578	PROF.; SCIENTIFIC; & TECH SVCS
96742	7	48	EXEC.; LEGIS.; & OTHER SUPPORT	96859	11	2937	HOSPITALS	97125	7	20	SPECIAL TRADE CONTRACTORS
96743	847	8726	ACCOMMODATION	96860	53	523	TRANSPORTATION EQUIPMENT MFG	97127	62	282	EDUCATIONAL SERVICES
96744	1418	10754	EDUCATIONAL SERVICES	96861	13	19	NAT'L SECURITY & INT'L AFFAIRS	97128	1390	15479	EDUCATIONAL SERVICES
96745	170	552	SPECIAL TRADE CONTRACTORS	96863	17	114	PERSONAL AND LAUNDRY SERVICES	97130	98	321	REAL ESTATE
96746	829	5516	FOOD SVCS & DRINKING PLACES	97001	10	61	ACCOMMODATION	97131	152	453	AMUSEMENT; GAMBLING;& RECREAT.
96747	10	50	FOOD AND BEVERAGE STORES	97002	364	4608	SUPPORT ACT. FOR TRANSPORT.	97132	1062	10886	MERCH. WHOLESALERS;DURABLE GDS
96748	240	1575	HOSPITALS	97004	174	677	MISCELLANEOUS STORE RETAILERS	97133	191	1519	AMUSEMENT; GAMBLING;& RECREAT.
96749	355	3183	EDUCATIONAL SERVICES	97005	2261	27912	LEATHER & ALLIED PRODUCT MFG	97134	3	2	POSTAL SERVICE
96750	302	2104	HOSPITALS	97006	1449	19099	EDUCATIONAL SERVICES	97135	79	350	FOOD SVCS & DRINKING PLACES
96751	6	9	PERSONAL AND LAUNDRY SERVICES	97007	1000	5805	EDUCATIONAL SERVICES	97136	51	191	EDUCATIONAL SERVICES
96752	55	369	EDUCATIONAL SERVICES	97008	881	10804	PROF.; SCIENTIFIC; & TECH SVCS	97137	103	1007	CROP PRODUCTION
96753	1652	14316	ACCOMMODATION	97009	364	3155	BLDG MATL & GARDEN EQPMT DLRS	97138	840	5356	FOOD SVCS & DRINKING PLACES
96754	199	600	EDUCATIONAL SERVICES	97010	4	83	FOOD SVCS & DRINKING PLACES	97140	754	6217	MERCH. WHOLESALERS;DURABLE GDS
96755	149	621	EDUCATIONAL SERVICES	97011	26	32	PETROLEUM & COAL PRODUCTS MFG	97141	266	2460	FOOD MANUFACTURING
96756	315	5406	ACCOMMODATION	97013	912	6803	BLDG MATL & GARDEN EQPMT DLRS	97143	2	1	UNCLASSIFIED ESTABLISHMENTS
96757	33	211	FOOD AND BEVERAGE STORES	97014	59	669	ADMIN. ENVIRO. QUALITY PROGRMS	97144	5	4	SPECIAL TRADE CONTRACTORS
96759	18	198	PROF.; SCIENTIFIC; & TECH SVCS	97015	1564	25907	AMBULATORY HEALTH CARE SVCS	97145	9	77	ACCOMMODATION
96760	53	466	BLDG MATL & GARDEN EQPMT DLRS	97016	202	2537	PAPER MANUFACTURING	97146	327	3076	HEALTH & PERSONAL CARE STORES
96761	1689	18823	ACCOMMODATION	97017	104	263	EDUCATIONAL SERVICES	97147	45	168	NURSING & RESID. CARE FACILIT.
96762	78	1976	MUSEUMS; HIST. SITES;& SIMILAR	97018	31	146	EDUCATIONAL SERVICES	97148	107	877	MERCH. WHOLESALERS;NONDUR. GDS
96763	125	2121	ACCOMMODATION	97019	77	432	ACCOMMODATION	97149	23	67	FOOD SVCS & DRINKING PLACES
96764	25	150	EDUCATIONAL SERVICES	97020	33	261	MACHINERY MANUFACTURING	97201	1287	19131	PROF.; SCIENTIFIC; & TECH SVCS
96765	40	143	FOOD SVCS & DRINKING PLACES	97021	52	209	MERCH. WHOLESALERS;NONDUR. GDS	97202	1690	19043	FOOD AND BEVERAGE STORES
96766	1467	14436	AMBULATORY HEALTH CARE SVCS	97022	63	349	PRIMARY METAL MANUFACTURING	97203	740	12337	PRIMARY METAL MANUFACTURING
96767	18	32	PUBLISHING INDUSTRIES	97023	387	1793	EDUCATIONAL SERVICES	97204	2413	33763	PROF.; SCIENTIFIC; & TECH SVCS
96768	584	2911	EDUCATIONAL SERVICES	97024	204	4092	FOOD MANUFACTURING	97205	1639	16643	PROF.; SCIENTIFIC; & TECH SVCS
96769	3	5	POSTAL SERVICE	97026	91	513	EDUCATIONAL SERVICES	97206	1278	8794	PRIMARY METAL MANUFACTURING
96770	29	39	REAL ESTATE	97027	360	3592	MOTOR VEHICLE & PARTS DEALERS	97207	62	63	PROF.; SCIENTIFIC; & TECH SVCS
96771	81	277	EDUCATIONAL SERVICES	97028	60	1473	ACCOMMODATION	97208	33	3092	POSTAL SERVICE
96772	117	343	EDUCATIONAL SERVICES	97029	22	53	EDUCATIONAL SERVICES	97209	1949	25198	AMBULATORY HEALTH CARE SVCS
96773	1	1	POSTAL SERVICE	97030	1725	14182	FOOD SVCS & DRINKING PLACES	97210	1405	23096	HOSPITALS
96774	5	11	MERCH. WHOLESALERS;DURABLE GDS	97031	1201	9860	MERCH. WHOLESALERS;NONDUR. GDS	97211	1107	12913	FOOD SVCS & DRINKING PLACES
96776	39	158	EDUCATIONAL SERVICES	97032	197	1472	MERCH. WHOLESALERS;NONDUR. GDS	97212	732	3922	EDUCATIONAL SERVICES
96777	46	277	EDUCATIONAL SERVICES	97033	4	3	SUPPORT ACT. FOR TRANSPORT.	97213	1228	14023	HOSPITALS
96778	268	1365	EDUCATIONAL SERVICES	97034	711	5154	EDUCATIONAL SERVICES	97214	2435	23999	EDUCATIONAL SERVICES
96779	209	1241	FOOD SVCS & DRINKING PLACES	97035	1815	15586	PROF.; SCIENTIFIC; & TECH SVCS	97215	459	2928	FOOD SVCS & DRINKING PLACES
96780	7	6	TRUCK TRANSPORTATION	97036	21	171	EDUCATIONAL SERVICES	97216	708	9175	HOSPITALS
96781	99	233	EDUCATIONAL SERVICES	97037	81	571	ACCOMMODATION	97217	1582	26404	TRUCK TRANSPORTATION
96782	840	9699	GENERAL MERCHANDISE STORES	97038	594	4421	CROP PRODUCTION	97218	658	10641	JUSTICE; PUBIC ORDER/SAFETY
96783	14	45	ADMINISTRATIVE & SUPPORT SVCS	97039	54	129	EXEC.; LEGIS.; & OTHER SUPPORT	97219	2043	12430	EDUCATIONAL SERVICES
96784	74	742	MERCH. WHOLESALERS;DURABLE GDS	97040	33	350	CROP PRODUCTION	97220	1667	17489	FOOD SVCS & DRINKING PLACES
96785	94	348	FOOD SVCS & DRINKING PLACES	97041	108	1388	ACCOMMODATION	97221	540	3779	ADMINISTRATIVE & SUPPORT SVCS
96786	581	5143	EDUCATIONAL SERVICES	97042	101	430	COMPUTER & ELECTRONIC PROD MFG	97222	1359	19974	BLDG MATL & GARDEN EQPMT DLRS
96788	28	147	ADMINISTRATIVE & SUPPORT SVCS	97044	15	20	HEAVY & CIVIL ENG. CONSTRUCT'N	97223	2934	27683	PROF.; SCIENTIFIC; & TECH SVCS
96789	637	5930	FOOD SVCS & DRINKING PLACES	97045	2229	17026	EDUCATIONAL SERVICES	97224	1181	15334	PROF.; SCIENTIFIC; & TECH SVCS
96790	298	1264	HOSPITALS	97048	202	1041	EDUCATIONAL SERVICES	97225	1654	19511	HOSPITALS
96791	126	716	EDUCATIONAL SERVICES	97049	34	316	ACCOMMODATION	97227	495	15274	AMBULATORY HEALTH CARE SVCS
96792	580	5604	EDUCATIONAL SERVICES	97050	19	62	FOOD SVCS & DRINKING PLACES	97228	27	32	PROF.; SCIENTIFIC; & TECH SVCS
96793	1823	15845	REAL ESTATE	97051	603	4423	PAPER MANUFACTURING	97229	916	6500	EDUCATIONAL SERVICES
96795	229	1784	EDUCATIONAL SERVICES	97053	78	371	PLASTICS & RUBBER PRODUCTS MFG	97230	1304	23579	TRANSPORTATION EQUIPMENT MFG
96796	127	1504	HOSPITALS	97054	23	172	CHEMICAL MANUFACTURING	97231	177	871	MERCH. WHOLESALERS;NONDUR. GDS
96797	1617	18059	FOOD SVCS & DRINKING PLACES	97055	608	3796	FOOD SVCS & DRINKING PLACES	97232	1723	27266	PROF.; SCIENTIFIC; & TECH SVCS
96801	12	68	PROF.; SCIENTIFIC; & TECH SVCS	97056	418	2506	FOOD SVCS & DRINKING PLACES	97233	775	6285	EXEC.; LEGIS.; & OTHER SUPPORT
96802	2	5	SOCIAL ASSISTANCE	97057	5	4	POSTAL SERVICE	97236	730	4375	EDUCATIONAL SERVICES
96803	3	8	PERSONAL AND LAUNDRY SERVICES	97058	1037	8074	HOSPITALS	97238	21	280	ADMINISTRATIVE & SUPPORT SVCS
96804	7	2	SPECIAL TRADE CONTRACTORS	97060	606	9164	GENERAL MERCHANDISE STORES	97239	1161	55868	AMBULATORY HEALTH CARE SVCS
96805	6	0	SPECIAL TRADE CONTRACTORS	97062	1343	18372	FABRICATED METAL PRODUCT MFG	97240	10	6	REPAIR AND MAINTENANCE
96806	5	9	INSURANCE CARRIERS & RELATED	97063	63	144	SPECIAL TRADE CONTRACTORS	97242	14	42	SOCIAL ASSISTANCE
96807	5	12	RELIG.; GRANT; CIVIC; PROF ORG	97064	124	532	EDUCATIONAL SERVICES	97258	76	690	PROF.; SCIENTIFIC; & TECH SVCS

ZIP CODE	2009 Total Firms	2009 Total Employ-ees	TOP INDUSTRY RANKED on 2009 EMPLOYMENT	ZIP CODE	2009 Total Firms	2009 Total Employ-ees	TOP INDUSTRY RANKED on 2009 EMPLOYMENT	ZIP CODE	2009 Total Firms	2009 Total Employ-ees	TOP INDUSTRY RANKED on 2009 EMPLOYMENT
97266	974	7099	GENERAL MERCHANDISE STORES	97402	3047	36154	MERCH. WHOLESALERS;DURABLE GDS	97523	321	1520	EDUCATIONAL SERVICES
97267	853	7044	PROF.; SCIENTIFIC; & TECH SVCS	97403	352	5011	MERCH. WHOLESALERS;DURABLE GDS	97524	389	1437	EDUCATIONAL SERVICES
97268	26	43	MISCELLANEOUS STORE RETAILERS	97404	772	4976	EDUCATIONAL SERVICES	97525	155	778	GENERAL MERCHANDISE STORES
97269	20	927	UNCLASSIFIED ESTABLISHMENTS	97405	1054	8734	PERFORM'G ARTS; SPEC. SPORTS	97526	2308	17182	FOOD SVCS & DRINKING PLACES
97280	48	119	TELECOMMUNICATIONS	97406	11	37	FOOD AND BEVERAGE STORES	97527	1051	6343	HOSPITALS
97281	63	136	PROF.; SCIENTIFIC; & TECH SVCS	97407	3	2	POSTAL SERVICE	97528	56	161	ADMINISTRATIVE & SUPPORT SVCS
97282	24	59	JUSTICE; PUBIC ORDER/SAFETY	97408	492	11695	TRANSPORTATION EQUIPMENT MFG	97530	344	1409	SPECIAL TRADE CONTRACTORS
97283	10	16	CONSTRUCTION OF BUILDINGS	97409	6	28	BLDG MATL & GARDEN EQPMT DLRS	97531	28	74	TRANSPORTATION EQUIPMENT MFG
97286	17	34	ADMINISTRATIVE & SUPPORT SVCS	97410	21	52	FOOD SVCS & DRINKING PLACES	97532	123	664	MOTOR VEHICLE & PARTS DEALERS
97290	33	58	ADMINISTRATIVE & SUPPORT SVCS	97411	424	2592	AMUSEMENT; GAMBLING;& RECREAT.	97533	15	24	CONSTRUCTION OF BUILDINGS
97291	18	36	ADMINISTRATIVE & SUPPORT SVCS	97412	17	118	MISCELLANEOUS MANUFACTURING	97534	14	22	FOOD SVCS & DRINKING PLACES
97292	41	78	AMBULATORY HEALTH CARE SVCS	97413	65	350	FOOD SVCS & DRINKING PLACES	97535	227	1621	EDUCATIONAL SERVICES
97293	21	32	SOCIAL ASSISTANCE	97414	6	38	WOOD PRODUCT MANUFACTURING	97536	41	311	EDUCATIONAL SERVICES
97294	36	52	SPECIAL TRADE CONTRACTORS	97415	790	4674	MERCH. WHOLESALERS;DURABLE GDS	97537	229	917	EDUCATIONAL SERVICES
97296	18	466	SPORTG GDS;HOBBY;BOOK; & MUSIC	97416	20	153	FORESTRY AND LOGGING	97538	63	159	FOOD AND BEVERAGE STORES
97298	43	71	CONSTRUCTION OF BUILDINGS	97417	111	1510	ACCOMMODATION	97539	146	415	FOOD SVCS & DRINKING PLACES
97301	3424	48457	AMBULATORY HEALTH CARE SVCS	97419	31	73	ACCOMMODATION	97540	246	1249	GENERAL MERCHANDISE STORES
97302	2037	21219	FOOD SVCS & DRINKING PLACES	97420	1222	12168	PROF.; SCIENTIFIC; & TECH SVCS	97541	32	111	ADMIN. ENVIRO. QUALITY PROGRMS
97303	952	7775	FOOD SVCS & DRINKING PLACES	97423	346	1869	WOOD PRODUCT MANUFACTURING	97543	29	58	FOOD SVCS & DRINKING PLACES
97304	632	4561	EDUCATIONAL SERVICES	97424	710	5032	BLDG MATL & GARDEN EQPMT DLRS	97544	62	260	CHEMICAL MANUFACTURING
97305	1020	12106	EDUCATIONAL SERVICES	97425	11	32	ACCOMMODATION	97601	1201	11641	HEALTH & PERSONAL CARE STORES
97306	437	3186	CROP PRODUCTION	97426	311	1558	FOOD MANUFACTURING	97602	7	8	SPECIAL TRADE CONTRACTORS
97307	40	104	PROF.; SCIENTIFIC; & TECH SVCS	97427	6	7	SPECIAL TRADE CONTRACTORS	97603	1134	10116	FOOD SVCS & DRINKING PLACES
97308	33	86	ADMINISTRATIVE & SUPPORT SVCS	97429	29	227	FURNITURE & RELATED PROD. MFG	97604	12	23	EXEC.; LEGIS.; & OTHER SUPPORT
97309	36	45	CONSTRUCTION OF BUILDINGS	97430	11	23	FORESTRY AND LOGGING	97620	6	23	EDUCATIONAL SERVICES
97310	85	9489	EXEC.; LEGIS.; & OTHER SUPPORT	97431	53	229	FORESTRY AND LOGGING	97621	6	14	MISCELLANEOUS MANUFACTURING
97311	2	2	FOOD SVCS & DRINKING PLACES	97432	11	3821	FORESTRY AND LOGGING	97622	17	83	ADMIN. OF ECONOMIC PROGRAMS
97312	1	850	INSURANCE CARRIERS & RELATED	97434	11	39	EDUCATIONAL SERVICES	97623	59	234	EDUCATIONAL SERVICES
97313	1	560	INSURANCE CARRIERS & RELATED	97435	114	1189	SPECIAL TRADE CONTRACTORS	97624	99	1470	BLDG MATL & GARDEN EQPMT DLRS
97314	2	1000	ADMIN. OF ECONOMIC PROGRAMS	97436	45	275	EXEC.; LEGIS.; & OTHER SUPPORT	97625	8	13	FOOD SVCS & DRINKING PLACES
97317	478	5696	OTHER INFORMATION SERVICES	97437	60	276	EDUCATIONAL SERVICES	97626	15	20	ACCOMMODATION
97321	1247	13618	EDUCATIONAL SERVICES	97438	25	305	RELIG.; GRANT; CIVIC; PROF ORG	97627	26	81	EDUCATIONAL SERVICES
97322	956	12140	FOOD SVCS & DRINKING PLACES	97439	733	5122	AMBULATORY HEALTH CARE SVCS	97630	331	1714	WOOD PRODUCT MANUFACTURING
97324	35	134	EDUCATIONAL SERVICES	97440	50	137	PERFORM'G ARTS; SPEC. SPORTS	97632	47	277	SOCIAL ASSISTANCE
97325	147	981	CONSTRUCTION OF BUILDINGS	97441	14	12	POSTAL SERVICE	97633	77	447	MERCH. WHOLESALERS;NONDUR. GDS
97326	20	27	FOOD AND BEVERAGE STORES	97442	74	1041	BLDG MATL & GARDEN EQPMT DLRS	97634	4	7	FOOD AND BEVERAGE STORES
97327	100	283	SPECIAL TRADE CONTRACTORS	97443	77	348	EDUCATIONAL SERVICES	97635	11	48	FORESTRY AND LOGGING
97329	2	5	REPAIR AND MAINTENANCE	97444	375	2061	ACCOMMODATION	97636	24	137	ANIMAL PRODUCTION
97330	1535	25078	PROF.; SCIENTIFIC; & TECH SVCS	97446	155	3867	TRANSPORTATION EQUIPMENT MFG	97637	4	6	EDUCATIONAL SERVICES
97331	36	945	EDUCATIONAL SERVICES	97447	34	183	EXEC.; LEGIS.; & OTHER SUPPORT	97638	25	82	EDUCATIONAL SERVICES
97333	845	9478	EDUCATIONAL SERVICES	97448	470	4992	TRANSPORTATION EQUIPMENT MFG	97639	9	10	ANIMAL PRODUCTION
97335	8	12	MERCH. WHOLESALERS;NONDUR. GDS	97449	58	191	ACCOMMODATION	97640	10	32	ACCOMMODATION
97336	5	39	EDUCATIONAL SERVICES	97450	21	67	EDUCATIONAL SERVICES	97641	58	156	FOOD SVCS & DRINKING PLACES
97338	612	4919	NURSING & RESID. CARE FACILIT.	97451	16	27	FOOD AND BEVERAGE STORES	97701	4894	41562	AMBULATORY HEALTH CARE SVCS
97339	58	132	AMBULATORY HEALTH CARE SVCS	97452	42	262	ADMIN. ENVIRO. QUALITY PROGRMS	97702	2265	19299	PROF.; SCIENTIFIC; & TECH SVCS
97341	171	673	FOOD SVCS & DRINKING PLACES	97453	35	170	FOOD SVCS & DRINKING PLACES	97707	320	3405	ACCOMMODATION
97342	25	169	ACCOMMODATION	97454	47	138	EDUCATIONAL SERVICES	97708	133	251	SPECIAL TRADE CONTRACTORS
97343	11	40	EDUCATIONAL SERVICES	97455	87	328	EDUCATIONAL SERVICES	97709	56	90	ACCOMMODATION
97344	25	92	JUSTICE; PUBIC ORDER/SAFETY	97456	120	568	EDUCATIONAL SERVICES	97710	6	16	ANIMAL PRODUCTION
97345	18	47	SOCIAL ASSISTANCE	97457	300	1780	RELIG.; GRANT; CIVIC; PROF ORG	97711	2	4	EDUCATIONAL SERVICES
97346	29	105	EDUCATIONAL SERVICES	97458	161	765	FOOD AND BEVERAGE STORES	97712	4	7	HEAVY & CIVIL ENG. CONSTRUCT'N
97347	41	1720	AMUSEMENT; GAMBLING;& RECREAT.	97459	666	6161	FOOD SVCS & DRINKING PLACES	97720	331	1690	EDUCATIONAL SERVICES
97348	72	1280	PAPER MANUFACTURING	97461	19	218	FORESTRY AND LOGGING	97721	8	106	ADMIN. ENVIRO. QUALITY PROGRMS
97350	13	47	FOOD SVCS & DRINKING PLACES	97462	119	584	GASOLINE STATIONS	97722	10	19	ACCOMMODATION
97351	245	2210	FURNITURE & RELATED PROD. MFG	97463	157	803	FOOD SVCS & DRINKING PLACES	97730	22	55	ACCOMMODATION
97352	130	618	EDUCATIONAL SERVICES	97464	6	15	UNCLASSIFIED ESTABLISHMENTS	97731	36	304	ACCOMMODATION
97355	888	7158	AMBULATORY HEALTH CARE SVCS	97465	135	516	UTILITIES	97732	7	29	EDUCATIONAL SERVICES
97357	6	12	FOOD AND BEVERAGE STORES	97466	33	167	EDUCATIONAL SERVICES	97733	34	264	SUPPORT ACTIVITIES: AGR./FOR.
97358	79	868	WOOD PRODUCT MANUFACTURING	97467	330	1849	FOOD SVCS & DRINKING PLACES	97734	64	549	TRANSPORTATION EQUIPMENT MFG
97360	69	273	EDUCATIONAL SERVICES	97469	64	1299	WOOD PRODUCT MANUFACTURING	97735	8	9	FOOD SVCS & DRINKING PLACES
97361	248	1578	CROP PRODUCTION	97470	1559	12928	EDUCATIONAL SERVICES	97736	6	27	ADMIN. ENVIRO. QUALITY PROGRMS
97362	165	2895	CROP PRODUCTION	97471	1053	11310	HOSPITALS	97737	29	285	WOOD PRODUCT MANUFACTURING
97364	9	12	CONSTRUCTION OF BUILDINGS	97473	6	13	FOOD SVCS & DRINKING PLACES	97738	68	730	TRANSPORTATION EQUIPMENT MFG
97365	1072	8213	FOOD SVCS & DRINKING PLACES	97476	8	17	MERCH. WHOLESALERS;NONDUR. GDS	97739	419	1948	EDUCATIONAL SERVICES
97366	111	482	ADMINISTRATIVE & SUPPORT SVCS	97477	1688	19516	AMBULATORY HEALTH CARE SVCS	97741	589	3859	EDUCATIONAL SERVICES
97367	825	5824	AMUSEMENT; GAMBLING;& RECREAT.	97478	806	6300	MERCH. WHOLESALERS;DURABLE GDS	97750	34	68	EDUCATIONAL SERVICES
97368	88	232	RELIG.; GRANT; CIVIC; PROF ORG	97479	368	2052	UTILITIES	97751	14	69	ADMIN. OF ECONOMIC PROGRAMS
97369	15	118	ACCOMMODATION	97480	6	51	WOOD PRODUCT MANUFACTURING	97752	4	4	ANIMAL PRODUCTION
97370	363	2324	WOOD PRODUCT MANUFACTURING	97481	9	42	EDUCATIONAL SERVICES	97753	72	224	HEAVY & CIVIL ENG. CONSTRUCT'N
97371	57	493	RELIG.; GRANT; CIVIC; PROF ORG	97484	13	57	ACCOMMODATION	97754	839	5789	WOOD PRODUCT MANUFACTURING
97373	2	59	EDUCATIONAL SERVICES	97486	22	56	CROP PRODUCTION	97756	1929	14184	HOSPITALS
97374	164	1037	EDUCATIONAL SERVICES	97487	292	1181	FOOD SVCS & DRINKING PLACES	97758	5	7	HEAVY & CIVIL ENG. CONSTRUCT'N
97375	28	60	EDUCATIONAL SERVICES	97488	37	195	EDUCATIONAL SERVICES	97759	551	3389	ACCOMMODATION
97376	53	127	ADMIN. OF ECONOMIC PROGRAMS	97489	35	82	FOOD SVCS & DRINKING PLACES	97760	200	747	TRUCK TRANSPORTATION
97377	31	85	WAREHOUSING AND STORAGE	97490	9	8	SPECIAL TRADE CONTRACTORS	97761	67	1354	ACCOMMODATION
97378	181	2529	CROP PRODUCTION	97491	4	8	FOOD MANUFACTURING	97801	1079	13031	EXEC.; LEGIS.; & OTHER SUPPORT
97380	58	305	EXEC.; LEGIS.; & OTHER SUPPORT	97492	17	527	SUPPORT ACTIVITIES: AGR./FOR.	97810	17	86	EXEC.; LEGIS.; & OTHER SUPPORT
97381	600	6091	HOSPITALS	97493	15	24	ACCOMMODATION	97812	53	400	SUPPORT ACT. FOR TRANSPORT.
97383	452	4687	FOOD MANUFACTURING	97494	4	16	MERCH. WHOLESALERS;DURABLE GDS	97813	41	166	EDUCATIONAL SERVICES
97384	13	43	WOOD PRODUCT MANUFACTURING	97495	33	175	MUSEUMS; HIST. SITES;& SIMILAR	97814	681	6036	FABRICATED METAL PRODUCT MFG
97385	112	891	NURSING & RESID. CARE FACILIT.	97496	180	1159	EDUCATIONAL SERVICES	97817	3	7	HEAVY & CIVIL ENG. CONSTRUCT'N
97386	361	2684	EDUCATIONAL SERVICES	97497	40	114	TEXTILE PRODUCT MILLS	97818	141	2834	MERCH. WHOLESALERS;NONDUR. GDS
97388	74	727	AMUSEMENT; GAMBLING;& RECREAT.	97498	143	537	FOOD SVCS & DRINKING PLACES	97819	3	15	ANIMAL PRODUCTION
97389	123	1984	PETROLEUM & COAL PRODUCTS MFG	97499	61	249	EDUCATIONAL SERVICES	97820	68	314	FORESTRY AND LOGGING
97390	28	69	FORESTRY AND LOGGING	97501	2680	25404	MERCH. WHOLESALERS;NONDUR. GDS	97823	127	389	EDUCATIONAL SERVICES
97391	190	1505	PAPER MANUFACTURING	97502	1093	8413	BLDG MATL & GARDEN EQPMT DLRS	97824	38	167	FOOD AND BEVERAGE STORES
97392	126	765	EDUCATIONAL SERVICES	97503	431	6719	WOOD PRODUCT MANUFACTURING	97825	24	69	CONSTRUCTION OF BUILDINGS
97394	299	990	FOOD AND BEVERAGE STORES	97504	2389	26685	HOSPITALS	97826	33	206	CROP PRODUCTION
97396	97	983	WOOD PRODUCT MANUFACTURING	97520	1529	11123	FOOD SVCS & DRINKING PLACES	97827	103	677	MERCH. WHOLESALERS;DURABLE GDS
97401	3891	44230	AMBULATORY HEALTH CARE SVCS	97522	26	68	JUSTICE; PUBIC ORDER/SAFETY	97828	286	1529	EXEC.; LEGIS.; & OTHER SUPPORT

BUSINESS DATA

ZIP CODE	2009 Total Firms	2009 Total Employ-ees	TOP INDUSTRY RANKED on 2009 EMPLOYMENT
97830	82	251	EXEC.; LEGIS.; & OTHER SUPPORT
97833	24	99	EDUCATIONAL SERVICES
97834	76	335	SUPPORT ACTIVITIES: AGR./FOR.
97835	26	113	EDUCATIONAL SERVICES
97836	144	954	EXEC.; LEGIS.; & OTHER SUPPORT
97837	3	3	FORESTRY AND LOGGING
97838	935	9537	FOOD MANUFACTURING
97839	22	77	MERCH. WHOLESALERS;DURABLE GDS
97840	8	109	WAREHOUSING AND STORAGE
97841	22	134	EDUCATIONAL SERVICES
97842	10	11	SPECIAL TRADE CONTRACTORS
97843	29	281	SPECIAL TRADE CONTRACTORS
97844	59	330	EDUCATIONAL SERVICES
97845	222	1786	SUPPORT ACTIVITIES: AGR./FOR.
97846	154	692	FOOD SVCS & DRINKING PLACES
97848	10	45	MUSEUMS; HIST. SITES;& SIMILAR
97850	954	8612	EDUCATIONAL SERVICES
97856	16	42	EDUCATIONAL SERVICES
97857	26	90	TRANSIT & GRND PASS. TRANSPORT
97859	10	44	PIPELINE TRANSPORTATION
97862	380	3134	PROF.; SCIENTIFIC; & TECH SVCS
97864	14	49	EDUCATIONAL SERVICES
97865	37	129	EDUCATIONAL SERVICES
97867	30	134	EDUCATIONAL SERVICES
97868	54	338	MERCH. WHOLESALERS;DURABLE GDS
97869	63	479	WOOD PRODUCT MANUFACTURING
97870	39	105	BLDG MATL & GARDEN EQPMT DLRS
97873	9	15	EDUCATIONAL SERVICES
97874	34	38	ANIMAL PRODUCTION
97875	64	332	CONSTRUCTION OF BUILDINGS
97876	12	27	CROP PRODUCTION
97877	29	104	RAIL TRANSPORTATION
97880	23	91	SUPPORT ACTIVITIES: AGR./FOR.
97882	149	1586	JUSTICE; PUBIC ORDER/SAFETY
97883	71	200	EDUCATIONAL SERVICES
97884	18	45	EDUCATIONAL SERVICES
97885	64	213	EDUCATIONAL SERVICES
97886	31	1152	FOOD MANUFACTURING
97901	21	154	EDUCATIONAL SERVICES
97902	2	6	EDUCATIONAL SERVICES
97903	5	9	SUPPORT ACTIVITIES: AGR./FOR.
97904	12	15	ANIMAL PRODUCTION
97905	10	124	NONMETALLIC MINERAL PROD. MFG
97906	8	26	EDUCATIONAL SERVICES
97907	17	127	GASOLINE STATIONS
97908	6	4	HEAVY & CIVIL ENG. CONSTRUCT'N
97909	3	3	POSTAL SERVICE
97910	43	113	FOOD SVCS & DRINKING PLACES
97911	12	23	FOOD SVCS & DRINKING PLACES
97913	152	1590	FOOD MANUFACTURING
97914	877	9075	FOOD MANUFACTURING
97917	1	0	UNCLASSIFIED ESTABLISHMENTS
97918	184	1454	EDUCATIONAL SERVICES
97920	3	2	MINING (EXCEPT OIL AND GAS)
98001	1399	24471	MERCH. WHOLESALERS;DURABLE GDS
98002	1566	15383	EXEC.; LEGIS.; & OTHER SUPPORT
98003	2483	26110	FOOD SVCS & DRINKING PLACES
98004	4395	73691	REPAIR AND MAINTENANCE
98005	2372	24601	PROF.; SCIENTIFIC; & TECH SVCS
98006	1112	12018	TELECOMMUNICATIONS
98007	1176	13008	EDUCATIONAL SERVICES
98008	576	4546	EDUCATIONAL SERVICES
98009	44	106	ADMINISTRATIVE & SUPPORT SVCS
98010	155	627	EDUCATIONAL SERVICES
98011	989	11412	PROF.; SCIENTIFIC; & TECH SVCS
98012	1130	7754	FOOD SVCS & DRINKING PLACES
98013	9	8	ADMINISTRATIVE & SUPPORT SVCS
98014	230	1271	EDUCATIONAL SERVICES
98015	29	94	ADMINISTRATIVE & SUPPORT SVCS
98019	318	1494	EDUCATIONAL SERVICES
98020	827	5550	FOOD SVCS & DRINKING PLACES
98021	720	9405	PROF.; SCIENTIFIC; & TECH SVCS
98022	823	5827	ACCOMMODATION
98023	535	4015	EDUCATIONAL SERVICES
98024	235	869	EDUCATIONAL SERVICES
98025	3	9	TRANSPORTATION EQUIPMENT MFG
98026	927	6950	HOSPITALS
98027	1738	17886	GENERAL MERCHANDISE STORES
98028	543	4316	EDUCATIONAL SERVICES
98029	355	4198	MISCELLANEOUS MANUFACTURING
98030	848	6287	EDUCATIONAL SERVICES
98031	719	6298	EDUCATIONAL SERVICES
98032	3040	53756	AMUSEMENT; GAMBLING;& RECREAT.
98033	2094	20576	PROF.; SCIENTIFIC; & TECH SVCS
98034	1547	16515	HOSPITALS
98035	25	69	SPECIAL TRADE CONTRACTORS
98036	2002	17164	FOOD SVCS & DRINKING PLACES
98037	917	9099	FOOD SVCS & DRINKING PLACES
98038	731	4178	EDUCATIONAL SERVICES
98039	66	314	EDUCATIONAL SERVICES
98040	878	6567	EDUCATIONAL SERVICES
98041	41	114	SPECIAL TRADE CONTRACTORS
98042	824	6179	EDUCATIONAL SERVICES
98043	580	4139	AMBULATORY HEALTH CARE SVCS
98045	669	3823	FOOD SVCS & DRINKING PLACES
98046	40	141	ADMINISTRATIVE & SUPPORT SVCS
98047	212	2696	TRUCK TRANSPORTATION
98050	41	402	FOOD AND BEVERAGE STORES
98051	93	381	EDUCATIONAL SERVICES
98052	2898	65135	PUBLISHING INDUSTRIES
98053	380	2324	ADMINISTRATIVE & SUPPORT SVCS
98054	3	5	CONSTRUCTION OF BUILDINGS
98055	521	4855	AMBULATORY HEALTH CARE SVCS
98056	556	3718	EDUCATIONAL SERVICES
98057	1791	29872	MOTOR VEHICLE & PARTS DEALERS
98058	530	3475	EDUCATIONAL SERVICES
98059	572	4408	EDUCATIONAL SERVICES
98061	12	17	PROF.; SCIENTIFIC; & TECH SVCS
98062	9	28	BLDG MATL & GARDEN EQPMT DLRS
98063	17	42	ADMINISTRATIVE & SUPPORT SVCS
98064	20	76	ADMINISTRATIVE & SUPPORT SVCS
98065	384	3313	EDUCATIONAL SERVICES
98068	48	239	ACCOMMODATION
98070	592	2419	EDUCATIONAL SERVICES
98071	37	109	HEAVY & CIVIL ENG. CONSTRUCT'N
98072	1594	18936	MERCH. WHOLESALERS;DURABLE GDS
98073	47	135	SPECIAL TRADE CONTRACTORS
98074	352	2209	EDUCATIONAL SERVICES
98075	283	1949	EDUCATIONAL SERVICES
98077	183	1045	EDUCATIONAL SERVICES
98082	46	111	SPECIAL TRADE CONTRACTORS
98083	41	312	EDUCATIONAL SERVICES
98087	623	4096	SPORTG GDS;HOBBY;BOOK; & MUSIC
98089	12	20	SPECIAL TRADE CONTRACTORS
98092	512	3913	EDUCATIONAL SERVICES
98093	22	39	SPECIAL TRADE CONTRACTORS
98101	4234	72499	PROF.; SCIENTIFIC; & TECH SVCS
98102	906	7016	FOOD SVCS & DRINKING PLACES
98103	2388	16845	FOOD SVCS & DRINKING PLACES
98104	3333	52624	PROF.; SCIENTIFIC; & TECH SVCS
98105	1541	19927	AMBULATORY HEALTH CARE SVCS
98106	638	12960	EDUCATIONAL SERVICES
98107	1656	15669	EDUCATIONAL SERVICES
98108	1935	31368	AMBULATORY HEALTH CARE SVCS
98109	2152	31502	PROF.; SCIENTIFIC; & TECH SVCS
98110	1389	6521	PROF.; SCIENTIFIC; & TECH SVCS
98111	44	63	PROF.; SCIENTIFIC; & TECH SVCS
98112	773	4586	FOOD SVCS & DRINKING PLACES
98113	13	14	PROF.; SCIENTIFIC; & TECH SVCS
98114	10	12	RELIG.; GRANT; CIVIC; PROF ORG
98115	1551	10446	EDUCATIONAL SERVICES
98116	950	4833	FOOD SVCS & DRINKING PLACES
98117	791	4166	PROF.; SCIENTIFIC; & TECH SVCS
98118	1243	8577	MERCH. WHOLESALERS;NONDUR. GDS
98119	1173	16897	PROF.; SCIENTIFIC; & TECH SVCS
98121	1581	23601	PROF.; SCIENTIFIC; & TECH SVCS
98122	1679	25609	HOSPITALS
98124	35	524	PERSONAL AND LAUNDRY SERVICES
98125	1544	10709	FOOD SVCS & DRINKING PLACES
98126	498	4620	FOOD SVCS & DRINKING PLACES
98127	36	43	SPECIAL TRADE CONTRACTORS
98133	1712	20484	AMBULATORY HEALTH CARE SVCS
98134	1118	29452	MERCH. WHOLESALERS;DURABLE GDS
98136	363	1606	FOOD SVCS & DRINKING PLACES
98138	16	161	FOOD MANUFACTURING
98139	20	247	RELIG.; GRANT; CIVIC; PROF ORG
98141	3	6	PROF.; SCIENTIFIC; & TECH SVCS
98144	970	9992	SOCIAL ASSISTANCE
98145	18	19	PERFORM'G ARTS; SPEC. SPORTS
98146	464	2601	EDUCATIONAL SERVICES
98148	478	4265	SUPPORT ACT. FOR TRANSPORT.
98151	1	1	ANIMAL PRODUCTION
98154	158	4381	INSURANCE CARRIERS & RELATED
98155	852	6443	ADMINISTRATIVE & SUPPORT SVCS
98158	150	24628	SUPPORT ACT. FOR TRANSPORT.
98160	8	10	PROF.; SCIENTIFIC; & TECH SVCS
98161	26	901	REAL ESTATE
98164	41	513	PROF.; SCIENTIFIC; & TECH SVCS
98165	27	72	ADMINISTRATIVE & SUPPORT SVCS
98166	1108	7594	HOSPITALS
98168	1193	12534	SPECIAL TRADE CONTRACTORS
98174	38	349	ADMIN. OF ECONOMIC PROGRAMS
98175	18	105	SOCIAL ASSISTANCE
98177	376	2133	ADMINISTRATIVE & SUPPORT SVCS
98178	319	2198	EDUCATIONAL SERVICES
98181	6	3546	GENERAL MERCHANDISE STORES
98185	4	10	OTHER INFORMATION SERVICES
98188	1944	34637	PROF.; SCIENTIFIC; & TECH SVCS
98191	3	20	PROF.; SCIENTIFIC; & TECH SVCS
98194	8	13	MOTOR VEHICLE & PARTS DEALERS
98195	184	9399	HOSPITALS
98198	839	6821	NURSING & RESID. CARE FACILIT.
98199	653	4572	CREDIT INTERMEDIATION & RELATD
98201	2161	32751	EXEC.; LEGIS.; & OTHER SUPPORT
98203	847	15137	COMPUTER & ELECTRONIC PROD MFG
98204	1124	11842	MOTOR VEHICLE & PARTS DEALERS
98205	225	1585	EDUCATIONAL SERVICES
98206	30	54	ADMINISTRATIVE & SUPPORT SVCS
98207	7	27	WASTE MANAGMT & REMEDIAT'N SVC
98208	1207	10117	FOOD SVCS & DRINKING PLACES
98213	17	36	ADMINISTRATIVE & SUPPORT SVCS
98220	24	105	EDUCATIONAL SERVICES
98221	978	8028	PETROLEUM & COAL PRODUCTS MFG
98222	5	8	RELIG.; GRANT; CIVIC; PROF ORG
98223	1331	13084	TRANSPORTATION EQUIPMENT MFG
98224	3	4	FOOD AND BEVERAGE STORES
98225	2984	29771	EDUCATIONAL SERVICES
98226	1666	20038	FOOD SVCS & DRINKING PLACES
98227	73	125	ADMINISTRATIVE & SUPPORT SVCS
98228	52	120	SPECIAL TRADE CONTRACTORS
98229	680	5750	REAL ESTATE
98230	501	4312	PETROLEUM & COAL PRODUCTS MFG
98231	7	9	RELIG.; GRANT; CIVIC; PROF ORG
98232	131	1173	ACCOMMODATION
98233	1002	10767	FOOD SVCS & DRINKING PLACES
98235	20	131	CONSTRUCTION OF BUILDINGS
98236	352	759	FOOD AND BEVERAGE STORES
98237	117	418	EDUCATIONAL SERVICES
98238	17	86	EDUCATIONAL SERVICES
98239	356	77845	PROF.; SCIENTIFIC; & TECH SVCS
98240	82	628	CROP PRODUCTION
98241	90	869	WOOD PRODUCT MANUFACTURING
98243	21	42	ACCOMMODATION
98244	108	887	AMUSEMENT; GAMBLING;& RECREAT.
98245	415	2013	ACCOMMODATION
98247	257	1819	MERCH. WHOLESALERS;DURABLE GDS
98248	715	6727	EDUCATIONAL SERVICES
98249	358	1570	TRANSPORTATION EQUIPMENT MFG
98250	884	3825	ACCOMMODATION
98251	69	353	JUSTICE; PUBIC ORDER/SAFETY
98252	189	1180	EDUCATIONAL SERVICES
98253	51	106	MERCH. WHOLESALERS;NONDUR. GDS
98255	14	50	EXEC.; LEGIS.; & OTHER SUPPORT
98256	12	36	SCENIC & SIGHTSEEING TRANSPORT
98257	270	1744	REPAIR AND MAINTENANCE
98258	635	5042	FOOD AND BEVERAGE STORES
98259	4	9	CONSTRUCTION OF BUILDINGS
98260	473	2176	EDUCATIONAL SERVICES
98261	175	669	EDUCATIONAL SERVICES
98262	30	89	FOOD SVCS & DRINKING PLACES
98263	13	63	FOOD SVCS & DRINKING PLACES
98264	789	7587	CROP PRODUCTION
98266	55	193	EDUCATIONAL SERVICES
98267	19	135	MUSEUMS; HIST. SITES;& SIMILAR
98270	1189	8945	FOOD SVCS & DRINKING PLACES
98271	637	9194	FOOD SVCS & DRINKING PLACES
98272	1004	10274	JUSTICE; PUBIC ORDER/SAFETY
98273	1650	15675	EXEC.; LEGIS.; & OTHER SUPPORT
98274	340	4392	HOSPITALS
98275	795	8120	SPECIAL TRADE CONTRACTORS
98276	7	14	MISCELLANEOUS MANUFACTURING
98277	1210	18263	NAT'L SECURITY & INT'L AFFAIRS
98278	25	2203	HOSPITALS
98279	30	133	ACCOMMODATION
98280	70	141	ACCOMMODATION
98281	102	405	FOOD SVCS & DRINKING PLACES
98282	286	1030	EDUCATIONAL SERVICES
98283	19	74	ACCOMMODATION
98284	560	5007	EDUCATIONAL SERVICES
98286	14	76	MERCH. WHOLESALERS;DURABLE GDS
98287	9	24	FOOD SVCS & DRINKING PLACES
98288	23	1025	ACCOMMODATION
98290	1012	6693	EDUCATIONAL SERVICES
98291	30	81	NONSTORE RETAILERS
98292	676	4800	NURSING & RESID. CARE FACILIT.
98293	11	35	CONSTRUCTION OF BUILDINGS
98294	194	1069	EDUCATIONAL SERVICES
98295	81	713	PETROLEUM & COAL PRODUCTS MFG
98296	515	3329	SPECIAL TRADE CONTRACTORS
98303	33	108	RELIG.; GRANT; CIVIC; PROF ORG
98304	55	436	MUSEUMS; HIST. SITES;& SIMILAR
98305	25	139	MERCH. WHOLESALERS;DURABLE GDS
98310	710	7911	SOCIAL ASSISTANCE
98311	410	3296	EDUCATIONAL SERVICES
98312	903	8911	NAT'L SECURITY & INT'L AFFAIRS
98314	25	186	FOOD SVCS & DRINKING PLACES
98315	38	636	NAT'L SECURITY & INT'L AFFAIRS
98320	55	229	ACCOMMODATION
98321	333	3493	SOCIAL ASSISTANCE
98322	21	71	MERCH. WHOLESALERS;DURABLE GDS

ZIP CODE	2009 Total Firms	2009 Total Employ-ees	TOP INDUSTRY RANKED on 2009 EMPLOYMENT	ZIP CODE	2009 Total Firms	2009 Total Employ-ees	TOP INDUSTRY RANKED on 2009 EMPLOYMENT	ZIP CODE	2009 Total Firms	2009 Total Employ-ees	TOP INDUSTRY RANKED on 2009 EMPLOYMENT
98323	16	50	EDUCATIONAL SERVICES	98438	54	489	RELIG.; GRANT; CIVIC; PROF ORG	98593	27	59	EDUCATIONAL SERVICES
98324	17	54	FOOD AND BEVERAGE STORES	98439	29	178	EDUCATIONAL SERVICES	98595	185	1213	MERCH. WHOLESALERS;NONDUR. GDS
98325	76	519	EDUCATIONAL SERVICES	98443	147	841	HEAVY & CIVIL ENG. CONSTRUCT'N	98596	141	765	WOOD PRODUCT MANUFACTURING
98326	45	559	JUSTICE; PUBIC ORDER/SAFETY	98444	1097	8967	FOOD SVCS & DRINKING PLACES	98597	742	3878	EDUCATIONAL SERVICES
98327	108	2030	INSURANCE CARRIERS & RELATED	98445	436	4073	EDUCATIONAL SERVICES	98601	83	238	EDUCATIONAL SERVICES
98328	293	1490	EDUCATIONAL SERVICES	98446	278	2509	MERCH. WHOLESALERS;DURABLE GDS	98602	3	4	REAL ESTATE
98329	205	922	SPORTG GDS;HOBBY;BOOK; & MUSIC	98447	63	1682	EDUCATIONAL SERVICES	98603	20	79	ADMIN. ENVIRO. QUALITY PROGRMS
98330	14	18	FOOD SVCS & DRINKING PLACES	98448	21	76	SPECIAL TRADE CONTRACTORS	98604	1011	5421	SPECIAL TRADE CONTRACTORS
98331	286	1829	HOSPITALS	98464	20	130	EDUCATIONAL SERVICES	98605	91	1138	MERCH. WHOLESALERS;NONDUR. GDS
98332	587	4627	EDUCATIONAL SERVICES	98465	166	1289	SOCIAL ASSISTANCE	98606	247	997	EDUCATIONAL SERVICES
98333	79	156	RELIG.; GRANT; CIVIC; PROF ORG	98466	1049	8263	EDUCATIONAL SERVICES	98607	634	8299	PAPER MANUFACTURING
98335	1997	8699	AMBULATORY HEALTH CARE SVCS	98467	196	1980	EDUCATIONAL SERVICES	98609	3	4	CONSTRUCTION OF BUILDINGS
98336	17	55	JUSTICE; PUBIC ORDER/SAFETY	98490	6	59	MERCH. WHOLESALERS;DURABLE GDS	98610	66	551	FORESTRY AND LOGGING
98337	412	5097	EDUCATIONAL SERVICES	98493	15	840	NURSING & RESID. CARE FACILIT.	98611	252	1304	ADMIN. ENVIRO. QUALITY PROGRMS
98338	418	1809	EDUCATIONAL SERVICES	98496	24	23	ADMINISTRATIVE & SUPPORT SVCS	98612	185	775	EXEC.; LEGIS.; & OTHER SUPPORT
98339	220	1138	FOOD SVCS & DRINKING PLACES	98497	5	7	WHOLESALE ELEC. MRKTS & AGENTS	98613	8	47	CONSTRUCTION OF BUILDINGS
98340	52	157	JUSTICE; PUBIC ORDER/SAFETY	98498	408	4584	HOSPITALS	98614	44	124	MERCH. WHOLESALERS;NONDUR. GDS
98342	12	37	ACCOMMODATION	98499	2084	17908	FOOD SVCS & DRINKING PLACES	98616	13	28	MERCH. WHOLESALERS;DURABLE GDS
98343	4	45	EDUCATIONAL SERVICES	98501	2591	32758	ADMIN. HUMAN RESOURCE PROGRAMS	98617	36	152	HEAVY & CIVIL ENG. CONSTRUCT'N
98344	5	11	CONSTRUCTION OF BUILDINGS	98502	1514	14049	EXEC.; LEGIS.; & OTHER SUPPORT	98619	23	137	EXEC.; LEGIS.; & OTHER SUPPORT
98345	18	344	COMPUTER & ELECTRONIC PROD MFG	98503	1153	13665	ADMIN. ENVIRO. QUALITY PROGRMS	98620	379	2034	EXEC.; LEGIS.; & OTHER SUPPORT
98346	352	2113	EDUCATIONAL SERVICES	98504	291	8822	EXEC.; LEGIS.; & OTHER SUPPORT	98621	11	45	JUSTICE; PUBIC ORDER/SAFETY
98348	3	18	UTILITIES	98505	3	569	EDUCATIONAL SERVICES	98622	2	2	AMBULATORY HEALTH CARE SVCS
98349	162	378	EDUCATIONAL SERVICES	98506	991	11421	AMBULATORY HEALTH CARE SVCS	98623	6	11	ACCOMMODATION
98350	21	171	ACCOMMODATION	98507	69	128	SPECIAL TRADE CONTRACTORS	98624	123	855	MERCH. WHOLESALERS;NONDUR. GDS
98351	17	121	MERCH. WHOLESALERS;NONDUR. GDS	98508	41	89	PROF.; SCIENTIFIC; & TECH SVCS	98625	193	1933	WOOD PRODUCT MANUFACTURING
98352	1	400	SPORTG GDS;HOBBY;BOOK; & MUSIC	98509	39	78	SPECIAL TRADE CONTRACTORS	98626	698	7282	FOOD MANUFACTURING
98353	14	43	FOOD SVCS & DRINKING PLACES	98511	13	73	WASTE MANAGMT & REMEDIAT'N SVC	98628	12	60	EDUCATIONAL SERVICES
98354	257	2367	FOOD SVCS & DRINKING PLACES	98512	890	7212	EDUCATIONAL SERVICES	98629	172	2652	FOOD SVCS & DRINKING PLACES
98355	18	66	MERCH. WHOLESALERS;DURABLE GDS	98513	320	2415	AMUSEMENT; GAMBLING;& RECREAT.	98631	289	1307	FOOD SVCS & DRINKING PLACES
98356	146	1115	WOOD PRODUCT MANUFACTURING	98516	785	8173	FOOD SVCS & DRINKING PLACES	98632	1958	23163	AMBULATORY HEALTH CARE SVCS
98357	76	451	SOCIAL ASSISTANCE	98520	1121	10583	EDUCATIONAL SERVICES	98635	58	116	EDUCATIONAL SERVICES
98358	30	37	AMUSEMENT; GAMBLING;& RECREAT.	98522	5	15	TRANSIT & GRND PASS. TRANSPORT	98637	14	82	FISHING; HUNTING AND TRAPPING
98359	116	269	RELIG.; GRANT; CIVIC; PROF ORG	98524	65	243	FOOD MANUFACTURING	98638	69	320	EDUCATIONAL SERVICES
98360	256	1775	EDUCATIONAL SERVICES	98526	32	219	EDUCATIONAL SERVICES	98639	33	279	ACCOMMODATION
98361	69	231	FOOD SVCS & DRINKING PLACES	98527	13	382	FISHING; HUNTING AND TRAPPING	98640	141	606	FOOD AND BEVERAGE STORES
98362	1471	12948	HOSPITALS	98528	406	1989	EDUCATIONAL SERVICES	98641	7	48	MUSEUMS; HIST. SITES;& SIMILAR
98363	346	3648	PROF.; SCIENTIFIC; & TECH SVCS	98530	11	14	RELIG.; GRANT; CIVIC; PROF ORG	98642	489	2787	MERCH. WHOLESALERS;DURABLE GDS
98364	22	49	FOOD SVCS & DRINKING PLACES	98531	1129	12350	UTILITIES	98643	17	28	DATA PROCESS'G
98365	125	419	ACCOMMODATION	98532	1129	11227	GENERAL MERCHANDISE STORES	98644	65	254	FOOD SVCS & DRINKING PLACES
98366	1268	10821	EXEC.; LEGIS.; & OTHER SUPPORT	98533	13	26	MISCELLANEOUS STORE RETAILERS	98645	20	60	SUPPORT ACTIVITIES: AGR./FOR.
98367	511	3804	EDUCATIONAL SERVICES	98535	20	51	ACCOMMODATION	98647	20	36	FOOD SVCS & DRINKING PLACES
98368	1231	6030	FOOD SVCS & DRINKING PLACES	98536	8	22	EXEC.; LEGIS.; & OTHER SUPPORT	98648	230	1446	ACCOMMODATION
98370	1416	8679	FOOD SVCS & DRINKING PLACES	98537	56	361	FORESTRY AND LOGGING	98649	33	243	EDUCATIONAL SERVICES
98371	914	9325	EDUCATIONAL SERVICES	98538	15	113	MISCELLANEOUS STORE RETAILERS	98650	35	184	EXEC.; LEGIS.; & OTHER SUPPORT
98372	794	9906	AMBULATORY HEALTH CARE SVCS	98539	4	5	FOOD AND BEVERAGE STORES	98651	23	60	EXEC.; LEGIS.; & OTHER SUPPORT
98373	1251	10401	FOOD SVCS & DRINKING PLACES	98540	6	33	EDUCATIONAL SERVICES	98660	1439	15205	PROF.; SCIENTIFIC; & TECH SVCS
98374	435	6280	EDUCATIONAL SERVICES	98541	310	1926	EDUCATIONAL SERVICES	98661	1854	19433	EDUCATIONAL SERVICES
98375	410	5169	GENERAL MERCHANDISE STORES	98542	27	105	FORESTRY AND LOGGING	98662	1484	18131	MERCH. WHOLESALERS;DURABLE GDS
98376	99	407	AMUSEMENT; GAMBLING;& RECREAT.	98544	2	4	POSTAL SERVICE	98663	566	4708	EDUCATIONAL SERVICES
98377	79	746	EDUCATIONAL SERVICES	98546	43	91	EDUCATIONAL SERVICES	98664	467	10220	AMBULATORY HEALTH CARE SVCS
98380	86	217	SPECIAL TRADE CONTRACTORS	98547	63	170	JUSTICE; PUBIC ORDER/SAFETY	98665	1265	10200	FOOD SVCS & DRINKING PLACES
98381	22	52	ACCOMMODATION	98548	88	230	REAL ESTATE	98666	27	116	JUSTICE; PUBIC ORDER/SAFETY
98382	1293	6714	EDUCATIONAL SERVICES	98550	382	3134	PAPER MANUFACTURING	98668	30	40	PROF.; SCIENTIFIC; & TECH SVCS
98383	1319	13746	FOOD SVCS & DRINKING PLACES	98552	16	57	WOOD PRODUCT MANUFACTURING	98670	4	10	SOCIAL ASSISTANCE
98384	10	26	ADMINISTRATIVE & SUPPORT SVCS	98554	6	6	CONSTRUCTION OF BUILDINGS	98671	451	3437	EDUCATIONAL SERVICES
98385	32	110	SPECIAL TRADE CONTRACTORS	98555	15	46	FOOD MANUFACTURING	98672	259	1403	EDUCATIONAL SERVICES
98386	8	5	POSTAL SERVICE	98556	14	159	JUSTICE; PUBIC ORDER/SAFETY	98673	11	118	RAIL TRANSPORTATION
98387	643	4199	EDUCATIONAL SERVICES	98557	76	1007	WOOD PRODUCT MANUFACTURING	98674	494	5075	EDUCATIONAL SERVICES
98388	102	1806	JUSTICE; PUBIC ORDER/SAFETY	98558	26	220	NURSING & RESID. CARE FACILIT.	98675	142	506	JUSTICE; PUBIC ORDER/SAFETY
98390	799	10062	PROF.; SCIENTIFIC; & TECH SVCS	98559	3	6	FOOD AND BEVERAGE STORES	98682	1066	9105	CREDIT INTERMEDIATION & RELATD
98391	742	5158	FOOD SVCS & DRINKING PLACES	98560	5	10	FOOD AND BEVERAGE STORES	98683	809	7430	FOOD SVCS & DRINKING PLACES
98392	74	1196	AMUSEMENT; GAMBLING;& RECREAT.	98561	10	53	EDUCATIONAL SERVICES	98684	924	9185	FOOD SVCS & DRINKING PLACES
98393	15	8	ADMINISTRATIVE & SUPPORT SVCS	98562	11	78	ACCOMMODATION	98685	620	3786	EDUCATIONAL SERVICES
98394	34	166	SPECIAL TRADE CONTRACTORS	98563	312	1868	JUSTICE; PUBIC ORDER/SAFETY	98686	609	5042	AMBULATORY HEALTH CARE SVCS
98395	21	46	POSTAL SERVICE	98564	89	541	BLDG MATL & GARDEN EQPMT DLRS	98687	32	47	FURNITURE & RELATED PROD. MFG
98396	15	88	EDUCATIONAL SERVICES	98565	45	225	EDUCATIONAL SERVICES	98801	2103	28038	MERCH. WHOLESALERS;NONDUR. GDS
98401	30	38	UTILITIES	98566	5	10	TRUCK TRANSPORTATION	98802	797	6964	FOOD SVCS & DRINKING PLACES
98402	1617	27414	EXEC.; LEGIS.; & OTHER SUPPORT	98568	62	311	EDUCATIONAL SERVICES	98807	51	1588	MERCH. WHOLESALERS;DURABLE GDS
98403	356	2001	EDUCATIONAL SERVICES	98569	327	1857	ACCOMMODATION	98811	2	22	EXEC.; LEGIS.; & OTHER SUPPORT
98404	499	6296	AMUSEMENT; GAMBLING;& RECREAT.	98570	104	375	EDUCATIONAL SERVICES	98812	172	3445	MERCH. WHOLESALERS;NONDUR. GDS
98405	1292	42167	HOSPITALS	98571	53	214	FOOD AND BEVERAGE STORES	98813	57	348	EDUCATIONAL SERVICES
98406	668	5031	FOOD SVCS & DRINKING PLACES	98572	32	374	FORESTRY AND LOGGING	98814	17	43	FOOD SVCS & DRINKING PLACES
98407	467	2845	FOOD SVCS & DRINKING PLACES	98575	11	136	ACCOMMODATION	98815	267	1828	MERCH. WHOLESALERS;NONDUR. GDS
98408	451	3781	FOOD SVCS & DRINKING PLACES	98576	170	557	EDUCATIONAL SERVICES	98816	434	4140	CROP PRODUCTION
98409	1937	30074	MOTOR VEHICLE & PARTS DEALERS	98577	252	1577	WOOD PRODUCT MANUFACTURING	98817	8	3	SPECIAL TRADE CONTRACTORS
98411	23	36	ADMINISTRATIVE & SUPPORT SVCS	98579	273	2876	RELIG.; GRANT; CIVIC; PROF ORG	98819	22	41	FOOD SVCS & DRINKING PLACES
98412	5	6	REPAIR AND MAINTENANCE	98580	176	731	CROP PRODUCTION	98821	18	101	WAREHOUSING AND STORAGE
98413	2	40	AMBULATORY HEALTH CARE SVCS	98581	10	32	JUSTICE; PUBIC ORDER/SAFETY	98822	59	405	EDUCATIONAL SERVICES
98415	9	46	PERSONAL AND LAUNDRY SERVICES	98582	32	89	MUSEUMS; HIST. SITES;& SIMILAR	98823	485	3967	UTILITIES
98416	2	7	SPORTG GDS;HOBBY;BOOK; & MUSIC	98583	18	52	SUPPORT ACT. FOR TRANSPORT.	98824	6	58	FOOD MANUFACTURING
98417	14	22	ADMINISTRATIVE & SUPPORT SVCS	98584	1170	10556	EDUCATIONAL SERVICES	98826	476	2813	ACCOMMODATION
98418	287	2537	ADMIN. HUMAN RESOURCE PROGRAMS	98585	22	139	EXEC.; LEGIS.; & OTHER SUPPORT	98827	11	15	ACCOMMODATION
98419	6	10	RELIG.; GRANT; CIVIC; PROF ORG	98586	200	1334	EXEC.; LEGIS.; & OTHER SUPPORT	98828	45	609	MERCH. WHOLESALERS;DURABLE GDS
98421	522	12235	MERCH. WHOLESALERS;DURABLE GDS	98587	29	785	RELIG.; GRANT; CIVIC; PROF ORG	98829	11	180	CROP PRODUCTION
98422	323	1935	EDUCATIONAL SERVICES	98588	25	99	ACCOMMODATION	98830	22	64	EDUCATIONAL SERVICES
98424	821	14978	SUPPORT ACT. FOR TRANSPORT.	98589	260	872	EDUCATIONAL SERVICES	98831	120	888	AMUSEMENT; GAMBLING;& RECREAT.
98430	8	621	NAT'L SECURITY & INT'L AFFAIRS	98590	14	204	AMUSEMENT; GAMBLING;& RECREAT.	98832	4	6	EDUCATIONAL SERVICES
98431	9	3127	AMBULATORY HEALTH CARE SVCS	98591	188	817	EDUCATIONAL SERVICES	98833	19	98	EDUCATIONAL SERVICES
98433	146	2335	MERCH. WHOLESALERS;DURABLE GDS	98592	82	744	ACCOMMODATION	98834	5	2	TRUCK TRANSPORTATION

BUSINESS DATA

ZIP CODE	2009 Total Firms	2009 Total Employ-ees	TOP INDUSTRY RANKED on 2009 EMPLOYMENT
98836	15	342	SUPPORT ACTIVITIES: AGR./FOR.
98837	1548	21861	ADMINISTRATIVE & SUPPORT SVCS
98840	307	2098	EXEC.; LEGIS.; & OTHER SUPPORT
98841	478	3935	EDUCATIONAL SERVICES
98843	40	1006	MERCH. WHOLESALERS;NONDUR. GDS
98844	198	1188	EDUCATIONAL SERVICES
98845	2	8	EDUCATIONAL SERVICES
98846	53	597	WAREHOUSING AND STORAGE
98847	62	975	SUPPORT ACTIVITIES: AGR./FOR.
98848	353	4685	FOOD MANUFACTURING
98849	23	60	MERCH. WHOLESALERS;NONDUR. GDS
98850	31	252	FOOD AND BEVERAGE STORES
98851	83	482	EDUCATIONAL SERVICES
98852	2	308	ACCOMMODATION
98853	2	4	MERCH. WHOLESALERS;NONDUR. GDS
98855	208	1220	HOSPITALS
98856	220	793	EXEC.; LEGIS.; & OTHER SUPPORT
98857	104	1066	MERCH. WHOLESALERS;NONDUR. GDS
98858	74	566	EDUCATIONAL SERVICES
98859	8	37	MERCH. WHOLESALERS;DURABLE GDS
98860	14	45	EDUCATIONAL SERVICES
98862	238	1236	ACCOMMODATION
98901	1299	13754	FOOD SVCS & DRINKING PLACES
98902	2022	23623	AMBULATORY HEALTH CARE SVCS
98903	793	12035	MERCH. WHOLESALERS;NONDUR. GDS
98904	5	3	REAL ESTATE
98907	22	46	SPECIAL TRADE CONTRACTORS
98908	915	7413	EDUCATIONAL SERVICES
98909	18	41	ADMINISTRATIVE & SUPPORT SVCS
98920	1	1	POSTAL SERVICE
98921	1	3	FOOD SVCS & DRINKING PLACES
98922	394	1949	FOOD SVCS & DRINKING PLACES
98923	37	316	EDUCATIONAL SERVICES
98925	36	117	EDUCATIONAL SERVICES
98926	1411	9518	FOOD SVCS & DRINKING PLACES
98930	335	3401	MERCH. WHOLESALERS;NONDUR. GDS
98932	75	820	MERCH. WHOLESALERS;NONDUR. GDS
98933	29	232	EDUCATIONAL SERVICES
98934	55	272	EDUCATIONAL SERVICES
98935	59	708	CROP PRODUCTION
98936	94	1466	MERCH. WHOLESALERS;NONDUR. GDS
98937	135	1275	ACCOMMODATION
98938	24	512	MERCH. WHOLESALERS;NONDUR. GDS
98939	7	94	HEAVY & CIVIL ENG. CONSTRUCT'N
98940	17	42	FOOD SVCS & DRINKING PLACES
98941	86	443	TELECOMMUNICATIONS
98942	430	4349	EDUCATIONAL SERVICES
98943	10	14	SPECIAL TRADE CONTRACTORS
98944	750	8399	FOOD MANUFACTURING
98946	26	177	RELIG.; GRANT; CIVIC; PROF ORG
98947	28	448	MERCH. WHOLESALERS;NONDUR. GDS
98948	353	5347	FOOD MANUFACTURING
98950	14	647	CROP PRODUCTION
98951	239	3414	MERCH. WHOLESALERS;NONDUR. GDS
98952	44	1358	CROP PRODUCTION
98953	171	1859	MERCH. WHOLESALERS;NONDUR. GDS
99001	204	3520	AMUSEMENT; GAMBLING;& RECREAT.
99003	89	508	EDUCATIONAL SERVICES
99004	425	3873	EDUCATIONAL SERVICES
99005	144	586	EDUCATIONAL SERVICES
99006	367	1742	EDUCATIONAL SERVICES
99008	14	70	MERCH. WHOLESALERS;NONDUR. GDS
99009	81	138	HEAVY & CIVIL ENG. CONSTRUCT'N
99011	53	5154	NAT'L SECURITY & INT'L AFFAIRS
99012	51	191	NURSING & RESID. CARE FACILIT.
99013	17	48	MINING (EXCEPT OIL AND GAS)
99014	8	37	MOTOR VEHICLE & PARTS DEALERS
99016	221	1148	EDUCATIONAL SERVICES
99017	6	32	EDUCATIONAL SERVICES
99018	8	115	MERCH. WHOLESALERS;NONDUR. GDS
99019	347	5716	SPECIAL TRADE CONTRACTORS
99020	4	4	SPECIAL TRADE CONTRACTORS
99021	220	1350	EDUCATIONAL SERVICES
99022	176	2955	HOSPITALS
99023	11	59	NONMETALLIC MINERAL PROD. MFG
99025	98	355	SPECIAL TRADE CONTRACTORS
99026	170	652	EDUCATIONAL SERVICES
99027	149	597	EDUCATIONAL SERVICES
99029	41	314	EDUCATIONAL SERVICES
99030	39	279	EDUCATIONAL SERVICES
99031	47	418	EDUCATIONAL SERVICES
99032	41	160	JUSTICE; PUBIC ORDER/SAFETY
99033	58	318	EDUCATIONAL SERVICES
99034	8	10	FABRICATED METAL PRODUCT MFG
99036	37	70	EXEC.; LEGIS.; & OTHER SUPPORT
99037	431	3525	GENERAL MERCHANDISE STORES
99039	7	4	MERCH. WHOLESALERS;NONDUR. GDS
99040	35	481	EXEC.; LEGIS.; & OTHER SUPPORT
99101	25	111	MERCH. WHOLESALERS;DURABLE GDS
99102	8	6	POSTAL SERVICE

ZIP CODE	2009 Total Firms	2009 Total Employ-ees	TOP INDUSTRY RANKED on 2009 EMPLOYMENT
99103	22	65	EDUCATIONAL SERVICES
99105	3	7	EDUCATIONAL SERVICES
99109	229	1798	ACCOMMODATION
99110	33	66	REPAIR AND MAINTENANCE
99111	277	2263	AMBULATORY HEALTH CARE SVCS
99113	41	187	EDUCATIONAL SERVICES
99114	645	5819	SOCIAL ASSISTANCE
99115	77	291	ACCOMMODATION
99116	56	349	EXEC.; LEGIS.; & OTHER SUPPORT
99117	18	106	EDUCATIONAL SERVICES
99118	26	194	EDUCATIONAL SERVICES
99119	25	114	EDUCATIONAL SERVICES
99121	10	6	GASOLINE STATIONS
99122	245	1557	HOSPITALS
99123	35	107	FOOD SVCS & DRINKING PLACES
99124	6	13	EXEC.; LEGIS.; & OTHER SUPPORT
99125	38	136	EDUCATIONAL SERVICES
99126	7	10	TRUCK TRANSPORTATION
99128	11	31	FOOD MANUFACTURING
99129	9	13	GASOLINE STATIONS
99130	34	137	EDUCATIONAL SERVICES
99131	4	17	EDUCATIONAL SERVICES
99133	111	1023	ADMIN. ENVIRO. QUALITY PROGRMS
99134	30	117	EDUCATIONAL SERVICES
99135	16	46	EDUCATIONAL SERVICES
99136	1	3	ANIMAL PRODUCTION
99137	23	111	EDUCATIONAL SERVICES
99138	48	255	EXEC.; LEGIS.; & OTHER SUPPORT
99139	41	117	EDUCATIONAL SERVICES
99140	53	99	EXEC.; LEGIS.; & OTHER SUPPORT
99141	165	1118	WOOD PRODUCT MANUFACTURING
99143	56	184	EDUCATIONAL SERVICES
99146	5	11	EXEC.; LEGIS.; & OTHER SUPPORT
99147	5	6	CONSTRUCTION OF BUILDINGS
99148	83	336	SOCIAL ASSISTANCE
99149	3	5	POSTAL SERVICE
99150	7	12	POSTAL SERVICE
99151	5	7	EXEC.; LEGIS.; & OTHER SUPPORT
99152	5	14	GASOLINE STATIONS
99153	29	139	MINING (EXCEPT OIL AND GAS)
99154	1	0	PERSONAL AND LAUNDRY SERVICES
99155	88	2623	AMUSEMENT; GAMBLING;& RECREAT.
99156	300	2395	EDUCATIONAL SERVICES
99157	43	264	EDUCATIONAL SERVICES
99158	35	204	EDUCATIONAL SERVICES
99159	89	472	EDUCATIONAL SERVICES
99160	11	40	EDUCATIONAL SERVICES
99161	43	200	EDUCATIONAL SERVICES
99163	686	6392	FOOD SVCS & DRINKING PLACES
99164	19	737	BROADCASTING
99166	199	1041	HOSPITALS
99167	11	21	AMBULATORY HEALTH CARE SVCS
99169	194	1010	FOOD SVCS & DRINKING PLACES
99170	52	245	MERCH. WHOLESALERS;NONDUR. GDS
99171	80	219	MERCH. WHOLESALERS;NONDUR. GDS
99173	42	426	EDUCATIONAL SERVICES
99174	4	17	EDUCATIONAL SERVICES
99176	3	21	WAREHOUSING AND STORAGE
99179	41	146	TELECOMMUNICATIONS
99180	21	434	PAPER MANUFACTURING
99181	72	223	MINING (EXCEPT OIL AND GAS)
99185	101	453	EDUCATIONAL SERVICES
99201	2671	34865	PROF.; SCIENTIFIC; & TECH SVCS
99202	1847	22791	AMBULATORY HEALTH CARE SVCS
99203	378	2052	EDUCATIONAL SERVICES
99204	506	15448	HOSPITALS
99205	1243	9784	EDUCATIONAL SERVICES
99206	1654	13702	ADMINISTRATIVE & SUPPORT SVCS
99207	1208	11171	FOOD SVCS & DRINKING PLACES
99208	1084	13375	SOCIAL ASSISTANCE
99209	46	127	ADMINISTRATIVE & SUPPORT SVCS
99210	29	56	MISCELLANEOUS MANUFACTURING
99211	7	16	HEAVY & CIVIL ENG. CONSTRUCT'N
99212	1380	16144	MERCH. WHOLESALERS;DURABLE GDS
99213	8	9	TRUCK TRANSPORTATION
99214	47	90	ADMINISTRATIVE & SUPPORT SVCS
99215	4	9	SPECIAL TRADE CONTRACTORS
99216	1156	17536	MERCH. WHOLESALERS;DURABLE GDS
99217	668	8062	SOCIAL ASSISTANCE
99218	791	8388	FOOD SVCS & DRINKING PLACES
99219	16	154	RENTAL AND LEASING SERVICES
99220	21	25	PROF.; SCIENTIFIC; & TECH SVCS
99223	711	5582	BROADCASTING
99224	557	8374	EDUCATIONAL SERVICES
99228	63	447	RELIG.; GRANT; CIVIC; PROF ORG
99252	3	1504	UTILITIES
99256	1	15	EXEC.; LEGIS.; & OTHER SUPPORT
99258	7	65	OTHER INFORMATION SERVICES
99260	61	869	JUSTICE; PUBIC ORDER/SAFETY
99301	1690	20908	EDUCATIONAL SERVICES

ZIP CODE	2009 Total Firms	2009 Total Employ-ees	TOP INDUSTRY RANKED on 2009 EMPLOYMENT
99302	27	51	CONSTRUCTION OF BUILDINGS
99320	144	1064	EDUCATIONAL SERVICES
99321	11	15	FOOD AND BEVERAGE STORES
99322	13	66	JUSTICE; PUBIC ORDER/SAFETY
99323	65	901	CROP PRODUCTION
99324	174	1216	EDUCATIONAL SERVICES
99326	118	1604	FOOD MANUFACTURING
99328	218	1050	HOSPITALS
99329	6	11	EDUCATIONAL SERVICES
99330	33	299	CROP PRODUCTION
99333	2	4	SUPPORT ACTIVITIES: AGR./FOR.
99335	14	65	EDUCATIONAL SERVICES
99336	2380	27838	FOOD SVCS & DRINKING PLACES
99337	285	3285	EDUCATIONAL SERVICES
99338	152	1184	EDUCATIONAL SERVICES
99341	61	276	MERCH. WHOLESALERS;NONDUR. GDS
99343	60	545	MERCH. WHOLESALERS;NONDUR. GDS
99344	471	5723	FOOD MANUFACTURING
99345	22	461	BEVERAGE & TOBACCO PRODUCT MFG
99346	7	102	CROP PRODUCTION
99347	145	805	MERCH. WHOLESALERS;NONDUR. GDS
99348	39	2881	CROP PRODUCTION
99349	141	2524	CROP PRODUCTION
99350	410	3871	CROP PRODUCTION
99352	1041	11057	PROF.; SCIENTIFIC; & TECH SVCS
99353	186	1046	EDUCATIONAL SERVICES
99354	563	14054	PROF.; SCIENTIFIC; & TECH SVCS
99356	16	224	WASTE MANAGMT & REMEDIAT'N SVC
99357	114	1152	EDUCATIONAL SERVICES
99359	9	26	EXEC.; LEGIS.; & OTHER SUPPORT
99360	43	223	EDUCATIONAL SERVICES
99361	64	177	EDUCATIONAL SERVICES
99362	1907	18399	EDUCATIONAL SERVICES
99363	11	1708	FOOD MANUFACTURING
99371	24	75	EDUCATIONAL SERVICES
99401	10	15	ACCOMMODATION
99402	71	286	EXEC.; LEGIS.; & OTHER SUPPORT
99403	645	5657	AMBULATORY HEALTH CARE SVCS
99501	3180	33684	PROF.; SCIENTIFIC; & TECH SVCS
99502	799	17013	SUPPORT ACT. FOR TRANSPORT.
99503	3182	32346	PROF.; SCIENTIFIC; & TECH SVCS
99504	998	6498	EDUCATIONAL SERVICES
99505	52	4868	NAT'L SECURITY & INT'L AFFAIRS
99506	99	927	EDUCATIONAL SERVICES
99507	1345	11186	SPECIAL TRADE CONTRACTORS
99508	1312	24222	HOSPITALS
99509	47	109	SPECIAL TRADE CONTRACTORS
99510	26	90	PROF.; SCIENTIFIC; & TECH SVCS
99511	84	217	SPECIAL TRADE CONTRACTORS
99513	55	1501	JUSTICE; PUBIC ORDER/SAFETY
99514	24	49	HOSPITALS
99515	1529	10817	GENERAL MERCHANDISE STORES
99516	368	1721	EDUCATIONAL SERVICES
99517	473	4525	FOOD AND BEVERAGE STORES
99518	1527	16672	SPECIAL TRADE CONTRACTORS
99519	25	1484	OIL AND GAS EXTRACTION
99520	19	30	PUBLISHING INDUSTRIES
99521	25	59	PROF.; SCIENTIFIC; & TECH SVCS
99522	42	107	SPECIAL TRADE CONTRACTORS
99523	42	74	ADMINISTRATIVE & SUPPORT SVCS
99524	39	50	RELIG.; GRANT; CIVIC; PROF ORG
99530	1	0	POSTAL SERVICE
99540	20	85	FOOD SVCS & DRINKING PLACES
99545	11	32	EXEC.; LEGIS.; & OTHER SUPPORT
99547	11	28	ACCOMMODATION
99548	6	9	EDUCATIONAL SERVICES
99549	13	22	EXEC.; LEGIS.; & OTHER SUPPORT
99550	23	59	RELIG.; GRANT; CIVIC; PROF ORG
99551	25	181	EDUCATIONAL SERVICES
99552	22	91	SOCIAL ASSISTANCE
99553	13	957	FOOD MANUFACTURING
99554	18	114	EDUCATIONAL SERVICES
99555	25	78	RELIG.; GRANT; CIVIC; PROF ORG
99556	91	251	EDUCATIONAL SERVICES
99557	67	225	AMBULATORY HEALTH CARE SVCS
99558	10	35	EXEC.; LEGIS.; & OTHER SUPPORT
99559	414	2594	EDUCATIONAL SERVICES
99561	16	130	EXEC.; LEGIS.; & OTHER SUPPORT
99563	27	176	EDUCATIONAL SERVICES
99564	16	295	FOOD MANUFACTURING
99565	11	18	EDUCATIONAL SERVICES
99566	23	58	EXEC.; LEGIS.; & OTHER SUPPORT
99567	304	1619	PERFORM'G ARTS; SPEC. SPORTS
99568	8	12	POSTAL SERVICE
99569	12	21	RELIG.; GRANT; CIVIC; PROF ORG
99571	41	266	MERCH. WHOLESALERS;NONDUR. GDS
99572	46	336	RELIG.; GRANT; CIVIC; PROF ORG
99573	53	314	ACCOMMODATION
99574	261	1538	FOOD MANUFACTURING
99575	7	22	EDUCATIONAL SERVICES

ZIP CODE	2009 Total Firms	2009 Total Employ-ees	TOP INDUSTRY RANKED on 2009 EMPLOYMENT
99576	273	2027	HOSPITALS
99577	886	3972	EDUCATIONAL SERVICES
99578	16	72	EDUCATIONAL SERVICES
99579	12	54	MERCH. WHOLESALERS;DURABLE GDS
99580	13	34	EDUCATIONAL SERVICES
99581	41	233	EDUCATIONAL SERVICES
99583	8	17	EXEC.; LEGIS.; & OTHER SUPPORT
99585	21	83	SOCIAL ASSISTANCE
99586	46	131	RELIG.; GRANT; CIVIC; PROF ORG
99587	180	1712	ACCOMMODATION
99588	168	896	REAL ESTATE
99589	13	60	EDUCATIONAL SERVICES
99590	13	41	EDUCATIONAL SERVICES
99591	17	43	EXEC.; LEGIS.; & OTHER SUPPORT
99599	1	30	POSTAL SERVICE
99602	14	43	EXEC.; LEGIS.; & OTHER SUPPORT
99603	873	4645	HOSPITALS
99604	32	237	EXEC.; LEGIS.; & OTHER SUPPORT
99605	17	41	MOTOR VEHICLE & PARTS DEALERS
99606	46	156	EXEC.; LEGIS.; & OTHER SUPPORT
99607	24	63	EDUCATIONAL SERVICES
99608	6	7	UTILITIES
99609	17	185	REAL ESTATE
99610	67	284	FORESTRY AND LOGGING
99611	853	6774	FOOD MANUFACTURING
99612	37	539	MERCH. WHOLESALERS;NONDUR. GDS
99613	118	618	RELIG.; GRANT; CIVIC; PROF ORG
99614	15	94	EDUCATIONAL SERVICES
99615	801	6020	FOOD MANUFACTURING
99619	9	444	NAT'L SECURITY & INT'L AFFAIRS
99620	30	165	RELIG.; GRANT; CIVIC; PROF ORG
99621	28	138	EDUCATIONAL SERVICES
99622	16	125	EXEC.; LEGIS.; & OTHER SUPPORT
99624	9	44	RELIG.; GRANT; CIVIC; PROF ORG
99625	15	25	EXEC.; LEGIS.; & OTHER SUPPORT
99626	7	27	EDUCATIONAL SERVICES
99627	54	215	EDUCATIONAL SERVICES
99628	18	104	CONSTRUCTION OF BUILDINGS
99629	14	19	COURIERS AND MESSENGERS
99630	16	75	FOOD AND BEVERAGE STORES
99631	28	178	SUPPORT ACTIVITIES: AGR./FOR.
99632	25	222	EDUCATIONAL SERVICES
99633	113	1732	FOOD MANUFACTURING
99634	15	100	EXEC.; LEGIS.; & OTHER SUPPORT
99635	61	538	FOOD MANUFACTURING
99636	19	111	EDUCATIONAL SERVICES
99637	27	185	EDUCATIONAL SERVICES
99638	5	6	GENERAL MERCHANDISE STORES
99639	111	333	FOOD MANUFACTURING
99640	9	27	EDUCATIONAL SERVICES
99641	17	250	EDUCATIONAL SERVICES
99643	16	38	RELIG.; GRANT; CIVIC; PROF ORG
99644	18	30	EXEC.; LEGIS.; & OTHER SUPPORT
99645	1294	11250	EXEC.; LEGIS.; & OTHER SUPPORT
99647	6	16	EXEC.; LEGIS.; & OTHER SUPPORT
99648	10	60	EXEC.; LEGIS.; & OTHER SUPPORT
99649	9	12	EXEC.; LEGIS.; & OTHER SUPPORT
99650	15	140	EXEC.; LEGIS.; & OTHER SUPPORT
99651	12	21	EXEC.; LEGIS.; & OTHER SUPPORT
99652	166	569	BLDG MATL & GARDEN EQPMT DLRS
99653	14	54	ACCOMMODATION
99654	2191	13002	EDUCATIONAL SERVICES
99655	29	287	RELIG.; GRANT; CIVIC; PROF ORG
99656	13	6	FORESTRY AND LOGGING
99657	16	60	EDUCATIONAL SERVICES
99658	53	208	EDUCATIONAL SERVICES
99659	17	140	EDUCATIONAL SERVICES
99660	24	164	EDUCATIONAL SERVICES
99661	59	813	FOOD MANUFACTURING
99662	25	72	SOCIAL ASSISTANCE
99663	51	146	RELIG.; GRANT; CIVIC; PROF ORG
99664	413	3621	ACCOMMODATION
99665	16	41	EXEC.; LEGIS.; & OTHER SUPPORT
99666	15	68	EXEC.; LEGIS.; & OTHER SUPPORT
99667	12	42	RELIG.; GRANT; CIVIC; PROF ORG
99668	12	10	EDUCATIONAL SERVICES
99669	1166	6388	EDUCATIONAL SERVICES
99670	19	20	EXEC.; LEGIS.; & OTHER SUPPORT
99671	17	164	EDUCATIONAL SERVICES
99672	123	396	AMUSEMENT; GAMBLING;& RECREAT.
99674	54	229	RELIG.; GRANT; CIVIC; PROF ORG
99675	7	17	RELIG.; GRANT; CIVIC; PROF ORG
99676	204	844	RENTAL AND LEASING SERVICES
99677	8	16	EDUCATIONAL SERVICES
99678	33	196	EXEC.; LEGIS.; & OTHER SUPPORT
99679	14	104	SOCIAL ASSISTANCE
99680	20	110	EDUCATIONAL SERVICES
99681	16	111	EDUCATIONAL SERVICES
99682	29	180	EXEC.; LEGIS.; & OTHER SUPPORT
99683	38	280	ACCOMMODATION
99684	55	298	EDUCATIONAL SERVICES
99685	117	1593	FOOD MANUFACTURING
99686	354	3002	RELIG.; GRANT; CIVIC; PROF ORG
99687	70	167	CONSTRUCTION OF BUILDINGS
99688	130	376	SPECIAL TRADE CONTRACTORS
99689	49	286	EDUCATIONAL SERVICES
99690	15	42	EDUCATIONAL SERVICES
99691	3	8	EDUCATIONAL SERVICES
99692	91	6509	FOOD MANUFACTURING
99693	44	108	EXEC.; LEGIS.; & OTHER SUPPORT
99694	73	307	EDUCATIONAL SERVICES
99695	3	6	RELIG.; GRANT; CIVIC; PROF ORG
99701	2554	21851	HOSPITALS
99702	25	350	EDUCATIONAL SERVICES
99703	48	6725	NAT'L SECURITY & INT'L AFFAIRS
99704	9	9	FOOD SVCS & DRINKING PLACES
99705	585	2862	EDUCATIONAL SERVICES
99706	20	50	PERFORM'G ARTS; SPEC. SPORTS
99707	54	86	CONSTRUCTION OF BUILDINGS
99708	82	180	PROF.; SCIENTIFIC; & TECH SVCS
99709	1297	10496	EXEC.; LEGIS.; & OTHER SUPPORT
99710	8	7	CONSTRUCTION OF BUILDINGS
99711	8	27	CONSTRUCTION OF BUILDINGS
99712	332	1329	MINING (EXCEPT OIL AND GAS)
99714	31	103	ACCOMMODATION
99716	9	11	PROF.; SCIENTIFIC; & TECH SVCS
99720	12	31	EXEC.; LEGIS.; & OTHER SUPPORT
99721	26	102	EXEC.; LEGIS.; & OTHER SUPPORT
99722	8	23	EDUCATIONAL SERVICES
99723	182	2174	EXEC.; LEGIS.; & OTHER SUPPORT
99724	6	15	EDUCATIONAL SERVICES
99725	14	54	REAL ESTATE
99726	20	43	RENTAL AND LEASING SERVICES
99727	18	68	EDUCATIONAL SERVICES
99729	26	73	ADMINISTRATIVE & SUPPORT SVCS
99730	8	24	ACCOMMODATION
99731	8	38	EDUCATIONAL SERVICES
99732	1	0	ACCOMMODATION
99733	7	16	EXEC.; LEGIS.; & OTHER SUPPORT
99734	89	2299	PROF.; SCIENTIFIC; & TECH SVCS
99736	14	39	EDUCATIONAL SERVICES
99737	247	1338	NAT'L SECURITY & INT'L AFFAIRS
99738	25	62	SCENIC & SIGHTSEEING TRANSPORT
99739	14	75	EDUCATIONAL SERVICES
99740	47	232	EXEC.; LEGIS.; & OTHER SUPPORT
99741	50	300	EDUCATIONAL SERVICES
99742	30	279	EDUCATIONAL SERVICES
99743	106	805	ACCOMMODATION
99744	19	49	EDUCATIONAL SERVICES
99745	9	26	EXEC.; LEGIS.; & OTHER SUPPORT
99746	18	39	EDUCATIONAL SERVICES
99747	26	99	EXEC.; LEGIS.; & OTHER SUPPORT
99748	12	32	EDUCATIONAL SERVICES
99749	27	97	RELIG.; GRANT; CIVIC; PROF ORG
99750	10	45	EDUCATIONAL SERVICES
99751	16	35	EXEC.; LEGIS.; & OTHER SUPPORT
99752	149	2410	RELIG.; GRANT; CIVIC; PROF ORG
99753	15	66	EDUCATIONAL SERVICES
99754	9	28	EXEC.; LEGIS.; & OTHER SUPPORT
99755	44	2308	ACCOMMODATION
99756	11	19	RELIG.; GRANT; CIVIC; PROF ORG
99757	3	1	RELIG.; GRANT; CIVIC; PROF ORG
99758	16	37	EDUCATIONAL SERVICES
99759	17	58	EXEC.; LEGIS.; & OTHER SUPPORT
99760	48	221	EDUCATIONAL SERVICES
99761	16	228	RELIG.; GRANT; CIVIC; PROF ORG
99762	265	2358	HOSPITALS
99763	22	91	EDUCATIONAL SERVICES
99764	13	47	EDUCATIONAL SERVICES
99765	15	61	EXEC.; LEGIS.; & OTHER SUPPORT
99766	20	239	EDUCATIONAL SERVICES
99767	4	2	AMBULATORY HEALTH CARE SVCS
99768	9	31	EXEC.; LEGIS.; & OTHER SUPPORT
99769	24	74	EXEC.; LEGIS.; & OTHER SUPPORT
99770	26	154	EDUCATIONAL SERVICES
99771	13	24	EXEC.; LEGIS.; & OTHER SUPPORT
99772	24	119	EDUCATIONAL SERVICES
99773	17	45	EDUCATIONAL SERVICES
99774	9	13	EXEC.; LEGIS.; & OTHER SUPPORT
99775	27	638	EDUCATIONAL SERVICES
99776	5	21	SOCIAL ASSISTANCE
99777	18	104	EXEC.; LEGIS.; & OTHER SUPPORT
99778	13	63	EDUCATIONAL SERVICES
99780	168	668	ACCOMMODATION
99781	11	43	EXEC.; LEGIS.; & OTHER SUPPORT
99782	25	184	EDUCATIONAL SERVICES
99783	12	45	EXEC.; LEGIS.; & OTHER SUPPORT
99784	11	60	EDUCATIONAL SERVICES
99785	13	76	EDUCATIONAL SERVICES
99786	20	52	EDUCATIONAL SERVICES
99788	5	18	JUSTICE; PUBIC ORDER/SAFETY
99789	22	140	EDUCATIONAL SERVICES
99791	18	62	EDUCATIONAL SERVICES
99801	2068	19658	EXEC.; LEGIS.; & OTHER SUPPORT
99802	26	26	MERCH. WHOLESALERS;DURABLE GDS
99803	49	321	MINING (EXCEPT OIL AND GAS)
99811	1	60	EXEC.; LEGIS.; & OTHER SUPPORT
99820	19	270	AMUSEMENT; GAMBLING;& RECREAT.
99821	12	23	SCENIC & SIGHTSEEING TRANSPORT
99824	54	415	ADMIN. ENVIRO. QUALITY PROGRMS
99825	9	39	RELIG.; GRANT; CIVIC; PROF ORG
99826	42	393	ACCOMMODATION
99827	301	1311	EDUCATIONAL SERVICES
99829	37	273	EDUCATIONAL SERVICES
99830	30	141	EDUCATIONAL SERVICES
99832	18	58	EDUCATIONAL SERVICES
99833	304	2016	FOOD MANUFACTURING
99835	719	5844	HOSPITALS
99836	8	57	POSTAL SERVICE
99840	225	1526	AIR TRANSPORTATION
99841	7	25	EXEC.; LEGIS.; & OTHER SUPPORT
99850	1	1	FOOD MANUFACTURING
99901	1065	10041	EXEC.; LEGIS.; & OTHER SUPPORT
99918	19	26	EXEC.; LEGIS.; & OTHER SUPPORT
99919	33	154	SUPPORT ACTIVITIES: AGR./FOR.
99921	147	856	EDUCATIONAL SERVICES
99922	23	89	EDUCATIONAL SERVICES
99923	1	0	RELIG.; GRANT; CIVIC; PROF ORG
99925	63	360	EDUCATIONAL SERVICES
99926	82	589	EDUCATIONAL SERVICES
99927	4	10	AMUSEMENT; GAMBLING;& RECREAT.
99928	14	17	CONSTRUCTION OF BUILDINGS
99929	210	1052	EDUCATIONAL SERVICES
99950	14	31	EDUCATIONAL SERVICES

Appendixes

Appendix I: Nonresidential ZIP Codes by State

Point ZIP Code		Enclosing Residential ZIP Code	
ZIP	Post Office Name	ZIP	Post Office Name
00501	HOLTSVILLE	11742	HOLTSVILLE
00544	HOLTSVILLE	11742	HOLTSVILLE
01004	AMHERST	01002	AMHERST
01009	BONDSVILLE	01069	PALMER
01014	CHICOPEE	01013	CHICOPEE
01021	CHICOPEE	01020	CHICOPEE
01029	EAST OTIS	01253	OTIS
01037	HARDWICK	01082	WARE
01041	HOLYOKE	01040	HOLYOKE
01059	NORTH AMHERST	01002	AMHERST
01061	NORTHAMPTON	01060	NORTHAMPTON
01066	NORTH HATFIELD	01038	HATFIELD
01074	SOUTH BARRE	01005	BARRE
01079	THORNDIKE	01069	PALMER
01083	WARREN	01585	WEST BROOKFIELD
01086	WESTFIELD	01085	WESTFIELD
01090	WEST SPRINGFIELD	01089	WEST SPRINGFIELD
01093	WHATELY	01373	SOUTH DEERFIELD
01094	WHEELWRIGHT	01031	GILBERTVILLE
01097	WORONOCO	01085	WESTFIELD
01101	SPRINGFIELD	01103	SPRINGFIELD
01102	SPRINGFIELD	01103	SPRINGFIELD
01111	SPRINGFIELD	01109	SPRINGFIELD
01115	SPRINGFIELD	01103	SPRINGFIELD
01116	LONGMEADOW	01106	LONGMEADOW
01138	SPRINGFIELD	01108	SPRINGFIELD
01139	SPRINGFIELD	01109	SPRINGFIELD
01144	SPRINGFIELD	01103	SPRINGFIELD
01152	SPRINGFIELD	01151	INDIAN ORCHARD
01199	SPRINGFIELD	01105	SPRINGFIELD
01202	PITTSFIELD	01201	PITTSFIELD
01203	PITTSFIELD	01201	PITTSFIELD
01227	DALTON	01226	DALTON
01229	GLENDALE	01266	WEST STOCKBRIDGE
01242	LENOX DALE	01238	LEE
01244	MILL RIVER	01230	GREAT BARRINGTON
01252	NORTH EGREMONT	01230	GREAT BARRINGTON
01260	SOUTH LEE	01238	LEE
01263	STOCKBRIDGE	01262	STOCKBRIDGE
01264	TYRINGHAM	01238	LEE
01302	GREENFIELD	01301	GREENFIELD
01347	LAKE PLEASANT	01349	MILLERS FALLS
01380	WENDELL DEPOT	01379	WENDELL
01438	EAST TEMPLETON	01468	TEMPLETON
01441	WESTMINSTER	01440	GARDNER
01467	STILL RIVER	01451	HARVARD
01471	GROTON	01450	GROTON
01472	WEST GROTON	01464	SHIRLEY
01477	WINCHENDON SPRINGS	01475	WINCHENDON
01508	CHARLTON CITY	01507	CHARLTON
01509	CHARLTON DEPOT	01507	CHARLTON
01517	EAST PRINCETON	01541	PRINCETON
01525	LINWOOD	01588	WHITINSVILLE
01526	MANCHAUG	01590	SUTTON
01538	NORTH UXBRIDGE	01569	UXBRIDGE
01546	SHREWSBURY	01545	SHREWSBURY
01561	SOUTH LANCASTER	01523	LANCASTER
01580	WESTBOROUGH	01581	WESTBOROUGH
01582	WESTBOROUGH	01581	WESTBOROUGH
01586	WEST MILLBURY	01527	MILLBURY
01601	WORCESTER	01608	WORCESTER
01613	WORCESTER	01604	WORCESTER
01614	WORCESTER	01608	WORCESTER
01615	WORCESTER	01605	WORCESTER
01653	WORCESTER	01605	WORCESTER
01654	WORCESTER	01605	WORCESTER
01655	WORCESTER	01605	WORCESTER
01703	FRAMINGHAM	01701	FRAMINGHAM
01704	FRAMINGHAM	01701	FRAMINGHAM
01705	FRAMINGHAM	01701	FRAMINGHAM
01784	WOODVILLE	01748	HOPKINTON
01805	BURLINGTON	01803	BURLINGTON
01807	WOBURN	01801	WOBURN
01812	ANDOVER	01810	ANDOVER
01813	WOBURN	01801	WOBURN
01815	WOBURN	01801	WOBURN
01822	BILLERICA	01824	CHELMSFORD
01831	HAVERHILL	01830	HAVERHILL
01842	LAWRENCE	01840	LAWRENCE
01853	LOWELL	01854	LOWELL
01865	NUTTING LAKE	01821	BILLERICA
01866	PINEHURST	01821	BILLERICA
01885	WEST BOXFORD	01921	BOXFORD
01888	WOBURN	01801	WOBURN
01889	NORTH READING	01864	NORTH READING
01899	ANDOVER	01810	ANDOVER
01903	LYNN	01901	LYNN
01910	LYNN	01905	LYNN
01931	GLOUCESTER	01930	GLOUCESTER
01936	HAMILTON	01982	SOUTH HAMILTON
01937	HATHORNE	01923	DANVERS
01961	PEABODY	01960	PEABODY
01965	PRIDES CROSSING	01915	BEVERLY
01971	SALEM	01970	SALEM
02018	ACCORD	02043	HINGHAM
02020	BRANT ROCK	02050	MARSHFIELD
02027	DEDHAM	02026	DEDHAM
02040	GREENBUSH	02066	SCITUATE
02041	GREEN HARBOR	02050	MARSHFIELD
02044	HINGHAM	02043	HINGHAM
02047	HUMAROCK	02050	MARSHFIELD
02051	MARSHFIELD HILLS	02050	MARSHFIELD
02055	MINOT	02066	SCITUATE
02059	NORTH MARSHFIELD	02050	MARSHFIELD
02060	NORTH SCITUATE	02066	SCITUATE
02065	OCEAN BLUFF	02050	MARSHFIELD
02070	SHELDONVILLE	02093	WRENTHAM
02112	BOSTON	02109	BOSTON
02117	BOSTON	02116	BOSTON
02123	BOSTON	02115	BOSTON
02133	BOSTON	02108	BOSTON
02137	READVILLE	02136	HYDE PARK
02156	WEST MEDFORD	02155	MEDFORD
02185	BRAINTREE	02184	BRAINTREE
02187	MILTON VILLAGE	02186	MILTON
02196	BOSTON	02111	BOSTON
02201	BOSTON	02108	BOSTON
02203	BOSTON	02114	BOSTON
02204	BOSTON	02150	CHELSEA
02205	BOSTON	02111	BOSTON
02206	BOSTON	02150	CHELSEA
02207	BOSTON	02110	BOSTON
02211	BOSTON	02109	BOSTON
02212	BOSTON	02109	BOSTON
02216	BOSTON	02109	BOSTON
02217	BOSTON	02116	BOSTON
02222	BOSTON	02114	BOSTON
02228	EAST BOSTON	02128	BOSTON
02238	CAMBRIDGE	02139	CAMBRIDGE
02239	CAMBRIDGE	02139	CAMBRIDGE
02241	BOSTON	02110	BOSTON
02266	BOSTON	02111	BOSTON
02269	QUINCY	02169	QUINCY
02283	BOSTON	02111	BOSTON
02284	BOSTON	02111	BOSTON
02293	BOSTON	02111	BOSTON
02295	BOSTON	02116	BOSTON
02297	BOSTON	02111	BOSTON
02298	BOSTON	02111	BOSTON
02303	BROCKTON	02302	BROCKTON
02304	BROCKTON	02301	BROCKTON
02305	BROCKTON	02301	BROCKTON
02327	BRYANTVILLE	02359	PEMBROKE
02331	DUXBURY	02332	DUXBURY
02334	EASTON	02356	NORTH EASTON
02337	ELMWOOD	02333	EAST BRIDGEWATER
02340	HANOVER	02339	HANOVER
02344	MIDDLEBORO	02346	MIDDLEBORO
02345	MANOMET	02360	PLYMOUTH
02348	LAKEVILLE	02347	LAKEVILLE
02349	MIDDLEBORO	02347	LAKEVILLE
02350	MONPONSETT	02341	HANSON
02355	NORTH CARVER	02330	CARVER
02358	NORTH PEMBROKE	02359	PEMBROKE
02361	PLYMOUTH	02360	PLYMOUTH
02362	PLYMOUTH	02360	PLYMOUTH
02366	SOUTH CARVER	02330	CARVER
02381	WHITE HORSE BEACH	02360	PLYMOUTH
02447	BROOKLINE VILLAGE	02445	BROOKLINE
02454	WALTHAM	02451	WALTHAM
02455	NORTH WALTHAM	02451	WALTHAM
02456	NEW TOWN	02472	WATERTOWN
02457	BABSON PARK	02481	WELLESLEY HILLS
02471	WATERTOWN	02472	WATERTOWN
02475	ARLINGTON HEIGHTS	02474	ARLINGTON
02477	WATERTOWN	02472	WATERTOWN
02479	WAVERLEY	02478	BELMONT
02495	NONANTUM	02458	NEWTON
02534	CATAUMET	02559	POCASSET
02541	FALMOUTH	02540	FALMOUTH
02552	MENEMSHA	02535	CHILMARK
02553	MONUMENT BEACH	02559	POCASSET
02557	OAK BLUFFS	02568	VINEYARD HAVEN
02558	ONSET	02538	EAST WAREHAM
02561	SAGAMORE	02532	BUZZARDS BAY
02564	SIASCONSET	02554	NANTUCKET
02565	SILVER BEACH	02556	NORTH FALMOUTH
02573	WEST CHOP	02568	VINEYARD HAVEN
02574	WEST FALMOUTH	02540	FALMOUTH
02584	NANTUCKET	02554	NANTUCKET
02634	CENTERVILLE	02632	CENTERVILLE
02637	CUMMAQUID	02675	YARMOUTH PORT
02641	EAST DENNIS	02660	SOUTH DENNIS
02643	EAST ORLEANS	02653	ORLEANS
02647	HYANNIS PORT	02601	HYANNIS
02651	NORTH EASTHAM	02642	EASTHAM

NONRESIDENTIAL ZIP CODES

MASSACHUSETTS

VERMONT

Point ZIP Code		Enclosing Residential ZIP Code	
ZIP	Post Office Name	ZIP	Post Office Name
02661	SOUTH HARWICH	02645	HARWICH
02662	SOUTH ORLEANS	02653	ORLEANS
02663	SOUTH WELLFLEET	02667	WELLFLEET
02669	WEST CHATHAM	02633	CHATHAM
02672	WEST HYANNISPORT	02601	HYANNIS
02712	CHARTLEY	02766	NORTON
02714	DARTMOUTH	02748	SOUTH DARTMOUTH
02722	FALL RIVER	02720	FALL RIVER
02741	NEW BEDFORD	02740	NEW BEDFORD
02742	NEW BEDFORD	02740	NEW BEDFORD
02761	NORTH ATTLEBORO	02760	NORTH ATTLEBORO
02768	RAYNHAM CENTER	02767	RAYNHAM
02783	TAUNTON	02379	WEST BRIDGEWATER
02791	WESTPORT POINT	02790	WESTPORT
02801	ADAMSVILLE	02837	LITTLE COMPTON
02802	ALBION	02865	LINCOLN
02823	FISKEVILLE	02831	HOPE
02824	FORESTDALE	02896	NORTH SMITHFIELD
02826	GLENDALE	02858	OAKLAND
02829	HARMONY	02814	CHEPACHET
02862	PAWTUCKET	02860	PAWTUCKET
02875	SHANNOCK	02812	CAROLINA
02876	SLATERSVILLE	02896	NORTH SMITHFIELD
02880	WAKEFIELD	02879	WAKEFIELD
02883	PEACE DALE	02879	WAKEFIELD
02887	WARWICK	02886	WARWICK
02901	PROVIDENCE	02903	PROVIDENCE
02902	PROVIDENCE	02903	PROVIDENCE
02940	PROVIDENCE	02904	PROVIDENCE
03040	EAST CANDIA	03034	CANDIA
03041	EAST DERRY	03038	DERRY
03061	NASHUA	03060	NASHUA
03073	NORTH SALEM	03079	SALEM
03105	MANCHESTER	03104	MANCHESTER
03108	MANCHESTER	03103	MANCHESTER
03215	WATERVILLE VALLEY	03285	THORNTON
03231	EAST ANDOVER	03216	ANDOVER
03233	ELKINS	03257	NEW LONDON
03238	GLENCLIFF	03279	WARREN
03247	LACONIA	03246	LACONIA
03252	LOCHMERE	03276	TILTON
03260	NORTH SUTTON	03278	WARNER
03272	SOUTH NEWBURY	03255	NEWBURY
03273	SOUTH SUTTON	03278	WARNER
03274	STINSON LAKE	03266	RUMNEY
03289	WINNISQUAM	03220	BELMONT
03293	WOODSTOCK	03262	NORTH WOODSTOCK
03298	TILTON	03253	MEREDITH
03299	TILTON	03253	MEREDITH
03302	CONCORD	03301	CONCORD
03305	CONCORD	03301	CONCORD
03435	KEENE	03431	KEENE
03468	WEST PETERBOROUGH	03458	PETERBOROUGH
03469	WEST SWANZEY	03446	SWANZEY
03575	BRETTON WOODS	03598	WHITEFIELD
03595	TWIN MOUNTAIN	03598	WHITEFIELD
03597	WEST STEWARTSTOWN	03576	COLEBROOK
03601	ACWORTH	03605	LEMPSTER
03604	DREWSVILLE	03602	ALSTEAD
03746	CORNISH FLAT	03745	CORNISH
03749	ENFIELD CENTER	03748	ENFIELD
03751	GEORGES MILLS	03782	SUNAPEE
03754	GUILD	03773	NEWPORT
03756	LEBANON	03766	LEBANON
03769	LYME CENTER	03768	LYME
03802	PORTSMOUTH	03801	PORTSMOUTH
03804	PORTSMOUTH	03904	KITTERY
03805	ROLLINSFORD	03869	ROLLINSFORD
03815	CENTER STRAFFORD	03884	STRAFFORD
03821	DOVER	03820	DOVER
03822	DOVER	03820	DOVER
03832	EATON CENTER	03849	MADISON
03843	HAMPTON	03842	HAMPTON
03847	KEARSARGE	03845	INTERVALE
03850	MELVIN VILLAGE	03816	CENTER TUFTONBORO
03859	NEWTON JUNCTION	03858	NEWTON
03866	ROCHESTER	03867	ROCHESTER
03896	WOLFEBORO FALLS	03894	WOLFEBORO
03897	WONALANCET	03886	TAMWORTH
03910	YORK BEACH	03909	YORK
03911	YORK HARBOR	03909	YORK
04004	BAR MILLS	04093	BUXTON
04007	BIDDEFORD	04005	BIDDEFORD
04014	CAPE PORPOISE	04046	KENNEBUNKPORT
04016	CENTER LOVELL	04051	LOVELL
04028	EAST PARSONSFIELD	04047	PARSONSFIELD
04033	FREEPORT	04032	FREEPORT
04034	FREEPORT	04032	FREEPORT
04054	MOODY	04090	WELLS
04056	NEWFIELD	04095	WEST NEWFIELD
04057	NORTH BRIDGTON	04040	HARRISON
04063	OCEAN PARK	04064	OLD ORCHARD BEACH
04070	SCARBOROUGH	04074	SCARBOROUGH

Point ZIP Code		Enclosing Residential ZIP Code	
ZIP	Post Office Name	ZIP	Post Office Name
04077	SOUTH CASCO	04015	CASCO
04078	SOUTH FREEPORT	04032	FREEPORT
04082	SOUTH WINDHAM	04062	WINDHAM
04094	WEST KENNEBUNK	04043	KENNEBUNK
04098	WESTBROOK	04092	WESTBROOK
04104	PORTLAND	04101	PORTLAND
04112	PORTLAND	04101	PORTLAND
04116	SOUTH PORTLAND	04101	PORTLAND
04122	PORTLAND	04102	PORTLAND
04123	PORTLAND	04102	PORTLAND
04124	PORTLAND	04102	PORTLAND
04211	AUBURN	04210	AUBURN
04212	AUBURN	04210	AUBURN
04223	DANVILLE	04210	AUBURN
04225	DRYDEN	04294	WILTON
04227	EAST DIXFIELD	04294	WILTON
04230	EAST POLAND	04274	POLAND
04234	EAST WILTON	04294	WILTON
04241	LEWISTON	04240	LEWISTON
04243	LEWISTON	04240	LEWISTON
04262	NORTH JAY	04239	JAY
04267	NORTH WATERFORD	04088	WATERFORD
04271	PARIS	04281	SOUTH PARIS
04286	WEST BETHEL	04217	BETHEL
04288	WEST MINOT	04258	MINOT
04291	WEST POLAND	04274	POLAND
04332	AUGUSTA	04330	AUGUSTA
04336	AUGUSTA	04330	AUGUSTA
04338	AUGUSTA	04330	AUGUSTA
04343	EAST WINTHROP	04364	WINTHROP
04359	SOUTH GARDINER	04345	GARDINER
04402	BANGOR	04401	BANGOR
04415	BROWNVILLE JUNCTION	04414	BROWNVILLE
04420	CASTINE	04421	CASTINE
04431	EAST ORLAND	04472	ORLAND
04485	SHIRLEY MILLS	04406	ABBOT
04489	STILLWATER	04468	OLD TOWN
04565	SEBASCO ESTATES	04562	PHIPPSBURG
04575	WEST BOOTHBAY HARBOR	04538	BOOTHBAY HARBOR
04629	EAST BLUE HILL	04614	BLUE HILL
04637	GRAND LAKE STREAM	04668	PRINCETON
04644	HULLS COVE	04609	BAR HARBOR
04662	NORTHEAST HARBOR	04609	BAR HARBOR
04664	SULLIVAN	04634	FRANKLIN
04672	SALSBURY COVE	04609	BAR HARBOR
04675	SEAL HARBOR	04609	BAR HARBOR
04686	WESLEY	04654	MACHIAS
04738	CROUSEVILLE	04786	WASHBURN
04739	EAGLE LAKE	04743	FORT KENT
04744	FORT KENT MILLS	04743	FORT KENT
04775	SHERIDAN	04732	ASHLAND
04846	GLEN COVE	04841	ROCKLAND
04850	LINCOLNVILLE CENTER	04849	LINCOLNVILLE
04855	PORT CLYDE	04860	TENANTS HARBOR
04865	WEST ROCKPORT	04856	ROCKPORT
04903	WATERVILLE	04901	WATERVILLE
04918	BELGRADE LAKES	04917	BELGRADE
04926	CHINA VILLAGE	04358	SOUTH CHINA
04933	EAST NEWPORT	04969	PLYMOUTH
04935	EAST VASSALBORO	04989	VASSALBORO
04940	FARMINGTON FALLS	04938	FARMINGTON
04944	HINCKLEY	04937	FAIRFIELD
04962	NORTH VASSALBORO	04358	SOUTH CHINA
04964	OQUOSSOC	04970	RANGELEY
04972	SANDY POINT	04981	STOCKTON SPRINGS
04975	SHAWMUT	04937	FAIRFIELD
04992	WEST FARMINGTON	04938	FARMINGTON
05009	WHITE RIVER JUNCTION	05001	WHITE RIVER JUNCTION
05030	ASCUTNEY	05089	WINDSOR
05031	BARNARD	05091	WOODSTOCK
05047	HARTFORD	05001	WHITE RIVER JUNCTION
05049	HARTLAND FOUR CORNER	05089	WINDSOR
05050	MC INDOE FALLS	05821	BARNET
05054	NORTH THETFORD	05043	EAST THETFORD
05059	QUECHEE	05001	WHITE RIVER JUNCTION
05074	THETFORD	05075	THETFORD CENTER
05085	WEST NEWBURY	05051	NEWBURY
05088	WILDER	05001	WHITE RIVER JUNCTION
05144	CHESTER DEPOT	05143	CHESTER
05159	WESTMINSTER STATION	05158	WESTMINSTER
05254	MANCHESTER	05255	MANCHESTER CENTER
05302	BRATTLEBORO	05301	BRATTLEBORO
05303	BRATTLEBORO	05301	BRATTLEBORO
05304	BRATTLEBORO	05301	BRATTLEBORO
05344	MARLBORO	05301	BRATTLEBORO
05357	WEST DUMMERSTON	05301	BRATTLEBORO
05402	BURLINGTON	05401	BURLINGTON
05406	BURLINGTON	05401	BURLINGTON
05407	SOUTH BURLINGTON	05403	SOUTH BURLINGTON
05439	COLCHESTER	05404	WINOOSKI
05449	COLCHESTER	05446	COLCHESTER
05451	ESSEX	05452	ESSEX JUNCTION
05453	ESSEX JUNCTION	05452	ESSEX JUNCTION

Point ZIP Code		Enclosing Residential ZIP Code		Point ZIP Code		Enclosing Residential ZIP Code	
ZIP	Post Office Name	ZIP	Post Office Name	ZIP	Post Office Name	ZIP	Post Office Name
05460	HIGHGATE SPRINGS	05488	SWANTON	06199	HARTFORD	06096	WINDSOR LOCKS
05466	JONESVILLE	05477	RICHMOND	06230	ABINGTON	06259	POMFRET CENTER
05469	MONKTON	05443	BRISTOL	06233	BALLOUVILLE	06241	DAYVILLE
05470	MONTGOMERY	05471	MONTGOMERY CENTER	06244	EAST WOODSTOCK	06281	WOODSTOCK
05479	SAINT ALBANS	05478	SAINT ALBANS	06245	FABYAN	06255	NORTH GROSVENORDALE
05481	SAINT ALBANS BAY	05478	SAINT ALBANS	06246	GROSVENOR DALE	06255	NORTH GROSVENORDALE
05485	SHELDON SPRINGS	05483	SHELDON	06251	MANSFIELD DEPOT	06268	STORRS MANSFIELD
05490	UNDERHILL CENTER	05489	UNDERHILL	06258	POMFRET	06259	POMFRET CENTER
05501	ANDOVER	01810	ANDOVER	06263	ROGERS	06241	DAYVILLE
05544	ANDOVER	01810	ANDOVER	06265	SOUTH WILLINGTON	06279	WILLINGTON
05601	MONTPELIER	05602	MONTPELIER	06267	SOUTH WOODSTOCK	06259	POMFRET CENTER
05603	MONTPELIER	05602	MONTPELIER	06332	CENTRAL VILLAGE	06374	PLAINFIELD
05604	MONTPELIER	05602	MONTPELIER	06338	MASHANTUCKET	06320	NEW LONDON
05609	MONTPELIER	05602	MONTPELIER	06350	HANOVER	06330	BALTIC
05620	MONTPELIER	05602	MONTPELIER	06372	OLD MYSTIC	06355	MYSTIC
05633	MONTPELIER	05602	MONTPELIER	06373	ONECO	06377	STERLING
05657	LAKE ELMORE	05680	WOLCOTT	06376	SOUTH LYME	06371	OLD LYME
05662	MOSCOW	05672	STOWE	06383	VERSAILLES	06330	BALTIC
05664	NORTHFIELD FALLS	05663	NORTHFIELD	06387	WAUREGAN	06239	DANIELSON
05665	NORTH HYDE PARK	05655	HYDE PARK	06388	WEST MYSTIC	06355	MYSTIC
05670	SOUTH BARRE	05641	BARRE	06389	YANTIC	06254	NORTH FRANKLIN
05671	WATERBURY	05676	WATERBURY	06404	BOTSFORD	06470	NEWTOWN
05678	WEBSTERVILLE	05654	GRANITEVILLE	06408	CHESHIRE	06410	CHESHIRE
05702	RUTLAND	05701	RUTLAND	06411	CHESHIRE	06410	CHESHIRE
05731	BENSON	05743	FAIR HAVEN	06414	COBALT	06424	EAST HAMPTON
05740	EAST MIDDLEBURY	05753	MIDDLEBURY	06439	HADLYME	06371	OLD LYME
05741	EAST POULTNEY	05764	POULTNEY	06440	HAWLEYVILLE	06470	NEWTOWN
05745	FOREST DALE	05733	BRANDON	06444	MARION	06479	PLANTSVILLE
05750	HYDEVILLE	05735	CASTLETON	06456	MIDDLE HADDAM	06424	EAST HAMPTON
05768	RUPERT	05776	WEST RUPERT	06467	MILLDALE	06479	PLANTSVILLE
05823	BEEBE PLAIN	05855	NEWPORT	06474	NORTH WESTCHESTER	06415	COLCHESTER
05838	EAST SAINT JOHNSBURY	05819	SAINT JOHNSBURY	06487	SOUTH BRITAIN	06488	SOUTHBURY
05840	GRANBY	05858	NORTH CONCORD	06491	STEVENSON	06468	MONROE
05848	LOWER WATERFORD	05819	SAINT JOHNSBURY	06493	WALLINGFORD	06492	WALLINGFORD
05849	LYNDON	05851	LYNDONVILLE	06494	WALLINGFORD	06492	WALLINGFORD
05861	PASSUMPSIC	05819	SAINT JOHNSBURY	06495	WALLINGFORD	06492	WALLINGFORD
05863	SAINT JOHNSBURY CENT	05819	SAINT JOHNSBURY	06501	NEW HAVEN	06510	NEW HAVEN
06006	WINDSOR	06095	WINDSOR	06502	NEW HAVEN	06510	NEW HAVEN
06011	BRISTOL	06010	BRISTOL	06503	NEW HAVEN	06510	NEW HAVEN
06020	CANTON CENTER	06019	CANTON	06504	NEW HAVEN	06510	NEW HAVEN
06025	EAST GLASTONBURY	06033	GLASTONBURY	06505	NEW HAVEN	06510	NEW HAVEN
06028	EAST WINDSOR HILL	06074	SOUTH WINDSOR	06506	NEW HAVEN	06511	NEW HAVEN
06030	FARMINGTON	06032	FARMINGTON	06507	NEW HAVEN	06510	NEW HAVEN
06034	FARMINGTON	06032	FARMINGTON	06508	NEW HAVEN	06510	NEW HAVEN
06041	MANCHESTER	06042	MANCHESTER	06509	NEW HAVEN	06510	NEW HAVEN
06045	MANCHESTER	06042	MANCHESTER	06520	NEW HAVEN	06510	NEW HAVEN
06050	NEW BRITAIN	06051	NEW BRITAIN	06521	NEW HAVEN	06510	NEW HAVEN
06061	PINE MEADOW	06057	NEW HARTFORD	06530	NEW HAVEN	06511	NEW HAVEN
06064	POQUONOCK	06095	WINDSOR	06531	NEW HAVEN	06511	NEW HAVEN
06072	SOMERSVILLE	06071	SOMERS	06532	NEW HAVEN	06511	NEW HAVEN
06075	STAFFORD	06076	STAFFORD SPRINGS	06533	NEW HAVEN	06511	NEW HAVEN
06077	STAFFORDVILLE	06076	STAFFORD SPRINGS	06534	NEW HAVEN	06511	NEW HAVEN
06079	TACONIC	06068	SALISBURY	06535	NEW HAVEN	06511	NEW HAVEN
06080	SUFFIELD	06078	SUFFIELD	06536	NEW HAVEN	06511	NEW HAVEN
06083	ENFIELD	06082	ENFIELD	06537	NEW HAVEN	06516	WEST HAVEN
06087	UNIONVILLE	06085	UNIONVILLE	06538	NEW HAVEN	06516	WEST HAVEN
06094	WINCHESTER CENTER	06098	WINSTED	06540	NEW HAVEN	06511	NEW HAVEN
06101	HARTFORD	06120	HARTFORD	06601	BRIDGEPORT	06604	BRIDGEPORT
06102	HARTFORD	06114	HARTFORD	06602	BRIDGEPORT	06604	BRIDGEPORT
06104	HARTFORD	06120	HARTFORD	06673	BRIDGEPORT	06615	STRATFORD
06115	HARTFORD	06105	HARTFORD	06699	BRIDGEPORT	06615	STRATFORD
06123	HARTFORD	06103	HARTFORD	06701	WATERBURY	06702	WATERBURY
06126	HARTFORD	06105	HARTFORD	06703	WATERBURY	06704	WATERBURY
06127	WEST HARTFORD	06107	WEST HARTFORD	06720	WATERBURY	06702	WATERBURY
06128	EAST HARTFORD	06106	HARTFORD	06721	WATERBURY	06702	WATERBURY
06129	WETHERSFIELD	06109	WETHERSFIELD	06722	WATERBURY	06702	WATERBURY
06131	NEWINGTON	06111	NEWINGTON	06723	WATERBURY	06702	WATERBURY
06132	HARTFORD	06112	HARTFORD	06724	WATERBURY	06702	WATERBURY
06133	WEST HARTFORD	06110	WEST HARTFORD	06725	WATERBURY	06702	WATERBURY
06134	HARTFORD	06114	HARTFORD	06726	WATERBURY	06702	WATERBURY
06137	WEST HARTFORD	06117	WEST HARTFORD	06749	WATERBURY	06762	MIDDLEBURY
06138	EAST HARTFORD	06118	EAST HARTFORD	06753	CORNWALL	06754	CORNWALL BRIDGE
06140	HARTFORD	06120	HARTFORD	06781	PEQUABUCK	06786	TERRYVILLE
06141	HARTFORD	06120	HARTFORD	06792	TORRINGTON	06790	TORRINGTON
06142	HARTFORD	06120	HARTFORD	06813	DANBURY	06810	DANBURY
06143	HARTFORD	06120	HARTFORD	06814	DANBURY	06810	DANBURY
06144	HARTFORD	06120	HARTFORD	06816	DANBURY	06810	DANBURY
06145	HARTFORD	06120	HARTFORD	06817	DANBURY	06810	DANBURY
06146	HARTFORD	06120	HARTFORD	06828	FAIRFIELD	06825	FAIRFIELD
06147	HARTFORD	06120	HARTFORD	06829	GEORGETOWN	06883	WESTON
06150	HARTFORD	06120	HARTFORD	06836	GREENWICH	06831	GREENWICH
06151	HARTFORD	06120	HARTFORD	06838	GREENS FARMS	06880	WESTPORT
06152	HARTFORD	06002	BLOOMFIELD	06852	NORWALK	06850	NORWALK
06153	HARTFORD	06032	FARMINGTON	06856	NORWALK	06854	NORWALK
06154	HARTFORD	06105	HARTFORD	06857	NORWALK	06854	NORWALK
06155	HARTFORD	06105	HARTFORD	06858	NORWALK	06850	NORWALK
06156	HARTFORD	06105	HARTFORD	06859	NORWALK	06851	NORWALK
06160	HARTFORD	06105	HARTFORD	06860	NORWALK	06854	NORWALK
06161	HARTFORD	06109	WETHERSFIELD	06875	REDDING CENTER	06896	REDDING
06167	HARTFORD	06110	WEST HARTFORD	06876	REDDING RIDGE	06896	REDDING
06176	HARTFORD	06103	HARTFORD	06879	RIDGEFIELD	06877	RIDGEFIELD
06180	HARTFORD	06107	WEST HARTFORD	06881	WESTPORT	06880	WESTPORT
06183	HARTFORD	06103	HARTFORD	06888	WESTPORT	06880	WESTPORT

Point ZIP Code		Enclosing Residential ZIP Code	
ZIP	Post Office Name	ZIP	Post Office Name
06889	WESTPORT	06880	WESTPORT
06904	STAMFORD	06901	STAMFORD
06910	STAMFORD	06902	STAMFORD
06911	STAMFORD	06902	STAMFORD
06912	STAMFORD	06902	STAMFORD
06913	STAMFORD	06902	STAMFORD
06920	STAMFORD	06902	STAMFORD
06921	STAMFORD	06901	STAMFORD
06922	STAMFORD	06902	STAMFORD
06925	STAMFORD	06902	STAMFORD
06926	STAMFORD	06902	STAMFORD
06927	STAMFORD	06902	STAMFORD
06928	STAMFORD	06902	STAMFORD
07007	CALDWELL	07006	CALDWELL
07015	CLIFTON	07011	CLIFTON
07019	EAST ORANGE	07017	EAST ORANGE
07051	ORANGE	07050	ORANGE
07061	PLAINFIELD	07060	PLAINFIELD
07091	WESTFIELD	07090	WESTFIELD
07096	SECAUCUS	07094	SECAUCUS
07097	JERSEY CITY	07307	JERSEY CITY
07099	KEARNY	07032	KEARNY
07101	NEWARK	07102	NEWARK
07175	NEWARK	07102	NEWARK
07184	NEWARK	07102	NEWARK
07188	NEWARK	07102	NEWARK
07189	NEWARK	07102	NEWARK
07191	NEWARK	07102	NEWARK
07192	NEWARK	07102	NEWARK
07193	NEWARK	07102	NEWARK
07195	NEWARK	07102	NEWARK
07198	NEWARK	07102	NEWARK
07199	NEWARK	07102	NEWARK
07207	ELIZABETH	07208	ELIZABETH
07303	JERSEY CITY	07302	JERSEY CITY
07308	JERSEY CITY	07302	JERSEY CITY
07309	JERSEY CITY	07304	JERSEY CITY
07311	JERSEY CITY	07302	JERSEY CITY
07395	JERSEY CITY	07302	JERSEY CITY
07399	JERSEY CITY	07306	JERSEY CITY
07428	MC AFEE	07462	VERNON
07451	RIDGEWOOD	07450	RIDGEWOOD
07474	WAYNE	07470	WAYNE
07495	MAHWAH	07430	MAHWAH
07507	HAWTHORNE	07506	HAWTHORNE
07509	PATERSON	07505	PATERSON
07510	PATERSON	07505	PATERSON
07511	TOTOWA	07512	TOTOWA
07533	PATERSON	07503	PATERSON
07538	HALEDON	07508	HALEDON
07543	PATERSON	07513	PATERSON
07544	PATERSON	07524	PATERSON
07602	HACKENSACK	07601	HACKENSACK
07653	PARAMUS	07652	PARAMUS
07699	TETERBORO	07601	HACKENSACK
07709	RED BANK	07711	ALLENHURST
07710	ADELPHIA	07728	FREEHOLD
07715	BELMAR	07719	BELMAR
07752	NAVESINK	07716	ATLANTIC HIGHLANDS
07754	NEPTUNE	07753	NEPTUNE
07763	TENNENT	07726	ENGLISHTOWN
07765	WICKATUNK	07751	MORGANVILLE
07799	EATONTOWN	07724	EATONTOWN
07802	DOVER	07801	DOVER
07806	PICATINNY ARSENAL	07801	DOVER
07820	ALLAMUCHY	07840	HACKETTSTOWN
07829	BUTTZVILLE	07823	BELVIDERE
07831	CHANGEWATER	08827	HAMPTON
07833	DELAWARE	07832	COLUMBIA
07837	GLASSER	07849	LAKE HOPATCONG
07839	GREENDELL	07821	ANDOVER
07842	HIBERNIA	07866	ROCKAWAY
07844	HOPE	07825	BLAIRSTOWN
07845	IRONIA	07945	MENDHAM
07846	JOHNSONBURG	07825	BLAIRSTOWN
07855	MIDDLEVILLE	07860	NEWTON
07870	SCHOOLEYS MOUNTAIN	07853	LONG VALLEY
07875	STILLWATER	07860	NEWTON
07877	SWARTSWOOD	07860	NEWTON
07878	MOUNT TABOR	07834	DENVILLE
07879	TRANQUILITY	07821	ANDOVER
07880	VIENNA	07840	HACKETTSTOWN
07881	WALLPACK CENTER	07826	BRANCHVILLE
07890	BRANCHVILLE	07826	BRANCHVILLE
07902	SUMMIT	07901	SUMMIT
07926	BROOKSIDE	07960	MORRISTOWN
07938	LIBERTY CORNER	07920	BASKING RIDGE
07939	LYONS	07920	BASKING RIDGE
07961	MORRISTOWN	07960	MORRISTOWN
07962	MORRISTOWN	07960	MORRISTOWN
07963	MORRISTOWN	07960	MORRISTOWN
07970	MOUNT FREEDOM	07945	MENDHAM
07977	PEAPACK	07934	GLADSTONE

Point ZIP Code		Enclosing Residential ZIP Code	
ZIP	Post Office Name	ZIP	Post Office Name
07978	PLUCKEMIN	07921	BEDMINSTER
07979	POTTERSVILLE	07830	CALIFON
07999	WHIPPANY	07981	WHIPPANY
08001	ALLOWAY	08079	SALEM
08006	BARNEGAT LIGHT	08008	BEACH HAVEN
08011	BIRMINGHAM	08088	SHAMONG
08018	CEDAR BROOK	08009	BERLIN
08023	DEEPWATER	08069	PENNS GROVE
08025	EWAN	08062	MULLICA HILL
08038	HANCOCKS BRIDGE	08079	SALEM
08039	HARRISONVILLE	08062	MULLICA HILL
08042	JULIUSTOWN	08068	PEMBERTON
08064	NEW LISBON	08088	SHAMONG
08072	QUINTON	08079	SALEM
08073	RANCOCAS	08060	MOUNT HOLLY
08074	RICHWOOD	08062	MULLICA HILL
08076	RIVERTON	08077	RIVERTON
08095	WINSLOW	08037	HAMMONTON
08099	BELLMAWR	08031	BELLMAWR
08101	CAMDEN	08102	CAMDEN
08212	CAPE MAY POINT	08204	CAPE MAY
08213	COLOGNE	08215	EGG HARBOR CITY
08214	DENNISVILLE	08270	WOODBINE
08217	ELWOOD	08215	EGG HARBOR CITY
08218	GOSHEN	08210	CAPE MAY COURT HOUSE
08219	GREEN CREEK	08204	CAPE MAY
08220	LEEDS POINT	08205	ABSECON
08224	NEW GRETNA	08087	LITTLE EGG HARBOR TW
08231	OCEANVILLE	08205	ABSECON
08240	POMONA	08215	EGG HARBOR CITY
08245	SOUTH DENNIS	08210	CAPE MAY COURT HOUSE
08246	SOUTH SEAVILLE	08230	OCEAN VIEW
08250	TUCKAHOE	08270	WOODBINE
08252	WHITESBORO	08210	CAPE MAY COURT HOUSE
08313	DEERFIELD STREET	08302	BRIDGETON
08315	DIVIDING CREEK	08349	PORT NORRIS
08316	DORCHESTER	08332	MILLVILLE
08320	FAIRTON	08302	BRIDGETON
08321	FORTESCUE	08345	NEWPORT
08329	MAURICETOWN	08349	PORT NORRIS
08342	MIZPAH	08330	MAYS LANDING
08347	NORMA	08318	ELMER
08348	PORT ELIZABETH	08332	MILLVILLE
08352	ROSENHAYN	08302	BRIDGETON
08362	VINELAND	08360	VINELAND
08404	ATLANTIC CITY	08401	ATLANTIC CITY
08504	BLAWENBURG	08558	SKILLMAN
08526	IMLAYSTOWN	08514	CREAM RIDGE
08541	PRINCETON	08540	PRINCETON
08543	PRINCETON	08540	PRINCETON
08557	SERGEANTSVILLE	08559	STOCKTON
08561	WINDSOR	08520	HIGHTSTOWN
08601	TRENTON	08611	TRENTON
08602	TRENTON	08691	TRENTON
08603	TRENTON	08691	TRENTON
08604	TRENTON	08691	TRENTON
08605	TRENTON	08691	TRENTON
08606	TRENTON	08691	TRENTON
08607	TRENTON	08691	TRENTON
08625	TRENTON	08608	TRENTON
08645	TRENTON	08608	TRENTON
08646	TRENTON	08608	TRENTON
08647	TRENTON	08608	TRENTON
08650	TRENTON	08691	TRENTON
08666	TRENTON	08608	TRENTON
08695	TRENTON	08608	TRENTON
08720	ALLENWOOD	07719	BELMAR
08739	NORMANDY BEACH	08738	MANTOLOKING
08754	TOMS RIVER	08753	TOMS RIVER
08756	TOMS RIVER	08721	BAYVILLE
08803	BAPTISTOWN	08825	FRENCHTOWN
08808	BROADWAY	07882	WASHINGTON
08818	EDISON	08817	EDISON
08821	FLAGTOWN	08844	HILLSBOROUGH
08834	LITTLE YORK	08848	MILFORD
08855	PISCATAWAY	08854	PISCATAWAY
08858	OLDWICK	08833	LEBANON
08862	PERTH AMBOY	08861	PERTH AMBOY
08868	QUAKERTOWN	08867	PITTSTOWN
08870	READINGTON	08889	WHITEHOUSE STATION
08871	SAYREVILLE	08872	SAYREVILLE
08875	SOMERSET	08873	SOMERSET
08885	STANTON	08822	FLEMINGTON
08888	WHITEHOUSE	08889	WHITEHOUSE STATION
08890	ZAREPHATH	08873	SOMERSET
08899	EDISON	08817	EDISON
08903	NEW BRUNSWICK	08901	NEW BRUNSWICK
08905	NEW BRUNSWICK	08902	NORTH BRUNSWICK
08906	NEW BRUNSWICK	08817	EDISON
08922	NEW BRUNSWICK	08902	NORTH BRUNSWICK
08933	NEW BRUNSWICK	08901	NEW BRUNSWICK
08988	NEW BRUNSWICK	08817	EDISON
08989	NEW BRUNSWICK	08817	EDISON

NEW YORK

Point ZIP Code		Enclosing Residential ZIP Code	
ZIP	Post Office Name	ZIP	Post Office Name
09001	APO	00000	NO ENCLOSING ZIP
09002	APO	00000	NO ENCLOSING ZIP
09003	APO	00000	NO ENCLOSING ZIP
09004	APO	00000	NO ENCLOSING ZIP
09005	APO	00000	NO ENCLOSING ZIP
09006	APO	00000	NO ENCLOSING ZIP
09007	APO	00000	NO ENCLOSING ZIP
09008	APO	00000	NO ENCLOSING ZIP
09009	APO	00000	NO ENCLOSING ZIP
09010	APO	00000	NO ENCLOSING ZIP
09011	APO	00000	NO ENCLOSING ZIP
09012	APO	00000	NO ENCLOSING ZIP
09013	APO	00000	NO ENCLOSING ZIP
09014	APO	00000	NO ENCLOSING ZIP
09020	APO	00000	NO ENCLOSING ZIP
09021	APO	00000	NO ENCLOSING ZIP
09028	APO	00000	NO ENCLOSING ZIP
09033	APO	00000	NO ENCLOSING ZIP
09034	APO	00000	NO ENCLOSING ZIP
09036	APO	00000	NO ENCLOSING ZIP
09038	APO	00000	NO ENCLOSING ZIP
09042	APO	00000	NO ENCLOSING ZIP
09046	APO	00000	NO ENCLOSING ZIP
09049	APO	00000	NO ENCLOSING ZIP
09051	APO	00000	NO ENCLOSING ZIP
09053	APO	00000	NO ENCLOSING ZIP
09054	APO	00000	NO ENCLOSING ZIP
09055	APO	00000	NO ENCLOSING ZIP
09056	APO	00000	NO ENCLOSING ZIP
09058	APO	00000	NO ENCLOSING ZIP
09059	APO	00000	NO ENCLOSING ZIP
09060	APO	00000	NO ENCLOSING ZIP
09063	APO	00000	NO ENCLOSING ZIP
09067	APO	00000	NO ENCLOSING ZIP
09069	APO	00000	NO ENCLOSING ZIP
09075	APO	00000	NO ENCLOSING ZIP
09079	APO	00000	NO ENCLOSING ZIP
09080	APO	00000	NO ENCLOSING ZIP
09081	APO	00000	NO ENCLOSING ZIP
09086	APO	00000	NO ENCLOSING ZIP
09088	APO	00000	NO ENCLOSING ZIP
09090	APO	00000	NO ENCLOSING ZIP
09092	APO	00000	NO ENCLOSING ZIP
09094	APO	00000	NO ENCLOSING ZIP
09095	APO	00000	NO ENCLOSING ZIP
09096	APO	00000	NO ENCLOSING ZIP
09099	APO	00000	NO ENCLOSING ZIP
09100	APO	00000	NO ENCLOSING ZIP
09102	APO	00000	NO ENCLOSING ZIP
09103	APO	00000	NO ENCLOSING ZIP
09104	APO	00000	NO ENCLOSING ZIP
09107	APO	00000	NO ENCLOSING ZIP
09110	APO	00000	NO ENCLOSING ZIP
09112	APO	00000	NO ENCLOSING ZIP
09114	APO	00000	NO ENCLOSING ZIP
09123	APO	00000	NO ENCLOSING ZIP
09126	APO	00000	NO ENCLOSING ZIP
09128	APO	00000	NO ENCLOSING ZIP
09131	APO	00000	NO ENCLOSING ZIP
09137	APO	00000	NO ENCLOSING ZIP
09138	APO	00000	NO ENCLOSING ZIP
09139	APO	00000	NO ENCLOSING ZIP
09140	APO	00000	NO ENCLOSING ZIP
09142	APO	00000	NO ENCLOSING ZIP
09143	APO	00000	NO ENCLOSING ZIP
09154	APO	00000	NO ENCLOSING ZIP
09165	APO	00000	NO ENCLOSING ZIP
09166	APO	00000	NO ENCLOSING ZIP
09172	APO	00000	NO ENCLOSING ZIP
09173	APO	00000	NO ENCLOSING ZIP
09175	APO	00000	NO ENCLOSING ZIP
09177	APO	00000	NO ENCLOSING ZIP
09180	APO	00000	NO ENCLOSING ZIP
09185	APO	00000	NO ENCLOSING ZIP
09186	APO	00000	NO ENCLOSING ZIP
09201	APO	00000	NO ENCLOSING ZIP
09211	APO	00000	NO ENCLOSING ZIP
09212	APO	00000	NO ENCLOSING ZIP
09213	APO	00000	NO ENCLOSING ZIP
09214	APO	00000	NO ENCLOSING ZIP
09226	APO	00000	NO ENCLOSING ZIP
09227	APO	00000	NO ENCLOSING ZIP
09229	APO	00000	NO ENCLOSING ZIP
09237	APO	00000	NO ENCLOSING ZIP
09245	APO	00000	NO ENCLOSING ZIP
09250	APO	00000	NO ENCLOSING ZIP
09261	APO	00000	NO ENCLOSING ZIP
09262	APO	00000	NO ENCLOSING ZIP
09263	APO	00000	NO ENCLOSING ZIP
09264	APO	00000	NO ENCLOSING ZIP
09265	APO	00000	NO ENCLOSING ZIP
09266	APO	00000	NO ENCLOSING ZIP
09267	APO	00000	NO ENCLOSING ZIP
09301	APO	00000	NO ENCLOSING ZIP
09302	APO	00000	NO ENCLOSING ZIP
09304	APO	00000	NO ENCLOSING ZIP
09305	APO	00000	NO ENCLOSING ZIP
09306	APO	00000	NO ENCLOSING ZIP
09307	APO	00000	NO ENCLOSING ZIP
09308	APO	00000	NO ENCLOSING ZIP
09309	APO	00000	NO ENCLOSING ZIP
09310	APO	00000	NO ENCLOSING ZIP
09311	APO	00000	NO ENCLOSING ZIP
09312	APO	00000	NO ENCLOSING ZIP
09313	APO	00000	NO ENCLOSING ZIP
09314	APO	00000	NO ENCLOSING ZIP
09315	APO	00000	NO ENCLOSING ZIP
09316	APO	00000	NO ENCLOSING ZIP
09317	APO	00000	NO ENCLOSING ZIP
09318	APO	00000	NO ENCLOSING ZIP
09320	APO	00000	NO ENCLOSING ZIP
09321	APO	00000	NO ENCLOSING ZIP
09322	APO	00000	NO ENCLOSING ZIP
09324	APO	00000	NO ENCLOSING ZIP
09327	APO	00000	NO ENCLOSING ZIP
09328	APO	00000	NO ENCLOSING ZIP
09330	APO	00000	NO ENCLOSING ZIP
09331	APO	00000	NO ENCLOSING ZIP
09332	APO	00000	NO ENCLOSING ZIP
09333	APO	00000	NO ENCLOSING ZIP
09334	APO	00000	NO ENCLOSING ZIP
09336	APO	00000	NO ENCLOSING ZIP
09337	APO	00000	NO ENCLOSING ZIP
09338	APO	00000	NO ENCLOSING ZIP
09339	APO	00000	NO ENCLOSING ZIP
09340	APO	00000	NO ENCLOSING ZIP
09342	APO	00000	NO ENCLOSING ZIP
09343	APO	00000	NO ENCLOSING ZIP
09344	APO	00000	NO ENCLOSING ZIP
09348	APO	00000	NO ENCLOSING ZIP
09350	APO	00000	NO ENCLOSING ZIP
09351	APO	00000	NO ENCLOSING ZIP
09353	APO	00000	NO ENCLOSING ZIP
09354	APO	00000	NO ENCLOSING ZIP
09355	APO	00000	NO ENCLOSING ZIP
09356	APO	00000	NO ENCLOSING ZIP
09357	APO	00000	NO ENCLOSING ZIP
09358	APO	00000	NO ENCLOSING ZIP
09359	APO	00000	NO ENCLOSING ZIP
09360	APO	00000	NO ENCLOSING ZIP
09361	APO	00000	NO ENCLOSING ZIP
09363	APO	00000	NO ENCLOSING ZIP
09365	APO	00000	NO ENCLOSING ZIP
09366	APO	00000	NO ENCLOSING ZIP
09367	APO	00000	NO ENCLOSING ZIP
09370	FPO	00000	NO ENCLOSING ZIP
09371	APO	00000	NO ENCLOSING ZIP
09375	APO	00000	NO ENCLOSING ZIP
09378	APO	00000	NO ENCLOSING ZIP
09381	APO	00000	NO ENCLOSING ZIP
09387	APO	00000	NO ENCLOSING ZIP
09388	APO	00000	NO ENCLOSING ZIP
09389	APO	00000	NO ENCLOSING ZIP
09390	APO	00000	NO ENCLOSING ZIP
09391	APO	00000	NO ENCLOSING ZIP
09393	APO	00000	NO ENCLOSING ZIP
09396	APO	00000	NO ENCLOSING ZIP
09402	FPO	00000	NO ENCLOSING ZIP
09409	FPO	00000	NO ENCLOSING ZIP
09421	FPO	00000	NO ENCLOSING ZIP
09447	APO	00000	NO ENCLOSING ZIP
09454	APO	00000	NO ENCLOSING ZIP
09456	APO	00000	NO ENCLOSING ZIP
09459	APO	00000	NO ENCLOSING ZIP
09461	APO	00000	NO ENCLOSING ZIP
09463	APO	00000	NO ENCLOSING ZIP
09464	APO	00000	NO ENCLOSING ZIP
09468	APO	00000	NO ENCLOSING ZIP
09469	APO	00000	NO ENCLOSING ZIP
09470	APO	00000	NO ENCLOSING ZIP
09494	APO	00000	NO ENCLOSING ZIP
09496	APO	00000	NO ENCLOSING ZIP
09498	FPO	00000	NO ENCLOSING ZIP
09501	FPO	00000	NO ENCLOSING ZIP
09502	FPO	00000	NO ENCLOSING ZIP
09503	FPO	00000	NO ENCLOSING ZIP
09504	FPO	00000	NO ENCLOSING ZIP
09505	FPO	00000	NO ENCLOSING ZIP
09506	FPO	00000	NO ENCLOSING ZIP
09507	FPO	00000	NO ENCLOSING ZIP
09508	FPO	00000	NO ENCLOSING ZIP
09509	FPO	00000	NO ENCLOSING ZIP
09510	FPO	00000	NO ENCLOSING ZIP
09513	FPO	00000	NO ENCLOSING ZIP
09517	FPO	00000	NO ENCLOSING ZIP
09524	FPO	00000	NO ENCLOSING ZIP

Point ZIP Code		Enclosing Residential ZIP Code	
ZIP	Post Office Name	ZIP	Post Office Name
09532	FPO	00000	NO ENCLOSING ZIP
09534	FPO	00000	NO ENCLOSING ZIP
09543	FPO	00000	NO ENCLOSING ZIP
09545	FPO	00000	NO ENCLOSING ZIP
09549	FPO	00000	NO ENCLOSING ZIP
09554	FPO	00000	NO ENCLOSING ZIP
09556	FPO	00000	NO ENCLOSING ZIP
09557	FPO	00000	NO ENCLOSING ZIP
09564	FPO	00000	NO ENCLOSING ZIP
09565	FPO	00000	NO ENCLOSING ZIP
09566	FPO	00000	NO ENCLOSING ZIP
09567	FPO	00000	NO ENCLOSING ZIP
09568	FPO	00000	NO ENCLOSING ZIP
09569	FPO	00000	NO ENCLOSING ZIP
09570	FPO	00000	NO ENCLOSING ZIP
09573	FPO	00000	NO ENCLOSING ZIP
09574	FPO	00000	NO ENCLOSING ZIP
09575	FPO	00000	NO ENCLOSING ZIP
09576	FPO	00000	NO ENCLOSING ZIP
09577	FPO	00000	NO ENCLOSING ZIP
09578	FPO	00000	NO ENCLOSING ZIP
09579	FPO	00000	NO ENCLOSING ZIP
09581	FPO	00000	NO ENCLOSING ZIP
09582	FPO	00000	NO ENCLOSING ZIP
09586	FPO	00000	NO ENCLOSING ZIP
09587	FPO	00000	NO ENCLOSING ZIP
09588	FPO	00000	NO ENCLOSING ZIP
09589	FPO	00000	NO ENCLOSING ZIP
09590	FPO	00000	NO ENCLOSING ZIP
09591	FPO	00000	NO ENCLOSING ZIP
09593	FPO	00000	NO ENCLOSING ZIP
09594	FPO	00000	NO ENCLOSING ZIP
09596	FPO	00000	NO ENCLOSING ZIP
09599	FPO	00000	NO ENCLOSING ZIP
09601	APO	00000	NO ENCLOSING ZIP
09602	APO	00000	NO ENCLOSING ZIP
09603	APO	00000	NO ENCLOSING ZIP
09604	APO	00000	NO ENCLOSING ZIP
09605	APO	00000	NO ENCLOSING ZIP
09606	APO	00000	NO ENCLOSING ZIP
09607	APO	00000	NO ENCLOSING ZIP
09609	FPO	00000	NO ENCLOSING ZIP
09610	APO	00000	NO ENCLOSING ZIP
09613	APO	00000	NO ENCLOSING ZIP
09617	APO	00000	NO ENCLOSING ZIP
09618	FPO	00000	NO ENCLOSING ZIP
09620	FPO	00000	NO ENCLOSING ZIP
09621	FPO	00000	NO ENCLOSING ZIP
09622	FPO	00000	NO ENCLOSING ZIP
09623	FPO	00000	NO ENCLOSING ZIP
09624	APO	00000	NO ENCLOSING ZIP
09625	FPO	00000	NO ENCLOSING ZIP
09626	FPO	00000	NO ENCLOSING ZIP
09627	FPO	00000	NO ENCLOSING ZIP
09630	APO	00000	NO ENCLOSING ZIP
09631	FPO	00000	NO ENCLOSING ZIP
09636	FPO	00000	NO ENCLOSING ZIP
09642	APO	00000	NO ENCLOSING ZIP
09643	APO	00000	NO ENCLOSING ZIP
09645	FPO	00000	NO ENCLOSING ZIP
09647	APO	00000	NO ENCLOSING ZIP
09648	FPO	00000	NO ENCLOSING ZIP
09649	FPO	00000	NO ENCLOSING ZIP
09701	APO	00000	NO ENCLOSING ZIP
09702	APO	00000	NO ENCLOSING ZIP
09703	APO	00000	NO ENCLOSING ZIP
09704	APO	00000	NO ENCLOSING ZIP
09705	APO	00000	NO ENCLOSING ZIP
09706	APO	00000	NO ENCLOSING ZIP
09707	APO	00000	NO ENCLOSING ZIP
09708	APO	00000	NO ENCLOSING ZIP
09709	APO	00000	NO ENCLOSING ZIP
09710	APO	00000	NO ENCLOSING ZIP
09711	APO	00000	NO ENCLOSING ZIP
09713	APO	00000	NO ENCLOSING ZIP
09714	APO	00000	NO ENCLOSING ZIP
09715	APO	00000	NO ENCLOSING ZIP
09716	APO	00000	NO ENCLOSING ZIP
09717	APO	00000	NO ENCLOSING ZIP
09718	APO	00000	NO ENCLOSING ZIP
09719	APO	00000	NO ENCLOSING ZIP
09720	APO	00000	NO ENCLOSING ZIP
09721	APO	00000	NO ENCLOSING ZIP
09722	APO	00000	NO ENCLOSING ZIP
09723	APO	00000	NO ENCLOSING ZIP
09724	APO	00000	NO ENCLOSING ZIP
09726	APO	00000	NO ENCLOSING ZIP
09727	FPO	00000	NO ENCLOSING ZIP
09729	FPO	00000	NO ENCLOSING ZIP
09730	FPO	00000	NO ENCLOSING ZIP
09731	APO	00000	NO ENCLOSING ZIP
09732	APO	00000	NO ENCLOSING ZIP
09733	FPO	00000	NO ENCLOSING ZIP
09734	APO	00000	NO ENCLOSING ZIP
09735	APO	00000	NO ENCLOSING ZIP
09736	APO	00000	NO ENCLOSING ZIP
09737	APO	00000	NO ENCLOSING ZIP
09738	APO	00000	NO ENCLOSING ZIP
09739	APO	00000	NO ENCLOSING ZIP
09741	APO	00000	NO ENCLOSING ZIP
09742	APO	00000	NO ENCLOSING ZIP
09743	APO	00000	NO ENCLOSING ZIP
09744	APO	00000	NO ENCLOSING ZIP
09746	APO	00000	NO ENCLOSING ZIP
09747	FPO	00000	NO ENCLOSING ZIP
09749	APO	00000	NO ENCLOSING ZIP
09750	APO	00000	NO ENCLOSING ZIP
09751	APO	00000	NO ENCLOSING ZIP
09752	APO	00000	NO ENCLOSING ZIP
09753	APO	00000	NO ENCLOSING ZIP
09754	APO	00000	NO ENCLOSING ZIP
09755	APO	00000	NO ENCLOSING ZIP
09756	APO	00000	NO ENCLOSING ZIP
09757	APO	00000	NO ENCLOSING ZIP
09777	APO	00000	NO ENCLOSING ZIP
09780	APO	00000	NO ENCLOSING ZIP
09790	APO	00000	NO ENCLOSING ZIP
09801	APO	00000	NO ENCLOSING ZIP
09803	APO	00000	NO ENCLOSING ZIP
09804	APO	00000	NO ENCLOSING ZIP
09806	APO	00000	NO ENCLOSING ZIP
09807	APO	00000	NO ENCLOSING ZIP
09808	APO	00000	NO ENCLOSING ZIP
09809	APO	00000	NO ENCLOSING ZIP
09811	APO	00000	NO ENCLOSING ZIP
09812	APO	00000	NO ENCLOSING ZIP
09814	APO	00000	NO ENCLOSING ZIP
09815	APO	00000	NO ENCLOSING ZIP
09817	APO	00000	NO ENCLOSING ZIP
09819	APO	00000	NO ENCLOSING ZIP
09821	APO	00000	NO ENCLOSING ZIP
09822	APO	00000	NO ENCLOSING ZIP
09823	APO	00000	NO ENCLOSING ZIP
09824	APO	00000	NO ENCLOSING ZIP
09825	APO	00000	NO ENCLOSING ZIP
09827	APO	00000	NO ENCLOSING ZIP
09828	APO	00000	NO ENCLOSING ZIP
09830	APO	00000	NO ENCLOSING ZIP
09831	APO	00000	NO ENCLOSING ZIP
09832	APO	00000	NO ENCLOSING ZIP
09833	APO	00000	NO ENCLOSING ZIP
09834	FPO	00000	NO ENCLOSING ZIP
09835	FPO	00000	NO ENCLOSING ZIP
09836	FPO	00000	NO ENCLOSING ZIP
09837	FPO	00000	NO ENCLOSING ZIP
09838	FPO	00000	NO ENCLOSING ZIP
09839	APO	00000	NO ENCLOSING ZIP
09840	FPO	00000	NO ENCLOSING ZIP
09841	APO	00000	NO ENCLOSING ZIP
09842	APO	00000	NO ENCLOSING ZIP
09843	APO	00000	NO ENCLOSING ZIP
09844	APO	00000	NO ENCLOSING ZIP
09852	APO	00000	NO ENCLOSING ZIP
09853	APO	00000	NO ENCLOSING ZIP
09855	APO	00000	NO ENCLOSING ZIP
09858	APO	00000	NO ENCLOSING ZIP
09865	FPO	00000	NO ENCLOSING ZIP
09868	APO	00000	NO ENCLOSING ZIP
09870	APO	00000	NO ENCLOSING ZIP
09880	APO	00000	NO ENCLOSING ZIP
09888	APO	00000	NO ENCLOSING ZIP
09890	APO	00000	NO ENCLOSING ZIP
09892	APO	00000	NO ENCLOSING ZIP
09898	APO	00000	NO ENCLOSING ZIP
10008	NEW YORK	10007	NEW YORK
10041	NEW YORK	10004	NEW YORK
10043	NEW YORK	10005	NEW YORK
10045	NEW YORK	10005	NEW YORK
10047	NEW YORK	10280	NEW YORK
10048	NEW YORK	10280	NEW YORK
10055	NEW YORK	10022	NEW YORK
10069	NEW YORK	10023	NEW YORK
10072	NEW YORK	10001	NEW YORK
10080	NEW YORK	10280	NEW YORK
10081	NEW YORK	10005	NEW YORK
10082	NEW YORK	10023	NEW YORK
10087	NEW YORK	10017	NEW YORK
10101	NEW YORK	10019	NEW YORK
10102	NEW YORK	10019	NEW YORK
10103	NEW YORK	10019	NEW YORK
10104	NEW YORK	10019	NEW YORK
10105	NEW YORK	10019	NEW YORK
10106	NEW YORK	10019	NEW YORK
10107	NEW YORK	10019	NEW YORK
10108	NEW YORK	10036	NEW YORK
10109	NEW YORK	10036	NEW YORK

NONRESIDENTIAL ZIP CODES

NEW YORK

Point ZIP Code		Enclosing Residential ZIP Code	
ZIP	Post Office Name	ZIP	Post Office Name
10110	NEW YORK	10017	NEW YORK
10113	NEW YORK	10011	NEW YORK
10114	NEW YORK	10003	NEW YORK
10115	NEW YORK	10024	NEW YORK
10116	NEW YORK	10027	NEW YORK
10117	NEW YORK	10001	NEW YORK
10118	NEW YORK	10016	NEW YORK
10119	NEW YORK	10001	NEW YORK
10120	NEW YORK	10001	NEW YORK
10121	NEW YORK	10001	NEW YORK
10122	NEW YORK	10001	NEW YORK
10123	NEW YORK	10001	NEW YORK
10124	NEW YORK	10022	NEW YORK
10125	NEW YORK	10001	NEW YORK
10126	NEW YORK	10022	NEW YORK
10129	NEW YORK	10018	NEW YORK
10130	NEW YORK	10001	NEW YORK
10131	NEW YORK	10021	NEW YORK
10132	NEW YORK	10024	NEW YORK
10133	NEW YORK	10023	NEW YORK
10138	NEW YORK	10016	NEW YORK
10149	NEW YORK	10019	NEW YORK
10150	NEW YORK	10022	NEW YORK
10151	NEW YORK	10022	NEW YORK
10152	NEW YORK	10022	NEW YORK
10153	NEW YORK	10022	NEW YORK
10154	NEW YORK	10022	NEW YORK
10155	NEW YORK	10022	NEW YORK
10156	NEW YORK	10016	NEW YORK
10157	NEW YORK	10016	NEW YORK
10158	NEW YORK	10016	NEW YORK
10159	NEW YORK	10010	NEW YORK
10160	NEW YORK	10010	NEW YORK
10161	NEW YORK	10011	NEW YORK
10162	NEW YORK	10021	NEW YORK
10163	NEW YORK	10017	NEW YORK
10164	NEW YORK	10017	NEW YORK
10165	NEW YORK	10017	NEW YORK
10166	NEW YORK	10017	NEW YORK
10167	NEW YORK	10017	NEW YORK
10168	NEW YORK	10017	NEW YORK
10169	NEW YORK	10017	NEW YORK
10170	NEW YORK	10017	NEW YORK
10171	NEW YORK	10017	NEW YORK
10172	NEW YORK	10010	NEW YORK
10173	NEW YORK	10017	NEW YORK
10174	NEW YORK	10017	NEW YORK
10175	NEW YORK	10017	NEW YORK
10176	NEW YORK	10036	NEW YORK
10177	NEW YORK	10017	NEW YORK
10178	NEW YORK	10016	NEW YORK
10179	NEW YORK	10017	NEW YORK
10185	NEW YORK	10036	NEW YORK
10197	NEW YORK	10022	NEW YORK
10199	NEW YORK	10001	NEW YORK
10213	NEW YORK	10013	NEW YORK
10242	NEW YORK	10007	NEW YORK
10249	NEW YORK	10007	NEW YORK
10256	NEW YORK	10006	NEW YORK
10259	NEW YORK	10017	NEW YORK
10260	NEW YORK	10005	NEW YORK
10261	NEW YORK	10017	NEW YORK
10265	NEW YORK	10005	NEW YORK
10268	NEW YORK	10005	NEW YORK
10269	NEW YORK	10005	NEW YORK
10270	NEW YORK	10005	NEW YORK
10271	NEW YORK	10005	NEW YORK
10272	NEW YORK	10038	NEW YORK
10273	NEW YORK	10038	NEW YORK
10274	NEW YORK	10004	NEW YORK
10275	NEW YORK	10004	NEW YORK
10276	NEW YORK	10003	NEW YORK
10277	NEW YORK	10007	NEW YORK
10278	NEW YORK	10007	NEW YORK
10279	NEW YORK	10007	NEW YORK
10281	NEW YORK	10280	NEW YORK
10282	NEW YORK	10007	NEW YORK
10285	NEW YORK	10280	NEW YORK
10286	NEW YORK	10005	NEW YORK
10292	NEW YORK	10038	NEW YORK
10311	STATEN ISLAND	10314	STATEN ISLAND
10313	STATEN ISLAND	10314	STATEN ISLAND
10499	BRONX	10465	BRONX
10503	ARDSLEY ON HUDSON	10533	IRVINGTON
10517	CROMPOND	10547	MOHEGAN LAKE
10519	CROTON FALLS	10560	NORTH SALEM
10521	CROTON ON HUDSON	10520	CROTON ON HUDSON
10540	LINCOLNDALE	10589	SOMERS
10542	MAHOPAC FALLS	10541	MAHOPAC
10545	MARYKNOLL	10562	OSSINING
10551	MOUNT VERNON	10550	MOUNT VERNON
10571	PLEASANTVILLE	10514	CHAPPAQUA
10572	PLEASANTVILLE	10570	PLEASANTVILLE
10587	SHENOROCK	10598	YORKTOWN HEIGHTS
10596	VERPLANCK	10548	MONTROSE
10602	WHITE PLAINS	10606	WHITE PLAINS
10610	WHITE PLAINS	10604	WEST HARRISON
10702	YONKERS	10701	YONKERS
10802	NEW ROCHELLE	10801	NEW ROCHELLE
10910	ARDEN	10975	SOUTHFIELDS
10912	BELLVALE	10990	WARWICK
10914	BLOOMING GROVE	10992	WASHINGTONVILLE
10915	BULLVILLE	10941	MIDDLETOWN
10922	FORT MONTGOMERY	10928	HIGHLAND FALLS
10932	HOWELLS	10940	MIDDLETOWN
10933	JOHNSON	10973	SLATE HILL
10943	MIDDLETOWN	10941	MIDDLETOWN
10949	MONROE	10950	MONROE
10953	MOUNTAINVILLE	12553	NEW WINDSOR
10959	NEW MILFORD	10990	WARWICK
10979	STERLING FOREST	10925	GREENWOOD LAKE
10981	SUGAR LOAF	10918	CHESTER
10982	TALLMAN	10901	SUFFERN
10988	UNIONVILLE	10998	WESTTOWN
10997	WEST POINT	10996	WEST POINT
11002	FLORAL PARK	11001	FLORAL PARK
11022	GREAT NECK	11021	GREAT NECK
11051	PORT WASHINGTON	11050	PORT WASHINGTON
11052	PORT WASHINGTON	11050	PORT WASHINGTON
11053	PORT WASHINGTON	11050	PORT WASHINGTON
11054	PORT WASHINGTON	11050	PORT WASHINGTON
11055	PORT WASHINGTON	11050	PORT WASHINGTON
11202	BROOKLYN	11201	BROOKLYN
11241	BROOKLYN	11201	BROOKLYN
11242	BROOKLYN	11201	BROOKLYN
11243	BROOKLYN	11217	BROOKLYN
11245	BROOKLYN	11201	BROOKLYN
11247	BROOKLYN	11216	BROOKLYN
11249	BROOKLYN	11201	BROOKLYN
11252	BROOKLYN	11209	BROOKLYN
11256	BROOKLYN	11208	BROOKLYN
11351	FLUSHING	11356	COLLEGE POINT
11352	FLUSHING	11355	FLUSHING
11380	ELMHURST	11373	ELMHURST
11381	FLUSHING	11379	MIDDLE VILLAGE
11386	RIDGEWOOD	11385	RIDGEWOOD
11405	JAMAICA	11433	JAMAICA
11424	JAMAICA	11415	KEW GARDENS
11425	JAMAICA	11434	JAMAICA
11431	JAMAICA	11432	JAMAICA
11451	JAMAICA	11433	JAMAICA
11499	JAMAICA	11430	JAMAICA
11531	GARDEN CITY	11530	GARDEN CITY
11535	GARDEN CITY	11530	GARDEN CITY
11547	GLENWOOD LANDING	11545	GLEN HEAD
11551	HEMPSTEAD	11550	HEMPSTEAD
11555	UNIONDALE	11553	UNIONDALE
11556	UNIONDALE	11553	UNIONDALE
11569	POINT LOOKOUT	11561	LONG BEACH
11571	ROCKVILLE CENTRE	11570	ROCKVILLE CENTRE
11582	VALLEY STREAM	11580	VALLEY STREAM
11594	WESTBURY	11590	WESTBURY
11597	WESTBURY	11590	WESTBURY
11599	GARDEN CITY	11530	GARDEN CITY
11690	FAR ROCKAWAY	11691	FAR ROCKAWAY
11695	FAR ROCKAWAY	11693	FAR ROCKAWAY
11707	WEST BABYLON	11702	BABYLON
11708	AMITYVILLE	11701	AMITYVILLE
11736	FARMINGDALE	11735	FARMINGDALE
11737	FARMINGDALE	11735	FARMINGDALE
11739	GREAT RIVER	11730	EAST ISLIP
11750	HUNTINGTON STATION	11747	MELVILLE
11760	ISLANDIA	11788	HAUPPAUGE
11773	SYOSSET	11791	SYOSSET
11774	FARMINGDALE	11735	FARMINGDALE
11775	MELVILLE	11747	MELVILLE
11802	HICKSVILLE	11801	HICKSVILLE
11815	HICKSVILLE	11801	HICKSVILLE
11854	HICKSVILLE	11801	HICKSVILLE
11855	HICKSVILLE	11801	HICKSVILLE
11930	AMAGANSETT	11937	EAST HAMPTON
11931	AQUEBOGUE	11901	RIVERHEAD
11932	BRIDGEHAMPTON	11963	SAG HARBOR
11947	JAMESPORT	11901	RIVERHEAD
11956	NEW SUFFOLK	11935	CUTCHOGUE
11959	QUOGUE	11942	EAST QUOGUE
11960	REMSENBURG	11941	EASTPORT
11962	SAGAPONACK	11963	SAG HARBOR
11969	SOUTHAMPTON	11968	SOUTHAMPTON
11970	SOUTH JAMESPORT	11901	RIVERHEAD
11972	SPEONK	11941	EASTPORT
11973	UPTON	11961	RIDGE
11975	WAINSCOTT	11937	EAST HAMPTON
12016	AURIESVILLE	12010	AMSTERDAM
12040	CHERRY PLAIN	12022	BERLIN
12045	COEYMANS	12143	RAVENA

NONRESIDENTIAL ZIP CODES

NEW YORK

Point ZIP Code		Enclosing Residential ZIP Code	
ZIP	Post Office Name	ZIP	Post Office Name
12050	COLUMBIAVILLE	12173	STUYVESANT
12055	DORMANSVILLE	12193	WESTERLO
12063	EAST SCHODACK	12123	NASSAU
12069	FORT HUNTER	12068	FONDA
12073	GALLUPVILLE	12157	SCHOHARIE
12082	GRAFTON	12052	CROPSEYVILLE
12085	GUILDERLAND CENTER	12009	ALTAMONT
12089	HOOSICK	12090	HOOSICK FALLS
12107	KNOX	12009	ALTAMONT
12124	NEW BALTIMORE	12192	WEST COXSACKIE
12128	NEWTONVILLE	12110	LATHAM
12132	NORTH CHATHAM	12123	NASSAU
12133	NORTH HOOSICK	12057	EAGLE BRIDGE
12141	QUAKER STREET	12053	DELANSON
12161	SOUTH BETHLEHEM	12054	DELMAR
12172	STOTTVILLE	12534	HUDSON
12174	STUYVESANT FALLS	12106	KINDERHOOK
12177	TRIBES HILL	12068	FONDA
12181	TROY	12180	TROY
12195	WEST LEBANON	12125	NEW LEBANON
12201	ALBANY	12205	ALBANY
12212	ALBANY	12205	ALBANY
12220	ALBANY	12206	ALBANY
12222	ALBANY	12206	ALBANY
12223	ALBANY	12207	ALBANY
12224	ALBANY	12207	ALBANY
12226	ALBANY	12206	ALBANY
12227	ALBANY	12207	ALBANY
12228	ALBANY	12202	ALBANY
12229	ALBANY	12208	ALBANY
12230	ALBANY	12207	ALBANY
12231	ALBANY	12210	ALBANY
12232	ALBANY	12206	ALBANY
12233	ALBANY	12207	ALBANY
12234	ALBANY	12207	ALBANY
12235	ALBANY	12207	ALBANY
12236	ALBANY	12207	ALBANY
12237	ALBANY	12207	ALBANY
12238	ALBANY	12207	ALBANY
12239	ALBANY	12207	ALBANY
12240	ALBANY	12207	ALBANY
12241	ALBANY	12207	ALBANY
12242	ALBANY	12207	ALBANY
12243	ALBANY	12207	ALBANY
12244	ALBANY	12207	ALBANY
12245	ALBANY	12207	ALBANY
12246	ALBANY	12203	ALBANY
12247	ALBANY	12207	ALBANY
12248	ALBANY	12207	ALBANY
12249	ALBANY	12207	ALBANY
12250	ALBANY	12204	ALBANY
12252	ALBANY	12207	ALBANY
12255	ALBANY	12207	ALBANY
12256	ALBANY	12207	ALBANY
12257	ALBANY	12207	ALBANY
12260	ALBANY	12206	ALBANY
12261	ALBANY	12206	ALBANY
12288	ALBANY	12205	ALBANY
12301	SCHENECTADY	12305	SCHENECTADY
12325	SCHENECTADY	12302	SCHENECTADY
12345	SCHENECTADY	12306	SCHENECTADY
12402	KINGSTON	12401	KINGSTON
12407	ASHLAND	12442	HUNTER
12417	CONNELLY	12466	PORT EWEN
12420	CRAGSMOOR	12566	PINE BUSH
12429	ESOPUS	12528	HIGHLAND
12432	GLASCO	12477	SAUGERTIES
12434	GRAND GORGE	12167	STAMFORD
12436	HAINES FALLS	12463	PALENVILLE
12438	HALCOTTSVILLE	12455	MARGARETVILLE
12441	HIGHMOUNT	12465	PINE HILL
12452	LEXINGTON	12492	WEST KILL
12453	MALDEN ON HUDSON	12477	SAUGERTIES
12459	NEW KINGSTON	12455	MARGARETVILLE
12471	RIFTON	12487	ULSTER PARK
12475	RUBY	12401	KINGSTON
12483	SPRING GLEN	12428	ELLENVILLE
12489	WAWARSING	12446	KERHONKSON
12490	WEST CAMP	12477	SAUGERTIES
12493	WEST PARK	12528	HIGHLAND
12504	ANNANDALE ON HUDSON	12571	RED HOOK
12506	BANGALL	12581	STANFORDVILLE
12510	BILLINGS	12540	LAGRANGEVILLE
12511	CASTLE POINT	12590	WAPPINGERS FALLS
12512	CHELSEA	12590	WAPPINGERS FALLS
12527	GLENHAM	12524	FISHKILL
12530	HOLLOWVILLE	12513	CLAVERACK
12537	HUGHSONVILLE	12590	WAPPINGERS FALLS
12541	LIVINGSTON	12502	ANCRAM
12544	MELLENVILLE	12075	GHENT
12551	NEWBURGH	12550	NEWBURGH
12552	NEWBURGH	12550	NEWBURGH
12555	NEWBURGH	12550	NEWBURGH
12565	PHILMONT	12534	HUDSON
12568	PLATTEKILL	12589	WALLKILL
12574	RHINECLIFF	12572	RHINEBECK
12584	VAILS GATE	12553	NEW WINDSOR
12588	WALKER VALLEY	12566	PINE BUSH
12602	POUGHKEEPSIE	12601	POUGHKEEPSIE
12722	BURLINGHAM	12721	BLOOMINGBURG
12724	CALLICOON CENTER	12776	ROSCOE
12749	KAUNEONGA LAKE	12786	WHITE LAKE
12767	OBERNBURG	12776	ROSCOE
12769	PHILLIPSPORT	12790	WURTSBORO
12778	SMALLWOOD	12701	MONTICELLO
12781	SUMMITVILLE	12790	WURTSBORO
12784	THOMPSONVILLE	12701	MONTICELLO
12785	WESTBROOKVILLE	12729	CUDDEBACKVILLE
12811	BAKERS MILLS	12843	JOHNSBURG
12820	CLEVERDALE	12845	LAKE GEORGE
12841	HULETTS LANDING	12819	CLEMONS
12848	MIDDLE FALLS	12834	GREENWICH
12856	NORTH RIVER	12843	JOHNSBURG
12862	RIPARIUS	12817	CHESTERTOWN
12864	SABAEL	12842	INDIAN LAKE
12874	SILVER BAY	12836	HAGUE
12879	NEWCOMB	12852	NEWCOMB
12884	VICTORY MILLS	12871	SCHUYLERVILLE
12915	BRAINARDSVILLE	12920	CHATEAUGAY
12927	CRANBERRY LAKE	13625	COLTON
12929	DANNEMORA	12981	SARANAC
12933	ELLENBURG	12934	ELLENBURG CENTER
12939	GABRIELS	12983	SARANAC LAKE
12949	LAWRENCEVILLE	12967	NORTH LAWRENCE
12975	PORT KENT	12944	KEESEVILLE
12976	RAINBOW LAKE	12989	VERMONTVILLE
12977	RAY BROOK	12983	SARANAC LAKE
12995	WHIPPLEVILLE	12953	MALONE
12998	WITHERBEE	12956	MINEVILLE
13020	APULIA STATION	13159	TULLY
13022	AUBURN	13021	AUBURN
13024	AUBURN	13021	AUBURN
13043	CLOCKVILLE	13032	CANASTOTA
13051	DELPHI FALLS	13104	MANLIUS
13056	EAST HOMER	13045	CORTLAND
13062	ETNA	14850	ITHACA
13064	FAIR HAVEN	13156	STERLING
13065	FAYETTE	14541	ROMULUS
13087	LITTLE YORK	13141	PREBLE
13089	LIVERPOOL	13090	LIVERPOOL
13093	LYCOMING	13126	OSWEGO
13102	MC LEAN	13068	FREEVILLE
13107	MAPLE VIEW	13114	MEXICO
13113	MERIDIAN	13033	CATO
13115	MINETTO	13126	OSWEGO
13117	MONTEZUMA	13140	PORT BYRON
13119	MOTTVILLE	13152	SKANEATELES
13121	NEW HAVEN	13114	MEXICO
13123	NORTH BAY	13316	CAMDEN
13134	PETERBORO	13408	MORRISVILLE
13137	PLAINVILLE	13027	BALDWINSVILLE
13138	POMPEY	13063	FABIUS
13139	POPLAR RIDGE	13026	AURORA
13153	SKANEATELES FALLS	13060	ELBRIDGE
13154	SOUTH BUTLER	13146	SAVANNAH
13157	SYLVAN BEACH	13308	BLOSSVALE
13162	VERONA BEACH	13308	BLOSSVALE
13163	WAMPSVILLE	13421	ONEIDA
13201	SYRACUSE	13202	SYRACUSE
13217	SYRACUSE	13210	SYRACUSE
13218	SYRACUSE	13204	SYRACUSE
13220	SYRACUSE	13212	SYRACUSE
13221	SYRACUSE	13212	SYRACUSE
13225	SYRACUSE	13212	SYRACUSE
13235	SYRACUSE	13210	SYRACUSE
13250	SYRACUSE	13212	SYRACUSE
13251	SYRACUSE	13212	SYRACUSE
13252	SYRACUSE	13202	SYRACUSE
13261	SYRACUSE	13202	SYRACUSE
13290	SYRACUSE	13204	SYRACUSE
13305	BEAVER FALLS	13620	CASTORLAND
13312	BRANTINGHAM	13345	GREIG
13313	BRIDGEWATER	13318	CASSVILLE
13321	CLARK MILLS	13323	CLINTON
13341	FRANKLIN SPRINGS	13323	CLINTON
13352	HINCKLEY	13438	REMSEN
13362	KNOXBORO	13425	ORISKANY FALLS
13364	LEONARDSVILLE	13485	WEST EDMESTON
13401	MC CONNELLSVILLE	13308	BLOSSVALE
13404	MARTINSBURG	13367	LOWVILLE
13410	NELLISTON	13428	PALATINE BRIDGE
13426	ORWELL	13144	RICHLAND
13435	PROSPECT	13438	REMSEN
13441	ROME	13440	ROME
13442	ROME	13440	ROME
13455	SANGERFIELD	13480	WATERVILLE

NONRESIDENTIAL ZIP CODES

Point ZIP Code		Enclosing Residential ZIP Code	
ZIP	Post Office Name	ZIP	Post Office Name
13457	SCHUYLER LAKE	13348	HARTWICK
13465	SOLSVILLE	13402	MADISON
13472	THENDARA	13331	EAGLE BAY
13479	WASHINGTON MILLS	13413	NEW HARTFORD
13484	WEST EATON	13334	EATON
13503	UTICA	13502	UTICA
13504	UTICA	13501	UTICA
13505	UTICA	13502	UTICA
13599	UTICA	13501	UTICA
13615	BROWNVILLE	13601	WATERTOWN
13623	CHIPPEWA BAY	13646	HAMMOND
13627	DEER RIVER	13619	CARTHAGE
13628	DEFERIET	13619	CARTHAGE
13631	DENMARK	13619	CARTHAGE
13632	DEPAUVILLE	13622	CHAUMONT
13641	FISHERS LANDING	13624	CLAYTON
13643	GREAT BEND	13619	CARTHAGE
13645	HAILESBORO	13642	GOUVERNEUR
13647	HANNAWA FALLS	13676	POTSDAM
13649	HELENA	13613	BRASHER FALLS
13651	HENDERSON HARBOR	13650	HENDERSON
13664	MORRISTOWN	13669	OGDENSBURG
13671	OXBOW	13608	ANTWERP
13674	PIERREPONT MANOR	13605	ADAMS
13677	PYRITES	13652	HERMON
13678	RAYMONDVILLE	13667	NORFOLK
13683	ROOSEVELTOWN	13655	HOGANSBURG
13692	THOUSAND ISLAND PARK	13640	WELLESLEY ISLAND
13737	BIBLE SCHOOL PARK	13760	ENDICOTT
13738	BLODGETT MILLS	13045	CORTLAND
13745	CHENANGO BRIDGE	13901	BINGHAMTON
13747	COLLIERSVILLE	12116	MARYLAND
13749	CORBETTSVILLE	13748	CONKLIN
13758	EAST PHARSALIA	13801	MC DONOUGH
13761	ENDICOTT	13760	ENDICOTT
13762	ENDWELL	13760	ENDICOTT
13763	ENDICOTT	13760	ENDICOTT
13774	FISHS EDDY	12760	LONG EDDY
13784	HARFORD	13835	RICHFORD
13794	KILLAWOG	13797	LISLE
13814	NORTH NORWICH	13815	NORWICH
13840	SMITHBORO	13734	BARTON
13845	TIOGA CENTER	13734	BARTON
13847	TROUT CREEK	13839	SIDNEY CENTER
13848	TUNNEL	13833	PORT CRANE
13851	VESTAL	13850	VESTAL
13860	WEST DAVENPORT	13820	ONEONTA
13902	BINGHAMTON	13901	BINGHAMTON
14010	ATHOL SPRINGS	14075	HAMBURG
14021	BATAVIA	14020	BATAVIA
14027	BRANT	14111	NORTH COLLINS
14029	CENTERVILLE	14065	FREEDOM
14035	COLLINS CENTER	14034	COLLINS
14038	CRITTENDEN	14004	ALDEN
14056	EAST PEMBROKE	14020	BATAVIA
14061	FARNHAM	14081	IRVING
14095	LOCKPORT	14094	LOCKPORT
14107	MODEL CITY	14092	LEWISTON
14110	NORTH BOSTON	14127	ORCHARD PARK
14112	NORTH EVANS	14057	EDEN
14126	OLCOTT	14028	BURT
14130	PIKE	14066	GAINESVILLE
14133	SANDUSKY	14065	FREEDOM
14135	SHERIDAN	14136	SILVER CREEK
14140	SPRING BROOK	14059	ELMA
14144	STELLA NIAGARA	14092	LEWISTON
14151	TONAWANDA	14150	TONAWANDA
14166	VAN BUREN POINT	14048	DUNKIRK
14168	VERSAILLES	14129	PERRYSBURG
14169	WALES CENTER	14052	EAST AURORA
14173	YORKSHIRE	14042	DELEVAN
14205	BUFFALO	14203	BUFFALO
14231	BUFFALO	14221	BUFFALO
14233	BUFFALO	14203	BUFFALO
14240	BUFFALO	14206	BUFFALO
14241	BUFFALO	14225	BUFFALO
14261	BUFFALO	14260	BUFFALO
14263	BUFFALO	14203	BUFFALO
14264	BUFFALO	14203	BUFFALO
14265	BUFFALO	14221	BUFFALO
14267	BUFFALO	14202	BUFFALO
14269	BUFFALO	14043	DEPEW
14270	BUFFALO	14203	BUFFALO
14272	BUFFALO	14043	DEPEW
14273	BUFFALO	14203	BUFFALO
14276	BUFFALO	14206	BUFFALO
14280	BUFFALO	14203	BUFFALO
14302	NIAGARA FALLS	14301	NIAGARA FALLS
14413	ALTON	14516	NORTH ROSE
14429	CLARENDON	14470	HOLLEY
14430	CLARKSON	14420	BROCKPORT
14443	EAST BLOOMFIELD	14469	BLOOMFIELD
14449	EAST WILLIAMSON	14589	WILLIAMSON
14452	FANCHER	14470	HOLLEY
14453	FISHERS	14564	VICTOR
14461	GORHAM	14561	STANLEY
14463	HALL	14456	GENEVA
14479	KNOWLESVILLE	14411	ALBION
14488	LIVONIA CENTER	14487	LIVONIA
14508	MORTON	14464	HAMLIN
14511	MUMFORD	14482	LE ROY
14515	NORTH GREECE	14468	HILTON
14518	OAKS CORNERS	14456	GENEVA
14520	ONTARIO CENTER	14519	ONTARIO
14529	PERKINSVILLE	14572	WAYLAND
14537	PORT GIBSON	14548	SHORTSVILLE
14538	PULTNEYVILLE	14589	WILLIAMSON
14539	RETSOF	14533	PIFFARD
14542	ROSE	14489	LYONS
14547	SENECA CASTLE	14561	STANLEY
14549	SILVER LAKE	14550	SILVER SPRINGS
14556	SONYEA	14510	MOUNT MORRIS
14557	SOUTH BYRON	14422	BYRON
14558	SOUTH LIMA	14487	LIVONIA
14563	UNION HILL	14519	ONTARIO
14585	WEST BLOOMFIELD	14469	BLOOMFIELD
14588	WILLARD	14521	OVID
14592	YORK	14533	PIFFARD
14602	ROCHESTER	14623	ROCHESTER
14603	ROCHESTER	14605	ROCHESTER
14638	ROCHESTER	14604	ROCHESTER
14639	ROCHESTER	14604	ROCHESTER
14643	ROCHESTER	14604	ROCHESTER
14644	ROCHESTER	14604	ROCHESTER
14646	ROCHESTER	14607	ROCHESTER
14647	ROCHESTER	14607	ROCHESTER
14649	ROCHESTER	14604	ROCHESTER
14650	ROCHESTER	14608	ROCHESTER
14651	ROCHESTER	14608	ROCHESTER
14652	ROCHESTER	14608	ROCHESTER
14653	ROCHESTER	14624	ROCHESTER
14673	ROCHESTER	14614	ROCHESTER
14683	ROCHESTER	14623	ROCHESTER
14692	ROCHESTER	14623	ROCHESTER
14694	ROCHESTER	14623	ROCHESTER
14702	JAMESTOWN	14701	JAMESTOWN
14707	ALLENTOWN	14895	WELLSVILLE
14720	CELORON	14701	JAMESTOWN
14722	CHAUTAUQUA	14757	MAYVILLE
14730	EAST RANDOLPH	14772	RANDOLPH
14732	ELLINGTON	14747	KENNEDY
14742	GREENHURST	14701	JAMESTOWN
14745	HUME	14735	FILLMORE
14751	LEON	14726	CONEWANGO VALLEY
14752	LILY DALE	14784	STOCKTON
14756	MAPLE SPRINGS	14712	BEMUS POINT
14758	NIOBE	14767	PANAMA
14766	OTTO	14719	CATTARAUGUS
14774	RICHBURG	14715	BOLIVAR
14778	SAINT BONAVENTURE	14706	ALLEGANY
14783	STEAMBURG	14772	RANDOLPH
14785	STOW	14710	ASHVILLE
14786	WEST CLARKSVILLE	14727	CUBA
14788	WESTONS MILLS	14760	OLEAN
14827	COOPERS PLAINS	14870	PAINTED POST
14831	CORNING	14830	CORNING
14851	ITHACA	14850	ITHACA
14852	ITHACA	14850	ITHACA
14854	JACKSONVILLE	14886	TRUMANSBURG
14856	KANONA	14810	BATH
14857	LAKEMONT	14837	DUNDEE
14863	MECKLENBURG	14886	TRUMANSBURG
14876	READING CENTER	14891	WATKINS GLEN
14887	TYRONE	14837	DUNDEE
14893	WAYNE	14837	DUNDEE
14902	ELMIRA	14901	ELMIRA
14925	ELMIRA	14901	ELMIRA
15004	ATLASBURG	15021	BURGETTSTOWN
15006	BAIRDFORD	15044	GIBSONIA
15020	BUNOLA	15063	MONONGAHELA
15028	COULTERS	15131	MCKEESPORT
15032	CURTISVILLE	15044	GIBSONIA
15038	ELRAMA	15025	CLAIRTON
15046	CRESCENT	15108	CORAOPOLIS
15047	GREENOCK	15135	MCKEESPORT
15053	JOFFRE	15021	BURGETTSTOWN
15054	LANGELOTH	15021	BURGETTSTOWN
15069	NEW KENSINGTON	15613	APOLLO
15072	PRICEDALE	15012	BELLE VERNON
15075	RURAL RIDGE	15024	CHESWICK
15081	SOUTH HEIGHTS	15001	ALIQUIPPA
15082	STURGEON	15071	OAKDALE
15087	WEBSTER	15012	BELLE VERNON
15088	WEST ELIZABETH	15025	CLAIRTON
15091	WILDWOOD	15044	GIBSONIA
15095	WARRENDALE	15090	WEXFORD

Point ZIP Code		Enclosing Residential ZIP Code		Point ZIP Code		Enclosing Residential ZIP Code	
ZIP	Post Office Name	ZIP	Post Office Name	ZIP	Post Office Name	ZIP	Post Office Name
15096	WARRENDALE	15086	WARRENDALE	15619	BOVARD	15601	GREENSBURG
15123	WEST MIFFLIN	15122	WEST MIFFLIN	15621	CALUMET	15666	MOUNT PLEASANT
15127	INGOMAR	15237	PITTSBURGH	15624	CRABTREE	15601	GREENSBURG
15134	MCKEESPORT	15132	MCKEESPORT	15629	EAST VANDERGRIFT	15690	VANDERGRIFT
15230	PITTSBURGH	15219	PITTSBURGH	15633	FORBES ROAD	15601	GREENSBURG
15231	PITTSBURGH	15108	CORAOPOLIS	15635	HANNASTOWN	15601	GREENSBURG
15240	PITTSBURGH	15206	PITTSBURGH	15638	HOSTETTER	15650	LATROBE
15242	PITTSBURGH	15220	PITTSBURGH	15640	HUTCHINSON	15637	HERMINIE
15244	PITTSBURGH	15136	MC KEES ROCKS	15660	LOWBER	15637	HERMINIE
15250	PITTSBURGH	15212	PITTSBURGH	15662	LUXOR	15601	GREENSBURG
15251	PITTSBURGH	15212	PITTSBURGH	15664	MAMMOTH	15666	MOUNT PLEASANT
15252	PITTSBURGH	15219	PITTSBURGH	15671	NEW DERRY	15627	DERRY
15253	PITTSBURGH	15212	PITTSBURGH	15673	NORTH APOLLO	15613	APOLLO
15254	PITTSBURGH	15219	PITTSBURGH	15674	NORVELT	15666	MOUNT PLEASANT
15255	PITTSBURGH	15212	PITTSBURGH	15676	PLEASANT UNITY	15601	GREENSBURG
15257	PITTSBURGH	15219	PITTSBURGH	15680	SALINA	15618	AVONMORE
15258	PITTSBURGH	15219	PITTSBURGH	15682	SCHENLEY	15656	LEECHBURG
15259	PITTSBURGH	15219	PITTSBURGH	15685	SOUTHWEST	15666	MOUNT PLEASANT
15262	PITTSBURGH	15219	PITTSBURGH	15689	UNITED	15666	MOUNT PLEASANT
15264	PITTSBURGH	15212	PITTSBURGH	15691	WENDEL	15601	GREENSBURG
15265	PITTSBURGH	15222	PITTSBURGH	15693	WHITNEY	15650	LATROBE
15267	PITTSBURGH	15233	PITTSBURGH	15695	WYANO	15089	WEST NEWTON
15268	PITTSBURGH	15212	PITTSBURGH	15696	YOUNGSTOWN	15650	LATROBE
15270	PITTSBURGH	15228	PITTSBURGH	15710	ALVERDA	15714	NORTHERN CAMBRIA
15272	PITTSBURGH	15222	PITTSBURGH	15712	ARCADIA	15724	CHERRY TREE
15274	PITTSBURGH	15212	PITTSBURGH	15715	BIG RUN	15767	PUNXSUTAWNEY
15276	PITTSBURGH	15205	PITTSBURGH	15723	CHAMBERSVILLE	15701	INDIANA
15277	PITTSBURGH	15205	PITTSBURGH	15727	CLUNE	15748	HOMER CITY
15278	PITTSBURGH	15222	PITTSBURGH	15731	CORAL	15748	HOMER CITY
15279	PITTSBURGH	15233	PITTSBURGH	15733	DE LANCEY	15767	PUNXSUTAWNEY
15281	PITTSBURGH	15219	PITTSBURGH	15734	DIXONVILLE	15759	MARION CENTER
15283	PITTSBURGH	15220	PITTSBURGH	15736	ELDERTON	15774	SHELOCTA
15286	PITTSBURGH	15212	PITTSBURGH	15737	ELMORA	15722	CARROLLTOWN
15290	PITTSBURGH	15212	PITTSBURGH	15738	EMEIGH	15714	NORTHERN CAMBRIA
15295	PITTSBURGH	15202	PITTSBURGH	15741	GIPSY	15742	GLEN CAMPBELL
15315	BOBTOWN	15327	DILLINER	15745	HEILWOOD	15728	CLYMER
15316	BRAVE	15362	SPRAGGS	15746	HILLSDALE	15759	MARION CENTER
15325	CRUCIBLE	15357	RICES LANDING	15750	JOSEPHINE	15717	BLAIRSVILLE
15334	GARARDS FORT	15320	CARMICHAELS	15752	KENT	15748	HOMER CITY
15336	GASTONVILLE	15332	FINLEYVILLE	15754	LUCERNEMINES	15748	HOMER CITY
15339	HENDERSONVILLE	15317	CANONSBURG	15756	MC INTYRE	15774	SHELOCTA
15347	MEADOW LANDS	15301	WASHINGTON	15761	MENTCLE	15714	NORTHERN CAMBRIA
15348	MILLSBORO	15357	RICES LANDING	15779	TORRANCE	15627	DERRY
15350	MUSE	15317	CANONSBURG	15781	WALSTON	15767	PUNXSUTAWNEY
15351	NEMACOLIN	15320	CARMICHAELS	15783	WEST LEBANON	15681	SALTSBURG
15358	RICHEYVILLE	15427	DAISYTOWN	15822	BRANDY CAMP	15853	RIDGWAY
15361	SOUTHVIEW	15057	MC DONALD	15831	DAGUS MINES	15846	KERSEY
15365	TAYLORSTOWN	15323	CLAYSVILLE	15841	FORCE	15868	WEEDVILLE
15366	VAN VOORHIS	15022	CHARLEROI	15847	KNOX DALE	15825	BROOKVILLE
15368	VESTABURG	15333	FREDERICKTOWN	15863	STUMP CREEK	15851	REYNOLDSVILLE
15378	WESTLAND	15340	HICKORY	15866	TROUTVILLE	15848	LUTHERSBURG
15379	WEST MIDDLETOWN	15312	AVELLA	15907	JOHNSTOWN	15901	JOHNSTOWN
15415	BRIER HILL	15442	GRINDSTONE	15921	BEAVERDALE	15955	SIDMAN
15416	BROWNFIELD	15401	UNIONTOWN	15922	BELSANO	15931	EBENSBURG
15420	CARDALE	15463	MERRITTSTOWN	15925	CASSANDRA	15938	LILLY
15421	CHALK HILL	15437	FARMINGTON	15929	DILLTOWN	15748	HOMER CITY
15422	CHESTNUT RIDGE	15442	GRINDSTONE	15930	DUNLO	15963	WINDBER
15429	DENBO	15417	BROWNSVILLE	15934	ELTON	15963	WINDBER
15430	DICKERSON RUN	15486	VANDERBILT	15937	JEROME	15935	HOLLSOPPLE
15435	FAIRBANK	15468	NEW SALEM	15948	REVLOC	15931	EBENSBURG
15439	GANS	15451	LAKE LYNN	15959	TIRE HILL	15904	JOHNSTOWN
15443	HIBBS	15458	MC CLELLANDTOWN	15962	WILMORE	15946	PORTAGE
15447	ISABELLA	15433	EAST MILLSBORO	16003	BUTLER	16001	BUTLER
15448	JACOBS CREEK	15479	SMITHTON	16016	BOYERS	16061	WEST SUNBURY
15449	KEISTERVILLE	15480	SMOCK	16017	BOYERS	16061	WEST SUNBURY
15454	LECKRONE	15458	MC CLELLANDTOWN	16018	BOYERS	16020	BOYERS
15455	LEISENRING	15486	VANDERBILT	16021	BRANCHTON	16038	HARRISVILLE
15460	MARTIN	15478	SMITHFIELD	16024	CALLERY	16033	EVANS CITY
15465	MOUNT BRADDOCK	15456	LEMONT FURNACE	16027	CONNOQUENESSING	16033	EVANS CITY
15466	NEWELL	15438	FAYETTE CITY	16029	EAST BUTLER	16001	BUTLER
15467	NEW GENEVA	15478	SMITHFIELD	16035	FORESTVILLE	16038	HARRISVILLE
15472	OLIVER	15401	UNIONTOWN	16039	HERMAN	16001	BUTLER
15476	RONCO	15461	MASONTOWN	16048	NORTH WASHINGTON	16050	PETROLIA
15484	ULEDI	15401	UNIONTOWN	16054	SAINT PETERSBURG	16036	FOXBURG
15485	URSINA	15424	CONFLUENCE	16058	TURKEY CITY	16373	EMLENTON
15489	WEST LEISENRING	15401	UNIONTOWN	16103	NEW CASTLE	16101	NEW CASTLE
15492	WICKHAVEN	15012	BELLE VERNON	16107	NEW CASTLE	16101	NEW CASTLE
15502	HIDDEN VALLEY	15501	SOMERSET	16108	NEW CASTLE	16101	NEW CASTLE
15510	SOMERSET	15501	SOMERSET	16113	CLARK	16125	GREENVILLE
15520	ACOSTA	15541	FRIEDENS	16132	HILLSVILLE	16116	EDINBURG
15532	BOYNTON	15552	MEYERSDALE	16136	KOPPEL	15010	BEAVER FALLS
15544	GRAY	15531	BOSWELL	16140	NEW BEDFORD	16143	PULASKI
15547	JENNERSTOWN	15531	BOSWELL	16151	SHEAKLEYVILLE	16130	HADLEY
15548	KANTNER	15563	STOYSTOWN	16155	VILLA MARIA	16143	PULASKI
15549	LISTIE	15541	FRIEDENS	16160	WEST PITTSBURG	16157	WAMPUM
15553	NEW BALTIMORE	15530	BERLIN	16161	WHEATLAND	16121	FARRELL
15555	QUECREEK	15501	SOMERSET	16211	BEYER	15747	HOME
15560	SHANKSVILLE	15541	FRIEDENS	16220	CROWN	16233	LEEPER
15561	SIPESVILLE	15501	SOMERSET	16221	CURLLSVILLE	16255	SLIGO
15564	WELLERSBURG	15545	HYNDMAN	16223	DISTANT	16242	NEW BETHLEHEM
15565	WEST SALISBURY	15558	SALISBURY	16228	FORD CLIFF	16226	FORD CITY
15605	GREENSBURG	15601	GREENSBURG	16230	HAWTHORN	16224	FAIRMOUNT CITY
15606	GREENSBURG	15601	GREENSBURG	16236	MC GRANN	16226	FORD CITY

NONRESIDENTIAL ZIP CODES

PENNSYLVANIA

Point ZIP Code ZIP	Point ZIP Code Post Office Name	Enclosing Residential ZIP Code ZIP	Enclosing Residential ZIP Code Post Office Name
16244	NU MINE	16249	RURAL VALLEY
16245	OAK RIDGE	16242	NEW BETHLEHEM
16246	PLUMVILLE	15747	HOME
16250	SAGAMORE	16249	RURAL VALLEY
16253	SEMINOLE	16242	NEW BETHLEHEM
16257	SNYDERSBURG	16235	LUCINDA
16261	WIDNOON	16259	TEMPLETON
16263	YATESBORO	16249	RURAL VALLEY
16312	CHANDLERS VALLEY	16350	SUGAR GROVE
16322	ENDEAVOR	16353	TIONESTA
16328	HYDETOWN	16354	TITUSVILLE
16343	RENO	16301	OIL CITY
16344	ROUSEVILLE	16301	OIL CITY
16352	TIONA	16365	WARREN
16361	TYLERSBURG	16233	LEEPER
16366	WARREN	16365	WARREN
16367	WARREN	16365	WARREN
16368	WARREN	16365	WARREN
16369	WARREN	16365	WARREN
16370	WEST HICKORY	16353	TIONESTA
16375	LAMARTINE	16232	KNOX
16388	MEADVILLE	16335	MEADVILLE
16413	ELGIN	16407	CORRY
16416	GARLAND	16340	PITTSFIELD
16422	HARMONSBURG	16316	CONNEAUT LAKE
16427	MILL VILLAGE	16441	WATERFORD
16432	RICEVILLE	16404	CENTERVILLE
16475	ALBION	16401	ALBION
16512	ERIE	16501	ERIE
16514	ERIE	16510	ERIE
16515	ERIE	16510	ERIE
16522	ERIE	16501	ERIE
16530	ERIE	16501	ERIE
16531	ERIE	16511	ERIE
16534	ERIE	16501	ERIE
16538	ERIE	16501	ERIE
16541	ERIE	16507	ERIE
16544	ERIE	16510	ERIE
16546	ERIE	16504	ERIE
16550	ERIE	16507	ERIE
16553	ERIE	16501	ERIE
16563	ERIE	16510	ERIE
16603	ALTOONA	16601	ALTOONA
16619	BLANDBURG	16639	FALLENTIMBER
16624	CHEST SPRINGS	16668	PATTON
16629	COUPON	16613	ASHVILLE
16631	CURRYVILLE	16662	MARTINSBURG
16633	DEFIANCE	16679	SIX MILE RUN
16638	ENTRIKEN	16657	JAMES CREEK
16644	GLASGOW	16639	FALLENTIMBER
16654	HUNTINGDON	16652	HUNTINGDON
16660	MC CONNELLSTOWN	16652	HUNTINGDON
16663	MORANN	16651	HOUTZDALE
16665	NEWRY	16635	DUNCANSVILLE
16670	QUEEN	16625	CLAYSBURG
16672	RIDDLESBURG	16679	SIX MILE RUN
16675	SAINT BONIFACE	16668	PATTON
16677	SANDY RIDGE	16866	PHILIPSBURG
16681	SMOKERUN	16661	MADERA
16682	SPROUL	16625	CLAYSBURG
16684	TIPTON	16617	BELLWOOD
16694	WOOD	16679	SIX MILE RUN
16698	HOUTZDALE	16651	HOUTZDALE
16699	CRESSON	16630	CRESSON
16725	CUSTER CITY	16701	BRADFORD
16728	DE YOUNG	16734	JAMES CITY
16730	EAST SMETHPORT	16749	SMETHPORT
16733	HAZEL HURST	16749	SMETHPORT
16804	STATE COLLEGE	16801	STATE COLLEGE
16805	STATE COLLEGE	16801	STATE COLLEGE
16825	BIGLER	16881	WOODLAND
16826	BLANCHARD	16841	HOWARD
16834	DRIFTING	16839	GRASSFLAT
16835	FLEMING	16844	JULIAN
16843	HYDE	16830	CLEARFIELD
16847	KYLERTOWN	16858	MORRISDALE
16848	LAMAR	17751	MILL HALL
16849	LANSE	16839	GRASSFLAT
16850	LECONTES MILLS	16836	FRENCHVILLE
16851	LEMONT	16801	STATE COLLEGE
16853	MILESBURG	16823	BELLEFONTE
16855	MINERAL SPRINGS	16881	WOODLAND
16856	MINGOVILLE	16823	BELLEFONTE
16868	PINE GROVE MILLS	16801	STATE COLLEGE
16873	SHAWVILLE	16830	CLEARFIELD
16876	WALLACETON	16858	MORRISDALE
16910	ALBA	17724	CANTON
16911	ARNOT	16912	BLOSSBURG
16945	SYLVANIA	16914	COLUMBIA CROSS ROADS
17001	CAMP HILL	17011	CAMP HILL
17010	CAMPBELLTOWN	17078	PALMYRA
17012	CAMP HILL	17055	MECHANICSBURG
17016	CORNWALL	17042	LEBANON

PENNSYLVANIA

Point ZIP Code ZIP	Point ZIP Code Post Office Name	Enclosing Residential ZIP Code ZIP	Enclosing Residential ZIP Code Post Office Name
17027	GRANTHAM	17055	MECHANICSBURG
17039	KLEINFELTERSVILLE	17073	NEWMANSTOWN
17041	LAWN	17078	PALMYRA
17054	MATTAWANA	17051	MC VEYTOWN
17056	MEXICO	17059	MIFFLINTOWN
17064	MOUNT GRETNA	17042	LEBANON
17069	NEW BUFFALO	17074	NEWPORT
17072	NEW KINGSTOWN	17050	MECHANICSBURG
17075	NEWTON HAMILTON	17066	MOUNT UNION
17077	ONO	17003	ANNVILLE
17081	PLAINFIELD	17015	CARLISLE
17083	QUENTIN	17042	LEBANON
17085	REXMONT	17042	LEBANON
17088	SCHAEFFERSTOWN	17073	NEWMANSTOWN
17089	CAMP HILL	17011	CAMP HILL
17093	SUMMERDALE	17025	ENOLA
17105	HARRISBURG	17101	HARRISBURG
17106	HARRISBURG	17110	HARRISBURG
17107	HARRISBURG	17110	HARRISBURG
17108	HARRISBURG	17101	HARRISBURG
17120	HARRISBURG	17101	HARRISBURG
17121	HARRISBURG	17101	HARRISBURG
17122	HARRISBURG	17104	HARRISBURG
17123	HARRISBURG	17101	HARRISBURG
17124	HARRISBURG	17101	HARRISBURG
17125	HARRISBURG	17101	HARRISBURG
17126	HARRISBURG	17101	HARRISBURG
17127	HARRISBURG	17101	HARRISBURG
17128	HARRISBURG	17101	HARRISBURG
17129	HARRISBURG	17101	HARRISBURG
17130	HARRISBURG	17101	HARRISBURG
17140	HARRISBURG	17111	HARRISBURG
17177	HARRISBURG	17110	HARRISBURG
17210	AMBERSON	17262	SPRING RUN
17231	LEMASTERS	17236	MERCERSBURG
17235	MARION	17202	CHAMBERSBURG
17247	QUINCY	17268	WAYNESBORO
17249	ROCKHILL FURNACE	17243	ORBISONIA
17250	ROUZERVILLE	17268	WAYNESBORO
17251	ROXBURY	17262	SPRING RUN
17253	SALTILLO	17264	THREE SPRINGS
17254	SCOTLAND	17202	CHAMBERSBURG
17256	SHADY GROVE	17225	GREENCASTLE
17261	SOUTH MOUNTAIN	17222	FAYETTEVILLE
17263	STATE LINE	17268	WAYNESBORO
17270	WILLIAMSON	17225	GREENCASTLE
17272	ZULLINGER	17268	WAYNESBORO
17303	ARENDTSVILLE	17307	BIGLERVILLE
17306	BENDERSVILLE	17304	ASPERS
17310	CASHTOWN	17353	ORRTANNA
17311	CODORUS	17362	SPRING GROVE
17312	CRALEY	17368	WRIGHTSVILLE
17317	EAST PROSPECT	17368	WRIGHTSVILLE
17318	EMIGSVILLE	17402	YORK
17323	FRANKLINTOWN	17019	DILLSBURG
17332	HANOVER	17331	HANOVER
17333	HANOVER	17331	HANOVER
17337	IDAVILLE	17324	GARDNERS
17342	LOGANVILLE	17403	YORK
17343	MC KNIGHTSTOWN	17307	BIGLERVILLE
17354	PORTERS SIDELING	17362	SPRING GROVE
17355	RAILROAD	17349	NEW FREEDOM
17358	ROSSVILLE	17019	DILLSBURG
17371	YORK NEW SALEM	17404	YORK
17375	PEACH GLEN	17324	GARDNERS
17405	YORK	17401	YORK
17415	YORK	17402	YORK
17503	BART	17562	PARADISE
17504	BAUSMAN	17601	LANCASTER
17506	BLUE BALL	17519	EAST EARL
17507	BOWMANSVILLE	17517	DENVER
17508	BROWNSTOWN	17522	EPHRATA
17521	ELM	17543	LITITZ
17528	GOODVILLE	17519	EAST EARL
17533	HOPELAND	17543	LITITZ
17534	INTERCOURSE	17529	GORDONVILLE
17537	LAMPETER	17602	LANCASTER
17549	MARTINDALE	17522	EPHRATA
17550	MAYTOWN	17547	MARIETTA
17564	PENRYN	17543	LITITZ
17567	REAMSTOWN	17578	STEVENS
17568	REFTON	17584	WILLOW STREET
17570	RHEEMS	17022	ELIZABETHTOWN
17573	RONKS	17572	RONKS
17575	SILVER SPRING	17512	COLUMBIA
17580	TALMAGE	17540	LEOLA
17583	WEST WILLOW	17584	WILLOW STREET
17585	WITMER	17505	BIRD IN HAND
17604	LANCASTER	17601	LANCASTER
17605	LANCASTER	17601	LANCASTER
17606	LANCASTER	17601	LANCASTER
17607	LANCASTER	17601	LANCASTER
17608	LANCASTER	17601	LANCASTER

PENNSYLVANIA

Point ZIP Code ZIP	Point ZIP Code Post Office Name	Enclosing Residential ZIP Code ZIP	Enclosing Residential ZIP Code Post Office Name
17611	LANCASTER	17601	LANCASTER
17622	LANCASTER	17601	LANCASTER
17703	WILLIAMSPORT	17701	WILLIAMSPORT
17705	WILLIAMSPORT	17701	WILLIAMSPORT
17720	ANTES FORT	17701	WILLIAMSPORT
17726	CASTANEA	17745	LOCK HAVEN
17727	CEDAR RUN	17723	CAMMAL
17730	DEWART	17777	WATSONTOWN
17731	EAGLES MERE	17758	MUNCY VALLEY
17735	GROVER	17724	CANTON
17738	HYNER	17764	RENOVO
17739	JERSEY MILLS	17723	CAMMAL
17748	MC ELHATTAN	17745	LOCK HAVEN
17749	MC EWENSVILLE	17777	WATSONTOWN
17750	MACKEYVILLE	17751	MILL HALL
17760	NORTH BEND	17764	RENOVO
17762	PICTURE ROCKS	17737	HUGHESVILLE
17767	SALONA	17751	MILL HALL
17769	SLATE RUN	17740	JERSEY SHORE
17773	TYLERSVILLE	17747	LOGANTON
17822	DANVILLE	17821	DANVILLE
17829	HARTLETON	17845	MILLMONT
17831	HUMMELS WHARF	17870	SELINSGROVE
17833	KREAMER	17842	MIDDLEBURG
17839	LIGHTSTREET	17815	BLOOMSBURG
17840	LOCUST GAP	17851	MOUNT CARMEL
17843	BEAVER SPRINGS	17812	BEAVER SPRINGS
17858	NUMIDIA	17820	CATAWISSA
17861	PAXTONVILLE	17842	MIDDLEBURG
17862	PENNS CREEK	17842	MIDDLEBURG
17865	POTTS GROVE	17847	MILTON
17880	SWENGEL	17845	MILLMONT
17882	TROXELVILLE	17813	BEAVERTOWN
17883	VICKSBURG	17844	MIFFLINBURG
17884	WASHINGTONVILLE	17821	DANVILLE
17885	WEIKERT	17845	MILLMONT
17886	WEST MILTON	17837	LEWISBURG
17887	WHITE DEER	17856	NEW COLUMBIA
17920	ARISTES	17888	WILBURTON
17930	CUMBOLA	17959	NEW PHILADELPHIA
17932	FRACKVILLE	17931	FRACKVILLE
17933	FRIEDENSBURG	17972	SCHUYLKILL HAVEN
17934	GILBERTON	17976	SHENANDOAH
17936	GORDON	17921	ASHLAND
17942	LANDINGVILLE	17922	AUBURN
17943	LAVELLE	17921	ASHLAND
17944	LLEWELLYN	17901	POTTSVILLE
17945	LOCUSTDALE	17921	ASHLAND
17946	LOST CREEK	17935	GIRARDVILLE
17949	MAHANOY PLANE	17976	SHENANDOAH
17951	MAR LIN	17901	POTTSVILLE
17952	MARY D	17925	BROCKTON
17953	MIDDLEPORT	17959	NEW PHILADELPHIA
17966	RAVINE	17963	PINE GROVE
17974	SELTZER	17901	POTTSVILLE
17979	SUMMIT STATION	17922	AUBURN
17982	TUSCARORA	17925	BROCKTON
18001	LEHIGH VALLEY	18101	ALLENTOWN
18002	LEHIGH VALLEY	18017	BETHLEHEM
18003	LEHIGH VALLEY	18017	BETHLEHEM
18010	ACKERMANVILLE	18013	BANGOR
18012	AQUASHICOLA	18071	PALMERTON
18016	BETHLEHEM	18018	BETHLEHEM
18025	BETHLEHEM	18018	BETHLEHEM
18030	BOWMANSTOWN	18071	PALMERTON
18039	DURHAM	18077	RIEGELSVILLE
18043	EASTON	18045	EASTON
18044	EASTON	18042	EASTON
18046	EAST TEXAS	18062	MACUNGIE
18050	FLICKSVILLE	18013	BANGOR
18060	LIMEPORT	18036	COOPERSBURG
18063	MARTINS CREEK	18040	EASTON
18065	NEFFS	18037	COPLAY
18068	OLD ZIONSVILLE	18092	ZIONSVILLE
18079	SLATEDALE	18080	SLATINGTON
18081	SPRINGTOWN	18055	HELLERTOWN
18083	STOCKERTOWN	18040	EASTON
18084	SUMNEYTOWN	18054	GREEN LANE
18085	TATAMY	18040	EASTON
18086	TREICHLERS	18088	WALNUTPORT
18098	EMMAUS	18049	EMMAUS
18099	EMMAUS	18049	EMMAUS
18105	ALLENTOWN	18101	ALLENTOWN
18195	ALLENTOWN	18106	ALLENTOWN
18212	ASHFIELD	18235	LEHIGHTON
18221	DRIFTON	18224	FREELAND
18223	EBERVALE	18201	HAZLETON
18225	HARLEIGH	18202	HAZLETON
18230	JUNEDALE	18216	BEAVER MEADOWS
18231	KELAYRES	18237	MCADOO
18234	LATTIMER MINES	18202	HAZLETON
18239	MILNESVILLE	18202	HAZLETON
18241	NUREMBERG	17985	ZION GROVE
18242	ONEIDA	18248	SHEPPTON
18244	PARRYVILLE	18071	PALMERTON
18247	SAINT JOHNS	18222	DRUMS
18251	SYBERTSVILLE	18249	SUGARLOAF
18254	TRESCKOW	18216	BEAVER MEADOWS
18256	WESTON	18246	ROCK GLEN
18320	ANALOMINK	18301	EAST STROUDSBURG
18323	BUCK HILL FALLS	18326	CRESCO
18335	MARSHALLS CREEK	18301	EAST STROUDSBURG
18341	MINISINK HILLS	18301	EAST STROUDSBURG
18342	MOUNTAINHOME	18326	CRESCO
18348	POCONO LAKE PRESERVE	18347	POCONO LAKE
18349	POCONO MANOR	18370	SWIFTWATER
18351	PORTLAND	18343	MOUNT BETHEL
18356	SHAWNEE ON DELAWARE	18302	EAST STROUDSBURG
18357	SKYTOP	18325	CANADENSIS
18410	CHINCHILLA	18411	CLARKS SUMMIT
18413	CLIFFORD	18421	FOREST CITY
18416	ELMHURST	18444	MOSCOW
18420	FLEETVILLE	18419	FACTORYVILLE
18440	LA PLUME	18414	DALTON
18448	OLYPHANT	18447	OLYPHANT
18449	ORSON	18439	LAKEWOOD
18454	POYNTELLE	18439	LAKEWOOD
18457	ROWLAND	18435	LACKAWAXEN
18459	SOUTH CANAAN	18436	LAKE ARIEL
18471	WAVERLY	18411	CLARKS SUMMIT
18473	WHITE MILLS	18431	HONESDALE
18501	SCRANTON	18505	SCRANTON
18502	SCRANTON	18503	SCRANTON
18515	SCRANTON	18508	SCRANTON
18601	BEACH HAVEN	18603	BERWICK
18602	BEAR CREEK	18702	WILKES BARRE
18611	CAMBRA	17814	BENTON
18625	LAKE WINOLA	18414	DALTON
18626	LAPORTE	17758	MUNCY VALLEY
18627	LEHMAN	18612	DALLAS
18653	RANSOM	18411	CLARKS SUMMIT
18654	SHAWANESE	18612	DALLAS
18703	WILKES BARRE	18701	WILKES BARRE
18710	WILKES BARRE	18701	WILKES BARRE
18711	WILKES BARRE	18706	WILKES BARRE
18762	WILKES BARRE	18702	WILKES BARRE
18764	WILKES BARRE	18705	WILKES BARRE
18765	WILKES BARRE	18706	WILKES BARRE
18766	WILKES BARRE	18701	WILKES BARRE
18767	WILKES BARRE	18702	WILKES BARRE
18769	WILKES BARRE	18702	WILKES BARRE
18773	WILKES BARRE	18701	WILKES BARRE
18813	BROOKLYN	18826	KINGSLEY
18814	BURLINGTON	18848	TOWANDA
18815	CAMPTOWN	18853	WYALUSING
18816	DIMOCK	18844	SPRINGVILLE
18820	GIBSON	18823	HARFORD
18827	LANESBORO	18847	SUSQUEHANNA
18843	SOUTH MONTROSE	18801	MONTROSE
18910	BEDMINSTER	18944	PERKASIE
18911	BLOOMING GLEN	18944	PERKASIE
18912	BUCKINGHAM	18902	DOYLESTOWN
18916	DANBORO	18901	DOYLESTOWN
18918	EARLINGTON	18969	TELFORD
18921	FERNDALE	18972	UPPER BLACK EDDY
18922	FOREST GROVE	18925	FURLONG
18924	FRANCONIA	18969	TELFORD
18926	GARDENVILLE	18947	PIPERSVILLE
18928	HOLICONG	18902	DOYLESTOWN
18931	LAHASKA	18938	NEW HOPE
18935	MILFORD SQUARE	18951	QUAKERTOWN
18943	PENNS PARK	18940	NEWTOWN
18946	PINEVILLE	18940	NEWTOWN
18949	PLUMSTEADVILLE	18947	PIPERSVILLE
18950	POINT PLEASANT	18947	PIPERSVILLE
18953	REVERE	18942	OTTSVILLE
18956	RUSHLAND	18929	JAMISON
18957	SALFORD	19438	HARLEYSVILLE
18958	SALFORDVILLE	19438	HARLEYSVILLE
18962	SILVERDALE	18944	PERKASIE
18963	SOLEBURY	18938	NEW HOPE
18968	SPINNERSTOWN	18951	QUAKERTOWN
18970	TRUMBAUERSVILLE	18951	QUAKERTOWN
18971	TYLERSPORT	18969	TELFORD
18979	WOXALL	19438	HARLEYSVILLE
18980	WYCOMBE	18940	NEWTOWN
18981	ZIONHILL	18951	QUAKERTOWN
18991	WARMINSTER	18974	WARMINSTER
19009	BRYN ATHYN	19006	HUNTINGDON VALLEY
19016	CHESTER	19013	CHESTER
19017	CHESTER HEIGHTS	19061	MARCUS HOOK
19019	PHILADELPHIA	19116	PHILADELPHIA
19028	EDGEMONT	19073	NEWTOWN SQUARE
19037	GLEN RIDDLE LIMA	19063	MEDIA
19039	GRADYVILLE	19342	GLEN MILLS
19048	FORT WASHINGTON	19053	FEASTERVILLE TREVOSE

NONRESIDENTIAL ZIP CODES

PENNSYLVANIA **DISTRICT OF COLUMBIA**

Point ZIP Code		Enclosing Residential ZIP Code		Point ZIP Code		Enclosing Residential ZIP Code	
ZIP	Post Office Name	ZIP	Post Office Name	ZIP	Post Office Name	ZIP	Post Office Name
19049	FORT WASHINGTON	19053	FEASTERVILLE TREVOSE	19480	UWCHLAND	19425	CHESTER SPRINGS
19052	LENNI	19063	MEDIA	19481	VALLEY FORGE	19460	PHOENIXVILLE
19058	LEVITTOWN	19055	LEVITTOWN	19482	VALLEY FORGE	19460	PHOENIXVILLE
19065	MEDIA	19063	MEDIA	19484	VALLEY FORGE	19406	KING OF PRUSSIA
19080	WAYNE	19087	WAYNE	19485	VALLEY FORGE	19406	KING OF PRUSSIA
19088	WAYNE	19087	WAYNE	19486	WEST POINT	19446	LANSDALE
19089	WAYNE	19087	WAYNE	19490	WORCESTER	19446	LANSDALE
19091	MEDIA	19063	MEDIA	19493	VALLEY FORGE	19355	MALVERN
19092	PHILADELPHIA	19104	PHILADELPHIA	19494	VALLEY FORGE	19355	MALVERN
19093	PHILADELPHIA	19104	PHILADELPHIA	19495	VALLEY FORGE	19355	MALVERN
19098	HOLMES	19043	HOLMES	19496	VALLEY FORGE	19355	MALVERN
19101	PHILADELPHIA	19104	PHILADELPHIA	19511	BOWERS	19530	KUTZTOWN
19105	PHILADELPHIA	19107	PHILADELPHIA	19516	CENTERPORT	19541	MOHRSVILLE
19108	PHILADELPHIA	19107	PHILADELPHIA	19519	EARLVILLE	19518	DOUGLASSVILLE
19109	PHILADELPHIA	19107	PHILADELPHIA	19523	GEIGERTOWN	19508	BIRDSBORO
19110	PHILADELPHIA	19107	PHILADELPHIA	19535	LIMEKILN	19547	OLEY
19155	PHILADELPHIA	19114	PHILADELPHIA	19536	LYON STATION	19522	FLEETWOOD
19160	PHILADELPHIA	19120	PHILADELPHIA	19538	MAXATAWNY	19530	KUTZTOWN
19161	PHILADELPHIA	19104	PHILADELPHIA	19542	MONOCACY STATION	19508	BIRDSBORO
19162	PHILADELPHIA	19104	PHILADELPHIA	19544	MOUNT AETNA	17087	RICHLAND
19170	PHILADELPHIA	19104	PHILADELPHIA	19545	NEW BERLINVILLE	19512	BOYERTOWN
19171	PHILADELPHIA	19107	PHILADELPHIA	19548	PINE FORGE	19512	BOYERTOWN
19172	PHILADELPHIA	19106	PHILADELPHIA	19550	REHRERSBURG	19507	BETHEL
19173	PHILADELPHIA	19103	PHILADELPHIA	19554	SHARTLESVILLE	19506	BERNVILLE
19175	PHILADELPHIA	19106	PHILADELPHIA	19559	STRAUSSTOWN	19506	BERNVILLE
19176	PHILADELPHIA	19104	PHILADELPHIA	19564	VIRGINVILLE	19530	KUTZTOWN
19177	PHILADELPHIA	19106	PHILADELPHIA	19603	READING	19604	READING
19178	PHILADELPHIA	19104	PHILADELPHIA	19612	READING	19604	READING
19181	PHILADELPHIA	19106	PHILADELPHIA	19708	KIRKWOOD	19701	BEAR
19182	PHILADELPHIA	19106	PHILADELPHIA	19710	MONTCHANIN	19807	WILMINGTON
19184	PHILADELPHIA	19104	PHILADELPHIA	19712	NEWARK	19711	NEWARK
19187	PHILADELPHIA	19102	PHILADELPHIA	19714	NEWARK	19711	NEWARK
19188	PHILADELPHIA	19123	PHILADELPHIA	19715	NEWARK	19711	NEWARK
19190	PHILADELPHIA	19104	PHILADELPHIA	19718	NEWARK	19713	NEWARK
19191	PHILADELPHIA	19102	PHILADELPHIA	19721	NEW CASTLE	19720	NEW CASTLE
19192	PHILADELPHIA	19102	PHILADELPHIA	19725	NEWARK	19711	NEWARK
19193	PHILADELPHIA	19104	PHILADELPHIA	19726	NEWARK	19711	NEWARK
19194	PHILADELPHIA	19104	PHILADELPHIA	19730	ODESSA	19709	MIDDLETOWN
19195	PHILADELPHIA	19104	PHILADELPHIA	19731	PORT PENN	19709	MIDDLETOWN
19196	PHILADELPHIA	19104	PHILADELPHIA	19732	ROCKLAND	19807	WILMINGTON
19197	PHILADELPHIA	19104	PHILADELPHIA	19733	SAINT GEORGES	19720	NEW CASTLE
19244	PHILADELPHIA	19154	PHILADELPHIA	19735	WINTERTHUR	19807	WILMINGTON
19255	PHILADELPHIA	19154	PHILADELPHIA	19850	WILMINGTON	19801	WILMINGTON
19316	BRANDAMORE	19320	COATESVILLE	19880	WILMINGTON	19801	WILMINGTON
19318	CHATHAM	19390	WEST GROVE	19884	WILMINGTON	19801	WILMINGTON
19331	CONCORDVILLE	19342	GLEN MILLS	19885	WILMINGTON	19801	WILMINGTON
19339	CONCORDVILLE	19373	THORNTON	19886	WILMINGTON	19801	WILMINGTON
19340	CONCORDVILLE	19373	THORNTON	19890	WILMINGTON	19801	WILMINGTON
19345	IMMACULATA	19355	MALVERN	19891	WILMINGTON	19713	NEWARK
19346	KELTON	19390	WEST GROVE	19892	WILMINGTON	19720	NEW CASTLE
19347	KEMBLESVILLE	19350	LANDENBERG	19893	WILMINGTON	19801	WILMINGTON
19351	LEWISVILLE	19350	LANDENBERG	19894	WILMINGTON	19801	WILMINGTON
19353	LIONVILLE	19341	EXTON	19895	WILMINGTON	19801	WILMINGTON
19354	LYNDELL	19335	DOWNINGTOWN	19896	WILMINGTON	19802	WILMINGTON
19357	MENDENHALL	19348	KENNETT SQUARE	19897	WILMINGTON	19803	WILMINGTON
19358	MODENA	19320	COATESVILLE	19898	WILMINGTON	19801	WILMINGTON
19360	NEW LONDON	19352	LINCOLN UNIVERSITY	19899	WILMINGTON	19801	WILMINGTON
19366	POCOPSON	19382	WEST CHESTER	19903	DOVER	19901	DOVER
19367	POMEROY	19365	PARKESBURG	19905	DOVER	19901	DOVER
19369	SADSBURYVILLE	19365	PARKESBURG	19906	DOVER	19901	DOVER
19371	SUPLEE	19344	HONEY BROOK	19936	CHESWOLD	19901	DOVER
19375	UNIONVILLE	19348	KENNETT SQUARE	19955	KENTON	19938	CLAYTON
19376	WAGONTOWN	19320	COATESVILLE	19961	LITTLE CREEK	19901	DOVER
19381	WEST CHESTER	19380	WEST CHESTER	19969	NASSAU	19958	LEWES
19388	WEST CHESTER	19380	WEST CHESTER	19980	WOODSIDE	19943	FELTON
19395	WESTTOWN	19382	WEST CHESTER	20013	WASHINGTON	20024	WASHINGTON
19397	SOUTHEASTERN	19087	WAYNE	20022	WASHINGTON	20002	WASHINGTON
19398	SOUTHEASTERN	19087	WAYNE	20023	WASHINGTON	20003	WASHINGTON
19399	SOUTHEASTERN	19087	WAYNE	20026	WASHINGTON	20019	WASHINGTON
19404	NORRISTOWN	19403	NORRISTOWN	20027	WASHINGTON	20007	WASHINGTON
19407	AUDUBON	19403	NORRISTOWN	20029	WASHINGTON	20019	WASHINGTON
19408	EAGLEVILLE	19403	NORRISTOWN	20030	WASHINGTON	20020	WASHINGTON
19409	FAIRVIEW VILLAGE	19403	NORRISTOWN	20033	WASHINGTON	20002	WASHINGTON
19415	EAGLEVILLE	19403	NORRISTOWN	20035	WASHINGTON	20036	WASHINGTON
19421	BIRCHRUNVILLE	19425	CHESTER SPRINGS	20038	WASHINGTON	20005	WASHINGTON
19423	CEDARS	19426	COLLEGEVILLE	20039	WASHINGTON	20011	WASHINGTON
19424	BLUE BELL	19422	BLUE BELL	20040	WASHINGTON	20011	WASHINGTON
19429	CONSHOHOCKEN	19428	CONSHOHOCKEN	20042	WASHINGTON	20018	WASHINGTON
19430	CREAMERY	19473	SCHWENKSVILLE	20043	WASHINGTON	20005	WASHINGTON
19432	DEVAULT	19355	MALVERN	20044	WASHINGTON	20004	WASHINGTON
19437	GWYNEDD VALLEY	19002	AMBLER	20045	WASHINGTON	20004	WASHINGTON
19441	HARLEYSVILLE	19438	HARLEYSVILLE	20046	WASHINGTON	20015	WASHINGTON
19442	KIMBERTON	19460	PHOENIXVILLE	20047	WASHINGTON	20015	WASHINGTON
19443	KULPSVILLE	19446	LANSDALE	20049	WASHINGTON	20004	WASHINGTON
19450	LEDERACH	19438	HARLEYSVILLE	20050	WASHINGTON	20018	WASHINGTON
19451	MAINLAND	19438	HARLEYSVILLE	20051	WASHINGTON	20004	WASHINGTON
19455	NORTH WALES	18936	MONTGOMERYVILLE	20052	WASHINGTON	20006	WASHINGTON
19456	OAKS	19460	PHOENIXVILLE	20053	WASHINGTON	20024	WASHINGTON
19457	PARKER FORD	19475	SPRING CITY	20055	WASHINGTON	20001	WASHINGTON
19470	SAINT PETERS	19520	ELVERSON	20056	WASHINGTON	20009	WASHINGTON
19472	SASSAMANSVILLE	19525	GILBERTSVILLE	20058	WASHINGTON	20817	BETHESDA
19474	SKIPPACK	19426	COLLEGEVILLE	20060	WASHINGTON	20001	WASHINGTON
19478	SPRING MOUNT	19473	SCHWENKSVILLE	20061	WASHINGTON	20018	WASHINGTON

NONRESIDENTIAL ZIP CODES

DISTRICT OF COLUMBIA

Point ZIP Code		Enclosing Residential ZIP Code		Point ZIP Code		Enclosing Residential ZIP Code	
ZIP	Post Office Name	ZIP	Post Office Name	ZIP	Post Office Name	ZIP	Post Office Name
20062	WASHINGTON	20006	WASHINGTON	20260	WASHINGTON	20024	WASHINGTON
20063	WASHINGTON	20037	WASHINGTON	20261	WASHINGTON	20024	WASHINGTON
20065	WASHINGTON	20024	WASHINGTON	20262	WASHINGTON	20018	WASHINGTON
20066	WASHINGTON	20018	WASHINGTON	20265	WASHINGTON	20024	WASHINGTON
20067	WASHINGTON	20006	WASHINGTON	20266	WASHINGTON	20024	WASHINGTON
20069	WASHINGTON	22031	FAIRFAX	20268	WASHINGTON	20005	WASHINGTON
20070	WASHINGTON	22031	FAIRFAX	20270	WASHINGTON	20001	WASHINGTON
20071	WASHINGTON	20005	WASHINGTON	20289	WASHINGTON	20024	WASHINGTON
20073	WASHINGTON	20004	WASHINGTON	20299	WASHINGTON	20018	WASHINGTON
20074	WASHINGTON	20018	WASHINGTON	20301	WASHINGTON	22202	ARLINGTON
20075	WASHINGTON	20018	WASHINGTON	20303	WASHINGTON	20018	WASHINGTON
20076	WASHINGTON	20015	WASHINGTON	20306	WASHINGTON	20012	WASHINGTON
20077	WASHINGTON	20018	WASHINGTON	20307	WASHINGTON	20012	WASHINGTON
20078	WASHINGTON	20018	WASHINGTON	20310	WASHINGTON	22202	ARLINGTON
20080	WASHINGTON	20005	WASHINGTON	20317	WASHINGTON	20011	WASHINGTON
20081	WASHINGTON	20005	WASHINGTON	20318	WASHINGTON	20018	WASHINGTON
20088	WASHINGTON	20016	WASHINGTON	20319	WASHINGTON	20024	WASHINGTON
20090	WASHINGTON	20018	WASHINGTON	20330	WASHINGTON	22202	ARLINGTON
20091	WASHINGTON	20001	WASHINGTON	20340	WASHINGTON	20032	WASHINGTON
20098	WASHINGTON	20018	WASHINGTON	20350	WASHINGTON	22202	ARLINGTON
20101	DULLES	20166	STERLING	20355	WASHINGTON	20018	WASHINGTON
20102	DULLES	20166	STERLING	20370	WASHINGTON	20003	WASHINGTON
20103	DULLES	20166	STERLING	20372	WASHINGTON	20037	WASHINGTON
20104	DULLES	20166	STERLING	20373	NAVAL ANACOST ANNEX	20020	WASHINGTON
20108	MANASSAS	20110	MANASSAS	20374	WASHINGTON NAVY YARD	20003	WASHINGTON
20113	MANASSAS	20111	MANASSAS	20375	WASHINGTON	20032	WASHINGTON
20116	MARSHALL	20115	MARSHALL	20376	WASHINGTON NAVY YARD	20003	WASHINGTON
20118	MIDDLEBURG	20117	MIDDLEBURG	20380	WASHINGTON	20003	WASHINGTON
20122	CENTREVILLE	20120	CENTREVILLE	20388	WASHINGTON NAVY YARD	20003	WASHINGTON
20128	ORLEAN	20115	MARSHALL	20389	WASHINGTON	20746	SUITLAND
20131	PHILOMONT	20132	PURCELLVILLE	20390	WASHINGTON	20003	WASHINGTON
20134	PURCELLVILLE	20132	PURCELLVILLE	20391	WASHINGTON NAVY YARD	20003	WASHINGTON
20138	CALVERTON	20119	CATLETT	20392	WASHINGTON	20007	WASHINGTON
20139	CASANOVA	20187	WARRENTON	20393	WASHINGTON	20016	WASHINGTON
20140	RECTORTOWN	20144	DELAPLANE	20394	WASHINGTON	20016	WASHINGTON
20142	ROUND HILL	20141	ROUND HILL	20395	WASHINGTON	20746	SUITLAND
20146	ASHBURN	20147	ASHBURN	20398	WASHINGTON NAVY YARD	20003	WASHINGTON
20153	CHANTILLY	20151	CHANTILLY	20401	WASHINGTON	20002	WASHINGTON
20156	GAINESVILLE	20155	GAINESVILLE	20402	WASHINGTON	20002	WASHINGTON
20159	HAMILTON	20158	HAMILTON	20403	WASHINGTON	20024	WASHINGTON
20160	LINCOLN	20132	PURCELLVILLE	20404	WASHINGTON	20002	WASHINGTON
20163	STERLING	20164	STERLING	20405	WASHINGTON	20006	WASHINGTON
20167	STERLING	20164	STERLING	20406	WASHINGTON	22202	ARLINGTON
20168	HAYMARKET	20169	HAYMARKET	20407	WASHINGTON	20002	WASHINGTON
20172	HERNDON	20170	HERNDON	20408	WASHINGTON	20004	WASHINGTON
20177	LEESBURG	20175	LEESBURG	20409	WASHINGTON	20746	SUITLAND
20178	LEESBURG	20175	LEESBURG	20410	WASHINGTON	20024	WASHINGTON
20182	NOKESVILLE	20181	NOKESVILLE	20411	WASHINGTON	20024	WASHINGTON
20185	UPPERVILLE	20184	UPPERVILLE	20412	WASHINGTON	20004	WASHINGTON
20188	WARRENTON	20186	WARRENTON	20413	WASHINGTON	20004	WASHINGTON
20189	DULLES	20166	STERLING	20414	WASHINGTON	20024	WASHINGTON
20195	RESTON	20190	RESTON	20415	WASHINGTON	20006	WASHINGTON
20196	RESTON	20191	RESTON	20416	WASHINGTON	20024	WASHINGTON
20201	WASHINGTON	20024	WASHINGTON	20418	WASHINGTON	20037	WASHINGTON
20202	WASHINGTON	20024	WASHINGTON	20419	WASHINGTON	20005	WASHINGTON
20203	WASHINGTON	20036	WASHINGTON	20420	WASHINGTON	20005	WASHINGTON
20204	WASHINGTON	20024	WASHINGTON	20421	WASHINGTON	20005	WASHINGTON
20206	WASHINGTON	22302	ALEXANDRIA	20422	WASHINGTON	20010	WASHINGTON
20207	WASHINGTON	20814	BETHESDA	20423	WASHINGTON	20024	WASHINGTON
20208	WASHINGTON	20001	WASHINGTON	20424	WASHINGTON	20004	WASHINGTON
20210	WASHINGTON	20004	WASHINGTON	20425	WASHINGTON	20001	WASHINGTON
20211	WASHINGTON	20001	WASHINGTON	20426	WASHINGTON	20002	WASHINGTON
20212	WASHINGTON	20002	WASHINGTON	20427	WASHINGTON	20006	WASHINGTON
20213	WASHINGTON	20004	WASHINGTON	20428	WASHINGTON	20009	WASHINGTON
20215	WASHINGTON	20004	WASHINGTON	20429	WASHINGTON	20006	WASHINGTON
20216	WASHINGTON	20004	WASHINGTON	20431	WASHINGTON	20006	WASHINGTON
20217	WASHINGTON	20001	WASHINGTON	20433	WASHINGTON	20006	WASHINGTON
20218	WASHINGTON	20006	WASHINGTON	20434	WASHINGTON	20006	WASHINGTON
20219	WASHINGTON	20024	WASHINGTON	20435	WASHINGTON	20007	WASHINGTON
20220	WASHINGTON	20005	WASHINGTON	20436	WASHINGTON	20004	WASHINGTON
20221	WASHINGTON	20004	WASHINGTON	20437	WASHINGTON	20037	WASHINGTON
20222	WASHINGTON	20005	WASHINGTON	20439	WASHINGTON	20006	WASHINGTON
20223	WASHINGTON	20036	WASHINGTON	20440	WASHINGTON	20009	WASHINGTON
20224	WASHINGTON	20004	WASHINGTON	20441	WASHINGTON	20009	WASHINGTON
20226	WASHINGTON	20006	WASHINGTON	20442	WASHINGTON	20001	WASHINGTON
20227	WASHINGTON	20004	WASHINGTON	20444	WASHINGTON	20001	WASHINGTON
20228	WASHINGTON	20024	WASHINGTON	20447	WASHINGTON	20024	WASHINGTON
20229	WASHINGTON	20004	WASHINGTON	20451	WASHINGTON	20006	WASHINGTON
20230	WASHINGTON	20005	WASHINGTON	20453	WASHINGTON	22202	ARLINGTON
20232	WASHINGTON	20009	WASHINGTON	20456	WASHINGTON	20006	WASHINGTON
20233	WASHINGTON	20746	SUITLAND	20460	WASHINGTON	20024	WASHINGTON
20235	WASHINGTON	20009	WASHINGTON	20463	WASHINGTON	20004	WASHINGTON
20237	WASHINGTON	20024	WASHINGTON	20469	WASHINGTON	20006	WASHINGTON
20238	WASHINGTON	20036	WASHINGTON	20472	WASHINGTON	20024	WASHINGTON
20239	WASHINGTON	20004	WASHINGTON	20500	WASHINGTON	20005	WASHINGTON
20240	WASHINGTON	20006	WASHINGTON	20502	WASHINGTON	20005	WASHINGTON
20241	WASHINGTON	20037	WASHINGTON	20503	WASHINGTON	20006	WASHINGTON
20242	WASHINGTON	20011	WASHINGTON	20504	WASHINGTON	20006	WASHINGTON
20244	WASHINGTON	20018	WASHINGTON	20505	WASHINGTON	20006	WASHINGTON
20245	WASHINGTON	20037	WASHINGTON	20506	WASHINGTON	20006	WASHINGTON
20250	WASHINGTON	20024	WASHINGTON	20507	WASHINGTON	20036	WASHINGTON
20251	WASHINGTON	20024	WASHINGTON	20508	WASHINGTON	20006	WASHINGTON
20254	WASHINGTON	20024	WASHINGTON	20509	WASHINGTON	20006	WASHINGTON

Point ZIP Code		Enclosing Residential ZIP Code	
ZIP	Post Office Name	ZIP	Post Office Name
20510	WASHINGTON	20004	WASHINGTON
20511	WASHINGTON	20018	WASHINGTON
20515	WASHINGTON	20004	WASHINGTON
20520	WASHINGTON	20037	WASHINGTON
20521	WASHINGTON	20037	WASHINGTON
20522	WASHINGTON	20037	WASHINGTON
20523	WASHINGTON	20006	WASHINGTON
20524	WASHINGTON	20005	WASHINGTON
20525	WASHINGTON	20005	WASHINGTON
20526	WASHINGTON	20006	WASHINGTON
20527	WASHINGTON	20005	WASHINGTON
20528	WASHINGTON	20018	WASHINGTON
20529	WASHINGTON	20001	WASHINGTON
20530	WASHINGTON	20004	WASHINGTON
20531	WASHINGTON	20004	WASHINGTON
20532	WASHINGTON	20001	WASHINGTON
20533	WASHINGTON	20005	WASHINGTON
20534	WASHINGTON	20001	WASHINGTON
20535	WASHINGTON	20004	WASHINGTON
20536	WASHINGTON	20001	WASHINGTON
20538	WASHINGTON	20001	WASHINGTON
20539	WASHINGTON	20005	WASHINGTON
20540	WASHINGTON	20003	WASHINGTON
20541	WASHINGTON	20003	WASHINGTON
20542	WASHINGTON	20011	WASHINGTON
20543	WASHINGTON	20003	WASHINGTON
20544	WASHINGTON	20002	WASHINGTON
20546	WASHINGTON	20024	WASHINGTON
20547	WASHINGTON	20024	WASHINGTON
20548	WASHINGTON	20001	WASHINGTON
20549	WASHINGTON	20001	WASHINGTON
20551	WASHINGTON	20037	WASHINGTON
20552	WASHINGTON	20006	WASHINGTON
20553	WASHINGTON	20024	WASHINGTON
20554	WASHINGTON	20009	WASHINGTON
20555	WASHINGTON	20006	WASHINGTON
20557	WASHINGTON	20003	WASHINGTON
20559	WASHINGTON	20003	WASHINGTON
20560	WASHINGTON	20004	WASHINGTON
20565	WASHINGTON	20004	WASHINGTON
20566	WASHINGTON	20037	WASHINGTON
20570	WASHINGTON	20006	WASHINGTON
20571	WASHINGTON	20005	WASHINGTON
20572	WASHINGTON	20005	WASHINGTON
20573	WASHINGTON	20002	WASHINGTON
20575	WASHINGTON	20006	WASHINGTON
20576	WASHINGTON	20005	WASHINGTON
20577	WASHINGTON	20006	WASHINGTON
20578	WASHINGTON	20001	WASHINGTON
20579	WASHINGTON	20036	WASHINGTON
20580	WASHINGTON	20004	WASHINGTON
20581	WASHINGTON	20036	WASHINGTON
20585	WASHINGTON	20024	WASHINGTON
20586	WASHINGTON	20037	WASHINGTON
20588	DHS	20623	CHELTENHAM
20590	WASHINGTON	20024	WASHINGTON
20591	WASHINGTON	20024	WASHINGTON
20593	WASHINGTON	20024	WASHINGTON
20594	WASHINGTON	20024	WASHINGTON
20597	WASHINGTON	20024	WASHINGTON
20598	DHS	22206	ARLINGTON
20599	WASHINGTON	20746	SUITLAND
20604	WALDORF	20602	WALDORF
20610	BARSTOW	20678	PRINCE FREDERICK
20612	BENEDICT	20637	HUGHESVILLE
20627	COMPTON	20650	LEONARDTOWN
20629	DOWELL	20688	SOLOMONS
20635	HELEN	20659	MECHANICSVILLE
20643	IRONSIDES	20640	INDIAN HEAD
20660	MORGANZA	20659	MECHANICSVILLE
20661	MOUNT VICTORIA	20664	NEWBURG
20682	ROCK POINT	20618	BUSHWOOD
20686	SAINT MARYS CITY	20653	LEXINGTON PARK
20703	LANHAM	20706	LANHAM
20704	BELTSVILLE	20705	BELTSVILLE
20709	LAUREL	20708	LAUREL
20717	BOWIE	20716	BOWIE
20718	BOWIE	20715	BOWIE
20719	BOWIE	20720	BOWIE
20725	LAUREL	20707	LAUREL
20726	LAUREL	20707	LAUREL
20731	CAPITOL HEIGHTS	20743	CAPITOL HEIGHTS
20738	RIVERDALE	20737	RIVERDALE
20741	COLLEGE PARK	20740	COLLEGE PARK
20749	FORT WASHINGTON	20744	FORT WASHINGTON
20750	OXON HILL	20745	OXON HILL
20752	SUITLAND	20746	SUITLAND
20753	DISTRICT HEIGHTS	20747	DISTRICT HEIGHTS
20757	TEMPLE HILLS	20748	TEMPLE HILLS
20765	GALESVILLE	20776	HARWOOD
20768	GREENBELT	20770	GREENBELT
20773	UPPER MARLBORO	20772	UPPER MARLBORO
20775	UPPER MARLBORO	20774	UPPER MARLBORO

Point ZIP Code		Enclosing Residential ZIP Code	
ZIP	Post Office Name	ZIP	Post Office Name
20787	HYATTSVILLE	20782	HYATTSVILLE
20788	HYATTSVILLE	20782	HYATTSVILLE
20790	CAPITOL HEIGHTS	20743	CAPITOL HEIGHTS
20791	CAPITOL HEIGHTS	20743	CAPITOL HEIGHTS
20792	UPPER MARLBORO	20774	UPPER MARLBORO
20797	SOUTHERN MD FACILITY	20743	CAPITOL HEIGHTS
20799	CAPITOL HEIGHTS	20743	CAPITOL HEIGHTS
20810	BETHESDA	20815	CHEVY CHASE
20811	BETHESDA	20815	CHEVY CHASE
20813	BETHESDA	20815	CHEVY CHASE
20824	BETHESDA	20814	BETHESDA
20825	CHEVY CHASE	20815	CHEVY CHASE
20827	BETHESDA	20817	BETHESDA
20830	OLNEY	20832	OLNEY
20847	ROCKVILLE	20852	ROCKVILLE
20848	ROCKVILLE	20851	ROCKVILLE
20849	ROCKVILLE	20850	ROCKVILLE
20857	ROCKVILLE	20852	ROCKVILLE
20859	POTOMAC	20854	POTOMAC
20875	GERMANTOWN	20874	GERMANTOWN
20880	WASHINGTON GROVE	20877	GAITHERSBURG
20883	GAITHERSBURG	20878	GAITHERSBURG
20884	GAITHERSBURG	20877	GAITHERSBURG
20885	GAITHERSBURG	20878	GAITHERSBURG
20889	BETHESDA	20814	BETHESDA
20891	KENSINGTON	20895	KENSINGTON
20892	BETHESDA	20814	BETHESDA
20894	BETHESDA	20814	BETHESDA
20896	GARRETT PARK	20895	KENSINGTON
20898	GAITHERSBURG	20855	DERWOOD
20899	GAITHERSBURG	20878	GAITHERSBURG
20907	SILVER SPRING	20910	SILVER SPRING
20908	SILVER SPRING	20906	SILVER SPRING
20911	SILVER SPRING	20910	SILVER SPRING
20913	TAKOMA PARK	20912	TAKOMA PARK
20914	SILVER SPRING	20904	SILVER SPRING
20915	SILVER SPRING	20902	SILVER SPRING
20916	SILVER SPRING	20906	SILVER SPRING
20918	SILVER SPRING	20901	SILVER SPRING
20993	SILVER SPRING	20904	SILVER SPRING
20997	SILVER SPRING	20910	SILVER SPRING
21018	BENSON	21014	BEL AIR
21020	BORING	21155	UPPERCO
21022	BROOKLANDVILLE	21093	LUTHERVILLE TIMONIUM
21023	BUTLER	21152	SPARKS GLENCOE
21027	CHASE	21220	MIDDLE RIVER
21041	ELLICOTT CITY	21043	ELLICOTT CITY
21052	FORT HOWARD	21219	SPARROWS POINT
21062	GLEN BURNIE	21061	GLEN BURNIE
21065	HUNT VALLEY	21031	HUNT VALLEY
21088	LINEBORO	21102	MANCHESTER
21092	LONG GREEN	21057	GLEN ARM
21094	LUTHERVILLE TIMONIUM	21093	LUTHERVILLE TIMONIUM
21105	MARYLAND LINE	21053	FREELAND
21106	MAYO	21037	EDGEWATER
21123	PASADENA	21122	PASADENA
21130	PERRYMAN	21001	ABERDEEN
21139	RIDERWOOD	21286	TOWSON
21150	SIMPSONVILLE	21044	COLUMBIA
21203	BALTIMORE	21202	BALTIMORE
21233	BALTIMORE	21202	BALTIMORE
21235	BALTIMORE	21207	GWYNN OAK
21241	BALTIMORE	21207	GWYNN OAK
21263	BALTIMORE	21202	BALTIMORE
21264	BALTIMORE	21218	BALTIMORE
21270	BALTIMORE	21215	BALTIMORE
21273	BALTIMORE	21202	BALTIMORE
21274	BALTIMORE	21202	BALTIMORE
21275	BALTIMORE	21202	BALTIMORE
21278	BALTIMORE	21218	BALTIMORE
21279	BALTIMORE	21202	BALTIMORE
21280	BALTIMORE	21202	BALTIMORE
21281	BALTIMORE	21224	BALTIMORE
21282	BALTIMORE	21208	PIKESVILLE
21284	BALTIMORE	21204	TOWSON
21285	BALTIMORE	21204	TOWSON
21287	BALTIMORE	21205	BALTIMORE
21288	BALTIMORE	21202	BALTIMORE
21289	BALTIMORE	21207	GWYNN OAK
21290	BALTIMORE	21201	BALTIMORE
21297	BALTIMORE	21202	BALTIMORE
21298	BALTIMORE	21202	BALTIMORE
21404	ANNAPOLIS	21401	ANNAPOLIS
21405	ANNAPOLIS	21401	ANNAPOLIS
21411	ANNAPOLIS	21401	ANNAPOLIS
21412	ANNAPOLIS	21402	ANNAPOLIS
21501	CUMBERLAND	21502	CUMBERLAND
21503	CUMBERLAND	21502	CUMBERLAND
21504	CUMBERLAND	21502	CUMBERLAND
21505	CUMBERLAND	21502	CUMBERLAND
21524	CORRIGANVILLE	21502	CUMBERLAND
21528	ECKHART MINES	21532	FROSTBURG
21529	ELLERSLIE	21502	CUMBERLAND

NONRESIDENTIAL ZIP CODES

MARYLAND — VIRGINIA

Point ZIP Code: ZIP	Point ZIP Code: Post Office Name	Enclosing Residential ZIP Code: ZIP	Enclosing Residential ZIP Code: Post Office Name
21542	MIDLAND	21532	FROSTBURG
21543	MIDLOTHIAN	21532	FROSTBURG
21556	PINTO	21557	RAWLINGS
21560	SPRING GAP	21502	CUMBERLAND
21609	BETHLEHEM	21655	PRESTON
21624	CLAIBORNE	21663	SAINT MICHAELS
21627	CROCHERON	21672	TODDVILLE
21641	HILLSBORO	21629	DENTON
21652	NEAVITT	21612	BOZMAN
21653	NEWCOMB	21663	SAINT MICHAELS
21656	PRICE	21623	CHURCH HILL
21664	SECRETARY	21631	EAST NEW MARKET
21670	TEMPLEVILLE	21649	MARYDEL
21690	CHESTERTOWN	21620	CHESTERTOWN
21705	FREDERICK	21702	FREDERICK
21709	FREDERICK	21701	FREDERICK
21714	BRADDOCK HEIGHTS	21702	FREDERICK
21715	BROWNSVILLE	21758	KNOXVILLE
21717	BUCKEYSTOWN	21704	FREDERICK
21720	CAVETOWN	21783	SMITHSBURG
21721	CHEWSVILLE	21783	SMITHSBURG
21734	FUNKSTOWN	21740	HAGERSTOWN
21741	HAGERSTOWN	21740	HAGERSTOWN
21746	HAGERSTOWN	21733	FAIRPLAY
21747	HAGERSTOWN	21742	HAGERSTOWN
21748	HAGERSTOWN	21742	HAGERSTOWN
21749	HAGERSTOWN	21742	HAGERSTOWN
21759	LADIESBURG	21757	KEYMAR
21762	LIBERTYTOWN	21701	FREDERICK
21775	NEW MIDWAY	21757	KEYMAR
21781	SAINT JAMES	21733	FAIRPLAY
21802	SALISBURY	21804	SALISBURY
21803	SALISBURY	21801	SALISBURY
21810	ALLEN	21822	EDEN
21836	MANOKIN	21871	WESTOVER
21843	OCEAN CITY	21842	OCEAN CITY
21852	POWELLVILLE	21850	PITTSVILLE
21857	REHOBETH	21871	WESTOVER
21862	SHOWELL	21811	BERLIN
21867	UPPER FAIRMOUNT	21871	WESTOVER
21890	WESTOVER	21871	WESTOVER
21902	PERRY POINT	21903	PERRYVILLE
21916	CHILDS	21921	ELKTON
21920	ELK MILLS	21921	ELKTON
21922	ELKTON	21921	ELKTON
21930	GEORGETOWN	21919	EARLEVILLE
22009	BURKE	22015	BURKE
22035	FAIRFAX	22030	FAIRFAX
22037	FAIRFAX	22042	FALLS CHURCH
22038	FAIRFAX	22030	FAIRFAX
22040	FALLS CHURCH	22046	FALLS CHURCH
22081	MERRIFIELD	22031	FAIRFAX
22082	MERRIFIELD	22031	FAIRFAX
22103	WEST MCLEAN	22182	VIENNA
22106	MC LEAN	22101	MC LEAN
22107	MC LEAN	22101	MC LEAN
22108	MC LEAN	22101	MC LEAN
22116	MERRIFIELD	22031	FAIRFAX
22118	MERRIFIELD	22031	FAIRFAX
22119	MERRIFIELD	22031	FAIRFAX
22121	MOUNT VERNON	22309	ALEXANDRIA
22122	NEWINGTON	22079	LORTON
22125	OCCOQUAN	22192	WOODBRIDGE
22135	QUANTICO	22134	QUANTICO
22156	SPRINGFIELD	22150	SPRINGFIELD
22158	SPRINGFIELD	22151	SPRINGFIELD
22159	SPRINGFIELD	22151	SPRINGFIELD
22160	SPRINGFIELD	22151	SPRINGFIELD
22161	SPRINGFIELD	22151	SPRINGFIELD
22183	VIENNA	22180	VIENNA
22185	VIENNA	22124	OAKTON
22194	WOODBRIDGE	22191	WOODBRIDGE
22195	WOODBRIDGE	22193	WOODBRIDGE
22199	LORTON	22079	LORTON
22210	ARLINGTON	22201	ARLINGTON
22214	ARLINGTON	22204	ARLINGTON
22215	ARLINGTON	22202	ARLINGTON
22216	ARLINGTON	22201	ARLINGTON
22217	ARLINGTON	22203	ARLINGTON
22219	ARLINGTON	22209	ARLINGTON
22222	ARLINGTON	22202	ARLINGTON
22226	ARLINGTON	22201	ARLINGTON
22227	ARLINGTON	22202	ARLINGTON
22230	ARLINGTON	22203	ARLINGTON
22240	ARLINGTON	22202	ARLINGTON
22242	ARLINGTON	22202	ARLINGTON
22243	ARLINGTON	22202	ARLINGTON
22244	ARLINGTON	22202	ARLINGTON
22245	ARLINGTON	22202	ARLINGTON
22246	ARLINGTON	22202	ARLINGTON
22313	ALEXANDRIA	22314	ALEXANDRIA
22320	ALEXANDRIA	22314	ALEXANDRIA
22331	ALEXANDRIA	22314	ALEXANDRIA
22332	ALEXANDRIA	22314	ALEXANDRIA
22333	ALEXANDRIA	22304	ALEXANDRIA
22334	ALEXANDRIA	22314	ALEXANDRIA
22402	FREDERICKSBURG	22401	FREDERICKSBURG
22403	FREDERICKSBURG	22405	FREDERICKSBURG
22404	FREDERICKSBURG	22401	FREDERICKSBURG
22412	FREDERICKSBURG	22406	FREDERICKSBURG
22428	BOWLING GREEN	22427	BOWLING GREEN
22430	BROOKE	22554	STAFFORD
22442	COLES POINT	22469	HAGUE
22446	CORBIN	22580	WOODFORD
22451	DOGUE	22485	KING GEORGE
22456	EDWARDSVILLE	22473	HEATHSVILLE
22463	GARRISONVILLE	22554	STAFFORD
22471	HARTWOOD	22406	FREDERICKSBURG
22472	HAYNESVILLE	22572	WARSAW
22481	JERSEY	22485	KING GEORGE
22501	LADYSMITH	22546	RUTHER GLEN
22507	LIVELY	22503	LANCASTER
22513	MERRY POINT	22503	LANCASTER
22517	MOLLUSK	22503	LANCASTER
22523	MORATTICO	22503	LANCASTER
22524	MOUNT HOLLY	22520	MONTROSS
22526	NINDE	22485	KING GEORGE
22528	NUTTSVILLE	22503	LANCASTER
22529	OLDHAMS	22469	HAGUE
22530	OPHELIA	22473	HEATHSVILLE
22544	ROLLINS FORK	22485	KING GEORGE
22545	RUBY	22556	STAFFORD
22547	SEALSTON	22485	KING GEORGE
22548	SHARPS	22572	WARSAW
22552	SPARTA	22514	MILFORD
22555	STAFFORD	22554	STAFFORD
22558	STRATFORD	22520	MONTROSS
22565	THORNBURG	22551	SPOTSYLVANIA
22570	VILLAGE	22435	CALLAO
22577	SANDY POINT	22488	KINSALE
22581	ZACATA	22520	MONTROSS
22604	WINCHESTER	22601	WINCHESTER
22622	BRUCETOWN	22624	CLEAR BROOK
22623	CHESTER GAP	22630	FRONT ROYAL
22626	FISHERS HILL	22657	STRASBURG
22646	MILLWOOD	22620	BOYCE
22711	BANCO	22727	MADISON
22721	GRAVES MILL	22727	MADISON
22723	HOOD	22727	MADISON
22739	SOMERVILLE	22728	MIDLAND
22746	VIEWTOWN	20106	AMISSVILLE
22748	WOLFTOWN	22727	MADISON
22803	HARRISONBURG	22801	HARRISONBURG
22833	LACEY SPRING	22802	HARRISONBURG
22848	PLEASANT VALLEY	22841	MOUNT CRAWFORD
22850	SINGERS GLEN	22834	LINVILLE
22905	CHARLOTTESVILLE	22903	CHARLOTTESVILLE
22906	CHARLOTTESVILLE	22901	CHARLOTTESVILLE
22908	CHARLOTTESVILLE	22903	CHARLOTTESVILLE
22909	CHARLOTTESVILLE	22911	CHARLOTTESVILLE
22910	CHARLOTTESVILLE	22903	CHARLOTTESVILLE
22924	BATESVILLE	22903	CHARLOTTESVILLE
22945	IVY	22901	CHARLOTTESVILLE
22957	MONTPELIER STATION	22960	ORANGE
22965	QUINQUE	22968	RUCKERSVILLE
22987	WHITE HALL	22932	CROZET
22989	WOODBERRY FOREST	22732	RADIANT
23001	ACHILLES	23072	HAYES
23003	ARK	23061	GLOUCESTER
23014	BEAUMONT	23102	MAIDENS
23018	BENA	23072	HAYES
23031	CHRISTCHURCH	23149	SALUDA
23058	GLEN ALLEN	23060	GLEN ALLEN
23064	GRIMSTEAD	23066	GWYNN
23067	HADENSVILLE	23093	LOUISA
23068	HALLIEFORD	23035	COBBS CREEK
23076	HUDGINS	23128	NORTH
23081	JAMESTOWN	23185	WILLIAMSBURG
23090	LIGHTFOOT	23188	WILLIAMSBURG
23101	MACON	23139	POWHATAN
23105	MANNBORO	23002	AMELIA COURT HOUSE
23107	MARYUS	23072	HAYES
23108	MASCOT	23156	SHACKLEFORDS
23115	MILLERS TAVERN	22560	TAPPAHANNOCK
23127	NORGE	23188	WILLIAMSBURG
23131	ORDINARY	23072	HAYES
23147	RUTHVILLE	23030	CHARLES CITY
23154	SCHLEY	23061	GLOUCESTER
23155	SEVERN	23061	GLOUCESTER
23162	STUDLEY	23116	MECHANICSVILLE
23170	TREVILIANS	23093	LOUISA
23178	WARE NECK	23061	GLOUCESTER
23183	WHITE MARSH	23061	GLOUCESTER
23184	WICOMICO	23072	HAYES
23187	WILLIAMSBURG	23185	WILLIAMSBURG
23190	WOODS CROSS ROADS	23061	GLOUCESTER

VIRGINIA

Point ZIP Code		Enclosing Residential ZIP Code		Point ZIP Code		Enclosing Residential ZIP Code	
ZIP	Post Office Name	ZIP	Post Office Name	ZIP	Post Office Name	ZIP	Post Office Name
23218	RICHMOND	23219	RICHMOND	23899	CLAREMONT	23881	SPRING GROVE
23232	RICHMOND	23220	RICHMOND	23939	EVERGREEN	24522	APPOMATTOX
23240	RICHMOND	23219	RICHMOND	23941	FORT MITCHELL	23924	CHASE CITY
23241	RICHMOND	23219	RICHMOND	23943	HAMPDEN SYDNEY	23901	FARMVILLE
23242	RICHMOND	23238	RICHMOND	23955	NOTTOWAY	23930	CREWE
23249	RICHMOND	23224	RICHMOND	24001	ROANOKE	24011	ROANOKE
23255	RICHMOND	23229	RICHMOND	24002	ROANOKE	24011	ROANOKE
23260	RICHMOND	23220	RICHMOND	24003	ROANOKE	24011	ROANOKE
23261	RICHMOND	23220	RICHMOND	24004	ROANOKE	24011	ROANOKE
23269	RICHMOND	23220	RICHMOND	24005	ROANOKE	24011	ROANOKE
23273	RICHMOND	23230	RICHMOND	24006	ROANOKE	24011	ROANOKE
23274	RICHMOND	23219	RICHMOND	24007	ROANOKE	24011	ROANOKE
23276	RICHMOND	23220	RICHMOND	24008	ROANOKE	24011	ROANOKE
23278	RICHMOND	23220	RICHMOND	24009	ROANOKE	24011	ROANOKE
23279	RICHMOND	23230	RICHMOND	24010	ROANOKE	24011	ROANOKE
23282	RICHMOND	23220	RICHMOND	24022	ROANOKE	24016	ROANOKE
23284	RICHMOND	23220	RICHMOND	24023	ROANOKE	24016	ROANOKE
23285	RICHMOND	23220	RICHMOND	24024	ROANOKE	24016	ROANOKE
23286	RICHMOND	23220	RICHMOND	24025	ROANOKE	24016	ROANOKE
23288	RICHMOND	23229	RICHMOND	24026	ROANOKE	24016	ROANOKE
23289	RICHMOND	23294	RICHMOND	24027	ROANOKE	24016	ROANOKE
23290	RICHMOND	23220	RICHMOND	24028	ROANOKE	24016	ROANOKE
23291	RICHMOND	23219	RICHMOND	24029	ROANOKE	24016	ROANOKE
23292	RICHMOND	23219	RICHMOND	24030	ROANOKE	24016	ROANOKE
23293	RICHMOND	23219	RICHMOND	24031	ROANOKE	24016	ROANOKE
23295	RICHMOND	23230	RICHMOND	24032	ROANOKE	24016	ROANOKE
23297	RICHMOND	23237	RICHMOND	24033	ROANOKE	24016	ROANOKE
23304	BATTERY PARK	23430	SMITHFIELD	24034	ROANOKE	24016	ROANOKE
23313	CAPEVILLE	23310	CAPE CHARLES	24035	ROANOKE	24016	ROANOKE
23316	CHERITON	23310	CAPE CHARLES	24036	ROANOKE	24016	ROANOKE
23326	CHESAPEAKE	23320	CHESAPEAKE	24037	ROANOKE	24016	ROANOKE
23327	CHESAPEAKE	23322	CHESAPEAKE	24038	ROANOKE	24016	ROANOKE
23328	CHESAPEAKE	23320	CHESAPEAKE	24040	ROANOKE	24016	ROANOKE
23341	CRADDOCKVILLE	23306	BELLE HAVEN	24042	ROANOKE	24016	ROANOKE
23345	DAVIS WHARF	23306	BELLE HAVEN	24044	ROANOKE	24016	ROANOKE
23347	EASTVILLE	23310	CAPE CHARLES	24048	ROANOKE	24018	ROANOKE
23358	HACKSNECK	23420	PAINTER	24050	ROANOKE	24019	ROANOKE
23389	HARBORTON	23420	PAINTER	24058	BELSPRING	24142	RADFORD
23397	ISLE OF WIGHT	23487	WINDSOR	24061	BLACKSBURG	24060	BLACKSBURG
23398	JAMESVILLE	23350	EXMORE	24062	BLACKSBURG	24060	BLACKSBURG
23399	JENKINS BRIDGE	23359	HALLWOOD	24063	BLACKSBURG	24060	BLACKSBURG
23401	KELLER	23410	MELFA	24068	CHRISTIANSBURG	24073	CHRISTIANSBURG
23407	MAPPSVILLE	23308	BLOXOM	24111	MC COY	24060	BLACKSBURG
23408	MARIONVILLE	23413	NASSAWADOX	24113	MARTINSVILLE	24112	MARTINSVILLE
23412	MODEST TOWN	23308	BLOXOM	24114	MARTINSVILLE	24112	MARTINSVILLE
23414	NELSONIA	23308	BLOXOM	24115	MARTINSVILLE	24112	MARTINSVILLE
23419	OYSTER	23310	CAPE CHARLES	24126	NEWBERN	24084	DUBLIN
23422	PUNGOTEAGUE	23420	PAINTER	24129	NEW RIVER	24142	RADFORD
23423	QUINBY	23420	PAINTER	24130	ORISKANY	24085	EAGLE ROCK
23424	RESCUE	23314	CARROLLTON	24132	PARROTT	24142	RADFORD
23427	SAXIS	23426	SANFORD	24143	RADFORD	24141	RADFORD
23429	SEAVIEW	23310	CAPE CHARLES	24146	REDWOOD	24092	GLADE HILL
23431	SMITHFIELD	23430	SMITHFIELD	24155	ROANOKE	24153	SALEM
23439	SUFFOLK	23434	SUFFOLK	24177	VESTA	24120	MEADOWS OF DAN
23441	TASLEY	23301	ACCOMAC	24178	VILLAMONT	24064	BLUE RIDGE
23443	TOWNSEND	23310	CAPE CHARLES	24203	BRISTOL	24201	BRISTOL
23450	VIRGINIA BEACH	23454	VIRGINIA BEACH	24205	BRISTOL	24201	BRISTOL
23458	VIRGINIA BEACH	23451	VIRGINIA BEACH	24209	BRISTOL	24201	BRISTOL
23465	VIRGINIA BEACH	23464	VIRGINIA BEACH	24212	ABINGDON	24210	ABINGDON
23466	VIRGINIA BEACH	23462	VIRGINIA BEACH	24215	ANDOVER	24216	APPALACHIA
23467	VIRGINIA BEACH	23464	VIRGINIA BEACH	24218	BEN HUR	24263	JONESVILLE
23471	VIRGINIA BEACH	23455	VIRGINIA BEACH	24246	EAST STONE GAP	24219	BIG STONE GAP
23479	VIRGINIA BEACH	23454	VIRGINIA BEACH	24327	EMORY	24361	MEADOWVIEW
23480	WACHAPREAGUE	23410	MELFA	24402	STAUNTON	24401	STAUNTON
23482	WARDTOWN	23350	EXMORE	24411	AUGUSTA SPRINGS	24430	CRAIGSVILLE
23483	WATTSVILLE	23337	WALLOPS ISLAND	24412	BACOVA	24484	WARM SPRINGS
23486	WILLIS WHARF	23350	EXMORE	24415	BROWNSBURG	24473	ROCKBRIDGE BATHS
23488	WITHAMS	23416	OAK HALL	24438	GLEN WILTON	24085	EAGLE ROCK
23501	NORFOLK	23510	NORFOLK	24448	IRON GATE	24422	CLIFTON FORGE
23506	NORFOLK	23502	NORFOLK	24457	LOW MOOR	24426	COVINGTON
23512	NORFOLK	23505	NORFOLK	24463	MINT SPRING	24401	STAUNTON
23514	NORFOLK	23510	NORFOLK	24469	NEW HOPE	24437	FORT DEFIANCE
23515	NORFOLK	23505	NORFOLK	24474	SELMA	24426	COVINGTON
23519	NORFOLK	23518	NORFOLK	24476	STEELES TAVERN	24483	VESUVIUS
23520	NORFOLK	23521	NORFOLK	24505	LYNCHBURG	24501	LYNCHBURG
23541	NORFOLK	23511	NORFOLK	24506	LYNCHBURG	24501	LYNCHBURG
23551	NORFOLK	23511	NORFOLK	24512	LYNCHBURG	24551	FOREST
23609	NEWPORT NEWS	23607	NEWPORT NEWS	24513	LYNCHBURG	24551	FOREST
23612	NEWPORT NEWS	23606	NEWPORT NEWS	24514	LYNCHBURG	24502	LYNCHBURG
23628	NEWPORT NEWS	23604	FORT EUSTIS	24515	LYNCHBURG	24502	LYNCHBURG
23630	HAMPTON	23661	HAMPTON	24533	CLIFFORD	24521	AMHERST
23667	HAMPTON	23668	HAMPTON	24535	CLUSTER SPRINGS	24592	SOUTH BOSTON
23670	HAMPTON	23661	HAMPTON	24543	DANVILLE	24541	DANVILLE
23681	HAMPTON	23665	HAMPTON	24544	DANVILLE	24541	DANVILLE
23691	YORKTOWN	23690	YORKTOWN	24576	NARUNA	24528	BROOKNEAL
23694	LACKEY	23690	YORKTOWN	24581	NORWOOD	24599	WINGINA
23705	PORTSMOUTH	23707	PORTSMOUTH	24595	SWEET BRIAR	24521	AMHERST
23804	PETERSBURG	23803	PETERSBURG	24601	AMONATE	24602	BANDY
23822	AMMON	23850	FORD	24604	BISHOP	24602	BANDY
23870	JARRATT	23847	EMPORIA	24606	BOISSEVAIN	24605	BLUEFIELD
23873	MEREDITHVILLE	23920	BRODNAX	24607	BREAKS	24256	HAYSI
23884	SUSSEX	23890	WAVERLY	24608	BURKES GARDEN	24651	TAZEWELL
23891	WAVERLY	23890	WAVERLY	24612	DORAN	24641	RICHLANDS

NONRESIDENTIAL ZIP CODES

VIRGINIA

WEST VIRGINIA

Point ZIP Code		Enclosing Residential ZIP Code		Point ZIP Code		Enclosing Residential ZIP Code	
ZIP	Post Office Name	ZIP	Post Office Name	ZIP	Post Office Name	ZIP	Post Office Name
24619	HORSEPEN	24602	BANDY	25324	CHARLESTON	25301	CHARLESTON
24624	KEEN MOUNTAIN	24631	OAKWOOD	25325	CHARLESTON	25301	CHARLESTON
24628	MAXIE	24614	GRUNDY	25326	CHARLESTON	25301	CHARLESTON
24635	POCAHONTAS	24605	BLUEFIELD	25327	CHARLESTON	25301	CHARLESTON
24640	RED ASH	24639	RAVEN	25328	CHARLESTON	25301	CHARLESTON
24647	SHORTT GAP	24639	RAVEN	25329	CHARLESTON	25301	CHARLESTON
24658	WOLFORD	24620	HURLEY	25330	CHARLESTON	25301	CHARLESTON
24716	BUD	24726	HERNDON	25331	CHARLESTON	25301	CHARLESTON
24719	COVEL	24726	HERNDON	25332	CHARLESTON	25301	CHARLESTON
24724	FREEMAN	24701	BLUEFIELD	25333	CHARLESTON	25301	CHARLESTON
24729	HIAWATHA	24736	MATOAKA	25334	CHARLESTON	25301	CHARLESTON
24732	KELLYSVILLE	24740	PRINCETON	25335	CHARLESTON	25301	CHARLESTON
24737	MONTCALM	24701	BLUEFIELD	25336	CHARLESTON	25301	CHARLESTON
24738	NEMOURS	24701	BLUEFIELD	25337	CHARLESTON	25301	CHARLESTON
24739	OAKVALE	24740	PRINCETON	25338	CHARLESTON	25301	CHARLESTON
24751	WOLFE	24701	BLUEFIELD	25339	CHARLESTON	25301	CHARLESTON
24808	ANAWALT	24801	WELCH	25350	CHARLESTON	25301	CHARLESTON
24811	AVONDALE	24844	IAEGER	25356	CHARLESTON	25313	CHARLESTON
24813	BARTLEY	24873	PAYNESVILLE	25357	CHARLESTON	25312	CHARLESTON
24816	BIG SANDY	24828	DAVY	25358	CHARLESTON	25309	CHARLESTON
24817	BRADSHAW	24850	JOLO	25360	CHARLESTON	25312	CHARLESTON
24826	CUCUMBER	24815	BERWIND	25361	CHARLESTON	25311	CHARLESTON
24829	ECKMAN	24801	WELCH	25362	CHARLESTON	25071	ELKVIEW
24830	ELBERT	24801	WELCH	25364	CHARLESTON	25304	CHARLESTON
24831	ELKHORN	24868	NORTHFORK	25365	CHARLESTON	25315	CHARLESTON
24836	GARY	24801	WELCH	25375	CHARLESTON	25312	CHARLESTON
24842	HEMPHILL	24801	WELCH	25387	CHARLESTON	25304	CHARLESTON
24843	HENSLEY	24828	DAVY	25389	CHARLESTON	25312	CHARLESTON
24845	IKES FORK	24839	HANOVER	25392	CHARLESTON	25301	CHARLESTON
24846	ISABAN	24862	MOHAWK	25396	CHARLESTON	25314	CHARLESTON
24847	ITMANN	25882	MULLENS	25402	MARTINSBURG	25401	MARTINSBURG
24848	JENKINJONES	24801	WELCH	25410	BAKERTON	25425	HARPERS FERRY
24851	JUSTICE	25621	GILBERT	25421	GLENGARY	25427	HEDGESVILLE
24853	KIMBALL	24801	WELCH	25423	HALLTOWN	25425	HARPERS FERRY
24854	KOPPERSTON	24870	OCEANA	25432	MILLVILLE	25425	HARPERS FERRY
24855	KYLE	24868	NORTHFORK	25440	RIDGEWAY	25413	BUNKER HILL
24857	LYNCO	24870	OCEANA	25441	RIPPON	25414	CHARLES TOWN
24861	MAYBEURY	24868	NORTHFORK	25507	CEREDO	25530	KENOVA
24866	NEWHALL	24884	SQUIRE	25562	SHOALS	25704	HUNTINGTON
24867	NEW RICHMOND	24874	PINEVILLE	25569	TEAYS	25526	HURRICANE
24871	PAGETON	24801	WELCH	25572	WOODVILLE	25501	ALKOL
24872	PANTHER	24862	MOHAWK	25606	ACCOVILLE	25635	MAN
24878	PREMIER	24801	WELCH	25611	BRUNO	25635	MAN
24880	ROCK VIEW	24874	PINEVILLE	25612	CHAUNCEY	25638	OMAR
24881	RODERFIELD	24828	DAVY	25614	CORA	25601	LOGAN
24887	SWITCHBACK	24868	NORTHFORK	25624	HENLAWSON	25601	LOGAN
24888	THORPE	24801	WELCH	25625	HOLDEN	25601	LOGAN
24892	WAR	24815	BERWIND	25628	KISTLER	25635	MAN
24894	WARRIORMINE	24815	BERWIND	25630	LORADO	25607	AMHERSTDALE
24895	WILCOE	24801	WELCH	25634	MALLORY	25617	DAVIN
24898	WYOMING	24874	PINEVILLE	25637	MOUNT GAY	25601	LOGAN
24902	FAIRLEA	24901	LEWISBURG	25639	PEACH CREEK	25601	LOGAN
24924	BUCKEYE	24954	MARLINTON	25644	SARAH ANN	25638	OMAR
25002	ALLOY	25136	MONTGOMERY	25646	STOLLINGS	25601	LOGAN
25011	BANCROFT	25159	POCA	25647	SWITZER	25047	CLOTHIER
25022	BLAIR	25654	YOLYN	25649	VERDUNVILLE	25508	CHAPMANVILLE
25026	BLUE CREEK	25071	ELKVIEW	25652	WHITMAN	25601	LOGAN
25031	BOOMER	25136	MONTGOMERY	25653	WILKINSON	25601	LOGAN
25036	CANNELTON	25136	MONTGOMERY	25665	BORDERLAND	25661	WILLIAMSON
25040	CHARLTON HEIGHTS	25136	MONTGOMERY	25667	CHATTAROY	25661	WILLIAMSON
25054	DAWES	25075	ESKDALE	25672	EDGARTON	25678	MATEWAN
25057	DEEP WATER	25136	MONTGOMERY	25685	NAUGATUCK	25676	LENORE
25061	DRYBRANCH	25015	BELLE	25686	NEWTOWN	25638	OMAR
25067	EAST BANK	25015	BELLE	25688	NORTH MATEWAN	25678	MATEWAN
25070	ELEANOR	25168	RED HOUSE	25690	RAGLAND	25670	DELBARTON
25076	ETHEL	25654	YOLYN	25691	RAWL	25661	WILLIAMSON
25086	GLASGOW	25039	CEDAR GROVE	25692	RED JACKET	25678	MATEWAN
25090	GLEN FERRIS	25136	MONTGOMERY	25696	VARNEY	25678	MATEWAN
25102	HANDLEY	25083	GALLAGHER	25706	HUNTINGTON	25701	HUNTINGTON
25109	HOMETOWN	25168	RED HOUSE	25707	HUNTINGTON	25701	HUNTINGTON
25110	HUGHESTON	25015	BELLE	25708	HUNTINGTON	25701	HUNTINGTON
25112	INSTITUTE	25143	NITRO	25709	HUNTINGTON	25701	HUNTINGTON
25126	LONDON	25039	CEDAR GROVE	25710	HUNTINGTON	25701	HUNTINGTON
25134	MIAMI	25075	ESKDALE	25711	HUNTINGTON	25701	HUNTINGTON
25149	OTTAWA	25114	JEFFREY	25712	HUNTINGTON	25701	HUNTINGTON
25152	PAGE	25136	MONTGOMERY	25713	HUNTINGTON	25701	HUNTINGTON
25156	PINCH	25071	ELKVIEW	25714	HUNTINGTON	25701	HUNTINGTON
25162	PRATT	25083	GALLAGHER	25715	HUNTINGTON	25701	HUNTINGTON
25183	SHARPLES	25654	YOLYN	25716	HUNTINGTON	25701	HUNTINGTON
25185	MOUNT OLIVE	25136	MONTGOMERY	25717	HUNTINGTON	25701	HUNTINGTON
25186	SMITHERS	25136	MONTGOMERY	25718	HUNTINGTON	25701	HUNTINGTON
25201	TAD	25306	CHARLESTON	25719	HUNTINGTON	25701	HUNTINGTON
25203	TURTLE CREEK	25053	DANVILLE	25720	HUNTINGTON	25701	HUNTINGTON
25205	UNEEDA	25130	MADISON	25721	HUNTINGTON	25701	HUNTINGTON
25206	VAN	25021	BIM	25722	HUNTINGTON	25701	HUNTINGTON
25211	WIDEN	26617	DILLE	25723	HUNTINGTON	25701	HUNTINGTON
25247	HARTFORD	25260	MASON	25724	HUNTINGTON	25701	HUNTINGTON
25265	NEW HAVEN	25253	LETART	25725	HUNTINGTON	25701	HUNTINGTON
25305	CHARLESTON	25311	CHARLESTON	25726	HUNTINGTON	25704	HUNTINGTON
25317	CHARLESTON	25311	CHARLESTON	25727	HUNTINGTON	25704	HUNTINGTON
25321	CHARLESTON	25301	CHARLESTON	25728	HUNTINGTON	25704	HUNTINGTON
25322	CHARLESTON	25301	CHARLESTON	25729	HUNTINGTON	25701	HUNTINGTON
25323	CHARLESTON	25301	CHARLESTON	25770	HUNTINGTON	25704	HUNTINGTON

Point ZIP Code		Enclosing Residential ZIP Code	
ZIP	Post Office Name	ZIP	Post Office Name
25771	HUNTINGTON	25704	HUNTINGTON
25772	HUNTINGTON	25704	HUNTINGTON
25773	HUNTINGTON	25704	HUNTINGTON
25774	HUNTINGTON	25704	HUNTINGTON
25775	HUNTINGTON	25704	HUNTINGTON
25776	HUNTINGTON	25704	HUNTINGTON
25777	HUNTINGTON	25704	HUNTINGTON
25778	HUNTINGTON	25704	HUNTINGTON
25779	HUNTINGTON	25704	HUNTINGTON
25802	BECKLEY	25801	BECKLEY
25810	ALLEN JUNCTION	25928	STEPHENSON
25818	BRADLEY	25880	MOUNT HOPE
25826	CORINNE	25811	AMIGO
25833	DOTHAN	25917	SCARBRO
25836	ECCLES	25801	BECKLEY
25846	GLEN JEAN	25880	MOUNT HOPE
25849	GLEN WHITE	25827	CRAB ORCHARD
25851	HARPER	25801	BECKLEY
25853	HELEN	25915	RHODELL
25855	HILLTOP	25901	OAK HILL
25860	LANARK	25801	BECKLEY
25866	LOCHGELLY	25901	OAK HILL
25871	MABSCOTT	25801	BECKLEY
25873	MAC ARTHUR	25801	BECKLEY
25875	MC GRAWS	25876	SAULSVILLE
25878	MIDWAY	25827	CRAB ORCHARD
25879	MINDEN	25901	OAK HILL
25904	PAX	25880	MOUNT HOPE
25906	PINEY VIEW	25801	BECKLEY
25907	PRINCE	25831	DANESE
25909	PROSPERITY	25880	MOUNT HOPE
25911	RALEIGH	25801	BECKLEY
25916	SABINE	25913	RAVENCLIFF
25919	SKELTON	25801	BECKLEY
25921	SOPHIA	25827	CRAB ORCHARD
25927	STANAFORD	25801	BECKLEY
25942	WINONA	25840	FAYETTEVILLE
25943	WYCO	25811	AMIGO
25972	LESLIE	25981	QUINWOOD
26030	BEECH BOTTOM	26070	WELLSBURG
26056	NEW MANCHESTER	26034	CHESTER
26058	SHORT CREEK	26070	WELLSBURG
26074	WEST LIBERTY	26003	WHEELING
26075	WINDSOR HEIGHTS	26070	WELLSBURG
26102	PARKERSBURG	26101	PARKERSBURG
26103	PARKERSBURG	26101	PARKERSBURG
26106	PARKERSBURG	26101	PARKERSBURG
26120	MINERAL WELLS	26150	MINERAL WELLS
26121	MINERAL WELLS	26150	MINERAL WELLS
26162	PORTERS FALLS	26167	READER
26209	SNOWSHOE	26291	SLATYFORK
26229	LORENTZ	26201	BUCKHANNON
26259	DAILEY	26293	VALLEY BEND
26275	JUNIOR	26250	BELINGTON
26285	NORTON	26257	COALTON
26298	BERGOO	26288	WEBSTER SPRINGS
26302	CLARKSBURG	26301	CLARKSBURG
26306	CLARKSBURG	26330	BRIDGEPORT
26323	ANMOORE	26301	CLARKSBURG
26349	GALLOWAY	26416	PHILIPPI
26361	GYPSY	26431	SHINNSTON
26366	HAYWOOD	26301	CLARKSBURG
26369	HEPZIBAH	26301	CLARKSBURG
26422	REYNOLDSVILLE	26301	CLARKSBURG
26424	ROSEMONT	26347	FLEMINGTON
26434	SHIRLEY	26320	ALMA
26435	SIMPSON	26347	FLEMINGTON
26436	SMITHBURG	26456	WEST UNION
26438	SPELTER	26330	BRIDGEPORT
26461	WILSONBURG	26301	CLARKSBURG
26463	WYATT	26568	ENTERPRISE
26502	MORGANTOWN	26501	MORGANTOWN
26504	MORGANTOWN	26505	MORGANTOWN
26507	MORGANTOWN	26501	MORGANTOWN
26520	ARTHURDALE	26547	REEDSVILLE
26524	BRETZ	26547	REEDSVILLE
26527	CASSVILLE	26501	MORGANTOWN
26531	DELLSLOW	26508	MORGANTOWN
26534	GRANVILLE	26501	MORGANTOWN
26543	OSAGE	26501	MORGANTOWN
26544	PENTRESS	26501	MORGANTOWN
26555	FAIRMONT	26554	FAIRMONT
26559	BARRACKVILLE	26554	FAIRMONT
26563	CAROLINA	26571	FARMINGTON
26566	COLFAX	26554	FAIRMONT
26572	FOUR STATES	26591	WORTHINGTON
26574	GRANT TOWN	26588	RIVESVILLE
26576	IDAMAY	26571	FARMINGTON
26578	KINGMONT	26554	FAIRMONT
26586	MONTANA MINES	26554	FAIRMONT
26671	GILBOA	26651	SUMMERSVILLE
26707	BAYARD	26720	GORMANIA
26823	CAPON SPRINGS	26808	HIGH VIEW
26886	ONEGO	26884	SENECA ROCKS
27010	BETHANIA	27106	WINSTON SALEM
27014	COOLEEMEE	27028	MOCKSVILLE
27031	WHITE PLAINS	27030	MOUNT AIRY
27049	TOAST	27030	MOUNT AIRY
27094	RURAL HALL	27045	RURAL HALL
27098	RURAL HALL	27045	RURAL HALL
27099	RURAL HALL	27045	RURAL HALL
27102	WINSTON SALEM	27105	WINSTON SALEM
27108	WINSTON SALEM	27101	WINSTON SALEM
27109	WINSTON SALEM	27106	WINSTON SALEM
27111	WINSTON SALEM	27101	WINSTON SALEM
27113	WINSTON SALEM	27103	WINSTON SALEM
27114	WINSTON SALEM	27103	WINSTON SALEM
27115	WINSTON SALEM	27105	WINSTON SALEM
27116	WINSTON SALEM	27106	WINSTON SALEM
27117	WINSTON SALEM	27107	WINSTON SALEM
27120	WINSTON SALEM	27105	WINSTON SALEM
27130	WINSTON SALEM	27103	WINSTON SALEM
27150	WINSTON SALEM	27101	WINSTON SALEM
27152	WINSTON SALEM	27101	WINSTON SALEM
27155	WINSTON SALEM	27101	WINSTON SALEM
27157	WINSTON SALEM	27103	WINSTON SALEM
27199	WINSTON SALEM	27105	WINSTON SALEM
27201	ALAMANCE	27215	BURLINGTON
27202	ALTAMAHAW	27244	ELON
27204	ASHEBORO	27203	ASHEBORO
27213	BONLEE	27207	BEAR CREEK
27216	BURLINGTON	27215	BURLINGTON
27228	BYNUM	27312	PITTSBORO
27230	CEDAR FALLS	27317	RANDLEMAN
27237	CUMNOCK	27330	SANFORD
27247	ETHER	27356	STAR
27256	GULF	27252	GOLDSTON
27259	HIGHFALLS	27325	ROBBINS
27261	HIGH POINT	27260	HIGH POINT
27264	HIGH POINT	27263	HIGH POINT
27285	KERNERSVILLE	27284	KERNERSVILLE
27289	EDEN	27288	EDEN
27293	LEXINGTON	27292	LEXINGTON
27294	LEXINGTON	27292	LEXINGTON
27323	REIDSVILLE	27320	REIDSVILLE
27331	SANFORD	27330	SANFORD
27340	SAXAPAHAW	27253	GRAHAM
27342	SEDALIA	27249	GIBSONVILLE
27351	SOUTHMONT	27292	LEXINGTON
27359	SWEPSONVILLE	27253	GRAHAM
27361	THOMASVILLE	27360	THOMASVILLE
27373	WALLBURG	27107	WINSTON SALEM
27374	WELCOME	27295	LEXINGTON
27375	WENTWORTH	27320	REIDSVILLE
27402	GREENSBORO	27401	GREENSBORO
27404	GREENSBORO	27408	GREENSBORO
27412	GREENSBORO	27403	GREENSBORO
27415	GREENSBORO	27405	GREENSBORO
27416	GREENSBORO	27406	GREENSBORO
27417	GREENSBORO	27407	GREENSBORO
27419	GREENSBORO	27409	GREENSBORO
27420	GREENSBORO	27401	GREENSBORO
27425	GREENSBORO	27409	GREENSBORO
27427	GREENSBORO	27407	GREENSBORO
27429	GREENSBORO	27408	GREENSBORO
27435	GREENSBORO	27401	GREENSBORO
27438	GREENSBORO	27408	GREENSBORO
27495	GREENSBORO	27407	GREENSBORO
27497	GREENSBORO	27407	GREENSBORO
27498	GREENSBORO	27401	GREENSBORO
27499	GREENSBORO	27401	GREENSBORO
27506	BUIES CREEK	27546	LILLINGTON
27512	CARY	27511	CARY
27515	CHAPEL HILL	27514	CHAPEL HILL
27528	CLAYTON	27520	CLAYTON
27532	GOLDSBORO	27530	GOLDSBORO
27533	GOLDSBORO	27530	GOLDSBORO
27543	KIPLING	27526	FUQUAY VARINA
27552	MAMERS	27546	LILLINGTON
27555	MICRO	27576	SELMA
27556	MIDDLEBURG	27537	HENDERSON
27564	CREEDMOOR	27522	CREEDMOOR
27568	PINE LEVEL	27569	PRINCETON
27570	RIDGEWAY	27563	NORLINA
27582	STOVALL	27565	OXFORD
27584	TOWNSVILLE	27537	HENDERSON
27586	VAUGHAN	27551	MACON
27588	WAKE FOREST	27587	WAKE FOREST
27593	WILSONS MILLS	27577	SMITHFIELD
27594	WISE	27563	NORLINA
27599	CHAPEL HILL	27516	CHAPEL HILL
27602	RALEIGH	27601	RALEIGH
27611	RALEIGH	27601	RALEIGH
27619	RALEIGH	27609	RALEIGH
27620	RALEIGH	27610	RALEIGH
27621	RALEIGH	27606	RALEIGH

Point ZIP Code		Enclosing Residential ZIP Code		Point ZIP Code		Enclosing Residential ZIP Code	
ZIP	Post Office Name	ZIP	Post Office Name	ZIP	Post Office Name	ZIP	Post Office Name
27622	RALEIGH	27612	RALEIGH	28111	MONROE	28112	MONROE
27623	RALEIGH	27560	MORRISVILLE	28123	MOUNT MOURNE	28117	MOORESVILLE
27624	RALEIGH	27615	RALEIGH	28126	NEWELL	28213	CHARLOTTE
27625	RALEIGH	27604	RALEIGH	28130	PAW CREEK	28214	CHARLOTTE
27626	RALEIGH	27601	RALEIGH	28136	POLKVILLE	28150	SHELBY
27627	RALEIGH	27606	RALEIGH	28145	SALISBURY	28144	SALISBURY
27628	RALEIGH	27608	RALEIGH	28151	SHELBY	28150	SHELBY
27629	RALEIGH	27604	RALEIGH	28169	WACO	28021	CHERRYVILLE
27634	RALEIGH	27601	RALEIGH	28201	CHARLOTTE	28202	CHARLOTTE
27635	RALEIGH	27604	RALEIGH	28218	CHARLOTTE	28205	CHARLOTTE
27636	RALEIGH	27607	RALEIGH	28219	CHARLOTTE	28208	CHARLOTTE
27640	RALEIGH	27604	RALEIGH	28220	CHARLOTTE	28209	CHARLOTTE
27650	RALEIGH	27607	RALEIGH	28221	CHARLOTTE	28269	CHARLOTTE
27656	RALEIGH	27612	RALEIGH	28222	CHARLOTTE	28211	CHARLOTTE
27658	RALEIGH	27616	RALEIGH	28223	CHARLOTTE	28213	CHARLOTTE
27661	RALEIGH	27616	RALEIGH	28224	CHARLOTTE	28210	CHARLOTTE
27668	RALEIGH	27609	RALEIGH	28228	CHARLOTTE	28208	CHARLOTTE
27675	RALEIGH	27617	RALEIGH	28229	CHARLOTTE	28212	CHARLOTTE
27676	RALEIGH	27601	RALEIGH	28230	CHARLOTTE	28202	CHARLOTTE
27690	RALEIGH	27612	RALEIGH	28231	CHARLOTTE	28202	CHARLOTTE
27697	RALEIGH	27601	RALEIGH	28232	CHARLOTTE	28202	CHARLOTTE
27698	RALEIGH	27601	RALEIGH	28233	CHARLOTTE	28202	CHARLOTTE
27699	RALEIGH	27601	RALEIGH	28234	CHARLOTTE	28202	CHARLOTTE
27702	DURHAM	27701	DURHAM	28235	CHARLOTTE	28202	CHARLOTTE
27708	DURHAM	27701	DURHAM	28236	CHARLOTTE	28202	CHARLOTTE
27710	DURHAM	27705	DURHAM	28237	CHARLOTTE	28202	CHARLOTTE
27711	DURHAM	27713	DURHAM	28241	CHARLOTTE	28273	CHARLOTTE
27715	DURHAM	27705	DURHAM	28242	CHARLOTTE	28202	CHARLOTTE
27717	DURHAM	27707	DURHAM	28243	CHARLOTTE	28208	CHARLOTTE
27722	DURHAM	27712	DURHAM	28244	CHARLOTTE	28202	CHARLOTTE
27802	ROCKY MOUNT	27801	ROCKY MOUNT	28246	CHARLOTTE	28202	CHARLOTTE
27811	BELLARTHUR	27834	GREENVILLE	28247	CHARLOTTE	28226	CHARLOTTE
27813	BLACK CREEK	27893	WILSON	28253	CHARLOTTE	28269	CHARLOTTE
27815	ROCKY MOUNT	27801	ROCKY MOUNT	28254	CHARLOTTE	28208	CHARLOTTE
27819	CONETOE	27886	TARBORO	28256	CHARLOTTE	28213	CHARLOTTE
27825	EVERETTS	27892	WILLIAMSTON	28258	CHARLOTTE	28208	CHARLOTTE
27827	FALKLAND	27834	GREENVILLE	28260	CHARLOTTE	28208	CHARLOTTE
27833	GREENVILLE	27834	GREENVILLE	28263	CHARLOTTE	28202	CHARLOTTE
27835	GREENVILLE	27858	GREENVILLE	28265	CHARLOTTE	28208	CHARLOTTE
27836	GREENVILLE	27858	GREENVILLE	28266	CHARLOTTE	28208	CHARLOTTE
27841	HASSELL	27857	OAK CITY	28271	CHARLOTTE	28202	CHARLOTTE
27861	PARMELE	27871	ROBERSONVILLE	28272	CHARLOTTE	28208	CHARLOTTE
27867	POTECASI	27897	WOODLAND	28275	CHARLOTTE	28208	CHARLOTTE
27868	RED OAK	27856	NASHVILLE	28280	CHARLOTTE	28202	CHARLOTTE
27873	SARATOGA	27883	STANTONSBURG	28281	CHARLOTTE	28202	CHARLOTTE
27877	SEVERN	27853	MARGARETTSVILLE	28282	CHARLOTTE	28202	CHARLOTTE
27878	SHARPSBURG	27803	ROCKY MOUNT	28284	CHARLOTTE	28202	CHARLOTTE
27879	SIMPSON	27837	GRIMESLAND	28285	CHARLOTTE	28202	CHARLOTTE
27881	SPEED	27843	HOBGOOD	28287	CHARLOTTE	28210	CHARLOTTE
27887	TILLERY	27839	HALIFAX	28289	CHARLOTTE	28208	CHARLOTTE
27894	WILSON	27893	WILSON	28290	CHARLOTTE	28208	CHARLOTTE
27895	WILSON	27893	WILSON	28296	CHARLOTTE	28208	CHARLOTTE
27906	ELIZABETH CITY	27909	ELIZABETH CITY	28297	CHARLOTTE	28216	CHARLOTTE
27907	ELIZABETH CITY	27909	ELIZABETH CITY	28299	CHARLOTTE	28205	CHARLOTTE
27915	AVON	27959	NAGS HEAD	28302	FAYETTEVILLE	28301	FAYETTEVILLE
27920	BUXTON	27959	NAGS HEAD	28309	FAYETTEVILLE	28314	FAYETTEVILLE
27930	DURANTS NECK	27944	HERTFORD	28319	BARNESVILLE	28369	ORRUM
27936	FRISCO	27959	NAGS HEAD	28325	CALYPSO	28365	MOUNT OLIVE
27943	HATTERAS	27959	NAGS HEAD	28329	CLINTON	28328	CLINTON
27967	POWELLSVILLE	27910	AHOSKIE	28330	CORDOVA	28379	ROCKINGHAM
27968	RODANTHE	27959	NAGS HEAD	28331	CUMBERLAND	28306	FAYETTEVILLE
27969	RODUCO	27937	GATES	28332	DUBLIN	28320	BLADENBORO
27972	SALVO	27959	NAGS HEAD	28335	DUNN	28334	DUNN
27982	WAVES	27959	NAGS HEAD	28342	FALCON	28344	GODWIN
27985	WINFALL	27944	HERTFORD	28350	LAKEVIEW	28394	VASS
28002	ALBEMARLE	28001	ALBEMARLE	28353	LAURINBURG	28352	LAURINBURG
28007	ANSONVILLE	28170	WADESBORO	28355	LEMON SPRINGS	27332	SANFORD
28009	BADIN	28001	ALBEMARLE	28359	LUMBERTON	28358	LUMBERTON
28010	BARIUM SPRINGS	28677	STATESVILLE	28362	MARIETTA	28340	FAIRMONT
28017	BOILING SPRINGS	28152	SHELBY	28367	NORMAN	28338	ELLERBE
28019	CAROLEEN	28043	FOREST CITY	28368	OLIVIA	27332	SANFORD
28024	CLIFFSIDE	28114	MOORESBORO	28370	PINEHURST	28374	PINEHURST
28026	CONCORD	28025	CONCORD	28375	PROCTORVILLE	28369	ORRUM
28035	DAVIDSON	28036	DAVIDSON	28378	REX	28384	SAINT PAULS
28038	EARL	28073	GROVER	28380	ROCKINGHAM	28379	ROCKINGHAM
28039	EAST SPENCER	28144	SALISBURY	28388	SOUTHERN PINES	28387	SOUTHERN PINES
28041	FAITH	28146	SALISBURY	28402	WILMINGTON	28401	WILMINGTON
28042	FALLSTON	28090	LAWNDALE	28404	WILMINGTON	28411	WILMINGTON
28053	GASTONIA	28052	GASTONIA	28406	WILMINGTON	28403	WILMINGTON
28055	GASTONIA	28054	GASTONIA	28407	WILMINGTON	28405	WILMINGTON
28070	HUNTERSVILLE	28078	HUNTERSVILLE	28408	WILMINGTON	28412	WILMINGTON
28072	GRANITE QUARRY	28146	SALISBURY	28410	WILMINGTON	28412	WILMINGTON
28074	HARRIS	28139	RUTHERFORDTON	28424	BRUNSWICK	28472	WHITEVILLE
28076	HENRIETTA	28114	MOORESBORO	28459	SHALLOTTE	28470	SHALLOTTE
28077	HIGH SHOALS	28034	DALLAS	28502	KINSTON	28501	KINSTON
28082	KANNAPOLIS	28081	KANNAPOLIS	28503	KINSTON	28501	KINSTON
28089	LATTIMORE	28150	SHELBY	28509	ALLIANCE	28515	BAYBORO
28093	LINCOLNTON	28092	LINCOLNTON	28519	BRIDGETON	28560	NEW BERN
28101	MC ADENVILLE	28056	GASTONIA	28522	COMFORT	28585	TRENTON
28102	MC FARLAN	28119	MORVEN	28524	DAVIS	28516	BEAUFORT
28106	MATTHEWS	28105	MATTHEWS	28533	CHERRY POINT	28532	HAVELOCK
28108	MINERAL SPRINGS	28112	MONROE	28541	JACKSONVILLE	28543	TARAWA TERRACE
28109	MISENHEIMER	28137	RICHFIELD	28545	MCCUTCHEON FIELD	28540	JACKSONVILLE

NONRESIDENTIAL ZIP CODES

NORTH CAROLINA

SOUTH CAROLINA

Point ZIP Code		Enclosing Residential ZIP Code	
ZIP	Post Office Name	ZIP	Post Office Name
28554	MAURY	28580	SNOW HILL
28561	NEW BERN	28562	NEW BERN
28563	NEW BERN	28560	NEW BERN
28564	NEW BERN	28560	NEW BERN
28575	SALTER PATH	28512	ATLANTIC BEACH
28583	STONEWALL	28556	MERRITT
28589	WILLISTON	28579	SMYRNA
28603	HICKORY	28602	HICKORY
28616	CROSSNORE	28657	NEWLAND
28619	DREXEL	28655	MORGANTON
28628	GLEN ALPINE	28655	MORGANTON
28629	GLENDALE SPRINGS	28640	JEFFERSON
28633	LENOIR	28645	LENOIR
28641	JONAS RIDGE	28657	NEWLAND
28646	LINVILLE	28657	NEWLAND
28647	LINVILLE FALLS	28657	NEWLAND
28652	MINNEAPOLIS	28657	NEWLAND
28653	MONTEZUMA	28657	NEWLAND
28656	NORTH WILKESBORO	28659	NORTH WILKESBORO
28661	PATTERSON	28645	LENOIR
28662	PINEOLA	28657	NEWLAND
28664	PLUMTREE	28657	NEWLAND
28666	ICARD	28612	CONNELLYS SPRINGS
28667	RHODHISS	28630	GRANITE FALLS
28671	RUTHERFORD COLLEGE	28612	CONNELLYS SPRINGS
28680	MORGANTON	28655	MORGANTON
28687	STATESVILLE	28677	STATESVILLE
28688	TURNERSBURG	28634	HARMONY
28691	VALLE CRUCIS	28604	BANNER ELK
28699	SCOTTS	28625	STATESVILLE
28707	BALSAM	28779	SYLVA
28710	BAT CAVE	28792	HENDERSONVILLE
28720	CHIMNEY ROCK	28746	LAKE LURE
28724	DANA	28792	HENDERSONVILLE
28725	DILLSBORO	28779	SYLVA
28727	EDNEYVILLE	28792	HENDERSONVILLE
28728	ENKA	28715	CANDLER
28737	GLENWOOD	28752	MARION
28738	HAZELWOOD	28786	WAYNESVILLE
28744	FRANKLIN	28734	FRANKLIN
28749	LITTLE SWITZERLAND	28752	MARION
28750	LYNN	28782	TRYON
28755	MICAVILLE	28714	BURNSVILLE
28757	MONTREAT	28711	BLACK MOUNTAIN
28758	MOUNTAIN HOME	28791	HENDERSONVILLE
28760	NAPLES	28791	HENDERSONVILLE
28765	PENLAND	28777	SPRUCE PINE
28770	RIDGECREST	28711	BLACK MOUNTAIN
28776	SKYLAND	28803	ASHEVILLE
28784	TUXEDO	28790	ZIRCONIA
28788	WEBSTER	28779	SYLVA
28793	HENDERSONVILLE	28739	HENDERSONVILLE
28802	ASHEVILLE	28801	ASHEVILLE
28810	ASHEVILLE	28806	ASHEVILLE
28813	ASHEVILLE	28803	ASHEVILLE
28814	ASHEVILLE	28804	ASHEVILLE
28815	ASHEVILLE	28805	ASHEVILLE
28816	ASHEVILLE	28806	ASHEVILLE
28903	CULBERSON	28906	MURPHY
29002	BALLENTINE	29063	IRMO
29021	CAMDEN	29020	CAMDEN
29041	DAVIS STATION	29102	MANNING
29062	HORATIO	29128	REMBERT
29071	LEXINGTON	29072	LEXINGTON
29074	LIBERTY HILL	29058	HEATH SPRINGS
29079	LYDIA	29550	HARTSVILLE
29116	ORANGEBURG	29115	ORANGEBURG
29122	PEAK	29075	LITTLE MOUNTAIN
29132	RION	29180	WINNSBORO
29143	SARDINIA	29051	GABLE
29147	STATE PARK	29203	COLUMBIA
29151	SUMTER	29150	SUMTER
29171	WEST COLUMBIA	29169	WEST COLUMBIA
29177	WHITE ROCK	29036	CHAPIN
29202	COLUMBIA	29201	COLUMBIA
29211	COLUMBIA	29201	COLUMBIA
29214	COLUMBIA	29201	COLUMBIA
29215	COLUMBIA	29201	COLUMBIA
29216	COLUMBIA	29201	COLUMBIA
29217	COLUMBIA	29201	COLUMBIA
29218	COLUMBIA	29201	COLUMBIA
29219	COLUMBIA	29223	COLUMBIA
29220	COLUMBIA	29201	COLUMBIA
29221	COLUMBIA	29210	COLUMBIA
29222	COLUMBIA	29201	COLUMBIA
29224	COLUMBIA	29223	COLUMBIA
29225	COLUMBIA	29208	COLUMBIA
29226	COLUMBIA	29210	COLUMBIA
29227	COLUMBIA	29210	COLUMBIA
29228	COLUMBIA	29201	COLUMBIA
29230	COLUMBIA	29203	COLUMBIA
29240	COLUMBIA	29204	COLUMBIA
29250	COLUMBIA	29205	COLUMBIA
29260	COLUMBIA	29206	COLUMBIA
29290	COLUMBIA	29209	COLUMBIA
29292	COLUMBIA	29201	COLUMBIA
29304	SPARTANBURG	29306	SPARTANBURG
29305	SPARTANBURG	29303	SPARTANBURG
29318	SPARTANBURG	29307	SPARTANBURG
29319	SPARTANBURG	29306	SPARTANBURG
29320	ARCADIA	29301	SPARTANBURG
29324	CLIFTON	29307	SPARTANBURG
29329	CONVERSE	29307	SPARTANBURG
29331	CROSS ANCHOR	29335	ENOREE
29333	DRAYTON	29307	SPARTANBURG
29336	FAIRFOREST	29301	SPARTANBURG
29338	FINGERVILLE	29349	INMAN
29342	GAFFNEY	29341	GAFFNEY
29346	GLENDALE	29307	SPARTANBURG
29348	GRAMLING	29349	INMAN
29364	LOCKHART	29379	UNION
29368	MAYO	29323	CHESNEE
29373	PACOLET MILLS	29372	PACOLET
29375	REIDVILLE	29388	WOODRUFF
29377	STARTEX	29385	WELLFORD
29378	UNA	29301	SPARTANBURG
29386	WHITE STONE	29302	SPARTANBURG
29390	DUNCAN	29334	DUNCAN
29391	DUNCAN	29334	DUNCAN
29395	JONESVILLE	29353	JONESVILLE
29402	CHARLESTON	29401	CHARLESTON
29409	CHARLESTON	29403	CHARLESTON
29413	CHARLESTON	29403	CHARLESTON
29415	NORTH CHARLESTON	29405	NORTH CHARLESTON
29416	CHARLESTON	29404	CHARLESTON AFB
29417	CHARLESTON	29407	CHARLESTON
29419	NORTH CHARLESTON	29406	CHARLESTON
29422	CHARLESTON	29412	CHARLESTON
29423	CHARLESTON	29418	NORTH CHARLESTON
29424	CHARLESTON	29401	CHARLESTON
29425	CHARLESTON	29401	CHARLESTON
29430	BETHERA	29461	MONCKS CORNER
29433	CANADYS	29488	WALTERBORO
29439	FOLLY BEACH	29412	CHARLESTON
29442	GEORGETOWN	29440	GEORGETOWN
29447	GROVER	29477	SAINT GEORGE
29452	JACKSONBORO	29474	ROUND O
29457	JOHNS ISLAND	29455	JOHNS ISLAND
29465	MOUNT PLEASANT	29464	MOUNT PLEASANT
29476	RUSSELLVILLE	29479	SAINT STEPHEN
29484	SUMMERVILLE	29483	SUMMERVILLE
29493	WILLIAMS	29475	RUFFIN
29502	FLORENCE	29501	FLORENCE
29503	FLORENCE	29501	FLORENCE
29504	FLORENCE	29505	FLORENCE
29519	CENTENARY	29571	MARION
29528	CONWAY	29526	CONWAY
29551	HARTSVILLE	29550	HARTSVILLE
29573	MINTURN	29536	DILLON
29578	MYRTLE BEACH	29577	MYRTLE BEACH
29587	MYRTLE BEACH	29582	NORTH MYRTLE BEACH
29589	RAINS	29571	MARION
29594	TATUM	29570	MC COLL
29597	NORTH MYRTLE BEACH	29582	NORTH MYRTLE BEACH
29598	NORTH MYRTLE BEACH	29582	NORTH MYRTLE BEACH
29602	GREENVILLE	29601	GREENVILLE
29603	GREENVILLE	29601	GREENVILLE
29604	GREENVILLE	29605	GREENVILLE
29606	GREENVILLE	29607	GREENVILLE
29608	GREENVILLE	29609	GREENVILLE
29610	GREENVILLE	29611	GREENVILLE
29612	GREENVILLE	29601	GREENVILLE
29614	GREENVILLE	29609	GREENVILLE
29616	GREENVILLE	29615	GREENVILLE
29622	ANDERSON	29621	ANDERSON
29623	ANDERSON	29621	ANDERSON
29633	CLEMSON	29631	CLEMSON
29634	CLEMSON	29632	CLEMSON
29636	CONESTEE	29605	GREENVILLE
29641	EASLEY	29640	EASLEY
29647	GREENWOOD	29653	HODGES
29648	GREENWOOD	29646	GREENWOOD
29652	GREER	29650	GREER
29656	LA FRANCE	29670	PENDLETON
29665	NEWRY	29672	SENECA
29675	RICHLAND	29672	SENECA
29677	SANDY SPRINGS	29670	PENDLETON
29679	SENECA	29678	SENECA
29683	SLATER	29661	MARIETTA
29695	HODGES	29653	HODGES
29698	GREENVILLE	29334	DUNCAN
29703	BOWLING GREEN	29710	CLOVER
29716	FORT MILL	29715	FORT MILL
29721	LANCASTER	29720	LANCASTER
29722	LANCASTER	29720	LANCASTER
29724	LANDO	29729	RICHBURG

NONRESIDENTIAL ZIP CODES

SOUTH CAROLINA

Point ZIP Code		Enclosing Residential ZIP Code	
ZIP	Post Office Name	ZIP	Post Office Name
29731	ROCK HILL	29730	ROCK HILL
29733	ROCK HILL	29730	ROCK HILL
29734	ROCK HILL	29730	ROCK HILL
29744	VAN WYCK	29720	LANCASTER
29802	AIKEN	29801	AIKEN
29804	AIKEN	29803	AIKEN
29813	HILDA	29812	BARNWELL
29816	BATH	29851	WARRENVILLE
29822	CLEARWATER	29842	BEECH ISLAND
29826	ELKO	29853	WILLISTON
29834	LANGLEY	29851	WARRENVILLE
29839	MONTMORENCI	29803	AIKEN
29844	PARKSVILLE	29845	PLUM BRANCH
29846	SYCAMORE	29849	ULMER
29850	VAUCLUSE	29801	AIKEN
29861	NORTH AUGUSTA	29841	NORTH AUGUSTA
29899	MC CORMICK	29835	MC CORMICK
29901	BEAUFORT	29902	BEAUFORT
29903	BEAUFORT	29906	BEAUFORT
29904	BEAUFORT	29906	BEAUFORT
29905	BEAUFORT	29902	BEAUFORT
29912	COOSAWHATCHIE	29936	RIDGELAND
29913	CROCKETVILLE	29924	HAMPTON
29914	DALE	29940	SEABROOK
29921	FURMAN	29918	ESTILL
29923	GIFFORD	29932	LURAY
29925	HILTON HEAD ISLAND	29926	HILTON HEAD ISLAND
29931	LOBECO	29940	SEABROOK
29933	MILEY	29924	HAMPTON
29938	HILTON HEAD ISLAND	29928	HILTON HEAD ISLAND
29939	SCOTIA	29918	ESTILL
30003	NORCROSS	30071	NORCROSS
30006	MARIETTA	30067	MARIETTA
30007	MARIETTA	30068	MARIETTA
30010	NORCROSS	30092	NORCROSS
30015	COVINGTON	30014	COVINGTON
30018	JERSEY	30014	COVINGTON
30023	ALPHARETTA	30009	ALPHARETTA
30026	NORTH METRO	30044	LAWRENCEVILLE
30029	NORTH METRO	30096	DULUTH
30031	DECATUR	30030	DECATUR
30036	DECATUR	30034	DECATUR
30037	DECATUR	30034	DECATUR
30042	LAWRENCEVILLE	30044	LAWRENCEVILLE
30046	LAWRENCEVILLE	30045	LAWRENCEVILLE
30048	LILBURN	30047	LILBURN
30049	LAWRENCEVILLE	30043	LAWRENCEVILLE
30061	MARIETTA	30060	MARIETTA
30065	MARIETTA	30062	MARIETTA
30070	PORTERDALE	30014	COVINGTON
30072	PINE LAKE	30083	STONE MOUNTAIN
30073	DECATUR	30030	DECATUR
30074	REDAN	30058	LITHONIA
30077	ROSWELL	30075	ROSWELL
30081	SMYRNA	30080	SMYRNA
30085	TUCKER	30084	TUCKER
30086	STONE MOUNTAIN	30083	STONE MOUNTAIN
30090	MARIETTA	30060	MARIETTA
30091	NORCROSS	30071	NORCROSS
30095	DULUTH	30096	DULUTH
30098	DULUTH	30097	DULUTH
30099	DULUTH	30096	DULUTH
30109	BOWDON JUNCTION	30117	CARROLLTON
30111	CLARKDALE	30127	POWDER SPRINGS
30112	CARROLLTON	30117	CARROLLTON
30119	CARROLLTON	30117	CARROLLTON
30123	CASSVILLE	30120	CARTERSVILLE
30129	COOSA	30165	ROME
30133	DOUGLASVILLE	30134	DOUGLASVILLE
30138	ESOM HILL	30125	CEDARTOWN
30140	FELTON	30113	BUCHANAN
30142	HOLLY SPRINGS	30115	CANTON
30146	LEBANON	30115	CANTON
30150	MOUNT ZION	30117	CARROLLTON
30151	NELSON	30107	BALL GROUND
30154	DOUGLASVILLE	30134	DOUGLASVILLE
30156	KENNESAW	30144	KENNESAW
30160	KENNESAW	30144	KENNESAW
30162	ROME	30161	ROME
30163	ROME	30161	ROME
30164	ROME	30165	ROME
30169	CANTON	30114	CANTON
30172	SHANNON	30161	ROME
30212	EXPERIMENT	30223	GRIFFIN
30219	GLENN	30217	FRANKLIN
30229	HARALSON	30276	SENOIA
30237	JONESBORO	30236	JONESBORO
30250	LOVEJOY	30228	HAMPTON
30261	LAGRANGE	30241	LAGRANGE
30264	NEWNAN	30263	NEWNAN
30266	ORCHARD HILL	30224	GRIFFIN
30270	PEACHTREE CITY	30269	PEACHTREE CITY
30271	NEWNAN	30263	NEWNAN

GEORGIA

Point ZIP Code		Enclosing Residential ZIP Code	
ZIP	Post Office Name	ZIP	Post Office Name
30272	RED OAK	30349	ATLANTA
30275	SARGENT	30263	NEWNAN
30284	SUNNY SIDE	30223	GRIFFIN
30287	MORROW	30260	MORROW
30289	TURIN	30276	SENOIA
30298	FOREST PARK	30297	FOREST PARK
30301	ATLANTA	30354	ATLANTA
30302	ATLANTA	30312	ATLANTA
30304	ATLANTA	30354	ATLANTA
30320	ATLANTA	30354	ATLANTA
30321	ATLANTA	30354	ATLANTA
30325	ATLANTA	30312	ATLANTA
30332	ATLANTA	30313	ATLANTA
30333	ATLANTA	30306	ATLANTA
30343	ATLANTA	30303	ATLANTA
30347	ATLANTA	30329	ATLANTA
30348	ATLANTA	30354	ATLANTA
30353	ATLANTA	30303	ATLANTA
30355	ATLANTA	30305	ATLANTA
30356	ATLANTA	30338	ATLANTA
30357	ATLANTA	30309	ATLANTA
30358	ATLANTA	30328	ATLANTA
30359	ATLANTA	30329	ATLANTA
30361	ATLANTA	30309	ATLANTA
30362	ATLANTA	30340	ATLANTA
30364	ATLANTA	30344	ATLANTA
30366	ATLANTA	30341	ATLANTA
30368	ATLANTA	30354	ATLANTA
30369	ATLANTA	30318	ATLANTA
30370	ATLANTA	30312	ATLANTA
30371	ATLANTA	30303	ATLANTA
30374	ATLANTA	30312	ATLANTA
30375	ATLANTA	30308	ATLANTA
30376	ATLANTA	30324	ATLANTA
30377	ATLANTA	30318	ATLANTA
30378	ATLANTA	30331	ATLANTA
30379	ATLANTA	30308	ATLANTA
30380	ATLANTA	30354	ATLANTA
30384	ATLANTA	30339	ATLANTA
30385	ATLANTA	30344	ATLANTA
30388	ATLANTA	30354	ATLANTA
30389	ATLANTA	30354	ATLANTA
30390	ATLANTA	30308	ATLANTA
30392	ATLANTA	30312	ATLANTA
30394	ATLANTA	30354	ATLANTA
30396	ATLANTA	30354	ATLANTA
30398	ATLANTA	30354	ATLANTA
30412	ALSTON	30473	UVALDA
30414	BELLVILLE	30417	CLAXTON
30423	DAISY	30417	CLAXTON
30424	DOVER	30467	SYLVANIA
30429	HAGAN	30417	CLAXTON
30447	NORRISTOWN	30401	SWAINSBORO
30448	NUNEZ	30401	SWAINSBORO
30449	OLIVER	30446	NEWINGTON
30451	PULASKI	30439	METTER
30459	STATESBORO	30458	STATESBORO
30460	STATESBORO	30458	STATESBORO
30464	STILLMORE	30471	TWIN CITY
30475	VIDALIA	30474	VIDALIA
30499	REIDSVILLE	30453	REIDSVILLE
30502	CHESTNUT MOUNTAIN	30542	FLOWERY BRANCH
30503	GAINESVILLE	30501	GAINESVILLE
30514	BLAIRSVILLE	30512	BLAIRSVILLE
30515	BUFORD	30518	BUFORD
30544	DEMOREST	30535	DEMOREST
30562	MOUNTAIN CITY	30525	CLAYTON
30573	TALLULAH FALLS	30552	LAKEMONT
30580	TURNERVILLE	30523	CLARKESVILLE
30581	WILEY	30576	TIGER
30598	TOCCOA FALLS	30577	TOCCOA
30599	COMMERCE	30529	COMMERCE
30603	ATHENS	30605	ATHENS
30604	ATHENS	30606	ATHENS
30608	ATHENS	30601	ATHENS
30612	ATHENS	30605	ATHENS
30623	BOSTWICK	30621	BISHOP
30638	FARMINGTON	30677	WATKINSVILLE
30639	FRANKLIN SPRINGS	30662	ROYSTON
30645	HIGH SHOALS	30621	BISHOP
30647	ILA	30633	DANIELSVILLE
30664	SHARON	30631	CRAWFORDVILLE
30665	SILOAM	30678	WHITE PLAINS
30671	MAXEYS	30667	STEPHENS
30703	CALHOUN	30701	CALHOUN
30719	DALTON	30721	DALTON
30722	DALTON	30720	DALTON
30724	ETON	30705	CHATSWORTH
30726	GRAYSVILLE	30736	RINGGOLD
30732	OAKMAN	30734	RANGER
30756	VARNELL	30710	COHUTTA
30806	BONEVILLE	30808	DEARING
30811	GOUGH	30816	KEYSVILLE

NONRESIDENTIAL ZIP CODES

GEORGIA

Point ZIP Code		Enclosing Residential ZIP Code	
ZIP	Post Office Name	ZIP	Post Office Name
30812	GRACEWOOD	30906	AUGUSTA
30819	MESENA	30828	WARRENTON
30903	AUGUSTA	30901	AUGUSTA
30914	AUGUSTA	30904	AUGUSTA
30916	AUGUSTA	30906	AUGUSTA
30917	AUGUSTA	30907	AUGUSTA
30919	AUGUSTA	30909	AUGUSTA
30999	AUGUSTA	30909	AUGUSTA
31004	BOLINGBROKE	31210	MACON
31010	CORDELE	31015	CORDELE
31013	CLINCHFIELD	31069	PERRY
31026	EATONTON	31024	EATONTON
31034	HARDWICK	31061	MILLEDGEVILLE
31039	HOWARD	31006	BUTLER
31040	DUBLIN	31021	DUBLIN
31051	LILLY	31092	VIENNA
31059	MILLEDGEVILLE	31061	MILLEDGEVILLE
31062	MILLEDGEVILLE	31061	MILLEDGEVILLE
31067	OCONEE	31089	TENNILLE
31083	SCOTLAND	31055	MC RAE
31084	SEVILLE	31072	PITTS
31086	SMARR	31029	FORSYTH
31095	WARNER ROBINS	31098	WARNER ROBINS
31099	WARNER ROBINS	31098	WARNER ROBINS
31106	ATLANTA	30306	ATLANTA
31107	ATLANTA	30306	ATLANTA
31119	ATLANTA	30319	ATLANTA
31126	ATLANTA	30096	DULUTH
31131	ATLANTA	30331	ATLANTA
31136	ATLANTA	30336	ATLANTA
31139	ATLANTA	30339	ATLANTA
31141	ATLANTA	30341	ATLANTA
31145	ATLANTA	30345	ATLANTA
31146	ATLANTA	30346	ATLANTA
31150	ATLANTA	30350	ATLANTA
31156	ATLANTA	30350	ATLANTA
31192	ATLANTA	30349	ATLANTA
31193	ATLANTA	30303	ATLANTA
31195	ATLANTA	30318	ATLANTA
31196	ATLANTA	30318	ATLANTA
31202	MACON	31201	MACON
31203	MACON	31204	MACON
31205	MACON	31206	MACON
31208	MACON	31201	MACON
31209	MACON	31204	MACON
31212	MACON	31206	MACON
31213	MACON	31201	MACON
31221	MACON	31201	MACON
31295	MACON	31217	MACON
31296	MACON	31217	MACON
31297	MACON	31210	MACON
31307	EDEN	31302	BLOOMINGDALE
31310	HINESVILLE	31313	HINESVILLE
31318	MELDRIM	31302	BLOOMINGDALE
31327	SAPELO ISLAND	31304	CRESCENT
31333	WALTHOURVILLE	31313	HINESVILLE
31402	SAVANNAH	31401	SAVANNAH
31403	SAVANNAH	31405	SAVANNAH
31412	SAVANNAH	31401	SAVANNAH
31414	SAVANNAH	31404	SAVANNAH
31416	SAVANNAH	31406	SAVANNAH
31418	SAVANNAH	31408	SAVANNAH
31420	SAVANNAH	31419	SAVANNAH
31421	SAVANNAH	31401	SAVANNAH
31502	WAYCROSS	31501	WAYCROSS
31515	BAXLEY	31513	BAXLEY
31521	BRUNSWICK	31520	BRUNSWICK
31524	BRUNSWICK	31525	BRUNSWICK
31534	DOUGLAS	31533	DOUGLAS
31556	OFFERMAN	31557	PATTERSON
31564	WARESBORO	31503	WAYCROSS
31598	JESUP	31546	JESUP
31599	JESUP	31545	JESUP
31603	VALDOSTA	31601	VALDOSTA
31604	VALDOSTA	31601	VALDOSTA
31627	CECIL	31620	ADEL
31702	ALBANY	31701	ALBANY
31703	ALBANY	31701	ALBANY
31706	ALBANY	31701	ALBANY
31708	ALBANY	31705	ALBANY
31720	BARWICK	31778	PAVO
31722	BERLIN	31788	MOULTRIE
31727	BROOKFIELD	31794	TIFTON
31739	COTTON	31779	PELHAM
31747	ELLENTON	31771	NORMAN PARK
31753	FUNSTON	31768	MOULTRIE
31758	THOMASVILLE	31792	THOMASVILLE
31769	MYSTIC	31774	OCILLA
31776	MOULTRIE	31768	MOULTRIE
31782	PUTNEY	31705	ALBANY
31799	THOMASVILLE	31792	THOMASVILLE
31810	GENEVA	31801	BOX SPRINGS
31814	LOUVALE	31821	OMAHA

FLORIDA

Point ZIP Code		Enclosing Residential ZIP Code	
ZIP	Post Office Name	ZIP	Post Office Name
31902	COLUMBUS	31907	COLUMBUS
31908	COLUMBUS	31907	COLUMBUS
31914	COLUMBUS	31904	COLUMBUS
31917	COLUMBUS	31907	COLUMBUS
31993	COLUMBUS	31907	COLUMBUS
31995	FORT BENNING	31907	COLUMBUS
31997	COLUMBUS	31907	COLUMBUS
31999	COLUMBUS	31906	COLUMBUS
32004	PONTE VEDRA BEACH	32082	PONTE VEDRA BEACH
32006	FLEMING ISLAND	32073	ORANGE PARK
32007	BOSTWICK	32177	PALATKA
32026	RAIFORD	32083	RAIFORD
32030	DOCTORS INLET	32068	MIDDLEBURG
32035	FERNANDINA BEACH	32034	FERNANDINA BEACH
32041	YULEE	32097	YULEE
32042	GRAHAM	32044	HAMPTON
32050	MIDDLEBURG	32068	MIDDLEBURG
32056	LAKE CITY	32055	LAKE CITY
32067	ORANGE PARK	32073	ORANGE PARK
32072	OLUSTEE	32087	SANDERSON
32079	PENNEY FARMS	32043	GREEN COVE SPRINGS
32085	SAINT AUGUSTINE	32084	SAINT AUGUSTINE
32099	JACKSONVILLE	32220	JACKSONVILLE
32105	BARBERVILLE	32180	PIERSON
32111	CANDLER	34472	OCALA
32115	DAYTONA BEACH	32114	DAYTONA BEACH
32116	DAYTONA BEACH	32118	DAYTONA BEACH
32120	DAYTONA BEACH	32114	DAYTONA BEACH
32121	DAYTONA BEACH	32119	DAYTONA BEACH
32122	DAYTONA BEACH	32114	DAYTONA BEACH
32123	PORT ORANGE	32119	DAYTONA BEACH
32125	DAYTONA BEACH	32117	DAYTONA BEACH
32126	DAYTONA BEACH	32118	DAYTONA BEACH
32133	EASTLAKE WEIR	32179	OCKLAWAHA
32135	PALM COAST	32136	FLAGLER BEACH
32138	GRANDIN	32666	MELROSE
32142	PALM COAST	32136	FLAGLER BEACH
32147	HOLLISTER	32148	INTERLACHEN
32149	EDGAR	32148	INTERLACHEN
32157	LAKE COMO	32181	POMONA PARK
32158	LADY LAKE	32159	LADY LAKE
32160	LAKE GENEVA	32656	KEYSTONE HEIGHTS
32163	THE VILLAGES	32162	LADY LAKE
32170	NEW SMYRNA BEACH	32169	NEW SMYRNA BEACH
32173	ORMOND BEACH	32174	ORMOND BEACH
32175	ORMOND BEACH	32174	ORMOND BEACH
32178	PALATKA	32177	PALATKA
32182	ORANGE SPRINGS	32134	FORT MC COY
32183	OCKLAWAHA	32179	OCKLAWAHA
32185	PUTNAM HALL	32666	MELROSE
32192	SPARR	32617	ANTHONY
32198	DAYTONA BEACH	32114	DAYTONA BEACH
32201	JACKSONVILLE	32202	JACKSONVILLE
32203	JACKSONVILLE	32209	JACKSONVILLE
32229	JACKSONVILLE	32218	JACKSONVILLE
32231	JACKSONVILLE	32207	JACKSONVILLE
32232	JACKSONVILLE	32209	JACKSONVILLE
32235	JACKSONVILLE	32206	JACKSONVILLE
32236	JACKSONVILLE	32205	JACKSONVILLE
32237	JACKSONVILLE	32257	JACKSONVILLE
32238	JACKSONVILLE	32244	JACKSONVILLE
32239	JACKSONVILLE	32277	JACKSONVILLE
32240	JACKSONVILLE BEACH	32250	JACKSONVILLE BEACH
32241	JACKSONVILLE	32223	JACKSONVILLE
32245	JACKSONVILLE	32216	JACKSONVILLE
32247	JACKSONVILLE	32207	JACKSONVILLE
32255	JACKSONVILLE	32207	JACKSONVILLE
32260	JACKSONVILLE	32259	SAINT JOHNS
32302	TALLAHASSEE	32301	TALLAHASSEE
32313	TALLAHASSEE	32304	TALLAHASSEE
32314	TALLAHASSEE	32301	TALLAHASSEE
32315	TALLAHASSEE	32303	TALLAHASSEE
32316	TALLAHASSEE	32304	TALLAHASSEE
32318	TALLAHASSEE	32305	TALLAHASSEE
32323	LANARK VILLAGE	32322	CARRABELLE
32326	CRAWFORDVILLE	32327	CRAWFORDVILLE
32329	APALACHICOLA	32320	APALACHICOLA
32330	GREENSBORO	32351	QUINCY
32337	LLOYD	32344	MONTICELLO
32341	MADISON	32340	MADISON
32345	MONTICELLO	32344	MONTICELLO
32353	QUINCY	32351	QUINCY
32357	SHADY GROVE	32331	GREENVILLE
32360	TELOGIA	32334	HOSFORD
32361	WACISSA	32344	MONTICELLO
32362	WOODVILLE	32305	TALLAHASSEE
32395	TALLAHASSEE	32301	TALLAHASSEE
32402	PANAMA CITY	32401	PANAMA CITY
32406	PANAMA CITY	32405	PANAMA CITY
32410	MEXICO BEACH	32401	PANAMA CITY
32411	PANAMA CITY	32408	PANAMA CITY
32412	PANAMA CITY	32401	PANAMA CITY
32417	PANAMA CITY	32407	PANAMA CITY BEACH

FLORIDA

Point ZIP Code ZIP	Point ZIP Code Post Office Name	Enclosing Residential ZIP Code ZIP	Enclosing Residential ZIP Code Post Office Name
32422	ARGYLE	32433	DEFUNIAK SPRINGS
32432	CYPRESS	32442	GRAND RIDGE
32434	MOSSY HEAD	32433	DEFUNIAK SPRINGS
32447	MARIANNA	32446	MARIANNA
32452	NOMA	32425	BONIFAY
32457	PORT SAINT JOE	32456	PORT SAINT JOE
32461	ROSEMARY BEACH	32413	PANAMA CITY BEACH
32463	WAUSAU	32428	CHIPLEY
32509	PENSACOLA	32526	PENSACOLA
32512	PENSACOLA	32507	PENSACOLA
32513	PENSACOLA	32503	PENSACOLA
32516	PENSACOLA	32506	PENSACOLA
32520	PENSACOLA	32502	PENSACOLA
32521	PENSACOLA	32507	PENSACOLA
32522	PENSACOLA	32502	PENSACOLA
32523	PENSACOLA	32501	PENSACOLA
32524	PENSACOLA	32501	PENSACOLA
32530	BAGDAD	32583	MILTON
32537	MILLIGAN	32536	CRESTVIEW
32538	PAXTON	32567	LAUREL HILL
32540	DESTIN	32541	DESTIN
32549	FORT WALTON BEACH	32548	FORT WALTON BEACH
32559	PENSACOLA	32526	PENSACOLA
32560	GONZALEZ	32533	CANTONMENT
32562	GULF BREEZE	32561	GULF BREEZE
32572	MILTON	32570	MILTON
32588	NICEVILLE	32578	NICEVILLE
32591	PENSACOLA	32501	PENSACOLA
32602	GAINESVILLE	32601	GAINESVILLE
32604	GAINESVILLE	32603	GAINESVILLE
32610	GAINESVILLE	32611	GAINESVILLE
32612	GAINESVILLE	32611	GAINESVILLE
32614	GAINESVILLE	32608	GAINESVILLE
32616	ALACHUA	32615	ALACHUA
32627	GAINESVILLE	32601	GAINESVILLE
32633	EVINSTON	32640	HAWTHORNE
32634	FAIRFIELD	32686	REDDICK
32635	GAINESVILLE	32605	GAINESVILLE
32639	GULF HAMMOCK	34449	INGLIS
32644	CHIEFLAND	32626	CHIEFLAND
32654	ISLAND GROVE	32640	HAWTHORNE
32655	HIGH SPRINGS	32643	HIGH SPRINGS
32658	LA CROSSE	32615	ALACHUA
32662	LOCHLOOSA	32640	HAWTHORNE
32663	LOWELL	32686	REDDICK
32664	MC INTOSH	32667	MICANOPY
32681	ORANGE LAKE	32667	MICANOPY
32683	OTTER CREEK	34449	INGLIS
32692	SUWANNEE	32680	OLD TOWN
32697	WORTHINGTON SPRINGS	32054	LAKE BUTLER
32704	APOPKA	32712	APOPKA
32706	CASSADAGA	32744	LAKE HELEN
32710	CLARCONA	32818	ORLANDO
32715	ALTAMONTE SPRINGS	32714	ALTAMONTE SPRINGS
32716	ALTAMONTE SPRINGS	32714	ALTAMONTE SPRINGS
32718	CASSELBERRY	32708	WINTER SPRINGS
32719	WINTER SPRINGS	32708	WINTER SPRINGS
32721	DELAND	32720	DELAND
32722	GLENWOOD	32720	DELAND
32723	DELAND	32724	DELAND
32727	EUSTIS	32726	EUSTIS
32728	DELTONA	32725	DELTONA
32733	GOLDENROD	32792	WINTER PARK
32739	DELTONA	32738	DELTONA
32745	MID FLORIDA	32746	LAKE MARY
32747	LAKE MONROE	32771	SANFORD
32752	LONGWOOD	32779	LONGWOOD
32753	DEBARY	32713	DEBARY
32756	MOUNT DORA	32757	MOUNT DORA
32762	OVIEDO	32765	OVIEDO
32768	PLYMOUTH	32712	APOPKA
32772	SANFORD	32771	SANFORD
32774	ORANGE CITY	32763	ORANGE CITY
32775	SCOTTSMOOR	32754	MIMS
32777	TANGERINE	32757	MOUNT DORA
32781	TITUSVILLE	32780	TITUSVILLE
32782	TITUSVILLE	32796	TITUSVILLE
32783	TITUSVILLE	32780	TITUSVILLE
32790	WINTER PARK	32789	WINTER PARK
32791	LONGWOOD	32779	LONGWOOD
32793	WINTER PARK	32792	WINTER PARK
32794	MAITLAND	32751	MAITLAND
32795	LAKE MARY	32746	LAKE MARY
32799	MID FLORIDA	32746	LAKE MARY
32802	ORLANDO	32801	ORLANDO
32816	ORLANDO	32826	ORLANDO
32834	ORLANDO	32828	ORLANDO
32853	ORLANDO	32803	ORLANDO
32854	ORLANDO	32804	ORLANDO
32855	ORLANDO	32805	ORLANDO
32856	ORLANDO	32806	ORLANDO
32857	ORLANDO	32807	ORLANDO
32858	ORLANDO	32808	ORLANDO
32859	ORLANDO	32809	ORLANDO
32860	ORLANDO	32810	ORLANDO
32861	ORLANDO	32811	ORLANDO
32862	ORLANDO	32827	ORLANDO
32867	ORLANDO	32817	ORLANDO
32868	ORLANDO	32818	ORLANDO
32869	ORLANDO	32809	ORLANDO
32872	ORLANDO	32822	ORLANDO
32877	ORLANDO	32837	ORLANDO
32878	ORLANDO	32828	ORLANDO
32885	ORLANDO	32827	ORLANDO
32886	ORLANDO	32801	ORLANDO
32887	ORLANDO	32821	ORLANDO
32891	ORLANDO	32803	ORLANDO
32896	ORLANDO	32801	ORLANDO
32897	ORLANDO	32801	ORLANDO
32902	MELBOURNE	32901	MELBOURNE
32906	PALM BAY	32905	PALM BAY
32910	PALM BAY	32907	PALM BAY
32911	PALM BAY	32905	PALM BAY
32912	MELBOURNE	32904	MELBOURNE
32919	MELBOURNE	32901	MELBOURNE
32923	COCOA	32922	COCOA
32924	COCOA	32922	COCOA
32932	COCOA BEACH	32931	COCOA BEACH
32936	MELBOURNE	32935	MELBOURNE
32941	MELBOURNE	32901	MELBOURNE
32954	MERRITT ISLAND	32953	MERRITT ISLAND
32956	ROCKLEDGE	32955	ROCKLEDGE
32957	ROSELAND	32958	SEBASTIAN
32959	SHARPES	32927	COCOA
32961	VERO BEACH	32960	VERO BEACH
32964	VERO BEACH	32960	VERO BEACH
32965	VERO BEACH	32962	VERO BEACH
32969	VERO BEACH	32966	VERO BEACH
32970	WABASSO	32967	VERO BEACH
32971	WINTER BEACH	32967	VERO BEACH
32978	SEBASTIAN	32958	SEBASTIAN
33001	LONG KEY	33050	MARATHON
33002	HIALEAH	33014	HIALEAH
33008	HALLANDALE	33009	HALLANDALE
33011	HIALEAH	33010	HIALEAH
33017	HIALEAH	33015	HIALEAH
33022	HOLLYWOOD	33020	HOLLYWOOD
33041	KEY WEST	33040	KEY WEST
33045	KEY WEST	33040	KEY WEST
33051	KEY COLONY BEACH	33050	MARATHON
33052	MARATHON SHORES	33050	MARATHON
33061	POMPANO BEACH	33060	POMPANO BEACH
33072	POMPANO BEACH	33069	POMPANO BEACH
33074	POMPANO BEACH	33064	POMPANO BEACH
33075	POMPANO BEACH	33067	POMPANO BEACH
33077	POMPANO BEACH	33071	POMPANO BEACH
33081	HOLLYWOOD	33021	HOLLYWOOD
33082	PEMBROKE PINES	33028	HOLLYWOOD
33083	HOLLYWOOD	33023	HOLLYWOOD
33084	HOLLYWOOD	33024	HOLLYWOOD
33090	HOMESTEAD	33030	HOMESTEAD
33092	HOMESTEAD	33032	HOMESTEAD
33093	COCONUT CREEK	33063	POMPANO BEACH
33097	POMPANO BEACH	33073	POMPANO BEACH
33101	MIAMI	33128	MIAMI
33111	MIAMI	33131	MIAMI
33114	MIAMI	33134	MIAMI
33116	MIAMI	33176	MIAMI
33119	MIAMI BEACH	33139	MIAMI BEACH
33124	MIAMI	33181	MIAMI
33151	MIAMI	33127	MIAMI
33153	MIAMI	33138	MIAMI
33159	MIAMI	33139	MIAMI BEACH
33163	MIAMI	33180	MIAMI
33164	MIAMI	33162	MIAMI
33197	MIAMI	33157	MIAMI
33231	MIAMI	33131	MIAMI
33233	MIAMI	33133	MIAMI
33234	MIAMI	33134	MIAMI
33238	MIAMI	33150	MIAMI
33239	MIAMI BEACH	33139	MIAMI BEACH
33242	MIAMI	33142	MIAMI
33243	MIAMI	33143	MIAMI
33245	MIAMI	33145	MIAMI
33255	MIAMI	33155	MIAMI
33256	MIAMI	33156	MIAMI
33257	MIAMI	33157	MIAMI
33261	MIAMI	33161	MIAMI
33265	MIAMI	33175	MIAMI
33266	MIAMI	33166	MIAMI
33269	MIAMI	33169	MIAMI
33280	MIAMI	33162	MIAMI
33283	MIAMI	33173	MIAMI
33296	MIAMI	33156	MIAMI
33302	FORT LAUDERDALE	33304	FORT LAUDERDALE
33303	FORT LAUDERDALE	33301	FORT LAUDERDALE

NONRESIDENTIAL ZIP CODES

FLORIDA

Point ZIP Code ZIP	Point ZIP Code Post Office Name	Enclosing Residential ZIP Code ZIP	Enclosing Residential ZIP Code Post Office Name
33307	FORT LAUDERDALE	33334	FORT LAUDERDALE
33310	FORT LAUDERDALE	33311	FORT LAUDERDALE
33318	FORT LAUDERDALE	33322	FORT LAUDERDALE
33320	FORT LAUDERDALE	33321	FORT LAUDERDALE
33329	FORT LAUDERDALE	33324	FORT LAUDERDALE
33335	FORT LAUDERDALE	33334	FORT LAUDERDALE
33336	FORT LAUDERDALE	33311	FORT LAUDERDALE
33337	FORT LAUDERDALE	33324	FORT LAUDERDALE
33338	FORT LAUDERDALE	33324	FORT LAUDERDALE
33339	FORT LAUDERDALE	33306	FORT LAUDERDALE
33340	FORT LAUDERDALE	33311	FORT LAUDERDALE
33345	FORT LAUDERDALE	33351	FORT LAUDERDALE
33346	FORT LAUDERDALE	33316	FORT LAUDERDALE
33348	FORT LAUDERDALE	33308	FORT LAUDERDALE
33349	FORT LAUDERDALE	33304	FORT LAUDERDALE
33355	FORT LAUDERDALE	33325	FORT LAUDERDALE
33359	FORT LAUDERDALE	33319	FORT LAUDERDALE
33388	FORT LAUDERDALE	33324	FORT LAUDERDALE
33394	FORT LAUDERDALE	33301	FORT LAUDERDALE
33402	WEST PALM BEACH	33480	PALM BEACH
33416	WEST PALM BEACH	33406	WEST PALM BEACH
33419	WEST PALM BEACH	33404	WEST PALM BEACH
33420	WEST PALM BEACH	33410	PALM BEACH GARDENS
33421	WEST PALM BEACH	33411	WEST PALM BEACH
33422	WEST PALM BEACH	33417	WEST PALM BEACH
33424	BOYNTON BEACH	33426	BOYNTON BEACH
33425	BOYNTON BEACH	33426	BOYNTON BEACH
33427	BOCA RATON	33486	BOCA RATON
33429	BOCA RATON	33432	BOCA RATON
33439	BRYANT	33438	CANAL POINT
33443	DEERFIELD BEACH	33441	DEERFIELD BEACH
33447	DELRAY BEACH	33444	DELRAY BEACH
33448	DELRAY BEACH	33446	DELRAY BEACH
33454	LAKE WORTH	33467	LAKE WORTH
33459	LAKE HARBOR	33440	CLEWISTON
33464	BOCA RATON	33460	LAKE WORTH
33465	LAKE WORTH	33462	LAKE WORTH
33466	LAKE WORTH	33461	LAKE WORTH
33468	JUPITER	33458	JUPITER
33474	BOYNTON BEACH	33436	BOYNTON BEACH
33475	HOBE SOUND	33455	HOBE SOUND
33481	BOCA RATON	33431	BOCA RATON
33482	DELRAY BEACH	33445	DELRAY BEACH
33488	BOCA RATON	33433	BOCA RATON
33497	BOCA RATON	33428	BOCA RATON
33499	BOCA RATON	33487	BOCA RATON
33503	BALM	33598	WIMAUMA
33508	BRANDON	33511	BRANDON
33509	BRANDON	33511	BRANDON
33521	COLEMAN	34785	WILDWOOD
33524	CRYSTAL SPRINGS	33540	ZEPHYRHILLS
33526	DADE CITY	33525	DADE CITY
33530	DURANT	33567	PLANT CITY
33537	LACOOCHEE	33523	DADE CITY
33539	ZEPHYRHILLS	33542	ZEPHYRHILLS
33550	MANGO	33584	SEFFNER
33564	PLANT CITY	33566	PLANT CITY
33568	RIVERVIEW	33569	RIVERVIEW
33571	SUN CITY CENTER	33573	SUN CITY CENTER
33574	SAINT LEO	33576	SAN ANTONIO
33575	RUSKIN	33570	RUSKIN
33583	SEFFNER	33584	SEFFNER
33586	SUN CITY	33570	RUSKIN
33587	SYDNEY	33527	DOVER
33593	TRILBY	33523	DADE CITY
33595	VALRICO	33594	VALRICO
33601	TAMPA	33602	TAMPA
33608	TAMPA	33621	TAMPA
33622	TAMPA	33607	TAMPA
33623	TAMPA	33607	TAMPA
33630	TAMPA	33607	TAMPA
33631	TAMPA	33607	TAMPA
33633	TAMPA	33607	TAMPA
33646	TAMPA	33602	TAMPA
33650	TAMPA	33607	TAMPA
33655	TAMPA	33602	TAMPA
33660	TAMPA	33619	TAMPA
33661	TAMPA	33619	TAMPA
33662	TAMPA	33619	TAMPA
33663	TAMPA	33607	TAMPA
33664	TAMPA	33607	TAMPA
33672	TAMPA	33602	TAMPA
33673	TAMPA	33603	TAMPA
33674	TAMPA	33604	TAMPA
33675	TAMPA	33605	TAMPA
33677	TAMPA	33607	TAMPA
33679	TAMPA	33629	TAMPA
33680	TAMPA	33610	TAMPA
33681	TAMPA	33611	TAMPA
33682	TAMPA	33612	TAMPA
33684	TAMPA	33634	TAMPA
33685	TAMPA	33615	TAMPA
33686	TAMPA	33616	TAMPA
33687	TAMPA	33617	TAMPA
33688	TAMPA	33618	TAMPA
33689	TAMPA	33619	TAMPA
33690	TAMPA	33609	TAMPA
33694	TAMPA	33624	TAMPA
33729	SAINT PETERSBURG	33716	SAINT PETERSBURG
33730	SAINT PETERSBURG	33713	SAINT PETERSBURG
33731	SAINT PETERSBURG	33701	SAINT PETERSBURG
33732	SAINT PETERSBURG	33702	SAINT PETERSBURG
33733	SAINT PETERSBURG	33713	SAINT PETERSBURG
33734	SAINT PETERSBURG	33704	SAINT PETERSBURG
33736	SAINT PETERSBURG	33706	SAINT PETERSBURG
33737	SAINT PETERSBURG	33707	SAINT PETERSBURG
33738	SAINT PETERSBURG	33708	SAINT PETERSBURG
33740	SAINT PETERSBURG	33706	SAINT PETERSBURG
33741	SAINT PETERSBURG	33706	SAINT PETERSBURG
33742	SAINT PETERSBURG	33702	SAINT PETERSBURG
33743	SAINT PETERSBURG	33710	SAINT PETERSBURG
33744	BAY PINES	33708	SAINT PETERSBURG
33747	SAINT PETERSBURG	33711	SAINT PETERSBURG
33757	CLEARWATER	33755	CLEARWATER
33758	CLEARWATER	33765	CLEARWATER
33766	CLEARWATER	33763	CLEARWATER
33769	CLEARWATER	33765	CLEARWATER
33775	SEMINOLE	33772	SEMINOLE
33779	LARGO	33771	LARGO
33780	PINELLAS PARK	33781	PINELLAS PARK
33784	SAINT PETERSBURG	33713	SAINT PETERSBURG
33802	LAKELAND	33803	LAKELAND
33804	LAKELAND	33805	LAKELAND
33806	LAKELAND	33803	LAKELAND
33807	LAKELAND	33813	LAKELAND
33820	ALTURAS	33830	BARTOW
33826	AVON PARK	33825	AVON PARK
33831	BARTOW	33830	BARTOW
33835	BRADLEY	33860	MULBERRY
33836	DAVENPORT	33837	DAVENPORT
33840	EATON PARK	33803	LAKELAND
33845	HAINES CITY	33844	HAINES CITY
33846	HIGHLAND CITY	33812	LAKELAND
33847	HOMELAND	33830	BARTOW
33848	INTERCESSION CITY	34758	KISSIMMEE
33851	LAKE HAMILTON	33844	HAINES CITY
33854	FEDHAVEN	33898	LAKE WALES
33855	INDIAN LAKE ESTATES	33898	LAKE WALES
33856	NALCREST	33898	LAKE WALES
33858	LOUGHMAN	33837	DAVENPORT
33862	LAKE PLACID	33852	LAKE PLACID
33863	NICHOLS	33860	MULBERRY
33867	RIVER RANCH	33853	LAKE WALES
33871	SEBRING	33870	SEBRING
33877	WAVERLY	33859	LAKE WALES
33882	WINTER HAVEN	33880	WINTER HAVEN
33883	WINTER HAVEN	33880	WINTER HAVEN
33885	WINTER HAVEN	33881	WINTER HAVEN
33888	WINTER HAVEN	33884	WINTER HAVEN
33900	FORT MYERS	33907	FORT MYERS
33902	FORT MYERS	33901	FORT MYERS
33906	FORT MYERS	33907	FORT MYERS
33910	CAPE CORAL	33990	CAPE CORAL
33911	FORT MYERS	33901	FORT MYERS
33915	CAPE CORAL	33990	CAPE CORAL
33918	NORTH FORT MYERS	33903	NORTH FORT MYERS
33929	ESTERO	33928	ESTERO
33930	FELDA	33935	LABELLE
33932	FORT MYERS BEACH	33931	FORT MYERS BEACH
33938	MURDOCK	33948	PORT CHARLOTTE
33944	PALMDALE	33471	MOORE HAVEN
33945	PINELAND	33922	BOKEELIA
33949	PORT CHARLOTTE	33950	PUNTA GORDA
33951	PUNTA GORDA	33950	PUNTA GORDA
33965	FORT MYERS	33967	FORT MYERS
33970	LEHIGH ACRES	33936	LEHIGH ACRES
33975	LABELLE	33935	LABELLE
33994	FORT MYERS	33905	FORT MYERS
34002	APO	00000	NO ENCLOSING ZIP
34004	APO	00000	NO ENCLOSING ZIP
34006	APO	00000	NO ENCLOSING ZIP
34007	APO	00000	NO ENCLOSING ZIP
34008	APO	00000	NO ENCLOSING ZIP
34020	APO	00000	NO ENCLOSING ZIP
34021	APO	00000	NO ENCLOSING ZIP
34022	APO	00000	NO ENCLOSING ZIP
34023	APO	00000	NO ENCLOSING ZIP
34024	APO	00000	NO ENCLOSING ZIP
34025	APO	00000	NO ENCLOSING ZIP
34030	APO	00000	NO ENCLOSING ZIP
34031	APO	00000	NO ENCLOSING ZIP
34032	APO	00000	NO ENCLOSING ZIP
34033	APO	00000	NO ENCLOSING ZIP
34034	APO	00000	NO ENCLOSING ZIP
34035	APO	00000	NO ENCLOSING ZIP
34036	APO	00000	NO ENCLOSING ZIP

NONRESIDENTIAL ZIP CODES

FLORIDA

Point ZIP Code		Enclosing Residential ZIP Code	
ZIP	Post Office Name	ZIP	Post Office Name
34037	APO	00000	NO ENCLOSING ZIP
34038	APO	00000	NO ENCLOSING ZIP
34039	APO	00000	NO ENCLOSING ZIP
34041	APO	00000	NO ENCLOSING ZIP
34042	APO	00000	NO ENCLOSING ZIP
34050	FPO	00000	NO ENCLOSING ZIP
34055	FPO	00000	NO ENCLOSING ZIP
34058	FPO	00000	NO ENCLOSING ZIP
34076	APO	00000	NO ENCLOSING ZIP
34078	APO	00000	NO ENCLOSING ZIP
34090	FPO	00000	NO ENCLOSING ZIP
34091	FPO	00000	NO ENCLOSING ZIP
34092	FPO	00000	NO ENCLOSING ZIP
34093	FPO	00000	NO ENCLOSING ZIP
34095	FPO	00000	NO ENCLOSING ZIP
34098	FPO	00000	NO ENCLOSING ZIP
34099	FPO	00000	NO ENCLOSING ZIP
34101	NAPLES	34102	NAPLES
34106	NAPLES	34102	NAPLES
34107	VANDERBILT BEACH	34102	NAPLES
34133	BONITA SPRINGS	34135	BONITA SPRINGS
34136	BONITA SPRINGS	34135	BONITA SPRINGS
34137	COPELAND	34114	NAPLES
34138	CHOKOLOSKEE	34141	OCHOPEE
34139	EVERGLADES CITY	34141	OCHOPEE
34143	IMMOKALEE	34142	IMMOKALEE
34146	MARCO ISLAND	34145	MARCO ISLAND
34204	BRADENTON	34203	BRADENTON
34206	BRADENTON	34205	BRADENTON
34216	ANNA MARIA	34217	BRADENTON BEACH
34218	HOLMES BEACH	34217	BRADENTON BEACH
34220	PALMETTO	34221	PALMETTO
34230	SARASOTA	34236	SARASOTA
34250	TERRA CEIA	34221	PALMETTO
34260	SARASOTA	34243	SARASOTA
34264	ONECO	34203	BRADENTON
34265	ARCADIA	34266	ARCADIA
34267	FORT OGDEN	34266	ARCADIA
34268	NOCATEE	34266	ARCADIA
34270	TALLEVAST	34243	SARASOTA
34272	LAUREL	34275	NOKOMIS
34274	NOKOMIS	34275	NOKOMIS
34276	SARASOTA	34236	SARASOTA
34277	SARASOTA	34231	SARASOTA
34278	SARASOTA	34234	SARASOTA
34280	BRADENTON	34209	BRADENTON
34281	BRADENTON	34207	BRADENTON
34282	BRADENTON	34207	BRADENTON
34284	VENICE	34285	VENICE
34290	NORTH PORT	34287	NORTH PORT
34295	ENGLEWOOD	34223	ENGLEWOOD
34421	BELLEVIEW	34420	BELLEVIEW
34423	CRYSTAL RIVER	34429	CRYSTAL RIVER
34430	DUNNELLON	34432	DUNNELLON
34445	HOLDER	34442	HERNANDO
34447	HOMOSASSA SPRINGS	34448	HOMOSASSA
34451	INVERNESS	34450	INVERNESS
34460	LECANTO	34461	LECANTO
34464	BEVERLY HILLS	34465	BEVERLY HILLS
34477	OCALA	34471	OCALA
34478	OCALA	34471	OCALA
34483	OCALA	34472	OCALA
34487	HOMOSASSA	34448	HOMOSASSA
34489	SILVER SPRINGS	34488	SILVER SPRINGS
34492	SUMMERFIELD	34491	SUMMERFIELD
34603	BROOKSVILLE	34601	BROOKSVILLE
34605	BROOKSVILLE	34601	BROOKSVILLE
34611	SPRING HILL	34606	SPRING HILL
34636	ISTACHATTA	34601	BROOKSVILLE
34656	NEW PORT RICHEY	34653	NEW PORT RICHEY
34660	OZONA	34683	PALM HARBOR
34661	NOBLETON	34601	BROOKSVILLE
34673	PORT RICHEY	34668	PORT RICHEY
34674	HUDSON	34667	HUDSON
34679	ARIPEKA	34667	HUDSON
34680	ELFERS	34652	NEW PORT RICHEY
34681	CRYSTAL BEACH	34683	PALM HARBOR
34682	PALM HARBOR	34683	PALM HARBOR
34692	HOLIDAY	34690	HOLIDAY
34697	DUNEDIN	34698	DUNEDIN
34712	CLERMONT	34711	CLERMONT
34713	CLERMONT	34714	CLERMONT
34729	FERNDALE	34715	CLERMONT
34740	KILLARNEY	34787	WINTER GARDEN
34742	KISSIMMEE	34741	KISSIMMEE
34745	KISSIMMEE	34741	KISSIMMEE
34749	LEESBURG	34748	LEESBURG
34755	MINNEOLA	34715	CLERMONT
34760	OAKLAND	34787	WINTER GARDEN
34770	SAINT CLOUD	34769	SAINT CLOUD
34777	WINTER GARDEN	34787	WINTER GARDEN
34778	WINTER GARDEN	34787	WINTER GARDEN
34789	LEESBURG	34788	LEESBURG

ALABAMA

Point ZIP Code		Enclosing Residential ZIP Code	
ZIP	Post Office Name	ZIP	Post Office Name
34948	FORT PIERCE	34950	FORT PIERCE
34954	FORT PIERCE	34983	PORT SAINT LUCIE
34958	JENSEN BEACH	34957	JENSEN BEACH
34973	OKEECHOBEE	34972	OKEECHOBEE
34979	FORT PIERCE	34950	FORT PIERCE
34985	PORT SAINT LUCIE	34952	PORT SAINT LUCIE
34991	PALM CITY	34990	PALM CITY
34992	PORT SALERNO	34997	STUART
34995	STUART	34994	STUART
35011	ALEXANDER CITY	35010	ALEXANDER CITY
35013	ALLGOOD	35121	ONEONTA
35015	ALTON	35210	BIRMINGHAM
35021	BESSEMER	35020	BESSEMER
35032	BON AIR	35044	CHILDERSBURG
35038	BURNWELL	35130	QUINTON
35048	CLAY	35173	TRUSSVILLE
35052	COOK SPRINGS	35128	PELL CITY
35056	CULLMAN	35055	CULLMAN
35060	DOCENA	35005	ADAMSVILLE
35070	GARDEN CITY	35077	HANCEVILLE
35074	GREEN POND	35184	WEST BLOCTON
35082	HOLLINS	35072	GOODWATER
35112	MARGARET	35120	ODENVILLE
35119	NEW CASTLE	35071	GARDENDALE
35123	PALMERDALE	35126	PINSON
35137	SAGINAW	35007	ALABASTER
35139	SAYRE	35071	GARDENDALE
35142	SHANNON	35022	BESSEMER
35144	SILURIA	35007	ALABASTER
35149	SYCAMORE	35150	SYLACAUGA
35161	TALLADEGA	35160	TALLADEGA
35181	WATSON	35117	MOUNT OLIVE
35182	WATTSVILLE	35125	PELL CITY
35185	WESTOVER	35078	HARPERSVILLE
35187	WILTON	35035	BRIERFIELD
35201	BIRMINGHAM	35203	BIRMINGHAM
35202	BIRMINGHAM	35207	BIRMINGHAM
35219	BIRMINGHAM	35209	BIRMINGHAM
35220	BIRMINGHAM	35215	BIRMINGHAM
35231	BIRMINGHAM	35214	BIRMINGHAM
35232	BIRMINGHAM	35212	BIRMINGHAM
35236	BIRMINGHAM	35244	BIRMINGHAM
35238	BIRMINGHAM	35242	BIRMINGHAM
35246	BIRMINGHAM	35203	BIRMINGHAM
35249	BIRMINGHAM	35233	BIRMINGHAM
35253	BIRMINGHAM	35223	BIRMINGHAM
35255	BIRMINGHAM	35205	BIRMINGHAM
35259	BIRMINGHAM	35209	BIRMINGHAM
35260	BIRMINGHAM	35226	BIRMINGHAM
35261	BIRMINGHAM	35206	BIRMINGHAM
35266	BIRMINGHAM	35216	BIRMINGHAM
35282	BIRMINGHAM	35205	BIRMINGHAM
35283	BIRMINGHAM	35203	BIRMINGHAM
35285	BIRMINGHAM	35234	BIRMINGHAM
35287	BIRMINGHAM	35203	BIRMINGHAM
35288	BIRMINGHAM	35203	BIRMINGHAM
35290	BIRMINGHAM	35212	BIRMINGHAM
35291	BIRMINGHAM	35203	BIRMINGHAM
35292	BIRMINGHAM	35203	BIRMINGHAM
35293	BIRMINGHAM	35209	BIRMINGHAM
35294	BIRMINGHAM	35233	BIRMINGHAM
35295	BIRMINGHAM	35233	BIRMINGHAM
35296	BIRMINGHAM	35226	BIRMINGHAM
35297	BIRMINGHAM	35223	BIRMINGHAM
35298	BIRMINGHAM	35205	BIRMINGHAM
35402	TUSCALOOSA	35401	TUSCALOOSA
35403	TUSCALOOSA	35401	TUSCALOOSA
35407	TUSCALOOSA	35405	TUSCALOOSA
35440	ABERNANT	35490	VANCE
35448	CLINTON	35462	EUTAW
35449	COALING	35453	COTTONDALE
35468	KELLERMAN	35490	VANCE
35471	MC SHAN	35461	ETHELSVILLE
35477	PANOLA	35442	ALICEVILLE
35478	PETERSON	35490	VANCE
35482	SAMANTHA	35475	NORTHPORT
35485	TUSCALOOSA	35401	TUSCALOOSA
35486	TUSCALOOSA	35487	TUSCALOOSA
35491	WEST GREENE	35462	EUTAW
35502	JASPER	35501	JASPER
35545	BELK	35555	FAYETTE
35551	DELMAR	35565	HALEYVILLE
35559	GLEN ALLEN	35594	WINFIELD
35560	GOODSPRINGS	35580	PARRISH
35573	KANSAS	35549	CARBON HILL
35577	NATURAL BRIDGE	35575	LYNN
35584	SIPSEY	35504	JASPER
35602	DECATUR	35601	DECATUR
35609	DECATUR	35601	DECATUR
35612	ATHENS	35611	ATHENS
35615	BELLE MINA	35671	TANNER
35617	CLOVERDALE	35633	FLORENCE
35631	FLORENCE	35630	FLORENCE

Point ZIP Code		Enclosing Residential ZIP Code	
ZIP	Post Office Name	ZIP	Post Office Name
35632	FLORENCE	35630	FLORENCE
35649	MOORESVILLE	35756	MADISON
35662	MUSCLE SHOALS	35661	MUSCLE SHOALS
35699	DECATUR	35601	DECATUR
35742	CAPSHAW	35757	MADISON
35762	NORMAL	35810	HUNTSVILLE
35767	RYLAND	35811	HUNTSVILLE
35804	HUNTSVILLE	35801	HUNTSVILLE
35807	HUNTSVILLE	35805	HUNTSVILLE
35809	HUNTSVILLE	35805	HUNTSVILLE
35812	HUNTSVILLE	35824	HUNTSVILLE
35813	HUNTSVILLE	35824	HUNTSVILLE
35814	HUNTSVILLE	35816	HUNTSVILLE
35815	HUNTSVILLE	35802	HUNTSVILLE
35893	HUNTSVILLE	35805	HUNTSVILLE
35894	HUNTSVILLE	35824	HUNTSVILLE
35896	HUNTSVILLE	35824	HUNTSVILLE
35897	HUNTSVILLE	35805	HUNTSVILLE
35899	HUNTSVILLE	35816	HUNTSVILLE
35902	GADSDEN	35901	GADSDEN
35964	DOUGLAS	35980	HORTON
35990	WALNUT GROVE	35952	ALTOONA
36008	BOOTH	36067	PRATTVILLE
36015	CHAPMAN	36033	GEORGIANA
36045	KENT	36078	TALLASSEE
36057	MOUNT MEIGS	36064	PIKE ROAD
36062	PETREY	36049	LUVERNE
36065	PINE LEVEL	36069	RAMER
36068	PRATTVILLE	36067	PRATTVILLE
36072	EUFAULA	36027	EUFAULA
36087	TUSKEGEE INSTITUTE	36088	TUSKEGEE INSTITUTE
36101	MONTGOMERY	36104	MONTGOMERY
36102	MONTGOMERY	36104	MONTGOMERY
36103	MONTGOMERY	36104	MONTGOMERY
36114	MONTGOMERY	36117	MONTGOMERY
36118	MONTGOMERY	36115	MONTGOMERY
36119	MONTGOMERY	36117	MONTGOMERY
36120	MONTGOMERY	36111	MONTGOMERY
36121	MONTGOMERY	36117	MONTGOMERY
36123	MONTGOMERY	36106	MONTGOMERY
36124	MONTGOMERY	36117	MONTGOMERY
36125	MONTGOMERY	36105	MONTGOMERY
36130	MONTGOMERY	36104	MONTGOMERY
36131	MONTGOMERY	36104	MONTGOMERY
36132	MONTGOMERY	36117	MONTGOMERY
36133	MONTGOMERY	36104	MONTGOMERY
36135	MONTGOMERY	36104	MONTGOMERY
36140	MONTGOMERY	36104	MONTGOMERY
36141	MONTGOMERY	36117	MONTGOMERY
36142	MONTGOMERY	36104	MONTGOMERY
36177	MONTGOMERY	36117	MONTGOMERY
36191	MONTGOMERY	36116	MONTGOMERY
36202	ANNISTON	36207	ANNISTON
36204	ANNISTON	36207	ANNISTON
36210	ANNISTON	36207	ANNISTON
36253	BYNUM	36260	EASTABOGA
36254	CHOCCOLOCCO	36207	ANNISTON
36257	DE ARMANVILLE	36207	ANNISTON
36261	EDWARDSVILLE	36264	HEFLIN
36275	SPRING GARDEN	35960	CENTRE
36302	DOTHAN	36303	DOTHAN
36304	DOTHAN	36303	DOTHAN
36313	BELLWOOD	36316	CHANCELLOR
36331	ENTERPRISE	36330	ENTERPRISE
36361	OZARK	36360	OZARK
36371	PINCKARD	36350	MIDLAND CITY
36427	BREWTON	36426	BREWTON
36429	BROOKLYN	36401	BURNT CORN
36439	EXCEL	36460	MONROEVILLE
36449	GOODWAY	36502	ATMORE
36455	LOCKHART	36442	FLORALA
36457	MEGARGEL	36445	FRISCO CITY
36458	MEXIA	36445	FRISCO CITY
36461	MONROEVILLE	36460	MONROEVILLE
36462	MONROEVILLE	36460	MONROEVILLE
36470	PERDUE HILL	36460	MONROEVILLE
36476	RIVER FALLS	36420	ANDALUSIA
36503	ATMORE	36502	ATMORE
36504	ATMORE	36502	ATMORE
36512	BUCKS	36560	MOUNT VERNON
36513	CALVERT	36553	MC INTOSH
36533	FAIRHOPE	36532	FAIRHOPE
36536	FOLEY	36535	FOLEY
36543	HUXFORD	36502	ATMORE
36547	GULF SHORES	36542	GULF SHORES
36556	MALCOLM	36553	MC INTOSH
36559	MONTROSE	36526	DAPHNE
36564	POINT CLEAR	36532	FAIRHOPE
36568	SAINT ELMO	36544	IRVINGTON
36577	SPANISH FORT	36526	DAPHNE
36581	SUNFLOWER	36585	WAGARVILLE
36590	THEODORE	36582	THEODORE
36601	MOBILE	36602	MOBILE
36616	MOBILE	36606	MOBILE
36622	MOBILE	36602	MOBILE
36625	MOBILE	36602	MOBILE
36628	MOBILE	36602	MOBILE
36633	MOBILE	36602	MOBILE
36640	MOBILE	36603	MOBILE
36652	MOBILE	36602	MOBILE
36660	MOBILE	36606	MOBILE
36663	MOBILE	36613	EIGHT MILE
36670	MOBILE	36607	MOBILE
36671	MOBILE	36611	MOBILE
36675	MOBILE	36602	MOBILE
36685	MOBILE	36608	MOBILE
36689	MOBILE	36608	MOBILE
36691	MOBILE	36609	MOBILE
36702	SELMA	36701	SELMA
36721	ANNEMANIE	36722	ARLINGTON
36723	BOYKIN	36720	ALBERTA
36741	FURMAN	36768	PINE APPLE
36745	JEFFERSON	36732	DEMOPOLIS
36753	MC WILLIAMS	36768	PINE APPLE
36762	MORVIN	36784	THOMASVILLE
36763	MYRTLEWOOD	36748	LINDEN
36764	NANAFALIA	36782	SWEET WATER
36766	OAK HILL	36768	PINE APPLE
36802	OPELIKA	36801	OPELIKA
36803	OPELIKA	36801	OPELIKA
36831	AUBURN	36830	AUBURN
36851	COTTONTON	36871	PITTSVIEW
36865	LOACHAPOKA	36830	AUBURN
36868	PHENIX CITY	36867	PHENIX CITY
36872	VALLEY	36854	VALLEY
36901	BELLAMY	36925	YORK
36913	MELVIN	36908	GILBERTOWN
37011	ANTIOCH	37013	ANTIOCH
37024	BRENTWOOD	37027	BRENTWOOD
37041	CLARKSVILLE	37040	CLARKSVILLE
37044	CLARKSVILLE	37040	CLARKSVILLE
37056	DICKSON	37055	DICKSON
37063	FOSTERVILLE	37020	BELL BUCKLE
37065	FRANKLIN	37064	FRANKLIN
37068	FRANKLIN	37064	FRANKLIN
37070	GOODLETTSVILLE	37072	GOODLETTSVILLE
37071	GLADEVILLE	37122	MOUNT JULIET
37077	HENDERSONVILLE	37075	HENDERSONVILLE
37088	LEBANON	37087	LEBANON
37111	MC MINNVILLE	37110	MC MINNVILLE
37116	MADISON	37115	MADISON
37119	MITCHELLVILLE	37148	PORTLAND
37121	MOUNT JULIET	37122	MOUNT JULIET
37131	MURFREESBORO	37129	MURFREESBORO
37133	MURFREESBORO	37130	MURFREESBORO
37136	NORENE	37184	WATERTOWN
37152	RIDGETOP	37072	GOODLETTSVILLE
37161	SHELBYVILLE	37160	SHELBYVILLE
37162	SHELBYVILLE	37160	SHELBYVILLE
37165	SLAYDEN	37051	CUMBERLAND FURNACE
37202	NASHVILLE	37214	NASHVILLE
37222	NASHVILLE	37211	NASHVILLE
37224	NASHVILLE	37214	NASHVILLE
37227	NASHVILLE	37214	NASHVILLE
37229	NASHVILLE	37214	NASHVILLE
37230	NASHVILLE	37203	NASHVILLE
37232	NASHVILLE	37212	NASHVILLE
37234	NASHVILLE	37203	NASHVILLE
37235	NASHVILLE	37240	NASHVILLE
37236	NASHVILLE	37203	NASHVILLE
37238	NASHVILLE	37201	NASHVILLE
37241	NASHVILLE	37214	NASHVILLE
37242	NASHVILLE	37219	NASHVILLE
37243	NASHVILLE	37203	NASHVILLE
37244	NASHVILLE	37219	NASHVILLE
37246	NASHVILLE	37203	NASHVILLE
37249	NASHVILLE	37217	NASHVILLE
37250	NASHVILLE	37214	NASHVILLE
37304	BAKEWELL	37373	SALE CREEK
37314	COKERCREEK	37385	TELLICO PLAINS
37315	COLLEGEDALE	37363	OOLTEWAH
37316	CONASAUGA	37362	OLDFORT
37320	CLEVELAND	37311	CLEVELAND
37326	DUCKTOWN	37317	COPPERHILL
37349	MANCHESTER	37355	MANCHESTER
37351	LUPTON CITY	37415	CHATTANOOGA
37364	CLEVELAND	37311	CLEVELAND
37371	ATHENS	37303	ATHENS
37378	SMARTT	37110	MC MINNVILLE
37382	SUMMITVILLE	37357	MORRISON
37384	SODDY DAISY	37379	SODDY DAISY
37389	ARNOLD A F B	37355	MANCHESTER
37394	VIOLA	37357	MORRISON
37401	CHATTANOOGA	37421	CHATTANOOGA
37414	CHATTANOOGA	37411	CHATTANOOGA
37422	CHATTANOOGA	37421	CHATTANOOGA

Point ZIP Code		Enclosing Residential ZIP Code	
ZIP	Post Office Name	ZIP	Post Office Name
37424	CHATTANOOGA	37421	CHATTANOOGA
37450	CHATTANOOGA	37402	CHATTANOOGA
37501	MEMPHIS	38118	MEMPHIS
37544	MEMPHIS	38126	MEMPHIS
37602	JOHNSON CITY	37604	JOHNSON CITY
37605	JOHNSON CITY	37601	JOHNSON CITY
37621	BRISTOL	37620	BRISTOL
37625	BRISTOL	37620	BRISTOL
37644	ELIZABETHTON	37643	ELIZABETHTON
37662	KINGSPORT	37660	KINGSPORT
37669	KINGSPORT	37660	KINGSPORT
37682	MILLIGAN COLLEGE	37601	JOHNSON CITY
37684	MOUNTAIN HOME	37604	JOHNSON CITY
37699	PINEY FLATS	37686	PINEY FLATS
37707	ARTHUR	37724	CUMBERLAND GAP
37717	CLINTON	37716	CLINTON
37719	COALFIELD	37840	OLIVER SPRINGS
37730	EAGAN	37715	CLAIRFIELD
37732	ELGIN	37852	ROBBINS
37733	RUGBY	37852	ROBBINS
37744	GREENEVILLE	37743	GREENEVILLE
37773	LONE MOUNTAIN	37825	NEW TAZEWELL
37802	MARYVILLE	37801	MARYVILLE
37815	MORRISTOWN	37813	MORRISTOWN
37816	MORRISTOWN	37813	MORRISTOWN
37822	NEWPORT	37821	NEWPORT
37824	NEW TAZEWELL	37825	NEW TAZEWELL
37828	NORRIS	37705	ANDERSONVILLE
37831	OAK RIDGE	37830	OAK RIDGE
37845	PETROS	37840	OLIVER SPRINGS
37851	PRUDEN	37715	CLAIRFIELD
37864	SEVIERVILLE	37862	SEVIERVILLE
37867	SHAWANEE	37752	HARROGATE
37868	PIGEON FORGE	37863	PIGEON FORGE
37901	KNOXVILLE	37902	KNOXVILLE
37927	KNOXVILLE	37917	KNOXVILLE
37928	KNOXVILLE	37918	KNOXVILLE
37929	KNOXVILLE	37902	KNOXVILLE
37930	KNOXVILLE	37923	KNOXVILLE
37933	KNOXVILLE	37934	KNOXVILLE
37939	KNOXVILLE	37919	KNOXVILLE
37940	KNOXVILLE	37920	KNOXVILLE
37950	KNOXVILLE	37909	KNOXVILLE
37995	KNOXVILLE	37909	KNOXVILLE
37996	KNOXVILLE	37916	KNOXVILLE
37997	KNOXVILLE	37915	KNOXVILLE
37998	KNOXVILLE	37920	KNOXVILLE
38007	BOGOTA	38080	RIDGELY
38010	BRADEN	38068	SOMERVILLE
38014	BRUNSWICK	38002	ARLINGTON
38021	CROCKETT MILLS	38034	FRIENDSHIP
38025	DYERSBURG	38024	DYERSBURG
38027	COLLIERVILLE	38017	COLLIERVILLE
38029	ELLENDALE	38134	MEMPHIS
38036	GALLAWAY	38068	SOMERVILLE
38045	LACONIA	38068	SOMERVILLE
38046	LA GRANGE	38057	MOSCOW
38047	LENOX	38024	DYERSBURG
38048	MACON	38060	OAKLAND
38050	MAURY CITY	38001	ALAMO
38054	MILLINGTON	38053	MILLINGTON
38055	MILLINGTON	38053	MILLINGTON
38070	TIGRETT	38059	NEWBERN
38071	TIPTON	38004	ATOKA
38077	WYNNBURG	38080	RIDGELY
38083	MILLINGTON	38053	MILLINGTON
38088	CORDOVA	38018	CORDOVA
38101	MEMPHIS	38126	MEMPHIS
38124	MEMPHIS	38117	MEMPHIS
38130	MEMPHIS	38118	MEMPHIS
38136	MEMPHIS	38106	MEMPHIS
38137	MEMPHIS	38117	MEMPHIS
38145	MEMPHIS	38103	MEMPHIS
38147	MEMPHIS	38103	MEMPHIS
38148	MEMPHIS	38103	MEMPHIS
38150	MEMPHIS	38126	MEMPHIS
38151	MEMPHIS	38112	MEMPHIS
38157	MEMPHIS	38117	MEMPHIS
38159	MEMPHIS	38103	MEMPHIS
38161	MEMPHIS	38134	MEMPHIS
38163	MEMPHIS	38105	MEMPHIS
38166	MEMPHIS	38120	MEMPHIS
38167	MEMPHIS	38127	MEMPHIS
38168	MEMPHIS	38128	MEMPHIS
38173	MEMPHIS	38103	MEMPHIS
38174	MEMPHIS	38104	MEMPHIS
38175	MEMPHIS	38115	MEMPHIS
38177	MEMPHIS	38117	MEMPHIS
38181	MEMPHIS	38118	MEMPHIS
38182	MEMPHIS	38112	MEMPHIS
38183	GERMANTOWN	38138	GERMANTOWN
38184	MEMPHIS	38134	MEMPHIS
38186	MEMPHIS	38116	MEMPHIS

Point ZIP Code		Enclosing Residential ZIP Code	
ZIP	Post Office Name	ZIP	Post Office Name
38187	MEMPHIS	38119	MEMPHIS
38188	MEMPHIS	38119	MEMPHIS
38190	MEMPHIS	38109	MEMPHIS
38193	MEMPHIS	38115	MEMPHIS
38194	MEMPHIS	38131	MEMPHIS
38197	MEMPHIS	38120	MEMPHIS
38223	COMO	38242	PARIS
38235	MC LEMORESVILLE	38258	TREZEVANT
38254	SAMBURG	38232	HORNBEAK
38271	WOODLAND MILLS	38261	UNION CITY
38281	UNION CITY	38261	UNION CITY
38302	JACKSON	38301	JACKSON
38303	JACKSON	38301	JACKSON
38308	JACKSON	38301	JACKSON
38314	JACKSON	38301	JACKSON
38324	CLARKSBURG	38344	HUNTINGDON
38331	EATON	38382	TRENTON
38336	FRUITVALE	38006	BELLS
38338	GIBSON	38343	HUMBOLDT
38346	IDLEWILD	38316	BRADFORD
38365	PICKWICK DAM	38326	COUNCE
38378	SPRING CREEK	38305	JACKSON
38389	YORKVILLE	38330	DYER
38393	CHEWALLA	38367	RAMER
38402	COLUMBIA	38401	COLUMBIA
38455	ELKTON	38449	ARDMORE
38502	COOKEVILLE	38501	COOKEVILLE
38503	COOKEVILLE	38501	COOKEVILLE
38550	CAMPAIGN	38581	ROCK ISLAND
38557	CROSSVILLE	38555	CROSSVILLE
38602	ARKABUTLA	38618	COLDWATER
38609	BELEN	38646	MARKS
38622	CROWDER	38643	LAMBERT
38623	DARLING	38670	SLEDGE
38628	FALCON	38670	SLEDGE
38630	FARRELL	38614	CLARKSDALE
38634	HOLLY SPRINGS	38635	HOLLY SPRINGS
38638	INDEPENDENCE	38668	SENATOBIA
38639	JONESTOWN	38617	COAHOMA
38644	LULA	38617	COAHOMA
38649	MOUNT PLEASANT	38635	HOLLY SPRINGS
38669	SHERARD	38614	CLARKSDALE
38675	TULA	38655	OXFORD
38679	VICTORIA	38611	BYHALIA
38686	WALLS	38680	WALLS
38702	GREENVILLE	38701	GREENVILLE
38704	GREENVILLE	38701	GREENVILLE
38722	ARCOLA	38701	GREENVILLE
38723	AVON	38748	HOLLANDALE
38738	PARCHMAN	38737	DREW
38739	DUBLIN	38614	CLARKSDALE
38745	GRACE	39113	MAYERSVILLE
38749	HOLLY RIDGE	38751	INDIANOLA
38760	METCALFE	38701	GREENVILLE
38764	PACE	38732	CLEVELAND
38765	PANTHER BURN	38721	ANGUILLA
38767	RENA LARA	38614	CLARKSDALE
38768	ROME	38737	DREW
38772	SCOTT	38725	BENOIT
38776	STONEVILLE	38703	GREENVILLE
38781	WINSTONVILLE	38762	MOUND BAYOU
38782	WINTERVILLE	38703	GREENVILLE
38802	TUPELO	38801	TUPELO
38803	TUPELO	38801	TUPELO
38820	ALGOMA	38863	PONTOTOC
38825	BECKER	38821	AMORY
38835	CORINTH	38834	CORINTH
38839	DERMA	38916	CALHOUN CITY
38869	SHERMAN	38841	ECRU
38874	TOCCOPOLA	38863	PONTOTOC
38875	TREBLOC	38851	HOUSTON
38877	VAN VLEET	38851	HOUSTON
38879	VERONA	38801	TUPELO
38880	WHEELER	38829	BOONEVILLE
38902	GRENADA	38901	GRENADA
38926	ELLIOTT	38901	GRENADA
38928	GLENDORA	38921	CHARLESTON
38935	GREENWOOD	38930	GREENWOOD
38945	MONEY	38930	GREENWOOD
38946	MORGAN CITY	38941	ITTA BENA
38947	NORTH CARROLLTON	38917	CARROLLTON
38955	SLATE SPRING	38916	CALHOUN CITY
38957	SUMNER	38963	TUTWILER
38958	SWAN LAKE	38921	CHARLESTON
38959	SWIFTOWN	38941	ITTA BENA
38960	TIE PLANT	38901	GRENADA
38962	TIPPO	38921	CHARLESTON
38966	WEBB	38963	TUTWILER
39043	BRANDON	39042	BRANDON
39054	CARY	39159	ROLLING FORK
39060	CLINTON	39056	CLINTON
39061	DELTA CITY	38721	ANGUILLA
39062	D LO	39114	MENDENHALL

NONRESIDENTIAL ZIP CODES

MISSISSIPPI — KENTUCKY

Point ZIP Code		Enclosing Residential ZIP Code	
ZIP	Post Office Name	ZIP	Post Office Name
39072	POCAHONTAS	39209	JACKSON
39077	GALLMAN	39059	CRYSTAL SPRINGS
39080	HARPERVILLE	39074	FOREST
39087	HILLSBORO	39117	MORTON
39098	LUDLOW	39117	MORTON
39107	MC ADAMS	39160	SALLIS
39109	MADDEN	39051	CARTHAGE
39115	MIDNIGHT	39097	LOUISE
39121	NATCHEZ	39120	NATCHEZ
39122	NATCHEZ	39120	NATCHEZ
39130	MADISON	39110	MADISON
39148	PINEY WOODS	39044	BRAXTON
39151	PUCKETT	39042	BRANDON
39158	RIDGELAND	39157	RIDGELAND
39161	SANDHILL	39047	BRANDON
39163	SHARON	39046	CANTON
39165	SIBLEY	39120	NATCHEZ
39167	STAR	39073	FLORENCE
39171	THOMASTOWN	39051	CARTHAGE
39173	TINSLEY	39194	YAZOO CITY
39174	TOUGALOO	39213	JACKSON
39181	VICKSBURG	39180	VICKSBURG
39182	VICKSBURG	39180	VICKSBURG
39190	WASHINGTON	39120	NATCHEZ
39193	WHITFIELD	39208	PEARL
39205	JACKSON	39201	JACKSON
39207	JACKSON	39203	JACKSON
39215	JACKSON	39201	JACKSON
39225	JACKSON	39201	JACKSON
39236	JACKSON	39211	JACKSON
39269	JACKSON	39201	JACKSON
39271	JACKSON	39201	JACKSON
39282	JACKSON	39212	JACKSON
39283	JACKSON	39213	JACKSON
39284	JACKSON	39204	JACKSON
39286	JACKSON	39206	JACKSON
39288	PEARL	39208	PEARL
39289	JACKSON	39209	JACKSON
39296	JACKSON	39216	JACKSON
39298	JACKSON	39232	FLOWOOD
39302	MERIDIAN	39301	MERIDIAN
39303	MERIDIAN	39301	MERIDIAN
39304	MERIDIAN	39307	MERIDIAN
39324	CLARA	39367	WAYNESBORO
39403	HATTIESBURG	39402	HATTIESBURG
39404	HATTIESBURG	39402	HATTIESBURG
39407	HATTIESBURG	39401	HATTIESBURG
39436	EASTABUCHIE	39459	MOSELLE
39441	LAUREL	39440	LAUREL
39442	LAUREL	39440	LAUREL
39457	MC NEILL	39426	CARRIERE
39460	MOSS	39443	LAUREL
39463	NICHOLSON	39466	PICAYUNE
39477	SANDERSVILLE	39439	HEIDELBERG
39502	GULFPORT	39501	GULFPORT
39505	GULFPORT	39501	GULFPORT
39506	GULFPORT	39507	GULFPORT
39521	BAY SAINT LOUIS	39520	BAY SAINT LOUIS
39533	BILOXI	39540	DIBERVILLE
39535	BILOXI	39531	BILOXI
39552	ESCATAWPA	39563	MOSS POINT
39555	HURLEY	39562	MOSS POINT
39558	LAKESHORE	39520	BAY SAINT LOUIS
39566	OCEAN SPRINGS	39564	OCEAN SPRINGS
39568	PASCAGOULA	39567	PASCAGOULA
39569	PASCAGOULA	39563	MOSS POINT
39595	PASCAGOULA	39567	PASCAGOULA
39602	BROOKHAVEN	39601	BROOKHAVEN
39603	BROOKHAVEN	39601	BROOKHAVEN
39632	CHATAWA	39652	MAGNOLIA
39635	FERNWOOD	39648	MCCOMB
39649	MCCOMB	39648	MCCOMB
39703	COLUMBUS	39705	COLUMBUS
39704	COLUMBUS	39705	COLUMBUS
39736	ARTESIA	39701	COLUMBUS
39737	BELLEFONTAINE	39744	EUPORA
39753	MAYHEW	39701	COLUMBUS
39754	MONTPELIER	39773	WEST POINT
39760	STARKVILLE	39759	STARKVILLE
39771	WALTHALL	39744	EUPORA
39818	BAINBRIDGE	39819	BAINBRIDGE
39829	CALVARY	39897	WHIGHAM
39832	CEDAR SPRINGS	39861	JAKIN
39852	FOWLSTOWN	39819	BAINBRIDGE
39885	SASSER	39842	DAWSON
39901	ATLANTA	30341	ATLANTA
40018	EASTWOOD	40245	LOUISVILLE
40020	FAIRFIELD	40013	COXS CREEK
40027	HARRODS CREEK	40059	PROSPECT
40032	LA GRANGE	40031	LA GRANGE
40041	MASONIC HOME	40207	LOUISVILLE
40048	NAZARETH	40004	BARDSTOWN
40049	NERINX	40037	LORETTO
40058	PORT ROYAL	40075	TURNERS STATION
40063	SAINT MARY	40033	LEBANON
40066	SHELBYVILLE	40065	SHELBYVILLE
40110	CLERMONT	40165	SHEPHERDSVILLE
40129	HILLVIEW	40229	LOUISVILLE
40153	MC QUADY	40119	FALLS OF ROUGH
40159	RADCLIFF	40160	RADCLIFF
40201	LOUISVILLE	40203	LOUISVILLE
40221	LOUISVILLE	40209	LOUISVILLE
40224	LOUISVILLE	40223	LOUISVILLE
40225	LOUISVILLE	40213	LOUISVILLE
40231	LOUISVILLE	40213	LOUISVILLE
40232	LOUISVILLE	40213	LOUISVILLE
40233	LOUISVILLE	40213	LOUISVILLE
40250	LOUISVILLE	40220	LOUISVILLE
40251	LOUISVILLE	40211	LOUISVILLE
40252	LOUISVILLE	40222	LOUISVILLE
40253	LOUISVILLE	40223	LOUISVILLE
40255	LOUISVILLE	40205	LOUISVILLE
40256	LOUISVILLE	40216	LOUISVILLE
40257	LOUISVILLE	40207	LOUISVILLE
40259	LOUISVILLE	40219	LOUISVILLE
40261	LOUISVILLE	40218	LOUISVILLE
40266	LOUISVILLE	40258	LOUISVILLE
40268	LOUISVILLE	40258	LOUISVILLE
40269	LOUISVILLE	40299	LOUISVILLE
40270	LOUISVILLE	40203	LOUISVILLE
40280	LOUISVILLE	40206	LOUISVILLE
40281	LOUISVILLE	40258	LOUISVILLE
40282	LOUISVILLE	40258	LOUISVILLE
40283	LOUISVILLE	40258	LOUISVILLE
40285	LOUISVILLE	40213	LOUISVILLE
40289	LOUISVILLE	40213	LOUISVILLE
40290	LOUISVILLE	40213	LOUISVILLE
40295	LOUISVILLE	40213	LOUISVILLE
40296	LOUISVILLE	40213	LOUISVILLE
40297	LOUISVILLE	40202	LOUISVILLE
40298	LOUISVILLE	40218	LOUISVILLE
40310	BURGIN	40330	HARRODSBURG
40317	ELLIOTTVILLE	40351	MOREHEAD
40319	FARMERS	40351	MOREHEAD
40334	HOPE	40337	JEFFERSONVILLE
40339	KEENE	40383	VERSAILLES
40340	NICHOLASVILLE	40356	NICHOLASVILLE
40348	MILLERSBURG	40361	PARIS
40357	NORTH MIDDLETOWN	40361	PARIS
40362	PARIS	40361	PARIS
40363	PERRY PARK	40359	OWENTON
40366	PRESTON	40360	OWINGSVILLE
40392	WINCHESTER	40391	WINCHESTER
40405	BIGHILL	40403	BEREA
40410	BRYANTSVILLE	40444	LANCASTER
40423	DANVILLE	40422	DANVILLE
40434	GRAY HAWK	40447	MC KEE
40448	MC KINNEY	40484	STANFORD
40452	MITCHELLSBURG	40422	DANVILLE
40473	RENFRO VALLEY	40456	MOUNT VERNON
40476	RICHMOND	40475	RICHMOND
40488	WANETA	40447	MC KEE
40492	WILDIE	40456	MOUNT VERNON
40495	WINSTON	40336	IRVINE
40512	LEXINGTON	40511	LEXINGTON
40522	LEXINGTON	40502	LEXINGTON
40523	LEXINGTON	40517	LEXINGTON
40524	LEXINGTON	40517	LEXINGTON
40526	LEXINGTON	40508	LEXINGTON
40533	LEXINGTON	40504	LEXINGTON
40536	LEXINGTON	40508	LEXINGTON
40544	LEXINGTON	40504	LEXINGTON
40546	LEXINGTON	40508	LEXINGTON
40555	LEXINGTON	40505	LEXINGTON
40574	LEXINGTON	40511	LEXINGTON
40575	LEXINGTON	40511	LEXINGTON
40576	LEXINGTON	40511	LEXINGTON
40577	LEXINGTON	40511	LEXINGTON
40578	LEXINGTON	40511	LEXINGTON
40579	LEXINGTON	40511	LEXINGTON
40580	LEXINGTON	40511	LEXINGTON
40581	LEXINGTON	40511	LEXINGTON
40582	LEXINGTON	40511	LEXINGTON
40583	LEXINGTON	40511	LEXINGTON
40588	LEXINGTON	40507	LEXINGTON
40591	LEXINGTON	40513	LEXINGTON
40598	LEXINGTON	40511	LEXINGTON
40602	FRANKFORT	40601	FRANKFORT
40603	FRANKFORT	40601	FRANKFORT
40604	FRANKFORT	40601	FRANKFORT
40702	CORBIN	40701	CORBIN
40724	BUSH	40744	LONDON
40730	EMLYN	40769	WILLIAMSBURG
40742	LONDON	40741	LONDON
40743	LONDON	40741	LONDON
40745	LONDON	40741	LONDON

NONRESIDENTIAL ZIP CODES

Point ZIP Code		Enclosing Residential ZIP Code	
ZIP	Post Office Name	ZIP	Post Office Name
40755	PITTSBURG	40741	LONDON
40803	ASHER	40858	MOZELLE
40827	ESSIE	40868	STINNETT
40830	GULSTON	40806	BAXTER
40844	HOSKINSTON	40858	MOZELLE
40849	LEJUNIOR	40828	EVARTS
40854	LOYALL	40831	HARLAN
40856	MIRACLE	40977	PINEVILLE
40874	WARBRANCH	40858	MOZELLE
40932	FALL ROCK	40983	SEXTONS CREEK
40939	FOURMILE	40977	PINEVILLE
40941	GARRARD	40962	MANCHESTER
40944	GOOSE ROCK	40962	MANCHESTER
40951	HIMA	40962	MANCHESTER
40955	INGRAM	40977	PINEVILLE
40981	SAUL	41721	BUCKHORN
41012	COVINGTON	41011	COVINGTON
41019	COVINGTON	41011	COVINGTON
41022	FLORENCE	41042	FLORENCE
41037	ELIZAVILLE	41039	EWING
41053	KENTON	41063	MORNING VIEW
41054	MASON	41097	WILLIAMSTOWN
41061	MILFORD	41004	BROOKSVILLE
41062	MINERVA	41034	DOVER
41065	MUSES MILLS	41093	WALLINGFORD
41072	NEWPORT	41071	NEWPORT
41081	PLUMMERS LANDING	41093	WALLINGFORD
41096	WASHINGTON	41056	MAYSVILLE
41105	ASHLAND	41101	ASHLAND
41128	CARTER	41164	OLIVE HILL
41142	GRAHN	41164	OLIVE HILL
41160	MAZIE	41159	MARTHA
41173	SOLDIER	41164	OLIVE HILL
41181	WILLARD	41143	GRAYSON
41203	BEAUTY	41267	WARFIELD
41264	ULYSSES	41232	LOWMANSVILLE
41268	WEST VAN LEAR	41260	THELMA
41307	ATHOL	41339	JACKSON
41310	BAYS	41385	VANCLEVE
41313	BETHANY	41301	CAMPTON
41333	HEIDELBERG	41311	BEATTYVILLE
41347	LONE	41311	BEATTYVILLE
41352	MIZE	41425	EZEL
41362	PRIMROSE	41311	BEATTYVILLE
41368	SAINT HELENS	41311	BEATTYVILLE
41408	CANNEL CITY	41301	CAMPTON
41413	CROCKETT	41472	WEST LIBERTY
41421	ELKFORK	41472	WEST LIBERTY
41426	FALCON	41465	SALYERSVILLE
41451	MALONE	41472	WEST LIBERTY
41459	OPHIR	41472	WEST LIBERTY
41477	WRIGLEY	41472	WEST LIBERTY
41502	PIKEVILLE	41501	PIKEVILLE
41517	BURDINE	41537	JENKINS
41520	DORTON	41537	JENKINS
41526	FORDS BRANCH	41501	PIKEVILLE
41534	HELLIER	41522	ELKHORN CITY
41538	JONANCY	41501	PIKEVILLE
41542	LOOKOUT	41522	ELKHORN CITY
41547	MAJESTIC	41568	STOPOVER
41549	MYRA	41537	JENKINS
41561	ROCKHOUSE	41522	ELKHORN CITY
41612	BYPRO	41650	MELVIN
41619	DRIFT	41631	GRETHEL
41651	MINNIE	41631	GRETHEL
41659	STANVILLE	41605	BETSY LAYNE
41663	TRAM	41642	IVEL
41667	WEEKSBURY	41606	BEVINSVILLE
41669	WHEELWRIGHT	41606	BEVINSVILLE
41702	HAZARD	41701	HAZARD
41713	AVAWAM	41701	HAZARD
41739	DWARF	41722	BULAN
41743	FISTY	41740	EMMALENA
41747	HARDBURLY	41722	BULAN
41751	JEFF	41701	HAZARD
41762	SIZEROCK	41714	BEAR BRANCH
41778	YERKES	41723	BUSY
41810	CROMONA	41840	NEON
41849	SECO	41840	NEON
42002	PADUCAH	42003	PADUCAH
42022	BANDANA	42056	LA CENTER
42033	CRAYNE	42064	MARION
42037	DYCUSBURG	42064	MARION
42060	LOVELACEVILLE	42053	KEVIL
42061	LOWES	42069	MELBER
42063	LYNNVILLE	42079	SEDALIA
42070	MILBURN	42021	ARLINGTON
42084	TOLU	42064	MARION
42102	BOWLING GREEN	42101	BOWLING GREEN
42128	DRAKE	42122	ALVATON
42135	FRANKLIN	42134	FRANKLIN
42142	GLASGOW	42141	GLASGOW
42152	HISEVILLE	42141	GLASGOW

Point ZIP Code		Enclosing Residential ZIP Code	
ZIP	Post Office Name	ZIP	Post Office Name
42201	ABERDEEN	42261	MORGANTOWN
42216	CLIFTY	42220	ELKTON
42219	DUNBAR	42261	MORGANTOWN
42221	FAIRVIEW	42266	PEMBROKE
42241	HOPKINSVILLE	42240	HOPKINSVILLE
42283	SOUTH UNION	42206	AUBURN
42288	WOODBURY	42261	MORGANTOWN
42302	OWENSBORO	42303	OWENSBORO
42304	OWENSBORO	42301	OWENSBORO
42322	BEECH GROVE	42327	CALHOUN
42332	CLEATON	42330	CENTRAL CITY
42334	CURDSVILLE	42301	OWENSBORO
42356	MAPLE MOUNT	42301	OWENSBORO
42364	PELLVILLE	42348	HAWESVILLE
42370	ROSINE	42349	HORSE BRANCH
42374	SOUTH CARROLLTON	42330	CENTRAL CITY
42375	STANLEY	42301	OWENSBORO
42377	WEST LOUISVILLE	42301	OWENSBORO
42402	BASKETT	42420	HENDERSON
42403	BLACKFORD	42404	CLAY
42419	HENDERSON	42420	HENDERSON
42440	MORTONS GAP	42431	MADISONVILLE
42444	POOLE	42455	SEBREE
42457	SMITH MILLS	42420	HENDERSON
42460	SULLIVAN	42459	STURGIS
42463	WHEATCROFT	42404	CLAY
42502	SOMERSET	42501	SOMERSET
42558	TATEVILLE	42553	SCIENCE HILL
42564	WEST SOMERSET	42503	SOMERSET
42631	MARSHES SIDING	42653	WHITLEY CITY
42702	ELIZABETHTOWN	42701	ELIZABETHTOWN
42719	CAMPBELLSVILLE	42718	CAMPBELLSVILLE
42720	CANE VALLEY	42728	COLUMBIA
42755	LEITCHFIELD	42754	LEITCHFIELD
42758	MANNSVILLE	42718	CAMPBELLSVILLE
42759	MARROWBONE	42717	BURKESVILLE
43005	BLADENSBURG	43080	UTICA
43007	BROADWAY	43040	MARYSVILLE
43010	CATAWBA	43044	MECHANICSBURG
43018	ETNA	43062	PATASKALA
43027	HOMER	43080	UTICA
43030	JACKSONTOWN	43076	THORNVILLE
43032	KILBOURNE	43015	DELAWARE
43033	KIRKERSVILLE	43062	PATASKALA
43036	MAGNETIC SPRINGS	43040	MARYSVILLE
43041	MARYSVILLE	43040	MARYSVILLE
43047	MINGO	43009	CABLE
43048	MOUNT LIBERTY	43011	CENTERBURG
43058	NEWARK	43055	NEWARK
43069	REYNOLDSBURG	43068	REYNOLDSBURG
43070	ROSEWOOD	43318	DE GRAFF
43073	SUMMIT STATION	43062	PATASKALA
43077	UNIONVILLE CENTER	43064	PLAIN CITY
43083	WESTVILLE	43078	URBANA
43086	WESTERVILLE	43081	WESTERVILLE
43093	NEWARK	43055	NEWARK
43101	ADELPHI	43135	LAURELVILLE
43109	BRICE	43110	CANAL WINCHESTER
43111	CARBON HILL	45764	NELSONVILLE
43117	DERBY	43146	ORIENT
43126	HARRISBURG	43146	ORIENT
43127	HAYDENVILLE	45764	NELSONVILLE
43136	LITHOPOLIS	43110	CANAL WINCHESTER
43142	MILLEDGEVILLE	43160	WASHINGTON COURT HOU
43144	MURRAY CITY	45732	GLOUSTER
43151	SEDALIA	43140	LONDON
43156	TARLTON	43135	LAURELVILLE
43157	THURSTON	43105	BALTIMORE
43158	UNION FURNACE	45764	NELSONVILLE
43163	WEST RUSHVILLE	43130	LANCASTER
43194	LOCKBOURNE	43137	LOCKBOURNE
43195	GROVEPORT	43125	GROVEPORT
43199	GROVEPORT	43125	GROVEPORT
43216	COLUMBUS	43215	COLUMBUS
43218	COLUMBUS	43215	COLUMBUS
43226	COLUMBUS	43229	COLUMBUS
43234	COLUMBUS	43235	COLUMBUS
43236	COLUMBUS	43219	COLUMBUS
43251	COLUMBUS	43222	COLUMBUS
43260	COLUMBUS	43215	COLUMBUS
43268	COLUMBUS	43215	COLUMBUS
43270	COLUMBUS	43215	COLUMBUS
43271	COLUMBUS	43215	COLUMBUS
43272	COLUMBUS	43215	COLUMBUS
43279	COLUMBUS	43215	COLUMBUS
43287	COLUMBUS	43215	COLUMBUS
43291	COLUMBUS	43228	COLUMBUS
43301	MARION	43302	MARION
43306	MARION	43302	MARION
43317	CHESTERVILLE	43019	FREDERICKTOWN
43322	GREEN CAMP	43302	MARION
43325	IBERIA	44833	GALION
43330	KIRBY	43351	UPPER SANDUSKY

NONRESIDENTIAL ZIP CODES

OHIO

Point ZIP Code: ZIP	Point ZIP Code: Post Office Name	Enclosing Residential ZIP Code: ZIP	Enclosing Residential ZIP Code: Post Office Name
43336	MIDDLEBURG	43319	EAST LIBERTY
43349	SHAUCK	44813	BELLVILLE
43350	SPARTA	43334	MARENGO
43408	CLAY CENTER	43430	GENOA
43414	DUNBRIDGE	43402	BOWLING GREEN
43433	GYPSUM	43452	PORT CLINTON
43434	HARBOR VIEW	43616	OREGON
43437	JERRY CITY	43413	CYGNET
43439	LACARNE	43452	PORT CLINTON
43441	LEMOYNE	43443	LUCKEY
43446	MIDDLE BASS	43452	PORT CLINTON
43458	ROCKY RIDGE	43449	OAK HARBOR
43463	STONY RIDGE	43551	PERRYSBURG
43467	WEST MILLGROVE	43466	WAYNE
43468	WILLISTON	43412	CURTICE
43505	BLAKESLEE	43518	EDON
43510	COLTON	43532	LIBERTY CENTER
43519	EVANSPORT	43512	DEFIANCE
43520	FARMER	43517	EDGERTON
43523	GRELTON	43534	MC CLURE
43529	HOYTVILLE	43516	DESHLER
43530	JEWELL	43512	DEFIANCE
43531	KUNKLE	43554	PIONEER
43541	MILTON CENTER	43511	CUSTAR
43547	NEAPOLIS	43522	GRAND RAPIDS
43550	OKOLONA	43545	NAPOLEON
43552	PERRYSBURG	43551	PERRYSBURG
43553	PETTISVILLE	43567	WAUSEON
43555	RIDGEVILLE CORNERS	43545	NAPOLEON
43565	TONTOGANY	43402	BOWLING GREEN
43601	TOLEDO	43604	TOLEDO
43603	TOLEDO	43604	TOLEDO
43635	TOLEDO	43615	TOLEDO
43652	TOLEDO	43604	TOLEDO
43654	TOLEDO	43619	NORTHWOOD
43656	TOLEDO	43623	TOLEDO
43657	TOLEDO	43612	TOLEDO
43659	TOLEDO	43604	TOLEDO
43660	TOLEDO	43604	TOLEDO
43661	TOLEDO	43607	TOLEDO
43666	TOLEDO	43604	TOLEDO
43667	TOLEDO	43604	TOLEDO
43681	TOLEDO	43604	TOLEDO
43682	TOLEDO	43604	TOLEDO
43697	TOLEDO	43604	TOLEDO
43699	TOLEDO	43604	TOLEDO
43702	SOUTH ZANESVILLE	43701	SOUTH ZANESVILLE
43711	AVA	43724	CALDWELL
43717	BELLE VALLEY	43724	CALDWELL
43721	BROWNSVILLE	43076	THORNVILLE
43722	BUFFALO	43780	SENECAVILLE
43733	DERWENT	43772	PLEASANT CITY
43735	EAST FULTONHAM	43777	ROSEVILLE
43736	FAIRVIEW	43773	QUAKER CITY
43738	FULTONHAM	43777	ROSEVILLE
43740	GRATIOT	43056	HEATH
43750	KIPLING	43725	CAMBRIDGE
43752	LAINGS	43793	WOODSFIELD
43757	MALAGA	43747	JERUSALEM
43759	MORRISTOWN	43718	BELMONT
43761	MOXAHALA	43730	CORNING
43768	OLD WASHINGTON	43755	LORE CITY
43786	STAFFORD	43754	LEWISVILLE
43789	SYCAMORE VALLEY	45734	GRAYSVILLE
43791	WHITE COTTAGE	43701	SOUTH ZANESVILLE
43803	BAKERSVILLE	43832	NEWCOMERSTOWN
43805	BLISSFIELD	43844	WARSAW
43828	KEENE	43812	COSHOCTON
43836	PLAINFIELD	43812	COSHOCTON
43842	TRINWAY	43821	DRESDEN
43905	BARTON	43912	BRIDGEPORT
43909	BLAINE	43950	SAINT CLAIRSVILLE
43914	CAMERON	43716	BEALLSVILLE
43916	COLERAIN	43912	BRIDGEPORT
43925	EAST SPRINGFIELD	43910	BLOOMINGDALE
43926	EMPIRE	43964	TORONTO
43927	FAIRPOINT	43950	SAINT CLAIRSVILLE
43928	GLENCOE	43950	SAINT CLAIRSVILLE
43931	HANNIBAL	43946	SARDIS
43934	LANSING	43935	MARTINS FERRY
43937	MAYNARD	43912	BRIDGEPORT
43939	MOUNT PLEASANT	43917	DILLONVALE
43940	NEFFS	43906	BELLAIRE
43941	PINEY FORK	43917	DILLONVALE
43948	SMITHFIELD	43917	DILLONVALE
43951	LAFFERTY	43977	FLUSHING
43961	STRATTON	43964	TORONTO
43962	SUMMITVILLE	43945	SALINEVILLE
43967	WARNOCK	43718	BELMONT
43970	WOLF RUN	43903	AMSTERDAM
43972	BANNOCK	43950	SAINT CLAIRSVILLE
43974	HARRISVILLE	43907	CADIZ
43981	NEW ATHENS	43907	CADIZ
43984	NEW RUMLEY	43986	JEWETT
43985	HOLLOWAY	43977	FLUSHING
44005	ASHTABULA	44004	ASHTABULA
44033	EAST CLARIDON	44024	CHARDON
44036	ELYRIA	44035	ELYRIA
44045	GRAND RIVER	44077	PAINESVILLE
44049	KIPTON	44090	WELLINGTON
44061	MENTOR	44060	MENTOR
44068	NORTH KINGSVILLE	44004	ASHTABULA
44073	NOVELTY	44072	NOVELTY
44080	PARKMAN	44021	BURTON
44088	UNIONVILLE	44041	GENEVA
44096	WILLOUGHBY	44094	WILLOUGHBY
44097	EASTLAKE	44095	EASTLAKE
44101	CLEVELAND	44115	CLEVELAND
44181	CLEVELAND	44135	CLEVELAND
44188	CLEVELAND	44115	CLEVELAND
44190	CLEVELAND	44106	CLEVELAND
44191	CLEVELAND	44113	CLEVELAND
44192	CLEVELAND	44115	CLEVELAND
44193	CLEVELAND	44113	CLEVELAND
44194	CLEVELAND	44114	CLEVELAND
44195	CLEVELAND	44106	CLEVELAND
44198	CLEVELAND	44115	CLEVELAND
44199	CLEVELAND	44114	CLEVELAND
44210	BATH	44333	AKRON
44211	BRADY LAKE	44240	KENT
44222	CUYAHOGA FALLS	44221	CUYAHOGA FALLS
44232	GREEN	44720	CANTON
44237	HUDSON	44236	HUDSON
44242	KENT	44240	KENT
44250	LAKEMORE	44312	AKRON
44251	WESTFIELD CENTER	44273	SEVILLE
44258	MEDINA	44256	MEDINA
44265	RANDOLPH	44201	ATWATER
44274	SHARON CENTER	44281	WADSWORTH
44282	WADSWORTH	44281	WADSWORTH
44285	WAYLAND	44266	RAVENNA
44309	AKRON	44311	AKRON
44315	AKRON	44312	AKRON
44316	AKRON	44305	AKRON
44317	AKRON	44301	AKRON
44322	AKRON	44320	AKRON
44326	AKRON	44308	AKRON
44328	AKRON	44308	AKRON
44334	FAIRLAWN	44312	AKRON
44372	AKRON	44311	AKRON
44393	AKRON	44310	AKRON
44396	AKRON	44311	AKRON
44398	AKRON	44311	AKRON
44399	AKRON	44308	AKRON
44415	ELKTON	44432	LISBON
44416	ELLSWORTH	44451	NORTH JACKSON
44422	GREENFORD	44406	CANFIELD
44424	HARTFORD	44418	FOWLER
44439	MESOPOTAMIA	44062	MIDDLEFIELD
44453	ORANGEVILLE	44404	BURGHILL
44482	WARREN	44481	WARREN
44486	WARREN	44481	WARREN
44492	WEST POINT	44432	LISBON
44493	WINONA	44423	HANOVERTON
44501	YOUNGSTOWN	44503	YOUNGSTOWN
44513	YOUNGSTOWN	44512	YOUNGSTOWN
44607	AUGUSTA	44427	KENSINGTON
44610	BERLIN	44654	MILLERSBURG
44617	CHARM	43804	BALTIC
44619	DAMASCUS	44460	SALEM
44630	GREENTOWN	44720	CANTON
44631	HARLEM SPRINGS	44615	CARROLLTON
44636	KIDRON	44606	APPLE CREEK
44639	LEESVILLE	44695	BOWERSTON
44640	LIMAVILLE	44601	ALLIANCE
44648	MASSILLON	44646	MASSILLON
44650	MAXIMO	44601	ALLIANCE
44652	MIDDLEBRANCH	44721	CANTON
44653	MIDVALE	44663	NEW PHILADELPHIA
44659	MOUNT EATON	44624	DUNDEE
44660	MOUNT HOPE	44654	MILLERSBURG
44661	NASHVILLE	44638	LAKEVILLE
44665	NORTH GEORGETOWN	44609	BELOIT
44670	ROBERTSVILLE	44669	PARIS
44671	SANDYVILLE	44656	MINERAL CITY
44678	SOMERDALE	44622	DOVER
44679	STILLWATER	44683	UHRICHSVILLE
44682	TUSCARAWAS	44629	GNADENHUTTEN
44687	WALNUT CREEK	44654	MILLERSBURG
44690	WINESBURG	44624	DUNDEE
44693	DEERSVILLE	44699	TIPPECANOE
44697	ZOAR	44612	BOLIVAR
44701	CANTON	44709	CANTON
44711	CANTON	44709	CANTON
44735	CANTON	44720	CANTON
44750	CANTON	44710	CANTON

NONRESIDENTIAL ZIP CODES

OHIO

Point ZIP Code ZIP	Point ZIP Code Post Office Name	Enclosing Residential ZIP Code ZIP	Enclosing Residential ZIP Code Post Office Name
44767	CANTON	44720	CANTON
44799	CANTON	44709	CANTON
44809	BASCOM	44883	TIFFIN
44815	BETTSVILLE	44841	KANSAS
44816	BIRMINGHAM	44889	WAKEMAN
44825	CHATFIELD	44818	BLOOMVILLE
44828	FLAT ROCK	44811	BELLEVUE
44838	HAYESVILLE	44805	ASHLAND
44845	MELMORE	44882	SYCAMORE
44848	NANKIN	44805	ASHLAND
44850	NEW HAVEN	44865	PLYMOUTH
44856	NORTH ROBINSON	44820	BUCYRUS
44860	OCEOLA	44849	NEVADA
44861	OLD FORT	44883	TIFFIN
44862	ONTARIO	44902	MANSFIELD
44871	SANDUSKY	44870	SANDUSKY
44874	SAVANNAH	44805	ASHLAND
44881	SULPHUR SPRINGS	44820	BUCYRUS
44888	WILLARD	44890	WILLARD
44901	MANSFIELD	44902	MANSFIELD
45004	COLLINSVILLE	45013	HAMILTON
45012	HAMILTON	45011	HAMILTON
45018	FAIRFIELD	45011	HAMILTON
45025	HAMILTON	45011	HAMILTON
45026	HAMILTON	45011	HAMILTON
45032	HARVEYSBURG	45068	WAYNESVILLE
45033	HOOVEN	45002	CLEVES
45041	MIAMITOWN	45002	CLEVES
45043	MIDDLETOWN	45042	MIDDLETOWN
45051	MOUNT SAINT JOSEPH	45233	CINCINNATI
45055	OVERPECK	45011	HAMILTON
45061	ROSS	45013	HAMILTON
45062	SEVEN MILE	45011	HAMILTON
45063	SHANDON	45013	HAMILTON
45070	WEST ELKTON	45064	SOMERVILLE
45071	WEST CHESTER	45069	WEST CHESTER
45105	BENTONVILLE	45144	MANCHESTER
45110	BUFORD	45171	SARDINIA
45112	CHILO	45120	FELICITY
45114	CUBA	45177	WILMINGTON
45115	DECATUR	45168	RUSSELLVILLE
45119	FEESBURG	45130	HAMERSVILLE
45131	HIGGINSPORT	45121	GEORGETOWN
45132	HIGHLAND	45135	LEESBURG
45138	LEES CREEK	45169	SABINA
45145	MARATHON	45176	WILLIAMSBURG
45147	MIAMIVILLE	45140	LOVELAND
45155	MOWRYSTOWN	45133	HILLSBORO
45156	NEVILLE	45153	MOSCOW
45158	NEWTONSVILLE	45122	GOSHEN
45164	PORT WILLIAM	45177	WILMINGTON
45166	REESVILLE	45169	SABINA
45172	SINKING SPRING	45133	HILLSBORO
45201	CINCINNATI	45203	CINCINNATI
45221	CINCINNATI	45219	CINCINNATI
45222	CINCINNATI	45212	CINCINNATI
45234	CINCINNATI	45214	CINCINNATI
45235	CINCINNATI	45241	CINCINNATI
45250	CINCINNATI	45214	CINCINNATI
45253	CINCINNATI	45251	CINCINNATI
45254	CINCINNATI	45255	CINCINNATI
45258	CINCINNATI	45248	CINCINNATI
45262	CINCINNATI	45241	CINCINNATI
45263	CINCINNATI	45202	CINCINNATI
45264	CINCINNATI	45203	CINCINNATI
45267	CINCINNATI	45219	CINCINNATI
45268	CINCINNATI	45220	CINCINNATI
45269	CINCINNATI	45225	CINCINNATI
45270	CINCINNATI	45203	CINCINNATI
45271	CINCINNATI	45225	CINCINNATI
45273	CINCINNATI	45214	CINCINNATI
45274	CINCINNATI	45225	CINCINNATI
45277	CINCINNATI	41015	LATONIA
45280	CINCINNATI	45214	CINCINNATI
45296	CINCINNATI	45203	CINCINNATI
45298	CINCINNATI	41011	COVINGTON
45299	CINCINNATI	45202	CINCINNATI
45301	ALPHA	45434	DAYTON
45307	BOWERSVILLE	45335	JAMESTOWN
45310	BURKETTSVILLE	45846	FORT RECOVERY
45316	CLIFTON	45387	YELLOW SPRINGS
45319	DONNELSVILLE	45344	NEW CARLISLE
45328	GETTYSBURG	45308	BRADFORD
45330	GRATIS	45381	WEST ALEXANDRIA
45336	KETTLERSVILLE	45306	BOTKINS
45343	MIAMISBURG	45342	MIAMISBURG
45349	NORTH HAMPTON	45502	SPRINGFIELD
45350	NORTH STAR	45348	NEW WESTON
45351	OSGOOD	45388	YORKSHIRE
45352	PALESTINE	45331	GREENVILLE
45353	PEMBERTON	45365	SIDNEY
45354	PHILLIPSBURG	45309	BROOKVILLE
45358	PITSBURG	45304	ARCANUM

INDIANA

Point ZIP Code ZIP	Point ZIP Code Post Office Name	Enclosing Residential ZIP Code ZIP	Enclosing Residential ZIP Code Post Office Name
45360	PORT JEFFERSON	45365	SIDNEY
45361	POTSDAM	45337	LAURA
45367	SIDNEY	45365	SIDNEY
45372	TREMONT CITY	45502	SPRINGFIELD
45374	TROY	45373	TROY
45378	VERONA	45338	LEWISBURG
45384	WILBERFORCE	45385	XENIA
45389	CHRISTIANSBURG	45312	CASSTOWN
45400	DAYTON	45402	DAYTON
45401	DAYTON	45410	DAYTON
45412	DAYTON	45402	DAYTON
45413	DAYTON	45414	DAYTON
45422	DAYTON	45402	DAYTON
45423	DAYTON	45402	DAYTON
45428	DAYTON	45417	DAYTON
45435	DAYTON	45324	FAIRBORN
45437	DAYTON	45431	DAYTON
45441	DAYTON	45459	DAYTON
45448	DAYTON	45342	MIAMISBURG
45454	DAYTON	45459	DAYTON
45463	DAYTON	45402	DAYTON
45470	DAYTON	45342	MIAMISBURG
45475	DAYTON	45459	DAYTON
45479	DAYTON	45409	DAYTON
45481	DAYTON	45430	DAYTON
45490	DAYTON	45377	VANDALIA
45501	SPRINGFIELD	45502	SPRINGFIELD
45617	BOURNEVILLE	45601	CHILLICOTHE
45618	CHERRY FORK	45697	WINCHESTER
45621	COALTON	45692	WELLSTON
45624	CYNTHIANA	45612	BAINBRIDGE
45630	FRIENDSHIP	45663	WEST PORTSMOUTH
45633	HALLSVILLE	45644	KINGSTON
45636	HAVERHILL	45629	FRANKLIN FURNACE
45642	JASPER	45661	PIKETON
45643	KERR	45614	BIDWELL
45674	RIO GRANDE	45631	GALLIPOLIS
45677	SCIOTO FURNACE	45694	WHEELERSBURG
45683	STOCKDALE	45613	BEAVER
45687	WAKEFIELD	45661	PIKETON
45698	ZALESKI	45651	MC ARTHUR
45699	LUCASVILLE	45648	LUCASVILLE
45712	BARLOW	45784	VINCENT
45713	BARTLETT	45724	CUTLER
45716	BUCHTEL	45764	NELSONVILLE
45719	CHAUNCEY	45761	MILLFIELD
45720	CHESTER	45743	LONG BOTTOM
45721	COAL RUN	45744	LOWELL
45739	HOCKINGPORT	45723	COOLVILLE
45740	JACKSONVILLE	45732	GLOUSTER
45777	SHARPSBURG	45711	AMESVILLE
45779	SYRACUSE	45771	RACINE
45782	TRIMBLE	45732	GLOUSTER
45783	TUPPERS PLAINS	45723	COOLVILLE
45787	WATERTOWN	45786	WATERFORD
45802	LIMA	45801	LIMA
45809	GOMER	45807	LIMA
45815	BELMORE	45856	LEIPSIC
45816	BENTON RIDGE	45840	FINDLAY
45819	BUCKLAND	45895	WAPAKONETA
45820	CAIRO	45807	LIMA
45826	CHICKASAW	45822	CELINA
45837	DUPONT	45827	CLOVERDALE
45838	ELGIN	45894	VENEDOCIA
45839	FINDLAY	45840	FINDLAY
45848	GLANDORF	45875	OTTAWA
45853	KALIDA	45844	FORT JENNINGS
45854	LAFAYETTE	45801	LIMA
45855	LATTY	45879	PAULDING
45859	MC GUFFEY	45812	ALGER
45861	MELROSE	45873	OAKWOOD
45864	MILLER CITY	45856	LEIPSIC
45866	MONTEZUMA	45822	CELINA
45870	NEW HAMPSHIRE	45895	WAPAKONETA
45876	OTTOVILLE	45844	FORT JENNINGS
45884	SAINT JOHNS	45895	WAPAKONETA
45888	UNIOPOLIS	45895	WAPAKONETA
45893	VAUGHNSVILLE	45830	COLUMBUS GROVE
45897	WILLIAMSTOWN	45843	FOREST
45899	WREN	45874	OHIO CITY
45999	CINCINNATI	41011	COVINGTON
46014	ANDERSON	46011	ANDERSON
46015	ANDERSON	46016	ANDERSON
46018	ANDERSON	46011	ANDERSON
46045	GOLDSMITH	46072	TIPTON
46047	HOBBS	46072	TIPTON
46061	NOBLESVILLE	46060	NOBLESVILLE
46063	ORESTES	46001	ALEXANDRIA
46067	SEDALIA	46041	FRANKFORT
46082	CARMEL	46032	CARMEL
46085	FISHERS	46038	FISHERS
46102	ADVANCE	46147	JAMESTOWN
46103	AMO	46121	COATESVILLE

INDIANA

Point ZIP Code ZIP	Point ZIP Code Post Office Name	Enclosing Residential ZIP Code ZIP	Enclosing Residential ZIP Code Post Office Name
46111	BROOKLYN	46158	MOORESVILLE
46125	EMINENCE	47456	QUINCY
46129	FINLY	46130	FOUNTAINTOWN
46144	GWYNNEVILLE	46161	MORRISTOWN
46146	HOMER	46150	MANILLA
46154	MAXWELL	46140	GREENFIELD
46155	MAYS	46148	KNIGHTSTOWN
46170	PUTNAMVILLE	46135	GREENCASTLE
46183	WEST NEWTON	46113	CAMBY
46206	INDIANAPOLIS	46225	INDIANAPOLIS
46207	INDIANAPOLIS	46225	INDIANAPOLIS
46209	INDIANAPOLIS	46225	INDIANAPOLIS
46211	INDIANAPOLIS	46268	INDIANAPOLIS
46230	INDIANAPOLIS	46220	INDIANAPOLIS
46242	INDIANAPOLIS	46241	INDIANAPOLIS
46244	INDIANAPOLIS	46204	INDIANAPOLIS
46247	INDIANAPOLIS	46227	INDIANAPOLIS
46249	INDIANAPOLIS	46216	INDIANAPOLIS
46251	INDIANAPOLIS	46241	INDIANAPOLIS
46253	INDIANAPOLIS	46254	INDIANAPOLIS
46255	INDIANAPOLIS	46204	INDIANAPOLIS
46262	INDIANAPOLIS	46204	INDIANAPOLIS
46266	INDIANAPOLIS	46204	INDIANAPOLIS
46274	INDIANAPOLIS	46268	INDIANAPOLIS
46275	INDIANAPOLIS	46268	INDIANAPOLIS
46277	INDIANAPOLIS	46204	INDIANAPOLIS
46282	INDIANAPOLIS	46204	INDIANAPOLIS
46283	INDIANAPOLIS	46225	INDIANAPOLIS
46285	INDIANAPOLIS	46221	INDIANAPOLIS
46291	INDIANAPOLIS	46219	INDIANAPOLIS
46295	INDIANAPOLIS	46225	INDIANAPOLIS
46296	INDIANAPOLIS	46225	INDIANAPOLIS
46298	INDIANAPOLIS	46268	INDIANAPOLIS
46301	BEVERLY SHORES	46304	CHESTERTON
46302	BOONE GROVE	46385	VALPARAISO
46308	CROWN POINT	46307	CROWN POINT
46325	HAMMOND	46320	HAMMOND
46345	KINGSBURY	46350	LA PORTE
46346	KINGSFORD HEIGHTS	46382	UNION MILLS
46352	LA PORTE	46350	LA PORTE
46355	LEROY	46307	CROWN POINT
46361	MICHIGAN CITY	46360	MICHIGAN CITY
46372	ROSELAWN	46310	DEMOTTE
46376	SCHNEIDER	46356	LOWELL
46377	SHELBY	46356	LOWELL
46379	SUMAVA RESORTS	46349	LAKE VILLAGE
46380	TEFFT	46392	WHEATFIELD
46381	THAYER	47943	FAIR OAKS
46384	VALPARAISO	46383	VALPARAISO
46393	WHEELER	46342	HOBART
46401	GARY	46407	GARY
46411	MERRILLVILLE	46410	MERRILLVILLE
46502	ATWOOD	46580	WARSAW
46513	DONALDSON	46563	PLYMOUTH
46515	ELKHART	46516	ELKHART
46527	GOSHEN	46526	GOSHEN
46537	LAPAZ	46563	PLYMOUTH
46546	MISHAWAKA	46544	MISHAWAKA
46572	TYNER	46563	PLYMOUTH
46581	WARSAW	46580	WARSAW
46595	WYATT	46506	BREMEN
46624	SOUTH BEND	46601	SOUTH BEND
46626	SOUTH BEND	46601	SOUTH BEND
46634	SOUTH BEND	46601	SOUTH BEND
46660	SOUTH BEND	46615	SOUTH BEND
46680	SOUTH BEND	46614	SOUTH BEND
46704	ARCOLA	46818	FORT WAYNE
46713	BIPPUS	46750	HUNTINGTON
46769	BERNE	46711	BERNE
46771	MONGO	46746	HOWE
46778	PETROLEUM	46759	KEYSTONE
46780	PLEASANT MILLS	46733	DECATUR
46782	PREBLE	46733	DECATUR
46786	SOUTH MILFORD	46795	WOLCOTTVILLE
46789	STROH	46747	HUDSON
46796	WOLFLAKE	46760	KIMMELL
46799	ZANESVILLE	46798	YODER
46801	FORT WAYNE	46802	FORT WAYNE
46850	FORT WAYNE	46802	FORT WAYNE
46851	FORT WAYNE	46802	FORT WAYNE
46852	FORT WAYNE	46802	FORT WAYNE
46853	FORT WAYNE	46802	FORT WAYNE
46854	FORT WAYNE	46802	FORT WAYNE
46855	FORT WAYNE	46802	FORT WAYNE
46856	FORT WAYNE	46802	FORT WAYNE
46857	FORT WAYNE	46802	FORT WAYNE
46858	FORT WAYNE	46802	FORT WAYNE
46859	FORT WAYNE	46802	FORT WAYNE
46860	FORT WAYNE	46802	FORT WAYNE
46861	FORT WAYNE	46802	FORT WAYNE
46862	FORT WAYNE	46802	FORT WAYNE
46863	FORT WAYNE	46802	FORT WAYNE
46864	FORT WAYNE	46802	FORT WAYNE

Point ZIP Code ZIP	Point ZIP Code Post Office Name	Enclosing Residential ZIP Code ZIP	Enclosing Residential ZIP Code Post Office Name
46865	FORT WAYNE	46802	FORT WAYNE
46866	FORT WAYNE	46802	FORT WAYNE
46867	FORT WAYNE	46802	FORT WAYNE
46868	FORT WAYNE	46802	FORT WAYNE
46869	FORT WAYNE	46802	FORT WAYNE
46885	FORT WAYNE	46835	FORT WAYNE
46895	FORT WAYNE	46805	FORT WAYNE
46896	FORT WAYNE	46806	FORT WAYNE
46897	FORT WAYNE	46819	FORT WAYNE
46898	FORT WAYNE	46808	FORT WAYNE
46899	FORT WAYNE	46809	FORT WAYNE
46903	KOKOMO	46902	KOKOMO
46904	KOKOMO	46902	KOKOMO
46912	ATHENS	46975	ROCHESTER
46915	BURLINGTON	46920	CUTLER
46916	BURROWS	46923	DELPHI
46921	DEEDSVILLE	46951	MACY
46922	DELONG	46975	ROCHESTER
46930	FOWLERTON	46928	FAIRMOUNT
46931	FULTON	46975	ROCHESTER
46937	HEMLOCK	46902	KOKOMO
46942	LAKE CICOTT	46947	LOGANSPORT
46943	LAKETON	46962	NORTH MANCHESTER
46945	LEITERS FORD	46975	ROCHESTER
46946	LIBERTY MILLS	46962	NORTH MANCHESTER
46957	MATTHEWS	46989	UPLAND
46958	MEXICO	46970	PERU
46959	MIAMI	46914	BUNKER HILL
46961	NEW WAVERLY	46947	LOGANSPORT
46965	OAKFORD	46902	KOKOMO
46967	ONWARD	46994	WALTON
46968	ORA	46960	MONTEREY
46971	GRISSOM ARB	46970	PERU
46977	ROCKFIELD	46923	DELPHI
46980	SERVIA	46962	NORTH MANCHESTER
46984	SOMERSET	46940	LA FONTAINE
46987	SWEETSER	46952	MARION
46995	WEST MIDDLETON	46979	RUSSIAVILLE
46998	YOUNG AMERICA	46932	GALVESTON
47019	EAST ENTERPRISE	47040	RISING SUN
47021	FRIENDSHIP	47042	VERSAILLES
47033	MORRIS	47006	BATESVILLE
47034	NAPOLEON	47037	OSGOOD
47035	NEW TRENTON	47060	WEST HARRISON
47039	PIERCEVILLE	47031	MILAN
47104	BETHLEHEM	47162	NEW WASHINGTON
47107	BRADFORD	47164	PALMYRA
47131	JEFFERSONVILLE	47130	JEFFERSONVILLE
47139	LITTLE YORK	47170	SCOTTSBURG
47146	MOUNT SAINT FRANCIS	47119	FLOYDS KNOBS
47151	NEW ALBANY	47150	NEW ALBANY
47190	JEFFERSONVILLE	47130	JEFFERSONVILLE
47199	JEFFERSONVILLE	47130	JEFFERSONVILLE
47202	COLUMBUS	47201	COLUMBUS
47225	CLARKSBURG	47240	GREENSBURG
47226	CLIFFORD	47203	COLUMBUS
47228	CORTLAND	47274	SEYMOUR
47245	HAYDEN	47265	NORTH VERNON
47247	JONESVILLE	47201	COLUMBUS
47249	KURTZ	47264	NORMAN
47261	MILLHOUSEN	47240	GREENSBURG
47263	NEW POINT	47240	GREENSBURG
47280	TAYLORSVILLE	47203	COLUMBUS
47307	MUNCIE	47302	MUNCIE
47308	MUNCIE	47302	MUNCIE
47322	BENTONVILLE	47331	CONNERSVILLE
47324	BOSTON	47374	RICHMOND
47335	DUBLIN	47327	CAMBRIDGE CITY
47337	DUNREITH	47385	SPICELAND
47344	GREENSBORO	46148	KNIGHTSTOWN
47351	KENNARD	47384	SHIRLEY
47361	MOUNT SUMMIT	47362	NEW CASTLE
47366	NEW LISBON	47387	STRAUGHN
47367	OAKVILLE	47302	MUNCIE
47370	PERSHING	47327	CAMBRIDGE CITY
47375	RICHMOND	47374	RICHMOND
47388	SULPHUR SPRINGS	47356	MIDDLETOWN
47402	BLOOMINGTON	47401	BLOOMINGTON
47407	BLOOMINGTON	47468	UNIONVILLE
47420	AVOCA	47462	SPRINGVILLE
47426	CLEAR CREEK	47403	BLOOMINGTON
47430	FORT RITNER	47421	BEDFORD
47434	HARRODSBURG	47462	SPRINGVILLE
47435	HELMSBURG	46160	MORGANTOWN
47437	HURON	47446	MITCHELL
47439	KOLEEN	47453	OWENSBURG
47445	MIDLAND	47441	LINTON
47455	PATRICKSBURG	47833	BOWLING GREEN
47457	SCOTLAND	47424	BLOOMFIELD
47458	SMITHVILLE	47401	BLOOMINGTON
47463	STANFORD	47403	BLOOMINGTON
47464	STINESVILLE	47429	ELLETTSVILLE
47467	TUNNELTON	47421	BEDFORD

INDIANA **MICHIGAN**

Point ZIP Code		Enclosing Residential ZIP Code		Point ZIP Code		Enclosing Residential ZIP Code	
ZIP	Post Office Name	ZIP	Post Office Name	ZIP	Post Office Name	ZIP	Post Office Name
47535	FREELANDVILLE	47561	OAKTOWN	48068	ROYAL OAK	48067	ROYAL OAK
47536	FULDA	47577	SAINT MEINRAD	48086	SOUTHFIELD	48033	SOUTHFIELD
47545	IRELAND	47546	JASPER	48090	WARREN	48092	WARREN
47547	JASPER	47546	JASPER	48099	TROY	48083	TROY
47549	JASPER	47546	JASPER	48106	ANN ARBOR	48103	ANN ARBOR
47573	RAGSDALE	47512	BICKNELL	48107	ANN ARBOR	48104	ANN ARBOR
47584	SPURGEON	47660	OAKLAND CITY	48110	AZALIA	48159	MAYBEE
47596	WESTPHALIA	47578	SANDBORN	48112	BELLEVILLE	48111	BELLEVILLE
47614	FOLSOMVILLE	47601	BOONVILLE	48113	ANN ARBOR	48103	ANN ARBOR
47617	HATFIELD	47634	RICHLAND	48115	BRIDGEWATER	48176	SALINE
47618	INGLEFIELD	47725	EVANSVILLE	48121	DEARBORN	48120	DEARBORN
47629	NEWBURGH	47630	NEWBURGH	48123	DEARBORN	48124	DEARBORN
47654	MACKEY	47613	ELBERFELD	48136	GARDEN CITY	48186	WESTLAND
47683	SOMERVILLE	47613	ELBERFELD	48139	HAMBURG	48189	WHITMORE LAKE
47701	EVANSVILLE	47708	EVANSVILLE	48143	LAKELAND	48169	PINCKNEY
47702	EVANSVILLE	47708	EVANSVILLE	48151	LIVONIA	48150	LIVONIA
47703	EVANSVILLE	47708	EVANSVILLE	48153	LIVONIA	48150	LIVONIA
47704	EVANSVILLE	47708	EVANSVILLE	48175	SALEM	48168	NORTHVILLE
47705	EVANSVILLE	47708	EVANSVILLE	48177	SAMARIA	48182	TEMPERANCE
47706	EVANSVILLE	47708	EVANSVILLE	48190	WHITTAKER	48160	MILAN
47716	EVANSVILLE	47715	EVANSVILLE	48222	DETROIT	48216	DETROIT
47719	EVANSVILLE	47712	EVANSVILLE	48231	DETROIT	48226	DETROIT
47721	EVANSVILLE	47712	EVANSVILLE	48232	DETROIT	48226	DETROIT
47724	EVANSVILLE	47710	EVANSVILLE	48233	DETROIT	48226	DETROIT
47727	EVANSVILLE	47711	EVANSVILLE	48243	DETROIT	48226	DETROIT
47728	EVANSVILLE	47714	EVANSVILLE	48244	DETROIT	48226	DETROIT
47730	EVANSVILLE	47708	EVANSVILLE	48255	DETROIT	48226	DETROIT
47731	EVANSVILLE	47708	EVANSVILLE	48260	DETROIT	48226	DETROIT
47732	EVANSVILLE	47708	EVANSVILLE	48264	DETROIT	48226	DETROIT
47733	EVANSVILLE	47708	EVANSVILLE	48265	DETROIT	48226	DETROIT
47734	EVANSVILLE	47708	EVANSVILLE	48266	DETROIT	48207	DETROIT
47735	EVANSVILLE	47708	EVANSVILLE	48267	DETROIT	48226	DETROIT
47736	EVANSVILLE	47708	EVANSVILLE	48268	DETROIT	48226	DETROIT
47737	EVANSVILLE	47708	EVANSVILLE	48269	DETROIT	48226	DETROIT
47740	EVANSVILLE	47710	EVANSVILLE	48272	DETROIT	48226	DETROIT
47744	EVANSVILLE	47712	EVANSVILLE	48275	DETROIT	48226	DETROIT
47747	EVANSVILLE	47710	EVANSVILLE	48277	DETROIT	48226	DETROIT
47750	EVANSVILLE	47714	EVANSVILLE	48278	DETROIT	48226	DETROIT
47801	TERRE HAUTE	47807	TERRE HAUTE	48279	DETROIT	48226	DETROIT
47808	TERRE HAUTE	47802	TERRE HAUTE	48288	DETROIT	48212	HAMTRAMCK
47811	TERRE HAUTE	47804	TERRE HAUTE	48303	BLOOMFIELD HILLS	48304	BLOOMFIELD HILLS
47812	TERRE HAUTE	47804	TERRE HAUTE	48308	ROCHESTER	48307	ROCHESTER
47830	BELLMORE	47872	ROCKVILLE	48311	STERLING HEIGHTS	48312	STERLING HEIGHTS
47831	BLANFORD	47842	CLINTON	48318	UTICA	48316	UTICA
47845	COALMONT	47438	JASONVILLE	48321	AUBURN HILLS	48326	AUBURN HILLS
47851	FONTANET	47834	BRAZIL	48325	WEST BLOOMFIELD	48322	WEST BLOOMFIELD
47852	GRAYSVILLE	47882	SULLIVAN	48330	DRAYTON PLAINS	48329	WATERFORD
47853	HARMONY	47834	BRAZIL	48332	FARMINGTON	48336	FARMINGTON
47855	HYMERA	47879	SHELBURN	48333	FARMINGTON	48334	FARMINGTON
47857	KNIGHTSVILLE	47834	BRAZIL	48343	PONTIAC	48341	PONTIAC
47860	MECCA	47872	ROCKVILLE	48347	CLARKSTON	48346	CLARKSTON
47863	NEW GOSHEN	47885	WEST TERRE HAUTE	48361	LAKE ORION	48362	LAKE ORION
47865	PAXTON	47838	CARLISLE	48366	LAKEVILLE	48367	LEONARD
47869	PRAIRIE CREEK	47802	TERRE HAUTE	48376	NOVI	48375	NOVI
47870	PRAIRIETON	47802	TERRE HAUTE	48387	UNION LAKE	48324	WEST BLOOMFIELD
47871	RILEY	47802	TERRE HAUTE	48391	WALLED LAKE	48390	WALLED LAKE
47875	SAINT BERNICE	47842	CLINTON	48397	WARREN	48092	WARREN
47876	SAINT MARY OF THE WO	47885	WEST TERRE HAUTE	48410	ARGYLE	48472	SNOVER
47878	SEELYVILLE	47803	TERRE HAUTE	48411	ATLAS	48439	GRAND BLANC
47880	SHEPARDSVILLE	47885	WEST TERRE HAUTE	48434	FORESTVILLE	48456	MINDEN CITY
47881	STAUNTON	47834	BRAZIL	48437	GENESEE	48458	MOUNT MORRIS
47884	UNIVERSAL	47842	CLINTON	48440	HADLEY	48455	METAMORA
47902	LAFAYETTE	47905	LAFAYETTE	48476	VERNON	48429	DURAND
47903	LAFAYETTE	47905	LAFAYETTE	48480	GRAND BLANC	48439	GRAND BLANC
47916	ALAMO	47933	CRAWFORDSVILLE	48501	FLINT	48503	FLINT
47924	BUCK CREEK	47905	LAFAYETTE	48531	FLINT	48504	FLINT
47925	BUFFALO	47960	MONTICELLO	48550	FLINT	48505	FLINT
47934	CRAWFORDSVILLE	47933	CRAWFORDSVILLE	48551	FLINT	48507	FLINT
47935	CRAWFORDSVILLE	47933	CRAWFORDSVILLE	48552	FLINT	48507	FLINT
47936	CRAWFORDSVILLE	47933	CRAWFORDSVILLE	48553	FLINT	48507	FLINT
47937	CRAWFORDSVILLE	47933	CRAWFORDSVILLE	48554	FLINT	48473	SWARTZ CREEK
47938	CRAWFORDSVILLE	47933	CRAWFORDSVILLE	48555	FLINT	48504	FLINT
47939	CRAWFORDSVILLE	47933	CRAWFORDSVILLE	48556	FLINT	48506	FLINT
47941	DAYTON	47905	LAFAYETTE	48557	FLINT	48507	FLINT
47958	MELLOTT	47987	VEEDERSBURG	48605	SAGINAW	48601	SAGINAW
47962	MONTMORENCI	47906	WEST LAFAYETTE	48606	SAGINAW	48607	SAGINAW
47964	MOUNT AYR	47963	MOROCCO	48608	SAGINAW	48603	SAGINAW
47965	NEW MARKET	47933	CRAWFORDSVILLE	48620	EDENVILLE	48628	HOPE
47966	NEWPORT	47928	CAYUGA	48627	HIGGINS LAKE	48653	ROSCOMMON
47969	NEWTOWN	47918	ATTICA	48630	HOUGHTON LAKE HEIGHT	48629	HOUGHTON LAKE
47982	STATE LINE	47932	COVINGTON	48633	LAKE GEORGE	48632	LAKE
47983	STOCKWELL	47909	LAFAYETTE	48641	MIDLAND	48640	MIDLAND
47984	TALBOT	47944	FOWLER	48663	SAGINAW	48603	SAGINAW
47986	TEMPLETON	47944	FOWLER	48667	MIDLAND	48640	MIDLAND
47988	WALLACE	47949	HILLSBORO	48670	MIDLAND	48640	MIDLAND
47996	WEST LAFAYETTE	47906	WEST LAFAYETTE	48674	MIDLAND	48642	MIDLAND
47997	YEOMAN	46923	DELPHI	48686	MIDLAND	48640	MIDLAND
48004	ANCHORVILLE	48023	FAIR HAVEN	48707	BAY CITY	48708	BAY CITY
48007	TROY	48083	TROY	48724	CARROLLTON	48604	SAGINAW
48012	BIRMINGHAM	48009	BIRMINGHAM	48736	GILFORD	48757	REESE
48037	SOUTHFIELD	48033	SOUTHFIELD	48758	RICHVILLE	48768	VASSAR
48046	MOUNT CLEMENS	48043	MOUNT CLEMENS	48764	TAWAS CITY	48763	TAWAS CITY
48061	PORT HURON	48060	PORT HURON	48769	TUSCOLA	48768	VASSAR

NONRESIDENTIAL ZIP CODES

MICHIGAN

IOWA

Point ZIP Code		Enclosing Residential ZIP Code	
ZIP	Post Office Name	ZIP	Post Office Name
48787	FRANKENMUTH	48734	FRANKENMUTH
48802	ALMA	48801	ALMA
48804	MOUNT PLEASANT	48858	MOUNT PLEASANT
48805	OKEMOS	48864	OKEMOS
48812	CEDAR LAKE	48891	VESTABURG
48816	COHOCTAH	48855	HOWELL
48826	EAST LANSING	48823	EAST LANSING
48830	ELM HALL	48877	RIVERDALE
48833	EUREKA	48879	SAINT JOHNS
48844	HOWELL	48843	HOWELL
48852	MCBRIDES	48829	EDMORE
48853	MAPLE RAPIDS	48879	SAINT JOHNS
48859	MOUNT PLEASANT	48858	MOUNT PLEASANT
48862	NORTH STAR	48847	ITHACA
48863	OAK GROVE	48855	HOWELL
48870	PALO	48834	FENWICK
48874	POMPEII	48806	ASHLEY
48882	SHAFTSBURG	48872	PERRY
48887	SMYRNA	48809	BELDING
48896	WINN	48858	MOUNT PLEASANT
48901	LANSING	48910	LANSING
48908	LANSING	48917	LANSING
48909	LANSING	48910	LANSING
48913	LANSING	48917	LANSING
48916	LANSING	48911	LANSING
48918	LANSING	48917	LANSING
48919	LANSING	48933	LANSING
48921	LANSING	48933	LANSING
48922	LANSING	48933	LANSING
48924	LANSING	48910	LANSING
48929	LANSING	48933	LANSING
48930	LANSING	48933	LANSING
48937	LANSING	48906	LANSING
48950	LANSING	48917	LANSING
48951	LANSING	48910	LANSING
48956	LANSING	48933	LANSING
48980	LANSING	48917	LANSING
49003	KALAMAZOO	49001	KALAMAZOO
49005	KALAMAZOO	49001	KALAMAZOO
49016	BATTLE CREEK	49017	BATTLE CREEK
49018	BATTLE CREEK	49017	BATTLE CREEK
49019	KALAMAZOO	49001	KALAMAZOO
49020	BEDFORD	49017	BATTLE CREEK
49023	BENTON HARBOR	49022	BENTON HARBOR
49027	BREEDSVILLE	49056	GRAND JUNCTION
49035	CLOVERDALE	49046	DELTON
49039	HAGAR SHORES	49038	COLOMA
49041	COMSTOCK	49001	KALAMAZOO
49062	KENDALL	49055	GOBLES
49063	LACOTA	49056	GRAND JUNCTION
49069	MARSHALL	49068	MARSHALL
49074	NAZARETH	49006	KALAMAZOO
49075	NOTTAWA	49091	STURGIS
49077	OSHTEMO	49009	KALAMAZOO
49081	PORTAGE	49024	PORTAGE
49084	RIVERSIDE	49038	COLOMA
49115	HARBERT	49125	SAWYER
49119	NEW TROY	49125	SAWYER
49121	NILES	49120	NILES
49204	JACKSON	49201	JACKSON
49239	FRONTIER	49242	HILLSDALE
49257	MOSCOW	49246	HORTON
49258	MOSHERVILLE	49250	JONESVILLE
49261	NAPOLEON	49201	JACKSON
49263	NORVELL	49230	BROOKLYN
49281	SOMERSET	49233	CEMENT CITY
49282	SOMERSET CENTER	49233	CEMENT CITY
49289	WESTON	49221	ADRIAN
49311	BRADLEY	49348	WAYLAND
49312	BROHMAN	49309	BITELY
49314	BURNIPS	49323	DORR
49317	CANNONSBURG	49301	ADA
49320	CHIPPEWA LAKE	49342	RODNEY
49335	MOLINE	49348	WAYLAND
49351	ROCKFORD	49341	ROCKFORD
49355	ADA	49301	ADA
49356	ADA	49301	ADA
49357	ADA	49301	ADA
49406	DOUGLAS	49453	SAUGATUCK
49409	FERRYSBURG	49456	SPRING LAKE
49413	FREMONT	49412	FREMONT
49416	GLENN	49408	FENNVILLE
49422	HOLLAND	49423	HOLLAND
49427	JAMESTOWN	49426	HUDSONVILLE
49429	JENISON	49428	JENISON
49430	LAMONT	49435	MARNE
49434	MACATAWA	49423	HOLLAND
49443	MUSKEGON	49440	MUSKEGON
49458	WALHALLA	49410	FOUNTAIN
49463	WABANINGO	49461	WHITEHALL
49468	GRANDVILLE	49418	GRANDVILLE
49501	GRAND RAPIDS	49503	GRAND RAPIDS
49502	GRAND RAPIDS	49503	GRAND RAPIDS

Point ZIP Code		Enclosing Residential ZIP Code	
ZIP	Post Office Name	ZIP	Post Office Name
49510	GRAND RAPIDS	49507	GRAND RAPIDS
49514	GRAND RAPIDS	49504	GRAND RAPIDS
49515	GRAND RAPIDS	49503	GRAND RAPIDS
49516	GRAND RAPIDS	49506	GRAND RAPIDS
49518	GRAND RAPIDS	49508	GRAND RAPIDS
49523	GRAND RAPIDS	49503	GRAND RAPIDS
49528	GRAND RAPIDS	49503	GRAND RAPIDS
49530	GRAND RAPIDS	49512	GRAND RAPIDS
49550	GRAND RAPIDS	49544	GRAND RAPIDS
49555	GRAND RAPIDS	49503	GRAND RAPIDS
49560	GRAND RAPIDS	49508	GRAND RAPIDS
49588	GRAND RAPIDS	49512	GRAND RAPIDS
49599	GRAND RAPIDS	49503	GRAND RAPIDS
49610	ACME	49690	WILLIAMSBURG
49611	ALBA	49659	MANCELONA
49626	EASTLAKE	49660	MANISTEE
49627	EASTPORT	49622	CENTRAL LAKE
49628	ELBERTA	49635	FRANKFORT
49634	FILER CITY	49660	MANISTEE
49666	MAYFIELD	49649	KINGSLEY
49673	OLD MISSION	49686	TRAVERSE CITY
49674	OMENA	49682	SUTTONS BAY
49685	TRAVERSE CITY	49684	TRAVERSE CITY
49696	TRAVERSE CITY	49686	TRAVERSE CITY
49711	BAY SHORE	49720	CHARLEVOIX
49717	BURT LAKE	49706	ALANSON
49722	CONWAY	49770	PETOSKEY
49723	CROSS VILLAGE	49740	HARBOR SPRINGS
49734	GAYLORD	49735	GAYLORD
49737	GOOD HART	49740	HARBOR SPRINGS
49739	GRAYLING	49738	GRAYLING
49748	HULBERT	49728	ECKERMAN
49761	MULLETT LAKE	49721	CHEBOYGAN
49764	ODEN	49706	ALANSON
49784	KINCHELOE	49783	SAULT SAINTE MARIE
49785	KINCHELOE	49788	KINCHELOE
49790	STRONGS	49728	ECKERMAN
49791	TOPINABEE	49749	INDIAN RIVER
49793	TROUT LAKE	49868	NEWBERRY
49796	WALLOON LAKE	49712	BOYNE CITY
49797	WATERS	49735	GAYLORD
49805	ALLOUEZ	49913	CALUMET
49808	BIG BAY	49861	MICHIGAMME
49819	ARNOLD	49833	LITTLE LAKE
49845	HARRIS	49896	WILSON
49852	LORETTO	49892	VULCAN
49863	NADEAU	49812	CARNEY
49864	NAHMA	49878	RAPID RIVER
49865	NATIONAL MINE	49849	ISHPEMING
49871	PALMER	49866	NEGAUNEE
49872	PERKINS	49880	ROCK
49877	RALPH	49834	FOSTER CITY
49901	AHMEEK	49913	CALUMET
49902	ALPHA	49920	CRYSTAL FALLS
49903	AMASA	49920	CRYSTAL FALLS
49915	CASPIAN	49935	IRON RIVER
49917	COPPER CITY	49913	CALUMET
49918	COPPER HARBOR	49913	CALUMET
49922	DOLLAR BAY	49930	HANCOCK
49929	GREENLAND	49953	ONTONAGON
49934	HUBBELL	49945	LAKE LINDEN
49942	KEARSARGE	49913	CALUMET
49955	PAINESDALE	49905	ATLANTIC MINE
49959	RAMSAY	49911	BESSEMER
49960	ROCKLAND	49953	ONTONAGON
49961	SIDNAW	49967	TROUT CREEK
49963	SOUTH RANGE	49905	ATLANTIC MINE
49964	STAMBAUGH	49935	IRON RIVER
49971	WHITE PINE	49953	ONTONAGON
50012	AMES	50014	AMES
50031	BEAVER	50212	OGDEN
50032	BERWICK	50021	ANKENY
50037	BOONE	50036	BOONE
50078	FERGUSON	50158	MARSHALLTOWN
50099	BOONE	50036	BOONE
50110	GRAY	50025	AUDUBON
50137	KILLDUFF	50251	SULLY
50145	LIBERTY CENTER	50166	MILO
50160	MARTENSDALE	50229	PROLE
50241	SAINT MARYS	50229	PROLE
50243	SHELDAHL	50226	POLK CITY
50255	THORNBURG	50136	KESWICK
50259	GIFFORD	50258	UNION
50269	WHITTEN	50258	UNION
50301	DES MOINES	50311	DES MOINES
50302	DES MOINES	50314	DES MOINES
50303	DES MOINES	50311	DES MOINES
50304	DES MOINES	50311	DES MOINES
50305	DES MOINES	50311	DES MOINES
50306	DES MOINES	50311	DES MOINES
50318	DES MOINES	50309	DES MOINES
50319	DES MOINES	50309	DES MOINES
50328	DES MOINES	50309	DES MOINES

NONRESIDENTIAL ZIP CODES

Point ZIP Code		Enclosing Residential ZIP Code	
ZIP	Post Office Name	ZIP	Post Office Name
50329	DES MOINES	50309	DES MOINES
50330	DES MOINES	50309	DES MOINES
50331	DES MOINES	50309	DES MOINES
50332	DES MOINES	50309	DES MOINES
50333	DES MOINES	50313	DES MOINES
50334	DES MOINES	50322	URBANDALE
50335	DES MOINES	50309	DES MOINES
50336	DES MOINES	50265	WEST DES MOINES
50339	DES MOINES	50266	WEST DES MOINES
50340	DES MOINES	50309	DES MOINES
50347	DES MOINES	50265	WEST DES MOINES
50359	DES MOINES	50266	WEST DES MOINES
50360	DES MOINES	50314	DES MOINES
50361	DES MOINES	50266	WEST DES MOINES
50362	DES MOINES	50266	WEST DES MOINES
50363	DES MOINES	50266	WEST DES MOINES
50364	DES MOINES	50266	WEST DES MOINES
50367	DES MOINES	50266	WEST DES MOINES
50368	DES MOINES	50266	WEST DES MOINES
50369	DES MOINES	50266	WEST DES MOINES
50381	DES MOINES	50309	DES MOINES
50391	DES MOINES	50265	WEST DES MOINES
50392	DES MOINES	50309	DES MOINES
50393	DES MOINES	50309	DES MOINES
50394	DES MOINES	50322	URBANDALE
50395	DES MOINES	50322	URBANDALE
50396	DES MOINES	50309	DES MOINES
50397	DES MOINES	50309	DES MOINES
50398	WEST DES MOINES	50266	WEST DES MOINES
50402	MASON CITY	50401	MASON CITY
50426	CARPENTER	50472	SAINT ANSGAR
50427	CHAPIN	50475	SHEFFIELD
50431	COULTER	50452	LATIMER
50481	TOETERVILLE	50472	SAINT ANSGAR
50526	CLARION	50525	CLARION
50592	TRUESDALE	50588	STORM LAKE
50593	VARINA	50540	FONDA
50620	COLWELL	50616	CHARLES CITY
50623	DEWAR	50703	WATERLOO
50631	FREDERIKA	50674	SUMNER
50657	MORRISON	50669	REINBECK
50661	NORTH WASHINGTON	50659	NEW HAMPTON
50664	ORAN	50629	FAIRBANK
50673	STOUT	50665	PARKERSBURG
50704	WATERLOO	50703	WATERLOO
50706	WATERLOO	50702	WATERLOO
50831	ARISPE	50830	AFTON
50839	CARBON	50841	CORNING
50842	CROMWELL	50801	CRESTON
50936	DES MOINES	50309	DES MOINES
50940	DES MOINES	50314	DES MOINES
50947	DES MOINES	50314	DES MOINES
50950	DES MOINES	50309	DES MOINES
50980	DES MOINES	50309	DES MOINES
50981	DES MOINES	50309	DES MOINES
51008	BRUNSVILLE	51031	LE MARS
51015	CLIMBING HILL	51026	HORNICK
51045	OYENS	51031	LE MARS
51102	SIOUX CITY	51101	SIOUX CITY
51242	LESTER	51241	LARCHWOOD
51244	MATLOCK	51201	SHELDON
51340	FOSTORIA	51301	SPENCER
51341	GILLETT GROVE	51343	GREENVILLE
51432	ASPINWALL	51455	MANNING
51459	RALSTON	51443	GLIDDEN
51502	COUNCIL BLUFFS	51503	COUNCIL BLUFFS
51554	MINEOLA	51534	GLENWOOD
51591	RED OAK	51566	RED OAK
51593	HARLAN	51537	HARLAN
51602	SHENANDOAH	51601	SHENANDOAH
51603	SHENANDOAH	51601	SHENANDOAH
52004	DUBUQUE	52001	DUBUQUE
52056	LUXEMBURG	52052	GUTTENBERG
52075	SPRINGBROOK	52031	BELLEVUE
52099	DUBUQUE	52001	DUBUQUE
52149	HIGHLANDVILLE	52101	DECORAH
52166	SAINT LUCAS	52175	WEST UNION
52168	SPILLVILLE	52132	CALMAR
52204	AMANA	52203	AMANA
52235	HILLS	52327	RIVERSIDE
52243	IOWA CITY	52240	IOWA CITY
52244	IOWA CITY	52240	IOWA CITY
52252	LANGWORTHY	52310	MONTICELLO
52312	MORLEY	52205	ANAMOSA
52319	OAKDALE	52240	IOWA CITY
52344	TROY MILLS	52218	COGGON
52350	VIOLA	52336	SPRINGVILLE
52351	WALFORD	52318	NORWAY
52406	CEDAR RAPIDS	52401	CEDAR RAPIDS
52407	CEDAR RAPIDS	52401	CEDAR RAPIDS
52408	CEDAR RAPIDS	52405	CEDAR RAPIDS
52409	CEDAR RAPIDS	52403	CEDAR RAPIDS
52410	CEDAR RAPIDS	52403	CEDAR RAPIDS
52497	CEDAR RAPIDS	52404	CEDAR RAPIDS
52498	CEDAR RAPIDS	52402	CEDAR RAPIDS
52499	CEDAR RAPIDS	52411	CEDAR RAPIDS
52562	HAYESVILLE	52591	SIGOURNEY
52568	MARTINSBURG	52563	HEDRICK
52595	UNIVERSITY PARK	52577	OSKALOOSA
52648	PILOT GROVE	52656	WEST POINT
52652	SWEDESBURG	52641	MOUNT PLEASANT
52733	CLINTON	52732	CLINTON
52734	CLINTON	52732	CLINTON
52736	CLINTON	52732	CLINTON
52737	COLUMBUS CITY	52738	COLUMBUS JUNCTION
52752	GRANDVIEW	52754	LETTS
52757	LOW MOOR	52742	DE WITT
52758	MC CAUSLAND	52748	ELDRIDGE
52759	MONTPELIER	52761	MUSCATINE
52767	PLEASANT VALLEY	52722	BETTENDORF
52771	TEEDS GROVE	52732	CLINTON
52805	DAVENPORT	52801	DAVENPORT
52808	DAVENPORT	52802	DAVENPORT
52809	DAVENPORT	52806	DAVENPORT
53003	ASHIPPUN	53036	IXONIA
53008	BROOKFIELD	53045	BROOKFIELD
53016	CLYMAN	53039	JUNEAU
53026	GREENBUSH	53023	GLENBEULAH
53031	HINGHAM	53085	SHEBOYGAN FALLS
53047	LEBANON	53094	WATERTOWN
53052	MENOMONEE FALLS	53051	MENOMONEE FALLS
53056	MERTON	53029	HARTLAND
53060	NEWBURG	53090	WEST BEND
53062	NEW HOLSTEIN	53061	NEW HOLSTEIN
53064	NORTH LAKE	53029	HARTLAND
53082	SHEBOYGAN	53081	SHEBOYGAN
53088	STOCKBRIDGE	53014	CHILTON
53099	WOODLAND	53035	IRON RIDGE
53101	BASSETT	53128	GENOA CITY
53102	BENET LAKE	53104	BRISTOL
53109	CAMP LAKE	53168	SALEM
53127	GENESEE DEPOT	53189	WAUKESHA
53138	HONEY CREEK	53105	BURLINGTON
53141	KENOSHA	53140	KENOSHA
53148	LYONS	53105	BURLINGTON
53152	NEW MUNSTER	53105	BURLINGTON
53157	PELL LAKE	53128	GENOA CITY
53159	POWERS LAKE	53128	GENOA CITY
53167	ROCHESTER	53185	WATERFORD
53171	SOMERS	53144	KENOSHA
53176	SPRINGFIELD	53121	ELKHORN
53187	WAUKESHA	53186	WAUKESHA
53192	WILMOT	53181	TWIN LAKES
53194	WOODWORTH	53104	BRISTOL
53195	ZENDA	53147	LAKE GENEVA
53199	SILVER LAKE	53170	SILVER LAKE
53201	MILWAUKEE	53203	MILWAUKEE
53234	MILWAUKEE	53219	MILWAUKEE
53237	MILWAUKEE	53207	MILWAUKEE
53244	MILWAUKEE	53203	MILWAUKEE
53259	MILWAUKEE	53203	MILWAUKEE
53263	MILWAUKEE	53222	MILWAUKEE
53267	MILWAUKEE	53202	MILWAUKEE
53268	MILWAUKEE	53203	MILWAUKEE
53274	MILWAUKEE	53203	MILWAUKEE
53278	MILWAUKEE	53202	MILWAUKEE
53288	MILWAUKEE	53202	MILWAUKEE
53290	MILWAUKEE	53203	MILWAUKEE
53293	MILWAUKEE	53203	MILWAUKEE
53295	MILWAUKEE	53214	MILWAUKEE
53401	RACINE	53403	RACINE
53407	RACINE	53403	RACINE
53408	RACINE	53406	RACINE
53501	AFTON	53548	JANESVILLE
53512	BELOIT	53511	BELOIT
53535	EDMUND	53533	DODGEVILLE
53537	FOOTVILLE	53545	JANESVILLE
53540	GOTHAM	53556	LONE ROCK
53542	HANOVER	53545	JANESVILLE
53547	JANESVILLE	53545	JANESVILLE
53571	MORRISONVILLE	53532	DE FOREST
53584	SEXTONVILLE	53556	LONE ROCK
53595	DODGEVILLE	53533	DODGEVILLE
53596	SUN PRAIRIE	53590	SUN PRAIRIE
53599	WOODFORD	53504	ARGYLE
53701	MADISON	53703	MADISON
53702	MADISON	53703	MADISON
53707	MADISON	53714	MADISON
53708	MADISON	53714	MADISON
53725	MADISON	53715	MADISON
53744	MADISON	53711	MADISON
53774	MADISON	53713	MADISON
53777	MADISON	53704	MADISON
53778	MADISON	53714	MADISON
53779	MADISON	53714	MADISON
53782	MADISON	53703	MADISON

Point ZIP Code		Enclosing Residential ZIP Code	
ZIP	Post Office Name	ZIP	Post Office Name
53783	MADISON	53718	MADISON
53784	MADISON	53713	MADISON
53785	MADISON	53703	MADISON
53786	MADISON	53703	MADISON
53788	MADISON	53703	MADISON
53789	MADISON	53703	MADISON
53790	MADISON	53703	MADISON
53792	MADISON	53726	MADISON
53793	MADISON	53714	MADISON
53794	MADISON	53714	MADISON
53802	BEETOWN	53806	CASSVILLE
53808	DICKEYVILLE	53807	CUBA CITY
53812	KIELER	53807	CUBA CITY
53817	PATCH GROVE	53804	BLOOMINGTON
53824	SINSINAWA	53811	HAZEL GREEN
53927	DELLWOOD	54613	ARKDALE
53928	DOYLESTOWN	53960	RIO
53931	FAIRWATER	53919	BRANDON
53935	FRIESLAND	53923	CAMBRIA
53940	LAKE DELTON	53965	WISCONSIN DELLS
53942	LIME RIDGE	53941	LA VALLE
53953	PACKWAUKEE	53949	MONTELLO
53957	RANDOLPH	53956	RANDOLPH
53958	REEDSBURG	53959	REEDSBURG
53962	UNION CENTER	53968	WONEWOC
53969	WYOCENA	53954	PARDEEVILLE
54010	EAST ELLSWORTH	54011	ELLSWORTH
54123	FOREST JUNCTION	54110	BRILLION
54127	GREEN VALLEY	54154	OCONTO FALLS
54131	FREEDOM	54130	KAUKAUNA
54152	NICHOLS	54165	SEYMOUR
54160	POTTER	53014	CHILTON
54182	ZACHOW	54107	BONDUEL
54207	COLLINS	53014	CHILTON
54211	EPHRAIM	54234	SISTER BAY
54214	FRANCIS CREEK	54220	MANITOWOC
54215	KELLNERSVILLE	54230	REEDSVILLE
54221	MANITOWOC	54220	MANITOWOC
54226	MAPLEWOOD	54235	STURGEON BAY
54232	SAINT NAZIANZ	53042	KIEL
54240	TISCH MILLS	54208	DENMARK
54305	GREEN BAY	54303	GREEN BAY
54306	GREEN BAY	54303	GREEN BAY
54307	GREEN BAY	54303	GREEN BAY
54308	GREEN BAY	54302	GREEN BAY
54324	GREEN BAY	54304	GREEN BAY
54344	GREEN BAY	54115	DE PERE
54402	WAUSAU	54403	WAUSAU
54404	MARSHFIELD	54449	MARSHFIELD
54415	BLENKER	54454	MILLADORE
54417	BROKAW	54403	WAUSAU
54429	ELDERON	54427	ELAND
54432	GALLOWAY	54499	WITTENBERG
54434	JUMP RIVER	54766	SHELDON
54439	HANNIBAL	54433	GILMAN
54450	MATTOON	54409	ANTIGO
54458	NELSONVILLE	54407	AMHERST JUNCTION
54464	PHLOX	54409	ANTIGO
54472	MARSHFIELD	54449	MARSHFIELD
54492	STEVENS POINT	54467	PLOVER
54525	GILE	54550	MONTREAL
54532	HEAFFORD JUNCTION	54487	TOMAHAWK
54543	MC NAUGHTON	54501	RHINELANDER
54561	STAR LAKE	54521	EAGLE RIVER
54602	LA CROSSE	54601	LA CROSSE
54620	CATARACT	54656	SPARTA
54637	HUSTLER	53950	NEW LISBON
54643	MILLSTON	54615	BLACK RIVER FALLS
54645	MOUNT STERLING	54631	GAYS MILLS
54649	OAKDALE	54660	TOMAH
54654	SENECA	54631	GAYS MILLS
54662	TUNNEL CITY	54660	TOMAH
54702	EAU CLAIRE	54703	EAU CLAIRE
54735	DOWNSVILLE	54751	MENOMONIE
54743	GILMANTON	54755	MONDOVI
54760	PIGEON FALLS	54758	OSSEO
54764	ROCK FALLS	54755	MONDOVI
54774	CHIPPEWA FALLS	54729	CHIPPEWA FALLS
54816	BENOIT	54856	MASON
54818	BRILL	54868	RICE LAKE
54834	EDGEWATER	54817	BIRCHWOOD
54841	HAUGEN	54868	RICE LAKE
54842	HAWTHORNE	54849	LAKE NEBAGAMON
54857	MIKANA	54817	BIRCHWOOD
54861	ODANAH	54806	ASHLAND
54890	WASCOTT	54859	MINONG
54903	OSHKOSH	54902	OSHKOSH
54906	OSHKOSH	54901	OSHKOSH
54912	APPLETON	54911	APPLETON
54919	APPLETON	54913	APPLETON
54926	BIG FALLS	54486	TIGERTON
54927	BUTTE DES MORTS	54963	OMRO
54931	DALE	54944	HORTONVILLE

Point ZIP Code		Enclosing Residential ZIP Code	
ZIP	Post Office Name	ZIP	Post Office Name
54933	EMBARRASS	54929	CLINTONVILLE
54934	EUREKA	54923	BERLIN
54936	FOND DU LAC	54935	FOND DU LAC
54946	KING	54981	WAUPACA
54957	NEENAH	54956	NEENAH
54969	READFIELD	54940	FREMONT
54976	SAXEVILLE	54984	WILD ROSE
54980	WAUKAU	54963	OMRO
54985	WINNEBAGO	54902	OSHKOSH
54990	IOLA	54945	IOLA
55010	CASTLE ROCK	55065	RANDOLPH
55029	GRANDY	55008	CAMBRIDGE
55078	STACY	55079	STACY
55083	STILLWATER	55082	STILLWATER
55085	VERMILLION	55033	HASTINGS
55090	WILLERNIE	55115	SAINT PAUL
55133	SAINT PAUL	55101	SAINT PAUL
55144	SAINT PAUL	55119	SAINT PAUL
55146	SAINT PAUL	55107	SAINT PAUL
55150	MENDOTA	55118	SAINT PAUL
55155	SAINT PAUL	55101	SAINT PAUL
55164	SAINT PAUL	55101	SAINT PAUL
55165	SAINT PAUL	55101	SAINT PAUL
55166	SAINT PAUL	55101	SAINT PAUL
55168	SAINT PAUL	55101	SAINT PAUL
55169	SAINT PAUL	55101	SAINT PAUL
55170	SAINT PAUL	55101	SAINT PAUL
55171	SAINT PAUL	55101	SAINT PAUL
55172	SAINT PAUL	55101	SAINT PAUL
55175	SAINT PAUL	55101	SAINT PAUL
55187	SAINT PAUL	55125	SAINT PAUL
55188	SAINT PAUL	55125	SAINT PAUL
55323	CRYSTAL BAY	55356	LONG LAKE
55348	MAPLE PLAIN	55359	MAPLE PLAIN
55361	MINNETONKA BEACH	55391	WAYZATA
55365	MONTICELLO	55362	MONTICELLO
55377	SANTIAGO	55319	CLEAR LAKE
55380	SILVER CREEK	55358	MAPLE LAKE
55383	NORWOOD	55368	NORWOOD YOUNG AMERIC
55392	NAVARRE	55391	WAYZATA
55393	MAPLE PLAIN	55359	MAPLE PLAIN
55394	YOUNG AMERICA	55397	YOUNG AMERICA
55399	YOUNG AMERICA	55397	YOUNG AMERICA
55440	MINNEAPOLIS	55401	MINNEAPOLIS
55458	MINNEAPOLIS	55401	MINNEAPOLIS
55459	MINNEAPOLIS	55401	MINNEAPOLIS
55460	MINNEAPOLIS	55401	MINNEAPOLIS
55467	MINNEAPOLIS	55401	MINNEAPOLIS
55470	MINNEAPOLIS	55401	MINNEAPOLIS
55472	MINNEAPOLIS	55401	MINNEAPOLIS
55473	MINNEAPOLIS	55401	MINNEAPOLIS
55474	MINNEAPOLIS	55402	MINNEAPOLIS
55479	MINNEAPOLIS	55401	MINNEAPOLIS
55480	MINNEAPOLIS	55401	MINNEAPOLIS
55483	MINNEAPOLIS	55409	MINNEAPOLIS
55484	MINNEAPOLIS	55401	MINNEAPOLIS
55485	MINNEAPOLIS	55406	MINNEAPOLIS
55486	MINNEAPOLIS	55402	MINNEAPOLIS
55487	MINNEAPOLIS	55415	MINNEAPOLIS
55488	MINNEAPOLIS	55415	MINNEAPOLIS
55550	YOUNG AMERICA	55397	YOUNG AMERICA
55551	YOUNG AMERICA	55397	YOUNG AMERICA
55552	YOUNG AMERICA	55397	YOUNG AMERICA
55553	YOUNG AMERICA	55397	YOUNG AMERICA
55554	NORWOOD	55368	NORWOOD YOUNG AMERIC
55555	YOUNG AMERICA	55368	NORWOOD YOUNG AMERIC
55556	YOUNG AMERICA	55397	YOUNG AMERICA
55557	YOUNG AMERICA	55397	YOUNG AMERICA
55558	YOUNG AMERICA	55397	YOUNG AMERICA
55559	YOUNG AMERICA	55397	YOUNG AMERICA
55560	YOUNG AMERICA	55397	YOUNG AMERICA
55561	MONTICELLO	55362	MONTICELLO
55562	YOUNG AMERICA	55397	YOUNG AMERICA
55563	MONTICELLO	55362	MONTICELLO
55564	YOUNG AMERICA	55397	YOUNG AMERICA
55565	MONTICELLO	55362	MONTICELLO
55566	YOUNG AMERICA	55397	YOUNG AMERICA
55567	YOUNG AMERICA	55397	YOUNG AMERICA
55568	YOUNG AMERICA	55397	YOUNG AMERICA
55569	OSSEO	55369	OSSEO
55570	MAPLE PLAIN	55359	MAPLE PLAIN
55571	MAPLE PLAIN	55359	MAPLE PLAIN
55572	ROCKFORD	55359	MAPLE PLAIN
55573	YOUNG AMERICA	55397	YOUNG AMERICA
55574	MAPLE PLAIN	55359	MAPLE PLAIN
55575	HOWARD LAKE	55349	HOWARD LAKE
55576	MAPLE PLAIN	55359	MAPLE PLAIN
55577	ROCKFORD	55359	MAPLE PLAIN
55578	MAPLE PLAIN	55359	MAPLE PLAIN
55579	MAPLE PLAIN	55359	MAPLE PLAIN
55580	MONTICELLO	55362	MONTICELLO
55581	MONTICELLO	55362	MONTICELLO
55582	MONTICELLO	55362	MONTICELLO

NONRESIDENTIAL ZIP CODES

MINNESOTA **MONTANA**

Point ZIP Code		Enclosing Residential ZIP Code		Point ZIP Code		Enclosing Residential ZIP Code	
ZIP	Post Office Name	ZIP	Post Office Name	ZIP	Post Office Name	ZIP	Post Office Name
55583	NORWOOD	55368	NORWOOD YOUNG AMERIC	57041	LYONS	57003	BALTIC
55584	MONTICELLO	55362	MONTICELLO	57061	SINAI	57071	VOLGA
55585	MONTICELLO	55362	MONTICELLO	57101	SIOUX FALLS	57104	SIOUX FALLS
55586	MONTICELLO	55362	MONTICELLO	57109	SIOUX FALLS	57105	SIOUX FALLS
55587	MONTICELLO	55362	MONTICELLO	57117	SIOUX FALLS	57104	SIOUX FALLS
55588	MONTICELLO	55362	MONTICELLO	57118	SIOUX FALLS	57104	SIOUX FALLS
55589	MONTICELLO	55362	MONTICELLO	57186	SIOUX FALLS	57104	SIOUX FALLS
55590	MONTICELLO	55362	MONTICELLO	57188	SIOUX FALLS	57104	SIOUX FALLS
55591	MONTICELLO	55362	MONTICELLO	57189	SIOUX FALLS	57104	SIOUX FALLS
55592	MAPLE PLAIN	55359	MAPLE PLAIN	57192	SIOUX FALLS	57104	SIOUX FALLS
55593	MAPLE PLAIN	55359	MAPLE PLAIN	57193	SIOUX FALLS	57104	SIOUX FALLS
55594	YOUNG AMERICA	55397	YOUNG AMERICA	57194	SIOUX FALLS	57104	SIOUX FALLS
55595	LORETTO	55357	LORETTO	57196	SIOUX FALLS	57110	SIOUX FALLS
55596	LORETTO	55357	LORETTO	57198	SIOUX FALLS	57030	GARRETSON
55597	LORETTO	55357	LORETTO	57214	BADGER	57212	ARLINGTON
55598	LORETTO	55357	LORETTO	57253	MILBANK	57252	MILBANK
55599	LORETTO	55357	LORETTO	57326	CHAMBERLAIN	57325	CHAMBERLAIN
55601	BEAVER BAY	55616	TWO HARBORS	57346	STEPHAN	57345	HIGHMORE
55609	KNIFE RIVER	55616	TWO HARBORS	57354	KAYLOR	57376	TRIPP
55701	ADOLPH GENERAL STORE	55810	DULUTH	57358	LANE	57385	WOONSOCKET
55708	BIWABIK	55741	GILBERT	57361	MARTY	57380	WAGNER
55713	BUHL	55719	CHISHOLM	57367	PICKSTOWN	57356	LAKE ANDES
55716	CALUMET	55709	BOVEY	57399	HURON	57350	HURON
55722	COLERAINE	55709	BOVEY	57402	ABERDEEN	57401	ABERDEEN
55730	GRAND RAPIDS	55744	GRAND RAPIDS	57426	BARNARD	57481	WESTPORT
55745	GRAND RAPIDS	55744	GRAND RAPIDS	57439	FERNEY	57434	CONDE
55747	HIBBING	55746	HIBBING	57563	OKREEK	57555	MISSION
55753	KEEWATIN	55769	NASHWAUK	57570	ROSEBUD	57572	SAINT FRANCIS
55758	KINNEY	55719	CHISHOLM	57621	BULLHEAD	57642	MC LAUGHLIN
55764	MARBLE	55709	BOVEY	57636	LANTRY	57633	ISABEL
55766	MELRUDE	55724	COTTON	57639	LITTLE EAGLE	57642	MC LAUGHLIN
55772	NETT LAKE	55771	ORR	57652	RIDGEVIEW	57625	EAGLE BUTTE
55777	VIRGINIA	55792	VIRGINIA	57659	WALKER	57642	MC LAUGHLIN
55782	SOUDAN	55790	TOWER	57661	WHITEHORSE	57656	TIMBER LAKE
55786	TACONITE	55709	BOVEY	57709	RAPID CITY	57701	RAPID CITY
55791	TWIG	55779	SAGINAW	57764	OGLALA	57770	PINE RIDGE
55796	WINTON	55731	ELY	57773	PRINGLE	57730	CUSTER
55814	DULUTH	55811	DULUTH	57776	REDIG	57720	BUFFALO
55815	DULUTH	55811	DULUTH	58001	ABERCROMBIE	58075	WAHPETON
55816	DULUTH	55806	DULUTH	58002	ABSARAKA	58007	AYR
55903	ROCHESTER	55901	ROCHESTER	58065	PILLSBURY	58046	HOPE
55905	ROCHESTER	55901	ROCHESTER	58074	WAHPETON	58075	WAHPETON
55931	EITZEN	55921	CALEDONIA	58105	FARGO	58102	FARGO
55942	HOMER	55987	WINONA	58106	FARGO	58103	FARGO
55950	LANSING	55912	AUSTIN	58107	FARGO	58102	FARGO
55988	STOCKTON	55987	WINONA	58108	FARGO	58102	FARGO
56002	MANKATO	56001	MANKATO	58109	FARGO	58103	FARGO
56006	MANKATO	56001	MANKATO	58121	FARGO	58103	FARGO
56046	HOPE	55060	OWATONNA	58122	FARGO	58102	FARGO
56056	LA SALLE	56081	SAINT JAMES	58124	FARGO	58103	FARGO
56084	SEARLES	56073	NEW ULM	58125	FARGO	58103	FARGO
56140	IHLEN	56144	JASPER	58126	FARGO	58103	FARGO
56177	TROSKY	56164	PIPESTONE	58202	GRAND FORKS	58203	GRAND FORKS
56302	SAINT CLOUD	56303	SAINT CLOUD	58206	GRAND FORKS	58201	GRAND FORKS
56317	BUCKMAN	56364	PIERZ	58207	GRAND FORKS	58205	GRAND FORKS AFB
56321	COLLEGEVILLE	56310	AVON	58208	GRAND FORKS	58201	GRAND FORKS
56325	ELROSA	56312	BELGRADE	58236	GLASSTON	58276	SAINT THOMAS
56333	GILMAN	56329	FOLEY	58310	AGATE	58353	MYLO
56335	GREENWALD	56352	MELROSE	58313	BALTA	58368	RUGBY
56344	LASTRUP	56364	PIERZ	58335	FORT TOTTEN	58370	SAINT MICHAEL
56356	NEW MUNICH	56352	MELROSE	58355	NEKOMA	58269	OSNABROCK
56369	ROCKVILLE	56301	SAINT CLOUD	58379	TOKIO	58370	SAINT MICHAEL
56371	ROSCOE	56368	RICHMOND	58402	JAMESTOWN	58401	JAMESTOWN
56372	SAINT CLOUD	56303	SAINT CLOUD	58452	JESSIE	58425	COOPERSTOWN
56376	SAINT MARTIN	56362	PAYNESVILLE	58502	BISMARCK	58504	BISMARCK
56388	WAITE PARK	56387	WAITE PARK	58505	BISMARCK	58501	BISMARCK
56393	SAINT CLOUD	56303	SAINT CLOUD	58506	BISMARCK	58504	BISMARCK
56395	SAINT CLOUD	56303	SAINT CLOUD	58507	BISMARCK	58504	BISMARCK
56396	SAINT CLOUD	56303	SAINT CLOUD	58602	DICKINSON	58601	DICKINSON
56397	SAINT CLOUD	56301	SAINT CLOUD	58644	MARSHALL	58652	RICHARDTON
56398	SAINT CLOUD	56301	SAINT CLOUD	58702	MINOT	58701	MINOT
56399	SAINT CLOUD	56387	WAITE PARK	58802	WILLISTON	58801	WILLISTON
56430	AH GWAH CHING	56484	WALKER	59004	ASHLAND	59003	ASHLAND
56436	FORT BENEDICT	56461	LAPORTE	59013	BOYD	59041	JOLIET
56459	LAKE HUBERT	56468	NISSWA	59018	CLYDE PARK	59086	WILSALL
56478	NIMROD	56477	SEBEKA	59020	COOKE CITY	59030	GARDINER
56502	DETROIT LAKES	56501	DETROIT LAKES	59026	EDGAR	59041	JOLIET
56538	FERGUS FALLS	56537	FERGUS FALLS	59035	YELLOWTAIL	59050	LODGE GRASS
56541	FLOM	56584	TWIN VALLEY	59036	HARLOWTON	59085	TWO DOT
56561	MOORHEAD	56560	MOORHEAD	59054	MELSTONE	59059	MUSSELSHELL
56591	WHITE EARTH	56521	CALLAWAY	59066	PRYOR	59050	LODGE GRASS
56619	BEMIDJI	56601	BEMIDJI	59073	ROUNDUP	59072	ROUNDUP
56631	BOWSTRING	56636	DEER RIVER	59081	SILVER GATE	59030	GARDINER
56658	MARGIE	56627	BIG FALLS	59082	SPRINGDALE	59047	LIVINGSTON
56679	SOUTH INTERNATIONAL	56649	INTERNATIONAL FALLS	59083	SUMATRA	59039	INGOMAR
56687	WILTON	56601	BEMIDJI	59084	TEIGEN	59087	WINNETT
56731	HUMBOLDT	56755	SAINT VINCENT	59103	BILLINGS	59101	BILLINGS
56901	WASHINGTON	20018	WASHINGTON	59104	BILLINGS	59102	BILLINGS
56915	WASHINGTON	20018	WASHINGTON	59107	BILLINGS	59101	BILLINGS
56920	WASHINGTON	20018	WASHINGTON	59108	BILLINGS	59102	BILLINGS
56933	WASHINGTON	20004	WASHINGTON	59116	BILLINGS	59105	BILLINGS
56944	WASHINGTON	20018	WASHINGTON	59217	CRANE	59262	SAVAGE
56972	WASHINGTON	20018	WASHINGTON	59231	SAINT MARIE	59230	GLASGOW

Point ZIP Code		Enclosing Residential ZIP Code	
ZIP	Post Office Name	ZIP	Post Office Name
59240	GLENTANA	59250	OPHEIM
59273	VANDALIA	59241	HINSDALE
59319	CAPITOL	57724	CAMP CROOK
59323	COLSTRIP	59347	ROSEBUD
59333	HATHAWAY	59347	ROSEBUD
59403	GREAT FALLS	59401	GREAT FALLS
59406	GREAT FALLS	59405	GREAT FALLS
59432	DUPUYER	59486	VALIER
59435	ETHRIDGE	59474	SHELBY
59461	LOTHAIR	59522	CHESTER
59477	SIMMS	59421	CASCADE
59485	ULM	59421	CASCADE
59547	ZURICH	59523	CHINOOK
59604	HELENA	59601	HELENA
59620	HELENA	59601	HELENA
59623	HELENA	59601	HELENA
59624	HELENA	59601	HELENA
59626	HELENA	59601	HELENA
59631	BASIN	59634	CLANCY
59636	FORT HARRISON	59602	HELENA
59638	JEFFERSON CITY	59634	CLANCY
59640	MARYSVILLE	59633	CANYON CREEK
59702	BUTTE	59701	BUTTE
59703	BUTTE	59701	BUTTE
59710	ALDER	59749	SHERIDAN
59713	AVON	59731	GARRISON
59716	BIG SKY	59730	GALLATIN GATEWAY
59719	BOZEMAN	59718	BOZEMAN
59728	ELLISTON	59731	GARRISON
59732	GLEN	59725	DILLON
59740	MC ALLISTER	59745	NORRIS
59743	MELROSE	59727	DIVIDE
59746	POLARIS	59725	DILLON
59760	WILLOW CREEK	59752	THREE FORKS
59771	BOZEMAN	59715	BOZEMAN
59772	BOZEMAN	59715	BOZEMAN
59806	MISSOULA	59801	MISSOULA
59807	MISSOULA	59802	MISSOULA
59830	DE BORGIA	59866	SAINT REGIS
59835	GRANTSDALE	59840	HAMILTON
59841	PINESDALE	59840	HAMILTON
59842	HAUGAN	59866	SAINT REGIS
59851	MILLTOWN	59802	MISSOULA
59855	PABLO	59864	RONAN
59856	PARADISE	59859	PLAINS
59863	RAVALLI	59821	ARLEE
59867	SALTESE	59866	SAINT REGIS
59903	KALISPELL	59901	KALISPELL
59904	KALISPELL	59901	KALISPELL
59913	CORAM	59901	KALISPELL
59918	FORTINE	59917	EUREKA
59919	HUNGRY HORSE	59901	KALISPELL
59921	LAKE MC DONALD	59916	ESSEX
59926	MARTIN CITY	59901	KALISPELL
59927	OLNEY	59937	WHITEFISH
59933	STRYKER	59917	EUREKA
59934	TREGO	59917	EUREKA
59936	WEST GLACIER	59901	KALISPELL
60001	ALDEN	60033	HARVARD
60006	ARLINGTON HEIGHTS	60005	ARLINGTON HEIGHTS
60009	ELK GROVE VILLAGE	60007	ELK GROVE VILLAGE
60011	BARRINGTON	60010	BARRINGTON
60017	DES PLAINES	60018	DES PLAINES
60019	DES PLAINES	60018	DES PLAINES
60038	PALATINE	60074	PALATINE
60039	CRYSTAL LAKE	60014	CRYSTAL LAKE
60049	LONG GROVE	60047	LAKE ZURICH
60055	PALATINE	60067	PALATINE
60065	NORTHBROOK	60062	NORTHBROOK
60075	RUSSELL	60099	ZION
60078	PALATINE	60067	PALATINE
60079	WAUKEGAN	60085	WAUKEGAN
60086	NORTH CHICAGO	60088	GREAT LAKES
60092	LIBERTYVILLE	60048	LIBERTYVILLE
60094	PALATINE	60067	PALATINE
60095	PALATINE	60074	PALATINE
60109	BURLINGTON	60140	HAMPSHIRE
60113	CRESTON	61068	ROCHELLE
60116	CAROL STREAM	60188	CAROL STREAM
60117	BLOOMINGDALE	60108	BLOOMINGDALE
60121	ELGIN	60120	ELGIN
60122	CAROL STREAM	60188	CAROL STREAM
60128	CAROL STREAM	60188	CAROL STREAM
60132	CAROL STREAM	60188	CAROL STREAM
60138	GLEN ELLYN	60137	GLEN ELLYN
60144	KANEVILLE	60119	ELBURN
60147	LAFOX	60119	ELBURN
60159	SCHAUMBURG	60194	SCHAUMBURG
60161	MELROSE PARK	60160	MELROSE PARK
60168	SCHAUMBURG	60194	SCHAUMBURG
60170	PLATO CENTER	60120	ELGIN
60179	HOFFMAN ESTATES	60192	HOFFMAN ESTATES
60183	WASCO	60175	SAINT CHARLES
60186	WEST CHICAGO	60185	WEST CHICAGO
60196	SCHAUMBURG	60173	SCHAUMBURG
60197	CAROL STREAM	60188	CAROL STREAM
60199	CAROL STREAM	60188	CAROL STREAM
60204	EVANSTON	60201	EVANSTON
60209	EVANSTON	60201	EVANSTON
60290	CHICAGO	60607	CHICAGO
60303	OAK PARK	60301	OAK PARK
60399	WOOD DALE	60106	BENSENVILLE
60412	CHICAGO HEIGHTS	60411	CHICAGO HEIGHTS
60434	JOLIET	60436	JOLIET
60454	OAK LAWN	60455	BRIDGEVIEW
60474	SOUTH WILMINGTON	60424	GARDNER
60499	BEDFORD PARK	60638	CHICAGO
60507	AURORA	60505	AURORA
60519	EOLA	60502	AURORA
60522	HINSDALE	60523	OAK BROOK
60536	MILLBROOK	60541	NEWARK
60557	WEDRON	61350	OTTAWA
60566	NAPERVILLE	60540	NAPERVILLE
60567	NAPERVILLE	60540	NAPERVILLE
60568	AURORA	60505	AURORA
60572	AURORA	60504	AURORA
60598	AURORA	60505	AURORA
60599	FOX VALLEY	60504	AURORA
60663	CHICAGO	60606	CHICAGO
60664	CHICAGO	60601	CHICAGO
60668	CHICAGO	60616	CHICAGO
60669	CHICAGO	60607	CHICAGO
60670	CHICAGO	60603	CHICAGO
60673	CHICAGO	60606	CHICAGO
60674	CHICAGO	60603	CHICAGO
60675	CHICAGO	60603	CHICAGO
60677	CHICAGO	60606	CHICAGO
60678	CHICAGO	60602	CHICAGO
60679	CHICAGO	60606	CHICAGO
60680	CHICAGO	60606	CHICAGO
60681	CHICAGO	60602	CHICAGO
60682	CHICAGO	60607	CHICAGO
60684	CHICAGO	60606	CHICAGO
60685	CHICAGO	60604	CHICAGO
60686	CHICAGO	60612	CHICAGO
60687	CHICAGO	60603	CHICAGO
60689	CHICAGO	60607	CHICAGO
60690	CHICAGO	60604	CHICAGO
60691	CHICAGO	60604	CHICAGO
60693	CHICAGO	60604	CHICAGO
60694	CHICAGO	60603	CHICAGO
60695	CHICAGO	60607	CHICAGO
60696	CHICAGO	60604	CHICAGO
60697	CHICAGO	60604	CHICAGO
60699	CHICAGO	60607	CHICAGO
60701	CHICAGO	60131	FRANKLIN PARK
60910	AROMA PARK	60964	SAINT ANNE
60920	CAMPUS	60420	DWIGHT
60926	CLAYTONVILLE	60924	CISSNA PARK
60932	EAST LYNN	60960	RANKIN
60933	ELLIOTT	60936	GIBSON CITY
60939	GOODWINE	60924	CISSNA PARK
60944	HOPKINS PARK	60964	SAINT ANNE
60945	IROQUOIS	60966	SHELDON
60956	PAPINEAU	60964	SAINT ANNE
60967	STOCKLAND	60953	MILFORD
60969	UNION HILL	60941	HERSCHER
60974	WOODLAND	60970	WATSEKA
61013	CEDARVILLE	61032	FREEPORT
61027	ELEROY	61048	LENA
61037	GALT	61081	STERLING
61043	HOLCOMB	61020	DAVIS JUNCTION
61057	NACHUSA	61021	DIXON
61059	NORA	61087	WARREN
61077	SEWARD	61063	PECATONICA
61079	SHIRLAND	61072	ROCKTON
61091	WOOSUNG	61021	DIXON
61105	ROCKFORD	61101	ROCKFORD
61106	ROCKFORD	61104	ROCKFORD
61110	ROCKFORD	61104	ROCKFORD
61125	ROCKFORD	61108	ROCKFORD
61126	ROCKFORD	61111	LOVES PARK
61130	LOVES PARK	61111	LOVES PARK
61131	LOVES PARK	61111	LOVES PARK
61132	LOVES PARK	61111	LOVES PARK
61204	ROCK ISLAND	61201	ROCK ISLAND
61233	ANDOVER	61238	CAMBRIDGE
61236	BARSTOW	61244	EAST MOLINE
61237	BUFFALO PRAIRIE	61259	ILLINOIS CITY
61239	CARBON CLIFF	61282	SILVIS
61258	HOOPPOLE	61277	PROPHETSTOWN
61266	MOLINE	61265	MOLINE
61276	PREEMPTION	61281	SHERRARD
61278	RAPIDS CITY	61275	PORT BYRON
61299	ROCK ISLAND	61201	ROCK ISLAND
61315	BUREAU	61356	PRINCETON

NONRESIDENTIAL ZIP CODES

ILLINOIS

Point ZIP Code: ZIP	Point ZIP Code: Post Office Name	Enclosing Residential ZIP Code: ZIP	Enclosing Residential ZIP Code: Post Office Name
61316	CEDAR POINT	61354	PERU
61317	CHERRY	61312	ARLINGTON
61322	DEPUE	61356	PRINCETON
61323	DOVER	61356	PRINCETON
61324	ELDENA	61021	DIXON
61328	KASBEER	61349	OHIO
61331	LEE CENTER	61310	AMBOY
61332	LEONORE	61370	TONICA
61338	MANLIUS	61361	SHEFFIELD
61340	MARK	61326	GRANVILLE
61359	SEATONVILLE	61356	PRINCETON
61363	STANDARD	61326	GRANVILLE
61371	TRIUMPH	61342	MENDOTA
61372	TROY GROVE	61342	MENDOTA
61374	VAN ORIN	61330	LA MOILLE
61402	GALESBURG	61401	GALESBURG
61416	BARDOLPH	61455	MACOMB
61419	BISHOP HILL	61434	GALVA
61424	CAMP GROVE	61421	BRADFORD
61426	CASTLETON	61421	BRADFORD
61439	HENDERSON	61401	GALESBURG
61468	OPHIEM	61262	LYNN CENTER
61539	KINGSTON MINES	61547	MAPLETON
61541	LA ROSE	61375	VARNA
61553	NORRIS	61531	FARMINGTON
61555	PEKIN	61554	PEKIN
61558	PEKIN	61554	PEKIN
61562	ROME	61523	CHILLICOTHE
61564	SOUTH PEKIN	61554	PEKIN
61601	PEORIA	61602	PEORIA
61612	PEORIA	61614	PEORIA
61613	PEORIA	61615	PEORIA
61629	PEORIA	61602	PEORIA
61630	PEORIA	61602	PEORIA
61633	PEORIA	61604	PEORIA
61634	PEORIA	61602	PEORIA
61636	PEORIA	61602	PEORIA
61637	PEORIA	61603	PEORIA
61638	PEORIA	61615	PEORIA
61639	PEORIA	61603	PEORIA
61641	PEORIA	61607	PEORIA
61643	PEORIA	61614	PEORIA
61650	PEORIA	61602	PEORIA
61651	PEORIA	61602	PEORIA
61652	PEORIA	61602	PEORIA
61653	PEORIA	61602	PEORIA
61654	PEORIA	61602	PEORIA
61655	PEORIA	61602	PEORIA
61656	PEORIA	61602	PEORIA
61702	BLOOMINGTON	61701	BLOOMINGTON
61709	BLOOMINGTON	61704	BLOOMINGTON
61710	BLOOMINGTON	61701	BLOOMINGTON
61750	LANE	61727	CLINTON
61751	LAWNDALE	62656	LINCOLN
61758	MERNA	61761	NORMAL
61791	BLOOMINGTON	61701	BLOOMINGTON
61799	BLOOMINGTON	61704	BLOOMINGTON
61803	URBANA	61801	URBANA
61815	BONDVILLE	61822	CHAMPAIGN
61824	CHAMPAIGN	61821	CHAMPAIGN
61825	CHAMPAIGN	61820	CHAMPAIGN
61826	CHAMPAIGN	61821	CHAMPAIGN
61848	HENNING	60963	ROSSVILLE
61857	MUNCIE	61844	FITHIAN
61871	ROYAL	61859	OGDEN
61936	LA PLACE	61818	CERRO GORDO
61941	MURDOCK	61956	VILLA GROVE
61949	REDMON	61944	PARIS
61955	VERMILION	61944	PARIS
62023	EAGARVILLE	62069	MOUNT OLIVE
62046	HAMEL	62025	EDWARDSVILLE
62058	LIVINGSTON	62074	NEW DOUGLAS
62059	LOVEJOY	62201	EAST SAINT LOUIS
62071	NATIONAL STOCK YARDS	62201	EAST SAINT LOUIS
62076	OHLMAN	62075	NOKOMIS
62077	PANAMA	62019	DONNELLSON
62078	PATTERSON	62050	HILLVIEW
62085	SAWYERVILLE	62009	BENLD
62089	TAYLOR SPRINGS	62049	HILLSBORO
62093	WILSONVILLE	62033	GILLESPIE
62098	WRIGHTS	62092	WHITE HALL
62202	EAST SAINT LOUIS	62201	EAST SAINT LOUIS
62216	AVISTON	62293	TRENTON
62219	BECKEMEYER	62231	CARLYLE
62222	BELLEVILLE	62220	BELLEVILLE
62247	HAGARSTOWN	62262	MULBERRY GROVE
62250	HOFFMAN	62801	CENTRALIA
62252	HUEY	62231	CARLYLE
62256	MAEYSTOWN	62244	FULTS
62259	MENARD	62233	CHESTER
62266	NEW MEMPHIS	62265	NEW BADEN
62273	PIERRON	62275	POCAHONTAS
62279	RENAULT	62277	PRAIRIE DU ROCHER

MISSOURI

Point ZIP Code: ZIP	Point ZIP Code: Post Office Name	Enclosing Residential ZIP Code: ZIP	Enclosing Residential ZIP Code: Post Office Name
62282	SAINT LIBORY	62258	MASCOUTAH
62289	SUMMERFIELD	62254	LEBANON
62292	TILDEN	62286	SPARTA
62306	QUINCY	62301	QUINCY
62329	COLUSA	62358	NIOTA
62336	FERRIS	62321	CARTHAGE
62435	JANESVILLE	62440	LERNA
62444	MODE	62414	BEECHER CITY
62459	SAINTE MARIE	62480	WILLOW HILL
62464	STOY	62454	ROBINSON
62519	CORNLAND	62634	ELKHART
62524	DECATUR	62526	DECATUR
62525	DECATUR	62523	DECATUR
62532	ELWIN	62521	DECATUR
62537	HARRISTOWN	62522	DECATUR
62540	KINCAID	62568	TAYLORVILLE
62541	LAKE FORK	62548	MOUNT PULASKI
62570	TOVEY	62568	TAYLORVILLE
62610	ALSEY	62694	WINCHESTER
62622	BLUFF SPRINGS	62618	BEARDSTOWN
62651	JACKSONVILLE	62650	JACKSONVILLE
62659	LINCOLNS NEW SALEM	62675	PETERSBURG
62660	LITERBERRY	62650	JACKSONVILLE
62662	LOWDER	62692	WAVERLY
62663	MANCHESTER	62694	WINCHESTER
62689	THAYER	62615	AUBURN
62695	WOODSON	62650	JACKSONVILLE
62705	SPRINGFIELD	62703	SPRINGFIELD
62706	SPRINGFIELD	62704	SPRINGFIELD
62708	SPRINGFIELD	62703	SPRINGFIELD
62715	SPRINGFIELD	62701	SPRINGFIELD
62716	SPRINGFIELD	62712	SPRINGFIELD
62719	SPRINGFIELD	62702	SPRINGFIELD
62721	SPRINGFIELD	62703	SPRINGFIELD
62722	SPRINGFIELD	62704	SPRINGFIELD
62723	SPRINGFIELD	62703	SPRINGFIELD
62726	SPRINGFIELD	62702	SPRINGFIELD
62736	SPRINGFIELD	62702	SPRINGFIELD
62739	SPRINGFIELD	62701	SPRINGFIELD
62746	SPRINGFIELD	62702	SPRINGFIELD
62756	SPRINGFIELD	62704	SPRINGFIELD
62757	SPRINGFIELD	62701	SPRINGFIELD
62761	SPRINGFIELD	62702	SPRINGFIELD
62762	SPRINGFIELD	62704	SPRINGFIELD
62763	SPRINGFIELD	62704	SPRINGFIELD
62764	SPRINGFIELD	62703	SPRINGFIELD
62765	SPRINGFIELD	62701	SPRINGFIELD
62766	SPRINGFIELD	62703	SPRINGFIELD
62767	SPRINGFIELD	62701	SPRINGFIELD
62769	SPRINGFIELD	62702	SPRINGFIELD
62776	SPRINGFIELD	62704	SPRINGFIELD
62777	SPRINGFIELD	62701	SPRINGFIELD
62781	SPRINGFIELD	62702	SPRINGFIELD
62786	SPRINGFIELD	62701	SPRINGFIELD
62791	SPRINGFIELD	62704	SPRINGFIELD
62794	SPRINGFIELD	62703	SPRINGFIELD
62796	SPRINGFIELD	62703	SPRINGFIELD
62805	AKIN	62890	THOMPSONVILLE
62811	BELLMONT	62863	MOUNT CARMEL
62825	COELLO	62812	BENTON
62834	EMMA	62821	CARMI
62840	FRANKFORT HEIGHTS	62896	WEST FRANKFORT
62841	FREEMAN SPUR	62948	HERRIN
62848	IRVINGTON	62877	RICHVIEW
62852	KEENSBURG	62863	MOUNT CARMEL
62856	LOGAN	62812	BENTON
62857	LOOGOOTEE	62880	SAINT PETER
62861	MAUNIE	62821	CARMI
62874	ORIENT	62896	WEST FRANKFORT
62876	RADOM	62831	DU BOIS
62879	SAILOR SPRINGS	62824	CLAY CITY
62891	VALIER	62822	CHRISTOPHER
62909	BOLES	62923	CYPRESS
62915	CAMBRIA	62918	CARTERVILLE
62921	COLP	62948	HERRIN
62927	DOWELL	62932	ELKVILLE
62949	HURST	62924	DE SOTO
62965	MUDDY	62946	HARRISBURG
62969	OLIVE BRANCH	62990	THEBES
62971	ORAVILLE	62966	MURPHYSBORO
62973	PERKS	62992	ULLIN
62993	UNITY	62988	TAMMS
63001	ALLENTON	63069	PACIFIC
63006	CHESTERFIELD	63017	CHESTERFIELD
63022	BALLWIN	63011	BALLWIN
63024	BALLWIN	63011	BALLWIN
63032	FLORISSANT	63033	FLORISSANT
63047	HEMATITE	63028	FESTUS
63053	KIMMSWICK	63052	IMPERIAL
63057	LIGUORI	63052	IMPERIAL
63065	MAPAVILLE	63050	HILLSBORO
63066	MORSE MILL	63050	HILLSBORO
63073	SAINT ALBANS	63069	PACIFIC

Point ZIP Code		Enclosing Residential ZIP Code	
ZIP	Post Office Name	ZIP	Post Office Name
63079	STANTON	63080	SULLIVAN
63099	FENTON	63026	FENTON
63150	SAINT LOUIS	63101	SAINT LOUIS
63151	SAINT LOUIS	63129	SAINT LOUIS
63155	SAINT LOUIS	63103	SAINT LOUIS
63156	SAINT LOUIS	63108	SAINT LOUIS
63157	SAINT LOUIS	63104	SAINT LOUIS
63158	SAINT LOUIS	63118	SAINT LOUIS
63160	SAINT LOUIS	63102	SAINT LOUIS
63163	SAINT LOUIS	63118	SAINT LOUIS
63164	SAINT LOUIS	63102	SAINT LOUIS
63166	SAINT LOUIS	63103	SAINT LOUIS
63167	SAINT LOUIS	63141	SAINT LOUIS
63169	SAINT LOUIS	63101	SAINT LOUIS
63171	SAINT LOUIS	63119	SAINT LOUIS
63177	SAINT LOUIS	63103	SAINT LOUIS
63178	SAINT LOUIS	63103	SAINT LOUIS
63179	SAINT LOUIS	63103	SAINT LOUIS
63180	SAINT LOUIS	63103	SAINT LOUIS
63182	SAINT LOUIS	63103	SAINT LOUIS
63188	SAINT LOUIS	63101	SAINT LOUIS
63190	SAINT LOUIS	63103	SAINT LOUIS
63195	SAINT LOUIS	63105	SAINT LOUIS
63197	SAINT LOUIS	63103	SAINT LOUIS
63198	SAINT LOUIS	63017	CHESTERFIELD
63199	SAINT LOUIS	63102	SAINT LOUIS
63302	SAINT CHARLES	63301	SAINT CHARLES
63338	COTTLEVILLE	63304	SAINT CHARLES
63342	DUTZOW	63357	MARTHASVILLE
63346	FLINTHILL	63385	WENTZVILLE
63365	NEW MELLE	63385	WENTZVILLE
63378	TRELOAR	63357	MARTHASVILLE
63387	WHITESIDE	63377	SILEX
63442	GRANGER	63432	ARBELA
63465	REVERE	63472	WAYLAND
63467	SAVERTON	63459	NEW LONDON
63651	KNOB LICK	63640	FARMINGTON
63663	PILOT KNOB	63650	IRONTON
63666	REYNOLDS	63638	ELLINGTON
63674	TIFF	63630	CADET
63702	CAPE GIRARDEAU	63701	CAPE GIRARDEAU
63737	BRAZEAU	63748	FROHNA
63738	BROWNWOOD	63730	ADVANCE
63742	COMMERCE	63780	SCOTT CITY
63745	DUTCHTOWN	63701	CAPE GIRARDEAU
63746	FARRAR	63748	FROHNA
63752	GORDONVILLE	63701	CAPE GIRARDEAU
63758	KELSO	63780	SCOTT CITY
63767	MORLEY	63771	ORAN
63774	PERKINS	63771	ORAN
63776	MC BRIDE	63775	PERRYVILLE
63779	POCAHONTAS	63755	JACKSON
63784	VANDUSER	63801	SIKESTON
63820	ANNISTON	63845	EAST PRAIRIE
63824	BLODGETT	63801	SIKESTON
63826	BRAGGADOCIO	63877	STEELE
63828	CANALOU	63867	MATTHEWS
63839	COOTER	63877	STEELE
63840	DEERING	63877	STEELE
63847	GIBSON	63837	CLARKTON
63850	GRAYRIDGE	63846	ESSEX
63853	HOLLAND	63877	STEELE
63860	KEWANEE	63869	NEW MADRID
63874	RISCO	63870	PARMA
63875	RIVES	63855	HORNERSVILLE
63878	TALLAPOOSA	63873	PORTAGEVILLE
63880	WHITEOAK	63852	HOLCOMB
63881	WOLF ISLAND	63845	EAST PRAIRIE
63882	WYATT	63834	CHARLESTON
63902	POPLAR BLUFF	63901	POPLAR BLUFF
63938	FAGUS	63961	QULIN
63962	ROMBAUER	63940	FISK
64002	LEES SUMMIT	64063	LEES SUMMIT
64013	BLUE SPRINGS	64015	BLUE SPRINGS
64028	FARLEY	64079	PLATTE CITY
64051	INDEPENDENCE	64055	INDEPENDENCE
64065	LEES SUMMIT	64064	LEES SUMMIT
64066	LEVASY	64088	SIBLEY
64069	LIBERTY	64068	LIBERTY
64072	MISSOURI CITY	64068	LIBERTY
64073	MOSBY	64068	LIBERTY
64090	STRASBURG	64080	PLEASANT HILL
64092	WALDRON	64152	KANSAS CITY
64121	KANSAS CITY	64127	KANSAS CITY
64141	KANSAS CITY	64108	KANSAS CITY
64144	KANSAS CITY	64161	KANSAS CITY
64148	KANSAS CITY	64108	KANSAS CITY
64168	KANSAS CITY	64150	RIVERSIDE
64170	KANSAS CITY	64137	KANSAS CITY
64171	KANSAS CITY	64111	KANSAS CITY
64172	KANSAS CITY	64108	KANSAS CITY
64179	KANSAS CITY	64108	KANSAS CITY
64180	KANSAS CITY	64106	KANSAS CITY
64183	KANSAS CITY	64108	KANSAS CITY
64184	KANSAS CITY	64106	KANSAS CITY
64187	KANSAS CITY	64106	KANSAS CITY
64188	KANSAS CITY	64118	KANSAS CITY
64190	KANSAS CITY	64152	KANSAS CITY
64191	KANSAS CITY	64124	KANSAS CITY
64192	KANSAS CITY	64137	KANSAS CITY
64193	KANSAS CITY	64153	KANSAS CITY
64195	KANSAS CITY	64152	KANSAS CITY
64196	KANSAS CITY	64105	KANSAS CITY
64197	KANSAS CITY	64131	KANSAS CITY
64198	KANSAS CITY	64106	KANSAS CITY
64199	KANSAS CITY	64106	KANSAS CITY
64420	ALLENDALE	64456	GRANT CITY
64502	SAINT JOSEPH	64501	SAINT JOSEPH
64508	SAINT JOSEPH	64505	SAINT JOSEPH
64680	STET	64668	NORBORNE
64743	EAST LYNNE	64701	HARRISONVILLE
64765	METZ	64778	RICHARDS
64766	MILFORD	64759	LAMAR
64781	ROSCOE	64776	OSCEOLA
64802	JOPLIN	64801	JOPLIN
64803	JOPLIN	64801	JOPLIN
64830	ALBA	64855	ORONOGO
64841	DUENWEG	64801	JOPLIN
64849	NECK CITY	64755	JASPER
64853	NEWTONIA	64866	STARK CITY
64857	PURCELL	64755	JASPER
64858	RACINE	64850	NEOSHO
64864	SAGINAW	64804	JOPLIN
64869	WACO	64832	ASBURY
64999	KANSAS CITY	64137	KANSAS CITY
65036	GASCONADE	65041	HERMANN
65038	LAURIE	65037	GRAVOIS MILLS
65055	MC GIRK	65018	CALIFORNIA
65102	JEFFERSON CITY	65101	JEFFERSON CITY
65103	JEFFERSON CITY	65101	JEFFERSON CITY
65104	JEFFERSON CITY	65101	JEFFERSON CITY
65105	JEFFERSON CITY	65101	JEFFERSON CITY
65106	JEFFERSON CITY	65101	JEFFERSON CITY
65107	JEFFERSON CITY	65101	JEFFERSON CITY
65108	JEFFERSON CITY	65101	JEFFERSON CITY
65110	JEFFERSON CITY	65109	JEFFERSON CITY
65111	JEFFERSON CITY	65101	JEFFERSON CITY
65205	COLUMBIA	65201	COLUMBIA
65212	COLUMBIA	65201	COLUMBIA
65217	COLUMBIA	65201	COLUMBIA
65218	COLUMBIA	65203	COLUMBIA
65278	RENICK	65243	CLARK
65299	COLUMBIA	65201	COLUMBIA
65302	SEDALIA	65301	SEDALIA
65320	ARROW ROCK	65347	NELSON
65327	EMMA	65351	SWEET SPRINGS
65402	ROLLA	65401	ROLLA
65532	LAKE SPRING	65401	ROLLA
65546	MONTIER	65438	BIRCH TREE
65607	CAPLINGER MILLS	65785	STOCKTON
65615	BRANSON	65616	BRANSON
65636	DIGGINS	65746	SEYMOUR
65645	EUDORA	65770	WALNUT GROVE
65664	HALLTOWN	65612	BOIS D ARC
65673	HOLLISTER	65739	RIDGEDALE
65726	POINT LOOKOUT	65672	HOLLISTER
65741	ROCKBRIDGE	65618	BRIXEY
65765	TURNERS	65809	SPRINGFIELD
65801	SPRINGFIELD	65802	SPRINGFIELD
65805	SPRINGFIELD	65806	SPRINGFIELD
65808	SPRINGFIELD	65804	SPRINGFIELD
65814	SPRINGFIELD	65804	SPRINGFIELD
65817	SPRINGFIELD	65807	SPRINGFIELD
65890	SPRINGFIELD	65804	SPRINGFIELD
65897	SPRINGFIELD	65807	SPRINGFIELD
65898	SPRINGFIELD	65807	SPRINGFIELD
65899	SPRINGFIELD	65804	SPRINGFIELD
66019	CLEARVIEW CITY	66018	DE SOTO
66024	ELWOOD	66090	WATHENA
66036	HILLSDALE	66071	PAOLA
66051	OLATHE	66061	OLATHE
66063	OLATHE	66062	OLATHE
66077	POTTER	66002	ATCHISON
66110	KANSAS CITY	66102	KANSAS CITY
66117	KANSAS CITY	66101	KANSAS CITY
66119	KANSAS CITY	66105	KANSAS CITY
66201	MISSION	66202	MISSION
66222	MISSION	66205	MISSION
66225	OVERLAND PARK	66210	OVERLAND PARK
66250	SHAWNEE MISSION	66219	LENEXA
66251	OVERLAND PARK	66202	MISSION
66276	SHAWNEE MISSION	66202	MISSION
66282	OVERLAND PARK	66202	MISSION
66283	OVERLAND PARK	66223	OVERLAND PARK
66285	LENEXA	66215	LENEXA
66286	SHAWNEE	66226	SHAWNEE

Point ZIP Code		Enclosing Residential ZIP Code	
ZIP	Post Office Name	ZIP	Post Office Name
66420	DOVER	66610	TOPEKA
66501	MC FARLAND	66401	ALMA
66505	MANHATTAN	66502	MANHATTAN
66601	TOPEKA	66603	TOPEKA
66620	TOPEKA	66619	TOPEKA
66621	TOPEKA	66604	TOPEKA
66622	TOPEKA	66614	TOPEKA
66624	TOPEKA	66619	TOPEKA
66625	TOPEKA	66612	TOPEKA
66626	TOPEKA	66612	TOPEKA
66628	TOPEKA	66612	TOPEKA
66629	TOPEKA	66612	TOPEKA
66636	TOPEKA	66603	TOPEKA
66647	TOPEKA	66604	TOPEKA
66667	TOPEKA	66604	TOPEKA
66675	TOPEKA	66608	TOPEKA
66683	TOPEKA	66603	TOPEKA
66699	TOPEKA	66612	TOPEKA
66741	GARLAND	66711	ARCADIA
66742	GAS	66749	IOLA
66760	OPOLIS	66762	PITTSBURG
66782	WEST MINERAL	66773	SCAMMON
66855	LAMONT	66860	MADISON
66863	NEAL	66870	VIRGIL
67012	BEAUMONT	67074	LEON
67041	ELBING	67114	NEWTON
67201	WICHITA	67202	WICHITA
67275	WICHITA	67209	WICHITA
67276	WICHITA	67209	WICHITA
67277	WICHITA	67209	WICHITA
67278	WICHITA	67209	WICHITA
67334	CHAUTAUQUA	67360	PERU
67340	DEARING	67337	COFFEYVILLE
67363	SYCAMORE	67301	INDEPENDENCE
67364	TYRO	67333	CANEY
67402	SALINA	67401	SALINA
67504	HUTCHINSON	67501	HUTCHINSON
67585	YODER	67543	HAVEN
67667	SCHOENCHEN	67601	HAYS
67674	WALKER	67671	VICTORIA
67747	MONUMENT	67764	WINONA
67836	COOLIDGE	67878	SYRACUSE
67843	FORT DODGE	67801	DODGE CITY
67905	LIBERAL	67901	LIBERAL
68009	BLAIR	68008	BLAIR
68016	CEDAR CREEK	68037	LOUISVILLE
68026	FREMONT	68025	FREMONT
68042	MEMPHIS	68003	ASHLAND
68056	ST COLUMBANS	68005	BELLEVUE
68058	SOUTH BEND	68037	LOUISVILLE
68063	UEHLING	68031	HOOPER
68068	WASHINGTON	68034	KENNARD
68072	WINSLOW	68031	HOOPER
68101	OMAHA	68102	OMAHA
68103	OMAHA	68108	OMAHA
68109	OMAHA	68107	OMAHA
68119	OMAHA	68110	OMAHA
68120	OMAHA	68110	OMAHA
68139	OMAHA	68137	OMAHA
68145	OMAHA	68137	OMAHA
68155	OMAHA	68105	OMAHA
68172	OMAHA	68131	OMAHA
68175	OMAHA	68131	OMAHA
68178	OMAHA	68102	OMAHA
68179	OMAHA	68102	OMAHA
68180	OMAHA	68124	OMAHA
68183	OMAHA	68102	OMAHA
68197	OMAHA	68102	OMAHA
68364	GOEHNER	68434	SEWARD
68382	LORTON	68346	DUNBAR
68403	MANLEY	68463	WEEPING WATER
68419	PANAMA	68317	BENNET
68438	SPRAGUE	68404	MARTELL
68501	LINCOLN	68508	LINCOLN
68509	LINCOLN	68508	LINCOLN
68529	LINCOLN	68507	LINCOLN
68542	LINCOLN	68502	LINCOLN
68602	COLUMBUS	68601	COLUMBUS
68634	DUNCAN	68601	COLUMBUS
68664	SNYDER	68633	DODGE
68702	NORFOLK	68701	NORFOLK
68738	HADAR	68701	NORFOLK
68802	GRAND ISLAND	68803	GRAND ISLAND
68848	KEARNEY	68847	KEARNEY
68902	HASTINGS	68901	HASTINGS
69103	NORTH PLATTE	69101	NORTH PLATTE
69135	ELSMERE	69214	JOHNSTOWN
69160	SIDNEY	69162	SIDNEY
69171	WILLOW ISLAND	69130	COZAD
69190	OSHKOSH	69154	OSHKOSH
69219	NENZEL	69216	KILGORE
69220	SPARKS	69201	VALENTINE
69353	MCGREW	69341	GERING
69355	MELBETA	69341	GERING
69363	SCOTTSBLUFF	69361	SCOTTSBLUFF
69365	WHITECLAY	69360	RUSHVILLE
70004	METAIRIE	70001	METAIRIE
70009	METAIRIE	70002	METAIRIE
70010	METAIRIE	70002	METAIRIE
70011	METAIRIE	70002	METAIRIE
70033	METAIRIE	70003	METAIRIE
70038	BOOTHVILLE	70041	BURAS
70044	CHALMETTE	70043	CHALMETTE
70050	EMPIRE	70041	BURAS
70054	GRETNA	70053	GRETNA
70055	METAIRIE	70005	METAIRIE
70059	HARVEY	70058	HARVEY
70060	METAIRIE	70002	METAIRIE
70063	KENNER	70062	KENNER
70064	KENNER	70065	KENNER
70069	LA PLACE	70068	LA PLACE
70073	MARRERO	70072	MARRERO
70078	NEW SARPY	70047	DESTREHAN
70082	POINTE A LA HACHE	70040	BRAITHWAITE
70093	BELLE CHASSE	70037	BELLE CHASSE
70096	WESTWEGO	70094	WESTWEGO
70097	KENNER	70062	KENNER
70139	NEW ORLEANS	70130	NEW ORLEANS
70140	NEW ORLEANS	70112	NEW ORLEANS
70141	NEW ORLEANS	70126	NEW ORLEANS
70142	NEW ORLEANS	70113	NEW ORLEANS
70143	NEW ORLEANS	70037	BELLE CHASSE
70145	NEW ORLEANS	70117	NEW ORLEANS
70146	NEW ORLEANS	70117	NEW ORLEANS
70149	NEW ORLEANS	70117	NEW ORLEANS
70150	NEW ORLEANS	70113	NEW ORLEANS
70151	NEW ORLEANS	70113	NEW ORLEANS
70152	NEW ORLEANS	70113	NEW ORLEANS
70153	NEW ORLEANS	70113	NEW ORLEANS
70154	NEW ORLEANS	70115	NEW ORLEANS
70156	NEW ORLEANS	70113	NEW ORLEANS
70157	NEW ORLEANS	70113	NEW ORLEANS
70158	NEW ORLEANS	70113	NEW ORLEANS
70159	NEW ORLEANS	70117	NEW ORLEANS
70160	NEW ORLEANS	70113	NEW ORLEANS
70161	NEW ORLEANS	70113	NEW ORLEANS
70162	NEW ORLEANS	70112	NEW ORLEANS
70163	NEW ORLEANS	70112	NEW ORLEANS
70164	NEW ORLEANS	70113	NEW ORLEANS
70165	NEW ORLEANS	70130	NEW ORLEANS
70166	NEW ORLEANS	70112	NEW ORLEANS
70167	NEW ORLEANS	70119	NEW ORLEANS
70170	NEW ORLEANS	70130	NEW ORLEANS
70172	NEW ORLEANS	70112	NEW ORLEANS
70174	NEW ORLEANS	70114	NEW ORLEANS
70175	NEW ORLEANS	70115	NEW ORLEANS
70176	NEW ORLEANS	70130	NEW ORLEANS
70177	NEW ORLEANS	70117	NEW ORLEANS
70178	NEW ORLEANS	70118	NEW ORLEANS
70179	NEW ORLEANS	70119	NEW ORLEANS
70181	NEW ORLEANS	70121	NEW ORLEANS
70182	NEW ORLEANS	70122	NEW ORLEANS
70183	NEW ORLEANS	70123	NEW ORLEANS
70184	NEW ORLEANS	70119	NEW ORLEANS
70185	NEW ORLEANS	70118	NEW ORLEANS
70186	NEW ORLEANS	70126	NEW ORLEANS
70187	NEW ORLEANS	70127	NEW ORLEANS
70189	NEW ORLEANS	70129	NEW ORLEANS
70190	NEW ORLEANS	70130	NEW ORLEANS
70195	NEW ORLEANS	70112	NEW ORLEANS
70302	THIBODAUX	70301	THIBODAUX
70310	THIBODAUX	70301	THIBODAUX
70340	AMELIA	70380	MORGAN CITY
70352	DONNER	70395	SCHRIEVER
70361	HOUMA	70360	HOUMA
70371	KRAEMER	70301	THIBODAUX
70373	LAROSE	70345	CUT OFF
70381	MORGAN CITY	70380	MORGAN CITY
70391	PAINCOURTVILLE	70390	NAPOLEONVILLE
70393	PLATTENVILLE	70341	BELLE ROSE
70404	HAMMOND	70401	HAMMOND
70421	AKERS	70454	PONCHATOULA
70429	BOGALUSA	70427	BOGALUSA
70434	COVINGTON	70433	COVINGTON
70451	NATALBANY	70401	HAMMOND
70457	SAINT BENEDICT	70435	COVINGTON
70459	SLIDELL	70458	SLIDELL
70463	SUN	70427	BOGALUSA
70464	TALISHEEK	70431	BUSH
70465	TANGIPAHOA	70444	KENTWOOD
70469	SLIDELL	70460	SLIDELL
70470	MANDEVILLE	70471	MANDEVILLE
70500	LAFAYETTE	70501	LAFAYETTE
70502	LAFAYETTE	70501	LAFAYETTE
70505	LAFAYETTE	70503	LAFAYETTE
70509	LAFAYETTE	70501	LAFAYETTE

NONRESIDENTIAL ZIP CODES

LOUISIANA

ARKANSAS

Point ZIP Code		Enclosing Residential ZIP Code	
ZIP	Post Office Name	ZIP	Post Office Name
70511	ABBEVILLE	70510	ABBEVILLE
70513	AVERY ISLAND	70560	NEW IBERIA
70519	CADE	70582	SAINT MARTINVILLE
70521	CECILIA	70517	BREAUX BRIDGE
70522	CENTERVILLE	70538	FRANKLIN
70523	CHARENTON	70514	BALDWIN
70524	CHATAIGNIER	70586	VILLE PLATTE
70527	CROWLEY	70526	CROWLEY
70534	ESTHERWOOD	70559	MORSE
70540	GARDEN CITY	70538	FRANKLIN
70541	GRAND COTEAU	70570	OPELOUSAS
70550	LAWTELL	70570	OPELOUSAS
70551	LEONVILLE	70570	OPELOUSAS
70556	MERMENTAU	70559	MORSE
70558	MILTON	70592	YOUNGSVILLE
70562	NEW IBERIA	70560	NEW IBERIA
70569	LYDIA	70560	NEW IBERIA
70571	OPELOUSAS	70570	OPELOUSAS
70575	PERRY	70510	ABBEVILLE
70576	PINE PRAIRIE	70586	VILLE PLATTE
70580	REDDELL	70554	MAMOU
70585	TURKEY CREEK	70586	VILLE PLATTE
70595	LAFAYETTE	70501	LAFAYETTE
70596	LAFAYETTE	70506	LAFAYETTE
70598	LAFAYETTE	70508	LAFAYETTE
70602	LAKE CHARLES	70601	LAKE CHARLES
70606	LAKE CHARLES	70605	LAKE CHARLES
70612	LAKE CHARLES	70611	LAKE CHARLES
70616	LAKE CHARLES	70615	LAKE CHARLES
70629	LAKE CHARLES	70601	LAKE CHARLES
70638	ELIZABETH	71463	OAKDALE
70640	FENTON	70648	KINDER
70644	GRANT	70654	MITTIE
70646	HAYES	70647	IOWA
70651	LEBLANC	70658	REEVES
70659	ROSEPINE	71446	LEESVILLE
70664	SULPHUR	70663	SULPHUR
70704	BAKER	70714	BAKER
70707	GONZALES	70737	GONZALES
70718	BRITTANY	70737	GONZALES
70727	DENHAM SPRINGS	70726	DENHAM SPRINGS
70728	DUPLESSIS	70737	GONZALES
70743	HESTER	70763	PAULINA
70747	INNIS	70715	BATCHELOR
70765	PLAQUEMINE	70764	PLAQUEMINE
70782	TUNICA	70775	SAINT FRANCISVILLE
70784	WAKEFIELD	70775	SAINT FRANCISVILLE
70786	WATSON	70706	DENHAM SPRINGS
70787	WEYANOKE	70775	SAINT FRANCISVILLE
70804	BATON ROUGE	70802	BATON ROUGE
70821	BATON ROUGE	70802	BATON ROUGE
70822	BATON ROUGE	70806	BATON ROUGE
70823	BATON ROUGE	70802	BATON ROUGE
70825	BATON ROUGE	70802	BATON ROUGE
70826	BATON ROUGE	70802	BATON ROUGE
70827	BATON ROUGE	70816	BATON ROUGE
70831	BATON ROUGE	70802	BATON ROUGE
70833	BATON ROUGE	70802	BATON ROUGE
70835	BATON ROUGE	70816	BATON ROUGE
70836	BATON ROUGE	70802	BATON ROUGE
70837	BATON ROUGE	70802	BATON ROUGE
70873	BATON ROUGE	70802	BATON ROUGE
70874	BATON ROUGE	70811	BATON ROUGE
70879	BATON ROUGE	70816	BATON ROUGE
70884	BATON ROUGE	70810	BATON ROUGE
70891	BATON ROUGE	70802	BATON ROUGE
70892	BATON ROUGE	70805	BATON ROUGE
70893	BATON ROUGE	70820	BATON ROUGE
70894	BATON ROUGE	70803	BATON ROUGE
70895	BATON ROUGE	70815	BATON ROUGE
70896	BATON ROUGE	70806	BATON ROUGE
70898	BATON ROUGE	70808	BATON ROUGE
71009	BLANCHARD	71107	SHREVEPORT
71021	CULLEN	71075	SPRINGHILL
71050	LONGSTREET	71049	LOGANSPORT
71058	MINDEN	71055	MINDEN
71066	POWHATAN	71457	NATCHITOCHES
71080	TAYLOR	71028	GIBSLAND
71102	SHREVEPORT	71103	SHREVEPORT
71113	BOSSIER CITY	71112	BOSSIER CITY
71120	SHREVEPORT	71101	SHREVEPORT
71130	SHREVEPORT	71103	SHREVEPORT
71133	SHREVEPORT	71103	SHREVEPORT
71134	SHREVEPORT	71104	SHREVEPORT
71135	SHREVEPORT	71105	SHREVEPORT
71136	SHREVEPORT	71106	SHREVEPORT
71137	SHREVEPORT	71107	SHREVEPORT
71138	SHREVEPORT	71118	SHREVEPORT
71148	SHREVEPORT	71108	SHREVEPORT
71149	SHREVEPORT	71103	SHREVEPORT
71150	SHREVEPORT	71103	SHREVEPORT
71151	SHREVEPORT	71108	SHREVEPORT
71152	SHREVEPORT	71108	SHREVEPORT

Point ZIP Code		Enclosing Residential ZIP Code	
ZIP	Post Office Name	ZIP	Post Office Name
71153	SHREVEPORT	71101	SHREVEPORT
71154	SHREVEPORT	71101	SHREVEPORT
71156	SHREVEPORT	71101	SHREVEPORT
71161	SHREVEPORT	71101	SHREVEPORT
71162	SHREVEPORT	71101	SHREVEPORT
71163	SHREVEPORT	71101	SHREVEPORT
71164	SHREVEPORT	71101	SHREVEPORT
71165	SHREVEPORT	71101	SHREVEPORT
71166	SHREVEPORT	71101	SHREVEPORT
71171	BOSSIER CITY	71111	BOSSIER CITY
71172	BOSSIER CITY	71112	BOSSIER CITY
71207	MONROE	71201	MONROE
71210	MONROE	71201	MONROE
71211	MONROE	71203	MONROE
71212	MONROE	71209	MONROE
71213	MONROE	71203	MONROE
71217	MONROE	71201	MONROE
71218	ARCHIBALD	71259	MANGHAM
71221	BASTROP	71220	BASTROP
71230	CROWVILLE	71295	WINNSBORO
71233	DELTA	71282	TALLULAH
71240	FAIRBANKS	71203	MONROE
71242	FOREST	71263	OAK GROVE
71247	HODGE	71251	JONESBORO
71249	JIGGER	71295	WINNSBORO
71253	KILBOURNE	71263	OAK GROVE
71272	RUSTON	71270	RUSTON
71273	RUSTON	71270	RUSTON
71279	START	71269	RAYVILLE
71281	SWARTZ	71203	MONROE
71284	TALLULAH	71282	TALLULAH
71294	WEST MONROE	71291	WEST MONROE
71306	ALEXANDRIA	71301	ALEXANDRIA
71307	ALEXANDRIA	71302	ALEXANDRIA
71309	ALEXANDRIA	71301	ALEXANDRIA
71315	ALEXANDRIA	71301	ALEXANDRIA
71320	BORDELONVILLE	71355	MOREAUVILLE
71324	CHASE	71295	WINNSBORO
71329	DUPONT	71362	PLAUCHEVILLE
71330	ECHO	71302	ALEXANDRIA
71339	HAMBURG	71369	SIMMESPORT
71345	LEBEAU	70589	WASHINGTON
71348	LIBUSE	71360	PINEVILLE
71359	PINEVILLE	71360	PINEVILLE
71361	PINEVILLE	71360	PINEVILLE
71363	RHINEHART	71340	HARRISONBURG
71365	RUBY	71360	PINEVILLE
71377	WILDSVILLE	71343	JONESVILLE
71410	CALVIN	71483	WINNFIELD
71414	CLARENCE	71457	NATCHITOCHES
71415	CLARKS	71435	GRAYSON
71428	FLORA	71469	ROBELINE
71431	GARDNER	71424	ELMER
71434	GORUM	71468	PROVENCAL
71440	JOYCE	71483	WINNFIELD
71443	KURTHWOOD	71446	LEESVILLE
71448	LONGLEAF	71430	FOREST HILL
71452	MELROSE	71456	NATCHEZ
71458	NATCHITOCHES	71457	NATCHITOCHES
71460	NEGREET	71429	FLORIEN
71471	SAINT MAURICE	71457	NATCHITOCHES
71474	SIMPSON	71446	LEESVILLE
71475	SLAGLE	71446	LEESVILLE
71477	TIOGA	71360	PINEVILLE
71480	URANIA	71479	TULLOS
71496	LEESVILLE	71446	LEESVILLE
71497	NATCHITOCHES	71457	NATCHITOCHES
71611	PINE BLUFF	71601	PINE BLUFF
71612	WHITE HALL	71602	WHITE HALL
71613	PINE BLUFF	71603	PINE BLUFF
71657	MONTICELLO	71655	MONTICELLO
71659	MOSCOW	71601	PINE BLUFF
71711	CAMDEN	71701	CAMDEN
71721	BEIRNE	71743	GURDON
71724	CALION	71730	EL DORADO
71728	CURTIS	71743	GURDON
71731	EL DORADO	71730	EL DORADO
71750	LAWSON	71730	EL DORADO
71754	MAGNOLIA	71753	MAGNOLIA
71759	NORPHLET	71730	EL DORADO
71768	URBANA	71730	EL DORADO
71772	WHELEN SPRINGS	71743	GURDON
71802	HOPE	71801	HOPE
71820	ALLEENE	71822	ASHDOWN
71823	BEN LOMOND	71846	LOCKESBURG
71840	GENOA	71837	FOUKE
71902	HOT SPRINGS NATIONAL	71901	HOT SPRINGS NATIONAL
71903	HOT SPRINGS NATIONAL	71901	HOT SPRINGS NATIONAL
71910	HOT SPRINGS VILLAGE	71909	HOT SPRINGS NATIONAL
71914	HOT SPRINGS NATIONAL	71913	HOT SPRINGS NATIONAL
71920	ALPINE	71921	AMITY
71932	BOARD CAMP	71953	MENA
72018	BENTON	72015	BENTON

NONRESIDENTIAL ZIP CODES

ARKANSAS

Point ZIP Code		Enclosing Residential ZIP Code	
ZIP	Post Office Name	ZIP	Post Office Name
72033	CONWAY	72032	CONWAY
72037	COY	72046	ENGLAND
72043	DIAZ	72112	NEWPORT
72053	COLLEGE STATION	72206	LITTLE ROCK
72059	GREGORY	72006	AUGUSTA
72061	GUY	72058	GREENBRIER
72074	HUNTER	72036	COTTON PLANT
72075	JACKSONPORT	72112	NEWPORT
72078	JACKSONVILLE	72076	JACKSONVILLE
72085	LETONA	72143	SEARCY
72089	BRYANT	72022	BRYANT
72107	MENIFEE	72127	PLUMERVILLE
72108	MONROE	72021	BRINKLEY
72115	NORTH LITTLE ROCK	72114	NORTH LITTLE ROCK
72119	NORTH LITTLE ROCK	72114	NORTH LITTLE ROCK
72123	PATTERSON	72101	MC CRORY
72124	NORTH LITTLE ROCK	72120	SHERWOOD
72139	RUSSELL	72010	BALD KNOB
72145	SEARCY	72143	SEARCY
72164	SWEET HOME	72206	LITTLE ROCK
72169	TUPELO	72112	NEWPORT
72178	WEST POINT	72143	SEARCY
72180	WOODSON	72065	HENSLEY
72181	WOOSTER	72058	GREENBRIER
72182	WRIGHT	72168	TUCKER
72183	WRIGHTSVILLE	72206	LITTLE ROCK
72190	NORTH LITTLE ROCK	72116	NORTH LITTLE ROCK
72198	NORTH LITTLE ROCK	72114	NORTH LITTLE ROCK
72203	LITTLE ROCK	72202	LITTLE ROCK
72214	LITTLE ROCK	72204	LITTLE ROCK
72215	LITTLE ROCK	72205	LITTLE ROCK
72216	LITTLE ROCK	72206	LITTLE ROCK
72217	LITTLE ROCK	72207	LITTLE ROCK
72219	LITTLE ROCK	72209	LITTLE ROCK
72221	LITTLE ROCK	72211	LITTLE ROCK
72222	LITTLE ROCK	72212	LITTLE ROCK
72225	LITTLE ROCK	72205	LITTLE ROCK
72231	LITTLE ROCK	72117	NORTH LITTLE ROCK
72260	LITTLE ROCK	72202	LITTLE ROCK
72295	LITTLE ROCK	72202	LITTLE ROCK
72303	WEST MEMPHIS	72301	WEST MEMPHIS
72312	BARTON	72355	LEXA
72316	BLYTHEVILLE	72315	BLYTHEVILLE
72319	GOSNELL	72315	BLYTHEVILLE
72322	CALDWELL	72326	COLT
72325	CLARKEDALE	72384	TURRELL
72332	EDMONDSON	72376	PROCTOR
72336	FORREST CITY	72335	FORREST CITY
72352	LA GRANGE	72355	LEXA
72353	LAMBROOK	72333	ELAINE
72359	MADISON	72335	FORREST CITY
72377	RIVERVALE	72365	MARKED TREE
72383	TURNER	72366	MARVELL
72387	VANNDALE	72396	WYNNE
72389	WABASH	72369	ONEIDA
72391	WEST RIDGE	72370	OSCEOLA
72402	JONESBORO	72401	JONESBORO
72403	JONESBORO	72401	JONESBORO
72427	EGYPT	72421	CASH
72431	GRUBBS	72112	NEWPORT
72439	LIGHT	72416	BONO
72451	PARAGOULD	72450	PARAGOULD
72462	REYNO	72413	BIGGERS
72474	WALCOTT	72450	PARAGOULD
72475	WALDENBURG	72429	FISHER
72503	BATESVILLE	72501	BATESVILLE
72525	CHEROKEE VILLAGE	72529	CHEROKEE VILLAGE
72526	CUSHMAN	72501	BATESVILLE
72545	HEBER SPRINGS	72543	HEBER SPRINGS
72575	SALADO	72501	BATESVILLE
72602	HARRISON	72601	HARRISON
72613	BEAVER	72632	EUREKA SPRINGS
72615	BERGMAN	72601	HARRISON
72630	DIAMOND CITY	72644	LEAD HILL
72636	GILBERT	72675	SAINT JOE
72654	MOUNTAIN HOME	72653	MOUNTAIN HOME
72657	TIMBO	72680	TIMBO
72672	PYATT	72687	YELLVILLE
72677	SUMMIT	72687	YELLVILLE
72702	FAYETTEVILLE	72701	FAYETTEVILLE
72711	AVOCA	72756	ROGERS
72716	BENTONVILLE	72712	BENTONVILLE
72728	ELM SPRINGS	72762	SPRINGDALE
72733	GATEWAY	72732	GARFIELD
72735	GOSHEN	72703	FAYETTEVILLE
72737	GREENLAND	72701	FAYETTEVILLE
72741	JOHNSON	72704	FAYETTEVILLE
72757	ROGERS	72756	ROGERS
72765	SPRINGDALE	72764	SPRINGDALE
72766	SPRINGDALE	72764	SPRINGDALE
72770	TONTITOWN	72762	SPRINGDALE
72811	RUSSELLVILLE	72801	RUSSELLVILLE
72812	RUSSELLVILLE	72802	RUSSELLVILLE

OKLAHOMA

Point ZIP Code		Enclosing Residential ZIP Code	
ZIP	Post Office Name	ZIP	Post Office Name
72829	CENTERVILLE	72834	DARDANELLE
72902	FORT SMITH	72903	FORT SMITH
72906	FORT SMITH	72903	FORT SMITH
72913	FORT SMITH	72903	FORT SMITH
72914	FORT SMITH	72904	FORT SMITH
72917	FORT SMITH	72903	FORT SMITH
72918	FORT SMITH	72908	FORT SMITH
72919	FORT SMITH	72903	FORT SMITH
72935	DYER	72921	ALMA
72945	MIDLAND	72940	HUNTINGTON
72957	VAN BUREN	72956	VAN BUREN
73001	ALBERT	73038	FORT COBB
73019	NORMAN	73072	NORMAN
73022	CONCHO	73036	EL RENO
73023	CHICKASHA	73018	CHICKASHA
73031	DIBBLE	73010	BLANCHARD
73032	DOUGHERTY	73030	DAVIS
73033	EAKLY	73048	HYDRO
73039	DAVIS	73030	DAVIS
73050	LANGSTON	73027	COYLE
73066	NICOMA PARK	73020	CHOCTAW
73070	NORMAN	73069	NORMAN
73083	EDMOND	73003	EDMOND
73085	YUKON	73099	YUKON
73097	WHEATLAND	73169	OKLAHOMA CITY
73101	OKLAHOMA CITY	73102	OKLAHOMA CITY
73113	OKLAHOMA CITY	73114	OKLAHOMA CITY
73123	OKLAHOMA CITY	73132	OKLAHOMA CITY
73124	OKLAHOMA CITY	73109	OKLAHOMA CITY
73125	OKLAHOMA CITY	73109	OKLAHOMA CITY
73126	OKLAHOMA CITY	73109	OKLAHOMA CITY
73136	OKLAHOMA CITY	73111	OKLAHOMA CITY
73137	OKLAHOMA CITY	73127	OKLAHOMA CITY
73140	OKLAHOMA CITY	73110	OKLAHOMA CITY
73143	OKLAHOMA CITY	73129	OKLAHOMA CITY
73144	OKLAHOMA CITY	73119	OKLAHOMA CITY
73146	OKLAHOMA CITY	73106	OKLAHOMA CITY
73147	OKLAHOMA CITY	73107	OKLAHOMA CITY
73148	OKLAHOMA CITY	73109	OKLAHOMA CITY
73152	OKLAHOMA CITY	73105	OKLAHOMA CITY
73153	OKLAHOMA CITY	73160	OKLAHOMA CITY
73154	OKLAHOMA CITY	73118	OKLAHOMA CITY
73155	OKLAHOMA CITY	73115	OKLAHOMA CITY
73156	OKLAHOMA CITY	73120	OKLAHOMA CITY
73157	OKLAHOMA CITY	73112	OKLAHOMA CITY
73167	OKLAHOMA CITY	73109	OKLAHOMA CITY
73172	OKLAHOMA CITY	73132	OKLAHOMA CITY
73178	OKLAHOMA CITY	73112	OKLAHOMA CITY
73184	OKLAHOMA CITY	73114	OKLAHOMA CITY
73185	OKLAHOMA CITY	73102	OKLAHOMA CITY
73189	OKLAHOMA CITY	73159	OKLAHOMA CITY
73190	OKLAHOMA CITY	73109	OKLAHOMA CITY
73194	OKLAHOMA CITY	73105	OKLAHOMA CITY
73195	OKLAHOMA CITY	73114	OKLAHOMA CITY
73196	OKLAHOMA CITY	73102	OKLAHOMA CITY
73198	OKLAHOMA CITY	73112	OKLAHOMA CITY
73301	AUSTIN	78741	AUSTIN
73344	AUSTIN	78744	AUSTIN
73402	ARDMORE	73401	ARDMORE
73403	ARDMORE	73401	ARDMORE
73425	COUNTYLINE	73533	DUNCAN
73435	FOX	73437	GRAHAM
73436	GENE AUTRY	73401	ARDMORE
73455	RAVIA	74856	MILL CREEK
73487	TATUMS	73444	HENNEPIN
73491	VELMA	73533	DUNCAN
73502	LAWTON	73501	LAWTON
73506	LAWTON	73505	LAWTON
73520	ADDINGTON	73573	WAURIKA
73522	ALTUS	73521	ALTUS
73534	DUNCAN	73533	DUNCAN
73536	DUNCAN	73533	DUNCAN
73555	MANITOU	73542	FREDERICK
73556	MARTHA	73521	ALTUS
73557	MEDICINE PARK	73507	LAWTON
73567	STERLING	73541	FLETCHER
73648	ELK CITY	73644	ELK CITY
73702	ENID	73701	ENID
73706	ENID	73703	ENID
73743	HILLSDALE	73727	CARRIER
73746	HOPETON	73731	DACOMA
73802	WOODWARD	73801	WOODWARD
73901	ADAMS	73945	HOOKER
74001	AVANT	74002	BARNSDALL
74005	BARTLESVILLE	74003	BARTLESVILLE
74013	BROKEN ARROW	74012	BROKEN ARROW
74018	CLAREMORE	74017	CLAREMORE
74031	FOYIL	74017	CLAREMORE
74034	HALLETT	74020	CLEVELAND
74043	LEONARD	74008	BIXBY
74046	MILFAY	74028	DEPEW
74050	OAKHURST	74107	TULSA
74052	OILTON	74030	DRUMRIGHT

NONRESIDENTIAL ZIP CODES

OKLAHOMA — TEXAS

Point ZIP Code		Enclosing Residential ZIP Code	
ZIP	Post Office Name	ZIP	Post Office Name
74067	SAPULPA	74066	SAPULPA
74068	SHAMROCK	74030	DRUMRIGHT
74071	SLICK	74010	BRISTOW
74076	STILLWATER	74074	STILLWATER
74082	VERA	74021	COLLINSVILLE
74101	TULSA	74103	TULSA
74102	TULSA	74103	TULSA
74121	TULSA	74103	TULSA
74141	TULSA	74129	TULSA
74147	TULSA	74145	TULSA
74148	TULSA	74106	TULSA
74149	TULSA	74127	TULSA
74150	TULSA	74104	TULSA
74152	TULSA	74114	TULSA
74153	TULSA	74135	TULSA
74155	TULSA	74145	TULSA
74156	TULSA	74126	TULSA
74157	TULSA	74107	TULSA
74158	TULSA	74115	TULSA
74159	TULSA	74104	TULSA
74169	TULSA	74134	TULSA
74170	TULSA	74136	TULSA
74172	TULSA	74103	TULSA
74182	TULSA	74103	TULSA
74186	TULSA	74103	TULSA
74187	TULSA	74103	TULSA
74192	TULSA	74103	TULSA
74193	TULSA	74136	TULSA
74335	CARDIN	74339	COMMERCE
74340	DISNEY	74367	STRANG
74345	GROVE	74344	GROVE
74349	KETCHUM	74301	VINITA
74350	LANGLEY	74367	STRANG
74355	MIAMI	74354	MIAMI
74362	PRYOR	74361	PRYOR
74402	MUSKOGEE	74401	MUSKOGEE
74430	CROWDER	74425	CANADIAN
74431	DEWAR	74437	HENRYETTA
74438	HITCHITA	74428	COUNCIL HILL
74439	BRAGGS	74423	BRAGGS
74440	HOYT	74472	WHITEFIELD
74444	MOODYS	74464	TAHLEQUAH
74446	OKAY	74467	WAGONER
74456	PRESTON	74447	OKMULGEE
74458	REDBIRD	74454	PORTER
74459	RENTIESVILLE	74426	CHECOTAH
74460	SCHULTER	74437	HENRYETTA
74465	TAHLEQUAH	74464	TAHLEQUAH
74468	WAINWRIGHT	74450	OKTAHA
74477	WAGONER	74467	WAGONER
74502	MCALESTER	74501	MCALESTER
74521	ALBION	74574	TUSKAHOMA
74522	ALDERSON	74501	MCALESTER
74529	BLOCKER	74561	QUINTON
74530	BROMIDE	73461	WAPANUCKA
74535	CLARITA	74572	TUPELO
74542	FARRIS	74525	ATOKA
74545	GOWEN	74578	WILBURTON
74546	HAILEYVILLE	74547	HARTSHORNE
74554	KREBS	74501	MCALESTER
74556	LEHIGH	74538	COALGATE
74559	PANOLA	74578	WILBURTON
74565	SAVANNA	74501	MCALESTER
74602	PONCA CITY	74601	PONCA CITY
74702	DURANT	74701	DURANT
74720	ACHILLE	74741	HENDRIX
74721	ALBANY	74726	BOKCHITO
74722	BATTIEST	74724	BETHEL
74737	GOLDEN	74728	BROKEN BOW
74747	KEMP	74741	HENDRIX
74750	MILLERTON	74764	VALLIANT
74752	PICKENS	74724	BETHEL
74753	PLATTER	74730	CALERA
74761	SWINK	74735	FORT TOWSON
74802	SHAWNEE	74801	SHAWNEE
74818	SEMINOLE	74868	SEMINOLE
74821	ADA	74820	ADA
74830	BOWLEGS	74854	MAUD
74836	CONNERVILLE	73460	TISHOMINGO
74837	CROMWELL	74884	WEWOKA
74844	FRANCIS	74825	ALLEN
74866	SAINT LOUIS	74854	MAUD
74935	FANSHAWE	74966	WISTER
74936	GANS	74948	MULDROW
74942	LEFLORE	74966	WISTER
74943	LEQUIRE	74944	MCCURTAIN
74945	MARBLE CITY	74955	SALLISAW
74946	MOFFETT	74954	ROLAND
74947	MONROE	74953	POTEAU
74951	PANAMA	74930	BOKOSHE
75011	CARROLLTON	75006	CARROLLTON
75014	IRVING	75062	IRVING
75015	IRVING	75061	IRVING
75016	IRVING	75062	IRVING
75017	IRVING	75060	IRVING
75026	PLANO	75075	PLANO
75027	FLOWER MOUND	75067	LEWISVILLE
75029	LEWISVILLE	75057	LEWISVILLE
75030	ROWLETT	75088	ROWLETT
75037	IRVING	75061	IRVING
75045	GARLAND	75044	GARLAND
75046	GARLAND	75040	GARLAND
75047	GARLAND	75041	GARLAND
75049	GARLAND	75043	GARLAND
75053	GRAND PRAIRIE	75051	GRAND PRAIRIE
75083	RICHARDSON	75080	RICHARDSON
75085	RICHARDSON	75081	RICHARDSON
75086	PLANO	75074	PLANO
75091	SHERMAN	75090	SHERMAN
75097	WESTON	75009	CELINA
75099	COPPELL	75019	COPPELL
75101	BARDWELL	75119	ENNIS
75106	CEDAR HILL	75104	CEDAR HILL
75118	ELMO	75161	TERRELL
75120	ENNIS	75119	ENNIS
75121	COPEVILLE	75173	NEVADA
75123	DESOTO	75115	DESOTO
75132	FATE	75189	ROYSE CITY
75138	DUNCANVILLE	75137	DUNCANVILLE
75151	CORSICANA	75110	CORSICANA
75157	ROSSER	75158	SCURRY
75164	JOSEPHINE	75173	NEVADA
75168	WAXAHACHIE	75165	WAXAHACHIE
75185	MESQUITE	75149	MESQUITE
75187	MESQUITE	75149	MESQUITE
75221	DALLAS	75206	DALLAS
75222	DALLAS	75208	DALLAS
75242	DALLAS	75202	DALLAS
75245	DALLAS	75235	DALLAS
75250	DALLAS	75202	DALLAS
75260	DALLAS	75208	DALLAS
75262	DALLAS	75208	DALLAS
75263	DALLAS	75208	DALLAS
75264	DALLAS	75208	DALLAS
75265	DALLAS	75208	DALLAS
75266	DALLAS	75208	DALLAS
75267	DALLAS	75208	DALLAS
75270	DALLAS	75202	DALLAS
75275	DALLAS	75205	DALLAS
75277	DALLAS	75215	DALLAS
75283	DALLAS	75208	DALLAS
75284	DALLAS	75208	DALLAS
75285	DALLAS	75208	DALLAS
75286	DALLAS	75208	DALLAS
75301	DALLAS	75237	DALLAS
75303	DALLAS	75217	DALLAS
75310	DALLAS	75219	DALLAS
75312	DALLAS	75208	DALLAS
75313	DALLAS	75201	DALLAS
75315	DALLAS	75215	DALLAS
75320	DALLAS	75208	DALLAS
75323	DALLAS	75208	DALLAS
75326	DALLAS	75208	DALLAS
75334	DALLAS	75208	DALLAS
75336	DALLAS	75253	DALLAS
75339	DALLAS	75216	DALLAS
75340	DALLAS	75208	DALLAS
75342	DALLAS	75212	DALLAS
75343	DALLAS	75208	DALLAS
75344	DALLAS	75208	DALLAS
75354	DALLAS	75220	DALLAS
75355	DALLAS	75238	DALLAS
75356	DALLAS	75247	DALLAS
75357	DALLAS	75228	DALLAS
75358	DALLAS	75235	DALLAS
75359	DALLAS	75214	DALLAS
75360	DALLAS	75206	DALLAS
75367	DALLAS	75230	DALLAS
75368	DALLAS	75063	IRVING
75370	DALLAS	75287	DALLAS
75371	DALLAS	75246	DALLAS
75372	DALLAS	75206	DALLAS
75373	DALLAS	75208	DALLAS
75374	DALLAS	75243	DALLAS
75376	DALLAS	75224	DALLAS
75378	DALLAS	75229	DALLAS
75379	DALLAS	75244	DALLAS
75380	DALLAS	75240	DALLAS
75381	DALLAS	75234	DALLAS
75382	DALLAS	75231	DALLAS
75387	DALLAS	75236	DALLAS
75389	DALLAS	75042	GARLAND
75390	DALLAS	75235	DALLAS
75391	DALLAS	75254	DALLAS
75392	DALLAS	75208	DALLAS
75393	DALLAS	75218	DALLAS

TEXAS

Point ZIP Code		Enclosing Residential ZIP Code		Point ZIP Code		Enclosing Residential ZIP Code	
ZIP	Post Office Name	ZIP	Post Office Name	ZIP	Post Office Name	ZIP	Post Office Name
75394	DALLAS	75218	DALLAS	76113	FORT WORTH	76102	FORT WORTH
75395	DALLAS	75201	DALLAS	76121	FORT WORTH	76116	FORT WORTH
75397	DALLAS	75208	DALLAS	76124	FORT WORTH	76112	FORT WORTH
75398	DALLAS	75211	DALLAS	76130	FORT WORTH	76109	FORT WORTH
75403	GREENVILLE	75401	GREENVILLE	76136	FORT WORTH	76179	FORT WORTH
75404	GREENVILLE	75402	GREENVILLE	76147	FORT WORTH	76107	FORT WORTH
75413	BAILEY	75452	LEONARD	76161	FORT WORTH	76106	FORT WORTH
75425	CHICOTA	75473	POWDERLY	76162	FORT WORTH	76133	FORT WORTH
75429	COMMERCE	75428	COMMERCE	76163	FORT WORTH	76133	FORT WORTH
75434	CUNNINGHAM	75435	DEPORT	76166	FORT WORTH	76102	FORT WORTH
75441	ENLOE	75432	COOPER	76181	FORT WORTH	76180	NORTH RICHLAND HILLS
75443	GOBER	75452	LEONARD	76182	NORTH RICHLAND HILLS	76180	NORTH RICHLAND HILLS
75444	GOLDEN	75410	ALBA	76185	FORT WORTH	76109	FORT WORTH
75456	MOUNT PLEASANT	75455	MOUNT PLEASANT	76191	FORT WORTH	76102	FORT WORTH
75458	MERIT	75423	CELESTE	76192	FORT WORTH	76179	FORT WORTH
75461	PARIS	75460	PARIS	76193	FORT WORTH	76102	FORT WORTH
75475	RANDOLPH	75418	BONHAM	76195	FORT WORTH	76102	FORT WORTH
75483	SULPHUR SPRINGS	75482	SULPHUR SPRINGS	76196	FORT WORTH	76102	FORT WORTH
75485	WESTMINSTER	75409	ANNA	76197	FORT WORTH	76102	FORT WORTH
75489	TOM BEAN	75090	SHERMAN	76198	FORT WORTH	76102	FORT WORTH
75504	TEXARKANA	75501	TEXARKANA	76199	FORT WORTH	76102	FORT WORTH
75505	TEXARKANA	75501	TEXARKANA	76202	DENTON	76201	DENTON
75507	TEXARKANA	75501	TEXARKANA	76203	DENTON	76201	DENTON
75562	KILDARE	75563	LINDEN	76204	DENTON	76201	DENTON
75564	LODI	75657	JEFFERSON	76206	DENTON	76201	DENTON
75565	MC LEOD	75555	BIVINS	76241	GAINESVILLE	76240	GAINESVILLE
75573	REDWATER	75567	MAUD	76244	KELLER	76248	KELLER
75606	LONGVIEW	75602	LONGVIEW	76246	GREENWOOD	76234	DECATUR
75607	LONGVIEW	75602	LONGVIEW	76253	MYRA	76252	MUENSTER
75608	LONGVIEW	75605	LONGVIEW	76267	SLIDELL	76234	DECATUR
75615	LONGVIEW	75602	LONGVIEW	76268	SOUTHMAYD	75092	SHERMAN
75636	CASON	75638	DAINGERFIELD	76307	WICHITA FALLS	76301	WICHITA FALLS
75637	CLAYTON	75633	CARTHAGE	76352	BLUEGROVE	76365	HENRIETTA
75641	EASTON	75603	LONGVIEW	76369	KAMAY	76360	ELECTRA
75642	ELYSIAN FIELDS	75672	MARSHALL	76370	MEGARGEL	76366	HOLLIDAY
75653	HENDERSON	75654	HENDERSON	76385	VERNON	76384	VERNON
75658	JOINERVILLE	75654	HENDERSON	76439	DENNIS	76087	WEATHERFORD
75659	JONESVILLE	75692	WASKOM	76452	ENERGY	76455	GUSTINE
75660	JUDSON	75605	LONGVIEW	76461	LINGLEVILLE	76401	STEPHENVILLE
75663	KILGORE	75662	KILGORE	76465	MORGAN MILL	76433	BLUFF DALE
75666	LAIRD HILL	75662	KILGORE	76466	OLDEN	76448	EASTLAND
75671	MARSHALL	75670	MARSHALL	76467	PALUXY	76433	BLUFF DALE
75680	MINDEN	75654	HENDERSON	76468	PROCTOR	76446	DUBLIN
75682	NEW LONDON	75684	OVERTON	76469	PUTNAM	79504	BAIRD
75685	PANOLA	75639	DE BERRY	76481	SOUTH BEND	76450	GRAHAM
75688	SCOTTSVILLE	75672	MARSHALL	76485	PEASTER	76088	WEATHERFORD
75694	WOODLAWN	75670	MARSHALL	76503	TEMPLE	76501	TEMPLE
75710	TYLER	75702	TYLER	76505	TEMPLE	76501	TEMPLE
75711	TYLER	75701	TYLER	76508	TEMPLE	76504	TEMPLE
75712	TYLER	75702	TYLER	76533	HEIDENHEIMER	76501	TEMPLE
75713	TYLER	75701	TYLER	76540	KILLEEN	76541	KILLEEN
75759	CUNEY	75766	JACKSONVILLE	76547	KILLEEN	76541	KILLEEN
75764	GALLATIN	75785	RUSK	76558	MOUND	76528	GATESVILLE
75772	MAYDELLE	75785	RUSK	76564	PENDLETON	76579	TROY
75779	NECHES	75801	PALESTINE	76573	SCHWERTNER	76511	BARTLETT
75780	NEW SUMMERFIELD	75789	TROUP	76596	GATESVILLE	76528	GATESVILLE
75782	POYNOR	75763	FRANKSTON	76597	GATESVILLE	76528	GATESVILLE
75788	SACUL	75760	CUSHING	76598	GATESVILLE	76528	GATESVILLE
75797	BIG SANDY	75755	BIG SANDY	76599	GATESVILLE	76528	GATESVILLE
75802	PALESTINE	75803	PALESTINE	76623	AVALON	75165	WAXAHACHIE
75832	CAYUGA	75861	TENNESSEE COLONY	76628	BRANDON	76666	MERTENS
75834	CENTRALIA	75926	APPLE SPRINGS	76644	LAGUNA PARK	76634	CLIFTON
75848	KIRVIN	76693	WORTHAM	76650	IRENE	76666	MERTENS
75849	LATEXO	75835	CROCKETT	76654	LEROY	76624	AXTELL
75858	RATCLIFF	75847	KENNARD	76684	ROSS	76691	WEST
75865	WOODLAKE	75845	GROVETON	76685	SATIN	76632	CHILTON
75880	TENNESSEE COLONY	75861	TENNESSEE COLONY	76686	TEHUACANA	76667	MEXIA
75882	PALESTINE	75803	PALESTINE	76702	WACO	76712	WOODWAY
75884	TENNESSEE COLONY	75861	TENNESSEE COLONY	76703	WACO	76712	WOODWAY
75886	TENNESSEE COLONY	75861	TENNESSEE COLONY	76714	WACO	76710	WACO
75902	LUFKIN	75904	LUFKIN	76715	WACO	76704	WACO
75903	LUFKIN	75904	LUFKIN	76716	WACO	76712	WOODWAY
75915	LUFKIN	75904	LUFKIN	76795	WACO	76710	WACO
75934	CAMDEN	75939	CORRIGAN	76797	WACO	76710	WACO
75942	DOUCETTE	75979	WOODVILLE	76798	WACO	76706	WACO
75944	ETOILE	75937	CHIRENO	76799	WACO	76710	WACO
75958	MARTINSVILLE	75961	NACOGDOCHES	76803	BROWNWOOD	76802	EARLY
75963	NACOGDOCHES	75965	NACOGDOCHES	76804	BROWNWOOD	76801	BROWNWOOD
75978	WODEN	75937	CHIRENO	76824	BEND	76877	SAN SABA
75990	WOODVILLE	75979	WOODVILLE	76855	LOWAKE	76866	PAINT ROCK
76003	ARLINGTON	76017	ARLINGTON	76886	VERIBEST	76905	SAN ANGELO
76004	ARLINGTON	76010	ARLINGTON	76902	SAN ANGELO	76903	SAN ANGELO
76005	ARLINGTON	76011	ARLINGTON	76906	SAN ANGELO	76904	SAN ANGELO
76007	ARLINGTON	76010	ARLINGTON	76939	KNICKERBOCKER	76904	SAN ANGELO
76061	LILLIAN	76009	ALVARADO	76953	TENNYSON	76933	BRONTE
76068	MINERAL WELLS	76067	MINERAL WELLS	76958	WATER VALLEY	76934	CARLSBAD
76094	ARLINGTON	76013	ARLINGTON	77001	HOUSTON	77002	HOUSTON
76095	BEDFORD	76021	BEDFORD	77052	HOUSTON	77002	HOUSTON
76096	ARLINGTON	76018	ARLINGTON	77201	HOUSTON	77002	HOUSTON
76097	BURLESON	76028	BURLESON	77202	HOUSTON	77014	HOUSTON
76098	AZLE	76020	AZLE	77203	HOUSTON	77002	HOUSTON
76099	GRAPEVINE	76051	GRAPEVINE	77204	HOUSTON	77004	HOUSTON
76101	FORT WORTH	76102	FORT WORTH	77205	HOUSTON	77032	HOUSTON

NONRESIDENTIAL ZIP CODES

TEXAS

Point ZIP Code		Enclosing Residential ZIP Code	
ZIP	Post Office Name	ZIP	Post Office Name
77206	HOUSTON	77018	HOUSTON
77207	HOUSTON	77017	HOUSTON
77208	HOUSTON	77002	HOUSTON
77209	HOUSTON	77002	HOUSTON
77210	HOUSTON	77002	HOUSTON
77212	HOUSTON	77002	HOUSTON
77213	HOUSTON	77013	HOUSTON
77215	HOUSTON	77042	HOUSTON
77216	HOUSTON	77034	HOUSTON
77217	HOUSTON	77017	HOUSTON
77218	HOUSTON	77094	HOUSTON
77219	HOUSTON	77019	HOUSTON
77220	HOUSTON	77020	HOUSTON
77221	HOUSTON	77021	HOUSTON
77222	HOUSTON	77022	HOUSTON
77223	HOUSTON	77023	HOUSTON
77224	HOUSTON	77079	HOUSTON
77225	HOUSTON	77025	HOUSTON
77226	HOUSTON	77026	HOUSTON
77227	HOUSTON	77027	HOUSTON
77228	HOUSTON	77078	HOUSTON
77229	HOUSTON	77013	HOUSTON
77230	HOUSTON	77054	HOUSTON
77231	HOUSTON	77035	HOUSTON
77233	HOUSTON	77033	HOUSTON
77234	HOUSTON	77075	HOUSTON
77235	HOUSTON	77035	HOUSTON
77236	HOUSTON	77036	HOUSTON
77237	HOUSTON	77036	HOUSTON
77238	HOUSTON	77088	HOUSTON
77240	HOUSTON	77040	HOUSTON
77241	HOUSTON	77040	HOUSTON
77242	HOUSTON	77077	HOUSTON
77243	HOUSTON	77055	HOUSTON
77244	HOUSTON	77077	HOUSTON
77245	HOUSTON	77089	HOUSTON
77246	HOUSTON	77002	HOUSTON
77247	HOUSTON	77002	HOUSTON
77248	HOUSTON	77008	HOUSTON
77249	HOUSTON	77009	HOUSTON
77250	HOUSTON	77002	HOUSTON
77251	HOUSTON	77036	HOUSTON
77252	HOUSTON	77002	HOUSTON
77253	HOUSTON	77002	HOUSTON
77254	HOUSTON	77054	HOUSTON
77255	HOUSTON	77055	HOUSTON
77256	HOUSTON	77027	HOUSTON
77257	HOUSTON	77057	HOUSTON
77258	HOUSTON	77062	HOUSTON
77259	HOUSTON	77062	HOUSTON
77260	HOUSTON	77002	HOUSTON
77261	HOUSTON	77017	HOUSTON
77262	HOUSTON	77012	HOUSTON
77263	HOUSTON	77071	HOUSTON
77265	HOUSTON	77005	HOUSTON
77266	HOUSTON	77006	HOUSTON
77267	HOUSTON	77067	HOUSTON
77268	HOUSTON	77014	HOUSTON
77269	HOUSTON	77070	HOUSTON
77270	HOUSTON	77002	HOUSTON
77271	HOUSTON	77071	HOUSTON
77272	HOUSTON	77072	HOUSTON
77273	HOUSTON	77090	HOUSTON
77274	HOUSTON	77074	HOUSTON
77275	HOUSTON	77075	HOUSTON
77276	HOUSTON	77002	HOUSTON
77277	HOUSTON	77027	HOUSTON
77278	HOUSTON	77002	HOUSTON
77279	HOUSTON	77079	HOUSTON
77280	HOUSTON	77080	HOUSTON
77282	HOUSTON	77077	HOUSTON
77284	HOUSTON	77084	HOUSTON
77285	HOUSTON	77002	HOUSTON
77286	HOUSTON	77002	HOUSTON
77287	HOUSTON	77017	HOUSTON
77288	HOUSTON	77004	HOUSTON
77289	HOUSTON	77062	HOUSTON
77290	HOUSTON	77014	HOUSTON
77291	HOUSTON	77091	HOUSTON
77292	HOUSTON	77018	HOUSTON
77293	HOUSTON	77091	HOUSTON
77294	HOUSTON	77002	HOUSTON
77296	HOUSTON	77002	HOUSTON
77297	HOUSTON	77002	HOUSTON
77298	HOUSTON	77002	HOUSTON
77299	HOUSTON	77007	HOUSTON
77305	CONROE	77301	CONROE
77315	NORTH HOUSTON	77032	HOUSTON
77325	KINGWOOD	77339	KINGWOOD
77326	ACE	77351	LIVINGSTON
77332	DALLARDSVILLE	77351	LIVINGSTON
77333	DOBBIN	77356	MONTGOMERY
77334	DODGE	77320	HUNTSVILLE
77341	HUNTSVILLE	77340	HUNTSVILLE
77342	HUNTSVILLE	77320	HUNTSVILLE
77347	HUMBLE	77338	HUMBLE
77348	HUNTSVILLE	77340	HUNTSVILLE
77350	LEGGETT	77351	LIVINGSTON
77353	MAGNOLIA	77355	MAGNOLIA
77367	RIVERSIDE	77320	HUNTSVILLE
77368	ROMAYOR	77327	CLEVELAND
77369	RYE	77327	CLEVELAND
77374	THICKET	77585	SARATOGA
77376	VOTAW	77585	SARATOGA
77383	SPRING	77379	SPRING
77387	SPRING	77380	SPRING
77391	SPRING	77379	SPRING
77393	SPRING	77381	SPRING
77399	LIVINGSTON	77351	LIVINGSTON
77402	BELLAIRE	77401	BELLAIRE
77404	BAY CITY	77414	BAY CITY
77410	CYPRESS	77429	CYPRESS
77411	ALIEF	77099	HOUSTON
77412	ALTAIR	77442	GARWOOD
77413	BARKER	77493	KATY
77415	CEDAR LANE	77414	BAY CITY
77428	COLLEGEPORT	77465	PALACIOS
77431	DANCIGER	77430	DAMON
77436	EGYPT	77435	EAST BERNARD
77443	GLEN FLORA	77435	EAST BERNARD
77446	PRAIRIE VIEW	77484	WALLER
77448	HUNGERFORD	77435	EAST BERNARD
77451	KENDLETON	77417	BEASLEY
77452	KENNEY	77418	BELLVILLE
77453	LANE CITY	77488	WHARTON
77454	LISSIE	77435	EAST BERNARD
77460	NADA	77442	GARWOOD
77463	OLD OCEAN	77480	SWEENY
77464	ORCHARD	77471	ROSENBERG
77466	PATTISON	77423	BROOKSHIRE
77467	PIERCE	77437	EL CAMPO
77470	ROCK ISLAND	78962	WEIMAR
77473	SAN FELIPE	77474	SEALY
77475	SHERIDAN	78962	WEIMAR
77476	SIMONTON	77485	WALLIS
77481	THOMPSONS	77469	RICHMOND
77487	SUGAR LAND	77478	SUGAR LAND
77491	KATY	77493	KATY
77492	KATY	77493	KATY
77496	SUGAR LAND	77479	SUGAR LAND
77497	STAFFORD	77477	STAFFORD
77501	PASADENA	77506	PASADENA
77508	PASADENA	77505	PASADENA
77512	ALVIN	77511	ALVIN
77516	ANGLETON	77515	ANGLETON
77522	BAYTOWN	77521	BAYTOWN
77533	DAISETTA	77564	HULL
77542	FREEPORT	77541	FREEPORT
77549	FRIENDSWOOD	77546	FRIENDSWOOD
77552	GALVESTON	77551	GALVESTON
77553	GALVESTON	77550	GALVESTON
77555	GALVESTON	77550	GALVESTON
77561	HARDIN	77575	LIBERTY
77572	LA PORTE	77571	LA PORTE
77574	LEAGUE CITY	77573	LEAGUE CITY
77580	MONT BELVIEU	77523	BAYTOWN
77582	RAYWOOD	77575	LIBERTY
77588	PEARLAND	77581	PEARLAND
77592	TEXAS CITY	77590	TEXAS CITY
77613	CHINA	77713	BEAUMONT
77615	EVADALE	77612	BUNA
77617	GILCHRIST	77650	PORT BOLIVAR
77623	HIGH ISLAND	77650	PORT BOLIVAR
77626	MAURICEVILLE	77632	ORANGE
77629	NOME	77713	BEAUMONT
77631	ORANGE	77630	ORANGE
77639	ORANGEFIELD	77630	ORANGE
77641	PORT ARTHUR	77640	PORT ARTHUR
77643	PORT ARTHUR	77640	PORT ARTHUR
77655	SABINE PASS	77640	PORT ARTHUR
77661	STOWELL	77665	WINNIE
77663	VILLAGE MILLS	77625	KOUNTZE
77670	VIDOR	77662	VIDOR
77704	BEAUMONT	77701	BEAUMONT
77709	BEAUMONT	77707	BEAUMONT
77720	BEAUMONT	77707	BEAUMONT
77725	BEAUMONT	77705	BEAUMONT
77726	BEAUMONT	77706	BEAUMONT
77805	BRYAN	77802	BRYAN
77806	BRYAN	77802	BRYAN
77834	BRENHAM	77833	BRENHAM
77838	CHRIESMAN	77836	CALDWELL
77841	COLLEGE STATION	77840	COLLEGE STATION
77842	COLLEGE STATION	77845	COLLEGE STATION
77844	COLLEGE STATION	77840	COLLEGE STATION
77852	DEANVILLE	77836	CALDWELL

NONRESIDENTIAL ZIP CODES

TEXAS

Point ZIP Code		Enclosing Residential ZIP Code	
ZIP	Post Office Name	ZIP	Post Office Name
77855	FLYNN	77865	MARQUEZ
77857	GAUSE	76556	MILANO
77862	KURTEN	77808	BRYAN
77863	LYONS	77879	SOMERVILLE
77866	MILLICAN	77845	COLLEGE STATION
77867	MUMFORD	77859	HEARNE
77870	NEW BADEN	77856	FRANKLIN
77875	ROANS PRAIRIE	77830	ANDERSON
77876	SHIRO	77830	ANDERSON
77878	SNOOK	77879	SOMERVILLE
77881	WELLBORN	77845	COLLEGE STATION
77882	WHEELOCK	77856	FRANKLIN
77902	VICTORIA	77901	VICTORIA
77903	VICTORIA	77904	VICTORIA
77950	AUSTWELL	77990	TIVOLI
77960	FANNIN	77963	GOLIAD
77961	FRANCITAS	77971	LOLITA
77967	HOCHHEIM	77995	YOAKUM
77969	LA SALLE	77957	EDNA
77970	LA WARD	77971	LOLITA
77973	MCFADDIN	77905	VICTORIA
77976	NURSERY	77904	VICTORIA
77977	PLACEDO	77951	BLOOMINGTON
77978	POINT COMFORT	77971	LOLITA
77986	SUBLIME	77964	HALLETTSVILLE
77987	SWEET HOME	77995	YOAKUM
77988	TELFERNER	77905	VICTORIA
77989	THOMASTON	77954	CUERO
77991	VANDERBILT	77957	EDNA
77993	WEESATCHE	77963	GOLIAD
78001	ARTESIA WELLS	78014	COTULLA
78012	CHRISTINE	78026	JOURDANTON
78029	KERRVILLE	78028	KERRVILLE
78042	LAREDO	78040	LAREDO
78044	LAREDO	78041	LAREDO
78049	LAREDO	78041	LAREDO
78050	LEMING	78064	PLEASANTON
78054	MACDONA	78002	ATASCOSA
78060	OAKVILLE	78071	THREE RIVERS
78062	PEGGY	78008	CAMPBELLTON
78104	BEEVILLE	78102	BEEVILLE
78107	BERCLAIR	77963	GOLIAD
78115	GERONIMO	78155	SEGUIN
78125	MINERAL	78102	BEEVILLE
78131	NEW BRAUNFELS	78130	NEW BRAUNFELS
78135	NEW BRAUNFELS	78130	NEW BRAUNFELS
78142	NORMANNA	78102	BEEVILLE
78143	PANDORA	78160	STOCKDALE
78144	PANNA MARIA	78116	GILLETT
78145	PAWNEE	78102	BEEVILLE
78146	PETTUS	78102	BEEVILLE
78156	SEGUIN	78155	SEGUIN
78162	TULETA	78102	BEEVILLE
78206	SAN ANTONIO	78210	SAN ANTONIO
78243	SAN ANTONIO	78236	SAN ANTONIO
78246	SAN ANTONIO	78216	SAN ANTONIO
78262	SAN ANTONIO	78217	SAN ANTONIO
78265	SAN ANTONIO	78217	SAN ANTONIO
78268	SAN ANTONIO	78238	SAN ANTONIO
78269	SAN ANTONIO	78249	SAN ANTONIO
78270	SAN ANTONIO	78232	SAN ANTONIO
78278	SAN ANTONIO	78230	SAN ANTONIO
78279	SAN ANTONIO	78216	SAN ANTONIO
78280	SAN ANTONIO	78233	SAN ANTONIO
78283	SAN ANTONIO	78204	SAN ANTONIO
78284	SAN ANTONIO	78233	SAN ANTONIO
78285	SAN ANTONIO	78217	SAN ANTONIO
78286	SAN ANTONIO	78217	SAN ANTONIO
78287	SAN ANTONIO	78219	SAN ANTONIO
78288	SAN ANTONIO	78230	SAN ANTONIO
78289	SAN ANTONIO	78233	SAN ANTONIO
78291	SAN ANTONIO	78205	SAN ANTONIO
78292	SAN ANTONIO	78205	SAN ANTONIO
78293	SAN ANTONIO	78205	SAN ANTONIO
78294	SAN ANTONIO	78205	SAN ANTONIO
78295	SAN ANTONIO	78205	SAN ANTONIO
78296	SAN ANTONIO	78205	SAN ANTONIO
78297	SAN ANTONIO	78205	SAN ANTONIO
78298	SAN ANTONIO	78205	SAN ANTONIO
78299	SAN ANTONIO	78205	SAN ANTONIO
78330	AGUA DULCE	78380	ROBSTOWN
78333	ALICE	78332	ALICE
78335	ARANSAS PASS	78336	ARANSAS PASS
78339	BANQUETE	78380	ROBSTOWN
78341	BENAVIDES	78349	CONCEPCION
78342	BEN BOLT	78332	ALICE
78347	CHAPMAN RANCH	78415	CORPUS CHRISTI
78350	DINERO	78022	GEORGE WEST
78351	DRISCOLL	78380	ROBSTOWN
78352	EDROY	78368	MATHIS
78358	FULTON	78382	ROCKPORT
78359	GREGORY	78374	PORTLAND
78364	KINGSVILLE	78363	KINGSVILLE

Point ZIP Code		Enclosing Residential ZIP Code	
ZIP	Post Office Name	ZIP	Post Office Name
78371	OILTON	78369	MIRANDO CITY
78381	ROCKPORT	78382	ROCKPORT
78403	CORPUS CHRISTI	78401	CORPUS CHRISTI
78426	CORPUS CHRISTI	78410	CORPUS CHRISTI
78427	CORPUS CHRISTI	78413	CORPUS CHRISTI
78460	CORPUS CHRISTI	78410	CORPUS CHRISTI
78463	CORPUS CHRISTI	78404	CORPUS CHRISTI
78465	CORPUS CHRISTI	78405	CORPUS CHRISTI
78466	CORPUS CHRISTI	78411	CORPUS CHRISTI
78467	CORPUS CHRISTI	78415	CORPUS CHRISTI
78468	CORPUS CHRISTI	78412	CORPUS CHRISTI
78469	CORPUS CHRISTI	78408	CORPUS CHRISTI
78470	CORPUS CHRISTI	78401	CORPUS CHRISTI
78471	CORPUS CHRISTI	78401	CORPUS CHRISTI
78472	CORPUS CHRISTI	78411	CORPUS CHRISTI
78473	CORPUS CHRISTI	78401	CORPUS CHRISTI
78474	CORPUS CHRISTI	78401	CORPUS CHRISTI
78475	CORPUS CHRISTI	78401	CORPUS CHRISTI
78476	CORPUS CHRISTI	78401	CORPUS CHRISTI
78477	CORPUS CHRISTI	78401	CORPUS CHRISTI
78478	CORPUS CHRISTI	78401	CORPUS CHRISTI
78480	CORPUS CHRISTI	78418	CORPUS CHRISTI
78502	MCALLEN	78501	MCALLEN
78505	MCALLEN	78501	MCALLEN
78522	BROWNSVILLE	78520	BROWNSVILLE
78523	BROWNSVILLE	78520	BROWNSVILLE
78535	COMBES	78552	HARLINGEN
78540	EDINBURG	78541	EDINBURG
78543	ELSA	78538	EDCOUCH
78545	FALCON HEIGHTS	78584	ROMA
78551	HARLINGEN	78550	HARLINGEN
78553	HARLINGEN	78550	HARLINGEN
78558	LA BLANCA	78537	DONNA
78561	LASARA	78580	RAYMONDVILLE
78562	LA VILLA	78538	EDCOUCH
78564	LOPENO	78076	ZAPATA
78565	LOS EBANOS	78595	SULLIVAN CITY
78567	LOS INDIOS	78586	SAN BENITO
78568	LOZANO	78583	RIO HONDO
78576	PENITAS	78560	LA JOYA
78579	PROGRESO	78570	MERCEDES
78585	SALINENO	78584	ROMA
78592	SANTA MARIA	78559	LA FERIA
78599	WESLACO	78596	WESLACO
78604	BELMONT	78629	GONZALES
78622	FENTRESS	78655	MARTINDALE
78627	GEORGETOWN	78626	GEORGETOWN
78630	CEDAR PARK	78613	CEDAR PARK
78646	LEANDER	78641	LEANDER
78651	MC NEIL	78728	AUSTIN
78658	OTTINE	78629	GONZALES
78661	PRAIRIE LEA	78655	MARTINDALE
78667	SAN MARCOS	78666	SAN MARCOS
78670	STAPLES	78638	KINGSBURY
78673	WALBURG	78626	GEORGETOWN
78674	WEIR	78626	GEORGETOWN
78680	ROUND ROCK	78681	ROUND ROCK
78682	ROUND ROCK	78681	ROUND ROCK
78683	ROUND ROCK	78664	ROUND ROCK
78691	PFLUGERVILLE	78660	PFLUGERVILLE
78708	AUSTIN	78758	AUSTIN
78709	AUSTIN	78749	AUSTIN
78710	AUSTIN	78754	AUSTIN
78711	AUSTIN	78701	AUSTIN
78713	AUSTIN	78705	AUSTIN
78714	AUSTIN	78701	AUSTIN
78715	AUSTIN	78745	AUSTIN
78716	AUSTIN	78746	AUSTIN
78718	AUSTIN	78758	AUSTIN
78720	AUSTIN	78759	AUSTIN
78755	AUSTIN	78759	AUSTIN
78760	AUSTIN	78744	AUSTIN
78761	AUSTIN	78752	AUSTIN
78762	AUSTIN	78702	AUSTIN
78763	AUSTIN	78703	AUSTIN
78764	AUSTIN	78704	AUSTIN
78765	AUSTIN	78751	AUSTIN
78766	AUSTIN	78757	AUSTIN
78767	AUSTIN	78701	AUSTIN
78768	AUSTIN	78701	AUSTIN
78769	AUSTIN	78701	AUSTIN
78772	AUSTIN	78741	AUSTIN
78773	AUSTIN	78701	AUSTIN
78774	AUSTIN	78701	AUSTIN
78778	AUSTIN	78701	AUSTIN
78779	AUSTIN	78731	AUSTIN
78780	AUSTIN	78746	AUSTIN
78781	AUSTIN	78747	AUSTIN
78783	AUSTIN	78723	AUSTIN
78785	AUSTIN	78751	AUSTIN
78789	AUSTIN	78757	AUSTIN
78799	AUSTIN	78721	AUSTIN
78802	UVALDE	78801	UVALDE

NONRESIDENTIAL ZIP CODES

TEXAS | **COLORADO**

Point ZIP Code ZIP	Point ZIP Code Post Office Name	Enclosing Residential ZIP Code ZIP	Enclosing Residential ZIP Code Post Office Name
78836	CATARINA	78827	ASHERTON
78841	DEL RIO	78840	DEL RIO
78842	DEL RIO	78840	DEL RIO
78847	DEL RIO	78840	DEL RIO
78853	EAGLE PASS	78852	EAGLE PASS
78860	EL INDIO	78852	EAGLE PASS
78871	LANGTRY	78837	COMSTOCK
78943	GLIDDEN	78934	COLUMBUS
78951	OAKLAND	78962	WEIMAR
78952	PLUM	78945	LA GRANGE
78960	WARDA	78945	LA GRANGE
78961	WARRENTON	78954	ROUND TOP
79002	ALANREED	79057	MCLEAN
79003	ALLISON	79011	BRISCOE
79008	BORGER	79007	BORGER
79010	BOYS RANCH	79092	VEGA
79012	BUSHLAND	79124	AMARILLO
79013	CACTUS	79029	DUMAS
79021	COTTON CENTER	79311	ABERNATHY
79024	DARROUZETT	79034	FOLLETT
79025	DAWN	79045	HEREFORD
79032	EDMONSON	79072	PLAINVIEW
79033	FARNSWORTH	79070	PERRYTON
79051	KERRICK	79022	DALHART
79053	LAZBUDDIE	79009	BOVINA
79054	LEFORS	79065	PAMPA
79066	PAMPA	79065	PAMPA
79073	PLAINVIEW	79072	PLAINVIEW
79077	SAM NORWOOD	79095	WELLINGTON
79078	SANFORD	79036	FRITCH
79091	UMBARGER	79015	CANYON
79093	WAKA	79070	PERRYTON
79105	AMARILLO	79101	AMARILLO
79114	AMARILLO	79109	AMARILLO
79116	AMARILLO	79106	AMARILLO
79117	AMARILLO	79107	AMARILLO
79120	AMARILLO	79103	AMARILLO
79159	AMARILLO	79124	AMARILLO
79166	AMARILLO	79101	AMARILLO
79168	AMARILLO	79104	AMARILLO
79172	AMARILLO	79101	AMARILLO
79174	AMARILLO	79101	AMARILLO
79185	AMARILLO	79119	AMARILLO
79189	AMARILLO	79103	AMARILLO
79221	AIKEN	79241	LOCKNEY
79223	CEE VEE	79248	PADUCAH
79231	DOUGHERTY	79235	FLOYDADA
79233	ESTELLINE	79245	MEMPHIS
79236	GUTHRIE	79248	PADUCAH
79258	SOUTH PLAINS	79241	LOCKNEY
79314	BLEDSOE	79346	MORTON
79330	JUSTICEBURG	79356	POST
79338	LEVELLAND	79336	LEVELLAND
79350	NEW DEAL	79403	LUBBOCK
79367	SMYER	79336	LEVELLAND
79369	SPADE	79339	LITTLEFIELD
79372	SUNDOWN	79336	LEVELLAND
79378	WELLMAN	79316	BROWNFIELD
79380	WHITHARRAL	79336	LEVELLAND
79383	NEW HOME	79373	TAHOKA
79402	LUBBOCK	79401	LUBBOCK
79406	LUBBOCK	79409	LUBBOCK
79408	LUBBOCK	79401	LUBBOCK
79430	LUBBOCK	79415	LUBBOCK
79452	LUBBOCK	79412	LUBBOCK
79453	LUBBOCK	79423	LUBBOCK
79457	LUBBOCK	79401	LUBBOCK
79464	LUBBOCK	79424	LUBBOCK
79490	LUBBOCK	79407	LUBBOCK
79491	LUBBOCK	79412	LUBBOCK
79493	LUBBOCK	79413	LUBBOCK
79499	LUBBOCK	79416	LUBBOCK
79505	BENJAMIN	76380	SEYMOUR
79516	DUNN	79526	HERMLEIGH
79550	SNYDER	79549	SNYDER
79604	ABILENE	79601	ABILENE
79608	ABILENE	79605	ABILENE
79702	MIDLAND	79701	MIDLAND
79704	MIDLAND	79701	MIDLAND
79708	MIDLAND	79707	MIDLAND
79710	MIDLAND	79705	MIDLAND
79711	MIDLAND	79706	MIDLAND
79712	MIDLAND	79705	MIDLAND
79721	BIG SPRING	79720	BIG SPRING
79733	FORSAN	79720	BIG SPRING
79740	GIRVIN	79743	IMPERIAL
79759	NOTREES	79741	GOLDSMITH
79760	ODESSA	79761	ODESSA
79768	ODESSA	79762	ODESSA
79769	ODESSA	79761	ODESSA
79770	ORLA	79772	PECOS
79776	PENWELL	79741	GOLDSMITH
79778	RANKIN	79755	MIDKIFF

Point ZIP Code ZIP	Point ZIP Code Post Office Name	Enclosing Residential ZIP Code ZIP	Enclosing Residential ZIP Code Post Office Name
79780	SARAGOSA	79718	BALMORHEA
79785	TOYAH	79772	PECOS
79786	TOYAHVALE	79718	BALMORHEA
79788	WICKETT	79756	MONAHANS
79831	ALPINE	79830	ALPINE
79838	FABENS	79836	CLINT
79845	PRESIDIO	79843	MARFA
79846	REDFORD	79843	MARFA
79848	SANDERSON	78851	DRYDEN
79853	TORNILLO	79836	CLINT
79910	EL PASO	79905	EL PASO
79911	EL PASO	79912	EL PASO
79913	EL PASO	79912	EL PASO
79914	EL PASO	79924	EL PASO
79917	EL PASO	79907	EL PASO
79920	EL PASO	79930	EL PASO
79923	EL PASO	79903	EL PASO
79926	EL PASO	79915	EL PASO
79929	EL PASO	79927	EL PASO
79931	EL PASO	79930	EL PASO
79937	EL PASO	79936	EL PASO
79940	EL PASO	79901	EL PASO
79941	EL PASO	79901	EL PASO
79942	EL PASO	79901	EL PASO
79943	EL PASO	79901	EL PASO
79944	EL PASO	79901	EL PASO
79945	EL PASO	79901	EL PASO
79946	EL PASO	79901	EL PASO
79947	EL PASO	79901	EL PASO
79948	EL PASO	79901	EL PASO
79949	EL PASO	79901	EL PASO
79950	EL PASO	79901	EL PASO
79951	EL PASO	79901	EL PASO
79952	EL PASO	79901	EL PASO
79953	EL PASO	79901	EL PASO
79954	EL PASO	79901	EL PASO
79955	EL PASO	79901	EL PASO
79958	EL PASO	79901	EL PASO
79960	EL PASO	79901	EL PASO
79961	EL PASO	79925	EL PASO
79976	EL PASO	79930	EL PASO
79978	EL PASO	79901	EL PASO
79980	EL PASO	79901	EL PASO
79990	EL PASO	79925	EL PASO
79995	EL PASO	79905	EL PASO
79996	EL PASO	79936	EL PASO
79997	EL PASO	79905	EL PASO
79998	EL PASO	79905	EL PASO
79999	EL PASO	79905	EL PASO
80001	ARVADA	80004	ARVADA
80006	ARVADA	80005	ARVADA
80024	DUPONT	80022	COMMERCE CITY
80025	ELDORADO SPRINGS	80305	BOULDER
80028	LOUISVILLE	80027	LOUISVILLE
80034	WHEAT RIDGE	80033	WHEAT RIDGE
80035	WESTMINSTER	80030	WESTMINSTER
80036	WESTMINSTER	80030	WESTMINSTER
80037	COMMERCE CITY	80022	COMMERCE CITY
80038	BROOMFIELD	80020	BROOMFIELD
80040	AURORA	80010	AURORA
80041	AURORA	80011	AURORA
80042	AURORA	80011	AURORA
80044	AURORA	80011	AURORA
80045	AURORA	80010	AURORA
80046	AURORA	80015	AURORA
80047	AURORA	80012	AURORA
80131	LOUVIERS	80125	LITTLETON
80150	ENGLEWOOD	80110	ENGLEWOOD
80151	ENGLEWOOD	80113	ENGLEWOOD
80155	ENGLEWOOD	80111	ENGLEWOOD
80160	LITTLETON	80120	LITTLETON
80161	LITTLETON	80121	LITTLETON
80162	LITTLETON	80123	LITTLETON
80163	LITTLETON	80126	LITTLETON
80165	LITTLETON	80120	LITTLETON
80166	LITTLETON	80120	LITTLETON
80201	DENVER	80202	DENVER
80217	DENVER	80202	DENVER
80243	DENVER	80205	DENVER
80244	DENVER	80202	DENVER
80248	DENVER	80202	DENVER
80250	DENVER	80210	DENVER
80251	DENVER	80014	AURORA
80252	DENVER	80216	DENVER
80256	DENVER	80202	DENVER
80257	DENVER	80202	DENVER
80259	DENVER	80202	DENVER
80261	DENVER	80210	DENVER
80263	DENVER	80237	DENVER
80264	DENVER	80203	DENVER
80265	DENVER	80202	DENVER
80266	DENVER	80216	DENVER
80271	DENVER	80202	DENVER

NONRESIDENTIAL ZIP CODES

COLORADO

WYOMING

Point ZIP Code		Enclosing Residential ZIP Code	
ZIP	Post Office Name	ZIP	Post Office Name
80273	DENVER	80204	DENVER
80274	DENVER	80202	DENVER
80279	DENVER	80216	DENVER
80280	DENVER	80230	DENVER
80281	DENVER	80202	DENVER
80290	DENVER	80202	DENVER
80291	DENVER	80202	DENVER
80293	DENVER	80202	DENVER
80294	DENVER	80202	DENVER
80295	DENVER	80203	DENVER
80299	DENVER	80202	DENVER
80306	BOULDER	80302	BOULDER
80307	BOULDER	80305	BOULDER
80308	BOULDER	80301	BOULDER
80310	BOULDER	80302	BOULDER
80314	BOULDER	80503	LONGMONT
80321	BOULDER	80303	BOULDER
80322	BOULDER	80303	BOULDER
80323	BOULDER	80303	BOULDER
80328	BOULDER	80303	BOULDER
80329	BOULDER	80303	BOULDER
80402	GOLDEN	80401	GOLDEN
80419	GOLDEN	80401	GOLDEN
80420	ALMA	80440	FAIRPLAY
80425	BUFFALO CREEK	80470	PINE
80426	BURNS	81637	GYPSUM
80427	CENTRAL CITY	80422	BLACK HAWK
80432	COMO	80440	FAIRPLAY
80434	COWDREY	80480	WALDEN
80436	DUMONT	80452	IDAHO SPRINGS
80437	EVERGREEN	80439	EVERGREEN
80438	EMPIRE	80452	IDAHO SPRINGS
80444	GEORGETOWN	80452	IDAHO SPRINGS
80448	GRANT	80421	BAILEY
80453	IDLEDALE	80401	GOLDEN
80454	INDIAN HILLS	80465	MORRISON
80457	KITTREDGE	80439	EVERGREEN
80469	PHIPPSBURG	80467	OAK CREEK
80471	PINECLIFFE	80466	NEDERLAND
80473	RAND	80480	WALDEN
80474	ROLLINSVILLE	80403	GOLDEN
80475	SHAWNEE	80421	BAILEY
80476	SILVER PLUME	80452	IDAHO SPRINGS
80477	STEAMBOAT SPRINGS	80487	STEAMBOAT SPRINGS
80483	YAMPA	80479	TOPONAS
80488	STEAMBOAT SPRINGS	80487	STEAMBOAT SPRINGS
80497	SILVERTHORNE	80498	SILVERTHORNE
80502	LONGMONT	80501	LONGMONT
80511	ESTES PARK	80517	ESTES PARK
80522	FORT COLLINS	80521	FORT COLLINS
80527	FORT COLLINS	80525	FORT COLLINS
80532	GLEN HAVEN	80515	DRAKE
80533	HYGIENE	80503	LONGMONT
80539	LOVELAND	80538	LOVELAND
80541	MASONVILLE	80538	LOVELAND
80544	NIWOT	80501	LONGMONT
80546	SEVERANCE	80550	WINDSOR
80551	WINDSOR	80550	WINDSOR
80553	FORT COLLINS	80525	FORT COLLINS
80614	EASTLAKE	80241	DENVER
80622	GALETON	80615	EATON
80623	GILCREST	80651	PLATTEVILLE
80632	GREELEY	80631	GREELEY
80633	GREELEY	80631	GREELEY
80638	GREELEY	80620	EVANS
80646	LUCERNE	80615	EATON
80732	HEREFORD	80729	GROVER
80746	PAOLI	80731	HAXTUN
80819	GREEN MOUNTAIN FALLS	80809	CASCADE
80826	LIMON	80828	LIMON
80841	U S A F ACADEMY	80840	U S A F ACADEMY
80860	VICTOR	80816	FLORISSANT
80862	WILD HORSE	80825	KIT CARSON
80866	WOODLAND PARK	80863	WOODLAND PARK
80901	COLORADO SPRINGS	80903	COLORADO SPRINGS
80912	COLORADO SPRINGS	80930	COLORADO SPRINGS
80931	COLORADO SPRINGS	80911	COLORADO SPRINGS
80932	COLORADO SPRINGS	80909	COLORADO SPRINGS
80933	COLORADO SPRINGS	80907	COLORADO SPRINGS
80934	COLORADO SPRINGS	80904	COLORADO SPRINGS
80935	COLORADO SPRINGS	80910	COLORADO SPRINGS
80936	COLORADO SPRINGS	80918	COLORADO SPRINGS
80937	COLORADO SPRINGS	80903	COLORADO SPRINGS
80938	COLORADO SPRINGS	80903	COLORADO SPRINGS
80939	COLORADO SPRINGS	80903	COLORADO SPRINGS
80940	COLORADO SPRINGS	80915	COLORADO SPRINGS
80941	COLORADO SPRINGS	80918	COLORADO SPRINGS
80942	COLORADO SPRINGS	80903	COLORADO SPRINGS
80943	COLORADO SPRINGS	80903	COLORADO SPRINGS
80944	COLORADO SPRINGS	80903	COLORADO SPRINGS
80945	COLORADO SPRINGS	80909	COLORADO SPRINGS
80946	COLORADO SPRINGS	80903	COLORADO SPRINGS
80947	COLORADO SPRINGS	80903	COLORADO SPRINGS
80949	COLORADO SPRINGS	80919	COLORADO SPRINGS
80950	COLORADO SPRINGS	80909	COLORADO SPRINGS
80960	COLORADO SPRINGS	80905	COLORADO SPRINGS
80962	COLORADO SPRINGS	80920	COLORADO SPRINGS
80970	COLORADO SPRINGS	80915	COLORADO SPRINGS
80977	COLORADO SPRINGS	80925	COLORADO SPRINGS
80995	COLORADO SPRINGS	80920	COLORADO SPRINGS
81002	PUEBLO	81003	PUEBLO
81009	PUEBLO	81001	PUEBLO
81010	PUEBLO	81003	PUEBLO
81011	PUEBLO	81003	PUEBLO
81012	PUEBLO	81003	PUEBLO
81024	BONCARBO	81082	TRINIDAD
81030	CHERAW	81050	LA JUNTA
81033	CROWLEY	81063	ORDWAY
81034	CROWLEY	81063	ORDWAY
81038	FORT LYON	81054	LAS ANIMAS
81046	HOEHNE	81082	TRINIDAD
81077	SWINK	81050	LA JUNTA
81124	CAPULIN	81140	LA JARA
81126	CHAMA	81152	SAN LUIS
81127	CHIMNEY ROCK	81147	PAGOSA SPRINGS
81128	CHROMO	81147	PAGOSA SPRINGS
81129	CONEJOS	81120	ANTONITO
81131	CRESTONE	81143	MOFFAT
81135	HOMELAKE	81144	MONTE VISTA
81138	JAROSO	81152	SAN LUIS
81141	MANASSA	81151	SANFORD
81148	ROMEO	81151	SANFORD
81157	PAGOSA SPRINGS	81147	PAGOSA SPRINGS
81215	CANON CITY	81212	CANON CITY
81221	COAL CREEK	81226	FLORENCE
81222	COALDALE	81233	HOWARD
81225	CRESTED BUTTE	81224	CRESTED BUTTE
81227	MONARCH	81201	SALIDA
81232	HILLSIDE	81223	COTOPAXI
81237	OHIO CITY	81239	PARLIN
81242	PONCHA SPRINGS	81201	SALIDA
81244	ROCKVALE	81226	FLORENCE
81248	SARGENTS	81149	SAGUACHE
81290	FLORENCE	81226	FLORENCE
81302	DURANGO	81301	DURANGO
81329	MARVEL	81326	HESPERUS
81330	MESA VERDE NATIONAL	81328	MANCOS
81332	RICO	81320	CAHONE
81402	MONTROSE	81401	MONTROSE
81414	CORY	81410	AUSTIN
81420	LAZEAR	81419	HOTCHKISS
81429	PARADOX	81411	BEDROCK
81502	GRAND JUNCTION	81501	GRAND JUNCTION
81602	GLENWOOD SPRINGS	81601	GLENWOOD SPRINGS
81612	ASPEN	81611	ASPEN
81626	CRAIG	81625	CRAIG
81636	BATTLEMENT MESA	81635	PARACHUTE
81645	MINTURN	81657	VAIL
81646	MOLINA	81624	COLLBRAN
81649	RED CLIFF	81657	VAIL
81655	WOLCOTT	81657	VAIL
81656	WOODY CREEK	81621	BASALT
81658	VAIL	81657	VAIL
82003	CHEYENNE	82009	CHEYENNE
82006	CHEYENNE	82009	CHEYENNE
82008	CHEYENNE	82007	CHEYENNE
82059	GRANITE CANON	82007	CHEYENNE
82060	HILLSDALE	82053	BURNS
82061	HORSE CREEK	82009	CHEYENNE
82073	LARAMIE	82072	LARAMIE
82218	HUNTLEY	82240	TORRINGTON
82324	ELK MOUNTAIN	82327	HANNA
82335	WALCOTT	82327	HANNA
82412	BYRON	82431	LOVELL
82420	COWLEY	82431	LOVELL
82422	EMBLEM	82426	GREYBULL
82423	FRANNIE	82421	DEAVER
82430	KIRBY	82401	WORLAND
82440	RALSTON	82435	POWELL
82450	WAPITI	82414	CODY
82515	HUDSON	82520	LANDER
82524	SAINT STEPHENS	82501	RIVERTON
82602	CASPER	82601	CASPER
82605	CASPER	82609	CASPER
82615	SHIRLEY BASIN	82327	HANNA
82630	ARMINTO	82604	CASPER
82635	EDGERTON	82643	MIDWEST
82638	HILAND	82649	SHOSHONI
82640	LINCH	82639	KAYCEE
82644	MILLS	82604	CASPER
82646	NATRONA	82604	CASPER
82648	POWDER RIVER	82604	CASPER
82711	ALVA	82720	HULETT
82717	GILLETTE	82716	GILLETTE
82833	BIG HORN	82801	SHERIDAN
82837	LEITER	82835	CLEARMONT

NONRESIDENTIAL ZIP CODES

WYOMING

UTAH

Point ZIP Code		Enclosing Residential ZIP Code	
ZIP	Post Office Name	ZIP	Post Office Name
82840	SADDLESTRING	82834	BUFFALO
82845	WYARNO	82801	SHERIDAN
82902	ROCK SPRINGS	82901	ROCK SPRINGS
82929	LITTLE AMERICA	82938	MC KINNON
82931	EVANSTON	82930	EVANSTON
82932	FARSON	82935	GREEN RIVER
82934	GRANGER	82935	GREEN RIVER
82939	MOUNTAIN VIEW	82933	FORT BRIDGER
82942	POINT OF ROCKS	82901	ROCK SPRINGS
82943	RELIANCE	82901	ROCK SPRINGS
82944	ROBERTSON	82933	FORT BRIDGER
82945	SUPERIOR	82901	ROCK SPRINGS
83002	JACKSON	83001	JACKSON
83025	TETON VILLAGE	83014	WILSON
83116	DIAMONDVILLE	83101	KEMMERER
83119	FAIRVIEW	83110	AFTON
83121	FRONTIER	83101	KEMMERER
83124	OPAL	83101	KEMMERER
83128	ALPINE	83118	ETNA
83205	POCATELLO	83201	POCATELLO
83206	POCATELLO	83201	POCATELLO
83215	ATOMIC CITY	83221	BLACKFOOT
83218	BASALT	83274	SHELLEY
83223	BLOOMINGTON	83261	PARIS
83229	COBALT	83469	SHOUP
83230	CONDA	83276	SODA SPRINGS
83233	DINGLE	83254	MONTPELIER
83239	GEORGETOWN	83254	MONTPELIER
83256	MORELAND	83221	BLACKFOOT
83277	SPRINGFIELD	83262	PINGREE
83281	SWANLAKE	83234	DOWNEY
83303	TWIN FALLS	83301	TWIN FALLS
83311	ALBION	83342	MALTA
83312	ALMO	83342	MALTA
83337	HILL CITY	83322	CORRAL
83353	SUN VALLEY	83340	KETCHUM
83354	SUN VALLEY	83340	KETCHUM
83403	IDAHO FALLS	83401	IDAHO FALLS
83405	IDAHO FALLS	83402	IDAHO FALLS
83415	IDAHO FALLS	83402	IDAHO FALLS
83421	CHESTER	83420	ASHTON
83433	MACKS INN	83429	ISLAND PARK
83438	PARKER	83445	SAINT ANTHONY
83441	REXBURG	83440	REXBURG
83454	UCON	83401	IDAHO FALLS
83465	LEMHI	83464	LEADORE
83468	TENDOY	83464	LEADORE
83531	FENN	83530	GRANGEVILLE
83606	CALDWELL	83605	CALDWELL
83630	HUSTON	83607	CALDWELL
83635	LAKE FORK	83638	MCCALL
83652	NAMPA	83651	NAMPA
83653	NAMPA	83651	NAMPA
83656	NOTUS	83607	CALDWELL
83666	PLACERVILLE	83629	HORSESHOE BEND
83671	WARREN	83549	RIGGINS
83680	MERIDIAN	83642	MERIDIAN
83701	BOISE	83702	BOISE
83707	BOISE	83702	BOISE
83708	BOISE	83702	BOISE
83711	BOISE	83704	BOISE
83715	BOISE	83705	BOISE
83717	BOISE	83716	BOISE
83719	BOISE	83702	BOISE
83720	BOISE	83702	BOISE
83722	BOISE	83702	BOISE
83724	BOISE	83702	BOISE
83726	BOISE	83706	BOISE
83728	BOISE	83702	BOISE
83729	BOISE	83712	BOISE
83731	BOISE	83705	BOISE
83732	BOISE	83702	BOISE
83735	BOISE	83702	BOISE
83756	BOISE	83702	BOISE
83799	BOISE	83709	BOISE
83806	BOVILL	83823	DEARY
83816	COEUR D ALENE	83815	COEUR D ALENE
83825	DOVER	83864	SANDPOINT
83826	EASTPORT	83845	MOYIE SPRINGS
83840	KOOTENAI	83864	SANDPOINT
83841	LACLEDE	83864	SANDPOINT
83844	MOSCOW	83843	MOSCOW
83849	OSBURN	83873	WALLACE
83865	COLBURN	83864	SANDPOINT
83866	SANTA	83861	SAINT MARIES
83867	SILVERTON	83873	WALLACE
83874	MURRAY	83837	KELLOGG
83877	POST FALLS	83854	POST FALLS
84008	BONANZA	84078	VERNAL
84011	BOUNTIFUL	84010	BOUNTIFUL
84016	CLEARFIELD	84015	CLEARFIELD
84024	ECHO	84017	COALVILLE
84027	FRUITLAND	84051	MOUNTAIN HOME

Point ZIP Code		Enclosing Residential ZIP Code	
ZIP	Post Office Name	ZIP	Post Office Name
84034	IBAPAH	84083	WENDOVER
84055	OAKLEY	84061	PEOA
84059	OREM	84057	OREM
84068	PARK CITY	84060	PARK CITY
84079	VERNAL	84078	VERNAL
84089	CLEARFIELD	84015	CLEARFIELD
84090	SANDY	84093	SANDY
84091	SANDY	84094	SANDY
84110	SALT LAKE CITY	84101	SALT LAKE CITY
84114	SALT LAKE CITY	84103	SALT LAKE CITY
84122	SALT LAKE CITY	84119	SALT LAKE CITY
84125	SALT LAKE CITY	84104	SALT LAKE CITY
84126	SALT LAKE CITY	84104	SALT LAKE CITY
84127	SALT LAKE CITY	84104	SALT LAKE CITY
84130	SALT LAKE CITY	84104	SALT LAKE CITY
84131	SALT LAKE CITY	84104	SALT LAKE CITY
84132	SALT LAKE CITY	84112	SALT LAKE CITY
84133	SALT LAKE CITY	84111	SALT LAKE CITY
84134	SALT LAKE CITY	84116	SALT LAKE CITY
84136	SALT LAKE CITY	84111	SALT LAKE CITY
84138	SALT LAKE CITY	84111	SALT LAKE CITY
84139	SALT LAKE CITY	84111	SALT LAKE CITY
84141	SALT LAKE CITY	84117	SALT LAKE CITY
84143	SALT LAKE CITY	84103	SALT LAKE CITY
84144	SALT LAKE CITY	84111	SALT LAKE CITY
84145	SALT LAKE CITY	84101	SALT LAKE CITY
84147	SALT LAKE CITY	84111	SALT LAKE CITY
84148	SALT LAKE CITY	84108	SALT LAKE CITY
84150	SALT LAKE CITY	84103	SALT LAKE CITY
84151	SALT LAKE CITY	84116	SALT LAKE CITY
84152	SALT LAKE CITY	84105	SALT LAKE CITY
84157	SALT LAKE CITY	84107	SALT LAKE CITY
84158	SALT LAKE CITY	84108	SALT LAKE CITY
84165	SALT LAKE CITY	84115	SALT LAKE CITY
84170	SALT LAKE CITY	84119	SALT LAKE CITY
84171	SALT LAKE CITY	84121	SALT LAKE CITY
84180	SALT LAKE CITY	84101	SALT LAKE CITY
84184	SALT LAKE CITY	84119	SALT LAKE CITY
84189	SALT LAKE CITY	84111	SALT LAKE CITY
84190	SALT LAKE CITY	84115	SALT LAKE CITY
84199	SALT LAKE CITY	84104	SALT LAKE CITY
84201	OGDEN	84404	OGDEN
84244	OGDEN	84404	OGDEN
84301	BEAR RIVER CITY	84314	HONEYVILLE
84304	CACHE JUNCTION	84335	SMITHFIELD
84316	HOWELL	84336	SNOWVILLE
84323	LOGAN	84321	LOGAN
84326	MILLVILLE	84332	PROVIDENCE
84327	NEWTON	84335	SMITHFIELD
84334	RIVERSIDE	84312	GARLAND
84402	OGDEN	84404	OGDEN
84407	OGDEN	84404	OGDEN
84409	OGDEN	84404	OGDEN
84412	OGDEN	84404	OGDEN
84415	OGDEN	84403	OGDEN
84512	BLUFF	84511	BLANDING
84513	CASTLE DALE	84528	HUNTINGTON
84515	CISCO	84540	THOMPSON
84516	CLAWSON	84523	FERRON
84518	CLEVELAND	84528	HUNTINGTON
84521	ELMO	84528	HUNTINGTON
84522	EMERY	84523	FERRON
84529	KENILWORTH	84526	HELPER
84530	LA SAL	84535	MONTICELLO
84534	MONTEZUMA CREEK	84510	ANETH
84537	ORANGEVILLE	84528	HUNTINGTON
84539	SUNNYSIDE	84520	EAST CARBON
84603	PROVO	84601	PROVO
84605	PROVO	84601	PROVO
84620	AURORA	84654	SALINA
84623	CHESTER	84647	MOUNT PLEASANT
84626	ELBERTA	84013	CEDAR VALLEY
84632	FOUNTAIN GREEN	84629	FAIRVIEW
84633	GOSHEN	84013	CEDAR VALLEY
84636	HOLDEN	84631	FILLMORE
84637	KANOSH	84631	FILLMORE
84638	LEAMINGTON	84624	DELTA
84639	LEVAN	84648	NEPHI
84640	LYNNDYL	84624	DELTA
84643	MAYFIELD	84642	MANTI
84644	MEADOW	84631	FILLMORE
84646	MORONI	84647	MOUNT PLEASANT
84649	OAK CITY	84624	DELTA
84652	REDMOND	84654	SALINA
84656	SCIPIO	84631	FILLMORE
84657	SIGURD	84701	RICHFIELD
84662	SPRING CITY	84647	MOUNT PLEASANT
84665	STERLING	84642	MANTI
84667	WALES	84647	MOUNT PLEASANT
84711	ANNABELLA	84701	RICHFIELD
84715	BICKNELL	84775	TORREY
84718	CANNONVILLE	84726	ESCALANTE
84723	CIRCLEVILLE	84743	KINGSTON

Point ZIP Code		Enclosing Residential ZIP Code	
ZIP	Post Office Name	ZIP	Post Office Name
84724	ELSINORE	84754	MONROE
84725	ENTERPRISE	84722	CENTRAL
84730	GLENWOOD	84701	RICHFIELD
84732	GREENWICH	84743	KINGSTON
84733	GUNLOCK	84782	VEYO
84735	HATCH	84759	PANGUITCH
84736	HENRIEVILLE	84726	ESCALANTE
84740	JUNCTION	84743	KINGSTON
84742	KANARRAVILLE	84721	CEDAR CITY
84744	KOOSHAREM	84701	RICHFIELD
84746	LEEDS	84737	HURRICANE
84749	LYMAN	84747	LOA
84752	MINERSVILLE	84751	MILFORD
84762	DUCK CREEK VILLAGE	84710	ALTON
84763	ROCKVILLE	84737	HURRICANE
84764	BRYCE	84726	ESCALANTE
84767	SPRINGDALE	84737	HURRICANE
84771	SAINT GEORGE	84770	SAINT GEORGE
84774	TOQUERVILLE	84745	LA VERKIN
84776	TROPIC	84726	ESCALANTE
84779	VIRGIN	84737	HURRICANE
84784	HILDALE	84737	HURRICANE
84791	SAINT GEORGE	84790	SAINT GEORGE
85001	PHOENIX	85003	PHOENIX
85002	PHOENIX	85003	PHOENIX
85005	PHOENIX	85009	PHOENIX
85010	PHOENIX	85008	PHOENIX
85011	PHOENIX	85014	PHOENIX
85025	PHOENIX	85003	PHOENIX
85026	PHOENIX	85008	PHOENIX
85030	PHOENIX	85003	PHOENIX
85036	PHOENIX	85008	PHOENIX
85038	PHOENIX	85008	PHOENIX
85046	PHOENIX	85032	PHOENIX
85055	PHOENIX	85008	PHOENIX
85060	PHOENIX	85018	PHOENIX
85061	PHOENIX	85017	PHOENIX
85062	PHOENIX	85008	PHOENIX
85063	PHOENIX	85031	PHOENIX
85064	PHOENIX	85033	PHOENIX
85065	PHOENIX	85034	PHOENIX
85066	PHOENIX	85040	PHOENIX
85067	PHOENIX	85013	PHOENIX
85068	PHOENIX	85020	PHOENIX
85069	PHOENIX	85021	PHOENIX
85070	PHOENIX	85247	SACATON
85071	PHOENIX	85029	PHOENIX
85072	PHOENIX	85008	PHOENIX
85074	PHOENIX	85034	PHOENIX
85075	PHOENIX	85033	PHOENIX
85076	PHOENIX	85044	PHOENIX
85078	PHOENIX	85020	PHOENIX
85079	PHOENIX	85017	PHOENIX
85080	PHOENIX	85018	PHOENIX
85082	PHOENIX	85008	PHOENIX
85098	PHOENIX	85008	PHOENIX
85099	PHOENIX	85008	PHOENIX
85211	MESA	85201	MESA
85214	MESA	85201	MESA
85216	MESA	85206	MESA
85217	APACHE JUNCTION	85220	APACHE JUNCTION
85221	BAPCHULE	85222	CASA GRANDE
85223	ARIZONA CITY	85222	CASA GRANDE
85227	CHANDLER HEIGHTS	85242	QUEEN CREEK
85230	CASA GRANDE	85222	CASA GRANDE
85235	HAYDEN	85292	WINKELMAN
85241	PICACHO	85231	ELOY
85244	CHANDLER	85225	CHANDLER
85246	CHANDLER	85224	CHANDLER
85252	SCOTTSDALE	85251	SCOTTSDALE
85261	SCOTTSDALE	85251	SCOTTSDALE
85267	SCOTTSDALE	85260	SCOTTSDALE
85269	FOUNTAIN HILLS	85268	FOUNTAIN HILLS
85271	SCOTTSDALE	85257	SCOTTSDALE
85274	MESA	85202	MESA
85275	MESA	85213	MESA
85277	MESA	85215	MESA
85278	APACHE JUNCTION	85220	APACHE JUNCTION
85280	TEMPE	85282	TEMPE
85285	TEMPE	85282	TEMPE
85290	TORTILLA FLAT	85264	FORT MCDOWELL
85291	VALLEY FARMS	85228	COOLIDGE
85299	GILBERT	85296	GILBERT
85311	GLENDALE	85301	GLENDALE
85312	GLENDALE	85306	GLENDALE
85318	GLENDALE	85301	GLENDALE
85320	AGUILA	85390	WICKENBURG
85325	BOUSE	85344	PARKER
85327	CAVE CREEK	85331	CAVE CREEK
85329	CASHION	85323	AVONDALE
85334	EHRENBERG	85328	CIBOLA
85336	GADSDEN	85350	SOMERTON
85346	QUARTZSITE	85344	PARKER
85349	SAN LUIS	85350	SOMERTON
85352	TACNA	85356	WELLTON
85357	WENDEN	85348	SALOME
85358	WICKENBURG	85390	WICKENBURG
85359	QUARTZSITE	85344	PARKER
85360	WIKIEUP	86406	LAKE HAVASU CITY
85366	YUMA	85364	YUMA
85369	YUMA	85364	YUMA
85371	POSTON	85344	PARKER
85372	SUN CITY	85373	SUN CITY
85376	SUN CITY WEST	85375	SUN CITY WEST
85377	CAREFREE	85331	CAVE CREEK
85378	SURPRISE	85374	SURPRISE
85380	PEORIA	85345	PEORIA
85385	PEORIA	85345	PEORIA
85502	GLOBE	85501	GLOBE
85531	CENTRAL	85552	THATCHER
85532	CLAYPOOL	85539	MIAMI
85536	FORT THOMAS	85535	EDEN
85547	PAYSON	85541	PAYSON
85548	SAFFORD	85546	SAFFORD
85551	SOLOMON	85546	SAFFORD
85553	TONTO BASIN	85541	PAYSON
85554	YOUNG	85541	PAYSON
85605	BOWIE	85632	SAN SIMON
85608	DOUGLAS	85607	DOUGLAS
85609	DRAGOON	85630	SAINT DAVID
85620	NACO	85603	BISBEE
85626	PIRTLEVILLE	85607	DOUGLAS
85627	POMERENE	85602	BENSON
85628	NOGALES	85621	NOGALES
85633	SASABE	85736	TUCSON
85636	SIERRA VISTA	85635	SIERRA VISTA
85639	TOPAWA	85634	SELLS
85644	WILLCOX	85643	WILLCOX
85646	TUBAC	85640	TUMACACORI
85652	CORTARO	85741	TUCSON
85654	RILLITO	85653	MARANA
85655	DOUGLAS	85607	DOUGLAS
85662	NOGALES	85621	NOGALES
85670	FORT HUACHUCA	85635	SIERRA VISTA
85702	TUCSON	85701	TUCSON
85703	TUCSON	85705	TUCSON
85717	TUCSON	85719	TUCSON
85722	TUCSON	85719	TUCSON
85723	TUCSON	85713	TUCSON
85724	TUCSON	85719	TUCSON
85725	TUCSON	85713	TUCSON
85726	TUCSON	85713	TUCSON
85728	TUCSON	85718	TUCSON
85731	TUCSON	85710	TUCSON
85732	TUCSON	85711	TUCSON
85733	TUCSON	85719	TUCSON
85734	TUCSON	85756	TUCSON
85738	CATALINA	85704	TUCSON
85740	TUCSON	85704	TUCSON
85744	TUCSON	85747	TUCSON
85751	TUCSON	85715	TUCSON
85752	TUCSON	85741	TUCSON
85754	TUCSON	85745	TUCSON
85902	SHOW LOW	85901	SHOW LOW
85911	CIBECUE	85901	SHOW LOW
85912	WHITE MOUNTAIN LAKE	85901	SHOW LOW
85923	CLAY SPRINGS	85901	SHOW LOW
85926	FORT APACHE	85901	SHOW LOW
85927	GREER	85925	EAGAR
85930	MCNARY	85901	SHOW LOW
85931	FOREST LAKES	85928	HEBER
85932	NUTRIOSO	85925	EAGAR
85933	OVERGAARD	85928	HEBER
85934	PINEDALE	85901	SHOW LOW
85939	TAYLOR	85937	SNOWFLAKE
85940	VERNON	85938	SPRINGERVILLE
85941	WHITERIVER	85901	SHOW LOW
85942	WOODRUFF	86025	HOLBROOK
86002	FLAGSTAFF	86001	FLAGSTAFF
86003	FLAGSTAFF	86001	FLAGSTAFF
86011	FLAGSTAFF	86001	FLAGSTAFF
86015	BELLEMONT	86001	FLAGSTAFF
86016	GRAY MOUNTAIN	86001	FLAGSTAFF
86017	MUNDS PARK	86001	FLAGSTAFF
86018	PARKS	86046	WILLIAMS
86020	CAMERON	86045	TUBA CITY
86023	GRAND CANYON	86046	WILLIAMS
86028	PETRIFIED FOREST NAT	86025	HOLBROOK
86029	SUN VALLEY	86025	HOLBROOK
86031	INDIAN WELLS	86047	WINSLOW
86032	JOSEPH CITY	86047	WINSLOW
86052	NORTH RIM	86022	FREDONIA
86302	PRESCOTT	86305	PRESCOTT
86304	PRESCOTT	86305	PRESCOTT
86312	PRESCOTT VALLEY	86314	PRESCOTT VALLEY
86313	PRESCOTT	86301	PRESCOTT

Point ZIP Code		Enclosing Residential ZIP Code	
ZIP	Post Office Name	ZIP	Post Office Name
86329	HUMBOLDT	86327	DEWEY
86330	IRON SPRINGS	86305	PRESCOTT
86331	JEROME	86324	CLARKDALE
86338	SKULL VALLEY	86305	PRESCOTT
86339	SEDONA	86336	SEDONA
86340	SEDONA	86336	SEDONA
86341	SEDONA	86351	SEDONA
86342	LAKE MONTEZUMA	86335	RIMROCK
86402	KINGMAN	86401	KINGMAN
86405	LAKE HAVASU CITY	86403	LAKE HAVASU CITY
86412	HUALAPAI	86409	KINGMAN
86427	FORT MOHAVE	86426	FORT MOHAVE
86430	BULLHEAD CITY	86429	BULLHEAD CITY
86431	CHLORIDE	86401	KINGMAN
86433	OATMAN	86442	BULLHEAD CITY
86437	VALENTINE	86401	KINGMAN
86438	YUCCA	86442	BULLHEAD CITY
86439	BULLHEAD CITY	86442	BULLHEAD CITY
86443	TEMPLE BAR MARINA	86445	WILLOW BEACH
86446	MOHAVE VALLEY	86442	BULLHEAD CITY
86504	FORT DEFIANCE	86505	GANADO
86506	HOUCK	86505	GANADO
86508	LUPTON	86505	GANADO
86511	SAINT MICHAELS	86505	GANADO
86512	SANDERS	86502	CHAMBERS
86515	WINDOW ROCK	86505	GANADO
86520	BLUE GAP	86510	PINON
86540	NAZLINI	86503	CHINLE
86544	RED VALLEY	86514	TEEC NOS POS
86545	ROCK POINT	86514	TEEC NOS POS
86547	ROUND ROCK	86538	MANY FARMS
87011	CLAUNCH	87801	SOCORRO
87022	ISLETA	87068	BOSQUE FARMS
87032	MC INTOSH	87016	ESTANCIA
87034	PUEBLO OF ACOMA	87014	CUBERO
87037	NAGEEZI	87401	FARMINGTON
87038	NEW LAGUNA	87007	CASA BLANCA
87040	PAGUATE	87014	CUBERO
87049	SAN FIDEL	87020	GRANTS
87051	SAN RAFAEL	87014	CUBERO
87061	TORREON	87016	ESTANCIA
87064	YOUNGSVILLE	87017	GALLINA
87070	CLINES CORNERS	87560	RIBERA
87072	COCHITI PUEBLO	87041	PENA BLANCA
87101	ALBUQUERQUE	87102	ALBUQUERQUE
87103	ALBUQUERQUE	87102	ALBUQUERQUE
87117	KIRTLAND AFB	87116	ALBUQUERQUE
87119	ALBUQUERQUE	87102	ALBUQUERQUE
87125	ALBUQUERQUE	87102	ALBUQUERQUE
87151	ALBUQUERQUE	87102	ALBUQUERQUE
87153	ALBUQUERQUE	87112	ALBUQUERQUE
87154	ALBUQUERQUE	87111	ALBUQUERQUE
87158	ALBUQUERQUE	87107	ALBUQUERQUE
87165	ALBUQUERQUE	87102	ALBUQUERQUE
87174	RIO RANCHO	87124	RIO RANCHO
87176	ALBUQUERQUE	87110	ALBUQUERQUE
87181	ALBUQUERQUE	87112	ALBUQUERQUE
87184	ALBUQUERQUE	87114	ALBUQUERQUE
87185	ALBUQUERQUE	87116	ALBUQUERQUE
87187	ALBUQUERQUE	87114	ALBUQUERQUE
87190	ALBUQUERQUE	87110	ALBUQUERQUE
87191	ALBUQUERQUE	87111	ALBUQUERQUE
87192	ALBUQUERQUE	87104	ALBUQUERQUE
87193	ALBUQUERQUE	87114	ALBUQUERQUE
87194	ALBUQUERQUE	87104	ALBUQUERQUE
87195	ALBUQUERQUE	87105	ALBUQUERQUE
87196	ALBUQUERQUE	87106	ALBUQUERQUE
87197	ALBUQUERQUE	87107	ALBUQUERQUE
87198	ALBUQUERQUE	87108	ALBUQUERQUE
87199	ALBUQUERQUE	87109	ALBUQUERQUE
87302	GALLUP	87301	GALLUP
87305	GALLUP	87301	GALLUP
87311	CHURCH ROCK	87301	GALLUP
87316	FORT WINGATE	87301	GALLUP
87317	GAMERCO	87301	GALLUP
87319	MENTMORE	87301	GALLUP
87322	REHOBOTH	87301	GALLUP
87326	VANDERWAGEN	87301	GALLUP
87347	JAMESTOWN	87312	CONTINENTAL DIVIDE
87357	PINEHILL	87014	CUBERO
87364	SHEEP SPRINGS	87420	SHIPROCK
87365	SMITH LAKE	87323	THOREAU
87375	YATAHEY	87301	GALLUP
87455	NEWCOMB	87420	SHIPROCK
87461	SANOSTEE	87420	SHIPROCK
87499	FARMINGTON	87401	FARMINGTON
87502	SANTA FE	87501	SANTA FE
87503	SANTA FE	87501	SANTA FE
87504	SANTA FE	87501	SANTA FE
87509	SANTA FE	87505	SANTA FE
87511	ALCALDE	87531	EMBUDO
87512	AMALIA	87524	COSTILLA
87515	CANJILON	87575	TIERRA AMARILLA

Point ZIP Code		Enclosing Residential ZIP Code	
ZIP	Post Office Name	ZIP	Post Office Name
87516	CANONES	87017	GALLINA
87517	CARSON	87549	OJO CALIENTE
87518	CEBOLLA	87575	TIERRA AMARILLA
87519	CERRO	87556	QUESTA
87523	CORDOVA	87522	CHIMAYO
87525	TAOS SKI VALLEY	87571	TAOS
87529	EL PRADO	87571	TAOS
87533	ESPANOLA	87532	ESPANOLA
87538	ILFELD	87552	PECOS
87543	LLANO	87579	VADITO
87545	LOS ALAMOS	87544	LOS ALAMOS
87548	MEDANALES	87510	ABIQUIU
87551	LOS OJOS	87575	TIERRA AMARILLA
87554	PETACA	87581	VALLECITOS
87558	RED RIVER	87556	QUESTA
87562	ROWE	87565	SAN JOSE
87569	SERAFINA	87560	RIBERA
87574	TESUQUE	87506	SANTA FE
87576	TRAMPAS	87553	PENASCO
87577	TRES PIEDRAS	87549	OJO CALIENTE
87578	TRUCHAS	87522	CHIMAYO
87582	VELARDE	87531	EMBUDO
87583	VILLANUEVA	87701	LAS VEGAS
87592	SANTA FE	87507	SANTA FE
87594	SANTA FE	87501	SANTA FE
87710	ANGEL FIRE	87714	CIMARRON
87712	BUENA VISTA	87732	MORA
87723	HOLMAN	87732	MORA
87735	OJO FELIZ	87722	GUADALUPITA
87736	RAINSVILLE	87732	MORA
87749	UTE PARK	87714	CIMARRON
87753	WATROUS	87750	VALMORA
87824	LUNA	87830	RESERVE
87832	SAN ANTONIO	87801	SOCORRO
87935	ELEPHANT BUTTE	87901	TRUTH OR CONSEQUENCES
87939	MONTICELLO	87901	TRUTH OR CONSEQUENCES
88004	LAS CRUCES	88001	LAS CRUCES
88006	LAS CRUCES	88001	LAS CRUCES
88009	PLAYAS	88045	LORDSBURG
88013	LAS CRUCES	88001	LAS CRUCES
88024	BERINO	88081	CHAPARRAL
88027	CHAMBERINO	88044	LA MESA
88028	CLIFF	88025	BUCKHORN
88029	COLUMBUS	88030	DEMING
88031	DEMING	88030	DEMING
88032	DONA ANA	88012	LAS CRUCES
88033	FAIRACRES	88007	LAS CRUCES
88034	FAYWOOD	88023	BAYARD
88036	FORT BAYARD	88061	SILVER CITY
88038	GILA	88061	SILVER CITY
88040	HACHITA	88043	HURLEY
88046	MESILLA	88005	LAS CRUCES
88051	MULE CREEK	88025	BUCKHORN
88052	ORGAN	88007	LAS CRUCES
88053	PINOS ALTOS	88061	SILVER CITY
88054	RADIUM SPRINGS	87940	RINCON
88055	REDROCK	88025	BUCKHORN
88056	RODEO	88020	ANIMAS
88058	SAN MIGUEL	88044	LA MESA
88062	SILVER CITY	88061	SILVER CITY
88065	TYRONE	88061	SILVER CITY
88102	CLOVIS	88101	CLOVIS
88115	DORA	88130	PORTALES
88122	KENNA	88116	ELIDA
88202	ROSWELL	88201	ROSWELL
88211	ARTESIA	88210	ARTESIA
88221	CARLSBAD	88220	CARLSBAD
88241	HOBBS	88240	HOBBS
88244	HOBBS	88240	HOBBS
88254	LAKEWOOD	88210	ARTESIA
88255	LOCO HILLS	88210	ARTESIA
88262	MC DONALD	88260	LOVINGTON
88263	MALAGA	88256	LOVING
88268	WHITES CITY	88220	CARLSBAD
88311	ALAMOGORDO	88310	ALAMOGORDO
88323	FORT STANTON	88316	CAPITAN
88325	HIGH ROLLS MOUNTAIN	88317	CLOUDCROFT
88342	OROGRANDE	88317	CLOUDCROFT
88349	SUNSPOT	88317	CLOUDCROFT
88350	TIMBERON	88317	CLOUDCROFT
88355	RUIDOSO	88345	RUIDOSO
88510	EL PASO	79906	EL PASO
88511	EL PASO	79906	EL PASO
88512	EL PASO	79906	EL PASO
88513	EL PASO	79906	EL PASO
88514	EL PASO	79906	EL PASO
88515	EL PASO	79906	EL PASO
88516	EL PASO	79925	EL PASO
88517	EL PASO	79906	EL PASO
88518	EL PASO	79906	EL PASO
88519	EL PASO	79906	EL PASO
88520	EL PASO	79906	EL PASO
88521	EL PASO	79906	EL PASO

NONRESIDENTIAL ZIP CODES

TEXAS

CALIFORNIA

Point ZIP Code		Enclosing Residential ZIP Code		Point ZIP Code		Enclosing Residential ZIP Code	
ZIP	Post Office Name	ZIP	Post Office Name	ZIP	Post Office Name	ZIP	Post Office Name
88523	EL PASO	79906	EL PASO	89125	LAS VEGAS	89101	LAS VEGAS
88524	EL PASO	79906	EL PASO	89126	LAS VEGAS	89102	LAS VEGAS
88525	EL PASO	79906	EL PASO	89127	LAS VEGAS	89106	LAS VEGAS
88526	EL PASO	79906	EL PASO	89132	LAS VEGAS	89119	LAS VEGAS
88527	EL PASO	79906	EL PASO	89133	LAS VEGAS	89128	LAS VEGAS
88528	EL PASO	79906	EL PASO	89136	LAS VEGAS	89119	LAS VEGAS
88529	EL PASO	79906	EL PASO	89137	LAS VEGAS	89144	LAS VEGAS
88530	EL PASO	79906	EL PASO	89140	LAS VEGAS	89119	LAS VEGAS
88531	EL PASO	79906	EL PASO	89150	LAS VEGAS	89103	LAS VEGAS
88532	EL PASO	79906	EL PASO	89151	LAS VEGAS	89146	LAS VEGAS
88533	EL PASO	79906	EL PASO	89152	LAS VEGAS	89107	LAS VEGAS
88534	EL PASO	79906	EL PASO	89153	LAS VEGAS	89102	LAS VEGAS
88535	EL PASO	79906	EL PASO	89155	LAS VEGAS	89101	LAS VEGAS
88536	EL PASO	79906	EL PASO	89157	LAS VEGAS	89119	LAS VEGAS
88538	EL PASO	79906	EL PASO	89159	LAS VEGAS	89119	LAS VEGAS
88539	EL PASO	79906	EL PASO	89160	LAS VEGAS	89121	LAS VEGAS
88540	EL PASO	79925	EL PASO	89161	LAS VEGAS	89119	LAS VEGAS
88541	EL PASO	79925	EL PASO	89162	LAS VEGAS	89122	LAS VEGAS
88542	EL PASO	79925	EL PASO	89163	THE LAKES	89117	LAS VEGAS
88543	EL PASO	79925	EL PASO	89164	LAS VEGAS	89117	LAS VEGAS
88544	EL PASO	79925	EL PASO	89170	LAS VEGAS	89154	LAS VEGAS
88545	EL PASO	79925	EL PASO	89173	LAS VEGAS	89103	LAS VEGAS
88546	EL PASO	79925	EL PASO	89177	LAS VEGAS	89106	LAS VEGAS
88547	EL PASO	79925	EL PASO	89180	LAS VEGAS	89103	LAS VEGAS
88548	EL PASO	79925	EL PASO	89185	LAS VEGAS	89104	LAS VEGAS
88549	EL PASO	79925	EL PASO	89193	LAS VEGAS	89119	LAS VEGAS
88550	EL PASO	79925	EL PASO	89199	LAS VEGAS	89119	LAS VEGAS
88553	EL PASO	79925	EL PASO	89314	DUCKWATER	89301	ELY
88554	EL PASO	79925	EL PASO	89315	ELY	89301	ELY
88555	EL PASO	79925	EL PASO	89318	MC GILL	89301	ELY
88556	EL PASO	79925	EL PASO	89319	RUTH	89301	ELY
88557	EL PASO	79925	EL PASO	89402	CRYSTAL BAY	89451	INCLINE VILLAGE
88558	EL PASO	79925	EL PASO	89407	FALLON	89406	FALLON
88559	EL PASO	79925	EL PASO	89411	GENOA	89413	GLENBROOK
88560	EL PASO	79925	EL PASO	89421	MC DERMITT	89425	OROVADA
88561	EL PASO	79925	EL PASO	89422	MINA	89420	LUNING
88562	EL PASO	79925	EL PASO	89428	SILVER CITY	89706	CARSON CITY
88563	EL PASO	79925	EL PASO	89432	SPARKS	89431	SPARKS
88565	EL PASO	79925	EL PASO	89435	SPARKS	89436	SPARKS
88566	EL PASO	79925	EL PASO	89438	VALMY	89414	GOLCONDA
88567	EL PASO	79925	EL PASO	89439	VERDI	89523	RENO
88568	EL PASO	79925	EL PASO	89446	WINNEMUCCA	89445	WINNEMUCCA
88569	EL PASO	79925	EL PASO	89448	ZEPHYR COVE	89413	GLENBROOK
88570	EL PASO	79925	EL PASO	89449	STATELINE	89413	GLENBROOK
88571	EL PASO	79925	EL PASO	89450	INCLINE VILLAGE	89451	INCLINE VILLAGE
88572	EL PASO	79925	EL PASO	89452	INCLINE VILLAGE	89451	INCLINE VILLAGE
88573	EL PASO	79925	EL PASO	89496	FALLON	89406	FALLON
88574	EL PASO	79925	EL PASO	89504	RENO	89501	RENO
88575	EL PASO	79925	EL PASO	89505	RENO	89501	RENO
88576	EL PASO	79925	EL PASO	89507	RENO	89503	RENO
88577	EL PASO	79925	EL PASO	89513	RENO	89503	RENO
88578	EL PASO	79925	EL PASO	89515	RENO	89502	RENO
88579	EL PASO	79925	EL PASO	89520	RENO	89503	RENO
88580	EL PASO	79925	EL PASO	89533	RENO	89523	RENO
88581	EL PASO	79925	EL PASO	89555	RENO	89502	RENO
88582	EL PASO	79925	EL PASO	89557	RENO	89503	RENO
88583	EL PASO	79925	EL PASO	89570	RENO	89502	RENO
88584	EL PASO	79925	EL PASO	89595	RENO	89502	RENO
88585	EL PASO	79925	EL PASO	89702	CARSON CITY	89701	CARSON CITY
88586	EL PASO	79925	EL PASO	89711	CARSON CITY	89701	CARSON CITY
88587	EL PASO	79925	EL PASO	89712	CARSON CITY	89701	CARSON CITY
88588	EL PASO	79925	EL PASO	89713	CARSON CITY	89701	CARSON CITY
88589	EL PASO	79925	EL PASO	89714	CARSON CITY	89701	CARSON CITY
88590	EL PASO	79925	EL PASO	89721	CARSON CITY	89701	CARSON CITY
88595	EL PASO	79905	EL PASO	89802	ELKO	89801	ELKO
88901	THE LAKES	89117	LAS VEGAS	89803	ELKO	89801	ELKO
88905	THE LAKES	89117	LAS VEGAS	89824	HALLECK	89823	DEETH
89004	BLUE DIAMOND	89124	LAS VEGAS	89826	JARBIDGE	89825	JACKPOT
89006	BOULDER CITY	89005	BOULDER CITY	89828	LAMOILLE	89815	SPRING CREEK
89007	BUNKERVILLE	89040	OVERTON	89830	MONTELLO	89835	WELLS
89009	HENDERSON	89015	HENDERSON	89832	OWYHEE	89831	MOUNTAIN CITY
89010	DYER	89047	SILVERPEAK	89883	WEST WENDOVER	89835	WELLS
89016	HENDERSON	89015	HENDERSON	90009	LOS ANGELES	90045	LOS ANGELES
89022	MANHATTAN	89049	TONOPAH	90030	LOS ANGELES	90012	LOS ANGELES
89023	MERCURY	89020	AMARGOSA VALLEY	90050	LOS ANGELES	90042	LOS ANGELES
89024	MESQUITE	89027	MESQUITE	90051	LOS ANGELES	90012	LOS ANGELES
89025	MOAPA	89040	OVERTON	90052	LOS ANGELES	90001	LOS ANGELES
89028	LAUGHLIN	89029	LAUGHLIN	90053	LOS ANGELES	90012	LOS ANGELES
89036	NORTH LAS VEGAS	89030	NORTH LAS VEGAS	90054	LOS ANGELES	90012	LOS ANGELES
89037	MOAPA	89040	OVERTON	90055	LOS ANGELES	90017	LOS ANGELES
89039	CAL NEV ARI	89046	SEARCHLIGHT	90060	LOS ANGELES	90012	LOS ANGELES
89041	PAHRUMP	89048	PAHRUMP	90070	LOS ANGELES	90010	LOS ANGELES
89042	PANACA	89043	PIOCHE	90072	LOS ANGELES	90028	LOS ANGELES
89053	HENDERSON	89044	HENDERSON	90074	LOS ANGELES	90071	LOS ANGELES
89067	MOAPA	89040	OVERTON	90075	LOS ANGELES	90020	LOS ANGELES
89070	INDIAN SPRINGS	89018	INDIAN SPRINGS	90076	LOS ANGELES	90020	LOS ANGELES
89077	HENDERSON	89015	HENDERSON	90078	LOS ANGELES	90028	LOS ANGELES
89087	NORTH LAS VEGAS	89030	NORTH LAS VEGAS	90079	LOS ANGELES	90015	LOS ANGELES
89105	LAS VEGAS	89119	LAS VEGAS	90080	LOS ANGELES	90045	LOS ANGELES
89111	LAS VEGAS	89119	LAS VEGAS	90081	LOS ANGELES	90017	LOS ANGELES
89112	LAS VEGAS	89110	LAS VEGAS	90082	LOS ANGELES	90037	LOS ANGELES
89114	LAS VEGAS	89106	LAS VEGAS	90083	LOS ANGELES	90045	LOS ANGELES
89116	LAS VEGAS	89104	LAS VEGAS	90084	LOS ANGELES	90017	LOS ANGELES

NONRESIDENTIAL ZIP CODES

CALIFORNIA

Point ZIP Code		Enclosing Residential ZIP Code	
ZIP	Post Office Name	ZIP	Post Office Name
90086	LOS ANGELES	90012	LOS ANGELES
90087	LOS ANGELES	90012	LOS ANGELES
90088	LOS ANGELES	90017	LOS ANGELES
90091	LOS ANGELES	90040	LOS ANGELES
90093	LOS ANGELES	90028	LOS ANGELES
90096	LOS ANGELES	90017	LOS ANGELES
90101	LOS ANGELES	90201	BELL
90103	LOS ANGELES	90201	BELL
90189	LOS ANGELES	90045	LOS ANGELES
90202	BELL GARDENS	90201	BELL
90209	BEVERLY HILLS	90210	BEVERLY HILLS
90213	BEVERLY HILLS	90210	BEVERLY HILLS
90223	COMPTON	90220	COMPTON
90224	COMPTON	90221	COMPTON
90231	CULVER CITY	90230	CULVER CITY
90233	CULVER CITY	90230	CULVER CITY
90239	DOWNEY	90241	DOWNEY
90251	HAWTHORNE	90250	HAWTHORNE
90261	LAWNDALE	90260	LAWNDALE
90264	MALIBU	90265	MALIBU
90267	MANHATTAN BEACH	90266	MANHATTAN BEACH
90294	VENICE	90291	VENICE
90295	MARINA DEL REY	90292	MARINA DEL REY
90296	PLAYA DEL REY	90293	PLAYA DEL REY
90306	INGLEWOOD	90301	INGLEWOOD
90307	INGLEWOOD	90301	INGLEWOOD
90308	INGLEWOOD	90301	INGLEWOOD
90309	INGLEWOOD	90302	INGLEWOOD
90310	INGLEWOOD	90250	HAWTHORNE
90311	INGLEWOOD	90094	LOS ANGELES
90312	INGLEWOOD	90066	LOS ANGELES
90406	SANTA MONICA	90401	SANTA MONICA
90407	SANTA MONICA	90401	SANTA MONICA
90408	SANTA MONICA	90403	SANTA MONICA
90409	SANTA MONICA	90405	SANTA MONICA
90410	SANTA MONICA	90401	SANTA MONICA
90411	SANTA MONICA	90401	SANTA MONICA
90507	TORRANCE	90501	TORRANCE
90508	TORRANCE	90501	TORRANCE
90509	TORRANCE	90503	TORRANCE
90510	TORRANCE	90503	TORRANCE
90607	WHITTIER	90605	WHITTIER
90608	WHITTIER	90601	WHITTIER
90609	WHITTIER	90603	WHITTIER
90610	WHITTIER	90606	WHITTIER
90622	BUENA PARK	90620	BUENA PARK
90624	BUENA PARK	90621	BUENA PARK
90632	LA HABRA	90631	LA HABRA
90633	LA HABRA	92821	BREA
90637	LA MIRADA	90638	LA MIRADA
90651	NORWALK	90650	NORWALK
90652	NORWALK	90650	NORWALK
90661	PICO RIVERA	90660	PICO RIVERA
90662	PICO RIVERA	90660	PICO RIVERA
90702	ARTESIA	90701	ARTESIA
90707	BELLFLOWER	90706	BELLFLOWER
90711	LAKEWOOD	90712	LAKEWOOD
90714	LAKEWOOD	90712	LAKEWOOD
90721	LOS ALAMITOS	90720	LOS ALAMITOS
90733	SAN PEDRO	90731	SAN PEDRO
90734	SAN PEDRO	90275	RANCHO PALOS VERDES
90748	WILMINGTON	90744	WILMINGTON
90749	CARSON	90745	CARSON
90801	LONG BEACH	90802	LONG BEACH
90809	LONG BEACH	90815	LONG BEACH
90831	LONG BEACH	90802	LONG BEACH
90832	LONG BEACH	90802	LONG BEACH
90833	LONG BEACH	90802	LONG BEACH
90834	LONG BEACH	90802	LONG BEACH
90835	LONG BEACH	90802	LONG BEACH
90842	LONG BEACH	90807	LONG BEACH
90844	LONG BEACH	90802	LONG BEACH
90846	LONG BEACH	90808	LONG BEACH
90847	LONG BEACH	90807	LONG BEACH
90848	LONG BEACH	90807	LONG BEACH
90853	LONG BEACH	90803	LONG BEACH
90895	CARSON	90810	LONG BEACH
90899	LONG BEACH	90802	LONG BEACH
91003	ALTADENA	91001	ALTADENA
91009	DUARTE	91010	DUARTE
91012	LA CANADA FLINTRIDGE	91011	LA CANADA FLINTRIDGE
91017	MONROVIA	91016	MONROVIA
91021	MONTROSE	91020	MONTROSE
91023	MOUNT WILSON	91011	LA CANADA FLINTRIDGE
91025	SIERRA MADRE	91024	SIERRA MADRE
91031	SOUTH PASADENA	91030	SOUTH PASADENA
91041	SUNLAND	91040	SUNLAND
91043	TUJUNGA	91042	TUJUNGA
91046	VERDUGO CITY	91214	LA CRESCENTA
91066	ARCADIA	91006	ARCADIA
91077	ARCADIA	91007	ARCADIA
91102	PASADENA	91103	PASADENA
91109	PASADENA	91103	PASADENA

Point ZIP Code		Enclosing Residential ZIP Code	
ZIP	Post Office Name	ZIP	Post Office Name
91110	PASADENA	91103	PASADENA
91114	PASADENA	91104	PASADENA
91115	PASADENA	91105	PASADENA
91116	PASADENA	91106	PASADENA
91117	PASADENA	91107	PASADENA
91118	SAN MARINO	91108	SAN MARINO
91121	PASADENA	91107	PASADENA
91124	PASADENA	91103	PASADENA
91125	PASADENA	91106	PASADENA
91126	PASADENA	91106	PASADENA
91129	PASADENA	91123	PASADENA
91182	PASADENA	91101	PASADENA
91184	PASADENA	91105	PASADENA
91185	PASADENA	91801	ALHAMBRA
91188	PASADENA	91101	PASADENA
91189	PASADENA	91105	PASADENA
91199	PASADENA	91101	PASADENA
91209	GLENDALE	91205	GLENDALE
91210	GLENDALE	91204	GLENDALE
91221	GLENDALE	91201	GLENDALE
91222	GLENDALE	91202	GLENDALE
91224	LA CRESCENTA	91214	LA CRESCENTA
91225	GLENDALE	91205	GLENDALE
91226	GLENDALE	91206	GLENDALE
91305	CANOGA PARK	91303	CANOGA PARK
91308	WEST HILLS	91307	WEST HILLS
91309	CANOGA PARK	91303	CANOGA PARK
91310	CASTAIC	91384	CASTAIC
91313	CHATSWORTH	91311	CHATSWORTH
91319	NEWBURY PARK	91320	NEWBURY PARK
91322	NEWHALL	91321	NEWHALL
91327	NORTHRIDGE	91326	PORTER RANCH
91328	NORTHRIDGE	91324	NORTHRIDGE
91329	NORTHRIDGE	91343	NORTH HILLS
91333	PACOIMA	91331	PACOIMA
91334	PACOIMA	91331	PACOIMA
91337	RESEDA	91335	RESEDA
91341	SAN FERNANDO	91340	SAN FERNANDO
91346	MISSION HILLS	91345	MISSION HILLS
91353	SUN VALLEY	91352	SUN VALLEY
91357	TARZANA	91356	TARZANA
91358	THOUSAND OAKS	91360	THOUSAND OAKS
91359	WESTLAKE VILLAGE	91362	THOUSAND OAKS
91365	WOODLAND HILLS	91367	WOODLAND HILLS
91372	CALABASAS	91302	CALABASAS
91376	AGOURA HILLS	91301	AGOURA HILLS
91380	SANTA CLARITA	91355	VALENCIA
91383	SANTA CLARITA	91355	VALENCIA
91385	VALENCIA	91355	VALENCIA
91386	CANYON COUNTRY	91350	SANTA CLARITA
91392	SYLMAR	91342	SYLMAR
91393	NORTH HILLS	91343	NORTH HILLS
91394	GRANADA HILLS	91326	PORTER RANCH
91395	MISSION HILLS	91345	MISSION HILLS
91396	WINNETKA	91306	WINNETKA
91404	VAN NUYS	91411	VAN NUYS
91407	VAN NUYS	91411	VAN NUYS
91408	VAN NUYS	91411	VAN NUYS
91409	VAN NUYS	91406	VAN NUYS
91410	VAN NUYS	91406	VAN NUYS
91412	PANORAMA CITY	91402	PANORAMA CITY
91413	SHERMAN OAKS	91403	SHERMAN OAKS
91416	ENCINO	91316	ENCINO
91426	ENCINO	91316	ENCINO
91470	VAN NUYS	91406	VAN NUYS
91482	VAN NUYS	91406	VAN NUYS
91495	SHERMAN OAKS	91403	SHERMAN OAKS
91496	VAN NUYS	91403	SHERMAN OAKS
91499	VAN NUYS	91405	VAN NUYS
91503	BURBANK	91502	BURBANK
91507	BURBANK	91505	BURBANK
91508	BURBANK	91504	BURBANK
91510	BURBANK	91505	BURBANK
91526	BURBANK	91505	BURBANK
91603	NORTH HOLLYWOOD	91601	NORTH HOLLYWOOD
91609	NORTH HOLLYWOOD	91606	NORTH HOLLYWOOD
91610	TOLUCA LAKE	91602	NORTH HOLLYWOOD
91611	NORTH HOLLYWOOD	91606	NORTH HOLLYWOOD
91612	NORTH HOLLYWOOD	91606	NORTH HOLLYWOOD
91614	STUDIO CITY	91604	STUDIO CITY
91615	NORTH HOLLYWOOD	91605	NORTH HOLLYWOOD
91616	NORTH HOLLYWOOD	91606	NORTH HOLLYWOOD
91617	VALLEY VILLAGE	91607	VALLEY VILLAGE
91715	CITY OF INDUSTRY	91745	HACIENDA HEIGHTS
91716	CITY OF INDUSTRY	91745	HACIENDA HEIGHTS
91729	RANCHO CUCAMONGA	91730	RANCHO CUCAMONGA
91734	EL MONTE	91731	EL MONTE
91735	EL MONTE	91731	EL MONTE
91743	GUASTI	91761	ONTARIO
91747	LA PUENTE	91744	LA PUENTE
91749	LA PUENTE	91745	HACIENDA HEIGHTS
91756	MONTEREY PARK	91754	MONTEREY PARK
91758	ONTARIO	91761	ONTARIO

Point ZIP Code		Enclosing Residential ZIP Code		Point ZIP Code		Enclosing Residential ZIP Code	
ZIP	Post Office Name	ZIP	Post Office Name	ZIP	Post Office Name	ZIP	Post Office Name
91769	POMONA	91768	POMONA	92202	INDIO	92201	INDIO
91771	ROSEMEAD	91770	ROSEMEAD	92222	BARD	92283	WINTERHAVEN
91772	ROSEMEAD	91770	ROSEMEAD	92226	BLYTHE	92225	BLYTHE
91778	SAN GABRIEL	91776	SAN GABRIEL	92232	CALEXICO	92231	CALEXICO
91785	UPLAND	91786	UPLAND	92235	CATHEDRAL CITY	92234	CATHEDRAL CITY
91788	WALNUT	91789	WALNUT	92244	EL CENTRO	92243	EL CENTRO
91793	WEST COVINA	91790	WEST COVINA	92247	LA QUINTA	92253	LA QUINTA
91795	WALNUT	91789	WALNUT	92248	LA QUINTA	92253	LA QUINTA
91802	ALHAMBRA	91801	ALHAMBRA	92255	PALM DESERT	92260	PALM DESERT
91804	ALHAMBRA	91801	ALHAMBRA	92258	NORTH PALM SPRINGS	92240	DESERT HOT SPRINGS
91896	ALHAMBRA	91801	ALHAMBRA	92261	PALM DESERT	92260	PALM DESERT
91903	ALPINE	91901	ALPINE	92263	PALM SPRINGS	92262	PALM SPRINGS
91908	BONITA	91902	BONITA	92266	PALO VERDE	92283	WINTERHAVEN
91909	CHULA VISTA	91911	CHULA VISTA	92268	PIONEERTOWN	92284	YUCCA VALLEY
91912	CHULA VISTA	91910	CHULA VISTA	92273	SEELEY	92243	EL CENTRO
91921	CHULA VISTA	91915	CHULA VISTA	92275	SALTON CITY	92274	THERMAL
91931	GUATAY	91962	PINE VALLEY	92286	YUCCA VALLEY	92284	YUCCA VALLEY
91933	IMPERIAL BEACH	91932	IMPERIAL BEACH	92292	PALM SPRINGS	92262	PALM SPRINGS
91943	LA MESA	91942	LA MESA	92312	BARSTOW	92311	BARSTOW
91944	LA MESA	91941	LA MESA	92318	BRYN MAWR	92354	LOMA LINDA
91946	LEMON GROVE	91945	LEMON GROVE	92323	CIMA	92364	NIPTON
91947	LINCOLN ACRES	91950	NATIONAL CITY	92326	CREST PARK	92407	SAN BERNARDINO
91948	MOUNT LAGUNA	91962	PINE VALLEY	92329	PHELAN	92371	PHELAN
91951	NATIONAL CITY	91950	NATIONAL CITY	92331	FONTANA	92335	FONTANA
91976	SPRING VALLEY	91977	SPRING VALLEY	92333	FAWNSKIN	92314	BIG BEAR CITY
91979	SPRING VALLEY	91977	SPRING VALLEY	92334	FONTANA	92335	FONTANA
91987	TECATE	91980	TECATE	92340	HESPERIA	92345	HESPERIA
92013	CARLSBAD	92011	CARLSBAD	92341	GREEN VALLEY LAKE	92314	BIG BEAR CITY
92018	CARLSBAD	92008	CARLSBAD	92357	LOMA LINDA	92354	LOMA LINDA
92022	EL CAJON	92020	EL CAJON	92366	MOUNTAIN PASS	92364	NIPTON
92023	ENCINITAS	92024	ENCINITAS	92369	PATTON	92346	HIGHLAND
92030	ESCONDIDO	92027	ESCONDIDO	92375	REDLANDS	92373	REDLANDS
92033	ESCONDIDO	92025	ESCONDIDO	92378	RIMFOREST	92407	SAN BERNARDINO
92038	LA JOLLA	92037	LA JOLLA	92386	SUGARLOAF	92314	BIG BEAR CITY
92039	LA JOLLA	92037	LA JOLLA	92391	TWIN PEAKS	92407	SAN BERNARDINO
92046	ESCONDIDO	92025	ESCONDIDO	92393	VICTORVILLE	92395	VICTORVILLE
92049	OCEANSIDE	92054	OCEANSIDE	92398	YERMO	92365	NEWBERRY SPRINGS
92051	OCEANSIDE	92054	OCEANSIDE	92402	SAN BERNARDINO	92401	SAN BERNARDINO
92052	OCEANSIDE	92054	OCEANSIDE	92403	SAN BERNARDINO	92401	SAN BERNARDINO
92060	PALOMAR MOUNTAIN	92059	PALA	92406	SAN BERNARDINO	92405	SAN BERNARDINO
92068	SAN LUIS REY	92058	OCEANSIDE	92412	SAN BERNARDINO	92401	SAN BERNARDINO
92072	SANTEE	92071	SANTEE	92413	SAN BERNARDINO	92404	SAN BERNARDINO
92074	POWAY	92064	POWAY	92414	SAN BERNARDINO	92404	SAN BERNARDINO
92079	SAN MARCOS	92069	SAN MARCOS	92415	SAN BERNARDINO	92404	SAN BERNARDINO
92085	VISTA	92083	VISTA	92418	SAN BERNARDINO	92401	SAN BERNARDINO
92088	FALLBROOK	92028	FALLBROOK	92423	SAN BERNARDINO	92408	SAN BERNARDINO
92090	EL CAJON	92020	EL CAJON	92424	SAN BERNARDINO	92404	SAN BERNARDINO
92092	LA JOLLA	92037	LA JOLLA	92427	SAN BERNARDINO	92407	SAN BERNARDINO
92093	LA JOLLA	92037	LA JOLLA	92502	RIVERSIDE	92501	RIVERSIDE
92112	SAN DIEGO	92101	SAN DIEGO	92513	RIVERSIDE	92503	RIVERSIDE
92132	SAN DIEGO	92101	SAN DIEGO	92514	RIVERSIDE	92504	RIVERSIDE
92137	SAN DIEGO	92110	SAN DIEGO	92515	RIVERSIDE	92503	RIVERSIDE
92138	SAN DIEGO	92110	SAN DIEGO	92516	RIVERSIDE	92506	RIVERSIDE
92142	SAN DIEGO	92124	SAN DIEGO	92517	RIVERSIDE	92507	RIVERSIDE
92143	SAN YSIDRO	92173	SAN YSIDRO	92519	RIVERSIDE	92509	RIVERSIDE
92147	SAN DIEGO	92106	SAN DIEGO	92522	RIVERSIDE	92501	RIVERSIDE
92149	SAN DIEGO	92139	SAN DIEGO	92531	LAKE ELSINORE	92530	LAKE ELSINORE
92150	SAN DIEGO	92128	SAN DIEGO	92546	HEMET	92543	HEMET
92153	SAN DIEGO	92154	SAN DIEGO	92552	MORENO VALLEY	92553	MORENO VALLEY
92158	SAN DIEGO	92154	SAN DIEGO	92554	MORENO VALLEY	92553	MORENO VALLEY
92159	SAN DIEGO	92119	SAN DIEGO	92556	MORENO VALLEY	92553	MORENO VALLEY
92160	SAN DIEGO	92120	SAN DIEGO	92564	MURRIETA	92562	MURRIETA
92161	SAN DIEGO	92037	LA JOLLA	92572	PERRIS	92570	PERRIS
92162	SAN DIEGO	92102	SAN DIEGO	92581	SAN JACINTO	92583	SAN JACINTO
92163	SAN DIEGO	92103	SAN DIEGO	92589	TEMECULA	92591	TEMECULA
92164	SAN DIEGO	92104	SAN DIEGO	92593	TEMECULA	92590	TEMECULA
92165	SAN DIEGO	92105	SAN DIEGO	92599	PERRIS	92571	PERRIS
92166	SAN DIEGO	92106	SAN DIEGO	92605	HUNTINGTON BEACH	92647	HUNTINGTON BEACH
92167	SAN DIEGO	92107	SAN DIEGO	92607	LAGUNA NIGUEL	92677	LAGUNA NIGUEL
92168	SAN DIEGO	92108	SAN DIEGO	92609	EL TORO	92630	LAKE FOREST
92169	SAN DIEGO	92109	SAN DIEGO	92615	HUNTINGTON BEACH	92646	HUNTINGTON BEACH
92170	SAN DIEGO	92113	SAN DIEGO	92616	IRVINE	92612	IRVINE
92171	SAN DIEGO	92111	SAN DIEGO	92619	IRVINE	92618	IRVINE
92172	SAN DIEGO	92129	SAN DIEGO	92623	IRVINE	92614	IRVINE
92174	SAN DIEGO	92102	SAN DIEGO	92628	COSTA MESA	92626	COSTA MESA
92175	SAN DIEGO	92115	SAN DIEGO	92650	EAST IRVINE	92618	IRVINE
92176	SAN DIEGO	92116	SAN DIEGO	92652	LAGUNA BEACH	92651	LAGUNA BEACH
92177	SAN DIEGO	92117	SAN DIEGO	92654	LAGUNA HILLS	92653	LAGUNA HILLS
92178	CORONADO	92118	CORONADO	92658	NEWPORT BEACH	92660	NEWPORT BEACH
92179	SAN DIEGO	92154	SAN DIEGO	92659	NEWPORT BEACH	92663	NEWPORT BEACH
92184	SAN DIEGO	92101	SAN DIEGO	92674	SAN CLEMENTE	92672	SAN CLEMENTE
92186	SAN DIEGO	92110	SAN DIEGO	92678	TRABUCO CANYON	92679	TRABUCO CANYON
92187	SAN DIEGO	92101	SAN DIEGO	92684	WESTMINSTER	92683	WESTMINSTER
92190	SAN DIEGO	92120	SAN DIEGO	92685	WESTMINSTER	92683	WESTMINSTER
92191	SAN DIEGO	92126	SAN DIEGO	92690	MISSION VIEJO	92691	MISSION VIEJO
92192	SAN DIEGO	92122	SAN DIEGO	92693	SAN JUAN CAPISTRANO	92675	SAN JUAN CAPISTRANO
92193	SAN DIEGO	92123	SAN DIEGO	92698	ALISO VIEJO	92612	IRVINE
92194	SAN DIEGO	92123	SAN DIEGO	92702	SANTA ANA	92701	SANTA ANA
92195	SAN DIEGO	92115	SAN DIEGO	92711	SANTA ANA	92701	SANTA ANA
92196	SAN DIEGO	92126	SAN DIEGO	92712	SANTA ANA	92701	SANTA ANA
92197	SAN DIEGO	92128	SAN DIEGO	92725	SANTA ANA	92707	SANTA ANA
92198	SAN DIEGO	92128	SAN DIEGO	92728	FOUNTAIN VALLEY	92708	FOUNTAIN VALLEY
92199	SAN DIEGO	92128	SAN DIEGO	92735	SANTA ANA	92705	SANTA ANA

Point ZIP Code ZIP	Point ZIP Code Post Office Name	Enclosing Residential ZIP Code ZIP	Enclosing Residential ZIP Code Post Office Name
92781	TUSTIN	92780	TUSTIN
92799	SANTA ANA	92704	SANTA ANA
92803	ANAHEIM	92801	ANAHEIM
92809	ANAHEIM	92807	ANAHEIM
92811	ATWOOD	92870	PLACENTIA
92812	ANAHEIM	92802	ANAHEIM
92814	ANAHEIM	92804	ANAHEIM
92815	ANAHEIM	92802	ANAHEIM
92816	ANAHEIM	92806	ANAHEIM
92817	ANAHEIM	92807	ANAHEIM
92822	BREA	92821	BREA
92825	ANAHEIM	92805	ANAHEIM
92834	FULLERTON	92831	FULLERTON
92836	FULLERTON	92832	FULLERTON
92837	FULLERTON	92833	FULLERTON
92838	FULLERTON	92835	FULLERTON
92842	GARDEN GROVE	92840	GARDEN GROVE
92846	GARDEN GROVE	92845	GARDEN GROVE
92850	ANAHEIM	92801	ANAHEIM
92856	ORANGE	92866	ORANGE
92857	ORANGE	92865	ORANGE
92859	ORANGE	92869	ORANGE
92863	ORANGE	92867	ORANGE
92864	ORANGE	92867	ORANGE
92871	PLACENTIA	92870	PLACENTIA
92877	CORONA	92881	CORONA
92878	CORONA	92882	CORONA
92885	YORBA LINDA	92886	YORBA LINDA
92899	ANAHEIM	92807	ANAHEIM
93002	VENTURA	93001	VENTURA
93005	VENTURA	93003	VENTURA
93006	VENTURA	93003	VENTURA
93007	VENTURA	93003	VENTURA
93009	VENTURA	93003	VENTURA
93011	CAMARILLO	93010	CAMARILLO
93014	CARPINTERIA	93013	CARPINTERIA
93016	FILLMORE	93015	FILLMORE
93020	MOORPARK	93021	MOORPARK
93024	OJAI	93023	OJAI
93031	OXNARD	93036	OXNARD
93032	OXNARD	93036	OXNARD
93034	OXNARD	93033	OXNARD
93040	PIRU	93015	FILLMORE
93044	PORT HUENEME	93043	PORT HUENEME CBC BAS
93061	SANTA PAULA	93060	SANTA PAULA
93062	SIMI VALLEY	93065	SIMI VALLEY
93064	BRANDEIS	93063	SIMI VALLEY
93094	SIMI VALLEY	93065	SIMI VALLEY
93099	SIMI VALLEY	93063	SIMI VALLEY
93102	SANTA BARBARA	93101	SANTA BARBARA
93107	SANTA BARBARA	93117	GOLETA
93116	GOLETA	93117	GOLETA
93118	GOLETA	93117	GOLETA
93120	SANTA BARBARA	93101	SANTA BARBARA
93121	SANTA BARBARA	93101	SANTA BARBARA
93130	SANTA BARBARA	93105	SANTA BARBARA
93140	SANTA BARBARA	93103	SANTA BARBARA
93150	SANTA BARBARA	93108	SANTA BARBARA
93160	SANTA BARBARA	93111	SANTA BARBARA
93190	SANTA BARBARA	93101	SANTA BARBARA
93199	GOLETA	93117	GOLETA
93201	ALPAUGH	93219	EARLIMART
93208	CAMP NELSON	93265	SPRINGVILLE
93216	DELANO	93215	DELANO
93218	DUCOR	93270	TERRA BELLA
93220	EDISON	93307	BAKERSFIELD
93222	FRAZIER PARK	93225	FRAZIER PARK
93227	GOSHEN	93291	VISALIA
93232	HANFORD	93230	HANFORD
93237	KAWEAH	93271	THREE RIVERS
93246	LEMOORE	93245	LEMOORE
93258	PORTERVILLE	93257	PORTERVILLE
93261	RICHGROVE	93219	EARLIMART
93275	TULARE	93274	TULARE
93278	VISALIA	93277	VISALIA
93279	VISALIA	93277	VISALIA
93290	VISALIA	93277	VISALIA
93302	BAKERSFIELD	93308	BAKERSFIELD
93303	BAKERSFIELD	93308	BAKERSFIELD
93380	BAKERSFIELD	93308	BAKERSFIELD
93383	BAKERSFIELD	93313	BAKERSFIELD
93384	BAKERSFIELD	93304	BAKERSFIELD
93385	BAKERSFIELD	93304	BAKERSFIELD
93386	BAKERSFIELD	93306	BAKERSFIELD
93387	BAKERSFIELD	93304	BAKERSFIELD
93388	BAKERSFIELD	93308	BAKERSFIELD
93389	BAKERSFIELD	93309	BAKERSFIELD
93390	BAKERSFIELD	93311	BAKERSFIELD
93403	SAN LUIS OBISPO	93401	SAN LUIS OBISPO
93406	SAN LUIS OBISPO	93401	SAN LUIS OBISPO
93408	SAN LUIS OBISPO	93401	SAN LUIS OBISPO
93409	SAN LUIS OBISPO	93405	SAN LUIS OBISPO
93410	SAN LUIS OBISPO	93407	SAN LUIS OBISPO
93412	LOS OSOS	93402	LOS OSOS
93421	ARROYO GRANDE	93445	OCEANO
93423	ATASCADERO	93422	ATASCADERO
93424	AVILA BEACH	93401	SAN LUIS OBISPO
93435	HARMONY	93430	CAYUCOS
93438	LOMPOC	93436	LOMPOC
93440	LOS ALAMOS	93455	SANTA MARIA
93443	MORRO BAY	93442	MORRO BAY
93447	PASO ROBLES	93446	PASO ROBLES
93448	PISMO BEACH	93449	PISMO BEACH
93456	SANTA MARIA	93454	SANTA MARIA
93457	SANTA MARIA	93455	SANTA MARIA
93464	SOLVANG	93463	SOLVANG
93475	OCEANO	93445	OCEANO
93483	GROVER BEACH	93433	GROVER BEACH
93502	MOJAVE	93501	MOJAVE
93504	CALIFORNIA CITY	93505	CALIFORNIA CITY
93515	BISHOP	93514	BISHOP
93522	DARWIN	93555	RIDGECREST
93530	KEELER	93545	LONE PINE
93539	LANCASTER	93534	LANCASTER
93542	LITTLE LAKE	93555	RIDGECREST
93549	OLANCHA	93545	LONE PINE
93556	RIDGECREST	93555	RIDGECREST
93558	RED MOUNTAIN	93555	RIDGECREST
93581	TEHACHAPI	93561	TEHACHAPI
93584	LANCASTER	93534	LANCASTER
93586	LANCASTER	93536	LANCASTER
93590	PALMDALE	93550	PALMDALE
93592	TRONA	93562	TRONA
93596	BORON	93516	BORON
93599	PALMDALE	93550	PALMDALE
93603	BADGER	93641	MIRAMONTE
93605	BIG CREEK	93664	SHAVER LAKE
93606	BIOLA	93723	FRESNO
93607	BURREL	93656	RIVERDALE
93613	CLOVIS	93612	CLOVIS
93624	FIVE POINTS	93234	HURON
93628	HUME	93633	KINGS CANYON NATIONA
93634	LAKESHORE	93664	SHAVER LAKE
93639	MADERA	93638	MADERA
93642	MONO HOT SPRINGS	93664	SHAVER LAKE
93649	PIEDRA	93654	REEDLEY
93661	SANTA RITA PARK	93620	DOS PALOS
93665	SOUTH DOS PALOS	93620	DOS PALOS
93666	SULTANA	93618	DINUBA
93670	YETTEM	93615	CUTLER
93673	TRAVER	93631	KINGSBURG
93707	FRESNO	93721	FRESNO
93708	FRESNO	93721	FRESNO
93709	FRESNO	93721	FRESNO
93712	FRESNO	93721	FRESNO
93714	FRESNO	93721	FRESNO
93715	FRESNO	93721	FRESNO
93716	FRESNO	93721	FRESNO
93717	FRESNO	93721	FRESNO
93718	FRESNO	93721	FRESNO
93724	FRESNO	93721	FRESNO
93729	FRESNO	93720	FRESNO
93744	FRESNO	93728	FRESNO
93745	FRESNO	93725	FRESNO
93747	FRESNO	93727	FRESNO
93750	FRESNO	93702	FRESNO
93755	FRESNO	93704	FRESNO
93760	FRESNO	93721	FRESNO
93761	FRESNO	93701	FRESNO
93764	FRESNO	93721	FRESNO
93765	FRESNO	93705	FRESNO
93771	FRESNO	93706	FRESNO
93772	FRESNO	93706	FRESNO
93773	FRESNO	93706	FRESNO
93774	FRESNO	93706	FRESNO
93775	FRESNO	93706	FRESNO
93776	FRESNO	93706	FRESNO
93777	FRESNO	93706	FRESNO
93778	FRESNO	93706	FRESNO
93779	FRESNO	93706	FRESNO
93780	FRESNO	93720	FRESNO
93784	FRESNO	93726	FRESNO
93786	FRESNO	93706	FRESNO
93790	FRESNO	93705	FRESNO
93791	FRESNO	93705	FRESNO
93792	FRESNO	93705	FRESNO
93793	FRESNO	93705	FRESNO
93794	FRESNO	93705	FRESNO
93844	FRESNO	93727	FRESNO
93888	FRESNO	93727	FRESNO
93902	SALINAS	93901	SALINAS
93912	SALINAS	93907	SALINAS
93915	SALINAS	93905	SALINAS
93921	CARMEL BY THE SEA	93923	CARMEL
93922	CARMEL	93923	CARMEL
93928	JOLON	93932	LOCKWOOD

NONRESIDENTIAL ZIP CODES

CALIFORNIA

Point ZIP Code		Enclosing Residential ZIP Code		Point ZIP Code		Enclosing Residential ZIP Code	
ZIP	Post Office Name	ZIP	Post Office Name	ZIP	Post Office Name	ZIP	Post Office Name
93942	MONTEREY	93940	MONTEREY	94289	SACRAMENTO	95814	SACRAMENTO
93944	MONTEREY	93940	MONTEREY	94290	SACRAMENTO	95818	SACRAMENTO
93954	SAN LUCAS	93930	KING CITY	94291	SACRAMENTO	95818	SACRAMENTO
93962	SPRECKELS	93908	SALINAS	94293	SACRAMENTO	95818	SACRAMENTO
94011	BURLINGAME	94010	BURLINGAME	94294	SACRAMENTO	95818	SACRAMENTO
94013	DALY CITY	94014	DALY CITY	94295	SACRAMENTO	95814	SACRAMENTO
94016	DALY CITY	94014	DALY CITY	94296	SACRAMENTO	95814	SACRAMENTO
94017	DALY CITY	94015	DALY CITY	94297	SACRAMENTO	95818	SACRAMENTO
94018	EL GRANADA	94019	HALF MOON BAY	94298	SACRAMENTO	95814	SACRAMENTO
94023	LOS ALTOS	94022	LOS ALTOS	94302	PALO ALTO	94303	PALO ALTO
94026	MENLO PARK	94025	MENLO PARK	94309	PALO ALTO	94305	STANFORD
94037	MONTARA	94038	MOSS BEACH	94497	SAN MATEO	94403	SAN MATEO
94039	MOUNTAIN VIEW	94043	MOUNTAIN VIEW	94511	BETHEL ISLAND	94561	OAKLEY
94042	MOUNTAIN VIEW	94041	MOUNTAIN VIEW	94516	CANYON	94563	ORINDA
94064	REDWOOD CITY	94063	REDWOOD CITY	94522	CONCORD	94520	CONCORD
94083	SOUTH SAN FRANCISCO	94080	SOUTH SAN FRANCISCO	94524	CONCORD	94520	CONCORD
94088	SUNNYVALE	94085	SUNNYVALE	94527	CONCORD	94520	CONCORD
94101	SAN FRANCISCO	94102	SAN FRANCISCO	94529	CONCORD	94520	CONCORD
94119	SAN FRANCISCO	94105	SAN FRANCISCO	94537	FREMONT	94536	FREMONT
94120	SAN FRANCISCO	94104	SAN FRANCISCO	94540	HAYWARD	94544	HAYWARD
94125	SAN FRANCISCO	94102	SAN FRANCISCO	94543	HAYWARD	94541	HAYWARD
94126	SAN FRANCISCO	94111	SAN FRANCISCO	94557	HAYWARD	94544	HAYWARD
94137	SAN FRANCISCO	94104	SAN FRANCISCO	94562	OAKVILLE	94574	SAINT HELENA
94139	SAN FRANCISCO	94104	SAN FRANCISCO	94570	MORAGA	94556	MORAGA
94140	SAN FRANCISCO	94109	SAN FRANCISCO	94573	RUTHERFORD	94574	SAINT HELENA
94141	SAN FRANCISCO	94103	SAN FRANCISCO	94575	MORAGA	94556	MORAGA
94142	SAN FRANCISCO	94103	SAN FRANCISCO	94581	NAPA	94558	NAPA
94143	SAN FRANCISCO	94117	SAN FRANCISCO	94604	OAKLAND	94612	OAKLAND
94144	SAN FRANCISCO	94118	SAN FRANCISCO	94614	OAKLAND	94621	OAKLAND
94145	SAN FRANCISCO	94104	SAN FRANCISCO	94615	OAKLAND	94607	OAKLAND
94146	SAN FRANCISCO	94114	SAN FRANCISCO	94617	OAKLAND	94607	OAKLAND
94147	SAN FRANCISCO	94123	SAN FRANCISCO	94620	PIEDMONT	94601	OAKLAND
94151	SAN FRANCISCO	94105	SAN FRANCISCO	94622	OAKLAND	94577	SAN LEANDRO
94156	SAN FRANCISCO	94104	SAN FRANCISCO	94623	OAKLAND	94607	OAKLAND
94159	SAN FRANCISCO	94118	SAN FRANCISCO	94624	OAKLAND	94603	OAKLAND
94160	SAN FRANCISCO	94124	SAN FRANCISCO	94649	OAKLAND	94612	OAKLAND
94161	SAN FRANCISCO	94111	SAN FRANCISCO	94659	OAKLAND	94612	OAKLAND
94162	SAN FRANCISCO	94104	SAN FRANCISCO	94660	OAKLAND	94607	OAKLAND
94163	SAN FRANCISCO	94104	SAN FRANCISCO	94661	OAKLAND	94611	OAKLAND
94164	SAN FRANCISCO	94109	SAN FRANCISCO	94662	EMERYVILLE	94608	EMERYVILLE
94172	SAN FRANCISCO	94122	SAN FRANCISCO	94666	OAKLAND	94612	OAKLAND
94177	SAN FRANCISCO	94105	SAN FRANCISCO	94701	BERKELEY	94704	BERKELEY
94188	SAN FRANCISCO	94124	SAN FRANCISCO	94712	BERKELEY	94704	BERKELEY
94199	SAN FRANCISCO	94105	SAN FRANCISCO	94802	RICHMOND	94801	RICHMOND
94203	SACRAMENTO	95814	SACRAMENTO	94807	RICHMOND	94801	RICHMOND
94204	SACRAMENTO	95815	SACRAMENTO	94808	RICHMOND	94804	RICHMOND
94205	SACRAMENTO	95823	SACRAMENTO	94820	EL SOBRANTE	94803	EL SOBRANTE
94206	SACRAMENTO	95823	SACRAMENTO	94850	RICHMOND	94804	RICHMOND
94207	SACRAMENTO	95814	SACRAMENTO	94912	SAN RAFAEL	94903	SAN RAFAEL
94208	SACRAMENTO	95814	SACRAMENTO	94913	SAN RAFAEL	94903	SAN RAFAEL
94209	SACRAMENTO	95814	SACRAMENTO	94914	KENTFIELD	94903	SAN RAFAEL
94211	SACRAMENTO	95814	SACRAMENTO	94915	SAN RAFAEL	94901	SAN RAFAEL
94229	SACRAMENTO	95814	SACRAMENTO	94926	COTATI	94928	ROHNERT PARK
94230	SACRAMENTO	95823	SACRAMENTO	94927	ROHNERT PARK	94928	ROHNERT PARK
94232	SACRAMENTO	95818	SACRAMENTO	94942	MILL VALLEY	94941	MILL VALLEY
94234	SACRAMENTO	95814	SACRAMENTO	94948	NOVATO	94947	NOVATO
94235	SACRAMENTO	95814	SACRAMENTO	94950	OLEMA	94946	NICASIO
94236	SACRAMENTO	95814	SACRAMENTO	94953	PETALUMA	94952	PETALUMA
94237	SACRAMENTO	95814	SACRAMENTO	94955	PETALUMA	94952	PETALUMA
94239	SACRAMENTO	95818	SACRAMENTO	94957	ROSS	94960	SAN ANSELMO
94240	SACRAMENTO	95811	SACRAMENTO	94966	SAUSALITO	94965	SAUSALITO
94244	SACRAMENTO	95814	SACRAMENTO	94974	SAN QUENTIN	94964	SAN QUENTIN
94246	SACRAMENTO	95815	SACRAMENTO	94975	PETALUMA	94952	PETALUMA
94247	SACRAMENTO	95823	SACRAMENTO	94976	CORTE MADERA	94925	CORTE MADERA
94248	SACRAMENTO	95814	SACRAMENTO	94977	LARKSPUR	94939	LARKSPUR
94249	SACRAMENTO	95816	SACRAMENTO	94978	FAIRFAX	94930	FAIRFAX
94250	SACRAMENTO	95814	SACRAMENTO	94979	SAN ANSELMO	94960	SAN ANSELMO
94252	SACRAMENTO	95814	SACRAMENTO	94999	PETALUMA	94954	PETALUMA
94254	SACRAMENTO	95823	SACRAMENTO	95001	APTOS	95003	APTOS
94256	SACRAMENTO	95823	SACRAMENTO	95007	BROOKDALE	95005	BEN LOMOND
94257	SACRAMENTO	95811	SACRAMENTO	95009	CAMPBELL	95008	CAMPBELL
94258	SACRAMENTO	95814	SACRAMENTO	95011	CAMPBELL	95008	CAMPBELL
94259	SACRAMENTO	95818	SACRAMENTO	95015	CUPERTINO	95014	CUPERTINO
94261	SACRAMENTO	95814	SACRAMENTO	95021	GILROY	95020	GILROY
94262	SACRAMENTO	95823	SACRAMENTO	95024	HOLLISTER	95023	HOLLISTER
94263	SACRAMENTO	95814	SACRAMENTO	95026	HOLY CITY	95033	LOS GATOS
94267	SACRAMENTO	95815	SACRAMENTO	95031	LOS GATOS	95030	LOS GATOS
94268	SACRAMENTO	95814	SACRAMENTO	95036	MILPITAS	95035	MILPITAS
94269	SACRAMENTO	95814	SACRAMENTO	95038	MORGAN HILL	95037	MORGAN HILL
94271	SACRAMENTO	95814	SACRAMENTO	95041	MOUNT HERMON	95018	FELTON
94273	SACRAMENTO	95814	SACRAMENTO	95042	NEW ALMADEN	95120	SAN JOSE
94274	SACRAMENTO	95814	SACRAMENTO	95044	REDWOOD ESTATES	95033	LOS GATOS
94277	SACRAMENTO	95814	SACRAMENTO	95052	SANTA CLARA	95050	SANTA CLARA
94278	SACRAMENTO	95814	SACRAMENTO	95055	SANTA CLARA	95051	SANTA CLARA
94279	SACRAMENTO	95814	SACRAMENTO	95056	SANTA CLARA	95054	SANTA CLARA
94280	SACRAMENTO	95822	SACRAMENTO	95061	SANTA CRUZ	95060	SANTA CRUZ
94282	SACRAMENTO	95823	SACRAMENTO	95063	SANTA CRUZ	95062	SANTA CRUZ
94283	SACRAMENTO	95823	SACRAMENTO	95067	SCOTTS VALLEY	95066	SCOTTS VALLEY
94284	SACRAMENTO	95818	SACRAMENTO	95071	SARATOGA	95070	SARATOGA
94285	SACRAMENTO	95818	SACRAMENTO	95075	TRES PINOS	95023	HOLLISTER
94286	SACRAMENTO	95818	SACRAMENTO	95077	WATSONVILLE	95076	WATSONVILLE
94287	SACRAMENTO	95814	SACRAMENTO	95101	SAN JOSE	95131	SAN JOSE
94288	SACRAMENTO	95814	SACRAMENTO	95103	SAN JOSE	95113	SAN JOSE

CALIFORNIA

Point ZIP Code		Enclosing Residential ZIP Code	
ZIP	Post Office Name	ZIP	Post Office Name
95106	SAN JOSE	95113	SAN JOSE
95108	SAN JOSE	95113	SAN JOSE
95109	SAN JOSE	95113	SAN JOSE
95115	SAN JOSE	95113	SAN JOSE
95150	SAN JOSE	95131	SAN JOSE
95151	SAN JOSE	95121	SAN JOSE
95152	SAN JOSE	95132	SAN JOSE
95153	SAN JOSE	95123	SAN JOSE
95154	SAN JOSE	95124	SAN JOSE
95155	SAN JOSE	95125	SAN JOSE
95156	SAN JOSE	95116	SAN JOSE
95157	SAN JOSE	95130	SAN JOSE
95158	SAN JOSE	95118	SAN JOSE
95159	SAN JOSE	95128	SAN JOSE
95160	SAN JOSE	95120	SAN JOSE
95161	SAN JOSE	95131	SAN JOSE
95164	SAN JOSE	95134	SAN JOSE
95170	SAN JOSE	95129	SAN JOSE
95172	SAN JOSE	95113	SAN JOSE
95173	SAN JOSE	95122	SAN JOSE
95190	SAN JOSE	95131	SAN JOSE
95191	SAN JOSE	95126	SAN JOSE
95193	SAN JOSE	95123	SAN JOSE
95194	SAN JOSE	95110	SAN JOSE
95196	SAN JOSE	95113	SAN JOSE
95201	STOCKTON	95206	STOCKTON
95208	STOCKTON	95206	STOCKTON
95213	STOCKTON	95206	STOCKTON
95221	ALTAVILLE	95222	ANGELS CAMP
95224	AVERY	95223	ARNOLD
95225	BURSON	95252	VALLEY SPRINGS
95226	CAMPO SECO	95252	VALLEY SPRINGS
95227	CLEMENTS	95220	ACAMPO
95229	DOUGLAS FLAT	95251	VALLECITO
95233	HATHAWAY PINES	95223	ARNOLD
95234	HOLT	95206	STOCKTON
95241	LODI	95240	LODI
95248	RAIL ROAD FLAT	95245	MOKELUMNE HILL
95250	SHEEP RANCH	95249	SAN ANDREAS
95253	VICTOR	95240	LODI
95254	WALLACE	95252	VALLEY SPRINGS
95267	STOCKTON	95207	STOCKTON
95269	STOCKTON	95207	STOCKTON
95296	STOCKTON	95206	STOCKTON
95297	STOCKTON	95204	STOCKTON
95305	BIG OAK FLAT	95321	GROVELAND
95312	CRESSEY	95388	WINTON
95314	DARDANELLE	95364	PINECREST
95319	EMPIRE	95357	MODESTO
95328	KEYES	95307	CERES
95343	MERCED	95340	MERCED
95344	MERCED	95340	MERCED
95347	MOCCASIN	95321	GROVELAND
95352	MODESTO	95350	MODESTO
95353	MODESTO	95354	MODESTO
95365	PLANADA	95340	MERCED
95373	STANDARD	95370	SONORA
95375	STRAWBERRY	95335	LONG BARN
95378	TRACY	95376	TRACY
95381	TURLOCK	95380	TURLOCK
95387	WESTLEY	95363	PATTERSON
95397	MODESTO	95350	MODESTO
95402	SANTA ROSA	95404	SANTA ROSA
95406	SANTA ROSA	95401	SANTA ROSA
95416	BOYES HOT SPRINGS	95476	SONOMA
95418	CALPELLA	95482	UKIAH
95419	CAMP MEEKER	95472	SEBASTOPOL
95424	CLEARLAKE PARK	95422	CLEARLAKE
95426	COBB	95461	MIDDLETOWN
95430	DUNCANS MILLS	95472	SEBASTOPOL
95431	ELDRIDGE	95442	GLEN ELLEN
95433	EL VERANO	95476	SONOMA
95435	FINLEY	95453	LAKEPORT
95463	NAVARRO	95466	PHILO
95471	RIO NIDO	95446	GUERNEVILLE
95473	SEBASTOPOL	95472	SEBASTOPOL
95481	TALMAGE	95482	UKIAH
95486	VILLA GRANDE	95421	CAZADERO
95487	VINEBURG	95476	SONOMA
95502	EUREKA	95501	EUREKA
95518	ARCATA	95521	ARCATA
95532	CRESCENT CITY	95531	CRESCENT CITY
95534	CUTTEN	95503	EUREKA
95537	FIELDS LANDING	95503	EUREKA
95538	FORT DICK	95531	CRESCENT CITY
95545	HONEYDEW	95542	GARBERVILLE
95553	MIRANDA	95554	MYERS FLAT
95559	PHILLIPSVILLE	95554	MYERS FLAT
95571	WEOTT	95569	REDCREST
95601	AMADOR CITY	95685	SUTTER CREEK
95604	AUBURN	95603	AUBURN
95609	CARMICHAEL	95608	CARMICHAEL
95611	CITRUS HEIGHTS	95621	CITRUS HEIGHTS
95613	COLOMA	95667	PLACERVILLE
95617	DAVIS	95618	DAVIS
95625	ELMIRA	95687	VACAVILLE
95639	HOOD	95757	ELK GROVE
95646	KIRKWOOD	95666	PIONEER
95654	MARTELL	95642	JACKSON
95656	MOUNT AUKUM	95684	SOMERSET
95671	REPRESA	95673	RIO LINDA
95675	RIVER PINES	95669	PLYMOUTH
95676	ROBBINS	95645	KNIGHTS LANDING
95680	RYDE	95690	WALNUT GROVE
95686	THORNTON	95242	LODI
95696	VACAVILLE	95688	VACAVILLE
95697	YOLO	95695	WOODLAND
95699	DRYTOWN	95685	SUTTER CREEK
95712	CHICAGO PARK	95945	GRASS VALLEY
95736	WEIMAR	95713	COLFAX
95741	RANCHO CORDOVA	95670	RANCHO CORDOVA
95759	ELK GROVE	95624	ELK GROVE
95763	FOLSOM	95630	FOLSOM
95798	WEST SACRAMENTO	95691	WEST SACRAMENTO
95799	WEST SACRAMENTO	95691	WEST SACRAMENTO
95812	SACRAMENTO	95814	SACRAMENTO
95813	SACRAMENTO	95815	SACRAMENTO
95840	SACRAMENTO	95811	SACRAMENTO
95851	SACRAMENTO	95815	SACRAMENTO
95852	SACRAMENTO	95815	SACRAMENTO
95853	SACRAMENTO	95815	SACRAMENTO
95860	SACRAMENTO	95821	SACRAMENTO
95865	SACRAMENTO	95825	SACRAMENTO
95866	SACRAMENTO	95825	SACRAMENTO
95867	SACRAMENTO	95811	SACRAMENTO
95887	SACRAMENTO	95821	SACRAMENTO
95894	SACRAMENTO	95818	SACRAMENTO
95899	SACRAMENTO	95691	WEST SACRAMENTO
95913	ARTOIS	95963	ORLAND
95924	CEDAR RIDGE	95945	GRASS VALLEY
95927	CHICO	95926	CHICO
95929	CHICO	95928	CHICO
95930	CLIPPER MILLS	95941	FORBESTOWN
95940	FEATHER FALLS	95965	OROVILLE
95950	GRIMES	95912	ARBUCKLE
95958	NELSON	95965	OROVILLE
95967	PARADISE	95969	PARADISE
95974	RICHVALE	95965	OROVILLE
95976	CHICO	95973	CHICO
95978	STIRLING CITY	95954	MAGALIA
95980	STORRIE	95915	BELDEN
95986	WASHINGTON	95959	NEVADA CITY
95992	YUBA CITY	95991	YUBA CITY
96009	BIEBER	96056	MCARTHUR
96011	BIG BEND	96065	MONTGOMERY CREEK
96017	CASTELLA	96051	LAKEHEAD
96029	FLOURNOY	96021	CORNING
96037	GREENVIEW	96032	FORT JONES
96049	REDDING	96002	REDDING
96061	MILL CREEK	96063	MINERAL
96068	NUBIEBER	96056	MCARTHUR
96070	OBRIEN	96051	LAKEHEAD
96074	PASKENTA	96021	CORNING
96078	PROBERTA	96035	GERBER
96079	SHASTA LAKE	96019	SHASTA LAKE
96084	ROUND MOUNTAIN	96065	MONTGOMERY CREEK
96089	SHASTA LAKE	96019	SHASTA LAKE
96090	TEHAMA	96035	GERBER
96092	VINA	96021	CORNING
96095	WHISKEYTOWN	96033	FRENCH GULCH
96099	REDDING	96001	REDDING
96110	EAGLEVILLE	96104	CEDARVILLE
96127	SUSANVILLE	96130	SUSANVILLE
96129	BECKWOURTH	96122	PORTOLA
96151	SOUTH LAKE TAHOE	96150	SOUTH LAKE TAHOE
96152	SOUTH LAKE TAHOE	96150	SOUTH LAKE TAHOE
96154	SOUTH LAKE TAHOE	96150	SOUTH LAKE TAHOE
96155	SOUTH LAKE TAHOE	96150	SOUTH LAKE TAHOE
96156	SOUTH LAKE TAHOE	96150	SOUTH LAKE TAHOE
96158	SOUTH LAKE TAHOE	96150	SOUTH LAKE TAHOE
96160	TRUCKEE	96161	TRUCKEE
96201	APO	00000	NO ENCLOSING ZIP
96202	APO	00000	NO ENCLOSING ZIP
96203	APO	00000	NO ENCLOSING ZIP
96204	APO	00000	NO ENCLOSING ZIP
96205	APO	00000	NO ENCLOSING ZIP
96206	APO	00000	NO ENCLOSING ZIP
96207	APO	00000	NO ENCLOSING ZIP
96209	APO	00000	NO ENCLOSING ZIP
96213	APO	00000	NO ENCLOSING ZIP
96214	APO	00000	NO ENCLOSING ZIP
96218	APO	00000	NO ENCLOSING ZIP
96224	APO	00000	NO ENCLOSING ZIP
96257	APO	00000	NO ENCLOSING ZIP
96258	APO	00000	NO ENCLOSING ZIP
96260	APO	00000	NO ENCLOSING ZIP

NONRESIDENTIAL ZIP CODES

CALIFORNIA

Point ZIP Code		Enclosing Residential ZIP Code	
ZIP	Post Office Name	ZIP	Post Office Name
96262	APO	00000	NO ENCLOSING ZIP
96264	APO	00000	NO ENCLOSING ZIP
96266	APO	00000	NO ENCLOSING ZIP
96267	APO	00000	NO ENCLOSING ZIP
96269	FPO	00000	NO ENCLOSING ZIP
96271	APO	00000	NO ENCLOSING ZIP
96275	APO	00000	NO ENCLOSING ZIP
96276	APO	00000	NO ENCLOSING ZIP
96278	APO	00000	NO ENCLOSING ZIP
96283	APO	00000	NO ENCLOSING ZIP
96284	APO	00000	NO ENCLOSING ZIP
96297	APO	00000	NO ENCLOSING ZIP
96303	APO	00000	NO ENCLOSING ZIP
96306	FPO	00000	NO ENCLOSING ZIP
96309	FPO	00000	NO ENCLOSING ZIP
96310	FPO	00000	NO ENCLOSING ZIP
96311	FPO	00000	NO ENCLOSING ZIP
96313	FPO	00000	NO ENCLOSING ZIP
96319	APO	00000	NO ENCLOSING ZIP
96321	FPO	00000	NO ENCLOSING ZIP
96322	FPO	00000	NO ENCLOSING ZIP
96323	APO	00000	NO ENCLOSING ZIP
96326	APO	00000	NO ENCLOSING ZIP
96328	APO	00000	NO ENCLOSING ZIP
96330	APO	00000	NO ENCLOSING ZIP
96336	APO	00000	NO ENCLOSING ZIP
96337	APO	00000	NO ENCLOSING ZIP
96338	APO	00000	NO ENCLOSING ZIP
96339	FPO	00000	NO ENCLOSING ZIP
96343	APO	00000	NO ENCLOSING ZIP
96346	FPO	00000	NO ENCLOSING ZIP
96347	FPO	00000	NO ENCLOSING ZIP
96348	FPO	00000	NO ENCLOSING ZIP
96349	FPO	00000	NO ENCLOSING ZIP
96350	FPO	00000	NO ENCLOSING ZIP
96351	FPO	00000	NO ENCLOSING ZIP
96362	FPO	00000	NO ENCLOSING ZIP
96365	APO	00000	NO ENCLOSING ZIP
96367	APO	00000	NO ENCLOSING ZIP
96368	APO	00000	NO ENCLOSING ZIP
96370	FPO	00000	NO ENCLOSING ZIP
96372	FPO	00000	NO ENCLOSING ZIP
96373	FPO	00000	NO ENCLOSING ZIP
96374	FPO	00000	NO ENCLOSING ZIP
96375	FPO	00000	NO ENCLOSING ZIP
96376	APO	00000	NO ENCLOSING ZIP
96377	APO	00000	NO ENCLOSING ZIP
96378	APO	00000	NO ENCLOSING ZIP
96379	FPO	00000	NO ENCLOSING ZIP
96384	APO	00000	NO ENCLOSING ZIP
96386	APO	00000	NO ENCLOSING ZIP
96387	FPO	00000	NO ENCLOSING ZIP
96388	FPO	00000	NO ENCLOSING ZIP
96401	APO	00000	NO ENCLOSING ZIP
96426	FPO	00000	NO ENCLOSING ZIP
96501	FPO	00000	NO ENCLOSING ZIP
96503	FPO	00000	NO ENCLOSING ZIP
96507	FPO	00000	NO ENCLOSING ZIP
96510	FPO	00000	NO ENCLOSING ZIP
96511	FPO	00000	NO ENCLOSING ZIP
96515	FPO	00000	NO ENCLOSING ZIP
96517	FPO	00000	NO ENCLOSING ZIP
96518	FPO	00000	NO ENCLOSING ZIP
96520	FPO	00000	NO ENCLOSING ZIP
96521	FPO	00000	NO ENCLOSING ZIP
96522	FPO	00000	NO ENCLOSING ZIP
96530	APO	00000	NO ENCLOSING ZIP
96531	FPO	00000	NO ENCLOSING ZIP
96534	FPO	00000	NO ENCLOSING ZIP
96535	APO	00000	NO ENCLOSING ZIP
96537	FPO	00000	NO ENCLOSING ZIP
96538	FPO	00000	NO ENCLOSING ZIP
96540	FPO	00000	NO ENCLOSING ZIP
96541	APO	00000	NO ENCLOSING ZIP
96542	APO	00000	NO ENCLOSING ZIP
96543	APO	00000	NO ENCLOSING ZIP
96544	FPO	00000	NO ENCLOSING ZIP
96546	APO	00000	NO ENCLOSING ZIP
96548	APO	00000	NO ENCLOSING ZIP
96549	APO	00000	NO ENCLOSING ZIP
96550	APO	00000	NO ENCLOSING ZIP
96551	APO	00000	NO ENCLOSING ZIP
96552	APO	00000	NO ENCLOSING ZIP
96553	APO	00000	NO ENCLOSING ZIP
96554	APO	00000	NO ENCLOSING ZIP
96555	APO	00000	NO ENCLOSING ZIP
96557	APO	00000	NO ENCLOSING ZIP
96562	APO	00000	NO ENCLOSING ZIP
96595	FPO	00000	NO ENCLOSING ZIP
96598	FPO	00000	NO ENCLOSING ZIP
96599	FPO	00000	NO ENCLOSING ZIP
96601	FPO	00000	NO ENCLOSING ZIP
96602	FPO	00000	NO ENCLOSING ZIP

HAWAII

Point ZIP Code		Enclosing Residential ZIP Code	
ZIP	Post Office Name	ZIP	Post Office Name
96603	FPO	00000	NO ENCLOSING ZIP
96604	FPO	00000	NO ENCLOSING ZIP
96605	FPO	00000	NO ENCLOSING ZIP
96606	FPO	00000	NO ENCLOSING ZIP
96607	FPO	00000	NO ENCLOSING ZIP
96608	FPO	00000	NO ENCLOSING ZIP
96609	FPO	00000	NO ENCLOSING ZIP
96610	FPO	00000	NO ENCLOSING ZIP
96611	FPO	00000	NO ENCLOSING ZIP
96612	FPO	00000	NO ENCLOSING ZIP
96615	FPO	00000	NO ENCLOSING ZIP
96616	FPO	00000	NO ENCLOSING ZIP
96617	FPO	00000	NO ENCLOSING ZIP
96619	FPO	00000	NO ENCLOSING ZIP
96620	FPO	00000	NO ENCLOSING ZIP
96622	FPO	00000	NO ENCLOSING ZIP
96624	FPO	00000	NO ENCLOSING ZIP
96628	FPO	00000	NO ENCLOSING ZIP
96634	FPO	00000	NO ENCLOSING ZIP
96643	FPO	00000	NO ENCLOSING ZIP
96650	FPO	00000	NO ENCLOSING ZIP
96657	FPO	00000	NO ENCLOSING ZIP
96660	FPO	00000	NO ENCLOSING ZIP
96661	FPO	00000	NO ENCLOSING ZIP
96662	FPO	00000	NO ENCLOSING ZIP
96663	FPO	00000	NO ENCLOSING ZIP
96664	FPO	00000	NO ENCLOSING ZIP
96665	FPO	00000	NO ENCLOSING ZIP
96666	FPO	00000	NO ENCLOSING ZIP
96667	FPO	00000	NO ENCLOSING ZIP
96668	FPO	00000	NO ENCLOSING ZIP
96669	FPO	00000	NO ENCLOSING ZIP
96670	FPO	00000	NO ENCLOSING ZIP
96671	FPO	00000	NO ENCLOSING ZIP
96672	FPO	00000	NO ENCLOSING ZIP
96673	FPO	00000	NO ENCLOSING ZIP
96674	FPO	00000	NO ENCLOSING ZIP
96675	FPO	00000	NO ENCLOSING ZIP
96677	FPO	00000	NO ENCLOSING ZIP
96678	FPO	00000	NO ENCLOSING ZIP
96679	FPO	00000	NO ENCLOSING ZIP
96681	FPO	00000	NO ENCLOSING ZIP
96682	FPO	00000	NO ENCLOSING ZIP
96683	FPO	00000	NO ENCLOSING ZIP
96686	FPO	00000	NO ENCLOSING ZIP
96687	FPO	00000	NO ENCLOSING ZIP
96698	FPO	00000	NO ENCLOSING ZIP
96703	ANAHOLA	96746	KAPAA
96709	KAPOLEI	96707	KAPOLEI
96714	HANALEI	96722	PRINCEVILLE
96715	HANAMAULU	96766	LIHUE
96721	HILO	96720	HILO
96733	KAHULUI	96732	KAHULUI
96737	OCEAN VIEW	96704	CAPTAIN COOK
96739	KEAUHOU	96740	KAILUA KONA
96745	KAILUA KONA	96740	KAILUA KONA
96751	KEALIA	96746	KAPAA
96759	KUNIA	96797	WAIPAHU
96765	LAWAI	96756	KOLOA
96767	LAHAINA	96761	LAHAINA
96784	PUUNENE	96732	KAHULUI
96788	PUKALANI	96768	MAKAWAO
96801	HONOLULU	96813	HONOLULU
96802	HONOLULU	96813	HONOLULU
96803	HONOLULU	96813	HONOLULU
96804	HONOLULU	96813	HONOLULU
96805	HONOLULU	96813	HONOLULU
96806	HONOLULU	96813	HONOLULU
96807	HONOLULU	96813	HONOLULU
96808	HONOLULU	96813	HONOLULU
96809	HONOLULU	96813	HONOLULU
96810	HONOLULU	96813	HONOLULU
96811	HONOLULU	96813	HONOLULU
96812	HONOLULU	96813	HONOLULU
96820	HONOLULU	96819	HONOLULU
96823	HONOLULU	96814	HONOLULU
96824	HONOLULU	96821	HONOLULU
96827	HONOLULU	96817	HONOLULU
96828	HONOLULU	96814	HONOLULU
96830	HONOLULU	96815	HONOLULU
96836	HONOLULU	96815	HONOLULU
96837	HONOLULU	96817	HONOLULU
96838	HONOLULU	96819	HONOLULU
96839	HONOLULU	96822	HONOLULU
96840	HONOLULU	96813	HONOLULU
96841	HONOLULU	96817	HONOLULU
96843	HONOLULU	96813	HONOLULU
96846	HONOLULU	96817	HONOLULU
96847	HONOLULU	96814	HONOLULU
96848	HONOLULU	96822	HONOLULU
96849	HONOLULU	96819	HONOLULU
96850	HONOLULU	96813	HONOLULU
96854	WHEELER ARMY AIRFIEL	96786	WAHIAWA

NONRESIDENTIAL ZIP CODES

HAWAII

Point ZIP Code ZIP	Point ZIP Code Post Office Name	Enclosing Residential ZIP Code ZIP	Enclosing Residential ZIP Code Post Office Name
96859	TAMC	96819	HONOLULU
96898	WAKE ISLAND	96819	HONOLULU
97020	DONALD	97002	AURORA
97036	MARYLHURST	97034	LAKE OSWEGO
97075	BEAVERTON	97005	BEAVERTON
97076	BEAVERTON	97006	BEAVERTON
97077	BEAVERTON	97005	BEAVERTON
97102	ARCH CAPE	97138	SEASIDE
97110	CANNON BEACH	97145	TOLOVANA PARK
97118	GARIBALDI	97136	ROCKAWAY BEACH
97130	MANZANITA	97131	NEHALEM
97134	OCEANSIDE	97141	TILLAMOOK
97135	PACIFIC CITY	97112	CLOVERDALE
97143	NETARTS	97141	TILLAMOOK
97147	WHEELER	97136	ROCKAWAY BEACH
97207	PORTLAND	97205	PORTLAND
97208	PORTLAND	97209	PORTLAND
97228	PORTLAND	97209	PORTLAND
97238	PORTLAND	97218	PORTLAND
97240	PORTLAND	97204	PORTLAND
97242	PORTLAND	97202	PORTLAND
97258	PORTLAND	97201	PORTLAND
97268	PORTLAND	97267	PORTLAND
97269	PORTLAND	97222	PORTLAND
97280	PORTLAND	97219	PORTLAND
97281	PORTLAND	97223	PORTLAND
97282	PORTLAND	97202	PORTLAND
97283	PORTLAND	97203	PORTLAND
97286	PORTLAND	97206	PORTLAND
97290	PORTLAND	97211	PORTLAND
97291	PORTLAND	97210	PORTLAND
97292	PORTLAND	97218	PORTLAND
97293	PORTLAND	97214	PORTLAND
97294	PORTLAND	97213	PORTLAND
97296	PORTLAND	97210	PORTLAND
97298	PORTLAND	97225	PORTLAND
97299	PORTLAND	97213	PORTLAND
97307	KEIZER	97303	SALEM
97308	SALEM	97301	SALEM
97309	SALEM	97301	SALEM
97310	SALEM	97301	SALEM
97311	SALEM	97301	SALEM
97312	SALEM	97302	SALEM
97314	SALEM	97301	SALEM
97335	CRABTREE	97374	SCIO
97336	CRAWFORDSVILLE	97386	SWEET HOME
97339	CORVALLIS	97333	CORVALLIS
97373	SAINT BENEDICT	97362	MOUNT ANGEL
97384	MEHAMA	97383	STAYTON
97388	GLENEDEN BEACH	97341	DEPOE BAY
97407	ALLEGANY	97420	COOS BAY
97409	ALVADORE	97448	JUNCTION CITY
97425	CRESCENT LAKE	97733	CRESCENT
97432	DILLARD	97496	WINSTON
97440	EUGENE	97404	EUGENE
97464	OPHIR	97444	GOLD BEACH
97472	SAGINAW	97424	COTTAGE GROVE
97491	WEDDERBURN	97444	GOLD BEACH
97494	WILBUR	97470	ROSEBURG
97528	GRANTS PASS	97526	GRANTS PASS
97533	MURPHY	97527	GRANTS PASS
97602	KLAMATH FALLS	97603	KLAMATH FALLS
97604	CRATER LAKE	97731	CHEMULT
97622	BLY	97623	BONANZA
97626	FORT KLAMATH	97624	CHILOQUIN
97634	MIDLAND	97603	KLAMATH FALLS
97641	CHRISTMAS VALLEY	97638	SILVER LAKE
97708	BEND	97701	BEND
97709	BEND	97701	BEND
97722	DIAMOND	97721	PRINCETON
97732	CRANE	97720	BURNS
97736	FRENCHGLEN	97721	PRINCETON
97819	BRIDGEPORT	97837	HEREFORD
97859	MEACHAM	97801	PENDLETON
97861	MIKKALO	97812	ARLINGTON
97880	UKIAH	97868	PILOT ROCK
97902	AROCK	97910	JORDAN VALLEY
97905	DURKEE	97907	HUNTINGTON
98009	BELLEVUE	98004	BELLEVUE
98013	BURTON	98070	VASHON
98015	BELLEVUE	98004	BELLEVUE
98025	HOBART	98027	ISSAQUAH
98035	KENT	98031	KENT
98041	BOTHELL	98011	BOTHELL
98046	LYNNWOOD	98036	LYNNWOOD
98050	PRESTON	98027	ISSAQUAH
98054	REDONDO	98198	SEATTLE
98061	ROLLINGBAY	98110	BAINBRIDGE ISLAND
98062	SEAHURST	98166	SEATTLE
98063	FEDERAL WAY	98003	FEDERAL WAY
98064	KENT	98031	KENT
98068	SNOQUALMIE PASS	98922	CLE ELUM
98071	AUBURN	98002	AUBURN

WASHINGTON

Point ZIP Code ZIP	Point ZIP Code Post Office Name	Enclosing Residential ZIP Code ZIP	Enclosing Residential ZIP Code Post Office Name
98073	REDMOND	98052	REDMOND
98082	BOTHELL	98012	BOTHELL
98083	KIRKLAND	98033	KIRKLAND
98089	KENT	98031	KENT
98093	FEDERAL WAY	98023	FEDERAL WAY
98111	SEATTLE	98101	SEATTLE
98113	SEATTLE	98103	SEATTLE
98114	SEATTLE	98104	SEATTLE
98124	SEATTLE	98108	SEATTLE
98127	SEATTLE	98107	SEATTLE
98129	SEATTLE	98121	SEATTLE
98131	SEATTLE	98188	SEATTLE
98132	SEATTLE	98188	SEATTLE
98138	SEATTLE	98188	SEATTLE
98139	SEATTLE	98199	SEATTLE
98141	SEATTLE	98101	SEATTLE
98145	SEATTLE	98105	SEATTLE
98154	SEATTLE	98104	SEATTLE
98160	SEATTLE	98177	SEATTLE
98161	SEATTLE	98101	SEATTLE
98164	SEATTLE	98104	SEATTLE
98165	SEATTLE	98125	SEATTLE
98170	SEATTLE	98101	SEATTLE
98171	SEATTLE	98188	SEATTLE
98174	SEATTLE	98104	SEATTLE
98175	SEATTLE	98125	SEATTLE
98181	SEATTLE	98101	SEATTLE
98184	SEATTLE	98104	SEATTLE
98185	SEATTLE	98105	SEATTLE
98190	SEATTLE	98168	SEATTLE
98191	SEATTLE	98101	SEATTLE
98194	SEATTLE	98104	SEATTLE
98206	EVERETT	98204	EVERETT
98207	EVERETT	98201	EVERETT
98213	EVERETT	98201	EVERETT
98222	BLAKELY ISLAND	98221	ANACORTES
98227	BELLINGHAM	98225	BELLINGHAM
98228	BELLINGHAM	98226	BELLINGHAM
98231	BLAINE	98230	BLAINE
98235	CLEARLAKE	98284	SEDRO WOOLLEY
98238	CONWAY	98273	MOUNT VERNON
98243	DEER HARBOR	98245	EASTSOUND
98255	HAMILTON	98284	SEDRO WOOLLEY
98256	INDEX	98294	SULTAN
98259	NORTH LAKEWOOD	98223	ARLINGTON
98263	LYMAN	98284	SEDRO WOOLLEY
98276	NOOKSACK	98247	EVERSON
98280	ORCAS	98245	EASTSOUND
98286	SHAW ISLAND	98261	LOPEZ ISLAND
98287	SILVANA	98292	STANWOOD
98291	SNOHOMISH	98290	SNOHOMISH
98293	STARTUP	98294	SULTAN
98297	WALDRON	98245	EASTSOUND
98322	BURLEY	98367	PORT ORCHARD
98324	CARLSBORG	98382	SEQUIM
98343	JOYCE	98363	PORT ANGELES
98344	KAPOWSIN	98338	GRAHAM
98348	LA GRANDE	98328	EATONVILLE
98350	LA PUSH	98331	FORKS
98352	SUMNER	98391	BONNEY LAKE
98353	MANCHESTER	98366	PORT ORCHARD
98357	NEAH BAY	98381	SEKIU
98364	PORT GAMBLE	98370	POULSBO
98378	RETSIL	98366	PORT ORCHARD
98384	SOUTH COLBY	98366	PORT ORCHARD
98385	SOUTH PRAIRIE	98321	BUCKLEY
98386	SOUTHWORTH	98366	PORT ORCHARD
98393	TRACYTON	98311	BREMERTON
98395	WAUNA	98329	GIG HARBOR
98396	WILKESON	98321	BUCKLEY
98397	LONGMIRE	98321	BUCKLEY
98398	PARADISE INN	98321	BUCKLEY
98401	TACOMA	98402	TACOMA
98411	TACOMA	98409	TACOMA
98412	TACOMA	98444	TACOMA
98413	TACOMA	98409	TACOMA
98415	TACOMA	98405	TACOMA
98417	TACOMA	98409	TACOMA
98419	TACOMA	98409	TACOMA
98431	TACOMA	98433	TACOMA
98442	TACOMA	98444	TACOMA
98448	TACOMA	98409	TACOMA
98464	TACOMA	98466	TACOMA
98471	TACOMA	98405	TACOMA
98481	TACOMA	98409	TACOMA
98490	TACOMA	98409	TACOMA
98492	LAKEWOOD	98498	LAKEWOOD
98493	TACOMA	98498	LAKEWOOD
98496	LAKEWOOD	98499	LAKEWOOD
98497	LAKEWOOD	98498	LAKEWOOD
98504	OLYMPIA	98501	OLYMPIA
98507	OLYMPIA	98501	OLYMPIA
98508	OLYMPIA	98502	OLYMPIA

NONRESIDENTIAL ZIP CODES

WASHINGTON

Point ZIP Code		Enclosing Residential ZIP Code	
ZIP	Post Office Name	ZIP	Post Office Name
98509	LACEY	98503	LACEY
98511	TUMWATER	98501	OLYMPIA
98522	ADNA	98532	CHEHALIS
98527	BAY CENTER	98586	SOUTH BEND
98530	BUCODA	98589	TENINO
98539	DOTY	98532	CHEHALIS
98540	EAST OLYMPIA	98501	OLYMPIA
98544	GALVIN	98531	CENTRALIA
98554	LEBAM	98577	RAYMOND
98556	LITTLEROCK	98512	OLYMPIA
98558	MCKENNA	98580	ROY
98559	MALONE	98541	ELMA
98561	MENLO	98577	RAYMOND
98565	NAPAVINE	98532	CHEHALIS
98566	NEILTON	98575	QUINAULT
98583	SATSOP	98563	MONTESANO
98599	OLYMPIA	98501	OLYMPIA
98609	CARROLLS	98626	KELSO
98614	CHINOOK	98638	NASELLE
98622	HEISSON	98604	BATTLE GROUND
98623	HUSUM	98672	WHITE SALMON
98637	NAHCOTTA	98640	OCEAN PARK
98639	NORTH BONNEVILLE	98648	STEVENSON
98641	OYSTERVILLE	98640	OCEAN PARK
98644	SEAVIEW	98631	LONG BEACH
98666	VANCOUVER	98661	VANCOUVER
98668	VANCOUVER	98661	VANCOUVER
98670	WAHKIACUS	98613	CENTERVILLE
98673	WISHRAM	98620	GOLDENDALE
98687	VANCOUVER	98684	VANCOUVER
98807	WENATCHEE	98801	WENATCHEE
98811	ARDENVOIR	98822	ENTIAT
98817	CHELAN FALLS	98816	CHELAN
98819	CONCONULLY	98849	RIVERSIDE
98821	DRYDEN	98815	CASHMERE
98824	GEORGE	98848	QUINCY
98829	MALOTT	98840	OKANOGAN
98836	MONITOR	98801	WENATCHEE
98853	STRATFORD	98851	SOAP LAKE
98860	WILSON CREEK	98832	MARLIN
98904	YAKIMA	98908	YAKIMA
98907	YAKIMA	98903	YAKIMA
98909	YAKIMA	98903	YAKIMA
98920	BROWNSTOWN	98933	HARRAH
98921	BUENA	98953	ZILLAH
98925	EASTON	98922	CLE ELUM
98929	GOOSE PRAIRIE	98937	NACHES
98934	KITTITAS	98926	ELLENSBURG
98939	PARKER	98951	WAPATO
98940	RONALD	98922	CLE ELUM
98941	ROSLYN	98922	CLE ELUM
98943	SOUTH CLE ELUM	98922	CLE ELUM
98950	VANTAGE	98926	ELLENSBURG
99014	FOUR LAKES	99004	CHENEY
99020	MARSHALL	99004	CHENEY
99039	WAVERLY	99012	FAIRFIELD
99102	ALBION	99163	PULLMAN
99104	BELMONT	99158	OAKESDALE
99124	ELMER CITY	99116	COULEE DAM
99144	LAMONA	99134	HARRINGTON
99146	LAURIER	99141	KETTLE FALLS
99149	MALDEN	99170	ROSALIA
99151	MARCUS	99141	KETTLE FALLS
99152	METALINE	99153	METALINE FALLS
99154	MOHLER	99134	HARRINGTON
99155	NESPELEM	99116	COULEE DAM
99160	ORIENT	99107	BOYDS
99174	STEPTOE	99111	COLFAX
99209	SPOKANE	99205	SPOKANE
99210	SPOKANE	99201	SPOKANE
99211	SPOKANE	99212	SPOKANE
99213	SPOKANE	99212	SPOKANE
99214	SPOKANE	99206	SPOKANE
99215	SPOKANE	99216	SPOKANE
99219	SPOKANE	99224	SPOKANE
99220	SPOKANE	99201	SPOKANE
99228	SPOKANE	99208	SPOKANE
99252	SPOKANE	99202	SPOKANE
99256	SPOKANE	99201	SPOKANE
99258	SPOKANE	99202	SPOKANE
99260	SPOKANE	99201	SPOKANE
99299	SPOKANE	99201	SPOKANE
99302	PASCO	99301	PASCO
99329	DIXIE	99361	WAITSBURG
99333	HOOPER	99143	LACROSSE
99335	KAHLOTUS	99301	PASCO
99345	PATERSON	99350	PROSSER
99346	PLYMOUTH	99338	KENNEWICK
99359	STARBUCK	99328	DAYTON
99363	WALLULA	99360	TOUCHET
99509	ANCHORAGE	99503	ANCHORAGE
99510	ANCHORAGE	99501	ANCHORAGE
99511	ANCHORAGE	99515	ANCHORAGE

ALASKA

Point ZIP Code		Enclosing Residential ZIP Code	
ZIP	Post Office Name	ZIP	Post Office Name
99513	ANCHORAGE	99501	ANCHORAGE
99514	ANCHORAGE	99508	ANCHORAGE
99519	ANCHORAGE	99502	ANCHORAGE
99520	ANCHORAGE	99501	ANCHORAGE
99521	ANCHORAGE	99504	ANCHORAGE
99522	ANCHORAGE	99502	ANCHORAGE
99523	ANCHORAGE	99507	ANCHORAGE
99524	ANCHORAGE	99502	ANCHORAGE
99529	ANCHORAGE	99501	ANCHORAGE
99530	ANCHORAGE	99501	ANCHORAGE
99545	KONGIGANAK	99559	BETHEL
99548	CHIGNIK LAKE	99564	CHIGNIK
99550	PORT LIONS	99615	KODIAK
99566	CHITINA	99573	COPPER CENTER
99599	ANCHORAGE	99503	ANCHORAGE
99605	HOPE	99631	MOOSE PASS
99608	KARLUK	99615	KODIAK
99609	KASIGLUK	99559	BETHEL
99619	KODIAK	99615	KODIAK
99624	LARSEN BAY	99615	KODIAK
99629	WASILLA	99654	WASILLA
99635	NIKISKI	99611	KENAI
99637	TOKSOOK BAY	99681	TUNUNAK
99641	NUNAPITCHUK	99559	BETHEL
99643	OLD HARBOR	99615	KODIAK
99644	OUZINKIE	99615	KODIAK
99652	BIG LAKE	99654	WASILLA
99663	SELDOVIA	99603	HOMER
99666	NUNAM IQUA	99554	ALAKANUK
99675	TAKOTNA	99627	MC GRATH
99677	TATITLEK	99686	VALDEZ
99678	TOGIAK	99576	DILLINGHAM
99680	TUNTUTULIAK	99559	BETHEL
99687	WASILLA	99654	WASILLA
99690	NIGHTMUTE	99559	BETHEL
99693	WHITTIER	99686	VALDEZ
99694	HOUSTON	99688	WILLOW
99695	ANCHORAGE	99502	ANCHORAGE
99697	KODIAK	99615	KODIAK
99706	FAIRBANKS	99709	FAIRBANKS
99707	FAIRBANKS	99701	FAIRBANKS
99708	FAIRBANKS	99709	FAIRBANKS
99710	FAIRBANKS	99712	FAIRBANKS
99711	FAIRBANKS	99705	NORTH POLE
99716	TWO RIVERS	99709	FAIRBANKS
99725	ESTER	99709	FAIRBANKS
99731	FORT GREELY	99737	DELTA JUNCTION
99732	CHICKEN	99780	TOK
99738	EAGLE	99780	TOK
99754	KOYUKUK	99765	NULATO
99764	NORTHWAY	99780	TOK
99775	FAIRBANKS	99709	FAIRBANKS
99776	TANACROSS	99780	TOK
99790	FAIRBANKS	99709	FAIRBANKS
99791	ATQASUK	99723	BARROW
99802	JUNEAU	99801	JUNEAU
99803	JUNEAU	99801	JUNEAU
99811	JUNEAU	99801	JUNEAU
99812	JUNEAU	99801	JUNEAU
99821	AUKE BAY	99801	JUNEAU
99830	KAKE	99833	PETERSBURG
99832	PELICAN	99829	HOONAH
99836	PORT ALEXANDER	99835	SITKA
99841	TENAKEE SPRINGS	99829	HOONAH
99850	JUNEAU	99801	JUNEAU
99918	COFFMAN COVE	99901	KETCHIKAN
99928	WARD COVE	99901	KETCHIKAN

Appendix II: NAICS Code Definitions

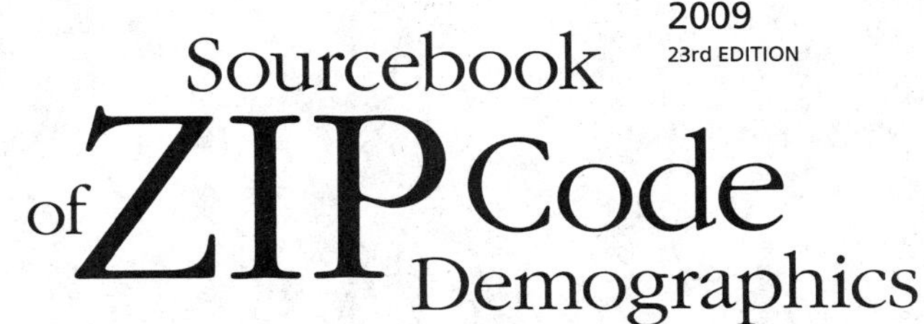

APPENDIX II
North American Industry Classification System (NAICS) Codes

111	Crop Production
112	Animal Production
113	Forestry and Logging
114	Fishing, Hunting and Trapping
115	Support Activities for Agriculture and Forestry
211	Oil and Gas Extraction
212	Mining (except Oil and Gas)
213	Support Activities for Mining
221	Utilities
236	Construction of Buildings
237	Heavy and Civil Engineering Construction
238	Specialty Trade Contractors
311	Food Manufacturing
312	Beverage and Tobacco Product Manufacturing
313	Textile Mills
314	Textile Product Mills
315	Apparel Manufacturing
316	Leather and Allied Product Manufacturing
321	Wood Product Manufacturing
322	Paper Manufacturing
323	Printing and Related Support Activities
324	Petroleum and Coal Products Manufacturing
325	Chemical Manufacturing
326	Plastics and Rubber Products Manufacturing
327	Nonmetallic Mineral Product Manufacturing
331	Primary Metal Manufacturing
332	Fabricated Metal Product Manufacturing
333	Machinery Manufacturing
334	Computer and Electronic Product Manufacturing
335	Electrical Equipment, Appliance, and Component Manufacturing
336	Transportation Equipment Manufacturing
337	Furniture and Related Product Manufacturing
339	Miscellaneous Manufacturing
423	Merchant Wholesalers, Durable Goods
424	Merchant Wholesalers, Nondurable Goods
425	Wholesale Electronic Markets and Agents and Brokers
441	Motor Vehicle and Parts Dealers
442	Furniture and Home Furnishings Stores
443	Electronics and Appliance Stores
444	Building Material and Garden Equipment and Supplies Dealers
445	Food and Beverage Stores
446	Health and Personal Care Stores
447	Gasoline Stations
448	Clothing and Clothing Accessories Stores
451	Sporting Goods, Hobby, Book, and Music Stores
452	General Merchandise Stores
453	Miscellaneous Store Retailers
454	Nonstore Retailers
481	Air Transportation
482	Rail Transportation
483	Water Transportation
484	Truck Transportation
485	Transit and Ground Passenger Transportation
486	Pipeline Transportation
487	Scenic and Sightseeing Transportation
488	Support Activities for Transportation
491	Postal Service
492	Couriers and Messengers
493	Warehousing and Storage
511	Publishing Industries (except Internet)
512	Motion Picture and Sound Recording Industries
515	Broadcasting (except Internet)
517	Telecommunications
518	Data Processing, Hosting and Related Services
519	Other Information Services
521	Monetary Authorities - Central Bank
522	Credit Intermediation and Related Activities
523	Securities/Commodity Contracts/Othr Fin. Inv./Related Activities
524	Insurance Carriers and Related Activities
525	Funds, Trusts, and Other Financial Vehicles
531	Real Estate
532	Rental and Leasing Services
533	Lessors of Nonfinancial Intangible Assets (except Copyrighted Works)
541	Professional, Scientific, and Technical Services
551	Management of Companies and Enterprises
561	Administrative and Support Services
562	Waste Management and Remediation Services
611	Educational Services
621	Ambulatory Health Care Services
622	Hospitals
623	Nursing and Residential Care Facilities
624	Social Assistance
711	Performing Arts, Spectator Sports, and Related Industries
712	Museums, Historical Sites, and Similar Institutions
713	Amusement, Gambling, and Recreation Industries
721	Accommodation
722	Food Services and Drinking Places
811	Repair and Maintenance
812	Personal and Laundry Services
813	Religious, Grantmaking, Civic, Professional, and Similar Organizations
814	Private Households
921	Executive, Legislative, and Other General Government Support
922	Justice, Public Order, and Safety Activities
923	Administration of Human Resource Programs
924	Administration of Environmental Quality Programs
925	Administration of Housing Programs, Urban Planning, & Community Dev.
926	Administration of Economic Programs
927	Space Research and Technology
928	National Security and International Affairs
999	Unclassified Establishments

Appendix III:
County FIPS Codes List

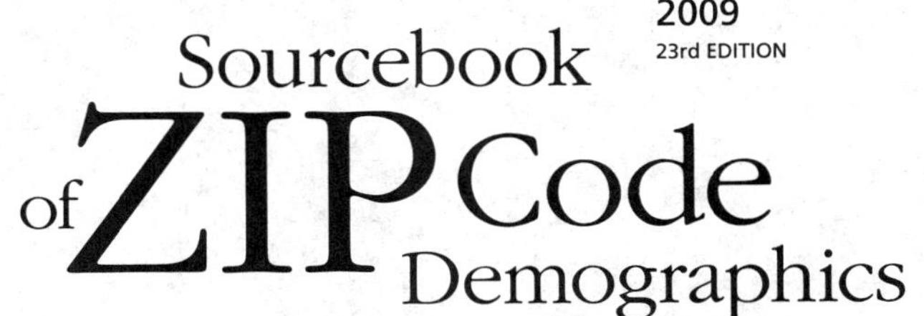

State Name: Alabama
State Abbreviation: AL
State Code: 01

County Name	Code
Autauga	001
Baldwin	003
Barbour	005
Bibb	007
Blount	009
Bullock	011
Butler	013
Calhoun	015
Chambers	017
Cherokee	019
Chilton	021
Choctaw	023
Clarke	025
Clay	027
Cleburne	029
Coffee	031
Colbert	033
Conecuh	035
Coosa	037
Covington	039
Crenshaw	041
Cullman	043
Dale	045
Dallas	047
DeKalb	049
Elmore	051
Escambia	053
Etowah	055
Fayette	057
Franklin	059
Geneva	061
Greene	063
Hale	065
Henry	067
Houston	069
Jackson	071
Jefferson	073
Lamar	075
Lauderdale	077
Lawrence	079
Lee	081
Limestone	083
Lowndes	085
Macon	087
Madison	089
Marengo	091
Marion	093
Marshall	095
Mobile	097
Monroe	099
Montgomery	101
Morgan	103
Perry	105
Pickens	107
Pike	109
Randolph	111
Russell	113
St. Clair	115
Shelby	117
Sumter	119
Talladega	121
Tallapoosa	123
Tuscaloosa	125
Walker	127
Washington	129
Wilcox	131
Winston	133

State Name: Alaska
State Abbreviation: AK
State Code: 02

County Name	Code
Aleutians East	013
Aleutians West	016
Anchorage	020
Bethel	050
Bristol Bay	060
Denali	068
Dillingham	070
Fairbanks North Star	090
Haines	100
Juneau City/Borough	110
Kenai Peninsula	122
Ketchikan Gateway	130
Kodiak Island	150
Lake and Peninsula	164
Matanuska-Susitna	170
Nome	180
North Slope	185
Northwest Arctic	188
Prince of Wales-Outer Ketchikan	201
Sitka City/Borough	220
Skagway-Hoonah-Angoon	232
Southeast Fairbanks	240
Valdez-Cordova	261
Wade Hampton	270
Wrangell-Petersburg	280
Yakutat City/Borough	282
Yukon-Koyukuk	290

State Name: Arizona
State Abbreviation: AZ
State Code: 04

County Name	Code
Apache	001
Cochise	003
Coconino	005
Gila	007
Graham	009
Greenlee	011
La Paz	012
Maricopa	013
Mohave	015
Navajo	017
Pima	019
Pinal	021
Santa Cruz	023
Yavapai	025
Yuma	027

State Name: Arkansas
State Abbreviation: AR
State Code: 05

County Name	Code
Arkansas	001
Ashley	003
Baxter	005
Benton	007
Boone	009
Bradley	011
Calhoun	013
Carroll	015
Chicot	017
Clark	019
Clay	021
Cleburne	023
Cleveland	025
Columbia	027
Conway	029
Craighead	031
Crawford	033
Crittenden	035
Cross	037
Dallas	039
Desha	041
Drew	043
Faulkner	045
Franklin	047
Fulton	049
Garland	051
Grant	053
Greene	055
Hempstead	057
Hot Spring	059
Howard	061
Independence	063
Izard	065
Jackson	067
Jefferson	069
Johnson	071
Lafayette	073
Lawrence	075
Lee	077
Lincoln	079
Little River	081
Logan	083
Lonoke	085
Madison	087
Marion	089
Miller	091
Mississippi	093
Monroe	095
Montgomery	097
Nevada	099
Newton	101
Ouachita	103
Perry	105
Phillips	107
Pike	109
Poinsett	111
Polk	113
Pope	115
Prairie	117
Pulaski	119
Randolph	121
St. Francis	123
Saline	125
Scott	127
Searcy	129
Sebastian	131
Sevier	133
Sharp	135
Stone	137
Union	139
Van Buren	141
Washington	143
White	145
Woodruff	147
Yell	149

State Name: California
State Abbreviation: CA
State Code: 06

County Name	Code
Alameda	001
Alpine	003
Amador	005
Butte	007
Calaveras	009
Colusa	011
Contra Costa	013
Del Norte	015
El Dorado	017
Fresno	019
Glenn	021
Humboldt	023
Imperial	025
Inyo	027
Kern	029
Kings	031

Lake	033
Lassen	035
Los Angeles	037
Madera	039
Marin	041
Mariposa	043
Mendocino	045
Merced	047
Modoc	049
Mono	051
Monterey	053
Napa	055
Nevada	057
Orange	059
Placer	061
Plumas	063
Riverside	065
Sacramento	067
San Benito	069
San Bernardino	071
San Diego	073
San Francisco	075
San Joaquin	077
San Luis Obispo	079
San Mateo	081
Santa Barbara	083
Santa Clara	085
Santa Cruz	087
Shasta	089
Sierra	091
Siskiyou	093
Solano	095
Sonoma	097
Stanislaus	099
Sutter	101
Tehama	103
Trinity	105
Tulare	107
Tuolumne	109
Ventura	111
Yolo	113
Yuba	115

State Name: **Colorado**
State Abbreviation: **CO**
State Code: **08**

County Name	Code
Adams	001
Alamosa	003
Arapahoe	005
Archuleta	007
Baca	009
Bent	011
Boulder	013
Broomfield	014
Chaffee	015
Cheyenne	017
Clear Creek	019
Conejos	021
Costilla	023
Crowley	025
Custer	027
Delta	029
Denver	031
Dolores	033
Douglas	035
Eagle	037
Elbert	039
El Paso	041
Fremont	043
Garfield	045
Gilpin	047
Grand	049
Gunnison	051
Hinsdale	053
Huerfano	055
Jackson	057
Jefferson	059
Kiowa	061
Kit Carson	063
Lake	065
La Plata	067
Larimer	069
Las Animas	071
Lincoln	073
Logan	075
Mesa	077
Mineral	079
Moffat	081
Montezuma	083
Montrose	085
Morgan	087
Otero	089
Ouray	091
Park	093
Phillips	095
Pitkin	097
Prowers	099
Pueblo	101
Rio Blanco	103
Rio Grande	105
Routt	107
Saguache	109
San Juan	111
San Miguel	113
Sedgwick	115
Summit	117
Teller	119
Washington	121
Weld	123
Yuma	125

State Name: **Connecticut**
State Abbreviation: **CT**
State Code: **09**

County Name	Code
Fairfield	001
Hartford	003
Litchfield	005
Middlesex	007
New Haven	009
New London	011
Tolland	013
Windham	015

State Name: **Delaware**
State Abbreviation: **DE**
State Code: **10**

County Name	Code
Kent	001
New Castle	003
Sussex	005

State Name: **D.C.**
State Abbreviation: **DC**
State Code: **11**

County Name	Code
District of Columbia	001

State Name: **Florida**
State Abbreviation: **FL**
State Code: **12**

County Name	Code
Alachua	001
Baker	003
Bay	005
Bradford	007
Brevard	009
Broward	011
Calhoun	013
Charlotte	015
Citrus	017
Clay	019
Collier	021
Columbia	023
DeSoto	027
Dixie	029
Duval	031
Escambia	033
Flagler	035
Franklin	037
Gadsden	039
Gilchrist	041
Glades	043
Gulf	045
Hamilton	047
Hardee	049
Hendry	051
Hernando	053
Highlands	055
Hillsborough	057
Holmes	059
Indian River	061
Jackson	063
Jefferson	065
Lafayette	067
Lake	069
Lee	071
Leon	073
Levy	075
Liberty	077
Madison	079
Manatee	081
Marion	083
Martin	085
Miami-Dade	086
Monroe	087
Nassau	089
Okaloosa	091
Okeechobee	093
Orange	095
Osceola	097
Palm Beach	099
Pasco	101
Pinellas	103
Polk	105
Putnam	107
St. Johns	109
St. Lucie	111
Santa Rosa	113
Sarasota	115
Seminole	117
Sumter	119
Suwannee	121
Taylor	123
Union	125
Volusia	127
Wakulla	129
Walton	131
Washington	133

State Name: **Georgia**
State Abbreviation: **GA**
State Code: **13**

County Name	Code
Appling	001
Atkinson	003
Bacon	005
Baker	007
Baldwin	009
Banks	011
Barrow	013
Bartow	015
Ben Hill	017
Berrien	019
Bibb	021

County Name	Code
Bleckley	023
Brantley	025
Brooks	027
Bryan	029
Bulloch	031
Burke	033
Butts	035
Calhoun	037
Camden	039
Candler	043
Carroll	045
Catoosa	047
Charlton	049
Chatham	051
Chattahoochee	053
Chattooga	055
Cherokee	057
Clarke	059
Clay	061
Clayton	063
Clinch	065
Cobb	067
Coffee	069
Colquitt	071
Columbia	073
Cook	075
Coweta	077
Crawford	079
Crisp	081
Dade	083
Dawson	085
Decatur	087
DeKalb	089
Dodge	091
Dooly	093
Dougherty	095
Douglas	097
Early	099
Echols	101
Effingham	103
Elbert	105
Emanuel	107
Evans	109
Fannin	111
Fayette	113
Floyd	115
Forsyth	117
Franklin	119
Fulton	121
Gilmer	123
Glascock	125
Glynn	127
Gordon	129
Grady	131
Greene	133
Gwinnett	135
Habersham	137
Hall	139
Hancock	141
Haralson	143
Harris	145
Hart	147
Heard	149
Henry	151
Houston	153
Irwin	155
Jackson	157
Jasper	159
Jeff Davis	161
Jefferson	163
Jenkins	165
Johnson	167
Jones	169
Lamar	171
Lanier	173
Laurens	175
Lee	177
Liberty	179
Lincoln	181
Long	183
Lowndes	185
Lumpkin	187
McDuffie	189
McIntosh	191
Macon	193
Madison	195
Marion	197
Meriwether	199
Miller	201
Mitchell	205
Monroe	207
Montgomery	209
Morgan	211
Murray	213
Muscogee	215
Newton	217
Oconee	219
Oglethorpe	221
Paulding	223
Peach	225
Pickens	227
Pierce	229
Pike	231
Polk	233
Pulaski	235
Putnam	237
Quitman	239
Rabun	241
Randolph	243
Richmond	245
Rockdale	247
Schley	249
Screven	251
Seminole	253
Spalding	255
Stephens	257
Stewart	259
Sumter	261
Talbot	263
Taliaferro	265
Tattnall	267
Taylor	269
Telfair	271
Terrell	273
Thomas	275
Tift	277
Toombs	279
Towns	281
Treutlen	283
Troup	285
Turner	287
Twiggs	289
Union	291
Upson	293
Walker	295
Walton	297
Ware	299
Warren	301
Washington	303
Wayne	305
Webster	307
Wheeler	309
White	311
Whitfield	313
Wilcox	315
Wilkes	317
Wilkinson	319
Worth	321

State Name: **Hawaii**
State Abbreviation: **HI**
State Code: **15**

County Name	Code
Hawaii	001
Honolulu	003
Kalawao	005
Kauai	007
Maui	009

State Name: **Idaho**
State Abbreviation: **ID**
State Code: **16**

County Name	Code
Ada	001
Adams	003
Bannock	005
Bear Lake	007
Benewah	009
Bingham	011
Blaine	013
Boise	015
Bonner	017
Bonneville	019
Boundary	021
Butte	023
Camas	025
Canyon	027
Caribou	029
Cassia	031
Clark	033
Clearwater	035
Custer	037
Elmore	039
Franklin	041
Fremont	043
Gem	045
Gooding	047
Idaho	049
Jefferson	051
Jerome	053
Kootenai	055
Latah	057
Lemhi	059
Lewis	061
Lincoln	063
Madison	065
Minidoka	067
Nez Perce	069
Oneida	071
Owyhee	073
Payette	075
Power	077
Shoshone	079
Teton	081
Twin Falls	083
Valley	085
Washington	087

State Name: **Illinois**
State Abbreviation: **IL**
State Code: **17**

County Name	Code
Adams	001
Alexander	003
Bond	005
Boone	007
Brown	009
Bureau	011
Calhoun	013
Carroll	015
Cass	017
Champaign	019
Christian	021
Clark	023
Clay	025
Clinton	027
Coles	029
Cook	031

Crawford	033
Cumberland	035
DeKalb	037
De Witt	039
Douglas	041
DuPage	043
Edgar	045
Edwards	047
Effingham	049
Fayette	051
Ford	053
Franklin	055
Fulton	057
Gallatin	059
Greene	061
Grundy	063
Hamilton	065
Hancock	067
Hardin	069
Henderson	071
Henry	073
Iroquois	075
Jackson	077
Jasper	079
Jefferson	081
Jersey	083
Jo Daviess	085
Johnson	087
Kane	089
Kankakee	091
Kendall	093
Knox	095
Lake	097
La Salle	099
Lawrence	101
Lee	103
Livingston	105
Logan	107
McDonough	109
McHenry	111
McLean	113
Macon	115
Macoupin	117
Madison	119
Marion	121
Marshall	123
Mason	125
Massac	127
Menard	129
Mercer	131
Monroe	133
Montgomery	135
Morgan	137
Moultrie	139
Ogle	141
Peoria	143
Perry	145
Piatt	147
Pike	149
Pope	151
Pulaski	153
Putnam	155
Randolph	157
Richland	159
Rock Island	161
St. Clair	163
Saline	165
Sangamon	167
Schuyler	169
Scott	171
Shelby	173
Stark	175
Stephenson	177
Tazewell	179
Union	181
Vermilion	183
Wabash	185
Warren	187
Washington	189
Wayne	191
White	193
Whiteside	195
Will	197
Williamson	199
Winnebago	201
Woodford	203

State Name: **Indiana**
State Abbreviation: **IN**
State Code: **18**

County Name	Code
Adams	001
Allen	003
Bartholomew	005
Benton	007
Blackford	009
Boone	011
Brown	013
Carroll	015
Cass	017
Clark	019
Clay	021
Clinton	023
Crawford	025
Daviess	027
Dearborn	029
Decatur	031
DeKalb	033
Delaware	035
Dubois	037
Elkhart	039
Fayette	041
Floyd	043
Fountain	045
Franklin	047
Fulton	049
Gibson	051
Grant	053
Greene	055
Hamilton	057
Hancock	059
Harrison	061
Hendricks	063
Henry	065
Howard	067
Huntington	069
Jackson	071
Jasper	073
Jay	075
Jefferson	077
Jennings	079
Johnson	081
Knox	083
Kosciusko	085
LaGrange	087
Lake	089
LaPorte	091
Lawrence	093
Madison	095
Marion	097
Marshall	099
Martin	101
Miami	103
Monroe	105
Montgomery	107
Morgan	109
Newton	111
Noble	113
Ohio	115
Orange	117
Owen	119
Parke	121
Perry	123
Pike	125
Porter	127
Posey	129
Pulaski	131
Putnam	133
Randolph	135
Ripley	137
Rush	139
St. Joseph	141
Scott	143
Shelby	145
Spencer	147
Starke	149
Steuben	151
Sullivan	153
Switzerland	155
Tippecanoe	157
Tipton	159
Union	161
Vanderburgh	163
Vermillion	165
Vigo	167
Wabash	169
Warren	171
Warrick	173
Washington	175
Wayne	177
Wells	179
White	181
Whitley	183

State Name: **Iowa**
State Abbreviation: **IA**
State Code: **19**

County Name	Code
Adair	001
Adams	003
Allamakee	005
Appanoose	007
Audubon	009
Benton	011
Black Hawk	013
Boone	015
Bremer	017
Buchanan	019
Buena Vista	021
Butler	023
Calhoun	025
Carroll	027
Cass	029
Cedar	031
Cerro Gordo	033
Cherokee	035
Chickasaw	037
Clarke	039
Clay	041
Clayton	043
Clinton	045
Crawford	047
Dallas	049
Davis	051
Decatur	053
Delaware	055
Des Moines	057
Dickinson	059
Dubuque	061
Emmet	063
Fayette	065
Floyd	067
Franklin	069
Fremont	071
Greene	073
Grundy	075
Guthrie	077
Hamilton	079
Hancock	081

Hardin	083
Harrison	085
Henry	087
Howard	089
Humboldt	091
Ida	093
Iowa	095
Jackson	097
Jasper	099
Jefferson	101
Johnson	103
Jones	105
Keokuk	107
Kossuth	109
Lee	111
Linn	113
Louisa	115
Lucas	117
Lyon	119
Madison	121
Mahaska	123
Marion	125
Marshall	127
Mills	129
Mitchell	131
Monona	133
Monroe	135
Montgomery	137
Muscatine	139
O'Brien	141
Osceola	143
Page	145
Palo Alto	147
Plymouth	149
Pocahontas	151
Polk	153
Pottawattamie	155
Poweshiek	157
Ringgold	159
Sac	161
Scott	163
Shelby	165
Sioux	167
Story	169
Tama	171
Taylor	173
Union	175
Van Buren	177
Wapello	179
Warren	181
Washington	183
Wayne	185
Webster	187
Winnebago	189
Winneshiek	191
Woodbury	193
Worth	195
Wright	197

State Name: Kansas
State Abbreviation: KS
State Code: 20

County Name	Code
Allen	001
Anderson	003
Atchison	005
Barber	007
Barton	009
Bourbon	011
Brown	013
Butler	015
Chase	017
Chautauqua	019
Cherokee	021
Cheyenne	023
Clark	025
Clay	027
Cloud	029
Coffey	031
Comanche	033
Cowley	035
Crawford	037
Decatur	039
Dickinson	041
Doniphan	043
Douglas	045
Edwards	047
Elk	049
Ellis	051
Ellsworth	053
Finney	055
Ford	057
Franklin	059
Geary	061
Gove	063
Graham	065
Grant	067
Gray	069
Greeley	071
Greenwood	073
Hamilton	075
Harper	077
Harvey	079
Haskell	081
Hodgeman	083
Jackson	085
Jefferson	087
Jewell	089
Johnson	091
Kearny	093
Kingman	095
Kiowa	097
Labette	099
Lane	101
Leavenworth	103
Lincoln	105
Linn	107
Logan	109
Lyon	111
McPherson	113
Marion	115
Marshall	117
Meade	119
Miami	121
Mitchell	123
Montgomery	125
Morris	127
Morton	129
Nemaha	131
Neosho	133
Ness	135
Norton	137
Osage	139
Osborne	141
Ottawa	143
Pawnee	145
Phillips	147
Pottawatomie	149
Pratt	151
Rawlins	153
Reno	155
Republic	157
Rice	159
Riley	161
Rooks	163
Rush	165
Russell	167
Saline	169
Scott	171
Sedgwick	173
Seward	175
Shawnee	177
Sheridan	179
Sherman	181
Smith	183
Stafford	185
Stanton	187
Stevens	189
Sumner	191
Thomas	193
Trego	195
Wabaunsee	197
Wallace	199
Washington	201
Wichita	203
Wilson	205
Woodson	207
Wyandotte	209

State Name: Kentucky
State Abbreviation: KY
State Code: 21

County Name	Code
Adair	001
Allen	003
Anderson	005
Ballard	007
Barren	009
Bath	011
Bell	013
Boone	015
Bourbon	017
Boyd	019
Boyle	021
Bracken	023
Breathitt	025
Breckinridge	027
Bullitt	029
Butler	031
Caldwell	033
Calloway	035
Campbell	037
Carlisle	039
Carroll	041
Carter	043
Casey	045
Christian	047
Clark	049
Clay	051
Clinton	053
Crittenden	055
Cumberland	057
Daviess	059
Edmonson	061
Elliott	063
Estill	065
Fayette	067
Fleming	069
Floyd	071
Franklin	073
Fulton	075
Gallatin	077
Garrard	079
Grant	081
Graves	083
Grayson	085
Green	087
Greenup	089
Hancock	091
Hardin	093
Harlan	095
Harrison	097
Hart	099
Henderson	101
Henry	103
Hickman	105
Hopkins	107
Jackson	109
Jefferson	111

Jessamine	113
Johnson	115
Kenton	117
Knott	119
Knox	121
Larue	123
Laurel	125
Lawrence	127
Lee	129
Leslie	131
Letcher	133
Lewis	135
Lincoln	137
Livingston	139
Logan	141
Lyon	143
McCracken	145
McCreary	147
McLean	149
Madison	151
Magoffin	153
Marion	155
Marshall	157
Martin	159
Mason	161
Meade	163
Menifee	165
Mercer	167
Metcalfe	169
Monroe	171
Montgomery	173
Morgan	175
Muhlenberg	177
Nelson	179
Nicholas	181
Ohio	183
Oldham	185
Owen	187
Owsley	189
Pendleton	191
Perry	193
Pike	195
Powell	197
Pulaski	199
Robertson	201
Rockcastle	203
Rowan	205
Russell	207
Scott	209
Shelby	211
Simpson	213
Spencer	215
Taylor	217
Todd	219
Trigg	221
Trimble	223
Union	225
Warren	227
Washington	229
Wayne	231
Webster	233
Whitley	235
Wolfe	237
Woodford	239

State Name: **Louisiana**
State Abbreviation: **LA**
State Code: **22**

County Name	Code
Acadia	001
Allen	003
Ascension	005
Assumption	007
Avoyelles	009
Beauregard	011
Bienville	013
Bossier	015
Caddo	017
Calcasieu	019
Caldwell	021
Cameron	023
Catahoula	025
Claiborne	027
Concordia	029
De Soto	031
East Baton Rouge	033
East Carroll	035
East Feliciana	037
Evangeline	039
Franklin	041
Grant	043
Iberia	045
Iberville	047
Jackson	049
Jefferson	051
Jefferson Davis	053
Lafayette	055
Lafourche	057
La Salle	059
Lincoln	061
Livingston	063
Madison	065
Morehouse	067
Natchitoches	069
Orleans	071
Ouachita	073
Plaquemines	075
Pointe Coupee	077
Rapides	079
Red River	081
Richland	083
Sabine	085
St. Bernard	087
St. Charles	089
St. Helena	091
St. James	093
St. John the Baptist	095
St. Landry	097
St. Martin	099
St. Mary	101
St. Tammany	103
Tangipahoa	105
Tensas	107
Terrebonne	109
Union	111
Vermilion	113
Vernon	115
Washington	117
Webster	119
West Baton Rouge	121
West Carroll	123
West Feliciana	125
Winn	127

State Name: **Maine**
State Abbreviation: **ME**
State Code: **23**

County Name	Code
Androscoggin	001
Aroostook	003
Cumberland	005
Franklin	007
Hancock	009
Kennebec	011
Knox	013
Lincoln	015
Oxford	017
Penobscot	019
Piscataquis	021
Sagadahoc	023
Somerset	025
Waldo	027
Washington	029
York	031

State Name: **Maryland**
State Abbreviation: **MD**
State Code: **24**

County Name	Code
Allegany	001
Anne Arundel	003
Baltimore	005
Calvert	009
Caroline	011
Carroll	013
Cecil	015
Charles	017
Dorchester	019
Frederick	021
Garrett	023
Harford	025
Howard	027
Kent	029
Montgomery	031
Prince George's	033
Queen Anne's	035
St. Mary's	037
Somerset	039
Talbot	041
Washington	043
Wicomico	045
Worcester	047
Baltimore city	510

State Name: **Massachusetts**
State Abbreviation: **MA**
State Code: **25**

County Name	Code
Barnstable	001
Berkshire	003
Bristol	005
Dukes	007
Essex	009
Franklin	011
Hampden	013
Hampshire	015
Middlesex	017
Nantucket	019
Norfolk	021
Plymouth	023
Suffolk	025
Worcester	027

State Name: **Michigan**
State Abbreviation: **MI**
State Code: **26**

County Name	Code
Alcona	001
Alger	003
Allegan	005
Alpena	007
Antrim	009
Arenac	011
Baraga	013
Barry	015
Bay	017
Benzie	019
Berrien	021
Branch	023
Calhoun	025
Cass	027
Charlevoix	029
Cheboygan	031
Chippewa	033
Clare	035
Clinton	037

Crawford	039
Delta	041
Dickinson	043
Eaton	045
Emmet	047
Genesee	049
Gladwin	051
Gogebic	053
Grand Traverse	055
Gratiot	057
Hillsdale	059
Houghton	061
Huron	063
Ingham	065
Ionia	067
Iosco	069
Iron	071
Isabella	073
Jackson	075
Kalamazoo	077
Kalkaska	079
Kent	081
Keweenaw	083
Lake	085
Lapeer	087
Leelanau	089
Lenawee	091
Livingston	093
Luce	095
Mackinac	097
Macomb	099
Manistee	101
Marquette	103
Mason	105
Mecosta	107
Menominee	109
Midland	111
Missaukee	113
Monroe	115
Montcalm	117
Montmorency	119
Muskegon	121
Newaygo	123
Oakland	125
Oceana	127
Ogemaw	129
Ontonagon	131
Osceola	133
Oscoda	135
Otsego	137
Ottawa	139
Presque Isle	141
Roscommon	143
Saginaw	145
St. Clair	147
St. Joseph	149
Sanilac	151
Schoolcraft	153
Shiawassee	155
Tuscola	157
Van Buren	159
Washtenaw	161
Wayne	163
Wexford	165

State Name: **Minnesota**
State Abbreviation: **MN**
State Code: **27**

County Name	Code
Aitkin	001
Anoka	003
Becker	005
Beltrami	007
Benton	009
Big Stone	011
Blue Earth	013
Brown	015
Carlton	017
Carver	019
Cass	021
Chippewa	023
Chisago	025
Clay	027
Clearwater	029
Cook	031
Cottonwood	033
Crow Wing	035
Dakota	037
Dodge	039
Douglas	041
Faribault	043
Fillmore	045
Freeborn	047
Goodhue	049
Grant	051
Hennepin	053
Houston	055
Hubbard	057
Isanti	059
Itasca	061
Jackson	063
Kanabec	065
Kandiyohi	067
Kittson	069
Koochiching	071
Lac qui Parle	073
Lake	075
Lake of the Woods	077
Le Sueur	079
Lincoln	081
Lyon	083
McLeod	085
Mahnomen	087
Marshall	089
Martin	091
Meeker	093
Mille Lacs	095
Morrison	097
Mower	099
Murray	101
Nicollet	103
Nobles	105
Norman	107
Olmsted	109
Otter Tail	111
Pennington	113
Pine	115
Pipestone	117
Polk	119
Pope	121
Ramsey	123
Red Lake	125
Redwood	127
Renville	129
Rice	131
Rock	133
Roseau	135
St. Louis	137
Scott	139
Sherburne	141
Sibley	143
Stearns	145
Steele	147
Stevens	149
Swift	151
Todd	153
Traverse	155
Wabasha	157
Wadena	159
Waseca	161
Washington	163
Watonwan	165
Wilkin	167
Winona	169
Wright	171
Yellow Medicine	173

State Name: **Mississippi**
State Abbreviation: **MS**
State Code: **28**

County Name	Code
Adams	001
Alcorn	003
Amite	005
Attala	007
Benton	009
Bolivar	011
Calhoun	013
Carroll	015
Chickasaw	017
Choctaw	019
Claiborne	021
Clarke	023
Clay	025
Coahoma	027
Copiah	029
Covington	031
DeSoto	033
Forrest	035
Franklin	037
George	039
Greene	041
Grenada	043
Hancock	045
Harrison	047
Hinds	049
Holmes	051
Humphreys	053
Issaquena	055
Itawamba	057
Jackson	059
Jasper	061
Jefferson	063
Jefferson Davis	065
Jones	067
Kemper	069
Lafayette	071
Lamar	073
Lauderdale	075
Lawrence	077
Leake	079
Lee	081
Leflore	083
Lincoln	085
Lowndes	087
Madison	089
Marion	091
Marshall	093
Monroe	095
Montgomery	097
Neshoba	099
Newton	101
Noxubee	103
Oktibbeha	105
Panola	107
Pearl River	109
Perry	111
Pike	113
Pontotoc	115
Prentiss	117
Quitman	119
Rankin	121
Scott	123
Sharkey	125
Simpson	127
Smith	129
Stone	131
Sunflower	133
Tallahatchie	135

Tate	137
Tippah	139
Tishomingo	141
Tunica	143
Union	145
Walthall	147
Warren	149
Washington	151
Wayne	153
Webster	155
Wilkinson	157
Winston	159
Yalobusha	161
Yazoo	163

State Name: **Missouri**
State Abbreviation: **MO**
State Code: **29**

County Name	Code
Adair	001
Andrew	003
Atchison	005
Audrain	007
Barry	009
Barton	011
Bates	013
Benton	015
Bollinger	017
Boone	019
Buchanan	021
Butler	023
Caldwell	025
Callaway	027
Camden	029
Cape Girardeau	031
Carroll	033
Carter	035
Cass	037
Cedar	039
Chariton	041
Christian	043
Clark	045
Clay	047
Clinton	049
Cole	051
Cooper	053
Crawford	055
Dade	057
Dallas	059
Daviess	061
DeKalb	063
Dent	065
Douglas	067
Dunklin	069
Franklin	071
Gasconade	073
Gentry	075
Greene	077
Grundy	079
Harrison	081
Henry	083
Hickory	085
Holt	087
Howard	089
Howell	091
Iron	093
Jackson	095
Jasper	097
Jefferson	099
Johnson	101
Knox	103
Laclede	105
Lafayette	107
Lawrence	109
Lewis	111
Lincoln	113
Linn	115
Livingston	117
McDonald	119
Macon	121
Madison	123
Maries	125
Marion	127
Mercer	129
Miller	131
Mississippi	133
Moniteau	135
Monroe	137
Montgomery	139
Morgan	141
New Madrid	143
Newton	145
Nodaway	147
Oregon	149
Osage	151
Ozark	153
Pemiscot	155
Perry	157
Pettis	159
Phelps	161
Pike	163
Platte	165
Polk	167
Pulaski	169
Putnam	171
Ralls	173
Randolph	175
Ray	177
Reynolds	179
Ripley	181
St. Charles	183
St. Clair	185
Ste. Genevieve	186
St. Francois	187
St. Louis	189
Saline	195
Schuyler	197
Scotland	199
Scott	201
Shannon	203
Shelby	205
Stoddard	207
Stone	209
Sullivan	211
Taney	213
Texas	215
Vernon	217
Warren	219
Washington	221
Wayne	223
Webster	225
Worth	227
Wright	229
St. Louis city	510

State Name: **Montana**
State Abbreviation: **MT**
State Code: **30**

County Name	Code
Beaverhead	001
Big Horn	003
Blaine	005
Broadwater	007
Carbon	009
Carter	011
Cascade	013
Chouteau	015
Custer	017
Daniels	019
Dawson	021
Deer Lodge	023
Fallon	025
Fergus	027
Flathead	029
Gallatin	031
Garfield	033
Glacier	035
Golden Valley	037
Granite	039
Hill	041
Jefferson	043
Judith Basin	045
Lake	047
Lewis and Clark	049
Liberty	051
Lincoln	053
McCone	055
Madison	057
Meagher	059
Mineral	061
Missoula	063
Musselshell	065
Park	067
Petroleum	069
Phillips	071
Pondera	073
Powder River	075
Powell	077
Prairie	079
Ravalli	081
Richland	083
Roosevelt	085
Rosebud	087
Sanders	089
Sheridan	091
Silver Bow	093
Stillwater	095
Sweet Grass	097
Teton	099
Toole	101
Treasure	103
Valley	105
Wheatland	107
Wibaux	109
Yellowstone	111

State Name: **Nebraska**
State Abbreviation: **NE**
State Code: **31**

County Name	Code
Adams	001
Antelope	003
Arthur	005
Banner	007
Blaine	009
Boone	011
Box Butte	013
Boyd	015
Brown	017
Buffalo	019
Burt	021
Butler	023
Cass	025
Cedar	027
Chase	029
Cherry	031
Cheyenne	033
Clay	035
Colfax	037
Cuming	039
Custer	041
Dakota	043
Dawes	045
Dawson	047
Deuel	049
Dixon	051
Dodge	053
Douglas	055

County Name	Code
Dundy	057
Fillmore	059
Franklin	061
Frontier	063
Furnas	065
Gage	067
Garden	069
Garfield	071
Gosper	073
Grant	075
Greeley	077
Hall	079
Hamilton	081
Harlan	083
Hayes	085
Hitchcock	087
Holt	089
Hooker	091
Howard	093
Jefferson	095
Johnson	097
Kearney	099
Keith	101
Keya Paha	103
Kimball	105
Knox	107
Lancaster	109
Lincoln	111
Logan	113
Loup	115
McPherson	117
Madison	119
Merrick	121
Morrill	123
Nance	125
Nemaha	127
Nuckolls	129
Otoe	131
Pawnee	133
Perkins	135
Phelps	137
Pierce	139
Platte	141
Polk	143
Red Willow	145
Richardson	147
Rock	149
Saline	151
Sarpy	153
Saunders	155
Scotts Bluff	157
Seward	159
Sheridan	161
Sherman	163
Sioux	165
Stanton	167
Thayer	169
Thomas	171
Thurston	173
Valley	175
Washington	177
Wayne	179
Webster	181
Wheeler	183
York	185

State Name: **Nevada**
State Abbreviation: **NV**
State Code: **32**

County Name	Code
Churchill	001
Clark	003
Douglas	005
Elko	007
Esmeralda	009
Eureka	011
Humboldt	013
Lander	015
Lincoln	017
Lyon	019
Mineral	021
Nye	023
Pershing	027
Storey	029
Washoe	031
White Pine	033
Carson City	510

State Name: **New Hampshire**
State Abbreviation: **NH**
State Code: **33**

County Name	Code
Belknap	001
Carroll	003
Cheshire	005
Coos	007
Grafton	009
Hillsborough	011
Merrimack	013
Rockingham	015
Strafford	017
Sullivan	019

State Name: **New Jersey**
State Abbreviation: **NJ**
State Code: **34**

County Name	Code
Atlantic	001
Bergen	003
Burlington	005
Camden	007
Cape May	009
Cumberland	011
Essex	013
Gloucester	015
Hudson	017
Hunterdon	019
Mercer	021
Middlesex	023
Monmouth	025
Morris	027
Ocean	029
Passaic	031
Salem	033
Somerset	035
Sussex	037
Union	039
Warren	041

State Name: **New Mexico**
State Abbreviation: **NM**
State Code: **35**

County Name	Code
Bernalillo	001
Catron	003
Chaves	005
Cibola	006
Colfax	007
Curry	009
De Baca	011
Dona Ana	013
Eddy	015
Grant	017
Guadalupe	019
Harding	021
Hidalgo	023
Lea	025
Lincoln	027
Los Alamos	028
Luna	029
McKinley	031
Mora	033
Otero	035
Quay	037
Rio Arriba	039
Roosevelt	041
Sandoval	043
San Juan	045
San Miguel	047
Santa Fe	049
Sierra	051
Socorro	053
Taos	055
Torrance	057
Union	059
Valencia	061

State Name: **New York**
State Abbreviation: **NY**
State Code: **36**

County Name	Code
Albany	001
Allegany	003
Bronx	005
Broome	007
Cattaraugus	009
Cayuga	011
Chautauqua	013
Chemung	015
Chenango	017
Clinton	019
Columbia	021
Cortland	023
Delaware	025
Dutchess	027
Erie	029
Essex	031
Franklin	033
Fulton	035
Genesee	037
Greene	039
Hamilton	041
Herkimer	043
Jefferson	045
Kings	047
Lewis	049
Livingston	051
Madison	053
Monroe	055
Montgomery	057
Nassau	059
New York	061
Niagara	063
Oneida	065
Onondaga	067
Ontario	069
Orange	071
Orleans	073
Oswego	075
Otsego	077
Putnam	079
Queens	081
Rensselaer	083
Richmond	085
Rockland	087
St. Lawrence	089
Saratoga	091
Schenectady	093
Schoharie	095
Schuyler	097
Seneca	099
Steuben	101
Suffolk	103
Sullivan	105
Tioga	107
Tompkins	109

Ulster	111
Warren	113
Washington	115
Wayne	117
Westchester	119
Wyoming	121
Yates	123

State Name: **North Carolina**
State Abbreviation: **NC**
State Code: **37**

County Name	Code
Alamance	001
Alexander	003
Alleghany	005
Anson	007
Ashe	009
Avery	011
Beaufort	013
Bertie	015
Bladen	017
Brunswick	019
Buncombe	021
Burke	023
Cabarrus	025
Caldwell	027
Camden	029
Carteret	031
Caswell	033
Catawba	035
Chatham	037
Cherokee	039
Chowan	041
Clay	043
Cleveland	045
Columbus	047
Craven	049
Cumberland	051
Currituck	053
Dare	055
Davidson	057
Davie	059
Duplin	061
Durham	063
Edgecombe	065
Forsyth	067
Franklin	069
Gaston	071
Gates	073
Graham	075
Granville	077
Greene	079
Guilford	081
Halifax	083
Harnett	085
Haywood	087
Henderson	089
Hertford	091
Hoke	093
Hyde	095
Iredell	097
Jackson	099
Johnston	101
Jones	103
Lee	105
Lenoir	107
Lincoln	109
McDowell	111
Macon	113
Madison	115
Martin	117
Mecklenburg	119
Mitchell	121
Montgomery	123
Moore	125
Nash	127
New Hanover	129
Northampton	131
Onslow	133
Orange	135
Pamlico	137
Pasquotank	139
Pender	141
Perquimans	143
Person	145
Pitt	147
Polk	149
Randolph	151
Richmond	153
Robeson	155
Rockingham	157
Rowan	159
Rutherford	161
Sampson	163
Scotland	165
Stanly	167
Stokes	169
Surry	171
Swain	173
Transylvania	175
Tyrrell	177
Union	179
Vance	181
Wake	183
Warren	185
Washington	187
Watauga	189
Wayne	191
Wilkes	193
Wilson	195
Yadkin	197
Yancey	199

State Name: **North Dakota**
State Abbreviation: **ND**
State Code: **38**

County Name	Code
Adams	001
Barnes	003
Benson	005
Billings	007
Bottineau	009
Bowman	011
Burke	013
Burleigh	015
Cass	017
Cavalier	019
Dickey	021
Divide	023
Dunn	025
Eddy	027
Emmons	029
Foster	031
Golden Valley	033
Grand Forks	035
Grant	037
Griggs	039
Hettinger	041
Kidder	043
LaMoure	045
Logan	047
McHenry	049
McIntosh	051
McKenzie	053
McLean	055
Mercer	057
Morton	059
Mountrail	061
Nelson	063
Oliver	065
Pembina	067
Pierce	069
Ramsey	071
Ransom	073
Renville	075
Richland	077
Rolette	079
Sargent	081
Sheridan	083
Sioux	085
Slope	087
Stark	089
Steele	091
Stutsman	093
Towner	095
Traill	097
Walsh	099
Ward	101
Wells	103
Williams	105

State Name: **Ohio**
State Abbreviation: **OH**
State Code: **39**

County Name	Code
Adams	001
Allen	003
Ashland	005
Ashtabula	007
Athens	009
Auglaize	011
Belmont	013
Brown	015
Butler	017
Carroll	019
Champaign	021
Clark	023
Clermont	025
Clinton	027
Columbiana	029
Coshocton	031
Crawford	033
Cuyahoga	035
Darke	037
Defiance	039
Delaware	041
Erie	043
Fairfield	045
Fayette	047
Franklin	049
Fulton	051
Gallia	053
Geauga	055
Greene	057
Guernsey	059
Hamilton	061
Hancock	063
Hardin	065
Harrison	067
Henry	069
Highland	071
Hocking	073
Holmes	075
Huron	077
Jackson	079
Jefferson	081
Knox	083
Lake	085
Lawrence	087
Licking	089
Logan	091
Lorain	093
Lucas	095
Madison	097
Mahoning	099
Marion	101
Medina	103
Meigs	105

Mercer	107
Miami	109
Monroe	111
Montgomery	113
Morgan	115
Morrow	117
Muskingum	119
Noble	121
Ottawa	123
Paulding	125
Perry	127
Pickaway	129
Pike	131
Portage	133
Preble	135
Putnam	137
Richland	139
Ross	141
Sandusky	143
Scioto	145
Seneca	147
Shelby	149
Stark	151
Summit	153
Trumbull	155
Tuscarawas	157
Union	159
Van Wert	161
Vinton	163
Warren	165
Washington	167
Wayne	169
Williams	171
Wood	173
Wyandot	175

State Name: **Oklahoma**
State Abbreviation: **OK**
State Code: **40**

County Name	Code
Adair	001
Alfalfa	003
Atoka	005
Beaver	007
Beckham	009
Blaine	011
Bryan	013
Caddo	015
Canadian	017
Carter	019
Cherokee	021
Choctaw	023
Cimarron	025
Cleveland	027
Coal	029
Comanche	031
Cotton	033
Craig	035
Creek	037
Custer	039
Delaware	041
Dewey	043
Ellis	045
Garfield	047
Garvin	049
Grady	051
Grant	053
Greer	055
Harmon	057
Harper	059
Haskell	061
Hughes	063
Jackson	065
Jefferson	067
Johnston	069
Kay	071
Kingfisher	073
Kiowa	075
Latimer	077
Le Flore	079
Lincoln	081
Logan	083
Love	085
McClain	087
McCurtain	089
McIntosh	091
Major	093
Marshall	095
Mayes	097
Murray	099
Muskogee	101
Noble	103
Nowata	105
Okfuskee	107
Oklahoma	109
Okmulgee	111
Osage	113
Ottawa	115
Pawnee	117
Payne	119
Pittsburg	121
Pontotoc	123
Pottawatomie	125
Pushmataha	127
Roger Mills	129
Rogers	131
Seminole	133
Sequoyah	135
Stephens	137
Texas	139
Tillman	141
Tulsa	143
Wagoner	145
Washington	147
Washita	149
Woods	151
Woodward	153

State Name: **Oregon**
State Abbreviation: **OR**
State Code: **41**

County Name	Code
Baker	001
Benton	003
Clackamas	005
Clatsop	007
Columbia	009
Coos	011
Crook	013
Curry	015
Deschutes	017
Douglas	019
Gilliam	021
Grant	023
Harney	025
Hood River	027
Jackson	029
Jefferson	031
Josephine	033
Klamath	035
Lake	037
Lane	039
Lincoln	041
Linn	043
Malheur	045
Marion	047
Morrow	049
Multnomah	051
Polk	053
Sherman	055
Tillamook	057
Umatilla	059
Union	061
Wallowa	063
Wasco	065
Washington	067
Wheeler	069
Yamhill	071

State Name: **Pennsylvania**
State Abbreviation: **PA**
State Code: **42**

County Name	Code
Adams	001
Allegheny	003
Armstrong	005
Beaver	007
Bedford	009
Berks	011
Blair	013
Bradford	015
Bucks	017
Butler	019
Cambria	021
Cameron	023
Carbon	025
Centre	027
Chester	029
Clarion	031
Clearfield	033
Clinton	035
Columbia	037
Crawford	039
Cumberland	041
Dauphin	043
Delaware	045
Elk	047
Erie	049
Fayette	051
Forest	053
Franklin	055
Fulton	057
Greene	059
Huntingdon	061
Indiana	063
Jefferson	065
Juniata	067
Lackawanna	069
Lancaster	071
Lawrence	073
Lebanon	075
Lehigh	077
Luzerne	079
Lycoming	081
McKean	083
Mercer	085
Mifflin	087
Monroe	089
Montgomery	091
Montour	093
Northampton	095
Northumberland	097
Perry	099
Philadelphia	101
Pike	103
Potter	105
Schuylkill	107
Snyder	109
Somerset	111
Sullivan	113
Susquehanna	115
Tioga	117
Union	119
Venango	121
Warren	123
Washington	125
Wayne	127
Westmoreland	129

Wyoming	131
York	133

State Name: **Rhode Island**
State Abbreviation: **RI**
State Code: **44**

County Name	Code
Bristol	001
Kent	003
Newport	005
Providence	007
Washington	009

State Name: **South Carolina**
State Abbreviation: **SC**
State Code: **45**

County Name	Code
Abbeville	001
Aiken	003
Allendale	005
Anderson	007
Bamberg	009
Barnwell	011
Beaufort	013
Berkeley	015
Calhoun	017
Charleston	019
Cherokee	021
Chester	023
Chesterfield	025
Clarendon	027
Colleton	029
Darlington	031
Dillon	033
Dorchester	035
Edgefield	037
Fairfield	039
Florence	041
Georgetown	043
Greenville	045
Greenwood	047
Hampton	049
Horry	051
Jasper	053
Kershaw	055
Lancaster	057
Laurens	059
Lee	061
Lexington	063
McCormick	065
Marion	067
Marlboro	069
Newberry	071
Oconee	073
Orangeburg	075
Pickens	077
Richland	079
Saluda	081
Spartanburg	083
Sumter	085
Union	087
Williamsburg	089
York	091

State Name: **South Dakota**
State Abbreviation: **SD**
State Code: **46**

County Name	Code
Aurora	003
Beadle	005
Bennett	007
Bon Homme	009
Brookings	011
Brown	013
Brule	015
Buffalo	017
Butte	019
Campbell	021
Charles Mix	023
Clark	025
Clay	027
Codington	029
Corson	031
Custer	033
Davison	035
Day	037
Deuel	039
Dewey	041
Douglas	043
Edmunds	045
Fall River	047
Faulk	049
Grant	051
Gregory	053
Haakon	055
Hamlin	057
Hand	059
Hanson	061
Harding	063
Hughes	065
Hutchinson	067
Hyde	069
Jackson	071
Jerauld	073
Jones	075
Kingsbury	077
Lake	079
Lawrence	081
Lincoln	083
Lyman	085
McCook	087
McPherson	089
Marshall	091
Meade	093
Mellette	095
Miner	097
Minnehaha	099
Moody	101
Pennington	103
Perkins	105
Potter	107
Roberts	109
Sanborn	111
Shannon	113
Spink	115
Stanley	117
Sully	119
Todd	121
Tripp	123
Turner	125
Union	127
Walworth	129
Yankton	135
Ziebach	137

State Name: **Tennessee**
State Abbreviation: **TN**
State Code: **47**

County Name	Code
Anderson	001
Bedford	003
Benton	005
Bledsoe	007
Blount	009
Bradley	011
Campbell	013
Cannon	015
Carroll	017
Carter	019
Cheatham	021
Chester	023
Claiborne	025
Clay	027
Cocke	029
Coffee	031
Crockett	033
Cumberland	035
Davidson	037
Decatur	039
DeKalb	041
Dickson	043
Dyer	045
Fayette	047
Fentress	049
Franklin	051
Gibson	053
Giles	055
Grainger	057
Greene	059
Grundy	061
Hamblen	063
Hamilton	065
Hancock	067
Hardeman	069
Hardin	071
Hawkins	073
Haywood	075
Henderson	077
Henry	079
Hickman	081
Houston	083
Humphreys	085
Jackson	087
Jefferson	089
Johnson	091
Knox	093
Lake	095
Lauderdale	097
Lawrence	099
Lewis	101
Lincoln	103
Loudon	105
McMinn	107
McNairy	109
Macon	111
Madison	113
Marion	115
Marshall	117
Maury	119
Meigs	121
Monroe	123
Montgomery	125
Moore	127
Morgan	129
Obion	131
Overton	133
Perry	135
Pickett	137
Polk	139
Putnam	141
Rhea	143
Roane	145
Robertson	147
Rutherford	149
Scott	151
Sequatchie	153
Sevier	155
Shelby	157
Smith	159
Stewart	161
Sullivan	163
Sumner	165
Tipton	167
Trousdale	169
Unicoi	171
Union	173
Van Buren	175

Warren	177
Washington	179
Wayne	181
Weakley	183
White	185
Williamson	187
Wilson	189

State Name: **Texas**
State Abbreviation: **TX**
State Code: **48**

County Name	Code
Anderson	001
Andrews	003
Angelina	005
Aransas	007
Archer	009
Armstrong	011
Atascosa	013
Austin	015
Bailey	017
Bandera	019
Bastrop	021
Baylor	023
Bee	025
Bell	027
Bexar	029
Blanco	031
Borden	033
Bosque	035
Bowie	037
Brazoria	039
Brazos	041
Brewster	043
Briscoe	045
Brooks	047
Brown	049
Burleson	051
Burnet	053
Caldwell	055
Calhoun	057
Callahan	059
Cameron	061
Camp	063
Carson	065
Cass	067
Castro	069
Chambers	071
Cherokee	073
Childress	075
Clay	077
Cochran	079
Coke	081
Coleman	083
Collin	085
Collingsworth	087
Colorado	089
Comal	091
Comanche	093
Concho	095
Cooke	097
Coryell	099
Cottle	101
Crane	103
Crockett	105
Crosby	107
Culberson	109
Dallam	111
Dallas	113
Dawson	115
Deaf Smith	117
Delta	119
Denton	121
DeWitt	123
Dickens	125
Dimmit	127
Donley	129
Duval	131
Eastland	133
Ector	135
Edwards	137
Ellis	139
El Paso	141
Erath	143
Falls	145
Fannin	147
Fayette	149
Fisher	151
Floyd	153
Foard	155
Fort Bend	157
Franklin	159
Freestone	161
Frio	163
Gaines	165
Galveston	167
Garza	169
Gillespie	171
Glasscock	173
Goliad	175
Gonzales	177
Gray	179
Grayson	181
Gregg	183
Grimes	185
Guadalupe	187
Hale	189
Hall	191
Hamilton	193
Hansford	195
Hardeman	197
Hardin	199
Harris	201
Harrison	203
Hartley	205
Haskell	207
Hays	209
Hemphill	211
Henderson	213
Hidalgo	215
Hill	217
Hockley	219
Hood	221
Hopkins	223
Houston	225
Howard	227
Hudspeth	229
Hunt	231
Hutchinson	233
Irion	235
Jack	237
Jackson	239
Jasper	241
Jeff Davis	243
Jefferson	245
Jim Hogg	247
Jim Wells	249
Johnson	251
Jones	253
Karnes	255
Kaufman	257
Kendall	259
Kenedy	261
Kent	263
Kerr	265
Kimble	267
King	269
Kinney	271
Kleberg	273
Knox	275
Lamar	277
Lamb	279
Lampasas	281
La Salle	283
Lavaca	285
Lee	287
Leon	289
Liberty	291
Limestone	293
Lipscomb	295
Live Oak	297
Llano	299
Loving	301
Lubbock	303
Lynn	305
McCulloch	307
McLennan	309
McMullen	311
Madison	313
Marion	315
Martin	317
Mason	319
Matagorda	321
Maverick	323
Medina	325
Menard	327
Midland	329
Milam	331
Mills	333
Mitchell	335
Montague	337
Montgomery	339
Moore	341
Morris	343
Motley	345
Nacogdoches	347
Navarro	349
Newton	351
Nolan	353
Nueces	355
Ochiltree	357
Oldham	359
Orange	361
Palo Pinto	363
Panola	365
Parker	367
Parmer	369
Pecos	371
Polk	373
Potter	375
Presidio	377
Rains	379
Randall	381
Reagan	383
Real	385
Red River	387
Reeves	389
Refugio	391
Roberts	393
Robertson	395
Rockwall	397
Runnels	399
Rusk	401
Sabine	403
San Augustine	405
San Jacinto	407
San Patricio	409
San Saba	411
Schleicher	413
Scurry	415
Shackelford	417
Shelby	419
Sherman	421
Smith	423
Somervell	425
Starr	427
Stephens	429
Sterling	431
Stonewall	433
Sutton	435

Swisher	437
Tarrant	439
Taylor	441
Terrell	443
Terry	445
Throckmorton	447
Titus	449
Tom Green	451
Travis	453
Trinity	455
Tyler	457
Upshur	459
Upton	461
Uvalde	463
Val Verde	465
Van Zandt	467
Victoria	469
Walker	471
Waller	473
Ward	475
Washington	477
Webb	479
Wharton	481
Wheeler	483
Wichita	485
Wilbarger	487
Willacy	489
Williamson	491
Wilson	493
Winkler	495
Wise	497
Wood	499
Yoakum	501
Young	503
Zapata	505
Zavala	507

State Name: **Utah**
State Abbreviation: **UT**
State Code: **49**

County Name	Code
Beaver	001
Box Elder	003
Cache	005
Carbon	007
Daggett	009
Davis	011
Duchesne	013
Emery	015
Garfield	017
Grand	019
Iron	021
Juab	023
Kane	025
Millard	027
Morgan	029
Piute	031
Rich	033
Salt Lake	035
San Juan	037
Sanpete	039
Sevier	041
Summit	043
Tooele	045
Uintah	047
Utah	049
Wasatch	051
Washington	053
Wayne	055
Weber	057

State Name: **Vermont**
State Abbreviation: **VT**
State Code: **50**

County Name	Code
Addison	001
Bennington	003
Caledonia	005
Chittenden	007
Essex	009
Franklin	011
Grand Isle	013
Lamoille	015
Orange	017
Orleans	019
Rutland	021
Washington	023
Windham	025
Windsor	027

State Name: **Virginia**
State Abbreviation: **VA**
State Code: **51**

County Name	Code
Accomack	001
Albemarle	003
Alleghany	005
Amelia	007
Amherst	009
Appomattox	011
Arlington	013
Augusta	015
Bath	017
Bedford	019
Bland	021
Botetourt	023
Brunswick	025
Buchanan	027
Buckingham	029
Campbell	031
Caroline	033
Carroll	035
Charles City	036
Charlotte	037
Chesterfield	041
Clarke	043
Craig	045
Culpeper	047
Cumberland	049
Dickenson	051
Dinwiddie	053
Essex	057
Fairfax	059
Fauquier	061
Floyd	063
Fluvanna	065
Franklin	067
Frederick	069
Giles	071
Gloucester	073
Goochland	075
Grayson	077
Greene	079
Greensville	081
Halifax	083
Hanover	085
Henrico	087
Henry	089
Highland	091
Isle of Wight	093
James City	095
King and Queen	097
King George	099
King William	101
Lancaster	103
Lee	105
Loudoun	107
Louisa	109
Lunenburg	111
Madison	113
Mathews	115
Mecklenburg	117
Middlesex	119
Montgomery	121
Nelson	125
New Kent	127
Northampton	131
Northumberland	133
Nottoway	135
Orange	137
Page	139
Patrick	141
Pittsylvania	143
Powhatan	145
Prince Edward	147
Prince George	149
Prince William	153
Pulaski	155
Rappahannock	157
Richmond	159
Roanoke	161
Rockbridge	163
Rockingham	165
Russell	167
Scott	169
Shenandoah	171
Smyth	173
Southampton	175
Spotsylvania	177
Stafford	179
Surry	181
Sussex	183
Tazewell	185
Warren	187
Washington	191
Westmoreland	193
Wise	195
Wythe	197
York	199
Alexandria city	510
Bedford city	515
Bristol city	520
Buena Vista city	530
Charlottesville city	540
Chesapeake city	550
Colonial Heights city	570
Covington city	580
Danville city	590
Emporia city	595
Fairfax city	600
Falls Church city	610
Franklin city	620
Fredericksburg city	630
Galax city	640
Hampton city	650
Harrisonburg city	660
Hopewell city	670
Lexington city	678
Lynchburg city	680
Manassas city	683
Manassas Park city	685
Martinsville city	690
Newport News city	700
Norfolk city	710
Norton city	720
Petersburg city	730
Poquoson city	735
Portsmouth city	740
Radford city	750
Richmond city	760
Roanoke city	770
Salem city	775
Staunton city	790
Suffolk city	800
Virginia Beach city	810
Waynesboro city	820
Williamsburg city	830
Winchester city	840

State Name: **Washington**
State Abbreviation: **WA**
State Code: **53**

County Name	Code
Adams	001
Asotin	003
Benton	005
Chelan	007
Clallam	009
Clark	011
Columbia	013
Cowlitz	015
Douglas	017
Ferry	019
Franklin	021
Garfield	023
Grant	025
Grays Harbor	027
Island	029
Jefferson	031
King	033
Kitsap	035
Kittitas	037
Klickitat	039
Lewis	041
Lincoln	043
Mason	045
Okanogan	047
Pacific	049
Pend Oreille	051
Pierce	053
San Juan	055
Skagit	057
Skamania	059
Snohomish	061
Spokane	063
Stevens	065
Thurston	067
Wahkiakum	069
Walla Walla	071
Whatcom	073
Whitman	075
Yakima	077

State Name: **West Virginia**
State Abbreviation: **WV**
State Code: **54**

County Name	Code
Barbour	001
Berkeley	003
Boone	005
Braxton	007
Brooke	009
Cabell	011
Calhoun	013
Clay	015
Doddridge	017
Fayette	019
Gilmer	021
Grant	023
Greenbrier	025
Hampshire	027
Hancock	029
Hardy	031
Harrison	033
Jackson	035
Jefferson	037
Kanawha	039
Lewis	041
Lincoln	043
Logan	045
McDowell	047
Marion	049
Marshall	051
Mason	053
Mercer	055
Mineral	057
Mingo	059
Monongalia	061
Monroe	063
Morgan	065
Nicholas	067
Ohio	069
Pendleton	071
Pleasants	073
Pocahontas	075
Preston	077
Putnam	079
Raleigh	081
Randolph	083
Ritchie	085
Roane	087
Summers	089
Taylor	091
Tucker	093
Tyler	095
Upshur	097
Wayne	099
Webster	101
Wetzel	103
Wirt	105
Wood	107
Wyoming	109

State Name: **Wisconsin**
State Abbreviation: **WI**
State Code: **55**

County Name	Code
Adams	001
Ashland	003
Barron	005
Bayfield	007
Brown	009
Buffalo	011
Burnett	013
Calumet	015
Chippewa	017
Clark	019
Columbia	021
Crawford	023
Dane	025
Dodge	027
Door	029
Douglas	031
Dunn	033
Eau Claire	035
Florence	037
Fond du Lac	039
Forest	041
Grant	043
Green	045
Green Lake	047
Iowa	049
Iron	051
Jackson	053
Jefferson	055
Juneau	057
Kenosha	059
Kewaunee	061
La Crosse	063
Lafayette	065
Langlade	067
Lincoln	069
Manitowoc	071
Marathon	073
Marinette	075
Marquette	077
Menominee	078
Milwaukee	079
Monroe	081
Oconto	083
Oneida	085
Outagamie	087
Ozaukee	089
Pepin	091
Pierce	093
Polk	095
Portage	097
Price	099
Racine	101
Richland	103
Rock	105
Rusk	107
St. Croix	109
Sauk	111
Sawyer	113
Shawano	115
Sheboygan	117
Taylor	119
Trempealeau	121
Vernon	123
Vilas	125
Walworth	127
Washburn	129
Washington	131
Waukesha	133
Waupaca	135
Waushara	137
Winnebago	139
Wood	141

State Name: **Wyoming**
State Abbreviation: **WY**
State Code: **56**

County Name	Code
Albany	001
Big Horn	003
Campbell	005
Carbon	007
Converse	009
Crook	011
Fremont	013
Goshen	015
Hot Springs	017
Johnson	019
Laramie	021
Lincoln	023
Natrona	025
Niobrara	027
Park	029
Platte	031
Sheridan	033
Sublette	035
Sweetwater	037
Teton	039
Uinta	041
Washakie	043
Weston	045

ZIP Code Maps

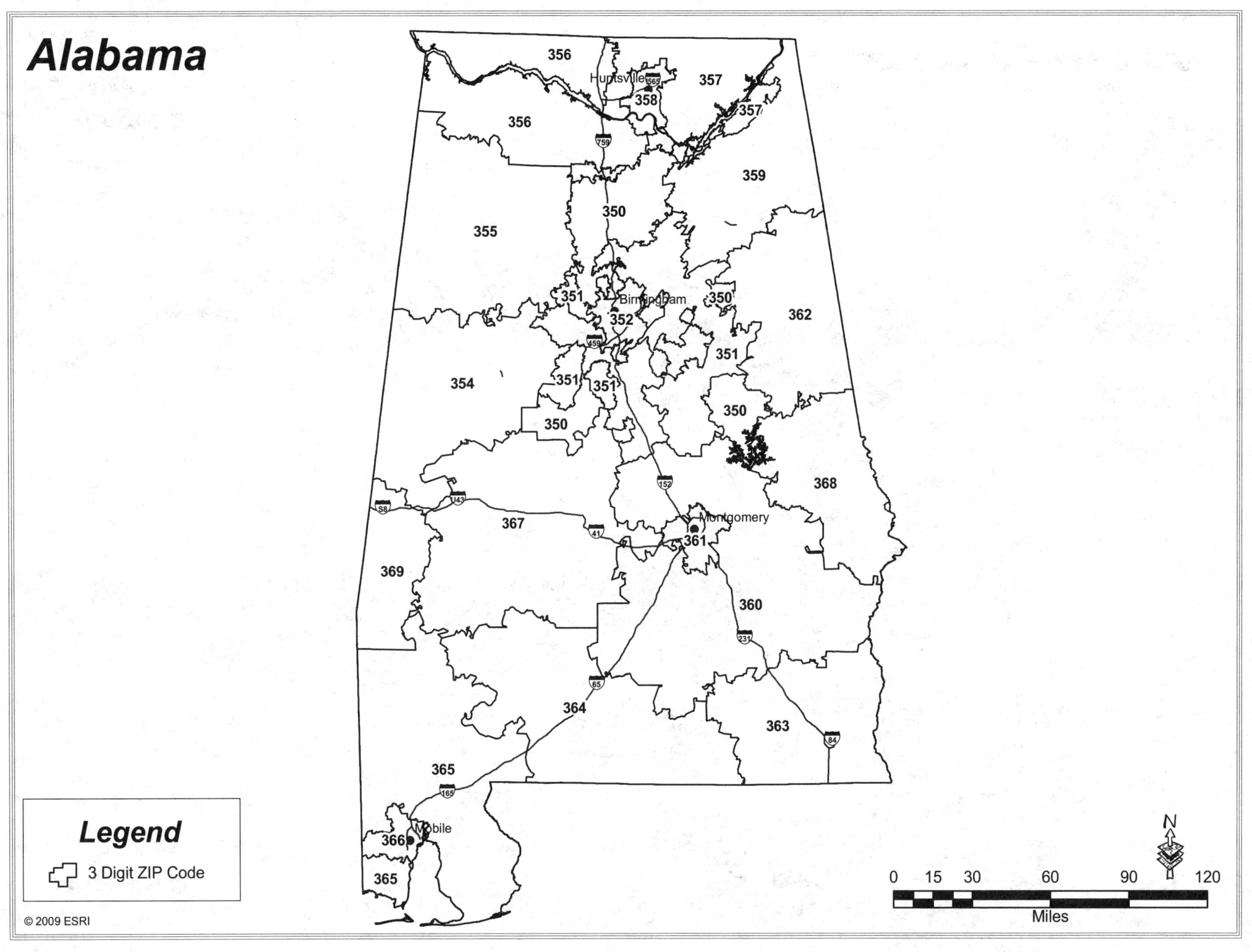
Alabama
356
Huntsville
357
358
357
356
359
350
355
351
Birmingham
350
352
362
351
354
351
351
350
350
368
367
Montgomery
361
369
360
364
363
365
Mobile
366
365
Legend
3 Digit ZIP Code
0 15 30 60 90 120
Miles
N
© 2009 ESRI

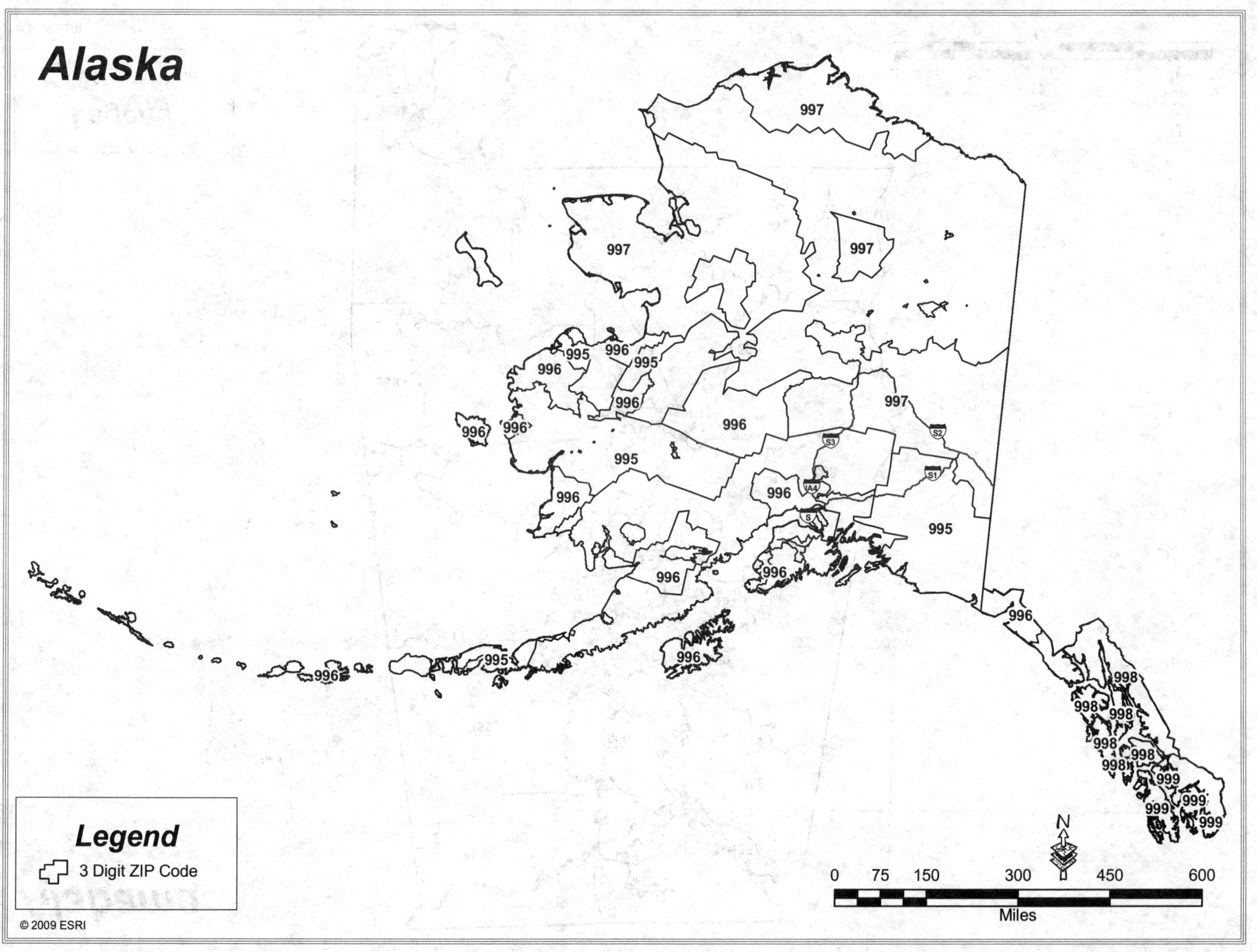

Alaska
997
997
997
995
996
996
995
996
996
996
997
996
995
996
996
995
996
995
996
996
996
995
998
998
998
998
998
998
999
999
999
999
Legend
3 Digit ZIP Code
N
0
75
150
300
450
600
Miles

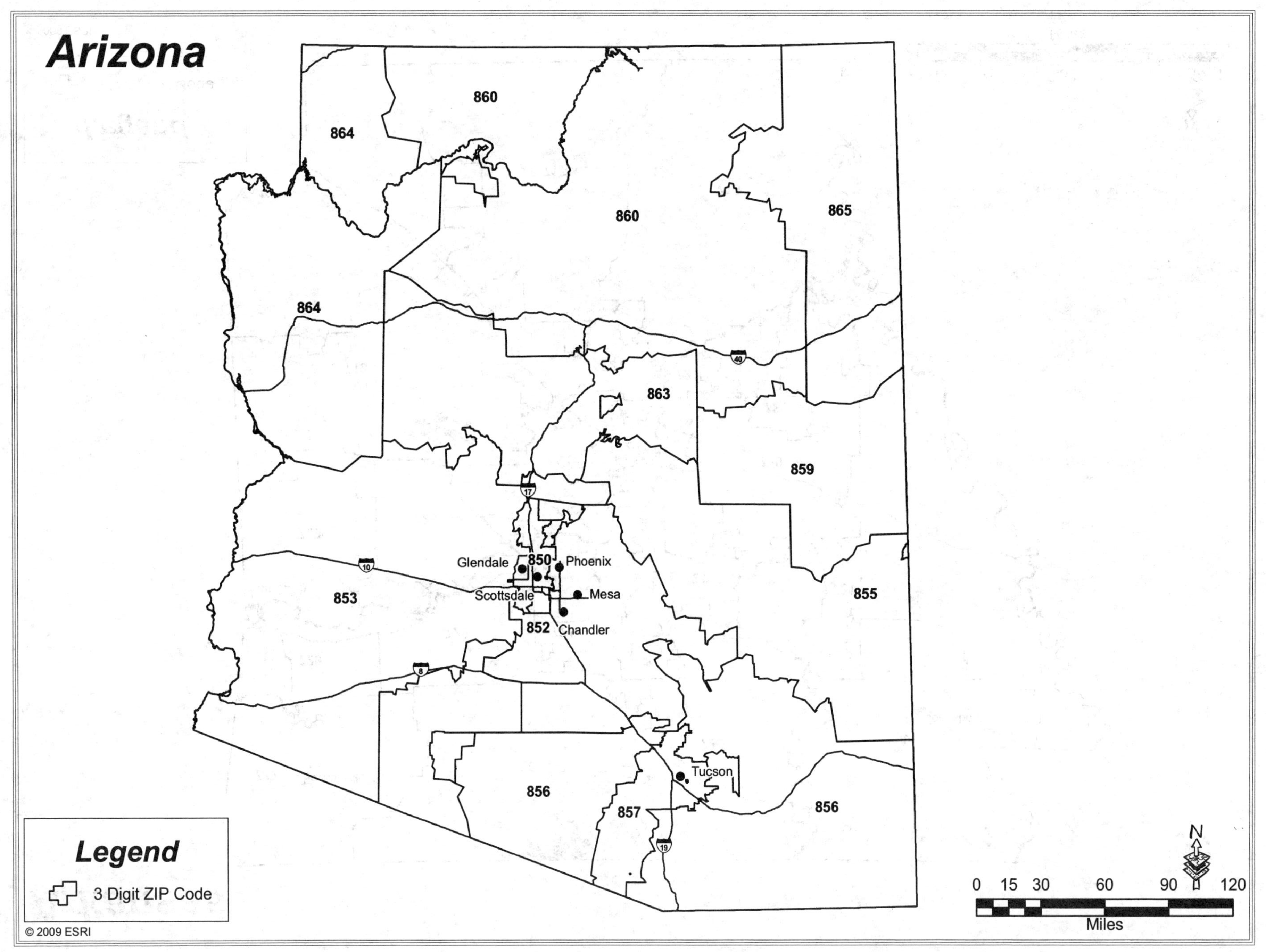

Arizona
860
864
860
865
864
863
859
850
Glendale
Phoenix
Scottsdale
Mesa
853
855
852
Chandler
Tucson
856
857
856
40
17
10
8
19
Legend
3 Digit ZIP Code
© 2009 ESRI
N
0 15 30 60 90 120
Miles

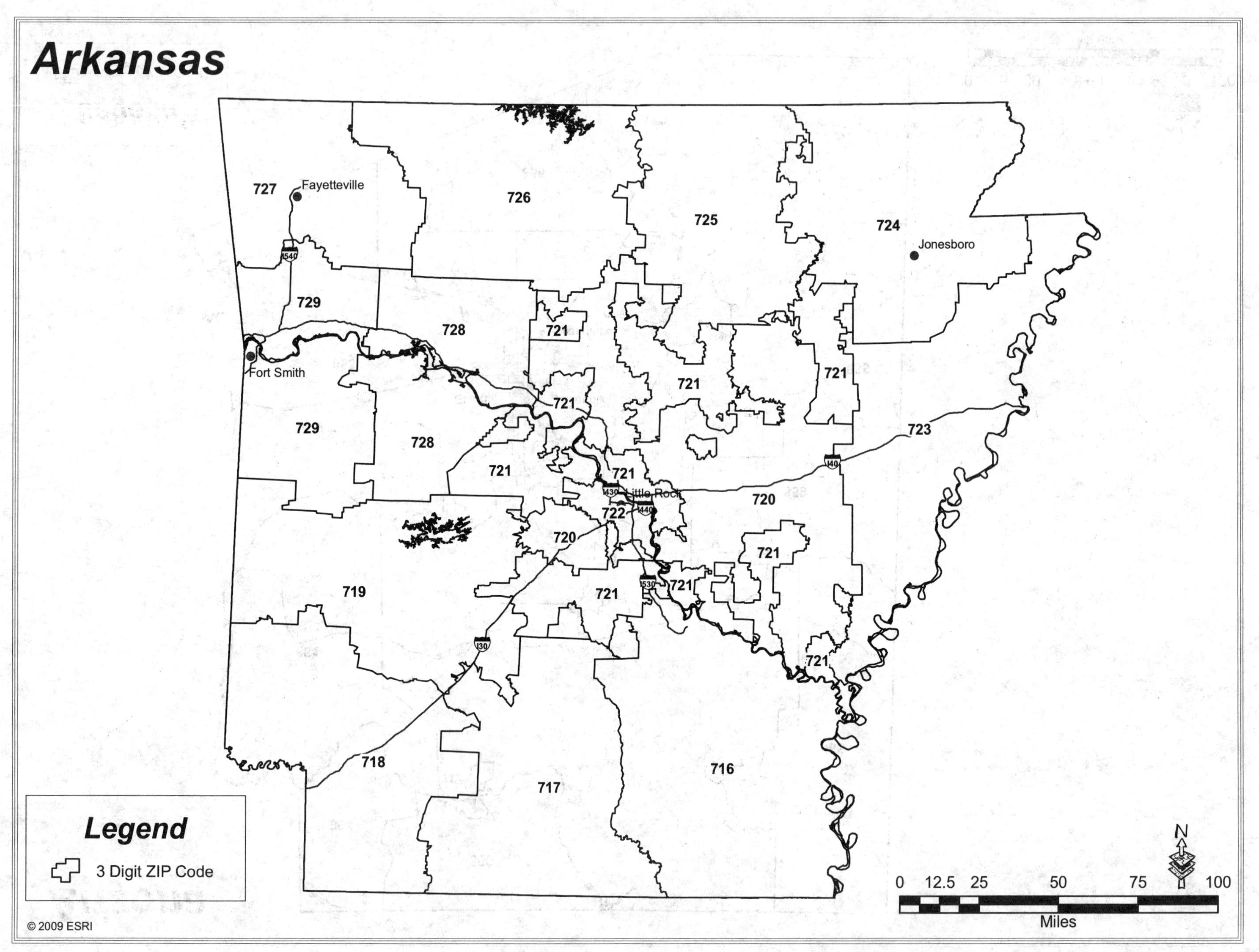
Arkansas
727
Fayetteville
726
725
724
Jonesboro
540
729
728
721
Fort Smith
721
721
721
729
728
723
721
721
440
430
Little Rock
720
722
720
721
719
721
530
721
30
721
718
716
717
Legend
3 Digit ZIP Code
N
0 12.5 25 50 75 100
Miles
© 2009 ESRI

Southern California

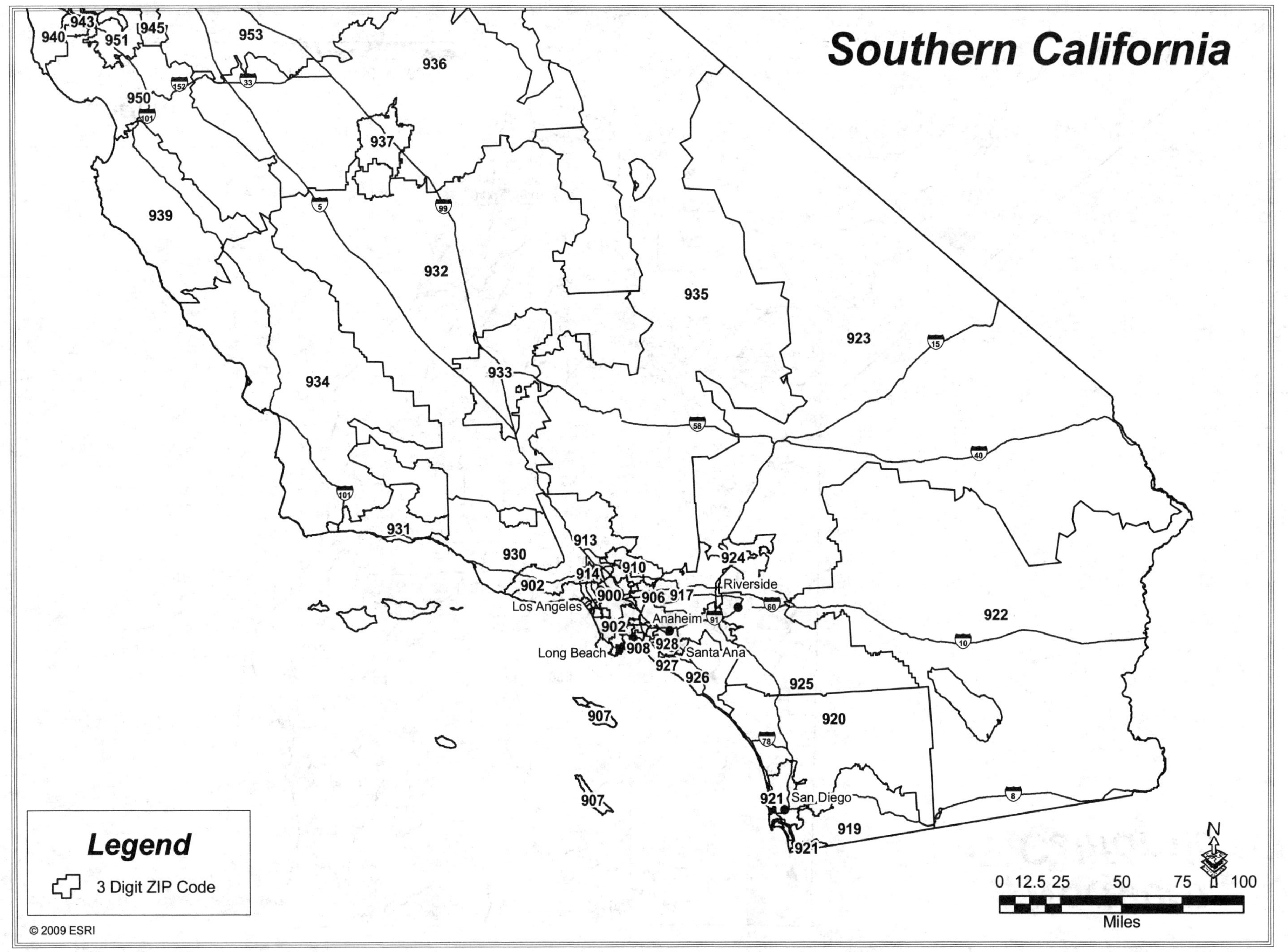

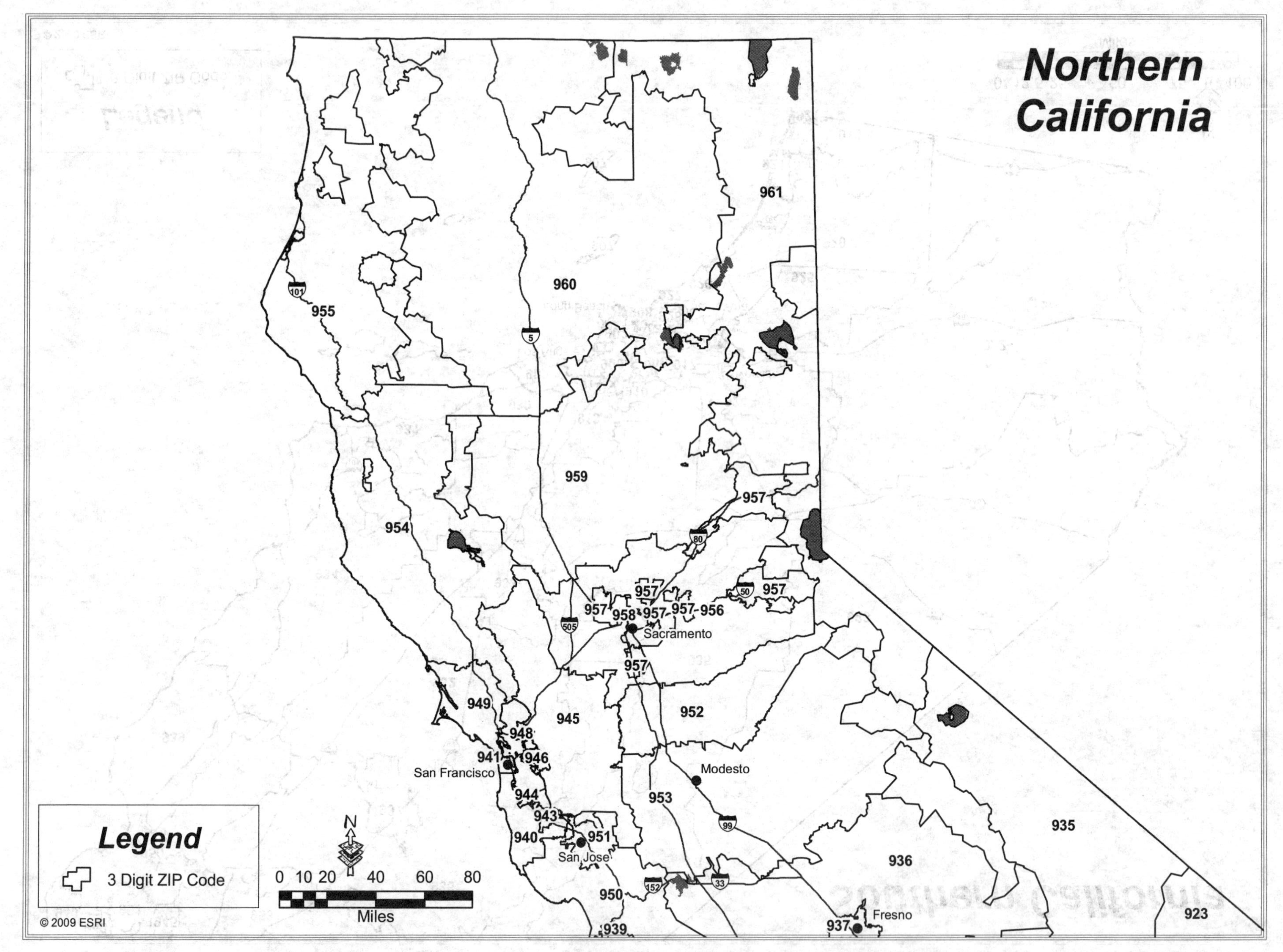
Northern
California
961
960
955
959
954
957
957
957
958
957
957
956
Sacramento
957
949
945
952
948
941
946
San Francisco
Modesto
944
953
943
940
951
San Jose
935
936
950
939
937
Fresno
923
Legend
3 Digit ZIP Code
N
0 10 20 40 60 80
Miles
© 2009 ESRI

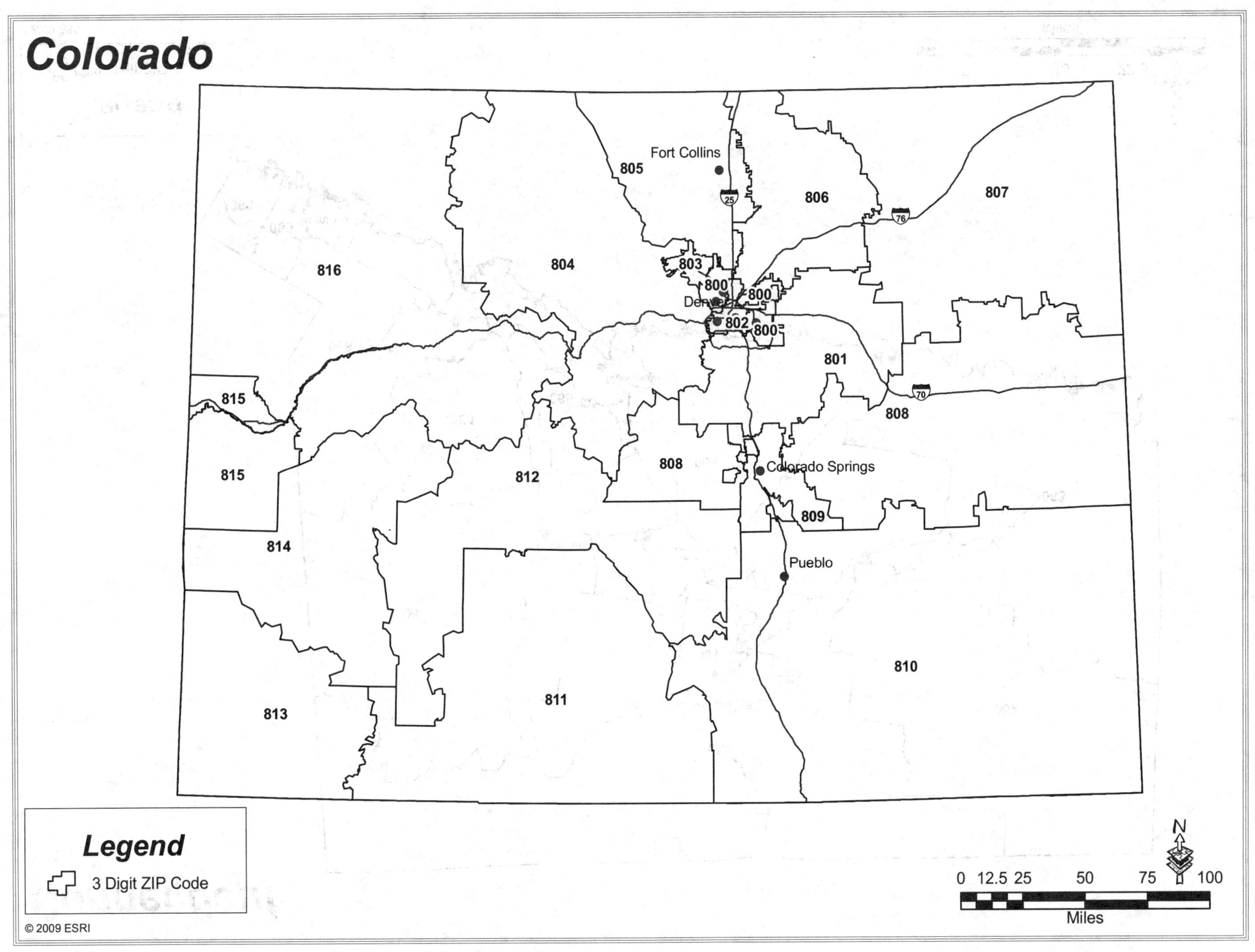
Colorado
805
Fort Collins
806
807
25
76
816
804
803
800
Denver
800
802
800
801
70
815
808
815
808
812
Colorado Springs
809
814
Pueblo
810
811
813
Legend
3 Digit ZIP Code
© 2009 ESRI
N
0 12.5 25 50 75 100
Miles

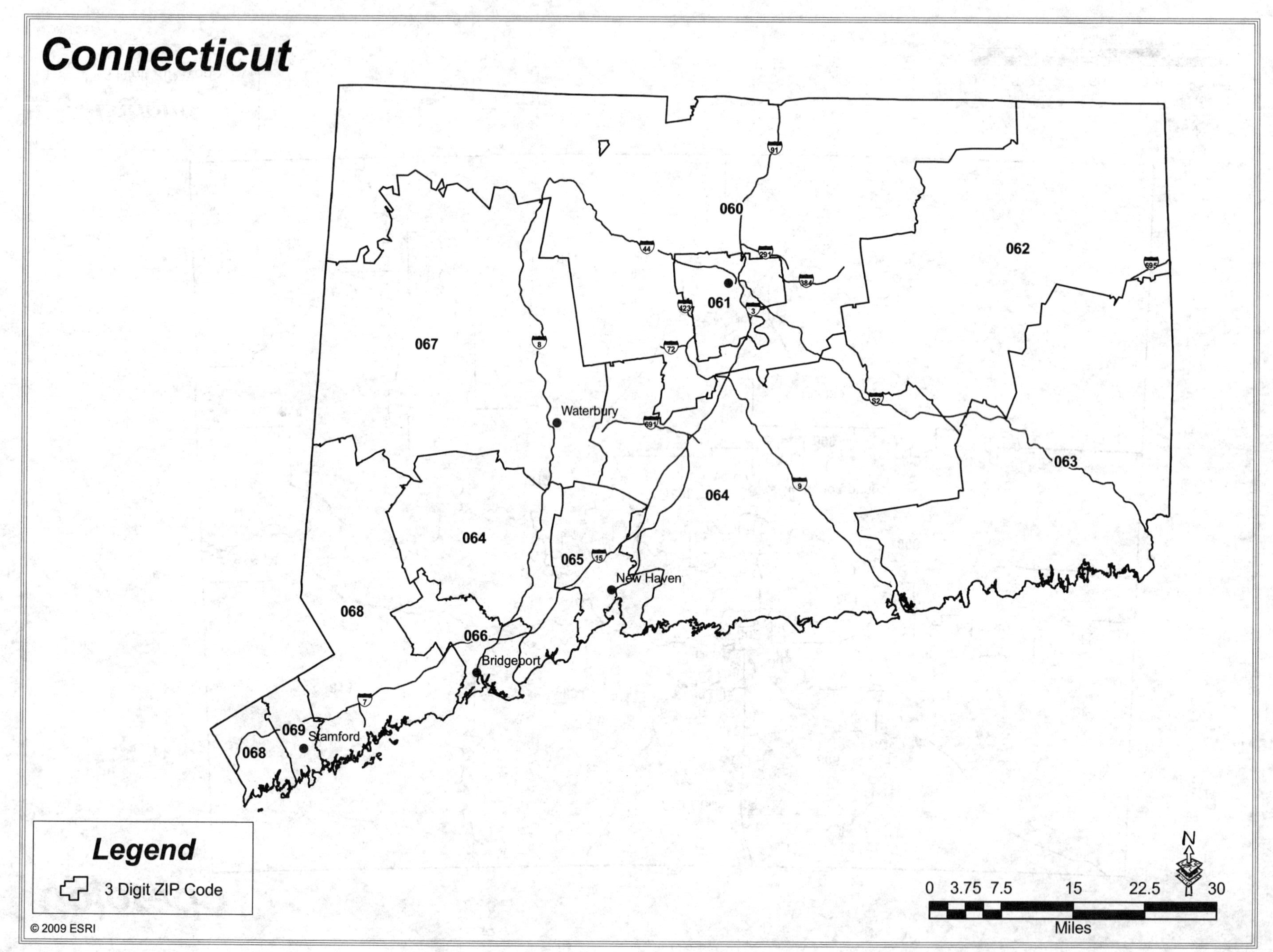
Connecticut
060
061
062
063
064
064
065
066
067
068
068
069
Waterbury
New Haven
Bridgeport
Stamford
91
291
384
395
44
423
3
72
8
691
84
9
15
7
Legend
3 Digit ZIP Code
© 2009 ESRI
0 3.75 7.5 15 22.5 30
Miles
N

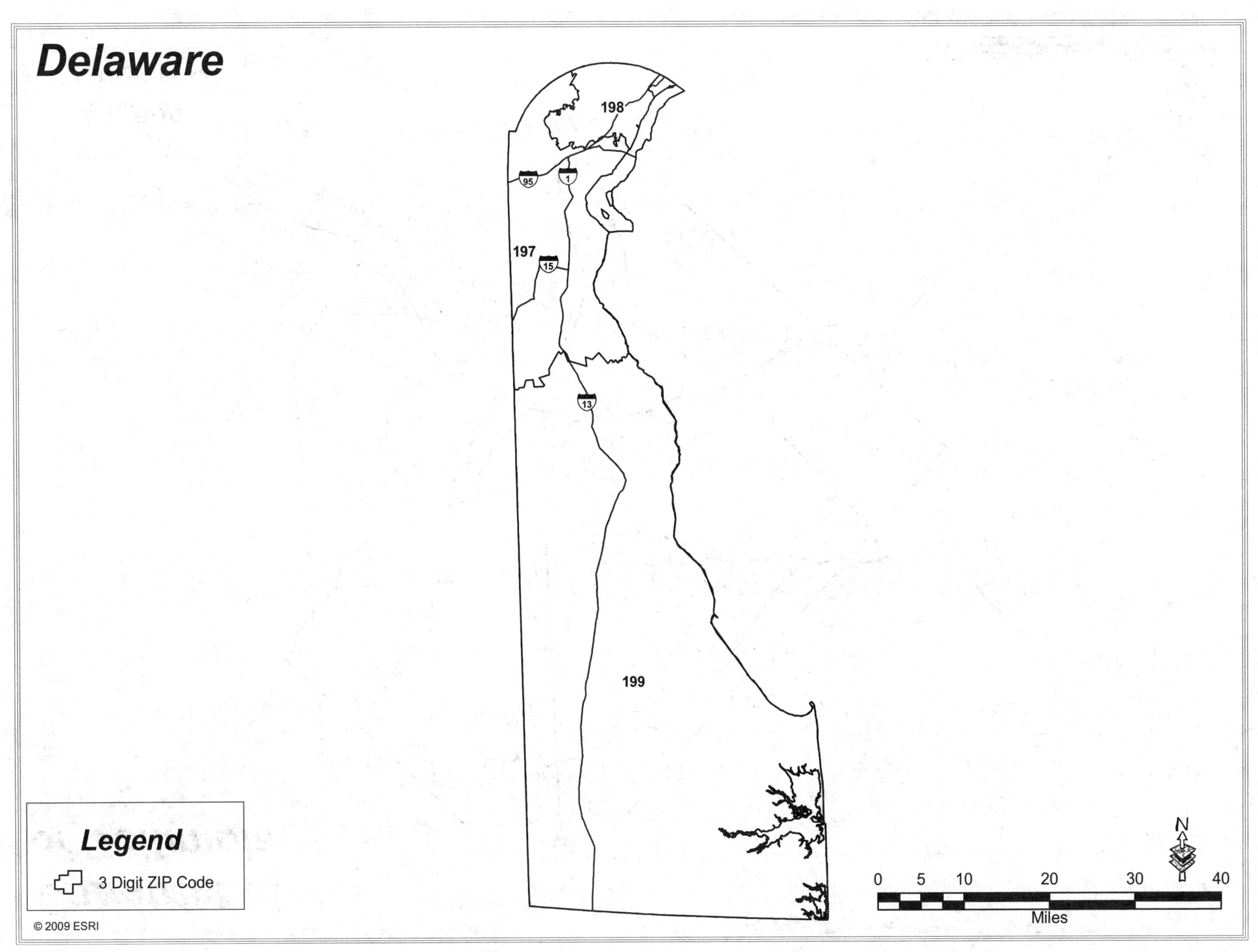
Delaware
198
95
1
197
15
13
199
Legend
3 Digit ZIP Code
© 2009 ESRI
0
5
10
20
30
40
Miles
N

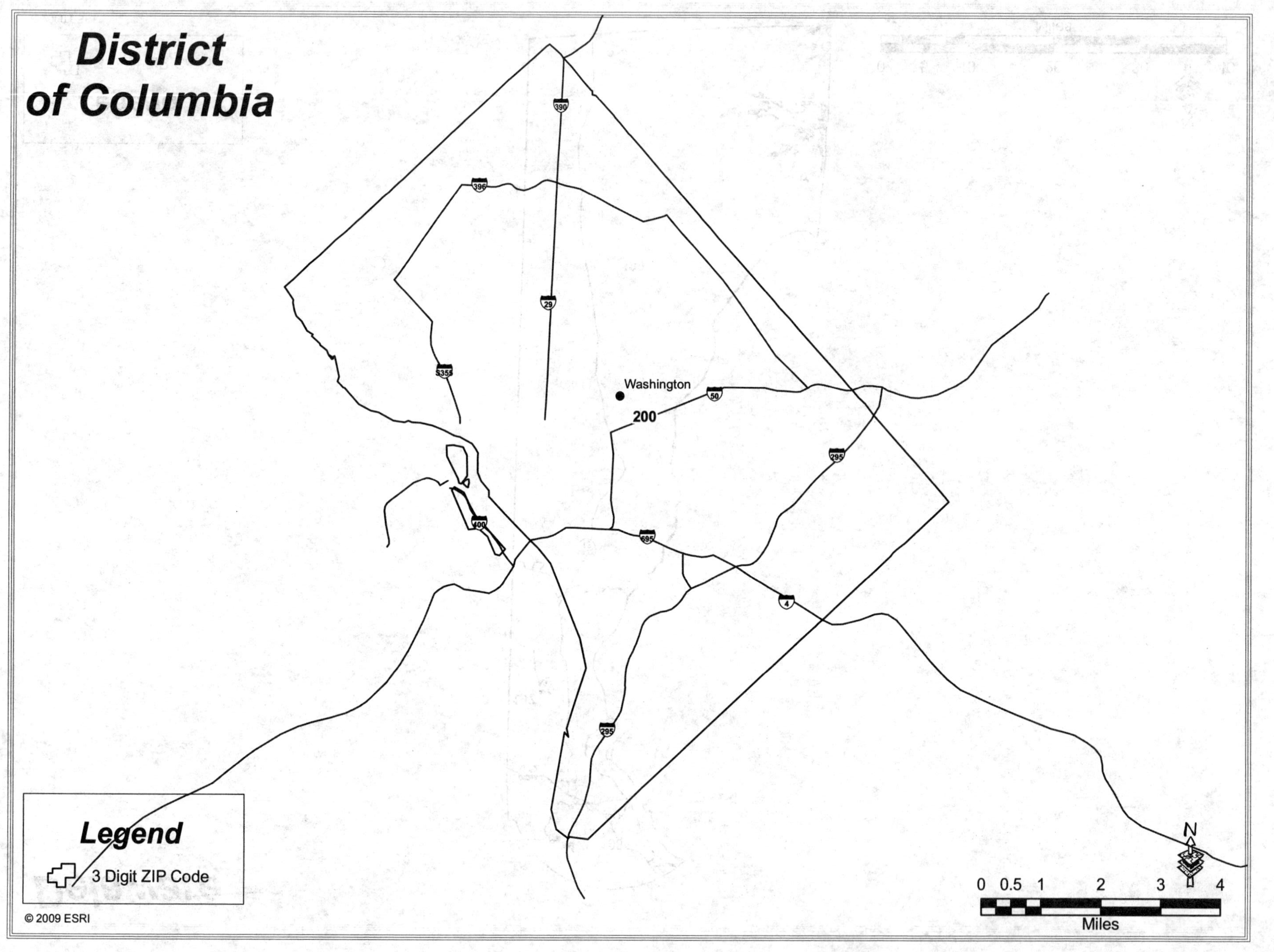
District
of Columbia
Washington
200
390
396
29
S355
50
295
695
4
400
Legend
3 Digit ZIP Code
© 2009 ESRI
0 0.5 1 2 3 4
Miles
N

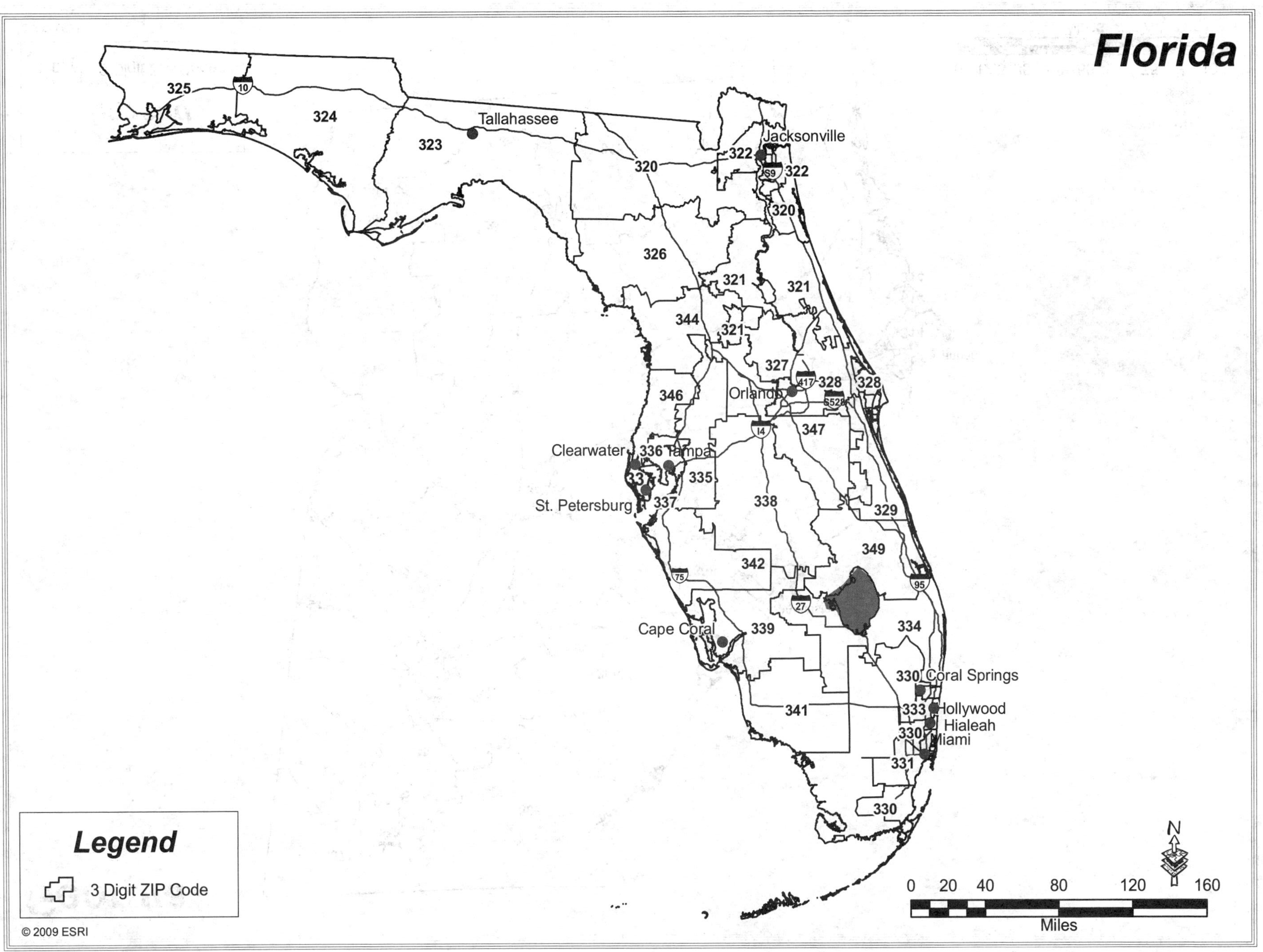
Florida
Tallahassee
Jacksonville
Orlando
Clearwater
Tampa
St. Petersburg
Cape Coral
Coral Springs
Hollywood
Hialeah
Miami
325
324
323
320
322
326
321
344
327
328
346
347
336
335
337
338
329
349
342
339
334
330
333
341
331
10
59
417
528
14
75
27
95
N
0 20 40 80 120 160
Miles
Legend
3 Digit ZIP Code
© 2009 ESRI

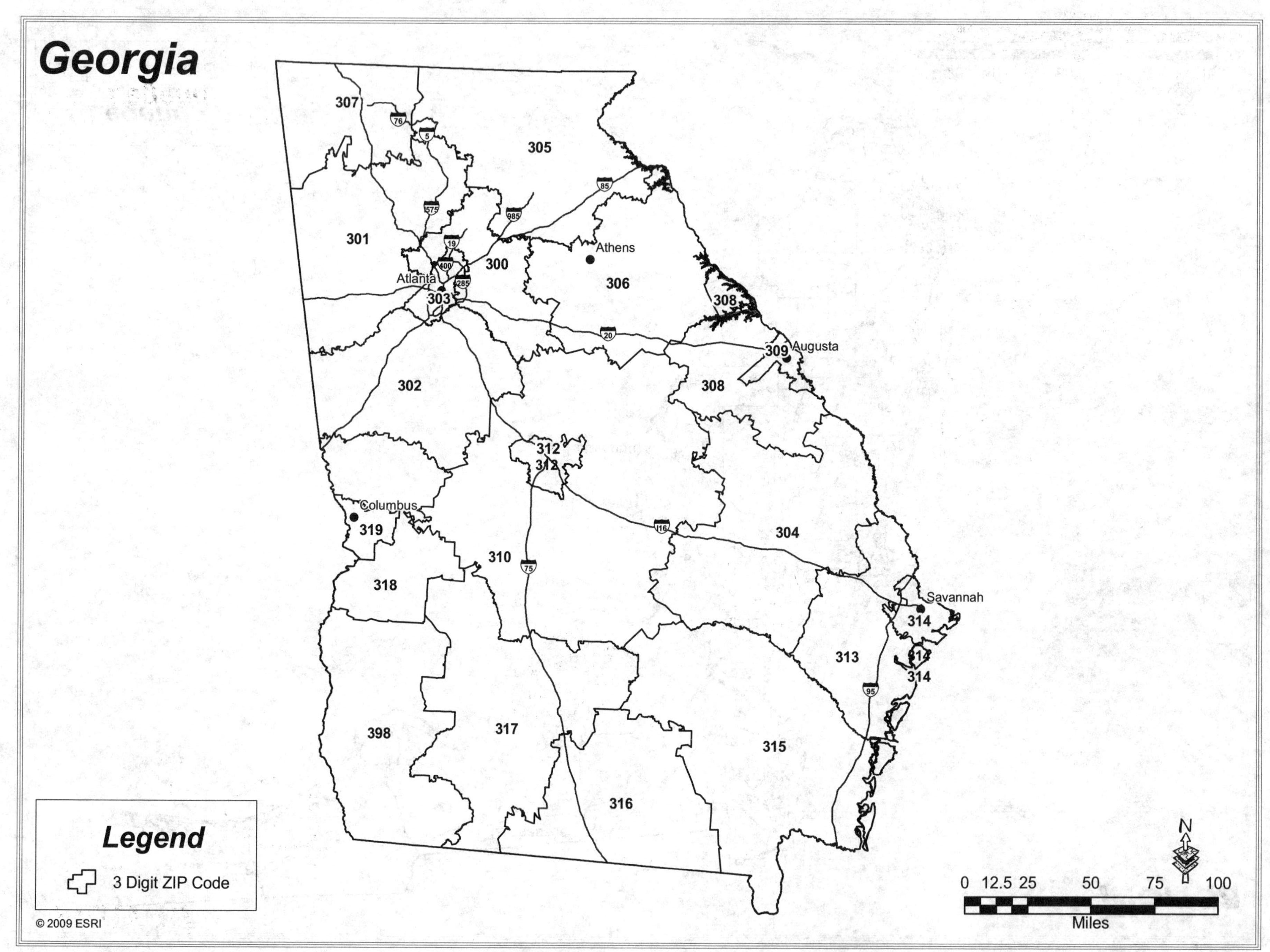
Georgia
307
305
301
300
Athens
306
Atlanta
303
308
309
Augusta
302
308
312
312
Columbus
319
304
310
318
Savannah
314
313
314
314
398
317
315
316
Legend
3 Digit ZIP Code
© 2009 ESRI
0 12.5 25 50 75 100
Miles
N
76
5
85
575
985
19
400
285
20
16
75
95

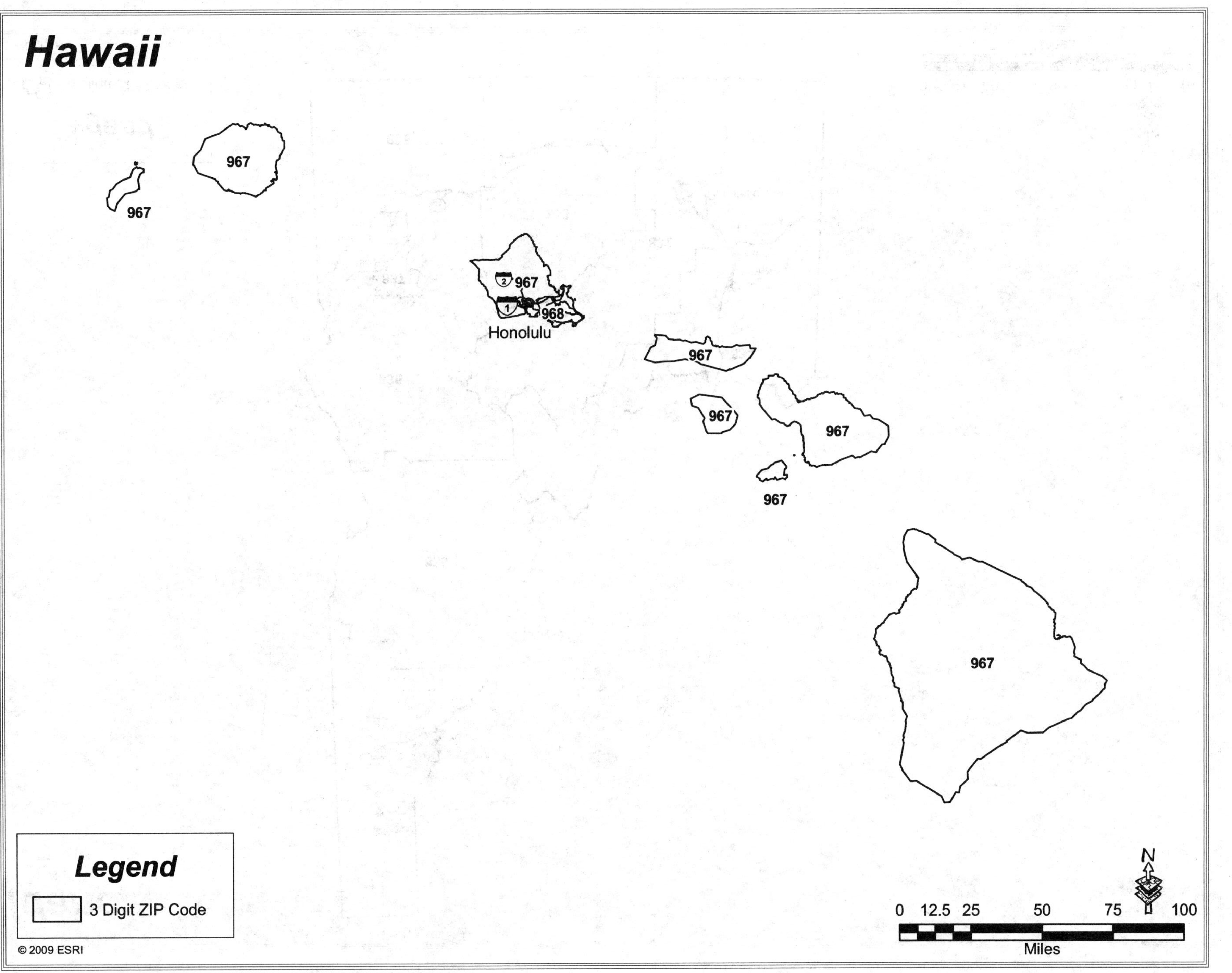

Hawaii
967
967
2
967
1
968
Honolulu
967
967
967
967
967
Legend
3 Digit ZIP Code
© 2009 ESRI
N
0
12.5
25
50
75
100
Miles

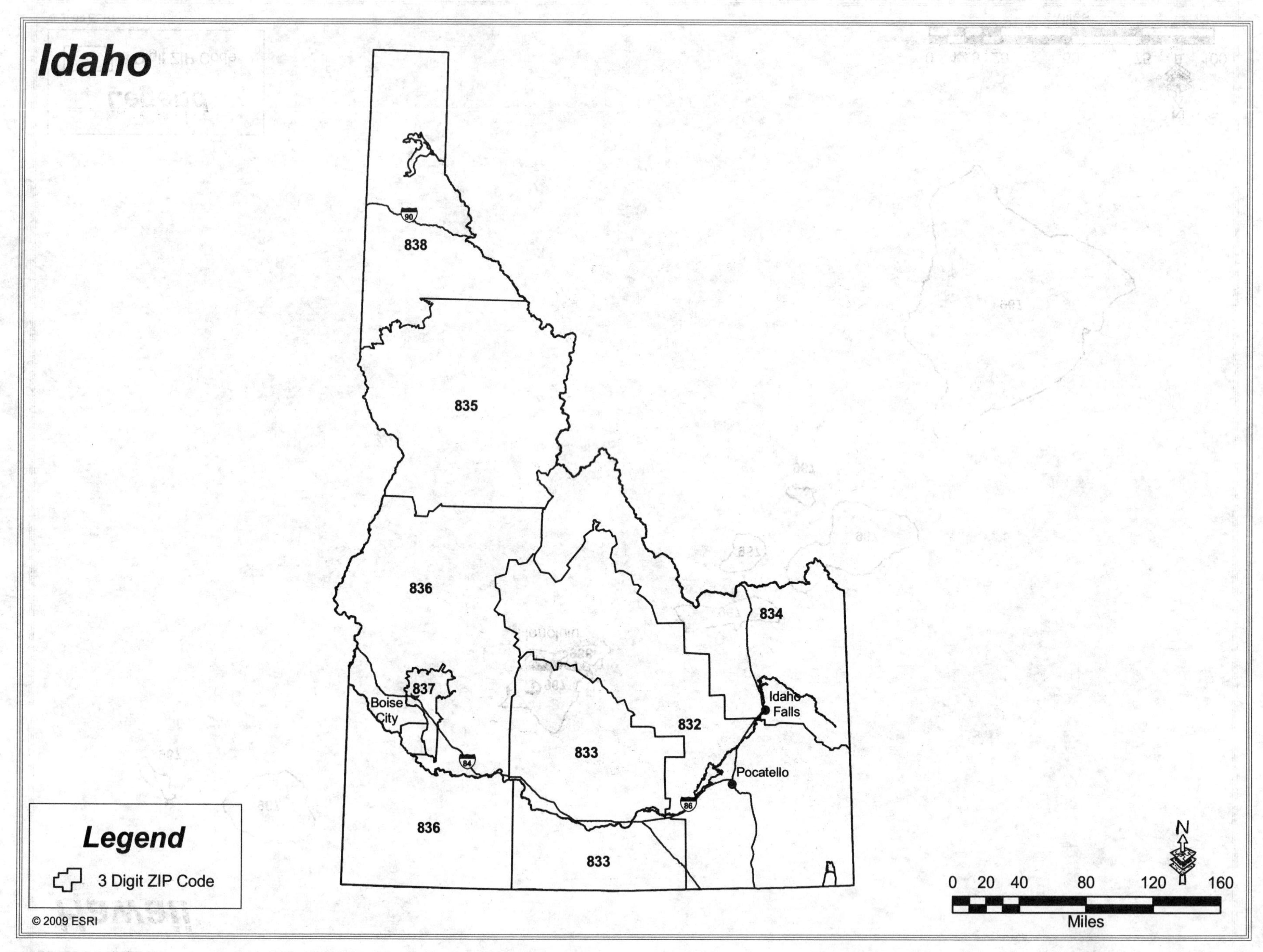
Idaho
90
838
835
836
837
Boise City
84
836
833
833
832
86
834
Idaho Falls
Pocatello
Legend
3 Digit ZIP Code
© 2009 ESRI
N
0 20 40 80 120 160
Miles

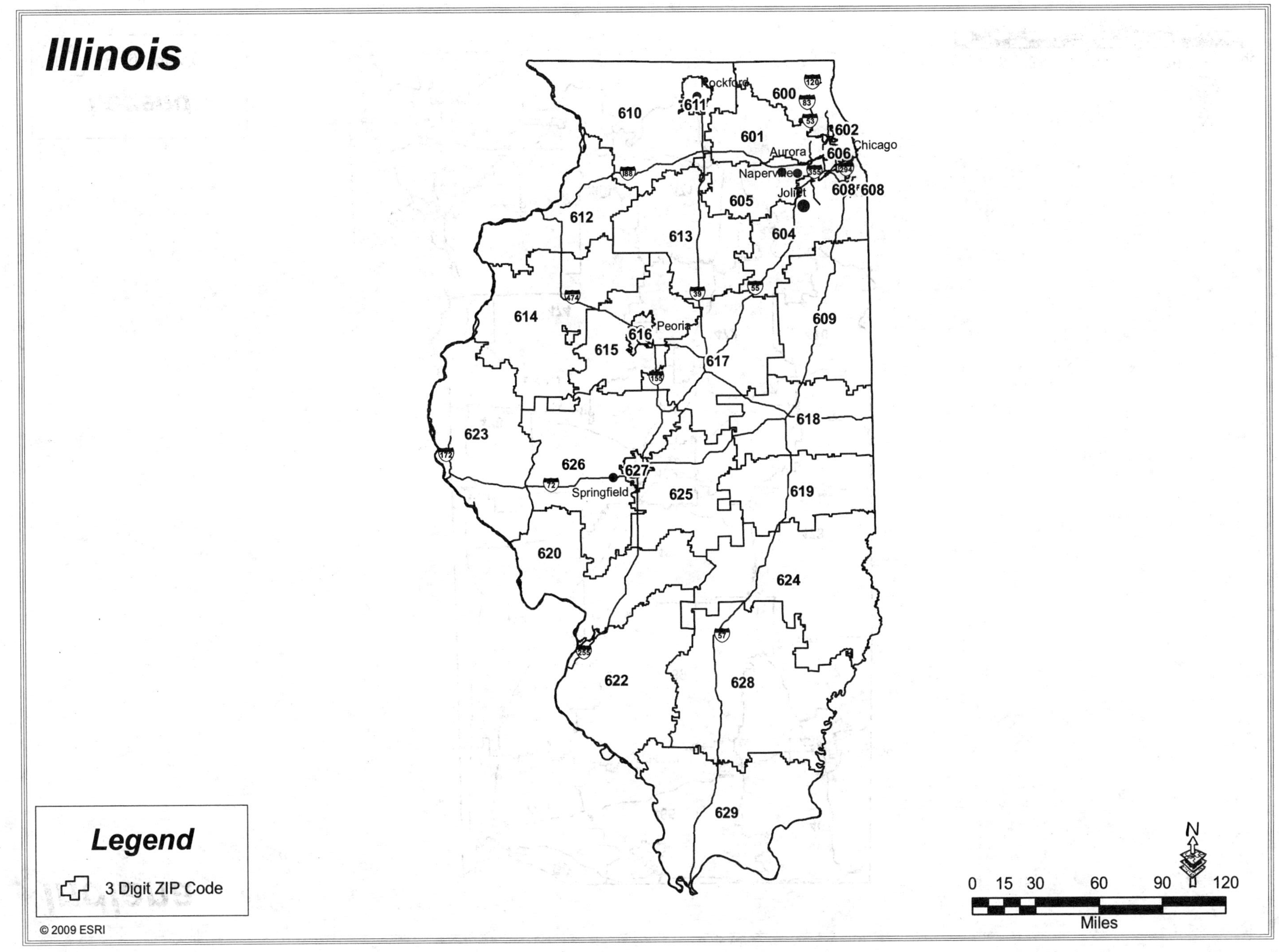
Illinois
Rockford
611
600
610
601
602
Chicago
Aurora
606
Naperville
608
608
Joliet
605
612
613
604
614
Peoria
616
609
615
617
618
623
626
627
Springfield
625
619
620
624
622
628
629
Legend
3 Digit ZIP Code
© 2009 ESRI
N
0 15 30 60 90 120
Miles

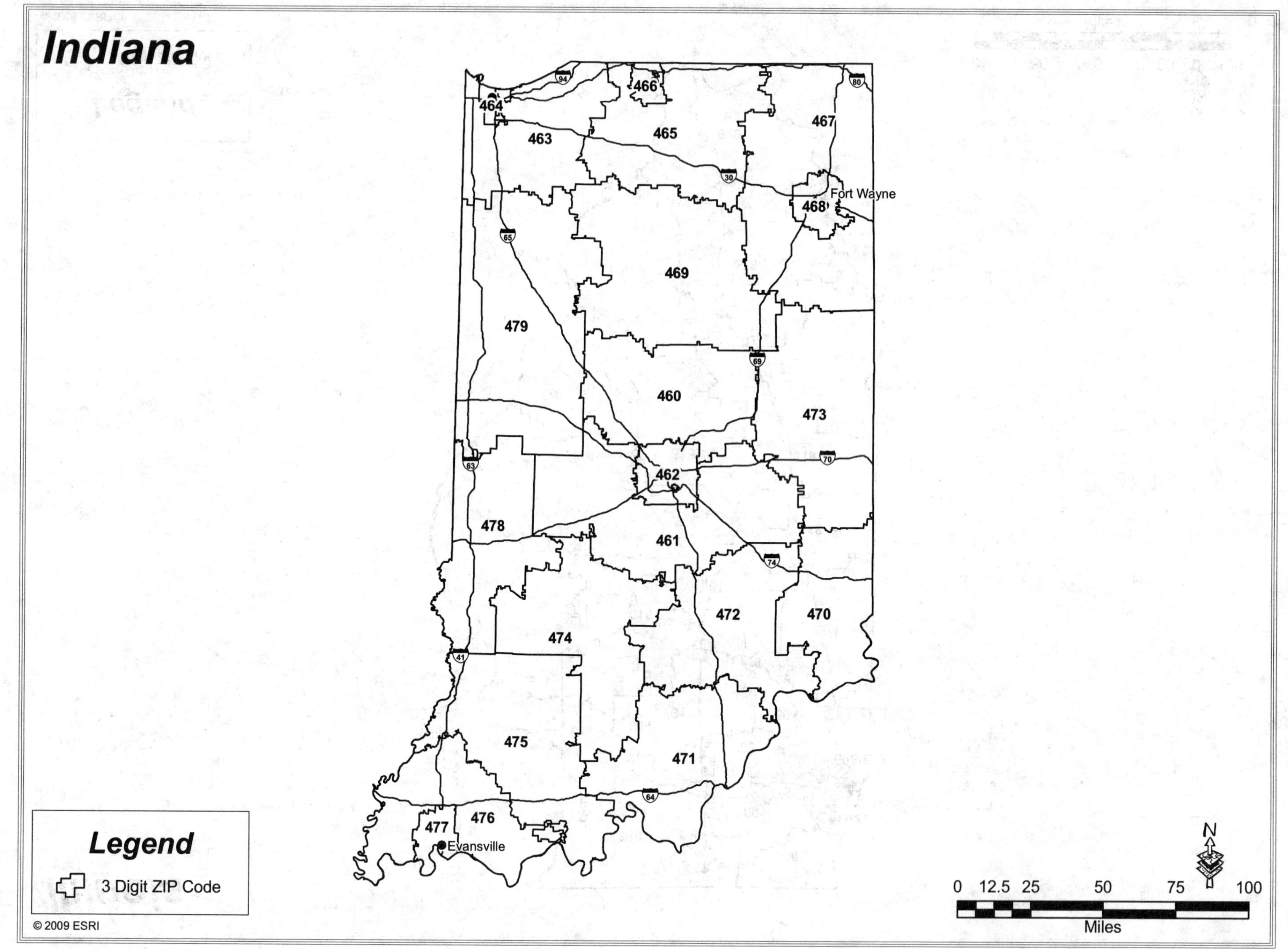

Indiana
94
466
464
80
467
465
463
30
Fort Wayne
468
65
469
479
69
460
473
70
63
462
478
461
74
472
470
474
41
475
471
64
476
477
Evansville
Legend
3 Digit ZIP Code
© 2009 ESRI
N
0 12.5 25 50 75 100
Miles

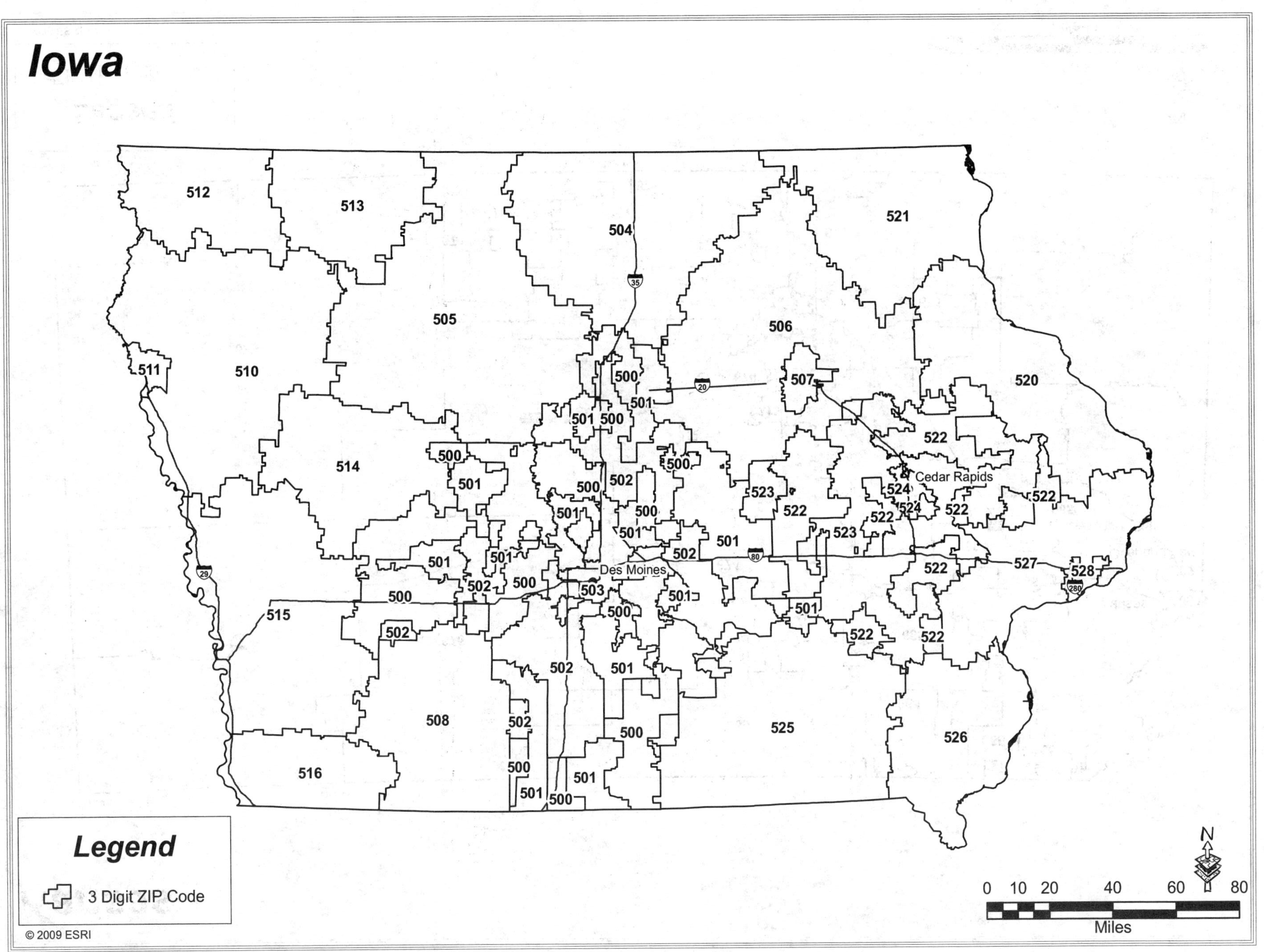

Iowa
512
513
504
521
505
506
511
510
500
507
520
501
514
522
502
Cedar Rapids
523
524
503
Des Moines
527
528
515
508
525
526
516
Legend
3 Digit ZIP Code
© 2009 ESRI
N
0 10 20 40 60 80
Miles

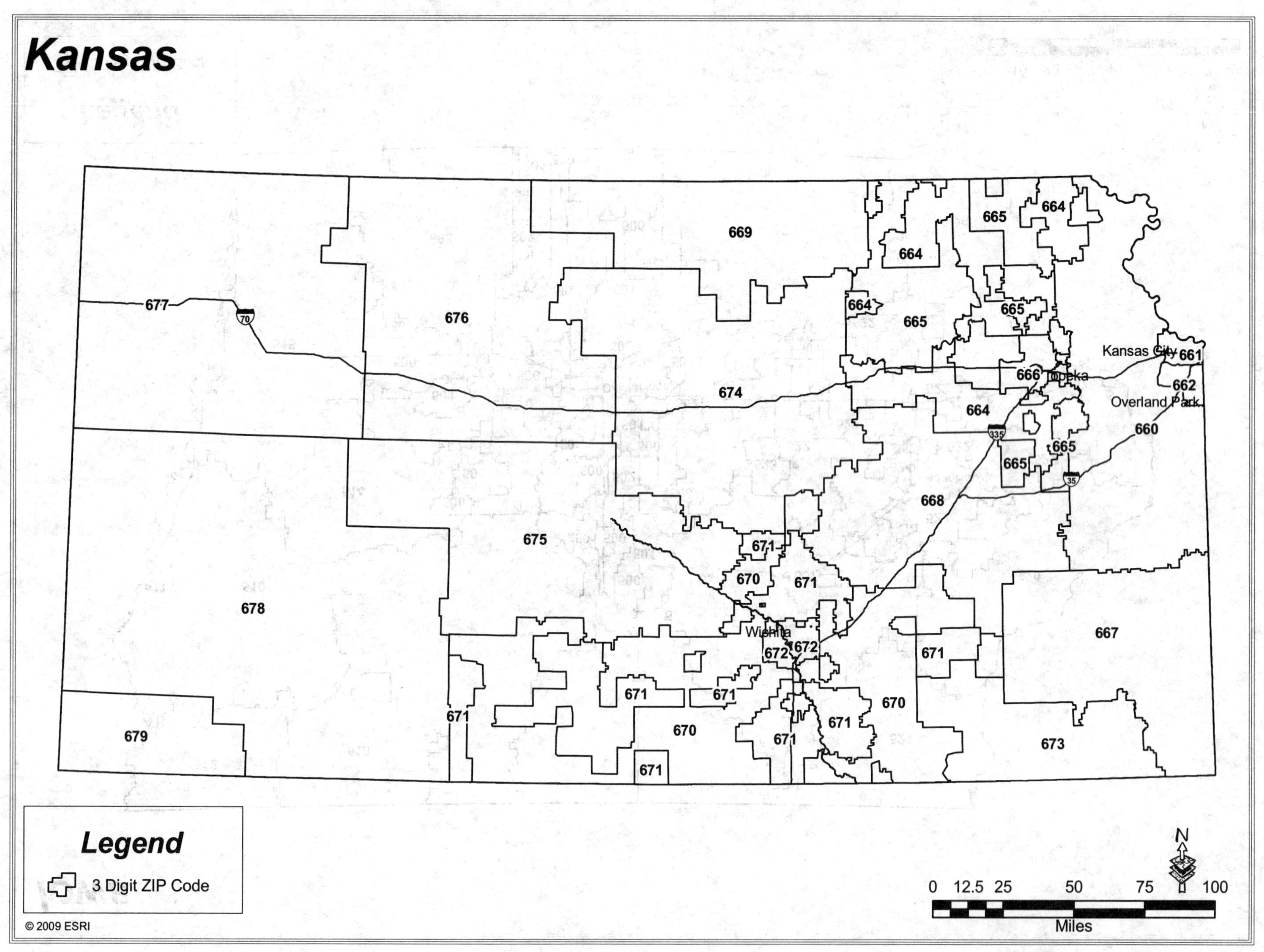

Kansas
Legend
3 Digit ZIP Code
© 2009 ESRI
N
0 12.5 25 50 75 100
Miles
Kansas City
Overland Park
Topeka
Wichita
660
661
662
664
665
666
667
668
669
670
671
672
673
674
675
676
677
678
679
70
35
335

Kentucky

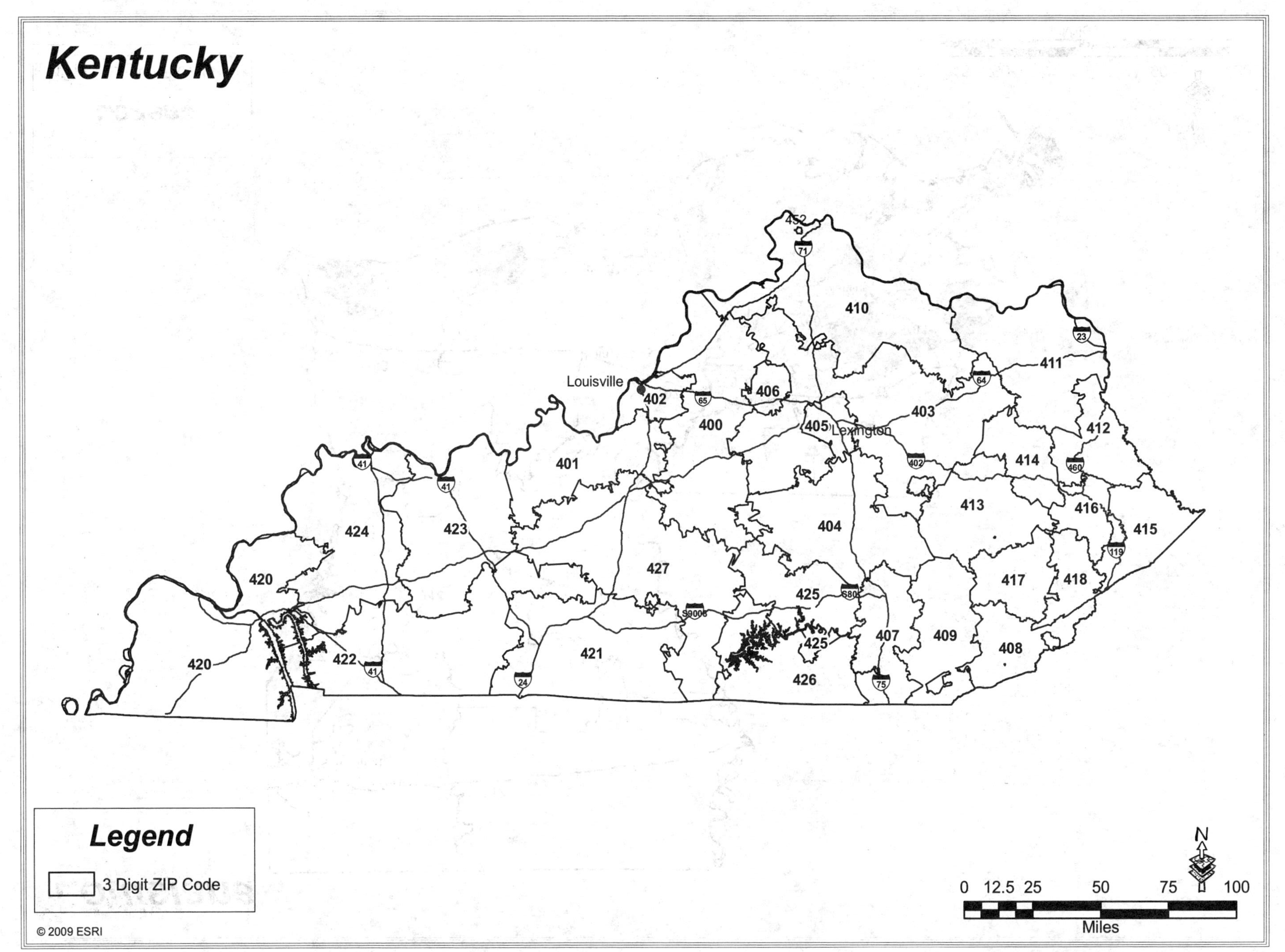

Kentucky
Louisville
Lexington
452
410
411
412
402
406
400
405
403
401
414
413
416
415
424
423
404
427
417
418
420
425
407
409
408
422
421
426
Legend
3 Digit ZIP Code
© 2009 ESRI
N
0 12.5 25 50 75 100
Miles

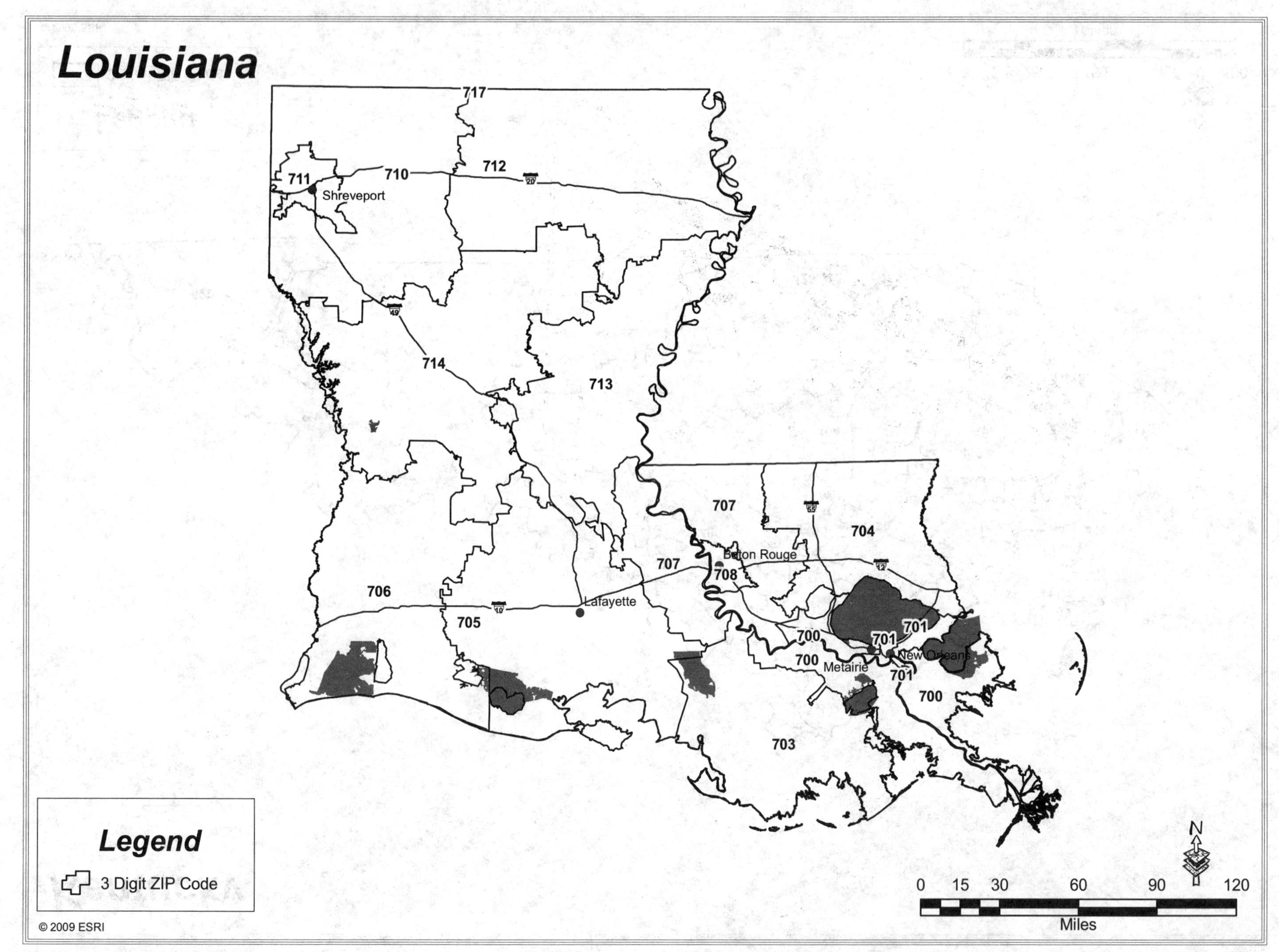
Louisiana
717
712
711
710
Shreveport
714
713
707
704
Baton Rouge
707
708
706
Lafayette
705
700
700
701
701
New Orleans
Metairie
701
700
703
Legend
3 Digit ZIP Code
0 15 30 60 90 120
Miles
N
© 2009 ESRI

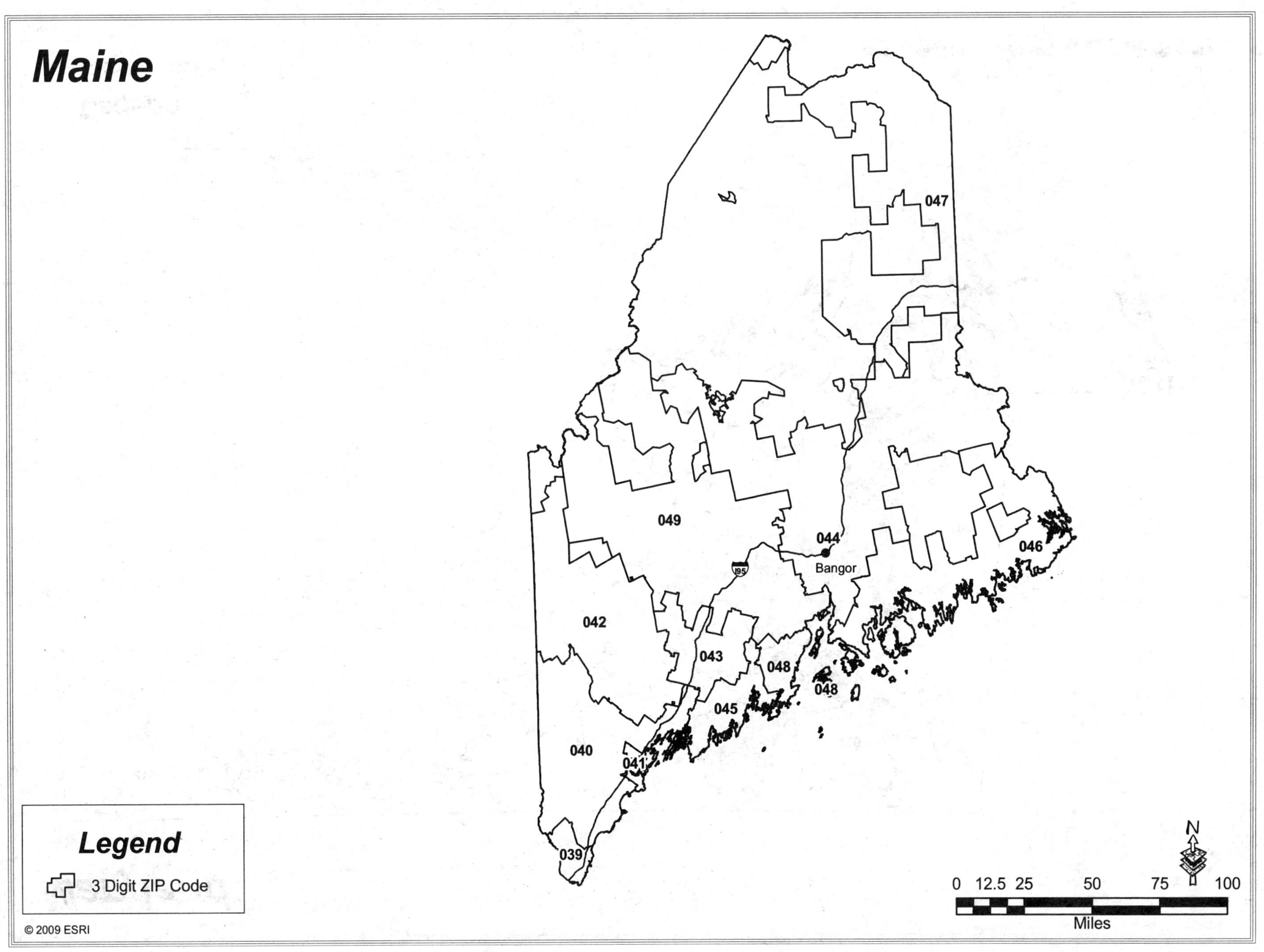
Maine
047
049
044
Bangor
95
046
042
043
048
048
045
040
041
039
Legend
3 Digit ZIP Code
© 2009 ESRI
N
0 12.5 25 50 75 100
Miles

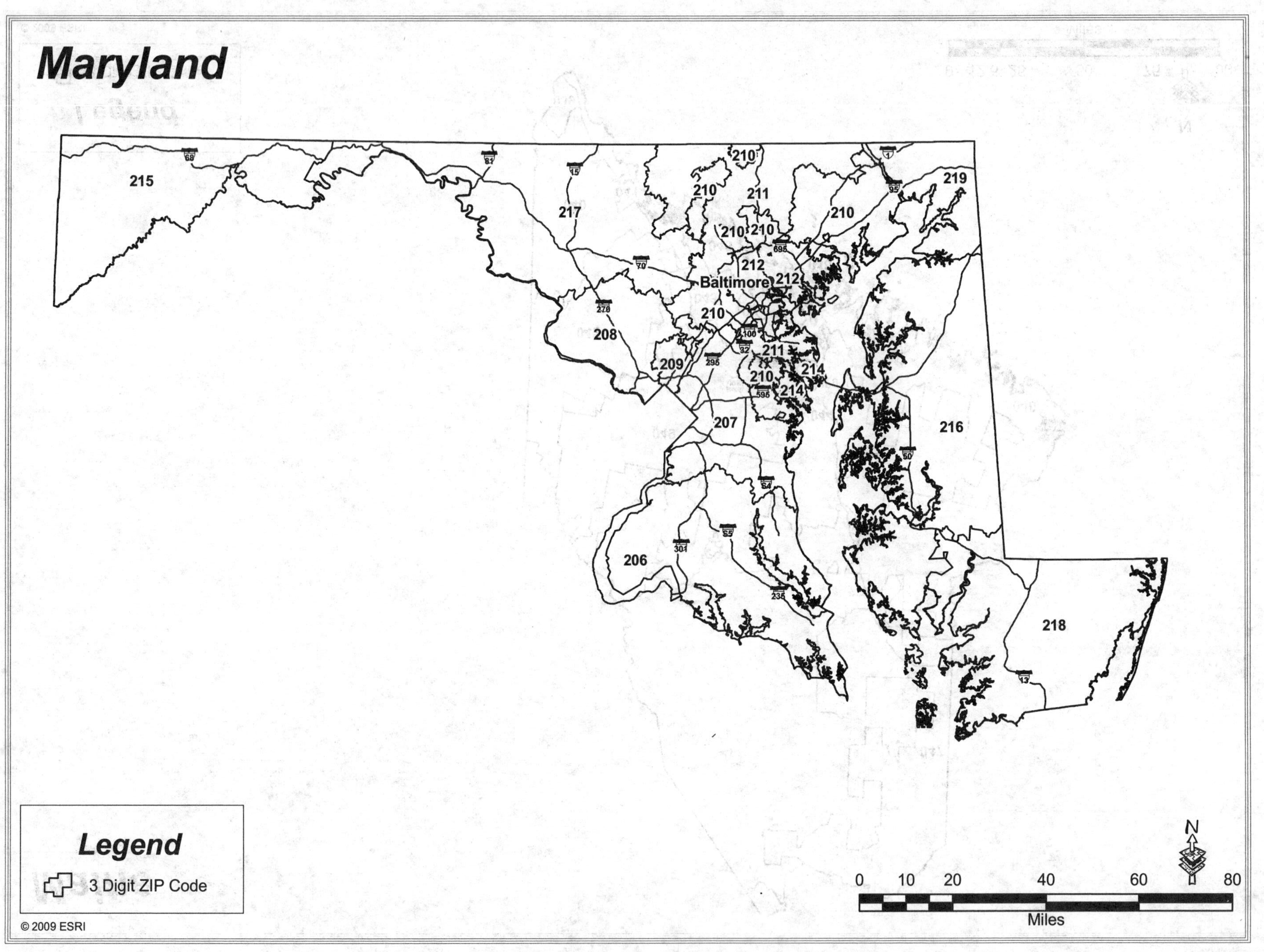

Maryland
215
217
208
209
210
211
212
Baltimore
214
207
206
216
218
219
Legend
3 Digit ZIP Code
© 2009 ESRI
0
10
20
40
60
80
Miles
N

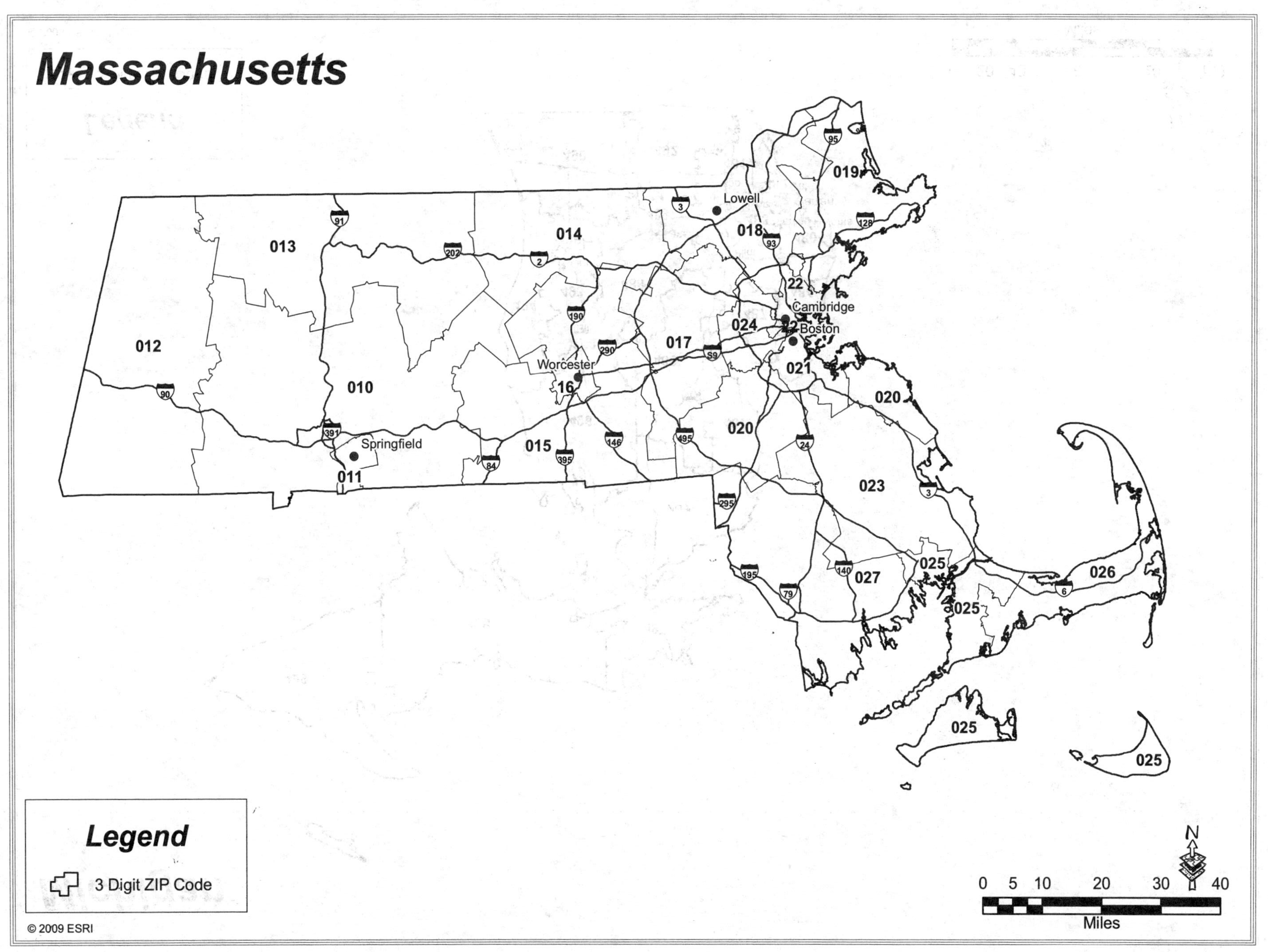

Massachusetts
Lowell
Cambridge
Boston
Worcester
Springfield
012
013
014
010
011
015
16
017
018
019
22
024
021
020
020
023
027
025
025
026
025
025
Legend
3 Digit ZIP Code
© 2009 ESRI
0 5 10 20 30 40
Miles
N

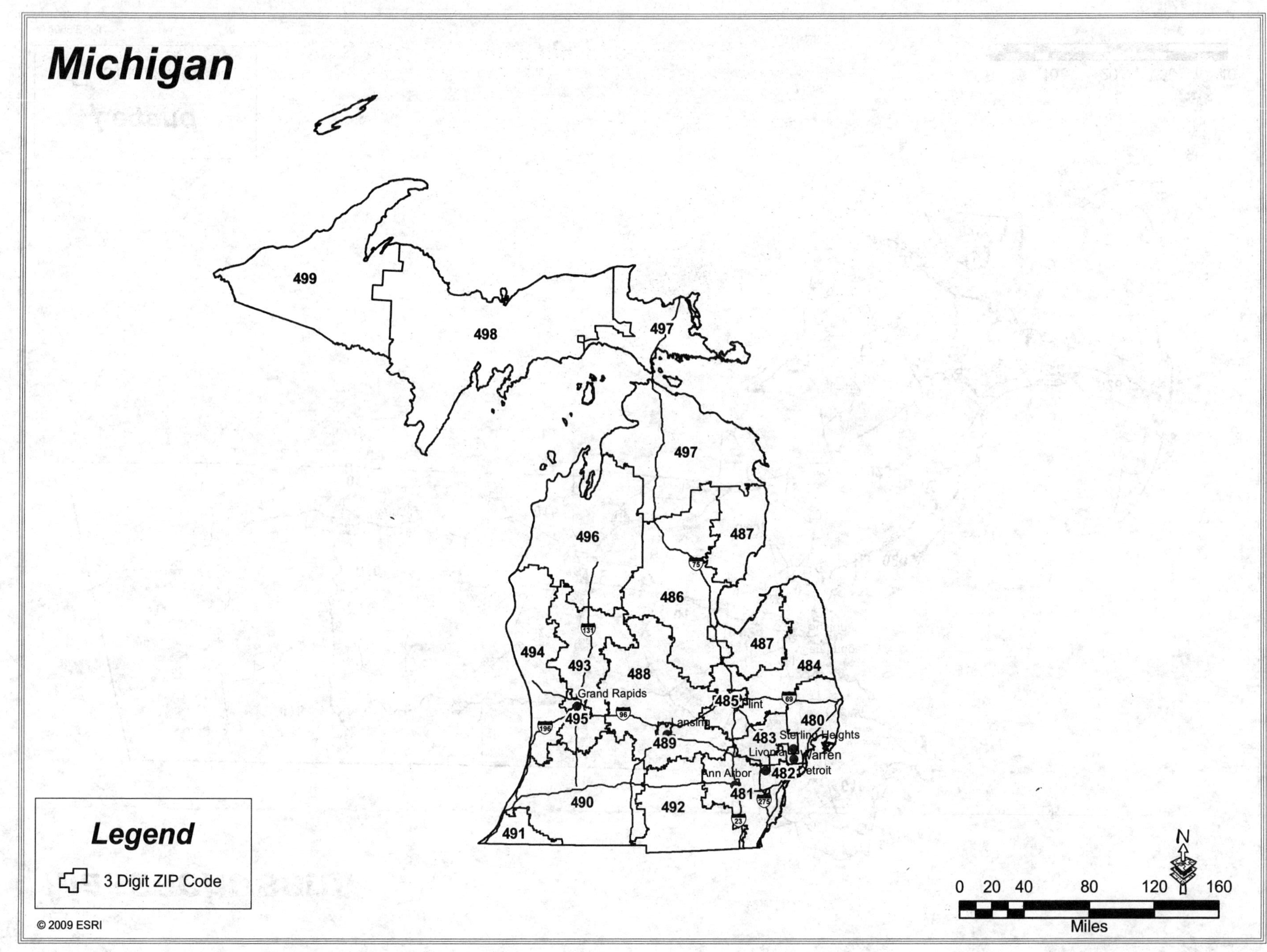
Michigan
499
498
497
497
496
487
486
487
484
494
493
488
Grand Rapids
485
Flint
495
480
Lansing
483
Sterling Heights
489
Livonia
Warren
Ann Arbor
482
Detroit
481
490
492
491
Legend
3 Digit ZIP Code
© 2009 ESRI
N
0 20 40 80 120 160
Miles

Minnesota

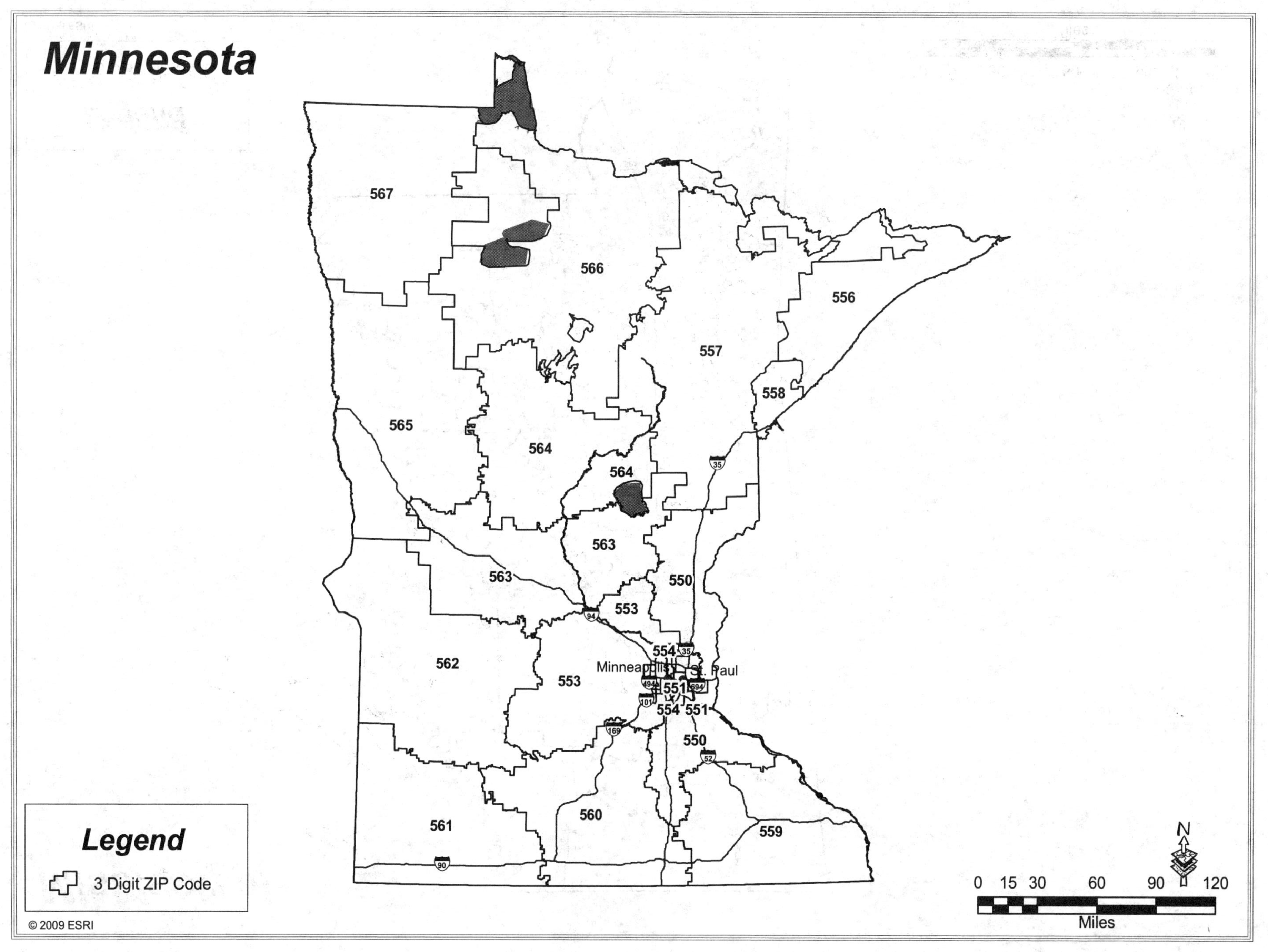

567
566
556
557
558
565
564
564
563
563
550
553
562
553
554
Minneapolis
St. Paul
551
554
551
550
560
561
559
35
94
494
694
101
169
52
90
Legend
3 Digit ZIP Code
0 15 30 60 90 120
Miles
N

Mississippi

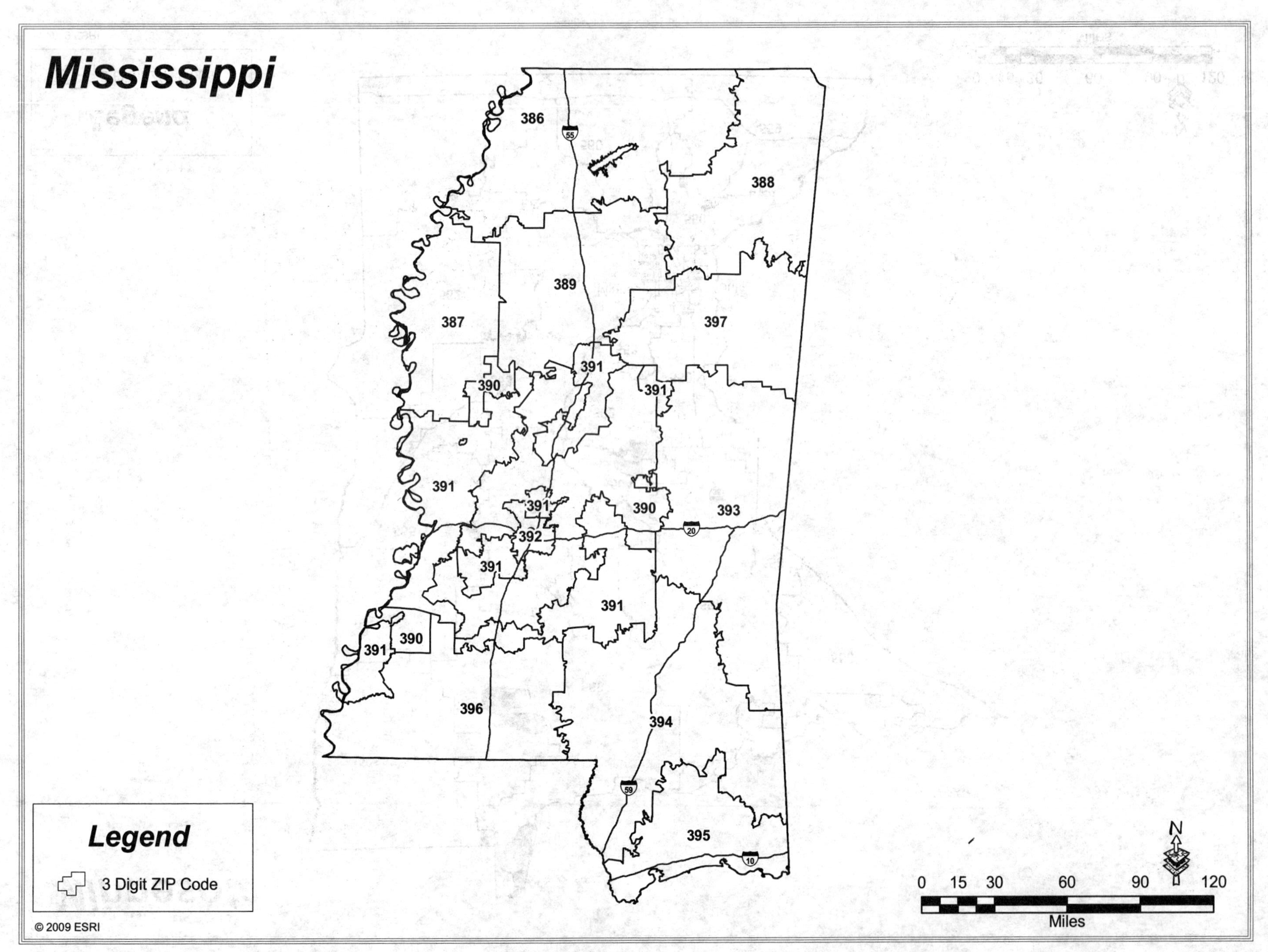

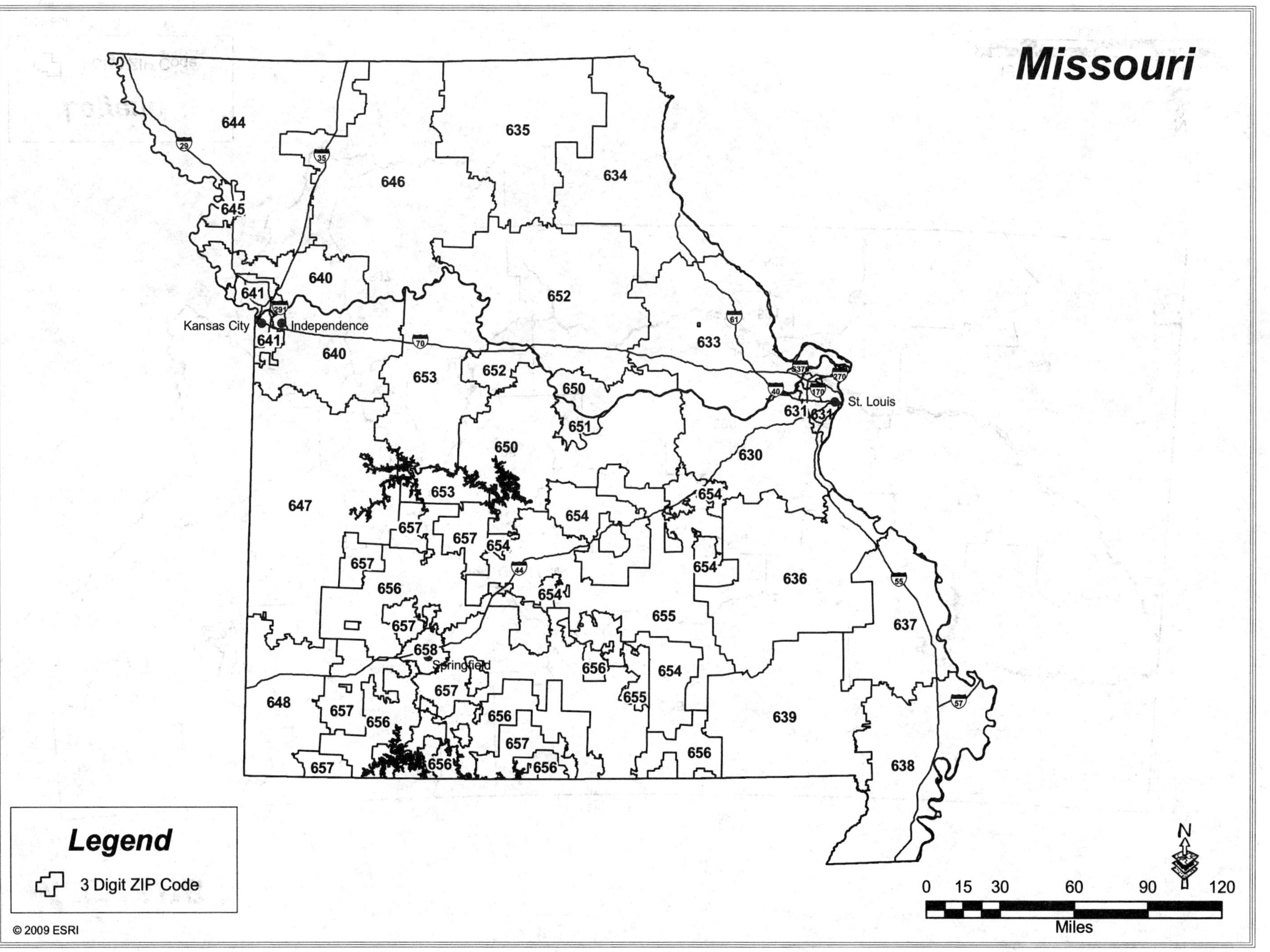
Missouri
Legend
3 Digit ZIP Code
© 2009 ESRI
N
0 15 30 60 90 120
Miles
Kansas City
Independence
St. Louis
Springfield
630
631
633
634
635
636
637
638
639
640
641
644
645
646
647
648
650
651
652
653
654
655
656
657
658

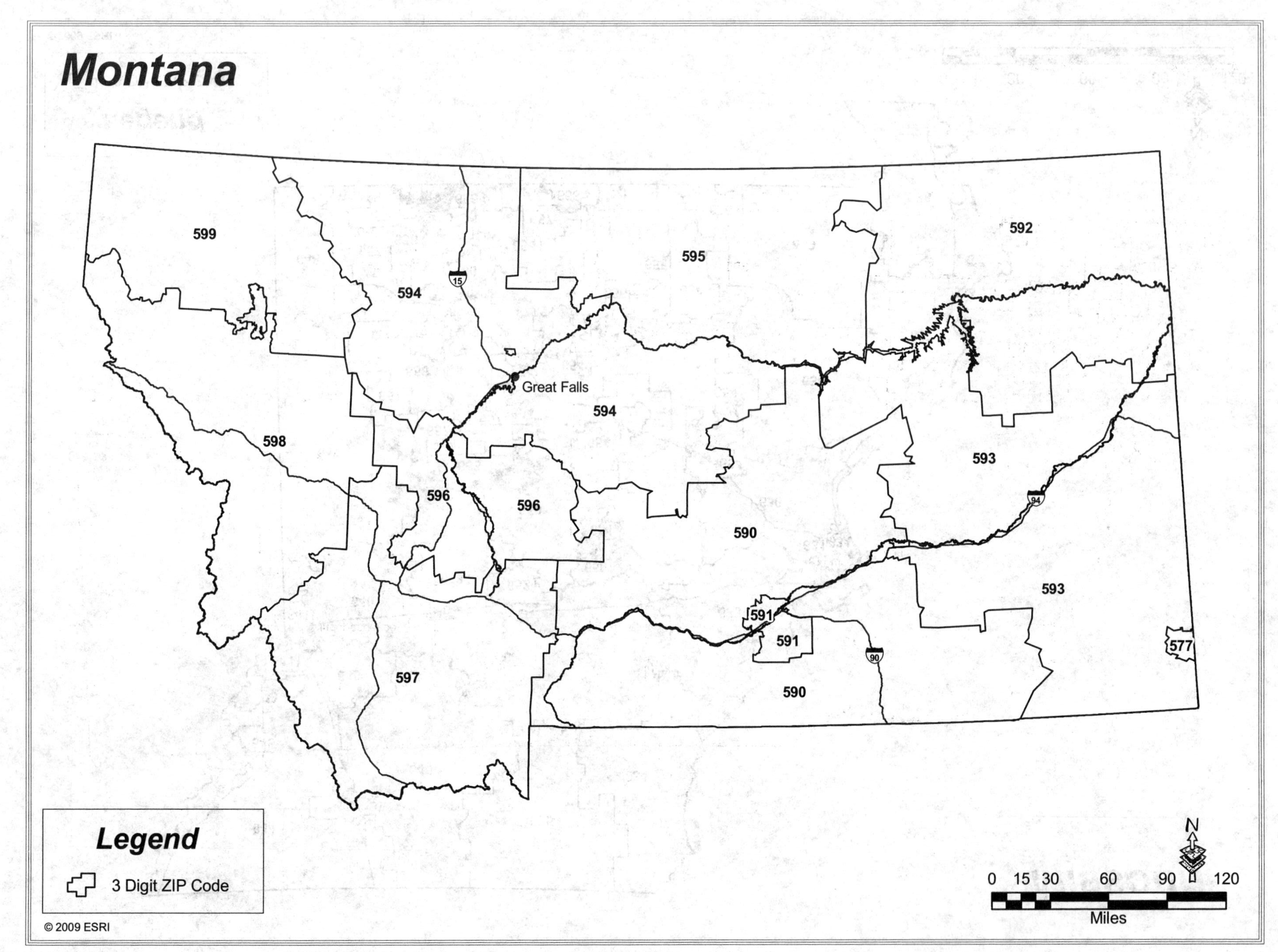

Montana
599
594
15
595
592
Great Falls
594
598
593
596
596
94
590
593
591
591
90
577
597
590
Legend
3 Digit ZIP Code
© 2009 ESRI
N
0 15 30 60 90 120
Miles

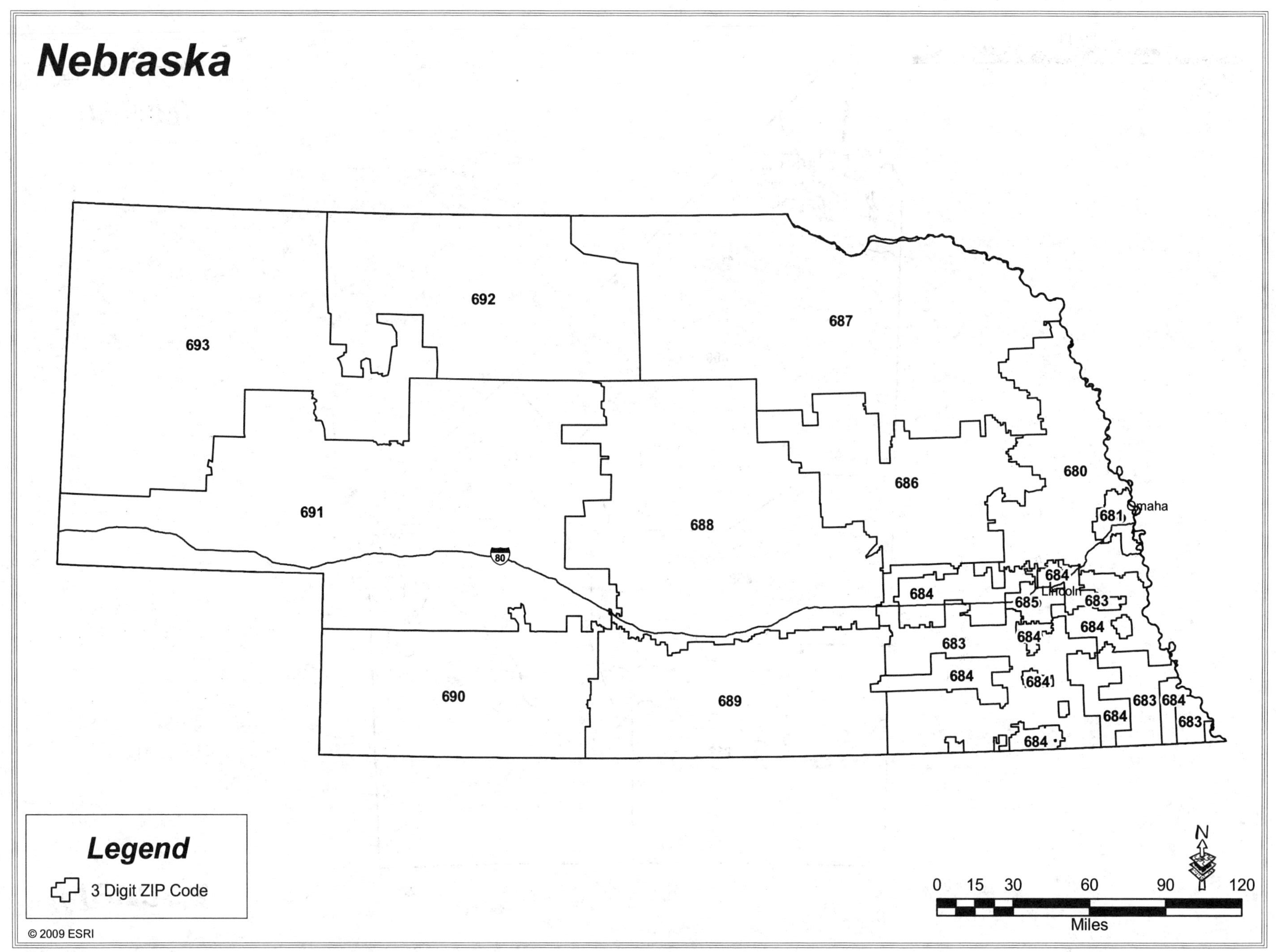
Nebraska
693
692
687
691
688
686
680
Omaha
681
684
Lincoln
685
683
80
690
689
Legend
3 Digit ZIP Code
© 2009 ESRI
N
0 15 30 60 90 120
Miles

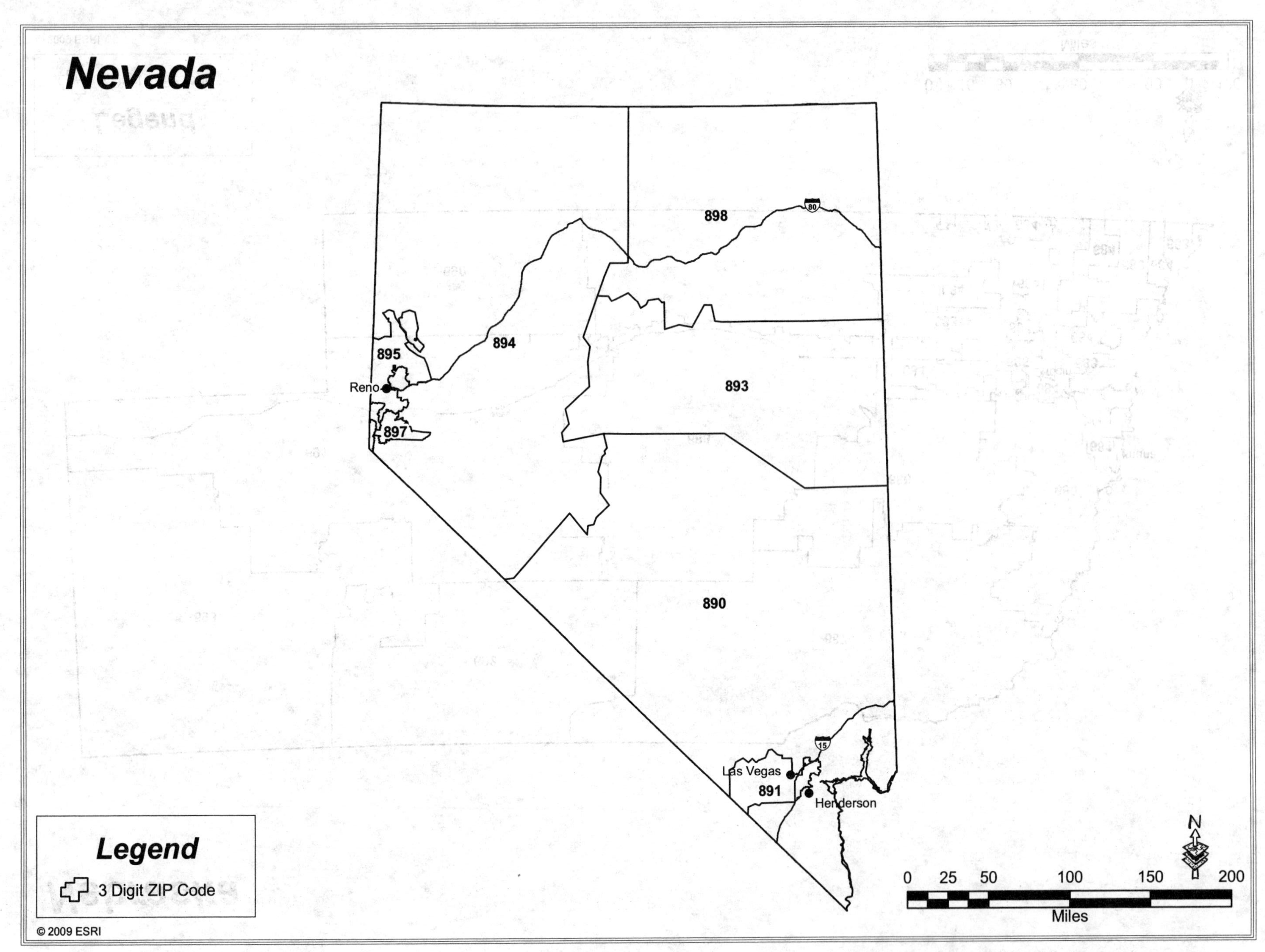
Nevada
898
80
894
895
Reno
893
897
890
15
Las Vegas
891
Henderson
Legend
3 Digit ZIP Code
© 2009 ESRI
N
0 25 50 100 150 200
Miles

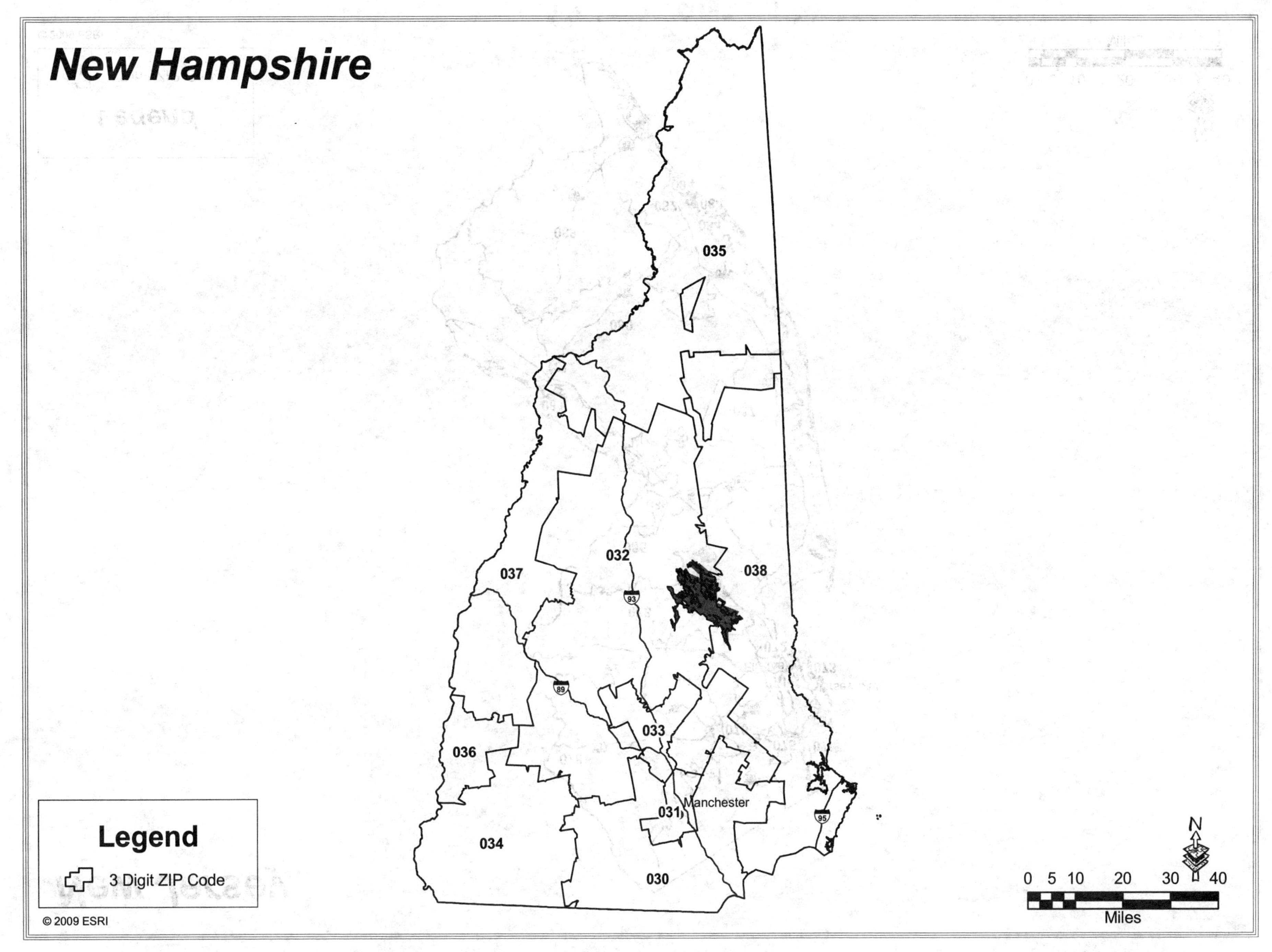
New Hampshire
035
038
032
037
033
036
Manchester
031
034
030
93
89
95
Legend
3 Digit ZIP Code
© 2009 ESRI
N
0 5 10 20 30 40
Miles

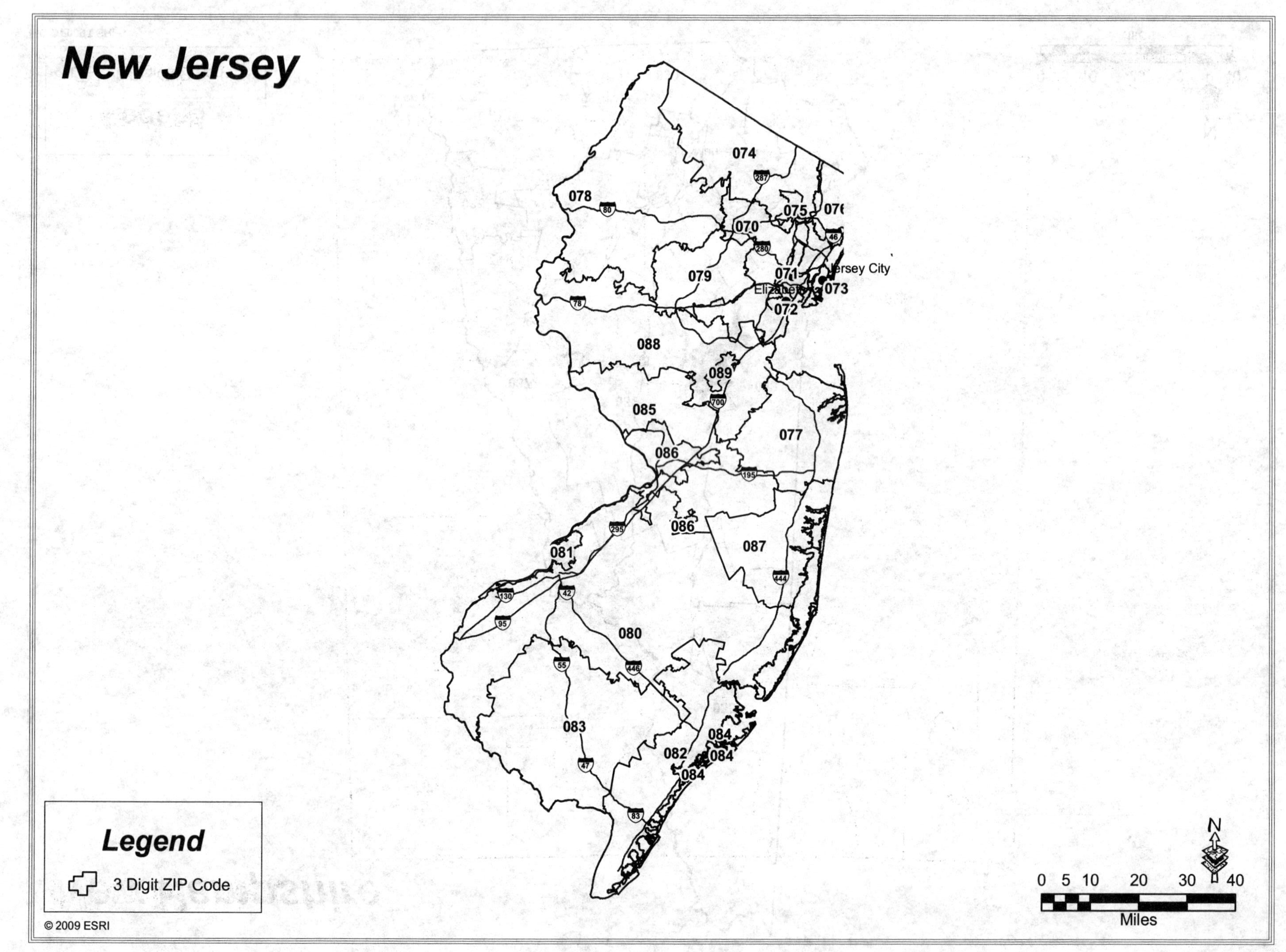
New Jersey
074
287
078
80
075
076
070
46
280
079
071
Jersey City
Elizabeth
073
072
78
088
089
700
085
077
086
195
086
295
087
081
444
42
130
95
080
55
446
083
084
082
084
084
47
83
Legend
3 Digit ZIP Code
N
0 5 10 20 30 40
Miles

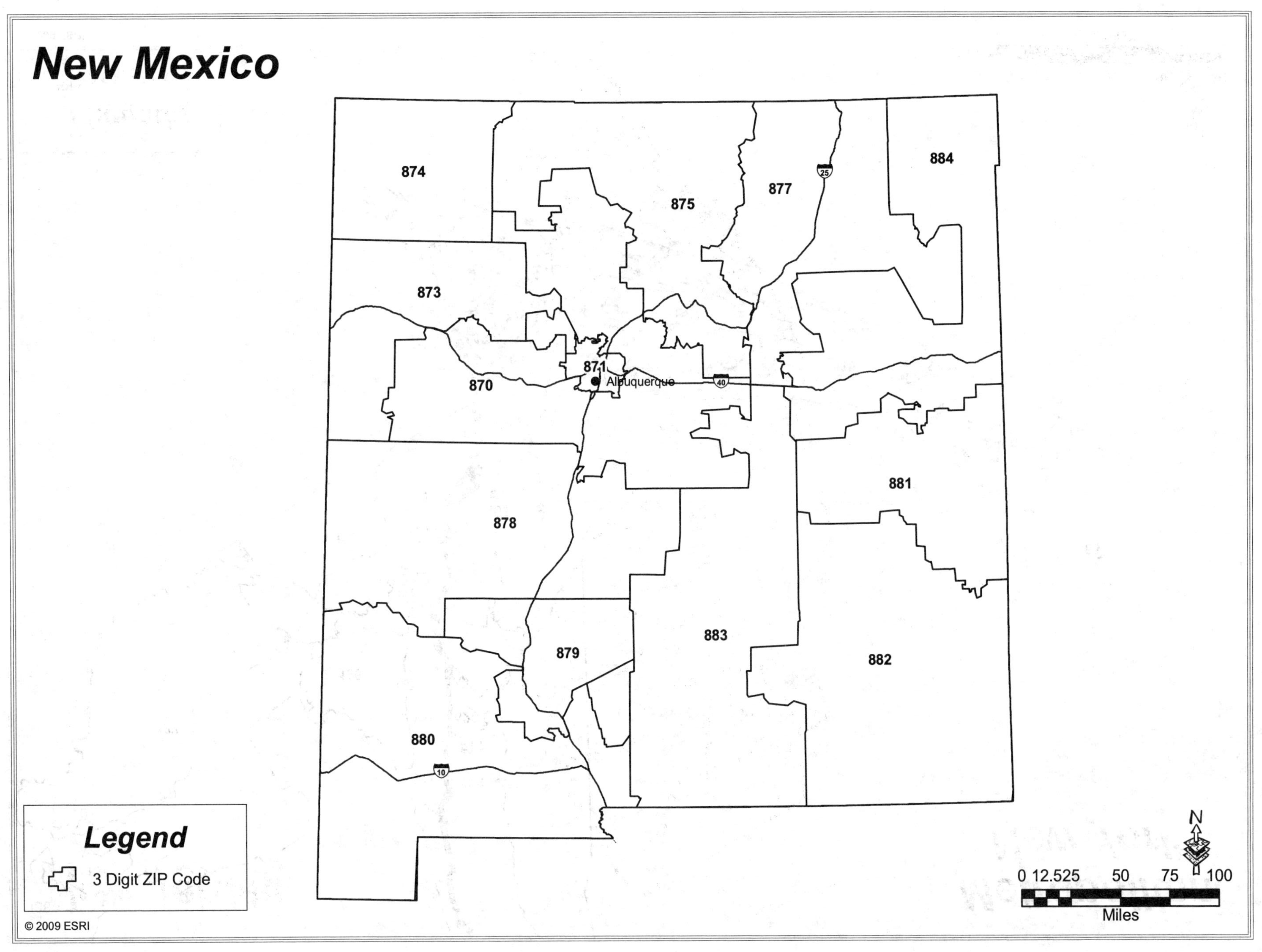
New Mexico
874
875
877
884
873
871
Albuquerque
870
878
881
879
883
882
880
25
40
10
Legend
3 Digit ZIP Code
© 2009 ESRI
N
0 12.525 50 75 100
Miles

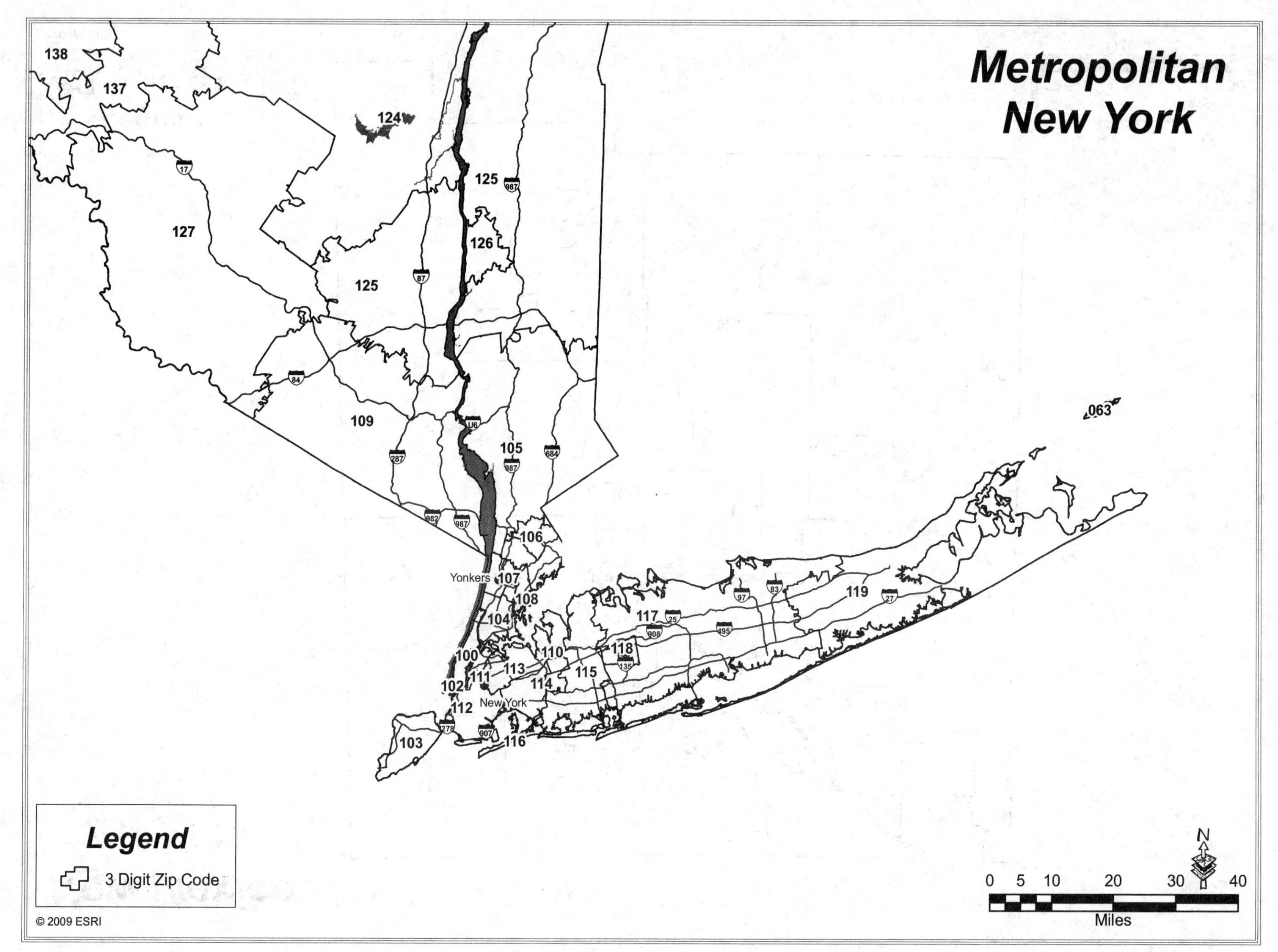
Metropolitan
New York
138
137
124
127
125
126
125
109
105
106
Yonkers
107
108
104
100
111
113
110
114
115
118
117
119
102
112
New York
116
103
063
Legend
3 Digit Zip Code
© 2009 ESRI
N
0 5 10 20 30 40
Miles

Upstate New York

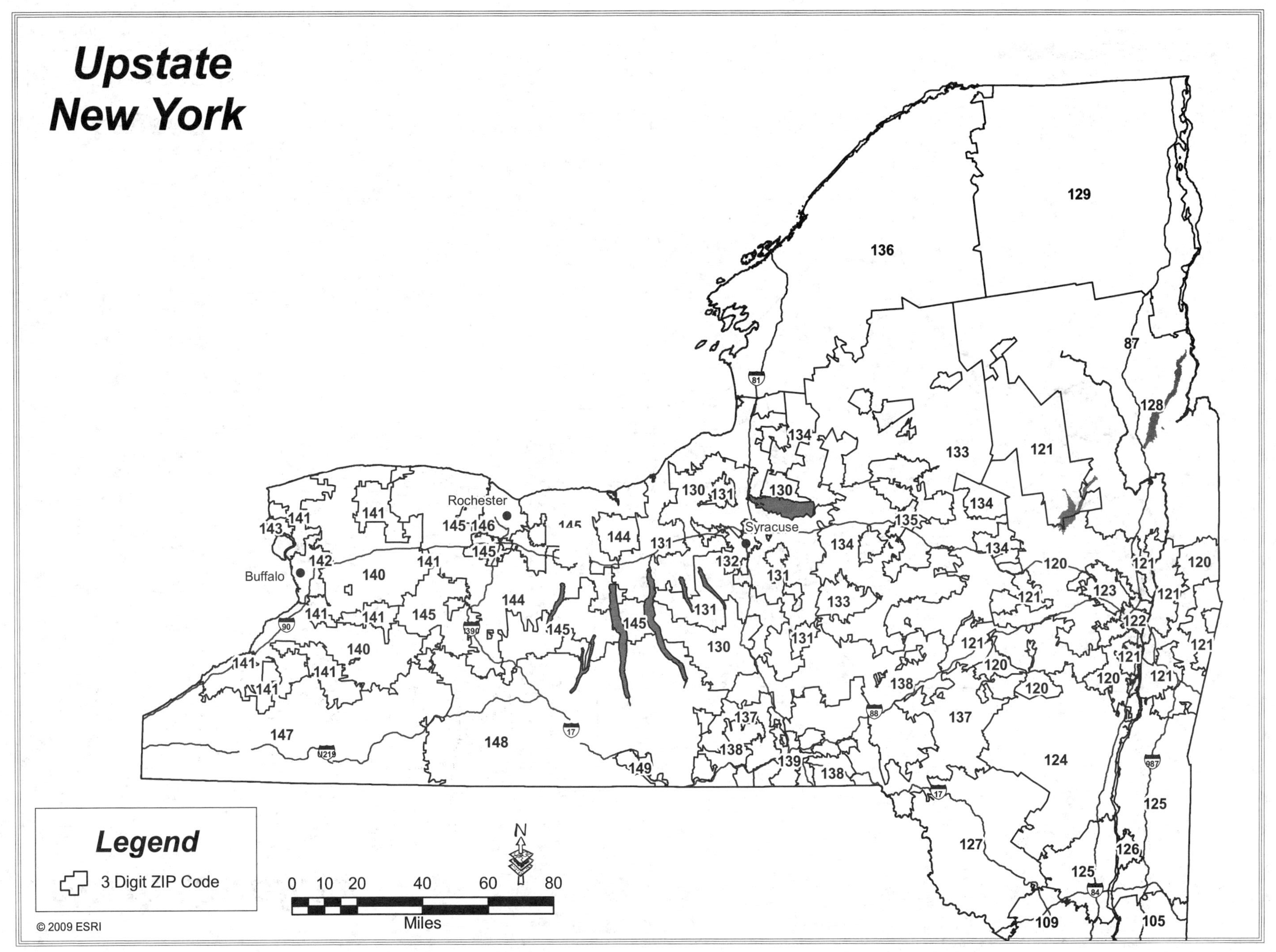

North Carolina

270
271
272
273
274
275
276
277
278
279
280
281
282
283
284
285
286
287
288
289
Greensboro
Durham
Raleigh
Charlotte
Fayetteville

Legend

3 Digit ZIP Code

0 12.5 25 50 75 100
Miles

N

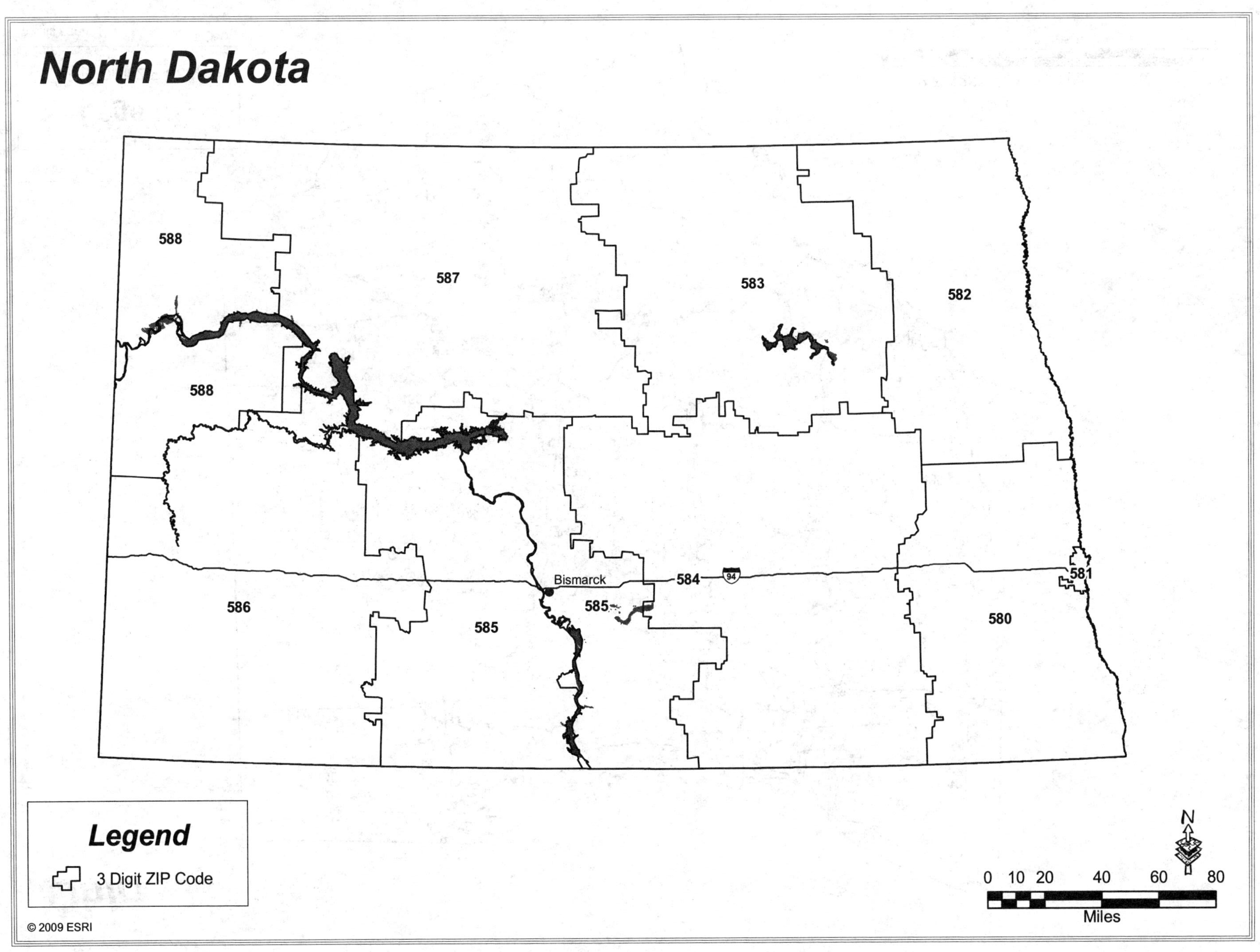
North Dakota
588
587
583
582
588
586
585
Bismarck
585
584
94
581
580
Legend
3 Digit ZIP Code
© 2009 ESRI
N
0 10 20 40 60 80
Miles

Ohio

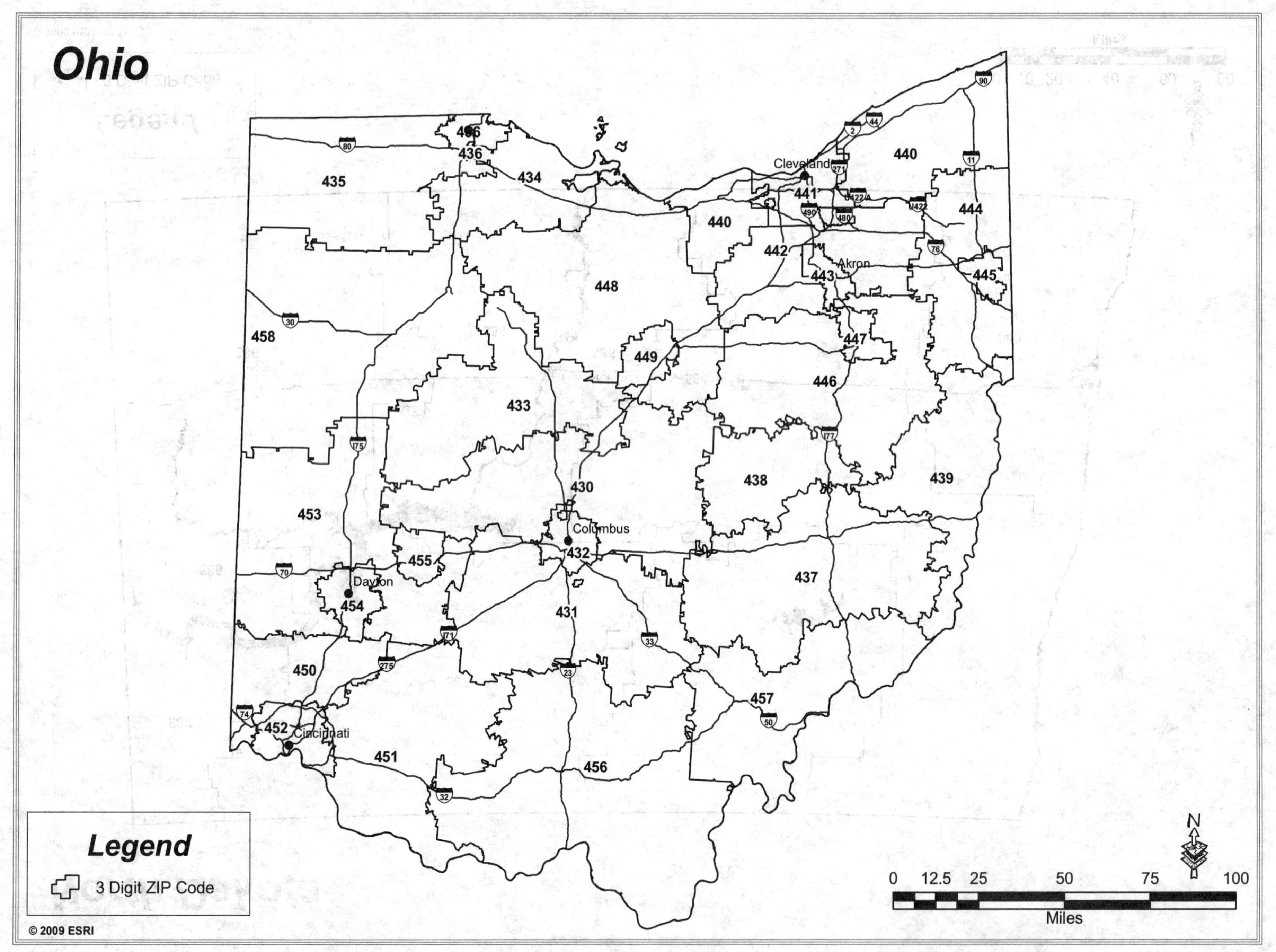

Cleveland
Akron
Columbus
Dayton
Cincinnati
435
436
434
440
441
442
443
444
445
446
447
448
449
433
430
432
431
437
438
439
453
454
455
458
450
451
452
456
457
Legend
3 Digit ZIP Code
0 12.5 25 50 75 100
Miles
N
© 2009 ESRI

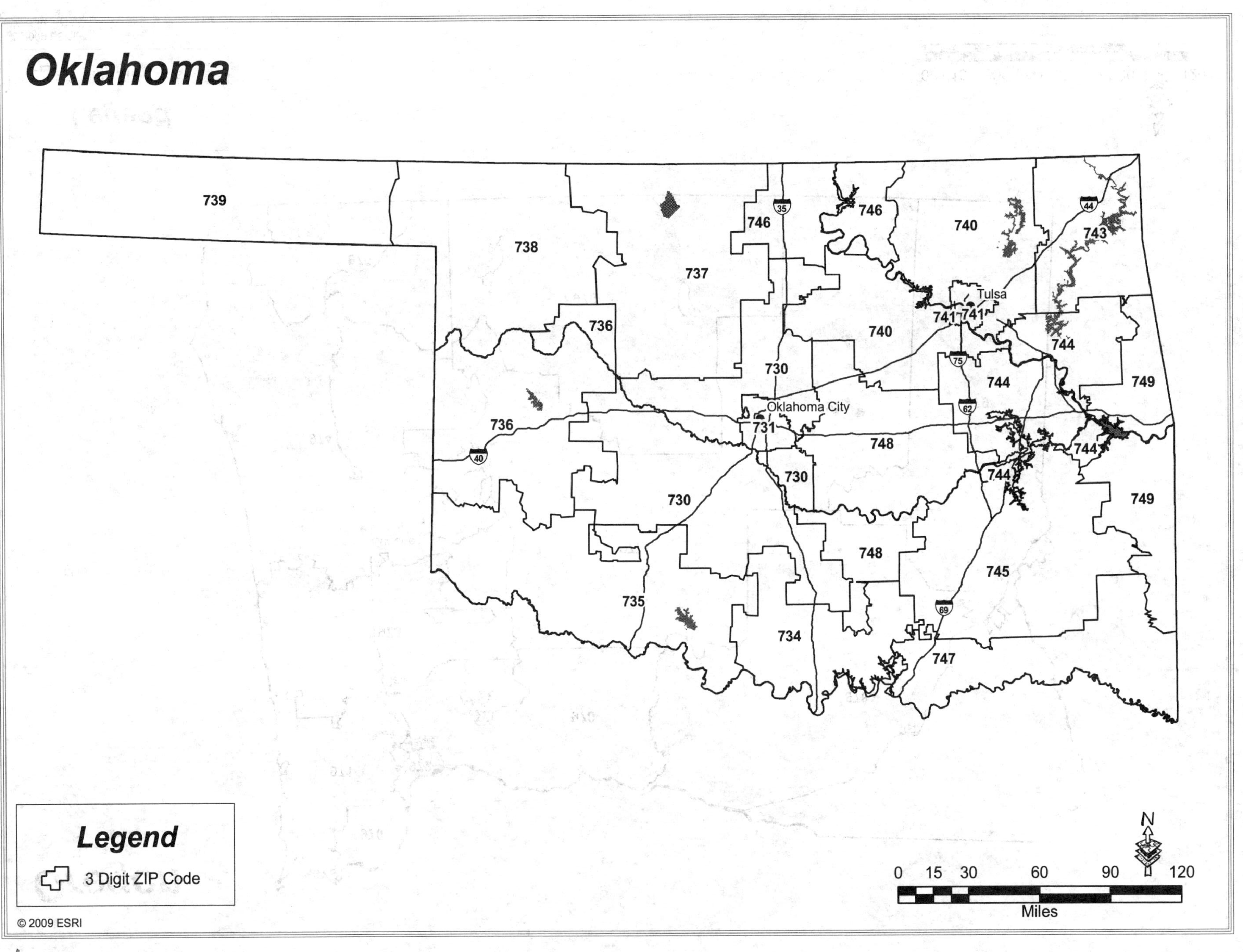

Oklahoma
739
738
737
736
746
746
740
743
741
741
Tulsa
740
744
730
744
749
Oklahoma City
731
748
744
744
730
730
749
748
745
735
734
747
35
44
75
62
40
69
Legend
3 Digit ZIP Code
© 2009 ESRI
N
0 15 30 60 90 120
Miles

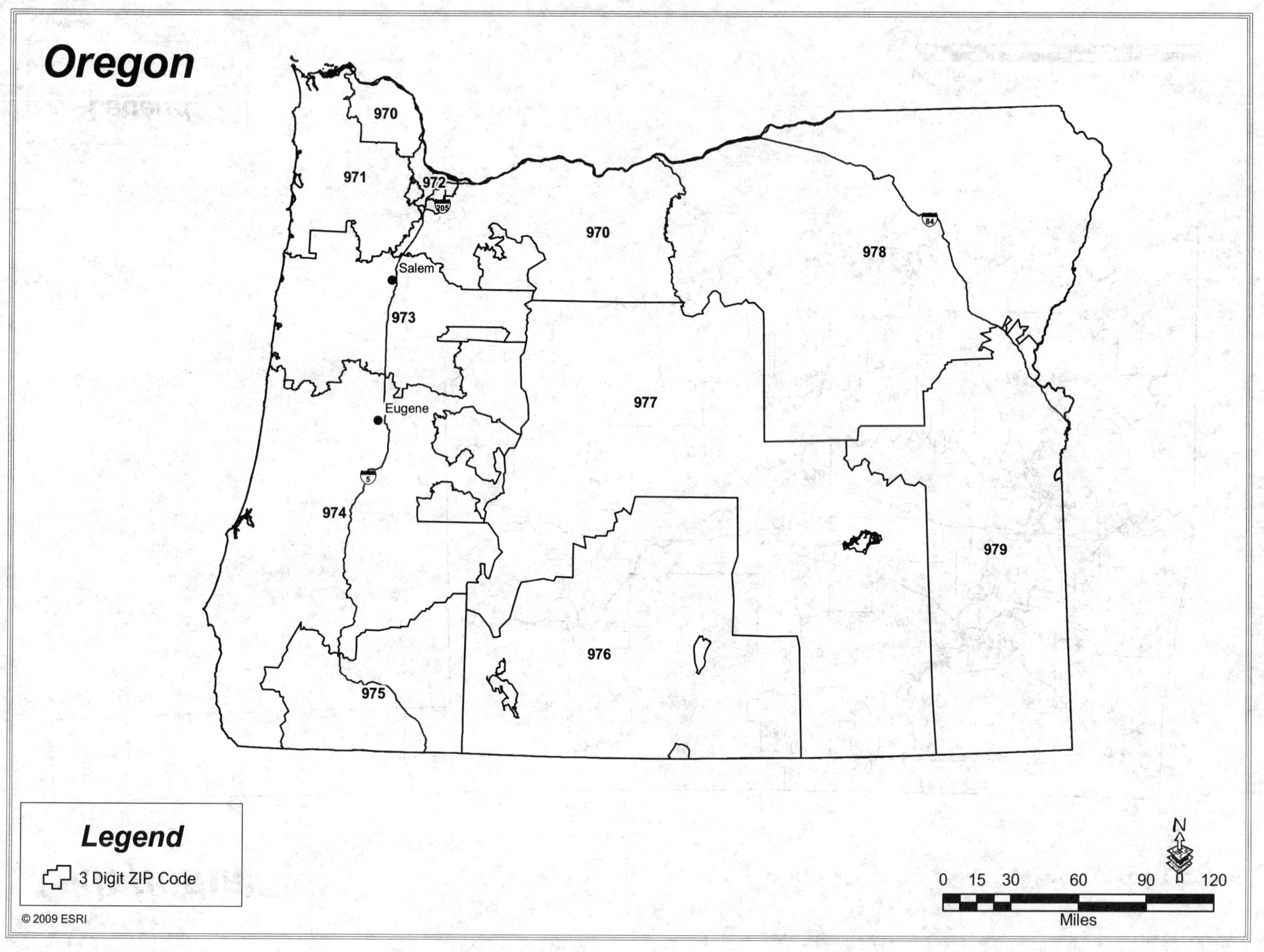
Oregon
970
971
972
205
970
978
84
Salem
973
977
Eugene
5
974
979
976
975
Legend
3 Digit ZIP Code
© 2009 ESRI
N
0 15 30 60 90 120
Miles

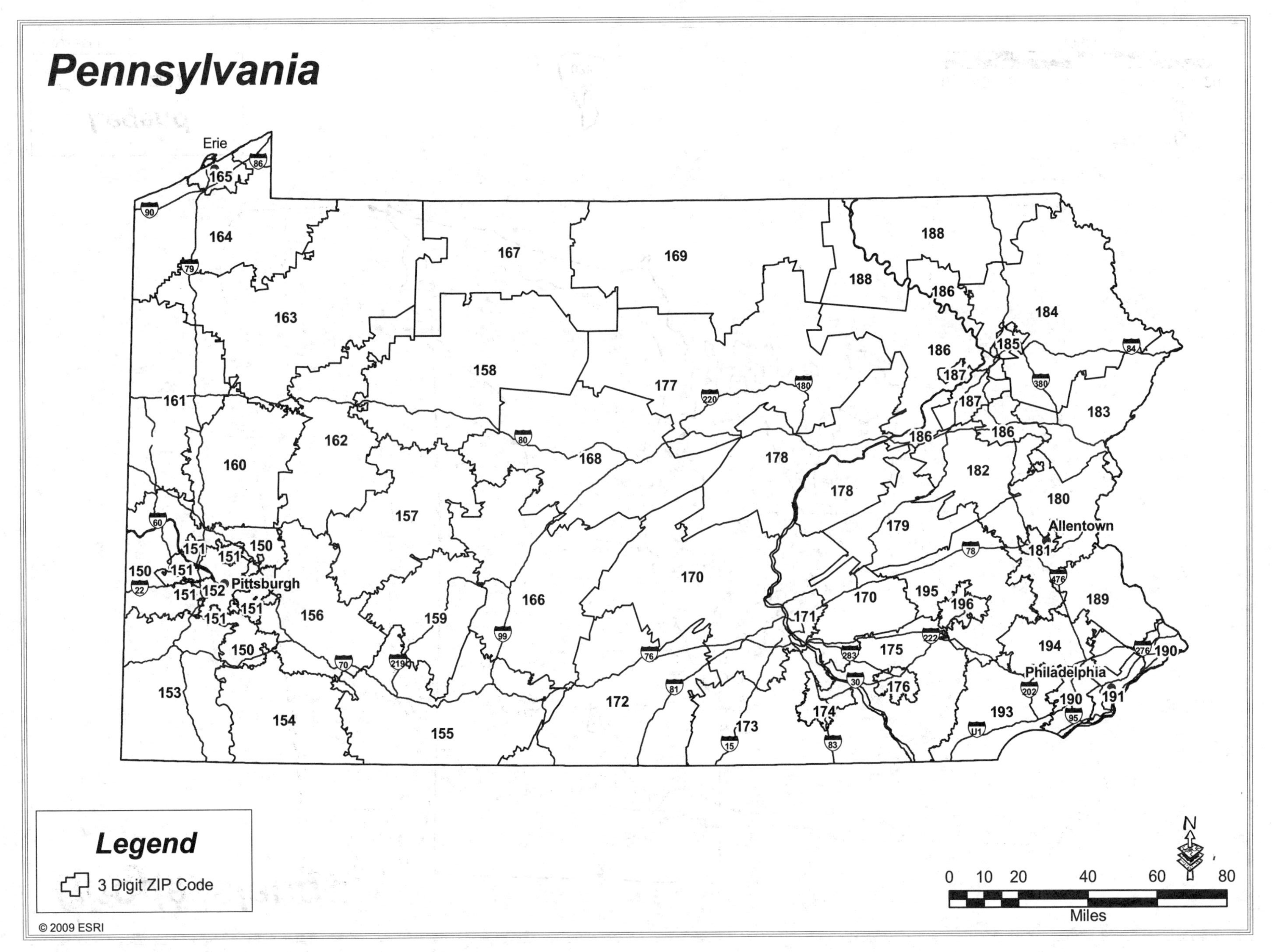
Pennsylvania
Erie
Allentown
Philadelphia
Pittsburgh
Legend
3 Digit ZIP Code
© 2009 ESRI
0 10 20 40 60 80
Miles
N
150
151
152
153
154
155
156
157
158
159
160
161
162
163
164
165
166
167
168
169
170
171
172
173
174
175
176
177
178
179
180
181
182
183
184
185
186
187
188
189
190
191
193
194
195
196

Rhode Island

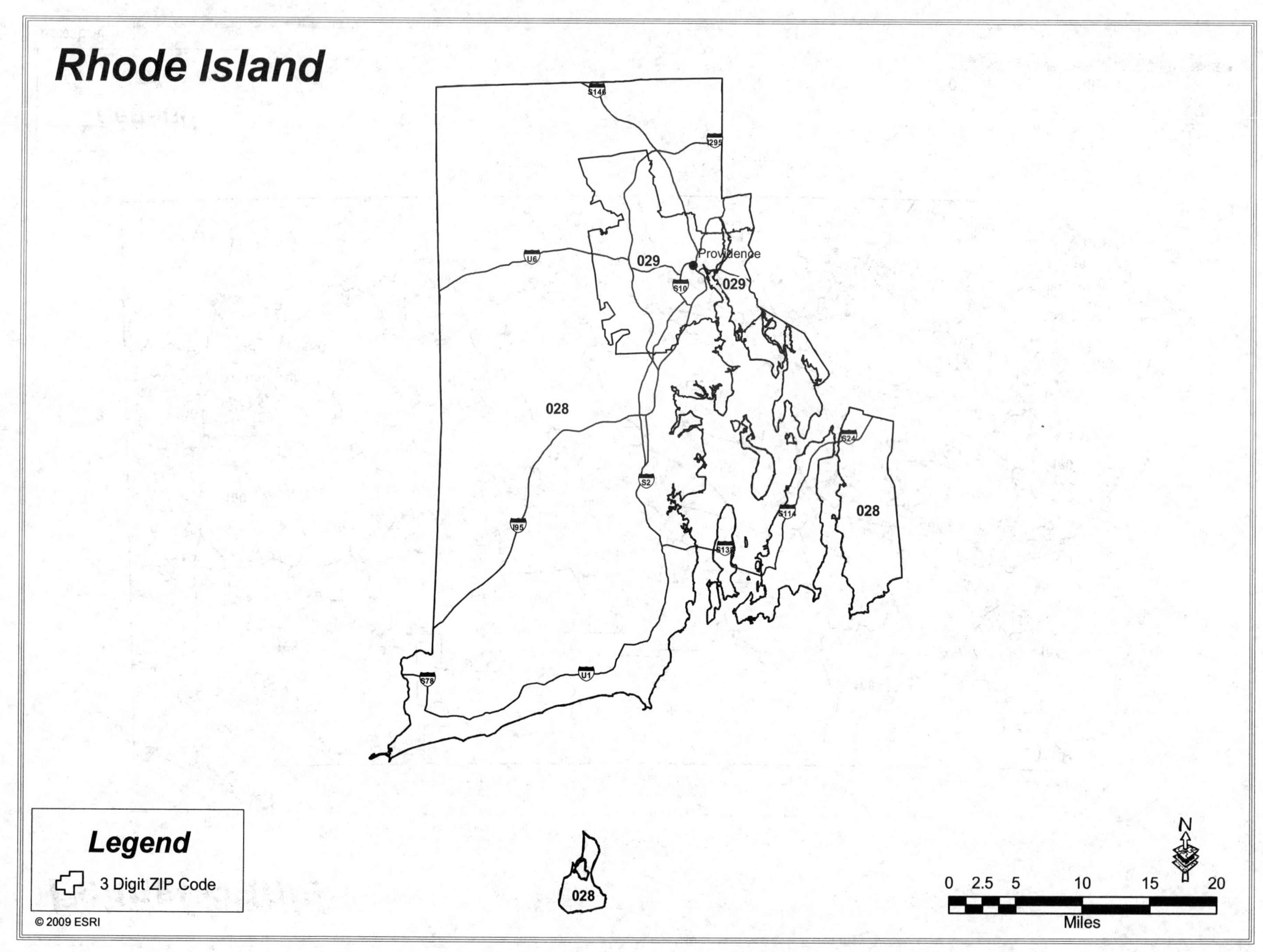

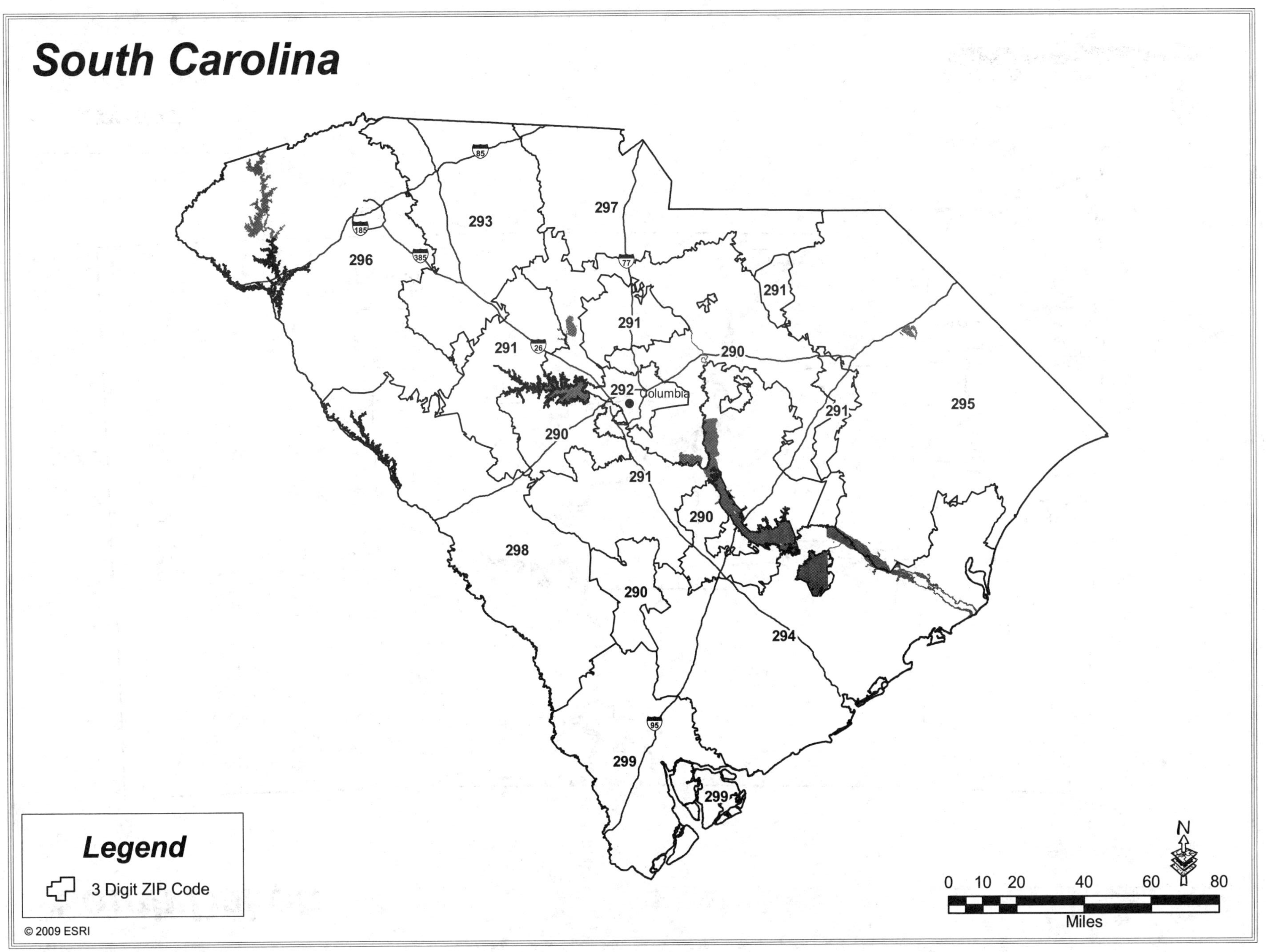
South Carolina
297
293
296
291
291
291
290
292
Columbia
295
291
290
291
290
298
290
294
299
299
85
185
385
77
26
95
Legend
3 Digit ZIP Code
© 2009 ESRI
N
0 10 20 40 60 80
Miles

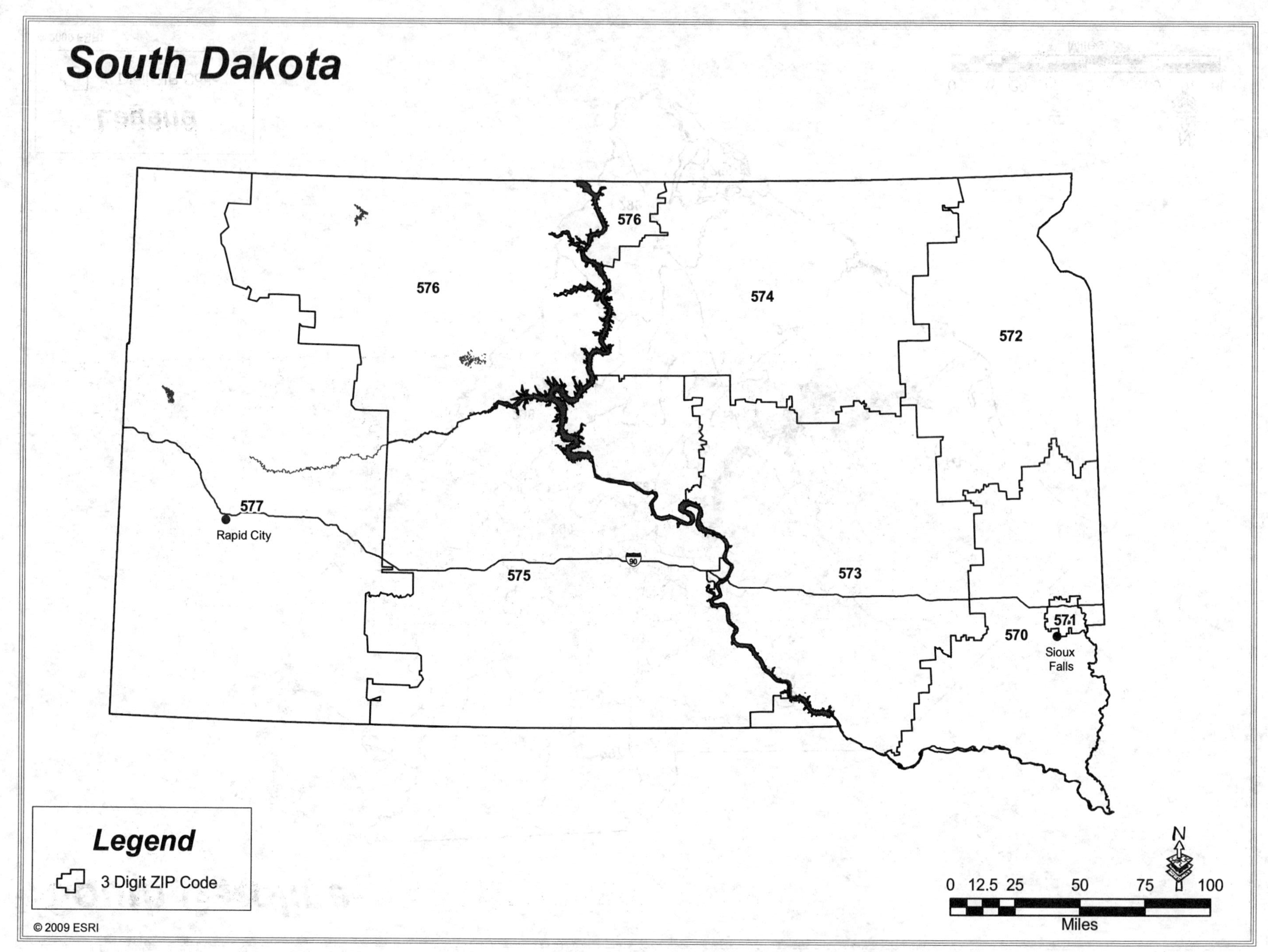
South Dakota
576
576
574
572
577
Rapid City
90
575
573
571
570
Sioux Falls
Legend
3 Digit ZIP Code
0 12.5 25 50 75 100
Miles
N
© 2009 ESRI

Tennessee

370 422 Clarksville 371 371 385 378 377 376
382 371 372 370 Nashville 385 378 377 Knoxville
380 383 370 371 378 379 377 377 378
723 370
381 Memphis 384 383 373 374 374 Chattanooga 373

51 155 40 840 65 24 75 81

Legend

3 Digit ZIP Code

N

0 12.5 25 50 75 100

Miles

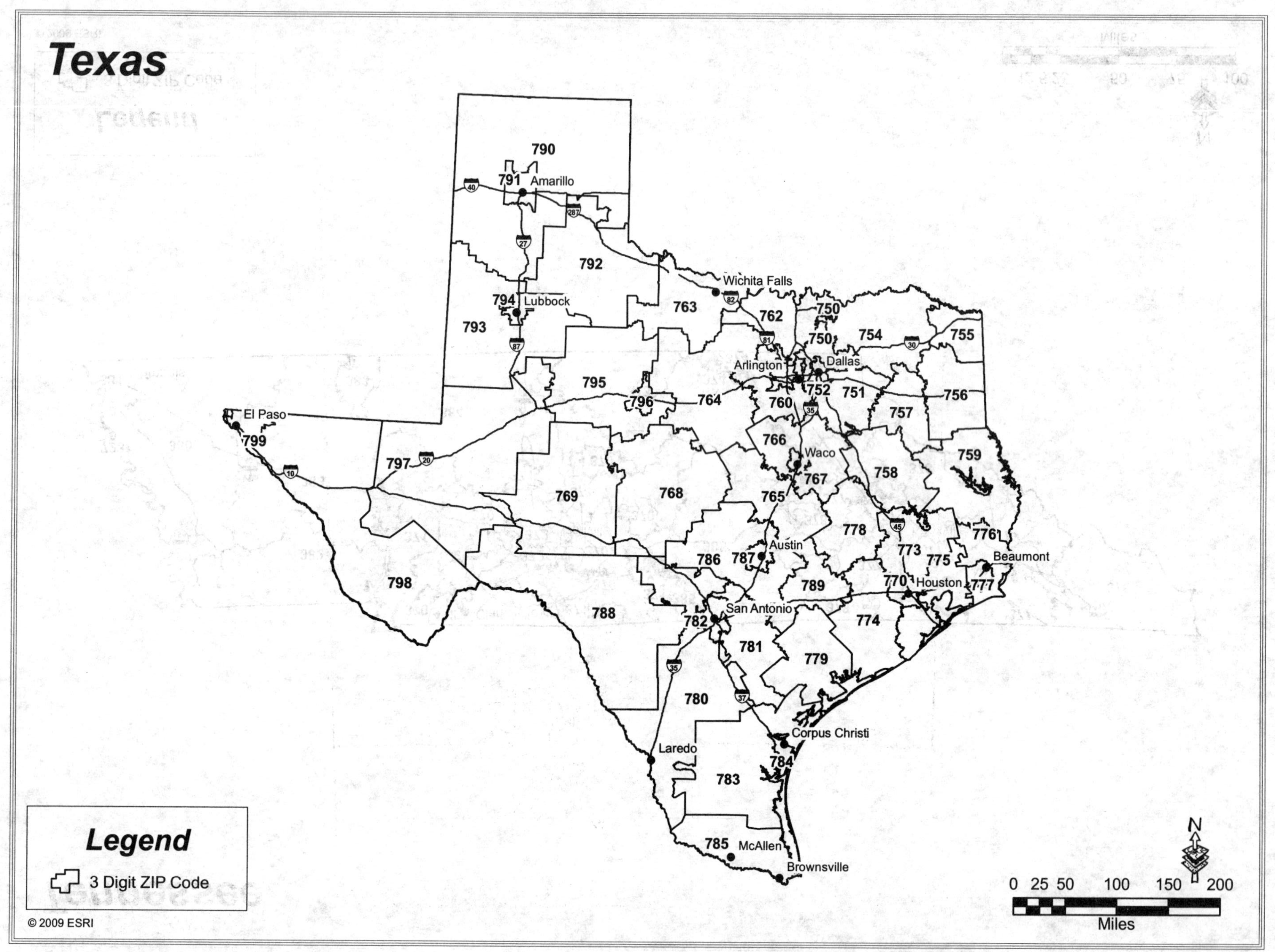
Texas
790
791
Amarillo
792
Wichita Falls
763
762
750
750
754
755
794
Lubbock
793
Arlington
Dallas
752
751
756
795
796
764
760
757
El Paso
799
766
Waco
759
797
767
758
769
768
765
778
776
Austin
773
775
Beaumont
786
787
789
770
Houston
777
798
788
San Antonio
782
774
781
779
780
Corpus Christi
Laredo
784
783
785
McAllen
Brownsville
Legend
3 Digit ZIP Code
© 2009 ESRI
N
0 25 50 100 150 200
Miles

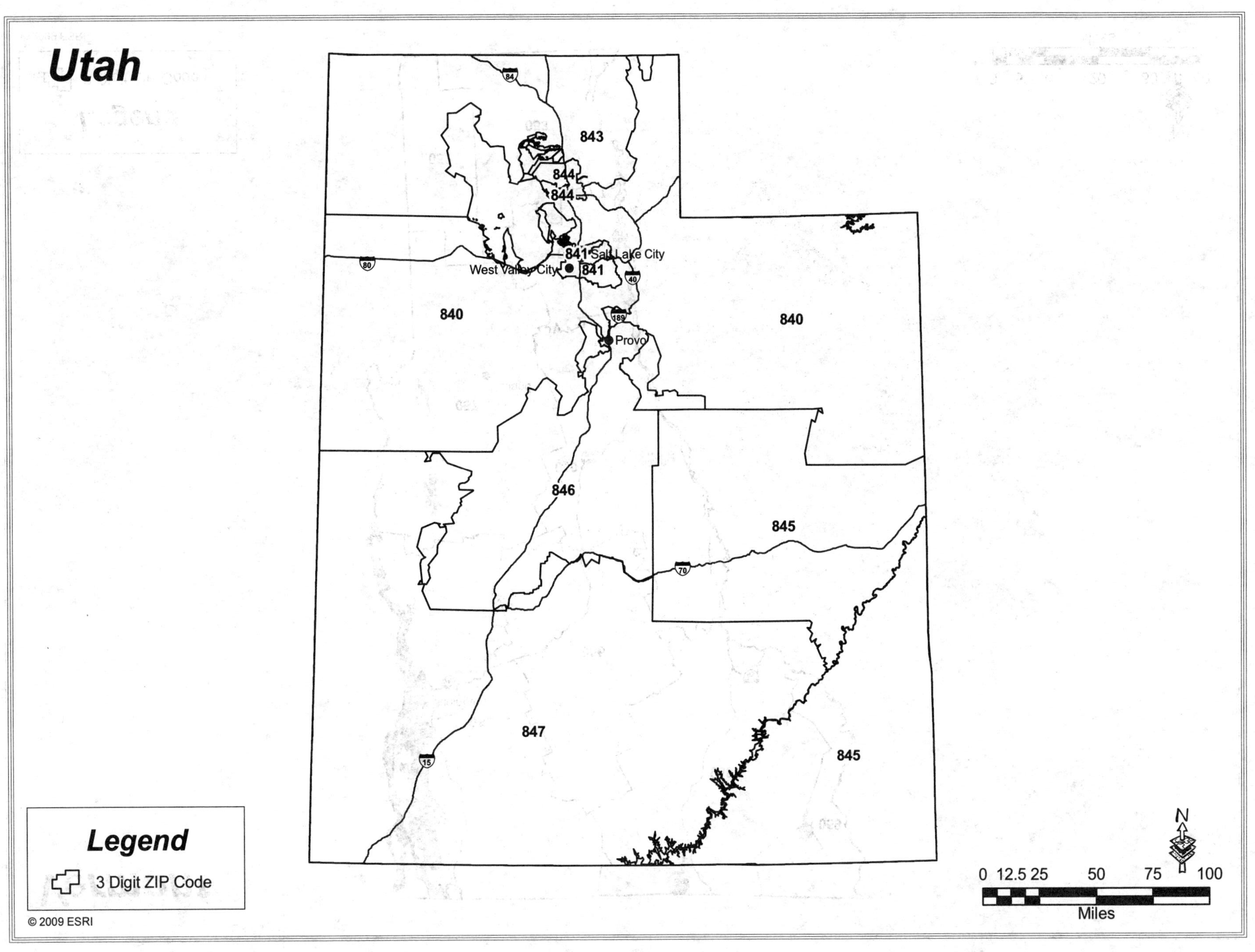

Utah
843
844
844
841
Salt Lake City
West Valley City
841
840
Provo
840
846
845
847
845
84
80
40
189
70
15
Legend
3 Digit ZIP Code
© 2009 ESRI
N
0 12.5 25 50 75 100
Miles

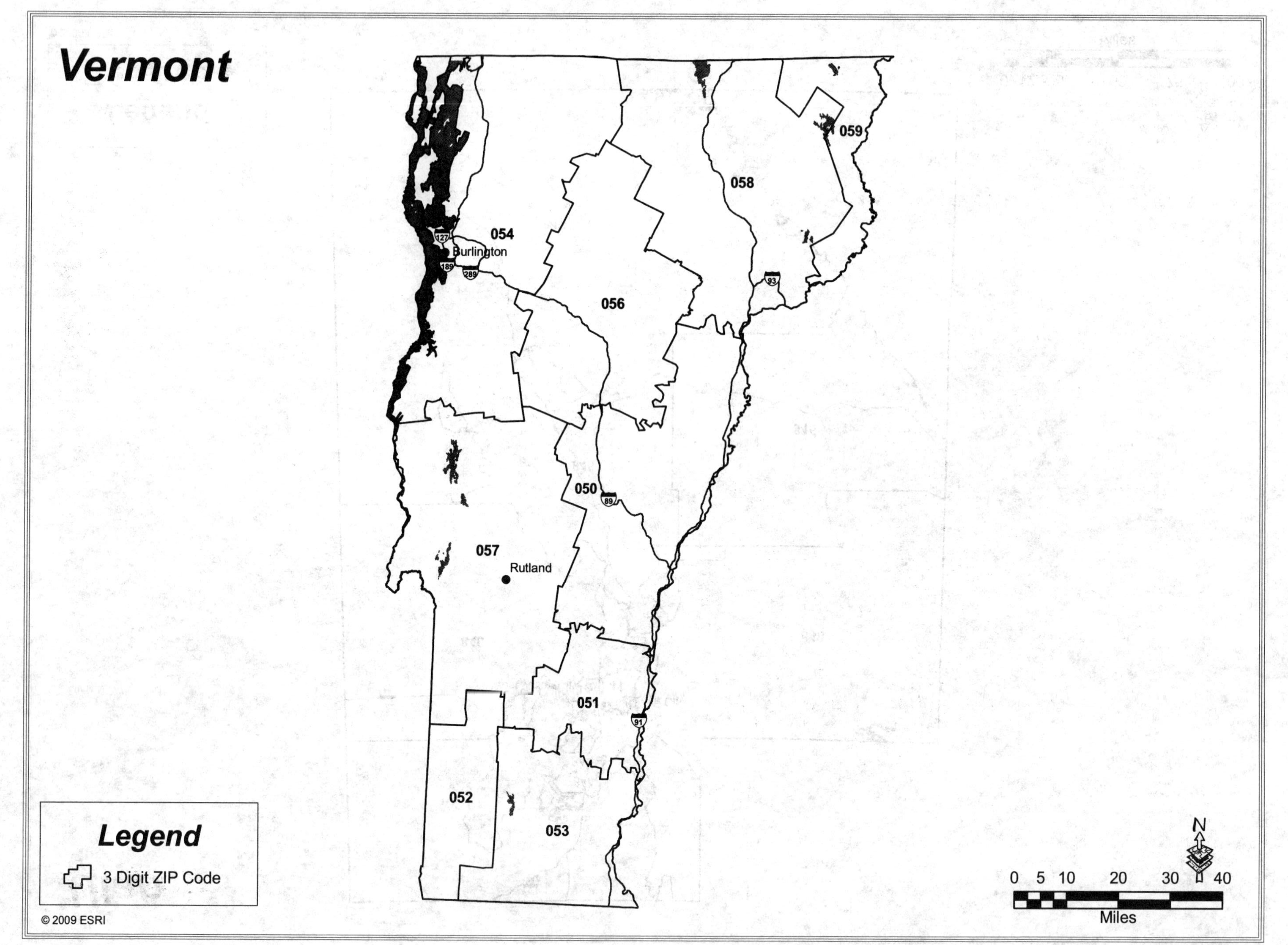

Vermont
054
Burlington
127
189
289
056
058
059
93
050
89
057
Rutland
051
91
052
053
Legend
3 Digit ZIP Code
© 2009 ESRI
N
0 5 10 20 30 40
Miles

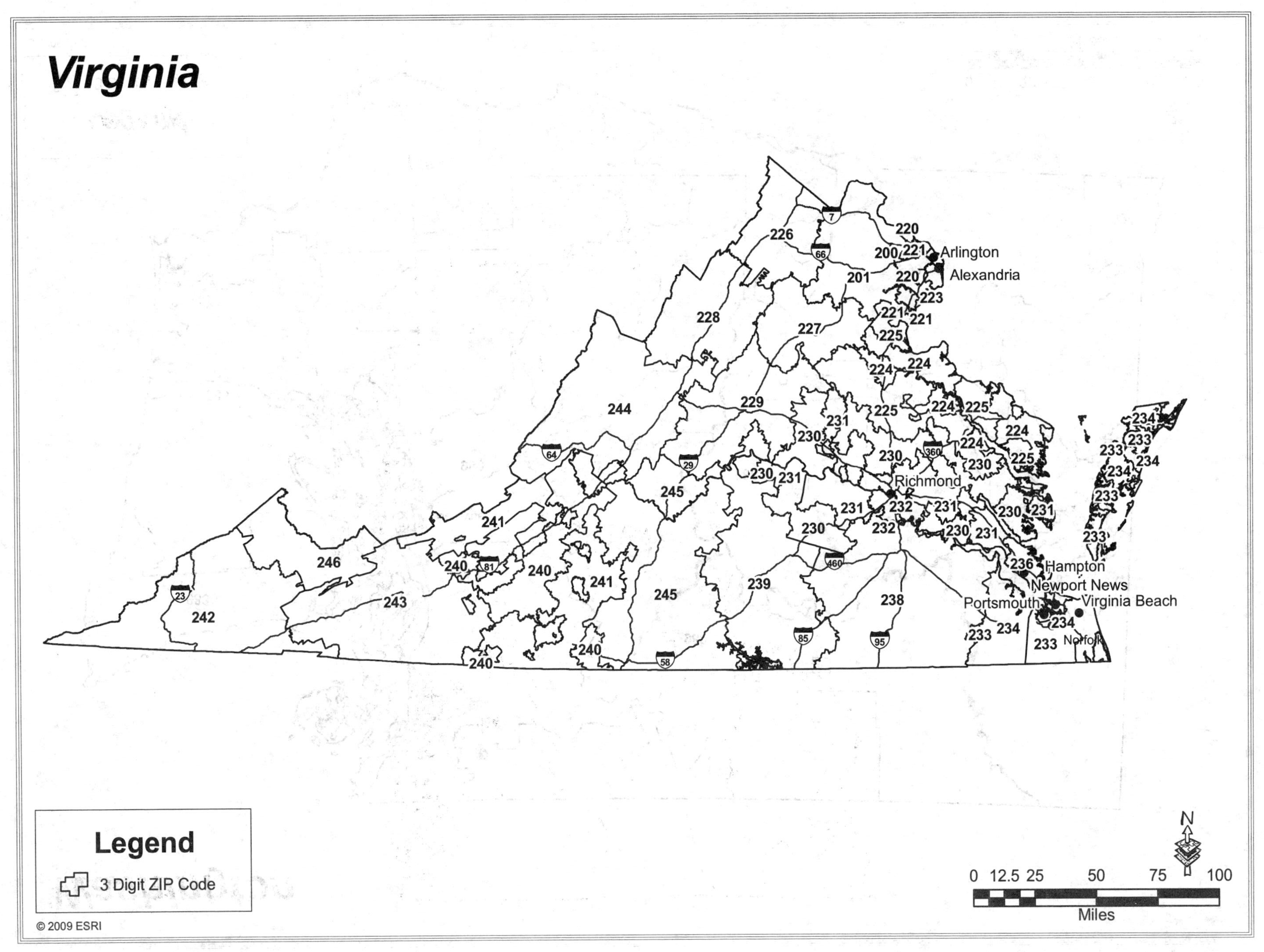
Virginia
Arlington
Alexandria
Richmond
Hampton
Newport News
Portsmouth
Virginia Beach
Norfolk
Legend
3 Digit ZIP Code
0 12.5 25 50 75 100
Miles
N
© 2009 ESRI

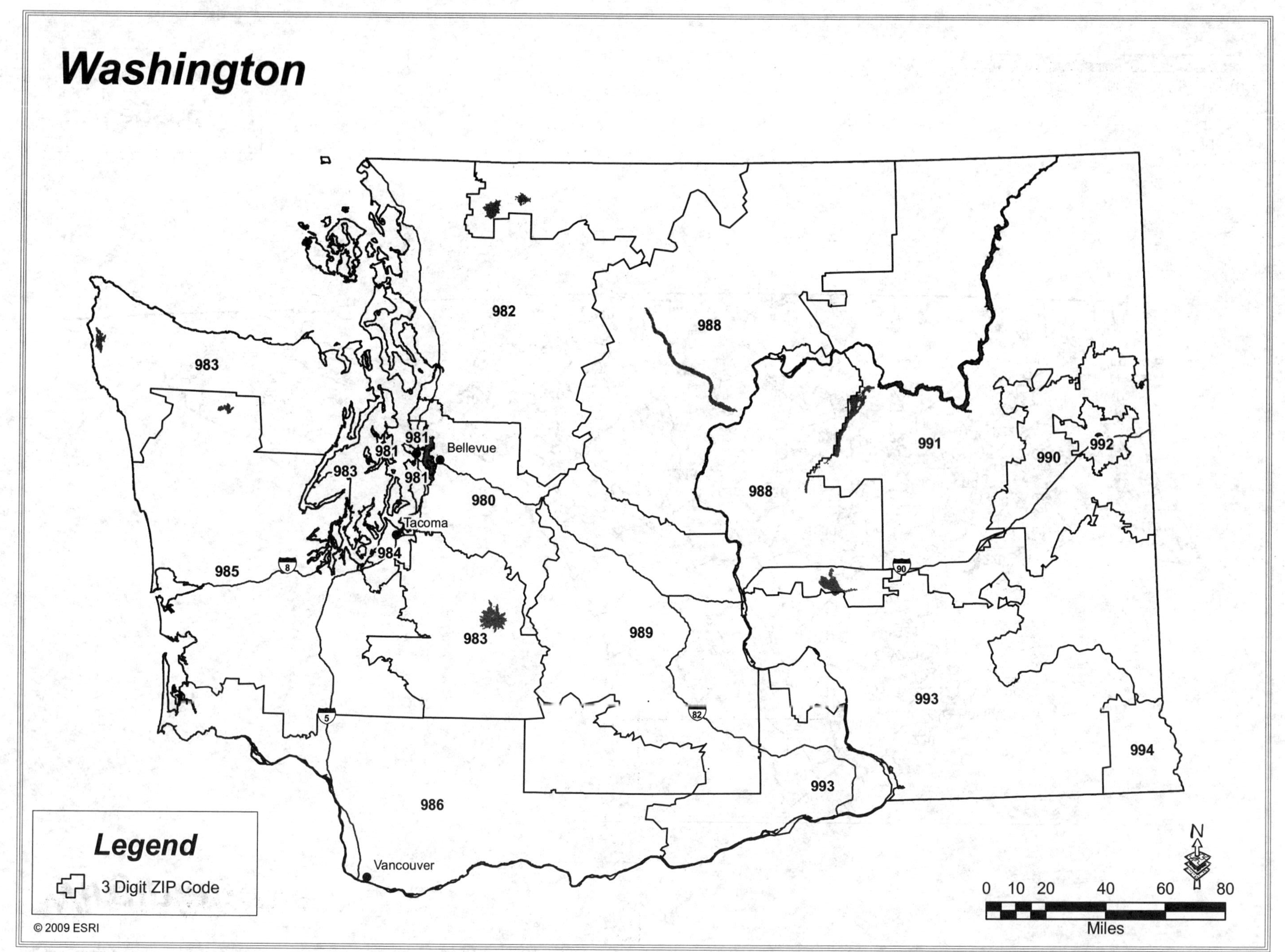

Washington
982
988
983
981
981
983
981
Bellevue
980
Tacoma
984
985
8
991
990
992
988
90
983
989
993
5
82
994
993
986
Vancouver
Legend
3 Digit ZIP Code
© 2009 ESRI
N
0 10 20 40 60 80
Miles

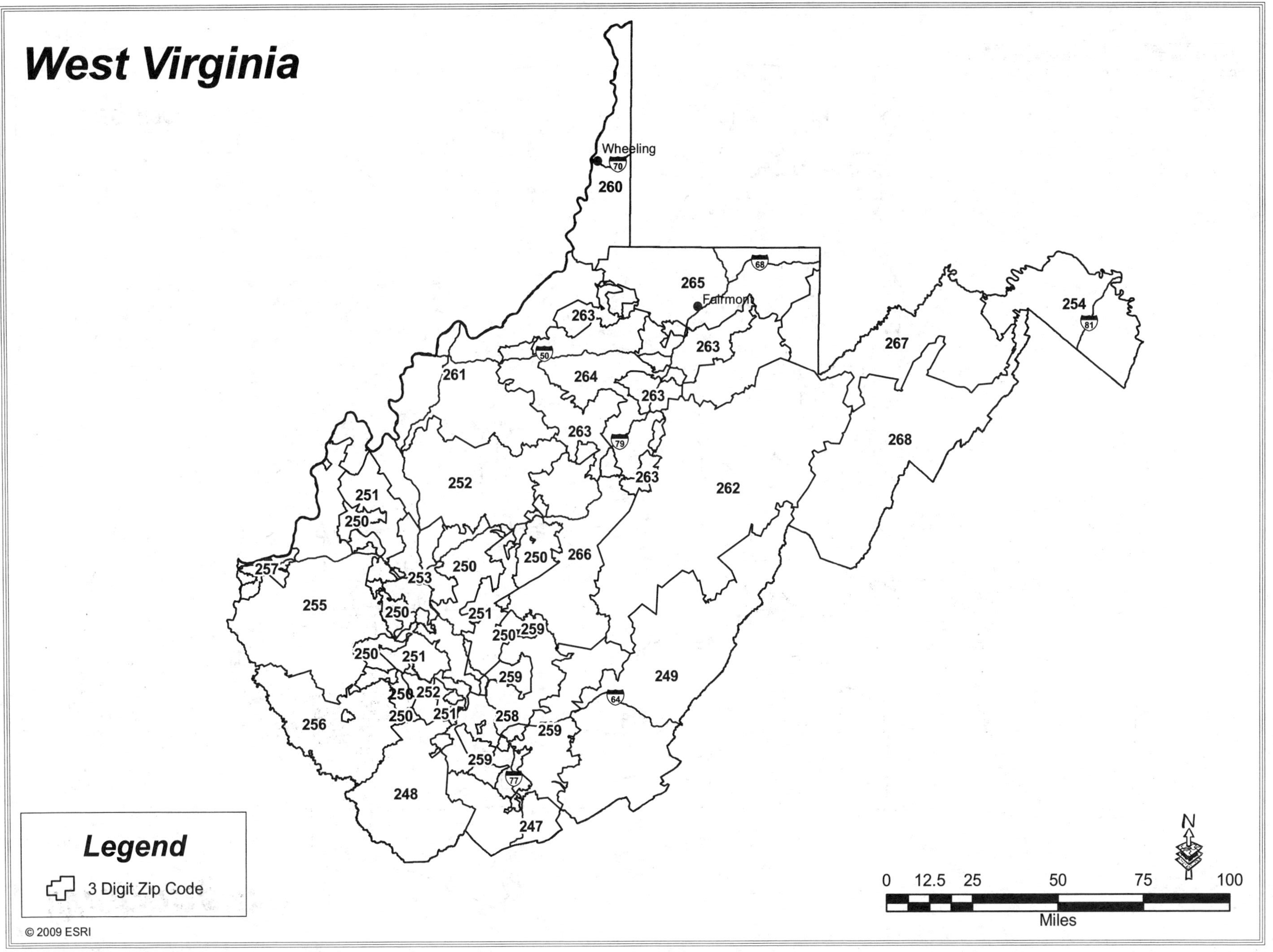
West Virginia
Wheeling
Fairmont
70
68
50
79
64
77
81
260
265
263
263
263
263
263
264
261
252
262
267
268
254
251
250
257
255
253
250
250
266
250
251
250
259
250
251
259
249
258
252
251
250
259
256
259
248
247
Legend
3 Digit Zip Code
© 2009 ESRI
N
0 12.5 25 50 75 100
Miles

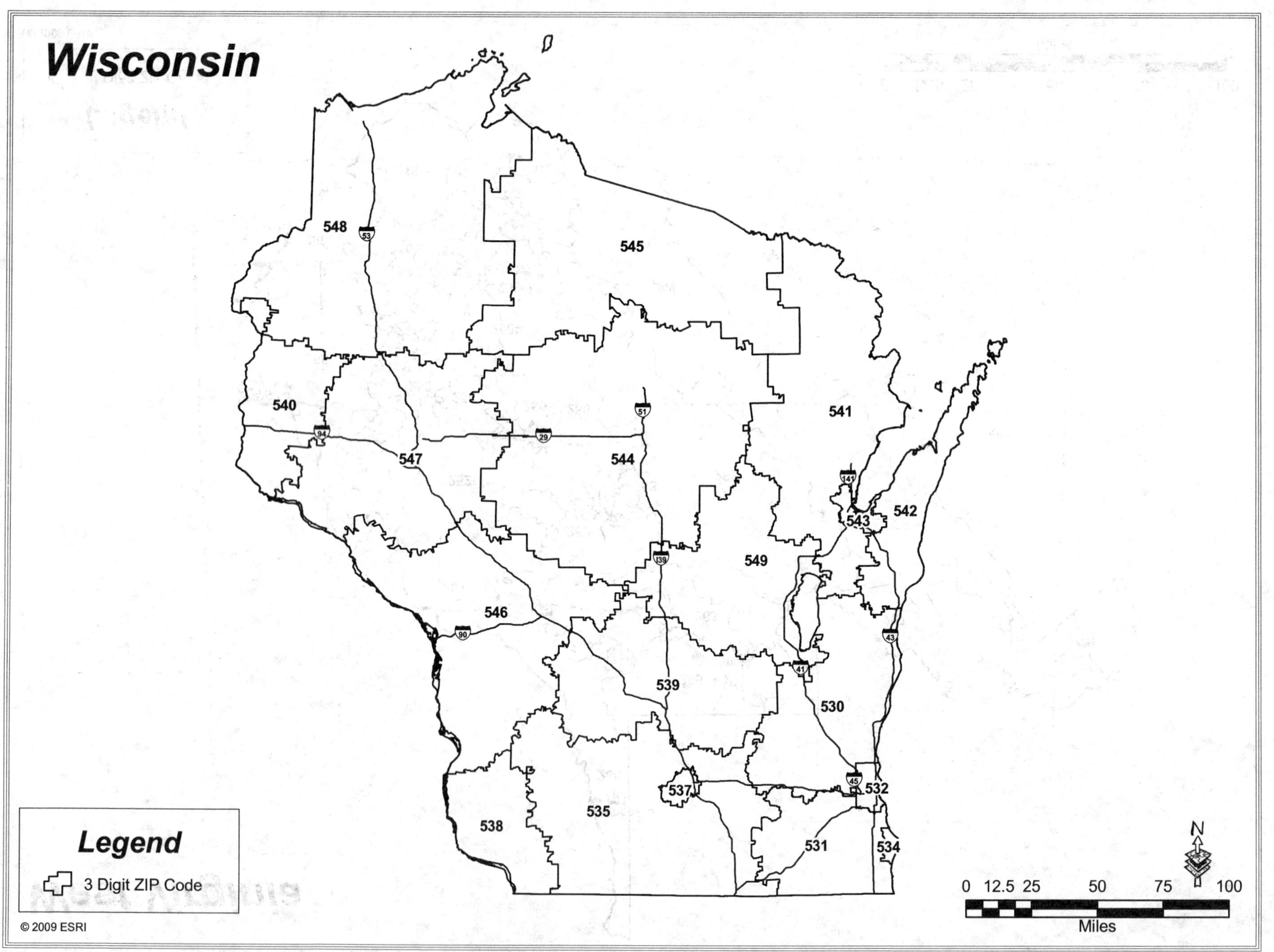
Wisconsin
548
53
545
540
94
29
51
541
547
544
141
543
542
549
139
546
90
43
41
539
530
45
532
537
535
538
531
534
Legend
3 Digit ZIP Code
© 2009 ESRI
N
0 12.5 25 50 75 100
Miles

Wyoming

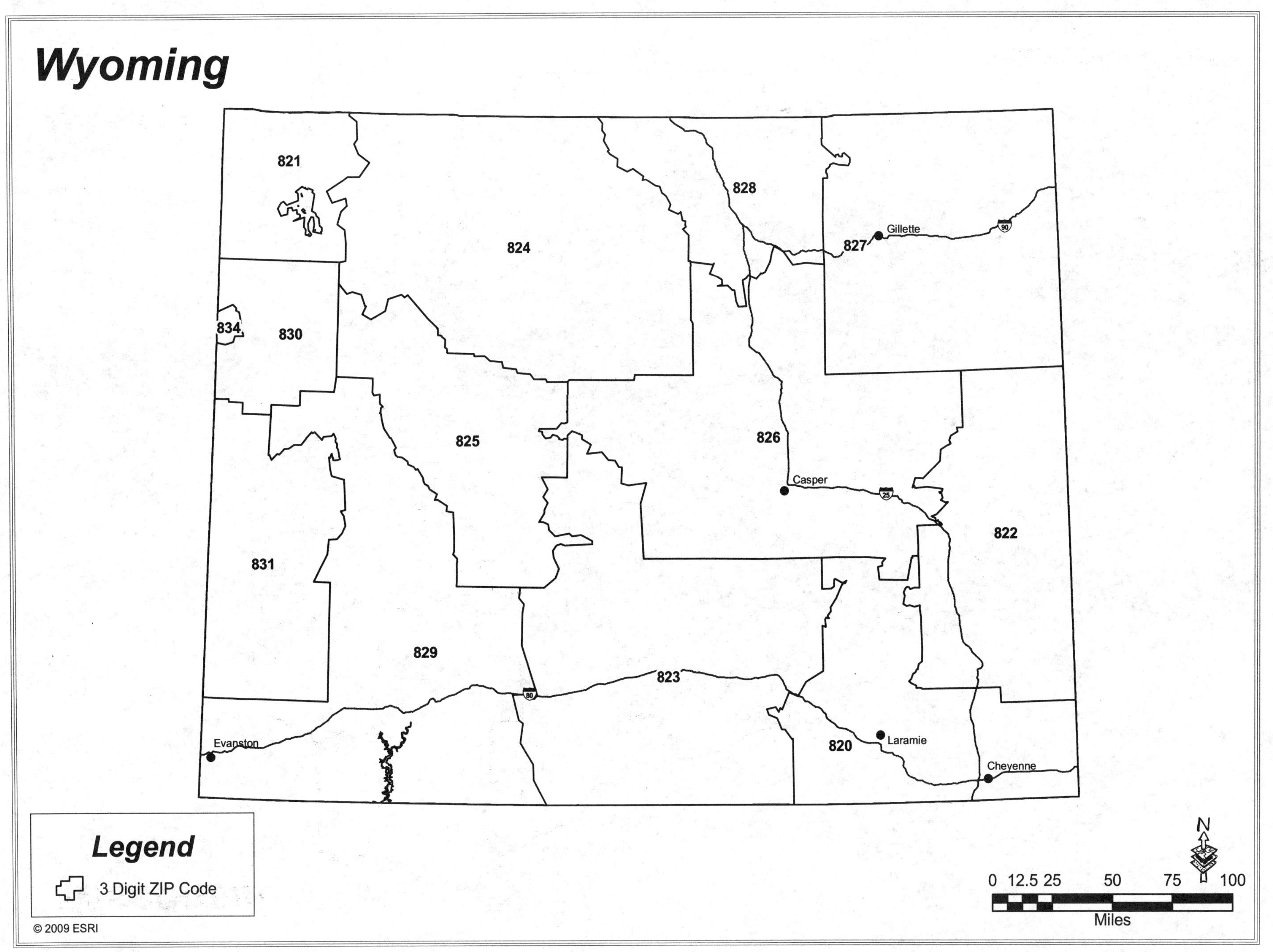

821
824
828
827
Gillette
90
834
830
825
826
Casper
25
822
831
829
823
80
Evanston
820
Laramie
Cheyenne
Legend
3 Digit ZIP Code
© 2009 ESRI
N
0 12.5 25 50 75 100
Miles